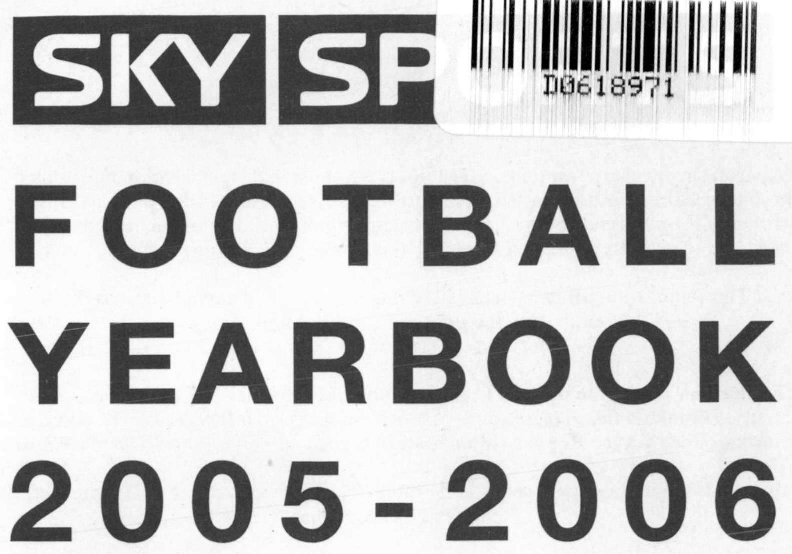

FOOTBALL YEARBOOK 2005-2006

EDITORS: GLENDA ROLLIN AND JACK ROLLIN

headline

First published in 2005
by HEADLINE BOOK PUBLISHING

1

Front cover photographs: (left) Francesc Fabregas (Arsenal) – *Empics/Joe Giddens*; (centre) Frank Lampard (Chelsea) – *Action Images/Darren Walsh Livepic*; (right and background) Wayne Rooney (Manchester United) – *Action Images/Darren Walsh*.

Spine photograph: Liverpool celebrating their 2005 UEFA Champions League victory – *Empics/Tony Marshall*.

Back cover photographs: (top) Dianbobo Balde (Celtic) and Steve Thompson (Rangers) – *Action Images/Lee Smith Livepic*; (bottom) Tim Cahill (Everton) – *Empics/Martin Rickett/PA*.

Cataloguing in Publication Data is available from the British Library

ISBN 0 7553 1384 4 (hardback)
ISBN 0 7553 1385 2 (trade paperback)

Typeset by Wearset Ltd, Boldon, Tyne and Wear

Printed and bound in Great Britain by
Mackays of Chatham PLC,
Chatham, Kent

Headline's policy is to use papers that are natural, renewable and recyclable products and made from wood grown in sustainable forests. The logging and manufacturing processes are expected to conform to the environmental regulations of the country of origin.

HEADLINE BOOK PUBLISHING
A division of Hodder Headline
338 Euston Road
London NW1 3BH

www.headline.co.uk
www.hodderheadline.com

CONTENTS

INTERNATIONAL FOOTBALL

NON-LEAGUE FOOTBALL

INFORMATION AND RECORDS

FOREWORD

The football 'bible' is a fixture on my bookshelf season after season.

When I was a young trainee journalist in local newspapers, the Yearbook was already established as football's preferred source of reference. From the *Wolverhampton Chronicle*, I moved to Hayters Sports Agency and then to local radio in Liverpool.

I still view myself primarily as a journalist and accuracy is a vital part of the job. The same key rules apply now as they did then – quite simply, you've got to get it right. You need the most reliable and comprehensive information resource whether you're in the front line reporting live from the match or preparing for one of the hundreds of live games we at Sky Sports broadcast every season.

These days I'm lucky enough to work with a highly professional team of producers and researchers and it's no surprise to see the famous blue and orange spine lining the desks here at Sky Sports. Now of course there's also a red, white and blue flash on the book and it seems the perfect partnership.

Long may it continue.

Richard Keys, presenter, Sky Sports

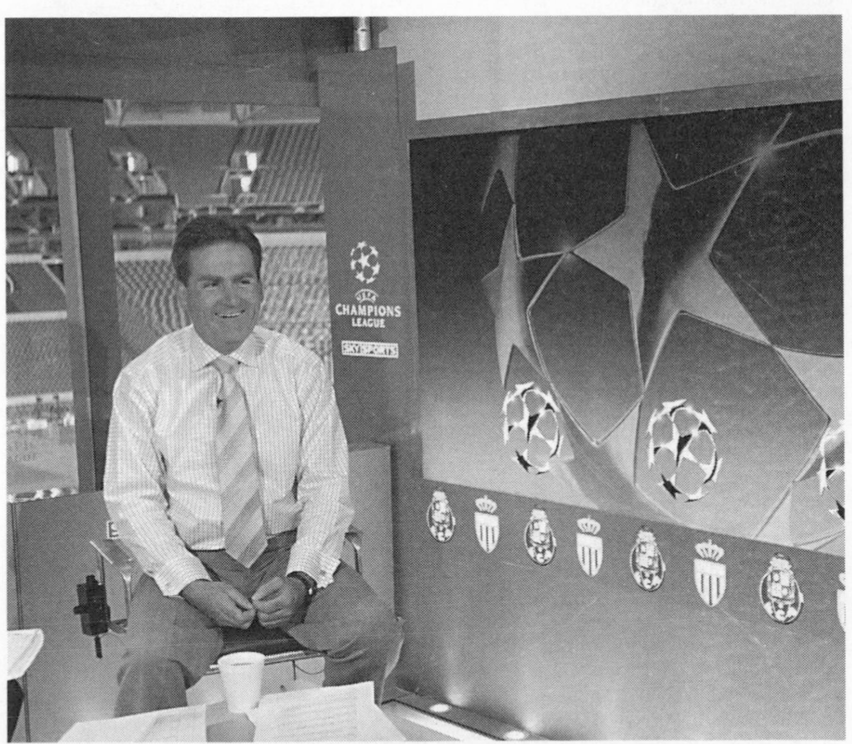

Richard Keys prepares for a Champions League match on Sky Sports.

INTRODUCTION

The 36th edition of the Yearbook, our third with new sponsors Sky Sports, has maintained its recent expansion to 1,056 pages. Once again, there is an A to Z index of names with a cross reference to the Players Directory, enabling readers to check on the whereabouts of any specific player during the 2004–05 season. The who's who style directory again provides a season-by-season account of individual player's appearances and goals. The fullest possible available details have been provided for players in this section, including all players who appeared in first-class matches.

With the continual increase in interest in non-League football, all Conference clubs have again been given the same style of recognition as the FA Premier League and Football League teams. In addition, the second echelon in the Conference North and South have featured as part of the non-league coverage.

As far as the club pages are concerned, a more uniform approach has been retained in respect of individual entries, without losing any of the essential information, including records over the previous ten seasons, latest sequences and runs of scoring and non-scoring.

Once more, every match played in the Champions League, including the qualifying competition, has full teams and line-ups. Also, with the expansion of the UEFA Cup with its group stage, there are full line-ups from that point onwards.

With the World Cup Finals to be held in Germany in 2006, the latest available results from the qualifying competition have been included, along with line-ups for all European and South American matches, plus results from all other areas of the world.

The usual detailed and varied coverage involves Scottish, Welsh and Irish football, amateur, schools, university, reserve team, extensive non-League information, awards, records and an international directory. Women's football, referees and the work of chaplains are also featured.

Transfer fees quoted in the Daily Round-up are invariably those initially mentioned when a deal is imminent. They may not reflect the figures which appear elsewhere in the edition. Moves during the summer months, together with any specific changes affecting the book appear in the Stop Press section .

The Editors would like to express their appreciation of the response from FA Premier League and Football League clubs when requesting information. Thanks are also due to Alan Elliott for the Scottish section, Tony Brown for sequences and instances of match results in the records section and Ian Nannestad for the obituaries and additional information on foreign players. Thanks are also due to John English, who provided invaluable and conscientious reading of the proofs.

ACKNOWLEDGEMENTS

The Editors would like to express appreciation of the following individuals and organisations for their co-operation: David Barber, Dawn Keleher and Gary Simmonds (Football Association), David C. Thomson (Scottish League), Heather Elliott, Dr Malcolm Brodie, Wally Goss (AFA), Rev. Nigel Sands, Ken Goldman, Grahame Lloyd, Marshall Gillespie, Valery Karpoushkin, Andrew Howe, Richard Beal, Mike Kelleher, Ester Kristiansson and Wendy McCance (Headline Book Publishing). The highest praise is due to the indefatigable and loquacious Lorraine Jerram, Headline's Managing Editor for her generosity, expertise, constant support, resilience, patience, sincerity, perspicacity and appreciation, not to mention her unfailing humour, stocism, quick-wittedness, courtesy, consideration and understated authority.

Finally sincere thanks to John Anderson, Simon Dunnington, Geoff Turner, Brian Tait, Robin Middlemiss and the staff at Wearset for their efforts in the production of this book, which was much appreciated throughout the year.

EDITORIAL

Money isn't everything, usually it isn't even enough, though you would think football had sufficient income to feed and clothe everyone in the game. Alas, too much drains away down the wrong channels when it should be filtered through to nourish the grass roots.

Yes, the finances have to be sorted. So has the lack of discipline on and off the field. There is too much verbal in-fighting among governing bodies who fail to understand we are all in the same game. Arrogance coupled with wealth can be another problem. Remember the arrogant man who said that he was never wrong. He thought he had been just once, but he was wrong! This type of attitude is also threatening the integrity of football.

Misbehaving people on and off the field are in a minority. But they are those who attract the publicity. Anti-social misdemeanours are unfortunately commonplace. Yet this is an area in which football can take the lead in restoring decent values. Players are role models whether they like it or not. What they do is seized upon by youngsters.

Despite massive publicity and desperately worthy efforts, racism remains an issue. Abuse of officials must stop, too. The pressures on everyone involved in football are enormous at the top level, but without referees it would be impossible to stage matches. Of course the man in the middle has to accept criticism. Everyone makes mistakes. However there are acceptable ways of making a point about them.

Serious concerns, too, over the number of matches players are required to play each season. Fifty years ago the European Cup of the Champions was an embryonic affair naively meant for the winners of various continental leagues. What a quaint old fashioned idea! Those misguided individuals responsible were they unaware that the rich countries could have multiple entries?

Those days the competition also started after domestic football and was almost top and tailed by the time leagues had been wrapped up. Now the Champions League and UEFA Cup start before domesticity and carries on relentlessly throughout the season. In 1955–56 there were the four divisions in England and an FA Cup competition. The old First Division had 42 matches. The FA Premier League now has 38.

True there are more domestic competitions with the League Cup and an Associate Members Cup, but the growth of the European competitions and proliferation of international matches drastically affects top players, who are invariably not included in these so-called minor competitions.

FIFA have only a partial interest in club football, UEFA simply when it applies to their own tournaments. Yet those responsible for finding the resources to pay players are being asked to reduce domestic football to accommodate more international fixtures for the very top players the governing bodies say need rest!

In 1955–56 Real Madrid played only seven games to win the European Cup. Liverpool last season needed 15. This season if they aim to repeat the feat, it will be 19, half the number of matches in the Premiership. All this after the result of the passing of the beautiful buck game between the FA and UEFA allowed the winners back in.

On 4 September it will be the 50th anniversary of the first European Cup match when Sporting Lisbon met Partizan Belgrade. Ironically that season Chelsea were denied the right to enter by an insular Football League with the excuse of fixture congestion. What a hoot given the present clutter.

Scrapping replays in cup competitions has brought in the penalty shoot-out lottery after extra time. But these additional half hours are becoming more and more irrelevant with neither team anxious to risk conceding a goal, relying on penalties as the better option. Scattered through the following pages this year are examples of finals being decided on penalties after extra time.

During normal play, the penalty kick is introduced as a sanction against a team committing a serious offence in the area. The goalkeeper must either gather the ball or dispatch it to safety, otherwise he is vulnerable to a follow-up strike. In the penalty shoot-out, the emphasis is on a reward for the successful. Moreover the goalkeeper has only to parry the ball with no fear of a rebound attempt. Because of the need to get the affair over as quickly as possible, Nelson's eye is in focus when viewing the goalkeeper's antics. So much for the spirit of the game and its Laws.

At least one player in one final and a manager in another last season admitted on the one hand that his team were holding on for penalties while on the other it was the only way in which they were going to win at all.

So, there is so little excitement in 90 or 120 minutes, penalty shoot-outs are crucial for entertainment value. Scrap extra time and double the number of penalty shots initially to ten each not five. Every outfield player has to take a kick. Also if a team has finished with ten men as a result of either injuries or dismissals, their available number has to be reduced accordingly. Arsenal were not handicapped against Manchester United despite finishing the match with ten players. Again where is the logic, the sense of fair play. It is all a circus act.

Is football heading the same way as cricket, which continually reduces the limit for matches? Will the willow game finally introduce French cricket with one batsman, four stumps and all over in no time?

UEFA are quite happy to draw lots to decide who gets in the UEFA Cup through the fair play award – are they having a joke! If not toss a coin to settle games. No, playing to a finish with the return of the golden goal or sudden death has to be the most sensible answer. Players are fitter today than ever before. It must be so – Gary Lineker has said it on television. Let them prove it. Also the approach to matches which have to be decided on play would change from the present reliance on the end lotte
The slogan should be: "On the day, but in a better way."

With Chelsea creating their own piece of club history and knocking for six a few Premier records in the process, it should be recorded that there were some other exceptional performances. Everton minus Wayne Rooney finished fourth against expectations from the experts, West Bromwich Albion avoided the curse of finishing bottom at the turn of the year.

Now here's a spooky one. At the start of the 2003–04 season, Wolves had been drawn to play Blackburn in the first game and subsequently found themselves relegated. In 2002–03 Rovers began against Sunderland who also went down. It had also happened the same way to Derby County in 2001–02. For 2004–05 the Baggies were paired with Blackburn and managed to exorcise that curse, too.

Manchester United's leading goalscorer managed only eleven goals last season. Yet Diego Forlan who was allowed to leave for Villarreal in Spain, finished the season over there not only as top scorer in the *La Liga* but also tying with Thierry Henry on 25 goals as Europe's ace marksman. Quiz question: How many League games did Forlan play for United in 2004–05. It's not a trick one – but no peeking until you guess.

A dip in attendance figures for the Premiership compared with the last couple of seasons has had the pessimists trying to find out if this is to be a trend, reciting the expense involved in a day's outing to see a match as a primary cause. Ticket pricing is just another of the problems facing supporters and merely adds to the equation of football finances touched on earlier with the solution tied up in who gets what from the revenue entering the sport. That is for all those who wish to see it.

There was much shaking of heads when Chelsea's wealth was said to have paid off with the capture of the Premiership title. The club bought foreign in abundance, but this was only part of the story. Most independent observers would agree that the improvement in the individual performances of England internationals like John Terry, Frank Lampard and Joe Cole, owed much to the shrewd coaching of Jose Mourinho. Success invariably produces jealousy and criticism in equal amounts and the Portuguese coach had it coming from all directions.

Both Sepp Blatter and Lennart Johansson, arguably two of the most powerful men in the game, have been in bother over allegations of sexism when it comes to discussing ladies playing football. Blatter suffered a verbal spanking that must have made his Herr stand on end when he said he wanted women to wear tighter kit, Johansson a similar lashing about his remarks asking female players to show off their sexual attributes on the pitch. Both might be accused of holding the wrong brief.

The disgraceful scenes at half-time during the Norwich City v Manchester City match in which one of the home officials indulged in rabble rousing was clearly the most disgraceful incident in the entire season – or so you would imagine from the publicity it received. This was no fag-ash Lil from the Pie and Mash in Letsby Avenue, Greasy Spoon or a short order nosh chef, but Delia Smith. A few more like her with spirit and passion for her team and the sport and it would be healthier for sure.

Not the best of seasons for the FA. Even before it started with "Alamgate" and finished if not with an action replay and reprise of sorts in the High Court. In the interim plenty of comings and goings at Soho Square. Lord Burns plans the third degree on the organisation while aiming to weald the chopper to the outfit and we await his recommendations with interest. However, revolutions are notorious for

Chelsea and England defender John Terry holds the PFA Player of the Year trophy. (PA/Empics)

Manchester United's Wayne Rooney (right) battles with Arsenal's Edu during the Barclays Premiership match at Old Trafford, Manchester. (PA/Empics)

axing at the top but invariably leaving few crumbs of comfort at the broken biscuit end of the food chain. The real grafters are more than likely to be the losers after any drastic measures.

The Women's European Championship held in England was not given the media coverage which one might have expected from such a competition. There remains an anti-female attitude to the sport in some quarters, though the Sports Minister was enthusiastic enough to want a professional league. Yet, one collapsed in the USA where it has a higher profile. Never fret, think of the Olympics in 2012.

Almost twenty-five years ago I said the next tactical move would be a kind of pyramid 4-3-2-1 system with a flexibility in defence when an extreme flank defender attacked and the defensive midfield player dropped back. The support strike players would tuck in the channels behind the spearhead. All this now seems positively progressive thinking gone loco with the advent of 4-5-1 with its midfield saturation.

Interesting to note that the members of the Football Writers' Association who voted on the Sky Sports Yearbook Team of the Season overwhelmingly kept their favoured system as 4-4-2. As far as 4-5-1 is concerned, when both teams adopt the formation it is scarcely white-knuckle watching stuff. Moreover our worthy scribes virtually ignored this one.

At the start of the 2004–05 season there was certainly a dearth of goals. By the end of it the chief concern was in the number of drawn matches in all four full-time professional divisions; 583 out of 2036 games. Three points for a win certainly reduced the number of games ending in stalemate in the first few years of its introduction, but doubtless the think-tank experts will be dreaming up another alteration to the points system, maybe rewarding away wins with four points.

If it was not already a difficult subject, the interpretation of the offside law continues to baffle onlookers. Successive tinkering with it has merely made a puzzle into an unsolvable problem. Just get back to where it was merely hard to follow, not impossible, please.

Next year it will be the 40th anniversary of when England triumphed at Wembley in the World Cup final against West Germany. Since then as we are painfully aware, such glory has eluded us at major international events outside of club football. There is wide opinion that at least on paper we have the best chance of emulating that feat since events of four decades ago.

We are promised a micro chip in the ball to end those goal-line disputes. What would Sir Geoff have said about that one! FIFA appear to have ruled out video evidence at present, so there will still be sufficient grey areas of controversy for the panellists to mull over. Can't wait for that.

What happens on the pitch is not so easy to predict in the wake of a series of near misses in the intervening years. There ought to be little room for error in terms of preparation. Sven has won his battle to have four weeks from the end of the domestic season until the opening of the finals. Failure and the knives will be honed at home. In Germany it will be a case of not mentioning the 5-1 or the war. Slim chance. We haven't forgotten Trafalgar.

SKY SPORTS FOOTBALL YEARBOOK HONOURS

Since Chelsea were convincing FA Premier League champions in 2004–05, it was obvious they would figure prominently in the Sky Sports Football Yearbook Honours. Nine of their players received votes, with five of them securing places in the final selection.

Forty-one different players were mentioned by the Football Writers Association members and Chelsea also had nine players among those recognised. The competition for places was as intense as ever, although there was unanimous recognition for Frank Lampard, who had been the recipient of the FWA Footballer of the Year award.

However, the fiercest competition was for the right-back position with Steve Finnan of Liverpool, Paulo Ferreira of Chelsea and Gary Neville of Manchester United evenly contesting the outcome. However, in the end, it was Finnan who narrowly gained a berth, ousting Neville from the team of the previous season.

Ashley Cole of Arsenal lost his place on the left flank to Gabriel Heinze of Manchester United. In midfield, Steven Gerrard of Liverpool retained his place but the Arsenal pairing of Patrick Vieira and Robert Pires gave way to Claude Makelele of Chelsea and his club colleague, Arjen Robben, a late arrival during the season. While John Terry kept his central defensive position, he was joined by Jamie Carragher of Liverpool, who took over from Arsenal's Sol Campbell. In goal, Petr Cech of Chelsea, who had an outstanding first season with the club, replaced Antti Niemi of Southampton. Thierry Henry was again a strong choice and was joined by Wayne Rooney of Manchester United, following his transfer from Everton.

On the managerial front, it was not surprising that Jose Mourinho became Manager of the Year, in view of Chelsea's outstanding performances, but there were votes too, for David Moyes of Everton, whose team finished fourth in the Championship, Arsene Wenger of Arsenal, who was the manager in 2003–04 and Bryan Robson, who achieved the feat of guiding West Bromwich Albion out of the relegation zone and thus defying history for a team bottom of the table at the turn of the year.

Sky Sports Football Yearbook Team of the Season 2004–05

Petr Cech
(Chelsea)

Steve Finnan *(Liverpool)* — John Terry *(Chelsea)* — Jamie Carragher *(Liverpool)* — Gabriel Heinze *(Manchester U)*

Steven Gerrard *(Liverpool)* — Frank Lampard *(Chelsea)* — Claude Makelele *(Chelsea)* — Arjen Robben *(Chelsea)*

Wayne Rooney *(Manchester U)* — Thierry Henry *(Arsenal)*

Manager:
Jose Mourinho *(Chelsea)*

Substitutes:
Ashley Cole (Arsenal)
Damien Duff (Chelsea)
Cristiano Ronaldo (Manchester U)

THE FOOTBALL RECORDS

LANDMARKS

Arsenal complete 49 unbeaten Premier League matches; Francesc Fabregas becomes the club's youngest League goalscorer at 17 years 113 days.
Thierry Henry overtakes Ian Wright's goal record and finishes the season with 137 League goals, 13 short of Cliff Bastin's record.
Chelsea record the most Premier League wins in a season at 29 and concede the fewest number of goals at 15.
Goalkeeper Petr Cech completes 1025 minutes without conceding a goal. The club also achieves the best points average of any Premier League club at 2.50 per game.
James Vaughan at 16 years 271 days is the youngest Premier League goalscorer and the youngest Everton debutant.
John McDermott extends his League appearance record at Grimsby Town to 592.
Liverpool become the first European Cup/Champions League team to retrieve a three goal deficit in the final and then win on penalties.
Ruud Van Nistelrooy overhauls Denis Law's European Cup goalscoring record of 28 goals. Record Premier League attendance at Old Trafford 67,989 v Portsmouth.
Ryan Giggs completes his 600th appearance in all matches. Sir Alex Ferguson his 1000th match in charge.
Alan Shearer becomes the first player to score 250 Premier League goals.
West Bromwich Albion complete the feat of escaping relegation, the first team in the Premier League to do so having been bottom at the turn of the year.
Michael Owen, with 32 goals, becomes England's fourth most prolific scorer.
David Healy extends his goalscoring record for Northern Ireland to 17, while Robbie Keane becomes the Republic of Ireland's leading goalscorer on 25.

THE EXPORT GAME

From the end of the 2003–04 season and into 2004–05, the movement of players has not only been incoming, but also outgoing. The following is a list of players who have moved abroad or to Scotland, either permanently, returning from loan periods or going on temporary transfers:

Alexandersson, Everton to IFK Gothenburg.
Ambrosio, Chelsea to Grasshoppers (loan).
Anderson, Grimsby T to Dundee.
Andresen, returned from loan to Stabaek from Blackburn R.
Anelka, Manchester C to Fenerbahce £7,000,000.
Armstrong, Rochdale to Q of S.
Arphexad, Coventry C to Marseille.
Babbel, Liverpool to Stuttgart.
Barnett, Portsmouth to Dundee.
Barthez, Manchester U to Marseille.
Berthelin, Crystal Palace to Mons.
Black, Blackburn R to Inverness Caley.
Brown, Colchester U to Hibernian.
Burchill, Portsmouth to Hearts.
Camara, returned from loan to Lens from Leeds U.
Carole, returned from loan to Monaco from West Ham U.
Contra, returned from loan to Atletico Madrid from WBA.
Cramb, Grimsby T to Hamilton A.
Delgado, Southampton to Aucas.
De Pedro, Blackburn R to Perugia.
Desailly, Chelsea to Al Ittihad.
Djetou, returned from loan to Parma from Fulham.
Djordjevic, Manchester U to Rangers.
Domi, returned from loan to Paris St Germain from Leeds U.
Drobny, Aston Villa to Strasbourg (loan).
Federici, Reading to Sardegna.
Forlan, Manchester U to Villarreal.
Freund, returned from loan to Kaiserslautern from Leicester C.
Garden, Notts Co to Ross Co.
Gravesen, Everton to Real Madrid £2,500,000.
Gudjonsson, returned from loan to Bursa from Wolverhampton W.
Haas, WBA to Bastia.
Hammond, Fulham to RBC (loan).
Hand, Watford to Livingston (loan).
Harte, Leeds U to Levante.
Herzig, Milton Keynes D to Berghausen.
Iversen, Wolverhampton W to Valerenga.
Iwelumo, Brighton & HA to Aachen.
Javi Moreno, returned from loan to Atletico Madrid from Bolton W.
Jeffs, Crewe Alex to IBV.
Johnston, Middlesbrough to Kilmarnock.
Kachloul, Aston Villa to Livingston
Kameni, returned from loan to Le Havre from Wolverhampton W.
Keller, Tottenham H to Moenchengladbach.
Kneissel, Chelsea to Westerlo (loan).
Konte, Cambridge U to Hibernian.
Kuduzovic, Notts Co to Sligo R.
Lilley, Boston U to Livingston.
Linderoth, Everton to FC Copenhagen.
Loran, Tranmere R to RBC.
Maccarone, Middlesbrough to Siena (loan).
Macho, Chelsea to Rapid Vienna.
Mair, Stockport Co to Dundee U.
Marshall, Aston Villa to St Johnstone.
McPhee, Port Vale to Beira Mar.
Mendieta, returned from loan to Lazio from Middlesbrough.
Miller, Bristol C to Hearts (loan).
Murphy, Middlesbrough to Hibernian.
Murray, Ipswich T to Hibernian.
Murray, Oldham Ath to Beira Mar.
Ndlovu, Sheffield U to Mamelodi Sundowns.
Owen, Liverpool to Real Madrid £8,000,000.
Pasanen, returned from loan to Ajax from Portsmouth.
Postiga, Tottenham H to Porto.
Rae, Wolverhampton W to Rangers.
Reid, Blackburn R to Ayr U.
Renton, Blackburn R to Elgin C.
Reuser, Ipswich T to Willem II.
Robertson, Bristol C to Hearts (loan).
Sakho, returned from loan to Marseille from Leeds U.
Scott, Sunderland to Q of S.
Shiels, Arsenal to Hibernian.
Silas, Wolverhampton W to Maritimo (loan).
Silva, Tottenham to Den Haag.
Skoubo, returned from loan to Moenchengladbach from WBA.
Sofiane, West Ham U to Roda JC (loan).

THE EXPORT GAME – *continued*

Stepanovs, Arsenal to Grasshoppers.
Stewart, Manchester U to Hibernian (loan).
Sutton, Millwall to Dundee (loan).
Tarnat, Manchester C to Hannover.
Tavlaridis, Arsenal to Lille.
Van Bronkhorst, Arsenal to Barcelona.
Van Buyten, returned from loan to Marseille from Manchester C.
Venus, Cambridge U to Hibernian.
Viana, Newcastle U to Sporting Lisbon (loan).
Vuoso, Manchester C to Santos Laguna.
Wales, Gillingham to Kilmarnock.
Wanchope, Manchester C to Malaga £500,000.
Wapenaar, Portsmouth to Vitesse.
Wattereus, Manchester C to Rangers £100,000.
Watt, Blackburn R to CS Brugge (loan).
Weaver, Blackburn R to CS Brugge (loan).
Whelan, Derby Co to Aberdeen.
Wiekens, Manchester C to Veendam.
Wilson, Middlesbrough to Livingston.
Wiltord, Arsenal to Lyon.
Winter, Leeds U to Aberdeen.
Woodgate, Newcastle U to Real Madrid £13,400,000.
Ziege, Tottenham H to Moenchengladbach.

Appearances and goals for players in Scotland can be found on the relevant Scottish pages.

CHAMPIONS LEAGUE AND EUROPEAN CUP RECORDS

ALL-TIME EUROPEAN CUP AND CHAMPIONS LEAGUE TOP SCORERS

Season	Player	Goals
1955–56	Milos Milutinovic (Partizan Belgrade)	8
1956–57	Dennis Viollet (Manchester United)	9
1957–58	Alfredo Di Stefano (Real Madrid)	10
1958–59	Just Fontaine (Reims)	10
1959–60	Ferenc Puskas (Real Madrid)	12
1960–61	Jose Aguas (Benfica)	11
1961–62	Alfredo Di Stefano (Real Madrid)	
	Ferenc Puskas (Real Madrid)	
	Justo Tejada (Real Madrid)	7
1962–63	Jose Altafini (AC Milan)	14
1963–64	Vladimir Kovacevic (Partizan Belgrade)	
	Ferenc Puskas (Real Madrid)	
	Alessandro Mazzola (Internazionale)	7
1964–65	Jose Torres (Benfica)	9
1965–66	Eusebio (Benfica)	
	Florian Albert (Ferencvaros)	7
1966–67	Paul Van Himst (Anderlecht)	
	Jurgen Piepenberg (Vorwaerts)	6
1967–68	Eusebio (Benfica)	6
1968–69	Denis Law (Manchester United)	9
1969–70	Mick Jones (Leeds United)	8
1970–71	Antonis Antoniadis (Panathinaikos)	10
1971–72	Sylvester Takac (Standard Liege)	
	Johan Cruyff (Ajax)	
	Lou Macari (Celtic)	5
1972–73	Gerd Muller (Bayern Munich)	11
1973–74	Gerd Muller (Bayern Munich)	9
1974–75	Gerd Muller (Bayern Munich)	6
1975–76	Josef Heynckes (Moenchengladbach)	
	Carlos Santillana (Real Madrid)	6
1976–77	Gerd Muller (Bayern Munich)	
	Franco Cucinotta (Zurich)	5
1977–78	Allan Simonsen (Moenchengladbach)	5
1978–79	Claudio Sulser (Grasshoppers)	11
1979–80	Soren Lerby (Ajax)	10
1980–81	Karl-Heinz Rummenigge (Bayern Munich)	
	Terry McDermott (Liverpool)	
	Graeme Souness (Liverpool)	6
1981–82	Dieter Hoeness (Bayern Munich)	7
1982–83	Paolo Rossi (Juventus)	6
1983–84	Viktor Sokol (Dynamo Minsk)	6
1984–85	Michel Platini (Juventus)	
	Torbjorn Nilsson (IFK Gothenburg)	7
1985–86	Torbjorn Nilsson (IFK Gothenburg)	7
1986–87	Borislav Cvetkovic (Red Star Belgrade)	7
1987–88	Rabah Madjer (Porto)	
	Jean-Marc Ferreri (Bordeaux)	
	Michel (Real Madrid)	
	Rui Aguas (Benfica)	
	Ally McCoist (Rangers)	
	Gheorghe Hagi (Steaua)	4
1988–89	Marco Van Basten (AC Milan)	10
1989–90	Romario (PSV Eindhoven)	
	Jean-Pierre Papin (Marseille)	6
1990–91	Peter Pacult (Tirol)	
	Jean-Pierre Papin (Marseille)	6
1991–92	Jean-Pierre Papin (Marseille)	7
1992–93	Romario (PSV Eindhoven)	7
1993–94	Ronald Koeman (Barcelona)	
	Wynton Rufer (Werder Bremen)	8
1994–95	George Weah (Paris St Germain)	7
1995–96	Jari Litmanen (Ajax)	9
1996–97	Ally McCoist (Rangers)	6
1997–98	Alessandro Del Piero (Juventus)	10
1998–99	Andrei Shevchenko (Dynamo Kiev)	10
1999–2000	Mario Jardel (Porto)	
	Rivaldo (Barcelona)	
	Raul (Real Madrid)	10
2000–01	Andrei Shevchenko (AC Milan)	
	Mario Jardel (Galatasaray)	9
2001–02	Ruud Van Nistelrooy (Manchester United)	10
2002–03	Ruud Van Nistelrooy (Manchester United)	14
2003–04	Fernando Morientes (Monaco)	9
2004–05	Adriano (Internazionale)	10

EUROPEAN CUP AND CHAMPIONS LEAGUE RECORDS

CHAMPIONS LEAGUE ATTENDANCES AND GOALS FROM GROUP STAGES ONWARDS

Season	*Attendances*	*Average*	*Goals*	*Games*
1992–93	873,251	34,930	56	25
1993–94	1,202,289	44,529	71	27
1994–95	2,328,515	38,172	140	61
1995–96	1,874,316	30,726	159	61
1996–97	2,093,228	34,315	161	61
1997–98	2,868,271	33,744	239	85
1998–99	3,608,331	42,451	238	85
1999–2000	5,490,709	34,973	442	157
2000–01	5,773,486	36,774	449	157
2001–02	5,417,716	34,508	393	157
2002–03	6,461,112	41,154	431	157
2003–04	4,611,214	36,890	309	125
2004–05	4,946,820	39,575	331	125

HIGHEST AVERAGE ATTENDANCE IN ONE EUROPEAN CUP SEASON
1959–60 50,545 from a total attendance of 2,780,000.

HIGHEST SCORE IN A EUROPEAN CUP MATCH
Feyenoord (Holland)12, KR Reykjavik (Iceland) 0
(First Round First Leg 1969–70)

HIGHEST AGGREGATE
Benfica (Portugal) 18, Dudelange (Luxembourg) 0
(Preliminary Round 1965–66)

MOST GOALS OVERALL
49 Alfredo Di Stefano (Real Madrid) *(1955–64)*
46 Eusebio (Benfica) *(1959–74)*
43 Raul (Real Madrid) *(1995–2003)*
36 Gerd Muller (Bayern Munich) *(1969–77)*

CHAMPIONS LEAGUE BIGGEST WINS
Juventus 7, Olympiakos 0 10.12.2003
Marseille 6, CKSA Moscow 0 17.3.93
Leeds U 6, Besiktas 0 26.9.2000
Real Madrid 6, Genk 0 25.9.2002

FIRST TEAM TO SCORE SEVEN GOALS
Paris St Germain 7, Rosenborg 2 24.10.2000

HIGHEST AGGREGATE OF GOALS
Monaco 8, La Coruna 3 05.11.2003

HIGHEST SCORING DRAW
Hamburg 4, Juventus 4 13.9.2000

GREATEST COMEBACKS
Werder Bremen beat Anderlecht 5-3 after being three goals down in 33 minutes on 8.12.1993. They scored five goals in 23 second-half minutes.
La Coruna beat Paris St Germain 4-3 after being three goals down in 55 minutes on 7.3.2001. They scored four goals in 27 second-half minutes.
Liverpool after being three goals down in the first half on 25.5.2005 in the Champions League Final. They scored three goals in five second-half minutes and won the penalty shoot-out after extra time 3-2.

MOST GOALS IN CHAMPIONS LEAGUE MATCH
4, Marco Van Basten AC Milan v IFK Gothenburg (33, 53 (pen), 61, 62 mins) 4-0 25.11.1992.
4, Simone Inzaghi Lazio v Marseille (17, 37, 38, 71 mins) 5-1 14.3.2000.
4, Ruud Van Nistelrooy Manchester U v Sparta Prague (14, 25 (pen), 60, 90 mins) 4-1 3.11.2004.

WINS WITH TWO DIFFERENT CLUBS
Miodrag Belodedici (Steaua) 1986; (Red Star Belgrade) 1991.
Ronald Koeman (PSV Eindhoven) 1988; (Barcelona) 1992.
Dejan Savicevic (Red Star Belgrade) 1991; (AC Milan) 1994.
Marcel Desailly (Marseille) 1993; (AC Milan) 1994.
Frank Rijkaard (AC Milan) 1989, 1990; (Ajax) 1995.
Vladimir Jugovic (Red Star Belgrade) 1991; (Juventus) 1996.
Didier Deschamps (Marseille) 1993; (Juventus) 1996.
Paulo Sousa (Juventus) 1996; (Borussia Dortmund) 1997.
Christian Panucci (AC Milan) 1994; (Real Madrid) 1998.
Jimmy Rimmer (Mancheser U) 1968, (Aston Villa) 1982 but as a non-playing substitute.

MOST WINS WITH DIFFERENT CLUBS
Clarence Seedorf (Ajax) 1995; (Real Madrid) 1998; (AC Milan) 2003.

MOST WINNERS MEDALS
6 Francisco Gento (Real Madrid) 1956, 1957, 1958, 1959, 1960, 1966.
5 Alfredo Di Stefano (Real Madrid) 1956, 1957, 1958, 1959, 1960.
5 Jose Maria Zarraga (Real Madrid) 1956, 1957, 1958, 1959, 1960.
4 Jose-Hector Rial (Real Madrid) 1956, 1957, 1958, 1959.
4 Marquitos (Real Madrid) 1956, 1957, 1959, 1960.
4 Phil Neal (Liverpool) 1977, 1978, 1981, 1984.

MOST GOALS SCORED IN FINALS
7 Alfredo Di Stefano (Real Madrid), 1956 (1), 1957 (1 pen), 1958 (1), 1959 (1), 1960 (3).
7 Ferenc Puskas (Real Madrid), 1960 (4), 1962 (3).

MOST FINAL APPEARANCES PER COUNTRY
Italy 24 (10 wins, 14 defeats).
Spain 19 (10 wins, 9 defeats).
Germany 13 (6 wins, 7 defeats).
England 12 (10 wins, 2 defeats).

MOST CLUB FINAL WINNERS

Real Madrid (Spain)	9	1956, 1957, 1958, 1959, 1960, 1966, 1998, 2000, 2002.
AC Milan (Italy)	6	1963, 1969, 1989, 1990, 1994, 2003.

MOST APPEARANCES IN FINAL
Real Madrid 12; AC Milan 10.

MOST EUROPEAN CUP APPEARANCES
Paolo Maldini (AC Milan)

Season	*European Cup*	*UEFA Cup*	*Super Cup*	*WCC*
1985–86	0	6	0	0
1987–88	0	2	0	0
1988–89	7	0	0	0
1989–90	8	0	2	1
1990–91	4	0	1	1
1992–93	10	0	0	0
1993–94	10	0	2	1
1994–95	11	0	1	1
1995–96	0	8	0	0
1996–97	6	0	0	0
1999–2000	6	0	0	0
2000–01	14	0	0	0
2001–02	0	4	0	0
2002–03	19	0	0	0
2003–04	9	0	1	1
2004–05	13	0	0	0
Total	117	20	7	5

MOST SUCCESSFUL MANAGER
Bob Paisley (Liverpool) 1977, 1978, 1981.

FASTEST GOALS SCORED IN CHAMPIONS LEAGUE

20.07 sec	Gilberto Silva for Arsenal at PSV Eindhoven 25 September 2002.
20.12 sec	Alessandro Del Piero for Juventus at Manchester United 1 October 1997.

MOST SUCCESSIVE CHAMPIONS LEAGUE APPEARANCES
Rosenborg (Norway) 10 1995–96 – 2004–05.

MOST SUCCESSIVE WINS IN THE CHAMPIONS LEAGUE
Barcelona (Spain) 11 2002–03.

OTHER BRITISH FOOTBALL RECORDS

ALL-TIME PREMIER LEAGUE CHAMPIONSHIP SEASONS ON POINTS AVERAGE

	Team	*Season*	*P*	*W*	*D*	*L*	*F*	*A*	*Pts*	*Pts Av*
1	Chelsea	2004–05	38	29	8	1	72	15	95	2.50
2	Manchester U	1999–2000	38	28	7	3	97	45	91	2.39
3	Arsenal	2003–04	38	26	12	0	73	26	90	2.36
4	Arsenal	2001–02	38	26	9	3	79	36	87	2.28
5	Manchester U	1993–94	42	27	11	4	80	38	92	2.19
6	Manchester U	2002–03	38	25	8	5	74	34	83	2.18
7	Manchester U	1995–96	38	25	7	6	73	35	82	2.15
8	Blackburn R	1994–95	42	27	8	7	80	39	89	2.11
9	Manchester U	2000–01	38	24	8	6	79	31	80	2.10
10	Manchester U	1998–99	38	22	13	3	80	37	79	2.07
11	Arsenal	1997–98	38	23	9	6	68	33	78	2.05
12	Manchester U	1992–93	42	24	12	6	67	31	84	2.00
13	Manchester U	1996–97	38	21	12	5	76	44	75	1.97

TOP TEN WORLD TRANSFERS

	Player	*Clubs*	*Fee (£m)*	*Year*
1	Zinedine Zidane	Juventus to Real Madrid	46.5	2001
2	Luis Figo	Barcelona to Real Madrid	37.4	2000
3	Hernan Crespo	Parma to Lazio	35.7	2000
4	Gianluigi Buffon	Parma to Juventus	34	2001
5	Christian Vieri	Lazio to Internationale	31	1999
6	Rio Ferdinand	Leeds U to Manchester U	30	2002
7	Giazka Mendieta	Valencia to Lazio	29	2001
8	Ronaldo	Internazionale to Real Madrid	28.9	2002
9	Juan Sebastian Veron	Lazio to Manchester U	28.1	2001
10	Rui Costa	Fiorentina to AC Milan	28	2001

Source: National Press.

TOP TEN BRITISH TRANSFERS (incoming only)

	Player	*Clubs*	*Fee (£m)*	*Year*
1	Rio Ferdinand	Leeds U to Manchester U	30	2002
2	Juan Sebastian Veron	Lazio to Manchester U	28.1	2001
3	Wayne Rooney	Everton to Manchester U	27	2004
4	Didier Drogba	Marseille to Chelsea	24	2004
5	Ruud Van Nistelrooy	PSV Eindhoven to Manchester U	19	2001
6	Rio Ferdinand	West Ham U to Leeds U	18	2000
7	José Antonio Reyes	Sevilla to Arsenal	17.6	2004
8	Damien Duff	Blackburn R to Chelsea	17	2003
9	Hernan Crespo	Inernazionale to Chelsea	16.8	2003
10	Ricardo Carvalho	Porto to Chelsea	16.5	2004

Source: National Press.

TOP TEN PREMIER LEAGUE AVERAGE ATTENDANCES 2004–05

1	Manchester U	67,871
2	Newcastle U	51,844
3	Manchester C	45,192
4	Liverpool	42,587
5	Chelsea	41,870
6	Arsenal	37,978
7	Aston Villa	37,354
8	Everton	36,834
9	Tottenham H	35,883
10	Middlesbrough	31,965

TOP TEN GOALSCORERS IN WORLD CUP FINAL TOURNAMENTS

1	Gerd Muller (West Germany)	1970, 74	14
2	Just Fontaine (France)	1958	13
3	Pele (Brazil)	1958, 70	12
4	Ronaldo (Brazil)	1998, 2002	12
5	Sandor Kocsis (Hungary)	1954	11
6	Jurgen Klinsmann (Germany)	1990, 98	11
7	Helmut Rahn (West Germany)	1954, 58	10
	Teofilo Cubillas (Peru)	1970, 78	10
	Grzegorz Lato (Poland)	1974, 82	10
	Gary Lineker (England)	1986, 90	10
	Gabriel Batistuta (Argentina)	1994, 2002	10

TOP TEN FOOTBALL LEAGUE AVERAGE ATTENDANCES 2004–05

1	Leeds U	29,207
2	Sunderland	28,821
3	West Ham U	27,403
4	Wolverhampton W	26,620
5	Ipswich T	25,651
6	Derby Co	25,219
7	Leicester C	24,137
8	Nottingham F	23,608
9	Sheffield W	23,100
10	Sheffield U	19,594

TOP TEN ALL-TIME ENGLAND GOALSCORERS

1	Bobby Charlton	49
2	Gary Lineker	48
3	Jimmy Greaves	44
4	Michael Owen	32
5	Tom Finney	30
6	Nat Lofthouse	30
7	Alan Shearer	30
8	Vivian Woodward	29
9	Steve Bloomer	28
10	David Platt	27

TOP TEN AVERAGE ATTENDANCES

1	Manchester United	2004–05	67,871
2	Manchester United	2003–04	67,641
3	Manchester United	2002–03	67,630
4	Manchester United	2001–02	67,586
5	Manchester United	2000–01	67,544
6	Manchester United	1999–2000	58,017
7	Manchester United	1967–68	57,552
8	Newcastle United	1947–48	56,283
9	Tottenham Hotspur	1950–51	55,509
10	Manchester United	1998–99	55,188

TOP TEN AVERAGE WORLD CUP FINAL CROWDS

1	In USA	1994	68,604
2	In Brazil	1950	60,772
3	In Mexico	1970	52,311
4	In England	1966	50,458
5	In Italy	1990	48,368
6	In Mexico	1986	46,956
7	In West Germany	1974	46,684
8	In France	1998	43,366
9	In Argentina	1978	42,374
10	In South Korea/Japan	2002	42,274

TOP TEN ALL-TIME ENGLAND CAPS

1	Peter Shilton	125
2	Bobby Moore	108
3	Bobby Charlton	106
4	Billy Wright	105
5	Bryan Robson	90
6	Kenny Sansom	86
7	Ray Wilkins	84
8	Gary Lineker	80
9	John Barnes	79
10	Stuart Pearce	78

TOP TEN PREMIERSHIP APPEARANCES

1	Gary Speed	452
2	Alan Shearer	409
3	Ryan Giggs	407
4	Gareth Southgate	402
5	David James	400
6	Teddy Sheringham	375
7	Sol Campbell	370
8	Andy Cole	367
9	Ray Parlour	366
10	Roy Keane	361

MOST GOALS FOR IN A SEASON

		Goals	Games
FA PREMIER LEAGUE			
1999–2000	Manchester U	97	38
FOOTBALL LEAGUE			
Championship			
2004–05	Ipswich T	85	46
Championship League One			
2004–05	Luton T	87	46
Championship League Two			
2004–05	Yeovil T	90	46
Division 1			
1930–31	Aston V	128	42
Division 2			
1926–27	Middlesbrough	122	42
Division 3(S)			
1927–28	Millwall	127	42
Division 3(N)			
1928–29	Bradford C	128	42
Division 3			
1961–62	QPR	111	46
Division 4			
1960–61	Peterborough U	134	46
SCOTTISH PREMIER LEAGUE			
2001–02	Celtic	94	38
SCOTTISH LEAGUE			
Premier Division			
2003–04	Celtic	105	38
1991–92	Rangers	101	44
1982–83	Dundee U	90	36
1982–83	Celtic	90	36
1986–87	Celtic	90	44
Division 1			
1957–58	Hearts	132	34
Division 2			
1937–38	Raith R	142	34
New Division 1			
1993–94	Dunfermline Ath	93	44
1981–82	Motherwell	92	39
New Division 2			
1987–88	Ayr U	95	39
New Division 3			
2004–05	Gretna	130	36

FEWEST GOALS AGAINST IN A SEASON

		Goals	Games
FA PREMIER LEAGUE			
2004–05	Chelsea	15	38
FOOTBALL LEAGUE (minimum 42 games)			
Championship			
2004–05	Wigan Ath	35	46
Championship League One			
2004–05	Luton T	48	46
Championship League Two			
2004–05	Scunthorpe U	42	46
Division 1			
1978–79	Liverpool	16	42
Division 2			
1924–25	Manchester U	23	42
2002–03	Wigan Ath	25	46
Division 3(S)			
1921–22	Southampton	21	42
Division 3(N)			
1953–54	Port Vale	21	46
Division 3			
1995–96	Gillingham	20	46
Division 4			
1980–81	Lincoln C	25	46
SCOTTISH PREMIER LEAGUE			
2001–02	Celtic	18	38
SCOTTISH LEAGUE (minimum 30 games)			
Premier Division			
1989–90	Rangers	19	36
1986–87	Rangers	23	44
1987–88	Celtic	23	44
Division 1			
1913–14	Celtic	14	38
Division 3			
1966–67	Morton	20	38
New Division 1			
1996–97	St Johnstone	23	36
1980–81	Hibernian	24	39
1993–94	Falkirk	32	44
New Division 2			
1987–88	St Johnstone	24	39
1990–91	Stirling Alb	24	39
New Division 3			
1995–96	Brechin C	21	36

FEWEST GOALS FOR IN A SEASON

		Goals	Games
FA PREMIER LEAGUE			
2002–03	Sunderland	21	38
FOOTBALL LEAGUE (minimum 42 games)			
Championship			
2004–05	Rotherham U	35	46
Championship League One			
2004–05	Port Vale	49	46
2004–05	Peterborough U	49	46
2004–05	Stockport Co	49	46
Championship League Two			
2004–05	Kidderminster H	39	46
2004–05	Cambridge U	39	46
Division 1			
1984–85	Stoke C	24	42
Division 2			
1971–72	Watford	24	42
1994–95	Leyton Orient	30	46
Division 3(S)			
1950–51	Crystal Palace	33	46
Division 3(N)			
1923–24	Crewe Alex	32	42
Division 3			
1969–70	Stockport Co	27	46
Division 4			
1981–82	Crewe Alex	29	46
SCOTTISH PREMIER LEAGUE			
2001–02	St Johnstone	24	38
SCOTTISH LEAGUE (minimum 30 games)			
Premier Division			
1988–89	Hamilton A	19	36
1991–92	Dunfermline Ath	22	44
Division 1			
1993–94	Brechin C	30	44
1966–67	Ayr U	20	34
Division 2			
1923–24	Lochgelly U	20	38
New Division 1			
1980–81	Stirling Alb	18	39
1995–96	Dumbarton	23	36
New Division 2			
1994–95	Brechin C	22	36
New Division 3			
1995–96	Alloa	26	36

MOST GOALS AGAINST IN A SEASON

		Goals	Games
FA PREMIER LEAGUE			
1993–94	Swindon T	100	42
FOOTBALL LEAGUE			
Championship			
2004–05	Crewe Alex	86	46
Championship League One			
2004–05	Stockport Co	98	46
Championship League Two			
2004–05	Kidderminster H	85	46
Division 1			
1930–31	Blackpool	125	42
Division 2			
1898–99	Darwen	141	34
Division 3(S)			
1929–30	Merthyr T	135	42
Division 3(N)			
1927–28	Nelson	136	42
Division 3			
1959–60	Accrington S	123	46
Division 4			
1959–60	Hartlepools U	109	46
SCOTTISH PREMIER LEAGUE			
1999–2000	Aberdeen	83	36
SCOTTISH LEAGUE			
Premier Division			
1984–85	Morton	100	36
1987–88	Morton	100	44
Division 1			
1931–32	Leith Ath	137	38
Division 2			
1931–32	Edinburgh C	146	38
New Division 1			
1988–89	Queen of the S	99	39
1992–93	Cowdenbeath	109	44
New Division 2			
1977–78	Meadowbank T	89	39
New Division 3			
2003–04	East Stirling	118	36

GOALS PER GAME (from 1992–93)

Goals per game	Premier Games	Premier Goals	Championship/Div 1 Games	Championship/Div 1 Goals	League One/Div 2 Games	League One/Div 2 Goals	League Two/Div 3 Games	League Two/Div 3 Goals
0	458	0	608	0	586	0	587	0
1	971	971	1346	1346	1330	1330	1328	1328
2	1283	2566	1806	3612	1823	3646	1755	3510
3	1048	3144	1501	4503	1566	4698	1509	4527
4	730	2920	1000	4000	998	3992	917	3668
5	371	1855	545	2725	522	2610	461	2305
6	195	1170	248	1488	212	1272	217	1302
7	86	602	83	581	98	686	90	630
8	36	288	29	232	26	208	31	248
9	8	72	5	45	12	108	8	72
10	0	0	3	30	3	30	2	20
11	0	0	2	22	0	0	1	11
	5186	**13588**	**7176**	**18584**	**7176**	**18580**	**6906**	**17621**

GOALS PER GAME (Football League to 1991–92)

Goals per game	Division 1 Games	Division 1 Goals	Division 2 Games	Division 2 Goals	Division 3 Games	Division 3 Goals	Division 4 Games	Division 4 Goals	Division 3(S) Games	Division 3(S) Goals	Division 3(N) Games	Division 3(N) Goals
0	2465	0	2665	0	1446	0	1438	0	997	0	803	0
1	5606	5606	5836	5836	3225	3225	3106	3106	2073	2073	1914	1914
2	8275	16550	8609	17218	4569	9138	4441	8882	3314	6628	2939	5878
3	7731	23193	7842	23526	3784	11352	4041	12123	2996	8988	2922	8766
4	6230	24920	5897	23588	2837	11348	2784	11136	2445	9780	2410	9640
5	3751	18755	3634	18170	1566	7830	1506	7530	1554	7770	1599	7995
6	2137	12822	2007	12042	769	4614	786	4716	870	5220	930	5580
7	1092	7644	1001	7007	357	2499	336	2352	451	3157	461	3227
8	542	4336	376	3008	135	1080	143	1144	209	1672	221	1768
9	197	1773	164	1476	64	576	35	315	76	684	102	918
10	83	830	68	680	13	130	8	80	33	330	45	450
11	37	407	19	209	2	22	7	77	15	165	15	165
12	12	144	17	204	1	12	0	0	7	84	8	96
13	4	52	4	52	0	0	0	0	2	26	4	52
14	2	28	1	14	0	0	0	0	0	0	0	0
17	0	0	0	0	0	0	0	0	0	0	1	17
	38164	**117060**	**38140**	**113030**	**18768**	**51826**	**18631**	**51461**	**15042**	**46577**	**14374**	**46466**

New Overall Totals (since 1992)		Totals (up to1991–92)		Complete Overall Totals (since 1888–89)	
Games	26444	Games	143119	Games	169563
Goals	68373	Goals	426420	Goals	494793

TOP TEN PREMIERSHIP GOALSCORERS

1	Alan Shearer	250	**6**	Thierry Henry	137
2	Andy Cole	175	**7**	Dwight Yorke	122
3	Robbie Fowler	154	**8**	Michael Owen	118
4	Les Ferdinand	149	**9**	Jimmy Floyd Hasselbaink	116
5	Teddy Sheringham	138	**10**	Ian Wright	113

MOST CUP GOALS IN A CAREER

FA CUP (Pre-Second World war)
Henry Cursham 48 (Notts Co)

FA CUP (post-war)
Ian Rush 43 (Chester, Liverpool)

LEAGUE CUP
Geoff Hurst 49 (West Ham U, Stoke C)
Ian Rush 49 (Chester, Liverpool, Newcastle U)

SCORED IN EVERY PREMIERSHIP GAME

Arsenal 2001–02 38 matches

MOST FA CUP FINAL GOALS

Ian Rush (Liverpool) 5: 1986(2), 1989(2), 1992(1)

MOST LEAGUE GOALS IN A SEASON

FA PREMIER LEAGUE		Goals	Games
1993–94	Andy Cole (Newcastle U)	34	40
1994–95	Alan Shearer (Blackburn R)	34	42
FOOTBALL LEAGUE			
Division 1			
1927–28	Dixie Dean (Everton)	60	39
Division 2			
1926–27	George Camsell (Middlesbrough)	59	37
Division 3(S)			
1936–37	Joe Payne (Luton T)	55	39
Division 3(N)			
1936–37	Ted Harston (Mansfield T)	55	41
Division 3			
1959–60	Derek Reeves (Southampton)	39	46
Division 4			
1960–61	Terry Bly (Peterborough U)	52	46
FA CUP			
1887–88	Jimmy Ross (Preston NE)	20	8
LEAGUE CUP			
1986–87	Clive Allen (Tottenham H)	12	9
SCOTTISH PREMIER LEAGUE			
2000–01	Henrik Larsson (Celtic)	35	37
SCOTTISH LEAGUE			
Division 1			
1931–32	William McFadyen (Motherwell)	52	34
Division 2			
1927–28	Jim Smith (Ayr U)	66	38

MOST LEAGUE GOALS IN A CAREER

FOOTBALL LEAGUE			
Arthur Rowley	*Goals*	*Games*	*Season*
WBA	4	24	1946–48
Fulham	27	56	1948–50
Leicester C	251	303	1950–58
Shrewsbury T	152	236	1958–65
	434	619	
SCOTTISH LEAGUE			
Jimmy McGrory			
Celtic	1	3	1922–23
Clydebank	13	30	1923–24
Celtic	396	375	1924–38
	410	408	

MOST HAT-TRICKS

Career
34 Dixie Dean (Tranmere R, Everton, Notts Co, England)

Division 1 (one season post-war)
6 Jimmy Greaves (Chelsea), 1960–61

Three for one team one match
West, Spouncer, Hooper, Nottingham F v Leicester Fosse, Division 1, 21 April 1909
Barnes, Ambler, Davies, Wrexham v Hartlepools U, Division 4, 3 March 1962
Adcock, Stewart, White, Manchester C v Huddersfield T, Division 2, 7 Nov 1987
Loasby, Smith, Wells, Northampton T v Walsall, Division 3S, 5 Nov 1927
Bowater, Hoyland, Readman, Mansfield T v Rotherham U, Division 3N, 27 Dec 1932

MOST GOALS IN A GAME

FA PREMIER LEAGUE	
19 Sept 1999	Alan Shearer (Newcastle U) 5 goals v Sheffield W
4 Mar 1995	Andy Cole (Manchester U) 5 goals v Ipswich T
FOOTBALL LEAGUE	
Division 1	
14 Dec 1935	Ted Drake (Arsenal) 7 goals v Aston V
Division 2	
5 Feb 1955	Tommy Briggs (Blackburn R) 7 goals v Bristol R
23 Feb 1957	Neville Coleman (Stoke C) 7 goals v Lincoln C
Division 3(S)	
13 April 1936	Joe Payne (Luton T) 10 goals v Bristol R
Division 3(N)	
26 Dec 1935	Bunny Bell (Tranmere R) 9 goals v Oldham Ath
Division 3	
16 Sept 1969	Steve Earle (Fulham) 5 goals v Halifax T
24 April 1965	Barrie Thomas (Scunthorpe U) 5 goals v Luton T
20 Nov 1965	Keith East (Swindon T) 5 goals v Mansfield T
2 Oct 1971	Alf Wood (Shrewsbury T) 5 goals v Blackburn R
10 Sept 1983	Tony Caldwell (Bolton W) 5 goals v Walsall
4 May 1987	Andy Jones (Port Vale) 5 goals v Newport Co
3 April 1990	Steve Wilkinson (Mansfield T) 5 goals v Birmingham C
5 Sept 1998	Giuliano Grazioli (Peterborough U) 5 goals v Barnet
6 April 2002	Lee Jones (Wrexham) 5 goals v Cambridge U
Division 4	
26 Dec 1962	Bert Lister (Oldham Ath) 6 goals v Southport
FA CUP	
20 Nov 1971	Ted MacDougall (Bournemouth) 9 goals v Margate (*1st Round*)
LEAGUE CUP	
25 Oct 1989	Frankie Bunn (Oldham Ath) 6 goals v Scarborough
SCOTTISH LEAGUE	
Premier Division	
17 Nov 1984	Paul Sturrock (Dundee U) 5 goals v Morton
Premier League	
23 Aug 1996	Marco Negri (Rangers) 5 goals v Dundee U
Division 1	
14 Sept 1928	Jimmy McGrory (Celtic) 8 goals v Dunfermline Ath
Division 2	
1 Oct 1927	Owen McNally (Arthurlie) 8 goals v Armadale
2 Jan 1930	Jim Dyet (King's Park) 8 goals v Forfar Ath
18 April 1936	John Calder (Morton) 8 goals v Raith R
20 Aug 1937	Norman Hayward (Raith R) 8 goals v Brechin C
SCOTTISH CUP	
12 Sept 1885	John Petrie (Arbroath) 13 goals v Bon Accord (*1st Round*)

HIGHEST WINS

Highest win in a First-Class Match
(Scottish Cup 1st Round)

Arbroath	36	Bon Accord	0	12 Sept 1885

Highest win in an International Match

England	13	Ireland	0	18 Feb 1882

Highest win in a FA Cup Match

Preston NE	26	Hyde U	0	15 Oct 1887

(1st Round)

Highest win in a League Cup Match

West Ham U	10	Bury	0	25 Oct 1983
(2nd Round, 2nd Leg)				
Liverpool	10	Fulham	0	23 Sept 1986
(2nd Round, 1st Leg)				

Highest win in an FA Premier League Match

Manchester U	9	Ipswich T	0	4 March 1995
Nottingham F	1	Manchester U	8	6 Feb 1999

Highest win in a Football League Match

Division 1 – highest home win

WBA	12	Darwen	0	4 April 1892
Nottingham F	12	Leicester Fosse	0	21 April 1909

Division 1 – highest away win

Newcastle U	1	Sunderland	9	5 Dec 1908
Cardiff C	1	Wolverhampton W	9	3 Sept 1955

Division 2 – highest home win

Newcastle U	13	Newport Co	0	5 Oct 1946

Division 2 – highest away win

Burslem PV	0	Sheffield U	10	10 Dec 1892

Division 3 – highest home win

Gillingham	10	Chesterfield	0	5 Sept 1987

Division 3 – highest away win

Barnet	1	Peterborough U	9	5 Sept 1998

Division 3(S) – highest home win

Luton T	12	Bristol R	0	13 April 1936

Division 3(S – highest away win

Northampton T	0	Walsall	8	2 Feb 1947

Division 3(N – highest home win

Stockport Co	13	Halifax T	0	6 Jan 1934

Division 3(N) – highest away win

Accrington S	0	Barnsley	9	3 Feb 1934

Division 4 – highest home win

Oldham Ath	11	Southport	0	26 Dec 1962

Division 4 – highest away win

Crewe Alex	1	Rotherham U	8	8 Sept 1973

Highest wins in a Scottish League Match

Scottish Premier Division – highest home win

Aberdeen	8	Motherwell	0	26 March 1979

Scottish Premier Division – highest away win

Hamilton A	0	Celtic	8	5 Nov 1988

Scottish Division 1 – highest home win

Celtic	11	Dundee	0	26 Oct 1895

Scottish Division 1 – highest away win

Airdrieonians	1	Hibernian	11	24 Oct 1950

Scottish Division 2 – highest home win

Airdrieonians	15	Dundee Wanderers	1	1 Dec 1894

Scottish Division 2 – highest away win

Alloa Ath	0	Dundee	10	8 March 1947

MOST HOME WINS IN A SEASON

Brentford won all 21 games in Division 3(S), 1929–30

RECORD AWAY WINS IN A SEASON

Doncaster R won 18 of 21 games in Division 3(N), 1946–47

CONSECUTIVE AWAY WINS

FA PREMIER LEAGUE

Chelsea 9 games 2004–05

FEWEST WINS IN A SEASON

FA PREMIER LEAGUE		*Wins*	*Games*
1993–94	Swindon T	5	42
2002–03	Sunderland	4	38
FOOTBALL LEAGUE			
Championship			
2004–05	Rotherham U	5	46
Championship League One			
2004–05	Stockport Co	6	46
Championship League Two			
2004–05	Cambridge U	8	46
Division 1			
1889–90	Stoke C	3	22
1912–13	Woolwich Arsenal	3	38
1984–85	Stoke C	3	42
Division 2			
1899–1900	Loughborough T	1	34
1983–84	Cambridge U	4	42
Division 3(S)			
1929–30	Merthyr T	6	42
1925–26	QPR	6	42
Division 3(N)			
1931–32	Rochdale	4	40
Division 3			
1973–74	Rochdale	2	46
Division 4			
1976–77	Southport	3	46
SCOTTISH PREMIER LEAGUE			
1998–99	Dunfermline Ath	4	36
SCOTTISH LEAGUE			
Premier Division			
1975–76	St Johnstone	3	36
1982–83	Kilmarnock	3	36
1987–88	Morton	3	44
Division 1			
1891–92	Vale of Leven	0	22
Division 2			
1905–06	East Stirlingshire	1	22
1974–75	Forfar Ath	1	38
New Division 1			
1988–89	Queen of the S	2	39
1992–93	Cowdenbeath	3	44
New Division 2			
1975–76	Forfar Ath	4	26
1987–88	Stranraer	4	39
New Division 3			
2002–03	East Stirling	2	36
2003–04	East Stirling	2	36

UNDEFEATED AT HOME OVERALL

Liverpool 85 games (63 League, 9 League Cup, 7 European, 6 FA Cup), Jan 1978–Jan 1981

UNDEFEATED IN A SEASON

FA PREMIER LEAGUE		
2003–04	Arsenal	38 games
FOOTBALL LEAGUE		
1889–90	Preston NE	22 games
Division 2		
1893–94	Liverpool	22 games

UNDEFEATED AWAY

Arsenal 19 games FA Premier League 2001–02 and 2003–04 (only Preston NE with 11 in 1888–89 had previously remained unbeaten away) in the top flight

HIGHEST AGGREGATE SCORES

Highest Aggregate Score England
Division 3(N)

Tranmere R	13	Oldham Ath	4	26 Dec 1935

Highest Aggregate Score Scotland
Division 2

Airdrieonians	15	Dundee Wanderers	1	1 Dec 1894

MOST WINS IN A SEASON

FA PREMIER LEAGUE		Wins	Games
2004–05	Chelsea	29	38
FOOTBALL LEAGUE			
Championship			
2004–05	Sunderland	29	46
Championship League One			
2004–05	Luton T	29	46
Championship League Two			
2004–05	Yeovil T	25	46
Division 1			
1960–61	Tottenham H	31	42
2001–02	Manchester C	31	46
Division 2			
1919–20	Tottenham H	32	42
Division 3(S)			
1927–28	Millwall	30	42
1929–30	Plymouth Arg	30	42
1946–47	Cardiff C	30	42
1950–51	Nottingham F	30	46
1954–55	Bristol C	30	46
Division 3(N)			
1946–47	Doncaster R	33	42
Division 3			
1971–72	Aston V	32	46
Division 4			
1975–76	Lincoln C	32	46
1985–86	Swindon T	32	46
SCOTTISH PREMIER LEAGUE			
2000–01	Celtic	31	38
2002–03	Rangers	31	38
	Celtic	31	38
2003–04	Celtic	31	38
SCOTTISH LEAGUE			
Premier Division			
1995–96	Rangers	27	36
1984–85	Aberdeen	27	36
1991–92	Rangers	33	44
1992–93	Rangers	33	44
Division 1			
1920–21	Rangers	35	42
Division 2			
1966–67	Morton	33	38
New Division 1			
1998–99	Hibernian	28	36
New Division 2			
1983–84	Forfar Ath	27	39
1987–88	Ayr U	27	39
New Division 3			
2004–05	Gretna	32	36

MOST POINTS IN A SEASON

(under old system of two points for a win)

FOOTBALL LEAGUE		Points	Games
Division 1			
1978–79	Liverpool	68	42
Division 2			
1919–20	Tottenham H	70	42
Division 3			
1971–72	Aston V	70	46
Division 3(S)			
1950–51	Nottingham F	70	46
1954–55	Bristol C	70	46
Division 3(N)			
1946–47	Doncaster R	72	42
Division 4			
1975–76	Lincoln C	74	46
SCOTTISH LEAGUE			
Premier Division			
1984–85	Aberdeen	59	36
1992–93	Rangers	73	44
Division 1			
1920–21	Rangers	76	42
Division 2			
1966–67	Morton	69	38
New Division 1			
1976–77	St Mirren	62	39
1993–94	Falkirk	66	44
New Division 2			
1983–84	Forfar Ath	63	39

MOST POINTS IN A SEASON

(three points for a win)

FA PREMIER LEAGUE		Points	Games
2004–05	Chelsea	95	38
FOOTBALL LEAGUE			
Championship			
2004–05	Sunderland	94	46
Championship League One			
2004–05	Luton T	98	46
Championship League Two			
2004–05	Yeovil T	83	46
Division 1			
1998–99	Sunderland	105	46
1984–85	Everton	90	42
1987–88	Liverpool	90	40
Division 2			
1998–99	Fulham	101	46
Division 3			
2001–02	Plymouth Arg	102	46
Division 4			
1985–86	Swindon T	102	46
SCOTTISH PREMIER LEAGUE			
2001–02	Celtic	103	38
SCOTTISH LEAGUE			
Premier League			
1995–96	Rangers	87	36
New Division 1			
1998–99	Hibernian	89	36
New Division 2			
1995–96	Stirling Alb	81	36
New Division 3			
2004–05	Gretna	98	36

FEWEST POINTS IN A SEASON

FA PREMIER LEAGUE		Points	Games
2002–03	Sunderland	19	38
FOOTBALL LEAGUE (minimum 34 games)			
Championship			
2004–05	Rotherham U	29	46
Championship League One			
2004–05	Stockport Co	26	46
Championship League Two			
2004–05	Kidderminster H	38	46
2004–05	Cambridge U*	30	46
**Deducted 10 points for entering administration.*			
Division 1			
1984–85	Stoke C	17	42
Division 2			
1904–05	Doncaster R	8	34
1899–1900	Loughborough T	8	34
Division 3			
1997–98	Doncaster R	20	46
Division 3(S)			
1924–25 & 1929–30	Merthyr T	21	42
1925–26	QPR	21	42
Division 3(N)			
1931–32	Rochdale	11	40
Division 4			
1976–77	Workington	19	46
SCOTTISH PREMIER LEAGUE			
2001–02	St Johnstone	21	38
SCOTTISH LEAGUE (minimum 30 games)			
Premier Division			
1975–76	St Johnstone	11	36
1987–88	Morton	16	44
Division 1			
1954–55	Stirling Alb	6	30
Division 2			
1936–37	Edinburgh C	7	34
New Division 1			
1988–89	Queen of the S	10	39
1992–93	Cowdenbeath	13	44
New Division 2			
1987–88	Berwick R	16	39
1987–88	Stranraer	16	39
New Division 3			
2003–04	East Stirling	8	36

FEWEST NUMBER OF DEFEATS IN A SEASON *(Minimum 20 games)*

FA PREMIER LEAGUE		Defeats	Games
2004–05	Chelsea	1	38
FOOTBALL LEAGUE			
Championship			
2004–05	Wigan Ath	9	46
2004–05	Ipswich T	9	46
Championship League One			
2004–05	Luton T	6	46
Championship League Two			
2004–05	Scunthorpe U	10	46
Division 1			
1990–91	Arsenal	1	38
1987–88	Liverpool	2	40
1968–69	Leeds U	2	42
Division 2			
1897–98	Burnley	2	30
1905–06	Bristol C	2	38
1963–64	Leeds U	3	42
2002–03	Wigan Ath	4	46
Division 3			
1966–67	QPR	5	46
1989–90	Bristol R	5	46
1997–98	Notts Co	5	46
Division 3(S)			
1921–22	Southampton	4	42
1929–30	Plymouth Arg	4	42
Division 3(N)			
1953–54	Port Vale	3	46
1946–47	Doncaster R	3	42
1923–24	Wolverhampton W	3	42
Division 4			
1975–76	Lincoln C	4	46
1981–82	Sheffield U	4	46
1981–82	Bournemouth	4	46
SCOTTISH PREMIER LEAGUE			
2001–02	Celtic	1	38
SCOTTISH LEAGUE			
Premier Division			
1995–96	Rangers	3	36
1987–88	Celtic	3	44
Division 1			
1920–21	Rangers	1	42
Division 2			
1956–57	Clyde	1	36
1962–63	Morton	1	36
1967–68	St Mirren	1	36
New Division 1			
1975–76	Partick T	2	26
1976–77	St Mirren	2	39
1992–93	Raith R	4	44
1993–94	Falkirk	4	44
New Division 2			
1975–76	Raith R	1	26
1975–76	Clydebank	3	26
1983–84	Forfar Ath	3	39
1986–87	Raith R	3	39
1998–99	Livingston	3	36
New Division 3			
2004–05	Gretna	2	36

NO DEFEATS IN A SEASON

FA PREMIER LEAGUE		
2003–04	Arsenal	won 26, drew 12
FOOTBALL LEAGUE		
Division 1		
1888–89	Preston NE	won 18, drew 4
Division 2		
1893–94	Liverpool	won 22, drew 6
SCOTTISH LEAGUE DIVISION 1		
1898–99	Rangers	won 18

MOST LEAGUE MEDALS

Phil Neal (Liverpool) 8: 1976, 1977, 1979, 1980, 1982, 1983, 1984, 1986
Alan Hansen (Liverpool) 8: 1979, 1980, 1982, 1983, 1984, 1986, 1988, 1990
Ryan Giggs (Manchester U) 8: 1993, 1994, 1996, 1997, 1999, 2000, 2001, 2003

MOST DEFEATS IN A SEASON

FA PREMIER LEAGUE		Defeats	Games
1994–95	Ipswich T	29	42
FOOTBALL LEAGUE			
Championship			
2004–05	Rotherham U	27	46
Championship League One			
2004–05	Stockport Co	32	46
Championship League Two			
2004–05	Kidderminster H	28	46
Division 1			
1984–85	Stoke C	31	42
2003–04	Wimbledon	33	46
Division 2			
1938–39	Tranmere R	31	42
1992–93	Chester C	33	46
2000–01	Oxford U	33	46
Division 3			
1997–98	Doncaster R	34	46
Division 3(S)			
1924–25	Merthyr T	29	42
1952–53	Walsall	29	46
1953–54	Walsall	29	46
Division 3(N)			
1931–32	Rochdale	33	40
Division 4			
1987–88	Newport Co	33	46
SCOTTISH PREMIER LEAGUE			
2001–02	St Johnstone	27	38
SCOTTISH LEAGUE			
Premier Division			
1984–85	Morton	29	36
Division 1			
1920–21	St Mirren	31	42
Division 2			
1962–63	Brechin C	30	36
1923–24	Lochgelly	30	38
New Division 1			
1988–89	Queen of the S	29	39
1995–96	Dumbarton	31	36
1992–93	Cowdenbeath	34	44
New Division 2			
1987–88	Berwick R	29	39
New Division 3			
2003–04	East Stirling	32	36

MOST DRAWN GAMES IN A SEASON

FA PREMIER LEAGUE		Draws	Games
1993–94	Manchester C	18	42
1993–94	Sheffield U	18	42
1994–95	Southampton	18	42
FOOTBALL LEAGUE			
Championship			
2004–05	Wolverhampton W	21	46
2004–05	Leicester C	21	46
Championship League One			
2004–05	Barnsley	19	46
Championship League Two			
2004–05	Bristol R	21	46
Division 1			
1978–79	Norwich C	23	42
Division 3			
1997–98	Cardiff C	23	46
1997–98	Hartlepool U	23	46
Division 4			
1986–87	Exeter C	23	46
SCOTTISH LEAGUE			
Premier Division			
1993–94	Aberdeen	21	44
New Division 1			
1986–87	East Fife	21	44

LONGEST WINNING SEQUENCE

FA PREMIER LEAGUE	*Team*	*Games*
2001–02 and 2002–03	Arsenal	14
FOOTBALL LEAGUE		
Division 1		
1959–60 (2) and 1960–61 (11)	Tottenham H	13
1891–92	Preston NE	13
1891–92	Sunderland	13
Division 2		
1904–05	Manchester U	14
1905–06	Bristol C	14
1950–51	Preston NE	14
Division 3		
1985–86	Reading	13
FROM SEASON'S START		
Division 1		
1960–61	Tottenham H	11
1992–93	Newcastle U	11
2000–01	Fulham	11
Division 3		
1985–86	Reading	13
SCOTTISH LEAGUE		
Premier League		
2003–04	Celtic	25

LONGEST SEQUENCE OF CONSECUTIVE SCORING (Individual)

FA PREMIER LEAGUE		
Ruud Van Nistelroy (Manchester U)	15 in 10 games	2003–04
FOOTBALL LEAGUE RECORD		
Tom Phillipson (Wolverhampton W)	23 in 13 games	1926–27

LONGEST UNBEATEN SEQUENCE

FA PREMIER LEAGUE	*Team*	*Games*
May 2003–October 2004	Arsenal	49
FOOTBALL LEAGUE		
Division 1		
Nov 1977–Dec 1978	Nottingham F	42

LONGEST UNBEATEN CUP SEQUENCE

Liverpool	25 rounds	League/Milk Cup	1980–84

LONGEST UNBEATEN SEQUENCE IN A SEASON

FA PREMIER LEAGUE	*Team*	*Games*
2003–04	Arsenal	38
FOOTBALL LEAGUE		
Division 1		
1920–21	Burnley	30

LONGEST UNBEATEN START TO A SEASON

FA PREMIER LEAGUE	*Team*	*Games*
2003–04	Arsenal	38
FOOTBALL LEAGUE	*Team*	*Games*
Division 1		
1973–74	Leeds U	29
1987–88	Liverpool	29

LONGEST SEQUENCE WITHOUT A WIN IN A SEASON

FOOTBALL LEAGUE	*Team*	*Games*
Division 2		
1983–84	Cambridge U	31

LEAGUE CHAMPIONSHIP HAT-TRICKS

Huddersfield T	1923–24 to 1925–26
Arsenal	1932–33 to 1934–35
Liverpool	1981–82 to 1983–84
Manchester U	1998–99 to 2000–01

LONGEST SEQUENCE WITHOUT A WIN FROM SEASON'S START

FOOTBALL LEAGUE	*Team*	*Games*
Championship		
2004–05	Rotherham U	20
Division 4		
1970–71	Newport Co	25

LONGEST SEQUENCE OF CONSECUTIVE DEFEATS

FOOTBALL LEAGUE	*Team*	*Games*
Division 2		
1898–99	Darwen	18

A CENTURY OF LEAGUE AND CUP GOALS IN CONSECUTIVE SEASONS

George Camsell	*League*	*Cup*	*Season*
Middlesbrough	59	5	1926–27
(101 goals)	33	4	1927–28

(Camsell's cup goals were all scored in the FA Cup.)

Steve Bull			
Wolverhampton W	34	18	1987–88
(102 goals)	37	13	1988–89

(Bull had 12 in the Sherpa Van Trophy, 3 Littlewoods Cup, 3 FA Cup in 1987–88; 11 Sherpa Van Trophy, 2 Littlewoods Cup in 1988–89.)

PENALTIES

Most in a Season (individual)

Division 1	*Goals*	*Season*
Francis Lee (Manchester C)	13	1971–72

Most awarded in one game

Five Crystal Palace (4 – 1 scored, 3 missed) v Brighton & HA (1 scored), Div 2 1988–89

Most saved in a Season

Division 1		
Paul Cooper (Ipswich T)	8 (of 10)	1979–80

GOALKEEPING RECORDS

(without conceding a goal)

BRITISH RECORD (all competitive games)
Chris Woods, Rangers, in 1196 minutes from 26 November 1986 to 31 January 1987.

FOOTBALL LEAGUE
Steve Death, Reading, 1103 minutes from 24 March to 18 August 1979.

MOST SUCCESSFUL MANAGERS

Sir Alex Ferguson CBE
Manchester U
16 major trophies in 14 seasons:
8 Premier League, 5 FA Cup, 1 European Cup, 1 Cup-Winners' Cup, 1 League Cup.

Aberdeen
1976–86 – 9 trophies:
3 League, 4 Scottish Cup, 1 League Cup, 1 Cup-Winners' Cup.

Bob Paisley
Liverpool
1974–83 – 13 trophies:
6 League, 3 European Cup, 3 League Cup, 1 UEFA Cup.

MOST LEAGUE APPEARANCES (750+ matches)

1005 Peter Shilton (286 Leicester City, 110 Stoke City, 202 Nottingham Forest, 188 Southampton, 175 Derby County, 34 Plymouth Argyle, 1 Bolton Wanderers, 9 Leyton Orient) 1966–97

931 Tony Ford (355 Grimsby T, 9 Sunderland (loan), 112 Stoke C, 114 WBA, 68 Grimsby T, 5 Bradford C (loan), 76 Scunthorpe U, 103 Mansfield T, 89 Rochdale) 1975–2002

909 Graeme Armstrong (204 Stirling A, 83 Berwick R, 353 Meadowbank T, 268 Stenhousemuir, 1 Alloa) 1975–2001

863 Tommy Hutchison (165 Blackpool, 314 Coventry City, 46 Manchester City, 92 Burnley, 178 Swansea City, 68 Alloa) 1965–91

824 Terry Paine (713 Southampton, 111 Hereford United) 1957–77

790 Neil Redfearn (35 Bolton W, 10 Lincoln C (loan), 90 Lincoln C, 46 Doncaster R, 57 Crystal Palace, 24 Watford, 62 Oldham Ath, 292 Barnsley, 30 Charlton Ath, 17 Bradford C, 22 Wigan Ath, 42 Halifax T, 54 Boston U, 9 Rochdale) 1982–2004

782 Robbie James (484 Swansea C, 48 Stoke C, 87 QPR, 23 Leicester C, 89 Bradford C, 51 Cardiff C) 1973–94

777 Alan Oakes (565 Manchester C, 211 Chester C, 1 Port Vale) 1959–84

771 John Burridge (27 Workington, 134 Blackpool, 65 Aston Villa, 6 Southend U (loan), 88 Crystal Palace, 39 QPR, 74 Wolverhampton W, 6 Derby Co (loan), 109 Sheffield U, 62 Southampton, 67 Newcastle U, 65 Hibernian, 3 Scarborough, 4 Lincoln C, 3 Aberdeen, 3 Dumbarton, 3 Falkirk, 4 Manchester C, 3 Darlington, 6 Queen of the South) 1968–96

770 John Trollope (all for Swindon Town) 1960–80†

764 Jimmy Dickinson (all for Portsmouth) 1946–65

761 Roy Sproson (all for Port Vale) 1950–72

760 Mick Tait (64 Oxford U, 106 Carlisle U, 33 Hull C, 240 Portsmouth, 99 Reading, 79 Darlington, 139 Hartlepool U) 1975–97

758 Ray Clemence (48 Scunthorpe United, 470 Liverpool, 240 Tottenham Hotspur) 1966–87

758 Billy Bonds (95 Charlton Ath, 663 West Ham U) 1964–88

757 Pat Jennings (48 Watford, 472 Tottenham Hotspur, 237 Arsenal) 1963–86

757 Frank Worthington (171 Huddersfield T, 210 Leicester C, 84 Bolton W, 75 Birmingham C, 32 Leeds U, 19 Sunderland, 34 Southampton, 31 Brighton & HA, 59 Tranmere R, 23 Preston NE, 19 Stockport Co) 1966–88

† record for one club

CONSECUTIVE
401 Harold Bell (401 Tranmere R; 459 in all games) 1946–55

FA CUP
88 Ian Callaghan (79 Liverpool, 7 Swansea C, 2 Crewe Alex)

MOST SENIOR MATCHES
1390 Peter Shilton (1005 League, 86 FA Cup, 102 League Cup, 125 Internationals, 13 Under-23, 4 Football League XI, 20 European Cup, 7 Texaco Cup, 5 Simod Cup, 4 European Super Cup, 4 UEFA Cup, 3 Screen Sport Super Cup, 3 Zenith Data Systems Cup, 2 Autoglass Trophy, 2 Charity Shield, 2 Full Members Cup, 1 Anglo-Italian Cup, 1 Football League play-offs, 1 World Club Championship)

YOUNGEST PLAYERS

FA Premier League appearance
Aaron Lennon, 16 years 129 days, Leeds U v Tottenham H, 23.8.2003.

FA Premier League scorer
James Vaughan, 16 years 271 days, Everton v Crystal Palace 10.4.2005

Football League appearance
Albert Geldard, 15 years 158 days, Bradford Park Avenue v Millwall, Division 2, 16.9.29; and
Ken Roberts, 15 years 158 days, Wrexham v Bradford Park Avenue, Division 3N, 1.9.51
If leap years are included, Ken Roberts was 157 days

Football League scorer
Ronnie Dix, 15 years 180 days, Bristol Rovers v Norwich City, Division 3S, 3.3.28.

Division 1 appearance
Derek Forster, 15 years 185 days, Sunderland v Leicester City, 22.8.64.

Division 1 scorer
Jason Dozzell, 16 years 57 days as substitute Ipswich Town v Coventry City, 4.2.84

Division 1 hat-tricks
Alan Shearer, 17 years 240 days, Southampton v Arsenal, 9.4.88
Jimmy Greaves, 17 years 10 months, Chelsea v Portsmouth, 25.12.57

FA Cup appearance (any round)
Andy Awford, 15 years 88 days as substitute Worcester City v Boreham Wood, 3rd Qual. rd, 10.10.87

FA Cup proper appearance
Lee Holmes, 15 years 277 days, Derby Co v Brentford 4.1.2003

FA Cup Final appearance
Curtis Weston, 17 years 119 days, Millwall v Manchester U, 2004

FA Cup Final scorer
Norman Whiteside, 18 years 18 days, Manchester United v Brighton & Hove Albion, 1983

FA Cup Final captain
David Nish, 21 years 212 days, Leicester City v Manchester City, 1969

League Cup Final scorer
Norman Whiteside, 17 years 324 days, Manchester United v Liverpool, 1983

League Cup Final captain
Barry Venison, 20 years 7 months 8 days, Sunderland v Norwich City, 1985

OLDEST PLAYERS

FA Premier League appearance
John Burridge 43 years 5 months, Manchester C v QPR 14.5.1995

Football League appearance
Neil McBain, 52 years 4 months, New Brighton v Hartlepools United, Div 3N, 15.3.47 (McBain was New Brighton's manager and had to play in an emergency)

Division 1 appearance
Stanley Matthews, 50 years 5 days, Stoke City v Fulham, 6.2.65

RECORD ATTENDANCES

FA PREMIER LEAGUE		
67,989	Manchester U v Portsmouth, Old Trafford	26.2.2005
FOOTBALL LEAGUE		
83,260	Manchester U v Arsenal, Maine Road	17.1.1948
SCOTTISH LEAGUE		
118,567	Rangers v Celtic, Ibrox Stadium	2.1.1939
FA CUP FINAL		
126,047*	Bolton W v West Ham U, Wembley	28.4.1923
EUROPEAN CUP		
135,826	Celtic v Leeds U, semi-final at Hampden Park	15.4.1970
SCOTTISH CUP		
146,433	Celtic v Aberdeen, Hampden Park	24.4.37
WORLD CUP		
199,854†	Brazil v Uruguay, Maracana, Rio	16.7.50

* It has been estimated that as many as 70,000 more broke in without paying.
† 173,830 paid.

SENDINGS-OFF

SEASON	
451 (League alone) *(Before rescinded cards taken into account)*	2003–04
DAY	
19 (League)	13 Dec 2003
FA CUP FINAL	
Kevin Moran, Manchester U v Everton	1985
Jose Antonio Reyes, Arsenal v Manchester U	2005
QUICKEST	
Walter Boyd, Swansea C v Darlington Div 3 as substitute in zero seconds	23 Nov 1999
MOST IN ONE GAME	
Five: Chesterfield (2) v Plymouth Arg (3)	22 Feb 1997
Five: Wigan Ath (1) v Bristol R (4)	2 Dec 1997
Five: Exeter C (3) v Cambridge U (2)	23 Nov 2002
MOST IN ONE TEAM	
Wigan Ath (1) v Bristol R (4)	2 Dec 1997
Hereford U (4) v Northampton T (0)	11 Nov 1992

RED CARD ANOMALIES 2004–05

Ferguson of Blackburn Rovers received two yellow cards on 21 August 2004 but the referee did not send him off.

On 5 February Roberts of Tranmere Rovers was dismissed. It was a case of mistaken identity as Taylor was disciplined.

There were four examples of players sent off who were not disciplined:

Clarke (Stoke C), 1 January
Gray (Southend U) 8 August
Lewis (Preston NE) 21 September (Carling Cup)
Pilkington (Port Vale) 18 September

PREMIER LEAGUE EVER-PRESENT CLUBS

	P	*W*	*D*	*L*	*F*	*A*	*Pts*
Manchester U	506	314	118	74	985	455	1060
Arsenal	506	269	139	98	843	451	946
Liverpool	506	240	129	137	811	527	849
Chelsea	506	232	143	131	776	534	839
Aston Villa	506	193	146	167	626	577	725
Tottenham H	506	177	132	197	663	694	663
Everton	506	163	138	205	617	690	627
Southampton	506	150	137	219	598	738	587

INTERNATIONAL RECORDS

MOST GOALS IN AN INTERNATIONAL

Record/World Cup	Archie Thompson (Australia) 13 goals v American Samoa	11.4.2001
England	Malcolm Macdonald (Newcastle U) 5 goals v Cyprus, at Wembley	16.4.1975
	Willie Hall (Tottenham H) 5 goals v Ireland, at Old Trafford	16.11.1938
	Steve Bloomer (Derby Co) 5 goals v Wales, at Cardiff	16.3.1896
	Howard Vaughton (Aston Villa) 5 goals v Ireland, at Belfast	18.2.1882
Northern Ireland	Joe Bambrick (Linfield) 6 goals v Wales, at Belfast	1.2.1930
Wales	John Price (Wrexham) 4 goals v Ireland, at Wrexham	25.2.1882
	Mel Charles (Cardiff C) 4 goals v Ireland, at Cardiff	11.4.1962
	Ian Edwards (Chester) 4 goals v Malta, at Wrexham	25.10.1978

MOST GOALS IN AN INTERNATIONAL CAREER

		Goals	*Games*
England	Bobby Charlton (Manchester U)	49	106
Scotland	Denis Law (Huddersfield T, Manchester C, Torino, Manchester U)	30	55
	Kenny Dalglish (Celtic, Liverpool)	30	102
Northern Ireland	David Healy (Manchester U, Preston NE)	17	43
Wales	Ian Rush (Liverpool, Juventus)	28	73
Republic of Ireland	Robbie Keane (Wolverhampton W, Coventry C, Internazionale, Leeds U, Tottenham H)	25	61

HIGHEST SCORES

Record/World Cup Match	Australia	31	American Samoa	0	2001
European Championship	Spain	12	Malta	1	1983
Olympic Games	Denmark	17	France	1	1908
	Germany	16	USSR	0	1912
Other International Match	Libya	21	Oman	0	1966
European Cup	Feyenoord	12	K R Reykjavik	2	1969
European Cup-Winners' Cup	Sporting Lisbon	16	Apoel Nicosia	1	1963
Fairs & UEFA Cups	Ajax	14	Red Boys	0	1984

GOALSCORING RECORDS

World Cup Final	Geoff Hurst (England) 3 goals v West Germany	1966
World Cup Final tournament	Just Fontaine (France) 13 goals	1958
Career	Artur Friedenreich (Brazil) 1329 goals	1910–30
	Pele (Brazil) 1281 goals	*1956–78
	Franz 'Bimbo' Binder (Austria, Germany) 1006 goals	1930–50
World Cup Finals fastest	Hakan Sukur (Turkey) 10.8 secs v South Korea	2002

**Pele subsequently scored two goals in Testimonial matches making his total 1283.*

MOST CAPPED INTERNATIONALS IN THE BRITISH ISLES

England	Peter Shilton	125 appearances	1970–90
Northern Ireland	Pat Jennings	119 appearances	1964–86
Scotland	Kenny Dalglish	102 appearances	1971–86
Wales	Neville Southall	92 appearances	1982–97
Republic of Ireland	Steve Staunton	102 appearances	1988–2002

LONDON INTERNATIONAL VENUES

Eleven different venues in the London area have staged full England international games: Kennington Oval, Richmond Athletic Ground, Queen's Club, Crystal Palace, Craven Cottage, The Den, Stamford Bridge, Highbury, Wembley, Selhurst Park and White Hart Lane.

DAILY ROUND-UP 2004–05

JULY 2004

FIFA sub-standard ... Comings and goings in FA scandal ... Drogba costs Chelsea £24m ... Copa win for Brazil on penalties ... Klinsmann in for Germany ... Van Basten for the Dutch.

5 Newcastle with Butt in their sights now go for Kluivert. Eric Black expected to join Birmingham as coach. MK Dons erase Wimbledon memories at last with new look. Trapattoni is new Benfica coach. Boston hope for Gascoigne. Bernard Stange, German coach of Iraq, resigns on insurgent worries. BBC easily won ratings war with ITV 3-1 over Euro 2004.

6 Everton tempt Rooney with record offer. Criticism forces Advocaat out as Dutch coach. Boro get Reiziger free from Barcelona. Desailly quits Chelsea.

7 FL clubs paid agents £1.4m in six months. Hoddle eyeing French connection. Roberto Mancini is new Inter coach. Everton–Liverpool share issue still on the cards.

8 With Viduka signed for £4.5m, Boro will add Hasselbaink. Venables back as Aussie boss. Peter Taylor to become England U-21 chief part-time. Stuart Pearce is Man City coach replacing retired Arthur Cox.

9 Spurs cop Sean Davis from Fulham, Pedro Mendes from Porto. Mass exodus at Leeds continues with Harte Spain bound at Levante. Didier Drogba might break English transfer record if Chelsea sign him from Marseille. Stanic retires with injury.

10 Man Utd discount Rooney bid as Everton hint at captain's role. Ref Walton quits Fulham–Watford friendly after 28 subs used!

11 Intertoto win for Cork against NEC Breda. Forlan hits spectacular Uruguay goal in Copa America and Mexico shake Argentina with 1-0 win. Greek coach Rehhagel snubs German approach.

12 Loan-star Carlton Cole goes to Villa. Florentino Perez re-elected as Real president, but denies Rooney interest. Leeds managing director David Richmond resigns. Hoddle fails to make the cut in France.

13 FIFA back down on unlimited subs in friendlies – outside of internationals. Mills moves from Leeds to Man City. Ch Lge and UEFA Cup opening salvos.

14 QPR bankrolled by foreign investment. Spurs ripe for takeover. Ch Lge: Linfield lose 1-0 to HJK, Rhyl 4-0 down in Riga, but Shelbourne draw 2-2 in Reykjavik.

15 UEFA Cup: Longford lose goal in Vaduz, Portadown held by Zalgiris and Icelanders edge Haverfordwest by the minimum. Bohs goalless with Levadia, TNS 2-0 down in Vaxjo and Glentoran all square with Allianssi. Paraguay beat Brazil 2-1 in Copa. FA to step up drug testing. Stoitchkov is new Bulgarian coach. Frei gets three man ban for Swiss spitting episode against Gerrard in Euro 2004.

16 Trevor Birch resigns after six weeks at Everton. Andy Cole joins Fulham. Copa: Ten-man Uruguay overturn Paraguay, ten-man Argentina edge hosts Peru and Colombia join them in semis after 2-0 v Costa Rica. Libyan interest in Liverpool.

17 Jeffers treble in Arsenal 10-1 romp at Barnet, Chelsea held at Oxford, Palace nap hand at Glentoran.

18 Wenger confident of keeping Vieira. Cork lose first leg 3-1 in Nantes. Celtic win 2-0 at Fulham, Newcastle held 1-1 by Kit Chee!

19 Drogba deal agreed at £24m, Tiago expected from Benfica for £10m taking Chelsea under Mourinho to £74.2m and Abramovich overall to £195m. Brazil coast to 4-0 win over Mexico and complete semi line-up. Simon Jordan not to sell Palace as Gaddafi link looks unlikely. Man Utd to court Glazer on US tour. FA secretary Faria Alam, through solicitor, denies affair with Eriksson.

20 Veterans Speed (to Bolton) and Keown (to Leicester) find new homes. Liverpool parade record £14m signing Djibril Cisse from Auxerre.

21 Kluivert said to be on £65,000 a week at Newcastle. Solskjaer knee injury nightmare. Argentina's 3-0 Copa win over Colombia. Ch Lge: Linfield and Rhyl out but Shelbourne go through on away goals. Man Utd likely to start without Olympic bound Heinze and Ronaldo.

22 Cahill signs for Everton for £2m. Thomas Helveg, Inter to Norwich. Parlour moves to Boro. England will play four of five home WC games at Old Trafford. FL want transfer window dispensation. Brazil beat Uruguay on penalties to reach Copa final against Argentina.

23 Scolari says he refused Everton offer, but the club denies it. Liverpool leave Diouf out of touring squad.

24 Santini still seeking first Spurs pre-season win after 2-2 at Hull. Chelsea win 4-2 at Celtic, Arsenal 2-1 at Graz. FA issue statement confirming Alam affairs with Mark Palios and Eriksson.

25 *News of the World* exposes alleged deal to protect Palios at Sven's expense. Brazil win on penalties again in Copa final, Uruguay take third place 2-1 over Colombia. Spain win UEFA U-19 title 1-0 v Turkey. Cork pop out of Intertoto. Man Utd lose on penalties themselves in Chicago against Bayern Munich.

26 Blatter warns top players could be driven to drugs by massive fixture commitments. Klinsmann, 49, is new German coach. Now Brooking questions Eriksson's football tactics.

27 FA to hold enquiry over 'Alamgate', as speculation grows over Sven's future. Gaunt Gascoigne has an hour with Boston. Ricardo Carvalho, Chelsea's latest £19.85 from Porto. Papa Bouba Diop joins Fulham. Instant ban for red cards. Rebrov now under the Hammers. Ch Lge: Georgia's WIT not in evidence as Wisla's eight goals testify there. UEFA Cup: Bohemians out after losing to Levadia at home.

28 Eriksson facing the chopper. Man Utd under fire in States for sub-standard approach to so-called Champions World series. Ch Lge: Shelbourne earn gritty draw in Split. Statistics on their head: though only a third of clubs in England and Scotland replied, a survey revealed two-thirds expect to make a loss! PL teams will shake hands before games.
29 Eriksson fights back in 'Alamgate' row as Becks pledges support. Van Basten is new Dutch coach. Sir Alex flies in stars. UEFA Cup: TNS, Longford, Haverfordwest all out but Glentoran get through.
30 Bookies make Sven odds-on to stay and LMA will back him in any legal battle. Chelsea win scrap with Roma 3-0 in Pittsburgh. Robbie Keane out with ankle injury for Spurs. Liverpool green light for new ground – not sharing with Everton.
31 Third successive defeat for Man Utd – on penalties again v AC Milan. Newcastle beat Rangers 4-2, Shearer withdrawn after booking. Spurs win at Forest. Palace lose 3-0 to QPR. Bell's Cup starts in Scotland: relegated Partick beat Brechin 3-0. In centenary re-match of Corinthians 11 Man Utd 3, a Utd Xl gain 3-1 revenge.

AUGUST 2004

Palios out, Sven survives at FA ... Owen gets Real ... Record Premier attendance ... Arsenal's unbeaten record ... Sir Bob axed ... Rooney to Man Utd for £27m.

1 Palios resigns and PR man Colin Gibson the alleged broker of the NOW revealed deal expected to go too. Gascoigne released from hospital after food poisoning scare.
2 Sir Bobby unlikely to be given further Newcastle tenure after this season.
3 Scholes quits England international scene. Real and Arsenal claim Vieira deal at £23m. Chelsea lose 3-2 to AC Milan in Philadelphia. Man Utd beat PSV 1-0 in Vodafone Cup game at Old Trafford, Van Nistelrooy returning to action.
4 Ch Lge: Shelbourne beat Hajduk. Liverpool beat Roma 2-1 in another Champions World game in New Jersey.
5 FA say no case to answer for Eriksson! Gibson resignation accepted. Now Van Nistelrooy has hernia problem. Kezman sending off in USA for Chelsea leads to three-match ban.
6 Rooney to miss crucial England games after his Euro injury. Mark Wright quits as Chester boss.
7 CCC starts: Leeds edge Derby with 30,459 present, Dublin red-carded against Hammers on Leicester bow before next best 30,231. Coventry two-timers shake Sunderland. CC1: Most of 24,138 at Sheff Wed unhappy with Colchester's 3-0 triumph. Only 4720 see MK Dons draw with Barnsley. CC2: Promoted Chester draw at Notts, but Shrewsbury lose at home to Lincoln. Goals in short supply – 84 in 35 games. SPL: Rangers drop points already in goalless draw at Aberdeen. SL: Partick losing opener, high fives for Stirling, Gretna and Peterhead. Early swipe by Sir Alex against Arsenal. Spurs and Palace suffer friendly fire against Cagliari and Sampdoria respectively.
8 First blood for Vieira-less Arsenal in 3-1 CM victory over Man Utd. CCC: demoted Wolves lose at Stoke.
9 Kezman red-card overturned – so much for instant suspension. Spurs Carr off to Newcastle. Leeds and Stoke suspended fines for indiscipline, but Man City–Leicester mass brawl in April receives £5000 and £3000 sanctions respectively. Webber double as Watford beat QPR 3-0.
10 Ch Lge: Owen bench mark leaves way open for Real move as Liverpool go 2-0 up in Graz; Rangers lose odd goal in three at CSKA Moscow. CCC: no 100 percent teams already. Veteran Sheringham scores for West Ham. CC1: Brentford finishing with ten men beat Doncaster 4-3. CC2: Second win for Wycombe. CIS Cup: Brechin 5-2 in extra time v Cowdenbeath, Forfar 5-2 at St Mirren. Outbreak of conjunctivitis threatens Newcastle opener. Di Canio off to Lazio. Charlton double-swoop for Murphy (Liverpool) £2.5m and Jeffers (Arsenal) £2.6m. Real closing on Vieira.
11 Ch Lge: Man Utd go 2-1 up at Dinamo Bucharest, Shelbourne hold La Coruna to goalless draw before 24,000 at Lansdowne Road. Real take 2-0 lead at Wisla Krakow. CCC: Wolves fail to beat ten-man Preston. Olympic start sees Argentina top scorers 6-0 over Serbia-Montenegro.
12 UEFA Cup: Glentoran lose to Elfsborg, but Dunfermline draw in Iceland. Spurs pick up Noureddine Naybet from La Coruna.
13 Owen a snip at £8m for Real, but Vieira declares undying love for the Gunners. Everton shareholders revolt. CCC: Plymouth continue confident start with 1-0 win at Cardiff. McClaren confirmed as No. 2 to Eriksson.
14 BPL: Okocha special double plus Pedersen brace for Bolton humbles Charlton, Villa 2-0 over sad Soton, but five 1-1 and one 2-2 draw – that courtesy of handball goal by Hasselbaink as Boro duel with the Toons, for whom Dyer unhappy with sub role and Sir Bobby under cloud from hierarchy. CCC: Veteran Saunders breaks leg as Gillingham go second after 2-1 over Preston. Wolves held by Leeds as Sullivan saves Miller penalty. CC1: Colchester and Luton maintain perfect start, Blackpool pointless, Oldham 5-3 revel with Walsall. CC2: Macclesfield sole 100 percent side after 1-0 v Swansea. Shrewsbury bottom, other promoted team Chester just above. Grimsby 5-1 winners over Bury. Conf: relegated York lose 2-0 at Aldershot, Carlisle held by Canvey. Other newcomers Crawley win at Leigh. SPL: Celtic already two points ahead of Rangers after 4-2 win over ten-man Killie. SL: Stenhousemuir hit six at Cowdenbeath.
15 Chelsea quiet in 1-0 success over Man Utd, but Arsenal carry on scoring in 4-1 at Everton. CCC: Wigan deliver hammer blow at Upton Park. SPL: Inverness get first points 2-0 over Dunfermline.
16 Rangers to appeal five-match ban on Rae dismissed in Russia for gross unsporting conduct.
17 U-21s: England 3-1 over Ukraine, Republic 3-2 against Bulgaria. Liverpool sign Xabi Alonso (Real Sociedad) and Antonio Nunez (Real Madrid).
18 Ints: England old guard wrap up Ukraine 3-0, Wales nicely thank you 2-0 in Latvia, Republic held by Bulgaria and six unbeaten for Northern Ireland after goalless in Switzerland, but Scotland humiliated by Hungary 3-0 at Hampden. Useful start for Klinsmann – 3-1 in Austria using 2-3-3-2 formation.

U-21s: Wales scoreless with Lativa, Northern Irish similarly with Swiss, but Scots – naturally – lose 4-2 to Hungary.

19 Russia beat England women 2-1. Olympic bound Ronaldo back for Man Utd after early elimination.

20 Woodgate becomes latest capture for Real at £15.7m, leaving with mixed Magpie reactions. Bradford out of administration, Sheff Wed to sell training ground. Forlan off to Villarreal. CCC: ten-man Sheff Utd win at Preston.

21 BPL: Chelsea need sub Cole to sink Brummies; record PL gate of 67,812 sees Smith spectacular for Man Utd against Norwich; Spurs' Atouba upsets off-key Toons; last ditch Beattie spot kick earns Saints win and Sturrock reprieve but ref D'Urso has senior moment booking Rovers Ferguson twice with no red; Palace crash to Everton seeking Russian roubles; Cole brace hits his double-ton and carries back-home Fulham to win over Bolton; Hislop blunder costs Pompey at Charlton. CCC: leaders Wigan attract only 8681 to 3-0 v cellar-dwellers Brighton, but Leeds draw with Forest has 31,808. CC1: Luton only 100% FL team after 1-0 v Torquay; first point for Blackpool. CC2: late Scunthorpe show gives them lead on goal difference – but where are the goals? – tally just 77 in 36 weekend. SL: eight-man St Johnstone lose 2-1 to St Mirren; another six goals for Stenbousemuir, this time against East Stirling.

22 Arsenal equal Forest's 42 match unbeaten run the hard way against Boro after being 3-1 down memorably to win 5-3. Albion held 1-1 in Villa derby.

23 'Mutual departure' by Sturrock at Soton! No. 2 Wigley appointed head coach. Birmingham Savage blow – three match ban after incident v Chelsea. Rangers Rae appeal fails. Carrick (£3.5m) and Nice defender Noe Pamarot (£1.7m) move to Spurs. C Cup: Wolves win at Rochdale after 2-1 down. £20m Rooney bid from Newcastle rejected. Olympic women: USA and Brazil to contest final.

24 BPL; Chelsea up a gear and double strike at the Palace; Heskey a head of the game for Brummies. Ch Lge: Liverpool let the Graz grow to one goal, but qualify; brave Shels beached at La Coruna; Monaco take six off Gorica. C Cup: MK Dons win 3-1 at Peterborough; impish Lincoln turn Derby over and extra time sees Yeovil edge Plymouth; another 30,115 pile into Elland Road for the Yorkshire derby as Leeds beat Huddersfield 1-0. CIS Cup: Falkirk 6-1 at Peterhead and Partick 5-2 at Stenhousemuir lead the high-scoring round. Rooney, exposed tabloid tales, hints at Merseyside exit. D'Urso dropped from Man Utd–Everton clash. Bolton make ninth capture with Nigerian Blessing Kaku. Olympics: Iraq fail in semis 3-1 to Paraguay, Argentina hit Italy 3-0. Intertoto winners: Lille, Schalke and Villarreal.

25 BPL: The New Invincibles become the Untouchables as Blackburn bow to Arsenal's historic 43rd without defeat while Fabregas becomes the club's youngest League scorer at 17 years 113 days; Saints slump under new management. Ch Lge: Smith double as Man Utd move on, but Rangers drawn to exit door. FA meet to discuss government pressure for independent inquiry with chairman Geoff Thompson under threat. Captain of industry is sought, alas with a corporal's salary. Man Utd said to be bidding £25m for Rooney.

26 UEFA Cup: Dunfermline and Glentoran out. Sir Bobby plans to fight on at St James' Park. Ch Lge draw throws up Mourinho against his old Porto mates while Abramovich's company links with CSKA Moscow hint at conflict of interest; Larsson faces Celtic for Barcelona; Man Utd and Arsenal in easier looking groups, Liverpool a tougher one.

27 Rooney asks for a move, Man Utd favourites. Albion's Hughes serving six years for dangerous driving is stabbed in prison. UEFA Cup draw links debut boys Millwall with Ferencvaros. Olympic bronze for Italy after 1-0 v Iraq; gold for USA women in extra time against Brazil 2-1. CC2: Bristol R go top after 2-1 over Southend. Irony as Ranieri wins the Super Cup with Valencia 2-1 against Porto – Mourinho's old outfit.

28 Rooney files flight plan, destination Old Trafford? Eta Tuesday latest. BPL: Arsenal power on to four and 44 – goals and unbeaten games; Chelsea suffer 12 second Beattie blow, then thanks to Beattie og and Lampard penalty, beat Saints; unbeaten Spurs third; Osman double lifts Roo-less Toffees; four for Man City; Smith overtime, overtime goal saves Man Utd at ten man Blackburn; Sir Bobby benches Shearer and loses lead to go down 4-2 at Villa. Whistlers trio Wiley–Riley–Poll under fire, respectively for missing Saha handball and mystery extra one minute, yellow only for handling Sorensen at Villa and similar colour coding for Lauren. CCC: Brighton first win, Wolves still searching. CC1: win-all Luton 3-1 at win-less Blackpool. MK Dons lose, too. CC2: Ian Rush begins managerial career for Chester losing 3-0 at home to Darlington; Gazza late sub debut for Boston. SPL: Dundee 4-1 down at Hibs share eight goals. Olympic gold for Argentina 1-0 over nine-man Paraguay.

29 BPL: Bolton hit Benitez Ranieri-like permutation at Liverpool to go third. CCC: Sheff Utd win Leeds derby. Craig Brown axed at Preston. Owen sub for hobbling Raul sets up Ronaldo goal for Real at Mallorca.

30 Sir Bob bounced out at Newcastle. BPL: Yakubu treble in Pompey's 4-3 over Fulham, but goalless Man Utd held by Roo-short Everton. CCC: Wolves fourth from bottom after 2-1 loss at Ipswich; Wigan and Stoke lead the pack, Brighton win again. CC1: Six out of six for Luton already six points ahead. MK Dons first win in front of 3015. CC2: Scunthorpe back on goal difference from Bristol R. Conf: Nine-man Woking beaten 2-1 in last minute by Aldershot. Transfers: WBA break club record in £3m deal for Earnshaw (Cardiff). Diomansy Kamara, Modena to Portsmouth £2m.

31 Rooney in arrival lounge after £27m Man Utd move, otherwise transfer window shuts quietly: Saints nab Andreas Jakobsson £1m from Brondby; Pompey get Valery Mezague (Montpellier), Jay Bothroyd once of Coventry moves to Blackburn from Perugia on loan as do Inter pair Nicola Ventola and Gonzalo Sorondo with Palace, while the last was Dwight Yorke Blackburn to Birmingham £250,000. Sir Clive Woodward expected to ditch handling code for job with Soton. CCC: Sheff Utd sneak it at QPR. Bell's Cup: Alloa nine go down 2-1 to Berwick, Falkirk beat Stirling 5-3.

SEPTEMBER 2004

Least said Souness mended at Toon ... Celtic's early advantage ... Mark Hughes for Rovers ... Van Nistelrooy new club Euro record ... Death of Brian Clough ... Wonder boy Rooney treble shot debut.

1 Newcastle thrashing around for new boss. D'Urso gets 28 day ban. Football League clubs to carry on signing.

2 Sir CW resigns at RFU. UEFA clear Abramovich of CSKA conflict. Gerrard injury worry ahead of Vienna WC game. Venners linked with Toon. Spain pain as Scots U-21's lose a man and 3-1.

3 Combative Scots holding Spain 1-1 when floodlights fail in 60 minutes. U-21s: part-time England boss Peter Taylor welcomes 2-0 win in Austria; ten-man Wales succeed 1-0 in Azerbaijan; Eire 3-0 over Cypriots. Newcastle in no hurry to replace Sir Bob.

4 WC: James gaffe, fit Gerrard sub error add up towards England being overdrawn in Vienna; Pole dancing as Irish reel in Belfast; Jones takes blame for Wales half-baked Baku stalemate; Robbie equalling Republic goal record is Keane enough against Cyprus. CC1: Luton drop first two points at Sheff Wed. CC2: Southend defender Barrett hits fourth goal in three games, equalling his 2003-04 total in 4-1 at Rushden. Conf: Barnet high five leads pack. Pointless: Alloa, Arbroath, East Stirling – naturally – and Forest Green.

6 Newcastle hope least said Souness mended as Graeme quits Rovers for Toon. Bradford hoping to come out of administration. Preston get 15 applicants for boss job. Wales report losing their balls in Baku – 20 of them. Boro Reiziger injury blow.

7 U21: Super sub Bent brace as England beat ten-man Poles; Republic go down 4-2 to Swiss; Scots held by ten-man Slovenia. Ahead of internationals: Sven under the cosh; Roy Keane back for Swiss game; Hughes linked with Blackburn job; Northern Ireland face defeat.

8 WC Pole vaulting England owe Defoe and an own goal to victory and boycott interviews. All square all-round the other British Isles teams results. Northern Ireland have Michael Hughes and Healy sent off, Wales Savage sees red for first time. Scots and Republic wasteful in their games. Vieira off in French win.

9 Sven backed England squad silence against the press gang. Gordon Taylor wants players to use PFA agency. Mark Hughes might be tempted to quit Wales for Blackburn. Tim Harris sacked at Forest Green.

10 Wenger and Mourinho among managers wanting end to back-to-back internationals. 50th anniversary of Roy of the Rovers debut.

11 BPL: Fulham boss Chris Coleman claims ex-cabbie ref Halsey gave short change over disallowed goal and penalty snub as Arsenal motor to 3-0 win. Whistler Styles earns Mourinho ire after Drogba 'diving' episode in Villa draw. Hunt og at the death saves point for Man Utd at Bolton. Everton match-winner Cahill dismissed for burying face in shirt on second card at Man City; ref Steve – not Gordon – Bennett. Caretaker Carver's Toon triumph as Souness watches old Rovers beaten 3-0. CCC: Wolves still drawing lots sharing six with table-topping Wigan. Peter Reid's Coventry lose 3-0 at Leeds. CC1: Luton open seven point gap. Bristol City hit five v Stockport. CC2: Wycombe overturn Southend lead to edge ahead. SPL: Five in a row Celtic making it hard for rest.

12 East Anglian joy as Norwich hold Spurs at WHL and Ipswich top CCC after 2-0 over Millwall. SPL: Rangers only draw at Hearts and are fourth, seven points adrift of Celtic.

13 Gary Megson in row at WBA. Soton make a point at Charlton whose Kiely clean sheet earns another £50 from him for Kent hospice. Blatter criticises Bennett over Cahill red. Leeds sign Gregan for £500,000. Mark Hughes denies Blackburn link. Gary Neville sidelined with hair-line knee cap fracture.

14 Ch Lge: Drogba double as Chelsea shine at PSG; Arsenal have to settle for own goal win; Old boy Larsson adds to Celtic woe for Barca. Keegan under fire. Wolves win at 8th attempt and Stoke top CCC after edging Ipswich 3-2 and ending with ten men. Hughes change of heart. Bielsa Marcelo resigns as Argentine coach.

15 Ch Lge: Van Nistelrooy double salvages point for Man Utd and with 30th Euro strike beats Law's 28 for the club; Swedish ref Anders Frisk hit by half-time missile at Roma, abandons game with Dynamo Kiev leading 1-0; little Luis Garcia stars as Liverpool beat Monaco. Zidane injury as Real rocked 3-0 by Leverkusen. FA Cup semis for Cardiff where City boss Lennie Lawrence faces chop. Hughes appointed at Rovers!

16 UEFA Cup: Butt and Israeli Suan off in ten-a-side Toon victory; Millwall hold Fenerbahce in Euro bow; Viduka double delights Boro over Banik; Shels leave it late for Lille draw; Schalke, having sacked coach Jupp Heynckes, hammer in five goals. Gordon Bennett! Toffees ref sticks to Cahill red decision.

17 Fabregas signs four-year contract with Arsenal. Keegan job said to be under serious threat.

18 BPL; Spiteful Hawthorns punch-up with Diop, Cole off for Fulham, Clement for WBA in brawl draw; Bolton twice come back to hold Arsenal at Highbury. Hughes off the mark in first Blackburn win. Anelka double saves Keegan. Promoted trio at bottom. CCC: Wigan take four off Sheff Utd; Stoke and Ipswich both draw; Wolves win again. CC1: Luton continue, 3-1 at Stockport; Chris Turner sacked by Sheff Wed after home defeat by Bournemouth; MK Dons win away. CC2: Yeovil six-hitters dump Oxford. SPL: Aberdeen go second after 1-0 at Killie. SL: Seventh pointless game for East Stirling. Conf: Forest Green first point under new boss Alan Leer. FA Cup: AFC Wimbledon win 1-0 at Dover and attract 2103.

19 BPL: Mourinho blasts Spurs for goalless negativity at the Bridge; Souness wins at old Saints mates; Roo-less Everton third. CCC: Watford sixth after 2-0 at Millwall. SPL: Celtic held 2-2 at Hibs, Rangers 1-0 over Inverness closes gap to five points. Real crisis: coach Camacho throws in towel after 1-0 defeat against Espanyol, Becks starts on bench, Owen replaced.

20 Brian Clough dies of cancer at 69. Rio back as Man Utd owe Silvestre brace for 2-1 win over Liverpool, who sustained Gerrard metatarsal misery, too. Real appoint little-known Mariano Garcia Remon as interim boss, but already speculation over eventual Eriksson destination.

21 C Cup: Colchester edge WBA in extra time; Barnsley slammed 7-1 by Man City; Wolves penalty shoot-out loss at Burnley. CIS Cup: Celtic thrash Falkirk 8-1. UEFA hit Roma with 3-0 statutory defeat against Kiev and remaining home games behind closed doors. Becks free-kick gives Real 1-0 win over Osasuna.

22 C Cup: Bournemouth 3-1 down in penalty shoot-out win it 7-6 at Blackburn; Spurs six send Latics packing; Wigley Saints win at Northampton; Everton scrape through on penalties at Bristol City. CIS Cup: Rangers 2-0 at Aberdeen.

23 Paul Sturrock becomes Sheff Wed's 10th boss in nine years. Roy Keane facing trial for alleged assault on teenager. FIFA likely to impose 14 May deadline for League games at end of 2005-06 season because of WC. Forssell injury may keep him out for season. Butt three game UEFA ban. Barry Davies to quit MOTD and the programme ratings are falling.

24 Now Hollywood cash tempts Liverpool as Man Utd to announce record profits. Sunderland win 1-0 at Leeds.

25 BPL: Spurs claim ref switch and unfair penalty for Man Utd win; Chelsea 'annihilate' Boro 1-0; similar wins for Arsenal at Man City and Fulham over Saints; late Newcastle revival floors ten-man WBA; Norwich ship three at vibrant Liverpool; Palace point at Villa. Bruised Steve Bruce after early home yob attack sees evening draw with Bolton. CCC: Wigan held at Derby, so Reading top after 1-0 at Watford; QPR two down against Leicester win 3-2 as do Ipswich over Plymouth. CC1: Luton nine point lead after edging Posh 2-1; Blackpool first win is 3-0 at Vale. CC2: Yeovil new leaders after 2-1 at Shrewsbury. Wrecks at the Recreation Grounds: Aldershot 0 Carlisle 5; Alloa l Morton 6. SL: East Stirling score three and get first point. Becks subbed as Real lose 2-1 at Athletic Bilbao.

26 BPL: Cahill strikes again as Everton stay third. CCC: Forest late at beating Hammers. SPL: Rangers 2-0 at Dundee close gap on Celtic to five points. FA dismiss Spurs ref comment.

27 BPL: Charlton minimum win over Rovers. Billy Davies steps up from caretaker to Preston job. Eamonn Dolan quits Exeter for Reading academy post. Surprise Man Utd £11.4m drop in profits with agents fees taking £8.5m.

28 Ch Lge: Wonder boy Wayne treble shoots Man Utd to 6-2 over Fenerbahce; a Rooney tune debut to savour; Liverpool disappoint in Olympiakos reverse; Real recover two against Roma to win 4-2; Makaay hat-trick in Ajax clean-up. CCC: Ipswich draw with Reading, Stoke and Wigan held away, only QPR with Cureton trio make ground. LDV Vans: Conf clubs get a nibble as Carlisle oust Grimsby, Hereford penalty success over Scunthorpe. Bell's Cup: Winters springs Ross Co into final with hat-trick against Forfar while Falkirk edge St Johnstone. Djorkaeff joins Blackburn.

29 Ch Lge: Chelsea unravel a Porto victory; Arsenal in a tangle as Strand equalises for Rosenborg; Celtic embroidery ruined as Milan hit two in last two minutes. CCC: Emergency striker Virgo pots another Brighton win; Hammers waste chances in Forest draw. LDV Vans: Conf take more chunks with Accrington and Exeter overturning FL clubs.

30 UEFA Cup: Shearer bags three, misses penalty, two goals for Kluivert in Toon Bnei romp; crowd trouble spoils ten-man Boro draw in Ostrava; four Millwall fans stabbed in Budapest as Lions go down; Hearts draw enough; Rangers need shoot-out; Shels bow to Lille. Vieira and Lauren allegedly in bus bust up.

OCTOBER 2004

Arsenal name new ground ... Racist fury of Luis Aragones ... Robbie Keane's Irish record ... Mutu drug shame ... Man Utd end Arsenal's run ... Spurs legend Bill Nicholson dies.

1 Ferencvaros and Banik Ostrava likely to be heavily dealt with. Man Utd may part with no-signing Brown in the summer. Leicester list Keown.

2 BPL: Four play enough for Arsenal against Charlton; Spurs stun Everton but Redknapp's tackle may be censured; Pompey twice squander lead at Norwich; WBA celebrate first win 2-1 over Bolton; Saints fall into bottom three after goalless with Man City. CCC: Wigan go top again as boss Jewell chalks up 150th League game in charge; Reading held by Burnley; super-sub Sheri tonic for Hammers; QPR roll on sixth win best for 20 years; two late Friio headers help Argyle pull socks up. Goalie Lonergan clearance equalises for Preston at Leicester. CC1: Luton held at Tranmere; six-goal sharing at Blackpool and Stockport. CC2; None of top three win while bottom pair Cambridge and Harriers in share issue. Conf: unbeaten Carlisle creep up to second. SL: another point for East Stirling.

3 BPL: Chelsea by the minimum again but Man Utd need sub Smith goal to save point against three-rookie Boro. CCC: Ipswich nip second after 2-1 at Coventry. Larsson goals take Barca top in Spain while second place Messina continue to surprise in Italy.

4 BPL: Palace down ten-man Fulham for first win. Glazer confirms serious interest in Man Utd. Redknapp charged after Cahill lunge.

5 Arsenal to call new ground Emirates Stadium after airline signs £100m sponsorship from 2006–07 and Wenger expected to sign new contract. UEFA Cup draw complicated – five teams in eight groups but only play four games. Spurs announce £1m loss. Becks, Ronaldo, Drogba, Gerrard, Giggs, Henry, Lampard, Owen, Pires, Rooney and Van Nistelrooy in FIFA player of the year nominees list. Ahead of WC games, Northern Ireland complain of withdrawals, Scots reduced to 19 squad. Gazza quits Boston for more coaching role. Conf: Exeter lose farewell match for Eamonn Dolan and Carlisle hit five second half goals at Leigh in 6-1 win.

6 FIFA threat to end domestic football 14 May 2006 ahead of WC finals. Jordan put Iraq forward as WC hosts one day! Andy Cole gets double punishment for Clement red card fight. Spain coach Luis Aragones alleged racist remark about Henry.

7 England threat to use three forwards; Wales row over money; Pressley out for Scots. Woodgate injury blow for Real.

8 U-21: Taylor revolution continues at Ewood 2-0 v Wales; Republic go down 1-0 in Troyes; Scots lose 2-0 to Norway at Cumbernauld. CC21: Luton stroll on taking three off Hartlepool.

9 WC: England ease it 2-0 v Wales but Becks 'deliberately' goes for yellow after injury; no goals for either Northern Ireland or Republic but they get a point each at Baku and Paris respectively, though scoreless Scots lose sent off McFadden and game to Norway. Poles win in Austria; Portugal only draw in Liechtenstein!; no 100% Euro teams. Brazil 5-2 romp in Venezuela, Uruguay go down 4-2 in Argentina, Paraguay held in Colombia.

10 CC2: Swadi Fayadh, first Iraqi in FL sub debut for Macclesfield.

11 Micky Adams quits at Leicester. Christian Damiano, one-time Fulham No. 2 moves in to assist Wigley at Soton.

12 U-21: Reo-Coker off in Baku ten-a-side draw; Poles hold Wales in Swansea; Scots point in Moldova's Chisinau. WC point for Uruguay in goalless Bolivia. German goalie Lehmann faces sack for using wrong gloves. Howard Wilkinson caretakes Leicester. Brown and Saha back from injury in Man Utd stiffs, but Man City Barton faces six-week knee agony.

13 The CO leads from the front; skipper Owen scores in rain-lashed Baku; Robbie Keane breaks Quinn's Republic overall scoring record; but Wales lose 3-2 to the Poles, Northern Ireland are held by Austria 3-3 and the Scots can only draw in Moldova. Other WC notes see minnows Andorra and Liechtenstein win; Portugal whack the Russians 7-1 and Gronkjaer is sent off as the Danes draw with Turkey. Home-based scorers include two each for Van Nistelrooy and Ronaldo, one apiece for Henry and Gudjohnsen plus Barca's Larsson gets a brace himself. Becks apologies. Celtic say a move out of Scotland is inevitable.

14 Glazer Man Utd takeover fails. Chris Coleman fancied for Wales, Gordon Strachan for Scots as Berti Vogts fears grow. Eriksson to speak to Becks. Alex Inglethorpe to get Exeter post. WC: three South American draws: Paraguay 1 Peru l; Chile 0 Argentina 0; Brazil 0 Colombia 0, but Venezuela improve with 3-1 win over Ecuador. Lowe under pressure at Soton, Turkish dosh interests Fulham.

15 Glazer buys up more shares. CCC: Wolves miss 5th of seven penalties this season in losing 1-0 to ten-man Forest. Coleman not interested in Wales job. Becks to face FA wrath. FA to put forward new Wembley for Ch Lge final, City of Manchester future UEFA Cup.

16 BPL: Arsenal's 49ers take Villa 3-1 and are the sole unbeaten Premier team surviving, as Chelsea lose to Anelka's spot kick for Man City. Liverpool give Fulham a two goals start and win second half 4-2. Depleted Saints late loss at third place Everton. Man Utd held goalless at Brummies. Hasselbaink treble in Boro 4-0 Ewood whacking of Blackburn. Bolton fourth still after 1-0 v Palace. CCC: Wigan, Reading and QPR win, no joy for Rotherham. CC1: unlucky 13 for Luton, defeated 2-1 at home by Huddersfield; goal rush at Tranmere 5-4 losers to Bradford. CC2: Grays loanee Eastwood makes Southend's day with debut hat-trick including 7.7 sec goal, costing Swansea top spot after Orient hit Shrewsbury 4-1. SL: East Stirling score first, lose 8-1 at Gretna. Conf: Barnet draw 9215 at Carlisle and end United run 3-1. Northwich ten points deducted for administration up to nil points! Real only draw at Betis. FA Cup: AFC Wimbledon pull in 3007 but lose 2-0 to Thurrock; Hornchurch slam Dulwich 9-0.

17 BPL: Subbed Bellamy rages as Newcastle draw at Charlton. Mutu drug allegations.

18 Yakubu goal as Pompey down Spurs. Glazer gears up again.

19 Ch Lge: La Coruna hold Liverpool at Anfield, Man Utd by Sparta in Prague – both goalless; but Owen on the goal standard for Real; troubled Roma have two sent off in 3-1 defeat to Leverkusen. CCC: Wolves beat ten-man Derby; one each off as Sheff Utd draw with Forest; Wigan hit Crewe 4-1, but QPR lose at Preston, Reading held by Leeds. CC1: Luton lose again lead down to five points as Brentford beat Hartlepool 2-1. CC2: Swans edged Orient 1-0 and leapfrog them to top.

20 Ch Lge: Lehmann lapses cost Arsenal two points in Greece; Chelsea overcome Abramovich's other team CSKA; Celtic eclipsed in Donetsk; AC Milan edge Barca; Inter thrash Ranieri's Valencia on their own patch. Mutu faces the couch and the game worries over extent of drug taking elsewhere. Claridge out at Weymouth. Gazza to become just G8.

21 UEFA Cup: minimum wins enough for away-day Boro and Newcastle; Rangers nap hand in Poland, but Hearts trumped in Holland. Allardyce seeks rugby kicking coach Dave Alred after introducing *tai chi*, darts and snooker to menu. Mutu changes cocaine admission. Thousands at Clough memorial.

22 Critics writing off Man Utd ahead of Arsenal game. Jimmy Quinn quits Shrewsbury.

23 BPL: Gudjohnsen two in Chelsea foursome over Rovers; Palace three against WBA; Bolton edge Spurs at WHL on day Bill Nicholson dies at 85; Vassell breaks ankle at Villa; Everton stay third after 3-2 at Norwich. CCC: Comfortable wins for Wigan and West Ham, Ipswich held at Watford. CC1: Luton crash to third in a row and Bradford close gap to four points in 3-1 derby win over Sheff Wed. CC2: Scunthorpe stay top with 1-0 against Yeovil; Orient win odd goal in seven at Lincoln. SL: Gretna 6-2 winners at Albion. Owen achieves winner for Real in Spain.

24 BPL: Controversy in Man Utd's surprise 2-0 win ending Arsenal's run: ref Riley awards United's eighth penalty in his eighth Old Trafford visit; Gunners claim for one against Ferdinand denied, Van Nistelrooy foul on Cole unpunished, Rooney celebrates 19th birthday with late goal and food and drink fly in the tunnel! But ex-whistler Elleray applauds official control. Newcastle odd goal in seven win over Man City. SPL: Rangers pegged by Dundee Utd equaliser, Celtic lead by seven points.

25 CCC: Rotherham club record 15 without a win. Caborn calls for two-year Mutu ban. Man Utd still opposing Glazer as Old Trafford feud with Arsenal rumbles on.

26 Van Nistelrooy gets three match ban. Gary Megson tenders resignation for season's end and is then sacked at WBA. C Cup: Burnley end Villa interest; crowd trouble at Millwall as Liverpool win. Kevin Keegan to apologise to ref for Sunday comments. Owen still on Real scoring roll.

27 C Cup: Spurs extra time revenge at Bolton; Palace stiffs stun Charlton; crowd disturbances at Chelsea in 1-0 v West Ham; super-sub baby Blackstock second half treble saves Saints against Colchester. SPL: Celtic stunned by Aberdeen last minute winner. Meeting of Davids – Gill and Dein – at Old Trafford over 'pie and pint', presumably not 'soup and pizza' to end hostilities.

28 Edu spills the beans on tunnel meals. Bolton's Fadiga with irregular heartbeat history recovering after his pre-match collapse. Jan Molby resigns at Kidderminster – again. Leeds seek USA cash influx. UEFA plan restriction on foreigners. Football League likely to lose window exemption. Bert Trautmann to receive OBE.

29 Chelsea sack Mutu. Toshack, Rush in line for Welsh job. Craig Levein ex-Hearts to take over Leicester vacancy. CCC: three in seven minutes early on give Sheff Utd edgy 3-2 over Crewe.

30 BPL: Van Persie pulls Arsenal out of defeat against Soton; Man Utd back to earth at Pompey, losing 2-0; Chelsea level on points with Gunners after second-half spree ends 4-1 at WBA; Palace's Johnson, top scorer now with eight, does in old Brummie mates; Liverpool's Cisse breaks left leg in two places, mirroring similar injuries to Baros and Carragher last season at Blackburn; Spurs 2-0 losers at Fulham, have poorest scoring record among the 92 – just six goals but 13 points. CCC: with Wigan absent, Ipswich consolidate with 3-0 win over Preston, but Reading go down 3-2 at Coventry and QPR's three early goals down Burnley. Rotherham squander two-goal lead at Derby and lose 3-2, Wolves lose 1-0 to ten-man Gillingham. CC1: Luton back to winning ways, four clear goals over Bradford. CC2: *status quo* as Scunthorpe draw at Orient. FA Cup: Thurrock bidding again after six-hit over Spalding; Stevenage five goals as Hendon finish with eight players!

31 BPL: Bolton end Souness run for Newcastle. CCC: Wigan restore six-point lead with 2-0 at Leeds. Owen makes in four in four for Real.

NOVEMBER 2004

Death of Emlyn Hughes ... Toshack back in Wales job ... Racism rife ... Sir Alex hits 1000th ... Harry Redknapp quits Pompey ... Ex-TV man Brian Barwick becomes FA supremo.

1 Bath rugby players deny Collymore assault and abuse charges from Sunday fracas in Dublin. Trevor Birch declines FA top job. Wolves axe Dave Jones, 11th English managerial change of the season. Berti Vogts resigns Scottish post Norwich make a point at Man City. Bradford complain to FA over ref Joe Ross' four fingers of scorn to red carded Windass on Saturday. Ranieri under fire at Valencia.

2 Ch Lge: Arsenal concede Cygan own goal as drawing Panathinaikos squander penalty; Robben bobs up for Chelsea in Moscow win; Celtic beat nine-man Donetsk 1-0; Barcelona take thriller 2-1 over AC Milan watched by 94,682. CCC: Wigan plough on, Ipswich hit five against Sheff Utd, Reading held at Plymouth, QPR by Millwall but West Ham ship four at Cardiff leaving Sunderland 3-1 winners over Wolves to move third. LDV: holders Blackpool 6-3 extra time win over ten-man Huddersfield; Hereford sole Conf survivors on penalties against Doncaster; Macclesfield boss Brian Horton celebrates 1000th career match in charge of a club with 4-0 win over Mansfield. Villa manager David O'Leary charged with making illegal approach to Saints Beattie in the summer.

3 Ch Lge: Ruud's solo four-play rakes Sparta for Man Utd; Liverpool grateful for og at La Coruna; Real fight back in Kiev to draw; 100 percent Juve late winner in Munich. CCC: Rotherham throw away another two-goal lead in draw at Forest. Brian Barwick controller of ITV Sport and ex-BBC, favourite to take FA post. George Best may get job at Pompey. England to play Holland at Villa Park in February. Bradford boss Colin Todd and striker Windass charged with misconduct to ref. Hearts appoint John Robertson as manager.

4 UEFA Cup: Newcastle ease to 2-0 over Tbilisi as do Boro with Zenden brace against Lazio, but Hearts give chief Robbo sad start, Mutu seven-month ban by FA riles Chelsea. Moneybags Hornchurch now skint on Carthium window pain. Tommy Burns is Scots caretaker. Notts sack Gary Mills and Ian Richardson gets the job. Joe Kinnear may go at Forest with Mick Harford taking over.

5 Not all right at Spurs as Jacques Santini jacks it in. Liverpool to announce record loss of £21.9m. Coventry losing £150,000 a week show loss of £8.1m with wage bill down to only £9m! Becks hopes to return next weekend. BPL to use yellow balls like FL in winter. CCC: Millwall celebrate Wise and Wilkins contract extension with 2-0 win over Sunderland.

6 BPL: Stumbling Arsenal held at Palace; Villa's first-half purr over Pompey; first away day wins for Birmingham at Liverpool, Charlton at Spurs; Robben robs Everton; Saints late saving point against Albion. CCC: Wigan fans clap Plymouth 2-0 winners at JJB; Ipswich and Reading make ground, Hammers edge QPR 2-1; still no win for Rotherham. CC1: Luton take five off Wrexham, Tranmere, Hull and Bournemouth also win. CC2: Scunthorpe, Swansea and Yeovil keep up pressure as six out of top seven win, Orient draw. SPL: Dundee in Tayside win over nine-man United. SL: goal glut in Divs 1 and 2, 47 in ten games with Gretna 8-0 winners at Cowdenbeath. Conf: Aldershot squander three-goal lead in Morecambe draw.

7 BPL: Newcastle blitz Fulham with 26 shots, 19 corners but lose 4-1 thanks to Crossley stops; faltering Man Utd goalless in Mancunian derby draw with Smith's 10th red; Boro late leveller with Bolton. Bell's Cup: Falkirk take trophy 2-1 over Ross.

8 FA keen to end Man Utd-Arsenal feud and Gunners field youth team in 2-0 reserve win over Chelsea at Aldershot with 5498 present! Martin Jol steps up for Spurs job. Stuart Murdoch axed by MK Dons, Chris Brass at York. Dons caretakers: Jimmy Gilligan and Steve Palmer. Harford arrival at Forest as assistant leads to dismissal of 'Clough' remnants Ian Bowyer and Liam O'Kane. Bryan Robson expected at WBA. Graeme Souness in bother over ref remarks. Mutu may get Romanian coaching offer! Jimmy Quinn new assistant at Posh.

Newcastle's talisman Alan Shearer battles with Dinamo Tbilisi goalkeeper Zurab Mamaladze during the UEFA Cup Group D victory at St James' Park. (PA/Empics)

9 C Cup: Wigley wobbles at Watford as Saints whacked 5-2; Spurs hit three at Burnley, Pompey two at Cardiff; Arsenal reserves beat Everton seniors 3-1 on day ex-skipper Tony Adams calls it a day at Wycombe. Robson in at WBA. Death of Emlyn 'Crazy Horse' Hughes, Liverpool and England at 57. Fadiga trains after heart op. EC fixture rebuff hits PL/FL cash. CC1: Tranmere ship four at Bristol C. CIS Cup: Dundee Utd and Motherwell through.

10 Lowe ready to hump Hoddle back to Saints? UEFA keen to restrict foreigners. C Cup: Chelsea extra time win at Newcastle, Fulham similarly at Forest; Man Utd win 'reserve' looking affair with Palace; Mellor brace lifts Liverpool. Harry Redknapp worries over story that Velimar Zajec may become Director of Football. Bells' Cup: Rangers at last beat Celtic; Hearts trump Dunfermline.

11 Pizza peace in doubt. Keith Curle mystery suspension at Mansfield, Carlton Palmer in temporary charge.

12 Shareholder Glazer strikes at Man Utd to oust directors Maurice Watkins and two others. John Toshack back at Wales helm. Leeds forced to sell Elland Road as Sainsbury deal rings up no sale. Mutu ban now world-wide. Tony Parkes 35 years at Blackburn sacked. Tigana wins High Court action against Fulham. FA Cup: Luton easily at Southend.

13 BPL: Nine-goal thriller at WHL with Arsenal edging Spurs 5-4; one enough for Everton again; Charlton hit four; Baros treble as Liverpool nudge Palace 3-2; Villa surprise Bolton; relief for Wiggies Saints over Pompey; Chelsea 4-1 at Fulham stay top. CCC: Ipswich catch Wigan after 1-0 v Leeds, Latics defeat at QPR leaves them with just goal difference lead. Veteran Claridge inspires Brighton at West Ham. Rotherham 19th game without a win. FA Cup: Hinckley, Histon and Slough giant-killing over Torquay, Shrewsbury and Walsall respectively; Exeter knock-out Grimsby; Alfreton hold Macclesfield as do Forest Green with Bournemouth; Bath win at Barnet, Halifax beat Cambridge. AFC Wimbledon create English record: 76 unbeaten league games to overtake St Blazey's run. SL; Gretna top Div 3 after 2-1 over Peterhead with 2200 present. Keith Weller dies at 58.

14 BPL: Rooney double as Man Utd win 3-1 at slipping Newcastle; Robbo bow for Albion hit by Kanu miss of the century from one yard helps Boro to victory. FA Cup: Thurrock go down to Oldham penalty. Owen's sixth in eight games as Real romp to 6-1.

15 Costcutting for WBA. Arnesen denies plot against Santini at Spurs. Walter Smith tipped for Scots. Parkes to get Rovers testimonial! One caretaker Peter Cawley leaves Wycombe, another moves in: Keith Ryan as player-caretaker. Bolton announce profit of £2.6m. Transfers: Luke Beckett, Stockport to Sheff Utd £50,000; Patrick Agyemang, Gillingham to Preston £350,000. Hollywood can wait says Becks. Glazer to menace Man Utd more. Gary Peters gets Shrewsbury post.

16 U-21s: England lose 1-0 to Spain and Chelsea's Johnson red-carded amid racist jibes; Scots lose 2-1 to Swedes. Republic beat Croatia 1-0 in a full international while Australia and Norway draw – at Fulham! Wrexham apply for administration. Diouf spitting allegations. Gerrard on way back.

17 Racism rules as Spanish crowd abuses England's black players, Luis Aragones under fire again, Rooney hauled off after yellow peril, Robinson saves Raul penalty in another 1-0 defeat for the

visitors to Madrid. WC scorers: Ronaldo (Portugal) and Gera (Hungary), but Djemba Djemba sent off for Cameroon and Baros injured with Czechs. Home wins in South America for Argentina, Colombia, Peru and Uruguay and Ecuador stun Brazil 1-0. Arie Haan quits as China boss after elimination despite 7-0 v Hong Kong. Third degree Burns night for Scots caretaker in 4-1 Swedish reverse.

18 FIFA likely to punish Spain, but Aragones unrepentant. Phil Starbuck quits Leigh RMI after budget cuts. Stuart Cash leaves St Albans after two games.

19 Taricco Spurs to West Ham on a free.

20 BPL: Arsenal, Chelsea caught in late home draws against Albion and Bolton respectively. Everton 1-0 – naturally – against Fulham edge within two points of Gunners. Boro, Man Utd and Newcastle also forge ahead with 2-0 wins. First win bonus for red underwear sporting Norwich over Soton. CCC: Goal-drought Wigan held, Leeds hammer QPR 6-1 with veteran Deane foursome but still no victory for Rotherham. CC1: Luton 4-1 at MK Dons and one goal enough for Tranmere at Blackpool. CC2: Scunthorpe hit three at Bristol Rovers, but Swansea have two sent off in Shrewsbury defeat. SPL: Rangers close gap to a point with rare League win against Celtic, who have two sent off in fiery affair. S Cup: only two survive frost. Barca slam Real 3-0 in La Liga.

21 BPL: Blackurn salvage 3-3 draw after Brummies lead 3-1, but Yorke suffers racist abuse. CCC: Sunderland make ground after beating Ipswich 2-0, but disturbances at Millwall in 1-0 win over Hammers.

22 BPL: Villa inflict Spurs sixth consecutive League defeat. Barca's Larsson out for rest of season with injury. Campbell fit again for Arsenal. Turkish teenager dies after stabbing at domestic game.

23 Ch Lge: Man Utd edge Lyon 2-1 in Sir Alex 1000th game in charge, but Liverpool go down to a Monaco goal; Leverkusen hold Real in Madrid, where more racial abuse is demonstrated. Juventus five 1-0 wins in succession! Conf Carlisle dump Bristol Rovers in FA Cup replay. Sheff Wed fans latest to have accusations of racism against them. Andy Hessenthaler steps down at Gillingham. Besiktas ordered to play three home games behind closed doors after Turkish stabbing. Leicester RFU Tigers to share Walkers with City.

24 Ch Lge: Double dismissal for Arsenal – Lauren and Vieira, but they draw in Eindhoven; gutsy Celtic hold Barca in Spain; Chelsea uninspired goalless affair with PSG. Harry Redknapp quits Portsmouth. Gunners add Emmanuel Eboue, Ivory Coast cap from Beveren.

25 UEFA Cup: Hearts nip in with a 2-1 win in Basle; Rangers ease three goals against Graz and Newcastle coast 4-0 at Sochaux, but Boro suffer 2-0 Villarreal reverse. Eriksson reckons time will turn Becks good again. Brian Barwick, controller of ITV Sport is the new chief executive at the FA. Sammy McIlroy leaves Stockport by mutual consent. Now Lazio hit with racist complaint. Sunderland reduce debt but it remains around £40m.

26 Sir Bobby tipped as Wolves boss. Ex-Liverpool manager Roy Evans is new Wales No. 2. Juventus club doctor jailed for giving drugs to players.

27 BPL: Terry inspired Chelsea four play win at Charlton; Man Utd take three off Albion; Blackburn's first away success at Fulham, similarly Velimir Zajec influence for Pompey at Bolton and Diouf in another spitting confrontation; Hendrie redded again in Villa reverse at Man City; Saints can only draw with Palace; as do Brummie against Norwich. CCC: Wigan held at Reading, so Ipswich 1-0 v Brighton ensures top; Sunderland third after edging Stoke and Hammers give Watford two goals start and beat them. CC1: Tranmere close gap to four points after 2-0 against MK Dons as Doncaster hold Luton. CC2: Scunthorpe open five point lead. Conf: As Barnet clip Shots 3-2, they stretch to seven points ahead of Carlisle beaten at York. S Cup: Huntly chop off Peterhead 3-1.

28 BPL: Mellor late strike blows out Arsenal at Liverpool; Everton draw at Newcastle; Spurs end losing run against ten-man Boro. SPL: Celtic held at Dundee, so Rangers take point lead. Diouf fined two weeks' wages. Becks and Owen score in Real win.

29 Dancing at Millmoor – first win in 21 attempts as Leeds beaten. Newcastle chairman Freddy Shepherd writes off all football below Premiership.

30 C Cup: After Saints, Watford complete south coast double: – with Pompey, but Redknapp and Mandaric make up; Lampard late one edges Chelsea home at Fulham. Dangers of blanket TV warning from David Dein, Arsenal vice-chairman. John Gorman, new manager of Wycombe, Stuart Watkiss at Peterborough, Richard Gough at Livingston. Oldham to quit Boundary Park. LDV: Conf Hereford oust holders Blackpool. Luis Aragones family want him to quit. Shadow of Ms Alam rises over FA again with new allegations. Becks officially Britain's richest player: £65m, but Roman Abramovich at £7.5b is wealthiest in our game. Death of Norwich's oldest surviving player Bernard Robinson at 92.

DECEMBER 2004

Walter Smith is Scots boss ... Wrexham get ten points deducted ... Porto are World Club Champions ... Shevchenko is European player, Rooney the young one ... Ronaldinho is FIFA's choice ... Another Henry milestone.

1 C Cup: 'Reserve' affair decided by 18.6 secs goal for Bellion as Man Utd beat Arsenal again; wasteful Spurs eventually pay the penalty against Liverpool. Spurs double hero goalkeeper Bill Brown dies at 73.

2 UEFA Cup: 100% AZ end Rangers unbeaten run at 16th game; betting scandal fear over Wednesday's Panionios 5-2 win over Dynamo Tbilisi, but Boro OK to stay in after Lazio only draw. Walter Smith gets Scotland post. Unhappy Liverpool AGM after £21.9m loss on year.

3 Wrexham minus ten points for administration, then ko in FA Cup at Scunthorpe.

4 BPL: another foursome for Chelsea as Blues doom Toon, but Arsenal revive with a Henry double inspired 3-0 win over Brummie; own goal gives Everton 3-2 win over Bolton; three second half goals cause Saints grief at Man Utd; late Pompey recovery beats Baggies; Fulham and Spurs each win

away, Liverpool draw at Villa. CCC: Ipswich draw at Crewe, West Ham win importantly at Sunderland and a welcome 4-1 for Wolves over Reading. FA Cup: giant-killers Exeter edge Doncaster, while Ryman Yeading head for plum pairing after 3-1 at Slough; Aldershot crash 5-1 at Hartlepools. SPL: Celtic regain leadership with Rangers inactive. Rory Howard, 69 year old Marine manager and window cleaner presented with certificate from the *Guinness Book of Records* as longest serving manager; 32 years and over 1800 matches in charge.

5 BPL: Rommedahl late winner for Charlton at Palace after hot-shot Johnson has penalty saved by Kiely. CCC: Wigan shake off goal-shyness, drill five past Preston. FA Cup: Salako penalty miss and Brentford must replay with Hinckley. SPL: Rangers only draw with Inverness, Celtic stay point ahead.

6 BPL: Viduka brace aids Boro to win over Man City. FA Cup draw has Yeading home to Newcastle, Exeter at Man Utd! News of Swiss player severing his ring finger on perimeter fence and getting booked for over-celebrating: Paulo Diogo (Servette).

7 Ch Lge: Arsenal cruise 5-1 over Rosenborg, but Mourinho suffers defeat against his old Porto mates and Celtic draw with AC Milan is not enough for even UEFA Cup status. Germany beat Scotland 3-0 in a B International. Wolves give Glenn Hoddle the nod on day Millwall beat them, CC1: ten-man Luton lose at Brentford, Tranmere 3-1 at Port Vale. CC2: Scunthorpe win again, 2-1 at Cambridge. Redknapp likely to move coastwards to Soton. Danny Wilson is new MK Dons boss, Stan Ternent at Gillingham. Sao Caetano deducted 24 points in Brazil for failing medical test standards after death of a player; club doctor and president receive bans.

8 Ch Lge: Liverpool put on the Mersey style against Olympiakos after going a goal down, but Tuncay treble trumps Man Utd at Fenerbahce; Monaco hit five at La Coruna; Juventus drop first point in Tel-Aviv; Real threesome at Roma; five, too, for Lyon over Sparta. Redknapp confirmed at Soton.

9 Oxford appoint Ramon Diaz, ex-Argentine international as manager. Gerrard hints at move from Anfield. Millwall anger at FA racism charge.

10 CCC: Injury-time penalty gives Leeds draw at West Ham. Tranmere back on track in CC1 after 2-0 against Bournemouth. Real fined £7000 for racist chanting; Luis Aragones to be investigated by anti-violence commission in Spain; Lazio ordered to play next Euro game behind closed doors. Two-match touchline ban for Neil Warnock. Pires fined £34,000 by French governing body for wearing his own sponsor on TV, not the Federation one!

11 BPL: Derby day delights Everton, disappoints Liverpool; Spurs win again, this time at Man City; Norwich edge out Bolton 3-2 once more; Redknapp riles as Saints concede two late goals and two points against Boro; Pompey draw at Newcastle; away day success for Charlton leaves Albion adrift; Palace and Blackburn settle for no goals. CCC: Leaders Wigan, Ipswich, Sunderland and Reading push on with wins. CC1: second place Hull keep pressure on leaders Luton. CC2: Crucial Scunthorpe win over Swansea and Yeovil slip into second spot. Herve Renard sacked by Cambridge after Oxford defeat. SPL: inactive Celtic overtaken by Rangers, 3-0 winners over Dundee. S Cup: Huntly hold East Fife, Morton win 7-1 at Cove. Conf: Barnet runaway leaders now have 13 point lead – unluckily for the rest.

12 Chelsea twice cancel out Arsenal lead in top-notch Highbury draw, but complain of quickly taken free-kick which led to Henry's second; Brummies win midlands derby at Villa. SPL: Celtic leapfrog top after 2-0 at Dunfermline. Real game with Sociedad abandoned because of ETA bomb scare with three minutes remaining at 1-1. Remaining time to be replayed later! Porto beat Once Caldas in last World Club Championship 8-7 on penalties after goalless draw in Yokohama; competition to be expanded later.

13 Late Diop strike robs Man Utd of Fulham win; Brummies win Midlands derby at Villa. Andriy Shevchenko is European Footballer of the Year, Henry finishes fourth. Deco, runner-up, Ronaldinho third. Earlier Rooney had become European Young Player of the Year.

14 Lua Lua denies Liverpool win at Anfield as Pompey chimes ring out again. Yeading tie to be live on BBC. FA to investigate Chelsea keeper Cech's remarks on whistler Poll. FA Cup: Brentford edge out Hinckley as do Swansea over Stockport in replays.

15 UEFA Cup: Boro ease through as group leaders, but Rangers blow it against Auxerre. FA Cup: Notts surprise Swindon. FA likely to crack down on Arsene Wenger over Van Nistelrooy 'cheating' accusation, while both Chelsea and West Ham to be charged over October disturbance. The *Daily Telegraph* reports encouraging attendance figures for all four divisions.

16 Wenger fined managerial record £15,000. UEFA Cup: Newcastle head group despite 1-1 with Sporting, but Hearts bow out to Ferencvaros. Joe Kinnear quits Forest, Mick Harford and Des Walker in caretaker roles. FA Youth Cup shock: Man Utd exit to Martin Paterson goal for Stoke.

17 Ch Lge: It's a Knock-out – Chelsea v Barca, Bayern v Arsenal, Man Utd v AC Milan and Leverkusen v Liverpool for Feb – March. Mansfield sack Keith Curle. Forest held by Leicester. Southend climb to fourth.

18 BPL: Baggies caught by Brummies four play; Bolton slump continues as Man City revive; another foursome for Chelsea; Man Utd best of season 5-2 thriller with Palace and Scholes carries on scoring after Rooney penalty fluff; five alive for Spurs with Defoe hat-trick against sad Saints; Boro consolidate fifth place, but Everton draw at Blackburn. CCC: with Wigan, Ipswich inactive, Sunderland, Reading and Sheff Utd progress. Rotherham even lose to Gillingham. CC1: Luton edge home at Bristol City, Hull take advantage of two injured keepers to beat Tranmere 6-1. Stockport caretaker Mark Lillis signs off with a win as new boss Chris Turner looks on. CC2: top six all win in two days. S Cup: East Fife need penalties to see off Huntly.

19 BPL: 75th minute, 76 mph Campbell goal for Arsenal wrecks Pompey; Liverpool recover to beat Newcastle 3-1 and Toon hit by three-week old row by some players antics at the Ritz. CCC: Morris

spot leveller for Millwall against old Leeds mates. CC1: Sheff Wed take four off Doncaster. Two-goal Totti breaks Roma scoring record with 108th Serie A goal.

20 Ronaldinho is FIFA World Player of the Year, Henry second, Shevchenko third. BPL: Charlton leap to seventh after 2-1 over Fulham. Window shopping Liverpool to chase Real's Morientes at £5m. Lord Burns to chair independent FA review.

21 CCC: Ipswich displace Wigan after Baines piledriver nullified by Naylor and Bent goals. Velimir Zajec confirmed as Portsmouth manager with Joe Jordan as coach. James, son of Trevor Francis costs Tamworth three point penalty after ineligible debut. Neville Southall is Hastings manager. Real appoint Arrigo Sacchi as director of football. Steve Morgan pulls out of Liverpool bid.

22 Newcastle £8m offer for Rangers Boumsong falls on deaf ears. Jim Smith re-unites with Redknapp at Soton. Real beaten 1-0 by Sevilla trail Barca by 13 points in La Liga. Sports minister Caborn wants fourth official to suspend games where racial abuse is evident.

23 Man City fine Joey Barton £90,000 for cigar-ash flicking Jamie Tandy who attempted to set light to his shirt at Xmas party.

24 Peter Ridsdale gives up his interest in Barnsley.

26 BPL: Slenderly Chelsea, confidently Arsenal and Man Utd plus edgingly Everton maintain momentum, but Boro slip up at Birmingham. Gunners Henry hits his 128th League goal to equal Ian Wright's tally. Liverpool hit sagging Baggies for five and Spurs make it a nap hand of wins to hoist 1000th post-war victory. Rovers and Toon share four goals. Home goal drought for Palace and Soton. CCC: Ipswich beaten 3-1 by improved Millwall, Wigan caught at home by Derby as are Sunderland by Leeds. Reading make the most of it 3-0 over Watford. First away win for Rotherham at Leicester. CC1: Away day successes for Luton and Hull. CC2: Scunny settle for point at Chester, but Yeovil close gap with 4-1 against Cheltenham. Frozen pitches postpone six FL games. Conf: red card costs Barnet defeat at Stevenage and four matches off. SPL: Celtic 2-0 at Hearts in sole fixture. SL: with Clyde frosted out, Falkirk extend lead to 14 points in Div 1.

27 Sir Alex riles over possible Rooney ban for shoving Ben Haim on Boxing Day. Ljungberg speaks of migraine misery after his return to duty. Leeds McMaster and Oster in bother over party antics. SPL: Rangers keep in touch 4-1 over Motherwell. SL: Alloa win costs Stranraer Div 2 lead to Brechin 3-1 victors at Forfar. Serie A: Giuseppe Papadopulo, match-fixer banned for five months, gets Lazio coaching job!

28 BPL: Chelsea late two goal show at Pompey, Giggs does it for Man Utd at Villa and just the two-goal Job for Boro. Spurs held by Palace and Everton – with Ferguson red – lose to resurging Charlton. Bolton suffer sixth straight defeat to Blackburn. Own goal gives WBA a point at Man City – Baggies only shot! Fourth win in a row for Brummies as Fulham wilt. Saints only concede one at Liverpool, Owen watching. CCC: Ipswich stay top with 1-0 against Stoke, but Wigan in the toils at Burnley and Sunderland's 2-1 win at Forest pushes them second. Reading leak three at Preston, but Sheff Utd and a Hayles inspired hat-trick for Millwall both impress. Leeds gate of 34,496 see another win. CCl: Luton held by Doncaster, Hull idle and Tranmere take advantage 2-0 at Walsall. Sheff Wed climb to fourth. CC2: Scunthorpe goalless with Notts as goal crazy Yeovil win 5-3 at new cellar dwellers and new boss man Steve Thompson's Cambridge. Harriers lift off bottom 2-0 at Oxford. Conf: Carlisle's 6712 see late equaliser against Aldershot. Serie A: Silvio Berlusconi resigns as AC Milan president because of new law affecting government officials. Brazil's Romario, 38, retires.

29 BPL: Arsenal owe it to Vieira at Newcastle. CC1: Hull do better against Donny than Luton in ten-a-side game 24,117 present. SL: Clyde now hit by waterlogged pitch as Falkirk suffer rebuff at Partick. Brummie Savage wants Blackburn move for personal reasons. Saints will flog Beattie.

30 Fergie rages at Rooney three game ban. Birmingham sign younger Kuqi, Njazi Finnish U-21 cap from Lahti for £400,000. Fourth coach in six months for Real as Brazilian Wanderley Luxemburgo moves in. Newcastle seek Babayaro and Boumsong could arrive on the Tyne from Rangers. Serie A: Inter and AC Milan accounts under scrutiny.

31 Now Luis Aragones calls Reyes a 'gypsy'. Brummie Dunn could be out for six months with injury. Leeds send Oster back to Sunderland and fine McMaster.

JANUARY

Call for technology after Spurs lose out ... Henry to have a rest ... Big day for Yeading ... Gravesen off to Real ... Ken Bates goes to Leeds ... Mourinho's birthday treat.

1 Late Cole delivery for Chelsea, Ljungberg brace for Gunners and Man Utd early and late strikes keep top three in contention, but Everton slump to worst defeat of season 5-2 at seven-in-a-row unbeaten Spurs for whom Marney is at the double. Seven without a win Newcastle end bleak spell 2-1 over Birmingham, ten man Norwich get a point at Pompey, but Saints suffer again at Man City. Cole brace in Fulham win against Palace and Diouf denies Albion first win in Bolton draw. Solano solo for Villa. CCC: Crucial win for Hammers at table-topping Ipswich, with 30,003 present. Wigan make up three points at Sheff Utd and Cresswell treble for Preston downs Sunderland. Rotherham throw away another lead. Nine-man Stoke crash at Forest. CC1: Top-Hatters held by Owls, 22,291 watch Hull edge Huddersfield. Stockport win at Torquay. CC2: Scunthorpe fall to Darlo, Yeovil close in with 2-0 at Swansea. Waterlogging causes two FL games abandoned. SPL: Rangers held at lowly Dundee Utd. Three SL matches postponed.

2 SPL: Celtic 2-1 over Livingston restores three-point advantage. Conf: Barnet maintain strong lead 2-1 over Stevenage. Beattie to move in at Everton in £6.5m switch.

3 BPL: Johnson double gives Palace victory over Villa, Blackburn ease to 1-0 against Charlton, Liverpool 2-1 at Norwich and point for Baggies in Norwich stalemate. CCC: Ipswich rely on Currie for sustenance at Plymouth, Sunderland held by the Gills, but Hammers bounce back at Sheff Utd. Rotherham stun the Lions. CC1: Hull's 3-1 at Stockport helps them as Luton are held at Posh.

Tranmere and Sheff Wed (24,253) foursomes also provide important wins, while Hartlepool hit five against the Dons. CC2: Scunthorpe in the toils again, Yeovil hit another four goals, Swans win at Rushden and Southend consolidate fourth 3-1 at Harriers. SL Alloa, having done for Stranraer, do same for Brechin in Div 2, while Peterhead make up ground on held leaders Gretna.

4 BPL: Early double Drogba aids Chelsea as Arsenal held by Man City and Man Utd goalless at home to Spurs who have goal disallowed with officials caught out by Mendes 50 yard lob. At the death, strike gives Bolton first win in 11 at Brummie and Everton beat Portsmouth 2-1 in stoppage time. CCC: Wigan oust Wolves 2-0 to close gap on Ipswich. Sunderland chairman Murray offers to buy up all cash-strapped Sunderland shares. Saints bag Harry's little boy Jamie Redknapp and Davenport (loan) from Spurs. Chelsea swoop for Jiri Jarosik, CSKA Moscow's Czech at £5.6m.

5 BPL: Saints have to settle for a point in 3-3 share with Fulham. Fresh calls for TV technology. Liverpool sign Mauricio Pellegrino from Valencia, but Alonso, Kirkland add to Cisse, Smicer and Nunez injury list. Dropped, transfer-seeking Savage to play for Brummie stiffs. Sporting Lisbon to complain over Chelsea tapping. Brighton and West Ham each fined £10,000 for November brawl. Rushden goalie Turley failed December drug test. Zidane adds penalty for Real in short-time extension to Sociedad game 4-1.

6 Peter Reid in mutual consent Coventry departure, 24th of season. Adrian Heath caretaker. Wrexham fail in appeal against ten-point reduction. Henry who has missed only eight minutes of 28 BPL games to have a rest. Blackburn secure two international skippers: Aaron Mokoena (South Africa) and Ryan Nelson (NZ). Veteran Ferdinand moves from Bolton to Reading.

7 Burnley fury at damp squib cup game ko against Liverpool. Shrewsbury to be fined for failing to fulfil Boxing Day fixture at Bury in time.

8 FA Cup: Exeter shock Man Utd in goalless Old Trafford draw; Man City lose to Oldham, Sheff Utd beat Villa 3-1, Palace lose 2-1 at Sunderland and Norwich beaten 1-0 at West Ham in Premiership casualty list; Blackburn and Fulham held at Cardiff and Watford respectively. But ahead of Yeading's clash with Newcastle at QPR, FA contemplating ground standard to threaten FA Cup minnows. CC1: Sheff Wed firm in on fourth spot 2-0 against Swindon. CC2: point for Cambridge at Bristol R but Harriers open gap at foot with 2-1 over Lincoln. Conf: Barnet draw at Woking. S Cup: Hearts held at Partick and three games off with waterlogged pitches.

9 FA Cup: Yeading not disgraced in 2-0 defeat, Arsenal recover to beat Stoke 2-1.

10 CC1: Tranmere fall to Bristol C. Don Megson is new Forest boss. Albion sign Campbell from Everton, Norwich pay club record £3m for Crewe's Ashton. More racist problems at Madrid derby. Toon chair Shepherd may give Yeading a friendly.

11 C Cup: narrow lead for Liverpool over Watford in first leg semi. Carlisle ground under water. No ground share on Merseyside. Claridge loan to Wycombe hoists 13th club. Boro boss Steve McClaren let off with warning after ref abuse.

12 C Cup: Chelsea held in goalless draw by Man Utd, but Mourinho alleges over Fergie influence with ref. Liverpool sign Fernando Morientes from Real for £6.3m. Mutu agrees deal with Juventus. Wigan rage over unfair police bill. Ian Richardson confirmed as Notts player-manager for the rest of the term.

13 FL chair Brian Mawhinney whines over agents fees. Sainsbury withdraws his offer for Leeds. Real to sign Gravesen for £2.5m. Vassell reserve comeback for Villa. Owen in scratch team Real cup draw. Paul Ashworth is new sporting director of Russia's Rostov.

14 CCC: Welcome win for Rangers over Stoke. Northern Ireland cap Quinn back from Holland with Sheff Wed.

15 BPL: Arsenal off the rails at Bolton in 1-0 defeat, allowing Chelsea to steam ten points ahead after 2-0 at Spurs. Rooney keeps Man Utd on track at Liverpool but riles the Kop with celebration resulting in mobile phone missile. Strugglers Norwich, Saints and Palace all lose again, but Blackburn edge it at nine-man Pompey. Charlton move up to seventh after 3-1 over Birmingham. CCC: Ipswich 3-2 against Coventry still in step with Wigan 2-0 winners at Rotherham a pace behind at the top. Wolves dent Hammers 4-2 with improved performance, but Sheff Utd lose at bome to Brighton and Reading held at Burnley. CC1: Luton move further ahead after beating Stockport 3-0 as Hull are held by Peterborough. Tranmere take five off Wrexham; Sheff Wed draw at Bournemouth. CC2: Yeovil's nine-game winning run comes to an end at Oxford; Scunthorpe take Bury 3-2, but Swansea, Southend, Northampton and Darlington all have to settle for a point each. SPL: Rangers ahead on goal difference 3-0 against Dunfermline with Celtic inactive. SL: Falkirk maintain massive 14 point lead in Div 1, Alloa keep on scoring in Div 2 as do Gretna in Div 3. Eight Conf sides out of Trophy, three others including Exeter must replay.

16 BPL: Diop drops WBA into last minute agony at Fulham, Everton draw at Boro, but melee spoils the spectacle. SPL: Celtic resume top spot after minimum win at Aberdeen. Conf: Aldershot latest to be dumped out of Trophy 1-0 at Thurrock; Carlisle playing at Workington because of persisting pitch problems beat Redditch 3-1. Owen on target for Real winners. Maldini celebrates 20th year as Serie A player.

17 FA Cup: Reading win Swansea replay 1-0. S Cup: gallant Gretna only beaten 4-3 by Dundee Utd before 3000. Saints Phillips likely to be out for a month with injury. FA ban two unnamed players for drug taking.

18 FA Cup: Traore own goal enough for Burnley against under-strength Liverpool. Villa guilty of Beattie illegal approach. Boro and Everton charged by FA. Ernie Tippett leaves Rushden.

19 FA Cup: Grecians 2005 application ends as Man Utd win 2-0; Blackburn pressed all the way by Cardiff win 3-2, Fulham 2-0 over Watford and Boyd redeems himself as Hartlepool winner after penalty miss in first game against Boston. Owen tenth goal for Real but they are out of the Spanish Cup. Mutu transfer to Juve on hold.

20 Peace to break out between Sir Alex and Wenger? New kit deal for Chelsea at £24.5m.

21 Ken Bates takes charge at Leeds; Micky Adams is the new Coventry boss. Arsenal to wear redcurrant shirts for last season at Highbury, their strip in 1913. Savage finally signs for Blackburn from Birmingham, Carson joins Liverpool from Leeds. Lawrie Sanchez to extend Northern Ireland contract. CC1: MacLean goal enough for Sheff Wed over Port Vale.

22 BPL: Chelsea see off Pompey by half-time; Man Utd beat Villa 3-1; Charlton surprise Everton at Goodison; Fulham win at Birmingham; Boro throw away three goal lead in 4-4 with Norwich; day of strugglers with Albion beating Man City 2-0, Saints similarly over Liverpool and Palace 3-0 against Spurs. CCC: Ipswich held at Reading, Wigan by Watford, but Sunderland 1-0 over Sheff Utd. CC1: Goalless Luton draw, but Hull lose at Doncaster. Ugarte all four for Wrexham in 4-2 at Chesterfield. CC2: Yeovil 2-1 against Cambridge, but Scunthorpe lose 2-0 at Notts. SPL: Celtic win again, 2-0 against Motherwell. SL: nine games hit by frozen pitches, but shock reverse for Gretna 4-2 at Peterhead in Div 3.

23 BPL: Arsenal just edge Given-inspired Magpies. CCC: Derby shake Hammers at Upton Park. SPL: own goal helps Rangers win at Dons.

24 BPL: Bolton's Diouf "dive" for penalty does in Blackburn – after Friedel blocks his penalty kick. McManaman to retire at season's end.

25 C Cup: Gerrard strike against Watford eases Liverpool into final. CC1: Colchester take five off Barnsley as do Macclesfield at Notts in CC2. LDV Vans: Wrexham and penalty winners Oldham are north finalists, Bristol Rovers and Southend in the south. Pennant facing jail for second driving offence. Steve McMahon gets Perth Glory job.

26 C Cup: Mourinho's 42nd birthday treat: Chelsea win 2-1 at Old Trafford with Duff freak effort to reach final. Mutu drops appeal against them. Spurs to loan Egyptian striker Mido and Slavia goalkeeper Cerny plus Moroccan El Hamdaoui permanently. Sinama-Pongolle out for rest of season. Man City land Musampa on loan from Atletico Madrid. Merson offer to resign refused at Walsall. Three face fraud inquiry at Exeter.

27 German referee Robert Hoyzer admits match fixing. European wide anti-racism campaign opens in London.

28 Mourinho faces "cheat" charge over C Cup first leg semi. Anelka off to Fenerbahce in £7m deal. Eriksson wins four-week cushion before WC finals.

29 FA Cup: controversial last gasp Crouch penalty ends south coast derby in Saints favour over ten-man Pompey; Another spot kick furore sees Spurs draw at Albion. Rooney back scoring with brace for Man Utd over Boro. Yeovil push Charlton all the way. CC1: Fryatt hat-trick lifts Walsall spirits; Tranmere draw at Luton. CC2: ten-man Harriers win cellar clash at Cambridge. SL; Div 2 sees Brechin five points clear as Stranraer crash 3-0 at home to Stirling. Another four goals for Gretna in Div 3 and East Stirling have their second win!. Conf: Barnet, Carlisle held in draws, Crawley go third.

30 FA Cup: Terry makes it 2-0 for Chelsea against Brum, Bolton win at Oldham tempered by loss of injured Hunt. SPL: Celtic spot on at Killie to go top. Conf: Shots hit by Hereford win. Becks free-kick in Real win.

31 Bellamy goes on loan to Celtic. Spurs get two for £8m from Forest as Reid and Dawson move; Rovers Ferguson is Rangers coup at £4.5m. Djemba-Djemba is a Villan at £1.35m. Vincent Candela French defender from Roma joins Bolton free. Everton get Mikel Arteta on loan from Sociedad. Soton have Camara on loan from Wolves and Bernard permanently from Newcastle. Pompey get Rodic a Slovenian international striker for £1m as transfer window shuts. Ronnie Moore leaves Rotherham. Barwick starts job at FA.

FEBRUARY

Man Utd double over Arsenal ... Another record for Shearer ... Euro Under-21 record score ... Glazer homing in on Old Trafford ... Newcastle shake Chelsea ... Trophy for Chelsea.

1 BPL: Man Utd virtually end Arsenal's title hopes with emphatic 4-2 win at Highbury. Late show gives Palace point at WBA. Bolton beat ten-man Spurs. Liverpool 2-1 at Charlton, Pompey similarly over Boro at Fratton. CIS Cup: Motherwell extra time winners over Hearts in semi. Opening hours of WC 2006 final tickets see half a million applications from 108 countries.

2 BPL: Chelsea reliant on Robben at Rovers; Everton edge Norwich. Angel falls from grace missing two Villa penalties at Fulham whose Cole is another on the missing spot in 1-1 draw. Newcastle manage draw at Man City as Shearer hits his 250th Premiership goal and 186th in all competitions for the Mags. Arsenal – Man Utd escape sanction over tunnel incident Tuesday. CIS Cup: Rangers semi slaughter of Dundee Utd 7-1. Ray Clemence has cancer.

3 UEFA to restrict foreign players in Euro competitions. Arsenal will get funds for players despite new ground finance. Man Utd go ahead for 70,000 capacity. Conf: Leigh RMI appoint Steve Bleasdale in succession to Geoff Lutley.

4 Cup Final switch next year to Wednesday has fans upset. CCC: Sunderland have to settle for draw at Wolves.

5 BPL: The Mido touch as the Egyptian double striker helps Spurs to win over Portsmouth; Arsenal stylish 3-1 winners at Villa and Henry breaks Wright's League total; Albion lose odd goal in five at Norwich, Palace hit by Bolton. Newcastle dull draw with Charlton. Boro edge Blackburn; Morientes inspires Liverpool win over Fulham; Keane scores 50th goal for Man Utd in 2-0 over Brummies. CCC: Ipswich five clear at top as Wigan lose at home to Stoke; bottom duo Rotherham and Forest in goalless draw. CC1: Top four all in drawn affairs, Hartlepool make ground 1-0 at Chesterfield. CC2: leaders Yeovil slump 3-1 at Macclesfield. S Cup: Aberdeen beat ex-tenants Caley 2-1. Trophy: Hucknall oust Conf Northwich.

Jose Mourinho looks on during Chelsea's Premiership match against Blackburn at Ewood Park. A fifth-minute Arjen Robben goal secured yet another victory for the Champions. (Actionimages)

6 BPL: Man City again prevent Chelsea scoring against them thanks to James the second clean-sheeter; Saints caught by injury-time Bent equaliser for Everton. S Cup: easy for Celtic over Fifers. Conf: Shots second after 2-0 at York. Trophy: Carlisle slam Barnet 4-1 at temporary Morecambe home. Barca lose at home to Atletico Madrid 2-0. UEFA want to stop anyone involved in football betting on matches.

7 Glazer homing in on Man Utd again.

8 U-21s: Dutch treat themselves to 2-1 over England with Derby gate of 33,184 a record at this level; Northern Ireland beat Scots 2-1 but Republic lose 2-0 in Portugal and Wales crash 4-0 to Germans. Euro U-21 record score: Spain 14 San Marino 0. But England win U-20 game with Russia. CC1: crucial MK Dons 4-1 win at Bradford. CC2: Swansea lose at Mansfield.

9 Ints: Sven's 4-3-3 only yields goalless draw with Holland; Irish all at sea as ten-man Canada's Occean dumps them; Duff inspired Republic edge Portugal 1-0 and Bellamy brace boosts Wales and boss Toshack 2-0. Glazer threats investigated. Fears of Wednesday cup final recede.

10 FA to pour cold water on revival of home championship internationals. Conf: new bosses: Liam Daish (Gravesend) and Bill McEwan (York).

11 Man Utd to give Glazer access. CC2: Southend and Scunny in goalless draw.

12 BPL: Beattie butt madness helps Chelsea as ten-man Everton lose it; Euro chasing teams find goals scarce: Bolton and Boro draw, Liverpool lose 2-0 at Birmingham; Villa win at Pompey, Blackburn take three off Norwich. FA Cup: Fulham need extra time against Derby; Brentford surprise Hartlepool and Defoe double hits Albion for Spurs. CCC: Stewart treble lifts Sunderland against Watford; Ipswich edge Leicester and Wigan win 3-1 at Crewe. CC1: Luton increase lead over Hull to four points after beating them 1-0, but Tranmere are held and Wednesday lose at home to Bradford. CC2: Yeovil recapture top spot as Jevons hat-trick sparks 4-2 win over Bristol Rovers. Conf: Barnet lose again as Hereford move fifth; Carlisle held by Gravesend. Crawley boss Francis Vines arrested after Woking game. SPL: Dundee Utd off bottom swapping places with Livingston after 2-0 win as Rangers lead on goal difference from Celtic following 3-0 v Hibs. SL: Stranraer close gap on Brechin to two points in Div 2 while another four goals for Div 3 Gretna.

13 Mancunian derby goes to Utd 2-0. FA Cup: Sheff Utd win penalty shoot-out with West Ham. Owen scores for Real again. Blatter rules out video evidence in matches.

14 BPL: Arsenal whack Palace 5-1 with squad of 16 foreigners. Turkish League game to be replayed after referee admits free-kick error.

15 CC1: Luton boss Mike Newall makes happy return to old club Hull in 3-2 win. CC2: Scunthorpe go own 2-1 to a Claridge inspired Wycombe. LDV Vans: Southend take 2-1 lead at Bristol Rovers and Ugarte strikes three as Wrexham win 5-3 at Oldham.

16 UEFA Cup: Valencia's 2-0 win over Steaua is the most decisive in the first leg knock-out round. CC2: useful 2-0 win for Lincoln at Boston. England beat Holland 3-0 in non-league international.

17 UEFA Cup: Newcastle take 2-1 lead at Heerenveen and Boro given hope with draw in Graz. CSKA Moscow look good in 2-0 against Benfica, even though game switched to Krasnodar.

18 CCC: Ipswich hold Preston at Deepdale. Djorkaeff joins New York MetroStars. Onandi Lowe cleared of cocaine smuggling.

19 FA Cup: last gasp penalty earns Sheff Utd draw at Arsenal; Rooney returns to Everton and scores in Man Utd win, though coin-throwing incident and after match disturbances cause concern; Saints throw away two-goal lead against Brentford and draw; veteran Dublin hits Leicester winner at Charlton; Davies goal for Bolton over Fulham. CCC: Sunderland shaken at Brighton, but Wigan take three off Leeds and Plymouth hammered 5-0 at Upton Park. CC1: Luton keep seven point lead as they win at Bradford and Hull beat Wrexham 2-1. CC2: Yeovil also retain two point lead over Scunthorpe. Conf: Barnet blip goes on losing 4-1 at Accrington – lead down to only 13 pts! SL: Div 2 jitters hit both Brechin and Stranraer – also nearest rivals Stirling and Morton who all lose. Div 3 sees statutory four goals for Gretna.

20 FA Cup: rare reverse for Chelsea at Newcastle; Forest surprise Spurs in draw at WHL while Burnley and Blackburn are goalless. SPL: Rangers end five year misery at Celtic with 2-0 win to go four ahead with game more played.

21 FA accept criticism over early evening kick-off at Goodison in cup.

22 Ch Lge: Toure late effort gives Arsenal some glimmer of hope after 3-1 defeat to Bayern, but Liverpool ease through Leverkusen 3-1 despite Dudek error and PSV and Real take 1-0 lead each against Monaco and Juventus respectively. BPL: Albion and Saints settle for a point. CCC: Ipswich surprised by Watford, but Hammers win at Gillingham and Sunderland hit Rotherham 4-1. CC1: Luton extend lead with 1-0 win over Walsall as Hull are held at MK Dons. CC2: Crucial 4-3 win for Yeovil over Scunthorpe. Rushden goalie Turley six month ban for drug taking.

23 Ch Lge: own goal gives Drogba dismissed Chelsea some hope in Barca's 2-1 win, Man Utd caught by Carroll gaffe and ex-Chelsea Crespo goal, Lyon impressive 3-0 win in Bremen while Porto and Inter draw 1-1. CCC: Wigan go top after 2-1 at Coventry. Hierro to quit playing at season's end. CC1: Sheff Wed keep up play-off chasing with 2-1 over Peterborough. Dr Malcolm Brodie, former Belfast Telegraph editor and SSFYB Northern Ireland correspondent receives Jules Rimet Award as only journalist to cover 13 World Cups.

24 UEFA Cup: Newcastle repeat 2-1 score and go through with Boro similar winners over Graz. Reyes banned for incident in cup game with Sheff Utd along with Bergkamp sent off in it. Millwall could be charged after Cardiff incident on Tuesday. Leeds to cull 15 players. WC final ticket total now 320,000. Conf: Dean Austin out as Farnborough boss.

25 Ranieri sacked by Valencia after UEFA Cup exit. Ten-yard advance experiment at free-kicks likely to be scrapped.

26 BPL: Arsenal held at Soton, Rooney brace helps Man Utd beat Pompey 2-1 with record 67,989 viewing, while two Johnson penalties give Palace points over Birmingham. Osman brace as Everton win at Villa and Spurs beat Fulham 2-0. CCC: Wigan, Ipswich, West Ham and Derby all lose –

Middlesbrough's Ray Parlour challenges Mario Bazina of Liebherr Grazer AK in the UEFA Cup First Knockout Round Second Leg at the Riverside Stadium. (Actionimages)

Heads you win! Steven Gerrard leaps to clear during the Carling Cup Final defeat by Chelsea. (Actionimages)

Sunderland and Preston are winners. CC1: Hull cut Luton lead after beating Colchester 2-0, as Hatters lose 3-1 at Port Vale. CC2: Yeovil lose 2-1 at Grimsby, Scunthorpe similarly at Swansea but Macclesfield and Southend win. Conf: Barnet back to winning ways 2-1 over Shots. Trophy: Conf Canvey and Hereford held in drawn games. SPL: Rangers have six point lead with two games more played after 2-1 over Killie. SL: Morton close on Stranraer in second place after 2-0 win. Real game with La Coruna halted by racial abuse.

27 C Cup final: Chelsea recover from 45 second Riise goal equalise with Gerrard own goal and edge home in extra time for Mourinho's first trophy of the season. S Cup: Celtic take five off Clyde.

28 BPL: Fowler breaks into the 150 goal club to turn deficit at Norwich into 3-2 win as Delia Smith and her half-time appeal for vocal support falls on deaf ears. Prutton faces lengthy ban. Everton will sign Ruddy from Cambridge at season's end.

MARCH

Euro exits for Arsenal and Real ... Keegan leaves Man City ... Chelsea streaking away ... Gretna create more records ... Ashley Cole "tapping" furore ... Sir Alex lifetime award.

1 FA Cup: Arsenal need penalties to beat Sheff Utd; Blackburn keep recent record over Burnley and Crouch brace pushes Saints through against Brentford. Conf: Barnet lose at York. Aragones fined £2000 for Henry outburst.

2 FA Cup: No trouble for Spurs at Forest. Mourinho escapes with FA warning. CCC: another Wolves draw 3-3 at Derby. SPL: last gasp penalty for Rangers breaks Hearts; Celtic beat Dundee 3-0.

3 FA Cup final on 13 May will give Eriksson four-week break before WC finals. Becks to end career at Real. Rinus Michels, legendary Dutch coach, dies at 77.

4 CCC: Sunderland top after Akinbiyi sub debut for Burnley lasts three minutes before seeing red. Mourinho promises lip service to end. Shaun W-P to miss England games with injury. Hearts complain over Rangers last minute penalty. Paul Hart to quit Barnsley post, Andy Ritchie stepping in. Cardiff transfer Kavanagh to Wigan for £450,000.

5 BPL: Chelsea extend lead to eight points after 3-1 at Norwich as Man Utd are held goalless by ten-man Palace. But Cech misses out on English league record of 11 consecutive clean sheets conceding his first goal in 1025 minutes. Henry treble inspires Arsenal over Pompey, Quashie squeezes crucial three points for Saints over Spurs; Liverpool lose at reviving Newcastle, Boro beaten 2-0 at Villa while Fulham and Charlton share no goals. CCC: Ellington spot kick lifts Wigan back top against Ipswich; West Ham lose red-carded Repka and 2-1 to visiting Preston; away wins for Gillingham and Forest further isolate Rotherham. CC1: Ugarte five in Wrexham's amazing 6-4 win at Hartlepool; Luton take five off Bristol C; Hull complete double over Tranmere. CC2: Yeovil, Scunthorpe find one goal enough for victory. SPL: Injury-time equaliser for Caley shakes Rangers; Livingston win at Dundee menaces Tayside duo at the bottom. Conf: 4181 see Shots local derby win over Farnborough while Halifax, Woking and Stevenage also register three points.

6 BPL: relegation-zone turn-ups: sub Stead hits Everton for Blackburn and WBA win midland derby with Brummies. CCC: point for Leeds at Millwall. CC1: Sheff Wed climb to third after 2-0 v Don caster. SPL: Celtic close gap on Rangers to four points with two games in hand after 3-1 at Hibs.

7 Ch Lge: war of words continues ahead of Chelsea – Barca clash; Mourinho and Rijkaard swapping swipes. BPL: Diouf strike hits Man City. Carlton Palmer to get official nod at Mansfield.

8 Ch Lge: Terry ends Barca dream for Chelsea in heart-stopping classic, after the Spaniards claw back two of the Blues rapid threesome while Stamford Bridge loanee at AC Milan Crespo does for Man Utd; Lyon rampant rattle seven up against Werder with ex-Arsenal Wiltord getting a hat-trick. CCC: Sheff Utd take four off Crewe; crucial win for Forest at Watford. CC1: one goal enough for Hull over Hartlepool. CC2: Northampton go down at Rochdale. SL: Peterhead promoted after 1-1 draw with Elgin. Conf: Halifax, Woking and Carlisle make ground. LDV: Southend reach final again to meet cash-strapped Wrexham. Wigan reach compromise with police. Ranieri tipped for Pompey post. Ipswich boss Joe Royle forced to pay back £423,000 compensation to Man City by Court of Appeal.

9 Ch Lge: Henry strike insufficient against Bayern, but Liverpool repeat 3-1 Leverkusen scoreline to reach last eight. Real exit in overtime in ten-a-side Juve match.

10 Kevin Keegan parts company with Man City. Mourinho rages over fines: £5000 for Carling Cup comments, £15,000 for failing to control players in Blackburn (hit for £10,000) game, while more problems might come from tunnel clash in Barca match. UEFA Cup: Newcastle take advantage of nine-man Olympiakos 3-1, but Boro bow 3-2 to Sporting. Disgraced German ref Robert Hoyzer turns supergrass in betting scandal.

11 Barcelona's Eto'o claims racial abuse at Chelsea. Oxford beat Cambridge to take series lead in Varsity match.

12 FA Cup: Ljungberg gives Arsenal victory at Bolton and Man Utd have easy passage at Soton 4-0. CCC: Ipswich six hitters over Forest, Plymouth get five against Brighton. Wigan and Sunderland level on points at the top. CC1: Luton, Hull retain leading roles. CC2: Yeovil lose 2-1 at Darlington. SPL: Dunferline crash 6-0 to Celtic. SL: third win for East Stirling. Raith relegated from Div 1.

13 FA Cup: Early Kluivert goal for Newcastle and late Dickov penalty for Blackburn dispose of Spurs and Leicester respectively. SPL: Rangers 2-0 at Dundee. Now Real lose 2-1 to Getafe. Mourinho dubbed "enemy of football" by Volker Roth, UEFA ref supremo.

14 Savage is 7th Welsh player to quit international team after Toshack post. Gilberto Silva on way back after reserve outing. Becks opens his Docklands soccer school.

15 BPL: Chelsea minimum win over WBA. CCC: Sunderland 5-1, Wigan 4-2 and Ipswich 1-0 stay leaders. Rotherham beat Reading 1-0! SL; East Stirling with fourth match. Leeds, Gillingham charged after brawl. Platini to press for UEFA presidency.

16 UEFA Cup: Magpies pick off Olympiakos 4-0 with comfort. BPL: Blackburn frustrate Liverpool, Spurs downed at Charlton.

17 UEFA Cup: Boro out as Sporting win 1-0. FA Cup semis to have early starts. Lawrie Sanchez to have N Ireland extension. Bill McGarry, ex-manager and England cap, dies at 77.

18 Ch Lge: draw revives Heysel in Liverpool v Juve clash; Chelsea get Bayern. UEFA Cup: Newcastle to play Sporting. Wenger unhappy with England USA tour. CCC: another draw for Hammers with ten man Leicester as Harewood fluffs penalty. CC1: Tranmere take five off Posh.

19 Slender, single goal wins for Arsenal at Blackburn and Man Utd edgy over Fulham, but Chelsea retain 11 point lead after 4-1 with Palace. Pompey make a point checking Newcastle's eight match winning streak; Spurs run Stuart Pearce's Man City boss debut and Bolton keep hopes of European football alive. Baggies kill off ten-man Charlton 4-1 at The Valley. CCC: Sunderland take over with 1-0 against Coventry, as Wigan and Ipswich are held by lowly Forest and Gillingham respectively, but Rotherham now 13 points adrift. CC1: Hull's 4-0 win closes Luton lead as Hatters held at Oldham. Huddersfield 5-3 over bottom club Stockport. CC2: Bury shake Yeovil, Scunthorpe only draw, but Macclesfield and Southend keep winning ways. Bristol Rovers and Mansfield share eight goals. Conf: Barnet 7-1 crushing of nine-man Farnborough. SPL: Bellamy hat-trick for Celtic in 3-2 at Dundee Utd. SL: Falkirk held by doomed Raith. Coasting Gretna whack fellow promoted Peterhead 6-1 in Div 2.

20 Liverpool win pulsating 201st Mersey derby 2-1 against Everton despite losing Baros sent off. Lifeline for Soton in 3-1 win at Boro and Brummies win Villa midland derby 2-0. CIS final: Rangers cruise 5-1 against Motherwell.

21 UEFA to crack down on Chelsea. FA to investigate 22 man melee in midland tunnel missed by ref Riley.

22 Man Utd profits £12.4m down by over half. Chelsea prepare UEFA defence. Baros "sorry" to Stubbs. Boss Ray Lewington axed by Watford. Ten-man Brentford lose at Blackpool.

23 BPL: Chelsea and Ashley Cole charged in "Tapgate". Becks hints at blighty return. Man Utd Ch Lge seeding scheme thrown out. Conf: Woking's nine-men slip to Scarborough in late draw.

24 Eriksson ally David Davies to quit FA in 2006. Chelsea's Peter Kenyon hit back in UEFA furore as Caborn complains of governing body's softness on racism. Mutu faces PL hearing. Last ever FL transfer deadline day.

25 WC eve: England confident, Irish prepared, Wales wary, Scots apprehensive and Republic ever ready. U21: Carson error in Germany's 2-2 draw with England; Scots down 2-0 in Italy, Republic lose 3-1 in Israel. CC1: shock for leaders Luton beaten 3-1 by Barnsley, only second defeat in 19. Hartlepool lose 1-0 to Huddersfield. CC2: Southend pressurise top two with 3-0 against Rochdale. Conf: Now Hereford take six off Farnborough.

26 WC: Joe Cole ignites burst of four in 15 second half minutes to ease England over N. Ireland; Wales succumb to two late Austrian strikes; Scots improve despite 2-0 Italian defeat and Republic caught in late Israel leveller. Poles hammer eight past Azerbaijan; France held scoreless by Swiss;

Liechtenstein surprisingly only 2-1 down to Russia; Robben injured again in Dutch game. Argentina 2-1 in Bolivia stay top in South America; Mali concede late goals to lose to Togo and riot ends match.

27 WC: Brazil just edge Peru 1-0, but Ecuador shake Paraguay with 5-2 victory; Eddie Lewis scores for USA but Mexico win 2-1. Conf: Sunday-best Shots hit four in Sky win over Woking.

28 CC1: Luton's 4-1 win at Torquay lifts them above Hull, 1-0 losers at Oldham. Doncaster stun Tranmere with 4-2 success. CC2: Southend equal 73 year old club record with 16th unbeaten game; Macclesfield held by Boston. Scunthorpe lose 2-0 at Lincoln. Conf: nine clubs in six-point range below Barnet. In Spain, Luis Aragones appeals against fine for verbal abuse on Henry.

29 U21: England 2-0 over Azerbaijan, Wales lose similarly in Austria. Republic beat China 1-0 in friendly. CC1: Huddersfield beat Sheff Wed 1-0 in Yorkshire derby. CC2: Yeovil shocked by Notts 3-1 victory. Edu may join Valencia. Watford appoint Adrian Boothroyd as manager with old-timer Keith Burkinshaw as No.2. After retirement of Dean Richards at Spurs, Brighton goalkeeper Ben Roberts is also forced out with injury. Sir Alex gets the Lifetime Achievement Award for 2005.

30 WC: Better Becks but brace and bit parts baulk Azers; Coyne slip costs Wales in Austria, Irish hit by late Pole. Van Nistelrooy a Dutch scorer, Trezeguet marksman and red-carder for France; Russia in danger of not qualifying. Mourinho waits for UEFA ruling.

31 Chelsea accept UEFA findings: £33,300 fine and two-match Mourinho ban plus £8900 fine for Barca incident at the Nou Camp. Carry on Shearer – one more year. WC: Brazil snatch draw in Uruguay, Argentina stay ahead 1-0 over Colombia.

APRIL

Shearer to carry on ... Norwich start to revive ... Vaughan is the youngest ... More Woodgate misery ... Henry to miss Cup Final ... Chelsea at last.

1 Shearer agrees to player-coach role next season. Query over Pennant playing tag. Atouba three match ban for violent conduct v Man City. Neil Sillett Farnborough boss goes after 34 days. CC2: Southend tops after club record 17 without defeat.

2 BPL: Three red Loony Toons with Bowyer fighting Dyer, Taylor for hands as Newcastle eight crash 3-0 to Villa. Chelsea 3-1 at Soton, Arsenal with Henry trio (now 181 goals) 4-1 over Norwich, Blackburn hold Man Utd but Palace fall to Boro. Charlton and Man City share four goals, Brummies, Spurs two, one goal enough for Liverpool against Bolton. CCC: Seven wins in a row Sunderland forge 3-1 at QPR as Ipswich edge to 3-2 victors over Derby, to plough level points behind Wigan, beaten by Hammers with Sheringham scoring on 39th birthday. Preston and Reading held to home draws. Rotherham cling on at the foot after 2-1 at ten-man Stoke. CC1: Shock for ten-man Sheff Wed, beaten by Tranmere, but Luton and Hull still pacesetters. Stockport first FL team to be relegated. CC2: Yeovil slip up 2-0 at Rushden, Scunthorpe and Macclesfield scoreless. SPL: Hearts stun Celtic at Parkhead. SL: Falkirk 14 points clear in Div 1 as stadium approval given, Morton making ground on second place Stranraer in Div 2, Gretna 15 points ahead in Div 3. Conf: Administration wrapped Northwich beat runaway leaders Barnet. Trophy semi-final sensation as Grays send Albion for a Burton 5-0.

3 BPL: Pompey fail after leading Fulham, Baggies shake Everton. SPL: ten-man Rangers claim top spot after 3-2 at Motherwell. Owen on the mark again for Real.

4 No sack but Bowyer fined six weeks wages, Dyer to appeal. Gordon Strachan tipped for Pompey role. FA to get streamlining.

5 Ch Lge: Carson gaffe leaves Liverpool just 2-1 ahead of Juve on emotional Anfield night. PSV draw in Lyon. Mourinho to watch Chelsea game on TV. Ian Rush quits at Chester. Water boy Lehmann gets two-game Euro ban. CCC: Eight on the spin Sunderland strike early at Wigan, Hammers win again with vintage Sheri. Ipswich relegate battling Rotherham after 4-3 win. Wolves register 20th draw only three short of FL record.

6 Ch Lge: Chelsea wary of Bayern second goal – the Ballack "dive" but take 4-2 lead while allegations that Mourinho "hat-trick" communications with Rui Faria; AC Milan 2-0 over Inter. Pompey to appoint Alain Perrin ex-PT teacher and Marseille coach as manager. Jordan stays as coach, David Pleat will be consultant. Viduka out for rest of season.

7 UEFA Cup: Shearer strike gives Mags advantage over Sporting, CSKA Moscow again look impressive with 4-0 win over Auxerre. Mick Harford is Rotherham boss. Leeds praise physio Dave Hancock for saving Paul Butler in Sheff Utd game Tuesday after the player swallowed his own tongue. Spanish Federation uphold fine on Aragones. Becks to stay in Spain.

8 Two referees Mike Dean and Matt Messias hit by suspensions. CC1: Tranmere 1-0 v Stockport keeps them in play-off frame.

9 BPL: Birmingham earn draw at Chelsea; Norwich sensationally beat Man Utd 2-0 as Soton lose 3-0 at Blackburn. Pires goal for Arsenal at Boro, Charlton beaten 4-2 at Pompey and Musampa goal 26 seconds from the end gives Man City 1-0 victory over Gerrard missing Liverpool. Bolton Euro hopes improve with 3-1 against Fulham. CCC: Reading dim Stadium of Light for Sunderland as Wigan close gap with 2-0 win at Cardiff; Hammers late threesome over Coventry. CC1: Luton take advantage of inactive Hull in 1-0 at Bournemouth. CC2: Yeovil in 5-2 gallop over Mansfield. Tennent's Cup: Dundee Utd reach final after 2-1 against Hibs. SL: Falkirk promoted as champions after 1-0 v Ross Co; Gretna do it in Div 3 by hammering Stenhousemuir 7-0. Conf: Barnet stretch lead to 16 pts as Carlisle fail at home to Forest Green.

10 BPL: Vaughan at 16 years 271 days becomes youngest Premier scorer as Everton beat Palace 4-0; lifeline for Baggies in dramatic draw at Villa; one goal enough for Spurs against Mags. CC1: Hull 2-0 at Bradford keep up pressure on Luton. Tennent's Cup: Celtic reach final, too, beating Hearts 2-1. LDV Vans: victory for cash and points strapped Wrexham in extra time against Southend. Owen ovation in his 13th goal for Real, 4-2 winners over Barca.

11 CCC: Wolves find winning formula against automatic hopefuls Ipswich. FA deny Sir Alex claim about Arsenal wanting Cardiff for semis.
12 Ch Lge: Chelsea rowing home comfortably almost catch a crab as Bayern strike back with two late goals; crowd trouble ends the Milan derby affair after 71 minutes with AC Milan leading 1-0. CCC: Forest hanging by a thread after tie with Sheff Utd. CC1: Luton gain promotion after Brentford beat Tranmere. Arsenal injury worries over Campbell and Clichy. SPL: shock for Rangers beaten 1-0 at Ibrox by Dundee Utd.
13 Ch Lge: Liverpool stalemate with Juventus is enough for semi-final place after night of unpleasantness in Turin; first penalty shoot-out in 13 years of knock-out stages sees PSV emerge against Lyon. SPL: Celtic joy as Hartson treble against Livingston leapfrogs them over Rangers. Stuttgart to sign Hitzlsperger in summer. Campbell surprise: lasts a full reserve game.
14 UEFA Cup: Newcastle take early lead then collapse in the last 19 minutes to lose 4-1 to Sporting; AZ draw ten-a-side game with Villarreal but go through along with away goal successes Parma against FK Austria. CSKA Moscow lose two goals in Auxerre but have two more to spare of course.
15 CCC: Derby still on road to play-offs after 1-0 – a club record 12th away win – over Sheff Utd. CC1: Hartlepool convincing 3-0 in play-off chasing win v Sheff Wed. CC2: blow to Southend automatic hopes as Orient win at Roots Hall while Swansea helped by 1-0 v Oxford. Inter fined £132,000 and behind closed doors six-match embargo for Euro games. Robben may be fit to return for Chelsea, Woodgate has op in Spain having never played out there since move.
16 FA Cup semi: Van Persie late double and a whack on the head still puts Arsenal 3-0 in front of Blackburn. BPL: Suicidal Saints lose 2-0 lead and game to Villa; six goal thriller shared by Palace and Norwich; Bolton firm up effort for Euro spot by winning 2-1 at Charlton as Liverpool are held by Spurs; Fulham and Man City share as do goalless Brum and Pompey. CCC: Wigan close gap on inactive Sunderland after 2-1 at Leicester; Hammers held in Millwall derby; draw 21 for Wolves; Preston 3-0 over Cardiff. CC1: own goal gives Luton three more points against MK Dons while Hull held by Swindon and having a penalty saved, gain promotion. CC2: As Yeovil held by Harriers, Scunny close gap with 4-0 win over Cambridge. SPL: Celtic lead by five points after 3-2 against the Dons prior to Sunday game for Rangers. SL: Falkirk win 1-0 at nearest rivals Clyde; Brechin stretching ahead in Div 2 and Morton close gap on Stranraer again. Gretna 6-2 at Elgin have now scored 120 League goals. Bundesliga: Hargreaves sub goal for Bayern gives them crucial lead in title race. Juventus three point lead over AC Milan.
17 FA Cup semi: Man Utd have no trouble in disposing of Newcastle 4-1 in second Cardiff affair on consecutive days. CCC: Sunderland close to winning at Ipswich but happy enough with draw. SPL: Rangers two points behind Celtic after 1-0 over Fifers.
18 Sir Alex unhappy about the meeting between Ferdinand and Chelsea's Peter Kenyon. Fair-play spots may go to English clubs in Europe. Youth Cup: Ipswich draw at Soton. Arthur Dunn Cup: Old Etonians (ex-FA Cup winners) 2 Old Brentwoods 1.
19 BPL: Saints managed a point at Bolton, as do Fulham at Boro. CCC: Zamora strike gets three points for Hammers at Stoke. CC2: Southend win away at Macclesfield. Conf: Shots share six goals at Accrington, Barnet held by Carlisle. Blackburn Todd charged over Van Persie elbow. Ronnie Moore expects Oldham post permanently. Ch Lge 2006 final Paris, UEFA Cup Eindhoven, but Hampden get UEFA in 2007. Scots lose B international 2-1 in Austria.
20 BPL: Chelsea title on hold again after draw with Arsenal, who resign themselves to losing crown. Everton importantly beat nine-man Man Utd 1-0 as Gary Neville and Scholes are dismissed; Norwich revival goes on: 2-1 over Newcastle; Liverpool 2-1 at Portsmouth, Albion hold Spurs at WHL, Palace go down at Blackburn, Stuart Pearce job prospects look good as Man City beat Birmingham 3-0; Villa and Charlton goalless. Birmingham to stage benefit game for MG Rover employees.
21 Todd in the clear. Leeds fined £3000 for failing to control players in Gillingham game. Hugh Dallas Scots whistler to retire at 47. England women beat Scots 2-1. Despite healthy play-off prospects West Ham bedevilled by takeover talk.
22 Bowyer gets four match ban over brawl with Dyer and police have investigated the incident. Henry may miss FA Cup final with groin problem. Marseille Barthez banned for three games for spitting at referee. Youth Cup: 15 year old sub Upson seals it for Ipswich over Saints.
23 BPL: Chelsea 3-1 over neighbours Fulham await inevitable; Palace living in hopes again after 1-0 over Liverpool as are Norwich with same scoreline against Charlton, but Albion crash 4-0 at Boro. Everton have to settle for draw with Brummies as do Man City at Blackburn and Bolton at Villa. CCC: Sunderland gain promotion after 2-1 over Leicester because Ipswich can only draw at Leeds. QPR hold Wigan; Derby beat Gills and Hammers draw at Brighton. CC1: Luton 2-1 at Wrexham, but Hull shaken up by Joachim hat-trick for Walsall. Peterborough relegated despite 1-0 win at Bournemouth who suffer fifth successive home defeat. CC2: Cambridge relegated after goalless draw with Rochdale. At the top Yeovil and Scunny held, Southend lose. Play-off berths look like Swansea, Macclesfield, Lincoln and either Darlington or Northampton now. SL: Partick relegated despite beating Clyde. Three top teams in Div 2 draw, Gretna restricted to four goal in Div 3. Conf: despite winning 2-0 at Carlisle, Exeter miss play-offs – the other three lucky ones are Hereford, Aldershot and Stevenage. Morecambe who missed last year again fail. Forest Green axe boss Alan Lewer. Belgrade derby Red Star and Partizan 1-1 but 27 injured and 67 arrested.
24 BPL: Saints 4-1 down in 27 minutes at Pompey; Man Utd 2-1 over Newcastle thanks to dipping swerving 25 yard Rooney volley prelude to receiving PFA Young Player award. John Terry gets the Player of the Year vote. CCC: Preston hit by 2-1 defeat at Millwall. SPL: Celtic 2-1 at Ibrox is ominous for Rangers five points adrift.

25 BPL: Chelsea on the brink as Arsenal beat Spurs. Birmingham sign out of jail Pennant. Arsenal Owusu-Abeyie arrested after PFA dinner fracas. FA to ask UEFA for extra Euro spot if Liverpool win Ch Lge. Chelsea clinch record £50m deal with Samsung starting June.

26 Ch Lge semi: AC Milan take 2-0 lead over PSV. BPL: another point for Albion against Blackburn. CCC: Derby lose ground in Leicester defeat. CC1: Wrexham still battling for survival after 1-0 win at Port Vale. UEFA turn down extra place. Coventry to move in to 32,500 Ricoh Arena next season after Japanese agree £10m sponsorship.

27 Ch Lge semi: Liverpool stifle Chelsea scoreless and the Bridge. BPL: 115th Tyne-Tees derby stalemate involving Mags and Boro, but Dyer injury puts him out for rest of season.

28 UEFA Cup semis: CSKA Moscow 0-0 in Parma, Sporting take 2-1 lead over AZ. Man Utd put figure on Glazer bid £800m. Keith Curle is Chester boss. Stoke put up for sale. Posh Legg quits through cancer. Conf: Forest Green may get reprieve as Northwich new ground has to be approved.

29 CCC: Sunderland 2-1 title winners at West Ham increase off-field pressures on the east Londoners. CC1: Tranmere important 1-0 win over Port Vale. Heinze out for rest of season with injury. Cambridge file for administration.

30 BPL: At last! Chelsea 2-0 at Bolton are champions 50 years after their last such title; Everton suffer 2-0 defeat at Fulham, but Liverpool are held by Boro; Palace draw at Newcastle and Soton comedy of defensive errors win 4-3 against Norwich; Man City take early two-goal lead over Pompey and Birmingham oust Blackburn. CCC: Wigan await automatic lift-off after 1-1 draw with Preston; Sheff Utd chances of play-offs look doomed after losing 1-0 to Millwall, leaving only Reading or West Ham to break into Ipswich, Preston and Derby bracket. Forest finally fall after 2-1 at QPR. Either Crewe or Gillingham to join them. Yet Derby swamped 6-2 at Coventry bidding farewell to Highfield Road. CC1: Huddersfield, Bristol City, Brentford and Bournemouth in hunt for last play-off place with Tranmere, Sheff Wed and Hartlepool already assured. Ugarte treble keeps Wrexham hoping to avoid the drop as do MK Dons 3-0 winners at Posh. CC2: Southend slipping out of automatic slot as Yeovil win 1-0 but Swansea beat Shrewsbury 1-0. Harriers jettisoned to Conference after losing 4-1 at home to Grimsby. SPL: Shock horror as Celtic lose 3-1 at home to Hibs. SL: Morton draw at Stranraer but not enough to prevent Blues promotion. East Stirling success: keep Gretna down to one goal!

MAY

Sunderland and West Ham back in the Premier ... Celtic stunned and O'Neill leaves ... WBA rewrite history and survive ... First penalty shoot-out in FA Cup Final ... Liverpool amazing Euro recovery and victory ... Owen becomes fourth all-time England scorer.

1 BPL: Spurs savouring Europe chance after 5-1 over Villa while Charlton ship four at home to Man Utd. SPL: Rangers two points behind Celtic after winning 3-1 at Aberdeen. Confusion over whether Liverpool can get Ch Lge place.

2 BPL: Arsenal late show sees off Baggies. Conf: Shots take slender lead over Carlisle, Stevenage late equaliser against Hereford. Becks 30th birthday gift – he has fractured his foot. Hartson is Scots FWA player of the year; Tony Mowbray of Hibs is the manager choice. Radebe retires at Leeds to coach. Women's cup final: Aluko (18) wins it for Charlton over Everton.

3 Ch Lge: Chelsea blow out to "no-to-over-the-line-goal" error having escaped Cech foul on Baros and red card as Liverpool reach European Cup final. Jose M says that best team lost. Belgian FA fined £5300 for fireworks in Bosnia game. CC1: Wrexham relegated as Brentford move into play-off spot.

4 Ch Lge: PSV scare AC Milan who win with late strike on away goals rule. BPL: Magpies back to winning ways at poorish Fulham. Mourinho new Chelsea deal to 2010 at £5m pa. Neale Cooper leaves Hartlepool, destination possibly Dunfermline. Ramon Diaz resigns at Oxford.

5 UEFA Cup: CSKA cruise through, but away goal agony for AZ at Sporting Lisbon. Mourinho may be in bother with UEFA over "no goal" comments. England U-17 lose to Turkey 3-2.

6 Conf: Shots pay the penalties at Carlisle while Stevenage snatch it at Hereford. Liverpool still hoping for Champions League place if finishing fifth. Chelsea may recall Crespo. Leicester unload six players. Oxford appoint Brian Talbot as boss.

7 Death dance marathon continues at the bottom with Norwich's turn to lead the foursome reel after 1-0 over Birmingham; ten-a-side game sees Palace and Saints draw, Baggies similarly at Man Utd. Everton consolidate fourth place with 2-0 over Newcastle, Bolton sixth place after 1-1 at Pompey, but Boro only a point behind after downing Spurs UEFA hopes. Man City in the frame for Europe place. Chelsea leave it late and Makelele has to put an unfair penalty away for his first goal for the Blues. CC1: Brentford shoot into fourth place 2-1 against Hull, Hartlepool draw ends Bournemouth's chances of play-off spot. MK Dons celebrate escape at the other end 2-1 over Tranmere to the chagrin of Torquay beaten by the same score at Colchester. CC2: Southend slip out of automatic promotion 1-1 at Grimsby while Swansea snatch third 1-0 at Bury in 25 secs, but bizarrely goalie Gueret arrested after fracas. Northampton sneak last play-off berth by goal difference of three as do Lincoln with plus 17, to the detriment of Darlington. SPL: Rangers edgy 2-1 over Hearts puts them top. Dundee slump to the foot after crashing 5-0 at Dunfermline.

8 Arsenal end Liverpool chance of fourth place with 3-1 win. Celtic regain lead in Scotland 2-0 against Aberdeen. Dennis Wise leaves Millwall. Owen scores 12th Real League goal.

9 Lennart Johansson urges FA to plead for Liverpool in classic buck passing game. Hierro to retire at 37.

10 BPL: Chelsea recover to beat Man Utd 3-1 at Old Trafford. FA dismiss England USA tour criticism. Steve Thompson leaves as boss of Cambridge United.

11 BPL: Season's best Arsenal classic 7-0 drubbing of Everton. Rooney rest gives Crouch USA chance. Baros unhappy with Benitez.

12 Stuart Pearce rewarded with tow-year Man City contract. Jon Obi Mikel tug-of-war teenager in Chelsea v Man Utd battle, fails to report for Lyn Oslo training. Blatter blasts Mourinho and Rooney. Play-off: slender lead for Sheff Wed against Brentford.
13 Formal offer by Glazer for Utd could mean heavy debt. Play-off: Boyd double gives Hartlepool the edge over Tranmere.
14 Play-offs: Hammers throw away two-goal lead in Ipswich draw. Lincoln take minimum lead over Macclesfield. Carlisle back in FL after 1-0 Conf final win over Stevenage.
15 BPL: Survival Sunday sees dramatic ending in drop zone: Canaries knocked off perch in six-goal rout at Fulham; Saints lose lead and their way against Man Utd; Palace draw at Charlton not enough, but Baggies defy history in great escape. Boro nab UEFA Cup spot from Man City in draw.
16 Will injured Henry absence be Arsenal's Achilles heel? Glazer will recoup after his £812m deal for Man Utd. Play-off: Sheff Wed book final place after 2-1 at Brentford. Yakubu moving to Boro from Pompey for £7.5m. Hoddle gets rolling contract at Wolves. Poll to referee UEFA Cup final.
17 Play-off: Hartlepool edge Tranmere on inevitable penalty shoot-out. Sheff Utd sign Nalis from Leicester.
18 UEFA Cup Final: CSKA Moscow become first Russian club to win a European trophy recovering to beat Sporting 3-1 in Lisbon. Play-off: Zamora at the double for Hammers at Ipswich. Harry Redknapp to carry on Sainting.
19 Second FA Cup trophy sold at Christie's for £478,000. Bidding described as "exciting." But 1936 final programme Arsenal v Sheff Utd goes for only £360. England may have nine clubs in Europe. Play-offs: Preston to meet West Ham in Championship final.
20 Everton hope to sign Spurs Davies. Hughes signed by Villa from Newcastle for £1.5m. Sheff Utd get Ifill from Millwall. Martin O'Neill hints at Celtic departure.
21 FAC Final: Frustrated. profligate Man Utd lose penalty shoot-out to shot shy Arsenal. SPL: Dundee can only draw at Livingston and are relegated. Play-offs: Southend and Lincoln will meet in the final.
22 SPL: Celtic disaster. They concede two in last two minutes at Motherwell and Rangers 1-0 winners at Hibs are champions! Wenger admits only hope was win on penalties. Trophy Final: Grays need penalties to beat Hucknall.
23 George Burley on collision course at Derby with board. Wise may go to QPR as player. Souness charged over ref criticism at Everton. Gullit resigns at Feyenoord. Liverpool call up Cisse for the big one.
24 Gordon Strachan to be Celtic boss. Rupert Lowe denies axing Jim Smith. NFL in USA question Glazer casino bid near Old Trafford. Wembley footbridge to be "White Horse Bridge" after 1923 steed.
25 Ch Lge final: night to remember as Liverpool fight back from 3-0 h-t deficit to level scores and with whirling Dervish antics of Pole dancing Dudek clinch the penalty shoot-out. Birmingham plan 50,000 all-sports stadium. Dave Jones is new Cardiff manager, Peter Ridsdale exec deputy chairman. Martin O'Neill reveals wife's ill-health as resignation issue.
26 Gerrard admits knackered Liverpool played for penalties. Groundswell opinion demands Anfield in Ch Lge next term. Man Utd board support Glazer bid. Spurs want Palace's Johnson, but transfer Davies to Everton for initial £3.5m. Wigley is Man City reserve team coach vice Hartford.
27 Man Utd release two goalies Carroll and Ricardo. Palace to sign Ward from Millwall for £1.5m.
28 Richardson bow double as England beat USA in Chicago. Play-offs: Eastwood sparks Southend in extra time against Lincoln. Houllier to coach Lyon next season.
29 Play-offs: Sheff Wed recover to beat Tranmere in extra time. UEFA to put Liverpool decision on priority list. Mutu finished with seven month drug ban is Juventus sub in 4-2 win over Cagliari (Zola two).
30 Play-offs: Zamora Hammers goal-king sinks Preston.
31 Owen treble lifts him fourth in England all time scorers as "he" beats Colombia 3-2 in New Jersey. Gordon Strachan unveiled as Celtic boss. Wise may join Soton. Mark Wright is Peterborough's new manager.

JUNE

Arnesen quits Spurs for Chelsea ... Liverpool allowed back in Europe ... Argentina qualify for World Cup ... England ladies exit ... Glazer gets United ... Brazil win Confederations Cup.

1 Cole fined record £100,000, Chelsea £300,000 and three-point deduction suspended for a year, Mourinho £200,000. Charlton sign Darren Bent from Ipswich in likely £3m deal.
2 Cole and advisers still unhappy over "Tapgate". Macken leaves Man City for Palace. Sheff Utd list seven players. Sam Ellis extends assistant job at Leeds by a year.
3 Ints: Republic confident, Scots hopeful, England Ladies aim is high.
4 WC: Irish wasteful in 2-2 draw with Israel, Scots late double over Moldova, England Euro Ladies late winner against Finns. England U-20s lose 1-0 to Portugal.
5 Man Utd grab Van der Sar from Fulham for £2m.
6 Spurs want two Chelsea players in compensation deal for Arnesen – Parker and Forssell. Cole to appeal tapping accusation. Millwall fined £25,000 for racism. Souness contests disrepute charge. Yakubu contracts malaria for second time. Coventry new ground delay to 26 August. Leicester sign Celtic keeper Douglas. Charlton get Davies from Oxford U.
7 Glazer brings on board his three sons – Joel, Bryan and Avi. Liverpool will no European fate on Friday. George Burley quits Derby and may head for Millwall. Report says Premiership clubs earned £1.3b in 2003–04. Sir Bobby Robson declines a post with Hearts. Carlos Alberto sacked as Azerbaijan manager. Scots struggling for players before Belarus WC game.

8 WC: Scots draw in Belarus may not be enough; Republic win in Faeroes gives them group lead; Spain scrape a last minute draw with Bosnia. Women's Euro: late Danish goals down England. Spurs may get £15m from Chelsea in package proposal for Arnesen. Man Utd board meetings may be in the USA. Benfica get Ronald Koeman as coach. England U-20s lose to France on penalties of course.

9 Liverpool expect Euro yes vote. Man Utd braced for Glazer ticket hike. Mourinho loses fine appeal. Martin van Geel likely Arnesen replacement at Spurs. Argentina confirmed as first South American WC qualifiers. C Cup final at Cardiff next 26 Feb. Britain may enter team for 2012 Olympics. Collina retires on 18 June at 45.

10 Liverpool report for training 27 June! Football League sign new Sky Sports deal £110m over three years, £35m more than at present. Fans groups unhappy with Glazer deal. Lord Burns to third degree FA.

11 Women's Euro exit for England 1-0 v Swedes. Park Ji-Sung latest tug-of-war between Chelsea and Man Utd. Robert may go to Bolton. Liverpool to haul in Jose Reina, 22, goalie of Villarreal. Last Conf ever-present Northwich lose place despite new ground because of late completion. Forest Green reprieved from drop.

12 Owen happy to stay to win things at Real.

13 Glazer 97.5% grip on Utd. Gerrard in contract extension talks with Liverpool. O'Brien moves from Newcastle to Pompey. Sunderland get Jon Stead from Blackburn. Utd's Carroll likely to become a Hammer. Blatter hints at micro chip WC finals.

14 Sunderland nap Davis Ipswich goalie for £1.25m. Death at 81 of Tommy Walker, Newcastle winger of the 1950s. Liverpool earned nearly £22m from Ch Lge run.

15 Chelsea not to fight Cole fine and suspended points deduction, but Mourinho to go ahead. Parker, Chelsea to Newcastle for £6.5m. Sheringham agrees one more year at West Ham. Diouf likely for permanent Bolton switch. Livingston reprieve after Dundee claim rejected over Kachloul "amateur" status. Women's Euro: Germany beat Finns 4-1 for final place. Confed Cup: Argentina edge Tunisia 2-1, Germans win best of seven goals v Aussies.

16 Anti-Bowyer Brummie fans put off Lee move. Graeme Souness ref rage over Knight lands £20,000 fine and two-match suspension. Sunderland aim for signing No. 5 with Miller from Ipswich, who expect Kuqi to join Blackburn. Confed Cup: Three goal Brazil down slip Greece, Mexicans surprise Japs.

17 Rooney agent on FA disrepute charge. Routledge Spurs target from Palace. Real failure in Ch Lge hits Utd in Becks original deal. Intertoto starts again! Bohs 1-0 over Gent.

18 Confed Cup: Figueroa treble as Argies beat Aussies 4-2.

19 Women's Euro: Germany 3 Norway 1 and fourth successive title for them. Young Redknapp retires. Intertoto: Bangor lose 2-1 at home to Dinaburg, Lisburn 1-0 defeat by Zalgiris.

20 Claridge gets Millwall job. Kluivert for Valencia. FC United the Glazer newly-formed protest club will play in N-W Counties Lge. "Alamgate" moves to High Court.

21 Asier Del Horno, left-back (!) from Bilbao latest Chelsea capture at £8m with Jonas Elmer, 17, Grasshoppers midfield player likely next. Repka re-signs for Hammers. Michael Appleton to sue surgeon who allegedly ruined his career at WBA. Confed Cup: Germany's draw with Argies puts them in semis, but Aussies lose to Tunisia. Alam alleges David Davies as third man.

22 Now seeding Liverpool is a Ch Lge problem. BPL first South Korean – Park Ji-Sung joines Man Utd from PSV. Sir Clive Woodward to become Saints Director of Football after life with the Lions. Pompey grab John Viafara, Colombian cap at £1.5m from Once Caldas. Midlands move sees Carter join Baggies from Brummies. Nicky Forster goes to Ipswich from Reading. Alam sex diary goes awol. Confed Cup sees two draws: Greece with Mexico, Japan and Brazil. Alam missing sex diaries

23 Chelsea and Spurs nearing Arnesen agreement fee. Leeds get Lewis (PNE) free. Ipswich pay Swindon £750,000 for Parkin.

24 Ch Lge: Liverpool drawn with TNS the Welsh club who had offered them a route back weeks ago! Spurs get £8m for Arnesen. Veron to stay loaned to Inter for two more years. Bellamy "no wish" to leave Newcastle. Roberto Carlos is robbed during car interview in Brazil! Derby appoint Bolton No. 2 Phil Brown as manager. Newcastle sign Belozoglu Emre – known in the trade as Emre B – from Inter. Sidibe goes to Stoke from Gillingham.

25 Confed Cup semi: Brazil with Adriano double beat Germany 3-2. Intertoto: Bohs go down 3-1 in Gent, Lisburn to a Zalgiris penalty.

26 Confed Cup semi: Argentina forced to penalties to oust Mexico. Intertoto: Bangor lose 2-0 to Dinaburg.

27 Alexander Hleb, Stuttgart midfield to Arsenal for £10m. Per Kroldrup, Udinese to Everton; Wise becomes a Saint. Helguson goes to Fulham £1.3m from Watford. Utd Shareholders United ask OFT to investigate Glazer takeover. Discipline on the agenda for FA on and off the field. Collina gets one more year. Chelsea to woo back Crespo.

28 Kezman likely to move to Atletico Madrid. Thomas Lyskov, 14, Reading academy midfield gets five year deal with Chelsea! Stoke push Pulis out for not signings foreigners. Stone goes to Leeds from Pompey. Barwick gets on the Wembley board.

29 Confed Cup: Adriano and Brazil turn on the style to whack Argentina 4-1 in the final. Germans edge Mexicans 4-3 for third spot. Zola retires. Villa get Phillips from Soton for £1m. Referees plan dissent meeting with Managers and PFA. Robert fined a second helping of two weeks wages at Newcastle. Stoke appoint Johan Boskamp as manager. Short journey Blackburn to Sheff Utd. Glazer boys set foot in Manchester and face some hostility.

30 Glazers meet Utd in Portugal. Sammy Lee is Bolton No. 2.

ENGLISH LEAGUE TABLES 2004–05

FA BARCLAYCARD PREMIERSHIP

			Home					Away					Total						
		P	*W*	*D*	*L*	*F*	*A*	*W*	*D*	*L*	*F*	*A*	*W*	*D*	*L*	*F*	*A*	*GD*	*Pts*
1	Chelsea	38	14	5	0	35	6	15	3	1	37	9	29	8	1	72	15	57	95
2	Arsenal	38	13	5	1	54	19	12	3	4	33	17	25	8	5	87	36	51	83
3	Manchester U	38	12	6	1	31	12	10	5	4	27	14	22	11	5	58	26	32	77
4	Everton	38	12	2	5	24	15	6	5	8	21	31	18	7	13	45	46	–1	61
5	Liverpool	38	12	4	3	31	15	5	3	11	21	26	17	7	14	52	41	11	58
6	Bolton W	38	9	5	5	25	18	7	5	7	24	26	16	10	12	49	44	5	58
7	Middlesbrough	38	9	6	4	29	19	5	7	7	24	27	14	13	11	53	46	7	55
8	Manchester C	38	8	6	5	24	14	5	7	7	23	25	13	13	12	47	39	8	52
9	Tottenham H	38	9	5	5	36	22	5	5	9	11	19	14	10	14	47	41	6	52
10	Aston Villa	38	8	6	5	26	17	4	5	10	19	35	12	11	15	45	52	–7	47
11	Charlton Ath	38	8	4	7	29	29	4	6	9	13	29	12	10	16	42	58	–16	46
12	Birmingham C	38	8	6	5	24	15	3	6	10	16	31	11	12	15	40	46	–6	45
13	Fulham	38	8	4	7	29	26	4	4	11	23	34	12	8	18	52	60	–8	44
14	Newcastle U	38	7	7	5	25	25	3	7	9	22	32	10	14	14	47	57	–10	44
15	Blackburn R	38	5	8	6	21	22	4	7	8	11	21	9	15	14	32	43	–11	42
16	Portsmouth	38	8	4	7	30	26	2	5	12	13	33	10	9	19	43	59	–16	39
17	WBA	38	5	8	6	17	24	1	8	10	19	37	6	16	16	36	61	–25	34
18	Crystal Palace	38	6	5	8	21	19	1	7	11	20	43	7	12	19	41	62	–21	33
19	Norwich C	38	7	5	7	29	32	0	7	12	13	45	7	12	19	42	77	–35	33
20	Southampton	38	5	9	5	30	30	1	5	13	15	36	6	14	18	45	66	–21	32

COCA-COLA FOOTBALL LEAGUE CHAMPIONSHIP

			Home					Away					Total						
		P	*W*	*D*	*L*	*F*	*A*	*W*	*D*	*L*	*F*	*A*	*W*	*D*	*L*	*F*	*A*	*GD*	*Pts*
1	Sunderland	46	16	4	3	45	21	13	3	7	31	20	29	7	10	76	41	35	94
2	Wigan Ath	46	13	5	5	42	15	12	7	4	37	20	25	12	9	79	35	44	87
3	Ipswich T	46	17	3	3	53	26	7	10	6	32	30	24	13	9	85	56	29	85
4	Derby Co	46	10	7	6	38	30	12	3	8	33	30	22	10	14	71	60	11	76
5	Preston NE	46	14	7	2	44	22	7	5	11	23	36	21	12	13	67	58	9	75
6	West Ham U	46	12	5	6	36	24	9	5	9	30	32	21	10	15	66	56	10	73
7	Reading	46	13	7	3	33	15	6	6	11	18	29	19	13	14	51	44	7	70
8	Sheffield U	46	9	7	7	28	23	9	6	8	29	33	18	13	15	57	56	1	67
9	Wolverhampton W	46	9	11	3	40	26	6	10	7	32	33	15	21	10	72	59	13	66
10	Millwall	46	12	5	6	33	22	6	7	10	18	23	18	12	16	51	45	6	66
11	QPR	46	10	7	6	32	26	7	4	12	22	32	17	11	18	54	58	–4	62
12	Stoke C	46	11	2	10	22	18	6	8	9	14	20	17	10	19	36	38	–2	61
13	Burnley	46	10	7	6	26	19	5	8	10	12	20	15	15	16	38	39	–1	60
14	Leeds U	46	7	10	6	28	26	7	8	8	21	26	14	18	14	49	52	–3	60
15	Leicester C	46	8	8	7	24	20	4	13	6	25	26	12	21	13	49	46	3	57
16	Cardiff C	46	10	4	9	24	19	3	11	9	24	32	13	15	18	48	51	–3	54
17	Plymouth Arg	46	9	8	6	31	23	5	3	15	21	41	14	11	21	52	64	–12	53
18	Watford	46	5	10	8	25	25	7	6	10	27	34	12	16	18	52	59	–7	52
19	Coventry C	46	8	7	8	32	28	5	6	12	29	45	13	13	20	61	73	–12	52
20	Brighton & HA	46	7	7	9	24	29	6	5	12	16	36	13	12	21	40	65	–25	51
21	Crewe Alex	46	6	8	9	37	38	6	6	11	29	48	12	14	20	66	86	–20	50
22	Gillingham	46	10	6	7	22	23	2	8	13	23	43	12	14	20	45	66	–21	50
23	Nottingham F	46	7	10	6	26	28	2	7	14	16	38	9	17	20	42	66	–24	44
24	Rotherham U	46	2	7	14	17	34	3	7	13	18	35	5	14	27	35	69	–34	29

COCA-COLA FOOTBALL LEAGUE DIVISION 1

			Home					*Away*					*Total*						
		P	*W*	*D*	*L*	*F*	*A*	*W*	*D*	*L*	*F*	*A*	*W*	*D*	*L*	*F*	*A*	*GD*	*Pts*
1	Luton T	46	17	4	2	46	16	12	7	4	41	32	29	11	6	87	48	39	98
2	Hull C	46	16	5	2	42	17	10	3	10	38	36	26	8	12	80	53	27	86
3	Tranmere R	46	14	5	4	43	23	8	8	7	30	32	22	13	11	73	55	18	79
4	Brentford	46	15	4	4	34	22	7	5	11	23	38	22	9	15	57	60	–3	75
5	Sheffield W	46	10	6	7	34	28	9	9	5	43	31	19	15	12	77	59	18	72
6	Hartlepool U	46	15	3	5	51	30	6	5	12	25	36	21	8	17	76	66	10	71
7	Bristol C	46	9	8	6	42	25	9	8	6	32	32	18	16	12	74	57	17	70
8	Bournemouth	46	9	7	7	40	30	11	3	9	37	34	20	10	16	77	64	13	70
9	Huddersfield T	46	12	6	5	42	28	8	4	11	32	37	20	10	16	74	65	9	70
10	Doncaster R	46	10	11	2	35	20	6	7	10	30	40	16	18	12	65	60	5	66
11	Bradford C	46	9	6	8	40	35	8	8	7	24	27	17	14	15	64	62	2	65
12	Swindon T	46	12	5	6	40	30	5	7	11	26	38	17	12	17	66	68	–2	63
13	Barnsley	46	7	11	5	38	31	7	8	8	31	33	14	19	13	69	64	5	61
14	Walsall	46	11	7	5	40	28	5	5	13	25	41	16	12	18	65	69	–4	60
15	Colchester U	46	8	6	9	27	23	6	11	6	33	27	14	17	15	60	50	10	59
16	Blackpool	46	8	7	8	28	30	7	5	11	26	29	15	12	19	54	59	–5	57
17	Chesterfield	46	9	8	6	32	28	5	7	11	23	34	14	15	17	55	62	–7	57
18	Port Vale	46	13	2	8	33	23	4	3	16	16	36	17	5	24	49	59	–10	56
19	Oldham Ath	46	10	5	8	42	34	4	5	14	18	39	14	10	22	60	73	–13	52
20	Milton Keynes Dons	46	8	10	5	33	28	4	5	14	21	40	12	15	19	54	68	–14	51
21	Torquay U	46	8	5	10	27	36	4	10	9	28	43	12	15	19	55	79	–24	51
22	Wrexham*	46	6	8	9	26	37	7	6	10	36	43	13	14	19	62	80	–18	43
23	Peterborough U	46	5	6	12	27	35	4	6	13	22	38	9	12	25	49	73	–24	39
24	Stockport Co	46	3	4	16	26	46	3	4	16	23	52	6	8	32	49	98	–49	26

**Wrexham deducted 10 points after entering administration.*

COCA-COLA FOOTBALL LEAGUE DIVISION 2

			Home					*Away*					*Total*						
		P	*W*	*D*	*L*	*F*	*A*	*W*	*D*	*L*	*F*	*A*	*W*	*D*	*L*	*F*	*A*	*GD*	*Pts*
1	Yeovil T	46	16	4	3	57	28	9	4	10	33	37	25	8	13	90	65	25	83
2	Scunthorpe U	46	16	5	2	43	16	6	9	8	26	26	22	14	10	69	42	27	80
3	Swansea C	46	15	5	3	36	16	9	3	11	26	27	24	8	14	62	43	19	80
4	Southend U	46	13	5	5	31	14	9	7	7	34	32	22	12	12	65	46	19	78
5	Macclesfield T	46	15	3	5	39	24	7	6	10	21	25	22	9	15	60	49	11	75
6	Lincoln C	46	11	8	4	37	22	9	4	10	27	25	20	12	14	64	47	17	72
7	Northampton T	46	11	9	3	35	20	9	3	11	27	31	20	12	14	62	51	11	72
8	Darlington	46	13	4	6	33	21	7	8	8	24	28	20	12	14	57	49	8	72
9	Rochdale	46	11	8	4	34	21	5	10	8	20	27	16	18	12	54	48	6	66
10	Wycombe W	46	8	7	8	28	26	9	7	7	30	26	17	14	15	58	52	6	65
11	Leyton Orient	46	10	8	5	40	30	6	7	10	25	37	16	15	15	65	67	–2	63
12	Bristol R	46	10	12	1	39	22	3	9	11	21	35	13	21	12	60	57	3	60
13	Mansfield T	46	9	8	6	29	24	6	7	10	27	32	15	15	16	56	56	0	60
14	Cheltenham T	46	10	5	8	27	23	6	7	10	24	31	16	12	18	51	54	–3	60
15	Oxford U	46	11	4	8	29	24	5	7	11	21	39	16	11	19	50	63	–13	59
16	Boston U	46	11	8	4	39	24	3	8	12	23	34	14	16	16	62	58	4	58
17	Bury	46	8	9	6	26	18	6	7	10	28	36	14	16	16	54	54	0	58
18	Grimsby T	46	8	10	5	28	19	6	6	11	23	33	14	16	16	51	52	–1	58
19	Notts Co	46	6	7	10	21	27	7	6	10	25	35	13	13	20	46	62	–16	52
20	Chester C	46	7	8	8	25	33	5	8	10	18	36	12	16	18	43	69	–26	52
21	Shrewsbury T	46	9	7	7	34	18	2	9	12	14	35	11	16	19	48	53	–5	49
22	Rushden & D	46	8	6	9	29	29	2	8	13	13	34	10	14	22	42	63	–21	44
23	Kidderminster H	46	6	6	11	21	39	4	2	17	18	46	10	8	28	39	85	–46	38
24	Cambridge U*	46	7	6	10	22	27	1	10	12	17	35	8	16	22	39	62	–23	30

**Cambridge U deducted 10 points after entering administration.*

FOOTBALL LEAGUE PLAY-OFFS 2004–05

▪ *Denotes player sent off.*

CHAMPIONSHIP FIRST LEG

Saturday, 14 May 2005

West Ham U (2) 2 *(Harewood 7, Zamora 13)*

Ipswich T (1) 2 *(Walker 45 (og), Kuqi 74)* 33,723

West Ham U: Walker; Repka, Powell C, Mullins, Ferdinand, Ward, Newton (Rebrov), Reo-Coker, Harewood, Zamora (Noble), Etherington.
Ipswich T: Davis; Diallo (Richards), Wilnis, Horlock (Currie), De Vos, Naylor, Miller, Magilton, Bent, Kuqi, Westlake.

Sunday, 15 May 2005

Preston NE (1) 2 *(Nugent 38, Cresswell 90)*

Derby Co (0) 0 20,315

Preston NE: Nash; Davis, Hill, O'Neil (Etuhu), Lucketti, Mawene, Sedgwick, McKenna, Cresswell, Nugent (Agyemang), Lewis (Broomes).
Derby Co: Camp; Kenna, Jackson, Huddlestone, Konjic, Johnson (Mills), Bisgaard, Taylor, Smith (Bolder), Peschisolido, Reich.

CHAMPIONSHIP SECOND LEG

Wednesday, 18 May 2005

Ipswich T (0) 0

West Ham U (0) 2 *(Zamora 61, 72)* 30,010

Ipswich T: Davis; Wilnis, Richards, Miller, De Vos, Naylor, Currie, Magilton (Bowditch), Bent, Kuqi, Westlake.
West Ham U: Walker; Repka (Dailly), Powell C, Mullins, Ferdinand, Ward, Fletcher, Reo-Coker, Harewood, Zamora (Newton), Etherington (Noble).

Thursday, 19 May 2005

Derby Co (0) 0

Preston NE (0) 0 31,310

Derby Co: Camp; Kenna (Taylor), Jackson, Huddlestone, Konjic, Bolder, Bisgaard, Peschisolido, Rasiak, Smith (Reich), Idiakez.
Preston NE: Nash; Davis, Hill, O'Neil (Etuhu), Lucketti, Mawene, Sedgwick, McKenna, Cresswell, Nugent (Agyemang), Lewis (Broomes).

CHAMPIONSHIP FINAL (at Millennium Stadium)

Monday, 30 May 2005

West Ham U (0) 1 *(Zamora 57)*

Preston NE (0) 0 70,275

West Ham U: Walker (Bywater); Repka, Powell C, Mullins, Ferdinand, Ward, Newton (Noble), Reo-Coker, Harewood, Zamora (Dailly), Etherington.
Preston NE: Nash; Davis, Hill, O'Neil (Etuhu), Lucketti, Mawene (Alexander), Sedgwick (Agyemang), McKenna, Cresswell, Nugent, Lewis.
Referee: M. Riley (Yorkshire).

LEAGUE 1 FIRST LEG

Thursday, 12 May 2005

Sheffield W (1) 1 *(McGovern 12)*

Brentford (0) 0 28,625

Sheffield W: Lucas; Bruce, Heckingbottom, Bullen, Wood, Whelan, Rocastle (McMahon), McGovern, Peacock (Talbot), Quinn (Brunt), Hamshaw.
Brentford: Nelson; O'Connor, Frampton, Talbot, Sodje, Turner, Pratley, Hargreaves, Burton, Gayle (Tabb), Hutchinson (Rankin).

Friday, 13 May 2005

Hartlepool U (1) 2 *(Boyd 32, 68)*

Tranmere R (0) 0 6604

Hartlepool U: Konstantopoulos; Barron, Robson, Nelson, Westwood, Strachan, Williams, Sweeney, Daly (Porter), Boyd (Tinkler), Humphreys.
Tranmere R: Achterberg; Taylor, Roberts, Sharps, Jackson, Goodison, Hall (Beresford), McAteer, Hume, Whitmore (Dadi), Rankine.

LEAGUE 1 SECOND LEG

Monday, 16 May 2005

Brentford (0) 1 *(Frampton 87)*

Sheffield W (1) 2 *(Peacock 27, Brunt 53)* 10,823

Brentford: Nelson; Hutchinson (Rankin), Frampton, Talbot, Sodje (Salako), Turner, Pratley, Hargreaves, Burton, Fitzgerald SP (Gayle), Tabb.
Sheffield W: Lucas; Bruce, Heckingbottom, Bullen, Wood, Whelan, Rocastle (Adams), McGovern, Peacock, Quinn (Talbot), Hamshaw (Brunt).

James Quinn of Sheffield Wednesday holds off Hartlepool's Chris Westwod during the League 1 Final at the Millennium Stadium. (Actionimages)

Southend United goalscorers Duncan Jupp (left) and Freddy Eastwood celebrate their team's League 2 play-off final success. (PA/Empics)

Tuesday, 17 May 2005

Tranmere R (0) 2 *(Taylor 70, Beresford 87)*

Hartlepool U (0) 0 13,356

Tranmere R: Achterberg; Taylor, Roberts, Sharps, Jackson, Goodison (Beresford), Hall, McAteer (Harrison), Hume, Dadi (Dagnall), Rankine.
Hartlepool U: Konstantopoulos; Barron (Tinkler), Robson, Nelson, Westwood, Strachan, Williams, Sweeney, Daly (Porter), Boyd (Butler), Humphreys.
aet; Hartlepool U won 6-5 on penalties: Taylor (saved), Strachan (scored), Hall (scored), Tinkler (saved), Roberts (scored), Porter (scored), Hume (scored), Robson (scored), Dagnall (scored), Westwood (scored), Beresford (scored), Sweeney (scored), Sharps (saved), Humphreys (scored).

LEAGUE 1 FINAL (at Millennium Stadium)

Sunday, 29 May 2005

Hartlepool U (0) 2 *(Williams 47, Daly 71)*

Sheffield W (1) 4 *(McGovern 45, MacLean 82 (pen), Whelan 94, Talbot 120)* 59,808

Hartlepool U: Konstantopoulos; Barron (Craddock), Robson, Nelson, Westwood■, Strachan, Butler (Williams), Sweeney, Porter (Daly), Boyd, Humphreys.
Sheffield W: Lucas; Bruce (Collins), Heckingbottom, Bullen, Wood, Whelan, Rocastle, McGovern, Peacock (Talbot), Quinn (MacLean), Brunt.
aet.
Referee: P. Crossley (Kent).

LEAGUE 2 FIRST LEG

Saturday, 14 May 2005

Lincoln C (1) 1 *(McAuley 11)*

Macclesfield T (0) 0 7032

Lincoln C: Marriott; McCombe, Sandwith, McAuley, Morgan, Futcher, Butcher, Asamoah, Taylor-Fletcher, Yeo, Gain.
Macclesfield T: Fetis; Bailey, Carragher, Morley, Swailes, Barras, Harsley, Whitaker (Townson), Tipton, Parkin, McIntyre.

Sunday, 15 May 2005

Northampton T (0) 0

Southend U (0) 0 6601

Northampton T: Harper; Togwell, Low (Sabin), Chambers, Willmott, Murray, Rowson, Hearn, McGleish, Kirk, Williamson (Smith).
Southend U: Flahavan; Jupp, Wilson, Maher, Barrett, Prior, Pettefer, Bentley, Bramble (Dudfield), Eastwood (Gray), Gower (Guttridge).

LEAGUE 2 SECOND LEG

Saturday, 21 May 2005

Macclesfield T (0) 1 *(Harsley 76)*

Lincoln C (1) 1 *(McAuley 15)* 5223

Macclesfield T: Fettis; Bailey (Whitaker), Carragher, Morley, Swailes, Barras, Harsley, Townson (Miles), Tipton (Briscoe), Parkin, McIntyre.
Lincoln C: Marriott; McCombe, Sandwith, McAuley, Morgan, Futcher, Butcher, Green (Beevers), Taylor-Fletcher (Asamoah), Yeo (Bloomer), Gain.

Southend U (0) 1 *(Eastwood 49 (pen))*

Northampton T (0) 0 9152

Southend U: Flahavan; Jupp, Wilson, Maher, Barrett, Prior, Pettefer, Bentley, Dudfield (Gray), Eastwood (Guttridge), Nicolau.
Northampton T: Harper; Togwell, Low, Chambers, Willmott, Murray (Hunt), Rowson (Richards), Hearn, McGleish, Kirk, Smith (Sabin).

LEAGUE 2 FINAL (at Millennium Stadium)

Saturday, 28 May 2005

Lincoln C (0) 0

Southend U (0) 2 *(Eastwood 105, Jupp 110)* 19,653

Lincoln C: Marriott; McCombe, Sandwith, McAuley, Morgan, Futcher, Butcher, Green (Beevers), Taylor-Fletcher (Bloomer), Yeo (Asamoah), Gain.
Southend U: Flahavan; Jupp, Wilson, Maher, Barrett, Prior, Pettefer, Bentley, Gray (Dudfield), Eastwood (Edwards), Nicolau (Gower).
aet.
Referee: M. Atkinson (West Yorkshire).

LEADING GOALSCORERS 2004–05

	League	Carling Cup	FA Cup	Other	Total
FA BARCLAYCARD PREMIERSHIP					
Players in this competition scoring ten or more League goals are listed. Other leading scorers classified by total number of goals in all competitions.					
Thierry Henry *(Arsenal)*	25	0	0	5	30
Andrew Johnson *(Crystal Palace)*	21	0	0	0	21
Robert Pires *(Arsenal)*	14	0	2	1	17
Jermain Defoe *(Tottenham H)*	13	5	4	0	22
Frank Lampard *(Chelsea)*	13	2	0	4	19
Jimmy Floyd Hasselbaink *(Middlesbrough)*	13	0	0	3	16
Ayegbeni Yakubu *(Portsmouth)*	12	2	2	0	16
Peter Crouch *(Southampton)*	12	0	4	0	16
Eidur Gudjohnsen *(Chelsea)*	12	1	1	2	16
Andy Cole *(Fulham)*	12	1	0	0	13
Wayne Rooney *(Manchester U)*	11	0	3	3	17
Robbie Keane *(Tottenham H)*	11	3	3	0	17
Robert Earnshaw *(WBA)*	11	0	3	0	14
Robbie Fowler *(Manchester C)*	11	1	0	0	12
Didier Drogba *(Chelsea)*	10	1	0	5	16
Emile Heskey *(Birmingham C)*	10	0	1	0	11
Freddie Ljungberg *(Arsenal)*	10	0	2	2	14
Kevin Phillips *(Southampton)*	10	1	2	0	13
Shaun Wright-Phillips *(Manchester C)*	10	1	0	0	11
In order of total goals:					
Alan Shearer *(Newcastle U)*	7	0	1	11	19
Ruud Van Nistelrooy *(Manchester U)*	6	0	2	8	16
COCA-COLA CHAMPIONSHIP					
Nathan Ellington *(Wigan Ath)*	24	0	0	0	24
Jason Roberts *(Wigan Ath)*	21	0	0	0	21
Teddy Sheringham *(West Ham U)*	20	0	1	0	21
Darren Bent *(Ipswich T)*	20	0	0	0	20
Kenny Miller *(Wolverhampton W)*	19	1	0	0	20
Shefki Kuqi *(Ipswich T)*	19	0	0	1	20
Dave Kitson *(Reading)*	19	0	0	0	19
Paul Furlong *(QPR)*	18	0	0	0	18
Marlon Harewood *(West Ham U)*	17	2	2	1	22
Dean Ashton *(Crewe Alex*)*	17	2	0	0	19
Heidar Helguson *(Watford)*	16	3	1	0	20
Richard Cresswell *(Preston NE)*	16	4	0	1	21
Grzegorz Rasiak *(Derby Co)*	16	0	1	0	17
Marcus Stewart *(Sunderland)*	16	0	1	0	17
Andy Gray *(Sheffield U)*	15	2	1	0	18
Carl Cort *(Wolverhampton W)*	15	0	1	0	16
Stephen Elliott *(Sunderland)*	15	1	0	0	16
Tommy Miller *(Ipswich T)*	13	1	1	0	15
David Connolly *(Leicester C)*	13	0	0	0	13
Gifton Noel-Williams *(Stoke C)*	13	0	0	0	13
**now Norwich C.*					
COCA-COLA LEAGUE 1					
Stuart Elliott *(Hull C)*	27	0	1	1	29
Dean Windass *(Bradford C)*	27	1	0	0	28
Pawel Abbott *(Huddersfield T)*	26	0	1	0	27
Leroy Lita *(Bristol C)*	24	2	1	2	29
Sam Parkin *(Swindon T)*	23	0	0	1	24
Adam Boyd *(Hartlepool U)*	22	1	3	3	29
Steve Brooker *(Bristol C)*	21	0	0	0	21
(Including 5 League goals for Port Vale).					
James Hayter *(Bournemouth)*	19	3	0	0	22
Luke Beckett *(Oldham Ath (on loan))*	19	0	0	0	19
(including 6 League goals for Huddersfield T (on loan) and 7 for Stockport Co).					
Steve Howard *(Luton T)*	18	0	4	0	22
Steve MacLean *(Sheffield W)*	18	0	0	2	20
Juan Ugarte *(Wrexham)*	17	0	0	6	23
Michael Chopra *(Barnsley (on loan))*	17	0	0	0	17
Izale McLeod *(Milton Keynes D)*	16	2	0	0	18
COCA-COLA LEAGUE 2					
Phil Jevons *(Yeovil T)*	27	0	2	0	29
Andy Kirk *(Northampton T)*	25	0	2	0	27
(including 18 League and 2 FA Cup goals for Boston U)					
Jon Parkin *(Macclesfield T)*	22	1	1	2	26
Lee Trundle *(Swansea C)*	22	0	1	0	23
Nathan Tyson *(Wycombe W)*	22	0	0	0	22
Simon Yeo *(Lincoln C)*	21	2	0	0	23
Freddy Eastwood *(Southend U)*	19	0	0	5	24
Junior Agogo *(Bristol R)*	19	0	0	2	21
Paul Hayes *(Scunthorpe U)*	18	0	2	0	20
Grant Holt *(Rochdale)*	17	1	5	1	24
Lee Steele *(Leyton Orient)*	16	1	0	0	17
Tommy Mooney *(Oxford U)*	15	0	0	0	15
Glynn Hurst *(Notts Co)*	14	0	0	1	15
Clive Wijnhard *(Darlington)*	14	0	0	0	14
Scott McGleish *(Northampton T)*	13	1	2	1	17

Other matches consist of European games, LDV Vans Trophy, Community Shield and Football League play-offs. Only goals scored in the respective divisions count in the table. Players listed in order of League goals total.

REVIEW OF THE SEASON

The 2004–05 season started with Arsenal on the heels of Nottingham Forest's long standing record of 42 unbeaten League games and finishing with the Gunners trailing in the wake of champions Chelsea who celebrated their centenary with their first title in 50 years.

Chelsea, with Jose Mourinho in charge, made a quiet, unspectacular start to the campaign winning seven, drawing two and losing only once 1-0 at Manchester City in the first ten matches. Significantly they conceded only two goals in the process.

But having hit the top in early November they were clearly there to stay. Defensively they were outstanding letting in only 15 goals in the entire season. They collected 25 clean sheets and only twice did they concede two goals in a match, in a 2-2 draw at home to Bolton Wanderers and in a similar score at Arsenal. Unbeaten at Stamford Bridge and only Manchester City managed to take more points off them. Having achieved a notable success at the City of Manchester, they held out for a goalless draw at the Bridge.

Though the wealth of Roman Abramovich was a key factor in finding the right type of foreign investment on the pitch, it should be recorded that the improved performances of the home grown players like John Terry, Frank Lampard and Joe Cole owed much to the shrewd coaching of Mourinho.

With enough competition for places to be envied by most other clubs, the two most successful additions from abroad were arguably goalkeeper Petr Cech and midfield anchor Claude Makelele. Lampard was the only ever present player, Terry missed the last two when he was to have some injury sorted out by the medicos.

Midway through the season the addition of Dutchman Arjen Robben injected more attacking potential, though he subsequently missed several games with injury. Eidur Gudjohnsen the Icelander was the most reliable striker, though it is interesting to note that he was only the second highest scorer, one less at 12 that Lampard, whose overall contribution was invaluable.

However Chelsea still had to wait until 30 April and a 2-0 win at Bolton before they were able to confirm what had been expected for many months.

On the way Chelsea collected the Carling Cup against Liverpool, but Rafael Benitez learned harsh lessons from these domestic encounters to plot the Blues execution in Europe.

So, Arsenal lost their unbeaten record but overtook Forest and established a milestone of their own by taking the run to 49 before they were beaten 2-0 by Manchester United at Old Trafford on Sunday 24 October. At that stage of the season Arsenal were still top with a two point lead over Chelsea, with United off the pace in fifth and already eight points adrift of the leaders.

Defeat certainly knocked Arsenal's confidence for a few games though they did win an amazing 5-4 affair with neighbours Tottenham Hotspur at White Hart Lane. And during this time Chelsea caught and passed them. Surprisingly a 4-2 home defeat in early February gave United a double over Arsenal, but prompted a resurgence of the fast-flowing football which has been the trade mark of the Highbury club in the Arsene Wenger years. This was epitomised by their 7-0 destruction of Everton on 11 May.

Chelsea's Frank Lampard (right) battles with Bolton Wanderers' Vincent Candela for the ball. (PA/Empics)

All this delayed the Chelsea crown of course, but these two victories by United over the former champions proved their best displays of the season. Having made such an indifferent start, United needed a strong run to close the gap and in fairness a 20 game unbeaten run from 7 November to 2 April still left them below Arsenal on goal difference and 13 points behind Chelsea.

Both Arsenal and Manchester United went out of the Champions League at the first knockout stage, the former to Bayern Munich, the latter by AC Milan. In the all-Reds FA Cup Final there was another first for the competition at this stage: a penalty shoot-out in which United's woeful finishing in the game was punished by Arsenal.

The arrival of Wayne Rooney at Old Trafford had been expected to hit his former club Everton badly enough. Yet to the credit of manager David Moyes and the players remaining, they battled together admirably and even managed in early December to not only beat Merseyside rivals Liverpool 1-0 at Goodison Park, but edge into second place.

They even recovered from a wobble at the turn of the year to hold on to fourth place and a return to the leading European competition in which they had last played in 1970. That shipping of seven goals at Highbury incidentally left them with a minus goal difference – for a team finishing fourth, an amazing fact.

Rivals Liverpool had to be content with fifth place, but it was succinctly said that they played below their best in domestic football, above it in Europe, culminating with their astonishing come-back in the Champions League final against AC Milan.

Actually fifth was the highest they hit all season and inconsistent results were spread throughout. Bolton survived a ten-match slump from November which threatened to derail them and recovered to finish sixth, enabling them to enter the UEFA Cup, the 31st English club so to do.

The remaining UEFA Cup place ended in a three-club struggle between Middlesbrough, Manchester City and Spurs. Moreover it was decided on the last day of the season. At the City of Manchester, Middlesbrough's 1-1 draw was enough to give them a three point lead over the other two clubs, Spurs having only managed a goalless draw with Blackburn Rovers. Boro thus had a ticket to Europe once again having reached the round before the quarter-finals in 2004–05.

Tottenham must have considered themselves hard done by the fates as they went on to lose a back-door entry to Europe by losing out in UEFA's fair-play draw!

Aston Villa had a mid-table look about them in the second half of the season, their best sequence being four wins and a draw from mid-October. Charlton Athletic won only one of their last 14 which scuppered any lingering hopes of getting into Europe on their own account.

Birmingham City had their moments ending the season with a 2-1 win over Arsenal, though ninth place in late December was the highest after beating Fulham 3-2. On their part, Fulham were menaced by thoughts of relegation at one time, but three wins from the last four banished any lingering fears.

Newcastle United had problems on and off the field, though they did well enough in the UEFA Cup reaching the quarter-finals before losing to Boro's conquerors Sporting Lisbon. But they failed to string more than two wins in a row in the Premier League. Blackburn were another team worried about the drop. Bottom in mid-November, a resolute defence frequently enabled them to pick up the necessary quota of points and they were out of the relegation area towards the close of the campaign.

Portsmouth were another of those wondering if a return to the Football League was on the cards. At one time six games provided just one point, but they, too, hauled themselves to safety. However the real drama was reserved for West Bromwich Albion, Crystal Palace, Norwich City and Southampton.

West Bromwich were the favourites to be one of the three unlucky teams. History said that no team at the bottom by the turn of the year had avoided the drop, but Albion did by beating Portsmouth on the last Sunday of the season, when fortunes fluctuated throughout the afternoon.

Liverpool's Luis Garcia scores in the Merseyside derby against Everton at Anfield in March. (Actionimages)

Kieran Richardson smashes the ball into the net to help West Bromwich Albion perform the great escape on the final day of the season – the only team to be bottom of the Premier League at Christmas and still survive. (Actionimages)

Norwich having revived incredibly after beating Manchester United 2-0 on 2 April but without an away win, collapsed 6-0 at Fulham to join Crystal Palace who were unable to sustain a revival which put them 14th at the end of October and could only draw 2-2 at Charlton while Southampton who continually lost matches after leading, did so ultimately against Manchester United.

For the first unveiling of the Football League under the Coca-Cola label and retitled as the Championship, Sunderland won a return to the Premiership with a well-timed run at the end in which they dropped only four points out of a possible 39. Wigan Athletic held on to the other automatic promotion slot after a disappointing second half of the season compared with the opening effort, unbeaten in the first 17.

Ipswich Town, having led in February slipped away and eventually lost to West Ham United in the play-offs. The Hammers who had their own problems off the field with talks of takeover produced their most consistent form at the death.

Derby County having beaten Preston North End 3-1 on the last day of the season, had the tables turned on them in the play-offs, Preston succumbing to West Ham in the final. But Reading who had appeared set for fourth place lost their last three and Sheffield United failed to win one of the last five.

Drawn matches cost Wolverhampton Wanderers dearly. They were only two short of the record 23 at the end. All this and unbeaten in the last 18. Millwall's best all season was fifth with no appreciable runs to back up a bid.

Queens Park Rangers were third in mid-October after seven successive wins but Stoke City were scratching around for goals and failed to score in 21 matches. Burnley's best period was eight without losing, but six of these were drawn and well supported Leeds United were another to suffer from too many draws – 18 of them including ten at home. Leicester City were even more level-headed in this respect, sharing 21 draws with Wolves!

Cardiff City won only one of the first nine but managed to pluck enough points thereafter, Plymouth Argyle won three and drew one of the first four, then never did as well again while Watford were in the draw cabinet with ten at home alone as well as being sixth after eight games.

Coventry City were never able to assemble more than two wins in a sequence but Brighton & Hove Albion having lost six in a row from March were undefeated in the last five and Crewe Alexandra escaped on the last day, recovering to beat Coventry 2-1 while Gillingham could only draw at Nottingham Forest despite only one reverse in the last 12.

Forest, already relegated with Rotherham United, could not maintain a February inspired return to form. But Rotherham registered their first win 1-0 over Leeds in the 21st game and realistically needed promotion form to survive.

The automatic promotion places in the League Championship One went to Luton Town and Hull City. Off to a flier, dropping only two points from the opening 12 games, Luton lost the next three but were never seriously troubled thereafter. Hull put it right half-way through and had eight wins on the trot at one time and were assured of going up when they lost their last three.

Play-off battles involved Tranmere Rovers, Brentford, Sheffield Wednesday and Hartlepool United. Wednesday achieved some stability with only one defeat in 18 from mid-December and ultimately took care of Brentford and then Hartlepool the conquerors of Tranmere in the final.

Brentford once held 3-3 by Wednesday in February seemed out of contention in 10th place, but rallied, though for Hartlepool they had won only three of their last 14. Tranmere for their part had looked a good bet for automatic promotion until losing 6-1 at Hull when both goalkeepers were injured during the game.

Bristol City, Bournemouth and Huddersfield Town missed out on the play-offs each by a point. Nine successive matches without defeat was City's best to the end of November, Bournemouth's home form was not as good as on their travels and Huddersfield misjudged the run-in despite dropping just two points in the last nine games.

Drawn matches also proved the downfall of Doncaster Rovers. They had 18 of them, while Bradford City hit second place in late October and slowly drifted out of it. Swindon Town were unable to shake off the mid-table look from the end of February and 19 drawn games spelled it out loud enough for Barnsley.

Walsall desperately needed their last five wins in a row and unbeaten in the last eleven was good enough for Colchester United bolstered with 17 draws of their own to ease concerns. Blackpool won for the first time in the ninth game, but did improve though Chesterfield had a poor second half of the season after still being sixth in December.

Port Vale managed to snap up enough wins to be safe after a tailing off following a better start which had them third in early September and Oldham Athletic needed that last gasp 2-1 win over Bradford City to escape the drop as did Milton Keynes Dons whose last two victories were priceless.

The relegated quartet were Torquay United, Wrexham, Peterborough United and Stockport County. Torquay appeared to have salvaged matters after four wins but lost 2-1 at Colchester on the last day and the ten point deduction for Wrexham was too much of a handicap. Their consolation was winning the LDV Vans Trophy.

Peterborough were undone when a mid-season stutter produced just four points out of a possible 30 and Stockport were never off the bottom after the end of September.

Yeovil Town followed in the wake of Doncaster Rovers who had capped promotion from the Conference by moving up again. After the turn of the year Yeovil had just one blip out of first place in early April, but always scored more than they let in – their matches producing 155 goals. Scunthorpe United joined them after losing top billing themselves in January after defeat in just three of their first 24.

Swansea City clinched the third automatic spot on the last day, winning 1-0 at Bury. This after a dreadful spell when just one win came in nine outings.

Having missed out when momentarily going top, Southend United won only one of the last five, but disposed first of Northampton Town, then Lincoln City in the play-off final. Macclesfield Town had been third as late as mid-March but lost to Lincoln.

Goal difference cost Darlington a play-off berth. Fifth in early December had been their highest placing. But Rochdale never better than seventh produced five draws in the last seven unbeaten from an overall total of 18.

Wycombe Wanderers, nine without a win to November had too much ground to make up and Leyton Orient had the consolation of being top in October after a 4-1 win over Shrewsbury Town. Bristol Rovers suffered from too many drawn games 21 in all, including 13 at home. Mansfield Town were hit by a goal famine in which only five came in ten matches and sixth place in November was Cheltenham Town's peak for the season.

Oxford United were 21st on 20 November but six in a row without defeat restored some balance from January. Boston United only once won two games in a row and Bury won only one game in a spell of 16.

Grimsby Town were heading in the wrong direction from mid-March with only one victory in the last ten yet Notts County produced a five game sequence without losing from mid-February which steered them out of danger.

Both newly restored Football League teams Chester City and Shrewsbury Town found the going tough at times though both survived. Only four goals in ten games spotlighted Chester's ills while Shrewsbury won only two of the first 15.

Rushden & Diamonds hovered above the relegation pairing from January, but Kidderminster Harriers and Cambridge United were not as fortunate. Harriers were unable to sustain a brave unbeaten run of six from mid-February and Cambridge ultimately docked ten points for late administration were never out of the bottom two from mid-October. Taking their places will be Barnet back after five years and Carlisle United with just one season's absence.

Bobby Zamora scores the winning goal at the Millennium Stadium to secure West Ham United's return to the Premiership. (Empics)

INTRODUCTION TO THE CLUB SECTION

The *Sky Sports Football Yearbook* features a who's who style players directory which incorporates the total appearances and goals for each player as in earlier editions of *Rothmans Football Yearbook*, but additionally, includes more personal information and a season-by-season account of the individual player's record. It is again presented in an A to Z form for easy reference (see pages 430 to 566). There is also each club's full record in the last ten seasons and the latest sequences recorded for wins, draws and defeats, etc. In addition, the individual club's record scoring and non-scoring runs are also included.

Again, an further A to Z of players has been included to enable readers to locate any player who appeared with a club during the 2004-05 season. Every club is given a number to facilitate easy reference.

Once again the club section comprises four pages, the first two feature new entries in the *Sky Sports Fact File* and *Did you know?* series. Record transfer fees are usually left to the discretion of the club concerned. The third and fourth pages of this section present a complete record of the League season, including date, venue, opponents, results, half-time score, League position, goalscorers, attendances and complete line-ups including substitutes where used. This comprises every League game in the 2004-05 season. Again, goal times have been added, though not official they give an indication of when goals were scored. These appear as superior figures $^{10, 20, 30}$

Players shown red cards are indicated thus ■

Squad numbers have not been included; those used are the familiar ones, 1-11, substitutes are recognised as follows: the first substitute number 12, the second number 13 and the third number 14. However, if there is a subsitute goalkeeper he is represented by number 15, *but only* if he replaces the first choice goalkeeper or another outfield player. Otherwise, he adopts one of the other three substitute numbers, as there have been several instances where a goalkeeper has been used as an outfield player because of injuries during the game. Players replaced are respectively noted with superior figures $^{1, 2, 3}$ and ^{g} for goalkeeper. These third and fourth pages also include consolidated lists of goalscorers for the club in League, Carling Cup, FA Cup, LDV Vans Trophy and European matches, plus a summary of results in all these major competitions.

The continued increase in the number of matches played on Sundays has resulted in the League positions after the weekend's results. Full holiday programmes are also recorded, but the position after mid-week fixtures will not normally have been updated. Attendance figures quoted for the FA Barclaycard Premiership and the Coca-Cola Football League are those that appeared in the Press at the time. The statistics published are unofficial. However, the total for the FA Premier League on page 599 is official. In the totals at the top of each column on page 4 of the club section, substitute appearances are listed separately by the '+', but have been amalgamated in the totals which feature in the players historical section in the directory mentioned above. Thus, these appearances include those as substitute. In fact, the directory features names of players who were with clubs during the 2004-05 season. Each player's height and weight where known, plus birth date and place plus source, together with total League goals and appearances for each club represented, can be found as in previous editions. The player's details remain under his last club. Appearances by players in the play-offs are not included in their career totals. International appearances with foreign players reflect latest information available. Players who in 2004-05 were transferred abroad, either on loan or permanently, can be located in the records section of the book from pages 11 to 24 under *The Export Game*.

ARSENAL FA Premiership

FOUNDATION

Formed by workers at the Royal Arsenal, Woolwich in 1886, they began as Dial Square (name of one of the workshops), and included two former Nottingham Forest players, Fred Beardsley and Morris Bates. Beardsley wrote to his old club seeking help and they provided the new club with a full set of red jerseys and a ball. The club became known as the 'Woolwich Reds' although their official title soon after formation was Woolwich Arsenal.

Arsenal Stadium, Highbury, London N5 1BU.

Telephone: (020) 7704 4000.

Fax: (020) 7704 4001.

Ticket Office: (020) 7704 4040.

Website: www.arsenal.com

Email: info@arsenal.com

Ground Capacity: 38,500 all seated.

Record Attendance: 73,295 v Sunderland, Div 1, 9 March 1935.

At Wembley: 73,707 v RC Lens, UEFA Champions League, 25 November 1998.

Pitch Measurements: 101m × 67m.

Chairman: Peter Hill-Wood.

Vice-chairman: David Dein.

Managing Director: Keith Edelman.

Secretary: David Miles.

Manager: Arsène Wenger.

Assistant Manager: Pat Rice.

Physio: Gary Lewin.

Colours: Redcurrant shirts, white shorts, redcurrant stockings.

Change Colours: Blue.

Year Formed: 1886.

Turned Professional: 1891.

Ltd Co: 1893.

Previous Names: 1886, Dial Square; 1886, Royal Arsenal; 1891, Woolwich Arsenal; 1914 Arsenal.

Club Nickname: 'Gunners'.

Previous Grounds: 1886, Plumstead Common; 1887, Sportsman Ground; 1888, Manor Ground; 1890, Invicta Ground; 1893, Manor Ground; 1913, Highbury.

HONOURS

FA Premier League: Champions 1997–98, 2001–02, 2003–04. Runners-up 1998–99, 1999–2000, 2000–01, 2002–03, 2004–05.

Football League: Division 1 – Champions 1930–31, 1932–33, 1933–34, 1934–35, 1937–38, 1947–48, 1952–53, 1970–71, 1988–89, 1990–91; Runners-up 1925–26, 1931–32, 1972–73; Division 2 – Runners-up 1903–04.

FA Cup: Winners 1930, 1936, 1950, 1971, 1979, 1993, 1998, 2002, 2003, 2005; Runners-up 1927, 1932, 1952, 1972, 1978, 1980, 2001.

Double performed: 1970–71, 1997–98, 2001–02.

Football League Cup: Winners 1987, 1993; Runners-up 1968, 1969, 1988.

European Competitions: *Fairs Cup:* 1963–64, 1969–70 (winners), 1970–71. *European Cup:* 1971–72, 1991–92. *UEFA Champions League:* 1998–99, 1999–2000, 2000–01, 2001–02, 2002–03, 2003–04, 2004–05. *UEFA Cup:* 1978–79, 1981–82, 1982–83, 1996–97, 1997–98, 1999–2000 (runners-up). *European Cup-Winners' Cup:* 1979–80 (runners-up), 1993–94 (winners), 1994–95 (runners-up).

SKY SPORTS FACT FILE

Arsenal extended their unbeaten run from 7 May 2003 to 49 matches until 24 October 2004 to establish a new Premier League record. Thirty-six games were won and 13 drawn. They also overhauled Nottingham Forest's 42 match unbeaten run.

First Football League Game: 2 September 1893, Division 2, v Newcastle U (h) D 2–2 – Williams; Powell, Jeffrey; Devine, Buist, Howat; Gemmell, Henderson, Shaw (1), Elliott (1), Booth.

Record League Victory: 12–0 v Loughborough T, Division 2, 12 March 1900 – Orr; McNichol, Jackson; Moir, Dick (2), Anderson (1); Hunt, Cottrell (2), Main (2), Gaudie (3), Tennant (2).

Record Cup Victory: 11–1 v Darwen, FA Cup 3rd rd, 9 January 1932 – Moss; Parker, Hapgood; Jones, Roberts, John; Hulme (2), Jack (3), Lambert (2), James, Bastin (4).

Record Defeat: 0–8 v Loughborough T, Division 2, 12 December 1896.

Most League Points (2 for a win): 66, Division 1, 1930–31.

Most League Points (3 for a win): 90, Premier League 2003–04.

Most League Goals: 127, Division 1, 1930–31.

Highest League Scorer in Season: Ted Drake, 42, 1934–35.

Most League Goals in Total Aggregate: Cliff Bastin, 150, 1930–47.

Most League Goals in One Match: 7, Ted Drake v Aston Villa, Division 1, 14 December 1935.

Most Capped Player: Patrick Vieira, 79, France.

Most League Appearances: David O'Leary, 558, 1975–93.

Youngest League Player: Gerry Ward, 16 years 321 days v Huddersfield T, 22 August 1953 (Jermaine Pennant, 16 years 319 days v Middlesbrough, League Cup, 30 November 1999).

Record Transfer Fee Received: A reported £22,900,000 from Real Madrid for Nicolas Anelka, August 1999.

Record Transfer Fee Paid: A reported £11,000,000 to Bordeaux for Sylvain Wiltord, August 2000.

Football League Record: 1893 Elected to Division 2; 1904–13 Division 1; 1913–19 Division 2; 1919–92 Division 1; 1992– FA Premier League.

MANAGERS

Sam Hollis 1894–97
Tom Mitchell 1897–98
George Elcoat 1898–99
Harry Bradshaw 1899–1904
Phil Kelso 1904–08
George Morrell 1908–15
Leslie Knighton 1919–25
Herbert Chapman 1925–34
George Allison 1934–47
Tom Whittaker 1947–56
Jack Crayston 1956–58
George Swindin 1958–62
Billy Wright 1962–66
Bertie Mee 1966–76
Terry Neill 1976–83
Don Howe 1984–86
George Graham 1986–95
Bruce Rioch 1995–96
Arsène Wenger September 1996–

LATEST SEQUENCES

Longest Sequence of League Wins: 14, 10.2.2002 – 18.8.2002.

Longest Sequence of League Defeats: 7, 12.2.1977 – 12.3.1977.

Longest Sequence of League Draws: 6, 4.3.1961 – 1.4.1961.

Longest Sequence of Unbeaten League Matches: 49, 7.5.2003 – 24.10.2004.

Longest Sequence Without a League Win: 23, 28.9.1912 – 1.3.1913.

Successive Scoring Runs: 55 from 19.5.2001.

Successive Non-scoring Runs: 6 from 25.2.1987.

TEN YEAR LEAGUE RECORD

		P	W	D	L	F	A	Pts	Pos
1995-96	PR Lge	38	17	12	9	49	32	63	5
1996-97	PR Lge	38	19	11	8	62	32	68	3
1997-98	PR Lge	38	23	9	6	68	33	78	1
1998-99	PR Lge	38	22	12	4	59	17	78	2
1999-2000	PR Lge	38	22	7	9	73	43	73	2
2000-01	PR Lge	38	20	10	8	63	38	70	2
2001-02	PR Lge	38	26	9	3	79	36	87	1
2002-03	PR Lge	38	23	9	6	85	42	78	2
2003-04	PR Lge	38	26	12	0	73	26	90	1
2004-05	PR Lge	38	25	8	5	87	36	83	2

DID YOU KNOW ?

On 14 February 2005 in a 5–1 win over Crystal Palace, Arsenal fielded a starting eleven without a single English player. There were four Frenchmen, one each from Brazil, Cameroon, Germany, Holland, Ivory Coast, Spain and Sweden.

ARSENAL 2004–05 LEAGUE RECORD

Match No.	*Date*	*Venue*	*Opponents*	*Result*		*H/T Score*	*Lg. Pos.*	*Goalscorers*	*Attendance*
1	Aug 15	A	Everton	W	4-1	2-0	—	Bergkamp ^{23}, Reyes ^{39}, Ljungberg ^{54}, Pires ^{83}	35,521
2	22	H	Middlesbrough	W	5-3	1-1	1	Henry 2 $^{25, 90}$, Bergkamp ^{54}, Pires ^{64}, Reyes ^{65}	37,415
3	25	H	Blackburn R	W	3-0	0-0	—	Henry ^{50}, Fabregas ^{58}, Reyes ^{79}	37,496
4	28	A	Norwich C	W	4-1	3-0	1	Reyes ^{22}, Henry ^{36}, Pires ^{40}, Bergkamp ^{90}	23,944
5	Sept 11	A	Fulham	W	3-0	0-0	1	Ljungberg ^{62}, Knight (og) ^{65}, Reyes ^{71}	21,681
6	18	H	Bolton W	D	2-2	1-0	1	Henry ^{31}, Pires ^{66}	37,010
7	25	A	Manchester C	W	1-0	1-0	1	Cole ^{14}	47,015
8	Oct 2	H	Charlton Ath	W	4-0	1-0	1	Ljungberg ^{33}, Henry 2 $^{48, 69}$, Reyes ^{70}	38,103
9	16	H	Aston Villa	W	3-1	2-1	1	Pires 2 (1 pen) $^{19 (p), 72}$, Henry ^{45}	38,137
10	24	A	Manchester U	L	0-2	0-0	1		67,862
11	30	H	Southampton	D	2-2	0-0	1	Henry ^{67}, Van Persie ^{90}	38,141
12	Nov 6	A	Crystal Palace	D	1-1	0-0	2	Henry ^{63}	26,193
13	13	A	Tottenham H	W	5-4	1-1	2	Henry ^{45}, Lauren (pen) ^{55}, Vieira ^{60}, Ljungberg ^{69}, Pires ^{81}	36,095
14	20	H	WBA	D	1-1	0-0	2	Pires ^{54}	38,109
15	28	A	Liverpool	L	1-2	0-1	2	Vieira ^{57}	43,730
16	Dec 4	H	Birmingham C	W	3-0	1-0	2	Pires ^{33}, Henry 2 $^{80, 86}$	38,064
17	12	H	Chelsea	D	2-2	2-1	3	Henry 2 $^{2, 29}$	38153
18	19	A	Portsmouth	W	1-0	0-0	2	Campbell ^{75}	20,170
19	26	H	Fulham	W	2-0	1-0	2	Henry ^{12}, Pires ^{71}	38,047
20	29	A	Newcastle U	W	1-0	1-0	—	Vieira ^{45}	52,320
21	Jan 1	A	Charlton Ath	W	3-1	1-1	2	Ljungberg 2 $^{35, 48}$, Van Persie ^{67}	26,711
22	4	H	Manchester C	D	1-1	0-1	2	Ljungberg ^{75}	38,066
23	15	A	Bolton W	L	0-1	0-1	2		27,514
24	23	H	Newcastle U	W	1-0	1-0	2	Bergkamp ^{19}	38,137
25	Feb 1	H	Manchester U	L	2-4	2-1	—	Vieira ^{8}, Bergkamp ^{36}	38,164
26	5	A	Aston Villa	W	3-1	3-0	3	Ljungberg ^{10}, Henry ^{14}, Cole ^{28}	42,593
27	14	H	Crystal Palace	W	5-1	3-0	—	Bergkamp ^{32}, Reyes ^{35}, Henry 2 $^{39, 77}$, Vieira ^{54}	38,056
28	26	A	Southampton	D	1-1	1-0	3	Ljungberg ^{45}	31,815
29	Mar 5	H	Portsmouth	W	3-0	1-0	3	Henry 3 $^{39, 53, 85}$	38,079
30	19	A	Blackburn R	W	1-0	1-0	3	Van Persie ^{43}	22,992
31	Apr 2	H	Norwich C	W	4-1	2-1	2	Henry 3 $^{19, 22, 66}$, Ljungberg ^{50}	38,066
32	9	A	Middlesbrough	W	1-0	0-0	2	Pires ^{73}	33,874
33	20	A	Chelsea	D	0-0	0-0	—		41,621
34	25	H	Tottenham H	W	1-0	1-0	—	Reyes ^{22}	38,147
35	May 2	A	WBA	W	2-0	0-0	—	Van Persie ^{66}, Edu ^{90}	27,351
36	8	H	Liverpool	W	3-1	2-0	2	Pires ^{25}, Reyes ^{29}, Fabregas ^{90}	38,119
37	11	H	Everton	W	7-0	3-0	—	Van Persie ^{8}, Pires 2 $^{12, 50}$, Vieira ^{37}, Edu (pen) ^{70}, Bergkamp ^{77}, Flamini ^{85}	38,073
38	15	A	Birmingham C	L	1-2	0-0	2	Bergkamp ^{88}	29,302

Final League Position: 2

GOALSCORERS

League (87): Henry 25, Pires 14 (1 pen), Ljungberg 10, Reyes 9, Bergkamp 8, Vieira 6, Van Persie 5, Cole 2, Edu 2 (1 pen), Fabregas 2, Campbell 1, Flamini 1, Lauren 1 (pen), own goal 1.
Carling Cup (5): Lupoli 2, Karbassiyoon 1, Owusu-Abeyie 1, Van Persie 1.
FA Cup (9): Van Persie 3, Ljungberg 2, Pires 2, Reyes 1, Vieira 1 (pen).
Community Shield (3): Silva 1, Reyes 1, own goal 1.
Champions League (13): Henry 5 (1 pen), Ljungberg 2, Fabregas 1, Pires 1 (pen), Reyes 1, Toure 1, Van Persie 1, own goal 1.

Lehmann J 28	Lauren E 32 + 1	Cole A 35	Silva G 13	Toure K 35	Cygan P 15	Ljungberg F 24 + 2	Fabregas F 24 + 9	Henry T 31 + 1	Bergkamp D 20 + 9	Reyes J 25 + 5	Pennant J 1 + 6	Pires R 26 + 7	Flamini M 9 + 12	Hoyte J 4 + 1	Edu6 + 6	Clichy G 7 + 8	Vieira P 32	Campbell S 16	Van Persie R 12 + 14	Almunia M 10	Senderos P 12 + 1	Eboue E — + 1	Owusu-Abeyie Q 1	Aliadiere J — + 4	*Match No.*
1	2	3	4[3]	5	6	7[1]	8	9	10	11[2]	12	13	14												1
1	2	3	4	5	6	7[1]	8	9	10	11[2]		12	13												2
1	2	3	4	5	6	12	8[2]	9	10[3]	14	7[1]	11	13												3
1	2	3	4	5		7	8[2]	10	12	9[1]		11[3]		6	13	14									4
1	2	3	8	5	6	7[2]	14	9	10	12	13	11[1]					4[3]								5
1	2	3	8[2]	5	6	7		10	12	9[1]		11[3]			13	14	4								6
1	2	3		5		7[1]	12	9	10[3]	11[2]					8	13	4	6	14						7
1	2			5		7[1]	8[2]	9[3]	10	11	12		13			3	4	6	14						8
1	2	3		5			8	9	10	7[1]	12	11[3]	13				4[2]	6	14						9
1	2	3		5		7		9	10	11[1]		12			8		4	6							10
1	2	3		5	6	7[3]	12	9	10	11[2]		13			8[1]		4		14						11
1	2	3		5	6	7[1]	8[2]	10	12	9		11[3]	13				4		14						12
1	2	3		5	6	7	8	9	10[2]	11[1]		12					4		13						13
1	2	3		5	6	7	8[1]	9	10[2]	12		11					4		13						14
1	2	3		5		7	8	10		9[1]		11					4	6	12						15
	2	3		5		7	8[2]	10		9[1]		11	13			12	4	6		1					16
	2	3		5			8	9	10[2]	11[1]		7	4			12		6	13	1					17
	2	3		5				9	12			7	8			11	4	6	10[1]	1					18
	2			5		7[1]	8	9	10[2]			11	12			3	4	6	13	1					19
	2	3		5		7		9				11	8			12	4	6	10[1]	1					20
		3		5		7[2]	8	9			13	12		2		11	4	6[3]	10[1]	1	14				21
		3		5		7	8[1]	9			12	11		2			4		10	1	6				22
		3		5		7	8[2]	9	12	13		11		2			4	6	10[1]	1					23
	2	3		5			12	9	10	7[1]		11	8				4	6		1					24
	2[1]	3			6	7	12	9	10	13		11	8[2]	14			4	5[3]		1					25
1	2	3			6	7	12	9	10[2]	11[1]		13	14		8[3]		4				5				26
1	2			5	6		12	9	10[3]	7		11[1]	13		8[2]	3	4		14						27
1		3		2[2]	6	7		10				11[1]	8			12	4		9[■]		5	13			28
1	12	3		2	6[1]	13	7[2]	9					8			11	4		14		5		10[3]		29
1	2	3		5			7			9			8			11	4		10		6				30
1	2	3	4	5	6	7	12	10		9[3]		11[2]	8[1]			13			14						31
1	2	3	8	5			7	10	12	9[1]		11					4				6				32
1	2	3	8	5			7[2]		10[1]	9		11					4		12		6			13	33
1	2	3	8	5			7[2]		12	9[3]		11			13		4		10[1]		6			14	34
1	2	3	8	5			7[1]		12	9		11			13		4		10[2]		6				35
1	2	3	8	5			7		12	9[3]		11[2]			13		4		10[1]		6			14	36
1	2	3					12	13	10	7		11[1]	14		8		4[3]	5	9[2]		6				37
1		3	8	2		11[3]	7[2]		10				13		12		4	5	9[1]		6			14	38

FA Cup

Third Round	Stoke C	(h)	2-1
Fourth Round	Wolverhampton W	(h)	2-0
Fifth Round	Sheffield U	(h)	1-1
		(a)	0-0
Sixth Round	Bolton W	(a)	1-0
Semi-Final	Blackburn R		3-0
(at Millennium Stadium)			
Final	Manchester U		0-0
(at Millennium Stadium)			

Carling Cup

Third Round	Manchester C	(a)	2-1
Fourth Round	Everton	(h)	3-1
Fifth Round			
	Manchester U	(a)	0-1

Champions League

Group E	PSV Eindhoven	(h)	1-0
	Rosenborg	(a)	1-1
	Panathinaikos	(a)	2-2
		(h)	1-1
	PSV Eindhoven	(a)	1-1
	Rosenborg	(h)	5-1
First Round	Bayern Munich	(a)	1-3
		(h)	1-0

ASTON VILLA — FA Premiership

FOUNDATION

Cricketing enthusiasts of Villa Cross Wesleyan Chapel, Aston, Birmingham decided to form a football club during the winter of 1874–75. Football clubs were few and far between in the Birmingham area and in their first game against Aston Brook St Mary's Rugby team they played one half rugby and the other soccer. In 1876 they were joined by a Scottish soccer enthusiast George Ramsay who was immediately appointed captain and went on to lead Aston Villa from obscurity to one of the country's top clubs in a period of less than 10 years.

Villa Park, Birmingham B6 6HE.

Telephone: (0121) 327 2299.

Fax: (0121) 322 2107.

Ticket Office: (0121) 327 5353.

Website: www.avfc.co.uk

Email: postmaster@astonvilla-fc.co.uk

Ground Capacity: 42,573 (subject to alteration).

Record Attendance: 76,588 v Derby Co, FA Cup 6th rd, 2 March 1946.

Pitch Measurements: 105m × 68m.

Chairman: H. D. Ellis OBE.

Chief Executive: Bruce Langham.

Club Secretary/Operations Director: Steven M. Stride.

Manager: David O'Leary.

Assistant Manager: Roy Aitken.

Physio: Alan Smith.

Sports Science Manager: Dr Stephen McGregor.

Colours: Claret shirt with blue sleeves, side panel of blue chevrons, yellow piping to side. White shorts with claret side panel and blue chevrons. Blue stockings with claret top.

Change Colours: Yellow shirts with navy side panel and yellow chevrons. Navy shorts with yellow side panel and navy chevrons. Navy stockings with yellow top.

Year Formed: 1874.

Turned Professional: 1885.

Ltd Co.: 1896.

Public Ltd Company: 1969.

Club Nickname: 'The Villans'.

Previous Grounds: 1874 Wilson Road and Aston Park (also used Aston Lower Grounds for some matches); 1876 Wellington Road, Perry Barr; 1897 Villa Park.

HONOURS

FA Premier League: Runners-up 1992–93.

Football League: Division 1 – Champions 1893–94, 1895–96, 1896–97, 1898–99, 1899–1900, 1909–10, 1980–81; Runners-up 1888–89, 1902–03, 1907–08, 1910–11, 1912–13, 1913–14, 1930–31, 1932–33, 1989–90; Division 2 – Champions 1937–38, 1959–60; Runners-up 1974–75, 1987–88; Division 3 – Champions 1971–72.

FA Cup: Winners 1887, 1895, 1897, 1905, 1913, 1920, 1957; Runners-up 1892, 1924, 2000.

Double Performed: 1896–97.

Football League Cup: Winners 1961, 1975, 1977, 1994, 1996; Runners-up 1963, 1971.

European Competitions: *European Cup:* 1981–82 (winners), 1982–83. *UEFA Cup:* 1975–76, 1977–78, 1983–84, 1990–91, 1993–94, 1994–95, 1996–97, 1997–98, 1998–99, 2001–02. *World Club Championship:* 1982. *European Super Cup:* 1982–83 (winners). *Intertoto Cup:* 2000, 2001 (winners), 2002.

SKY SPORTS FACT FILE

On 22 October 1888 Aston Villa entertained foreign opposition for the first time with the visit of the Canadian touring team to Perry Barr. A crowd of 4000 saw Villa win 4–2. Three years later Canada lost 6–1 to England in an unofficial international.

First Football League Game: 8 September 1888, Football League, v Wolverhampton W (a) D 1–1 – Warner; Cox, Coulton; Yates, H. Devey, Dawson; A. Brown, Green (1), Allen, Garvey, Hodgetts.

Record League Victory: 12–2 v Accrington S, Division 1, 12 March 1892 – Warner; Evans, Cox; Harry Devey, Jimmy Cowan, Baird; Athersmith (1), Dickson (2), John Devey (4), L. Campbell (4), Hodgetts (1).

Record Cup Victory: 13–0 v Wednesbury Old Ath, FA Cup 1st rd, 30 October 1886 – Warner; Coulton, Simmonds; Yates, Robertson, Burton (2); R. Davis (1), A. Brown (3), Hunter (3), Loach (2), Hodgetts (2).

Record Defeat: 1–8 v Blackburn R, FA Cup 3rd rd, 16 February 1889.

Most League Points (2 for a win): 70, Division 3, 1971–72.

Most League Points (3 for a win): 78, Division 2, 1987–88.

Most League Goals: 128, Division 1, 1930–31.

Highest League Scorer in Season: 'Pongo' Waring, 49, Division 1, 1930–31.

Most League Goals in Total Aggregate: Harry Hampton, 215, 1904–15.

Most League Goals in One Match: 5, Harry Hampton v Sheffield W, Division 1, 5 October 1912; 5, Harold Halse v Derby Co, Division 1, 19 October 1912; 5, Len Capewell v Burnley, Division 1, 29 August 1925; 5, George Brown v Leicester C, Division 1, 2 January 1932; 5, Gerry Hitchens v Charlton Ath, Division 2, 18 November 1959.

Most Capped Player: Steve Staunton 64 (102), Republic of Ireland.

Most League Appearances: Charlie Aitken, 561, 1961–76.

Youngest League Player: Jimmy Brown, 15 years 349 days v Bolton W, 17 September 1969.

Record Transfer Fee Received: £12,600,000 from Manchester U for Dwight Yorke, August 1998.

Record Transfer Fee Paid: £9,500,000 to River Plate for Juan Pablo Angel, January 2001.

Football League Record: 1888 Founder Member of the League; 1936–38 Division 2; 1938–59 Division 1; 1959–60 Division 2; 1960–67 Division 1; 1967–70 Division 2; 1970–72 Division 3; 1972–75 Division 2; 1975–87 Division 1; 1987–88 Division 2; 1988–92 Division 1; 1992– FA Premier League.

MANAGERS

George Ramsay 1884–1926
(Secretary-Manager)
W. J. Smith 1926–34
(Secretary-Manager)
Jimmy McMullan 1934–35
Jimmy Hogan 1936–44
Alex Massie 1945–50
George Martin 1950–53
Eric Houghton 1953–58
Joe Mercer 1958–64
Dick Taylor 1964–67
Tommy Cummings 1967–68
Tommy Docherty 1968–70
Vic Crowe 1970–74
Ron Saunders 1974–82
Tony Barton 1982–84
Graham Turner 1984–86
Billy McNeill 1986–87
Graham Taylor 1987–90
Dr Jozef Venglos 1990–91
Ron Atkinson 1991–94
Brian Little 1994–98
John Gregory 1998–2002
Graham Taylor OBE 2002–03
David O'Leary May 2003–

LATEST SEQUENCES

Longest Sequence of League Wins: 9, 15.10.1910 – 10.12.1910.

Longest Sequence of League Defeats: 11, 23.3.1963 – 4.5.1963.

Longest Sequence of League Draws: 6, 12.9.1981 – 10.10.1981.

Longest Sequence of Unbeaten League Matches: 15, 12.3.1949 – 27.8.1949.

Longest Sequence Without a League Win: 12, 27.12.1986 – 25.3.1987.

Successive Scoring Runs: 35 from 10.11.1895.

Successive Non-scoring Runs: 5 from 29.2.1992.

TEN YEAR LEAGUE RECORD

		P	*W*	*D*	*L*	*F*	*A*	*Pts*	*Pos*
1995-96	PR Lge	38	18	9	11	52	35	63	4
1996-97	PR Lge	38	17	10	11	47	34	61	5
1997-98	PR Lge	38	17	6	15	49	48	57	7
1998-99	PR Lge	38	15	10	13	51	46	55	6
1999-2000	PR Lge	38	15	13	10	46	35	58	6
2000-01	PR Lge	38	13	15	10	46	43	54	8
2001-02	PR Lge	38	12	14	12	46	47	50	8
2002-03	PR Lge	38	12	9	17	42	47	45	16
2003-04	PR Lge	38	15	11	12	48	44	56	6
2004-05	PR Lge	38	12	11	15	45	52	47	10

DID YOU KNOW ?

The first player to score a hat-trick for Aston Villa in a European Cup match was Gary Shaw against Dinamo Bucharest in a second leg second round match at Villa Park on 3 November 1982 in a 4–2 win. He had also scored both goals in Romania.

ASTON VILLA 2004–05 LEAGUE RECORD

Match No.	Date	Venue	Opponents	Result		H/T Score	Lg. Pos.	Goalscorers	Attendance
1	Aug 14	H	Southampton	W	2-0	2-0	—	Vassell 12, Cole 34	36,690
2	22	A	WBA	D	1-1	1-1	3	Mellberg 4	26,601
3	25	A	Charlton Ath	L	0-3	0-2	—		26,190
4	28	H	Newcastle U	W	4-2	1-2	6	Mellberg 4, Cole 53, Barry 71, Angel 82	36,305
5	Sept 11	H	Chelsea	D	0-0	0-0	7		36,691
6	18	A	Norwich C	D	0-0	0-0	7		23,805
7	25	H	Crystal Palace	D	1-1	1-1	8	Hendrie 36	34,843
8	Oct 2	A	Blackburn R	D	2-2	1-1	8	Angel 25, Mellberg 80	20,502
9	16	A	Arsenal	L	1-3	1-2	12	Hendrie 3	38,137
10	23	H	Fulham	W	2-0	1-0	9	Solano 29, Hendrie 75	34,460
11	30	A	Everton	D	1-1	1-1	10	Hendrie 26	37,816
12	Nov 6	H	Portsmouth	W	3-0	3-0	6	Whittingham 18, Angel 25, Solano 40	32,633
13	13	A	Bolton W	W	2-1	1-1	6	McCann 41, Hitzlsperger 89	25,779
14	22	H	Tottenham H	W	1-0	0-0	—	Solano 57	35,702
15	27	A	Manchester C	L	0-2	0-2	6		44,530
16	Dec 4	H	Liverpool	D	1-1	1-1	6	Solano 44	42,593
17	12	H	Birmingham C	L	1-2	0-1	6	Barry 90	41,329
18	18	A	Middlesbrough	L	0-3	0-1	8		30,338
19	26	A	Chelsea	L	0-1	0-1	10		41,950
20	28	H	Manchester U	L	0-1	0-1	11		42,593
21	Jan 1	H	Blackburn R	W	1-0	0-0	9	Solano 88	34,265
22	3	A	Crystal Palace	L	0-2	0-1	9		24,140
23	15	H	Norwich C	W	3-0	2-0	10	Ashton (og) 9, Hendrie 27, Solano 76	38,172
24	22	A	Manchester U	L	1-3	0-1	10	Barry 53	67,859
25	Feb 2	A	Fulham	D	1-1	0-0	—	Angel 55	17,624
26	5	H	Arsenal	L	1-3	0-3	11	Angel 74	42,593
27	12	A	Portsmouth	W	2-1	1-1	10	De Zeeuw (og) 17, Hitzlsperger 73	20,160
28	26	H	Everton	L	1-3	0-1	10	Solano 46	40,248
29	Mar 5	H	Middlesbrough	W	2-0	0-0	10	Laursen 64, Moore L 79	34,201
30	20	A	Birmingham C	L	0-2	0-0	11		29,382
31	Apr 2	A	Newcastle U	W	3-0	1-0	10	Angel 5, Barry 2 (2 pens) 73, 80	52,306
32	10	H	WBA	D	1-1	1-0	10	Vassell 27	39,402
33	16	A	Southampton	W	3-2	0-2	9	Cole 55, Solano 70, Davis 72	31,926
34	20	H	Charlton Ath	D	0-0	0-0	—		31,312
35	23	H	Bolton W	D	1-1	1-0	9	Hierro (og) 26	36,053
36	May 1	A	Tottenham H	L	1-5	1-3	10	Barry (pen) 45	36,078
37	7	H	Manchester C	L	1-2	0-2	10	Angel 61	39,645
38	15	A	Liverpool	L	1-2	0-2	10	Barry 67	43,406

Final League Position: 10

GOALSCORERS

League (45): Solano 8, Angel 7, Barry 7 (3 pens), Hendrie 5, Cole 3, Mellberg 3, Hitzlsperger 2, Vassell 2, Davis 1, Laursen 1, McCann 1, Moore L 1, Whittingham 1, own goals 3.
Carling Cup (4): Angel 2, Solano 1, Vassell 1.
FA Cup (1): Barry 1.

Sorensen T 36	Delaney M 30	Samuel J 34 + 1	McCann G 20	Mellberg O 30	Laursen M 12	Hendrie L 25 + 4	Hitzlsperger T 17 + 11	Cole C 18 + 9	Vassell D 17 + 4	Barry G 33 + 1	Whittingham P 5 + 8	De la Cruz U 30 + 4	Moore L 5 + 20	Solano N 32 + 4	Angel J 30 + 5	Postma S 2 + 1	Davis S 19 + 9	Ridgewell L 12 + 3	Berson M 7 + 4	Moore S — + 1	Djemba-Djemba E 4 + 2	*Match No.*
1	2	3	4	5	6	7[1]	8	9	10[3]	11	12[2]	13	14									1
1	2	3	4	5	6		8	9	10[3]	11[1]	12	13		7[2]	14							2
1[6]	2	3	4	5	6		8	9[1]	10	11				7	12	15						3
1	6	3	4	5		12	8[1]	9[3]	10[2]	11		2	13	7	14							4
1	6	3	4	5		12	8		10[2]	11	13	2	14	7[1]	9[3]							5
1	6	3	4	5			8[1]	9[2]	10	11	12	2		7[3]	13		14					6
1	6	3	4	5		8[1]	12	13	10[2]	11[3]	14	2		7	9							7
1	6	3	4	5		8	12	10	13	11[1]		2		7[2]	9							8
	6	3	4	5		7	8[3]	9[2]	10	11[1]	12	2			13	1	14					9
1	6	3	4	5		8[1]	12	13	10[2]		11[3]	2		7	9		14					10
1	6[3]	3	4	5		11	8[2]	10			12	2		7[1]	9		13	14				11
1	6	3	4	5		8[3]	12	10[2]			11	2	13	7[1]	9		14					12
1	6	3	4	5		8[3]	12	9			11[1]	2	13	7[2]	10			14				13
1	6	3	4	5			8[1]	9		12		2	13	7[2]	10		11					14
1	6	3	4	5		8■	12	9[2]		11[1]		2	13	7	10							15
1	6	3	4[2]	5				9[1]		11		2	12	7	10		8		13			16
1	6	3	4	5				9		11		2		7	10		8					17
1	6	3	4[1]	5				12		11	10[2]	2		7	9		8		13			18
1	6[1]			5		7[2]				11	10	2	13	12	9		8	3	4			19
1				5		11[1]		9[2]		3	12	2	13	7	10		8	6	4[3]	14		20
1		3	4	5		8				11		2	9[1]	7	10		12	6				21
1	6	3	4			10[1]				11		2	12	7	9		8	5				22
1	2	3		5		8	12	9[2]		11			13	7[3]	10		14	6	4[1]			23
1	2[2]	3		5		10	12			11		13	14	7[3]	9		8	6	4[1]			24
1				5		11[2]	8	9[1]		3		2	12	7[3]	10		13	6	4		14	25
1		3[1]		5			12			11		2	9	7	10		4	6	13		8[2]	26
1		3		5		4[1]	12			11		2	9[3]	7[2]	10		13	6	14		8	27
1		3		5		12	8		13	11		2	9[2]	7	10			6			4[1]	28
1		3		5	6	9			10[1]	11		2	12	7			8		4			29
1		3		5	6	10	12	13	14	11		2	9[2]	7[1]			8		4[3]			30
1	2	3		5[3]	6	7[2]	8	12	10	11				13	9[1]		4	14				31
1	2	3			6	8		12	10	11		13		7[2]	9[1]		4	5■				32
1	5	3			6[2]	7	8	12	10[1]	11		2	14	13	9[3]		4					33
1	5	6				11[1]	8	9[2]	12	3		2	13	7	10		4					34
1	5	3			6		8	12	10	11		2		7[1]	9		4					35
	2	3			6	12	8[1]		10	11			13	7	9[2]	1	4	5				36
1	5	3[3]			6	7[2]	8[1]		10	11		2	13	12	9		4				14	37
1	5	12			6	11[1]		13	10[3]	3		2	14	7	9[2]		4				8	38

FA Cup

Third Round	Sheffield U	(a)	1-3

Carling Cup

Second Round	QPR	(h)	3-1
Third Round	Burnley	(a)	1-3

BARNET FL Championship 2

FOUNDATION

Barnet Football Club was formed in 1888 as an amateur organisation and they played at a ground in Queen's Road until they disbanded in 1901. A club known as Alston Works FC was then formed and they played at Totteridge Lane until changing to Barnet Alston FC in 1906. They moved to their present ground a year later, combining with The Avenue to form Barnet and Alston in 1912. The club progressed to senior amateur football by way of the Athenian and Isthmian Leagues, turning professional in 1965. It was as a Southern League and Conference club that they made their name.

Underhill Stadium, Barnet Lane, Barnet, Herts EN5 2BE.

Telephone: (020) 8441 6932.

Fax: (020) 8447 0655.

Ticket Office: (020) 8449 6325.

Website: www.barnetfc.com

Email: info@barnetfc.com

Ground Capacity: 4800.

Record Attendance: 11,026 v Wycombe Wanderers, FA Amateur Cup 4th Round 1951–52.

Record Receipts: £31,202 v Portsmouth, FA Cup 3rd Round, 5 January 1991.

Pitch Measurements: 113yd × 72yd.

Chairman: Anthony Kleanthous.

Chief Executive/Secretary: Andrew Adie.

Manager: Paul Fairclough.

Physio: TBC.

Colours: Black and amber.

Change Colours: Amber and black.

Year Formed: 1888.

Turned Professional: 1965.

Previous Names: 1906, Barnet Alston FC; 1919 Barnet.

Club Nickname: The Bees.

Previous Grounds: 1888, Queens Road; 1901, Totteridge Lane, 1907 Barnet Lane.

HONOURS

Football League: Division 2 best season: 24th, 1993–94.

FA Amateur Cup: Winners 1946.

FA Trophy: Finalists 1972.

GM Vauxhall Conference: Winners 1990–91. *Conference:* Winners 2004–05

FA Cup: never past 3rd rd.

League Cup: never past 2nd rd.

SKY SPORTS FACT FILE

When Barnet graduated from the Athenian League to the Southern League in 1965–66 they achieved promotion to the Premier Division after an impressive start with a 10–1 win over Hinckley Athletic and just one point dropped in ten games.

First Football League Game: 17 August 1991, Division 4, v Crewe Alex (h) L 4–7 – Phillips; Blackford, Cooper (Murphy), Horton, Bodley (Stein), Johnson, Showler, Carter (2), Bull (2), Lowe, Evans.

Record League Victory: 7–0 v Blackpool, Division 3, 11 November 2000 – Naisbitt; Stockley, Sawyers, Niven (Brown), Heald, Arber (1), Currie (3), Doolan, Richards (2) (McGleish), Cottee (1) (Riza), Toms.

Record Cup Victory: 6–1 v Newport Co, FA Cup 1st rd, 21 November 1970 – McClelland; Lye, Jenkins, Ward, Embery, King, Powell (1), Ferry, Adams (1), Gray, George (3), (1 og).

Record Defeat: 1–9 v Peterborough U, Division 3, 5 September 1998.

Most League Points (3 for a win): 79, Division 3, 1992–93.

Most League Goals: 81, Division 4, 1991–92.

Highest League Scorer in Season: Dougie Freedman, 24, Division 3, 1994–95.

Most League Goals in Total Aggregate: Sean Devine, 47, 1995–99.

Most League Goals in One Match: 4, Dougie Freedman v Rochdale, Division 3, 13 September 1994; 4, Lee Hodges v Rochdale, Division 3, 8 April 1996.

Most Capped Player: Ken Charlery, 4, St. Lucia.

Most League Appearances: Paul Wilson, 263, 1991–2000.

Youngest League Player: Kieran Adams, 17 years 71 days v Mansfield T, 31 December 1994.

Record Transfer Fee Received: £800,000 from Crystal Palace for Dougie Freedman, September 1995.

Record Transfer Fee Paid: £130,000 to Peterborough U for Greg Heald, August 1997.

Football League Record: Promoted to Division 4 from GMVC 1991; 1991–92 Division 4; 1992–93 Division 3; 1993–94 Division 2; 1994–2001 Division 3; 2001– Conference.

MANAGERS

Lester Finch
George Wheeler
Dexter Adams
Tommy Coleman
Gerry Ward
Gordon Ferry
Brian Kelly
Bill Meadows
Barry Fry
Roger Thompson
Don McAllister
Barry Fry
Edwin Stein
Gary Phillips *(Player-Manager)* 1993–94
Ray Clemence 1994–96
Alan Mullery *(Director of Football)* 1996–97
Terry Bullivant 1997
John Still 1997–2000
Tony Cottee 2000–01
John Still 2001–02
Peter Shreeves 2002–04
Paul Fairclough March 2004–

LATEST SEQUENCES

Longest Sequence of League Wins: 6, 28.8.93 – 25.9.99.

Longest Sequence of League Defeats: 11, 8.5.93 – 2.10.93.

Longest Sequence of League Draws: 4, 22.1.94 – 12.2.94.

Longest Sequence of Unbeaten League Matches: 12, 5.12.92 – 2.3.93.

Longest Sequence Without a League Win: 14, 24.4.93 – 10.10.93.

TEN YEAR LEAGUE RECORD

		P	W	D	L	F	A	Pts	Pos
1995-96	Div 3	46	18	16	12	65	45	70	9
1996-97	Div 3	46	14	16	16	46	51	58	15
1997-98	Div 3	46	19	13	14	61	51	70	7
1998-99	Div 3	46	14	13	19	54	71	55	16
1999-2000	Div 3	46	21	12	13	59	53	75	6
2000–01	Div 3	46	12	9	25	67	81	45	24
2001–02	Conf	42	19	10	13	64	48	67	5
2002–03	Conf	42	13	14	15	65	68	53	11
2003–04	Conf	42	19	14	9	60	48	71	4
2004–05	Conf	42	26	8	8	90	44	86	1

DID YOU KNOW

At the end of the 1931–32 season, the annual report produced by Barnet drew attention to the feat achieved by Arthur Morris in scoring his 250th goal in his fifth season with the Athenian League club.

BARNSLEY FL Championship 1

FOUNDATION

Many clubs owe their inception to the church and Barnsley are among them, for they were formed in 1887 by the Rev. T. T. Preedy, curate of Barnsley St Peter's and went under that name until it was dropped in 1897 a year before being admitted to the Second Division of the Football League.

Oakwell Stadium, Grove Street, Barnsley, South Yorkshire S71 1ET.

Telephone: (01226) 211 211.

Fax: (01226) 211 444.

Ticket Office: (01226) 211 211.

Website: www.barnsleyfc.co.uk

Email: thereds@barnsleyfc.co.uk

Ground Capacity: 25,000.

Record Attendance: 40,255 v Stoke C, FA Cup 5th rd, 15 February 1936.

Pitch Measurements: 110yd × 75yd.

Chairman: Gordon Shepherd.

Secretary: Don Roling.

Manager: Andy Ritchie.

Assistant Manager: Rick Holden.

Physio: Rick Holden.

Colours: Red shirts, white shorts, red stockings.

Change Colours: Navy and sky shirts, navy and sky shorts, navy and sky stockings.

Year Formed: 1887.

Turned Professional: 1888.

Ltd Co.: 1899.

Previous Name: 1887, Barnsley St Peter's; 1897, Barnsley.

Club Nickname: 'The Tykes', 'Reds' or 'Colliers'.

First Football League Game: 1 September 1898, Division 2, v Lincoln C (a) L 0–1 – Fawcett; McArtney, Nixon; King, Burleigh, Porteous; Davis, Lees, Murray, McCullough, McGee.

Record League Victory: 9–0 v Loughborough T, Division 2, 28 January 1899 – Greaves; McArtney, Nixon; Porteous, Burleigh, Howard; Davis (4), Hepworth (1), Lees (1), McCullough (1), Jones (2). 9–0 v Accrington S, Division 3 (N), 3 February 1934 – Ellis; Cookson, Shotton; Harper, Henderson, Whitworth; Spence (2), Smith (1), Blight (4), Andrews (1), Ashton (1).

Record Cup Victory: 6–0 v Blackpool, FA Cup 1st rd replay, 20 January 1910 – Mearns; Downs, Ness; Glendinning, Boyle (1), Utley; Bartrop, Gadsby (1), Lillycrop (2), Tufnell (2), Forman. 6–0 v Peterborough U, League Cup 1st rd 2nd leg, 15 September 1981 – Horn; Joyce, Chambers, Glavin (2), Banks, McCarthy, Evans, Parker (2), Aylott (1), McHale, Barrowclough (1).

HONOURS

Football League: Division 1 – Runners-up 1996–97; Division 3 (N) – Champions 1933–34, 1938–39, 1954–55; Runners-up 1953–54; Division 3 – Runners-up 1980–81; Division 4 – Runners-up 1967–68; Promoted 1978–79.

FA Cup: Winners 1912; Runners-up 1910.

Football League Cup: best season: 5th rd, 1982.

SKY SPORTS FACT FILE

Third place in 1914–15 for Barnsley came after an erratic opening. Hammered 7–0 at Derby County on the first day they managed a 3–1 win then failed to score in the next three. Later on they revenged themselves on Derby with a Dickie Downs penalty.

Record Defeat: 0–9 v Notts Co, Division 2, 19 November 1927.

Most League Points (2 for a win): 67, Division 3 (N), 1938–39.

Most League Points (3 for a win): 82, Division 1, 1999–2000.

Most League Goals: 118, Division 3 (N), 1933–34.

Highest League Scorer in Season: Cecil McCormack, 33, Division 2, 1950–51.

Most League Goals in Total Aggregate: Ernest Hine, 123, 1921–26 and 1934–38.

Most League Goals in One Match: 5, Frank Eaton v South Shields, Division 3N, 9 April 1927; 5, Peter Cunningham v Darlington, Division 3N, 4 February 1933; 5, Beau Asquith v Darlington, Division 3N, 12 November 1938; 5, Cecil McCormack v Luton T, Division 2, 9 September 1950.

Most Capped Player: Gerry Taggart, 35 (50), Northern Ireland.

Most League Appearances: Barry Murphy, 514, 1962–78.

Youngest League Player: Alan Ogley, 16 years 226 days v Bristol R, 18 September 1962.

Record Transfer Fee Received: £4,500,000 from Blackburn R for Ashley Ward, December 1998.

Record Transfer Fee Paid: £1,500,000 to Partizan Belgrade for Georgi Hristov, July 1997.

Football League Record: 1898 Elected to Division 2; 1932–34 Division 3 (N); 1934–38 Division 2; 1938–39 Division 3 (N); 1946–53 Division 2; 1953–55 Division 3 (N); 1955–59 Division 2; 1959–65 Division 3; 1965–68 Division 4; 1968–72 Division 3; 1972–79 Division 4; 1979–81 Division 3; 1981–92 Division 2; 1992–97 Division 1; 1997–98 FA Premier League; 1998–2002 Division 1; 2002–04 Division 2; 2004– FL1.

MANAGERS

Arthur Fairclough 1898–1901 *(Secretary-Manager)*
John McCartney 1901–04 *(Secretary-Manager)*
Arthur Fairclough 1904–12
John Hastie 1912–14
Percy Lewis 1914–19
Peter Sant 1919–26
John Commins 1926–29
Arthur Fairclough 1929–30
Brough Fletcher 1930–37
Angus Seed 1937–53
Tim Ward 1953–60
Johnny Steele 1960–71 *(continued as General Manager)*
John McSeveney 1971–72
Johnny Steele *(General Manager)* 1972–73
Jim Iley 1973–78
Allan Clarke 1978–80
Norman Hunter 1980–84
Bobby Collins 1984–85
Allan Clarke 1985–89
Mel Machin 1989–93
Viv Anderson 1993–94
Danny Wilson 1994–98
John Hendrie 1998–99
Dave Bassett 1999–2000
Nigel Spackman 2001
Steve Parkin 2001–02
Glyn Hodges 2002–03
Gudjon Thordarson 2003–04
Paul Hart 2004–05
Andy Ritchie March 2005–

LATEST SEQUENCES

Longest Sequence of League Wins: 10, 5.3.1955 – 23.4.1955.

Longest Sequence of League Defeats: 9, 14.3.1953 – 25.4.1953.

Longest Sequence of League Draws: 7, 28.3.1911 – 22.4.1911.

Longest Sequence of Unbeaten League Matches: 21, 1.1.1934 – 5.5.1934.

Longest Sequence Without a League Win: 26, 13.12.1952 – 26.8.1953.

Successive Scoring Runs: 44 from 2.10.1926.

Successive Non-scoring Runs: 6 from 7.10.1899.

TEN YEAR LEAGUE RECORD

		P	*W*	*D*	*L*	*F*	*A*	*Pts*	*Pos*
1995-96	Div 1	46	14	18	14	60	66	60	10
1996-97	Div 1	46	22	14	10	76	55	80	2
1997-98	PR Lge	38	10	5	23	37	82	35	19
1998-99	Div 1	46	14	17	15	59	56	59	13
1999-2000	Div 1	46	24	10	12	88	67	82	4
2000-01	Div 1	46	15	9	22	49	62	54	16
2001-02	Div 1	46	11	15	20	59	86	48	23
2002-03	Div 2	46	13	13	20	51	64	52	19
2003-04	Div 2	46	15	17	14	54	58	62	12
2004-05	FL 1	46	14	19	13	69	64	61	13

DID YOU KNOW ?

Harry Holdcroft joined Barnsley in 1945. An experienced veteran goalkeeper aged 36, he took part in six FA Cup matches and 14 regional league games before joining Morecambe.

BARNSLEY 2004–05 LEAGUE RECORD

Match No.	*Date*	*Venue*	*Opponents*	*Result*		*H/T Score*	*Lg. Pos.*	*Goalscorers*	*Atten-dance*
1	Aug 7	A	Milton Keynes D	D	1-1	1-0	—	Reid [22]	4720
2	10	H	Bristol C	W	2-1	0-0	—	Shuker 2 [68, 76]	10,435
3	14	H	Luton T	L	3-4	1-3	12	Boulding 2 [2, 90], McPhail [72]	10,057
4	21	A	Walsall	D	2-2	1-1	15	Vaughan [16], Conlon [49]	6059
5	28	H	Hull C	L	1-2	1-0	18	Conlon [12]	13,175
6	30	A	Wrexham	L	1-2	0-1	19	Nardiello [62]	4223
7	Sept 4	A	Hartlepool U	D	1-1	1-0	20	Chopra [38]	5119
8	11	H	Tranmere R	D	0-0	0-0	20		8615
9	18	A	Huddersfield T	W	2-0	2-0	19	Conlon [10], Mirfin (og) [21]	14,794
10	25	H	Chesterfield	W	1-0	0-0	14	Kay [87]	9792
11	Oct 2	A	Bradford C	L	0-1	0-0	16		8715
12	9	H	Brentford	D	0-0	0-0	16		8453
13	17	A	Sheffield W	L	0-1	0-1	17		25,391
14	20	H	Doncaster R	L	1-3	0-1	—	Chopra [71]	12,478
15	23	H	Swindon T	D	2-2	1-1	19	Chopra [41], Reid [66]	8837
16	30	A	Bournemouth	W	3-1	2-0	17	Conlon 2 (1 pen) [20 (p), 36], Chopra [69]	7709
17	Nov 6	H	Port Vale	L	1-2	1-0	17	Conlon (pen) [44]	8642
18	20	A	Oldham Ath	L	2-3	1-1	19	Boulding [11], Chopra [55]	5593
19	27	H	Blackpool	W	1-0	0-0	19	Burns [75]	9084
20	Dec 7	A	Colchester U	W	2-0	1-0	—	Kay 2 [34, 54]	2927
21	11	A	Torquay U	W	1-0	1-0	16	Boulding [45]	2983
22	18	H	Peterborough U	W	4-0	1-0	12	Chopra 3 [14, 57, 77], Shuker [51]	8536
23	26	A	Tranmere R	D	1-1	0-0	14	Kay [90]	11,519
24	28	H	Stockport Co	D	3-3	2-0	13	Vaughan 2 [14, 47], Shuker [43]	10,236
25	Jan 1	H	Hartlepool U	D	0-0	0-0	12		9595
26	3	A	Chesterfield	D	2-2	2-0	12	Boulding 2 [38, 45]	5985
27	15	H	Huddersfield T	W	4-2	3-0	12	Chopra 3 (1 pen) [9, 24, 87 (p)], Boulding [38]	11,725
28	22	A	Stockport Co	D	2-2	1-1	12	Boulding [31], Vaughan [63]	5326
29	25	A	Brentford	D	1-1	1-0	—	Boulding [34]	4835
30	31	H	Bradford C	D	2-2	0-2	—	Chopra [54], Kay [88]	8729
31	Feb 5	H	Sheffield W	D	0-0	0-0	12		19,659
32	12	A	Swindon T	L	1-2	1-1	14	Burns [30]	5511
33	19	H	Bournemouth	L	0-1	0-0	15		8153
34	22	A	Doncaster R	L	0-4	0-2	—		7286
35	26	H	Torquay U	W	4-1	3-0	14	McPhail [24], Chopra [27], Reid [29], Boulding [64]	7466
36	Mar 5	A	Peterborough U	W	3-1	0-0	12	Chopra (pen) [67], Nardiello [89], Shuker [90]	3485
37	12	A	Bristol C	D	0-0	0-0	13		9321
38	19	H	Milton Keynes D	D	1-1	1-0	13	Nardiello [45]	8111
39	25	A	Luton T	W	3-1	3-0	—	Shuker [33], Davies (og) [37], Chopra [42]	7548
40	28	H	Walsall	W	3-2	1-0	12	Kay [37], Nardiello [48], Chopra [80]	8358
41	Apr 2	A	Hull C	L	1-2	0-1	13	Nardiello [64]	19,341
42	5	H	Wrexham	D	2-2	1-0	—	Nardiello [26], Chopra [72]	7753
43	16	H	Oldham Ath	D	2-2	1-1	13	Johnson 2 [6, 79]	8856
44	23	A	Port Vale	L	0-5	0-2	13		4324
45	30	H	Colchester U	D	1-1	1-0	13	Nardiello [41]	8162
46	May 7	A	Blackpool	W	2-0	1-0	13	Shuker [38], Williams R [85]	7571

Final League Position: 13

GOALSCORERS

League (69): Chopra 17 (2 pens), Boulding 10, Nardiello 7, Shuker 7, Conlon 6 (2 pens), Kay 6, Vaughan 4, Reid 3, Burns 2, Johnson 2, McPhail 2, Williams R 1, own goals 2.
Carling Cup (3): Conlon 1, Reid 1 (pen), Shuker 1.
FA Cup (0).
LDV Vans Trophy (0).

Colgan N 12 + 1	Hassell B 37 + 2	Williams T 38 + 1	Burns J 33 + 1	Carbon M 16 + 10	Vaughan T 25 + 1	Reid P 38 + 3	Conlon B 17 + 7	Boulding M 22 + 7	Shuker C 39 + 6	McPhail S 36	Wroe N 26 + 5	Onibuje F — + 3	Austin N 9 + 6	Nardiello D 11 + 17	Kay A 37 + 2	Stallard M — + 5	Chopra M 38 + 1	Williams R 13 + 4	Turnbull R 23	Tonge D 14	Jarman N 1 + 5	Baker T — + 3	Johnson S 10 + 1	Flinders S 11	Joynes N — + 1	Atkinson R — + 1	*Match No.*
1	2	3	4^{1}	5	6	7	8	9^{2}	10	11	12	13															1
1	2	3		5^{1}	6	7	8	9^{2}	10	11	4		12	13													2
1	2	3		5	6	7	8	9	10^{2}	11				12	4^{1}	13											3
1	2	3		5	6	7	8	9	10	11^{1}	12				4												4
1	2	3		5	6	7	8^{3}	12	10^{1}		4			14	11	13	9^{2}										5
1	2	3		5	6	7	12	13	10^{2}		11^{1}			8^{3}	4	14	9										6
1	2	3		5	6■	7	8	12	10^{3}		11^{1}		14	13	4		9^{2}										7
1	2	3	4	5		6	8		10		11^{1}			12	7		9										8
1	2	3	12			6	8^{2}		10^{1}	7	4				5	13	9	11									9
1	2	3			6	5	8		12	11	7^{1}			10	4		9										10
1	2	3		12	6	5^{1}	8	13	14	11^{2}	7			10^{3}	4		9										11
		3	4	5^{3}	6		8^{2}		10	11	7	13		12	2		9^{1}	14	1								12
		2	4		6	12	8	13	10^{3}	11			5	14	7^{1}		9	3^{2}	1								13
	12		4■		6^{1}	7	8	11^{2}	10	2^{3}	14		5	13			9	3	1								14
	2	3				7	8^{2}	12	10■		4		5^{1}	13			9	11	1	6							15
	2	11		5		4	8^{1}				10	12			7		9	3	1	6							16
	2	3		5		6	8		12		7^{1}			13	10		9	11	1	4^{2}							17
	2	3	4	5	6	7		9^{1}	10		11						8		1		12						18
	2^{2}	3	4		6	5	12	9	10		11		13		7		8^{1}		1								19
	2	3	4	12	6	5	13	9^{2}	10^{1}	11					7		8		1								20
	2	3	4		6	5		9	10	11					7		8		1								21
	2	3	4	12	6	7^{1}	13	9^{3}	10	11^{2}				14	5		8		1								22
	2	3	4	12	6	5	13	9^{2}	10^{1}	11^{3}				14	7		8		1								23
	2	3^{3}	4	12	6	7^{1}		9	10	11^{2}			14	13	5		8		1								24
	2	3	4		6	7	9^{2}		12	11	8^{1}			10	5		13		1								25
	2	3	4	12	6	7	13	9	10^{1}	11^{2}					5		8		1								26
15	2	3	4	12	6	7		9^{1}	10^{G}	11^{2}			13		5		8		1■								27
1	2	3	4	12	6	7		9	10	11					5^{1}	13	8^{2}										28
	2	3	4	12	6^{1}	7		9	10	11					5		8		1								29
	2	3	4	5		7		9	10	11					6		8		1								30
		3	4	5		7		9	10	11^{1}	12		2		6		8		1								31
	12	3	4	5		7		9	10^{1}		11^{2}		2	8	6				1		13						32
		3	4	5^{1}	12	7		9	10^{2}	11			2		6		8		1			13					33
	2	12	4		6■	7		9	10^{1}	11			3		5		8		1								34
	2	3	4			6		9^{2}	12	11	7			13	5		8		1				10^{1}				35
	2	3	4			6			10	11^{2}	7			12	14		8^{1}	13		5^{3}			9	1			36
	2	3	4			6			10	11	7			12			8■			5			9^{1}	1			37
	2	6	4					12	10	11	7			8^{1}				3		5			9	1			38
	2	3^{1}	4						10	11	7			13	6		8	12		5			9^{2}	1			39
	2		4			12			10	11	7^{3}			9^{2}	6		8	3		5^{1}		13	14	1			40
	2	3^{2}	4			12			10	11				9	6		8	13		5^{1}		14	7^{3}	1			41
	2		4			6			10	11	7^{1}			9^{2}	12		8	3		5	13			1			42
	2^{1}		4	12		7^{2}			10	11	13				6		8	3		5^{3}	14		9	1			43
			4			6^{1}			10	11	7		12		5			3		2	8		9^{2}	1	13^{3}	14	44
			4^{1}						12	11	7		5	9^{2}	6		8	3		2	13		10	1			45
							12		10^{1}	11	7		5	9	6		8	3		2			4	1			46

FA Cup
First Round Northampton T (a) 0-1

Carling Cup
First Round Darlington (a) 2-0
Second Round Manchester C (a) 1-7

LDV Vans Trophy
First Round Port Vale (a) 0-1

BIRMINGHAM CITY FA Premiership

FOUNDATION

In 1875, cricketing enthusiasts who were largely members of Trinity Church, Bordesley, determined to continue their sporting relationships throughout the year by forming a football club which they called Small Heath Alliance. For their earliest games played on waste land in Arthur Street, the team included three Edden brothers and two James brothers.

St Andrews Stadium, Birmingham B9 4NH.

Telephone: 0870 066 1875.

Fax: 0870 226 1975.

Ticket Office: (0121) 773 3803.

Website: www.bcfc.com

Email: reception@bcfc.com

Ground Capacity: 29,949.

Record Attendance: 66,844 v Everton, FA Cup 5th rd, 11 February 1939.

Pitch Measurements: 100m × 68m.

Chairman: David Gold.

Vice-chairman: Jack Wiseman.

Managing Director: Karren Brady.

Secretary: Julia Shelton.

Manager: Steve Bruce.

Assistant Manager: Eric Black.

Physio: Steve Brannigan.

Colours: Royal blue shirts, white shorts, blue stockings.

Change Colours: All white with red trim.

Year Formed: 1875.

Turned Professional: 1885.

Ltd Co.: 1888.

Previous Names: 1875, Small Heath Alliance; 1888, dropped 'Alliance'; 1905, Birmingham; 1945, Birmingham City.

Club Nickname: 'Blues'.

Previous Grounds: 1875, waste ground near Arthur St; 1877, Muntz St, Small Heath; 1906, St Andrews.

First Football League game: 3 September 1892, Division 2, v Burslem Port Vale (h) W 5–1 – Charsley; Bayley, Speller; Ollis, Jenkyns, Devey; Hallam (1), Edwards (1), Short (1), Wheldon (2), Hands.

Record League Victory: 12–0 v Walsall T Swifts, Division 2, 17 December 1892 – Charsley; Bayley, Jones; Ollis, Jenkyns, Devey; Hallam (2), Walton (3), Mobley (3), Wheldon (2), Hands (2). 12–0 v Doncaster R, Division 2, 11 April 1903 – Dorrington; Goldie, Wassell; Beer, Dougherty (1), Howard; Athersmith (1), Leonard (3), McRoberts (1), Wilcox (4), Field (1). Aston, (1 og).

HONOURS

Football League: Promoted from Division 1 (play offs) 2001–02; Division 2 – Champions 1892–93, 1920–21, 1947–48, 1954–55, 1994–95; Runners-up 1893–94, 1900–01, 1902–03, 1971–72, 1984–85; Division 3 Runners-up 1991–92.

FA Cup: Runners-up 1931, 1956.

Football League Cup: Winners 1963; Runners-up 2001.

Leyland Daf Cup: Winners 1991.

Auto Windscreens Shield: Winners 1995.

European Competitions: *European Fairs Cup:* 1955–58, 1958–60 (runners-up), 1960–61 (runners-up), 1961–62.

SKY SPORTS FACT FILE

In their Football Alliance days before entry to the Football League, Birmingham City enjoyed their best season in 1891–92 finishing third. Still known as Small Heath they even defeated Crewe Alexandra on 20 April with a man short throughout.

Record Cup Victory: 9–2 v Burton W, FA Cup 1st rd, 31 October 1885 – Hedges; Jones, Evetts (1); F. James, Felton, A. James (1); Davenport (2), Stanley (4), Simms, Figures, Morris (1).

Record Defeat: 1–9 v Sheffield W, Division 1, 13 December 1930. 1–9 v Blackburn R, Division 1, 5 January 1895.

Most League Points (2 for a win): 59, Division 2, 1947–48.

Most League Points (3 for a win): 89, Division 2, 1994–95.

Most League Goals: 103, Division 2, 1893–94 (only 28 games).

Highest League Scorer in Season: Joe Bradford, 29, Division 1, 1927–28.

Most League Goals in Total Aggregate: Joe Bradford, 249, 1920–35.

Most League Goals in One Match: 5, Walter Abbott v Darwen, Division 2, 26 November, 1898; 5, John McMillan v Blackpool, Division 2, 2 March 1901; 5, James Windridge v Glossop, Division 2, 23 January 1915.

Most Capped Player: Malcolm Page, 28, Wales.

Most League Appearances: Frank Womack, 491, 1908–28.

Youngest League Player: Trevor Francis, 16 years 7 months v Cardiff C, 5 September 1970.

Record Transfer Fee Received: £3,500,000 from Leicester C for Gary Rowett, July 2000.

Record Transfer Fee Paid: £5,875,000 to Liverpool for Emile Heskey, July 2004.

Football League Record: 1892 elected to Division 2; 1894–96 Division 1; 1896–1901 Division 2; 1901–02 Division 1; 1902–03 Division 2; 1903–08 Division 1; 1908–21 Division 2; 1921–39 Division 1; 1946–48 Division 2; 1948–50 Division 1; 1950–55 Division 2; 1955–65 Division 1; 1965–72 Division 2; 1972–79 Division 1; 1979–80 Division 2; 1980–84 Division 1; 1984–85 Division 2; 1985–86 Division 1; 1986–89 Division 2; 1989–92 Division 3; 1992–94 Division 1; 1994–95 Division 2; 1995–2002 Division 1; 2002– FA Premier League.

MANAGERS

Alfred Jones 1892–1908
(Secretary-Manager)
Alec Watson 1908–10
Bob McRoberts 1910–15
Frank Richards 1915–23
Billy Beer 1923–27
Leslie Knighton 1928–33
George Liddell 1933–39
Harry Storer 1945–48
Bob Brocklebank 1949–54
Arthur Turner 1954–58
Pat Beasley 1959–60
Gil Merrick 1960–64
Joe Mallett 1965
Stan Cullis 1965–70
Fred Goodwin 1970–75
Willie Bell 1975–77
Jim Smith 1978–82
Ron Saunders 1982–86
John Bond 1986–87
Garry Pendrey 1987–89
Dave Mackay 1989–91
Lou Macari 1991
Terry Cooper 1991–93
Barry Fry 1993–96
Trevor Francis 1996–2001
Steve Bruce December 2001–

LATEST SEQUENCES

Longest Sequence of League Wins: 13, 17.12.1892 – 16.9.1893.

Longest Sequence of League Defeats: 8, 28.9.1985 – 23.11.1985.

Longest Sequence of League Draws: 8, 18.9.1990 – 23.10.1990.

Longest Sequence of Unbeaten League Matches: 20, 3.9.1994 – 2.1.1995.

Longest Sequence Without a League Win: 17, 28.9.1985 – 18.1.1986.

Successive Scoring Runs: 24 from 24.9.1892.

Successive Non-scoring Runs: 6 from 1.10.1949.

TEN YEAR LEAGUE RECORD

		P	W	D	L	F	A	Pts	Pos
1995-96	Div 1	46	15	13	18	61	64	58	15
1996-97	Div 1	46	17	15	14	52	48	66	10
1997-98	Div 1	46	19	17	10	60	35	74	7
1998-99	Div 1	46	23	12	11	66	37	81	4
1999-2000	Div 1	46	22	11	13	65	44	77	5
2000-01	Div 1	46	23	9	14	59	48	78	5
2001-02	Div 1	46	21	13	12	70	49	76	5
2002-03	PR Lge	38	13	9	16	41	49	48	13
2003-04	PR Lge	38	12	14	12	43	48	50	10
2004-05	PR Lge	38	11	12	15	40	46	45	12

DID YOU KNOW ?

Birmingham were third again in the Second Division in 1919–20. The following season they won the championship of the division with two spells of 12 and 10 matches without defeat.

BIRMINGHAM CITY 2004–05 LEAGUE RECORD

Match No.	Date	Venue	Opponents	Result	H/T Score	Lg. Pos.	Goalscorers	Attendance
1	Aug 14	A	Portsmouth	D 1-1	1-1	—	Savage [10]	20,021
2	21	H	Chelsea	L 0-1	0-0	18		28,559
3	24	H	Manchester C	W 1-0	1-0	—	Heskey [8]	28,551
4	28	A	Tottenham H	L 0-1	0-1	13		35,290
5	Sept 11	A	Middlesbrough	L 1-2	1-1	14	Heskey [42]	30,252
6	18	H	Charlton Ath	D 1-1	0-0	14	Yorke [68]	27,400
7	25	A	Bolton W	D 1-1	0-1	15	Izzet [49]	23,692
8	Oct 3	H	Newcastle U	D 2-2	1-1	15	Yorke [23], Upson [57]	29,021
9	16	H	Manchester U	D 0-0	0-0	14		29,221
10	24	A	Southampton	D 0-0	0-0	14		27,568
11	30	H	Crystal Palace	L 0-1	0-1	16		28,916
12	Nov 6	A	Liverpool	W 1-0	0-0	15	Anderton [77]	42,669
13	13	H	Everton	L 0-1	0-0	15		28,388
14	21	A	Blackburn R	D 3-3	3-1	14	Anderton [17], Savage [38], Dunn [45]	20,290
15	27	H	Norwich C	D 1-1	1-0	14	Morrison [9]	29,120
16	Dec 4	A	Arsenal	L 0-3	0-1	15		38,064
17	12	A	Aston Villa	W 2-1	1-0	14	Morrison [9], Dunn [18]	41,329
18	18	H	WBA	W 4-0	3-0	14	Savage (pen) [4], Morrison [23], Heskey [30], Anderton [80]	28,880
19	26	H	Middlesbrough	W 2-0	2-0	12	Morrison [10], Heskey [45]	29,082
20	28	A	Fulham	W 3-2	2-1	9	Heskey [25], Carter [41], Savage [53]	18,706
21	Jan 1	A	Newcastle U	L 1-2	0-2	12	Heskey [64]	52,222
22	4	H	Bolton W	L 1-2	0-1	13	Upson [66]	27,177
23	15	A	Charlton Ath	L 1-3	0-1	14	Melchiot [55]	26,111
24	22	H	Fulham	L 1-2	0-0	15	Volz (og) [51]	28,512
25	Feb 2	H	Southampton	W 2-1	2-0	—	Pandiani [12], Blake (pen) [41]	28,797
26	5	A	Manchester U	L 0-2	0-0	14		67,838
27	12	H	Liverpool	W 2-0	2-0	12	Pandiani (pen) [38], Gray [45]	29,318
28	26	A	Crystal Palace	L 0-2	0-1	13		23,376
29	Mar 6	A	WBA	L 0-2	0-0	13		25,749
30	20	H	Aston Villa	W 2-0	0-0	13	Heskey [52], Gray [89]	29,382
31	Apr 2	H	Tottenham H	D 1-1	0-0	13	Carter [66]	29,304
32	9	A	Chelsea	D 1-1	0-0	13	Pandiani [65]	42,031
33	16	H	Portsmouth	D 0-0	0-0	12		28,883
34	20	A	Manchester C	L 0-3	0-0	—		42,453
35	23	A	Everton	D 1-1	1-0	13	Heskey [5]	36,828
36	30	H	Blackburn R	W 2-1	0-1	12	Blake [61], Heskey [80]	28,621
37	May 7	A	Norwich C	L 0-1	0-1	13		25,477
38	15	H	Arsenal	W 2-1	0-0	12	Pandiani [80], Heskey [90]	29,302

Final League Position: 12

GOALSCORERS

League (40): Heskey 10, Morrison 4, Pandiani 4 (1 pen), Savage 4 (1 pen), Anderton 3, Blake 2 (1 pen), Carter 2, Dunn 2, Gray 2, Upson 2, Yorke 2, Izzet 1, Melchiot 1, own goal 1.
Carling Cup (3): Gronkjaer 1, Morrison 1, Savage 1 (pen).
FA Cup (3): Carter 2, Heskey 1.

Taylor Maik 38	Melchiot M 33 + 1	Lazaridis S 15 + 5	Savage R 18	Upson M 36	Taylor Martin 4 + 3	Johnson D 36	Izzet M 10	Forssell M 4	Heskey E 34	Gronkjaer J 13 + 3	Gray J 18 + 14	Morrison C 13 + 13	John S — + 3	Clemence S 13 + 9	Tebily O 9 + 6	Cunningham K 36	Yorke D 4 + 9	Dunn D 9 + 2	Clapham J 18 + 9	Anderton D 9 + 11	Carter D 12 + 3	Blake R 2 + 9	Diao S 2	Nafti M 7 + 3	Pennant J 12	Pandiani W 13 + 1	*Match No.*
1	2	3	4	5	6	7	8	9^{2}	10	11^{1}	12	13															1
1	2	3	4	5	6	7	8		9	11^{1}	10		12														2
1	2	3^{2}		5		4	8	9^{3}	10^{1}	7	11		12	13	14	6											3
1	2			5		7	8	9^{2}	10	11	3	13	12	4^{1}		6											4
1	2			5		7^{1}	4	9	10	11	3	12				6	8										5
1	2		4	5		7■	8		10	11	3	9^{2}				6^{1}	12	13									6
1	2		4	5		7	8^{1}		9	11^{2}	12			10		6		13	3								7
1	2		4	5		7	8^{3}		9^{2}	11	12			14		6	13	10^{1}	3								8
1	2		4	5		7^{2}			9	11^{3}	3				13	6	10^{1}	8	12	14							9
1	2		4	5		11			9	12	3					6	10^{1}	8^{2}	13	7							10
1	2	3^{3}	4	5		8^{2}			9	7	11			13		6^{1}	10		12	14							11
1	2	12	4	5		7	8^{2}		9	11^{1}	3			10^{3}		6			13	14							12
1	2	12	4	5		7	8■		9	11^{3}	3			10^{1}		6^{2}	13			14							13
1	2		4	5		8				11	3	9^{1}		13		6	14	10^{2}	12	7^{3}							14
1	2^{1}		4	5		7			10	12		9^{2}		14		6	13	11^{3}	3	8							15
1	2^{1}		4	5	12	7			9	13	11	14				6		10^{3}	3	8^{2}							16
1		3^{2}	4	5		7			10		12	9^{3}			2	6		11^{1}	13	14	8						17
1		3	4^{2}	5		7^{3}			10^{1}		12	9			2	6		11	13	14	8						18
1	12	3	4	5		7			10^{2}		13	9^{1}			2	6		11^{3}	14		8						19
1	2		4^{3}	5		7			10^{1}		12	9^{2}		13	3	6			11	14	8						20
1	2	11	4	5		7			10		12	9			3^{1}	6^{2}	13			14	8^{3}						21
1	2	11		5		7			10		12	9^{2}		4^{3}	3^{1}	6	13		14	8							22
1	2			5		7			10^{3}		12	9		4^{1}	3	6	13			11^{2}	8	14					23
1	2				5^{1}	7^{2}			10		11	9^{3}				6	12		3	13	8	14	4				24
1	2			5		8					11	12		4	13	6			3		14	10^{1}			7^{3}	9^{2}	25
1	2				5^{2}	8					11	12			13	6			3		14	10^{1}		4^{3}	7	9	26
1	2^{1}			5		8			10		11			4	12	6			3			13		14	7^{3}	9^{2}	27
1				5		8					11	10^{1}		4	2^{2}	6			3	12		13			7	9	28
1		12		5		7			10		11^{3}			4	2^{1}	6			3	13		14	8^{2}			9	29
1	2	11^{2}		5		7			10		13	12		4^{3}		6			3		8			14		9^{1}	30
1	2	11^{3}		5		8			10		12	13				6			3		4			14	7^{1}	9^{2}	31
1	2	12		5		8			10		13	14				6			3		4^{1}			11	7^{2}	9^{3}	32
1	2	11^{2}		5		8			10		13	12				6			3		14			4^{3}	7	9^{1}	33
1	2	12		5					10			9		11^{2}		6			3^{1}	8^{3}	4	13			7	14	34
1	2	3		5	12	8			10					13		6				11^{2}		14		4	7^{1}	9^{3}	35
1	2	3		5		8			10			12		13		6				11^{2}		14		4^{3}	7	9^{1}	36
1	2	11^{2}		5		8■			10			12		13		6^{3}			3			14		4	7	9^{1}	37
1	2^{3}			5	12				10			13		8	14	6			3		11^{2}			4	7	9^{1}	38

FA Cup

Third Round	Leeds U	(h)	3-0
Fourth Round	Chelsea	(a)	0-2

Carling Cup

Second Round	Lincoln C	(h)	3-1
Third Round	Fulham	(h)	0-1

BLACKBURN ROVERS FA Premiership

FOUNDATION

It was in 1875 that some Public School old boys called a meeting at which the Blackburn Rovers club was formed and the colours blue and white adopted. The leading light was John Lewis, later to become a founder of the Lancashire FA, a famous referee who was in charge of two FA Cup Finals, and a vice-president of both the FA and the Football League.

Ewood Park, Blackburn BB2 4JF.

Telephone: 0870 111 3232.

Fax: (01254) 671 042.

Ticket Office: 0870 112 3456.

Website: www.rovers.co.uk

Email: enquiries@rovers.co.uk

Ground Capacity: 31,367.

Record Attendance: 62,522 v Bolton W, FA Cup 6th rd, 2 March 1929.

Pitch Measurements: 105m × 65m.

Chairman: Robert D. Coar BSC.

Vice-chairman: Richard L. Matthewman.

Chief Executive: John Williams.

Manager: Mark Hughes.

Physio: Dave Fevre.

Assistant Manager: Alan Murray.

Secretary: Tom Finn.

Colours: Blue and white halved shirts.

Change Colours: Red and black.

Year Formed: 1875.

Turned Professional: 1880.

Ltd Co.: 1897.

Club Nickname: Rovers.

Previous Grounds: 1875, all matches played away; 1876, Oozehead Ground; 1877, Pleasington Cricket Ground; 1878, Alexandra Meadows; 1881, Leamington Road; 1890, Ewood Park.

First Football League Game: 15 September 1888, Football League, v Accrington (h) D 5–5 – Arthur; Beverley, James Southworth; Douglas, Almond, Forrest; Beresford (1), Walton, John Southworth (1), Fecitt (1), Townley (2).

Record League Victory: 9–0 v Middlesbrough, Division 2, 6 November 1954 – Elvy; Suart, Eckersley; Clayton, Kelly, Bell; Mooney (3), Crossan (2), Briggs, Quigley (3), Langton (1).

HONOURS

FA Premier League: Champions 1994–95; Runners-up 1993–94.

Football League: Division 1 – Champions 1911–12, 1913–14; 1991–92 (play-offs); Runners-up 2000–01; Division 2 – Champions 1938–39; Runners-up 1957–58; Division 3 – Champions 1974–75; Runners-up 1979–80.

FA Cup: Winners 1884, 1885, 1886, 1890, 1891, 1928; Runners-up 1882, 1960.

Football League Cup: Winners 2002.

Full Members' Cup: Winners 1987.

European Competitions: *European Cup:* 1995–96. *UEFA Cup:* 1994–95, 1998–99, 2002–03, 2003–04.

SKY SPORTS FACT FILE

Jack Southworth joined Blackburn Rovers from Blackburn Olympic in 1887 making his debut against his former club on 24 September and scored the winning goal in a 3–2 success. It was the season before they entered the Football League.

Record Cup Victory: 11–0 v Rossendale, FA Cup 1st rd, 13 October 1884 – Arthur; Hopwood, McIntyre; Forrest, Blenkhorn, Lofthouse; Sowerbutts (2), J. Brown (1), Fecitt (4), Barton (3), Birtwistle (1).

Record Defeat: 0–8 v Arsenal, Division 1, 25 February 1933.

Most League Points (2 for a win): 60, Division 3, 1974–75.

Most League Points (3 for a win): 91, Division 1, 2000–01.

Most League Goals: 114, Division 2, 1954–55.

Highest League Scorer in Season: Ted Harper, 43, Division 1, 1925–26.

Most League Goals in Total Aggregate: Simon Garner, 168, 1978–92.

Most League Goals in One Match: 7, Tommy Briggs v Bristol R, Division 2, 5 February 1955.

Most Capped Player: Henning Berg, 58 (100), Norway.

Most League Appearances: Derek Fazackerley, 596, 1970–86.

Youngest League Player: Harry Dennison, 16 years 155 days v Bristol C, 8 April 1911.

Record Transfer Fee Received: £16,000,000 from Chelsea for Damian Duff, July 2003.

Record Transfer Fee Paid: £7,500,000 to Manchester U for Andy Cole, December 2001.

Football League Record: 1888 Founder Member of the League; 1936–39 Division 2; 1946–48 Division 1; 1948–58 Division 2; 1958–66 Division 1; 1966–71 Division 2; 1971–75 Division 3; 1975–79 Division 2; 1979–80 Division 3; 1980–92 Division 2; 1992–99 FA Premier League; 1999–2001 Division 1; 2001– FA Premier League.

MANAGERS

Thomas Mitchell 1884–96
(Secretary-Manager)
J. Walmsley 1896–1903
(Secretary-Manager)
R. B. Middleton 1903–25
Jack Carr 1922–26
(Team Manager under Middleton to 1925)
Bob Crompton 1926–30
(Hon. Team Manager)
Arthur Barritt 1931–36
(had been Secretary from 1927)
Reg Taylor 1936–38
Bob Crompton 1938–41
Eddie Hapgood 1944–47
Will Scott 1947
Jack Bruton 1947–49
Jackie Bestall 1949–53
Johnny Carey 1953–58
Dally Duncan 1958–60
Jack Marshall 1960–67
Eddie Quigley 1967–70
Johnny Carey 1970–71
Ken Furphy 1971–73
Gordon Lee 1974–75
Jim Smith 1975–78
Jim Iley 1978
John Pickering 1978–79
Howard Kendall 1979–81
Bobby Saxton 1981–86
Don Mackay 1987–91
Kenny Dalglish 1991–95
Ray Harford 1995–97
Roy Hodgson 1997–98
Brian Kidd 1998–99
Tony Parkes 1999–2000
Graeme Souness 2000–04
Mark Hughes September 2004–

LATEST SEQUENCES

Longest Sequence of League Wins: 8, 1.3.1980 – 7.4.1980.

Longest Sequence of League Defeats: 7, 12.3.1966 – 16.4.1966.

Longest Sequence of League Draws: 5, 11.10.1975 – 1.11.1975.

Longest Sequence of Unbeaten League Matches: 23, 30.9.1987 – 27.3.1988.

Longest Sequence Without a League Win: 16, 11.11.1978 – 24.3.1979.

Successive Scoring Runs: 32 from 24.4.1954.

Successive Non-scoring Runs: 4 from 12.12.1908.

TEN YEAR LEAGUE RECORD

		P	W	D	L	F	A	Pts	Pos
1995-96	PR Lge	38	18	7	13	61	47	61	7
1996-97	PR Lge	38	9	15	14	42	43	42	13
1997-98	PR Lge	38	16	10	12	57	52	58	6
1998-99	PR Lge	38	7	14	17	38	52	35	19
1999-2000	Div 1	46	15	17	14	55	51	62	11
2000-01	Div 1	46	26	13	7	76	39	91	2
2001-02	PR Lge	38	12	10	16	55	51	46	10
2002-03	PR Lge	38	16	12	10	52	43	60	6
2003-04	PR Lge	38	12	8	18	51	59	44	15
2004-05	PR Lge	38	9	15	14	32	43	42	15

DID YOU KNOW?

In the 1930s within three years of each other Blackburn Rovers won two matches in which the opposing team scored five times against them! They won 7–5 at Sheffield United on 3 January 1930 and 6–5 v Blackpool on 2 January 1933.

BLACKBURN ROVERS 2004–05 LEAGUE RECORD

Match No.	*Date*	*Venue*	*Opponents*	*Result*		*H/T Score*	*Lg. Pos.*	*Goalscorers*	*Attendance*
1	Aug 14	H	WBA	D	1-1	0-1	—	Short 70	23,475
2	21	A	Southampton	L	2-3	0-1	13	Ferguson 50, Dickov 68	27,492
3	25	A	Arsenal	L	0-3	0-0	—		37,496
4	28	H	Manchester U	D	1-1	1-0	18	Dickov 17	26,155
5	Sept 11	A	Newcastle U	L	0-3	0-2	19		52,015
6	18	H	Portsmouth	W	1-0	0-0	16	Jansen 75	20,647
7	27	A	Charlton Ath	L	0-1	0-0	—		26,193
8	Oct 2	H	Aston Villa	D	2-2	1-1	17	Ferguson 30, Emerton 63	20,502
9	16	H	Middlesbrough	L	0-4	0-0	18		20,385
10	23	A	Chelsea	L	0-4	0-2	20		41,546
11	30	H	Liverpool	D	2-2	2-1	19	Bothroyd 16, Emerton 45	26,314
12	Nov 6	A	Norwich C	D	1-1	0-0	20	Dickov 86	23,834
13	13	A	Manchester C	D	1-1	0-1	19	Dickov (pen) 78	45,504
14	21	H	Birmingham C	D	3-3	1-3	20	Jansen 4, Reid S 57, Gallagher 63	20,290
15	27	A	Fulham	W	2-0	1-0	17	Gallagher 10, Dickov (pen) 77	19,103
16	Dec 4	H	Tottenham H	L	0-1	0-0	17		22,182
17	11	A	Crystal Palace	D	0-0	0-0	18		22010
18	18	H	Everton	D	0-0	0-0	16		25,191
19	26	H	Newcastle U	D	2-2	1-2	16	Dickov 26, Todd 54	29,271
20	28	A	Bolton W	W	1-0	1-0	15	Dickov 6	27,038
21	Jan 1	A	Aston Villa	L	0-1	0-0	16		34,265
22	3	H	Charlton Ath	W	1-0	1-0	15	Emerton 41	19,809
23	15	A	Portsmouth	W	1-0	0-0	16	Pedersen 55	19,904
24	24	H	Bolton W	L	0-1	0-0	—		20,056
25	Feb 2	H	Chelsea	L	0-1	0-1	—		23,414
26	5	A	Middlesbrough	L	0-1	0-1	16		30,564
27	12	H	Norwich C	W	3-0	2-0	16	Pedersen 17, Dickov 2 39, 62	20,923
28	Mar 6	A	Everton	W	1-0	0-0	14	Stead 71	32,406
29	15	A	Liverpool	D	0-0	0-0	—		37,763
30	19	H	Arsenal	L	0-1	0-1	14		22,992
31	Apr 2	A	Manchester U	D	0-0	0-0	14		67,939
32	9	H	Southampton	W	3-0	1-0	14	Pedersen 11, Jakobsson (og) 48, Reid S 55	20,726
33	20	H	Crystal Palace	W	1-0	1-0	—	Pedersen 45	18,006
34	23	H	Manchester C	D	0-0	0-0	12		24,646
35	26	A	WBA	D	1-1	0-1	—	Emerton 64	25,154
36	30	A	Birmingham C	L	1-2	1-0	13	Stead 13	28,621
37	May 7	H	Fulham	L	1-3	1-1	14	Neill 6	18,991
38	15	A	Tottenham H	D	0-0	0-0	15		35,797

Final League Position: 15

GOALSCORERS

League (32): Dickov 9 (2 pens), Emerton 4, Pedersen 4, Ferguson 2, Gallagher 2, Jansen 2, Reid S 2, Stead 2, Bothroyd 1, Neill 1, Short 1, Todd 1, own goal 1.
Carling Cup (3): Emerton 1, Gallagher 1, Pedersen 1.
FA Cup (10): Pedersen 3, Thompson 2, Dickov 1 (pen), Johnson 1, Matteo 1, Tugay 1, own goal 1.

Friedel B 38	Emerton B 33 + 4	Gresko V 2 + 1	Short C 13 + 1	Amoruso L 5 + 1	Matteo D 25 + 3	De Pedro J 1 + 1	Ferguson B 21	Stead J 19 + 10	Yorke D 2 + 2	Gray M 9	Gallagher P 5 + 11	Tugay K 13 + 8	Dickov P 27 + 2	Johansson N 18 + 4	Flitcroft G 17 + 2	Neill L 34 + 2	Pedersen M 19	Thompson D 11 + 13	Bothroyd J 6 + 5	Douglas J — + 1	Jansen M 3 + 4	Djorkaeff Y 3	Reid S 23 + 5	McEveley J 5	Todd A 26	Nelsen R 15	Mokoena A 16	Savage R 9	Johnson J — + 3	Derbyshire M — + 1	*Match No.*
1	2^{1}	3^{3}	4	5	6	7^{2}	8	9	10	11	12	13	14																		1
1	2	12	4		3^{1}		8	9	10^{3}	11		6	14	5	7^{2}	13															2
1	7	3	4		6	13		9^{1}	12	11		8^{2}	10	5		2															3
1	12		4	5■	3		8	9^{2}	13			6	10^{3}	14		2	11	7^{1}													4
1	7^{1}		5		6		4	9		3			10		8	2	11^{2}		12	13											5
1	7		5^{1}	12	6		4	9^{2}		3			10		8	2	11^{3}		13		14										6
1	7			5	6		4	9^{2}		3		12	10		8^{1}	2			13		11										7
1	7			5	6		8	12		3		4	10		13	2					11^{2}	9^{1}									8
1	7		12	5^{1}	6		8	13		3		4■	9^{2}			2					14	10^{3}	11								9
1	7		5		6		4	12		3^{2}			9^{3}	13	8	2			14			10^{1}	11								10
1	7		4				8	12				6	10	5		2			9^{1}				11	3							11
1	7						8	12				4^{2}	10^{1}	5	13	2			9■				11	3	6						12
1	7						8	9^{1}				4^{2}	10	5		2		13			12		11	3	6						13
1	7						8				12	4^{2}	9	5		2		13			10^{1}		11	3	6						14
1	7		5		12		8				9^{2}	4	10	3^{1}		2		13					11		6						15
1	7		5^{1}		12		8				9^{3}	4^{2}	10	3		2		13	14				11		6						16
1	7		5		3		4	12					10		8	2		13■	9^{1}				11^{2}		6						17
1	7		5^{1}		3		4				13		10	12	8	2			9^{2}				11		6						18
1	7				3		4	9^{1}			12		10	5	8	2		13					11^{2}		6						19
1	7				3		4	12					10	5	8	2			9^{1}				11		6						20
1	7				3		4	9^{1}			12		10	5	8	2		13					11^{2}		6						21
1	7				3		4	9^{1}			12		10	5	8	2		11^{2}					13		6						22
1	7										9^{2}	4^{1}	10	3			8	11			13		12		6	2	5				23
1	7				3			12			9^{1}					2	8	11	10^{2}						6		5	4	13		24
1	7				3								9			2	10	11^{1}					12		5	6	4	8			25
1	7				3								9			2	10	11^{1}					12		5	6	4^{2}	8	13		26
1	7^{3}										9	4	10	3		12	11	13					14		5	2	6^{1}	8^{2}			27
1								12					10^{1}	3	8	2	9	7					11		5	6	4				28
1	7				12			9^{2}			13			3^{1}	8	2	10						11		5	6	4				29
1	12				3^{3}							13	9	14	8^{1}	2	10	7					11		5^{2}	6	4				30
1	12				3			9			13				8	2	10^{2}	7					11		5	6	4^{1}				31
1	12				3			13				14	9		8^{3}	2	10	7^{1}					11^{2}		5	6	4				32
1	7				3			9				12				2	10^{2}	13					11		5	6	4	8^{1}			33
1	7				3			9			12					2	10^{1}	13					11		5	6	4	8^{2}			34
1	7				3			9			12	13				2	10^{3}	14					11		5	6	4^{2}	8^{1}			35
1	7^{1}							9			12	13		3^{2}	8	2	10^{3}	14					11		5	6	4				36
1	7		5■					9				12		3		2	10^{3}	13					11^{2}			6	4^{1}	8		14	37
1	7							9^{1}								2	10	11						3	5	6	4	8	12		38

FA Cup

Third Round	Cardiff C	(a)	1-1
		(h)	3-2
Fourth Round	Colchester U	(h)	3-0
Fifth Round	Burnley	(a)	0-0
		(h)	2-1
Sixth Round	Leicester C	(h)	1-0
Semi-Final (at Millennium Stadium)	Arsenal		0-3

Carling Cup

Second Round	Bournemouth	(h)	3-3

BLACKPOOL FL Championship 1

FOUNDATION

Old boys of St John's School who had formed themselves into a football club decided to establish a club bearing the name of their town and Blackpool FC came into being at a meeting at the Stanley Arms Hotel in the summer of 1887. In their first season playing at Raikes Hall Gardens, the club won both the Lancashire Junior Cup and the Fylde Cup.

Bloomfield Road Ground, Seasiders Way, Blackpool FY1 6JJ.

Telephone: 0870 443 1953.

Fax: (01253) 405 011.

Ticket Office: 0870 443 1953.

Website: www.blackpoolfc.co.uk

Email: info@blackpoolfc.co.uk, secretary@blackpoolfc.co.uk

Ground Capacity: 9,491.

Record Attendance: 38,098 v Wolverhampton W, Division 1, 17 September 1955.

Pitch Measurements: 112yd × 74yd.

Chairman: Karl Oyston.

Secretary: Peter Collins.

Manager: Colin Hendry.

Assistant Manager: Billy Dearden.

Physio: Phil Horner.

Colours: Tangerine and white.

Change Colours: All black.

Year Formed: 1887.

Turned Professional: 1887.

Ltd Co.: 1896.

Previous Name: 'South Shore' combined with Blackpool in 1899, twelve years after the latter had been formed on the breaking up of the old 'Blackpool St John's' club.

Club Nickname: 'The Seasiders'.

Previous Grounds: 1887, Raikes Hall Gardens; 1897, Athletic Grounds; 1899, Raikes Hall Gardens; 1899, Bloomfield Road.

First Football League game: 5 September 1896, Division 2, v Lincoln C (a) L 1–3 – Douglas; Parr, Bowman; Stuart, Stirzaker, Norris; Clarkin, Donnelly, R. Parkinson, Mount (1), J. Parkinson.

Record League Victory: 7–0 v Reading, Division 2, 10 November 1928 – Mercer; Gibson, Hamilton, Watson, Wilson, Grant, Ritchie, Oxberry (2), Hampson (5), Tufnell, Neal. 7–0 v Preston NE (away), Division 1, 1 May 1948 – Robinson; Shimwell, Crosland; Buchan, Hayward, Kelly; Hobson, Munro (1), McIntosh (5), McCall, Rickett (1). 7–0 v Sunderland, Division 1, 5 October 1957 – Farm; Armfield, Garrett, Kelly (J), Gratrix, Kelly (H), Matthews, Taylor (2), Charnley (2), Durie (2), Perry (1).

HONOURS

Football League: Division 1 – Runners-up 1955–56; Division 2 – Champions 1929–30; Runners-up 1936–37, 1969–70; Promoted from Division 3 – 2000–01 (play-offs); Division 4 – Runners-up 1984–85.

FA Cup: Winners 1953; Runners-up 1948, 1951.

Football League Cup: Semi-final 1962.

Anglo-Italian Cup: Winners 1971; Runners-up 1972.

LDV Vans Trophy: Winners 2002, 2004.

SKY SPORTS FACT FILE

In 1914–15 Blackpool only finished tenth in the Second Division but for the first time in the club's history one of their players was leading scorer in the division. Joe Lane hit 28 of the team's 58 League goals. Later in his career he had a spell with Barcelona!

Record Cup Victory: 7–1 v Charlton Ath, League Cup 2nd rd, 25 September 1963 – Harvey; Armfield, Martin; Crawford, Gratrix, Cranston; Lea, Ball (1), Charnley (4), Durie (1), Oates (1).

Record Defeat: 1–10 v Small Heath, Division 2, 2 March 1901 and v Huddersfield T, Division 1, 13 December 1930.

Most League Points (2 for a win): 58, Division 2, 1929–30 and Division 2, 1967–68.

Most League Points (3 for a win): 86, Division 4, 1984–85.

Most League Goals: 98, Division 2, 1929–30.

Highest League Scorer in Season: Jimmy Hampson, 45, Division 2, 1929–30.

Most League Goals in Total Aggregate: Jimmy Hampson, 246, 1927–38.

Most League Goals in One Match: 5, Jimmy Hampson v Reading, Division 2, 10 November 1928; 5, Jimmy McIntosh v Preston NE, Division 1, 1 May 1948.

Most Capped Player: Jimmy Armfield, 43, England.

Most League Appearances: Jimmy Armfield, 568, 1952–71.

Youngest League Player: Trevor Sinclair, 16 years 170 days v Wigan Ath, 19 August 1989.

Record Transfer Fee Received: £1,500,000 from Southampton for Brett Ormerod, December 2001.

Record Transfer Fee Paid: £275,000 to Millwall for Chris Malkin, October 1996.

Football League Record: 1896 Elected to Division 2; 1899 Failed re-election; 1900 Re-elected; 1900–30 Division 2; 1930–33 Division 1; 1933–37 Division 2; 1937–67 Division 1; 1967–70 Division 2; 1970–71 Division 1; 1971–78 Division 2; 1978–81 Division 3; 1981–85 Division 4; 1985–90 Division 3; 1990–92 Division 4; 1992–2000 Division 2; 2000–01 Division 3; 2001–04 Division 2; 2004– FL1.

MANAGERS

Tom Barcroft 1903–33
(Secretary-Manager)
John Cox 1909–11
Bill Norman 1919–23
Maj. Frank Buckley 1923–27
Sid Beaumont 1927–28
Harry Evans 1928–33
(Hon. Team Manager)
Alex 'Sandy' Macfarlane 1933–35
Joe Smith 1935–58
Ronnie Suart 1958–67
Stan Mortensen 1967–69
Les Shannon 1969–70
Bob Stokoe 1970–72
Harry Potts 1972–76
Allan Brown 1976–78
Bob Stokoe 1978–79
Stan Ternent 1979–80
Alan Ball 1980–81
Allan Brown 1981–82
Sam Ellis 1982–89
Jimmy Mullen 1989–90
Graham Carr 1990
Bill Ayre 1990–94
Sam Allardyce 1994–96
Gary Megson 1996–97
Nigel Worthington 1997–99
Steve McMahon 2000–04
Colin Hendry June 2004–

LATEST SEQUENCES

Longest Sequence of League Wins: 9, 21.11.1936 – 1.1.1937.

Longest Sequence of League Defeats: 8, 26.11.1898 – 7.1.1899.

Longest Sequence of League Draws: 5, 4.12.1976 – 1.1.1977.

Longest Sequence of Unbeaten League Matches: 17, 6.4.1968 – 21.9.1968.

Longest Sequence Without a League Win: 19, 19.12.1970 – 24.4.1971.

Successive Scoring Runs: 33 from 23.2.1929.

Successive Non-scoring Runs: 5 from 12.4.1975.

TEN YEAR LEAGUE RECORD

		P	*W*	*D*	*L*	*F*	*A*	*Pts*	*Pos*
1995-96	Div 2	46	23	13	10	67	40	82	3
1996-97	Div 2	46	18	15	13	60	47	69	7
1997-98	Div 2	46	17	11	18	59	67	62	12
1998-99	Div 2	46	14	14	18	44	54	56	14
1999-2000	Div 2	46	8	17	21	49	77	41	22
2000-01	Div 2	46	22	6	18	74	58	72	7
2001-02	Div 2	46	14	14	18	66	69	56	16
2002-03	Div 2	46	15	13	18	56	64	58	13
2003-04	Div 2	46	16	11	19	58	65	59	14
2004-05	FL 1	46	15	12	19	54	59	57	16

DID YOU KNOW ?

There were only four survivors from the Blackpool team which lost the FA Cup to Manchester United in 1948 who became winners in 1953 against Bolton Wanderers: Eddie Shimwell, Harry Johnston, Stanley Matthews and treble-shooter Stan Mortensen.

BLACKPOOL 2004–05 LEAGUE RECORD

Match No.	Date	Venue	Opponents	Result		H/T Score	Lg. Pos.	Goalscorers	Attendance
1	Aug 7	A	Doncaster R	L	0-2	0-1	—		7082
2	10	H	Sheffield W	L	1-2	0-1	—	Edwards R 74	6713
3	14	H	Stockport Co	L	0-4	0-2	24		6334
4	21	A	Hartlepool U	D	1-1	0-1	24	Taylor 72	5144
5	28	H	Luton T	L	1-3	1-0	24	Taylor 4	5793
6	30	A	Peterborough U	D	0-0	0-0	24		4142
7	Sept 11	A	Hull C	L	1-2	1-1	24	Taylor 37	15,568
8	18	H	Swindon T	D	1-1	1-0	24	Taylor 33	5229
9	25	A	Port Vale	W	3-0	2-0	22	Taylor 6, Vernon 2 27, 47	5347
10	Oct 2	H	Bournemouth	D	3-3	3-2	22	Clarke 2, Vernon 10, Edwards P 42	5525
11	10	A	Oldham Ath	W	2-1	1-1	22	Murphy 43, Wellens 68	7125
12	16	H	Colchester U	D	1-1	1-0	22	Murphy 10	6464
13	19	A	Bradford C	L	1-2	0-1	—	Taylor (pen) 76	7622
14	23	A	Brentford	W	3-0	1-0	20	Murphy 2 14, 53, Taylor 79	6722
15	30	H	Huddersfield T	D	1-1	0-1	21	Murphy 51	7676
16	Nov 6	A	Chesterfield	L	0-1	0-0	21		4978
17	9	H	Wrexham	W	2-1	0-1	—	Clarke 46, Taylor (pen) 66	5054
18	20	H	Tranmere R	L	0-1	0-1	20		6490
19	27	A	Barnsley	L	0-1	0-0	22		9084
20	Dec 7	H	Torquay U	W	4-0	1-0	—	Taylor 20, Parker 3 67, 87, 90	4179
21	11	H	Bristol C	D	1-1	1-1	19	Taylor (pen) 45	5220
22	18	A	Walsall	L	2-3	1-1	19	Taylor 32, Parker 57	5476
23	26	H	Hull C	L	0-2	0-0	20		8774
24	28	A	Milton Keynes D	L	1-3	0-1	20	Taylor (pen) 81	4943
25	Jan 1	A	Wrexham	W	2-1	0-1	20	Murphy 2 64, 77	5601
26	3	H	Port Vale	L	0-2	0-0	20		5115
27	15	A	Swindon T	D	2-2	1-2	20	Parker 18, Clarke 90	5526
28	22	H	Milton Keynes D	W	1-0	1-0	19	Edwards P 8	5798
29	Feb 5	A	Colchester U	W	1-0	0-0	19	Grayson 75	3526
30	8	H	Oldham Ath	W	2-0	0-0	—	Clarke 72, Edwards P 86	5563
31	19	A	Huddersfield T	L	0-1	0-1	20		10,614
32	22	H	Bradford C	W	2-1	0-0	—	Southern 48, Parker 90	4805
33	26	A	Bristol C	D	1-1	0-1	18	Wellens 60	10,977
34	Mar 5	H	Walsall	W	2-0	0-0	16	Murphy 57, Southern 70	6844
35	8	A	Bournemouth	W	3-2	2-1	—	Parker 2 1, 51, Maher (og) 26	5390
36	12	A	Sheffield W	L	2-3	0-1	14	Southern 47, Wellens 90	21,539
37	19	H	Doncaster R	D	1-1	0-1	15	Murphy 53	6548
38	22	H	Brentford	W	2-1	2-0	—	Southern 2 7, 15	5478
39	28	H	Hartlepool U	D	2-2	1-2	16	Southern (pen) 3, Clarke 82	6853
40	Apr 2	A	Luton T	L	0-1	0-1	16		7806
41	9	H	Peterborough U	L	0-1	0-1	16		5090
42	12	A	Stockport Co	W	1-0	1-0	—	Parker 6	4302
43	16	A	Tranmere R	D	0-0	0-0	15		8568
44	23	H	Chesterfield	W	1-0	1-0	14	Grayson 18	5613
45	30	A	Torquay U	L	0-2	0-1	14		5347
46	May 7	H	Barnsley	L	0-2	0-1	16		7571

Final League Position: 16

GOALSCORERS

League (54): Taylor 12 (4 pens), Murphy 9, Parker 9, Southern 6 (1 pen), Clarke 5, Edwards P 3, Vernon 3, Wellens 3, Grayson 2, Edwards R 1, own goal 1.
Carling Cup (1): Taylor 1.
FA Cup (6): Wellens 2, Clarke 1, Parker 1, Southern 1, Taylor 1.
LDV Vans Trophy (9): Blinkhorn 3, Burns 2, Parker 2 (1 pen), Coid 1, Murphy 1.

Ilic S 3	Richardson L 20 + 3	Clare R 19 + 4	Grayson S 32 + 4	Flynn Mike 5 + 1	Livesey D 1	Wellens R 27 + 1	Bullock M 24 + 4	Murphy J 30 + 1	Taylor S 24	Edwards R 24 + 2	Parker K 26 + 9	McGregor M 36 + 2	Barrowman A — + 2	Burns J 19 + 4	Jones L 29	Edwards P 22 + 6	Coid D 33 + 2	Flynn Michael 6	Vernon S 4	Evans G 22	Clarke P 38	Gorre D — + 1	Blinkhorn M 2 + 2	Jones B 12	Southern K 25 + 2	Paterson S — + 2	Lynch S 5 + 2	Ellegaard K 2	Grabovac Z 1 + 2	Warhurst P 2 + 2	Anderson S 1 + 3	Butler T 6 + 2	Shaw M 2 + 8	Donnelly C 4 + 4	Boyack S — + 1	*Match No.*
1	2^{1}	3	4	5	6^{2}	7	8	9	10	11	12	13																								1
1	3	6		5		7	8	9	10	11	4^{1}	2	12																							2
1	3	6	12	5		7^{1}	8	9	10^{2}	11	4^{3}	2	13	14																						3
	2	6	4				8		10	3	9	7			1	5^{1}	12	11																		4
	2^{1}	6	4^{2}	13			8	9	10	3	12	7			1	11		5																		5
		6		5			8	9	10	3		7			1	11	2	4																		6
		6		5			8		10	3	12	7			1	11^{1}	2	4	9																	7
	12					7	8^{2}		10			5			1	11	2^{1}	4	9	3	6	13														8
	2					8			10			4			1	11	7	5	9	3	6															9
	2		4			8		12	10			5			1	11	7		9^{1}	3	6															10
	2		4			8		9	10			5			1	11	7			3	6															11
	2		4			8		9	10		12	5			1	11	7^{1}			3	6															12
	2	12	4			8		9	10			5^{1}			1	11	7			3	6															13
	2	5	4			8		9	10						1	11	7			3	6															14
	2	5	4			8		9	10					11	1		7			3	6															15
	2		4			8			10	12	13	5		14		11^{1}	7			3^{3}	6		9^{2}	1												16
	2^{1}	12	4			8			10		13	5		14		11^{3}	7			3	6		9^{2}	1												17
	7^{1}	2	4			8		9^{2}	10	3	12	5				11					6		13	1												18
	2	3^{2}	4^{1}			8			10	11	9	5		7							6		12	1	13											19
	12	2	4			7			10		9^{2}	5		11						3	6			1	8^{1}	13										20
		2	4^{1}			7			10		9	5		11			12			3	6			1	8											21
	2	6	4^{2}			7	12		10		9	5		11^{1}						3				1	8		13									22
	12	2^{1}	4			11	7^{2}		10			5		13	1					3	6				8		9									23
	2^{1}		4^{2}			8	12	9	10		13	5		7^{3}	1		11			3	6				14											24
		2	4					9			12	5		7			11			3	6				8		10^{1}	1								25
		2^{2}	4				12	9			10	5		7^{1}			11			3	6				8		13	1								26
		2	4							3	9	5		7^{2}			11				6			1			10		13	8^{1}	12					27
	2^{1}	12	4					9^{2}		3	10	5				11	7				6			1	8				13							28
		2	4			7				5	9^{1}					11				3	6			1	8		10			12						29
			4			7				5	9					12	2			3	6			1	8		10^{2}		11^{1}	13						30
			4^{3}			12	13	9		11	10					7^{2}	2			3	6			1	8					5^{1}		14				31
						11	7	9			10			4	1		2			3	6				8							5				32
						11	7	9			10			4	1		2			3	6				8							5				33
	2^{1}		13			11■	7	9			10^{3}	12		4^{2}	1	14	3				6				8							5				34
			4				7	9			10	2		11	1	12	3^{1}				6				8							5				35
						7	11	9		3^{1}	10	2		4^{2}	1	12					6				8							5	13			36
						7■	11	9		12	10^{1}	2		4^{2}	1		3				6				8							5		13		37
			12				7	9^{3}		5	10	2		11^{2}	1	13	3				6				8^{1}								14	4		38
		12	13				7			5	10	2■		11^{3}	1	14	3				6				8								9^{1}	4^{2}		39
			2				7	9		5	10			11^{1}	1		3				6				8								12	4		40
							7	9		5	10	2		11^{1}	1		3				6				8						13		12	4^{2}		41
			4				7	9		5	10^{1}	2			1	11	3				6				8								12			42
			4^{1}				7	9		5	10^{2}	2			1	11	3				6				8								12	13		43
			4^{2}				7	9		5	10^{1}	2			1	11	3				6				8							13	12			44
			4				7^{2}	9		5		2			1	11^{3}	3				6				8						10^{1}		12	13	14	45
			4^{1}				7^{2}	9		5		2			1	11	3				6				8	14					12		10^{3}	13		46

FA Cup

First Round	Tamworth	(h)	3-0
Second Round	Port Vale	(h)	1-0
Third Round	Leicester C	(a)	2-2
		(h)	0-1

Carling Cup

First Round	Crewe Alex	(a)	1-4

LDV Vans Trophy

First Round	York C	(a)	2-0
Second Round	Huddersfield T	(h)	6-3
Quarter-Final	Hereford U	(a)	1-2

BOLTON WANDERERS FA Premiership

FOUNDATION

In 1874 boys of Christ Church Sunday School, Blackburn Street, led by their master Thomas Ogden, established a football club which went under the name of the school and whose president was Vicar of Christ Church. Membership was 6d (two and a half pence). When their president began to lay down too many rules about the use of church premises, the club broke away and formed Bolton Wanderers in 1877, holding their earliest meetings at the Gladstone Hotel.

Reebok Stadium, Burnden Way, Lostock, Bolton BL6 6JW.

Telephone: (01204) 673 673.

Fax: (01204) 673 773.

Ticket Office: 0871 871 2932.

Website: www.bwfc.co.uk

Email: reception@bwfc.co.uk

Ground Capacity: 27,879.

Record Attendance: 69,912 v Manchester C, FA Cup 5th rd, 18 February 1933.

Pitch Measurements: 100m × 65m.

Chairman: Phil A. Gartside.

Vice-chairman: Brett Warburton.

Chief Executive: Allan Duckworth.

Secretary: Simon Marland.

Manager: Sam Allardyce.

Assistant Manager: Sammy Lee.

Physio: Mark Taylor.

Colours: White shirts, white shorts, white stockings.

Change Colours: Navy shirts, navy shorts, navy stockings.

Year Formed: 1874.

Turned Professional: 1880.

Ltd Co.: 1895.

Previous Name: 1874, Christ Church FC; 1877, Bolton Wanderers.

Club Nickname: 'The Trotters'.

Previous Grounds: Park Recreation Ground and Cockle's Field before moving to Pike's Lane ground 1881; 1895, Burnden Park; 1997, Reebok Stadium.

First Football League Game: 8 September 1888, Football League, v Derby Co (h) L 3–6 – Harrison; Robinson, Mitchell; Roberts, Weir, Bullough, Davenport (2), Milne, Coupar, Barbour, Brogan (1).

Record League Victory: 8–0 v Barnsley, Division 2, 6 October 1934 – Jones; Smith, Finney; Goslin, Atkinson, George Taylor; George T. Taylor (2), Eastham, Milsom (1), Westwood (4), Cook, (1 og).

HONOURS

Football League: Division 1 – Champions 1996–97; Promoted from Division 1 (play-offs) 2000–01. Division 2 – Champions 1908–09, 1977–78; Runners-up 1899–1900, 1904–05, 1910–11, 1934–35, 1992–93; Division 3 – Champions 1972–73.

FA Cup: Winners 1923, 1926, 1929, 1958; Runners-up 1894, 1904, 1953.

Football League Cup: Runners-up 1995, 2004.

Freight Rover Trophy: Runners-up 1986.

Sherpa Van Trophy: Winners 1989.

SKY SPORTS FACT FILE

On 18 April 1951 Bolton Wanderers opened their League programme at home to Aston Villa, who though temporarily down to ten men led 2–0. But the Trotters tore into the game, equalised before the break and won 5–2 with a Bobby Langton penalty.

Record Cup Victory: 13–0 v Sheffield U, FA Cup 2nd rd, 1 February 1890 – Parkinson; Robinson (1), Jones; Bullough, Davenport, Roberts; Rushton, Brogan (3), Cassidy (5), McNee, Weir (4).

Record Defeat: 1–9 v Preston NE, FA Cup 2nd rd, 10 December 1887.

Most League Points (2 for a win): 61, Division 3, 1972–73.

Most League Points (3 for a win): 98, Division 1, 1996–97.

Most League Goals: 100, Division 1, 1996–97.

Highest League Scorer in Season: Joe Smith, 38, Division 1, 1920–21.

Most League Goals in Total Aggregate: Nat Lofthouse, 255, 1946–61.

Most League Goals in One Match: 5, Tony Caldwell v Walsall, Division 3, 10 September 1983.

Most Capped Player: Mark Fish, 34 (62), South Africa.

Most League Appearances: Eddie Hopkinson, 519, 1956–70.

Youngest League Player: Ray Parry, 15 years 267 days v Wolverhampton W, 13 October 1951.

Record Transfer Fee Received: £4,500,000 from Liverpool for Jason McAteer, September 1995.

Record Transfer Fee Paid: £3,500,000 for Dean Holdsworth from Wimbledon, October 1997.

Football League Record: 1888 Founder Member of the League; 1899–1900 Division 2; 1900–03 Division 1; 1903–05 Division 2; 1905–08 Division 1; 1908–09 Division 2; 1909–10 Division 1; 1910–11 Division 2; 1911–33 Division 1; 1933–35 Division 2; 1935–64 Division 1; 1964–71 Division 2; 1971–73 Division 3; 1973–78 Division 2; 1978–80 Division 1; 1980–83 Division 2; 1983–87 Division 3; 1987–88 Division 4; 1988–92 Division 3; 1992–93 Division 2; 1993–95 Division 1; 1995–96 FA Premier League; 1996–97 Division 1; 1997–98 FA Premier League; 1998–2001 Division 1; 2001– FA Premier League.

MANAGERS

Tom Rawthorne 1874–85 *(Secretary)*
J. J. Bentley 1885–86 *(Secretary)*
W. G. Struthers 1886–87 *(Secretary)*
Fitzroy Norris 1887 *(Secretary)*
J. J. Bentley 1887–95 *(Secretary)*
Harry Downs 1895–96 *(Secretary)*
Frank Brettell 1896–98 *(Secretary)*
John Somerville 1898–1910
Will Settle 1910–15
Tom Mather 1915–19
Charles Foweraker 1919–44
Walter Rowley 1944–50
Bill Ridding 1951–68
Nat Lofthouse 1968–70
Jimmy McIlroy 1970
Jimmy Meadows 1971
Nat Lofthouse 1971 *(then Admin. Manager to 1972)*
Jimmy Armfield 1971–74
Ian Greaves 1974–80
Stan Anderson 1980–81
George Mulhall 1981–82
John McGovern 1982–85
Charlie Wright 1985
Phil Neal 1985–92
Bruce Rioch 1992–95
Roy McFarland 1995–96
Colin Todd 1996–99
Sam Allardyce October 1999–

LATEST SEQUENCES

Longest Sequence of League Wins: 11, 5.11.1904 – 2.1.1905.

Longest Sequence of League Defeats: 11, 7.4.1902 – 18.10.1902.

Longest Sequence of League Draws: 6, 25.1.1913 – 8.3.1913.

Longest Sequence of Unbeaten League Matches: 23, 13.10.1990 – 9.3.1991.

Longest Sequence Without a League Win: 26, 7.4.1902 – 10.1.1903.

Successive Scoring Runs: 24 from 22.11.1996.

Successive Non-scoring Runs: 5 from 3.1.1898.

TEN YEAR LEAGUE RECORD

		P	W	D	L	F	A	Pts	Pos
1995-96	PR Lge	38	8	5	25	39	71	29	20
1996-97	Div 1	46	28	14	4	100	53	98	1
1997-98	PR Lge	38	9	13	16	41	61	40	18
1998-99	Div 1	46	20	16	10	78	59	76	6
1999-2000	Div 1	46	21	13	12	69	50	76	6
2000-01	Div 1	46	24	15	7	76	45	87	3
2001-02	PR Lge	38	9	13	16	44	62	40	16
2002-03	PR Lge	38	10	14	14	41	51	44	17
2003-04	PR Lge	38	14	11	13	48	56	53	8
2004-05	PR Lge	38	16	10	12	49	44	58	6

DID YOU KNOW?

In 1972–73 Bolton Wanderers equalled a club record with 18 home wins in Division Three. Their previous such total had been achieved in the First Division in 1924–25 while finishing third. In both seasons they lost just once at home.

BOLTON WANDERERS 2004–05 LEAGUE RECORD

Match No.	*Date*	*Venue*	*Opponents*	*Result*		*H/T Score*	*Lg. Pos.*	*Goalscorers*	*Atten-dance*
1	Aug 14	H	Charlton Ath	W	4-1	2-0	—	Okocha 2 [11, 59], Pedersen 2 [30, 72]	24,100
2	21	A	Fulham	L	0-2	0-1	7		17,541
3	25	A	Southampton	W	2-1	2-0	—	Pedersen [7], Okocha (pen) [27]	30,713
4	29	H	Liverpool	W	1-0	1-0	3	Davies [38]	27,880
5	Sept 11	H	Manchester U	D	2-2	0-1	3	Nolan [52], Ferdinand [90]	27,766
6	18	A	Arsenal	D	2-2	0-1	4	Jaidi [63], Pedersen [85]	37,010
7	25	H	Birmingham C	D	1-1	1-0	4	Jaidi [16]	23,692
8	Oct 2	A	WBA	L	1-2	0-0	7	Giannakopoulos [73]	23,849
9	16	H	Crystal Palace	W	1-0	1-0	4	Davies [45]	25,501
10	23	A	Tottenham H	W	2-1	1-1	4	Jaidi [11], Pedersen [75]	36,025
11	31	H	Newcastle U	W	2-1	0-0	4	Diouf [52], Davies [70]	27,196
12	Nov 7	A	Middlesbrough	D	1-1	0-0	4	Pedersen [72]	29,656
13	13	H	Aston Villa	L	1-2	1-1	5	Diouf [21]	25,779
14	20	A	Chelsea	D	2-2	0-1	6	Davies [52], Jaidi [87]	42,203
15	27	H	Portsmouth	L	0-1	0-1	8		25,008
16	Dec 4	A	Everton	L	2-3	1-1	8	Davies 2 [16, 59]	35,929
17	11	A	Norwich C	L	2-3	2-1	9	Okocha (pen) [19], Hierro [23]	23,549
18	18	H	Manchester C	L	0-1	0-0	11		27,274
19	26	A	Manchester U	L	0-2	0-1	13		67,867
20	28	H	Blackburn R	L	0-1	0-1	13		27,038
21	Jan 1	H	WBA	D	1-1	0-1	14	Diouf [85]	25,205
22	4	A	Birmingham C	W	2-1	1-0	11	Diouf [17], Nolan [90]	27,177
23	15	H	Arsenal	W	1-0	1-0	11	Giannakopoulos [41]	27,514
24	24	A	Blackburn R	W	1-0	0-0	—	Diouf [77]	20,056
25	Feb 1	H	Tottenham H	W	3-1	0-0	—	Diouf (pen) [49], Ben Haim [86], Davies [87]	24,780
26	5	A	Crystal Palace	W	1-0	1-0	7	Nolan [31]	23,163
27	12	H	Middlesbrough	D	0-0	0-0	7		24,322
28	27	A	Newcastle U	L	1-2	1-1	7	Giannakopoulos [41]	50,430
29	Mar 7	A	Manchester C	W	1-0	1-0	—	Diouf [45]	43,050
30	19	H	Norwich C	W	1-0	1-0	6	Giannakopoulos [42]	25,081
31	Apr 2	A	Liverpool	L	0-1	0-0	6		43,755
32	9	H	Fulham	W	3-1	2-0	6	Okocha (pen) [13], Nolan [33], Giannakopoulos [54]	25,493
33	16	A	Charlton Ath	W	2-1	1-1	5	Okocha (pen) [7], Diouf [58]	26,708
34	19	H	Southampton	D	1-1	1-0	—	Giannakopoulos [25]	25,125
35	23	A	Aston Villa	D	1-1	0-1	6	Speed [54]	36,053
36	30	H	Chelsea	L	0-2	0-0	6		27,653
37	May 7	A	Portsmouth	D	1-1	1-0	6	Diouf [11]	20,188
38	15	H	Everton	W	3-2	0-1	6	Jaidi [53], Davies [61], Giannakopoulos [66]	27,701

Final League Position: 6

GOALSCORERS

League (49): Diouf 9 (1 pen), Davies 8, Giannakopoulos 7, Okocha 6 (4 pens), Pedersen 6, Jaidi 5, Nolan 4, Ben Haim 1, Ferdinand 1, Hierro 1, Speed 1.
Carling Cup (5): Cesar 1, Ferdinand 1, Okocha 1 (pen), Pedersen 1, own goal 1.
FA Cup (5): Pedersen 2, Davies 1, Giannakopoulos 1, Vaz Te 1.

Jaaskelainen J 36	Hunt N 29	Gardner R 30 + 3	Campo I 20 + 7	N'Gotty B 37	Julio Cesar4 + 1	Okocha J 29 + 2	Nolan K 27 + 9	Pedersen H 13 + 14	Davies K 33 + 2	Speed G 37 + 1	Ben Haim T 19 + 2	Ferdinand L 1 + 11	Giannakopoulos S 28 + 6	Hierro F 15 + 14	Barness A 5 + 3	Jaidi R 20 + 7	Diouf E 23 + 4	Kaku B — + 1	Fadiga K — + 5	Poole K 1 + 1	Vaz Te R 1 + 6	Oakes A 1	Candela V 9 + 1	O'Brien J — + 1	*Match No.*
1	2^1	3	4	5	6	7	8^3	9	10^2	11	12	13	14												1
1	2	3^1	4^2	5	6	7	8	9^3	10	11			14	12	13										2
1	2	3	4	5		7	12	9^2	10^3	8		14	11^1	13		6									3
1	2	3	4	5		7^3	12	9	10^2	8		13	11^1	14		6									4
1	2		4	5		7	8	9^3	10^1	11^2		12		13	3	6	14								5
1	2	3	4^3	5		7	8	12	10^1	11		13		14		6	9^2								6
1	2	3	4	5			8	9	10^1	11		12	13			6	7^2								7
1		3	4^3	5		7^2	8	9^1		11	2	10	12			6	13	14							8
1	2	3	4^1	5			7^2	12	10	8			11		13	6	9^3		14						9
1	2	3		5		7	8^1	12	9	4			11	13		6	10^2								10
1	2	3		5		7	8	12	10	4			11^1	13	14	6^2	9^3								11
1■	2^2	3		5			7	12	10	8	13		11^1	4		6	9^G			15					12
	2	3	12	5			7^2	9	10	11				4^1		6	8				13	1			13
1	2	3	12	5		7^3	8^1	9	10	4			13	14		6	11^2								14
1	2	3^3	4^1	5^2		7	12	13	10	8			11	14		6	9								15
1	2		4	5		7^2	12	9	10	8		13	11^1	3		6									16
1	2		4^2	3^1	12	7^3	13	9	10	8		14	11	5		6									17
1				5	2	7^2	8	9^1	10	4	6	12	11		3						13				18
1	2		4		3	12	8		10^3	11	5	14	13			6	7^1				9^2				19
1	2	3		5		7		9^3	10	4^2		12	11^1	13		6	8				14				20
	2	3	4	5		7	8		10^1	11						6	9			1	12				21
1	2	3	4	5		7	8	12		10^2			11^1	13		6	9								22
1	2	3	4	5		7^1	8^2	12		10	6		11	13			9								23
1	2	3	4	5		7^2	8	12	13	10	6		11^1				9^3		14						24
1		3	4	5			7	12	10^1	8	6		11^2	13	2^3		9		14						25
1		3	4^2	5			7	12	10	8	6		11^1	13	2	14	9^3								26
1		3	4^1	5		7	8		10	11	6		9^2		2		13				12				27
1	2^2	3	12	5		7^3			9	10	6		11	4^1					13		14		8		28
1		3	12	5		7^2	8		10	13	6		11	4^1		14	9						2^3		29
1	2	11		5			8		9	10	6		7	4		12							3^1		30
1	2^2	11	12	5		13	8	14	9	10	6		7^3	4^1									3		31
1	2	12		5		7	8		9	10	6		11	4^2					13				3^1		32
1	2	12	13	5		7^2	8		9^3	10	6		11	4			14						3^1		33
1	2	12		5		7	8^2		13	10	6		11^3	4		14	9						3^1		34
1	2^3	3	12	5		7^2	13		10	8	6		11	4^1		14	9								35
1		3		5		7^1	12	13	10	8	6		11^2	4		14	9						2^3		36
1		3		5		7	12	13	10	8	6		11^1	4		14	9^2						2^3		37
1		3		5■		7	12		10	8	2		11^1	4^2		6	9^3						13	14	38

FA Cup

Third Round	Ipswich T	(a)	3-1
Fourth Round	Oldham Ath	(a)	1-0
Fifth Round	Fulham	(h)	1-0
Sixth Round	Arsenal	(h)	0-1

Carling Cup

Second Round	Yeovil T	(a)	2-0
Third Round	Tottenham H	(h)	3-4

BOSTON UNITED FL Championship 2

FOUNDATION

Although it was 1934 before the name Boston United first appeared, football had been played in the town since the late 1800s and indeed, always on the same site as the present York Street stadium. In fact Boston Football Club was established in March 1870 playing their first match against Louth the following month. Before the First World War, there were two clubs, Boston Town, whose headquarters were The Coach and Horses, and Boston Swifts, who used The Indian Queen. In fact, as both public houses were situated on Main Ridge and the pitch was virtually just opposite, it was not surprising that for the first forty years or so, that was what the ground was called. Swifts never reappeared after the First World War and it was left to the club called simply Boston to achieve the first giant-killing in the FA Cup by beating Bradford Park Avenue 1-0 on 12 December 1925. The club was now competing in the Midland League and subsequently reformed under the new title of Boston United.

York Street Ground, York Street, Boston, Lincolnshire.

Telephone: (01205) 364 406, (01205) 365 525.

Fax: (01205) 354 063.

Ticket Office: (01205) 364 406.

Website: www.bostonunited.co.uk

Email: jan.mclucas1@playing4success.org.uk

Ground Capacity: 6,868.

Record Attendance: 10,086 v Corby Town, Friendly, 1955.

Chairman: Jon Sotnick.

Vice-chairman: Nigel Clempson.

Chief Executive: James Rodwell.

Secretary: John Blackwell.

Manager: Steve Evans.

Assistant Manager: Paul Raynor.

HONOURS

FA Cup: best season: 3rd rd, 1926, 1956, 1972, 1974.
Football League Cup: never past 1st rd.
Conference: Champions 2001–02.
Dr. Martens: Champions 1999–2000. Runners-up: 1998–99.
Unibond League: Runners-up 1995–96, 1997–98.
Unibond Challenge Cup: Runners-up 1996–97.
FA Trophy: Runners-up 1984–85.
Northern Premier League: Champions 1972–73, 1973–74, 1976–77, 1977–78.
Northern Premier League Cup: Winners 1974, 1976.
Northern Premier League Challenge Shield: Winners 1974, 1975, 1977, 1978.
Lincolnshire Senior Cup: Winners 1935, 1937, 1938, 1946, 1950, 1955, 1956, 1960, 1977, 1979, 1986, 1988, 1989.
Non-League Champions of Champions Cup: Winners 1973, 1977.
East Anglian Cup: Winners 1961.
Central Alliance League: Champions 1961–62.
United Counties League: Champions 1965–66.
West Midlands League: Champions 1966–67, 1967–68.
Eastern Professional Floodlit Cup: Winners 1972.

SKY SPORTS FACT FILE

Paul Gascoigne was not the first famous player-coach to be associated with Boston United. In the mid-1970s Howard Wilkinson held a similar role with the Pilgrims prior to a managerial career which included taking charge of England.

Physio: Lee Taylor.

Colours: Amber and black shirts, black shorts, black stockings.

Change Colours: All white with blue edgings or all royal blue

Year formed: 1934.

Club Nickname: 'The Pilgrims'.

MANAGERS

George Kerr/Dave Cusack
Dave Cusack
Peter Morris
Mel Sterland
Greg Fee
Steve Evans 1998–2002
Neil Thompson 2002–04
Steve Evans March 2004–

First Football League Game: 10 August 2002, Division 3, v Bournemouth (h), D 2–2 – Bastock; Hocking, Chapman, Morley (Rodwell), Warburton, Ellender, Gould (1), Bennett, Clare, Elding (Cook), Weatherstone S. (1 og).

Record League Victory: 6–0 v Shrewsbury T, Division 3, 21 December 2002 – Bastock; Costello, Chapman, Redfearn (1), Balmer, Hocking (McCarthy), Weatherstone S, Higgins, Douglas (1), Logan (2) (Thompson L), Angel (Gould (1)). (1 og).

Most League Points (3 for a win): 59, Division 3 2003–04

Most League Goals: 62, FL Championship 2, 2004–05.

Most Capped Player: Andy Kirk, 1, Northern Ireland.

Record Transfer Fee Received: £125,000 from Northampton T for Andy Kirk, March 2005.

Record Transfer Fee Paid: £30,000 to Scarborough for Paul Ellender, August 2001.

Football League Record: 2002 Promoted to Division 3; 2004– FL2.

LATEST SEQUENCES

Longest Sequence of League Wins: 4, 19.4.2003 – 3.5.2003.

Longest Sequence of League Defeats: 6, 29.10.2002 – 14.12.2002.

Longest Sequence of League Draws: 3, 29.3.2003 – 2.4.2003.

Longest Sequence of Unbeaten League Matches: 6, 19.4.2002 – 16.8.2003.

Longest Sequence Without a League Win: 6, 28.12.2002 – 1.2.2003.

Successive Scoring Runs: 8 from 26.3.2005 – continuing.

Successive Non-scoring Runs: 5 from 29.10.2002.

TEN YEAR LEAGUE RECORD

		P	W	D	L	F	A	Pts	Pos
1995-96	NP pr	42	23	6	13	86	59	75	2
1996-97	NP pr	44	22	13	9	74	47	79	6
1997-98	NP pr	42	22	12	8	55	40	78	2
1998-99	SL pr	42	17	16	9	69	51	67	2
1999-2000	SL pr	42	27	11	4	102	39	92	1
2000-01	Conf.	42	13	17	12	74	63	56	12
2001-02	Conf.	42	25	9	8	84	42	84	1
2002-03	Div 3	46	15	13	18	55	56	54*	15
2003-04	Div 3	46	16	11	19	50	54	59	11
2004-05	FL 2	46	14	16	16	62	58	58	16

**4 pts deducted at start of season.*

DID YOU KNOW ?

One of the other honours achieved by Boston United in the 1970s was the Watneys Challenge Shield. On 13 August 1973 they defeated Northwich Victoria 2–0 with goals from Wilkinson and Matt Tees during United's Northern Premier League days.

BOSTON UNITED 2004–05 LEAGUE RECORD

Match No.	*Date*	*Venue*	*Opponents*	*Result*	*H/T Score*	*Lg. Pos.*	*Goalscorers*	*Attendance*
1	Aug 7	H	Oxford U	W 1-0	0-0	—	Thompson [82]	3596
2	10	A	Grimsby T	D 1-1	1-0	—	Melton [9]	6737
3	14	A	Yeovil T	L 0-2	0-0	15		5178
4	21	H	Macclesfield T	D 1-1	0-0	14	Lee [81]	2736
5	28	A	Cheltenham T	L 0-1	0-0	19		3596
6	30	H	Chester C	W 3-1	2-0	12	Thomas [3], Abbey Z [45], Pitt (pen) [73]	2698
7	Sept 4	H	Cambridge U	W 2-1	1-0	10	Lee [40], McCann [87]	3026
8	11	A	Lincoln C	D 2-2	0-1	11	Pitt (pen) [65], Lee [88]	7142
9	18	H	Shrewsbury T	D 2-2	2-2	9	Lee [31], Kirk [42]	2593
10	25	A	Leyton Orient	D 0-0	0-0	10		4753
11	Oct 2	H	Scunthorpe U	W 2-1	0-1	9	Pitt [68], O'Halloran [90]	3640
12	8	A	Southend U	L 1-2	0-2	—	Kirk [49]	5688
13	16	H	Wycombe W	W 2-0	1-0	7	Kirk 2 [14, 51]	2635
14	19	A	Bury	D 1-1	1-1	—	Challinor (og) [35]	2001
15	23	A	Notts Co	L 1-2	0-1	10	Ellender [54]	5434
16	30	H	Bristol R	D 2-2	0-0	11	Miller (og) [68], Kirk [74]	2723
17	Nov 6	A	Kidderminster H	W 4-0	0-0	7	Beevers [50], Kirk 3 (2 pens) [56 (p), 81 (p), 90]	2208
18	20	H	Mansfield T	D 0-0	0-0	9		3354
19	27	A	Rochdale	L 0-2	0-0	14		2474
20	Dec 8	H	Rushden & D	W 1-0	1-0	—	Thomas [27]	2334
21	11	A	Northampton T	L 1-2	0-0	13	Kirk [74]	5245
22	18	H	Darlington	W 3-1	3-0	9	Kirk (pen) [20], Clare [41], Thomas [45]	2428
23	28	A	Swansea C	L 1-3	0-3	11	Lee [86]	10,162
24	Jan 1	A	Cambridge U	W 1-0	0-0	10	Kirk [83]	3507
25	3	H	Leyton Orient	D 2-2	0-1	10	Kirk [50], Ellender [88]	3183
26	12	H	Southend U	W 2-0	0-0	—	Kirk 2 [65, 84]	2389
27	15	A	Shrewsbury T	D 0-0	0-0	8		3789
28	22	H	Swansea C	L 2-3	1-0	9	Kirk [15], Rusk [72]	2545
29	29	A	Scunthorpe U	D 1-1	0-0	11	Lee [57]	5056
30	Feb 5	A	Wycombe W	W 2-1	1-1	9	Kirk 2 [4, 85]	4091
31	12	H	Bury	D 2-2	2-1	10	Kirk [9], Rusk [13]	2351
32	16	H	Lincoln C	L 0-2	0-1	—		6445
33	19	A	Bristol R	D 1-1	0-0	12	Kirk [59]	5563
34	26	H	Northampton T	L 0-1	0-0	13		2749
35	Mar 5	A	Darlington	L 0-1	0-0	15		3219
36	12	H	Grimsby T	D 1-1	1-0	15	Clare [1]	3941
37	16	H	Notts Co	W 4-0	0-0	—	Noble [76], Easter 2 [84, 90], Thompson [89]	2229
38	19	A	Oxford U	L 0-2	0-1	11		5176
39	26	H	Yeovil T	L 1-2	1-1	13	Rusk [23]	3069
40	28	A	Macclesfield T	D 1-1	1-0	14	Noble (pen) [15]	2501
41	Apr 2	H	Cheltenham T	W 2-1	1-0	12	Lee 2 [15, 88]	2192
42	9	A	Chester C	L 1-2	1-1	13	Noble [9]	2040
43	16	A	Rushden & D	L 2-4	2-1	16	Clare (pen) [13], Maylett [34]	3671
44	23	H	Kidderminster H	W 3-0	2-0	14	Easter [15], Lee [28], Maylett [69]	2053
45	30	A	Mansfield T	L 2-3	0-0	16	Maylett [49], Thompson [90]	3223
46	May 7	H	Rochdale	D 1-1	0-0	16	Pitt [71]	2528

Final League Position: 16

GOALSCORERS

League (62): Kirk 19 (3 pens), Lee 9, Pitt 4 (2 pens), Clare 3 (1 pen), Easter 3, Maylett 3, Noble 3 (1 pen), Rusk 3, Thomas 3, Thompson 3, Ellender 2, Abbey Z 1, Beevers 1, McCann 1, Melton 1, O'Halloran 1, own goals 2.
Carling Cup (5): Thompson 2, Beevers 1, Lee 1, Pitt 1.
FA Cup (8): Kirk 2, McManus 2, Ellender 1, Lee 1, Noble 1, Thompson 1.
LDV Vans Trophy (0).

Abbey N 44	Beevers L 31	McCann A 45	Bennett T 11	Greaves M 21+1	Strong G 8+1	Melton S 5+4	Noble D 30+2	Carruthers M 4+2	Lee J 32+7	Jelleyman G 3	Pitt C 20+12	Thompson L 8+37	Holland C 30+2	Ellender P 39	Staff D —+5	Rusk S 22+9	Thomas D 32+7	Abbey Z 3+2	Gascoigne P 2+2	McManus T 5+3	Kirk A 25	West D 22+2	O'Halloran M 5+3	McCormick L 2	Norris R 1+1	Clare D 14+5	James K 6	Gabrieli E 4	O'Donnell S 2+2	Boyack S 2+2	Roma D 2	Wiseman S 1+1	White A 11	Easter J 5+4	Maylett B 8+1	Hurst T —+1	Brooks L 1+1	*Match No.*
1	2	3	4	5	6	7	8	9^1	10	11^2	12	13																										1
1	2	3	4	5	6	7	8^3	9^2	10^1	11	12	13	14																									2
1	2	3	4	5▮	6	7^2	8^3	9	10	11^1	13	12	14																									3
1	2	3	4		6		8^3	9^1	10		11	7^2		5	13	14	12																					4
1	2	3	4		6			12	10^1		11^3	7^2		5		8	13	9	14																			5
1	2	3	4	5				12	10		13	14	7	6			11^1	9^2	8^3																			6
1	2	3	4^2	5^1					10		13	12	7	6			11^3	9	8	14																		7
1	2	3	4^2	5					10		11	12	7	6		8^1		14	13	9^3																		8
1	2	3	4	5			12		10		11	13	7^1	6				14		9^2	8^3																	9
1	2	3		13			8		9		11	12	4	6						14	10^3	7^2	5^1															10
1	5	3	4				8		9		11	12		6			7^2				10^1	2	13															11
1	5	3	4				8		9		11	12		6			7^3			13	10^2	2^1	14															12
1	5	3		4			8^2				11	12		6		13	14			9^1	10^3	2	7															13
1	5	3		4			8		12		11	13		6						9^1	10	2	7^2															14
	5	3		4^1			8		9		11	13		6		12	14				10	2^3	7^2	1														15
	5	3		4			8^1		9			13		6		12	11				10	2		1	7^2													16
1	5	3		4			8		9			7		6		12	11				10^1	2																17
1	5▮	3		4		12	8^2		10			7		6		13	11			9^3		2^1				14												18
1		3		5		12	8		9			7	4^1	6			11					2^2	13			10												19
1	5	3		4					9			12	8	6			11				10^2	2	7^1			13												20
1	5	3		4					9			12	8	6		7^1	11				10	2^2				13												21
1	5	3		4		7^1					13	12	8	6		14	11^2				10	2				9^3												22
1	5	3				7^2			12			11	4	6		13	8				10^1	2				9												23
1	5	3		4					12			13	8^3	6		14	11				10^2	2^1				9	7											24
1	5	3		4					12			13	8	6			11				10	2^1				9^2	7											25
1	2	3		4	5							12	8	6			11				10					9^1	7											26
1	2	3		4	5^1				12		13	14	8	6			11				10^3					9^2	7											27
1	2	3			9^1		8		12			13	4^3	6		7	11				10	14					5^2											28
1	5	3			12		4		9			13		6^1	14	7	11				10^3					8^2	2											29
1	2	3					8		9		12	13	7			11	6^1				10^2							5	4^3	14								30
1	2	3					8		9		12	13	4		14	7	11^1				10^3							5	6^2									31
1		3					8^1		9			12	4	6		7	11				10	2^2						5		13								32
1	5								9		12	13	4	6		7	11				10									8^1	2	3^2						33
1		3					8^3		9		12	13		6		7	11^1				10							5		4	2^2	14						34
1		3					8		9^1		12	11	4	6	13	2^2	7				10												5					35
1		3				12	8				10^1	13	4	6	14	7^2	11					2				9^3							5					36
1		3				12	8				10^3	13	4^2	6		7	11					2				9^1							5	14				37
1		3					4		12		10	8^3		6		7	11					2^2				9^1							5	13	14			38
1		3					8^1		10			12	4	6		2	11									9^2							5	13	7			39
1		3					8^3		9		11	12	4	6		2	13												14				5	10^2	7^1			40
1		3					8		9		11^2	12	4^3	6		2	13					14											5	10^1	7			41
1		3					8^3		9		11^2	12	4	6		2	13												14				5	10^1	7			42
1		3					6		9		11^2	12	4			2	8									10^1							5		7	13		43
1		3							9▮		11		4			2	8					6			12	13							5^3	10^2	7^1		14	44
1		3					12				10	13	4	6		11	8^1					2				14								9^3	7		5^2	45
1		3					8				10	12	4	6		2	11^1									9^2							5	13	7			46

FA Cup

First Round	Hornchurch	(h)	5-2
Second Round	Hereford U	(a)	3-2
Third Round	Hartlepool U	(a)	0-0
		(h)	0-1

Carling Cup

First Round	Luton T	(h)	4-3
Second Round	Fulham	(h)	1-4

LDV Vans Trophy

First Round	Cambridge U	(h)	0-1

AFC BOURNEMOUTH FL Championship 1

FOUNDATION

There was a Bournemouth FC as early as 1875, but the present club arose out of the remnants of the Boscombe St John's club (formed 1890). The meeting at which Boscombe FC came into being was held at a house in Gladstone Road in 1899. They began by playing in the Boscombe and District Junior League.

The Fitness First Stadium at Dean Court, Bournemouth, Dorset BH7 7AF.

Telephone: (01202) 726 300.

Fax: (01202) 726 301.

Ticket Office: (01202) 726 303. ***Hotline:*** 0845 330 1000

Website: www.afcb.co.uk

Email: admin@afcb.co.uk

Ground Capacity: 9,300 seats, rising to 12,000 all-seater.

Record Attendance: 28,799 v Manchester U, FA Cup 6th rd, 2 March 1957.

Pitch Measurements: 105m × 78m.

Chairman: P. I. Phillips.

Vice-chairman: A. H. Kaye.

Secretary: K. R. J. MacAlister.

Manager: Sean O'Driscoll.

Assistant Manager: Richard O'Kelly.

Physio: Jim Marshall.

HONOURS

Football League: Division 3 – Champions 1986–87; Promoted from Division 3, 2002–03 (play-offs); Division 3 (S) – Runners-up 1947–48; Division 4 – Runners-up 1970–71; Promotion from Division 4 1981–82 (4th).

FA Cup: best season: 6th rd, 1957.

Football League Cup: best season: 4th rd, 1962, 1964.

Associate Members' Cup: Winners 1984.

Auto Windscreens Shield: Runners-up 1998.

Colours: Red shirts with black side panels, black shorts, black stockings.

Change Colours: Navy and sky blue shirts, navy shorts, navy stockings.

Year Formed: 1899.

Turned Professional: 1912.

Ltd Co.: 1914.

Previous Names: 1890, Boscombe St Johns; 1899, Boscombe FC; 1923, Bournemouth & Boscombe Ath FC; 1971, AFC Bournemouth.

Club Nickname: 'Cherries'.

Previous Grounds: 1899, Castlemain Road, Pokesdown; 1910, Dean Court.

First Football League Game: 25 August 1923, Division 3 (S), v Swindon T (a) L 1–3 – Heron; Wingham, Lamb; Butt, C. Smith, Voisey; Miller, Lister (1), Davey, Simpson, Robinson.

Record League Victory: 7–0 v Swindon T, Division 3 (S), 22 September 1956 – Godwin; Cunningham, Keetley; Clayton, Crosland, Rushworth; Siddall (1), Norris (2), Arnott (1), Newsham (2), Cutler (1). 10–0 win v Northampton T at start of 1939–40 expunged from the records on outbreak of war.

Record Cup Victory: 11–0 v Margate, FA Cup 1st rd, 20 November 1971 – Davies; Machin (1), Kitchener, Benson, Jones, Powell, Cave (1), Boyer, MacDougall (9 incl. 1p), Miller, Scott (De Garis).

SKY SPORTS FACT FILE

An alarming goal famine in 1968–69 hit Bournemouth badly in the second half of the season when only 19 goals came from the last 22 matches, in ten of which they failed to score at all. Fourth place cost them promotion at the end.

Record Defeat: 0–9 v Lincoln C, Division 3, 18 December 1982.

Most League Points (2 for a win): 62, Division 3, 1971–72.

Most League Points (3 for a win): 97, Division 3, 1986–87.

Most League Goals: 88, Division 3 (S), 1956–57.

Highest League Scorer in Season: Ted MacDougall, 42, 1970–71.

Most League Goals in Total Aggregate: Ron Eyre, 202, 1924–33.

Most League Goals in One Match: 4, Jack Russell v Clapton Orient, Division 3S, 7 January 1933; 4, Jack Russell v Bristol C, Division 3S, 28 January 1933; 4, Harry Mardon v Southend U, Division 3S, 1 January 1938; 4, Jack McDonald v Torquay U, Division 3S, 8 November 1947; 4, Ted MacDougall v Colchester U, 18 September 1970; 4, Brian Clark v Rotherham U, 10 October 1972, 4, Luther Blissett v Hull C, 29 November 1988; 4, James Hayter v Bury, Division 2, 21 October 2000.

Most Capped Player: Gerry Peyton, 7 (33), Republic of Ireland.

Most League Appearances: Steve Fletcher, 425, 1992–.

Youngest League Player: Jimmy White, 15 years 321 days v Brentford, 30 April 1958.

Record Transfer Fee Received: £800,000 from Everton for Joe Parkinson, March 1994.

Record Transfer Fee Paid: £210,000 to Gillingham for Gavin Peacock, August 1989.

Football League Record: 1923 Elected to Division 3 (S) and remained a Third Division club for record number of years until 1970; 1970–71 Division 4; 1971–75 Division 3; 1975–82 Division 4; 1982–87 Division 3; 1987–90 Division 2; 1990–92 Division 3; 1992–2002 Division 2; 2002–03 Division 3; 2003–04 Division 2; 2004– FL1.

MANAGERS

Vincent Kitcher 1914–23
(Secretary-Manager)
Harry Kinghorn 1923–25
Leslie Knighton 1925–28
Frank Richards 1928–30
Billy Birrell 1930–35
Bob Crompton 1935–36
Charlie Bell 1936–39
Harry Kinghorn 1939–47
Harry Lowe 1947–50
Jack Bruton 1950–56
Fred Cox 1956–58
Don Welsh 1958–61
Bill McGarry 1961–63
Reg Flewin 1963–65
Fred Cox 1965–70
John Bond 1970–73
Trevor Hartley 1974–75
John Benson 1975–78
Alec Stock 1979–80
David Webb 1980–82
Don Megson 1983
Harry Redknapp 1983–92
Tony Pulis 1992–94
Mel Machin 1994–2000
Sean O'Driscoll August 2000–

LATEST SEQUENCES

Longest Sequence of League Wins: 7, 22.8.1970 – 23.9.1970.

Longest Sequence of League Defeats: 7, 13.8.1994 – 13.9.1994.

Longest Sequence of League Draws: 5, 25.4.2000 – 12.8.2000.

Longest Sequence of Unbeaten League Matches: 18, 6.3.1982 – 28.8.1982.

Longest Sequence Without a League Win: 14, 6.3.1974 – 27.4.1974.

Successive Scoring Runs: 31 from 28.10.2000.

Successive Non-scoring Runs: 6 from 1.2.1975.

TEN YEAR LEAGUE RECORD

		P	W	D	L	F	A	Pts	Pos
1995-96	Div 2	46	16	10	20	51	70	58	14
1996-97	Div 2	46	15	15	16	43	45	60	16
1997-98	Div 2	46	18	12	16	57	52	66	9
1998-99	Div 2	46	21	13	12	63	41	76	7
1999-2000	Div 2	46	16	9	21	59	62	57	16
2000-01	Div 2	46	20	13	13	79	55	73	7
2001-02	Div 2	46	10	14	22	56	71	44	21
2002-03	Div 3	46	20	14	12	60	48	74	4
2003-04	Div 2	46	17	15	14	56	51	66	9
2004-05	FL 1	46	20	10	16	77	64	70	8

DID YOU KNOW?

In the two seasons prior to their election to the Football League in 1923, Bournemouth enjoyed decent runs in the FA Cup from the preliminary round. But with the 28 votes giving them new status they had to scratch the tie against Portsea Island Gas Co!

AFC BOURNEMOUTH 2004–05 LEAGUE RECORD

Match No.	Date	Venue	Opponents	Result	H/T Score	Lg. Pos.	Goalscorers	Atten-dance
1	Aug 7	A	Hull C	L 0-1	0-1	—		17,569
2	10	H	Walsall	D 2-2	0-1	—	Hayter [72], Elliott [74]	6485
3	14	H	Bristol C	D 2-2	1-0	20	Fletcher C [38], Hayter [88]	6918
4	21	A	Milton Keynes D	W 3-1	1-0	14	Hayter 2 [21, 76], Fletcher C [90]	3230
5	28	H	Wrexham	W 1-0	1-0	10	Connell [28]	5774
6	30	A	Luton T	L 0-1	0-0	14		7404
7	Sept 4	A	Brentford	L 1-2	0-1	17	Holmes [50]	5682
8	11	H	Colchester U	L 1-3	0-2	19	Stockley (og) [74]	5944
9	18	A	Sheffield W	W 1-0	1-0	18	Spicer [41]	19,203
10	25	H	Doncaster R	W 5-0	4-0	9	Rodrigues [3], Hayter 2 [5, 70], Howe [19], O'Connor G [25]	6588
11	Oct 2	A	Blackpool	D 3-3	2-3	12	Hayter [12], Rodrigues 2 [28, 64]	5525
12	8	H	Stockport Co	W 2-1	1-0	—	Stock [22], Hayter [45]	6925
13	16	H	Port Vale	W 4-0	3-0	5	Spicer [9], Stock 2 [39, 45], Cummings [46]	6119
14	19	A	Torquay U	W 2-1	0-0	—	Fletcher S [57], O'Connor G [62]	3055
15	23	A	Oldham Ath	W 2-1	0-1	4	Hayter 2 [59, 76]	5335
16	30	H	Barnsley	L 1-3	0-2	5	Elliott [52]	7709
17	Nov 6	A	Peterborough U	W 1-0	1-0	4	Hayter [4]	4004
18	20	H	Chesterfield	D 0-0	0-0	5		6565
19	27	A	Hartlepool U	L 2-3	2-1	5	Holmes [34], Stock [45]	4376
20	Dec 7	H	Bradford C	W 2-0	2-0	—	Broadhurst [12], Connell [18]	5578
21	10	A	Tranmere R	L 0-2	0-1	—		8557
22	18	H	Swindon T	W 2-1	0-0	4	O'Connor G [51], Maher [77]	7110
23	28	H	Huddersfield T	D 2-2	1-1	6	Spicer 2 [17, 51]	8448
24	Jan 1	H	Brentford	W 3-2	2-0	4	Fletcher S 3 [5, 35, 58]	8072
25	3	A	Doncaster R	D 1-1	1-0	6	Spicer [44]	6016
26	15	H	Sheffield W	D 1-1	1-0	7	O'Connor G [11]	8847
27	22	A	Huddersfield T	L 2-3	1-3	8	Hayter 2 [45, 62]	9754
28	Feb 1	A	Stockport Co	D 2-2	1-1	—	Spicer [6], O'Connor G [83]	3850
29	5	A	Port Vale	L 1-2	1-2	10	O'Connor G [13]	4186
30	12	H	Oldham Ath	W 4-0	1-0	9	Fletcher S [28], O'Connor G 2 [60, 90], Hayter [81]	6622
31	15	A	Colchester U	L 1-3	0-0	—	Cummings [47]	2820
32	19	A	Barnsley	W 1-0	0-0	6	O'Connor G [77]	8153
33	22	H	Torquay U	W 3-0	1-0	—	Maher [29], O'Connor G (pen) [48], Fletcher S [84]	5867
34	26	H	Tranmere R	D 1-1	1-1	6	Mills [43]	7305
35	Mar 5	A	Swindon T	W 3-0	1-0	6	Elliott [1], Hayter [56], Mills [74]	8275
36	8	H	Blackpool	L 2-3	1-2	—	Stock [7], Hayter (pen) [90]	5390
37	12	A	Walsall	W 2-1	1-1	5	Fletcher S [40], O'Connor G [53]	5126
38	19	H	Hull C	L 0-4	0-2	6		8895
39	28	H	Milton Keynes D	L 0-1	0-0	6		7064
40	Apr 2	A	Wrexham	W 2-1	0-0	6	Purches S [58], Elliott [67]	3801
41	5	A	Bristol C	W 2-0	0-0	—	O'Connor G 2 (1 pen) [60, 77 (p)]	12,008
42	9	H	Luton T	L 0-1	0-0	6		9058
43	16	A	Chesterfield	W 3-2	0-1	5	Fletcher S 2 [47, 90], Stock [63]	4009
44	23	H	Peterborough U	L 0-1	0-1	6		7929
45	30	A	Bradford C	L 2-4	0-2	6	Hayter [61], Mills [63]	10,263
46	May 7	H	Hartlepool U	D 2-2	2-1	8	Hayter 2 [12, 31]	8620

Final League Position: 8

GOALSCORERS

League (77): Hayter 19 (1 pen), O'Connor G 13 (2 pens), Fletcher S 9, Spicer 6, Stock 6, Elliott 4, Mills 3, Rodrigues 3, Connell 2, Cummings 2, Fletcher C 2, Holmes 2, Maher 2, Broadhurst 1, Howe 1, Purches S 1, own goal 1.
Carling Cup (9): Hayter 3, Broadhurst 1, Browning 1, Cummings 1, O'Connor G 1, Spicer 1, Stock 1.
FA Cup (8): Connell 2, Elliott 1, Fletcher S 1, Holmes 1, Maher 1, Rodrigues 1, Spicer 1.
LDV Vans Trophy (2): Stock 1, own goal 1.

Moss N 46	Young N 23 + 7	Cummings W 30	Broadhurst K 29	Fletcher C 6	Browning M 17 + 23	Elliott W 43	Stock B 39 + 2	Holmes D 8 + 15	Rodrigues D 10 + 13	Hayter J 37 + 2	Howe E 33 + 2	Fletcher S 30 + 6	Connell A 7 + 27	Maher S 29 + 7	Rowe J — + 2	O'Connor G 39 + 1	Moss R — + 1	Purches S 10 + 4	Coutts J — + 1	Spicer J 39	Cranie M 2 + 1	O'Connor J 6	Mills M 12	Green A 3	Simek F 8	*Match No.*
1	2■	3	4	5	6^{1}	7	8	9^{2}	10	11^{3}	12	13	14													1
1		3	4	9	6	7	8^{2}		10^{1}	11	2	13	12	5												2
1	2	3	4	10	6	7^{2}	8^{3}	9^{1}		11	5		12	13	14											3
1	2	3	4	10	6	7	8^{2}	9^{1}		11	5		12	13												4
1	12	3	2	10	6^{3}	7^{2}	8	9^{1}		11	5		13	4		14										5
1	2^{1}	3	4	9			8	12		11	5		10^{2}	6		7	13									6
1	2■	3	4^{2}		7		8^{1}	9		10	5			6	12	11^{3}		13	14							7
1		3	4		12		8	9^{1}	10^{2}	11	5		13	6		7				2						8
1		3	4			7	8	12	10^{1}	9	5		13	6		2^{2}				11						9
1		3	4		12	7	8	13	10^{2}	9^{3}	5		14	6^{1}		2				11						10
1	12	3	4			7	8		10^{2}	9	5	13		6		2^{1}				11						11
1	2	3	4			7	8		10^{1}	9	5	12				6				11						12
1	2	3	4			7	8	14	10^{2}	9	5^{1}	13^{3}		12		6				11						13
1	2	3	4		13	7	6	12		9^{3}	5	10^{1}	14			8				11^{2}						14
1	2		4		12	7	8	13		9^{3}	5	10^{2}	14	6		3^{1}				11						15
1	2^{2}		4		12	7	8	13		9	5	10		6		3^{3}				11^{1}	14					16
1	2		4		12	7	8			9^{2}	5	10	13			6^{1}				11	3					17
1	2	3	4		12	7	6	13	14		5	10^{2}	9^{3}			8^{1}				11						18
1	2		4		12	7	6	9^{3}	13		5		10^{2}	14		8^{1}				11	3					19
1	2	3	4		12	7	6^{1}	9^{2}			5^{3}	13	10	14		8				11						20
1	2	3^{2}	4		6	7		12	9^{1}			10	13	5		8				11						21
1	2		3^{3}		12	7	6		10^{1}	13	5		9^{2}	4		8		14		11						22
1	2	3^{3}	4		12	7	6		13			10	9^{2}	5		8^{1}		14		11						23
1	2	3	4		12	7	6		13			10	9^{1}	5		8^{3}		14		11^{2}						24
1	2	3	4		6	7	8■	12	13			10^{2}		5		9^{1}				11						25
1	2	3	4		6	7				9		10		5		8				11						26
1		3	4		6^{3}	7		14		9	12	10	13	5		8		2^{1}		11^{2}						27
1		3	2		12	7^{1}	6^{2}	13		9^{3}	5	10	14	4		8				11						28
1		3	2^{1}		12	7	6	13		9^{2}	5	10^{3}	14	4		8				11						29
1		3			12	7	6^{1}	13		9^{3}	5	10^{2}	14	4		8		2		11						30
1		3			12	7	6^{3}		13	9^{1}	5	10	14	4		8		2^{2}		11						31
1		3			12	7	6	13		9^{2}	5^{1}	10		4		8				11		2				32
1		3			12	7^{2}	6^{1}		13	9^{3}		10	14	4		8				11		2	5			33
1		3			6	7	8			12		10		4		9^{1}				11		2	5			34
1		3^{1}			12	7	6		13	9^{3}		10^{2}	14	4		8				11		2	5			35
1	2^{3}				12	7	6^{1}		13	9		10	14	4		8^{2}				11		3	5			36
1	12				6	7				9		10		4		8				11		2	5	3^{1}		37
1	2				6	7	12		13	9		10^{2}	14	4■		8				11^{1}			5	3^{3}		38
1	3				4	7	12		13	9	5^{1}	10	14			8^{2}				11				2^{3}	6	39
1	12				13	7	6			9^{2}	5	10				8		3^{1}		11			2		4	40
1					12	7^{1}	6			9	5	10				8		3		11			2		4	41
1					6^{1}	7^{2}			12	9	5	10	13			8		3		11			2		4	42
1	12					7^{2}	6			9	5	10	14	13		8^{3}		3		11			2		4^{1}	43
1	12				6^{1}	7	8			9	5	10	13	14				3^{2}		11			2		4^{3}	44
1	12				6	7	8^{1}			9	5	10^{2}	13					3		11			2		4	45
1					12	7	6		13	9	5	10	14	4		8^{3}		2^{2}		11					3^{1}	46

FA Cup

First Round	Forest Green R	(a)	1-1
		(h)	3-1
Second Round	Carlisle U	(h)	2-1
Third Round	Chester C	(h)	2-1
Fourth Round	Burnley	(a)	0-2

Carling Cup

First Round	Leyton Orient	(a)	3-1
Second Round	Blackburn R	(a)	3-3
Third Round	Cardiff C	(h)	3-3

LDV Vans Trophy

First Round	Shrewsbury T	(a)	2-3

BRADFORD CITY — FL Championship 1

FOUNDATION

Bradford was a rugby stronghold around the turn of the century but after Manningham RFC held an archery contest to help them out of financial difficulties in 1903, they were persuaded to give up the handling code and turn to soccer. So they formed Bradford City and continued at Valley Parade. Recognising this as an opportunity of spreading the dribbling code in this part of Yorkshire, the Football League immediately accepted the new club's first application for membership of the Second Division.

Valley Parade, Bradford, West Yorkshire BD8 7DY.
Telephone: (01274) 773 355.
Fax: (01274) 773 356.
Ticket Office: (01274) 770 022.
Website: www.bradfordcityfc.co.uk
Email: bradfordcityfc@compuserve.com
Ground Capacity: 25,136.
Record Attendance: 39,146 v Burnley, FA Cup 4th rd, 11 March 1911.
Pitch Measurements: 110yd × 73yd.
Chairman: Julian Rhodes.
Vice-chairman: Jim Brown.
Chief Executive: Julian Rhodes.
Secretary: Jon Pollard.
Manager: Colin Todd.
Assistant Manager: Bobby Davison.
Physio: Steve Redmond.
Colours: Claret and amber.
Change Colours: All silver.
Year Formed: 1903.
Turned Professional: 1903.
Ltd Co.: 1908.
Club Nickname: 'The Bantams'.

HONOURS

Football League: Division 1 – Runners-up 1998–99; Division 2 – Champions 1907–08; Promoted from Division 2 1995–96 (play-offs); Division 3 – Champions 1984–85; Division 3 (N) – Champions 1928–29; Division 4 – Runners-up 1981–82.

FA Cup: Winners 1911.

Football League Cup: best season: 5th rd, 1965, 1989.

European Competitions: *Intertoto Cup:* 2000.

First Football League Game: 1 September 1903, Division 2, v Grimsby T (a) L 0–2 – Seymour; Wilson, Halliday; Robinson, Millar, Farnall; Guy, Beckram, Forrest, McMillan, Graham.

Record League Victory: 11–1 v Rotherham U, Division 3 (N), 25 August 1928 – Sherlaw; Russell, Watson; Burkinshaw (1), Summers, Bauld; Harvey (2), Edmunds (3), White (3), Cairns, Scriven (2).

Record Cup Victory: 11–3 v Walker Celtic, FA Cup 1st rd (replay), 1 December 1937 – Parker; Rookes, McDermott; Murphy, Mackie, Moore; Bagley (1), Whittingham (1), Deakin (4 incl. 1p), Cooke (1), Bartholomew (4).

SKY SPORTS FACT FILE

Bradford City had the same two ever-present players in four successive seasons. From 1955–56 to 1958–59 full-back George Mulholland and goalkeeper Geoff Smith had consistent records and both received benefit payments at the same time.

Record Defeat: 1–9 v Colchester U, Division 4, 30 December 1961.

Most League Points (2 for a win): 63, Division 3 (N), 1928–29.

Most League Points (3 for a win): 94, Division 3, 1984–85.

Most League Goals: 128, Division 3 (N), 1928–29.

Highest League Scorer in Season: David Layne, 34, Division 4, 1961–62.

Most League Goals in Total Aggregate: Bobby Campbell, 121, 1981–84, 1984–86.

Most League Goals in One Match: 7, Albert Whitehurst v Tranmere R, Division 3N, 6 March 1929.

Most Capped Player: Jamie Lawrence, Jamaica.

Most League Appearances: Cec Podd, 502, 1970–84.

Youngest League Player: Robert Cullingford, 16 years 141 days v Mansfield T, 22 April 1970.

Record Transfer Fee Received: £2,000,000 from Newcastle U for Des Hamilton, July 1997 and £2,000,000 from Newcastle U for Andrew O'Brien, March 2001.

Record Transfer Fee Paid: £2,500,000 to Leeds U for David Hopkin, July 2000.

Football League Record: 1903 Elected to Division 2; 1908–22 Division 1; 1922–27 Division 2; 1927–29 Division 3 (N); 1929–37 Division 2; 1937–61 Division 3; 1961–69 Division 4; 1969–72 Division 3; 1972–77 Division 4; 1977–78 Division 3; 1978–82 Division 4; 1982–85 Division 3; 1985–90 Division 2; 1990–92 Division 3; 1992–96 Division 2; 1996–99 Division 1; 1999–2001 FA Premier League; 2001–04 Division 1; 2004– FL1.

MANAGERS

Robert Campbell 1903–05
Peter O'Rourke 1905–21
David Menzies 1921–26
Colin Veitch 1926–28
Peter O'Rourke 1928–30
Jack Peart 1930–35
Dick Ray 1935–37
Fred Westgarth 1938–43
Bob Sharp 1943–46
Jack Barker 1946–47
John Milburn 1947–48
David Steele 1948–52
Albert Harris 1952
Ivor Powell 1952–55
Peter Jackson 1955–61
Bob Brocklebank 1961–64
Bill Harris 1965–66
Willie Watson 1966–69
Grenville Hair 1967–68
Jimmy Wheeler 1968–71
Bryan Edwards 1971–75
Bobby Kennedy 1975–78
John Napier 1978
George Mulhall 1978–81
Roy McFarland 1981–82
Trevor Cherry 1982–87
Terry Dolan 1987–89
Terry Yorath 1989–90
John Docherty 1990–91
Frank Stapleton 1991–94
Lennie Lawrence 1994–95
Chris Kamara 1995–98
Paul Jewell 1998–2000
Chris Hutchings 2000
Jim Jefferies 2000–01
Nicky Law 2002–03
Bryan Robson 2003–04
Colin Todd June 2004–

LATEST SEQUENCES

Longest Sequence of League Wins: 10, 26.11.1983 – 3.2.1984.

Longest Sequence of League Defeats: 8, 21.1.1933 – 11.3.1933.

Longest Sequence of League Draws: 6, 30.1.1976 – 13.3.1976.

Longest Sequence of Unbeaten League Matches: 21, 11.1.1969 – 2.5.1969.

Longest Sequence Without a League Win: 16, 28.8.1948 – 20.11.1948.

Successive Scoring Runs: 30 from 26.12.1961.

Successive Non-scoring Runs: 7 from 18.4.1925.

TEN YEAR LEAGUE RECORD

		P	*W*	*D*	*L*	*F*	*A*	*Pts*	*Pos*
1995-96	Div 2	46	22	7	17	71	69	73	6
1996-97	Div 1	46	12	12	22	47	72	48	21
1997-98	Div 1	46	14	15	17	46	59	57	13
1998-99	Div 1	46	26	9	11	82	47	87	2
1999-2000	PR Lge	38	9	9	20	38	68	36	17
2000-01	PR Lge	38	5	11	22	30	70	26	20
2001-02	Div 1	46	15	10	21	69	76	55	15
2002-03	Div 1	46	14	10	22	51	73	52	19
2003-04	Div 1	46	10	6	30	38	69	36	23
2004-05	FL 1	46	17	14	15	64	62	65	11

DID YOU KNOW 

Promotion for Bradford City in fourth place in 1976–77 was aided by a fine unbeaten home record for the first time in the club's history. Included in this period was a run of 25 games at Valley Parade without loss.

BRADFORD CITY 2004–05 LEAGUE RECORD

Match No.	Date	Venue	Opponents	Result		H/T Score	Lg. Pos.	Goalscorers	Attendance
1	Aug 7	A	Hartlepool U	L	1-2	0-0	—	Windass [54]	6032
2	10	H	Peterborough U	D	2-2	1-1	—	Windass [9], Wetherall [84]	6929
3	14	H	Doncaster R	W	2-0	2-0	9	Bower [8], Crooks [45]	10,444
4	21	A	Stockport Co	W	1-0	0-0	6	Windass [76]	5338
5	28	H	Chesterfield	L	2-3	1-0	12	Windass 2 [41, 54]	7590
6	31	A	Hull C	W	1-0	0-0	—	Holloway [77]	16,865
7	Sept 4	H	Port Vale	L	0-2	0-1	13		7043
8	11	A	Wrexham	L	0-1	0-1	17		3712
9	18	H	Bristol C	W	4-1	2-0	12	Schumacher [30], Roberts [38], Wetherall [61], Adebola [80]	7235
10	25	A	Swindon T	L	0-1	0-0	15		5189
11	Oct 2	H	Barnsley	W	1-0	0-0	10	Windass (pen) [63]	8715
12	8	A	Milton Keynes D	W	2-1	0-1	—	Kearney [55], Adebola [90]	4532
13	16	A	Tranmere R	W	5-4	1-1	3	Schumacher [33], Summerbee [53], Windass [70], Muirhead [81], Wetherall [90]	8901
14	19	H	Blackpool	W	2-1	1-0	—	Adebola [36], Summerbee [89]	7622
15	23	H	Sheffield W	W	3-1	0-0	2	Symes 2 [59, 78], Windass [62]	13,717
16	30	A	Luton T	L	0-4	0-3	4		7975
17	Nov 6	H	Colchester U	D	2-2	1-2	5	Windass 2 [23, 81]	7851
18	20	A	Brentford	W	2-1	1-0	4	Abbey [2], Forrest [78]	5909
19	27	H	Oldham Ath	L	1-3	1-1	4	Windass [27]	8647
20	Dec 7	A	Bournemouth	L	0-2	0-2	—		5578
21	11	H	Walsall	D	1-1	0-0	7	Wetherall [83]	6732
22	18	A	Huddersfield T	W	1-0	1-0	6	Morrison [42]	17,281
23	26	H	Wrexham	D	1-1	0-0	`6	Schumacher [54]	10,268
24	28	A	Torquay U	D	0-0	0-0	7		4119
25	Jan 1	A	Port Vale	W	1-0	0-0	5	Forrest [61]	5001
26	3	H	Swindon T	L	1-2	0-0	7	Windass [56]	8239
27	15	A	Bristol C	D	0-0	0-0	9		11,605
28	22	H	Torquay U	D	2-2	2-2	6	Cooke [33], Windass [36]	8209
29	31	A	Barnsley	D	2-2	2-0	—	Windass 2 (1 pen) [27, 32 (p)]	8729
30	Feb 5	H	Tranmere R	D	1-1	0-1	9	Windass [77]	8129
31	8	H	Milton Keynes D	L	1-4	0-2	—	Windass [50]	6409
32	12	A	Sheffield W	W	2-1	1-0	8	Summerbee [6], Morrison [90]	23,232
33	19	H	Luton T	L	0-1	0-1	10		8702
34	22	A	Blackpool	L	1-2	0-0	—	Cooke [54]	4805
35	26	A	Walsall	D	1-1	1-0	11	Schumacher [20]	4966
36	Mar 5	H	Huddersfield T	W	2-0	1-0	10	Cooke [44], Windass [54]	15,417
37	12	A	Peterborough U	D	2-2	0-2	10	Windass 2 [64, 73]	3472
38	19	H	Hartlepool U	L	1-2	0-1	11	Bower [60]	7509
39	24	A	Doncaster R	D	1-1	1-1	—	Bridge-Wilkinson [10]	6688
40	28	H	Stockport Co	W	3-1	2-1	10	Cooke [2], Schumacher [5], Windass [64]	7263
41	Apr 2	A	Chesterfield	D	0-0	0-0	10		4663
42	10	H	Hull C	L	0-2	0-1	11		13,631
43	16	H	Brentford	W	4-1	4-0	11	Windass 2 [6, 37], Bridge-Wilkinson 2 [23, 45]	6743
44	23	A	Colchester U	D	0-0	0-0	12		3351
45	30	H	Bournemouth	W	4-2	2-0	11	Windass 3 [19, 75, 90], Schumacher [38]	10,263
46	May 7	A	Oldham Ath	L	1-2	1-2	11	Windass [10]	9381

Final League Position: 11

GOALSCORERS

League (64): Windass 27 (2 pens), Schumacher 6, Cooke 4, Wetherall 4, Adebola 3, Bridge-Wilkinson 3, Summerbee 3, Bower 2, Forrest 2, Morrison 2, Symes 2, Abbey 1, Crooks 1, Holloway 1, Kearney 1, Muirhead 1, Roberts 1.
Carling Cup (1): Windass 1 (pen).
FA Cup (0).
LDV Vans Trophy (1): Adebola 1.

Turnbull R 2	Holloway D 33	Jacobs W 13+1	Schumacher S 42+1	Wetherall D 45	Bower M 46	Summerbee N 31+2	Crooks L 30+2	Windass D 39+2	Symes M 5+7	Emanuel L 28+8	Atherton P 12+4	Sanasy K —+3	Muirhead B 26+14	Penford T —+3	Henderson P 40	Adebola D 14+1	Kearney T 13	Roberts N 3	Forrest D 4+16	Gavin J 1+2	Swift J 2+3	Abbey Z 6	Morrison O 17+5	Tierney P 14+2	Cooke A 20	Armstrong C 4+3	Bentham C —+2	Bridge-Wilkinson M 12	Ricketts D 4	*Match No.*
1	2^1	3	4	5	6	7	8	9	10^2	11^3	12	13	14																	1
1	2	3	4	5	6	7^2	8	9^1	10			12	11	13																2
	2	3^1	4	5	6	7	8	9			12		11^2	13	1	10														3
	2		4	5	6	7	8	9		3			11^1	12	1	10														4
	2	3	4	5	6			9		11			7		1	10	8													5
	2	3		5	6	12	4	9		11^1			7		1	10	8													6
	2	3^3	12	5	6	13	4	9	14	11^2			7		1	10	8^1													7
	2	3^1	4	5	6		11■	9	12	13			7		1	10^2	8													8
	2	3	4	5	6	7			12				11		1	10	8	9^1												9
	2	3	4^1	5	6	7	13	14		12			11^2		1	10^3	8	9												10
	2	3	4	5	6	7		9^1					11		1	12	8	10												11
	2	3	4	5	6	7		9		12			11^1		1	10	8													12
	2		4	5	6	7		9		3			11		1	10	8													13
	2		4	5	6	7		9		3			11		1	10	8													14
	2		4	5	6	7^1	12	9	13	3			11		1	10^2	8													15
	2		4	5	6		7^2	9	12	3			11		1	10^1	8		13											16
	2^1			5	6		4	9		3			11		1	10	8			12	7									17
	2^1		4	5	6	7	8	9		3			11^2		1				13	12		10■								18
			4^1	5	6	7■	8	9	12	3	13		11		1				10	2^2										19
		3	4	5	6		8		10^1	11	2	12	7		1				9											20
		3^1	4	5	6	7	8^3		10	11	2^2		12		1				9		13		14							21
	2		4	5	6	7	8	9	12	3			13		1							10^1	11^2							22
	2		4	5	6	7	8	9■		3					1							10	11							23
	2		4	5	6	7	8			11^1			12		1				13			9	10^2	3						24
	2		4	5	6	7	8		10^1	11					1				12			9	13	3^2						25
	2		4	5	6	7	8	9		3			12		1				13			10^2	11^1							26
	2		4	5	6	7	8	9		3^3			12		1				13				11^1	14	10^2					27
	2^2		4	5	6	7	8	9			13		12		1				14				11^1	3	10^3					28
			4	5	6	7	8	9		3	2				1				12					11^2	10^1	13				29
			4	5	6	7	8^1	9			2		12		1									3	10	11				30
				5	6	7	8	9		3	2		12		1				13				11^1	14	10^2	4^3				31
			4	5	6	7	8^3	9		11	2		12^2		1								13	3^1	10	14				32
			4	5	6	7	8	9		3	2		12		1				13				11^1		10^2					33
			4	5	6	7^1	8	9			2		12		1								11		10	3				34
			4		6		8	9			5		7^1		1						2				10	3	12	11		35
			4	5	6	7	8^1	9^2		3	2		12		1				13						10			11		36
			4	5	6	7		9		3	2		11^1		1				13				12		10^2			8		37
			4	5	6	7		9		3	2^2				1				12		13		11^3		10^1	14		8		38
	2		4	5	6		8	9		12					1								11^1	3	10			7		39
	2		4	5	6		8^2	12					13		1				9				11	3	10^1			7		40
	2		4	5	6	7^1		9		12					1				13				11	3	10^2			8		41
	2		4	5	6			9		3			7		1								12	11^1	10			8		42
	2^2		4^3	5	6			9		12			7								13		11^1	3	10		14	8	1	43
	2		4	5	6			9		12			7						13				11^1	3	10^2			8	1	44
	2	12	4	5	6			9^2					11						13				7	3^1	10			8	1	45
	2		4	5	6			9		12			7										11	3^1	10			8	1	46

FA Cup
First Round Rushden & D (h) 0-1

Carling Cup
First Round Notts Co (h) 1-2

LDV Vans Trophy
First Round Accrington S (h) 1-2

BRENTFORD — FL Championship 1

FOUNDATION

Formed as a small amateur concern in 1889 they were very successful in local circles. They won the championship of the West London Alliance in 1893 and a year later the West Middlesex Junior Cup before carrying off the Senior Cup in 1895. After winning both the London Senior Amateur Cup and the Middlesex Senior Cup in 1898 they were admitted to the Second Division of the Southern League.

Griffin Park, Braemar Road, Brentford, TW8 0NT.
Telephone: 0845 3456 442.
Fax: (0208) 380 9937.
Ticket Office: 0845 3456 442.
Website: www.brentfordfc.co.uk
E-mail: enquiries@brentfordfc.co.uk
Ground Capacity: 12,763.
Record Attendance: 38,678 v Leicester C, FA Cup 6th rd, 26 February 1949.
Pitch Measurements: 111yd × 74yd.
Chairman: Eddie Rogers.
Chief Executive: Andrew Finch.
Secretary: Lisa Hall.
Manager: Martin Allen.
First Team Coach: Adrian Whitbread.
Physio: Matt Hirons. ***Sports Therapist:*** Damien Doyle.
Colours: Red and white striped shirts, black shorts, black stockings.
Change Colours: White shirts with red trim, white shorts, white stockings.
Year Formed: 1889.
Turned Professional: 1899.
Ltd Co.: 1901.
Club Nickname: 'The Bees'.
Previous Grounds: 1889, Clifden Road; 1891, Benns Fields, Little Ealing; 1895, Shotters Field; 1898, Cross Road, S. Ealing; 1900, Boston Park; 1904, Griffin Park.
First Football League Game: 28 August 1920, Division 3, v Exeter C (a) L 0–3 – Young; Hodson, Rosier, Elliott J, Levitt, Amos, Smith, Thompson, Spreadbury, Morley, Henery.
Record League Victory: 9–0 v Wrexham, Division 3, 15 October 1963 – Cakebread; Coote, Jones; Slater, Scott, Higginson; Summers (1), Brooks (2), McAdams (2), Ward (2), Hales (1), (1 og).
Record Cup Victory: 7–0 v Windsor & Eton (away), FA Cup 1st rd, 20 November 1982 – Roche; Rowe, Harris (Booker), McNichol (1), Whitehead, Hurlock (2), Kamara, Joseph (1), Mahoney (3), Bowles, Roberts. *N.B.* 8–0 v Uxbridge, FA Cup, 3rd Qual rd, 31 October 1903.

HONOURS

Football League: Division 1 best season: 5th, 1935–36; Division 2 – Champions 1934–35; Division 3 – Champions 1991–92, 1998–99; Division 3 (S) – Champions 1932–33, Runners-up 1929–30, 1957–58; Division 4 – Champions 1962–63.
FA Cup: best season: 6th rd, 1938, 1946, 1949, 1989.
Football League Cup: best season: 4th rd, 1983.
Freight Rover Trophy: Runners-up 1985.
LDV Vans Trophy: Runners-up 2001.

SKY SPORTS FACT FILE

Brentford's 2–0 victory at Oldham Athletic on 15 March 2005 was the first time in 70 seasons that they had recorded a League win at Boundary Park. On 10 November 1934 they won 3–1 with goals from Jack Holliday, Charlie Fletcher and Billy Scott.

Record Defeat: 0–7 v Swansea T, Division 3 (S), 8 November 1924 and v Walsall, Division 3 (S), 19 January 1957.

Most League Points (2 for a win): 62, Division 3 (S), 1932–33 and Division 4, 1962–63.

Most League Points (3 for a win): 85, Division 2, 1994–95 and Division 3, 1998–99.

Most League Goals: 98, Division 4, 1962–63.

Highest League Scorer in Season: Jack Holliday, 38, Division 3 (S), 1932–33.

Most League Goals in Total Aggregate: Jim Towers, 153, 1954–61.

Most League Goals in One Match: 5, Jack Holliday v Luton T, Division 3S, 28 January 1933; Billy Scott v Barnsley, Division 2, 15 December 1934; Peter McKennan v Bury, Division 2, 18 February 1949.

Most Capped Player: John Buttigieg, 22 (98), Malta.

Most League Appearances: Ken Coote, 514, 1949–64.

Youngest League Player: Danis Salman, 15 years 243 days v Watford, 15 November 1975.

Record Transfer Fee Received: £2,500,000 from Wimbledon for Hermann Hreidarsson, October 1999.

Record Transfer Fee Paid: £750,000 to Crystal Palace for Hermann Hreidarsson, September 1998.

Football League Record: 1920 Original Member of Division 3; 1921–33 Division 3 (S); 1933–35 Division 2; 1935–47 Division 1; 1947–54 Division 2; 1954–62 Division 3 (S); 1962–63 Division 4; 1963–66 Division 3; 1966–72 Division 4; 1972–73 Division 3; 1973–78 Division 4; 1978–92 Division 3; 1992–93 Division 1; 1993–98 Division 2; 1998–99 Division 3; 1999–04 Division 2; 2004– FL1.

MANAGERS

Will Lewis 1900–03
(Secretary-Manager)
Dick Molyneux 1902–06
W. G. Brown 1906–08
Fred Halliday 1908–12, 1915–21, 1924–26
(only Secretary to 1922)
Ephraim Rhodes 1912–15
Archie Mitchell 1921–24
Harry Curtis 1926–49
Jackie Gibbons 1949–52
Jimmy Blain 1952–53
Tommy Lawton 1953
Bill Dodgin Snr 1953–57
Malcolm Macdonald 1957–65
Tommy Cavanagh 1965–66
Billy Gray 1966–67
Jimmy Sirrel 1967–69
Frank Blunstone 1969–73
Mike Everitt 1973–75
John Docherty 1975–76
Bill Dodgin Jnr 1976–80
Fred Callaghan 1980–84
Frank McLintock 1984–87
Steve Perryman 1987–90
Phil Holder 1990–93
David Webb 1993–97
Eddie May 1997
Micky Adams 1997–98
Ron Noades 1998–2000
Ray Lewington 2001
Steve Coppell 2001–02
Wally Downes 2002–04
Martin Allen March 2004–

LATEST SEQUENCES

Longest Sequence of League Wins: 9, 30.4.1932 – 24.9.1932.

Longest Sequence of League Defeats: 9, 20.10.1928 – 25.12.1928.

Longest Sequence of League Draws: 5, 16.3.1957 – 6.4.1957.

Longest Sequence of Unbeaten League Matches: 26, 20.2.1999 – 16.10.1999.

Longest Sequence Without a League Win: 16, 19.2.1994 – 7.5.1994.

Successive Scoring Runs: 26 from 4.3.1963.

Successive Non-scoring Runs: 7 from 7.3.2000.

TEN YEAR LEAGUE RECORD

		P	*W*	*D*	*L*	*F*	*A*	*Pts*	*Pos*
1995-96	Div 2	46	15	13	18	43	49	58	15
1996-97	Div 2	46	20	14	12	56	43	74	4
1997-98	Div 2	46	11	17	18	50	71	50	21
1998-99	Div 3	46	26	7	13	79	56	85	1
1999-2000	Div 2	46	13	13	20	47	61	52	17
2000-01	Div 2	46	14	17	15	56	70	59	14
2001-02	Div 2	46	24	11	11	77	43	83	3
2002-03	Div 2	46	14	12	20	47	56	54	16
2003-04	Div 2	46	14	11	21	52	69	53	17
2004-05	FL 1	46	22	9	15	57	60	75	4

DID YOU KNOW?

Brentford can claim to have had a player on their books who went on to achieve more than a century of caps for his country. Brian Turner, brought up in New Zealand, made his Bees bow in 1969–70 and in the 1982 World Cup reached his 100th international.

BRENTFORD 2004–05 LEAGUE RECORD

Match No.	Date	Venue	Opponents	Result		H/T Score	Lg. Pos.	Goalscorers	Attendance
1	Aug 7	A	Chesterfield	L	1-3	0-1	—	Rhodes 70	4651
2	10	H	Doncaster R	W	4-3	1-2	—	Rankin 35, Hargreaves 52, Burton 54, Tabb 63	5621
3	14	H	Wrexham	W	1-0	0-0	7	O'Connor 85	5091
4	21	A	Peterborough U	L	0-3	0-1	13		4868
5	28	H	Stockport Co	W	3-0	3-0	8	Dobson 4, Salako 16, Burton 30	4643
6	30	A	Bristol C	L	1-4	0-1	12	O'Connor 61	10,296
7	Sept 4	H	Bournemouth	W	2-1	1-0	7	Talbot 32, Rankin 47	5682
8	11	A	Torquay U	D	2-2	0-1	9	Hargreaves 69, Sodje 77	3458
9	18	H	Port Vale	W	1-0	1-0	5	Salako (pen) 25	5442
10	25	A	Walsall	W	1-0	1-0	4	Salako (pen) 30	5302
11	Oct 2	H	Oldham Ath	W	2-0	1-0	2	Rankin 45, Burton 47	5818
12	9	A	Barnsley	D	0-0	0-0	2		8453
13	16	A	Milton Keynes D	D	0-0	0-0	2		5924
14	19	H	Hartlepool U	W	2-1	1-1	—	Rankin 35, Burton 90	4797
15	23	H	Blackpool	L	0-3	0-1	5		6722
16	30	A	Tranmere R	L	0-1	0-0	6		8740
17	Nov 7	A	Huddersfield T	D	1-1	0-0	6	Sodje 62	10,810
18	20	H	Bradford C	L	1-2	0-1	8	Rhodes 90	5909
19	27	A	Hull C	L	0-2	0-1	11		15,710
20	Dec 7	H	Luton T	W	2-0	1-0	—	Burton 41, May 62	6393
21	11	A	Sheffield W	W	2-1	0-1	5	Rhodes 81, Burton 82	21,592
22	18	H	Colchester U	W	1-0	1-0	5	Salako 45	5634
23	26	H	Torquay U	L	1-3	1-0	7	Sodje 26	6419
24	28	A	Swindon T	L	0-3	0-1	8		6875
25	Jan 1	A	Bournemouth	L	2-3	0-2	9	Rankin 2 50, 65	8072
26	3	H	Walsall	W	1-0	1-0	9	Broad (og) 25	5084
27	15	A	Port Vale	W	1-0	1-0	8	Hutchinson 29	4230
28	22	H	Swindon T	W	2-1	1-1	6	Burton 44, Hunt 81	5857
29	25	H	Barnsley	D	1-1	0-1	—	Sodje 59	4835
30	Feb 5	H	Milton Keynes D	W	1-0	0-0	6	Hunt (pen) 78	5077
31	22	A	Hartlepool U	L	1-3	0-0	—	Rankin 50	4206
32	26	H	Sheffield W	D	3-3	1-2	10	Burton 42, Peters 82, Hunt 90	8323
33	Mar 5	A	Colchester U	W	1-0	0-0	7	Tabb 58	3066
34	12	A	Doncaster R	D	0-0	0-0	7		5525
35	15	A	Oldham Ath	W	2-0	0-0	—	Fitzgerald SP 2 52, 63	4291
36	19	H	Chesterfield	D	2-2	0-1	7	Burton 68, Tabb 77	6097
37	22	A	Blackpool	L	1-2	0-2	—	Pratley 84	5478
38	28	H	Peterborough U	D	0-0	0-0	7		6341
39	Apr 2	A	Stockport Co	W	2-1	0-0	7	Fitzgerald SP 57, Sodje 86	4408
40	9	H	Bristol C	W	1-0	1-0	7	Sodje 12	6780
41	12	H	Tranmere R	W	1-0	0-0	—	Turner 69	6005
42	16	A	Bradford C	L	1-4	0-4	6	Tabb 79	6743
43	23	H	Huddersfield T	L	0-1	0-1	7		7703
44	30	A	Luton T	L	2-4	2-1	7	Sodje 21, Burton 26	9313
45	May 3	A	Wrexham	W	2-1	0-1	—	Rankin 68, Fitzgerald SP 90	4374
46	7	H	Hull C	W	2-1	1-1	4	Sobers 43, Tabb 86	9604

Final League Position: 4

GOALSCORERS

League (57): Burton 10, Rankin 8, Sodje 7, Tabb 5, Fitzgerald SP 4, Salako 4 (2 pens), Hunt 3 (1 pen), Rhodes 3, Hargreaves 2, O'Connor 2, Dobson 1, Hutchinson 1, May 1, Peters 1, Pratley 1, Sobers 1, Talbot 1, Turner 1, own goal 1.
Carling Cup (0).
FA Cup (10): Rankin 2, Frampton 1, Hargreaves 1, Hutchinson 1, Rhodes 1 (pen), Salako 1, Sodje 1, Tabb 1, Talbot 1.
LDV Vans Trophy (0).
Play-offs (1): Frampton 1.

Nelson S 43	Dobson M 13 + 5	Myers A 6 + 4	Talbot S 35 + 2	Fitzgerald SB 12	Turner M 45	Tabb J 29 + 11	Hargreaves C 30	Rankin I 33 + 8	Burton D 38 + 2	Salako J 30 + 5	O'Connor K 32 + 5	Frampton A 34 + 1	Rhodes A 4 + 18	Sommer M 1 + 1	Smith J — + 2	Peters R 1 + 8	Sodje S 40	Hunt S 13 + 6	Lawrence J 8 + 6	Harrold M 6 + 13	Pacquette R 1	May B 7 + 3	Claridge S 3 + 1	Hutchinson E 14 + 1	Bankole A 3	Pratley D 11 + 3	Fitzgerald SP 7 + 5	Gayle M 4 + 2	Osborne K 1	Ide C — + 1	Sobers J 1	Moleski G — + 1	Watts R — + 1	Charles D 1	Match No.
1	2^{1}	3^{2}	4^{3}	5	6	7	8	9	10	11	12	13	14																						1
1	2		4	5	6	7^{1}	8	9^{2}	10	11	12	3^{3}	13	14■																					2
1	2		4^{2}	5	6	7	8^{3}	9	10	11^{1}	14	3	12		13																				3
1	2		4^{1}	5	6	7^{3}	8	9	10	11^{2}	12	3	13			14																			4
1	2		4^{1}	5	6	7	8^{3}	9	10	11^{2}	14	3	13		12																				5
1	2^{1}		12	5	6		8	9^{3}	10	13	7	3	14	4^{2}			11																		6
1			4	5	6		8	9		7	10	3	12				2	11^{1}																	7
1			4	5	6	12	8	9	13	7	10^{2}	3^{1}					2	11																	8
1			4^{3}		6	12	8	9	10^{2}	7	2	3	13				5	11^{1}	14																9
1			4		6	7	8	9	10^{1}	11	2	3					5			12															10
1			4		6	7	8^{2}	9	10^{3}	11^{1}	2	3					5	12	13	14															11
1		12	4		6		8	9		7^{2}	2	3	13				5	11		10^{1}															12
1		3■	4		6	7	8	9^{2}	10^{1}		2		12				5^{3}	11	14	13															13
1					6	7^{1}	8	9	10	3	2		12				5	11^{2}	4	13															14
1		3^{3}			6	12	8	9	10^{2}	7	2		13				5	11^{1}	4	14															15
1			4		6	12		9	10	11	2	3	13				5		7^{2}	8^{1}															16
1			4^{1}		6	7^{2}	8	9	10	11	2	3					5		12	13															17
1			4		6	7^{2}	8^{1}	9	10■	11^{3}	2	3	13				5		12	14															18
1		11			6	7	8			12	2	3^{3}	9			13	5^{1}		4^{2}	14	10														19
1			4		6	7	8^{1}	12	10^{3}	11^{2}	2	3	13				5			14		9													20
1		12	4		6■	7	8^{2}	13	10	11	2	3^{1}	14				5					9^{3}													21
1			4		6		8	12	10	11^{2}	2	3	7				5		13				9^{1}												22
1			4		6	12		13	10^{3}	11	2	3^{2}	8^{1}				5		7			14	9												23
1			4^{1}		6	7	8	9	10			3	12				5		2			13	11^{2}												24
1				5^{3}	6	12	8	9	10^{2}	11^{1}		3	13				2					7	14	4											25
1					6	7	8	9	10			3	11^{1}				5		2			12		4											26
1	2	3^{1}	4^{2}		6	13	8	9	10	12							5					11		7											27
1	2		4		6	7	8^{1}		10	3							5	12				9		11											28
1	2		12	5^{1}	6	7		9^{2}	10	3						13	4	14		8^{3}				11											29
	2		4	5^{1}	6				10	11						12	3	7		8		9			1										30
1	2				6	12		9	13	3						14	5	11		8^{3}		10^{2}		7		4^{1}									31
	12		4^{3}		6	7		9^{2}	10	3	2					13	5^{1}	11						8	1	14									32
1	12		4		6	7^{1}			10^{2}		2	3					5	9						8		11	13								33
1	12		4		6	7^{2}		9	10^{1}	11	2	3^{3}					5	13						8		14									34
1	12		4^{1}		6	7		13	10^{2}		2	3					5	14						8		11	9^{3}								35
1					6	7	8	9	10	12	2	3^{1}					5	13						4			11^{2}								36
1	12		4^{3}		6^{1}	11	8^{2}	9	10■		2	3					5							13		7	14								37
1	2		4		6	12		9			3					13	5	11^{1}						8^{2}		7	10								38
1	2^{2}	12	4		6	7		13			8	3				14	5	10^{3}								11	9^{1}								39
1			4		6	7		12	10^{1}		2	3					5			13						11	9^{2}	8							40
1			4		6	12		8	10^{2}	11^{1}	2	3					5			13						7	9^{3}	14							41
1		12			6	13		8	10^{3}	11	2	3					5^{1}			14						7	9	4^{2}							42
1			4		6	7^{1}		8	10	12	2	3					5									11	13	9^{2}							43
1			4^{2}		6			12	10^{1}	11^{3}	2	3					5			13				8		7	14	9							44
1			4		6	7^{3}	8^{2}	9	10^{1}		2	3					5							11		13	12	14							45
		3		5		7^{1}	8									9^{3}			6	10^{2}					1				2	12	4	14	13	11	46

FA Cup

First Round	Bristol C	(a)	1-1
		(h)	1-1
Second Round	Hinckley U	(a)	0-0
		(h)	2-1
Third Round	Luton T	(a)	2-0
Fourth Round	Hartlepool U	(h)	0-0
		(a)	1-0
Fifth Round	Southampton	(a)	2-2
		(h)	1-3

Carling Cup

First Round	Ipswich T	(a)	0-2

LDV Vans Trophy

First Round	Milton Keynes D	(h)	0-3

Play-offs

Semi-Final	Sheffield W	(a)	0-1
		(h)	1-2

BRIGHTON & HOVE ALBION FL Championship

FOUNDATION

A professional club Brighton United was formed in November 1897 at the Imperial Hotel, Queen's Road, but folded in March 1900 after less than two seasons in the Southern League at the County Ground. An amateur team, Brighton & Hove Rangers was then formed by some prominent United supporters and after one season at Withdean, decided to turn semi-professional and play at the County Ground. Rangers were accepted into the Southern League but then also folded June 1901. John Jackson the former United manager organised a meeting at the Seven Stars public house, Ship Street on 24 June 1901 at which a new third club Brighton & Hove United was formed. They took over Rangers' place in the Southern League and pitch at County Ground. The name was changed to Brighton & Hove Albion before a match was played because of objections by Hove FC.

Withdean Stadium, Tongdean Lane, Brighton, East Sussex BN1 5JD.

Telephone: (01273) 695 400.

Fax: (01273) 648 179.

Ticket Office: (01273) 776 992.

Website: www.seagulls.co.uk

Email: seagulls@bhafc.co.uk

Ground Capacity: 6,973.

Record Attendance: 36,747 v Fulham, Division 2, 27 December 1958.

Pitch Measurements: 110yd × 70yd.

Chairman: Dick Knight.

Chief Executive: Martin Perry.

Secretary: Derek J. Allan.

Manager: Mark McGhee.

Assistant Manager: Bob Booker.

Physio: Malcolm Stuart.

Colours: Blue and white vertical striped shirts, white shorts, white stockings.

Change Colours: Burgundy shirts, burgundy shorts, burgundy stockings.

Year Formed: 1901.

Turned Professional: 1901.

Ltd Co.: 1904.

Previous Grounds: 1901, County Ground; 1902, Goldstone Ground.

Club Nickname: 'The Seagulls'.

First Football League Game: 28 August 1920, Division 3, v Southend U (a) L 0–2 – Hayes; Woodhouse, Little; Hall, Comber, Bentley; Longstaff, Ritchie, Doran, Rodgerson, March.

HONOURS

Football League: Division 1 best season: 13th, 1981–82; Division 2 – Champions 2001–02; Runners-up 1978–79; Promoted from Division 2 2003–04 (play-offs); Division 3 (S) – Champions 1957–58; Runners-up 1953–54, 1955–56; Division 3 – Champions 2000–01; Runners-up 1971–72, 1976–77, 1987–88; Division 4 – Champions 1964–65.

FA Cup: Runners-up 1983.

Football League Cup: best season: 5th rd, 1979.

SKY SPORTS FACT FILE

Few players have made such an early scoring impact on their debut in the Football League as Maheta Molango did for Brighton & Hove Albion against Reading on 7 August 2004 when he was on the scoresheet after 19 seconds.

Record League Victory: 9–1 v Newport Co, Division 3 (S), 18 April 1951 – Ball; Tennant (1p), Mansell (1p); Willard, McCoy, Wilson; Reed, McNichol (4), Garbutt, Bennett (2), Keene (1). 9–1 v Southend U, Division 3, 27 November 1965 – Powney; Magill, Baxter; Leck, Gall, Turner; Gould (1), Collins (1), Livesey (2), Smith (3), Goodchild (2).

Record Cup Victory: 10–1 v Wisbech, FA Cup 1st rd, 13 November 1965 – Powney; Magill, Baxter; Collins (1), Gall, Turner; Gould, Smith (2), Livesey (3), Cassidy (2), Goodchild (1), (1 og).

Record Defeat: 0–9 v Middlesbrough, Division 2, 23 August 1958.

Most League Points (2 for a win): 65, Division 3 (S), 1955–56 and Division 3, 1971–72.

Most League Points (3 for a win): 92, Division 3, 2000–01.

Most League Goals: 112, Division 3 (S), 1955–56.

Highest League Scorer in Season: Peter Ward, 32, Division 3, 1976–77.

Most League Goals in Total Aggregate: Tommy Cook, 114, 1922–29.

Most League Goals in One Match: 5, Jack Doran v Northampton T, Division 3S, 5 November 1921; 5, Adrian Thorne v Watford, Division 3S, 30 April 1958.

Most Capped Player: Steve Penney, 17, Northern Ireland.

Most League Appearances: 'Tug' Wilson, 509, 1922–36.

Youngest League Player: Ian Chapman, 16 years 259 days v Birmingham C, 14 February 1987.

Record Transfer Fee Received: £1,500,000 from Tottenham H for Bobby Zamora, July 2003.

Record Transfer Fee Paid: £500,000 to Manchester U for Andy Ritchie, October 1980.

Football League Record: 1920 Original Member of Division 3; 1921–58 Division 3 (S); 1958–62 Division 2; 1962–63 Division 3; 1963–65 Division 4; 1965–72 Division 3; 1972–73 Division 2; 1973–77 Division 3; 1977–79 Division 2; 1979–83 Division 1; 1983–87 Division 2; 1987–88 Division 3; 1988–96 Division 2; 1996–2001 Division 3; 2001–02 Division 2; 2002–03 Division 1; 2003–04 Division 2; 2004– FLC.

MANAGERS

John Jackson 1901–05
Frank Scott-Walford 1905–08
John Robson 1908–14
Charles Webb 1919–47
Tommy Cook 1947
Don Welsh 1947–51
Billy Lane 1951–61
George Curtis 1961–63
Archie Macaulay 1963–68
Fred Goodwin 1968–70
Pat Saward 1970–73
Brian Clough 1973–74
Peter Taylor 1974–76
Alan Mullery 1976–81
Mike Bailey 1981–82
Jimmy Melia 1982–83
Chris Cattlin 1983–86
Alan Mullery 1986–87
Barry Lloyd 1987–93
Liam Brady 1993–95
Jimmy Case 1995–96
Steve Gritt 1996–98
Brian Horton 1998–99
Jeff Wood 1999
Micky Adams 1999–2001
Peter Taylor 2001–02
Martin Hinshelwood 2002
Steve Coppell 2002–03
Mark McGhee October 2003–

LATEST SEQUENCES

Longest Sequence of League Wins: 9, 2.10.1926 – 20.11.1926.

Longest Sequence of League Defeats: 12, 17.8.2002 – 26.10.2002.

Longest Sequence of League Draws: 6, 16.2.1980 – 15.3.1980.

Longest Sequence of Unbeaten League Matches: 16, 8.10.1930 – 28.1.1931.

Longest Sequence Without a League Win: 15, 21.10.1972 – 27.1.1973

Successive Scoring Runs: 31 from 4.2.1956.

Successive Non-scoring Runs: 6 from 8.11.1924.

TEN YEAR LEAGUE RECORD

		P	*W*	*D*	*L*	*F*	*A*	*Pts*	*Pos*
1995-96	Div 2	46	10	10	26	46	69	40	23
1996-97	Div 3	46	13	10	23	53	70	47	23
1997-98	Div 3	46	6	17	23	38	66	35	23
1998-99	Div 3	46	16	7	23	49	66	55	17
1999-2000	Div 3	46	17	16	13	64	46	67	11
2000-01	Div 3	46	28	8	10	73	35	92	1
2001-02	Div 2	46	25	15	6	66	42	90	1
2002-03	Div 1	46	11	12	23	49	67	45	23
2003-04	Div 2	46	22	11	13	64	43	77	4
2004-05	FL C	46	13	12	21	40	65	51	20

DID YOU KNOW ?

In 1938–39 Brighton & Hove Albion experienced problems in attack with a lack of consistent goalscoring. They failed to score in 11 matches but as the defence kept no fewer than 17 clean sheets they were able to finished a respectable third.

BRIGHTON & HOVE ALBION 2004–05 LEAGUE RECORD

Match No.	Date	Venue	Opponents	Result		H/T Score	Lg. Pos.	Goalscorers	Attendance
1	Aug 7	A	Reading	L	2-3	1-2	—	Molango [1], Robinson [63]	15,641
2	10	H	Plymouth Arg	L	0-2	0-2	—		6387
3	14	H	Coventry C	D	1-1	0-0	24	Virgo [89]	6368
4	21	A	Wigan Ath	L	0-3	0-1	24		8681
5	28	H	Preston NE	W	1-0	1-0	23	Broomes (og) [30]	5996
6	30	A	Leicester C	W	1-0	1-0	13	Virgo [41]	22,263
7	Sept 11	A	Watford	D	1-1	0-0	19	Virgo [85]	14,148
8	14	H	Wolverhampton W	L	0-1	0-1	—		6804
9	18	H	QPR	L	2-3	2-1	20	Hinshelwood [23], Currie [44]	6612
10	25	A	Gillingham	W	1-0	0-0	19	Knight (pen) [79]	8365
11	29	A	Nottingham F	W	1-0	1-0	—	Virgo [25]	20,109
12	Oct 2	H	Sheffield U	D	1-1	1-0	16	Currie [22]	6418
13	16	A	Crewe Alex	L	1-3	0-2	18	Jarrett [79]	6811
14	19	H	Cardiff C	D	1-1	1-0	—	Knight [10]	6112
15	23	H	Leeds U	W	1-0	0-0	15	Carlisle (og) [58]	6716
16	30	A	Sunderland	L	0-2	0-0	15		25,532
17	Nov 3	A	Derby Co	L	0-3	0-1	—		22,480
18	6	H	Crewe Alex	L	1-3	0-1	21	Reid [85]	6163
19	13	A	West Ham U	W	1-0	0-0	18	Butters [68]	29,514
20	20	H	Burnley	L	0-1	0-0	20		6109
21	27	A	Ipswich T	L	0-1	0-1	20		26,269
22	Dec 4	H	Rotherham U	W	1-0	0-0	20	Harding [82]	6076
23	11	A	Millwall	L	0-2	0-1	20		12,196
24	17	H	Stoke C	L	0-1	0-0	—		6208
25	26	H	Gillingham	W	2-1	0-1	20	Carpenter [79], Virgo [88]	6420
26	28	A	Wolverhampton W	D	1-1	1-1	20	Hart [4]	28,516
27	Jan 1	A	QPR	D	0-0	0-0	20		15,898
28	3	H	Watford	W	2-1	1-1	18	Mayo [15], Knight [69]	6335
29	15	A	Sheffield U	W	2-1	1-0	17	Carpenter [45], Knight [90]	21,482
30	22	H	Nottingham F	D	0-0	0-0	18		6704
31	29	A	Leeds U	D	1-1	0-1	—	Butters [81]	27,033
32	Feb 5	H	Derby Co	L	2-3	1-2	18	McCammon 2 [14, 60]	6587
33	12	A	Cardiff C	L	0-2	0-2	18		11,435
34	19	H	Sunderland	W	2-1	2-0	15	Carpenter [26], McCammon [43]	6647
35	26	H	Millwall	W	1-0	0-0	15	Hart [90]	6608
36	Mar 5	A	Stoke C	L	0-2	0-2	16		14,908
37	12	A	Plymouth Arg	L	1-5	1-4	17	Oatway [11]	15,606
38	15	H	Wigan Ath	L	2-4	1-4	—	Virgo [36], Hammond [83]	6306
39	21	H	Reading	L	0-1	0-0	—		6108
40	Apr 2	A	Coventry C	L	1-2	0-0	20	Virgo [62]	18,606
41	5	A	Preston NE	L	0-3	0-2	—		14,234
42	9	H	Leicester C	D	1-1	0-1	22	Reid [80]	6638
43	16	A	Burnley	D	1-1	0-1	22	Hammond [52]	11,611
44	23	H	West Ham U	D	2-2	0-1	22	Hammond 2 [54, 90]	6819
45	30	A	Rotherham U	W	1-0	1-0	20	McLaren (og) [19]	6549
46	May 8	H	Ipswich T	D	1-1	1-1	20	Virgo [10]	6848

Final League Position: 20

GOALSCORERS

League (40): Virgo 8, Hammond 4, Knight 4 (1 pen), Carpenter 3, McCammon 3, Butters 2, Currie 2, Hart 2, Reid 2, Harding 1, Hinshelwood 1, Jarrett 1, Mayo 1, Molango 1, Oatway 1, Robinson 1, own goals 3.
Carling Cup (1): Butters 1.
FA Cup (1): Carpenter 1.

Kuipers M 30	Virgo A 36	Harding D 39 + 4	Cullip D 18	Butters G 41	Reid P 33 + 1	Nicolas A 29 + 4	Oatway C 31 + 3	Jarrett A 3 + 9	Molango M 4 + 1	Currie D 21 + 1	Robinson J 1 + 9	Jones N 3 + 16	Hinshelwood A 37 + 1	Mayo K 21 + 6	Hart G 16 + 10	Knight L 33 + 6	Hammond D 20 + 10	El-Abd A 14 + 2	McPhee C 6 + 10	Carpenter R 28 + 4	Piercy J 1 + 1	Claridge S 5	Watson P 1 + 3	McCammon M 16 + 2	May C — + 1	Yelldell D 3	Shaaban R 6	Blayney A 7	Dolan J 3	*Match No.*
1	2^{1}	3	4	5	6	7	8^{2}	9^{3}	10	11	12	14	13																	1
1	2	3■	4	5	6^{1}	7		9^{2}	10^{3}	11	13	12		8	14															2
1	2		4	5		7		9^{1}	10^{2}	11	8	12	6	3	13															3
1	2	3	4	5		7		12	10^{2}	11	13		6	8^{1}		9														4
1	10	3	4	5		7				8		11^{1}	2	12		9	6													5
1	10^{2}		4	5		7			13	11^{1}		12	3	8	14	9^{3}	6	2												6
1	10	13	4	5		7		12^{2}		11			6	3		9^{3}	8	2^{1}	14											7
1	10	12	4	5^{1}		7^{2}		13		11			6	3		9	8	2^{3}	14											8
1	10	5	4			7^{1}		13		11			6	3		12	8^{3}	2^{2}	9	14										9
1	10	3	4			7^{1}	12			11			5			9	8	2^{2}	13	6										10
1	10	3	4			7	8^{3}	13		11			5	12		9^{2}	2^{1}		14	6										11
1	10	3			6	7	8	12		11			5	4		9	2^{1}													12
1	10	3			6	7	8^{3}	12		11	13		5	2		9^{2}	4^{1}			14										13
1	10	3		5	6	7^{2}	8	12		11^{1}			2			9	4			13										14
1	10	3		5			8^{1}			11			4		12	9	7	2		6										15
1		3	4	5			8	12		11			10		13	9	7^{2}	2^{1}		6										16
1	10	3	4	5			8^{1}			11			6	12		9	7^{3}	2^{2}		13	14									17
1		8	4	5	6	7				11			2	3		9	12				10^{1}									18
1	10■	3	4	5	6	7	8			12			2							11		9^{1}								19
1		3^{1}		5	6	7^{2}	8			11		14	2	12	13	9^{3}				4		10								20
1		3^{2}	4	5	10	7^{1}	8			11		13	2			12	14			6^{3}		9								21
1		3	4	5	6	7	8			11			2			9						10								22
1	10	3	4	5	6^{1}	7^{2}	8						2^{3}			12	13			11		9	14							23
1	10	3^{1}		5	2	7^{2}	8					12	4			9	13			6				11						24
1	10			5	2	7^{1}	8					12	4	3	9					6				11						25
1	4	11^{3}		5	2		8					12	7	3	9^{2}	13	14			6				10^{1}						26
1	10	11		5	2^{1}	12	8						4	3	7	13				6				9^{2}						27
1	2	12		5	14	13	8						4	11	7^{2}	9				6			3^{1}	10^{3}						28
1	2	3		5	7		8						4	11	10^{1}	9				6				12						29
1^{6}		11		5	7		8					12	4	3	10^{1}	9		2		6					15					30
	2	11^{2}		5	7	12	8■					13	4	3	14	9^{1}				6				10^{3}		1				31
	2	11^{2}		5	8^{1}	7^{3}						13	4	3	12	9	14			6				10		1				32
	2	12		5	8^{1}	7						11^{3}	4	3^{2}	13	9				6			14	10		1				33
	11■	3		5	2	7							4		8	9	12			6				10^{1}			1			34
		3		5	2	7	12						4	13	8	9			11^{2}	6				10^{1}			1			35
		3		5	2	7^{3}	12					13	4		11	9		14	8^{1}	6				10^{2}			1			36
		11^{1}		5	2	7^{2}	8						4	3	10	9	12		13	6■							1			37
	6	3		5	2^{3}	7^{1}	8						4		11	9	12		13				14	10^{2}			1			38
	6	3		5	2		8					12	4^{2}	11^{1}	7	9	13		14					10^{3}			1			39
	11	3^{2}		5	2	12	8					13			7	9	4^{1}		14					10^{3}				1	6	40
	10	3		5	2		8					11^{1}			9■	12	7^{3}	13		6				14				1	4^{2}	41
	10	3		5	2		8				12	13					7^{2}	4	14	11				9^{3}				1	6^{1}	42
	2	3		5	7		8				12						11	4	9	6				10^{1}				1		43
	4	3		5	7		8^{2}				13				12	9	11	2^{1}	10	6								1		44
		3		5	4		8				12			13	7^{1}	9	11	2	10^{2}	6								1		45
	10	3		5	4		8				12				7^{2}	9^{1}	11	2	13	6								1		46

FA Cup
Third Round — Tottenham H — (a) — 1-2

Carling Cup
First Round — Bristol R — (h) — 1-2

BRISTOL CITY FL Championship 1

FOUNDATION

The name Bristol City came into being in 1897 when the Bristol South End club, formed three years earlier, decided to adopt professionalism and apply for admission to the Southern League after competing in the Western League. The historic meeting was held at The Albert Hall, Bedminster. Bristol City employed Sam Hollis from Woolwich Arsenal as manager and gave him £40 to buy players. In 1900 they merged with Bedminster, another leading Bristol club.

Ashton Gate Stadium, Bristol, North Somerset, BS3 2EJ.

Telephone: (0117) 9630 630.

Fax: (0117) 9630 700.

Ticket Office: 0870 112 1897.

Website: www.bcfc.co.uk

Ground Capacity: 21,497.

Record Attendance: 43,335 v Preston NE, FA Cup 5th rd, 16 February 1935.

Pitch Measurements: 115yd × 75yd.

Chairman: Stephen Lansdown.

Chief Executive: Colin Sexstone.

Secretary: Michelle McDonald.

Player Manager: Brian Tinnion.

Assistant Manager: Keith Millen.

Physio: Anna Eason.

Colours: Red shirts, red shorts, red stockings.

Change Colours: White shirts, white shorts, white stockings.

Year Formed: 1894.

Turned Professional: 1897.

Ltd Co.: 1897. Bristol City Football Club Ltd.

Previous Name: 1894, Bristol South End; 1897, Bristol City.

Club Nickname: 'Robins'.

Previous Grounds: 1894, St John's Lane; 1904, Ashton Gate.

First Football League Game: 7 September 1901, Division 2, v Blackpool (a) W 2–0 – Moles; Tuft, Davies; Jones, McLean, Chambers; Bradbury, Connor, Boucher, O'Brien (2), Flynn.

Record League Victory: 9–0 v Aldershot, Division 3 (S), 28 December 1946 – Eddols; Morgan, Fox; Peacock, Roberts, Jones (1); Chilcott, Thomas, Clark (4 incl. 1p), Cyril Williams (1), Hargreaves (3).

HONOURS

Football League: Division 1 – Runners-up 1906–07; Division 2 – Champions 1905–06; Runners-up 1975–76, 1997–98; Division 3 (S) – Champions 1922–23, 1926–27, 1954–55; Runners-up 1937–38; Division 3 – Runners-up 1964–65, 1989–90.

FA Cup: Runners-up 1909.

Football League Cup: Semi-final 1971, 1989.

Welsh Cup: Winners 1934.

Anglo-Scottish Cup: Winners 1978.

Freight Rover Trophy: Winners 1986; Runners-up 1987.

Auto Windscreens Shield: Runners-up 2000.

LDV Vans Trophy: Winners 2003.

SKY SPORTS FACT FILE

In 2004–05 Leroy Lita became the youngest Bristol City player to score 25 goals in a season for the club. In addition to his goalscoring for City he came on as a substitute for England Under-21s against Holland and scored on his debut.

Record Cup Victory: 11–0 v Chichester C, FA Cup 1st rd, 5 November 1960 – Cook; Collinson, Thresher; Connor, Alan Williams, Etheridge; Tait (1), Bobby Williams (1), Atyeo (5), Adrian Williams (3), Derrick, (1 og).

Record Defeat: 0–9 v Coventry C, Division 3 (S), 28 April 1934.

Most League Points (2 for a win): 70, Division 3 (S), 1954–55.

Most League Points (3 for a win): 91, Division 3, 1989–90.

Most League Goals: 104, Division 3 (S), 1926–27.

Highest League Scorer in Season: Don Clark, 36, Division 3 (S), 1946–47.

Most League Goals in Total Aggregate: John Atyeo, 314, 1951–66.

Most League Goals in One Match: 6, Tommy 'Tot' Walsh v Gillingham, Division 3S, 15 January 1927.

Most Capped Player: Billy Wedlock, 26, England.

Most League Appearances: John Atyeo, 597, 1951–66.

Youngest League Player: Marvin Brown, 16 years 105 days v Bristol R, 17 October 1999.

Record Transfer Fee Received: £3,000,000 from Wolverhampton W for Ade Akinbiyi, September 1999.

Record Transfer Fee Paid: £1,200,000 to Gillingham for Ade Akinbiyi, May 1998.

Football League Record: 1901 Elected to Division 2; 1906–11 Division 1; 1911–22 Division 2; 1922–23 Division 3 (S); 1923–24 Division 2; 1924–27 Division 3 (S); 1927–32 Division 2; 1932–55 Division 3 (S); 1955–60 Division 2; 1960–65 Division 3; 1965–76 Division 2; 1976–80 Division 1; 1980–81 Division 2; 1981–82 Division 3; 1982–84 Division 4; 1984–90 Division 3; 1990–92 Division 2; 1992–95 Division 1; 1995–98 Division 2; 1998–99 Division 1; 1999–04 Division 2; 2004– FL1.

MANAGERS

Sam Hollis 1897–99
Bob Campbell 1899–1901
Sam Hollis 1901–05
Harry Thickett 1905–10
Sam Hollis 1911–13
George Hedley 1913–17
Jack Hamilton 1917–19
Joe Palmer 1919–21
Alex Raisbeck 1921–29
Joe Bradshaw 1929–32
Bob Hewison 1932–49
(under suspension 1938–39)
Bob Wright 1949–50
Pat Beasley 1950–58
Peter Doherty 1958–60
Fred Ford 1960–67
Alan Dicks 1967–80
Bobby Houghton 1980–82
Roy Hodgson 1982
Terry Cooper 1982–88
(Director from 1983)
Joe Jordan 1988–90
Jimmy Lumsden 1990–92
Denis Smith 1992–93
Russell Osman 1993–94
Joe Jordan 1994–97
John Ward 1997–98
Benny Lennartsson 1998–99
Tony Pulis 1999
Tony Fawthrop 2000
Danny Wilson 2000–04
Brian Tinnion June 2004–

LATEST SEQUENCES

Longest Sequence of League Wins: 14, 9.9.1905 – 2.12.1905.

Longest Sequence of League Defeats: 7, 3.10.1970 – 7.11.1970.

Longest Sequence of League Draws: 4, 6.11.1999 – 27.11.1999.

Longest Sequence of Unbeaten League Matches: 24, 9.9.1905 – 10.2.1906.

Longest Sequence Without a League Win: 15, 29.4.1933 – 4.11.1933.

Successive Scoring Runs: 25 from 26.12.1905.

Successive Non-scoring Runs: 6 from 10.9.1910.

TEN YEAR LEAGUE RECORD

		P	*W*	*D*	*L*	*F*	*A*	*Pts*	*Pos*
1995-96	Div 2	46	15	15	16	55	60	60	13
1996-97	Div 2	46	21	10	15	69	51	73	5
1997-98	Div 2	46	25	10	11	69	39	85	2
1998-99	Div 1	46	9	15	22	57	80	42	24
1999-2000	Div 2	46	15	19	12	59	57	64	9
2000-01	Div 2	46	18	14	14	70	56	68	9
2001-02	Div 2	46	21	10	15	68	53	73	7
2002-03	Div 2	46	24	11	11	79	48	83	3
2003-04	Div 2	46	23	13	10	58	37	82	3
2004-05	FL 1	46	18	16	12	74	57	70	7

DID YOU KNOW ?

On 21 August 1976 Bristol City made a return to the First Division for the first time in 65 years with an away game against an Arsenal complete with new £330,000 signing Malcolm Macdonald. But City won with a Paul Cheesley goal in the 65th minute.

BRISTOL CITY 2004–05 LEAGUE RECORD

Match No.	*Date*	*Venue*	*Opponents*	*Result*		*H/T Score*	*Lg. Pos.*	*Goalscorers*	*Attendance*
1	Aug 7	H	Torquay U	D	1-1	0-0	—	Lita [59]	14,275
2	10	A	Barnsley	L	1-2	0-0	—	Lita [88]	10,435
3	14	A	Bournemouth	D	2-2	0-1	21	Lita [77], Smith [90]	6918
4	21	H	Swindon T	L	1-2	1-1	21	Doherty [45]	13,389
5	28	A	Port Vale	L	0-3	0-2	21		5377
6	30	H	Brentford	W	4-1	1-0	20	Wilkshire 2 [25, 69], Murray 2 [48, 73]	10,296
7	Sept 4	A	Peterborough U	W	1-0	0-0	18	Lita [72]	4227
8	11	H	Stockport Co	W	5-0	3-0	13	Tinnion [11], Roberts [24], Lita 2 [31, 80], Heffernan [79]	10,811
9	18	A	Bradford C	L	1-4	0-2	15	Murray [88]	7235
10	25	H	Huddersfield T	D	3-3	1-2	17	Murray [9], Lita (pen) [82], Mirfin (og) [90]	10,783
11	Oct 2	A	Chesterfield	D	2-2	0-1	15	Murray [47], Coles [54]	4854
12	16	H	Hull C	W	3-1	1-0	13	Brooker [38], Wilkshire [58], Butler [85]	12,011
13	19	A	Oldham Ath	D	0-0	0-0	—		5090
14	23	A	Walsall	W	2-1	0-0	10	Lita 2 [64, 90]	7105
15	30	H	Colchester U	D	0-0	0-0	12		11,678
16	Nov 6	H	Milton Keynes D	W	4-1	3-0	11	Lita 2 [4, 25], Brooker [29], Wilkshire [63]	10,717
17	9	H	Tranmere R	W	4-0	2-0	—	Brooker 2 [19, 57], Wilkshire 2 (1 pen) [41, 90 (p)]	11,098
18	20	A	Wrexham	W	3-1	2-0	6	Bell (pen) [36], Murray [44], Brooker [52]	7833
19	27	H	Sheffield W	L	1-4	0-1	6	Murray [56]	14,852
20	Dec 7	A	Doncaster R	D	1-1	1-1	—	Brooker [45]	5608
21	11	A	Blackpool	D	1-1	1-1	8	Wilkshire [21]	5220
22	18	H	Luton T	L	1-2	0-1	10	Lita [66]	13,414
23	26	A	Stockport Co	W	2-1	1-1	9	Butler [5], Heffernan [55]	5071
24	28	H	Hartlepool U	D	0-0	0-0	9		13,034
25	Jan 1	H	Peterborough U	W	2-0	2-0	8	Brooker [30], Heffernan [34]	10,873
26	3	A	Huddersfield T	D	2-2	0-1	8	Lita [71], Clarke (og) [90]	11,151
27	10	A	Tranmere R	W	1-0	1-0	—	Lita [10]	8183
28	15	H	Bradford C	D	0-0	0-0	6		11,605
29	22	A	Hartlepool U	L	1-2	1-1	7	Brooker [26]	5399
30	28	H	Chesterfield	L	2-3	0-2	—	Brooker [67], Smith [70]	10,103
31	Feb 5	A	Hull C	D	1-1	0-0	7	Lita [76]	17,637
32	11	H	Walsall	L	0-1	0-0	—		10,820
33	19	A	Colchester U	W	2-0	0-0	9	Brooker [51], Lita [71]	3412
34	22	H	Oldham Ath	W	5-1	3-0	—	Lita 2 [8, 23], Wilkshire [45], Brooker [52], Branston (og) [87]	9007
35	26	H	Blackpool	D	1-1	1-0	8	Brooker [21]	10,977
36	Mar 5	A	Luton T	L	0-5	0-3	9		8330
37	12	H	Barnsley	D	0-0	0-0	8		9321
38	19	A	Torquay U	W	4-0	3-0	8	Lita 3 [9, 12, 21], Heffernan [54]	4299
39	Apr 2	H	Port Vale	W	2-0	1-0	8	Lita [14], Heffernan [68]	10,284
40	5	H	Bournemouth	L	0-2	0-0	—		12,008
41	9	A	Brentford	L	0-1	0-1	9		6780
42	13	A	Swindon T	D	0-0	0-0	—		6977
43	16	H	Wrexham	W	1-0	0-0	8	Murray [66]	8267
44	23	A	Milton Keynes D	W	2-1	1-1	8	Lita 2 [45, 70]	5656
45	30	H	Doncaster R	D	2-2	0-1	8	Brooker 2 [62, 90]	12,375
46	May 7	A	Sheffield W	W	3-2	2-0	7	Brooker 2 [25, 45], Wilkshire (pen) [81]	28,798

Final League Position: 7

GOALSCORERS

League (74): Lita 24 (1 pen), Brooker 16, Wilkshire 9 (2 pens), Murray 8, Heffernan 5, Butler 2, Smith 2, Bell 1 (pen), Coles 1, Doherty 1, Roberts 1, Tinnion 1, own goals 3.
Carling Cup (3): Lita 2, own goal 1.
FA Cup (2): Heffernan 1, Lita 1.
LDV Vans Trophy(3): Lita 2, Heffernan 1.

Phillips S 46	Smith J 35 + 4	Woodman C 3	Fortune C 17 + 13	Coles D 37 + 1	Hill M 23	Murray S 31 + 11	Orr B 23 + 14	Lita L 42 + 2	Heffernan P 10 + 17	Tinnion B 15 + 7	Doherty T 25 + 4	Roberts C 6 + 2	Anyinsah J 2 + 5	Miller L 2 + 5	Goodfellow M 1 + 4	Gillespie S 1 + 7	Bell M 26 + 5	Butler T 22	Harley R 1 + 1	Wilkshire L 35 + 2	Brooker S 33	Amankwaah K 1 + 4	Brown S 13 + 6	Cotterill D 8 + 4	Dinning T 15 + 4	Ireland C 5	Carey L 14	Skuse C 4 + 3	Golbourne S 7 + 2	Keith J 3	Wring D — + 1	*Match No.*
1	2	3	4^{1}	5	6	7	8	9	10^{2}	11^{3}	12	14	13																			1
1	2	3		5	6	7	8	9	10^{2}	11^{1}	4		12	13																		2
1	2		4	5	3	7^{2}	8	9	10^{1}		6		11^{3}	12	13	14																3
1	2	3^{3}		5	6	12	8	9		11^{1}	4	7^{2}		10		13	14															4
1	2		4		3		6	9	12	13		14		10^{1}		11^{3}		5	8^{2}	7												5
1	2			5	3	7	12	9		8	4^{1}	10						6		11												6
1	2		12	5	3	7	4	9		8^{1}		10^{2}		13				6		11												7
1	2		12	5	3^{1}	7	13	9	14	8^{2}	4	10^{3}						6		11												8
1	2			5	3	7	12	9	13	8	4	10^{2}						6		11^{1}												9
1	2^{3}			5	3	7	8^{2}	9	12	13	4	10^{1}		14				6		11												10
1	2▪		12	5	3	7	13	9^{3}		8	4						14	6^{1}		11^{2}	10											11
1			12	2	6	7^{2}	4	9		8^{3}							3	5		11^{1}	10	13	14									12
1				4	6	7	8	9^{1}	12								3	5		11	10	2										13
1			12	2	6	7	8^{2}	9		13^{3}	4						3	5		11^{1}	10		14									14
1	2		12		6	7^{2}	8	9								13	3^{3}	5		11	10			14	4^{1}							15
1	12			2	6	7	13	9^{3}			4^{2}					14	3^{1}	5		11	10				8							16
1	12			2	6	7	13	9			4^{2}					14	3^{1}	5		11	10^{3}				8							17
1	13		12	2	6	7^{2}	14	9^{1}			4						3	5		11^{3}	10				8							18
1	2^{3}		12	5▪	6	7		9		13	4^{2}						3			11	10	14			8^{1}							19
1	2				6	7^{2}	12	9			4^{1}						3	5		11^{3}	10	14	13		8							20
1	2		12		6^{1}	7		9	13		4						3	5		11	10^{2}				8							21
1	2^{2}			13	6	7		9	12	14	4						3	5		11	10^{1}				8^{3}							22
1	2		12	5		7^{1}	4	9	10	13							3	6		11^{3}		14			8^{2}							23
1	2			4	3	12	6	9	10^{2}	8				13			11^{3}	5		7^{1}				14								24
1	2		12	6		7	4	13	10		14						3	5^{1}		11	9^{2}				8^{3}							25
1	2		6	5		7^{2}	8	12	10	13					14		3			11^{1}	9^{3}				4							26
1	2		6	5		12	8	9		7^{3}	13						3			11^{2}	10^{1}				14	4						27
1	2		6	5		12	8^{2}	9		7^{3}					13		3^{1}			11	10				14	4						28
1	2		6	4		12	8	9	13		14						3^{2}	5		11^{1}	10				7^{3}							29
1	2		12	5		7		9		11^{2}	4^{3}				8		3	6^{1}		13	10				14							30
1	2		3			7	4	9		8							12				10		11^{1}			6	5					31
1	2		3^{1}			7	4	9	13	8^{3}							12				10		11^{2}		14	6	5					32
1				5				9^{1}			4		12				3			11^{3}	10		8	7^{2}		6	2	13	14			33
1	2			5		12	13	9	14								3			11^{1}	10^{3}		8	7^{2}	4		6					34
1	2			5		12		9^{2}	13				14				3			11^{1}	10		8	7^{3}	4		6					35
1	2		7	5^{3}			12	9							13		3			11	10		8^{2}		4^{1}		6	14				36
1	2^{1}		13	6		12		9	14		4									11	10		8^{3}	7			5^{2}		3			37
1	2^{3}		5	6		7	14	9^{1}	12		4									13	10^{2}		8						3	11		38
1	2			6		7^{3}	12	9^{2}	13		4						3				10		8	14			5			11^{1}		39
1	2			6		7		9	12		4						3^{2}				10^{1}		8	14			5		13	11^{3}		40
1	2		5	6		13	11	9	12		4^{3}										10		8^{2}	7^{1}				14	3			41
1	2		5			12	8	9	13		4									11^{3}	10^{2}		14	7^{1}			6		3			42
1			6			12	8^{1}	9	10		4^{2}								14	11			13	7^{3}			5	2	3			43
1	12		5	6		7	13	9												11^{2}	10^{1}		14	8^{3}			2	4	3			44
1			5	6		7^{3}			10				14			13	12			11	9		8^{2}				2	4	3^{1}			45
1			5	6			12		10^{2}				4^{3}			13	3^{1}			11	9		8				2	7			14	46

FA Cup

First Round	Brentford	(h)	1-1
		(a)	1-1

Carling Cup

First Round	Wycombe W	(a)	1-0
Second Round	Everton	(h)	2-2

LDV Vans Trophy

First Round	Peterborough U	(h)	1-0
Second Round	Milton Keynes D	(h)	2-1
Quarter-Final	Swindon T	(a)	0-1

BRISTOL ROVERS FL Championship 2

FOUNDATION

Bristol Rovers were formed at a meeting in Stapleton Road, Eastville, in 1883. However, they first went under the name of the Black Arabs (wearing black shirts). Changing their name to Eastville Rovers in their second season, they won the Gloucestershire Senior Cup in 1888–89. Original members of the Bristol & District League in 1892, this eventually became the Western League and Eastville Rovers adopted professionalism in 1897.

The Memorial Stadium, Filton Avenue, Horfield, Bristol BS7 0BF.

Telephone: (0117) 909 6648.

Fax: (0117) 908 5530.

Ticket Office: (0117) 909 8848.

Website: www.bristolrovers.co.uk

Email: admin@bristolrovers.co.uk

Ground Capacity: 11,626.

Record Attendance: 11,433 v Sunderland, Worthington Cup 3rd rd, 31 October 2000 (Memorial Stadium). 9464 v Liverpool, FA Cup 4th rd, 8 February 1992 (Twerton Park). 38,472 v Preston NE, FA Cup 4th rd, 30 January 1960 (Eastville).

Pitch Measurements: 101m × 68m.

Chairman: Geoff Dunford.

Vice-chairman: Ron Craig.

Managing Director: Mike Turl.

Secretary: Rod Wesson.

Manager: Ian Atkins.

Assistant Manager: Kevan Broadhurst.

Physio: Phil Kite.

HONOURS

Football League: Division 2 best season: 4th, 1994–95; Division 3 (S) – Champions 1952–53; Division 3 – Champions 1989–90; Runners-up 1973–74.

FA Cup: best season: 6th rd, 1951, 1958.

Football League Cup: best season: 5th rd, 1971, 1972.

Colours: Blue and white quartered shirts, blue shorts, white stockings.

Change Colours: Yellow shirts, navy shorts, yellow stockings.

Year Formed: 1883. ***Turned Professional:*** 1897. ***Ltd Co.:*** 1896.

Previous Names: 1883, Black Arabs; 1884, Eastville Rovers; 1897, Bristol Eastville Rovers; 1898, Bristol Rovers. ***Club Nickname:*** 'Pirates'.

Previous Grounds: 1883, Purdown; Three Acres, Ashley Hill; Rudgeway, Fishponds; 1897, Eastville; 1986, Twerton Park; 1996, The Memorial Stadium.

First Football League Game: 28 August 1920, Division 3, v Millwall (a) L 0–2 – Stansfield; Bethune, Panes; Boxley, Kenny, Steele; Chance, Bird, Sims, Bell, Palmer.

Record League Victory: 7–0 v Brighton & HA, Division 3 (S), 29 November 1952 – Hoyle; Bamford, Fox; Pitt, Warren, Sampson; McIlvenny, Roost (2), Lambden (1), Bradford (1), Petherbridge (2), (1 og). 7–0 v Swansea T, Division 2, 2 October 1954 – Radford; Bamford, Watkins; Pitt, Muir, Anderson; Petherbridge, Bradford (2), Meyer, Roost (1), Hooper (2), (2 og). 7–0 v Shrewsbury T, Division 3, 21 March 1964 – Hall; Hillard, Gwyn Jones; Oldfield, Stone (1), Mabbutt; Jarman (2), Brown (1), Biggs (1p), Hamilton, Bobby Jones (2).

SKY SPORTS FACT FILE

In 1929–30 Bristol Rovers escaped having to seek re-election on goal average by beating Brentford 4–1 on the last day. Two of their goals were scored by Jack Phillips, top scorer with 24 League goals and previously with Brentford!

Record Cup Victory: 6–0 v Merthyr Tydfil, FA Cup 1st rd, 14 November 1987 – Martyn; Alexander (Dryden), Tanner, Hibbitt, Twentyman, Jones, Holloway, Meacham (1), White (2), Penrice (3) (Reece), Purnell.

Most League Points (2 for a win): 64, Division 3 (S), 1952–53.

Most League Points (3 for a win): 93, Division 3, 1989–90.

Most League Goals: 92, Division 3 (S), 1952–53.

Highest League Scorer in Season: Geoff Bradford, 33, Division 3 (S), 1952–53.

Most League Goals in Total Aggregate: Geoff Bradford, 242, 1949–64.

Most League Goals in One Match: 4, Sidney Leigh v Exeter C, Division 3S, 2 May 1921; 4, Jonah Wilcox v Bournemouth, Division 3S, 12 December 1925; 4, Bill Culley v QPR, Division 3S, 5 March 1927; Frank Curran v Swindon T, Division 3S, 25 March 1939; Vic Lambden v Aldershot, Division 3S, 29 March 1947; George Petherbridge v Torquay U, Division 3S, 1 December 1951; Vic Lambden v Colchester U, Division 3S, 14 May 1952; Geoff Bradford v Rotherham U, Division 2, 14 March 1959; Robin Stubbs v Gillingham, Division 2, 10 October 1970; Alan Warboys v Brighton & HA, Division 3, 1 December 1973; Jamie Cureton v Reading, Division 2, 16 January 1999.

Most Capped Player: Vitalijs Astafjevs, 31 (105), Latvia.

Most League Appearances: Stuart Taylor, 546, 1966–80.

Youngest League Player: Ronnie Dix, 15 years 173 days v Charlton Ath, 25 February 1928.

Record Transfer Fee Received: £2,000,000 from Fulham for Barry Hayles, November 1998 and £2,000,000 from WBA for Jason Roberts, July 2000.

Record Transfer Fee Paid: £370,000 to QPR for Andy Tillson, November 1992.

Football League Record: 1920 Original Member of Division 3; 1921–53 Division 3 (S); 1953–62 Division 2; 1962–74 Division 3; 1974–81 Division 2; 1981–90 Division 3; 1990–92 Division 2. 1992–93 Division 1; 1993–2001 Division 2; 2001–04 Division 3; 2004– FL2.

MANAGERS

Alfred Homer 1899–1920 *(continued as Secretary to 1928)*
Ben Hall 1920–21
Andy Wilson 1921–26
Joe Palmer 1926–29
Dave McLean 1929–30
Albert Prince-Cox 1930–36
Percy Smith 1936–37
Brough Fletcher 1938–49
Bert Tann 1950–68 *(continued as General Manager to 1972)*
Fred Ford 1968–69
Bill Dodgin Snr 1969–72
Don Megson 1972–77
Bobby Campbell 1978–79
Harold Jarman 1979–80
Terry Cooper 1980–81
Bobby Gould 1981–83
David Williams 1983–85
Bobby Gould 1985–87
Gerry Francis 1987–91
Martin Dobson 1991
Dennis Rofe 1992
Malcolm Allison 1992–93
John Ward 1993–96
Ian Holloway 1996–2001
Garry Thompson 2001
Gerry Francis 2001
Garry Thompson 2001–02
Ray Graydon 2002–04
Ian Atkins April 2004–

LATEST SEQUENCES

Longest Sequence of League Wins: 12, 18.10.1952 – 17.1.1953.

Longest Sequence of League Defeats: 8, 26.10.2002 – 21.12.2002.

Longest Sequence of League Draws: 5, 1.11.1975 – 22.11.1975.

Longest Sequence of Unbeaten League Matches: 32, 7.4.1973 – 27.1.1974.

Longest Sequence Without a League Win: 20, 5.4.1980 – 1.11.1980.

Successive Scoring Runs: 26 from 26.3.1927.

Successive Non-scoring Runs: 6 from 14.10.1922.

TEN YEAR LEAGUE RECORD

		P	W	D	L	F	A	Pts	Pos
1995-96	Div 2	46	20	10	16	57	60	70	10
1996-97	Div 2	46	15	11	20	47	50	56	17
1997-98	Div 2	46	20	10	16	70	64	70	5
1998-99	Div 2	46	13	17	16	65	56	56	13
1999-2000	Div 2	46	23	11	12	69	45	80	7
2000-01	Div 2	46	12	15	19	53	57	51	21
2001-02	Div 3	46	11	12	23	40	60	45	23
2002-03	Div 3	46	12	15	19	50	57	51	20
2003-04	Div 3	46	14	13	19	50	61	55	15
2004-05	FL 2	46	13	21	12	60	57	60	12

DID YOU KNOW ?

On 29 August 1960 Bristol Rovers found themselves 4–0 down at home to Leeds United. But they scored a minute after half-time and made it three in eight minutes. Pressing for an equaliser it finally came two minutes from the end at 4–4.

BRISTOL ROVERS 2004–05 LEAGUE RECORD

Match No.	*Date*	*Venue*	*Opponents*	*Result*	*H/T Score*	*Lg. Pos.*	*Goalscorers*	*Attendance*
1	Aug 7	A	Mansfield T	W 2-0	1-0	—	Agogo 2 [31, 52]	5709
2	10	H	Bury	D 2-2	1-1	—	Forrester (pen) [43], Anderson J [50]	8705
3	14	H	Notts Co	W 2-1	0-0	3	Edwards [62], Agogo [81]	8225
4	21	A	Darlington	W 1-0	0-0	3	Agogo [77]	3661
5	27	H	Southend U	W 2-1	1-0	—	Thorpe [13], Hunt [86]	9287
6	30	A	Rushden & D	D 0-0	0-0	2		3367
7	Sept 4	H	Shrewsbury T	D 0-0	0-0	2		8381
8	11	A	Leyton Orient	L 2-4	1-1	4	Forrester [28], Trollope [53]	3972
9	18	H	Lincoln C	D 0-0	0-0	6		7004
10	25	A	Northampton T	L 1-2	0-2	7	Savage [81]	5645
11	Oct 2	H	Oxford U	W 2-0	1-0	4	Agogo 2 [44, 82]	8049
12	9	A	Cambridge U	L 0-1	0-0	5		2748
13	16	A	Grimsby T	D 0-0	0-0	8		4691
14	19	H	Yeovil T	D 2-2	0-1	—	Hunt [64], Agogo [86]	9295
15	23	H	Kidderminster H	W 2-0	1-0	4	Agogo 2 [21, 74]	7020
16	30	A	Boston U	D 2-2	0-0	5	Forrester [88], Agogo [90]	2723
17	Nov 6	A	Swansea C	L 0-1	0-0	8		8778
18	20	H	Scunthorpe U	L 0-3	0-2	11		7039
19	27	A	Wycombe W	L 0-1	0-0	15		4999
20	Dec 7	H	Chester C	W 4-1	2-1	—	Disley [3], Forrester (pen) [45], Thorpe [71], Trollope [74]	5524
21	11	H	Macclesfield T	D 0-0	0-0	14		6504
22	18	A	Rochdale	D 0-0	0-0	15		2623
23	26	H	Leyton Orient	D 1-1	0-1	14	Forrester (pen) [51]	8414
24	29	A	Cheltenham T	D 1-1	1-1	—	Forrester [4]	5511
25	Jan 1	A	Shrewsbury T	L 0-2	0-0	14		5043
26	3	H	Northampton T	W 3-1	1-0	12	Hunt [39], Edwards [51], Agogo [90]	6961
27	8	H	Cambridge U	D 1-1	1-1	11	Agogo (pen) [25]	6510
28	15	A	Lincoln C	D 1-1	0-0	11	Agogo [67]	3929
29	22	H	Cheltenham T	D 1-1	1-1	11	Thorpe [45]	6954
30	29	A	Oxford U	L 2-3	0-2	15	Agogo [46], Walker [90]	7830
31	Feb 5	H	Grimsby T	W 3-0	3-0	13	Hunt [27], Williams [38], Walker [45]	6134
32	12	A	Yeovil T	L 2-4	1-1	15	Disley [17], Walker [88]	9153
33	19	H	Boston U	D 1-1	0-0	16	Agogo [74]	5563
34	22	A	Kidderminster H	D 1-1	0-1	—	Agogo [53]	2082
35	26	A	Macclesfield T	L 1-2	0-1	17	Elliott [55]	2114
36	Mar 5	H	Rochdale	D 0-0	0-0	16		5464
37	12	A	Bury	D 1-1	1-0	17	Disley [30]	2132
38	19	H	Mansfield T	D 4-4	2-1	17	Williams [21], Walker (pen) [45], Agogo (pen) [82], Forrester [88]	5294
39	26	A	Notts Co	W 2-1	1-1	17	Baudet (og) [44], Walker [53]	4258
40	28	H	Darlington	D 3-3	1-1	17	Walker 2 [45, 71], Elliott [69]	5918
41	Apr 1	A	Southend U	L 0-2	0-2	—		7858
42	9	H	Rushden & D	W 3-0	1-0	16	Walker [22], Disley [59], Shearer (og) [83]	5740
43	16	A	Chester C	D 2-2	2-0	15	Williams [23], Agogo [30]	2475
44	23	H	Swansea C	W 2-0	2-0	13	Walker [14], Agogo [26]	7433
45	30	A	Scunthorpe U	L 0-4	0-2	17		6925
46	May 7	H	Wycombe W	W 1-0	1-0	12	Walker [12]	7358

Final League Position: 12

GOALSCORERS

League (60): Agogo 19 (2 pens), Walker 10 (1 pen), Forrester 7 (3 pens), Disley 4, Hunt 4, Thorpe 3, Williams 3, Edwards 2, Elliott 2, Trollope 2, Anderson J 1, Savage 1, own goals 2.
Carling Cup (2): Thorpe 1, Walker 1.
FA Cup (1): Walker 1.
LDV Vans Trophy (9): Agogo 2, Forrester 2, Walker 2, Disley 1, Haldane 1, Thorpe 1.

Miller K 28	Gibb A 16 + 7	Ryan R 39 + 1	Edwards C 39 + 3	Anderson J 28 + 6	Hinton C 33 + 5	Trollope P 26 + 4	Hunt J 41	Forrester J 20 + 15	Agogo J 37 + 6	Campbell S 21 + 4	Savage D 21 + 6	Walker R 20 + 7	Elliott S 40 + 1	Williams R 9 + 8	Thorpe L 17 + 8	Disley C 18 + 10	Lescott A 24 + 2	Haldane L 1 + 12	Burns L 3	Sinclair S — + 2	Ward E — + 3	Clarke R 18	Cash B — + 1	Shakes R — + 1	Carruthers C 2 + 3	Bass J 3	Jeannin A 1	Louis J 1	Soares L — + 1	Match No.
1	2	3	4	5	6	7	8	9^{1}	10^{2}	11^{3}	12	13	14																	1
1	2	3	4	5		7^{1}	8	9^{2}	10	11^{3}	12	13	6	14																2
1	2^{1}	3	4	5	12	7	8	9^{3}	10	11^{2}	13		6		14															3
1	2	3	4	5	12	7^{2}	8	9^{3}	10^{1}	11	13		6		14															4
1	2^{3}	3	4	12	6	7	8	13	10	11^{1}	14		5		9^{2}															5
1	2	3	4	12	6	7	8	13	10	11^{1}			5		9^{2}															6
1	12	3	4	13	6^{2}	7^{3}	8	9	10	2		14	5		11^{1}															7
1	2	3	4		6	7^{1}	8	9	12	11^{3}		13	5		10^{2}	14														8
1	2	3	4	5		7^{2}	8	9^{1}	10	12			6		11	13														9
1	2^{2}	3	4	5	6	7^{1}	8■	9^{3}	10	11	12				13		14													10
1	2	3	4	5	12				10	11^{1}	7		6		9		8													11
1	2	3^{2}	4	5	6^{1}	13		12	10		8	14	7		9^{3}		11													12
1	2	3	4	5			8	12	10^{2}		7	9^{1}	6				11	13												13
1	2^{2}	3	4	5	12		8		10	13	7■	9^{1}	6■		14		11^{3}													14
1		3	4	5	2	7	8	12	10^{1}	6^{3}		9^{2}			13	14	11													15
1		3	4	5	2	7	8	12	10			9^{2}			13	14	11^{1}		6^{3}											16
1	12	3	4		2	7^{1}	8	13	10^{2}	6^{3}		14			9		11		5											17
1	12	3	4		2	7	8	9	10				6		13	11^{1}			5^{2}											18
1		3	4		2	7^{1}	8	12	10^{3}	5^{2}	11		6	13	9			14												19
1			4		2	12	8	9^{2}	13	11^{1}	7		6		10	5	3													20
1			4		2	7^{1}	8	9	12		11		6		10	5	3													21
1	13	12	4		2	7	8	9^{2}	14		11		6		10	5^{3}	3^{1}													22
1	12	3■	4	13	2	7	8	9^{2}	10^{3}	5^{1}	11		6							14										23
1			4	5	2	7^{1}	8	9^{2}	10	6^{3}	11		3		13	12					14									24
	12		4	5■	2	7^{3}	8	9^{2}	13	6^{1}	11		3		10			14				1								25
	2	3	4		6	7	8	9^{2}	12		11^{1}		5		10						14	1	13^{3}							26
	2	3	4		6	7	8^{2}	12	9	13			5		10^{3}	11^{1}		14				1								27
	2^{1}	3	4		6	7	8	9^{3}	10■	12^{2}			5		11	14					13	1								28
		3	4	12	2	7^{2}	8	9^{1}		11			5	13	10	6						1								29
		3		5	2		8	9^{3}	10	4^{2}	7^{1}	12	6			11	13	14				1								30
		3	4		12	7^{2}	8		10^{3}	6^{1}		9	5	13		11	2	14				1								31
		3	4^{1}		2	7	8		10	5^{2}		9		12		11	6	13				1								32
		3^{1}	4	12	2		8	13	10			9	5	11		7^{2}	6					1								33
1		3	4	5^{1}	2		8		10			9^{2}	6	11		12	7	13												34
1		3	4^{2}	5	2		8		10			9	6	12		11^{1}	7							13						35
1		3		5	4		8	12	10^{2}			9	6	11^{1}		7	2	13												36
1		3	12	5	2		8		10		7^{1}	9	6			11^{2}	4	13												37
		3		5	2^{2}		8	12	10			9	6	7		13	4	11^{1}				1								38
		3	12	5	2		8		10^{2}		7	9	6^{1}			4^{3}	11	13				1			14					39
		3	12	5	2^{3}		8^{1}	13	10		7	9	6	14		4^{2}	11					1								40
		3		5	2^{3}		8	12	10^{1}		7	9	6	13		4^{2}	11					1			14					41
		3	4	5					10		7	9	6	11^{1}		8	2			12		1								42
		3	4	5			8		10		7^{1}	9	6	11		12	2					1								43
		3^{3}	4	5			8■	12	10^{1}		7	9	6	11^{2}		13						1			14	2				44
	12		4	5		13		9^{1}			7^{2}	10	6	11		2■						1			8	3				45
			4^{1}	5		12						9	6	11^{3}			7	13				1			8	2	3	10^{2}	14	46

FA Cup

First Round	Carlisle U	(h)	1-1
		(a)	0-1

Carling Cup

First Round	Brighton & HA	(a)	2-1
Second Round	Norwich C	(a)	0-1

LDV Vans Trophy

First Round	Kidderminster H	(h)	1-0
Second Round	Barnet	(h)	2-0
Quarter-Final	Wycombe W	(h)	1-0
Semi-Final	Leyton Orient	(a)	2-1
Southern Final	Southend U	(h)	1-2
		(a)	2-2

BURNLEY FL Championship

FOUNDATION

The majority of those responsible for the formation of the Burnley club in 1881 were from the defunct rugby club Burnley Rovers. Indeed, they continued to play rugby for a year before changing to soccer and dropping 'Rovers' from their name. The changes were decided at a meeting held in May 1882 at the Bull Hotel.

Turf Moor, Harry Potts Way, Burnley, Lancashire BB10 4BX.

Telephone: 0870 443 1882.

Fax: (01282) 700 014.

Ticket Office: 0870 443 1914.

Website: www.burnleyfc.com

Email: info@burnleyfootballclub.net

Ground Capacity: 22,516.

Record Attendance: 54,775 v Huddersfield T, FA Cup 3rd rd, 23 February 1924.

Pitch Measurements: 112yd × 70yd.

Chairman: Barry Kilby.

Vice-chairman: Ray Ingleby.

Chief Executive: Dave Edmundson.

Secretary: Cathy Pickup.

Manager: Steve Cotterill.

Assistant Manager: Dave Kevan.

Physio: Andy Mitchell.

Colours: Claret and blue shirts, white shorts, white stockings.

Change Colours: White shirts with blue trim.

Year Formed: 1882.

Turned Professional: 1883.

Ltd Co.: 1897.

Previous Name: 1881, Burnley Rovers; 1882, Burnley.

Club Nickname: 'The Clarets'.

Previous Grounds: 1881, Calder Vale; 1882, Turf Moor.

First Football League Game: 8 September 1888, Football League, v Preston NE (a) L 2–5 – Smith; Lang, Bury, Abrams, Friel, Keenan, Brady, Tait, Poland (1), Gallocher (1), Yates.

Record League Victory: 9–0 v Darwen, Division 1, 9 January 1892 – Hillman; Walker, McFettridge, Lang, Matthews, Keenan, Nicol (3), Bowes, Espie (1), McLardie (3), Hill (2).

Record Cup Victory: 9–0 v Crystal Palace, FA Cup 2nd rd (replay), 10 February 1909 – Dawson; Barron, McLean; Cretney (2), Leake, Moffat; Morley, Ogden, Smith (3), Abbott (2), Smethams (1). 9–0 v New Brighton, FA Cup 4th rd, 26 January 1957 – Blacklaw; Angus, Winton; Seith, Adamson, Miller; Newlands (1), McIlroy (3), Lawson (3), Cheesebrough (1), Pilkington (1). 9–0 v Penrith, FA Cup 1st rd, 17 November 1984 – Hansbury; Miller, Hampton, Phelan, Overson (Kennedy), Hird (3 incl. 1p), Grewcock (1), Powell (2), Taylor (3), Biggins, Hutchison.

HONOURS

Football League: Division 1 – Champions 1920–21, 1959–60; Runners-up 1919–20, 1961–62; Division 2 – Champions 1897–98, 1972–73; Runners-up 1912–13, 1946–47, 1999–2000; Promoted from Division 2, 1993–94 (play-offs); Division 3 – Champions 1981–82; Division 4 – Champions 1991–92. Record 30 consecutive Division 1 games without defeat 1920–21.

FA Cup: Winners 1914; Runners-up 1947, 1962.

Football League Cup: Semi-final 1961, 1969, 1983.

Anglo-Scottish Cup: Winners 1979.

Sherpa Van Trophy: Runners-up 1988.

European Competitions: *European Cup:* 1960–61. *European Fairs Cup:* 1966–67.

SKY SPORTS FACT FILE

The season after suffering relegation from the First Division through Test Matches in 1897–98, Burnley gained promotion via the same route and beating neighbours Blackburn Rovers in the process. One 9–3 win in the season was against Loughborough.

Record Defeat: 0–10 v Aston Villa, Division 1, 29 August 1925 and v Sheffield U, Division 1, 19 January 1929.

Most League Points (2 for a win): 62, Division 2, 1972–73.

Most League Points (3 for a win): 88, Division 2, 1999–2000.

Most League Goals: 102, Division 1, 1960–61.

Highest League Scorer in Season: George Beel, 35, Division 1, 1927–28.

Most League Goals in Total Aggregate: George Beel, 178, 1923–32.

Most League Goals in One Match: 6, Louis Page v Birmingham C, Division 1, 10 April 1926.

Most Capped Player: Jimmy McIlroy, 51 (55), Northern Ireland.

Most League Appearances: Jerry Dawson, 522, 1907–28.

Youngest League Player: Tommy Lawton, 16 years 174 days v Doncaster R, 28 March 1936.

Record Transfer Fee Received: £1,500,000 from WBA for Richard Chaplow, June 2005.

Record Transfer Fee Paid: £1,000,000 to Stockport C for Ian Moore, November 2000 and £1,000,000 to Bradford C for Robbie Blake, January 2002.

Football League Record: 1888 Original Member of the Football League; 1897–98 Division 2; 1898–1900 Division 1; 1900–13 Division 2; 1913–30 Division 1; 1930–47 Division 2; 1947–71 Division 1; 1971–73 Division 2; 1973–76 Division 1; 1976–80 Division 2; 1980–82 Division 3; 1982–83 Division 2; 1983–85 Division 3; 1985–92 Division 4; 1992–94 Division 2; 1994–95 Division 1; 1995–2000 Division 2; 2000–04 Division 1; 2004– FLC.

MANAGERS

Arthur F. Sutcliffe 1893–96 *(Secretary-Manager)*
Harry Bradshaw 1896–99 *(Secretary-Manager)*
Ernest Magnall 1899–1903 *(Secretary-Manager)*
Spen Whittaker 1903–10
R. H. Wadge 1910–11 *(Secretary-Manager)*
John Haworth 1911–25
Albert Pickles 1925–32
Tom Bromilow 1932–35
Alf Boland 1935–39 *(Secretary-Manager)*
Cliff Britton 1945–48
Frank Hill 1948–54
Alan Brown 1954–57
Billy Dougall 1957–58
Harry Potts 1958–70 *(General Manager to 1972)*
Jimmy Adamson 1970–76
Joe Brown 1976–77
Harry Potts 1977–79
Brian Miller 1979–83
John Bond 1983–84
John Benson 1984–85
Martin Buchan 1985
Tommy Cavanagh 1985–86
Brian Miller 1986–89
Frank Casper 1989–91
Jimmy Mullen 1991–96
Adrian Heath 1996–97
Chris Waddle 1997–98
Stan Ternent 1998–2004
Steve Cotterill June 2004–

LATEST SEQUENCES

Longest Sequence of League Wins: 10, 16.11.1912 – 18.1.1913.

Longest Sequence of League Defeats: 8, 2.1.1995 – 25.2.1995.

Longest Sequence of League Draws: 6, 21.2.1931 – 28.3.1931.

Longest Sequence of Unbeaten League Matches: 30, 6.9.1920 – 25.3.1921.

Longest Sequence Without a League Win: 24, 16.4.1979 – 17.11.1979.

Successive Scoring Runs: 27 from 13.2.1926.

Successive Non-scoring Runs: 6 from 9.8.1997.

TEN YEAR LEAGUE RECORD

		P	*W*	*D*	*L*	*F*	*A*	*Pts*	*Pos*
1995-96	Div 2	46	14	13	19	56	68	55	17
1996-97	Div 2	46	19	11	16	71	55	68	9
1997-98	Div 2	46	13	13	20	55	65	52	20
1998-99	Div 2	46	13	16	17	54	73	55	15
1999-2000	Div 2	46	25	13	8	69	47	88	2
2000-01	Div 2	46	21	9	16	50	54	72	7
2001-02	Div 1	46	21	12	13	70	62	75	7
2002-03	Div 1	46	15	10	21	65	89	55	16
2003-04	Div 1	46	13	14	19	60	77	53	19
2004-05	FL C	46	15	15	16	38	39	60	13

DID YOU KNOW ?

In four of his five seasons with Burnley Irish international striker Billy Hamilton was top scorer including his first season 1979–80 when playing in only the last 25 matches. His total of 58 goals with the club came from 200 League games.

BURNLEY 2004–05 LEAGUE RECORD

Match No.	Date	Venue	Opponents	Result	H/T Score	Lg. Pos.	Goalscorers	Attendance
1	Aug 7	H	Sheffield U	D 1-1	1-0	—	Hyde [16]	16,956
2	10	A	Rotherham U	D 0-0	0-0	—		6243
3	14	A	Watford	W 1-0	0-0	6	Moore [64]	12,048
4	21	H	Wolverhampton W	D 1-1	1-1	10	Blake [24]	13,869
5	28	A	West Ham U	L 0-1	0-0	11		22,119
6	30	H	Gillingham	L 1-2	0-1	14	Moore [87]	11,574
7	Sept 11	H	Crewe Alex	W 3-0	2-0	12	McGreal [12], Blake [42], Chaplow [49]	11,274
8	14	A	Wigan Ath	D 0-0	0-0	—		9746
9	18	A	Leicester C	D 0-0	0-0	14		22,495
10	25	H	Stoke C	D 2-2	2-1	14	Moore [3], Blake (pen) [19]	12,981
11	28	H	Cardiff C	W 1-0	0-0	—	Chaplow [88]	7200
12	Oct 2	A	Reading	D 0-0	0-0	11		15,400
13	16	A	Ipswich T	D 1-1	1-0	10	Blake [19]	23,183
14	19	H	Coventry C	D 2-2	0-0	—	Blake (pen) [65], Branch [73]	10,919
15	22	H	Derby Co	L 0-2	0-0	—		13,703
16	30	A	QPR	L 0-3	0-3	17		15,638
17	Nov 3	A	Leeds U	W 2-1	2-1	—	Roche [10], Duffy [31]	27,490
18	6	H	Ipswich T	L 0-2	0-1	16		11,969
19	13	H	Nottingham F	W 1-0	1-0	14	Blake [6]	11,622
20	20	A	Brighton & HA	W 1-0	0-0	12	Blake [70]	6109
21	27	H	Millwall	W 1-0	0-0	8	Blake (pen) [61]	11,471
22	Dec 4	A	Plymouth Arg	L 0-1	0-0	11		13,508
23	11	H	Preston NE	W 2-0	1-0	11	Blake 2 [45, 85]	15,318
24	18	A	Sunderland	L 1-2	1-1	12	Branch [36]	27,102
25	28	H	Wigan Ath	W 1-0	1-0	11	Branch [24]	16,485
26	Jan 3	A	Stoke C	W 1-0	0-0	11	Cahill [79]	15,689
27	15	H	Reading	D 0-0	0-0	10		11,392
28	22	A	Cardiff C	L 0-2	0-1	13		11,562
29	Feb 5	H	Leeds U	L 0-1	0-0	16		17,789
30	12	A	Coventry C	W 2-0	0-0	12	Oster [64], Moore [69]	13,236
31	15	A	Crewe Alex	D 1-1	0-1	—	Grant [53]	7718
32	23	A	Derby Co	D 1-1	1-0	—	Valois [34]	23,701
33	26	A	Preston NE	L 0-1	0-0	13		18,202
34	Mar 4	H	Sunderland	L 0-2	0-1	—		12,103
35	8	H	Leicester C	D 0-0	0-0	—		10,933
36	12	H	Rotherham U	W 2-1	2-1	13	Grant [11], Sinclair [14]	10,539
37	15	A	Wolverhampton W	L 0-2	0-1	—		24,336
38	19	A	Sheffield U	L 1-2	0-1	14	Akinbiyi [84]	19,374
39	Apr 2	H	Watford	W 3-1	2-0	14	Bowditch [20], O'Connor [43], Valois [90]	11,507
40	5	H	West Ham U	L 0-1	0-0	—		12,209
41	9	A	Gillingham	L 0-1	0-0	14		9447
42	16	H	Brighton & HA	D 1-1	1-0	14	Akinbiyi [23]	11,611
43	19	H	QPR	W 2-0	1-0	—	Akinbiyi 2 [43, 81]	10,396
44	23	A	Nottingham F	L 0-1	0-0	14		24,165
45	30	H	Plymouth Arg	W 2-0	0-0	13	Valois (pen) [87], O'Connor [90]	12,893
46	May 8	A	Millwall	D 0-0	0-0	13		12,171

Final League Position: 13

GOALSCORERS

League (38): Blake 10 (3 pens), Akinbiyi 4, Moore 4, Branch 3, Valois 3 (1 pen), Chaplow 2, Grant 2, O'Connor 2, Bowditch 1, Cahill 1, Duffy 1, Hyde 1, McGreal 1, Oster 1, Roche 1, Sinclair 1.
Carling Cup (7): Blake 3 (1 pen), Branch 1, Camara 1, Valois 1, own goal 1.
FA Cup (4): Moore 2, Hyde 1, own goal 1.

Coyne D 20	Duff M 37 + 5	Camara M 45	Grant T 37 + 5	McGreal J 38 + 1	Sinclair F 36	Hyde M 37 + 1	Chaplow R 16 + 5	Moore I 30 + 5	Blake R 24	Branch G 39 + 4	Roche L 17 + 12	Valois J 18 + 12	O'Neill M — + 2	Pilkington J — + 1	Duffy R 3 + 4	Sanokho A — + 3	Jensen B 26 + 1	O'Connor J 20 + 1	Cahill G 27	Oster J 12 + 3	Whittingham P 7	Akinbiyi A 9 + 1	Bowditch D 8 + 2	*Match No.*
1	2	3	4^{1}	5	6	7	8	9	10	11	12													1
1	2	3	4	5	6	7	8	9	10	11														2
1	2	3	4	5	6	7	8^{1}	9	10	11	12													3
1	2	3	4	5	6	7	8	9	10	11														4
1	2	3	4	5	6	7	8	9	10	11^{1}	12													5
1	2	3	4	5	6	7■	8	9	10	11														6
1	2	3	4	5	6		8^{1}	9	10^{3}	11	7^{2}	13	12	14										7
1	2	3	4	5	6		8	9	10	11	7^{1}	12												8
1	2	3	4	5	6		8	9	10	11		7												9
1	2■	3	4^{1}	5	6	7	8	9	10	11					12									10
1		3	4^{1}	5	6	12	8	9	10	11		7^{2}			2	13								11
1	2	3		5	6	4	8	9	10	11		7												12
1	2^{2}	3	4	5	6	7	8^{3}	9^{1}	10	11	12	14			13									13
1	2	3	12	5	6	4	8^{1}	9	10	11	13	7^{2}												14
1	2	3	12	5	6	4	8^{2}	9	10	11		7^{1}			13									15
1^{6}	11	3	4	5	6	8	12		9	10^{2}	2	7^{1}					15	13						16
	2	3	4	5^{2}	6	8			9		7		12		11^{1}	13	1	10						17
		3	4	5	6^{1}	8			9	10	2				11	12	1	7						18
	2	3	4	5		8^{2}		12	9		7	11^{1}			13		1	10	6					19
	5	3	8		6			9	10	11	2						1	7	4					20
	2	3	4		6			9	10	11	7						1	8	5					21
	2	3	4	12	6			9	10	11	7^{1}						1	8	5					22
	2	3	4^{1}		6	8		9	10		7	12					1	11	5					23
	2	3		5		4	12	9	10	11^{1}	13	7^{2}					1	8	6					24
	2	3	4	5		8	12	9		10	7^{1}						1	11	6					25
	2^{1}	3	4	5	6	7	13	9		11	12						1	10^{2}	8					26
	2^{1}	3	4	5	6		8	9		10^{2}	12	13					1	11	7					27
		3	4	5	6^{1}	7	13	9		12	2	11^{2}					1	10	8					28
		3	4	5	6■	7		9		10	2	12					1		8	11^{1}				29
	2	3	4	5		8		9		10	12	11					1		6	7^{1}				30
	2	3	4	5	6	8		12		9^{1}		11					1			7	10			31
	5	3	4			8		9^{1}		12	2	11					1		6	7	10			32
	5	3	4					9		8	2	11					1		6	7	10			33
	2^{2}	3	4^{1}		6	8		9		7	12	11					1		5		10	13■		34
	2			5	3	4		9		8		11					1		6	7	10			35
	14	3	4	5	2	8		12		13		11^{1}					1		6	7	10^{2}		9^{3}	36
	13	3	4	5■	2	8		12		14		11^{1}					1		6	7	10^{3}		9^{2}	37
	5	3			4	8		12		11^{2}	2	13					1		6	7^{1}		9	10	38
	12	3	13	5	6	4				11^{1}		14					1	8	2	7^{3}		10	9^{2}	39
1	12	3	13	5	2^{2}	4				11^{1}		14						8	6	7^{3}		10	9	40
	2	3	12	5		4				9		11^{2}					1	8	6	7^{1}		10	13	41
1	2^{1}	3	4	5		8				11	12							7	6			10	9	42
	2	3	4^{3}	5		8				11	12	13					1	7	6	14		10^{2}	9^{1}	43
1	2	3	4^{3}	5		8				11^{1}	9^{2}	12						7	6	13		10	14	44
	12	3	4^{2}	5	2	8				11		13					1	7	6^{1}	14		10	9^{3}	45
1	2	3	4	5	6	7				11								8	10			9		46

FA Cup

Third Round	Liverpool	(h)	1-0
Fourth Round	Bournemouth	(h)	2-0
Fifth Round	Blackburn R	(h)	0-0
		(a)	1-2

Carling Cup

First Round	Bury	(a)	3-2
Second Round	Wolverhampton W	(h)	1-1
Third Round	Aston Villa	(h)	3-1
Fourth Round	Tottenham H	(h)	0-3

BURY FL Championship 2

FOUNDATION

A meeting at the Waggon & Horses Hotel, attended largely by members of Bury Wesleyans and Bury Unitarians football clubs, decided to form a new Bury club. This was officially formed at a subsequent gathering at the Old White Horse Hotel, Fleet Street, Bury on 24 April 1885.

Gigg Lane, Bury BL9 9HR.

Telephone: (0161) 764 4881.

Fax: (0161) 764 5521.

Ticket Office: (0161) 764 4881.

Website: www.buryfc.co.uk

Email: admin@buryfc.co.uk

Ground Capacity: 11,669.

Record Attendance: 35,000 v Bolton W, FA Cup 3rd rd, 9 January 1960.

Pitch Measurements: 112yd × 70yd.

Secretary: Jill Neville.

Manager: Graham Barrow.

Assistant Manager: Kelham O'Hanlon.

Physio: Joe Hinnigan.

Colours: White shirts, royal blue shorts, royal blue stockings.

Change Colours: All yellow.

Year Formed: 1885.

Turned Professional: 1885.

Ltd Co.: 1897.

Club Nickname: 'Shakers'.

First Football League Game: 1 September 1894, Division 2, v Manchester C (h) W 4–2 – Lowe; Gillespie, Davies; White, Clegg, Ross; Wylie, Barbour (2), Millar (1), Ostler (1), Plant.

Record League Victory: 8–0 v Tranmere R, Division 3, 10 January 1970 – Forrest; Tinney, Saile; Anderson, Turner, McDermott; Hince (1), Arrowsmith (1), Jones (4), Kerr (1), Grundy, (1 og).

Record Cup Victory: 12–1 v Stockton, FA Cup 1st rd (replay), 2 February 1897 – Montgomery; Darroch, Barbour; Hendry (1), Clegg, Ross (1); Wylie (3), Pangbourn, Millar (4), Henderson (2), Plant, (1 og).

Record Defeat: 0–10 v Blackburn R, FA Cup pr rd, 1 October 1887. 0–10 v West Ham U, Milk Cup 2nd rd 2nd leg, 25 October 1983.

HONOURS

Football League: Division 1 best season: 4th, 1925–26; Division 2 – Champions 1894–95, 1996–97; Runners-up 1923–24; Division 3 – Champions 1960–61; Runners-up 1967–68; Promoted from Division 3 (3rd) 1995–96.

FA Cup: Winners 1900, 1903.

Football League Cup: Semi-final 1963.

SKY SPORTS FACT FILE

In 1900 the FA Cup Final victory for Bury was conveyed to crowds congregating back home in Lancashire where the result was wired to G.R. Barker Football Requisites in Broad Street!

Most League Points (2 for a win): 68, Division 3, 1960–61.

Most League Points (3 for a win): 84, Division 4, 1984–85 and Division 2, 1996–97.

Most League Goals: 108, Division 3, 1960–61.

Highest League Scorer in Season: Craig Madden, 35, Division 4, 1981–82.

Most League Goals in Total Aggregate: Craig Madden, 129, 1978–86.

Most League Goals in One Match: 5, Eddie Quigley v Millwall, Division 2, 15 February 1947; 5, Ray Pointer v Rotherham U, Division 2, 2 October 1965.

Most Capped Player: Bill Gorman, 11 (13), Republic of Ireland and (4), Northern Ireland.

Most League Appearances: Norman Bullock, 506, 1920–35.

Youngest League Player: Brian Williams, 16 years 133 days v Stockport Co, 18 March 1972.

Record Transfer Fee Received: £1,100,000 from Ipswich T for David Johnson, November 1997.

Record Transfer Fee Paid: £200,000 to Ipswich T for Chris Swailes, November 1997 and £200,000 to Swindon T for Darren Bullock, February 1999.

Football League Record: 1894 Elected to Division 2; 1895–1912 Division 1; 1912–24 Division 2; 1924–29 Division 1; 1929–57 Division 2; 1957–61 Division 3; 1961–67 Division 2; 1967–68 Division 3; 1968–69 Division 2; 1969–71 Division 3; 1971–74 Division 4; 1974–80 Division 3; 1980–85 Division 4; 1985–96 Division 3; 1996–97 Division 2; 1997–99 Division 1; 1999–2002 Division 2; 2002–04 Division 3; 2004– FL2.

MANAGERS

T. Hargreaves 1887
(Secretary-Manager)
H. S. Hamer 1887–1907
(Secretary-Manager)
Archie Montgomery 1907–15
William Cameron 1919–23
James Hunter Thompson 1923–27
Percy Smith 1927–30
Arthur Paine 1930–34
Norman Bullock 1934–38
Jim Porter 1944–45
Norman Bullock 1945–49
John McNeil 1950–53
Dave Russell 1953–61
Bob Stokoe 1961–65
Bert Head 1965–66
Les Shannon 1966–69
Jack Marshall 1969
Les Hart 1970
Tommy McAnearney 1970–72
Alan Brown 1972–73
Bobby Smith 1973–77
Bob Stokoe 1977–78
David Hatton 1978–79
Dave Connor 1979–80
Jim Iley 1980–84
Martin Dobson 1984–89
Sam Ellis 1989–90
Mike Walsh 1990–95
Stan Ternent 1995–98
Neil Warnock 1998–99
Andy Preece 2000–04
Graham Barrow January 2004–

LATEST SEQUENCES

Longest Sequence of League Wins: 9, 26.9.1960 – 19.11.1960.

Longest Sequence of League Defeats: 8, 18.8.2001 – 25.9.2001.

Longest Sequence of League Draws: 6, 6.3.1999 – 3.4.1999.

Longest Sequence of Unbeaten League Matches: 18, 4.2.1961 – 29.4.1961.

Longest Sequence Without a League Win: 19, 1.4.1911 – 2.12.1911.

Successive Scoring Runs: 24 from 1.9.1894.

Successive Non-scoring Runs: 6 from 11.1.1969.

TEN YEAR LEAGUE RECORD

		P	W	D	L	F	A	Pts	Pos
1995-96	Div 3	46	22	13	11	66	48	79	3
1996-97	Div 2	46	24	12	10	62	38	84	1
1997-98	Div 1	46	11	19	16	42	58	52	17
1998-99	Div 1	46	10	17	19	35	60	47	22
1999-2000	Div 2	46	13	18	15	61	64	57	15
2000-01	Div 2	46	16	10	20	45	59	58	16
2001-02	Div 2	46	11	11	24	43	75	44	22
2002-03	Div 3	46	18	16	12	57	56	70	7
2003-04	Div 3	46	15	11	20	54	64	56	12
2004-05	FL 2	46	14	16	16	54	54	58	17

DID YOU KNOW?

In February 1961 championship-chasing Bury transferred centre-half John McGrath to Newcastle United for £24,000 but received Bob Stokoe in part of the deal. After that they were unbeaten in 18 matches while taking the title.

BURY 2004–05 LEAGUE RECORD

Match No.	Date	Venue	Opponents	Result	H/T Score	Lg. Pos.	Goalscorers	Attendance
1	Aug 7	H	Yeovil T	W 3-1	0-1	—	Nugent 2 [66, 77], Jones [81]	3171
2	10	A	Bristol R	D 2-2	1-1	—	Mattis [7], Barry-Murphy [68]	8705
3	14	A	Grimsby T	L 1-5	1-1	16	Barry-Murphy [2]	4277
4	21	H	Chester C	D 1-1	0-1	15	Porter [60]	2870
5	28	A	Rochdale	W 3-0	1-0	7	Mattis [27], Swailes [52], Nugent [77]	3912
6	30	H	Kidderminster H	W 4-0	2-0	4	Nugent [33], Porter 2 [45, 64], Flitcroft [60]	2504
7	Sept 4	H	Lincoln C	L 0-1	0-1	8		3188
8	11	A	Shrewsbury T	D 2-2	1-0	10	Mattis [16], Nugent [54]	3801
9	18	H	Scunthorpe U	L 0-1	0-0	11		2846
10	25	A	Oxford U	L 1-3	0-1	14	Nugent [70]	4308
11	Oct 2	H	Macclesfield T	W 2-1	1-1	11	Newby [23], Nugent [72]	2859
12	9	A	Leyton Orient	D 1-1	0-1	13	Porter [75]	3398
13	16	A	Darlington	W 2-1	2-0	10	Porter [35], Dunfield [39]	4642
14	19	H	Boston U	D 1-1	1-1	—	Challinor [10]	2001
15	23	H	Rushden & D	D 1-1	0-0	9	Mattis [65]	2672
16	30	A	Mansfield T	D 0-0	0-0	10		4147
17	Nov 6	A	Cheltenham T	L 0-1	0-0	14		3061
18	20	H	Notts Co	W 1-0	1-0	10	Porter [22]	2938
19	27	A	Swansea C	W 3-1	2-1	7	Nugent [3], Mattis [7], Barry-Murphy [83]	6971
20	Dec 7	H	Wycombe W	D 2-2	1-0	—	Nugent 2 [8, 66]	1866
21	11	H	Southend U	L 0-1	0-1	12		2522
22	18	A	Cambridge U	D 1-1	0-0	14	Nugent [49]	2875
23	28	A	Northampton T	L 0-2	0-1	16		6041
24	Jan 1	A	Lincoln C	L 0-1	0-1	17		3962
25	3	H	Oxford U	D 0-0	0-0	17		2783
26	8	H	Leyton Orient	D 0-0	0-0	17		2192
27	15	A	Scunthorpe U	L 2-3	1-1	18	Porter [31], Keogh [48]	5365
28	22	H	Northampton T	W 2-0	1-0	18	Newby [42], Keogh [58]	2687
29	29	A	Macclesfield T	L 1-2	1-0	18	Unsworth [14]	2513
30	Feb 5	H	Darlington	L 0-1	0-1	18		2971
31	8	H	Shrewsbury T	D 0-0	0-0	—		2233
32	12	A	Boston U	D 2-2	1-2	18	Kennedy (pen) [36], Newby [51]	2351
33	19	H	Mansfield T	L 0-2	0-1	18		2529
34	22	A	Rushden & D	L 0-3	0-3	—		1803
35	26	A	Southend U	L 0-1	0-1	20		5553
36	Mar 5	H	Cambridge U	W 2-1	0-1	20	Newby [56], Flitcroft [90]	2437
37	12	H	Bristol R	D 1-1	0-1	20	Whaley [78]	2132
38	19	A	Yeovil T	W 1-0	1-0	18	Whaley [14]	6269
39	25	H	Grimsby T	W 3-1	2-0	—	Porter [1], Barry-Murphy [12], Kazim-Richards [53]	5671
40	28	A	Chester C	L 1-2	1-0	18	Kazim-Richards [12]	3107
41	Apr 2	H	Rochdale	D 0-0	0-0	19		4606
42	9	A	Kidderminster H	D 2-2	1-1	18	Porter [9], Shakes [90]	2474
43	16	A	Wycombe W	W 2-1	1-1	18	Whaley [34], Flitcroft [81]	4703
44	23	H	Cheltenham T	W 3-1	3-0	17	Barry-Murphy [3], Kazim-Richards [21], Shakes [38]	2490
45	30	A	Notts Co	W 1-0	0-0	15	Barry-Murphy [47]	6424
46	May 7	H	Swansea C	L 0-1	0-1	18		7575

Final League Position: 18

GOALSCORERS

League (54): Nugent 11, Porter 9, Barry-Murphy 6, Mattis 5, Newby 4, Flitcroft 3, Kazim-Richards 3, Whaley 3, Keogh 2, Shakes 2, Challinor 1, Dunfield 1, Jones 1, Kennedy 1 (pen), Swailes 1, Unsworth 1.
Carling Cup (2): Challinor 1, Mattis 1.
FA Cup (5): Mattis 2, Challinor 1, Nugent 1, Porter 1.
LDV Vans Trophy (1): Scott 1.

Garner G 27	Barrass M 8 + 1	Kennedy T 46	Unsworth L 34 + 2	Challinor D 43	Woodthorpe C 29 + 1	Flitcroft D 32 + 4	Mattis D 39	Newby J 17 + 19	Nugent D 26	Barry-Murphy B 43 + 2	Jones G 1 + 2	Whaley S 22 + 16	Porter C 29 + 3	Dunfield T 7 + 8	Scott P 20 + 3	Swailes D 20	Kazim-Richards C 10 + 20	Marriott A 19	Keogh A 4	Fitzgerald J 14	Moore D — + 3	Harkins G 4 + 1	Savage B 5	Cartledge J 1 + 4	Shakes R 4 + 3	Boshell D 2 + 4	Buchanan D — + 3	*Match No.*
1	2	3	4	5	6	7^1	8	9^2	10^3	11	12	13	14															1
1	2^2	3	4	5	6■	7	8	12	10^1	11	9^3	13	14															2
1	2	3	4	5		7	8^2	12	10	11		6	9^1	13														3
1		3	2^1	5	6■	7	8		10	11		12	9^2	13	4													4
1		3	2	5		7	8^3	12	10^1	11^2		14	9	13	4	6												5
1		3	2	5	12	7■	8	13	10^2	11^3			9	14	4	6^1												6
1		3	2^2	5			8		10	11	12	13	9^1	7	4	6												7
1	2	3		5		7	8	12	10	11^1			9		4	6												8
1		3	2	5		7	8	12	10	11			9^1		4	6												9
1		3^1	2^2	5	6	7	8	12	10	11		13	9		4													10
1		3	2	5	6	7^2	8	9^3	10^1	11		13		12		4	14											11
1		3	2	5	6	7^1	8	9^2	10^3	11		13	12			4	14											12
1		3	2	5	6		8	12	10^1	11			9	7^2	13	4												13
1		3	2	5	6		8	12	10	11		13	9^2	7^1		4												14
1	2	3		5	6		8	7^1	10	11			9^2	12		4	13											15
1		3	2	5	6	12	8	13	10	11^3		14	9^2	7^1		4												16
		3	2	5	6^1		8	12	10	11		13	9^3	7^2		4	14	1										17
	2	3	5		6	7	8	12	10^2	11			9^1			4	13	1										18
	2	3	5		6	7	8	12	10^1	11			9^2			4	13	1										19
		3	2	5	6■	7^2		12	10^1	11		8	9^3		13	4	14	1										20
		3^1	2	5		7^2	8	12	10	11		13	9^3		6	4	14	1										21
	12	3	2	5		7		13	10^2	11^3		8	9^1		6	4■	14	1										22
	2	3^1	4	5		7■	8^2	9^3	10	11		14		12	6		13	1										23
		3	2^2	5	6		8		10	11		13	9	12	7^1	4		1										24
		3		5	6		8	12	10^2	11		2	9^1	7		4	13	1										25
		3	12	5	6		8	13	10	11		2	9^2	7^1		4		1										26
		3	12	5	6^1	13	8	10^2		11		2	9^3		4		14	1	7									27
		3	2	5	6		8	9^2		11		7					12	1	10^1	4	13							28
		3	2	5	6	12	8	9^2		11^1		7					13	1	10^3	4	14							29
		3	4^2	5	6	12	8^1	9		11		7					13	1	10	2								30
		3	4	5	6	7		9		11		2^1					10	1			12	8						31
		3	4	5	6	7		9^1		11							12	1		2		8	10					32
		3	2	5	6^1	7		9		11		12					13	1		4		8	10^2					33
		3	2	5		7		9		11		12						1		4		8^1	10	6				34
		3	4	5		7		9		11^1		2					8	1		6		12	10					35
1		3	4		6	7	8	12				2	9				11			5			10^1					36
1		3^2	4	5	6	7	8	10		12		2	9				13			11^1								37
1		3	4	5	6	7	8	10^1		12		2^3	9^2		14		13			11								38
1		3	4^2	5		7	8	10^1		11		2	9^3		6		12							13	14			39
1		3		5		7	8			11		2	9		4		10								6^1	12		40
1		3^2		5		7	8			11		2	9		6		10			4^1				12		13		41
1		3		5		7	8			11		2^3	9^1		4		10^2			6					13	12	14	42
1		3		5		7	8			11		2			4		9^2			6				12	13	10^1		43
1		3		5			8			11		2			4		9			6				12	7^2	10^1	13	44
1		3		5	6	7	8^1			11		2			4		9								10	12		45
1		3^1		5	6	7	8			11		2			4		9								10		12	46

FA Cup

First Round	Vauxhall M	(h)	5-2
Second Round	Northampton T	(a)	0-1

Carling Cup

First Round	Burnley	(h)	2-3

LDV Vans Trophy

First Round	Stockport Co	(a)	1-3

CAMBRIDGE UNITED Conference National

FOUNDATION

The football revival in Cambridge began soon after World War II when the Abbey United club (formed 1912) decided to turn professional in 1949. In 1951 they changed their name to Cambridge United. They were competing in the United Counties League before graduating to the Eastern Counties League in 1951 and the Southern League in 1958.

Abbey Stadium, Newmarket Road, Cambridge CB5 8LN.

Telephone: (01223) 566 500.

Fax: (01223) 566 502.

Website: www.cambridgeunited.com

Email: web@cambridge-united.co.uk

Ground Capacity: 8,696.

Record Attendance: 14,000 v Chelsea, Friendly, 1 May 1970.

Pitch Measurements: 110yd × 74yd.

Chairman: Roger Hunt.

Vice-chairman: John Howard.

Secretary: Andrew Pincher.

Caretaker Manager: Rob Newman.

Physio: Greg Reid.

Colours: Amber shirts, black shorts, amber stockings.

Change Colours: Navy and sky blue shirts, sky blue shorts, sky blue stockings.

Year Formed: 1912.

Turned Professional: 1949.

Ltd Co.: 1948.

Previous Name: 1919, Abbey United; 1951, Cambridge United.

Club Nickname: The 'U's'.

First Football League Game: 15 August 1970, Division 4, v Lincoln C (h) D 1–1 – Roberts; Thompson, Meldrum (1), Slack, Eades, Hardy, Leggett, Cassidy, Lindsey, McKinven, Harris.

Record League Victory: 6–0 v Darlington, Division 4, 18 September 1971 – Roberts; Thompson, Akers, Guild, Eades, Foote, Collins (1p), Horrey, Hollett, Greenhalgh (4), Phillips, (1 og). 6–0 v Hartlepool U, Division 4, 11 February 1989 – Vaughan; Beck, Kimble, Turner, Chapple (1), Daish, Clayton, Holmes, Taylor (3 incl. 1p), Bull (1), Leadbitter (1).

HONOURS

Football League: Division 2 best season: 5th, 1991–92; Division 3 – Champions 1990–91; Runners-up 1977–78, 1998–99; Division 4 – Champions 1976–77; Promoted from Division 4 1989–90 (play-offs).

FA Cup: best season: 6th rd, 1990 (shared record for Fourth Division club), 1991.

Football League Cup: best season: 5th rd, 1993.

LDV Vans Trophy: Runners-up 2002.

SKY SPORTS FACT FILE

Given his debut in goal on 8 May 2004 in the last match of the season John Ruddy had the satisfaction of keeping a clean sheet against Leyton Orient and saving a twice taken penalty to enable his team to win the match 1–0.

Record Cup Victory: 5–1 v Bristol C, FA Cup 5th rd second replay, 27 February 1990 – Vaughan; Fensome, Kimble, Bailie (O'Shea), Chapple, Daish, Cheetham (Robinson), Leadbitter (1), Dublin (2), Taylor (1), Philpott (1).

Record Defeat: 0–7 v Sunderland, League Cup 2nd rd, 1 October 2002.

Most League Points (2 for a win): 65, Division 4, 1976–77.

Most League Points (3 for a win): 86, Division 3, 1990–91.

Most League Goals: 87, Division 4, 1976–77.

Highest League Scorer in Season: David Crown, 24, Division 4, 1985–86.

Most League Goals in Total Aggregate: John Taylor, 86, 1988–92; 1996–2001.

Most League Goals in One Match: 5, Steve Butler v Exeter C, Division 2, 4 April 1994.

Most Capped Player: Tom Finney, 7 (15), Northern Ireland.

Most League Appearances: Steve Spriggs, 416, 1975–87.

Youngest League Player: Andy Sinton, 16 years 228 days v Wolverhampton W, 2 November 1982.

Record Transfer Fee Received: £1,000,000 from Manchester U for Dion Dublin, August 1992 and £1,000,000 from Leicester C for Trevor Benjamin, July 2000.

MANAGERS

Bill Whittaker 1949–55
Gerald Williams 1955
Bert Johnson 1955–59
Bill Craig 1959–60
Alan Moore 1960–63
Roy Kirk 1964–66
Bill Leivers 1967–74
Ron Atkinson 1974–78
John Docherty 1978–83
John Ryan 1984–85
Ken Shellito 1985
Chris Turner 1985–90
John Beck 1990–92
Ian Atkins 1992–93
Gary Johnson 1993–95
Tommy Taylor 1995–96
Roy McFarland 1996–2001
John Beck 2001
John Taylor 2002–04
Claude Le Roy 2004
Herve Renard 2004
Steve Thompson 2004–05
Rob Newman May 2005–
(Caretaker Manager)

Record Transfer Fee Paid: £192,000 to Luton T for Steve Claridge, November 1992.

Football League Record: 1970 Elected to Division 4; 1973–74 Division 3; 1974–77 Division 4; 1977–78 Division 3; 1978–84 Division 2; 1984–85 Division 3; 1985–90 Division 4; 1990–91 Division 3; 1991–92 Division 2; 1992–93 Division 1; 1993–95 Division 2; 1995–99 Division 3; 1999– 2002 Division 2; 2002–04 Division 3; 2004–05 FL2; 2005– Conference.

LATEST SEQUENCES

Longest Sequence of League Wins: 7, 19.2.1977 – 1.4.1977.

Longest Sequence of League Defeats: 7, 8.4.1985 – 30.4.1985.

Longest Sequence of League Draws: 6, 6.9.1986 – 30.9.1986.

Longest Sequence of Unbeaten League Matches: 14, 9.9.1972 – 10.11.1972.

Longest Sequence Without a League Win: 31, 8.10.1983 – 23.4.1984.

Successive Scoring Runs: 26 from 9.4.2002.

Successive Non-scoring Runs: 5 from 29.9.1973.

TEN YEAR LEAGUE RECORD

		P	*W*	*D*	*L*	*F*	*A*	*Pts*	*Pos*
1995-96	Div 3	46	14	12	20	61	71	54	16
1996-97	Div 3	46	18	11	17	53	59	65	10
1997-98	Div 3	46	14	18	14	63	57	60	16
1998-99	Div 3	46	23	12	11	78	48	81	2
1999-2000	Div 2	46	12	12	22	64	65	48	19
2000-01	Div 2	46	14	11	21	61	77	53	19
2001-02	Div 2	46	7	13	26	47	93	34	24
2002-03	Div 3	46	16	13	17	67	70	61	12
2003-04	Div 3	46	14	14	18	55	67	56	13
2004-05	FL 2	46	8	16	22	39	62	30	24

10 points deducted for entering administration.

DID YOU KNOW ?

On 7 September 1954 Cambridge United played a pre-season friendly at Fakenham and recorded a 14–3 victory. Peter Dobson scored six times and Percy Anderson five. Dobson was the club's leading marksman for two seasons.

CAMBRIDGE UNITED 2004–05 LEAGUE RECORD

Match No.	Date	Venue	Opponents	Result		H/T Score	Lg. Pos.	Goalscorers	Attendance
1	Aug 7	A	Wycombe W	L	1-2	0-0	—	Easter 70	4726
2	10	H	Leyton Orient	D	1-1	0-1	—	Walker 53	4114
3	14	H	Shrewsbury T	W	1-0	0-0	10	Chillingworth 53	3135
4	21	A	Southend U	D	0-0	0-0	10		3941
5	28	H	Swansea C	L	0-1	0-1	18		2949
6	30	A	Darlington	D	1-1	0-0	17	Chillingworth 58	3350
7	Sept 4	A	Boston U	L	1-2	0-1	21	Easter 51	3026
8	11	H	Mansfield T	D	2-2	1-1	22	Oli 17, Easter 54	3549
9	18	A	Chester C	D	0-0	0-0	22		2771
10	25	H	Grimsby T	L	0-2	0-0	23		3824
11	Oct 2	A	Kidderminster H	D	1-1	0-0	23	Mbome 90	2356
12	9	H	Bristol R	W	1-0	0-0	20	Turner 46	2748
13	15	H	Northampton T	L	0-1	0-1	—		4118
14	19	A	Macclesfield T	D	1-1	1-0	—	Easter 39	1436
15	23	A	Cheltenham T	L	1-2	1-1	22	Tann 2	3315
16	30	H	Lincoln C	L	0-1	0-0	23		3604
17	Nov 6	A	Rochdale	L	1-2	0-1	23	Konte 47	2353
18	20	H	Rushden & D	W	3-1	2-1	23	Turner 3 5, 10, 52	3466
19	27	A	Notts Co	L	1-2	0-1	23	Tudor 53	5080
20	Dec 7	H	Scunthorpe U	L	1-2	1-0	—	Hodgson 35	2666
21	11	A	Oxford U	L	1-2	0-2	23	Easter 79	4844
22	18	H	Bury	D	1-1	0-0	23	Konte 64	2875
23	28	H	Yeovil T	L	3-5	1-0	24	Hodgson 37, Konte 50, Easter 87	3828
24	Jan 1	H	Boston U	L	0-1	0-0	24		3507
25	3	A	Grimsby T	L	0-3	0-2	24		4148
26	8	A	Bristol R	D	1-1	1-1	24	Tudor 26	6510
27	11	A	Mansfield T	D	0-0	0-0	—		3557
28	15	H	Chester C	D	0-0	0-0	24		3185
29	22	A	Yeovil T	L	1-2	0-0	24	Tudor 77	6204
30	29	H	Kidderminster H	L	1-3	1-1	24	Tudor 16	3948
31	Feb 4	A	Northampton T	D	2-2	0-1	—	Chillingworth 2 48, 60	6615
32	12	H	Macclesfield T	L	0-1	0-0	24		2926
33	19	A	Lincoln C	L	1-2	0-2	24	Webb 52	4672
34	22	H	Cheltenham T	W	1-0	0-0	—	Tudor 61	2021
35	26	H	Oxford U	W	2-1	0-1	23	Turner 69, Tudor 90	3765
36	Mar 5	A	Bury	L	1-2	1-0	24	Roberts 28	2437
37	12	A	Leyton Orient	D	1-1	0-0	24	Bramble 75	3759
38	19	H	Wycombe W	W	2-1	2-1	24	Bramble 13, Roberts 38	4649
39	25	A	Shrewsbury T	D	0-0	0-0	—		5309
40	28	H	Southend U	L	0-2	0-2	24		6715
41	Apr 2	A	Swansea C	L	0-3	0-0	24		8664
42	9	H	Darlington	W	3-1	1-1	24	Roberts 24, Duncan 48, Turner 83	3116
43	16	A	Scunthorpe U	L	0-4	0-1	24		5642
44	23	H	Rochdale	D	0-0	0-0	24		3738
45	30	A	Rushden & D	W	1-0	1-0	24	Bramble (pen) 28	5104
46	May 7	H	Notts Co	D	0-0	0-0	24		4723

Final League Position: 24

GOALSCORERS

League (39): Easter 6, Tudor 6, Turner 6, Chillingworth 4, Bramble 3 (1 pen), Konte 3, Roberts 3, Hodgson 2, Duncan 1, Mbome 1, Oli 1, Tann 1, Walker 1, Webb 1.
Carling Cup (0).
FA Cup (1): Tudor 1.
LDV Vans Trophy (1): Easter 1.

Ruddy J 38	Latte-Yedo I 5+6	El Kholti A 13+2 / Blackburn L —+3	Duncan A 40+2	Angus S 14 / Roberts I 11	Walker J 36	Tudor S 22+4	Guttridge L 14+3	Webb D 15+7	Chillingworth D 22+6	Nicholls A 25+3	Quinton D 14+17	Easter J 15+9	Tann A 34+2	Turner J 16+22	Gleeson D 21+9	Robinson M —+4	Beech T —+4	Hutton R —+2 / Bramble T 9	Mbome K 12+1	Marshall S 1 / Toner C 6+2	Oli D 4	Jowsey J 1	Goodhind W 25+1	Davies A —+2	Konte A 6+3	Hodgson R 9+1	Price L 6	Fuller A —+2	Bimson S 16+3	Anselin C 2	Sonmer M 24	Heath C 5+1	Johnson B —+1	Rea S 4	Wardley S 1+2	Newey T 15+1	Carruthers M 5	*Match No.*
1	2■	3	4	5	6	7[1]	8	9	10[2]	11[3]	14	13	12																									1
1	2	3	12	5	6	7	8	9	10[2]	11[1]			4	13																								2
1	2[1]	3	4	5	6	12	8	9	10[2]	11	7[3]			13	14																							3
1		3	4	5	6	11		9[2]	10[1]	8	7[3]		2		12	14	13																					4
1		3[3]	4	5[1]	6		8	9[2]	10	11	13	7	2		12			14																				5
1	2[3]	3	4[2]	5	6[1]			12	10	11	7	9	8		13			14																				6
1	2	3[3]	4	5	11			9		7	12	10[2]	6		13		14		8[1]																			7
		3		5	6				10	11		7	4	12	2				8	1	9[1]																	8
1		3	12	5	6				10[3]	7[1]		11	4	13	2		14		8		9[2]																	9
		3		5	6				10[1]	7[2]	13	11	4	12	2				8		9	1																10
1		11	4		6[3]				12	7	14	10	5	13	2				8		9[2]		3[1]															11
1		11	4		6[3]				10[1]	7			5	9[2]	2	12	13		8				3	14														12
1		12	4	5	11				10	7[3]		13	6	9	2[1]	14			8[2]				3															13
1			4	5	11				12	7		9[1]	6	10	2				8				3															14
1			4	5	11	12			13	2		7[1]	6	10[2]		14			8				3		9[3]													15
1			4	5	11	12			13	7		14	6	10[3]	2[1]								3		9[2]	8												16
1			4		6■	7			12	13		9[1]	5	14	2[3]				8[2]				3		10	11												17
			4			7	8[3]	9			11		5[1]	10[2]	12				13				2			6	1	14	3									18
			4			7	8	9				12		10	6[1]								2			11	1	13	3	5[2]								19
			4				8				7			10[3]					6				2■	13	12	11[2]	1			5	3	9[1]	14					20
			5			7	8				6	12		10[1]					4[3]				3		13	11[2]	1		14		2	9						21
			5		6		8				12	9		13									2		10	11	1		3		4[2]	7[1]						22
			4		6					12	7	9		13									2		10	11[2]	1		3		5	8[1]						23
1		11[2]	4		6	7[1]						9	5	12	2										10[3]	13			3		8	14						24
1					6	7[1]		13		12	8[2]	9	4	14	2											11[3]			3		5	10						25
1		12	4		6	7		9[1]			8[3]	13		10[2]	2														3		11			5	14			26
1			4		6			9[1]			7	8		10	2										12				3		11[2]			5	13			27
1			4		6	7[1]		9[2]	13		8	12	14	10	2														3					5	11[3]			28
1	12		4		6	7		9[2]	10		14		5[1]	13	8								2						3							11[3]		29
1			4		6	7	8		10		12		11[1]	13	2[3]								14						3[2]					5			9	30
1			4		6	7[2]	8[1]		10		14		5	13	12														3		2					11[3]	9	31
1			4		6	7	8[2]		10		13	12	5										2						3[3]		11					14	9[1]	32
1	12		4		6	7	8[3]	9[1]	10[2]		14	13	5										2						3		11							33
1	12		4		6	7	13	9[3]			11		5	14															3		2					8[2]	10[1]	34
1	12		4		6	7	13	9[3]					5	14									2						3		11					8[2]	10[1]	35
1	12	13		9	6	7	8[2]				11		5	10[1]									4								2					3		36
1			4	9[2]	6[1]	7	12	13			14		5	8[3]				10					2								3					11		37
1		14	4	9[1]	6[2]	7		12		8	13		5		2[3]			10													11					3		38
1			4	9[1]	6			12		7			5	8[2]	2			10		13											11					3		39
1			4	9	6[1]	7			10[2]	8	12		5	13	2					14											11[3]					3		40
1	12		4	9[2]		13			10[3]	7			5	14				8		6[1]			2								11					3		41
1		14	4	9[1]					10[2]	8	7			12	13			11[3]		6			2								5					3		42
1			4	9[2]					10	8	12		5	13				7		6[1]			2								11					3		43
1			4	9[2]				12	10	7	13		5	14				8		6[3]			2								11[1]					3		44
1			4	9					10[1]	7			5	13	12			8[2]		6			2						14		11					3[3]		45
1			4	9[3]				12		7	13			10[1]	2[2]			8		6			5						14		11					3		46

FA Cup
First Round Halifax T (a) 1-3

Carling Cup
First Round Watford (a) 0-1

LDV Vans Trophy
First Round Boston U (a) 1-0
Second Round Leyton Orient (h) 0-2

CARDIFF CITY FL Championship

FOUNDATION

Credit for the establishment of a first class professional football club in such a rugby stronghold as Cardiff, is due to members of the Riverside club formed in 1899 out of a cricket club of that name. Cardiff became a city in 1905 and in 1908 the South Wales and Monmouthshire FA granted Riverside permission to call themselves Cardiff City. The club turned professional under that name in 1910.

Ninian Park, Sloper Road, Cardiff CF11 8SX.

Telephone: (029) 2022 1011.

Fax: (029) 2034 1148.

Ticket Office: 0845 345 1400.

Website: www.cardiffcityfc.co.uk

Ground Capacity: 21,432.

Record Attendance: 62,634, Wales v England, 17 October 1959.

Club Record Attendance: 57,893 v Arsenal, Division 1, 22 April 1953.

Pitch Measurements: 110yd × 75yd.

Owner: Sam Hammam.

Vice-chairman: Michael Isaac.

Chief Executive: David Temme.

Club Secretary: Jason Turner.

Manager: Dave Jones.

Assistant Manager: Terry Burton.

Physio: Steve Allen.

Colours: Royal blue shirts, royal blue shorts, royal blue stockings.

Change Colours: Yellow shirts, blue shorts, yellow stockings.

Year Formed: 1899.

Turned Professional: 1910.

Ltd Co.: 1910.

Previous Names: 1899, Riverside; 1902, Riverside Albion; 1908, Cardiff City.

Club Nickname: 'Bluebirds'.

Previous Grounds: Riverside, Sophia Gardens, Old Park and Fir Gardens. Moved to Ninian Park, 1910.

First Football League Game: 28 August 1920, Division 2, v Stockport Co (a) W 5–2 – Kneeshaw; Brittan, Leyton; Keenor (1), Smith, Hardy; Grimshaw (1), Gill (2), Cashmore, West, Evans (1).

Record League Victory: 9–2 v Thames, Division 3 (S), 6 February 1932 – Farquharson; E. L. Morris, Roberts; Galbraith, Harris, Ronan; Emmerson (1), Keating (1), Jones (1), McCambridge (1), Robbins (5).

HONOURS

Football League: Division 1 – Runners-up 1923–24; Division 2 – Runners-up 1920–21, 1951–52, 1959–60; Division 2 – 2002–03 (play-offs); Division 3 (S) – Champions 1946–47; Division 3 – Champions 1992–93. Runners-up 1975–76, 1982–83, 2000–01; Division 4 – Runners-up 1987–88.

FA Cup: Winners 1927 (only occasion the Cup has been won by a club outside England); Runners-up 1925.

Football League Cup: Semi-final 1966.

Welsh Cup: Winners 22 times (joint record).

Charity Shield: Winners 1927.

European Competitions: *European Cup-Winners' Cup:* 1964–65, 1965–66, 1967–68 (semi-finalists), 1968–69, 1969–70, 1970–71, 1971–72, 1973–74, 1974–75, 1976–77, 1977–78, 1988–89, 1992–93, 1993–94.

SKY SPORTS FACT FILE

John Toshack scored his 100th first team goal for Cardiff City in a European Cup-Winners' Cup match against Nantes in France on 4 November 1971. Number one had arrived as a 16 year old substitute on 13 November 1965.

Record Cup Victory: 8–0 v Enfield, FA Cup 1st rd, 28 November 1931 – Farquharson; Smith, Roberts; Harris (1), Galbraith, Ronan; Emmerson (2), Keating (3); O'Neill (2), Robbins, McCambridge.

Record Defeat: 2–11 v Sheffield U, Division 1, 1 January 1926.

Most League Points (2 for a win): 66, Division 3 (S), 1946–47.

Most League Points (3 for a win): 86, Division 3, 1982–83.

Most League Goals: 95, Division 3, 2000–01.

Highest League Scorer in Season: Robert Earnshaw, 31, Division 2, 2002–03.

Most League Goals in Total Aggregate: Len Davies, 128, 1920–31.

Most League Goals in One Match: 5, Hugh Ferguson v Burnley, Division 1, 1 September 1928; 5, Walter Robbins v Thames, Division 3S, 6 February 1932; 5, William Henderson v Northampton T, Division 3S, 22 April 1933.

Most Capped Player: Alf Sherwood, 39 (41), Wales.

Most League Appearances: Phil Dwyer, 471, 1972–85.

Youngest League Player: John Toshack, 16 years 236 days v Leyton Orient, 13 November 1965.

Record Transfer Fee Received: £3,000,000 from WBA for Robert Earnshaw, August 2004.

Record Transfer Fee Paid: £1,700,000 to Stoke C for Peter Thorne, September 2001.

Football League Record: 1920 Elected to Division 2; 1921–29 Division 1; 1929–31 Division 2; 1931–47 Division 3 (S); 1947–52 Division 2; 1952–57 Division 1; 1957–60 Division 2; 1960–62 Division 1; 1962–75 Division 2; 1975–76 Division 3; 1976–82 Division 2; 1982–83 Division 3; 1983–85 Division 2; 1985–86 Division 3; 1986–88 Division 4; 1988–90 Division 3; 1990–92 Division 4; 1992–93 Division 3; 1993–95 Division 2; 1995–99 Division 3; 1999–2000 Division 2; 2000–01 Division 3; 2001–03 Division 2; 2003–04 Division 1; 2004– FLC.

MANAGERS

Davy McDougall 1910–11
Fred Stewart 1911–33
Bartley Wilson 1933–34
B. Watts-Jones 1934–37
Bill Jennings 1937–39
Cyril Spiers 1939–46
Billy McCandless 1946–48
Cyril Spiers 1948–54
Trevor Morris 1954–58
Bill Jones 1958–62
George Swindin 1962–64
Jimmy Scoular 1964–73
Frank O'Farrell 1973–74
Jimmy Andrews 1974–78
Richie Morgan 1978–82
Len Ashurst 1982–84
Jimmy Goodfellow 1984
Alan Durban 1984–86
Frank Burrows 1986–89
Len Ashurst 1989–91
Eddie May 1991–94
Terry Yorath 1994–95
Eddie May 1995
Kenny Hibbitt *(Chief Coach)* 1995
Phil Neal 1996
Russell Osman 1996–97
Kenny Hibbitt 1996–98
Frank Burrows 1998–99
Billy Ayre 1999–2000
Bobby Gould 2000
Alan Cork 2000–02
Lennie Lawrence 2002–05
Dave Jones May 2005–

LATEST SEQUENCES

Longest Sequence of League Wins: 9, 26.10.1946 – 28.12.1946.

Longest Sequence of League Defeats: 7, 4.11.1933 – 25.12.1933.

Longest Sequence of League Draws: 6, 29.11.1980 – 17.1.1981.

Longest Sequence of Unbeaten League Matches: 21, 21.9.1946 – 1.3.1947.

Longest Sequence Without a League Win: 15, 21.11.1936 – 6.3.1937.

Successive Scoring Runs: 23 from 24.10.1992.

Successive Non-scoring Runs: 8 from 20.12.1952.

TEN YEAR LEAGUE RECORD

		P	*W*	*D*	*L*	*F*	*A*	*Pts*	*Pos*
1995-96	Div 3	46	11	12	23	41	64	45	22
1996-97	Div 3	46	20	9	17	56	54	69	7
1997-98	Div 3	46	9	23	14	48	52	50	21
1998-99	Div 3	46	22	14	10	60	39	80	3
1999-2000	Div 2	46	9	17	20	45	67	44	21
2000-01	Div 3	46	23	13	10	95	58	82	2
2001-02	Div 2	46	23	14	9	75	50	83	4
2002-03	Div 2	46	23	12	11	68	43	81	6
2003-04	Div 1	46	17	14	15	68	58	65	13
2004-05	FL C	46	13	15	18	48	51	54	16

DID YOU KNOW?

In 1912–13 Cardiff City enjoyed their best season in the Southern League finishing as champions with just one defeat. That season saw the advent of Fred Keenor signed as an amateur from Roath Wednesdays. He turned professional on 28 November.

CARDIFF CITY 2004–05 LEAGUE RECORD

Match No.	Date	Venue	Opponents	Result		H/T Score	Lg. Pos.	Goalscorers	Attendance
1	Aug 7	A	Crewe Alex	D	2-2	1-1	—	Robinson [44], Lee [59]	7339
2	10	H	Coventry C	W	2-1	0-1	—	Earnshaw [54], Bullock [61]	14,031
3	13	H	Plymouth Arg	L	0-1	0-1	—		12,697
4	21	A	Ipswich T	L	1-3	0-1	18	Lee [55]	21,828
5	28	H	Stoke C	L	0-1	0-1	22		12,929
6	30	A	Wigan Ath	L	1-2	0-2	23	Lee (pen) [66]	9004
7	Sept 11	A	Nottingham F	D	0-0	0-0	23		21,607
8	14	H	Watford	L	0-3	0-2	—		10,606
9	18	H	Derby Co	L	0-2	0-1	23		12,008
10	25	A	Wolverhampton W	W	3-2	1-1	22	Parry [11], Thorne [48], Kavanagh [59]	27,896
11	28	A	Burnley	L	0-1	0-0	—		7200
12	Oct 2	H	Leeds U	D	0-0	0-0	23		17,006
13	16	H	Rotherham U	W	2-0	0-0	21	Thorne 2 [56, 75]	11,004
14	19	A	Brighton & HA	D	1-1	0-1	—	Bullock [81]	6112
15	23	A	Millwall	D	2-2	1-0	21	O'Neil [40], Lee [68]	10,476
16	30	H	Leicester C	D	0-0	0-0	20		13,759
17	Nov 2	H	West Ham U	W	4-1	2-0	—	Lee [3], Ledley [16], Parry [54], McAnuff [77]	14,222
18	6	A	Rotherham U	D	2-2	0-0	18	Ledley [70], Parry [74]	5093
19	13	A	Reading	L	1-2	0-2	20	Jerome [87]	16,107
20	19	H	Preston NE	L	0-1	0-1	—		10,950
21	27	A	QPR	L	0-1	0-1	21		15,146
22	Dec 4	H	Gillingham	W	3-1	2-1	21	Jerome [13], Thorne 2 (1 pen) [41 (p), 55]	10,623
23	11	H	Sunderland	L	0-2	0-0	21		12,528
24	18	A	Sheffield U	L	1-2	1-0	21	Harris [41]	18,240
25	26	H	Wolverhampton W	D	1-1	1-0	21	Jerome [17]	16,699
26	28	A	Watford	D	0-0	0-0	21		13,409
27	Jan 1	A	Derby Co	W	1-0	1-0	21	Thorne [27]	22,800
28	3	H	Nottingham F	W	3-0	0-0	21	Thorne 2 (1 pen) [55 (p), 86], Kavanagh [90]	13,545
29	15	A	Leeds U	D	1-1	0-1	21	Thorne (pen) [52]	29,548
30	22	H	Burnley	W	2-0	1-0	19	Langley [13], Kavanagh [74]	11,562
31	Feb 6	A	West Ham U	L	0-1	0-0	19		23,716
32	12	H	Brighton & HA	W	2-0	2-0	19	Thorne (pen) [16], Collins [19]	11,435
33	22	H	Millwall	L	0-1	0-1	—		11,424
34	26	A	Sunderland	L	1-2	0-2	20	Vidmar [85]	32,788
35	Mar 5	H	Sheffield U	W	1-0	0-0	20	Ledley [75]	12,250
36	12	A	Coventry C	D	1-1	1-1	20	Bullock [19]	17,059
37	15	H	Ipswich T	L	0-1	0-0	—		11,768
38	19	H	Crewe Alex	D	1-1	1-0	20	Gabbidon [21]	10,007
39	Apr 2	A	Plymouth Arg	D	1-1	1-0	21	Langley [22]	18,045
40	5	A	Stoke C	W	3-1	1-1	—	Jerome 2 [26, 58], Thorne (pen) [60]	12,785
41	9	H	Wigan Ath	L	0-2	0-0	19		16,858
42	16	A	Preston NE	L	0-3	0-0	21		15,141
43	19	A	Leicester C	D	1-1	0-1	—	Ardley [58]	21,336
44	23	H	Reading	W	2-0	2-0	17	Thorne [12], Jerome [30]	14,821
45	30	A	Gillingham	D	1-1	0-0	19	Parry [85]	10,810
46	May 8	H	QPR	W	1-0	1-0	16	McAnuff [27]	15,722

Final League Position: 16

GOALSCORERS

League (48): Thorne 12 (5 pens), Jerome 6, Lee 5 (1 pen), Parry 4, Bullock 3, Kavanagh 3, Ledley 3, Langley 2, McAnuff 2, Ardley 1, Collins 1, Earnshaw 1, Gabbidon 1, Harris 1, O'Neil 1, Robinson 1, Vidmar 1.
Carling Cup (8): Bullock 2, Thorne 2, Anthony 1, Earnshaw 1, Jerome 1, Lee 1.
FA Cup (3): Collins 1, Lee 1, McAnuff 1.

Margetson M 3 + 1	Weston R 23 + 2	Vidmar T 23 + 5	Kavanagh G 28	Gabbidon D 45	Page R 8 + 1	Langley R 24 + 1	Bullock L 8 + 13	Earnshaw R 4	Lee A 24 + 14	Robinson J 8	Croft G — + 1	Campbell A 6 + 6	Collins J 32 + 2	Parry P 12 + 12	Warner T 26	McAnuff J 42 + 1	Boland W 18 + 3	Thorne P 28 + 3	Barker C 38 + 1	Fleetwood S 1 + 5	Williams D 17 + 3	O'Neil G 8 + 1	Jerome C 21 + 8	Ledley J 20 + 8	Thomas D — + 1	Harris N 1 + 2	Inamoto J 13 + 1	Alexander N 17	Koskela T — + 2	Ardley N 8	Boulding M — + 4	*Match No.*
1	2^{1}	3	4	5	6	7	8	9^{2}	10	11^{3}	12	13	14																			1
1	2	3	4	5	6	7	8	9^{1}	10	11		12																				2
1	2^{1}	3	4	5	6	7^{3}	8^{2}	9	10	11		13	12	14																		3
	12	3	4	2^{1}	6	7		9^{2}	10	11		13	5	14	1	8^{3}																4
	2		4	5	6		12		10	11^{1}		9	3	13	1	8	7^{2}															5
	2	3	4	5	6		12		10	11^{2}		9		13	1	8	7^{1}															6
15	2	3	4	5	6				10	11^{1}		9^{2}		12	1^{6}	8	7	13														7
	2	3	4	5	6^{1}				10	11		9^{3}		13	1	8	7^{2}	14	12													8
	2	6	4	5			8		12			13		11^{2}	1	7		10	3	9^{1}												9
		6	4	5			12		9^{1}					11	1	8^{2}	7	10	3		2	13										10
		6	4	5			12		9^{1}					11	1	7		10	3		2	8										11
		6		5								9^{1}		11	1	8	7	10	3		2	4	12									12
		6	4	5					9					11^{1}	1	7		10	3		2	8		12								13
		6	4	5			12		9^{2}			13			1	7		10	3		2	8		11^{1}								14
		6	4	5					9						1	7		10	3		2	8		11								15
			4	5			12		9^{2}				6	11^{1}	1	7			3		2	8	13	10								16
			4	5					9				6	10^{2}	1	7	12		3		2	8^{1}	13	11								17
			4	5					9				6	10^{2}	1	7^{1}	12		3		2	8	13	11								18
			4■	5			12		9^{2}				6	10^{3}	1	7^{1}	8		3	13	2		14	11								19
	12			5			8		9				6	10	1	7	4^{2}		3^{3}		2^{1}		13	11	14							20
				5			8		9^{1}				6	10	1	7	4	12	3		2		13	11^{2}								21
				5									6	10	1	7	4	8	3		2		9^{1}	11		12						22
		6	4										5	12	1	7^{2}	8^{1}	10	3		2		9	11		13						23
			4■	5									6	12	1	13	8	10	3		2		11^{2}	7^{1}		9						24
	2	4		5		12							6		1	7^{3}	8	10	3	13			9^{2}	11^{1}			14					25
	2	11		5	12		13		14				6^{1}		1	7	4	10	3				9^{3}				8^{2}					26
	2		4	5		11			12				6	13	1	7^{2}		10	3				9^{1}				8					27
	2	14	4	5		11			12				6	13^{3}	1	7		10	3				9^{1}				8^{2}					28
	2		4	5		11			12				6		1	7		10	3				9^{1}	13			8^{2}					29
	2	12	4	5		11			9			10^{2}	6			7			3^{1}					13			8	1				30
	2^{1}	12	4	5		11			9				6			7		10	3					13			8^{2}	1				31
	2		4	5		11	12		9^{2}				6			7		10	3					13			8^{1}	1				32
	2^{1}		4	5		11^{2}	12		9^{3}				6■			7		10	3				14	13			8	1				33
	2^{3}	6	4	5		11			12■							7		10	3		14		9^{1}	13			8^{2}	1				34
	2			5		11	12						6			7		10^{1}	3	13			9^{2}	8			4	1				35
	2^{2}			5		11	10						6			7			3	12	13		9^{1}	8			4	1				36
	2			5		11^{1}	10						6			7			3	12			9	8			4^{2}	1	13			37
	2			5		11	12		9^{1}				6			7			3				10	8			4^{2}	1	13			38
	2^{1}	12		5		8			13				6			11		10^{2}	3				9^{3}	4				1		7	14	39
		2		5		8			12				6			11		10^{1}	3				9^{2}	4				1		7	13	40
		2		5		8			12				6			11^{2}		10^{1}	3				9	4				1		7	13	41
		2		5		8			12				6			11^{1}	13	10^{2}	3				9^{3}	4				1		7	14	42
		2		5		8			12				6			11	4	10	3				9^{1}	13				1		7^{2}		43
		2^{2}		5		8			12				6			11	4	10	3		13		9^{1}					1		7		44
				5		8	14		12				6	13		11^{2}	4	10	3		2^{3}		9^{1}					1		7		45
		12		5		8			14				6	13		11	4	10^{3}	3		2^{1}		9^{2}					1		7		46

FA Cup

Third Round	Blackburn R	(h)	1-1
		(a)	2-3

Carling Cup

First Round	Kidderminster H	(a)	1-1
Second Round	Milton Keynes D	(a)	4-1
Third Round	Bournemouth	(a)	3-3
Fourth Round	Portsmouth	(h)	0-2

CARLISLE UNITED FL Championship 2

FOUNDATION

Carlisle United came into being in 1903 through the amalgamation of Shaddongate United and Carlisle Red Rose. The new club was admitted to the Second Division of the Lancashire Combination in 1905–06, winning promotion the following season. Devonshire Park was officially opened on 2 September 1905, when St Helens Town were the visitors. Despite defeat in a disappointing 3-2 start, a respectable mid-table position was achieved.

Brunton Park, Warwick Road, Carlisle CA1 1LL.

Telephone: (01228) 526 237.

Fax: (01228) 554 141.

Ticket Office: (01228) 526 237.

Website: www.carlisleunited.co.uk

Email: enquiries@carlisleunited.co.uk

Ground Capacity: 16,063.

Record Attendance: 27,500 v Birmingham C, FA Cup 3rd rd, 5 January 1957 and v Middlesbrough, FA Cup 5th rd, 7 February 1970.

Pitch Measurements: 117yd × 72yd.

Chairman: H. A. Jenkins.

Secretary: Sarah McKnight.

Manager: Paul Simpson.

Assistant Manager: Dennis Booth.

Physio: Neil Dalton.

Colours: Blue shirts, white shorts, blue stockings.

Change Colours: White shirts, blue shorts, white stockings.

Year Formed: 1903.

Ltd Co.: 1921.

Previous Name: 1903, Shaddongate United; 1904, Carlisle United.

Club Nicknames: 'Cumbrians' or 'The Blues'.

Previous Grounds: 1903, Milholme Bank; 1905, Devonshire Park; 1909, Brunton Park.

First Football League Game: 25 August 1928, Division 3 (N), v Accrington S (a) W 3–2 – Prout; Coulthard, Cook; Harrison, Ross, Pigg; Agar (1), Hutchison, McConnell (1), Ward (1), Watson.

Record League Victory: 8–0 v Hartlepool U, Division 3 (N), 1 September 1928 – Prout; Smiles, Cook; Robinson (1) Ross, Pigg; Agar (1), Hutchison (1), McConnell (4), Ward (1), Watson. 8–0 v Scunthorpe U, Division 3 (N), 25 December 1952 – MacLaren; Hill, Scott; Stokoe, Twentyman, Waters; Harrison (1), Whitehouse (5), Ashman (2), Duffett, Bond.

Record Cup Victory: 6–0 v Shepshed Dynamo, FA Cup 1st rd, 16 November 1996 – Caig; Hopper, Archdeacon (pen), Walling, Robinson, Pounewatchy, Peacock (1), Conway (1) (Jansen), Smart (McAlindon (1)), Hayward, Aspinall (Thorpe), (2 og).

HONOURS

Football League: Division 1 best season: 22nd, 1974–75; Promoted from Division 2 (3rd) 1973–74; Division 3 – Champions 1964–65, 1994–95; Runners-up 1981–82; Promoted from Division 3 1996–97; Division 4 – Runners-up 1963–64. Promoted from Conference (play-offs) 2004–05.

FA Cup: best season: 6th rd 1975.

Football League Cup: Semi-final 1970.

Auto Windscreens Shield: Winners 1997; Runners-up 1995.

LDV Vans Trophy: Runners-up 2003.

SKY SPORTS FACT FILE

In 1970–71 Carlisle United beat Portsmouth 6–0 on 5 December, Bob Hatton scoring four goals and Bobby Owen two. It was their highest score of the season and with the highest total (65) of teams not promoted, qualified for the Watney Cup.

Record Defeat: 1–11 v Hull C, Division 3 (N), 14 January 1939.

Most League Points (2 for a win): 62, Division 3 (N), 1950–51.

Most League Points (3 for a win): 91, Division 3, 1994–95.

Most League Goals: 113, Division 4, 1963–64.

Highest League Scorer in Season: Jimmy McConnell, 42, Division 3 (N), 1928–29.

Most League Goals in Total Aggregate: Jimmy McConnell, 126, 1928–32.

Most League Goals in One Match: 5, Hugh Mills v Halifax T, Division 3N, 11 September 1937; 5, Jim Whitehouse v Scunthorpe U, Division 3N, 25 December 1952.

Most Capped Player: Eric Welsh, 4, Northern Ireland.

Most League Appearances: Allan Ross, 466, 1963–79.

Youngest League Player: John Slaven, 16 years 162 days v Scunthorpe U, 16 March 2002.

Record Transfer Fee Received: £1,500,000 from Crystal Palace for Matt Jansen, February 1998.

Record Transfer Fee Paid: £121,000 to Notts Co for David Reeves, December 1993.

Football League Record: 1928 Elected to Division 3 (N); 1958–62 Division 4; 1962–63 Division 3; 1963–64 Division 4; 1964–65 Division 3; 1965–74 Division 2; 1974–75 Division 1; 1975–77 Division 2; 1977–82 Division 3; 1982–86 Division 2; 1986–87 Division 3; 1987–92 Division 4; 1992–95 Division 3; 1995–96 Division 2; 1996–97 Division 3; 1997–98 Division 2; 1998–04 Division 3; 2004–05 Conference; 2005– FL2.

LATEST SEQUENCES

Longest Sequence of League Wins: 6, 27.8.1994 – 17.9.1994.

Longest Sequence of League Defeats: 12, 27.9.2003 – 13.12.2003.

Longest Sequence of League Draws: 6, 11.2.1978 – 11.3.1978.

Longest Sequence of Unbeaten League Matches: 19, 1.10.1994 – 11.2.1995.

Longest Sequence Without a League Win: 14, 19.1.1935 – 19.4.1935.

Successive Scoring Runs: 26 from 23.8.1947.

Successive Non-scoring Runs: 5 from 24.8.1968.

MANAGERS

Harry Kirkbride 1904–05 *(Secretary-Manager)*
McCumiskey 1905–06 *(Secretary-Manager)*
Jack Houston 1906–08 *(Secretary-Manager)*
Bert Stansfield 1908–10
Jack Houston 1910–12
Davie Graham 1912–13
George Bristow 1913–30
Billy Hampson 1930–33
Bill Clarke 1933–35
Robert Kelly 1935–36
Fred Westgarth 1936–38
David Taylor 1938–40
Howard Harkness 1940–45
Bill Clark 1945–46 *(Secretary-Manager)*
Ivor Broadis 1946–49
Bill Shankly 1949–51
Fred Emery 1951–58
Andy Beattie 1958–60
Ivor Powell 1960–63
Alan Ashman 1963–67
Tim Ward 1967–68
Bob Stokoe 1968–70
Ian MacFarlane 1970–72
Alan Ashman 1972–75
Dick Young 1975–76
Bobby Moncur 1976–80
Martin Harvey 1980
Bob Stokoe 1980–85
Bryan 'Pop' Robson 1985
Bob Stokoe 1985–86
Harry Gregg 1986–87
Cliff Middlemass 1987–91
Aidan McCaffery 1991–92
David McCreery 1992–93
Mick Wadsworth *(Director of Coaching)* 1993–96
Mervyn Day 1996–97
David Wilkes and John Halpin (*Directors of Coaching*), and Michael Knighton 1997–99
Martin Wilkinson 1999–2000
Ian Atkins 2000–01
Roddy Collins 2001–02; 2002–03
Paul Simpson October 2003–

TEN YEAR LEAGUE RECORD

		P	W	D	L	F	A	Pts	Pos
1995-96	Div 2	46	12	13	21	57	72	49	21
1996-97	Div 3	46	24	12	10	67	44	84	3
1997-98	Div 2	46	12	8	26	57	73	44	23
1998-99	Div 3	46	11	16	19	43	53	49	23
1999-2000	Div 3	46	9	12	25	42	75	39	23
2000-01	Div 3	46	11	15	20	42	65	48	22
2001-02	Div 3	46	12	16	18	49	56	52	17
2002-03	Div 3	46	13	10	23	52	78	49	22
2003-04	Div 3	46	12	9	25	46	69	45	23
2004-05	Conf	42	20	13	9	74	37	73	3

DID YOU KNOW ?

On 14 February 1955 Carlisle United entertained foreign visitors for the first time when the Austrian club Columbia Wien provided the opposition. Carlisle won 3–2. Ironically that same season because of a protracted spell of bad weather no fewer than eleven League games had to be played in April.

CHARLTON ATHLETIC FA Premiership

FOUNDATION

The club was formed on 9 June 1905, by a group of 14- and 15-year-old youths living in streets by the Thames in the area which now borders the Thames Barrier. The club's progress through local leagues was so rapid that after the First World War they joined the Kent League where they spent a season before turning professional and joining the Southern League in 1920. A year later they were elected to the Football League's Division 3 (South).

The Valley, Floyd Road, Charlton, London SE7 8BL.

Telephone: (020) 8333 4000.

Fax: (020) 8333 4001.

Website: www.cafc.co.uk

Email: info@cafc.co.uk

Ground Capacity: 27,111.

Record Attendance: 75,031 v Aston Villa, FA Cup 5th rd, 12 February 1938 (at The Valley).

Pitch Measurements: 101.5m × 65.8m.

Chairman: M. A. Simons.

Vice Chairman: R. A. Murray.

Chief Executive: P. D. Varney.

Secretary: Chris Parkes.

Manager: Alan Curbishley.

Assistant Manager: Keith Peacock.

Physio: George Cooper.

Colours: Red shirts, white shorts, red stockings.

Change Colours: White shirts, black shorts, white stockings.

Year Formed: 1905.

Turned Professional: 1920.

Ltd Co.: 1919.

Club Nickname: 'Addicks'.

Previous Grounds: 1906, Siemen's Meadow; 1907, Woolwich Common; 1909, Pound Park; 1913, Horn Lane; 1920, The Valley; 1923, Catford (The Mount); 1924, The Valley; 1985, Selhurst Park; 1991, Upton Park; 1992, The Valley.

First Football League Game: 27 August 1921, Division 3 (S), v Exeter C (h) W 1–0 – Hughes; Mitchell, Goodman; Dowling (1), Hampson, Dunn; Castle, Bailey, Halse, Green, Wilson.

Record League Victory: 8–1 v Middlesbrough, Division 1, 12 September 1953 – Bartram; Campbell, Ellis; Fenton, Ufton, Hammond; Hurst (2), O'Linn (2), Leary (1), Firmani (3), Kiernan.

HONOURS

Football League: Division 1 – Champions 1999–2000; Runners-up 1936–37; Promoted from Division 1, 1997–98 (play-offs); Division 2 – Runners-up 1935–36, 1985–86; Division 3 (S) – Champions 1928–29, 1934–35; Promoted from Division 3 (3rd) 1974–75, 1980–81.

FA Cup: Winners 1947; Runners-up 1946.

Football League Cup: best season: 4th rd, 1963, 1966, 1979.

Full Members' Cup: Runners-up 1987.

SKY SPORTS FACT FILE

On Easter Monday 19 April 1954 a goal by Eddie Firmani for Charlton Athletic was enough to defeat Manchester United at the Valley. It was a red letter day in other respects as the club announced financial solvency for the first time.

Record Cup Victory: 7–0 v Burton A, FA Cup 3rd rd, 7 January 1956 – Bartram; Campbell, Townsend; Hewie, Ufton, Hammond; Hurst (1), Gauld (1), Leary (3), White, Kiernan (2).

Record Defeat: 1–11 v Aston Villa, Division 2, 14 November 1959.

Most League Points (2 for a win): 61, Division 3 (S), 1934–35.

Most League Points (3 for a win): 91, Division 1, 1999–2000.

Most League Goals: 107, Division 2, 1957–58.

Highest League Scorer in Season: Ralph Allen, 32, Division 3 (S), 1934–35.

Most League Goals in Total Aggregate: Stuart Leary, 153, 1953–62.

Most League Goals in One Match: 5, Wilson Lennox v Exeter C, Division 3S, 2 February 1929; 5, Eddie Firmani v Aston Villa, Division 1, 5 February 1955; 5, John Summers v Huddersfield T, Division 2, 21 December 1957; 5, John Summers v Portsmouth, Division 2, 1 October 1960.

MANAGERS

Bill Rayner 1920–25
Alex McFarlane 1925–27
Albert Lindon 1928
Alex McFarlane 1928–32
Jimmy Seed 1933–56
Jimmy Trotter 1956–61
Frank Hill 1961–65
Bob Stokoe 1965–67
Eddie Firmani 1967–70
Theo Foley 1970–74
Andy Nelson 1974–79
Mike Bailey 1979–81
Alan Mullery 1981–82
Ken Craggs 1982
Lennie Lawrence 1982–91
Steve Gritt/Alan Curbishley 1991–95
Alan Curbishley June 1995–

Most Capped Player: Mark Kinsella, 33 (48), Republic of Ireland.

Most League Appearances: Sam Bartram, 583, 1934–56.

Youngest League Player: Paul Konchesky, 16 years 93 days v Oxford U, 16 August 1997.

Record Transfer Fee Received: £10,000,000 from Chelsea for Scott Parker, January 2004.

Record Transfer Fee Paid: £4,750,000 to Wimbledon for Jason Euell, July 2001.

Football League Record: 1921 Elected to Division 3 (S); 1929–33 Division 2; 1933–35 Division 3 (S); 1935–36 Division 2; 1936–57 Division 1; 1957–72 Division 2; 1972–75 Division 3; 1975–80 Division 2; 1980–81 Division 3; 1981–86 Division 2; 1986–90 Division 1; 1990–92 Division 2; 1992–98 Division 1; 1998–99 FA Premier League; 1999–2000 Division 1; 2000– FA Premier League.

LATEST SEQUENCES

Longest Sequence of League Wins: 12, 26.12.1999 – 7.3.2000.

Longest Sequence of League Defeats: 10, 11.4.1990 – 15.9.1990.

Longest Sequence of League Draws: 6, 13.12.1992 – 16.1.1993.

Longest Sequence of Unbeaten League Matches: 15, 4.10.1980 – 20.12.1980.

Longest Sequence Without a League Win: 16, 26.2.1955 – 22.8.1955.

Successive Scoring Runs: 25 from 26.12.1935.

Successive Non-scoring Runs: 5 from 6.9.1922.

TEN YEAR LEAGUE RECORD

		P	*W*	*D*	*L*	*F*	*A*	*Pts*	*Pos*
1995-96	Div 1	46	17	20	9	57	45	71	6
1996-97	Div 1	46	16	11	19	52	66	59	15
1997-98	Div 1	46	26	10	10	80	49	88	4
1998-99	PR Lge	38	8	12	18	41	56	36	18
1999-2000	Div 1	46	27	10	9	79	45	91	1
2000-01	PR Lge	38	14	10	14	50	57	52	9
2001-02	PR Lge	38	10	14	14	38	49	44	14
2002-03	PR Lge	38	14	7	17	45	56	49	12
2003-04	PR Lge	38	14	11	13	51	51	53	7
2004-05	PR Lge	38	12	10	16	42	58	46	11

DID YOU KNOW ?

When Charlton Athletic defeated Exeter City 1–0 at The Valley on 21 February 1981 it was their 28th League and Cup win in a season, a club record. By the end of it 32 had been recorded and 20 clean sheets for another League record alone.

CHARLTON ATHLETIC 2004–05 LEAGUE RECORD

Match No.	*Date*	*Venue*	*Opponents*	*Result*		*H/T Score*	*Lg. Pos.*	*Goalscorers*	*Attendance*
1	Aug 14	A	Bolton W	L	1-4	0-2	—	Lisbie [67]	24,100
2	21	H	Portsmouth	W	2-1	1-0	11	Euell [23], Unsworth (og) [87]	25,204
3	25	H	Aston Villa	W	3-0	2-0	—	Jeffers 2 [29, 34], Young [58]	26,190
4	28	A	Manchester C	L	0-4	0-2	8		43,593
5	Sept 13	H	Southampton	D	0-0	0-0	—		24,263
6	18	A	Birmingham C	D	1-1	0-0	9	Young [49]	27,400
7	27	H	Blackburn R	W	1-0	0-0	—	El Karkouri [49]	26,193
8	Oct 2	A	Arsenal	L	0-4	0-1	10		38,103
9	17	H	Newcastle U	D	1-1	0-1	10	Carr (og) [51]	26,553
10	23	A	Liverpool	L	0-2	0-0	12		41,625
11	30	H	Middlesbrough	L	1-2	0-1	12	Johansson [46]	26,031
12	Nov 6	A	Tottenham H	W	3-2	2-0	11	Bartlett 2 [17, 39], Thomas [50]	35,423
13	13	H	Norwich C	W	4-0	2-0	9	Johansson 2 [15, 21], Konchesky [75], Euell [88]	27,057
14	20	A	Manchester U	L	0-2	0-1	10		67,704
15	27	H	Chelsea	L	0-4	0-1	12		26,355
16	Dec 5	A	Crystal Palace	W	1-0	0-0	10	Rommedahl [90]	20,705
17	11	A	WBA	W	1-0	1-0	8	Holland [30]	24,697
18	20	H	Fulham	W	2-1	1-0	—	Thomas [27], El Karkouri [66]	26,108
19	26	A	Southampton	D	0-0	0-0	8		31,195
20	28	H	Everton	W	2-0	0-0	7	El Karkouri [82], Hreidarsson [85]	27,001
21	Jan 1	H	Arsenal	L	1-3	1-1	8	El Karkouri [45]	26,711
22	3	A	Blackburn R	L	0-1	0-1	8		19,809
23	15	H	Birmingham C	W	3-1	1-0	7	El Karkouri [9], Bartlett [67], Murphy [75]	26,111
24	22	A	Everton	W	1-0	1-0	7	Holland [45]	36,041
25	Feb 1	H	Liverpool	L	1-2	1-0	—	Bartlett [20]	27,102
26	5	A	Newcastle U	D	1-1	0-0	8	Rommedahl [53]	51,114
27	27	A	Middlesbrough	D	2-2	1-0	9	Holland [14], Bartlett [80]	29,603
28	Mar 5	A	Fulham	D	0-0	0-0	8		18,290
29	15	H	Tottenham H	W	2-0	1-0	—	Thomas [4], Murphy [85]	26,870
30	19	H	WBA	L	1-4	1-1	7	Johansson [24]	27,104
31	Apr 2	H	Manchester C	D	2-2	1-2	8	Bartlett [10], Perry [90]	26,436
32	9	A	Portsmouth	L	2-4	2-2	9	Fortune [22], Murphy [45]	20,108
33	16	H	Bolton W	L	1-2	1-1	10	Jeffers [29]	26,708
34	20	A	Aston Villa	D	0-0	0-0	—		31,312
35	23	A	Norwich C	L	0-1	0-0	11		25,459
36	May 1	H	Manchester U	L	0-4	0-2	11		26,789
37	7	A	Chelsea	L	0-1	0-0	11		42,065
38	15	H	Crystal Palace	D	2-2	1-0	11	Hughes [30], Fortune [82]	26,870

Final League Position: 11

GOALSCORERS

League (42): Bartlett 6, El Karkouri 5, Johansson 4, Holland 3, Jeffers 3, Murphy 3, Thomas 3, Euell 2, Fortune 2, Rommedahl 2, Young 2, Hreidarsson 1, Hughes 1, Konchesky 1, Lisbie 1, Perry 1, own goals 2.
Carling Cup (3): Hreidarsson 1, Jeffers 1, Murphy 1.
FA Cup (8): Hughes 3, Bartlett 2, Fortune 1, Jeffers 1, Murphy 1.

Kiely D 36	Young L 36	Hreidarsson H 33 + 1	Holland M 31 + 1	Fortune J 28 + 3	Fish M 6 + 1	Murphy D 37 + 1	Euell J 7 + 19	Bartlett S 25	Lisbie K 12 + 5	Konchesky P 15 + 13	Hughes B 10 + 7	Jeffers F 9 + 11	Rommedahl D 19 + 7	Kishishev R 27 + 4	El Karkouri T 28 + 4	Johansson J 15 + 11	Perry C 17 + 2	Stuart G 4	Thomas J 21 + 3	Andersen S 2	Sam L — + 1	*Match No.*
1	2	3	4[1]	5	6	7[2]	8	9	10	11[3]	12	13	14									1
1	2	3		5	6	4[1]	8	9[2]	10	12		13	11[3]	7	14							2
1	2	3		5	6	4	8		10	12	13	9[1]	11[2]	7[3]	14							3
1	2	3		5[2]	6	4	8		10	12		9	11[3]	7[1]	13	14						4
1	2	3		5		4	8		10		12	9[2]	11[3]	7[1]	14	13	6					5
1	2	3		5		8	12		10[1]		11		13	7	4[2]	9	6					6
1	2	3		5		8	13		10		11[3]	9[1]		14	4	12[2]	6	7				7
1	2	3	12	5		8	9[2]		10				14	7[3]	4	13	6	11[1]				8
1	2	3	4	5		8		9	10[1]			12	11				6	7				9
1	2	3	4	5		8	12	9[1]	10[3]		14	13	11[2]				6	7				10
1	2	3	4			12	8	9[2]	13	14				7[1]	5	10	6		11[3]			11
1	2	3	4	12		8[1]	14	9■		13				7	5	10[3]	6		11[2]			12
1	2	3	4			8[1]	12		9[2]	13		14		7	5	10	6		11[3]			13
1	2	3	4	12		8		9[2]		14		13		7	5	10	6[1]		11[3]			14
1	2	12	4	5		8[2]	13	9		3			14	7[3]	6	10			11[1]			15
1	2	3	4	5		8		9[2]				13	12	7	6	10[1]			11			16
1	2	3	4	5		8		9		12	13		10[1]	7	6				11[2]			17
1	2	3	4	5		8	12	9[2]		14		13	7[3]	10	6				11[1]			18
1	2	3	4	5		8		9					7	10	6				11			19
1	2	3	4	5		8	12	9		13			10[2]	7	6				11[1]			20
1	2	3	4	5		8	12	9[3]		13			10	7[1]	6	14			11[2]			21
1	2	3[3]	4	5		8	12			13	14		10	7[1]	6	9			11[2]			22
1	2	3	4	5		8		9		12	7[1]	14	10[3]	13	6				11[2]			23
1	2	3	4	5		8		9		11	10[1]				6	12			7			24
1	2	3	4[2]	5		8	12	9		11	10[1]	13		14	6				7[3]			25
1	2	3	4			8[1]	12	9	13	11			10[2]	7	5		6					26
1	2	3	4			8[1]	12	9		11				7	5	13	6		10[2]			27
1	2	3	4			8		9		11				7	5	12	6		10[1]			28
1	2	3	4		12	8	13	9[2]		11			10[3]		5	14	6		7[1]			29
1	2	3	4		6	8[3]	12	9[2]		11	13		14		5■	10[1]			7			30
1	2	3[2]	4	12	5[1]	8		9	13	11		14				10[3]	6		7			31
1	2	3	4	5		8		9[1]	12	11		10		7[2]		14	6[3]		13			32
1		3	4	5		8	12			2[3]	11[1]	9	10	14		13	6		7[2]			33
1		3[2]	4	5		8	12				7	9	11[1]	2	6	10	13					34
1	3		4	5		8	12				7[1]	9	11	2	6	10[2]			13			35
	2		4	5		8	12		13	3		9[2]	11[1]	7[3]	6	10	14■			1		36
	2		4	5		8			9	3	11			7	6	10				1		37
1	2		4[2]	5		8[3]		9[1]		3	11		12	7	6	10			13		14	38

FA Cup

Third Round	Rochdale	(h)	4-1
Fourth Round	Yeovil T	(h)	3-2
Fifth Round	Leicester C	(h)	1-2

Carling Cup

Second Round	Grimsby T	(a)	2-0
Third Round	Crystal Palace	(h)	1-2

CHELSEA FA Premiership

FOUNDATION

Chelsea may never have existed but for the fact that Fulham rejected an offer to rent the Stamford Bridge ground from Mr H. A. Mears who had owned it since 1904. Fortunately he was determined to develop it as a football stadium rather than sell it to the Great Western Railway and got together with Frederick Parker, who persuaded Mears of the financial advantages of developing a major sporting venue. Chelsea FC was formed in 1905, and when admission to the Southern League was denied, they immediately gained admission to the Second Division of the Football League.

Stamford Bridge, Fulham Road, London SW6 1HS.

Telephone: 0870 300 1212.

Fax: (020) 7381 4831.

Ticket Office: 0870 300 2322.

Website: www.chelseafc.com

Ground Capacity: 42,522.

Record Attendance: 82,905 v Arsenal, Division 1, 12 October 1935.

Pitch Measurements: 103m × 67m.

Chairman: Bruce Buck.

Director: Eugene Tenenbaum.

Chief Executive: Peter Kenyon.

Club Secretary: David Barnard.

Head Coach: José Mourinho.

Assistant Managers: Steve Clarke and Baltemar Brito.

Physio: Mike Banks.

Colours: Royal blue and white.

Change Colours: Black and silver.

Year Formed: 1905.

Turned Professional: 1905.

Ltd Co.: 1905.

Club Nickname: 'The Blues'.

First Football League Game: 2 September 1905, Division 2, v Stockport Co (a) L 0–1 – Foulke; Mackie, McEwan; Key, Harris, Miller; Moran, J. T. Robertson, Copeland, Windridge, Kirwan.

Record League Victory: 9–2 v Glossop N E, Division 2, 1 September 1906 – Byrne; Walton, Miller; Key (1), McRoberts, Henderson; Moran, McDermott (1), Hilsdon (5), Copeland (1), Kirwan (1).

HONOURS

FA Premier League: Champions 2004–05. Runners-up 2003–04.

Football League: Division 1 – Champions 1954–55; Division 2 – Champions 1983–84, 1988–89; Runners-up 1906–07, 1911–12, 1929–30, 1962–63, 1976–77.

FA Cup: Winners 1970, 1997, 2000; Runners-up 1915, 1967, 1994, 2002.

Football League Cup: Winners 1965, 1998, 2005; Runners-up 1972.

Full Members' Cup: Winners 1986.

Zenith Data Systems Cup: Winners 1990.

European Competitions: *Champions League:* 1999–2000, 2003–04 (semi-finals), 2004–05 (semi-finals). *European Fairs Cup:* 1958–60, 1965–66, 1968–69. *European Cup-Winners' Cup:* 1970–71 (winners), 1971–72, 1994–95, 1997–98 (winners), 1998–99 (semi-finals). *UEFA Cup:* 2000–01, 2001–02, 2002–03. *Super Cup:* 1998–99 (winners).

SKY SPORTS FACT FILE

Chelsea clinched their first championship success in half a century with a 2–0 win at Bolton Wanderers on 30 April 2005. Their best previous scoreline there had been 5–2 on New Year's Day 1955 en route to the First Division title.

Record Cup Victory: 13–0 v Jeunesse Hautcharage, ECWC, 1st rd 2nd leg, 29 September 1971 – Bonetti; Boyle, Harris (1), Hollins (1p), Webb (1), Hinton, Cooke, Baldwin (3), Osgood (5), Hudson (1), Houseman (1).

Record Defeat: 1–8 v Wolverhampton W, Division 1, 26 September 1953.

Most League Points (2 for a win): 57, Division 2, 1906–07.

Most League Points (3 for a win): 99, Division 2, 1988–89.

Most League Goals: 98, Division 1, 1960–61.

Highest League Scorer in Season: Jimmy Greaves, 41, 1960–61.

Most League Goals in Total Aggregate: Bobby Tambling, 164, 1958–70.

Most League Goals in One Match: 5, George Hilsdon v Glossop, Division 2, 1 September 1906; 5, Jimmy Greaves v Wolverhampton W, Division 1, 30 August 1958; 5, Jimmy Greaves v Preston NE, Division 1, 19 December 1959; 5, Jimmy Greaves v WBA, Division 1, 3 December 1960; 5, Bobby Tambling v Aston Villa, Division 1, 17 September 1966; 5, Gordon Durie v Walsall, Division 2, 4 February 1989.

Most Capped Player: Marcel Desailly, 67 (116), France.

Most League Appearances: Ron Harris, 655, 1962–80.

Youngest League Player: Ian Hamilton, 16 years 138 days v Tottenham H, 18 March 1967.

Record Transfer Fee Received: £12,000,000 from Rangers for Tore Andre Flo, November 2000.

Record Transfer Fee Paid: £24,000,000 to Olympique Marseille for Didier Drogba, June 2004.

Football League Record: 1905 Elected to Division 2; 1907–10 Division 1; 1910–12 Division 2; 1912–24 Division 1; 1924–30 Division 2; 1930–62 Division 1; 1962–63 Division 2; 1963–75 Division 1; 1975–77 Division 2; 1977–79 Division 1; 1979–84 Division 2; 1984–88 Division 1; 1988–89 Division 2; 1989–92 Division 1; 1992– FA Premier League.

MANAGERS

John Tait Robertson 1905–07
David Calderhead 1907–33
Leslie Knighton 1933–39
Billy Birrell 1939–52
Ted Drake 1952–61
Tommy Docherty 1962–67
Dave Sexton 1967–74
Ron Suart 1974–75
Eddie McCreadie 1975–77
Ken Shellito 1977–78
Danny Blanchflower 1978–79
Geoff Hurst 1979–81
John Neal 1981–85 *(Director to 1986)*
John Hollins 1985–88
Bobby Campbell 1988–91
Ian Porterfield 1991–93
David Webb 1993
Glenn Hoddle 1993–96
Ruud Gullit 1996–98
Gianluca Vialli 1998–2000
Claudio Ranieri 2000–04
Jose Mourinho June 2004–

LATEST SEQUENCES

Longest Sequence of League Wins: 8, 15.3.1989 – 8.4.1989.

Longest Sequence of League Defeats: 7, 1.11.1952 – 20.12.1952.

Longest Sequence of League Draws: 6, 20.8.1969 – 13.9.1969.

Longest Sequence of Unbeaten League Matches: 29, 23.10.2004 – continuing.

Longest Sequence Without a League Win: 21, 3.11.1987 – 2.4.1988.

Successive Scoring Runs: 27 from 29.10.1988.

Successive Non-scoring Runs: 9 from 14.3.1981.

TEN YEAR LEAGUE RECORD

		P	W	D	L	F	A	Pts	Pos
1995-96	PR Lge	38	12	14	12	46	44	50	11
1996-97	PR Lge	38	16	11	11	58	55	59	6
1997-98	PR Lge	38	20	3	15	71	43	63	4
1998-99	PR Lge	38	20	15	3	57	30	75	3
1999-2000	PR Lge	38	18	11	9	53	34	65	5
2000-01	PR Lge	38	17	10	11	68	45	61	6
2001-02	PR Lge	38	17	13	8	66	38	64	6
2002-03	PR Lge	38	19	10	9	68	38	67	4
2003-04	PR Lge	38	24	7	7	67	30	79	2
2004-05	PR Lge	38	29	8	1	72	15	95	1

DID YOU KNOW ?

Premier League records tumbled for Chelsea in 2004–05. They produced the most wins (29) and fewest goals conceded (15). There were 25 clean sheets. Of the 30 players called upon in the competition 22 were full internationals.

CHELSEA 2004–05 LEAGUE RECORD

Match No.	*Date*	*Venue*	*Opponents*	*Result*	*H/T Score*	*Lg. Pos.*	*Goalscorers*	*Attendance*
1	Aug 15	H	Manchester U	W 1-0	1-0	—	Gudjohnsen [15]	41,813
2	21	A	Birmingham C	W 1-0	0-0	2	Cole [68]	28,559
3	24	A	Crystal Palace	W 2-0	1-0	—	Drogba [28], Tiago [72]	24,953
4	28	H	Southampton	W 2-1	2-1	2	Beattie (og) [34], Lampard (pen) [43]	40,864
5	Sept 11	A	Aston Villa	D 0-0	0-0	2		36,691
6	19	H	Tottenham H	D 0-0	0-0	2		42,246
7	25	A	Middlesbrough	W 1-0	0-0	2	Drogba [81]	32,341
8	Oct 3	H	Liverpool	W 1-0	0-0	2	Cole [64]	42,028
9	16	A	Manchester C	L 0-1	0-1	2		45,047
10	23	H	Blackburn R	W 4-0	2-0	2	Gudjohnsen 3 (1 pen) [37, 38, 51 (p)], Duff [74]	41,546
11	30	A	WBA	W 4-1	1-0	2	Gallas [45], Gudjohnsen [51], Duff [59], Lampard [81]	27,399
12	Nov 6	H	Everton	W 1-0	0-0	1	Robben [72]	41,965
13	13	A	Fulham	W 4-1	1-0	1	Lampard [33], Robben [59], Gallas [73], Tiago [81]	21,877
14	20	H	Bolton W	D 2-2	1-0	1	Duff [1], Tiago [48]	42,203
15	27	A	Charlton Ath	W 4-0	1-0	1	Duff [4], Terry 2 [47, 50], Gudjohnsen [59]	26,355
16	Dec 4	H	Newcastle U	W 4-0	0-0	1	Lampard [63], Drogba [69], Robben [89], Kezman (pen) [90]	42,328
17	12	A	Arsenal	D 2-2	1-2	1	Terry [17], Gudjohnsen [46]	38153
18	18	H	Norwich C	W 4-0	3-0	1	Duff [10], Lampard [34], Robben [44], Drogba [83]	42,071
19	26	H	Aston Villa	W 1-0	1-0	1	Duff [30]	41,950
20	28	A	Portsmouth	W 2-0	0-0	1	Robben [79], Cole [90]	20,210
21	Jan 1	A	Liverpool	W 1-0	0-0	1	Cole [80]	43,886
22	4	H	Middlesbrough	W 2-0	2-0	1	Drogba 2 [15, 17]	40,982
23	15	A	Tottenham H	W 2-0	1-0	1	Lampard 2 (1 pen) [39 (p), 90]	36,105
24	22	H	Portsmouth	W 3-0	3-0	1	Drogba 2 [15, 39], Robben [21]	42,267
25	Feb 2	A	Blackburn R	W 1-0	1-0	—	Robben [5]	23,414
26	6	H	Manchester C	D 0-0	0-0	1		42,093
27	12	A	Everton	W 1-0	0-0	1	Gudjohnsen [69]	40,270
28	Mar 5	A	Norwich C	W 3-1	1-0	1	Cole [22], Kezman [71], Ricardo Carvalho [79]	24,506
29	15	H	WBA	W 1-0	1-0	—	Drogba [26]	41,713
30	19	H	Crystal Palace	W 4-1	1-1	1	Lampard [29], Cole [54], Kezman 2 [78, 90]	41,667
31	Apr 2	A	Southampton	W 3-1	2-0	1	Lampard [22], Gudjohnsen 2 [39, 83]	31,949
32	9	H	Birmingham C	D 1-1	0-0	1	Drogba [82]	42,031
33	20	H	Arsenal	D 0-0	0-0	—		41,621
34	23	H	Fulham	W 3-1	1-1	1	Cole [17], Lampard [64], Gudjohnsen [87]	42,081
35	30	A	Bolton W	W 2-0	0-0	1	Lampard 2 [60, 76]	27,653
36	May 7	H	Charlton Ath	W 1-0	0-0	1	Makelele [90]	42,065
37	10	A	Manchester U	W 3-1	1-1	—	Tiago [17], Gudjohnsen [61], Cole [82]	67,832
38	15	A	Newcastle U	D 1-1	1-1	1	Lampard (pen) [35]	52,326

Final League Position: 1

GOALSCORERS

League (72): Lampard 13 (3 pens), Gudjohnsen 12 (1 pen), Drogba 10, Cole 8, Robben 7, Duff 6, Kezman 4 (1 pen), Tiago 4, Terry 3, Gallas 2, Makelele 1, Ricardo Carvalho 1, own goal 1.
Carling Cup (10): Duff 2, Kezman 2, Lampard 2, Drogba 1, Gudjohnsen 1, Robben 1, own goal 1.
FA Cup (5): Gudjohnsen 1, Huth 1, Kezman 1, Terry 1, own goal 1.
Champions League (21): Drogba 5, Lampard 4, Terry 4, Duff 2, Gudjohnsen 2, Robben 1, Smertin 1, own goals 2.

Cech P 35	Paulo Ferreira 29	Bridge W 12 + 3	Makelele C 36	Terry J 36	Gallas W 28	Geremi 6 + 7	Lampard F 38	Drogba D 18 + 8	Gudjohnsen E 30 + 7	Smertin A 11 + 5	Kezman M 6 + 19	Ricardo Carvalho 22 + 3	Parker S 1 + 3	Tiago 21 + 13	Cole J 19 + 9	Babayaro C 3 + 1	Mutu A — + 2	Duff D 28 + 2	Huth R 6 + 4	Johnson G 13 + 4	Robben A 14 + 4	Jarosik J 3 + 11	Cudicini C 3	Pidgeley L — + 1	Forssell M — + 1	Grant A — + 1	Nuno Morais — + 2	Watt S — + 1	Oliveira F — + 1	*Match No.*
1	2	3	4	5	6	7^2	8	9^1	10^3	11	12	13	14																	1
1	2	3	4	5		7^3	8	9	10^1	11^2	12	6		13	14															2
1	2		4	5	6	12	8	9^2	13		10^3			7	11^1	3	14													3
1	2	3	4^1	5		12	8	9	10^2		13	6		7	11^3			14												4
1	2		4	5			8	9	12	13	10^1	6		7^2	11^3	3	14													5
1	2	3^1	4	5			8	9	10	12	13	6		7^2	11^3			14												6
1	2		4	5	3		8	9	10^1	7^2	12	6		13				11^3	14											7
1	2		4	5	3	12	8	9^2	10	7^3		6		14	13			11^1												8
1	2	12	4	5	3^1	13	8		10		9	6^2		7^3	14			11												9
1		3		5			8		10^2	7^1	13	6	4	12	9^3			11		2	14									10
1	2	3^1	4	5	6		8^2		10	7		12		13	9^3			11			14									11
1	2		4	5		12	8		10^1		13	6		7^2		3		11^3	14		9									12
1	2		4	5	3		8		10^3	7^1	13	6		12				11^2	14		9									13
1	2		4	5	3		8		10^2		12	6		7				11^1		13	9									14
1	2		4	5	3	12	8	13	10^2			6		7		14		11^1			9^3									15
1	2	12	4	5	3^1		8	13	10^2		14	6		7^3				11			9									16
1	2	12	4	5	3		8	13	10^3			6^2	14	7^1				11			9									17
1	2	3	4	5	6		8	12	10^1		13		14	7^3				11			9^2									18
1	2	3	4	5	6		8	12	10^1	13				7				11^2		14	9^3									19
1	2		4	5	6	12	8	10^2	13	7^3					14			11		3	9^1									20
1	2		4	5	6		8	12	10^1		13			7	14			11^3		3	9^2									21
1	2		4	5	6		8	10^1		3^3	12			13	7^2			11		14	9									22
1	2		4	5	6		8	10^1	12	7^3					13			11^2		3	9	14								23
1	2	3	4	5	6		8	10^1	12		13			14	7			11^3			9^2									24
1	2	3	4	5	6		8		10^1		12			7	13^3			11			9^2	14								25
1	2	3	4	5	6		8		10		9^2			12	13			11				7^1								26
1	2	3	4	5	6		8		10			12		7^2	9^3			11^1		13		14								27
1	3		4	5			8	10^1	12		13	6		7^2	9			11^3		2		14								28
1	2		4	5	3		8	9	10^3	12	13				7^2			11^1	6			14								29
1	2		4	5			8	9^2	10^1		12	6		13	7			11^3		3	14									30
1			4	5	3		8	12	10		9^1			13	7^2			11^3	6	2		14								31
1				5	3		8	12	13	4^2	9^1			7	10			11	6	2^3		14								32
1			4	5	3		8	9	10^3		12	6		13	7^2			11^1		2		14								33
1			4	5			8	9^1	10			6		12	7^2			11	3^3	2	13	14								34
1			4^3	5	3	2	8	9^2	10^1	14		6		7	12				13			11								35
			4	5	3	2	8		10			6		11^2	9					7^1		12	1^G	15	13					36
			4		3	2	8		10^3			6		11	9^2				5	7^1		12	1			13	14			37
			4			2	8		10^3			6		11	9^1				5	3		7^2	1				12	13	14	38

FA Cup

Third Round	Scunthorpe U	(h)	3-1
Fourth Round	Birmingham C	(h)	2-0
Fifth Round	Newcastle U	(a)	0-1

Carling Cup

Third Round	West Ham U	(h)	1-0
Fourth Round	Newcastle U	(a)	2-0
Fifth Round	Fulham	(a)	2-1
Semi-Final	Manchester U	(h)	0-0
		(a)	2-1
Final	Liverpool		3-2
(at Millennium Stadium)			

Champions League

Group H	Paris St Germain	(a)	3-0
	Porto	(h)	3-1
	CSKA Moscow	(h)	2-0
		(a)	1-0
	Paris St Germain	(h)	0-0
	Porto	(a)	1-2
First Round	Barcelona	(a)	1-2
		(h)	4-2
Quarter-Final	Bayern Munich	(h)	4-2
		(a)	2-3
Semi-Final	Liverpool	(h)	0-0
		(a)	0-1

CHELTENHAM TOWN FL Championship 2

FOUNDATION

Although a scratch team representing Cheltenham played a match against Gloucester in 1884, the earliest recorded match for Cheltenham Town FC was a friendly against Dean Close School on 12 March 1892. The School won 4–3 and the match was played at Prestbury (half a mile from Whaddon Road). Cheltenham Town played Wednesday afternoon friendlies at a local cricket ground until entering the Mid Gloucester League. In those days the club played in deep red coloured shirts and were nicknamed 'the Rubies'. The club moved to Whaddon Lane for season 1901–02 and changed to red and white colours two years later.

Whaddon Road, Cheltenham, Gloucester GL52 5NA.

Telephone: (01242) 573 558.

Fax: (01242) 224 675.

Website: www.ctfc.com

Email: info@ctfc.com

Ground Capacity: 7,289.

Record Attendance: at Whaddon Road: 8,326 v Reading, FA Cup 1st rd, 17 November 1956; at Cheltenham Athletic Ground: 10,389 v Blackpool, FA Cup 3rd rd, 13 January 1934.

Pitch Measurements: 111yd × 72yd.

Chairman: Paul Baker.

Vice-chairman: Colin Farmer.

Secretary: Paul Godfrey.

Manager: John Ward.

Assistant Manager: Keith Downing.

Physio: Ian Weston.

Colours: Red and white striped shirts, black shorts, black stockings.

Change Colours: All yellow with blue trim.

Year Formed: 1892.

Turned Professional: 1932.

Ltd Co.: 1937.

Club Nickname: 'The Robins'.

Previous Grounds: Grafton Cricket Ground, Whaddon Lane, Carter's Field (pre 1932).

HONOURS

Football League: Promoted from Division 3 (play-offs) 2001–02.

FA Cup: best season: 5th rd 2002.

Football League Cup: never past 2nd rd.

Football Conference: Champions 1998–99, runners-up 1997–98.

Trophy: Winners 1997–98.

Southern League: Champions 1984–85; *Southern League Cup:* Winners 1957–58, runners-up 1968–69, 1984–85; *Southern League Merit Cup:* Winners 1984–85; *Southern League Championship Shield:* Winners 1985.

Gloucestershire Senior Cup: Winners 1998–99; *Gloucestershire Northern Senior Professional Cup:* Winners 30 times; *Midland Floodlit Cup:* Winners 1985–86, 1986–87, 1987–88; *Mid Gloucester League:* Champions 1896–97; *Gloucester and District League:* Champions 1902–03, 1905–06; *Cheltenham League:* Champions 1910–11, 1913–14; *North Gloucestershire League:* Champions 1913–14; *Gloucestershire Northern Senior League:* Champions 1928–29, 1932–33; *Gloucestershire Northern Senior Amateur Cup:* Winners 1929–30, 1930–31, 1932–33, 1933–34, 1934–35; *Leamington Hospital Cup:* Winners 1934–35.

SKY SPORTS FACT FILE

Dave Lewis was leading goalscorer for Cheltenham Town in nine successive seasons during the club's Southern League and Conference days with 290 goals in all competitions between 1970 and 1983 in two spells sandwiching a period with Gloucester City.

Record League Victory: 11–0 v Bourneville Ath, Birmingham Combination, 29 April 1933 – Davis; Jones, Williams; Lang (1), Blackburn, Draper; Evans, Hazard (4), Haycox (4), Goodger (1), Hill (1).

Record Cup Victory: 12–0 v Chippenham R, FA Cup 3rd qual. rd, 2 November 1935 – Bowles; Whitehouse, Williams; Lang, Devonport (1), Partridge (2); Perkins, Hackett, Jones (4), Black (4), Griffiths (1).

Record Defeat: 0–7 v Crystal Palace, League Cup 2nd rd, 2 October 2002.
N.B. 1–10 v Merthyr T, Southern League, 8 March 1952.

Most League Points (2 for a win): 60, Southern League Division 1, 1963–64.

Most League Points (3 for a win): 78, Division 3, 2001–02.

Most League Goals: 66, Division 3, 2001–02.

Highest League Scorer in Season: Julian Alsop, 20, Division 3, 2001–02.

Most League Goals in Total Aggregate: Martin Devaney, 38, 1999–2005.

Most Capped Player: Grant McCann, 4 (9), Northern Ireland.

Most League Appearances: Jamie Victory, 226, 1999–.

Record Transfer Fee Received: £60,000 from Southampton for Christer Warren, March 1995.

Record Transfer Fee Paid: £50,000 to West Ham U for Grant McCann, January 2003 and £50,000 to Stoke C for Brian Wilson, March 2004.

Football League Record: 1999 Promoted to Division 3; 2002 Division 2; 2003–04 Division 3; 2004– FL2.

MANAGERS

George Blackburn 1932–34
George Carr 1934–37
Jimmy Brain 1937–48
Cyril Dean 1948–50
George Summerbee 1950–52
William Raeside 1952–53
Arch Anderson 1953–58
Ron Lewin 1958–60
Peter Donnelly 1960–61
Tommy Cavanagh 1961
Arch Anderson 1961–65
Harold Fletcher 1965–66
Bob Etheridge 1966–73
Willie Penman 1973–74
Dennis Allen 1974–79
Terry Paine 1979
Alan Grundy 1979–82
Alan Wood 1982–83
John Murphy 1983–88
Jim Barron 1988–90
John Murphy 1990
Dave Lewis 1990–91
Ally Robertson 1991–92
Lindsay Parsons 1992–95
Chris Robinson 1995–97
Steve Cotterill 1997–2002
Graham Allner 2002–03
Bobby Gould 2003
John Ward November 2003–

LATEST SEQUENCES

Longest Sequence of League Wins: not more than 3.

Longest Sequence of League Defeats: 5, 13.1.2001 – 13.2.2001.

Longest Sequence of League Draws: 5, 5.4.2003 – 21.4.2003.

Longest Sequence of Unbeaten League Matches: 16, 1.12.2001 – 12.3.2002.

Longest Sequence Without a League Win: 10, 16.4.2002 – 14.9.2002.

Successive Scoring Runs: 15 from 15.2.2003.

Successive Non-scoring Runs: 4 from 12.9.1999.

TEN YEAR LEAGUE RECORD

		P	*W*	*D*	*L*	*F*	*A*	*Pts*	*Pos*
1995–96	Sth L	42	21	11	10	76	57	74	3
1996–97	Sth L	42	21	11	10	76	44	74	2
1997–98	Conf.	42	23	9	10	63	43	78	2
1998-99	Conf.	42	22	14	6	71	36	80	1
1999-2000	Div 3	46	20	10	16	50	42	70	8
2000-01	Div 3	46	18	14	14	59	52	68	9
2001-02	Div 3	46	21	15	10	66	49	78	4
2002-03	Div 2	46	10	18	18	53	68	48	21
2003-04	Div 3	46	14	14	18	57	71	56	14
2004-05	FL 2	46	16	12	18	51	54	60	14

DID YOU KNOW?

In 1982–83 when Cheltenham Town were Midland Division champions of the Southern League they had had the longest continuous membership of the competition. Top scorer Paul Tester was transferred to Shrewsbury Town for £10,000.

CHELTENHAM TOWN 2004–05 LEAGUE RECORD

Match No.	*Date*	*Venue*	*Opponents*	*Result*		*H/T Score*	*Lg. Pos.*	*Goalscorers*	*Atten-dance*
1	Aug 7	A	Southend U	W	2-0	2-0	—	Melligan [18], Odejayi [29]	5332
2	10	H	Scunthorpe U	L	0-2	0-1	—		3647
3	14	H	Leyton Orient	L	1-2	0-1	18	Devaney [75]	3346
4	21	A	Swansea C	D	1-1	1-0	17	McCann [25]	6874
5	28	H	Boston U	W	1-0	0-0	11	Victory [57]	3596
6	31	A	Shrewsbury T	L	0-2	0-1	—		3862
7	Sept 4	A	Notts Co	D	0-0	0-0	15		4302
8	11	H	Yeovil T	D	1-1	1-1	14	Guinan [25]	3966
9	18	A	Rushden & D	L	0-1	0-1	20		2601
10	25	H	Wycombe W	D	1-1	1-0	19	Victory [37]	3663
11	Oct 1	A	Grimsby T	D	1-1	0-1	—	Spencer [85]	6133
12	8	H	Chester C	D	0-0	0-0	—		3670
13	16	A	Rochdale	W	2-1	0-0	18	Melligan [63], Wilson [84]	2778
14	19	H	Mansfield T	W	2-0	1-0	—	Guinan [45], Devaney [87]	2706
15	23	H	Cambridge U	W	2-1	1-1	11	Vincent [28], Spencer [90]	3315
16	30	A	Oxford U	L	0-1	0-1	15		5163
17	Nov 6	H	Bury	W	1-0	0-0	11	McCann (pen) [68]	3061
18	20	A	Macclesfield T	W	2-0	0-0	6	Guinan [60], McCann [71]	1796
19	26	H	Darlington	L	0-2	0-1	—		3578
20	Dec 7	A	Northampton T	D	1-1	0-0	—	Spencer [84]	4373
21	11	A	Lincoln C	D	0-0	0-0	15		4097
22	18	H	Kidderminster H	W	2-0	0-0	10	Guinan [53], Bennett (og) [90]	3718
23	26	A	Yeovil T	L	1-4	1-2	12	Devaney [17]	7320
24	29	H	Bristol R	D	1-1	1-1	—	Caines [37]	5511
25	Jan 1	H	Notts Co	L	0-2	0-0	13		3375
26	3	A	Wycombe W	D	1-1	1-0	15	Caines [37]	4394
27	15	H	Rushden & D	W	4-1	2-1	13	Wilson [9], Gillespie [26], Devaney [58], McCann (pen) [69]	3160
28	22	A	Bristol R	D	1-1	1-1	13	Gillespie [38]	6954
29	28	H	Grimsby T	L	2-3	1-1	—	Guinan [17], Devaney [76]	3327
30	Feb 1	A	Chester C	W	3-0	1-0	—	Wilson [14], Gillespie 2 (1 pen) [55, 90 (p)]	1643
31	5	H	Rochdale	W	2-0	1-0	10	Devaney 2 (1 pen) [20, 89 (p)]	2951
32	12	A	Mansfield T	W	2-1	0-0	8	Devaney [61], Finnigan [89]	3665
33	19	H	Oxford U	L	0-1	0-0	9		5044
34	22	A	Cambridge U	L	0-1	0-0	—		2021
35	26	H	Lincoln C	W	1-0	0-0	9	Guinan [63]	3187
36	Mar 5	A	Kidderminster H	L	0-1	0-0	10		2879
37	12	A	Scunthorpe U	L	1-4	0-1	12	Victory [48]	4659
38	19	H	Southend U	L	0-3	0-2	13		3341
39	25	A	Leyton Orient	W	3-2	2-0	—	Finnigan 2 [17, 53], Duff [19]	3261
40	28	H	Swansea C	L	1-2	1-1	12	Devaney [26]	4669
41	Apr 2	A	Boston U	L	1-2	0-1	14	Devaney (pen) [90]	2192
42	8	H	Shrewsbury T	D	1-1	0-0	—	Spencer [66]	3769
43	16	H	Northampton T	W	1-0	1-0	12	Spencer [22]	3689
44	23	A	Bury	L	1-3	0-3	16	Gillespie (pen) [80]	2490
45	30	H	Macclesfield T	W	3-0	1-0	12	Morley (og) [34], Spencer 2 [64, 77]	3622
46	May 7	A	Darlington	L	1-3	1-1	14	Spencer [29]	5575

Final League Position: 14

GOALSCORERS

League (51): Devaney 10 (2 pens), Spencer 8, Guinan 6, Gillespie 5 (2 pens), McCann 4 (2 pens), Finnigan 3, Victory 3, Wilson 3, Caines 2, Melligan 2, Duff 1, Odejayi 1, Vincent 1, own goals 2.
Carling Cup (1): Devaney 1.
FA Cup (1): Spencer 1.
LDV Vans Trophy (7): Vincent 2, Brough 1, Finnigan 1, Guinan 1, McCann 1 (pen), Spencer 1.

Higgs S 46	Wilson B 35 + 8	Victory J 40 + 2	Duff S 45	Brough J 11 + 2	McCann G 39	Melligan J 23 + 6	Bird D 26 + 8	Odejayi K 10 + 22	Fyfe G 1 + 2	Devaney M 37 + 1	Gill J 43 + 1	Vincent A 14 + 12	Guinan S 35 + 8	Taylor M 10 + 3	Spencer D 14 + 27	Ward G — + 2	Finnigan J 31 + 1	Caines G 27 + 2	Murphy C — + 4	Gillespie S 10 + 2	Morgan A 8	Connolly A 1 + 3	*Match No.*
1	2^{1}	3	4	5	6	7^{3}	8	9^{2}	10	11	12	14	13										1
1	2	3	4	5	6^{1}	7	8	9		11		10	12										2
1		3	4	5^{1}	6	7^{3}	8	13		11	2	14	10	12	9^{2}								3
1		3	4		6	7	8	9^{2}	12	11	2	10^{1}	13	5									4
1	2^{2}	3	4		6	7^{3}	8	9^{1}		11	10	13		5	12	14							5
1	2^{1}	3	4		6	7^{2}	8	9^{3}		11	10	14	13	5	12								6
1	2	3	4^{1}	12	6			13		11	8	14	10^{3}	5	9^{2}		7						7
1	2	3	4		6			12		11	8		10^{1}	5	9		7						8
1	2^{2}	3	4	12	6	13				11	8	14	10^{3}	5^{1}	9		7						9
1		3	4	5	6	7		12^{2}		11	2	9	10^{1}		13		8						10
1	2^{2}	3	4	5	6		8				11	9	10^{1}		12		7	13					11
1	12	3	4	5	6	7				11	2	10^{1}	13		9^{2}		8						12
1	12	3	4	5	6	7^{2}	13			11	2	9^{1}	10^{3}		14		8						13
1	12	3	4	5	6	7^{2}	13			11	2	9^{1}	10^{3}		14		8						14
1	12	3	4	5	6	7^{3}	13			11	2	9^{1}	10^{2}		14		8						15
1	12	3	4	5	6^{3}	7	8			11^{1}	2	9^{2}	10		13				14				16
1	2	3	4	5	6	7^{1}	8			11^{3}	9		10^{2}		13		12	14					17
1	2	3	4		6		8			9	11		10^{1}		12	13	7^{2}	5					18
1	2	3	4		6	12	8^{2}			9^{3}	11^{1}	14	10		13		7	5					19
1	2^{3}	3	4		6	7	12				11	9^{2}	10^{1}		13		8	5	14				20
1	2	3	4		6	7^{1}	12	13			11	9^{2}	10^{3}		14		8	5					21
1	12	3	4^{1}		6	7		13		11	2	9^{3}	10^{2}		14		8	5					22
1	2^{3}	3	4		6	7^{1}		14		9	11	12	10^{2}		13		8	5					23
1	2	3	4		6	7	12	13		9	11^{2}		10^{3}		14		8^{1}	5					24
1	2	3	4		6		8^{1}	13		9	11^{2}	12	14		10^{3}		7	5					25
1	2	3	4		6		12	13		11	7	9^{2}	10				8^{1}	5					26
1	2^{1}	3	4		6	12	8		13	7^{2}	11		10		14			5		9^{3}			27
1	2	3	4		6▮	12	8			7	11		10^{2}		13			5		9^{1}			28
1	2	3	4			7	8	12		11	6^{2}		10^{1}		13			5		9			29
1	2^{1}	3	4			7	8			11	6	12	10^{2}		13			5		9			30
1	2	3	4				8	12		11	6		10^{2}		13		7	5		9^{1}			31
1	2	3	4		6			12		11	8		10^{1}		9		7	5					32
1	2	3	4		6			12		8	11		10		9^{1}		7	5					33
1	2	3	4		6			12		8^{2}	11^{3}	13	10	14	9^{1}		7	5					34
1	2	3	4		6			12		8	11		10^{1}		13		7	5		9^{2}			35
1	2^{1}	3			6		12	13			11	8^{2}	10^{3}	4	14		7	5		9			36
1	2	3	4		6	12	8^{1}	13			11		10^{3}		14		7	5		9^{2}			37
1	2^{1}	3	4		6	12		10		8^{2}	11			14	13		7	5^{3}		9			38
1	12	13	4		6		8	9^{1}		11	2		10^{3}	5^{2}	14		7				3		39
1	12	3	4		6▮		8	13		11	2		10^{2}	5			7^{1}			14	9^{3}		40
1	2	3	4^{3}				8	9		12				6	13		7	5		10^{2}	11^{1}	14	41
1	2		4				8^{2}	12		11	3		10^{1}		9		7	5			6	13	42
1	2	12	4				8	13		11^{1}	3		10^{2}		9^{3}		7	5			6	14	43
1	2		4			7	8	12			3		10^{1}		9^{2}			5	14	13	6^{3}	11	44
1	2^{2}		4		6	7	8	9^{1}			3		12		10			5	13		11		45
1	2		4		6	7	8	9^{1}			11	12	13		10^{2}			5			3		46

FA Cup

First Round	Swansea C	(h)	1-3

Carling Cup

First Round	Colchester U	(a)	1-2

LDV Vans Trophy

First Round	Dagenham & R	(h)	5-1
Second Round	Walsall	(h)	2-2

CHESTER CITY FL Championship 2

FOUNDATION

All students of soccer history have read about the medieval games of football in Chester, but the present club was not formed until 1884 through the amalgamation of King's School Old Boys with Chester Rovers. For many years Chester were overshadowed in Cheshire by Northwich Victoria and Crewe Alexandra who had both won the Senior Cup several times before Chester's first success in 1894–95. The final against Macclesfield saw Chester face the team that had not only beaten them in the previous year's final, but also knocked them out of the FA Cup two seasons in succession. The final was held at the Drill Field, Northwich and Chester had the support of more than 1000 fans. Chester won 2-1.

Saunders Honda Stadium, Bumpers Lane, Chester CH1 4LT.

Telephone: (01244) 371 376.

Fax: (01244) 390 265.

Ticket Offfice: (01244) 371 376.

Website: www.chestercityfc.net

Email: info@chestercityfc.net

Ground Capacity: 6,000.

Record Attendance: 20,500 v Chelsea, FA Cup 3rd rd (replay), 16 January 1952 (at Sealand Road).

Pitch Measurements: 115yd × 75yd.

Chairman: Stephen Vaughan.

Chief Executive: David Burford.

Secretary: Tony Allan.

Manager: Keith Curle.

Assistant Managers: J. Gannon, D. Bell.

Physio: C. Goodyear.

Colours: Blue and white striped shirts, blue shorts, blue stockings.

Change Colours: Yellow shirts, yellow shorts, yellow stockings.

Year Formed: 1885.

Turned Professional: 1902.

Ltd Co.: 1909.

Previous Name: Chester until 1983.

Club Nickname: 'Blues' and 'City'.

Previous Grounds: 1885, Faulkner Street; 1898, The Old Showground; 1901, Whipcord Lane; 1906, Sealand Road; 1990, Moss Rose Ground, Macclesfield; 1992, Deva Stadium, Bumpers Lane.

HONOURS

Football League: Division 3 – Runners-up 1993–94; Division 3 (N) – Runners-up 1935–36; Division 4 – Runners-up 1985–86.

Conference: Champions 2003–04.

FA Cup: best season: 5th rd, 1977, 1980.

Football League Cup: Semi-final 1975.

Welsh Cup: Winners 1908, 1933, 1947.

Debenhams Cup: Winners 1977.

SKY SPORTS FACT FILE

On the opening day of the 1935–36 season, Welsh international Ron Williams scored a hat-trick for Chester in the space of eight minutes against Southport in a 5–1 win. Williams hit 14 goals in the first 11 matches in which Chester scored.

First Football League Game: 2 September 1931, Division 3 (N), v Wrexham (a) D 1–1 – Johnson; Herod, Jones; Keeley, Skitt, Reilly; Thompson, Ranson, Jennings (1), Cresswell, Hedley.

Record League Victory: 12–0 v York C, Division 3 (N), 1 February 1936 – Middleton; Common, Hall; Wharton, Wilson, Howarth; Horsman (2), Hughes, Wrightson (4), Cresswell (2), Sargeant (4).

Record Cup Victory: 6–1 v Darlington, FA Cup 1st rd, 25 November 1933 – Burke; Bennett, Little; Pitcairn, Skitt, Duckworth; Armes (3), Whittam, Mantle (2), Cresswell (1), McLachlan.

Record Defeat: 2–11 v Oldham Ath, Division 3 (N), 19 January 1952.

Most League Points (2 for a win): 56, Division 3 (N), 1946–47 and Division 4, 1964–65.

Most League Points (3 for a win): 84, Division 4, 1985–86.

Most League Goals: 119, Division 4, 1964–65.

Highest League Scorer in Season: Dick Yates, 36, Division 3 (N), 1946–47.

Most League Goals in Total Aggregate: Stuart Rimmer, 135, 1985–88, 1991–98.

Most League Goals in One Match: 5, Tom Jennings v Walsall, Division 3N, 30 January 1932; 5, Barry Jepson v York C, Division 4, 8 February 1958.

Most Capped Player: Trevor Eve, 35, Trinidad & Tobago.

Most League Appearances: Ray Gill, 406, 1951–62.

Youngest League Player: Aidan Newhouse, 15 years 350 days v Bury, 7 May 1988.

Record Transfer Fee Received: £300,000 from Liverpool for Ian Rush, May 1980.

Record Transfer Fee Paid: £95,000 to Boston U for Daryl Clare, November 2002.

Football League Record: 1931 Elected Division 3 (N); 1958–75 Division 4; 1975–82 Division 3; 1982–86 Division 4; 1986–92 Division 3; 1992–93 Division 2; 1993–94 Division 3; 1994–95 Division 2; 1995–2000 Division 3; 2000–04 Conference; 2004– FL2.

MANAGERS

Charlie Hewitt 1930–36
Alex Raisbeck 1936–38
Frank Brown 1938–53
Louis Page 1953–56
John Harris 1956–59
Stan Pearson 1959–61
Bill Lambton 1962–63
Peter Hauser 1963–68
Ken Roberts 1968–76
Alan Oakes 1976–82
Cliff Sear 1982
John Sainty 1982–83
John McGrath 1984
Harry McNally 1985–92
Graham Barrow 1992–94
Mike Pejic 1994–95
Derek Mann 1995
Kevin Ratcliffe 1995–99
Terry Smith 1999
Ian Atkins 2000
Graham Barrow 2000–01
Gordon Hill 2001
Steve Mungall 2001
Andy Porter/Dean Spink 2001–02
Mark Wright 2002–04
Ian Rush 2004–05
Keith Curle May 2005–

LATEST SEQUENCES

Longest Sequence of League Wins: 8, 12.4.78 – 26.8.78.

Longest Sequence of League Defeats: 9, 30.4.94 – 13.9.94.

Longest Sequence of League Draws: 6, 11.10.86 – 1.11.86.

Longest Sequence of Unbeaten League Matches: 18, 27.10.34 – 16.2.35.

Longest Sequence Without a League Win: 25, 19.9.61 – 3.3.62.

TEN YEAR LEAGUE RECORD

		P	W	D	L	F	A	Pts	Pos
1995-96	Div 3	46	18	16	12	72	53	70	8
1996-97	Div 3	46	18	16	12	55	43	70	6
1997-98	Div 3	46	17	10	19	60	61	61	14
1998-99	Div 3	46	13	18	15	57	66	57	14
1999-2000	Div 3	46	10	9	27	44	79	39	24
2000-01	Conf.	42	16	14	12	49	43	62	8
2001-02	Conf.	42	15	9	18	54	51	54	14
2002-03	Conf.	42	21	12	9	59	31	75	4
2003-04	Conf.	42	27	11	4	85	34	92	1
2004-05	FL 2	46	12	16	18	43	69	52	20

DID YOU KNOW?

After five successive seasons finishing as runners-up in the Combination, Chester finally won the title in 1908–09. Joe Freeman scored 25 goals in 25 matches. Later in his career he played for Hamilton Academical.

CHESTER CITY 2004–05 LEAGUE RECORD

Match No.	Date	Venue	Opponents	Result	H/T Score	Lg. Pos.	Goalscorers	Attendance
1	Aug 7	A	Notts Co	D 1-1	0-0	—	Rapley 87	6432
2	10	H	Wycombe W	L 0-2	0-1	—		2881
3	14	H	Mansfield T	L 0-3	0-0	23		2648
4	21	A	Bury	D 1-1	1-0	24	Branch 21	2870
5	28	H	Darlington	L 0-3	0-2	4		2392
6	30	A	Boston U	L 1-3	0-2	24	Branch (pen) 84	2698
7	Sept 4	H	Macclesfield T	W 1-0	0-0	24	Collins 90	2913
8	11	A	Scunthorpe U	W 2-1	2-0	20	Ellison 24, Bolland 31	4203
9	18	H	Cambridge U	D 0-0	0-0	21		2771
10	25	A	Lincoln C	D 1-1	1-1	21	Ellison 36	3985
11	Oct 2	H	Swansea C	D 1-1	1-0	20	Rapley 19	3847
12	8	A	Cheltenham T	D 0-0	0-0	—		3670
13	16	A	Rushden & D	W 1-0	0-0	19	Drummond 77	2735
14	23	H	Grimsby T	W 2-1	2-1	18	Branch 2 39, 42	3233
15	26	H	Kidderminster H	W 3-0	1-0	—	Branch 28, Ellison 52, Davies 64	2968
16	30	A	Yeovil T	L 1-4	0-1	17	Clare (pen) 73	5741
17	Nov 6	H	Leyton Orient	D 1-1	0-1	15	Belle 83	3125
18	19	A	Northampton T	D 1-1	1-1	—	Ellison 26	5625
19	27	H	Oxford U	L 1-3	1-1	19	Ellison 35	2791
20	Dec 7	A	Bristol R	L 1-4	1-2	—	Ellison 27	5524
21	11	H	Shrewsbury T	D 1-1	0-0	19	Branch (pen) 90	3219
22	17	A	Southend U	L 0-1	0-0	—		4837
23	26	H	Scunthorpe U	D 1-1	1-1	19	Ellison 19	3216
24	28	A	Rochdale	D 2-2	1-0	19	Ellison 6, Branch 83	3724
25	Jan 1	A	Macclesfield T	W 2-1	0-1	19	Drummond 77, Ellison 81	3076
26	3	H	Lincoln C	L 0-1	0-0	21		2839
27	15	A	Cambridge U	D 0-0	0-0	19		3185
28	22	H	Rochdale	D 0-0	0-0	20		2985
29	29	A	Swansea C	L 0-3	0-1	20		8989
30	Feb 1	H	Cheltenham T	L 0-3	0-1	—		1643
31	5	H	Rushden & D	W 3-1	2-0	19	Atieno 15, Hessey 38, O'Neill 74	2340
32	12	A	Kidderminster H	W 1-0	0-0	19	Drummond 76	2779
33	19	H	Yeovil T	L 0-2	0-2	21		3072
34	22	A	Grimsby T	L 0-1	0-0	—		3144
35	26	A	Shrewsbury T	L 0-5	0-2	21		4859
36	Mar 5	H	Southend U	D 2-2	1-1	21	Walsh 9, Davies 49	2396
37	12	A	Wycombe W	L 2-4	1-1	21	Branch 2 (1 pen) 26, 88 (p)	8124
38	19	H	Notts Co	W 3-2	1-1	21	Drummond 28, Branch 2 58, 77	2324
39	25	A	Mansfield T	D 0-0	0-0	—		3437
40	28	H	Bury	W 2-1	0-1	19	Lowe 2 59, 70	3107
41	Apr 2	A	Darlington	L 0-1	0-0	21		3778
42	9	H	Boston U	W 2-1	1-1	20	Booth 45, Lowe 77	2040
43	16	H	Bristol R	D 2-2	0-2	20	Drummond 2 60, 72	2475
44	23	A	Leyton Orient	L 0-2	0-2	20		3192
45	30	H	Northampton T	L 0-2	0-1	20		3455
46	May 7	A	Oxford U	W 1-0	0-0	18	Lowe 90	5055

Final League Position: 18

GOALSCORERS

League (43): Branch 11 (3 pens), Ellison 9, Drummond 6, Lowe 4, Davies 2, Rapley 2, Atieno 1, Belle 1, Bolland 1, Booth 1, Clare 1 (pen), Collins 1, Hessey 1, O'Neill 1, Walsh 1.
Carling Cup (0).
FA Cup (6): Branch 2 (1 pen), Rapley 2, Belle 1, Ellison 1.
LDV Vans Trophy (3): Ellison 1, Hessey 1, Hope 1.

Brown W 23	Edmondson D 26 + 1	Vaughan S 14 + 7	Collins D 12	Bolland P 42	Harris A 9 + 10	Drummond S 44 + 1	Davies B 38 + 6	Clare D 3 + 4	Branch M 31 + 2	Ellison K 24	Rapley K 12 + 9	McIntyre K 9 + 1	Carden P 36 + 4	Hessey S 31 + 3	Navarro A 3	Belle C 17 + 5	Stamp D 2 + 2	Whalley S — + 3	Hope R 26 + 2	MacKenzie C 23 + 1	Booth R 7 + 4	Hillier I 7 + 1	Bayliss D 9	Brown M 11 + 7	Walsh2 + 3	Elokobi G 4 + 1	O'Neill J 5 + 6	Lynch G — + 1	Atieno T 3 + 1	Foy R 13	Sestanovich A 3 + 4	Nicholas A 5	Lowe R 8	Regan C 4 + 2	*Match No.*
1	2	3	4	5	6	7	8^{2}	9	10^{1}	11	12		13																						1
1	2^{1}	3	4	5	6	7	8^{2}	9	10	11	13		12																						2
1		2	4	5	6^{1}	7	13	12	10	11	9	3	8^{2}																						3
1		2	4	5		7			10	11	9^{2}	3	12	6	8^{1}	13																			4
1		2	4	5		7^{2}	13		10	11	9^{3}	3	12	6	8^{1}	14																			5
1		2	4	5		12	7		10	11^{1}		3		6	8	9																			6
1	2^{1}		4	5	12	7	8		10	11		3	6			9																			7
1	2		4	5	12	7	6			11	9^{2}		8^{1}	3		10■	13																		8
1	2	12	4	5	13	7^{1}	6^{2}			11	9		8	3			10^{3}	14																	9
1	2	12	4	5		7	6			11	9^{1}		8	3			10^{2}		13																10
1	2		4	5	12	7	6		13		9	11	8^{1}	3		10^{2}																			11
1	2		4	5		7	6		12	11	9^{1}		8	3		10																			12
	2			5		7	4		10^{1}	11	12		8	3		9			6	1															13
	2			5	12	7	6^{1}	13	10^{2}	11	14		8	3		9^{3}			4	1															14
	2	12		5		7^{2}	6	14	10	11	13		8	3^{1}		9^{3}			4	1															15
	2^{1}			5	12	7	6	13	10^{2}	11	14		8	3		9^{3}			4	1															16
	2^{1}	12		5	13	7^{3}	6^{2}	10		11	14		8	3		9			4	1															17
	2			5	6^{1}	7	12			11	9	3	8	4^{2}		10■			13	1															18
	2			5	6	7	8			11	9	3							4	1	10														19
1		2		5		7	6^{2}		10	11	9	12	8	3					4^{1}		13														20
1				5	6	7	12		9	11■	13	3^{1}	4			10^{3}	14		2		8^{2}														21
1		12		5	6	7	4^{1}		10^{2}		14		8	11		9					13^{3}	2	3												22
1^{6}				4		7	6^{1}		10	11			8	3		9				15		2	5	12											23
				4	12	7	13		10	11			6	3^{1}		9^{3}		14		1		2	5	8^{2}											24
				4		7	12		10	11			6	3		9				1		2	5	8^{1}											25
		12		4	13	7			10^{3}	11			8	3^{1}		9		14		1		2^{2}	5	6											26
		11				7	2		10				8	3^{2}		12			6	1	9^{1}		5	4	13										27
		3^{2}		4		7	2		10		9^{1}		8■	13		12■			6	1			5	11											28
		3		4	6		2		10					12						1		7^{2}	5	8^{1}	9^{3}	11	13	14							29
		11^{1}		4	8^{2}	7	2		10					12						1		6^{3}	5■		13	3	9		14						30
1	2^{1}			4		7	6		10				8	3					5			12					9		11						31
1	2			4		7	6		9^{1}				8	3					5					12			11		10						32
1	2■			4^{1}		7	6						8	3					5					11^{3}		12	13		9^{2}	10	14				33
1						7	6						8	3					5		12			4		2	9^{1}			10	11				34
1	2					7	6						8	3		12			5					13		4■	9^{2}			10	11^{1}				35
1	2			4		7	6		11				8	3					5						9					10					36
1	2	11		4		7	6		9					3					5					8^{1}						10	12				37
	2			4		7	6		9										5	1	12			8			13			10^{2}	11^{1}	3			38
	2^{1}			5		7	6		9				8						4	1										10		3	11	12	39
	12			5		7	6		9				8						4	1										10	13	3	11^{2}	2^{1}	40
	2			5■		7	6^{1}		9				8^{2}						4	1				12			13			10	14	3	11^{3}		41
	2					7	6						8	5					4	1	9									10		3	11		42
	2^{3}			5		7	6						8	3					4	1	9^{2}			12			13			10^{1}			11	14	43
		12		5^{3}		7	6		9^{3}				8	3■					4	1				13			14■			10			11^{2}	2	44
		3		5		7	6						8						4	1	9^{1}			12						10			11	2	45
		3		5	12	7	6						8^{1}						4	1	9^{2}			11	13								10	2	46

FA Cup

First Round	Stafford R	(a)	2-0
Second Round	Halifax T	(a)	3-1
Third Round	Bournemouth	(a)	1-2

Carling Cup

First Round	Sunderland	(a)	0-3

LDV Vans Trophy

First Round	Sheffield W	(a)	2-1
Second Round	Rochdale	(h)	1-0
Quarter-Final	Wrexham	(h)	0-1

CHESTERFIELD FL Championship 1

FOUNDATION

Chesterfield are fourth only to Stoke, Notts County and Nottingham Forest in age for they can trace their existence as far back as 1866, although it is fair to say that they were somewhat casual in the first few years of their history playing only a few friendlies a year. However, their rules of 1871 are still in existence showing an annual membership of 2s (10p), but it was not until 1891 that they won a trophy (the Barnes Cup) and followed this a year later by winning the Sheffield Cup, Barnes Cup and the Derbyshire Junior Cup.

Recreation Ground, St Margarets Drive, Saltergate, Chesterfield, Derbyshire S40 4SX.

Telephone: (01246) 209 765.

Fax: (01246) 556 799.

Ticket Office: (01246) 209 765.

Website: www.chesterfieldfc.co.uk

Email: reception@cfc2fsnet.co.uk

Ground Capacity: 8,502.

Record Attendance: 30,968 v Newcastle U, Division 2, 7 April 1939.

Pitch Measurements: 113yd × 71yd.

Chairman: Barrie Hubbard.

Vice-chairman: Jason Elliott.

Chief Executive/Secretary: Alan Walters.

Manager: Roy McFarland.

Assistant Manager: Lee Richardson.

Physio: Jamie Hewitt.

Colours: Blue shirts, white shorts, blue stockings.

Change Colours: Sky blue shirts, sky blue shorts, sky blue stockings.

Year Formed: 1866.

Turned Professional: 1891.

Ltd Co: 1871.

Previous Name: Chesterfield Town.

Club Nicknames: 'Blues' or 'Spireites'.

First Football League Game: 2 September 1899, Division 2, v Sheffield W (a) L 1–5 – Hancock; Pilgrim, Fletcher; Ballantyne, Bell, Downie; Morley, Thacker, Gooing, Munday (1), Geary.

Record League Victory: 10–0 v Glossop NE, Division 2, 17 January 1903 – Clutterbuck; Thorpe, Lerper; Haig, Banner, Thacker; Tomlinson (2), Newton (1), Milward (3), Munday (2), Steel (2).

Record Cup Victory: 5–0 v Wath Ath (a), FA Cup 1st rd, 28 November 1925 – Birch; Saxby, Dennis; Wass, Abbott, Thompson; Fisher (1), Roseboom (1), Cookson (2), Whitfield (1), Hopkinson.

HONOURS

Football League: Division 2 best season: 4th, 1946–47; Division 3 (N) – Champions 1930–31, 1935–36; Runners-up 1933–34; Promoted to Division 2 (3rd) – 2000–01; Division 4 – Champions 1969–70, 1984–85.

FA Cup: Semi-final 1997.

Football League Cup: best season: 4th rd, 1965.

Anglo-Scottish Cup: Winners 1981.

SKY SPORTS FACT FILE

The year 1926 was a vintage one for Jimmy Cookson in scoring goals for Chestefield. Three times he managed to score as many as four times in a match: January v Accrington Stanley; May v Ashington and September v Wigan Borough.

Record Defeat: 0–10 v Gillingham, Division 3, 5 September 1987.

Most League Points (2 for a win): 64, Division 4, 1969–70.

Most League Points (3 for a win): 91, Division 4, 1984–85.

Most League Goals: 102, Division 3 (N), 1930–31.

Highest League Scorer in Season: Jimmy Cookson, 44, Division 3 (N), 1925–26.

Most League Goals in Total Aggregate: Ernie Moss, 161, 1969–76, 1979–81 and 1984–86.

Most League Goals in One Match: 4, Jimmy Cookson v Accrington S, Division 3N, 16 January 1926; 4, Jimmy Cookson v Ashington, Division 3N, 1 May 1926; 4, Jimmy Cookson v Wigan Borough, Division 3N, 4 September 1926; 4, Tommy Lyon v Southampton, Division 2, 3 December 1938.

Most Capped Player: Walter McMillen, 4 (7), Northern Ireland; Mark Williams, 4 (30), Northern Ireland.

Most League Appearances: Dave Blakey, 613, 1948–67.

Youngest League Player: Dennis Thompson, 16 years 160 days v Notts Co, 26 December 1950.

Record Transfer Fee Received: £750,000 from Southampton for Kevin Davies, May 1997.

Record Transfer Fee Paid: £250,000 to Watford for Jason Lee, August 1998.

Football League Record: 1899 Elected to Division 2; 1909 failed re-election; 1921–31 Division 3 (N); 1931–33 Division 2; 1933–36 Division 3 (N); 1936–51 Division 2; 1951–58 Division 3 (N); 1958–61 Division 3; 1961–70 Division 4; 1970–83 Division 3; 1983–85 Division 4; 1985–89 Division 3; 1989–92 Division 4; 1992–95 Division 3; 1995–2000 Division 2; 2000–01 Division 3; 2001–04 Division 2; 2004– FL1.

MANAGERS

E. Russell Timmeus 1891–95 *(Secretary-Manager)*
Gilbert Gillies 1895–1901
E. F. Hind 1901–02
Jack Hoskin 1902–06
W. Furness 1906–07
George Swift 1907–10
G. H. Jones 1911–13
R. L. Weston 1913–17
T. Callaghan 1919
J. J. Caffrey 1920–22
Harry Hadley 1922
Harry Parkes 1922–27
Alec Campbell 1927
Ted Davison 1927–32
Bill Harvey 1932–38
Norman Bullock 1938–45
Bob Brocklebank 1945–48
Bobby Marshall 1948–52
Ted Davison 1952–58
Duggie Livingstone 1958–62
Tony McShane 1962–67
Jimmy McGuigan 1967–73
Joe Shaw 1973–76
Arthur Cox 1976–80
Frank Barlow 1980–83
John Duncan 1983–87
Kevin Randall 1987–88
Paul Hart 1988–91
Chris McMenemy 1991–93
John Duncan 1993–2000
Nicky Law 2000–02
Dave Rushbury 2002–03
Roy McFarland May 2003–

LATEST SEQUENCES

Longest Sequence of League Wins: 10, 6.9.1933 – 4.11.1933.

Longest Sequence of League Defeats: 9, 22.10.1960 – 27.12.1960.

Longest Sequence of League Draws: 5, 19.9.1990 – 6.10.1990.

Longest Sequence of Unbeaten League Matches: 21, 26.12.1994 – 29.4.1995.

Longest Sequence Without a League Win: 18, 11.9.1999 – 3.1.2000.

Successive Scoring Runs: 46 from 25.12.1929.

Successive Non-scoring Runs: 7 from 23.9.1977.

TEN YEAR LEAGUE RECORD

		P	W	D	L	F	A	Pts	Pos
1995-96	Div 2	46	20	12	14	56	51	72	7
1996-97	Div 2	46	18	14	14	42	39	68	10
1997-98	Div 2	46	16	17	13	46	44	65	10
1998-99	Div 2	46	17	13	16	46	44	64	9
1999-2000	Div 2	46	7	15	24	34	63	36	24
2000-01	Div 3	46	25	14	7	79	42	80*	3
2001-02	Div 2	46	13	13	20	53	65	52	18
2002-03	Div 2	46	14	8	24	43	73	50	20
2003-04	Div 2	46	12	15	19	49	71	51	20
2004-05	FL 1	46	14	15	17	55	62	57	17

**9 pts deducted.*

DID YOU KNOW ?

Versatile defender Alan Pringle and right-winger Robert Sinclair were the only two Chesterfield players whose first-class careers there came from the abortive 1939–40 season and FA Cup ties in 1945–46, though both assisted the club in wartime matches.

CHESTERFIELD 2004–05 LEAGUE RECORD

Match No.	*Date*	*Venue*	*Opponents*	*Result*	*H/T Score*	*Lg. Pos.*	*Goalscorers*	*Attendance*
1	Aug 7	H	Brentford	W 3-1	1-0	—	Allison [17], Folan [64], N'Toya [90]	4651
2	10	A	Huddersfield T	D 0-0	0-0	—		11,942
3	14	A	Tranmere R	L 0-1	0-1	10		8287
4	21	H	Colchester U	W 2-1	1-1	8	N'Toya 2 [9, 55]	4028
5	28	A	Bradford C	W 3-2	0-1	5	Nicholson (pen) [78], Folan 2 [79, 88]	7590
6	31	H	Port Vale	W 1-0	0-0	—	N'Toya [53]	5150
7	Sept 4	H	Milton Keynes D	D 2-2	1-0	2	N'Toya [31], Downes [48]	4537
8	11	A	Luton T	L 0-1	0-0	4		7532
9	18	H	Walsall	W 1-0	1-0	3	Hudson [21]	4755
10	25	A	Barnsley	L 0-1	0-0	5		9792
11	Oct 2	H	Bristol C	D 2-2	1-0	6	Nicholson (pen) [33], Bailey [88]	4854
12	10	A	Hull C	L 0-1	0-0	8		15,500
13	16	A	Hartlepool U	L 2-3	1-2	12	Nicholson (pen) [25], Stallard [50]	4617
14	20	H	Stockport Co	W 4-0	2-0	—	Clingan [16], N'Toya [21], Blatherwick [51], Allott [84]	4567
15	23	H	Doncaster R	D 0-0	0-0	8		6219
16	30	A	Sheffield W	D 2-2	1-2	9	Blatherwick [13], Clingan [55]	24,271
17	Nov 6	H	Blackpool	W 1-0	0-0	7	Folan [90]	4978
18	20	A	Bournemouth	D 0-0	0-0	9		6565
19	27	H	Swindon T	W 1-0	0-0	8	Allison [63]	4244
20	Dec 7	A	Oldham Ath	L 1-4	0-2	—	Folan [76]	5207
21	11	A	Peterborough U	W 2-1	1-0	6	Downes [24], Evatt [54]	3865
22	18	H	Torquay U	D 1-1	0-0	8	Allison [73]	4133
23	26	H	Luton T	L 0-1	0-0	10		7158
24	28	A	Wrexham	L 1-3	1-2	11	Stallard [44]	4273
25	Jan 1	A	Milton Keynes D	D 1-1	0-1	11	Evatt [84]	4214
26	3	H	Barnsley	D 2-2	0-2	11	Folan [50], Nicholson [88]	5985
27	15	A	Walsall	L 0-3	0-2	13		5177
28	22	H	Wrexham	L 2-4	1-2	15	Evatt [40], Nicholson (pen) [75]	3966
29	28	A	Bristol C	W 3-2	2-0	—	Hudson 2 [1, 87], Allison [14]	10,103
30	Feb 1	H	Hull C	D 1-1	0-0	—	Myhill (og) [82]	5517
31	5	H	Hartlepool U	L 0-1	0-0	13		4606
32	12	A	Doncaster R	W 1-0	0-0	12	N'Toya [87]	6765
33	19	H	Sheffield W	L 1-3	0-1	12	De Bolla [90]	7831
34	22	A	Stockport Co	W 2-1	0-1	—	De Bolla [51], Allott [81]	4201
35	26	H	Peterborough U	L 1-3	1-2	12	Davies [24]	3715
36	Mar 5	A	Torquay U	D 2-2	1-1	13	Niven [31], Hudson [50]	2746
37	12	H	Huddersfield T	W 2-1	0-0	12	Nicholson 2 (2 pens) [53, 78]	4827
38	19	A	Brentford	D 2-2	1-0	12	De Bolla [38], Allison [66]	6097
39	26	H	Tranmere R	D 2-2	1-0	13	Blatherwick [45], Logan [90]	4293
40	28	A	Colchester U	L 0-1	0-0	13		3471
41	Apr 2	H	Bradford C	D 0-0	0-0	14		4663
42	9	A	Port Vale	L 0-1	0-0	15		4489
43	16	H	Bournemouth	L 2-3	1-0	16	Allison [17], Blatherwick [76]	4009
44	23	A	Blackpool	L 0-1	0-1	17		5613
45	30	H	Oldham Ath	W 1-0	0-0	17	Evatt [69]	5421
46	May 7	A	Swindon T	D 1-1	1-1	17	N'Toya [21]	6044

Final League Position: 17

GOALSCORERS

League (55): N'Toya 8, Nicholson 7 (6 pens), Allison 6, Folan 6, Blatherwick 4, Evatt 4, Hudson 4, De Bolla 3, Allott 2, Clingan 2, Downes 2, Stallard 2, Bailey 1, Davies 1, Logan 1, Niven 1, own goal 1.
Carling Cup (1): Allott 1.
FA Cup (0).
LDV Vans Trophy (1): Campbell-Ryce 1.

Muggleton C 37	Bailey A 45	Nicholson S 42 + 1	Niven D 38	Blatherwick S 33 + 2	Evatt I 41	Allott M 45	Hudson M 32 + 2	De Bolla M 15 + 13	Allison W 27 + 11	Innes M 18 + 3	N'Toya T 18 + 20	Folan C 17 + 15	Davies G 9 + 10	Smith A 6 + 10	O'Hare A 14 + 7	Campbell-Ryce J 14	Downes A 7 + 2	Stallard M 7 + 2	Clingan S 15	Richmond A 1	Dawson K 1	Fowler J 4 + 2	McMaster J 6 + 2	Fulop M 7	Logan C 6 + 3	Thompson G 1	Fox M — + 1	*Match No.*
1	2	3	4	5	6	7	8	9^1	10^2	11^3	12	13	14															1
1	2	3	4	5	6	7	8	9^1		11	12	10																2
1	2	3	4	5	6	7	8	9		11^2	12	10^1		13														3
1	2	3	4		6	7		9^1		11	10	12		13	5	8^2												4
1	2	3	4	5	6^3	7		9^1	12	11	10^2	13			14	8												5
1	2	3	4	5		7^2	13		9	11	12	10^1			6	8												6
1	2	3	4	5^3		7	12	13	9	11	10^2				6	8^1	14											7
1	2	3■	4	5■		7	8^2	12	9^1	13	10^3				6	11	14											8
1	2		4^2		6	7	8	9^1	12	3	10		13^3	14	5	11												9
1	2	3		5	6	7	8	9^2	12	4■	10^1		13			11												10
1	2	3		5	6	7	8	12			10^1		4^2	13		11		9										11
1	2	3		5	6	7		12	10		13		4	8^2				9^1	11									12
1	2	3	4^3	5	6	7		12	10^2		13		14			11		9^1	8									13
1	2	3	4^3	5	6	7		12	9^1		10^2	13	14			11			8									14
1	2	3	4^2	5	6	7		12		13	10^3	14				11		9^1	8									15
1	2	3		5	6	7			10			12	4^2		13	11		9^1	8									16
1	2	3	4	5	6	7			9		10^1	12				11			8									17
	2	3	4	5	6	7			10							11		9	8	1								18
1	2	3	4^2	5	6	7	11		9		10^1	12		13					8									19
1	2	3		5^2	6	7	4		9	11^3	10^1	12		14	13				8									20
1		12			6	7	4		10^2	11		9^1	2		3		5	13	8									21
1	2	3			6	7	4		12	11^2	10^1	9		13			5		8									22
1	2	3	4	5	6				10^2	11	12	9^1		7				13	8									23
1	2	3	4^3	5	6	7	11	12	13			9^2		14				10^1	8									24
1	2	3	4^1		6	7	11	12	10^2		13			9			5		8									25
1	2	3	4^1	5^3		7	11	12	10			13		9^2	14		6		8									26
1	2	3	4			7	8	12	10^1		13	14	11^3	9^2	6						5							27
1	2	3	4		6	7	8^2	9^1	12	11^3	13	10	14		5													28
1	2	3	4		6	7	8		10	11^2	12	9^1			5							13						29
1	2	3	4■		6	7	8		10^1	12	13	9			5							11^2						30
1	2^1	3			6	7	8	12	10	11	13	9^2			5							4■						31
1	2	11	4		6	7	8		10^1		12	9			3		5											32
1	2	3	4^2	5	6	7	8	12		11^3	10	9^1			13							14						33
1	2	3	4	12	6	7	8	9^2			13	10					5^1					11						34
1	2		4	12	6	7	8	9		3	10^2	13■	14				5^1					11^3						35
1	2	3	4	5	6	7	8^1	9	12				11										10					36
	2	3	4	5	6	7	8^1	9^2	12				13		11								10	1				37
	2	3	4	5	6	7		9^1	10		12		11	13										1	8^2			38
1	2^2	3	4	5	6	7	8	9^3	10^1			12			13								11		14			39
1	2	3	4	5	6	7			12		13	10^1	11^3		14								8^2		9			40
	2	3	4	5	6	7	8	9^1	10^2		12	13											11^3	1	14			41
	2	3	4	5	6	7	8		12		10^2	13		14									11^1	1	9^3			42
	2	3	4	5	6	7	8^3		10^1		12	9		11^2									14	1	13			43
	2	3	4^2	5	6	7	8^3		10		12	9^1	13										14	1	11			44
	2	3	4^1	5	6	7	8		10		9		12											1	11			45
	2		4	5	6	7	8		12		10^1		11		3										9^2	1	13	46

FA Cup
First Round — Scunthorpe U — (a) — 0-2

Carling Cup
First Round — Rotherham U — (a) — 1-2

LDV Vans Trophy
First Round — Macclesfield T — (a) — 1-2

COLCHESTER UNITED FL Championship 1

FOUNDATION

Colchester United was formed in 1937 when a number of enthusiasts of the much older Colchester Town club decided to establish a professional concern as a limited liability company. The new club continued at Layer Road which had been the amateur club's home since 1909.

Layer Road Ground, Colchester, Essex CO2 7JJ.

Telephone: 0871 226 2161.

Fax: (01206) 715 327.

Ticket Office: 0871 226 2161.

Website: www.cu-fc.com

Email: caroline@colchesterunited.net

Ground Capacity: 6,143.

Record Attendance: 19,072 v Reading, FA Cup 1st rd, 27 November 1948.

Pitch Measurements: 110yd × 71yd.

Chairman: Peter J. Heard.

Chief Executive: Marie Partner.

Secretary: Caroline Pugh.

Manager: Phil Parkinson.

Assistant Manager: Geraint Williams.

Physio: Stuart Ayles.

Colours: Blue and white vertical striped shirts, white shorts, white stockings.

Change Colours: Yellow with royal trim, royal shorts with yellow trim.

Year Formed: 1937.

Turned Professional: 1937.

Ltd Co.: 1937.

Club Nickname: 'The U's'.

First Football League Game: 19 August 1950, Division 3 (S), v Gillingham (a) D 0–0 – Wright; Kettle, Allen; Bearryman, Stewart, Elder; Jones, Curry, Turner, McKim, Church.

Record League Victory: 9–1 v Bradford C, Division 4, 30 December 1961 – Ames; Millar, Fowler; Harris, Abrey, Ron Hunt; Foster, Bobby Hunt (4), King (4), Hill (1), Wright.

Record Cup Victory: 7–1 v Yeovil T (away), FA Cup 2nd rd (replay), 11 December 1958 – Ames; Fisher, Fowler; Parker, Milligan, Hammond; Williams (1), McLeod (2), Langman (4), Evans, Wright. 7–1 v Yeading, FA Cup 1st rd (replay), 22 November 1994 – Cheesewright; Betts, English, Cawley, Caesar, Locke (Dennis), Fry, Brown (2), Whitton (2) (Thompson), Kinsella (1), Abrahams (2).

HONOURS

Football League: Promoted from Division 3 – 1997–98 (play-offs); Division 4 – Runners-up 1961–62.

FA Cup: best season: 6th rd, 1971.

Football League Cup: best season: 5th rd, 1975.

Auto Windscreens Shield: Runners-up 1997.

GM Vauxhall Conference: Winners 1991–92.

FA Trophy: Winners 1992.

SKY SPORTS FACT FILE

On the last day of the 1949–50 season, Colchester United led the Southern League by a point with an inferior goal average to Merthyr Tydfil. United drew at Bury, Merthyr beat Bedford Town 5–1, but Colchester were elected to the Football League.

Record Defeat: 0–8 v Leyton Orient, Division 4, 15 October 1989.

Most League Points (2 for a win): 60, Division 4, 1973–74.

Most League Points (3 for a win): 81, Division 4, 1982–83.

Most League Goals: 104, Division 4, 1961–62.

Highest League Scorer in Season: Bobby Hunt, 38, Division 4, 1961–62.

Most League Goals in Total Aggregate: Martyn King, 130, 1956–64.

Most League Goals in One Match: 4, Bobby Hunt v Bradford C, Division 4, 30 December 1961; 4, Martyn King v Bradford C, Division 4, 30 December 1961; 4, Bobby Hunt v Doncaster R, Division 4, 30 April 1962.

Most Capped Player: None.

Most League Appearances: Micky Cook, 613, 1969–84.

Youngest League Player: Lindsay Smith, 16 years 218 days v Grimsby T, 24 April 1971.

Record Transfer Fee Received: £2,250,000 from Newcastle U for Lomano Lua-Lua, September 2000.

Record Transfer Fee Paid: £50,000 to Peterborough U for Neil Gregory, March 1998 and £50,000 to Norwich C for Adrian Coote, December 2001.

MANAGERS

Ted Fenton 1946–48
Jimmy Allen 1948–53
Jack Butler 1953–55
Benny Fenton 1955–63
Neil Franklin 1963–68
Dick Graham 1968–72
Jim Smith 1972–75
Bobby Roberts 1975–82
Allan Hunter 1982–83
Cyril Lea 1983–86
Mike Walker 1986–87
Roger Brown 1987–88
Jock Wallace 1989
Mick Mills 1990
Ian Atkins 1990–91
Roy McDonough 1991–94
George Burley 1994
Steve Wignall 1995–99
Mick Wadsworth 1999
Steve Whitton 1999–2003
Phil Parkinson February 2003–

Football League Record: 1950 Elected to Division 3 (S); 1958–61 Division 3; 1961–62 Division 4; 1962–65 Division 3; 1965–66 Division 4; 1966–68 Division 3; 1968–74 Division 4; 1974–76 Division 3, 1976–77 Division 4; 1977–81 Division 3; 1981–90 Division 4; 1990–92 GM Vauxhall Conference; 1992–98 Division 3; 1998–04 Division 2; 2004– FL1.

LATEST SEQUENCES

Longest Sequence of League Wins: 7, 29.11.1968 – 1.2.1969.

Longest Sequence of League Defeats: 8, 9.10.1954 – 4.12.1954.

Longest Sequence of League Draws: 6, 21.3.1977 – 11.4.1977.

Longest Sequence of Unbeaten League Matches: 20, 22.12.1956 – 19.4.1957.

Longest Sequence Without a League Win: 20, 2.3.1968 – 31.8.1968.

Successive Scoring Runs: 24 from 15.9.1962.

Successive Non-scoring Runs: 5 from 7.4.1981.

TEN YEAR LEAGUE RECORD

		P	W	D	L	F	A	Pts	Pos
1995-96	Div 3	46	18	18	10	61	51	72	7
1996-97	Div 3	46	17	17	12	62	51	68	8
1997-98	Div 3	46	21	11	14	72	60	74	4
1998-99	Div 2	46	12	16	18	52	70	52	18
1999-2000	Div 2	46	14	10	22	59	82	52	18
2000-01	Div 2	46	15	12	19	55	59	57	17
2001-02	Div 2	46	15	12	19	65	76	57	15
2002-03	Div 2	46	14	16	16	52	56	58	12
2003-04	Div 2	46	17	13	16	52	56	64	11
2004-05	FL 1	46	14	17	15	60	50	59	15

DID YOU KNOW ?

Colchester United had a successful first season in the Southern League during 1937–38 losing only once at home and finishing sixth, runners-up in the Midweek Section and winners of the Southern League Cup on aggregate against Yeovil.

COLCHESTER UNITED 2004–05 LEAGUE RECORD

Match No.	*Date*	*Venue*	*Opponents*	*Result*	*H/T Score*	*Lg. Pos.*	*Goalscorers*	*Attendance*
1	Aug 7	A	Sheffield W	W 3-0	0-0	—	Fagan ^{85}, Stockley ^{89}, Keith J ^{90}	24,138
2	10	H	Stockport Co	W 3-2	3-0	—	Watson ^{19}, Andrews ^{30}, Fagan ^{41}	3346
3	14	H	Peterborough U	W 2-1	0-1	1	Andrews (pen) ^{58}, Ireland (og) ^{64}	3754
4	21	A	Chesterfield	L 1-2	1-1	3	Johnson ^{44}	4028
5	28	H	Doncaster R	W 4-1	3-1	2	Fagan ^{16}, Johnson ^{22}, Halford ^{27}, Keith J ^{70}	3803
6	30	A	Hartlepool U	L 1-2	0-1	2	Keith J ^{90}	4371
7	Sept 4	H	Swindon T	L 0-1	0-1	4		3868
8	11	A	Bournemouth	W 3-1	2-0	2	Fagan ^{10}, Williams ^{24}, May ^{79}	5944
9	18	H	Milton Keynes D	L 0-1	0-1	6		3460
10	25	A	Oldham Ath	D 1-1	0-1	6	Halford ^{56}	5166
11	Oct 2	H	Port Vale	W 2-1	2-0	4	Danns 2 $^{10,\,19}$	3230
12	9	A	Walsall	L 1-2	0-0	5	Garcia ^{71}	5203
13	16	A	Blackpool	D 1-1	0-1	6	Watson ^{80}	6464
14	19	H	Wrexham	L 1-2	0-0	—	Danns ^{49}	2866
15	23	H	Tranmere R	L 1-2	0-1	11	Halford ^{83}	3420
16	30	A	Bristol C	D 0-0	0-0	13		11,678
17	Nov 6	A	Bradford C	D 2-2	2-1	15	Johnson 2 $^{8,\,39}$	7851
18	20	H	Huddersfield T	D 0-0	0-0	14		3972
19	27	A	Torquay U	W 3-1	0-0	13	Fagan 2 $^{67,\,72}$, Garcia ^{78}	2984
20	Dec 7	H	Barnsley	L 0-2	0-1	—		2927
21	11	H	Hull C	L 1-2	0-1	17	Williams ^{73}	4046
22	18	A	Brentford	L 0-1	0-1	18		5634
23	28	A	Luton T	D 2-2	1-1	18	Garcia ^{34}, Halford ^{62}	8806
24	Jan 1	A	Swindon T	W 3-0	2-0	17	Johnson ^{31}, Danns ^{38}, Garcia ^{47}	6468
25	3	H	Oldham Ath	D 0-0	0-0	18		3873
26	15	A	Milton Keynes D	L 0-2	0-2	18		3833
27	22	H	Luton T	D 0-0	0-0	17		4309
28	25	H	Walsall	W 5-0	4-0	—	Fagan 2 (1 pen) $^{18\,(p),\,22}$, Johnson ^{34}, Williams ^{44}, Hunt ^{90}	2616
29	Feb 5	H	Blackpool	L 0-1	0-0	17		3526
30	12	A	Tranmere R	D 1-1	0-1	17	Keith J ^{65}	8098
31	15	H	Bournemouth	W 3-1	0-0	—	Johnson ^{54}, N'Dumbu Nsungu ^{82}, Danns ^{83}	2820
32	19	H	Bristol C	L 0-2	0-0	16		3412
33	22	A	Wrexham	D 2-2	0-0	—	Danns ^{60}, Brown W ^{71}	2391
34	26	A	Hull C	L 0-2	0-2	17		16,484
35	Mar 5	H	Brentford	L 0-1	0-0	18		3066
36	8	A	Port Vale	D 0-0	0-0	—		3496
37	12	A	Stockport Co	W 2-1	1-1	16	Danns 2 (1 pen) $^{30\,(p),\,90}$	4004
38	19	H	Sheffield W	D 1-1	0-0	17	Heckingbottom (og) ^{48}	4169
39	25	A	Peterborough U	W 3-0	1-0	—	Goodfellow ^{45}, Danns ^{70}, Keith M (pen) ^{83}	4084
40	28	H	Chesterfield	W 1-0	0-0	14	Keith M ^{75}	3471
41	Apr 1	A	Doncaster R	D 1-1	1-0	—	Keith M ^{14}	6774
42	9	H	Hartlepool U	D 1-1	1-0	14	Johnson ^{39}	3148
43	16	A	Huddersfield T	D 2-2	1-1	14	Danns ^{19}, Chilvers ^{90}	10,831
44	23	H	Bradford C	D 0-0	0-0	15		3351
45	30	A	Barnsley	D 1-1	0-1	16	Johnson ^{88}	8162
46	May 7	H	Torquay U	W 2-1	1-0	15	Danns ^{42}, Keith M ^{89}	4834

Final League Position: 15

GOALSCORERS

League (60): Danns 11 (1 pen), Johnson 9, Fagan 8 (1 pen), Garcia 4, Halford 4, Keith J 4, Keith M 4 (1 pen), Williams 3, Andrews 2 (1 pen), Watson 2, Brown W 1, Chilvers 1, Goodfellow 1, Hunt 1, May 1, N'Dumbu Nsungu 1, Stockley 1, own goals 2.
Carling Cup (6): Fagan 2, Danns 1, Halford 1, Johnson 1, May 1.
FA Cup (12): Fagan 4 (1 pen), Halford 4, Williams 2 (1 pen), Garcia 1, own goal 1.
LDV Vans Trophy (1): Garcia 1.

Davison A 33	Stockley S 33 + 4	Halford G 43 + 1	Brown W 38 + 2	Chilvers L 40 + 1	Watson K 44	Johnson G 36 + 1	Bowry B 7 + 4	Andrews W 4 + 1	Fagan C 25 + 1	Keith J 27 + 4	Cade J 4 + 5	May B 5 + 9	Baldwin P 35 + 3	Hunt S 16 + 4	White J 16 + 4	Bowditch B — + 5	Garcia R 20 + 4	Williams G 12 + 17	Danns N 32	Gerken D 13	Izzet K 3 + 1	N'Dumbu Nsungu G 2 + 6	Guy J — + 2	Keith M 12	Goodfellow M 4 + 1	Jarvis R 2 + 4	*Match No.*
1	2	3	4	5	6	7^1	8	9^2	10	11	12	13															1
1	2	3	4	5	6	7^1	8	9^2	10	11	12	13															2
1	2	3		5	6	7		9	10	11	8^1	12	4														3
1	2	3	4	5	6	7^2		9	10	11^1	8	12		13■													4
1	2	3	4	5^2	6^1	7		12	10	11		9	13		8^3	14											5
1	2	3	4	5^1		7			10	11	8	9	12		6^2	13											6
1	2	3	4	5	6				10	11	12	9^3		13	8^1		7^2	14									7
1	2	3^1	4	5	6				10	11		13	12			14	7^2	9	8^3								8
1		3	4	5	6				10	11		12		2^1		13	7	9	8^2								9
1		3	4		6	7^1	12			11		9^2	5	2			10	13	8								10
1		3	4		6	7^1	12			11		13	5	2			10	9^2	8								11
	12	3^1	4		6	7^2	14			11		13	5	2			10	9	8^3	1							12
	2		4	5	6		8^1		12	11		9^2	3					13	10	1	7						13
	2^1		4	5	6	13			10	11		12	3				9^2		8	1	7						14
	12	13	4	5	6					11	14		2^1	3			10^3	9^2	8	1	7						15
	2	10	4	5	6	7			9	11			3						8	1							16
	2	10	4	5	6	7			9	11			3						8	1							17
1	2	10		5	6	7^1	12		9	3			8		4		11										18
1	2	10		5	6	7^1	8		9	12			3		4		11										19
1	2	3		5	6		8^2		10■	11	12		7		4^1		9	13									20
1	2	10	4	5	6		8^2			11	7^1				3	13	9	12									21
1	2	10	4	5	6	7	8^1		9				3				11	12									22
1	2	10	4	5	6	7			9				3				11		8								23
	2	10	4	5	6	7^2			9				3	13	12		11^1		8	1							24
	2	10	4	5	6	7			9				3				11^1	12	8	1							25
	2	3	4	5	6	7			9	12			11^2				13	10^1	8	1							26
1	2	10	4		6	7			9	11^1			5	3					8			12					27
1	2	11	4	12	6^2	7^1			10	13			5	3				9^3	8			14					28
1	2^2	11	4	5		7			10	3^1			6					9	8			12	13				29
		10	4	5	6	7				11			2	3				12	8	1		9^1					30
		10	4	5	6	7				11			2	3				9^1	8	1		12					31
		10	4	5	6	7			9	11^2			2	3^1				12	8	1		13					32
		10	4	5	6	7			9				2	3	11				8	1							33
1	12	3	4	5	6	7				11			2		8			9^2				10^1	13				34
1	12	11	4	5	6	7				13			2^1	3	8^3			9				14		10^2			35
1		10	4	5■	6	7							2	3	11			12	8					9^1			36
1		10	4		6	7				11			2	3	5^1			12	8					9			37
1	2	3	4	5	6	7							11		12			13	8^2					9	10^1		38
1	2	10	4	5	6	7^2							3	12	13			14	8^3					9	11^1		39
1	2	10	4	5	6								3^2		7		13	12	8					9	11^1		40
1	2	10	4	5	6									3	7^2		12		8					9	11^1	13	41
1	2	10		5	6	7								3	4		12		8					9		11^1	42
1	2^1	3		5	6	7							4		11^2		10^3	12	8					9	13	14	43
1	2	3	12	5^1	6	7							4		13		11^2	14	8					9		10^3	44
1	2	10	4^1	5	6	7							3				11^2	12	8					9		13	45
1	2	3	12	5	6	7							4				11^3	10^1	8^2		13			9		14	46

FA Cup

First Round	Mansfield T	(a)	1-1
		(h)	4-1
Second Round	Rushden & D	(a)	5-2
Third Round	Hull C	(a)	2-0
Fourth Round	Blackburn R	(a)	0-3

Carling Cup

First Round	Cheltenham T	(h)	2-1
Second Round	WBA	(h)	2-1
Third Round	Southampton	(a)	2-3

LDV Vans Trophy

First Round	Southend U	(h)	1-1

COVENTRY CITY FL Championship

FOUNDATION

Workers at Singers' cycle factory formed a club in 1883. The first success of Singers' FC was to win the Birmingham Junior Cup in 1891 and this led in 1894 to their election to the Birmingham and District League. Four years later they changed their name to Coventry City and joined the Southern League in 1908 at which time they were playing in blue and white quarters.

Ricoh Arena, Coventry CV6 6AQ.

Telephone: 0870 421 1987.

Fax: 0870 421 1988.

Ticket Office: 0870 421 1987.

Website: www.ccfc.co.uk

Email: info@ccfc.co.uk

Ground Capacity: 32,500.

Record Attendance: 51,455 v Wolverhampton W, Division 2, 29 April 1967.

Pitch Measurements: 110yd × 75yd (at Highfield Road).

Chairman: Mike McGinnity.

Chief Executive/Secretary: Graham Hover.

Manager: Micky Adams.

Assistant Manager: Adrian Heath.

Physio: Michael McBride.

Colours: Sky blue and white striped shirts with plain sky blue panels on either side, sky blue shorts with white panel on one side and along the top on back, sky blue stockings with white stripe down each calf.

Change Colours: Black shirts with sky blue piping, black shorts with sky blue piping, black stockings with sky blue stripe down either side of calf muscle.

Year Formed: 1883.

Turned Professional: 1893.

Ltd Co.: 1907.

Previous Names: 1883, Singers FC; 1898, Coventry City FC.

Club Nickname: 'Sky Blues'.

Previous Grounds: 1883, Binley Road; 1887, Stoke Road; 1899, Highfield Road.

First Football League Game: 30 August 1919, Division 2, v Tottenham H (h) L 0–5 – Lindon; Roberts, Chaplin, Allan, Hawley, Clarke, Sheldon, Mercer, Sambrooke, Lowes, Gibson.

Record League Victory: 9–0 v Bristol C, Division 3 (S), 28 April 1934 – Pearson; Brown, Bisby; Perry, Davidson, Frith; White (2), Lauderdale, Bourton (5), Jones (2), Lake.

Record Cup Victory: 8–0 v Rushden & D, League Cup 2nd rd, 2 October 2002 – Debec; Caldwell, Quinn, Betts (1p), Konjic (Shaw), Davenport, Pipe, Safri (Stanford), Mills (2) (Bothroyd (2)), McSheffery (3), Partridge.

HONOURS

Football League: Division 1 best season: 6th, 1969–70; Division 2 – Champions 1966–67; Division 3 – Champions 1963–64; Division 3 (S) – Champions 1935–36; Runners-up 1933–34; Division 4 – Runners-up 1958–59.

FA Cup: Winners 1987.

Football League Cup: Semi-final 1981, 1990.

European Competitions: *European Fairs Cup:* 1970–71.

SKY SPORTS FACT FILE

On successive Saturdays at the turn of the year in 1933–34, Arthur Bacon scored five at Gillingham and four times at home to Crystal Palace. His 11 goals that season came in a spell of seven games in which Coventry scored.

Record Defeat: 2–10 v Norwich C, Division 3 (S), 15 March 1930.

Most League Points (2 for a win): 60, Division 4, 1958–59 and Division 3, 1963–64.

Most League Points (3 for a win): 66, Division 1, 2001–02.

Most League Goals: 108, Division 3 (S), 1931–32.

Highest League Scorer in Season: Clarrie Bourton, 49, Division 3 (S), 1931–32.

Most League Goals in Total Aggregate: Clarrie Bourton, 171, 1931–37.

Most League Goals in One Match: 5, Clarrie Bourton v Bournemouth, Division 3S, 17 October 1931; 5, Arthur Bacon v Gillingham, Division 3S, 30 December 1933.

Most Capped Player: Magnus Hedman 44 (56), Sweden.

Most League Appearances: Steve Ogrizovic, 507, 1984–2000.

Youngest League Player: Ben Mackey, 16 years 167 days v Ipswich T, 12 April 2003.

Record Transfer Fee Received: £12,500,000 from Internazionale for Robbie Keane, July 2000.

Record Transfer Fee Paid: £6,000,000 to Wolverhampton W for Robbie Keane, August 1999.

Football League Record: 1919 Elected to Division 2; 1925–26 Division 3 (N); 1926–36 Division 3 (S); 1936–52 Division 2; 1952–58 Division 3 (S); 1958–59 Division 4; 1959–64 Division 3; 1964–67 Division 2; 1967–92 Division 1; 1992–2001 FA Premier League; 2001–04 Division 1; 2004– FLC.

LATEST SEQUENCES

Longest Sequence of League Wins: 6, 25.4.1964 – 5.9.1964.

Longest Sequence of League Defeats: 9, 30.8.1919 – 11.10.1919.

Longest Sequence of League Draws: 6, 1.11.2003 – 29.11.2003.

Longest Sequence of Unbeaten League Matches: 25, 26.11.1966 – 13.5.1967.

Longest Sequence Without a League Win: 19, 30.8.1919 – 20.12.1919.

Successive Scoring Runs: 25 from 10.9.1966.

Successive Non-scoring Runs: 11 from 11.10.1919.

MANAGERS

H. R. Buckle 1909–10
Robert Wallace 1910–13
(Secretary-Manager)
Frank Scott-Walford 1913–15
William Clayton 1917–19
H. Pollitt 1919–20
Albert Evans 1920–24
Jimmy Kerr 1924–28
James McIntyre 1928–31
Harry Storer 1931–45
Dick Bayliss 1945–47
Billy Frith 1947–48
Harry Storer 1948–53
Jack Fairbrother 1953–54
Charlie Elliott 1954–55
Jesse Carver 1955–56
Harry Warren 1956–57
Billy Frith 1957–61
Jimmy Hill 1961–67
Noel Cantwell 1967–72
Bob Dennison 1972
Joe Mercer 1972–75
Gordon Milne 1972–81
Dave Sexton 1981–83
Bobby Gould 1983–84
Don Mackay 1985–86
George Curtis 1986–87
(became Managing Director)
John Sillett 1987–90
Terry Butcher 1990–92
Don Howe 1992
Bobby Gould 1992–93
Phil Neal 1993–95
Ron Atkinson 1995–96
(became Director of Football)
Gordon Strachan 1996–2001
Roland Nilsson 2001–02
Gary McAllister 2002–04
Eric Black 2004
Peter Reid 2004–05
Micky Adams January 2005–

TEN YEAR LEAGUE RECORD

		P	W	D	L	F	A	Pts	Pos
1995-96	PR Lge	38	8	14	16	42	60	38	16
1996-97	PR Lge	38	9	14	15	38	54	41	17
1997-98	PR Lge	38	12	16	10	46	44	52	11
1998-99	PR Lge	38	11	9	18	39	51	42	15
1999-2000	PR Lge	38	12	8	18	47	54	44	14
2000-01	PR Lge	38	8	10	20	36	63	34	19
2001-02	Div 1	46	20	6	20	59	53	66	11
2002-03	Div 1	46	12	14	20	46	62	50	20
2003-04	Div 1	46	17	14	15	67	54	65	12
2004-05	FL C	46	13	13	20	61	73	52	19

DID YOU KNOW ?

In 1907–08 Coventry City had a lengthy run in the FA Cup while members of the Birmingham & District League. In eight games to reach the first round proper they scored 31 goals shared by eight different players.

COVENTRY CITY 2004–05 LEAGUE RECORD

Match No.	*Date*	*Venue*	*Opponents*	*Result*	*H/T Score*	*Lg. Pos.*	*Goalscorers*	*Attendance*
1	Aug 7	H	Sunderland	W 2-0	0-0	—	Suffo (pen) 84, Johnson 90	16,460
2	10	A	Cardiff C	L 1-2	1-0	—	Barrett 29	14,031
3	14	A	Brighton & HA	D 1-1	0-0	7	Hughes 69	6368
4	21	H	Millwall	L 0-1	0-0	15		13,910
5	28	A	Nottingham F	W 4-1	1-0	10	Morrell 2 41, 52, Johnson 59, Hughes 70	23,041
6	30	H	West Ham U	W 2-1	1-1	5	Doyle 45, Morrell 76	17,404
7	Sept 11	A	Leeds U	L 0-3	0-1	10		26,725
8	15	H	Gillingham	D 2-2	1-0	—	Morrell 31, John (pen) 49	11,966
9	18	H	Rotherham U	D 0-0	0-0	11		13,834
10	25	A	Sheffield U	D 1-1	1-1	10	Morrell 15	16,337
11	28	A	QPR	L 1-4	0-2	—	Barrett 49	14,680
12	Oct 3	H	Ipswich T	L 1-2	0-0	18	Suffo 77	12,608
13	16	H	Leicester C	D 1-1	0-0	19	Makin (og) 80	18,054
14	19	A	Burnley	D 2-2	0-0	—	Johnson 62, Barrett 70	10,919
15	23	A	Wigan Ath	L 1-4	1-1	19	Johnson 32	9632
16	30	H	Reading	W 3-2	1-1	18	John (pen) 14, Morrell 51, Johnson 66	13,663
17	Nov 3	H	Preston NE	D 1-1	0-0	—	Suffo (pen) 49	12,478
18	8	A	Leicester C	L 0-3	0-2	—		22,479
19	13	H	Plymouth Arg	W 2-1	2-0	17	Hughes 9, Barrett 15	15,314
20	20	A	Wolverhampton W	W 1-0	0-0	16	McSheffrey 61	26,291
21	27	H	Crewe Alex	L 0-1	0-1	18		12,823
22	Dec 4	A	Derby Co	D 2-2	1-0	18	Hughes 22, Adebola 80	22,648
23	11	A	Stoke C	L 0-1	0-1	19		15,744
24	18	H	Watford	W 1-0	1-0	18	McSheffrey 45	14,493
25	26	H	Sheffield U	L 1-2	1-2	19	John 19	21,146
26	28	A	Gillingham	L 1-3	1-1	19	Adebola 37	8734
27	Jan 1	A	Rotherham U	W 2-1	0-1	19	John 58, Williams 75	5742
28	3	H	Leeds U	L 1-2	0-1	20	McSheffrey 82	19,084
29	15	A	Ipswich T	L 2-3	1-1	20	John 12, McSheffrey (pen) 61	23,670
30	22	H	QPR	L 1-2	0-1	21	Williams 59	16,595
31	Feb 5	A	Preston NE	L 2-3	1-2	21	Jorgensen 14, McSheffrey 72	13,691
32	12	H	Burnley	L 0-2	0-0	21		13,236
33	19	A	Reading	W 2-1	0-1	20	McSheffrey 63, John 72	15,904
34	23	H	Wigan Ath	L 1-2	1-1	—	McSheffrey (pen) 22	12,130
35	26	H	Stoke C	D 0-0	0-0	21		13,871
36	Mar 5	A	Watford	W 3-2	1-1	21	Benjamin 14, Jorgensen 54, Doyle 78	13,794
37	12	H	Cardiff C	D 1-1	1-1	21	John 16	17,059
38	15	A	Millwall	D 1-1	0-0	—	Jorgensen 89	8835
39	19	A	Sunderland	L 0-1	0-0	22		29,424
40	Apr 2	H	Brighton & HA	W 2-1	0-0	19	McSheffrey (pen) 47, Staunton 84	18,606
41	6	H	Nottingham F	W 2-0	2-0	—	McSheffrey (pen) 24, Adebola 41	22,221
42	9	A	West Ham U	L 0-3	0-0	17		26,839
43	16	H	Wolverhampton W	D 2-2	1-1	18	McSheffrey (pen) 19, John 90	19,412
44	23	A	Plymouth Arg	D 1-1	1-0	19	John 45	18,443
45	30	H	Derby Co	W 6-2	4-0	17	McSheffrey 2 (1 pen) 20, 29 (p), Adebola 37, John 2 40, 55, Whing 68	22,728
46	May 8	A	Crewe Alex	L 1-2	1-0	19	Adebola 23	9269

Final League Position: 19

GOALSCORERS

League (61): McSheffrey 12 (6 pens), John 11 (2 pens), Morrell 6, Adebola 5, Johnson 5, Barrett 4, Hughes 4, Jorgensen 3, Suffo 3 (2 pens), Doyle 2, Williams 2, Benjamin 1, Staunton 1, Whing 1, own goal 1.
Carling Cup (5): Suffo 2, Doyle 1, Hughes 1, Morrell 1.
FA Cup (4): McSheffrey 2, Adebola 1, John 1.

Shearer S 8	Carey L 23	Staunton S 32 + 3	Hughes S 39 + 1	Shaw R 30 + 3	Davenport C 6	Doyle M 43 + 1	Gudjonsson B 3 + 7	McSheffrey G 31 + 6	Johnson E 20 + 6	Barrett G 12 + 12	Sherwood T 10 + 1	Morrell A 24 + 10	Suffo P 2 + 19	Wood N 6 + 7	Leacock D 12 + 1	Whing A 9 + 7	Steele L 32	Mills M 4	John S 25 + 5	Jorgensen C 11 + 6	Ricketts R 5 + 1	Giddings S 11 + 1	Laville F 5 + 1	Deloumeaux E 1 + 1	Williams A 21	Adebola D 18 + 7	Osbourne I 7 + 2	Duffy R 14	Negouai C 1	Bennett I 6	Benjamin T 6 + 6	Hall M 10	Page R 9	Dyer L 6	Goater S 4 + 2	Match No.
1	2	3	4^1	5	6	7	8^2	9^3	10	11	12	13	14																							1
1	2	3	4	5	6	7	8^1	13	10^3	11	9^2	12	14																							2
1	2	3	4	5	6	7	8^1	9^2	10	11		12	13																							3
1	2	3	4^1	5	6	7	12	13	10^3	11	8	14	9^2																							4
1	2	3	4	5	6	7	12	13	10^3	11^2	8	9^1	14																							5
1	2	3	4	5	6	7	12		10^3	13	8	9^1	14	11^2																						6
1	2■	3^1	4	5		7			10^2	12	8	9	13	11^3	6	14																				7
		3	4^1	5		7	12			11^2	8	9	13		6	2	1		10																	8
	2	3	4^1	5		7	12			11^2	8	9	13				1	6	10																	9
	2	3^3		5		7				12	4	9	13	8^2		14	1	6	10	11^1																10
	2	3		5		7			12	11	4	9^1	13			14	1	6^3	10	8^2																11
		3	4	5		7	12			11^1	8^2	9^3	13			2	1	6	10	14																12
		3	4	5		7			8	12		9	13		6	2	1		10^2		11^1															13
		3	4	5		7			8	12		9^1	13		6	2	1		10^2		11															14
	2	3■	4	5		7	12	13	8			9^2	14		6		1		10^3		11^1															15
	2		4			7		12	8^1			9	13		6		1		10^2		11^3	3	5	14												16
			4	12		7		13	8			9	10		2		1				11^2	3	6^1		5											17
			11	12		7		10				9	13	8^3	2		1				14	3	6^1	4^2	5											18
	2		4	6		7		10	8^1	11^2		9	12				1					3			5	13										19
	2		4	6		7		10^1	8	12		9					1					3			5	11										20
	2	3	4	6		7		10	8			9^1	12				1								5	11										21
	2	3	4	6		7		10^1	8^2	12		9	13				1								5	11										22
	2	3	4	6		7		10	8^1			9					1		12				13		5^2	11										23
	2		4	5				10^1	12			9		13			1		8^2			3	6			11	7									24
	2		4			7		10	12			9^1		13			1		8^2			3	6		5	11										25
	2	3	4	6		12		10	8	11^2				7^1			1		13						5	9										26
	2^3	12	4^2	6		7		10	8					13	14		1		11			3^1			5	9										27
	2	14	4	6		7		10	8^1	12				13			1		9			3^3			5	11^2										28
		3	4	6		7		10				9^2			2^1	12	1		8	13					5	14	11^3									29
	2	3	4			7		10	12			9		11^2	6		1		8^1						5	13										30
			4	6^1		7		10		12				13	8	2	1			11^2					5	9		3								31
		3^3	4^1			7		10		11				12	6	2	1		13			14			5	9			8^2							32
				6		7		10		12				13					9	11^1		3			5	14	4^2	2		1	8^3					33
			12	6^3		7		10								13			9	14		3^2			5		4^1	2		1	8	11				34
		6	4			7		10	12							2			9^1	11					5			3		1■	8					35
1		6	4			7		10^2	12										9^1	11					5		13	2			8	3				36
		6	4			7		10		12		13							9^1	11^2					5	14		2		1	8^3	3				37
			4	6				10				7^2							8	12						9^1	11	2		1	13	3	5			38
		6		12		7		10^3		13									9	11						14	4	2^1		1	8^2	3	5			39
		6	4			7		10				12					1			11^1						13		2			14	3	5	8^2	9^3	40
		6	4^2			7		10								12	1									11	13	2			14	3	5	8^1	9^3	41
		14		6		7		10				12					1		13							11^1	4^3	2				3	5	8	9^2	42
		6				7		10				12					1		13	11^3						8		2			14	3	5	4^1	9^2	43
		6	4			7		10								2	1		9^3	12						11^2		3			14		5	8^1	13	44
		6	4			7		10^1				12				13	1		8	11^2						9^3		2			14	3	5			45
		3^2	4^1			7		10				12				2	1		9	13					5	11^3							6	8	14	46

FA Cup

Third Round	Crewe Alex	(h)	3-0
Fourth Round	Newcastle U	(a)	1-3

Carling Cup

First Round	Torquay U	(h)	4-1
Second Round	Sheffield W	(h)	1-0
Third Round	Middlesbrough	(a)	0-3

CREWE ALEXANDRA FL Championship

FOUNDATION

The first match played at Crewe was on 1 December 1877 against Basford, the leading North Staffordshire team of that time. During the club's history they have also played in a number of other leagues including the Football Alliance, Football Combination, Lancashire League, Manchester League, Central League and Lancashire Combination. Two former players, Aaron Scragg in 1899 and Jackie Pearson in 1911, had the distinction of refereeing FA Cup finals. Pearson was also capped for England against Ireland in 1892.

The Alexandra Stadium, Gresty Road, Crewe, Cheshire CW2 6EB.

Telephone: (01270) 213 014.

Fax: (01270) 216 320.

Ticket Office: (01270) 252 610.

Website: www.crewealex.net

Email: info@crewealex.net

Ground Capacity: 10,046.

Record Attendance: 20,000 v Tottenham H, FA Cup 4th rd, 30 January 1960.

Pitch Measurements: 112yd × 74yd.

Chairman: John Bowler.

Vice-chairman: Norman Hassall.

Secretary: Alison Bowler.

Manager: Dario Gradi MBE.

Assistant Manager: Neil Baker.

Physio: Matt Radcliffe.

Colours: Red shirts, white shorts, red stockings.

Change Colours: Blue shirts, blue shorts, white stockings.

Year Formed: 1877.

Turned Professional: 1893.

Ltd Co.: 1892.

Club Nickname: 'Railwaymen'.

First Football League Game: 3 September 1892, Division 2, v Burton Swifts (a) L 1–7 – Hickton; Moore, Cope; Linnell, Johnson, Osborne; Bennett, Pearson (1), Bailey, Barnett, Roberts.

Record League Victory: 8–0 v Rotherham U, Division 3 (N), 1 October 1932 – Foster; Pringle, Dawson; Ward, Keenor (1), Turner (1); Gillespie, Swindells (1), McConnell (2), Deacon (2), Weale (1).

HONOURS

Football League: Divison 2 – Runners-up 2002–03; Promoted from Division 2 1996–97 (play-offs).

FA Cup: Semi-final 1888.

Football League Cup: best season: 3rd rd, 1975, 1976, 1979, 1993, 1999, 2000, 2002.

Welsh Cup: Winners 1936, 1937.

SKY SPORTS FACT FILE

Phil Smith was a prolific goalscorer for Crewe Alexandra during their wilderness days outside the Football League. Chelsea paid £250 for him in 1910 and after a short spell with Burnley he returned to Crewe scoring 38 in 1911–12.

Record Cup Victory: 8–0 v Hartlepool U, Auto Windscreens Shield 1st rd, 17 October 1995 – Gayle; Collins (1), Booty, Westwood (Unsworth), Macauley (1), Whalley (1), Garvey (1), Murphy (1), Savage (1) (Rivers (1p)), Lennon, Edwards, (1 og). 8–0 v Doncaster R, LDV Vans Trophy 3rd rd, 10 November 2002 – Bankole; Wright, Walker, Foster, Tierney; Lunt (1), Brammer, Sorvel, Vaughan (1) (Bell); Ashton (3) (Miles), Jack (2) (Jones (1)).

Record Defeat: 2–13 v Tottenham H, FA Cup 4th rd replay, 3 February 1960.

Most League Points (2 for a win): 59, Division 4, 1962–63.

Most League Points (3 for a win): 86, Division 2, 2002–03.

Most League Goals: 95, Division 3 (N), 1931–32.

Highest League Scorer in Season: Terry Harkin, 35, Division 4, 1964–65.

Most League Goals in Total Aggregate: Bert Swindells, 126, 1928–37.

Most League Goals in One Match: 5, Tony Naylor v Colchester U, Division 3, 24 April 1993.

Most Capped Player: Clayton Ince, 38, Trinidad & Tobago.

Most League Appearances: Tommy Lowry, 436, 1966–78.

Youngest League Player: Steve Walters, 16 years 119 days v Peterborough U, 6 May 1988.

Record Transfer Fee Received: £3,000,000 from Derby Co for Seth Johnson, May 1999.

Record Transfer Fee Paid: £650,000 to Torquay U for Rodney Jack, June 1998.

Football League Record: 1892 Original Member of Division 2; 1896 Failed re-election; 1921 Re-entered Division 3 (N); 1958–63 Division 4; 1963–64 Division 3; 1964–68 Division 4; 1968–69 Division 3; 1969–89 Division 4; 1989–91 Division 3; 1991–92 Division 4; 1992–94 Division 3; 1994–97 Division 2; 1997–2002 Division 1; 2002–03 Division 2; 2003–04 Division 1; 2004– FLC.

MANAGERS

W. C. McNeill 1892–94 *(Secretary-Manager)*
J. G. Hall 1895–96 *(Secretary-Manager)*
R. Roberts *(1st team Secretary-Manager)* 1897
J. B. Blomerley 1898–1911 *(Secretary-Manager, continued as Hon. Secretary to 1925)*
Tom Bailey *(Secretary only)* 1925–38
George Lillycrop *(Trainer)* 1938–44
Frank Hill 1944–48
Arthur Turner 1948–51
Harry Catterick 1951–53
Ralph Ward 1953–55
Maurice Lindley 1956–57
Willie Cook 1957–58
Harry Ware 1958–60
Jimmy McGuigan 1960–64
Ernie Tagg 1964–71 *(continued as Secretary to 1972)*
Dennis Viollet 1971
Jimmy Melia 1972–74
Ernie Tagg 1974
Harry Gregg 1975–78
Warwick Rimmer 1978–79
Tony Waddington 1979–81
Arfon Griffiths 1981–82
Peter Morris 1982–83
Dario Gradi June 1983–

LATEST SEQUENCES

Longest Sequence of League Wins: 7, 30.4.1994 – 3.9.1994.

Longest Sequence of League Defeats: 10, 16.4.1979 – 22.8.1979.

Longest Sequence of League Draws: 5, 31.8.1987 – 18.9.1987.

Longest Sequence of Unbeaten League Matches: 17, 25.3.1995 – 16.9.1995.

Longest Sequence Without a League Win: 30, 22.9.1956 – 6.4.1957.

Successive Scoring Runs: 26 from 7.4.1934.

Successive Non-scoring Runs: 9 from 6.11.1974.

TEN YEAR LEAGUE RECORD

		P	*W*	*D*	*L*	*F*	*A*	*Pts*	*Pos*
1995-96	Div 2	46	22	7	17	77	60	73	5
1996-97	Div 2	46	22	7	17	56	47	73	6
1997-98	Div 1	46	18	5	23	58	65	59	11
1998-99	Div 1	46	12	12	22	54	78	48	18
1999-2000	Div 1	46	14	9	23	46	67	51	19
2000-01	Div 1	46	15	10	21	47	62	55	14
2001-02	Div 1	46	12	13	21	47	76	49	22
2002-03	Div 2	46	25	11	10	76	40	86	2
2003-04	Div 1	46	14	11	21	57	66	53	18
2004-05	FL C	46	12	14	20	66	86	50	21

DID YOU KNOW

On the last day of the 2004–05 season Crewe Alexandra needed to better any victory and scoreline achieved by Gillingham to avoid relegation. Trailing 1–0 at home to Coventry City they managed to score twice in the second half to ensure survival.

CREWE ALEXANDRA 2004–05 LEAGUE RECORD

Match No.	Date	Venue	Opponents	Result		H/T Score	Lg. Pos.	Goalscorers	Attendance
1	Aug 7	H	Cardiff C	D	2-2	1-1	—	Ashton (pen) [5], Higdon [85]	7339
2	10	A	Sunderland	L	1-3	1-1	—	Rivers [43]	22,341
3	14	A	Nottingham F	D	2-2	2-1	22	Rivers 2 [21, 44]	24,201
4	21	H	West Ham U	L	2-3	1-3	22	Ashton 2 [31, 82]	7857
5	28	A	Derby Co	W	4-2	2-1	14	Jones S 2 [5, 83], Vaughan [12], Ashton [74]	24,436
6	Sept 11	A	Burnley	L	0-3	0-2	21		11,274
7	14	H	QPR	L	0-2	0-1	—		5682
8	18	H	Leeds U	D	2-2	0-0	21	Ashton (pen) [48], Jones S [83]	9095
9	25	A	Preston NE	L	0-1	0-1	23		11,823
10	28	A	Rotherham U	W	3-2	1-1	—	Ashton 2 (1 pen) [19 (p), 71], Lunt [61]	4498
11	Oct 2	H	Watford	W	3-0	3-0	19	Jones S [20], Sorvel 2 [23, 38]	6382
12	16	H	Brighton & HA	W	3-1	2-0	16	Lunt [9], White [34], Higdon [69]	6811
13	19	A	Wigan Ath	L	1-4	0-2	—	Jones S [56]	7547
14	23	A	Reading	L	0-4	0-3	20		13,630
15	29	H	Sheffield U	L	2-3	1-3	—	Foster [24], Thirlwell (og) [90]	7131
16	Nov 2	H	Leicester C	D	2-2	0-1	—	Rivers [49], Otsemobor [61]	6849
17	6	A	Brighton & HA	W	3-1	1-0	20	Ashton 2 [40, 59], Rivers [50]	6163
18	13	A	Stoke C	L	0-1	0-0	21		17,640
19	20	H	Gillingham	W	4-1	1-0	19	Vaughan [35], Ashton 2 [71, 80], Jones S [89]	6128
20	27	A	Coventry C	W	1-0	1-0	17	Ashton (pen) [26]	12,823
21	30	H	Millwall	W	2-1	1-0	—	Ashton [1], Varney [76]	5409
22	Dec 4	H	Ipswich T	D	2-2	2-0	14	Ashton 2 [24, 27]	7236
23	11	H	Plymouth Arg	W	3-0	1-0	12	Lunt [42], Ashton [57], Doumbe (og) [80]	6823
24	18	A	Wolverhampton W	D	1-1	1-0	11	Lescott (og) [38]	25,340
25	28	A	QPR	W	2-1	2-0	10	Walker [39], Rivers [45]	15,770
26	Jan 1	A	Leeds U	W	2-0	1-0	8	Ashton [16], Rivers [54]	32,302
27	3	H	Preston NE	L	1-2	0-1	10	Walker [81]	8667
28	15	A	Watford	L	1-3	0-2	12	Varney [68]	11,223
29	22	H	Rotherham U	D	1-1	0-1	12	White [79]	6382
30	Feb 5	A	Leicester C	D	1-1	1-0	12	White [36]	27,011
31	12	H	Wigan Ath	L	1-3	1-1	13	White [45]	7981
32	15	H	Burnley	D	1-1	1-0	—	Jones S [18]	7718
33	22	H	Reading	D	1-1	1-0	—	Varney [12]	5703
34	26	A	Plymouth Arg	L	0-3	0-1	16		14,918
35	Mar 5	H	Wolverhampton W	L	1-4	1-3	17	Lunt (pen) [11]	8212
36	8	A	Sheffield U	L	0-4	0-2	—		16,079
37	12	H	Sunderland	L	0-1	0-0	18		7949
38	15	A	West Ham U	D	1-1	0-0	—	Jones S [90]	26,593
39	19	A	Cardiff C	D	1-1	0-1	16	Vaughan [57]	10,007
40	Apr 2	H	Nottingham F	D	1-1	0-1	16	Sorvel [71]	8458
41	5	H	Derby Co	L	1-2	0-1	—	Vaughan [90]	8026
42	9	A	Millwall	L	3-4	0-1	20	Lunt (pen) [62], Jones S [68], Varney [81]	10,767
43	16	A	Gillingham	D	1-1	0-0	20	Vaughan [73]	10,315
44	23	H	Stoke C	L	0-2	0-0	21		9166
45	30	A	Ipswich T	L	1-5	0-2	22	Vaughan [90]	28,244
46	May 8	H	Coventry C	W	2-1	0-1	21	Higdon [54], Jones S [72]	9269

Final League Position: 21

GOALSCORERS

League (66): Ashton 17 (4 pens), Jones S 10, Rivers 7, Vaughan 6, Lunt 5 (2 pens), Varney 4, White 4, Higdon 3, Sorvel 3, Walker 2, Foster 1, Otsemobor 1, own goals 3.
Carling Cup (7): Jones S 3, Ashton 2, Foster 1, Rivers 1.
FA Cup (0).

Williams B 23	Briggs K 3	Jones B 20	Lunt K 46	Walker R 15 + 8	Foster S 34	Sorvel N 45 + 1	Cochrane J 21 + 8	Ashton D 23 + 1	Rivers M 26 + 8	Vaughan D 43 + 1	Higdon M 1 + 19	Jones S 24 + 12	Tonkin A 33 + 2	Moses A 19 + 2	Varney L 17 + 9	Roberts M 3 + 3	Bignot P 3 + 2	Otsemobor J 14	White A 11 + 11	Ince C 23	McCready C 19 + 1	Bell L 17	Murdock C 15 + 1	Moss D 6	Platt M — + 1	Roberts G 2	*Match No.*
1	2	3	4	5	6	7	8^{1}	9	10^{2}	11	12	13															1
1		3	4	5	6	7	8	9	10^{1}	11	12	13	2^{2}														2
1	2^{3}	3	4	5	6	7	8	9^{1}	10^{2}	11	12	13	14														3
1	2^{3}	3	4	5	6	7	8^{1}	9	10^{2}	11	13	12	14														4
1		3	4		6	7		9	10^{1}	11	12	8	2	5													5
1		3^{1}	4	12	6	7		9^{3}	10^{2}	11	13	8	2	5	14												6
1		3^{1}	4	12	6	7		9	10^{2}	11	13	8^{3}	2	5	14												7
1			4	5	6	7	12	9^{2}		11	13	8	3	2	10^{1}												8
1		5	4		6	7	8	9	12	11		10	3^{1}			2											9
1		6	4	5		7	8	9		11		10				2	3										10
1		5	4		6	7	8	9^{2}	12	11	13	10^{1}	3^{3}			14		2									11
1		5	4^{1}		6	7	8		12	11	13^{3}	10	3			14		2	9^{2}								12
1		5^{1}	4	12	6	7	8		13	11		10				3		2	9^{2}								13
1		5^{2}	4		6	7	8^{3}	12	9	11^{1}		10	3			13		2	14								14
1		5	4		6	7	8		12	11		10	3^{1}		13			2	9^{2}								15
		5	4	12	6^{1}	7	8	9^{3}	10^{2}	11		13	3					2	14	1							16
		5	4		6	7	8	9	10	11			3					2		1							17
		5	4		6	7	8^{1}	9^{2}	10	11		12	3		13			2		1							18
			4	5^{3}	6	7	8^{1}	9^{2}	10	11		12	3					2	13	1	14						19
			4	12	6	7	8	9	10^{2}	11^{1}		13	3					2		1	5						20
			4		6	7	8	9	10^{1}			11		5	12			2		1	3						21
			4	12	6	7	8	9		11		10		5			2			1	3^{1}						22
		3	4^{1}	12	6	7	8	9^{3}	13	11		10^{2}		5	14			2		1							23
			4	5	6	7		9	10	11				3				2		1		8					24
			4	5	6	7	12	9^{2}	10^{3}	11				3	14			2	13	1		8^{1}					25
			4	5	6	7	12	9^{2}	10^{1}	11				3	13		14			1	2^{3}	8					26
			4	5	6	7		9^{1}		11	12	10^{2}	3	2	13					1		8					27
			4	5		7			10^{1}	11	12			2	9		3			1	6	8					28
			4		6	7			12	11		10	3	5	9^{2}				13	1	2	8^{1}					29
			4^{1}		6	7	12			11			3		9				10	1	2	8	5				30
			4		6	7	12		10^{2}	11	14	13	3						9^{3}	1	2	8^{1}	5				31
			4		6	12	8			13		11^{2}	3		9				10	1	2^{1}	7	5				32
			4		6	7				11	12		3		9				10^{1}	1	2	8	5				33
			4		6■	7			12	11		10^{1}	3	13	9					1	2	8	5^{2}				34
1			4			7			10^{3}	11	12	8	3	5					9^{1}		6		13	2^{2}	14		35
1			4		6	7			10	11	9^{1}		3						12				5	2		8	36
1			4		6	7			10^{1}	11		12	3		9				13			8^{2}	5	2			37
1			4	6		7	12		10^{2}			13	3		9				14		2	8^{1}	5			11^{3}	38
1			4	6		7			10^{1}	11		12	3		9						2	8	5				39
1			4			7				11		10	3	6	9				12		2	8^{1}	5				40
1			4			7				11		10	3	2	9				12		6	8^{1}	5				41
1			4			7				11		8	3	2	9				10		6		5				42
			4			7	12			11	13	8^{1}	3	6	9				10^{2}	1	2		5				43
			4	12		7			10	11	13		3		9				8^{2}	1	6		5^{1}	2			44
		6^{2}	4	5		7^{1}	12		10	11	14			3	9		13			1		8^{3}		2			45
		6	4			7^{1}	8^{2}			11	12	10^{3}	3	13	9				14	1			5	2			46

FA Cup

Third Round	Coventry C	(a)	0-3

Carling Cup

First Round	Blackpool	(h)	4-1
Second Round	Sunderland	(h)	3-3
Third Round	Manchester U	(h)	0-3

CRYSTAL PALACE FL Championship

FOUNDATION

There was a Crystal Palace club as early as 1861 but the present organisation was born in 1905 after the formation of a club by the company that controlled the Crystal Palace (building), had been rejected by the FA who did not like the idea of the Cup Final hosts running their own club. A separate company had to be formed and they had their home on the old Cup Final ground until 1915.

Selhurst Park Stadium, Whitehorselane, London SE25 6PU.

Telephone: (020) 8768 6000.

Fax: (020) 8771 5311.

Ticket Office: 0871 200 0071

Website: www.cpfc.co.uk

Email: info@cpfc.co.uk

Ground Capacity: 26,257.

Record Attendance: 51,482 v Burnley, Division 2, 11 May 1979.

Pitch Measurements: 110yd × 74yd.

Chairman: Simon Jordan.

Vice-chairman: Dominic Jordan.

Chief Executive: Phil Alexander.

Assistant Secretary: Christine Dowdeswell.

Manager: Iain Dowie.

Assistant Manager: Kit Symons.

Physio: Paul Caton.

Colours: Red and royal blue shirts, royal blue shorts, royal blue stockings.

Change Colours: All black.

Year Formed: 1905.

Turned Professional: 1905.

Ltd Co.: 1905.

Club Nickname: 'The Eagles'.

Previous Grounds: 1905, Crystal Palace; 1915, Herne Hill; 1918, The Nest; 1924, Selhurst Park.

First Football League Game: 28 August 1920, Division 3, v Merthyr T (a) L 1–2 – Alderson; Little, Rhodes; McCracken, Jones, Feebury; Bateman, Conner, Smith, Milligan (1), Whibley.

Record League Victory: 9–0 v Barrow, Division 4, 10 October 1959 – Rouse; Long, Noakes; Truett, Evans, McNichol; Gavin (1), Summersby (4 incl. 1p), Sexton, Byrne (2), Colfar (2).

Record Cup Victory: 8–0 v Southend U, Rumbelows League Cup 2nd rd (1st leg), 25 September 1989 – Martyn; Humphrey (Thompson (1)), Shaw, Pardew, Young, Thorn, McGoldrick, Thomas, Bright (3), Wright (3), Barber (Hodges (1)).

HONOURS

Football League: Division 1 – Champions 1993–94; Promoted from Division 1, 1996–97 (play-offs), 2003–04 (play-offs); Division 2 – Champions 1978–79; Runners-up 1968–69; Division 3 – Runners-up 1963–64; Division 3 (S) – Champions 1920–21; Runners-up 1928–29, 1930–31, 1938–39; Division 4 – Runners-up 1960–61.

FA Cup: Runners-up 1990.

Football League Cup: Semi-final 1993, 1995, 2001.

Zenith Data Systems Cup: Winners 1991.

European Competition: *Intertoto Cup:* 1998.

SKY SPORTS FACT FILE

Cam Burgess hit a rich vein of goalscoring shortly after joining Crystal Palace in September 1951. In a run of 14 matches he scored 18 of the team's 27 goals. His final haul for the season was 21 from only 22 games.

Record Defeat: 0–9 v Burnley, FA Cup 2nd rd replay, 10 February 1909. 0–9 v Liverpool, Division 1, 12 September 1990.

Most League Points (2 for a win): 64, Division 4, 1960–61.

Most League Points (3 for a win): 90, Division 1, 1993–94.

Most League Goals: 110, Division 4, 1960–61.

Highest League Scorer in Season: Peter Simpson, 46, Division 3 (S), 1930–31.

Most League Goals in Total Aggregate: Peter Simpson, 153, 1930–36.

Most League Goals in One Match: 6, Peter Simpson v Exeter C, Division 3S, 4 October 1930.

Most Capped Player: Aleksandrs Kolinko 23 (51), Latvia.

Most League Appearances: Jim Cannon, 571, 1973–88.

Youngest League Player: Phil Hoadley, 16 years 112 days v Bolton W, 27 April 1968.

Record Transfer Fee Received: £4,500,000 from Tottenham H for Chris Armstrong, June 1995.

Record Transfer Fee Paid: £2,750,000 to RC Strasbourg for Valerien Ismael, January 1998.

Football League Record: 1920 Original Members of Division 3; 1921–25 Division 2; 1925–58 Division 3 (S); 1958–61 Division 4; 1961–64 Division 3; 1964–69 Division 2; 1969–73 Division 1; 1973–74 Division 2; 1974–77 Division 3; 1977–79 Division 2; 1979–81 Division 1; 1981–89 Division 2; 1989–92 Division 1; 1992–93 FA Premier League; 1993–94 Division 1; 1994–95 FA Premier League; 1995–97 Division 1; 1997–98 FA Premier League; 1998–2004 Division 1; 2004–05 FA Premier League; 2005– FLC.

LATEST SEQUENCES

Longest Sequence of League Wins: 8, 9.2.1921 – 26.3.1921.

Longest Sequence of League Defeats: 8, 10.1.1998 – 14.3.1998.

Longest Sequence of League Draws: 5, 21.9.2002 – 19.10.2002.

Longest Sequence of Unbeaten League Matches: 18, 22.2.1969 – 13.8.1969.

Longest Sequence Without a League Win: 20, 3.3.1962 – 8.9.1962.

Successive Scoring Runs: 24 from 27.4.1929.

Successive Non-scoring Runs: 9 from 19.11.1994.

MANAGERS

John T. Robson 1905–07
Edmund Goodman 1907–25 *(had been Secretary since 1905 and afterwards continued in this position to 1933)*
Alec Maley 1925–27
Fred Mavin 1927–30
Jack Tresadern 1930–35
Tom Bromilow 1935–36
R. S. Moyes 1936
Tom Bromilow 1936–39
George Irwin 1939–47
Jack Butler 1947–49
Ronnie Rooke 1949–50
Charlie Slade and Fred Dawes *(Joint Managers)* 1950–51
Laurie Scott 1951–54
Cyril Spiers 1954–58
George Smith 1958–60
Arthur Rowe 1960–62
Dick Graham 1962–66
Bert Head 1966–72 *(continued as General Manager to 1973)*
Malcolm Allison 1973–76
Terry Venables 1976–80
Ernie Walley 1980
Malcolm Allison 1980–81
Dario Gradi 1981
Steve Kember 1981–82
Alan Mullery 1982–84
Steve Coppell 1984–93
Alan Smith 1993–95
Steve Coppell *(Technical Director)* 1995–96
Dave Bassett 1996–97
Steve Coppell 1997–98
Attilio Lombardo 1998
Terry Venables *(Head Coach)* 1998–99
Steve Coppell 1999–2000
Alan Smith 2000–01
Steve Bruce 2001
Trevor Francis 2001–03
Steve Kember 2003
Iain Dowie December 2003–

TEN YEAR LEAGUE RECORD

		P	W	D	L	F	A	Pts	Pos
1995-96	Div 1	46	20	15	11	67	48	75	3
1996-97	Div 1	46	19	14	13	78	48	71	6
1997-98	PR Lge	38	8	9	21	37	71	33	20
1998-99	Div 1	46	14	16	16	58	71	58	14
1999-2000	Div 1	46	13	15	18	57	67	54	15
2000-01	Div 1	46	12	13	21	57	70	49	21
2001-02	Div 1	46	20	6	20	70	62	66	10
2002-03	Div 1	46	14	17	15	59	52	59	14
2003-04	Div 1	46	21	10	15	72	61	73	6
2004-05	PR Lge	38	7	12	19	41	62	33	18

DID YOU KNOW ?

Andy Johnson became the first Premier League player to score more than half of his team's total number of goals in a season. In 2004–05 his 11th successful penalty of the season in the 2–2 draw with Charlton Athletic on 15 May made it 21 of 41 goals.

CRYSTAL PALACE 2004–05 LEAGUE RECORD

Match No.	Date	Venue	Opponents	Result		H/T Score	Lg. Pos.	Goalscorers	Attendance
1	Aug 14	A	Norwich C	D	1-1	0-1	—	Johnson 73	23,717
2	21	H	Everton	L	1-3	1-1	20	Hudson 9	23,666
3	24	H	Chelsea	L	0-2	0-1	—		24,953
4	28	A	Middlesbrough	L	1-2	0-0	20	Johnson (pen) 52	31,560
5	Sept 11	A	Portsmouth	L	1-3	1-1	20	Granville 43	20,019
6	18	H	Manchester C	L	1-2	0-0	20	Johnson (pen) 77	25,052
7	25	A	Aston Villa	D	1-1	1-1	20	Johnson 6	34,843
8	Oct 4	H	Fulham	W	2-0	0-0	—	Johnson 53, Riihilahti 69	21,825
9	16	A	Bolton W	L	0-1	0-1	24		25,501
10	23	H	WBA	W	3-0	2-0	15	Hall 5, Johnson 2 (1 pen) 12 (p), 50	22,922
11	30	A	Birmingham C	W	1-0	1-0	14	Johnson 41	28,916
12	Nov 6	H	Arsenal	D	1-1	0-0	16	Riihilahti 65	26,193
13	13	A	Liverpool	L	2-3	1-2	16	Kolkka 44, Hughes 52	42,862
14	20	H	Newcastle U	L	0-2	0-0	16		22,937
15	27	A	Southampton	D	2-2	0-0	16	Johnson 48, Jakobsson (og) 54	31,833
16	Dec 5	H	Charlton Ath	L	0-1	0-0	16		20,705
17	11	H	Blackburn R	D	0-0	0-0	17		22010
18	18	A	Manchester U	L	2-5	1-2	18	Granville 27, Kolkka 46	67,814
19	26	H	Portsmouth	L	0-1	0-0	18		25,238
20	28	A	Tottenham H	D	1-1	0-0	17	Johnson 79	36,100
21	Jan 1	A	Fulham	L	1-3	1-1	18	Johnson (pen) 35	18,680
22	3	H	Aston Villa	W	2-0	1-0	17	Johnson 2 (1 pen) 33, 66 (p)	24,140
23	15	A	Manchester C	L	1-3	1-2	17	Powell 32	44,010
24	22	H	Tottenham H	W	3-0	0-0	17	Leigertwood 66, Granville 70, Johnson (pen) 77	23,723
25	Feb 1	A	WBA	D	2-2	0-0	—	Johnson 47, Riihilahti 90	25,092
26	5	H	Bolton W	L	0-1	0-1	17		23,163
27	14	A	Arsenal	L	1-5	0-3	—	Johnson (pen) 63	38,056
28	26	H	Birmingham C	W	2-0	1-0	17	Johnson 2 (2 pens) 41, 68	23,376
29	Mar 5	H	Manchester U	D	0-0	0-0	17		26,021
30	19	A	Chelsea	L	1-4	1-1	18	Riihilahti 42	41,667
31	Apr 2	H	Middlesbrough	L	0-1	0-1	19		24,274
32	10	A	Everton	L	0-4	0-1	19		36,519
33	16	H	Norwich C	D	3-3	1-1	19	Kolkka 5, Hughes 73, Johnson (pen) 83	25,754
34	20	A	Blackburn R	L	0-1	0-1	—		18,006
35	23	H	Liverpool	W	1-0	1-0	17	Johnson 34	26,043
36	30	A	Newcastle U	D	0-0	0-0	18		52,123
37	May 7	H	Southampton	D	2-2	1-1	19	Hall 34, Ventola 72	26,066
38	15	A	Charlton Ath	D	2-2	0-1	18	Freedman 58, Johnson (pen) 71	26,870

Final League Position: 18

GOALSCORERS

League (41): Johnson 21 (11 pens), Riihilahti 4, Granville 3, Kolkka 3, Hall 2, Hughes 2, Freedman 1, Hudson 1, Leigertwood 1, Powell 1, Ventola 1, own goal 1.
Carling Cup (4): Freedman 2, Soares 1, Torghelle 1.
FA Cup (1): own goal 1.

Speroni J 6	Boyce E 26 + 1	Granville D 35	Hudson M 7	Popovic T 21 + 2	Hall F 36	Routledge W 38	Hughes M 34 + 2	Johnson A 37	Torghelle S 3 + 9	Kolkka J 20 + 3	Freedman D 10 + 10	Riihilahti A 28 + 4	Derry S 1 + 6	Kaviedes I 1 + 3	Ventola N — + 3	Watson B 16 + 5	Kiraly G 32	Sorondo G 16 + 4	Soares T 16 + 6	Lakis V 6 + 12	Leigertwood M 16 + 4	Andrews W — + 9	Butterfield D 7	Powell D 4 + 2	Shipperley N — + 1	Borrowdale G 2 + 5	*Match No.*
1	2	3	4	5	6^{3}	7	8^{1}	9	10	11^{2}	12	13	14														1
1	2^{2}	3	4	5	6	7		9		11	10	8^{1}	12	13													2
1	2	3	4	5	6	7	12	9		11		8		10^{1}													3
1	2	3	4	5	6	7^{2}	8	9		11		10^{1}	12	13													4
1	2	3	4	5	6	7^{2}	12	9	10	11^{3}		8^{1}	13		14												5
1	2	3	4		6	7	8	9	10^{1}	12		5^{3}	11^{2}		13	14											6
	2	3		5	6^{1}	7	8	9		11^{2}		10				4	1	12	13								7
	2	3		5	6^{2}	7^{3}	8	9		11		10^{1}		12		4	1	13		14							8
	2	3		5	6	7	8	9		11^{3}	12	10^{2}	13			4^{1}	1			14							9
	2	3		5	6	7	8^{2}	9		10^{1}	12	11				4^{3}	1	14		13							10
	2	3		5^{3}	6	7	8^{1}	9		10^{2}	13	4	12			11	1	14									11
	2	3		5		7^{2}	8	9		10^{1}	12	6				11	1	4^{3}		13	14						12
	2	3		5		7^{1}	8			10	9	6^{2}				11	1		13	12	4						13
	2	3		5	6	7	8	9		10^{2}	12	4^{1}				11	1			13							14
	2	3		5	6	7	8	9		10		4				11	1										15
	2	3		5	6	7	8	9		10^{2}	12	4^{1}				11	1			13							16
	2	3		5	6	7^{1}	8	9	12	10^{2}		4^{3}				11	1			13		14					17
	2	3			6	7^{3}	8^{1}	9		10		4^{2}				11	1	5	12	13		14					18
		3			6	7^{1}	8	9		10	12	4^{3}				11^{2}	1	5	13			14	2				19
		3			6	7^{1}	8	9	12			4					1	5	11	10			2				20
		3		5	6	7	8^{2}	9	12			4^{1}					1		11	10^{3}	13	14	2				21
	12	3			6	7	8	9				4				11^{2}	1			10	13		2^{1}	5			22
	2				6	7^{2}		9								11^{1}	1	3	8	10^{3}	4	12		5	13	14	23
	2	3			6	7	8	9^{1}			10						1	5	11^{2}		4	12				13	24
	2				6	7	8^{1}	9			10^{2}	14					1	5■	11		4	12		13^{3}		3	25
	2	3			6	7^{1}	8	9		12	10	13					1		11^{3}		4^{2}	14		5			26
	2	3			6	7^{2}	8	9		12	10^{1}	4^{3}					1	5	11	13	14						27
	2	3			6	7^{2}	8	9	12		10^{1}						1	5	11^{3}	13	4					14	28
	2	3			6	7^{1}	8	9									1	5	11	10■	4					12	29
	2	3			6	7^{1}	8	9	12		13	4^{3}				14	1	5^{2}	11		10						30
		3^{3}	5		6	7	8	9			10	4^{2}					1		11^{1}	12	2	13				14	31
		3			6	7	8	9	12			4^{2}				13	1		11	10^{1}	2			5			32
		3		12	6	7	8	9	13	11^{1}	10						1	5	14		4^{3}		2^{2}				33
				12	6	7	8	9	13	11^{3}	10^{2}						1	5	14		4		2^{1}			3	34
		3		5	6	7	8	9				11				12	1	2	10^{1}		4						35
		3		5	6	7^{1}	8	9	12			11					1	2	10		4						36
		3		5^{2}	2	7	8	9				11^{1}			13	12	1	4■	10		6						37
		3		5	6	7	8	9			12	13				11^{2}	1		10^{3}		4		2^{1}	14			38

FA Cup

Third Round	Sunderland	(a)	1-2

Carling Cup

Second Round	Hartlepool U	(h)	2-1
Third Round	Charlton Ath	(a)	2-1
Fourth Round	Manchester U	(a)	0-2

DARLINGTON FL Championship 2

FOUNDATION

A football club was formed in Darlington as early as 1861 but the present club began in 1883 and reached the final of the Durham Senior Cup in their first season, losing to Sunderland in a replay after complaining that they had suffered from intimidation in the first. On 5 April 1884, Sunderland had defeated Darlington 4-3. Darlington's objection was upheld by the referee and the replay took place on 3 May. The new referee for the match was Major Marindin, appointed by the Football Association to ensure fair play. Sunderland won 2-0. The following season Darlington won this trophy and for many years were one of the leading amateur clubs in their area.

Williamson Motors Stadium, Neasham Road, Darlington DL2 1GR.

Telephone: (01325) 387 000.

Fax: (01325) 387 050.

Ticket Office: (01325) 387 030.

Website: darlington-fc.net

Email: info@darlington-fc.net

Ground Capacity: 25,000.

Record Attendance: 21,023 v Bolton W, League Cup 3rd rd, 14 November 1960.

Pitch Measurements: 105m × 68m.

Chairman: Stewart Davies.

Secretary: Lisa Charlton.

Manager: David Hodgson.

Assistant Manager: Mark Proctor.

Physio: Paul Gough.

Colours: Black and white hoops.

Change Colours: All black.

Year Formed: 1883. ***Turned Professional:*** 1908. ***Ltd Co.:*** 1891.

Previous Grounds: Feethams Ground; 2003, Reynolds Arena, Hurworth Moor.

Club Nickname: 'The Quakers'.

First Football League Game: 27 August 1921, Division 3 (N), v Halifax T (h) W 2–0 – Ward; Greaves, Barbour; Dickson (1), Sutcliffe, Malcolm; Dolphin, Hooper (1), Edmunds, Wolstenholme, Winship.

Record League Victory: 9–2 v Lincoln C, Division 3 (N), 7 January 1928 – Archibald; Brooks, Mellen; Kelly, Waugh, McKinnell; Cochrane (1), Gregg (1), Ruddy (3), Lees (3), McGiffen (1).

Record Cup Victory: 7–2 v Evenwood T, FA Cup 1st rd, 17 November 1956 – Ward; Devlin, Henderson; Bell (1p), Greener, Furphy; Forster (1), Morton (3), Tulip (2), Davis, Moran.

HONOURS

Football League: Division 2 best season: 15th, 1925–26; Division 3 (N) – Champions 1924–25; Runners-up 1921–22; Division 4 – Champions 1990–91; Runners-up 1965–66.

FA Cup: best season: 5th rd, 1958.

Football League Cup: best season: 5th rd, 1968.

GM Vauxhall Conference: Champions 1989–90.

SKY SPORTS FACT FILE

Erratic form in 1929–30 prevented Darlington from achieving honours though they were third in Division Three (North). Their record 108 goals included two 8s, a 7 and two 6s. Maurice Wellock plundered 34 of the total himself.

Record Defeat: 0–10 v Doncaster R, Division 4, 25 January 1964.

Most League Points (2 for a win): 59, Division 4, 1965–66.

Most League Points (3 for a win): 85, Division 4, 1984–85.

Most League Goals: 108, Division 3 (N), 1929–30.

Highest League Scorer in Season: David Brown, 39, Division 3 (N), 1924–25.

Most League Goals in Total Aggregate: Alan Walsh, 90, 1978–84.

Most League Goals in One Match: 5, Tom Ruddy v South Shields, Division 2, 23 April 1927; 5, Maurice Wellock v Rotherham U, Division 3N, 15 February 1930.

Most Capped Player: Jason Devos, 3 (46), Canada.

Most League Appearances: Ron Greener, 442, 1955–68.

Youngest League Player: Dale Anderson, 16 years 254 days v Chesterfield, 4 May 1987.

Record Transfer Fee Received: £400,000 from Dundee U for Jason Devos, October 1998.

Record Transfer Fee Paid: £95,000 to Motherwell for Nick Cusack, January 1992.

Football League Record: 1921 Original Member Division 3 (N); 1925–27 Division 2; 1927–58 Division 3 (N); 1958–66 Division 4; 1966–67 Division 3; 1967–85 Division 4; 1985–87 Division 3; 1987–89 Division 4; 1989–90 GM Vauxhall Conference; 1990–91 Division 4; 1991–2004 Division 3; 2004– FL2.

LATEST SEQUENCES

Longest Sequence of League Wins: 6, 6.2.2000 – 7.3.2000.

Longest Sequence of League Defeats: 8, 31.8.1985 – 19.10.1985.

Longest Sequence of League Draws: 5, 31.12.1988 – 28.1.1989.

Longest Sequence of Unbeaten League Matches: 17, 27.4.1968 – 19.10.1968.

Longest Sequence Without a League Win: 19, 27.4.1988 – 8.11.1988.

Successive Scoring Runs: 22 from 3.12.1932.

Successive Non-scoring Runs: 7 from 5.9.1975.

MANAGERS

Tom McIntosh 1902–11
W. L. Lane 1911–12
(Secretary-Manager)
Dick Jackson 1912–19
Jack English 1919–28
Jack Fairless 1928–33
George Collins 1933–36
George Brown 1936–38
Jackie Carr 1938–42
Jack Surtees 1942
Jack English 1945–46
Bill Forrest 1946–50
George Irwin 1950–52
Bob Gurney 1952–57
Dick Duckworth 1957–60
Eddie Carr 1960–64
Lol Morgan 1964–66
Jimmy Greenhalgh 1966–68
Ray Yeoman 1968–70
Len Richley 1970–71
Frank Brennan 1971
Ken Hale 1971–72
Allan Jones 1972
Ralph Brand 1972–73
Dick Conner 1973–74
Billy Horner 1974–76
Peter Madden 1976–78
Len Walker 1978–79
Billy Elliott 1979–83
Cyril Knowles 1983–87
Dave Booth 1987–89
Brian Little 1989–91
Frank Gray 1991–92
Ray Hankin 1992
Billy McEwan 1992–93
Alan Murray 1993–95
Paul Futcher 1995
David Hodgson/Jim Platt
(Director of Coaching) 1995
Jim Platt 1995–96
David Hodgson 1996–2000
Gary Bennett 2000–01
Tommy Taylor 2001–02
Mick Tait 2003
David Hodgson November 2003–

TEN YEAR LEAGUE RECORD

		P	W	D	L	F	A	Pts	Pos
1995-96	Div 3	46	20	18	8	60	42	78	5
1996-97	Div 3	46	14	10	22	64	78	52	18
1997-98	Div 3	46	14	12	20	56	72	54	19
1998-99	Div 3	46	18	11	17	69	58	65	11
1999-2000	Div 3	46	21	16	9	66	36	79	4
2000-01	Div 3	46	12	13	21	44	56	49	20
2001-02	Div 3	46	15	11	20	60	71	56	15
2002-03	Div 3	46	12	18	16	58	59	54	14
2003-04	Div 3	46	14	11	21	53	61	53	18
2004-05	FL 2	46	20	12	14	57	49	72	8

DID YOU KNOW 

Harry Clarke, a pre-war teenager for Rotherham United, joined Darlington in 1946. He was to have three goalscoring spells with the club after moves to Leeds United and Hartlepool United and he rattled in over 50 goals for the Quakers.

DARLINGTON 2004–05 LEAGUE RECORD

Match No.	Date	Venue	Opponents	Result		H/T Score	Lg. Pos.	Goalscorers	Attendance
1	Aug 7	H	Grimsby T	W	1-0	0-0	—	Clark [83]	4807
2	10	A	Yeovil T	D	1-1	0-1	—	Clarke [53]	5116
3	14	A	Kidderminster H	L	0-1	0-0	11		2303
4	21	H	Bristol R	L	0-1	0-0	19		3661
5	28	A	Chester C	W	3-0	2-0	10	Wainwright [16], Kendrick [25], Clarke [64]	2392
6	30	H	Cambridge U	D	1-1	0-0	11	Valentine [76]	3350
7	Sept 4	H	Scunthorpe U	D	0-0	0-0	12		3983
8	11	A	Rochdale	D	1-1	0-1	12	Hignett [87]	2616
9	18	H	Northampton T	D	1-1	1-0	13	Hignett [23]	4028
10	25	A	Macclesfield T	L	0-1	0-0	16		1872
11	Oct 2	H	Southend U	W	4-0	3-0	12	Armstrong 3 [15, 40, 52], Wijnhard [24]	3901
12	10	A	Oxford U	W	2-1	0-1	8	Wijnhard [51], Clark [74]	5881
13	16	H	Bury	L	1-2	0-2	13	Wijnhard [89]	4642
14	19	A	Notts Co	D	1-1	0-1	—	Armstrong [69]	3620
15	30	H	Wycombe W	W	1-0	1-0	12	Wijnhard (pen) [35]	4292
16	Nov 6	A	Rushden & D	W	2-1	1-0	9	Hignett 2 [21, 82]	3036
17	17	A	Swansea C	L	1-2	1-0	—	Liddle [26]	7824
18	20	H	Lincoln C	L	0-3	0-2	13		4035
19	26	A	Cheltenham T	W	2-0	1-0	—	Gill (og) [40], Armstrong [57]	3578
20	Dec 7	H	Mansfield T	W	2-1	0-1	—	Wijnhard [63], Hignett [74]	3686
21	11	H	Leyton Orient	W	3-0	1-0	5	White (og) [5], Wijnhard [59], Armstrong [74]	3702
22	18	A	Boston U	L	1-3	0-3	8	Hignett (pen) [57]	2428
23	26	H	Rochdale	L	0-3	0-1	9		7028
24	28	A	Shrewsbury T	L	0-4	0-3	10		3915
25	Jan 1	A	Scunthorpe U	W	1-0	0-0	8	Armstrong [60]	5131
26	3	H	Macclesfield T	W	3-1	2-1	6	Wijnhard [26], Maddison [40], Armstrong [81]	3677
27	8	H	Oxford U	D	1-1	1-1	6	Gregorio [8]	3735
28	15	A	Northampton T	D	1-1	1-0	6	Gregorio [7]	5762
29	22	H	Shrewsbury T	W	3-0	1-0	5	Wainwright [28], Hignett 2 [67, 74]	3934
30	29	A	Southend U	L	0-2	0-0	8		7358
31	Feb 5	A	Bury	W	1-0	1-0	7	Petta [29]	2971
32	12	H	Notts Co	L	1-2	1-0	9	McGurk [21]	4213
33	19	A	Wycombe W	D	1-1	1-1	8	Wijnhard [34]	4326
34	22	H	Swansea C	W	2-1	1-1	—	Clarke [34], Wainwright [84]	2709
35	26	A	Leyton Orient	L	0-1	0-1	8		3430
36	Mar 5	H	Boston U	W	1-0	0-0	8	McGurk [69]	3219
37	12	H	Yeovil T	W	2-1	1-0	6	Wijnhard [13], Armstrong [61]	4121
38	19	A	Grimsby T	W	1-0	1-0	6	St'Juste [11]	4578
39	26	H	Kidderminster H	L	0-2	0-0	7		6972
40	28	A	Bristol R	D	3-3	1-1	8	Russell C [1], Hignett (pen) [50], St'Juste [63]	5918
41	Apr 2	H	Chester C	W	1-0	0-0	7	Wijnhard (pen) [76]	3778
42	9	A	Cambridge U	L	1-3	1-1	7	Wijnhard [9]	3116
43	16	A	Mansfield T	D	1-1	0-0	7	Wijnhard [66]	3569
44	23	H	Rushden & D	W	2-0	0-0	7	Wijnhard 2 (2 pens) [49, 54]	4579
45	30	A	Lincoln C	D	0-0	0-0	8		7753
46	May 7	H	Cheltenham T	W	3-1	1-1	8	Dickman [43], Wainwright [89], Sodje [90]	5575

Final League Position: 8

GOALSCORERS

League (57): Wijnhard 14 (4 pens), Armstrong 9, Hignett 9 (2 pens), Wainwright 4, Clarke 3, Clark 2, Gregorio 2, McGurk 2, St'Juste 2, Dickman 1, Kendrick 1, Liddle 1, Maddison 1, Petta 1, Russell C 1, Sodje 1, Valentine 1, own goals 2.
Carling Cup (0).
FA Cup (3): Armstrong 2, Keltie 1.
LDV Vans Trophy (0).

Russell S 46	Valentine R 32 + 4	Kendrick J 19 + 12	Liddle C 19 + 1	Hutchinson J 8	Keltie C 10 + 11	Convery M 10 + 13	Close B 37 + 1	Clarke M 42 + 1	Russell C 15 + 13	Thomas S 11 + 1	Wainwright N 26 + 12	Clark I 13 + 11	Hughes C 5 + 10	Fleming C 24 + 3	Maddison N 21 + 3	Hignett C 17 + 2	Armstrong A 31 + 1	Gregorio A 19 + 5	Wijnhard C 31	Webster A 16 + 6	McGurk D 9 + 1	St Juste J 9 + 6	Petta B 12	Gilroy K 1 + 1	Logan R — + 1	Dickman J 8	Appleby M 10	Sodje A 1 + 6	Bates M 4	*Match No.*
1	2	3	4	5	6	7^{1}	8	9^{2}	10	11^{3}	12	13	14																	1
1	2	3	4	5	6^{2}			9	10^{1}	11	7	12		8	13															2
1	2	3^{2}	4	5	6	12		9	10	8^{1}	11^{3}	13		7	14															3
1	2^{1}	3^{2}	4	5	6^{3}	12	8	9	10		11	13	14	7																4
1	2	3	4^{1}	5	6^{3}		8	9	10	14	7^{2}	11	13	12																5
1	2	3	4	5	12	13	6^{1}	9	10^{2}	8	7	11																		6
1	2	12	4	5	13	7^{3}	8	9^{1}	10	11^{2}	14	3		6																7
1	2		4	5^{1}	6^{3}	7^{2}	8	12	10		13	11		3	14	9														8
1	2	3^{3}	4		6	12^{2}	8	5			14	11		7		9^{1}	10	13												9
1	2	12	4			13	8^{2}	5	14		11		3	6	10		9^{1}	7^{3}												10
1	2	3			12		6	5	13	11		14			4^{1}	8	9^{2}	7^{3}	10											11
1	2	3	12				6	5		11^{2}		13	4^{1}		8		9	7	10											12
1	2^{3}	3				12	4	5	14	11^{2}		13			6	8^{1}	9	7	10											13
1	2	3			12		4	5				11			6	8	9^{1}	7	10											14
1	2	3			12		4	5			13	11			6^{1}	8	9	7^{2}	10											15
1	2	3					4	5	9		12	11			6	8^{2}		7^{1}	10	13										16
1	2^{2}	12	4		6		8	5			7	13			11		9		10		3^{1}									17
1		3^{1}	4		6^{3}	12	2	5	7^{2}		11	13			8		9		10	14										18
1	2	3	5		12		4				7	11			6^{1}		9		10	8^{2}		13								19
1		3			12			5^{3}	13		7	11^{2}		2	6	8	9		10	4^{1}	14									20
1	12				13	14	4	5			7	3^{1}		2	6^{2}	8	9		10	11^{3}										21
1	2^{3}	12			13		4	5				11^{1}		3	6^{2}	8	9	14	10	7										22
1		12			6^{1}	13	4	5^{2}			7	3^{3}		2		8	9	14	10	11										23
1		3					4^{1}	5	13		12			2	6	8	9^{2}	7	10	11										24
1	3						4■	5	12		8^{1}		13	2^{2}	6	14	9^{3}	7	10	11										25
1	2	12						5			3^{2}		13	4	6	9^{3}	14	7^{1}	10	11		8								26
1	2						4	5	12		3		13	6			9	7	10^{1}	11		8^{2}								27
1	2				12		4	5	13		11		14	3	6^{1}		9	7^{3}	10^{2}	8										28
1	2				12	13	4^{3}	5			11		14	3	6^{1}	10	9	7		8^{2}										29
1	3	12	4				2	5			11		13		6^{1}	8	9	7^{2}	10											30
1	2	3	4				6	5	12		11^{2}		14			13	9	7^{3}	10				8^{1}							31
1	3		4				7	5	12		13					8^{2}	9		10	6^{1}	2	14	11^{3}							32
1		12	4			8	6	5			3						9	7^{1}	10		2	13	11^{2}							33
1	12	13	4^{1}			8	6	5			3			14			9	7^{2}	10		2^{3}		11							34
1	12	13	4			8	2^{2}	5	14		7				6		9		10^{3}		3^{1}		11							35
1		12				8	2	5	9						6^{2}			13			3	10^{1}	11	7^{3}	14	4				36
1	3					7^{3}	6	5	12		13						9^{1}		10■	14	2		11^{2}			4	8			37
1	3					7^{1}	6	5	10		12			13			9			14	2^{2}	11				4^{3}	8			38
1	3^{2}					7^{3}	6	5	12		13						9^{1}			14	2	11				4	8	10		39
1		12						5	9		13		3	2		10^{2}		7^{1}		6		11^{3}		14		4	8			40
1	12					13		5	9^{3}				3	2				7^{2}	10	6		11				4^{1}	8	14		41
1						12		5	9^{2}	7		13	3^{1}	2					10	6		8^{3}	11				4	14		42
1	2	3					12			8	7			4			9^{3}		10			13	11^{2}				6^{1}	14	5	43
1	3						2			8^{1}	7			4			9^{3}		10	12		13	11^{2}				6	14	5	44
1							2	9			7			3^{2}				12	10	8^{3}		13	11^{1}			4	6	14	5	45
1						12		5			2	13		4			9^{3}		10			3	11^{2}			7	8^{1}	14	6	46

FA Cup
First Round Yeovil T (h) 3-3
(a) 0-1

Carling Cup
First Round Barnsley (h) 0-2

LDV Vans Trophy
First Round Mansfield T (a) 0-0

DERBY COUNTY FL Championship

FOUNDATION

Derby County was formed by members of the Derbyshire County Cricket Club in 1884, when football was booming in the area and the cricketers thought that a football club would help boost finances for the summer game. To begin with, they sported the cricket club's colours of amber, chocolate and pale blue, and went into the game at the top immediately entering the FA Cup.

Pride Park Stadium, Pride Park, Derby DE24 8XL.

Telephone: 0870 444 1884.

Fax: (01332) 667 519.

Ticket Office: 0870 444 1884.

Website: www.dcfc.co.uk

Email: derby.county@dcfc.co.uk

Ground Capacity: 33,597.

Record Attendance: 41,826 v Tottenham H, Division 1, 20 September 1969.

Pitch Measurements: 110yd × 72yd.

Chairman: John Sleightholme.

Chief Executive: Jeremy Keith.

Secretary: Marian McMinn.

Manager: Phil Brown.

Assistant Manager: Steve Taylor.

Physio: Peter Melville.

Colours: White shirts, black shorts, white stockings.

Change Colours: Blue shirts, white shorts, blue stockings.

Year Formed: 1884.

Turned Professional: 1884.

Ltd Co.: 1896.

Club Nickname: 'The Rams'.

Previous Grounds: 1884, Racecourse Ground; 1895, Baseball Ground; 1997, Pride Park.

First Football League Game: 8 September 1888, Football League, v Bolton W (a) W 6–3 – Marshall; Latham, Ferguson, Williamson; Monks, W. Roulstone; Bakewell (2), Cooper (2), Higgins, H. Plackett, L. Plackett (2).

Record League Victory: 9–0 v Wolverhampton W, Division 1, 10 January 1891 – Bunyan; Archie Goodall, Roberts; Walker, Chalmers, Roulstone (1); Bakewell, McLachlan, Johnny Goodall (1), Holmes (2), McMillan (5). 9–0 v Sheffield W, Division 1, 21 January 1899 – Fryer; Methven, Staley; Cox, Archie Goodall, May; Oakden (1), Bloomer (6), Boag, McDonald (1), Allen, (1 og).

HONOURS

Football League: Division 1 – Champions 1971–72, 1974–75; Runners-up 1895–96, 1929–30, 1935–36, 1995–96; Division 2 – Champions 1911–12, 1914–15, 1968–69, 1986–87; Runners-up 1925–26; Division 3 (N) Champions 1956–57; Runners-up 1955–56.

FA Cup: Winners 1946; Runners-up 1898, 1899, 1903.

Football League Cup: Semi-final 1968.

Texaco Cup: Winners 1972.

European Competitions: *European Cup:* 1972–73, 1975–76. *UEFA Cup:* 1974–75, 1976–77. *Anglo-Italian Cup:* Runners-up 1993.

SKY SPORTS FACT FILE

The pivotal point of their promotion season in 1914–15 for Derby County was an unbeaten 16 game spell from mid-October. It cushioned a bleak end to the season when the goals dried up in the last seven matches producing just five goals.

Record Cup Victory: 12–0 v Finn Harps, UEFA Cup 1st rd 1st leg, 15 September 1976 – Moseley; Thomas, Nish, Rioch (1), McFarland, Todd (King), Macken, Gemmill, Hector (5), George (3), James (3).

Record Defeat: 2–11 v Everton, FA Cup 1st rd, 1889–90.

Most League Points (2 for a win): 63, Division 2, 1968–69 and Division 3 (N), 1955–56 and 1956–57.

Most League Points (3 for a win): 84, Division 3, 1985–86 and Division 3, 1986–87.

Most League Goals: 111, Division 3 (N), 1956–57.

Highest League Scorer in Season: Jack Bowers, 37, Division 1, 1930–31; Ray Straw, 37 Division 3 (N), 1956–57.

Most League Goals in Total Aggregate: Steve Bloomer, 292, 1892–1906 and 1910–14.

Most League Goals in One Match: 6, Steve Bloomer v Sheffield W, Division 1, 2 January 1899.

Most Capped Players: Deon Burton, 41 (98), Jamaica and Mart Poom, 41 (48), Estonia`.

Most League Appearances: Kevin Hector, 486, 1966–78 and 1980–82.

Youngest League Player: Lee Holmes, 15 years 268 days v Grimsby T, 26 December 2002.

Record Transfer Fee Received: £7,000,000 rising to £9,000,000 for Seth Johnson from Leeds U, October 2001.

Record Transfer Fee Paid: £3,000,000 rising to £4,000,000 for Lee Morris from Sheffield U, October 1999.

Football League Record: 1888 Founder Member of the Football League; 1907–12 Division 2; 1912–14 Division 1; 1914–15 Division 2; 1915–21 Division 1; 1921–26 Division 2; 1926–53 Division 1; 1953–55 Division 2; 1955–57 Division 3 (N); 1957–69 Division 2; 1969–80 Division 1; 1980–84 Division 2; 1984–86 Division 3; 1986–87 Division 2; 1987–91 Division 1; 1991–92 Division 2; 1992–96 Division 1; 1996–2002 FA Premier League; 2002–04 Division 1; 2004– FLC.

MANAGERS

W. D. Clark 1896–1900
Harry Newbould 1900–06
Jimmy Methven 1906–22
Cecil Potter 1922–25
George Jobey 1925–41
Ted Magner 1944–46
Stuart McMillan 1946–53
Jack Barker 1953–55
Harry Storer 1955–62
Tim Ward 1962–67
Brian Clough 1967–73
Dave Mackay 1973–76
Colin Murphy 1977
Tommy Docherty 1977–79
Colin Addison 1979–82
Johnny Newman 1982
Peter Taylor 1982–84
Roy McFarland 1984
Arthur Cox 1984–93
Roy McFarland 1993–95
Jim Smith 1995–2001
Colin Todd 2001–02
John Gregory 2002–03
George Burley 2003–05
Phil Brown June 2005–

LATEST SEQUENCES

Longest Sequence of League Wins: 9, 15.3.1969 – 19.4.1969.

Longest Sequence of League Defeats: 8, 12.12.1987 – 10.2.1988.

Longest Sequence of League Draws: 6, 26.3.1927 – 18.4.1927.

Longest Sequence of Unbeaten League Matches: 22, 8.3.1969 – 20.9.1969.

Longest Sequence Without a League Win: 20, 15.12.1990 – 23.4.1991.

Successive Scoring Runs: 29 from 3.12.1960.

Successive Non-scoring Runs: 8 from 30.10.1920.

TEN YEAR LEAGUE RECORD

		P	*W*	*D*	*L*	*F*	*A*	*Pts*	*Pos*
1995-96	Div 1	46	21	16	9	71	51	79	2
1996-97	PR Lge	38	11	13	14	45	58	46	12
1997-98	PR Lge	38	16	7	15	52	49	55	9
1998-99	PR Lge	38	13	13	12	40	45	52	8
1999-2000	PR Lge	38	9	11	18	44	57	38	16
2000-01	PR Lge	38	10	12	16	37	59	42	17
2001-02	PR Lge	38	8	6	24	33	63	30	19
2002-03	Div 1	46	15	7	24	55	74	52	18
2003-04	Div 1	46	13	13	20	53	67	52	20
2004-05	FL C	46	22	10	14	71	60	76	4

DID YOU KNOW ?

In December 1930 Derby County were impressed by wing-half Errington "Ernie" Keen's debut for Newcastle United against them and signed him. He won England caps and though moving non-league with Chelmsford City in 1938 was a much sought-after wartime guest.

DERBY COUNTY 2004–05 LEAGUE RECORD

Match No.	Date	Venue	Opponents	Result		H/T Score	Lg. Pos.	Goalscorers	Attendance
1	Aug 7	A	Leeds U	L	0-1	0-0	—		30,459
2	11	H	Leicester C	L	1-2	0-1	—	Tudgay ^{69}	26,650
3	14	H	Ipswich T	W	3-2	1-2	19	Reich 2 $^{36, 65}$, Idiakez ^{58}	22,234
4	21	A	QPR	W	2-0	2-0	9	Smith ^{8}, Tudgay ^{17}	15,295
5	28	H	Crewe Alex	L	2-4	1-2	12	Tudgay ^{16}, Idiakez ^{46}	24,436
6	30	A	Stoke C	L	0-1	0-0	15		18,673
7	Sept 11	H	Reading	W	2-1	0-0	13	Smith ^{70}, Tudgay ^{83}	22,096
8	18	A	Cardiff C	W	2-0	1-0	12	Reich ^{34}, Taylor ^{49}	12,008
9	22	A	Millwall	L	1-3	0-1	—	Reich ^{49}	9132
10	25	H	Wigan Ath	D	1-1	1-1	12	Smith ^{17}	26,113
11	29	H	West Ham U	D	1-1	1-1	—	Johnson ^{6}	23,112
12	Oct 2	A	Sunderland	D	0-0	0-0	15		29,881
13	16	H	Watford	D	2-2	1-2	15	Smith ^{39}, Rasiak ^{85}	23,253
14	19	A	Wolverhampton W	L	0-2	0-1	—		26,465
15	22	A	Burnley	W	2-0	0-0	—	Tudgay ^{57}, Reich ^{63}	13,703
16	30	H	Rotherham U	W	3-2	1-2	10	Rasiak ^{39}, Peschisolido ^{58}, Vincent ^{66}	25,096
17	Nov 3	H	Brighton & HA	W	3-0	1-0	—	Smith ^{9}, Rasiak 2 $^{49, 80}$	22,480
18	6	A	Watford	D	2-2	0-1	8	Taylor ^{58}, Peschisolido ^{73}	13,689
19	13	A	Gillingham	W	2-0	1-0	7	Rasiak ^{42}, Taylor ^{90}	8015
20	20	H	Sheffield U	L	0-1	0-0	8		25,725
21	27	A	Preston NE	L	0-3	0-2	10		12,702
22	Dec 4	H	Coventry C	D	2-2	0-1	10	Rasiak ^{88}, Peschisolido ^{90}	22,648
23	11	H	Nottingham F	W	3-0	0-0	10	Smith ^{4}, Rasiak 2 $^{75, 89}$	30,793
24	18	A	Plymouth Arg	W	2-0	1-0	8	Coughlan (og) ^{3}, Peschisolido ^{62}	15,335
25	26	A	Wigan Ath	W	2-1	0-1	7	Rasiak ^{64}, Smith ^{82}	12,420
26	28	H	Millwall	L	0-3	0-1	8		27,725
27	Jan 1	H	Cardiff C	L	0-1	0-1	9		22,800
28	3	A	Reading	W	1-0	1-0	8	Smith ^{45}	15,491
29	16	H	Sunderland	L	0-2	0-0	9		22,995
30	23	A	West Ham U	W	2-1	1-1	8	Rasiak 2 $^{10, 63}$	30,347
31	26	H	Leeds U	W	2-0	0-0	—	Smith ^{64}, Bolder ^{90}	25,648
32	Feb 5	A	Brighton & HA	W	3-2	2-1	5	Bisgaard ^{13}, Tudgay 2 $^{43, 72}$	6587
33	19	A	Rotherham U	W	3-1	1-1	4	Rasiak ^{32}, Tudgay ^{47}, Idiakez (pen) ^{77}	7937
34	23	H	Burnley	D	1-1	0-1	—	Peschisolido ^{70}	23,701
35	26	A	Nottingham F	D	2-2	1-1	4	Rasiak 2 $^{12, 78}$	26,160
36	Mar 2	H	Wolverhampton W	D	3-3	1-1	—	Idiakez 2 (1 pen) $^{9, 77 (p)}$, Reich ^{90}	24,109
37	5	H	Plymouth Arg	W	1-0	1-0	4	Idiakez ^{24}	27,581
38	16	H	QPR	D	0-0	0-0	—		24,486
39	Apr 2	A	Ipswich T	L	2-3	1-1	6	Tudgay ^{7}, Idiakez ^{85}	28,796
40	5	A	Crewe Alex	W	2-1	1-0	—	Rasiak ^{16}, Smith ^{74}	8026
41	9	H	Stoke C	W	3-1	2-1	5	Rasiak ^{8}, Bisgaard ^{45}, Idiakez ^{79}	27,640
42	15	A	Sheffield U	W	1-0	0-0	—	Bisgaard ^{74}	20,794
43	23	H	Gillingham	W	2-0	1-0	5	Bisgaard ^{33}, Peschisolido ^{72}	27,481
44	26	A	Leicester C	L	0-1	0-0	—		25,762
45	30	A	Coventry C	L	2-6	0-4	5	Bolder ^{51}, Peschisolido ^{63}	22,728
46	May 8	H	Preston NE	W	3-1	1-0	4	Idiakez ^{45}, Smith ^{49}, Peschisolido ^{90}	31,237

Final League Position: 4

GOALSCORERS

League (71): Rasiak 16, Smith 11, Idiakez 9 (2 pens), Tudgay 9, Peschisolido 8, Reich 6, Bisgaard 4, Taylor 3, Bolder 2, Johnson 1, Vincent 1, own goal 1.
Carling Cup (1): Idiakez 1.
FA Cup (5): Idiakez 1, Junior 1, Peschisolido 1, Rasiak 1, Tudgay 1.
Play-offs (0).

Camp L 45	Kenna J 40	Jackson R 18 + 1	Huddlestone T 42 + 3	Mills P 15 + 7	Johnson M 35 + 1	Bisgaard M 31 + 5	Taylor I 25 + 14	Tudgay M 22 + 12	Smith T 41 + 1	Idiakez I 41	Reich M 27 + 10	Bolder A 24 + 12	Junior5 + 13	Peschisolido P 10 + 22	Doyle N 3	Vincent J 15	Konjic M 13 + 3	Holmes L — + 3	Talbot J 2	Rasiak G 35	Grant L 1 + 1	Kaku B 3 + 1	Makin C 13	*Match No.*
1	2^{1}	3	4^{2}	5	6	7	8	9^{3}	10	11	12	13	14											1
1	2	3	4		6	7	8	12	10	5	11^{1}		9^{2}	13										2
1		3	4		6	7	8	12	10^{3}	5	11^{2}	13	9^{1}	14	2									3
1		3	4		6	7	8^{1}	9	10^{3}	5	11^{2}	12	13	14	2									4
1			4		6	7	8	9	10	5	11^{1}		12		2	3								5
1	2		4		6	7^{2}	8	9^{1}	10	5		11	12	13		3								6
1	2		12		6		4^{1}	9	10	11	7		8^{2}	13		3	5							7
1	2		4		6		8	9^{2}	10	11	7^{1}	13	12			3	5							8
1	2		4		6^{1}		8		10	11	7	12	9^{2}			3■	5	13						9
1	2		4	12			8^{2}		10	11	7	6		13			5		3^{1}	9				10
1	2		4		6		12		10	11^{1}	7^{2}	8		13			5		3	9				11
1	2		12	5	6		8		10	11^{1}	7	4				3				9				12
1	2^{1}	12	4^{2}	5	6		8^{3}	9	10		7	13	14			3				11				13
1■		2	12	5	6^{1}		8	9	10^{2}		7^{G}	4				3		13		11	15			14
		2	4	5		12	8	9		11	7^{1}	6				3				10	1			15
1	2		4		6	7^{2}	12	9^{1}		5	11	8		13		3				10				16
1	2		4	12	6		13	14	10^{3}	5^{1}	11	7^{2}		8		3				9				17
1	2		4	12	6^{1}	13	8		10^{2}	5	11^{3}	7		14		3				9				18
1		2^{1}	4	12	6	13	8		10^{3}	5	14	7		11^{2}		3				9				19
1	2		4		6	12	13	14	10	5	11^{3}	7^{2}		8		3^{1}				9				20
1	2		4		6	12	8	13	10	5	11^{3}			14		3				9^{2}		7^{1}		21
1	2	3	4	5	6^{1}	7	12	13	10^{2}	8	11^{3}			14						9				22
1	2	3	4	12	6^{1}	7	8		10	5^{2}	14	13		11^{3}						9				23
1	2	3	4		6	7	5	12	10^{2}		13			11^{1}						9		8		24
1	2	3	4		6	7	8		12	5	11^{2}			10^{1}						9		13		25
1	2	3	4		6	7	12	13	10^{2}	5	11^{3}			14						9		8^{1}		26
1	2^{2}	3	4		6	7	8	12	10	5	13			11^{1}						9				27
1	2	3	4	5	6	7^{2}		12	10^{1}	8	11	13								9				28
1	2	3	4	5	6^{2}	7^{1}	12		10	8	11^{3}		13	14						9				29
1	2	3	4	5		7^{1}	8	12	10^{2}	11	13	6	14							9^{3}				30
1	2	3^{1}	4	5	12	7^{2}	8	14	10	6	11^{3}	13								9				31
1	2		4	5	6	7	8■	11^{2}	10	3		13	12							9^{1}				32
1	2		4	5		7		8	10^{1}	11^{2}	12	6					13			9			3	33
1	2		4	5^{2}		7		10		8	11^{1}	6		12			13			9			3	34
1	2		4			7^{1}	12	10		11		6	13	8^{2}			5			9			3	35
1	2		4	5			12	8^{1}	10^{2}	11	13	6	7^{3}	14						9			3	36
1	2		4			7^{1}	12	8^{2}	10	11		6		13			5			9			3	37
1	2		4			7		8^{1}	10^{2}	11	12	6		13			5			9			3	38
1	2		4	5		7		8^{1}	10	11		6		12						9			3	39
1	2		4	12	5^{1}	7		8	10	11		6	13							9^{2}			3	40
1	2		4^{1}		6	7		8	10	11		12		13			5			9^{2}			3	41
1	2		4		6^{1}	7	12	8^{3}	10	11^{2}		13		14			5			9			3	42
1	2		4	12	6^{1}	7^{2}	13		10^{3}		14	11		8			5			9			3	43
1	2		4		6	7	12		10		11	8^{1}	13	14			5^{2}			9^{3}			3	44
1	2				6	7	8^{2}	9^{1}	10	11		4	12	13			5						3	45
1	2	3	4		5	7	12		10^{3}	11^{1}	9^{2}	6		8			13	14						46

FA Cup

Third Round	Wigan Ath	(h)	2-1
Fourth Round	Fulham	(h)	1-1
		(a)	2-4

Carling Cup

First Round	Lincoln C	(a)	1-3

Play-offs

Semi-Final	Preston NE	(a)	0-2
		(h)	0-0

DONCASTER ROVERS FL Championship 1

FOUNDATION

In 1879, Mr Albert Jenkins assembled a team to play a match against the Yorkshire Institution for the Deaf. The players remained together as Doncaster Rovers, joining the Midland Alliance in 1889 and the Midland Counties League in 1891.

The Earth Stadium, Belle Vue, Bawtry Road, Doncaster, South Yorkshire DN4 5HT.

Telephone: (01302) 539 441.

Fax: (01302) 539 679.

Ticket Office: 0845 450 6250.

Website: www.doncasterroversfc.co.uk

Email: info@doncasterroversfc.co.uk

Ground Capacity: 10,593.

Record Attendance: 3,7149 v Hull C, Division 3 (N), 2 October 1948.

Pitch Measurements: 110yd × 76yd.

Chairman: John Ryan.

Vice-chairman: Stuart Highfield JP.

Chief Executive: David Morris.

Secretary: David Morris.

Manager: Dave Penney.

Assistant Manager: Mickey Walker.

Physio: Barrie Windle.

Colours: Red and white hoops.

Change Colours: All blue.

Year Formed: 1879.

Turned Professional: 1885.

Ltd Co.: 1905 & 1920.

Club Nickname: 'Rovers'.

Previous Grounds: Intake Ground 1880–1916; Benetthorpe Ground 1920–1922; Low Pasture, Belle Vue 1922.

Record League Victory: 10–0 v Darlington, Division 4, 25 January 1964: Potter; Raine, Meadows, Windross (1), White, Ripley (2), Robinson, Book (2), Hale (4), Jeffrey, Broadbent (1).

Record Cup Victory: 7–0 v Blyth Spartans, FA Cup 1st rd, 27 November 1937: Imrie; Shaw, Rodgers, McFarlane, Bycroft, Cyril Smith, Burton (1), Killourhy (4), Morgan (2), Malam, Dutton.

HONOURS

Football League: Division 2 best season: 7th, 1901–02; Division 3 Champions 2003–04; Division 3 (N) Champions – 1934–35, 1946–47, 1949–50; Runners-up: 1937–38, 1938–39; Division 4 Champions 1965–66, 1968–69; Runners-up: 1983–84. Promoted 1980–81 (3rd).

FA Cup: best season 5th rd, 1952, 1954, 1955, 1956.

Football League Cup: best season: 5th rd, 1976.

Sheffield County Cup: Winners 1891, 1912, 1936, 1938, 1956, 1968, 1976, 1986.

Midland Counties League: Champions 1897, 1899.

Conference Trophy: Winners 1999, 2000.

Sheffield & Hallamshire Senior Cup: Winners 2001, 2002.

SKY SPORTS FACT FILE

In April 1949 Doncaster Rovers paid £8000 for the transfer of Irish international Peter Doherty to act as player-manager. An innovative coach he experimented with having players line up out of position to cause consternation among the opposition.

Record Defeat: 0–12 v Small Heath, Division 2, 11 April 1903.

Most League Points (2 for a win): 72, Division 3 (N), 1946–47.

Most League Points (3 for a win): 92, Division 3, 2003–04.

Most League Goals: 123, Division 3 (N), 1946–47.

Highest League Scorer in Season: Clarrie Jordan, 42, Division 3 (N), 1946–47.

Most League Goals in Total Aggregate: Tom Keetley, 180, 1923–29.

Most Capped Player: Len Graham, 14, Northern Ireland.

Most League Appearances: Fred Emery, 417, 1925–36.

Record Transfer Fee Received: £275,000 from QPR for Rufus Brevett, February 1991.

Record Transfer Fee Paid: £125,000 to Bristol C for Paul Heffernan, July 2005.

Football League Record: 1901 Elected to Division 2; 1903 Failed re-election; 1904 Re-elected; 1905 Failed re-election; 1923 Re-elected to Divison 3 (N); 1935–37 Division 2; 1937–47 Division 3 (N); 1947–48 Division 2; 1948–50 Division 3 (N); 1950–58 Division 2; 1958–59 Division 3; 1959–66 Division 4; 1966–67 Division 3; 1967–69 Division 4; 1969–71 Division 3; 1971–81 Division 4; 1981–83 Division 3; 1983–84 Division 4; 1984–88 Division 3; 1988–92 Division 4; 1992–98 Division 3; 1998–2003 Conference; 2003–04 Division 3; 2004– FL1.

LATEST SEQUENCES

Longest Sequence of League Wins: 10, 22.1.1947 – 4.4.1947.

Longest Sequence of League Defeats: 9, 14.1.1905 – 1.4.1905.

Longest Sequence of League Draws: 4, 29.10.1932 – 19.11.1932.

Longest Sequence of Unbeaten League Matches: 20, 26.12.1968 – 12.4.1969.

Longest Sequence Without a League Win: 20, 9.8.1997 – 29.11.1997.

Successive Scoring Runs: 27 from 10.11.1934.

Successive Non-scoring Runs: 7 from 27.9.1947.

MANAGERS

Arthur Porter 1920–21
Harry Tufnell 1921–22
Arthur Porter 1922–23
Dick Ray 1923–27
David Menzies 1928–36
Fred Emery 1936–40
Bill Marsden 1944–46
Jackie Bestall 1946–49
Peter Doherty 1949–58
Jack Hodgson & Sid Bycroft (*Joint Managers*) 1958
Jack Crayston 1958–59 (*continued as Secretary-Manager to 1961*)
Jackie Bestall (TM) 1959–60
Norman Curtis 1960–61
Danny Malloy 1961–62
Oscar Hold 1962–64
Bill Leivers 1964–66
Keith Kettleborough 1966–67
George Raynor 1967–68
Lawrie McMenemy 1968–71
Morris Setters 1971–74
Stan Anderson 1975–78
Billy Bremner 1978–85
Dave Cusack 1985–87
Dave Mackay 1987–89
Billy Bremner 1989–91
Steve Beaglehole 1991–93
Ian Atkins 1994
Sammy Chung 1994–96
Kerry Dixon (*Player–Manager*) 1996–97
Dave Cowling 1997
Mark Weaver 1997–98
Ian Snodin 1998–99
Steve Wignall 1999–2001
Dave Penney March 2002–

TEN YEAR LEAGUE RECORD

		P	*W*	*D*	*L*	*F*	*A*	*Pts*	*Pos*
1995-96	Div 3	46	16	11	19	49	60	59	13
1996-97	Div 3	46	14	10	22	52	65	52	19
1997-98	Div 3	46	4	8	34	30	113	20	24
1998-99	Conf.	42	12	12	18	51	55	48	16
1999-2000	Conf.	42	15	9	18	46	48	54	12
2000-01	Conf.	42	15	13	14	47	43	58	9
2001-02	Conf.	42	18	13	11	68	46	67	4
2002-03	Conf.	42	22	12	8	73	47	78	3
2003-04	Div 3	46	27	11	8	79	37	92	1
2004-05	FL 1	46	16	18	12	65	60	66	10

DID YOU KNOW ?

Leslie Lievesley was an 18 year old debutant centre-forward for Doncaster Rovers in 1929 but lasted only five minutes before injury. Returning in February he hit 12 goals in 14 matches. As coach to Torino he was killed in the 1949 Superga air disaster.

DONCASTER ROVERS 2004–05 LEAGUE RECORD

Match No.	Date	Venue	Opponents	Result	H/T Score	Lg. Pos.	Goalscorers	Atten-dance
1	Aug 7	H	Blackpool	W 2-0	1-0	—	Ryan [8], Fortune-West [81]	7082
2	10	A	Brentford	L 3-4	2-1	—	McIndoe 2 (1 pen) [4, 45 (p)], Green [84]	5621
3	14	A	Bradford C	L 0-2	0-2	18		10,444
4	21	H	Tranmere R	D 0-0	0-0	17		6040
5	28	A	Colchester U	L 1-4	1-3	19	Doolan [45]	3803
6	30	H	Huddersfield T	W 2-1	1-0	18	Fortune-West [28], Green [56]	7068
7	Sept 4	H	Walsall	W 3-1	1-0	14	Fenton [20], McIndoe [50], Blundell [88]	6146
8	11	A	Milton Keynes D	W 1-0	0-0	8	Albrighton [66]	4334
9	18	H	Oldham Ath	D 1-1	1-1	9	McIndoe (pen) [45]	6774
10	25	A	Bournemouth	L 0-5	0-4	13		6588
11	Oct 2	H	Wrexham	D 0-0	0-0	14		7567
12	8	A	Port Vale	L 0-2	0-2	—		5314
13	16	H	Torquay U	D 2-2	2-1	16	McIndoe 2 [18, 27]	5529
14	20	A	Barnsley	W 3-1	1-0	—	Reid (og) [45], Blundell [57], Vaughan (og) [59]	12,478
15	23	A	Chesterfield	D 0-0	0-0	15		6219
16	30	H	Peterborough U	W 2-1	1-1	11	McIndoe [4], Green [87]	6039
17	Nov 6	A	Hartlepool U	L 1-2	1-0	14	Roberts [30]	5495
18	20	H	Stockport Co	W 3-1	1-0	12	Blundell 2 [9, 67], Ryan [65]	6697
19	27	A	Luton T	D 1-1	0-0	12	Roberts [82]	8142
20	Dec 7	H	Bristol C	D 1-1	1-1	—	Roberts [34]	5608
21	11	A	Swindon T	D 1-1	1-0	13	Blundell [39]	5452
22	19	H	Sheffield W	L 0-4	0-2	16		10,131
23	26	H	Milton Keynes D	W 3-0	1-0	13	Edds (og) [8], Johnson 2 [60, 62]	6153
24	29	A	Hull C	L 1-2	1-1	—	Mulligan [45]	24,117
25	Jan 1	A	Walsall	D 1-1	1-1	14	Bennett (og) [11]	6021
26	3	H	Bournemouth	D 1-1	0-1	14	Green [69]	6016
27	8	H	Port Vale	W 2-0	1-0	11	Ryan [45], Green [90]	5209
28	15	A	Oldham Ath	W 2-1	1-0	10	Blundell [1], McSporran [81]	7401
29	22	H	Hull C	W 1-0	0-0	10	McIndoe [59]	9633
30	29	A	Wrexham	D 0-0	0-0	8		6115
31	Feb 5	A	Torquay U	L 1-2	0-2	11	Johnson [87]	3157
32	12	H	Chesterfield	L 0-1	0-0	11		6765
33	19	A	Peterborough U	W 2-0	0-0	11	Roberts [55], Foster [81]	4983
34	22	H	Barnsley	W 4-0	2-0	—	Blundell 2 [16, 31], Doolan [69], Green [84]	7286
35	26	H	Swindon T	D 1-1	1-1	9	Roberts [30]	7696
36	Mar 6	A	Sheffield W	L 0-2	0-1	11		28,712
37	12	H	Brentford	D 0-0	0-0	11		5525
38	19	A	Blackpool	D 1-1	1-0	10	Ryan [40]	6548
39	24	H	Bradford C	D 1-1	1-1	—	Bower (og) [22]	6688
40	28	A	Tranmere R	W 4-2	2-2	9	McIndoe [3], Blundell [5], Ravenhill [52], Roberts [81]	9730
41	Apr 1	H	Colchester U	D 1-1	0-1	—	Guy [76]	6774
42	9	A	Huddersfield T	L 1-3	1-2	10	Fortune-West [15]	12,972
43	16	A	Stockport Co	W 4-2	1-2	10	Ravenhill [2], Green [72], McIndoe [82], Brown [87]	4508
44	23	H	Hartlepool U	W 2-0	0-0	9	Ravenhill [59], Fortune-West [90]	7024
45	30	A	Bristol C	D 2-2	1-0	10	Fortune-West 2 [34, 88]	12,375
46	May 7	H	Luton T	D 3-3	1-2	10	Guy 2 [1, 65], Robinson (og) [51]	8928

Final League Position: 10

GOALSCORERS

League (65): McIndoe 10 (2 pens), Blundell 9, Green 7, Fortune-West 6, Roberts 6, Ryan 4, Guy 3, Johnson 3, Ravenhill 3, Doolan 2, Albrighton 1, Brown 1, Fenton 1, Foster 1, McSporran 1, Mulligan 1, own goals 6.
Carling Cup (5): Doolan 1, Fortune-West 1, McIndoe 1, McSporran 1, Ravenhill 1.
FA Cup (4): Blundell 2, Fenton 1, McIndoe 1.
LDV Vans Trophy (2): Beardsley 1, Rigoglioso 1.

Warrington A 34	Marples S 12	Ryan T 38 + 1	Foster S 34	Fenton N 37 + 1	Green P 38 + 4	Mulligan D 27 + 4	Doolan J 32 + 6	Blundell G 33 + 8	Fortune-West L 16 + 8	McIndoe M 43 + 1	Ravenhill R 21 + 14	Rigoglioso A 2 + 10	Beardsley C 1 + 3	Coppinger J 27 + 4	Ipoua G 1 + 8	Albrighton M 15 + 2	McSporran J 15 + 11	Wilson M 1 + 2	Priet N 7	Jackson B — + 1	Roberts N 30 + 1	Morley D 9	Price J 5 + 1	Ingham M 1	Johnson S 8 + 3	Jones S 3 + 1	Beech C 2	Campbell A 1 + 2	Guy L 4 + 5	Turner I 8	Maloney J 1 + 1	Brown A — + 3	Nelthorpe C — + 1	*Match No.*
1	2	3	4	5	6^{1}	7^{2}	8	9	10	11	12	13																						1
1	2	3	4	5	6	7^{2}	8^{1}	9	10^{3}	11	12	13	14																					2
1	2	3	4	5	6		8^{2}	9	10^{3}	11	12	13■		7^{1}	14																			3
1	2	3	4	5	6	12	8	9^{2}	10	11				7^{1}	13																			4
1	2	3	4	5	6	12	8^{2}	9^{3}	10	11	13			7^{1}	14																			5
1	2	3	4	5	6		8	9^{3}	10^{1}	11				7^{2}	12	13	14																	6
1	2	3^{3}	4	5	6^{2}		8	9	10^{1}	11	12			7		14		13																7
1			4	5			8	9^{2}	10	11	12			13		6	7	3^{1}	2															8
1			4	5	6^{3}		8^{1}		10	11	12		13	7^{2}		3	9	14	2															9
1			4	5	12	13	8^{1}		10	11	6			14	9^{3}	3	7		2^{2}															10
1		12		5	6	2			10^{2}	11	8		9^{3}	7		4	13		3^{1}	14														11
1				5	6	7	12	9	13	11	4^{1}			8^{3}		3	14		2^{2}		10													12
1	2	3		5	6			9		11	8			7^{1}		4	12				10													13
1	2	3		5	12		8^{3}	9^{1}	13	11	6■						7				10^{2}	4	14											14
1	2^{1}	3		5	6	12	8	9^{2}	13	11							7				10	4												15
1		3		5	6		8■	9^{1}	12	11							7				10	4	2											16
		3		5	6			9		11	8		12	7^{1}							10	4	2	1										17
1		3		5	6		12	9		11	8^{1}			7			13				10	4	2^{2}											18
1	2	3		5	6			9^{1}		11	8				12		7				10	4												19
1		3		5	6		12	9^{2}		11	8^{1}				13						10	4	2		7									20
1		3		5	6		12	9		11	8^{1}						13				10	4	2		7^{2}									21
1	2	3		5	6		12	9^{3}		11	8^{1}			13	14						10	4			7^{2}									22
1		3	4		6^{2}	2	8^{1}			11	12	13		7^{3}		5	14				9				10									23
1		3	4		6	2	8	12		11						5^{1}	7■				9				10									24
1^{6}		3	4		6	2	8	12		11^{1}	7					5					9				10	15								25
			4		6	2	8	12						7^{1}	13	5	11				9				10	1	3^{2}							26
		3	4		6	2		12		11	8^{2}	13				5	7				9				10^{1}	1								27
		3	4	2	6			9^{3}		11	8^{1}	12		13		5	7^{2}				10				14	1								28
1		3	4		6	2	8	9^{1}		11							7				10				12		5							29
1		3	4	12	6	2	8^{2}	9^{1}		11	13					5	7^{3}				10							14						30
1		3	4		6	2	8	9^{2}		11		12		7		5									13			10^{1}						31
1		3	4		6^{2}	2	8^{1}	9^{3}		11	12	13		7		5					10							14						32
1		3	4	5	6	2	8^{1}	9^{2}		11	12	13		7							10													33
1		3	4	5	6^{1}	2	8	9		11^{3}	12	13		7			14				10^{2}													34
1		3	4	5	6	2^{1}	8	9		11				7			12				10													35
1		3	4	5	6^{1}	2^{2}	8	9		11	12			7			13				10^{3}								14					36
1		3	4	5		2^{2}	8	12	13	11^{3}		6		7			14				9								10^{1}					37
		3	4	5		2	8	12	13	14	10^{3}	6^{1}		7			11				9^{2}									1				38
1		3	4	5	6^{1}	2	8	9			12			7			11^{2}				10								13					39
		3	4	5		2	8	9	12	11	6			7							10^{1}									1				40
			4	5	12	2	8	9	13	11	6^{1}			7^{3}					3^{2}		10								14	1				41
			4	5	12	2	8^{1}	7	10	11	6								3^{3}		9^{2}								13	1	14			42
		3	4	5	6	7^{2}		9^{1}	10	11	8																		12	1	2	13		43
		3	4	5	6	2		12	10	11	8			7^{2}															9^{1}	1		13		44
		3	4	5	6	2	12	13	10	11	8■			7^{1}															9^{2}	1				45
		3	4^{3}	5	6	2	8		10^{2}	11				7^{1}							13								9	1		12	14	46

FA Cup

First Round	Tiverton T	(a)	3-1
Second Round	Exeter C	(a)	1-2

Carling Cup

First Round	Port Vale	(h)	3-1
Second Round	Ipswich T	(h)	2-0
Third Round	Nottingham F	(h)	0-2

LDV Vans Trophy

First Round	Lincoln C	(a)	1-0
Second Round	Hereford U	(a)	1-1

EVERTON

FA Premiership

FOUNDATION

St Domingo Church Sunday School formed a football club in 1878 which played at Stanley Park. Enthusiasm was so great that in November 1879 they decided to expand membership and changed the name to Everton playing in black shirts with a scarlet sash and nicknamed the 'Black Watch'. After wearing several other colours, royal blue was adopted in 1901.

Goodison Park, Goodison Road, Liverpool L4 4EL.

Telephone: (0151) 330 2200.

Fax: (0151) 286 9114.

Ticket Office: 0870 442 1878.

Website: www.evertonfc.com

Email: everton@evertonfc.com

Ground Capacity: 40,565.

Record Attendance: 78,299 v Liverpool, Division 1, 18 September 1948.

Pitch Measurements: 100.58m × 68m.

Chairman: Bill Kenwright CBE.

Vice chairman: Jon Woods.

Chief Executive: Keith Wyness.

Secretary: David Harrison.

Manager: David Moyes.

Assistant Manager: Alan Irvine.

Head of Physiotherapy: Mick Rathbone, Bsc (Hons), MCSP.

Colours: Blue shirts, white shorts, white stockings.

Change Colours: Silver shirts, black shorts, black stockings.

Year Formed: 1878.

Turned Professional: 1885.

Ltd Co.: 1892.

Previous Name: 1878, St Domingo FC; 1879, Everton.

Club Nickname: 'The Toffees'.

Previous Grounds: 1878, Stanley Park; 1882, Priory Road; 1884, Anfield Road; 1892, Goodison Park.

First Football League Game: 8 September 1888, Football League, v Accrington (h) W 2–1 – Smalley; Dick, Ross; Holt, Jones, Dobson; Fleming (2), Waugh, Lewis, E. Chadwick, Farmer.

HONOURS

Football League: Division 1 – Champions 1890–91, 1914–15, 1927–28, 1931–32, 1938–39, 1962–63, 1969–70, 1984–85, 1986–87; Runners-up 1889–90, 1894–95, 1901–02, 1904–05, 1908–09, 1911–12, 1985–86; Division 2 – Champions 1930–31; Runners-up 1953–54.

FA Cup: Winners 1906, 1933, 1966, 1984, 1995; Runners-up 1893, 1897, 1907, 1968, 1985, 1986, 1989.

Football League Cup: Runners-up 1977, 1984.

League Super Cup: Runners-up 1986.

Simod Cup: Runners-up 1989.

Zenith Data Systems Cup: Runners-up 1991.

European Competitions: *European Cup:* 1963–64, 1970–71. *European Cup-Winners' Cup:* 1966–67, 1984–85 (winners), 1995–96. *European Fairs Cup:* 1962–63, 1964–65, 1965–66. *UEFA Cup:* 1975–76, 1978–79, 1979–80.

SKY SPORTS FACT FILE

Everton won their first six League games at the start of the 1938–39 championship winning season, a First Division record between the wars. Tommy Lawton scored in each of them.

Record League Victory: 9–1 v Manchester C, Division 1, 3 September 1906 – Scott; Balmer, Crelley; Booth, Taylor (1), Abbott (1); Sharp, Bolton (1), Young (4), Settle (2), George Wilson. 9–1 v Plymouth Arg, Division 2, 27 December 1930 – Coggins; Williams, Cresswell; McPherson, Griffiths, Thomson; Critchley, Dunn, Dean (4), Johnson (1), Stein (4).

Record Cup Victory: 11–2 v Derby Co, FA Cup 1st rd, 18 January 1890 – Smalley; Hannah, Doyle (1); Kirkwood, Holt (1), Parry; Latta, Brady (3), Geary (3), Chadwick, Millward (3).

Record Defeat: 4–10 v Tottenham H, Division 1, 11 October 1958.

Most League Points (2 for a win): 66, Division 1, 1969–70.

Most League Points (3 for a win): 90, Division 1, 1984–85.

Most League Goals: 121, Division 2, 1930–31.

Highest League Scorer in Season: William Ralph 'Dixie' Dean, 60, Division 1, 1927–28 (All-time League record).

Most League Goals in Total Aggregate: William Ralph 'Dixie' Dean, 349, 1925–37.

Most League Goals in One Match: 6, Jack Southworth v WBA, Division 1, 30 December 1893.

Most Capped Player: Neville Southall, 92, Wales.

Most League Appearances: Neville Southall, 578, 1981–98.

Youngest League Player: James Vaughan, 16 years 271 days v Crystal Palace, 10 April 2005.

Record Transfer Fee Received: up to £30,000,000 from Manchester U for Wayne Rooney, August 2004.

Record Transfer Fee Paid: £6,000,000 to Southampton for James Beattie, January 2005.

Football League Record: 1888 Founder Member of the Football League; 1930–31 Division 2; 1931–51 Division 1; 1951–54 Division 2; 1954–92 Division 1; 1992– FA Premier League.

MANAGERS

W. E. Barclay 1888–89
(Secretary-Manager)
Dick Molyneux 1889–1901
(Secretary-Manager)
William C. Cuff 1901–18
(Secretary-Manager)
W. J. Sawyer 1918–19
(Secretary-Manager)
Thomas H. McIntosh 1919–35
(Secretary-Manager)
Theo Kelly 1936–48
Cliff Britton 1948–56
Ian Buchan 1956–58
Johnny Carey 1958–61
Harry Catterick 1961–73
Billy Bingham 1973–77
Gordon Lee 1977–81
Howard Kendall 1981–87
Colin Harvey 1987–90
Howard Kendall 1990–93
Mike Walker 1994
Joe Royle 1994–97
Howard Kendall 1997–98
Walter Smith 1998–2002
David Moyes March 2002–

LATEST SEQUENCES

Longest Sequence of League Wins: 12, 24.3.1894 – 13.10.1894.

Longest Sequence of League Defeats: 6, 26.12.1996 – 29.1.1997.

Longest Sequence of League Draws: 5, 4.5.1977 – 16.5.1977.

Longest Sequence of Unbeaten League Matches: 20, 29.4.1978 – 16.12.1978.

Longest Sequence Without a League Win: 14, 6.3.1937 – 4.9.1937.

Successive Scoring Runs: 40 from 15.3.1930.

Successive Non-scoring Runs: 6 from 3.3.1951.

TEN YEAR LEAGUE RECORD

		P	*W*	*D*	*L*	*F*	*A*	*Pts*	*Pos*
1995-96	PR Lge	38	17	10	11	64	44	61	6
1996-97	PR Lge	38	10	12	16	44	57	42	15
1997-98	PR Lge	38	9	13	16	41	56	40	17
1998-99	PR Lge	38	11	10	17	42	47	43	14
1999-2000	PR Lge	38	12	14	12	59	49	50	13
2000-01	PR Lge	38	11	9	18	45	59	42	16
2001-02	PR Lge	38	11	10	17	45	57	43	15
2002-03	PR Lge	38	17	8	13	48	49	59	7
2003-04	PR Lge	38	9	12	17	45	57	39	17
2004-05	PR Lge	38	18	7	13	45	46	61	4

DID YOU KNOW ?

In 2004–05 Everton qualified for the Champions League, the first time since they played in the European Cup in 1970–71 reaching the quarter-final stage and losing on the away goals rule to Panathinaikos.

EVERTON 2004–05 LEAGUE RECORD

Match No.	*Date*	*Venue*	*Opponents*	*Result*		*H/T Score*	*Lg. Pos.*	*Goalscorers*	*Attendance*
1	Aug 15	H	Arsenal	L	1-4	0-2	—	Carsley [64]	35,521
2	21	A	Crystal Palace	W	3-1	1-1	9	Gravesen 2 (1 pen) [19 (p), 62], Bent [82]	23,666
3	28	H	WBA	W	2-1	1-1	7	Osman 2 [2, 70]	34,510
4	30	A	Manchester U	D	0-0	0-0	—		67,803
5	Sept 11	A	Manchester C	W	1-0	0-0	5	Cahill [60]	47,006
6	19	H	Middlesbrough	W	1-0	0-0	3	Bent [47]	34,078
7	26	A	Portsmouth	W	1-0	0-0	3	Cahill [80]	20,125
8	Oct 2	H	Tottenham H	L	0-1	0-0	3		38,264
9	16	H	Southampton	W	1-0	0-0	3	Osman [88]	35,256
10	23	A	Norwich C	W	3-2	2-0	3	Kilbane [10], Bent [40], Ferguson [73]	23,871
11	30	H	Aston Villa	D	1-1	1-1	3	Bent [33]	37,816
12	Nov 6	A	Chelsea	L	0-1	0-0	3		41,965
13	13	A	Birmingham C	W	1-0	0-0	3	Gravesen (pen) [69]	28,388
14	20	H	Fulham	W	1-0	0-0	3	Ferguson [67]	34,763
15	28	A	Newcastle U	D	1-1	0-1	3	Carsley [56]	51,247
16	Dec 4	H	Bolton W	W	3-2	1-1	3	Ferguson [45], Gravesen [75], Jaidi (og) [85]	35,929
17	11	H	Liverpool	W	1-0	0-0	2	Carsley [68]	40552
18	18	A	Blackburn R	D	0-0	0-0	3		25,191
19	26	H	Manchester C	W	2-1	1-1	3	Cahill [22], Bent [63]	40,530
20	28	A	Charlton Ath	L	0-2	0-0	4		27,001
21	Jan 1	A	Tottenham H	L	2-5	1-2	4	Cahill [40], McFadden [87]	36,102
22	4	H	Portsmouth	W	2-1	1-1	4	Stubbs [29], Osman [90]	35,480
23	16	A	Middlesbrough	D	1-1	0-1	4	Cahill [76]	31,794
24	22	H	Charlton Ath	L	0-1	0-1	4		36,041
25	Feb 2	H	Norwich C	W	1-0	0-0	—	Doherty (og) [78]	37,485
26	6	A	Southampton	D	2-2	1-1	4	Beattie [4], Bent [90]	31,509
27	12	H	Chelsea	L	0-1	0-0	4		40,270
28	26	A	Aston Villa	W	3-1	1-0	4	Osman 2 [17, 67], Cahill [48]	40,248
29	Mar 6	H	Blackburn R	L	0-1	0-0	4		32,406
30	20	A	Liverpool	L	1-2	0-2	4	Cahill [82]	44,224
31	Apr 3	A	WBA	L	0-1	0-0	4		26,805
32	10	H	Crystal Palace	W	4-0	1-0	4	Arteta [7], Cahill 2 [47, 54], Vaughan [87]	36,519
33	20	H	Manchester U	W	1-0	0-0	—	Ferguson [55]	37,160
34	23	H	Birmingham C	D	1-1	0-1	4	Ferguson [86]	36,828
35	30	A	Fulham	L	0-2	0-2	4		21,881
36	May 7	H	Newcastle U	W	2-0	1-0	4	Weir [43], Cahill [59]	40,438
37	11	A	Arsenal	L	0-7	0-3	—		38,073
38	15	A	Bolton W	L	2-3	1-0	4	Cahill [9], Carsley [63]	27,701

Final League Position: 4

GOALSCORERS

League (45): Cahill 11, Bent 6, Osman 6, Ferguson 5, Carsley 4, Gravesen 4 (2 pens), Arteta 1, Beattie 1, Kilbane 1, McFadden 1, Stubbs 1, Vaughan 1, Weir 1, own goals 2.
Carling Cup (5): Bent 1, Carsley 1, Chadwick 1, Ferguson 1 (pen), Gravesen 1.
FA Cup (6): McFadden 2, Beattie 1, Cahill 1, Chadwick 1, Osman 1.

Martyn N 32	Pistone A 32 + 1	Naysmith G 5 + 6	Stubbs A 29 + 2	Yobo J 19 + 8	Carsley L 35 + 1	Osman L 24 + 5	Gravesen T 20 + 1	Campbell K 4 + 2	McFadden J 7 + 16	Kilbane K 37 + 1	Hibbert T 35 + 1	Ferguson D 6 + 29	Bent M 31 + 6	Watson S 12 + 13	Weir D 34	Cahill T 33	Chadwick N — + 1	Wright R 6 + 1	Beattie J 7 + 4	Arteta M 10 + 2	Vaughan J — + 2	*Match No.*
1	2	3	4^{1}	5	6	7^{2}	8	9	10^{3}	11	12	13	14									1
1	12	3■	4	5	6	7^{1}	8	9^{2}		11	2	13	10^{3}	14								2
1	3		4	5	6	7	8	9^{1}		11	2	12	10									3
1	3	12	4		6	7				11	2	13	9^{2}	8	5	10^{1}						4
1	3	12	4		6	7^{2}	13			11^{1}	2	14	9^{3}	8	5	10■						5
1	3		4		6	7	8		12	11	2	13	9^{2}	10^{1}	5							6
1	3		4^{1}	12	6		8			11	2	13	9	7^{2}	5	10						7
1	3^{1}		4		6^{2}	7	8		12	11	2	13	9	14	5	10^{3}						8
1	3		4		6	7	8		12	11^{1}	2	13	9^{3}	14	5	10^{2}						9
1	3		4	12	6	7^{2}	8			11	2	14	9^{1}	13	5	10^{3}						10
1	3		4			7^{1}	6		12	11	2	13	9	8^{2}	5	10						11
1	3^{1}		4			7^{3}	6	13	12	11	2		9	8^{2}	5	10	14					12
1	3		4		6	7^{1}	8			11	2	12	9^{2}	13	5	10						13
1	3		4		6	7^{2}	8^{1}		12	11	2	13	9^{3}	14	5	10						14
1	3		4	12	6	7	8^{1}			11	2	13	9^{2}	14	5	10^{3}						15
1	3		4	12	6	13	8		14	11^{3}	2	10^{1}	9		5	7^{2}						16
1	3		4	12	6	7^{3}	8^{1}			11	2	13	9^{2}	14	5	10						17
1	3		4		6	7^{1}	8		12	11	2	13	9^{3}	14	5	10^{2}						18
1	3		4	12	6		8^{1}		13	11	2	14	9^{2}	7^{3}	5	10						19
1^{6}	3		4	6^{1}	7		8		12	11	2	13■	9^{2}		5	10		15				20
	3^{1}	12		4	6	13	8	14	7	11^{3}	2		9^{2}		5	10		1				21
		3	4	5	6	7	8	9^{2}	11^{1}	12	2		13			10		1				22
	3	12	4	6^{2}	7				14	11	2	13	9		5	10^{1}		1	8^{3}			23
	3^{1}		4	12	6	7			13	11^{2}	2	14	9^{3}		5	10		1	8			24
1	3	12	4	6	7				8^{1}	11	2	13	14		5^{2}	10			9^{3}			25
1	3		4^{3}	6	7^{1}				8	11^{2}	2	13	12		5	10			9	14		26
1	2	3^{1}	4	6	7^{2}					11		12	9		5	10			8■	13		27
1	3	12		4	6	7				11	2	13	9^{2}		5	10^{1}				8		28
1	3^{1}			4	6	7			12	11	2	13	9		5	10				8^{2}		29
1	3^{1}		4	8^{3}	6	7				11	2	13	9^{2}	12	5	10			14			30
1	3^{1}		4^{3}	12	6^{2}	7				11	2	13	9	14	5	10				8		31
1		3^{3}	4^{2}		12	7				11	2	10	9^{1}	13	5	8				6	14	32
1				4	6	12			13	11	2	10^{3}	9^{1}	3	5	7^{2}			14	8		33
1	3^{3}			4	6^{2}	7				11	2	13	12	14	5	10			9^{1}	8		34
1	3			4	6	12			13	11		10	9^{3}	2	5	7^{1}			14	8^{2}		35
1			12	4	6				13	11	2	10^{3}	9^{2}	3	5	7^{1}			14	8		36
	3			4	6				10	11	2	12	13	7	5			1	9^{2}	8^{1}		37
			12	4	6	13			7	11	2^{3}	9		3	5	10^{2}		1		8^{1}	14	38

FA Cup

Third Round	Plymouth Arg	(a)	3-1
Fourth Round	Sunderland	(h)	3-0
Fifth Round	Manchester U	(h)	0-2

Carling Cup

Second Round	Bristol C	(a)	2-2
Third Round	Preston NE	(h)	2-0
Fourth Round	Arsenal	(a)	1-3

FULHAM

FA Premiership

FOUNDATION

Churchgoers were responsible for the foundation of Fulham, which first saw the light of day as Fulham St Andrew's Church Sunday School FC in 1879. They won the West London Amateur Cup in 1887 and the championship of the West London League in its initial season of 1892–93. The name Fulham had been adopted in 1888.

Craven Cottage, Stevenage Road, London SW6 6HH
Telephone: 0870 442 1222.
Fax: (020) 8336 0514.
Ticket Office: 0870 442 1234
Website: www.fulhamfc.co.uk
Email: enquiries@fulhamfc.com
Ground Capacity: 22,150.
Record Attendance: 49,335 v Millwall, Division 2, 8 October 1938.
Pitch Measurements: 100m × 68m.
Chairman: Mohammed Al Fayed.
Acting Chief Executive: Mark Collins.
Secretary: Lee Hoos.
Manager: Chris Coleman.
Assistant Manager: Steve Kean.
Physio: Jason Palmer
Colours: White shirts, black shorts, white stockings.
Change Colours: Red shirts, red shorts, red stockings.
Year Formed: 1879.
Turned Professional: 1898.
Ltd Co.: 1903.
Reformed: 1987.
Previous Name: 1879, Fulham St Andrew's; 1888, Fulham.
Club Nickname: 'Cottagers'.
Previous Grounds: 1879, Star Road, Fulham; c.1883, Eel Brook Common, 1884, Lillie Road; 1885, Putney Lower Common; 1886, Ranelagh House, Fulham; 1888, Barn Elms, Castelnau; 1889, Purser's Cross (Roskell's Field), Parsons Green Lane; 1891, Eel Brook Common; 1891, Half Moon, Putney; 1895, Captain James Field, West Brompton; 1896, Craven Cottage.
First Football League Game: 3 September 1907, Division 2, v Hull C (h) L 0–1 – Skene; Ross, Lindsay; Collins, Morrison, Goldie; Dalrymple, Freeman, Bevan, Hubbard, Threlfall.
Record League Victory: 10–1 v Ipswich T, Division 1, 26 December 1963 – Macedo; Cohen, Langley; Mullery (1), Keetch, Robson (1); Key, Cook (1), Leggat (4), Haynes, Howfield (3).
Record Cup Victory: 7–0 v Swansea C, FA Cup 1st rd, 11 November 1995 – Lange; Jupp (1), Herrera, Barkus (Brooker (1)), Moore, Angus, Thomas (1), Morgan, Brazil (Hamill), Conroy (3) (Bolt), Cusack (1).

HONOURS

Football League: Division 1 – Champions 2000–01; Division 2 – Champions 1948–49, 1998–99; Runners-up 1958–59; Division 3 (S) – Champions 1931–32; Division 3 – Runners-up 1970–71, 1996–97.

FA Cup: Runners-up 1975.

Football League Cup: best season: 5th rd, 1968, 1971, 2000.

European Competitions: *UEFA Cup:* 2002–03. *Intertoto Cup:* 2002 (winners)

SKY SPORTS FACT FILE

Frank Penn made his debut for Fulham at the start of the 1919–20 season. He spent nearly 50 years at the club, finishing as a trainer and even turning out as a player again in a wartime regional league game.

Record Defeat: 0–10 v Liverpool, League Cup 2nd rd 1st leg, 23 September 1986.

Most League Points (2 for a win): 60, Division 2, 1958–59 and Division 3, 1970–71.

Most League Points (3 for a win): 101, Division 2, 1998–99.

Most League Goals: 111, Division 3 (S), 1931–32.

Highest League Scorer in Season: Frank Newton, 43, Division 3 (S), 1931–32.

Most League Goals in Total Aggregate: Gordon Davies, 159, 1978–84, 1986–91.

Most League Goals in One Match: 5, Fred Harrison v Stockport Co, Division 2, 5 September 1908; 5, Bedford Jezzard v Hull C, Division 2, 8 October 1955; 5, Jimmy Hill v Doncaster R, Division 2, 15 March 1958; 5, Steve Earle v Halifax T, Division 3, 16 September 1969.

Most Capped Player: Johnny Haynes, 56, England.

Most League Appearances: Johnny Haynes, 594, 1952–70.

Youngest League Player: Tony Mahoney, 17 years 38 days v Cardiff C, 6 November 1976.

Record Transfer Fee Received: £11,500,000 from Manchester U for Louis Saha, January 2004.

Record Transfer Fee Paid: £11,500,000 to Lyon for Steve Marlet, August 2001.

Football League Record: 1907 Elected to Division 2; 1928–32 Division 3 (S); 1932–49 Division 2; 1949–52 Division 1; 1952–59 Division 2; 1959–68 Division 1; 1968–69 Division 2; 1969–71 Division 3; 1971–80 Division 2; 1980–82 Division 3; 1982–86 Division 2; 1986–92 Division 3; 1992–94 Division 2; 1994–97 Division 3; 1997–99 Division 2; 1999–2001 Division 1; 2001– FA Premier League.

MANAGERS

Harry Bradshaw 1904–09
Phil Kelso 1909–24
Andy Ducat 1924–26
Joe Bradshaw 1926–29
Ned Liddell 1929–31
Jim MacIntyre 1931–34
Jimmy Hogan 1934–35
Jack Peart 1935–48
Frank Osborne 1948–64
(was Secretary-Manager or General Manager for most of this period)
Bill Dodgin Snr 1949–53
Duggie Livingstone 1956–58
Bedford Jezzard 1958–64
(General Manager for last two months)
Vic Buckingham 1965–68
Bobby Robson 1968
Bill Dodgin Jnr 1969–72
Alec Stock 1972–76
Bobby Campbell 1976–80
Malcolm Macdonald 1980–84
Ray Harford 1984–96
Ray Lewington 1986–90
Alan Dicks 1990–91
Don Mackay 1991–94
Ian Branfoot 1994–96
(continued as General Manager)
Micky Adams 1996–97
Ray Wilkins 1997–98
Kevin Keegan 1998–99
(Chief Operating Officer)
Paul Bracewell 1999–2000
Jean Tigana 2000–03
Chris Coleman April 2003–

LATEST SEQUENCES

Longest Sequence of League Wins: 12, 7.5.2000 – 18.10.2000.

Longest Sequence of League Defeats: 11, 2.12.1961 – 24.2.1962.

Longest Sequence of League Draws: 6, 14.10.1995 – 18.11.1995.

Longest Sequence of Unbeaten League Matches: 15, 26.1.1999 – 13.4.1999.

Longest Sequence Without a League Win: 15, 25.2.1950 – 23.8.1950.

Successive Scoring Runs: 26 from 28.3.1931.

Successive Non-scoring Runs: 6 from 21.8.1971.

TEN YEAR LEAGUE RECORD

		P	*W*	*D*	*L*	*F*	*A*	*Pts*	*Pos*
1995-96	Div 3	46	12	17	17	57	63	53	17
1996-97	Div 3	46	25	12	9	72	38	87	2
1997-98	Div 2	46	20	10	16	60	43	70	6
1998-99	Div 2	46	31	8	7	79	32	101	1
1999-2000	Div 1	46	17	16	13	49	41	67	9
2000-01	Div 1	46	30	11	5	90	32	101	1
2001-02	PR Lge	38	10	14	14	36	44	44	13
2002-03	PR Lge	38	13	9	16	41	50	48	14
2003-04	PR Lge	38	14	10	14	52	46	52	9
2004-05	PR Lge	38	12	8	18	52	60	44	13

DID YOU KNOW ?

Gibraltar-born Fulham goalkeeper Tony Macedo was serving in the RAF in Germany. After saving two penalties in a reserve match he kept five clean sheets in his first seven senior games. Fulham had to pay £14 air fare to fly him to games.

FULHAM 2004–05 LEAGUE RECORD

Match No.	*Date*	*Venue*	*Opponents*	*Result*	*H/T Score*	*Lg. Pos.*	*Goalscorers*	*Attendance*
1	Aug 14	A	Manchester C	D 1-1	0-1	—	John[56]	44,026
2	21	H	Bolton W	W 2-0	1-0	4	Cole 2[5, 82]	17,541
3	25	H	Middlesbrough	L 0-2	0-0	—		17,759
4	30	A	Portsmouth	L 3-4	2-3	—	Cole[39], Boa Morte[41], Bocanegra[75]	19,728
5	Sept 11	H	Arsenal	L 0-3	0-0	15		21,681
6	18	A	WBA	D 1-1	0-0	15	Cole[72]	24,128
7	25	H	Southampton	W 1-0	1-0	11	Radzinski[24]	19,237
8	Oct 4	A	Crystal Palace	L 0-2	0-0	—		21,825
9	16	H	Liverpool	L 2-4	2-0	16	Boa Morte 2[24, 30]	21,884
10	23	A	Aston Villa	L 0-2	0-1	17		34,460
11	30	H	Tottenham H	W 2-0	1-0	15	Boa Morte[33], Cole[61]	21,317
12	Nov 7	A	Newcastle U	W 4-1	1-0	12	John[28], Malbranque 2 (1 pen)[65, 71 (p)], Boa Morte[76]	51,118
13	13	H	Chelsea	L 1-4	0-1	13	Diop[57]	21,877
14	20	A	Everton	L 0-1	0-0	13		34,763
15	27	H	Blackburn R	L 0-2	0-1	15		19,103
16	Dec 4	A	Norwich C	W 1-0	1-0	14	Cole[7]	23,755
17	13	H	Manchester U	D 1-1	0-1	—	Diop[87]	21,940
18	20	A	Charlton Ath	L 1-2	0-1	—	Radzinski[82]	26,108
19	26	A	Arsenal	L 0-2	0-1	15		38,047
20	28	H	Birmingham C	L 2-3	1-2	16	Legwinski[34], Radzinski[90]	18,706
21	Jan 1	H	Crystal Palace	W 3-1	1-1	15	Cole 2[4, 60], Radzinski[73]	18,680
22	5	A	Southampton	D 3-3	2-2	—	Diop[20], Malbranque[43], Radzinski[50]	27,343
23	16	H	WBA	W 1-0	0-0	15	Diop[90]	16,180
24	22	A	Birmingham C	W 2-1	0-0	13	Cole (pen)[79], Diop[83]	28,512
25	Feb 2	H	Aston Villa	D 1-1	0-0	—	Clark[90]	17,624
26	5	A	Liverpool	L 1-3	1-1	15	Cole[16]	43,534
27	26	A	Tottenham H	L 0-2	0-0	15		35,885
28	Mar 5	H	Charlton Ath	D 0-0	0-0	15		18,290
29	19	A	Manchester U	L 0-1	0-1	16		67,959
30	Apr 3	H	Portsmouth	W 3-1	0-1	15	Cole[63], McBride[81], Boa Morte[90]	20,502
31	9	A	Bolton W	L 1-3	0-2	16	Boa Morte[47]	25,493
32	16	H	Manchester C	D 1-1	0-1	16	Boa Morte[76]	21,796
33	19	A	Middlesbrough	D 1-1	0-0	—	McBride[82]	30,650
34	23	A	Chelsea	L 1-3	1-1	16	John[41]	42,081
35	30	H	Everton	W 2-0	2-0	15	John[15], McBride[39]	21,881
36	May 4	H	Newcastle U	L 1-3	0-1	—	Radzinski[86]	19,003
37	7	A	Blackburn R	W 3-1	1-1	15	Malbranque 2[20, 77], McBride[53]	18,991
38	15	H	Norwich C	W 6-0	2-0	13	McBride 2[10, 86], Diop[35], Knight[54], Malbranque[72], Cole[90]	21,927

Final League Position: 13

GOALSCORERS

League (52): Cole 12 (1 pen), Boa Morte 8, Diop 6, Malbranque 6 (1 pen), McBride 6, Radzinski 6, John 4, Bocanegra 1, Clark 1, Knight 1, Legwinski 1.
Carling Cup (10): Radzinski 4, McBride 3, Cole 1, Malbranque 1, Pembridge 1.
FA Cup (8): John 2, Boa Morte 1, Diop 1 (pen), Jensen 1, Knight 1, Radzinski 1, Volz 1.

Van der Sar E 33 + 1	Volz M 31	Bocanegra C 26 + 2	Diop P 29	Knight Z 35	Pearce I 11	John C 13 + 14	Jensen C 10 + 2	Cole A 29 + 2	Radzinski T 25 + 10	Legwinski S 13 + 2	McBride B 15 + 16	Pembridge M 26 + 2	Goma A 15 + 1	Boa Morte L 29 + 2	Green A 4	Malbranque S 22 + 4	McKinlay B 1 + 1	Rehman Z 15 + 2	Crossley M 5 + 1	Rosenior L 16 + 1	Hammond E — + 1	Clark L 15 + 2	Fontaine L — + 1	*Match No.*
1	2	3	4	5	6	7[1]	8	9	10[2]	11	12	13												1
1	2	3	4	5		7[3]	8[1]	9	10[2]	11	13	12	6	14										2
1	2	3	4[2]	5		7[1]	8	9	10	11	12		6	13										3
1	2	3	4	5		13	8	9	10[2]	7[1]	12		6	11										4
1	2	3	4	5	6	7		9	12	11[1]	13	8		10[2]										5
1	2		4■	5	6	7[1]		9■	12	11		8		10	3									6
1	2			5	6	12			8[1]	7	9	4		10	3	11[2]	13							7
1	2	13		5	6■	14			8[1]		9[3]	11	12[2]	10	3	7	4							8
1	2	6	4	5		12			8[1]		9	11		10	3	7								9
1	2	3	4	5	6[3]	12	8[1]	9[2]			13	11		10		7		14						10
	2	3	4	5		8[1]		9	12			11		10		7		6	1					11
	2	3	4	5		8[1]		9	12			11		10		7		6	1					12
	2	3	4	5				9	8		12	11[1]		10		7		6	1					13
	2	3	4[1]	5				9	8	13	12	11		10[2]		7		6	1					14
15	2	3	4	5■				9	10	8[1]	12	11				7		6	1[6]					15
1	2	3	4		5			9		8	10	11				7		6						16
1		3	4		5	12		9	13	8[2]	10	11				7[1]		6		2				17
1		3	4		5	12		9	13	8[1]	10	11				7[2]		6		2				18
1	2	3	4	5	6	7		9[1]	10		12	11				13		8[2]						19
1	2	3	4	5	6[1]	7[3]		9	8	11	10[2]					13		12			14			20
1	2[2]	3	4	5		12		9	8			11		10[1]		7[3]		6		13		14		21
1		3	4	5		12		9[2]	8[1]		13	11		10		7		6		2[3]			14	22
1	2	3	4	5		9[1]			8		12	11		10		7[2]		6				13		23
1	2	3	4	5				9[1]	8		12	11		10				6				7		24
1	2		4	5		12		9[2]	8[1]		13	11		10				6		3		7		25
1		3	4	5				9	8			11		10				6		2		7		26
1		3	4	5		12	10[2]	9[1]	8		13		6	11						2		7		27
1		3	4	5		12	8[1]	9					6	10		11				2		7		28
1		3	4[2]	5			8[1]	9	12	13			6	10		11				2		7		29
1	2	12		5			8[3]	9	13	7[2]	14		6	10		11				3		4[1]		30
1	2			5		12	8■	9[1]	13		10		6	11		7[2]				3		4		31
1	2			5		12		9[1]	13		10	11	6	8		7[2]				3		4		32
1	2			5		7[1]			8		9	11	6	10		12				3		4		33
1	2			5		7			8		9	11[1]	6	10		12				3		4		34
1	2		4■	5		11[1]	13	12	8[2]		9		6	10						3		7		35
1[6]	2			5			12	9[1]	7		10	11	6	8					15	3		4		36
1	2			5					8		9	11	6	10		7				3■		4		37
1	2	3	4	5				12	8		9		6	10[1]		11						7		38

FA Cup

Third Round	Watford	(a)	1-1
		(h)	2-0
Fourth Round	Derby Co	(a)	1-1
		(h)	4-2
Fifth Round	Bolton W	(a)	0-1

Carling Cup

Second Round	Boston U	(a)	4-1
Third Round	Birmingham C	(a)	1-0
Fourth Round	Nottingham F	(a)	4-2
Fifth Round	Chelsea	(h)	1-2

GILLINGHAM FL Championship 1

FOUNDATION

The success of the pioneering Royal Engineers of Chatham excited the interest of the residents of the Medway Towns and led to the formation of many clubs including Excelsior. After winning the Kent Junior Cup and the Chatham District League in 1893, Excelsior decided to go for bigger things and it was at a meeting in the Napier Arms, Brompton, in 1893 that New Brompton FC came into being, buying and developing the ground which is now Priestfield Stadium. Changed name to Gillingham in 1913, when they also changed their strip from black and white stripes to predominantly blue.

Priestfield Stadium, Redfern Avenue, Gillingham, Kent ME7 4DD.

Telephone: (01634) 300 000.

Fax: (01634) 850 986.

Ticket Office: (01634) 300 000.

Website: www.gillinghamfootballclub.com

Email: info@gillinghamfootballclub.com

Ground Capacity: 11,400.

Record Attendance: 23,002 v QPR, FA Cup 3rd rd, 10 January 1948.

Pitch Measurements: 114yd × 75yd.

Chairman/Chief Executive: P. D. P. Scally.

Vice-chairman: P. A. Spokes.

Chief Executive: P. D. P. Scally.

Secretary: Mrs G. E. Poynter.

Manager: Neale Cooper.

Assistant Manager: R. Jepson.

Physio: S. Webster.

Colours: Blue shirts, blue shorts, blue stockings.

Change Colours: Yellow shirts, yellow shorts, yellow stockings.

Year Formed: 1893.

Turned Professional: 1894.

Ltd Co.: 1893.

Previous Name: 1893, New Brompton; 1913, Gillingham.

Club Nickname: 'The Gills'.

First Football League Game: 28 August 1920, Division 3, v Southampton (h) D 1–1 – Branfield; Robertson, Sissons; Battiste, Baxter, Wigmore; Holt, Hall, Gilbey (1), Roe, Gore.

Record League Victory: 10–0 v Chesterfield, Division 3, 5 September 1987 – Kite; Haylock, Pearce, Shipley (2) (Lillis), West, Greenall (1), Pritchard (2), Shearer (2), Lovell, Elsey (2), David Smith (1).

HONOURS

Football League: Promoted from Division 2 1999–2000 (play-offs); Division 3 – Runners-up 1995-96; Division 4 – Champions 1963–64; Runners-up 1973–74.

FA Cup: best season: 6th rd, 2000.

Football League Cup: best season: 4th rd, 1964, 1997.

SKY SPORTS FACT FILE

Gillingham had the perfect start to the post-war period in 1945–46 as Kent League champions, Kent League Cup winners, Senior Cup and Kent Senior Shield victors. They even won the Kent Challenge Cup on a coin toss with Millwall after a 2–2 draw!

Record Cup Victory: 10–1 v Gorleston, FA Cup 1st rd, 16 November 1957 – Brodie; Parry, Hannaway; Riggs, Boswell, Laing; Payne, Fletcher (2), Saunders (5), Morgan (1), Clark (2).

Record Defeat: 2–9 v Nottingham F, Division 3 (S), 18 November 1950.

Most League Points (2 for a win): 62, Division 4, 1973–74.

Most League Points (3 for a win): 85, Division 2, 1999–2000.

Most League Goals: 90, Division 4, 1973–74.

Highest League Scorer in Season: Ernie Morgan, 31, Division 3 (S), 1954–55; Brian Yeo, 31, Division 4, 1973–74.

Most League Goals in Total Aggregate: Brian Yeo, 135, 1963–75.

Most League Goals in One Match: 6, Fred Cheesmur v Merthyr T, Division 3S, 26 April 1930.

Most Capped Player: Mamady Sidibe, 7, Mali.

Most League Appearances: John Simpson, 571, 1957–72.

Youngest League Player: Billy Hughes, 15 years 275 days v Southend U, 13 April 1976.

Record Transfer Fee Received: £1,500,000 from Manchester C for Robert Taylor, November 1999.

Record Transfer Fee Paid: £600,000 to Reading for Carl Asaba, August 1998.

Football League Record: 1920 Original Member of Division 3; 1921 Division 3 (S); 1938 Failed re-election; Southern League 1938–44; Kent League 1944–46; Southern League 1946–50; 1950 Re-elected to Division 3 (S); 1958–64 Division 4; 1964–71 Division 3; 1971–74 Division 4; 1974–89 Division 3; 1989–92 Division 4; 1992–96; Division 3; 1996–2000 Division 2; 2000–04 Division 1; 2004–05 FLC; 2005– FL1.

MANAGERS

W. Ironside Groombridge 1896–1906 *(Secretary-Manager) (previously Financial Secretary)*
Steve Smith 1906–08
W. I. Groombridge 1908–19 *(Secretary-Manager)*
George Collins 1919–20
John McMillan 1920–23
Harry Curtis 1923–26
Albert Hoskins 1926–29
Dick Hendrie 1929–31
Fred Mavin 1932–37
Alan Ure 1937–38
Bill Harvey 1938–39
Archie Clark 1939–58
Harry Barratt 1958–62
Freddie Cox 1962–65
Basil Hayward 1966–71
Andy Nelson 1971–74
Len Ashurst 1974–75
Gerry Summers 1975–81
Keith Peacock 1981–87
Paul Taylor 1988
Keith Burkinshaw 1988–89
Damien Richardson 1989–93
Mike Flanagan 1993–95
Neil Smillie 1995
Tony Pulis 1995–99
Peter Taylor 1999–2000
Andy Hessenthaler 2000–04
Stan Ternent 2004–05
Neale Cooper May 2005–

LATEST SEQUENCES

Longest Sequence of League Wins: 7, 18.12.1954 – 29.1.1955.

Longest Sequence of League Defeats: 10, 20.9.1988 – 5.11.1988.

Longest Sequence of League Draws: 5, 28.8.1993 – 18.9.1993.

Longest Sequence of Unbeaten League Matches: 20, 13.10.1973 – 10.2.1974.

Longest Sequence Without a League Win: 15, 1.4.1972 – 2.9.1972.

Successive Scoring Runs: 20 from 31.10.1959.

Successive Non-scoring Runs: 6 from 11.2.1961.

TEN YEAR LEAGUE RECORD

		P	*W*	*D*	*L*	*F*	*A*	*Pts*	*Pos*
1995-96	Div 3	46	22	17	7	49	20	83	2
1996-97	Div 2	46	19	10	17	60	59	67	11
1997-98	Div 2	46	19	13	14	52	47	70	8
1998-99	Div 2	46	22	14	10	75	44	80	4
1999-2000	Div 2	46	25	10	11	79	48	85	3
2000-01	Div 1	46	13	16	17	61	66	55	13
2001-02	Div 1	46	18	10	18	64	67	64	12
2002-03	Div 1	46	16	14	16	56	65	62	11
2003-04	Div 1	46	14	9	23	48	67	51	21
2004-05	FL C	46	12	14	20	45	66	50	22

DID YOU KNOW?

Bounced out of the Football League in 1938, Gillingham made a strong bid for Southern League honours finishing third, three points behind Colchester United. Ex-Manchester United forward Harry Rowley was switched to lead the attack and scored 38 goals.

GILLINGHAM 2004–05 LEAGUE RECORD

Match No.	Date	Venue	Opponents	Result	H/T Score	Lg. Pos.	Goalscorers	Attendance
1	Aug 7	A	Ipswich T	L 1-2	1-1	—	Smith 24	23,130
2	10	H	Leeds U	W 2-1	2-0	—	Byfield 4, Roberts 45	10,739
3	14	H	Preston NE	W 2-1	1-1	3	Byfield 16, Roberts 78	7073
4	21	A	Stoke C	L 0-2	0-1	11		13,234
5	27	H	QPR	L 0-1	0-1	—		7391
6	30	A	Burnley	W 2-1	1-0	10	Roberts 5, Byfield 69	11,574
7	Sept 11	H	Sunderland	L 0-4	0-3	14		8775
8	15	A	Coventry C	D 2-2	0-1	—	Agyemang 2 65, 76	11,966
9	18	A	Reading	L 1-3	0-3	19	Byfield 55	13,867
10	25	H	Brighton & HA	L 0-1	0-0	20		8365
11	28	H	Leicester C	L 0-2	0-0	—		6089
12	Oct 2	A	Plymouth Arg	L 1-2	0-0	21	Henderson 47	13,665
13	17	H	Sheffield U	L 1-3	0-1	23	Bromby (og) 75	6964
14	19	A	Millwall	L 1-2	0-2	—	Nowland 47	10,722
15	23	A	West Ham U	L 1-3	1-3	23	Byfield 45	25,247
16	30	H	Wolverhampton W	W 1-0	1-0	23	Jarvis 18	9112
17	Nov 2	H	Watford	D 0-0	0-0	—		7009
18	6	A	Sheffield U	D 0-0	0-0	22		16,598
19	13	H	Derby Co	L 0-2	0-1	22		8015
20	20	A	Crewe Alex	L 1-4	0-1	23	Henderson 73	6128
21	27	H	Nottingham F	W 2-1	0-1	22	Henderson (pen) 76, Johnson T 82	8784
22	Dec 4	A	Cardiff C	L 1-3	1-2	23	Johnson T 33	10,623
23	11	A	Wigan Ath	L 0-2	0-1	23		8451
24	18	H	Rotherham U	W 3-1	0-0	23	Hope 70, Jarvis 80, Vernazza (og) 90	8576
25	26	A	Brighton & HA	L 1-2	1-0	23	Crofts 34	6420
26	28	H	Coventry C	W 3-1	1-1	22	Byfield 15, Cox 2 48, 49	8734
27	Jan 1	H	Reading	D 0-0	0-0	22		8570
28	3	A	Sunderland	D 1-1	1-1	22	Henderson 15	27,147
29	15	H	Plymouth Arg	W 1-0	0-0	22	Crofts 61	8451
30	22	A	Leicester C	L 0-2	0-2	22		23,457
31	Feb 5	A	Watford	L 0-2	0-1	22		15,188
32	12	H	Millwall	D 0-0	0-0	22		9127
33	19	A	Wolverhampton W	D 2-2	0-0	22	Henderson 55, Flynn 89	24,949
34	22	H	West Ham U	L 0-1	0-1	—		9510
35	26	H	Wigan Ath	W 2-1	0-0	22	Henderson 2 53, 65	7209
36	Mar 5	A	Rotherham U	W 3-1	1-0	22	Flynn 26, Sidibe 72, Henderson 82	4367
37	12	A	Leeds U	D 1-1	1-0	22	Hope 43	27,995
38	15	H	Stoke C	W 2-1	1-0	—	McEveley 2, Smith 70	7766
39	19	H	Ipswich T	D 0-0	0-0	21		9311
40	Apr 2	A	Preston NE	D 1-1	0-1	22	Smith 90	15,054
41	5	A	QPR	D 1-1	1-0	—	Flynn 17	16,431
42	9	H	Burnley	W 1-0	0-0	18	Henderson 56	9447
43	16	H	Crewe Alex	D 1-1	0-0	19	Southall 80	10,315
44	23	A	Derby Co	L 0-2	0-1	20		27,481
45	30	H	Cardiff C	D 1-1	0-0	21	Jarvis 72	10,810
46	May 8	A	Nottingham F	D 2-2	0-1	22	Melville (og) 61, Sidibe 77	24,800

Final League Position: 22

GOALSCORERS

League (45): Henderson 9 (1 pen), Byfield 6, Flynn 3, Jarvis 3, Roberts 3, Smith 3, Agyemang 2, Cox 2, Crofts 2, Hope 2, Johnson T 2, Sidibe 2, McEveley 1, Nowland 1, Southall 1, own goals 3.
Carling Cup (1): Sidibe 1.
FA Cup (0).

Banks S 26	Nosworthy N 36 + 1	Hills J 20 + 3	Smith P 40 + 1	Ashby B 22	Hope C 35 + 2	Saunders M 3	Agyemang P 9 + 4	Roberts I 11 + 9	Byfield D 27 + 11	Spiller D 19 + 3	Sidibe M 22 + 13	Jarvis M 12 + 18	Southall N 30 + 3	Hessenthaler A 14 + 3	Rose R 16 + 2	Cox I 29 + 2	Johnson L 6 + 2	Crofts A 25 + 2	Perpetuini D 3	Henderson D 27 + 5	Nowland A 3	Robinson J 2 + 2	Pouton A 8 + 4	Brown J 16	Johnson T 2 + 6	Marney D 3	Bossu B 1 + 1	Gallacher P 3	Bodkin M — + 2	Flynn M 16	Beckwith D — + 1	McEveley J 10	Douglas J 10	Match No.
1	2	3	4	5	6	7	8	9[1]	10[2]	11[3]	12	13	14																					1
1	2[1]	3	4	5	6	7	8[2]	9	10[3]	11	14	13		12																				2
1		3	4	5	6	2[3]	8[2]	9	10[1]	11	12	13		7	14																			3
1		3■	4	5	6		8[3]	9	10[1]	11	12	14	13	7	2[2]																			4
1		3	8	5	6		12	9	10[1]	11	13	2[2]		7		4																		5
1		3	8	5	6			9	10	11		2		7		4																		6
1		3	4		6		12	9[3]	10	11		8		7[1]	13	2	5[2]	14																7
1		3	4		6		8	9[2]	10[1]	7	12		2			5		13	11															8
1	12	3	4		6		8	9[1]	10	7	13		2			5			11[2]															9
1	2	3	4		6		8	9[1]	10		12		7			5			11															10
1	2	3	4		6		12		10		13	8[1]	7■				5	11		9[2]														11
1	2	3[3]	4		6				10	12	13			7[1]		14	5	11		9[2]	8													12
1	3				6		12		10[1]	7	13		2	8[3]			5	11[2]		9	4	14												13
1	2						10[1]		12	11	9		13	7[3]	3	4	5[2]				6	8	14											14
	2				6		10[1]		12	7	9[3]	13	5[2]	8	3	4		11		14				1										15
	2				6					7	9	4		8[1]	3	5■	12	11		10[2]				1	13									16
	2				6			12		7	9[1]	4		8[2]	3		5	11		10				1	13									17
	2		12		6			13		7	9	4[1]		8[3]	3			11		10[2]				1	14	5								18
	2		4		6			12		7	9[1]	8[3]			3			11[2]		10		13		1	14	5								19
	2		4		6				10	7		12			3			11		9		8[2]		1	13	5[1]								20
	2		4	5	6			9[1]	10[2]	7	12	14			3			11[3]		8				1	13									21
	2	3	4	5	6			12		7[2]	9	8						11[1]					13		10		1							22
	2	11	4	5	6			12			9	13	7		3								8[2]		10[1]			1						23
	2	3	4	5	6				10[1]		9	13	7	12				11[2]					8					1						24
	2	3[2]	4	5	6[1]				10		9[3]	13	7			12		11		14			8					1						25
1	2	3	4	5					10		9[1]		7			6		11		12			8											26
1	2	3	4	5					10		9[1]		7			6		11		12			8											27
1		3[2]	4	5				12	10			13	7	8	2	6		11		9[1]														28
1		12	4		6				10				2	7[2]	3	5		11		9[1]			8						13					29
1	2		4		6			12	10[1]				7	13	3	5		11[2]		9			8[3]						14					30
	2		8	5				12	10				7		3[1]	6		11		9				1						4				31
1	2		8	5				12	10[1]			13	7		3[2]	6		11		9										4				32
1	2		7	5					10	12		8[1]	3			6		11[2]		9			13							4				33
1	2	12	7	5					10[1]	13		8	3			6		11[2]		9			14							4[3]				34
1	2	3	8	5	12						13	10[2]	7			6[1]		11		9										4				35
1			7	5[1]	6						10	13[3]	2		3		12	11		9			8[2]							4	14			36
1	2		8		6				12		10[1]		7			5				9■										4		3	11	37
1[6]	2		8		6				12		10		7			5				9[1]							15			4		3	11	38
	2		8		6				12		10		7			5				9[1]				1						4		3	11	39
	2	12	8		6[2]				13		10	14	7			5				9[3]				1						4[1]		3	11	40
	2		8		6				12		10		7			5				9[1]				1						4		3	11	41
	2		8		6				12		10		7			5				9[1]				1						4		3	11	42
	2		8		6[1]				12		10	13	7			5				9				1						4[2]		3	11	43
	2		8		6[1]				10			12	7			5				9				1						4		3	11	44
	2		8	5	12				13		10	14	7			6				9[2]				1						4[3]		3[1]	11	45
	2		8	5[1]					12		9	13	7			6		10[2]		14				1						4[3]		3	11	46

FA Cup
Third Round Portsmouth (a) 0-1

Carling Cup
First Round Northampton T (h) 1-2

GRIMSBY TOWN FL Championship 2

FOUNDATION

Grimsby Pelham FC, as they were first known, came into being at a meeting held at the Wellington Arms in September 1878. Pelham is the family name of big landowners in the area, the Earls of Yarborough. The receipts for their first game amounted to 6s. 9d. (approx. 39p). After a year, the club name was changed to Grimsby Town.

Blundell Park, Cleethorpes, North East Lincolnshire DN35 7PY.

Telephone: (01472) 605 050.

Fax: (01472) 693 665.

Ticket Office: (01472) 608 026.

Website: www.gtfc.co.uk.

Email: commercial@gtfc.co.uk.

Ground Capacity: 10,033.

Record Attendance: 31,657 v Wolverhampton W, FA Cup 5th rd, 20 February 1937.

Pitch Measurements: 111yd × 75yd.

Chairman: John Fenty.

Chief Executive: Ian Fleming.

Manager: Russell Slade.

Assistant Manager: Graham Rodger.

Physio: David Moore.

Colours: Black and white striped shirts, black shorts, black stockings.

Change Colours: Yellow shirts, white shorts, yellow stockings.

Year Formed. 1878.

Turned Professional: 1890. ***Ltd Co.:*** 1890.

Previous Name: 1878, Grimsby Pelham; 1879, Grimsby Town.

Club Nickname: 'The Mariners'.

Previous Grounds: 1880, Clee Park; 1889, Abbey Park; 1899, Blundell Park.

First Football League Game: 3 September 1892, Division 2, v Northwich Victoria (h) W 2–1 – Whitehouse; Lundie, T. Frith; C. Frith, Walker, Murrell; Higgins, Henderson, Brayshaw, Riddoch (2), Ackroyd.

Record League Victory: 9–2 v Darwen, Division 2, 15 April 1899 – Bagshaw; Lockie, Nidd; Griffiths, Bell (1), Nelmes; Jenkinson (3), Richards (1), Cockshutt (3), Robinson, Chadburn (1).

Record Cup Victory: 8–0 v Darlington, FA Cup 2nd rd, 21 November 1885 – G. Atkinson; J. H. Taylor, H. Taylor; Hall, Kimpson, Hopewell; H. Atkinson (1), Garnham, Seal (3), Sharman, Monument (4).

HONOURS

Football League: Division 1 best season: 5th, 1934–35; Division 2 – Champions 1900–01, 1933–34; Runners-up 1928–29; Promoted from Division 2 1997–98 (play-offs); Division 3 (N) – Champions 1925–26, 1955–56; Runners-up 1951–52; Division 3 – Champions 1979–80; Runners-up 1961–62; Division 4 – Champions 1971–72; Runners-up 1978–79; 1989–90.

FA Cup: Semi-finals, 1936, 1939.

Football League Cup: best season: 5th rd, 1980, 1985.

League Group Cup: Winners 1982.

Auto Windscreen Shield: Winners 1998.

SKY SPORTS FACT FILE

On 6 November 1937 Grimsby Town were the only First Division team to win at home. In fact there were only 14 home wins in the League, 13 defeats and 17 draws. Grimsby's 2–1 win over champions elect Arsenal ultimately saved them from relegation.

Record Defeat: 1–9 v Arsenal, Division 1, 28 January 1931.

Most League Points (2 for a win): 68, Division 3 (N), 1955–56.

Most League Points (3 for a win): 83, Division 3, 1990–91.

Most League Goals: 103, Division 2, 1933–34.

Highest League Scorer in Season: Pat Glover, 42, Division 2, 1933–34.

Most League Goals in Total Aggregate: Pat Glover, 180, 1930–39.

Most League Goals in One Match: 6, Tommy McCairns v Leicester Fosse, Division 2, 11 April 1896.

Most Capped Player: Pat Glover, 7, Wales.

Most League Appearances: John McDermott, 592, 1987– .

Youngest League Player: Tony Ford, 16 years 143 days v Walsall, 4 October 1975.

Record Transfer Fee Received: £1,500,000 from Everton for John Oster, July 1997.

Record Transfer Fee Paid: £500,000 to Preston NE for Lee Ashcroft, August 1998.

Football League Record: 1892 Original Member Division 2; 1901–03 Division 1; 1903 Division 2; 1910 Failed re-election; 1911 re-elected Division 2; 1920–21 Division 3; 1921–26 Division 3 (N); 1926–29 Division 2; 1929–32 Division 1; 1932–34 Division 2; 1934–48 Division 1; 1948–51 Division 2; 1951–56 Division 3 (N); 1956–59 Division 2; 1959–62 Division 3; 1962–64 Division 2; 1964–68 Division 3; 1968–72 Division 4; 1972–77 Division 3; 1977–79 Division 4; 1979–80 Division 3; 1980–87 Division 2; 1987–88 Division 3; 1988–90 Division 4; 1990–91 Division 3; 1991–92 Division 2; 1992–97 Division 1; 1997–98 Division 2; 1998–2003 Division 1; 2003–04 Division 2; 2004– FL2.

MANAGERS

H. N. Hickson 1902–20
(Secretary-Manager)
Haydn Price 1920
George Fraser 1921–24
Wilf Gillow 1924–32
Frank Womack 1932–36
Charles Spencer 1937–51
Bill Shankly 1951–53
Billy Walsh 1954–55
Allenby Chilton 1955–59
Tim Ward 1960–62
Tom Johnston 1962–64
Jimmy McGuigan 1964–67
Don McEvoy 1967–68
Bill Harvey 1968–69
Bobby Kennedy 1969–71
Lawrie McMenemy 1971–73
Ron Ashman 1973–75
Tom Casey 1975–76
Johnny Newman 1976–79
George Kerr 1979–82
David Booth 1982–85
Mike Lyons 1985–87
Bobby Roberts 1987–88
Alan Buckley 1988–94
Brian Laws 1994–96
Kenny Swain 1997
Alan Buckley 1997–2000
Lennie Lawrence 2000–01
Paul Groves 2001–04
Nicky Law 2004
Russell Slade May 2004

LATEST SEQUENCES

Longest Sequence of League Wins: 11, 19.1.1952 – 29.3.1952.

Longest Sequence of League Defeats: 9, 30.11.1907 – 18.1.1908.

Longest Sequence of League Draws: 5, 6.2.1965 – 6.3.1965.

Longest Sequence of Unbeaten League Matches: 19, 16.2.1980 – 30.8.1980.

Longest Sequence Without a League Win: 18, 10.10.1981 – 16.3.1982.

Successive Scoring Runs: 33 from 6.10.1928.

Successive Non-scoring Runs: 6 from 11.3.2000.

TEN YEAR LEAGUE RECORD

		P	*W*	*D*	*L*	*F*	*A*	*Pts*	*Pos*
1995-96	Div 1	46	14	14	18	55	69	56	17
1996-97	Div 1	46	11	13	22	60	81	46	22
1997-98	Div 2	46	19	15	12	55	37	72	3
1998-99	Div 1	46	17	10	19	40	52	61	11
1999-2000	Div 1	46	13	12	21	41	67	51	20
2000-01	Div 1	46	14	10	22	43	62	52	18
2001-02	Div 1	46	12	14	20	50	72	50	19
2002-03	Div 1	46	9	12	25	48	85	39	24
2003-04	Div 2	46	13	11	22	55	81	50	21
2004-05	FL 2	46	14	16	16	51	52	58	18

DID YOU KNOW?

Despite suffering relegation from Division Two in 1950–51 there was some consolation for Grimsby Town in the figure seven. A convincing season's best 7–2 win was recorded over Brentford and Billy Cairns scored in seven consecutive matches.

GRIMSBY TOWN 2004–05 LEAGUE RECORD

Match No.	*Date*	*Venue*	*Opponents*	*Result*		*H/T Score*	*Lg. Pos.*	*Goalscorers*	*Attendance*
1	Aug 7	A	Darlington	L	0-1	0-0	—		4807
2	10	H	Boston U	D	1-1	0-1	—	Reddy [71]	6737
3	14	H	Bury	W	5-1	1-1	7	Mansaram [17], Sestanovich [49], Pinault 2 [64, 73], Reddy [78]	4277
4	21	A	Rushden & D	L	0-1	0-0	16		2924
5	28	H	Mansfield T	W	2-0	1-0	9	Pinault [5], Crowe [86]	5693
6	30	A	Wycombe W	L	0-2	0-1	15		4320
7	Sept 4	H	Rochdale	L	0-1	0-0	18		4795
8	11	A	Macclesfield T	L	1-3	1-0	21	Crowe [13]	2128
9	18	H	Leyton Orient	W	2-0	0-0	15	Crowe [57], Pinault (pen) [90]	5082
10	25	A	Cambridge U	W	2-0	0-0	12	Parkinson [65], McDermott [72]	3824
11	Oct 1	H	Cheltenham T	D	1-1	1-0	—	Parkinson [16]	6133
12	8	A	Northampton T	W	1-0	0-0	—	Gordon [86]	5805
13	16	H	Bristol R	D	0-0	0-0	12		4691
14	19	A	Shrewsbury T	D	1-1	1-0	—	Fleming [5]	2956
15	23	A	Chester C	L	1-2	1-2	14	Daly [45]	3233
16	30	H	Swansea C	D	1-1	0-0	18	Cramb [56]	4618
17	Nov 6	A	Scunthorpe U	L	0-2	0-1	19		8054
18	20	H	Kidderminster H	W	2-1	2-0	17	Gordon [9], Pinault [24]	3605
19	26	A	Southend U	D	1-1	1-0	—	McDermott [32]	5192
20	Dec 7	H	Notts Co	W	3-2	1-1	—	Bull [7], Parkinson [49], Whittle [79]	4030
21	11	A	Yeovil T	L	1-2	0-1	16	Sestanovich [86]	5733
22	17	H	Oxford U	D	1-1	1-0	—	Cramb [18]	4777
23	26	H	Macclesfield T	D	0-0	0-0	14		5108
24	29	A	Lincoln C	D	0-0	0-0	—		8056
25	Jan 3	H	Cambridge U	W	3-0	2-0	16	Pinault [34], Bull [38], Gritton [90]	4148
26	11	H	Northampton T	L	1-2	1-0	—	Reddy [22]	3774
27	15	A	Leyton Orient	W	2-1	1-0	14	Parkinson [19], Gritton [71]	3816
28	22	H	Lincoln C	L	2-4	0-2	17	Pinault [50], Coidicott [59]	7091
29	28	A	Cheltenham T	W	3-2	1-1	—	Fleming [13], Reddy 2 [56, 85]	3327
30	Feb 5	A	Bristol R	L	0-3	0-3	17		6134
31	12	H	Shrewsbury T	L	0-1	0-1	17		4781
32	19	A	Swansea C	D	0-0	0-0	17		7760
33	22	H	Chester C	W	1-0	0-0	—	Gritton [81]	3144
34	26	H	Yeovil T	W	2-1	0-1	14	Gritton [60], Parkinson [87]	4414
35	Mar 1	A	Rochdale	L	0-2	0-1	—		2312
36	5	A	Oxford U	W	2-1	0-1	12	Harrold [46], Parkinson [71]	5625
37	12	A	Boston U	D	1-1	0-1	11	Harrold [69]	3941
38	19	H	Darlington	L	0-1	0-1	12		4578
39	25	A	Bury	L	1-3	0-2	—	Reddy [48]	5671
40	28	H	Rushden & D	D	0-0	0-0	15		4566
41	Apr 2	A	Mansfield T	L	0-2	0-1	16		3424
42	9	H	Wycombe W	D	0-0	0-0	17		3452
43	16	A	Notts Co	D	2-2	1-0	17	Parkinson [27], Crowe [50]	5478
44	23	H	Scunthorpe U	D	0-0	0-0	18		7941
45	30	A	Kidderminster H	W	4-1	2-0	18	Jones [8], Reddy 2 [13, 78], Parkinson [48]	2340
46	May 7	H	Southend U	D	1-1	0-0	18	Reddy [57]	6259

Final League Position: 18

GOALSCORERS

League (51): Reddy 9, Parkinson 8, Pinault 7 (1 pen), Crowe 4, Gritton 4, Bull 2, Cramb 2, Fleming 2, Gordon 2, Harrold 2, McDermott 2, Sestanovich 2, Coldicott 1, Daly 1, Jones 1, Mansaram 1, Whittle 1.
Carling Cup (1): Parkinson 1.
FA Cup (0).
LDV Vans Trophy (1): Cramb 1.

Williams A 46	Crowe J 37	Bull R 22 + 5	Jones R 18 + 2	Ramsden S 23 + 2	Whittle J 39 + 1	Fleming T 43	Pinault T 32 + 11	Parkinson A 43 + 2	Mansaram D 3 + 5	Sestanovich A 17 + 5	Reddy M 24 + 16	Marcelle C — + 3	McDermott J 39	Young G 2 + 4	Coldicott S 20 + 12	Gordon D 20	Williams C 1 + 2	Robinson P 1 + 1	Forbes T 33	Cramb C 7 + 4	Daly J 3	Gritton M 22 + 1	North D — + 1	Hockless G 3 + 3	Crane T 2 + 1	Soames D — + 4	Harrold M 6	Downey G — + 1	Hegarty N — + 1	*Match No.*
1	2	3	4	5	6	7	8	9	10¹	11²	12	13																		1
1	2		4³	5	6	7	8	9	10¹	11²	12	13	3	14																2
1	2	12		5	6	7	8³	9	10²	11	13		3¹		14	4														3
1	2	12		5	6	7	8³	9	13	10²	11		3¹		14	4														4
1	2			5³	6	7	8	9	12	10²	11¹		3	14	13	4														5
1	2	12		5	6	7	8²	9		10³	14	13	3¹		11	4														6
1	2			5¹	6	7	8	9		10²	11		3		12	4	13													7
1	2				6	7²	8	9			12		3	5	13	4	11¹	10												8
1	2				6	7	8	9		10	11		3			4			5											9
1	2				6	7		9		10¹	11²		3		8	4	13	12	5											10
1	2				6	7	8	9		10	11		3			4			5											11
1	2				6	7	8	9		12	11¹				3	4			5	10										12
1	2				6	7	8	9		10¹	11²		3		12	4			5	13										13
1	2¹	12			6	7		9		10²	11		3		8	4			5	13										14
1					6	7²	8	3		11	12		2		13	4			5	10¹	9									15
1	2¹		3		6	7	12	9			11²				8	4			5	13	10									16
1	2		4		6	7	12	9		11²	13		3³		8¹	5				14	10■									17
1	2	3	4		6		8	9		11			7		12	5¹				10										18
1	2²	11	4		6	7	8	9			12		3		13	5				10¹										19
1	2	11²			6	7	8	9		12	13		3			4			5	10¹										20
1	2	11¹			6	7	8	9²	14	12	13		3			4			5	10³										21
1	2	11¹			6	7	8	9²	14	12	13		3			4			5	10³										22
1	2	11	4		6	7		9¹		8	12		3						5			10								23
1	2	11	4	5	6¹	7	12	9²		10	13		3									8								24
1	2	11	4	5		7	8	9¹	12				3						6			10								25
1	2	11²	4	5			8	9¹		12■	7		3	13					6			10								26
1		3■	4	5		7	12	9²			11		2	13	8¹				6			10								27
1			4	5		7	12	9			11		2	3¹	8				6			10								28
1			4	5		7	8	9			11		2		6				3			10								29
1			4¹	5	12	7	8	9²			11		2		6				3			10³	13	14						30
1		3		5		7	8	9			11		2						6			10		4						31
1	2²	3		5	6	7	12				9				8				4			10		11¹	13					32
1	2¹	3		5	6	7	13	12			9				8				4			10		11²						33
1	2	3		5	6	7¹	12	9			11				8				4			10								34
1	3²		13	5	6	7	12	9			11¹		2³		8				4			10				14				35
1		3		5¹	6	7	8	9					2		11				4			12					10			36
1		3			6	7¹	8	9			12		2		4				5			10					11			37
1		3			6	7■	8	9¹			11		2						5			10		12			4			38
1	4	3¹	12		6		8	9			7		2³		13				5			10²				14	11			39
1	3				6	7	8	9					2		4²				5			10¹		13		12	11			40
1	3			12	6	7	8²	9					2		4				5			10¹				13	11			41
1	3	12	4	11¹	6	7²	13	9					2		8				5			10								42
1	3		4	5	6	7	12	9			13		2		8¹				11			10²								43
1	3	11	4		6	7	8	9			12		2						5			10¹								44
1	3¹	11	4²	5	6	7	8	9³			10				12										2			13	14	45
1	3	11		12	6	7²	8	14			9³		2¹		13				5			10			4					46

FA Cup

First Round	Exeter C	(a)	0-1

Carling Cup

First Round	Wigan Ath	(h)	1-0
Second Round	Charlton Ath	(h)	0-2

LDV Vans Trophy

First Round	Carlisle U	(a)	1-2

HARTLEPOOL UNITED FL Championship 1

FOUNDATION

The inspiration for the launching of Hartlepool United was the West Hartlepool club which won the FA Amateur Cup in 1904–05. They had been in existence since 1881 and their Cup success led in 1908 to the formation of the new professional concern which first joined the North-Eastern League. In those days they were Hartlepools United and won the Durham Senior Cup in their first two seasons.

Victoria Park, Clarence Road, Hartlepool TS24 8BZ.

Telephone: (01429) 272 584.

Fax: (01429) 863 007.

Ticket Office: (01429) 272 584.

Website: www.hartlepoolunited.co.uk

Email: info@hartlepoolunited.co.uk

Ground Capacity: 7,629.

Record Attendance: 17,426 v Manchester U, FA Cup 3rd rd, 5 January 1957.

Pitch Measurements: 100 × 66 metres.

Chairman: Ken Hodcroft.

Chief Executive: Russ Green.

Secretary: Maureen Smith.

Manager: Martin Scott.

Assistant Manager: Steve Agnew.

Physio: John Murray.

Colours: Blue and white stripes.

Change Colours: Black.

Year Formed: 1908.

Turned Professional: 1908.

Ltd Co.: 1908.

Previous Names: 1908, Hartlepools United; 1968, Hartlepool; 1977, Hartlepool United.

Club Nickname: 'The Pool'.

First Football League Game: 27 August 1921, Division 3 (N), v Wrexham (a) W 2–0 – Gill; Thomas, Crilly; Dougherty, Hopkins, Short; Kessler, Mulholland (1), Lister (1), Robertson, Donald.

Record League Victory: 10–1 v Barrow, Division 4, 4 April 1959 – Oakley; Cameron, Waugh; Johnson, Moore, Anderson; Scott (1), Langland (1), Smith (3), Clark (2), Luke (2), (1 og).

Record Cup Victory: 6–0 v North Shields, FA Cup 1st rd, 30 November 1946 – Heywood; Brown, Gregory; Spelman, Lambert, Jones; Price, Scott (2), Sloan (4), Moses, McMahon.

HONOURS

Football League: Division 3 – Runners-up 2002–03; Division 3 (N) – Runners-up 1956–57.

FA Cup: best season: 4th rd, 1955, 1978, 1989, 1993.

Football League Cup, best season: 4th rd, 1975.

SKY SPORTS FACT FILE

Tommy Yews was a part-time professional with Hartlepools United in the 1920s and played outside-right. He turned full-time and was transferred to West Ham United in 1923 where he made well over 300 League appearances for the club.

Record Defeat: 1–10 v Wrexham, Division 4, 3 March 1962.

Most League Points (2 for a win): 60, Division 4, 1967–68.

Most League Points (3 for a win): 85, Division 3, 2002–03.

Most League Goals: 90, Division 3 (N), 1956–57.

Highest League Scorer in Season: William Robinson, 28, Division 3 (N), 1927–28; Joe Allon, 28, Division 4, 1990–91.

Most League Goals in Total Aggregate: Ken Johnson, 98, 1949–64.

Most League Goals in One Match: 5, Harry Simmons v Wigan Borough, Division 3N, 1 January 1931; 5, Bobby Folland v Oldham Ath, Division 3N, 15 April 1961.

Most Capped Player: Ambrose Fogarty, 1 (11), Republic of Ireland.

Most League Appearances: Wattie Moore, 447, 1948–64.

Youngest League Player: David Foley, 16 years 105 days v Port Vale, 25 August 2003.

Record Transfer Fee Received: £750,000 from Ipswich T for Tommy Miller, July 2001.

Record Transfer Fee Paid: £75,000 to Notts Co for Gary Jones, March 1999; £75,000 to Mansfield T for Darrell Clarke, July 2001.

Football League Record: 1921 Original Member of Division 3 (N); 1958–68 Division 4; 1968–69 Division 3; 1969–91 Division 4; 1991–92 Division 3; 1992–94 Division 2; 1994–2003 Division 3; 2003–04 Division 2; 2004– FL1.

LATEST SEQUENCES

Longest Sequence of League Wins: 7, 30.3.2002 – 13.8.2002.

Longest Sequence of League Defeats: 8, 27.1.1993 – 27.2.1993.

Longest Sequence of League Draws: 5, 24.2.2001 – 17.3.2001.

Longest Sequence of Unbeaten League Matches: 21, 2.12.2000 – 31.3.2001.

Longest Sequence Without a League Win: 18, 9.1.1993 – 3.4.1993.

Successive Scoring Runs: 17 from 28.2.1964.

Successive Non-scoring Runs: 11 from 9.1.1993.

MANAGERS

Alfred Priest 1908–12
Percy Humphreys 1912–13
Jack Manners 1913–20
Cecil Potter 1920–22
David Gordon 1922–24
Jack Manners 1924–27
Bill Norman 1927–31
Jack Carr 1932–35
(had been Player-Coach since 1931)
Jimmy Hamilton 1935–43
Fred Westgarth 1943–57
Ray Middleton 1957–59
Bill Robinson 1959–62
Allenby Chilton 1962–63
Bob Gurney 1963–64
Alvan Williams 1964–65
Geoff Twentyman 1965
Brian Clough 1965–67
Angus McLean 1967–70
John Simpson 1970–71
Len Ashurst 1971–74
Ken Hale 1974–76
Billy Horner 1976–83
Johnny Duncan 1983
Mike Docherty 1983
Billy Horner 1984–86
John Bird 1986–88
Bobby Moncur 1988–89
Cyril Knowles 1989–91
Alan Murray 1991–93
Viv Busby 1993
John MacPhail 1993–94
David McCreery 1994–95
Keith Houchen 1995–96
Mick Tait 1996–99
Chris Turner 1999–2002
Mike Newell 2002–03
Neale Cooper 2003–05
Martin Scott June 2005–

TEN YEAR LEAGUE RECORD

		P	W	D	L	F	A	Pts	Pos
1995-96	Div 3	46	12	13	21	47	67	49	20
1996-97	Div 3	46	14	9	23	53	66	51	20
1997-98	Div 3	46	12	23	11	61	53	59	17
1998-99	Div 3	46	13	12	21	52	65	51	22
1999-2000	Div 3	46	21	9	16	60	49	72	7
2000-01	Div 3	46	21	14	11	71	54	77	4
2001-02	Div 3	46	20	11	15	74	48	71	7
2002-03	Div 3	46	24	13	9	71	51	85	2
2003-04	Div 2	46	20	13	13	76	61	73	6
2004-05	FL 1	46	21	8	17	76	66	71	6

DID YOU KNOW ?

In the League Cup during 1974–75 Hartlepool United had a four match second round marathon with Bournemouth, drawing 1–1 away, 2–2 at home 1–1 away again and finally winning 1–0 on their own ground with a goal from winger Billy Ward.

HARTLEPOOL UNITED 2004–05 LEAGUE RECORD

Match No.	Date	Venue	Opponents	Result	H/T Score	Lg. Pos.	Goalscorers	Attendance
1	Aug 7	H	Bradford C	W 2-1	0-0	—	Boyd (pen) [75], Robertson [81]	6032
2	10	A	Tranmere R	L 1-2	1-1	—	Robertson [23]	8128
3	16	A	Huddersfield T	W 2-0	0-0	—	Betsy [68], Tinkler [70]	9968
4	21	H	Blackpool	D 1-1	1-0	7	Williams E [24]	5144
5	28	A	Swindon T	L 0-3	0-3	14		5365
6	30	H	Colchester U	W 2-1	1-0	8	Williams E [38], Boyd [70]	4371
7	Sept 4	H	Barnsley	D 1-1	0-1	9	Boyd [77]	5119
8	11	A	Oldham Ath	L 2-3	0-1	15	Westwood [78], Griffin (og) [90]	5805
9	18	H	Torquay U	W 4-1	1-1	7	Porter [6], Sweeney [64], Tinkler [73], Humphreys [83]	4485
10	25	A	Milton Keynes D	L 2-4	1-1	11	Boyd 2 [20, 87]	3685
11	Oct 2	H	Hull C	W 2-0	1-0	9	Porter [8], Boyd [50]	5768
12	8	A	Luton T	L 0-3	0-1	—		7865
13	16	H	Chesterfield	W 3-2	2-1	10	Sweeney 3 [3, 8, 83]	4617
14	19	A	Brentford	L 1-2	1-1	—	Robson [31]	4797
15	23	A	Peterborough U	L 0-3	0-2	13		3841
16	30	H	Port Vale	W 1-0	1-0	10	Williams E [24]	4755
17	Nov 6	H	Doncaster R	W 2-1	0-1	8	Porter 2 [78, 89]	5495
18	20	A	Sheffield W	L 0-2	0-0	13		19,919
19	27	H	Bournemouth	W 3-2	1-2	9	Westwood [23], Nelson [88], Appleby [90]	4376
20	Dec 7	A	Walsall	L 1-2	1-0	—	Boyd [33]	5522
21	11	H	Stockport Co	W 3-1	1-1	9	Westwood 2 [28, 51], Porter [55]	4572
22	18	A	Wrexham	W 5-1	4-1	7	Humphreys [8], Sweeney 2 [18, 72], Porter [35], Boyd [37]	3582
23	26	H	Oldham Ath	W 2-1	2-0	4	Boyd 2 (2 pens) [7, 23]	6520
24	28	A	Bristol C	D 0-0	0-0	5		13,034
25	Jan 1	A	Barnsley	D 0-0	0-0	7		9595
26	3	H	Milton Keynes D	W 5-0	1-0	5	Sweeney [21], Boyd 2 [49, 57], Porter [80], Appleby [90]	5060
27	15	A	Torquay U	W 2-1	0-1	5	Porter [68], Sweeney [71]	2543
28	22	H	Bristol C	W 2-1	1-1	5	Boyd (pen) [16], Sweeney [71]	5399
29	Feb 5	A	Chesterfield	W 1-0	0-0	5	Boyd [55]	4606
30	15	H	Luton T	L 2-3	0-1	—	Davis (og) [62], Robson [90]	5542
31	19	A	Port Vale	W 1-0	1-0	5	Porter [2]	4366
32	22	H	Brentford	W 3-1	0-0	—	Boyd (pen) [54], Williams E [74], Sweeney [87]	4206
33	26	A	Stockport Co	L 0-1	0-1	5		4548
34	Mar 5	H	Wrexham	L 4-6	2-3	5	Strachan [4], Porter 2 [31, 84], Boyd [62]	4707
35	8	A	Hull C	L 0-1	0-1	—		17,112
36	12	H	Tranmere R	L 0-1	0-0	6		4887
37	19	A	Bradford C	W 2-1	1-0	5	Williams E [42], Porter [73]	7509
38	25	H	Huddersfield T	L 0-1	0-1	—		6205
39	28	A	Blackpool	D 2-2	2-1	5	Boyd 2 [27, 28]	6853
40	Apr 2	H	Swindon T	W 3-0	1-0	5	Porter [31], Butler [49], Humphreys [83]	4536
41	5	H	Peterborough U	D 2-2	2-0	—	Porter [22], Sweeney [36]	4579
42	9	A	Colchester U	D 1-1	0-1	5	Sweeney [54]	3148
43	15	H	Sheffield W	W 3-0	2-0	—	Boyd 3 [2, 18, 58]	6429
44	23	A	Doncaster R	L 0-2	0-0	4		7024
45	30	H	Walsall	L 1-3	0-3	5	Boyd (pen) [77]	6389
46	May 7	A	Bournemouth	D 2-2	1-2	6	Daly [20], Sweeney [65]	8620

Final League Position: 6

GOALSCORERS

League (76): Boyd 22 (6 pens), Porter 14, Sweeney 13, Williams E 5, Westwood 4, Humphreys 3, Appleby 2, Robertson 2, Robson 2, Tinkler 2, Betsy 1, Butler 1, Daly 1, Nelson 1, Strachan 1, own goals 2.
Carling Cup (3): Boyd 1, Sweeney 1, Williams 1.
FA Cup (9): Boyd 3, Westwood 2, Porter 1, Robson 1, Tinkler 1, Williams 1.
LDV Vans Trophy (5): Boyd 1, Porter 1, Pouton 1, Strachan 1 (pen), Sweeney 1.
Play-offs (4): Boyd 2, Daly 1, Williams 1.

Provett J 21	Ross J 21 + 3	Robertson H 17 + 3	Nelson M 42 + 1	Westwood C 36 + 1	Tinkler M 30 + 3	Williams E 31 + 7	Sweeney A 44	Porter J 36 + 3	Boyd A 43 + 2	Humphreys R 46	Betsy K 3 + 3	Istead S — + 17	Brackstone J 8 + 1	Strachan G 21 + 8	Konstantopoulos D 25	Robson M 22 + 5	Appleby A — + 15	Craddock D 9 + 1	Woods M 3 + 3	Pouton A 5	Foley D 1 + 1	Barron M 10 + 3	Turnbull S — + 2	Wilkinson J 1 + 2	Clark B 21 + 4	Maidens M — + 1	Gobern L 1	Daly J 4 + 8	Butler T 5 + 4	Howey S — + 1	Match No.
1	2	3	4	5	6	7^1	8	9^2	10	11	12	13																			1
1	2^1	3	4	5	6	7	8	9	10	11	12																				2
1	2	3	4	5	6	7	8		10	11	9																				3
1	2^3	3	4	5	6	7	8	12	10	11^2	9^1	13	14																		4
1	2	3	4	5	6^2	7	8	9^1	10	11	12			13																	5
	2		4	5		7	8		10	11	9			6	1	3															6
1	2		4	5		7^1	8	9^2	10	11		12		6		3	13														7
1			4^1	5	12		8		10	11		13				3	14	2	6^3	7	9^2										8
1			4		5	12	8	9^1	10	11		13		6		3^2		2	14	7^3											9
1			4	5	6	9	8■	12	10	11				13		3			2^1	7^2											10
1			4	12	5	7		9^2	10	11		13		6^3		3			14	8		2^1									11
1			4		5	7		9	10	11				6		3				8		2									12
1			4		5	7^1	8	9	10	11				6^2		3			12			2	13								13
1			4	5	6	12	8	9^1	10	11						3			7			2									14
1			4	5	6	12	8	9^3	10	11^2				7^1		3						2		14	13						15
	12			5	6	7	8	9^3		11					1	3						2^1	13	10^2	4	14					16
	12		13	5	6	7	8	14	10^2	11					1	3						2^1			4		9^3				17
	2^1		4	5	6	7^3	8	9^2	10	11					1	3					13	12		14							18
			4	5	6		8	9	10	11			3^1	7	1		12					2									19
	2	12		5	6		8	9	10	11			3^1	7^2	1		13								4						20
	2	3		5	6	12	8	9	10^2	11		13		7^3	1		14								4^1						21
	2	3	4	5	6	7^2	8	9^3	10^1	11		13		12	1		14														22
	2	3	4	5	6	7^2	8	9^1	10^3	11		12		13	1		14														23
	2	3	4	5	6	7	8	9^3	10^1	11		12^2		13	1		14														24
	2	3	4	5	6	7	8	9^1	10	11		13			1		12^2														25
	2	3	4	5	6^2	7^1	8	9	10^3	11				12	1		14								13						26
	2		4	5	6	7^3	8	9^1	10^2	11		12		13	1		14								3						27
	2	3	4	5	6		8^1	9^2	10	11		12			1		13								7						28
	2	3	4	5	6	12	8	9^1	10	11					1										7						29
	12		4	5^2	6	13	8	9	10	11				3^1	1	14									2			7^3			30
	2		4			7	8	9^1	10	11			3	6	1		12								5						31
	2		4			7	8	9	10	11			3	6^1	1	12									5						32
	2^1		4			7	8	9	10	11			3	6^2	1							12			5			13			33
			4			7	8	9	10	11			3	6	1	12						2^2			5^1			13			34
1			4			7	8	9	10	11			3^1	6^2		12		14				2^3			5			13			35
1			4			7	8	9	10	11		12	3^2	6^1		13		2							5						36
1		3^2	4	5	6^1	7	8	9^3	12	11		13				10		2							14						37
1		3^3	4	5	6^2	7^1	8	9	12	11						10		2							13				14		38
1		3	4	5			8^2	9	10	11						7		2^1							6			12	13		39
1		12	4	5			8	9^1	10	11						3		2							7			13	6^2		40
1			4	5			8	9	10	11		12				3		2^1							6			13	7^2		41
		3	4^3	5			8		10	11		12		6	1		13								2			9^2	7^1	14	42
			4	5	12	13	8	9^2	10	11				6	1	3									2^1			14	7^3		43
			4	5		9	8		10	11				6^2	1	3	13								2			12	7^1		44
		13	4	5	6^1	7	8		10	11				12	1	3		2^3										9^2	14		45
			4	5	12	7	8		10	11				6^1	1	3^3						13			2^2			9	14		46

FA Cup

First Round	Lincoln C	(h)	3-0
Second Round	Aldershot T	(h)	5-1
Third Round	Boston U	(h)	0-0
		(a)	1-0
Fourth Round	Brentford	(a)	0-0
		(h)	0-1

Carling Cup

First Round	Macclesfield T	(h)	2-1
Second Round	Crystal Palace	(a)	1-2

LDV Vans Trophy

First Round	Hull C	(h)	3-3
Second Round	Carlisle U	(a)	1-0
Quarter-Final	Oldham Ath	(a)	1-3

Play-offs

Semi-Final	Tranmere R	(h)	2-0
		(a)	0-2
Final	Sheffield W		2-4
(at Millennium Stadium)			

HUDDERSFIELD TOWN FL Championship 1

FOUNDATION

A meeting, attended largely by members of the Huddersfield & District FA, was held at the Imperial Hotel in 1906 to discuss the feasibility of establishing a football club in this rugby stronghold. However, it was not until a man with both the enthusiasm and the money to back the scheme came on the scene, that real progress was made. This benefactor was Mr Hilton Crowther and it was at a meeting at the Albert Hotel in 1908, that the club formally came into existence with a capital of £2,000 and joined the North-Eastern League.

The Galpharm Stadium, Stadium Way, Leeds Road, Huddersfield HD1 6PX.

Telephone: (01484) 484 100.

Fax: (01484) 484 101.

Ticket Office: (01484) 484 100.

Website: www.htafc.com

Email: info@htafc.com

Ground Capacity: 24,500.

Record Attendance: 67,037 v Arsenal, FA Cup 6th rd, 27 February 1932 (at Leeds Road); 23,678 v Liverpool, FA Cup 3rd rd, 12 December 1999 (at Alfred McAlpine Stadium).

Pitch Measurements: 115yd × 76yd.

Chairman: Ken Davy.

Chief Executive: Andrew Watson.

Secretary: Ann Hough.

Manager: Peter Jackson.

Assistant Manager: Terry Yorath.

Physio: Lee Martin.

Colours: Blue and white striped shirts, white shorts, white stockings.

Change Colours: White shirt, blue shorts, blue stockings.

Year Formed: 1908. ***Turned Professional:*** 1908. ***Ltd Co.:*** 1908.

Club Nickname: 'The Terriers'.

Previous Grounds: 1908, Leeds Road; 1994, The Alfred McAlpine Stadium.

First Football League Game: 3 September 1910, Division 2, v Bradford PA (a) W 1–0 – Mutch; Taylor, Morris; Beaton, Hall, Bartlett; Blackburn, Wood, Hamilton (1), McCubbin, Jee.

Record League Victory: 10–1 v Blackpool, Division 1, 13 December 1930 – Turner; Goodall, Spencer; Redfern, Wilson, Campbell; Bob Kelly (1), McLean (4), Robson (3), Davies (1), Smailes (1).

Record Cup Victory: 7–0 v Lincoln U, FA Cup 1st rd, 16 November 1991 – Clarke; Trevitt, Charlton, Donovan (2), Mitchell, Doherty, O'Regan (1), Stapleton (1) (Wright), Roberts (2), Onuora (1), Barnett

HONOURS

Football League: Division 1 – Champions 1923–24, 1924–25, 1925–26; Runners-up 1926–27, 1927–28, 1933–34; Division 2 – Champions 1969–70; Runners-up 1919–20, 1952–53; Promoted from Division 2 1994–95 (play-offs); Promoted from Division 3 2003–04 (play-offs); Division 4 – Champions 1979–80.

FA Cup: Winners 1922; Runners-up 1920, 1928, 1930, 1938.

Football League Cup: Semi-final 1968.

Autoglass Trophy: Runners-up 1994.

SKY SPORTS FACT FILE

On 13 January 1960 Eddie Boot as caretaker-manager of Huddersfield Town took his team to West Ham United and following a sparkling 5–1 victory on.snow and ice inspired by Denis Law he was given the job permanently shortly afterwards.

(Ireland).*N.B.* 11-0 v Heckmondwike (a), FA Cup pr rd, 18 September 1909 – Doggart; Roberts, Ewing; Hooton, Stevenson, Randall; Kenworthy (2), McCreadie (1), Foster (4), Stacey (4), Jee.

Record Defeat: 1–10 v Manchester C, Division 2, 7 November 1987.

Most League Points (2 for a win): 66, Division 4, 1979–80.

Most League Points (3 for a win): 82, Division 3, 1982–83.

Most League Goals: 101, Division 4, 1979–80.

Highest League Scorer in Season: Sam Taylor, 35, Division 2, 1919–20; George Brown, 35, Division 1, 1925–26.

Most League Goals in Total Aggregate: George Brown, 142, 1921–29; Jimmy Glazzard, 142, 1946–56.

Most League Goals in One Match: 5, Dave Mangnall v Derby Co, Division 1, 21 November 1931; 5, Alf Lythgoe v Blackburn R, Division 1, 13 April 1935.

Most Capped Player: Jimmy Nicholson, 31 (41), Northern Ireland.

Most League Appearances: Billy Smith, 520, 1914–34.

Youngest League Player: Denis Law, 16 years 303 days v Notts Co, 24 December 1956.

Record Transfer Fee Received: £2,750,000 from Ipswich T for Marcus Stewart, February 2000.

Record Transfer Fee Paid: £1,200,000 to Bristol R for Marcus Stewart, July 1996.

Football League Record: 1910 Elected to Division 2; 1920–52 Division 1; 1952–53 Division 2; 1953–56 Division 1; 1956–70 Division 2; 1970–72 Division 1; 1972–73 Division 2; 1973–75 Division 3; 1975–80 Division 4; 1980–83 Division 3; 1983–88 Division 2; 1988–92 Division 3; 1992–95 Division 2; 1995–2001 Division 1; 2001–03 Division 2; 2003–04 Division 3; 2004– FL1.

MANAGERS

Fred Walker 1908–10
Richard Pudan 1910–12
Arthur Fairclough 1912–19
Ambrose Langley 1919–21
Herbert Chapman 1921–25
Cecil Potter 1925–26
Jack Chaplin 1926–29
Clem Stephenson 1929–42
David Steele 1943–47
George Stephenson 1947–52
Andy Beattie 1952–56
Bill Shankly 1956–59
Eddie Boot 1960–64
Tom Johnston 1964–68
Ian Greaves 1968–74
Bobby Collins 1974
Tom Johnston 1975–78
(had been General Manager since 1975)
Mike Buxton 1978–86
Steve Smith 1986–87
Malcolm Macdonald 1987–88
Eoin Hand 1988–92
Ian Ross 1992–93
Neil Warnock 1993–95
Brian Horton 1995–97
Peter Jackson 1997–99
Steve Bruce 1999–2000
Lou Macari 2000–02
Mick Wadsworth 2002–03
Peter Jackson June 2003–

LATEST SEQUENCES

Longest Sequence of League Wins: 11, 5.4.1920 – 4.9.1920.

Longest Sequence of League Defeats: 7, 8.10.1955 – 19.11.1955.

Longest Sequence of League Draws: 6, 3.3.1987 – 3.4.1987.

Longest Sequence of Unbeaten League Matches: 27, 24.1.1925 – 17.10.1925.

Longest Sequence Without a League Win: 22, 4.12.1971 – 29.4.1972.

Successive Scoring Runs: 21 from 5.12.1931.

Successive Non-scoring Runs: 7 from 22.1.1972.

TEN YEAR LEAGUE RECORD

		P	W	D	L	F	A	Pts	Pos
1995-96	Div 1	46	17	12	17	61	58	63	8
1996-97	Div 1	46	13	15	18	48	61	54	20
1997-98	Div 1	46	14	11	21	50	72	53	16
1998-99	Div 1	46	15	16	15	62	71	61	10
1999-2000	Div 1	46	21	11	14	62	49	74	8
2000-01	Div 1	46	11	15	20	48	57	48	22
2001-02	Div 2	46	21	15	10	65	47	78	6
2002-03	Div 2	46	11	12	23	39	61	45	22
2003-04	Div 3	46	23	12	11	68	52	81	4
2004-05	FL 1	46	20	10	16	74	65	70	9

DID YOU KNOW ?

In 1919–20 Huddersfield Town were disappointed to finish second in the Second Division but had the satisfaction of promotion and creating three club records: most wins overall (28), at home (16) and away (12). This after losing three of the first seven.

HUDDERSFIELD TOWN 2004–05 LEAGUE RECORD

Match No.	Date	Venue	Opponents	Result	H/T Score	Lg. Pos.	Goalscorers	Attendance
1	Aug 7	A	Stockport Co	W 3-2	1-0	—	Carss [45], Booth [87], Abbott [90]	7473
2	10	H	Chesterfield	D 0-0	0-0	—		11,942
3	16	H	Hartlepool U	L 0-2	0-0	—		9968
4	21	A	Sheffield W	L 0-1	0-1	18		26,264
5	28	H	Peterborough U	W 2-1	1-1	15	McAliskey [16], Worthington [48]	9531
6	30	A	Doncaster R	L 1-2	0-1	17	Worthington [83]	7068
7	Sept 5	H	Hull C	W 4-0	2-0	11	Abbott [7], Edwards [19], Brandon [74], Booth [87]	13,452
8	11	A	Port Vale	W 3-0	0-0	5	Abbott 3 [62, 67, 75]	6298
9	18	H	Barnsley	L 0-2	0-2	10		14,794
10	25	A	Bristol C	D 3-3	2-1	10	Schofield [28], Abbott [35], Brandon [60]	10,783
11	Oct 2	H	Walsall	W 3-1	2-0	7	Abbott 2 [29, 68], Mendes [30]	11,324
12	9	A	Torquay U	L 1-2	1-0	9	Mendes [39]	3033
13	16	A	Luton T	W 2-1	2-0	7	Mendes 2 [14, 36]	8192
14	19	H	Tranmere R	L 1-3	1-1	—	Abbott [33]	10,324
15	23	H	Milton Keynes D	W 3-1	3-0	7	Abbott 2 (1 pen) [33, 45 (p)], Mendes [44]	10,709
16	30	A	Blackpool	D 1-1	1-0	8	Booth [15]	7676
17	Nov 7	H	Brentford	D 1-1	0-0	9	Abbott [71]	10,810
18	20	A	Colchester U	D 0-0	0-0	11		3972
19	27	H	Wrexham	L 1-2	1-1	14	Schofield [41]	11,127
20	Dec 8	A	Swindon T	W 2-1	2-0	—	Abbott [19], Brandon [34]	4828
21	11	A	Oldham Ath	L 1-2	1-0	11	Abbott [7]	8389
22	18	H	Bradford C	L 0-1	0-1	13		17,281
23	26	H	Port Vale	W 2-1	2-1	12	Schofield [4], Abbott [8]	12,243
24	28	A	Bournemouth	D 2-2	1-1	12	McAliskey [38], Mirfin [60]	8448
25	Jan 1	A	Hull C	L 1-2	1-1	13	Brandon [40]	22,291
26	3	H	Bristol C	D 2-2	1-0	13	Orr (og) [18], Abbott [58]	11,151
27	8	H	Torquay U	D 1-1	1-0	13	Sodje E [24]	9194
28	15	A	Barnsley	L 2-4	0-3	14	Abbott (pen) [55], Booth [70]	11,725
29	22	H	Bournemouth	W 3-2	3-1	13	Abbott (pen) [8], Beckett 2 [35, 45]	9754
30	29	A	Walsall	L 3-4	3-2	14	Booth [7], Beckett 2 [11, 33]	5727
31	Feb 5	H	Luton T	D 1-1	0-1	14	Beckett [90]	12,611
32	12	A	Milton Keynes D	L 1-2	1-1	15	Booth [30]	4793
33	19	H	Blackpool	W 1-0	1-0	14	Beckett [2]	10,614
34	22	A	Tranmere R	L 0-3	0-2	—		7613
35	26	H	Oldham Ath	W 2-1	2-0	13	Abbott 2 [4, 29]	11,161
36	Mar 5	A	Bradford C	L 0-2	0-1	14		15,417
37	12	A	Chesterfield	L 1-2	0-0	15	Mirfin [79]	4827
38	19	H	Stockport Co	W 5-3	1-1	14	Booth [4], Abbott [51], Mirfin [82], Ahmed [83], Dolan (og) [90]	11,180
39	25	A	Hartlepool U	W 1-0	1-0	—	Booth [42]	6205
40	29	H	Sheffield W	W 1-0	1-0	—	Worthington [7]	17,292
41	Apr 2	A	Peterborough U	W 2-1	1-1	12	Brandon [21], Schofield [84]	3976
42	9	H	Doncaster R	W 3-1	2-1	8	Abbott [1], Booth [43], Brandon [56]	12,972
43	16	H	Colchester U	D 2-2	1-1	9	Abbott [20], Schofield [62]	10,831
44	23	A	Brentford	W 1-0	1-0	10	Abbott [26]	7703
45	30	H	Swindon T	W 4-0	0-0	9	Abbott 2 [62, 80], Booth [79], Edwards [85]	13,559
46	May 7	A	Wrexham	W 1-0	1-0	9	Mirfin [43]	7151

Final League Position: 9

GOALSCORERS

League (74): Abbott 26 (3 pens), Booth 10, Beckett 6, Brandon 6, Mendes 5, Schofield 5, Mirfin 4, Worthington 3, Edwards 2, McAliskey 2, Ahmed 1, Carss 1, Sodje E 1, own goals 2.
Carling Cup (0).
FA Cup (1): Abbott 1.
LDV Vans Trophy (6): Ahmed 1, Fowler 1, McAliskey 1, Mendes 1 (pen), Mirfin 1, Schofield 1.

Gray I 12	Holdsworth A 38 + 2	Edwards R 21 + 3	Mirfin D 38 + 3	Yates S 15 + 2	Sodje E 24 + 4	Worthington J 39	Schofield D 21 + 12	Booth A 25 + 4	Mendes J 13 + 12	Carss T 23 + 4	Senior P 5 + 1	Abbott P 36 + 8	Brandon C 42 + 2	Clarke N 37	McAliskey J 7 + 11	Brown N 7 + 10	Fowler A 8 + 12	Sodje A 1 + 6	Lloyd A 10 + 1	Rachubka P 29	Beckett L 7	Ahmed A 16 + 2	McCombe J 4 + 1	Clarke T 12	Collins M 7 + 1	Facey D 4	Adams D 5	*Match No.*
1[0]	2	3	4	5	6[1]	7	8[2]	9	10	11	15	12	13															1
	2	3	4	5	6	7	8[2]	9	10[1]	11	1	12	13															2
	2	3	4		6	7	12	9	10[2]	11	1	13	8	5[1]														3
1	2	3	4		6	7	12	9	10[2]	11		13	8[1]	5														4
1	2	3	4		6	7				11[2]		10	8	5	9[1]	12	13											5
1	2	3	4			11	12	9[2]				10	7	5[1]	13	6	8											6
1	2[2]	3	4	5	6	7	8	9[3]	12			10[1]	11		14	13												7
1	2	3	4	5	6[1]	7	8	9[2]				10	11			12		13										8
1	2	3	4	5[1]	6■	7	8[2]	9	12			10	11					13										9
1	2[1]		4	5		7	8	9[2]				10	11	6		12		13	3									10
1	2		4	5					9[2]	12		10	11	6	13	8	7[1]		3									11
1	2		4[2]	5	13	7			9	12		10[3]	11	6	14	8[1]			3									12
1	2		12	5	6	7		14	9[2]	11		10[3]	8[1]	4			13		3									13
1	2			5[1]	6	7		12	9	11		10	8	4					3									14
	2		4[1]	12	6	7	13	14	9[3]	11	1	10	8[2]	5					3									15
	2		4		6	7		9		11	1	10[1]	8	5				12	3									16
	2		4	5[2]		7	3		9	11		10	8[1]	6	13		12			1								17
	2	12	4	5		7	10			11		9	8	6					3[1]	1								18
	2	12	4	5[3]		7	3[1]	9[2]	13	11		10	8	6		14				1								19
	2	3	4		6	7				11		9	8	5			10■			1								20
	2	10	4[1]		6	7	12		13	11		9	8	5					3[2]	1								21
	2	3	4[1]		6	7	12		9[2]	11		10	8	5				13		1								22
	2	3[1]	12		6	7	4			11		10	8	5	9[2]	13				1								23
	2		4		6	7	3			11		10	8	5	9					1								24
	2				6	7[1]	4[2]		13	11		10	8	5	9		12		3	1								25
	2		4[2]		6	7	3		12	11		10	8	5	9[1]	13				1								26
	2				6	7	4			11			8	5	9	3	12	10[1]		1								27
	2[2]			12	6	7	3[3]	13		11		9	8	5[1]		4	14			1	10							28
		3		5	6	7	12	9		11		10[1]				2	4[2]			1	8	13						29
		3	12	5[2]	6	7	13	9				10	8			2[1]	4[3]			1	11	14						30
		3[1]	4		6	7	11	9	12			13	8[2]	5			14			1	10	2[3]						31
		3[3]	4[2]			7	11	9[1]				12	8	5			13			1	10	2	14	6				32
			4			7							8■	5	9[2]			12	13	1	10[1]	2	3	6	11			33
			4[1]			7	8[2]					9		5	13	12				1	10	2	11	6	3			34
	2[1]		4		12	7				13		9[3]	8	5	14					1		3		6[2]	11	10		35
	2		4		12	7			13	14		9	8	5[1]						1		3[3]		6	11[2]	10		36
	2[1]		4		13■			9		11		12	8	5						1		7		6■	3[2]	10		37
	2	3	4					9	12			10[2]	8	5	13		14			1		11			6[3]	7[1]		38
	2	3	4			7		9	12			10[2]	8	5■		13	14			1		11[1]		6[3]				39
	2	3	4			7	12	9	11			10[1]	8							1		5		6				40
	2[2]	3	4			7	13	9	10[1]		1	12	8	5			14					11[3]		6				41
	12		4			7	11	9				10[2]	8	5	13					1		2		6			3[1]	42
	12		4				11	9	13			10	8	5[2]			7[3]			1		2		6[1]	14		3	43
	2		4				12	9				10	8			13	11			1		7[1]	5	6			3[2]	44
	2	12	4				11[2]	9[3]	13			10	8	5	14		6			1		7					3[1]	45
	2		4				12	9[2]				10	8	5	13		14			1		3[3]	7		6		11[1]	46

FA Cup
First Round — Stockport Co — (a) — 1-3

Carling Cup
First Round — Leeds U — (a) — 0-1

LDV Vans Trophy
First Round — Morecambe — (h) — 3-0
Second Round — Blackpool — (a) — 3-6

HULL CITY FL Championship

FOUNDATION

The enthusiasts who formed Hull City in 1904 were brave men indeed. More than that they were audacious for they immediately put the club on the map in this Rugby League fortress by obtaining a three-year agreement with the Hull Rugby League club to rent their ground! They had obtained quite a number of conversions to the dribbling code, before the Rugby League forbade the use of any of their club grounds by Association Football clubs. By that time, Hull City were well away having entered the FA Cup in their initial season and the Football League, Second Division after only a year.

Koveston Communications Stadium, The Circle, Walton Street, Anlaby Road, Hull HU3 6HU.

Telephone: 0870 837 0003.

Fax: (01482) 304 882.

Ticket Office: 0870 837 0004.

Website: www.hullcityafc.net

Email: info@hulltigers.com

Ground Capacity: 25,404.

Record Attendance: KC Stadium: 23,495 v Huddersfield T, Division 3, 24 April 2004. Boothferry Park: 55,019 v Manchester U, FA Cup 6th rd, 26 February 1949.

Pitch Measurements: 105m × 68m.

Chairman: Adam Pearson.

Football Secretary: Phil Hough.

Manager: Peter Taylor.

Assistant Manager: Colin Murphy.

Physio: Simon Maltby.

Colours: Black and amber striped shirts, black shorts, amber stockings.

Change Colours: Black shirts with amber trim, white shorts, black stockings.

Year Formed: 1904. ***Turned Professional:*** 1905.

Ltd Co.: 1905.

Club Nickname: 'The Tigers'.

Previous Grounds: 1904, Boulevard Ground (Hull RFC); 1905, Anlaby Road (Hull CC); 1944, Boulevard Ground; 1946, Boothferry Park; 2002, Kingston Communications Stadium.

First Football League Game: 2 September 1905, Division 2, v Barnsley (h) W 4–1 – Spendiff; Langley, Jones; Martin, Robinson, Gordon (2); Rushton, Spence (1), Wilson (1), Howe, Raisbeck.

Record League Victory: 11–1 v Carlisle U, Division 3 (N), 14 January 1939 – Ellis; Woodhead, Dowen; Robinson (1), Blyth, Hardy; Hubbard (2), Richardson (2), Dickinson (2), Davies (2), Cunliffe (2).

HONOURS

Football League: Championship 1 runners-up 2004–05; Division 2 best season: 3rd, 1909–10; Division 3 (N) – Champions 1932–33, 1948–49; Division 3 – Champions 1965–66; Runners-up 1958–59, 2003–04; Division 4 – Runners-up 1982–83.

FA Cup: Semi-final 1930.

Football League Cup: best season: 4th, 1974, 1976, 1978.

Associate Members' Cup: Runners-up 1984.

SKY SPORTS FACT FILE

The Browell brothers from Walbottle – Andy, George and Tommy – played for Hull City before the first World War, though only in two matches early in the 1910–11 season did all three of them appear together in the first team.

Record Cup Victory: 8–2 v Stalybridge Celtic (a), FA Cup 1st rd, 26 November 1932 – Maddison; Goldsmith, Woodhead; Gardner, Hill (1), Denby; Forward (1), Duncan, McNaughton (1), Wainscoat (4), Sargeant (1).

Record Defeat: 0–8 v Wolverhampton W, Division 2, 4 November 1911.

Most League Points (2 for a win): 69, Division 3, 1965–66.

Most League Points (3 for a win): 90, Division 4, 1982–83.

Most League Goals: 109, Division 3, 1965–66.

Highest League Scorer in Season: Bill McNaughton, 39, Division 3 (N), 1932–33.

Most League Goals in Total Aggregate: Chris Chilton, 195, 1960–71.

Most League Goals in One Match: 5, Ken McDonald v Bristol C, Division 2, 17 November 1928; 5, Simon 'Slim' Raleigh v Halifax T, Division 3N, 26 December 1930.

Most Capped Player: Theo Whitmore, Jamaica.

Most League Appearances: Andy Davidson, 520, 1952–67.

Youngest League Player: Matthew Edeson, 16 years 63 days v Fulham, 10 October 1992.

Record Transfer Fee Received: £750,000 from Middlesbrough for Andy Payton, November 1991.

Record Transfer Fee Paid: £200,000 to Leeds U for Peter Swan, March 1989.

Football League Record: 1905 Elected to Division 2; 1930–33 Division 3 (N); 1933–36 Division 2; 1936–49 Division 3 (N); 1949–56 Division 2; 1956–58 Division 3 (N); 1958–59 Division 3; 1959–60 Division 2; 1960–66 Division 3; 1966–78 Division 2; 1978–81 Division 3; 1981–83 Division 4; 1983–85 Division 3; 1985–91 Division 2; 1991–92 Division 3; 1992–96 Division 2; 1996–2004 Division 3; 2004–05 FL1; 2005– FLC.

MANAGERS

James Ramster 1904–05
(Secretary-Manager)
Ambrose Langley 1905–13
Harry Chapman 1913–14
Fred Stringer 1914–16
David Menzies 1916–21
Percy Lewis 1921–23
Bill McCracken 1923–31
Haydn Green 1931–34
John Hill 1934–36
David Menzies 1936
Ernest Blackburn 1936–46
Major Frank Buckley 1946–48
Raich Carter 1948–51
Bob Jackson 1952–55
Bob Brocklebank 1955–61
Cliff Britton 1961–70
(continued as General Manager to 1971)
Terry Neill 1970–74
John Kaye 1974–77
Bobby Collins 1977–78
Ken Houghton 1978–79
Mike Smith 1979–82
Bobby Brown 1982
Colin Appleton 1982–84
Brian Horton 1984–88
Eddie Gray 1988–89
Colin Appleton 1989
Stan Ternent 1989–91
Terry Dolan 1991–97
Mark Hateley 1997–98
Warren Joyce 1998–2000
Brian Little 2000–02
Jan Molby 2002
Peter Taylor October 2002–

LATEST SEQUENCES

Longest Sequence of League Wins: 10, 23.2.1966 – 20.4.1966.

Longest Sequence of League Defeats: 8, 7.4.1934 – 8.9.1934.

Longest Sequence of League Draws: 5, 30.3.1929 – 15.4.1929.

Longest Sequence of Unbeaten League Matches: 19, 13.3.2001 – 22.9.2001.

Longest Sequence Without a League Win: 27, 27.3.1989 – 4.11.1989.

Successive Scoring Runs: 26 from 10.4.1990.

Successive Non-scoring Runs: 6 from 13.11.1920.

TEN YEAR LEAGUE RECORD

		P	W	D	L	F	A	Pts	Pos
1995-96	Div 2	46	5	16	25	36	78	31	24
1996-97	Div 3	46	13	18	15	44	50	57	17
1997-98	Div 3	46	11	8	27	56	83	41	22
1998-99	Div 3	46	14	11	21	44	62	53	21
1999-2000	Div 3	46	15	14	17	43	43	59	14
2000-01	Div 3	46	19	17	10	47	39	74	6
2001-02	Div 3	46	16	13	17	57	51	61	11
2002-03	Div 3	46	14	17	15	58	53	59	13
2003-04	Div 3	46	25	13	8	82	44	88	2
2004-05	FL 1	46	26	8	12	80	53	86	2

DID YOU KNOW 

Automatic promotion for Hull City in 2004–05 was fashioned by a run of eight successive wins from the end of November and reinforced by an unbeaten sequence of eight from mid-February. And their 3–0 win over Luton was the champions' heaviest loss.

HULL CITY 2004–05 LEAGUE RECORD

Match No.	*Date*	*Venue*	*Opponents*	*Result*	*H/T Score*	*Lg. Pos.*	*Goalscorers*	*Attendance*
1	Aug 7	H	Bournemouth	W 1-0	1-0	—	Green (pen) [3]	17,569
2	10	A	Torquay U	W 3-0	2-0	—	Green [9], Elliott 2 [19, 57]	3973
3	14	A	Port Vale	L 2-3	1-1	3	Barmby [14], Elliott [90]	6736
4	21	H	Oldham Ath	W 2-0	2-0	2	Allsopp [27], Green [45]	16,916
5	28	A	Barnsley	W 2-1	0-1	3	Elliott [58], Keane [88]	13,175
6	31	H	Bradford C	L 0-1	0-0	—		16,865
7	Sept 5	A	Huddersfield T	L 0-4	0-2	6		13,452
8	11	H	Blackpool	W 2-1	1-1	3	Green [14], Elliott [57]	15,568
9	18	A	Peterborough U	W 3-2	1-1	2	Elliott 2 [22, 65], Cort [53]	5745
10	25	H	Stockport Co	D 0-0	0-0	3		16,182
11	Oct 2	A	Hartlepool U	L 0-2	0-1	5		5768
12	10	H	Chesterfield	W 1-0	0-0	3	Green [64]	15,500
13	16	A	Bristol C	L 1-3	0-1	4	Facey [54]	12,011
14	20	H	Milton Keynes D	W 3-2	1-1	—	Green 2 [1, 90], Keane [88]	14,317
15	23	H	Luton T	W 3-0	3-0	3	Elliott 2 [11, 33], Facey [22]	18,575
16	30	A	Wrexham	D 2-2	1-2	3	Cort [36], Facey [55]	5601
17	Nov 6	H	Walsall	W 3-1	3-0	3	Barmby [1], Elliott [34], Lewis [39]	16,010
18	20	A	Swindon T	L 2-4	1-1	3	Walters [36], Elliott [90]	6348
19	27	H	Brentford	W 2-0	1-0	3	Elliott 2 [32, 82]	15,710
20	Dec 8	A	Sheffield W	W 4-2	3-1	—	Keane (pen) [14], Barmby 2 [22, 43], Allsopp [83]	28,701
21	11	A	Colchester U	W 2-1	1-0	2	France [11], Elliott [50]	4046
22	18	H	Tranmere R	W 6-1	1-0	2	Ashbee [34], Elliott 3 (1 pen) [54, 68, 75 (p)], Barmby [56], Allsopp [88]	20,064
23	26	A	Blackpool	W 2-0	0-0	2	Elliott 2 [60, 85]	8774
24	29	H	Doncaster R	W 2-1	1-1	—	Allsopp [21], Elliott [86]	24,117
25	Jan 1	H	Huddersfield T	W 2-1	1-1	2	Elliott [42], Wilbraham [49]	22,291
26	3	A	Stockport Co	W 3-1	1-1	1	Wilbraham [10], Price [61], Allsopp [65]	6670
27	15	H	Peterborough U	D 2-2	0-1	2	Barmby [46], Green [60]	16,149
28	22	A	Doncaster R	L 0-1	0-0	2		9633
29	Feb 1	A	Chesterfield	D 1-1	0-0	—	Lewis [74]	5517
30	5	H	Bristol C	D 1-1	0-0	2	Barmby [59]	17,637
31	12	A	Luton T	L 0-1	0-0	2		9500
32	19	H	Wrexham	W 2-1	1-0	2	Allsopp 2 [35, 58]	15,995
33	22	A	Milton Keynes D	D 1-1	0-0	—	Facey [86]	4407
34	26	H	Colchester U	W 2-0	2-0	2	Cort [16], Barmby [33]	16,484
35	Mar 5	A	Tranmere R	W 3-1	1-1	2	Ellison [43], Price [63], Fagan [69]	12,684
36	8	H	Hartlepool U	W 1-0	1-0	—	Elliott [14]	17,112
37	12	H	Torquay U	W 2-0	0-0	2	Fagan (pen) [61], Elliott (pen) [73]	17,147
38	19	A	Bournemouth	W 4-0	2-0	2	France [26], Elliott 2 [31, 58], Delaney [64]	8895
39	26	H	Port Vale	D 2-2	1-1	1	Cort [33], Fagan (pen) [90]	17,678
40	28	A	Oldham Ath	L 0-1	0-0	2		8562
41	Apr 2	H	Barnsley	W 2-1	1-0	2	Cort [4], Fagan [69]	19,341
42	10	A	Bradford C	W 2-0	1-0	2	Elliott [4], Barmby [68]	13,631
43	16	H	Swindon T	D 0-0	0-0	2		23,125
44	23	A	Walsall	L 0-3	0-1	2		7958
45	30	H	Sheffield W	L 1-2	0-1	2	Elliott (pen) [60]	24,277
46	May 7	A	Brentford	L 1-2	1-1	2	Cort [1]	9604

Final League Position: 2

GOALSCORERS

League (80): Elliott 27 (3 pens), Barmby 9, Green 8 (1 pen), Allsopp 7, Cort 6, Facey 4, Fagan 4 (2 pens), Keane 3 (1 pen), France 2, Lewis 2, Price 2, Wilbraham 2, Ashbee 1, Delaney 1, Ellison 1, Walters 1.
Carling Cup (2): France 1, Keane 1.
FA Cup (7): Facey 2, Elliott 1, France 1, Green 1, Keane 1, Walters 1.
LDV Vans Trophy (3): Elliott 1, Green 1, Price 1.

Myhill B 45	Hinds R 6	Dawson A 34	Ashbee I 40	Joseph M 25 + 4	Delaney D 43	Green S 26 + 3	Barmby N 38 + 1	Allsopp D 14 + 14	Elliott S 35 + 1	Lewis J 31 + 8	Cort L 43 + 1	Wilbraham A 10 + 9	Walters J 4 + 17	France R 22 + 9	Facey D 12 + 9	Duke M 1 + 1	Keane M 12 + 8	Price J 6 + 21	Thelwell A 2 + 1	Wiseman S 2 + 1	Edge R 13 + 1	Angus S 1 + 1	Ellison K 11 + 5	Stockdale R 12 + 2	Hessenthaler A 6 + 4	Fagan C 11 + 1	Burgess B — + 2	Fry R 1	*Match No.*
1	2	3	4	5^{1}	6	7	8^{2}	9^{3}	10	11	12	13	14																1
1	2	3	4		6	7^{3}	8^{2}	9^{1}	10	11	5	13■	12	14															2
1	2^{3}	3	4		6	7^{2}	8	9^{1}	10	11	5		12	13	14														3
1^{6}		3	4	2	6	7	8	9^{1}	10^{2}	11	5		12		13	15													4
1		3	4	2^{3}	6	7^{2}	8^{1}	12	10	11	5	9		13			14												5
1		3	4	2	6	7^{3}	8^{1}	12	10	11	5	9^{2}	13	14															6
1	2^{2}	3	4	6			8	9		11	5	10^{1}	12	7				13											7
1		3	4	2	6	7	8^{1}	9^{2}	10		5		12	11				13											8
1		3	4	2^{2}				9^{1}	10	11	5	8^{3}	14	7			6	12	13										9
1		3	4			12		9^{3}	10	11	5	8^{1}	13	7			6	14	2^{2}										10
		3	4		6	7		9^{2}	10	5		8^{3}		12	14	1	11	13	2^{1}										11
1		3	4■	12	6	7				11	5		10^{2}	2	13		8	9^{1}											12
1		3		2	6	7		12	10	11	5			8^{1}	9		4^{2}	13											13
1		3		5	6	4	8^{3}	12	10^{2}	11				7^{1}	9		13	14		2									14
1				2	6	4	8^{1}	12	10	11	5		13		9^{2}		14	7^{3}			3								15
1		3^{3}	4	2	6	7	8	12	10^{1}	11	5				9^{2}			13			14								16
1		3	4	2	6	7^{3}	8^{1}	9^{2}	10	11	5		12				13	14											17
1		3^{2}	4	2	6	7	8	12	10	11	5		13				9^{1}												18
1		3	4	2	6	7^{2}	8^{1}		10	11	5		9^{3}	13	14		12												19
1		3	4	2	6		8^{2}	12	10	14	5	13		7	9^{1}		11^{3}												20
1		3	4	2	6		8^{3}	12	10	13	5	14		7	9^{1}		11^{2}												21
1			4	2	6	7	8^{3}	12	10^{2}		5	14		11	9^{1}		13				3								22
1			4	2	6	7^{3}	8^{2}	12	10		5	13			9^{1}		11	14			3								23
1			4	2^{3}	6	7	8■	9^{2}	10		5		13				11^{1}	12			3	14							24
1		3	4		6	7^{1}			10^{2}	13	5	14	8^{3}		9		11	12				2							25
1		3	4	2	6			9^{2}		8	5	10			13		12	7^{3}		14	11^{1}								26
1		3	4	2	6	7^{3}	8^{2}	12		13	5			10	9^{1}		14						11						27
1	2	3	4■		6	12	8^{3}	13			5			7	9^{2}		10^{1}	14					11						28
1		3			6	12	10^{3}			8	5	9		13	14			7^{2}					11^{1}	2	4				29
1					6	7	10^{1}	12		8	5	9^{2}		4	13						3		11	2^{3}	14				30
1			4		6	7	10			11	5	9^{1}			12			13			3			2	8^{2}				31
1		3	4		6	7	8	9	10		5							11						2					32
1			4		6	7^{3}	12	9^{2}	13		5			14	10						3		11^{1}	2	8				33
1		3	4		6	7^{1}	10		9	12	5			8				13					11^{2}	2					34
1			4		6		10^{2}		9^{1}	8	5			12				7			3		11	2		13			35
1		3^{1}	4		6		10^{2}		11	12	5			7									13	2	8	9			36
1	2^{1}		4		6		10^{3}		11	8	5		13	7				12			3		14			9^{2}			37
1			4		6		10^{1}		11	8	5		13	7				12			3^{3}			2	14	9^{2}			38
1		3	4		6		10^{3}			12	5		14	7				13					11	2^{2}	8^{1}	9			39
1			4	2^{2}	6		10^{3}			8	5	12	14	7				13			3		11^{1}			9			40
1		3^{3}		2^{1}	6		10		11^{2}	8	5			7				12					13	14	4	9			41
1		3	4	2^{1}	6		10		11	8	5			7										12		9			42
1		3	4	12	6		10		11	8^{3}	5			7^{2}				13					14	2^{1}		9			43
1		3	4^{2}	2	6		10		11	8	5	12	7^{1}										14		13	9^{3}			44
1			4	12	6		7^{3}		10	8^{2}	5										3		11	2^{1}	13	9	14		45
1		3	4^{1}	12	6		8		10	13	5									2			11^{3}			9	14	7^{2}	46

FA Cup

First Round	Morecambe	(h)	3-2
Second Round	Macclesfield T	(h)	4-0
Third Round	Colchester U	(h)	0-2

Carling Cup

First Round	Wrexham	(h)	2-2

LDV Vans Trophy

First Round	Hartlepool U	(a)	3-3

IPSWICH TOWN — FL Championship

FOUNDATION

Considering that Ipswich Town only reached the Football League in 1938, many people outside of East Anglia may be surprised to learn that this club was formed at a meeting held in the Town Hall as far back as 1878 when Mr T. C. Cobbold, MP, was voted president. Originally it was the Ipswich Association FC to distinguish it from the older Ipswich Football Club which played rugby. These two amalgamated in 1888 and the handling game was dropped in 1893.

Portman Road, Ipswich, Suffolk IP1 2DA.

Telephone: (01473) 400 500.

Fax: (01473) 400 040.

Ticket Office: 0870 1110 555.

Website: www.itfc.co.uk

Email: enquiries@itfc.co.uk

Ground Capacity: 30,311.

Record Attendance: 38,010 v Leeds U, FA Cup 6th rd, 8 March 1975.

Pitch Measurements: 101m × 65m.

Chairman: David Sheepshanks.

Chief Executive: Derek Bowden.

Secretary: Sally Webb.

Manager: Joe Royle.

Assistant Manager: Willie Donachie.

Physio: David Williams.

Colours: Blue and white.

Change Colours: Orange and black.

Year Formed: 1878.

Turned Professional: 1936.

Ltd Co.: 1936.

Club Nicknames: 'Blues' or 'Town' or 'Tractor Boys'.

First Football League Game: 27 August 1938, Division 3 (S), v Southend U (h) W 4–2 – Burns; Dale, Parry; Perrett, Fillingham, McLuckie; Williams, Davies (1), Jones (2), Alsop (1), Little.

HONOURS

Football League: Division 1 – Champions 1961–62; Runners-up 1980–81, 1981–82; Promoted from Division 1 1999–2000 (play-offs); Division 2 – Champions 1960–61, 1967–68, 1991–92; Division 3 (S) – Champions 1953–54, 1956–57.

FA Cup: Winners 1978.

Football League Cup: Semi-final 1982, 1985.

Texaco Cup: Winners 1973.

European Competitions: *European Cup:* 1962–63. *European Cup-Winners' Cup:* 1978–79. *UEFA Cup:* 1973–74, 1974–75, 1975–76, 1977–78, 1979–80, 1980–81 (winners), 1981–82, 1982–83, 2001–02, 2002–03.

SKY SPORTS FACT FILE

Before full-back Mick Mills established a record number of appearances for Ipswich Town, the honour was held by Tom Parker who between 1946 and 1957 played 428 times at inside-forward and wing-half after his debut in the transitional 1945–46 term.

MANAGERS

Mick O'Brien 1936–37
Scott Duncan 1937–55
(continued as Secretary)
Alf Ramsey 1955–63
Jackie Milburn 1963–64
Bill McGarry 1964–68
Bobby Robson 1969–82
Bobby Ferguson 1982–87
Johnny Duncan 1987–90
John Lyall 1990–94
George Burley 1994–2002
Joe Royle October 2002–

Record League Victory: 7–0 v Portsmouth, Division 2, 7 November 1964 – Thorburn; Smith, McNeil; Baxter, Bolton, Thompson; Broadfoot (1), Hegan (2), Baker (1), Leadbetter, Brogan (3). 7–0 v Southampton, Division 1, 2 February 1974 – Sivell; Burley, Mills (1), Morris, Hunter, Beattie (1), Hamilton (2), Viljoen, Johnson, Whymark (2), Lambert (1) (Woods). 7–0 v WBA, Division 1, 6 November 1976 – Sivell; Burley, Mills, Talbot, Hunter, Beattie (1), Osborne, Wark (1), Mariner (1) (Bertschin), Whymark (4), Woods.

Record Cup Victory: 10–0 v Floriana, European Cup prel. rd, 25 September 1962 – Bailey; Malcolm, Compton; Baxter, Laurel, Elsworthy (1); Stephenson, Moran (2), Crawford (5), Phillips (2), Blackwood.

Record Defeat: 1–10 v Fulham, Division 1, 26 December 1963.

Most League Points (2 for a win): 64, Division 3 (S), 1953–54 and 1955–56.

Most League Points (3 for a win): 87, Division 1, 1999–2000.

Most League Goals: 106, Division 3 (S), 1955–56.

Highest League Scorer in Season: Ted Phillips, 41, Division 3 (S), 1956–57.

Most League Goals in Total Aggregate: Ray Crawford, 203, 1958–63 and 1966–69.

Most League Goals in One Match: 5, Alan Brazil v Southampton, Division 1, 16 February 1981.

Most Capped Player: Allan Hunter, 47 (53), Northern Ireland.

Most League Appearances: Mick Mills, 591, 1966–82.

Youngest League Player: Jason Dozzell, 16 years 56 days v Coventry C, 4 February 1984.

Record Transfer Fee Received: £6,000,000 from Newcastle U for Kieron Dyer, July 1999 and £6,000,000 from Arsenal for Richard Wright, July 2001.

Record Transfer Fee Paid: £4,750,000 to Sampdoria for Matteo Sereni, July 2001.

Football League Record: 1938 Elected to Division 3 (S); 1954–55 Division 2; 1955–57 Division 3 (S); 1957–61 Division 2; 1961–64 Division 1; 1964–68 Division 2; 1968–86 Division 1; 1986–92 Division 2; 1992–95 FA Premier League; 1995–2000 Division 1; 2000–02 FA Premier League; 2002–04 Division 1; 2004– FLC.

LATEST SEQUENCES

Longest Sequence of League Wins: 8, 23.9.1953 – 31.10.1953.

Longest Sequence of League Defeats: 10, 4.9.1954 – 16.10.1954.

Longest Sequence of League Draws: 7, 10.11.1990 – 21.12.1990.

Longest Sequence of Unbeaten League Matches: 23, 8.12.1979 – 26.4.1980.

Longest Sequence Without a League Win: 21, 28.8.1963 – 14.12.1963.

Successive Scoring Runs: 31 from 7.3.2004.

Successive Non-scoring Runs: 7 from 28.2.1995.

TEN YEAR LEAGUE RECORD

		P	*W*	*D*	*L*	*F*	*A*	*Pts*	*Pos*
1995-96	Div 1	46	19	12	15	79	69	69	7
1996-97	Div 1	46	20	14	12	68	50	74	4
1997-98	Div 1	46	23	14	9	77	43	83	5
1998-99	Div 1	46	26	8	12	69	32	86	3
1999-2000	Div 1	46	25	12	9	71	42	87	3
2000-01	PR Lge	38	20	6	12	57	42	66	5
2001-02	PR Lge	38	9	9	20	41	64	36	18
2002-03	Div 1	46	19	13	14	80	64	70	7
2003-04	Div 1	46	21	10	15	84	72	73	5
2004-05	FL C	46	24	13	9	85	56	85	3

DID YOU KNOW ?

As a prelude to returning to European cup competition, Ipswich Town enjoyed success in the 1972–73 Texaco Cup beating St Johnstone, Wolverhampton Wanderers, Newcastle United and neighbours Norwich City.

IPSWICH TOWN 2004–05 LEAGUE RECORD

Match No.	*Date*	*Venue*	*Opponents*	*Result*		*H/T Score*	*Lg. Pos.*	*Goalscorers*	*Attendance*
1	Aug 7	H	Gillingham	W	2-1	1-1	—	Naylor [35], Bowditch [46]	23,130
2	11	A	Nottingham F	D	1-1	0-1	—	Bent [54]	21,125
3	14	A	Derby Co	L	2-3	2-1	8	Miller (pen) [41], Bowditch [43]	22,234
4	21	H	Cardiff C	W	3-1	1-0	5	Bent [21], Miller [67], Westlake [86]	21,828
5	28	A	Rotherham U	W	2-0	1-0	3	Kuqi 2 [43, 47]	5504
6	30	H	Wolverhampton W	W	2-1	1-0	3	Bent [28], Miller (pen) [50]	24,590
7	Sept 12	H	Millwall	W	2-0	0-0	1	Bent [83], Counago [90]	21,246
8	14	A	Stoke C	L	2-3	1-1	—	De Vos [41], Westlake [62]	23,029
9	18	A	West Ham U	D	1-1	0-1	4	Counago [57]	28,812
10	25	H	Plymouth Arg	W	3-2	1-2	3	De Vos [24], Kuqi 2 [82, 85]	23,270
11	28	H	Reading	D	1-1	1-1	—	Kuqi [10]	23,167
12	Oct 3	A	Coventry C	W	2-1	0-0	2	Bowditch [70], Mills (og) [87]	12,608
13	16	H	Burnley	D	1-1	0-1	4	Richards [90]	23,183
14	19	A	Leicester C	D	2-2	1-1	—	Westlake [2], Heath (og) [89]	22,497
15	23	A	Watford	D	2-2	0-0	3	Westlake [50], Bent [63]	15,894
16	30	H	Preston NE	W	3-0	2-0	2	Kuqi [44], Miller [45], Bent [72]	23,745
17	Nov 2	H	Sheffield U	W	5-1	2-1	—	Miller (pen) [22], Kuqi 2 [23, 68], Naylor [62], Westlake [71]	22,977
18	6	A	Burnley	W	2-0	1-0	2	Bent 2 [15, 65]	11,969
19	13	H	Leeds U	W	1-0	0-0	2	Bent [51]	29,955
20	21	A	Sunderland	L	0-2	0-0	2		31,723
21	27	H	Brighton & HA	W	1-0	1-0	1	Kuqi [22]	26,269
22	Dec 4	A	Crewe Alex	D	2-2	0-2	2	Naylor [55], Bent [59]	7236
23	11	A	QPR	W	4-2	1-2	2	De Vos [25], Bent [58], Currie [72], Kuqi [77]	18,231
24	21	H	Wigan Ath	W	2-1	0-0	—	Naylor [66], Bent [89]	28,286
25	26	A	Millwall	L	1-3	0-1	1	Kuqi [62]	14,532
26	28	H	Stoke C	W	1-0	1-0	1	Kuqi [34]	26,217
27	Jan 1	H	West Ham U	L	0-2	0-1	1		30,003
28	3	A	Plymouth Arg	W	2-1	0-0	1	Currie 2 (1 pen) [67 (p), 85]	17,923
29	15	H	Coventry C	W	3-2	1-1	1	Bent 2 [45, 59], Kuqi [77]	23,670
30	22	A	Reading	D	1-1	0-0	1	Bent [89]	23,203
31	Feb 5	A	Sheffield U	W	2-0	1-0	1	Unsworth [20], Kuqi [61]	20,680
32	12	H	Leicester C	W	2-1	2-0	1	Kuqi [2], De Vries (og) [24]	27,392
33	18	A	Preston NE	D	1-1	0-1	—	Miller [69]	14,418
34	22	H	Watford	L	1-2	0-1	—	Miller (pen) [87]	23,993
35	26	H	QPR	L	0-2	0-1	3		29,008
36	Mar 5	A	Wigan Ath	L	0-1	0-1	3		16,744
37	12	H	Nottingham F	W	6-0	2-0	3	Naylor [27], Westlake [35], Miller 2 (1 pen) [50, 64 (p)], Kuqi [67], Bent [71]	25,765
38	15	A	Cardiff C	W	1-0	0-0	—	Miller (pen) [62]	11,768
39	19	A	Gillingham	D	0-0	0-0	3		9311
40	Apr 2	H	Derby Co	W	3-2	1-1	3	Magilton [24], Bent [46], Miller [71]	28,796
41	5	H	Rotherham U	W	4-3	2-1	—	Westlake [6], Bent 2 [25, 57], Magilton [60]	26,017
42	11	A	Wolverhampton W	L	0-2	0-2	—		25,882
43	17	H	Sunderland	D	2-2	0-0	3	Naylor [66], Bent [89]	29,230
44	23	A	Leeds U	D	1-1	1-1	3	Kuqi [11]	29,607
45	30	H	Crewe Alex	W	5-1	2-0	3	Kuqi [6], Magilton [12], Miller 2 [51, 81], Counago [82]	28,244
46	May 8	A	Brighton & HA	D	1-1	1-1	3	Kuqi [4]	6848

Final League Position: 3

GOALSCORERS

League (85): Bent 20, Kuqi 19, Miller 13 (6 pens), Westlake 7, Naylor 6, Bowditch 3, Counago 3, Currie 3 (1 pen), De Vos 3, Magilton 3, Richards 1, Unsworth 1, own goals 3.
Carling Cup (2): Miller 1, Westlake 1.
FA Cup (1): Miller 1.
Play-offs (2): Kuqi 1, own goal 1.

Davis K 39	Diallo D 23 + 3	Richards M 15 + 9	Horlock K 33 + 8	De Vos J 45	Naylor R 46	Miller T 45	Bowditch D 6 + 15	Bent D 45	Kuqi S 40 + 3	Westlake I 41 + 4	Counago P 4 + 15	Dinning T 3 + 4	Wilnis F 40 + 1	Magilton J 33 + 6	Price L 7 + 1	Knights D — + 1	Currie D 19 + 5	Karbassiyon D 3 + 2	Unsworth D 16	Scowcroft J 3 + 6	*Match No.*
1	2	3	4	5	6	7	8^{1}	9	10	11	12										1
1	2	3	4	5	6	7	12	9	10^{1}	11		8									2
1	2	3^{2}	4	5	6	7^{1}	8^{3}	9	12	11	13	10	14								3
1	2		4	5	6	7	8^{2}	9	10^{1}	11	12	13	3								4
1	2		4	5	6	7	12	9^{1}	10	11		13	3	8^{2}							5
1	2		4	5	6	7		9	10	11		12	3	8^{1}							6
1	2		4	5	6	7		9	10^{1}	11	12		3	8							7
1	2		4	5	6	7	12	9	10^{2}	11	13		3^{1}	8							8
1	2		4	5	6	7		9	12	11	10^{1}	13	3	8^{2}							9
1	2	12	4	5	6	7		9	13	14	10^{2}	11^{1}	3■	8^{3}							10
1^{6}	2	3	4	5	6	7		9	10	11				8	15						11
	2	3	4	5	6	7	11	9	10^{1}	12				8	1						12
	2	3	4	5	6	7	9^{1}		10	11	12			8	1						13
	2		4	5	6	7	12	9^{1}	10	11	13		3	8^{2}	1						14
	2		4	5	6	7	12	9	10	11	8^{1}		3		1						15
	2	12	4	5	6	7^{1}	13	9	10	11	14		3^{3}	8^{2}	1						16
	2	12	4	5^{1}	6	7		9	10	11			3	8	1						17
1	2	12	4	5	6	7		9	10	11			3	8^{1}							18
1	2		4	5	6	7^{1}	12	9	10	11			3	8							19
1	2		4	5	6		7^{1}	9	10^{2}	11	12		3	8		13					20
1	2	12	4	5	6	7		9	10	11			3	8^{1}							21
1	2^{1}	12	4	5	6	7		9	10	11			3	8							22
1	2^{1}	12	4^{2}	5	6	7		9	10	11			3	8			13				23
1		3		5	6	4		9	10	11			2	8			7				24
1		3^{2}	4^{3}	5	6	8	12	9^{1}	10	11			2	13			7	14			25
1		3	12	5	6	4		9	10	11			2	8^{1}			7				26
1		3		5	6	4	12	9^{1}	10	11			2	8			7				27
1		12	4	5	6	8^{2}		9	10	11			2	13			7	3^{1}			28
1			4	5	6	7	12	9	10				2	8^{1}			11	3			29
1			4	5	6	8		9	10	11			2				7	3			30
1			12	5	6	4	13	9^{2}	10	11			2	8			7^{1}		3		31
1			12	5	6	4		9	10^{1}	11			2	8^{2}			7	13	3		32
1			4^{1}	5	6	8	12	9		11			2	13			7^{2}		3	10	33
1			4	5	6	7	12	9		11^{2}			2^{1}	8			13		3	10	34
1			4	5	6	7	12	9		13	14		2	8^{3}			11^{1}		3	10^{2}	35
1		3	4^{2}		6	8	12	9^{1}	10	11	13		2	14			7^{3}		5		36
1		3	12	5	6^{1}	7		9	10^{3}	11			2	8^{2}			13		4	14	37
1		3	12	5	6	8		9^{1}	10^{2}	11			2				7		4	13	38
1		3^{2}	12	5	6	8		9	10^{3}	11^{1}			2	13			7		4	14	39
1			12	5	6	4		9	10	11			2	8^{1}			7		3		40
1		12	13	5	6	4^{1}		9	10	11			2	8			7^{2}		3		41
1		3^{2}		5	6	7		9	10^{3}	11^{1}	12		2	8			13		4	14	42
1			4^{2}	5	6	8		9	10	11	12		2	13			7^{1}		3		43
	12		4^{2}	5	6	7		9	10	13	11^{3}		2	8	1		14		3^{1}		44
1	12			5	6^{1}	4		9^{3}	10^{2}	11	13		2	8			7		3	14	45
1	12^{2}			5	6	4		9	10	11	14		2^{1}	8			7^{3}		3	13	46

FA Cup
Third Round | Bolton W | (h) | 1-3

Carling Cup
First Round | Brentford | (h) | 2-0
Second Round | Doncaster R | (a) | 0-2

Play-offs
Semi-Final | West Ham U | (a) | 2-2
| | (h) | 0-2

KIDDERMINSTER HARRIERS Conference National

FOUNDATION

Kidderminster Harriers were originally formed as a rugby team and played their first game as a soccer club on 18 September 1886 away to Wilden. Harriers won 2-1 with goals from Arthur Millward and William Colsey. Millward was vice-captain and later Kidderminster's first representative on the executive of the Birmingham County FA in 1897. Colsey was to die in tragic circumstances following an accidental injury sustained in a match only two months later.

Aggborough Stadium, Hoo Road, Kidderminster DY10 1NB.

Telephone: (01562) 823 931.

Fax: (01562) 827 329.

Ticket Office: (01562) 823 931.

Website: www.harriers.co.uk

Email: info@harriers.co.uk

Ground Capacity: 6,444.

Record Attendance: 9,155 v Hereford U, 27 November 1948.

Chairman: Colin Youngjohns.

Vice-chairman: Barry Norgrove.

Secretary: Roger Barlow.

Manager: Stuart Watkiss.

Assistant Manager: Garry Barnett.

Physio: Jim Conway.

Colours: Red shirts, white shorts, red stockings.

Change Colours: White with red and black trim.

Year Formed: 1886.

Club Nickname: 'Harriers'.

HONOURS

FA Cup: best season: 5th rd 1994
Football League Cup: never past 2nd rd.
Conference: Champions 1993–94, 1999–2000; Runners-up 1996–97.
FA Trophy: 1986–87 (winners); 1990–91, 1994–95 (runners-up).
Spalding Challenge Cup: Winners 1996–97.
Welsh FA Cup: Runners-up 1985–86, 1988–89.
Southern League Cup: Winners 1979–80.
Worcester Senior Cup: (22)
Birmingham Senior Cup: (7)
Staffordshire Senior Cup: (4)
West Midland League: Champions (6); Runners-up (3)
Southern Premier: Runners-up (1)
West Midland League Cup: Winners (7)
Keys Cup: Winners (7)
Border Counties Floodlit League: Champions: (3)
Camkin Floodlit Cup: Winners (3)
Bass County Vase: Winners (1)
Conference Fair Play Trophy: (5)

SKY SPORTS FACT FILE

Ambrose Mulvaney starred for Kidderminster Harriers in their first Southern League season in 1948–49. On Birmingham City's transfer list at the time, he was quickly snapped up by Aston Villa and promoted to their first team.

First Football League Game: 12 August 2000, Division 3, v Torquay U (h) W 2–0 – Clarke; Clarkson, Stamps, Webb, Hinton, Smith, Bennett, Horne (1), Foster, Hadley (1), Ducros (Bird).

Record League Victory: 4–0 v Swansea C (a), Division 3, 29 October 2002 – Brock; Coleman, Shilton (1), Stamps, Hinton (Bennett), Ayres, Melligan (1), Flynn, Broughton (1) (Foster), Henriksen (1), Williams (Parrish).

Record Cup Victory: 4–0 v Halesowen T, FA Cup 1st rd replay, 16 November 1987.
N.B. 25–0 v Hereford, Birmingham Senior Cup, 1889–90.

Record Defeat: 0–13 v Darwen, FA Cup 1st rd replay, 24 January 1891.

Most League Points (3 for a win): 66, Division 3, 2001–02.

Most League Goals: 62, Division 3, 2002–03.

Record Transfer Fee Received: £380,000 from WBA for Lee Hughes, July 1997.

Record Transfer Fee Paid: £80,000 to Nuneaton Borough for Andy Ducros, July 2000.

Football League Record: 2000 Promoted to Division 3; 2004–05 FL2; 2005– Conference.

MANAGERS

Leslie Smith
Amos Moss
John Spilsbury
Dudley Kernick
Archie Styles
Stan Lloyd
Harold Cox
Stan Jones
Ron Whitehouse
Alan Grundy
John Chambers
Graham Allner 1983–99
Jan Molby 1999–2002
Ian Britton 2002–03
Jan Molby 2003–04
Stuart Watkiss November 2004–

LATEST SEQUENCES

Longest Sequence of League Wins: 4, 3.11.2001 – 24.11.2001.

Longest Sequence of League Defeats: 4, 16.9.2003 – 30.9.2003.

Longest Sequence Without a League Win: 9, 23.8.2003 – 30.9.2003.

Longest Sequence of League Draws: 4, 26.8.2002 – 14.9.2002.

Longest Sequence of Unbeaten League Matches: 9, 24.8.2002 – 5.10.2002.

Successive Scoring Runs: 10 from 3.11.2001.

Successive Non-scoring Runs: 4 from 10.3.2001.

TEN YEAR LEAGUE RECORD

		P	*W*	*D*	*L*	*F*	*A*	*Pts*	*Pos*
1995-96	Conf.	42	18	10	14	78	66	64	7
1996-97	Conf.	42	26	7	9	84	42	85	2
1997-98	Conf.	42	11	14	17	56	63	47	17
1998-99	Conf.	42	14	9	19	56	52	51	15
1999-2000	Conf.	42	26	7	9	75	40	85	1
2000-01	Div 3	46	13	14	19	47	61	53	16
2001-02	Div 3	46	19	9	18	56	47	66	10
2002-03	Div 3	46	16	15	15	62	63	63	11
2003-04	Div 3	46	14	13	19	45	59	55	16
2004-05	FL 2	46	10	8	28	39	85	38	23

DID YOU KNOW ?

Kidderminster Harriers pulled off a scoop in March 1925 when signing Stan Fazackerley and his Wolves captain George Getgood, both in dispute with the Molineux club. They made their debut against Hednesford in a 3–0 success.

KIDDERMINSTER HARRIERS 2004–05 LEAGUE RECORD

Match No.	*Date*	*Venue*	*Opponents*	*Result*		*H/T Score*	*Lg. Pos.*	*Goalscorers*	*Attendance*
1	Aug 7	A	Rushden & D	D	0-0	0-0	—		2699
2	10	H	Notts Co	D	0-0	0-0	—		2927
3	14	H	Darlington	W	1-0	0-0	6	Foster I (pen) [51]	2303
4	21	A	Mansfield T	L	1-2	1-1	11	Roberts [1]	3859
5	28	H	Wycombe W	L	0-2	0-1	20		2444
6	30	A	Bury	L	0-4	0-2	21		2504
7	Sept 4	H	Leyton Orient	L	1-2	0-1	23	Foster I [89]	2367
8	11	A	Swansea C	L	0-3	0-1	24		6462
9	18	H	Macclesfield T	W	1-0	0-0	23	Appleby (pen) [80]	2290
10	25	A	Southend U	L	0-1	0-1	24		4087
11	Oct 2	H	Cambridge U	D	1-1	0-0	24	Hatswell [67]	2356
12	9	A	Lincoln C	L	0-3	0-1	24		3605
13	16	H	Scunthorpe U	W	3-2	1-1	23	Foster I 2 [26, 69], Langmead [90]	2167
14	23	A	Bristol R	L	0-2	0-1	24		7020
15	26	A	Chester C	L	0-3	0-1	—		2968
16	30	H	Shrewsbury T	L	0-1	0-0	24		3830
17	Nov 6	H	Boston U	L	0-4	0-0	24		2208
18	20	A	Grimsby T	L	1-2	0-2	24	Matias [71]	3605
19	27	H	Northampton T	L	0-2	0-1	24		2701
20	Dec 7	A	Yeovil T	L	1-2	1-1	—	Stamp [33]	4639
21	11	H	Rochdale	W	2-1	1-1	24	Keates [5], Foster I (pen) [69]	2337
22	18	A	Cheltenham T	L	0-2	0-0	24		3718
23	26	H	Swansea C	L	1-5	0-2	24	Birch [82]	4288
24	28	A	Oxford U	W	2-0	1-0	23	Sturrock [37], Russell [68]	5947
25	Jan 1	A	Leyton Orient	L	1-2	1-0	23	Foster I [11]	3573
26	3	H	Southend U	L	1-3	0-1	23	Beardsley [79]	2755
27	8	H	Lincoln C	W	2-1	1-1	23	Sturrock [16], Russell [51]	2283
28	15	A	Macclesfield T	L	0-2	0-1	23		2001
29	22	H	Oxford U	L	1-3	0-2	23	Ashton (og) [66]	3143
30	29	A	Cambridge U	W	3-1	1-1	23	Beardsley [30], Mullins [61], Birch [86]	3948
31	Feb 5	A	Scunthorpe U	L	1-2	0-1	23	Birch [59]	5023
32	12	H	Chester C	L	0-1	0-0	23		2779
33	19	A	Shrewsbury T	L	2-4	2-3	23	Beardsley [13], Sturrock [27]	5309
34	22	H	Bristol R	D	1-1	1-0	—	Sturrock [29]	2082
35	26	A	Rochdale	D	1-1	1-1	24	Beardsley [18]	2385
36	Mar 5	H	Cheltenham T	W	1-0	0-0	23	Mullins [48]	2879
37	12	A	Notts Co	W	3-1	0-0	23	Keates 2 (2 pens) [76, 86], Beardsley [90]	4358
38	19	H	Rushden & D	D	0-0	0-0	23		3860
39	26	A	Darlington	W	2-0	0-0	23	Keates [81], Rawle [90]	6972
40	28	H	Mansfield T	L	1-3	1-0	23	Rawle [41]	3237
41	Apr 2	A	Wycombe W	L	0-3	0-2	23		4608
42	9	H	Bury	D	2-2	1-1	23	Sturrock [12], Keates [80]	2474
43	16	H	Yeovil T	D	1-1	0-0	23	Rawle [83]	4014
44	23	A	Boston U	L	0-3	0-2	23		2053
45	30	H	Grimsby T	L	1-4	0-2	23	Birch [47]	2340
46	May 7	A	Northampton T	L	0-3	0-0	23		6786

Final League Position: 23

GOALSCORERS

League (39): Foster I 6 (2 pens), Beardsley 5, Keates 5 (2 pens), Sturrock 5, Birch 4, Rawle 3, Mullins 2, Russell 2, Appleby 1 (pen), Hatswell 1, Langmead 1, Matias 1, Roberts 1, Stamp 1, own goal 1.
Carling Cup (1): Brown 1.
FA Cup (1): Hatswell 1.
LDV Vans Trophy (0).

Danby J 37	Jenkins L 31+1	Burton S 15+1	Viveash A 7	Hatswell W 38+2	McHale C 11+3	Mellon M 5+2 / Cozic B 13+2	Brown S 11+2	Christiansen J 11+6	Diop Y 7+3	Advice-Desruisseaux F 9	Keates D 40+1	Rickards S —+4 / Jackson M 13	Russell S 18+10	Foster I 15+12	Appleby R 6+3	Roberts S 4+1 / Rawle M 5+6	Langmead K 9+1	McMahon S 3+2 / Chambers A 2	Sall A 13+1	Christie I 1+7	Cooper S 10	Keene J 5 / Lewis D 1	Foster B 2	Beswetherick J 10 / Hollis J —+1	Stamp D 4	Clarke R 6	Bennett T 24	Matias P 4+1	Gleeson J 2+5	Weaver S 22+1	Beardsley C 15+10	Mullins J 21	Birch G 11+3	Burns L —+1	Sturrock B 17+5	Jones B 10+2	McGrath J 18+1	*Match No.*
1	2	3	4	5	6	7^1	8	9	10^2	11^3	12	13	14																									1
1	2	3	4	5		7^3	8	12	10^1	11	6	13	14	9^2																								2
1	2	3	4	5		7^2	8■	12	10^1	11	6	13		9																								3
1	2	3	4	5		7		9		11	6^2	12		10^1	13	8																						4
1	2	3	4	5		12	8	9		11^1	6		7^3	13	14	10^2																						5
1	2^1	3	4	5	12	7■	8^2	9		11	6				13	10																						6
1	2	3	4	5	6		8			11^2				12	7	10^1	9	13																				7
1	2^1	3		5	6	12	8	9						7^2	4	13	10	11																				8
1	2	3		5			12	13	10^3		11			7^1	8		9^2	4	6	14																		9
1	2	3		5	12		13	14	10^1		7^2				8		9^3	11	6■		4																	10
1	2	3		5	6		8	12	10^2		11			9	7^1		13				4																	11
1	2^1	3		5	6		8	9			11			12	7		10				4																	12
1	2			5			8^1	9		11^2	4		12	7			10	13	6		3																	13
1	2			5	6			9			7			8			10^1		4	12	3	11																14
1	2	3		5■	12			9	13	11^1	4			14			10^2		6		7	8^3																15
	2	3			6			12	13		4		8	10^1			9		5		7	11^2	1															16
	2^2			5				9^1	12		7		4	13					6		8	11	1	3	10													17
					6		8	9^2	10^1		7		12						5		2			3	11	1	4	13										18
				5							8		7						6		2	9		3	10	1	4	11^1	12									19
	2^1			5	6						10		7	12					4					3	9	1	8	11^2	13									20
	2			5	6						9		7	10^3					12					3		1	8	11^2	13	4^1	14							21
	2^1			5■							11		7	12										3		1	8	10^2		4	13	6	9					22
	2				6								7^1	10^3					5^2					3		1	8		11		12	4	9	13	14			23
1	2										11		7^2	12										3			8		4^1	5	13	6	9		10			24
1	2										11		7	8										3			4		13	5	12	6	9^2		10^1			25
1	2										11		7^1	10^2										3			4		13	5	12	6	9		8			26
1	2			5							11		7														8			6	12	4	9		10^1	3		27
1	2■			5							11		7^1														8^2			6	12	4	9		10	3	13	28
1				5							7		8	12													4^1			6	13	2	9		10^2	3	11	29
1				5							7		8^1	12													4■			6	10^2	2	9		13	3	11	30
1				5		7					4^2		12	8^1					6											2	10		9		13	3	11	31
1	2^3			5		14							8^1	12													7			6	10	4	9^2		13	3	11	32
1				3		7						5	12	8^1													4			6	9	2			10		11	33
1	12			3		7					8	5															4			6	9	2^1			10		11	34
1	2			3		7					8	5				12											4				9^1	6			10		11	35
1	2^1			3		7					8	5															4			12	9	6			10		11	36
1				6		7					8	5				12											4			2	9	3			10^1		11	37
1	2^1			6		7					8	5	12			14				13										4	9^2	3			10^3		11	38
1	2■			6		7					8	5				14				12^2										4	9^1	3			10^3	13	11	39
1				6^3		7^1					8	5	12			10^2				13							4			2	9	3	14				11	40
1				6^3		7					8	5				10^1				12							4			2	9^2	3	13			14	11	41
1				12		14					8	5	7^2			13											4			2^1	9	3			10	6	11^3	42
1				12		7					8	5	13			14											4			2	9^3	3^1			10	6	11^2	43
1				6		7					8	5	12			9				13							4^1			2^3	14				10^2	3	11	44
1		12		6		7					4	5	8^2			9		2													10^3		14		13	3^1	11	45
		3		6							4			12		9		7	5	8^1		1		13						2					10^2		11■	46

FA Cup
First Round Port Vale (a) 1-3

Carling Cup
First Round Cardiff C (h) 1-1

LDV Vans Trophy
First Round Bristol R (a) 0-1

LEEDS UNITED FL Championship

FOUNDATION

Immediately the Leeds City club (founded in 1904) was wound up by the FA in October 1919, following allegations of illegal payments to players, a meeting was called by a Leeds solicitor, Mr Alf Masser, at which Leeds United was formed. They joined the Midland League playing their first game in that competition in November 1919. It was in this same month that the new club had discussions with the directors of a virtually bankrupt Huddersfield Town who wanted to move to Leeds in an amalgamation. But Huddersfield survived even that crisis.

Elland Road, Leeds, West Yorkshire LS11 0ES.

Telephone: (0113) 367 6000.

Fax: (0113) 367 6050.

Ticket Office: 0845 121 1992.

Website: www.leedsunited.com

Email: football@leedsunited.com

Ground Capacity: 40,232.

Record Attendance: 57,892 v Sunderland, FA Cup 5th rd (replay), 15 March 1967.

Pitch Measurements: 105m × 68m.

Chairman: Ken Bates.

Vice-chairman: Jayne McGuinness.

Chief Executive: Shaun Harvey.

Manager: Kevin Blackwell.

Assistant Manager: Sam Ellis.

Physio: Dave Hancock.

Colours: White shirts with fine blue and yellow pinstripe, white shorts, white stockings.

Change Colours: Navy shirts, sky blue shorts, navy stockings.

Year Formed: 1919, as Leeds United after disbandment (by FA order) of Leeds City (formed in 1904).

Turned Professional: 1920.

Ltd Co.: 1920.

Club Nickname: 'The Whites'.

First Football League Game: 28 August 1920, Division 2, v Port Vale (a) L 0–2 – Down; Duffield, Tillotson; Musgrove, Baker, Walton; Mason, Goldthorpe, Thompson, Lyon, Best.

HONOURS

Football League: Division 1 – Champions 1968–69, 1973–74, 1991–92; Runners-up 1964–65, 1965–66, 1969–70, 1970–71, 1971–72; Division 2 – Champions 1923–24, 1963–64, 1989–90; Runners-up 1927–28, 1931–32, 1955–56.

FA Cup: Winners 1972; Runners-up 1965, 1970, 1973.

Football League Cup: Winners 1968; Runners-up 1996.

European Competitions: *European Cup:* 1969–70, 1974–75 (runners-up). *Champions League:* 1992–93, 2000–01 (semi-finalists). *European Cup-Winners' Cup:* 1972–73 (runners-up). *European Fairs Cup:* 1965–66, 1966–67 (runners-up), 1967–68 (winners), 1968–69, 1970–71 (winners). *UEFA Cup:* 1971–72, 1973–74, 1979–80, 1995–96, 1998–99, 1999–2000 (semi-finalists), 2001–02, 2002–03.

SKY SPORTS FACT FILE

The Second Division championship in 1923–24 came to Leeds United only after an indifferent start in which just one win and two draws were derived from five games. However by the end of the season they had seven points to spare at the top.

Record League Victory: 8–0 v Leicester C, Division 1, 7 April 1934 – Moore; George Milburn, Jack Milburn; Edwards, Hart, Copping; Mahon (2), Firth (2), Duggan (2), Furness (2), Cochrane.

Record Cup Victory: 10–0 v Lyn (Oslo), European Cup 1st rd 1st leg, 17 September 1969 – Sprake; Reaney, Cooper, Bremner (2), Charlton, Hunter, Madeley, Clarke (2), Jones (3), Giles (2) (Bates), O'Grady (1).

Record Defeat: 1–8 v Stoke C, Division 1, 27 August 1934.

Most League Points (2 for a win): 67, Division 1, 1968–69.

Most League Points (3 for a win): 85, Division 2, 1989–90.

Most League Goals: 98, Division 2, 1927–28.

Highest League Scorer in Season: John Charles, 42, Division 2, 1953–54.

Most League Goals in Total Aggregate: Peter Lorimer, 168, 1965–79 and 1983–86.

Most League Goals in One Match: 5, Gordon Hodgson v Leicester C, Division 1, 1 October 1938.

Most Capped Player: Lucas Radebe, 58 (70), South Africa.

Most League Appearances: Jack Charlton, 629, 1953–73.

Youngest League Player: Peter Lorimer, 15 years 289 days v Southampton, 29 September 1962.

Record Transfer Fee Received: £28,250,000 from Manchester U for Rio Ferdinand, July 2002 (see Manchester United page 251).

Record Transfer Fee Paid: £18,000,000 to West Ham United for Rio Ferdinand, November 2000.

Football League Record: 1920 Elected to Division 2; 1924–27 Division 1; 1927–28 Division 2; 1928–31 Division 1; 1931–32 Division 2; 1932–47 Division 1; 1947–56 Division 2; 1956–60 Division 1; 1960–64 Division 2; 1964–82 Division 1; 1982–90 Division 2; 1990–92 Division 1; 1992–2004 FA Premier League; 2004– FLC.

MANAGERS

Dick Ray 1919–20
Arthur Fairclough 1920–27
Dick Ray 1927–35
Bill Hampson 1935–47
Willis Edwards 1947–48
Major Frank Buckley 1948–53
Raich Carter 1953–58
Bill Lambton 1958–59
Jack Taylor 1959–61
Don Revie OBE 1961–74
Brian Clough 1974
Jimmy Armfield 1974–78
Jock Stein CBE 1978
Jimmy Adamson 1978–80
Allan Clarke 1980–82
Eddie Gray MBE 1982–85
Billy Bremner 1985–88
Howard Wilkinson 1988–96
George Graham 1996–98
David O'Leary 1998–2002
Terry Venables 2002–03
Peter Reid 2003
Eddie Gray *(Caretaker)* 2003–04
Kevin Blackwell May 2004–

LATEST SEQUENCES

Longest Sequence of League Wins: 9, 26.9.1931 – 21.11.1931.

Longest Sequence of League Defeats: 6, 28.12.2003 – 7.2.2004.

Longest Sequence of League Draws: 5, 19.4.1997 – 9.8.1997.

Longest Sequence of Unbeaten League Matches: 34, 26.10.1968 – 26.8.1969.

Longest Sequence Without a League Win: 17, 1.2.1947 – 26.5.1947.

Successive Scoring Runs: 30 from 27.8.1927.

Successive Non-scoring Runs: 6 from 30.1.1982.

TEN YEAR LEAGUE RECORD

		P	*W*	*D*	*L*	*F*	*A*	*Pts*	*Pos*
1995-96	PR Lge	38	12	7	19	40	57	43	13
1996-97	PR Lge	38	11	13	14	28	38	46	11
1997-98	PR Lge	38	17	8	13	57	46	59	5
1998-99	PR Lge	38	18	13	7	62	34	67	4
1999-2000	PR Lge	38	21	6	11	58	43	69	3
2000-01	PR Lge	38	20	8	10	64	43	68	4
2001-02	PR Lge	38	18	12	8	53	37	66	5
2002-03	PR Lge	38	14	5	19	58	57	47	15
2003-04	PR Lge	38	8	9	21	40	79	33	19
2004-05	FL C	46	14	18	14	49	52	60	14

DID YOU KNOW ?

In nine seasons as a midfield player for Leeds United over nine years from 1975 Gwyn Thomas was selected for the full Welsh international team only to be injured and not asked again. He had been capped by his country at schoolboy and Under-21 level.

LEEDS UNITED 2004–05 LEAGUE RECORD

Match No.	Date	Venue	Opponents	Result	H/T Score	Lg. Pos.	Goalscorers	Attendance
1	Aug 7	H	Derby Co	W 1-0	0-0	—	Richardson [72]	30,459
2	10	A	Gillingham	L 1-2	0-2	—	Pugh [80]	10,739
3	14	A	Wolverhampton W	D 0-0	0-0	12		28,397
4	21	H	Nottingham F	D 1-1	1-0	12	Guppy [25]	31,808
5	29	A	Sheffield U	L 0-2	0-0	16		22,959
6	Sept 11	H	Coventry C	W 3-0	1-0	16	Carlisle [40], Joachim [71], Pugh [90]	26,725
7	14	A	Plymouth Arg	W 1-0	1-0	—	Keith (og) [43]	20,555
8	18	A	Crewe Alex	D 2-2	0-0	10	Pugh 2 [53, 89]	9095
9	24	H	Sunderland	L 0-1	0-0	—		28,926
10	28	H	Stoke C	D 0-0	0-0	—		25,759
11	Oct 2	A	Cardiff C	D 0-0	0-0	17		17,006
12	16	H	Preston NE	W 1-0	0-0	11	Pugh [78]	30,458
13	19	A	Reading	D 1-1	1-1	—	Walton [1]	22,230
14	23	A	Brighton & HA	L 0-1	0-0	17		6716
15	31	H	Wigan Ath	L 0-2	0-0	16		27,432
16	Nov 3	H	Burnley	L 1-2	1-2	—	Wright [1]	27,490
17	6	A	Preston NE	W 4-2	3-0	15	Deane [13], Healy 2 [15, 44], Walton [72]	18,531
18	13	A	Ipswich T	L 0-1	0-0	19		29,955
19	20	H	QPR	W 6-1	5-1	17	Healy [9], Deane 4 [13, 42, 44, 72], Wright [23]	29,739
20	24	H	Watford	D 2-2	1-1	—	Wright [21], Carlisle [86]	24,585
21	29	A	Rotherham U	L 0-1	0-0	—		8860
22	Dec 4	H	Leicester C	L 0-2	0-0	19		27,384
23	10	A	West Ham U	D 1-1	0-0	—	Healy (pen) [90]	30,684
24	19	H	Millwall	D 1-1	1-0	19	Oster [43]	26,265
25	26	A	Sunderland	W 3-2	1-1	16	Lennon [30], Deane [61], Joachim [85]	43,253
26	28	H	Plymouth Arg	W 2-1	0-0	14	Gilbert (og) [46], Healy [90]	34,496
27	Jan 1	H	Crewe Alex	L 0-2	0-1	14		32,302
28	3	A	Coventry C	W 2-1	1-0	14	Blake [28], Healy [65]	19,084
29	15	H	Cardiff C	D 1-1	1-0	14	Walton [14]	29,548
30	22	A	Stoke C	W 1-0	0-0	11	Thomas (og) [72]	18,372
31	26	A	Derby Co	L 0-2	0-0	—		25,648
32	29	H	Brighton & HA	D 1-1	1-0	—	Carlisle [43]	27,033
33	Feb 5	A	Burnley	W 1-0	0-0	10	Einarsson [66]	17,789
34	12	H	Reading	W 3-1	1-0	10	Healy [36], Hulse 2 [56, 63]	30,034
35	19	A	Wigan Ath	L 0-3	0-1	10		17,177
36	26	H	West Ham U	W 2-1	0-0	10	Hulse [51], Derry [86]	34,115
37	Mar 6	A	Millwall	D 1-1	0-1	9	Hulse [78]	12,510
38	12	H	Gillingham	D 1-1	0-1	10	Hulse [81]	27,995
39	16	A	Nottingham F	D 0-0	0-0	—		25,101
40	Apr 2	H	Wolverhampton W	D 1-1	0-1	12	Derry [50]	29,773
41	5	H	Sheffield U	L 0-4	0-2	—		28,936
42	9	A	Watford	W 2-1	1-1	10	Hulse [28], Carlisle [67]	16,306
43	16	A	QPR	D 1-1	1-0	10	Johnson Seth [24]	18,182
44	23	H	Ipswich T	D 1-1	1-1	12	Spring [12]	29,607
45	May 1	A	Leicester C	L 0-2	0-2	14		26,593
46	8	H	Rotherham U	D 0-0	0-0	14		30,900

Final League Position: 14

GOALSCORERS

League (49): Healy 7 (1 pen), Deane 6, Hulse 6, Pugh 5, Carlisle 4, Walton 3, Wright 3, Derry 2, Joachim 2, Blake 1, Einarsson 1, Guppy 1, Johnson Seth 1, Lennon 1, Oster 1, Richardson 1, Spring 1, own goals 3.
Carling Cup (3): Deane 1, Pugh 1, Ricketts 1.
FA Cup (0).

Sullivan N 46	Kelly G 43	Kilgallon M 26	Walton S 23 + 7	Butler P 39	Duberry M 4	Richardson F 28 + 10	Pugh D 33 + 5	Ricketts M 9 + 12	Joachim J 10 + 17	Wright J 33 + 2	Radebe L 1 + 2	Deane B 23 + 8	Guppy S 1 + 2	Crainey S 9	Carlisle C 29 + 6	McMaster J — + 7	Lennon A 19 + 8	Spring M 4 + 9	Gregan S 34 + 1	Ormerod B 6	Healy D 27 + 1	Johnson Simon 1 + 1	Oster J 8	Woods M — + 1	Einarsson G 6 + 2	Blake N 2	Griffit L — + 1	Bakke E — + 1	Gray M 10	Hulse R 13	Derry S 7	King M 4 + 5	Johnson Seth 4 + 2	Moore I 4 + 2	*Match No.*
1	2	3	4^1	5	6	7	8	9^2	10	11	12	13																							1
1	2	3	4^2	5	6	7	8	9^1	10	11		12	13																						2
1	2		12	5	6■	7^2	8	9^3	14	11	4^1	10	13	3																					3
1	2		12	5		7	4	13	10^3	8		9^2	11^1	3	6	14																			4
1	2			5	6	7	4	9^1	10^2	11		8		3		12	13																		5
1	2		4	5		7	8	12	10^1	11		9^2		3	6	13																			6
1	2		4^3	5		7	8	12	10^2	11		9^1		3	6	13		14																	7
1	2			5		7^2	8	12	10^1	11		9		3	6	13			4																8
1	2			5		7^2	8	12	13	11		9^1		3	6				4	10															9
1	2			5		7^1	8		12	11		9		3	6				4	10															10
1	2			5		7^2	8	12	13	11		9^1		3	6				4	10															11
1	2	3	11	5		7^2	8	9^1				12			6		13	14	4	10^3															12
1	2	3	11^3	5		7	8	9^1	13			12			6			14	4	10^2															13
1	2	3■	11^3	5■		7^2	8	9^1				12			6		13	14	4	10															14
1	2	3	5^2			7^1	8		13	12		9			6		14		4		10	11^3													15
1	2	3		5			8^3	12	11	7		9^1			6^2		13		4		10	14													16
1	2		3	5		12	8			7		9			6				4		10		11^1												17
1	2		3	5			8		12	11^1		9			6				4		10		7												18
1	2		3^1	5		12	8		13	7		9^3			6		14		4		10^2		11												19
1	2		3	5			8		12	7		9^1			6				4		10		11												20
1	2	3	8^1	5		13		9	12	7					6^2		14		4		10		11^3												21
1	2	3^3	8	5		12			13	7		9			6^2	14			4		10		11^1												22
1	2	3	12	5		7	8		13	6		9^2				14			4^1		10		11^3												23
1	2	6	12	5		7	3		13	8^1		9^2							4		10		11												24
1	2	6		5		7	3	12	13	11		9^1					8^2	4			10^3			14											25
1	2	6		5		7^1	3		13	11		9^2			12		8		4		10														26
1	2^2	6	12	5■		7	3^3	13		11^1							8		4		10				14	9									27
1		6	7			2	3		12	11					5■		8^2	13	4		10					9^1									28
1	2	6	4^2	5		7	3		9	11					12		8^1	13			10														29
1	2			5		7	3	12	13	11		9^1			6		8^2		4		10														30
1	2		12	5		3	8	9^2	11^3	7^1		13			6				4		10						14								31
1	2		7^2	5		3						9			6		8^1	12	4		10				11			13							32
1	2			5			12	13		11		9^2			6		8		4		10				7^1				3						33
1	2			5		12	13	14		11					6		8^1		4		10^2				7				3	9^3					34
1	2			5		12				11^1					6		8		4		10								3	9	7				35
1	2	6	11^1	5			12								13		8^2		4		10								3	9	7				36
1	2^1	6	11^2	5											12		8		4		10^3								3	9	7	13	14		37
1	2^1	6	11	5		12				7^3		13					8		4		10								3■	9^2		14			38
1	2	6	11	5		4^2	3			7^3		12			13		8				10^1									9			14		39
1		6	2	5			3										8	12			13				14					9^2	4	7^1	11^3	10	40
1		6	2^2	5^1			3								12		8		13		10									9	4	7^3	11	14	41
1	2	6				12									5		8^2		4		10^3								3	9^1	7	13	11	14	42
1	2					12	13								5		8^1	14	4						7				3	9	6■	10^2	11^3		43
1	2	6	12^2			11^3				13					5			8	4						7^1				3	9		14		10	44
1	2	6				11^2	12								5		13	8	4						7^3				3^1	9		14		10	45
1	2	5				12	3^2			7	13						8	6	4											9		11^1		10	46

FA Cup

Third Round	Birmingham C	(a)	0-3

Carling Cup

First Round	Huddersfield T	(h)	1-0
Second Round	Swindon T	(h)	1-0
Third Round	Portsmouth	(a)	1-2

LEICESTER CITY FL Championship

FOUNDATION

In 1884 a number of young footballers who were mostly old boys of Wyggeston School, held a meeting at a house on the Roman Fosse Way and formed Leicester Fosse FC. They collected 9d (less than 4p) towards the cost of a ball, plus the same amount for membership. Their first professional, Harry Webb from Stafford Rangers, was signed in 1888 for 2s 6d (12p) per week, plus travelling expenses.

The Walkers Stadium, Filbert Way, Leicester LE2 7FL.

Telephone: 0870 040 6000.

Ticket Office: 0870 499 1884.

Website: www.lcfc.co.uk

Ground Capacity: 32,500.

Record Attendance: 47,298 v Tottenham H, FA Cup 5th rd, 18 February 1928.

Pitch Measurements: 110yd × 76yd.

Chairman: Jim McCahill.

Chief Executive: Tim Davies.

Secretary: Andrew Neville.

Manager: Craig Levein.

Assistant Manager: Robert Kelly.

Physio: David Rennie.

HONOURS

Football League: Division 1 – Runners-up 1928–29; Promoted from Division 1 1993–94 (play-offs) and 1995–96 (play-offs); Division 2 – Champions 1924–25, 1936–37, 1953–54, 1956–57, 1970–71, 1979–80; Runners-up 1907–08.

FA Cup: Runners-up 1949, 1961, 1963, 1969.

Football League Cup: Winners 1964, 1997, 2000; Runners-up 1965, 1999.

European Competitions: *European Cup-Winners' Cup:* 1961–62. *UEFA Cup:* 1997–98, 2000–01.

Colours: Blue shirts, white shorts, blue stockings.

Change Colours: White shirts, blue shorts, blue stockings; or all gold.

Year Formed: 1884.

Turned Professional: 1888.

Ltd Co: 1897.

Previous Name: 1884, Leicester Fosse; 1919, Leicester City.

Club Nickname: 'Foxes'.

Previous Grounds: 1884, Victoria Park; 1887, Belgrave Road; 1888, Victoria Park; 1891, Filbert Street; 2002, Walkers Stadium.

First Football League Game: 1 September 1894, Division 2, v Grimsby T (a) L 3–4 – Thraves; Smith, Bailey; Seymour, Brown, Henrys; Hill, Hughes, McArthur (1), Skea (2), Priestman.

Record League Victory: 10–0 v Portsmouth, Division 1, 20 October 1928 – McLaren; Black, Brown; Findlay, Carr, Watson; Adcock, Hine (3), Chandler (6), Lochhead, Barry (1).

Record Cup Victory: 8–1 v Coventry C (a), League Cup 5th rd, 1 December 1964 – Banks; Sjoberg, Norman (2); Roberts, King, McDerment; Hodgson (2), Cross, Goodfellow, Gibson (1), Stringfellow (2), (1 og).

SKY SPORTS FACT FILE

Dave Buchanan was not only the youngest player to turn out for Leicester City but the youngest goalscorer in the same game. Then two months later Neil Grewcock became the second youngest goalscorer for the club v Cardiff City!

Record Defeat: 0–12 (as Leicester Fosse) v Nottingham F, Division 1, 21 April 1909.

Most League Points (2 for a win): 61, Division 2, 1956–57.

Most League Points (3 for a win): 92, Division 1, 2002–03.

Most League Goals: 109, Division 2, 1956–57.

Highest League Scorer in Season: Arthur Rowley, 44, Division 2, 1956–57.

Most League Goals in Total Aggregate: Arthur Chandler, 259, 1923–35.

Most League Goals in One Match: 6, John Duncan v Port Vale, Division 2, 25 December 1924; 6, Arthur Chandler v Portsmouth, Division 1, 20 October 1928.

Most Capped Player: John O'Neill, 39, Northern Ireland.

Most League Appearances: Adam Black, 528, 1920–35.

Youngest League Player: Dave Buchanan, 16 years 192 days v Oldham Ath, 1 January 1979.

Record Transfer Fee Received: £11,500,000 from Liverpool for Emile Heskey, February 2000.

Record Transfer Fee Paid: £5,500,000 to Wolverhampton W for Ade Akinbiyi, July 2000.

Football League Record: 1894 Elected to Division 2; 1908–09 Division 1; 1909–25 Division 2; 1925–35 Division 1; 1935–37 Division 2; 1937–39 Division 1; 1946–54 Division 2; 1954–55 Division 1; 1955–57 Division 2; 1957–69 Division 1; 1969–71 Division 2; 1971–78 Division 1; 1978–80 Division 2; 1980–81 Division 1; 1981–83 Division 2; 1983–87 Division 1; 1987–92 Division 2; 1992–94 Division 1; 1994–95 FA Premier League; 1995–96 Division 1; 1996–2002 FA Premier League; 2002–03 Division 1; 2003–04 FA Premier League; 2004– FLC.

MANAGERS

Frank Gardner 1884–92
Ernest Marson 1892–94
J. Lee 1894–95
Henry Jackson 1895–97
William Clark 1897–98
George Johnson 1898–1912
Jack Bartlett 1912–14
Louis Ford 1914–15
Harry Linney 1915–19
Peter Hodge 1919–26
Willie Orr 1926–32
Peter Hodge 1932–34
Arthur Lochhead 1934–36
Frank Womack 1936–39
Tom Bromilow 1939–45
Tom Mather 1945–46
John Duncan 1946–49
Norman Bullock 1949–55
David Halliday 1955–58
Matt Gillies 1958–68
Frank O'Farrell 1968–71
Jimmy Bloomfield 1971–77
Frank McLintock 1977–78
Jock Wallace 1978–82
Gordon Milne 1982–86
Bryan Hamilton 1986–87
David Pleat 1987–91
Gordon Lee 1991
Brian Little 1991–94
Mark McGhee 1994–95
Martin O'Neill 1995–2000
Peter Taylor 2000–01
Dave Bassett 2001–02
Micky Adams 2002–04
Craig Levein November 2004–

LATEST SEQUENCES

Longest Sequence of League Wins: 7, 28.2.1993 – 27.3.1993.

Longest Sequence of League Defeats: 8, 17.3.2001 – 28.4.2001.

Longest Sequence of League Draws: 6, 21.8.1976 – 18.9.1976.

Longest Sequence of Unbeaten League Matches: 19, 6.2.1971 – 18.8.1971.

Longest Sequence Without a League Win: 18, 12.4.1975 – 1.11.1975.

Successive Scoring Runs: 31 from 12.11.1932.

Successive Non-scoring Runs: 7 from 21.11.1987.

TEN YEAR LEAGUE RECORD

		P	*W*	*D*	*L*	*F*	*A*	*Pts*	*Pos*
1995-96	Div 1	46	19	14	13	66	60	71	5
1996-97	PR Lge	38	12	11	15	46	54	47	9
1997-98	PR Lge	38	13	14	11	51	41	53	10
1998-99	PR Lge	38	12	13	13	40	46	49	10
1999-2000	PR Lge	38	16	7	15	55	55	55	8
2000-01	PR Lge	38	14	6	18	39	51	48	13
2001-02	PR Lge	38	5	13	20	30	64	28	20
2002-03	Div 1	46	26	14	6	73	40	92	2
2003-04	PR Lge	38	6	15	17	48	65	33	18
2004-05	FL C	46	12	21	13	49	46	57	15

DID YOU KNOW 

In addition to his six goals in one match, Leicester City top scorer Arthur Chandler also hit five goals on three occasions, plus a four and any number of hat-tricks. In two of the five-goal feats he scored all City goals.

LEICESTER CITY 2004–05 LEAGUE RECORD

Match No.	Date	Venue	Opponents	Result		H/T Score	Lg. Pos.	Goalscorers	Attendance
1	Aug 7	H	West Ham U	D	0-0	0-0	—		30,231
2	11	A	Derby Co	W	2-1	1-0	—	Nalis [41], Benjamin [76]	26,650
3	14	A	Millwall	L	0-2	0-1	9		11,754
4	21	H	Watford	L	0-1	0-0	19		22,478
5	28	A	Wolverhampton W	D	1-1	1-0	17	Scowcroft [4]	27,550
6	30	H	Brighton & HA	L	0-1	0-1	19		22,263
7	Sept 11	A	Rotherham U	W	2-0	1-0	17	Nalis [44], Dublin [59]	6272
8	14	H	Sheffield U	W	3-2	2-0	—	Scowcroft [8], Dabizas [29], Wilcox [52]	23,422
9	18	H	Burnley	D	0-0	0-0	13		22,495
10	25	A	QPR	L	2-3	2-0	16	Scowcroft [29], Connolly [45]	15,535
11	28	A	Gillingham	W	2-0	0-0	—	Heath [49], Dublin [71]	6089
12	Oct 2	H	Preston NE	D	1-1	1-1	12	Benjamin [4]	21,249
13	16	A	Coventry C	D	1-1	0-0	12	Dublin [70]	18,054
14	19	H	Ipswich T	D	2-2	1-1	—	Connolly [34], Heath [60]	22,497
15	23	H	Stoke C	D	1-1	1-1	13	Halls (og) [21]	22,882
16	30	A	Cardiff C	D	0-0	0-0	14		13,759
17	Nov 2	A	Crewe Alex	D	2-2	1-0	—	Nalis [45], Gudjonsson [53]	6849
18	8	H	Coventry C	W	3-0	2-0	—	Nalis [26], Tiatto [45], Heath [72]	22,479
19	13	H	Sunderland	L	0-1	0-0	13		25,897
20	20	A	Wigan Ath	D	0-0	0-0	15		10,924
21	27	H	Plymouth Arg	W	2-1	0-1	13	Scowcroft [49], Dublin [52]	23,799
22	Dec 4	A	Leeds U	W	2-0	0-0	8	Nalis [48], Kelly (og) [78]	27,384
23	11	H	Reading	L	0-2	0-0	13		24,068
24	17	A	Nottingham F	D	1-1	0-0	—	Connolly [90]	22,415
25	26	H	Rotherham U	L	0-1	0-1	14		27,014
26	28	A	Sheffield U	L	0-2	0-0	15		22,100
27	Jan 3	H	QPR	W	1-0	1-0	15	Connolly (pen) [9]	23,754
28	15	A	Preston NE	D	1-1	1-0	16	Connolly [25]	12,677
29	22	H	Gillingham	W	2-0	2-0	14	Connolly [19], Nosworthy (og) [29]	23,457
30	Feb 5	H	Crewe Alex	D	1-1	0-1	15	Gillespie [58]	27,011
31	12	A	Ipswich T	L	1-2	0-2	15	Stewart [82]	27,392
32	22	A	Stoke C	L	2-3	1-2	—	Williams [15], Gudjonsson [86]	14,076
33	26	A	Reading	D	0-0	0-0	18		14,651
34	Mar 5	H	Nottingham F	L	0-1	0-1	18		27,277
35	8	A	Burnley	D	0-0	0-0	—		10,933
36	15	A	Watford	D	2-2	0-2	—	Connolly [56], Hughes [72]	11,084
37	18	A	West Ham U	D	2-2	2-1	—	Connolly (pen) [25], Gillespie [44]	22,031
38	Apr 2	H	Millwall	W	3-1	1-0	15	Stearman [15], Connolly (pen) [74], De Vries [83]	22,338
39	5	H	Wolverhampton W	D	1-1	0-0	—	Maybury [73]	22,950
40	9	A	Brighton & HA	D	1-1	1-0	16	Connolly (pen) [34]	6638
41	16	H	Wigan Ath	L	0-2	0-1	16		23,894
42	19	H	Cardiff C	D	1-1	1-0	—	Connolly [33]	21,336
43	23	A	Sunderland	L	1-2	1-1	16	Maybury [5]	34,815
44	26	H	Derby Co	W	1-0	0-0	—	Connolly [50]	25,762
45	May 1	H	Leeds U	W	2-0	2-0	15	Dublin [6], Connolly [39]	26,593
46	8	A	Plymouth Arg	D	0-0	0-0	15		19,199

Final League Position: 15

GOALSCORERS

League (49): Connolly 13 (4 pens), Dublin 5, Nalis 5, Scowcroft 4, Heath 3, Benjamin 2, Gillespie 2, Gudjonsson 2, Maybury 2, Dabizas 1, De Vries 1, Hughes 1, Stearman 1, Stewart 1, Tiatto 1, Wilcox 1, Williams 1, own goals 3.
Carling Cup (2): Blake 1, Gudjonsson 1 (pen).
FA Cup (7): Williams 2, Dabizas 1, Dublin 1, Gudjonsson 1, Scowcroft 1, own goal 1.

Walker I 22	Makin C 21	Wilcox J 11 + 3	Williams G 25 + 8	Heath M 17 + 5	Dabizas N 33	Scowcroft J 30 + 1	Nalis L 32 + 7	Dublin D 34 + 3	Connolly D 43 + 1	Stewart J 33 + 2	Blake N 4 + 10	Keown M 16 + 1	Gillespie K 19 + 11	Gudjonsson J 26 + 9	Benjamin T 2 + 8	Canero P 6	Tiatto D 25 + 5	Gemmill S 11 + 6	Pressman K 13	Harper K 2	Wright T 1 + 6	Elliott M 1 + 1	Stearman R 3 + 5	Morris L 2 + 8	Taylor S 10	Maybury A 17	De Vries M 9 + 7	Hughes S 13 + 3	Kenton D 9 + 1	McCarthy P 12	Moore S 2 + 5	Hirschfeld L 1	Sheehan A 1	Match No.
1	2	3^1	4	5^2	6	7	8	9▮	10	11	12	13																						1
1	2	3^1	4		6	7	8^2		10	11	9^3	5	12	13	14																			2
1	2▮	3	4		6	7	8^3		10	11^1	9^2	5	12	13	14																			3
1		3^1	4	2	6	9			10	12		5^2		8^3	13	7	11	14																4
1				6		7	8	9	10^2	3	13	5	14	12		2	11^3	4^1																5
1		12		5	6^1	7	8	9	10	3	13		14	4^3		2	11^2																	6
	2	12	4		6	7	8	9^2	10	11		5							1	3^1	13													7
	2	11^2	4		6	7	8	9	10^1	3	12	5					13		1															8
	2	11^2	4^3		6	7	8	9	10^1	3▮	12	5					13	14	1															9
	2	3			6	7	8	9^3	10▮		11^2	5		12	13			4^1	1		14													10
	2	3	4	5	6	7		9^1						8	10		11		1		12													11
	2	3	4^1	5	6	7	12	9	13^3					8	10^2		11		1		14													12
	2	3^2	12	5		14	8	9	10	11		4			13			6^1	1	7^3														13
	2		4^1	5		7	8	9^2	10	3		6		12	13		11		1															14
	2			5		7	8	9^1	10	3		6^2			12		11	4	1			13												15
	2			5		7	8	9^2	10	3	13		12				11^1	4^3	1			6	14											16
				5	6	9	8		10	3^1			7	4		2	11		1					12										17
				5	6	9	8^1		10	3			7^2	4		2	11	12	1					13										18
				5	6	9	8	12	10	3			7^3	4^2		2^1	11	13	1					14										19
	2				6	9	8		10^1	3	12	5	7^3	4			11^2	13						14	1									20
	2		12		6	9	8	5	10	3	13		7^2					4						11^1	1									21
	2		12		6	9	11	5	10^3	3	13		7^2	8				4^1						14	1									22
			12		6	9	11	5		3	10		7	8^1				4^2					2	13	1									23
	2		12			9	8^1	5	10	11^3	13	6	7	4			3^2							14	1									24
	2					9	11^1	5	10	3		6	7	4	13			12						8^2	1									25
	2		12	6		9	11^1	5	10^3	3			7▮	8^2				4			13			14	1									26
	3		4	14	6	9	8^1	5	10^3	11		2		13			12	7^2							1									27
			4		6	9	8	5	10	11		2		7											1	3								28
				5	6	9^2	8	12	10^1	3			7	4			11								1	2	13							29
1			4^1	5	6	9^3	12^2		10	3			7	8			11									2	14	13						30
1	2^3				6	9^2	12	5	10	3			7	8^1			13						14				11	4						31
1			4	12	6			5	10	3			7	8			11									2^1	13	9^2						32
1			4^3	12	6		13	5^1	10	3			7	8			11^2						2				9	14						33
1			4	5^1	6		8		10				7				11				12					3^2	9	13	2					34
1			4		6		12		10^1	3^2			13					8			11^3					9	14	7	2	5				35
1			4		6			9	10				12	8^2			13									3^3	14	7	2	5	11^1			36
1			12		6▮			9^3	10^2	13			7	8			11^1									3	14	4	2	5				37
1		11^3	4^2	12			8	5	10				14	13									2^1			3	9	7		6				38
1		12	4		6		13	5	10^2				7^3	8^1												3	9	11		2	14			39
1			4		6		12	5	10					8			11^1									3	9	7▮		2				40
1			4		6			5	10				7^1	8			11^2									3	9		12	2	13			41
1			4		6▮		8	9	10^2				12				11						14			3	13	7^1	2^3	5				42
1			12				8^2	5	10					4^1			11						13			3	9^3	7	2	6	14			43
1			4^2				8	9	10	3			12	13			11^3									2		7^1	5	6	14			44
1			4				8	9^3	10	3			12	13			11^1									2		7^2	5	6	14			45
				12				13	10	11				4									14			2	9^2	7	5^3	6^1	8	1	3	46

FA Cup

Third Round	Blackpool	(h)	2-2
		(a)	1-0
Fourth Round	Reading	(a)	2-1
Fifth Round	Charlton Ath	(a)	2-1
Sixth Round	Blackburn R	(a)	0-1

Carling Cup

Second Round	Preston NE	(h)	2-3

LEYTON ORIENT FL Championship 2

FOUNDATION

There is some doubt about the foundation of Leyton Orient, and, indeed, some confusion with clubs like Leyton and Clapton over their early history. As regards the foundation, the most favoured version is that Leyton Orient was formed originally by members of Homerton Theological College who established Glyn Cricket Club in 1881 and then carried on through the following winter playing football. Eventually many employees of the Orient Shipping Line became involved and so the name Orient was chosen in 1888.

Matchroom Stadium, Brisbane Road, Leyton, London E10 5NE.

Telephone: (020) 8926 1111.

Fax: (020) 8926 1110.

Ticket Office: (020) 8926 1010.

Website: www.leytonorient.com

Email: info@leytonorient.net

Ground Capacity: 7,804.

Record Attendance: 34,345 v West Ham U, FA Cup 4th rd, 25 January 1964.

Pitch Measurements: 110yd × 80yd.

Chairman: Barry Hearn.

Vice-chairman: Nick Levene.

Chief Executive: Steve Dawson.

Manager: Martin Ling.

Assistant Manager: Dean Smith.

Secretary: Lindsey Freeman.

HONOURS

Football League: Division 1 best season: 22nd, 1962–63; Division 2 – Runners-up 1961–62; Division 3 – Champions 1969–70; Division 3 (S) – Champions 1955–56; Runners-up 1954–55; Promoted from Division 4 1988–89 (play-offs).

FA Cup: Semi-final 1978.

Football League Cup: best season: 5th rd, 1963.

Colours: Red shirts, red shorts, red stockings. ***Change Colours:*** Black shirts, black shorts, black stockings.

Year Formed: 1881. ***Turned Professional:*** 1903.

Ltd Co.: 1906.

Previous Names: 1881, Glyn Cricket and Football Club; 1886, Eagle Football Club; 1888, Orient Football Club; 1898, Clapton Orient; 1946, Leyton Orient; 1966, Orient; 1987, Leyton Orient.

Club Nickname: 'The O's'.

Previous Grounds: 1884, Glyn Road; 1896, Whittles Athletic Ground; 1900, Millfields Road; 1930, Lea Bridge Road; 1937, Brisbane Road.

First Football League Game: 2 September 1905, Division 2, v Leicester Fosse (a) L 1–2 – Butler; Holmes, Codling; Lamberton, Boden, Boyle; Kingaby (1), Wootten, Leigh, Evenson, Bourne.

Record League Victory: 8–0 v Crystal Palace, Division 3 (S), 12 November 1955 – Welton; Lee, Earl; Blizzard, Aldous, McKnight; White (1), Facey (3), Burgess (2), Heckman, Hartburn (2). 8–0 v Rochdale, Division 4, 20 October 1987 – Wells; Howard, Dickenson (1), Smalley (1), Day, Hull, Hales (2), Castle (Sussex), Shinners (2), Godfrey (Harvey), Comfort (2). 8–0 v Colchester U,

SKY SPORTS FACT FILE

Highlights of a disappointing 1951–52 season for Leyton Orient came from a 7–0 win over Colchester United on 5 January and two hat-tricks from Billy Rees in League and FA Cup games plus another treble in the Cup from Dennis Pacey.

Division 4, 15 October 1988 – Wells; Howard, Dickenson, Hales (1p), Day (1), Sitton (1), Baker (1), Ward, Hull (3), Juryeff, Comfort (1). 8–0 v Doncaster R, Division 3, 28 December 1997 – Hyde; Channing, Naylor, Smith (1p), Hicks, Clark, Ling, Joseph R, Griffiths (3) (Harris), Richards (2) (Baker (1)), Inglethorpe (1) (Simpson).

Record Cup Victory: 9–2 v Chester, League Cup 3rd rd, 15 October 1962 – Robertson; Charlton, Taylor; Gibbs, Bishop, Lea; Deeley (1), Waites (3), Dunmore (2), Graham (3), Wedge.

Record Defeat: 0–8 v Aston Villa, FA Cup 4th rd, 30 January 1929.

Most League Points (2 for a win): 66, Division 3 (S), 1955–56.

Most League Points (3 for a win): 75, Division 4, 1988–89.

Most League Goals: 106, Division 3 (S), 1955–56.

Highest League Scorer in Season: Tom Johnston, 35, Division 2, 1957–58.

Most League Goals in Total Aggregate: Tom Johnston, 121, 1956–58, 1959–61.

Most League Goals in One Match: 4, Wally Leigh v Bradford C, Division 2, 13 April 1906; 4, Albert Pape v Oldham Ath, Division 2, 1 September 1924; 4, Peter Kitchen v Millwall, Division 3, 21 April 1984.

Most Capped Players: Tunji Banjo, 7 (7), Nigeria; John Chiedozie, 7 (9), Nigeria; Tony Grealish, 7 (45), Eire.

Most League Appearances: Peter Allen, 432, 1965–78.

Youngest League Player: Paul Went, 15 years 327 days v Preston NE, 4 September 1965.

Record Transfer Fee Received: £600,000 from Notts Co for John Chiedozie, August 1981.

Record Transfer Fee Paid: £175,000 to Wigan Ath for Paul Beesley, October 1989.

Football League Record: 1905 Elected to Division 2; 1929–56 Division 3 (S); 1956–62 Division 2; 1962–63 Division 1; 1963–66 Division 2; 1966–70 Division 3; 1970–82 Division 2; 1982–85 Division 3; 1985–89 Division 4; 1989–92 Division 3; 1992–95 Division 2; 1995–2004 Division 3; 2004– FL2.

LATEST SEQUENCES

Longest Sequence of League Wins: 10, 21.1.1956 – 30.3.1956.

Longest Sequence of League Defeats: 9, 1.4.1995 – 6.5.1995.

Longest Sequence of League Draws: 6, 30.11.1974 – 28.12.1974.

Longest Sequence of Unbeaten League Matches: 13, 30.10.1954 – 19.2.1955.

Longest Sequence Without a League Win: 23, 6.10.1962 – 13.4.1963.

Successive Scoring Runs: 24 from 3.5.2003.

Successive Non-scoring Runs: 8 from 19.11.1994.

MANAGERS

Sam Omerod 1905–06
Ike Ivenson 1906
Billy Holmes 1907–22
Peter Proudfoot 1922–29
Arthur Grimsdell 1929–30
Peter Proudfoot 1930–31
Jimmy Seed 1931–33
David Pratt 1933–34
Peter Proudfoot 1935–39
Tom Halsey 1939
Bill Wright 1939–45
Willie Hall 1945
Bill Wright 1945–46
Charlie Hewitt 1946–48
Neil McBain 1948–49
Alec Stock 1949–59
Les Gore 1959–61
Johnny Carey 1961–63
Benny Fenton 1963–64
Dave Sexton 1965
Dick Graham 1966–68
Jimmy Bloomfield 1968–71
George Petchey 1971–77
Jimmy Bloomfield 1977–81
Paul Went 1981
Ken Knighton 1981
Frank Clark 1982–91 *(Managing Director)*
Peter Eustace 1991–94
Chris Turner/John Sitton 1994–95
Pat Holland 1995–96
Tommy Taylor 1996–2001
Paul Brush 2001–03
Martin Ling January 2004–

TEN YEAR LEAGUE RECORD

		P	W	D	L	F	A	Pts	Pos
1995-96	Div 3	46	12	11	23	44	63	47	21
1996-97	Div 3	46	15	12	19	50	58	57	16
1997-98	Div 3	46	19	12	15	62	47	66	11
1998-99	Div 3	46	19	15	12	68	59	72	6
1999-2000	Div 3	46	13	13	20	47	52	52	19
2000-01	Div 3	46	20	15	11	59	51	75	5
2001-02	Div 3	46	13	13	20	55	71	52	18
2002-03	Div 3	46	14	11	21	51	61	53	18
2003-04	Div 3	46	13	14	19	48	65	53	19
2004-05	FL 2	46	16	15	15	65	67	63	11

DID YOU KNOW ?

In the 1976–77 season Leyton Orient enjoyed a splendid run in the Anglo-Scottish Cup disposing of Norwich City, Chelsea, Aberdeen and Partick Thistle before reaching the final and losing to Nottingham Forest.

LEYTON ORIENT 2004–05 LEAGUE RECORD

Match No.	*Date*	*Venue*	*Opponents*	*Result*	*H/T Score*	*Lg. Pos.*	*Goalscorers*	*Attendance*
1	Aug 7	H	Macclesfield T	L 1-3	0-1	—	Purser [83]	4540
2	10	A	Cambridge U	D 1-1	1-0	—	Scott [41]	4114
3	14	A	Cheltenham T	W 2-1	1-0	13	Steele [35], Ibehre [68]	3346
4	21	H	Oxford U	D 0-0	0-0	13		3426
5	28	A	Northampton T	D 2-2	1-1	14	Carlisle 2 [6, 62]	5577
6	30	H	Rochdale	W 2-1	1-0	10	Steele [26], Newey [77]	3243
7	Sept 4	A	Kidderminster H	W 2-1	1-0	7	Alexander [20], Lockwood (pen) [69]	2367
8	11	H	Bristol R	W 4-2	1-1	3	Simpson [34], Steele [63], Alexander 2 [65, 70]	3972
9	18	A	Grimsby T	L 0-2	0-0	7		5082
10	25	H	Boston U	D 0-0	0-0	8		4753
11	Oct 2	A	Notts Co	W 2-1	1-1	6	Steele [20], Alexander [71]	5141
12	9	H	Bury	D 1-1	1-0	4	Steele [9]	3398
13	16	H	Shrewsbury T	W 4-1	3-0	1	Steele 2 [17, 85], Scott 2 [19, 25]	3718
14	19	A	Swansea C	L 0-1	0-1	—		8485
15	23	A	Lincoln C	W 4-3	2-2	2	Steele 3 [11, 78, 89], Ibehre [37]	4246
16	30	H	Scunthorpe U	D 1-1	0-0	2	Scott [51]	4359
17	Nov 6	A	Chester C	D 1-1	1-0	4	Steele [38]	3125
18	20	H	Wycombe W	L 1-2	1-0	4	Carlisle [29]	4047
19	27	A	Mansfield T	W 1-0	0-0	4	Scott [51]	3803
20	Dec 7	H	Southend U	D 2-2	1-2	—	Lockwood (pen) [15], Scott [59]	3852
21	11	A	Darlington	L 0-3	0-1	7		3702
22	18	H	Yeovil T	L 2-3	0-2	11	Echanomi [67], Chillingworth [74]	3867
23	26	A	Bristol R	D 1-1	1-0	10	Lockwood (pen) [6]	8414
24	28	H	Rushden & D	D 2-2	0-1	8	Echanomi [88], Chillingworth [90]	3777
25	Jan 1	H	Kidderminster H	W 2-1	0-1	7	Scott 2 [74, 84]	3573
26	3	A	Boston U	D 2-2	1-0	8	McMahon 2 [32, 90]	3183
27	8	A	Bury	D 0-0	0-0	7		2192
28	15	H	Grimsby T	L 1-2	0-1	10	Echanomi [81]	3816
29	22	A	Rushden & D	L 0-2	0-0	10		3288
30	29	H	Notts Co	W 2-0	0-0	10	Youngs [56], Barnard D [85]	3440
31	Feb 5	A	Shrewsbury T	L 1-4	0-1	12	Echanomi [90]	3496
32	12	H	Swansea C	W 3-1	2-0	12	Scott [15], McMahon [34], Lockwood (pen) [52]	4050
33	19	A	Scunthorpe U	L 0-1	0-0	14		5162
34	22	H	Lincoln C	D 1-1	0-1	—	Mackie [83]	2436
35	26	H	Darlington	W 1-0	1-0	11	Steele [26]	3430
36	Mar 5	A	Yeovil T	L 0-1	0-1	13		6545
37	12	H	Cambridge U	D 1-1	0-0	13	Lockwood [72]	3759
38	19	A	Macclesfield T	L 1-3	0-1	14	Steele [50]	2234
39	25	H	Cheltenham T	L 2-3	0-2	—	Alexander [50], Mackie [84]	3261
40	28	A	Oxford U	D 2-2	1-1	16	Steele [1], Simpson [72]	5320
41	Apr 2	H	Northampton T	W 3-2	1-0	13	Mackie [16], Steele 2 [63, 90]	3585
42	9	A	Rochdale	L 0-2	0-0	15		2255
43	15	A	Southend U	W 1-0	1-0	—	Mackie [22]	9189
44	23	H	Chester C	W 2-0	2-0	11	Echanomi [14], Lockwood (pen) [31]	3192
45	30	A	Wycombe W	L 2-3	0-3	13	Alexander 2 [48, 49]	5333
46	May 7	H	Mansfield T	W 2-1	2-0	11	Alexander 2 [26, 33]	3882

Final League Position: 11

GOALSCORERS

League (65): Steele 16, Alexander 9, Scott 9, Lockwood 6 (5 pens), Echanomi 5, Mackie 4, Carlisle 3, McMahon 3, Chillingworth 2, Ibehre 2, Simpson 2, Barnard D 1, Newey 1, Purser 1, Youngs 1.
Carling Cup (1): Steele 1.
FA Cup (3): Carlisle 1, Hunt 1, Lockwood 1.
LDV Vans Trophy (7): Ibehre 2, Alexander 1, Carlisle 1, Miller 1, Saah 1, own goal 1.

Morris G 12	Barnard D 22 + 11	Lockwood M 42 + 1	Hunt D 22 + 5	White A 26	Mackie J 26 + 1	Carlisle W 24 + 4	Simpson M 45	Alexander G 25 + 3	Steele L 37 + 2	Scott A 37 + 2	Purser W — + 2	Ibehre J 10 + 9	Newey T 3 + 17	Miller J 43	Zakuani G 32 + 1	Harrison L 34	Saah B 9 + 3	Peters M — + 2	Wardley S 4 + 2	Barnard L 3 + 5	Chillingworth D 8	Echanomi E 4 + 14	McMahon D 22 + 2	Duncan D 6 + 9	Fitzgerald S 1	Youngs T 6 + 4	Palmer A 3 + 2	Wallis S — + 3	*Match No.*
1	2	3	4	5	6	7^1	8	9^2	10	11^3	12	13	14																1
1		3	4	5		7	8		10	11^2	12	9^1	13	2	6														2
1		3	4	5		7	8	12	10	11^2	*	9^1	13	2	6														3
1		3	4	5		7^1	8	12	10	11		9		2	6														4
1		3	4	5		7	8	9	10^1	11^2		12	13	2	6														5
1	12	3	4	5		7^1	8	9^2	10	11^3		13	14	2	6														6
	12	3	4^3	5		7^1	8	9	10	11^2			13	2	6	1	14												7
	12	3	4	5		7^1	8	9	10^3	11^2		14	13	2	6	1													8
		3	4	5		7^2	8	9^1	10	11		12	13	2	6	1													9
	2	3	4	5■		7^3	8	9	10^1	11^2		12	13	6		1		14											10
	2	3	4			7	8	9	10	11				5	6^1	1		12											11
	2	3	4^1			7	8	9^2	10	11^3		13	12	5	6	1			14										12
	2	3	12	5		7	8	9^2	10	11^3		13	14	4		1			6^1										13
	2^3	3	12	5		7	8	9	10	11^2		13		4	14	1			6^1										14
		3	12	5		7^2	8		10	11		9	13	2	6	1			4^1										15
	12	3		5		7^2	8		10	11		9	13	2	6	1			4^1										16
		3	4	5		7	8		10	11		9		2	6	1													17
		3	4■	5		7^1	8		10	11^3		9	12	2^2	6	1			13	14									18
	2	3		5	6	7	8			11		9				1	4			10									19
	2	3^1	4	5	6	7	8			11		9	12			1					10^2	13							20
1		3	4	5	6	7^1	8			11^2		9	12	2						13	10								21
1		3	7^2		5		8			11			9	2	6		4^1				10	12	13						22
	2	3		5		12	8			11^2			13	7	6^1	1	4			9^3	10	14							23
		3		5	12		8			7			11	2	6^1	1	4^2			9^3	10	14	13						24
		3	12	5	6^1		8		13	11				2		1				14	10	9^3	7	4^2					25
	2	3	4		6				12	11				5		1	7			13	10^2	9^1	8						26
	2	3	12	5	6		8		9^3	11				4		1				13	10^2	14	7^1						27
		3		5	6		8		10	11^1			7^2	2		1						13	4	12	9■				28
	2	3	4	5	6		8	12	10	13				7		1						9^1	11^2						29
	12	3	4		6		8	9	10	11^2				5		1							7	13		2^1			30
	12	3	4^3		5		8	9	10	11				2		1						14	6^1	13		7^2			31
	12	3			5		8	9	10	11				2	6	1							4			7^1			32
	2				5		8	9■	10	11				3	6	1						12	4			7^1			33
	12	3			5		8		9	11				2	6	1						13	4	10^2		7^1			34
	2^3	3	4^2	5			8		9	11^1				7	6	1						13	10	12		14			35
	12	3^1			5	7^2	8		9	11				2	6	1						13■	4			10			36
	12	3			5	7^3	8	9	10	11^2				2	6	1							4^1	13		14			37
	2^2	3^1			5	12	8	9	10	13				4	6	1	11						7						38
1	12	3^1			5	7^3	8	9	10	11^2				2	6								4	13		14			39
1	3^2				5		8	9	10					2	6		11						4^1	12			7	13	40
1	3	12			5		8	9	10					2^1	6		11^2						4^3	13			7	14	41
1	3^3				5		8	9	10					2	6		11					12	7^2	13			4^1	14	42
	2	3^1			5		8	9	10					4	6	1							7	11			12		43
	2	3			5	12	8	9						4	6	1						10^2	7	11^1		13			44
	2	3^1			5		8	9	10					4	6	1	12					13	7^2	11^3			14		45
	2	3			5^1	12	8	9	10^3					4	6	1	13					14	7	11^2					46

FA Cup
First Round Dagenham & R (h) 3-1
Second Round Oldham Ath (a) 0-4

Carling Cup
First Round Bournemouth (h) 1-3

LDV Vans Trophy
First Round Woking (a) 3-0
Second Round Cambridge U (a) 2-0
Quarter-Final Walsall (h) 1-0
Semi-Final Bristol R (h) 1-2

LINCOLN CITY — FL Championship 2

FOUNDATION

The original Lincoln Football Club was established in the early 1860's and was one of the first provisional clubs to affiliate to the Football Association. In their early years, they regularly played matches against the famous Sheffield Club and later became known as Lincoln Lindum. The present organisation was formed at a public meeting held in the Monson Arms Hotel in June 1884 and won the Lincolnshire Cup in only their third season. They were founder members of the Midland League in 1889 and that competition's first champions.

Sincil Bank Stadium, Sincil Bank, Lincoln LN5 8LD.

Telephone: 0870 899 2005.

Fax: (01522) 880 020.

Ticket Office: 0870 899 2005.

Website: www.redimps.com

Email: lcfc@redimps.com

Ground Capacity: 10,127.

Record Attendance: 23,196 v Derby Co, League Cup 4th rd, 15 November 1967.

Pitch Measurements: 110yd × 71yd.

Vice-chairman: Steff Wright.

Cheif Executive: Dave Roberts.

Secretary: Fran Martin.

Manager: Keith Alexander.

Assistant Manager: Gary Simpson.

Physio: Keith Oakes.

Colours: Red and white.

Change Colours: Black.

Year Formed: 1884.

Turned Professional: 1892.

Ltd Co.: 1895.

Club Nickname: 'The Red Imps'.

Previous Grounds: 1883, John O'Gaunt's; 1894, Sincil Bank.

First Football League Game: 3 September 1892, Division 2, v Sheffield U (a) L 2–4 – W. Gresham; Coulton, Neill; Shaw, Mettam, Moore; Smallman, Irving (1), Cameron (1), Kelly, J. Gresham.

Record League Victory: 11–1 v Crewe Alex, Division 3 (N), 29 September 1951 – Jones; Green (1p), Varney; Wright, Emery, Grummett (1); Troops (1), Garvey, Graver (6), Whittle (1), Johnson (1).

Record Cup Victory: 8–1 v Bromley, FA Cup 2nd rd, 10 December 1938 – McPhail; Hartshorne, Corbett; Bean, Leach, Whyte (1); Hancock, Wilson (1), Ponting (3), Deacon (1), Clare (2).

HONOURS

Football League: Division 2 best season: 5th, 1901–02; Promotion from Division 3, 1997–98; Division 3 (N) – Champions 1931–32, 1947–48, 1951–52; Runners-up 1927–28, 1930–31, 1936–37; Division 4 – Champions 1975–76; Runners-up 1980–81.

FA Cup: best season: 1st rd of Second Series (5th rd equivalent), 1887, 2nd rd (5th rd equivalent), 1890, 1902.

Football League Cup: best season: 4th rd, 1968.

GM Vauxhall Conference: Champions 1987–88.

SKY SPORTS FACT FILE

The most successful season at the turnstiles for Lincoln City occurred in 1952–53 when an average attendance of 16,774 was recorded at Sincil Bank. The season after promotion they finished 15th in Division Two. Even the reserves averaged 5000.

Record Defeat: 3–11 v Manchester C, Division 2, 23 March 1895.

Most League Points (2 for a win): 74, Division 4, 1975–76.

Most League Points (3 for a win): 77, Division 3, 1981–82.

Most League Goals: 121, Division 3 (N), 1951–52.

Highest League Scorer in Season: Allan Hall, 41, Division 3 (N), 1931–32.

Most League Goals in Total Aggregate: Andy Graver, 143, 1950–55 and 1958–61.

Most League Goals in One Match: 6, Frank Keetley v Halifax T, Division 3N, 16 January 1932; 6, Andy Graver v Crewe Alex, Division 3N, 29 September 1951.

Most Capped Player: David Pugh, 3 (7), Wales; George Moulson, 3, Republic of Ireland.

Most League Appearances: Grant Brown, 407, 1989–2002.

Youngest League Player: Shane Nicholson, 16 years 172 days v Burnley, 22 November 1986.

Record Transfer Fee Received: £500,000 from Port Vale for Gareth Ainsworth, September 1997.

Record Transfer Fee Paid: £75,000 to Carlisle U for Dean Walling, September 1997 and £75,000 to Bury for Tony Battersby, August 1998.

Football League Record: 1892 Founder member of Division 2. Remained in Division 2 until 1920 when they failed re-election but also missed seasons 1908–09 and 1911–12 when not re-elected. 1921–32 Division 3 (N); 1932–34 Division 2; 1934–48 Division 3 (N); 1948–49 Division 2; 1949–52 Division 3 (N); 1952–61 Division 2; 1961–62 Division 3; 1962–76 Division 4; 1976–79 Division 3; 1979–81 Division 4; 1981–86 Division 3; 1986–87 Division 4; 1987–88 GM Vauxhall Conference; 1988–92 Division 4; 1992–98 Division 3; 1998–99 Division 2; 1999–2004 Division 3; 2004– FL2.

MANAGERS

David Calderhead 1900–07
John Henry Strawson 1907–14
(had been Secretary)
George Fraser 1919–21
David Calderhead Jnr. 1921–24
Horace Henshall 1924–27
Harry Parkes 1927–36
Joe McClelland 1936–46
Bill Anderson 1946–65
(General Manager to 1966)
Roy Chapman 1965–66
Ron Gray 1966–70
Bert Loxley 1970–71
David Herd 1971–72
Graham Taylor 1972–77
George Kerr 1977–78
Willie Bell 1977–78
Colin Murphy 1978–85
John Pickering 1985
George Kerr 1985–87
Peter Daniel 1987
Colin Murphy 1987–90
Allan Clarke 1990
Steve Thompson 1990–93
Keith Alexander 1993–94
Sam Ellis 1994–95
Steve Wicks *(Head Coach)* 1995
John Beck 1995–98
Shane Westley 1998
John Reames 1998–99
Phil Stant 2000–01
Alan Buckley 2001–02
Keith Alexander May 2002–

LATEST SEQUENCES

Longest Sequence of League Wins: 10, 1.9.1930 – 18.10.1930.

Longest Sequence of League Defeats: 12, 21.9.1896 – 9.1.1897.

Longest Sequence of League Draws: 5, 21.2.1981 – 7.3.1981.

Longest Sequence of Unbeaten League Matches: 18, 11.3.1980 – 13.9.1980.

Longest Sequence Without a League Win: 19, 22.8.1978 – 23.12.1978.

Successive Scoring Runs: 37 from 1.3.1930.

Successive Non-scoring Runs: 5 from 15.11.1913.

TEN YEAR LEAGUE RECORD

		P	W	D	L	F	A	Pts	Pos
1995-96	Div 3	46	13	14	19	57	73	53	18
1996-97	Div 3	46	18	12	16	70	69	66	9
1997-98	Div 3	46	20	15	11	60	51	72	3
1998-99	Div 2	46	13	7	26	42	74	46	23
1999-2000	Div 3	46	15	14	17	67	69	59	15
2000-01	Div 3	46	12	15	19	58	66	51	18
2001-02	Div 3	46	10	16	20	44	62	46	22
2002-03	Div 3	46	18	16	12	46	37	70	6
2003-04	Div 3	46	19	17	10	68	47	74	7
2004-05	FL 2	46	20	12	14	64	47	72	6

DID YOU KNOW ?

Ninth place out of 12 clubs in 1892–93 might not have astonished the football world but Lincoln City managed to score in each of their 22 Second Division games. Frank Smallman managed four in one and a hat-trick in another among his 17 League goals.

LINCOLN CITY 2004–05 LEAGUE RECORD

Match No.	*Date*	*Venue*	*Opponents*	*Result*		*H/T Score*	*Lg. Pos.*	*Goalscorers*	*Attendance*
1	Aug 7	A	Shrewsbury T	W	1-0	0-0	—	Taylor-Fletcher [52]	4843
2	10	H	Southend U	D	1-1	1-1	—	Taylor-Fletcher [9]	3991
3	14	H	Rushden & D	L	1-3	0-1	14	Taylor-Fletcher [55]	4127
4	21	A	Scunthorpe U	L	2-3	0-1	20	Taylor-Fletcher (pen) [76], Futcher [90]	5215
5	28	H	Notts Co	L	1-2	0-1	21	Taylor-Fletcher [90]	5173
6	30	A	Swansea C	L	0-1	0-1	22		6948
7	Sept 4	A	Bury	W	1-0	1-0	20	Bloomer [45]	3188
8	11	H	Boston U	D	2-2	1-0	19	McCombe [33], Green [59]	7142
9	18	A	Bristol R	D	0-0	0-0	19		7004
10	25	H	Chester C	D	1-1	1-1	18	Green [27]	3985
11	Oct 2	A	Mansfield T	D	2-2	2-1	17	McAuley [15], Yeo [45]	5349
12	9	H	Kidderminster H	W	3-0	1-0	16	Yeo [43], Sandwith [58], Taylor-Fletcher [74]	3605
13	16	A	Oxford U	W	1-0	1-0	14	Green [45]	4089
14	19	H	Rochdale	D	1-1	0-0	—	Bloomer [50]	3274
15	23	H	Leyton Orient	L	3-4	2-2	16	McAuley 2 [3, 48], Yeo [14]	4246
16	30	A	Cambridge U	W	1-0	0-0	13	Green [73]	3604
17	Nov 6	H	Northampton T	W	3-2	0-2	10	Yeo 2 [54, 57], Richardson [90]	4808
18	20	A	Darlington	W	3-0	2-0	5	Yeo [36], Richardson [45], Butcher [70]	4035
19	27	H	Yeovil T	W	3-1	2-0	5	Richardson 2 [30, 78], Taylor-Fletcher [45]	4714
20	Dec 7	A	Macclesfield T	L	1-2	0-0	—	McCombe [90]	1633
21	11	H	Cheltenham T	D	0-0	0-0	8		4097
22	18	A	Wycombe W	L	0-1	0-0	12		4277
23	29	H	Grimsby T	D	0-0	0-0	—		8056
24	Jan 1	H	Bury	W	1-0	1-0	9	Westcarr [24]	3962
25	3	A	Chester C	W	1-0	0-0	7	Yeo [90]	2839
26	8	A	Kidderminster H	L	1-2	1-1	8	Green [7]	2283
27	15	H	Bristol R	D	1-1	0-0	9	Green [62]	3929
28	22	A	Grimsby T	W	4-2	2-0	7	Yeo 3 [13, 27, 60], Toner [71]	7091
29	29	H	Mansfield T	W	2-0	0-0	6	Toner [54], Yeo [82]	5511
30	Feb 5	H	Oxford U	W	3-0	1-0	6	Yeo 2 (1 pen) [31 (p), 90], Taylor-Fletcher [57]	4535
31	12	A	Rochdale	L	1-3	1-1	6	Yeo (pen) [24]	2847
32	16	A	Boston U	W	2-0	1-0	—	Hanlon [36], Yeo [70]	6445
33	19	H	Cambridge U	W	2-1	2-0	5	Yeo [17], Taylor-Fletcher [26]	4672
34	22	A	Leyton Orient	D	1-1	1-0	—	Yeo [3]	2436
35	26	A	Cheltenham T	L	0-1	0-0	6		3187
36	Mar 5	H	Wycombe W	L	2-3	0-3	7	Sandwith [63], Yeo (pen) [68]	4250
37	12	A	Southend U	D	1-1	0-0	7	Futcher [87]	5824
38	19	H	Shrewsbury T	W	2-0	2-0	7	Green [4], Yeo [17]	4255
39	25	A	Rushden & D	W	4-1	1-1	—	Yeo [20], Futcher [75], McCombe [79], Taylor-Fletcher [83]	4213
40	28	H	Scunthorpe U	W	2-0	1-0	6	Yeo [1], Taylor-Fletcher [78]	6729
41	Apr 2	A	Notts Co	L	0-1	0-1	6		7103
42	9	H	Swansea C	W	1-0	0-0	6	Monk (og) [90]	5207
43	16	H	Macclesfield T	W	2-0	1-0	5	Butcher [33], Green [68]	5289
44	23	A	Northampton T	L	0-1	0-0	6		6435
45	30	H	Darlington	D	0-0	0-0	5		7753
46	May 7	A	Yeovil T	L	0-3	0-1	6		8855

Final League Position: 6

GOALSCORERS

League (64): Yeo 21 (3 pens), Taylor-Fletcher 11 (1 pen), Green 8, Richardson 4, Futcher 3, McAuley 3, McCombe 3, Bloomer 2, Butcher 2, Sandwith 2, Toner 2, Hanlon 1, Westcarr 1, own goal 1.
Carling Cup (4): Yeo 2 (1 pen), McCombe 1, Taylor-Fletcher 1 (pen).
FA Cup (0).
LDV Vans Trophy (0).
Play-offs (2): McAuley 2.

Marriott A 45	West D 4	Blackwood M 5 + 4	Weaver S 5	Morgan P 39	Futcher B 35	Butcher R 46	Green F 28 + 9	Taylor-Fletcher G 35 + 3	Yeo S 38 + 6	Gain P 36 + 4	McNamara N — + 1	Toner C 10 + 5	McAuley G 32 + 5	Richardson M 7 + 7	Littlejohn A 1 + 7	McCombe J 37 + 4	Bloomer M 31 + 6	Pearson G 1 + 2	Peat N 6 + 4	Sandwith K 34 + 3	Rayner S 1	Carruthers M 7 + 4	Kerley A — + 1	Ryan O — + 6	Hanlon R 6 + 6	Westcarr C 5 + 1	Hobbs J — + 1	Ipoua G — + 6	Bermingham K — + 2	Frecklington L — + 3	Beevers L 4 + 4	Asamoah D 8 + 2	Match No.
1	2	3	4	5	6	7	8^{1}	9^{2}	10^{3}	11	13	14	12																				1
1	2	3	4	5	6	7	8^{1}	9	10^{2}	11		12	13																				2
1	2^{2}	3	4	5	6	7	8^{1}	9	12	11			13	10^{3}	14																		3
1	2^{1}	3	4^{3}		6	7		9	10	11			12		13	14	5	8^{2}															4
1		3^{3}	4^{1}		6	7	12	9	10	11			2			8^{2}	5	13	14														5
1				5	6	7	12	9	13	11		8^{1}	2		10^{2}	14	3^{3}		4														6
1				5	6	7		9^{1}	10^{2}	11		12	4		13	3	2		8														7
1				5	6	7	8		10	11			4			9	2		3														8
1				5	6	7	8^{1}		10^{2}	11			4	12		9	2	13	3^{3}	14													9
				5	6	7	8^{2}	9	13	11			4	12■		10^{1}	2^{3}		3		1	14											10
1				5	6	7	12	9^{1}	10	11			4			13	2		3^{3}	14		8^{2}											11
1				5	6	7	12	9^{3}	10^{2}	11		13	4				2			3		8^{1}	14										12
1				5	6	7	8		10^{3}	11		14	4^{2}	12		13	2			3		9^{1}											13
1				5	6	7	8	12	10^{1}	11			4	13			2			3		9^{2}											14
1				5		7	8		10^{2}	11			4	12		6	2		13	3		9^{1}											15
1					6	7	8		10	11			4			5	2			3		9											16
1					6	7	8^{1}	12	10^{3}	11			4	13	14	5	2			3		9^{2}											17
1				5	6	7		9	10^{3}	11^{2}			4	8^{1}	12	2			13	3				14									18
1				5	6■	7		9	10^{2}	11^{1}			4	8	13	2	12			3													19
1				5	6	7		9	10	11				8^{1}		4	2			3		12											20
1				5	6	7	12	9^{3}	10^{2}	11				8^{1}	13	4	2		14	3													21
1				5	6	7			10			11^{2}	4^{1}	9		8	2			3		12			13								22
1				5	6	7	8		10			11^{2}		9^{1}		4	2			3		12			13								23
1				5	6	7	8	9^{1}	12			11				4	2			3					13	10^{2}							24
1				5	6	7	8	9	12			11				4	2			3						10^{1}							25
1		13		5	6	7	8	9	12^{2}			11		14		4	2			3^{1}						10^{3}							26
1				5		7	8	9		12		11	4			6	2^{2}			3						10^{1}	13						27
1				5		7		9	8^{1}	12		11	4			6	2			3						10							28
1		12		5		7	8^{1}	9	10^{3}	13		11	4			6^{2}	2			3						14							29
1				5		7	8^{2}	9	10	12		11^{1}	4			6	2			3				13									30
1				5		7	8	9	10				4^{3}			6	2^{1}			3^{2}					11			12	13	14			31
1				5		7	8	9^{1}	10	11						4	2			3					6			12					32
1				5		7	8	9^{1}	10	11						4	2			3					6			12					33
1				5		7	8	9^{1}	10	11						4	2			3					6						12		34
1				5		7	8	9^{3}	10	11			12			4^{1}	2			3					6^{2}			13		14			35
1		12				7	8^{2}	9	10	11			4			6	2^{3}			3^{1}								14	13		5		36
1					6	7	12	9	10^{1}	11			4			2				3								13			5	8^{2}	37
1		12			6	7	8^{2}		10^{3}	11			4			2	13			3				14							5	9^{1}	38
1				5	6	7	8^{3}	12	10	11			4^{2}			2	13			3					14							9^{1}	39
1				5	6	7	8^{3}	9^{1}	10^{2}	11			4			2	12			3				13								14	40
1				5	6	7	8^{2}	9	10	11			4			2				3^{1}				12								13	41
1				5	6	7	12	9	10	11			4			2				3												8^{1}	42
1				5	6	7	12	9^{2}	10	11			4			2	13			3^{3}											14	8^{1}	43
1				5	6	7	12	9^{2}	10	11			4			2				3^{1}					13						14	8^{3}	44
1				5	6	7		9^{1}	10^{2}	11			4			2	12			3					13						14	8^{3}	45
1				5	6	7		9		11^{1}			4			2				12				13	8^{3}					14	3	10^{2}	46

FA Cup
First Round | Hartlepool U | (a) | 0-3

Carling Cup
First Round | Derby Co | (h) | 3-1
Second Round | Birmingham C | (a) | 1-3

LDV Vans Trophy
First Round | Doncaster R | (h) | 0-1

Play-offs
Semi-Final | Macclesfield T | (h) | 1-0
| | (a) | 1-1
Final | Southend U | | 0-2
(at Millennium Stadium)

LIVERPOOL — FA Premiership

FOUNDATION

But for a dispute between Everton FC and their landlord at Anfield in 1892, there may never have been a Liverpool club. This dispute persuaded the majority of Evertonians to quit Anfield for Goodison Park, leaving the landlord, Mr John Houlding, to form a new club. He originally tried to retain the name 'Everton' but when this failed, he founded Liverpool Association FC on 15 March 1892.

Anfield Stadium, Anfield Road, Liverpool L4 0TH.

Telephone: (0151) 263 2361.

Fax: (0151) 260 8813.

Ticket Office: 0870 220 2345.

Website: www.liverpoolfc.tv

Email: customercontact@liverpoolfc.tv

Ground Capacity: 45,362.

Record Attendance: 61,905 v Wolverhampton W, FA Cup 4th rd, 2 February 1952.

Pitch Measurements: 101m × 68m.

Chairman: David Moores.

Chief Executive: Rick Parry BSC, FCA.

Secretary: Bryce Morrison.

Manager: Rafael Benitez.

Assistant Manager: Pako Ayestaran.

Physio: Dave Galley.

Colours: Red shirts, red shorts, red stockings.

Change Colours: White shirts, black shorts, white stockings.

Year Formed: 1892.

Turned Professional: 1892.

Ltd Co.: 1892.

Club Nicknames: 'Reds' or 'Pool'.

First Football League Game: 2 September 1893, Division 2, v Middlesbrough Ironopolis (a) W 2–0 – McOwen; Hannah, McLean; Henderson, McQue (1), McBride; Gordon, McVean (1), M. McQueen, Stott, H. McQueen.

Record League Victory: 10–1 v Rotherham T, Division 2, 18 February 1896 – Storer; Goldie, Wilkie; McCartney, McQue, Holmes; McVean (3), Ross (2), Allan (4), Becton (1), Bradshaw.

HONOURS

Football League: Division 1 – Champions 1900–01, 1905–06, 1921–22, 1922–23, 1946–47, 1963–64, 1965–66, 1972–73, 1975–76, 1976–77, 1978–79, 1979–80, 1981–82, 1982–83, 1983–84, 1985–86, 1987–88, 1989–90 (Liverpool have a record number of 18 League Championship wins); Runners-up 1898–99, 1909–10, 1968–69, 1973–74, 1974–75, 1977–78, 1984–85, 1986–87, 1988–89, 1990–91, 2001–02; Division 2 – Champions 1893–94, 1895–96, 1904–05, 1961–62.

FA Cup: Winners 1965, 1974, 1986, 1989, 1992, 2001; Runners-up 1914, 1950, 1971, 1977, 1988, 1996;

Football League Cup: Winners 1981, 1982, 1983, 1984, 1995, 2001, 2003; Runners-up 1978, 1987, 2005.

League Super Cup: Winners 1986.

European Competitions: *European Cup:* 1964–65, 1966–67, 1973–74, 1976–77 (winners), 1977–78 (winners), 1978–79, 1979–80, 1980–81 (winners), 1981–82, 1982–83, 1983–84 (winners), 1984–85 (runners-up). *Champions League:* 2001–02, 2002–03, 2004–05 (winners). *European Cup-Winners' Cup:* 1965–66 (runners-up), 1971–72, 1974–75, 1992–93, 1996–97 (s-f.). *European Fairs Cup:* 1967–68, 1968–69, 1969–70, 1970–71. *UEFA Cup:* 1972–73 (winners), 1975–76 (winners), 1991–92, 1995–96, 1997–98, 1998–99, 2000–01 (winners), 2002–03, 2003–04. *Super Cup:* 1977 (winners), 1978, 1984, 2001 (winners). *World Club Championship:* 1981 (runners-up), 1984 (runners-up).

SKY SPORTS FACT FILE

On 25 May 2005 Liverpool staged the most dramatic recovery in the history of the European Cup final. Having conceded three first half goals to AC Milan in Istanbul they hit three in a five minute spell and won the subsequent penalty shoot-out 3-2.

Record Cup Victory: 11–0 v Stromsgodset Drammen, ECWC 1st rd 1st leg, 17 September 1974 – Clemence; Smith (1), Lindsay (1p), Thompson (2), Cormack (1), Hughes (1), Boersma (2), Hall, Heighway (1), Kennedy (1), Callaghan (1).

Record Defeat: 1–9 v Birmingham C, Division 2, 11 December 1954.

Most League Points (2 for a win): 68, Division 1, 1978–79.

Most League Points (3 for a win): 90, Division 1, 1987–88.

Most League Goals: 106, Division 2, 1895–96.

Highest League Scorer in Season: Roger Hunt, 41, Division 2, 1961–62.

Most League Goals in Total Aggregate: Roger Hunt, 245, 1959–69.

Most League Goals in One Match: 5, Andy McGuigan v Stoke C, Division 1, 4 January 1902; 5, John Evans v Bristol R, Division 2, 15 September 1954; 5, Ian Rush v Luton T, Division 1, 29 October 1983.

Most Capped Player: Ian Rush, 67 (73), Wales.

Most League Appearances: Ian Callaghan, 640, 1960–78.

Youngest League Player: Max Thompson, 17 years 128 days v Tottenham H, 8 May 1974.

Record Transfer Fee Received: £12,500,000 from Leeds U for Robbie Fowler, November 2001.

Record Transfer Fee Paid: £14,000,000 (reported figure) to Auxerre for Djibril Cisse, July 2004.

Football League Record: 1893 Elected to Division 2; 1894–95 Division 1; 1895–96 Division 2; 1896–1904 Division 1; 1904–05 Division 2; 1905–54 Division 1; 1954–62 Division 2; 1962–92 Division 1; 1992– FA Premier League.

MANAGERS

W. E. Barclay 1892–96
Tom Watson 1896–1915
David Ashworth 1920–23
Matt McQueen 1923–28
George Patterson 1928–36
(continued as Secretary)
George Kay 1936–51
Don Welsh 1951–56
Phil Taylor 1956–59
Bill Shankly 1959–74
Bob Paisley 1974–83
Joe Fagan 1983–85
Kenny Dalglish 1985–91
Graeme Souness 1991–94
Roy Evans 1994–98
(then Joint Manager)
Gerard Houllier 1998–2004
Rafael Benitez June 2004–

LATEST SEQUENCES

Longest Sequence of League Wins: 12, 21.4.1990 – 6.10.1990.

Longest Sequence of League Defeats: 9, 29.4.1899 – 14.10.1899.

Longest Sequence of League Draws: 6, 19.2.1975 – 19.3.1975.

Longest Sequence of Unbeaten League Matches: 31, 4.5.1987 – 16.3.1988.

Longest Sequence Without a League Win: 14, 12.12.1953 – 20.3.1954.

Successive Scoring Runs: 29 from 27.4.1957.

Successive Non-scoring Runs: 5 from 22.12.1906.

TEN YEAR LEAGUE RECORD

		P	W	D	L	F	A	Pts	Pos
1995-96	PR Lge	38	20	11	7	70	34	71	3
1996-97	PR Lge	38	19	11	8	62	37	68	4
1997-98	PR Lge	38	18	11	9	68	42	65	3
1998-99	PR Lge	38	15	9	14	68	49	54	7
1999-2000	PR Lge	38	19	10	9	51	30	67	4
2000-01	PR Lge	38	20	9	9	71	39	69	3
2001-02	PR Lge	38	24	8	6	67	30	80	2
2002-03	PR Lge	38	18	10	10	61	41	64	5
2003-04	PR Lge	38	16	12	10	55	37	60	4
2004-05	PR Lge	38	17	7	14	52	41	58	5

DID YOU KNOW ?

Bob Paisley has the best record of any manager in Europe in the European Cup or the Champions League. His European Cup successes for Liverpool came in 1977, 1978 and 1981.

LIVERPOOL 2004–05 LEAGUE RECORD

Match No.	Date	Venue	Opponents	Result	H/T Score	Lg. Pos.	Goalscorers	Attendance
1	Aug 14	A	Tottenham H	D 1-1	1-0	—	Cisse [38]	35,105
2	21	H	Manchester C	W 2-1	0-1	5	Baros [48], Gerrard [75]	42,831
3	29	A	Bolton W	L 0-1	0-1	11		27,880
4	Sept 11	H	WBA	W 3-0	2-0	8	Gerrard [16], Finnan [42], Luis Garcia [60]	42,947
5	20	A	Manchester U	L 1-2	0-1	—	O'Shea (og) [54]	67,857
6	25	H	Norwich C	W 3-0	2-0	7	Baros [23], Luis Garcia [26], Cisse [64]	43,152
7	Oct 3	A	Chelsea	L 0-1	0-0	11		42,028
8	16	A	Fulham	W 4-2	0-2	7	Knight (og) [50], Baros [71], Alonso [79], Biscan [90]	21,884
9	23	H	Charlton Ath	W 2-0	0-0	6	Riise [52], Luis Garcia [74]	41,625
10	30	A	Blackburn R	D 2-2	1-2	6	Riise [7], Baros [54]	26,314
11	Nov 6	H	Birmingham C	L 0-1	0-0	8		42,669
12	13	H	Crystal Palace	W 3-2	2-1	8	Baros 3 (2 pens) [23 (p), 45, 90 (p)]	42,862
13	20	A	Middlesbrough	L 0-2	0-1	8		34,751
14	28	H	Arsenal	W 2-1	1-0	7	Alonso [41], Mellor [90]	43,730
15	Dec 4	A	Aston Villa	D 1-1	1-1	7	Kewell [16]	42,593
16	11	A	Everton	L 0-1	0-0	7		40552
17	14	H	Portsmouth	D 1-1	0-0	—	Gerrard [70]	35,064
18	19	H	Newcastle U	W 3-1	2-1	6	Bramble (og) [33], Mellor [38], Baros [61]	43,856
19	26	A	WBA	W 5-0	1-0	6	Riise 2 [17, 82], Sinama-Pongolle [51], Gerrard [55], Luis Garcia [89]	27,533
20	28	H	Southampton	W 1-0	1-0	6	Sinama-Pongolle [44]	42,382
21	Jan 1	H	Chelsea	L 0-1	0-0	6		43,886
22	3	A	Norwich C	W 2-1	0-0	5	Luis Garcia [58], Riise [64]	24,583
23	15	H	Manchester U	L 0-1	0-1	5		44,183
24	22	A	Southampton	L 0-2	0-2	5		32,017
25	Feb 1	A	Charlton Ath	W 2-1	0-1	—	Morientes [61], Riise [79]	27,102
26	5	H	Fulham	W 3-1	1-1	5	Morientes [9], Hyypia [63], Baros [77]	43,534
27	12	A	Birmingham C	L 0-2	0-2	5		29,318
28	Mar 5	A	Newcastle U	L 0-1	0-0	5		52,323
29	15	H	Blackburn R	D 0-0	0-0	—		37,763
30	20	H	Everton	W 2-1	2-0	5	Gerrard [27], Luis Garcia [32]	44,224
31	Apr 2	H	Bolton W	W 1-0	0-0	5	Biscan [86]	43,755
32	9	A	Manchester C	L 0-1	0-1	5		47,203
33	16	H	Tottenham H	D 2-2	1-1	6	Luis Garcia [44], Hyypia [63]	44,029
34	20	A	Portsmouth	W 2-1	2-1	—	Morientes [4], Luis Garcia [45]	20,205
35	23	A	Crystal Palace	L 0-1	0-1	5		26,043
36	30	H	Middlesbrough	D 1-1	0-1	5	Gerrard [52]	43,250
37	May 8	A	Arsenal	L 1-3	0-2	5	Gerrard [51]	38,119
38	15	H	Aston Villa	W 2-1	2-0	5	Cisse 2 (1 pen) [20 (p), 27]	43,406

Final League Position: 5

GOALSCORERS

League (52): Baros 9 (2 pens), Luis Garcia 8, Gerrard 7, Riise 6, Cisse 4 (1 pen), Morientes 3, Alonso 2, Biscan 2, Hyypia 2, Mellor 2, Sinama-Pongolle 2, Finnan 1, Kewell 1, own goals 3.
Carling Cup (10): Baros 2, Gerrard 2, Mellor 2, Diao 1, Nunez 1, Riise 1, Sinama-Pongolle 1 (pen).
FA Cup (0).
Champions League (20): Luis Garcia 5, Gerrard 4, Baros 2, Alonso 1, Cisse 1, Hamann 1, Hyypia 1, Mellor 1, Riise 1, Sinama-Pongolle 1, Smicer 1, own goal 1.

Dudek J 24	Josemi13 + 2	Riise J 34 + 3	Hamann D 23 + 7	Carragher J 38	Hyypia S 32	Finnan S 29 + 4	Gerrard S 28 + 2	Baros M 22 + 4	Cisse D 10 + 6	Kewell H 15 + 3	Biscan I 8 + 11	Sinama-Pongolle F 6 + 10	Warnock S 11 + 8	Diao S 4 + 4	Traore D 18 + 8	Luis Garcia26 + 3	Alonso X 20 + 4	Kirkland C 10	Mellor N 6 + 3	Nunez A 8 + 10	Pellegrino M 11 + 1	Morientes F 12 + 1	Raven D — + 1	Potter D — + 2	Smicer V 2 + 8	Carson S 4	Le Tallec A 2 + 2	Welsh J 2 + 1	Match No.
1	2	3	4^{1}	5	6	7	8	9^{3}	10^{2}	11	12	13	14																1
1	2^{3}	3	4	5	6	7^{2}	8	9	10	11^{1}	12		13	14															2
1	2	3	4	5	6^{2}		8	9	12				11^{1}		13	10	7												3
1	2	3	4	5	6	7	8^{3}	12	10	11^{1}					13	9^{2}	14												4
1	2	3	12	5	6	7	4^{1}	13	10^{2}	11						9	8												5
1		3	4	5	6	2		9	10^{1}		13		11^{2}	14	12	7	8^{3}												6
	2^{3}	11	12	5	6	13		14	9	10				4^{1}	3	8^{2}	7	1											7
	2■	11	4	5	6			9^{2}	10		13		12	8^{3}	3	7^{1}	14	1											8
		11^{1}	4	5	6	2		9^{3}	10	12		14	13		3^{2}	7	8	1											9
	2	11	4^{2}	5	6	7^{1}		9	10^{3}	12				13	3	14	8	1											10
	2	11^{3}	4^{2}	5	6	12				10	13	9^{1}			3	7	8	1	14										11
	2^{3}	11^{1}	4	5	6	12		9^{2}		10		13			3	7	8	1	14										12
	2^{3}	11	4^{1}	5	6	7	12			10	13	14			3	9	8^{2}	1											13
		3	4	5	6	2	7			11		10^{1}					8	1	9	12									14
	12	3	4	5	6	2	8^{2}			10		13			14		11	1	9^{3}	7^{1}									15
	2	3	4^{3}	5	6		8			11		10^{1}		7^{2}	12		13	1	9	14									16
1	12		4	5	6	2	8	9^{2}		10		13			3		11			7^{1}									17
1		3		5	6	2	4	9		11^{2}		12			13	7^{3}	8		10^{1}	14									18
1		11	4	5	6	2^{3}	8^{2}	9^{1}				10	14		3	12	13			7									19
1		3	12	5	6	2^{2}	4					10	11	13		7^{1}	8		9^{3}	14									20
1		11^{1}	4	5	6	2	8					10			3	7	9^{2}		12	13									21
1		3^{3}	12	5	6	2	8					13	11	4	14	10			9^{2}	7^{1}									22
1		11^{1}	4^{2}	2	6		8	9			13	12			3	7				14	5	10^{3}							23
1		11	4^{2}	2	6^{3}		8	9			13	12	3^{1}			7					5	10	14						24
1		11^{1}		5	6	2	8	9			4		12		3	7^{2}						10^{3}		13	14				25
1		11^{2}	12	5	6	2	8	9^{3}			4^{1}		13		3	7						10			14				26
1		11^{1}	4	5	6	2^{2}	8	9			7^{3}				3					12	13	10			14				27
		11		3	6	2	8	9^{1}			4		12			7				13	5^{3}				10^{2}	1	14		28
1		12	4	5		2	8	9^{3}			13		3^{2}			7				14	6	10			11^{1}				29
1		11	4^{1}	5		2	8	9■			12		3^{3}			7				14	6	10^{2}			13				30
		11^{1}		5		2	8				7				3	9				4^{3}	6	14			13	1	12	10^{2}	31
		11^{1}		5		2	8				4		3		12	7^{2}					6	10^{3}			13	1	9	14	32
1		12		3	6.	2	8		13		14		11^{1}			9	4^{3}			7^{2}	5	10							33
1		11		5	6	2	12	9^{2}	13		4^{1}				3	7^{3}	8					10			14				34
1		12		3	6	2	8	9^{3}	13						4^{2}						5^{1}	10		14			7	11	35
1		11	12	5		2	8		13	9			3^{1}			14	4			7^{2}	6^{3}	10							36
1		11^{2}	4^{3}	5	6	2	8	9^{1}	12	13					3	10	7								14				37
	2	11	12	5		13		14	9	10^{3}	4^{1}		3				8			7^{2}	6					1			38

FA Cup

Third Round	Burnley	(a)	0-1

Carling Cup

Third Round	Millwall	(a)	3-0
Fourth Round	Middlesbrough	(h)	2-0
Fifth Round	Tottenham H	(a)	1-1
Semi-Final	Watford	(h)	1-0
		(a)	1-0
Final (at Millennium Stadium)	Chelsea		2-3

Champions League

Third Qualifying Round	Graz	(a)	2-0
		(h)	0-1
Group A	Monaco	(h)	2-0
	Olympiakos	(a)	0-1
	La Coruna	(h)	0-0
		(a)	1-0
	Monaco	(a)	0-1
	Olympiakos	(h)	3-1
First Round	Leverkusen	(h)	3-1
		(a)	3-1
Quarter-Final	Juventus	(h)	2-1
		(a)	0-0
Semi-Final	Chelsea	(a)	0-0
		(h)	1-0
Final (in Istanbul)	AC Milan		3-3

LUTON TOWN FL Championship

FOUNDATION

Formed by an amalgamation of two leading local clubs, Wanderers and Excelsior a works team, at a meeting in Luton Town Hall in April 1885. The Wanderers had three months earlier changed their name to Luton Town Wanderers and did not take too kindly to the formation of another Town club but were talked around at this meeting. Wanderers had already appeared in the FA Cup and the new club entered in its inaugural season.

Kenilworth Stadium, 1 Maple Road, Luton, Beds LU4 8AW.

Telephone: (01582) 411 622.

Fax: (01582) 405 070.

Ticket Office: 0870 017 0656.

Website: www.lutontown.co.uk

Email: clubsec@lutontown.co.uk

Ground Capacity: 10,155.

Record Attendance: 30,069 v Blackpool, FA Cup 6th rd replay, 4 March 1959.

Pitch Measurements: 110yd × 72yd.

Chairman: Bill Tomlins.

Secretary: Cherry Newbery.

Manager: Mike Newell.

First Team Coach: Brian Stein.

Physio: Jon Bowden.

Colours: White shirts, black shorts, black stockings.

Change Colours: Black shirts, black shorts, black stockings.

Year Formed: 1885.

Turned Professional: 1890.

Ltd Co.: 1897.

Club Nickname: 'The Hatters'.

Previous Grounds: 1885, Excelsior, Dallow Lane; 1897, Dunstable Road; 1905, Kenilworth Road.

First Football League Game: 4 September 1897, Division 2, v Leicester Fosse (a) D 1–1 – Williams; McCartney, McEwen; Davies, Stewart, Docherty; Gallacher, Coupar, Birch, McInnes, Ekins (1).

Record League Victory: 12–0 v Bristol R, Division 3 (S), 13 April 1936 – Dolman; Mackey, Smith; Finlayson, Nelson, Godfrey; Rich, Martin (1), Payne (10), Roberts (1), Stephenson.

HONOURS

Football League: Championship 1 – Winners 2004–05; Division 1 best season: 7th, 1986–87; Division 2 – Champions 1981–82; Runners-up 1954–55, 1973–74; Division 3 – Runners-up 1969–70, 2001–02; Division 4 – Champions 1967–68; Division 3 (S) – Champions 1936–37; Runners-up 1935–36.

FA Cup: Runners-up 1959.

Football League Cup: Winners 1988; Runners-up 1989.

Simod Cup: Runners-up 1988.

SKY SPORTS FACT FILE

When Paul Walsh achieved a trio of hat-tricks for Luton Town in 1982–83, it was the first time one of their players had managed such a treble since Gordon Turner in 1957–58 who struck four hat-tricks the previous season.

Record Cup Victory: 9–0 v Clapton, FA Cup 1st rd (replay after abandoned game), 30 November 1927 – Abbott; Kingham, Graham; Black, Rennie, Fraser; Pointon, Yardley (4), Reid (2), Woods (1), Dennis (2).

Record Defeat: 0–9 v Small Heath, Division 2, 12 November 1898.

Most League Points (2 for a win): 66, Division 4, 1967–68.

Most League Points (3 for a win): 98, Championship 1 2004–05.

Most League Goals: 103, Division 3 (S), 1936–37.

Highest League Scorer in Season: Joe Payne, 55, Division 3 (S), 1936–37.

Most League Goals in Total Aggregate: Gordon Turner, 243, 1949–64.

Most League Goals in One Match: 10, Joe Payne v Bristol R, Division 3S, 13 April 1936.

Most Capped Player: Mal Donaghy, 58 (91), Northern Ireland.

Most League Appearances: Bob Morton, 495, 1948–64.

Youngest League Player: Mike O'Hara, 16 years 32 days v Stoke C, 1 October 1960.

Record Transfer Fee Received: £2,500,000 from Arsenal for John Hartson, January 1995.

Record Transfer Fee Paid: £850,000 to Odense for Lars Elstrup, August 1989.

Football League Record: 1897 Elected to Division 2; 1900 Failed re-election; 1920 Division 3; 1921–37 Division 3 (S); 1937–55 Division 2; 1955–60 Division 1; 1960–63 Division 2; 1963–65 Division 3; 1965–68 Division 4; 1968–70 Division 3; 1970–74 Division 2; 1974–75 Division 1; 1975–82 Division 2; 1982–96 Division 1; 1996–2001 Division 2; 2001–02 Division 3; 2002–04 Division 2; 2004–05 FL1; 2005– FLC.

MANAGERS

Charlie Green 1901–28
(Secretary-Manager)
George Thomson 1925
John McCartney 1927–29
George Kay 1929–31
Harold Wightman 1931–35
Ted Liddell 1936–38
Neil McBain 1938–39
George Martin 1939–47
Dally Duncan 1947–58
Syd Owen 1959–60
Sam Bartram 1960–62
Bill Harvey 1962–64
George Martin 1965–66
Allan Brown 1966–68
Alec Stock 1968–72
Harry Haslam 1972–78
David Pleat 1978–86
John Moore 1986–87
Ray Harford 1987–89
Jim Ryan 1900–91
David Pleat 1991–95
Terry Westley 1995
Lennie Lawrence 1995–2000
Ricky Hill 2000
Lil Fuccillo 2000
Joe Kinnear 2001–03
Mike Newell June 2003–

LATEST SEQUENCES

Longest Sequence of League Wins: 12, 19.2.2002 – 6.4.2002.

Longest Sequence of League Defeats: 8, 11.11.1899 – 6.1.1900.

Longest Sequence of League Draws: 5, 28.8.1971 – 18.9.1971.

Longest Sequence of Unbeaten League Matches: 19, 8.4.1969 – 7.10.1969.

Longest Sequence Without a League Win: 16, 9.9.1964 – 6.11.1964.

Successive Scoring Runs: 25 from 24.10.1931.

Successive Non-scoring Runs: 5 from 10.4.1973.

TEN YEAR LEAGUE RECORD

		P	W	D	L	F	A	Pts	Pos
1995-96	Div 1	46	11	12	23	40	64	45	24
1996-97	Div 2	46	21	15	10	71	45	78	3
1997-98	Div 2	46	14	15	17	60	64	57	17
1998-99	Div 2	46	16	10	20	51	60	58	12
1999-2000	Div 2	46	17	10	19	61	65	61	13
2000-01	Div 2	46	9	13	24	52	80	40	22
2001-02	Div 3	46	30	7	9	96	48	97	2
2002-03	Div 2	46	17	14	15	67	62	65	9
2003-04	Div 2	46	17	15	14	69	66	66	10
2004-05	FL 1	46	29	11	6	87	48	98	1

DID YOU KNOW ?

Luton Town suffered only one real spell of poor form during their championship winning season of 2004–05 and incredibly this came after the first dozen unbeaten games. They then lost three in a row but were able to get back on course.

LUTON TOWN 2004–05 LEAGUE RECORD

Match No.	Date	Venue	Opponents	Result	H/T Score	Lg. Pos.	Goalscorers	Attendance
1	Aug 7	H	Oldham Ath	W 2-1	1-1	—	Howard [19], Underwood [65]	6634
2	11	A	Swindon T	W 3-2	2-1	—	Nicholls (pen) [24], Fallon (og) [37], Howard [51]	6286
3	14	A	Barnsley	W 4-3	3-1	2	Howard [4], Vine [44], Brkovic [45], Robinson [66]	10,057
4	21	H	Torquay U	W 1-0	1-0	1	Howard [36]	6664
5	28	A	Blackpool	W 3-1	0-1	1	Howard [58], Brkovic 2 [59, 90]	5793
6	30	H	Bournemouth	W 1-0	0-0	1	Nicholls [81]	7404
7	Sept 4	A	Sheffield W	D 0-0	0-0	1		20,806
8	11	H	Chesterfield	W 1-0	0-0	1	Vine [49]	7532
9	18	A	Stockport Co	W 3-1	2-0	1	Robinson [33], Vine [35], Brkovic [54]	5128
10	25	H	Peterborough U	W 2-1	1-0	1	Vine [31], Underwood [57]	7694
11	Oct 2	A	Tranmere R	D 1-1	0-1	1	Coyne [76]	10,884
12	8	H	Hartlepool U	W 3-0	1-0	—	Howard [36], Brkovic [51], McSheffrey [84]	7865
13	16	H	Huddersfield T	L 1-2	0-2	1	Underwood [57]	8192
14	19	A	Walsall	L 0-2	0-1	—		5963
15	23	A	Hull C	L 0-3	0-3	1		18,575
16	30	H	Bradford C	W 4-0	3-0	1	Brkovic 2 [14, 69], Howard [33], Underwood [37]	7975
17	Nov 6	H	Wrexham	W 5-1	4-0	1	Robinson [13], Davis [17], O'Leary [22], Howard [44], Brkovic [62]	7144
18	20	A	Milton Keynes D	W 4-1	2-1	1	Vine [8], Howard 3 [44, 66, 83]	7620
19	27	H	Doncaster R	D 1-1	0-0	1	Nicholls [60]	8142
20	Dec 7	A	Brentford	L 0-2	0-1	—		6393
21	11	H	Port Vale	W 1-0	0-0	1	Brkovic [84]	6974
22	18	A	Bristol C	W 2-1	1-0	1	Coyne [34], Showunmi [90]	13,414
23	26	A	Chesterfield	W 1-0	0-0	1	Showunmi [87]	7158
24	28	H	Colchester U	D 2-2	1-1	1	Vine 2 [37, 48]	8806
25	Jan 1	H	Sheffield W	D 1-1	0-1	1	Howard [47]	9500
26	3	A	Peterborough U	D 2-2	0-0	2	Nicholls [54], Howard [85]	7662
27	15	H	Stockport Co	W 3-0	1-0	1	Coyne [29], Howard [54], Nicholls (pen) [74]	6603
28	22	A	Colchester U	D 0-0	0-0	1		4309
29	29	H	Tranmere R	D 1-1	0-1	1	Nicholls (pen) [54]	8594
30	Feb 5	A	Huddersfield T	D 1-1	1-0	1	Brkovic [34]	12,611
31	12	H	Hull C	W 1-0	0-0	1	Brkovic [89]	9500
32	15	A	Hartlepool U	W 3-2	1-0	—	Coyne [21], Showunmi [58], Foley [64]	5542
33	19	A	Bradford C	W 1-0	1-0	1	Vine [10]	8702
34	22	H	Walsall	W 1-0	0-0	—	Nicholls (pen) [88]	7236
35	26	A	Port Vale	L 1-3	1-1	1	Foley [6]	5353
36	Mar 5	H	Bristol C	W 5-0	3-0	1	Brkovic 2 [10, 79], Nicholls (pen) [26], Davis [45], Holmes [61]	8330
37	12	H	Swindon T	W 3-1	2-1	1	Nicholls (pen) [13], Brkovic [27], Holmes [84]	8173
38	19	A	Oldham Ath	D 2-2	1-1	1	Underwood [6], Howard [90]	5809
39	25	H	Barnsley	L 1-3	0-3	—	Showunmi [67]	7548
40	28	A	Torquay U	W 4-1	2-1	1	Nicholls [23], Holmes [32], Howard [51], Vine [71]	4264
41	Apr 2	H	Blackpool	W 1-0	1-0	1	Howard [15]	7806
42	9	A	Bournemouth	W 1-0	0-0	1	Showunmi [84]	9058
43	16	H	Milton Keynes D	W 1-0	1-0	1	Chorley (og) [31]	9000
44	23	A	Wrexham	W 2-1	0-1	1	Davies [52], Coyne [59]	6614
45	30	H	Brentford	W 4-2	1-2	1	Brkovic [5], Nicholls (pen) [84], Showunmi [89], Robinson [90]	9313
46	May 7	A	Doncaster R	D 3-3	2-1	1	Perrett [32], Howard [36], Nicholls [63]	8928

Final League Position: 1

GOALSCORERS

League (87): Howard 18, Brkovic 15, Nicholls 12 (7 pens), Vine 9, Showunmi 6, Coyne 5, Underwood 5, Robinson 4, Holmes 3, Davis 2, Foley 2, Davies 1, McSheffrey 1, O'Leary 1, Perrett 1, own goals 2.
Carling Cup (3): Nicholls 1 (pen), Showunmi 1, own goal 1.
FA Cup (6): Howard 4, Brkovic 1, Nicholls 1.
LDV Vans Trophy (0).

Beresford M 38	Foley K 38 + 1	Davis S 45	Robinson S 28 + 3	Davies C 44	Coyne C 39 + 1	O'Leary S 12 + 5	Nicholls K 44	Howard S 40	Vine R 43 + 2	Underwood P 37	Brkovic A 39 + 3	Showunmi E 7 + 28	Neilson A 6 + 3	Keane K 11 + 6	Leary M 1 + 7	McSheffrey G 1 + 4	Seremet D 6 + 1	Holmes P 13 + 6	Blinkhorn M — + 2	Royce S 2	Perrett R 9 + 3	Andrew C 2 + 6	Mansell L — + 1	Feeney W 1 + 5	*Match No.*
1	2	3	4	5	6	7^{1}	8	9	10^{2}	11	12	13													1
1	2^{3}	3	4	5	6	7^{1}	8	9	10^{2}	11	12	13	14												2
1	2^{3}	3	4	5	6	7^{1}	8	9	10^{2}	11	12	13	14												3
1		3	4	5	6		8	9	10^{1}	7	11	12		2											4
1		3	4	5	6		8	9	10	7	11			2											5
1	2	3	4	5	6		8	9	10^{1}	7	11	12													6
1		3	4	5	6		8	9	10	7	11			2											7
1	2	3	4^{2}	5	6		8	9	10^{1}	7	11	12			13										8
1	2	3	4^{1}	5	6		8	9	10^{3}	7	11^{2}			13	12	14									9
1^{6}	2	3	4	5	6		8	9	10^{1}	7	11					12	15								10
	2	3	4	5	6		8		10	7	11					9	1								11
		3	4	5	6	12	8	9^{3}	10^{2}	7	11^{1}	14		2		13	1								12
	2^{1}	3		5	6	13	8	9	10	7^{2}	11	12			4^{3}	14	1								13
	2	3	4	5	6	12	8	9	10^{2}	7	11^{1}	13					1								14
	2	3^{1}	4	5	6	7^{2}	8■	9^{3}	10	11		12					1	13	14						15
	2	3	4	5	6^{2}	7		9	10^{1}	11	8								12	1	13				16
	2	3	4^{2}	5	6	7		9	10^{1}	11	8	12			13					1					17
1	2	3^{2}		5	6	4	8	9	10	7	11^{1}			12				13							18
1	2	3		5	6	4^{2}	8	9	10	7^{3}	11^{1}	12		13				14							19
1		3		5	6	4	8	9■	10^{1}	7	11^{2}	12		2								13			20
1	2	3		5	6	4	8		10	7	11	12										9^{1}			21
1	2	3		5	6		8		10	7	11	9						4							22
1	2	3			6		8			7	11	10						4			5	9			23
1	2	3	4	5	6^{2}		8	9	10		11	12						7^{1}			13				24
1	2	3	4	5	6		8	9	10	7	11														25
1	2	3	12	5		7^{1}	8	9	13	11		10^{2}						4^{3}			6	14			26
1	2		4	3	6		8^{2}	9^{1}	10	7^{3}	11	12	5	14				13							27
1	2	3	4	5	6		8	9	10^{1}	11^{2}		12		7				13							28
1	2	3	4	5	6		8	9	10		11			7											29
1	2	3	4	5			8	9	10^{2}		11^{1}		12	7							6	13			30
1	7	3	4	5	6	12	8		10		11^{1}	9^{2}	2									13			31
1	7	3	4	5	6		8		10		11	9	2^{1}	12											32
1	7	3	4	5	6		8	9	10^{1}		11	12	2												33
1	7	3	4^{1}	5	6	12	8	9	10		11	13	2^{2}												34
1	7^{1}	3		5	6^{2}	4^{3}	8	9	10		11	12	2					14			13				35
1		3^{1}		5			8	9	10^{3}	7	11	12		2	13			4^{2}			6	14			36
1	12	3		5			8	9	10^{2}	7	11^{1}	13		2^{3}	14			4			6				37
1	2	3		5	6		8	9	10^{1}	7^{2}	11	12		13				4							38
1		3		5	6■		8	9	10	11		7^{2}		2	12			4^{1}				13			39
1	2	3		5			8	9	10	7^{1}	11							4			6		12		40
1	2	3		5			8	9	10^{3}	7^{1}	11^{2}	12			13			4			6			14	41
1	2	3		5	12		8	9	10^{1}	7	11^{3}	13						4^{2}			6■			14	42
1	2	3	12	5	6		8	9	10^{3}	7	11^{2}	13						4^{1}						14	43
1	2	3	12	5	6		8	9	10^{2}		11	7^{1}						4						13	44
1	2	3	4	5	6		8	9	12	7	11^{2}	13												10^{1}	45
	2	3	4		6		8	9	10^{2}	7	11^{1}	12					1				5			13	46

FA Cup

First Round	Southend U	(a)	3-0
Second Round	Wycombe W	(a)	3-0
Third Round	Brentford	(h)	0-2

Carling Cup

First Round	Boston U	(a)	3-4

LDV Vans Trophy

First Round	Swansea C	(a)	0-2

MACCLESFIELD TOWN FL Championship 2

FOUNDATION

From the mid-19th Century until 1874, Macclesfield Town FC played under rugby rules. In 1891 they moved to the Moss Rose and finished champions of the Manchester & District League in 1906 and 1908. By 1911, they had carried off the Cheshire Senior Cup five times. Macclesfield were founder members of the Cheshire County League in 1919.

Moss Rose Ground, London Road, Macclesfield, Cheshire SK11 7SP.

Telephone: (01625) 264 686.

Fax: (01625) 264 692.

Ticket Office: (01625) 264 686.

Website: www.mtfc.co.uk

Email: admin@mtfc.co.uk

Ground Capacity: 6,208.

Record Attendance: 9008 v Winsford U, Cheshire Senior Cup 2nd rd, 4 February 1948.

Pitch Measurements: 100m × 66m.

Chairman: Robert Bickerton.

Deputy Chairman: Alan Cash.

Chief Executive/Secretary: Colin Garlick.

Manager: Brian Horton.

Assistant Manager: John Askey.

Physio: Paul Lake.

Colours: Blue shirts, white shorts, blue stockings.

Change Colours: White shirts, blue shorts, white stockings.

Year formed: 1874.

Club Nickname: 'The Silkmen'.

Previous Ground: 1874, Rostron Field; 1891, Moss Rose.

First Football League Game: 9 August 1997, Division 3, v Torquay U (h) W 2–1 – Price; Tinson, Rose, Payne (Edey), Howarth, Sodje (1), Askey, Wood, Landon (1) (Power), Mason, Sorvel.

Record League Victory: 5–2 v Mansfield T, Division 3, 2 November 1999 – Martin; Ingram, Rioch, Collins, Tinson, Sedgemore (1), Askey (1), Priest (1), Barker (2), Davies (Wood), Durkan.

HONOURS

Football League: Division 3 – Runners-up 1997–98.

FA Cup: best season: 3rd rd, 1968, 1988, 2002, 2003, 2004.

Football League Cup: never past 2nd rd.

Vauxhall Conference: Champions 1994–95, 1996–97.

FA Trophy: Winners 1969–70, 1995–96; Runners-up 1988–89.

Bob Lord Trophy: Winners 1993–94; Runners-up 1995–96, 1996–97.

Vauxhall Conference Championship Shield: Winners 1996, 1997, 1998.

Northern Premier League: Winners 1968–69, 1969–70, 1986–87; Runners-up 1984–85.

Northern Premier League Challenge Cup: Winners 1986–87; Runners-up 1969–70, 1970–71, 1982–83.

Northern Premier League Presidents Cup: Winners 1986–87; Runners-up 1984–85.

Cheshire Senior Cup: Winners 20 times; Runners-up 11.

SKY SPORTS FACT FILE

In August 1949 Macclesfield Town secured the services from Sheffield United of Eric Barber, a 23 year old centre-forward. In six months they were able to transfer him to Bolton Wanderers for a then club record fee of £1500.

Record Win: 15–0 v Chester St Marys, Cheshire Senior Cup, 2nd rd, 16 February 1886.

Record Defeat: 1–13 v Tranmere R reserves, 3 May 1929.

Most League Points (3 for a win): 82, Division 3, 1997–98.

Most League Goals: 66, Division 3, 1999–2000.

Highest League Scorer in Season: Richard Barker, 16, Division 3, 1999–2000.

Most League Goals in Total Aggregate: John Askey, 31, 1997–2003.

Most Capped Player: George Abbey, 10, Nigeria.

Most League Appearances: Darren Tinson, 263, 1997–2003.

Youngest League Player: Peter Griffiths, 18 years 44 days v Reading, 26 September 1998.

Record Transfer Fee Received: £250,000 from Stockport Co for Rickie Lambert, April 2002.

Record Transfer Fee Paid: £40,000 to Bury for Danny Swailes, January 2005.

Football League Record: 1997 Promoted to Division 3; 1998–99 Division 2; 1999–2004 Division 3; 2004– FL2.

MANAGERS

Since 1967
Keith Goalen 1967–68
Frank Beaumont 1968–72
Billy Haydock 1972–74
Eddie Brown 1974
John Collins 1974
Willie Stevenson 1974
John Collins 1975–76
Tony Coleman 1976
John Barnes 1976
Brian Taylor 1976
Dave Connor 1976–78
Derek Partridge 1978
Phil Staley 1978–80
Jimmy Williams 1980–81
Brian Booth 1981–85
Neil Griffiths 1985–86
Roy Campbell 1986
Peter Wragg 1986–93
Sammy McIlroy 1993–2000
Peter Davenport 2000
Gil Prescott 2001
David Moss 2001–03
John Askey 2003–04
Brian Horton April 2004–

LATEST SEQUENCES

Longest Sequence of League Wins: 6, 25.1.2005 – 26.2.2005.

Longest Sequence of League Defeats: 6, 26.12.1998 –6.2.1999.

Longest Sequence of League Draws: 3, 27.9.1997 – 11.10.1997.

Longest Sequence of Unbeaten League Matches: 8, 16.10.1999 – 27.11.1999.

Longest Sequence Without a League Win: 10, 21.11.1998 – 6.2.1999.

Successive Scoring Runs: 14 from 11.10.2003.

Successive Non-scoring Runs: 5 from 18.12.1998.

TEN YEAR LEAGUE RECORD

		P	*W*	*D*	*L*	*F*	*A*	*Pts*	*Pos*
1995-96	Conf.	42	22	9	11	66	49	75	4
1996-97	Conf.	42	27	9	6	80	30	90	1
1997-98	Div 3	46	23	13	10	63	44	82	2
1998-99	Div 2	46	11	10	25	43	63	43	24
1999-2000	Div 3	46	18	11	17	66	61	65	13
2000-01	Div 3	46	14	14	18	51	62	56	14
2001-02	Div 3	46	15	13	18	41	52	58	13
2002-03	Div 3	46	14	12	20	57	63	54	16
2003-04	Div 3	46	13	13	20	54	69	52	20
2004-05	FL 2	46	22	9	15	60	49	75	5

DID YOU KNOW ?

The 1994–95 season saw Macclesfield Town set a Conference record at the time of ten consecutive victories on the way to the title. This despite a slump in the last third of the campaign which produced only two wins in 13 fixtures.

MACCLESFIELD TOWN 2004–05 LEAGUE RECORD

Match No.	Date	Venue	Opponents	Result		H/T Score	Lg. Pos.	Goalscorers	Attendance
1	Aug 7	A	Leyton Orient	W	3-1	1-0	—	Tipton [40], Parkin 2 [74, 82]	4540
2	10	H	Shrewsbury T	W	2-1	2-0	—	Parkin [18], Barras [28]	2641
3	14	H	Swansea C	W	1-0	1-0	1	Parkin [17]	2164
4	21	A	Boston U	D	1-1	0-0	2	Parkin [79]	2736
5	28	H	Scunthorpe U	D	2-2	1-1	3	Harsley [45], Tipton (pen) [71]	2321
6	30	A	Southend U	L	1-2	0-1	5	Whitaker [51]	3753
7	Sept 4	A	Chester C	L	0-1	0-0	9		2913
8	11	H	Grimsby T	W	3-1	0-1	5	Harsley [67], Miles [71], Potter [83]	2128
9	18	A	Kidderminster H	L	0-1	0-0	8		2290
10	25	H	Darlington	W	1-0	0-0	6	Bailey [47]	1872
11	Oct 2	A	Bury	L	1-2	1-1	8	Tipton [9]	2859
12	10	H	Notts Co	L	1-2	1-0	10	Parkin [17]	2456
13	16	A	Yeovil T	W	2-1	1-0	6	Skiverton (og) [24], Parkin [86]	5313
14	19	H	Cambridge U	D	1-1	0-1	—	Tipton [49]	1436
15	23	H	Oxford U	W	1-0	0-0	5	Sheron [50]	2007
16	30	A	Rochdale	L	0-3	0-1	6		2704
17	Nov 6	A	Mansfield T	W	1-0	1-0	6	Sheron [41]	3816
18	20	H	Cheltenham T	L	0-2	0-0	8		1796
19	27	A	Rushden & D	W	2-0	1-0	6	Potter [44], Parkin [89]	2643
20	Dec 7	H	Lincoln C	W	2-1	0-0	—	Parkin 2 [82, 89]	1633
21	11	A	Bristol R	D	0-0	0-0	4		6504
22	18	H	Northampton T	L	1-3	0-0	7	Potter [64]	2073
23	26	A	Grimsby T	D	0-0	0-0	5		5108
24	28	H	Wycombe W	W	2-1	1-0	5	Whitaker [6], Navarro [90]	1908
25	Jan 1	H	Chester C	L	1-2	1-0	6	Sheron [19]	3076
26	3	A	Darlington	L	1-3	1-2	9	Parkin [42]	3677
27	15	H	Kidderminster H	W	2-0	1-0	7	Tipton [18], Parkin [54]	2001
28	22	A	Wycombe W	D	1-1	1-0	8	Parkin [36]	4105
29	25	A	Notts Co	W	5-0	2-0	—	Tipton [26], Parkin 3 (1 pen) [38, 57, 90 (p)], Welch [83]	3586
30	29	H	Bury	W	2-1	0-1	5	Welch [48], Parkin [89]	2513
31	Feb 5	H	Yeovil T	W	3-1	1-0	4	Tipton [38], Potter 2 [46, 83]	2471
32	12	A	Cambridge U	W	1-0	0-0	4	Potter [80]	2926
33	19	H	Rochdale	W	3-0	2-0	4	Tipton 3 [8, 12, 90]	3031
34	26	H	Bristol R	W	2-1	1-0	3	Parkin 2 [45, 62]	2114
35	Mar 5	A	Northampton T	L	0-1	0-1	4		5804
36	12	A	Shrewsbury T	W	1-0	0-0	3	Miles [81]	4262
37	19	H	Leyton Orient	W	3-1	1-0	3	Parkin [33], Tipton (pen) [53], Harsley [74]	2234
38	25	A	Swansea C	L	0-2	0-2	—		9809
39	28	H	Boston U	D	1-1	0-1	5	Bailey [84]	2501
40	Apr 2	A	Scunthorpe U	D	0-0	0-0	5		5536
41	6	A	Oxford U	D	1-1	0-1	—	Miles [87]	4273
42	16	A	Lincoln C	L	0-2	0-1	6		5289
43	19	H	Southend U	L	1-2	1-1	—	Morley [28]	2768
44	23	H	Mansfield T	W	3-1	1-0	5	Parkin [6], Tipton [58], Morley [62]	2456
45	30	A	Cheltenham T	L	0-3	0-1	6		3622
46	May 7	H	Rushden & D	W	1-0	0-0	5	Parkin [60]	2658

Final League Position: 5

GOALSCORERS

League (60): Parkin 22 (1 pen), Tipton 12 (2 pens), Potter 6, Harsley 3, Miles 3, Sheron 3, Bailey 2, Morley 2, Welch 2, Whitaker 2, Barras 1, Navarro 1, own goal 1.
Carling Cup (1): Parkin 1.
FA Cup (3): Parkin 1, Sheron 1, Whitaker 1.
LDV Vans Trophy (6): Parkin 2, Tipton 2, Barras 1, Whitaker 1.
Play-offs (1): Harsley 1.

Fettis A 28	Bailey M 20 + 1	Potter G 39 + 2	Welch M 31	Barras T 22 + 2	Briscoe M 12 + 2	Whitaker D 26 + 10	Widdrington T 21 + 2	Tipton M 40 + 4	Parkin J 42	Harsley P 44 + 2	Sheron M 14 + 12	Wilson S 18 + 1	Brightwell I 3 + 3	Miles J 14 + 16	Carragher M 26 + 5	Swadi-Fayadh J — + 1	Weaver S 7	Rooney T — + 1	MacKenzie N 16 + 2	Teague A 5	Navarro A 11	Strong G 4	McIntyre K 21 + 2	Morley D 19	Swailes D 17	Boyd M 4 + 1	Townson K 2 + 4	*Match No.*
1	2	3	4	5	6	7	8	9^1	10	11	12																	1
1	2	3	4	5	6	7	8^1	9	10	11	12																	2
1	2	3	4	5	6	7	8	9	10	11																		3
1	2	3	4	5	6	7	8	9	10	11																		4
1	2	3	4	5	6	7	8^1	9	10	11	12																	5
1^6	2^2	3	4	5	6	7	8^1	9	10	11	12	15	13															6
	2	3	4	5^2	6	7	8	9	10	11^1	12	1	13															7
	2	3	4	5	6	7^1	8	9	10	12	11^2	1		13														8
	2	3■	4	5	6	7^1	8	9^2	10	12	13	1		11														9
1	2		4	5	6	7	8	9	10	11				3														10
1	2	12	4^2	5^3	6	7	8^1	9	10	11	13			3	14													11
1	2	3		5	6^1	7		9	10	11	12			8^2	4	13												12
1	2	3		5		7	8^1	9	10	11	12				4		6											13
1	2	3		5		7^1	8	9	10	11	12				6		4											14
1		3		5		7	8	9^1	10	2	11			12	6		4											15
1		3		5	12	7^2	8	9	10^1	2	11			13	6		4											16
1		3		5		7	8	9^1	10	2	11			12	6		4											17
1		3		5		7	8^1	9		2	10		12	11	6		4^2	13										18
		3	4			7^1	12		10	2	9	1		11	6		5		8									19
		3	4			7	8	12	10	11	9	1	2^1		5					6								20
		3	4			7^1	8	12	10	11	9	1	2		5					6								21
		3	4			12	8^2	13	10	11	9	1	2	14	5^3					6	7^1							22
		3	4				12	9	10	11	8^1	1			5					2	7^2	6	13					23
		3	4			7		9^2	10	11	8^1	1		12	5						6	2	13					24
		3	4		12	7		9	10	11	8^2	1		13	5^1						6	2						25
		12	4				8^1	13	10	3	9^3	1		14	5					6	7	2^2	11					26
1		3	4			12		9	10	7									6^1		8		11	2	5			27
1		3	4					9	10	7	12								8^1		6		11	2	5			28
1		3	4			12		9	10	7									6^1		8		11	2	5			29
1		3	4			12		9	10	2				13	6				8^2		7^1		11		5			30
1		3				12		9	10	8					4				6^1		7		11	2	5			31
1		3						9	10	4				12	6				8^1		7		11	2	5			32
1		3						9	10	2				7	6				8				11	4	5			33
1		3				12			9	2	10^1			7	6				8				11	4	5			34
1		3				12		9	10	2	13			7^3	6				8^1				11^2	4	5	14		35
1		3	4					9	10	7				12	6				8^1				11	2	5			36
1		3	4	12				9	10	7				13	6				8^2				11	2	5^1			37
1	12	3	4^1	5				9	10■	7				13	6^2				8^3				11	2			14	38
	2	3	4^2	5		12		9		7		1		10					8^1				11	6			13	39
	2^1	3	4	5				9		7		1		8	12								11	6			10	40
		3	4	12		13		9		7		1		8	6^1								11^2	2	5		10	41
	2		4^2	6^1		12		9	10	7		1		8^3					13				11	3	5		14	42
	2	3						9	10	7^2		1		12	6^1				13				11	4	5	8		43
	2^2					7^1		9	10	3		1		12	13				4				11	6	5	8		44
			4			7		9	10	2		1		12	13				8^1				11	6	5	3^2		45
1	2					8		9^2	10	7				11	12								3	6	5	4^1	13	46

FA Cup

First Round	Alfreton T	(a)	1-1
		(h)	2-0
Second Round	Hull C	(a)	0-4

Carling Cup

First Round	Hartlepool U	(a)	1-2

LDV Vans Trophy

First Round	Chesterfield	(h)	2-1
Second Round	Mansfield T	(h)	4-0
Quarter-Final	Tranmere R	(h)	0-1

Play-offs

Semi-Final	Lincoln C	(a)	0-1
		(h)	1-1

MANCHESTER CITY FA Premiership

FOUNDATION

Manchester City was formed as a Limited Company in 1894 after their predecessors Ardwick had been forced into bankruptcy. However, many historians like to trace the club's lineage as far back as 1880 when St Mark's Church, West Gorton added a football section to their cricket club. They amalgamated with Gorton Athletic in 1884 as Gorton FC. Because of a change of ground they became Ardwick in 1887.

City of Manchester Stadium, SportCity, Manchester M11 3FF.

Telephone: 0870 062 1894.

Fax: (0161) 438 7999.

Ticket Office: 0870 062 1894.

Website: www.mcfc.co.uk

Email: mcfc@mcfc.co.uk

Ground Capacity: 47,500.

Record Attendance: 85,569 v Stoke C, FA Cup 6th rd, 3 March 1934 (British record for any game outside London or Glasgow).

Pitch Measurements: 105m × 68m.

Chairman: John Wardle.

Deputy chairman: Bryan Bodek.

Chief Executive: Alistair Mackintosh.

Secretary: J. B. Halford.

Manager: Stuart Pearce.

Assistant Manager: TBA.

Physio: Jim Webb.

Colours: Sky blue shirts, white shorts, sky blue stockings.

Change Colours: Navy blue, navy blue shorts, navy blue stockings.

Year Formed: 1887 as Ardwick FC; 1894 as Manchester City.

Turned Professional: 1887 as Ardwick FC.

Ltd Co.: 1894.

Previous Names: 1887, Ardwick FC (formed through the amalgamation of West Gorton and Gorton Athletic, the latter having been formed in 1880); 1894, Manchester City.

Club Nicknames: 'Blues' or 'The Citizens'.

Previous Grounds: 1880, Clowes Street; 1881, Kirkmanshulme Cricket Ground; 1882, Queens Road; 1884, Pink Bank Lane; 1887, Hyde Road (1894–1923 as City); 1923, Maine Road; 2003, City of Manchester Stadium.

First Football League Game: 3 September 1892, Division 2, v Bootle (h) W 7–0 – Douglas; McVickers, Robson; Middleton, Russell, Hopkins; Davies (3), Morris (2), Angus (1), Weir (1), Milarvie.

Record League Victory: 10–1 v Huddersfield T, Division 2, 7 November 1987 – Nixon; Gidman, Hinchcliffe, Clements, Lake, Redmond, White (3), Stewart (3), Adcock (3), McNab (1), Simpson.

HONOURS

Football League: Division 1 – Champions 1936–37, 1967–68, 2001–02; Runners-up 1903–04, 1920–21, 1976–77, 1999–2000; Division 2 – Champions 1898–99, 1902–03, 1909–10, 1927–28, 1946–47, 1965–66; Runners-up 1895–96, 1950–51, 1987–88; Promoted from Division 2 (play-offs) 1998–99.

FA Cup: Winners 1904, 1934, 1956, 1969; Runners-up 1926, 1933, 1955, 1981.

Football League Cup: Winners 1970, 1976; Runners-up 1974.

European Competitions: *European Cup:* 1968–69. *European Cup-Winners' Cup:* 1969–70 (winners), 1970–71. *UEFA Cup:* 1972–73, 1976–77, 1977–78, 1978–79, 2003–04.

SKY SPORTS FACT FILE

Manchester City became the only Premier League team to prevent champions Chelsea from scoring against them in the competition during 2004–05, with goalkeeper David James claiming the two shut-outs as City took four points off them.

Record Cup Victory: 10–1 v Swindon T, FA Cup 4th rd, 29 January 1930 – Barber; Felton, McCloy; Barrass, Cowan, Heinemann; Toseland, Marshall (5), Tait (3), Johnson (1), Brook (1).

Record Defeat: 1–9 v Everton, Division 1, 3 September 1906.

Most League Points (2 for a win): 62, Division 2, 1946–47.

Most League Points (3 for a win): 99, Division 1, 2001–02.

Most League Goals: 108, Division 2, 1926–27, 108, Division 1, 2001–02.

Highest League Scorer in Season: Tommy Johnson, 38, Division 1, 1928–29.

Most League Goals in Total Aggregate: Tommy Johnson, 158, 1919–30.

Most League Goals in One Match: 5, Fred Williams v Darwen, Division 2, 18 February 1899; 5, Tom Browell v Burnley, Division 2, 24 October 1925; 5, Tom Johnson v Everton, Division 1, 15 September 1928; 5, George Smith v Newport Co, Division 2, 14 June 1947.

Most Capped Player: Colin Bell, 48, England.

Most League Appearances: Alan Oakes, 565, 1959–76.

Youngest League Player: Glyn Pardoe, 15 years 314 days v Birmingham C, 11 April 1962.

Record Transfer Fee Received: £7,000,000 from Fenerbahce for Nicolas Anelka, January 2005.

Record Transfer Fee Paid: £10,000,000 to Paris St Germain for Nicolas Anelka, June 2002.

Football League Record: 1892 Ardwick elected founder member of Division 2; 1894 Newly-formed Manchester C elected to Division 2; Division 1 1899–1902, 1903–09, 1910–26, 1928–38, 1947–50, 1951–63, 1966–83, 1985–87, 1989–92; Division 2 1902–03, 1909–10, 1926–28, 1938–47, 1950–51, 1963–66, 1983–85, 1987–89; 1992–96 FA Premier League; 1996–98 Division 1; 1998–99 Division 2; 1999–2000 Division 1; 2000–01 FA Premier League; 2001–02 Division 1; 2002– FA Premier League.

MANAGERS

Joshua Parlby 1893–95
(Secretary-Manager)
Sam Omerod 1895–1902
Tom Maley 1902–06
Harry Newbould 1906–12
Ernest Magnall 1912–24
David Ashworth 1924–25
Peter Hodge 1926–32
Wilf Wild 1932–46
(continued as Secretary to 1950)
Sam Cowan 1946–47
John 'Jock' Thomson 1947–50
Leslie McDowall 1950–63
George Poyser 1963–65
Joe Mercer 1965–71
(continued as General Manager to 1972)
Malcolm Allison 1972–73
Johnny Hart 1973
Ron Saunders 1973–74
Tony Book 1974–79
Malcolm Allison 1979–80
John Bond 1980–83
John Benson 1983
Billy McNeill 1983–86
Jimmy Frizzell 1986–87
(continued as General Manager)
Mel Machin 1987–89
Howard Kendall 1990
Peter Reid 1990–93
Brian Horton 1993–95
Alan Ball 1995–96
Steve Coppell 1996
Frank Clark 1996–98
Joe Royle 1998–2001
Kevin Keegan 2001–05
Stuart Pearce March 2005–

LATEST SEQUENCES

Longest Sequence of League Wins: 9, 8.4.1912 – 28.9.1912.

Longest Sequence of League Defeats: 8, 23.8.1995 – 14.10.1995.

Longest Sequence of League Draws: 6, 5.4.1913 – 6.9.1913.

Longest Sequence of Unbeaten League Matches: 22, 16.11.1946 – 19.4.1947.

Longest Sequence Without a League Win: 17, 26.12.1979 – 7.4.1980.

Successive Scoring Runs: 44 from 3.10.1936.

Successive Non-scoring Runs: 6 from 30.1.1971.

TEN YEAR LEAGUE RECORD

		P	W	D	L	F	A	Pts	Pos
1995-96	PR Lge	38	9	11	18	33	58	38	18
1996-97	Div 1	46	17	10	19	59	60	61	14
1997-98	Div 1	46	12	12	22	56	57	48	22
1998-99	Div 2	46	22	16	8	69	33	82	3
1999-2000	Div 1	46	26	11	9	78	40	89	2
2000-01	PR Lge	38	8	10	20	41	65	34	18
2001-02	Div 1	46	31	6	9	108	52	99	1
2002-03	PR Lge	38	15	6	17	47	54	51	9
2003-04	PR Lge	38	9	14	15	55	54	41	16
2004-05	PR Lge	38	13	13	12	47	39	52	8

DID YOU KNOW ?

Already assured of a place in the First Division the following season, Manchester City entertained Newport County on 14 June 1947 and had a 5–1 win. It was a personal triumph for George Smith who scored all five goals and finished as top scorer with 23.

MANCHESTER CITY 2004–05 LEAGUE RECORD

Match No.	Date	Venue	Opponents	Result		H/T Score	Lg. Pos.	Goalscorers	Attendance
1	Aug 14	H	Fulham	D	1-1	1-0	—	Fowler ^{28}	44,026
2	21	A	Liverpool	L	1-2	1-0	14	Anelka ^{45}	42,831
3	24	A	Birmingham C	L	0-1	0-1	—		28,551
4	28	H	Charlton Ath	W	4-0	2-0	9	Anelka 2 $^{13, 60}$, Sinclair ^{34}, Wright-Phillips S ^{78}	43,593
5	Sept 11	H	Everton	L	0-1	0-0	13		47,006
6	18	A	Crystal Palace	W	2-1	0-0	11	Anelka 2 (1 pen) $^{55, 64 (p)}$	25,052
7	25	H	Arsenal	L	0-1	0-1	13		47,015
8	Oct 2	A	Southampton	D	0-0	0-0	12		28,605
9	16	H	Chelsea	W	1-0	1-0	11	Anelka (pen) ^{11}	45,047
10	24	A	Newcastle U	L	3-4	0-0	13	Wright-Phillips S 2 $^{64, 77}$, Fowler (pen) ^{67}	52,316
11	Nov 1	H	Norwich C	D	1-1	1-0	—	Flood ^{11}	42,803
12	7	A	Manchester U	D	0-0	0-0	13		67,863
13	13	H	Blackburn R	D	1-1	1-0	12	Sibierski ^{45}	45,504
14	20	A	Portsmouth	W	3-1	1-1	11	Wright-Phillips S ^{6}, Sibierski ^{79}, Bosvelt ^{87}	20,101
15	27	H	Aston Villa	W	2-0	2-0	9	Macken ^{29}, Wright-Phillips S ^{38}	44,530
16	Dec 6	A	Middlesbrough	L	2-3	1-1	—	Fowler ^{39}, Wright-Phillips B ^{80}	29,787
17	11	H	Tottenham H	L	0-1	0-0	13		45805
18	18	A	Bolton W	W	1-0	0-0	10	Barton ^{52}	27,274
19	26	A	Everton	L	1-2	1-1	11	Fowler ^{42}	40,530
20	28	H	WBA	D	1-1	1-0	12	Anelka ^{32}	47,177
21	Jan 1	H	Southampton	W	2-1	2-0	10	Bosvelt ^{19}, Wright-Phillips S ^{40}	42,895
22	4	A	Arsenal	D	1-1	1-0	9	Wright-Phillips S ^{31}	38,066
23	15	H	Crystal Palace	W	3-1	2-1	9	Wright-Phillips S 2 $^{12, 90}$, Fowler ^{15}	44,010
24	22	A	WBA	L	0-2	0-1	9		25,348
25	Feb 2	H	Newcastle U	D	1-1	0-1	—	Fowler (pen) ^{49}	45,752
26	6	A	Chelsea	D	0-0	0-0	10		42,093
27	13	H	Manchester U	L	0-2	0-0	11		47,111
28	28	A	Norwich C	W	3-2	2-2	—	Sibierski ^{25}, Fowler 2 $^{37, 90}$	24,302
29	Mar 7	H	Bolton W	L	0-1	0-1	—		43,050
30	19	A	Tottenham H	L	1-2	1-1	12	Reyna ^{44}	35,681
31	Apr 2	A	Charlton Ath	D	2-2	2-1	12	Dunne ^{4}, Fowler ^{38}	26,436
32	9	H	Liverpool	W	1-0	1-0	11	Musampa ^{90}	47,203
33	16	A	Fulham	D	1-1	1-0	11	Reyna ^{20}	21,796
34	20	H	Birmingham C	W	3-0	0-0	—	Fowler ^{55}, Dunne ^{80}, Sibierski (pen) ^{86}	42,453
35	23	A	Blackburn R	D	0-0	0-0	10		24,646
36	30	H	Portsmouth	W	2-0	2-0	9	Distin ^{4}, Fowler ^{16}	46,454
37	May 7	A	Aston Villa	W	2-1	2-0	8	Wright-Phillips S ^{5}, Musampa ^{12}	39,645
38	15	H	Middlesbrough	D	1-1	0-1	8	Musampa ^{46}	47,221

Final League Position: 8

GOALSCORERS

League (47): Fowler 11 (2 pens), Wright-Phillips S 10, Anelka 7 (2 pens), Sibierski 4 (1 pen), Musampa 3, Bosvelt 2, Dunne 2, Reyna 2, Barton 1, Distin 1, Flood 1, Macken 1, Sinclair 1, Wright-Phillips B 1.
Carling Cup (8): Macken 2, Sibierski 2, Barton 1, Flood 1, Fowler 1, Wright-Phillips S 1.
FA Cup (0).

James D 38	Mills D 29 + 3	Thatcher B 17 + 1	Dunne R 35	Distin S 38	Bosvelt P 28	Wright-Phillips S 33 + 1	Reyna C 16 + 1	Anelka N 18 + 1	Fowler R 28 + 4	Sibierski A 34 + 1	Barton J 28 + 3	Macken J 16 + 7	Sinclair T 2 + 2	Jihai S 4 + 2	McManaman S 5 + 8	Flood W 4 + 5	Jordan S 19	Onuoha N 11 + 6	Wright-Phillips B — + 14	Negouai C — + 1	Musampa K 14	Sommeil D 1	Croft L — + 7	Weaver N — + 1	Match No.
1	2	3	4	5	6^{1}	7	8	9	10^{2}	11	12	13													1
1	2	3	4■	5	6^{1}	7	8	9	10	11^{2}	12		13												2
1	4	3		5	6^{1}	7	8	9	10^{2}	11^{3}	12	13	14	2											3
1	2	3	4	5		7	8	9	10		6^{2}	12	11^{1}		13										4
1	2	3^{1}	4	5		7	8	9	10^{3}	13	6	14	11^{2}	12											5
1	2	3	4	5		7	8	9		11	6	10^{1}		12											6
1	2		4	5	8^{1}	7		9		11	6	10^{2}		3	12	13									7
1	2	3	4	5	8	7		9			6	10		11											8
1	2	3	4	5	8	7		9	13	11		10^{2}		6^{1}	12										9
1	2	3	4	5	6	7		9^{1}	12	11		10^{2}			8	13									10
1	2		4^{2}	5	6	10		9	12	11					8^{1}	7	3	13							11
1	2		4	5	6	10		9		11					8	7	3								12
1	2■		4	5	6	10	12	9		11					8	7^{1}	3								13
1			4	5	8	7		9^{1}	12	11	6	10					3	2							14
1	2		4	5^{1}	8	7			9	11	6	10					3	12							15
1	2		4	5	8	7			10	11^{1}	6	9^{2}				12	3		13						16
1	2		4	5	8	7		12	10^{1}	11	6	9^{2}					3		13						17
1	2		4	5	8	7		9	10	11	6						3								18
1	2^{1}		4	5	6	7		9	10	11		8^{2}					3	12		13■					19
1	2		4	5	8	7		9	10	11	6						3^{1}	12							20
1	2	3^{3}	4	5	8	7		9^{1}	10^{2}	11	6	12			13			14							21
1		3	4	5	8	7			10	11	6^{1}	9^{2}				12		2	13						22
1	2	3	4	5	8	7			10^{3}	11^{1}	6	9^{2}			12			14	13						23
1	2		4	5	8	7			10	11^{1}	6	9^{2}			12		3		13						24
1	2	3	4	5	8	7			10		6	9^{1}							12		11				25
1	2	3	4	5	8	7			10	11^{1}	6				12						9				26
1	2^{2}	3	4	5		7			10	11	6^{1}	12			8				13		9				27
1	2		4	5	8	7			10	11	6						3				9				28
1	2		4	5	6^{2}		8		10	11^{3}					12	7^{1}			13		9	3	14		29
1	12		4	5	8^{2}		7		10	11^{3}	6	13				14	3	2^{1}			9				30
1			4	5			8		10	11	6	9					2	3			7				31
1	12		4	5	8^{3}		7		10	11^{2}	6						3	2^{1}	13		9		14		32
1			4	5	8	12	7		10^{1}	11	6						3	2	13		9^{2}				33
1			4	5		7^{2}	8		10^{1}	11	6						3	2	12		9		13		34
1			4	5		7	8		10^{1}	11	6						3	2	12		9^{2}		13		35
1	12	13	4	5		7	8		10^{3}	11	6						3^{2}	2			9^{1}		14		36
1	2	3		5		7	8			11^{1}	6	10^{2}						4	12		9		13		37
1	2^{2}	3		5		7	8^{G}		10	11^{1}	6							4	12		9		13	15	38

FA Cup

Third Round	Oldham Ath	(a)	0-1

Carling Cup

Second Round	Barnsley	(h)	7-1
Third Round	Arsenal	(h)	1-2

MANCHESTER UNITED FA Premiership

FOUNDATION

Manchester United was formed as comparatively recently as 1902 after their predecessors, Newton Heath, went bankrupt. However, it is usual to give the date of the club's foundation as 1878 when the dining room committee of the carriage and waggon works of the Lancashire and Yorkshire Railway Company formed Newton Heath L and YR Cricket and Football Club. They won the Manchester Cup in 1886 and as Newton Heath FC were admitted to the Second Division in 1892.

Old Trafford, Sir Matt Busby Way, Manchester M16 0RA.

Telephone: (0161) 868 8000.

Fax: (0161) 868 8804.

Ticket Office: 0870 442 1994.

Website: www.manutd.com

Email: enquiries@manutd.co.uk

Ground Capacity: 68,210.

Record Attendance: 76,962 Wolverhampton W v Grimsby T, FA Cup semi-final, 25 March 1939.
Club Record Attendance: 70,504 v Aston Villa, Division 1, 27 December 1920.

Pitch Measurements: 105m × 68m.

Chairman: Sir Roy Gardner.

Chief Executive: David Gill.

Secretary: Kenneth R. Merrett.

Manager: Sir Alex Ferguson CBE.

Assistant Manager: Carlos Queiroz. ***Physio:*** Robert Swire.

Colours: Red shirts, white shorts, black or white stockings.

Change Colours: All black.

Year Formed: 1878 as Newton Heath LYR; 1902, Manchester United.

Turned Professional: 1885. ***Ltd Co.:*** 1907.

Previous Name: 1880, Newton Heath; 1902, Manchester United.

Club Nickname: 'Red Devils'.

Previous Grounds: 1880, North Road, Monsall Road; 1893, Bank Street; 1910, Old Trafford (played at Maine Road 1941–49).

First Football League Game: 3 September 1892, Division 1, v Blackburn R (a) L 3–4 – Warner; Clements, Brown; Perrins, Stewart, Erentz; Farman (1), Coupar (1), Donaldson (1), Carson, Mathieson.

HONOURS

FA Premier League – Champions 1992–93, 1993–94, 1995–96, 1996–97, 1998–99, 1999–2000, 2000–01, 2002–03; Runners-up 1994–95, 1997–98.

Football League: Division 1 – Champions 1907–08, 1910–11, 1951–52, 1955–56, 1956–57, 1964–65, 1966–67; Runners-up 1946–47, 1947–48, 1948–49, 1950–51, 1958–59, 1963–64, 1967–68, 1979–80, 1987–88, 1991–92. Division 2 – Champions 1935–36, 1974–75; Runners-up 1896–97, 1905–06, 1924–25, 1937–38.

FA Cup: Winners 1909, 1948, 1963, 1977, 1983, 1985, 1990, 1994, 1996, 1999, 2004; Runners-up 1957, 1958, 1976, 1979, 1995, 2005.

Football League Cup: Winners 1992; Runners-up 1983, 1991, 1994, 2003.

European Competitions: *European Cup:* 1956–57 (s-f), 1957–58 (s-f), 1965–66 (s-f), 1967–68 (winners), 1968–69 (s-f). *Champions League:* 1993–94, 1994–95, 1996–97 (s-f), 1997–98, 1998–99 (winners), 1999–2000, 2000–01, 2001–02 (s-f), 2002–03, 2003–04, 2004–05. *European Cup-Winners' Cup:* 1963–64, 1977–78, 1983–84, 1990–91 (winners). 1991–92. *Inter Cities Fairs Cup:* 1964–65. *UEFA Cup:* 1976–77, 1980–81, 1982–83, 1984–85, 1992–93, 1995–96. *Super Cup:* 1991 (winners), 1999 (runners-up). *Inter-Continental Cup:* 1999 (winners), 1968 (runners-up).

SKY SPORTS FACT FILE

When Wayne Rooney scored a hat-trick on his Manchester United debut on 28 September 2004 in a 6–2 win over Fenerbahce, it was the second such treble-shooting bow in the club's history after Charlie Sagar on 2 September 1905 v Bristol City.

Record League Victory (as Newton Heath): 10–1 v Wolverhampton W, Division 1, 15 October 1892 – Warner; Mitchell, Clements; Perrins, Stewart (3), Erentz; Farman (1), Hood (1), Donaldson (3), Carson (1), Hendry (1).

Record League Victory (as Manchester U): 9–0 v Ipswich T, FA Premier League, 4 March 1995 – Schmeichel; Keane (1) (Sharpe), Irwin, Bruce (Butt), Kanchelskis, Pallister, Cole (5), Ince (1), McClair, Hughes (2), Giggs.

Record Cup Victory: 10–0 v RSC Anderlecht, European Cup prel. rd 2nd leg, 26 September 1956 – Wood; Foulkes, Byrne; Colman, Jones, Edwards; Berry (1), Whelan (2), Taylor (3), Viollet (4), Pegg.

Record Defeat: 0–7 v Blackburn R, Division 1, 10 April 1926. 0–7 v Aston Villa, Division 1, 27 December 1930. 0–7 v Wolverhampton W, Division 2, 26 December 1931.

Most League Points (2 for a win): 64, Division 1, 1956–57.

Most League Points (3 for a win): 92, FA Premier League, 1993–94.

Most League Goals: 103, Division 1, 1956–57 and 1958–59.

Highest League Scorer in Season: Dennis Viollet, 32, 1959–60.

Most League Goals in Total Aggregate: Bobby Charlton, 199, 1956–73.

Most Capped Player: Bobby Charlton, 106, England.

Most League Appearances: Bobby Charlton, 606, 1956–73.

Youngest League Player: Jeff Whitefoot, 16 years 105 days v Portsmouth, 15 April 1950.

Record Transfer Fee Received: £25,000,000 from Real Madrid for David Beckham, July 2003.

Record Transfer Fee Paid: £30,000,000 to Leeds U for Rio Ferdinand, July 2002 (see also Leeds United page 217).

Football League Record: 1892 Newton Heath elected to Division 1; 1894–1906 Division 2; 1906–22 Division 1; 1922–25 Division 2; 1925–31 Division 1; 1931–36 Division 2; 1936–37 Division 1; 1937–38 Division 2; 1938–74 Division 1; 1974–75 Division 2; 1975–92 Division 1; 1992– FA Premier League.

MANAGERS

J. Ernest Mangnall 1903–12
John Bentley 1912–14
John Robson 1914–21
(Secretary-Manager from 1916)
John Chapman 1921–26
Clarence Hilditch 1926–27
Herbert Bamlett 1927–31
Walter Crickmer 1931–32
Scott Duncan 1932–37
Walter Crickmer 1937–45
(Secretary-Manager)
Matt Busby 1945–69
(continued as General Manager then Director)
Wilf McGuinness 1969–70
Sir Matt Busby 1970–71
Frank O'Farrell 1971–72
Tommy Docherty 1972–77
Dave Sexton 1977–81
Ron Atkinson 1981–86
Sir Alex Ferguson November 1986–

LATEST SEQUENCES

Longest Sequence of League Wins: 14, 15.10.1904 – 3.1.1905.

Longest Sequence of League Defeats: 14, 26.4.1930 – 25.10.1930.

Longest Sequence of League Draws: 6, 30.10.1988 – 27.11.1988.

Longest Sequence of Unbeaten League Matches: 29, 26.12.1998 – 25.9.1999.

Longest Sequence Without a League Win: 16, 19.4.1930 – 25.10.1930.

Successive Scoring Runs: 27 from 11.10.1958.

Successive Non-scoring Runs: 5 from 22.2.1902.

TEN YEAR LEAGUE RECORD

		P	*W*	*D*	*L*	*F*	*A*	*Pts*	*Pos*
1995-96	PR Lge	38	25	7	6	73	35	82	1
1996-97	PR Lge	38	21	12	5	76	44	75	1
1997-98	PR Lge	38	23	8	7	73	26	77	2
1998-99	PR Lge	38	22	13	3	80	37	79	1
1999-2000	PR Lge	38	28	7	3	97	45	91	1
2000-01	PR Lge	38	24	8	6	79	31	80	1
2001-02	PR Lge	38	24	5	9	87	45	77	3
2002-03	PR Lge	38	25	8	5	74	34	83	1
2003-04	PR Lge	38	23	6	9	64	35	75	3
2004-05	PR Lge	38	22	11	5	58	26	77	3

DID YOU KNOW ?

Ruud Van Nistelrooy overtook Denis Law as the highest scorer in European matches during 2004–05. All four goals against Sparta Prague on 3 November took his total to a club record 35 in 36 European matches.

MANCHESTER UNITED 2004–05 LEAGUE RECORD

Match No.	*Date*	*Venue*	*Opponents*	*Result*		*H/T Score*	*Lg. Pos.*	*Goalscorers*	*Attendance*
1	Aug 15	A	Chelsea	L	0-1	0-1	—		41,813
2	21	H	Norwich C	W	2-1	1-0	8	Bellion [32], Smith [52]	67,812
3	28	A	Blackburn R	D	1-1	0-1	12	Smith [90]	26,155
4	30	H	Everton	D	0-0	0-0	—		67,803
5	Sept 11	A	Bolton W	D	2-2	1-0	10	Heinze [44], Hunt (og) [90]	27,766
6	20	H	Liverpool	W	2-1	1-0	—	Silvestre 2 [20, 66]	67,857
7	25	A	Tottenham H	W	1-0	1-0	5	Van Nistelrooy (pen) [42]	36,103
8	Oct 3	H	Middlesbrough	D	1-1	0-1	4	Smith [81]	67,988
9	16	A	Birmingham C	D	0-0	0-0	6		29,221
10	24	H	Arsenal	W	2-0	0-0	5	Van Nistelrooy (pen) [73], Rooney [90]	67,862
11	30	A	Portsmouth	L	0-2	0-0	7		20,190
12	Nov 7	H	Manchester C	D	0-0	0-0	7		67,863
13	14	A	Newcastle U	W	3-1	1-0	7	Rooney 2 [7, 90], Van Nistelrooy (pen) [74]	52,320
14	20	H	Charlton Ath	W	2-0	1-0	5	Giggs [41], Scholes [50]	67,704
15	27	A	WBA	W	3-0	0-0	4	Scholes 2 [53, 82], Van Nistelrooy [72]	27,709
16	Dec 4	H	Southampton	W	3-0	0-0	4	Scholes [53], Rooney [58], Ronaldo [87]	67,921
17	13	A	Fulham	D	1-1	1-0	—	Smith [33]	21,940
18	18	H	Crystal Palace	W	5-2	2-1	4	Scholes 2 [22, 49], Smith [35], Boyce (og) [48], O'Shea [90]	67,814
19	26	H	Bolton W	W	2-0	1-0	4	Giggs [10], Scholes [89]	67,867
20	28	A	Aston Villa	W	1-0	1-0	3	Giggs [41]	42,593
21	Jan 1	A	Middlesbrough	W	2-0	1-0	3	Fletcher [9], Giggs [79]	34,299
22	4	H	Tottenham H	D	0-0	0-0	3		67,962
23	15	A	Liverpool	W	1-0	1-0	3	Rooney [21]	44,183
24	22	H	Aston Villa	W	3-1	1-0	3	Ronaldo [8], Saha [69], Scholes [70]	67,859
25	Feb 1	A	Arsenal	W	4-2	1-2	—	Cole (og) [18], Ronaldo 2 [54, 58], O'Shea [89]	38,164
26	5	H	Birmingham C	W	2-0	0-0	2	Keane [55], Rooney [78]	67,838
27	13	A	Manchester C	W	2-0	0-0	2	Rooney [68], Dunne (og) [75]	47,111
28	26	H	Portsmouth	W	2-1	1-0	2	Rooney 2 [8, 81]	67,989
29	Mar 5	A	Crystal Palace	D	0-0	0-0	2		26,021
30	19	H	Fulham	W	1-0	1-0	2	Ronaldo [21]	67,959
31	Apr 2	H	Blackburn R	D	0-0	0-0	3		67,939
32	9	A	Norwich C	L	0-2	0-0	3		25,522
33	20	A	Everton	L	0-1	0-0	—		37,160
34	24	H	Newcastle U	W	2-1	0-1	3	Rooney [57], Brown [75]	67,845
35	May 1	A	Charlton Ath	W	4-0	2-0	3	Scholes [34], Fletcher [44], Smith [62], Rooney [67]	26,789
36	7	H	WBA	D	1-1	1-0	3	Giggs [21]	67,827
37	10	H	Chelsea	L	1-3	1-1	—	Van Nistelrooy [7]	67,832
38	15	A	Southampton	W	2-1	1-1	3	Fletcher [19], Van Nistelrooy [63]	32,066

Final League Position: 3

GOALSCORERS

League (58): Rooney 11, Scholes 9, Smith 6, Van Nistelrooy 6 (3 pens), Giggs 5, Ronaldo 5, Fletcher 3, O'Shea 2, Silvestre 2, Bellion 1, Brown 1, Heinze 1, Keane 1, Saha 1, own goals 4.
Carling Cup (7): Bellion 1, Giggs 1, Miller 1, Richardson 1, Saha 1, Smith 1, own goal 1.
FA Cup (15): Ronaldo 4, Rooney 3, Scholes 3, Van Nistelrooy 2, Fortune 1, Keane 1, O'Shea 1.
Champions League (19): Van Nistelrooy 8 (1 pen), Rooney 3, Bellion 2, Giggs 2, Smith 2, Neville G 1, own goal 1.
Community Shield (1): Smith 1.

Howard T 12	Neville G 22	Fortune Q 12 + 5	Keane R 28 + 3	Miller L 3 + 5	Silvestre M 33 + 2	O'Shea J 16 + 7	Djemba-Djemba E 3 + 2	Smith A 22 + 9	Scholes P 29 + 4	Giggs R 26 + 6	Bellion D 1 + 9	Forlan D — + 1	Richardson K — + 2	Ronaldo C 25 + 8	Neville P 12 + 7	Spector J 2 + 1	Kleberson J 6 + 2	Saha L 7 + 7	Fletcher D 18	Heinze G 26	Van Nistelrooy R 16 + 1	Brown W 18 + 3	Carroll R 26	Ferdinand R 31	Rooney W 24 + 5	*Match No.*
1	2	3^1	4	5^3	6	7	8^2	9	10	11	12	13	14													1
1	2^3		4	5^1	6	3	8	9	10	11	7^2		13	12	14											2
1	2			12	6	4	8^2	9	10	11	13			7		3^1	5^3	14								3
1	2				6	4	13	9	8	12	14			11^3		3	5^1	10	7^2							4
1			5		6			9	8	11	12			13	2		7^2			3	10^1	4				5
			5		6	8		12	10^1	11				7						3	9	2	1	4		6
			5	12	6	8		10		11^1	13			7						3	9^2	2	1	4		7
	2		5		6	8^1		12		11				7						3	9		1	4	10	8
	2	3	5					8	12					11^1			7^2	10			9	4	1	6	13	9
	2				6			12	8	11				7^1	5			13		3	9^2		1	4	10	10
	2^1		13		6			9^3	8	11				7	5^2			14		3		12	1	4	10	11
	2		5	7^1	6			9■	8^2	12				11				10		3			1	4	13	12
	2		5		6^3			12	8	13				11^1					7^2	3	9	14	1	4	10	13
		3	5^2		6	12		14	8	11					13				7^1		9^3	2	1	4	10	14
			5		6			12	8	11				13					7^2	3	9^1	2	1	4	10	15
	2		5		6			9^1	8	11	12			7						3			1	4	10	16
	2		5		6			9	8	11				7						3			1	4	10	17
	2	3^1	5		6	12		9	8	11									7				1	4	10	18
			5	12	6	2		9	13	11				7^2					8	3			1	4	10^1	19
			12		6	2^1		9	8	11				13	5				7	3			1	4	10^2	20
			5		6		12	9	10	11^2	13			7^1	2				8	3			1	4		21
			5	12	6			9	10	11^2	13			7^3	2	14			8^1	3			1	4		22
		12	5		6	13			8		14			11^2	2			9^1	7	3		4■	1		10^3	23
	2	12	5		6	13			8^2	14				11				9	7^1	3			1	4	10^3	24
	2		5		6■	12			8	9^2				11^3				13	7^1	3		14	1	4	10	25
	2	13	5	12		8				11^3				7	14			9^2		3		6	1	4	10^1	26
	2	11	5			7^2			9^3	12				13	14				8^1	3		6	1	4	10	27
1	2^2	12			6	5		13	11^3	14				7	8					3	9^1	4			10	28
1		7^1	5		6			10^3	12	11				13	8^2					3	9	2		4	14	29
1		11	5		6	12		13	8^3					7	14					3	9^2	2		4	10^1	30
1	2	5	12		6	3		13	8	11^1				7							9^2			4	10	31
1	2	11^1			6			9	8					13	5		7^3	10^2		3	14			4	12	32
1	2■		5		12	13			8■					11					7^2	3	9	6^1		4	10	33
1		11	5^1		12			9		8				13	2		14		7^3	3^2		6		4	10	34
		12	5^3		3	2		9	8^2	11					13		14		7			6	1	4	10^1	35
		11			6	3		9^2	12	10				7	5^1		8^3	13				2	1	4	14	36
	2		5		3				8					11				12	7^1		9	6	1	4	10	37
		11			6	3		5		8					12			13	7		9^1	2	1	4	10^2	38

FA Cup

Third Round	Exeter C	(h)	0-0
		(a)	2-0
Fourth Round	Middlesbrough	(h)	3-0
Fifth Round	Everton	(a)	2-0
Sixth Round	Southampton	(a)	4-0
Semi-Final	Newcastle U		4-1
(at Millennium Stadium)			
Final	Arsenal		0-0
(at Millennium Stadium)			

Carling Cup

Third Round	Crewe Alex	(a)	3-0
Fourth Round	Crystal Palace	(h)	2-0
Fifth Round	Arsenal	(h)	1-0
Semi-Final	Chelsea	(a)	0-0
		(h)	1-2

Champions League

Third Qualifying Round	Dinamo Bucharest	(a)	2-1
		(h)	3-0
Group D	Lyon	(a)	2-0
	Fenerbahce	(h)	6-2
	Sparta Prague	(a)	0-0
		(h)	4-1
	Lyon	(h)	2-1
	Fenerbahce	(a)	0-3
First Round	AC Milan	(h)	0-1
		(a)	0-1

MANSFIELD TOWN FL Championship 2

FOUNDATION

The club was formed as Mansfield Wesleyans in 1897, and changed their name to Mansfield Wesley in 1906 and Mansfield Town in 1910. This was after the Mansfield Wesleyan Chapel trustees had requested that the club change its name as 'it has no longer had any connection with either the chapel or school'. The new club participated in the Notts and Derby District League, but in the following season 1911–12 joined the Central Alliance.

Field Mill Ground, Quarry Lane, Mansfield, Notts NG18 5DA.

Telephone: 0870 756 3160.

Fax: (01623) 482 495.

Ticket Office: (01623) 482 482.

Website: www.mansfieldtown.net

Email: mtfc@stags.plus.com

Ground Capacity: 9,954.

Record Attendance: 24,467 v Nottingham F, FA Cup 3rd rd, 10 January 1953.

Pitch Measurements: 114yd × 70yd.

Chairman/Chief Executive: Keith Haslam.

Secretary: Rita Stringfellow.

Manager: Calton Palmer.

Assistant Manager: Peter Shirtliff.

Physio: Paul Madin.

Colours: Amber shirts, royal blue shorts, royal blue stockings.

Change Colours: White shirts with amber and blue trim, white shorts with amber and blue stripe, amber stockings with blue trim.

Year Formed: 1897.

Turned Professional: 1906.

Ltd Co.: 1922.

Previous Name: 1897, Mansfield Wesleyans; 1906, Mansfield Wesley; 1910, Mansfield Town.

Previous Grounds: 1897–99, Westfield Lane; 1899–1901, Ratcliffe Gate; 1901–12, Newgate Lane; 1912–16, Ratcliffe Gate; Field Mill.

Club Nickname: 'The Stags'.

First Football League Game: 29 August 1931, Division 3 (S), v Swindon T (h) W 3–2 – Wilson; Clifford, England; Wake, Davis, Blackburn; Gilhespy, Readman (1), Johnson, Broom (2), Baxter.

Record League Victory: 9–2 v Rotherham U, Division 3 (N), 27 December 1932 – Wilson; Anthony, England; Davies, S. Robinson, Slack; Prior, Broom, Readman (3), Hoyland (3), Bowater (3).

HONOURS

Football League: Division 2 best season: 21st, 1977–78; Division 3 – Champions 1976–77; Promoted to Division 2 (3rd) 2001–02; Division 4 – Champions 1974–75; Division 3 (N) – Runners-up 1950–51.

FA Cup: best season: 6th rd, 1969.

Football League Cup: best season: 5th rd, 1976.

Freight Rover Trophy: Winners 1987.

SKY SPORTS FACT FILE

Eli Siviter only made two peacetime League appearances for Mansfield Town but unusually they were against the same Hartlepools United opposition and in the last game of 1932–33 and first of 1933–34, though he was a wartime guest for them.

Record Cup Victory: 8–0 v Scarborough (a), FA Cup 1st rd, 22 November 1952 – Bramley; Chessell, Bradley; Field, Plummer, Lewis; Scott, Fox (3), Marron (2), Sid Watson (1), Adam (2).

Record Defeat: 1–8 v Walsall, Division 3 (N), 19 January 1933.

Most League Points (2 for a win): 68, Division 4, 1974–75.

Most League Points (3 for a win): 81, Division 4, 1985–86.

Most League Goals: 108, Division 4, 1962–63.

Highest League Scorer in Season: Ted Harston, 55, Division 3 (N), 1936–37.

Most League Goals in Total Aggregate: Harry Johnson, 104, 1931–36.

Most League Goals in One Match: 7, Ted Harston v Hartlepools U, Division 3N, 23 January 1937.

Most Capped Player: John McClelland, 6 (53), Northern Ireland.

Most League Appearances: Rod Arnold, 440, 1970–83.

Youngest League Player: Cyril Poole, 15 years 351 days v New Brighton, 27 February 1937.

Record Transfer Fee Received: £655,000 from Tottenham H for Colin Calderwood, July 1993.

Record Transfer Fee Paid: £150,000 to Carlisle U for Lee Peacock, October 1997.

Football League Record: 1931 Elected to Division 3 (S); 1932–37 Division 3 (N); 1937–47 Division 3 (S); 1947–58 Division 3 (N); 1958–60 Division 3; 1960–63 Division 4; 1963–72 Division 3; 1972–75 Division 4; 1975–77 Division 3; 1977–78 Division 2; 1978–80 Division 3; 1980–86 Division 4; 1986–91 Division 3; 1991–92 Division 4; 1992–93 Division 2; 1993–2002 Division 3; 2002–03 Division 2; 2003–04 Division 3; 2004– FL2.

MANAGERS

John Baynes 1922–25
Ted Davison 1926–28
Jack Hickling 1928–33
Henry Martin 1933–35
Charlie Bell 1935
Harold Wightman 1936
Harold Parkes 1936–38
Jack Poole 1938–44
Lloyd Barke 1944–45
Roy Goodall 1945–49
Freddie Steele 1949–51
George Jobey 1952–53
Stan Mercer 1953–55
Charlie Mitten 1956–58
Sam Weaver 1958–60
Raich Carter 1960–63
Tommy Cummings 1963–67
Tommy Eggleston 1967–70
Jock Basford 1970–71
Danny Williams 1971–74
Dave Smith 1974–76
Peter Morris 1976–78
Billy Bingham 1978–79
Mick Jones 1979–81
Stuart Boam 1981–83
Ian Greaves 1983–89
George Foster 1989–93
Andy King 1993–96
Steve Parkin 1996–99
Bill Dearden 1999–2002
Stuart Watkiss 2002
Keith Curle 2002–05
Carlton Palmer March 2005–

LATEST SEQUENCES

Longest Sequence of League Wins: 7, 13.9.1991 – 26.10.1991.

Longest Sequence of League Defeats: 7, 18.1.1947 – 15.3.1947.

Longest Sequence of League Draws: 5, 18.10.1986 – 22.11.1986.

Longest Sequence of Unbeaten League Matches: 20, 14.2.1976 – 21.8.1976.

Longest Sequence Without a League Win: 14, 25.3.2000 – 2.9.2000.

Successive Scoring Runs: 27 from 1.10.1962.

Successive Non-scoring Runs: 8 from 25.3.2000.

TEN YEAR LEAGUE RECORD

		P	*W*	*D*	*L*	*F*	*A*	*Pts*	*Pos*
1995-96	Div 3	46	11	20	15	54	64	53	19
1996-97	Div 3	46	16	16	14	47	45	64	11
1997-98	Div 3	46	16	17	13	64	55	65	12
1998-99	Div 3	46	19	10	17	60	58	67	8
1999-2000	Div 3	46	16	8	22	50	65	56	17
2000-01	Div 3	46	15	13	18	64	72	68	13
2001-02	Div 3	46	24	7	15	72	60	79	3
2002-03	Div 2	46	12	8	26	66	97	44	23
2003-04	Div 3	46	22	9	15	76	62	75	5
2004-05	FL 2	46	15	15	16	56	56	60	13

DID YOU KNOW ?

Mansfield Town made several applications to join Division Three (North) from 1925 without success. In 1931 the club decided to change tack and apply to the Southern Section. They succeeded. But the following year were transferred north!

MANSFIELD TOWN 2004–05 LEAGUE RECORD

Match No.	*Date*	*Venue*	*Opponents*	*Result*	*H/T Score*	*Lg. Pos.*	*Goalscorers*	*Attendance*
1	Aug 7	H	Bristol R	L 0-2	0-1	—		5709
2	11	A	Oxford U	L 0-1	0-1	—		5029
3	14	A	Chester C	W 3-0	0-0	17	Asamoah [46], Buxton [62], Larkin [78]	2648
4	21	H	Kidderminster H	W 2-1	1-1	9	Larkin 2 [16, 48]	3859
5	28	A	Grimsby T	L 0-2	0-1	15		5693
6	30	H	Yeovil T	W 4-1	1-1	9	Asamoah [8], Artell [67], Larkin [69], Corden [71]	3826
7	Sept 5	H	Northampton T	W 4-1	2-1	5	Asamoah [12], Corden 2 [44, 86], Larkin [55]	5173
8	11	A	Cambridge U	D 2-2	1-1	7	Larkin [44], MacKenzie [63]	3549
9	18	H	Rochdale	W 1-0	0-0	4	Larkin [85]	4266
10	25	A	Scunthorpe U	D 1-1	0-1	5	Artell [70]	5463
11	Oct 2	H	Lincoln C	D 2-2	1-2	7	Murray [45], John-Baptiste [51]	5349
12	8	A	Swansea C	L 0-1	0-0	—		8868
13	16	H	Notts Co	W 3-1	2-0	4	Day [25], Woodman [45], Larkin [69]	7682
14	19	A	Cheltenham T	L 0-2	0-1	—		2706
15	23	A	Wycombe W	D 1-1	0-0	7	Asamoah [46]	4215
16	30	H	Bury	D 0-0	0-0	8		4147
17	Nov 6	H	Macclesfield T	L 0-1	0-1	12		3816
18	20	A	Boston U	D 0-0	0-0	12		3354
19	27	H	Leyton Orient	L 0-1	0-0	16		3803
20	Dec 7	A	Darlington	L 1-2	1-0	—	Barker [36]	3686
21	11	H	Rushden & D	D 0-0	0-0	17		3776
22	18	A	Shrewsbury T	W 2-0	1-0	16	Asamoah [22], Murray [74]	3469
23	28	A	Southend U	W 1-0	0-0	14	Warne [80]	7082
24	Jan 1	A	Northampton T	L 1-2	1-0	15	Rowson (og) [45]	6122
25	3	H	Scunthorpe U	W 1-0	1-0	14	Murray [19]	5315
26	11	H	Cambridge U	D 0-0	0-0	—		3557
27	15	A	Rochdale	D 1-1	1-1	15	Barker [38]	2576
28	22	H	Southend U	D 1-1	0-0	15	Murray [53]	3894
29	29	A	Lincoln C	L 0-2	0-0	17		5511
30	Feb 5	A	Notts Co	W 1-0	1-0	15	Barker [21]	10,005
31	8	H	Swansea C	W 1-0	1-0	—	Barker [45]	3829
32	12	H	Cheltenham T	L 1-2	0-0	13	Larkin (pen) [73]	3665
33	19	A	Bury	W 2-0	1-0	11	Murray [38], Rundle [82]	2529
34	22	H	Wycombe W	L 1-4	0-0	—	Barker [54]	2497
35	26	A	Rushden & D	D 0-0	0-0	12		3096
36	Mar 5	H	Shrewsbury T	D 1-1	0-0	14	Neil [64]	3278
37	12	H	Oxford U	L 1-3	0-2	14	Larkin (pen) [90]	3030
38	19	A	Bristol R	D 4-4	1-2	16	Barker 2 [19, 49], Larkin [46], Lloyd [68]	5294
39	25	H	Chester C	D 0-0	0-0	—		3437
40	28	A	Kidderminster H	W 3-1	0-1	11	Barker 2 [48, 85], Brown [51]	3237
41	Apr 2	H	Grimsby T	W 2-0	1-0	11	Brown [36], Rundle [85]	3424
42	9	A	Yeovil T	L 2-5	1-1	11	Rundle [32], Day (pen) [51]	6471
43	16	H	Darlington	D 1-1	0-0	11	Day [90]	3569
44	23	A	Macclesfield T	L 1-3	0-1	15	Lloyd [54]	2456
45	30	H	Boston U	W 3-2	0-0	11	Barker [53], Lloyd [65], Rundle [70]	3223
46	May 7	A	Leyton Orient	L 1-2	0-2	13	Lloyd [88]	3882

Final League Position: 13

GOALSCORERS

League (56): Larkin 11 (2 pens), Barker 10, Asamoah 5, Murray 5, Lloyd 4, Rundle 4, Corden 3, Day 3 (1 pen), Artell 2, Brown 2, Buxton 1, John-Baptiste 1, MacKenzie 1, Neil 1, Warne 1, Woodman 1, own goal 1.
Carling Cup (0).
FA Cup (2): John-Baptiste 1, Neil 1.
LDV Vans Trophy (0).

Pilkington K 42	McNiven S 24 + 1	Eaton A 2	Murray A 27 + 5	Artell D 19	John-Baptiste A 41	Williamson L 3 + 1	Neil A 40 + 1	Larkin C 29 + 4	Asamoah D 24 + 6	Corden W 19 + 5	Tate C — + 4	O'Neill J 3 + 12	Day R 11 + 7	MacKenzie N 9 + 6	Buxton J 29 + 1	Curtis T 26 + 6	Woodman C 8	Dimech L 19 + 6	Ipoua G 4 + 1	Talbot J 2	McLachlan F 16 + 5	Barker R 28	Warne P 7	Brown S 16 + 5	Kitamirike J 2	Maxwell L 1	Wood C — + 1	Smeltz S 1 + 4	Jelleyman G 14	Rundle A 18	Lambu G 1	Lloyd C 7 + 3	Barrowman A 1 + 2	Coke G 7 + 2	Heron D 1 + 2	White J 4	McIntosh A 1	*Match No.*
1	2	3^3	4	5	6	7^1	8	9	10	11^2	12	13	14																									1
1	2	3^3	4	5	6	7■	8^1	9	10^2	11		12	13	14																								2
1	2		4	5	6			9	10		12	11^1		8	3	7																						3
1	2		4^1	5	6	12		9	10	13		3^2		8	11	7																						4
1	2		4	5	6	3^1	13	9	10	12	14	11^3		8^2		7																						5
1	2		12	5	6^1		7^2	9	10^3	11	14		4	8	3	13																						6
1	2		12	5	6^2		8	9^3	10	11		14	4	7^1	3	13																						7
1	2		12	5	6		7^1	9	10^3	11		14	4	8^2	3	13																						8
1	2		12	5	6		7	9	10	11^2		13		8^1	3	4																						9
1	2		4	5	6		7	9	10^1	11			12			8	3																					10
1	2		4^1	5	6		8^2	9	10^3	11		14	13	12		7	3																					11
1	2			5	6		7	9	10	11^2		13	4	8^1		12	3																					12
1	2		4	5			7^1	9	10			13	6^3	12		11	3	14	8^2																			13
1	2		4	5			7^1	9	10			13	6^3	12		11	3^2	14	8																			14
1	2			5	6		7^1	9	10	12		13				11	3	4	8^2																			15
1	2			5	6		7^2	9	10	12		14		13		11^3	3	4	8^1																			16
1	2			5	6		7	9	10^1	11^2		12		13		8	3	4^3	14																			17
1			12	5	6		7	9		11				8	2	4				3	10^1																	18
1			4	5			8			11					2	7		6		3		9	10															19
1			4		6		3		10^1	11					2	7		5				9	8	12														20
1			4		6		7		10	11					2	3		5				9	8															21
1			4		6		2		10^1	11					3	7		5				9	8	12														22
1			4^1		6				10						3	7		5			12	9	11	8	2													23
1			4		6			12	10■	13					3	7^3		5			14	9	11	8^2	2^1													24
1			4		6		3	10^1		7					2			5			8	9	11	12														25
1			4		6		3	10		11					2			5			8	9		7														26
1					6		3	10^1	12	11					2			5			4	9		8^3		7^2	13	14										27
1			4		6		7	10^1	12	11					2			5				9		8					3									28
1			4		6		7	12	13						2	8^2		5■			14	9		11^1					3	10^3								29
1			4		6		7		8						2	5						9		12				10^1	3	11								30
1			4		6		2	12	10^1						5	7						9^2		8■				13	3	11								31
1			4		6		2	10	12						5	7						9							3	11	8^1							32
1			4^3		6		2	10^1	12						5	7					8	9^2						13	3	11		14						33
1			4		6		2	10	12						5	7					8^1	9							3	11								34
1			4		6		7	10^1							2			5			8	9						12	3	11								35
1			4		6^1		2	10^3							5	13		12			8^2	9		7					3	11			14					36
1	2		4				7^3	12					6			8		5			13	9		14					3	11^2			10^1					37
1	2						3	10							6			5			4	9								11		7		8				38
1	2				6		3								5			12			4	9		10						11^1		8		7				39
1	3				6		2^1						12		5						8	9		10						11		7^2	13	4				40
1					6		4	10^2					5		2						8^1	9		7					3	11^3		12		13	14			41
1	2				6								5								8	9		10					3	11		7		4				42
					6		2^3						5		12			13			8	9		10					3	11		7^1		4^2	14	1		43
	12				6		2						5					13			8^2	9		10					3^1	11		7		4		1		44
	3				6		2						12			13		5			8^3	9		10						11		14		4^2	7^1	1		45
	3^3				6		7^1						14			4		5			12	9		10						11		8		13		1	2^2	46

FA Cup
First Round — Colchester U — (h) 1-1
(a) 1-4

Carling Cup
First Round — Preston NE — (h) 0-4

LDV Vans Trophy
First Round — Darlington — (h) 0-0
Second Round — Macclesfield T — (a) 0-4

MIDDLESBROUGH FA Premiership

FOUNDATION

A previous belief that Middlesbrough Football Club was founded at a tripe supper at the Corporation Hotel has proved to be erroneous. In fact, members of Middlesbrough Cricket Club were responsible for forming it at a meeting in the gymnasium of the Albert Park Hotel in 1875.

Riverside Stadium, Middlesbrough TS3 6RS.

Telephone: 0870 421 1986.

Fax: (01642) 877 731.

Ticket Office: 0870 421 1986.

Website: www.mfc.co.uk

Email: enquiries@mfc.co.uk

Ground Capacity: 35,120.

Record Attendance: Ayresome Park: 53,536 v Newcastle U, Division 1, 27 December 1949. Riverside Stadium: 34,814 v Newcastle U, FA Premier League, 5 March 2003.

Pitch Measurements: 105m × 68m.

Chairman: Steve Gibson.

Chief Executive: Keith Lamb.

Secretary: Karen Nelson.

Manager: Steve McClaren.

Physio: Grant Downie.

HONOURS

Football League: Division 1 – Champions 1994–95; Runners-up 1997–98; Division 2 – Champions 1926–27, 1928–29, 1973–74; Runners-up 1901–02, 1991–92; Division 3 – Runners-up 1966–67, 1986–87.

FA Cup: Runners-up 1997.

Football League Cup: Winners 2004; Runners-up 1997, 1998.

Amateur Cup: Winners 1895, 1898.

Anglo-Scottish Cup: Winners 1976.

Zenith Data Systems Cup: Runners-up 1990.

European Competitions: *UEFA Cup:* 2004–05.

Colours: Red shirts with white chest band, red shorts, red stockings.

Change Colours: Royal blue shirts with navy trim, royal blue shorts with navy trim, royal blue stockings.

Year Formed: 1876; re-formed 1986.

Turned Professional: 1889; became amateur 1892, and professional again, 1899.

Ltd Co: 1892.

Club Nickname: 'Boro'.

Previous Grounds: 1877, Old Archery Ground, Albert Park; 1879, Breckon Hill; 1882, Linthorpe Road Ground; 1903, Ayresome Park; 1995, Cellnet Riverside Stadium.

First Football League Game: 2 September 1899, Division 2, v Lincoln C (a) L 0–3 – Smith; Shaw, Ramsey; Allport, McNally, McCracken; Wanless, Longstaffe, Gettins, Page, Pugh.

Record League Victory: 9–0 v Brighton & HA, Division 2, 23 August 1958 – Taylor; Bilcliff, Robinson; Harris (2p), Phillips, Walley; Day, McLean, Clough (5), Peacock (2), Holliday.

Record Cup Victory: 7–0 v Hereford U, Coca-Cola Cup 2nd rd, 1st leg, 18 September 1996 – Miller; Fleming (1), Branco (1), Whyte, Vickers, Whelan, Emerson (1), Mustoe, Stamp, Juninho, Ravanelli (4).

SKY SPORTS FACT FILE

Brian Clough was particularly harsh on Brighton & Hove Albion and Scunthorpe United for Middlesbrough in 1958–59, scoring five and three against Albion and two separate hat-tricks over United. The respective scores in these matches were 9–0, 6–4, 6–1 and 3–0.

Record Defeat: 0–9 v Blackburn R, Division 2, 6 November 1954.

Most League Points (2 for a win): 65, Division 2, 1973–74.

Most League Points (3 for a win): 94, Division 3, 1986–87.

Most League Goals: 122, Division 2, 1926–27.

Highest League Scorer in Season: George Camsell, 59, Division 2, 1926–27 (Second Division record).

Most League Goals in Total Aggregate: George Camsell, 325, 1925–39.

Most League Goals in One Match: 5, Andy Wilson v Nottingham F, Division 1, 6 October 1923; 5, George Camsell v Manchester C, Division 2, 25 December 1926; 5, George Camsell v Aston Villa, Division 1, 9 September 1935; 5, Brian Clough v Brighton & HA, Division 2, 22 August 1958.

Most Capped Player: Wilf Mannion, 26, England.

Most League Appearances: Tim Williamson, 563, 1902–23.

Youngest League Player: Stephen Bell, 16 years 323 days v Southampton, 30 January 1982; Sam Lawrie, 16 years 323 days v Arsenal, 3 November 1951.

Record Transfer Fee Received: £12,000,000 from Atletico Madrid for Juninho, July 1997.

Record Transfer Fee Paid: £8,100,500 to Empoli for Massimo Maccarone, July 2002.

Football League Record: 1899 Elected to Division 2; 1902–24 Division 1; 1924–27 Division 2; 1927–28 Division 1; 1928–29 Division 2; 1929–54 Division 1; 1954–66 Division 2; 1966–67 Division 3; 1967–74 Division 2; 1974–82 Division 1; 1982–86 Division 2; 1986–87 Division 3; 1987–88 Division 2; 1988–89 Division 1; 1989–92 Division 2; 1992–93 FA Premier League; 1993–95 Division 1; 1995–97 FA Premier League; 1997–98 Division 1; 1998– FA Premier League.

MANAGERS

John Robson 1899–1905
Alex Mackie 1905–06
Andy Aitken 1906–09
J. Gunter 1908–10
(Secretary-Manager)
Andy Walker 1910–11
Tom McIntosh 1911–19
Jimmy Howie 1920–23
Herbert Bamlett 1923–26
Peter McWilliam 1927–34
Wilf Gillow 1934–44
David Jack 1944–52
Walter Rowley 1952–54
Bob Dennison 1954–63
Raich Carter 1963–66
Stan Anderson 1966–73
Jack Charlton 1973–77
John Neal 1977–81
Bobby Murdoch 1981–82
Malcolm Allison 1982–84
Willie Maddren 1984–86
Bruce Rioch 1986–90
Colin Todd 1990–91
Lennie Lawrence 1991–94
Bryan Robson 1994–2001
Steve McClaren July 2001–

LATEST SEQUENCES

Longest Sequence of League Wins: 9, 16.2.1974 – 6.4.1974.

Longest Sequence of League Defeats: 8, 26.12.1995 – 17.2.1996.

Longest Sequence of League Draws: 8, 3.4.1971 – 1.5.1971.

Longest Sequence of Unbeaten League Matches: 24, 8.9.1973 – 19.1.1974.

Longest Sequence Without a League Win: 19, 3.10.1981 – 6.3.1982.

Successive Scoring Runs: 26 from 21.9.1946.

Successive Non-scoring Runs: 4 from 24.11.1923.

TEN YEAR LEAGUE RECORD

		P	*W*	*D*	*L*	*F*	*A*	*Pts*	*Pos*
1995-96	PR Lge	38	11	10	17	35	50	43	12
1996-97	PR Lge	38	10	12	16	51	60	39	19
1997-98	Div 1	46	27	10	9	77	41	91	2
1998-99	PR Lge	38	12	15	11	48	54	51	9
1999-2000	PR Lge	38	14	10	14	46	52	52	12
2000-01	PR Lge	38	9	15	14	44	44	42	14
2001-02	PR Lge	38	12	9	17	35	47	45	12
2002-03	PR Lge	38	13	10	15	48	44	49	11
2003-04	PR Lge	38	13	9	16	44	52	48	11
2004-05	PR Lge	38	14	13	11	53	46	55	7

DID YOU KNOW

Before the advent of the Premier League Middlesbrough achieved average attendances over 30,000 in five successive seasons from 1946–47. The 36,123 in 1950–51 was the highest in the club's history when they finished sixth.

MIDDLESBROUGH 2004–05 LEAGUE RECORD

Match No.	Date	Venue	Opponents	Result		H/T Score	Lg. Pos.	Goalscorers	Attendance
1	Aug 14	H	Newcastle U	D	2-2	0-1	—	Downing [73], Hasselbaink [90]	34,268
2	22	A	Arsenal	L	3-5	1-1	19	Job [43], Hasselbaink [50], Queudrue [53]	37,415
3	25	A	Fulham	W	2-0	0-0	—	Viduka [54], Nemeth [79]	17,759
4	28	H	Crystal Palace	W	2-1	0-0	5	Poovic (og) [61], Hasselbaink [78]	31,560
5	Sept 11	H	Birmingham C	W	2-1	1-1	4	Viduka 2 [27, 48]	30,252
6	19	A	Everton	L	0-1	0-0	6		34,078
7	25	H	Chelsea	L	0-1	0-0	10		32,341
8	Oct 3	A	Manchester U	D	1-1	1-0	9	Downing [33]	67,988
9	16	A	Blackburn R	W	4-0	0-0	5	Hasselbaink 3 [46, 57, 90], Boateng [50]	20,385
10	24	H	Portsmouth	D	1-1	0-1	8	Downing [74]	30,964
11	30	A	Charlton Ath	W	2-1	1-0	5	El Karkouri (og) [21], Zenden [58]	26,031
12	Nov 7	H	Bolton W	D	1-1	0-0	5	Boateng [90]	29,656
13	14	A	WBA	W	2-1	1-1	4	Purse (og) [32], Zenden [52]	24,008
14	20	H	Liverpool	W	2-0	1-0	4	Riggott [36], Zenden [62]	34,751
15	28	A	Tottenham H	L	0-2	0-0	5		35,772
16	Dec 6	H	Manchester C	W	3-2	1-1	—	Viduka 2 [9, 54], Hasselbaink [65]	29,787
17	11	A	Southampton	D	2-2	0-1	5	Higginbotham (og) [89], Downing [90]	29018
18	18	H	Aston Villa	W	3-0	1-0	5	Hasselbaink [20], Job [68], Reiziger [88]	30,338
19	26	A	Birmingham C	L	0-2	0-2	5		29,082
20	28	H	Norwich C	W	2-0	0-0	5	Job 2 [52, 54]	34,836
21	Jan 1	H	Manchester U	L	0-2	0-1	6		34,299
22	4	A	Chelsea	L	0-2	0-2	6		40,982
23	16	H	Everton	D	1-1	1-0	6	Zenden [26]	31,794
24	22	A	Norwich C	D	4-4	1-1	6	Hasselbaink 2 [34, 78], Queudrue 2 [49, 55]	24,547
25	Feb 1	A	Portsmouth	L	1-2	1-1	—	Christie [35]	19,620
26	5	H	Blackburn R	W	1-0	1-0	6	Queudrue [35]	30,564
27	12	A	Bolton W	D	0-0	0-0	6		24,322
28	27	H	Charlton Ath	D	2-2	0-1	6	Riggott [74], Graham [86]	29,603
29	Mar 5	A	Aston Villa	L	0-2	0-0	6		34,201
30	20	H	Southampton	L	1-3	1-1	9	Hasselbaink [41]	30,082
31	Apr 2	A	Crystal Palace	W	1-0	1-0	7	Queudrue [35]	24,274
32	9	H	Arsenal	L	0-1	0-0	8		33,874
33	19	H	Fulham	D	1-1	0-0	—	Zenden (pen) [90]	30,650
34	23	H	WBA	W	4-0	3-0	7	Nemeth 2 [27, 37], Hasselbaink [33], Downing [90]	32,951
35	27	A	Newcastle U	D	0-0	0-0	—		52,047
36	30	A	Liverpool	D	1-1	1-0	8	Nemeth [4]	43,250
37	May 7	H	Tottenham H	W	1-0	1-0	7	Boateng [11]	34,766
38	15	A	Manchester C	D	1-1	1-0	7	Hasselbaink [23]	47,221

Final League Position: 7

GOALSCORERS

League (53): Hasselbaink 13, Downing 5, Queudrue 5, Viduka 5, Zenden 5 (1 pen), Job 4, Nemeth 4, Boateng 3, Riggott 2, Christie 1, Graham 1, Reiziger 1, own goals 4.
Carling Cup (3): Graham 1, Morrison 1, Nemeth 1.
FA Cup (2): Doriva 1, Job 1.
UEFA Cup (16): Hasselbaink 3, Morrison 3, Zenden 3, Job 2, Viduka 2, Downing 1, Nemeth 1, Riggott 1.

Schwarzer M 31	Reiziger M 15 + 3	Parnaby S 16 + 3	Riggott C 20 + 1	Ehiogu U 9 + 1	Boateng G 25	Mendieta G 7	Parlour R 32 + 1	Hasselbaink J 36	Job J 10 + 13	Zenden B 36	Downing S 28 + 7	Nemeth S 18 + 13	Queudrue F 31	Cooper C 11 + 4	Southgate G 36	Doriva15 + 11	Viduka M 15 + 1	Morrison J 4 + 10	McMahon A 12 + 1	Graham D — + 11	Bates M — + 2	Christie M 2	Nash C 2	Jones B 5	Kennedy J — + 1	Davies A 2 + 1	*Match No.*
1	2	3[1]	4	5	6	7	8	9	10[2]	11	12	13															1
1	2[1]	12	4		6	7	8	9	10	11[2]		13	3	5													2
1		2	4		6[1]	7[2]	8	9	14	11		13	3		5	12	10[3]										3
1		2	4		6	7[2]	8	9		11[1]	12	13	3		5		10										4
1		2	12	5[1]	6		8	9	13	11		7[2]	3		4	14	10[3]										5
1		2	4		6		8	9	12	11[2]	13	7[3]	3		5	14	10[1]										6
1		2			8		7[1]	9	12[2]	11	13		3	4	5	6	10[3]	14									7
1		3[1]	4		6	8				11	10[3]	9		12	5	13		7[2]	2	14							8
1		3[1]	4		6	7[2]	8	9		11	10	12			5			13	2								9
1			4		6[2]	7[1]	8	9		3	11	12		13	5		10		2								10
1			4		6		8	9	12	11	7[2]		3		5	13	10[1]		2								11
1			4		6		8	9	10[1]	11	7		3		5		12	13	2[2]								12
1			4		6		8	9		11[1]	7		3		5	12	10		2								13
1			4		6		8	9[1]	12	11[2]	7	13	3		5		10		2								14
1	12		4		6		8	9		11	7	13	3■		5		10[2]		2[1]								15
1	3						6	9[2]		11	7	8[1]		4	5	12	10		2		13						16
1	3				6		8[1]	9	12	11	7	13		4	5		10		2[2]								17
1	3		4[2]		6			9	12	11	7	8[3]		13	5	14	10[1]		2								18
1	2						8	9	12	11	7	13	3	4[3]	5	6[2]	10[1]	14									19
1	2						6	9	10	11	7	8[1]	3	4	5			12									20
1	2						8	9	10[1]	11	7	12	3	4	5	6[2]		13									21
1	2						8	9	12	11	7	10[1]	3	4	5	6[2]		13									22
1	2			5[1]				9	10	11	7	8[2]	3	12	4	6		13									23
1	2						8	9	10[2]	11	7		3		5	6[1]		12	4	13							24
1	2						6	9	12	11	7		3	4[2]	5			8	13[3]	14		10[1]					25
1	4	2					6■		10[1]	11	7		3		5	12		8[3]		13	14	9[2]					26
1	2	8	4					9	10[1]		11	12	3		5	6		7									27
	2[3]	12	4				8[2]	9	13	11	7	10[1]	3		5	6				14			1				28
		2	4				8	9	12	11	7[1]	10[2]	3		5	6				13			1				29
1	12	2[1]	4					9	10	11	7	8[2]	3		5	6				13							30
1		2	4		6		8	9		11[3]	7	12[2]	3		5	14	10[1]			13							31
		2	4	12	6		8[1]	9			7	10	3		5	11[2]				13				1			32
				5	6		8	9		11	7	10	3	2[1]	4									1	12		33
				5	8		12	9		11[1]	7	10[2]	3	2[3]	4	6				13				1		14	34
				5	8		7	9		11[1]	12	10[2]	3		4	6				13				1		2	35
		12		5	8		7[1]	9		11	13	10[2]	3		4	6								1		2	36
1		2		5	6		8	9		11[1]	7	10	3		4	12											37
1	13	2		5	8		7[1]	9		11	14	10[3]	3		4	6		12[2]									38

FA Cup

Third Round	Notts Co	(a)	2-1
Fourth Round	Manchester U	(a)	0-3

Carling Cup

Third Round	Coventry C	(h)	3-0
Fourth Round	Liverpool	(a)	0-2

UEFA Cup

First Round	Banik Ostrava	(h)	3-0
		(a)	1-1
Group E	Aigalio	(a)	1-0
	Lazio	(h)	2-0
	Villarreal	(a)	0-2
	Partizan Belgrade	(h)	3-0
Third Round	Graz	(a)	2-2
		(h)	2-1
Fourth Round	Sporting Lisbon	(h)	2-3
		(a)	0-1

MILLWALL FL Championship

FOUNDATION

Formed in 1885 as Millwall Rovers by employees of Morton & Co, a jam and marmalade factory in West Ferry Road. The founders were predominantly Scotsmen. Their first headquarters was The Islanders pub in Tooke Street, Millwall. Their first trophy was the East End Cup in 1887.

The Den, Zampa Road, London SE16 3LN.

Telephone: (020) 7232 1222.

Fax: (020) 7231 3663.

Ticket Office: (020) 7231 9999.

Website: www.millwallfc.co.uk

Email: info@millwallplc.com

Ground Capacity: 20,146.

Record Attendance: 20,093 v Arsenal, FA Cup 3rd rd, 10 January 1994.

Pitch Measurements: 100m × 68m.

Chief Executive: Ken Brown

Secretary: Yvonne Haines.

Manager: Steve Claridge.

Assistant Manager: TBA.

Physio: Gerry Docherty.

Colours: Blue and white shirts, blue shorts, blue stockings.

Change Colours: All yellow.

Year Formed: 1885.

Turned Professional: 1893.

Ltd Co.: 1894.

Previous Names: 1885, Millwall Rovers; 1889, Millwall Athletic; 1899, Millwall; 1985, Millwall Football & Athletic Company.

Club Nickname: 'The Lions'.

Previous Grounds: 1885, Glengall Road, Millwall; 1886, Back of 'Lord Nelson'; 1890, East Ferry Road; 1901, North Greenwich; 1910, The Den, Cold Blow Lane; 1993, The Den, Bermondsey.

First Football League Game: 28 August 1920, Division 3, v Bristol R (h) W 2–0 – Lansdale; Fort, Hodge; Voisey (1), Riddell, McAlpine; Waterall, Travers, Broad (1), Sutherland, Dempsey.

Record League Victory: 9–1 v Torquay U, Division 3 (S), 29 August 1927 – Lansdale, Tilling, Hill, Amos, Bryant (3), Graham, Chance, Hawkins (3), Landells (1), Phillips (2), Black. 9–1 v Coventry C, Division 3 (S), 19 November 1927 – Lansdale, Fort, Hill, Amos, Collins (1), Graham, Chance, Landells (4), Cock (2), Phillips (2), Black.

HONOURS

Football League: Division 1 best season: 3rd, 1993–94; Division 2 – Champions 1987–88, 2000–01; Division 3 (S) – Champions 1927–28, 1937–38; Runners-up 1952–53; Division 3 – Runners-up 1965–66, 1984–85; Division 4 – Champions 1961–62; Runners-up 1964–65.

FA Cup: Runners-up 2004; Semi-final 1900, 1903, 1937 (first Division 3 side to reach semi-final).

Football League Cup: best season: 5th rd, 1974, 1977, 1995.

Football League Trophy: Winners 1983.

Auto Windscreens Shield: Runners-up 1999.

European Competitions: *UEFA Cup:* 2004–05.

SKY SPORTS FACT FILE

Though they lost their opening two fixtures in 1961–62 and a blip in late September when just a point came from four outings, Millwall clinched the Fourth Division title thanks to Peter Burridge (23 goals), David Jones (22) and Pat Terry (13).

Record Cup Victory: 7–0 v Gateshead, FA Cup 2nd rd, 12 December 1936 – Yuill; Ted Smith, Inns; Brolly, Hancock, Forsyth; Thomas (1), Mangnall (1), Ken Burditt (2), McCartney (2), Thorogood (1).

Record Defeat: 1–9 v Aston Villa, FA Cup 4th rd, 28 January 1946.

Most League Points (2 for a win): 65, Division 3 (S), 1927–28 and Division 3, 1965–66.

Most League Points (3 for a win): 93, Division 2, 2000–01.

Most League Goals: 127, Division 3 (S), 1927–28.

Highest League Scorer in Season: Richard Parker, 37, Division 3 (S), 1926–27.

Most League Goals in Total Aggregate: Teddy Sheringham, 93, 1984–91.

Most League Goals in One Match: 5, Richard Parker v Norwich C, Division 3S, 28 August 1926.

Most Capped Player: Eamonn Dunphy, 22 (23), Republic of Ireland.

Most League Appearances: Barry Kitchener, 523, 1967–82.

Youngest League Player: Moses Ashikodi, 15 years 240 days v Brighton & HA, 22 February 2003.

Record Transfer Fee Received: £2,300,000 from Liverpool for Mark Kennedy, March 1995.

Record Transfer Fee Paid: £800,000 to Derby Co for Paul Goddard, December 1989.

Football League Record: 1920 Original Members of Division 3; 1921 Division 3 (S); 1928–34 Division 2; 1934–38 Division 3 (S); 1938–48 Division 2; 1948–58 Division 3 (S); 1958–62 Division 4; 1962–64 Division 3; 1964–65 Division 4; 1965–66 Division 3; 1966–75 Division 2; 1975–76 Division 3; 1976–79 Division 2; 1979–85 Division 3; 1985–88 Division 2; 1988–90 Division 1; 1990–92 Division 2; 1992–96 Division 1; 1996–2001 Division 2; 2001–04 Division 1; 2004– FLC.

MANAGERS

F. B. Kidd 1894–99
(Hon. Treasurer/Manager)
E. R. Stopher 1899–1900
(Hon. Treasurer/Manager)
George Saunders 1900–11
(Hon. Treasurer/Manager)
Herbert Lipsham 1911–19
Robert Hunter 1919–33
Bill McCracken 1933–36
Charlie Hewitt 1936–40
Bill Voisey 1940–44
Jack Cock 1944–48
Charlie Hewitt 1948–56
Ron Gray 1956–57
Jimmy Seed 1958–59
Reg Smith 1959–61
Ron Gray 1961–63
Billy Gray 1963–66
Benny Fenton 1966–74
Gordon Jago 1974–77
George Petchey 1978–80
Peter Anderson 1980–82
George Graham 1982–86
John Docherty 1986–90
Bob Pearson 1990
Bruce Rioch 1990–92
Mick McCarthy 1992–96
Jimmy Nicholl 1996–97
John Docherty 1997
Billy Bonds 1997–98
Keith Stevens May 1998–2000
(then Joint Manager)
(*plus* Alan McLeary 1999–2000)
Mark McGhee 2000–03
Dennis Wise 2003–05
Steve Claridge June 2005–

LATEST SEQUENCES

Longest Sequence of League Wins: 10, 10.3.1928 – 25.4.1928.

Longest Sequence of League Defeats: 11, 10.4.1929 – 16.9.1929.

Longest Sequence of League Draws: 5, 22.12.1973 – 12.1.1974.

Longest Sequence of Unbeaten League Matches: 19, 22.8.1959 – 31.10.1959.

Longest Sequence Without a League Win: 20, 26.12.1989 – 5.5.1990.

Successive Scoring Runs: 22 from 8.12.1923.

Successive Non-scoring Runs: 6 from 20.12.1947.

TEN YEAR LEAGUE RECORD

		P	*W*	*D*	*L*	*F*	*A*	*Pts*	*Pos*
1995-96	Div 1	46	13	13	20	43	63	52	22
1996-97	Div 2	46	16	13	17	50	55	61	14
1997-98	Div 2	46	14	13	19	43	54	55	18
1998-99	Div 2	46	17	11	18	52	59	62	10
1999-2000	Div 2	46	23	13	10	76	50	82	5
2000-01	Div 2	46	28	9	9	89	38	93	1
2001-02	Div 1	46	22	11	13	69	48	77	4
2002-03	Div 1	46	19	9	18	59	69	66	9
2003-04	Div 1	46	18	15	13	55	48	69	10
2004-05	FL C	46	18	12	16	51	45	66	10

DID YOU KNOW ?

The youngest ever first team player for Millwall was Will Jones at 15 years 168 days v Tottenham Hotspur in a London Senior Cup tie on 31 January 1891, scoring twice. Tragically he died at 23 after serious injury scoring in a Ryde v Sandown match.

MILLWALL 2004–05 LEAGUE RECORD

Match No.	*Date*	*Venue*	*Opponents*	*Result*	*H/T Score*	*Lg. Pos.*	*Goalscorers*	*Attendance*
1	Aug 7	A	Plymouth Arg	D 0-0	0-0	—		16,063
2	10	H	Wigan Ath	L 0-2	0-0	—		10,660
3	14	H	Leicester C	W 2-0	1-0	13	Morris ^{37}, Dichio ^{76}	11,754
4	21	A	Coventry C	W 1-0	0-0	6	Dichio ^{80}	13,910
5	28	H	Reading	W 1-0	0-0	5	Dichio ^{79}	12,098
6	Sept 12	A	Ipswich T	L 0-2	0-0	11		21,246
7	19	H	Watford	L 0-2	0-0	18		10,865
8	22	H	Derby Co	W 3-1	1-0	—	Wise ^{2}, Simpson ^{48}, Ifill ^{90}	9132
9	25	A	Rotherham U	D 1-1	0-0	9	Ifill ^{77}	5062
10	Oct 3	H	Nottingham F	W 1-0	1-0	9	Livermore ^{45}	11,233
11	16	A	Sunderland	L 0-1	0-0	13		23,839
12	19	H	Gillingham	W 2-1	2-0	—	Hayles ^{33}, Dunne ^{44}	10,722
13	23	H	Cardiff C	D 2-2	0-1	9	Tessem ^{47}, Harris ^{74}	10,476
14	30	A	Stoke C	L 0-1	0-0	11		14,125
15	Nov 2	A	QPR	D 1-1	0-0	—	Hayles ^{51}	16,685
16	5	H	Sunderland	W 2-0	2-0	—	Wise (pen) ^{33}, Livermore ^{45}	10,513
17	13	A	Preston NE	D 1-1	0-1	11	Hayles ^{87}	10,339
18	21	H	West Ham U	W 1-0	0-0	9	Dichio ^{78}	15,025
19	27	A	Burnley	L 0-1	0-0	9		11,471
20	30	A	Crewe Alex	L 1-2	0-1	—	Ifill ^{71}	5409
21	Dec 4	H	Sheffield U	L 1-2	0-0	13	Phillips ^{58}	11,207
22	7	A	Wolverhampton W	W 2-1	1-0	—	Dobie ^{9}, Dichio ^{72}	24,748
23	11	H	Brighton & HA	W 2-0	1-0	8	Dobie ^{21}, Ifill ^{78}	12,196
24	19	A	Leeds U	D 1-1	0-1	9	Morris (pen) ^{86}	26,265
25	26	H	Ipswich T	W 3-1	1-0	8	Hayles ^{45}, Dichio ^{52}, Dobie ^{79}	14,532
26	28	A	Derby Co	W 3-0	1-0	6	Hayles 3 $^{18, 52, 58}$	27,725
27	Jan 1	A	Watford	L 0-1	0-0	7		13,158
28	3	H	Rotherham U	L 1-2	1-1	7	Dunne ^{16}	11,725
29	15	A	Nottingham F	W 2-1	2-0	6	Hayles ^{11}, Dunne ^{37}	25,949
30	22	H	Wolverhampton W	L 1-2	0-1	7	Wise (pen) ^{77}	13,145
31	Feb 5	H	QPR	D 0-0	0-0	9		15,603
32	12	A	Gillingham	D 0-0	0-0	9		9127
33	19	H	Stoke C	L 0-1	0-1	9		11,036
34	22	A	Cardiff C	W 1-0	1-0	—	Dichio (pen) ^{20}	11,424
35	26	A	Brighton & HA	L 0-1	0-0	9		6608
36	Mar 6	H	Leeds U	D 1-1	1-0	8	Robinson T ^{17}	12,510
37	12	A	Wigan Ath	L 0-2	0-0	12		9614
38	15	H	Coventry C	D 1-1	0-0	—	Morris (pen) ^{69}	8835
39	20	H	Plymouth Arg	W 3-0	1-0	10	Sweeney ^{15}, Hayles ^{56}, Dichio ^{63}	11,465
40	Apr 2	A	Leicester C	L 1-3	0-1	10	Dichio ^{68}	22,338
41	5	A	Reading	L 1-2	1-0	—	Dichio ^{39}	14,379
42	9	H	Crewe Alex	W 4-3	1-0	9	Hayles ^{27}, Elliott ^{49}, Morris ^{50}, May (pen) ^{85}	10,767
43	16	A	West Ham U	D 1-1	1-1	9	Hayles ^{12}	28,221
44	24	H	Preston NE	W 2-1	1-0	9	Sweeney ^{9}, Hayles ^{76}	11,417
45	30	A	Sheffield U	W 1-0	1-0	9	Morris ^{5}	19,797
46	May 8	H	Burnley	D 0-0	0-0	10		12,171

Final League Position: 10

GOALSCORERS

League (51): Hayles 12, Dichio 10 (1 pen), Morris 5 (2 pens), Ifill 4, Dobie 3, Dunne 3, Wise 3 (2 pens), Livermore 2, Sweeney 2, Elliott 1, Harris 1, May 1 (pen), Phillips 1, Robinson T 1, Simpson 1, Tessem 1.
Carling Cup (0).
FA Cup (0).
UEFA Cup (2): Wise 2.

Stack G 25+1	Dunne A 15+4	Livermore D 41	Elliott M 32+9	Lawrence M 40+4	Ward D 43	Sweeney P 23+1	Morris J 35+2	Moore S 3+3	Dichio D 27+4	Ifill P 9+9	Wise D 16+9	Cogan B 2+5	Simpson J 22+8	McCammon M 5+3	Harris N 5+7	Serioux A 10+9	Muscat K 25+1	Hayles B 28+4	Phillips M 25	Tessem J 11+1	Marshall A 21+1	Dobie S 15+1	Healy J —+2	Braniff K 1	Craig T 9+1	Quigley M 4+4	Robinson T 8+1	Weston C 2+1	May B 4+4	Peeters B —+3	Impey A —+5	*Match No.*
1	2^1	3	4	5	6	7^2	8	9	10	11^3	12	13	14																			1
1	2	3	4^1	5	6	7	8	9^2	10		12		11^3	13	14																	2
1		3	4	5	6		8	12	10		7		11	9^1		2																3
1		3	4	5	6		8	12	10		7^2		11	9^1	13	2																4
1		3	4	5	6		8		10		7		11	9^1	12	2																5
1		3	4	5	6		8	12			7^3		11	9^2	13	2	14	10^1														6
1			4	5	6	7^2		9^1	10■	12	14	11	3		13	8^3	2															7
1		3	4	5	6					10	7	8^1	11	12	9		2															8
1	12	3	4^3	5	6^1		13		10^2	11	7	14	8		9		2															9
1	3■	11	4		6		8			7^2		13	12		9^1		2		5	10												10
1		3	4	5	6		8				7	12		11^2	9^1		2	13		10												11
1^G	2	3	4	5	6		8				7^1	13	11^2			12		9		10	15											12
1	4	3		5	6		8				7		11^1		12		2	9		10												13
1	2^2	3	4	5	6		8				7		12	13	9^1			11		10												14
1		3		5	6		8^1				7		12			11■	2	9	4	10												15
1	12	3	4	5	6				13		7		11				2^1	9^2	8	10												16
1		3	4	5	6				12	13			11				2^1	10	7	8^2		9										17
1		3	12	5^2	6				14	13	7^1		11				2	10	4	8^3		9										18
1		3	4^2	5	6				12	13			11^1			14	2	10	7	8		9^3										19
1		3	12	5	6					13			11^2		14	7	2	10^1	4	8^3		9										20
1		3	12	13	6	7	8			11						5^1	2■	10^3	4	14		9^2										21
	2	3	4	12	6	7	8		10^2							13		11^1	5		1	9										22
	2^3	3	4^1	12	6	7	8		10	13	14							11^2	5		1	9										23
	12	3	2^2		6	7	8		10	4						13		11^1	5		1	9										24
		3	4	12	6^1	7^2	8		10	11^3	13						2	14	5		1	9										25
		3	4	5		11	8		10		7^1					12	2	9	6		1											26
	12	3	4	5		7^2	8^1		10■				13			11^3	2	9	6		1		14									27
	7	3	4	5			12				8^1		11				2		6		1	9	13	10^2								28
1	7	3	12	5	6		8^1		10							13	2	11	4			9^2										29
1	7	3		5	6		8^2		10	12	13						2	11	4			9^1										30
	7	3	12	5	6		8		10^3		11^1		13				2^2	9	4		1	14										31
	7^2	3	4	5	6		8		10				11^1			12	2	13			1	9										32
	7		12	5	6	13			10							8^1		11	2		1	9			3^3	14	4^2					33
	7■	3■	12	5	6	8			10									11^1	4		1	9			2							34
			4	5	6	7^2	8		10							12			2■		1				3	9^3	13	11^1	14			35
			4	5	6	7^1	8		10				11								1				3	9^2	2	12		13		36
			4	5	6	7^1	8^3		10							12		9			1				3	11^2	2			13	14	37
		11		5	6	7	8											9			1				3	10^1	2	4^2	12		13	38
		11	12	5	6	7	8^1		10^2				4^3					9			1				3	14	2		13			39
		11		5	6	7	8		10				4^2								1				3	12	2		9^1		13	40
		11	12	5	6	7^3	8		10				4^1					13			1				3		2		9^2		14	41
		3	4	5	6	7^2	8^1				12		11^3					10			1				13		2		9		14	42
		3	4	5	6	7	8^1		10	13			12				2	9^2	11		1											43
15		11	4	5	6	7^2	8^1		10	13	12						2	9	3		1^G											44
1		3	4	5	6	7^1	8			11			12				2	9^2	10										13			45
1		11	4	5	6	7	8^1			10	12						3^2		2							13			9^3	14		46

FA Cup
Third Round Wolverhampton W (a) 0-2

Carling Cup
Third Round Liverpool (h) 0-3

UEFA Cup
First Round Ferencvaros (h) 1-1
(a) 1-3

MILTON KEYNES DONS FL Championship 1

FOUNDATION

Old boys from Central School formed this club as Wimbledon Old Centrals in 1889. Their earliest successes were in the Clapham League before switching to the Southern Suburban League in 1902.

The National Hockey Stadium, Silbury Boulevard, Milton Keynes, Buckinghamshire MK9 1FA.

Telephone: (01908) 607 090.

Fax: (01908) 209 449.

Ticket Office: (01908) 609 000.

Website: www.mkdons.com

Ground Capacity: 8,500.

Record Attendance: 30,115 v Manchester U, FA Premier League, 9 May 1993.

Pitch Measurements: 110yd × 74yd.

Chairman: Pete Winkelman.

Acting Chief Executive: John Cove.

Football Operations Manager: Kirstine Nicholson.

Manager: Danny Wilson.

Coach: Ian Bowyer.

Physio: Tony Flynn.

Colours: White shirts, white shorts, white stockings.

Change Colours: All red with gold and black trim.

Year Formed: 1889.

Turned Professional: 1964.

Ltd Co.: 1964.

Previous Names: Wimbledon Old Centrals, 1899–1905; Wimbledon 1905–2004.

Previous Grounds: 1899, Plough Lane; 1991, Selhurst Park.

Club Nicknames: 'The Dons', 'The Crazy Gang'.

First Football League Game: 20 August 1977, Division 4, v Halifax T (h) D 3–3 – Guy; Bryant (1), Galvin, Donaldson, Aitken, Davies, Galliers, Smith, Connell (1), Holmes, Leslie (1).

HONOURS

FA Premier League: best season: 6th, 1993–94.

Football League: Division 3 – Runners-up 1983–84; Division 4 – Champions 1982–83.

FA Cup: Winners 1988.

Football League Cup: Semi-final 1996–97, 1998–99.

League Group Cup: Runners-up 1982.

Amateur Cup: Winners 1963; Runners-up 1935, 1947.

European Competitions: *Intertoto Cup:* 1995.

SKY SPORTS FACT FILE

Even though Milton Keynes Dons recorded only three wins in their opening 20 League games during 2004–05, a run of 11 matches without defeat from early February was the foundation for a spirited escape from relegation.

Record League Victory: 6–0 v Newport Co, Division 3, 3 September 1983 – Beasant; Peters, Winterburn, Galliers, Morris, Hatter, Evans (2), Ketteridge (1), Cork (3 incl. 1p), Downes, Hodges (Driver).

Record Cup Victory: 7–2 v Windsor & Eton, FA Cup 1st rd, 22 November 1980 – Beasant; Jones, Armstrong, Galliers, Mick Smith (2), Cunningham (1), Ketteridge, Hodges, Leslie, Cork (1), Hubbick (3).

Record Defeat: 0–8 v Everton, League Cup 2nd rd, 29 August 1978.

Most League Points (2 for a win): 61, Division 4, 1978–79.

Most League Points (3 for a win): 98, Division 4, 1982–83.

Most League Goals: 97, Division 3, 1983–84.

Highest League Scorer in Season: Alan Cork, 29, 1983–84.

Most League Goals in Total Aggregate: Alan Cork, 145, 1977–92.

Most League Goals in One Match: 4, Alan Cork v Torquay U, Division 4, 28 February 1979.

Most Capped Player: Kenny Cunningham, 40 (68), Republic of Ireland.

Most League Appearances: Alan Cork, 430, 1977–92.

Youngest League Player: Kevin Gage, 17 years 15 days v Bury, 2 May 1981.

Record Transfer Fee Received: £7,000,000 from Newcastle U for Carl Cort, July 2000.

Record Transfer Fee Paid: £7,500,000 to West Ham U for John Hartson, January 1999.

Football League Record: 1977 Elected to Division 4; 1979–80 Division 3; 1980–81 Division 4; 1981–82 Division 3; 1982–83 Division 4; 1983–84 Division 3; 1984–86 Division 2; 1986–92 Division 1; 1992–2000 FA Premier League; 2000–04 Division 1; 2004– FL1.

MANAGERS

Les Henley 1955–71
Mike Everitt 1971–73
Dick Graham 1973–74
Allen Batsford 1974–78
Dario Gradi 1978–81
Dave Bassett 1981–87
Bobby Gould 1987–90
Ray Harford 1990–91
Peter Withe 1991
Joe Kinnear 1992–99
Egil Olsen 1999–2000
Terry Burton 2000–02
Stuart Murdock 2002–04
Danny Wilson December 2004–

LATEST SEQUENCES

Longest Sequence of League Wins: 7, 4.9.1996 – 19.10.1996.

Longest Sequence of League Defeats: 14, 19.3.2000 – 28.8.2000.

Longest Sequence of League Draws: 4, 24.4.2001 – 6.5.2001.

Longest Sequence of Unbeaten League Matches: 22, 15.1.1983 – 14.5.1983.

Longest Sequence Without a League Win: 14, 19.3.2000 – 28.8.2000.

Successive Scoring Runs: 23 from 18.2.1984.

Successive Non-scoring Runs: 5 from 13.4.1995.

TEN YEAR LEAGUE RECORD

		P	*W*	*D*	*L*	*F*	*A*	*Pts*	*Pos*
1995-96	PR Lge	38	10	11	17	55	70	41	14
1996-97	PR Lge	38	15	11	12	49	46	56	8
1997-98	PR Lge	38	10	14	14	34	46	44	15
1998-99	PR Lge	38	10	12	16	40	63	42	16
1999-2000	PR Lge	38	7	12	19	46	74	33	18
2000-01	Div 1	46	17	18	11	71	50	69	8
2001-02	Div 1	46	18	13	15	63	57	67	9
2002-03	Div 1	46	18	11	17	76	73	65	10
2003-04	Div 1	46	8	5	33	41	89	29	24
2004-05	FL 1	46	12	15	19	54	68	51	20

DID YOU KNOW

Wimbledon were out on their own in 1982–83 with their unbeaten start to the season of eleven matches spearheading a rush to win the championship of the Fourth Division. It also confirmed their progress which later shot them to the Premiership.

MILTON KEYNES DONS 2004–05 LEAGUE RECORD

Match No.	Date	Venue	Opponents	Result	H/T Score	Lg. Pos.	Goalscorers	Atten-dance
1	Aug 7	H	Barnsley	D 1-1	0-1	—	McLeod [76]	4720
2	10	A	Port Vale	L 2-3	1-1	—	Harding 2 [19, 75]	4602
3	14	A	Swindon T	L 1-2	1-1	22	Smart [42]	5060
4	21	H	Bournemouth	L 1-3	0-1	22	Smart (pen) [49]	3230
5	28	A	Oldham Ath	L 0-3	0-2	23		5066
6	30	H	Torquay U	W 1-0	1-0	22	Puncheon [45]	3015
7	Sept 4	A	Chesterfield	D 2-2	0-1	22	McLeod [64], Small [88]	4537
8	11	H	Doncaster R	L 0-1	0-0	22		4334
9	18	A	Colchester U	W 1-0	1-0	21	McLeod [45]	3460
10	25	H	Hartlepool U	W 4-2	1-1	20	McLeod 2 [31, 57], Small [46], Smith (pen) [50]	3685
11	Oct 2	A	Sheffield W	D 1-1	0-0	20	McLeod [89]	20,245
12	8	H	Bradford C	L 1-2	1-0	—	McLeod [20]	4532
13	16	H	Brentford	D 0-0	0-0	19		5924
14	20	A	Hull C	L 2-3	1-1	—	McLeod [33], Chorley [76]	14,317
15	23	A	Huddersfield T	L 1-3	0-3	22	Chorley (pen) [86]	10,709
16	30	H	Walsall	D 1-1	1-1	22	Kamara [36]	4247
17	Nov 6	A	Bristol C	L 1-4	0-3	23	Small [52]	10,717
18	20	H	Luton T	L 1-4	1-2	23	Small [45]	7620
19	27	A	Tranmere R	L 0-2	0-0	23		8402
20	Dec 7	H	Peterborough U	D 1-1	0-0	—	Small [53]	3913
21	11	H	Wrexham	W 3-0	1-0	22	Rizzo [7], Small 2 [50, 84]	3601
22	18	A	Stockport Co	L 1-3	0-2	22	Tapp [77]	3902
23	26	A	Doncaster R	L 0-3	0-1	23		6153
24	28	H	Blackpool	W 3-1	1-0	23	McLeod [40], Palmer [73], Smart [82]	4943
25	Jan 1	H	Chesterfield	D 1-1	1-0	21	Smart (pen) [5]	4214
26	3	A	Hartlepool U	L 0-5	0-1	22		5060
27	15	H	Colchester U	W 2-0	2-0	21	Harding [2], Small [18]	3833
28	22	A	Blackpool	L 0-1	0-1	22		5798
29	29	H	Sheffield W	D 2-2	0-1	22	Platt [58], McLeod [85]	7325
30	Feb 5	A	Brentford	L 0-1	0-0	23		5077
31	8	A	Bradford C	W 4-1	2-0	—	Small [32], McLeod 2 [44, 57], Harding [55]	6409
32	12	H	Huddersfield T	W 2-1	1-1	21	McLeod [33], Platt [90]	4793
33	19	A	Walsall	D 0-0	0-0	21		5888
34	22	H	Hull C	D 1-1	0-0	—	Lewington [50]	4407
35	26	A	Wrexham	D 0-0	0-0	21		3406
36	Mar 5	H	Stockport Co	W 2-1	1-0	20	Lewington [34], Edds [59]	4146
37	12	H	Port Vale	D 1-1	0-0	20	Platt [72]	4676
38	19	A	Barnsley	D 1-1	0-1	20	Pensee-Bilong [55]	8111
39	25	H	Swindon T	D 1-1	1-1	—	Small [14]	7019
40	28	A	Bournemouth	W 1-0	0-0	20	Edds [73]	7064
41	Apr 2	H	Oldham Ath	D 1-1	0-1	20	Edds [84]	5426
42	9	A	Torquay U	L 0-1	0-0	20		3509
43	16	A	Luton T	L 0-1	0-1	20		9000
44	23	H	Bristol C	L 1-2	1-1	21	McLeod [8]	5656
45	30	A	Peterborough U	W 3-0	2-0	21	Rizzo [9], McLeod 2 [22, 85]	3742
46	May 7	H	Tranmere R	W 2-1	1-0	20	Edds 2 [6, 84]	7359

Final League Position: 20

GOALSCORERS

League (54): McLeod 16, Small 10, Edds 5, Harding 4, Smart 4 (2 pens), Platt 3, Chorley 2 (1 pen), Lewington 2, Rizzo 2, Kamara 1, Palmer 1, Pensee-Bilong 1, Puncheon 1, Smith 1 (pen), Tapp 1.
Carling Cup (4): McLeod 2, Kamara 1, Smart 1.
FA Cup (2): Small 1, Smart 1.
LDV Vans Trophy (4): Lewington 1, Makofo 1, Pacquette 1, Small 1.

Rachubka P 4	Palmer S 27 + 5	Lewington D 43	Harding B 21 + 5	Williams M 11 + 2	Oyedele S 18 + 7	Kamara M 16 + 9	Smith G 20 + 3	Smart A 15 + 3	McLeod I 39 + 4	Small W 41 + 3	Herve L 15 + 5	Hornuss J — + 3	Edds G 37 + 2	Ntimban-Zeh H 11	Chorley B 41	Crooks L 15 + 2	Martin D 15	Koo-Boothe N 1	Puncheon J 8 + 17	Bevan S 7	Mackie J — + 3	Pacquette R 1 + 4	Tapp A 5 + 7	Johnson R 2	Makofo S — + 1	Rizzo N 13 + 5	Mitchell P 13	Baker M 20	Danze A 2	Platt C 20	Pensee-Bilong M 18	McClenahan T 7 + 1	Westcarr C — + 4	*Match No.*
1	2	3	4	5	6	7	8	9[1]	10[2]	11	12	13																						1
1	2	3	4	5	6	7[1]	8	12	10	11	9																							2
1	2	3[3]	4[2]	5	6	7[1]	8	9	10	11	13	12	14																					3
1	2		4[2]	5	3	12		9	10	11	7[1]			6	8	13																		4
	3[1]					12		9[2]	10	11	7	13	2	6	4	8	1	5[3]	14															5
	5	3	12			7		9	10	13	8[1]		2	6	4				11[2]	1														6
	5	3	12			7		9[1]	10	13	8		2	6	4				11[2]	1														7
	5	3	12	13				9	10	7	8[3]		2	6[2]	4				11[1]	1	14													8
		3		5	12	7[2]		9	10	11[1]	8		2	6	4				13	1														9
	7	3		5	6		8		10	9[2]	12		2		4[1]				11	1		13												10
	6	3		5	7				10	9	8[1]		2		4		1		11[2]			12	13											11
	5	3				7[1]	8		10	9			2	6	4		1		11			12												12
	7	3		5	6[1]	12	8[2]			9			2		4		1		11			10	13											13
	5	3				7			10	9	8		2	6	4		1		12				11[1]											14
	5	3			12	7			10[3]	9	8		2[1]	6	4		1		13			14	11[2]											15
	6	3		5		7			10	9			2		4		1		12				11[1]	8										16
	6	3		5		7			10	9			2		4					1			11[1]	8	12									17
	5					7	8	12	10	9[1]			2	6	4		1		3				13			11[2]								18
	5	3				7	11		10	9	8[1]		2	6	4					1	12													19
	5	3				7[3]	8	9[1]	12	10	11		2		4		1		13				14			6[2]								20
	5	3		12	13		8[3]	9[1]	10[2]	11			2		4		1						14			6	7							21
	5	3					8	9	10		11[2]		2		4		1				12		13			6[1]	7							22
	12	3		5	13		8[3]	9[1]	10				2		4								7[2]			14	11	1	6					23
	5	3					12	9	10	11			2		4								13			6[2]	7	1	8[1]					24
	5	3			12		8	9	10[2]	11			2		4				13							6[1]	7	1						25
	5	3			12	13		9	10[2]	11	8		2		4											6[1]	7	1						26
	12	3	11[1]		5		8		13	10[2]			2		4		1		14							6[3]	7			9				27
		3	11				8		10[1]	12			2		4		1									6	7			9	5			28
	12	3	11				8[2]		13	10			2[1]		4		1		14							6[3]	7			9	5			29
		3	11		2		8[1]		12	10					4		1		13							6[2]	7			9	5			30
	12	3	6[2]		2				10	11	13				4	8											7	1		9	5[1]			31
		3	6		2	12			10	11[1]					4	8[2]			13								7	1		9	5			32
	12	3	6		2	13			10	11[2]	8[1]				4	7												1		9	5			33
		3	6		2				10	11			12		4	8											7[1]	1		9	5			34
		3	6		2				10	11[1]			7		4	8			12									1		9	5			35
		3	7		6				10[1]	11			2		4	8			12									1		9	5			36
		3	11		6	7[2]		12		10			2[1]		4	8[3]			13							14		1		9	5			37
	4	3	11		6	7[2]				10[1]			2			8			12							13		1		9	5			38
	6	3	7		4[2]	12			10	11			2			8[1]												1		9	5	13		39
	5	3	7		12				10	11[1]			2		4	8												1		9		6		40
		3	7[1]				12		10	11[3]			2		4	8[2]										13		1		9	5	6	14	41
		3	7[1]				12		10	11[3]			2		4	8[2]										13		1		9	5	6	14	42
		3	7[1]			13			10[2]	11	12		2		4	8[3]			14									1		9	5	6		43
		3	12			13	7		10	11			2[1]		4	8[2]												1		9	5	6[3]	14	44
		3					8		10[2]	11			2		4	12										7[1]		1		9	5	6	13	45
		3	12				8[1]		10	11			2		4				13							7[2]		1		9	5	6		46

FA Cup

First Round	Lancaster C	(h)	1-0
Second Round	Cambridge C	(a)	1-0
Third Round	Peterborough U	(h)	0-2

Carling Cup

First Round	Peterborough U	(a)	3-0
Second Round	Cardiff C	(h)	1-4

LDV Vans Trophy

First Round	Brentford	(a)	3-0
Second Round	Bristol C	(a)	1-2

NEWCASTLE UNITED FA Premiership

FOUNDATION

It stemmed from a newly formed club called Stanley in 1881. In October 1882 they changed their name to Newcastle East End to avoid confusion with two other local clubs, Stanley Nops and Stanley Albion. Shortly afterwards another club Rosewood merged with them. Newcastle West End had been formed in August 1882 and they played on a pitch which was part of the Town Moor. Moved to Brandling Park 1885 and St James' Park 1886 (home of Newcastle Rangers). West End went out of existence after a bad run and the remaining committee men invited East End to move to St James' Park. They accepted and, at a meeting in Bath Lane Hall in 1892, changed their name to Newcastle United.

St James' Park, Newcastle-upon-Tyne NE1 4ST.

Telephone: (0191) 201 8400.

Fax: (0191) 201 8600.

Ticket Office: (0191) 261 1571.

Website: www.nufc.co.uk

Email: admin@nufc.co.uk

Ground Capacity: 52,387.

Record Attendance: 68,386 v Chelsea, Division 1, 3 September 1930.

Pitch Measurements: 105m × 68m.

Chairman: W. F. Shepherd.

Deputy Chairman: D. S. Hall.

Chief Operating Officer: R. Cushing.

Manager: Graeme Souness.

Coaches: Alan Murray.

Physios: Derek Wright.

Colours: Black and white striped shirts, black shorts, black stockings.

Change Colours: Cypress green shirts, white shorts, white stockings.

Year Formed: 1881.

Turned Professional: 1889.

Ltd Co.: 1890.

Previous Names: 1881, Stanley; 1882, Newcastle East End; 1892, Newcastle United.

Club Nickname: 'The Magpies'.

Previous Grounds: 1881, South Byker; 1886, Chillingham Road, Heaton, 1892, St James' Park.

First Football League Game: 2 September 1893, Division 2, v Royal Arsenal (a) D 2–2 – Ramsay; Jeffery, Miller; Crielly, Graham, McKane; Bowman, Crate (1), Thompson, Sorley (1), Wallace. Graham and not Crate scored according to some reports.

HONOURS

FA Premier League: Runners-up 1995–96, 1996–97; *Football League:* Division 1 – Champions 1904–05, 1906–07, 1908–09, 1926–27, 1992–93; Division 2 – Champions 1964–65; Runners-up 1897–98, 1947–48.

FA Cup: Winners 1910, 1924, 1932, 1951, 1952, 1955; Runners-up 1905, 1906, 1908, 1911, 1974, 1998, 1999.

Football League Cup: Runners-up 1976.

Texaco Cup: Winners 1974, 1975.

European Competitions: *Champions League:* 1997–98, 2002–03, 2003–04. *European Fairs Cup:* 1968–69 (winners), 1969–70, 1970–71. *UEFA Cup:* 1977–78, 1994–95, 1996–97, 1999–2000, 2003–04 (semi-final), 2004–05. *European Cup Winners' Cup:* 1998–99. *Anglo-Italian Cup:* Winners 1972–73. *Intertoto Cup:* 2001 (runners-up).

SKY SPORTS FACT FILE

The first Newcastle United player to captain England was centre-half Jack Hill, an £8100 signing from Burnley in October 1928. Winner of 11 caps he led his country three times on their continental tour in May 1929.

Record League Victory: 13–0 v Newport Co, Division 2, 5 October 1946 – Garbutt; Cowell, Graham; Harvey, Brennan, Wright; Milburn (2), Bentley (1), Wayman (4), Shackleton (6), Pearson.

Record Cup Victory: 9–0 v Southport (at Hillsborough), FA Cup 4th rd, 1 February 1932 – McInroy; Nelson, Fairhurst; McKenzie, Davidson, Weaver (1); Boyd (1), Jimmy Richardson (3), Cape (2), McMenemy (1), Lang (1).

Record Defeat: 0–9 v Burton Wanderers, Division 2, 15 April 1895.

Most League Points (2 for a win): 57, Division 2, 1964–65.

Most League Points (3 for a win): 96, Division 1, 1992–93.

Most League Goals: 98, Division 1, 1951–52.

Highest League Scorer in Season: Hughie Gallacher, 36, Division 1, 1926–27.

Most League Goals in Total Aggregate: Jackie Milburn, 177, 1946–57.

Most League Goals in One Match: 6, Len Shackleton v Newport Co, Division 2, 5 October 1946.

Most Capped Player: Shay Given, 61 (70), Republic of Ireland.

Most League Appearances: Jim Lawrence, 432, 1904–22.

Youngest League Player: Steve Watson, 16 years 223 days v Wolverhampton W, 10 November 1990.

Record Transfer Fee Received: £13,650,000 from Real Madrid for Jonathan Woodgate, August 2004.

Record Transfer Fee Paid: £15,000,000 to Blackburn R for Alan Shearer, July 1996.

Football League Record: 1893 Elected to Division 2; 1898–1934 Division 1; 1934–48 Division 2; 1948–61 Division 1; 1961–65 Division 2; 1965–78 Division 1; 1978–84 Division 2; 1984–89 Division 1; 1989–92 Division 2; 1992–93 Division 1; 1993– FA Premier League.

MANAGERS

Frank Watt 1895–32
(Secretary-Manager)
Andy Cunningham 1930–35
Tom Mather 1935–39
Stan Seymour 1939–47
(Hon. Manager)
George Martin 1947–50
Stan Seymour 1950–54
(Hon. Manager)
Duggie Livingstone 1954–56
Stan Seymour 1956–58
(Hon. Manager)
Charlie Mitten 1958–61
Norman Smith 1961–62
Joe Harvey 1962–75
Gordon Lee 1975–77
Richard Dinnis 1977
Bill McGarry 1977–80
Arthur Cox 1980–84
Jack Charlton 1984
Willie McFaul 1985–88
Jim Smith 1988–91
Ossie Ardiles 1991–92
Kevin Keegan 1992–97
Kenny Dalglish 1997–98
Ruud Gullit 1998–99
Sir Bobby Robson 1999–2004
Graeme Souness September 2004–

LATEST SEQUENCES

Longest Sequence of League Wins: 13, 25.4.1992 – 18.10.1992.

Longest Sequence of League Defeats: 10, 23.8.1977 – 15.10.1977.

Longest Sequence of League Draws: 4, 20.1.1990 – 24.2.1990.

Longest Sequence of Unbeaten League Matches: 14, 22.4.1950 – 30.9.1950.

Longest Sequence Without a League Win: 21, 14.1.1978 – 23.8.1978.

Successive Scoring Runs: 25 from 15.4.1939.

Successive Non-scoring Runs: 6 from 31.12.1938.

TEN YEAR LEAGUE RECORD

		P	*W*	*D*	*L*	*F*	*A*	*Pts*	*Pos*
1995-96	PR Lge	38	24	6	8	66	37	78	2
1996-97	PR Lge	38	19	11	8	73	40	68	2
1997-98	PR Lge	38	11	11	16	35	44	44	13
1998-99	PR Lge	38	11	13	14	48	54	46	13
1999-2000	PR Lge	38	14	10	14	63	54	52	11
2000-01	PR Lge	38	14	9	15	44	50	51	11
2001-02	PR Lge	38	21	8	9	74	52	71	4
2002-03	PR Lge	38	21	6	11	63	48	69	3
2003-04	PR Lge	38	13	17	8	52	40	56	5
2004-05	PR Lge	38	10	14	14	47	57	44	14

DID YOU KNOW?

Although finishing only tenth in the First Division in 1967–68, Newcastle United qualified for the Fairs Cup through the "one club per city" ruling and went on to win the trophy, accounting for Ujpest Dozsa in the final.

NEWCASTLE UNITED 2004–05 LEAGUE RECORD

Match No.	Date	Venue	Opponents	Result		H/T Score	Lg. Pos.	Goalscorers	Attendance
1	Aug 14	A	Middlesbrough	D	2-2	1-0	—	Bellamy [14], Shearer (pen) [82]	34,268
2	21	H	Tottenham H	L	0-1	0-0	15		52,185
3	25	H	Norwich C	D	2-2	1-0	—	Bellamy [40], Hughes [50]	51,574
4	28	A	Aston Villa	L	2-4	2-1	16	Kluivert [28], O'Brien [36]	36,305
5	Sept 11	H	Blackburn R	W	3-0	2-0	12	Flitcroft (og) [9], Shearer [16], O'Brien [83]	52,015
6	19	A	Southampton	W	2-1	1-0	8	Prutton (og) [45], Carr [57]	30,709
7	25	H	WBA	W	3-1	0-0	6	Kluivert [70], Milner [78], Shearer [86]	52,308
8	Oct 3	A	Birmingham C	D	2-2	1-1	6	Jenas [3], Butt [67]	29,021
9	17	A	Charlton Ath	D	1-1	1-0	8	Bellamy [39]	26,553
10	24	H	Manchester C	W	4-3	0-0	7	Robert [49], Shearer (pen) [58], Elliott [69], Bellamy [89]	52,316
11	31	A	Bolton W	L	1-2	0-0	8	Ambrose [55]	27,196
12	Nov 7	H	Fulham	L	1-4	0-1	9	Bellamy [77]	51,118
13	14	H	Manchester U	L	1-3	0-1	10	Shearer [71]	52,320
14	20	A	Crystal Palace	W	2-0	0-0	9	Kluivert [79], Bellamy [88]	22,937
15	28	H	Everton	D	1-1	1-0	10	Bellamy [5]	51,247
16	Dec 4	A	Chelsea	L	0-4	0-0	12		42,328
17	11	H	Portsmouth	D	1-1	1-1	12	Bowyer [3]	51480
18	19	A	Liverpool	L	1-3	1-2	13	Kluivert [32]	43,856
19	26	A	Blackburn R	D	2-2	2-1	14	Dyer [6], Robert [34]	29,271
20	29	H	Arsenal	L	0-1	0-1	—		52,320
21	Jan 1	H	Birmingham C	W	2-1	2-0	12	Ameobi [6], Bowyer [44]	52,222
22	3	A	WBA	D	0-0	0-0	13		25,259
23	15	H	Southampton	W	2-1	2-1	12	Shearer (pen) [9], Bramble [38]	51,266
24	23	A	Arsenal	L	0-1	0-1	12		38,137
25	Feb 2	A	Manchester C	D	1-1	1-0	—	Shearer [9]	45,752
26	5	H	Charlton Ath	D	1-1	0-0	12	Dyer [52]	51,114
27	27	H	Bolton W	W	2-1	1-1	11	Bowyer [35], Dyer [69]	50,430
28	Mar 5	H	Liverpool	W	1-0	0-0	11	Robert [70]	52,323
29	19	A	Portsmouth	D	1-1	1-1	10	Dyer [43]	20,165
30	Apr 2	H	Aston Villa	L	0-3	0-1	11		52,306
31	10	A	Tottenham H	L	0-1	0-1	12		35,885
32	20	A	Norwich C	L	1-2	0-0	—	Kluivert [89]	25,503
33	24	A	Manchester U	L	1-2	1-0	14	Ambrose [27]	67,845
34	27	H	Middlesbrough	D	0-0	0-0	—		52,047
35	30	H	Crystal Palace	D	0-0	0-0	14		52,123
36	May 4	A	Fulham	W	3-1	1-0	—	Ambrose [18], Kluivert [62], Ameobi [75]	19,003
37	7	A	Everton	L	0-2	0-1	12		40,438
38	15	H	Chelsea	D	1-1	1-1	14	Geremi (og) [33]	52,326

Final League Position: 14

GOALSCORERS

League (47): Bellamy 7, Shearer 7 (3 pens), Kluivert 6, Dyer 4, Ambrose 3, Bowyer 3, Robert 3, Ameobi 2, O'Brien 2, Bramble 1, Butt 1, Carr 1, Elliott 1, Hughes 1, Jenas 1, Milner 1, own goals 3.
Carling Cup (2): Ameobi 1 (pen), Jenas 1.
FA Cup (8): Ameobi 3, Kluivert 2, Babayaro 1, Bowyer 1, Shearer 1,
UEFA Cup (28): Shearer 11 (3 pens), Kluiver 5, Bellamy 3, Bowyer 3, Dyer 2, Robert 2, Ameobi 1, own goal 1.

Given S 36	Carr S 26	Bernard O 19 + 2	Butt N 16 + 2	Hughes A 18 + 4	Elliott R 15 + 2	Milner J 13 + 12	Jenas J 28 + 3	Shearer A 26 + 2	Bellamy C 21	Robert L 20 + 11	Dyer K 20 + 3	Kluivert P 15 + 10	Ameobi F 17 + 14	O'Brien A 21 + 2	Bowyer L 26 + 1	N'Zogbia C 8 + 6	Ambrose D 8 + 4	Harper S 2	Johnsen R 3	Bramble T 18 + 1	Taylor S 11 + 2	Babayaro C 7	Boumsong J 14	Faye A 8 + 1	Ramage P 2 + 2	Chopra M — + 1	Match No.
1	2	3	4	5	6	7^{1}	8	9^{2}	10	11^{3}	12	13	14														1
1	2	3	4	5		7^{2}	8^{1}	9	10	11^{3}	12	13	14	6													2
1	2	3	4	5		7^{1}		9	10	11	8^{2}		12	6	13												3
1	2	3	4	5	12		8	14	10	11		9^{3}	13	6^{1}	7^{2}												4
1	2			3	6	12	4	9	10^{2}	11^{3}	7^{1}		13	5	8	14											5
1	2	3	4		6	12	8	9	10			11^{1}		5	7												6
1	2	3	4		6	12	8	9	10^{2}	13		11^{1}		5	7												7
1	2	3^{3}	4	12	6	13	8	9	10	14		11^{2}		5	7^{1}												8
1	2	3	4^{1}		6	12	8	9	10^{3}	13			14	5	7		11^{2}										9
1	2^{1}	3	4	12	6	13	8	9	10^{3}	11^{2}			14	5	7												10
1	2^{1}	12	4	3	6			9	10	13		11^{2}	14	5	7		8^{3}										11
		3^{2}	4	2^{1}	6		8	9	10	12		11	13	5	7			1									12
1	2^{3}	3	4				8	9	10	12	13	11^{1}		14	7^{2}				5	6							13
1		3		2	12	13	4		10	11	8	9			7^{2}				5^{1}	6							14
1		3		5			4		10	11	8	9	12		7^{1}					6	2						15
1				3			4		10	11^{1}	8	9	12		7				5	6	2						16
1		3		5		11^{1}	4		10	12	8		9		7^{2}		13			6	2						17
1		3			6	11^{3}	4			12	8^{2}	10^{1}	9	2	7■	14	13			5							18
1		12		5	3^{3}	7^{1}	4		10	11	8	9^{2}	13	6						14	2						19
1		3^{1}		5			4		10	11	8		9		7	12				6	2						20
1		3		5		12	4		10^{2}	11^{1}	8		9		7	13				6	2						21
1		3		5		12	4			11	10		9		8	7^{1}				6	2						22
1				12		13	4	9^{3}	10^{2}		8	14	11		7					6	2	3^{1}	5				23
1		3		12			4	9		11^{3}	8		10	13	7	14				6	2^{1}		5^{2}				24
1	2		12				8	9			7^{1}	13	10^{2}	5	11					6		3		4			25
1	2						8	9		12	7	13	10^{2}	5	11^{1}					6		3		4			26
1	2						12	9		11^{1}	7		10		8					6		3	5	4			27
1	2		12	3			13	9		11	7^{1}	14	10^{3}		8^{2}					6			5	4			28
1	2		8^{3}	3		12	13	9		11^{1}	10	14		5	7								6	4^{2}			29
1	2		4	3			8^{1}	9		11^{3}	10■		12	5^{2}	7■						13■		6	14			30
	2		8^{2}			12	7	9^{1}		11^{3}			10	5		14	13	1				3	6	4			31
1	2		4		3	8^{2}		9		11		12	10^{1}	5		7	13						6				32
1	2				3	8		9^{2}		12		13	10	5		11	7						6		4^{1}		33
1	2				3	8		9			10^{1}		12	5		11	7						6		4		34
1	2				3^{3}	8		9		12		13	10^{1}			11	7^{2}				5		6	4	14		35
1	2					8						9	10			11	7			5	3		6	4			36
1	2^{2}					8^{1}	4	12				9	10■			11	7			5		3	6		13		37
1	2^{1}					8	4	9				10^{2}				11	7			5	12	3	6			13	38

FA Cup

Third Round	Yeading	(a)	2-0
Fourth Round	Coventry C	(h)	3-1
Fifth Round	Chelsea	(h)	1-0
Sixth Round	Tottenham H	(h)	1-0
Semi-Final	Manchester U		1-4
(at Millennium Stadium)			

Carling Cup

Third Round	Norwich C	(h)	2-1
Fourth Round	Chelsea	(h)	0-2

UEFA Cup

First Round	Hapoel Bnei	(h)	2-0
		(a)	5-1
Group D	Panionios	(a)	1-0
	Dinamo Tbilisi	(h)	2-0
	Sochaux	(a)	4-0
	Sporting Lisbon	(h)	1-1
Third Round	Heerenveen	(a)	2-1
		(h)	2-1
Fourth Round	Olympiakos	(a)	3-1
		(h)	4-0
Quarter-Final	Sporting Lisbon	(h)	1-0
		(a)	1-4

NORTHAMPTON TOWN FL Championship 2

FOUNDATION

Formed in 1897 by school teachers connected with the Northampton and District Elementary Schools' Association, they survived a financial crisis at the end of their first year when they were £675 in the red and became members of the Midland League – a fast move indeed for a new club. They achieved Southern League membership in 1901.

Sixfields Stadium, Upton Way, Northampton NN5 5QA.

Telephone: (01604) 757 773.

Fax: (01604) 751 613.

Ticket Office: (01604) 588 338.

Website: www.ntfc.co.uk

Email: info@ntfc.co.uk

Ground Capacity: 7,653.

Record Attendance: (at County Ground): 24,523 v Fulham, Division 1, 23 April 1966; (at Sixfields Stadium): 7,557 v Manchester C, Division 2, 26 September 1998.

Pitch Measurements: 116yd × 72yd.

Chairman: David Cardoza.

Secretary: Norman Howells.

Manager: Colin Calderwood.

Director of Football: John Deehan.

Physio: Denis Casey.

Colours: Claret shirts with white sides and sleeves, white shorts, claret stockings.

Change Colours: Black shirts, black shorts, black stockings.

Year Formed: 1897.

Turned Professional: 1901.

Ltd Co.: 1901.

Previous Ground: 1897, County Ground; 1994, Sixfields Stadium.

Club Nickname: 'The Cobblers'.

First Football League Game: 28 August 1920, Division 3, v Grimsby T (a) L 0–2 – Thorpe; Sproston, Hewison; Jobey, Tomkins, Pease; Whitworth, Lockett, Thomas, Freeman, MacKechnie.

Record League Victory: 10–0 v Walsall, Division 3 (S), 5 November 1927 – Hammond; Watson, Jeffs; Allen, Brett, Odell; Daley, Smith (3), Loasby (3), Hoten (1), Wells (3).

Record Cup Victory: 10–0 v Sutton T, FA Cup prel rd, 7 December 1907 – Cooch; Drennan, Lloyd Davies, Tirrell (1), McCartney, Hickleton, Badenock (3), Platt (3), Lowe (1), Chapman (2), McDiarmid.

HONOURS

Football League: Division 1 best season: 21st, 1965–66; Division 2 – Runners-up 1964–65; Division 3 – Champions 1962–63; Promoted from Division 3 1996–97 (play-offs); Division 3 (S) – Runners-up 1927–28, 1949–50; Division 4 – Champions 1986–87; Runners-up 1975–76.

FA Cup: best season: 5th rd, 1934, 1950, 1970.

Football League Cup: best season: 5th rd, 1965, 1967.

SKY SPORTS FACT FILE

Disappointed runners-up in Division Three (South) in 1927–28, consolation for Northampton Town came from some high-scoring matches, notably 6–5 v Luton Town, 10–0 v Walsall, 6–0 v Merthyr plus 8–0 in the FA Cup against amateurs Leyton.

Record Defeat: 0–11 v Southampton, Southern League, 28 December 1901.

Most League Points (2 for a win): 68, Division 4, 1975–76.

Most League Points (3 for a win): 99, Division 4, 1986–87.

Most League Goals: 109, Division 3, 1962–63 and Division 3 (S), 1952–53.

Highest League Scorer in Season: Cliff Holton, 36, Division 3, 1961–62.

Most League Goals in Total Aggregate: Jack English, 135, 1947–60.

Most League Goals in One Match: 5, Ralph Hoten v Crystal Palace, Division 3S, 27 October 1928.

Most Capped Player: E. Lloyd Davies, 12 (16), Wales.

Most League Appearances: Tommy Fowler, 521, 1946–61.

Youngest League Player: Adrian Mann, 16 years 297 days v Bury, 5 May 1984.

Record Transfer Fee Received: £265,000 from Watford for Richard Hill, July 1987.

Record Transfer Fee Paid: £165,000 to Oldham Ath for Josh Low, July 2003.

Football League Record: 1920 Original Member of Division 3; 1921 Division 3 (S); 1958–61 Division 4; 1961–63 Division 3; 1963–65 Division 2; 1965–66 Division 1; 1966–67 Division 2; 1967–69 Division 3; 1969–76 Division 4; 1976–77 Division 3; 1977–87 Division 4; 1987–90 Division 3; 1990–92 Division 4; 1992–97 Division 3; 1997–99 Division 2; 1999–2000 Division 3; 2000–03 Division 2; 2003–04 Division 3; 2004– FL2.

MANAGERS

Arthur Jones 1897–1907
(Secretary-Manager)
Herbert Chapman 1907–12
Walter Bull 1912–13
Fred Lessons 1913–19
Bob Hewison 1920–25
Jack Tresadern 1925–30
Jack English 1931–35
Syd Puddefoot 1935–37
Warney Cresswell 1937–39
Tom Smith 1939–49
Bob Dennison 1949–54
Dave Smith 1954–59
David Bowen 1959–67
Tony Marchi 1967–68
Ron Flowers 1968–69
Dave Bowen 1969–72
(continued as General Manager and Secretary to 1985 when joined the board)
Billy Baxter 1972–73
Bill Dodgin Jnr 1973–76
Pat Crerand 1976–77
Bill Dodgin Jnr 1977
John Petts 1977–78
Mike Keen 1978–79
Clive Walker 1979–80
Bill Dodgin Jnr 1980–82
Clive Walker 1982–84
Tony Barton 1984–85
Graham Carr 1985–90
Theo Foley 1990–92
Phil Chard 1992–93
John Barnwell 1993–95
Ian Atkins 1995–99
Kevin Wilson 1999–2001
Kevan Broadhurst 2001–03
Terry Fenwick 2003
Martin Wilkinson 2003
Colin Calderwood October 2003–

LATEST SEQUENCES

Longest Sequence of League Wins: 8, 27.8.1960 – 19.9.1960.

Longest Sequence of League Defeats: 8, 26.10.1935 – 21.12.1935.

Longest Sequence of League Draws: 6, 18.9.1983 – 15.10.1983.

Longest Sequence of Unbeaten League Matches: 21, 27.9.1986 – 6.2.1987.

Longest Sequence Without a League Win: 18, 26.3.1969 – 20.9.1969.

Successive Scoring Runs: 27 from 23.8.1986.

Successive Non-scoring Runs: 7 from 7.4.1939.

TEN YEAR LEAGUE RECORD

		P	W	D	L	F	A	Pts	Pos
1995-96	Div 3	46	18	13	15	51	44	67	11
1996-97	Div 3	46	20	12	14	67	44	72	4
1997-98	Div 2	46	18	17	11	52	37	71	4
1998-99	Div 2	46	10	18	18	43	57	48	22
1999-2000	Div 3	46	25	7	14	63	45	82	3
2000-01	Div 2	46	15	12	19	46	59	57	18
2001-02	Div 2	46	14	7	25	54	79	49	20
2002-03	Div 2	46	10	9	27	40	79	39	24
2003-04	Div 3	46	22	9	15	58	51	75	6
2004-05	FL 2	46	20	12	14	62	51	72	7

DID YOU KNOW 

Few clubs have made their Football League debut with a player-manager in charge. Yet Bob Hewison led Northampton Town from right-half before moving variously to inside-forward, full-back and centre-half from 1920 until 1924.

NORTHAMPTON TOWN 2004–05 LEAGUE RECORD

Match No.	Date	Venue	Opponents	Result		H/T Score	Lg. Pos.	Goalscorers	Attendance
1	Aug 7	A	Swansea C	W	2-0	1-0	—	McGleish [3], Ricketts (og) [82]	9578
2	10	H	Rushden & D	W	1-0	0-0	—	Sabin [75]	7107
3	14	H	Wycombe W	D	1-1	0-1	5	Richards [46]	6049
4	21	A	Shrewsbury T	L	0-2	0-0	6		3980
5	28	H	Leyton Orient	D	2-2	1-1	8	Richards [37], McGleish [65]	5577
6	30	A	Scunthorpe U	L	0-2	0-1	14		4201
7	Sept 5	A	Mansfield T	L	1-4	1-2	17	Sabin [37]	5173
8	11	H	Notts Co	D	0-0	0-0	16		5471
9	18	A	Darlington	D	1-1	0-1	17	Morison [53]	4028
10	25	H	Bristol R	W	2-1	2-0	13	McGleish 2 [4, 23]	5645
11	Oct 2	A	Yeovil T	D	1-1	0-1	14	Sabin [79]	5944
12	8	H	Grimsby T	L	0-1	0-0	—		5805
13	15	A	Cambridge U	W	1-0	1-0	—	Sabin [41]	4118
14	19	H	Oxford U	W	1-0	0-0	—	McGleish [83]	5455
15	23	H	Rochdale	W	5-1	3-0	6	Burgess (og) [9], Smith 2 (1 pen) [21 (p), 28], Edwards (og) [63], Low [90]	5342
16	30	A	Southend U	L	1-2	0-1	9	Sabin [87]	5696
17	Nov 6	A	Lincoln C	L	2-3	2-0	13	Sabin [6], McGleish [38]	4808
18	19	H	Chester C	D	1-1	1-1	—	Smith [7]	5625
19	27	A	Kidderminster H	W	2-0	1-0	10	McGleish [16], Alsop [76]	2701
20	Dec 7	H	Cheltenham T	D	1-1	0-0	—	McGleish [64]	4373
21	11	H	Boston U	W	2-1	0-0	9	Smith [72], McGleish [86]	5245
22	18	A	Macclesfield T	W	3-1	0-0	5	Low 2 [50, 86], Hearn [78]	2073
23	28	H	Bury	W	2-0	1-0	6	Rowson [40], Low [73]	6041
24	Jan 1	H	Mansfield T	W	2-1	0-1	5	Benjamin [53], Smith [77]	6122
25	3	A	Bristol R	L	1-3	0-1	5	Sabin [81]	6961
26	11	A	Grimsby T	W	2-1	0-1	—	McGleish [49], Benjamin [55]	3774
27	15	H	Darlington	D	1-1	0-1	5	Galbraith [87]	5762
28	22	A	Bury	L	0-2	0-1	6		2687
29	Feb 4	H	Cambridge U	D	2-2	1-0	—	Rowson [3], McGleish [82]	6615
30	12	A	Oxford U	W	2-1	0-0	7	Sabin [64], McGleish [70]	7032
31	15	A	Notts Co	D	0-0	0-0	—		4645
32	19	H	Southend U	L	1-2	1-0	7	Smith [7]	6602
33	26	A	Boston U	W	1-0	0-0	7	Smith [73]	2749
34	Mar 1	H	Yeovil T	D	1-1	0-1	—	Crow [88]	5630
35	5	H	Macclesfield T	W	1-0	1-0	6	Crow [2]	5804
36	8	A	Rochdale	L	0-1	0-0	—		2107
37	12	A	Rushden & D	L	2-3	1-1	9	Smith [45], Kirk [52]	5520
38	19	H	Swansea C	D	2-2	2-1	8	Smith [35], Kirk [40]	5799
39	25	A	Wycombe W	W	1-0	1-0	—	McGleish [44]	7417
40	28	H	Shrewsbury T	W	2-0	2-0	7	Smith [16], Westwood [38]	6514
41	Apr 2	A	Leyton Orient	L	2-3	0-1	8	Kirk [68], Westwood [75]	3585
42	9	H	Scunthorpe U	L	1-2	1-2	8	Kirk [4]	6523
43	16	A	Cheltenham T	L	0-1	0-1	8		3689
44	23	H	Lincoln C	W	1-0	0-0	8	Low [69]	6435
45	30	A	Chester C	W	2-0	1-0	7	Kirk 2 [22, 47]	3455
46	May 7	H	Kidderminster H	W	3-0	0-0	7	Kirk [68], Low 2 [85, 87]	6786

Final League Position: 7

GOALSCORERS

League (62): McGleish 13, Smith 10 (1 pen), Sabin 8, Kirk 7, Low 7, Benjamin 2, Crow 2, Richards 2, Rowson 2, Westwood 2, Alsop 1, Galbraith 1, Hearn 1, Morison 1, own goals 3.
Carling Cup (2): McGleish 1, Sabin 1.
FA Cup (3): McGleish 2, Williamson 1.
LDV Vans Trophy (3): Alsop 1, McGleish 1, Williamson 1.
Play-offs (0).

Harper L 36	Low J 33 + 1	Galbraith D 9 + 16	Chambers L 19 + 8	Willmott C 45	Murray F 38	Rowson D 35 + 2	Richards M 8 + 4	McGleish S 43 + 1	Smith M 31 + 3	Cozic B 8 + 6	Bojic P 25 + 11	Sabin E 28 + 12	Youngs T 4 + 5	Jaszczun T 24 + 8	Amoo R 2 + 3	Morison S 1 + 3	Reeves M — + 1	Westwood A 19	Hughes M 3	Haslam S 2 + 1	Hicks D 1 + 2	Rachubka P 10	Williamson L 31 + 6	Alsop J 1 + 6	Hearn C 21 + 3	Benjamin T 5	Cross S — + 1	Noble S — + 4	Crow D 4 + 6	Carruthers C — + 1	Barnard L 3 + 2	Kirk A 8	Hunt D 2 + 2	Togwell S 7 + 1	*Match No.*
1	2^{1}	3	4	5	6	7	8^{2}	9	10^{3}	11	12	13	14																						1
1	2	3^{3}	4	5	6	7	8	9		11^{1}	12	10^{2}	13	14																					2
1	2	3^{2}	4	5	6■		8^{3}	9^{1}		11	12	10		13	7	14																			3
1	2^{2}	3^{1}	4	5			8	9^{3}		7■	12	10		6	11■	13	14																		4
1	2		4	5			8	9^{1}			7	10	12	6^{2}				3	11^{3}	14	13														5
1	2		4	5	6		8^{1}	9		13		12	10^{3}			14		3	7^{2}	11															6
	2	12	4	5	6		8	9^{1}			13	10						3	7^{2}	11		1													7
	2	12		5	4		8^{2}	9		11	3^{1}	10	13					6			14	1	7^{3}												8
	2	3^{1}		5	6					7	4	10	11	12	13	9						1	8^{2}												9
	2	3^{2}	14	5	6			9	12	7^{1}		10	8	13				4^{3}				1	11												10
	2	3^{3}		5	6	12		9	13	7^{2}	14	10	8^{1}	11								1	4												11
	2	12		5	6	7		9^{1}	10		4	8		11								1	3												12
	2^{2}	12		5	6	7		9	10^{1}	13	4	8		3								1	11												13
	2^{1}		12	5	6	7		9	10		4	8		3								1	11												14
	2	12	13	5	6	7		9	10		4	8^{3}		3^{2}								1	11^{1}	14											15
	2			5	6	7		9	10	12	4	8		3^{2}								1	11^{1}	13											16
1	2^{1}		13	5	6	7		9^{3}	10	12	4^{2}	8		3									11	14											17
1		12		5	6	7	13^{3}	9	10		4	8^{2}	14	3^{1}									2	11											18
1		11^{1}		5	6	7		9	10	12	4	8^{3}		3	13								2^{2}	14											19
1	12		4	5	6	7		9	10	13	2	8											3^{1}		11^{2}										20
1	2		12	5	6	7		9	10^{2}		3^{1}	8^{3}		13				4						14	11										21
1	2	11^{2}			6	7		9			4	8		3				5					12	13	10^{1}										22
1	2			5		7		9	10^{1}		4	8^{2}		3				6					12		11		13								23
1	2			5		7		9	10		4	12		3				6					13		11^{2}	8^{1}									24
1	2	12		5		7		9	10		4^{2}	13		3				6					11^{1}			8									25
1	2		4	5		7		9	10^{2}		12			3				6^{1}					11		13	8									26
1		12	4	5		7		9			2	8		3^{1}									11		6	10									27
1		12		5		7		9	13		2	8		3^{2}				6					11		4^{1}	10■									28
1		12^{2}	13	5	3	7		9	10^{1}		2	8^{3}						6					11		4			14							29
1			4	5	6	7		9	10		2	8^{2}		12							3^{1}				11			13							30
1			2	5	6	7		9	10		12	8^{3}		3^{2}									11		4^{1}			14	13						31
1			2	5	6	7		9	10		13	8^{1}		3									11^{3}		4^{2}			14	12						32
1		12	2^{3}	5	6	7		9	10		13	14		3									11		4^{2}				8^{1}						33
1		12	2^{2}	5	6	7		9^{3}	10		13	8^{1}		3									11		4				14						34
1		12		5	6	7			10		2			3^{3}	13								11^{2}		4				9^{1}	14	8				35
1			12	5	6	7		13	10		2	14		3^{1}									11		4				9^{2}		8^{3}				36
1	2^{1}	12	3	5	6			9	10		4												11		7				13			8^{2}			37
1	2^{3}			5	6	7		9	10		3^{1}			12				4					11						13		14	8^{2}			38
1	2^{2}			5	6	7		9	10			12						4					11		13						8^{1}		3^{3}	14	39
1	2^{3}			5	6	7^{1}		9	10									4					11		12				8^{2}		13		14	3	40
1	2	12		5^{1}	6	13		9	10									4					11^{3}						14			8	7^{2}	3	41
1	2	12		5^{2}	6	7^{3}		9	10^{1}			13						4					14		11							8		3	42
1	2		12	5	6^{3}	7		9	10			13						4^{1}					14		11^{2}							8		3	43
1	2^{1}		4	5	6	7	12	9				13		14									11^{3}		8							10^{2}		3	44
1	2		4	5	6	7^{1}	12	9	10^{3}			13											14		11							8^{2}		3	45
1	2		4	5	6	7	12	9^{1}				13											11		8^{2}							10^{3}	14	3	46

FA Cup

First Round	Barnsley	(h)	1-0
Second Round	Bury	(h)	1-0
Third Round	Southampton	(h)	1-3

Carling Cup

First Round	Gillingham	(a)	2-1
Second Round	Southampton	(h)	0-3

LDV Vans Trophy

First Round			
Second Round	Torquay U	(a)	3-1
Quarter-Final	Southend U	(h)	0-2

Play-offs

Semi-Final	Southend U	(h)	0-0
		(a)	0-1

NORWICH CITY FL Championship

FOUNDATION

Formed in 1902, largely through the initiative of two local schoolmasters who called a meeting at the Criterion Cafe, they were shocked by an FA Commission which in 1904 declared the club professional and ejected them from the FA Amateur Cup. However, this only served to strengthen their determination. New officials were appointed and a professional club established at a meeting in the Agricultural Hall in March 1905.

Carrow Road, Norwich NR1 1JE.

Telephone: (01603) 760 760.

Fax: (01603) 613 886.

Ticket Office: 0870 444 1902.

Website: www.canaries.co.uk

Email: reception@ncfc-canaries.co.uk

Ground Capacity: 26,034.

Record Attendance: 43,984 v Leicester C, FA Cup 6th rd, 30 March 1963.

Pitch Measurements: 105m × 67m.

Chairman: Roger Munby.

Vice-chairman: Barry Skipper.

Chief Executive: Neil Doncaster.

Secretary: Kevan Platt.

Manager: Nigel Worthington.

Assistant Manager: Doug Livermore.

Physio: Neil Reynolds, MCSP, SRP.

Colours: Yellow shirts, green shorts, yellow stockings.

Change Colours: Green shirts, green shorts, green stockings.

Year Formed: 1902.

Turned Professional: 1905.

Ltd Co.: 1905.

Club Nickname: 'The Canaries'.

Previous Grounds: 1902, Newmarket Road; 1908, The Nest, Rosary Road; 1935, Carrow Road.

First Football League Game: 28 August 1920, Division 3, v Plymouth Arg (a) D 1–1 – Skermer; Gray, Gadsden; Wilkinson, Addy, Martin; Laxton, Kidger, Parker, Whitham (1), Dobson.

Record League Victory: 10–2 v Coventry C, Division 3 (S), 15 March 1930 – Jarvie; Hannah, Graham; Brown, O'Brien, Lochhead (1); Porter (1), Anderson, Hunt (5), Scott (2), Slicer (1).

HONOURS

FA Premier League: best season: 3rd 1992–93.

Football League: Division 1 – Champions 2003–04; Division 2 – Champions 1971–72, 1985–86; Division 3 (S) – Champions 1933–34; Division 3 – Runners-up 1959–60.

FA Cup: Semi-finals 1959, 1989, 1992.

Football League Cup: Winners 1962, 1985; Runners-up 1973, 1975.

European Competitions: *UEFA Cup:* 1993–94.

SKY SPORTS FACT FILE

In 1981–82 the change in the points system to three for a win helped Norwich City gain promotion to the First Division having won 22 and drawn five games. Under the old system Sheffield Wednesday with 20 wins and ten draws would have triumphed.

Record Cup Victory: 8–0 v Sutton U, FA Cup 4th rd, 28 January 1989 – Gunn; Culverhouse, Bowen, Butterworth, Linighan, Townsend (Crook), Gordon, Fleck (3), Allen (4), Phelan, Putney (1).

Record Defeat: 2–10 v Swindon T, Southern League, 5 September 1908.

Most League Points (2 for a win): 64, Division 3 (S), 1950–51.

Most League Points (3 for a win): 94, Division 1, 2003–04.

Most League Goals: 99, Division 3 (S), 1952–53.

Highest League Scorer in Season: Ralph Hunt, 31, Division 3 (S), 1955–56.

Most League Goals in Total Aggregate: Johnny Gavin, 122, 1945–54, 1955–58.

Most League Goals in One Match: 5, Tommy Hunt v Coventry C, Division 3S, 15 March 1930; 5, Roy Hollis v Walsall, Division 3S, 29 December 1951.

Most Capped Player: Mark Bowen, 35 (41), Wales.

Most League Appearances: Ron Ashman, 592, 1947–64.

Youngest League Player: Ryan Jarvis, 16 years 282 days v Walsall, 19 April 2003.

Record Transfer Fee Received: £5,000,000 from Blackburn R for Chris Sutton, July 1994 and £5,000,000 from Coventry C for Craig Bellamy, August 2000.

Record Transfer Fee Paid: £3,000,000 to Crewe Alex for Dean Ashton, January 2005.

Football League Record: 1920 Original Member of Division 3; 1921 Division 3 (S): 1934–39 Division 2; 1946–58 Division 3 (S); 1958–60 Division 3; 1960–72 Division 2; 1972–74 Division 1; 1974–75 Division 2; 1975–81 Division 1; 1981–82 Division 2; 1982–85 Division 1; 1985–86 Division 2; 1986–92 Division 1; 1992–95 FA Premier League; 1995–2004 Division 1; 2004–05 FA Premier League; 2005– FLC.

MANAGERS

John Bowman 1905–07
James McEwen 1907–08
Arthur Turner 1909–10
Bert Stansfield 1910–15
Major Frank Buckley 1919–20
Charles O'Hagan 1920–21
Albert Gosnell 1921–26
Bert Stansfield 1926
Cecil Potter 1926–29
James Kerr 1929–33
Tom Parker 1933–37
Bob Young 1937–39
Jimmy Jewell 1939
Bob Young 1939–45
Cyril Spiers 1946–47
Duggie Lochhead 1947–50
Norman Low 1950–55
Tom Parker 1955–57
Archie Macaulay 1957–61
Willie Reid 1961–62
George Swindin 1962
Ron Ashman 1962–66
Lol Morgan 1966–69
Ron Saunders 1969–73
John Bond 1973–80
Ken Brown 1980–87
Dave Stringer 1987–92
Mike Walker 1992–94
John Deehan 1994–95
Martin O'Neill 1995
Gary Megson 1995–96
Mike Walker 1996–98
Bruce Rioch 1998–2000
Bryan Hamilton 2000
Nigel Worthington January 2001–

LATEST SEQUENCES

Longest Sequence of League Wins: 10, 23.11.1985 – 25.1.1986.

Longest Sequence of League Defeats: 7, 1.4.1995 – 6.5.1995.

Longest Sequence of League Draws: 7, 15.1.1994 – 26.2.1994.

Longest Sequence of Unbeaten League Matches: 20, 31.8.1950 – 30.12.1950.

Longest Sequence Without a League Win: 25, 22.9.1956 – 23.2.1957.

Successive Scoring Runs: 25 from 31.8.1963.

Successive Non-scoring Runs: 5 from 21.2.1925.

TEN YEAR LEAGUE RECORD

		P	*W*	*D*	*L*	*F*	*A*	*Pts*	*Pos*
1995-96	Div 1	46	14	15	17	59	55	57	16
1996-97	Div 1	46	17	12	17	63	68	63	13
1997-98	Div 1	46	14	13	19	52	69	55	15
1998-99	Div 1	46	15	17	14	62	61	62	9
1999-2000	Div 1	46	14	15	17	45	50	57	12
2000-01	Div 1	46	14	12	20	46	58	54	15
2001-02	Div 1	46	22	9	15	60	51	75	6
2002-03	Div 1	46	19	12	15	60	49	69	8
2003-04	Div 1	46	28	10	8	79	39	94	1
2004-05	PR Lge	38	7	12	19	42	77	33	19

DID YOU KNOW ?

Argentine born centre-forward Francisco Enrique Gonsalez had changed his name to Frank Peed before signing for Norwich City in October 1930 having been with Aston Villa and Bournemouth prior to moving to the East Anglian club.

NORWICH CITY 2004–05 LEAGUE RECORD

Match No.	Date	Venue	Opponents	Result		H/T Score	Lg. Pos.	Goalscorers	Attendance
1	Aug 14	H	Crystal Palace	D	1-1	1-0	—	Huckerby [16]	23,717
2	21	A	Manchester U	L	1-2	0-1	16	McVeigh [75]	67,812
3	25	A	Newcastle U	D	2-2	0-1	—	Bentley [52], Doherty [74]	51,574
4	28	H	Arsenal	L	1-4	0-3	17	Huckerby (pen) [50]	23,944
5	Sept 12	A	Tottenham H	D	0-0	0-0	17		36,095
6	18	H	Aston Villa	D	0-0	0-0	18		23,805
7	25	A	Liverpool	L	0-3	0-2	19		43,152
8	Oct 2	H	Portsmouth	D	2-2	0-1	19	Huckerby [63], Charlton [67]	23,853
9	16	A	WBA	D	0-0	0-0	17		26,257
10	23	H	Everton	L	2-3	0-2	19	McKenzie [48], Francis [57]	23,871
11	Nov 1	A	Manchester C	D	1-1	0-1	—	Francis [46]	42,803
12	6	H	Blackburn R	D	1-1	0-0	19	Svensson [56]	23,834
13	13	A	Charlton Ath	L	0-4	0-2	20		27,057
14	20	H	Southampton	W	2-1	1-1	18	Francis 2 [28, 52]	23,706
15	27	A	Birmingham C	D	1-1	0-1	19	Huckerby [64]	29,120
16	Dec 4	H	Fulham	L	0-1	0-1	19		23,755
17	11	H	Bolton W	W	3-2	1-2	16	Svensson 2 [19, 84], Huckerby (pen) [69]	23,549
18	18	A	Chelsea	L	0-4	0-3	17		42,071
19	26	H	Tottenham H	L	0-2	0-0	17		24,508
20	28	A	Middlesbrough	L	0-2	0-0	18		34,836
21	Jan 1	A	Portsmouth	D	1-1	1-0	17	Francis [9]	20,015
22	3	H	Liverpool	L	1-2	0-0	18	Jarvis [88]	24,583
23	15	A	Aston Villa	L	0-3	0-2	18		38,172
24	22	H	Middlesbrough	D	4-4	1-1	19	Francis [18], Ashton [80], McKenzie [89], Drury [90]	24,547
25	Feb 2	A	Everton	L	0-1	0-0	—		37,485
26	5	H	WBA	W	3-2	1-1	18	Fleming [45], Doherty [62], Francis [85]	24,292
27	12	A	Blackburn R	L	0-3	0-2	18		20,923
28	28	H	Manchester C	L	2-3	2-2	—	Ashton [12], McKenzie [16]	24,302
29	Mar 5	H	Chelsea	L	1-3	0-1	20	McKenzie [64]	24,506
30	19	A	Bolton W	L	0-1	0-1	20		25,081
31	Apr 2	A	Arsenal	L	1-4	1-2	20	Huckerby [30]	38,066
32	9	H	Manchester U	W	2-0	0-0	20	Ashton [55], McKenzie [66]	25,522
33	16	A	Crystal Palace	D	3-3	1-1	20	Ashton 2 [22, 46], McKenzie [53]	25,754
34	20	H	Newcastle U	W	2-1	0-0	—	Safri [68], Ashton [90]	25,503
35	23	H	Charlton Ath	W	1-0	0-0	18	Svensson [88]	25,459
36	30	A	Southampton	L	3-4	3-3	20	Bentley [3], Higginbotham (og) [31], McKenzie [45]	31,944
37	May 7	H	Birmingham C	W	1-0	1-0	17	Ashton (pen) [45]	25,477
38	15	A	Fulham	L	0-6	0-2	19		21,927

Final League Position: 19

GOALSCORERS

League (42): Ashton 7 (1 pen), Francis 7, McKenzie 7, Huckerby 6 (2 pens), Svensson 4, Bentley 2, Doherty 2, Charlton 1, Drury 1, Fleming 1, Jarvis 1, McVeigh 1, Safri 1, own goal 1.
Carling Cup (2): Huckerby 1 (pen), Safri 1.
FA Cup (0).

Green R 38	Helveg T 16 + 4	Drury A 31 + 2	Fleming C 38	Charlton S 22 + 2	Holt G 21 + 6	Jonson M 19 + 9	Francis D 32	Huckerby D 36 + 1	Svensson M 10 + 12	Bentley D 22 + 4	McVeigh P 3 + 14	Edworthy M 27 + 1	McKenzie L 24 + 13	Doherty G 17 + 3	Safri Y 13 + 5	Brennan J 6 + 4	Henderson I — + 3	Ward D — + 1	Mulryne P 8 + 2	Jarvis R 1 + 3	Crow D — + 3	Ashton D 16	Stuart G 7 + 1	Shackell J 11	*Match No.*
1	2	3	4	5	6	7^{1}	8	9	10^{3}	11^{2}	12	13	14												1
1	2	3	4	5	6	7^{1}	8	9	10^{3}	11^{2}	12		13	14											2
1		3	4	5	6	12	8	9		11^{2}	7^{1}	2	13	10											3
1		3	4	5	6	7^{3}	8	9	13		11^{1}	2	12	10^{2}	14										4
1	12	3	4	5	6		8	9		11^{1}	13	2	14	10^{3}	7^{2}										5
1		3	4	5	6	12	8	9		11^{3}	13	2	14	10^{1}	7^{2}										6
1		3	4	5	6	12	11	9		13	7^{1}	2	14	10^{3}	8^{2}										7
1		3	4	5	6	7^{1}	8	9	13	11	12	2	10^{2}												8
1	12	3	4	5	6	7^{1}	8	9	13	11^{3}	14	2	10^{2}												9
1	7^{2}	3	4	5	6	11^{3}	8	9	13	12		2	10^{1}	14											10
1			4	5	6	7^{2}	8	9	10		12	2	11^{1}			3	13								11
1		3	4	5	6	7^{2}	8	9	10		12	2	11^{1}				13								12
1^{6}		3	4	5	6^{2}	7^{1}	8	9	10	12		2	11					15	13						13
1		3	4	5			8	9	10	7		2	11						6						14
1	12	3	4	5	6^{1}			9	10	7		2	13			11^{2}			8						15
1	7	3	4			12		9	10^{1}	11		2	8	5	13				6^{2}						16
1	8		4	3		7^{1}		9	10	11	12	2		5	6										17
1	8		4	3		7		9	10^{1}	11	13	2	12	5	6^{2}										18
1	8	12	4	3^{1}		7^{2}		9		11	13	2	10	5	6^{3}				14						19
1	7^{1}	3	4					9		11		2	10	5		12			6	8^{2}	13				20
1		12	4	3		7	8	9^{1}		11		2■	10^{3}	5		13			6^{2}	14					21
1	2		4	3		7	8^{2}	9		11			10^{3}	5		12			6^{1}	13	14				22
1		3	4			7	8	9^{3}				2	12	5		11			6^{1}	13	14	10^{2}			23
1		3	4		12	7^{3}	8	9			14	2	13	5		11^{2}			6^{1}			10			24
1		3^{2}	4		6	7^{1}	8	9				2	12	5		11						10	13		25
1			4	3^{2}	6		8	9			12	2	11	5		13						10	7^{1}		26
1		3	4	2^{1}	6		8	9					13	5	12	11^{2}						10	7		27
1		3	4		6	7■	8					2	9		12							10	11^{1}	5	28
1		3	4		6		8	9			12	2	11^{2}				13					10	7^{1}	5	29
1		3	4		6	12	8	9				2^{2}	11	13								10	7^{1}	5	30
1	12	3	4		6^{3}		8	9	13			2^{1}	11^{2}		14							10	7	5	31
1	2	3	4			12	8	9^{1}	13	14			11		6							10^{2}	7^{3}	5	32
1	2	3	4		12	13	8^{1}	9^{2}	14	7			11^{3}		6							10		5	33
1	2	3	4		12	13	8	9^{2}	14	7^{1}			11^{3}		6							10		5	34
1	2	3	4		12	7^{2}	8	13	14	11^{3}			9^{1}		6							10		5	35
1	2	3	4	12			8	9^{1}	13	7			11		6							10^{2}		5	36
1	2	3^{1}	4	12	13		8	9	14	7			11^{3}		6^{2}							10		5	37
1	2^{1}	3	4		13	12	8	9	14	7^{3}			11		6^{2}							10		5	38

FA Cup

Third Round	West Ham U	(a)	0-1

Carling Cup

Second Round	Bristol R	(h)	1-0
Third Round	Newcastle U	(a)	1-2

NOTTINGHAM FOREST FL Championship 1

FOUNDATION

One of the oldest football clubs in the world, Nottingham Forest was formed at a meeting in the Clinton Arms in 1865. Known originally as the Forest Football Club, the game which first drew the founders together was 'shinney', a form of hockey. When they determined to change to football in 1865, one of their first moves was to buy a set of red caps to wear on the field.

The City Ground, Nottingham NG2 5FJ.

Telephone: (0115) 982 4444.

Fax: (0115) 982 4455.

Ticket Office: 0871 226 1980.

Website: www.nottinghamforest.co.uk

Email: enquiries@nottinghamforest.co.uk

Ground Capacity: 30,602.

Record Attendance: 49,946 v Manchester U, Division 1, 28 October 1967.

Pitch Measurements: 112yd × 74yd.

Chairman: Nigel Doughty.

Chief Executive: Mark Arthur.

Secretary: Paul White.

Manager: Gary Megson.

Assistant Manager: Frank Barlow.

Physios: Gary Fleming and Steve Devine.

Colours: Red shirts, white shorts, red stockings.

Change Colours: Yellow shirts, blue shorts, white stockings.

Year Formed: 1865.

Turned Professional: 1889.

Ltd Co.: 1982.

Club Nickname: 'Reds'.

Previous Grounds: 1865, Forest Racecourse; 1879, The Meadows; 1880, Trent Bridge Cricket Ground; 1882, Parkside, Lenton; 1885, Gregory, Lenton; 1890, Town Ground; 1898, City Ground.

First Football League Game: 3 September 1892, Division 1, v Everton (a) D 2–2 – Brown; Earp, Scott; Hamilton, A. Smith, McCracken; McCallum, W. Smith, Higgins (2), Pike, McInnes.

Record League Victory: 12–0 v Leicester Fosse, Division 1, 12 April 1909 – Iremonger; Dudley, Maltby; Hughes (1), Needham, Armstrong; Hooper (3), Marrison, West (3), Morris (2), Spouncer (3 incl. 1p).

Record Cup Victory: 14–0 v Clapton (away), FA Cup 1st rd, 17 January 1891 – Brown; Earp, Scott; A. Smith, Russell, Jeacock; McCallum (2), 'Tich' Smith (1), Higgins (5), Lindley (4), Shaw (2).

Record Defeat: 1–9 v Blackburn R, Division 2, 10 April 1937.

HONOURS

Football League: Division 1 – Champions 1977–78, 1997–98; Runners-up 1966–67, 1978–79; Division 2 – Champions 1906–07, 1921–22; Runners-up 1956–57; Division 3 (S) – Champions 1950–51.

FA Cup: Winners 1898, 1959; Runners-up 1991.

Football League Cup: Winners 1978, 1979, 1989, 1990; Runners-up 1980, 1992.

Anglo-Scottish Cup: Winners 1977;

Simod Cup: Winners 1989.

Zenith Data Systems Cup: Winners: 1992.

European Competitions: *European Fairs Cup:* 1961–62, 1967–68. *European Cup:* 1978–79 (winners), 1979–80 (winners), 1980–81. *Super Cup:* 1979–80 (winners), 1980–81 (runners-up). *World Club Championship:* 1980. *UEFA Cup:* 1983–84, 1984–85, 1995–96.

SKY SPORTS FACT FILE

Billy McKinlay was a between-the-wars wing-half for Nottingham Forest making 356 League and Cup appearances for them. Later he scouted for them and recommended his nephew Bobby McKinlay who went on to become the club's appearance record holder.

Most League Points (2 for a win): 70, Division 3 (S), 1950–51.

Most League Points (3 for a win): 94, Division 1, 1997–98.

Most League Goals: 110, Division 3 (S), 1950–51.

Highest League Scorer in Season: Wally Ardron, 36, Division 3 (S), 1950–51.

Most League Goals in Total Aggregate: Grenville Morris, 199, 1898–1913.

Most League Goals in One Match: 4, Enoch West v Sunderland, Division 1, 9 November 1907; 4, Tommy Gibson v Burnley, Division 2, 25 January 1913; 4, Tom Peacock v Port Vale, Division 2, 23 December 1933; 4, Tom Peacock v Barnsley, Division 2, 9 November 1935; 4, Tom Peacock v Port Vale, Division 2, 23 November 1935; 4, Tom Peacock v Doncaster R, Division 2, 26 December 1935; 4, Tommy Capel v Gillingham, Division 3S, 18 November 1950; 4, Wally Ardron v Hull C, Division 2, 26 December 1952; 4, Tommy Wilson v Barnsley, Division 2, 9 February 1957; 4, Peter Withe v Ipswich T, Division 1, 4 October 1977.

Most Capped Player: Stuart Pearce, 76 (78), England.

Most League Appearances: Bob McKinlay, 614, 1951–70.

Youngest League Player: Craig Westcarr, 16 years 257 days v Burnley, 13 October 2001.

Record Transfer Fee Received: £8,500,000 from Liverpool for Stan Collymore, June 1995.

Record Transfer Fee Paid: £3,500,000 to Celtic for Pierre van Hooijdonk, March 1997.

Football League Record: 1892 Elected to Division 1; 1906–07 Division 2; 1907–11 Division 1; 1911–22 Division 2; 1922–25 Division 1; 1925–49 Division 2; 1949–51 Division 3 (S); 1951–57 Division 2; 1957–72 Division 1; 1972–77 Division 2; 1977–92 Division 1; 1992–93 FA Premier League; 1993–94 Division 1; 1994–97 FA Premier League; 1997–98 Division 1; 1998–99 FA Premier League; 1999–2004 Division 1; 2004–05 FLC; 2005– FL1.

MANAGERS

Harry Radford 1889–97 *(Secretary-Manager)*
Harry Haslam 1897–1909 *(Secretary-Manager)*
Fred Earp 1909–12
Bob Masters 1912–25
John Baynes 1925–29
Stan Hardy 1930–31
Noel Watson 1931–36
Harold Wightman 1936–39
Billy Walker 1939–60
Andy Beattie 1960–63
Johnny Carey 1963–68
Matt Gillies 1969–72
Dave Mackay 1972
Allan Brown 1973–75
Brian Clough 1975–93
Frank Clark 1993–96
Stuart Pearce 1996–97
Dave Bassett 1997–98 *(previously General Manager from February)*
Ron Atkinson 1998–99
David Platt 1999–2001
Paul Hart 2001–04
Joe Kinnear 2004
Gary Megson January 2005–

LATEST SEQUENCES

Longest Sequence of League Wins: 7, 9.5.1979 – 1.9.1979.

Longest Sequence of League Defeats: 14, 21.3.1913 – 27.9.1913.

Longest Sequence of League Draws: 7, 29.4.1978 – 2.9.1978.

Longest Sequence of Unbeaten League Matches: 42, 26.11.1977 – 25.11.1978.

Longest Sequence Without a League Win: 19, 8.9.1998 – 16.1.1999.

Successive Scoring Runs: 22 from 28.3.1931.

Successive Non-scoring Runs: 7 from 13.12.2003.

TEN YEAR LEAGUE RECORD

		P	W	D	L	F	A	Pts	Pos
1995-96	PR Lge	38	15	13	10	50	54	58	9
1996-97	PR Lge	38	6	16	16	31	59	34	20
1997-98	Div 1	46	28	10	8	82	42	94	1
1998-99	PR Lge	38	7	9	22	35	69	30	20
1999-2000	Div 1	46	14	14	18	53	55	56	14
2000-01	Div 1	46	20	8	18	55	53	68	11
2001-02	Div 1	46	12	18	16	50	51	54	16
2002-03	Div 1	46	20	14	12	82	50	74	6
2003-04	Div 1	46	15	15	16	61	58	60	14
2004-05	FL C	46	9	17	20	42	66	44	23

DID YOU KNOW ?

On 7 May 1938 Nottingham Forest were due at Barnsley in a relegation clash. Points level, Forest had a slightly better goal average. See-sawing fortunes ended when Forest equalised in the last few minutes at 2–2 to escape by a fraction.

NOTTINGHAM FOREST 2004–05 LEAGUE RECORD

Match No.	Date	Venue	Opponents	Result	H/T Score	Lg. Pos.	Goalscorers	Attendance
1	Aug 7	A	Wigan Ath	D 1-1	0-1	—	Taylor G 55	12,035
2	11	H	Ipswich T	D 1-1	1-0	—	Evans 25	21,125
3	14	H	Crewe Alex	D 2-2	1-2	17	Taylor G 39, King 71	24,201
4	21	A	Leeds U	D 1-1	0-1	14	Reid (pen) 78	31,808
5	28	H	Coventry C	L 1-4	0-1	21	Johnson 74	23,041
6	30	A	Plymouth Arg	L 2-3	1-2	22	Jess 2 44, 80	17,538
7	Sept 11	H	Cardiff C	D 0-0	0-0	22		21,607
8	14	A	Sunderland	L 0-2	0-2	—		23,540
9	18	A	Stoke C	D 0-0	0-0	22		21,115
10	26	H	West Ham U	W 2-1	0-0	21	Evans 84, King 90	25,615
11	29	H	Brighton & HA	L 0-1	0-1	—		20,109
12	Oct 3	A	Millwall	L 0-1	0-1	22		11,233
13	15	H	Wolverhampton W	W 1-0	1-0	—	Reid 42	21,856
14	19	A	Sheffield U	D 1-1	0-1	—	Johnson 84	19,445
15	23	A	Preston NE	L 2-3	0-2	22	King 2 78, 80	12,439
16	30	H	Watford	L 1-2	1-2	22	Reid 45	24,473
17	Nov 3	H	Rotherham U	D 2-2	0-2	—	Johnson 52, King (pen) 63	21,619
18	6	A	Wolverhampton W	L 1-2	1-2	23	Johnson 25	27,605
19	13	A	Burnley	L 0-1	0-1	23		11,622
20	20	H	Reading	W 1-0	1-0	22	Taylor G 26	21,138
21	27	A	Gillingham	L 1-2	1-0	23	Taylor G 14	8784
22	Dec 4	H	QPR	W 2-1	1-0	22	Reid 15, Lester 58	26,099
23	11	A	Derby Co	L 0-3	0-0	22		30,793
24	17	H	Leicester C	D 1-1	0-0	—	Dawson 57	22,415
25	26	A	West Ham U	L 2-3	0-2	22	Johnson 2 65, 68	32,270
26	28	H	Sunderland	L 1-2	0-0	23	Reid 55	27,457
27	Jan 1	H	Stoke C	W 1-0	0-0	23	Bopp 68	22,051
28	3	A	Cardiff C	L 0-3	0-0	23		13,545
29	15	H	Millwall	L 1-2	0-2	23	Commons 87	25,949
30	22	A	Brighton & HA	D 0-0	0-0	23		6704
31	Feb 5	A	Rotherham U	D 0-0	0-0	23		8448
32	23	H	Preston NE	W 2-0	0-0	—	Evans 77, Commons 82	19,209
33	26	H	Derby Co	D 2-2	1-1	23	Evans (pen) 36, Taylor G 69	26,160
34	Mar 5	A	Leicester C	W 1-0	1-0	23	Taylor G 41	27,277
35	8	A	Watford	W 2-0	1-0	—	Commons 2 45, 79	12,118
36	12	A	Ipswich T	L 0-6	0-2	23		25,765
37	16	H	Leeds U	D 0-0	0-0	—		25,101
38	19	H	Wigan Ath	D 1-1	0-0	23	Taylor G 85	24,008
39	Apr 2	A	Crewe Alex	D 1-1	1-0	23	Dobie 37	8458
40	6	A	Coventry C	L 0-2	0-2	—		22,221
41	9	H	Plymouth Arg	L 0-3	0-2	23		28,887
42	12	H	Sheffield U	D 1-1	0-0	—	Commons 47	21,903
43	16	A	Reading	L 0-1	0-0	23		17,905
44	23	H	Burnley	W 1-0	0-0	23	Commons 70	24,165
45	30	A	QPR	L 1-2	0-1	23	Bopp 77	17,834
46	May 8	H	Gillingham	D 2-2	1-0	23	Morgan 29, Bopp 85	24,800

Final League Position: 23

GOALSCORERS

League (42): Taylor G 7, Commons 6, Johnson 6, King 5 (1 pen), Reid 5 (1 pen), Evans 4 (1 pen), Bopp 3, Jess 2, Dawson 1, Dobie 1, Lester 1, Morgan 1.
Carling Cup (8): King 3, Taylor G 3, Perch 1, Reid 1.
FA Cup (5): Commons 1, Folly 1, King 1, Reid 1, Taylor G 1.

Gerrard P 42	Louis-Jean M 22 + 3	Rogers A 32 + 1	Evans P 34 + 5	Doig C 20 + 1	Perch J 17 + 5	Impey A 18 + 2	Jess E 16 + 4	Johnson D 24 + 7	Taylor G 33 + 3	Reid A 25	Walker D — + 1	Hjelde J 13 + 1	James K 2 + 5	Morgan W 42 + 1	King M 17 + 9	Roche B 2	Commons K 19 + 11	Gardner R 9 + 5	Robertson G 13 + 7	Bopp E 6 + 12	Dawson M 13 + 1	Thompson J 14 + 6	Nowland A 5	Lester J 3	Westcarr C — + 1	Derry S 7	Harris N 5 + 8	Folly Y — + 1	Curtis J 11	Melville A 13	Powell D 11	Friio D 5	Dobie S 11 + 1	Doyle C 2 + 1	*Match No.*
1	2	3	4	5	6^1	7	8	9	10	11	12																								1
1	2	3	4	5		7	8^1	9	10	11		6	12																						2
1	2	3	4	5^1		7	8^2	9	10	11		6		12	13																				3
1	2	3	4			7	8^1	9	10	11		6		5	12																				4
	2^1	3	4			7	8^3	9	10■	11		6		5	14	1	12^2	13																	5
		3^1	4	6		2	8	9		11				5	10	1	7		12																6
1		3	4			2	8^1	9		11		6		5	10		7			12															7
1		11	4	12		2	8	9		7		6^1		5	10^2		13		3																8
1		3	4	6	2	7	8	9	10					5			11^1		12																9
1		3	4		2	7^1	8^2	9	10	11		6		5	12					13															10
1		3	4		2	7^2	8^1	9	10	11		6		5	12					13															11
1	2^1	3	4			7	8	9		11		6		5	10					12															12
1	2	3	4			7	8^2	9^1		11■		6		5	10				12		13														13
1	2	11	4		12	7■	8^1	9						6	10		13^3	14	3^2		5														14
1	2	11^2	4		14		8^3	9	12■					6	10		13		3	7^1	5														15
1	2	3	4		7^2		8^1	9		11				6	10		12				5	13													16
1	2	3	4^1			7^2	12	9		11				6	10		13				5	8													17
1	2^3	3	4		14		12	9		11				6	10		13				5	7^1	8^2												18
1		3^3	4^1		2^2		13	12	10	11				6	9			8	14		5	7													19
1			4			12		14	10	11			13	6	9^3			8^2	3		5	2	7^1												20
1			4			13	12^2	14	10	11		6		5	9^3				3			2	7^1	8											21
1		11	4					9^1	10	7		5		6				12	3			2		8											22
1		3	4			2		9^2	10	11				6	12				13		5	14	7^1	8^3											23
1		11				7		9^1	12^2	8		13		6	10				3	14	5	2	4^3												24
1		11				2^1		9						6			12		3	4	5	7^2			13	8	10								25
1		11						9^2	12	7				6	13		14		2■	4	5	3^3				8	10^1								26
1	12	11^1		2					10	7				6	13					4	5	3				8	9^2								27
1	12	11^3		3				13	10	7		5■		6	14					4		2^1				8	9^2								28
1	2	12	4^2	6				9^1	10						8		11		3^3		5					7	13	14							29
1	2	3	4	5				12	10	11				6	9^1		7									8									30
1		3	4^1	5					10				13	2	9^2		11^3		14	12						8			7	6					31
1		3^1	12	5	8^2			13	9					6			10^3					14							2	4	7	11			32
1			4	5				12	10					6			11												2	3	8	7	9^1		33
1		11^2	12	3	13				10					5			7^3										14		2	6	8	4^1	9		34
1			4^1	3	7				10					5			11					12							2	6	8		9		35
1		11^2	12	3	13				10					5			7										14		2	6	8^1	4	9^3		36
1	2			3	7^3				10				9	5			12	8	13	11^1		6					14		4^2						37
1	2^3		4^2	6	7				10				14	5			12	11^1	3	13		8											9		38
1	2		12	6	7				10				13	5			11^1					14							3^2		8	4^3	9		39
1	2			6	7				10					5			11	12	3^2	13										4	8^1		9		40
1	2		12	3	7				10				4^1	5			11	8				13					14			6^2			9^3		41
1	2	11^1	4^2		7				10					5			9	12		13		3^3								6	8		14		42
1■	2		4		7				10					5			11^6	3		12							13			6	8^2		9^1	15	43
			4		7				10					5			11^1	8									12		2	6	3		9	1	44
1	12		4^2						10					5			11	8	3^1	13							14		2	6	7■		9^3		45
	2		4		7^1				10					5			11	8		12							9		3	6				1	46

FA Cup

Third Round	QPR	(a)	3-0
Fourth Round	Peterborough U	(h)	1-0
Fifth Round	Tottenham H	(a)	1-1
		(h)	0-3

Carling Cup

First Round	Scunthorpe U	(h)	2-0
Second Round	Rotherham U	(h)	2-1
Third Round	Doncaster R	(a)	2-0
Fourth Round	Fulham	(h)	2-4

NOTTS COUNTY FL Championship 2

FOUNDATION

According to the official history of Notts County 'the true date of Notts' foundation has to be the meeting at the George Hotel on 7 December 1864'. However, in the same opening chapter is the following: *The Nottingham Guardian* on 28 November 1862 carried the following report: 'The opening of the Nottingham Football Club commenced on Tuesday last at Cremorne Gardens. A side was chosen by W. Arkwright and Chas Deakin. A very spirited game resulted in the latter scoring two goals and two rouges against one and one.'

The Meadow Lane Stadium, Meadow Lane, Nottingham NG2 3HJ.

Telephone: (0115) 952 9000.

Fax: (0115) 955 3994.

Ticket Office: (0115) 955 7204.

Website: www.nottscountyfc.co.uk

Email: info@nottscountyfc.co.uk

Ground Capacity: 20,300.

Record Attendance: 47,310 v York C, FA Cup 6th rd, 12 March 1955.

Pitch Measurements: 113yd × 72yd.

Chief Executive: Patrick Nelson.

Secretary: Tony Cuthbert.

Manager: Gudjon Thordarson.

Physio: John Haselden.

Colours: Black with white striped shirts, white shorts, white stockings.

Change Colours: Pale blue.

Year Formed: 1862* (*see Foundation*).

Turned Professional: 1885.

Ltd Co.: 1888.

Club Nickname: 'Magpies'.

Previous Grounds: 1862, The Park; 1864, The Meadows; 1877, Beeston Cricket Ground; 1880, Castle Ground; 1883, Trent Bridge; 1910, Meadow Lane.

First Football League Game: 15 September 1888, Football League, v Everton (a) L 1–2 – Holland; Guttridge, McLean; Brown, Warburton, Shelton; Hodder, Harker, Jardine, Moore (1), Wardle.

Record League Victory: 11–1 v Newport Co, Division 3 (S), 15 January 1949 – Smith; Southwell, Purvis; Gannon, Baxter, Adamson; Houghton (1), Sewell (4), Lawton (4), Pimbley, Johnston (2).

Record Cup Victory: 15–0 v Rotherham T (at Trent Bridge), FA Cup 1st rd, 24 October 1885 – Sherwin; Snook, H. T. Moore; Dobson (1), Emmett (1), Chapman; Gunn (1), Albert Moore (2), Jackson (3), Daft (2), Cursham (4), (1 og).

HONOURS

Football League: Division 1 best season: 3rd, 1890–91, 1900–01; Division 2 – Champions 1896–97, 1913–14, 1922–23; Runners-up 1894–95, 1980–81; Promoted from Division 2 1990–91 (play-offs); Division 3 (S) – Champions 1930–31, 1949–50; Runners-up 1936–37; Division 3 – Champions 1997–98; Runners-up 1972–73; Promoted from Division 3 1989–90 (play-offs); Division 4 – Champions 1970–71; Runners-up 1959–60.

FA Cup: Winners 1894; Runners-up 1891.

Football League Cup: best season: 5th rd, 1964, 1973, 1976.

Anglo-Italian Cup: Winners 1995; Runners-up 1994.

SKY SPORTS FACT FILE

In 1985–86 the combination of 6ft 5in Mick Waitt and pint-sized Ian McParland produced 39 goals in League and Cup matches out of 91 scored. That season Notts County also won the Notts FA County Cup beating neighbours Nottingham Forest 2–1.

Record Defeat: 1–9 v Blackburn R, Division 1, 16 November 1889. 1–9 v Aston Villa, Division 1, 29 September 1888. 1–9 v Portsmouth, Division 2, 9 April 1927.

Most League Points (2 for a win): 69, Division 4, 1970–71.

Most League Points (3 for a win): 99, Division 3, 1997–98.

Most League Goals: 107, Division 4, 1959–60.

Highest League Scorer in Season: Tom Keetley, 39, Division 3 (S), 1930–31.

Most League Goals in Total Aggregate: Les Bradd, 124, 1967–78.

Most League Goals in One Match: 5, Robert Jardine v Burnley, Division 1, 27 October 1888; 5, Daniel Bruce v Port Vale, Division 2, 26 February 1895; 5, Bertie Mills v Barnsley, Division 2, 19 November 1927.

Most Capped Player: Kevin Wilson, 15 (42), Northern Ireland.

Most League Appearances: Albert Iremonger, 564, 1904–26.

Youngest League Player: Tony Bircumshaw, 16 years 54 days v Brentford, 3 April 1961.

Record Transfer Fee Received: £2,500,000 from Derby Co for Craig Short, September 1992.

Record Transfer Fee Paid: £685,000 to Sheffield U for Tony Agana, November 1991.

Football League Record: 1888 Founder Member of the Football League; 1893–97 Division 2; 1897–1913 Division 1; 1913–14 Division 2; 1914–20 Division 1; 1920–23 Division 2; 1923–26 Division 1; 1926–30 Division 2; 1930–31 Division 3 (S); 1931–35 Division 2; 1935–50 Division 3 (S); 1950–58 Division 2; 1958–59 Division 3; 1959–60 Division 4; 1960–64 Division 3; 1964–71 Division 4; 1971–73 Division 3; 1973–81 Division 2; 1981–84 Division 1; 1984–85 Division 2; 1985–90 Division 3; 1990–91 Division 2; 1991–95 Division 1; 1995–97 Division 2; 1997–98 Division 3; 1998–2004 Division 2; 2004– FL2.

LATEST SEQUENCES

Longest Sequence of League Wins: 10, 3.12.1997 – 31.1.1998.

Longest Sequence of League Defeats: 7, 3.9.1983 – 16.10.1983.

Longest Sequence of League Draws: 5, 2.12.1978 – 26.12.1978.

Longest Sequence of Unbeaten League Matches: 19, 26.4.1930 – 6.12.1930.

Longest Sequence Without a League Win: 20, 3.12.1996 – 31.3.1997.

Successive Scoring Runs: 35 from 26.4.1930.

Successive Non-scoring Runs: 5 from 30.11.1912.

MANAGERS

Edwin Browne 1883–93 *(Secretary-Manager)*
Tom Featherstone 1893 *(Secretary-Manager)*
Tom Harris 1893–1913 *(Secretary-Manager)*
Albert Fisher 1913–27
Horace Henshall 1927–34
Charlie Jones 1934–35
David Pratt 1935
Percy Smith 1935–36
Jimmy McMullan 1936–37
Harry Parkes 1938–39
Tony Towers 1939–42
Frank Womack 1942–43
Major Frank Buckley 1944–46
Arthur Stollery 1946–49
Eric Houghton 1949–53
George Poyser 1953–57
Tommy Lawton 1957–58
Frank Hill 1958–61
Tim Coleman 1961–63
Eddie Lowe 1963–65
Tim Coleman 1965–66
Jack Burkitt 1966–67
Andy Beattie *(General Manager)* 1967
Billy Gray 1967–68
Jimmy Sirrel 1969–75
Ron Fenton 1975–77
Jimmy Sirrel 1978–82 *(continued as General Manager to 1984)*
Howard Wilkinson 1982–83
Larry Lloyd 1983–84
Richie Barker 1984–85
Jimmy Sirrel 1985–87
John Barnwell 1987–88
Neil Warnock 1989–93
Mick Walker 1993–94
Russell Slade 1994–95
Howard Kendall 1995
Colin Murphy 1995 *(continued as General Manager to 1996)*
Steve Thompson 1996
Sam Allardyce 1997–99
Gary Brazil 1999–2000
Jocky Scott 2000–01
Gary Brazil 2001
Billy Dearden 2002–04
Gary Mills 2004
Ian Richardson 2004–05
Gudjon Thordarson May 2005–

TEN YEAR LEAGUE RECORD

		P	W	D	L	F	A	Pts	Pos
1995-96	Div 2	46	21	15	10	63	39	78	4
1996-97	Div 2	46	7	14	25	33	59	35	24
1997-98	Div 3	46	29	12	5	82	43	99	1
1998-99	Div 2	46	14	12	20	52	61	54	16
1999-2000	Div 2	46	18	11	17	61	55	65	8
2000-01	Div 2	46	19	12	15	62	66	69	8
2001-02	Div 2	46	13	11	22	59	71	50	19
2002-03	Div 2	46	13	16	17	62	70	55	15
2003-04	Div 2	46	10	12	24	50	78	42	23
2004-05	FL 2	46	13	13	20	46	62	52	19

DID YOU KNOW

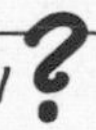

A fine start to 1930–31 saw Notts County go 18 matches before defeat. Then in 1970–71 though their opening run lasted exactly half as many games as previously it was again the best in the entire four Football League divisions.

NOTTS COUNTY 2004–05 LEAGUE RECORD

Match No.	*Date*	*Venue*	*Opponents*	*Result*	*H/T Score*	*Lg. Pos.*	*Goalscorers*	*Attendance*
1	Aug 7	H	Chester C	D 1-1	0-0	—	Baudet (pen) [65]	6432
2	10	A	Kidderminster H	D 0-0	0-0	—		2927
3	14	A	Bristol R	L 1-2	0-0	21	Hurst [66]	8225
4	21	H	Yeovil T	L 1-2	0-0	22	Gordon [56]	5024
5	28	A	Lincoln C	W 2-1	1-0	17	Scully 2 [27, 63]	5173
6	30	H	Oxford U	L 0-1	0-1	19		5288
7	Sept 4	H	Cheltenham T	D 0-0	0-0	22		4302
8	11	A	Northampton T	D 0-0	0-0	23		5471
9	18	H	Southend U	L 1-2	0-1	24	Hurst [86]	4487
10	25	A	Rochdale	W 3-0	1-0	17	Hurst 3 [40, 65, 90]	2370
11	Oct 2	H	Leyton Orient	L 1-2	1-1	21	Baudet (pen) [7]	5141
12	10	A	Macclesfield T	W 2-1	0-1	19	Hurst 2 [66, 71]	2456
13	16	A	Mansfield T	L 1-3	0-2	21	Gordon [90]	7682
14	19	H	Darlington	D 1-1	1-0	—	Hurst [28]	3620
15	23	H	Boston U	W 2-1	1-0	19	Gordon [17], Palmer [51]	5434
16	30	A	Rushden & D	L 1-5	0-3	21	Pipe [55]	3504
17	Nov 6	H	Shrewsbury T	W 3-0	1-0	20	Bolland [39], Hurst [70], Palmer [90]	5745
18	20	A	Bury	L 0-1	0-1	20		2938
19	27	H	Cambridge U	W 2-1	1-0	18	Williams [39], Palmer [74]	5080
20	Dec 7	A	Grimsby T	L 2-3	1-1	—	Oakes [18], Gordon [71]	4030
21	11	H	Wycombe W	L 0-1	0-1	20		6529
22	18	A	Swansea C	L 0-4	0-1	20		6609
23	28	A	Scunthorpe U	D 0-0	0-0	21		6399
24	Jan 1	A	Cheltenham T	W 2-0	0-0	20	Hurst [58], Palmer [69]	3375
25	3	H	Rochdale	D 0-0	0-0	20		5258
26	15	A	Southend U	D 0-0	0-0	20		5304
27	22	H	Scunthorpe U	W 2-0	1-0	19	Hurst [30], Gordon [57]	6429
28	25	H	Macclesfield T	L 0-5	0-2	—		3586
29	29	A	Leyton Orient	L 0-2	0-0	19		3440
30	Feb 5	H	Mansfield T	L 0-1	0-1	20		10,005
31	12	A	Darlington	W 2-1	0-1	20	Pipe [59], Wilson [67]	4213
32	15	H	Northampton T	D 0-0	0-0	—		4645
33	19	H	Rushden & D	D 1-1	0-0	20	Baudet (pen) [54]	4556
34	26	A	Wycombe W	W 2-1	1-1	19	Wilson [13], Oakes [71]	4199
35	Mar 5	H	Swansea C	W 1-0	0-0	18	Stallard [50]	4644
36	12	H	Kidderminster H	L 1-3	0-0	18	Stallard [88]	4358
37	16	A	Boston U	L 0-4	0-0	—		2229
38	19	A	Chester C	L 2-3	1-1	19	Hurst [23], Zadkovich [82]	2324
39	26	H	Bristol R	L 1-2	1-1	19	Hurst [9]	4258
40	29	A	Yeovil T	W 3-1	2-0	—	Oakes [6], Hurst [25], Stallard [58]	7221
41	Apr 2	H	Lincoln C	W 1-0	1-0	18	Baudet (pen) [41]	7103
42	9	A	Oxford U	L 1-2	1-0	19	Baudet [28]	4436
43	16	H	Grimsby T	D 2-2	0-1	19	Oakes 2 [76, 88]	5478
44	23	A	Shrewsbury T	D 1-1	1-0	19	Harrad [24]	4202
45	30	H	Bury	L 0-1	0-0	19		6424
46	May 7	A	Cambridge U	D 0-0	0-0	19		4723

Final League Position: 19

GOALSCORERS

League (46): Hurst 14, Baudet 5 (4 pens), Gordon 5, Oakes 5, Palmer 4, Stallard 3, Pipe 2, Scully 2, Wilson 2, Bolland 1, Harrad 1, Williams 1, Zadkovich 1.
Carling Cup (4): Richardson 2, Ullathorne 1, Wilson 1.
FA Cup (6): Gordon 3, Baudet 1 (pen), Oakes 1, Scully 1.
LDV Vans Trophy (2): Hurst 1, Sofiane 1.

Mildenhall S 1	Richardson I 10	Ullathorne R 34 + 2	Edwards M 8 + 1	Whitlow M 22 + 2	Baudet J 38 + 1	Pipe D 38 + 3	Bolland P 38 + 2	Gordon G 23 + 4	Hurst G 36 + 5	Gill M 38 + 5	Harrad S 4 + 12	Henderson W 11	Wilson K 36 + 5	McFaul S 17 + 7	Williams M 8 + 10	Scully T 20 + 11	Deeney S 31 + 1	Kuduzovic F — + 3	Sofiane Y 2 + 2	Robinson M 1 + 1	Pead C 4 + 1	O'Grady C 3 + 6	Oakes S 28 + 3	Palmer C 23 + 2	Friars E 4 + 5	Stallard M 16	Elliot R 3 + 1	Zadkovich R 6 + 2	Scoffham S 3 + 4	*Match No.*
1	2	3	4	5	6	7	8	9	10^{1}	11	12																			1
	2	3	4^{3}		6	7^{1}	8	9	10^{2}	11		1	5	12	13	14														2
	2^{2}	3	4		6	7	8	9	10	5		1	13		12	11^{1}														3
	2	3	4		6	7	8	9^{1}	10	11		1	13		12	5^{2}														4
	2	3	4		6	7	8		10^{1}	11	12	1^{6}	13		9	5^{2}	15													5
	2	3	4^{2}	12	6^{1}	7	8^{3}		10	11			13	14	9	5	1													6
	2	3	12	5^{1}	6		8	9		11^{2}	13		4^{3}		10	7	1	14												7
		3	4	12	6^{1}	7	8	13^{3}	10	11		1				5			9^{2}	14	2									8
	2	3	4	5		7	8		12	13		1			14	11^{2}			9	10^{1}	6^{3}									9
	2	3^{1}		5	6	7	8		10	11		1	4			9^{2}			13^{3}		12	14								10
		3		5	6	7^{1}	8	13	10	11		1	2			12			14		4^{3}	9^{2}								11
		3		5	6		8	9^{1}	10			1	2								4	12	7	11						12
		3		5	6	7	8	14	10	2^{1}			12			13	1					9^{3}	11	4^{2}						13
		3		5^{2}	6		8	9^{1}	10				2			11	1					12	7	4	13					14
		3		5	6	12	8^{2}	9^{3}	10	13			2			11	1					14	7^{1}	4						15
		3^{3}		5		12	8	9	10	2^{2}			6	13		11	1						7	4^{1}	14					16
				5	6	7	8	9	10	12			2	3^{1}			1						11	4						17
	2				6	7	8	9	$10^{■}$	12			5	3^{2}		11^{1}	1	13						4						18
		12		5	6	7	$8^{■}$	9^{3}		13			3	2^{1}	10^{2}		1					14	11	4						19
				5	6	7^{2}		9	12	11		1	2	3^{3}	10^{1}	13						14	8	4						20
				5		3			10	11		1		2^{2}	9	6		12				8^{1}	7	4	13					21
		12			6	2	8	9	13	3	10^{2}		5		11^{3}	7^{1}	1						14	4						22
		3		5	6	7	8	9		11	10		2				1							4						23
		3		5	6	7	8	9	10	11			2				1							4						24
		3		5	6	7^{1}	8	9	10				2		13	12	1						11	4^{2}						25
				5^{1}	6	7		9	10	3			2	12		11	1						8	4						26
		3			6	7^{3}	12	9	10^{2}	11			5	4	13	2	1						8^{1}	14						27
		3			6	7	12	9^{2}	10	2			5	4	13	11^{1}	1						8							28
		3			6	7	8	9	10	2	12		5			11^{2}	1						13	4^{1}						29
		3^{1}			6^{3}	7	8	9	12	4			5	2		11^{2}	1						14	13		10				30
		3		5		7^{1}	8		10	11			4	2	12		1						6			9				31
		3		5	12	7	8	13	10	11			2	6^{1}			1						4			9^{2}				32
		3		5^{2}	6	7	8^{1}	9^{3}	10	11	14		2	13		12	1						4							33
		3			6	7	8		10^{1}	11	12		2	5			1						4			9				34
		3			6^{2}	7	8		10	11	12		5	2			1						4		13	9^{1}				35
		2				7	8		10^{1}	11	12		5	4	13		$1^{■}$						6^{2}		3^{6}	9	15			36
		3		5		7	8		10^{1}	11	12		2	6^{2}		13							4			9	1			37
		3				7	8^{1}		10	11	12		5	6^{2}									4		2	9	1	13		38
		3			6		8		10	11			5	2^{1}		12							4			9^{2}	1	7	13	39
		3			6		8		10	2			5	12			1						11	4^{1}		9^{2}		7	13	40
		3^{1}			6	12	8		10	11			5			13	1						$2^{■}$	4		9^{3}		7^{2}	14	41
					6	7	8		10	2	12		5	13	11^{1}		1							4		9		3^{2}		42
					6	7	8		10^{2}	11				2		12	1						3	4		9		5^{1}	13	43
					6	7				2	11^{1}		5			12	1						8	4	3	9			10	44
					6	7				11	8^{2}		5		12		1						3	4	2^{1}	9		13	10	45
					6	7			12	2	13		5^{3}			11	1						3	4	14	9		8^{1}	10^{2}	46

FA Cup

First Round	Woking	(h)	2-0
Second Round	Swindon T	(a)	1-1
		(h)	2-0
Third Round	Middlesbrough	(h)	1-2

Carling Cup

First Round	Bradford C	(a)	2-1
Second Round	West Ham U	(a)	2-3

LDV Vans Trophy

First Round	Wrexham	(h)	2-3

OLDHAM ATHLETIC FL Championship 1

FOUNDATION

It was in 1895 that John Garland, the landlord of the Featherstall and Junction Hotel, decided to form a football club. As Pine Villa they played in the Oldham Junior League. In 1899 the local professional club, Oldham County, went out of existence and one of the liquidators persuaded Pine Villa to take over their ground at Sheepfoot Lane and change their name to Oldham Athletic.

Boundary Park, Furtherwood Road, Oldham OL1 2PA.

Telephone: 0871 226 2235.

Fax: 0871 226 1715.

Ticket Office: 0871 226 2235.

Website: www.oldhamathletic.co.uk

Email: info@oldhamathletic.co.uk

Ground Capacity: 13,624.

Record Attendance: 46,471 v Sheffield W, FA Cup 4th rd, 25 January 1930.

Pitch Measurements: 110yd × 74yd.

Chairman: Barry Chayton.

Managing Director: Simon Corney.

Chief Executive/Secretary: Alan Hardy.

Manager: Ronnie Moore.

Assistant Manager: John Breckin.

Physio: Lee Nobes.

Colours: Royal blue shirts, royal blue shorts, white stockings.

Change Colours: All black.

Year Formed: 1895.

Turned Professional: 1899.

Ltd Co.: 1906.

Previous Name: 1895, Pine Villa; 1899, Oldham Athletic.

Club Nickname: 'The Latics'.

Previous Grounds: 1895, Sheepfoot Lane; 1900, Hudson Field; 1906, Sheepfoot Lane; 1907, Boundary Park.

First Football League Game: 9 September 1907, Division 2, v Stoke (a) W 3–1 – Hewitson; Hodson, Hamilton; Fay, Walders, Wilson; Ward, W. Dodds (1), Newton (1), Hancock, Swarbrick (1).

Record League Victory: 11–0 v Southport, Division 4, 26 December 1962 – Bollands; Branagan, Marshall; McCall, Williams, Scott; Ledger (1), Johnstone, Lister (6), Colquhoun (1), Whitaker (3).

HONOURS

Football League: Division 1 – Runners-up 1914–15; Division 2 – Champions 1990–91; Runners-up 1909–10; Division 3 (N) – Champions 1952–53; Division 3 – Champions 1973–74; Division 4 – Runners-up 1962–63.

FA Cup: Semi-final 1913, 1990, 1994.

Football League Cup: Runners-up 1990.

SKY SPORTS FACT FILE

Promotion to the Second Division for champions Oldham Athletic was achieved in 1952–53 after recovering from a disastrous spell from mid-February to the end of March when only one win was registered from a sequence of 11 matches.

Record Cup Victory: 10–1 v Lytham, FA Cup 1st rd, 28 November 1925 – Gray; Wynne, Grundy; Adlam, Heaton, Naylor (1), Douglas, Pynegar (2), Ormston (2), Barnes (3), Watson (2).

Record Defeat: 4–13 v Tranmere R, Division 3 (N), 26 December 1935.

Most League Points (2 for a win): 62, Division 3, 1973–74.

Most League Points (3 for a win): 88, Division 2, 1990–91.

Most League Goals: 95, Division 4, 1962–63.

Highest League Scorer in Season: Tom Davis, 33, Division 3 (N), 1936–37.

Most League Goals in Total Aggregate: Roger Palmer, 141, 1980–94.

Most League Goals in One Match: 7, Eric Gemmell v Chester, Division 3N, 19 January 1952.

Most Capped Player: Gunnar Halle, 24 (64), Norway.

Most League Appearances: Ian Wood, 525, 1966–80.

Youngest League Player: Wayne Harrison, 15 years 11 months v Notts Co, 27 October 1984.

Record Transfer Fee Received: £1,700,000 from Aston Villa for Earl Barrett, February 1992.

Record Transfer Fee Paid: £750,000 to Aston Villa for Ian Olney, June 1992.

Football League Record: 1907 Elected to Division 2; 1910–23 Division 1; 1923–35 Division 2; 1935–53 Division 3 (N); 1953–54 Division 2; 1954–58 Division 3 (N); 1958–63 Division 4; 1963–69 Division 3; 1969–71 Division 4; 1971–74 Division 3; 1974–91 Division 2; 1991–92 Division 1; 1992–94 FA Premier League; 1994–97 Division 1; 1997–2004 Division 2; 2004– FL1.

MANAGERS

David Ashworth 1906–14
Herbert Bamlett 1914–21
Charlie Roberts 1921–22
David Ashworth 1923–24
Bob Mellor 1924–27
Andy Wilson 1927–32
Jimmy McMullan 1933–34
Bob Mellor 1934–45
(continued as Secretary to 1953)
Frank Womack 1945–47
Billy Wootton 1947–50
George Hardwick 1950–56
Ted Goodier 1956–58
Norman Dodgin 1958–60
Jack Rowley 1960–63
Les McDowall 1963–65
Gordon Hurst 1965–66
Jimmy McIlroy 1966–68
Jack Rowley 1968–69
Jimmy Frizzell 1970–82
Joe Royle 1982–94
Graeme Sharp 1994–97
Neil Warnock 1997–98
Andy Ritchie 1998–2001
Mick Wadsworth 2001–02
Iain Dowie 2002–03
Brian Talbot 2004–05
Ronnie Moore March 2005–

LATEST SEQUENCES

Longest Sequence of League Wins: 10, 12.1.1974 – 12.3.1974.

Longest Sequence of League Defeats: 8, 15.12.1934 – 2.2.1935.

Longest Sequence of League Draws: 5, 26.12.1982 – 15.1.1983.

Longest Sequence of Unbeaten League Matches: 20, 1.5.1990 – 10.11.1990.

Longest Sequence Without a League Win: 17, 4.9.1920 – 18.12.1920.

Successive Scoring Runs: 25 from 15.1.1927.

Successive Non-scoring Runs: 6 from 4.2.1922.

TEN YEAR LEAGUE RECORD

		P	W	D	L	F	A	Pts	Pos
1995-96	Div 1	46	14	14	18	54	50	56	18
1996-97	Div 1	46	10	13	23	51	66	43	23
1997-98	Div 2	46	15	16	15	62	54	61	13
1998-99	Div 2	46	14	9	23	48	66	51	20
1999-2000	Div 2	46	16	12	18	50	55	60	14
2000-01	Div 2	46	15	13	18	53	65	58	15
2001-02	Div 2	46	18	16	12	77	65	70	9
2002-03	Div 2	46	22	16	8	68	38	82	5
2003-04	Div 2	46	12	21	13	66	60	57	15
2004-05	FL 1	46	14	10	22	60	73	52	19

DID YOU KNOW ?

Oldham Athletic celebrated their 3000th Football League match on 7 May 1988 when they defeated Bournemouth 2–0 at Boundary Park. It was their 1122nd victory in the competition and registered their 4380th goal in finishing tenth in the table.

OLDHAM ATHLETIC 2004–05 LEAGUE RECORD

Match No.	*Date*	*Venue*	*Opponents*	*Result*		*H/T Score*	*Lg. Pos.*	*Goalscorers*	*Attendance*
1	Aug 7	A	Luton T	L	1-2	1-1	—	Haining [10]	6634
2	10	H	Wrexham	L	2-3	0-2	—	Boshell [71], Jack [79]	6143
3	14	H	Walsall	W	5-3	2-2	16	Eyres 2 [42, 45], Holden [50], Jack [54], Griffin [90]	5654
4	21	A	Hull C	L	0-2	0-2	20		16,916
5	28	H	Milton Keynes D	W	3-0	2-0	16	Johnson [39], Killen [43], Arber [61]	5066
6	30	A	Sheffield W	D	1-1	0-0	15	Johnson [75]	21,530
7	Sept 11	H	Hartlepool U	W	3-2	1-0	16	Eyre [43], Betsy [60], Johnson [82]	5805
8	14	A	Tranmere R	L	0-2	0-0	—		8437
9	18	A	Doncaster R	D	1-1	1-1	17	Johnson [39]	6774
10	25	H	Colchester U	D	1-1	1-0	18	Eyres [22]	5166
11	Oct 2	A	Brentford	L	0-2	0-1	19		5818
12	10	H	Blackpool	L	1-2	1-1	20	Haining [39]	7125
13	16	A	Swindon T	L	0-1	0-1	21		5522
14	19	H	Bristol C	D	0-0	0-0	—		5090
15	23	H	Bournemouth	L	1-2	1-0	21	Vernon (pen) [3]	5335
16	30	A	Stockport Co	W	2-1	2-1	20	Wilbraham 2 [13, 39]	6146
17	Nov 6	A	Torquay U	L	0-2	0-1	20		3183
18	20	H	Barnsley	W	3-2	1-1	18	Killen 2 [17, 90], Vernon [89]	5593
19	27	A	Bradford C	W	3-1	1-1	18	Kilkenny 2 [12, 82], Killen [63]	8647
20	Dec 7	H	Chesterfield	W	4-1	2-0	—	Killen 2 (1 pen) [3, 19 (p)], Betsy [55], Kilkenny [62]	5207
21	11	H	Huddersfield T	W	2-1	0-1	14	Haining [4], Betsy [38]	8389
22	18	A	Port Vale	L	1-3	1-1	17	Vernon [34]	4849
23	26	A	Hartlepool U	L	1-2	0-2	17	Holden [64]	6520
24	28	H	Peterborough U	W	2-1	0-0	15	Vernon [46], Kilkenny [54]	5618
25	Jan 1	H	Tranmere R	D	2-2	1-1	15	Griffin [39], Vernon [71]	6876
26	3	A	Colchester U	D	0-0	0-0	15		3873
27	15	H	Doncaster R	L	1-2	0-1	16	Vernon [87]	7401
28	22	A	Peterborough U	W	2-1	1-1	14	Betsy 2 [7, 63]	4047
29	Feb 5	H	Swindon T	L	1-2	1-0	15	Cooper [14]	5810
30	8	A	Blackpool	L	0-2	0-0	—		5563
31	12	A	Bournemouth	L	0-4	0-1	18		6622
32	19	H	Stockport Co	L	1-2	0-1	18	Vernon [70]	5924
33	22	A	Bristol C	L	1-5	0-3	—	Haining [57]	9007
34	26	A	Huddersfield T	L	1-2	0-2	19	Branston [75]	11,161
35	Mar 5	H	Port Vale	W	3-0	1-0	19	Haining [27], Cooper 2 [52, 54]	5799
36	12	A	Wrexham	L	0-1	0-0	19		4170
37	15	H	Brentford	L	0-2	0-0	—		4291
38	19	H	Luton T	D	2-2	1-1	19	Killen [39], Beckett [48]	5809
39	26	A	Walsall	W	1-0	0-0	19	Beckett [72]	6794
40	28	H	Hull C	W	1-0	0-0	18	Killen [71]	8562
41	Apr 2	A	Milton Keynes D	D	1-1	1-0	17	Beckett [5]	5426
42	9	H	Sheffield W	D	1-1	1-0	18	Beckett [28]	9645
43	16	A	Barnsley	D	2-2	1-1	19	Killen [37], Beckett [66]	8856
44	23	H	Torquay U	L	1-2	1-1	19	Eyres [25]	8941
45	30	A	Chesterfield	L	0-1	0-0	20		5421
46	May 7	H	Bradford C	W	2-1	2-1	19	Killen [3], Beckett [22]	9381

Final League Position: 19

GOALSCORERS

League (60): Killen 10 (1 pen), Vernon 7 (1 pen), Beckett 6, Betsy 5, Haining 5, Eyres 4, Johnson 4, Kilkenny 4, Cooper 3, Griffin 2, Holden 2, Jack 2, Wilbraham 2, Arber 1, Boshell 1, Branston 1, Eyre 1.
Carling Cup (2): Eyre 1 (pen), Eyres 1.
FA Cup (6): Killen 4 (2 pens), Croft 1, Vernon 1.
LDV Vans Trophy (10): Eyres 2, Vernon 2 (1 pen), Appleby 1 (pen), Croft 1, Griffin 1, Holden 1, Kilkenny 1, Killen 1 (pen).

Pogliacomi L 37	Holden D 39 + 1	Griffin A 33 + 2	Bonner M 15 + 4	Haining W 34 + 1	Arber M 13 + 1	Jack R 5 + 5 Facey D 1 + 5	Eyre J 18 + 6	Vernon S 13 + 9	Johnson J 13 + 6	Cooksey E 1	Barlow M 1 + 8	Appleby M 9 + 8	Boshell D 10 + 6	Eyres D 40 + 2	Hall D 20 + 1	Killen C 25 + 1	Betsy K 34 + 2	Mawson C 3 + 1	Lomax K 7 + 2	Tierney M 7 + 4	Lee D 5 + 2	Winn A — + 2 Sanokho A — +	Hall C 2 + 4	Wilbraham A 4	Beharall D 3	Hughes M 25 + 2	Croft L 11 + 1	Kilkenny N 24 + 3	Bruce A 8 + 4	Wolfenden M — + 1	Cooper K 5 + 2	Branston G 6 + 1	Stam S 11 + 2	Mildenhall S 6	Wilkinson W — + 1	Owen G 9	Beckett L 9	*Match No.*
1	2	3	4	5	6	7^1	8	9^2	10	11^3	12	13	14																									1
1	2	3	4	5	6	7	8^2	9^1	10			11	12	13																								2
1	2	3	4	5	6	9	7		10^1		12	13	8^2	11																								3
1	2	3	4	5	6	9^2	7		10^1		12	13	8	11																								4
1	2	3	4	5	6	12	7^3		10^1		13		8	11	14	9^2																						5
1	2	3	4	5	6	9	7		10^1		12		8	11																								6
1	2	3	4^1	5	6		7		12		13		8	11		9^2	10																					7
1^6	2	3		5	6	12	7		8				4	11		9^1	10	15																				8
	2	3		5	6	12	7		8			13	4^2	11^1		9	10	1																				9
	2	3		5	6	12	7^1		8			13	4	11		9^2	10	1																				10
	2	3^1		5	6	12	7		8			13	4^3	11^2		9	10	1	14																			11
1	2	3^2	4^3	5	6		7				12		8^1	11		9	10			13	14																	12
1	2	12		5			7	9			8^1			11^3	4		10		3		6^2	13	14															13
1	2			5				9	$8^■$			7		11	6		10		3		4																	14
1	2	13		5				9			12	7		11^2	6		10		3		4^3	14	8^1															15
1	2			5^1	12		7^3	13	8^2			4		11	6		10		3		14			9														16
1	2	3			6			10^2				8		11	5				12		7		13	9	4^1													17
1	2	3		12				13						11	6	9					7^3			10^2	5^1	4	8	14										18
1	2	3		5				12					13	11	6	9^1	14							10^3		4	7	8^2										19
1	2	3		5				12					13	11^3	6	9^1	10			14						4	7	8^2										20
1	2	3		5				12					13	11	6	9^1	10									4	7	8^2										21
1		3	13	5			14	9	12^2					11	6		10								2	4^3	7^1	8										22
1	2	3		5			9	12						11^2	6		10^1									4	7	8	13									23
1	2	3^3		5			9^1	12				13		11	6		10									4	7^2	8	14									24
1	2	3		5				9						11^1	6		10									4	7^2	8	12	13								25
1	2^3	3	12	5			13	9				7			6		10									4^1	14	8^2	11									26
1		3		5				9						11	6	12	10									4	7^1	8	2									27
1		3		5			12	9				13		11	6		10									4	7^1	8^2	2									28
1		3					12							11	6		10		9							4	7^1	8	2		5							29
1		3	4				9	12				7^2		11	6		10		2				13						5		8^1							30
1	12	3^1	4				7	9							6		10		2				11^3			8^2		13	5		14							31
1	2	3		5				9^3						11		7^2	10^1									4		8	12		13	6	14					32
	7^1	3		5										11^2		9	12									4		8	2		10^3	6	13	1	14			33
1		3^1	4^2	5								8	13	12	6^3	9	10									7			2			14	11					34
1	2	3	4	5								7		11		9												8			10	6						35
1	2	3	7	5			12							11		9	10									4		8^1					6					36
1	2	3		5										11		9	10^1						12			4		8			7		6					37
	2		7				12		13					11		9				3						4		8^1					6	1		5	10^2	38
	2		12	4					13					11^3		9^2	10			3						14		8^1					6	1		5	7	39
	2			4^1										11		9	10			3						12		8					6	1		5	7	40
	2		12			14			13					11^2		9^3	10			3						4		8					6	1		5	7^1	41
	2					12								11		9^1	10			3		13				4^2		8					6	1		5	7	42
1	2					12								11		9^1	10			3						4		8					6			5	7	43
1	2					13			12					11^1		9^2	10			3						4		8				6				5	7	44
1	2		8			9		12	11^1								10			14						4^2		13				5	6^3			3	7	45
1	2					13								11		9^2	10			12						4		8				5	6			3^1	7	46

FA Cup

First Round	Thurrock	(a)	1-0
Second Round	Leyton Orient	(h)	4-0
Third Round	Manchester C	(h)	1-0
Fourth Round	Bolton W	(h)	0-1

Carling Cup

First Round	Stoke C	(h)	2-1
Second Round	Tottenham H	(h)	0-6

LDV Vans Trophy

First Round			
Second Round	Accrington S	(h)	3-2
Quarter-Final	Hartlepool U	(h)	3-1
Semi-Final	Tranmere R	(h)	1-1
Northern Final	Wrexham	(h)	3-5
		(a)	0-1

OXFORD UNITED FL Championship 2

FOUNDATION

There had been an Oxford United club around the time of World War I but only in the Oxfordshire Thursday League and there is no connection with the modern club which began as Headington in 1893, adding 'United' a year later. Playing first on Quarry Fields and subsequently Wootten's Fields, they owe much to a Dr Hitchings for their early development.

The Kassam Stadium, Grenoble Road, Oxford OX4 4XP.

Telephone: (01865) 337 500.

Fax: (01865) 337 555.

Ticket Office: (01865) 337 533.

Website: www.oufc.co.uk

Email: admin@oufc.co.uk

Ground Capacity: 12,450.

Record Attendance: 22,730 v Preston NE, FA Cup 6th rd, 29 February 1964.

Pitch Measurements: 115yd × 74yd.

Chairman: Firoz Kassam.

Secretary: Mick Brown.

Manager: Brian Talbot.

Colours: Yellow shirts, navy shorts, navy stockings.

Change Colours: Navy shirts, navy shorts, navy stockings.

Year Formed: 1893.

Turned Professional: 1949.

Ltd Co.: 1949.

Club Nickname: 'The U's'.

Previous Names: 1893, Headington; 1894, Headington United; 1960, Oxford United.

Previous Grounds: 1893, Headington Quarry; 1894, Wootten's Field; 1898, Sandy Lane Ground; 1902, Britannia Field; 1909, Sandy Lane; 1910, Quarry Recreation Ground; 1914, Sandy Lane; 1922, The Paddock Manor Road; 1925, Manor Ground; 2001, The Kassam Stadium.

First Football League Game: 18 August 1962, Division 4, v Barrow (a) L 2–3 – Medlock; Beavon, Quartermain; R. Atkinson, Kyle, Jones; Knight, G. Atkinson (1), Houghton (1), Cornwell, Colfar.

Record League Victory: 7–0 v Barrow, Division 4, 19 December 1964 – Fearnley; Beavon, Quartermain; R. Atkinson (1), Kyle, Jones; Morris, Booth (3), Willey (1), G. Atkinson (1), Harrington (1).

HONOURS

Football League: Division 1 best season: 12th, 1997–98; Division 2 – Champions 1984–85; Runners-up 1995–96; Division 3 – Champions 1967–68, 1983–84; Division 4 – Promoted 1964–65 (4th).

FA Cup: best season: 6th rd, 1964 (shared record for 4th Division club).

Football League Cup: Winners 1986.

SKY SPORTS FACT FILE

When Oxford United were elected to the Football League to fill the vacancy caused by Accrington Stanley's resignation in 1962, they received 39 votes, easily the highest number received by a club being elected for the first time.

Record Cup Victory: 9–1 v Dorchester T, FA Cup 1st rd, 11 November 1995 – Whitehead; Wood (2), Ford M (1), Smith, Elliott, Gilchrist, Rush (1), Massey (Murphy), Moody (3), Ford R (1), Angel (Beauchamp (1)).

Record Defeat: 0–7 v Sunderland, Division 1, 19 September 1998.

Most League Points (2 for a win): 61, Division 4, 1964–65.

Most League Points (3 for a win): 95, Division 3, 1983–84.

Most League Goals: 91, Division 3, 1983–84.

Highest League Scorer in Season: John Aldridge, 30, Division 2, 1984–85.

Most League Goals in Total Aggregate: Graham Atkinson, 77, 1962–73.

Most League Goals in One Match: 4, Tony Jones v Newport Co, Division 4, 22 September 1962; 4, Arthur Longbottom v Darlington, Division 4, 26 October 1963; 4, Richard Hill v Walsall, Division 2, 26 December 1988; 4, John Durnin v Luton T, 14 November 1992.

Most Capped Player: Jim Magilton, 18 (52), Northern Ireland.

Most League Appearances: John Shuker, 478, 1962–77.

Youngest League Player: Jason Seacole, 16 years 149 days v Mansfield T, 7 September 1976.

Record Transfer Fee Received: £1,600,000 from Leicester C for Matt Elliott, January 1997.

Record Transfer Fee Paid: £475,000 to Aberdeen for Dean Windass, August 1998.

Football League Record: 1962 Elected to Division 4; 1965–68 Division 3; 1968–76 Division 2; 1976–84 Division 3; 1984–85 Division 2; 1985–88 Division 1; 1988–92 Division 2; 1992–94 Division 1; 1994–96 Division 2; 1996–99 Division 1; 1999–2001 Division 2; 2001–04 Division 3; 2004– FL2.

MANAGERS

Harry Thompson 1949–58
(Player-Manager) 1949-51
Arthur Turner 1959–69
(continued as General Manager to 1972)
Ron Saunders 1969
Gerry Summers 1969–75
Mick Brown 1975–79
Bill Asprey 1979–80
Ian Greaves 1980–82
Jim Smith 1982–85
Maurice Evans 1985–88
Mark Lawrenson 1988
Brian Horton 1988–93
Denis Smith 1993–97
Malcolm Crosby 1997
Malcolm Shotton 1998–99
Denis Smith 2000
David Kemp 2000–01
Mark Wright 2001
Ian Atkins 2001–04
Graham Rix 2004
Ramon Diaz 2004–05
Brian Talbot May 2005–

LATEST SEQUENCES

Longest Sequence of League Wins: 6, 6.4.1985 – 24.4.1985.

Longest Sequence of League Defeats: 7, 4.5.1991 – 7.9.1991.

Longest Sequence of League Draws: 5, 7.10.1978 – 28.10.1978.

Longest Sequence of Unbeaten League Matches: 20, 17.3.1984 – 29.9.1984.

Longest Sequence Without a League Win: 27, 14.11.1987 – 27.8.1988.

Successive Scoring Runs: 17 from 10.9.1983.

Successive Non-scoring Runs: 6 from 26.3.1988.

TEN YEAR LEAGUE RECORD

		P	W	D	L	F	A	Pts	Pos
1995-96	Div 2	46	24	11	11	76	39	83	2
1996-97	Div 1	46	16	9	21	64	68	57	17
1997-98	Div 1	46	16	10	20	60	64	58	12
1998-99	Div 1	46	10	14	22	48	71	44	23
1999-2000	Div 2	46	12	9	25	43	73	45	20
2000-01	Div 2	46	7	6	33	53	100	27	24
2001-02	Div 3	46	11	14	21	53	62	47	21
2002-03	Div 3	46	19	12	15	57	47	69	8
2003-04	Div 3	46	18	17	11	55	44	71	9
2004-05	FL 2	46	16	11	19	50	63	59	15

DID YOU KNOW ?

In 1984–85 Oxford United were able to recover from a poor spell from 5 February when they took only two points from five matches, scoring just three goals. John Aldridge's 30 goals were more than three times any other player in the team.

OXFORD UNITED 2004–05 LEAGUE RECORD

Match No.	*Date*	*Venue*	*Opponents*	*Result*		*H/T Score*	*Lg. Pos.*	*Goalscorers*	*Attendance*
1	Aug 7	A	Boston U	L	0-1	0-0	—		3596
2	11	H	Mansfield T	W	1-0	1-0	—	Mooney 36	5029
3	14	H	Scunthorpe U	D	1-1	0-1	12	Mooney 54	4920
4	21	A	Leyton Orient	D	0-0	0-0	12		3426
5	28	H	Shrewsbury T	W	2-0	1-0	6	Bradbury 3, Mooney 48	4430
6	30	A	Notts Co	W	1-0	1-0	6	Bradbury (pen) 16	5288
7	Sept 3	A	Wycombe W	D	1-1	1-1	—	Roget 20	6348
8	11	H	Rushden & D	D	0-0	0-0	9		4756
9	18	A	Yeovil T	L	1-6	0-1	10	E'Beyer 73	5467
10	25	H	Bury	W	3-1	1-0	9	Basham 40, Scott (og) 62, Mooney 72	4308
11	Oct 2	A	Bristol R	L	0-2	0-1	10		8049
12	10	H	Darlington	L	1-2	1-0	15	Woozley 45	5881
13	16	H	Lincoln C	L	0-1	0-1	17		4089
14	19	A	Northampton T	L	0-1	0-0	—		5455
15	23	A	Macclesfield T	L	0-1	0-0	20		2007
16	30	H	Cheltenham T	W	1-0	1-0	19	Mooney 45	5163
17	Nov 6	A	Southend U	L	0-4	0-0	21		5608
18	20	H	Rochdale	L	0-1	0-0	21		4204
19	27	A	Chester C	W	3-1	1-1	20	E'Beyer 16, Robinson 67, Basham 84	2791
20	Dec 8	H	Swansea C	L	0-1	0-0	—		4767
21	11	H	Cambridge U	W	2-1	2-0	18	Mooney 19, Davies 29	4844
22	17	A	Grimsby T	D	1-1	0-1	—	Mooney 52	4777
23	26	A	Rushden & D	D	3-3	2-1	18	Hackett 14, Bradbury 43, Davies 77	4140
24	28	H	Kidderminster H	L	0-2	0-1	18		5947
25	Jan 1	H	Wycombe W	W	2-1	1-0	18	Brooks 23, Basham 87	7195
26	3	A	Bury	D	0-0	0-0	18		2783
27	8	A	Darlington	D	1-1	1-1	18	Brooks 31	3735
28	15	H	Yeovil T	W	2-1	1-0	17	Mooney 20, Davies 57	6778
29	22	A	Kidderminster H	W	3-1	2-0	14	Hackett 22, Davies 38, Basham 90	3143
30	29	H	Bristol R	W	3-2	2-0	12	Bradbury (pen) 15, Roget 19, Davies 74	7830
31	Feb 5	A	Lincoln C	L	0-3	0-1	14		4535
32	12	H	Northampton T	L	1-2	0-0	16	Mooney 58	7032
33	19	A	Cheltenham T	W	1-0	0-0	15	Mooney 90	5044
34	26	A	Cambridge U	L	1-2	1-0	16	Basham 45	3765
35	Mar 5	H	Grimsby T	L	1-2	1-0	17	Cominelli 34	5625
36	12	A	Mansfield T	W	3-1	2-0	16	Basham 7, Hackett 2 33, 52	3030
37	19	H	Boston U	W	2-0	1-0	15	Basham 2 39, 63	5176
38	25	A	Scunthorpe U	D	1-1	1-0	—	Mooney 32	5977
39	28	H	Leyton Orient	D	2-2	1-1	13	Basham 17, Mooney 54	5320
40	Apr 2	A	Shrewsbury T	L	0-3	0-0	15		3974
41	6	H	Macclesfield T	D	1-1	1-0	—	Wanless 3	4273
42	9	H	Notts Co	W	2-1	0-1	12	Mooney 2 (2 pens) 75, 82	4436
43	15	A	Swansea C	L	0-1	0-1	—		10,602
44	23	H	Southend U	W	2-1	2-0	12	Davies 20, Mooney 40	5916
45	30	A	Rochdale	L	1-5	0-4	14	Robinson 81	2579
46	May 7	H	Chester C	L	0-1	0-0	15		5055

Final League Position: 15

GOALSCORERS

League (50): Mooney 15 (2 pens), Basham 9, Davies 6, Bradbury 4 (2 pens), Hackett 4, Brooks 2, E'Beyer 2, Robinson 2, Roget 2, Cominelli 1, Wanless 1, Woozley 1, own goal 1.
Carling Cup (0).
FA Cup (1): Bradbury 1.
LDV Vans Trophy (2): Hand 1, Winters 1.

Tardif C 40	Mackay D 44	Robinson M 45	Brown D 3 + 1	Roget L 35	Ashton J 30	Hackett C 31 + 6	Wanless P 18 + 9	Mooney T 42	Bradbury L 39 + 2	Wolleaston R 14 + 6	Parker T 6 + 2	Louis J — + 1	Molyneaux L 6 + 10	Basham S 29 + 10	Quinn B 34 + 2	Alsop J 3 + 2	Winters T — + 4	Hand J 11	Davies C 13 + 15	Woozley D 11 + 2	E'Beyer M 6 + 4	Rawle M — + 6	Cox S 2 + 1	Togwell S 3 + 1	Judge A 1	Brooks J 6 + 6	Morgan D — + 3	Clarke B 3 + 1	Dodou E — + 1	Corbo M 13	Cominelli L 11 + 5	Beechers B — + 3	Raponi J 5 + 5	Diaz E 2 + 5	Karam A — + 2	Burton P — + 1	Match No.
1	2	3	4^{1}	5	6	7^{2}	8	9	10	11	12	13																									1
1	2	3	12	5■	6	7^{3}	8^{1}	9	10	11	4^{2}		13	14																							2
1	2	3	4^{1}		6	12		9	10	11	13		7	14	5^{2}	8^{3}																					3
1	2^{2}	3		5	6	7^{1}	8	9	10	11			13	12	4^{3}	14																					4
1	2	3	4^{2}	5^{1}	6			9	10	11			12	7			13	8																			5
1	2	3		5	6		12	9	10^{2}	11^{1}	4			7				8	13																		6
1	2	3^{1}		5	6			9		11	4			7		10	12	8																			7
1	2	3^{1}			6			9		11	5		4^{3}	7		10^{2}	12	8	13	14																	8
1	2	3^{3}		5	6^{2}			9	10	11^{1}	4		13	7		12		8			14																9
1	2	3		5		12	13	9	10	11^{2}	4^{1}			7				8		6																	10
1	2	3		5		7	8^{1}	9	10	12				11				4		6																	11
1	2	3		5		7	8^{2}	9	10^{1}	12				11	13			4		6																	12
1	2	3		5		7	8^{1}	9		11^{2}				10	12			4		6		13															13
1^{6}	2	3		5		7		9^{1}	12	11				10^{2}	4			8		6		13	15														14
	2	3		5^{3}	6	12		9	10					7^{2}	4			8			11^{1}	13	1	14													15
	2	3		5	6	12		9^{2}	10					7	8						11^{1}	13	1	4													16
	2	3		5	6■	12	13	9	10					7^{2}	8^{1}						11^{3}	14		4	1												17
1		3		5	6	7^{1}	8		10					9	4				12		11^{2}			2		13											18
1	2	3		5	6		8	9^{1}	10					7	4				12		11																19
1	2	3		5	6■	12	8^{1}	9^{2}	10					7	4				13		11^{3}					14											20
	2	3		5		7		9^{3}	10	12					4				8^{1}	6		13				11^{2}	14	1									21
	2	3		5		7^{1}	12	9^{2}	10	13					4				8	6						11^{3}	14	1									22
	2	3		5		7^{2}		9■	10^{3}	12			13		4				8	6	14					11^{1}		1									23
1	2	3		5		7	12		9	11^{1}					4				10	6						8^{2}	13										24
1	2	3		5		7■		9^{2}	8	12			14	13	4				10^{3}	6						11^{1}											25
1	2	3		5	6		12	9	10^{1}	11^{3}			8	7^{2}	4											13			14								26
1	2	3		5	6^{2}		8	9	10				4	12					7^{1}	13	14					11^{3}											27
1	2	3		5	6		8^{2}	9^{3}	10				13	12	4				7^{1}		14									11							28
1	2	3		5	6	7^{2}		9	10^{3}					12	4				8^{1}							13				11	14						29
1	2	3		5	6	7^{2}		9^{3}	10					12	4				8^{1}							13				11	14						30
1	2	3		5	6	7^{2}		9	10^{1}						4				8											11	12	13					31
1	2	3		5		7^{2}		9	10					12	4				8							13				11	6^{1}						32
1	2	3			6	7	12	9	10^{1}					13	4				11^{2}											5	14		8^{3}				33
1	2			5	6	7		9^{1}	10					11	4				12	3													8				34
1	2^{1}	3			6	7	12	9						10^{2}	4				13											11	5		8^{3}	14			35
1	2	3^{2}		5	6	7			10					9^{1}	4				12											11	8^{3}		13	14			36
1	2	3		5	6	7^{1}		9^{2}	10					8^{3}	4				12												11		13	14			37
1	2	3		5	6	7^{2}	12	9	10				13	8	4																11^{1}						38
1		3		5	6	7		9	12				2	10	4																11^{2}	13	8^{1}				39
1	2	3			6^{1}	7	5	9^{3}	10				12	11	4				13												14		8^{2}				40
1	2	3				7	5	9^{1}	8^{2}					10^{3}	4				12											6	11		13	14			41
1	2	3				7	5^{1}	9						10	4				12											6	11^{3}		13	8^{2}	14		42
1^{6}	2	3				7	5		8					9	4				12									15		6■	11^{2}			10^{1}	13		43
1	2	3			6	7^{1}	5	9^{3}	8				12		4				10^{2}												11		13	14			44
1	2	3				7	5	9^{2}	8^{1}					10	4		12		13											6	11						45
1	2^{3}	3				7	5	9^{2}	8				6	10	4				12											11^{1}		13				14	46

FA Cup
First Round Rochdale (a) 1-2

Carling Cup
First Round Reading (h) 0-2

LDV Vans Trophy
First Round Exeter C (h) 2-2

PETERBOROUGH UNITED FL Championship 2

FOUNDATION

The old Peterborough & Fletton club, founded in 1923, was suspended by the FA during season 1932–33 and disbanded. Local enthusiasts determined to carry on and in 1934 a new professional club, Peterborough United, was formed and entered the Midland League the following year. Peterborough's first success came in 1939–40, but from 1955–56 to 1959–60 they won five successive titles. During the 1958–59 season they were undefeated in the Midland League. They reached the third round of the FA Cup, won the Northamptonshire Senior Cup, the Maunsell Cup and were runners-up in the East Anglian Cup.

London Road Stadium, Peterborough PE2 8AL.

Telephone: (01733) 563 947.

Fax: (01733) 344 140.

Ticket Office: (01733) 865 674.

Website: www.theposh.com

Email: info@theposh.com

Ground Capacity: 15,460.

Record Attendance: 30,096 v Swansea T, FA Cup 5th rd, 20 February 1965.

Pitch Measurements: 112yd × 71yd.

Chairman: Steve Holt.

Director of Football: Barry Fry.

Executive Director: Bob Symns.

Secretary: Julie Etherington.

Manager: Mark Wright.

Assistant Manager: Steve Bleasdale.

Physio: TBC.

Colours: All blue.

Change Colours: All yellow.

Year Formed: 1934.

Turned Professional: 1934.

Ltd Co.: 1934.

Club Nickname: 'The Posh'.

First Football League Game: 20 August 1960, Division 4, v Wrexham (h) W 3–0 – Walls; Stafford, Walker; Rayner, Rigby, Norris; Hails, Emery (1), Bly (1), Smith, McNamee (1).

Record League Victory: 9–1 v Barnet (a) Division 3, 5 September 1998 – Griemink; Hooper (1), Drury (Farell), Gill, Bodley, Edwards, Davies, Payne, Grazioli (5), Quinn (2) (Rowe), Houghton (Etherington) (1).

HONOURS

Football League: Division 1 best season: 10th, 1992–93; Division 2 1991–92 (play-offs). Promoted from Division 3 1999–2000 (play-offs); Division 4 – Champions 1960–61, 1973–74.

FA Cup: best season: 6th rd, 1965.

Football League Cup: Semi-final 1966.

SKY SPORTS FACT FILE

On 20 April 1964 Peterborough United entertained Coventry City who were Division Three title contenders. A record League gate of 26,307 saw Posh win 2–0 with Colin Thompson scoring on his debut and Derek Dougan adding the second.

Record Cup Victory: 7–0 v Harlow T, FA Cup 1st rd, 16 November 1991 – Barber; Luke, Johnson, Halsall (1), Robinson D, Welsh, Sterling (1) (Butterworth), Cooper G (2 incl. 1p), Riley (1) (Culpin (1)), Charlery (1), Kimble.

Record Defeat: 1–8 v Northampton T, FA Cup 2nd rd (2nd replay), 18 December 1946.

Most League Points (2 for a win): 66, Division 4, 1960–61.

Most League Points (3 for a win): 82, Division 4, 1981–82.

Most League Goals: 134, Division 4, 1960–61.

Highest League Scorer in Season: Terry Bly, 52, Division 4, 1960–61.

Most League Goals in Total Aggregate: Jim Hall, 122, 1967–75.

Most League Goals in One Match: 5, Guiliano Grazioli v Barnet, Division 3, 5 September 1998.

Most Capped Player: Tony Millington, 8 (21), Wales.

Most League Appearances: Tommy Robson, 482, 1968–81.

Youngest League Player: Matthew Etherington, 15 years 262 days v Brentford, 3 May 1997.

Record Transfer Fee Received: £700,000 from Tottenham H for Simon Davies, December 1999.

Record Transfer Fee Paid: £350,000 to Walsall for Martin O'Connor, July 1996.

Football League Record: 1960 Elected to Division 4; 1961–68 Division 3, when they were demoted for financial irregularities; 1968–74 Division 4; 1974–79 Division 3; 1979–91 Division 4; 1991–92 Division 3; 1992–94 Division 1; 1994–97 Division 2; 1997–2000 Division 3; 2000–04 Division 2; 2004–05 FL1, 2005– FL2.

MANAGERS

Jock Porter 1934–36
Fred Taylor 1936–37
Vic Poulter 1937–38
Sam Madden 1938–48
Jack Blood 1948–50
Bob Gurney 1950–52
Jack Fairbrother 1952–54
George Swindin 1954–58
Jimmy Hagan 1958–62
Jack Fairbrother 1962–64
Gordon Clark 1964–67
Norman Rigby 1967–69
Jim Iley 1969–72
Noel Cantwell 1972–77
John Barnwell 1977–78
Billy Hails 1978–79
Peter Morris 1979–82
Martin Wilkinson 1982–83
John Wile 1983–86
Noel Cantwell 1986–88 *(continued as General Manager)*
Mick Jones 1988–89
Mark Lawrenson 1989–90
Chris Turner 1991–92
Lil Fuccillo 1992–93
John Still 1994–95
Mick Halsall 1995–96
Barry Fry 1996–2005
Mark Wright May 2005–

LATEST SEQUENCES

Longest Sequence of League Wins: 9, 1.2.1992 – 14.3.1992.

Longest Sequence of League Defeats: 5, 8.10.1996 – 26.10.1996.

Longest Sequence of League Draws: 8, 18.12.1971 – 12.2.1972.

Longest Sequence of Unbeaten League Matches: 17, 17.12.1960 – 8.4.1961.

Longest Sequence Without a League Win: 17, 23.9.1978 – 30.12.1978.

Successive Scoring Runs: 33 from 20.9.1960.

Successive Non-scoring Runs: 6 from 13.8.2002.

TEN YEAR LEAGUE RECORD

		P	*W*	*D*	*L*	*F*	*A*	*Pts*	*Pos*
1995-96	Div 2	46	13	13	20	59	66	52	19
1996-97	Div 2	46	11	14	21	55	73	47	21
1997-98	Div 3	46	18	13	15	63	51	67	10
1998-99	Div 3	46	18	12	16	72	56	66	9
1999-2000	Div 3	46	22	12	12	63	54	78	5
2000-01	Div 2	46	15	14	17	61	66	59	12
2001-02	Div 2	46	15	10	21	64	59	55	17
2002-03	Div 2	46	14	16	16	51	54	58	11
2003-04	Div 2	46	12	16	18	58	58	52	18
2004-05	FL 1	46	9	12	25	49	73	39	23

DID YOU KNOW?

Peterborough United played their first Midland League game against Gainsborough Trinity on 1 September 1934. Watched by a crowd of 4035, Len Hargreaves a former Luton Town player scored the first goal in a subsequent 4–0 win.

PETERBOROUGH UNITED 2004–05 LEAGUE RECORD

Match No.	Date	Venue	Opponents	Result	H/T Score	Lg. Pos.	Goalscorers	Attendance
1	Aug 7	H	Tranmere R	W 1-0	0-0	—	Burton [80]	5390
2	10	A	Bradford C	D 2-2	1-1	—	Platt [20], Kennedy [56]	6929
3	14	A	Colchester U	L 1-2	1-0	13	Farrell [10]	3754
4	21	H	Brentford	W 3-0	1-0	5	Platt [20], Legg [46], Clarke [53]	4868
5	28	A	Huddersfield T	L 1-2	1-1	11	Woodhouse (pen) [45]	9531
6	30	H	Blackpool	D 0-0	0-0	13		4142
7	Sept 4	H	Bristol C	L 0-1	0-0	16		4227
8	11	A	Swindon T	W 1-0	1-0	14	Jenkins [34]	5777
9	18	H	Hull C	L 2-3	1-1	16	Willock [2], Clarke [90]	5745
10	25	A	Luton T	L 1-2	0-1	19	Woodhouse [48]	7694
11	Oct 2	H	Torquay U	D 1-1	1-1	18	Clarke [42]	3828
12	16	A	Stockport Co	L 0-1	0-0	20		4119
13	19	H	Sheffield W	D 1-1	1-0	—	Platt [21]	5875
14	23	H	Hartlepool U	W 3-0	2-0	18	Kennedy [15], Willock [18], Legg [55]	3841
15	26	A	Wrexham	D 1-1	0-0	—	Willock [69]	3009
16	30	A	Doncaster R	L 1-2	1-1	19	Platt [27]	6039
17	Nov 6	H	Bournemouth	L 0-1	0-1	19		4004
18	20	A	Walsall	L 1-2	1-0	22	Purser [11]	5465
19	27	H	Port Vale	W 4-0	1-0	22	Purser [36], Farrell [62], Boucaud [69], Woodhouse (pen) [83]	3785
20	Dec 7	A	Milton Keynes D	D 1-1	0-0	—	Constantine [26]	3913
21	11	H	Chesterfield	L 1-2	0-1	20	Woodhouse [76]	3865
22	18	A	Barnsley	L 0-4	0-1	21		8536
23	26	H	Swindon T	L 0-2	0-0	21		4212
24	28	A	Oldham Ath	L 1-2	0-0	21	Logan [48]	5618
25	Jan 1	A	Bristol C	L 0-2	0-2	22		10,873
26	3	H	Luton T	D 2-2	0-0	21	Willock 2 [73, 82]	7662
27	11	H	Wrexham	D 2-2	2-1	—	Willock [2], Branston [12]	3048
28	15	A	Hull C	D 2-2	1-0	22	Thomson [26], Willock [90]	16,149
29	22	H	Oldham Ath	L 1-2	1-1	22	Legg [20]	4047
30	Feb 5	H	Stockport Co	W 2-1	1-0	21	Willock [24], Logan [60]	3719
31	15	A	Torquay U	L 1-2	0-1	—	Willock [64]	2769
32	19	H	Doncaster R	L 0-2	0-0	23		4983
33	23	A	Sheffield W	L 1-2	1-1	—	Purser [21]	19,648
34	26	A	Chesterfield	W 3-1	2-1	22	Logan [12], Purser 2 [14, 62]	3715
35	Mar 5	H	Barnsley	L 1-3	0-0	23	Legg [73]	3485
36	12	H	Bradford C	D 2-2	2-0	23	Thomson [28], Legg [31]	3472
37	18	A	Tranmere R	L 0-5	0-3	—		8401
38	25	H	Colchester U	L 0-3	0-1	—		4084
39	28	A	Brentford	D 0-0	0-0	23		6341
40	Apr 2	H	Huddersfield T	L 1-2	1-1	23	Purser [45]	3976
41	5	A	Hartlepool U	D 2-2	0-2	—	Logan [49], Willock [56]	4579
42	9	A	Blackpool	W 1-0	1-0	23	Willock [42]	5090
43	16	H	Walsall	L 0-2	0-0	23		3841
44	23	A	Bournemouth	W 1-0	1-0	22	Willock [17]	7929
45	30	H	Milton Keynes D	L 0-3	0-2	23		3742
46	May 7	A	Port Vale	L 0-1	0-0	23		4815

Final League Position: 23

GOALSCORERS

League (49): Willock 12, Purser 6, Legg 5, Logan 4, Platt 4, Woodhouse 4 (2 pens), Clarke 3, Farrell 2, Kennedy 2, Thomson 2, Boucaud 1, Branston 1, Burton 1, Constantine 1, Jenkins 1.
Carling Cup (0).
FA Cup (6): Willock 2, Arber 1, Kennedy 1, Logan 1, Woodhouse 1.
LDV Vans Trophy (0).

Tyler M 46	Newton A 27 + 3	Legg A 38 + 1	Woodhouse C 32 + 2	Ireland C 22 + 1	Burton S 16	Farrell D 22 + 9	Thomson S 30 + 1	Platt C 18 + 1	Willock C 29 + 6	Kennedy P 15 + 2	Clarke A 13 + 20	Constantine L 5 + 6	Rea S 13 + 1	Sonner D 11 + 4	Semple R 2 + 6	Jenkins S 5 + 1	Kanu C 9 + 4	Plummer C 21	Logan R 15 + 11	Jelleyman G 11 + 3	St Ledger-Hall S 33	Boucaud A 13 + 9	Purser W 15 + 11	Caskey D 2 + 2	Arber M 21	Branston G 4	McMaster J 3	Deen A 4 + 1	Day J — + 1	Huke S 6 + 2	Coulson M 2 + 5	Onibuje F — + 2	Fry A 3	*Match No.*
1	2	3	4	5	6	7^{1}	8	9^{2}	10	11	12	13																						1
1	2	3	4	5	6	7^{1}	8	9	10^{2}	11	12	13																						2
1	2	3	4	5	6^{2}	7^{3}	8	9	10^{1}	11	12		13	14																				3
1	2	3^{3}	4	5		7	8^{2}	9		11	10^{1}	12	6	13	14																			4
1	2	3^{1}	4	5		12		9	10^{3}	11	13	8^{2}	6	7		14																		5
1	2	3^{3}	4	5		7	8^{1}	9		11	10^{2}	13	6	12			14																	6
1	2	3	4	5		12		9^{2}		11^{1}	13	10^{3}	6					8	14	7														7
1		3		5			8	9			12		6	7		2		4	10^{1}	11														8
1		3	12	5			8	9^{1}	10^{2}		13		6^{3}	7	14	2		4		11														9
1		3	4	5		12	8^{3}				10^{1}	13	6^{2}	7		2	14	9		11														10
1	7^{2}	3	4			12					9	10^{1}	6			2	13			11	5	8												11
1	12	3	8				7^{2}	9	10^{3}	11	14	13	6			2^{1}		4			5													12
1	2	3	8	5	6			9	10^{1}	11^{2}	12			7				4		13														13
1	2	3	8^{2}	5	6			9^{3}	10^{1}	11	12			7				4■	14			13												14
1	2	3		5	6			9	10	11				7							4	8												15
1	2	3^{3}	8	5	6			9	10^{2}	11^{1}	12			7					13		4	14												16
1	2	3	8		6	12		9		11^{3}	13			7^{1}				4	10^{2}	14	5													17
1		3	6	12		13	14	9	10^{3}	8^{1}							2^{2}	4		11	5		7											18
1	2	3	4		6	7^{2}			12		13	10								11	5	8^{1}	9											19
1	2	3	6			12			10^{2}			8						4	13	11	5	7^{3}	9^{1}	14										20
1	2	3^{1}	6			7			12						13			4	10^{2}	11	5	8^{3}	9	14										21
1	2		4			7^{2}			12		13			11^{1}				6	10	3	5	14	9	8^{3}										22
1	2	3	8		6		7	9^{3}	10^{1}										12	13	5		14	11^{2}	4									23
1	2	3	8	4	6	12		13							14				10^{3}	11^{1}	5	7	9^{2}											24
1	2	3^{2}			6	7		9^{1}	12		13			11	14				10^{3}			8			4	5								25
1	2^{3}	3		5		7	8^{1}		10					12	14			4	13		11		9^{2}			6								26
1	2	3				7	8		10									11	9^{1}		5		12		4	6								27
1	2	3^{2}				7	8		10		9						12	11^{1}			5	13	14		4	6^{3}								28
1	2	3■	12		6	7	8		10^{2}	11^{1}	13										5		14		4		9^{3}							29
1	2		3		6		8		10	12	11^{1}								9^{2}		5		13		4		7							30
1	2		3			7^{1}	11		10				6						9		5		12		4		8^{2}	13						31
1	2	12	6			11^{3}	8^{1}		10^{2}						7				13		5		9		4			3	14					32
1		3	8	6		11^{2}	7^{3}			13	12		2						9		5	14	10^{1}		4									33
1		3^{1}	8	6		7	11						2						9		5	12	10		4									34
1	12	3		6		11	8^{1}						2						9		5	7	10		4									35
1		3		5	6		8		10^{1}		12								13^{3}		2	7	9^{2}		4			11		14				36
1		3^{2}	7	5			8		10		12							6			2		9^{1}		4			11^{3}		13	14			37
1		3	11	5^{2}			8		10^{3}		9				7^{1}			6			2		12		4						13	14		38
1		3	7				8		10^{2}		9^{1}						2				5		12		4					6	11	13		39
1		3	7^{3}			12	8		13		9						2				5	14	10^{2}		4					6	11^{1}			40
1		3				11	8		12		9^{1}						2		13		5	7	10^{2}		4					6				41
1		3				11	8		10								2		9		5	7			4					6				42
1						11^{3}	8		10		12						2	3	9^{1}		5	7^{2}	13		4					6	14			43
1			7				8		10^{1}		9^{3}						2	3	12		5	13	14		4					6^{2}			11	44
1			7			11^{3}	8^{2}		10		9						3	5^{1}	12		2	13			4						14		6	45
1	12				6				10		9						2	4	11^{2}		5	8	13					3^{3}			14		7^{1}	46

FA Cup

First Round	Tranmere R	(h)	2-1
Second Round	Bath C	(h)	2-0
Third Round	Milton Keynes D	(a)	2-0
Fourth Round	Nottingham F	(a)	0-1

Carling Cup

First Round	Milton Keynes D	(h)	0-3

LDV Vans Trophy

First Round	Bristol C	(a)	0-1

PLYMOUTH ARGYLE FL Championship

FOUNDATION

The club was formed in September 1886 as the Argyle Football Club by former public and private school pupils who wanted to continue playing the game. The meeting was held in a room above the Borough Arms (a Coffee House), Bedford Street, Plymouth. It was common then to choose a local street/terrace as a club name and Argyle or Argyll was a fashionable name throughout the land due to Queen Victoria's great interest in Scotland.

Home Park, Plymouth, Devon PL2 3DQ.

Telephone: (01752) 562 561.

Fax: (01752) 606 167.

Ticket Office: 0871 222 1288.

Website: www.pafc.co.uk

Email: argyle@pafc.co.uk

Ground Capacity: 20,922.

Record Attendance: 43,596 v Aston Villa, Division 2, 10 October 1936.

Pitch Measurements: 110yd × 72yd.

Chairman: Paul Stapleton.

Vice-chairman: Robert Dennerly.

Chief Executive: Michael Dunford.

Secretary: Carole Rowntree.

Manager: Bobby Williamson.

Assistant Managers: Gerry McCabe and Jocky Soctt.

Physio: Paul Maxwell.

Colours: Green shirts, white shorts, green stockings.

Change Colours: White shirts, green shorts, white stockings.

Year Formed: 1886.

Turned Professional: 1903.

Ltd Co.: 1903.

Previous Name: 1886, Argyle Athletic Club; 1903, Plymouth Argyle.

Club Nickname: 'The Pilgrims'.

First Football League Game: 28 August 1920, Division 3, v Norwich C (h) D 1–1 – Craig; Russell, Atterbury; Logan, Dickinson, Forbes; Kirkpatrick, Jack, Bowler, Heeps (1), Dixon.

Record League Victory: 8–1 v Millwall, Division 2, 16 January 1932 – Harper; Roberts, Titmuss; Mackay, Pullan, Reed; Grozier, Bowden (2), Vidler (3), Leslie (1), Black (1), (1 og). 8–1 v Hartlepool U (a), Division 2, 7 May 1994 – Nicholls; Patterson (Naylor), Hill, Burrows, Comyn, McCall (1), Barlow, Castle (1), Landon (3), Marshall (1), Dalton (2).

HONOURS

Football League: Division 2 – Champions 2003–04; Division 3 (S) – Champions 1929–30, 1951–52; Runners-up 1921–22, 1922–23, 1923–24, 1924–25, 1925–26, 1926–27 (record of six consecutive years); Division 3 – Champions 1958–59, 2001–02; Runners-up 1974–75, 1985–86, Promoted 1995–96 (play-offs).

FA Cup: Semi-final 1984.

Football League Cup: Semi-final 1965, 1974.

SKY SPORTS FACT FILE

It is rare for any team to be involved in games aggregating ten goals and in successive seasons against the same opposition. However after Plymouth Argyle had beaten Charlton Athletic 6–4 in 1959–60 they repeated the scoreline in 1960–61.

Record Cup Victory: 6–0 v Corby T, FA Cup 3rd rd, 22 January 1966 – Leiper; Book, Baird; Williams, Nelson, Newman; Jones (1), Jackson (1), Bickle (3), Piper (1), Jennings.

Record Defeat: 0–9 v Stoke C, Division 2, 17 December 1960.

Most League Points (2 for a win): 68, Division 3 (S), 1929–30.

Most League Points (3 for a win): 102, Division 3, 2001–02.

Most League Goals: 107, Division 3 (S), 1925–26 and 1951–52.

Highest League Scorer in Season: Jack Cock, 32, Division 3 (S), 1926–27.

Most League Goals in Total Aggregate: Sammy Black, 180, 1924–38.

Most League Goals in One Match: 5, Wilf Carter v Charlton Ath, Division 2, 27 December 1960.

Most Capped Player: Moses Russell, 20 (23), Wales.

Most League Appearances: Kevin Hodges, 530, 1978–92.

Youngest League Player: Lee Phillips, 16 years 43 days v Gillingham, 29 October 1996.

Record Transfer Fee Received: £750,000 from Southampton for Mickey Evans, March 1997.

Record Transfer Fee Paid: £250,000 to Hartlepool U for Paul Dalton, June 1992.

Football League Record: 1920 Original Member of Division 3; 1921–30 Division 3 (S); 1930–50 Division 2; 1950–52 Division 3 (S); 1952–56 Division 2; 1956–58 Division 3 (S); 1958–59 Division 3; 1959–68 Division 2; 1968–75 Division 3; 1975–77 Division 2; 1977–86 Division 3; 1986–95 Division 2; 1995–96 Division 3; 1996–98 Division 2; 1998–2002 Division 3; 2002–04 Division 2; 2004– FLC.

MANAGERS

Frank Brettell 1903–05
Bob Jack 1905–06
Bill Fullerton 1906–07
Bob Jack 1910–38
Jack Tresadern 1938–47
Jimmy Rae 1948–55
Jack Rowley 1955–60
Neil Dougall 1961
Ellis Stuttard 1961–63
Andy Beattie 1963–64
Malcolm Allison 1964–65
Derek Ufton 1965–68
Billy Bingham 1968–70
Ellis Stuttard 1970–72
Tony Waiters 1972–77
Mike Kelly 1977–78
Malcolm Allison 1978–79
Bobby Saxton 1979–81
Bobby Moncur 1981–83
Johnny Hore 1983–84
Dave Smith 1984–88
Ken Brown 1988–90
David Kemp 1990–92
Peter Shilton 1992–95
Steve McCall 1995
Neil Warnock 1995–97
Mick Jones 1997–98
Kevin Hodges 1998–2000
Paul Sturrock 2000–04
Bobby Williamson April 2004–

LATEST SEQUENCES

Longest Sequence of League Wins: 9, 8.3.1986 – 12.4.1986.

Longest Sequence of League Defeats: 9, 12.10.1963 – 7.12.1963.

Longest Sequence of League Draws: 5, 26.2.2000 – 14.3.2000.

Longest Sequence of Unbeaten League Matches: 22, 20.4.1929 – 21.12.1929.

Longest Sequence Without a League Win: 13, 27.4.1963 – 2.10.1963.

Successive Scoring Runs: 39 from 15.4.1939.

Successive Non-scoring Runs: 5 from 20.9.1947.

TEN YEAR LEAGUE RECORD

		P	W	D	L	F	A	Pts	Pos
1995-96	Div 3	46	22	12	12	68	49	79	4
1996-97	Div 2	46	12	18	16	47	58	54	19
1997-98	Div 2	46	12	13	21	55	70	49	22
1998-99	Div 3	46	17	10	19	58	54	61	13
1999-2000	Div 3	46	16	18	12	55	51	66	12
2000-01	Div 3	46	15	13	18	54	61	58	12
2001-02	Div 3	46	31	9	6	71	28	102	1
2002-03	Div 2	46	17	14	15	63	52	65	8
2003-04	Div 2	46	26	12	8	85	41	90	1
2004-05	FL C	46	14	11	21	52	64	53	17

DID YOU KNOW ?

In 1946–47 Dave Thomas scored in 10 successive League matches for Plymouth Argyle. A pre-war signing from Romford in 1938 he spent ten years at Home Park bridging the war period during which he guested for other clubs before joining Watford.

PLYMOUTH ARGYLE 2004–05 LEAGUE RECORD

Match No.	Date	Venue	Opponents	Result		H/T Score	Lg. Pos.	Goalscorers	Attendance
1	Aug 7	H	Millwall	D	0-0	0-0	—		16,063
2	10	A	Brighton & HA	W	2-0	2-0	—	Cullip (og) [11], Wotton (pen) [45]	6387
3	13	A	Cardiff C	W	1-0	1-0	—	Bullock (og) [24]	12,697
4	21	H	Sunderland	W	2-1	2-0	2	Wotton [1], Crawford [40]	16,874
5	28	A	Watford	L	1-3	1-1	4	Evans [18]	13,104
6	30	H	Nottingham F	W	3-2	2-1	4	Norris [26], Coughlan [40], Wotton (pen) [90]	17,538
7	Sept 11	A	QPR	L	2-3	1-1	4	Friio [7], Keith [90]	15,425
8	14	H	Leeds U	L	0-1	0-1	—		20,555
9	18	H	Wolverhampton W	L	1-2	0-0	9	Friio [62]	18,635
10	25	A	Ipswich T	L	2-3	2-1	13	Adams [12], Crawford [13]	23,270
11	28	A	Preston NE	D	1-1	1-0	—	Doumbe [19]	11,445
12	Oct 2	H	Gillingham	W	2-1	0-0	10	Friio 2 [89, 90]	13,665
13	16	H	Wigan Ath	L	1-2	0-0	14	Crawford [78]	14,443
14	19	A	Rotherham U	W	1-0	0-0	—	Doumbe [65]	5088
15	23	A	Sheffield U	L	1-2	0-0	12	Friio [87]	18,893
16	30	H	West Ham U	D	1-1	0-1	12	Wotton [76]	20,220
17	Nov 2	H	Reading	D	2-2	2-0	—	Ingimarsson (og) [18], Crawford [41]	14,336
18	6	A	Wigan Ath	W	2-0	1-0	11	Wotton [40], Crawford [69]	10,294
19	13	A	Coventry C	L	1-2	0-2	12	Evans [48]	15,314
20	20	H	Stoke C	D	0-0	0-0	13		15,264
21	27	A	Leicester C	L	1-2	1-0	15	Capaldi [9]	23,799
22	Dec 4	H	Burnley	W	1-0	0-0	12	Wotton (pen) [90]	13,508
23	11	A	Crewe Alex	L	0-3	0-1	15		6823
24	18	H	Derby Co	L	0-2	0-1	17		15,335
25	26	H	QPR	W	2-1	1-0	15	Wotton [13], Evans [49]	19,535
26	28	A	Leeds U	L	1-2	0-0	16	Crawford [89]	34,496
27	Jan 1	A	Wolverhampton W	D	1-1	0-1	15	Friio [58]	27,564
28	3	H	Ipswich T	L	1-2	0-0	17	Evans [87]	17,923
29	15	A	Gillingham	L	0-1	0-0	19		8451
30	22	H	Preston NE	L	0-2	0-2	20		13,663
31	Feb 5	A	Reading	D	0-0	0-0	20		19,783
32	12	H	Rotherham U	D	1-1	0-1	20	Wotton (pen) [51]	14,798
33	19	A	West Ham U	L	0-5	0-3	21		25,490
34	22	H	Sheffield U	W	3-0	1-0	—	Coughlan [3], Wotton [47], Blackstock [88]	13,953
35	26	H	Crewe Alex	W	3-0	1-0	19	Wotton [25], Blackstock [68], Taylor [90]	14,918
36	Mar 5	A	Derby Co	L	0-1	0-1	19		27,581
37	12	H	Brighton & HA	W	5-1	4-1	16	Chadwick [8], Wotton 2 (1 pen) [13 (p), 21], Norris [36], Taylor [88]	15,606
38	15	A	Sunderland	L	1-5	0-3	—	Taylor [88]	25,258
39	20	A	Millwall	L	0-3	0-1	18		11,465
40	Apr 2	H	Cardiff C	D	1-1	0-1	18	Aljofree [60]	18,045
41	5	H	Watford	W	1-0	1-0	—	Buzsaky [10]	15,333
42	9	A	Nottingham F	W	3-0	2-0	15	Blackstock 2 [3, 59], Norris [23]	28,887
43	16	A	Stoke C	L	0-2	0-2	15		13,017
44	23	H	Coventry C	D	1-1	0-1	15	Capaldi [90]	18,443
45	30	A	Burnley	L	0-2	0-0	18		12,893
46	May 8	H	Leicester C	D	0-0	0-0	17		19,199

Final League Position: 17

GOALSCORERS

League (52): Wotton 12 (5 pens), Crawford 6, Friio 6, Blackstock 4, Evans 4, Norris 3, Taylor 3, Capaldi 2, Coughlan 2, Doumbe 2, Adams 1, Aljofree 1, Buzsaky 1, Chadwick 1, Keith 1, own goals 3.
Carling Cup (2): Crawford 1, Wotton 1 (pen).
FA Cup (1): Gudjonsson 1.

McCormick L 23	Worrell D 30	Gilbert P 38	Adams S 17+3	Wotton P 38+2	Coughlan G 43	Lasley K 14+10	Hodges L 11+8	Crawford S 19+7	Evans M 33+9	Capaldi T 24+11	Milne S —+12	Keith M 6+11	Lowndes N 1+3	Friio D 23+5	Makel L 13+6	Norris D 33+2	Larrieu R 23	Connolly P 19	Doumbe S 24+2	Dickson R 2+1	Yetton S —+1	Gudjonsson B 12+3	Taylor S 9+7	Buzsaky A 14+1	Blackstock D 10+4	Chadwick N 11+4	Aljofree H 12	Dodd J 4	Summerfield L —+1	*Match No.*
1	2	3	4	5	6	7	8	9¹	10²	11	12	13																		1
1	2	3	4	5	6	7	8²	9¹		11	12	10	13																	2
1	2	3	4	5	6	7	8³	9¹	10²	11		12	13	14																3
1	2	3	4²	5	6	7³	8	9	10¹	11		12		13	14															4
1	2	3		5	6	12	8³	9	10²	11¹		13		4	14	7														5
1	2	3		5	6	12	13	9³	10	11²	14			4	8¹	7														6
1	2	3		5	6	12	13	9	10³	11²		14		4	8	7¹														7
		3		5	6		12	13	9²	11¹	14	10		4	8	7³	1	2												8
		3¹	8	5	6		12	13	9³		14	10²		4	11	7	1	2												9
		3²	8	5	6	7	12	9		11¹				4	10		1	2	13											10
	2		3		6	7	12	9³	10²		14	13		4	8¹		1	5	11											11
	3		8		6	7³	11¹	9²	13		14		12	4	10		1	2	5											12
	2³		3		6	12		9	13				10²	4	8	7¹	1	5	11	14										13
	2	3	4¹	12	6	13		9	10						8	7	1		5	11²										14
	2	3			6	12	8	9³	13					4	10	7²	1		5	11¹	14									15
	2	3		12	6		8¹	9²	10		13			4	11	7	1		5											16
	2	3	12	8	6	11³		9	10²		13			4¹	14	7	1		5											17
	2	3²	12	8	6	11	13	14	9³					4¹	10	7	1		5											18
	2³	3		8	6	11¹		12	9	13	14			4	10²	7	1		5											19
	2	3		8	6			9	10	11				4¹	12	7	1		5											20
	2	3	12	8	6			9	10	11²		13		4³	14	7¹	1		5											21
	2	3	8¹	5	6		12	9	10²	11		13		4		7	1													22
	2	3	10	8	6			12	9²	11¹		13		4	14	7³	1		5											23
	2²	3¹		8	6			9	10	11		12		4		7	1		5			13								24
		3		8	6▮			12	9¹	11		10		4			1	2	5			7								25
		3	4¹	6			8	13	12	11³		9²		14		7	1	2	5			10								26
		3		6			8		9¹	12		11²		4		7	1	2	5			10	13							27
		3	8¹	6					9	11		12		4		7²	1	2	5			13	10							28
		3		8	6		11¹		9	12				4			1	2▮	5			7	10							29
	2	3²			6	7			9	11				12		13	1		5			4	10	8¹						30
1	2	11		5	6	8			12	13				14					3			4	10¹	7³	9²					31
1	2	3¹		4	6	7²			12	13									5			8		11	9	10				32
1	2		11		6	7²				12						13			5▮			4¹		8	9	10	3			33
1		3		4	6				9¹	11						7		2						8	12	10	5			34
1		3	11	4	6				9²							7		2				14	12	8³	13	10¹	5			35
1		3	8²	4	6				12	11¹						7		2						13	9	10	5			36
1		3		4	6	12			13	11¹						7		2				8	14		9²	10³	5			37
1		3		4	6				12	11						7		2				8¹	13		9²	10	5			38
1		3		4	6				9²	12						7³		2				11¹	10	8	14	13	5			39
1				4	6				9	11						7		2					12	8²	13	10¹	5	3		40
1				4	6	12			9²	11³						7		2					14	8	10¹	13	5	3		41
1	2			4	6	12			9³	13						7							11²	8¹	10	14	5	3		42
1	2			4¹	6	12			9³	13						7							11²	8	10	14	5	3		43
1	2³	3		4	6				9	12						7			13				14	8	10	11¹	5²			44
1	2	3		4	6				9²	12	13					7			5				11¹	8		10				45
1	2²	3		4	6						12					7			5			10	11¹	8		9			13	46

FA Cup
Third Round Everton (h) 1-3

Carling Cup
First Round Yeovil T (a) 2-3

PORTSMOUTH FA Premiership

FOUNDATION

At a meeting held in his High Street, Portsmouth offices in 1898, solicitor Alderman J. E. Pink and five other business and professional men agreed to buy some ground close to Goldsmith Avenue for £4,950 which they developed into Fratton Park in record breaking time. A team of professionals was signed up by manager Frank Brettell and entry to the Southern League obtained for the new club's September 1899 kick-off.

Fratton Park, Frogmore Road, Portsmouth, Hampshire PO4 8RA.

Telephone: (02392) 731 204.

Fax: (02392) 734 129.

Ticket Office: 0871 230 1898

Website: www.pompeyfc.co.uk

Email: info@pompeyfc.co.uk

Ground Capacity: 20,288.

Record Attendance: 51,385 v Derby Co, FA Cup 6th rd, 26 February 1949.

Pitch Measurements: 100m × 65m.

Chairman: Milan Mandaric.

Chief Executive: Peter Storrie.

Secretary: Paul Weld.

Manager: Alain Perrin.

Physio: Gary Sadler.

Colours: Blue shirts, white shorts, red stockings.

Change Colours: Red shirts, white shorts, blue stockings.

Year Formed: 1898.

Turned Professional: 1898.

Ltd Co.: 1898.

Club Nickname: 'Pompey'.

First Football League Game: 28 August 1920, Division 3, v Swansea T (h) W 3–0 – Robson; Probert, Potts; Abbott, Harwood, Turner; Thompson, Stringfellow (1), Reid (1), James (1), Beedie.

Record League Victory: 9–1 v Notts Co, Division 2, 9 April 1927 – McPhail; Clifford, Ted Smith; Reg Davies (1), Foxall, Moffat; Forward (1), Mackie (2), Haines (3), Watson, Cook (2).

Record Cup Victory: 7–0 v Stockport Co, FA Cup 3rd rd, 8 January 1949 – Butler; Rookes, Ferrier; Scoular, Flewin, Dickinson; Harris (3), Barlow, Clarke (2), Phillips (2), Froggatt.

HONOURS

Football League: Division 1 – Champions 1948–49, 1949–50, 2002–03; Division 2 – Runners-up 1926–27, 1986–87; Division 3 (S) – Champions 1923–24; Division 3 – Champions 1961–62, 1982–83.

FA Cup: Winners 1939; Runners-up 1929, 1934.

Football League Cup: best season: 5th rd, 1961, 1986.

SKY SPORTS FACT FILE

Between 1909 and 1920 Arthur Egerton Knight played in 21 amateur internationals for England and the 1912 Olympics. In his last two games he was captain and he also won a full England cap against Northern Ireland while with Portsmouth.

Record Defeat: 0–10 v Leicester C, Division 1, 20 October 1928.

Most League Points (2 for a win): 65, Division 3, 1961–62.

Most League Points (3 for a win): 98, Division 1, 2002–03.

Most League Goals: 97, Division 1, 2002–03.

Highest League Scorer in Season: Guy Whittingham, 42, Division 1, 1992–93.

Most League Goals in Total Aggregate: Peter Harris, 194, 1946–60.

Most League Goals in One Match: 5, Alf Strange v Gillingham, Division 3, 27 January 1923; 5, Peter Harris v Aston Villa, Division 1, 3 September 1958.

Most Capped Player: Jimmy Dickinson, 48, England.

Most League Appearances: Jimmy Dickinson, 764, 1946–65.

Youngest League Player: Clive Green, 16 years 259 days v Wrexham, 21 August 1976.

Record Transfer Fee Received: £4,500,000 from Aston Villa for Peter Crouch, March 2002.

Record Transfer Fee Paid: £1,800,000 to Vitesse Arnhem for Dejan Stefanovic, July 2003.

Football League Record: 1920 Original Member of Division 3; 1921 Division 3 (S); 1924–27 Division 2; 1927–59 Division 1; 1959–61 Division 2; 1961–62 Division 3; 1962–76 Division 2; 1976–78 Division 3; 1978–80 Division 4; 1980–83 Division 3; 1983–87 Division 2; 1987–88 Division 1; 1988–92 Division 2; 1992–2003 Division 1; 2003– FA Premier League.

MANAGERS

Frank Brettell 1898–1901
Bob Blyth 1901–04
Richard Bonney 1905–08
Bob Brown 1911–20
John McCartney 1920–27
Jack Tinn 1927–47
Bob Jackson 1947–52
Eddie Lever 1952–58
Freddie Cox 1958–61
George Smith 1961–70
Ron Tindall 1970–73
(General Manager to 1974)
John Mortimore 1973–74
Ian St John 1974–77
Jimmy Dickinson 1977–79
Frank Burrows 1979–82
Bobby Campbell 1982–84
Alan Ball 1984–89
John Gregory 1989–90
Frank Burrows 1990–91
Jim Smith 1991–95
Terry Fenwick 1995–98
Alan Ball 1998–99
Tony Pulis 2000
Steve Claridge 2000–01
Graham Rix 2001–02
Harry Redknapp 2002–04
Velimir Zajec 2004–05
Alain Perrin April 2005–

LATEST SEQUENCES

Longest Sequence of League Wins: 7, 17.8.2002 – 17.9.2002.

Longest Sequence of League Defeats: 9, 21.10.1975 – 6.12.1975.

Longest Sequence of League Draws: 5, 16.12.2000 – 13.1.2001.

Longest Sequence of Unbeaten League Matches: 15, 18.4.1924 – 18.10.1924.

Longest Sequence Without a League Win: 25, 29.11.1958 – 22.8.1959.

Successive Scoring Runs: 23 from 30.8.1930.

Successive Non-scoring Runs: 6 from 14.1.1939.

TEN YEAR LEAGUE RECORD

		P	W	D	L	F	A	Pts	Pos
1995-96	Div 1	46	13	13	20	61	69	52	21
1996-97	Div 1	46	20	8	18	59	53	68	7
1997-98	Div 1	46	13	10	23	51	63	49	20
1998-99	Div 1	46	11	14	21	57	73	47	19
1999-2000	Div 1	46	13	12	21	55	66	51	18
2000-01	Div 1	46	10	19	17	47	59	49	20
2001-02	Div 1	46	13	14	19	60	72	53	17
2002-03	Div 1	46	29	11	6	97	45	98	1
2003-04	PR Lge	38	12	9	17	47	54	45	13
2004-05	PR Lge	38	10	9	19	43	59	39	16

DID YOU KNOW ?

Comparing the two First Division titles by Portsmouth in 1948–49 and 1949–50 they used 18 players in the former, 25 in the latter, While they had a five point cushion in the first, it was just .396 of goal average over Wolves in the second.

PORTSMOUTH 2004–05 LEAGUE RECORD

Match No.	Date	Venue	Opponents	Result		H/T Score	Lg. Pos.	Goalscorers	Atten-dance
1	Aug 14	H	Birmingham C	D	1-1	1-1	—	Unsworth (pen) [16]	20,021
2	21	A	Charlton Ath	L	1-2	0-1	17	Berger [53]	25,204
3	30	H	Fulham	W	4-3	3-2	—	Berkovic [19], Yakubu 3 (1 pen) [22 (p), 28, 72]	19,728
4	Sept 11	H	Crystal Palace	W	3-1	1-1	9	Fuller [3], Berger [47], Popovic (og) [85]	20,019
5	18	A	Blackburn R	L	0-1	0-0	12		20,647
6	26	H	Everton	L	0-1	0-0	14		20,125
7	Oct 2	A	Norwich C	D	2-2	1-0	13	Yakubu [37], Berger [65]	23,853
8	18	H	Tottenham H	W	1-0	0-0	—	Yakubu [63]	20,121
9	24	A	Middlesbrough	D	1-1	1-0	11	Kamara [5]	30,964
10	30	H	Manchester U	W	2-0	0-0	9	Unsworth (pen) [53], Yakubu [72]	20,190
11	Nov 6	A	Aston Villa	L	0-3	0-3	10		32,633
12	13	A	Southampton	L	1-2	1-1	11	Jakobsson (og) [12]	30,921
13	20	H	Manchester C	L	1-3	1-1	12	O'Neil [8]	20,101
14	27	A	Bolton W	W	1-0	1-0	11	De Zeeuw [45]	25,008
15	Dec 4	H	WBA	W	3-2	1-2	9	Purse (og) [35], De Zeeuw [85], Lua-Lua [89]	20,110
16	11	A	Newcastle U	D	1-1	1-1	10	Stone [30]	51480
17	14	A	Liverpool	D	1-1	0-0	—	Lua-Lua [90]	35,064
18	19	H	Arsenal	L	0-1	0-0	12		20,170
19	26	A	Crystal Palace	W	1-0	0-0	9	Primus [69]	25,238
20	28	H	Chelsea	L	0-2	0-0	10		20,210
21	Jan 1	H	Norwich C	D	1-1	0-1	11	Yakubu (pen) [61]	20,015
22	4	A	Everton	L	1-2	1-1	12	Yakubu [31]	35,480
23	15	H	Blackburn R	L	0-1	0-0	13		19,904
24	22	A	Chelsea	L	0-3	0-3	14		42,267
25	Feb 1	H	Middlesbrough	W	2-1	1-1	—	Taylor [40], Queudrue (og) [58]	19,620
26	5	A	Tottenham H	L	1-3	1-1	13	Kamara [28]	36,105
27	12	H	Aston Villa	L	1-2	1-1	14	Yakubu (pen) [24]	20,160
28	26	A	Manchester U	L	1-2	0-1	14	O'Neil [47]	67,989
29	Mar 5	A	Arsenal	L	0-3	0-1	16		38,079
30	19	H	Newcastle U	D	1-1	1-1	15	Stone [45]	20,165
31	Apr 3	A	Fulham	L	1-3	1-0	16	Lua-Lua [32]	20,502
32	9	H	Charlton Ath	W	4-2	2-2	15	Yakubu [3], Stone [20], Kamara [83], Lua-Lua [90]	20,108
33	16	A	Birmingham C	D	0-0	0-0	15		28,883
34	20	H	Liverpool	L	1-2	1-2	—	Kamara [34]	20,205
35	24	H	Southampton	W	4-1	4-1	15	Yakubu (pen) [4], De Zeeuw [17], Lua-Lua 2 [22, 27]	20,210
36	30	A	Manchester C	L	0-2	0-2	16		46,454
37	May 7	H	Bolton W	D	1-1	0-1	16	Yakubu [72]	20,188
38	15	A	WBA	L	0-2	0-0	16		27,751

Final League Position: 16

GOALSCORERS

League (43): Yakubu 12 (4 pens), Lua-Lua 6, Kamara 4, Berger 3, De Zeeuw 3, Stone 3, O'Neil 2, Unsworth 2 (2 pens), Berkovic 1, Fuller 1, Primus 1, Taylor 1, own goals 4.
Carling Cup (5): Kamara 2, Yakubu 2 (1 pen), Berkovic 1 (pen).
FA Cup (2): Yakubu 2.

Hislop S 17	Primus L 31 + 4	Unsworth D 15	Hughes R 13 + 3	Stefanovic D 32	De Zeeuw A 32	Stone S 22 + 1	Quashie N 19	Yakubu A 29 + 1	Lua-Lua L 20 + 5	Berger P 30 + 2	Griffin A 18 + 4	Taylor M 21 + 11	Curtis J — + 1	Berkovic E 6 + 5	O'Neil G 21 + 3	Fuller R 13 + 18	Faye A 17 + 3	Kamara D 15 + 10	Cisse A 12 + 8	Mezague V 3 + 8	Ashdown J 16	Skopelitis G 9 + 4	Chalkias K 5	Rodic A 1 + 3	Keene J 1 + 1	*Match No.*
1	2	3	4	5	6	7^1	8	9	10	11^2	12	13														1
1	2^2	3		5	6		8	9	10	11	7^1	13	12	4^3	14											2
1	2	3		5	6	7	8	9^2	12	11		13		4^1		10										3
1	2	3		5	6^1	7	8	9		11		12		4^2		10^3	13	14								4
1	6	3		5		12	8	9		11^2	2			7^1		10	4	13								5
1	6	3		5			7	9	12	11	2			8^1		10^2	4	13								6
1	5	6	12				8	9	13	11	2	3				14	4^1	10^3	7^2							7
1	5	3		6			7	9^2	10	11	2			8^1		12	4^3	13	14							8
1	5	3^2		6			7	9	10^1	11	2	13				12	4	8^3	14							9
1	5	2		3	6		7	9	10	11^2						12	4	8^1		13						10
1	2^2	3	12	5	6		8	9	10		13					11	4^3		14	7^1						11
1	2	3^1		5	6		8	9^3	10	11^2	13	12			7	14	4									12
	2^2	3		5	6		8		10^3	11^1	13	12		14	7	9	4				1					13
	2			5	6	7	8			11	4	3^1			10	9	12				1					14
	12	3^1		5	6	7	8^3		13	10	2	11^2		14		9	4				1					15
	2			5	6	7			10^2	11	3	12			8	9^1	4		13		1					16
	5			3	6	7			10	11	2	12		13	8	9^1	4^2				1					17
	5				6	7		12	10	11	2	3		13	8	9^1	4^2				1					18
1	5				6	7	8	9^2		11	2	3				13	4	12		10^1						19
1	5				6	7^2	8^1	9			2	3		12	11	14	4	10^3	13							20
1	5				6	7	8	9		11^2	2	3^3			4	12	13	10^1		14						21
1	2			5	6	7	8	9^1		11		12			3		4^2	10	13							22
1	5			3	6	2^1		9	10■	11		12			7	13	4■	8^2								23
	6	3^2	4	5				9^1		10		11			7	12		8	2	13	1					24
	2		4	5	6			9		11^2		3			7	10^1			8			12	1	13		25
	2^3		4	5	6			9		11^1		3			7^2	12		10	8	13		14	1			26
			4	5	6	7		9^1	12	11		3				13		10	2			8^2	1			27
			4^2	5	6	7		9	10		2	3			11^1			12		13		8	1			28
	12			5	6	7		9	10	11^2	2^1	3			4			13				8	1			29
	2		12	5	6	7^2		9^3	10	11^1		3			13	14			4		1	8				30
	2			5	6	7^1		9^3	10	11^2		3			12	14		13	4		1	8				31
	12		4	5	6	7		9	10	11^3		3^1						13	2		1	8^2		14		32
	5		11		6	7^1			10	12	3				4	13		9^2	2	14	1	8^3				33
	12		4	5	6^1	7^2			10^3	13		3			11	14		9	2		1	8				34
			4	5	6	7		9^3	10^1	11^2	2	3			8			12	13		1	14				35
	2		4	5	6			9				3			8	12		10	7^2	13	1			11^1		36
	2		4	5	6			9				3			11	12		10^3	13	7^2	1	8^1			14	37
	2		4^2	5	6							3			7	10		11^3	8	12	1	13		14	9^1	38

FA Cup

Third Round	Gillingham	(h)	1-0
Fourth Round	Southampton	(a)	1-2

Carling Cup

Second Round	Tranmere R	(a)	1-0
Third Round	Leeds U	(h)	2-1
Fourth Round	Cardiff C	(a)	2-0
Fifth Round	Watford	(a)	0-3

PORT VALE FL Championship 1

FOUNDATION

Formed in 1876 as Port Vale, adopting the prefix 'Burslem' in 1884 upon moving to that part of the city. It was dropped in 1909.

Vale Park, Hamil Road, Burslem, Stoke-on-Trent ST6 1AW.

Telephone: (01782) 655 800.

Fax: (01782) 834 981.

Ticket Office: (01782) 655 832.

Website: www.port-vale.co.uk

Email: lodey@port-vale.co.uk

Ground Capacity: 19,892.

Record Attendance: 49,768 v Aston Villa, FA Cup 5th rd, 20 February 1960.

Pitch Measurements: 114yd × 75yd.

Chairman: William A. Bratt.

Vice-chairmen: David Smith, Peter Jackson.

Secretary: Bill Lodey.

Manager: Martin Foyle.

Assistant Manager: Dean Glover.

Physio: Ian Baddiley.

Colours: White shirts, black shorts, black stockings.

Change Colours: Black and amber striped shirts, amber and black shorts, black and amber stockings.

Year Formed: 1876.

Turned Professional: 1885.

Ltd Co.: 1911.

Previous Names: 1876, Port Vale; 1884, Burslem Port Vale; 1909, Port Vale.

Club Nickname: 'Valiants'.

Previous Grounds: 1876, Limekin Lane, Longport; 1881, Westport; 1884, Moorland Road, Burslem; 1886, Athletic Ground, Cobridge; 1913, Recreation Ground, Hanley; 1950, Vale Park.

First Football League Game: 3 September 1892, Division 2, v Small Heath (a) L 1–5 – Frail; Clutton, Elson; Farrington, McCrindle, Delves; Walker, Scarratt, Bliss (1), Jones. (Only 10 men).

Record League Victory: 9–1 v Chesterfield, Division 2, 24 September 1932 – Leckie; Shenton, Poyser; Sherlock, Round, Jones; McGrath, Mills, Littlewood (6), Kirkham (2), Morton (1).

Record Cup Victory: 7–1 v Irthlingborough, FA Cup 1st rd, 12 January 1907 – Matthews; Dunn, Hamilton; Eardley, Baddeley, Holyhead; Carter, Dodds (2), Beats, Mountford (2), Coxon (3).

Record Defeat: 0–10 v Sheffield U, Division 2, 10 December 1892. 0–10 v Notts Co, Division 2, 26 February 1895.

HONOURS

Football League: Division 2 – Runners-up 1993–94; Division 3 (N) – Champions 1929–30, 1953–54; Runners-up 1952–53; Division 4 – Champions 1958–59; Promoted 1969–70 (4th).

FA Cup: Semi-final 1954, when in Division 3.

Football League Cup: best season: 3rd rd 1992, 1997.

Autoglass Trophy: Winners 1993.

Anglo-Italian Cup: Runners-up 1996.

LDV Vans Trophy: Winners 2001.

SKY SPORTS FACT FILE

Mid-way through their successful 1929–30 season the directors of Port Vale decided to recharge the players' batteries with a week's rest in Llandudno. It worked. The Valiants went on to win their next six matches.

Most League Points (2 for a win): 69, Division 3 (N), 1953–54.

Most League Points (3 for a win): 89, Division 2, 1992–93.

Most League Goals: 110, Division 4, 1958–59.

Highest League Scorer in Season: Wilf Kirkham 38, Division 2, 1926–27.

Most League Goals in Total Aggregate: Wilf Kirkham, 154, 1923–29, 1931–33.

Most League Goals in One Match: 6, Stewart Littlewood v Chesterfield, Division 2, 24 September 1922.

Most Capped Player: Tony Rougier, Trinidad & Tobago.

Most League Appearances: Roy Sproson, 761, 1950–72.

Youngest League Player: Malcolm McKenzie, 15 years 347 days v Newport Co, 12 April 1966.

Record Transfer Fee Received: £2,000,000 from Wimbledon for Gareth Ainsworth, October 1998.

Record Transfer Fee Paid: £500,000 to York C for Jon McCarthy, August 1995 and £500,000 to Lincoln C for Gareth Ainsworth, September 1997.

Football League Record: 1892 Original Member of Division 2. Failed re-election in 1896; Re-elected 1898; Resigned 1907; Returned in Oct, 1919, when they took over the fixtures of Leeds City; 1929–30 Division 3 (N); 1930–36 Division 2; 1936–38 Division 3 (N); 1938–52 Division 3 (S); 1952–54 Division 3 (N); 1954–57 Division 2; 1957–58 Division 3 (S); 1958–59 Division 4; 1959–65 Division 3; 1965–70 Division 4; 1970–78 Division 3; 1978–83 Division 4; 1983–84 Division 3; 1984–86 Division 4; 1986–89 Division 3; 1989–94 Division 2; 1994–2000 Division 1; 2000–04 Division 2; 2004– FL1.

MANAGERS

Sam Gleaves 1896–1905
(Secretary-Manager)
Tom Clare 1905–11
A. S. Walker 1911–12
H. Myatt 1912–14
Tom Holford 1919–24
(continued as Trainer)
Joe Schofield 1924–30
Tom Morgan 1930–32
Tom Holford 1932–35
Warney Cresswell 1936–37
Tom Morgan 1937–38
Billy Frith 1945–46
Gordon Hodgson 1946–51
Ivor Powell 1951
Freddie Steele 1951–57
Norman Low 1957–62
Freddie Steele 1962–65
Jackie Mudie 1965–67
Sir Stanley Matthews
(General Manager) 1965–68
Gordon Lee 1968–74
Roy Sproson 1974–77
Colin Harper 1977
Bobby Smith 1977–78
Dennis Butler 1978–79
Alan Bloor 1979
John McGrath 1980–83
John Rudge 1984–99
Brian Horton 1999–2004
Martin Foyle February 2004–

LATEST SEQUENCES

Longest Sequence of League Wins: 8, 8.4.1893 – 30.9.1893.

Longest Sequence of League Defeats: 9, 9.3.1957 – 20.4.1957.

Longest Sequence of League Draws: 6, 26.4.1981 – 12.9.1981.

Longest Sequence of Unbeaten League Matches: 19, 5.5.1969 – 8.11.1969.

Longest Sequence Without a League Win: 17, 7.12.1991 – 21.3.1992.

Successive Scoring Runs: 22 from 12.9.1992.

Successive Non-scoring Runs: 4 from 10.2.1896.

TEN YEAR LEAGUE RECORD

		P	*W*	*D*	*L*	*F*	*A*	*Pts*	*Pos*
1995-96	Div 1	46	15	15	16	59	66	60	12
1996-97	Div 1	46	17	16	13	58	55	67	8
1997-98	Div 1	46	13	10	23	56	66	49	19
1998-99	Div 1	46	13	8	25	45	75	47	21
1999-2000	Div 1	46	7	15	24	48	69	36	23
2000-01	Div 2	46	16	14	16	55	49	62	11
2001-02	Div 2	46	16	10	20	51	62	58	14
2002-03	Div 2	46	14	11	21	54	70	53	17
2003-04	Div 2	46	21	10	15	73	63	73	7
2004-05	FL 1	46	17	5	24	49	59	56	18

DID YOU KNOW?

Not only did Port Vale create a defensive record in 1953–54 conceding only 21 goals in 46 matches, five of them at home, but the next best defensive performance by another team was to let in 30 more than the winners.

PORT VALE 2004–05 LEAGUE RECORD

Match No.	*Date*	*Venue*	*Opponents*	*Result*		*H/T Score*	*Lg. Pos.*	*Goalscorers*	*Attendance*
1	Aug 7	A	Walsall	L	2-3	0-1	—	Paynter [61], Matthews [90]	8225
2	10	H	Milton Keynes D	W	3-2	1-1	—	Brooker [43], Armstrong 2 [46, 64]	4602
3	14	H	Hull C	W	3-2	1-1	4	Collins [26], Brooker 2 [51, 90]	6736
4	21	A	Wrexham	D	1-1	0-0	9	Brooker [64]	5005
5	28	H	Bristol C	W	3-0	2-0	4	James [37], Brooker [45], Armstrong [66]	5377
6	31	A	Chesterfield	L	0-1	0-0	—		5150
7	Sept 4	A	Bradford C	W	2-0	1-0	3	Paynter [40], Smith J [49]	7043
8	11	H	Huddersfield T	L	0-3	0-0	6		6298
9	18	A	Brentford	L	0-1	0-1	13		5442
10	25	H	Blackpool	L	0-3	0-2	16		5347
11	Oct 2	A	Colchester U	L	1-2	0-2	17	Matthews [84]	3230
12	8	H	Doncaster R	W	2-0	2-0	—	Paynter [15], Matthews [29]	5314
13	16	A	Bournemouth	L	0-4	0-3	15		6119
14	19	H	Swindon T	W	1-0	0-0	—	Birchall [76]	3872
15	23	H	Stockport Co	D	0-0	0-0	14		5025
16	30	A	Hartlepool U	L	0-1	0-1	16		4755
17	Nov 6	A	Barnsley	W	2-1	0-1	13	Paynter [65], Williams R (og) [65]	8642
18	20	H	Torquay U	L	1-2	0-1	15	Cummins [50]	4763
19	27	A	Peterborough U	L	0-4	0-1	17		3785
20	Dec 7	H	Tranmere R	W	3-1	2-0	—	Birchall 2 [9, 52], Paynter [17]	4027
21	11	A	Luton T	L	0-1	0-0	18		6974
22	18	H	Oldham Ath	W	3-1	1-1	15	Paynter [36], Birchall [62], Matthews (pen) [79]	4849
23	26	A	Huddersfield T	L	1-2	1-2	16	Eldershaw [38]	12,243
24	28	H	Sheffield W	L	0-2	0-2	17		8671
25	Jan 1	H	Bradford C	L	0-1	0-0	18		5001
26	3	A	Blackpool	W	2-0	0-0	17	Matthews 2 (1 pen) [72, 78 (p)]	5115
27	8	A	Doncaster R	L	0-2	0-1	17		5209
28	15	H	Brentford	L	0-1	0-1	17		4230
29	21	A	Sheffield W	L	0-1	0-1	—		18,465
30	Feb 5	H	Bournemouth	W	2-1	2-1	18	Paynter [17], Birchall [34]	4186
31	12	A	Stockport Co	W	2-1	1-0	16	Lowndes [22], Paynter [52]	4587
32	19	H	Hartlepool U	L	0-1	0-1	17		4366
33	23	A	Swindon T	L	0-1	0-1	—		4724
34	26	H	Luton T	W	3-1	1-1	16	Hibbert 2 [42, 59], Matthews [81]	5353
35	Mar 5	A	Oldham Ath	L	0-3	0-1	17		5799
36	8	H	Colchester U	D	0-0	0-0	—		3496
37	12	A	Milton Keynes D	D	1-1	0-0	18	Matthews [69]	4676
38	19	H	Walsall	W	2-0	0-0	16	Cummins [51], Matthews [57]	5085
39	26	A	Hull C	D	2-2	1-1	17	Matthews [13], Delaney (og) [67]	17,678
40	Apr 2	A	Bristol C	L	0-2	0-1	18		10,284
41	9	H	Chesterfield	W	1-0	0-0	17	Matthews [49]	4489
42	16	A	Torquay U	L	0-1	0-0	18		3592
43	23	H	Barnsley	W	5-0	2-0	18	Birchall [16], Paynter 2 [41, 50], Dinning 2 [57, 70]	4324
44	26	H	Wrexham	L	0-2	0-2	—		4151
45	29	A	Tranmere R	L	0-1	0-1	—		8940
46	May 7	H	Peterborough U	W	1-0	0-0	18	Dinning [63]	4815

Final League Position: 18

GOALSCORERS

League (49): Matthews 11 (2 pens), Paynter 10, Birchall 6, Brooker 5, Armstrong 3, Dinning 3, Cummins 2, Hibbert 2, Collins 1, Eldershaw 1, James 1, Lowndes 1, Smith J 1, own goals 2.
Carling Cup (1): Smith D 1.
FA Cup (3): Paynter 2, Reid 1.
LDV Vans Trophy (2): Birchall 1, Paynter 1 (pen).

Brain J 26 + 1	Rowland S 17 + 7	James C 23 + 7	Collins S 33	Smith D 12 + 1	Hulbert R 23 + 1	Reid L 21 + 9	Cummins M 39	Brooker S 9	Paynter B 43 + 2	Armstrong I 6 + 3	Smith J 23 + 11	Matthews L 21 + 10	Pilkington G 42 + 1	Brown R 16 + 4	Goodlad M 20	Lipa A — + 2	Hibbert D 2 + 7	O'Connor J 13	McMahon D 1 + 4	Birchall C 29 + 5	Goodfellow M 4 + 1	Eldershaw S 5 + 8	Walsh M 22 + 1	Lowndes N 7 + 5	Porter A — + 2	Hanson C 3 + 2	Loran T 6	Abbey G 16 + 2	Widdrington T 2 + 4	Sonner D 13	Dinning T 7	Innes M 2 + 3	*Match No.*
1	2	3	4	5	6^{1}	7	8	9^{2}	10■	11	12	13																					1
1	2	3	4	5^{1}	6	7	8	9		11		10	12																				2
1	12	3	4	5	6	7	8	9	13	11^{2}	14	10^{3}	2^{1}																				3
1	2	3	4	5	6^{1}	7		9	11			10	8	12																			4
	2	3	4		6^{3}	7	8	9	12	11^{2}	13	10^{1}	5		1	14																	5
	2^{2}	3	4	5■	6	7	8		9		12	10	11^{1}		1		13																6
		3	4		6	7^{2}	8	9^{1}	10		11	12	5		1	13		2															7
		3	4		6	7^{2}	8	9	10^{1}	13	11	12	5		1			2															8
15		3	4		6	7	8	9	10		11^{1}	12	5■		1^{G}			2															9
1		3	4		6	7	8^{2}	9	10	11	12		5				13	2^{1}															10
1		3	4			7	8		9		11	10	5					2^{1}	12	6													11
1		3	4		6^{1}	12	8		9		13	10^{2}	5					2	14	7	11^{3}												12
1		3^{1}		5		7	8		9		11^{2}		6	12				2	13	4^{3}	10	14											13
1				5	11		8		9				6	3				2	7^{1}	12	10		4										14
1		12	4		6	13	8^{2}		9				5	3^{1}				2		7	10		11■										15
1		3	4	5^{1}	6		8		9	12			11	7^{2}				2		10	13												16
1			5			7	8^{2}		9	11^{1}	12		6	3				2	13	4		14		10^{3}									17
1	12		4^{1}		13	7	8		9		11		5	3^{2}				2		6				10									18
1	12			13		7^{2}	8		9		11		6	3^{1}				2		4			5	10									19
1	2			5		7^{1}	8		9		11		6	3						4		13^{3}		10^{2}	12	14							20
1	2	12		5			8		9		11		6	3^{1}						4		10					7						21
1	2	12		5			8		9		11^{1}	13	6	3^{3}						7		10^{2}					4	14					22
1	2				6^{1}	12	8		9		11	13	5	3						7		10^{2}					4						23
1				5^{2}	7	12	8		9		11	10^{1}	6	3^{3}						4		14	13				2						24
1	12				6		8		9		11	10	5	3^{2}								13	2^{1}				4	7					25
1	14				6^{1}	12	8		9		11	10^{2}	4	3^{3}								13	5				2	7					26
1			4		6		8		9		11	10^{2}	2	3						12		13	5					7^{1}					27
1			4		6^{3}	7			9		11		5	3						12		10^{2}	2^{1}	13				8	14				28
1			4		6	7^{3}			9		11	12	2	3^{2}						10^{1}			5	13				8	14				29
1	3				6^{2}		8		9		11		4				12			7			5	10^{1}				2	13				30
	2^{3}	12	4				3		9		11		6		1		13			8^{2}			5	10^{1}				7	14				31
		3^{2}	4			12	8^{1}		9		11^{3}		2	13	1		14			6			5					7	10				32
		3^{1}	4				8		9		12		2		1		14			13		10^{3}	5					7	6^{2}	11			33
			4			12	8		9		11	13	3		1		10^{2}			6^{1}			5					2		7			34
			4			12	8^{2}		9	13	11^{1}	14	3		1		10^{3}			6			5					2		7			35
	12	3^{3}	4			13■	8■		9		11^{2}	10^{1}	6		1					14			5					2		7			36
	7	3	4						9			10^{1}	6^{3}		1		12^{2}			8			5		14	13		2		11			37
	5	3	4		6^{1}		8		9			10^{2}		12	1					7		13						2		11			38
	2	3	4				8		9			10	5		1					6										11	7		39
	2	3^{1}	4			7^{2}	8		9			10	5		1					6								12		11		13	40
	12		4				8		9			10	3		1					6			5					2^{1}		11	7		41
	2	12	4				8		9			10	3		1					6			5^{1}							11^{2}	7	13	42
		12	4				8^{2}		9			10^{3}	3		1					7			5	13				2^{1}		11	6	14	43
1		3	4			7			9		12	13								6			5	10^{2}		2					8^{1}	11	44
	3^{1}	12				7^{2}			9		13	10^{3}	4		1					6			5	14		2				11	8		45
		3							9		12	10^{2}	4		1					6			5	13		2				7	8	11^{1}	46

FA Cup

First Round	Kidderminster H	(h)	3-1
Second Round	Blackpool	(a)	0-1

Carling Cup

First Round	Doncaster R	(a)	1-3

LDV Vans Trophy

First Round	Barnsley	(h)	1-0
Second Round	Tranmere R	(a)	1-2

PRESTON NORTH END FL Championship

FOUNDATION

North End Cricket and Rugby Club which was formed in 1863, indulged in most sports before taking up soccer in about 1879. In 1881 they decided to stick to football to the exclusion of other sports and even a 16–0 drubbing by Blackburn Rovers in an invitation game at Deepdale, a few weeks after taking this decision, did not deter them for they immediately became affiliated to the Lancashire FA.

Deepdale, Sir Tom Finney Way, Deepdale, Preston PR1 6RU.

Telephone: 0870 442 1964.

Fax: (01772) 693 366.

Ticket Office: 0870 442 1966.

Website: www.pne.com

Email: enquiries@pne.com

Ground Capacity: 20,600.

Record Attendance: 42,684 v Arsenal, Division 1, 23 April 1938.

Pitch Measurements: 110yd × 77yd.

Chairman: Derek Shaw.

Vice-chairman: David Taylor.

Chief Executive: Steve Jackson.

Secretary: Janet Parr.

Manager: Billy Davies.

Assistant Manager: David Kelly.

Physio: Andrew Balderston.

Colours: White shirts, navy shorts, white stockings.

Change Colours: Grey with white trim.

Year Formed: 1881.

Turned Professional: 1885.

Ltd Co.: 1893.

Club Nicknames: 'The Lilywhites' or 'North End'.

First Football League Game: 8 September 1888, Football League, v Burnley (h) W 5–2 – Trainer; Howarth, Holmes; Robertson, W. Graham, J. Graham; Gordon (1), Ross (2), Goodall, Dewhurst (2), Drummond.

Record League Victory: 10–0 v Stoke, Division 1, 14 September 1889 – Trainer; Howarth, Holmes; Kelso, Russell (1), Graham; Gordon, Jimmy Ross (2), Nick Ross (3), Thomson (2), Drummond (2).

Record Cup Victory: 26–0 v Hyde, FA Cup 1st rd, 15 October 1887 – Addision; Howarth, Nick Ross; Russell (1), Thomson (5), Graham (1); Gordon (5), Jimmy Ross (8), John Goodall (1), Dewhurst (3), Drummond (2).

Record Defeat: 0–7 v Blackpool, Division 1, 1 May 1948.

Most League Points (2 for a win): 61, Division 3, 1970–71.

HONOURS

Football League: Division 1 – Champions 1888–89 (first champions) 1889–90; Runners-up 1890–91, 1891–92, 1892–93, 1905–06, 1952–53, 1957–58; Division 2 – Champions 1903–04, 1912–13, 1950–51, 1999–2000; Runners-up 1914–15, 1933–34; Division 3 – Champions 1970–71, 1995–96; Division 4 – Runners-up 1986–87.

FA Cup: Winners 1889, 1938; Runners-up 1888, 1922, 1937, 1954, 1964.

Football League Cup: best season: 4th rd, 2003.

Double Performed: 1888–89.

Football League Cup: best season: 4th rd, 1963, 1966, 1972, 1981.

SKY SPORTS FACT FILE

In 1921–22 Preston North End signed Alf Quantrill, a Punjab born England international winger from Derby County. He was the son-in-law of Steve Bloomer. Aged 23 when capped, one appearance was against Scotland when the average age of the side was 30.

Most League Points (3 for a win): 95, Division 2, 1999–2000.

Most League Goals: 100, Division 2, 1927–28 and Division 1, 1957–58.

Highest League Scorer in Season: Ted Harper, 37, Division 2, 1932–33.

Most League Goals in Total Aggregate: Tom Finney, 187, 1946–60.

Most League Goals in One Match: 4, Jimmy Ross v Stoke, Division 1, 6 October 1888; 4, Nick Ross v Derby Co, Division 1, 11 January 1890; 4, George Drummond v Notts Co, Division 1, 12 December 1891; 4, Frank Becton v Notts Co, Division 1, 31 March 1893; 4, George Harrison v Grimsby T, Division 2, 3 November 1928; 4, Alex Reid v Port Vale, Division 2, 23 February 1929; 4, James McClelland v Reading, Division 2, 6 September 1930; 4, Dick Rowley v Notts Co, Division 2, 16 April 1932; 4, Ted Harper v Burnley, Division 2, 29 August 1932; 4, Ted Harper v Lincoln C, Division 2, 11 March 1933; 4, Charlie Wayman v QPR, Division 2, 25 December 1950; 4, Alex Bruce v Colchester U, Division 3, 28 February 1978.

Most Capped Player: Tom Finney, 76, England.

Most League Appearances: Alan Kelly, 447, 1961–75.

Youngest League Player: Steve Doyle, 16 years 166 days v Tranmere R, 15 November 1974.

Record Transfer Fee Received: £5,000,000 from Manchester C for Jon Macken March 2002.

Record Transfer Fee Paid: £1,500,000 to Manchester U for David Healy, December 2000.

Football League Record: 1888 Founder Member of League; 1901–04 Division 2; 1904–12 Division 1; 1912–13 Division 2; 1913–14 Division 1; 1914–15 Division 2; 1919–25 Division 1; 1925–34 Division 2; 1934–49 Division 1; 1949–51 Division 2; 1951–61 Division 1; 1961–70 Division 2; 1970–71 Division 3; 1971–74 Division 2; 1974–78 Division 3; 1978–81 Division 2; 1981–85 Division 3; 1985–87 Division 4; 1987–92 Division 3; 1992–93 Division 2; 1993–96 Division 3; 1996–2000 Division 2; 2000–04 Division 1; 2004– FLC.

MANAGERS

Charlie Parker 1906–15
Vincent Hayes 1919–23
Jim Lawrence 1923–25
Frank Richards 1925–27
Alex Gibson 1927–31
Lincoln Hayes 1931–32
Run by committee 1932–36
Tommy Muirhead 1936–37
Run by committee 1937–49
Will Scott 1949–53
Scot Symon 1953–54
Frank Hill 1954–56
Cliff Britton 1956–61
Jimmy Milne 1961–68
Bobby Seith 1968–70
Alan Ball Sr 1970–73
Bobby Charlton 1973–75
Harry Catterick 1975–77
Nobby Stiles 1977–81
Tommy Docherty 1981
Gordon Lee 1981–83
Alan Kelly 1983–85
Tommy Booth 1985–86
Brian Kidd 1986
John McGrath 1986–90
Les Chapman 1990–92
Sam Allardyce 1992 (*Caretaker*)
John Beck 1992–94
Gary Peters 1994–98
David Moyes 1998–2002
Kelham O'Hanlon 2002 (*Caretaker*)
Craig Brown 2002–04
Billy Davies August 2004–

LATEST SEQUENCES

Longest Sequence of League Wins: 14, 25.12.1950 – 27.3.1951.

Longest Sequence of League Defeats: 8, 22.9.1984 – 27.10.1984.

Longest Sequence of League Draws: 6, 24.2.1979 – 20.3.1979.

Longest Sequence of Unbeaten League Matches: 23, 8.9.1888 – 14.9.1889.

Longest Sequence Without a League Win: 15, 14.4.1923 – 20.10.1923.

Successive Scoring Runs: 30 from 15.11.1952.

Successive Non-scoring Runs: 6 from 8.4.1897.

TEN YEAR LEAGUE RECORD

		P	W	D	L	F	A	Pts	Pos
1995-96	Div 3	46	23	17	6	78	38	86	1
1996-97	Div 2	46	18	7	21	49	55	61	15
1997-98	Div 2	46	15	14	17	56	56	59	15
1998-99	Div 2	46	22	13	11	78	50	79	5
1999-2000	Div 2	46	28	11	7	74	37	95	1
2000-01	Div 1	46	23	9	14	64	52	78	4
2001-02	Div 1	46	20	12	14	71	59	72	8
2002-03	Div 1	46	16	13	17	68	70	61	12
2003-04	Div 1	46	15	14	17	69	71	59	15
2004-05	FL C	46	21	12	13	67	58	75	5

DID YOU KNOW?

On the last day of the 1933–34 season Preston North End needed to win at Southampton to be certain of promotion from the Second Division. Supporters at the home reserve game were kept informed but left thinking it was 0–0 at The Dell. Preston had won 1–0.

PRESTON NORTH END 2004–05 LEAGUE RECORD

Match No.	Date	Venue	Opponents	Result	H/T Score	Lg. Pos.	Goalscorers	Attendance
1	Aug 7	H	Watford	W 2-1	1-0	—	Cresswell [34], Healy (pen) [77]	12,208
2	11	A	Wolverhampton W	D 2-2	2-0	—	Lucketti [4], Healy [15]	26,115
3	14	A	Gillingham	L 1-2	1-1	9	Fuller [34]	7073
4	20	H	Sheffield U	L 0-1	0-1	—		12,084
5	28	A	Brighton & HA	L 0-1	0-1	20		5996
6	30	H	Rotherham U	W 2-0	2-0	12	Etuhu 2 [15, 45]	11,439
7	Sept 11	H	Stoke C	W 3-0	1-0	9	Cresswell 2 [27, 79], Healy [80]	12,759
8	14	A	Reading	L 1-3	1-2	—	Healy [45]	11,857
9	18	A	Sunderland	L 1-3	1-2	17	Alexander (pen) [39]	24,264
10	25	H	Crewe Alex	W 1-0	1-0	11	Davidson [40]	11,823
11	28	H	Plymouth Arg	D 1-1	0-1	—	Cresswell [66]	11,445
12	Oct 2	A	Leicester C	D 1-1	1-1	14	Lonergan [39]	21,249
13	16	A	Leeds U	L 0-1	0-0	17		30,458
14	19	H	QPR	W 2-1	1-1	—	Healy [11], Cresswell (pen) [78]	10,548
15	23	H	Nottingham F	W 3-2	2-0	8	McKenna [11], Lucketti [36], Etuhu [57]	12,439
16	30	A	Ipswich T	L 0-3	0-2	13		23,745
17	Nov 3	A	Coventry C	D 1-1	0-0	—	Lewis [68]	12,478
18	6	H	Leeds U	L 2-4	0-3	13	Cresswell 2 [54, 83]	18,531
19	13	H	Millwall	D 1-1	1-0	16	Lewis [15]	10,339
20	19	A	Cardiff C	W 1-0	1-0	—	Mawene [14]	10,950
21	27	H	Derby Co	W 3-0	2-0	11	Alexander 2 (1 pen) [13, 43 (p)], Cresswell [88]	12,702
22	Dec 5	A	Wigan Ath	L 0-5	0-1	15		10,565
23	11	A	Burnley	L 0-2	0-1	16		15,318
24	18	H	West Ham U	W 2-1	2-0	14	Lewis [9], O'Neil [45]	13,451
25	26	A	Stoke C	D 0-0	0-0	13		20,350
26	28	H	Reading	W 3-0	2-0	9	Agyemang [17], Hughes (og) [26], Lewis [67]	12,795
27	Jan 1	H	Sunderland	W 3-2	3-0	10	Cresswell 3 [13, 30, 43]	16,940
28	3	A	Crewe Alex	W 2-1	1-0	9	Sedgwick [9], O'Neil [59]	8667
29	15	H	Leicester C	D 1-1	0-1	8	McKenna [64]	12,677
30	22	A	Plymouth Arg	W 2-0	2-0	6	Sedgwick [29], Agyemang [34]	13,663
31	Feb 5	H	Coventry C	W 3-2	2-1	6	Alexander (pen) [22], Cresswell [23], Lucketti [48]	13,691
32	12	A	QPR	W 2-1	0-1	4	Nugent [67], Lucketti [75]	15,620
33	18	H	Ipswich T	D 1-1	1-0	—	Nugent [36]	14,418
34	23	A	Nottingham F	L 0-2	0-0	—		19,209
35	26	H	Burnley	W 1-0	0-0	5	Alexander (pen) [82]	18,202
36	Mar 5	A	West Ham U	W 2-1	1-0	5	Nugent [17], Agyemang [81]	26,442
37	12	H	Wolverhampton W	D 2-2	1-1	5	Cresswell [3], Alexander (pen) [53]	16,296
38	15	A	Sheffield U	D 1-1	0-1	—	Cresswell [48]	18,647
39	19	A	Watford	W 2-0	0-0	4	Nugent [60], McKenna [71]	19,649
40	Apr 2	H	Gillingham	D 1-1	1-0	4	Brown (og) [28]	15,054
41	5	H	Brighton & HA	W 3-0	2-0	—	Alexander (pen) [31], Cresswell [45], Nugent [51]	14,234
42	9	A	Rotherham U	W 2-1	0-1	4	Sedgwick [51], Mawene [64]	6312
43	16	H	Cardiff C	W 3-0	0-0	4	Nugent 2 [67, 79], Cresswell [85]	15,141
44	24	A	Millwall	L 1-2	0-1	4	Nugent [58]	11,417
45	30	H	Wigan Ath	D 1-1	1-1	4	O'Neil [41]	20,221
46	May 8	A	Derby Co	L 1-3	0-1	5	Agyemang [69]	31,237

Final League Position: 5

GOALSCORERS

League (67): Cresswell 16 (1 pen), Nugent 8, Alexander 7 (6 pens), Healy 5 (1 pen), Agyemang 4, Lewis 4, Lucketti 4, Etuhu 3, McKenna 3, O'Neil 3, Sedgwick 3, Mawene 2, Davidson 1, Fuller 1, Lonergan 1, own goals 2.
Carling Cup (7): Cresswell 4 (1 pen), Alexander 1, Daley 1, Lynch 1.
FA Cup (0).
Play-offs (2): Cresswell 1, Nugent 1.

Lonergan A 23	Skora E 5 + 4	Lewis E 37 + 3	Davis C 21 + 11	Lucketti C 41	Mawene Y 46	Etuhu D 22 + 13	Healy D 11	Cresswell R 46	Fuller R 2	O'Neil B 40 + 3	Smith A 3 + 11	McCormack A — + 3	Alexander G 41 + 1	Broomes M 8 + 3	Davidson C 16 + 3	McKenna P 37 + 2	Lynch S 2 + 7	Daley O 1 + 13	Curtis J 12	Jackson M — + 2	N'Dumbu Nsungu G 4 + 2	Ward G 6 + 1	Gould J 4	Langmead K — + 1	Agyemang P 15 + 12	Sedgwick C 24	Oliveira F 1 + 4	O'Neill J — + 2	Hill M 11 + 3	Nugent D 13 + 5	Kozluk R — + 1	Neal C — + 1	Day C 6	Nash C 7	Folly Y — + 2	Mears T 1 + 3	*Match No.*
1	2^1	3	4	5	6	7	8	9	10^2	11	12	13																									1
1	3	11	4^1	5	6	7■	10^2	9		8	13	12	2																								2
1	12	11	4	5	6		8	9	10^2	13			2	3^3	14	7^1																					3
1	3^2	11	4^1	5	6		10	9		8			2	12		7	13																				4
1	2^1	11	4	5	6^2		10	9		8	12			3		7		13																			5
1		11^3	4	5	6	2	10^1	9^2		8	12			3		7	13	14																			6
1	12			5	6	11	8^3	9		4^1	13		2			7	10^2		3	14																	7
1	12	11		5	6	3	10	9		8			2			7^1			4																		8
1	3^1	11		5^2	6	7	10^3	9		8	12		2		13		14		4																		9
1		11	4		6	7		9		8^1	10^2	12	2		5		13■		3																		10
1		11	4		6	7		9		8^1			2		5^2	12		13	3	14	10^3																11
1		12	4		6	7		9		11	13		2	5	3^1				8		10^2																12
1		12		5	6	11	10^3	9			13		2	3^1	8^2	7			4		14																13
1^6		11	4	5	6	3	10	9		8			2^1			7		12				15															14
		11^3	4	5	6	3		9^2			12		2			7	13	14	8		10^1	1															15
	12	11		5	6	3		9		8^1			2			7	13	14	4^3		10^2	1															16
		11	4	5	6	3		9		8^1	10^2		2			7		12			13	1															17
		11	4	5	6^1	3		9		12	10^2		2			7		13	8			1															18
		11		5	6	3		9					2			7	10^1	8	4				1	12													19
		11		5	6			9		8			2	3	12	7		13	4^2				1		10^1												20
		11		5	6	12		9^2		4			2	3		7^1	13	14					1		10	8^3											21
		12	4	5	6^1	11		9		8			2	3									1		10	7											22
		11	4	5	6	3		9		8^1					2	7		12				1			10												23
1		11	4	5	6	12		9		8^1			13		3	2									10^3	7^2	14										24
1		11	4		6	13		9		8			2	12^2	5^1	7		14							10		3^3										25
1		3	4	5	6	12		9^3		8			2			11^1									10	7^2	13	14									26
1		3	4	5	6	12		9		8^1			2			11		13							10^2	7^3	14										27
1		3	4^1	5	6	12		9		8■			2			11									10^2	7		13									28
1				5	6	3		9		8			2			11									10^2	7^1	12		4	13							29
1		11		5	6	12		9		4^1			2			8									10^2	7^3			3	13	14						30
1		11	12	5	6	8		9^3		4	13		2												10^2	7^1			3	14							31
1		11■	12	5	6	4^2		9		8			2^1			13									10^3	7			3	14							32
				5	6	12		9		8			2		3^1	11						1^6			13	7			4	10^2		15					33
		11	12	5	6			9		4			2			8									13	7			3^1	10^2			1				34
		11	12	5	6			9^2		4			2^1		3	8									13	7				10			1				35
		11^1	12	5	6	13		9		4^2			2			8									14	7			3	10^3			1				36
		11^3	12	5	6	13		9		4^2			2		3	8^1									14	7				10			1				37
		11^1	12	5	6			9		4			2		3	8^3									13	7			14	10^2			1				38
		11^3	12	5	6			9		4			2		3	8									13	7^1			14	10^2			1				39
		11^1	12	5	6			9		4			2		3	8									13	7^3				10^2				1	14		40
		11	12	5	6			9		4^3			2^1		3	8									13	7^2				10				1	14		41
		11^3	12	5	6			9^2		4			2		3	8									13	7^1			14	10				1			42
		11		5	6	12		9		4^1			2			8									13	7^3			3	10^2				1		14	43
				5	6	12		9		4	13		2			8									11^1	7^3			3^2	10				1		14	44
				5	6	12		9		4^3			2		11^1	8									13	7			3	10^2				1		14	45
			4		6^1	11		9^3		13			2	12		8									10	7^2			3	14				1		5	46

FA Cup

Third Round	WBA	(h)	0-2

Carling Cup

First Round	Mansfield T	(a)	4-0
Second Round	Leicester C	(a)	3-2
Third Round	Everton	(a)	0-2

Play-offs

Semi-Final	Derby Co	(h)	2-0
		(a)	0-0
Final (at Millennium Stadium)	West Ham U		0-1

QUEENS PARK RANGERS FL Championship

FOUNDATION

There is an element of doubt about the date of the foundation of this club, but it is believed that in either 1885 or 1886 it was formed through the amalgamation of Christchurch Rangers and St Jude's Institute FC. The leading light was George Wodehouse, whose family maintained a connection with the club until comparatively recent times. Most of the players came from the Queen's Park district so this name was adopted after a year as St Jude's Institute.

Loftus Road Stadium, South Africa Road, Shepherds Bush, London W12 7PA.

Telephone: (020) 8743 0262.

Fax: (020) 8749 0994.

Ticket Office: 0870 112 1967.

Website: www.qpr.co.uk

Email: qpr.co.uk

Ground Capacity: 18,200 (subject to confirmation due to alterations during the close season).

Record Attendance: 35,353 v Leeds U, Division 1, 27 April 1974.

Pitch Measurements: 112yd × 72yd.

Chairman: Bill Power.

Chief Executive: Mark Devlin.

Secretary: Sheila Marson.

Manager: Ian Holloway.

Physio: Prabhat Mathema.

Colours: Blue and white hooped shirts, white shorts, white stockings.

Change Colours: Red and black hooped shirts, red or black shorts, red or black stockings.

Year Formed: 1885* (*see Foundation*).

Turned Professional: 1898. ***Ltd Co.:*** 1899.

Previous Names: 1885, St Jude's; 1887, Queens Park Rangers. ***Club Nicknames:*** 'Rangers' or 'Rs'.

Previous Grounds: 1885* (*see Foundation*), Welford's Fields; 1888–99; London Scottish Ground, Brondesbury, Home Farm, Kensal Rise Green, Gun Club Wormwood Scrubs, Kilburn Cricket Ground; 1899, Kensal Rise Athletic Ground; 1901, Latimer Road, Notting Hill; 1904, Agricultural Society, Park Royal; 1907, Park Royal Ground; 1917, Loftus Road; 1931, White City; 1933, Loftus Road; 1962, White City; 1963, Loftus Road.

First Football League Game: 28 August 1920, Division 3, v Watford (h) L 1–2 – Price; Blackman, Wingrove; McGovern, Grant, O'Brien; Faulkner, Birch (1), Smith, Gregory, Middlemiss.

Record League Victory: 9–2 v Tranmere R, Division 3, 3 December 1960 – Drinkwater; Woods, Ingham; Keen, Rutter, Angell; Lazarus (2), Bedford (2), Evans (2), Andrews (1), Clark (2).

Record Cup Victory: 8–1 v Bristol R (away), FA Cup 1st rd, 27 November 1937 – Gilfillan; Smith, Jefferson; Lowe, James, March; Cape, Mallett, Cheetham (3), Fitzgerald (3) Bott (2). 8–1 v Crewe Alex, Milk Cup 1st rd, 3 October 1983 – Hucker; Neill, Dawes, Waddock (1), McDonald (1), Fenwick, Micklewhite (1), Stewart (1), Allen (1), Stainrod (3), Gregory.

HONOURS

Football League: Division 1 – Runners-up 1975–76; Division 2 – Champions 1982–83; Runners-up 1967–68, 1972–73, 2003–04; Division 3 (S) – Champions 1947–48; Runners-up 1946–47; Division 3 – Champions 1966–67.

FA Cup: Runners-up 1982.

Football League Cup: Winners 1967; Runners-up 1986. (In 1966–67 won Division 3 and Football League Cup).

European Competitions: *UEFA Cup:* 1976–77, 1984–85.

SKY SPORTS FACT FILE

In 1920–21 three Queens Park Rangers players were responsible for all but 13 of the 61 League goals: Jack Smith 18, Jimmy Birch and Jack Gregory 15 each. Birch even missed most of the second half and had scored against his old club Aston Villa the previous term.

Record Defeat: 1–8 v Mansfield T, Division 3, 15 March 1965. 1–8 v Manchester U, Division 1, 19 March 1969.

Most League Points (2 for a win): 67, Division 3, 1966–67.

Most League Points (3 for a win): 85, Division 2, 1982–83.

Most League Goals: 111, Division 3, 1961–62.

Highest League Scorer in Season: George Goddard, 37, Division 3 (S), 1929–30.

Most League Goals in Total Aggregate: George Goddard, 172, 1926–34.

Most League Goals in One Match: 4, George Goddard v Merthyr T, Division 3S, 9 March 1929; 4, George Goddard v Swindon T, Division 3S, 12 April 1930; 4, George Goddard v Exeter C, Division 3S, 20 December 1930; 4, George Goddard v Watford, Division 3S, 19 September 1931; 4, Tom Cheetham v Aldershot, Division 3S, 14 September 1935; 4, Tom Cheetham v Aldershot, Division 3S, 12 November 1938.

Most Capped Player: Alan McDonald, 52, Northern Ireland.

Most League Appearances: Tony Ingham, 519, 1950–63.

Youngest League Player: Frank Sibley, 16 years 97 days v Bristol C, 10 March 1964.

Record Transfer Fee Received: £6,000,000 from Newcastle U for Les Ferdinand, June 1995.

Record Transfer Fee Paid: £2,750,000 to Stoke C for Mike Sheron, July 1997.

Football League Record: 1920 Original Members of Division 3; 1921–48 Division 3 (S); 1948–52 Division 2; 1952–58 Division 3 (S); 1958–67 Division 3; 1967–68 Division 2; 1968–69 Division 1; 1969–73 Division 2; 1973–79 Division 1; 1979–83 Division 2; 1983–92 Division 1; 1992–96 FA Premier League; 1996–2001 Division 1; 2001–04 Division 2; 2004– FLC.

LATEST SEQUENCES

Longest Sequence of League Wins: 8, 7.11.1931 – 28.12.1931.

Longest Sequence of League Defeats: 9, 25.2.1969 – 5.4.1969.

Longest Sequence of League Draws: 6, 29.1.2000 – 5.3.2000.

Longest Sequence of Unbeaten League Matches: 20, 11.3.1972 – 23.9.1972.

Longest Sequence Without a League Win: 20, 7.12.1968 – 7.4.1969.

Successive Scoring Runs: 33 from 9.12.1961.

Successive Non-scoring Runs: 6 from 18.3.1939.

MANAGERS

James Cowan 1906–13
Jimmy Howie 1913–20
Ted Liddell 1920–24
Will Wood 1924–25 *(had been Secretary since 1903)*
Bob Hewison 1925–30
John Bowman 1930–31
Archie Mitchell 1931–33
Mick O'Brien 1933–35
Billy Birrell 1935–39
Ted Vizard 1939–44
Dave Mangnall 1944–52
Jack Taylor 1952–59
Alec Stock 1959–65 *(General Manager to 1968)*
Bill Dodgin Jnr 1968
Tommy Docherty 1968
Les Allen 1968–71
Gordon Jago 1971–74
Dave Sexton 1974–77
Frank Sibley 1977–78
Steve Burtenshaw 1978–79
Tommy Docherty 1979–80
Terry Venables 1980–84
Gordon Jago 1984
Alan Mullery 1984
Frank Sibley 1984–85
Jim Smith 1985–88
Trevor Francis 1988–90
Don Howe 1990–91
Gerry Francis 1991–94
Ray Wilkins 1994–96
Stewart Houston 1996–97
Ray Harford 1997–98
Gerry Francis 1998–2001
Ian Holloway February 2001–

TEN YEAR LEAGUE RECORD

		P	W	D	L	F	A	Pts	Pos
1995-96	PR Lge	38	9	6	23	38	57	33	19
1996-97	Div 1	46	18	12	16	64	60	66	9
1997-98	Div 1	46	10	19	17	51	63	49	21
1998-99	Div 1	46	12	11	23	52	61	47	20
1999-2000	Div 1	46	16	18	12	62	53	66	10
2000-01	Div 1	46	7	19	20	45	75	40	23
2001-02	Div 2	46	19	14	13	60	49	71	8
2002-03	Div 2	46	24	11	11	69	45	83	4
2003-04	Div 2	46	22	17	7	80	45	83	2
2004-05	FL C	46	17	11	18	54	58	62	11

DID YOU KNOW 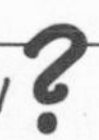

Queens Park Rangers introduced no fewer than eight players to Football League experience in 2004–05, most of them in the last half dozen matches of the season. Of 36 players called upon only Keith Gallen appeared in every League match.

QUEENS PARK RANGERS 2004–05 LEAGUE RECORD

Match No.	Date	Venue	Opponents	Result		H/T Score	Lg. Pos.	Goalscorers	Attendance
1	Aug 7	H	Rotherham U	D	1-1	1-1	—	Ainsworth [5]	14,547
2	9	A	Watford	L	0-3	0-2	—		14,737
3	14	A	Sunderland	D	2-2	1-1	23	Furlong [12], Rowlands [71]	26,063
4	21	H	Derby Co	L	0-2	0-2	23		15,295
5	27	A	Gillingham	W	1-0	1-0	—	Bean [29]	7391
6	31	H	Sheffield U	L	0-1	0-1	—		13,804
7	Sept 11	H	Plymouth Arg	W	3-2	1-1	18	Furlong 2 [29, 72], Gallen [89]	15,425
8	14	A	Crewe Alex	W	2-0	1-0	—	Furlong [22], Santos [68]	5682
9	18	A	Brighton & HA	W	3-2	1-2	8	Gallen [16], Furlong [74], Rose [90]	6612
10	25	H	Leicester C	W	3-2	0-2	7	Cook [58], Furlong 2 [70, 90]	15,535
11	28	H	Coventry C	W	4-1	2-0	—	Cureton 3 [32, 41, 74], Furlong [90]	14,680
12	Oct 2	A	Stoke C	W	1-0	0-0	4	Gallen [69]	16,877
13	16	H	West Ham U	W	1-0	1-0	3	Rose [22]	18,363
14	19	A	Preston NE	L	1-2	1-1	—	Santos [8]	10,548
15	23	A	Wolverhampton W	L	1-2	0-1	5	Gallen [90]	27,070
16	30	H	Burnley	W	3-0	3-0	4	Gallen (pen) [13], Santos [16], Furlong [24]	15,638
17	Nov 2	H	Millwall	D	1-1	0-0	—	Furlong [87]	16,685
18	6	A	West Ham U	L	1-2	0-1	6	McLeod [72]	31,365
19	13	H	Wigan Ath	W	1-0	0-0	5	Furlong [86]	15,804
20	20	A	Leeds U	L	1-6	1-5	5	Ainsworth [2]	29,739
21	27	H	Cardiff C	W	1-0	1-0	5	Shittu [23]	15,146
22	Dec 4	A	Nottingham F	L	1-2	0-1	6	Santos [49]	26,099
23	11	H	Ipswich T	L	2-4	2-1	7	Furlong 2 [27, 30]	18,231
24	18	A	Reading	L	0-1	0-0	10		20,272
25	26	A	Plymouth Arg	L	1-2	0-1	10	Furlong [53]	19,535
26	28	H	Crewe Alex	L	1-2	0-2	12	Shittu [81]	15,770
27	Jan 1	H	Brighton & HA	D	0-0	0-0	12		15,898
28	3	A	Leicester C	L	0-1	0-1	13		23,754
29	14	H	Stoke C	W	1-0	1-0	—	Cook [18]	13,559
30	22	A	Coventry C	W	2-1	1-0	10	Cureton [13], Santos [90]	16,595
31	Feb 5	A	Millwall	D	0-0	0-0	11		15,603
32	12	H	Preston NE	L	1-2	1-0	11	Furlong [26]	15,620
33	22	H	Wolverhampton W	D	1-1	1-0	—	Gallen [11]	15,029
34	26	A	Ipswich T	W	2-0	1-0	12	Furlong [4], Shittu [75]	29,008
35	Mar 5	H	Reading	D	0-0	0-0	12		16,971
36	12	H	Watford	W	3-1	2-0	11	Furlong [34], Gallen 2 [45, 58]	16,638
37	16	A	Derby Co	D	0-0	0-0	—		24,486
38	19	A	Rotherham U	W	1-0	0-0	9	Rowlands [53]	5387
39	Apr 2	H	Sunderland	L	1-3	1-0	9	Shittu [22]	18,198
40	5	H	Gillingham	D	1-1	0-1	—	Furlong [54]	16,431
41	9	A	Sheffield U	L	2-3	1-1	11	Rowlands [26], Gallen [66]	20,426
42	16	H	Leeds U	D	1-1	0-1	12	Gallen [85]	18,182
43	19	A	Burnley	L	0-2	0-1	—		10,396
44	23	A	Wigan Ath	D	0-0	0-0	13		12,007
45	30	H	Nottingham F	W	2-1	1-0	11	Curtis (og) [45], Bircham [51]	17,834
46	May 8	A	Cardiff C	L	0-1	0-1	11		15,722

Final League Position: 11

GOALSCORERS

League (54): Furlong 18, Gallen 10 (1 pen), Santos 5, Cureton 4, Shittu 4, Rowlands 3, Ainsworth 2, Cook 2, Rose 2, Bean 1, Bircham 1, McLeod 1, own goal 1.
Carling Cup (4): Cureton 1, Gallen 1, McLeod 1, Rowlands 1.
FA Cup (0).

Day C 30	Bignot M 41 + 2	Padula G 28 + 5	Johnson R 6	Rose M 24 + 4	Gnohere A 3	Ainsworth G 14 + 8	Bean M 13 + 7	Furlong P 39 + 1	Gallen K 46	Rowlands M 31 + 4	Santos G 39 + 4	McLeod K 4 + 20	Thorpe T 4 + 6	Cook L 38 + 4	Forbes T 2 + 1	Cureton J 18 + 12	Bircham M 32 + 3	Edghill R 13 + 7	Shittu D 33 + 1	Branco S 3 + 4	Donnelly S — + 2	Simek F 5	Miller A 9 + 5	Best L 2 + 3	Royce S 13	Davies A 9	Sturridge D — + 2	Baidoo S 2 + 2	Bailey S 1 + 1	Hamilton L — + 1	Townsend L — + 2	Kanyuka P 1	Mulholland S — + 1	Rossi G 3	Brown A — + 1	Match No.
1	2^{1}	3	4	5	6	7	8^{2}	9	10	11^{3}	12	13	14																							1
1	2	3	4	7	6		12	13	9	8^{3}	5^{2}	11^{1}	10	14																						2
1	2^{3}	3	4^{1}	5	6	7^{2}	8	9	10	11	12			13	14																					3
1	2^{2}	3	4	5^{1}			8	9	10	7	12	13		11^{3}	6	14																				4
1	2	3	4^{2}				8	9	10	7	5			11^{1}	6^{3}	12	13	14																		5
1	2	3	4^{3}	12			8^{2}		10	7	6	13		11		9	14	5^{1}																		6
1	2	3		5			8	9	10	7^{2}	6	12		11^{1}		13	4																			7
1	2	3		5			8	9	10	7	6			11			4																			8
1	2	3^{2}		5				9	10	7^{1}	6	12		11^{3}		8	4	13	14																	9
1	2			3				9	10	7^{1}	6	12		11^{2}		8	4		5	13																10
1	2			12				9	10	7	6^{1}	13		11^{3}		8^{2}	4	3	5	14																11
1	2			3			12	9	10	7^{1}	6	13		11^{3}		8	4^{2}		5	14																12
1	2	12		3				9	10	7	6	13		11		8^{2}	4^{3}		5^{1}	14																13
1	2	3^{1}						9	10	8	6	7		11			4				12	5														14
1	2			3			8^{2}		10	9	6	12		11			4			7	13	5^{1}														15
1	2	12		3^{1}			13	9	10	8^{2}	6	14		11			4			7^{3}		5														16
1	2	3^{1}		4				9	10		6	12	13	11			8			7^{2}		5														17
1		12		3		13		9	10		6	14	7^{2}	11^{3}		8	4		2			5^{1}														18
1	2	12		3		7^{2}	4	9	10		6	13		11^{1}		8			5																	19
1	2	12		3^{1}		7	13	9	10		6	11^{3}		14		8^{2}	4		5																	20
1	2	3				7	12	9	10		6	13		11^{2}		8^{1}	4		5																	21
1	2	3				7^{2}	4	9	10		6	12		11^{1}		13			5				8													22
1	2	3				7^{3}	4^{2}	9	10	13	6	12				14	8^{1}		5				11													23
1	2	3^{3}				12		9	10	7^{2}	6			13		8■	4		5				11^{1}	14												24
1	2	3^{2}				12		9	10	4	6■			11^{1}			8	13	5				7^{3}	14												25
1	2	3^{2}				12		9	10	7		13		11^{1}			4^{3}	6	5				14	8												26
1	2					7	8	9■	10	11	6	12						3	5					4^{1}												27
1	2							9	10^{2}	7	6	11				12	4	3	5				8^{1}	13												28
		3		12		7	13	9	10		6	14		11^{3}		8^{2}		2	5						1	4^{1}										29
	12	3^{1}				7^{2}		9	10	13	6		14	11		8^{3}		2	5						1	4										30
		3		14		7^{1}		9	10	12	6		13^{3}	11		8^{2}		2	5						1	4										31
	12	3				7		9	10	13	6			11^{2}		8^{3}	14	2^{1}	5						1	4										32
	2			4		12		9	10	7	6			11^{1}			8^{2}	3	5				13		1											33
	2			4^{2}		12		9	10	7	6			11^{1}			8	3	5				13		1											34
	2			4		12		9	10	7	6		13	11^{2}		14	8^{3}	3^{1}	5						1											35
	2			3^{1}		7		9^{3}	10	4	6		13	11^{2}			8	12	5				14		1											36
	2			3^{2}		12		9	10	7	6			11			8^{1}	13	5						1	4										37
	2			3		7^{2}		9	10	6	12			11^{3}		13	8^{1}		5						1	4	14									38
	2	3						9	10	7^{2}	6			11		14	8^{1}		5				12		1	4	13^{3}									39
	2			3				9^{1}	10		6			11		12	8		5				7^{2}		1	4		13								40
	2	3^{1}							10	9^{2}	6			11		12	8		5				7		1	4■			13							41
1	2	3		6^{1}				9^{2}	10					11		13	8	12	5				7■					14	4^{3}							42
1	2	3							10					11		9	7^{1}	6	5									4^{2}		13^{3}	14	8	12			43
	2	3					8		10		6			11^{3}		9		12	5				7^{1}					4^{2}			13			1	14	44
	2	3					12	9	10	4	6		8	11			7^{1}		5															1		45
	2	3							10	4	6		9	11		8	7		5															1		46

FA Cup

Third Round	Nottingham F	(h)	0-3

Carling Cup

First Round	Swansea C	(h)	3-0
Second Round	Aston Villa	(a)	1-3

READING FL Championship

FOUNDATION

Reading was formed as far back as 1871 at a public meeting held at the Bridge Street Rooms. They first entered the FA Cup as early as 1877 when they amalgamated with the Reading Hornets. The club was further strengthened in 1889 when Earley FC joined them. They were the first winners of the Berks and Bucks Cup in 1878–79.

Madejski Stadium, Junction 11, M4, Reading, Berks RG2 0FL.

Telephone: (0118) 968 1100.

Fax: (0118) 968 1101.

Ticket Office: (0118) 968 1000.

Website: www.readingfc.co.uk

Email: comments@readingfc.co.uk

Ground Capacity: 24,200.

Record Attendance: 33,042 v Brentford, FA Cup 5th rd, 19 February 1927.

Pitch Measurements: 102m × 68m.

Chairman: John Madejski OBE, DL.

Chief Executive: Nigel Howe.

Secretary: Sue Hewett.

Manager: Steve Coppell.

Assistant Manager: Kevin Dillon.

Physio: Jon Fearn MSC, MMACP, MCSP.

Colours: Royal blue and white hooped shirts, royal blue shorts, royal blue stockings.

Change Colours: All dark blue with silver trim.

Year Formed: 1871.

Turned Professional: 1895.

Ltd Co.: 1895.

Club Nickname: 'The Royals'.

Previous Grounds: 1871, Reading Recreation; Reading Cricket Ground; 1882, Coley Park; 1889, Caversham Cricket Ground; 1896, Elm Park; 1998, Madejski Stadium.

First Football League Game: 28 August 1920, Division 3, v Newport Co (a) W 1–0 – Crawford; Smith, Horler; Christie, Mavin, Getgood; Spence, Weston, Yarnell, Bailey (1), Andrews.

Record League Victory: 10–2 v Crystal Palace, Division 3 (S), 4 September 1946 – Groves; Glidden, Gulliver; McKenna, Ratcliffe, Young; Chitty, Maurice Edelston (3), McPhee (4), Barney (1), Deverell (2).

HONOURS

Football League: Division 1 – Runners-up 1994–95; Division 2 – Champions 1993–94; Runners-up 2001–02; Division 3 – Champions 1985–86; Division 3 (S) – Champions 1925–26; Runners-up 1931–32, 1934–35, 1948–49, 1951–52; Division 4 – Champions 1978–79.

FA Cup: Semi-final 1927.

Football League Cup: best season: 5th rd, 1996.

Simod Cup: Winners 1988.

SKY SPORTS FACT FILE

In 1946–47 Maurice Edelston scored hat-tricks in each of two consecutive matches for Reading against Crystal Palace and Southend United. He entered the record books as the only amateur to achieve this feat.

Record Cup Victory: 6–0 v Leyton, FA Cup 2nd rd, 12 December 1925 – Duckworth; Eggo, McConnell; Wilson, Messer, Evans; Smith (2), Braithwaite (1), Davey (1), Tinsley, Robson (2).

Record Defeat: 0–18 v Preston NE, FA Cup 1st rd, 1893–94.

Most League Points (2 for a win): 65, Division 4, 1978–79.

Most League Points (3 for a win): 94, Division 3, 1985–86.

Most League Goals: 112, Division 3 (S), 1951–52.

Highest League Scorer in Season: Ronnie Blackman, 39, Division 3 (S), 1951–52.

Most League Goals in Total Aggregate: Ronnie Blackman, 158, 1947–54.

Most League Goals in One Match: 6, Arthur Bacon v Stoke C, Division 2, 3 April 1931.

Most Capped Player: Jimmy Quinn, 17 (46), Northern Ireland.

Most League Appearances: Martin Hicks, 500, 1978–91.

Youngest League Player: Peter Castle, 16 years 49 days v Watford, 30 April 2003.

Record Transfer Fee Received: £1,575,000 from Newcastle U for Shaka Hislop, August 1995.

Record Transfer Fee Paid: £800,000 to Brentford for Carl Asaba, August 1997.

Football League Record: 1920 Original Member of Division 3; 1921–26 Division 3 (S); 1926–31 Division 2; 1931–58 Division 3 (S); 1958–71 Division 3; 1971–76 Division 4; 1976–77 Division 3; 1977–79 Division 4; 1979–83 Division 3; 1983–84 Division 4; 1984–86 Division 3; 1986–88 Division 2; 1988–92 Division 3; 1992–94 Division 2; 1994–98 Division 1; 1998–2002 Division 2; 2002–04 Division 1; 2004– FLC.

MANAGERS

Thomas Sefton 1897–1901
(Secretary-Manager)
James Sharp 1901–02
Harry Matthews 1902–20
Harry Marshall 1920–22
Arthur Chadwick 1923–25
H. S. Bray 1925–26
(Secretary only since 1922 and 1926–35)
Andrew Wylie 1926–31
Joe Smith 1931–35
Billy Butler 1935–39
John Cochrane 1939
Joe Edelston 1939–47
Ted Drake 1947–52
Jack Smith 1952–55
Harry Johnston 1955–63
Roy Bentley 1963–69
Jack Mansell 1969–71
Charlie Hurley 1972–77
Maurice Evans 1977–84
Ian Branfoot 1984–89
Ian Porterfield 1989–91
Mark McGhee 1991–94
Jimmy Quinn/Mick Gooding 1994–97
Terry Bullivant 1997–98
Tommy Burns 1998–99
Alan Pardew 1999–2003
Steve Coppell October 2003–

LATEST SEQUENCES

Longest Sequence of League Wins: 13, 17.8.1985 – 19.10.1985.

Longest Sequence of League Defeats: 7, 10.4.1998 – 15.8.1998.

Longest Sequence of League Draws: 6, 23.3.2002 – 20.4.02.

Longest Sequence of Unbeaten League Matches: 19, 21.4.1973 – 27.10.1973.

Longest Sequence Without a League Win: 14, 30.4.1927 – 29.10.1927.

Successive Scoring Runs: 32 from 1.10.1932.

Successive Non-scoring Runs: 6 from 13.4.1925.

TEN YEAR LEAGUE RECORD

		P	*W*	*D*	*L*	*F*	*A*	*Pts*	*Pos*
1995-96	Div 1	46	13	17	16	54	63	56	19
1996-97	Div 1	46	15	12	19	58	67	57	18
1997-98	Div 1	46	11	9	26	39	78	42	24
1998-99	Div 2	46	16	13	17	54	63	61	11
1999-2000	Div 2	46	16	14	16	57	63	62	10
2000-01	Div 2	46	25	11	10	86	52	86	3
2001-02	Div 2	46	23	15	8	70	43	84	2
2002-03	Div 1	46	25	4	17	61	46	79	4
2003-04	Div 1	46	20	10	16	55	57	70	9
2004-05	FL C	46	19	13	14	51	44	70	7

DID YOU KNOW?

When Andy Proudlove, a 16 year old apprentice, made his first class debut for Reading against Bridgwater in a 3–0 FA Cup win for Reading in November 1971 his record lasted only a few months before it was beaten by Steve Hetzke at 16 years 184 days.

READING 2004–05 LEAGUE RECORD

Match No.	Date	Venue	Opponents	Result		H/T Score	Lg. Pos.	Goalscorers	Attendance
1	Aug 7	H	Brighton & HA	W	3-2	2-1	—	Kitson [2], Harper [41], Forster [59]	15,641
2	10	A	West Ham U	L	0-1	0-0	—		26,242
3	14	A	Sheffield U	W	1-0	1-0	4	Harper [41]	22,429
4	21	H	Rotherham U	W	1-0	1-0	3	Kitson (pen) [45]	11,404
5	28	A	Millwall	L	0-1	0-0	8		12,098
6	31	H	Sunderland	W	1-0	1-0	—	Forster [2]	15,792
7	Sept 11	A	Derby Co	L	1-2	0-0	6	Shorey [88]	22,096
8	14	H	Preston NE	W	3-1	2-1	—	Kitson [11], Forster 2 [34, 85]	11,857
9	18	H	Gillingham	W	3-1	3-0	2	Kitson 3 (2 pens) [1, 16 (p), 28 (p)]	13,867
10	25	A	Watford	W	1-0	0-0	1	Sidwell [65]	13,389
11	28	A	Ipswich T	D	1-1	1-1	—	Kitson [26]	23,167
12	Oct 2	H	Burnley	D	0-0	0-0	3		15,400
13	16	A	Stoke C	W	1-0	1-0	2	Shorey [41]	15,574
14	19	H	Leeds U	D	1-1	1-1	—	Owusu [45]	22,230
15	23	H	Crewe Alex	W	4-0	3-0	2	Sidwell [21], Kitson [25], Owusu [45], Ingimarsson [47]	13,630
16	30	A	Coventry C	L	2-3	1-1	3	Owusu [11], Kitson [71]	13,663
17	Nov 2	A	Plymouth Arg	D	2-2	0-2	—	Coughlan (og) [51], Kitson [90]	14,336
18	6	H	Stoke C	W	1-0	1-0	3	Kitson [23]	14,831
19	13	H	Cardiff C	W	2-1	2-0	3	Morgan [13], Kitson [39]	16,107
20	20	A	Nottingham F	L	0-1	0-1	4		21,138
21	27	H	Wigan Ath	D	1-1	1-1	4	Owusu [42]	22,114
22	Dec 4	A	Wolverhampton W	L	1-4	0-2	4	Morgan [47]	25,572
23	11	A	Leicester C	W	2-0	0-0	4	Sidwell [68], Ingimarsson [82]	24,068
24	18	H	QPR	W	1-0	0-0	4	Shorey [64]	20,272
25	26	H	Watford	W	3-0	1-0	3	Sonko [3], Sidwell [76], Owusu [88]	18,757
26	28	A	Preston NE	L	0-3	0-2	4		12,795
27	Jan 1	A	Gillingham	D	0-0	0-0	4		8570
28	3	H	Derby Co	L	0-1	0-1	4		15,491
29	15	A	Burnley	D	0-0	0-0	4		11,392
30	22	H	Ipswich T	D	1-1	0-0	4	Ingimarsson [90]	23,203
31	Feb 5	H	Plymouth Arg	D	0-0	0-0	4		19,783
32	12	A	Leeds U	L	1-3	0-1	5	Owusu [89]	30,034
33	19	H	Coventry C	L	1-2	1-0	7	Ferdinand [8]	15,904
34	22	A	Crewe Alex	D	1-1	0-1	—	Kitson [70]	5703
35	26	H	Leicester C	D	0-0	0-0	7		14,651
36	Mar 5	A	QPR	D	0-0	0-0	6		16,971
37	12	H	West Ham U	W	3-1	2-0	6	Kitson 3 [13, 27, 57]	22,268
38	15	A	Rotherham U	L	0-1	0-0	—		3804
39	21	A	Brighton & HA	W	1-0	0-0	—	Forster [64]	6108
40	Apr 2	H	Sheffield U	D	0-0	0-0	5		18,899
41	5	H	Millwall	W	2-1	0-1	—	Kitson [73], Forster [83]	14,379
42	9	A	Sunderland	W	2-1	0-0	6	Kitson 2 (1 pen) [76, 82 (p)]	34,237
43	16	H	Nottingham F	W	1-0	0-0	6	Harper [74]	17,905
44	23	A	Cardiff C	L	0-2	0-2	7		14,821
45	30	H	Wolverhampton W	L	1-2	1-0	7	Forster [8]	20,495
46	May 8	A	Wigan Ath	L	1-3	0-2	7	Sidwell [90]	19,662

Final League Position: 7

GOALSCORERS

League (51): Kitson 19 (4 pens), Forster 7, Owusu 6, Sidwell 5, Harper 3, Ingimarsson 3, Shorey 3, Morgan 2, Ferdinand 1, Sonko 1, own goal 1.
Carling Cup (2): Goater 1, Hughes 1.
FA Cup (3): Forster 2, Ingimarsson 1.

Hahnemann M 46	Murty G 41	Shorey N 44	Ingimarsson I 43 + 1	Williams A 11	Harper J 39 + 2	Little G 29 + 6	Sidwell S 44	Kitson D 37	Forster N 27 + 3	Hughes A 40 + 1	Newman R 11 + 6	Convey B 4 + 14	Goater S 2 + 7	Brooker P 22 + 9	Sonko I 35 + 4	Owusu L 14 + 11	Morgan D 10 + 8	Ferdinand L 4 + 8	Keown M 3 + 2	*Match No.*
1	2[1]	3	4	5	6	7	8	9	10	11	12									1
1	2	3	4	5	6	7[1]	8	9	10	11[2]		12	13							2
1	2	3	4	5	6		8	9	10	11		7[1]		12						3
1	2	3	4	5	6		8	9	10[1]	11		7	12							4
1	2[3]	3	4	5	6	7[1]	8	9[2]	10	11		12	13		14					5
1	2	3	4	5	6		8	9[2]	10[1]	11				7	12	13				6
1	2	3	4	5	6		8	9	10	11[1]		12	13	7[2]						7
1	2	3	4	5	6		8	9	10	11[1]		12		7						8
1	2	3	4	5	6		8	9	10[1]	11			12	7						9
1	2	3	4	5	6		8	9[1]	10	11				7	12					10
1	2	3	4	5[2]	6		8	9	10	11		12		7[1]	13					11
1	2	3	4		6	12	8	9	10[3]	11[1]		13	14	7[2]	5					12
1	2	3	4		6	7[1]		9[2]		11	14	12	10[3]	8	5	13				13
1	2	3	4		6	7[1]	8	9		11		12	10[2]		5	13				14
1	2	3	4		6	7[1]	8	9[3]		11[2]		12		13	5	10	14			15
1	2	3	4		6	7	8	9				12		11[1]	5	10				16
1	2	3	4		6	7	8	9				11[1]			5	10	12			17
1	2	3	4		6	7	8	9						12	5	10	11[1]			18
1	2	3	4		6		8	9[2]		11[1]	13	12		14	5	10	7[3]			19
1	2	3	4		6	12	8	9[2]		11				13	5	10[1]	7			20
1	2	3	4		6	7	8			11					5	9	10			21
1	2[2]	3	4		6	7	8	9[3]		11[1]	13	12			5	14	10			22
1		3	4		6	7	8	9		2				11	5	12	10[1]			23
1		3	4		6	7	8	9[2]	12	2				11	5	13	10[1]			24
1		3	4		6[2]	7[1]	8		10	2	13	12		11	5	9				25
1		3	4		6	7	8[2]		10	2	13	12	14	11[1]	5	9[3]				26
1	2	3	4		6	7	8		10[1]	11					5	9	12			27
1	2	3	4		6	7	8		10	11[1]					5	9	12			28
1	2	3	4		6	7	8		10	11		9			5					29
1	2	3	4		6	7			10	11	8				5	9[1]	12			30
1	2	3	4		6	7	8[1]		10[2]	11				12	5	13		9[3]	14	31
1	2	3	4		6[1]	7[2]	8		10	11				12	5	14	13	9[3]		32
1	2	3	4		6	7[2]	8	9	12	11					5		13	10[1]		33
1	2	3	4		6[1]	12	8	9		11				7	5	10				34
1	2	3	4			12	8	9		11	6			7[1]	5	10[2]		13		35
1		3	4			7	8	9		2	6			11	5		12	10[1]		36
1	2	3	4		12	7[1]	8	9		11	6[3]			14	5	13	10[2]			37
1	2	3	4			7	8	9		11	6				5	12	10[1]			38
1	2	3	4			7	8	9	12	11	6				5		10[1]			39
1	2	3	4				8	9	10[1]	11	6			7	5			12		40
1	2	3	4		12	7[3]	8	9	10	11[2]	6[1]			13	5			14		41
1	2	3	4[2]		6		8	9	10		7[1]			11	5			12	13	42
1	2	3			6	12	8	9[2]	10	13	7[1]			11[3]	5			14	4	43
1	2	3			6	12	8	9	10		7[2]			11[1]	5			13	4	44
1	2		12		6	7[2]	8	9	10	3				11[1]	5			13	4	45
1	2		4		6	7[1]	8	9	10	3				11[2]	5	12		13		46

FA Cup

Third Round	Swansea C	(h)	1-1
		(a)	1-0
Fourth Round	Leicester C	(h)	1-2

Carling Cup

First Round	Oxford U	(a)	2-0
Second Round	Watford	(h)	0-3

ROCHDALE FL Championship 2

FOUNDATION

Considering the love of rugby in their area, it is not surprising that Rochdale had difficulty in establishing an Association Football club. The earlier Rochdale Town club formed in 1900 went out of existence in 1907 when the present club was immediately established and joined the Manchester League, before graduating to the Lancashire Combination in 1908.

Spotland Stadium, Sandy Lane, Rochdale OL11 5DS.

Telephone: (01706) 644 648.

Fax: (01706) 648 466.

Ticket Office: (01706) 644 648.

Website: www.rochdaleafc.co.uk

Email: office@rochdaleafc.co.uk

Ground Capacity: 10,200.

Record Attendance: 24,231 v Notts Co, FA Cup 2nd rd, 10 December 1949.

Pitch Measurements: 114yd × 76yd.

Chairman: D. F. Kilpatrick.

Secretary: Hilary Molyneux Dearden.

Manager: Steve Parkin.

Assistant Manager: Tony Ford

Physio: Andy Thorpe.

Colours: Blue.

Change Colours: Yellow.

Year Formed: 1907.

Turned Professional: 1907.

Ltd Co.: 1910.

Club Nickname: 'The Dale'.

First Football League Game: 27 August 1921, Division 3 (N), v Accrington Stanley (h) W 6–3 – Crabtree; Nuttall, Sheehan; Hill, Farrer, Yarwood; Hoad, Sandiford, Dennison (2), Owens (3), Carney (1).

Record League Victory: 8–1 v Chesterfield, Division 3 (N), 18 December 1926 – Hill; Brown, Ward; Hillhouse, Parkes, Braidwood; Hughes, Bertram, Whitehurst (5), Schofield (2), Martin (1).

Record Cup Victory: 8–2 v Crook T, FA Cup 1st rd, 26 November 1927 – Moody; Hopkins, Ward; Braidwood, Parkes, Barker; Tompkinson, Clennell (3) Whitehurst (4), Hall, Martin (1).

HONOURS

Football League: Division 3 best season: 9th, 1969–70; Division 3 (N) – Runners-up 1923–24, 1926–27.

FA Cup: best season: 5th rd, 1990, 2003.

Football League Cup: Runners-up 1962 (record for 4th Division club).

SKY SPORTS FACT FILE

Promotion from the Fourth Division in 1968–69 for Rochdale came after a bizarre first half of the season in which they failed to score in 12 of 22 games, though seven of them were goalless draws. The defence was outstanding having conceded just 35 goals overall.

Record Defeat: 1–9 v Tranmere R, Division 3 (N), 25 December 1931.

Most League Points (2 for a win): 62, Division 3 (N), 1923–24.

Most League Points (3 for a win): 78, Division 3, 2001–02.

Most League Goals: 105, Division 3 (N), 1926–27.

Highest League Scorer in Season: Albert Whitehurst, 44, Division 3 (N), 1926–27.

Most League Goals in Total Aggregate: Reg Jenkins, 119, 1964–73.

Most League Goals in One Match: 6, Tommy Tippett v Hartlepools U, Division 3N, 21 April 1930.

Most Capped Player: Leo Bertos, 6 (7), New Zealand.

Most League Appearances: Graham Smith, 317, 1966–74.

Youngest League Player: Zac Hughes, 16 years 105 days v Exeter C, 19 September 1987.

Record Transfer Fee Received: £400,000 from West Ham U for Stephen Bywater, August 1998.

Record Transfer Fee Paid: £150,000 to Stoke C for Paul Connor, March 2001.

Football League Record: 1921 Elected to Division 3 (N); 1958–59 Division 3; 1959–69 Division 4; 1969–74 Division 3; 1974–92 Division 4; 1992–2004 Division 3; 2004– FL2.

MANAGERS

Billy Bradshaw 1920
Run by committee 1920–22
Tom Wilson 1922–23
Jack Peart 1923–30
Will Cameron 1930–31
Herbert Hopkinson 1932–34
Billy Smith 1934–35
Ernest Nixon 1935–37
Sam Jennings 1937–38
Ted Goodier 1938–52
Jack Warner 1952–53
Harry Catterick 1953–58
Jack Marshall 1958–60
Tony Collins 1960–68
Bob Stokoe 1967–68
Len Richley 1968–70
Dick Conner 1970–73
Walter Joyce 1973–76
Brian Green 1976–77
Mike Ferguson 1977–78
Doug Collins 1979
Bob Stokoe 1979–80
Peter Madden 1980–83
Jimmy Greenhoff 1983–84
Vic Halom 1984–86
Eddie Gray 1986–88
Danny Bergara 1988–89
Terry Dolan 1989–91
Dave Sutton 1991–94
Mick Docherty 1995–96
Graham Barrow 1996–99
Steve Parkin 1999–2001
John Hollins 2001–02
Paul Simpson 2002–03
Alan Buckley 2003–04
Steve Parkin January 2004–

LATEST SEQUENCES

Longest Sequence of League Wins: 8, 29.9.1969 – 3.11.1969.

Longest Sequence of League Defeats: 17, 14.11.1931 – 12.3.1932.

Longest Sequence of League Draws: 6, 17.8.1968 – 14.9.1968.

Longest Sequence of Unbeaten League Matches: 20, 15.9.1923 – 19.1.1924.

Longest Sequence Without a League Win: 28, 14.11.1931 – 29.8.1932.

Successive Scoring Runs: 29 from 8.1.1927.

Successive Non-scoring Runs: 9 from 14.3.1980.

TEN YEAR LEAGUE RECORD

		P	*W*	*D*	*L*	*F*	*A*	*Pts*	*Pos*
1995-96	Div 3	46	14	13	19	57	61	55	15
1996-97	Div 3	46	14	16	16	58	58	58	14
1997-98	Div 3	46	17	7	22	56	55	58	18
1998-99	Div 3	46	13	15	18	42	55	54	19
1999-2000	Div 3	46	18	14	14	57	54	68	10
2000-01	Div 3	46	18	17	11	59	48	71	8
2001-02	Div 3	46	21	15	10	65	52	78	5
2002-03	Div 3	46	12	16	18	63	70	52	19
2003-04	Div 3	46	12	14	20	49	58	50	21
2004-05	FL 2	46	16	18	12	54	48	66	9

DID YOU KNOW ?

Jim Dailey was already a seasoned traveller in the Football League with Sheffield Wednesday, Birmingham City, Exeter City and Workington when he joined Rochdale in October 1957. The following month he scored five against Hartlepools United.

ROCHDALE 2004–05 LEAGUE RECORD

Match No.	Date	Venue	Opponents	Result		H/T Score	Lg. Pos.	Goalscorers	Attendance
1	Aug 7	A	Scunthorpe U	L	1-3	1-0	—	Bertos (pen) [45]	4409
2	10	H	Swansea C	L	0-2	0-1	—		2514
3	14	H	Southend U	W	2-0	1-0	20	Jones 2 (1 pen) [3, 60 (p)]	2218
4	21	A	Wycombe W	W	3-0	0-0	8	Holt [70], Jones (pen) [89], McGivern [90]	4440
5	28	H	Bury	L	0-3	0-1	16		3912
6	30	A	Leyton Orient	L	1-2	0-1	18	Holt [70]	3243
7	Sept 4	A	Grimsby T	W	1-0	0-0	13	Holt [80]	4795
8	11	H	Darlington	D	1-1	1-0	13	Holt [30]	2616
9	18	A	Mansfield T	L	0-1	0-0	16		4266
10	25	H	Notts Co	L	0-3	0-1	20		2370
11	Oct 2	A	Rushden & D	D	0-0	0-0	19		2619
12	8	H	Yeovil T	W	2-1	0-0	—	Holt [68], Jones [82]	2402
13	16	H	Cheltenham T	L	1-2	0-0	20	Jones (pen) [88]	2778
14	19	A	Lincoln C	D	1-1	0-0	—	Clarke [86]	3274
15	23	A	Northampton T	L	1-5	0-3	21	Griffiths [77]	5342
16	30	H	Macclesfield T	W	3-0	1-0	20	Holt [42], Cooksey [55], Jones [67]	2704
17	Nov 6	H	Cambridge U	W	2-1	1-0	18	Holt 2 [31, 83]	2353
18	20	A	Oxford U	W	1-0	0-0	16	Tardif (og) [90]	4204
19	27	H	Boston U	W	2-0	0-0	13	Bertos [62], Cooksey [84]	2474
20	Dec 7	A	Shrewsbury T	W	2-0	0-0	—	Tait [53], Holt [66]	3677
21	11	A	Kidderminster H	L	1-2	1-1	11	Holt [36]	2337
22	18	H	Bristol R	D	0-0	0-0	13		2623
23	26	A	Darlington	W	3-0	1-0	7	Atieno [18], Holt 2 [62, 78]	7028
24	28	H	Chester C	D	2-2	0-1	7	Bertos [58], Atieno [64]	3724
25	Jan 3	A	Notts Co	D	0-0	0-0	11		5258
26	15	H	Mansfield T	D	1-1	1-1	12	Tait [4]	2576
27	22	A	Chester C	D	0-0	0-0	12		2985
28	25	A	Yeovil T	D	2-2	1-0	—	Goodall [8], Bertos [77]	5180
29	29	H	Rushden & D	W	2-0	0-0	9	Cooksey [56], Holt [82]	2664
30	Feb 5	A	Cheltenham T	L	0-2	0-1	11		2951
31	12	H	Lincoln C	W	3-1	1-1	11	Holt [7], Heald [59], Goodall [74]	2847
32	19	A	Macclesfield T	L	0-3	0-2	13		3031
33	26	H	Kidderminster H	D	1-1	1-1	15	Lambert [40]	2385
34	Mar 1	H	Grimsby T	W	2-0	1-0	—	Lambert [27], Jones [90]	2312
35	5	A	Bristol R	D	0-0	0-0	11		5464
36	8	H	Northampton T	W	1-0	0-0	—	Lambert [56]	2107
37	12	A	Swansea C	D	2-2	1-0	10	Holt [31], Lambert [90]	6804
38	19	H	Scunthorpe U	D	0-0	0-0	10		3605
39	25	A	Southend U	L	0-3	0-1	—		7656
40	28	H	Wycombe W	D	1-1	1-0	10	Jones (pen) [16]	2707
41	Apr 2	A	Bury	D	0-0	0-0	10		4606
42	9	H	Leyton Orient	W	2-0	0-0	10	Richards 2 [47, 59]	2255
43	16	H	Shrewsbury T	D	1-1	1-1	10	Lambert [40]	3142
44	23	A	Cambridge U	D	0-0	0-0	10		3738
45	30	H	Oxford U	W	5-1	4-0	10	Heald [3], Cooksey [11], Holt 2 [14, 69], Lambert [25]	2579
46	May 7	A	Boston U	D	1-1	0-0	9	Cooksey [50]	2528

Final League Position: 9

GOALSCORERS

League (54): Holt 17, Jones 8 (4 pens), Lambert 6, Cooksey 5, Bertos 4 (1 pen), Atieno 2, Goodall 2, Heald 2, Richards 2, Tait 2, Clarke 1, Griffiths 1, McGivern 1, own goal 1.
Carling Cup (2): Holt 1, Tait 1.
FA Cup (5): Holt 5.
LDV Vans Trophy (4): Griffiths 3 (1 pen), Holt 1.

Edwards N 16	Evans W 40	Goodall A 27 + 7	Brisco N 6 + 5	Burgess D 19 + 2	Heald G 29	Probets A 4 + 5	Warner S 25 + 3	Tait P 27 + 9	Holt G 40	Bertos L 33 + 9	McCourt P 3 + 3	McGivern L 2 + 23	Griffiths G 36 + 3	Clarke J 32 + 9	Townson K 1	Jones G 39	Gallimore T 32 + 2	Cash B 6	Cooksey E 27 + 7	Weller P 5	Atieno T 6 + 7	Gilks M 30	Richardson M 1 + 1	Lambert R 15	Richards M 4 + 1	Brown G 1	Williams M — + 1	Kitchen B — + 1	*Match No.*
1	2	3	4	5	6	7^{1}	8	9	10^{2}	11	12	13																	1
1	2	3	4	5^{2}	6		8^{3}		10	7	11	12	13	14	9^{1}														2
1	2	3	12	5	6	13		9^{3}	10	7■	11^{2}	14		4		8^{1}													3
1	2			5	6	11^{2}		9^{1}	10		13	12		4		8	3	7											4
1	2	12		5	6^{3}			9	10		11^{2}	13	14	4		8	3^{1}	7											5
1	2		12	5		11^{2}		9^{3}	10	13		14	6	4		8^{1}	3	7											6
1	2	12	4	5				13	10^{2}	11			6	8		9	3	7^{1}											7
1	2		4	5		12		13	10^{2}	11^{1}		14	6	8^{3}		9	3	7											8
1	2^{1}	3	4	5^{2}				12	10	13		14	6	8		9		7^{3}	11										9
1	2		4^{1}			12		9	10	7^{2}		13	6	5		8	3		11										10
1	2		12				8^{1}	13	10^{2}	7			6	5		9	3		11	4									11
1	2			5			8	12	10	7			6^{2}	13		9	3		11^{1}	4									12
1	2			5	6	12	8^{1}	9^{2}		7		13				10	3		11	4									13
1	2			5	6	12	4^{1}		10	13		8^{3}		14		9	3		11^{2}	7									14
1	2			5■	6	11	4^{1}		10	12		8^{2}	13			9	3			7^{3}	14								15
1	2	3		5				9	10		12		6	4		8			11		7^{1}								16
	2	3		5■			12	9^{2}	10	13			6	4		8			11		7^{1}	1							17
	2	3						9	10	12			6	4		8	5		11		7^{1}	1							18
	2				5			9^{2}	10^{1}	7		12	6	4		8	3		11		13	1							19
	2				6		8	9	10^{1}	7			5	4			3		11		12	1							20
	2	12			6		8^{2}	9^{3}	10	7		13	5	4			3^{1}		11		14	1							21
	2	12		5	6		8	9^{2}	10	7				4		11	3^{1}				13	1							22
	2	3			6				10	7		12	5	4		8			11		9^{1}	1							23
	2	3			6				10	7			5	4		8			11		9	1							24
	2	3		12	6			9^{2}	10	7			5■	4^{1}		8			11■		13	1							25
	2	3		5	6			9	10	7^{2}		12		4		8			11^{1}		13	1							26
	2	3			6		8	9		7		13	5	12		4			11^{1}		10^{2}	1							27
	2	11^{1}		13	6		8^{3}	9		7		12	5^{2}	4		10	3		14			1							28
	2	3			6		8	9	10	7			5	4					11			1							29
	2■	3			6		8	9^{1}	10	7		12	5	4			13		11^{2}			1							30
		12		2	6		8	9^{1}	10	7			5	4			3		11■			1							31
				2	6		8	12	10^{1}	11			5	4^{2}		7	3					1	13	9					32
	2	12			6		8^{2}	13	10^{3}	14			5			4	3		11^{1}			1	7	9					33
	2■	3			6^{2}		8^{1}	9^{3}	10	11			5	12		4	13		14			1		7					34
		3					8	9	10	7^{1}		12	5	2		4	6					1		11					35
		3					8	9	10	7			5	2		4	6		12			1		11^{1}					36
		3	12				8^{3}	9■	10	7^{2}		13	5	2		4	6^{1}		14			1		11					37
	2	3					8^{2}		10	7		12	5	4^{1}		9	6		13			1		11					38
	2	3	12						10^{2}	7			5	13		4^{1}	6		11			1		8	9				39
	2	3^{1}					8		10	11^{2}		12	5	14		4	6		13			1		7	9^{3}				40
	2	12			6		8^{3}	9	10	13			5			4	3		14			1		7^{2}	11^{1}				41
	2	8^{1}			6		12	9^{3}		7			5^{2}	13		4	3		11			1		10	14				42
	2	8^{1}			6					7^{2}		12	5	13		4	3		11			1		10	9				43
	2	8^{2}			6			12		7		13	5	4		10	3		11^{1}			1		9					44
	2	8^{2}			6		12		10	13			5	4		7^{1}	3		11			1		9					45
		3					8^{3}	12	10^{1}				5	4		7	6		11			1		9		2^{2}	13	14	46

FA Cup

First Round	Oxford U	(h)	2-1
Second Round	Stevenage B	(a)	2-0
Third Round	Charlton Ath	(a)	1-4

Carling Cup

First Round	Wolverhampton W	(h)	2-4

LDV Vans Trophy

First Round	Scarborough	(h)	4-1
Second Round	Chester C	(a)	0-1

ROTHERHAM UNITED FL Championship 1

FOUNDATION

Rotherham were formed in 1870 before becoming Town in the late 1880s. Thornhill United were founded in 1877 and changed their name to Rotherham County in 1905. The Town amalgamated with Rotherham County to form Rotherham United in 1925.

Millmoor Ground, Rotherham S60 1HR.
Telephone: (01709) 512 434.
Fax: (01709) 512 762.
Ticket Office: 0870 443 1884.
Website: www.themillers.co.uk
Email: office@rotherhamunited.net
Ground Capacity: 9,624.
Record Attendance: 25,170 v Sheffield U, Division 2, 13 December 1952.
Pitch Measurements. 115yd × 70yd.
Chairman: Peter Ruchniewicz.
Vice-chairman: David Veal.
Chief Executive: Phil Henson.
Manager: Mick Harford.
Assistant Manager: Alan Knill.
Physio: Denis Circuit.
Colours: Red shirts with white sleeves, white shorts with red stripe, red stockings.

HONOURS

Football League: Division 2 – runners-up 2000–01; Division 3 – Champions 1980–81; Runners-up 1999–2000; Division 3 (N) – Champions 1950–51; Runners-up 1946–47, 1947–48, 1948–49; Division 4 – Champions 1988–89; Runners-up 1991–92.

FA Cup: best season: 5th rd, 1953, 1968.

Football League Cup: Runners-up 1961.

Auto Windscreens Shield: Winners 1996.

Change Colours: Black shirts with white stripe, black shorts, black stockings.
Year Formed: 1870.
Turned Professional: 1905.
Ltd Co.: 1920.
Club Nickname: 'The Merry Millers'.
Previous Names: 1877, Thornhill United; 1905, Rotherham County; 1925, amalgamated with Rotherham Town under Rotherham United.
Previous Ground: 1870, Red House Ground; 1907, Millmoor.
First Football League Game: 2 September 1893, Division 2, Rotherham T v Lincoln C (a) D 1–1 – McKay; Thickett, Watson; Barr, Brown, Broadhead; Longden, Cutts, Leatherbarrow, McCormick, Pickering, (1 og). 30 August 1919, Division 2, Rotherham Co v Nottingham F (h) W 2–0 – Branston; Alton, Baines; Bailey, Coe, Stanton; Lee (1), Cawley (1), Glennon, Lees, Lamb.
Record League Victory: 8–0 v Oldham Ath, Division 3 (N), 26 May 1947 – Warnes; Selkirk, Ibbotson; Edwards, Horace Williams, Danny Williams; Wilson (2), Shaw (1), Ardron (3), Guest (1), Hainsworth (1).
Record Cup Victory: 6–0 v Spennymoor U, FA Cup 2nd rd, 17 December 1977 – McAlister; Forrest, Breckin, Womble, Stancliffe, Green, Finney, Phillips (3), Gwyther (2) (Smith), Goodfellow, Crawford (1). 6–0 v Wolverhampton W, FA Cup 1st rd, 16 November 1985 – O'Hanlon; Forrest, Dungworth, Gooding (1), Smith (1), Pickering, Birch (2), Emerson, Tynan (1), Simmons (1), Pugh. 6–0 v Kings Lynn, FA Cup 2nd rd, 6 December 1997 – Mimms; Clark, Hurst (Goodwin), Garner (1) (Hudson) (1), Warner (Bass), Richardson (1), Berry (1), Thompson, Druce (1), Glover (1), Roscoe.

SKY SPORTS FACT FILE

With 18 goals in 35 games for Rotherham United, former Bevin Boy Stuart McLean was missed when he had to return to Glasgow for family reasons in October 1947. He carried on as a part-timer in Scotland and also won the World Award for Display Achievement.

Record Defeat: 1–11 v Bradford C, Division 3 (N), 25 August 1928.

Most League Points (2 for a win): 71, Division 3 (N), 1950–51.

Most League Points (3 for a win): 91, Division 2, 2000–01.

Most League Goals: 114, Division 3 (N), 1946–47.

Highest League Scorer in Season: Wally Ardron, 38, Division 3 (N), 1946–47.

Most League Goals in Total Aggregate: Gladstone Guest, 130, 1946–56.

Most League Goals in One Match: 4, Roland Bastow v York C, Division 3N, 9 November 1935; 4, Roland Bastow v Rochdale, Division 3N, 7 March 1936; 4, Wally Ardron v Crewe Alex, Division 3N, 5 October 1946; 4, Wally Ardron v Carlisle U, Division 3N, 13 September 1947; 4, Wally Ardron v Hartlepools U, Division 3N, 13 October 1948; 4, Ian Wilson v Liverpool, Division 2, 2 May 1955; 4, Carl Gilbert v Swansea C, Division 3, 28 September 1971; 4, Carl Airey v Chester, Division 3, 31 August 1987; 4, Shaun Goater v Hartlepool U, Division 3, 9 April 1994; 4, Lee Glover v Hull C, Division 3, 28 December 1997; 4, Darren Byfield v Millwall, Division 1, 10 August 2002.

Most Capped Player: Shaun Goater 14 (19), Bermuda.

Most League Appearances: Danny Williams, 459, 1946–62.

Youngest League Player: Kevin Eley, 16 years 72 days v Scunthorpe U, 15 May 1984.

Record Transfer Fee Received: £900,000 from Cardiff C for Alan Lee, August 2003.

Record Transfer Fee Paid: £150,000 to Millwall for Tony Towner, August 1980; £150,000 to Port Vale for Lee Glover, August 1996; £150,000 to Burnley for Alan Lee, September 2000; £150,000 to Reading for Martin Butler, September 2003.

Football League Record: 1893 Rotherham Town elected to Division 2; 1896 Failed re-election; 1919 Rotherham County elected to Division 2; 1923–51 Division 3 (N); 1951–68 Division 2; 1968–73 Division 3; 1973–75 Division 4; 1975–81 Division 3; 1981–83 Division 2; 1983–88 Division 3; 1988–89 Division 4; 1989–91 Division 3; 1991–92 Division 4; 1992–97 Division 2; 1997–2000 Division 3; 2000–01 Division 2; 2001–04 Division 1; 2004–05 FLC; 2005– FL1.

MANAGERS

Billy Heald 1925–29 *(Secretary only for long spell)*
Stanley Davies 1929–30
Billy Heald 1930–33
Reg Freeman 1934–52
Andy Smailes 1952–58
Tom Johnston 1958–62
Danny Williams 1962–65
Jack Mansell 1965–67
Tommy Docherty 1967–68
Jimmy McAnearney 1968–73
Jimmy McGuigan 1973–79
Ian Porterfield 1979–81
Emlyn Hughes 1981–83
George Kerr 1983–85
Norman Hunter 1985–87
Dave Cusack 1987–88
Billy McEwan 1988–91
Phil Henson 1991–94
Archie Gemmill/John McGovern 1994–96
Danny Bergara 1996–97
Ronnie Moore 1997–2005
Mick Harford April 2005–

LATEST SEQUENCES

Longest Sequence of League Wins: 9, 2.2.1982 – 6.3.1982.

Longest Sequence of League Defeats: 8, 7.4.1956 – 18.8.1956.

Longest Sequence of League Draws: 6, 13.10.1969 – 22.11.1969.

Longest Sequence of Unbeaten League Matches: 18, 13.10.1969 – 7.2.1970.

Longest Sequence Without a League Win: 21, 9.5.2004 – 20.11.2004.

Successive Scoring Runs: 30 from 3.4.1954.

Successive Non-scoring Runs: 6 from 21.8.2004.

TEN YEAR LEAGUE RECORD

		P	*W*	*D*	*L*	*F*	*A*	*Pts*	*Pos*
1995-96	Div 2	46	14	14	18	54	62	56	16
1996-97	Div 2	46	7	14	25	39	70	35	23
1997-98	Div 3	46	16	19	11	67	61	67	9
1998-99	Div 3	46	20	13	13	79	61	73	5
1999-2000	Div 3	46	24	12	10	72	36	84	2
2000-01	Div 2	46	27	10	9	79	55	91	2
2001-02	Div 1	46	10	19	17	52	66	49	21
2002-03	Div 1	46	15	14	17	62	62	59	15
2003-04	Div 1	46	13	15	18	53	61	54	17
2004-05	FL C	46	5	14	27	35	69	29	24

DID YOU KNOW ?

As champions of Division Three in 1980–81 Rotherham United scored almost twice as many goals as they conceded. Of the 24 wins exactly half were achieved by more than a two-goal margin. Defensively sound they had 24 clean sheets.

ROTHERHAM UNITED 2004–05 LEAGUE RECORD

Match No.	Date	Venue	Opponents	Result		H/T Score	Lg. Pos.	Goalscorers	Attendance
1	Aug 7	A	QPR	D	1-1	1-1	—	Shaw [15]	14,547
2	10	H	Burnley	D	0-0	0-0	—		6243
3	14	H	Stoke C	D	1-1	0-0	18	Shaw [56]	5925
4	21	A	Reading	L	0-1	0-1	21		11,404
5	28	H	Ipswich T	L	0-2	0-1	24		5504
6	30	A	Preston NE	L	0-2	0-2	24		11,439
7	Sept 11	H	Leicester C	L	0-2	0-1	24		6272
8	14	A	West Ham U	L	0-1	0-0	—		26,233
9	18	A	Coventry C	D	0-0	0-0	24		13,834
10	25	H	Millwall	D	1-1	0-0	24	Sedgwick [87]	5062
11	28	H	Crewe Alex	L	2-3	1-1	—	Burchill [17], Barker S [87]	4498
12	Oct 2	A	Wigan Ath	L	0-2	0-1	24		7937
13	16	A	Cardiff C	L	0-2	0-0	24		11,004
14	19	H	Plymouth Arg	L	0-1	0-0	—		5088
15	25	H	Sunderland	L	0-1	0-0	—		6026
16	30	A	Derby Co	L	2-3	2-1	24	Swailes [8], Scott [34]	25,096
17	Nov 3	A	Nottingham F	D	2-2	2-0	—	Sedgwick [19], Junior [27]	21,619
18	6	H	Cardiff C	D	2-2	0-0	24	McLaren [76], Proctor [80]	5093
19	13	H	Wolverhampton W	L	1-2	1-0	24	McIntosh [36]	6693
20	20	A	Watford	D	0-0	0-0	24		17,780
21	29	H	Leeds U	W	1-0	0-0	—	McIntosh [77]	8860
22	Dec 4	A	Brighton & HA	L	0-1	0-0	24		6076
23	11	H	Sheffield U	D	2-2	0-1	24	Swailes [54], McIntosh [71]	8195
24	18	A	Gillingham	L	1-3	0-0	24	Hoskins [89]	8576
25	26	A	Leicester C	W	1-0	1-0	24	Barker S [37]	27,014
26	28	H	West Ham U	D	2-2	2-0	24	Butler [13], McIntosh [37]	7769
27	Jan 1	H	Coventry C	L	1-2	1-0	24	Junior [39]	5742
28	3	A	Millwall	W	2-1	1-1	24	Butler [43], Scott [69]	11,725
29	15	H	Wigan Ath	L	0-2	0-0	24		9050
30	22	A	Crewe Alex	D	1-1	1-0	24	Mullin [33]	6382
31	Feb 5	H	Nottingham F	D	0-0	0-0	24		8448
32	12	A	Plymouth Arg	D	1-1	1-0	24	Monkhouse [26]	14,798
33	19	H	Derby Co	L	1-3	1-1	24	Butler (pen) [24]	7937
34	22	A	Sunderland	L	1-4	0-2	—	Monkhouse [77]	22,267
35	26	A	Sheffield U	L	0-1	0-0	24		18,431
36	Mar 5	H	Gillingham	L	1-3	0-1	24	Butler [56]	4367
37	12	A	Burnley	L	1-2	1-2	24	Gilchrist [4]	10,539
38	15	H	Reading	W	1-0	0-0	—	Warne [90]	3804
39	19	H	QPR	L	0-1	0-0	24		5387
40	Apr 2	A	Stoke C	W	2-1	1-0	24	Butler [23], Noel-Williams (og) [90]	16,552
41	5	A	Ipswich T	L	3-4	1-2	—	Thorpe [26], Butler [67], McIntosh [79]	26,017
42	9	H	Preston NE	L	1-2	1-0	24	Hoskins [23]	6312
43	16	H	Watford	L	0-1	0-1	24		5438
44	23	A	Wolverhampton W	L	0-2	0-0	24		25,177
45	30	H	Brighton & HA	L	0-1	0-1	24		6549
46	May 8	A	Leeds U	D	0-0	0-0	24		30,900

Final League Position: 24

GOALSCORERS

League (35): Butler 6 (1 pen), McIntosh 5, Barker S 2, Hoskins 2, Junior 2, Monkhouse 2, Scott 2, Sedgwick 2, Shaw 2, Swailes 2, Burchill 1, Gilchrist 1, McLaren 1, Mullin 1, Proctor 1, Thorpe 1, Warne 1, own goal 1.
Carling Cup (3): Barker R 1, Proctor 1, Sedgwick 1.
FA Cup (0).

Pollitt M 45	Stockdale R 27	Minto S 13+1	Garner D 17+1	Swailes C 37	Gilchrist P 21+3	Sedgwick C 19+1	Mullin J 26+5	Proctor M 16+12	Barker R 16+1	Shaw P 9	Scott R 17+7	Vernazza P 14+13	Warne P 13+11	Barker S 30+3	Hurst P 38+1	McLaren P 32+1	Hoskins W 6+16	Burchill M 3	McIntosh M 23	Junior 12	Butler M 21	Monkhouse A 11+3	Campbell-Ryce J 23+1	Duncum S 1+1	Griffit L 1+1	Keane M 9+1	Newsham M —+4	Thorpe T 5	Montgomery G 1	Match No.
1	2	3	4	5	6	7[1]	8[2]	9[3]	10	11	12	13	14																	1
1	2	3	4	5	6	7	8	9	10	11																				2
1	2	3	4	5	6	7	8	9[1]	10	11			12																	3
1	2	3	4[1]	5		7[2]	8	12	10[3]	9	14	11	13	6																4
1	2	3[1]	4[3]	5	6	7[2]	8	9	10	11	12	14	13																	5
1	2			5	6	7[1]	12	13	10	11		4			3	8	9[2]													6
1	2	3	11	5	6	7	8[2]	12	10	9		4[1]	13																	7
1	2	3	11	5	6	7	8	12	10[1]	9[3]		4[2]	13		14															8
1	2	3	4	5	6	7	8	9	10	11																				9
1	2		4	5	6[1]	7	8[2]		10		12	13	11[3]		3		14	9												10
1	2		4			7			10		5	11		6	3	8	12	9[1]												11
1	2		11[1]	5	6	7		9[2]	10[3]		13		12	4	3	8	14													12
1	2			5	6	7	8	9			11		12	4	3			10[1]												13
1	2		10[3]	5	12	7	8[2]	13	9			14	11	4	3				6[1]											14
1	2			5	12	7	8	9[2]	13				11	4[3]	3	14			6[1]	10										15
1	2			5		12	8	13	10		7[1]		11[2]	9	3	4			6											16
1	2			5		7[1]			9		11		12	8	3	4			6	10■										17
1	2			5		7	12	13	9[1]		11	14	10[2]	8[3]	3	4			6											18
1	2					7	8	9						5	3	4			6	11	10[1]	12								19
1	2			5		7		9				12		11	3	4[1]			6	10	8									20
1	2			5			12	11						4	3	8			6	10	9		7[1]							21
1	2			5				12			11	7		4[1]	3	8			6	10[2]	9		13							22
1	2			5				10				12		4[1]	3	8			6	11	9[2]	13	7							23
1	2		12	5				9[2]			4[3]	8			3	7[1]	13		6	10		14	11							24
1	2[1]			5							12			4	3	7			6	10	9	8	11							25
1				5				12			2			4	3	8	13		6	10[1]	9	7[2]	11							26
1				5							2	12		4[1]	3	8	13		6	10[2]	9	7	11							27
1				5	12						2	4			3	8	13		6[1]	10[2]	9	7	11							28
1	2		4[1]	5				12				13	10		3	8[2]	14		6		9	7[3]	11							29
1	2	6	4[1]		5		8					12	10		3						9	7	11							30
1			4[1]	5	6		12	10[2]						2	3	8	13				9	7	11							31
1			4	5	6		10							2	3	8	12				9	7	11[1]							32
1			4[2]	5	6		10[1]	12				13		2	3	8	14				9	7[3]	11							33
1				5	6							4	12	2	3	8	10[1]				9	7	11							34
1		12		5[1]	6							4		2	3	8	10				9	7	11							35
1		3			6							4	7[1]	5	2	8	10				9		11	12						36
1					6		12				2	4	10	5	3	8	9[1]						11		7[2]	13				37
1					4[1]		7				2		10	5	3	8	12		6				11			9				38
1					4		7				2		10[3]	5[1]	3	8	12		6				11[2]		13	9	14			39
1				5			7				2			12	3	8	13		6		9		11			4[1]		10[2]		40
1				5			7				2	12		13	3	8[2]			6		9		11[1]			4		10		41
1				5			7[1]	13			2[2]	4		12	3		11		6		9					8		10		42
1							7				2	4[2]	12	5	3[1]	8			6		9					11	13	10		43
		6		5			7						10	2	3[2]	8	12						11			4[1]	13	9	1	44
1		2		5[1]			7[3]	9[2]			12		10	6	3	8	13						11			4	14			45
1		2					7	9				12		5	3	8			6				11	10[1]		4				46

FA Cup

Third Round	Yeovil T	(h)	0-3

Carling Cup

First Round	Chesterfield	(h)	2-1
Second Round	Nottingham F	(a)	1-2

RUSHDEN & DIAMONDS FL Championship 2

FOUNDATION

Rushden & Diamonds were formed in 1992 from an amalgamation of Rushden Town and Irthlingborough Diamonds. At the end of 1990–91, Rushden Town had been relegated to the Southern League Midland Division as their ground was unfit for Premier Division football. Irthlingborough Diamonds were competing in the United Counties League at the time. The idea for this merger came from Max Griggs (owner of Dr Martens), a local multi-millionaire businessman. He invested several million pounds and they were able to achieve Football League status in nine years.

Nene Park, Diamond Way, Irthlingborough, Northants NN9 5QF.

Telephone: (01933) 652 000.

Fax: (01933) 650 418.

Ticket Office: (01933) 625 936.

Website: www.thediamondsfc.com

Email: dave.joyce@airwair.co.uk

Ground Capacity: 6,441.

Record Attendance: 6,431 v Leeds U, FA Cup 3rd rd, 2 January 1999.

Pitch Measurements: 111yd × 75yd.

Secretary: David Joyce.

Manager: Barry Hunter.

Assistant Manager: Neville Hamilton.

Physio: Simon Parsell.

Colours: Red.

Change Colours: Blue.

Year formed: 1992.

Turned Professional: 1992.

Ltd Co.: 1992.

Club Nickname: 'The Diamonds'.

HONOURS

Football League: Division 3 – Champions 2002–03

FA Cup: best season 3rd rd 1999.

Football League Cup: never past 2nd rd.

Conference: Champions 2000–01.

Conference Championship Shield: Winners 2001.

Southern League Midland Division: Champions 1993–94.

Premier Division: Champions 1995–96.

FA Trophy: Semi-finalists 1994.

Northants FA Hillier Senior Cup: Winners 1993–94, 1998–99.

Maunsell Premier Cup: Winners 1994–95, 1998–99; Finalists 2001–02.

SKY SPORTS FACT FILE

In their late Southern League days David Collins was a prolific goalscorer for the Rushden & Diamonds club. In 1995–96 he registered 30 in League games alone. During the period from 1994 to 2000 and into the Conference he hit 112.

MANAGERS

Roger Ashby 1992–97
Brian Talbot 1997–2004
Ernie Tippett 2004–05
Barry Hunter March 2005–

First Football League Match: 11 August 2001, Division 3, v York C (a) W 1–0 – Turley; Mustafa, Underwood, Talbot (Setchell), Peters, Rodwell, Butterworth, Brady, Patmore (1) (Darby), Jackson, Mills (Carey).

Record League Victory: 7–0 v Redditch U, Southern League, Midland Division, 7 May 1994 – Fox; Wooding (1), Johnson, Flower (1), Beech, Page, Coe, Mann (2), Nuttell (1), Watkins (1), Keast (1).

Record Cup Victory: 8–0 v Desborough T, Northants FA Hillier Senior Cup, 1st rd, 27 September 1994 – Fox; Wooding, Johnson, Flower, Keast, Page, Collins, Butterworth, Nuttell (2), Watkins (2), Mann (2). Subs:– Capone (2), Mason.

Record Defeat: 0–8 v Coventry C, League Cup 2nd rd, 2 October 2002.

Most League Points (3 for a win): 87, Division 3, 2002–03.

Most League Goals: 73, Division 3, 2002–03.

Highest League Scorer in Season: Onandi Lowe, 19, Division 3, 2001–02.

Most League Goals in Total Aggregate: Onandi Lowe, 49, 2001–05.

Most Capped Player: Onandi Lowe, 9, Jamaica.

Most League Appearances: Andy Burgess, 138, 2001–.

Record Transfer Fee Received: Undisclosed for Justin Jackson from Doncaster R, May 2003.

Record Transfer Fee Paid: Undisclosed to Morecambe for Justin Jackson, June 2000.

Football League Record: 2001 Promoted to Division 3; 2003–04 Division 2; 2004– FL2.

LATEST SEQUENCES

Longest Sequence of League Wins: 6, 29.10.2002 – 14.12.2002.

Longest Sequence of League Defeats: 4, 27.8.2001 – 15.9.2001.

Longest Sequence of League Draws: not more than 2.

Longest Sequence of Unbeaten League Matches: 12, 18.9.2001 – 20.11.2001.

Longest Sequence Without a League Win: 12, 6.11.2004 – 22.1.2005.

Successive Scoring Runs: 16 from 26.1.2002.

Successive Non-scoring Runs: 7 from 12.4.2004.

TEN YEAR LEAGUE RECORD

		P	W	D	L	F	A	Pts	Pos
1995-96	SL pr	42	29	7	6	99	41	94	1
1996-97	Conf.	42	14	11	17	61	63	53	12
1997-98	Conf.	42	23	5	14	79	57	74	4
1998-99	Conf.	42	20	12	10	71	42	72	4
1999-2000	Conf.	42	21	13	8	71	42	76	2
2000-01	Conf.	42	25	11	6	78	36	86	1
2001-02	Div 3	46	20	13	13	69	53	73	6
2002-03	Div 3	46	24	15	7	73	47	87	1
2003-04	Div 2	46	13	9	24	60	74	48	22
2004-05	FL 2	46	10	14	22	42	63	44	22

DID YOU KNOW?

Survival for Rushden & Diamonds in 2004–05 came despite a run of 12 matches mid-season in which only four points were taken from drawn games. But they did not slip into the bottom two places throughout the campaign.

RUSHDEN & DIAMONDS 2004–05 LEAGUE RECORD

Match No.	Date	Venue	Opponents	Result	H/T Score	Lg. Pos.	Goalscorers	Attendance
1	Aug 7	H	Kidderminster H	D 0-0	0-0	—		2699
2	10	A	Northampton T	L 0-1	0-0	—		7107
3	14	A	Lincoln C	W 3-1	1-0	8	Braniff [39], Hay [68], Dove [89]	4127
4	21	H	Grimsby T	W 1-0	0-0	4	Braniff [72]	2924
5	28	A	Yeovil T	L 1-3	0-3	12	Mills [83]	5088
6	30	H	Bristol R	D 0-0	0-0	13		3367
7	Sept 4	H	Southend U	L 1-4	0-1	16	Burgess [50]	2804
8	11	A	Oxford U	D 0-0	0-0	15		4756
9	18	H	Cheltenham T	W 1-0	1-0	12	Braniff [31]	2601
10	25	A	Swansea C	L 0-1	0-1	15		7410
11	Oct 2	H	Rochdale	D 0-0	0-0	16		2619
12	8	A	Shrewsbury T	W 1-0	1-0	—	Dove [45]	3882
13	16	H	Chester C	L 0-1	0-0	16		2735
14	19	A	Wycombe W	D 1-1	1-1	—	Mulligan [18]	3844
15	23	A	Bury	D 1-1	0-0	17	Hay [58]	2672
16	30	H	Notts Co	W 5-1	3-0	14	Broughton 3 (1 pen) [1, 11, 68 (p)], Dove 2 [41, 53]	3504
17	Nov 6	H	Darlington	L 1-2	0-1	16	Mulligan [85]	3036
18	20	A	Cambridge U	L 1-3	1-2	19	Broughton [41]	3466
19	27	H	Macclesfield T	L 0-2	0-1	21		2643
20	Dec 8	A	Boston U	L 0-1	0-1	—		2334
21	11	A	Mansfield T	D 0-0	0-0	21		3776
22	18	H	Scunthorpe U	L 1-3	1-1	21	Mulligan [4]	3198
23	26	H	Oxford U	D 3-3	1-2	20	Dove [37], Bell David [51], Taylor [62]	4140
24	28	A	Leyton Orient	D 2-2	1-0	20	Hay [28], Dove [63]	3777
25	Jan 1	A	Southend U	L 0-3	0-1	22		5930
26	3	H	Swansea C	L 0-2	0-2	22		3382
27	8	H	Shrewsbury T	D 0-0	0-0	22		2829
28	15	A	Cheltenham T	L 1-4	1-2	22	Taylor [30]	3160
29	22	H	Leyton Orient	W 2-0	0-0	21	Gier [86], Bell David [90]	3288
30	29	A	Rochdale	L 0-2	0-0	21		2664
31	Feb 5	A	Chester C	L 1-3	0-2	22	Sharp [86]	2340
32	12	H	Wycombe W	L 1-2	0-0	22	Allen [50]	3490
33	19	A	Notts Co	D 1-1	0-0	22	Sharp [52]	4556
34	22	H	Bury	W 3-0	3-0	—	Sharp [30], Gier [43], Bell David [45]	1803
35	26	H	Mansfield T	D 0-0	0-0	22		3096
36	Mar 5	A	Scunthorpe U	L 0-1	0-0	22		4932
37	12	H	Northampton T	W 3-2	1-1	22	Hawkins [7], Broughton (pen) [57], Sharp [90]	5520
38	19	A	Kidderminster H	D 0-0	0-0	22		3860
39	25	H	Lincoln C	L 1-4	1-1	—	Sharp [14]	4213
40	28	A	Grimsby T	D 0-0	0-0	22		4566
41	Apr 2	H	Yeovil T	W 2-0	0-0	22	Gray [82], Sharp [88]	3726
42	9	A	Bristol R	L 0-3	0-1	22		5740
43	16	H	Boston U	W 4-2	1-2	22	Broughton [27], Sharp 3 [54, 65, 84]	3671
44	23	A	Darlington	L 0-2	0-0	22		4579
45	30	H	Cambridge U	L 0-1	0-1	22		5104
46	May 7	A	Macclesfield T	L 0-1	0-0	22		2658

Final League Position: 22

GOALSCORERS

League (42): Sharp 9, Broughton 6 (2 pens), Dove 6, Bell David 3, Braniff 3, Hay 3, Mulligan 3, Gier 2, Taylor 2, Allen 1, Burgess 1, Gray 1, Hawkins 1, Mills 1.
Carling Cup (0).
FA Cup (3): Broughton 1, Gray 1, Robinson 1.
LDV Vans Trophy (0).

Turley B 22	Connelly S 40 + 2	Hawkins P 41	Gray S 37 + 1	Allen G 25 + 1	Gier R 30 + 2	Bell David 39 + 1	Mills G 7	Braniff K 11 + 1	Hay A 29 + 13	Burgess A 42	Kelly M 3 + 8	Dove C 31 + 5	Gulliver P 29 + 3	Jackson S — + 3	Sambrook A 3 + 5	Dempster J 9 + 6	Taylor J 4 + 16	Mulligan G 12 + 1	Broughton D 20 + 1	Robinson M — + 2	Worgan L 7	Kennedy L 1 + 2	Duffy R — + 1	Blayney A 4	Littlejohn A 8 + 7	Sharp B 16	McCafferty N 16	Shearer S 13	Williams M 7	Hunter B — + 1	Wark S — + 1	*Match No.*
1	2	3	4	5	6	7	8^{1}	9	10^{2}	11	12	13																				1
1	2	3	4	5			8	9	10	11		7^{1}	6	12																		2
1	2	3	4	5			8	9	10	11		7	6																			3
1	2	3	4	5	6	7^{1}	8	9	10	11		12																				4
1	2	3	4		6	7	8	9	10^{2}	11^{1}		12	5	13																		5
1	2	3	4		6	7	8	9	10	11			5																			6
1	2^{3}	3	4^{1}	12	6■	7		9	10	11	8^{2}	13	5		14																	7
1	2	3	4	5		7	8^{1}	9^{2}	10			11	6			12	13															8
1	2	3		5		7		9^{1}	10	11		8	6			4	12															9
1	2	3		5		7		9	10	11		8	6		12	4^{1}																10
1	2	3		5		7		9^{1}	10	11	12	8^{2}	6		4		13															11
1	2	3	4^{1}	5		7			10	11		8	6			12	9															12
1	2		4	5^{1}	12	7			10	11		8^{2}	6			3		13	9													13
1	2	3	4	5■	12	7				11^{2}		8^{1}	6			13		10	9													14
1	2	3	4	5				12	10			8	6		13	7		11^{1}	9^{2}													15
1		3	4	5	2	7			11		12	8^{1}	6				13	10	9^{2}													16
1	12		4	5	2^{1}	7			11	3		8	6					10	9													17
1	2	3	4	5		12			7^{1}	11		8^{2}	6					10	9	13												18
1	2	3	4	5		7^{1}			12	11		8^{2}	6					10	9	13												19
1	2^{3}	3	4		5	7^{2}			12	11		8^{1}	6		13		14	10	9													20
1	2	3	4		5	7^{2}			12	11		8^{1}	6		13		14	10	9^{3}													21
1		3	4		5	7			9	11		8	6		2			10														22
	12	3	4	5	6	7			9	11		8			2^{1}		13	10^{2}			1											23
	2■	3	4	5	6	7			9	11		8^{1}	12				10				1											24
		3	4^{1}	5	6	7			9	11		8	12			2^{2}	10				1	13										25
	2	3		5	6	7			9^{3}	11	12	8^{1}					14	10			1	4^{2}	13									26
	2	3		5	6	8^{1}			7	11	13	4^{2}				12	14	10^{3}						1	9							27
	2	3		5	6	4			7^{1}	11	13	8^{2}					10					12		1	9							28
	2	3			6	7				11	4	8	5				12							1	9	10^{1}						29
	2	3			6	7			12	11		8^{1}	5				13							1	9^{2}	10	4					30
	2	3	12	5		7			13	11		8^{1}	6								1				9^{2}	10	4					31
	2	3	4	5		7			12	11			6^{2}			13			9		1					10	8^{1}					32
	2	3	4	5^{1}	6	7				11						12			9							10	8	1				33
	2	3	4^{1}		6	7			12	11						5			9^{2}						13	10	8	1				34
	2	3	4		6	7				11						5			9						12	10^{1}	8	1				35
	2	3	4		6				7	11^{1}									9		1				12	10	8		5			36
	2	3	4		6	7^{2}			12			11^{1}					14		9^{3}						13	10	8	1	5			37
	2		4		6				7	3	12	11^{1}							9						13	10^{2}	8	1	5			38
	2		4		6				7	3^{1}	12	11^{2}	5						9■						13	10	8	1				39
	2	3	4		6	7			12	11		9^{1}	5												13	10^{2}	8	1				40
	2	3	4		6	7^{1}			12	11							13								9^{2}	10	8	1	5			41
	2	3	4		6	7			12	11							13								9^{2}	10^{1}	8	1	5			42
	2	3	4		6■	7^{1}			12	11			13						14						9^{3}	10^{2}	8	1	5			43
	2	3	4			7^{1}			12	11			6				13		9^{2}							10	8	1	5			44
	2	3	4			7			10	11		12	6			5^{2}			9								8^{1}	1		13		45
			4		6	7			10	3	11	8^{2}	5	13		2^{3}	12		9^{1}									1			14	46

FA Cup

First Round	Bradford C	(a)	1-0
Second Round	Colchester U	(h)	2-5

Carling Cup

First Round	Swindon T	(h)	0-1

LDV Vans Trophy

First Round	Walsall	(a)	0-1

SCUNTHORPE UNITED FL Championship 1

FOUNDATION

The year of foundation for Scunthorpe United has often been quoted as 1910, but the club can trace its history back to 1899 when Brumby Hall FC, who played on the Old Showground, consolidated their position by amalgamating with some other clubs and changing their name to Scunthorpe United. The year 1910 was when that club amalgamated with North Lindsey United as Scunthorpe and Lindsey United. The link is Mr W. T. Lockwood whose chairmanship covers both years.

Glanford Park, Doncaster Road, Scunthorpe DN15 8TD.

Telephone: (01724) 848 077.

Fax: (01724) 857 986.

Ticket Office: (01724) 747 670.

Website: www.scunthorpe-united.co.uk

Email: admin@scunthorpe-united.co.uk

Ground Capacity: 9,088.

Record Attendance: Old Showground: 23,935 v Portsmouth, FA Cup 4th rd, 30 January 1954. Glanford Park: 8,775 v Rotherham U, Division 4, 1 May 1989.

Pitch Measurements: 110yd × 71yd.

Chairman: J. S. Wharton.

Vice-chairman: R. Garton.

Chief Executive/Secretary: J. Hammond.

Manager: Brian Laws.

Assistant Manager: R. Wilcox.

Physio: N. Adkins.

Colours: Claret and blue.

Change Colours: Black with blue trim.

Year Formed: 1899.

Turned Professional: 1912.

Ltd Co.: 1912.

Club Nickname: 'The Iron'.

Previous Names: Amalgamated first with Brumby Hall then North Lindsey United to become Scunthorpe & Lindsey United, 1910; dropped '& Lindsey' in 1958.

Previous Ground: 1899, Old Showground; 1988, Glanford Park.

First Football League Game: 19 August 1950, Division 3 (N), v Shrewsbury T (h) D 0–0 – Thompson; Barker, Brownsword; Allen, Taylor, McCormick; Mosby, Payne, Gorin, Rees, Boyes.

HONOURS

Football League: Division 2 best season: 4th, 1961–62; Championship 2 – Runners-up 2004–05; Division 3 (N) – Champions 1957–58. Promoted from Division 3 1998–99 (play-offs).

FA Cup: best season: 5th rd, 1958, 1970.

Football League Cup: never past 3rd rd.

SKY SPORTS FACT FILE

In 1950–51 Scunthorpe United finished a creditable 12th in their first season in the Football League. Only one home defeat and an amazing 18 draws overall kept them out of trouble. Scoreless in 15 games the defence recorded 17 clean sheets.

Record League Victory: 8–1 v Luton T, Division 3, 24 April 1965 – Sidebottom; Horstead, Hemstead; Smith, Neale, Lindsey; Bramley (1), Scott, Thomas (5), Mahy (1), Wilson (1). 8–1 v Torquay U (a), Division 3, 28 October 1995 – Samways; Housham, Wilson, Ford (1), Knill (1), Hope (Nicholson), Thornber, Bullimore (Walsh), McFarlane (4) (Young), Eyre (2), Paterson.

Record Cup Victory: 9–0 v Boston U, FA Cup 1st rd, 21 November 1953 – Malan; Hubbard, Brownsword; Sharpe, White, Bushby; Mosby (1), Haigh (3), Whitfield (2), Gregory (1), Mervyn Jones (2).

Record Defeat: 0–8 v Carlisle U, Division 3 (N), 25 December 1952.

Most League Points (2 for a win): 66, Division 3 (N), 1956–57, 1957–58.

Most League Points (3 for a win): 83, Division 4, 1982–83.

Most League Goals: 88, Division 3 (N), 1957–58.

Highest League Scorer in Season: Barrie Thomas, 31, Division 2, 1961–62.

Most League Goals in Total Aggregate: Steve Cammack, 110, 1979–81, 1981–86.

Most League Goals in One Match: 5, Barrie Thomas v Luton T, Division 3, 24 April 1965.

Most Capped Player: None.

Most League Appearances: Jack Brownsword, 595, 1950–65.

Youngest League Player: Mike Farrell, 16 years 240 days v Workington, 8 November 1975.

Record Transfer Fee Received: £350,000 from Aston Villa for Neil Cox, February 1991.

Record Transfer Fee Paid: £175,000 to Bristol C for Steve Torpey, February 2000.

Football League Record: 1950 Elected to Division 3 (N); 1958–64 Division 2; 1964–68 Division 3; 1968–72 Division 4; 1972–73 Division 3; 1973–83 Division 4; 1983–84 Division 3; 1984–92 Division 4; 1992–99 Division 3; 1999–2000 Division 2; 2000–04 Division 3; 2004–05 FL2; 2005– FL1.

MANAGERS

Harry Allcock 1915–53
(Secretary-Manager)
Tom Crilly 1936–37
Bernard Harper 1946–48
Leslie Jones 1950–51
Bill Corkhill 1952–56
Ron Suart 1956–58
Tony McShane 1959
Bill Lambton 1959
Frank Soo 1959–60
Dick Duckworth 1960–64
Fred Goodwin 1964–66
Ron Ashman 1967–73
Ron Bradley 1973–74
Dick Rooks 1974–76
Ron Ashman 1976–81
John Duncan 1981–83
Allan Clarke 1983–84
Frank Barlow 1984–87
Mick Buxton 1987–91
Bill Green 1991–93
Richard Money 1993–94
David Moore 1994–96
Mick Buxton 1996–97
Brian Laws February 1997–

LATEST SEQUENCES

Longest Sequence of League Wins: 6, 18.10.1969 – 25.11.1969.

Longest Sequence of League Defeats: 8, 29.11.1997 – 20.1.1998.

Longest Sequence of League Draws: 6, 2.1.1984 – 25.2.1984.

Longest Sequence of Unbeaten League Matches: 15, 13.11.1971 – 26.2.1972.

Longest Sequence Without a League Win: 14, 22.3.1975 – 6.9.1975.

Successive Scoring Runs: 23 from 18.8.1951.

Successive Non-scoring Runs: 7 from 19.4.1975.

TEN YEAR LEAGUE RECORD

		P	W	D	L	F	A	Pts	Pos
1995-96	Div 3	46	15	15	16	67	61	60	12
1996-97	Div 3	46	18	9	19	59	62	63	13
1997-98	Div 3	46	19	12	15	56	52	69	8
1998-99	Div 3	46	22	8	16	69	58	74	4
1999-2000	Div 2	46	9	12	25	40	74	39	23
2000-01	Div 3	46	18	11	17	62	52	65	10
2001-02	Div 3	46	19	14	13	74	56	71	8
2002-03	Div 3	46	19	15	12	68	49	72	5
2003-04	Div 3	46	11	16	19	69	72	49	22
2004-05	FL 2	46	22	14	10	69	42	80	2

DID YOU KNOW?

Scunthorpe United received their first ever transfer fee when inside-right Jack Spaven moved to Nottingham Forest for £340, a useful sum of money in 1920. The former Goole Town player spent six successful seasons with Forest.

SCUNTHORPE UNITED 2004–05 LEAGUE RECORD

Match No.	Date	Venue	Opponents	Result		H/T Score	Lg. Pos.	Goalscorers	Attendance
1	Aug 7	H	Rochdale	W	3-1	0-1	—	Taylor [68], Hayes [75], Sparrow [90]	4409
2	10	A	Cheltenham T	W	2-0	1-0	—	Kell [10], Keogh [88]	3647
3	14	A	Oxford U	D	1-1	1-0	2	Hayes [38]	4920
4	21	H	Lincoln C	W	3-2	1-0	1	Kell [6], Butler 2 [58, 90]	5215
5	28	A	Macclesfield T	D	2-2	1-1	2	Sparrow [29], Hayes [51]	2321
6	30	H	Northampton T	W	2-0	1-0	1	Keogh [43], Crosby (pen) [73]	4201
7	Sept 4	A	Darlington	D	0-0	0-0	1		3983
8	11	H	Chester C	L	1-2	0-2	2	Butler [76]	4203
9	18	A	Bury	W	1-0	0-0	1	Rankine [89]	2846
10	25	H	Mansfield T	D	1-1	1-0	2	Baraclough [3]	5463
11	Oct 2	A	Boston U	L	1-2	1-0	3	Hayes [42]	3640
12	8	H	Wycombe W	W	2-0	2-0	—	Hayes [27], Crosby (pen) [39]	4373
13	16	A	Kidderminster H	L	2-3	1-1	3	Torpey [18], Hayes [58]	2167
14	19	H	Southend U	W	3-2	2-1	—	Torpey [35], Hayes 2 [44, 72]	3402
15	23	H	Yeovil T	W	1-0	0-0	1	Butler [78]	4470
16	30	A	Leyton Orient	D	1-1	0-0	1	Torpey [52]	4359
17	Nov 6	H	Grimsby T	W	2-0	1-0	1	Hayes 2 [16, 69]	8054
18	20	A	Bristol R	W	3-0	2-0	1	Hayes 2 [18, 53], Torpey [20]	7039
19	27	H	Shrewsbury T	W	3-1	1-0	1	Beagrie (pen) [32], Hayes [71], Taylor [76]	4418
20	Dec 7	A	Cambridge U	W	2-1	0-1	—	Torpey [88], Taylor [90]	2666
21	11	H	Swansea C	W	1-0	1-0	1	Torpey [1]	5075
22	18	A	Rushden & D	W	3-1	1-1	1	Butler 2 [31, 49], Torpey [90]	3198
23	26	A	Chester C	D	1-1	1-1	1	Torpey [3]	3216
24	28	H	Notts Co	D	0-0	0-0	1		6399
25	Jan 1	H	Darlington	L	0-1	0-0	1		5131
26	3	A	Mansfield T	L	0-1	0-1	2		5315
27	15	H	Bury	W	3-2	1-1	2	Butler [6], Torpey 2 [64, 87]	5365
28	22	A	Notts Co	L	0-2	0-1	2		6429
29	29	H	Boston U	D	1-1	0-0	3	Butler [60]	5056
30	Feb 5	H	Kidderminster H	W	2-1	1-0	2	Baraclough [20], Hayes [78]	5023
31	11	A	Southend U	D	0-0	0-0	—		8224
32	15	A	Wycombe W	L	1-2	0-2	—	Sparrow [87]	4089
33	19	H	Leyton Orient	W	1-0	0-0	2	Keogh [68]	5162
34	22	A	Yeovil T	L	3-4	2-1	—	Hayes 2 [36, 90], Butler [45]	7598
35	26	A	Swansea C	L	1-2	1-1	2	Butler [33]	7249
36	Mar 5	H	Rushden & D	W	1-0	0-0	2	Beagrie [90]	4932
37	12	H	Cheltenham T	W	4-1	1-0	2	Sparrow 2 [44, 55], Kell [85], Byrne [90]	4659
38	19	A	Rochdale	D	0-0	0-0	2		3605
39	25	H	Oxford U	D	1-1	0-1	—	Baraclough [90]	5977
40	28	A	Lincoln C	L	0-2	0-1	3		6729
41	Apr 2	H	Macclesfield T	D	0-0	0-0	4		5536
42	9	A	Northampton T	W	2-1	2-1	3	Hayes [14], Kell [21]	6523
43	16	H	Cambridge U	W	4-0	1-0	2	Kell [34], Crosby [63], Taylor 2 [81, 83]	5642
44	23	A	Grimsby T	D	0-0	0-0	3		7941
45	30	H	Bristol R	W	4-0	2-0	2	Torpey 2 [8, 14], Hayes [46], Taylor [69]	6925
46	May 7	A	Shrewsbury T	D	0-0	0-0	2		6285

Final League Position: 2

GOALSCORERS

League (69): Hayes 18, Torpey 12, Butler 10, Taylor 6, Kell 5, Sparrow 5, Baraclough 3, Crosby 3 (2 pens), Keogh 3, Beagrie 2 (1 pen), Byrne 1, Rankine 1.
Carling Cup (0).
FA Cup (5): Hayes 2, Baraclough 1, Ridley 1, Sparrow 1.
LDV Vans Trophy (1): Torpey 1.

Musselwhite P 46	Stanton N 18 + 3	Ridley L 43 + 1	Crosby A 43 + 1	Butler A 36 + 1	Baraclough I 45	Taylor C 18 + 26	Kell R 43	Hayes P 41 + 5	Bailey M 2 + 2	Beagrie P 36	Sparrow M 35 + 9	Keogh A 13 + 12	Brighton T 2 + 3	Featherstone L — + 1	Rankine M 1 + 20	Torpey S 33 + 1	Byrne C 24 + 5	Jackson M 1 + 2	Teggart N 1	Sharp K 4 + 2	Parton A — + 1	Walters J 3	Angus S 9	Corden W 3 + 5	Williams M — + 4	Hinds R 6 + 1	Match No.
1	2	3	4	5	6	7	8^{1}	9	10^{2}	11	12	13															1
1	2	3	4	5	6	7	8	9	10^{1}	11^{2}	13	12															2
1	2	3	4	5	6	7	8^{2}	9	12	11	13	10^{1}															3
1	2	3	4	5	6	7^{1}	8	9	13	11	12	10^{2}															4
1	2	3	4	5	6	12	8	9		11^{1}	7	10															5
1	2	3	4	5	6	11	8	9			7	10															6
1	2	3	4	5	6	11^{1}	8	9			7	10	12														7
1	2	3	4	5	6	11	8	9			7^{1}	10^{2}	12	13													8
1	2	3	4	5	6	12	8	9^{2}		11	7^{1}	10			13												9
1	2	3	4	5	6	12	8^{2}	9		11^{1}	7	10^{3}	13		14												10
1	2	3	4	5	6	7	8^{1}	9^{2}		11	12	10^{3}			13	14											11
1	2^{3}	3	4	5	6	11	8	9^{2}			12	13	7^{1}			10	14										12
1	2^{3}	3	4	5	6	11^{2}	8	9			12		7^{1}		13	10	14										13
1	2	3	4	5	6	7^{1}	8	9^{2}		11	12				13	10											14
1	2	3	4	5	6	7^{1}	8	9^{2}		11	12				13	10											15
1	2■	3	4	5	6	12	8^{1}	9^{3}		11	7				13	10^{2}		14									16
1		3	4	5	6	12	8	9^{2}		11	7^{1}				13	10	2										17
1		3	4	5	6	12	8^{1}	9		11	7					10	2										18
1		3	4	5	6	12	8	9		11	7^{1}				13	10^{2}	2										19
1	12	3^{3}	4	5	6	13	8	9		11	7^{2}				14	10	2^{1}										20
1		3	4	5	6	12	8^{1}	9^{2}		11	7				13	10	2										21
1	12	3	4	5	6	13	8^{2}	9		11	7					10	2^{1}										22
1	12	3	4	5	6	7		9		11	8					10	2^{1}										23
1	2	3	4	5	6	12	8^{1}	9^{2}		11	7				13	10■											24
1	2	3	4	5■	6	12	8^{1}	9^{2}		11	7				13			14	10^{3}								25
1		3			6	12	8	9^{2}		11	7^{1}				10		4	5		2	13						26
1		3	4	5	6	12	8^{1}	9^{2}		11	7				13	10	2										27
1		3^{3}	4	5	6	12	8^{1}	9^{2}		11	7				13	10	2			14							28
1		3^{3}	4	5	6	12	8	9^{2}		11	7^{1}				13	10	2			14							29
1			4	5	6^{1}	12	8	13		11	7					10	2			3		9^{2}					30
1			4		6	11	8	12			7					10	2			3		9^{1}	5				31
1		12	4			7^{3}	8	13		11	6	14				10	2			3^{1}		9^{2}	5				32
1		3	4	5	6	12	8	9^{2}		11^{3}	7^{1}	13				10							2	14			33
1		3	4^{1}	5	6^{3}	7		9			8	13				10	12						2	11^{2}	14		34
1		3		5	6	12	8	9^{2}			7^{1}	13				10	2						4■	11^{3}	14		35
1		3	4	5^{1}	6		8	9^{2}		11		7^{3}			13	10	12						2	14			36
1		3	4		6	12	8	9^{2}		11	7^{1}	13				10	2						5^{3}		14		37
1		3	12		6		8	9^{2}		11^{3}	7	13				10	2^{1}						5	14		4	38
1		3	4		6	12	8	13		11	7^{1}	9^{2}				10	14						5^{3}			2	39
1		3	4^{3}		6	12	8	13		11^{1}	7	9^{2}				10	5								14	2	40
1		3	4		6	12	8^{1}	9			7	11^{2}			13	10	5									2	41
1		3	4		6	12	8	9			7				13	10^{2}	5							11^{1}		2	42
1		3	4	12	6	13	8^{2}	9		11	7	14				10^{3}	5									2^{1}	43
1		3	4	5	6	12	8	9^{2}		11^{3}	7^{1}				13	10	2							14			44
1		3	4	5	6	7^{1}	8^{3}	9		11^{2}		12				10	2							13		14	45
1		3	4	5	6	7		9^{1}		11	8	12				10	2										46

FA Cup

First Round	Chesterfield	(h)	2-0
Second Round	Wrexham	(h)	2-0
Third Round	Chelsea	(a)	1-3

Carling Cup

First Round	Nottingham F	(a)	0-2

LDV Vans Trophy

First Round	Hereford U	(a)	1-1

SHEFFIELD UNITED — FL Championship

FOUNDATION

In March 1889, Yorkshire County Cricket Club formed Sheffield United six days after an FA Cup semi-final between Preston North End and West Bromwich Albion had finally convinced Charles Stokes, a member of the cricket club, that the formation of a professional football club would prove successful at Bramall Lane. The United's first secretary, Mr J. B. Wostinholm was also secretary of the cricket club.

Bramall Lane Ground, Cherry Street, Bramall Lane, Sheffield S2 4SU.

Telephone: 0870 787 1960.

Fax: 0870 787 3345.

Ticket Office: 0870 787 1799.

Website: www.sufc.co.uk

Email: info@sufc.co.uk

Ground Capacity: 28,000.

Record Attendance: 68,287 v Leeds U, FA Cup 5th rd, 15 February 1936.

Pitch Measurements: 112yd × 72yd.

Chairman: Derek Dooley MBE.

Vice-chairman: Terry Robinson.

Secretary: Donna Fletcher.

Manager: Neil Warnock.

Assistant Manager: Stuart McCall.

Physio: Dennis Pettitt.

Colours: Red and white stripes.

Change Colours: White.

Year Formed: 1889.

Turned Professional: 1889.

Ltd Co.: 1899.

Club Nickname: 'The Blades'.

First Football League Game: 3 September 1892, Division 2, v Lincoln C (h) W 4–2 – Lilley; Witham, Cain; Howell, Hendry, Needham (1); Wallace, Dobson, Hammond (3), Davies, Drummond.

Record League Victory: 10–0 v Burslem Port Vale (a), Division 2, 10 December 1892 – Howlett; Witham, Lilley; Howell, Hendry, Needham; Drummond (1), Wallace (1), Hammond (4), Davies (2), Watson (2).

HONOURS

Football League: Division 1 – Champions 1897–98; Runners-up 1896–97, 1899–1900; Division 2 – Champions 1952–53; Runners-up 1892–93, 1938–39, 1960–61, 1970–71, 1989–90; Division 4 – Champions 1981–82.

FA Cup: Winners 1899, 1902, 1915, 1925; Runners-up 1901, 1936.

Football League Cup: semi-final 2003.

SKY SPORTS FACT FILE

On the way to winning the FA Cup in 1925 Sheffield United had a measure of good fortune in the semi-final against Southampton at Stamford Bridge. One of the two goals was from an opponent and goalkeeper Charlie Sutcliffe saved a penalty.

Record Cup Victory: 6–1 v Lincoln C, League Cup, 22 August 2000 – Tracey; Uhlenbeek, Weber, Woodhouse (Ford), Murphy, Sandford, Devlin (pen), Ribeiro (Santos), Bent (3), Kelly (1) (Thompson), Jagielka, og (1). 6–1 v Loughborough, FA Cup 4th qualifying rd, 6 December 1890; 6–1 v Scarborough (a), FA Cup 1st qualifying rd, 5 October 1889.

Record Defeat: 0–13 v Bolton W, FA Cup 2nd rd, 1 February 1890.

Most League Points (2 for a win): 60, Division 2, 1952–53.

Most League Points (3 for a win): 96, Division 4, 1981–82.

Most League Goals: 102, Division 1, 1925–26.

Highest League Scorer in Season: Jimmy Dunne, 41, Division 1, 1930–31.

Most League Goals in Total Aggregate: Harry Johnson, 205, 1919–30.

Most League Goals in One Match: 5, Harry Hammond v Bootle, Division 2, 26 November 1892; 5, Harry Johnson v West Ham U, Division 1, 26 December 1927.

Most Capped Player: Billy Gillespie, 25, Northern Ireland.

Most League Appearances: Joe Shaw, 629, 1948–66.

Youngest League Player: Steve Hawes, 17 years 47 days v WBA, 2 September 1995.

Record Transfer Fee Received: £3,000,000 (dependant on appearances) from Derby Co for Lee Morris, October 1999.

Record Transfer Fee Paid: £1,200,000 to West Ham U for Don Hutchison, January 1996.

Football League Record: 1892 Elected to Division 2; 1893–1934 Division 1; 1934–39 Division 2; 1946–49 Division 1; 1949–53 Division 2; 1953–56 Division 1; 1956–61 Division 2; 1961–68 Division 1; 1968–71 Division 2; 1971–76 Division 1; 1976–79 Division 2; 1979–81 Division 3; 1981–82 Division 4; 1982–84 Division 3; 1984–88 Division 2; 1988–89 Division 3; 1989–90 Division 2; 1990–92 Division 1; 1992–94 FA Premier League; 1994–2004 Division 1; 2004– FLC.

MANAGERS

J. B. Wostinholm 1889–99 *(Secretary-Manager)*
John Nicholson 1899–1932
Ted Davison 1932–52
Reg Freeman 1952–55
Joe Mercer 1955–58
Johnny Harris 1959–68 *(continued as General Manager to 1970)*
Arthur Rowley 1968–69
Johnny Harris *(General Manager resumed Team Manager duties)* 1969–73
Ken Furphy 1973–75
Jimmy Sirrel 1975–77
Harry Haslam 1978–81
Martin Peters 1981
Ian Porterfield 1981–86
Billy McEwan 1986–88
Dave Bassett 1988–95
Howard Kendall 1995–97
Nigel Spackman 1997–98
Steve Bruce 1998–99
Adrian Heath 1999
Neil Warnock December 1999–

LATEST SEQUENCES

Longest Sequence of League Wins: 8, 14.9.1960 – 22.10.1960.

Longest Sequence of League Defeats: 7, 19.8.1975 – 20.9.1975.

Longest Sequence of League Draws: 6, 6.5.2001 – 8.9.2001.

Longest Sequence of Unbeaten League Matches: 22, 2.9.1899 – 13.1.1900.

Longest Sequence Without a League Win: 19, 27.9.1975 – 7.2.1976.

Successive Scoring Runs: 34 from 30.3.1956.

Successive Non-scoring Runs: 6 from 4.12.1993.

TEN YEAR LEAGUE RECORD

		P	W	D	L	F	A	Pts	Pos
1995-96	Div 1	46	16	14	16	57	54	62	9
1996-97	Div 1	46	20	13	13	75	52	73	5
1997-98	Div 1	46	19	17	10	69	54	74	6
1998-99	Div 1	46	18	13	15	71	66	67	8
1999-2000	Div 1	46	13	15	18	59	71	54	16
2000-01	Div 1	46	19	11	16	52	49	68	10
2001-02	Div 1	46	15	15	16	53	54	60	13
2002-03	Div 1	46	23	11	12	72	52	80	3
2003-04	Div 1	46	20	11	15	65	56	71	8
2004-05	FL C	46	18	13	15	57	56	67	8

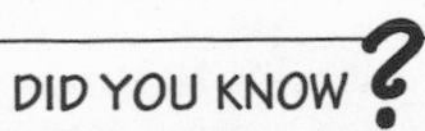

In the early 1950s Sheffield United had two players called Fred Smith in attack. One 6ft known as Big Fred, the other 5ft 7in as Little Fred. Both were born in 1926, though the latter a Scot was inevitably often called Jock.

SHEFFIELD UNITED 2004–05 LEAGUE RECORD

Match No.	Date	Venue	Opponents	Result		H/T Score	Lg. Pos.	Goalscorers	Atten-dance
1	Aug 7	A	Burnley	D	1-1	0-1	—	Gray[52]	16,956
2	10	H	Stoke C	D	0-0	0-0	—		19,723
3	14	H	Reading	L	0-1	0-1	21		22,429
4	20	A	Preston NE	W	1-0	1-0	—	Gray[4]	12,084
5	29	H	Leeds U	W	2-0	0-0	9	Ward[50], Harley[64]	22,959
6	31	A	QPR	W	1-0	1-0	—	Gray[17]	13,804
7	Sept11	H	West Ham U	L	1-2	0-1	7	Quinn A[65]	21,058
8	14	A	Leicester C	L	2-3	0-2	—	Morgan[75], Forte[84]	23,422
9	18	A	Wigan Ath	L	0-4	0-3	16		10,682
10	25	H	Coventry C	D	1-1	1-1	17	Black[30]	16,337
11	28	H	Sunderland	W	1-0	0-0	—	Shaw[67]	17,908
12	Oct 2	A	Brighton & HA	D	1-1	0-1	13	Shaw[62]	6418
13	17	A	Gillingham	W	3-1	1-0	8	Shaw 2[9, 59], Tonge[71]	6964
14	19	H	Nottingham F	D	1-1	1-0	—	Liddell[26]	19,445
15	23	H	Plymouth Arg	W	2-1	0-0	6	Bromby[78], Gray[85]	18,893
16	29	A	Crewe Alex	W	3-2	3-1	—	Harley[5], Gray[10], Cadamarteri[12]	7131
17	Nov 2	A	Ipswich T	L	1-5	1-2	—	Bromby[45]	22,977
18	6	H	Gillingham	D	0-0	0-0	7		16,598
19	13	H	Watford	D	1-1	1-0	8	Quinn A[30]	18,454
20	20	A	Derby Co	W	1-0	0-0	7	Quinn A[61]	25,725
21	27	H	Wolverhampton W	D	3-3	1-1	7	Bromby[28], Thirlwell[53], Shaw[72]	18,946
22	Dec 4	A	Millwall	W	2-1	0-0	7	Liddell[77], Geary[84]	11,207
23	11	A	Rotherham U	D	2-2	1-0	6	Tonge[45], Shaw[47]	8195
24	18	H	Cardiff C	W	2-1	0-1	5	Liddell[69], Gray[79]	18,240
25	26	A	Coventry C	W	2-1	2-1	5	Morgan[33], Gray[40]	21,146
26	28	H	Leicester C	W	2-0	0-0	5	Gray[52], Quinn A[65]	22,100
27	Jan 1	H	Wigan Ath	L	0-2	0-1	6		21,869
28	3	A	West Ham U	W	2-0	1-0	5	Repka (og)[40], Bromby[60]	27,424
29	15	H	Brighton & HA	L	1-2	0-1	5	Mayo (og)[59]	21,482
30	22	A	Sunderland	L	0-1	0-1	5		27,337
31	Feb 5	H	Ipswich T	L	0-2	0-1	8		20,680
32	22	A	Plymouth Arg	L	0-3	0-1	—		13,953
33	26	H	Rotherham U	W	1-0	0-0	8	Shaw[51]	18,431
34	Mar 5	A	Cardiff C	L	0-1	0-0	11		12,250
35	8	H	Crewe Alex	W	4-0	2-0	—	Kabba 2[14, 66], Gray 2[39, 75]	16,079
36	12	A	Stoke C	L	0-2	0-0	9		17,019
37	15	H	Preston NE	D	1-1	1-0	—	Bromby[31]	18,647
38	19	H	Burnley	W	2-1	1-0	6	Quinn A[29], Gray[49]	19,374
39	Apr 2	A	Reading	D	0-0	0-0	8		18,899
40	5	A	Leeds U	W	4-0	2-0	—	Webber[2], Montgomery[30], Gray 2[47, 74]	28,936
41	9	H	QPR	W	3-2	1-1	8	Webber 2[43, 53], Gray (pen)[90]	20,426
42	12	A	Nottingham F	D	1-1	0-0	—	Quinn A[71]	21,903
43	15	H	Derby Co	L	0-1	0-0	—		20,794
44	23	A	Watford	D	0-0	0-0	8		17,138
45	30	H	Millwall	L	0-1	0-1	8		19,797
46	May 8	A	Wolverhampton W	L	2-4	2-2	8	Quinn A[13], Gray[37]	27,454

Final League Position: 8

GOALSCORERS

League (57): Gray 15 (1 pen), Quinn A 7, Shaw 7, Bromby 5, Liddell 3, Webber 3, Harley 2, Kabba 2, Morgan 2, Tonge 2, Black 1, Cadamarteri 1, Forte 1, Geary 1, Montgomery 1, Thirlwell 1, Ward 1, own goals 2.
Carling Cup (7): Gray 2, Jagielka 1, Lester 1, Morgan 1, Tonge 1, own goal 1.
FA Cup (6): Liddell 3, Cullip 1, Gray 1 (pen), Jagielka 1.

Kenny P 40	Jagielka P 46	Wright A 11 + 3	Montgomery N 16 + 9	Bromby L 46	Morgan C 40 + 1	Liddell A 26 + 7	Tonge M 33 + 1	Gray A 41 + 2	Hayles B 4	Harley J 44	Forte J 1 + 21	Ward A 5 + 5	Quinn A 38 + 5	Thirlwell P 24 + 6	Lester J 1 + 11	Francis S 2 + 4	Black T 3 + 1	Shaw P 16 + 5	Hurst K — + 1	Cadamarteri D 14 + 7	Gabrieli E — + 1	Geary D 15 + 4	Sharp B — + 2	Beckett L 1 + 4	Bennett I 5	Cullip D 11	Barnes P 1	Kozluk R 9	Kabba S 6 + 5	Johnson T 1 + 4	Webber D 6 + 1	Match No.
1	2	3	4	5	6	7^{1}	8	9	10^{2}	11	12	13																				1
1	2	3	4^{3}	5	6	7^{1}	8	9	10^{2}	11	12	13	14																			2
1	2	3^{3}		5	6	7^{1}	8	9	10^{2}	11	12	13	14	4																		3
1	2■	3		5	6		8	9^{1}	10^{2}	11	13	12	7	4																		4
1	2	3	12	5	6		8	9^{1}		11^{2}		10	7	4	13																	5
1	2	3	12	5	6		8^{1}	9^{2}		11		10	7^{3}	4	13	14																6
1	2	3		5	6		8^{1}	9		11		10	7	4	12																	7
1	2	3^{1}	8	5	6			9^{2}		11	12	10	7	4	13																	8
1	2	3	8^{3}	5	6			12		11	13	10^{1}	7	4	9^{2}		14															9
1	2			5	6		8	9		3	12		7	4			10^{2}	11^{1}	13													10
1	2	12	13	5	6^{1}		8	9■		3	14		7^{2}	4			10^{3}	11														11
1	6	2		5		12	8^{2}			3	13		7	4			10^{1}	11		9												12
1	2		12	5	6■	7	8^{1}			3			11	4	13			9^{2}		10^{3}	14											13
1	2		6	5		7	8			3			11■	4	12			9		10^{1}												14
1	2			5	6	7	8	9		3				4	12			11		10^{1}												15
1	8		12	5	6	7^{1}		9		3	13			4	14			11		10^{3}		2^{2}										16
1	2		12	5	6	7		9		3	13		8^{1}	4	14			11^{2}		10^{3}												17
1	3			5	6	7		12		11^{2}	13		8	4	14			9^{1}		10^{3}		2										18
1	3			5	6	7		9			12		8	4^{3}	13			11^{2}		10^{1}		2	14									19
1	3		12	5	6	7^{1}	13	9		11			8	4						10^{2}		2										20
1	2		12	5	6	7	11^{1}	9^{2}		3			8	4				10						13								21
1■	7			5	6	12	11	9^{2}		3			8	4^{1}				10		13		2										22
	2	12		5	6	7	11	9^{2}		3			8^{1}	4				10		13					1							23
	7			5	6	12	11	9		3			8^{3}	14				10^{2}		13		2^{1}			1	4						24
	2			5	6	7	11	9		3			8^{2}	12						10^{1}		13			1	4						25
	2			5	6	7	11^{2}	9		3	12		8^{1}	13				14		10^{3}					1	4						26
	2			5	6	7	11	9		3	12		8^{1}					13		10^{2}					1	4						27
1	3	13	12	5	6	10^{1}	7^{2}	9^{3}		11			8							14		2				4						28
1	2	3^{2}		5	6	10^{1}	7	9		11	12		8							13						4						29
1	2			5	6	10^{2}	7	9		11	12		8^{1}					14		13		3				4^{3}						30
1	3		7^{2}	5	6	12	8	9		11		14	13							10^{3}		2^{1}				4						31
1^{6}	6		7	5		11	8^{2}	9		3	12		13	15				10^{1}				2				4						32
	4			5	6	12	11	9^{2}		3			8					10^{3}						13			1	2	14	7^{1}		33
1	8		7^{1}	5	6	11^{2}		9		3			12			13						2		10^{3}		4			14			34
1	2			5	6	11		9^{3}		3			8	7						12		13		14		4^{2}			10^{1}			35
1	4			5	6			9^{1}		3			11	7		8				10^{2}		2		12						13		36
1	6		4	5		7	11	9		3			8^{2}					12										2	10^{1}	13		37
1	6		4	5		7^{2}	11	9		3			8^{1}	12		13												2	10^{3}	14		38
1	4		7	5	6		11	9		3			8															2	10^{1}		12	39
1	4		7	5	6		11^{1}	9		3			8									12						2	13		10^{2}	40
1	4		7	5	6	11^{2}		9		3			8	12														2	13		10^{1}	41
1	4		11	5	6	12		9		3			8			7^{1}						13						2^{2}			10	42
1	4		11^{1}	5	6	7^{3}		9		3	12		8			13						2^{2}							14		10	43
1	4			5	6^{1}		11	9		3	12		8^{2}	7								2							10	13		44
1	6			5	13	12	11	9		3	4^{1}		8															2	10^{2}		7	45
1	4		7	5	6		11	9^{3}			12		8^{2}					13				3	14					2			10^{1}	46

FA Cup

Third Round	Aston Villa	(h)	3-1
Fourth Round	West Ham U	(a)	1-1
		(h)	1-1
Fifth Round	Arsenal	(a)	1-1
		(h)	0-0

Carling Cup

First Round	Stockport Co	(h)	4-1
Second Round	Wrexham	(a)	3-2
Third Round	Watford	(h)	0-0

SHEFFIELD WEDNESDAY FL Championship

FOUNDATION

Sheffield being one of the principal centres of early Association Football, this club was formed as long ago as 1867 by the Sheffield Wednesday Cricket Club (formed 1825) and their colours from the start were blue and white. The inaugural meeting was held at the Adelphi Hotel and the original committee included Charles Stokes who was subsequently a founder member of Sheffield United.

Hillsborough, Sheffield S6 1SW.

Telephone: (0114) 221 2121.

Fax: (0114) 221 2122.

Ticket Office: 0870 999 12867.

Website: www.swfc.co.uk

Email: enquiries@swfc.co.uk

Ground Capacity: 39,814.

Record Attendance: 72,841 v Manchester C, FA Cup 5th rd, 17 February 1934.

Pitch Measurements: 115yd × 74yd.

Chairman: Dave E. D. Allen.

Chief Executive/Secretary: Kaven Walker.

Manager: Paul Sturrock.

Assistant Manager: Kevin Summerfield.

Defensive Co-ordinator: John Blackley.

Physio: John Dickens.

Colours: Blue and white striped shirts, black shorts, blue stockings.

Change Colours: All black.

Year Formed: 1867 (fifth oldest League club).

Turned Professional: 1887.

Ltd Co.: 1899.

Former Names: The Wednesday until 1929.

Club Nickname: 'The Owls'.

Previous Grounds: 1867, Highfield; 1869, Myrtle Road; 1877, Sheaf House; 1887, Olive Grove; 1899, Owlerton (since 1912 known as Hillsborough). Some games were played at Endcliffe in the 1880s. Until 1895 Bramall Lane was used for some games.

First Football League Game: 3 September 1892, Division 1, v Notts Co (a) W 1–0 – Allan; Tom Brandon (1), Mumford; Hall, Betts, Harry Brandon; Spiksley, Brady, Davis, R. N. Brown, Dunlop.

Record League Victory: 9–1 v Birmingham, Division 1, 13 December 1930 – Brown; Walker, Blenkinsop; Strange, Leach, Wilson; Hooper (3), Seed (2), Ball (2), Burgess (1), Rimmer (1).

HONOURS

Football League: Division 1 – Champions 1902–03, 1903–04, 1928–29, 1929–30; Runners-up 1960–61; Promotion from Championship 1 2004–05 (play-offs); Division 2 – Champions 1899–1900, 1925–26, 1951–52, 1955–56, 1958–59; Runners-up 1949–50, 1983–84.

FA Cup: Winners 1896, 1907, 1935; Runners-up 1890, 1966, 1993.

Football League Cup: Winners 1991; Runners-up 1993.

European Competitions: *European Fairs Cup:* 1961–62, 1963–64. *UEFA Cup:* 1992–93. *Intertoto Cup:* 1995.

SKY SPORTS FACT FILE

The 1950s provided more than their share of ups and downs for Sheffield Wednesday with four promotions and four relegations to and from the First Division. The highest average crowd was 42,634 during 1952–53 when avoiding the drop by a point!

Record Cup Victory: 12–0 v Halliwell, FA Cup 1st rd, 17 January 1891 – Smith; Thompson, Brayshaw; Harry Brandon (1), Betts, Cawley (2); Winterbottom, Mumford (2), Bob Brandon (1), Woolhouse (5), Ingram (1).

Record Defeat: 0–10 v Aston Villa, Division 1, 5 October 1912.

Most League Points (2 for a win): 62, Division 2, 1958–59.

Most League Points (3 for a win): 88, Division 2, 1983–84.

Most League Goals: 106, Division 2, 1958–59.

Highest League Scorer in Season: Derek Dooley, 46, Division 2, 1951–52.

Most League Goals in Total Aggregate: Andrew Wilson, 199, 1900–20.

Most League Goals in One Match: 6, Doug Hunt v Norwich C, Division 2, 19 November 1938.

Most Capped Player: Nigel Worthington, 50 (66), Northern Ireland.

Most League Appearances: Andrew Wilson, 501, 1900–20.

Youngest League Player: Peter Fox, 15 years 269 days v Orient, 31 March 1973.

Record Transfer Fee Received: £2,750,000 from Blackburn R for Paul Warhurst, September 1993.

Record Transfer Fee Paid: £4,500,000 to Celtic for Paolo Di Canio, August 1997.

Football League Record: 1892 Elected to Division 1; 1899–1900 Division 2; 1900–20 Division 1; 1920–26 Division 2; 1926–37 Division 1; 1937–50 Division 2; 1950–51 Division 1; 1951–52 Division 2; 1952–55 Division 1; 1955–56 Division 2; 1956–58 Division 1; 1958–59 Division 2; 1959–70 Division 1; 1970–75 Division 2; 1975–80 Division 3; 1980–84 Division 2; 1984–90 Division 1; 1990–91 Division 2; 1991–92 Division 1; 1992–2000 FA Premier League; 2000–03 Division 1; 2003–04 Division 2; 2004–05 FL1; 2005– FLC.

MANAGERS

Arthur Dickinson 1891–1920
(Secretary-Manager)
Robert Brown 1920–33
Billy Walker 1933–37
Jimmy McMullan 1937–42
Eric Taylor 1942–58
(continued as General Manager to 1974)
Harry Catterick 1958–61
Vic Buckingham 1961–64
Alan Brown 1964–68
Jack Marshall 1968–69
Danny Williams 1969–71
Derek Dooley 1971–73
Steve Burtenshaw 1974–75
Len Ashurst 1975–77
Jackie Charlton 1977–83
Howard Wilkinson 1983–88
Peter Eustace 1988–89
Ron Atkinson 1989–91
Trevor Francis 1991–95
David Pleat 1995–97
Ron Atkinson 1997–98
Danny Wilson 1998–2000
Peter Shreeves (Acting) 2000
Paul Jewell 2000–01
Peter Shreeves 2001
Terry Yorath 2001–02
Chris Turner 2002–04
Paul Sturrock September 2004–

LATEST SEQUENCES

Longest Sequence of League Wins: 9, 23.4.1904 – 15.10.1904.

Longest Sequence of League Defeats: 8, 9.9.2000 – 17.10.2000.

Longest Sequence of League Draws: 5, 24.10.1992 – 28.11.1992.

Longest Sequence of Unbeaten League Matches: 19, 10.12.1960 – 8.4.1961.

Longest Sequence Without a League Win: 20, 11.1.1975 – 30.8.1975.

Successive Scoring Runs: 40 from 14.11.1959.

Successive Non-scoring Runs: 8 from 8.3.1975.

TEN YEAR LEAGUE RECORD

		P	*W*	*D*	*L*	*F*	*A*	*Pts*	*Pos*
1995-96	PR Lge	38	10	10	18	48	61	40	15
1996-97	PR Lge	38	14	15	9	50	51	57	7
1997-98	PR Lge	38	12	8	18	52	67	44	16
1998-99	PR Lge	38	13	7	18	41	42	46	12
1999-2000	PR Lge	38	8	7	23	38	70	31	19
2000-01	Div 1	46	15	8	23	52	71	53	17
2001-02	Div 1	46	12	14	20	49	71	50	20
2002-03	Div 1	46	10	16	20	56	73	46	22
2003-04	Div 2	46	13	14	19	48	64	53	16
2004-05	FL 1	46	19	15	12	77	59	72	5

DID YOU KNOW?

As low as 15th at the end of October 2004, Sheffield Wednesday revived with a run of ten games without defeat, consolidated into a play-off slot and were boosted by the ultimate return of injury hit striker Steve MacLean who had been out for three months.

SHEFFIELD WEDNESDAY 2004–05 LEAGUE RECORD

Match No.	*Date*	*Venue*	*Opponents*	*Result*	*H/T Score*	*Lg. Pos.*	*Goalscorers*	*Atten-dance*
1	Aug 7	H	Colchester U	L 0-3	0-0	—		24,138
2	10	A	Blackpool	W 2-1	1-0	—	Bullen [44], McMahon [80]	6713
3	14	A	Torquay U	W 4-2	1-1	8	MacLean (pen) [8], Lee [51], Peacock [74], Heckingbottom [80]	5005
4	21	H	Huddersfield T	W 1-0	1-0	4	MacLean [21]	26,264
5	27	A	Tranmere R	L 2-4	2-3	—	MacLean [27], N'Dumbu Nsungu [45]	9506
6	30	H	Oldham Ath	D 1-1	0-0	9	Brunt [70]	21,530
7	Sept 4	H	Luton T	D 0-0	0-0	10		20,806
8	11	A	Walsall	D 1-1	1-1	12	Whelan [16]	6493
9	18	H	Bournemouth	L 0-1	0-1	14		19,203
10	25	A	Wrexham	W 3-0	1-0	8	MacLean [25], Brunt [55], Proudlock [62]	5688
11	Oct 2	H	Milton Keynes D	D 1-1	0-0	11	McGovern [65]	20,245
12	17	H	Barnsley	W 1-0	1-0	11	Proudlock [24]	25,391
13	19	A	Peterborough U	D 1-1	0-1	—	Bullen [85]	5875
14	23	A	Bradford C	L 1-3	0-0	12	Bullen [73]	13,717
15	27	A	Swindon T	L 2-3	1-0	—	Bullen [4], MacLean [63]	6972
16	30	H	Chesterfield	D 2-2	2-1	15	Proudlock [9], MacLean (pen) [15]	24,271
17	Nov 6	A	Stockport Co	W 3-0	1-0	12	Proudlock [40], McGovern [50], McMahon [88]	7222
18	20	H	Hartlepool U	W 2-0	0-0	10	MacLean [59], Hamshaw [85]	19,919
19	27	A	Bristol C	W 4-1	1-0	7	Proudlock 2 [15, 63], Brunt [61], Collins [84]	14,852
20	Dec 8	H	Hull C	L 2-4	1-3	—	O'Brien [9], McGovern [81]	28,701
21	11	H	Brentford	L 1-2	1-0	10	MacLean (pen) [22]	21,592
22	19	A	Doncaster R	W 4-0	2-0	9	MacLean 3 [9, 59, 76], Jones [22]	10,131
23	26	H	Walsall	W 3-2	1-1	8	Jones [30], Wright (og) [65], MacLean (pen) [73]	26,996
24	28	A	Port Vale	W 2-0	2-0	4	Jones [27], McGovern [43]	8671
25	Jan 1	A	Luton T	D 1-1	1-0	6	Jones [45]	9500
26	3	H	Wrexham	W 4-0	0-0	4	MacLean (pen) [49], Jones 2 [55, 59], Heckingbottom [84]	24,253
27	8	H	Swindon T	W 2-0	1-0	4	O'Brien [40], Jones [69]	20,804
28	15	A	Bournemouth	D 1-1	0-1	4	Heckingbottom [90]	8847
29	21	H	Port Vale	W 1-0	1-0	—	MacLean [15]	18,465
30	29	A	Milton Keynes D	D 2-2	1-0	4	Quinn [11], Chorley (og) [62]	7325
31	Feb 5	A	Barnsley	D 0-0	0-0	4		19,659
32	12	H	Bradford C	L 1-2	0-1	4	MacLean [71]	23,232
33	19	A	Chesterfield	W 3-1	1-0	4	MacLean 2 [15, 55], Peacock [78]	7831
34	23	H	Peterborough U	W 2-1	1-1	—	MacLean (pen) [36], Heckingbottom [52]	19,648
35	26	A	Brentford	D 3-3	2-1	4	Peacock 2 [4, 41], Bullen [49]	8323
36	Mar 6	H	Doncaster R	W 2-0	1-0	3	Bullen [45], Talbot [78]	28,712
37	12	H	Blackpool	W 3-2	1-0	3	Rocastle [27], Talbot 2 [84, 89]	21,539
38	19	A	Colchester U	D 1-1	0-0	4	McGovern [63]	4169
39	26	H	Torquay U	D 2-2	0-1	4	Bullen [54], Barrett [60]	21,526
40	29	A	Huddersfield T	L 0-1	0-1	—		17,292
41	Apr 2	H	Tranmere R	L 1-2	1-1	4	Brunt (pen) [31]	22,925
42	9	A	Oldham Ath	D 1-1	0-1	4	Whelan [54]	9645
43	15	A	Hartlepool U	L 0-3	0-2	—		6429
44	23	H	Stockport Co	D 0-0	0-0	5		22,331
45	30	A	Hull C	W 2-1	1-0	4	Talbot [19], Quinn [90]	24,277
46	May 7	H	Bristol C	L 2-3	0-2	5	McGovern [52], Wood [61]	28,798

Final League Position: 5

GOALSCORERS

League (77): MacLean 18 (6 pens), Bullen 7, Jones 7, McGovern 6, Proudlock 6, Brunt 4 (1 pen), Heckingbottom 4, Peacock 4, Talbot 4, McMahon 2, O'Brien 2, Quinn 2, Whelan 2, Barrett 1, Collins 1, Hamshaw 1, Lee 1, N'Dumbu Nsungu 1, Rocastle 1, Wood 1, own goals 2.
Carling Cup (1): Peacock 1.
FA Cup (1): Whelan 1.
LDV Vans Trophy (1): MacLean 1.
Play-offs (7): McGovern 2, Brunt 1, MacLean 1 (pen), Peacock 1, Talbot 1, Whelan 1.

Lucas D 34	Bullen L 46	Heckingbottom P 37 + 1	Lee G 19 + 3	Collins P 25 + 3	McMahon L 13 + 2	Marsden C 15	McGovern J 46	MacLean S 36	Proudlock A 11 + 3	Brunt C 27 + 15	Branston G 10 + 1	Hamshaw M 9 + 11	Peacock L 18 + 11	Smith P 7 + 1	Shaw J 1 + 2	N'Dumbu Nsungu G 4 + 7	Whelan G 36	Wood R 33 + 1	Aljofree H 2	Greenwood R — + 2	Tidman O 3 + 1	Talbot D 3 + 18	O'Brien J 14 + 1	Jones K 7	Quinn J 10 + 5	Green A 3	Rocastle C 9 + 2	Adamson C 1 + 1	Bruce A 5 + 1	Adams S 8 + 1	Gallacher P 8	Barrett G 5 + 1	Aranalde Z 1 + 1	*Match No.*
1	2	3	4^{1}	5	6^{2}	7	8	9	10^{3}	11	12	13	14																					1
1	2		4	5	6	7	8	9		12^{2}	3		10	11^{1}	13																			2
1	2	12	4	5	6^{2}	7	8	9		13	3		10^{3}	11^{1}		14																		3
1	2	3		5		7	8	9^{2}	13	11^{3}	4	12	10			14	6^{1}																	4
1	2	3		5		7	8^{1}	9	12		4■		10			11^{2}	6	13																5
1	2	3		5	6		8	9	12	13			10			11^{2}	4^{1}	7																6
1	2	3		5		7	8	9^{2}	6	11^{1}			10	12		13		4																7
1	2			5		7	8	9	6^{1}	12				11	10^{2}	13	4	3																8
1	2			5		7	8	9^{2}		12	4		10	11^{1}		13	6	3																9
1	2			5	6	7	8^{2}	9^{1}	10	11				3	12				4	13														10
1	2			5	6	7	8	9	10	11^{1}		12		4					3															11
1	2		12	5	6	7	8	9	10	11				3^{1}				4																12
1^{6}	2	3	12	5	6	7	8^{2}	9		11^{1}							10	4			15	13												13
	2	3	12	5	6^{2}	7	8^{3}	9	10^{1}			14					11	4			1	13												14
	2	3		5	6	7	8	9	10								11	4			1													15
	2	3		5	12	7	8^{2}	9^{3}	10	11^{1}		13					6	4			1	14												16
1	2	3		5	6		8	9	10	11^{1}	4	12					7																	17
1	2	3		5	6		8	9		11	4	12				10^{1}	7																	18
1	2	3		5	6^{1}		8	9	10^{2}	11	4	12				13	7																	19
1	2	3		5			8	9		11	4		12			10^{1}	6						7											20
1	2	3		5			8	9		11	4^{2}	12	10^{1}				6					13	7											21
1	2	3	4				8	9^{2}		12		7^{1}	14			13	6	5					11	10^{3}										22
1	2	3	4				8	9		12		7^{1}					6	5					11	10										23
1	2	3	4				8	9		12		7^{1}					6	5				13	11	10^{2}										24
1	2	3	4				8	9		12		7^{1}					6	5					11	10										25
1	2^{3}	3	4				8	9^{2}		12		7					6	5		14		13	11	10^{1}										26
1	2	3	4				8	9		12		7^{1}					6	5					11	10										27
1	2	3	4				8	9		7							6	5^{1}				12	11^{2}	10	13									28
1	2	3	4				8	9		7			12				6	5					11		10^{1}									29
1	2		4				8	9		7			12				6	5					11		10^{1}	3								30
1	2	3	4				8	9^{2}		12			13				6	5				14	11		10^{3}	7^{1}								31
1	2	3	4				8^{1}	9		12			13				6	5					11		10^{2}	7^{3}	14							32
1	2	3	4				8	9^{1}		11			10^{2}				6	5				12			13		7							33
1	2	3	4				8	9		11			10^{1}				6	5				12	13				7^{2}							34
1	2	3	4				8	9		7			10^{1}				6	5					11		12									35
1	2	3	4				8	9^{1}		11			10				6	5				12					7							36
1^{6}	2	3	4^{2}				8			11			9				6	5				12			10^{1}		7	15	13					37
	2	3		12			8			11			9				6	5				13			10^{2}		7^{3}	1	4^{1}	14				38
	2	3					8					4	9^{1}					5				12			13		7		11	6	1	10^{2}		39
	2			12			8^{1}			13			9				6	5				14					7^{2}		4■	11	1	10^{3}	3	40
	2	3		4			8			7			12				6	5^{2}				10								11	1	9^{1}	13■	41
	2	3^{1}		5			8			11		12	9				6■					13			10^{2}		7			4	1			42
	2	3		5	12		8			7^{1}		4	9^{3}					6				13			14					11	1	10^{2}		43
	2	3		5			8			12		7^{1}	13					6				14			10^{2}		11			4	1	9^{3}		44
	2	3					8			11^{1}		12	13				6	5				9^{2}			10		14		4	7^{3}	1			45
	2	3		12			8			11			15				6	5				9^{2}			10^{6}				4	7^{1}	1■	13		46

FA Cup

First Round	Swindon T	(a)	1-4

Carling Cup

First Round	Walsall	(h)	1-0
Second Round	Coventry C	(a)	0-1

LDV Vans Trophy

First Round	Chester C	(h)	1-2

Play-offs

Semi-Final	Brentford	(h)	1-0
		(a)	2-1
Final (at Millennium Stadium)	Hartlepool U		4-2

SHREWSBURY TOWN FL Championship 2

FOUNDATION

Shrewsbury School having provided a number of the early England and Wales international players it is not surprising that there was a Town club as early as 1876 which won the Birmingham Senior Cup in 1879. However, the present Shrewsbury Town club was formed in 1886 and won the Welsh FA Cup as early as 1891.

Gay Meadow, Abbey Foregate, Shrewsbury SY2 6AB.

Telephone: (01743) 360 111.

Ticket Office: (01743) 360 111.

Website: www.shrewsburytown.com

Email: info@shrewsburytown.co.uk

Ground Capacity: 8,000.

Record Attendance: 18,917 v Walsall, Division 3, 26 April 1961.

Pitch Measurements: 114yd × 74yd.

Chairman: Roland Wycherley.

Vice-chairman: Keith Sayfritz.

Secretary: Judy Shone.

Manager: Gary Peters.

Assistant Manager: Mick Wadsworth.

Physio: Rachel Greenley MCSP.

HONOURS

Football League: Division 2 best season: 8th, 1983–84, 1984–85; Division 3 – Champions 1978–79, 1993–94; Division 4 – Runners-up 1974–75.

Conference: Promotion 2003–04 (play-offs)

FA Cup: best season: 6th rd, 1979, 1982.

Football League Cup: Semi-final 1961.

Welsh Cup: Winners 1891, 1938, 1977, 1979, 1984, 1985; Runners-up 1931, 1948, 1980.

Auto Windscreens Shield: Runners-up 1996

Colours: Blue and amber shirts, blue shorts, blue stockings.

Change Colours: Red and white shirts, white shorts, white stockings.

Year Formed: 1886.

Turned Professional: 1896.

Ltd Co.: 1936.

Club Nickname: 'Town', 'Blues' or 'Salop'. The name 'Salop' is a colloquialism for the county of Shropshire. Since Shrewsbury is the only club in Shropshire, cries of 'Come on Salop' are frequently used!

Previous Ground: 1886, Old Shrewsbury Racecourse; 1910, Gay Meadow.

First Football League Game: 19 August 1950, Division 3 (N), v Scunthorpe U (a) D 0–0 – Egglestone; Fisher, Lewis; Wheatley, Depear, Robinson; Griffin, Hope, Jackson, Brown, Barker.

Record League Victory: 7–0 v Swindon T, Division 3 (S), 6 May 1955 – McBride; Bannister, Skeech; Wallace, Maloney, Candlin; Price, O'Donnell (1), Weigh (4), Russell, McCue (2).

Record Cup Victory: 11–2 v Marine, FA Cup 1st rd, 11 November 1995 – Edwards, Seabury (Dempsey (1)), Withe (1), Evans (1), Whiston (2), Scott (1), Woods, Stevens (1), Spink (3) (Anthrobus), Walton, Berkley, (1 og).

SKY SPORTS FACT FILE

Terry Harkin signed for Shrewsbury Town from Southport in March 1969. On 2 May he scored a hat-trick against his former club in a 5–1 victory and went on to win two further caps for Northern Ireland while with them.

Record Defeat: 1–8 v Norwich C, Division 3 (S), 13 September 1952. 1–8 v Coventry C, Division 3, 22 October 1963.

Most League Points (2 for a win): 62, Division 4, 1974–75.

Most League Points (3 for a win): 79, Division 3, 1993–94.

Most League Goals: 101, Division 4, 1958–59.

Highest League Scorer in Season: Arthur Rowley, 38, Division 4, 1958–59.

Most League Goals in Total Aggregate: Arthur Rowley, 152, 1958–65 (thus completing his League record of 434 goals).

Most League Goals in One Match: 5, Alf Wood v Blackburn R, Division 3, 2 October 1971.

Most Capped Player: Jimmy McLaughlin, 5 (12), Northern Ireland; Bernard McNally, 5, Northern Ireland.

Most League Appearances: Mickey Brown, 418, 1986–91; 1992–94; 1996–2001.

Youngest League Player: Graham French, 16 years 177 days v Reading, 30 September 1961.

Record Transfer Fee Received: £700,000 from Crewe Alex for Dave Walton, December 1997.

Record Transfer Fee Paid: £100,000 to Aldershot for John Dungworth, November 1979 and £100,000 to Southampton for Mark Blake, August 1990.

Football League Record: 1950 Elected to Division 3 (N); 1951–58 Division 3 (S); 1958–59 Division 4; 1959–74 Division 3; 1974–75 Division 4; 1975–79 Division 3; 1979–89 Division 2; 1989–94 Division 3; 1994–97 Division 2; 1997–2003 Division 3; 2003–04 Conference; 2004– FL2.

MANAGERS

W. Adams 1905–12
(Secretary-Manager)
A. Weston 1912–34
(Secretary-Manager)
Jack Roscamp 1934–35
Sam Ramsey 1935–36
Ted Bousted 1936–40
Leslie Knighton 1945–49
Harry Chapman 1949–50
Sammy Crooks 1950–54
Walter Rowley 1955–57
Harry Potts 1957–58
Johnny Spuhler 1958
Arthur Rowley 1958–68
Harry Gregg 1968–72
Maurice Evans 1972–73
Alan Durban 1974–78
Richie Barker 1978
Graham Turner 1978–84
Chic Bates 1984–87
Ian McNeill 1987–90
Asa Hartford 1990–91
John Bond 1991–93
Fred Davies 1994–97
(previously Caretaker-Manager 1993–94)
Jake King 1997–99
Kevin Ratcliffe 1999–2003
Jimmy Quinn 2003–04
Gary Peters November 2004–

LATEST SEQUENCES

Longest Sequence of League Wins: 7, 28.10.1995 – 16.12.1995.

Longest Sequence of League Defeats: 11, 9.4.2003 – 14.8.2004.

Longest Sequence of League Draws: 6, 30.10.1963 – 14.12.1963.

Longest Sequence of Unbeaten League Matches: 16, 30.10.1993 – 26.2.1994.

Longest Sequence Without a League Win: 18, 8.3.2003 – 14.8.2004.

Successive Scoring Runs: 28 from 7.9.1960.

Successive Non-scoring Runs: 6 from 1.1.1991.

TEN YEAR LEAGUE RECORD

		P	W	D	L	F	A	Pts	Pos
1995-96	Div 2	46	13	14	19	58	70	53	18
1996-97	Div 2	46	11	13	22	49	74	46	22
1997-98	Div 3	46	16	13	17	61	62	61	13
1998-99	Div 3	46	14	14	18	52	63	56	15
1999-2000	Div 3	46	9	13	24	40	67	40	22
2000-01	Div 3	46	15	10	21	49	65	55	15
2001-02	Div 3	46	20	10	16	64	53	70	9
2002-03	Div 3	46	9	14	23	62	92	41	24
2003-04	Conf.	42	20	14	8	67	42	74	3
2004-05	FL 2	46	11	16	19	48	53	49	21

DID YOU KNOW 

In 1950–51 Shrewsbury Town began with a goalless draw with fellow newcomers Scunthorpe United and finished 21st in their first season. In 2004–05 back in the Football League they were 21st. In the last game they drew 0–0 with Scunthorpe!

SHREWSBURY TOWN 2004–05 LEAGUE RECORD

Match No.	Date	Venue	Opponents	Result	H/T Score	Lg. Pos.	Goalscorers	Attendance
1	Aug 7	H	Lincoln C	L 0-1	0-0	—		4843
2	10	A	Macclesfield T	L 1-2	0-2	—	Smith [66]	2641
3	14	A	Cambridge U	L 0-1	0-0	24		3135
4	21	H	Northampton T	W 2-0	0-0	21	Grant [50], Smith [78]	3980
5	28	A	Oxford U	L 0-2	0-1	22		4430
6	31	H	Cheltenham T	W 2-0	1-0	—	Lowe [35], Rodgers [88]	3862
7	Sept 4	A	Bristol R	D 0-0	0-0	19		8381
8	11	H	Bury	D 2-2	0-1	17	Moss [70], Challinor (og) [76]	3801
9	18	A	Boston U	D 2-2	2-2	18	Logan [25], Smith [34]	2593
10	25	H	Yeovil T	L 1-2	1-0	22	Rodgers [40]	4196
11	Oct 2	A	Wycombe W	D 1-1	1-0	22	Moss [37]	4634
12	8	H	Rushden & D	L 0-1	0-1	—		3882
13	16	A	Leyton Orient	L 1-4	0-3	24	Fox [90]	3718
14	19	H	Grimsby T	D 1-1	0-1	—	Sedgemore [77]	2956
15	23	H	Southend U	D 1-1	1-0	23	Street [14]	3719
16	30	A	Kidderminster H	W 1-0	0-0	22	Lowe [82]	3830
17	Nov 6	A	Notts Co	L 0-3	0-1	22		5745
18	20	H	Swansea C	W 2-0	1-0	22	Sedgemore [21], Walton [81]	5055
19	27	A	Scunthorpe U	L 1-3	0-1	22	Tolley J [70]	4418
20	Dec 7	H	Rochdale	L 0-2	0-0	—		3677
21	11	A	Chester C	D 1-1	0-0	22	Langmead [62]	3219
22	18	H	Mansfield T	L 0-2	0-1	22		3469
23	28	H	Darlington	W 4-0	3-0	22	Aiston [34], Tolley J 2 [38, 44], Edwards [90]	3915
24	Jan 1	H	Bristol R	W 2-0	0-0	21	Edwards [64], Grant [71]	5043
25	3	A	Yeovil T	L 2-4	0-1	21	Sedgemore (pen) [64], Edwards [74]	7250
26	8	A	Rushden & D	D 0-0	0-0	21		2829
27	15	H	Boston U	D 0-0	0-0	21		3789
28	22	A	Darlington	L 0-3	0-1	22		3934
29	29	H	Wycombe W	L 0-1	0-1	22		3884
30	Feb 5	H	Leyton Orient	W 4-1	1-0	21	Walton [43], Darby [52], Moss 2 [68, 75]	3496
31	8	A	Bury	D 0-0	0-0	—		2233
32	12	A	Grimsby T	W 1-0	1-0	21	Sedgemore [26]	4781
33	19	H	Kidderminster H	W 4-2	3-2	19	Moss 2 [33, 40], Langmead [45], Rodgers [56]	5309
34	22	A	Southend U	L 0-1	0-0	—		4219
35	26	H	Chester C	W 5-0	2-0	18	Tolley J [28], Rodgers [41], Sedgemore (pen) [57], Lowe [65], Langmead [78]	4859
36	Mar 5	A	Mansfield T	D 1-1	0-0	19	Rodgers [75]	3278
37	12	H	Macclesfield T	L 0-1	0-0	19		4262
38	19	A	Lincoln C	L 0-2	0-2	20		4255
39	25	H	Cambridge U	D 0-0	0-0	—		5309
40	28	A	Northampton T	L 0-2	0-2	21		6514
41	Apr 2	H	Oxford U	W 3-0	0-0	20	Edwards [47], Wanless (og) [57], Rodgers [71]	3974
42	8	A	Cheltenham T	D 1-1	0-0	—	Sheron [79]	3769
43	16	A	Rochdale	D 1-1	1-1	21	Sheron (pen) [6]	3142
44	23	H	Notts Co	D 1-1	0-1	21	Edwards [60]	4202
45	30	A	Swansea C	L 0-1	0-1	21		11,469
46	May 7	H	Scunthorpe U	D 0-0	0-0	21		6285

Final League Position: 21

GOALSCORERS

League (48): Moss 6, Rodgers 6, Edwards 5, Sedgemore 5 (2 pens), Tolley J 4, Langmead 3, Lowe 3, Smith 3, Grant 2, Sheron 2 (1 pen), Walton 2, Aiston 1, Darby 1, Fox 1, Logan 1, Street 1, own goals 2.
Carling Cup (1): Rodgers 1.
FA Cup (0).
LDV Vans Trophy (4): Logan 1, Rodgers 1, Tolley J 1, own goal 1.

Howie S 40	Sedgemore J 25+6	Challis T 38	Walton D 20+2	Tinson D 42+1	Ridler D 6+3	Edwards D 16+11	Tolley J 33+3	Rodgers L 35+1	Darby D 8+8	Smith B 10+2	Lowe R 19+11	Aiston S 26+9	Grant J 10+9	O'Connor M 13+8	Moss D 26	Cramb C —+2	Street K 15+6	Whitehead S 37+3	McGrath J 7+1	Stephens R —+2	Logan R 5	Fox D 2+2	Langmead K 24+4	Ashton N 22+2	Burns L 1+1	Lyng C —+4	Wilkinson A 9	Sheron M 6+1	Hart J 6	Adaggio M —+5	Cowan G 5	Match No.
1	2^{1}	3	4	5	6	7^{2}	8	9	10	11^{3}	12	13	14																			1
1	2^{1}	3	4	5	6^{3}	7^{2}	8	9	10	11	13	12	14																			2
1		3	4	5	6^{2}		8■	9	10^{1}	7	2	11	12	13																		3
1	12	3	4	5	13	7^{1}		9		6	8^{2}	11	10^{3}		2	14																4
1	12	3	4	5				9		6	8^{1}	11^{3}	10^{2}		2	13	7	14														5
1	12	3		5				9		6	8^{1}		10		2		7	4	11													6
1	8	3		5				9		6	12		10^{1}		2		7	4	11													7
1	12	3		5			13	9^{1}		6	8^{3}	14■	10		2		7^{2}	4	11													8
1	11	3	12	5			8	9^{2}		6			13		2		7^{3}	4		14	10^{1}											9
1	7^{2}	3^{3}	12	5			8	9	13	6					2			4	11^{1}	14	10											10
1	6^{1}	3		5			8	9^{3}	14		13	12			2		7	4	11^{2}		10											11
1		3^{1}		5	12			9	13		8	14			2		7	4	11^{3}		10^{2}	6										12
1				5	6		8	9	12		7^{3}	13			2		14	4	11^{2}		10^{1}	3										13
1	3			5			8^{1}	9	10		12	11		6^{2}	2		7^{3}	4	13			14										14
1	3			5				9	10		8	11		6^{1}	2		7	4				12										15
1	12	3		5			8		10		9^{2}	11	13	6^{1}	2		7	4														16
1		3		5		12	8	9			10	11	7	6^{1}	2■			4														17
1	11	3	4	5				9			10			6	2		7	8														18
1	11^{1}	3	4■	5		13	12	9			10			8^{3}	2		7	6^{2}					14									19
1		3		5			8	9	12		11			6	2		7^{1}	4					10									20
1		3^{1}		5		13	8	9^{3}			7^{2}			6■	2■		12	4					10	11	14							21
1	2	3^{2}		5			8	9			7^{1}		13				12	4					10	11	6							22
1	7		4	5		6	8		12		13	11^{3}	10^{2}					2					9^{1}	3		14						23
1	7			5	6	4	8^{1}					11^{2}	10	12				2					9	3		13						24
1	7	3^{3}		5	6	8	4	12■				11^{2}	10^{1}	13				2					9			14						25
1	7			5		8	4				12	11	10^{1}		2			6					9	3								26
1	7			5		8	6				10	11		12	2			4					9	3^{1}								27
1	7	3		5		10^{1}	8		12		13	11		6^{2}	2			4					9									28
1	7	3^{2}		5		8	6	9	12			11			2			4					10^{1}	13								29
1	7		4	5			8	9	10^{1}			11			2			3					12	6								30
1	7	3	4	5^{1}		12		9	10^{2}			11			2			6					13	8								31
1	7	3	4		12	13	6	9^{3}			14	11^{2}			2^{1}			5					10	8								32
1	7	3	4	12		13	8	9				11^{3}		14	2^{2}			5^{1}					10	6								33
1		3	4	5		7	8	9^{2}			13	11^{3}	12	6				2					10^{1}	14								34
1	7	3	4	5		12	8^{3}	9^{1}			11^{2}		13	14				2					10	6								35
1	11^{3}	3^{1}	4	5		13	6	9			7^{2}	12		14				2					10	8								36
1		3	4	5		12	8				9^{1}	11	13	6				2					10	7^{2}								37
1		3	4				8				12	11		6^{1}			13	5					10	7			2	9^{2}				38
1	12	3	4			13	8	9				11^{2}		6^{1}				5					14	7			2	10^{3}				39
1	11^{1}	3	4	5			8	9				12						6■					10^{2}	7			2	13				40
		3	4	5		12	8^{1}	9^{3}				11^{2}					13						10	6			2	7	1	14		41
		3		5		7^{1}	8	9^{2}				12											10	4			2	11	1	13	6	42
		3		5		7^{3}	4^{1}	9						12			13	14					10	8^{2}			2	11	1		6	43
		3		5		7						11					8^{2}	12					10	4			2	9^{1}	1	13	6	44
		3		5^{1}		7				12		11^{2}					9^{3}	4					10	8		13	2		1	14	6	45
		3		5		4	12	9^{3}		13		11^{2}						2					10	8			7^{1}		1	14	6	46

FA Cup
First Round Histon (a) 0-2

Carling Cup
First Round Tranmere R (a) 1-2

LDV Vans Trophy
First Round Bournemouth (h) 3-2
Second Round Southend U (a) 1-4

SOUTHAMPTON FL Championship

FOUNDATION

Formed largely by players from the Deanery FC, which had been established by school teachers in 1880. Most of the founders were connected with the young men's association of St Mary's Church. At the inaugural meeting held in November 1885 the club was named Southampton St Mary's and the church's curate was elected president.

St Mary's Stadium, Britannia Road, Southampton SO14 5FP.

Telephone: 0870 220 0000.

Fax: (02380) 727 727.

Ticket Office: 0870 220 0155.

Website: www.saintsfc.co.uk

Email: sfc@saintsfc.co.uk

Ground Capacity: 32,689.

Record Attendance: 32,104 v Liverpool, FA Premier League, 18 January 2003.

Pitch Measurements: 102.6m × 65.8m.

Chairman: Rupert Lowe.

Vice-chairman: Brian Hunt.

Managing Director: Andrew Cowen.

Secretary: Liz Coley.

Manager: Harry Redknapp.

Physio: Jim Joyce.

Colours: Red and white striped shirts, black shorts, white stockings.

Change Colours: Sky blue shirts with navy trim, navy shorts with sky blue trim, sky blue stockings with navy trim.

Year Formed: 1885.

Turned Professional: 1894.

Ltd Co.: 1897.

Previous Name: 1885, Southampton St Mary's; 1897, Southampton.

Club Nickname: 'The Saints'.

Previous Grounds: 1885, Antelope Ground; 1897, County Cricket Ground; 1898, The Dell; 2001, St Mary's.

First Football League Game: 28 August 1920, Division 3, v Gillingham (a) D 1–1 – Allen; Parker, Titmuss; Shelley, Campbell, Turner; Barratt, Dominy (1), Rawlings, Moore, Foxall.

Record League Victory: 9–3 v Wolverhampton W, Division 2, 18 September 1965 – Godfrey; Jones, Williams; Walker, Knapp, Huxford; Paine (2), O'Brien (1), Melia, Chivers (4), Sydenham (2).

HONOURS

Football League: Division 1 – Runners-up 1983–84; Division 2 – Runners-up 1965–66, 1977–78; Division 3 (S) – Champions 1921–22; Runners-up 1920–21; Division 3 – Champions 1959–60.

FA Cup: Winners 1976; Runners-up 1900, 1902, 2003.

Football League Cup: Runners-up 1979.

Zenith Data Systems Cup: Runners-up 1992.

European Competitions: *European Fairs Cup:* 1969–70. *UEFA Cup:* 1971–72, 1981–82, 1982–83, 1984–85, 2003–04. *European Cup-Winners' Cup:* 1976–77.

SKY SPORTS FACT FILE

In their Southern League days Southampton won the championship six times in eight years up to 1903–04. Right-half Sammy Meston was a regular choice for these years and his half a dozen medals represented a club record of its kind.

Record Cup Victory: 7–1 v Ipswich T, FA Cup 3rd rd, 7 January 1961 – Reynolds; Davies, Traynor; Conner, Page, Huxford; Paine (1), O'Brien (3 incl. 1p), Reeves, Mulgrew (2), Penk (1).

Record Defeat: 0–8 v Tottenham H, Division 2, 28 March 1936. 0–8 v Everton, Division 1, 20 November 1971.

Most League Points (2 for a win): 61, Division 3 (S), 1921–22 and Division 3, 1959–60.

Most League Points (3 for a win): 77, Division 1, 1983–84.

Most League Goals: 112, Division 3 (S), 1957–58.

Highest League Scorer in Season: Derek Reeves, 39, Division 3, 1959–60.

Most League Goals in Total Aggregate: Mike Channon, 185, 1966–77, 1979–82.

Most League Goals in One Match: 5, Charlie Wayman v Leicester C, Division 2, 23 October 1948.

Most Capped Player: Peter Shilton, 49 (125), England.

Most League Appearances: Terry Paine, 713, 1956–74.

Youngest League Player: Danny Wallace, 16 years 313 days v Manchester U, 29 November 1980.

Record Transfer Fee Received: £8,000,000 from Tottenham H for Dean Richards, October 2001.

Record Transfer Fee Paid: £4,000,000 to Derby Co for Rory Delap, July 2001.

Football League Record: 1920 Original Member of Division 3; 1921–22 Division 3 (S); 1922–53 Division 2; 1953–58 Division 3 (S); 1958–60 Division 3; 1960–66 Division 2; 1966–74 Division 1; 1974–78 Division 2; 1978–92 Division 1; 1992–2005 FA Premier League; 2005– FLC.

MANAGERS

Cecil Knight 1894–95
(Secretary-Manager)
Charles Robson 1895–97
E. Arnfield 1897–1911
(Secretary-Manager)
(continued as Secretary)
George Swift 1911–12
Ernest Arnfield 1912–19
Jimmy McIntyre 1919–24
Arthur Chadwick 1925–31
George Kay 1931–36
George Gross 1936–37
Tom Parker 1937–43
J. R. Sarjantson stepped down from the board to act as Secretary-Manager 1943–47 with the next two listed being team Managers during this period
Arthur Dominy 1943–46
Bill Dodgin Snr 1946–49
Sid Cann 1949–51
George Roughton 1952–55
Ted Bates 1955–73
Lawrie McMenemy 1973–85
Chris Nicholl 1985–91
Ian Branfoot 1991–94
Alan Ball 1994–95
Dave Merrington 1995–96
Graeme Souness 1996–97
Dave Jones 1997–2000
Glenn Hoddle 2000–01
Stuart Gray 2001
Gordon Strachan 2001–04
Paul Sturrock 2004
Steve Wigley 2004
Harry Redknapp December 2004–

LATEST SEQUENCES

Longest Sequence of League Wins: 6, 3.3.1992 – 4.4.1992.

Longest Sequence of League Defeats: 5, 16.8.1998 – 12.9.1998.

Longest Sequence of League Draws: 7, 28.12.1994 – 11.2.1995.

Longest Sequence of Unbeaten League Matches: 19, 5.9.1921 – 31.12.1921.

Longest Sequence Without a League Win: 20, 30.8.1969 – 27.12.1969.

Successive Scoring Runs: 24 from 5.9.1966.

Successive Non-scoring Runs: 5 from 1.9.1937.

TEN YEAR LEAGUE RECORD

		P	*W*	*D*	*L*	*F*	*A*	*Pts*	*Pos*
1995-96	PR Lge	38	9	11	18	34	52	38	17
1996-97	PR Lge	38	10	11	17	50	56	41	16
1997-98	PR Lge	38	14	6	18	50	55	48	12
1998-99	PR Lge	38	11	8	19	37	64	41	17
1999-2000	PR Lge	38	12	8	18	45	62	44	15
2000-01	PR Lge	38	14	10	14	40	48	52	10
2001-02	PR Lge	38	12	9	17	46	54	45	11
2002-03	PR Lge	38	13	13	12	43	46	52	8
2003-04	PR Lge	38	12	11	15	44	45	47	12
2004-05	PR Lge	38	6	14	18	45	66	32	20

DID YOU KNOW ?

The well documented failure to achieve promotion in 1948–49, when with seven matches remaining Southampton led the Second Division by eight points, was mainly due to injury to Charlie Wayman who at the time had scored 32 goals in 35 matches.

SOUTHAMPTON 2004–05 LEAGUE RECORD

Match No.	*Date*	*Venue*	*Opponents*	*Result*	*H/T Score*	*Lg. Pos.*	*Goalscorers*	*Attendance*
1	Aug 14	A	Aston Villa	L 0-2	0-2	—		36,690
2	21	H	Blackburn R	W 3-2	1-0	10	Phillips 32, Svensson A 74, Beattie (pen) 90	27,492
3	25	H	Bolton W	L 1-2	0-2	—	Crouch 85	30,713
4	28	A	Chelsea	L 1-2	1-2	15	Beattie 1	40,864
5	Sept 13	A	Charlton Ath	D 0-0	0-0	—		24,263
6	19	H	Newcastle U	L 1-2	0-1	17	Svensson A 53	30,709
7	25	A	Fulham	L 0-1	0-1	17		19,237
8	Oct 2	H	Manchester C	D 0-0	0-0	18		28,605
9	16	A	Everton	L 0-1	0-0	19		35,256
10	24	H	Birmingham C	D 0-0	0-0	18		27,568
11	30	A	Arsenal	D 2-2	0-0	18	Delap 2 80, 85	38,141
12	Nov 6	H	WBA	D 2-2	1-2	18	Svensson A 28 Robinson (og) 87	31,057
13	13	H	Portsmouth	W 2-1	1-1	17	Blackstock 18, Phillips 71	30,921
14	20	A	Norwich C	L 1-2	1-1	17	Beattie 24	23,706
15	27	H	Crystal Palace	D 2-2	0-0	18	Phillips 50, Jakobsson 76	31,833
16	Dec 4	A	Manchester U	L 0-3	0-0	18		67,921
17	11	H	Middlesbrough	D 2-2	1-0	19	Phillips 45, Crouch 54	29018
18	18	A	Tottenham H	L 1-5	0-3	19	Crouch 47	36,254
19	26	H	Charlton Ath	D 0-0	0-0	19		31,195
20	28	A	Liverpool	L 0-1	0-1	19		42,382
21	Jan 1	A	Manchester C	L 1-2	0-2	19	Phillips (pen) 90	42,895
22	5	H	Fulham	D 3-3	2-2	—	Phillips 2 21, 29, Rosenior (og) 71	27,343
23	15	A	Newcastle U	L 1-2	1-2	19	Crouch 42	51,266
24	22	H	Liverpool	W 2-0	2-0	18	Prutton 5, Crouch 22	32,017
25	Feb 2	A	Birmingham C	L 1-2	0-2	—	Camara 52	28,797
26	6	H	Everton	D 2-2	1-1	19	Crouch 36, Camara 55	31,509
27	22	A	WBA	D 0-0	0-0	—		25,865
28	26	H	Arsenal	D 1-1	0-1	18	Crouch 67	31,815
29	Mar 5	H	Tottenham H	W 1-0	0-0	18	Quashie 51	31,903
30	20	A	Middlesbrough	W 3-1	1-1	17	Jakobsson 14, Crouch 2 60, 67	30,082
31	Apr 2	H	Chelsea	L 1-3	0-2	17	Phillips 69	31,949
32	9	A	Blackburn R	L 0-3	0-1	18		20,726
33	16	H	Aston Villa	L 2-3	2-0	18	Phillips 4, Crouch 13	31,926
34	19	A	Bolton W	D 1-1	0-1	—	Phillips 69	25,125
35	24	A	Portsmouth	L 1-4	1-4	20	Camara 20	20,210
36	30	H	Norwich C	W 4-3	3-3	17	Oakley 7, Crouch 20, Le Saux 39, Camara 88	31,944
37	May 7	A	Crystal Palace	D 2-2	1-1	18	Crouch (pen) 37, Higginbotham 90	26,066
38	15	H	Manchester U	L 1-2	1-1	20	O'Shea (og) 10	32,066

Final League Position: 20

GOALSCORERS

League (45): Crouch 12 (1 pen), Phillips 10 (1 pen), Camara 4, Beattie 3 (1 pen), Svensson A 3, Delap 2, Jakobsson 2, Blackstock 1, Higginbotham 1, Le Saux 1, Oakley 1, Prutton 1, Quashie 1, own goals 3.
Carling Cup (8): Blackstock 4, McCann 1, Ormerod 1, Phillips 1, Prutton 1.
FA Cup (10): Crouch 4 (1 pen), Camara 2, Phillips 2, Oakley 1, Redknapp 1.

Niemi A 28	Dodd J 4 + 1	Le Saux G 24 + 1	Folly Y 1 + 2	Lundekvam C 33 + 1	Higginbotham D 20 + 1	Fernandes F 14 + 2	Prutton D 19 + 4	Ormerod B 5 + 4	Phillips K 21 + 9	Nilsson M 12 + 4	Delap R 34 + 3	Svensson A 21 + 9	Crouch P 18 + 9	Telfer P 26 + 4	Beattie J 11	Van Damme J 4 + 2	Kenton D 9	Jakobsson A 24 + 3	Best L 1 + 2	McCann N 5 + 6	Blackstock D 8 + 1	Blayney A 1	Keller K 4	Griffit L — + 2	Cranie M 3	Oakley M 6 + 1	Davenport C 5 + 2	Redknapp J 16	Smith P 5 + 1	Jones K 1 + 1	Bernard O 12 + 1	Quashie N 13	Camara H 10 + 3	*Match No.*
1	2	3	4^{2}	5	6	7	8	9^{3}	10	11^{1}	12	13	14																					1
1		3		5	6	7	8		10		4	11		2	9																			2
1		3		5	6	7	8		10		4^{1}	11	12	2	9																			3
1		3	12^{2}	5	6	7^{1}	8		10		4	11^{3}	13	2	9	14																		4
1		3		5		7^{2}	8		10	12	4	11	13		9		2^{1}	6																5
1		3		5		7	8		10^{1}	2	4	11^{2}	12		9			6	13															6
1		3		5		7	8		10	2	4	11^{1}			9			6		12														7
1		3^{3}		5		7^{2}	8		10	2	4	11	12		9^{1}	14		6		13														8
1							8			2	4	7		12		3	5	6	9^{1}	11	10													9
1				5		7^{1}	12	13		8^{2}	4	10				3	2	6		11	9													10
1				5	3		12	10^{2}		11	4	8^{1}		7			2	6	14	13	9^{3}													11
				5			12	13	10	11^{1}	4	8		7		3	2	6^{3}		14	9^{2}	1												12
	12	3		5		11^{3}			13		4	8		7	9^{2}		2	6^{1}			10		1	14										13
	2^{3}	3		5		7			12	13	4	8	14	11^{2}	9		6				10^{1}		1											14
	2^{2}	3				11			10		4	8	12	7			5	6			9^{1}		1	13										15
		3		5	11	12			10	2	4^{1}	8		7	9^{2}			6			13		1											16
1		11		5	3	7^{1}			10	2	4	8	9	12				6																17
1	2^{1}		12	5	3		4		10	11^{2}		8	9	7			6	13																18
1				5	3		12	13	10		4	14	8^{3}	7	9^{2}			6							2	11^{1}								19
1					6		7	9	12		4	13		2				5		11	10^{1}				3	8^{2}								20
1					6	12	7	9^{1}	10		4		13	2				5		11					3	8^{2}								21
1				5	3	7^{1}			10		4	11	9	2				13		12							6^{2}	8						22
1^{G}				5	3		7	12	10^{1}		4	13	9	2						11^{2}							6	8	15					23
1				5	3		11			7^{1}	4	10^{2}	9	2				12									6	8		13				24
1				5			7				4	12	9	2		11^{1}											6	8		10^{2}	3		13	25
		11		5			2				4		9														6	8	1		3	7	10	26
		11		5			7				2		9					6										4	1		3	8	10	27
		11^{2}		5			$7^{\blacksquare}$		12		2		9	13				6										4	1		3	8	10^{1}	28
		11^{2}		5	6					12	2^{1}	13	9	7														4	1		3	8	10	29
1		11^{1}		5					13		2	12	9	7				6										4			3	8	10^{2}	30
1		11^{1}		5					13		2	12	9	7				6										4			3	8	10^{2}	31
		11^{2}		5	12				13		2	14	9	7				6										4	1		3^{1}	8	10^{3}	32
1		12		5					10		2	11^{1}	9	7^{3}				6^{2}									13	4			3	8	14	33
1		11^{2}		5	3				10	12	2	4^{1}	9	7				6								13						8		34
1				5	3				9		2			7				6								8^{1}		4			12	11	10	35
1		11^{3}		12	5				10		2^{2}		9	13				6^{1}								7		4			3	8	14	36
1		11^{2}		5	6				13		12		$9^{\blacksquare}$	2						14						7^{1}		4^{3}			3	8	10	37
1		11^{1}		5	6		7^{2}	9	12		13			2													14	4			3^{3}	8	10	38

FA Cup

Third Round	Northampton T	(a)	3-1
Fourth Round	Portsmouth	(h)	2-1
Fifth Round	Brentford	(h)	2-2
		(a)	3-1
Sixth Round	Manchester U	(h)	0-4

Carling Cup

Second Round	Northampton T	(a)	3-0
Third Round	Colchester U	(h)	3-2
Fourth Round	Watford	(a)	2-5

SOUTHEND UNITED FL Championship 1

FOUNDATION

The leading club in Southend around the turn of the century was Southend Athletic, but they were an amateur concern. Southend United was a more ambitious professional club when they were founded in 1906, employing Bob Jack as secretary-manager and immediately joining the Second Division of the Southern League.

Roots Hall, Victoria Avenue, Southend-on-Sea, Essex SS2 6NQ.

Telephone: (01702) 304 050.

Fax: (01702) 304 124.

Ticket Office: (01702) 304 090.

Website: www.southendunited.co.uk

Email: info@southend-united.co.uk

Ground Capacity: 12,343.

Record Attendance: 31,090 v Liverpool, FA Cup 3rd rd, 10 January 1979.

Pitch Measurements: 110yd × 74yd.

Chairman: Ron Martin.

Vice-chairman: Geoffrey King.

Secretary: Helen Norbury.

Manager: Steve Tilson.

Assistant Manager: Paul Brush.

Physio: John Stannard.

Club Nickname: 'The Blues' or 'The Shrimpers'.

Colours: Navy blue shirts, navy blue shorts, navy blue stockings.

Change Colours: White shirts with black sleeves, white shorts, white stockings

Year Formed: 1906.

Turned Professional: 1906.

Ltd Co.: 1919.

Previous Grounds: 1906, Roots Hall, Prittlewell; 1920, Kursaal; 1934, Southend Stadium; 1955, Roots Hall Football Ground.

First Football League Game: 28 August 1920, Division 3, v Brighton & HA (a) W 2–0 – Capper; Reid, Newton; Wileman, Henderson, Martin; Nicholls, Nuttall, Fairclough (2), Myers, Dorsett.

Record League Victory: 9–2 v Newport Co, Division 3 (S), 5 September 1936 – McKenzie; Nelson, Everest (1); Deacon, Turner, Carr; Bolan, Lane (1), Goddard (4), Dickinson (2), Oswald (1).

Record Cup Victory: 10–1 v Golders Green, FA Cup 1st rd, 24 November 1934 – Moore; Morfitt, Kelly; Mackay, Joe Wilson, Carr (1); Lane (1), Johnson (5), Cheesmuir (2), Deacon (1), Oswald. 10–1 v Brentwood, FA Cup 2nd rd, 7 December 1968 – Roberts; Bentley, Birks; McMillan (1) Beesley, Kurila; Clayton, Chisnall, Moore (4), Best (5), Hamilton. 10–1 v Aldershot, Leyland Daf Cup Prel rd,

HONOURS

Football League: Division 1 best season: 13th, 1994–95; Promoted from Championship 2 2004–05 (play-offs); Division 3 – Runners-up 1990–91; Division 4 – Champions 1980–81; Runners-up 1971–72, 1977–78.

FA Cup: best season: old 3rd rd, 1921; 5th rd, 1926, 1952, 1976, 1993.

Football League Cup: never past 3rd rd.

LDV Vans Trophy: Runners-up 2004, 2005.

SKY SPORTS FACT FILE

There was a debut hat-trick by Freddy Eastwood on 16 October 2004 for Southend United against Swansea City while he was on loan from Grays Athletic. Subsequently signed he scored in seven consecutive matches and finished top scorer.

6 November 1990 – Sansome; Austin, Powell, Cornwell, Prior (1), Tilson (3), Cawley, Butler, Ansah (1), Benjamin (1), Angell (4).

Record Defeat: 1–9 v Brighton & HA, Division 3, 27 November 1965.

Most League Points (2 for a win): 67, Division 4, 1980–81.

Most League Points (3 for a win): 85, Division 3, 1990–91.

Most League Goals: 92, Division 3 (S), 1950–51.

Highest League Scorer in Season: Jim Shankly, 31, 1928–29; Sammy McCrory, 1957–58, both in Division 3 (S).

Most League Goals in Total Aggregate: Roy Hollis, 122, 1953–60.

Most League Goals in One Match: 5, Jim Shankly v Merthyr T, Division 3S, 1 March 1930.

Most Capped Player: George Mackenzie, 9, Eire.

Most League Appearances: Sandy Anderson, 452, 1950–63.

Youngest League Player: Phil O'Connor, 16 years 76 days v Lincoln C, 26 December 1969.

Record Transfer Fee Received: £3,570,000 from Nottingham F for Stan Collymore, June 1993.

Record Transfer Fee Paid: £750,000 to Crystal Palace for Stan Collymore, November 1992.

Football League Record: 1920 Original Member of Division 3; 1921–58 Division 3 (S); 1958–66 Division 3; 1966–72 Division 4; 1972–76 Division 3; 1976–78 Division 4; 1978–80 Division 3; 1980–81 Division 4; 1981–84 Division 3; 1984–87 Division 4; 1987–89 Division 3; 1989–90 Division 4; 1990–91 Division 3; 1991–92 Division 2; 1992–97 Division 1; 1997–98 Division 2; 1998–2004 Division 3; 2004–05 FL2; 2005– FL1.

MANAGERS

Bob Jack 1906–10
George Molyneux 1910–11
O. M. Howard 1911–12
Joe Bradshaw 1912–19
Ned Liddell 1919–20
Tom Mather 1920–21
Ted Birnie 1921–34
David Jack 1934–40
Harry Warren 1946–56
Eddie Perry 1956–60
Frank Broome 1960
Ted Fenton 1961–65
Alvan Williams 1965–67
Ernie Shepherd 1967–69
Geoff Hudson 1969–70
Arthur Rowley 1970–76
Dave Smith 1976–83
Peter Morris 1983–84
Bobby Moore 1984–86
Dave Webb 1986–87
Dick Bate 1987
Paul Clark 1987–88
Dave Webb *(General Manager)* 1988–92
Colin Murphy 1992–93
Barry Fry 1993
Peter Taylor 1993–95
Steve Thompson 1995
Ronnie Whelan 1995–97
Alvin Martin 1997–99
Alan Little 1999–2000
David Webb 2000–01
Rob Newman 2001–03
Steve Wignall 2003–04
Steve Tilson May 2004–

LATEST SEQUENCES

Longest Sequence of League Wins: 7, 27.4.1990 – 18.9.1990.

Longest Sequence of League Defeats: 6, 29.8.1987 – 19.9.1987.

Longest Sequence of League Draws: 6, 30.1.1982 – 19.2.1982.

Longest Sequence of Unbeaten League Matches: 16, 20.2.1932 – 29.8.1932.

Longest Sequence Without a League Win: 17, 31.12.1983 – 14.4.1984.

Successive Scoring Runs: 24 from 23.3.1929.

Successive Non-scoring Runs: 6 from 28.10.1933.

TEN YEAR LEAGUE RECORD

		P	W	D	L	F	A	Pts	Pos
1995-96	Div 1	46	15	14	17	52	61	59	14
1996-97	Div 1	46	8	15	23	42	86	39	24
1997-98	Div 2	46	11	10	25	47	79	43	24
1998-99	Div 3	46	14	12	20	52	58	54	18
1999-2000	Div 3	46	15	11	20	53	61	56	16
2000-01	Div 3	46	15	18	13	55	53	63	11
2001-02	Div 3	46	15	13	18	51	54	58	12
2002-03	Div 3	46	17	3	26	47	59	54	17
2003-04	Div 3	46	14	12	20	51	63	54	17
2004-05	FL 2	46	22	12	12	65	46	78	4

DID YOU KNOW?

During 2004–05 Southend United had a run of 14 unbeaten League matches, the third best in the club's history. There was also a personal best for central defender Adam Barrett who scored 11 League goals, two more than in his entire previous career.

SOUTHEND UNITED 2004–05 LEAGUE RECORD

Match No.	Date	Venue	Opponents	Result		H/T Score	Lg. Pos.	Goalscorers	Attendance
1	Aug 7	H	Cheltenham T	L	0-2	0-2	—		5332
2	10	A	Lincoln C	D	1-1	1-1	—	Gray (pen) [34]	3991
3	14	A	Rochdale	L	0-2	0-1	22		2218
4	21	H	Cambridge U	D	0-0	0-0	23		3941
5	27	A	Bristol R	L	1-2	0-1	—	Barrett [71]	9287
6	30	H	Macclesfield T	W	2-1	1-0	20	Barrett 2 [42, 55]	3753
7	Sept 4	A	Rushden & D	W	4-1	1-0	14	Dudfield 2 (1 pen) [19, 54 (p)], Bramble [70], Barrett [90]	2804
8	11	H	Wycombe W	L	1-2	1-0	18	Bentley [42]	4771
9	18	A	Notts Co	W	2-1	1-0	14	Barrett 2 [28, 55]	4487
10	25	H	Kidderminster H	W	1-0	1-0	11	Gower [27]	4087
11	Oct 2	A	Darlington	L	0-4	0-3	15		3901
12	8	H	Boston U	W	2-1	2-0	—	Gower [15], Gray [22]	5688
13	16	H	Swansea C	W	4-2	2-1	9	Eastwood 3 [1, 58, 87], Prior [42]	4940
14	19	A	Scunthorpe U	L	2-3	1-2	—	Eastwood [30], Corbett [63]	3402
15	23	A	Shrewsbury T	D	1-1	0-1	13	Gray [59]	3719
16	30	H	Northampton T	W	2-1	1-0	7	Gower [27], Gray [76]	5696
17	Nov 6	H	Oxford U	W	4-0	0-0	5	Gower [47], Eastwood [75], Barrett [81], Dudfield (pen) [90]	5608
18	20	A	Yeovil T	L	1-3	0-1	7	Barrett [62]	5839
19	26	H	Grimsby T	D	1-1	0-1	—	Eastwood [60]	5192
20	Dec 7	A	Leyton Orient	D	2-2	2-1	—	Eastwood [28], Gray [55]	3852
21	11	A	Bury	W	1-0	1-0	6	Gray (pen) [27]	2522
22	17	H	Chester C	W	1-0	0-0	—	Dudfield [88]	4837
23	26	A	Wycombe W	W	1-0	1-0	4	Eastwood [17]	5669
24	28	H	Mansfield T	L	0-1	0-0	4		7082
25	Jan 1	H	Rushden & D	W	3-0	1-0	4	Maher [17], Edwards [59], Bentley [90]	5930
26	3	A	Kidderminster H	W	3-1	1-0	4	Eastwood 2 [10, 84], Nicolau [82]	2755
27	12	A	Boston U	L	0-2	0-0	—		2389
28	15	H	Notts Co	D	0-0	0-0	4		5304
29	22	A	Mansfield T	D	1-1	0-0	4	Gower [59]	3894
30	29	H	Darlington	W	2-0	0-0	4	Bentley [77], Eastwood [90]	7358
31	Feb 4	A	Swansea C	D	1-1	0-0	—	Gray [59]	10,190
32	11	H	Scunthorpe U	D	0-0	0-0	—		8224
33	19	A	Northampton T	W	2-1	0-1	6	Barrett 2 [72, 90]	6602
34	22	H	Shrewsbury T	W	1-0	0-0	—	Eastwood [78]	4219
35	26	H	Bury	W	1-0	1-0	5	Eastwood [42]	5553
36	Mar 5	A	Chester C	D	2-2	1-1	3	Gower [38], Eastwood [85]	2396
37	12	H	Lincoln C	D	1-1	0-0	4	Eastwood (pen) [90]	5824
38	19	A	Cheltenham T	W	3-0	2-0	4	Gray 2 [16, 45], Eastwood [66]	3341
39	25	H	Rochdale	W	3-0	1-0	—	Eastwood [44], Bentley [55], Gray [60]	7656
40	28	A	Cambridge U	W	2-0	2-0	2	Prior [23], Barrett [45]	6715
41	Apr 1	H	Bristol R	W	2-0	2-0	—	Bentley [14], Gray (pen) [26]	7858
42	15	H	Leyton Orient	L	0-1	0-1	—		9189
43	19	A	Macclesfield T	W	2-1	1-1	—	McCormack 2 [31, 90]	2768
44	23	A	Oxford U	L	1-2	0-2	2	Eastwood [60]	5916
45	30	H	Yeovil T	L	0-1	0-0	3		11,735
46	May 7	A	Grimsby T	D	1-1	0-0	4	Eastwood [70]	6259

Final League Position: 4

GOALSCORERS

League (65): Eastwood 19 (1 pen), Barrett 11, Gray 11 (3 pens), Gower 6, Bentley 5, Dudfield 4 (2 pens), McCormack 2, Prior 2, Bramble 1, Corbett 1, Edwards 1, Maher 1, Nicolau 1.
Carling Cup (0).
FA Cup (0).
LDV Vans Trophy (13): Dudfield 3, Eastwood 3, Gray 2 (1 pen), Bentley 1, Bramble 1, Gower 1, Nicolau 1, Pettefer 1.
Play-offs (3): Eastwood 2 (1 pen), Jupp 1.

Griemink B 19	Jupp D 28 + 3	Nicolau N 15 + 7	Maher K 42	Edwards A 9 + 3	Prior S 41	Gower M 32 + 6	Hunt L 27 + 4	Gray W 33 + 11	Dudfield L 16 + 20	Pettefer C 46	Husbands M — + 2	Bramble T 10 + 10	Bentley M 35 + 4	Broughton D 4 + 5	Barrett A 42 + 1	Wilson C 40	Flahavan D 26 + 2	Corbett J 1 + 5	Clarke R 1	Eastwood F 31 + 2	Kightly M — + 1	Lawson J — + 1	McCormack A 5 + 2	Blewitt D — + 1	Guttridge L 3 + 2	*Match No.*
1	2	3	4	5	6	7	8	9	10^{1}	11^{2}	12	13■														1
1	2	3	4	5	6	7	12	9^{2}	13	11^{1}			8	10												2
1	2	3^{1}	4	5	6^{2}	7		9	12	11			8	10	13											3
1	2	3	4	5	6	7		9	12	11^{2}	13		8	10^{1}												4
1	2	3	4		6	7^{1}	12	13	10^{2}	11^{3}		14	8	9	5											5
1	2		4		6	7^{1}	12		10	11		9^{2}	8	13	5	3										6
1^{G}	2		4		6	7^{2}			10	11		9^{1}	8	12	5	3	15	13								7
	2^{2}			13	6	7^{1}	4	12	10	11		9^{3}	8	14	5	3	1									8
	2		4		6	7^{2}		12	10	11		9^{1}	8		5	3	1	13								9
	2		4		6	7^{1}		12	10^{2}	11		9	8	13	5	3	1									10
	2		4		6	7	13	9^{3}		11		10^{1}	8	12^{2}	5	3	1	14								11
	2		4		6	7	8	9^{1}		11		10			5	3	1■	12								12
	2		4		6	7^{1}	8	9		11					5	3		12	1	10^{2}	13					13
	2	12	4	13	6^{2}		8	9	14	11^{3}					5	3	1	7^{1}		10						14
	2		4		6	7^{1}	8	9		11			12		5	3	1			10						15
	2		4		6	7^{1}	8	9	13	11			12		5	3	1			10^{2}						16
1	2		4		6	7^{2}	8	9^{1}	12	11		14	13		5	3				10^{3}						17
1	12		4■	5^{1}		7	2	9		11		13	8		6	3				10^{2}						18
1	2^{1}				6	7	4	9		11		12	8		5	3				10						19
1			4		6		2	9		11		7	8		5	3				10						20
1		12	4		6	7^{1}	2	9	13	11			8		5	3				10^{2}						21
1			4		6	7^{2}	2	9	12	11		13	8		5	3				10^{1}						22
1			4	5		7^{1}	2	9	12	11			8		6	3				10						23
1			4	5			2	9	12	11		7^{1}	8		6	3				10						24
1		11^{2}	4	5			2	12	10^{1}	7		9	8		6	3						13				25
1		11	4	12	6		2	9	14	7		13^{3}	8^{2}		5	3				10^{1}						26
1		11^{1}	4	5			2	9	12	7			8		6	3				10						27
1^{G}		11	4		6	12	2	13	9^{2}	7			8^{1}		5	3	15			10						28
		11	4		6	8^{1}	2	12	9	7		13			5	3	1			10^{2}						29
		11	4		6	12	2	9^{2}	10^{1}	7			8		5	3	1			13						30
	12	11	4		6^{1}		2	9	10^{2}	7			8		5	3	1			13						31
		11^{1}	4		6	12	2	9^{2}	13	7			8		5	3	1			10						32
		11^{1}	4		6	12	2	13	9	7			8		5	3	1			10^{2}						33
	12	13	4		6	11^{2}	2^{1}	14	9^{3}	7			8		5	3	1			10						34
		12	4		6	11^{1}	2	9^{2}		7		13	8		5	3	1			10						35
		12	4		6	11^{1}	2	9		7^{2}		13	8		5	3	1			10						36
	2	12	4		6	11^{1}		9^{2}	13	7			8		5	3	1			10						37
	2				6^{2}	11^{3}		9	12	7			8		5	3	1			10^{1}			4	13	14	38
	2	12			6	11^{1}		9	13	7^{3}			8		5	3	1			10^{2}			4		14	39
	2		4		6	11		9		7			8		5	3	1			10						40
	2		4		6	11^{2}		9	12	7			8		5	3	1			10^{1}			13			41
	2		4		6	11^{2}		9	12	7^{1}			8		5	3	1			10			13			42
	2		4		6			12	9^{1}	7					5	3	1			10			11		8	43
	2	3^{2}	4		6	13		12	9^{1}	7					5		1			10			11		8	44
	2		4		6	11^{2}		9	13	7			12		5	3	1			10					8^{1}	45
	2^{2}		4		6	12		9	13	7			8		5	3	1			10			11^{1}			46

FA Cup

First Round	Luton T	(h)	0-3

Carling Cup

First Round	West Ham U	(a)	0-2

Play-offs

Semi-Final	Northampton T	(a)	0-0
		(h)	1-0
Final (at Millennium Stadium)	Lincoln C		2-0

LDV Vans Trophy

First Round	Colchester U	(a)	1-1
Second Round	Shrewsbury T	(h)	4-1
Quarter-Final	Northampton T	(a)	2-0
Semi-Final	Swindon T	(h)	2-0
Southern Final	Bristol R	(a)	2-1
		(h)	2-2
Final (at Millennium Stadium)	Wrexham		0-2

STOCKPORT COUNTY FL Championship 2

FOUNDATION

Formed at a meeting held at Wellington Road South by members of Wycliffe Congregational Chapel in 1883, they called themselves Heaton Norris Rovers until changing to Stockport County in 1890, a year before joining the Football Combination.

Edgeley Park, Hardcastle Road, Edgeley, Stockport, Cheshire SK3 9DD.

Telephone: (0161) 286 8888.

Fax: (0161) 286 8900.

Ticket Office: (0161) 286 8888.

Website: www.stockportcounty.com

Ground Capacity: 10,817.

Record Attendance: 27,833 v Liverpool, FA Cup 5th rd, 11 February 1950.

Pitch Measurements: 111yd × 72yd.

Chairman: Mike Baker.

Vice-chairman: Michael Rains.

Chief Executive/Secretary: Kevan Taylor.

Manager: Chris Turner.

Reserve Team Manager: Colin West.

Physio: Rodger Wylde.

Colours: Blue shirt, blue shorts, white stockings.

Change Colours: Black shirt with yellow trim, yellow shorts with black trim, yellow stockings with black trim.

Year Formed: 1883.

Turned Professional: 1891.

Ltd Co.: 1908.

Previous Names: 1883, Heaton Norris Rovers; 1888, Heaton Norris; 1890, Stockport County.

Club Nicknames: 'County' or 'Hatters'.

Previous Grounds: 1883 Heaton Norris Recreation Ground; 1884 Heaton Norris Wanderers Cricket Ground; 1885 Chorlton's Farm, Chorlton's Lane; 1886 Heaton Norris Cricket Ground; 1887 Wilkes' Field, Belmont Street; 1889 Nursery Inn, Green Lane; 1902 Edgeley Park.

First Football League Game: 1 September 1900, Division 2, v Leicester Fosse (a) D 2–2 – Moores; Earp, Wainwright; Pickford, Limond, Harvey; Stansfield, Smith (1), Patterson, Foster, Betteley (1).

Record League Victory: 13–0 v Halifax T, Division 3 (N), 6 January 1934 – McGann; Vincent (1p), Jenkinson; Robinson, Stevens, Len Jones; Foulkes (1), Hill (3), Lythgoe (2), Stevenson (2), Downes (4).

Record Cup Victory: 5–0 v Lincoln C, FA Cup 1st rd, 11 November 1995 – Edwards; Connelly, Todd, Bennett, Flynn, Gannon (Dinning), Beaumont, Oliver, Ware, Eckhardt (3), Armstrong (1) (Mike), Chalk, (1 og).

HONOURS

Football League: Division 1 best season: 8th, 1997–98; Division 2 – Runners-up 1996–97; Division 3 (N) – Champions 1921–22, 1936–37; Runners-up 1928–29, 1929-30, 1996–97; Division 4 – Champions 1966–67; Runners-up 1990–91.

FA Cup: best season: 5th rd, 1935, 1950, 2001.

Football League Cup: Semi-final 1997.

Autoglass Trophy: Runners-up 1992, 1993.

SKY SPORTS FACT FILE

During his ten seasons with Stockport County, outside-right Harold Crossthwaite had the unusual experience of playing in 142 of 144 regional league matches during the First World War. His missing duo saw him playing in fund raising games elsewhere.

Record Defeat: 1–8 v Chesterfield, Division 2, 19 April 1902.

Most League Points (2 for a win): 64, Division 4, 1966–67.

Most League Points (3 for a win): 85, Division 2, 1993–94.

Most League Goals: 115, Division 3 (N), 1933–34.

Highest League Scorer in Season: Alf Lythgoe, 46, Division 3 (N), 1933–34.

Most League Goals in Total Aggregate: Jack Connor, 132, 1951–56.

Most League Goals in One Match: 5, Joe Smith v Southport, Division 3N, 7 January 1928; 5, Joe Smith v Lincoln C, Division 3N, 15 September 1928; 5, Frank Newton v Nelson, Division 3N, 21 September 1929; 5, Alf Lythgoe v Southport, Division 3N, 25 August 1934; 5, Billy McNaughton v Mansfield T, Division 3N, 14 December 1935; 5, Jack Connor v Workington, Division 3N, 8 November 1952; 5, Jack Connor v Carlisle U, Division 3N, 7 April 1956.

Most Capped Player: Jarkko Wiss, 9 (36), Finland.

Most League Appearances: Andy Thorpe, 489, 1978–86, 1988–92.

Youngest League Player: Jimmy Collier, 16 years 227 days v Bristol R, 8 April 1969.

Record Transfer Fee Received: £1,600,000 from Middlesbrough for Alun Armstrong, February 1998.

Record Transfer Fee Paid: £800,000 to Nottingham F for Ian Moore, July 1998.

Football League Record: 1900 Elected to Division 2; 1904 Failed re-election; 1905–21 Division 2; 1921–22 Division 3 (N); 1922–26 Division 2; 1926–37 Division 3 (N); 1937–38 Division 2; 1938–58 Division 3 (N); 1958–59 Division 3; 1959–67 Division 4; 1967–70 Division 3; 1970–91 Division 4; 1991–92 Division 3; 1992–97 Division 2; 1997–2002 Division 1; 2002–04 Division 2; 2004–05 FL1; 2005– FL2.

MANAGERS

Fred Stewart 1894–1911
Harry Lewis 1911–14
David Ashworth 1914–19
Albert Williams 1919–24
Fred Scotchbrook 1924–26
Lincoln Hyde 1926–31
Andrew Wilson 1932–33
Fred Westgarth 1934–36
Bob Kelly 1936–38
George Hunt 1938–39
Bob Marshall 1939–49
Andy Beattie 1949–52
Dick Duckworth 1952–56
Billy Moir 1956–60
Reg Flewin 1960–63
Trevor Porteous 1963–65
Bert Trautmann *(General Manager)* 1965–66
Eddie Quigley *(Team Manager)* 1965–66
Jimmy Meadows 1966–69
Wally Galbraith 1969–70
Matt Woods 1970–71
Brian Doyle 1972–74
Jimmy Meadows 1974–75
Roy Chapman 1975–76
Eddie Quigley 1976–77
Alan Thompson 1977–78
Mike Summerbee 1978–79
Jimmy McGuigan 1979–82
Eric Webster 1982–85
Colin Murphy 1985
Les Chapman 1985–86
Jimmy Melia 1986
Colin Murphy 1986–87
Asa Hartford 1987–89
Danny Bergara 1989–95
Dave Jones 1995–97
Gary Megson 1997–99
Andy Kilner 1999–2001
Carlton Palmer 2001–03
Sammy McIlroy 2003–04
Chris Turner December 2004–

LATEST SEQUENCES

Longest Sequence of League Wins: 8, 26.12.1927 – 28.1.1928.

Longest Sequence of League Defeats: 10, 24.11.2001 – 13.01.2002

Longest Sequence of League Draws: 7, 17.3.1989 – 14.4.1989.

Longest Sequence of Unbeaten League Matches: 18, 28.1.1933 – 28.8.1933.

Longest Sequence Without a League Win: 19, 28.12.1999 – 22.4.2000.

Successive Scoring Runs: 24 from 8.9.1928.

Successive Non-scoring Runs: 7 from 10.3.1923.

TEN YEAR LEAGUE RECORD

		P	W	D	L	F	A	Pts	Pos
1995-96	Div 2	46	19	13	14	61	47	70	9
1996-97	Div 2	46	23	13	10	59	41	82	2
1997-98	Div 1	46	19	8	19	71	69	65	8
1998-99	Div 1	46	12	17	17	49	60	53	16
1999-2000	Div 1	46	13	15	18	55	67	54	17
2000-01	Div 1	46	11	18	17	58	65	51	19
2001-02	Div 1	46	6	8	32	42	102	26	24
2002-03	Div 2	46	15	10	21	65	70	55	14
2003-04	Div 2	46	11	19	16	62	70	52	19
2004-05	FL 1	46	6	8	32	49	98	26	24

DID YOU KNOW 

Despite the disappointment of relegation from the Second Division at the end of 1937–38, Stockport County had their highest aggregate attendance, 14,399. Moreover 24,386 witnessed a Joe Mantle goal beating Manchester United 1–0.

STOCKPORT COUNTY 2004–05 LEAGUE RECORD

Match No.	*Date*	*Venue*	*Opponents*	*Result*		*H/T Score*	*Lg. Pos.*	*Goalscorers*	*Attendance*
1	Aug 7	H	Huddersfield T	L	2-3	0-1	—	Beckett [57], Feeney [68]	7473
2	10	A	Colchester U	L	2-3	0-3	—	Cartwright [66], Beckett [79]	3346
3	14	A	Blackpool	W	4-0	2-0	15	Jackman [10], Feeney [31], Beckett 2 [50, 64]	6334
4	21	H	Bradford C	L	0-1	0-0	19		5338
5	28	A	Brentford	L	0-3	0-3	20		4643
6	30	H	Tranmere R	D	1-1	0-0	21	Feeney [81]	5502
7	Sept 4	H	Torquay U	L	0-2	0-1	23		4372
8	11	A	Bristol C	L	0-5	0-3	23		10,811
9	18	H	Luton T	L	1-3	0-2	23	Lambert [80]	5128
10	25	A	Hull C	D	0-0	0-0	24		16,182
11	Oct 2	H	Swindon T	D	3-3	0-2	24	Beckett 2 [72, 80], Barlow [83]	4394
12	8	A	Bournemouth	L	1-2	0-1	—	Feeney [85]	6925
13	16	H	Peterborough U	W	1-0	0-0	24	Beckett [64]	4119
14	20	A	Chesterfield	L	0-4	0-2	—		4567
15	23	A	Port Vale	D	0-0	0-0	24		5025
16	30	H	Oldham Ath	L	1-2	1-2	24	Bridge-Wilkinson [43]	6146
17	Nov 6	H	Sheffield W	L	0-3	0-1	24		7222
18	20	A	Doncaster R	L	1-3	0-1	24	Feeney [50]	6697
19	27	H	Walsall	L	0-1	0-1	24		4448
20	Dec 7	A	Wrexham	L	1-2	1-1	—	Bridge-Wilkinson [17]	3984
21	11	A	Hartlepool U	L	1-3	1-1	24	Daly [26]	4572
22	18	H	Milton Keynes D	W	3-1	2-0	24	Daly 2 [1, 41], Williams A [87]	3902
23	26	H	Bristol C	L	1-2	1-1	24	Feeney [19]	5071
24	28	A	Barnsley	D	3-3	0-2	24	Feeney [60], Barlow [73], Lambert [81]	10,236
25	Jan 1	A	Torquay U	W	2-1	0-1	24	Lambert 2 (1 pen) [47, 89 (p)]	3456
26	3	H	Hull C	L	1-3	1-1	24	Adams [24]	6670
27	15	A	Luton T	L	0-3	0-1	24		6603
28	22	H	Barnsley	D	2-2	1-1	24	Briggs [5], Feeney (pen) [90]	5326
29	29	A	Swindon T	L	0-3	0-0	24		5090
30	Feb 1	H	Bournemouth	D	2-2	1-1	—	Armstrong [26], Dolan [78]	3850
31	5	A	Peterborough U	L	1-2	0-1	24	Jackman [49]	3719
32	12	H	Port Vale	L	1-2	0-1	24	Le Fondre [88]	4587
33	19	A	Oldham Ath	W	2-1	1-0	24	Hurst [37], Feeney [60]	5924
34	22	H	Chesterfield	L	1-2	1-0	—	Feeney [45]	4201
35	26	H	Hartlepool U	W	1-0	1-0	24	Feeney [19]	4548
36	Mar 5	A	Milton Keynes D	L	1-2	0-1	24	Briggs [74]	4146
37	12	H	Colchester U	L	1-2	1-1	24	Feeney [4]	4004
38	19	A	Huddersfield T	L	3-5	1-1	24	Feeney 3 (1 pen) [2, 57 (p), 65]	11,180
39	28	A	Bradford C	L	1-3	1-2	24	Le Fondre [40]	7263
40	Apr 2	H	Brentford	L	1-2	0-0	24	Le Fondre (pen) [80]	4408
41	8	A	Tranmere R	L	0-1	0-0	—		8757
42	12	H	Blackpool	L	0-1	0-1	—		4302
43	16	H	Doncaster R	L	2-4	2-1	24	Allen [28], Le Fondre [45]	4508
44	23	A	Sheffield W	D	0-0	0-0	24		22,331
45	30	H	Wrexham	L	1-4	1-4	24	Barlow [27]	5480
46	May 7	A	Walsall	L	0-3	0-0	24		6971

Final League Position: 24

GOALSCORERS

League (49): Feeney 15 (2 pens), Beckett 7, Lambert 4 (1 pen), Le Fondre 4 (1 pen), Barlow 3, Daly 3, Bridge-Wilkinson 2, Briggs 2, Jackman 2, Adams 1, Allen 1, Armstrong 1, Cartwright 1, Dolan 1, Hurst 1, Williams A 1.
Carling Cup (1): own goal 1.
FA Cup (4): Feeney 2, Griffin 1, Williams A 1.
LDV Vans Trophy (3): Barlow 1, Daly 1, Le Fondre 1.

Cutler N 22	Geary D 12 + 1	Adams D 27	Robertson M 18 + 2	Williams A 44	Mair L 9 + 5	Cartwright L 18 + 1	Lambert R 27 + 2	Feeney W 31	Beckett L 15	Bridge-Wilkinson M 19 + 3	Jackman D 24 + 9	Barlow S 11 + 20	Welsh A 4 + 9	Goodwin J 30 + 6	Hardiker J 26 + 3	Daly J 10 + 4	Spencer J 24	Morrison O — + 1	Griffin D 16	Williams C 6 + 3	Le Fondre A 11 + 9	Smith A 1	Allen D 14 + 7	Raynes M 15 + 4	Armstrong C 9 + 2	Clarke D 1	Briggs K 14 + 2	Dolan J 11	Hurst K 14	Singh H 5 + 1	Bailey M — + 1	Hadfield J 1	Horwood E 10	Tomlinson E 2 + 3	Dje L 2 + 1	Robinson M 3	Turnbull P — + 1	*Match No.*
1	2	3	4	5	6	7	8	9^{2}	10	11^{1}	12	13																										1
1	2	3	4^{3}	5	6	7	8^{2}	9	10	11^{1}		13	12	14																								2
1	2	3	4^{3}	5		7	8	9^{2}	10		11^{1}	13	12	14	6																							3
1	2	3	4	5		7^{1}	8	9^{3}	10	12	11^{2}		13		6	14																						4
1	2	3	4^{3}	5	12	7	8	9		11^{2}			13	10	6^{1}	14																						5
	2	3	4	5	6		8^{2}	9	10	11		12	7^{1}	13			1																					6
	2	3^{2}	4^{3}	5	6	7	8	9		11	13	12				10^{1}	1	14																				7
	2	3		5		7	8	9	10		11			4	6		1																					8
	2	7		5	6^{3}		8	9^{1}	10	11	3	13	12	14			1		4^{2}																			9
1		3	4	5	6	7	8^{2}		10		12		9	11		13			2^{1}																			10
1	12		4^{1}	5	6	7	8	9	10		3	13	11^{2}						2																			11
1	2^{2}	3		5	6	7	8	9	10		11	4^{1}	12			13																						12
1	2	4		5		7	8	9	10	11^{1}	3			12					6																			13
1	2^{2}	3		5		7	8	9	10		11	12	13	4^{1}					6																			14
		3■		5		7	8	9	10	11			12		2		1		6	4^{1}																		15
				5		7	8	9	10	11	3	12	4^{1}		2		1		6																			16
				5	6	7^{1}	8	9	10		3	11^{2}	12	4	2		1				13																	17
		3	6	5		7		9			12			8	2		1		4	11^{1}		10																18
		3	6	5		7	8^{1}	9		12		13		14	2		1		4		11^{2}		10^{3}															19
1		3	4	5	12		13			11		10^{3}		8^{2}	2^{1}	9			6		14		7															20
1		3	4	5	12		8			11^{3}		13		7	2	9			6^{2}	14			10^{1}															21
1		3	4	5	12		8^{2}	9^{1}		11		13		7	2	10^{3}			6					14														22
1		3		5			8	9		11^{1}	7	12			2	10			4				6															23
1		3		5	12		8	9		11^{2}	7^{3}	13			2^{1}	10			6				4	14														24
1		3		5			8	9						7	2	10			6				4	11														25
1		3^{3}		5			8^{1}	9		12	14	13		11	2	10			6^{2}				4	7														26
1		3		5			8^{1}	9			12			7	2	10^{2}							4	6	13	11^{3}	14											27
				5				9		11	3			7	4		1			8^{1}			12		10		2	6										28
				5			12			11^{1}	7	13		3	2^{2}	10	1			8			14		9		4^{3}	6										29
		3		5			8			11	7	10		2			1			4^{2}	12		13		9^{1}			6										30
1		3	12	5			8			11^{1}	7^{3}	10^{2}		2						4	13			14	9			6										31
1		2	12	5						11^{1}	3^{2}	10		7						14	13		4	9	8^{3}			6										32
			6					9						2	3		1				12			4	10^{1}		7	5	8	11								33
			4^{1}					9						2	3		1				13			6	10^{2}		7	5	8	11	12							34
			4	5				9^{3}			12	13		2	3		1				14				10^{2}		7	6	8	11^{1}								35
			4	5^{3}				9			12			2	3■		1				13			14	10^{1}		7	6	8			11^{2}						36
				5				9^{2}			11^{1}			2			1				10		12	4	13		7	6	8				3					37
				5				9			12			2			1				10			4			7^{2}	6	8	11^{1}			3	13				38
				5								9		2			1				10		12	6					8	11			3	7	4^{1}			39
				5							11^{3}	12		2	13		1				10		4	6			14		8				3	7^{1}		9^{2}		40
				5							11	12		2	4		1				10^{3}		13	6			7		8^{2}				3^{1}		14	9		41
				5		7^{2}						12		2	4^{3}		1				10		13	6			11		8				3	14		9^{1}		42
1				5							11	9		2							10		4	6			7		8				3					43
				5							11	9		2	12		1			14	10^{1}		4	6			7		8	13^{3}			3^{2}					44
				5							3	9^{3}		2	12		1				10		4	6			7		8^{2}				11^{1}	13			14	45
1				5		12					11	9			2						10		4				7		8^{1}				3		6			46

FA Cup

First Round	Huddersfield T	(h)	3-1
Second Round	Swansea C	(h)	0-0
		(a)	1-2

Carling Cup

First Round	Sheffield U	(a)	1-4

LDV Vans Trophy

First Round	Bury	(h)	3-1
Second Round	Wrexham	(a)	0-2

STOKE CITY FL Championship

FOUNDATION

The date of the formation of this club has long been in doubt. The year 1863 was claimed, but more recent research by Wade Martin has uncovered nothing earlier than 1868, when a couple of Old Carthusians, who were apprentices at the local works of the old North Staffordshire Railway Company, met with some others from that works, to form Stoke Ramblers. It should also be noted that the old Stoke club went bankrupt in 1908 when a new club was formed.

Britannia Stadium, Stanley Matthews Way, Stoke-on-Trent, Staffs ST4 4EG.

Telephone: (01782) 592 222.

Fax: (01782) 592 221.

Ticket Office: (01782) 592 200.

Website: www.stokecityfc.com

Email: info@stokecityfc.com

Ground Capacity: 28,218.

Record Attendance: 51,380 v Arsenal, Division 1, 29 March 1937.

Pitch Measurements: 116yd × 70yd.

Chairman: Gunnar Por Gislason.

Vice-chairman: Stefan Geir Thorisson.

Chief Executive: Tony Scholes.

Secretary: Diane Richardson.

Manager: Johan Boskamp.

Director of Football: John Rudge.

Physio: Dave Watson.

Colours: Red and white striped shirts, white shorts, white stockings with red trim.

Change Colours: Black shirts with red trim, black shorts with red trim, black stockings with red trim.

Year Formed: 1863 *(*see Foundation*). ***Turned Professional:*** 1885. ***Ltd Co.:*** 1908.

Previous Names: 1868, Stoke Ramblers; 1870, Stoke; 1925, Stoke City.

Club Nickname: 'The Potters'.

Previous Grounds: 1875, Sweeting's Field; 1878, Victoria Ground (previously known as the Athletic Club Ground); 1997, Britannia Stadium.

First Football League Game: 8 September 1888, Football League, v WBA (h) L 0–2 – Rowley; Clare, Underwood; Ramsey, Shutt, Smith; Sayer, McSkimming, Staton, Edge, Tunnicliffe.

Record League Victory: 10–3 v WBA, Division 1, 4 February 1937 – Doug Westland; Brigham, Harbot; Tutin, Turner (1p), Kirton; Matthews, Antonio (2), Freddie Steele (5), Jimmy Westland, Johnson (2).

HONOURS

Football League: Division 1 best season: 4th, 1935–36, 1946–47; Division 2 – Champions 1932–33, 1962–63, 1992–93; Runners-up 1921–22; Promoted 1978–79 (3rd), Promoted from Division 2 (play-offs) 2001–02; Division 3 (N) – Champions 1926–27.

FA Cup: Semi-finals 1899, 1971, 1972.

Football League Cup: Winners 1972.

Autoglass Trophy: Winners: 1992.

Auto Windscreens Shield: Winners: 2000.

European Competitions: *UEFA Cup:* 1972–73, 1974–75.

SKY SPORTS FACT FILE

Eight days after his 20th birthday Garth Crooks scored a hat-trick for Stoke City against Blackburn Rovers in March 1978. He was also a treble shooter on his debut for England Under-21s against Bulgaria on 20 November 1979.

Record Cup Victory: 7–1 v Burnley, FA Cup 2nd rd (replay), 20 February 1896 – Clawley; Clare, Eccles; Turner, Grewe, Robertson; Willie Maxwell, Dickson, A. Maxwell (3), Hyslop (4), Schofield.

Record Defeat: 0–10 v Preston NE, Division 1, 14 September 1889.

Most League Points (2 for a win): 63, Division 3 (N), 1926–27.

Most League Points (3 for a win): 93, Division 2, 1992–93.

Most League Goals: 92, Division 3 (N), 1926–27.

Highest League Scorer in Season: Freddie Steele, 33, Division 1, 1936–37.

Most League Goals in Total Aggregate: Freddie Steele, 142, 1934–49.

Most League Goals in One Match: 7, Neville Coleman v Lincoln C, Division 2, 23 February 1957.

Most Capped Player: Gordon Banks, 36 (73), England.

Most League Appearances: Eric Skeels, 506, 1958–76.

Youngest League Player: Peter Bullock, 16 years 163 days v Swansea C, 19 April 1958.

Record Transfer Fee Received: £2,750,000 from QPR for Mike Sheron, July 1997.

Record Transfer Fee Paid: £600,000 to Orgryte for Brynjar Gunnarsson, December 1999.

Football League Record: 1888 Founder Member of Football League; 1890 Not re-elected; 1891 Re-elected; relegated in 1907, and after one year in Division 2, resigned for financial reasons; 1919 re-elected to Division 2; 1922–23 Division 1; 1923–26 Division 2; 1926–27 Division 3 (N); 1927–33 Division 2; 1933–53 Division 1; 1953–63 Division 2; 1963–77 Division 1; 1977–79 Division 2; 1979–85 Division 1; 1985–90 Division 2; 1990–92 Division 3; 1992–93 Division 2; 1993–98 Division 1; 1998–2002 Division 2; 2002–04 Division 1; 2004– FLC.

MANAGERS

Tom Slaney 1874–83 *(Secretary-Manager)*
Walter Cox 1883–84 *(Secretary-Manager)*
Harry Lockett 1884–90
Joseph Bradshaw 1890–92
Arthur Reeves 1892–95
William Rowley 1895–97
H. D. Austerberry 1897–1908
A. J. Barker 1908–14
Peter Hodge 1914–15
Joe Schofield 1915–19
Arthur Shallcross 1919–23
John 'Jock' Rutherford 1923
Tom Mather 1923–35
Bob McGrory 1935–52
Frank Taylor 1952–60
Tony Waddington 1960–77
George Eastham 1977–78
Alan A'Court 1978
Alan Durban 1978–81
Richie Barker 1981–83
Bill Asprey 1984–85
Mick Mills 1985–89
Alan Ball 1989–91
Lou Macari 1991–93
Joe Jordan 1993–94
Lou Macari 1994–97
Chic Bates 1997–98
Chris Kamara 1998
Brian Little 1998–99
Gary Megson 1999
Gudjon Thordarson 1999–2002
Steve Cotterill 2002
Tony Pulis 2002–05
Johan Boskamp June 2005–

LATEST SEQUENCES

Longest Sequence of League Wins: 8, 30.3.1895 – 21.9.1895.

Longest Sequence of League Defeats: 11, 6.4.1985 – 17.8.1985.

Longest Sequence of League Draws: 5, 21.3.1987 – 11.4.1987.

Longest Sequence of Unbeaten League Matches: 25, 5.9.1992 – 20.2.1993.

Longest Sequence Without a League Win: 17, 22.4.1989 – 14.10.1989.

Successive Scoring Runs: 21 from 24.12.1921.

Successive Non-scoring Runs: 8 from 29.12.1984.

TEN YEAR LEAGUE RECORD

		P	*W*	*D*	*L*	*F*	*A*	*Pts*	*Pos*
1995-96	Div 1	46	20	13	13	60	49	73	4
1996-97	Div 1	46	18	10	18	51	57	64	12
1997-98	Div 1	46	11	13	22	44	74	46	23
1998-99	Div 2	46	21	6	19	59	63	69	8
1999-2000	Div 2	46	23	13	10	68	42	82	6
2000-01	Div 2	46	21	14	11	74	49	77	5
2001-02	Div 2	46	23	11	12	67	40	80	5
2002-03	Div 1	46	12	14	20	45	69	50	21
2003-04	Div 1	46	18	12	16	58	55	66	11
2004-05	FL C	46	17	10	19	36	38	61	12

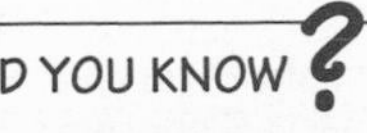

Stoke City fielded an unchanged team in 15 consecutive League games in Division Two between 19 September and Christmas Day 1931. At the end of the season they were just two points off promotion in third place.

STOKE CITY 2004–05 LEAGUE RECORD

Match No.	Date	Venue	Opponents	Result		H/T Score	Lg. Pos.	Goalscorers	Attendance
1	Aug 8	H	Wolverhampton W	W	2-1	0-0	—	Russell [55], Clarke (pen) [70]	17,086
2	10	A	Sheffield U	D	0-0	0-0	—		19,723
3	14	A	Rotherham U	D	1-1	0-0	5	Akinbiyi [85]	5925
4	21	H	Gillingham	W	2-0	1-0	4	Noel-Williams [42], Akinbiyi [72]	13,234
5	28	A	Cardiff C	W	1-0	1-0	2	Noel-Williams [37]	12,929
6	30	H	Derby Co	W	1-0	0-0	2	Hall [90]	18,673
7	Sept 11	A	Preston NE	L	0-3	0-1	3		12,759
8	14	H	Ipswich T	W	3-2	1-1	—	Thomas 2 [45, 75], Akinbiyi [85]	23,029
9	18	H	Nottingham F	D	0-0	0-0	3		21,115
10	25	A	Burnley	D	2-2	1-2	4	Akinbiyi 2 [34, 50]	12,981
11	28	A	Leeds U	D	0-0	0-0	—		25,759
12	Oct 2	H	QPR	L	0-1	0-0	6		16,877
13	16	H	Reading	L	0-1	0-1	7		15,574
14	19	A	West Ham U	L	0-2	0-1	—		29,808
15	23	A	Leicester C	D	1-1	1-1	10	Asaba [37]	22,882
16	30	H	Millwall	W	1-0	0-0	8	Greenacre [86]	14,125
17	Nov 2	H	Wigan Ath	L	0-1	0-0	—		15,882
18	6	A	Reading	L	0-1	0-1	12		14,831
19	13	H	Crewe Alex	W	1-0	0-0	9	Noel-Williams [64]	17,640
20	20	A	Plymouth Arg	D	0-0	0-0	10		15,264
21	27	H	Sunderland	L	0-1	0-0	14		16,980
22	Dec 4	A	Watford	W	1-0	1-0	9	Noel-Williams [24]	12,169
23	11	H	Coventry C	W	1-0	1-0	9	Akinbiyi [21]	15,744
24	17	A	Brighton & HA	W	1-0	0-0	—	Akinbiyi [85]	6208
25	26	H	Preston NE	D	0-0	0-0	9		20,350
26	28	A	Ipswich T	L	0-1	0-1	9		26,217
27	Jan 1	A	Nottingham F	L	0-1	0-0	11		22,051
28	3	H	Burnley	L	0-1	0-0	12		15,689
29	14	A	QPR	L	0-1	0-1	—		13,559
30	22	H	Leeds U	L	0-1	0-0	16		18,372
31	Feb 5	A	Wigan Ath	W	1-0	1-0	13	Noel-Williams [39]	9938
32	19	A	Millwall	W	1-0	1-0	12	Jones [15]	11,036
33	22	H	Leicester C	W	3-2	2-1	—	Brammer [24], Noel-Williams [34], Taggart [59]	14,076
34	26	A	Coventry C	D	0-0	0-0	11		13,871
35	Mar 5	H	Brighton & HA	W	2-0	2-0	10	Noel-Williams 2 (2 pens) [39, 44]	14,908
36	12	H	Sheffield U	W	2-0	0-0	8	Noel-Williams 2 [57, 59]	17,019
37	15	A	Gillingham	L	1-2	0-1	—	Jones [54]	7766
38	19	A	Wolverhampton W	D	1-1	1-0	11	Noel-Williams [41]	28,103
39	Apr 2	H	Rotherham U	L	1-2	0-1	11	Noel-Williams [83]	16,552
40	5	H	Cardiff C	L	1-3	1-1	—	Hill [40]	12,785
41	9	A	Derby Co	L	1-3	1-2	12	Taggart [7]	27,640
42	16	H	Plymouth Arg	W	2-0	2-0	11	Jones [28], Russell [41]	13,017
43	19	H	West Ham U	L	0-1	0-0	—		14,534
44	23	A	Crewe Alex	W	2-0	0-0	10	Neal [79], Noel-Williams [89]	9166
45	30	H	Watford	L	0-1	0-0	12		15,229
46	May 8	A	Sunderland	L	0-1	0-0	12		47,350

Final League Position: 12

GOALSCORERS

League (36): Noel-Williams 13 (2 pens), Akinbiyi 7, Jones 3, Russell 2, Taggart 2, Thomas 2, Asaba 1, Brammer 1, Clarke 1 (pen), Greenacre 1, Hall 1, Hill 1, Neal 1.
Carling Cup (1): Asaba 1.
FA Cup (1): Thomas 1.

De Goey E 17	Halls J 20 + 2	Clarke C 42	Thomas W 35	Taggart G 31	Neal L 10 + 13	Russell D 45	Brammer D 42 + 1	Akinbiyi A 29	Noel-Williams G 41 + 5	Hall M 19 + 1	Henry K 14 + 20	Greenacre C 18 + 14	Asaba C 14 + 19	Barker C 4	Hill C 31 + 1	Simonsen S 29 + 2	Guppy S — + 4	Duberry M 25	Palmer J — + 1	Eustace J 2 + 5	Dickinson C — + 1	Owen G — + 2	Buxton L 14 + 2	Jarrett J 2	Harper K 8 + 1	Wilkinson A — + 1	Jones K 13	Ricketts M 1 + 10	Gudjonsson T — + 2	Clark C — + 2	Paterson M — + 3	Match No.
1	2	3	4	5	6[1]	7	8	9[2]	10[3]	11	12	13	14																			1
1	2	3	4	5		7	8[1]	9	10■	11[2]	12		13	6																		2
1	2	3	4	5	12	7	8[1]	9[2]	10	11[3]	13		14	6																		3
1	2	3	4	5	6[2]	7	8	9[1]	10[3]		12	14	13	11																		4
1	2	3		5	12	7	8	9[2]	10	11	4[1]		13		6																	5
1	2	3	4	5	6[2]	7	8	9	10[1]	11		12	13																			6
1	2	3	4	5		7[1]	8	9[3]	10	11	12	14	13	6[2]																		7
1[G]	2■	3	4	5		7	8[2]	9	10[1]	11	6		12			15	13															8
		3	2	5		7	8[2]	9	10	11	6[1]		12		4	1	13															9
1	2	3	4	5		7	8[2]	9[1]	10	11	13		12		6[3]		14															10
1	2	3	4	5		7	8	9[2]	10[1]	11		13	12		6																	11
1	2	3	4	5■	6[3]	7	8[2]	9	10[1]	11	13		12		14																	12
1	2		4		6[1]	7	8	9	10	11	3[2]		12		5		13															13
1	2	3	4			7	12	9	10	11[2]	8[1]		13		5			6														14
1	2	3	4		12	7	8	9	13	11[1]			10[2]		5			6														15
1		3	2	5	11[1]	7	8[3]	9[2]	12		13	14	10		4			6														16
1		3	2	5		7	8	9	12		13	11	10[1]		6[2]			4														17
1[G]	2	3	4		12	8	6	9	10			7	11[1]			15		5														18
	2	3	4			7	8	9	10	5		11				1		6														19
		3	2		12	7	8	9	10		13	4[1]	11[2]		5	1		6														20
	2	3	4		12	7	8		10			11[1]	9		5[2]	1		6	13													21
	2	3	4			7	8	9[1]	10		12	13	11[2]		5	1		6														22
		3			6[1]	7		9	10		2	11	8[3]		5	1		4		13	14	12[2]										23
	2	3	4			7	8	9	10	12			11[1]		5	1		6														24
	2[3]	3	4			7	8	9	10[1]		12	13	11[2]		5	1		6					14									25
		3	4			7[3]	8[1]	9	10[2]		12	13	11		5	1		6		14			2									26
		3■	4			7		9	12		8	10[2]	11[1]		5■	1		6		13			2									27
		3[1]	4		12	7		9	10	11	6	13				1		5		8[2]			2									28
		3	4	5		7	8	9	12	11[2]		10[1]	13			1				14			2	6[3]								29
		3	4	5		7	8[3]	9	10[2]			13	12		6[1]	1				14			2	11								30
		3		5			8		10	11	12	7	9		6	1				4[1]			2									31
					12	7	8		10	3	4	9			5	1						14	2		6[2]	13[3]	11[1]					32
				5		7	8		10		2	11	12		6	1							3		4[1]		9[2]	13				33
		3		5	12	7	8		10			11[1]			6	1							2		4		9[2]	13[3]	14			34
		3[2]	2	5		7	8		10[3]		12	13			11	1		4							6[1]		9			14		35
		3	2	5		7	8		10[3]		12	13			6	1		4							11[1]		9[2]	14				36
		3[1]	2	5[2]		7	8		10[3]			12			6	1		4					13		11		9	14				37
		3	2	5		7	8		10[2]		11				6	1		4							12		9[1]	13				38
		3[1]	2	5	12	7	8[3]		10		14		13		6	1		4■							11			9[2]				39
			4	5	6[1]	7	8		10		13		12		3	1							2		11[2]		9[3]		14			40
		3	4[1]	5	12	7	8		10[2]			9[3]	6		11	1							2					13		14		41
		3[1]		5	12	7	8		10		13	11[3]			6	1		4					2				9[2]				14	42
		3		5	12	7	8		10		13	11[1]			6	1		4					2[2]				9[3]	14				43
		3		5	6	7	8		10		2	11				1		4									9[1]	12				44
	12	3[1]		5	6[2]	7	8		10		2	11				1		4									9[3]	13			14	45
	12	3		5		7	8		10[3]		6[1]	11				1		4					2				9[2]	13			14	46

FA Cup
Third Round Arsenal (a) 1-2

Carling Cup
First Round Oldham Ath (a) 1-2

SUNDERLAND FA Premiership

FOUNDATION

A Scottish schoolmaster named James Allan, working at Hendon Board School, took the initiative in the foundation of Sunderland in 1879 when they were formed as The Sunderland and District Teachers' Association FC at a meeting in the Adults School, Norfolk Street. Due to financial difficulties, they quickly allowed members from outside the teaching profession and so became Sunderland AFC in October 1880.

Stadium of Light, Sunderland, Tyne and Wear SR5 1SU.

Telephone: (0191) 551 5000.

Fax: (0191) 551 5123.

Ticket Office: (0191) 551 5151.

Website: www.safc.com

Ground Capacity: 49,000.

Record Attendance: Stadium of Light: 48,353 v Liverpool, FA Premier League, 13 April 2002. FA Premier League figure (46,062). Roker Park: 75,118 v Derby Co, FA Cup 6th rd replay, 8 March 1933.

Pitch Measurements: 105m × 68m.

Chairman: Bob Murray CBE.

Vice-chairman: John Fickling.

Chief Executive: Peter Walker.

Manager: Mick McCarthy.

Assistant Manager: Ian Evans.

Physio: Pete Friar.

HONOURS

Football League: Championship – Winners 2004–05; Division 1 – Champions 1891–92, 1892–93, 1894–95, 1901–02, 1912–13, 1935–36, 1995–96, 1998–99; Runners-up 1893–94, 1897–98, 1900–01, 1922–23, 1934–35; Division 2 – Champions 1975–76; Runners-up 1963–64, 1979–80; 1989–90 (play-offs). Division 3 – Champions 1987–88.

FA Cup: Winners 1937, 1973; Runners-up 1913, 1992.

Football League Cup: Runners-up 1985.

European Competitions: *European Cup-Winners' Cup:* 1973–74.

Colours: Red and white striped shirts, black shorts, black stockings.

Change Colours: Black shirts, black shorts, black stockings.

Year Formed: 1879.

Turned Professional: 1886.

Ltd Co.: 1906.

Previous Name: 1879, Sunderland and District Teacher's AFC; 1880, Sunderland.

Previous Grounds: 1879, Blue House Field, Hendon; 1882, Groves Field, Ashbrooke; 1883, Horatio Street; 1884, Abbs Field, Fulwell; 1886, Newcastle Road; 1898, Roker Park; 1997, Stadium of Light.

First Football League Game: 13 September 1890, Football League, v Burnley (h) L 2–3 – Kirtley; Porteous, Oliver; Wilson, Auld, Gibson; Spence (1), Miller, Campbell (1), Scott, D. Hannah.

Record League Victory: 9–1 v Newcastle U (a), Division 1, 5 December 1908 – Roose; Forster, Melton; Daykin, Thomson, Low; Mordue (1), Hogg (3), Brown, Holley (3), Bridgett (2).

SKY SPORTS FACT FILE

Even though his League debut in 1890 v WBA cost Sunderland a £50 fine and two points deducted for a registration error, goalkeeper Ted Doig missed only 12 League and Cup matches in the next 14 largely successful seasons with the club.

Record Cup Victory: 11–1 v Fairfield, FA Cup 1st rd, 2 February 1895 – Doig; McNeill, Johnston; Dunlop, McCreadie (1), Wilson; Gillespie (1), Millar (5), Campbell, Hannah (3), Scott (1).

Record Defeat: 0–8 v Sheff Wed, Division 1, 26 December 1911. 0–8 v West Ham U, Division 1, 19 October 1968. 0–8 v Watford, Division 1, 25 September 1982.

Most League Points (2 for a win): 61, Division 2, 1963–64.

Most League Points (3 for a win): 105, Division 1, 1998–99 (Football League Record).

Most League Goals: 109, Division 1, 1935–36.

Highest League Scorer in Season: Dave Halliday, 43, Division 1, 1928–29.

Most League Goals in Total Aggregate: Charlie Buchan, 209, 1911–25.

Most League Goals in One Match: 5, Charlie Buchan v Liverpool, Division 1, 7 December 1919; 5, Bobby Gurney v Bolton W, Division 1, 7 December 1935; 5, Dominic Sharkey v Norwich C, Division 2, 20 February 1962.

Most Capped Player: Charlie Hurley, 38 (40), Republic of Ireland.

Most League Appearances: Jim Montgomery, 537, 1962–77.

Youngest League Player: Derek Forster, 15 years 184 days v Leicester C, 22 August 1964.

MANAGERS

Tom Watson 1888–96
Bob Campbell 1896–99
Alex Mackie 1899–1905
Bob Kyle 1905–28
Johnny Cochrane 1928–39
Bill Murray 1939–57
Alan Brown 1957–64
George Hardwick 1964–65
Ian McColl 1965–68
Alan Brown 1968–72
Bob Stokoe 1972–76
Jimmy Adamson 1976–78
Ken Knighton 1979–81
Alan Durban 1981–84
Len Ashurst 1984–85
Lawrie McMenemy 1985–87
Denis Smith 1987–91
Malcolm Crosby 1992–93
Terry Butcher 1993
Mick Buxton 1993–95
Peter Reid 1995–2002
Howard Wilkinson 2002–03
Mick McCarthy March 2003–

Record Transfer Fee Received: £5,500,000 from Leeds U for Michael Bridges, July 1999.

Record Transfer Fee Paid: £8,000,000 to Rangers for Tore Andre Flo, August 2002.

Football League Record: 1890 Elected to Division 1; 1958–64 Division 2; 1964–70 Division 1; 1970–76 Division 2; 1976–77 Division 1; 1977–80 Division 2; 1980–85 Division 1; 1985–87 Division 2; 1987–88 Division 3; 1988–90 Division 2; 1990–91 Division 1; 1991–92 Division 2; 1992–96 Division 1; 1996–97 FA Premier League; 1997–99 Division 1; 1999–2003 FA Premier League; 2003–04 Division 1; 2004–05 FLC; 2005– FA Premier League.

LATEST SEQUENCES

Longest Sequence of League Wins: 13, 14.11.1891 – 2.4.1892.

Longest Sequence of League Defeats: 17, 18.1.2003 – 16.8.2003.

Longest Sequence of League Draws: 6, 26.3.1949 – 19.4.1949.

Longest Sequence of Unbeaten League Matches: 19, 3.5.1998 – 14.11.1998.

Longest Sequence Without a League Win: 22, 21.12.2002 – 16.8.2003.

Successive Scoring Runs: 29 from 8.11.1997

Successive Non-scoring Runs: 10 from 27.11.1976.

TEN YEAR LEAGUE RECORD

		P	W	D	L	F	A	Pts	Pos
1995-96	Div 1	46	22	17	7	59	33	83	1
1996-97	PR Lge	38	10	10	18	35	53	40	18
1997-98	Div 1	46	26	12	8	86	50	90	3
1998-99	Div 1	46	31	12	3	91	28	105	1
1999-2000	PR Lge	38	16	10	12	57	56	58	7
2000-01	PR Lge	38	15	12	11	46	41	57	7
2001-02	PR Lge	38	10	10	18	29	51	40	17
2002-03	PR Lge	38	4	7	27	21	65	19	20
2003-04	Div 1	46	22	13	11	62	45	79	3
2004-05	FL C	46	29	7	10	76	41	94	1

DID YOU KNOW ?

On 5 December 1998 Sunderland began a sequence of 12 consecutive home League wins on the way to the First Division championship. In 1891–92 they had won all 13 home fixtures during the season on the way to their first such triumph.

SUNDERLAND 2004–05 LEAGUE RECORD

Match No.	*Date*	*Venue*	*Opponents*	*Result*	*H/T Score*	*Lg. Pos.*	*Goalscorers*	*Attendance*
1	Aug 7	A	Coventry C	L 0-2	0-0	—		16,460
2	10	H	Crewe Alex	W 3-1	1-1	—	Robinson [12], Stewart [67], Elliott [90]	22,341
3	14	H	QPR	D 2-2	1-1	10	Stewart [33], Caldwell [90]	26,063
4	21	A	Plymouth Arg	L 1-2	0-2	16	Stewart [71]	16,874
5	28	H	Wigan Ath	D 1-1	0-1	15	Elliott [82]	26,330
6	31	A	Reading	L 0-1	0-1	—		15,792
7	Sept 11	A	Gillingham	W 4-0	3-0	15	Stewart 3 [4, 20, 68], Elliott [17]	8775
8	14	H	Nottingham F	W 2-0	2-0	—	Arca [4], Wright [11]	23,540
9	18	H	Preston NE	W 3-1	2-1	7	Elliott 2 [27, 52], Carter [45]	24,264
10	24	A	Leeds U	W 1-0	0-0	—	Robinson [65]	28,926
11	28	A	Sheffield U	L 0-1	0-0	—		17,908
12	Oct 2	H	Derby Co	D 0-0	0-0	7		29,881
13	16	H	Millwall	W 1-0	0-0	5	Muscat (og) [72]	23,839
14	19	A	Watford	D 1-1	1-1	—	Elliott [22]	13,198
15	25	A	Rotherham U	W 1-0	0-0	—	Whitehead [61]	6026
16	30	H	Brighton & HA	W 2-0	0-0	5	Arca [64], Lawrence (pen) [82]	25,532
17	Nov 2	H	Wolverhampton W	W 3-1	0-1	—	Lawrence 2 [57, 80], Elliott [68]	23,925
18	5	A	Millwall	L 0-2	0-2	—		10,513
19	13	A	Leicester C	W 1-0	0-0	4	Caldwell [69]	25,897
20	21	H	Ipswich T	W 2-0	0-0	3	Elliott [60], Brown [75]	31,723
21	27	A	Stoke C	W 1-0	0-0	3	Bridges [83]	16,980
22	Dec 4	H	West Ham U	L 0-2	0-0	3		29,510
23	11	A	Cardiff C	W 2-0	0-0	3	Whitehead [67], Lawrence [77]	12,528
24	18	H	Burnley	W 2-1	1-1	3	Arca [35], Lawrence [52]	27,102
25	26	H	Leeds U	L 2-3	1-1	4	Lawrence (pen) [43], Arca [90]	43,253
26	28	A	Nottingham F	W 2-1	0-0	2	Elliott [49], Stewart [90]	27,457
27	Jan 1	A	Preston NE	L 2-3	0-3	3	Elliott [72], Thornton [81]	16,940
28	3	H	Gillingham	D 1-1	1-1	3	Brown [19]	27,147
29	16	A	Derby Co	W 2-0	0-0	3	Elliott [51], Whitehead [66]	22,995
30	22	H	Sheffield U	W 1-0	1-0	3	Stewart [44]	27,337
31	Feb 4	A	Wolverhampton W	D 1-1	1-1	—	Elliott [12]	26,968
32	12	H	Watford	W 4-2	2-0	3	Stewart 3 (1 pen) [18, 33 (p), 51], Brown [73]	24,948
33	19	A	Brighton & HA	L 1-2	0-2	3	Arca [80]	6647
34	22	H	Rotherham U	W 4-1	2-0	—	Whitehead [13], Thornton 2 [36, 73], Breen [49]	22,267
35	26	H	Cardiff C	W 2-1	2-0	2	Breen [4], Stewart [42]	32,788
36	Mar 4	A	Burnley	W 2-0	1-0	—	Lawrence [26], Stewart [89]	12,103
37	12	A	Crewe Alex	W 1-0	0-0	2	Elliott [58]	7949
38	15	H	Plymouth Arg	W 5-1	3-0	—	Whitehead [31], Arca [40], Stewart (pen) [45], Caldwell [75], Thornton [90]	25,258
39	19	H	Coventry C	W 1-0	0-0	1	Brown [76]	29,424
40	Apr 2	A	QPR	W 3-1	0-1	1	Welsh [46], Brown [63], Arca [75]	18,198
41	5	A	Wigan Ath	W 1-0	1-0	—	Stewart [3]	20,745
42	9	H	Reading	L 1-2	0-0	1	Arca [52]	34,237
43	17	A	Ipswich T	D 2-2	0-0	1	Elliott [71], Robinson [84]	29,230
44	23	H	Leicester C	W 2-1	1-1	1	Stewart [23], Caldwell [60]	34,815
45	29	A	West Ham U	W 2-1	0-1	—	Arca [52], Elliott [87]	33,482
46	May 8	H	Stoke C	W 1-0	0-0	1	Robinson [57]	47,350

Final League Position: 1

GOALSCORERS

League (76): Stewart 16 (2 pens), Elliott 15, Arca 9, Lawrence 7 (2 pens), Brown 5, Whitehead 5, Caldwell 4, Robinson 4, Thornton 4, Breen 2, Bridges 1, Carter 1, Welsh 1, Wright 1, own goal 1.
Carling Cup (6): Brown 2, Caldwell 1, Elliott 1, Kyle 1, own goal 1.
FA Cup (2): Stewart 1 (pen), Welsh 1.

Poom M 11	Wright S 39	Arca J 39 + 1	Robinson C 40	Breen G 40	McCartney G 35 + 1	Clark B 1 + 1	Whitley J 32 + 3	Elliott S 29 + 13	Stewart M 40 + 3	Oster J 6 + 3	Whitehead D 39 + 3	Kyle K 5 + 1	Lawrence L 20 + 12	Myhre T 31	Caldwell S 41	Thornton S 3 + 13	Lynch M 5 + 6	Williams D 1	Collins N 8 + 3	Johnson S 1 + 4	Carter D 8 + 2	Brown C 13 + 24	Bridges M 5 + 14	Collins D 6 + 8	Piper M 1 + 1	Welsh A 3 + 4	Ingham M 1 + 1	Deane B — + 4	Alnwick B 3	*Match No.*
1	2	3	4	5	6	7^1	8	9^2	10	11^3	12	13	14																	1
	2	3	4	5		14	8	12	10^1	11		9^3	7^2	1	6	13														2
	2	3	4	5			8	12	10^3	11^1		9	7^2	1	6	13	14													3
	2^3	3	4	5				12	10	11^2	8	9	7^1	1	6	13	14													4
1		3^3	4	5	12		8	13	10	11^2	7	9			6^1	14	2													5
1		11		5	3		8^2	12	10^1	7^3	4	9	14			13		2	6											6
1	2	11	4^1	5	3		8	9^2	10^3	12	7				6		13			14										7
1	2	11^1	4	5	3		8	9^2	10^3	12	7		13		6					14										8
1	2	11	4^2	5	3			9^1	10		7		13		6					12	8									9
1	2		4	5	3		8	9^1			7		12		6						11	10^2	13							10
1	2		4	5■	3		8^3	9		12	7				6		13			14	11^1	10^2								11
1	2	11	4		3		8^1	9	10^2		7		12		6				5			13								12
1		11	4		3		8				7^1		12		6		2		5	10^2		9	13							13
1	2	11	4		3		8^1	9^2	10^3		7		12		6				5			13	14							14
	2	3	4	5			8	9	10^2		7			1	6						11^1	13		12						15
	2	11	4	5			8^1	9^2	10^3		12		7	1	6							13	14	3						16
	2	11^3	4	5			8	9^1	10^2				7	1	6						14	12	13	3						17
		11^3	4				8		10		12		7^2	1	6		2^1		5		14	13	9	3						18
		3	4	5			8^3	9	10^2		7		12	1	6		2^1				11	13		14						19
	2	11		5	3		8^1	9^3	10^2		4		12	1	6						7	13	14							20
	2	3		5	4			9^2	10^1		11		7^3	1	6		14				8	12	13							21
	2			5	3			9^1	10^2		4		7	1	6■						8	12	13	11						22
	2	11	4	5	3			9^1	12		8		7^3	1	6		14					10^2	13							23
	2	11^1	4	5	3		12	13	14		8		7	1					6			10^3	9^2							24
	2	11	4	5	3			12	13		8		7^2	1	6							10	9^1							25
	2	11	4^1	5	3		12	9	10^3		8		7^2	1	6				14			13								26
	2	11^2		5	3		8	9	10^3		7			1	6	12						13			4^1	14				27
	2			5^1	3		8^3	9	10		4			1	6	7			12			11^2	13		14					28
	2	11	4		3		8	9^1	10		7			1					5			12		6						29
	2	11	4		3		8^3	9^1	10^2		7			1		14			5			12	13	6						30
	2	11^3	4	5	3		8	9^2	10^1		7			1	6							12	13	14						31
	2	11	4	5	3		8	9	10^1		7			1	6							12								32
	2	11	4	5	3		8^3	9^2	10		7^1			1	6	14						12	13							33
	2^3	11^1	4	5	3		8	9^2	10		7			1	6	12						14	13							34
			4	5	3		8	9^1	10		7		13	1	6		2^2					12		14		11^3				35
			4	5	3		8		10		2		7	1	6	11^2						12	9^1			13				36
	2	12	4	5	3		8	13	10^3		7			1	6	11^1						14	9^2							37
	2	11	4	5	3		8^1	9	10^2		7^3		12	1	6	14						13								38
	2	11^3	4	5	3		8^1	9	10				7^2	1	6	12						13				14				39
	2	3	4	5			8^3	9	10^1		7			1	6	12						14		13		11^2				40
	2	11	4	5	3^2			12	10^1		8		7	1	6							9		13						41
	2	11	4	5	3		12		10		8		7^1	1^6	6							9^2					15	13		42
	2	11	4	5	3			12	10^1		8		7^2		6	13						9^3					1	14		43
	2	3	4	5				12	10^1		8		7		6							9^3		13		11^2		14	1	44
	2	11	4	5^2	3			12	10^1		8		7		6							9^3		13				14	1	45
	2	11	4	5^2	3			12	10^3		8		7		6				13			9^1				14			1	46

FA Cup
Third Round — Crystal Palace — (h) — 2-1
Fourth Round — Everton — (a) — 0-3

Carling Cup
First Round — Chester C — (h) — 3-0
Second Round — Crewe Alex — (a) — 3-3

SWANSEA CITY FL Championship 1

FOUNDATION

The earliest Association Football in Wales was played in the Northern part of the country and no international took place in the South until 1894, when a local paper still thought it necessary to publish an outline of the rules and an illustration of the pitch markings. There had been an earlier Swansea club, but this has no connection with Swansea Town (now City) formed at a public meeting in June 1912.

The New Stadium, Landure, Swansea SA1 2FA.

Telephone: (01792) 616 600.

Fax: (01792) 616 606.

Ticket Office: (0870) 040 0004.

Website: www.swanseacity.net

Email: dawn@swanseacityfc.co.uk

Ground Capacity: 20,000.

Record Attendance: 32,796 v Arsenal, FA Cup 4th rd, 17 February 1968 (at Vetch Field).

Pitch Measurements: 112yd × 74yd.

Chairman: Huw Jenkins.

Vice-chairman: Leigh Dineen.

Secretary: Jackie Rockey.

Manager: Kenny Jackett.

Assistant Manager: Kevin Nugent.

Physio: Richard Evans.

Colours: All white.

Change Colours: All black.

Year Formed: 1912.

Turned Professional: 1912.

Ltd Co.: 1912.

Previous Name: 1912, Swansea Town; 1970, Swansea City.

Club Nicknames: 'The Swans', 'The Jacks'.

First Football League Game: 28 August 1920, Division 3, v Portsmouth (a) L 0–3 – Crumley; Robson, Evans; Smith, Holdsworth, Williams; Hole, I. Jones, Edmundson, Rigsby, Spottiswood.

Record League Victory: 8–0 v Hartlepool U, Division 4, 1 April 1978 – Barber; Evans, Bartley, Lally (1) (Morris), May, Bruton, Kevin Moore, Robbie James (3 incl. 1p), Curtis (3), Toshack (1), Chappell.

Record Cup Victory: 12–0 v Sliema W (Malta), ECWC 1st rd 1st leg, 15 September 1982 – Davies; Marustik, Hadziabdic (1), Irwin (1), Kennedy, Rajkovic (1), Loveridge (2) (Leighton James), Robbie James, Charles (2), Stevenson (1), Latchford (1) (Walsh (3)).

HONOURS

Football League: Championship 2 – promoted 2004–05 (3rd); Division 1 best season: 6th, 1981–82; Division 2 – Promoted 1980–81 (3rd); Division 3 (S) – Champions 1924–25, 1948–49; Division 3 – Champions 1999–2000; Promoted 1978–79 (3rd); Division 4 – Promoted 1969–70 (3rd), 1977–78 (3rd), 1987–88 (play-offs).

FA Cup: Semi-finals 1926, 1964.

Football League Cup: best season: 4th rd, 1965, 1977.

Welsh Cup: Winners 10 times; Runners-up 8 times.

Autoglass Trophy: Winners 1994.

European Competitions: *European Cup-Winners' Cup:* 1961–62, 1966–67, 1981–82, 1982–83, 1983–84, 1989–90,

SKY SPORTS FACT FILE

Thirteen matches, 13 goals including five in one game and only nine points might have been an unlucky start for Swansea in 1920–21, but they improved to finish a highly respectable fifth. John Edmondson scored 20 goals in only 32 League games in what was their inaugural season in the League.

Record Defeat: 0–8 v Liverpool, FA Cup 3rd rd, 9 January 1990. 0–8 v Monaco, ECWC, 1st rd 2nd leg, 1 October 1991.

Most League Points (2 for a win): 62, Division 3 (S), 1948–49.

Most League Points (3 for a win): 85, Division 3, 1999–2000.

Most League Goals: 90, Division 2, 1956–57.

Highest League Scorer in Season: Cyril Pearce, 35, Division 2, 1931–32.

Most League Goals in Total Aggregate: Ivor Allchurch, 166, 1949–58, 1965–68.

Most League Goals in One Match: 5, Jack Fowler v Charlton Ath, Division 3S, 27 December 1924.

Most Capped Player: Ivor Allchurch, 42 (68), Wales.

Most League Appearances: Wilfred Milne, 585, 1919–37.

Youngest League Player: Nigel Dalling, 15 years 289 days v Southport, 6 December 1974.

Record Transfer Fee Received: £400,000 from Bristol C for Steve Torpey, August 1997.

Record Transfer Fee Paid: £340,000 to Liverpool for Colin Irwin, August 1981.

Football League Record: 1920 Original Member of Division 3; 1921–25 Division 3 (S); 1925–47 Division 2; 1947–49 Division 3 (S); 1949–65 Division 2; 1965–67 Division 3; 1967–70 Division 4; 1970–73 Division 3; 1973–78 Division 4; 1978–79 Division 3; 1979–81 Division 2; 1981–83 Division 1; 1983–84 Division 2; 1984–86 Division 3; 1986–88 Division 4; 1988–92 Division 3; 1992–96 Division 2; 1996–2000 Division 3; 2000–01 Division 2; 2001–04 Division 3; 2004–05 FL2; 2005– FL1.

MANAGERS

Walter Whittaker 1912–14
William Bartlett 1914–15
Joe Bradshaw 1919–26
Jimmy Thomson 1927–31
Neil Harris 1934–39
Haydn Green 1939–47
Bill McCandless 1947–55
Ron Burgess 1955–58
Trevor Morris 1958–65
Glyn Davies 1965–66
Billy Lucas 1967–69
Roy Bentley 1969–72
Harry Gregg 1972–75
Harry Griffiths 1975–77
John Toshack 1978–83
(resigned October re-appointed in December) 1983–84
Colin Appleton 1984
John Bond 1984–85
Tommy Hutchison 1985–86
Terry Yorath 1986–89
Ian Evans 1989–90
Terry Yorath 1990–91
Frank Burrows 1991–95
Bobby Smith 1995
Kevin Cullis 1996
Jan Molby 1996–97
Micky Adams 1997
Alan Cork 1997–98
John Hollins 1998–2001
Colin Addison 2001–02
Nick Cusack 2002
Brian Flynn 2002–04
Kenny Jackett April 2004–

LATEST SEQUENCES

Longest Sequence of League Wins: 9, 27.11.1999 – 22.01.2000.

Longest Sequence of League Defeats: 9, 26.1.1991 – 19.3.1991.

Longest Sequence of League Draws: 5, 5.1.1993 – 5.2.1993.

Longest Sequence of Unbeaten League Matches: 19, 19.10.1970 – 9.3.1971.

Longest Sequence Without a League Win: 15, 25.3.1989 – 2.9.1989.

Successive Scoring Runs: 27 from 28.8.1947.

Successive Non-scoring Runs: 6 from 6.2.1996.

TEN YEAR LEAGUE RECORD

		P	*W*	*D*	*L*	*F*	*A*	*Pts*	*Pos*
1995-96	Div 2	46	11	14	21	43	79	47	22
1996-97	Div 3	46	21	8	17	62	58	71	5
1997-98	Div 3	46	13	11	22	49	62	50	20
1998-99	Div 3	46	19	14	13	56	48	71	7
1999-2000	Div 3	46	24	13	9	51	30	85	1
2000-01	Div 2	46	8	13	25	47	73	37	23
2001-02	Div 3	46	13	12	21	53	77	51	20
2002-03	Div 3	46	12	13	21	48	65	49	21
2003-04	Div 3	46	15	14	17	58	61	59	10
2004-05	FL 2	46	24	8	14	62	43	80	3

DID YOU KNOW

In their last match at the Vetch Field on 30 April 2005, Swansea City had a season's best attendance of 11,469 for the 1–0 win over Shrewsbury Town. The following week they clinched automatic promotion with a similar success at Bury.

SWANSEA CITY 2004–05 LEAGUE RECORD

Match No.	*Date*	*Venue*	*Opponents*	*Result*		*H/T Score*	*Lg. Pos.*	*Goalscorers*	*Attendance*
1	Aug 7	H	Northampton T	L	0-2	0-1	—		9578
2	10	A	Rochdale	W	2-0	1-0	—	Nugent [21], Robinson [61]	2514
3	14	A	Macclesfield T	L	0-1	0-1	19		2164
4	21	H	Cheltenham T	D	1-1	0-1	18	Trundle [76]	6874
5	28	A	Cambridge U	W	1-0	1-0	13	Trundle [22]	2949
6	30	H	Lincoln C	W	1-0	1-0	7	Iriekpen [3]	6948
7	Sept 4	A	Yeovil T	L	0-1	0-0	11		5826
8	11	H	Kidderminster H	W	3-0	1-0	8	Connor 2 [16, 87], Trundle [53]	6462
9	18	A	Wycombe W	W	1-0	1-0	5	Robinson [14]	5247
10	25	H	Rushden & D	W	1-0	1-0	3	Nugent [36]	7410
11	Oct 2	A	Chester C	D	1-1	0-1	2	Trundle (pen) [55]	3847
12	8	H	Mansfield T	W	1-0	0-0	—	Forbes [89]	8868
13	16	A	Southend U	L	2-4	1-2	2	Connor [11], Forbes [82]	4940
14	19	H	Leyton Orient	W	1-0	1-0	—	Forbes [44]	8485
15	30	A	Grimsby T	D	1-1	0-0	3	Trundle (pen) [70]	4618
16	Nov 6	H	Bristol R	W	1-0	0-0	2	Trundle (pen) [88]	8778
17	17	H	Darlington	W	2-1	0-1	—	Trundle [55], Robinson [59]	7824
18	20	A	Shrewsbury T	L	0-2	0-1	2		5055
19	27	H	Bury	L	1-3	1-2	2	Nugent [2]	6971
20	Dec 8	A	Oxford U	W	1-0	0-0	—	Goodfellow [61]	4767
21	11	A	Scunthorpe U	L	0-1	0-1	3		5075
22	18	H	Notts Co	W	4-0	1-0	3	Trundle 3 (1 pen) [42, 71, 90 (p)], Connor [76]	6609
23	26	A	Kidderminster H	W	5-1	2-0	3	Connor [1], Iriekpen [9], Robinson 2 (1 pen) [88 (p), 90], Goodfellow [89]	4288
24	28	H	Boston U	W	3-1	3-0	3	Trundle [4], Forbes [21], Goodfellow [27]	10,162
25	Jan 1	H	Yeovil T	L	0-2	0-0	3		11,225
26	3	A	Rushden & D	W	2-0	2-0	3	Connor [4], Robinson [22]	3382
27	15	H	Wycombe W	D	2-2	0-0	3	Connor [51], Trundle (pen) [59]	6793
28	22	A	Boston U	W	3-2	0-1	3	Trundle 2 (1 pen) [52, 90 (p)], Robinson [62]	2545
29	29	H	Chester C	W	3-0	1-0	2	Trundle 2 [42, 61], Connor [50]	8989
30	Feb 4	H	Southend U	D	1-1	0-0	—	Trundle [55]	10,190
31	8	A	Mansfield T	L	0-1	0-1	—		3829
32	12	A	Leyton Orient	L	1-3	0-2	3	Thorpe [81]	4050
33	19	H	Grimsby T	D	0-0	0-0	3		7760
34	22	A	Darlington	L	1-2	1-1	—	Forbes [37]	2709
35	26	H	Scunthorpe U	W	2-1	1-1	4	Trundle 2 (1 pen) [25, 60 (p)]	7249
36	Mar 5	A	Notts Co	L	0-1	0-0	5		4644
37	12	H	Rochdale	D	2-2	0-1	5	Gurney [46], Holt (og) [52]	6804
38	19	A	Northampton T	D	2-2	1-2	5	Connor [30], Trundle [70]	5799
39	25	H	Macclesfield T	W	2-0	2-0	—	Thorpe [25], Connor [32]	9809
40	28	A	Cheltenham T	W	2-1	1-1	3	Thorpe [3], Britton [82]	4669
41	Apr 2	H	Cambridge U	W	3-0	0-0	3	Robinson [66], Trundle 2 [83, 88]	8664
42	9	A	Lincoln C	L	0-1	0-0	4		5207
43	15	H	Oxford U	W	1-0	1-0	—	O'Leary [44]	10,602
44	23	A	Bristol R	L	0-2	0-2	4		7433
45	30	H	Shrewsbury T	W	1-0	1-0	4	Forbes [8]	11,469
46	May 7	A	Bury	W	1-0	1-0	3	Forbes [1]	7575

Final League Position: 3

GOALSCORERS

League (62): Trundle 22 (7 pens), Connor 10, Robinson 8 (1 pen), Forbes 7, Goodfellow 3, Nugent 3, Thorpe 3, Iriekpen 2, Britton 1, Gurney 1, O'Leary 1, own goal 1.
Carling Cup (0).
FA Cup (6): Connor 3, Goodfellow 1, O'Leary 1, Trundle 1.
LDV Vans Trophy (2): Nugent 1, Ricketts 1.

Gueret W 44	Jones S 2 + 2	Ricketts S 42	O'Leary K 32	Tate A 17 + 6	Monk G 34	Britton L 16 + 14	Martinez R 34 + 3	Forbes A 36 + 4	Connor P 34 + 6	Robinson A 29 + 8	Maylett B 4 + 12	Oli D — + 1	Austin K 41 + 1	Fisken G 1 + 4	Thomas J — + 2	Nugent K 7 + 12	Trundle L 41 + 1	Iriekpen E 29	Gurney A 25 + 3	Fitzgerald S — + 3	Anderson I 8 + 5	Goodfellow M 6	Murphy B 2	Thorpe L 9 + 6	McLeod K 7 + 4	Bean M 6 + 2	Match No.
1	2	3	4	5	6	7	8^1	9^2	10	11	12	13															1
1		3	4	5	6	7		9	10^2	11^1			2	12	13	8											2
1		3	4	5	6	7		9^1	10^2	11	12		2		13	8											3
1	2	3	4	5	6	7		9^1	10^2	11	12					8	13										4
1		3	4^2	2	6	12	8	14	9	11^1	7^3			13			10	5									5
1		3	4		6	12	8	7^2	9	11^1			2	13			10	5									6
1		3	4^1		6■		8	7	9^3	11	12^2		2			13	10	5	14								7
1		3	4	12		13	8	7^2	9^3	11			2			14	10	5^1	6								8
1		3	4		6	7	8	9	10^2	11^1	12		5			13			2								9
1		3	4		6	12	8	7^1		11^2	13		5			9	10		2								10
1		3	4	5	6^1	12	8	7^2	9^3	11	13		2			14	10										11
1		3	4	5		12	8	13	9^3	11^1	7^2		6			14	10		2								12
1		3	2	5	6		8	12	9^2	11	7^1		4				10			13							13
1		3	4		6	12	8	7	9^2	11^1			5				10		2	13							14
1		3	4	12	6	7^2	8	11^1	9^3				5			13	10		2	14							15
1		3	4		6	7	8	11^1	9^2		12		5			13	10		2								16
1		3	4		6	12	8	7^1	9^2	11			5			13	10		2								17
1		3	4	12	6■		8	7^3	9^2	11■			5	14		13	10		2^1								18
1	12	3		5		13		9^2					6	4^1		8	10		2		11	7					19
1		3	4		6		8	7	12				5			9^2	10^1		2		13	11					20
1		3	4		6		8	7	12	13			5			9^1	10		2			11^2					21
1		3		4			8	7	9				5				10	6	2			11					22
1	12			4			8	7^1	9^3	13			5			14	10^2	6	2■		3	11					23
1		3		4			8	7^2	9^1	13			5			12	10	6			2	11					24
1		3		4		12	8	7^1	9	11			5				10	6			2						25
1		3		4	5		8	7	9^2	11	12		2			13	10^1	6^3			14						26
1		3		4	5	7			9	11^2	12		2				10	6	8^1		13						27
		3		12	5	8		7^1	9	13			2				10	6	4		11^2		1				28
1		3			5	8		7	9	11			4				10	6	2								29
1		3			5	8	12		9	11	7		4				10	6	2^1								30
				2	5■	4	8		9^2	7	12		3				10	6			11^1		1	13			31
1		3		2		4^1	8		9	7			5				10	6			11			12			32
1		3		12			8	7^3	9^2	11			5				10	6^1	2					13	14	4	33
1		3				7	8	9^1					5				10	6	2					12	11	4	34
1		3	4	12	5			7					2^2				10^1	6	13					9	11	8	35
1		3	4			12		7^1	13	14							10	6	2		5^3			9^2	11	8	36
1		3	4				12	7^2	9	14	13		5				10■	6	2						11^3	8^1	37
1		3	4^1		5		12	7^2	9	13			2				10	6						14	11^3	8	38
1			4^2		5		8	12	9	11			3				10^1	6	2		13			7			39
1			4		5	12	8^2		9^3	11^1			3				10	6	2					7	14	13	40
1		3^2	4		5	7	8			12			2				10	6	13					9	11^1		41
1		3	4		5		8	7^1		11			2				10	6						9		12	42
1		3	4		5		8	7	12	11			2				10	6						9^1			43
1		3	4		5	12	8^1	7^2	13	11■			2				10	6						9^3	14		44
1		3	4		5	12	8	7	9^1				13				10	6	2^2					14	11^3		45
1		3	4^2		5	7	8	11	12				2				10^3	6			13			9^1	14		46

FA Cup

First Round	Cheltenham T	(a)	3-1
Second Round	Stockport Co	(a)	0-0
		(h)	2-1
Third Round	Reading	(a)	1-1
		(h)	0-1

Carling Cup

First Round	QPR	(a)	0-3

LDV Vans Trophy

First Round	Luton T	(h)	2-0
Second Round	Wycombe W	(a)	0-1

SWINDON TOWN FL Championship 1

FOUNDATION

It is generally accepted that Swindon Town came into being in 1881, although there is no firm evidence that the club's founder, Rev. William Pitt, captain of the Spartans (an offshoot of a cricket club) changed his club's name to Swindon Town before 1883, when the Spartans amalgamated with St Mark's Young Men's Friendly Society.

County Ground, County Road, Swindon SN1 2ED.

Telephone: 0870 443 1969.

Fax: (01793) 333 703.

Ticket Office: 0870 443 1894.

Website: www.swindontownfc.co.uk

Email: enquiries@swindontownfc.co.uk

Ground Capacity: 14,540.

Record Attendance: 32,000 v Arsenal, FA Cup 3rd rd, 15 January 1972.

Pitch Measurements: 110yd × 70yd.

Chairman: Willie Carson.

Chief Executive: Sandy Gray.

Secretary: Linda Birrell.

Manager: Andy King.

Assistant Manager: Alan Reeves.

Physio: Dick Mackey.

Colours: Red and white shirts, white shorts, red and white stockings.

Change Colours: Blue and white shirts, blue shorts, blue and white stockings.

Year Formed: 1881* (*see Foundation*).

Turned Professional: 1894.

Ltd Co.: 1894.

Club Nickname: 'Robins'.

Previous Ground: 1881, The Croft; 1896, County Ground.

First Football League Game: 28 August 1920, Division 3, v Luton T (h) W 9–1 – Nash; Kay, Macconachie; Langford, Hawley, Wareing; Jefferson (1), Fleming (4), Rogers, Batty (2), Davies (1), (1 og).

Record League Victory: 9–1 v Luton T, Division 3 (S), 28 August 1920 – Nash; Kay, Macconachie; Langford, Hawley, Wareing; Jefferson (1), Fleming (4), Rogers, Batty (2), Davies (1), (1 og).

HONOURS

FA Premier League: best season: 22nd 1993–94; Division 1 – 1992–93 (play-offs).

Football League: Division 2 – Champions 1995–96; Division 3 – Runners-up 1962–63, 1968–69; Division 4 – Champions 1985–86 (with record 102 points).

FA Cup: Semi-finals 1910, 1912.

Football League Cup: Winners 1969.

Anglo-Italian Cup: Winners 1970.

SKY SPORTS FACT FILE

In their successful 1968–69 season Swindon Town enjoyed an average League attendance of 17,856. Seven times the crowd exceeded 20,000. They were particularly strong at home and goalkeeper Peter Downsborough conceded only seven goals there.

Record Cup Victory: 10–1 v Farnham U Breweries (away), FA Cup 1st rd (replay), 28 November 1925 – Nash; Dickenson, Weston, Archer, Bew, Adey; Denyer (2), Wall (1), Richardson (4), Johnson (3), Davies.

Record Defeat: 1–10 v Manchester C, FA Cup 4th rd (replay), 25 January 1930.

Most League Points (2 for a win): 64, Division 3, 1968–69.

Most League Points (3 for a win): 102, Division 4, 1985–86.

Most League Goals: 100, Division 3 (S), 1926–27.

Highest League Scorer in Season: Harry Morris, 47, Division 3 (S), 1926–27.

Most League Goals in Total Aggregate: Harry Morris, 216, 1926–33.

Most League Goals in One Match: 5, Harry Morris v QPR, Division 3S, 18 December 1926; 5, Harry Morris v Norwich C, Division 3S, 26 April 1930; 5, Keith East v Mansfield T, Division 3, 20 November 1965.

Most Capped Player: Rod Thomas, 30 (50), Wales.

Most League Appearances: John Trollope, 770, 1960–80.

Youngest League Player: Paul Rideout, 16 years 107 days v Hull C, 29 November 1980.

Record Transfer Fee Received: £1,500,000 from Manchester C for Kevin Horlock, January 1997.

Record Transfer Fee Paid: £800,000 to West Ham U for Joey Beauchamp, August 1994.

Football League Record: 1920 Original Member of Division 3; 1921–58 Division 3 (S); 1958–63 Division 3; 1963–65 Division 2; 1965–69 Division 3; 1969–74 Division 2; 1974–82 Division 3; 1982–86 Division 4; 1986–87 Division 3; 1987–92 Division 2; 1992–93 Division 1; 1993–94 FA Premier League; 1994–95 Division 1; 1995–96 Division 2; 1996–2000 Division 1; 2000–04 Division 2; 2004– FL1.

MANAGERS

Sam Allen 1902–33
Ted Vizard 1933–39
Neil Harris 1939–41
Louis Page 1945–53
Maurice Lindley 1953–55
Bert Head 1956–65
Danny Williams 1965–69
Fred Ford 1969–71
Dave Mackay 1971–72
Les Allen 1972–74
Danny Williams 1974–78
Bobby Smith 1978–80
John Trollope 1980–83
Ken Beamish 1983–84
Lou Macari 1984–89
Ossie Ardiles 1989–91
Glenn Hoddle 1991–93
John Gorman 1993–94
Steve McMahon 1994–99
Jimmy Quinn 1999–2000
Colin Todd 2000
Andy King 2000–01
Roy Evans 2001
Andy King January 2002–

LATEST SEQUENCES

Longest Sequence of League Wins: 8, 12.1.1986 – 15.3.1986.

Longest Sequence of League Defeats: 6, 2.5.1993 – 25.8.1993.

Longest Sequence of League Draws: 6, 22.11.1991 – 28.12.1991.

Longest Sequence of Unbeaten League Matches: 22, 12.1.1986 – 23.8.86.

Longest Sequence Without a League Win: 19, 30.10.1999 – 4.3.2000.

Successive Scoring Runs: 31 from 17.4.1926.

Successive Non-scoring Runs: 5 from 16.11.1963.

TEN YEAR LEAGUE RECORD

		P	*W*	*D*	*L*	*F*	*A*	*Pts*	*Pos*
1995-96	Div 2	46	25	17	4	71	34	92	1
1996-97	Div 1	46	15	9	22	52	71	54	19
1997-98	Div 1	46	14	10	22	42	73	52	18
1998-99	Div 1	46	13	11	22	59	81	50	17
1999-2000	Div 1	46	8	12	26	38	77	36	24
2000-01	Div 2	46	13	13	20	47	65	52	20
2001-02	Div 2	46	15	14	17	46	56	59	13
2002-03	Div 2	46	16	12	18	59	63	60	10
2003-04	Div 2	46	20	13	13	76	58	73	5
2004-05	FL 1	46	17	12	17	66	68	63	12

DID YOU KNOW ?

The first player signed by Swindon Town for a four-figure transfer fee was Ben Morton who arrived from Torquay United on 30 October 1937 in a £1000 move. The following season he was top scorer for them with 28 League goals.

SWINDON TOWN 2004–05 LEAGUE RECORD

Match No.	Date	Venue	Opponents	Result	H/T Score	Lg. Pos.	Goalscorers	Atten-dance
1	Aug 7	A	Wrexham	L 1-2	0-1	—	Caton [90]	5099
2	11	H	Luton T	L 2-3	1-2	—	Parkin [45], Reeves [65]	6286
3	14	H	Milton Keynes D	W 2-1	1-1	19	Parkin [23], Howard [63]	5060
4	21	A	Bristol C	W 2-1	1-1	12	Henderson 2 [23, 60]	13,389
5	28	H	Hartlepool U	W 3-0	3-0	7	Henderson [17], Parkin [37], Nelson (og) [40]	5365
6	30	A	Walsall	L 2-3	2-2	10	Howard [5], Henderson [25]	5951
7	Sept 4	A	Colchester U	W 1-0	1-0	5	Parkin [7]	3868
8	11	H	Peterborough U	L 0-1	0-1	11		5777
9	18	A	Blackpool	D 1-1	0-1	11	Henderson [69]	5229
10	25	H	Bradford C	W 1-0	0-0	7	Igoe [87]	5189
11	Oct 2	A	Stockport Co	D 3-3	2-0	8	Fallon 2 [13, 66], McMaster [45]	4394
12	16	H	Oldham Ath	W 1-0	1-0	9	Roberts [14]	5522
13	19	A	Port Vale	L 0-1	0-0	—		3872
14	23	A	Barnsley	D 2-2	1-1	9	Igoe [28], Roberts [82]	8837
15	27	H	Sheffield W	W 3-2	0-1	—	Howard [78], Parkin [86], Fallon [88]	6972
16	30	H	Torquay U	D 3-3	3-1	7	Parkin [27], Igoe [32], Howard [36]	6724
17	Nov 6	A	Tranmere R	L 1-2	0-1	10	Duke [69]	8419
18	20	H	Hull C	W 4-2	1-1	7	Parkin 2 [22, 87], O'Hanlon [74], Roberts [89]	6348
19	27	A	Chesterfield	L 0-1	0-0	10		4244
20	Dec 8	H	Huddersfield T	L 1-2	0-2	—	Smith G [89]	4828
21	11	H	Doncaster R	D 1-1	0-1	12	Parkin [72]	5452
22	18	A	Bournemouth	L 1-2	0-0	14	O'Hanlon [60]	7110
23	26	A	Peterborough U	W 2-0	0-0	11	Igoe [54], Parkin [85]	4212
24	28	H	Brentford	W 3-0	1-0	10	Hewlett [42], Howard [67], Parkin [76]	6875
25	Jan 1	H	Colchester U	L 0-3	0-2	10		6468
26	3	A	Bradford C	W 2-1	0-0	10	Smith G 2 [46, 47]	8239
27	8	A	Sheffield W	L 0-2	0-1	10		20,804
28	15	H	Blackpool	D 2-2	2-1	11	Parkin 2 [36, 45]	5526
29	22	A	Brentford	L 1-2	1-1	11	Smith G [20]	5857
30	29	H	Stockport Co	W 3-0	0-0	11	Heywood [61], O'Hanlon [63], Smith G [64]	5090
31	Feb 5	A	Oldham Ath	W 2-1	0-1	8	Parkin [60], Smith G [69]	5810
32	12	H	Barnsley	W 2-1	1-1	7	Parkin 2 [13, 76]	5511
33	19	A	Torquay U	D 2-2	1-1	8	Parkin 2 [38, 58]	4190
34	23	H	Port Vale	W 1-0	1-0	—	Proctor [25]	4724
35	26	A	Doncaster R	D 1-1	1-1	7	Holmes [5]	7696
36	Mar 5	H	Bournemouth	L 0-3	0-1	8		8275
37	12	A	Luton T	L 1-3	1-2	9	Proctor [34]	8173
38	19	H	Wrexham	W 4-2	1-2	9	Parkin 3 (1 pen) [40, 76, 90 (p)], Smith G [80]	5123
39	25	A	Milton Keynes D	D 1-1	1-1	—	Smith G [43]	7019
40	Apr 2	A	Hartlepool U	L 0-3	0-1	11		4536
41	9	H	Walsall	L 1-2	0-1	12	Parkin (pen) [84]	5592
42	13	H	Bristol C	D 0-0	0-0	—		6977
43	16	A	Hull C	D 0-0	0-0	12		23,125
44	23	H	Tranmere R	W 2-1	0-1	11	Smith G 2 [57, 59]	4484
45	30	A	Huddersfield T	L 0-4	0-0	12		13,559
46	May 7	H	Chesterfield	D 1-1	1-1	12	Parkin [13]	6044

Final League Position: 12

GOALSCORERS

League (66): Parkin 23 (2 pens), Smith G 10, Henderson 5, Howard 5, Igoe 4, Fallon 3, O'Hanlon 3, Roberts 3, Proctor 2, Caton 1, Duke 1, Hewlett 1, Heywood 1, Holmes 1, McMaster 1, Reeves 1, own goal 1.
Carling Cup (1): Hewlett 1.
FA Cup (5): Duke 1, Howard 1, Jenkins 1, O'Hanlon 1, Roberts 1.
LDV Vans Trophy (3): Fallon 1, Nicolas 1, Parkin 1.

Evans R 45	Gurney A 6	Duke D 42 + 2	Smith G 23 + 7	O'Hanlon S 40	Hewlett M 30 + 1	Igoe S 42 + 1	Miglioranzi S 16 + 5	Fallon R 12 + 19	Parkin S 41	Howard B 28 + 7	Reeves A 6 + 2	Caton A 1 + 7	Robinson M 11 + 7	Ifil J 31 + 4	Henderson D 6	Nicolas A 8 + 8	Yeates M 3 + 1	Mitchell P 7	Heywood M 28 + 4	McMaster J 2 + 2	Roberts C 18 + 3	Jenkins S 24	Garrard L 8 + 1	Pook M 3 + 2	Holmes L 14 + 1	Slabber J 4 + 5	Proctor M 4	Book S 1 + 1	Lapham K 2	Wells B — + 1	Holgate A — + 2	*Match No.*
1	2	3^{1}	4^{2}	5	6	7	8	9^{3}	10	11	12	13	14																			1
1	2	3		5	6	7	8	9^{1}	10	11	4	12																				2
1	2	3	13	5	6	7	8	12	10	11^{2}			9^{1}	4																		3
1	2	3■		5	6	7	8^{2}	12	10	11^{3}			13	4	9^{1}	14																4
1	2^{1}	3	12	5	6			13	10	11			14	4	9^{2}	7	8^{3}															5
1	2	3	12	5	6			13	10	11^{1}			14	4	9	7^{2}	8^{3}															6
1		3		5	6	7	8^{1}		10	11				4	9	12		2														7
1		3	12	5	6	7		13	10	11^{1}				4	9		8^{2}	2														8
1		3		5	6^{2}	7	8^{1}		10	11			12	4	9		13	2														9
1		3		5	12	7	8^{1}	9	10■	11			6	4				2														10
1		3^{2}		5	6	7		9		11		12	8	4				2	13	10^{1}												11
1		3^{1}		5	6	7		9		11				4		8		2		12	10											12
1		3		5	6	7^{1}		9		11				4				2	12	8	10											13
1		3	13	5		7		9^{1}	10	11			8	4		2				12^{2}	6											14
1		3^{1}	6	5		7		12	10	11			8	4		2^{2}			13		9											15
1		3^{3}	12	5	6	7			10	11			8^{1}	4		13			14		9	2^{2}										16
1		3^{1}		5	6	7		12	10	11				4					2		9	8										17
1		3		5		7			10	11			8	4					6		9	2										18
1		3^{1}		5		7		13	10	11^{2}			8	4		12			6		9	2										19
1		3^{1}	12	5	7^{2}			13	10	11			8	4■					6		9	2										20
1		12		5	6	7			10	11						8^{1}			4		9	2	3									21
1		3		5		7^{2}		12	10	11^{1}	4		8			13			6		9^{3}		2	14								22
1		3		5	11	7			10		6			4							9^{1}	2	12		8							23
1		3			6	7		12	10^{1}	11	5			4								2	8		9							24
1		3			6	7			10	11^{1}			8^{2}	4		12			5				2		9	13						25
1		3	8		6^{1}	7		13^{3}	10	11	14		12^{2}	4■					5				2		9							26
1		3	8	5^{2}		7		12	10	11^{1}	6					13			4				2		9							27
1		3^{2}	4			7	12	9	10	13	5								6			2^{1}	11		8							28
1			3	5		7^{2}	8	12	10					4					6			2	11^{1}		9	13						29
1		3	8^{3}	5	6	7^{1}	12	13	10	14									4			2			9	11^{2}						30
1		3	8^{3}	5	11	12	7^{1}	13	10	14				4					6			2				9^{2}						31
1		3	8	5	6	7^{1}	12	13	10										4			2			11	9^{2}						32
1		3	8	5	6	7			10										4			2			11	9						33
1		3	8	5	6	7	12		10										4			2			11^{1}	13	9^{2}					34
1		3	8	5	6	7^{2}			10	12				13					4			2			11^{1}	14	9^{3}					35
1^{G}		3	8	5	6^{1}	7	12		10										4			2			11^{2}	13	9	15				36
1		3	8	5		11	7^{1}		10					4					6		13	2			12		9^{2}					37
		3^{2}	8	5		11^{1}	7		10	12		14		13					6		9^{3}	2			4			1				38
1		3	8	5	6	11	7^{2}		10	12				13					4		9^{1}	2										39
1		3^{3}	8	5	6^{1}	11	7	13	10	12				2					4		9^{2}			14								40
1		3^{2}	8	5	6^{1}	11	7	12	10			14		13					4		9^{3}	2										41
1		12	8	5		7	3^{1}	9	10	11				4					6			2										42
1		3	8	5		7		9^{1}	10	11				4					6		12	2										43
1		3	8	5^{1}		11		9				13		4		12			6		10^{2}	2		7								44
1		11■	8^{1}			7		9■				13^{3}		4		2			5		10^{2}			6					3	12	14	45
1			8			11^{3}	7		10			9^{2}	12	4		5^{1}			6		13			2					3		14	46

FA Cup

First Round	Sheffield W	(h)	4-1
Second Round	Notts Co	(h)	1-1
		(a)	0-2

Carling Cup

First Round	Rushden & D	(a)	1-0
Second Round	Leeds U	(a)	0-1

LDV Vans Trophy

First Round			
Second Round	Exeter C	(a)	2-1
Quarter-Final	Bristol C	(h)	1-0
Semi-Final	Southend U	(a)	0-2

TORQUAY UNITED FL Championship 2

FOUNDATION

The idea of establishing a Torquay club was agreed by old boys of Torquay College and Torbay College, while sitting in Princess Gardens listening to the band. A proper meeting was subsequently held at Tor Abbey Hotel at which officers were elected. This was on 1 May 1899 and the club's first competition was the Eastern League (later known as the East Devon League). As an amateur club it played at Teignmouth Road, Torquay Recreation Ground and Cricket Field Road before settling down for four years at Torquay Cricket Ground where the rugby club now plays. They became Torquay United in 1921 after merging with Babbacombe FC.

Plainmoor Ground, Torquay, Devon TQ1 3PS.

Telephone: (01803) 328 666.

Fax: (01803) 323 976.

Ticket Office: (01803) 328 666.

Website: www.torquayunited.com

Email: gullsfc@aol.com

Ground Capacity: 6,104.

Record Attendance: 21,908 v Huddersfield T, FA Cup 4th rd, 29 January 1955.

Pitch Measurements: 110yd × 74yd.

Chairman: Michael Bateson.

Vice-chairman: Mervyn Benney.

Secretary: Deborah Hancox.

Manager: Leroy Rosenior.

Colours: Yellow and blue.

Change Colours: White.

Year Formed: 1899.

Turned Professional: 1921.

Ltd Co.: 1921.

Previous Name: 1910, Torquay Town; 1921, Torquay United.

Club Nickname: 'The Gulls'.

Previous Grounds: 1899, Teignmouth Road; 1900, Torquay Recreation Ground; 1904, Cricket Field Road; 1906, Torquay Cricket Ground; 1910, Plainmoor Ground.

First Football League Game: 27 August 1927, Division 3 (S), v Exeter C (h) D 1–1 – Millsom; Cook, Smith; Wellock, Wragg, Connor, Mackey, Turner (1), Jones, McGovern, Thomson.

HONOURS

Football League: Division 3 – Promoted 2003–04 (3rd); Division 3 (S) – Runners-up 1956–57; Division 4 – Promoted 1959–60 (3rd), 1965–66 (3rd), 1990–91 (play-offs).

FA Cup: best season: 4th rd, 1949, 1955, 1971, 1983, 1990.

Football League Cup: never past 3rd rd.

Sherpa Van Trophy: Runners-up 1989.

SKY SPORTS FACT FILE

Promotion from the play-offs courtesy of a penalty shoot-out success at Wembley over Blackpool came only after an amazing slump in fortunes for Torquay United from 3 November 1990 to 26 March when they failed to score in 13 of 21 matches.

Record League Victory: 9–0 v Swindon T, Division 3 (S), 8 March 1952 – George Webber; Topping, Ralph Calland; Brown, Eric Webber, Towers; Shaw (1), Marchant (1), Northcott (2), Collins (3), Edds (2).

Record Cup Victory: 7–1 v Northampton T, FA Cup 1st rd, 14 November 1959 – Gill; Penford, Downs; Bettany, George Northcott, Rawson; Baxter, Cox, Tommy Northcott (1), Bond (3), Pym (3).

Record Defeat: 2–10 v Fulham, Division 3 (S), 7 September 1931. 2–10 v Luton T, Division 3 (S), 2 September 1933.

Most League Points (2 for a win): 60, Division 4, 1959–60.

Most League Points (3 for a win): 81, Division 3, 2003–04.

Most League Goals: 89, Division 3 (S), 1956–57.

Highest League Scorer in Season: Sammy Collins, 40, Division 3 (S), 1955–56.

Most League Goals in Total Aggregate: Sammy Collins, 204, 1948–58.

Most League Goals in One Match: 5, Robin Stubbs v Newport Co, Division 4, 19 October 1963.

Most Capped Player: Rodney Jack, St Vincent.

Most League Appearances: Dennis Lewis, 443, 1947–59.

Youngest League Player: David Byng, 16 years 36 days v Walsall, 14 August 1993.

Record Transfer Fee Received: £500,000 from Crewe Alex for Rodney Jack, July 1998.

Record Transfer Fee Paid: £75,000 to Peterborough U for Leon Constantine, December 2004.

Football League Record: 1927 Elected to Division 3 (S); 1958–60 Division 4; 1960–62 Division 3; 1962–66 Division 4; 1966–72 Division 3; 1972–91 Division 4; 1991–2004 Division 3; 2004–05 FL1; 2005– FL2.

MANAGERS

Percy Mackrill 1927–29
A. H. Hoskins 1929 *(Secretary-Manager)*
Frank Womack 1929–32
Frank Brown 1932–38
Alf Steward 1938–40
Billy Butler 1945–46
Jack Butler 1946–47
John McNeil 1947–50
Bob John 1950
Alex Massie 1950–51
Eric Webber 1951–65
Frank O'Farrell 1965–68
Alan Brown 1969–71
Jack Edwards 1971–73
Malcolm Musgrove 1973–76
Mike Green 1977–81
Frank O'Farrell 1981–82 *(continued as General Manager to 1983)*
Bruce Rioch 1982–84
Dave Webb 1984–85
John Sims 1985
Stuart Morgan 1985–87
Cyril Knowles 1987–89
Dave Smith 1989–91
John Impey 1991–92
Ivan Golac 1992
Paul Compton 1992–93
Don O'Riordan 1993–95
Eddie May 1995–96
Kevin Hodges *(Head Coach)* 1996–98
Wes Saunders 1998–2001
Roy McFarland 2001–02
Leroy Rosenior June 2002–

LATEST SEQUENCES

Longest Sequence of League Wins: 8, 24.1.1998 – 3.3.1998.

Longest Sequence of League Defeats: 8, 30.9.1995 – 18.11.1995.

Longest Sequence of League Draws: 8, 25.10.1969 – 13.12.1969.

Longest Sequence of Unbeaten League Matches: 15, 5.5.1990 – 3.11.1990.

Longest Sequence Without a League Win: 17, 5.3.1938 – 10.9.1938.

Successive Scoring Runs: 19 from 3.10.1953.

Successive Non-scoring Runs: 7 from 8.1.1972.

TEN YEAR LEAGUE RECORD

		P	*W*	*D*	*L*	*F*	*A*	*Pts*	*Pos*
1995-96	Div 3	46	5	14	27	30	84	29	24
1996-97	Div 3	46	13	11	22	46	62	50	21
1997-98	Div 3	46	21	11	14	68	59	74	5
1998-99	Div 3	46	12	17	17	47	58	53	20
1999-2000	Div 3	46	19	12	15	62	52	69	9
2000-01	Div 3	46	12	13	21	52	77	49	21
2001-02	Div 3	46	12	15	19	46	63	51	19
2002-03	Div 3	46	16	18	12	71	71	66	9
2003-04	Div 3	46	23	12	11	68	44	81	3
2004-05	FL 1	46	12	15	19	55	79	51	21

DID YOU KNOW?

During 1925–26 improved form in the Southern League was hampered when winter storms blew away the club's grandstand roof. Generous public donations and fund-raising games by Plymouth Argyle and Exeter City helped the finances.

TORQUAY UNITED 2004–05 LEAGUE RECORD

Match No.	Date	Venue	Opponents	Result	H/T Score	Lg. Pos.	Goalscorers	Attendance
1	Aug 7	A	Bristol C	D 1-1	0-0	—	Woods (pen) 72	14,275
2	10	H	Hull C	L 0-3	0-2	—		3973
3	14	H	Sheffield W	L 2-4	1-1	23	Osei-Kuffour 44, Gritton 60	5005
4	21	A	Luton T	L 0-1	0-1	23		6664
5	28	H	Walsall	D 0-0	0-0	22		3791
6	30	A	Milton Keynes D	L 0-1	0-1	23		3015
7	Sept 4	A	Stockport Co	W 2-0	1-0	21	Gritton 2 30, 58	4372
8	11	H	Brentford	D 2-2	1-0	21	Wardley 2 38, 48	3458
9	18	A	Hartlepool U	L 1-4	1-1	22	Gritton 10	4485
10	25	H	Tranmere R	L 1-2	0-1	23	Russell 55	2922
11	Oct 2	A	Peterborough U	D 1-1	1-1	23	Russell 34	3828
12	9	H	Huddersfield T	W 2-1	0-1	23	Hill 49, Osei-Kuffour 84	3033
13	16	A	Doncaster R	D 2-2	1-2	23	Akinfenwa 9, Osei-Kuffour 90	5529
14	19	H	Bournemouth	L 1-2	0-0	—	Hill 54	3055
15	30	A	Swindon T	D 3-3	1-3	23	Constantine 16, Akinfenwa 2 66, 84	6724
16	Nov 6	H	Oldham Ath	W 2-0	1-0	22	Constantine 9, Gritton 71	3183
17	20	A	Port Vale	W 2-1	1-0	21	Hill 42, Constantine 65	4763
18	23	H	Wrexham	W 1-0	1-0	—	Bedeau 26	2384
19	27	H	Colchester U	L 1-3	0-0	20	Gritton (pen) 74	2984
20	Dec 7	A	Blackpool	L 0-4	0-1	—		4179
21	11	H	Barnsley	L 0-1	0-1	21		2983
22	18	A	Chesterfield	D 1-1	0-0	20	Gosling 48	4133
23	26	A	Brentford	W 3-1	0-1	19	Constantine 3 55, 70, 83	6419
24	28	H	Bradford C	D 0-0	0-0	19		4119
25	Jan 1	H	Stockport Co	L 1-2	1-0	19	Hill 45	3456
26	3	A	Tranmere R	L 1-4	1-1	19	Akinfenwa 21	8792
27	8	A	Huddersfield T	D 1-1	0-1	19	Hill 56	9194
28	15	H	Hartlepool U	L 1-2	1-0	19	Osei-Kuffour 13	2543
29	22	A	Bradford C	D 2-2	2-2	20	Bedeau 40, Akinfenwa 42	8209
30	Feb 5	H	Doncaster R	W 2-1	2-0	20	Constantine 7, Akinfenwa 19	3157
31	12	A	Wrexham	D 1-1	1-0	20	Osei-Kuffour 20	3608
32	15	H	Peterborough U	W 2-1	1-0	—	Akinfenwa 2 24, 75	2769
33	19	H	Swindon T	D 2-2	1-1	19	Constantine 25, Osei-Kuffour 63	4190
34	22	A	Bournemouth	L 0-3	0-1	—		5867
35	26	A	Barnsley	L 1-4	0-3	20	Phillips 88	7466
36	Mar 5	H	Chesterfield	D 2-2	1-1	21	Akinfenwa 20, Phillips 88	2746
37	12	A	Hull C	L 0-2	0-0	21		17,147
38	19	H	Bristol C	L 0-4	0-3	21		4299
39	26	A	Sheffield W	D 2-2	1-0	21	Akinfenwa 25, Woods 49	21,526
40	28	H	Luton T	L 1-4	1-2	21	Akinfenwa 6	4264
41	Apr 2	A	Walsall	D 1-1	0-0	21	Akinfenwa 59	5694
42	9	H	Milton Keynes D	W 1-0	0-0	21	Abbey 82	3509
43	16	H	Port Vale	W 1-0	0-0	21	Constantine (pen) 90	3592
44	23	A	Oldham Ath	W 2-1	1-1	20	Hockley 41, Akinfenwa 49	8941
45	30	H	Blackpool	W 2-0	1-0	19	Akinfenwa 16, Russell 54	5347
46	May 7	A	Colchester U	L 1-2	0-1	21	Woodman 90	4834

Final League Position: 21

GOALSCORERS

League (55): Akinfenwa 14, Constantine 9 (1 pen), Gritton 6 (1 pen), Osei-Kuffour 6, Hill 5, Russell 3, Bedeau 2, Phillips 2, Wardley 2, Woods 2 (1 pen), Abbey 1, Gosling 1, Hockley 1, Woodman 1.
Carling Cup (1): Osei-Kuffour 1.
FA Cup (0).
LDV Vans Trophy (5): Akinfenwa 2, Bedeau 1, Osei-Kuffour 1, Taylor 1.

Bossu B 2	Canoville L 29 + 2	McGlinchey B 32 + 1	Hockley M 20 + 14	Taylor C 35 + 1	Woods S 36	Fowler J 7 + 5	Russell A 38	Akinfenwa A 28 + 9	Osei-Kuffour J 26 + 8	Hill K 36 + 3	Phillips M 19 + 11	Owen G 2 + 3	Gritton M 16 + 3	Bedeau A 31 + 4	Dearden K 5	Villis M 12 + 10	Van Heusden A 7	Meirelles B 5 + 4	Wardley S 5 + 2	Noble S 2 + 1	Bond K — + 1	Gottskalksson O 15	Boardley S 2 + 4	Constantine L 24 + 3	Woodman C 20 + 2	Gosling J 6 + 1	Robinson P 12	Pulis A 1 + 2	Story O — + 2	Lopes O 1	Barnes P 5	Jarvie P 1	Marriott A 11	Abbey Z 2 + 4	Garner D 8 + 1	Brown A 5	Match No.
1	2	3	4^1	5	6	7^2	8	9	10	11^3	12	13	14																								1
1	2	3	4^2	5■	6	7^3	8	9^1	10	11	13		12	14																							2
	2^3	3	4^1			7	8^2	12	10	13	6	5	9	11	1	14																					3
		3	4		6	7^2		12	10	11	8^1	5	9	2			1	13																			4
		3	4	5	6				11		7	12	9	2			1	8^2	13	10^1																	5
		3	4	5	6				11		7^2	12	9	2			1	8	13	10^1																	6
	2	3	12	5	6				10		11		9^2	7			1	8^1	4	13																	7
	2	3	12	5	6				10^3	13	11^1		9	7			1	8^2	4		14																8
	2	3		5	6	12		13	10^2	14	11^1		9	7^3			1	8	4																		9
	2	3		5	6	12	8^1	13	10	11^3	14		9^2	7			1		4																		10
		3^1	12	5	6	13	8		10		11^3		9	2				14	4			1	7^2														11
		3	12	5	6	4^1	8	10	13	11	7^3		9^2	2		14						1															12
		3	12	5	6	4^1	8	9	10	11^3	7^2			2				13				1	14														13
		3	4	5	6	7^2	8	9	10	11^1				2				12				1	13														14
	2^2	3		5	6		4	9	10^1	11	13		12	7								1		8													15
	2	3	12	5	6	13	4	9^2		11			10^1	7								1		8													16
	2	3	4	5		12	8	13	14	11			9^2	7^3	1	6								10^1													17
	2	3	4	5			8	12		11			9^1	7	1	6								10													18
	2	3	4^2	5			8	12	10^1	11			9	7	1	6							13														19
	2	3	4^1	5■	6		8	13	12	11			9^2	7	1	14									10^3												20
	2	3	4^1		6		8	13	12	11	7^3		9^2			5						1		10		14											21
	2	3	12		6		8			10				7		5						1		9	11	4^1											22
	2				6		8			10				7		3						1		9	11	4	5										23
	2				6		8			10				7		3						1		9	11	4	5										24
	2	12		13	6		8^3	9		10				7		3						1			11^1	4^2	5	14									25
	2	3^1	12	5	6			9			13			7^3								1	8		11	4^2	10		14								26
		3	12	5	6			9		10	13					2^2						1			11	4^1	8		14	7^3							27
	12	3^2		5	6		7	9	10^1	11	13			2								1		8			4										28
			12	5	6		4	9	10^1	11				7								1		8	3		2										29
	12	3	13	5	6^1		4	9	10^2	11				7										8			2				1						30
	2	3	12	5			7	9	10^1	11														8	6		4				1						31
	2	3	12	5			4	9	10^2	11				7										8^1	13		6				1						32
	2	3		5^1			4	9	10	11				7		12								8			6				1						33
	2	3^1	12				4^2	9	10	7						5								8	11		6	13			1						34
	2	3	4^2				7	9	10^3	11	12					13							14	8	6			5^1				1					35
	2	3^2					4	9	12	11	13			7		5								8	6								1	10^1			36
	2		4		6		11	9	10	3	7^1					5								8									1	12			37
	2			5	6		4	9	10^1	3	7^3			12										8^2	13								1	14	11		38
	2			5	6		8	9^1		11	13			7		14								12	3								1		4^3	10^2	39
	2^2			5	6		4	9	10^3	11	12			7^1										13	3								1		14	8	40
			2	5	6		8	9		11	7													12	3								1		4	10^1	41
			2	5	6		8	9^1	12		7^2					13								10	3								1	14	4	11^3	42
			2	5	6		8		12		7^2					13								10	3								1	9	4	11^1	43
			2	5	6		8	9		11	7^1					12								10	3								1		4		44
			2	5	6		8^3	9^2	12	11	7^1			13		14								10	3								1		4		45
			2	5	6		8	9		11	7			12										10^1	3								1	13	4^2		46

FA Cup
First Round Hinckley (a) 0-2

Carling Cup
First Round Coventry C (a) 1-4

LDV Vans Trophy
First Round Yeovil T (h) 4-3
Second Round Northampton T (h) 1-3

TOTTENHAM HOTSPUR FA Premiership

FOUNDATION

The Hotspur Football Club was formed from an older cricket club in 1882. Most of the founders were old boys of St John's Presbyterian School and Tottenham Grammar School. The Casey brothers were well to the fore as the family provided the club's first goalposts (painted blue and white) and their first ball. They soon adopted the local YMCA as their meeting place, but after a couple of moves settled at the Red House, which is still their headquarters, although now known simply as 748 High Road.

Bill Nicholson Way, 748 High Road, Tottenham, London N17 0AP.

Telephone: 0870 420 5000.

Fax: (020) 8365 5175.

Ticket Office: 0870 420 5000.

Website: www.spurs.co.uk

Email: email@spurs.co.uk

Ground Capacity: 36,237.

Record Attendance: 75,038 v Sunderland, FA Cup 6th rd. 5 March 1938.

Pitch Measurements: 100m × 67m.

Chairman: Daniel Levy.

Vice-chairman: David Buchler.

Secretary: John Alexander.

Head Coach: Martin Jol.

First Team Coach: Chris Hughton.

Head of Medical Services: Dr Charlotte Cowie.

Colours: White shirts, navy shorts, white stockings.

Change Colours: Royal blue shirts, royal blue shorts, royal blue stockings, all with yellow trim.

Year Formed: 1882.

Turned Professional: 1895.

Ltd Co.: 1898.

Previous Names: 1882, Hotspur Football Club; 1884, Tottenham Hotspur.

Club Nickname: 'Spurs'.

Previous Grounds: 1882, Tottenham Marshes; 1888, Northumberland Park; 1899, White Hart Lane.

First Football League Game: 1 September 1908, Division 2, v Wolverhampton W (h) W 3–0 – Hewitson; Coquet, Burton; Morris (1), D. Steel, Darnell; Walton, Woodward (2), Macfarlane, R. Steel, Middlemiss.

Record League Victory: 9–0 v Bristol R, Division 2, 22 October 1977 – Daines; Naylor, Holmes, Hoddle (1), McAllister, Perryman, Pratt, McNab, Moores (3), Lee (4), Taylor (1).

HONOURS

Football League: Division 1 – Champions 1950–51, 1960–61; Runners-up 1921–22, 1951–52, 1956–57, 1962–63; Division 2 – Champions 1919–20, 1949–50; Runners-up 1908–09, 1932–33; Promoted 1977–78 (3rd).

FA Cup: Winners 1901 (as non-League club), 1921, 1961, 1962, 1967, 1981, 1982, 1991; Runners-up 1987.

Football League Cup: Winners 1971, 1973, 1999; Runners-up 1982, 2002.

European Competitions: *European Cup:* 1961–62. *European Cup-Winners' Cup:* 1962–63 (winners), 1963–64, 1967–68, 1981–82, 1982–83, 1991–92. *UEFA Cup:* 1971–72 (winners), 1972–73, 1973–74 (runners-up), 1983–84 (winners), 1984–85, 1999–2000. *Intertoto Cup:* 1995.

SKY SPORTS FACT FILE

Arthur Rowe's "push and run" style brought Tottenham Hotspur the title in 1950–51. It was never better demonstrated than on the visit of Newcastle United on 18 November. Spurs won 7–0 against the then league leaders before a crowd of 70,026.

Record Cup Victory: 13–2 v Crewe Alex, FA Cup 4th rd (replay), 3 February 1960 – Brown; Hills, Henry; Blanchflower, Norman, Mackay; White, Harmer (1), Smith (4), Allen (5), Jones (3 incl. 1p).

Record Defeat: 0–8 v Cologne, UEFA Intertoto Cup, 22 July 1995.

Most League Points (2 for a win): 70, Division 2, 1919–20.

Most League Points (3 for a win): 77, Division 1, 1984–85.

Most League Goals: 115, Division 1, 1960–61.

Highest League Scorer in Season: Jimmy Greaves, 37, Division 1, 1962–63.

Most League Goals in Total Aggregate: Jimmy Greaves, 220, 1961–70.

Most League Goals in One Match: 5, Ted Harper v Reading, Division 2, 30 August 1930; 5, Alf Stokes v Birmingham C, Division 1, 18 September 1957; 5, Bobby Smith v Aston Villa, Division 1, 29 March 1958.

Most Capped Player: Pat Jennings, 74 (119), Northern Ireland.

Most League Appearances: Steve Perryman, 655, 1969–86.

Youngest League Player: Ally Dick, 16 years 301 days v Manchester C, 20 February 1982.

Record Transfer Fee Received: £5,500,000 from Lazio for Paul Gascoigne, May 1992.

Record Transfer Fee Paid: £11,000,000 to Dynamo Kiev for Sergei Rebrov, May 2000.

Football League Record: 1908 Elected to Division 2; 1909–15 Division 1; 1919–20 Division 2; 1920–28 Division 1; 1928–33 Division 2; 1933–35 Division 1; 1935–50 Division 2; 1950–77 Division 1; 1977–78 Division 2; 1978–92 Division 1; 1992– FA Premier League.

MANAGERS

Frank Brettell 1898–99
John Cameron 1899–1906
Fred Kirkham 1907–08
Peter McWilliam 1912–27
Billy Minter 1927–29
Percy Smith 1930–35
Jack Tresadern 1935–38
Peter McWilliam 1938–42
Arthur Turner 1942–46
Joe Hulme 1946–49
Arthur Rowe 1949–55
Jimmy Anderson 1955–58
Bill Nicholson 1958–74
Terry Neill 1974–76
Keith Burkinshaw 1976–84
Peter Shreeves 1984–86
David Pleat 1986–87
Terry Venables 1987–91
Peter Shreeves 1991–92
Ossie Ardiles 1993–94
Gerry Francis 1994–97
Christian Gross *(Head Coach)* 1997–98
George Graham 1998–2001
Glenn Hoddle 2001–03
David Pleat (*Caretaker*) 2003–04
Jacques Santini 2004
Martin Jol November 2004–

LATEST SEQUENCES

Longest Sequence of League Wins: 13, 23.4.1960 – 1.10.1960.

Longest Sequence of League Defeats: 7, 1.1.1994 – 27.2.1994.

Longest Sequence of League Draws: 6, 9.1.1999 – 27.2.1999.

Longest Sequence of Unbeaten League Matches: 22, 31.8.1949 – 31.12.1949.

Longest Sequence Without a League Win: 16, 29.12.1934 – 13.4.1935.

Successive Scoring Runs: 32 from 24.2.1962.

Successive Non-scoring Runs: 6 from 28.12.1985.

TEN YEAR LEAGUE RECORD

		P	*W*	*D*	*L*	*F*	*A*	*Pts*	*Pos*
1995-96	PR Lge	38	16	13	9	50	38	61	8
1996-97	PR Lge	38	13	7	18	44	51	46	10
1997-98	PR Lge	38	11	11	16	44	56	44	14
1998-99	PR Lge	38	11	14	13	47	50	47	11
1999-2000	PR Lge	38	15	8	15	57	49	53	10
2000-01	PR Lge	38	13	10	15	47	54	49	12
2001-02	PR Lge	38	14	8	16	49	53	50	9
2002-03	PR Lge	38	14	8	16	51	62	50	10
2003-04	PR Lge	38	13	6	19	47	57	45	14
2004-05	PR Lge	38	14	10	14	47	41	52	9

DID YOU KNOW ?

Application to the Football League having been rejected to Tottenham Hotspur in 1896, they were granted admission to the First Division of the Southern League without having to play in Division 2. They finished fourth in the eleven team competition.

TOTTENHAM HOTSPUR 2004–05 LEAGUE RECORD

Match No.	Date	Venue	Opponents	Result		H/T Score	Lg. Pos.	Goalscorers	Attendance
1	Aug 14	H	Liverpool	D	1-1	0-1	—	Defoe [71]	35,105
2	21	A	Newcastle U	W	1-0	0-0	6	Atouba [51]	52,185
3	25	A	WBA	D	1-1	1-1	—	Defoe [34]	27,191
4	28	H	Birmingham C	W	1-0	1-0	4	Defoe [35]	35,290
5	Sept 12	H	Norwich C	D	0-0	0-0	6		36,095
6	19	A	Chelsea	D	0-0	0-0	5		42,246
7	25	H	Manchester U	L	0-1	0-1	9		36,103
8	Oct 2	A	Everton	W	1-0	0-0	5	Pamarot [53]	38,264
9	18	A	Portsmouth	L	0-1	0-0	—		20,121
10	23	H	Bolton W	L	1-2	1-1	10	Keane [41]	36,025
11	30	A	Fulham	L	0-2	0-1	11		21,317
12	Nov 6	H	Charlton Ath	L	2-3	0-2	14	Keane (pen) [69], Defoe [79]	35,423
13	13	H	Arsenal	L	4-5	1-1	14	Naybet [37], Defoe [61], King [74], Kanoute [88]	36,095
14	22	A	Aston Villa	L	0-1	0-0	—		35,702
15	28	H	Middlesbrough	W	2-0	0-0	13	Defoe [49], Kanoute [76]	35,772
16	Dec 4	A	Blackburn R	W	1-0	0-0	13	Keane [56]	22,182
17	11	A	Manchester C	W	1-0	0-0	11	Kanoute [57]	45805
18	18	H	Southampton	W	5-1	3-0	7	Defoe 3 [8, 27, 61], Kanoute [44], Keane [88]	36,254
19	26	A	Norwich C	W	2-0	0-0	7	Keane [73], Brown [77]	24,508
20	28	H	Crystal Palace	D	1-1	0-0	8	Defoe [54]	36,100
21	Jan 1	H	Everton	W	5-2	2-1	7	Marney 2 [16, 80], Ziegler [27], Pedro Mendes [59], Keane [68]	36,102
22	4	A	Manchester U	D	0-0	0-0	7		67,962
23	15	H	Chelsea	L	0-2	0-1	8		36,105
24	22	A	Crystal Palace	L	0-3	0-0	8		23,723
25	Feb 1	A	Bolton W	L	1-3	0-0	—	Defoe [66]	24,780
26	5	H	Portsmouth	W	3-1	1-1	9	Mido 2 [34, 57], Keane [83]	36,105
27	26	H	Fulham	W	2-0	0-0	8	Kanoute [78], Keane [90]	35,885
28	Mar 5	A	Southampton	L	0-1	0-0	9		31,903
29	15	A	Charlton Ath	L	0-2	0-1	—		26,870
30	19	H	Manchester C	W	2-1	1-1	8	Defoe [16], Keane [84]	35,681
31	Apr 2	A	Birmingham C	D	1-1	0-0	9	Kelly [59]	29,304
32	10	H	Newcastle U	W	1-0	1-0	7	Defoe [42]	35,885
33	16	A	Liverpool	D	2-2	1-1	7	Edman [12], Keane [55]	44,029
34	20	H	WBA	D	1-1	0-1	—	Keane [52]	35,885
35	25	A	Arsenal	L	0-1	0-1	—		38,147
36	May 1	H	Aston Villa	W	5-1	3-1	7	Kanoute 2 [6, 27], King [19], Reid [67], Kelly [90]	36,078
37	7	A	Middlesbrough	L	0-1	0-1	9		34,766
38	15	H	Blackburn R	D	0-0	0-0	9		35,797

Final League Position: 9

GOALSCORERS

League (47): Defoe 13, Keane 11 (1 pen), Kanoute 7, Kelly 2, King 2, Marney 2, Mido 2, Atouba 1, Brown 1, Edman 1, Naybet 1, Pamarot 1, Pedro Mendes 1, Reid 1, Ziegler 1.
Carling Cup (14): Defoe 5, Keane 3, Bunjevcevic 2, Kanoute 2, Brown 1, Gardner 1.
FA Cup (10): Defoe 4 (1 pen), Keane 3, King 1, Mido 1, Pamarot 1.

Robinson P 36	Ifil P 2	Edman E 28	Davis S 11 + 4	Naybet N 27	King L 38	Pedro Mendes22 + 2	Redknapp J 9 + 5	Kanoute F 22 + 10	Defoe J 28 + 7	Jackson J 3 + 5	Doherty G — + 1	Atouba T 15 + 3	Brown M 20 + 4	Gardner A 8 + 9	Pamarot N 23	Keane R 23 + 12	Davies S 17 + 4	Mabizela M 1	Ziegler R 12 + 11	Carrick M 26 + 3	Bunjevcevic G 2 + 1	Davenport C — + 1	Ricketts R 5 + 1	Kelly S 13 + 4	Marney D 3 + 2	Yeates M — + 2	Mido4 + 5	Reid A 13	Dawson M 5	Cerny R 2 + 1	*Match No.*
1	2	3	4	5^{2}	6	7	8^{3}	9	10	11^{1}	12	13	14																		1
1	2	3	4	5	6	7	8^{2}	9^{3}	10	12		11^{1}	13	14																	2
1		3	4	5	6	7	8^{2}	9	10^{3}	12		11^{1}	13		2	14															3
1		3	4	5	6	7	12	13	10^{1}	11^{3}			8	14	2	9^{2}															4
1		3		5	6	7	8	9^{2}	10	12		11^{1}	4^{3}		2	13	14														5
1		3		5	6	7	8	12	10^{1}			4^{2}	13		2	9	11														6
1		3		5	6	7	8	9^{2}	10	12					2	11	13	4^{1}													7
1		3^{1}		5	6	7	8		10^{2}			4		12	2	9	11		13												8
1				5	6	7		12	10	13		8^{2}	4^{3}	3^{1}	2	9	11			14											9
1			12	5	6	7	8^{1}	10	13	11^{2}				3	2	9	4^{3}		14												10
1			4^{3}	5	6	7		12	10				8^{2}		2	9	13		11^{1}	14	3										11
1				5	6	7	4^{2}	8	10						2	9	11^{1}		12	13	3										12
1		3		5	6	7^{2}		12	10				4^{1}	14	2	9^{3}	13		11	8											13
1		3^{2}		5	6	7^{1}		9	10			11^{3}	4		2	12			13	8		14									14
1				5	6	8		12	10			3			2	9^{1}			11	4			7								15
1				5	6	7	12	13	10^{2}			3	4	14		9^{3}			11^{1}	8				2							16
1				5^{2}	6	7^{3}	12	10				3	4	13	2	9				8			11^{1}	14							17
1					6	12		9	10			3	4	5	2	13			11^{2}	8			7^{1}								18
1		3		5	6	7	12	10^{2}	13			11^{3}	4^{1}		2	9			14	8											19
1		3			6	12		9^{2}	10				4	5	2	13			11	8			7^{1}								20
1		3		5	6	7	12	10							2	9			11^{2}	4^{1}			13		8						21
1		3		5	6	7								12	2	9			10	4			11^{1}		8						22
1		3		5	6	7^{3}			10				4	12	2^{2}	9			11^{1}	8					13	14					23
1		3		5	6	7			10			12			2^{3}	9			11^{1}	4				13	8^{2}	14					24
1		3^{1}			6			10[illegible]	12			11	4	5		9	7			8				2							25
1				5^{2}	6				10			3	4			12	7			8	13			2			9^{1}	11			26
1		3		5	6			12	10^{1}				4			13	7			8				2			9^{2}	11			27
1		3			6			12	10				4	5		13	7		14	8				2^{3}			9^{1}	11^{2}			28
1		3	12		6			10	13				4	5	2^{3}	9			11^{2}	8^{1}				14				7			29
1				5^{3}	6			12	10			3	4	14		13	7			8				2			9^{1}	11^{2}			30
1		3	12	5^{3}	6			9	10				4		2^{2}				11^{1}	8				13			14	7			31
1		3	12		6			9	10^{2}				4^{1}	5		13	7^{3}		14	8				2				11			32
1		3	4		6			10	12							9^{1}	7		13	8				2				11^{2}	5		33
1		3^{1}	4^{3}		6				10^{2}			12				9	7		13	8				2			14	11	5		34
1		3	4^{2}		6			9^{3}	10^{1}							12	7		13	8				2			14	11	5		35
1^{G}		3	4		6			10^{2}	12							9^{1}	7			8				2			13	11	5	15	36
		3	4		6			9^{2}	10^{1}							12	7		13	8				2			14	11^{3}	5	1	37
		3	4^{2}	5	6			10	12							9	7			8				2	13			11^{1}		1	38

FA Cup

Third Round	Brighton & HA	(h)	2-1
Fourth Round	WBA	(a)	1-1
		(h)	3-1
Fifth Round	Nottingham F	(h)	1-1
		(a)	3-0
Sixth Round	Newcastle U	(a)	0-1

Carling Cup

Second Round	Oldham Ath	(a)	6-0
Third Round	Bolton W	(a)	4-3
Fourth Round	Burnley	(a)	3-0
Fifth Round	Liverpool	(h)	1-1

TRANMERE ROVERS FL Championship 1

FOUNDATION

Formed in 1884 as Belmont they adopted their present title the following year and eventually joined their first league, the West Lancashire League in 1889–90, the same year as their first success in the Wirral Challenge Cup. The club almost folded in 1899–1900 when all the players left en bloc to join a rival club, but they survived the crisis and went from strength to strength winning the 'Combination' title in 1907–08 and the Lancashire Combination in 1913–14. They joined the Football League in 1921 from the Central League.

Prenton Park, Prenton Road West, Birkenhead, Wirral CH42 9PY.

Telephone: 0870 460 3333.

Fax: Main reception: (0151) 608 6114; Matchday reception: (0151) 608 4385; Commerical: (0151) 609 0606; Ticket Office: (0151) 609 3355.

Ticket Office: 0870 460 3332.

Website: www.tranmererovers.co.uk

Email: Main: info@tranmererovers.co.uk; Ticket office: tickets@tranmererovers.co.uk; Club shop: shop@tranmererovers.co.uk

Ground Capacity: 16,789.

Record Attendance: 24,424 v Stoke C, FA Cup 4th rd, 5 February 1972.

Pitch Measurements: 110yd × 70yd.

Chairperson: Lorraine Rogers.

Chief Executive/Secretary: Mick Horton.

Manager: Brian Little.

Assistant Manager: Richard Hill.

Physio: Les Parry.

Colours: White shirts with reflex blue trim, white shorts with reflex blue trim, white stockings with reflex blue trim.

Change Colours: Amber shirts with black trim, amber shorts with black trim, amber stockings with black trim.

Year Formed: 1884.

Turned Professional: 1912.

Ltd Co.: 1920.

Previous Name: 1884, Belmont AFC; 1885, Tranmere Rovers.

Club Nickname: 'The Rovers'.

Previous Grounds: 1884, Steeles Field; 1887, Ravenshaws Field/Old Prenton Park; 1912, Prenton Park.

HONOURS

Football League Division 1 best season: 4th, 1992–93; Promoted from Division 3 1990–91 (play-offs); Division 3 (N) – Champions 1937–38; Promotion to 3rd Division: 1966–67, 1975–76; Division 4 – Runners-up 1988–89.

FA Cup: best season: 6th rd, 2000, 2001, 2004.

Football League Cup: Runners-up, 2000.

Welsh Cup: Winners 1935; Runners-up 1934.

Leyland Daf Cup: Winners 1990; Runners-up 1991.

SKY SPORTS FACT FILE

An early season stutter in which they scored in only three of 11 matches threatened Tranmere Rovers in 1922–23 before a spirited second half revival lifted them out of the danger area when five wins were recorded in the last seven matches.

First Football League Game: 27 August 1921, Division 3 (N), v Crewe Alex (h) W 4–1 – Bradshaw; Grainger, Stuart (1); Campbell, Milnes (1), Heslop; Moreton, Groves (1), Hyam, Ford (1), Hughes.

Record League Victory: 13–4 v Oldham Ath, Division 3 (N), 26 December 1935 – Gray; Platt, Fairhurst; McLaren, Newton, Spencer; Eden, MacDonald (1), Bell (9), Woodward (2), Urmson (1).

Record Cup Victory: 13–0 v Oswestry U, FA Cup 2nd prel rd, 10 October 1914 – Ashcroft; Stevenson, Bullough, Hancock, Taylor, Holden (1), Moreton (1), Cunningham (2), Smith (5), Leck (3), Gould (1).

Record Defeat: 1–9 v Tottenham H, FA Cup 3rd rd (replay), 14 January 1953.

Most League Points (2 for a win): 60, Division 4, 1964–65.

Most League Points (3 for a win): 80, Division 4, 1988–89; Division 3, 1989–90; Division 2, 2002–03.

Most League Goals: 111, Division 3 (N), 1930–31.

Highest League Scorer in Season: Bunny Bell, 35, Division 3 (N), 1933–34.

Most League Goals in Total Aggregate: Ian Muir, 142, 1985–95.

MANAGERS

Bert Cooke 1912–35
Jackie Carr 1935–36
Jim Knowles 1936–39
Bill Ridding 1939–45
Ernie Blackburn 1946–55
Noel Kelly 1955–57
Peter Farrell 1957–60
Walter Galbraith 1961
Dave Russell 1961–69
Jackie Wright 1969–72
Ron Yeats 1972–75
John King 1975–80
Bryan Hamilton 1980–85
Frank Worthington 1985–87
Ronnie Moore 1987
John King 1987–96
John Aldridge 1996–2001
Dave Watson 2001–02
Ray Mathias 2002–03
Brian Little October 2003–

Most League Goals in One Match: 9, Bunny Bell v Oldham Ath, Division 3N, 26 December 1935.

Most Capped Player: John Aldridge, 30 (69), Republic of Ireland.

Most League Appearances: Harold Bell, 595, 1946–64 (incl. League record 401 consecutive appearances).

Youngest League Player: Iain Hume, 16 years 167 days v Swindon T, 15 April 2000.

Record Transfer Fee Received: £3,300,000 from Everton for Steve Simonsen, September 1998.

Record Transfer Fee Paid: £450,000 to Aston Villa for Shaun Teale, August 1995.

Football League Record: 1921 Original Member of Division 3 (N): 1938–39 Division 2; 1946–58 Division 3 (N); 1958–61 Division 3; 1961–67 Division 4; 1967–75 Division 3; 1975–76 Division 4; 1976–79 Division 3; 1979–89 Division 4; 1989–91 Division 3; 1991–92 Division 2; 1992–2001 Division 1; 2001–04 Division 2; 2004– FL1.

LATEST SEQUENCES

Longest Sequence of League Wins: 9, 9.2.1990 – 19.3.1990.

Longest Sequence of League Defeats: 8, 29.10.1938 – 17.12.1938.

Longest Sequence of League Draws: 5, 26.12.1997 – 31.1.1998.

Longest Sequence of Unbeaten League Matches: 18, 16.3.1970 – 4.9.1970.

Longest Sequence Without a League Win: 16, 8.11.1969 – 14.3.1970.

Successive Scoring Runs: 32 from 24.2.1934.

Successive Non-scoring Runs: 7 from 20.12.1997.

TEN YEAR LEAGUE RECORD

		P	W	D	L	F	A	Pts	Pos
1995-96	Div 1	46	14	17	15	64	60	59	13
1996-97	Div 1	46	17	14	15	63	56	65	11
1997-98	Div 1	46	14	14	18	54	57	56	14
1998-99	Div 1	46	12	20	14	63	61	56	15
1999-2000	Div 1	46	15	12	19	57	68	57	13
2000-01	Div 1	46	9	11	26	46	77	38	24
2001-02	Div 2	46	16	15	15	63	60	63	12
2002-03	Div 2	46	23	11	12	66	57	80	7
2003-04	Div 2	46	17	16	13	59	56	67	8
2004-05	FL 1	46	22	13	11	73	55	79	3

DID YOU KNOW ?

The loss of centre-forward Bunny Bell transferred to Everton on 13 March was unlucky for Tranmere Rovers in 1935–36. He had scored in a 4–2 win over Crewe Alexandra when the table toppers led by a point. They won only three more games.

TRANMERE ROVERS 2004–05 LEAGUE RECORD

Match No.	Date	Venue	Opponents	Result		H/T Score	Lg. Pos.	Goalscorers	Attendance
1	Aug 7	A	Peterborough U	L	0-1	0-0	—		5390
2	10	H	Hartlepool U	W	2-1	1-1	—	Taylor (pen) [27], Dagnall [68]	8128
3	14	H	Chesterfield	W	1-0	1-0	6	Dadi [44]	8287
4	21	A	Doncaster R	D	0-0	0-0	11		6040
5	27	H	Sheffield W	W	4-2	3-2	—	Zola Makongo [12], Jackson [18], Taylor (pen) [30], Hume [64]	9506
6	30	A	Stockport Co	D	1-1	0-0	4	Jackson [54]	5502
7	Sept 11	A	Barnsley	D	0-0	0-0	10		8615
8	14	H	Oldham Ath	W	2-0	0-0	—	Dadi [65], Hume [73]	8437
9	18	H	Wrexham	D	1-1	0-1	4	Roberts [59]	9826
10	25	A	Torquay U	W	2-1	1-0	2	Hume 2 [2, 87]	2922
11	Oct 2	H	Luton T	D	1-1	1-0	3	Taylor [32]	10,884
12	16	H	Bradford C	L	4-5	1-1	8	Taylor (pen) [45], Hume 2 [66, 87], Beresford [82]	8901
13	19	A	Huddersfield T	W	3-1	1-1	—	Whitmore 2 [15, 61], Dagnall [65]	10,324
14	23	A	Colchester U	W	2-1	1-0	6	Dagnall [29], Zola Makongo [81]	3420
15	30	H	Brentford	W	1-0	0-0	2	Sharps [53]	8740
16	Nov 6	H	Swindon T	W	2-1	1-0	2	Hall 2 [34, 74]	8419
17	9	A	Bristol C	L	0-4	0-2	—		11,098
18	20	A	Blackpool	W	1-0	1-0	2	Goodison [38]	6490
19	27	H	Milton Keynes D	W	2-0	0-0	2	Hall [53], Whitmore [84]	8402
20	Dec 7	A	Port Vale	L	1-3	0-2	—	Jackson [73]	4027
21	10	H	Bournemouth	W	2-0	1-0	—	Hume [45], Hall [89]	8557
22	18	A	Hull C	L	1-6	0-1	3	Dadi [55]	20,064
23	26	H	Barnsley	D	1-1	0-0	3	Hume [73]	11,519
24	28	A	Walsall	W	2-0	0-0	3	McAteer [57], Taylor [81]	7217
25	Jan 1	A	Oldham Ath	D	2-2	1-1	3	Taylor (pen) [37], Hume [52]	6876
26	3	H	Torquay U	W	4-1	1-1	3	Dadi [8], McAteer [66], Jones [77], Hall [90]	8792
27	10	H	Bristol C	L	0-1	0-1	—		8183
28	15	A	Wrexham	W	5-1	2-0	3	Dagnall [21], Hume [42], Roberts [49], Whitmore [79], Hall [81]	6221
29	22	H	Walsall	W	2-1	1-0	3	Hume [8], Dagnall [50]	8651
30	29	A	Luton T	D	1-1	1-0	3	Dadi [5]	8594
31	Feb 5	A	Bradford C	D	1-1	1-0	3	Hume [1]	8129
32	12	H	Colchester U	D	1-1	1-0	3	Dadi [8]	8098
33	22	H	Huddersfield T	W	3-0	2-0	—	Dadi [16], Hume [24], Roberts [90]	7613
34	26	A	Bournemouth	D	1-1	1-1	3	Hall [22]	7305
35	Mar 5	H	Hull C	L	1-3	1-1	4	Taylor [7]	12,684
36	12	A	Hartlepool U	W	1-0	0-0	4	Dagnall [53]	4887
37	18	H	Peterborough U	W	5-0	3-0	—	Hall 2 [16, 80], Hume [29], McAteer [45], Whitmore [60]	8401
38	26	A	Chesterfield	D	2-2	0-1	3	Jackson [72], Dadi [86]	4293
39	28	H	Doncaster R	L	2-4	2-2	3	Dadi [11], Hall [44]	9730
40	Apr 2	A	Sheffield W	W	2-1	1-1	3	Jackson [42], Hume [60]	22,925
41	8	H	Stockport Co	W	1-0	0-0	—	McAteer [66]	8757
42	12	A	Brentford	L	0-1	0-0	—		6005
43	16	H	Blackpool	D	0-0	0-0	3		8568
44	23	A	Swindon T	L	1-2	1-0	3	Taylor [20]	4484
45	29	H	Port Vale	W	1-0	1-0	—	Hall [40]	8940
46	May 7	A	Milton Keynes D	L	1-2	0-1	3	Beresford [65]	7359

Final League Position: 3

GOALSCORERS

League (73): Hume 15, Hall 11, Dadi 9, Taylor 8 (4 pens), Dagnall 6, Jackson 5, Whitmore 5, McAteer 4, Roberts 3, Beresford 2, Zola Makongo 2, Goodison 1, Jones 1, Sharps 1.
Carling Cup (2): McAteer 1, Zola 1.
FA Cup (1): Taylor 1.
LDV Vans Trophy (4): Hall 1, Hume 1, Roberts 1, Zola 1.
Play-Offs (2): Beresford 1, Taylor 1.

Achterberg J 39	Taylor R 43	Roberts G 40	McAteer J 32 + 2	Jackson M 43	Goodison I 43 + 1	Hall P 40 + 6	Rankine M 41	Hume I 40 + 2	Jones G 5 + 5	Zola Makongo C 7 + 8	Beresford D 8 + 11	Dadi E 15 + 16	Dagnall C 13 + 10	Sharps I 44	Harrison D 16 + 16	Whitmore T 17 + 16	Loran T — + 2	Jennings S 4 + 7	Haworth S 2 + 1	Brown P 1 + 3	Howarth R 7 + 1	Linwood P 4 + 6	Tremarco C 2 + 1	Match No.
1	2	3	4	5	6	7	8	9[1]	10[2]	11	12	13												1
1	2	3	4[2]	5	6	7	8			12		9[1]	10■	11	13									2
1	2	3	4[2]	5	6	7	8	9[3]		12		10[1]		11	13	14								3
1	2	3	4	5		7[1]	8	12		13	11	9[2]	10[3]	6	14									4
1	2	3		5	6[1]	7	8	9		10[2]	12	13		4	11[3]	14								5
1	2	3		5	6[1]	7	8	9		10[2]	12	13		4		11[3]	14							6
1	2	3		5	6[2]	7	8	12		10	11[1]			4			13	9						7
1	2	3	12	5	6	7	8	9[2]		10[3]	13	14		4				11[1]						8
1	2[2]	3	4	5■	6	7	8	9				10[1]	12	11		13								9
1	2	3	4[3]		6	7	8	9		10[1]	11[2]	12		5		13		14						10
1	2	3			6	7	8	9		12	11[2]	10[1]		5	4	13								11
1	2	3	4	5	6	7	8	9		12	13	10[1]		11[2]										12
1	2	3	4[3]	5	6	12	8	9[2]		13			10[1]	11	14	7								13
1	2	3	4	5	6	12	8	9[1]		13			10[2]	11	14	7[3]								14
1	2	3	4	5	6	7	8	9		12			10[1]	11										15
1	2	3	4	5	6	7		9		10[1]		12		11	8									16
1	2	3	4[2]	5	6[1]	7	8	9[3]	10		12			11	13				14					17
1	2	3	12	5[2]	6	7	8	9				13		11	4[1]	14			10[3]					18
1	2	3		5	6[2]	7	8	9						11	4	12			10[1]	13				19
1	2	3		5	6[2]	7[3]	8	9	12		13	14		11	4	10[1]								20
1	2	3	4	5[1]	12	7	8[2]	9	10		11[3]			6	13	14								21
1[6]		3		5	6	7	8	9	10[1]		11	12		2	4	13					15[2]			22
	2	3	4	5	6[2]	7	8	9			13	12	10[1]	11							1			23
	2	3	4	5	6	12	8	9[1]				13	10[3]	11	14	7[2]					1			24
	2	3	4	5	6	12	8[3]	9			13		10[2]	11	14	7[1]					1			25
	2	3	4[1]	5	6	7			10			9[2]		11	8	12		13			1			26
	2	3	4	5	6	10[1]	8	9	13			12		11[2]	7[3]	14					1			27
	2	3	4[2]	5	6[3]	12	8	9					10[1]	11	13	7					1	14		28
	2	3		5	6	12	8[3]	9[2]				13	10		11	7[1]		14			1	4		29
1	2	3		5	6[2]	7	8	9[1]				10		4	11	12						13		30
1	2	3■		5	6	7[1]	8	9				10[2]		11	4			13				12		31
1		3	4	5	6	7[3]			12		11[2]	10[1]	9	2	8	13		14						32
1	2	3	4	5	6	7	8	9				10[1]	12	11										33
1	2	3	4[2]	5	6	7	8	9[1]	12				10[3]	11	13	14								34
1	2	3	4		6	7	8	9	12			10[2]	13	5		11[1]								35
1	2	3	4	5	6[3]	7	8	9[2]				10[1]	12	11		13						14		36
1	2	3	4	5	6[3]	7	8	9[2]					12	11	13	10[1]						14		37
1	2		4	5	6[3]	10	8	9[2]				12	13	3	7[1]					14		11		38
1	2		4[2]	5	6	7	8	9				10■		3	12	13				11[1]				39
1	2	3	4[2]	5	6	7	8	9[1]					12	11	13	10[3]		14						40
1	2	3	4	5	6	7	8	9						11		10								41
1	2	3	4[3]	5	6	7	8	9[1]					12	11	13	10[2]		14						42
1	2		4	5	6	7	8	9			11[1]	13	12	3		10[2]								43
1	2		4	5	6	7	8[2]	9				10[3]		3	12	11[1]						13	14	44
1	2[1]			5		7		9			13		12	3	11	10[2]		8				4	6	45
1				5[1]	6	9[3]					13	12	10	3	7[2]	11		8		14		4	2	46

FA Cup

First Round	Peterborough U	(a)	1-2

LDV Vans Trophy

First Round			
Second Round	Port Vale	(h)	2-1
Quarter-Final	Macclesfield T	(a)	1-0
Semi-Final	Oldham Ath	(a)	1-1

Carling Cup

First Round	Shrewsbury T	(h)	2-1
Second Round	Portsmouth	(h)	0-1

Play-offs

Semi-Final	Hartlepool U	(a)	0-2
		(h)	2-0

WALSALL FL Championship 1

FOUNDATION

Two of the leading clubs around Walsall in the 1880s were Walsall Swifts (formed 1877) and Walsall Town (formed 1879). The Swifts were winners of the Birmingham Senior Cup in 1881, while the Town reached the 4th round (5th round modern equivalent) of the FA Cup in 1883. These clubs amalgamated as Walsall Town Swifts in 1888, becoming simply Walsall in 1895.

Bescot Stadium, Bescot Crescent, Walsall WS1 4SA.

Telephone: 0870 442 0442.

Fax: (01922) 613 202.

Ticket Office: 0870 442 0111/0222.

Website: www.saddlers@walsallfc.co.uk

Email: info@walsallfc.co.uk

Ground Capacity: 11,200.

Record Attendance: 11,037 v Wolverhampton W, Division 1, 11 January 2003.

Pitch Measurements: 110yd × 73yd.

Chairman: Jeff Bonser.

Chief Executive/Secretary: K. R. Whalley.

Manager: Paul Merson.

Physio: John Whitney.

Colours: Red shirts, white shorts, red stockings.

Change Colours: Navy shirts, navy shorts, navy stockings.

Year Formed: 1888.

Turned Professional: 1888.

Ltd Co.: 1921.

Previous Names: Walsall Swifts (founded 1877) and Walsall Town (founded 1879) amalgamated in 1888 and were known as Walsall Town Swifts until 1895.

Club Nickname: 'The Saddlers'.

Previous Ground: 1888, Fellows Park; 1990, Bescot Stadium.

First Football League Game: 3 September 1892, Division 2, v Darwen (h) L 1–2 – Hawkins; Withington, Pinches; Robinson, Whitrick, Forsyth; Marshall, Holmes, Turner, Gray (1), Pangbourn.

Record League Victory: 10–0 v Darwen, Division 2, 4 March 1899 – Tennent; E. Peers (1), Davies; Hickinbotham, Jenkyns, Taggart; Dean (3), Vail (2), Aston (4), Martin, Griffin.

Record Cup Victory: 7–0 v Macclesfield T (a), FA Cup 2nd rd, 6 December 1997 – Walker; Evans, Marsh, Viveash (1), Ryder, Peron, Boli (2 incl. 1p) (Ricketts), Porter (2), Keates, Watson (Platt), Hodge (2 incl. 1p).

Record Defeat: 0–12 v Small Heath, 17 December 1892. 0–12 v Darwen, 26 December 1896, both Division 2.

HONOURS

Football League: Division 2: Runners-up, 1998–99, Promoted to Division 1 – 2000–01 (play-offs); Division 3 – Runners-up 1960–61, 1994–95; Division 4 – Champions 1959–60; Runners-up 1979–80.

FA Cup: best season: 5th rd, 1939, 1975, 1978, 1987, 2002, 2003 and last 16 1889.

Football League Cup: Semi-final 1984.

SKY SPORTS FACT FILE

Despite a woefully ineffective start to the 1922–23 season in which only one win was gained from the first ten games, Walsall finished a creditable third, their best ever performance in the Northern Section of Division Three.

Most League Points (2 for a win): 65, Division 4, 1959–60.

Most League Points (3 for a win): 87, Division 2, 1998–99.

Most League Goals: 102, Division 4, 1959–60.

Highest League Scorer in Season: Gilbert Alsop, 40, Division 3 (N), 1933–34 and 1934–35.

Most League Goals in Total Aggregate: Tony Richards, 184, 1954–63; Colin Taylor, 184, 1958–63, 1964–68, 1969–73.

Most League Goals in One Match: 5, Gilbert Alsop v Carlisle U, Division 3N, 2 February 1935; 5, Bill Evans v Mansfield T, Division 3N, 5 October 1935; 5, Johnny Devlin v Torquay U, Division 3S, 1 September 1949.

Most Capped Player: Mick Kearns, 15 (18), Republic of Ireland.

Most League Appearances: Colin Harrison, 467, 1964–82.

Youngest League Player: Geoff Morris, 16 years 218 days v Scunthorpe U, 14 September 1965.

Record Transfer Fee Received: £600,000 from West Ham U for David Kelly, July 1988.

Record Transfer Fee Paid: £175,000 to Birmingham C for Alan Buckley, June 1979.

Football League Record: 1892 Elected to Division 2; 1895 Failed re-election; 1896–1901 Division 2; 1901 Failed re-election; 1921 Original Member of Division 3 (N); 1927–31 Division 3 (S); 1931–36 Division 3 (N); 1936–58 Division 3 (S); 1958–60 Division 4; 1960–61 Division 3; 1961–63 Division 2; 1963–79 Division 3; 1979–80 Division 4; 1980–88 Division 3; 1988–89 Division 2; 1989–90 Division 3; 1990–92 Division 4; 1992–95 Division 3; 1995–99 Division 2; 1999–2000 Division 1; 2000–01 Division 2; 2001–04 Division 1; 2004– FL1.

LATEST SEQUENCES

Longest Sequence of League Wins: 7, 10.10.1959 – 21.11.1959.

Longest Sequence of League Defeats: 15, 29.10.1988 – 4.2.1989.

Longest Sequence of League Draws: 5, 7.5.1988 – 17.9.1988.

Longest Sequence of Unbeaten League Matches: 21, 6.11.1979 – 22.3.1980.

Longest Sequence Without a League Win: 18, 15.10.1988 – 4.2.1989.

Successive Scoring Runs: 27 from 9.2.1928.

Successive Non-scoring Runs: 5 from 8.10.1927.

MANAGERS

H. Smallwood 1888–91 *(Secretary-Manager)*
A. G. Burton 1891–93
J. H. Robinson 1893–95
C. H. Ailso 1895–96 *(Secretary-Manager)*
A. E. Parsloe 1896–97 *(Secretary-Manager)*
L. Ford 1897–98 *(Secretary-Manager)*
G. Hughes 1898–99 *(Secretary-Manager)*
L. Ford 1899–1901 *(Secretary-Manager)*
J. E. Shutt 1908–13 *(Secretary-Manager)*
Haydn Price 1914–20
Joe Burchell 1920–26
David Ashworth 1926–27
Jack Torrance 1927–28
James Kerr 1928–29
Sid Scholey 1929–30
Peter O'Rourke 1930–32
Bill Slade 1932–34
Andy Wilson 1934–37
Tommy Lowes 1937–44
Harry Hibbs 1944–51
Tony McPhee 1951
Brough Fletcher 1952–53
Major Frank Buckley 1953–55
John Love 1955–57
Billy Moore 1957–64
Alf Wood 1964
Reg Shaw 1964–68
Dick Graham 1968
Ron Lewin 1968–69
Billy Moore 1969–72
John Smith 1972–73
Doug Fraser 1973–77
Dave Mackay 1977–78
Alan Ashman 1978
Frank Sibley 1979
Alan Buckley 1979–86
Neil Martin *(Joint Manager with Buckley)* 1981–82
Tommy Coakley 1986–88
John Barnwell 1989–90
Kenny Hibbitt 1990–94
Chris Nicholl 1994–97
Jan Sorensen 1997–98
Ray Graydon 1998–2002
Colin Lee 2002–04
Paul Merson May 2004–

TEN YEAR LEAGUE RECORD

		P	W	D	L	F	A	Pts	Pos
1995-96	Div 2	46	19	12	15	60	45	69	11
1996-97	Div 2	46	19	10	17	54	53	67	12
1997-98	Div 2	46	14	12	20	43	52	54	19
1998-99	Div 2	46	26	9	11	63	47	87	2
1999-2000	Div 1	46	11	13	22	52	77	46	22
2000-01	Div 2	46	23	12	11	79	50	81	4
2001-02	Div 1	46	13	12	21	51	71	51	18
2002-03	Div 1	46	15	9	22	57	69	54	17
2003-04	Div 1	46	13	12	21	45	65	51	22
2004-05	FL 1	46	16	12	18	65	69	60	14

DID YOU KNOW

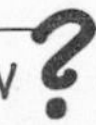

From the 19 April 1960 until 2 September 1961 Walsall completed a run of 26 unbeaten home League games which included the club's two most highly successful consecutive seasons with promotion from first Division Four then Division Three.

WALSALL 2004–05 LEAGUE RECORD

Match No.	Date	Venue	Opponents	Result	H/T Score	Lg. Pos.	Goalscorers	Attendance
1	Aug 7	H	Port Vale	W 3-2	1-0	—	Fryatt (pen) 12, Williams 82, Taylor D 86	8225
2	10	A	Bournemouth	D 2-2	1-0	—	Taylor D 37, Taylor K 51	6485
3	14	A	Oldham Ath	L 3-5	2-2	14	Fryatt 2 (1 pen) 29, 78 (p), Taylor D 34	5654
4	21	H	Barnsley	D 2-2	1-1	16	Fryatt 36, Wrack 90	6059
5	28	A	Torquay U	D 0-0	0-0	17		3791
6	30	H	Swindon T	W 3-2	2-2	11	Leitao 2 28, 34, Birch 87	5951
7	Sept 4	A	Doncaster R	L 1-3	0-1	15	Fryatt 73	6146
8	11	H	Sheffield W	D 1-1	1-1	18	Standing 39	6493
9	18	A	Chesterfield	L 0-1	0-1	20		4755
10	25	H	Brentford	L 0-1	0-1	21		5302
11	Oct 2	A	Huddersfield T	L 1-3	0-2	21	Clarke (og) 73	11,324
12	9	H	Colchester U	W 2-1	0-0	18	Bennett 73, Emblen 84	5203
13	16	A	Wrexham	D 1-1	0-1	18	Bennett 74	3803
14	19	H	Luton T	W 2-0	1-0	—	Merson 7, Fryatt 72	5963
15	23	H	Bristol C	L 1-2	0-0	17	Fryatt (pen) 49	7105
16	30	A	Milton Keynes D	D 1-1	1-1	18	Wrack 13	4247
17	Nov 6	A	Hull C	L 1-3	0-3	18	Standing 49	16,010
18	20	H	Peterborough U	W 2-1	0-1	16	Wrack 62, Birch 68	5465
19	27	A	Stockport Co	W 1-0	1-0	15	Wrack 14	4448
20	Dec 7	H	Hartlepool U	W 2-1	0-1	—	Fryatt 51, Leitao 69	5522
21	11	A	Bradford C	D 1-1	0-0	15	Robinson 61	6732
22	18	H	Blackpool	W 3-2	1-1	11	Leitao 45, Robinson 2 55, 70	5476
23	26	A	Sheffield W	L 2-3	1-1	15	Robinson 42, McShane 81	26,996
24	28	H	Tranmere R	L 0-2	0-0	16		7217
25	Jan 1	H	Doncaster R	D 1-1	1-1	16	Standing 21	6021
26	3	A	Brentford	L 0-1	0-1	16		5084
27	15	H	Chesterfield	W 3-0	2-0	15	Wrack 14, Leitao 26, Fryatt 90	5177
28	22	A	Tranmere R	L 1-2	0-1	16	Leitao 62	8651
29	25	A	Colchester U	L 0-5	0-4	—		2616
30	29	H	Huddersfield T	W 4-3	2-3	15	Merson 16, Fryatt 3 (1 pen) 45, 50 (p), 74	5727
31	Feb 5	H	Wrexham	D 2-2	2-2	15	Wrack 20, Leitao 42	5659
32	11	A	Bristol C	W 1-0	0-0	—	Surman 75	10,820
33	19	H	Milton Keynes D	D 0-0	0-0	13		5888
34	22	A	Luton T	L 0-1	0-0	—		7236
35	26	H	Bradford C	D 1-1	0-1	15	Emblen 72	4966
36	Mar 5	A	Blackpool	L 0-2	0-0	15		6844
37	12	H	Bournemouth	L 1-2	1-1	17	Fryatt 1	5126
38	19	A	Port Vale	L 0-2	0-0	18		5085
39	26	H	Oldham Ath	L 0-1	0-0	18		6794
40	28	A	Barnsley	L 2-3	0-1	19	Joachim 51, Leitao 53	8358
41	Apr 2	H	Torquay U	D 1-1	0-0	19	Fryatt 80	5694
42	9	A	Swindon T	W 2-1	1-0	19	Joachim 44, Wright 90	5592
43	16	A	Peterborough U	W 2-0	0-0	17	Standing 64, Wrack 76	3841
44	23	H	Hull C	W 3-0	1-0	16	Joachim 3 34, 53, 68	7958
45	30	A	Hartlepool U	W 3-1	3-0	15	Robson (og) 10, Joachim 14, Surman 42	6389
46	May 7	H	Stockport Co	W 3-0	0-0	14	Fryatt 86, Taylor K 89, Wright 90	6971

Final League Position: 14

GOALSCORERS

League (65): Fryatt 15 (4 pens), Leitao 8, Wrack 7, Joachim 6, Robinson 4, Standing 4, Taylor D 3, Bennett 2, Birch 2, Emblen 2, Merson 2, Surman 2, Taylor K 2, Wright 2, McShane 1, Williams 1, own goals 2.
Carling Cup (0).
FA Cup (1): Wrack 1.
LDV Vans Trophy (3): Leitao 3.

McKinney R 3	Bazeley D 7	Bennett J 30 + 1	Kinsella M 21 + 1	Emblen N 34 + 2	Roper I 25 + 1	Standing M 27 + 5	Merson P 31 + 5	Birch G 11 + 2	Fryatt M 22 + 14	Wrack D 43	Leitao J 34 + 8	Taylor D 10 + 9	Williams L 2 + 5	Taylor K 11 + 1	Osborn S 32 + 6	Paston M 8 + 1	Atieno T — + 3	Aranalde Z 28 + 2	Broad J 5 + 5	Bewers J 1	Dakinah K 1	Wright M 35 + 2	Murphy J 25	Robinson M 4 + 6	McShane P 3 + 1	Herivelto H — + 1	Dann S — + 1	Surman A 10 + 4	Coleman D 1 + 1	Oakes A 9	Perpetuini D 7	Pead C 8	Joachim J 8	Gerrard A 8	Bradley M 1	Harkness J 1	*Match No.*
1	2	3	4	5	6■	7^{1}	8^{2}	9^{3}	10	11	14	12	13																								1
1	2	3	4	5			8^{1}	9	10^{2}	11	13	7	12	6																							2
1	2^{2}	3	4	5	6		8	9^{3}	10	11^{1}	14	7	12		13																						3
	2^{1}	3	4^{2}	5	6	13			10^{3}	11	9	7	12		8	1	14																				4
	2	3	4^{3}	5	6■	7	12		10^{1}	11	9^{2}	13			8	1		14																			5
	2	6		5		12	8	9		11	10				4	1		3	7^{1}																		6
	2^{2}	6		5		13	8	9^{1}	12	11	10	14			4	1		3	7^{3}																		7
		6	4	12		7	13		14	11	10		9^{3}		8^{2}	1		3		2	5^{1}																8
		3	4^{3}	5^{1}	12	7^{2}	8		10	11	9	13	14		6	1						2															9
		3	4^{2}		6	7			10	11	9	8		5^{1}	12	1	13					2															10
		6			5		8	12	10	11	9	13		3^{2}	4	1			7^{1}			2															11
		6	4	5			8		10	11	9				7	15		3				2	1^{G}														12
		6	4	5			8	12	10^{1}	11	9				7			3				2	1														13
		6		5		7	8	9	12	11	10^{1}				4			3				2	1														14
		6		5		7	8	9	10	11					4			3				2	1														15
		6		5		7	8	9^{1}		11	10	12			4			3				2	1														16
		6		5		7	8		9	11	10				4			3				2	1														17
			4	5	6	12	8	9		11	10				7^{1}			3				2	1														18
		12	4	5	6^{1}	7	8^{3}	9^{2}	13	11	10				14			3				2	1														19
		6	4		5	7	8	9^{1}	12	11	10							3				2	1														20
		6	4		5^{1}	7	8		9^{2}	11	10				12			3				2	1	13													21
		6	4^{3}	5		7^{1}	8			11	9	13			12			3	14			2	1	10^{2}													22
			4^{1}	5		7^{2}	8			11	10				12			3	13			2	1	9	6												23
		6		5		7	8			11	10				4			3				12	1	9	2^{1}												24
		6^{2}		5		7	8		12		10				4			13	11			3	1	9^{1}	2												25
		6	4	5		7^{1}	8				9^{2}	11^{3}						3	10			2	1	13	12	14											26
		6	4	5^{2}		7	8		9	11	10^{1}							3				2	1	12			13										27
		6	4^{1}	5		7^{2}	8			11	9				10			3	12			2	1	13													28
		6	4	5			8			11	10^{2}		9^{1}		7			3	12			2	1	13													29
		6	4	5			8		9	11	10			7				3				2	1														30
		6		5			8		9	11	10^{2}			7^{3}	4^{1}			3	12			2	1	13				14									31
				5	6				12	11	9^{1}	10		7	4			3				2	1					8									32
				5	6		12		13	11	9	7		8	4^{2}			3				2	1					10^{1}									33
				5	6				9	11		7		8	4			3				2	1					10									34
				5	6	7	12		9	11^{2}	10	13			4			3				2	1					8^{1}									35
		3^{G}		5	6	7^{1}	12		9		10	4		11								2	1■					8	15								36
				5	6	7^{3}			9	11	10	12		8^{2}	4^{1}		14	3				2						13	1								37
		6^{1}		12	5	13	8		9	11	14	7^{2}			4			3				2						10^{3}		1							38
					6		8		9^{1}	11	12			7^{2}	4													13		1	3	2	10	5			39
				5^{2}	6		8		12	7	9^{1}											2						13		1	11	3	10	4			40
				5^{2}	6		8		12	7	9^{1}				4							13								1	11	3	10	2			41
					6	7^{2}			12	11	13				4							2						9		1	3	8	10^{1}	5			42
					6	7				11					4							2						9		1	3	8	10	5			43
					6	8			12	11					4							7						10		1	3	2	9^{1}	5			44
			12		6	8			13	11	14				4^{1}							7^{3}						10		1	3	2	9^{2}	5			45
					6^{3}	8			12	10	13			14	7							11								1		3	9	5	2^{1}	4^{2}	46

FA Cup

First Round	Slough T	(a)	1-2

Carling Cup

First Round	Sheffield W	(a)	0-1

LDV Vans Trophy

First Round	Rushden & D	(h)	1-0
Second Round	Cheltenham T	(a)	2-2
Quarter-Final	Leyton Orient	(a)	0-1

WATFORD FL Championship

FOUNDATION

The club was formed as Watford Rovers in 1881. The name was changed to West Herts in 1893 and then the name Watford was adopted after rival club Watford St Mary's was absorbed in 1898.

Vicarage Road Stadium, Vicarage Road, Watford, Herts WD18 0ER.

Telephone: 0870 111 1881.

Fax: (01923) 496 001.

Ticket Office: 0870 111 1881.

Website: www.watfordfc.com

Email: yourvoice@watfordfc.com

Ground Capacity: 19,500 (under development).

Record Attendance: 34,099 v Manchester U, FA Cup 4th rd (replay), 3 February 1969.

Pitch Measurements: 113yd × 73yd.

Chairman: Graham Simpson.

Vice-chairman: Jimmy Russo.

Chief Executive: Mark Ashton.

Secretary: Michelle Ives.

Manager: Adrian Boothroyd.

Assistant Manager: Keith Burkinshaw.

Physio: Luke Anthony.

Colours: Yellow shirts, black shorts, black stockings.

Change Colours: Red shirts, red shorts, red stockings.

Year Formed: 1881.

Turned Professional: 1897.

Ltd Co.: 1909.

Club Nickname: 'The Hornets'.

Previous Names: 1881, Watford Rovers; 1893, West Herts; 1898, Watford.

Previous Grounds: 1883, Vicarage Meadow, Rose and Crown Meadow; 1889, Colney Butts; 1890, Cassio Road; 1922, Vicarage Road.

First Football League Game: 28 August 1920, Division 3, v QPR (a) W 2–1 – Williams; Horseman, F. Gregory; Bacon, Toone, Wilkinson; Bassett, Ronald (1), Hoddinott, White (1), Waterall.

Record League Victory: 8–0 v Sunderland, Division 1, 25 September 1982 – Sherwood; Rice, Rostron, Taylor, Terry, Bolton, Callaghan (2), Blissett (4), Jenkins (2), Jackett, Barnes.

Record Cup Victory: 10–1 v Lowestoft T, FA Cup 1st rd, 27 November 1926 – Yates; Prior, Fletcher (1); F. Smith, 'Bert' Smith, Strain; Stephenson, Warner (3), Edmonds (3), Swan (1), Daniels (1), (1 og).

HONOURS

Football League: Division 1 – Runners-up 1982–83, promoted from Division 1 1998–99 (play-offs); Division 2 – Champions 1997–98; Runners-up 1981–82; Division 3 – Champions 1968–69; Runners-up 1978–79; Division 4 – Champions 1977–78; Promoted 1959–60 (4th).

FA Cup: Runners-up 1984, semi-finals 1970, 1984, 1987, 2003.

Football League Cup: Semi-final 1979.

European Competitions: *UEFA Cup:* 1983–84.

SKY SPORTS FACT FILE

Thanks chiefly to the goalscoring of Bill Sheppard with 15 in 40 matches, local amateur Joe Groome 14 in 16 and one-time Manchester City forward Jack Warner with 12 in 36, Watford were able to haul themselves out of trouble in 1927–28.

Record Defeat: 0–10 v Wolverhampton W, FA Cup 1st rd (replay), 24 January 1912.

Most League Points (2 for a win): 71, Division 4, 1977–78.

Most League Points (3 for a win): 88, Division 2, 1997–98.

Most League Goals: 92, Division 4, 1959–60.

Highest League Scorer in Season: Cliff Holton, 42, Division 4, 1959–60.

Most League Goals in Total Aggregate: Luther Blissett, 148, 1976–83, 1984–88, 1991–92.

Most League Goals in One Match: 5, Eddie Mummery v Newport Co, Division 3S, 5 January 1924.

Most Capped Player: John Barnes, 31 (79), England and Kenny Jackett, 31, Wales.

Most League Appearances: Luther Blissett, 415, 1976–83, 1984–88, 1991–92.

Youngest League Player: Keith Mercer, 16 years 125 days v Tranmere R, 16 February 1973.

Record Transfer Fee Received: £2,300,000 from Chelsea for Paul Furlong, May 1994.

Record Transfer Fee Paid: £2,250,000 to Tottenham H for Allan Nielsen, August 2000.

Football League Record: 1920 Original Member of Division 3; 1921–58 Division 3 (S); 1958–60 Division 4; 1960–69 Division 3; 1969–72 Division 2; 1972–75 Division 3; 1975–78 Division 4; 1978–79 Division 3; 1979–82 Division 2; 1982–88 Division 1; 1988–92 Division 2; 1992–96 Division 1; 1996–98 Division 2; 1998–99 Division 1; 1999–2000 FA Premier League; 2000–04 Division 1; 2004– FLC.

MANAGERS

John Goodall 1903–10
Harry Kent 1910–26
Fred Pagnam 1926–29
Neil McBain 1929–37
Bill Findlay 1938–47
Jack Bray 1947–48
Eddie Hapgood 1948–50
Ron Gray 1950–51
Haydn Green 1951–52
Len Goulden 1952–55
(General Manager to 1956)
Johnny Paton 1955–56
Neil McBain 1956–59
Ron Burgess 1959–63
Bill McGarry 1963–64
Ken Furphy 1964–71
George Kirby 1971–73
Mike Keen 1973–77
Graham Taylor 1977–87
Dave Bassett 1987–88
Steve Harrison 1988–90
Colin Lee 1990
Steve Perryman 1990–93
Glenn Roeder 1993–96
Kenny Jackett 1996–97
Graham Taylor 1997–2001
Gianluca Vialli 2001–02
Ray Lewington 2002–05
Adrian Boothroyd March 2005–

LATEST SEQUENCES

Longest Sequence of League Wins: 7, 28.8.2000 – 14.10.2000.

Longest Sequence of League Defeats: 9, 26.12.1972 – 27.2.1973.

Longest Sequence of League Draws: 7, 30.11.1996 – 27.1.1997.

Longest Sequence of Unbeaten League Matches: 22, 1.10.1996 – 1.3.1997.

Longest Sequence Without a League Win: 19, 27.11.1971 – 8.4.1972.

Successive Scoring Runs: 22 from 20.8.1985.

Successive Non-scoring Runs: 7 from 18.12.1971.

TEN YEAR LEAGUE RECORD

		P	W	D	L	F	A	Pts	Pos
1995-96	Div 1	46	10	18	18	62	70	48	23
1996-97	Div 2	46	16	19	11	45	38	67	13
1997-98	Div 2	46	24	16	6	67	41	88	1
1998-99	Div 1	46	21	14	11	65	56	77	5
1999-2000	PR Lge	38	6	6	26	35	77	24	20
2000-01	Div 1	46	20	9	17	76	67	69	9
2001-02	Div 1	46	16	11	19	62	56	59	14
2002-03	Div 1	46	17	9	20	54	70	60	13
2003-04	Div 1	46	15	12	19	54	68	57	16
2004-05	FL C	46	12	16	18	52	59	52	18

DID YOU KNOW?

During the 1977–78 season when Watford won the Fourth Division title, defender Alan Garner scored the club's 2000th home League goal. His career total of League games for Watford was exactly 200 from 1974–75 to 1979–80.

WATFORD 2004–05 LEAGUE RECORD

Match No.	Date	Venue	Opponents	Result		H/T Score	Lg. Pos.	Goalscorers	Attendance
1	Aug 7	A	Preston NE	L	1-2	0-1	—	Devlin [47]	12,208
2	9	H	QPR	W	3-0	2-0	—	Webber 2 [12, 59], Dyer [45]	14,737
3	14	H	Burnley	L	0-1	0-0	16		12,048
4	21	A	Leicester C	W	1-0	0-0	8	Webber [90]	22,478
5	28	H	Plymouth Arg	W	3-1	1-1	7	Ardley [33], Webber 2 [46, 58]	13,104
6	Sept 11	H	Brighton & HA	D	1-1	0-0	8	Webber [53]	14,148
7	14	A	Cardiff C	W	3-0	2-0	—	Webber 2 [11, 86], Ardley [45]	10,606
8	19	A	Millwall	W	2-0	0-0	6	Webber [65], Helguson [76]	10,865
9	25	H	Reading	L	0-1	0-0	8		13,389
10	28	H	Wigan Ath	D	0-0	0-0	—		11,161
11	Oct 2	A	Crewe Alex	L	0-3	0-3	8		6382
12	16	A	Derby Co	D	2-2	2-1	9	Helguson 2 [7, 14]	23,253
13	19	H	Sunderland	D	1-1	1-1	—	Ardley [9]	13,198
14	23	H	Ipswich T	D	2-2	0-0	11	Helguson [67], Bouazza [73]	15,894
15	30	A	Nottingham F	W	2-1	2-1	9	Helguson 2 [20, 27]	24,473
16	Nov 2	A	Gillingham	D	0-0	0-0	—		7009
17	6	H	Derby Co	D	2-2	1-0	9	Helguson [41], Gunnarsson [82]	13,689
18	13	A	Sheffield U	D	1-1	0-1	10	Gunnarsson [65]	18,454
19	20	H	Rotherham U	D	0-0	0-0	11		17,780
20	24	A	Leeds U	D	2-2	1-1	—	Dyer 2 [9, 71]	24,585
21	27	A	West Ham U	L	2-3	2-2	12	Gunnarsson [5], Dyer [21]	24,541
22	Dec 4	H	Stoke C	L	0-1	0-1	16		12,169
23	11	H	Wolverhampton W	D	1-1	1-1	14	Helguson [4]	14,605
24	18	A	Coventry C	L	0-1	0-1	15		14,493
25	26	A	Reading	L	0-3	0-1	18		18,757
26	28	H	Cardiff C	D	0-0	0-0	18		13,409
27	Jan 1	H	Millwall	W	1-0	0-0	15	Helguson [75]	13,158
28	3	A	Brighton & HA	L	1-2	1-1	16	Helguson [11]	6335
29	15	H	Crewe Alex	W	3-1	2-0	15	Helguson 2 [9, 29], Demerit [46]	11,223
30	22	A	Wigan Ath	D	2-2	2-1	17	Dyer [13], Webber [27]	9008
31	Feb 5	H	Gillingham	W	2-0	1-0	14	Ashby (og) [23], Eagles [90]	15,188
32	12	A	Sunderland	L	2-4	0-2	16	Dyer 2 [76, 90]	24,948
33	22	A	Ipswich T	W	2-1	1-0	—	Demerit [45], Dyer [81]	23,993
34	26	A	Wolverhampton W	D	0-0	0-0	14		25,060
35	Mar 5	H	Coventry C	L	2-3	1-1	15	Dyer [32], Webber [84]	13,794
36	8	H	Nottingham F	L	0-2	0-1	—		12,118
37	12	A	QPR	L	1-3	0-2	15	Ardley [80]	16,638
38	15	H	Leicester C	D	2-2	2-0	—	Demerit [40], Webber (pen) [44]	11,084
39	19	H	Preston NE	L	0-2	0-0	15		19,649
40	Apr 2	A	Burnley	L	1-3	0-2	17	Blizzard [77]	11,507
41	5	A	Plymouth Arg	L	0-1	0-1	—		15,333
42	9	H	Leeds U	L	1-2	1-1	21	Helguson [41]	16,306
43	16	A	Rotherham U	W	1-0	1-0	17	Helguson [32]	5438
44	23	H	Sheffield U	D	0-0	0-0	18		17,138
45	30	A	Stoke C	W	1-0	0-0	16	Helguson [51]	15,229
46	May 8	H	West Ham U	L	1-2	0-1	18	Helguson (pen) [89]	19,673

Final League Position: 18

GOALSCORERS

League (52): Helguson 16 (1 pen), Webber 12 (1 pen), Dyer 9, Ardley 4, Demerit 3, Gunnarsson 3, Blizzard 1, Bouazza 1, Devlin 1, Eagles 1, own goal 1.
Carling Cup (12): Helguson 3, Bouazza 2, Chambers 2, Dyer 2, Cox 1 (pen), Ferrell 1, own goal 1.
FA Cup (1): Helguson 1 (pen).

Lee R 33	Smith J 7	Mayo P 13	Cox N 38 + 1	Dyche S 23	Mahon G 42 + 1	Ardley N 28 + 2	Gunnarsson B 34 + 2	Webber D 24 + 4	Dyer B 21 + 15	Devlin P 15 + 2	Bouazza H 10 + 18	Young A 15 + 19	Helguson H 36 + 3	Chambers J 40	Darlington J 25 + 1	Doyley L 25 + 4	Blizzard D 12 + 5	Demerit J 22 + 2	Fitzgerald S — + 7	Gayle M — + 3	Chamberlain A 4 + 1	Jones P 9	Jackson J 14 + 1	McNamee A 1 + 13	Eagles C 10 + 3	Cullip D 4	Bangura A 1 + 1	Osborne J — + 1	*Match No.*
1	2^{1}	3	4	5	6	7^{2}	8	9	10^{3}	11	12	13	14																1
1		3	4	5	6	7^{3}	8	9^{1}	10^{2}	11	12	14	13	2															2
1		3	4		6	7^{3}	8	9	10^{1}	11^{2}	13	14	12	5	2														3
1		3	4	5	6	7	8^{2}	9	12	11		13	10^{1}	2															4
1		3	4	5	6	7	8^{2}	9^{1}	12	11		13	10	2															5
1		3	4	5	6	7^{1}	8	9		11	13	12	10			2^{2}													6
1		3	4	5	6	7	8	9		11^{1}		12	10			2													7
1		3	4	5	6	7	8	9^{1}	13		12	11	10^{2}			2													8
1		3^{1}	4	5^{2}	6	7	8	9			12	11	10	2		13													9
1		3	4		6	7^{1}	8	9			12	11	10	2		5													10
1		3^{2}	4		6	7	8	9	13		12	11^{1}	10	2		5													11
1			4	5	6	7	8	9	12			11^{1}	10	3^{2}	2	13													12
1			4	5	6	7		9	12		13	11^{1}	10	3	2		8^{2}												13
1			4^{2}	5	6	7		9^{1}	12		14	13	10	3	2	8	11^{3}												14
1				5	6	7	8^{3}	9^{1}	12			13	10	3^{2}	2	4	14	11											15
1				5	6	7	8	9^{1}	12				10	3	2	4		11											16
1				5	6	7	8		9^{2}		12	2^{1}	10		3	4		11	13										17
1	3		4	5	6	7	8		10		9^{2}	12		11^{1}	2				13										18
1	3^{1}		4	5	6	7	8		9^{2}		13^{3}	12	10	11	2				14										19
1	2		4	5	6	7^{1}	8		9^{2}			12	10	11	3				13										20
1			4	5	6	7^{1}	8^{2}		9	12		13	10	11	3^{3}	2				14									21
1				5	6		8		9^{2}	12		7^{3}	10	11	3	2^{1}		4	13	14									22
1			4		6	7^{2}	8		9^{1}	11		12	10	3	2			5	13										23
1^{6}			4	5	6	7	8		9^{1}	11		12	10	2^{2}	3					13	15								24
			4	5	6^{2}		8		9^{1}	7		12	10	2	3^{3}		13	14				1	11						25
			4	5	6		8			9			10	11^{1}	3	2^{2}		12	13			1	7^{3}	14					26
			4	5^{1}	6		8	12		9			10	11	3	2						1	7^{2}	13					27
		3	4				8	12		9^{2}	13		10	7		2^{1}	6	5				1	11^{3}	14					28
			4		6^{2}	7	8^{1}			11	9^{3}		10	2	3		12	5				1	13	14					29
		3			12		13	9	10		14	7		2		4	8^{1}	5				1	11^{2}		6^{3}				30
			4		6	7		9^{1}	12	8^{2}			10		3	2		5				1	11		13				31
			4		6	7^{2}		9	12			13	10^{1}	11	2	3^{3}		5				1	8		14				32
			4		6			9^{1}	12		10			2	3	13	8	5				1	11		7^{2}				33
1			4		6			9^{1}	12		10			2	3		8	5					11		7				34
1			4				12	9	10		13	11^{3}		2	3^{2}		8^{1}	5					6	14	7				35
1			4		6	12	8	13	10		9			2	3^{1}			5					11^{2}	14	7^{3}				36
1			4		6	12	8■	13	10^{1}		9^{2}		7	2	3^{3}	14		5					11						37
1	3		4		6	7		9^{1}			12		10	2^{2}		8		5					11	13					38
1	3^{2}		4		6	7^{3}	8	9^{1}	12				10	2		5							11	13	14				39
1	2^{1}		4		6		8^{2}		10		9	11		3	12		13	5						14	7^{3}				40
1			4^{1}		6		8^{3}		9^{2}		13	12	10	3		2	11	5						14	7				41
1					6		8^{1}		12		9^{3}	13	10	3		2	11	5■						14	7^{2}	4			42
			5		6		8		9			11^{1}	10	3		2	12				1			13	7^{2}	4			43
			4		6				9		12	11	10	3		2	8	5			1				7^{1}				44
			12		6^{3}				9		11^{2}	7	10	3		2	8	5^{1}			1			13		4	14		45
											9^{1}	7	10	3		2	11	5			1			6		4	8	12	46

FA Cup

Third Round	Fulham	(h)	1-1
		(a)	0-2

Carling Cup

First Round	Cambridge U	(h)	1-0
Second Round	Reading	(a)	3-0
Third Round	Sheffield U	(a)	0-0
Fourth Round	Southampton	(h)	5-2
Fifth Round	Portsmouth	(h)	3-0
Semi-Final	Liverpool	(a)	0-1
		(h)	0-1

WEST BROMWICH ALBION FA Premiership

FOUNDATION

There is a well known story that when employees of Salter's Spring Works in West Bromwich decided to form a football club, they had to send someone to the nearby Association Football stronghold of Wednesbury to purchase a football. A weekly subscription of 2d (less than 1p) was imposed and the name of the new club was West Bromwich Strollers.

The Hawthorns, West Bromwich, West Midlands B71 4LF.

Telephone: 0870 066 8888.

Fax: 0870 066 2861.

Ticket Office: 0870 066 2800.

Website: www.wbafc.co.uk

Email: enquiries@wbafc.co.uk

Ground Capacity: 28,000.

Record Attendance: 64,815 v Arsenal, FA Cup 6th rd, 6 March 1937.

Pitch Measurements: 115yd × 74yd.

Chairman: Jeremy Peace.

Secretary: Dr John J. Evans BA, PHD.

Manager: Bryan Robson.

Assistant Manager: Nigel Pearson.

Physio: Nick Worth.

Colours: Navy blue and white striped shirts, white shorts, navy blue stockings.

Change Colours: Red shirts, blue shorts, red stockings.

Year Formed: 1878.

Turned Professional: 1885.

Ltd Co.: 1892.

Plc: 1996.

Previous Name: 1878, West Bromwich Strollers; 1881, West Bromwich Albion.

Club Nicknames: 'Throstles', 'Baggies', 'Albion'.

Previous Grounds: 1878, Coopers Hill; 1879, Dartmouth Park; 1881, Bunns Field, Walsall Street; 1882, Four Acres (Dartmouth Cricket Club); 1885, Stoney Lane; 1900, The Hawthorns.

First Football League Game: 8 September 1888, Football League, v Stoke (a) W 2–0 – Roberts; J. Horton, Green; E. Horton, Perry, Bayliss; Bassett, Woodhall (1), Hendry, Pearson, Wilson (1).

Record League Victory: 12–0 v Darwen, Division 1, 4 April 1892 – Reader; J. Horton, McCulloch; Reynolds (2), Perry, Groves; Bassett (3), McLeod, Nicholls (1), Pearson (4), Geddes (1), (1 og).

HONOURS

Football League: Division 1 – Champions 1919–20; Runners-up 1924–25, 1953–54, 2001–02, 2003–04; Division 2 – Champions 1901–02, 1910–11; Runners-up 1930–31, 1948–49; Promoted to Division 1 1975–76 (3rd); 1992–93 (play-offs); Promoted to FA Premier League 2001–02.

FA Cup: Winners 1888, 1892, 1931, 1954, 1968; Runners-up 1886, 1887, 1895, 1912, 1935.

Football League Cup: Winners 1966; Runners-up 1967, 1970.

European Competitions: *European Cup-Winners' Cup:* 1968–69. *European Fairs Cup:* 1966–67. *UEFA Cup:* 1978–79, 1979–80, 1981–82.

SKY SPORTS FACT FILE

The first player to score a hat-trick in the FA Cup for West Bromwich Albion was Jem Bayliss on 13 February 1886 in a 6–0 win over Old Westminsters. Later capped by England, while holidaying abroad he read his own premature obituary notice!

Record Cup Victory: 10–1 v Chatham (away), FA Cup 3rd rd, 2 March 1889 – Roberts; J. Horton, Green; Timmins (1), Charles Perry, E. Horton; Bassett (2), Perry (1), Bayliss (2), Pearson, Wilson (3), (1 og).

Record Defeat: 3–10 v Stoke C, Division 1, 4 February 1937.

Most League Points (2 for a win): 60, Division 1, 1919–20.

Most League Points (3 for a win): 89, Division 1, 2001–02.

Most League Goals: 105, Division 2, 1929–30.

Highest League Scorer in Season: William 'Ginger' Richardson, 39, Division 1, 1935–36.

Most League Goals in Total Aggregate: Tony Brown, 218, 1963–79.

Most League Goals in One Match: 6, Jimmy Cookson v Blackpool, Division 2, 17 September 1927.

Most Capped Player: Stuart Williams, 33 (43), Wales.

Most League Appearances: Tony Brown, 574, 1963–80.

Youngest League Player: Charlie Wilson, 16 years 73 days v Oldham Ath, 1 October 1921.

Record Transfer Fee Received: £5,000,001 from Coventry C for Lee Hughes, July 2001.

Record Transfer Fee Paid: £3,000,000 to Cardiff C for Robert Earnshaw, August 2004.

Football League Record: 1888 Founder Member of Football League; 1901–02 Division 2; 1902–04 Division 1; 1904–11 Division 2; 1911–27 Division 1; 1927–31 Division 2; 1931–38 Division 1; 1938–49 Division 2; 1949–73 Division 1; 1973–76 Division 2; 1976–86 Division 1; 1986–91 Division 2; 1991–92 Division 3; 1992–93 Division 2; 1993–2002 Division 1; 2002–03 FA Premier League; 2003–04 Division 1; 2004– FA Premier League.

MANAGERS

Louis Ford 1890–92
(Secretary-Manager)
Henry Jackson 1892–94
(Secretary-Manager)
Edward Stephenson 1894–95
(Secretary-Manager)
Clement Keys 1895–96
(Secretary-Manager)
Frank Heaven 1896–1902
(Secretary-Manager)
Fred Everiss 1902–48
Jack Smith 1948–52
Jesse Carver 1952
Vic Buckingham 1953–59
Gordon Clark 1959–61
Archie Macaulay 1961–63
Jimmy Hagan 1963–67
Alan Ashman 1967–71
Don Howe 1971–75
Johnny Giles 1975–77
Ronnie Allen 1977
Ron Atkinson 1978–81
Ronnie Allen 1981–82
Ron Wylie 1982–84
Johnny Giles 1984–85
Ron Saunders 1986–87
Ron Atkinson 1987–88
Brian Talbot 1988–91
Bobby Gould 1991–92
Ossie Ardiles 1992–93
Keith Burkinshaw 1993–94
Alan Buckley 1994–97
Ray Harford 1997
Denis Smith 1997–2000
Brian Little 2000
Gary Megson 2000–04
Bryan Robson November 2004–

LATEST SEQUENCES

Longest Sequence of League Wins: 11, 5.4.1930 – 8.9.1930.

Longest Sequence of League Defeats: 11, 28.10.1995 – 26.12.1995.

Longest Sequence of League Draws: 5, 30.8.1999 – 3.10.1999.

Longest Sequence of Unbeaten League Matches: 17, 7.9.1957 – 7.12.1957.

Longest Sequence Without a League Win: 15, 16.10.2004 – 25.9.2004.

Successive Scoring Runs: 36 from 26.4.1958.

Successive Non-scoring Runs: 4 from 15.2.1913.

TEN YEAR LEAGUE RECORD

		P	*W*	*D*	*L*	*F*	*A*	*Pts*	*Pos*
1995-96	Div 1	46	16	12	18	60	68	60	11
1996-97	Div 1	46	14	15	17	68	72	57	16
1997-98	Div 1	46	16	12	17	50	56	61	10
1998-99	Div 1	46	16	11	19	69	76	59	12
1999-2000	Div 1	46	10	19	17	43	60	49	21
2000-01	Div 1	46	21	11	14	60	52	74	6
2001-02	Div 1	46	27	8	11	61	29	89	2
2002-03	PR Lge	38	6	8	24	29	65	26	19
2003-04	Div 1	46	25	11	10	64	42	86	2
2004-05	PR Lge	38	6	16	16	36	61	34	17

DID YOU KNOW?

In 2004–05 West Bromwich Albion became the first Premier League team to avoid relegation after being placed bottom of the table at the turn of the year. The 2–0 victory over Portsmouth on 15 May completed the great escape.

WEST BROMWICH ALBION 2004–05 LEAGUE RECORD

Match No.	Date	Venue	Opponents	Result		H/T Score	Lg. Pos.	Goalscorers	Attendance
1	Aug 14	A	Blackburn R	D	1-1	1-0	—	Clement [33]	23,475
2	22	H	Aston Villa	D	1-1	1-1	12	Clement [38]	26,601
3	25	H	Tottenham H	D	1-1	1-1	—	Gera [3]	27,191
4	28	A	Everton	L	1-2	1-1	14	Dobie [7]	34,510
5	Sept 11	A	Liverpool	L	0-3	0-2	18		42,947
6	18	H	Fulham	D	1-1	0-0	19	Kanu [88]	24,128
7	25	A	Newcastle U	L	1-3	0-0	18	Horsfield [87]	52,308
8	Oct 2	H	Bolton W	W	2-1	0-0	16	Kanu [57], Gera [65]	23,849
9	16	H	Norwich C	D	0-0	0-0	15		26,257
10	23	A	Crystal Palace	L	0-3	0-2	16		22,922
11	30	H	Chelsea	L	1-4	0-1	17	Gera [56]	27,399
12	Nov 6	A	Southampton	D	2-2	2-1	17	Earnshaw 2 [29, 37]	31,057
13	14	H	Middlesbrough	L	1-2	1-1	18	Earnshaw [37]	24,008
14	20	A	Arsenal	D	1-1	0-0	19	Earnshaw [79]	38,109
15	27	H	Manchester U	L	0-3	0-0	20		27,709
16	Dec 4	A	Portsmouth	L	2-3	2-1	20	Stefanovic (og) [14], Earnshaw [45]	20,110
17	11	H	Charlton Ath	L	0-1	0-1	20		24,697
18	18	A	Birmingham C	L	0-4	0-3	20		28,880
19	26	H	Liverpool	L	0-5	0-1	20		27,533
20	28	A	Manchester C	D	1-1	0-1	20	Dunne (og) [85]	47,177
21	Jan 1	A	Bolton W	D	1-1	1-0	20	Gera [13]	25,205
22	3	H	Newcastle U	D	0-0	0-0	20		25,259
23	16	A	Fulham	L	0-1	0-0	20		16,180
24	22	H	Manchester C	W	2-0	1-0	20	Campbell [5], Wallwork [81]	25,348
25	Feb 1	H	Crystal Palace	D	2-2	0-0	—	Campbell [82], Earnshaw [89]	25,092
26	5	A	Norwich C	L	2-3	1-1	20	Earnshaw [41], Richardson [49]	24,292
27	22	H	Southampton	D	0-0	0-0	—		25,865
28	Mar 6	H	Birmingham C	W	2-0	0-0	19	Clement [53], Campbell [64]	25,749
29	15	A	Chelsea	L	0-1	0-1	—		41,713
30	19	A	Charlton Ath	W	4-1	1-1	19	Horsfield [9], Earnshaw 3 (1 pen) [73, 84, 90 (p)]	27,104
31	Apr 3	H	Everton	W	1-0	0-0	18	Gera [63]	26,805
32	10	A	Aston Villa	D	1-1	0-1	17	Robinson [90]	39,402
33	20	A	Tottenham H	D	1-1	1-0	—	Gera [24]	35,885
34	23	A	Middlesbrough	L	0-4	0-3	19		32,951
35	26	H	Blackburn R	D	1-1	1-0	—	Richardson [32]	25,154
36	May 2	H	Arsenal	L	0-2	0-0	—		27,351
37	7	A	Manchester U	D	1-1	0-1	20	Earnshaw (pen) [63]	67,827
38	15	H	Portsmouth	W	2-0	0-0	17	Horsfield [58], Richardson [75]	27,751

Final League Position: 17

GOALSCORERS

League (36): Earnshaw 11 (2 pens), Gera 6, Campbell 3, Clement 3, Horsfield 3, Richardson 3, Kanu 2, Dobie 1, Robinson 1, Wallwork 1, own goals 2.
Carling Cup (1): Horsfield 1.
FA Cup (4): Earnshaw 3, Kanu 1.

Hoult R 36	Haas B 9 + 1	Robinson P 28 + 2	Scimeca R 27 + 6	Gaardsoe T 25 + 4	Purse D 22	Greening J 32 + 2	Johnson A 22	Kanu N 21 + 7	Horsfield G 18 + 11	Clement N 35	Gera Z 31 + 7	Moore D 10 + 6	Dobie S 1 + 4	Dyer L — + 4	Albrechtsen M 20 + 4	Earnshaw R 18 + 13	Koumas J 5 + 5	Kuszczak T 2 + 1	Contra C 5	Hulse R — + 5	Sakiri A 2 + 1	Wallwork R 19 + 1	Campbell K 16	Richardson K 11 + 1	Chaplow R 3 + 1	Inamoto J — + 3	*Match No.*
1	2	3	4	5	6	7	8^{1}	9	10^{3}	11^{2}	12	13	14														1
1	2^{1}	3	4	5	6	7	8	9	10^{2}	11	12		13														2
1		3	2	5	6	7	8^{3}	9	10^{1}	11	4^{2}	13	12	14													3
1	12	3^{2}	2	5^{3}	6	7	8	9		11	4^{1}	13	10		14												4
1	7^{1}	3	2		6	11		9	10^{2}	4	12				5	13	8										5
		3^{2}	2	5	6	7	8^{1}	9		4▮	14			12	13^{3}	10	11	1									6
1			2	5	6▮	7	8	9	12	4	13				3	10^{1}	11^{2}										7
1	2		4	5		11	8	9	10		7	6		12	3^{1}												8
1	2	12	4	5		11^{2}	8	9^{3}	10		7^{1}	6			3	14	13										9
1	2	3	4	5		12	8	9			7	6			11^{1}	10											10
1		3	2	5		11^{3}	8	9		4^{2}	7	6	12	14		10^{1}	13										11
1		3	2		6	11	8	9^{1}	12	4	7^{2}	5				10	13										12
1			2		5	11	8	9	12	3	7^{1}	6				10^{2}			4	13							13
1			2	12	5	11	8	9^{2}	13	3	7	6				14			4^{3}		10^{1}						14
1		14	2	12	5	11	8		13	3	7	6^{1}				9			4^{3}		10^{2}						15
1	7^{1}		2	12	5	11	8	9		3	4^{3}	6				10^{2}				13	14						16
1	2		4		5	7	8	9	12	3	11^{1}					10	13		6^{2}								17
1	2^{2}		4	5	6	11	8	9		3	7^{1}					12	10					13					18
1			2	5	6	11	8^{1}		9	3	12					10^{2}	7		4▮	13							19
1		3	2^{2}	5▮	6	7^{3}	8		10	11	9^{1}				13	14				12		4					20
1		3	2		5	11^{2}	8	9^{3}	10^{1}	6	7				13	14				12		4					21
1		3	7		5		8	9^{1}	10	6	12				2	11						4					22
1		3	12		5	7	8^{1}			6	11				2	10						4	9				23
1		3	8	12	5	11			13	6	7				2	10^{2}						4	9^{1}				24
1		3	4		5	11			10^{1}	6	7				2^{2}	12						8	9	13			25
1		3	2		5	11^{1}			12	6	7					10						4	9	8			26
1		3	12	5		11				6	7^{1}				2	10	13					4	9	8^{2}			27
1		3	12	5		11		13	10^{2}	6	7				2							4	9	8^{1}			28
1		3		5		12		11	10^{2}	6	7				2	13						4	9	8^{1}			29
1		3		5^{2}		11			10	6	7^{3}	13			2	12						4	9	8^{1}	14		30
1		3	12	5		11			10	6	7	13			2^{1}							4	9	8^{2}			31
1		3	12	5		11▮		13	10^{3}	6	7				2^{1}	14						4	9^{2}	8			32
1		3	2	5				10^{1}		6	7	13				12						4	9^{2}	8^{3}	11	14	33
1		3	8	5				12	13	6	7^{2}				2^{3}	10						4	9^{1}		11	14	34
1		3	12	5				13	10^{3}	6	7				2	14						4	9^{1}	8	11^{2}		35
1		3		5		11		12	13	6	7^{1}	10			2^{3}	14						4	9^{2}	8			36
1^{6}		3		5		11		12	10^{1}	6	7^{2}				2	8		15				4	9			13	37
		3		5		11^{1}		13	12	6	7				2	10^{2}		1				4	9	8			38

FA Cup

Third Round	Preston NE	(a)	2-0
Fourth Round	Tottenham H	(h)	1-1
		(a)	1-3

Carling Cup

Second Round	Colchester U	(a)	1-2

WEST HAM UNITED FA Premiership

FOUNDATION

Thames Iron Works FC was formed by employees of this famous shipbuilding company in 1895 and entered the FA Cup in their initial season at Chatham and the London League in their second. The committee wanted to introduce professional players, so Thames Iron Works was wound up in June 1900 and relaunched a month later as West Ham United.

The Boleyn Ground, Green Street, Upton Park, London E13 9AZ.

Telephone: (020) 8548 2748.

Fax: (020) 8548 2758.

Ticket Office: 0870 112 2700.

Website: www.whufc.co.uk

Ground Capacity: 34,500.

Record Attendance: 42,322 v Tottenham H, Division 1, 17 October 1970.

Pitch Measurements: 112yd × 72yd.

Chairman: Terence Brown FCIS, AII, FCCA.

Vice-chairman: Martin Cearns ACIB.

Chief Executive: Paul Aldridge.

Secretary: Peter Barnes.

Manager: Alan Pardew.

Assistant Manager: Peter Grant.

Physio: John Green.

Colours: Claret shirts with sky blue sleeves, white shorts, white stockings.

Change Colours: Sky blue shirts, sky blue shorts, sky blue stockings.

Year Formed: 1895.

Turned Professional: 1900.

Ltd Co.: 1900.

Previous Names: 1895, Thames Iron Works FC; 1900, West Ham United.

Club Nicknames: 'The Hammers', 'The Irons'.

Previous Grounds: 1895, Memorial Recreation Ground, Canning Town; 1904, Boleyn Ground.

First Football League Game: 30 August 1919, Division 2, v Lincoln C (h) D 1–1 – Hufton; Cope, Lee; Lane, Fenwick, McCrae; D. Smith, Moyes (1), Puddefoot, Morris, Bradshaw.

HONOURS

Football League: Promotion from Championship 2004–05 (play-offs); Division 2 – Champions 1957–58, 1980–81; Runners-up 1922–23, 1990–91.

FA Cup: Winners 1964, 1975, 1980; Runners-up 1923.

Football League Cup: Runners-up 1966, 1981.

European Competitions: *European Cup-Winners' Cup:* 1964–65 (winners), 1965–66, 1975–76 (runners-up), 1980–81. *UEFA Cup:* 1999–2000. *Intertoto Cup:* 1999 (winners).

SKY SPORTS FACT FILE

The successful nine game Cup-Winners' Cup campaign by West Ham United in pre-substitute 1964–65 season saw only 16 players used, five of whom were ever-present. The 16 goals scored were distributed among seven different players.

Record League Victory: 8–0 v Rotherham U, Division 2, 8 March 1958 – Gregory; Bond, Wright; Malcolm, Brown, Lansdowne; Grice, Smith (2), Keeble (2), Dick (4), Musgrove. 8–0 v Sunderland, Division 1, 19 October 1968 – Ferguson; Bonds, Charles; Peters, Stephenson, Moore (1); Redknapp, Boyce, Brooking (1), Hurst (6), Sissons.

Record Cup Victory: 10–0 v Bury, League Cup 2nd rd (2nd leg), 25 October 1983 – Parkes; Stewart (1), Walford, Bonds (Orr), Martin (1), Devonshire (2), Allen, Cottee (4), Swindlehurst, Brooking (2), Pike.

Record Defeat: 2–8 v Blackburn R, Division 1, 26 December 1963.

Most League Points (2 for a win): 66, Division 2, 1980–81.

Most League Points (3 for a win): 88, Division 1, 1992–93.

Most League Goals: 101, Division 2, 1957–58.

Highest League Scorer in Season: Vic Watson, 42, Division 1, 1929–30.

Most League Goals in Total Aggregate: Vic Watson, 298, 1920–35.

Most League Goals in One Match: 6, Vic Watson v Leeds U, Division 1, 9 February 1929; 6, Geoff Hurst v Sunderland, Division 1, 19 October 1968.

Most Capped Player: Bobby Moore, 108, England.

Most League Appearances: Billy Bonds, 663, 1967–88.

Youngest League Player: Neil Finn, 17 years 3 days v Manchester C, 1 January 1996.

Record Transfer Fee Received: £18,000,000 from Leeds U for Rio Ferdinand, November 2000.

Record Transfer Fee Paid: £5,000,000 to Sunderland for Don Hutchison, August 2001 and £5,000,000 to Fiorentina for Tomas Repka, September 2001.

Football League Record: 1919 Elected to Division 2; 1923–32 Division 1; 1932–58 Division 2; 1958–78 Division 1; 1978–81 Division 2; 1981–89 Division 1; 1989–91 Division 2; 1991–93 Division 1; 1993–2003 FA Premier League; 2003–04 Division 1; 2004–05 FLC; 2005– FA Premier League.

MANAGERS

Syd King 1902–32
Charlie Paynter 1932–50
Ted Fenton 1950–61
Ron Greenwood 1961–74
(continued as General Manager to 1977)
John Lyall 1974–89
Lou Macari 1989–90
Billy Bonds 1990–94
Harry Redknapp 1994–2001
Glenn Roeder 2001–03
Alan Pardew October 2003–

LATEST SEQUENCES

Longest Sequence of League Wins: 9, 19.10.1985 – 14.12.1985.

Longest Sequence of League Defeats: 9, 28.3.1932 – 29.8.1932.

Longest Sequence of League Draws: 5, 15.10.2003 – 1.11.2003.

Longest Sequence of Unbeaten League Matches: 27, 27.12.80 – 10.10.81.

Longest Sequence Without a League Win: 17, 31.1.1976 – 21.8.1976.

Successive Scoring Runs: 27 from 5.10.1957.

Successive Non-scoring Runs: 5 from 1.5.1971.

TEN YEAR LEAGUE RECORD

		P	W	D	L	F	A	Pts	Pos
1995-96	PR Lge	38	14	9	15	43	52	51	10
1996-97	PR Lge	38	10	12	16	39	48	42	14
1997-98	PR Lge	38	16	8	14	56	57	56	8
1998-99	PR Lge	38	16	9	13	46	53	57	5
1999-2000	PR Lge	38	15	10	13	52	53	55	9
2000-01	PR Lge	38	10	12	16	45	50	42	15
2001-02	PR Lge	38	15	8	15	48	57	53	7
2002-03	PR Lge	38	10	12	16	42	59	42	18
2003-04	Div 1	46	19	17	10	67	45	74	4
2004-05	FL C	46	21	10	15	66	56	73	6

DID YOU KNOW ?

On 30 May 2005 West Ham United secured a return to the Premier League after two years with a Bobby Zamora goal defeating Preston North End in Cardiff. It was third time lucky for the Hammers who had twice lost 2–1 to Preston in the Championship.

WEST HAM UNITED 2004–05 LEAGUE RECORD

Match No.	*Date*	*Venue*	*Opponents*	*Result*		*H/T Score*	*Lg. Pos.*	*Goalscorers*	*Attendance*
1	Aug 7	A	Leicester C	D	0-0	0-0	—		30,231
2	10	H	Reading	W	1-0	0-0	—	Sheringham [81]	26,242
3	15	H	Wigan Ath	L	1-3	0-2	14	Zamora [69]	23,271
4	21	A	Crewe Alex	W	3-2	3-1	7	Sheringham 2 [16, 22], Brevett [30]	7857
5	28	H	Burnley	W	1-0	0-0	6	Nowland [62]	22,119
6	30	A	Coventry C	L	1-2	1-1	7	Sheringham [42]	17,404
7	Sept 11	A	Sheffield U	W	2-1	1-0	5	Harewood [9], Sheringham [85]	21,058
8	14	H	Rotherham U	W	1-0	0-0	—	Etherington [69]	26,233
9	18	H	Ipswich T	D	1-1	1-0	5	MacKay [11]	28,812
10	26	A	Nottingham F	L	1-2	0-0	6	Harewood [58]	25,615
11	29	A	Derby Co	D	1-1	1-1	—	Etherington [11]	23,112
12	Oct 2	H	Wolverhampton W	W	1-0	0-0	5	Sheringham [75]	29,585
13	16	A	QPR	L	0-1	0-1	6		18,363
14	19	H	Stoke C	W	2-0	1-0	—	Harewood [31], Sheringham [59]	29,808
15	23	H	Gillingham	W	3-1	3-1	4	Zamora [18], Harewood [25], Mullins [39]	25,247
16	30	A	Plymouth Arg	D	1-1	1-0	6	Lomas [43]	20,220
17	Nov 2	A	Cardiff C	L	1-4	0-2	—	Harewood (pen) [69]	14,222
18	6	H	QPR	W	2-1	1-0	5	Harewood 2 (1 pen) [36 (p), 84]	31,365
19	13	H	Brighton & HA	L	0-1	0-0	6		29,514
20	21	A	Millwall	L	0-1	0-0	6		15,025
21	27	H	Watford	W	3-2	2-2	6	Reo-Coker [28], Powell D [30], Rebrov [58]	24,541
22	Dec 4	A	Sunderland	W	2-0	0-0	5	Harewood [59], Sheringham [90]	29,510
23	10	H	Leeds U	D	1-1	0-0	—	Chadwick [50]	30,684
24	18	A	Preston NE	L	1-2	0-2	6	Reo-Coker [50]	13,451
25	26	H	Nottingham F	W	3-2	2-0	7	Etherington [17], Sheringham 2 [39, 82]	32,270
26	28	A	Rotherham U	D	2-2	0-2	7	Sheringham (pen) [71], Harewood (pen) [76]	7769
27	Jan 1	A	Ipswich T	W	2-0	1-0	5	Harewood [1], Etherington [90]	30,003
28	3	H	Sheffield U	L	0-2	0-1	6		27,424
29	15	A	Wolverhampton W	L	2-4	1-1	7	Zamora 2 [36, 57]	28,411
30	23	H	Derby Co	L	1-2	1-1	9	Fletcher [26]	30,347
31	Feb 6	H	Cardiff C	W	1-0	0-0	7	Fletcher [89]	23,716
32	19	H	Plymouth Arg	W	5-0	3-0	6	Harewood (pen) [10], McCormick (og) [23], MacKay [40], Sheringham 2 (1 pen) [76, 84 (p)]	25,490
33	22	A	Gillingham	W	1-0	1-0	—	Harewood [13]	9510
34	26	A	Leeds U	L	1-2	0-0	6	Williams [68]	34,115
35	Mar 5	H	Preston NE	L	1-2	0-1	7	Zamora [87]	26,442
36	12	A	Reading	L	1-3	0-2	7	Sheringham [82]	22,268
37	15	H	Crewe Alex	D	1-1	0-0	—	Sheringham [76]	26,593
38	18	H	Leicester C	D	2-2	1-2	—	Sheringham 2 [28, 62]	22,031
39	Apr 2	A	Wigan Ath	W	2-1	0-0	7	Sheringham [55], Harewood [67]	12,993
40	5	A	Burnley	W	1-0	0-0	—	Sheringham [83]	12,209
41	9	H	Coventry C	W	3-0	0-0	7	Shaw (og) [76], Sheringham (pen) [89], Zamora [90]	26,839
42	16	H	Millwall	D	1-1	1-1	7	Harewood [35]	28,221
43	19	A	Stoke C	W	1-0	0-0	—	Zamora [78]	14,534
44	23	A	Brighton & HA	D	2-2	1-0	6	Reo-Coker [8], Harewood [55]	6819
45	29	H	Sunderland	L	1-2	1-0	—	Harewood [43]	33,482
46	May 8	A	Watford	W	2-1	1-0	6	Ferdinand [42], Harewood (pen) [70]	19,673

Final League Position: 6

GOALSCORERS

League (66): Sheringham 20 (3 pens), Harewood 17 (5 pens), Zamora 7, Etherington 4, Reo-Coker 3, Fletcher 2, MacKay 2, Brevett 1, Chadwick 1, Ferdinand 1, Lomas 1, Mullins 1, Nowland 1, Powell D 1, Rebrov 1, Williams 1, own goals 2.
Carling Cup (5): Harewood 2, Zamora 2, Rebrov 1.
FA Cup (3): Harewood 2, Sheringham 1 (pen).
Play-offs (5): Zamora 4, Harewood 1.

Bywater S 36	Repka T 42	Brevett R 10	Mullins H 32 + 5	Melville A 3	Dailly C 2 + 1	Rebrov S 12 + 14	Reo-Coker N 34 + 5	Harewood M 45	Sheringham T 26 + 7	Etherington M 37 + 2	Cohen C 1 + 10	McAnuff J — + 1	Zamora B 15 + 19	Ferdinand A 24 + 5	Chadwick L 22 + 10	McClenahan T — + 2	Nowland A 3 + 1	Lomas S 18 + 5	Garcia R — + 1	Fletcher C 26 + 6	Davenport C 10	MacKay M 17 + 1	Powell C 35 + 1	Hutchison D 2 + 3	Taricco M 1	Powell D 5	Williams G 7 + 3	Walker J 10	Noble M 10 + 3	Newton S 11	Ward E 10 + 1	*Match No.*
1	2	3■	4	5	6	7^{2}	8	9^{3}	10^{1}	11	12	13	14																			1
1	2		4	5^{1}	6	7^{2}	8	9^{3}	10	11	3		14	12	13																	2
1	2	3^{1}	4	5		7^{3}	8	9^{2}	10	11	12		13	6	14																	3
1	2	3	4^{2}				6	9	10	11^{1}	12			5	7	13	8															4
1	2	3	4				6	9	10^{1}	11	12■			5	7^{2}		8	13														5
1	2	3^{3}	4			7^{1}	6	9	10	11				5	12		8^{2}	13■	14													6
1	2	3	4^{3}			12	8	9^{1}	10	11					7^{2}		13			5	6	14										7
1	2		12			13	8	9	10	11^{1}					7^{2}					4	6	5	3									8
1	2		12			13	8	9	10^{1}	11					7^{2}					4	6	5	3									9
1	2						8	9	10	11					7^{1}			12		4	6	5	3									10
1	2		5				8	9	10^{1}	11			12		7					4	6		3									11
1	2		5			12	8	9	13	11^{3}			10^{2}		7^{1}			14		4	6		3									12
1	2		4			7	8	9			12		10^{2}	5	11^{1}			6					3	13								13
1	2	3	4			12	8	9	13	11^{2}			10^{1}		7^{3}			6		14		5										14
1	2	3	4			7	8^{3}	9		11^{1}	12		10^{2}		13			6		14		5										15
1	2	3	4				8	9		11			10^{1}					7		5	6			12								16
1	2	3^{2}	5^{1}			12		9		11			10		7^{3}			8		4	6		13	14								17
1	2		5					9		11			12	13	10^{1}			7		4	6		3	8^{2}								18
1	2		5■			12	13	9		11^{3}			14		7^{2}			8		4	6		3	10^{1}								19
1	5						8	9■		11			12	13	10^{1}			7		4			3		2^{2}	6						20
1	2					9	8			11^{1}			10	12	7			6		4			3			5						21
1	2					10^{1}		9	12	11			13	5	7^{2}			8		4			3			6						22
1	5					10^{2}	12	9	13	11				2	7^{1}			8		4			3			6						23
1	2					12	13	9	10	11				5	7^{2}			8		4			3			6^{1}						24
1	2		12				8	9	10	11				4^{1}	7^{2}			6				5	3				13					25
1	2		4				8	9	10^{1}	11			12		13			6^{2}				5	3				7					26
1	2		4			12	8^{2}	9		11^{3}			10^{1}	13		14				6		5	3				7					27
1	2		4			12	8	9		11^{2}	14		10^{1}		13					6		5^{3}	3				7					28
	2		4			11		9			12		10	6	7^{1}							5	3				13	1	8^{2}			29
	2		4			7^{1}	8	9	12						10					6		5	3				11^{2}	1	13			30
1			2			12	8	9	10				11^{2}	4	13					6		5	3						7^{1}			31
1	2		4^{3}			7^{1}	12	9	10				13	6				14		8		5	3						11^{2}			32
1	2						8^{3}	9	12	11^{1}	13		10^{2}	6				7		4		5	3				14					33
1	2		12					9	10	11^{3}	14		13	6^{1}				4		8		5	3^{2}				7					34
1	2■		4				12	9	10^{2}	11			13					6		8		5^{1}	3				7					35
1			4^{3}					9	12	11			10^{1}		13			6		8^{2}		5	3						7	2	14	36
1			12					9	10^{1}	11^{3}			13	5	14					4			3				7^{2}		8	2	6	37
1						12^{2}	8	9	10				13	5	11^{1}					4			3						7	2	6	38
	2		4				8	9	10					5						12			3					1	11	7^{1}	6	39
	2		4^{3}				8	9^{2}	10	12			13	5						14			3					1	11^{1}	7	6	40
	2		4^{1}				8	9^{2}	10	12			13	5									3					1	11	7	6	41
	2						8	9	10	11			12	5									3					1	4	7^{1}	6	42
	2^{1}		4^{3}				8	9^{2}	10	11			12	5	13					14			3					1		7	6	43
	2		4				8	9	10^{1}	11^{2}			12	5						13			3					1		7	6	44
	2		4			12	8	9		11^{2}			10	5									3					1	13	7^{1}	6	45
	2		4		12	13	8^{1}	9		11^{3}			10	5									3					1	14	7^{2}	6	46

FA Cup

Third Round	Norwich C	(h)	1-0
Fourth Round	Sheffield U	(h)	1-1
		(a)	1-1

Carling Cup

First Round	Southend U	(h)	2-0
Second Round	Notts Co	(h)	3-2
Third Round	Chelsea	(a)	0-1

Play-offs

Semi-Final	Ipswich T	(h)	2-2
		(a)	2-0
Final (at Millennium Stadium)	Preston NE		1-0

WIGAN ATHLETIC FA Premiership

FOUNDATION

Following the demise of Wigan Borough and their resignation from the Football League in 1931, a public meeting was called in Wigan at the Queen's Hall in May 1932 at which a new club, Wigan Athletic, was founded in the hope of carrying on in the Football League. With this in mind, they bought Springfield Park for £2,250, but failed to gain admission to the Football League until 46 years later.

JJB Stadium, Wigan WN5 0UZ.

Telephone: (01942) 774 000.

Fax: (01942) 770 477.

Ticket Office: 0870 112 2552.

Website: www.wiganathletic.tv

Email: latics@jjbstadium.co.uk

Ground Capacity: 25,000.

Record Attendance: 27,526 v Hereford U, 12 December 1953 (at Springfield Park).

Pitch Measurements: 115yd × 75yd.

Chairman: David Whelan.

Vice-chairman: Philip Williams.

Chief Executive: Brenda Spencer.

Secretary: Stuart Hayton.

Manager: Paul Jewell.

Assistant Manager: Chris Hutchings.

Physio: Alex Cribley.

Colours: Reflex blue and white vertical striped shirts, reflex blue shorts, white stockings.

Change Colours: Amber shirt with navy side panels, navy shorts, amber stockings.

Year Formed: 1932.

Previous Grounds: 1932, Springfield Park; 1999, JJB Stadium.

Club Nickname: 'The Latics'.

First Football League Game: 19 August 1978, Division 4, v Hereford U (a) D 0–0 – Brown; Hinnigan, Gore, Gillibrand, Ward, Davids, Corrigan, Purdie, Houghton, Wilkie, Wright.

Record League Victory: 7–1 v Scarborough, Division 3, 11 March 1997 – Butler L, Butler J, Sharp (Morgan), Greenall, McGibbon (Biggins (1)), Martinez (1), Diaz (2), Jones (Lancashire (1)), Lowe (2), Rogers, Kilford.

Record Cup Victory: 6–0 v Carlisle U (away), FA Cup 1st rd, 24 November 1934 – Caunce; Robinson, Talbot; Paterson, Watson, Tufnell; Armes (2), Robson (1), Roberts (2), Felton, Scott (1).

HONOURS

Football League: Championship – Runners-up 2004–05; Division 2 Champions, 2002–03; Division 3 Champions, 1996–97; Division 4 – Promoted (3rd) 1981–82.

FA Cup: best season: 6th rd, 1987.

Football League Cup: best season: 5th rd, 2003.

Freight Rover Trophy: Winners 1985.

Auto Windscreens Shield: Winners 1999.

SKY SPORTS FACT FILE

Wigan Athletic made 34 unsuccessful applications to be admitted to the Football League before achieving it in 1978 with 29 votes while Southport were not re-elected with 20. In 1936 Wigan's initial attempt received six votes.

Record Defeat: 1–6 v Bristol R, Division 3, 3 March 1990.

Most League Points (2 for a win): 55, Division 4, 1978–79 and 1979–80.

Most League Points (3 for a win): 100, Division 2, 2002–03.

Most League Goals: 84, Division 3, 1996–97.

Highest League Scorer in Season: Graeme Jones, 31, Division 3, 1996–97.

Most League Goals in Total Aggregate: Andy Liddell, 70, 1998–2004.

Most League Goals in One Match: Not more than three goals by one player.

Most Capped Player: Roy Carroll, 9 (17), Northern Ireland.

Most League Appearances: Kevin Langley, 317, 1981–86, 1990–94.

Youngest League Player: Steve Nugent, 16 years 132 days v Leyton Orient, 16 September 1989.

Record Transfer Fee Received: £3,000,000 from Manchester U for Roy Carroll, July 2001.

Record Transfer Fee Paid: £1,400,000 to WBA for Jason Roberts, January 2004.

Football League Record: 1978 Elected to Division 4; 1982–92 Division 3; 1992–93 Division 2; 1993–97 Division 3; 1997–2003 Division 2; 2003–04 Division 1; 2004–05 FLC; 2005– FA Premier League.

LATEST SEQUENCES

Longest Sequence of League Wins: 11, 2.11.2002 – 18.1.2003.

Longest Sequence of League Defeats: 7, 6.4.1993 – 4.5.1993.

Longest Sequence of League Draws: 6, 11.12.2001 – 5.1.2002.

Longest Sequence of Unbeaten League Matches: 25, 8.5.1999 – 3.1.2000.

Longest Sequence Without a League Win: 14, 9.5.1989 – 17.10.1989.

Successive Scoring Runs: 24 from 27.4.1996.

Successive Non-scoring Runs: 4 from 15.4.1995.

MANAGERS

Charlie Spencer 1932–37
Jimmy Milne 1946–47
Bob Pryde 1949–52
Ted Goodier 1952–54
Walter Crook 1954–55
Ron Suart 1955–56
Billy Cooke 1956
Sam Barkas 1957
Trevor Hitchen 1957–58
Malcolm Barrass 1958–59
Jimmy Shirley 1959
Pat Murphy 1959–60
Allenby Chilton 1960
Johnny Ball 1961–63
Allan Brown 1963–66
Alf Craig 1966–67
Harry Leyland 1967–68
Alan Saunders 1968
Ian McNeill 1968–70
Gordon Milne 1970–72
Les Rigby 1972–74
Brian Tiler 1974–76
Ian McNeill 1976–81
Larry Lloyd 1981–83
Harry McNally 1983–85
Bryan Hamilton 1985–86
Ray Mathias 1986–89
Bryan Hamilton 1989–93
Dave Philpotts 1993
Kenny Swain 1993–94
Graham Barrow 1994–95
John Deehan 1995–98
Ray Mathias 1998–99
John Benson 1999–2000
Bruce Rioch 2000–01
Steve Bruce 2001
Paul Jewell June 2001–

TEN YEAR LEAGUE RECORD

		P	W	D	L	F	A	Pts	Pos
1995-96	Div 3	46	20	10	16	62	56	70	10
1996-97	Div 3	46	26	9	11	84	51	87	1
1997-98	Div 2	46	17	11	18	64	66	62	11
1998-99	Div 2	46	22	10	14	75	48	76	6
1999-2000	Div 2	46	22	17	7	72	38	83	4
2000-01	Div 2	46	19	18	9	53	42	75	6
2001-02	Div 2	46	16	16	14	66	51	64	10
2002-03	Div 2	46	29	13	4	68	25	100	1
2003-04	Div 1	46	18	17	11	60	45	71	7
2004-05	FL C	46	25	12	9	79	35	87	2

DID YOU KNOW ?

A solid start to 2004–05 was a prelude to promotion to the Premier League after 17 unbeaten matches. Defensively only once were as many as three goals conceded and there were 20 clean sheets to stress their capabilities.

WIGAN ATHLETIC 2004–05 LEAGUE RECORD

Match No.	Date	Venue	Opponents	Result	H/T Score	Lg. Pos.	Goalscorers	Atten-dance
1	Aug 7	H	Nottingham F	D 1-1	1-0	—	McCulloch [38]	12,035
2	10	A	Millwall	W 2-0	0-0	—	McCulloch [51], Roberts [75]	10,660
3	15	A	West Ham U	W 3-1	2-0	1	Ellington 2 [5, 58], Roberts [45]	23,271
4	21	H	Brighton & HA	W 3-0	1-0	1	Ellington 2 [45, 49], Frandsen [77]	8681
5	28	A	Sunderland	D 1-1	1-0	1	Roberts [18]	26,330
6	30	H	Cardiff C	W 2-1	2-0	1	Ellington (pen) [16], Roberts [36]	9004
7	Sept 11	A	Wolverhampton W	D 3-3	2-1	2	Jackson [23], Ellington [28], Roberts (pen) [75]	26,790
8	14	H	Burnley	D 0-0	0-0	—		9746
9	18	H	Sheffield U	W 4-0	3-0	1	Ellington 2 [29, 35], Roberts 2 [33, 90]	10,682
10	25	A	Derby Co	D 1-1	1-1	2	McCulloch [19]	26,113
11	28	A	Watford	D 0-0	0-0	—		11,161
12	Oct 2	H	Rotherham U	W 2-0	1-0	1	Roberts [11], Mahon [63]	7937
13	16	A	Plymouth Arg	W 2-1	0-0	1	Roberts 2 [54, 69]	14,443
14	19	H	Crewe Alex	W 4-1	2-0	—	McCulloch [18], Ellington 2 [25, 48], Bullard [84]	7547
15	23	H	Coventry C	W 4-1	1-1	1	Mahon [15], Graham [53], Ellington [63], Flynn [90]	9632
16	31	A	Leeds U	W 2-0	0-0	1	Mahon [46], Bullard [52]	27,432
17	Nov 2	A	Stoke C	W 1-0	0-0	—	McCulloch [87]	15,882
18	6	H	Plymouth Arg	L 0-2	0-1	1		10,294
19	13	A	QPR	L 0-1	0-0	1		15,804
20	20	H	Leicester C	D 0-0	0-0	1		10,924
21	27	A	Reading	D 1-1	1-1	2	Mahon [26]	22,114
22	Dec 5	H	Preston NE	W 5-0	1-0	1	McCulloch [27], Mahon [52], Ellington 2 [57, 72], Roberts (pen) [79]	10,565
23	11	H	Gillingham	W 2-0	1-0	1	Ellington [17], McCulloch [88]	8451
24	21	A	Ipswich T	L 1-2	0-0	—	Baines [57]	28,286
25	26	H	Derby Co	L 1-2	1-0	2	Roberts [27]	12,420
26	28	A	Burnley	L 0-1	0-1	3		16,485
27	Jan 1	A	Sheffield U	W 2-0	1-0	2	McCulloch [7], Ellington [73]	21,869
28	4	H	Wolverhampton W	W 2-0	2-0	—	Ellington 2 (1 pen) [17, 26 (p)]	10,335
29	15	A	Rotherham U	W 2-0	0-0	2	Teale [69], Roberts [90]	9050
30	22	H	Watford	D 2-2	1-2	2	McCulloch 2 [25, 52]	9008
31	Feb 5	H	Stoke C	L 0-1	0-1	2		9938
32	12	A	Crewe Alex	W 3-1	1-1	2	Roberts 2 [3, 76], Ellington (pen) [68]	7981
33	19	H	Leeds U	W 3-0	1-0	2	Ellington [10], Roberts [56], Mahon [75]	17,177
34	23	A	Coventry C	W 2-1	1-1	—	Teale [9], Ellington [68]	12,130
35	26	A	Gillingham	L 1-2	0-0	1	Ellington [55]	7209
36	Mar 5	H	Ipswich T	W 1-0	1-0	1	Ellington (pen) [43]	16,744
37	12	H	Millwall	W 2-0	0-0	1	Ellington (pen) [58], Roberts [82]	9614
38	15	A	Brighton & HA	W 4-2	4-1	—	Bullard [2], McCulloch [4], Teale [17], Roberts [34]	6306
39	19	A	Nottingham F	D 1-1	0-0	2	McCulloch [46]	24,008
40	Apr 2	H	West Ham U	L 1-2	0-0	2	Roberts [51]	12,993
41	5	H	Sunderland	L 0-1	0-1	—		20,745
42	9	A	Cardiff C	W 2-0	0-0	2	Roberts [51], Mahon [86]	16,858
43	16	A	Leicester C	W 2-0	1-0	2	Ormerod 2 [25, 59]	23,894
44	23	H	QPR	D 0-0	0-0	2		12,007
45	30	A	Preston NE	D 1-1	1-1	2	McCulloch [24]	20,221
46	May 8	H	Reading	W 3-1	2-0	2	McCulloch [18], Roberts [21], Ellington [85]	19,662

Final League Position: 2

GOALSCORERS

League (79): Ellington 24 (5 pens), Roberts 21 (2 pens), McCulloch 14, Mahon 7, Bullard 3, Teale 3, Ormerod 2, Baines 1, Flynn 1, Frandsen 1, Graham 1, Jackson 1.
Carling Cup (0).
FA Cup (1): Mahon 1.

Filan J 46	Wright D 19 + 12	Baines L 41	Frandsen P 9	Breckin I 42	Jackson M 35 + 1	Teale G 29 + 8	Bullard J 46	Ellington N 43 + 2	Roberts J 45	McCulloch L 42	Graham D 13 + 17	Eaden N 33 + 6	Emerson11 + 4	Mahon A 21 + 6	Whalley G 7 + 1	McMillan S 5 + 3	Flynn M 1 + 12	Mitchell P — + 1	Johansson A — + 1	Jarrett J 4 + 10	Kavanagh G 11	Ormerod B 3 + 3	*Match No.*
1	2	3	4	5	6	7	8	9^1	10	11	12												1
1	2	3	4	5	6	7^1	8	9	10	11		12											2
1	2	3	4	5	6	7	8	9	10^1	11^2	12	13											3
1	2	3	4	5^3	6	7^2	8	9	10^1	11	12	13	14										4
1	2	3	4	5	6	7	8	9	10	11													5
1	2	3	4	5	6	7^1	8	9	10	11		12											6
1	2	3	4	5	6	7^1	8	9^2	10	11		12	13										7
1	2	3	4	5	6	7^1	8	9	10	11	12												8
1	12	3	4^3	5	6^2	7	8	9	10	11^1		2	13	14									9
1		3		5	6^1	7	8	9	10	11▪		2	12	4									10
1	12	3		5		7^2	8	9	10		13	2	4	6	11^1								11
1		3		5			8	9	10	11	7	2	4	6									12
1	12	3		5			8	9	10	11	7	2^1	4	6									13
1	2	3		5			8^1	9	10	11	7		4^2	6	12	13							14
1	2	3		5	6		8	9^1	10	11	7			4			12						15
1	2	3		5	6		8	9^2	10	11	7^1			4			12	13					16
1	2	3		5	6		8	9^1	10	11	7			4			12						17
1	2	3		5	6	7^1	8		10	11^2	9	14		4		13^3	12						18
1	2	3^2		5	6	12	8	9^3	10		11^1	7		4		13	14						19
1	2^1	3		5	6	12	8	9	10	11^2	13	7		4									20
1	12	3		5	6	7^3	8	9	10	11^2	13	2		4^1			14						21
1	12	3		5	6	7	8^1	9^2	10	11	13	2		4^3			14						22
1		3		5	6	7^1	8	9^2	10	11	12	2		4			13						23
1	12	3		5	6	7^2	8	9	10	11	13	2		4^1									24
1		3		5	6	12	8	9	10	11	7^1	2		4									25
1		3^1		5		12	8	9		11	10	2	6	4^2	7		13						26
1		3		5			8^1	9	10	11	7	2	6		4		12						27
1	12	3			6	13	8	9^3	10	11	7^2	2^1	5		4		14						28
1		3			6	12	8	9	10	11	7^1	2	5		4^2		13						29
1		3			6	7	8	9	10	11		2	5	12			4^1						30
1		3^1			6	7^2	8	9	10	11	12	2	5	4					13				31
1		3		5	12	7	8	9	10	11		2	6^1	4^2						13			32
1		3		5	6	7	8	9^2	10^1	11	12	2		4						13			33
1	12	3		5	6	7	8	9	10^2	11	13	2^1			4^3					14			34
1		3^1		5	6	7	8	9	10	11	12	2			4^2					13			35
1	12	3		5	6^1	7^2	8	9	10	11	13	2								14	4^3		36
1	6	3		5		7	8	9^2	10^1	11	12	2								13	4		37
1	6	3		5		7	8^1	9	10	11		2								12	4		38
1	6	3		5		7^1	8	9^2	10	11		2								12	4	13	39
1	6	3^1		5		7	8	9	10	11^2		2		12							4	13	40
1		3		5	6	7^1	8	9	10			2		11^2						12	4	13	41
1	12			5	6		8^1	9^2	10			2		13		3				7	4	11	42
1	13			5	6		8	12	10^1	11^2		2				3				7	4	9	43
1				5	6	12	8	13	10	11		2				3				7^1	4	9^2	44
1				5	6	7^3	8^2	9^1	10	11	12	2		13		3				14	4		45
1	13			5	6	12	8^1	9^2	10^3	11		2		14		3				7	4		46

FA Cup
Third Round Derby Co (a) 1-2

Carling Cup
First Round Grimsby T (a) 0-1

WOLVERHAMPTON WANDERERS FL Championship

FOUNDATION

Enthusiasts of the game at St Luke's School, Blakenhall formed a club in 1877. In the same neighbourhood a cricket club called Blakenhall Wanderers had a football section. Several St Luke's footballers played cricket for them and shortly before the start of the 1879–80 season the two amalgamated and Wolverhampton Wanderers FC was brought into being.

Molineux, Waterloo Road, Wolverhampton WV1 4QR.

Telephone: 0870 442 0123.

Fax: (01902) 687 006.

Ticket Office: 0870 442 0123.

Website: wolves.co.uk

Email: info@wolves.co.uk

Ground Capacity: 29,277.

Record Attendance: 61,315 v Liverpool, FA Cup 5th rd, 11 February 1939.

Pitch Measurements: 110yd × 75yd.

Chairman: Rick Hayward.

Vice-chairman: Derek Harrington CBE.

Chief Executive: Jez Moxey.

Secretary: Richard Skirrow.

Manager: Glen Hoddle.

Coach: Stuart Gray.

Physio: Barry Holmes.

Colours: Gold and black.

Change Colours: Black with gold trim.

Year Formed: 1877* (*see Foundation*).

Turned Professional: 1888.

Ltd Co.: 1923 (but current club is WWFC (1986) Ltd).

Previous Names: 1879, St Luke's combined with Wanderers Cricket Club to become Wolverhampton Wanderers (1923) Ltd. New limited companies followed in 1982 and 1986 (current).

Club Nickname: 'Wolves'.

Previous Grounds: 1877, Windmill Field; 1879, John Harper's Field; 1881, Dudley Road; 1889, Molineux.

First Football League Game: 8 September 1888, Football League, v Aston Villa (h) D 1–1 – Baynton; Baugh, Mason; Fletcher, Allen, Lowder; Hunter, Cooper, Anderson, White, Cannon, (1 og).

Record League Victory: 10–1 v Leicester C, Division 1, 15 April 1938 – Sidlow; Morris, Dowen; Galley, Cullis, Gardiner; Maguire (1), Horace Wright, Westcott (4), Jones (1), Dorsett (4).

HONOURS

Football League: Division 1 – Champions 1953–54, 1957–58, 1958–59; Runners-up 1937–38, 1938–39, 1949–50, 1954–55, 1959–60; 2002–03 (play-offs). Division 2 – Champions 1931–32, 1976–77; Runners-up 1966–67, 1982–83; Division 3 (N) – Champions 1923–24; Division 3 – Champions 1988–89; Division 4 – Champions 1987–88.

FA Cup: Winners 1893, 1908, 1949, 1960; Runners-up 1889, 1896, 1921, 1939.

Football League Cup: Winners 1974, 1980.

Texaco Cup: Winners 1971.

Sherpa Van Trophy: Winners 1988.

European Competitions: *European Cup:* 1958–59, 1959–60. *European Cup-Winners' Cup:* 1960–61. *UEFA Cup:* 1971–72 (runners-up), 1973–74, 1974–75, 1980–81.

SKY SPORTS FACT FILE

Billy Hartill scored 15 hat-tricks for Wolverhampton Wanderers in the Football League from 1929–30 to 1934–35, including five on two occasions and one foursome. An ex-bombardier in the Royal Horse Artillery he was nicknamed "Hartillery".

Record Cup Victory: 14–0 v Crosswell's Brewery, FA Cup 2nd rd, 13 November 1886 – I. Griffiths; Baugh, Mason; Pearson, Allen (1), Lowder; Hunter (4), Knight (2), Brodie (4), B. Griffiths (2), Wood. Plus one goal 'scrambled through'.

Record Defeat: 1–10 v Newton Heath, Division 1, 15 October 1892.

Most League Points (2 for a win): 64, Division 1, 1957–58.

Most League Points (3 for a win): 92, Division 3, 1988–89.

Most League Goals: 115, Division 2, 1931–32.

Highest League Scorer in Season: Dennis Westcott, 38, Division 1, 1946–47.

Most League Goals in Total Aggregate: Steve Bull, 250, 1986–99.

Most League Goals in One Match: 5, Joe Butcher v Accrington, Division 1, 19 November 1892; 5, Tom Phillipson v Barnsley, Division 2, 26 April 1926; 5, Tom Phillipson v Bradford C, Division 2, 25 December 1926; 5, Billy Hartill v Notts Co, Division 2, 12 October 1929; 5, Billy Hartill v Aston Villa, Division 1, 3 September 1934.

Most Capped Player: Billy Wright, 105, England (70 consecutive).

Most League Appearances: Derek Parkin, 501, 1967–82.

Youngest League Player: Jimmy Mullen, 16 years 43 days v Leeds U, 18 February 1939.

Record Transfer Fee Received: £6,000,000 from Coventry C for Robbie Keane, August 1999.

Record Transfer Fee Paid: £3,500,000 to Bristol C for Ade Akinbiyi, September 1999.

Football League Record: 1888 Founder Member of Football League: 1906–23 Division 2; 1923–24 Division 3 (N); 1924–32 Division 2; 1932–65 Division 1; 1965–67 Division 2; 1967–76 Division 1; 1976–77 Division 2; 1977–82 Division 1; 1982–83 Division 2; 1983–84 Division 1; 1984–85 Division 2; 1985–86 Division 3; 1986–88 Division 4; 1988–89 Division 3; 1989–92 Division 2; 1992–2003 Division 1; 2003–04 FA Premier League; 2004– FLC.

MANAGERS

George Worrall 1877–85
(Secretary-Manager)
John Addenbrooke 1885–1922
George Jobey 1922–24
Albert Hoskins 1924–26
(had been Secretary since 1922)
Fred Scotchbrook 1926–27
Major Frank Buckley 1927–44
Ted Vizard 1944–48
Stan Cullis 1948–64
Andy Beattie 1964–65
Ronnie Allen 1966–68
Bill McGarry 1968–76
Sammy Chung 1976–78
John Barnwell 1978–81
Ian Greaves 1982
Graham Hawkins 1982–84
Tommy Docherty 1984–85
Bill McGarry 1985
Sammy Chapman 1985–86
Brian Little 1986
Graham Turner 1986–94
Graham Taylor 1994–95
Mark McGhee 1995–98
Colin Lee 1998–2000
Dave Jones 2001–04
Glen Hoddle December 2004–

LATEST SEQUENCES

Longest Sequence of League Wins: 8, 15.10.1988 – 26.11.1988.

Longest Sequence of League Defeats: 8, 5.12.1981 – 13.2.1982.

Longest Sequence of League Draws: 6, 22.4.1995 – 20.8.1995.

Longest Sequence of Unbeaten League Matches: 20, 24.11.1923 – 5.4.1924.

Longest Sequence Without a League Win: 19, 1.12.1984 – 6.4.1985.

Successive Scoring Runs: 41 from 20.12.1958.

Successive Non-scoring Runs: 7 from 2.2.1985.

TEN YEAR LEAGUE RECORD

		P	W	D	L	F	A	Pts	Pos
1995-96	Div 1	46	13	16	17	56	62	55	20
1996-97	Div 1	46	22	10	14	68	51	76	3
1997-98	Div 1	46	18	11	17	57	53	65	9
1998-99	Div 1	46	19	16	11	64	43	73	7
1999-2000	Div 1	46	21	11	14	64	48	74	7
2000-01	Div 1	46	14	13	19	45	48	55	12
2001-02	Div 1	46	25	11	10	76	43	86	3
2002-03	Div 1	46	20	16	10	81	44	76	5
2003-04	PR Lge	38	7	12	19	38	77	33	20
2004-05	FL C	46	15	21	10	72	59	66	9

DID YOU KNOW

An erratic start to the 1957–58 season for Wolverhampton Wanderers was transformed in a run of 18 matches without defeat from 14 September and despite a hiccup at the end they were champions with five points to spare.

WOLVERHAMPTON WANDERERS 2004–05 LEAGUE RECORD

Match No.	Date	Venue	Opponents	Result		H/T Score	Lg. Pos.	Goalscorers	Atten-dance
1	Aug 8	A	Stoke C	L	1-2	0-0	—	Miller (pen) [88]	17,086
2	11	H	Preston NE	D	2-2	0-2	—	Clarke [76], Miller [79]	26,115
3	14	H	Leeds U	D	0-0	0-0	20		28,397
4	21	A	Burnley	D	1-1	1-1	20	Newton [15]	13,869
5	28	H	Leicester C	D	1-1	0-1	19	Miller [52]	27,550
6	30	A	Ipswich T	L	1-2	0-1	21	Olofinjana [54]	24,590
7	Sept 11	H	Wigan Ath	D	3-3	1-2	20	Miller 2 [15, 65], Cameron [90]	26,790
8	14	A	Brighton & HA	W	1-0	1-0	—	Miller [22]	6804
9	18	A	Plymouth Arg	W	2-1	0-0	15	Cort (pen) [77], Sturridge [85]	18,635
10	25	H	Cardiff C	L	2-3	1-1	18	Cort [12], Ince [85]	27,896
11	Oct 2	A	West Ham U	L	0-1	0-0	20		29,585
12	15	A	Nottingham F	L	0-1	0-1	—		21,856
13	19	H	Derby Co	W	2-0	1-0	—	Cooper 2 (1 pen) [19 (p), 50]	26,465
14	23	H	QPR	W	2-1	1-0	18	Cort 2 [22, 70]	27,070
15	30	A	Gillingham	L	0-1	0-1	19		9112
16	Nov 2	A	Sunderland	L	1-3	1-0	—	Miller [18]	23,925
17	6	H	Nottingham F	W	2-1	2-1	17	Cooper (pen) [19], Bischoff [43]	27,605
18	13	A	Rotherham U	W	2-1	0-1	15	Cooper [69], Cort [79]	6693
19	20	H	Coventry C	L	0-1	0-0	18		26,291
20	27	A	Sheffield U	D	3-3	1-1	19	Olofinjana [7], Cort [50], Lescott [87]	18,946
21	Dec 4	H	Reading	W	4-1	2-0	17	Cameron [31], Olofinjana [45], Clarke 2 [77, 90]	25,572
22	7	H	Millwall	L	1-2	0-1	—	Cooper (pen) [57]	24,748
23	11	A	Watford	D	1-1	1-1	17	Olofinjana [35]	14,605
24	18	H	Crewe Alex	D	1-1	0-1	16	Cort [90]	25,340
25	26	A	Cardiff C	D	1-1	0-1	17	Miller [75]	16,699
26	28	H	Brighton & HA	D	1-1	1-1	17	Miller [33]	28,516
27	Jan 1	H	Plymouth Arg	D	1-1	1-0	18	Seol [24]	27,564
28	4	A	Wigan Ath	L	0-2	0-2	—		10,335
29	15	H	West Ham U	W	4-2	1-1	18	Miller 2 [29, 54], Ince [72], Cort [75]	28,411
30	22	A	Millwall	W	2-1	1-0	15	Olofinjana [37], Seol [90]	13,145
31	Feb 4	H	Sunderland	D	1-1	1-1	—	Seol [13]	26,968
32	19	H	Gillingham	D	2-2	0-0	18	Miller [60], Clarke [90]	24,949
33	22	A	QPR	D	1-1	0-1	—	Cort [85]	15,029
34	26	H	Watford	D	0-0	0-0	17		25,060
35	Mar 2	A	Derby Co	D	3-3	1-1	—	Miller [12], Lescott [72], Cort [89]	24,109
36	5	A	Crewe Alex	W	4-1	3-1	13	Cort 2 [13, 45], Miller 2 (1 pen) [35 (p), 60]	8212
37	12	A	Preston NE	D	2-2	1-1	14	Craddock [10], Seol [73]	16,296
38	15	H	Burnley	W	2-0	1-0	—	Miller [38], Ince [60]	24,336
39	19	H	Stoke C	D	1-1	0-1	13	Cort [90]	28,103
40	Apr 2	A	Leeds U	D	1-1	1-0	13	Cort [40]	29,773
41	5	A	Leicester C	D	1-1	0-0	—	Lescott [88]	22,950
42	11	H	Ipswich T	W	2-0	2-0	—	Cameron [5], Cort [22]	25,882
43	16	A	Coventry C	D	2-2	1-1	13	Clarke [15], Naylor [79]	19,412
44	23	H	Rotherham U	W	2-0	0-0	11	Miller 2 [55, 90]	25,177
45	30	A	Reading	W	2-1	0-1	10	Clarke [53], Ricketts [84]	20,495
46	May 8	H	Sheffield U	W	4-2	2-2	9	Lescott [12], Clarke [23], Cooper [50], Miller [60]	27,454

Final League Position: 9

GOALSCORERS

League (72): Miller 19 (2 pens), Cort 15 (1 pen), Clarke 7, Cooper 6 (3 pens), Olofinjana 5, Lescott 4, Seol 4, Cameron 3, Ince 3, Bischoff 1, Craddock 1, Naylor 1, Newton 1, Ricketts 1, Sturridge 1.
Carling Cup (5): Andrews 1, Clarke 1, Ince 1, Miller 1, Seol 1.
FA Cup (2): Cort 1, Seol 1.

Jones P 10	Clyde M 17 + 1	Naylor L 36 + 2	Olofinjana S 41 + 1	Craddock J 40 + 2	Bjorklund J 2 + 1	Newton S 21 + 3	Cameron C 24 + 13	Sturridge D 5 + 6	Miller K 41 + 3	Kennedy M 27 + 3	Cooper K 15 + 15	Edwards R 15 + 2	Clarke L 11 + 17	Ince P 25 + 3	Andrews K 14 + 6	Lescott J 41	Mulligan G — + 1	Cort C 34 + 3	Seol K 28 + 9	Lowe K 11	Oakes M 35	Bischoff M 9 + 2	Murray M 1	Ricketts R 3 + 4	*Match No.*
1	2	3^{1}	4	5	6^{2}	7	8	9^{3}	10	11	12	13	14												1
1	2	12	8	5	6^{1}	7	13		10	11^{2}	14	3^{3}	9	4											2
1	2	3^{2}	6	5		7	8^{1}		10		12	11	9	4	13										3
1	2		8	5		7	11		10^{1}			3	9	4		6	12								4
1	2	3	8	5		7	11^{1}		10		12		9	4		6									5
1	2^{1}	3^{3}	8	5		7	11^{2}	12	10		13		9	4	14	6									6
1	2	3^{3}	8^{1}	5		7	12	13	10		14			4		6		9	11^{2}						7
1	2	3	8	5		7			10		12			4		6		9	11^{1}						8
1	2	3	8	5		7		13^{3}	10^{2}		12■			4	14	6		9	11^{1}						9
1	6^{1}	3	8	5	12	7	13		10					4				9	11	2^{2}					10
	2	3^{2}	8^{3}	5		7	12		10				13	4	14	6		9	11^{1}		1				11
						7	12		10	3	11			4^{1}	8	6		9	13	2^{2}	1	5			12
			4	5		12	8		10	3	7		13					9^{2}	11^{1}	2	1	6			13
			4			12	8		10■	3	7					6		9	11^{1}	2	1	5			14
			4	14		7	8^{2}	12		3	11			13		6		9	10	2^{1}	1	5^{3}			15
			4			7	8^{1}	13	10	3	11^{2}			12		6		9		2	1	5			16
		3	4			7	8	12	10^{1}		11					6		9		2	1	5			17
		3	4	12		7^{2}	8		10^{3}		11		14			6		9	13	2	1	5^{1}			18
		3^{1}	4^{3}	5		7	8		10	12	11				14	6		9	13	2^{2}	1				19
	2		8	5			7^{2}	10^{1}	12	3	11				4	6		9	13		1				20
		12	8^{1}	5			7	10^{2}		3	11		13		4	6		9		2	1				21
	2		8	5			7	10^{2}	12	3	11^{1}		13		4^{3}	6		9	14		1				22
		3	8	5				10^{1}	12	11	7^{2}				4	6		9	13	2	1				23
		3^{2}	8^{3}	5		2	12		10	11	7^{1}		13		4	6		9	14		1				24
	12	3	8^{3}	5		2^{1}	13		10	11	7^{2}				4	6		9	14		1				25
		3^{1}		5		2	8^{2}		10	11	12		13		4	6		9	7		1				26
		3		5		2	8^{1}		10	11			12		4	6		9	7		1				27
	2	3	8	5			12		10^{2}	11^{1}			13	14	4^{3}	6		9	7		1				28
	2	3	8^{1}	5			12		10	11				4		6		9	7				1		29
	2	3	8^{2}	5					10^{1}	11			12	4	13	6		9	7		1				30
	2	3	8^{2}	5		12	13		10	11^{1}				4		6		9	7		1				31
		3	8^{1}	5			11		10		12	2	13		4	6		9	7^{2}		1				32
		3	12	5			8^{2}		10		13	2	9	4	7^{3}	6		14	11^{1}		1				33
		3		5			12		10	13	7^{3}	2	9	4	8^{2}	6		14	11^{1}		1				34
		3	8	5					10	11		2		4		6		9	7		1				35
		3	8	5					10^{1}	11	12		13	4	2	6		9	7^{2}		1				36
		3^{1}	8	5					10^{2}	11	12	2	13	4		6		9	7		1				37
		3	8	5					10^{1}	11		2		4		6		9	7		1			12	38
		3	8	5					10^{2}	11^{1}		2	12	4		6		9	7		1			13	39
		3	8	5			12		10	11^{1}		2		4		6		9	13		1			7^{2}	40
		3	8	5			12		10	11^{1}		2	13	4		6		9	7^{2}		1				41
		3	8	5			11		10			2	12	4		6		9^{1}	7		1				42
		3	8	5			11^{1}		10	12			9^{2}	4		6			7		1	2		13	43
		3^{2}	4	5			8		10	11	13	12	9			6			7^{3}		1	2^{1}		14	44
		3	4	5			7		10			2	9^{1}			6			11		1	12		8	45
		3	4^{1}	5			7^{2}		10		12	2^{3}	9			6		13	11		1	14		8	46

FA Cup

Third Round	Millwall	(h)	2-0
Fourth Round	Arsenal	(a)	0-2

Carling Cup

First Round	Rochdale	(a)	4-2
Second Round	Burnley	(a)	1-1

WREXHAM — FL Championship 2

FOUNDATION

The club was formed on 28 September 1872 by members of Wrexham Cricket Club, so they could continue playing a sport during the winter months. This meeting was held at the Turf Hotel, which although rebuilt since, still stands at one corner of the present ground. Their first game was a few weeks later and matches often included 17 players on either side! By 1875 team formations were reduced to 11 men and a year later the club was among the founder members of the Cambrian Football Association, which quickly changed its title to the Football Association of Wales.

Racecourse Ground, Mold Road, Wrexham LL11 2AH.

Telephone: (01978) 262 190.

Fax: (01978) 357 821.

Ticket Office: (01978) 262 190.

Website: www.wrexhamafc.co.uk

Email: geraint@wrexhamafc.co.uk

Ground Capacity: 15,500.

Record Attendance: 34,445 v Manchester U, FA Cup 4th rd, 26 January 1957.

Pitch Measurements: 111yd × 71yd.

Secretary: Geraint Parry.

Manager: Denis Smith.

Assistant Manager: Kevin Russell.

Physio: Mel Pejic BSc (Hons).

Colours: Red shirts, white shorts, red stockings.

Change Colours: All light blue.

Year Formed: 1872 (oldest club in Wales).

Turned Professional: 1912.

Ltd Co.: 1912.

Club Nickname: 'Red Dragons'.

Previous Grounds: 1872, Racecourse Ground; 1883, Rhosddu Recreation Ground; 1887, Racecourse Ground.

First Football League Game: 27 August 1921, Division 3 (N), v Hartlepools U (h) L 0–2 – Godding; Ellis, Simpson; Matthias, Foster, Griffiths; Burton, Goode, Cotton, Edwards, Lloyd.

Record League Victory: 10–1 v Hartlepool U, Division 4, 3 March 1962 – Keelan; Peter Jones, McGavan; Tecwyn Jones, Fox, Ken Barnes; Ron Barnes (3), Bennion (1), Davies (3), Ambler (3), Ron Roberts.

HONOURS

Football League: Division 3 – Champions 1977–78; Runners-up 1992–93; Promoted (3rd) 2002–03; Division 3 (N) – Runners-up 1932–33; Division 4 – Runners-up 1969–70.

FA Cup: best season: 6th rd, 1974, 1978, 1997.

Football League Cup: best season: 5th rd, 1961, 1978.

Welsh Cup: Winners 22 times (joint record); Runners-up 22 times (record).

FAW Premier Cup: Winners 1998, 2000, 2001, 2003.

LDV Vans Trophy: Winners 2005

European Competition: *European Cup-Winners' Cup:* 1972–73, 1975–76, 1978–79, 1979–80, 1984–85, 1986–87, 1990–91, 1995–96.

SKY SPORTS FACT FILE

While the ten-point deduction ultimately proved too great a handicap despite a gallant effort, the goalscoring of Juan Ugarte with a 5, 4 and hat-trick plus another treble on the way to winning the LDV Vans Trophy was an outstanding effort.

Record Cup Victory: 11–1 v New Brighton, Football League Northern Section Cup 1st rd, 3 January 1934 – Foster; Alfred Jones, Hamilton, Bulling, McMahon, Lawrence, Bryant (3), Findlay (1), Bamford (5), Snow, Waller (1), (o.g. 1).

Record Defeat: 0–9 v Brentford, Division 3, 15 October 1963.

Most League Points (2 for a win): 61, Division 4, 1969–70 and Division 3, 1977–78.

Most League Points (3 for a win): 84, Division 3, 2002–03.

Most League Goals: 106, Division 3 (N), 1932–33.

Highest League Scorer in Season: Tom Bamford, 44, Division 3 (N), 1933–34.

Most League Goals in Total Aggregate: Tom Bamford, 175, 1928–34.

Most League Goals in One Match: 5, Tom Bamford v Carlisle U, Division 3N, 17 March 1934; 5, Lee Jones v Cambridge U, Division 2, 6 April 2002; 5 Juan Ugarte v Hartlepool U, League Championship 1, 5 March 2005.

Most Capped Player: Joey Jones, 29 (72), Wales.

Most League Appearances: Arfon Griffiths, 592, 1959–61, 1962–79.

Youngest League Player: Ken Roberts, 15 years 158 days v Bradford PA, 1 September 1951.

Record Transfer Fee Received: £800,000 from Birmingham C for Bryan Hughes, March 1997.

Record Transfer Fee Paid: £210,000 to Liverpool for Joey Jones, October 1978.

Football League Record: 1921 Original Member of Division 3 (N); 1958–60 Division 3; 1960–62 Division 4; 1962–64 Division 3; 1964–70 Division 4; 1970–78 Division 3; 1978–82 Division 2; 1982–83 Division 3; 1983–92 Division 4; 1992–93 Division 3; 1993–2002 Division 2; 2002–03 Division 3; 2003–04 Division 2; 2004–05 FL1; 2005– FL2.

MANAGERS

Selection Committee 1872–1924
Charlie Hewitt 1924–25
Selection Committee 1925–29
Jack Baynes 1929–31
Ernest Blackburn 1932–37
James Logan 1937–38
Arthur Cowell 1938
Tom Morgan 1938–42
Tom Williams 1942–49
Les McDowell 1949–50
Peter Jackson 1950–55
Cliff Lloyd 1955–57
John Love 1957–59
Cliff Lloyd 1959–60
Billy Morris 1960–61
Ken Barnes 1961–65
Billy Morris 1965
Jack Rowley 1966–67
Alvan Williams 1967–68
John Neal 1968–77
Arfon Griffiths 1977–81
Mel Sutton 1981–82
Bobby Roberts 1982–85
Dixie McNeil 1985–89
Brian Flynn 1989–2001
Denis Smith October 2001–

LATEST SEQUENCES

Longest Sequence of League Wins: 8, 5.4.2003 – 3.5.2003.

Longest Sequence of League Defeats: 9, 2.10.1963 – 30.10.1963.

Longest Sequence of League Draws: 6, 12.11.1999 – 26.12.1999.

Longest Sequence of Unbeaten League Matches: 18, 8.3.2003 – 25.8.2003.

Longest Sequence Without a League Win: 16, 25.9.1999 – 3.1.2000.

Successive Scoring Runs: 25 from 5.5.1928.

Successive Non-scoring Runs: 6 from 12.9.1973.

TEN YEAR LEAGUE RECORD

		P	*W*	*D*	*L*	*F*	*A*	*Pts*	*Pos*
1995-96	Div 2	46	18	16	12	76	55	70	8
1996-97	Div 2	46	17	18	11	54	50	69	8
1997-98	Div 2	46	18	16	12	55	51	70	7
1998-99	Div 2	46	13	14	19	43	62	53	17
1999-2000	Div 2	46	17	11	18	52	61	62	11
2000-01	Div 2	46	17	12	17	65	71	63	10
2001-02	Div 2	46	11	10	25	56	89	43	23
2002-03	Div 3	46	23	15	8	84	50	84	3
2003-04	Div 2	46	17	9	20	50	60	60	13
2004-05	FL 1	46	13	14	19	62	80	43	22

10 points deducted for entering administration.

DID YOU KNOW?

Wrexham shared something with Manchester United in 1966–67 when they were the only two teams in the Football League to remain unbeaten at home. United finished First Division champions while Wrexham had to be content with seventh place after 20 draws!

WREXHAM 2004–05 LEAGUE RECORD

Match No.	Date	Venue	Opponents	Result		H/T Score	Lg. Pos.	Goalscorers	Atten-dance
1	Aug 7	H	Swindon T	W	2-1	1-0	—	Lawrence [24], Armstrong (pen) [73]	5099
2	10	A	Oldham Ath	W	3-2	2-0	—	Sam 3 [2, 24, 62]	6143
3	14	A	Brentford	L	0-1	0-0	5		5091
4	21	H	Port Vale	D	1-1	0-0	10	Holt [72]	5005
5	28	A	Bournemouth	L	0-1	0-1	13		5774
6	30	H	Barnsley	W	2-1	1-0	7	Armstrong [45], Roberts [61]	4223
7	Sept 11	H	Bradford C	W	1-0	1-0	7	Lawrence [2]	3712
8	18	A	Tranmere R	D	1-1	1-0	8	Armstrong [38]	9826
9	25	H	Sheffield W	L	0-3	0-1	12		5688
10	Oct 2	A	Doncaster R	D	0-0	0-0	13		7567
11	16	H	Walsall	D	1-1	1-0	14	Lawrence [16]	3803
12	19	A	Colchester U	W	2-1	0-0	—	Roberts [59], Llewellyn [90]	2866
13	26	H	Peterborough U	D	1-1	0-0	—	Lawrence [87]	3009
14	30	H	Hull C	D	2-2	2-1	14	Llewellyn [13], Ferguson [29]	5601
15	Nov 6	A	Luton T	L	1-5	0-4	16	Sam [73]	7144
16	9	A	Blackpool	L	1-2	1-0	—	Holt [23]	5054
17	20	H	Bristol C	L	1-3	0-2	17	Armstrong [77]	7833
18	23	A	Torquay U	L	0-1	0-1	—		2384
19	27	A	Huddersfield T	W	2-1	1-1	16	Holt [9], Armstrong (pen) [50]	11,127
20	Dec 7	H	Stockport Co	W	2-1	1-1	—	Holt [45], Sam [61]	3984
21	11	A	Milton Keynes D	L	0-3	0-1	23		3601
22	18	H	Hartlepool U	L	1-5	1-4	23	Ugarte [25]	3582
23	26	A	Bradford C	D	1-1	0-0	22	Armstrong (pen) [90]	10,268
24	28	H	Chesterfield	W	3-1	2-1	22	Roberts [14], Jones Mark [36], Llewellyn [61]	4273
25	Jan 1	H	Blackpool	L	1-2	1-0	23	Llewellyn [18]	5601
26	3	A	Sheffield W	L	0-4	0-0	23		24,253
27	11	A	Peterborough U	D	2-2	1-2	—	Ugarte 2 [45, 79]	3048
28	15	H	Tranmere R	L	1-5	0-2	23	Armstrong [67]	6221
29	22	A	Chesterfield	W	4-2	2-1	21	Ugarte 4 [44, 45, 59, 64]	3966
30	29	H	Doncaster R	D	0-0	0-0	21		6115
31	Feb 5	A	Walsall	D	2-2	2-2	22	Ferguson [12], Llewellyn [22]	5659
32	12	H	Torquay U	D	1-1	0-1	22	Ugarte [87]	3608
33	19	A	Hull C	L	1-2	0-1	22	Sam [75]	15,995
34	22	H	Colchester U	D	2-2	0-0	—	Jones Mark [50], Sam [80]	2391
35	26	H	Milton Keynes D	D	0-0	0-0	23		3406
36	Mar 5	A	Hartlepool U	W	6-4	3-2	22	Ugarte 5 (1 pen) [11, 21, 35 (p), 68, 89], Jones Mark [86]	4707
37	12	H	Oldham Ath	W	1-0	0-0	22	Sam [90]	4170
38	19	A	Swindon T	L	2-4	2-1	22	Ugarte [16], Sam [32]	5123
39	Apr 2	H	Bournemouth	L	1-2	0-0	22	Armstrong [69]	3801
40	5	A	Barnsley	D	2-2	0-1	—	Ferguson [58], Llewellyn [64]	7753
41	16	A	Bristol C	L	0-1	0-0	22		8267
42	23	H	Luton T	L	1-2	1-0	23	Holt [31]	6614
43	26	A	Port Vale	W	2-0	2-0	—	Holt [21], Llewellyn [42]	4151
44	30	A	Stockport Co	W	4-1	4-1	22	Ugarte 3 [5, 11, 29], Edwards C [14]	5480
45	May 3	H	Brentford	L	1-2	1-0	—	Hutchinson (og) [6]	4374
46	7	H	Huddersfield T	L	0-1	0-1	22		7151

Final League Position: 22

GOALSCORERS

League (62): Ugarte 17 (1 pen), Sam 9, Armstrong 8 (3 pens), Llewellyn 7, Holt 6, Lawrence 4, Ferguson 3, Jones Mark 3, Roberts 3, Edwards C 1, own goal 1.
Carling Cup (4): Ferguson 1, Llewellyn 1, Morgan 1, Sam 1.
FA Cup (4): Holt 1, Lawrence 1, Llewellyn 1, Sam 1.
LDV Vans Trophy (16): Ugarte 6, Llewellyn 3, Ferguson 2, Jones Mark 1, Lawrence 1, Pejic 1, Sam 1, Williams 1.

Dibble A 15	Smith A 17 + 7	Holt A 45	Lawrence D 44	Roberts S 34	Carey B 10	Whitley J 13 + 3	Ferguson D 40	Sam H 19 + 19	Llewellyn C 45	Williams D 21	Pejic S 30 + 5	Armstrong C 18 + 15	Bennett D 7 + 7	Spender S 9 + 4	Crowell M 22 + 6	Jones Mark 17 + 9	Baker M 11 + 2	Morgan C 18 + 8	Shaw M — + 1	Mackin L 5 + 5	Ugarte J 23 + 7	Green S 5 + 7	Valero V 3	Edwards C 18	Jones Michael — + 1	Foster B 17	*Match No.*
1	2	3	4	5	6[1]	7	8	9[2]	10	11	12	13															1
1	2	3	4	5	6[1]	7	8	9	10[2]	11	12	13															2
1	2	3	4	5	6	7[2]	8	9	10[1]	11		12	13														3
1	7	3	4	5	6		8	9	10[1]	11		12	2														4
1		3[1]	4	5	6		8[2]	9	11	7		10[3]	2	12	13	14											5
1		3	4[1]	5	6			9	11[2]	7	12	10	2	14	8[3]	13											6
1[G]		3	4	5[2]		12	8	10[1]	11	7	6	9	2				15	13									7
1[G]	12	3	4[2]		6	2	8	10	11[1]	7	5	9■					15	13									8
	11[1]	3		5	6	12	8[2]	9	10	7	4		2			13	1										9
	2	3	4	5	6	7	8	9[1]	10	11			12				1										10
	2	3	4	5	6[2]	7[3]	8	12	10	11	13	9[1]	14				1										11
	2	3	4	5			8	9[2]	10	11[1]	6		7		12		1		13								12
	2[2]	3	4	5			8	9[1]	10		6	12		7[3]	11	13	1	14									13
		3	4	5			8		10	11[1]	6	9		2	7	12	1										14
	2[2]	3	4	5			8	12	10[1]		6	9[3]		7	11		1			13	14						15
		3	4	5			8	10[1]	11		6	9[3]		2	7[2]	12	1			13	14						16
		3	4[1]	5			8	10[2]	11		6	9		2		7	1	12			13						17
		3	4	5[3]			8	12	11		6	9[1]		2	13	7[2]	1	14			10						18
		3[2]	4				8	12■	9		6	13		2	14	11	1	5			10[1]	7[3]					19
1		3	4	5			8	9	11		6	12		2	13						10[1]	7[2]					20
1	12	3	4	5				9[2]	11		6	13		2	14					8	10[1]	7[3]					21
1		3	4	5		7[3]	8[2]	9	11			12		14		13		6		2	10[1]						22
1	2	3	4	5		7	8	12	10[1]		6	9								11[2]	13						23
1	2	3	4	5		7	8		10		6	9[1]				11[2]				13	12						24
1	2[1]	3	4	5		7	8[3]	12	10		6	9[2]				11					13	14					25
1	2[1]	3	4	5■		7	8		10		6	9[2]				11[3]		12			13	14					26
		3	4			7[1]	8[2]	9	11		6			12	2			5			10	13	1				27
		3	4	5		7		12	11		6[2]	9			8			13			10[1]		1	2			28
		3	4	5		12			10	11[1]					7[2]	8		6			9	13	1[G]	2	15		29
		3	4	5			8	12	10	11		9[1]				7		6						2		1	30
		3	4	5			8	12	10				13		11	7[2]		6			9[1]			2		1	31
	3		4	5			8	12	10	11			13			7[1]		6			9			2[2]		1	32
	2	3	4				8	12			5	9	6[2]		7	11					10[1]	13				1	33
	3[2]	6	4				8	12	10[1]		5	9			7	11		13						2		1	34
		3	4	5[2]			8	12	10[1]		13				7[3]	11		6		14	9			2		1	35
		3	4	5			8	12	10[1]		6				7	11[2]					9	13		2		1	36
		3	4	5			8	12	10						7			6		11[2]	9[1]	13		2		1	37
		3	4					9	11		5	12			7			6		13	10[1]	8[2]		2		1	38
	12	3		5					10		6	13	14		11	8[1]		4			9	7[2]		2[3]		1	39
	12	3	4	5			8	13	10			14			7[1]			6		11[2]	9[3]			2		1	40
	12	3[1]	4				8	13	10		6	14			7[2]	11[3]		5			9			2		1	41
	12	3	4				8	13	10[2]	11	6	14				7[3]		5			9[1]			2		1	42
	12	3[1]	4				8		10	11	6				7			5			9			2		1	43
		3	4				8		10	11	6		12		7[1]			5			9			2		1	44
		3	4				8		10[2]	11	6	12			7[1]	13		5			9			2		1	45
		3	4				8	12	10[1]	11	6				7[2]	13		5			9			2		1	46

FA Cup

First Round	Hayes	(a)	4-0
Second Round	Scunthorpe U	(a)	0-2

Carling Cup

First Round	Hull C	(a)	2-2
Second Round	Sheffield U	(h)	2-3

LDV Vans Trophy

First Round	Notts Co	(a)	3-2
Second Round	Stockport Co	(h)	2-0
Quarter-Final	Chester C	(a)	1-0
Semi-Final	Hereford U	(a)	2-1
Northern Final	Oldham Ath	(a)	5-3
		(h)	1-0
Final (at Millennium Stadium)	Southend U		2-0

WYCOMBE WANDERERS FL Championship 2

FOUNDATION

In 1887 a group of young furniture trade workers called a meeting at the Steam Engine public house with the aim of forming a football club and entering junior football. It is thought that they were named after the famous FA Cup winners, The Wanderers who had visited the town in 1877 for a tie with the original High Wycombe club. It is also possible that they played informally before their formation, although there is no proof of this.

Causeway Stadium, Hillbottom Road, Sands, High Wycombe HP12 4HJ.

Telephone: (01494) 472 100.

Fax: (01494) 527 633.

Ticket Office: (01494) 441 118.

Website: www.wwfc.org

Email: wwfc@wycombewanderers.co.uk

Ground Capacity: 10,000.

Record Attendance: 9,650 v Wimbledon, FA Cup 5th rd, 17 February 2001.

Pitch Measurements: 115yd × 75yd.

Chairman: Ivor L. Beeks.

Vice-chairman: Brian Kane.

Chief Executive: John Harrison.

Secretary: Keith J. Allen.

Manager: John Gorman.

Assistant Manager: Steve Brown.

Physio: Shay Connolly.

Colours: Light blue and dark blue.

Change Colours: All white.

Year Formed: 1887.

Turned Professional: 1974.

Club Nicknames: 'Chairboys' (after High Wycombe's tradition of furniture making), 'The Blues'.

Previous Grounds: 1887, The Rye; 1893, Spring Meadow; 1895, Loakes Park; 1899, Daws Hill Park; 1901, Loakes Park; 1990, Adams Park.

First Football League Game: 14 August 1993, Division 3 v Carlisle U (a) D 2–2: Hyde; Cousins, Horton (Langford), Kerr, Crossley, Ryan, Carroll, Stapleton, Thompson, Scott, Guppy (1) (Hutchinson), (1 og).

HONOURS

Football League: Division 2 best season: 6th, 1994–95. Division 3 1993–94 (play-offs).

FA Amateur Cup: Winners 1931.

FA Trophy: Winners 1991, 1993.

GM Vauxhall Conference: Winners 1992–93.

FA Cup: semi-final 2001.

Football League Cup: never beyond 2nd rd.

SKY SPORTS FACT FILE

When Wycombe Wanderers won the Conference title in 1992–93 they were catapulted by a determined start to their programme. After a draw at Macclesfield Town they won the next nine matches to establish themselves and had 15 points to spare at the end.

Record League Victory: 5–0 v Burnley, Division 2, 15 April 1997 – Parkin; Cousins, Bell, Kavanagh, McCarthy, Forsyth, Carroll (2p) (Simpson), Scott (Farrell), Stallard (1), McGavin (1) (Read (1)), Brown.

Record Cup Victory: 5–0 v Hitchin T (a), FA Cup 2nd rd, 3 December 1994 – Hyde; Cousins, Brown, Crossley, Evans, Ryan (1), Carroll, Bell (1), Thompson, Garner (3) (Hemmings), Stapleton (Langford).

Record Defeat: 0–5 v Walsall, Auto Windscreens Shield 1st rd, 7 November 1995.

Most League Points (3 for a win): 78, Division 2, 1994–95.

Most League Goals: 67, Division 3, 1993–94.

Highest League Goalscorer in Season: Sean Devine, 23, 1999–2000.

Most League Goals in Total Aggregate: Dave Carroll, 41, 1993–2002.

Most League Goals in One Match: 3, Miguel Desouza v Bradford C, Division 2, 26 March 1996; 3, Mark Stallard v Walsall, Division 2, 21 October 1997; 3, Sean Devine v Reading, Division 2, 2 October 1999; 3, Sean Divine v Bury, Division 2, 26 February 2000.

Most Capped Player: Mark Rogers, 7, Canada.

Most League Appearances: Steve Brown, 371, 1994–2004.

Youngest League Player: Roger Johnson, 17 years 8 days v Cambridge U, 6 May 2000.

Record Transfer Fee Received: £295,000 from Swindon T for Keith Scott, November 1993.

Record Transfer Fee Paid: £200,000 to Barnet for Sean Devine, 15 April 1999.

Football League Record: Promoted to Division 3 from GM Vauxhall Conference in 1993; 1993–94 Division 3; 1994–2004 Division 2; 2004– FL2.

MANAGERS

First coach appointed 1951.
Prior to Brian Lee's appointment in 1969 the team was selected by a Match Committee which met every Monday evening.

James McCormack 1951–52
Sid Cann 1952–61
Graham Adams 1961–62
Don Welsh 1962–64
Barry Darvill 1964–68
Brian Lee 1969–76
Ted Powell 1976–77
John Reardon 1977–78
Andy Williams 1978–80
Mike Keen 1980–84
Paul Bence 1984–86
Alan Gane 1986–87
Peter Suddaby 1987–88
Jim Kelman 1988–90
Martin O'Neill 1990–95
Alan Smith 1995–96
John Gregory 1996–98
Neil Smillie 1998–99
Lawrie Sanchez 1999–2003
Tony Adams 2003–04
John Gorman November 2004–

LATEST SEQUENCES

Longest Sequence of League Wins: 4, 26.2.1994 – 19.3.1994.

Longest Sequence of League Defeats: 4, 2.1.1999 – 30.1.1999.

Longest Sequence of League Draws: 5, 24.1.2004 – 21.2.2004

Longest Sequence of Unbeaten League Matches: 14, 29.8.1995 – 18.11.1995.

Longest Sequence Without a League Win: 13, 16.8.2003 – 18.10.2003 and 10.1.2004 – 20.3.2004.

Successive Scoring Runs: 15 from 28.12.2004.

Successive Non-scoring Runs: 5 from 15.10.1996

TEN YEAR LEAGUE RECORD

		P	*W*	*D*	*L*	*F*	*A*	*Pts*	*Pos*
1995-96	Div 2	46	15	15	16	63	59	60	12
1996-97	Div 2	46	15	10	21	51	56	55	18
1997-98	Div 2	46	14	18	14	51	53	60	14
1998-99	Div 2	46	13	12	21	52	58	51	19
1999-2000	Div 2	46	16	13	17	56	53	61	12
2000-01	Div 2	46	15	14	17	46	53	59	13
2001-02	Div 2	46	17	13	16	58	64	64	11
2002-03	Div 2	46	13	13	20	59	66	52	18
2003-04	Div 2	46	6	19	21	50	75	37	24
2004-05	FL 2	46	17	14	15	58	52	65	10

DID YOU KNOW ?

For their FA Amateur Cup quarter-final against St Albans City on 25 February 1950 a then record crowd of 15,850 were attracted to Loakes Park. Polish centre-forward Henrik Mikrut was outstanding, scoring twice and making another goal in a 4–1 win.

WYCOMBE WANDERERS 2004–05 LEAGUE RECORD

Match No.	*Date*	*Venue*	*Opponents*	*Result*		*H/T Score*	*Lg. Pos.*	*Goalscorers*	*Attendance*
1	Aug 7	H	Cambridge U	W	2-1	0-0	—	Tyson 2 [55, 81]	4726
2	10	A	Chester C	W	2-0	1-0	—	Williamson [23], Senda [84]	2881
3	14	A	Northampton T	D	1-1	1-0	4	Stonebridge [42]	6049
4	21	H	Rochdale	L	0-3	0-0	7		4440
5	28	A	Kidderminster H	W	2-0	1-0	5	Tyson [21], Ahmed [90]	2444
6	30	H	Grimsby T	W	2-0	1-0	3	Birchall 2 [43, 51]	4320
7	Sept 3	H	Oxford U	D	1-1	1-1	—	Tyson (pen) [45]	6348
8	11	A	Southend U	W	2-1	0-1	1	Tyson [60], Senda [82]	4771
9	18	H	Swansea C	L	0-1	0-1	3		5247
10	25	A	Cheltenham T	D	1-1	0-1	4	Ryan [74]	3663
11	Oct 2	H	Shrewsbury T	D	1-1	0-1	5	Senda [74]	4634
12	8	A	Scunthorpe U	L	0-2	0-2	—		4373
13	16	A	Boston U	L	0-2	0-1	11		2635
14	19	H	Rushden & D	D	1-1	1-1	—	Birchall [14]	3844
15	23	H	Mansfield T	D	1-1	0-0	12	Birchall [60]	4215
16	30	A	Darlington	L	0-1	0-1	16		4292
17	Nov 6	H	Yeovil T	L	0-1	0-0	17		5453
18	20	A	Leyton Orient	W	2-1	0-1	15	Tyson [49], Johnson [67]	4047
19	27	H	Bristol R	W	1-0	0-0	12	Tyson (pen) [54]	4999
20	Dec 7	A	Bury	D	2-2	0-1	—	Tyson 2 [61, 79]	1866
21	11	A	Notts Co	W	1-0	1-0	10	Stonebridge [42]	6529
22	18	H	Lincoln C	W	1-0	0-0	6	Ryan [89]	4277
23	26	H	Southend U	L	0-1	0-1	8		5669
24	28	A	Macclesfield T	L	1-2	0-1	9	Johnson [89]	1908
25	Jan 1	A	Oxford U	L	1-2	0-1	12	Senda (pen) [90]	7195
26	3	H	Cheltenham T	D	1-1	0-1	13	Tyson [70]	4394
27	15	A	Swansea C	D	2-2	0-0	16	Johnson [77], Guppy [83]	6793
28	22	H	Macclesfield T	D	1-1	0-1	16	Johnson [55]	4105
29	29	A	Shrewsbury T	W	1-0	1-0	13	Tyson (pen) [29]	3884
30	Feb 5	H	Boston U	L	1-2	1-1	16	Dixon (pen) [39]	4091
31	12	A	Rushden & D	W	2-1	0-0	14	Bloomfield [74], Tyson [90]	3490
32	15	H	Scunthorpe U	W	2-1	2-0	—	Claridge [13], Tyson [43]	4089
33	19	H	Darlington	D	1-1	1-1	10	Claridge [36]	4326
34	22	A	Mansfield T	W	4-1	0-0	—	Claridge 2 (1 pen) [59 (p), 90], Stonebridge [62], Uhlenbeek [87]	2497
35	26	H	Notts Co	L	1-2	1-1	10	Stonebridge [14]	4199
36	Mar 5	A	Lincoln C	W	3-2	3-0	9	Tyson 3 [12, 30, 40]	4250
37	12	H	Chester C	W	4-2	1-1	8	Tyson 2 [43, 52], Uhlenbeek [57], Johnson [59]	8124
38	19	A	Cambridge U	L	1-2	1-2	9	Uhlenbeek [18]	4649
39	25	H	Northampton T	L	0-1	0-1	—		7417
40	28	A	Rochdale	D	1-1	0-1	9	Tyson [47]	2707
41	Apr 2	H	Kidderminster H	W	3-0	2-0	9	Tyson 3 [25, 36, 67]	4608
42	9	A	Grimsby T	D	0-0	0-0	9		3452
43	16	H	Bury	L	1-2	1-1	9	Johnson [10]	4703
44	23	A	Yeovil T	D	1-1	1-1	9	Easton [23]	7421
45	30	H	Leyton Orient	W	3-2	3-0	9	Bloomfield [2], Williamson [23], Uhlenbeek [30]	5333
46	May 7	A	Bristol R	L	0-1	0-1	10		7358

Final League Position: 10

GOALSCORERS

League (58): Tyson 22 (3 pens), Johnson 6, Birchall 4, Claridge 4 (1 pen), Senda 4 (1 pen), Stonebridge 4, Uhlenbeek 4, Bloomfield 2, Ryan 2, Williamson 2, Ahmed 1, Dixon 1 (pen), Easton 1, Guppy 1.
Carling Cup (0).
FA Cup (1): Johnson 1.
LDV Vans Trophy (2): Birchall 1, Dixon 1.

Talia F 45	Uhlenbeek G 36 + 6	Silk G 19 + 3	Johnson R 40 + 2	Nethercott S 27 + 2	Williamson M 32 + 5	Easton C 29 + 4	Burnell J 23 + 1	Stonebridge I 31 + 7	Tyson N 40 + 2	Ryan K 35 + 3	Martin R 1 + 6	Ahmed S — + 4	Senda D 42 + 2	Birchall A 11 + 1	Savage B 2 + 2	Comyn-Platt C 3 + 1	Abbey Z 3 + 2	Dixon J 4 + 12	Anya I — + 3	Bloomfield M 20 + 6	Craig T 14	Williams S — + 1	Guppy S 12 + 2	Cooke S 4 + 2	Faulconbridge C 6 + 2	Broughton D 2 + 1	Claridge S 14 + 5	Perpetuini D 1 + 1	Lee R 6 + 1	Philo M 2 + 3	Caceres A 1 + 2	Cronin L 1	*Match No.*
1	2	3	4	5	6	7	8[1]	9	10[2]	11[3]	12	13	14																				1
1	2[1]	3	4	5	6	7	8	9	10	11			12																				2
1	12	3	4	5[1]	6	7	8	9	10[3]	11[2]	13	14	2																				3
1	12	3	4	5	6	7[2]	8[3]	9	10	11[1]	13		2	14																			4
1	2	3		5	6	7		9	10	11		12	4	8[1]																			5
1	2	3		5	6	7		9	10[1]	11		12	4	8																			6
1	2	3■	12	5	6	7		9	10	11[1]			4		8																		7
1	2		4[1]	5	6	7		9	10	11			3	8	12																		8
1	12	3	4	5		7		13	10	11			2	8	9[2]	6[1]																	9
1	2	3	4	5		7		9	10	11			6	8[1]	12																		10
1	2[1]	3	12	5		7		9	10	11			4	8		6																	11
1	2	3	4	5		7		9	10[1]	11[3]			8			6[2]	13	12	14														12
1	2[1]	3	4		6	12	8	9	10	13			5				11			7[2]													13
1		3	4		6	7[1]	8		10				5	11		12	9			2													14
1		3		5	6		4	9	10				2	8						11	7												15
1	2			5	6		4	9[3]	10[1]	11[2]			7	8			13	14		12	3												16
1[6]		3	4		6			9	12	13	7		5	8			10[1]			11[2]	2	15											17
1	2	3	4		6			9	10	11[1]			7	8						12	5												18
1	2	3	4		6			9	10	8[2]	13		7							12	5		11[1]										19
1	2	12	4	5[1]	6			13	10	8			7								3		11[2]		9								20
1		3	4		6			7	10[2]	5			8							12	2		13	11[1]	9								21
1	2		4		6			9[2]		5			8							12	3		11	7[1]	10	13							22
1	2		4		6	12		9	10	11			5								3			7[1]	8								23
1	2		4		6	12		13	10[1]	11			5								3			7[2]	8	9							24
1	2	3[3]	4		6			8[2]	10[1]	11			5								7		14	13	12	9							25
1	2[2]		4	5	12				10	6			7							8[1]	3		11	13	9								26
1	12		4	5[1]	6	13	8[2]		10	7			2								3		11				9						27
1	12		4	5[1]	6		8[2]		10	7			2								3		11		13		9						28
1	2		4		6	7	8		10[1]	3			5					12					11				9						29
1	2	12	4		6	3	8[1]	13	10	5								7[3]	14				11[2]				9						30
1	2[2]		4	5		7		12	10	6			8					14		13			11[3]				9	3[1]					31
1	3		4■	5	12	6		11	10[2]	7			2					13		8							9[1]						32
1	3[2]		4	5	12	6		10		7			2					13		8[1]			11[3]				9	14					33
1	2	12	4	5		6		10		7			3							8			11[1]				9						34
1	2[3]		4	5		6	12	10	13	3			7					14		8[1]			11[2]				9						35
1	2		4	5		6	8	9	10	11			3							7[1]							12						36
1	2		4	5	12	3	7[3]	9	10	11[1]			6					13		8[2]							14						37
1	2[1]		4	5		3	7	9	10	11[2]			6					12		8[3]							13		14				38
1	2		4	5[1]	12	3	8	9[2]	10				6							7[3]							13		11	14			39
1	12		4	13	5[2]	3	7		10				2					11[1]		8							9		6				40
1	3		4		5	6[1]	7[2]	12	10				2					13		8							9[3]		11		14		41
1	3[1]		4		5		7	9[2]	10				2					12		8							11		6	13			42
1	3		4		5		7	9	10	12			2							8[1]							11		6				43
1	2		4		5	3[1]	7	12	10	11[3]								13		8							9		6[2]	14			44
1	2		4		5	6	7[2]		10[3]		12		3					9[1]		8							13			11	14		45
	3[1]		4	12	5	6	7				13		2					9	14	8[3]										11[2]	10	1	46

FA Cup

First Round	Coalville T	(h)	1-0
Second Round	Luton T	(h)	0-3

Carling Cup

First Round	Bristol C	(h)	0-1

LDV Vans Trophy

First Round	Aldershot T	(a)	1-0
Second Round	Swansea C	(h)	1-0
Quarter-Final	Bristol R	(a)	0-1

YEOVIL TOWN — FL Championship 1

FOUNDATION

One of the prime movers of Yeovil football was Ernest J. Sercombe. His association with the club began in 1895 as a playing member of Yeovil Casuals, of which team he became vice-captain and in his last season 1899–1900, he was chosen to play for Somerset against Devon. Upon the reorganisation of the club, he became secretary of the old Yeovil Town FC and with the amalgamation with Petters United in 1914, he continued to serve until his resignation in 1930.

Huish Park, Lufton Way, Yeovil, Somerset BA22 8YF.

Telephone: (01935) 423 662.

Fax: (01935) 473 956.

Ticket Office: (01935) 847 888.

Website: www.ytfc.net

Email: jcotton@ytfc.co.uk

Ground Capacity: 9,634.

Record Attendance: 8,612 v Arsenal, F.A. Cup 3rd rd, 2 January 1993 (16,318 v Sunderland at Huish).

Chairman/Chief Executive: John R. Fry.

Secretary: Jean Cotton

Manager: Gary Johnson.

Assistant Manager: Steve Thompson.

Physio: Glen Schmidt.

Colours: Green and white shirts, white or green shorts, white or green stockings.

Change Colours: Red and black shirts, black shorts, black or red stockings.

Year formed: 1895.

Turned Professional: 1921.

HONOURS

FL Championship 2 winners 2004–05.

Conference: Champions 2002–03.

FA Cup: 5th rd 1949.

League Cup: 1st rd 2004.

Southern League: Champions 1954–55, 1963–64, 1970–71; Runners-up: 1923–24, 1931–32, 1934–35, 1969–70, 1972–73.

Southern League Cup: Winners 1948–49, 1954–55, 1960–61, 1965–66; Runners-up: 1946–47, 1955–56.

Isthmian League: Winners 1987–88; Runners-up: 1985–86, 1986–87, 1996–97.

AC Delco Cup: Winners 1987–88.

Bob Lord Trophy: Winners 1989–90.

FA Trophy: Winners 2002.

London Combination: Runners-up 1930–31, 1932–33.

SKY SPORTS FACT FILE

Rarely have two brothers won championship medals with different clubs in the same season. But when Paul Terry accepted his winners' medal for Yeovil Town in 2004–05 he emulated the achievement of brother John who lifted the Premier League title for runaway winners Chelsea.

MANAGERS

(since 1990)
Clive Whitehead
Steve Rutter
Brian Hall
Graham Roberts
Colin Lippiatt
Steve Thompson
Dave Webb
Gary Johnson June 2001–

Ltd Co.: 1923.

Club Nickname: "Glovers".

Previous names: 1895, Yeovil; 1907, Yeovil Town; 1914, Yeovil & Petters United; 1946, Yeovil Town.

Previous grounds: 1895–1921, Pen Mill Ground; 1921–1990, Huish; 1990, Huish Park.

First Football League Game: 9 August 2003, Division 3 v Rochdale (h) W 3-1: Weale; Williams (Lindegaard), Crittenden, Lockwood, O'Brien, Pluck (Rodrigues), Gosling (El Kholti), Way, Jackson, Gall (2), Johnson (1).

Record League Victory: 10–0 v Kidderminster H, Southern League, 27 December 1955. 10–0 v Bedford T, Southern League, 4 March 1961.

Record Cup Victory: 12–1 v Westbury United, FA Cup 1st qual rd, 1923–24.

Record Defeat: 0–8 v Manchester United, FA Cup 5th rd, 12 February 1949.

Most League Goals: 90, FL Championship 2, 2004–05.

Highest League Goalscorer in Season: Phil Jevons, 27, 2004–05

Most League Goals in Total Aggregate: Phil Jevons, 27, 2004–05

Most Capped Player: None.

Most League Appearances: Lee Johnson, 89, 2003–05

Record Transfer Fee Received: Undisclosed from West Ham U for Gavin Williams, December 2004.

Record Transfer Fee Paid: Undisclosed to Hereford U for Michael McIndoe, December 2001.

Football League Record: 2003 Promoted to Division 3 from Conference; 2003–04 Division 3; 2004–05 FL2; 2005– FL1.

LATEST SEQUENCES

Longest Sequence of League Wins: 7, 7.12.2004 – 15.1.2005.

Longest Sequence of Unbeaten League Matches: 7, 7.12.2004 – 15.1.2005.

Longest Sequence Without a League Win: 5, 16.3.2004 – 17.4.2004.

Successive Scoring Runs: 22 from 30.10.2004.

TEN YEAR LEAGUE RECORD

		P	*W*	*D*	*L*	*F*	*A*	*Pts*	*Pos*
1995–96	Isth.	42	23	11	8	83	51	80	4
1996–97	Isth.	42	31	8	3	83	34	101	1
1997–98	Conf.	42	17	8	17	73	63	59	11
1998–99	Conf.	42	20	11	11	68	54	71	5
1999–2000	Conf.	42	18	10	14	60	63	64	7
2000–01	Conf.	42	24	8	10	73	50	80	2
2001–02	Conf.	42	19	13	10	66	53	70	3
2002–03	Conf.	42	28	11	3	100	37	95	1
2003-04	Div 3	46	23	5	18	70	57	74	8
2004-05	FL 2	46	25	8	13	90	65	83	1

DID YOU KNOW ?

One of the earliest sponsorships must have concerned Yeovil Town during their FA Cup run in 1948–49 when the official club programme prominently displayed above the players names "Equipped by Templemans", a local footwear company.

YEOVIL TOWN 2004–05 LEAGUE RECORD

Match No.	Date	Venue	Opponents	Result	H/T Score	Lg. Pos.	Goalscorers	Atten-dance
1	Aug 7	A	Bury	L 1-3	1-0	—	Caceres [39]	3171
2	10	H	Darlington	D 1-1	1-0	—	Jevons [6]	5116
3	14	H	Boston U	W 2-0	0-0	9	Jevons [49], Tarachulski [65]	5178
4	21	A	Notts Co	W 2-1	0-0	5	Terry [68], Jevons [81]	5024
5	28	H	Rushden & D	W 3-1	3-0	4	Johnson [18], Tarachulski [44], Jevons [45]	5088
6	30	A	Mansfield T	L 1-4	1-1	8	Skiverton [24]	3826
7	Sept 4	H	Swansea C	W 1-0	0-0	4	Williams (pen) [85]	5826
8	11	A	Cheltenham T	D 1-1	1-1	6	Way [29]	3966
9	18	H	Oxford U	W 6-1	1-0	2	Stolcers 2 [38, 49], Jevons 3 [59, 69, 79], Gall [75]	5467
10	25	A	Shrewsbury T	W 2-1	0-1	1	Johnson [69], Tarachulski [72]	4196
11	Oct 2	H	Northampton T	D 1-1	1-0	1	Jevons [14]	5944
12	8	A	Rochdale	L 1-2	0-0	—	Jevons [48]	2402
13	16	H	Macclesfield T	L 1-2	0-1	5	Way [51]	5313
14	19	A	Bristol R	D 2-2	1-0	—	Terry [27], Williams [57]	9295
15	23	A	Scunthorpe U	L 0-1	0-0	8		4470
16	30	H	Chester C	W 4-1	1-0	4	Jevons 3 (2 pens) [25 (p), 66 (p), 90], Caceres [56]	5741
17	Nov 6	A	Wycombe W	W 1-0	0-0	3	Tarachulski [84]	5453
18	20	H	Southend U	W 3-1	1-0	3	Jevons [43], Guyett [83], Tarachulski [85]	5839
19	27	A	Lincoln C	L 1-3	0-2	3	Skiverton [81]	4714
20	Dec 7	H	Kidderminster H	W 2-1	1-1	—	Lindegaard [38], Stolcers [83]	4639
21	11	H	Grimsby T	W 2-1	1-0	2	Johnson [43], Tarachulski [47]	5733
22	18	A	Leyton Orient	W 3-2	2-0	2	Tarachulski [26], Terry [45], Davies [77]	3867
23	26	H	Cheltenham T	W 4-1	2-1	2	Gall [30], Jevons [44], Davies [80], Terry [86]	7320
24	28	A	Cambridge U	W 5-3	0-1	2	Jevons 2 (2 pens) [55, 81], Way [56], Johnson [69], Stolcers [90]	3828
25	Jan 1	A	Swansea C	W 2-0	0-0	2	Stolcers [78], Jevons [90]	11,225
26	3	H	Shrewsbury T	W 4-2	1-0	1	Way [34], Terry [78], Caceres [84], Gall [89]	7250
27	15	A	Oxford U	L 1-2	0-1	1	Guyett [82]	6778
28	22	H	Cambridge U	W 2-1	0-0	1	Terry [46], Jevons (pen) [86]	6204
29	25	H	Rochdale	D 2-2	0-1	—	Tarachulski [54], Johnson (pen) [85]	5180
30	Feb 5	A	Macclesfield T	L 1-3	0-1	1	Whittaker (og) [90]	2471
31	12	H	Bristol R	W 4-2	1-1	1	Jevons 3 (1 pen) [26, 53 (p), 64], Tarachulski [72]	9153
32	19	A	Chester C	W 2-0	2-0	1	Davies [12], Jevons (pen) [32]	3072
33	22	H	Scunthorpe U	W 4-3	1-2	—	Tarachulski [16], Johnson [47], Fallon [82], Davies [86]	7598
34	26	A	Grimsby T	L 1-2	1-0	1	Davies [11]	4414
35	Mar 1	A	Northampton T	D 1-1	1-0	—	Davies [31]	5630
36	5	H	Leyton Orient	W 1-0	1-0	1	Jevons (pen) [9]	6545
37	12	A	Darlington	L 1-2	0-1	1	Way [81]	4121
38	19	H	Bury	L 0-1	0-1	1		6269
39	26	A	Boston U	W 2-1	1-1	1	Skiverton 2 [10, 82]	3069
40	29	H	Notts Co	L 1-3	0-2	—	Jevons (pen) [86]	7221
41	Apr 2	A	Rushden & D	L 0-2	0-0	2		3726
42	9	H	Mansfield T	W 5-2	1-1	1	Davies [5], Way 2 [53, 81], Rose [71], Jevons [72]	6471
43	16	A	Kidderminster H	D 1-1	0-0	1	Davies [61]	4014
44	23	H	Wycombe W	D 1-1	1-1	1	Johnson [25]	7421
45	30	A	Southend U	W 1-0	0-0	1	Jevons [83]	11,735
46	May 7	H	Lincoln C	W 3-0	1-0	1	Sodje 2 [45, 78], Jevons (pen) [54]	8855

Final League Position: 1

GOALSCORERS

League (90): Jevons 27 (10 pens), Tarachulski 10, Davies 8, Johnson 7 (1 pen), Way 7, Terry 6, Stolcers 5, Skiverton 4, Caceres 3, Gall 3, Guyett 2, Sodje 2, Williams 2 (1 pen), Fallon 1, Lindegaard 1, Rose 1, own goal 1.
Carling Cup (3): Johnson 3.
FA Cup (12): Jevons 2 (2 pens), Tarachulski 2, Way 2, Davies 1, Johnson 1, Miles 1, Odubade 1, Stolcers 1, Terry 1.
LDV Vans Trophy (3): Caceres 1, Stolcers 1, Tarachulski 1.

Collis S 9	Rose M 37 + 3	O'Brien R 10 + 4	Way D 45	Skiverton T 36 + 2	Miles C 20 + 1	Caceres A 7 + 14	Johnson L 44	Gall K 30 + 13	Tarachulski B 27 + 15	Williams G 12 + 1	Weatherstone S — + 6	Mirza N — + 3	Jevons P 45 + 1	Lindegaard A 19 + 10	Weale C 37 + 1	Fontaine L 15	Terry P 35 + 4	Ibe K — + 3	Lockwood A 6 + 4	Stolcers A 23 + 13	Guyett S 13 + 5	Odubade Y — + 4	Reed S 1 + 2	Davies A 15 + 8	Amankwaah K 10 + 5	Fallon R 2 + 4	Woozley D — + 1	Richardson M 2 + 2	Brown M — + 2	Sodje E 6	*Match No.*
1	2	3	4^1	5	6	7	8^2	9	10^3	11	12	13	14																		1
1	2^1	12	4	5	6^2	7^3	8	14	10	11	13		9	3																	2
	2		4	5		7^1	8	11^2	10		12		9^3	3	1	6	13	14													3
	2		4	5		7^2	8	11	10		14		9^3	3^1	1	6	12		13												4
	2	12	4	5		13	8	11	10^3				9^2		1	6	7	14	3^1												5
	2	3	4	5	14	12	8	11	10^2		13		9		1	6^1	7^3														6
	2	3	4	5			8	11^2	10^3	13	12		9		1	6	7^1			14											7
	2	3	4	5		12	8		13	11			9		1	6^1	7			10^2											8
	2	3	4	5		7^3	8	12	13			14	9		1	6	11^1			10^2											9
	2	3	4		5^1		8	12	13	11		14	9^2		1	6	7			10^3											10
	2	3	4			12	8	11^3	13	7^1			9^2	14	1	6	5			10											11
	2	3	4	12	5^1		8	11^2	14				9	13	1	6^3	7			10											12
	2	12	4	5^1		13	8	11^2	14	7			9		1	6	3			10^3											13
	2^1	3	4		5	12	8	13	14	11			9		1	6	7^2			10^3											14
	2		4		5^3	12	8		13	11			9	3	1	6	7^2			10^1	14										15
	2		4		5^3	7^2	8	12		11			9	13	1	6	3			10^1	14										16
	2	12	4			7^2	8	13	14	11			9		1	6^1	5			10^3	3										17
	2		4		5		8	12	7	11			9	13	1		3^1			10^2	6										18
	2		4	12	5^1	13	8		10^2	11■			9		1		3			7	6										19
	2^3		4	5	6^1	12	8	7	10				9	11^2	1				13	14	3										20
	2		4	5	6		8	7	10^3				9		1				12	11^2	3^1	14	13								21
	2^2		4	5	6		8	7	10				9^1		1		3			11	12			13							22
	2		4	5	6		8	7	10^2				9^3	12	1		3			11^1	13			14							23
	2		4	5	6		8	7^3	10^1				9^2	12	1		3			11	13			14							24
	2^2		4	5		12	8^1	7^3	10				9	13	1		3			11	6			14							25
			4	5	6■	12		7	10^1				9^3	2	1		3			11	8^2		13	14							26
		3^2	4	5		12		7	10				9^1	2	1		8			11	6			13							27
			4	5		12	8	7^2	10^3				9		1		2			11^1	6	14	3	13							28
			4	5	3^1		8	7	10^3				9^2	12	1		2			11	6	14		13							29
	12		4	5		13	8	7^1					9	3^3	1					11^2	6	14		10	2						30
	3		4	5	6		8	7^1	10^2				9	2^3	1			13		12				11	14						31
	3		4^2		6^3		8	7	10				9^1	2	1		12			13	5			11	14						32
	3		4	5			8	7^1	10^3				9	2	1					12^2	6			11	13	14					33
	3^2		4	5			8	7^3	10^1				9	2	1		12			13				11	6	14					34
	3		4	5			8	12	13				9^1	2	1		7							11	6	10^2					35
	3		4	5			8	12	10^2				9	2^1	1		7							11	6	13					36
	3^1		4	5			8	12	13				9^3	2	1		7			14				11	6	10^2					37
1	3		4	5			8	12	10				9	2^2			7		13					11^3	6^1	14					38
	3^2		4	5			8	7	12				9		1		11		2	13					6^3		14	10^1			39
	12		4	5			8	7^1	10^2				9	3	1		2^3		6	11								13	14		40
1			4	5			8	13	12^2				9^3	3			7		2	14				11				10^1		6	41
1	3		4	5			8	7^1					9^2				11		2^3	12				10	14				13	6	42
1	3		4	5			8	7^2	12				9^1				11		2^3	13				10	14					6	43
1	3^1		4	5			8	7^3	12				9^2	14			11			13				10	2					6	44
1				5	6^1		8	12	10^2				9	3			7			14				11	2			13^3		4	45
1^6	12		4	5	3^1		8	7^2					9	13	15		11							10	2					6	46

FA Cup

First Round	Darlington	(a)	3-3
		(h)	1-0
Second Round	Histon	(a)	3-1
Third Round	Rotherham U	(a)	3-0
Fourth Round	Charlton Ath	(a)	2-3

Carling Cup

First Round	Plymouth Arg	(h)	3-2
Second Round	Bolton W	(h)	0-2

LDV Vans Trophy

First Round	Torquay U	(a)	3-4

ENGLISH LEAGUE PLAYERS DIRECTORY

Players listed represent those with their clubs during the 2004–05 season.

Players are listed alphabetically on pages 566–572.
The number alongside each player corresponds to the team number heading. (Aaritalo, Mika 2 = team 2 (Aston Villa))

ARSENAL (1)

ALIADIERE, Jeremie (F) 18 1
H: 6 0 W: 11 00 b.Rambouillet 30-3-83
Source: Scholarship. *Honours:* France Under-21.

1999–2000	Arsenal	0	0		
2000–01	Arsenal	0	0		
2001–02	Arsenal	1	0		
2002–03	Arsenal	3	1		
2003–04	Arsenal	10	0		
2004–05	Arsenal	4	0	**18**	**1**

ALMUNIA, Manuel (G) 143 0
H: 6 3 W: 13 00 b.Pamplona 19-5-77

1997–98	Osasuna B	31	0		
1998–99	Osasuna B	13	0	**44**	**0**
1999–2000	Cartagonova	3	0	**3**	**0**
2000–01	Sabadell	25	0	**25**	**0**
2001–02	Celta Vigo	0	0		
2001–02	*Eibar*	35	0	**35**	**0**
2002–03	*Recreativo*	2	0	**2**	**0**
2003–04	Albacete	24	0	**24**	**0**
2004–05	Arsenal	10	0	**10**	**0**

BENTLEY, David (F) 27 2
H: 5 10 W: 11 03 b.Peterborough 27-8-84
Source: Scholar. *Honours:* England Youth, Under-20, Under-21.

2001–02	Arsenal	0	0		
2002–03	Arsenal	0	0		
2003–04	Arsenal	1	0		
2004–05	Arsenal	0	0	**1**	**0**
2004–05	*Norwich C*	26	2	**26**	**2**

BERGKAMP, Dennis (F) 528 199
H: 6 0 W: 12 10 b.Amsterdam 18-5-69
Honours: Holland 79 full caps, 36 goals.

1986–87	Ajax	14	2		
1987–88	Ajax	25	5		
1988–89	Ajax	30	13		
1989–90	Ajax	25	8		
1990–91	Ajax	33	25		
1991–92	Ajax	30	24		
1992–93	Ajax	28	26	**185**	**103**
1993–94	Internazionale	31	8		
1994–95	Internazionale	21	3	**52**	**11**
1995–96	Arsenal	33	11		
1996–97	Arsenal	29	12		
1997–98	Arsenal	28	16		
1998–99	Arsenal	29	12		
1999–2000	Arsenal	28	6		
2000–01	Arsenal	25	3		
2001–02	Arsenal	33	9		
2002–03	Arsenal	29	4		
2003–04	Arsenal	28	4		
2004–05	Arsenal	29	8	**291**	**85**

BIRCHALL, Adam (F) 12 4
H: 5 7 W: 11 08 b.Maidstone 2-12-84
Source: Trainee. *Honours:* Wales Under-21.

2002–03	Arsenal	0	0		
2003–04	Arsenal	0	0		
2004–05	Arsenal	0	0		
2004–05	*Wycombe W*	12	4	**12**	**4**

CAMPBELL, Sol (D) 370 16
H: 6 2 W: 15 07 b.Newham 18-9-74
Source: Trainee. *Honours:* England Youth, Under-21, B, 65 full caps, 1 goal.

1992–93	Tottenham H	1	1		
1993–94	Tottenham H	34	0		
1994–95	Tottenham H	30	0		
1995–96	Tottenham H	31	1		
1996–97	Tottenham H	38	0		
1997–98	Tottenham H	34	0		
1998–99	Tottenham H	37	6		
1999–2000	Tottenham H	29	0		
2000–01	Tottenham H	21	2	**255**	**10**
2001–02	Arsenal	31	2		
2002–03	Arsenal	33	2		
2003–04	Arsenal	35	1		
2004–05	Arsenal	16	1	**115**	**6**

CLICHY, Gael (D) 27 0
H: 5 9 W: 10 04 b.Toulouse 26-7-85
Source: Cannes. *Honours:* France Under-21.

2003–04	Arsenal	12	0		
2004–05	Arsenal	15	0	**27**	**0**

COLE, Ashley (D) 159 9
H: 5 8 W: 10 05 b.Stepney 20-12-80
Source: Trainee. *Honours:* England Youth, Under-21, 41 full caps.

1998–99	Arsenal	0	0		
1999–2000	Arsenal	1	0		
1999–2000	*Crystal Palace*	14	1	**14**	**1**
2000–01	Arsenal	17	3		
2001–02	Arsenal	29	2		
2002–03	Arsenal	31	1		
2003–04	Arsenal	32	0		
2004–05	Arsenal	35	2	**145**	**8**

CREGG, Patrick (M) 0 0
H: 5 9 W: 10 04 b.Dublin 21-2-86
Source: Trainee. *Honours:* Eire Youth, Under-21.

2002–03	Arsenal	0	0		
2003–04	Arsenal	0	0		
2004–05	Arsenal	0	0		

CYGAN, Pascal (D) 230 10
H: 6 4 W: 13 12 b.Lens 19-4-74
Source: Wasquehal.

1995–96	Lille	27	0		
1996–97	Lille	14	0		
1997–98	Lille	26	3		
1998–99	Lille	21	1		
1999–2000	Lille	33	2		
2000–01	Lille	29	2		
2001–02	Lille	29	1	**179**	**9**
2002–03	Arsenal	18	1		
2003–04	Arsenal	18	0		
2004–05	Arsenal	15	0	**51**	**1**

DJOUROU, Johan (D) 0 0
H: 6 3 W: 13 01 b.Ivory Coast 18-1-87
Source: Scholar. *Honours:* Switzerland Youth.

2004–05	Arsenal	0	0		

EBOUE, Emmanuel (D) 71 4
H: 5 10 W: 10 03 b.Abidjan 4-6-83
Honours: Ivory Coast full caps.

2002–03	Beveren	23	0		
2003–04	Beveren	30	2		
2004–05	Beveren	17	2	**70**	**4**
2004–05	Arsenal	1	0	**1**	**0**

EDU (M) 107 7
H: 6 1 W: 12 06 b.Sao Paulo 15-5-78
Honours: Brazil 15 full caps.

1998	Corinthians	1	0		
1999	Corinthians	19	0		
2000	Corinthians	8	0	**28**	**0**
2000–01	Arsenal	5	0		
2001–02	Arsenal	14	1		
2002–03	Arsenal	18	2		
2003–04	Arsenal	30	2		
2004–05	Arsenal	12	2	**79**	**7**

FABREGAS, Francesc (M) 33 2
H: 5 11 W: 11 01 b.Arenys de Mar 4-5-87
Source: Barcelona. *Honours:* Spain Youth, Under-21.

2003–04	Arsenal	0	0		
2004–05	Arsenal	33	2	**33**	**2**

FLAMINI, Mathieu (M) 35 1
H: 5 11 W: 11 10 b.Marseille 7-3-84
Source: Marseille. *Honours:* France Under-21.

2003–04	Marseille	14	0	**14**	**0**
2004–05	Arsenal	21	1	**21**	**1**

FOWLER, Jordan (M) 6 0
H: 5 9 W: 11 00 b.Barking 1-10-84
Source: Trainee.

2002–03	Arsenal	0	0		
2003–04	Arsenal	0	0		
2004–05	Arsenal	0	0		
2004–05	*Chesterfield*	6	0	**6**	**0**

GARRY, Ryan (D) 1 0
H: 6 2 W: 13 00 b.Hornchurch 29-9-83
Source: Scholar. *Honours:* England Youth, Under-20.

2001–02	Arsenal	0	0		
2002–03	Arsenal	1	0		
2003–04	Arsenal	0	0		
2004–05	Arsenal	0	0	**1**	**0**

HENRY, Thierry (F) 326 160
H: 6 2 W: 13 05 b.Paris 17-8-77
Honours: France 70 full caps, 28 goals.

1994–95	Monaco	8	3		
1995–96	Monaco	18	3		
1996–97	Monaco	36	9		
1997–98	Monaco	30	4		
1998–99	Monaco	13	1	**105**	**20**
1998–99	Juventus	16	3	**16**	**3**
1999–2000	Arsenal	31	17		
2000–01	Arsenal	35	17		
2001–02	Arsenal	33	24		
2002–03	Arsenal	37	24		
2003–04	Arsenal	37	30		
2004–05	Arsenal	32	25	**205**	**137**

HOLLOWAY, Craig (G) 0 0
b.Blackheath 10-8-84
Source: Trainee.

2002–03	Arsenal	0	0		
2003–04	Arsenal	0	0		
2004–05	Arsenal	0	0		

HOWARD, Mark (G) 0 0
Source: Scholar.

2004–05	Arsenal	0	0		

HOYTE, Justin (D) 7 0
H: 5 11 W: 11 00 b.Waltham Forest 20-11-84
Source: From Scholar. *Honours:* England Youth, Under-20, Under-21.

2002–03	Arsenal	1	0		
2003–04	Arsenal	1	0		
2004–05	Arsenal	5	0	**7**	**0**

JORDAN, Michael (G) 0 0
H: 6 2 W: 13 02 b.Enfield 7-4-86
Source: Scholar.

2003–04	Arsenal	0	0		
2004–05	Arsenal	0	0		

JUAN (D) 3 0
H: 5 6 W: 9 07 b.Sao Paulo 6-2-82
Source: Sao Paulo.

2001–02	Arsenal	0	0		
2002–03	Arsenal	0	0		
2003–04	Arsenal	0	0		
2003–04	*Millwall*	3	0	**3**	**0**
2004–05	Arsenal	0	0		

KARBASSIYON, Daniel (F) 5 0
H: 5 8 W: 11 07 b.Virginia 10-8-84
Source: Roanoke Star. *Honours:* USA Youth.

2003–04	Arsenal	0	0		
2004–05	Arsenal	0	0		
2004–05	*Ipswich T*	5	0	**5**	**0**

LARSSON, Sebastian (M) 0 0
H: 5 10 W: 11 00 b.Eskilstuna 6-6-85
Source: Trainee. *Honours:* Sweden Under-21.

2002–03	Arsenal	0	0		
2003–04	Arsenal	0	0		
2004–05	Arsenal	0	0		

LAUREN, Etame-Mayer (D) **280 24**
H: 5 11 W: 11 07 b.Londi Kribi 19-1-77
Honours: Cameroon 25 full caps, 1 goal.
1995–96 Utrera 30 5 **30 5**
1996–97 Sevilla B 17 3 **17 3**
1997–98 Levante 34 6 **34 6**
1998–99 Mallorca 32 1
1999–2000 Mallorca 30 3 **62 4**
2000–01 Arsenal 18 2
2001–02 Arsenal 27 2
2002–03 Arsenal 27 1
2003–04 Arsenal 32 0
2004–05 Arsenal 33 1 **137 6**

LEHMANN, Jens (G) **400 2**
H: 6 4 W: 13 05 b.Essen 10-11-69
Honours: Germany 25 full caps.
1991–92 Schalke 37 0
1992–93 Schalke 8 0
1993–94 Schalke 21 0
1994–95 Schalke 34 1
1995–96 Schalke 32 0
1996–97 Schalke 34 0
1997–98 Schalke 34 1 **200 2**
1998–99 AC Milan 5 0 **5 0**
1998–99 Borussia Dortmd 13 0
1999–2000 Borussia Dortmd 31 0
2000–01 Borussia Dortmd 31 0
2001–02 Borussia Dortmd 30 0
2002–03 Borussia Dortmd 24 0 **129 0**
2003–04 Arsenal 38 0
2004–05 Arsenal 28 0 **66 0**

LJUNGBERG, Frederik (M) **252 55**
H: 5 9 W: 11 00 b.Vittsjo 16-4-77
Honours: Sweden 52 full caps, 10 goals.
1994 Halmstad 1 0
1995 Halmstad 16 1
1996 Halmstad 20 2
1997 Halmstad 24 5
1998 Halmstad 18 2 **79 10**
1998–99 Arsenal 16 1
1999–2000 Arsenal 26 6
2000–01 Arsenal 30 6
2001–02 Arsenal 25 12
2002–03 Arsenal 20 6
2003–04 Arsenal 30 4
2004–05 Arsenal 26 10 **173 45**

LUPOLI, Arturo (F) **0 0**
H: 5 9 W: 10 07 b.Brescia 24-6-87
Source: Parma. *Honours:* Italy Youth.
2004–05 Arsenal 0 0

O'DONNELL, Stephen (M) **0 0**
H: 5 9 W: 11 07 b.Galway 15-1-86
Source: Trainee.
2002–03 Arsenal 0 0
2003–04 Arsenal 0 0
2004–05 Arsenal 0 0

OWUSU-ABEYIE, Quincy (F) **1 0**
H: 5 11 W: 11 10 b.Amsterdam 15-4-86
Source: Scholar. *Honours:* Holland Youth.
2003–04 Arsenal 0 0
2004–05 Arsenal 1 0 **1 0**

PIRES, Robert (M) **384 106**
H: 6 1 W: 12 09 b.Reims 29-10-73
Honours: France 79 full caps, 14 goals.
1992–93 Metz 2 0
1993–94 Metz 24 1
1994–95 Metz 35 9
1995–96 Metz 38 11
1996–97 Metz 32 11
1997–98 Metz 31 11 **162 43**
1998–99 Marseille 34 6
1999–2008 Marseille 32 2 **66 8**
2000–01 Arsenal 33 4
2001–02 Arsenal 28 9
2002–03 Arsenal 26 14
2003–04 Arsenal 36 14
2004–05 Arsenal 33 14 **156 55**

REYES, Jose Antonio (F) **160 34**
H: 5 9 W: 12 01 b.Utrera 1-9-83
Honours: Spain 12 full caps, 2 goals.
1999–2000 Sevilla B 32 1
1999–2000 Sevilla 1 0
2000–01 Sevilla B 0 0 **32 1**
2000–01 Sevilla 1 0
2001–02 Sevilla 29 8
2002–03 Sevilla 34 9
2003–04 Sevilla 20 5 **85 22**
2003–04 Arsenal 13 2
2004–05 Arsenal 30 9 **43 11**

SENDEROS, Philippe (D) **39 3**
H: 6 1 W: 13 10 b.Geneva 14-2-85
Honours: Switzerland Youth, Under-21, 2 full caps.
2001–02 Servette 3 0
2002–03 Servette 23 3 **26 3**
2003–04 Arsenal 0 0
2004–05 Arsenal 13 0 **13 0**

SILVA, Gilberto (M) **107 7**
H: 6 3 W: 12 04 b.Lagoa da Prata 7-10-76
Honours: Brazil 31 full caps, 3 goals.
2000 Atletico Mineiro 1 0
2001 Atletico Mineiro 26 3 **27 3**
2002–03 Arsenal 35 0
2003–04 Arsenal 32 4
2004–05 Arsenal 13 0 **80 4**

SIMEK, Franklin (D) **13 0**
H: 6 0 W: 11 06 b.St Louis 13-10-84
Source: Trainee.
2002–03 Arsenal 0 0
2003–04 Arsenal 0 0
2004–05 Arsenal 0 0
2004–05 *QPR* 5 0 **5 0**
2004–05 *Bournemouth* 8 0 **8 0**

SKULASON, Olafur-Ingi (M) **0 0**
H: 6 0 W: 12 04 b.Reykjavik 1-4-83
Source: Fylkir. *Honours:* Iceland 1 full cap, Under-21.
2001–02 Arsenal 0 0
2002–03 Arsenal 0 0
2003–04 Arsenal 0 0
2004–05 Arsenal 0 0

SMITH, Ryan (M) **0 0**
H: 5 10 W: 10 07 b.Islington 10-11-86
Source: Scholar. *Honours:* England Youth.
2004–05 Arsenal 0 0

STACK, Graham (G) **26 0**
H: 6 2 W: 13 02 b.Hampstead 26-9-81
Honours: Eire Under-21.
2000–01 Arsenal 0 0
2001–02 Arsenal 0 0
2002–03 Arsenal 0 0
2003–04 Arsenal 0 0
2004–05 Arsenal 0 0
2004–05 *Millwall* 26 0 **26 0**

SVARD, Sebastian (M) **23 1**
H: 6 0 W: 12 06 b.Hvidovre 15-1-83
Honours: Denmark Youth, Under-21.
2000–01 Arsenal 0 0
2001–02 Arsenal 0 0
2002–03 Arsenal 0 0
2003–04 *FC Copenhagen* 10 0 **10 0**
2003–04 *Stoke C* 13 1 **13 1**
2004–05 Arsenal 0 0

TAYLOR, Stuart (G) **48 0**
H: 6 5 W: 14 07 b.Romford 28-11-80
Source: Trainee. *Honours:* FA Schools, England Youth, Under-21.
1998–99 Arsenal 0 0
1999–2000 Arsenal 0 0
1999–2000 *Bristol R* 4 0 **4 0**
2000–01 Arsenal 0 0
2000–01 *Crystal Palace* 10 0 **10 0**
2000–01 *Peterborough U* 6 0 **6 0**
2001–02 Arsenal 10 0
2002–03 Arsenal 8 0
2003–04 Arsenal 0 0
2004–05 Arsenal 0 0 **18 0**
2004–05 *Leicester C* 10 0 **10 0**

TOURE, Kolo (D) **98 3**
H: 5 10 W: 13 08 b.Ivory Coast 19-3-81
Source: ASEC Mimosas. *Honours:* Ivory Coast full caps.
2001–02 Arsenal 0 0
2002–03 Arsenal 26 2
2003–04 Arsenal 37 1
2004–05 Arsenal 35 0 **98 3**

VAN PERSIE, Robin (F) **87 19**
H: 6 0 W: 11 00 b.Rotterdam 6-8-83
Honours: Holland Under-21, 2 full caps, 1 goal.
2001–02 Feyenoord 10 0
2002–03 Feyenoord 23 8
2003–04 Feyenoord 28 6 **61 14**
2004–05 Arsenal 26 5 **26 5**

VIEIRA, Patrick (M) **330 30**
H: 6 4 W: 13 09 b.Dakar 23-6-76
Honours: France Under-21, 79 full caps, 4 goals.
1993–94 Cannes 5 0
1994–95 Cannes 31 2
1995–96 Cannes 13 0 **49 2**
1995–96 AC Milan 2 0 **2 0**
1996–97 Arsenal 31 2
1997–98 Arsenal 33 2
1998–99 Arsenal 34 3
1999–2000 Arsenal 30 2
2000–01 Arsenal 30 5
2001–02 Arsenal 36 2
2002–03 Arsenal 24 3
2003–04 Arsenal 29 3
2004–05 Arsenal 32 6 **279 28**

Scholars
Bendtner, Nicklas; Connolly, Matthew Thomas Martin; Gilbert, Kerrea Kuche; Gill, Benjamin David; Kelly, Sean; Muamba, Fabrice Ndala; Murphy, Mitchell Alan; Stokes, Anthony

ASTON VILLA (2)

AARITALO, Mika (F) **0 0**
H: 6 1 W: 12 13 b.Taivassalo 25-7-85
Source: TPS Turku.
2002–03 Aston Villa 0 0
2003–04 Aston Villa 0 0
2004–05 Aston Villa 0 0

AGBONLOHOR, Gabriel (F) **0 0**
H: 5 11 W: 12 05 b.Birmingham 13-10-86
Source: Scholar.
2004–05 Aston Villa 0 0

ANGEL, Juan Pablo (F) **212 82**
H: 6 0 W: 12 10 b.Medellin 24-10-75
Source: From Nacional. *Honours:* Colombia 30 caps, 7 goals.
1997–98 River Plate 12 2
1998–99 River Plate 27 11
1999–2000 River Plate 34 19
2000–01 River Plate 18 13 **91 45**
2000–01 Aston Villa 9 1
2001–02 Aston Villa 29 12
2002–03 Aston Villa 15 1
2003–04 Aston Villa 33 16
2004–05 Aston Villa 35 7 **121 37**

BARRY, Gareth (D) **219 16**
H: 5 11 W: 12 06 b.Hastings 23-2-81
Source: Trainee. *Honours:* England Youth, Under-21, 8 full caps.
1997–98 Aston Villa 2 0
1998–99 Aston Villa 32 2
1999–2000 Aston Villa 30 1
2000–01 Aston Villa 30 0
2001–02 Aston Villa 20 0
2002–03 Aston Villa 35 3
2003–04 Aston Villa 36 3
2004–05 Aston Villa 34 7 **219 16**

BERSON, Mathieu (M) **133 7**
H: 5 9 W: 11 06 b.Vannes 23-2-80
Honours: France Under-21.
1999–2000 Nantes 12 0
2000–01 Nantes 28 0
2001–02 Nantes 29 3
2002–03 Nantes 29 2
2003–04 Nantes 24 2 **122 7**
2004–05 Aston Villa 11 0 **11 0**

BRAZIL, Alan (M) **0 0**
H: 5 7 W: 12 02 b.Edinburgh 5-7-85
Source: Trainee.
2002–03 Aston Villa 0 0
2003–04 Aston Villa 0 0
2004–05 Aston Villa 0 0

BRIDGES, Stuart (D) 0 0
H: 5 9 W: 11 09 b.Oxford 6-1-86
Source: Trainee. *Honours:* FA Schools, England Youth.
2002–03 Aston Villa 0 0
2003–04 Aston Villa 0 0
2004–05 Aston Villa 0 0

CAHILL, Gary (D) 27 1
H: 6 2 W: 12 06 b.Dronfield 19-12-85
Source: Trainee. *Honours:* England Youth.
2003–04 Aston Villa 0 0
2004–05 Aston Villa 0 0
2004–05 *Burnley* 27 1 **27 1**

COOKE, Stephen (M) 19 0
H: 5 7 W: 9 00 b.Walsall 15-2-83
Source: Scholar. *Honours:* England Youth, Under-20.
1999–2000 Aston Villa 0 0
2000–01 Aston Villa 0 0
2001–02 Aston Villa 0 0
2001–02 *Bournemouth* 7 0
2002–03 Aston Villa 3 0
2003–04 Aston Villa 0 0
2003–04 *Bournemouth* 3 0 **10 0**
2004–05 Aston Villa 0 0 **3 0**
2004–05 *Wycombe W* 6 0 **6 0**

DAVIS, Steven (M) 28 1
H: 5 7 W: 9 07 b.Ballymena 1-1-85
Source: Scholar. *Honours:* Northern Ireland Schools, Youth, Under-21, Under-23, 4 full caps.
2001–02 Aston Villa 0 0
2002–03 Aston Villa 0 0
2003–04 Aston Villa 0 0
2004–05 Aston Villa 28 1 **28 1**

DE LA CRUZ, Ulises (D) 282 26
H: 5 8 W: 12 10 b.Bolivar 8-2-74
Source: Cruzeiro. *Honours:* Ecuador 78 full caps, 4 goals.
1996 Aucas 32 3 **32 3**
1997 LDU Quito 38 4
1998 LDU Quito 42 7
1999 LDU Quito 22 4
1999 Cruzeiro 4 0 **4 0**
2000 LDU Quito 30 5 **132 20**
2001–02 Hibernian 32 2 **32 2**
2002–03 Aston Villa 20 1
2003–04 Aston Villa 28 0
2004–05 Aston Villa 34 0 **82 1**

DELANEY, Mark (D) 174 1
H: 6 1 W: 11 07 b.Haverfordwest 13-5-76
Source: Carmarthen T. *Honours:* Wales 33 full caps.
1998–99 Cardiff C 28 0 **28 0**
1998–99 Aston Villa 2 0
1999–2000 Aston Villa 28 1
2000–01 Aston Villa 19 0
2001–02 Aston Villa 30 0
2002–03 Aston Villa 12 0
2003–04 Aston Villa 25 0
2004–05 Aston Villa 30 0 **146 1**

DJEMBA-DJEMBA, Eric (M) 68 1
H: 5 9 W: 11 13 b.Douala 4-5-81
Source: Kadji Sport, UCB Douala. *Honours:* Cameroon 26 full caps.
2001–02 Nantes 14 0
2002–03 Nantes 28 1 **42 1**
2003–04 Manchester U 15 0
2004–05 Manchester U 5 0 **20 0**
2004–05 Aston Villa 6 0 **6 0**

DROBNY, Vaclav (D) 126 1
H: 6 3 W: 13 03 b.Melink 9-9-80
1998–99 Chmel Blany 9 0
1999–2000 Chmel Blany 20 0
From Bolislav
2000–01 Chmel Blany 28 1
2001–02 Chmel Blany 27 0 **84 1**
2002–03 Strasbourg 17 0
2003–04 Strasbourg 25 0 **42 0**
2004–05 Aston Villa 0 0

FOLEY-SHERIDAN, Steven (M) 0 0
H: 5 4 W: 9 02 b.Dublin 10-2-86
Source: Trainee.
2002–03 Aston Villa 0 0
2003–04 Aston Villa 0 0
2004–05 Aston Villa 0 0

GARDNER, Craig (M) 0 0
H: 5 10 W: 11 13 b.Solihull 25-11-86
Source: Scholar.
2004–05 Aston Villa 0 0

GRANT, Lee (M) 0 0
H: 6 2 W: 12 02 b.York 31-12-85
Source: Trainee.
2003–04 Aston Villa 0 0
2004–05 Aston Villa 0 0

HENDERSON, Wayne (G) 14 0
H: 5 11 W: 12 02 b.Dublin 16-9-83
Source: Scholar. *Honours:* Eire Youth, Under-21.
2000–01 Aston Villa 0 0
2001–02 Aston Villa 0 0
2002–03 Aston Villa 0 0
2003–04 Aston Villa 0 0
2003–04 *Wycombe W* 3 0 **3 0**
2004–05 Aston Villa 0 0
2004–05 *Notts Co* 11 0 **11 0**

HENDRIE, Lee (M) 234 26
H: 5 10 W: 11 00 b.Birmingham 18-5-77
Source: Trainee. *Honours:* England Youth, Under-21, B, 1 full cap.
1993–94 Aston Villa 0 0
1994–95 Aston Villa 0 0
1995–96 Aston Villa 3 0
1996–97 Aston Villa 4 0
1997–98 Aston Villa 17 3
1998–99 Aston Villa 32 3
1999–2000 Aston Villa 29 1
2000–01 Aston Villa 32 6
2001–02 Aston Villa 29 2
2002–03 Aston Villa 27 4
2003–04 Aston Villa 32 2
2004–05 Aston Villa 29 5 **234 26**

HITZLSPERGER, Thomas (M) 104 8
H: 6 0 W: 11 12 b.Munich 5-4-82
Source: Bayern Munich. *Honours:* Germany Youth, Under-21, 9 full caps.
2000–01 Aston Villa 1 0
2001–02 *Chesterfield* 5 0 **5 0**
2001–02 Aston Villa 12 1
2002–03 Aston Villa 26 2
2003–04 Aston Villa 32 3
2004–05 Aston Villa 28 2 **99 8**

KACHLOUL, Hassan (M) 249 48
H: 6 1 W: 12 01 b.Agadir 19-2-73
Honours: Morocco 12 full caps.
1992–93 Nimes 17 1
1993–94 Nimes 37 17
1994–95 Nimes 32 8 **86 26**
1995–96 Dunkerque 28 6 **28 6**
1996–97 Metz 7 0 **7 0**
1997–98 St Etienne 16 0 **16 0**
1998–99 Southampton 22 5
1999–2000 Southampton 32 5
2000–01 Southampton 32 4 **86 14**
2001–02 Aston Villa 22 2
2002–03 Aston Villa 0 0
2003–04 Aston Villa 0 0
2003–04 *Wolverhampton W* 4 0 **4 0**
2004–05 Aston Villa 0 0 **22 2**

KOUMAN, Amadou (F) 0 0
H: 5 9 W: 11 00 b.Marcory 14-4-86
Source: Trainee.
2002–03 Aston Villa 0 0
2003–04 Aston Villa 0 0
2004–05 Aston Villa 0 0

LAURSEN, Martin (D) 145 6
H: 6 2 W: 12 05 b.Silkeborg 26-7-77
Honours: Denmark Youth, Under-21, 41 full caps.
1995–96 Silkeborg 1 0
1996–97 Silkeborg 12 0
1997–98 Silkeborg 22 1 **35 1**
1998–99 Verona 6 0
1999–2000 Verona 19 2
2000–01 Verona 31 0 **56 2**
2001–02 AC Milan 22 2
2002–03 AC Milan 10 0
2003–04 AC Milan 10 0 **42 2**
2004–05 Aston Villa 12 1 **12 1**

MASALIN, Jon (G) 0 0
H: 6 2 W: 14 06 b.Helsinki 29-1-86
2002–03 Aston Villa 0 0
2003–04 Aston Villa 0 0
2004–05 Aston Villa 0 0

McCANN, Gavin (M) 175 9
H: 5 11 W: 11 00 b.Blackpool 10-1-78
Source: Trainee. *Honours:* England 1 full cap.
1995–96 Everton 0 0
1996–97 Everton 0 0
1997–98 Everton 11 0
1998–99 Everton 0 0 **11 0**
1998–99 Sunderland 11 0
1999–2000 Sunderland 24 4
2000–01 Sunderland 22 3
2001–02 Sunderland 29 0
2002–03 Sunderland 30 1 **116 8**
2003–04 Aston Villa 28 0
2004–05 Aston Villa 20 1 **48 1**

MELLBERG, Olof (D) 295 5
H: 6 1 W: 12 10 b.Amncharad 3-9-77
Honours: Sweden 56 full caps, 1 goal.
1996 Degerfors 22 0
1997 Degerfors 25 0 **47 0**
1998 AIK Stockholm 17 0 **17 0**
1998–99 Santander 25 0
1999–2000 Santander 37 0
2000–01 Santander 36 0 **98 0**
2001–02 Aston Villa 32 0
2002–03 Aston Villa 38 1
2003–04 Aston Villa 33 1
2004–05 Aston Villa 30 3 **133 5**

MOORE, Luke (F) 38 5
H: 5 11 W: 11 13 b.Birmingham 13-2-86
Source: Trainee. *Honours:* FA Schools, England Youth.
2002–03 Aston Villa 0 0
2003–04 Aston Villa 7 0
2003–04 *Wycombe W* 6 4 **6 4**
2004–05 Aston Villa 25 1 **32 1**

MOORE, Stefan (F) 37 2
H: 5 10 W: 10 12 b.Birmingham 28-9-83
Source: Scholar. *Honours:* England Youth.
2000–01 Aston Villa 0 0
2001–02 Aston Villa 0 0
2001–02 *Chesterfield* 2 0 **2 0**
2002–03 Aston Villa 13 1
2003–04 Aston Villa 8 1
2004–05 Aston Villa 1 0 **22 2**
2004–05 *Millwall* 6 0 **6 0**
2004–05 *Leicester C* 7 0 **7 0**

MULCAHY, Kevin (D) 0 0
H: 5 10 W: 11 00 b.Cork 2-3-86
Source: Trainee.
2002–03 Aston Villa 0 0
2003–04 Aston Villa 0 0
2004–05 Aston Villa 0 0

NIX, Kyle (F) 0 0
H: 5 6 W: 9 10 b.Sydney 21-1-86
Source: Manchester U Trainee. *Honours:* FA Schools, England Youth.
2002–03 Aston Villa 0 0
2003–04 Aston Villa 0 0
2004–05 Aston Villa 0 0

OLEJNIK, Robert (G) 0 0
H: 6 0 W: 15 06 b.Vienna 26-11-86
Source: Scholar.
2004–05 Aston Villa 0 0

PAUL, Shane (F) 0 0
H: 5 6 W: 10 07 b.Walsall 25-1-87
Source: From Scholar. *Honours:* England Youth.
2004–05 Aston Villa 0 0

POSTMA, Stefan (G) 111 0
H: 6 4 W: 15 04 b.Utrecht 6-10-76
1995–96 Utrecht 5 0
1996–97 Utrecht 12 0
1997–98 Utrecht 13 0
1998–99 Utrecht 1 0
1999–2000 Utrecht 2 0 **33 0**
2000–01 De Graafschap 34 0
2001–02 De Graafschap 33 0 **67 0**
2002–03 Aston Villa 6 0
2003–04 Aston Villa 2 0
2004–05 Aston Villa 3 0 **11 0**

RIDGEWELL, Liam (D) **31** **0**
H: 5 10 W: 10 03 b.Bexley 21-7-84
Source: Scholar. *Honours:* England Youth, Under-20, Under-21.

2001–02	Aston Villa	0	0		
2002–03	Aston Villa	0	0		
2002–03	*Bournemouth*	5	0	**5**	**0**
2003–04	Aston Villa	11	0		
2004–05	Aston Villa	15	0	**26**	**0**

SAMUEL, J Lloyd (D) **154** **2**
H: 5 11 W: 11 04 b.Trinidad 29-3-81
Source: Charlton Ath Trainee. *Honours:* England Youth, Under-20, Under-21.

1998–99	Aston Villa	0	0		
1999–2000	Aston Villa	9	0		
2000–01	Aston Villa	3	0		
2001–02	*Gillingham*	8	0	**8**	**0**
2001–02	Aston Villa	23	0		
2002–03	Aston Villa	38	0		
2003–04	Aston Villa	38	2		
2004–05	Aston Villa	35	0	**146**	**2**

SOLANO, Nolberto (M) **325** **74**
H: 5 9 W: 11 06 b.Callao 12-12-74
Honours: Peru 75 full caps, 20 goals.

1994–95	Sporting Cristal	38	12		
1995–96	Sporting Cristal	26	13		
1996–97	Sporting Cristal	11	7	**75**	**32**
1997–98	Boca Juniors	32	5	**32**	**5**
1998–99	Newcastle U	29	6		
1999–2000	Newcastle U	30	3		
2000–01	Newcastle U	33	6		
2001–02	Newcastle U	37	7		
2002–03	Newcastle U	31	7		
2003–04	Newcastle U	12	0	**172**	**29**
2003–04	Aston Villa	10	0		
2004–05	Aston Villa	36	8	**46**	**8**

SORENSEN, Thomas (G) **245** **0**
H: 6 4 W: 13 10 b.Fredericia 12-6-76
Source: Odense. *Honours:* Denmark Under-21, B, 48 full caps.

1998–99	Sunderland	45	0		
1999–2000	Sunderland	37	0		
2000–01	Sunderland	34	0		
2001–02	Sunderland	34	0		
2002–03	Sunderland	21	0	**171**	**0**
2003–04	Aston Villa	38	0		
2004–05	Aston Villa	36	0	**74**	**0**

TROEST, Magnus (D) **0** **0**
H: 6 2 W: 12 07 b.Copenhagen 5-6-87
Source: Scholar.

2004–05	Aston Villa	0	0

TSHIMANGA, Christian (M) **0** **0**
H: 5 9 W: 11 10 b.Kinshasa 16-6-87
Source: Scholar.

2004–05	Aston Villa	0	0

VASSELL, Darius (F) **162** **35**
H: 5 7 W: 12 00 b.Birmingham 13-6-80
Source: From Trainee. *Honours:* England Youth, Under-21, 22 full caps, 6 goals.

1998–99	Aston Villa	6	0		
1999–2000	Aston Villa	11	0		
2000–01	Aston Villa	23	4		
2001–02	Aston Villa	36	12		
2002–03	Aston Villa	33	8		
2003–04	Aston Villa	32	9		
2004–05	Aston Villa	21	2	**162**	**35**

WARD, Jamie (M) **0** **0**
H: 5 5 W: 9 04 b.Birmingham 12-5-86
Source: Scholar.

2003–04	Aston Villa	0	0
2004–05	Aston Villa	0	0

WARD, Jamie (M) **0** **0**
H: 5 5 W: 9 04 b.Birmingham 12-5-86
Source: Scholar.

2004–05	Aston Villa	0	0

WHITTINGHAM, Peter (D) **56** **1**
H: 5 10 W: 9 13 b.Nuneaton 8-9-84
Source: From Trainee. *Honours:* England Youth, Under-20, Under-21.

2002–03	Aston Villa	4	0		
2003–04	Aston Villa	32	0		
2004–05	Aston Villa	13	1	**49**	**1**
2004–05	*Burnley*	7	0	**7**	**0**

WILLIAMS, Sam (M) **0** **0**
H: 5 11 W: 10 08 b.London 9-6-87
Source: Scholar.

2004–05	Aston Villa	0	0

Scholars
Boyle, Lee; Bridges, Scott Ashley; Green, Phillip Richard; Henderson, Stephen; Morgan, Oluwaseyi; O'Halloran, Stephen Edward; Osbourne, Isaiah; Saunders, Matthew; Williams, Sam

BARNSLEY (3)

ALCOCK, Danny (G) **1** **0**
H: 5 11 W: 11 03 b.Staffordshire 15-2-84
Source: Scholar.

2001–02	Stoke C	0	0		
2002–03	Stoke C	0	0		
2003–04	Barnsley	1	0		
2004–05	Barnsley	0	0	**1**	**0**

ATKINSON, Rob (M) **2** **0**
H: 6 1 W: 12 00 b.Beverley 29-4-87
Source: Scholar.

2003–04	Barnsley	1	0		
2004–05	Barnsley	1	0	**2**	**0**

AUSTIN, Neil (D) **86** **0**
H: 5 10 W: 11 09 b.Barnsley 26-4-83
Source: Trainee. *Honours:* England Youth, Under-20.

1999–2000	Barnsley	0	0		
2000–01	Barnsley	0	0		
2001–02	Barnsley	0	0		
2002–03	Barnsley	34	0		
2003–04	Barnsley	37	0		
2004–05	Barnsley	15	0	**86**	**0**

BAKER, Tom (F) **4** **0**
H: 5 5 W: 9 02 b.Salford 28-3-85
Source: Scholar.

2003–04	Barnsley	1	0		
2004–05	Barnsley	3	0	**4**	**0**

BOULDING, Mick (F) **185** **49**
H: 5 10 W: 11 05 b.Sheffield 8-2-76
Source: Hallam.

1999–2000	Mansfield T	33	6		
2000–01	Mansfield T	33	6		
2001–02	Mansfield T	0	0	**66**	**12**
2001–02	Grimsby T	35	11		
2002–03	Aston Villa	0	0		
2002–03	*Sheffield U*	6	0	**6**	**0**
2002–03	Grimsby T	12	4		
2003–04	Grimsby T	27	12	**74**	**27**
2003–04	Barnsley	6	0		
2004–05	Barnsley	29	10	**35**	**10**
2004–05	*Cardiff C*	4	0	**4**	**0**

BURNS, Jacob (M) **144** **11**
H: 5 10 W: 11 08 b.Sydney 21-1-78
Honours: Australia Under-23, 2 full caps.

1996–97	Sydney U	5	0		
1997–98	Sydney U	25	2		
1998–99	Sydney U	27	3	**57**	**5**
1999–2000	Parramatta Power	25	3	**25**	**3**
2000–01	Leeds U	4	0		
2001–02	Leeds U	0	0		
2002–03	Leeds U	2	0		
2003–04	Leeds U	0	0	**6**	**0**
2003–04	Barnsley	22	1		
2004–05	Barnsley	34	2	**56**	**3**

CARBON, Matt (D) **284** **17**
H: 6 2 W: 11 13 b.Nottingham 8-6-75
Source: Trainee. *Honours:* England Under-21.

1992–93	Lincoln C	1	0		
1993–94	Lincoln C	9	0		
1994–95	Lincoln C	33	7		
1995–96	Lincoln C	26	3		
1995–96	Derby Co	6	0		
1996–97	Derby Co	10	0		
1997–98	Derby Co	4	0	**20**	**0**
1997–98	WBA	16	1		
1998–99	WBA	39	2		
1999–2000	WBA	34	2		
2000–01	WBA	24	0	**113**	**5**
2001–02	Walsall	22	1		
2002–03	Walsall	25	1		
2003–04	Walsall	8	0	**55**	**2**
2003–04	*Lincoln C*	1	0	**70**	**10**
2004–05	Barnsley	26	0	**26**	**0**

COLGAN, Nick (G) **160** **0**
H: 6 1 W: 13 06 b.Drogheda 19-9-73
Source: Drogheda. *Honours:* Eire Under-21, 8 full caps.

1992–93	Chelsea	0	0		
1993–94	Chelsea	0	0		
1993–94	*Crewe Alex*	0	0		
1994–95	Chelsea	0	0		
1994–95	*Grimsby T*	0	0		
1995–96	Chelsea	0	0		
1995–96	*Millwall*	0	0		
1996–97	Chelsea	1	0		
1997–98	Chelsea	0	0	**1**	**0**
1997–98	*Brentford*	5	0	**5**	**0**
1997–98	*Reading*	5	0	**5**	**0**
1998–99	Bournemouth	0	0		
1999–2000	Hibernian	24	0		
2000–01	Hibernian	37	0		
2001–02	Hibernian	30	0		
2002–03	Hibernian	30	0		
2003–04	Hibernian	0	0	**121**	**0**
2003–04	*Stockport Co*	15	0	**15**	**0**
2004–05	Barnsley	13	0	**13**	**0**

CONLON, Barry (F) **267** **73**
H: 6 3 W: 14 00 b.Drogheda 1-10-78
Source: QPR Trainee. *Honours:* Eire Under-21.

1997–98	Manchester C	7	0		
1997–98	*Plymouth Arg*	13	2	**13**	**2**
1998–99	Manchester C	0	0	**7**	**0**
1998–99	Southend U	34	7	**34**	**7**
1999–2000	York C	40	11		
2000–01	York C	8	0	**48**	**11**
2000–01	*Colchester U*	26	8	**26**	**8**
2001–02	Darlington	35	10		
2002–03	Darlington	41	15		
2003–04	Darlington	39	14	**115**	**39**
2004–05	Barnsley	24	6	**24**	**6**

FLINDERS, Scott (G) **11** **0**
H: 6 4 W: 14 00 b.Rotherham 12-6-86
Source: Scholar. *Honours:* England Youth, Under-20.

2004–05	Barnsley	11	0	**11**	**0**

HASSELL, Bobby (D) **199** **3**
H: 5 10 W: 12 00 b.Derby 4-6-80
Source: Trainee.

1997–98	Mansfield T	9	0		
1998–99	Mansfield T	3	0		
1999–2000	Mansfield T	11	1		
2000–01	Mansfield T	40	1		
2001–02	Mansfield T	43	1		
2002–03	Mansfield T	20	0		
2003–04	Mansfield T	34	0	**160**	**3**
2004–05	Barnsley	39	0	**39**	**0**

JACK, Darren (M) **3** **0**
H: 6 3 W: 13 03 b.Norwich 9-9-83

2000–01	Ross Co	0	0		
2001–02	Ross Co	1	0	**1**	**0**
2002–03	Motherwell	2	0	**2**	**0**
2003–04	Barnsley	0	0		
2004–05	Barnsley	0	0		

JARMAN, Nathan (F) **6** **0**
H: 5 11 W: 11 03 b.Scunthorpe 19-9-86
Source: Scholar.

2004–05	Barnsley	6	0	**6**	**0**

JOYNES, Nathan (M) **1** **0**
H: 6 1 W: 12 00 b.Hoyland 7-8-85
Source: Scholar.

2004–05	Barnsley	1	0	**1**	**0**

KAY, Antony (D) **106** **9**
H: 5 11 W: 11 08 b.Barnsley 21-10-82
Source: From Trainee. *Honours:* England Youth.

1999–2000	Barnsley	0	0		
2000–01	Barnsley	7	0		
2001–02	Barnsley	1	0		
2002–03	Barnsley	16	0		
2003–04	Barnsley	43	3		
2004–05	Barnsley	39	6	**106**	**9**

LAIGHT, Ryan (D)				**0**	**0**
H: 6 0 W: 11 09 b.Barnsley 16-11-85					
Source: Scholar.					
2002–03	Barnsley	0	0		
2003–04	Barnsley	0	0		
2004–05	Barnsley	0	0		

LUMSDON, Chris (M)				**109**	**14**
H: 5 11 W: 10 03 b.Newcastle 15-12-79					
Source: Trainee.					
1997–98	Sunderland	1	0		
1998–99	Sunderland	0	0		
1999–2000	Sunderland	1	0		
1999–2000	*Blackpool*	6	1	**6**	**1**
2000–01	Sunderland	0	0		
2000–01	*Crewe Alex*	16	0	**16**	**0**
2001–02	Sunderland	0	0	**2**	**0**
2001–02	Barnsley	32	7		
2002–03	Barnsley	25	3		
2003–04	Barnsley	28	3		
2004–05	Barnsley	0	0	**85**	**13**

McPHAIL, Stephen (M)				**131**	**5**
H: 5 8 W: 11 04 b.Westminster 9-12-79					
Source: Trainee. *Honours:* Eire Under-21, 10 full caps, 1 goal.					
1996–97	Leeds U	0	0		
1997–98	Leeds U	4	0		
1998–99	Leeds U	17	0		
1999–2000	Leeds U	24	2		
2000–01	Leeds U	7	0		
2001–02	Leeds U	1	0		
2001–02	*Millwall*	3	0	**3**	**0**
2002–03	Leeds U	13	0		
2003–04	Leeds U	12	1	**78**	**3**
2003–04	*Nottingham F*	14	0	**14**	**0**
2004–05	Barnsley	36	2	**36**	**2**

REID, Paul (D)				**113**	**6**
H: 6 2 W: 11 08 b.Carlisle 18-2-82					
Source: Trainee. *Honours:* England Youth, Under-20.					
1998–99	Carlisle U	0	0		
1999–2000	Carlisle U	19	0	**19**	**0**
2000–01	Rangers	0	0		
2001–02	Rangers	0	0		
2001–02	*Preston NE*	1	1	**1**	**1**
2002–03	Rangers	0	0		
2002–03	*Northampton T*	19	0		
2003–04	Northampton T	33	2	**52**	**2**
2004–05	Barnsley	41	3	**41**	**3**

SCARSELLA, David (G)				**0**	**0**
H: 6 1 W: 11 03 b.Australia 2-10-82					
Honours: Australia Schools.					
2004–05	Barnsley	0	0		

SCOTHERN, Ashley (F)				**1**	**0**
H: 6 0 W: 11 00 b.Pontefract 11-9-84					
Source: Scholar. *Honours:* England Youth.					
2001–02	Barnsley	1	0		
2002–03	Barnsley	0	0		
2003–04	Barnsley	0	0		
2004–05	Barnsley	0	0	**1**	**0**

SHUKER, Chris (M)				**101**	**10**
H: 5 5 W: 9 03 b.Liverpool 9-5-82					
Source: Scholarship.					
1999–2000	Manchester C	0	0		
2000–01	Manchester C	0	0		
2000–01	*Macclesfield T*	9	1	**9**	**1**
2001–02	Manchester C	2	0		
2002–03	Manchester C	3	0		
2002–03	*Walsall*	5	0	**5**	**0**
2003–04	Manchester C	0	0	**5**	**0**
2003–04	*Rochdale*	14	1	**14**	**1**
2003–04	*Hartlepool U*	14	1	**14**	**1**
2003–04	Barnsley	9	0		
2004–05	Barnsley	45	7	**54**	**7**

STALLARD, Mark (F)				**373**	**112**
H: 6 0 W: 13 09 b.Derby 24-10-74					
Source: Trainee.					
1991–92	Derby Co	3	0		
1992–93	Derby Co	5	0		
1993–94	Derby Co	0	0		
1994–95	Derby Co	16	2		
1994–95	*Fulham*	4	3	**4**	**3**
1995–96	Derby Co	3	0	**27**	**2**
1995–96	Bradford C	21	9		
1996–97	Bradford C	22	1	**43**	**10**
1996–97	*Preston NE*	4	1	**4**	**1**
1996–97	Wycombe W	12	4		
1997–98	Wycombe W	43	17		
1998–99	Wycombe W	15	2	**70**	**23**
1998–99	Notts Co	14	4		
1999–2000	Notts Co	36	14		
2000–01	Notts Co	42	17		
2001–02	Notts Co	26	4		
2002–03	Notts Co	45	24		
2003–04	Notts Co	22	4		
2003–04	Barnsley	10	1		
2004–05	Barnsley	5	0	**15**	**1**
2004–05	*Chesterfield*	9	2	**9**	**2**
2004–05	*Notts Co*	16	3	**201**	**70**

TONGE, Dale (D)				**15**	**0**
H: 5 10 W: 10 06 b.Doncaster 7-5-85					
Source: Scholar.					
2003–04	Barnsley	1	0		
2004–05	Barnsley	14	0	**15**	**0**

VAUGHAN, Tony (D)				**249**	**12**
H: 6 1 W: 11 02 b.Manchester 11-10-75					
Source: Trainee. *Honours:* England Schools.					
1994–95	Ipswich T	10	0		
1995–96	Ipswich T	25	1		
1996–97	Ipswich T	32	2	**67**	**3**
1997–98	Manchester C	19	1		
1998–99	Manchester C	38	1		
1999–2000	Manchester C	1	0	**58**	**2**
1999–2000	*Cardiff C*	14	0	**14**	**0**
1999–2000	Nottingham F	10	0		
2000–01	Nottingham F	25	1		
2001–02	Nottingham F	8	0		
2001–02	*Scunthorpe U*	5	0	**5**	**0**
2002–03	Nottingham F	0	0	**43**	**1**
2002–03	*Mansfield T*	4	0		
2003–04	Mansfield T	32	2	**36**	**2**
2004–05	Barnsley	26	4	**26**	**4**

WILLIAMS, Robbie (D)				**29**	**2**
H: 5 10 W: 11 13 b.Pontefract 2-10-84					
Source: Scholar.					
2002–03	Barnsley	8	0		
2003–04	Barnsley	4	1		
2004–05	Barnsley	17	1	**29**	**2**

WILLIAMS, Tom (D)				**131**	**4**
H: 5 11 W: 12 05 b.Carshalton 8-7-80					
Source: Walton & Hersham.					
1999–2000	West Ham U	0	0		
2000–01	West Ham U	0	0		
2000–01	*Peterborough U*	2	0		
2001–02	Peterborough U	34	2		
2001–02	Birmingham C	4	0		
2002–03	Birmingham C	0	0		
2002–03	*QPR*	26	1		
2003–04	Birmingham C	0	0	**4**	**0**
2003–04	*QPR*	5	0	**31**	**1**
2003–04	*Peterborough U*	21	1	**57**	**3**
2004–05	Barnsley	39	0	**39**	**0**

WROE, Nicky (M)				**34**	**1**
H: 5 11 W: 10 02 b.Sheffield 28-9-85					
Source: Scholar.					
2002–03	Barnsley	1	0		
2003–04	Barnsley	2	1		
2004–05	Barnsley	31	0	**34**	**1**

BIRMINGHAM C (4)

ALSOP, Sam (D)				**0**	**0**
H: 5 11 W: 11 07 b.Birmingham 7-3-85					
Source: Scholar.					
2004–05	Birmingham C	0	0		

ANDERTON, Darren (M)				**381**	**44**
H: 6 1 W: 12 05 b.Southampton 3-3-72					
Source: From Trainee. *Honours:* England Youth, Under-21, B, 30 full caps, 7 goals.					
1989–90	Portsmouth	0	0		
1990–91	Portsmouth	20	0		
1991–92	Portsmouth	42	7	**62**	**7**
1992–93	Tottenham H	34	6		
1993–94	Tottenham H	37	6		
1994–95	Tottenham H	37	5		
1995–96	Tottenham H	8	2		
1996–97	Tottenham H	16	3		
1997–98	Tottenham H	15	0		
1998–99	Tottenham H	32	3		
1999–2000	Tottenham H	22	3		
2000–01	Tottenham H	23	2		
2001–02	Tottenham H	35	3		
2002–03	Tottenham H	20	0		
2003–04	Tottenham H	20	1	**299**	**34**
2004–05	Birmingham C	20	3	**20**	**3**

BENNETT, Ian (G)				**370**	**0**
H: 6 0 W: 13 01 b.Worksop 10-10-71					
Source: Newcastle U Trainee.					
1991–92	Peterborough U	7	0		
1992–93	Peterborough U	46	0		
1993–94	Peterborough U	19	0	**72**	**0**
1993–94	Birmingham C	22	0		
1994–95	Birmingham C	46	0		
1995–96	Birmingham C	24	0		
1996–97	Birmingham C	40	0		
1997–98	Birmingham C	45	0		
1998–99	Birmingham C	10	0		
1999–2000	Birmingham C	21	0		
2000–01	Birmingham C	45	0		
2001–02	Birmingham C	18	0		
2002–03	Birmingham C	10	0		
2003–04	Birmingham C	6	0		
2004–05	Birmingham C	0	0	**287**	**0**
2004–05	*Sheffield U*	5	0	**5**	**0**
2004–05	*Coventry C*	6	0	**6**	**0**

BLAKE, Robbie (F)				**363**	**106**
H: 5 7 W: 12 07 b.Middlesbrough 4-3-76					
Source: Trainee.					
1994–95	Darlington	9	0		
1995–96	Darlington	29	11		
1996–97	Darlington	30	10	**68**	**21**
1996–97	Bradford C	5	0		
1997–98	Bradford C	34	8		
1998–99	Bradford C	39	16		
1999–2000	Bradford C	28	2		
2000–01	Bradford C	21	4		
2000–01	*Nottingham F*	11	1	**11**	**1**
2001–02	Bradford C	26	10	**153**	**40**
2001–02	Burnley	10	0		
2002–03	Burnley	41	13		
2003–04	Burnley	45	19		
2004–05	Burnley	24	10	**120**	**42**
2004–05	Birmingham C	11	2	**11**	**2**

BRUCE, Alex (D)				**18**	**0**
H: 6 0 W: 11 06 b.Norwich 28-9-84					
Source: Trainee.					
2002–03	Blackburn R	0	0		
2003–04	Blackburn R	0	0		
2004–05	Blackburn R	0	0		
2004–05	*Oldham Ath*	12	0	**12**	**0**
2004–05	Birmingham C	0	0		
2004–05	*Sheffield W*	6	0	**6**	**0**

CARTER, Darren (M)				**55**	**4**
H: 6 2 W: 12 11 b.Solihull 18-12-83					
Source: Scholar. *Honours:* England Youth, Under-20.					
2001–02	Birmingham C	13	1		
2002–03	Birmingham C	12	0		
2003–04	Birmingham C	5	0		
2004–05	Birmingham C	15	2	**45**	**3**
2004–05	*Sunderland*	10	1	**10**	**1**

CLAPHAM, Jamie (M)				**287**	**10**
H: 5 9 W: 11 09 b.Lincoln 7-12-75					
Source: Trainee.					
1994–95	Tottenham H	0	0		
1995–96	Tottenham H	0	0		
1996–97	Tottenham H	1	0		
1996–97	*Leyton Orient*	6	0	**6**	**0**
1996–97	*Bristol R*	5	0	**5**	**0**
1997–98	Tottenham H	0	0	**1**	**0**
1997–98	Ipswich T	22	0		
1998–99	Ipswich T	46	3		
1999–2000	Ipswich T	46	2		
2000–01	Ipswich T	35	2		
2001–02	Ipswich T	32	2		
2002–03	Ipswich T	26	1	**207**	**10**
2002–03	Birmingham C	16	0		
2003–04	Birmingham C	25	0		
2004–05	Birmingham C	27	0	**68**	**0**

CLEMENCE, Stephen (M)				**162**	**6**
H: 6 0 W: 12 09 b.Liverpool 31-3-78					
Source: Trainee. *Honours:* England Schools, Youth, Under-21.					
1994–95	Tottenham H	0	0		
1995–96	Tottenham H	0	0		
1996–97	Tottenham H	0	0		

1997–98 Tottenham H 17 0
1998–99 Tottenham H 18 0
1999–2000 Tottenham H 20 1
2000–01 Tottenham H 29 1
2001–02 Tottenham H 6 0
2002–03 Tottenham H 0 0 **90 2**
2002–03 Birmingham C 15 2
2003–04 Birmingham C 35 2
2004–05 Birmingham C 22 0 **72 4**

COTTRILL, Chris (M) 0 0
H: 5 10 W: 11 00 b.Birmingham 4-9-84
Source: Scholar.
2004–05 Birmingham C 0 0

CUNNINGHAM, Kenny (D) 489 1
H: 5 11 W: 12 07 b.Dublin 28-6-71
Source: From Tolka R. *Honours:* Eire Youth, Under-21, B, 68 full caps.
1989–90 Millwall 5 0
1990–91 Millwall 23 0
1991–92 Millwall 17 0
1992–93 Millwall 37 0
1993–94 Millwall 39 1
1994–95 Millwall 15 0 **136 1**
1994–95 Wimbledon 28 0
1995–96 Wimbledon 33 0
1996–97 Wimbledon 36 0
1997–98 Wimbledon 32 0
1998–99 Wimbledon 35 0
1999–2000 Wimbledon 37 0
2000–01 Wimbledon 15 0
2001–02 Wimbledon 34 0 **250 0**
2002–03 Birmingham C 31 0
2003–04 Birmingham C 36 0
2004–05 Birmingham C 36 0 **103 0**

DOYLE, Colin (G) 3 0
H: 6 5 W: 14 05 b.Cork 12-8-85
Honours: Eire Youth
2004–05 Birmingham C 0 0
2004–05 *Chester C* 0 0
2004–05 *Nottingham F* 3 0 **3 0**

DUNN, David (M) 168 34
H: 5 9 W: 12 03 b.Gt Harwood 27-12-79
Source: Trainee. *Honours:* England Youth, Under-21, 1 full cap.
1997–98 Blackburn R 0 0
1998–99 Blackburn R 15 1
1999–2000 Blackburn R 22 2
2000–01 Blackburn R 42 12
2001–02 Blackburn R 29 7
2002–03 Blackburn R 28 8 **136 30**
2003–04 Birmingham C 21 2
2004–05 Birmingham C 11 2 **32 4**

FIGUEROA, Luciano (F) 58 35
H: 6 0 W: 12 02 b.Argentina 19-5-81
Honours: Argentina 1 full cap.
2001–02 Rosario Central 20 8
2002–03 Rosario Central 37 27 **57 35**
2003–04 Birmingham C 1 0
2004–05 Birmingham C 0 0 **1 0**

GRAINGER, Martin (D) 380 44
H: 5 10 W: 12 11 b.Enfield 23-8-72
Source: Trainee.
1989–90 Colchester U 7 2
1990–91 Colchester U 0 0
1991–92 Colchester U 0 0
1992–93 Colchester U 31 3
1993–94 Colchester U 8 2 **46 7**
1993–94 Brentford 31 2
1994–95 Brentford 37 7
1995–96 Brentford 33 3 **101 12**
1995–96 Birmingham C 8 0
1996–97 Birmingham C 23 3
1997–98 Birmingham C 33 2
1998–99 Birmingham C 40 4
1999–2000 Birmingham C 34 5
2000–01 Birmingham C 35 6
2001–02 Birmingham C 40 4
2002–03 Birmingham C 9 0
2003–04 Birmingham C 4 1
2003–04 *Coventry C* 7 0 **7 0**
2004–05 Birmingham C 0 0 **226 25**

GRAY, Julian (M) 167 12
H: 6 1 W: 11 00 b.Lewisham 21-9-79
Source: Trainee.
1998–99 Arsenal 0 0
1999–2000 Arsenal 1 0 **1 0**
2000–01 Crystal Palace 23 1
2001–02 Crystal Palace 43 2
2002–03 Crystal Palace 35 5
2003–04 Crystal Palace 24 2 **125 10**
2003–04 *Cardiff C* 9 0 **9 0**
2004–05 Birmingham C 32 2 **32 2**

GRONKJAER, Jesper (M) 246 28
H: 5 11 W: 11 00 b.Nuuk 12-8-77
Honours: Denmark Under-21, 55 full caps, 5 goals.
1995–96 Aalborg 29 3
1996–97 Aalborg 28 1
1997–98 Aalborg 29 6 **86 10**
1998–99 Ajax 25 8
1999–2000 Ajax 25 3
2000–01 Ajax 6 0 **56 11**
2000–01 Chelsea 14 1
2001–02 Chelsea 13 0
2002–03 Chelsea 30 4
2003–04 Chelsea 31 2 **88 7**
2004–05 Birmingham C 16 0 **16 0**

HALL, Asa (M) 0 0
H: 6 2 W: 11 09 b.Sandwell 29-11-86
Source: Scholar. *Honours:* England Youth.
2004–05 Birmingham C 0 0

HESKEY, Emile (F) 338 89
H: 6 2 W: 13 12 b.Leicester 11-1-78
Source: Trainee. *Honours:* England Youth, Under-21, B, 43 full caps, 5 goals.
1994–95 Leicester C 1 0
1995–96 Leicester C 30 7
1996–97 Leicester C 35 10
1997–98 Leicester C 35 10
1998–99 Leicester C 30 6
1999–2000 Leicester C 23 7 **154 40**
1999–2000 Liverpool 12 3
2000–01 Liverpool 36 14
2001–02 Liverpool 35 9
2002–03 Liverpool 32 6
2003–04 Liverpool 35 7 **150 39**
2004–05 Birmingham C 34 10 **34 10**

HOWLAND, David (M) 0 0
H: 5 11 W: 10 08 b.Ballynahinch 17-9-86
Source: Scholar.
2004–05 Birmingham C 0 0

IZZET, Muzzy (M) 279 39
H: 5 10 W: 10 03 b.Mile End 31-10-74
Source: From Trainee. *Honours:* Turkey 9 full caps.
1993–94 Chelsea 0 0
1994–95 Chelsea 0 0
1995–96 Chelsea 0 0
1995–96 *Leicester C* 9 1
1996–97 Leicester C 35 3
1997–98 Leicester C 36 4
1998–99 Leicester C 31 5
1999–2000 Leicester C 32 8
2000–01 Leicester C 27 7
2001–02 Leicester C 31 4
2002–03 Leicester C 38 4
2003–04 Leicester C 30 2 **269 38**
2004–05 Birmingham C 10 1 **10 1**

JOHNSON, Damien (M) 175 6
H: 5 9 W: 11 09 b.Lisburn 18-11-78
Source: Trainee. *Honours:* Northern Ireland Youth, Under-21, 43 full caps.
1995–96 Blackburn R 0 0
1996–97 Blackburn R 0 0
1997–98 Blackburn R 0 0
1997–98 *Nottingham F* 6 0 **6 0**
1998–99 Blackburn R 21 1
1999–2000 Blackburn R 16 1
2000–01 Blackburn R 16 0
2001–02 Blackburn R 7 1 **60 3**
2001–02 Birmingham C 8 1
2002–03 Birmingham C 30 1
2003–04 Birmingham C 35 1
2004–05 Birmingham C 36 0 **109 3**

KILKENNY, Neil (M) 27 4
H: 5 8 W: 10 08 b.Middlesex 19-12-85
Source: Arsenal Trainee. *Honours:* England Youth, Under-20.
2003–04 Birmingham C 0 0
2004–05 Birmingham C 0 0
2004–05 *Oldham Ath* 27 4 **27 4**

KUQI, Njazi (F) 0 0
H: 6 3 W: 13 05 b.Vushtrri 25-3-83
Source: Lahti.
2004–05 Birmingham C 0 0

LAZARIDIS, Stan (M) 316 16
H: 5 9 W: 11 12 b.Perth 16-8-72
Honours: Australia Youth, Under-23, 56 full caps.
1992–93 Adelaide Sharks 28 2
1993–94 Adelaide Sharks 23 3
1994–95 Adelaide Sharks 22 0 **73 5**
1995–96 West Ham U 4 0
1996–97 West Ham U 22 1
1997–98 West Ham U 28 2
1998–99 West Ham U 15 0 **69 3**
1999–2000 Birmingham C 31 2
2000–01 Birmingham C 31 2
2001–02 Birmingham C 32 0
2002–03 *Portsmouth* 0 0
2002–03 Birmingham C 30 2
2003–04 Birmingham C 30 2
2004–05 Birmingham C 20 0 **174 8**

MELCHIOT, Mario (D) 237 6
H: 6 2 W: 11 09 b.Amsterdam 4-11-76
Honours: Holland 13 full caps.
1996–97 Ajax 23 0
1997–98 Ajax 26 0
1998–99 Ajax 24 1 **73 1**
1999–2000 Chelsea 5 0
2000–01 Chelsea 31 0
2001–02 Chelsea 37 2
2002–03 Chelsea 34 0
2003–04 Chelsea 23 2 **130 4**
2004–05 Birmingham C 34 1 **34 1**

MORRISON, Clinton (F) 243 76
H: 6 1 W: 11 13 b.Tooting 14-5-79
Source: Trainee. *Honours:* Eire Under-21, 30 full caps, 9 goals.
1996–97 Crystal Palace 0 0
1997–98 Crystal Palace 1 1
1998–99 Crystal Palace 37 12
1999–2000 Crystal Palace 29 13
2000–01 Crystal Palace 45 14
2001–02 Crystal Palace 45 22 **157 62**
2002–03 Birmingham C 28 6
2003–04 Birmingham C 32 4
2004–05 Birmingham C 26 4 **86 14**

MOTTERAM, Carl (M) 0 0
H: 5 8 W: 9 11 b.Birmingham 3-9-84
Source: Scholar.
2004–05 Birmingham C 0 0

NAFTI, Mehdi (M) 155 4
H: 5 9 W: 11 03 b.Toulouse 28-11-78
Honours: Tunisia full caps.
1998–99 Toulouse 0 0
1999–2000 Toulouse 13 1 **13 1**
2000–01 Santander B 21 0 **21 0**
2000–01 Santander 3 0
2001–02 Santander 30 0
2002–03 Santander 31 2
2003–04 Santander 31 1
2004–05 Santander 16 0 **111 3**
2004–05 Birmingham C 10 0 **10 0**

OJI, Samuel (D) 0 0
H: 6 0 W: 14 05 b.Westminster 9-10-85
2003–04 Birmingham C 0 0
2004–05 Birmingham C 0 0

PANDIANI, Walter (F) 204 73
H: 6 0 W: 11 09 b.Montevideo 27-4-76
Honours: Uruguay 3 full caps.
1996 Progreso 0 0
1997 Basanez 0 0
1998 Penarol 21 3
1999 Penarol 35 17
2000 Penarol 15 9 **71 29**
2000–01 La Coruna 25 7
2001–02 La Coruna 18 0
2002–03 Mallorca 33 13 **33 13**
2003–04 La Coruna 28 14
2004–05 La Coruna 15 6 **86 27**
2004–05 Birmingham C 14 4 **14 4**

PENNANT, Jermaine (M) 88 7
H: 5 9 W: 10 06 b.Nottingham 15-1-83
Honours: England Schools, Youth, England Under-21.

1998–99	Notts Co	0	0		
1998–99	Arsenal	0	0		
1999–2000	Arsenal	0	0		
2000–01	Arsenal	0	0		
2001–02	Arsenal	0	0		
2001–02	*Watford*	9	2		
2002–03	Arsenal	5	3		
2002–03	*Watford*	12	0	**21**	**2**
2003–04	Arsenal	7	0		
2003–04	*Leeds U*	36	2	**36**	**2**
2004–05	Arsenal	7	0	**19**	**3**
2004–05	Birmingham C	12	0	**12**	**0**

SADLER, Matthew (D) 9 0
H: 5 11 W: 11 08 b.Birmingham 26-2-85
Source: Scholar. *Honours:* England Youth.

2001–02	Birmingham C	0	0		
2002–03	Birmingham C	2	0		
2003–04	Birmingham C	0	0		
2003–04	*Northampton T*	7	0	**7**	**0**
2004–05	Birmingham C	0	0	**2**	**0**

TAYLOR, Maik (G) 344 0
H: 6 4 W: 14 02 b.Hildeshein 4-9-71
Source: Farnborough T. *Honours:* Northern Ireland Under-21, B, 45 full caps.

1995–96	Barnet	45	0		
1996–97	Barnet	25	0	**70**	**0**
1996–97	Southampton	18	0		
1997–98	Southampton	0	0	**18**	**0**
1997–98	Fulham	28	0		
1998–99	Fulham	46	0		
1999–2000	Fulham	46	0		
2000–01	Fulham	44	0		
2001–02	Fulham	1	0		
2002–03	Fulham	19	0		
2003–04	Fulham	0	0	**184**	**0**
2003–04	Birmingham C	34	0		
2004–05	Birmingham C	38	0	**72**	**0**

TAYLOR, Martin (D) 118 6
H: 6 4 W: 15 00 b.Ashington 9-11-79
Source: Trainee. *Honours:* England Youth, Under-21.

1997–98	Blackburn R	0	0		
1998–99	Blackburn R	3	0		
1999–2000	Blackburn R	6	0		
1999–2000	*Darlington*	4	0	**4**	**0**
1999–2000	*Stockport Co*	7	0	**7**	**0**
2000–01	Blackburn R	16	3		
2001–02	Blackburn R	19	0		
2002–03	Blackburn R	33	2		
2003–04	Blackburn R	11	0	**88**	**5**
2003–04	Birmingham C	12	1		
2004–05	Birmingham C	7	0	**19**	**1**

TEBILY, Oliver (D) 118 1
H: 6 0 W: 13 05 b.Abidjan 19-12-75
Source: Chateauroux. *Honours:* France Under-21. Ivory Coast full caps.

1997–98	Chateauroux	11	1	**11**	**1**
1998–99	Sheffield U	8	0	**8**	**0**
1999–2000	Celtic	23	0		
2000–01	Celtic	4	0		
2001–02	Celtic	11	0	**38**	**0**
2001–02	Birmingham C	7	0		
2002–03	Birmingham C	12	0		
2003–04	Birmingham C	27	0		
2004–05	Birmingham C	15	0	**61**	**0**

UPSON, Matthew (D) 137 2
H: 6 1 W: 11 04 b.Hartismere 18-4-79
Source: Trainee. *Honours:* England Youth, Under-21, 7 full caps.

1995–96	Luton T	0	0		
1996–97	Luton T	1	0	**1**	**0**
1996–97	Arsenal	0	0		
1997–98	Arsenal	5	0		
1998–99	Arsenal	5	0		
1999–2000	Arsenal	8	0		
2000–01	Arsenal	2	0		
2000–01	*Nottingham F*	1	0	**1**	**0**
2000–01	*Crystal Palace*	7	0	**7**	**0**
2001–02	Arsenal	14	0		
2002–03	Arsenal	0	0	**34**	**0**
2002–03	*Reading*	14	0	**14**	**0**
2002–03	Birmingham C	14	0		
2003–04	Birmingham C	30	0		
2004–05	Birmingham C	36	2	**80**	**2**

VAESEN, Nico (G) 255 0
H: 6 3 W: 12 13 b.Hasselt 28-9-69
Source: Tongeren.

1993–94	CS Brugge	13	0		
1994–95	CS Brugge	3	0	**16**	**0**
1995–96	Aalst	20	0		
1996–97	Aalst	0	0		
1997–98	Aalst	14	0	**34**	**0**
1998–99	Huddersfield T	43	0		
1999–2000	Huddersfield T	46	0		
2000–01	Huddersfield T	45	0	**134**	**0**
2001–02	Birmingham C	23	0		
2002–03	Birmingham C	27	0		
2003–04	Birmingham C	0	0		
2003–04	*Gillingham*	5	0	**5**	**0**
2003–04	*Bradford C*	6	0	**6**	**0**
2003–04	*Crystal Palace*	10	0	**10**	**0**
2004–05	Birmingham C	0	0	**50**	**0**

YORKE, Dwight (F) 400 135
H: 5 10 W: 12 04 b.Canaan 3-11-71
Source: St Clair's, Tobago. *Honours:* Trinidad & Tobago full caps.

1989–90	Aston Villa	2	0		
1990–91	Aston Villa	18	2		
1991–92	Aston Villa	32	11		
1992–93	Aston Villa	27	6		
1993–94	Aston Villa	12	2		
1994–95	Aston Villa	37	6		
1995–96	Aston Villa	35	17		
1996–97	Aston Villa	37	17		
1997–98	Aston Villa	30	12		
1998–99	Aston Villa	1	0	**231**	**73**
1998–99	Manchester U	32	18		
1999–2000	Manchester U	32	20		
2000–01	Manchester U	22	9		
2001–02	Manchester U	10	1	**96**	**48**
2002–03	Blackburn R	33	8		
2003–04	Blackburn R	23	4		
2004–05	Blackburn R	4	0	**60**	**12**
2004–05	Birmingham C	13	2	**13**	**2**

Scholars
Bagnall, Andrew Brian; Birley, Matthew Mark; Blake, James; Davies, Craig; Dormand, James; Hall, Mark Stephen John; Hinks, Brett; Howell, Michael Robert; Legzdins, Adam Richard; Luckett, Stephen Paul; Meredith, Jake Leslie; Painter, Marcos; Price, Jamie Michael; Till, Peter; Wright, Nicholas

BLACKBURN R (5)

AMORUSO, Lorenzo (D) 216 17
H: 6 2 W: 13 10 b.Palese 28-6-71

1988–89	Bari	3	0		
1989–90	Bari	3	0		
1990–91	Bari	5	1		
1991–92	Bari	0	0		
1991–92	Mantova	13	1	**13**	**1**
1992–93	Bari	0	0		
1992–93	Pescavo	19	1	**19**	**1**
1993–94	Bari	37	3		
1994–95	Bari	27	4	**75**	**8**
1995–96	Fiorentina	31	2		
1996–97	Fiorentina	23	1	**54**	**3**
1997–98	Rangers	4	0		
1998–99	Rangers	33	1		
1999–2000	Rangers	0	0		
2000–01	Rangers	0	0		
2001–02	Rangers	0	0	**37**	**1**
2003–04	Blackburn R	12	3		
2004–05	Blackburn R	6	0	**18**	**3**

BARKER, Keith (F) 0 0
H: 6 2 W: 12 12 b.Accrington 21-10-86
Source: Scholar. *Honours:* England Youth.

2004–05	Blackburn R	0	0		

BOTHROYD, Jay (F) 109 19
H: 6 3 W: 13 01 b.Islington 7-5-82
Source: Trainee. *Honours:* England Youth, Under-20, Under-21.

1999–2000	Arsenal	0	0		
2000–01	Coventry C	8	0		
2001–02	Coventry C	31	6		
2002–03	Coventry C	33	8	**72**	**14**
2003–04	*Perugia*	26	4	**26**	**4**
2004–05	Blackburn R	11	1	**11**	**1**

BYROM, Joel (M) 0 0
H: 6 0 W: 12 04 b.Oswaldtwistle 14-9-86
Source: Scholar.

2004–05	Blackburn R	0	0		

DE PEDRO, Javier (M) 320 51
H: 5 11 W: 12 03 b.Logrono 4-8-73
Honours: Spain 12 full caps.

1992–93	Real Sociedad B	14	6	**14**	**6**
1993–94	Real Sociedad	14	0		
1994–95	Real Sociedad	29	3		
1995–96	Real Sociedad	38	5		
1996–97	Real Sociedad	37	8		
1997–98	Real Sociedad	30	5		
1998–99	Real Sociedad	27	6		
1999–2000	Real Sociedad	27	3		
2000–01	Real Sociedad	30	5		
2001–02	Real Sociedad	30	3		
2002–03	Real Sociedad	29	6		
2003–04	Real Sociedad	13	1	**304**	**45**
2004–05	Blackburn R	2	0	**2**	**0**

DERBYSHIRE, Matt (F) 1 0
H: 5 10 W: 11 01 b.Gt Harwood 14-4-86
Source: Gt Harwood T.

2003–04	Blackburn R	0	0		
2004–05	Blackburn R	1	0	**1**	**0**

DICKOV, Paul (F) 318 83
H: 5 6 W: 10 06 b.Livingston 1-11-72
Source: Trainee. *Honours:* Scotland Schools, Youth, Under-21, 10 full caps, 1 goal.

1992–93	Arsenal	3	2		
1993–94	Arsenal	1	0		
1993–94	*Luton T*	15	1	**15**	**1**
1993–94	*Brighton & HA*	8	5	**8**	**5**
1994–95	Arsenal	9	0		
1995–96	Arsenal	7	1		
1996–97	Arsenal	1	0	**21**	**3**
1996–97	Manchester C	29	5		
1997–98	Manchester C	30	9		
1998–99	Manchester C	35	10		
1999–2000	Manchester C	34	5		
2000–01	Manchester C	21	4		
2001–02	Manchester C	7	0	**156**	**33**
2001–02	Leicester C	12	4		
2002–03	Leicester C	42	17		
2003–04	Leicester C	35	11	**89**	**32**
2004–05	Blackburn R	29	9	**29**	**9**

DJORKAEFF, Youri (M) 526 184
H: 5 10 W: 11 02 b.Lyon 9-3-68
Honours: France 82 full caps, 28 goals.

1984–85	Grenoble	2	0		
1985–86	Grenoble	6	0		
1986–87	Grenoble	26	4		
1987–88	Grenoble	19	8		
1988–89	Grenoble	25	11		
1989–90	Grenoble	3	0	**81**	**23**
1989–90	Strasbourg	28	21		
1990–91	Strasbourg	7	4	**35**	**25**
1990–91	Monaco	20	5		
1991–92	Monaco	35	9		
1992–93	Monaco	32	12		
1993–94	Monaco	35	20		
1994–95	Monaco	33	14	**155**	**60**
1995–96	Paris St Germain	35	13	**35**	**13**
1996–97	Internazionale	33	14		
1997–98	Internazionale	29	8		
1998–99	Internazionale	25	8	**87**	**30**
1999–2000	Kaiserslautern	25	11		
2000–01	Kaiserslautern	26	3		
2001–02	Kaiserslautern	4	0	**55**	**14**
2001–02	Bolton W	12	4		
2002–03	Bolton W	36	7		
2003–04	Bolton W	27	8		
2004–05	Bolton W	0	0	**75**	**19**
2004–05	Blackburn R	3	0	**3**	**0**

DOUGLAS, Jonathan (M) 49 5
H: 6 0 W: 12 07 b.Clones 22-11-81
Source: Trainee. *Honours:* Eire 2 full caps, Under-21.

1999–2000	Blackburn R	0	0		
2000–01	Blackburn R	0	0		
2001–02	Blackburn R	0	0		
2002–03	Blackburn R	1	0		
2002–03	*Chesterfield*	7	1	**7**	**1**
2003–04	Blackpool	16	3	**16**	**3**

2003–04	Blackburn R	14	1		
2004–05	Blackburn R	1	0	**16**	**1**
2004–05	*Gillingham*	10	0	**10**	**0**

DRENCH, Steven (G) **0** **0**
H: 5 11 W: 12 08 b.Salford 11-9-85
Source: Trainee.

2002–03	Blackburn R	0	0		
2003–04	Blackburn R	0	0		
2004–05	Blackburn R	0	0		

EMERTON, Brett (M) **260** **33**
H: 6 1 W: 13 05 b.Bankstown 22-2-79
Honours: Australia Youth, Under-20, Under-23, 40 full caps, 9 goals.

1996–97	Sydney Olympic	18	2		
1997–98	Sydney Olympic	24	3		
1998–99	Sydney Olympic	21	2		
1999–2000	Sydney Olympic	31	9	**94**	**16**
2000–01	Feyenoord	28	2		
2001–02	Feyenoord	31	6		
2002–03	Feyenoord	33	3	**92**	**11**
2003–04	Blackburn R	37	2		
2004–05	Blackburn R	37	4	**74**	**6**

ENCKELMAN, Peter (G) **133** **0**
H: 6 2 W: 12 05 b.Turku 10-3-77
Source: TPS Turku. *Honours:* Finland Under-21, 6 full caps.

1995	TPS Turku	6	0		
1996	TPS Turku	24	0		
1997	TPS Turku	25	0		
1998	TPS Turku	24	0	**79**	**0**
1998–99	Aston Villa	0	0		
1999–2000	Aston Villa	10	0		
2000–01	Aston Villa	0	0		
2001–02	Aston Villa	9	0		
2002–03	Aston Villa	33	0		
2003–04	Aston Villa	0	0	**52**	**0**
2003–04	Blackburn R	2	0		
2004–05	Blackburn R	0	0	**2**	**0**

FERGUSON, Barry (M) **189** **27**
H: 5 7 W: 9 10 b.Glasgow 2-2-78
Source: Rangers SABC. *Honours:* Scotland Under-21, 29 full caps, 2 goals.

1994–95	Rangers	0	0		
1995–96	Rangers	0	0		
1996–97	Rangers	1	0		
1997–98	Rangers	7	0		
1998–99	Rangers	23	1		
1999–2000	Rangers	31	4		
2000–01	Rangers	30	2		
2001–02	Rangers	22	1		
2002–03	Rangers	36	16		
2003–04	Rangers	3	0	**153**	**24**
2003–04	Blackburn R	15	1		
2004–05	Blackburn R	21	2	**36**	**3**

FITZGERALD, John (D) **14** **0**
H: 6 2 W: 12 13 b.Dublin 10-2-84
Source: Scholar. *Honours:* Eire Youth, Under-21.

2000–01	Blackburn R	0	0		
2001–02	Blackburn R	0	0		
2002–03	Blackburn R	0	0		
2003–04	Blackburn R	0	0		
2004–05	Blackburn R	0	0		
2004–05	*Bury*	14	0	**14**	**0**

FLITCROFT, Garry (M) **371** **27**
H: 6 0 W: 11 08 b.Bolton 6-11-72
Source: Trainee. *Honours:* England Schools, Under-21.

1991–92	Manchester C	0	0		
1991–92	*Bury*	12	0	**12**	**0**
1992–93	Manchester C	32	5		
1993–94	Manchester C	21	3		
1994–95	Manchester C	37	5		
1995–96	Manchester C	25	0	**115**	**13**
1995–96	Blackburn R	3	0		
1996–97	Blackburn R	28	3		
1997–98	Blackburn R	33	0		
1998–99	Blackburn R	8	2		
1999–2000	Blackburn R	19	0		
2000–01	Blackburn R	41	3		
2001–02	Blackburn R	29	1		
2002–03	Blackburn R	33	2		
2003–04	Blackburn R	31	3		
2004–05	Blackburn R	19	0	**244**	**14**

FRIEDEL, Brad (G) **237** **1**
H: 6 3 W: 14 00 b.Lakewood 18-5-71
Honours: USA 82 full caps.

1996	Columbus Crew	9	0		
1997	Columbus Crew	29	0	**38**	**0**
1997–98	Liverpool	11	0		
1998–99	Liverpool	12	0		
1999–2000	Liverpool	2	0		
2000–01	Liverpool	0	0	**25**	**0**
2000–01	Blackburn R	27	0		
2001–02	Blackburn R	36	0		
2002–03	Blackburn R	37	0		
2003–04	Blackburn R	36	1		
2004–05	Blackburn R	38	0	**174**	**1**

GALLAGHER, Paul (F) **43** **5**
H: 6 1 W: 12 00 b.Glasgow 9-8-84
Source: Trainee. *Honours:* Scotland Under-21, 1 full cap.

2002–03	Blackburn R	1	0		
2003–04	Blackburn R	26	3		
2004–05	Blackburn R	16	2	**43**	**5**

GARNER, Joseph (F) **0** **0**
b.Blackburn 12-4-88
Source: Scholar. *Honours:* England Schools, Youth.

2004–05	Blackburn R	0	0		

GRAY, Michael (D) **396** **16**
H: 5 8 W: 10 07 b.Sunderland 3-8-74
Source: Trainee. *Honours:* England 3 full caps.

1992–93	Sunderland	27	2		
1993–94	Sunderland	22	1		
1994–95	Sunderland	16	0		
1995–96	Sunderland	46	4		
1996–97	Sunderland	34	3		
1997–98	Sunderland	44	2		
1998–99	Sunderland	37	2		
1999–2000	Sunderland	33	0		
2000–01	Sunderland	36	1		
2001–02	Sunderland	35	0		
2002–03	Sunderland	32	1		
2003–04	Sunderland	1	0	**363**	**16**
2003–04	Blackburn R	14	0		
2004–05	Blackburn R	9	0	**23**	**0**
2004–05	*Leeds U*	10	0	**10**	**0**

GRESKO, Vratislav (D) **158** **6**
H: 6 0 W: 11 05 b.Bratislava 24-7-77
Honours: Slovakia 24 full caps, 1 goal.

1995–96	Dukla Banska	1	0		
1996–97	Dukla Banska	7	0	**8**	**0**
1997–98	Internazionale	22	0		
1998–99	Internazionale	29	5		
1999–2000	Leverkusen	9	0		
2000–01	Leverkusen	7	0	**16**	**0**
2000–01	Internazionale	18	0		
2001–02	Internazionale	23	0	**92**	**5**
2002–03	Parma	5	0	**5**	**0**
2002–03	Blackburn R	10	0		
2003–04	Blackburn R	24	1		
2004–05	Blackburn R	3	0	**37**	**1**

HARKINS, Gary (M) **8** **0**
H: 6 2 W: 12 10 b.Greenock 2-1-85
Source: Trainee.

2003–04	Blackburn R	0	0		
2003–04	*Huddersfield T*	3	0	**3**	**0**
2004–05	Blackburn R	0	0		
2004–05	*Bury*	5	0	**5**	**0**

HODGE, Bryan (M) **0** **0**
H: 5 10 W: 12 02 b.Hamilton 23-9-87
Source: Scholar.

2004–05	Blackburn R	0	0		

JANSEN, Matt (F) **226** **65**
H: 5 11 W: 11 03 b.Carlisle 20-10-77
Source: From Trainee. *Honours:* England Under-21.

1995–96	Carlisle U	0	0		
1996–97	Carlisle U	19	1		
1997–98	Carlisle U	23	9	**42**	**10**
1997–98	Crystal Palace	8	3		
1998–99	Crystal Palace	18	7	**26**	**10**
1998–99	Blackburn R	11	2		
1999–2000	Blackburn R	30	4		
2000–01	Blackburn R	40	23		
2001–02	Blackburn R	35	10		
2002–03	Blackburn R	7	0		
2002–03	*Coventry C*	9	2	**9**	**2**
2003–04	Blackburn R	19	2		
2004–05	Blackburn R	7	2	**149**	**43**

JOHANSSON, Nils-Eric (D) **96** **0**
H: 6 1 W: 12 10 b.Stockholm 13-1-80
Source: Viksjo, Brommapojkana. *Honours:* Sweden 4 full caps.

1998	AIK Stockholm	0	0		
1998–99	Bayern Munich	2	0		
1999–2000	Bayern Munich	0	0		
2000–01	Bayern Munich	0	0	**2**	**0**
2001–02	Nuremberg	8	0	**8**	**0**
2001–02	Blackburn R	20	0		
2002–03	Blackburn R	30	0		
2003–04	Blackburn R	14	0		
2004–05	Blackburn R	22	0	**86**	**0**

JOHNSON, Jemal (F) **3** **0**
H: 5 8 W: 11 09 b.New Jersey 3-5-84

2001–02	Blackburn R	0	0		
2002–03	Blackburn R	0	0		
2003–04	Blackburn R	0	0		
2004–05	Blackburn R	3	0	**3**	**0**

KANE, Anthony (D) **0** **0**
H: 5 11 W: 11 00 b.Belfast 29-8-87
Source: Scholar.

2004–05	Blackburn R	0	0		

MATTEO, Dominic (D) **271** **3**
H: 6 1 W: 13 08 b.Dumfries 28-4-74
Source: From Trainee. *Honours:* England Youth, Under-21, B, Scotland 6 full caps.

1992–93	Liverpool	0	0		
1993–94	Liverpool	11	0		
1994–95	Liverpool	7	0		
1994–95	*Sunderland*	1	0	**1**	**0**
1995–96	Liverpool	5	0		
1996–97	Liverpool	26	0		
1997–98	Liverpool	26	0		
1998–99	Liverpool	20	1		
1999–2000	Liverpool	32	0		
2000–01	Liverpool	0	0	**127**	**1**
2000–01	Leeds U	30	0		
2001–02	Leeds U	32	0		
2002–03	Leeds U	20	0		
2003–04	Leeds U	33	2	**115**	**2**
2004–05	Blackburn R	28	0	**28**	**0**

McEVELEY, James (D) **28** **1**
H: 6 1 W: 13 03 b.Liverpool 11-2-85
Source: Trainee. *Honours:* England Under-20, Under-21.

2002–03	Blackburn R	9	0		
2003–04	Blackburn R	0	0		
2003–04	*Burnley*	4	0	**4**	**0**
2004–05	Blackburn R	5	0	**14**	**0**
2004–05	*Gillingham*	10	1	**10**	**1**

MOKOENA, Aaron (D) **82** **2**
H: 6 2 W: 14 00 b.Johannesburg 25-11-80
Honours: South Africa 50 full caps.

2000–01	Ajax	0	0		
2000–01	Antwerp	6	0		
2001–02	Antwerp	13	1		
2002–03	Antwerp	29	1	**48**	**2**
2003–04	Genk	18	0	**18**	**0**
2004–05	Blackburn R	16	0	**16**	**0**

MORGAN, Alan (M) **13** **1**
H: 6 0 W: 12 06 b.Edinburgh 27-11-83
Source: Scholar.

2000–01	Blackburn R	0	0		
2001–02	Blackburn R	0	0		
2002–03	Blackburn R	0	0		
2003–04	Blackburn R	0	0		
2003–04	*Darlington*	5	1	**5**	**1**
2004–05	Blackburn R	0	0		
2004–05	*Cheltenham T*	8	0	**8**	**0**

NEILL, Lucas (D) **285** **17**
H: 6 0 W: 12 03 b.Sydney 9-3-78
Source: NSW Soccer Academy. *Honours:* Australia Youth, Under-20, Under-23, 13 full caps.

1995–96	Millwall	13	0		
1996–97	Millwall	39	3		
1997–98	Millwall	6	0		
1998–99	Millwall	35	6		
1999–2000	Millwall	31	1		
2000–01	Millwall	24	2		
2001–02	Millwall	4	1	**152**	**13**

2001–02 Blackburn R 31 1
2002–03 Blackburn R 34 0
2003–04 Blackburn R 32 2
2004–05 Blackburn R 36 1 **133 4**

NELSEN, Ryan (D) 96 7
H: 5 11 W: 14 02 b.Christchurch, NZ 18-10-77
Honours: New Zealand 29 full caps, 3 goals.
2001 DC United 19 0
2002 DC United 20 4
2003 DC United 25 1
2004 DC United 17 2 **81 7**
2004–05 Blackburn R 15 0 **15 0**

PEDERSEN, Morten (F) 182 49
H: 5 11 W: 11 00 b.Vadso 8-9-81
Honours: Norway 15 full caps, 3 goals.
2004 Tromso 18 7
1997 Norlid 21 0
1998 Pola 20 4 **20 4**
1999 Norlid 19 0 **40 0**
2000 Tromso 10 3
2001 Tromso 26 5
2002 Tromso 23 18
2003 Tromso 26 8 **103 41**
2004–05 Blackburn R 19 4 **19 4**

PEERS, Gavin (D) 0 0
H: 5 11 W: 13 05 b.Dublin 10-11-85
Source: Trainee.
2002–03 Blackburn R 0 0
2003–04 Blackburn R 0 0
2004–05 Blackburn R 0 0

REID, Andrew (M) 0 0
H: 6 0 W: 11 07 b.Kilmarnock 26-9-85
2002–03 Blackburn R 0 0
2003–04 Blackburn R 0 0
2004–05 Blackburn R 0 0

REID, Steven (M) 183 20
H: 6 0 W: 12 07 b.Kingston 10-3-81
Source: Trainee. *Honours:* England Youth. Eire 13 full caps, 2 goals.
1997–98 Millwall 1 0
1998–99 Millwall 25 0
1999–2000 Millwall 21 0
2000–01 Millwall 37 7
2001–02 Millwall 35 5
2002–03 Millwall 20 6 **139 18**
2003–04 Blackburn R 16 0
2004–05 Blackburn R 28 2 **44 2**

SAKALI, Abdeltareck (F) 0 0
H: 5 10 W: 12 02 b.Torcy 25-4-86
Source: Trainee.
2002–03 Blackburn R 0 0
2003–04 Blackburn R 0 0
2004–05 Blackburn R 0 0

SAVAGE, Robbie (M) 340 29
H: 5 11 W: 11 00 b.Wrexham 18-10-74
Source: Trainee. *Honours:* Wales Schools, Youth, Under-21, 39 full caps, 2 goals.
1993–94 Manchester U 0 0
1994–95 Crewe Alex 6 2
1995–96 Crewe Alex 30 7
1996–97 Crewe Alex 41 1 **77 10**
1997–98 Leicester C 35 2
1998–99 Leicester C 34 1
1999–2000 Leicester C 35 1
2000–01 Leicester C 33 4
2001–02 Leicester C 35 0 **172 8**
2002–03 Birmingham C 33 4
2003–04 Birmingham C 31 3
2004–05 Birmingham C 18 4 **82 11**
2004–05 Blackburn R 9 0 **9 0**

SHORT, Craig (D) 542 30
H: 6 3 W: 14 06 b.Bridlington 25-6-68
Source: Pickering T. *Honours:* England Schools.
1987–88 Scarborough 21 2
1988–89 Scarborough 42 5 **63 7**
1989–90 Notts Co 44 2
1990–91 Notts Co 0 0
1990–91 Notts Co 43 0
1991–92 Notts Co 38 3
1992–93 Notts Co 3 1 **128 6**
1992–93 Derby Co 38 3
1993–94 Derby Co 43 3
1994–95 Derby Co 37 3 **118 9**
1995–96 Everton 23 2
1996–97 Everton 23 2
1997–98 Everton 31 0
1998–99 Everton 22 0 **99 4**
1999–2000 Blackburn R 17 0
2000–01 Blackburn R 35 1
2001–02 Blackburn R 22 0
2002–03 Blackburn R 27 1
2003–04 Blackburn R 19 1
2004–05 Blackburn R 14 1 **134 4**

STEAD, Jon (F) 110 30
H: 6 3 W: 12 00 b.Huddersfield 7-4-83
Source: Scholar. *Honours:* England Under-21.
2001–02 Huddersfield T 0 0
2002–03 Huddersfield T 42 6
2003–04 Huddersfield T 26 16 **68 22**
2003–04 Blackburn R 13 6
2004–05 Blackburn R 29 2 **42 8**

TAYLOR, Andrew (D) 0 0
H: 5 11 W: 11 07 b.Blackburn 14-3-86
Source: Scholar. *Honours:* England Youth.
2004–05 Blackburn R 0 0

THOMPSON, David (M) 182 25
H: 5 7 W: 10 00 b.Birkenhead 12-9-77
Source: Trainee. *Honours:* England Youth, Under-21.
1994–95 Liverpool 0 0
1995–96 Liverpool 0 0
1996–97 Liverpool 2 0
1997–98 Liverpool 5 1
1997–98 *Swindon T* 10 0 **10 0**
1998–99 Liverpool 14 1
1999–2000 Liverpool 27 3 **48 5**
2000–01 Coventry C 25 3
2001–02 Coventry C 37 12
2002–03 Coventry C 4 0 **66 15**
2002–03 Blackburn R 23 4
2003–04 Blackburn R 11 1
2004–05 Blackburn R 24 0 **58 5**

TODD, Andy (D) 221 8
H: 5 11 W: 13 04 b.Derby 21-9-74
Source: Trainee.
1991–92 Middlesbrough 0 0
1992–93 Middlesbrough 0 0
1993–94 Middlesbrough 3 0
1994–95 Middlesbrough 5 0 **8 0**
1994–95 *Swindon T* 13 0 **13 0**
1995–96 Bolton W 12 2
1996–97 Bolton W 15 0
1997–98 Bolton W 25 0
1998–99 Bolton W 20 0
1999–2000 Bolton W 12 0 **84 2**
1999–2000 Charlton Ath 12 0
2000–01 Charlton Ath 23 1
2001–02 Charlton Ath 5 0 **40 1**
2001–02 *Grimsby T* 12 3 **12 3**
2002–03 Blackburn R 12 1
2003–04 Blackburn R 19 0
2003–04 *Burnley* 7 0 **7 0**
2004–05 Blackburn R 26 1 **57 2**

TUGAY, Kerimoglu (M) 444 43
H: 5 9 W: 11 07 b.Istanbul 24-8-70
Honours: Turkey 92 full caps, 2 goals.
1988–89 Galatasaray 16 0
1989–90 Galatasaray 23 0
1990–91 Galatasaray 12 0
1991–92 Galatasaray 26 3
1992–93 Galatasaray 25 6
1993–94 Galatasaray 25 12
1994–95 Galatasaray 23 1
1995–96 Galatasaray 30 3
1996–97 Galatasaray 33 4
1997–98 Galatasaray 30 2
1998–99 Galatasaray 22 2
1999–2000 Galatasaray 10 1 **275 34**
1999–2000 Rangers 16 1
2000–01 Rangers 26 3 **42 4**
2001–02 Blackburn R 33 3
2002–03 Blackburn R 37 1
2003–04 Blackburn R 36 1
2004–05 Blackburn R 21 0 **127 5**

WATT, Jerome (M) 0 0
b.Preston 20-10-84
Source: Scholar. *Honours:* England Youth.
2001–02 Blackburn R 0 0
2002–03 Blackburn R 0 0
2003–04 Blackburn R 0 0
2004–05 Blackburn R 0 0

WEAVER, Paul (M) 0 0
b.Irvine 27-2-86
Source: Trainee.
2002–03 Blackburn R 0 0
2003–04 Blackburn R 0 0
2004–05 Blackburn R 0 0

WELCH, Ralph (M) 0 0
b.Liverpool 10-3-87
Source: Scholar.
2004–05 Blackburn R 0 0

YELLDELL, David (G) 3 0
H: 6 5 W: 12 11 b.Stuttgart 1-10-81
2003–04 Blackburn R 0 0
2004–05 Blackburn R 0 0
2004–05 *Brighton & HA* 3 0 **3 0**

Scholars
Barr, Craig John; De Vita, Raffaele; Fielding, Francis David; Griffiths, Rostyn; Jones, Luke Joseph; King, Mark; Nolan, Edward William; Rowntree, Gari Richard; Stopforth, Gary; Thomas, Adam Hamilton; Thomson, Stephen; Woods, Ryan Alexander

BLACKPOOL (6)

ANDERSON, Stuart (M) 4 0
H: 6 0 W: 11 09 b.Banff 22-4-86
Source: Scholar. *Honours:* Scotland Youth.
2003–04 Southampton 0 0
2004–05 Southampton 0 0
2004–05 Blackpool 4 0 **4 0**

BLINKHORN, Matthew (F) 28 3
H: 5 11 W: 10 10 b.Blackpool 2-3-85
Source: Scholar.
2001–02 Blackpool 3 0
2002–03 Blackpool 7 2
2003–04 Blackpool 12 1
2004–05 Blackpool 4 0 **26 3**
2004–05 *Luton T* 2 0 **2 0**

BOYACK, Steven (M) 132 7
H: 5 10 W: 10 07 b.Edinburgh 4-9-76
Source: Rangers BC. *Honours:* Scotland Under-21.
1996–97 Rangers 1 0
1997–98 Rangers 0 0
1997–98 *Hull C* 12 3 **12 3**
1998–99 Rangers 0 0 **1 0**
1998–99 Dundee 8 2
1999–2000 Dundee 36 1 **44 3**
2000–01 Hearts 12 0
2001–02 Hearts 19 0
2002–03 Hearts 25 1
2003–04 Hearts 8 0 **64 1**
2004–05 Livingston 6 0 **6 0**
2004–05 Boston U 4 0 **4 0**
2004–05 Blackpool 1 0 **1 0**

BULLOCK, Martin (M) 344 9
H: 5 5 W: 10 07 b.Derby 5-3-75
Source: Eastwood T. *Honours:* England Under-21.
1993–94 Barnsley 0 0
1994–95 Barnsley 29 0
1995–96 Barnsley 41 1
1996–97 Barnsley 28 0
1997–98 Barnsley 33 0
1998–99 Barnsley 32 2
1999–2000 Barnsley 4 0
1999–2000 *Port Vale* 6 1 **6 1**
2000–01 Barnsley 18 1
2001–02 Barnsley 0 0 **185 4**
2001–02 Blackpool 43 2
2002–03 Blackpool 38 1
2003–04 Blackpool 44 1
2004–05 Blackpool 28 0 **153 4**

BURNS, Jamie (M) 41 0
H: 5 9 W: 10 11 b.Blackpool 6-3-84
Source: Scholar.
2002–03 Blackpool 7 0
2003–04 Blackpool 11 0
2004–05 Blackpool 23 0 **41 0**

BUTLER, Tony (D) 442 10
H: 6 2 W: 13 07 b.Stockport 28-9-72
Source: Trainee.
1990–91 Gillingham 6 0
1991–92 Gillingham 5 0
1992–93 Gillingham 41 0
1993–94 Gillingham 27 1
1994–95 Gillingham 33 2
1995–96 Gillingham 36 2 **148 5**
1996–97 Blackpool 42 0
1997–98 Blackpool 37 0
1998–99 Blackpool 20 0
1998–99 Port Vale 4 0
1999–2000 Port Vale 15 0 **19 0**
1999–2000 WBA 7 0
2000–01 WBA 44 1
2001–02 WBA 19 0
2002–03 WBA 0 0 **70 1**
2002–03 Bristol C 38 1
2003–04 Bristol C 38 1
2004–05 Bristol C 22 2 **98 4**
2004–05 Blackpool 8 0 **107 0**

CLANCY, Sean (M) 2 0
H: 5 8 W: 9 12 b.Liverpool 16-9-87
Source: School.
2003–04 Blackpool 2 0
2004–05 Blackpool 0 0 **2 0**

CLARE, Rob (D) 140 3
H: 6 1 W: 11 07 b.Belper 28-2-83
Source: Trainee. *Honours:* England Under-20.
1999–2000 Stockport Co 0 0
2000–01 Stockport Co 22 0
2001–02 Stockport Co 23 0
2002–03 Stockport Co 36 0
2003–04 Stockport Co 36 3 **117 3**
2004–05 Blackpool 23 0 **23 0**

CLARKE, Peter (D) 81 9
H: 6 0 W: 12 00 b.Southport 3-1-82
Source: Trainee. *Honours:* England Youth, Under-20, Under-21.
1998–99 Everton 0 0
1999–2000 Everton 0 0
2000–01 Everton 1 0
2001–02 Everton 7 0
2002–03 Everton 0 0
2002–03 *Blackpool* 16 3
2002–03 *Port Vale* 13 1 **13 1**
2003–04 Everton 1 0
2003–04 *Coventry C* 5 0 **5 0**
2004–05 Everton 0 0 **9 0**
2004–05 Blackpool 38 5 **54 8**

COID, Danny (D) 201 9
H: 5 11 W: 11 07 b.Liverpool 3-10-81
Source: Trainee.
1998–99 Blackpool 1 0
1999–2000 Blackpool 21 1
2000–01 Blackpool 46 1
2001–02 Blackpool 27 3
2002–03 Blackpool 36 1
2003–04 Blackpool 35 3
2004–05 Blackpool 35 0 **201 9**

DAVIS, Steve (D) 503 64
H: 6 2 W: 14 07 b.Hexham 30-10-68
Source: Trainee.
1987–88 Southampton 0 0
1988–89 Southampton 0 0
1989–90 Southampton 4 0
1989–90 *Burnley* 9 0
1990–91 Southampton 3 0 **7 0**
1990–91 *Notts Co* 2 0 **2 0**
1991–92 Burnley 40 6
1992–93 Burnley 37 2
1993–94 Burnley 42 7
1994–95 Burnley 43 7
1995–96 Luton T 36 2
1996–97 Luton T 44 8
1997–98 Luton T 38 5
1998–99 Luton T 20 6 **138 21**
1998–99 Burnley 19 3
1999–2000 Burnley 42 7
2000–01 Burnley 44 5
2001–02 Burnley 23 1
2002–03 Burnley 28 4 **327 42**
2003–04 Blackpool 29 1
2004–05 Blackpool 0 0 **29 1**

DONNELLY, Ciaran (M) 17 0
H: 5 9 W: 11 09 b.Blackpool 2-4-84
Source: Scholar. *Honours:* England Youth.
2001–02 Blackburn R 0 0
2002–03 Blackburn R 0 0
2003–04 *Blackpool* 9 0
2004–05 Blackburn R 0 0
2004–05 Blackpool 8 0 **17 0**

DOUGHTY, Phil (M) 0 0
H: 6 2 W: 13 02 b.Kirkham 6-9-86
2003–04 Blackpool 0 0
2004–05 Blackpool 0 0

EDGE, Lewis (G) 1 0
H: 6 1 W: 12 10 b.Lancaster 12-1-87
Source: Scholar.
2003–04 Blackpool 1 0
2004–05 Blackpool 0 0 **1 0**

EDWARDS, Paul (M) 127 7
H: 5 11 W: 10 12 b.Manchester 1-1-80
Source: Altrincham.
2001–02 Swindon T 20 0 **20 0**
2002–03 Wrexham 38 4
2003–04 Wrexham 41 0 **79 4**
2004–05 Blackpool 28 3 **28 3**

EDWARDS, Rob (D) 459 15
H: 6 0 W: 12 02 b.Kendal 1-7-73
Source: Trainee. *Honours:* Wales Youth, Under-21, B, 4 full caps.
1989–90 Carlisle U 12 0
1990–91 Carlisle U 36 5 **48 5**
1990–91 Bristol C 0 0
1991–92 Bristol C 20 1
1992–93 Bristol C 18 0
1993–94 Bristol C 38 2
1994–95 Bristol C 30 0
1995–96 Bristol C 19 0
1996–97 Bristol C 31 0
1997–98 Bristol C 37 2
1998–99 Bristol C 23 0 **216 5**
1999–2000 Preston NE 41 2
2000–01 Preston NE 42 0
2001–02 Preston NE 36 2
2002–03 Preston NE 26 0
2003–04 Preston NE 24 0 **169 4**
2004–05 Blackpool 26 1 **26 1**

EVANS, Gareth (D) 81 0
H: 6 0 W: 11 12 b.Leeds 15-2-81
Source: Trainee. *Honours:* England Youth.
1997–98 Leeds U 0 0
1998–99 Leeds U 0 0
1999–2000 Leeds U 0 0
2000–01 Leeds U 1 0 **1 0**
2001–02 Huddersfield T 35 0
2002–03 Huddersfield T 0 0 **35 0**
2003–04 Blackpool 23 0
2004–05 Blackpool 22 0 **45 0**

FLYNN, Mike (D) 654 25
H: 6 0 W: 11 00 b.Oldham 23-2-69
Source: Trainee.
1986–87 Oldham Ath 0 0
1987–88 Oldham Ath 31 1
1988–89 Oldham Ath 9 0 **40 1**
1988–89 Norwich C 0 0
1989–90 Norwich C 0 0
1989–90 Preston NE 23 1
1990–91 Preston NE 35 1
1991–92 Preston NE 43 3
1992–93 Preston NE 35 2 **136 7**
1992–93 Stockport Co 10 0
1993–94 Stockport Co 46 1
1994–95 Stockport Co 43 2
1995–96 Stockport Co 46 6
1996–97 Stockport Co 46 2
1997–98 Stockport Co 34 1
1998–99 Stockport Co 46 1
1999–2000 Stockport Co 46 1
2000–01 Stockport Co 44 0
2001–02 Stockport Co 26 2 **387 16**
2001–02 *Stoke C* 13 0 **13 0**
2001–02 Barnsley 7 0
2002–03 Barnsley 14 0 **21 0**
2002–03 Blackpool 21 0
2003–04 Blackpool 30 1
2004–05 Blackpool 6 0 **57 1**

GORRE, Dean (M) 317 51
H: 5 8 W: 11 04 b.Surinam 10-9-70
1991–92 SVV/Dordrecht 32 8 **32 8**
1992–93 Feyenoord 25 2
1993–94 Feyenoord 12 3
1994–95 Feyenoord 5 1 **42 6**
1994–95 Groningen 12 3
1995–96 Groningen 34 4
1996–97 Groningen 34 11 **80 18**
1997–98 Ajax 21 3
1998–99 Ajax 14 1 **35 4**
1999–2000 Huddersfield T 28 4
2000–01 Huddersfield T 34 2 **62 6**
2001–02 Barnsley 19 2
2002–03 Barnsley 27 0
2003–04 Barnsley 19 7
2004–05 Barnsley 0 0 **65 9**
From Breidablik.
2004–05 Blackpool 1 0 **1 0**

GRABOVAC, Zarko (F) 3 0
H: 6 5 W: 14 09 b.Ruma 16-3-83
Source: Geldrup.
2004–05 Blackpool 3 0 **3 0**

GRAYSON, Simon (D) 421 11
H: 6 0 W: 13 07 b.Ripon 16-12-69
Source: Trainee.
1987–88 Leeds U 2 0
1988–89 Leeds U 0 0
1989–90 Leeds U 0 0
1990–91 Leeds U 0 0
1991–92 Leeds U 0 0 **2 0**
1991–92 Leicester C 13 0
1992–93 Leicester C 24 1
1993–94 Leicester C 40 1
1994–95 Leicester C 34 0
1995–96 Leicester C 41 2
1996–97 Leicester C 36 0 **188 4**
1997–98 Aston Villa 33 0
1998–99 Aston Villa 15 0 **48 0**
1999–2000 Blackburn R 34 0
2000–01 Blackburn R 0 0
2000–01 *Sheffield W* 5 0 **5 0**
2000–01 *Stockport Co* 13 0 **13 0**
2001–02 Blackburn R 0 0 **34 0**
2001–02 *Notts Co* 10 1 **10 1**
2001–02 *Bradford C* 7 0 **7 0**
2002–03 Blackpool 45 3
2003–04 Blackpool 33 1
2004–05 Blackpool 36 2 **114 6**

HERZIG, Denny (M) 0 0
b.Pobneck 13-11-84
2001–02 Wimbledon 0 0
2002–03 Wimbledon 0 0
2002–03 Blackpool 0 0
2003–04 Blackpool 0 0
2004–05 Blackpool 0 0

JONES, Lee (G) 207 0
H: 6 3 W: 14 04 b.Pontypridd 9-8-70
Source: Porth.
1993–94 Swansea C 0 0
1994–95 Swansea C 2 0
1995–96 Swansea C 1 0
1995–96 *Crewe Alex* 0 0
1996–97 Swansea C 1 0
1997–98 Swansea C 2 0 **6 0**
1997–98 Bristol R 8 0
1998–99 Bristol R 32 0
1999–2000 Bristol R 36 0 **76 0**
2000–01 Stockport Co 27 0
2001–02 Stockport Co 24 0
2002–03 Stockport Co 24 0
2003–04 Stockport Co 0 0 **75 0**
2003–04 Blackpool 21 0
2004–05 Blackpool 29 0 **50 0**

MANGAN, Andrew (M) 2 0
H: 5 9 W: 10 03 b.Liverpool 30-8-86
Source: Scholar.
2003–04 Blackpool 2 0
2004–05 Blackpool 0 0 **2 0**

McGREGOR, Mark (D) 336 13
H: 5 11 W: 11 05 b.Chester 16-2-77
Source: Trainee.
1994–95 Wrexham 1 0
1995–96 Wrexham 32 1
1996–97 Wrexham 38 1

1997–98	Wrexham	42	2		
1998–99	Wrexham	43	1		
1999–2000	Wrexham	45	1		
2000–01	Wrexham	43	5		
2001–02	Wrexham	0	0	**244**	**11**
2001–02	Burnley	1	0		
2002–03	Burnley	30	1		
2003–04	Burnley	23	1	**54**	**2**
2004–05	Blackpool	38	0	**38**	**0**

McMAHON, Steve (M) **23** **0**
H: 5 9 W: 10 05 b.Southport 31-7-84
Source: Scholar.

2002–03	Blackpool	6	0		
2003–04	Blackpool	12	0		
2004–05	Blackpool	0	0	**18**	**0**
2004–05	*Kidderminster H*	5	0	**5**	**0**

MURPHY, John (F) **321** **95**
H: 6 2 W: 14 00 b.Whiston 18-10-76
Source: Trainee.

1994–95	Chester C	5	0		
1995–96	Chester C	18	3		
1996–97	Chester C	11	1		
1997–98	Chester C	27	4		
1998–99	Chester C	42	12	**103**	**20**
1999–2000	Blackpool	39	10		
2000–01	Blackpool	46	18		
2001–02	Blackpool	37	13		
2002–03	Blackpool	35	16		
2003–04	Blackpool	30	9		
2004–05	Blackpool	31	9	**218**	**75**

PARKER, Keigan (F) **37** **9**
H: 5 7 W: 10 05 b.Livingston 8-6-82
Source: St Johnstone BC. *Honours:* Scotland Youth, Under-21.

1998–99	St Johnstone	2	0		
1999–2000	St Johnstone	0	0		
2000–01	St Johnstone	0	0		
2001–02	St Johnstone	0	0	**2**	**0**
2004–05	Blackpool	35	9	**35**	**9**

PATERSON, Sean (M) **2** **0**
H: 5 11 W: 11 05 b.Greenock 26-3-87

2004–05	Blackpool	2	0	**2**	**0**

RICHARDSON, Leam (D) **105** **0**
H: 5 7 W: 11 04 b.Leeds 19-11-79
Source: Trainee.

1997–98	Blackburn R	0	0		
1998–99	Blackburn R	0	0		
1999–2000	Blackburn R	0	0		
2000–01	Bolton W	12	0		
2001–02	Bolton W	1	0		
2001–02	*Notts Co*	21	0	**21**	**0**
2002–03	Bolton W	0	0	**13**	**0**
2002–03	*Blackpool*	20	0		
2003–04	Blackpool	28	0		
2004–05	Blackpool	23	0	**71**	**0**

SHAW, Matthew (F) **11** **0**
H: 6 1 W: 11 09 b.Blackpool 17-5-84

2001–02	Sheffield W	0	0		
2002–03	Sheffield W	0	0		
2003–04	Sheffield W	0	0		
2004–05	Sheffield W	0	0		
2004–05	Wrexham	1	0	**1**	**0**
2004–05	Blackpool	10	0	**10**	**0**

SOUTHERN, Keith (M) **93** **9**
H: 5 10 W: 12 06 b.Gateshead 24-4-81
Source: Trainee.

1998–99	Everton	0	0		
1999–2000	Everton	0	0		
2000–01	Everton	0	0		
2001–02	Everton	0	0		
2002–03	Everton	0	0		
2002–03	Blackpool	38	1		
2003–04	Blackpool	28	2		
2004–05	Blackpool	27	6	**93**	**9**

WARHURST, Paul (M) **333** **17**
H: 6 0 W: 13 00 b.Stockport 26-9-69
Source: Trainee. *Honours:* England Under-21.

1987–88	Manchester C	0	0		
1988–89	Oldham Ath	4	0		
1989–90	Oldham Ath	30	1		
1990–91	Oldham Ath	33	1	**67**	**2**
1991–92	Sheffield W	33	0		
1992–93	Sheffield W	29	6		
1993–94	Sheffield W	4	0	**66**	**6**
1993–94	Blackburn R	9	0		
1994–95	Blackburn R	27	2		
1995–96	Blackburn R	10	0		
1996–97	Blackburn R	11	2	**57**	**4**
1997–98	Crystal Palace	22	3		
1998–99	Crystal Palace	5	1	**27**	**4**
1998–99	Bolton W	20	0		
1999–2000	Bolton W	19	0		
2000–01	Bolton W	20	0		
2001–02	Bolton W	25	0		
2002–03	Bolton W	7	0	**91**	**0**
2002–03	*Stoke C*	5	1	**5**	**1**
2003–04	Chesterfield	4	0	**4**	**0**
2003–04	Barnsley	4	0	**4**	**0**
2003–04	Carlisle U	1	0	**1**	**0**
2003–04	Grimsby T	7	0		
2004–05	Grimsby T	0	0	**7**	**0**
2004–05	Blackpool	4	0	**4**	**0**

WELLENS, Richard (M) **188** **16**
H: 5 9 W: 11 06 b.Manchester 26-3-80
Source: Trainee. *Honours:* England Youth.

1996–97	Manchester U	0	0		
1997–98	Manchester U	0	0		
1998–99	Manchester U	0	0		
1999–2000	Manchester U	0	0		
1999–2000	Blackpool	8	0		
2000–01	Blackpool	36	8		
2001–02	Blackpool	36	1		
2002–03	Blackpool	39	1		
2003–04	Blackpool	41	3		
2004–05	Blackpool	28	3	**188**	**16**

WHITTAKER, Danny (M) **0** **0**
H: 6 0 W: 11 10 b.Blackpool 13-1-87
Source: Scholar.

2004–05	Blackpool	0	0		

WILES, Simon (M) **4** **0**
H: 5 11 W: 11 04 b.Preston 22-4-85
Source: Scholar.

2003–04	Blackpool	4	0		
2004–05	Blackpool	0	0	**4**	**0**

BOLTON W (7)

BARNESS, Anthony (D) **235** **4**
H: 5 10 W: 12 06 b.Lewisham 25-2-73
Source: Trainee.

1990–91	Charlton Ath	0	0		
1991–92	Charlton Ath	22	1		
1992–93	Charlton Ath	5	0		
1992–93	Chelsea	2	0		
1993–94	Chelsea	0	0		
1993–94	*Middlesbrough*	0	0		
1994–95	Chelsea	12	0		
1995–96	Chelsea	0	0	**14**	**0**
1995–96	*Southend U*	5	0	**5**	**0**
1996–97	Charlton Ath	45	2		
1997–98	Charlton Ath	29	1		
1998–99	Charlton Ath	3	0		
1999–2000	Charlton Ath	19	0	**123**	**4**
2000–01	Bolton W	20	0		
2001–02	Bolton W	25	0		
2002–03	Bolton W	25	0		
2003–04	Bolton W	15	0		
2004–05	Bolton W	8	0	**93**	**0**

BEN HAIM, Tal (D) **21** **1**
H: 5 11 W: 11 09 b.Rishon Le Zion 31-3-82
Source: Maccabi Tel Aviv. *Honours:* Israel 21 full caps.

2004–05	Bolton W	21	1	**21**	**1**

BUVAL, Bedi (F) **0** **0**
H: 5 11 W: 11 01 b.Domont 16-6-86
Source: Scholar.

2004–05	Bolton W	0	0		

CAMPO, Ivan (M) **265** **13**
H: 6 1 W: 12 11 b.San Sebastian 21-2-74
Honours: Spain 4 full caps.

1993–94	Alaves	11	1		
1994–95	Alaves	23	1		
1995–96	Alaves	11	0	**45**	**2**
1995–96	Valladolid	24	2	**24**	**2**
1996–97	Valencia	7	1	**7**	**1**
1997–98	Mallorca	33	1	**33**	**1**
1998–99	Real Madrid	27	1		
1999–2000	Real Madrid	20	0		
2000–01	Real Madrid	10	0		
2001–02	Real Madrid	3	0	**60**	**1**
2002–03	Bolton W	31	2		
2003–04	Bolton W	38	4		
2004–05	Bolton W	27	0	**96**	**6**

CANDELA, Vincent (D) **325** **19**
H: 5 10 W: 11 10 b.Bedarieux 24-10-73
Honours: France 40 full caps, 2 goals.

1992–93	Toulouse	3	0		
1993–94	Toulouse	27	1		
1994–95	Toulouse	27	2	**57**	**3**
1995–96	Guingamp	27	1		
1996–97	Guingamp	21	1	**48**	**2**
1996–97	Roma	15	2		
1997–98	Roma	32	2		
1998–99	Roma	30	1		
1999–2000	Roma	26	3		
2000–01	Roma	33	3		
2001–02	Roma	31	2		
2002–03	Roma	23	1		
2003–04	Roma	12	0		
2004–05	Roma	8	0	**210**	**14**
2004–05	Bolton W	10	0	**10**	**0**

COMYN-PLATT, Charlie (D) **4** **0**
H: 6 1 W: 11 08 b.Salford 2-10-85
Source: Scholar.

2003–04	Bolton W	0	0		
2004–05	Bolton W	0	0		
2004–05	*Wycombe W*	4	0	**4**	**0**

DAVIES, Kevin (F) **341** **62**
H: 6 0 W: 12 10 b.Sheffield 26-3-77
Source: Trainee. *Honours:* England Youth, Under-21.

1993–94	Chesterfield	24	4		
1994–95	Chesterfield	41	11		
1995–96	Chesterfield	30	4		
1996–97	Chesterfield	34	3	**129**	**22**
1996–97	Southampton	0	0		
1997–98	Southampton	25	9		
1998–99	Blackburn R	21	1		
1999–2000	Blackburn R	2	0	**23**	**1**
1999–2000	Southampton	23	6		
2000–01	Southampton	27	1		
2001–02	Southampton	23	2		
2002–03	Southampton	9	1	**107**	**19**
2002–03	*Millwall*	9	3	**9**	**3**
2003–04	Bolton W	38	9		
2004–05	Bolton W	35	8	**73**	**17**

FADIGA, Khalilou (F) **207** **25**
H: 6 0 W: 12 02 b.Dakar 30-12-74
Honours: Senegal full caps.

1995–96	Lommel	20	0		
1996–97	Lommel	28	2	**48**	**2**
1997–98	FC Brugge	31	3		
1998–99	FC Brugge	21	4		
1999–2000	FC Brugge	17	2		
2000–01	FC Brugge	3	4	**72**	**13**
2000–01	Auxerre	21	1		
2001–02	Auxerre	27	8		
2002–03	Auxerre	34	1	**82**	**10**
2004–05	Bolton W	5	0	**5**	**0**

GARDNER, Ricardo (D) **209** **15**
H: 5 9 W: 11 00 b.St Andrews 25-9-78
Source: Harbour View. *Honours:* Jamaica 60 full caps, 5 goals.

1998–99	Bolton W	30	2		
1999–2000	Bolton W	29	5		
2000–01	Bolton W	32	3		
2001–02	Bolton W	31	3		
2002–03	Bolton W	32	2		
2003–04	Bolton W	22	0		
2004–05	Bolton W	33	0	**209**	**15**

GIANNAKOPOULOS, Stelios (M) **371** **105**
H: 5 8 W: 11 00 b.Athens 12-7-74
Honours: Greece 54 full caps, 9 goals.

1992–93	Ethnikos	32	6	**32**	**6**
1993–94	Paniliakos	26	9		
1994–95	Paniliakos	31	10		
1995–96	Paniliakos	27	7	**84**	**26**
1996–97	Olympiakos	31	7		
1997–98	Olympiakos	31	3		
1998–99	Olympiakos	23	7		
1999–2000	Olympiakos	29	10		
2000–01	Olympiakos	26	11		
2001–02	Olympiakos	21	11		
2002–03	Olympiakos	29	15	**190**	**64**
2003–04	Bolton W	31	2		
2004–05	Bolton W	34	7	**65**	**9**

HIERRO, Fernando (M) **525 105**

H: 6 2 W: 13 03 b.Velez, Malaga 23-3-68

Honours: Spain 89 full caps, 29 goals.

1987–88	Valladolid	28	0		
1988–89	Valladolid	29	2	**57**	**2**
1989–90	Real Madrid	37	7		
1990–91	Real Madrid	35	7		
1991–92	Real Madrid	37	21		
1992–93	Real Madrid	33	13		
1993–94	Real Madrid	34	10		
1994–95	Real Madrid	33	7		
1995–96	Real Madrid	31	7		
1996–97	Real Madrid	39	6		
1997–98	Real Madrid	28	3		
1998–99	Real Madrid	28	6		
1999–2000	Real Madrid	20	5		
2000–01	Real Madrid	29	5		
2001–02	Real Madrid	30	5		
2002–03	Real Madrid	25	0	**439**	**102**

From Al-Rayyan.

2004–05	Bolton W	29	1	**29**	**1**

HUNT, Nicky (D) **61 1**

H: 6 1 W: 13 08 b.Westhoughton 3-9-83

Source: Scholar. *Honours:* England Under-21.

2000–01	Bolton W	1	0		
2001–02	Bolton W	0	0		
2002–03	Bolton W	0	0		
2003–04	Bolton W	31	1		
2004–05	Bolton W	29	0	**61**	**1**

JAASKELAINEN, Jussi (G) **359 0**

H: 6 3 W: 12 10 b.Mikkeli 19-4-75

Honours: Finland Youth, Under-21, 21 full caps.

1992	MP	6	0		
1993	MP	6	0		
1994	MP	26	0		
1995	MP	26	0	**64**	**0**
1996	VPS	27	0		
1997	VPS	27	0	**54**	**0**
1997–98	Bolton W	0	0		
1998–99	Bolton W	34	0		
1999–2000	Bolton W	34	0		
2000–01	Bolton W	27	0		
2001–02	Bolton W	34	0		
2002–03	Bolton W	38	0		
2003–04	Bolton W	38	0		
2004–05	Bolton W	36	0	**241**	**0**

JAIDI, Radhi (D) **27 5**

H: 6 4 W: 14 00 b.Tunis 30-8-75

Source: Esperance. *Honours:* Tunisia full caps.

2004–05	Bolton W	27	5	**27**	**5**

JULIO CESAR (D) **168 11**

H: 6 1 W: 12 04 b.Sao Luis de Maranhao 18-11-78

1996–97	Valladolid	28	0		
1997–98	Valladolid	16	2		
1998–99	Valladolid	16	2		
1999–2000	Real Madrid	26	0		
2000–01	Real Madrid	0	0	**26**	**0**
2000–01	AC Milan	4	0	**4**	**0**
2000–01	Real Sociedad	8	1	**8**	**1**
2001–02	Benfica	30	3	**30**	**3**
2002–03	FK Austria	9	1	**9**	**1**
2003–04	Valladolid	26	2	**86**	**6**
2004–05	Bolton W	5	0	**5**	**0**

KAKU, Blessing (M) **114 19**

H: 5 11 W: 12 04 b.Ughelli 5-3-78

Source: Invincible Leopards, DLC, Sharks, Branau, Molenbeek. *Honours:* Nigeria full caps.

1999–2000	Harelbeke	27	5	**27**	**5**
2000–01	Genk	21	0		
2001–02	Genk	0	0	**21**	**0**
2002–03	Hapoel Beer Sheva	31	9		
2003–04	Hapoel Beer Sheva	11	2	**42**	**11**
2003–04	Ashdod	19	3	**19**	**3**
2004–05	Bolton W	1	0	**1**	**0**
2004–05	*Derby Co*	4	0	**4**	**0**

LAVILLE, Florent (D) **226 2**

H: 6 1 W: 11 11 b.Valence 7-8-83

1993–94	Lyon	8	0		
1994–95	Lyon	28	0		
1995–96	Lyon	28	0		
1996–97	Lyon	27	1		
1997–98	Lyon	29	0		
1998–99	Lyon	29	0		
1999–2000	Lyon	29	0		
2000–01	Lyon	9	0		
2001–02	Lyon	13	0		
2002–03	Lyon	5	1	**205**	**2**
2002–03	Bolton W	10	0		
2003–04	Bolton W	5	0		
2004–05	Bolton W	0	0	**15**	**0**
2004–05	*Coventry C*	6	0	**6**	**0**

LIVESEY, Danny (D) **27 0**

H: 6 3 W: 12 10 b.Salford 31-12-84

Source: Trainee.

2002–03	Bolton W	2	0		
2003–04	Bolton W	0	0		
2003–04	*Notts Co*	11	0	**11**	**0**
2003–04	*Rochdale*	13	0	**13**	**0**
2004–05	Bolton W	0	0	**2**	**0**
2004–05	*Blackpool*	1	0	**1**	**0**

N'GOTTY, Bruno (D) **486 24**

H: 6 1 W: 13 08 b.Lyon 10-6-71

Honours: France 6 full caps.

1989–90	Lyon	27	0		
1990–91	Lyon	37	2		
1991–92	Lyon	36	1		
1992–93	Lyon	36	3		
1993–94	Lyon	36	3		
1994–95	Lyon	35	3	**207**	**12**
1995–96	Paris St Germain	24	1		
1996–97	Paris St Germain	30	4		
1997–98	Paris St Germain	26	2	**80**	**7**
1998–99	AC Milan	25	1		
1999–2000	AC Milan	9	0	**34**	**1**
1999–2000	Venezia	16	0	**16**	**0**
2000–01	Marseille	30	0	**30**	**0**
2001–02	Bolton W	26	1		
2002–03	Bolton W	23	1		
2003–04	Bolton W	33	2		
2004–05	Bolton W	37	0	**119**	**4**

NOLAN, Kevin (M) **176 23**

H: 6 0 W: 14 00 b.Liverpool 24-6-82

Source: Scholar. *Honours:* England Youth, Under-20, Under-21.

1999–2000	Bolton W	4	0		
2000–01	Bolton W	31	1		
2001–02	Bolton W	35	8		
2002–03	Bolton W	33	1		
2003–04	Bolton W	37	9		
2004–05	Bolton W	36	4	**176**	**23**

O'BRIEN, Joey (M) **16 2**

H: 6 0 W: 10 13 b.Dublin 17-2-86

Source: Scholar. *Honours:* Eire Youth, Under-21.

2004–05	Bolton W	1	0	**1**	**0**
2004–05	*Sheffield W*	15	2	**15**	**2**

OKOCHA, Jay-Jay (M) **333 72**

H: 5 8 W: 11 00 b.Enugu 14-8-73

Source: Enugu Rangers, Neunkirchen. *Honours:* Nigeria 65 full caps, 12 goals.

1992–93	Eintracht Frankfurt	20	2		
1993–94	Eintracht Frankfurt	19	2		
1994–95	Eintracht Frankfurt	27	6		
1995–96	Eintracht Frankfurt	24	7	**90**	**17**
1996–97	Fenerbahce	33	16		
1997–98	Fenerbahce	30	14	**63**	**30**
1998–99	Paris St Germain	25	4		
1999–2000	Paris St Germain	23	2		
2000–01	Paris St Germain	15	2		
2001–02	Paris St Germain	20	4	**83**	**12**
2002–03	Bolton W	31	7		
2003–04	Bolton W	35	0		
2004–05	Bolton W	31	6	**97**	**13**

PEDERSEN, Henrik (F) **226 82**

H: 6 1 W: 13 03 b.Jutland 10-6-75

Honours: Denmark 3 full caps.

1995–96	Silkeborg	12	4		
1996–97	Silkeborg	2	0		
1997–98	Silkeborg	15	9		
1998–99	Silkeborg	33	16		
1999–2000	Silkeborg	28	13		
2000–01	Silkeborg	32	20	**122**	**62**
2001–02	Bolton W	11	0		
2002–03	Bolton W	33	7		
2003–04	Bolton W	33	7		
2004–05	Bolton W	27	6	**104**	**20**

POOLE, Kevin (G) **301 0**

H: 5 10 W: 12 11 b.Bromsgrove 21-7-63

Source: Apprentice.

1981–82	Aston Villa	0	0		
1982–83	Aston Villa	0	0		
1983–84	Aston Villa	0	0		
1984–85	Aston Villa	7	0		
1984–85	*Northampton T*	3	0	**3**	**0**
1985–86	Aston Villa	11	0		
1986–87	Aston Villa	10	0	**28**	**0**
1987–88	Middlesbrough	1	0		
1988–89	Middlesbrough	12	0		
1989–90	Middlesbrough	21	0		
1990–91	Middlesbrough	0	0	**34**	**0**
1990–91	*Hartlepool U*	12	0	**12**	**0**
1991–92	Leicester C	42	0		
1992–93	Leicester C	19	0		
1993–94	Leicester C	14	0		
1994–95	Leicester C	36	0		
1995–96	Leicester C	45	0		
1996–97	Leicester C	7	0	**163**	**0**
1997–98	Birmingham C	1	0		
1998–99	Birmingham C	36	0		
1999–2000	Birmingham C	18	0		
2000–01	Birmingham C	1	0		
2001–02	Birmingham C	0	0	**56**	**0**
2001–02	Bolton W	3	0		
2002–03	Bolton W	0	0		
2003–04	Bolton W	0	0		
2004–05	Bolton W	2	0	**5**	**0**

POWELL, Rhys (D) **0 0**

H: 5 8 W: 11 08 b.Cardiff 25-2-87

Source: Scholar.

2004–05	Bolton W	0	0		

SHAKES, Ricky (M) **8 2**

H: 5 10 W: 12 00 b.Brixton 26-1-85

Source: Scholar.

2003–04	Bolton W	0	0		
2004–05	Bolton W	0	0		
2004–05	*Bristol R*	1	0	**1**	**0**
2004–05	*Bury*	7	2	**7**	**2**

SPEED, Gary (M) **557 85**

H: 5 10 W: 12 11 b.Deeside 8-9-69

Source: Trainee. *Honours:* Wales Youth, Under-21, 85 full caps, 7 goals.

1988–89	Leeds U	1	0		
1989–90	Leeds U	25	3		
1990–91	Leeds U	38	7		
1991–92	Leeds U	41	7		
1992–93	Leeds U	39	7		
1993–94	Leeds U	36	10		
1994–95	Leeds U	39	3		
1995–96	Leeds U	29	2	**248**	**39**
1996–97	Everton	37	9		
1997–98	Everton	21	7	**58**	**16**
1997–98	Newcastle U	13	1		
1998–99	Newcastle U	38	4		
1999–2000	Newcastle U	36	9		
2000–01	Newcastle U	35	5		
2001–02	Newcastle U	29	5		
2002–03	Newcastle U	24	2		
2003–04	Newcastle U	38	3	**213**	**29**
2004–05	Bolton W	38	1	**38**	**1**

TALBOT, Jason (D) **4 0**

H: 5 9 W: 10 08 b.Irlam 30-9-85

Source: Scholar.

2004–05	Bolton W	0	0		
2004–05	*Derby Co*	2	0	**2**	**0**
2004–05	*Mansfield T*	2	0	**2**	**0**

THACH, Duong (F) **0 0**

b.Minh Hai 9-12-85

Source: Trainee.

2003–04	Bolton W	0	0		
2004–05	Bolton W	0	0		

VAZ TE, Ricardo (F) **8 0**

H: 6 2 W: 12 07 b.Lisbon 1-10-86

Source: From Trainee. *Honours:* Portugal Youth.

2003–04	Bolton W	1	0		
2004–05	Bolton W	7	0	**8**	**0**

Scholars

Ashton, Samuel Seth; Fojut, Jaroslaw; Hill, Bradley; Howarth, Christopher; Kazimierczak, Prezemek; Luisi, Karl Marlo; Sinclair, James Alexander; Smith, Johann Anwar Ryan; Stott, Daniel Adam; Whitehead, Dale Andrew

BOSTON U (8)

ABBEY, Nathan (G) 150 0
H: 6 0 W: 11 03 b.Islington 11-7-78
Source: Trainee.

1995–96	Luton T	0	0		
1996–97	Luton T	0	0		
1997–98	Luton T	0	0		
1998–99	Luton T	2	0		
1999–2000	Luton T	33	0		
2000–01	Luton T	20	0		
2001–02	Chesterfield	46	0	**46**	**0**
2002–03	Northampton T	5	0	**5**	**0**
2003–04	Luton T	0	0	**55**	**0**
2003–04	Macclesfield T	0	0		
2003–04	Ipswich T	0	0		
2003–04	Burnley	0	0		
2004–05	Boston U	44	0	**44**	**0**

BASTOCK, Paul (G) 104 0
H: 5 8 W: 10 00 b.Leamington Spa 19-5-70
Source: Trainee.

1986–87	Coventry C	0	0		
1987–88	Cambridge U	10	0		
1988–89	Cambridge U	2	0	**12**	**0**
From Fisher, Kettering					
2002–03	Boston U	46	0		
2003–04	Boston U	46	0		
2004–05	Boston U	0	0	**92**	**0**

BROOKS, Lewis (M) 2 0
H: 5 10 W: 11 06 b.Boston 4-9-87

2004–05	Boston U	2	0	**2**	**0**

BROUGH, Scott (M) 46 3
H: 5 5 W: 9 11 b.Doncaster 10-2-83

2000–01	Scunthorpe U	4	0		
2001–02	Scunthorpe U	19	1		
2002–03	Scunthorpe U	23	2	**46**	**3**
2003–04	Boston U	0	0		
2004–05	Boston U	0	0		

CLARE, Daryl (F) 130 17
H: 5 9 W: 12 08 b.Jersey 1-8-78
Source: Trainee. *Honours:* Eire Under-21.

1995–96	Grimsby T	1	0		
1996–97	Grimsby T	0	0		
1997–98	Grimsby T	22	3		
1998–99	Grimsby T	22	3		
1999–2000	Grimsby T	17	3		
1999–2000	*Northampton T*	10	3		
2000–01	Grimsby T	17	0	**79**	**9**
2000–01	*Northampton T*	4	0	**14**	**3**
2000–01	*Cheltenham T*	4	0	**4**	**0**
2002–03	Boston U	7	1		
2003–04	Boston U	0	0		
2004–05	Chester C	7	1	**7**	**1**
2004–05	Boston U	19	3	**26**	**4**

CLARKE, Ryan (D) 4 0
H: 5 11 W: 12 04 b.Sutton Coldfield 22-1-84
Source: Scholar.

2003–04	Boston U	4	0		
2004–05	Boston U	0	0	**4**	**0**

EASTER, Jermaine (F) 75 13
H: 5 10 W: 12 03 b.Cardiff 15-1-82
Source: Trainee. *Honours:* Wales Youth.

2000–01	Wolverhampton W	0	0		
2000–01	Hartlepool U	4	0		
2001–02	Hartlepool U	12	2		
2002–03	Hartlepool U	8	0		
2003–04	Hartlepool U	3	0	**27**	**2**
2003–04	*Cambridge U*	15	2		
2004–05	Cambridge U	24	6	**39**	**8**
2004–05	Boston U	9	3	**9**	**3**

ELLENDER, Paul (D) 107 6
H: 6 1 W: 12 07 b.Scunthorpe 21-10-74
Source: Trainee.

1992–93	Scunthorpe U	0	0		
1993–94	Scunthorpe U	0	0		
From Altrincham, Scarborough					
2002–03	Boston				
2003–04	Boston U	42	4		
2004–05	Boston U	39	2	**107**	**6**

GASCOIGNE, Paul (M) 382 81
H: 5 10 W: 11 11 b.Gateshead 27-5-67
Source: Apprentice. *Honours:* England, Under-21 B, 57 full caps, 10 goals.

1984–85	Newcastle U	2	0		
1985–86	Newcastle U	31	9		
1986–87	Newcastle U	24	5		
1987–88	Newcastle U	35	7	**92**	**21**
1988–89	Tottenham H	32	6		
1989–90	Tottenham H	34	6		
1990–91	Tottenham H	26	7		
1991–92	Tottenham H	0	0	**92**	**19**
1992–93	Lazio	22	4		
1993–94	Lazio	17	2		
1994–95	Lazio	2	0	**41**	**6**
1995–96	Rangers	28	14		
1996–97	Rangers	26	13		
1997–98	Rangers	20	3	**74**	**30**
1997–98	Middlesbrough	7	0		
1998–99	Middlesbrough	26	3		
1999–2000	Middlesbrough	8	1	**41**	**4**
2000–01	Everton	14	0		
2001–02	Everton	18	1	**32**	**1**
2001–02	Burnley	6	0	**6**	**0**
2004–05	Boston U	4	0	**4**	**0**

GREAVES, Mark (D) 262 11
H: 6 1 W: 13 00 b.Hull 22-1-75
Source: Brigg Town.

1996–97	Hull C	30	2		
1997–98	Hull C	25	2		
1998–99	Hull C	25	0		
1999–2000	Hull C	38	3		
2000–01	Hull C	30	2		
2001–02	Hull C	26	1		
2002–03	Hull C	3	0	**177**	**10**
2002–03	Boston U	26	1		
2003–04	Boston U	37	0		
2004–05	Boston U	22	0	**85**	**1**

HOLLAND, Chris (M) 231 2
H: 5 9 W: 12 13 b.Clitheroe 11-9-75
Source: Trainee. *Honours:* England Youth, Under-21.

1993–94	Preston NE	1	0	**1**	**0**
1993–94	Newcastle U	3	0		
1994–95	Newcastle U	0	0		
1995–96	Newcastle U	0	0		
1996–97	Newcastle U	0	0	**3**	**0**
1996–97	Birmingham C	32	0		
1997–98	Birmingham C	10	0		
1998–99	Birmingham C	14	0		
1999–2000	Birmingham C	14	0	**70**	**0**
1999–2000	Huddersfield T	17	1		
2000–01	Huddersfield T	29	0		
2001–02	Huddersfield T	37	1		
2002–03	Huddersfield T	34	0		
2003–04	Huddersfield T	3	0	**120**	**2**
2003–04	Boston U	5	0		
2004–05	Boston U	32	0	**37**	**0**

HURST, Tom (M) 1 0
H: 6 1 W: 11 00 b.Leicester 23-9-87
Source: Scholar.

2004–05	Boston U	1	0	**1**	**0**

LEE, Jason (F) 393 80
H: 6 3 W: 13 03 b.Newham 9-5-71
Source: Trainee.

1989–90	Charlton Ath	1	0		
1990–91	Charlton Ath	0	0		
1990–91	*Stockport Co*	2	0	**2**	**0**
1990–91	Lincoln C	17	3		
1991–92	Lincoln C	35	6		
1992–93	Lincoln C	41	12	**93**	**21**
1993–94	Southend U	24	3	**24**	**3**
1993–94	Nottingham F	13	2		
1994–95	Nottingham F	22	3		
1995–96	Nottingham F	28	8		
1996–97	Nottingham F	13	1	**76**	**14**
1996–97	*Charlton Ath*	8	3	**9**	**3**
1996–97	*Grimsby T*	7	1	**7**	**1**
1997–98	Watford	36	10		
1998–99	Watford	1	1	**37**	**11**
1998–99	Chesterfield	22	1		
1999–2000	Chesterfield	6	0	**28**	**1**
1999–2000	Peterborough U	23	6		
2000–01	Peterborough U	30	8		
2001–02	Peterborough U	0	0		
2002–03	Peterborough U	25	3		
2003–04	Peterborough U	0	0	**78**	**17**
2004–05	Boston U	39	9	**39**	**9**

LILLEY, Derek (F) 385 95
H: 5 9 W: 11 10 b.Paisley 9-2-74
Source: Everton BC.

1991–92	Morton	25	3		
1992–93	Morton	22	4		
1993–94	Morton	38	5		
1994–95	Morton	35	16		
1995–96	Morton	35	14		
1996–97	Morton	25	15	**180**	**57**
1996–97	Leeds U	6	0		
1997–98	Leeds U	13	1		
1998–99	Leeds U	2	0	**21**	**1**
1998–99	*Bury*	5	1	**5**	**1**
1998–99	*Hearts*	4	1	**4**	**1**
1999–2000	Oxford U	44	7		
2000–01	Oxford U	19	2	**63**	**9**
2000–01	Dundee U	18	6		
2001–02	Dundee U	26	6		
2002–03	Dundee U	33	2	**77**	**14**
2003–04	Livingston	35	12	**35**	**12**
2004–05	Boston U	0	0		

McCANN, Austin (D) 184 9
H: 5 9 W: 11 13 b.Alexandria 21-1-80
Source: Wolverhampton W Trainee.

1997–98	Airdrieonians	14	0		
1998–99	Airdrieonians	31	4		
1999–2000	Airdrieonians	29	2		
2000–01	Airdrieonians	20	1	**94**	**7**
2000–01	Hearts	10	0		
2001–02	Hearts	6	0		
2002–03	Hearts	17	1		
2003–04	Hearts	6	0	**39**	**1**
2003–04	Clyde	6	0	**6**	**0**
2004–05	Boston U	45	1	**45**	**1**

McMANUS, Tom (M) 118 19
H: 5 9 W: 10 02 b.Glasgow 28-2-81
Source: S Form. *Honours:* Scotland Under-21.

1997–98	Hibernian	0	0		
1998–99	Hibernian	1	0		
1999–2000	Hibernian	2	0		
2000–01	Hibernian	16	2		
2000–01	Airdrieonians	1	0	**1**	**0**
2001–02	Hibernian	21	3		
2002–03	Hibernian	35	11		
2003–04	Hibernian	32	3		
2004–05	Hibernian	2	0	**109**	**19**
2004–05	Boston U	8	0	**8**	**0**

MELTON, Steve (M) 102 5
H: 5 11 W: 12 03 b.Lincoln 3-10-78
Source: Trainee.

1995–96	Nottingham F	0	0		
1996–97	Nottingham F	0	0		
1997–98	Nottingham F	0	0		
1998–99	Nottingham F	1	0		
1999–2000	Nottingham F	2	0	**3**	**0**
1999–2000	Stoke C	5	0	**5**	**0**
2000–01	Brighton & HA	28	1		
2001–02	Brighton & HA	10	1		
2002–03	Brighton & HA	8	1	**46**	**3**
2002–03	Hull C	25	0		
2003–04	Hull C	5	0	**30**	**0**
2003–04	Boston U	9	1		
2004–05	Boston U	9	1	**18**	**2**

NOBLE, David (M) 64 6
H: 6 0 W: 12 04 b.Hitchin 2-2-82
Source: Scholar. *Honours:* England Youth, Under-20. Scotland Under-21.

2000–01	Arsenal	0	0		
2001–02	Arsenal	0	0		
2001–02	*Watford*	15	1	**15**	**1**
2002–03	Arsenal	0	0		
2002–03	West Ham U	0	0		
2003–04	West Ham U	3	0	**3**	**0**
2003–04	Boston U	14	2		
2004–05	Boston U	32	3	**46**	**5**

NORRIS, Rob (M) 2 0
H: 5 9 W: 10 03 b.Nottingham 12-10-87
Source: Scholar.

2004–05	Boston U	2	0	**2**	**0**

O'DONNELL, Stephen (M) 47 3
H: 5 11 W: 12 02 b.Bellshill 10-7-83

2001–02	Dundee U	6	0		
2002–03	Dundee U	11	0		

2003–04	*Ross Co*	26	3	**26**	**3**
2004–05	Dundee U	0	0	**17**	**0**
2004–05	Boston U	4	0	**4**	**0**

O'HALLORAN, Matt (F) 24 2
H: 5 10 W: 11 06 b.Nottingham 18-11-82
Source: Trainee.

2002–03	Derby Co	0	0		
2003–04	Oldham Ath	13	1	**13**	**1**
2003–04	Chesterfield	3	0	**3**	**0**
2004–05	Boston U	8	1	**8**	**1**

PITT, Courtney (F) 92 7
H: 5 7 W: 10 08 b.Westminster 17-12-81
Source: Scholar.

2000–01	Chelsea	0	0		
2001–02	Portsmouth	39	3		
2002–03	Portsmouth	0	0		
2003–04	Portsmouth	0	0	**39**	**3**
2003–04	*Luton T*	12	0	**12**	**0**
2003–04	*Coventry C*	1	0	**1**	**0**
2003–04	Oxford U	8	0	**8**	**0**
2004–05	Boston U	32	4	**32**	**4**

RUSK, Simon (M) 68 5
H: 5 11 W: 12 08 b.Peterborough 17-12-81
Source: Peterborough U.

2002–03	Boston U	18	2		
2003–04	Boston U	19	0		
2004–05	Boston U	31	3	**68**	**5**

STAFF, David (F) 5 0
H: 6 1 W: 11 07 b.Market Harborough 8-11-79
Source: Kings Lynn.

2004–05	Boston U	5	0	**5**	**0**

STRONG, Greg (D) 174 9
H: 6 2 W: 11 12 b.Bolton 5-9-75
Source: From Trainee. *Honours:* England Schools, Youth.

1992–93	Wigan Ath	0	0		
1993–94	Wigan Ath	18	1		
1994–95	Wigan Ath	17	2	**35**	**3**
1995–96	Bolton W	1	0		
1996–97	Bolton W	0	0		
1997–98	Bolton W	0	0		
1997–98	*Blackpool*	11	1	**11**	**1**
1998–99	Bolton W	5	1		
1998–99	*Stoke C*	5	1	**5**	**1**
1999–2000	Bolton W	6	0	**12**	**1**
1999–2000	*Motherwell*	10	0		
2000–01	Motherwell	32	1		
2001–02	Motherwell	32	2	**74**	**3**
2002–03	Hull C	3	0		
2002–03	*Cheltenham T*	4	0	**4**	**0**
2002–03	*Scunthorpe U*	7	0	**7**	**0**
2003–04	Hull C	0	0	**3**	**0**
2003–04	*Bury*	10	0	**10**	**0**
2003–04	Boston U	0	0		
2004–05	Boston U	9	0	**9**	**0**
2004–05	*Macclesfield T*	4	0	**4**	**0**

THOMAS, Danny (M) 109 8
H: 5 7 W: 10 10 b.Leamington Spa 1-5-81
Source: Trainee.

1997–98	Nottingham F	0	0		
1997–98	Leicester C	0	0		
1998–99	Leicester C	0	0		
1999–2000	Leicester C	3	0		
2000–01	Leicester C	0	0		
2001–02	Leicester C	0	0	**3**	**0**
2001–02	Bournemouth	12	0		
2002–03	Bournemouth	37	2		
2003–04	Bournemouth	10	0	**59**	**2**
2003–04	Boston U	8	3		
2004–05	Boston U	39	3	**47**	**6**

THOMPSON, Lee (F) 95 12
H: 5 7 W: 10 10 b.Sheffield 25-3-83
Honours: England Schools.

2000–01	Sheffield U	0	0		
2001–02	Sheffield U	0	0		
2002–03	Sheffield U	0	0		
2002–03	Boston U	15	4		
2003–04	Boston U	35	5		
2004–05	Boston U	45	3	**95**	**12**

WEST, Dean (D) 415 33
H: 5 10 W: 11 07 b.Wakefield 5-12-72
Source: Leeds U Schoolboy.

1990–91	Lincoln C	1	1		
1991–92	Lincoln C	32	3		
1992–93	Lincoln C	19	3		
1993–94	Lincoln C	18	6		
1994–95	Lincoln C	41	6		
1995–96	Lincoln C	8	1		
1995–96	Bury	37	1		
1996–97	Bury	46	4		
1997–98	Bury	4	0		
1998–99	Bury	23	3	**110**	**8**
1999–2000	Burnley	34	0		
2000–01	Burnley	7	0		
2001–02	Burnley	44	0		
2002–03	Burnley	41	4		
2003–04	Burnley	32	1	**158**	**5**
2004–05	Lincoln C	4	0	**123**	**20**
2004–05	Boston U	24	0	**24**	**0**

WHITE, Alan (D) 260 7
H: 6 3 W: 12 05 b.Darlington 22-3-76
Source: Derby Co Schoolboy.

1994–95	Middlesbrough	0	0		
1995–96	Middlesbrough	0	0		
1996–97	Middlesbrough	0	0		
1997–98	Middlesbrough	0	0		
1997–98	Luton T	28	1		
1998–99	Luton T	33	1		
1999–2000	Luton T	19	1	**80**	**3**
1999–2000	*Colchester U*	4	0		
2000–01	Colchester U	32	0		
2001–02	Colchester U	33	3		
2002–03	Colchester U	41	0		
2003–04	Colchester U	33	1	**143**	**4**
2004–05	Leyton Orient	26	0	**26**	**0**
2004–05	Boston U	11	0	**11**	**0**

BOURNEMOUTH (9)

ANDRADE, Diogo (M) 0 0
H: 5 9 W: 12 00 b.Lisbon 23-7-85
Honours: Portugal Youth.

2004–05	Bournemouth	0	0		

BROADHURST, Karl (D) 158 3
H: 6 1 W: 11 07 b.Portsmouth 18-3-80
Source: Trainee.

1998–99	Bournemouth	0	0		
1999–2000	Bournemouth	16	0		
2000–01	Bournemouth	30	0		
2001–02	Bournemouth	23	0		
2002–03	Bournemouth	21	1		
2003–04	Bournemouth	39	1		
2004–05	Bournemouth	29	1	**158**	**3**

BROWNING, Marcus (M) 417 22
H: 6 1 W: 12 12 b.Bristol 22-4-71
Source: Trainee. *Honours:* Wales 5 full caps.

1989–90	Bristol R	1	0		
1990–91	Bristol R	0	0		
1991–92	Bristol R	11	0		
1992–93	Bristol R	19	1		
1992–93	*Hereford U*	7	5	**7**	**5**
1993–94	Bristol R	31	4		
1994–95	Bristol R	41	2		
1995–96	Bristol R	45	4		
1996–97	Bristol R	26	2	**174**	**13**
1996–97	Huddersfield T	13	0		
1997–98	Huddersfield T	14	0		
1998–99	Huddersfield T	6	0	**33**	**0**
1998–99	Gillingham	4	0		
1999–2000	Gillingham	1	0		
2000–01	Gillingham	31	0		
2001–02	Gillingham	42	3	**78**	**3**
2002–03	Bournemouth	43	1		
2003–04	Bournemouth	42	0		
2004–05	Bournemouth	40	0	**125**	**1**

CONNELL, Alan (F) 54 8
H: 6 0 W: 10 10 b.Enfield 5-2-83
Source: Ipswich T Trainee.

2002–03	Bournemouth	13	6		
2003–04	Bournemouth	7	0		
2004–05	Bournemouth	34	2	**54**	**8**

COUTTS, James (M) 1 0
H: 5 6 W: 9 07 b.Weymouth 15-4-87

2004–05	Bournemouth	1	0	**1**	**0**

CUMMINGS, Warren (D) 119 5
H: 5 9 W: 11 08 b.Aberdeen 15-10-80
Source: Trainee. *Honours:* Scotland Under-21, 1 full cap.

1999–2000	Chelsea	0	0		
2000–01	Chelsea	0	0		
2000–01	*Bournemouth*	10	1		
2000–01	*WBA*	3	0		
2001–02	Chelsea	0	0		
2001–02	*WBA*	14	0	**17**	**0**
2002–03	Chelsea	0	0		
2002–03	Bournemouth	20	0		
2003–04	Bournemouth	42	2		
2004–05	Bournemouth	30	2	**102**	**5**

ELLIOTT, Wade (M) 220 31
H: 5 10 W: 11 01 b.Southampton 14-12-78

1999–2000	Bournemouth	12	3		
2000–01	Bournemouth	36	9		
2001–02	Bournemouth	46	8		
2002–03	Bournemouth	44	4		
2003–04	Bournemouth	39	3		
2004–05	Bournemouth	43	4	**220**	**31**

FLETCHER, Steve (F) 457 87
H: 6 2 W: 14 09 b.Hartlepool 26-7-72
Source: Trainee.

1990–91	Hartlepool U	14	2		
1991–92	Hartlepool U	18	2	**32**	**4**
1992–93	Bournemouth	31	4		
1993–94	Bournemouth	36	6		
1994–95	Bournemouth	40	6		
1995–96	Bournemouth	7	1		
1996–97	Bournemouth	35	7		
1997–98	Bournemouth	42	12		
1998–99	Bournemouth	39	8		
1999–2000	Bournemouth	36	7		
2000–01	Bournemouth	45	9		
2001–02	Bournemouth	2	0		
2002–03	Bournemouth	35	5		
2003–04	Bournemouth	41	9		
2004–05	Bournemouth	36	9	**425**	**83**

HAYTER, James (F) 270 64
H: 5 9 W: 10 13 b.Newport (IW) 9-4-79
Source: Trainee.

1996–97	Bournemouth	2	0		
1997–98	Bournemouth	5	0		
1998–99	Bournemouth	20	2		
1999–2000	Bournemouth	31	2		
2000–01	Bournemouth	40	11		
2001–02	Bournemouth	44	7		
2002–03	Bournemouth	45	9		
2003–04	Bournemouth	44	14		
2004–05	Bournemouth	39	19	**270**	**64**

HOLMES, Derek (F) 161 30
H: 6 2 W: 13 07 b.Lanark 18-10-78
Source: Royal Albert.

1995–96	Hearts	0	0		
1996–97	Hearts	1	0		
1997–98	Hearts	1	1		
1997–98	Cowdenbeath	13	5	**13**	**5**
1998–99	Hearts	6	0	**8**	**1**
1999–2000	Ross Co	25	8		
2000–01	Ross Co	0	0	**25**	**8**
2001–02	Bournemouth	37	9		
2002–03	Bournemouth	29	3		
2003–04	Bournemouth	26	2		
2004–05	Bournemouth	23	2	**115**	**16**

HOWE, Eddie (D) 237 11
H: 5 11 W: 11 07 b.Amersham 29-11-77
Source: Trainee.

1995–96	Bournemouth	5	0		
1996–97	Bournemouth	13	0		
1997–98	Bournemouth	40	1		
1998–99	Bournemouth	45	2		
1999–2000	Bournemouth	28	1		
2000–01	Bournemouth	31	2		
2001–02	Bournemouth	38	4		
2001–02	Portsmouth	1	0		
2002–03	Portsmouth	1	0		
2003–04	Portsmouth	0	0		
2003–04	*Swindon T*	0	0		
2004–05	Portsmouth	0	0	**2**	**0**
2004–05	Bournemouth	35	1	**235**	**11**

MAHER, Shaun (D) **170 7**
H: 6 1 W: 13 02 b.Dublin 20-6-78
Source: Bohemians.

1996–97	Bohemians	2	0		
1997–98	Fulham	0	0		
1997–98	Bohemians	11	0		
1998–99	Bohemians	25	1		
1999–2000	Bohemians	28	1		
2000–01	Bohemians	0	0	**66**	**2**
2001–02	Bournemouth	31	0		
2002–03	Bournemouth	8	2		
2003–04	Bournemouth	29	1		
2004–05	Bournemouth	36	2	**104**	**5**

MOSS, Neil (G) **181 0**
H: 6 2 W: 13 10 b.New Milton 10-5-75
Source: Trainee.

1992–93	Bournemouth	1	0		
1993–94	Bournemouth	6	0		
1994–95	Bournemouth	8	0		
1995–96	Bournemouth	7	0		
1995–96	Southampton	0	0		
1996–97	Southampton	3	0		
1997–98	Southampton	0	0		
1997–98	*Gillingham*	10	0	**10**	**0**
1998–99	Southampton	7	0		
1999–2000	Southampton	9	0		
2000–01	Southampton	3	0		
2001–02	Southampton	2	0		
2002–03	Southampton	0	0	**24**	**0**
2002–03	Bournemouth	33	0		
2003–04	Bournemouth	46	0		
2004–05	Bournemouth	46	0	**147**	**0**

MOSS, Ryan (M) **1 0**
H: 5 11 W: 12 04 b.Dorchester 14-11-86

2004–05	Bournemouth	1	0	**1**	**0**

O'CONNOR, Gareth (F) **198 28**
H: 5 10 W: 11 00 b.Dublin 10-11-78
Source: Bohemians.

1998–99	Shamrock R	8	0	**8**	**0**
1999–2000	Bohemians	22	4	**22**	**4**
2000–01	Bournemouth	22	1		
2001–02	Bournemouth	28	0		
2002–03	Bournemouth	41	8		
2003–04	Bournemouth	37	2		
2004–05	Bournemouth	40	13	**168**	**24**

O'CONNOR, James (D) **19 0**
H: 5 10 W: 12 05 b.Birmingham 20-11-84
Source: Scholar.

2003–04	Aston Villa	0	0		
2004–05	Aston Villa	0	0		
2004–05	*Port Vale*	13	0	**13**	**0**
2004–05	Bournemouth	6	0	**6**	**0**

PURCHES, Stephen (M) **175 9**
H: 5 11 W: 11 09 b.Ilford 14-1-80
Source: Trainee.

1998–99	West Ham U	0	0		
1999–2000	West Ham U	0	0		
2000–01	Bournemouth	34	0		
2001–02	Bournemouth	41	2		
2002–03	Bournemouth	44	3		
2003–04	Bournemouth	42	3		
2004–05	Bournemouth	14	1	**175**	**9**

RODRIGUES, Dani (F) **57 8**
H: 5 11 W: 12 00 b.Madeira 3-3-80
Source: Farense.

1998–99	Bournemouth	5	0		
1998–99	Southampton	0	0		
1999–2000	Southampton	2	0		
2000–01	Southampton	0	0		
2000–01	*Bristol C*	4	0		
2001–02	Southampton	0	0	**2**	**0**
2001–02	*Bristol C*	4	0	**8**	**0**
2002–03	Walsall	1	0	**1**	**0**
2002–03	Ionikos	14	1	**14**	**1**
2003–04	Yeovil T	4	4	**4**	**4**
2004–05	Bournemouth	23	3	**28**	**3**

ROWE, James (M) **2 0**
H: 5 9 W: 10 00 b.Frimley 10-3-87

2004–05	Bournemouth	2	0	**2**	**0**

SPICER, John (M) **39 6**
H: 5 11 W: 11 08 b.Romford 13-9-83
Source: Scholar. *Honours:* England Youth, Under-20.

2001–02	Arsenal	0	0		
2002–03	Arsenal	0	0		
2003–04	Arsenal	0	0		
2004–05	Arsenal	0	0		
2004–05	Bournemouth	39	6	**39**	**6**

STEWART, Gareth (G) **84 0**
H: 6 0 W: 12 08 b.Preston 3-2-80
Source: Trainee. *Honours:* England Schools, Youth.

1996–97	Blackburn R	0	0		
1997–98	Blackburn R	0	0		
1998–99	Blackburn R	0	0		
1999–2000	Bournemouth	3	0		
2000–01	Bournemouth	35	0		
2001–02	Bournemouth	45	0		
2002–03	Bournemouth	1	0		
2003–04	Bournemouth	0	0		
2004–05	Bournemouth	0	0	**84**	**0**

STOCK, Brian (M) **119 13**
H: 5 11 W: 11 02 b.Winchester 24-12-81
Source: Trainee. *Honours:* Wales Under-21.

1999–2000	Bournemouth	5	0		
2000–01	Bournemouth	1	0		
2001–02	Bournemouth	26	2		
2002–03	Bournemouth	27	2		
2003–04	Bournemouth	19	3		
2004–05	Bournemouth	41	6	**119**	**13**

TINDALL, Jason (M) **160 6**
H: 6 1 W: 12 13 b.Stepney 15-11-77
Source: Trainee.

1996–97	Charlton Ath	0	0		
1997–98	Charlton Ath	0	0		
1998–99	Bournemouth	17	1		
1999–2000	Bournemouth	8	0		
2000–01	Bournemouth	45	1		
2001–02	Bournemouth	44	3		
2002–03	Bournemouth	27	1		
2003–04	Bournemouth	19	0		
2004–05	Bournemouth	0	0	**160**	**6**

YOUNG, Neil (D) **332 4**
H: 5 9 W: 12 00 b.Harlow 31-8-73
Source: Trainee.

1991–92	Tottenham H	0	0		
1992–93	Tottenham H	0	0		
1993–94	Tottenham H	0	0		
1994–95	Bournemouth	32	0		
1995–96	Bournemouth	41	0		
1996–97	Bournemouth	44	0		
1997–98	Bournemouth	44	2		
1998–99	Bournemouth	44	1		
1999–2000	Bournemouth	37	0		
2000–01	Bournemouth	7	0		
2001–02	Bournemouth	11	0		
2002–03	Bournemouth	32	1		
2003–04	Bournemouth	10	0		
2004–05	Bournemouth	30	0	**332**	**4**

BRADFORD C (10)

ARMSTRONG, Craig (M) **241 7**
H: 5 11 W: 12 09 b.South Shields 23-5-75
Source: Trainee.

1992–93	Nottingham F	0	0		
1993–94	Nottingham F	0	0		
1994–95	Nottingham F	0	0		
1994–95	*Burnley*	4	0	**4**	**0**
1995–96	Nottingham F	0	0		
1995–96	*Bristol R*	14	0	**14**	**0**
1996–97	Nottingham F	0	0		
1996–97	*Gillingham*	10	0	**10**	**0**
1996–97	*Watford*	15	0	**15**	**0**
1997–98	Nottingham F	18	0		
1998–99	Nottingham F	22	0	**40**	**0**
1998–99	Huddersfield T	13	1		
1999–2000	Huddersfield T	39	0		
2000–01	Huddersfield T	44	3		
2001–02	Huddersfield T	11	1	**107**	**5**
2001–02	Sheffield W	8	0		
2002–03	Sheffield W	17	1		
2003–04	Sheffield W	10	0		
2003–04	*Grimsby T*	9	1	**9**	**1**
2004–05	Sheffield W	0	0	**35**	**1**
2004–05	Bradford C	7	0	**7**	**0**

ATHERTON, Peter (D) **581 13**
H: 5 11 W: 13 12 b.Wigan 6-4-70
Source: Trainee. *Honours:* England Schools, Under-21.

1987–88	Wigan Ath	16	0		
1988–89	Wigan Ath	40	1		
1989–90	Wigan Ath	46	0		
1990–91	Wigan Ath	46	0		
1991–92	Wigan Ath	1	0	**149**	**1**
1991–92	Coventry C	35	0		
1992–93	Coventry C	39	0		
1993–94	Coventry C	40	0	**114**	**0**
1994–95	Sheffield W	41	1		
1995–96	Sheffield W	36	0		
1996–97	Sheffield W	37	2		
1997–98	Sheffield W	27	3		
1998–99	Sheffield W	38	2		
1999–2000	Sheffield W	35	1	**214**	**9**
2000–01	Bradford C	25	0		
2000–01	*Birmingham C*	10	0	**10**	**0**
2001–02	Bradford C	1	0		
2002–03	Bradford C	25	1		
2003–04	Bradford C	27	2		
2004–05	Bradford C	16	0	**94**	**3**

BENTHAM, Craig (D) **2 0**
H: 5 9 W: 11 06 b.Bingley 7-3-85
Source: Scholar.

2004–05	Bradford C	2	0	**2**	**0**

BOWER, Mark (D) **146 6**
H: 5 10 W: 11 00 b.Bradford 23-1-80
Source: Trainee.

1997–98	Bradford C	3	0		
1998–99	Bradford C	0	0		
1999–2000	Bradford C	0	0		
1999–2000	*York C*	15	1		
2000–01	Bradford C	0	0		
2000–01	*York C*	21	1	**36**	**2**
2001–02	Bradford C	10	2		
2002–03	Bradford C	37	0		
2003–04	Bradford C	14	0		
2004–05	Bradford C	46	2	**110**	**4**

COLBECK, Joe (M) **0 0**
H: 5 10 W: 10 12 b.Bradford 29-11-86
Source: Scholar.

2004–05	Bradford C	0	0		

COMBE, Alan (G) **247 0**
H: 6 1 W: 12 05 b.Edinburgh 3-4-74
Source: Kelty Hearts.

1992–93	Cowdenbeath	18	0	**18**	**0**
1993–94	St Mirren	16	0		
1994–95	St Mirren	21	0		
1995–96	St Mirren	21	0		
1996–97	St Mirren	36	0		
1997–98	St Mirren	30	0	**124**	**0**
1998–99	Dundee U	10	0		
1999–2000	Dundee U	35	0		
2000–01	Dundee U	23	0		
2001–02	Dundee U	0	0	**68**	**0**
2001–02	Bradford C	16	0		
2002–03	Bradford C	0	0		
2003–04	Bradford C	21	0		
2004–05	Bradford C	0	0	**37**	**0**

COOKE, Andy (F) **279 77**
H: 6 0 W: 12 07 b.Shrewsbury 20-1-74
Source: Newtown.

1994–95	Burnley	0	0		
1995–96	Burnley	23	5		
1996–97	Burnley	31	13		
1997–98	Burnley	34	16		
1998–99	Burnley	36	9		
1999–2000	Burnley	36	7		
2000–01	Burnley	11	2	**171**	**52**
2000–01	Stoke C	22	6		
2001–02	Stoke C	35	9		
2002–03	Stoke C	31	6		
2003–04	Stoke C	0	0	**88**	**21**
From Pusan Icons.					
2004–05	Bradford C	20	4	**20**	**4**

CORNWALL, Luke (F) **20 5**
H: 5 10 W: 12 01 b.Lambeth 23-7-80
Source: Trainee.

1998–99	Fulham	4	1		
1999–2000	Fulham	0	0		
2000–01	Fulham	0	0		
2000–01	*Grimsby T*	10	4	**10**	**4**

2001–02 Fulham 0 0
2002–03 Fulham 0 0 **4** **1**
2002–03 *Lincoln C* 3 0 **3** **0**
2003–04 Bradford C 3 0
2004–05 Bradford C 0 0 **3** **0**

CROOKS, Lee (M) **178** **3**
H: 6 2 W: 13 01 b.Wakefield 14-1-78
Source: Trainee. *Honours:* England Youth.
1994–95 Manchester C 0 0
1995–96 Manchester C 0 0
1996–97 Manchester C 15 0
1997–98 Manchester C 5 0
1998–99 Manchester C 34 1
1999–2000 Manchester C 20 1
2000–01 Manchester C 2 0 **76** **2**
2000–01 *Northampton T* 3 0 **3** **0**
2000–01 Barnsley 0 0
2001–02 Barnsley 26 0
2002–03 Barnsley 18 0
2003–04 Barnsley 23 0 **67** **0**
2004–05 Bradford C 32 1 **32** **1**

DENTON, Sam (M) **0** **0**
H: 6 2 W: 13 02 b.Kippax
Source: Scholar.
2004–05 Bradford C 0 0

EMANUEL, Lewis (D) **102** **2**
H: 5 8 W: 12 01 b.Bradford 14-10-83
Source: From Scholar. *Honours:* England Youth.
2001–02 Bradford C 9 0
2002–03 Bradford C 29 0
2003–04 Bradford C 28 2
2004–05 Bradford C 36 0 **102** **2**

FLYNN, Liam (M) **0** **0**
H: 5 9 W: 11 00 b.Bradford 9-11-84
Source: Scholar.
2004–05 Bradford C 0 0

FOLKES, Peter (D) **0** **0**
H: 5 11 W: 12 08 b.Birmingham 16-11-84
Source: Bristol C Scholar.
2003–04 Bradford C 0 0
2004–05 Bradford C 0 0

FORREST, Danny (M) **50** **5**
H: 5 10 W: 11 07 b.Keighley 23-10-84
Source: Trainee. *Honours:* England Youth.
2002–03 Bradford C 17 3
2003–04 Bradford C 13 0
2004–05 Bradford C 20 2 **50** **5**

GAVIN, Jason (D) **92** **1**
H: 6 0 W: 11 13 b.Dublin 14-3-80
Source: Trainee. *Honours:* Eire Under-21.
1996–97 Middlesbrough 0 0
1997–98 Middlesbrough 0 0
1998–99 Middlesbrough 2 0
1999–2000 Middlesbrough 6 0
2000–01 Middlesbrough 14 0
2001–02 Middlesbrough 9 0
2002–03 Middlesbrough 0 0 **31** **0**
2002–03 *Grimsby T* 10 0 **10** **0**
2002–03 *Huddersfield T* 10 1 **10** **1**
2003–04 Bradford C 38 0
2004–05 Bradford C 3 0 **41** **0**

HENDERSON, Paul (G) **174** **0**
H: 6 1 W: 12 06 b.Sydney 22-4-76
1998–99 Northern Spirit 30 0
1999–2000 Northern Spirit 14 0
2000–01 Northern Spirit 21 0
2001–02 Northern Spirit 13 0
2002–03 Northern Spirit 33 0
2003–04 Northern Spirit 23 0 **134** **0**
2004–05 Bradford C 40 0 **40** **0**

HOLLOWAY, Darren (D) **197** **2**
H: 6 0 W: 12 05 b.Crook 3-10-77
Source: Trainee. *Honours:* England Under-21.
1995–96 Sunderland 0 0
1996–97 Sunderland 0 0
1997–98 Sunderland 32 0
1997–98 *Carlisle U* 5 0 **5** **0**
1998–99 Sunderland 6 0
1999–2000 Sunderland 15 0
1999–2000 *Bolton W* 4 0 **4** **0**
2000–01 Sunderland 5 0 **58** **0**
2000–01 Wimbledon 31 0
2001–02 Wimbledon 32 0
2002–03 Wimbledon 16 0
2003–04 Wimbledon 13 0 **92** **0**
2003–04 *Scunthorpe U* 5 1 **5** **1**
2004–05 Bradford C 33 1 **33** **1**

JACOBS, Wayne (D) **495** **18**
H: 5 9 W: 11 02 b.Sheffield 3-2-69
Source: Apprentice.
1986–87 Sheffield W 0 0
1987–88 Sheffield W 6 0 **6** **0**
1987–88 Hull C 6 0
1988–89 Hull C 33 0
1989–90 Hull C 46 3
1990–91 Hull C 19 1
1991–92 Hull C 25 0
1992–93 Hull C 0 0 **129** **4**
1993–94 Rotherham U 42 2 **42** **2**
1994–95 Bradford C 38 1
1995–96 Bradford C 28 0
1996–97 Bradford C 39 3
1997–98 Bradford C 36 2
1998–99 Bradford C 44 3
1999–2000 Bradford C 24 0
2000–01 Bradford C 21 2
2001–02 Bradford C 38 1
2002–03 Bradford C 23 0
2003–04 Bradford C 13 0
2004–05 Bradford C 14 0 **318** **12**

KEARNEY, Tom (M) **39** **1**
H: 5 11 W: 10 08 b.Liverpool 7-10-81
Source: Trainee.
1999–2000 Everton 0 0
2000–01 Everton 0 0
2001–02 Everton 0 0
2001–02 Bradford C 5 0
2002–03 Bradford C 4 0
2003–04 Bradford C 17 0
2004–05 Bradford C 13 1 **39** **1**

MORRISON, Owen (M) **111** **11**
H: 5 8 W: 11 12 b.Derry 8-12-81
Source: Trainee. *Honours:* Northern Ireland Schools, Youth, Under-21.
1998–99 Sheffield W 1 0
1999–2000 Sheffield W 0 0
2000–01 Sheffield W 30 6
2001–02 Sheffield W 24 2
2002–03 Sheffield W 1 0 **56** **8**
2002–03 *Hull C* 2 0 **2** **0**
2002–03 Sheffield U 8 0 **8** **0**
2003–04 Stockport Co 22 1
2004–05 Stockport Co 1 0 **23** **1**
2004–05 Bradford C 22 2 **22** **2**

MUIRHEAD, Ben (M) **76** **3**
H: 5 9 W: 11 02 b.Doncaster 5-1-83
Source: Trainee. *Honours:* England Youth.
1999–2000 Manchester U 0 0
2000–01 Manchester U 0 0
2001–02 Manchester U 0 0
2002–03 Manchester U 0 0
2002–03 Bradford C 8 0
2003–04 Bradford C 28 2
2004–05 Bradford C 40 1 **76** **3**

PENFORD, Thomas (M) **10** **0**
H: 5 10 W: 11 03 b.Leeds 5-1-85
Source: Scholar.
2002–03 Bradford C 3 0
2003–04 Bradford C 4 0
2004–05 Bradford C 3 0 **10** **0**

RICKETTS, Donovan (G) **4** **0**
H: 6 1 W: 11 05 b.St James 6-7-77
Source: Village U. *Honours:* Jamaica full caps.
2003–04 Bolton W 0 0
2004–05 Bolton W 0 0
2004–05 Bradford C 4 0 **4** **0**

SANASY, Kevin (M) **9** **1**
H: 5 8 W: 10 05 b.Leeds 2-11-84
Source: Scholar.
2002–03 Bradford C 1 0
2003–04 Bradford C 5 1
2004–05 Bradford C 3 0 **9** **1**

SCHUMACHER, Steven (M) **47** **6**
H: 5 10 W: 11 00 b.Liverpool 30-4-84
Source: Scholar. *Honours:* England Youth.
2000–01 Everton 0 0
2001–02 Everton 0 0
2002–03 Everton 0 0
2003–04 Everton 0 0
2003–04 *Carlisle U* 4 0 **4** **0**
2004–05 Bradford C 43 6 **43** **6**

SUMMERBEE, Nicky (M) **462** **26**
H: 5 11 W: 12 08 b.Altrincham 26-8-71
Source: Trainee. *Honours:* England Under-21.
1989–90 Swindon T 1 0
1990–91 Swindon T 7 0
1991–92 Swindon T 27 0
1992–93 Swindon T 39 3
1993–94 Swindon T 38 3 **112** **6**
1994–95 Manchester C 41 1
1995–96 Manchester C 37 1
1996–97 Manchester C 44 4
1997–98 Manchester C 9 0
1997–98 Sunderland 25 3
1998–99 Sunderland 36 3
1999–2000 Sunderland 32 1
2000–01 Sunderland 0 0 **93** **7**
2000–01 Bolton W 12 1 **12** **1**
2001–02 Manchester C 0 0 **131** **6**
2001–02 Nottingham F 17 2 **17** **2**
2002–03 Leicester C 29 0 **29** **0**
2003–04 Bradford C 35 1
2004–05 Bradford C 33 3 **68** **4**

SWIFT, John (M) **5** **0**
H: 5 7 W: 10 06 b.Leeds 20-9-84
Source: Scholar.
2004–05 Bradford C 5 0 **5** **0**

SYMES, Michael (F) **16** **3**
H: 6 3 W: 12 04 b.Gt Yarmouth 31-10-83
Source: Scholar.
2001–02 Everton 0 0
2002–03 Everton 0 0
2003–04 Everton 0 0
2003–04 *Crewe Alex* 4 1 **4** **1**
2004–05 Bradford C 12 2 **12** **2**
2004–05 *Darlington* 0 0

WETHERALL, David (D) **373** **22**
H: 6 3 W: 13 12 b.Sheffield 14-3-71
Source: School. *Honours:* England Schools.
1989–90 Sheffield W 0 0
1990–91 Sheffield W 0 0
1991–92 Leeds U 1 0
1992–93 Leeds U 13 1
1993–94 Leeds U 32 1
1994–95 Leeds U 38 3
1995–96 Leeds U 34 4
1996–97 Leeds U 29 0
1997–98 Leeds U 34 3
1998–99 Leeds U 21 0 **202** **12**
1999–2000 Bradford C 38 2
2000–01 Bradford C 18 1
2001–02 Bradford C 19 2
2002–03 Bradford C 17 0
2003–04 Bradford C 34 1
2004–05 Bradford C 45 4 **171** **10**

WINDASS, Dean (F) **492** **151**
H: 5 10 W: 12 03 b.North Ferriby 1-4-69
Source: N Ferriby U.
1991–92 Hull C 32 6
1992–93 Hull C 41 7
1993–94 Hull C 43 23
1994–95 Hull C 44 17
1995–96 Hull C 16 4 **176** **57**
1995–96 Aberdeen 20 6
1996–97 Aberdeen 29 10
1997–98 Aberdeen 24 5 **73** **21**
1998–99 Oxford U 33 15 **33** **15**
1998–99 Bradford C 12 3
1999–2000 Bradford C 38 10
2000–01 Bradford C 24 3
2000–01 Middlesbrough 8 2
2001–02 Middlesbrough 27 1
2001–02 *Sheffield W* 2 0 **2** **0**
2002–03 Middlesbrough 2 0 **37** **3**
2002–03 Sheffield U 20 6 **20** **6**
2003–04 Bradford C 36 6
2004–05 Bradford C 41 27 **151** **49**

BRENTFORD (11)

BANKOLE, Ademola (G) **62 0**
H: 6 3 W: 14 00 b.Lagos 9-9-69
Source: Leyton Orient.

1996–97	Crewe Alex	3	0		
1997–98	Crewe Alex	3	0		
1998–99	QPR	0	0		
1998–99	*Grimsby T*	0	0		
1999–2000	QPR	1	0	**1**	**0**
1999–2000	*Bradford C*	0	0		
2000–01	Crewe Alex	21	0		
2001–02	Crewe Alex	28	0		
2002–03	Crewe Alex	3	0		
2003–04	Crewe Alex	0	0	**58**	**0**
2004–05	Brentford	3	0	**3**	**0**

BURTON, Deon (F) **270 54**
H: 5 9 W: 11 09 b.Reading 25-10-77
Source: Trainee. *Honours:* Jamaica 49 full caps, 8 goals.

1993–94	Portsmouth	2	0		
1994–95	Portsmouth	7	2		
1995–96	Portsmouth	32	7		
1996–97	Portsmouth	21	1		
1996–97	*Cardiff C*	5	2	**5**	**2**
1997–98	Derby Co	29	3		
1998–99	Derby Co	21	9		
1998–99	*Barnsley*	3	0	**3**	**0**
1999–2000	Derby Co	19	4		
2000–01	Derby Co	32	5		
2001–02	Derby Co	17	1		
2001–02	*Stoke C*	12	2	**12**	**2**
2002–03	Derby Co	7	3	**125**	**25**
2002–03	Portsmouth	15	4		
2003–04	Portsmouth	1	0	**78**	**14**
2003–04	*Walsall*	3	0	**3**	**0**
2003–04	*Swindon T*	4	1	**4**	**1**
2004–05	Brentford	40	10	**40**	**10**

CHARLES, Darius (M) **1 0**
H: 5 11 W: 11 10 b.Ealing 10-12-87

2004–05	Brentford	1	0	**1**	**0**

CLARIDGE, Steve (F) **606 188**
H: 6 0 W: 12 10 b.Portsmouth 10-4-66
Source: Portsmouth, Fareham T.

1984–85	Bournemouth	6	1		
1985–86	Bournemouth	1	0	**7**	**1**
From Weymouth					
1988–89	Crystal Palace	0	0		
1988–89	Aldershot	37	9		
1989–90	Aldershot	25	10	**62**	**19**
1989–90	Cambridge U	20	4		
1990–91	Cambridge U	30	12		
1991–92	Cambridge U	29	12		
1992–93	Luton T	16	2	**16**	**2**
1992–93	Cambridge U	29	7		
1993–94	Cambridge U	24	11	**132**	**46**
1993–94	Birmingham C	18	7		
1994–95	Birmingham C	42	20		
1995–96	Birmingham C	28	8	**88**	**35**
1995–96	Leicester C	14	5		
1996–97	Leicester C	32	11		
1997–98	Leicester C	17	0	**63**	**16**
1997–98	*Portsmouth*	10	2		
1997–98	Wolverhampton W	5	0	**5**	**0**
1998–99	Portsmouth	39	9		
1999–2000	Portsmouth	34	14		
2000–01	Portsmouth	31	11	**114**	**36**
2000–01	*Millwall*	6	3		
2001–02	Millwall	41	17		
2002–03	Millwall	44	9		
2003–04	Millwall	0	0	**91**	**29**
2004–05	Brighton & HA	5	0	**5**	**0**
2004–05	Brentford	4	0	**4**	**0**
2004–05	*Wycombe W*	19	4	**19**	**4**

DOBSON, Michael (D) **171 3**
H: 5 11 W: 12 04 b.Isleworth 9-4-81
Source: Trainee.

1999–2000	Brentford	0	0		
2000–01	Brentford	26	0		
2001–02	Brentford	39	0		
2002–03	Brentford	46	1		
2003–04	Brentford	42	1		
2004–05	Brentford	18	1	**171**	**3**

FITZGERALD, Scott B (D) **338 2**
H: 6 1 W: 13 00 b.Westminster 13-8-69
Source: Trainee. *Honours:* Eire Under-21, B.

1988–89	Wimbledon	0	0		
1989–90	Wimbledon	1	0		
1990–91	Wimbledon	0	0		
1991–92	Wimbledon	36	1		
1992–93	Wimbledon	20	0		
1993–94	Wimbledon	28	0		
1994–95	Wimbledon	17	0		
1995–96	Wimbledon	4	0		
1995–96	*Sheffield U*	6	0	**6**	**0**
1996–97	Wimbledon	0	0	**106**	**1**
1996–97	*Millwall*	7	0		
1997–98	Millwall	18	0		
1998–99	Millwall	32	1		
1999–2000	Millwall	31	0		
2000–01	Millwall	1	0	**89**	**1**
2000–01	Colchester U	30	0		
2001–02	Colchester U	37	0		
2002–03	Colchester U	26	0		
2003–04	Colchester U	23	0	**116**	**0**
2003–04	*Brentford*	9	0		
2004–05	Brentford	12	0	**21**	**0**

FITZGERALD, Scott P (F) **71 15**
H: 5 11 W: 12 00 b.Hillingdon 18-11-79
Source: Northwood.

2002–03	Watford	4	1		
2003–04	Watford	44	10		
2004–05	Watford	7	0	**55**	**11**
2004–05	*Swansea C*	3	0	**3**	**0**
2004–05	*Leyton Orient*	1	0	**1**	**0**
2004–05	Brentford	12	4	**12**	**4**

FRAMPTON, Andrew (D) **94 0**
H: 5 11 W: 10 10 b.Wimbledon 3-9-79
Source: Trainee.

1998–99	Crystal Palace	6	0		
1999–2000	Crystal Palace	9	0		
2000–01	Crystal Palace	10	0		
2001–02	Crystal Palace	2	0		
2002–03	Crystal Palace	1	0	**28**	**0**
2002–03	Brentford	15	0		
2003–04	Brentford	16	0		
2004–05	Brentford	35	0	**66**	**0**

GAYLE, Marcus (D) **504 64**
H: 6 3 W: 14 03 b.Hammersmith 28-9-70
Source: Trainee. *Honours:* England Youth. Jamaica 14 full caps, 3 goals.

1988–89	Brentford	3	0		
1989–90	Brentford	9	0		
1990–91	Brentford	33	6		
1991–92	Brentford	38	6		
1992–93	Brentford	38	4		
1993–94	Brentford	35	6		
1993–94	Wimbledon	10	0		
1994–95	Wimbledon	23	2		
1995–96	Wimbledon	34	5		
1996–97	Wimbledon	36	8		
1997–98	Wimbledon	30	2		
1998–99	Wimbledon	35	10		
1999–2000	Wimbledon	36	7		
2000–01	Wimbledon	32	3	**236**	**37**
2000–01	Rangers	4	0	**4**	**0**
2001–02	Watford	36	4		
2002–03	Watford	31	0		
2003–04	Watford	32	1		
2004–05	Watford	3	0	**102**	**5**
2004–05	Brentford	6	0	**162**	**22**

HARGREAVES, Chris (M) **422 24**
H: 5 11 W: 13 02 b.Cleethorpes 12-5-72
Source: Trainee.

1989–90	Grimsby T	19	2		
1990–91	Grimsby T	18	3		
1991–92	Grimsby T	10	0		
1992–93	Grimsby T	4	0		
1992–93	*Scarborough*	3	0	**3**	**0**
1993–94	Grimsby T	0	0	**51**	**5**
1993–94	Hull C	28	0		
1994–95	Hull C	21	0	**49**	**0**
1995–96	WBA	1	0	**1**	**0**
1995–96	*Hereford U*	17	2		
1996–97	Hereford U	44	4		
1997–98	Hereford U	0	0	**61**	**6**
From Hereford U.					
1998–99	Plymouth Arg	32	2		
1999–2000	Plymouth Arg	44	3	**76**	**5**
2000–01	Northampton T	31	0		
2001–02	Northampton T	39	3		
2002–03	Northampton T	39	0		
2003–04	Northampton T	42	3	**151**	**6**
2004–05	Brentford	30	2	**30**	**2**

HARROLD, Matt (F) **38 4**
H: 6 1 W: 11 10 b.Leyton 24-7-84
Source: Harlow T.

2003–04	Brentford	13	2		
2004–05	Brentford	19	0	**32**	**2**
2004–05	*Grimsby T*	6	2	**6**	**2**

HILLIER, Sean (D) **0 0**
H: 5 10 W: 11 10 b.Hanwell 19-4-86
Source: Colchester U Trainee.

2004–05	Brentford	0	0		

HUNT, Steve (M) **139 25**
H: 5 7 W: 12 06 b.Port Laoise 1-8-80
Source: Trainee.

1999–2000	Crystal Palace	3	0		
2000–01	Crystal Palace	0	0	**3**	**0**
2001–02	Brentford	35	4		
2002–03	Brentford	42	7		
2003–04	Brentford	40	11		
2004–05	Brentford	19	3	**136**	**25**

HUTCHINSON, Eddie (M) **90 6**
H: 6 1 W: 12 07 b.Kingston 23-2-82
Source: Sutton U.

2000–01	Brentford	7	0		
2001–02	Brentford	9	0		
2002–03	Brentford	23	0		
2003–04	Brentford	36	5		
2004–05	Brentford	15	1	**90**	**6**

IDE, Charlie (M) **1 0**
H: 5 8 W: 10 06 b.Sunbury 10-5-88

2004–05	Brentford	1	0	**1**	**0**

JULIAN, Alan (G) **16 0**
H: 6 2 W: 13 07 b.Ashford 11-3-83
Source: Trainee. *Honours:* Northern Ireland Youth, Under-21.

2001–02	Brentford	0	0		
2002–03	Brentford	3	0		
2003–04	Brentford	13	0		
2004–05	Brentford	0	0	**16**	**0**

LAWRENCE, Jamie (M) **276 18**
H: 5 9 W: 12 10 b.Balham 8-3-70
Source: Cowes. *Honours:* Jamaica 23 full caps.

1993–94	Sunderland	4	0	**4**	**0**
1993–94	Doncaster R	9	1		
1994–95	Doncaster R	16	2	**25**	**3**
1994–95	Leicester C	17	1		
1995–96	Leicester C	15	0		
1996–97	Leicester C	15	0	**47**	**1**
1997–98	Bradford C	43	3		
1998–99	Bradford C	35	2		
1999–2000	Bradford C	23	3		
2000–01	Bradford C	17	1		
2001–02	Bradford C	21	2		
2002–03	Bradford C	16	1	**155**	**12**
2002–03	Walsall	5	0		
2003–04	Walsall	17	1	**22**	**1**
2003–04	*Wigan Ath*	4	0	**4**	**0**
2003–04	Grimsby T	5	1		
2004–05	Grimsby T	0	0	**5**	**1**
2004–05	Brentford	14	0	**14**	**0**

LENNIE, Josh (G) **0 0**
H: 6 1 W: 13 03 b.Greenford 25-3-86

2004–05	Brentford	0	0		

MOLESKI, George (M) **1 0**
H: 5 6 W: 10 08 b.Hillingdon 27-7-87
Source: Scholar.

2004–05	Brentford	1	0	**1**	**0**

MULDOWNEY, Luke (D) **0 0**
H: 5 7 W: 10 06 b.Feltham 31-7-86
Source: Scholar.

2004–05	Brentford	0	0		

MYERS, Andy (D) **212 5**
H: 5 8 W: 11 00 b.Hounslow 3-11-73
Source: From Trainee. *Honours:* England Schools, Youth, Under-21.

1990–91	Chelsea	3	0		
1991–92	Chelsea	11	1		
1992–93	Chelsea	3	0		
1993–94	Chelsea	6	0		
1994–95	Chelsea	10	0		

1995–96 Chelsea 20 0
1996–97 Chelsea 18 1
1997–98 Chelsea 12 0
1998–99 Chelsea 1 0 **84 2**
1999–2000 Bradford C 13 0
1999–2000 *Portsmouth* 8 0 **8 0**
2000–01 Bradford C 20 1
2001–02 Bradford C 32 2
2002–03 Bradford C 24 0 **89 3**
2003–04 Colchester U 21 0 **21 0**
2004–05 Brentford 10 0 **10 0**

NELSON, Stuart (G) 52 0
H: 6 1 W: 12 12 b.Stroud 17-9-81
Source: Doncaster R, Hucknall T.
2003–04 Brentford 9 0
2004–05 Brentford 43 0 **52 0**

O'CONNOR, Kevin (F) 167 9
H: 5 11 W: 12 00 b.Blackburn 24-2-82
Source: Trainee. *Honours:* Eire Under-21.
1999–2000 Brentford 6 0
2000–01 Brentford 11 1
2001–02 Brentford 25 0
2002–03 Brentford 45 5
2003–04 Brentford 43 1
2004–05 Brentford 37 2 **167 9**

OSBORNE, Karleigh (M) 1 0
H: 6 2 W: 12 08 b.Southall 19-3-88
2004–05 Brentford 1 0 **1 0**

PACQUETTE, Richard (F) 42 7
H: 5 11 W: 12 12 b.Paddington 28-1-83
Source: Trainee.
1999–2000 QPR 0 0
2000–01 QPR 2 0
2001–02 QPR 16 2
2002–03 QPR 11 4
2003–04 QPR 2 0
2003–04 *Mansfield T* 5 1 **5 1**
2004–05 QPR 0 0 **31 6**
2004–05 Milton Keynes D 5 0 **5 0**
2004–05 Brentford 1 0 **1 0**

PALMER, Jamie (M) 0 0
H: 5 9 W: 11 10 b.Feltham 25-11-85
Source: Scholar.
2004–05 Brentford 0 0

PETERS, Ryan (F) 9 1
H: 5 8 W: 10 08 b.Wandsworth 21-8-87
Source: Scholar.
2004–05 Brentford 9 1 **9 1**

RANKIN, Isiah (F) 178 35
H: 5 10 W: 11 00 b.London 22-5-78
Source: Trainee.
1995–96 Arsenal 0 0
1996–97 Arsenal 0 0
1997–98 Arsenal 1 0 **1 0**
1997–98 *Colchester U* 11 5 **11 5**
1998–99 Bradford C 27 4
1999–2000 Bradford C 9 0
1999–2000 *Birmingham C* 13 4 **13 4**
2000–01 Bradford C 1 0 **37 4**
2000–01 *Bolton W* 16 2 **16 2**
2000–01 Barnsley 9 1
2001–02 Barnsley 9 1
2002–03 Barnsley 9 1
2003–04 Barnsley 20 5 **47 8**
2003–04 Grimsby T 12 4 **12 4**
2004–05 Brentford 41 8 **41 8**

RHODES, Alex (F) 25 4
H: 5 9 W: 10 04 b.Cambridge 23-1-82
Source: Newmarket T.
2003–04 Brentford 3 1
2004–05 Brentford 22 3 **25 4**

SALAKO, John (M) 510 49
H: 5 10 W: 12 08 b.Nigeria 11-2-69
Source: Trainee. *Honours:* England 5 full caps.
1986–87 Crystal Palace 4 0
1987–88 Crystal Palace 31 0
1988–89 Crystal Palace 28 0
1989–90 Crystal Palace 17 2
1989–90 *Swansea C* 13 3 **13 3**
1990–91 Crystal Palace 35 6
1991–92 Crystal Palace 10 2
1992–93 Crystal Palace 13 0
1993–94 Crystal Palace 38 8
1994–95 Crystal Palace 39 4 **215 22**
1995–96 Coventry C 37 3
1996–97 Coventry C 24 1
1997–98 Coventry C 11 0 **72 4**
1997–98 Bolton W 7 0 **7 0**
1998–99 Fulham 10 1
1999–2000 Fulham 0 0 **10 1**
1999–2000 Charlton Ath 27 2
2000–01 Charlton Ath 17 0
2001–02 Charlton Ath 3 0 **47 2**
2001–02 Reading 31 6
2002–03 Reading 43 4
2003–04 Reading 37 3 **111 13**
2004–05 Brentford 35 4 **35 4**

SMITH, Jay (M) 48 0
H: 5 11 W: 11 07 b.Hammersmith 29-12-81
Source: Trainee.
2000–01 Brentford 3 0
2001–02 Brentford 0 0
2002–03 Brentford 26 0
2003–04 Brentford 17 0
2004–05 Brentford 2 0 **48 0**

SODJE, Sam (D) 40 7
H: 6 0 W: 12 00 b.Greenwich 29-5-79
Source: Stevenage B, Margate.
2004–05 Brentford 40 7 **40 7**

TABB, Jay (M) 86 14
H: 5 5 W: 9 07 b.Tooting 21-2-84
Source: From Trainee. *Honours:* Eire Under-21.
2000–01 Brentford 2 0
2001–02 Brentford 3 0
2002–03 Brentford 5 0
2003–04 Brentford 36 9
2004–05 Brentford 40 5 **86 14**

TALBOT, Stuart (M) 308 21
H: 6 0 W: 13 12 b.Birmingham 14-6-73
Source: Doncaster R, Moor Green.
1994–95 Port Vale 2 0
1995–96 Port Vale 20 0
1996–97 Port Vale 34 4
1997–98 Port Vale 42 6
1998–99 Port Vale 33 0
1999–2000 Port Vale 6 0 **137 10**
2000–01 Rotherham U 38 5
2001–02 Rotherham U 38 1
2002–03 Rotherham U 15 1
2002–03 *Shrewsbury T* 5 0 **5 0**
2003–04 Rotherham U 23 1 **114 8**
2003–04 Brentford 15 2
2004–05 Brentford 37 1 **52 3**

TURNER, Michael (D) 52 2
H: 6 4 W: 12 06 b.Lewisham 9-11-83
Source: Scholar.
2001–02 Charlton Ath 0 0
2002–03 Charlton Ath 0 0
2002–03 *Leyton Orient* 7 1 **7 1**
2003–04 Charlton Ath 0 0
2004–05 Charlton Ath 0 0
2004–05 Brentford 45 1 **45 1**

WATTS, Ryan (M) 1 0
H: 5 9 W: 10 10 b.Greenford 18-5-88
2004–05 Brentford 1 0 **1 0**

WEIGHT, Scott (M) 0 0
H: 5 11 W: 10 04 b.Hounslow 3-4-87
2004–05 Brentford 0 0

BRIGHTON & HA (12)

BECK, Dan (F) 1 0
H: 5 10 W: 10 06 b.Worthing 14-11-83
Source: Scholar.
2003–04 Brighton & HA 1 0
2004–05 Brighton & HA 0 0 **1 0**

BLACKWELL, Dean (D) 233 3
H: 6 1 W: 12 09 b.Camden 5-12-69
Source: Trainee. *Honours:* England Under-21.
1988–89 Wimbledon 0 0
1989–90 Wimbledon 3 0
1989–90 *Plymouth Arg* 7 0 **7 0**
1990–91 Wimbledon 35 0
1991–92 Wimbledon 4 1
1992–93 Wimbledon 24 0
1993–94 Wimbledon 18 0
1994–95 Wimbledon 0 0
1995–96 Wimbledon 8 0
1996–97 Wimbledon 27 0
1997–98 Wimbledon 35 0
1998–99 Wimbledon 28 0
1999–2000 Wimbledon 17 0
2000–01 Wimbledon 6 0
2001–02 Wimbledon 0 0
2002–03 Wimbledon 0 0 **205 1**
2002–03 Brighton & HA 21 2
2003–04 Brighton & HA 0 0
2004–05 Brighton & HA 0 0 **21 2**

BUTTERS, Guy (D) 457 32
H: 6 1 W: 15 05 b.Hillingdon 30-10-69
Source: Trainee. *Honours:* England Under-21.
1988–89 Tottenham H 28 1
1989–90 Tottenham H 7 0 **35 1**
1989–90 *Southend U* 16 3 **16 3**
1990–91 Portsmouth 23 0
1991–92 Portsmouth 33 2
1992–93 Portsmouth 15 1
1993–94 Portsmouth 15 1
1994–95 Portsmouth 24 0
1994–95 *Oxford U* 3 1 **3 1**
1995–96 Portsmouth 37 2
1996–97 Portsmouth 7 0 **154 6**
1996–97 Gillingham 30 0
1997–98 Gillingham 31 7
1998–99 Gillingham 23 3
1999–2000 Gillingham 40 2
2000–01 Gillingham 12 3
2001–02 Gillingham 23 1 **159 16**
2002–03 Brighton & HA 6 0
2003–04 Brighton & HA 43 3
2004–05 Brighton & HA 41 2 **90 5**

CARPENTER, Richard (M) 460 31
H: 6 0 W: 13 03 b.Sheppey 30-9-72
Source: Trainee.
1990–91 Gillingham 9 1
1991–92 Gillingham 3 0
1992–93 Gillingham 28 0
1993–94 Gillingham 40 3
1994–95 Gillingham 29 0
1995–96 Gillingham 12 0
1996–97 Gillingham 1 0 **122 4**
1996–97 Fulham 34 5
1997–98 Fulham 24 2 **58 7**
1998–99 Cardiff C 42 1
1999–2000 Cardiff C 33 1 **75 2**
2000–01 Brighton & HA 42 6
2001–02 Brighton & HA 45 3
2002–03 Brighton & HA 44 2
2003–04 Brighton & HA 42 4
2004–05 Brighton & HA 32 3 **205 18**

EL-ABD, Adam (D) 27 0
H: 5 10 W: 13 05 b.Brighton 11-9-84
Source: Scholar.
2003–04 Brighton & HA 11 0
2004–05 Brighton & HA 16 0 **27 0**

HAMMOND, Dean (M) 42 4
H: 6 1 W: 11 02 b.Hastings 7-3-83
Source: Scholar.
2002–03 Brighton & HA 4 0
2003–04 Brighton & HA 0 0
2003–04 *Leyton Orient* 8 0 **8 0**
2004–05 Brighton & HA 30 4 **34 4**

HARDING, Daniel (D) 67 1
H: 6 0 W: 11 11 b.Gloucester 23-12-83
Source: Scholar. *Honours:* England Under-21.
2002–03 Brighton & HA 1 0
2003–04 Brighton & HA 23 0
2004–05 Brighton & HA 43 1 **67 1**

HART, Gary (F) 275 41
H: 5 9 W: 12 07 b.Harlow 21-9-76
Source: Stansted.
1998–99 Brighton & HA 44 12
1999–2000 Brighton & HA 43 9
2000–01 Brighton & HA 45 7
2001–02 Brighton & HA 39 4
2002–03 Brighton & HA 36 4
2003–04 Brighton & HA 42 3
2004–05 Brighton & HA 26 2 **275 41**

HINSHELWOOD, Adam (D) 62 1
H: 5 11 W: 13 00 b.Oxford 8-1-84
Source: Scholar.

2002–03	Brighton & HA	7	0		
2003–04	Brighton & HA	17	0		
2004–05	Brighton & HA	38	1	**62**	**1**

JARRETT, Albert (M) 21 1
H: 5 11 W: 11 02 b.Sierra Leone 23-10-84
Source: Dulwich Hamlet.

2002–03	Wimbledon	0	0		
2003–04	Wimbledon	9	0	**9**	**0**
2004–05	Brighton & HA	12	1	**12**	**1**

JONES, Nathan (M) 267 9
H: 5 6 W: 10 06 b.Rhondda 28-5-73
Source: Cardiff C Trainee, Maesteg Park, Ton Pentre, Merthyr T.

1995–96	Luton T	0	0		
Badajoz, Numaicia					
1997–98	Southend U	39	0		
1998–99	Southend U	17	0		
1998–99	*Scarborough*	9	0	**9**	**0**
1999–2000	Southend U	43	2	**99**	**2**
2000–01	Brighton & HA	40	4		
2001–02	Brighton & HA	36	2		
2002–03	Brighton & HA	28	1		
2003–04	Brighton & HA	36	0		
2004–05	Brighton & HA	19	0	**159**	**7**

KNIGHT, Leon (F) 149 48
H: 5 5 W: 10 02 b.Hackney 16-9-82
Source: Trainee. *Honours:* England Youth, Under-20.

1999–2000	Chelsea	0	0		
2000–01	Chelsea	0	0		
2000–01	*QPR*	11	0	**11**	**0**
2001–02	Chelsea	0	0		
2001–02	*Huddersfield T*	31	16	**31**	**16**
2002–03	Chelsea	0	0		
2002–03	*Sheffield W*	24	3	**24**	**3**
2003–04	Chelsea	0	0		
2003–04	Brighton & HA	44	25		
2004–05	Brighton & HA	39	4	**83**	**29**

KUIPERS, Michels (G) 138 0
H: 6 2 W: 15 00 b.Amsterdam 26-6-74

1998–99	Bristol R	1	0		
1999–2000	Bristol R	0	0	**1**	**0**
2000–01	Brighton & HA	34	0		
2001–02	Brighton & HA	39	0		
2002–03	Brighton & HA	21	0		
2003–04	Brighton & HA	10	0		
2003–04	*Hull C*	3	0	**3**	**0**
2004–05	Brighton & HA	30	0	**134**	**0**

MAY, Christopher (G) 1 0
H: 5 11 W: 11 08 b.Wakefield 2-9-85
Source: Scholar.

2004–05	Brighton & HA	1	0	**1**	**0**

MAYO, Kerry (D) 303 11
H: 5 9 W: 13 10 b.Cuckfield 21-9-77
Source: Trainee.

1996–97	Brighton & HA	24	0		
1997–98	Brighton & HA	44	6		
1998–99	Brighton & HA	25	1		
1999–2000	Brighton & HA	31	1		
2000–01	Brighton & HA	45	1		
2001–02	Brighton & HA	33	0		
2002–03	Brighton & HA	41	1		
2003–04	Brighton & HA	33	0		
2004–05	Brighton & HA	27	1	**303**	**11**

McARTHUR, Duncan (M) 3 0
H: 5 9 W: 12 06 b.Brighton 6-5-81
Source: Trainee.

1998–99	Brighton & HA	3	0		
1999–2000	Brighton & HA	0	0		
2000–01	Brighton & HA	0	0		
2001–02	Brighton & HA	0	0		
2002–03	Brighton & HA	0	0		
2003–04	Brighton & HA	0	0		
2004–05	Brighton & HA	0	0	**3**	**0**

McCAMMON, Mark (F) 127 15
H: 6 3 W: 15 02 b.Barnet 7-8-78
Source: Cambridge C.

1997–98	Cambridge U	2	0		
1998–99	Cambridge U	2	0	**4**	**0**
1998–99	Charlton Ath	0	0		
1999–2000	Charlton Ath	4	0	**4**	**0**
1999–2000	*Swindon T*	4	0	**4**	**0**
2000–01	Brentford	24	3		
2001–02	Brentford	14	0		
2002–03	Brentford	37	7	**75**	**10**
2002–03	Millwall	7	2		
2003–04	Millwall	7	0		
2004–05	Millwall	8	0	**22**	**2**
2004–05	Brighton & HA	18	3	**18**	**3**

McPHEE, Christopher (F) 53 4
H: 6 0 W: 11 11 b.Eastbourne 20-3-83
Source: Scholarship.

1999–2000	Brighton & HA	4	0		
2000–01	Brighton & HA	0	0		
2001–02	Brighton & HA	2	0		
2002–03	Brighton & HA	2	0		
2003–04	Brighton & HA	29	4		
2004–05	Brighton & HA	16	0	**53**	**4**

MOLANGO, Maheta (F) 5 1
H: 6 1 W: 12 00 b.St Imier 24-7-82
Source: SV Burghausen.

2004–05	Brighton & HA	5	1	**5**	**1**

NICOLAS, Alexis (M) 35 0
H: 5 8 W: 9 13 b.Westminster 13-2-83
Source: Scholar. *Honours:* Cyprus Under-21.

2000–01	Aston Villa	0	0		
2001–02	Aston Villa	0	0		
2001–02	Chelsea	0	0		
2002–03	Chelsea	0	0		
2003–04	Chelsea	2	0		
2004–05	Chelsea	0	0	**2**	**0**
2004–05	Brighton & HA	33	0	**33**	**0**

OATWAY, Charlie (M) 365 9
H: 5 7 W: 11 11 b.Hammersmith 28-11-73
Source: Yeading.

1994–95	Cardiff C	30	0		
1995–96	Cardiff C	2	0	**32**	**0**
1995–96	Torquay U	24	0		
1996–97	Torquay U	41	1		
1997–98	Torquay U	2	0	**67**	**1**
1997–98	Brentford	33	0		
1998–99	Brentford	24	0	**57**	**0**
1998–99	*Lincoln C*	3	0	**3**	**0**
1999–2000	Brighton & HA	42	4		
2000–01	Brighton & HA	38	0		
2001–02	Brighton & HA	32	1		
2002–03	Brighton & HA	29	1		
2003–04	Brighton & HA	31	1		
2004–05	Brighton & HA	34	1	**206**	**8**

PIERCY, John (M) 38 4
H: 5 9 W: 13 00 b.Forest Gate 18-9-79
Source: Trainee. *Honours:* England Youth.

1998–99	Tottenham H	0	0		
1999–2000	Tottenham H	3	0		
2000–01	Tottenham H	5	0		
2001–02	Tottenham H	0	0		
2002–03	Tottenham H	0	0	**8**	**0**
2002–03	Brighton & HA	4	0		
2003–04	Brighton & HA	24	4		
2004–05	Brighton & HA	2	0	**30**	**4**

REID, Paul (M) 145 19
H: 5 8 W: 12 09 b.Sydney 6-7-79
Honours: Australia Under-20.

1998–99	Wollongong Wolves	22	2		
1999–2000	Wollongong Wolves	31	3		
2000–01	Wollongong Wolves	30	7		
2001–02	Wollongong Wolves	15	3	**98**	**15**
2002–03	Bradford C	8	2		
2003–04	Bradford C	0	0	**8**	**2**
2003–04	Brighton & HA	5	0		
2004–05	Brighton & HA	34	2	**39**	**2**

ROBERTS, Ben (G) 109 0
H: 6 2 W: 13 05 b.Bishop Auckland 22-6-75
Source: Trainee. *Honours:* England Under-21.

1992–93	Middlesbrough	0	0		
1993–94	Middlesbrough	0	0		
1994–95	Middlesbrough	0	0		
1995–96	Middlesbrough	0	0		
1995–96	*Hartlepool U*	4	0	**4**	**0**
1995–96	*Wycombe W*	15	0	**15**	**0**
1996–97	Middlesbrough	10	0		
1996–97	*Bradford C*	2	0	**2**	**0**
1997–98	Middlesbrough	6	0		
1998–99	Middlesbrough	0	0		
1998–99	*Millwall*	11	0	**11**	**0**
1999–2000	Middlesbrough	0	0	**16**	**0**
1999–2000	*Luton T*	14	0		
2000–01	Charlton Ath	0	0		
2001–02	Charlton Ath	0	0		
2001–02	*Reading*	6	0	**6**	**0**
2002–03	Charlton Ath	1	0	**1**	**0**
2002–03	*Luton T*	5	0	**19**	**0**
2002–03	*Brighton & HA*	3	0		
2003–04	Brighton & HA	32	0		
2004–05	Brighton & HA	0	0	**35**	**0**

ROBINSON, Jake (F) 19 1
H: 5 7 W: 10 10 b.Brighton 23-10-86
Source: Scholar.

2003–04	Brighton & HA	9	0		
2004–05	Brighton & HA	10	1	**19**	**1**

SHAABAN, Rami (G) 152 0
H: 6 4 W: 14 02 b.Sweden 30-6-75

1994	Saltsjobadens	26	0		
1995	Saltsjobadens	13	0	**39**	**0**
1995–96	Zamalek	4	0	**4**	**0**
1995–96	Thadodosman	5	0	**5**	**0**
1997–	Nacka	2	0		
1998–	Nacka	20	0		
1999–	Nacka	26	0	**48**	**0**
2000	Djurgaarden	29	0		
2001	Djurgaarden	5	0		
2001	Djurgaarden	5	0		
2001	Vartan	2	0	**2**	**0**
2002	Djurgaarden	6	0	**45**	**0**
2002–03	Arsenal	3	0		
2003–04	Arsenal	0	0		
2003–04	*West Ham U*	0	0		
2004–05	Arsenal	0	0	**3**	**0**
2004–05	Brighton & HA	6	0	**6**	**0**

VIRGO, Adam (D) 82 9
H: 6 2 W: 13 12 b.Brighton 25-1-83
Source: Juniors. *Honours:* Scotland B.

2000–01	Brighton & HA	6	0		
2001–02	Brighton & HA	6	0		
2002–03	Brighton & HA	3	0		
2002–03	*Exeter C*	9	0	**9**	**0**
2003–04	Brighton & HA	22	1		
2004–05	Brighton & HA	36	8	**73**	**9**

WATSON, Paul (D) 346 20
H: 5 8 W: 11 04 b.Hastings 4-1-75
Source: Trainee.

1992–93	Gillingham	1	0		
1993–94	Gillingham	14	0		
1994–95	Gillingham	39	2		
1995–96	Gillingham	8	0	**62**	**2**
1996–97	Fulham	44	3		
1997–98	Fulham	6	1	**50**	**4**
1997–98	Brentford	25	0		
1998–99	Brentford	12	0	**37**	**0**
1999–2000	Brighton & HA	42	4		
2000–01	Brighton & HA	46	5		
2001–02	Brighton & HA	45	5		
2002–03	Brighton & HA	45	0		
2003–04	Brighton & HA	15	0		
2004–05	Brighton & HA	4	0	**197**	**14**

BRISTOL C (13)

ANYINSAH, Joseph (M) 7 0
H: 5 8 W: 11 00 b.Bristol 8-10-84
Source: Scholar.

2001–02	Bristol C	0	0		
2002–03	Bristol C	0	0		
2003–04	Bristol C	0	0		
2004–05	Bristol C	7	0	**7**	**0**

BELL, Mickey (M) 563 50
H: 5 10 W: 12 09 b.Newcastle 15-11-71
Source: Trainee.

1989–90	Northampton T	6	0		
1990–91	Northampton T	28	0		
1991–92	Northampton T	30	4		
1992–93	Northampton T	39	5		
1993–94	Northampton T	38	0		
1994–95	Northampton T	12	1	**153**	**10**
1994–95	Wycombe W	31	3		
1995–96	Wycombe W	41	1		
1996–97	Wycombe W	46	2	**118**	**6**
1997–98	Bristol C	44	10		
1998–99	Bristol C	33	5		
1999–2000	Bristol C	36	5		

2000–01 Bristol C 41 4
2001–02 Bristol C 42 7
2002–03 Bristol C 38 2
2003–04 Bristol C 27 0
2004–05 Bristol C 31 1 **292 34**

BROOKER, Stephen (F) 165 52
H: 5 11 W: 13 13 b.Newport Pagnell 21-5-81
Source: Trainee.
1999–2000 Watford 1 0
2000–01 Watford 0 0 **1 0**
2000–01 Port Vale 23 9
2001–02 Port Vale 41 9
2002–03 Port Vale 26 5
2003–04 Port Vale 32 8
2004–05 Port Vale 9 5 **131 36**
2004–05 Bristol C 33 16 **33 16**

BROWN, Scott (M) 19 0
H: 5 9 W: 11 00 b.Runcorn 8-5-85
Source: Scholar. *Honours:* England Youth.
2001–02 Everton 0 0
2002–03 Everton 0 0
2003–04 Everton 0 0
2004–05 Bristol C 19 0 **19 0**

CAREY, Louis (D) 349 5
H: 5 10 W: 12 09 b.Bristol 20-1-77
Source: Trainee. *Honours:* Scotland Under-21.
1995–96 Bristol C 23 0
1996–97 Bristol C 42 0
1997–98 Bristol C 38 0
1998–99 Bristol C 41 0
1999–2000 Bristol C 22 0
2000–01 Bristol C 46 3
2001–02 Bristol C 35 0
2002–03 Bristol C 24 1
2003–04 Bristol C 41 1
2004–05 Coventry C 23 0 **23 0**
2004–05 Bristol C 14 0 **326 5**

COLES, Daniel (D) 148 5
H: 6 1 W: 13 05 b.Bristol 31-10-81
Source: Scholarship.
1999–2000 Bristol C 1 0
2000–01 Bristol C 2 0
2001–02 Bristol C 23 0
2002–03 Bristol C 39 2
2003–04 Bristol C 45 2
2004–05 Bristol C 38 1 **148 5**

COTTERILL, David (F) 12 0
H: 5 10 W: 10 11 b.Cardiff 4-12-87
Source: Scholar. *Honours:* Wales Youth, Under-21.
2004–05 Bristol C 12 0 **12 0**

DAVIES, Clint (G) 2 0
H: 6 3 W: 12 07 b.Perth 24-4-83
Source: Scholar. *Honours:* Australia Under-23.
2002–03 Birmingham C 0 0
2003–04 Bradford C 2 0 **2 0**
2004–05 Bristol C 0 0

DOHERTY, Tom (M) 188 7
H: 5 8 W: 11 12 b.Bristol 17-3-79
Source: Trainee. *Honours:* Northern Ireland 9 full caps.
1997–98 Bristol C 30 2
1998–99 Bristol C 23 1
1999–2000 Bristol C 1 0
2000–01 Bristol C 0 0
2001–02 Bristol C 34 1
2002–03 Bristol C 38 0
2003–04 Bristol C 33 2
2004–05 Bristol C 29 1 **188 7**

FORTUNE, Clayton (D) 47 0
H: 6 3 W: 14 04 b.Forest Gate 10-11-82
Source: Tottenham H Scholar.
2000–01 Bristol C 0 0
2001–02 Bristol C 1 0
2002–03 Bristol C 10 0
2003–04 Bristol C 6 0
2004–05 Bristol C 30 0 **47 0**

GILLESPIE, Steven (F) 20 5
H: 5 9 W: 11 05 b.Liverpool 4-6-84
Source: Liverpool Scholar.
2004–05 Bristol C 8 0 **8 0**
2004–05 *Cheltenham T* 12 5 **12 5**

GOLBOURNE, Scott (M) 9 0
H: 5 8 W: 11 08 b.Bristol 29-2-88
Source: Scholar. *Honours:* England Youth.
2004–05 Bristol C 9 0 **9 0**

GOODFELLOW, Marc (M) 90 14
H: 5 7 W: 11 00 b.Swadlincote 20-9-81
1998–99 Stoke C 0 0
1999–2000 Stoke C 0 0
2000–01 Stoke C 7 0
2001–02 Stoke C 23 5
2002–03 Stoke C 20 1
2003–04 Stoke C 4 0 **54 6**
2003–04 Bristol C 15 4
2004–05 Bristol C 5 0 **20 4**
2004–05 *Port Vale* 5 0 **5 0**
2004–05 *Swansea C* 6 3 **6 3**
2004–05 *Colchester U* 5 1 **5 1**

GOULD, Jonathan (G) 214 0
H: 6 1 W: 13 01 b.Paddington 18-7-68
Source: Clevedon T. *Honours:* Scotland B, 2 full caps..
1990–91 Halifax T 23 0
1991–92 Halifax T 9 0 **32 0**
1991–92 WBA 0 0
1992–93 Coventry C 9 0
1993–94 Coventry C 9 0
1994–95 Coventry C 7 0
1995–96 Coventry C 0 0 **25 0**
1995–96 *Bradford C* 9 0
1996–97 Bradford C 9 0 **18 0**
1996–97 *Gillingham* 3 0 **3 0**
1997–98 Celtic 35 0
1998–99 Celtic 28 0
1999–2000 Celtic 0 0
2000–01 Celtic 15 0
2001–02 Celtic 1 0
2002–03 Celtic 2 0 **81 0**
2002–03 Preston NE 14 0
2003–04 Preston NE 37 0
2004–05 Preston NE 4 0 **55 0**
2004–05 Bristol C 0 0

HARLEY, Ryan (M) 2 0
H: 5 9 W: 11 00 b.Bristol 22-1-85
Source: Scholar.
2004–05 Bristol C 2 0 **2 0**

HAWKINS, Darren (M) 0 0
H: 5 8 W: 11 09 b.Bristol 25-4-84
Source: Scholar.
2003–04 Bristol C 0 0
2004–05 Bristol C 0 0

HEFFERNAN, Paul (F) 127 41
H: 5 9 W: 11 00 b.Dublin 29-12-81
Source: Newton.
1999–2000 Notts Co 2 0
2000–01 Notts Co 1 0
2001–02 Notts Co 23 6
2002–03 Notts Co 36 10
2003–04 Notts Co 38 20 **100 36**
2004–05 Bristol C 27 5 **27 5**

LITA, Leroy (F) 85 31
H: 5 8 W: 11 12 b.DR Congo 28-12-84
Source: Scholar. *Honours:* England Under-21.
2002–03 Bristol C 15 2
2003–04 Bristol C 26 5
2004–05 Bristol C 44 24 **85 31**

LOXTON, Craig (M) 0 0
H: 5 9 W: 11 00 b.Bristol 14-9-84
Source: Scholar.
2001–02 Bristol C 0 0
2002–03 Bristol C 0 0
2003–04 Bristol C 0 0
2004–05 Bristol C 0 0

MILLER, Lee (F) 110 36
H: 6 0 W: 11 07 b.Lanark 18-5-83
Source: Form S.
2000–01 Falkirk 0 0
2001–02 Falkirk 27 11
2002–03 Falkirk 34 17 **61 28**
2003–04 Bristol C 42 8
2004–05 Bristol C 7 0 **49 8**

MURRAY, Scott (M) 310 59
H: 5 8 W: 11 02 b.Aberdeen 26-5-74
Source: Fraserburgh. *Honours:* Scotland B.
1993–94 Aston Villa 0 0
1994–95 Aston Villa 0 0
1995–96 Aston Villa 3 0
1996–97 Aston Villa 1 0
1997–98 Aston Villa 0 0 **4 0**
1997–98 Bristol C 23 0
1998–99 Bristol C 32 3
1999–2000 Bristol C 41 6
2000–01 Bristol C 46 10
2001–02 Bristol C 37 8
2002–03 Bristol C 45 19
2003–04 Reading 34 5 **34 5**
2003–04 Bristol C 6 0
2004–05 Bristol C 42 8 **272 54**

ORR, Bradley (M) 41 0
H: 6 0 W: 11 11 b.Liverpool 1-11-82
Source: Scholar.
2001–02 Newcastle U 0 0
2002–03 Newcastle U 0 0
2003–04 Newcastle U 0 0
2003–04 *Burnley* 4 0 **4 0**
2004–05 Bristol C 37 0 **37 0**

PHILLIPS, Steve (G) 238 0
H: 6 1 W: 13 06 b.Bath 6-5-78
Source: Paulton R.
1996–97 Bristol C 0 0
1997–98 Bristol C 0 0
1998–99 Bristol C 15 0
1999–2000 Bristol C 21 0
2000–01 Bristol C 42 0
2001–02 Bristol C 22 0
2002–03 Bristol C 46 0
2003–04 Bristol C 46 0
2004–05 Bristol C 46 0 **238 0**

SIMPSON, Sekani (M) 0 0
H: 5 9 W: 11 10 b.Bristol 11-3-84
Source: Scholar.
2003–04 Bristol C 0 0
2004–05 Bristol C 0 0

SKUSE, Cole (M) 7 0
H: 6 1 W: 11 05 b.Bristol 29-3-86
Source: Scholar.
2004–05 Bristol C 7 0 **7 0**

SMITH, Jamie (M) 284 7
H: 5 8 W: 11 02 b.Birmingham 17-9-74
Source: Trainee.
1993–94 Wolverhampton W 0 0
1994–95 Wolverhampton W 25 0
1995–96 Wolverhampton W 13 0
1996–97 Wolverhampton W 38 0
1997–98 Wolverhampton W 11 0 **87 0**
1997–98 Crystal Palace 18 0
1998–99 Crystal Palace 26 0
1998–99 *Fulham* 9 1 **9 1**
1999–2000 Crystal Palace 27 0
2000–01 Crystal Palace 29 0
2001–02 Crystal Palace 32 4
2002–03 Crystal Palace 2 0
2003–04 Crystal Palace 15 0 **149 4**
2004–05 Bristol C 39 2 **39 2**

STOWELL, Mike (G) 453 0
H: 6 2 W: 14 01 b.Preston 19-4-65
Source: Leyland Motors.
1984–85 Preston NE 0 0
1985–86 Preston NE 0 0
1985–86 Everton 0 0
1986–87 Everton 0 0
1987–88 *Chester C* 14 0 **14 0**
1987–88 *York C* 6 0 **6 0**
1987–88 *Manchester C* 14 0 **14 0**
1988–89 Everton 0 0
1988–89 *Port Vale* 7 0 **7 0**
1988–89 *Wolverhampton W* 7 0
1989–90 Everton 0 0
1989–90 *Preston NE* 2 0 **2 0**
1990–91 Wolverhampton W 39 0
1991–92 Wolverhampton W 46 0
1992–93 Wolverhampton W 26 0
1993–94 Wolverhampton W 46 0
1994–95 Wolverhampton W 37 0
1995–96 Wolverhampton W 38 0
1996–97 Wolverhampton W 46 0
1997–98 Wolverhampton W 35 0
1998–99 Wolverhampton W 46 0
1999–2000 Wolverhampton W 18 0
2000–01 Wolverhampton W 1 0 **385 0**
2001–02 Bristol C 25 0

2002–03 Bristol C 0 0
2003–04 Bristol C 0 0
2004–05 Bristol C 0 0 **25** **0**

TINNION, Brian (M) **635** **60**
H: 6 0 W: 13 05 b.Stanley 23-3-68
Source: Apprentice.
1985–86 Newcastle U 0 0
1986–87 Newcastle U 3 0
1987–88 Newcastle U 16 1
1988–89 Newcastle U 13 1 **32** **2**
1988–89 Bradford C 14 1
1989–90 Bradford C 37 5
1990–91 Bradford C 41 5
1991–92 Bradford C 26 8
1992–93 Bradford C 27 3 **145** **22**
1992–93 Bristol C 11 2
1993–94 Bristol C 41 5
1994–95 Bristol C 35 2
1995–96 Bristol C 30 3
1996–97 Bristol C 32 1
1997–98 Bristol C 44 3
1998–99 Bristol C 35 1
1999–2000 Bristol C 43 3
2000–01 Bristol C 42 1
2001–02 Bristol C 38 3
2002–03 Bristol C 40 9
2003–04 Bristol C 45 2
2004–05 Bristol C 22 1 **458** **36**

WILKSHIRE, Luke (M) **95** **11**
H: 5 9 W: 11 00 b.Wollongong 2-10-81
Honours: Australia Youth, Under-20, Under-23, 4 full caps.
1998–99 Middlesbrough 0 0
1999–2000 Middlesbrough 0 0
2000–01 Middlesbrough 0 0
2001–02 Middlesbrough 7 0
2002–03 Middlesbrough 14 0 **21** **0**
2003–04 Bristol C 37 2
2004–05 Bristol C 37 9 **74** **11**

WILSON, Cameron (M) **0** **0**
H: 5 10 W: 11 00 b.Delta, Canada 21-1-86
Honours: Canada Youth.
2004–05 Bristol C 0 0

WOODMAN, Craig (D) **72** **2**
H: 5 8 W: 11 00 b.Tiverton 22-12-82
Source: Trainee.
1999–2000 Bristol C 0 0
2000–01 Bristol C 2 0
2001–02 Bristol C 6 0
2002–03 Bristol C 10 0
2003–04 Bristol C 21 0
2004–05 Bristol C 3 0 **42** **0**
2004–05 *Mansfield T* 8 1 **8** **1**
2004–05 *Torquay U* 22 1 **22** **1**

WRING, Danny (M) **1** **0**
H: 5 10 W: 10 03 b.Portishead 26-10-86
Source: Scholar.
2004–05 Bristol C 1 0 **1** **0**

BRISTOL R (14)

AGOGO, Junior (F) **104** **32**
H: 5 10 W: 11 07 b.Accra 1-8-79
Source: Willesden.
1996–97 Sheffield W 0 0
1997–98 Sheffield W 1 0
1998–99 Sheffield W 1 0
1999–2000 Sheffield W 0 0 **2** **0**
1999–2000 *Oldham Ath* 2 0 **2** **0**
1999–2000 *Chester C* 10 6 **10** **6**
1999–2000 *Chesterfield* 4 0 **4** **0**
1999–2000 *Lincoln C* 3 1 **3** **1**
From Colorado R, San Jose E.
2001–02 QPR 2 0 **2** **0**
2002–03 Barnet 0 0
2003–04 Bristol R 38 6
2004–05 Bristol R 43 19 **81** **25**

ANDERSON, John (D) **331** **33**
H: 6 2 W: 12 02 b.Greenock 2-10-72
Source: Gourock YAC.
1993–94 Morton 19 2
1994–95 Morton 30 3
1995–96 Morton 30 4
1996–97 Morton 31 4
1997–98 Morton 33 4
1998–99 Morton 33 6
1999–2000 Morton 29 5 **205** **28**
2000–01 Livingston 30 3
2001–02 Livingston 11 0 **41** **3**
2002–03 Hull C 43 1
2003–04 Hull C 0 0 **43** **1**
2003–04 Bristol R 8 0
2004–05 Bristol R 34 1 **42** **1**

ARNDALE, Neil (D) **5** **0**
H: 5 7 W: 10 07 b.Bristol 26-4-84
Source: Scholar. *Honours:* England Youth.
2001–02 Bristol R 1 0
2002–03 Bristol R 1 0
2003–04 Bristol R 3 0
2004–05 Bristol R 0 0 **5** **0**

BASS, Jon (D) **105** **1**
H: 6 0 W: 12 02 b.Weston-Super-Mare 1-1-76
Source: Trainee. *Honours:* England Schools.
1994–95 Birmingham C 0 0
1995–96 Birmingham C 5 0
1996–97 Birmingham C 13 0
1996–97 *Carlisle U* 3 0 **3** **0**
1997–98 Birmingham C 30 0
1998–99 Birmingham C 11 0
1999–2000 Birmingham C 8 0
1999–2000 *Gillingham* 7 0 **7** **0**
2000–01 Birmingham C 1 0 **68** **0**
2001–02 Hartlepool U 20 1
2002–03 Hartlepool U 4 0
2003–04 Hartlepool U 0 0 **24** **1**
2004–05 Bristol R 3 0 **3** **0**

BRYANT, Simon (M) **87** **2**
H: 5 11 W: 13 04 b.Bristol 22-11-82
Source: Scholarship. *Honours:* England Youth.
1999–2000 Bristol R 15 0
2000–01 Bristol R 30 1
2001–02 Bristol R 8 0
2002–03 Bristol R 22 1
2003–04 Bristol R 12 0
2004–05 Bristol R 0 0 **87** **2**

CAMPBELL, Stuart (M) **219** **12**
H: 5 10 W: 10 00 b.Corby 9-12-77
Source: Trainee. *Honours:* Scotland Under-21.
1996–97 Leicester C 10 0
1997–98 Leicester C 11 0
1998–99 Leicester C 12 0
1999–2000 Leicester C 4 0
1999–2000 *Birmingham C* 2 0 **2** **0**
2000–01 Leicester C 0 0 **37** **0**
2000–01 *Grimsby T* 38 2
2001–02 Grimsby T 33 3
2002–03 Grimsby T 45 6
2003–04 Grimsby T 39 1 **155** **12**
2004–05 Bristol R 25 0 **25** **0**

CASH, Brian (M) **19** **0**
H: 5 9 W: 11 01 b.Dublin 24-11-82
Source: Trainee. *Honours:* Eire Under-21.
1999–2000 Nottingham F 0 0
2000–01 Nottingham F 0 0
2001–02 Nottingham F 5 0
2002–03 Nottingham F 1 0
2002–03 *Swansea C* 5 0 **5** **0**
2003–04 Nottingham F 1 0
2004–05 Nottingham F 0 0 **7** **0**
2004–05 *Rochdale* 6 0 **6** **0**
2004–05 Bristol R 1 0 **1** **0**

CLARKE, Ryan (G) **30** **0**
H: 6 3 W: 13 00 b.Bristol 30-4-82
Source: Scholar.
2001–02 Bristol R 1 0
2002–03 Bristol R 2 0
2003–04 Bristol R 2 0
2004–05 Bristol R 18 0 **23** **0**
2004–05 *Southend U* 1 0 **1** **0**
2004–05 *Kidderminster H* 6 0 **6** **0**

DISLEY, Craig (M) **169** **20**
H: 5 10 W: 10 13 b.Worksop 24-8-81
Source: Trainee.
1999–2000 Mansfield T 5 0
2000–01 Mansfield T 24 0
2001–02 Mansfield T 36 7
2002–03 Mansfield T 42 4
2003–04 Mansfield T 34 5 **141** **16**
2004–05 Bristol R 28 4 **28** **4**

EDWARDS, Christian (D) **288** **10**
H: 6 2 W: 12 08 b.Caerphilly 23-11-75
Source: Trainee. *Honours:* Wales Under-21, B, 1 full cap.
1994–95 Swansea C 9 0
1995–96 Swansea C 38 2
1996–97 Swansea C 36 0
1997–98 Swansea C 32 2 **115** **4**
1997–98 Nottingham F 0 0
1998–99 Nottingham F 12 0
1998–99 *Bristol C* 3 0 **3** **0**
1999–2000 Nottingham F 0 0
1999–2000 *Oxford U* 5 1
2000–01 Nottingham F 36 3
2001–02 Nottingham F 6 0
2001–02 *Crystal Palace* 9 0 **9** **0**
2002–03 Nottingham F 0 0 **54** **3**
2002–03 *Tranmere R* 12 0 **12** **0**
2002–03 *Oxford U* 6 0 **11** **1**
2003–04 Bristol R 42 0
2004–05 Bristol R 42 2 **84** **2**

ELLIOTT, Steve (D) **142** **3**
H: 6 1 W: 14 00 b.Derby 29-10-78
Source: Trainee.
1996–97 Derby Co 0 0
1997–98 Derby Co 3 0
1998–99 Derby Co 11 0
1999–2000 Derby Co 20 0
2000–01 Derby Co 6 0
2001–02 Derby Co 6 0
2002–03 Derby Co 23 1
2003–04 Derby Co 4 0 **73** **1**
2003–04 Blackpool 28 0 **28** **0**
2004–05 Bristol R 41 2 **41** **2**

FORRESTER, Jamie (F) **359** **103**
H: 5 7 W: 11 00 b.Bradford 1-11-74
Source: Auxerre. *Honours:* England Schools, Youth.
1992–93 Leeds U 6 0
1993–94 Leeds U 3 0
1994–95 Leeds U 0 0
1994–95 *Southend U* 5 0 **5** **0**
1994–95 *Grimsby T* 9 1
1995–96 Leeds U 0 0 **9** **0**
1995–96 Grimsby T 28 5
1996–97 Grimsby T 13 1 **50** **7**
1996–97 Scunthorpe U 10 6
1997–98 Scunthorpe U 45 11
1998–99 Scunthorpe U 46 20 **101** **37**
1999–2000 Utrecht 1 0 **1** **0**
1999–2000 Walsall 5 0 **5** **0**
1999–2000 *Northampton T* 10 6
2000–01 Northampton T 43 17
2001–02 Northampton T 43 17
2002–03 Northampton T 25 5 **121** **45**
2002–03 Hull C 11 3
2003–04 Hull C 21 4 **32** **7**
2004–05 Bristol R 35 7 **35** **7**

GIBB, Ali (M) **327** **6**
H: 5 9 W: 11 07 b.Salisbury 17-2-76
Source: Trainee.
1994–95 Norwich C 0 0
1995–96 Norwich C 0 0
1995–96 Northampton T 23 2
1996–97 Northampton T 18 1
1997–98 Northampton T 35 1
1998–99 Northampton T 41 0
1999–2000 Northampton T 14 0 **131** **4**
1999–2000 Stockport Co 14 0
2000–01 Stockport Co 39 0
2001–02 Stockport Co 41 0
2002–03 Stockport Co 45 1
2003–04 Stockport Co 26 0 **165** **1**
2003–04 Bristol R 8 1
2004–05 Bristol R 23 0 **31** **1**

GREAVES, Danny (G) **0** **0**
H: 6 2 W: 12 06 b.Bristol 7-12-83
2003–04 Bristol R 0 0
2004–05 Bristol R 0 0

HALDANE, Lewis (F) **40** **5**
H: 6 0 W: 11 03 b.Trowbridge 13-3-85
Source: Scholar.
2003–04 Bristol R 27 5
2004–05 Bristol R 13 0 **40** **5**

HINTON, Craig (D) **211 3**
H: 6 0 W: 12 00 b.Wolverhampton 26-11-77
Source: Trainee.

1996–97	Birmingham C	0	0		
1997–98	Birmingham C	0	0		
2000–01	Kidderminster H	46	2		
2001–02	Kidderminster H	41	0		
2002–03	Kidderminster H	44	0		
2003–04	Kidderminster H	42	1	**173**	**3**
2004–05	Bristol R	38	0	**38**	**0**

HOBBS, Shane (M) **2 0**
H: 5 7 W: 10 07 b.Bristol 30-4-85
Source: Scholar.

2003–04	Bristol R	2	0		
2004–05	Bristol R	0	0	**2**	**0**

HODGES, Lee (M) **187 23**
H: 5 5 W: 10 02 b.Plaistow 2-3-78
Source: Trainee. *Honours:* England Schools.

1994–95	West Ham U	0	0		
1995–96	West Ham U	0	0		
1996–97	West Ham U	0	0		
1996–97	*Exeter C*	17	0	**17**	**0**
1996–97	*Leyton Orient*	3	0	**3**	**0**
1997–98	West Ham U	2	0		
1997–98	*Plymouth Arg*	9	0	**9**	**0**
1998–99	West Ham U	1	0	**3**	**0**
1998–99	*Ipswich T*	4	0	**4**	**0**
1998–99	*Southend U*	10	1	**10**	**1**
1999–2000	Scunthorpe U	40	6		
2000–01	Scunthorpe U	38	8		
2001–02	Scunthorpe U	35	6	**113**	**20**
2002–03	Rochdale	7	0	**7**	**0**
2002–03	*Bristol R*	8	0		
2003–04	Bristol R	13	2		
2004–05	Bristol R	0	0	**21**	**2**

HUNT, James (M) **312 16**
H: 5 8 W: 10 03 b.Derby 17-12-76
Source: Trainee.

1994–95	Notts Co	0	0		
1995–96	Notts Co	10	1		
1996–97	Notts Co	9	0	**19**	**1**
1997–98	Northampton T	21	0		
1998–99	Northampton T	35	2		
1999–2000	Northampton T	37	1		
2000–01	Northampton T	41	1		
2001–02	Northampton T	38	4	**172**	**8**
2002–03	Oxford U	39	1		
2003–04	Oxford U	41	2	**80**	**3**
2004–05	Bristol R	41	4	**41**	**4**

JEANNIN, Alex (D) **23 0**
H: 6 0 W: 11 06 b.Troyes 30-12-77
Source: Troyes.

2000–01	Darlington	11	0		
2001–02	Darlington	11	0	**22**	**0**
From Exeter C.					
2004–05	Bristol R	1	0	**1**	**0**

LESCOTT, Aaron (M) **148 1**
H: 5 8 W: 10 09 b.Birmingham 2-12-78
Source: Trainee. *Honours:* England Schools.

1996–97	Aston Villa	0	0		
1997–98	Aston Villa	0	0		
1998–99	Aston Villa	0	0		
1999–2000	Aston Villa	0	0		
1999–2000	*Lincoln C*	5	0	**5**	**0**
2000–01	Aston Villa	0	0		
2000–01	Sheffield W	30	0		
2001–02	Sheffield W	7	0	**37**	**0**
2001–02	Stockport Co	17	0		
2002–03	Stockport Co	41	1		
2003–04	Stockport Co	14	0	**72**	**1**
2003–04	*Bristol R*	8	0		
2004–05	Bristol R	26	0	**34**	**0**

LOUIS, Jefferson (F) **57 8**
H: 6 2 W: 15 00 b.Harrow 22-2-79
Source: Thame U, from Forest Green R, Woking.

2001–02	Oxford U	1	0		
2002–03	Oxford U	34	6		
2003–04	Oxford U	20	2		
2004–05	Oxford U	1	0	**56**	**8**
From For GR, Woking					
2004–05	Bristol R	1	0	**1**	**0**

MILLER, Kevin (G) **614 0**
H: 6 1 W: 13 00 b.Falmouth 15-3-69
Source: Newquay.

1988–89	Exeter C	3	0		
1989–90	Exeter C	28	0		
1990–91	Exeter C	46	0		
1991–92	Exeter C	42	0		
1992–93	Exeter C	44	0		
1993–94	Birmingham C	24	0	**24**	**0**
1994–95	Watford	44	0		
1995–96	Watford	42	0		
1996–97	Watford	42	0	**128**	**0**
1997–98	Crystal Palace	38	0		
1998–99	Crystal Palace	28	0		
1999–2000	Crystal Palace	0	0	**66**	**0**
1999–2000	Barnsley	41	0		
2000–01	Barnsley	46	0		
2001–02	Barnsley	28	0	**115**	**0**
2002–03	Exeter C	46	0	**209**	**0**
2003–04	Bristol R	44	0		
2004–05	*Derby Co*	0	0		
2004–05	Bristol R	28	0	**72**	**0**

PARKER, Sonny (D) **30 1**
H: 5 11 W: 11 11 b.Middlesbrough 28-2-83
Source: Trainee. *Honours:* England Youth.

1999–2000	Birmingham C	0	0		
2000–01	Birmingham C	0	0		
2001–02	Birmingham C	0	0		
2002–03	Birmingham C	0	0		
2002–03	Bristol R	15	0		
2003–04	Bristol R	15	1		
2004–05	Bristol R	0	0	**30**	**1**

RYAN, Robbie (D) **281 2**
H: 5 10 W: 12 05 b.Dublin 16-5-77
Source: Belvedere. *Honours:* Eire Youth, Under-21.

1994–95	Huddersfield T	0	0		
1995–96	Huddersfield T	0	0		
1996–97	Huddersfield T	5	0		
1997–98	Huddersfield T	10	0	**15**	**0**
1997–98	Millwall	16	0		
1998–99	Millwall	26	0		
1999–2000	Millwall	34	0		
2000–01	Millwall	42	0		
2001–02	Millwall	37	0		
2002–03	Millwall	41	2		
2003–04	Millwall	30	0	**226**	**2**
2004–05	Bristol R	40	0	**40**	**0**

SAVAGE, David (M) **395 32**
H: 6 2 W: 12 07 b.Dublin 30-7-73
Source: Longford T. *Honours:* Eire Under-21, 5 full caps.

1994–95	Millwall	37	2		
1995–96	Millwall	27	0		
1996–97	Millwall	35	3		
1997–98	Millwall	31	1		
1998–99	Millwall	2	0	**132**	**6**
1998–99	Northampton T	27	5		
1999–2000	Northampton T	43	5		
2000–01	Northampton T	43	8	**113**	**18**
2001–02	Oxford U	42	1		
2002–03	Oxford U	43	4	**85**	**5**
2003–04	Bristol R	38	2		
2004–05	Bristol R	27	1	**65**	**3**

SINCLAIR, Scott (F) **2 0**
H: 5 10 W: 10 00 b.Bath 26-3-89

2004–05	Bristol R	2	0	**2**	**0**

SOARES, Louie (D) **1 0**
H: 5 11 W: 11 05 b.Reading 8-1-85
Source: Scholar.

2004–05	Reading	0	0		
2004–05	Bristol R	1	0	**1**	**0**

TROLLOPE, Paul (M) **383 37**
H: 6 0 W: 12 06 b.Swindon 3-6-72
Source: Trainee. *Honours:* Wales B, 9 full caps.

1989–90	Swindon T	0	0		
1990–91	Swindon T	0	0		
1991–92	Swindon T	0	0		
1991–92	*Torquay U*	10	0		
1992–93	Torquay U	36	2		
1993–94	Torquay U	42	10		
1994–95	Torquay U	18	4	**106**	**16**
1994–95	Derby Co	24	4		
1995–96	Derby Co	17	0		
1996–97	Derby Co	14	1		
1996–97	*Grimsby T*	7	1	**7**	**1**
1996–97	*Crystal Palace*	9	0	**9**	**0**
1997–98	Derby Co	10	0	**65**	**5**
1997–98	Fulham	24	3		
1998–99	Fulham	20	2		
1999–2000	Fulham	22	0		
2000–01	Fulham	10	0		
2001–02	Fulham	0	0	**76**	**5**
2001–02	Coventry C	6	0	**6**	**0**
2002–03	Northampton T	41	2		
2003–04	Northampton T	43	6	**84**	**8**
2004–05	Bristol R	30	2	**30**	**2**

WALKER, Richard (F) **162 37**
H: 6 0 W: 12 04 b.Sutton Coldfield 8-11-77
Source: Trainee.

1995–96	Aston Villa	0	0		
1996–97	Aston Villa	0	0		
1997–98	Aston Villa	1	0		
1998–99	Aston Villa	0	0		
1998–99	*Cambridge U*	21	3	**21**	**3**
1999–2000	Aston Villa	5	2		
2000–01	Aston Villa	0	0		
2000–01	*Blackpool*	18	3		
2001–02	Aston Villa	0	0	**6**	**2**
2001–02	*Wycombe W*	12	3	**12**	**3**
2001–02	Blackpool	21	8		
2002–03	Blackpool	32	4		
2003–04	Blackpool	9	0	**80**	**15**
2003–04	*Northampton T*	12	4	**12**	**4**
2003–04	Oxford U	4	0	**4**	**0**
2004–05	Bristol R	27	10	**27**	**10**

WILLIAMS, Ryan (M) **194 22**
H: 5 5 W: 11 04 b.Sutton-in-Ashfield 31-8-78
Source: Trainee. *Honours:* England Youth.

1995–96	Mansfield T	10	3		
1996–97	Mansfield T	16	0	**26**	**3**
1997–98	Tranmere R	0	0		
1998–99	Tranmere R	5	0		
1999–2000	Tranmere R	0	0	**5**	**0**
1999–2000	Chesterfield	30	5		
2000–01	Chesterfield	45	8	**75**	**13**
2001–02	Hull C	29	2		
2002–03	Hull C	23	0		
2003–04	Hull C	0	0	**52**	**2**
2003–04	Bristol R	19	1		
2004–05	Bristol R	17	3	**36**	**4**

BURNLEY (15)

AKINBIYI, Ade (F) **362 111**
H: 6 1 W: 13 08 b.Hackney 10-10-74
Source: Trainee. *Honours:* Nigeria full caps.

1992–93	Norwich C	0	0		
1993–94	Norwich C	2	0		
1993–94	*Hereford U*	4	2	**4**	**2**
1994–95	Norwich C	13	0		
1994–95	*Brighton & HA*	7	4	**7**	**4**
1995–96	Norwich C	22	3		
1996–97	Norwich C	12	0	**49**	**3**
1996–97	Gillingham	19	7		
1997–98	Gillingham	44	21	**63**	**28**
1998–99	Bristol C	44	19		
1999–2000	Bristol C	3	2	**47**	**21**
1999–2000	Wolverhampton W	37	16	**37**	**16**
2000–01	Leicester C	37	9		
2001–02	Leicester C	21	2	**58**	**11**
2001–02	Crystal Palace	14	2		
2002–03	Crystal Palace	10	1		
2002–03	*Stoke C*	4	2		
2003–04	Crystal Palace	0	0	**24**	**3**
2003–04	Stoke C	30	10		
2004–05	Stoke C	29	7	**63**	**19**
2004–05	Burnley	10	4	**10**	**4**

BRANCH, Graham (M) **345 29**
H: 6 3 W: 13 11 b.Liverpool 12-2-72
Source: Heswall.

1991–92	Tranmere R	4	0		
1992–93	Tranmere R	3	0		
1992–93	*Bury*	4	1	**4**	**1**
1993–94	Tranmere R	13	0		
1994–95	Tranmere R	1	0		
1995–96	Tranmere R	21	2		
1996–97	Tranmere R	35	5		

1997–98	Tranmere R	25	3	**102**	**10**
1997–98	*Wigan Ath*	3	0	**3**	**0**
1998–99	Stockport Co	14	3	**14**	**3**
1998–99	Burnley	20	1		
1999–2000	Burnley	44	3		
2000–01	Burnley	35	5		
2001–02	Burnley	10	0		
2002–03	Burnley	32	0		
2003–04	Burnley	38	3		
2004–05	Burnley	43	3	**222**	**15**

CAMARA, Mo (D) **252** **2**
H: 5 11 W: 11 03 b.Conakry 25-6-75

1993–94	Beauvais	19	0		
1994–95	Beauvais	0	0		
1995–96	Troyes	13	0	**13**	**0**
1996–97	Beauvais	35	0	**54**	**0**
1997–98	Le Havre	14	0		
1998–99	Lille	34	2	**34**	**2**
1999–2000	Le Havre	2	0	**16**	**0**
2000–01	Wolverhampton W	18	0		
2001–02	Wolverhampton W	27	0		
2002–03	Wolverhampton W	0	0	**45**	**0**
2003–04	Burnley	45	0		
2004–05	Burnley	45	0	**90**	**0**

COYNE, Danny (G) **316** **0**
H: 6 0 W: 12 11 b.Prestatyn 27-8-73
Source: Trainee. *Honours:* Wales Schools, Youth, Under-21, B, 8 full caps.

1991–92	Tranmere R	0	0		
1992–93	Tranmere R	1	0		
1993–94	Tranmere R	5	0		
1994–95	Tranmere R	5	0		
1995–96	Tranmere R	46	0		
1996–97	Tranmere R	21	0		
1997–98	Tranmere R	16	0		
1998–99	Tranmere R	17	0	**111**	**0**
1999–2000	Grimsby T	44	0		
2000–01	Grimsby T	46	0		
2001–02	Grimsby T	45	0		
2002–03	Grimsby T	46	0	**181**	**0**
2003–04	Leicester C	4	0	**4**	**0**
2004–05	Burnley	20	0	**20**	**0**

DUFF, Michael (D) **243** **12**
H: 6 3 W: 12 10 b.Belfast 11-1-78
Source: Trainee. *Honours:* Northern Ireland 4 full caps.

1999–2000	Cheltenham T	31	2		
2000–01	Cheltenham T	39	5		
2001–02	Cheltenham T	45	3		
2002–03	Cheltenham T	44	2		
2003–04	Cheltenham T	42	0	**201**	**12**
2004–05	Burnley	42	0	**42**	**0**

GRANT, Tony (M) **240** **6**
H: 5 9 W: 11 00 b.Liverpool 14-11-74
Source: Trainee. *Honours:* England Under-21.

1993–94	Everton	0	0		
1994–95	Everton	5	0		
1995–96	Everton	13	1		
1995–96	*Swindon T*	3	1	**3**	**1**
1996–97	Everton	18	0		
1997–98	Everton	7	1		
1998–99	Everton	16	0		
1999–2000	Everton	2	0	**61**	**2**
1999–2000	*Tranmere R*	9	0	**9**	**0**
1999–2000	Manchester C	8	0		
2000–01	Manchester C	10	0		
2000–01	*WBA*	5	0	**5**	**0**
2001–02	Manchester C	3	0	**21**	**0**
2001–02	Burnley	28	0		
2002–03	Burnley	34	1		
2003–04	Burnley	37	0		
2004–05	Burnley	42	2	**141**	**3**

HYDE, Micah (M) **398** **38**
H: 5 11 W: 12 03 b.Newham 10-11-74
Source: Trainee. *Honours:* Jamaica 16 full caps.

1993–94	Cambridge U	18	2		
1994–95	Cambridge U	27	0		
1995–96	Cambridge U	24	4		
1996–97	Cambridge U	38	7	**107**	**13**
1997–98	Watford	40	4		
1998–99	Watford	44	2		
1999–2000	Watford	34	3		
2000–01	Watford	26	6		
2001–02	Watford	39	4		
2002–03	Watford	37	4		
2003–04	Watford	33	1	**253**	**24**
2004–05	Burnley	38	1	**38**	**1**

JENSEN, Brian (G) **120** **0**
H: 6 4 W: 16 09 b.Copenhagen 8-6-75

1997–98	AZ	0	0		
1998–99	AZ	1	0	**1**	**0**
1999–2000	WBA	12	0		
2000–01	WBA	33	0		
2001–02	WBA	1	0		
2002–03	WBA	0	0	**46**	**0**
2003–04	Burnley	46	0		
2004–05	Burnley	27	0	**73**	**0**

JOHNROSE, Lenny (M) **430** **49**
H: 5 10 W: 12 06 b.Preston 29-11-69
Source: Trainee.

1987–88	Blackburn R	1	0		
1988–89	Blackburn R	0	0		
1989–90	Blackburn R	8	3		
1990–91	Blackburn R	26	7		
1991–92	Blackburn R	7	1	**42**	**11**
1991–92	*Preston NE*	3	1	**3**	**1**
1991–92	Hartlepool U	15	2		
1992–93	Hartlepool U	38	6		
1993–94	Hartlepool U	13	3	**66**	**11**
1993–94	Bury	14	0		
1994–95	Bury	26	4		
1995–96	Bury	34	6		
1996–97	Bury	43	4		
1997–98	Bury	44	3		
1998–99	Bury	27	2		
1998–99	Burnley	12	1		
1999–2000	Burnley	35	2		
2000–01	Burnley	19	1		
2001–02	Burnley	6	0		
2002–03	Burnley	6	0		
2002–03	Bury	6	0	**194**	**19**
2002–03	Swansea C	15	3		
2003–04	Swansea C	25	0	**40**	**3**
2003–04	Burnley	7	0		
2004–05	Burnley	0	0	**85**	**4**

McGREAL, John (D) **357** **6**
H: 6 0 W: 12 06 b.Birkenhead 2-6-72
Source: Trainee.

1990–91	Tranmere R	3	0		
1991–92	Tranmere R	0	0		
1992–93	Tranmere R	0	0		
1993–94	Tranmere R	15	1		
1994–95	Tranmere R	43	0		
1995–96	Tranmere R	32	0		
1996–97	Tranmere R	24	0		
1997–98	Tranmere R	42	0		
1998–99	Tranmere R	36	0	**195**	**1**
1999–2000	Ipswich T	34	0		
2000–01	Ipswich T	28	1		
2001–02	Ipswich T	27	1		
2002–03	Ipswich T	16	1		
2003–04	Ipswich T	18	1	**123**	**4**
2004–05	Burnley	39	1	**39**	**1**

O'CONNOR, James (M) **227** **18**
H: 5 8 W: 11 06 b.Dublin 1-9-79
Source: Trainee. *Honours:* Eire Under-21.

1996–97	Stoke C	0	0		
1997–98	Stoke C	0	0		
1998–99	Stoke C	4	0		
1999–2000	Stoke C	42	6		
2000–01	Stoke C	44	8		
2001–02	Stoke C	43	2		
2002–03	Stoke C	43	0	**176**	**16**
2003–04	WBA	30	0		
2004–05	WBA	0	0	**30**	**0**
2004–05	Burnley	21	2	**21**	**2**

O'NEILL, Matt (F) **13** **0**
H: 5 10 W: 10 11 b.Accrington 25-6-84
Source: Scholar.

2002–03	Burnley	7	0		
2003–04	Burnley	4	0		
2004–05	Burnley	2	0	**13**	**0**

OSTER, John (M) **174** **17**
H: 5 9 W: 11 05 b.Boston 8-12-78
Source: Trainee. *Honours:* Wales Youth, Under-21, B, 13 full caps.

1996–97	Grimsby T	24	3		
1997–98	Everton	31	1		
1998–99	Everton	9	0	**40**	**1**
1999–2000	Sunderland	10	0		
2000–01	Sunderland	8	0		
2001–02	Sunderland	0	0		
2001–02	*Barnsley*	2	0	**2**	**0**
2002–03	Sunderland	3	0		
2002–03	*Grimsby T*	17	6	**41**	**9**
2003–04	Sunderland	38	5		
2004–05	Sunderland	9	0	**68**	**5**
2004–05	*Leeds U*	8	1	**8**	**1**
2004–05	Burnley	15	1	**15**	**1**

PILKINGTON, Joel (M) **2** **0**
H: 5 7 W: 11 00 b.Accrington 1-8-84
Source: Scholar.

2003–04	Burnley	1	0		
2004–05	Burnley	1	0	**2**	**0**

ROCHE, Lee (D) **96** **2**
H: 5 11 W: 12 00 b.Bolton 28-10-80
Source: Trainee. *Honours:* England Youth, Under-21.

1998–99	Manchester U	0	0		
1999–2000	Manchester U	0	0		
2000–01	Manchester U	0	0		
2000–01	*Wrexham*	41	0	**41**	**0**
2001–02	Manchester U	0	0		
2002–03	Manchester U	1	0	**1**	**0**
2003–04	Burnley	25	1		
2004–05	Burnley	29	1	**54**	**2**

SCOTT, Paul (D) **2** **0**
H: 5 11 W: 12 05 b.Burnley 29-1-85
Source: Scholar.

2003–04	Burnley	2	0		
2004–05	Burnley	0	0	**2**	**0**

SINCLAIR, Frank (D) **375** **12**
H: 5 9 W: 12 03 b.Lambeth 3-12-71
Source: Trainee. *Honours:* Jamaica 24 full caps, 1 goal.

1989–90	Chelsea	0	0		
1990–91	Chelsea	4	0		
1991–92	Chelsea	8	1		
1991–92	*WBA*	6	1	**6**	**1**
1992–93	Chelsea	32	0		
1993–94	Chelsea	35	0		
1994–95	Chelsea	35	3		
1995–96	Chelsea	13	1		
1996–97	Chelsea	20	1		
1997–98	Chelsea	22	1	**169**	**7**
1998–99	Leicester C	31	1		
1999–2000	Leicester C	34	0		
2000–01	Leicester C	17	0		
2001–02	Leicester C	35	0		
2002–03	Leicester C	33	1		
2003–04	Leicester C	14	1	**164**	**3**
2004–05	Burnley	36	1	**36**	**1**

TOWNSEND, Ryan (M) **1** **0**
H: 6 0 W: 12 05 b.Tameside 2-9-85
Source: Scholar. *Honours:* Australia Under-20.

2003–04	Burnley	1	0		
2004–05	Burnley	0	0	**1**	**0**

VALOIS, Jean-Louis (F) **217** **32**
H: 5 11 W: 12 03 b.Saint-Priest 15-10-73

1996–97	Auxerre	2	0	**2**	**0**
1997–98	Gueugnon	40	11	**40**	**11**
1998–99	Lille	29	5		
1999–2000	Lille	24	4		
2000–01	Lille	9	1	**62**	**10**
2001–02	Luton T	34	6	**34**	**6**
2002–03	Hearts	38	2		
2003–04	Hearts	11	0	**49**	**2**
2004–05	Burnley	30	3	**30**	**3**

BURY (16)

BARRASS, Matt (D) **84** **2**
H: 5 10 W: 12 05 b.Bury 28-2-80
Source: Trainee.

1999–2000	Bury	25	1		
2000–01	Bury	5	0		
2001–02	Bury	7	0		
2002–03	Bury	16	0		
2003–04	Bury	22	1		
2004–05	Bury	9	0	**84**	**2**

BARRY-MURPHY, Brian (M) 219 9
H: 6 1 W: 13 01 b.Cork 27-7-78
Honours: Eire Under-21.

1995–96	Cork City	13	0		
1996–97	Cork City	25	0		
1997–98	Cork City	15	1		
1998–99	Cork City	27	1	**80**	**2**
1999–2000	Preston NE	1	0		
2000–01	Preston NE	14	0		
2001–02	Preston NE	4	0		
2001–02	*Southend U*	8	1	**8**	**1**
2002–03	Preston NE	2	0	**21**	**0**
2002–03	*Hartlepool U*	7	0	**7**	**0**
2002–03	Sheffield W	17	0		
2003–04	Sheffield W	41	0	**58**	**0**
2004–05	Bury	45	6	**45**	**6**

BUCHANAN, David (M) 3 0
H: 5 8 W: 10 08 b.Rochdale 6-5-86
Source: Scholar. *Honours:* Northern Ireland Youth.

2004–05	Bury	3	0	**3**	**0**

CARTLEDGE, Jon (D) 16 1
H: 6 2 W: 13 00 b.Carshalton 27-11-84
Source: Scholar.

2003–04	Bury	11	1		
2004–05	Bury	5	0	**16**	**1**

CHALLINOR, Dave (D) 279 8
H: 6 1 W: 12 06 b.Chester 2-10-75
Source: Bromborough Pool. *Honours:* England Schools.

1994–95	Tranmere R	0	0		
1995–96	Tranmere R	0	0		
1996–97	Tranmere R	5	0		
1997–98	Tranmere R	32	1		
1998–99	Tranmere R	34	2		
1999–2000	Tranmere R	41	3		
2000–01	Tranmere R	22	0		
2001–02	Tranmere R	6	0	**140**	**6**
2001–02	Stockport Co	18	0		
2002–03	Stockport Co	46	1		
2003–04	Stockport Co	17	0	**81**	**1**
2003–04	*Bury*	15	0		
2004–05	Bury	43	1	**58**	**1**

DOUGLAS-PRINGLE, Daniel (F) 0 0
H: 5 10 W: 11 07 b.Manchester 8-12-84
Source: Scholar.

2004–05	Bury	0	0		

DUNFIELD, Terry (M) 75 5
H: 5 11 W: 12 04 b.Vancouver 20-2-82
Source: From Trainee. *Honours:* Canada Under-23, England Youth.

1998–99	Manchester C	0	0		
1999–2000	Manchester C	0	0		
2000–01	Manchester C	1	0		
2001–02	Manchester C	0	0		
2002–03	Manchester C	0	0	**1**	**0**
2002–03	Bury	29	2		
2003–04	Bury	30	2		
2004–05	Bury	15	1	**74**	**5**

DUXBURY, Lee (M) 596 66
H: 5 10 W: 10 09 b.Keighley 7-10-69
Source: Trainee.

1988–89	Bradford C	1	0		
1989–90	Bradford C	12	1		
1989–90	*Rochdale*	10	0	**10**	**0**
1990–91	Bradford C	45	5		
1991–92	Bradford C	46	5		
1992–93	Bradford C	42	5		
1993–94	Bradford C	43	9		
1994–95	Bradford C	20	0		
1994–95	Huddersfield T	26	2		
1995–96	Huddersfield T	3	0	**29**	**2**
1995–96	Bradford C	30	4		
1996–97	Bradford C	33	3	**272**	**32**
1996–97	Oldham Ath	12	1		
1997–98	Oldham Ath	38	5		
1998–99	Oldham Ath	41	6		
1999–2000	Oldham Ath	43	4		
2000–01	Oldham Ath	40	8		
2001–02	Oldham Ath	40	4		
2002–03	Oldham Ath	34	4	**248**	**32**
2003–04	Bury	37	0		
2004–05	Bury	0	0	**37**	**0**

FLITCROFT, David (M) 405 27
H: 5 11 W: 14 05 b.Bolton 14-1-74
Source: Trainee.

1991–92	Preston NE	0	0		
1992–93	Preston NE	8	2		
1993–94	Preston NE	0	0	**8**	**2**
1993–94	*Lincoln C*	2	0	**2**	**0**
1993–94	Chester C	8	1		
1994–95	Chester C	32	0		
1995–96	Chester C	9	1		
1996–97	Chester C	32	6		
1997–98	Chester C	44	4		
1998–99	Chester C	42	6	**167**	**18**
1999–2000	Rochdale	43	2		
2000–01	Rochdale	41	0		
2001–02	Rochdale	35	0		
2002–03	Rochdale	41	2	**160**	**4**
2003–04	Macclesfield T	15	0	**15**	**0**
2003–04	Bury	17	0		
2004–05	Bury	36	3	**53**	**3**

GARNER, Glyn (G) 126 0
H: 6 2 W: 13 04 b.Pontypool 9-12-76
Source: Llanelli.

2000–01	Bury	0	0		
2001–02	Bury	7	0		
2002–03	Bury	46	0		
2003–04	Bury	46	0		
2004–05	Bury	27	0	**126**	**0**

JONES, Graeme (F) 289 87
H: 6 1 W: 13 06 b.Gateshead 13-3-70
Source: Bridlington T.

1993–94	Doncaster R	28	4		
1994–95	Doncaster R	32	12		
1995–96	Doncaster R	32	10	**92**	**26**
1996–97	Wigan Ath	40	31		
1997–98	Wigan Ath	33	9		
1998–99	Wigan Ath	20	3		
1999–2000	Wigan Ath	3	1	**96**	**44**
1999–2000	St Johnstone	19	3		
2000–01	St Johnstone	9	3		
2001–02	St Johnstone	13	1	**41**	**7**
2002–03	Southend U	21	2	**21**	**2**
2002–03	Boston U	3	1		
2003–04	Boston U	33	6	**36**	**7**
2004–05	Bury	3	1	**3**	**1**

KAZIM-RICHARDS, Colin (F) 30 3
H: 6 1 W: 10 10 b.Leyton 26-8-86
Source: Scholar.

2004–05	Bury	30	3	**30**	**3**

KENNEDY, Tom (D) 73 1
H: 5 10 W: 11 01 b.Bury 24-6-85
Source: Scholar.

2002–03	Bury	0	0		
2003–04	Bury	27	0		
2004–05	Bury	46	1	**73**	**1**

MADEN, Steven (M) 0 0
H: 5 11 W: 11 09 b.Bury 12-12-84
Source: Scholar.

2004–05	Bury	0	0		

MATTIS, Dwayne (M) 108 7
H: 6 1 W: 11 12 b.Huddersfield 31-7-81
Source: From Trainee. *Honours:* Eire Under-21.

1998–99	Huddersfield T	2	0		
1999–2000	Huddersfield T	0	0		
2000–01	Huddersfield T	0	0		
2001–02	Huddersfield T	29	1		
2002–03	Huddersfield T	33	1		
2003–04	Huddersfield T	5	0	**69**	**2**
2004–05	Bury	39	5	**39**	**5**

NEWBY, Jon (F) 186 25
H: 5 11 W: 11 00 b.Warrington 28-11-78
Source: Trainee.

1998–99	Liverpool	0	0		
1999–2000	Liverpool	1	0		
1999–2000	*Crewe Alex*	6	0	**6**	**0**
2000–01	Liverpool	0	0	**1**	**0**
2000–01	*Sheffield U*	13	0	**13**	**0**
2000–01	Bury	17	5		
2001–02	Bury	46	6		
2002–03	Bury	46	10		
2003–04	Huddersfield T	14	0	**14**	**0**
2003–04	*York C*	7	0	**7**	**0**
2004–05	Bury	36	4	**145**	**25**

PORTER, Chris (F) 71 18
H: 6 1 W: 12 08 b.Wigan 12-12-83
Source: School.

2002–03	Bury	2	0		
2003–04	Bury	37	9		
2004–05	Bury	32	9	**71**	**18**

RICKERS, Paul (M) 272 20
H: 5 11 W: 12 04 b.Pontefract 9-5-75
Source: Trainee.

1993–94	Oldham Ath	0	0		
1994–95	Oldham Ath	4	1		
1995–96	Oldham Ath	23	0		
1996–97	Oldham Ath	46	4		
1997–98	Oldham Ath	40	4		
1998–99	Oldham Ath	45	4		
1999–2000	Oldham Ath	41	3		
2000–01	Oldham Ath	38	2		
2001–02	Oldham Ath	24	2	**261**	**20**
2002–03	Northampton T	11	0		
2003–04	Northampton T	0	0	**11**	**0**
2003–04	Bury	0	0		
2004–05	Bury	0	0		

SCOTT, Paul (D) 55 2
H: 5 11 W: 12 00 b.Wakefield 5-11-79
Source: Trainee.

1998–99	Huddersfield T	0	0		
1999–2000	Huddersfield T	0	0		
2000–01	Huddersfield T	0	0		
2001–02	Huddersfield T	0	0		
2002–03	Huddersfield T	13	0		
2003–04	Huddersfield T	19	2		
2004–05	Huddersfield T	0	0	**32**	**2**
2004–05	Bury	23	0	**23**	**0**

UNSWORTH, Lee (D) 274 6
H: 5 11 W: 11 09 b.Eccles 25-2-73
Source: Ashton U.

1994–95	Crewe Alex	0	0		
1995–96	Crewe Alex	29	0		
1996–97	Crewe Alex	29	0		
1997–98	Crewe Alex	36	0		
1998–99	Crewe Alex	24	0		
1999–2000	Crewe Alex	8	0	**126**	**0**
2000–01	Bury	15	0		
2001–02	Bury	35	1		
2002–03	Bury	35	2		
2003–04	Bury	27	2		
2004–05	Bury	36	1	**148**	**6**

WHALEY, Simon (F) 50 4
H: 5 10 W: 11 11 b.Bolton 7-6-85
Source: Scholar.

2002–03	Bury	2	0		
2003–04	Bury	10	1		
2004–05	Bury	38	3	**50**	**4**

WOODTHORPE, Colin (D) 500 12
H: 6 0 W: 11 08 b.Ellesmere Pt 13-1-69
Source: Apprentice.

1986–87	Chester C	30	2		
1987–88	Chester C	35	0		
1988–89	Chester C	44	3		
1989–90	Chester C	46	1	**155**	**6**
1990–91	Norwich C	1	0		
1991–92	Norwich C	15	1		
1992–93	Norwich C	7	0		
1993–94	Norwich C	20	0	**43**	**1**
1994–95	Aberdeen	14	0		
1995–96	Aberdeen	15	1		
1996–97	Aberdeen	19	0	**48**	**1**
1997–98	Stockport Co	32	1		
1998–99	Stockport Co	37	2		
1999–2000	Stockport Co	26	0		
2000–01	Stockport Co	24	1		
2001–02	Stockport Co	34	0		
2002–03	Stockport Co	0	0	**153**	**4**
2002–03	Bury	32	0		
2003–04	Bury	39	0		
2004–05	Bury	30	0	**101**	**0**

CAMBRIDGE U (17)

ANGUS, Stevland (D) 155 1
H: 6 0 W: 12 00 b.Westminster 16-9-80
Source: Trainee.

1999–2000	West Ham U	0	0		
2000–01	West Ham U	0	0		

2000–01 *Bournemouth* 9 0 **9 0**
2001–02 Cambridge U 41 0
2002–03 Cambridge U 40 0
2003–04 Cambridge U 40 1
2004–05 Cambridge U 14 0 **135 1**
2004–05 *Hull C* 2 0 **2 0**
2004–05 *Scunthorpe U* 9 0 **9 0**

ANSELIN, Cedric (M) 51 2
H: 5 7 W: 11 02 b.Lens 24-7-77
1995–96 Bordeaux 3 0
1996–97 Bordeaux 5 0
1997–98 Lille 14 1 **14 1**
1998–99 Bordeaux 1 0 **9 0**
1998–99 Norwich C 7 1
1999–2000 Norwich C 19 0 **26 1**
From Ross Co.
2004–05 Cambridge U 2 0 **2 0**

BEECH, Tom (F) 4 0
H: 6 4 W: 15 00 b.Potton 2-12-85
Source: St Albans C.
2004–05 Cambridge U 4 0 **4 0**

BIMSON, Stuart (D) 254 4
H: 5 11 W: 11 12 b.Liverpool 29-9-69
Source: Macclesfield T.
1994–95 Bury 19 0
1995–96 Bury 16 0
1996–97 Bury 1 0 **36 0**
1996–97 Lincoln C 15 1
1997–98 Lincoln C 12 0
1998–99 Lincoln C 31 2
1999–2000 Lincoln C 20 0
2000–01 Lincoln C 20 0
2001–02 Lincoln C 35 0
2002–03 Lincoln C 42 1 **175 4**
2003–04 Cambridge U 24 0
2004–05 Cambridge U 19 0 **43 0**

BLACKBURN, Lee (M) 3 0
H: 5 8 W: 10 07 b.Hornchurch 1-10-85
Source: Norwich C Trainee.
2004–05 Cambridge U 3 0 **3 0**

BRENNAN, Martin (G) 1 0
H: 6 1 W: 12 00 b.Whipps Cross 14-9-82
2000–01 Charlton Ath 0 0
2001–02 Charlton Ath 0 0
2002–03 Cambridge U 1 0
2003–04 Cambridge U 0 0
2004–05 Cambridge U 0 0 **1 0**

BRIDGES, David (M) 45 5
H: 6 0 W: 12 00 b.Huntingdon 22-9-82
Source: Scholar.
2001–02 Cambridge U 7 1
2002–03 Cambridge U 17 2
2003–04 Cambridge U 21 2
2004–05 Cambridge U 0 0 **45 5**

CHILLINGWORTH, Daniel (F) 99 16
H: 6 1 W: 12 06 b.Cambridge 13-9-81
Source: Scholarship.
1999–2000 Cambridge U 3 0
2000–01 Cambridge U 1 0
2001–02 *Darlington* 4 1 **4 1**
2001–02 Cambridge U 12 2
2002–03 Cambridge U 30 0
2003–04 Cambridge U 13 7
2004–05 Cambridge U 28 4 **87 13**
2004–05 *Leyton Orient* 8 2 **8 2**

DANIELS, David (M) 1 0
H: 5 8 W: 10 10 b.Bedford 14-9-85
Source: Scholar.
2003–04 Cambridge U 1 0
2004–05 Cambridge U 0 0 **1 0**

DAVIES, Adam (D) 2 0
H: 6 2 W: 13 05 b.Peterborough 27-3-87
Source: Scholar. *Honours:* Wales Youth.
2004–05 Cambridge U 2 0 **2 0**

DUNCAN, Andy (D) 242 6
H: 5 11 W: 13 00 b.Hexham 20-10-77
Source: From Trainee. *Honours:* England Schools.
1996–97 Manchester U 0 0
1997–98 Manchester U 0 0
1997–98 Cambridge U 19 0
1998–99 Cambridge U 45 1
1999–2000 Cambridge U 13 1
2000–01 Cambridge U 39 1
2001–02 Cambridge U 24 0
2002–03 Cambridge U 23 0
2003–04 Cambridge U 37 2
2004–05 Cambridge U 42 1 **242 6**

EL KHOLTI, Abdelhalim (M) 38 1
H: 5 10 W: 11 00 b.Annesse 17-10-80
Source: Raja.
2003–04 Yeovil T 23 1 **23 1**
2004–05 Cambridge U 15 0 **15 0**

FULLER, Ashley (M) 3 0
H: 5 9 W: 10 10 b.Bedford 14-11-86
Source: Scholar.
2003–04 Cambridge U 1 0
2004–05 Cambridge U 2 0 **3 0**

GLEESON, Dan (M) 37 0
H: 6 3 W: 13 02 b.Cambridge 17-2-85
Source: Scholar.
2003–04 Cambridge U 7 0
2004–05 Cambridge U 30 0 **37 0**

GOODHIND, Warren (D) 196 3
H: 5 11 W: 11 02 b.Johannesburg 16-8-77
Source: Trainee.
1996–97 Barnet 3 0
1997–98 Barnet 35 1
1998–99 Barnet 15 1
1999–2000 Barnet 9 0
2000–01 Barnet 31 1
2001–02 Barnet 0 0 **93 3**
2001–02 Cambridge U 14 0
2002–03 Cambridge U 37 0
2003–04 Cambridge U 26 0
2004–05 Cambridge U 26 0 **103 0**

HODGSON, Richard (M) 109 8
H: 5 10 W: 11 08 b.Sunderland 1-10-79
Source: Trainee.
1996–97 Nottingham F 0 0
1997–98 Nottingham F 0 0
1998–99 Nottingham F 0 0
1999–2000 Nottingham F 0 0
1999–2000 Scunthorpe U 1 0 **1 0**
2000–01 Darlington 35 2
2001–02 Darlington 36 2
2002–03 Darlington 27 2
2003–04 Darlington 0 0 **98 6**
2004–05 Cambridge U 10 2 **10 2**

HUTTON, Rory (D) 2 0
H: 5 9 W: 10 04 b.Ely 3-5-85
Source: Peterborough U. *Honours:* Eire Youth.
2004–05 Cambridge U 2 0 **2 0**

JOHNSON, Brad (M) 1 0
H: 6 0 W: 12 10 b.London 28-4-87
2004–05 Cambridge U 1 0 **1 0**

JOWSEY, James (G) 1 0
H: 6 0 W: 12 04 b.Filey 24-11-83
Source: Scholar.
2000–01 Manchester U 0 0
2001–02 Manchester U 0 0
2002–03 Manchester U 0 0
2003–04 Manchester U 0 0
From Scarborough
2004–05 Cambridge U 1 0 **1 0**

KELLY, Gavin (G) 0 0
H: 6 0 W: 13 07 b.Hammersmith 3-6-81
Source: Trainee.
1999–2000 Tottenham H 0 0
2000–01 Tottenham H 0 0
2001–02 Tottenham H 0 0
2002–03 Tottenham H 0 0
2003–04 Cambridge U 0 0
2004–05 Cambridge U 0 0

KONTE, Amadou (F) 9 3
H: 6 3 W: 13 08 b.Mali 23-1-81
Source: Strasbourg, Porto, Vilanovense, Palermo. *Honours:* Mali Youth.
2004–05 Cambridge U 9 3 **9 3**

LATTE-YEDO, Igor (D) 11 0
H: 6 3 W: 13 00 b.Dabou 14-12-78
Source: Gap, Beaucaire, Cannes, Estoril, Endoume.
2004–05 Cambridge U 11 0 **11 0**

LOCKETT, Ryan (F) 2 0
H: 5 10 W: 11 08 b.Cambridge 11-11-86
Source: Scholar.
2003–04 Cambridge U 2 0
2004–05 Cambridge U 0 0 **2 0**

MARSHALL, Shaun (G) 155 0
H: 6 1 W: 13 03 b.Fakenham 3-10-78
Source: Trainee.
1996–97 Cambridge U 1 0
1997–98 Cambridge U 2 0
1998–99 Cambridge U 19 0
1999–2000 Cambridge U 24 0
2000–01 Cambridge U 11 0
2001–02 Cambridge U 7 0
2002–03 Cambridge U 45 0
2003–04 Cambridge U 45 0
2004–05 Cambridge U 1 0 **155 0**

MBOME, Kingsley (M) 13 1
H: 6 2 W: 13 06 b.Yaounde 21-11-81
Honours: Cameroon Youth.
1999–2000 Sheffield U 0 0
2000–01 Sheffield U 0 0
2001–02 Sheffield U 0 0
2004–05 Cambridge U 13 1 **13 1**

NACCA, Franco (D) 26 0
H: 5 6 W: 10 00 b.Venezuela 9-11-82
Source: Scholar.
2000–01 Cambridge U 0 0
2001–02 Cambridge U 0 0
2002–03 Cambridge U 17 0
2003–04 Cambridge U 9 0
2004–05 Cambridge U 0 0 **26 0**

NICHOLLS, Ashley (M) 111 7
H: 5 11 W: 11 11 b.Ipswich 30-10-81
Source: Ipswich W. *Honours:* England Schools.
2000–01 Ipswich T 0 0
2001–02 Ipswich T 0 0
2002–03 Darlington 41 6
2003–04 Darlington 26 0 **67 6**
2003–04 *Cambridge U* 16 1
2004–05 Cambridge U 28 0 **44 1**

OLI, Dennis (F) 28 1
H: 6 0 W: 12 00 b.Newham 28-1-84
2001–02 QPR 2 0
2002–03 QPR 18 0
2003–04 QPR 3 0 **23 0**
2004–05 Swansea C 1 0 **1 0**
2004–05 Cambridge U 4 1 **4 1**

QUINTON, Darren (M) 32 0
H: 5 10 W: 10 10 b.Romford 28-4-86
Source: Scholar.
2003–04 Cambridge U 1 0
2004–05 Cambridge U 31 0 **32 0**

ROBINSON, Matthew (F) 7 0
H: 6 0 W: 11 06 b.Ipswich 22-3-84
Source: Scholar.
2003–04 Ipswich T 0 0
2003–04 Bournemouth 0 0
2003–04 Cambridge U 3 0
2004–05 Cambridge U 4 0 **7 0**

RUDDY, John (G) 39 0
H: 6 4 W: 15 04 b.St Ives 24-10-86
Source: Scholar.
2003–04 Cambridge U 1 0
2004–05 Cambridge U 38 0 **39 0**

SMITH, Stephen (M) 2 0
H: 5 8 W: 11 07 b.Harlow 19-9-86
Source: Scholar.
2003–04 Cambridge U 2 0
2004–05 Cambridge U 0 0 **2 0**

SOMNER, Matt (D) 108 1
H: 6 0 W: 13 00 b.Isleworth 8-12-82
Source: Trainee. *Honours:* Wales Under-21.
2000–01 Brentford 3 0
2001–02 Brentford 0 0
2002–03 Brentford 40 1
2003–04 Brentford 39 0
2004–05 Brentford 2 0 **84 1**
2004–05 Cambridge U 24 0 **24 0**

TANN, Adam (D) 121 4
H: 6 0 W: 11 05 b.Fakenham 12-5-82
Source: Scholar. *Honours:* England Youth.
1999–2000 Cambridge U 0 0
2000–01 Cambridge U 1 0

2001–02	Cambridge U	25	0		
2002–03	Cambridge U	25	1		
2003–04	Cambridge U	34	2		
2004–05	Cambridge U	36	1	**121**	**4**

TUDOR, Shane (M) **122 21**
H: 5 8 W: 11 00 b.Wolverhampton 10-2-82
Source: Trainee.

1999–2000	Wolverhampton W	0	0		
2000–01	Wolverhampton W	1	0		
2001–02	Wolverhampton W	0	0	**1**	**0**
2001–02	Cambridge U	32	3		
2002–03	Cambridge U	27	9		
2003–04	Cambridge U	36	3		
2004–05	Cambridge U	26	6	**121**	**21**

TURNER, John (F) **75 10**
H: 5 10 W: 11 00 b.Harrow 12-2-86
Source: Scholar.

2002–03	Cambridge U	1	1		
2003–04	Cambridge U	36	3		
2004–05	Cambridge U	38	6	**75**	**10**

WALKER, Justin (M) **315 13**
H: 5 11 W: 12 04 b.Nottingham 6-9-75
Source: Trainee. *Honours:* England Schools, Youth.

1992–93	Nottingham F	0	0		
1993–94	Nottingham F	0	0		
1994–95	Nottingham F	0	0		
1995–96	Nottingham F	0	0		
1996–97	Nottingham F	0	0		
1996–97	Scunthorpe U	9	0		
1997–98	Scunthorpe U	40	1		
1998–99	Scunthorpe U	41	1		
1999–2000	Scunthorpe U	42	0	**132**	**2**
2000–01	Lincoln C	45	1		
2001–02	Lincoln C	31	3	**76**	**4**
2002–03	Exeter C	39	5	**39**	**5**
2003–04	Cambridge U	23	1		
2003–04	*York C*	9	0	**9**	**0**
2004–05	Cambridge U	36	1	**59**	**2**

WARDLEY, Stuart (M) **160 26**
H: 5 11 W: 13 00 b.Cambridge 10-9-75
Source: Saffron Walden T.

1999–2000	QPR	43	11		
2000–01	QPR	34	3		
2001–02	QPR	10	0	**87**	**14**
2001–02	Rushden & D	18	4		
2002–03	Rushden & D	39	6		
2003–04	Rushden & D	0	0	**57**	**10**
2004–05	Torquay U	7	2	**7**	**2**
2004–05	Leyton Orient	6	0	**6**	**0**
2004–05	Cambridge U	3	0	**3**	**0**

WEBB, Daniel (F) **110 9**
H: 6 1 W: 11 08 b.Poole 2-7-83

2000–01	Southend U	15	1		
2001–02	Southend U	16	2		
2001–02	*Brighton & HA*	12	1		
2002–03	Southend U	0	0	**31**	**3**
2002–03	*Brighton & HA*	3	0	**15**	**1**
2002–03	Hull C	12	0		
2002–03	*Lincoln C*	5	1	**5**	**1**
2003–04	Hull C	4	0	**16**	**0**
2003–04	Cambridge U	21	3		
2004–05	Cambridge U	22	1	**43**	**4**

CARDIFF C (18)

ALEXANDER, Neil (G) **236 0**
H: 6 1 W: 12 08 b.Edinburgh 10-3-78
Source: Edina Hibs. *Honours:* Scotland Under-21.

1996–97	Stenhousemuir	12	0		
1997–98	Stenhousemuir	36	0	**48**	**0**
1998–99	Livingston	21	0		
1999–2000	Livingston	13	0		
2000–01	Livingston	26	0	**60**	**0**
2001–02	Cardiff C	46	0		
2002–03	Cardiff C	40	0		
2003–04	Cardiff C	25	0		
2004–05	Cardiff C	17	0	**128**	**0**

ANTHONY, Byron (D) **0 0**
H: 6 1 W: 11 02 b.Newport 20-9-84
Source: Scholar. *Honours:* Wales Youth, Under-21.

2003–04	Cardiff C	0	0		
2004–05	Cardiff C	0	0		

ARDLEY, Neal (M) **364 26**
H: 5 10 W: 12 12 b.Epsom 1-9-72
Source: Trainee. *Honours:* England Under-21.

1990–91	Wimbledon	1	0		
1991–92	Wimbledon	8	0		
1992–93	Wimbledon	26	4		
1993–94	Wimbledon	16	1		
1994–95	Wimbledon	14	1		
1995–96	Wimbledon	6	0		
1996–97	Wimbledon	34	2		
1997–98	Wimbledon	34	2		
1998–99	Wimbledon	23	0		
1999–2000	Wimbledon	17	2		
2000–01	Wimbledon	37	3		
2001–02	Wimbledon	29	3	**245**	**18**
2002–03	Watford	43	2		
2003–04	Watford	38	1		
2004–05	Watford	30	4	**111**	**7**
2004–05	Cardiff C	8	1	**8**	**1**

BARKER, Chris (D) **235 3**
H: 6 2 W: 13 08 b.Sheffield 2-3-80
Source: Alfreton.

1998–99	Barnsley	0	0		
1999–2000	Barnsley	29	0		
2000–01	Barnsley	40	0		
2001–02	Barnsley	44	3	**113**	**3**
2002–03	Cardiff C	40	0		
2003–04	Cardiff C	39	0		
2004–05	*Stoke C*	4	0	**4**	**0**
2004–05	Cardiff C	39	0	**118**	**0**

BOLAND, Willie (M) **257 3**
H: 5 9 W: 12 04 b.Ennis 6-8-75
Source: Trainee. *Honours:* Eire Youth, Under-21.

1992–93	Coventry C	1	0		
1993–94	Coventry C	27	0		
1994–95	Coventry C	12	0		
1995–96	Coventry C	3	0		
1996–97	Coventry C	1	0		
1997–98	Coventry C	19	0		
1998–99	Coventry C	0	0	**63**	**0**
1999–2000	Cardiff C	28	1		
2000–01	Cardiff C	25	1		
2001–02	Cardiff C	42	1		
2002–03	Cardiff C	41	0		
2003–04	Cardiff C	37	0		
2004–05	Cardiff C	21	0	**194**	**3**

BULLOCK, Lee (M) **203 30**
H: 6 0 W: 13 01 b.Stockton 22-5-81
Source: Trainee.

1999–2000	York C	24	0		
2000–01	York C	33	3		
2001–02	York C	40	8		
2002–03	York C	39	6		
2003–04	York C	35	7	**171**	**24**
2003–04	*Cardiff C*	11	3		
2004–05	Cardiff C	21	3	**32**	**6**

CAMPBELL, Andy (F) **149 19**
H: 5 11 W: 12 04 b.Middlesbrough 18-4-79
Source: Trainee. *Honours:* England Youth, Under-21.

1995–96	Middlesbrough	2	0		
1996–97	Middlesbrough	3	0		
1997–98	Middlesbrough	7	0		
1998–99	Middlesbrough	8	0		
1998–99	*Sheffield U*	11	3	**11**	**3**
1999–2000	Middlesbrough	25	4		
2000–01	Middlesbrough	7	0		
2000–01	*Bolton W*	6	0	**6**	**0**
2001–02	Middlesbrough	4	0	**56**	**4**
2001–02	Cardiff C	8	7		
2002–03	Cardiff C	28	3		
2003–04	Cardiff C	25	2		
2004–05	Cardiff C	12	0	**73**	**12**
2004–05	*Doncaster R*	3	0	**3**	**0**

COLLINS, James (D) **66 3**
H: 6 2 W: 14 05 b.Newport 23-8-83
Source: Scholar. *Honours:* Wales Youth, Under-21, 6 full caps.

2000–01	Cardiff C	3	0		
2001–02	Cardiff C	7	1		
2002–03	Cardiff C	2	0		
2003–04	Cardiff C	20	1		
2004–05	Cardiff C	34	1	**66**	**3**

CROFT, Gary (D) **302 8**
H: 5 9 W: 11 11 b.Burton-on-Trent 17-2-74
Source: Trainee. *Honours:* England Under-21.

1990–91	Grimsby T	1	0		
1991–92	Grimsby T	0	0		
1992–93	Grimsby T	32	0		
1993–94	Grimsby T	36	1		
1994–95	Grimsby T	44	1		
1995–96	Grimsby T	36	1	**149**	**3**
1995–96	Blackburn R	0	0		
1996–97	Blackburn R	5	0		
1997–98	Blackburn R	23	1		
1998–99	Blackburn R	12	0		
1999–2000	Blackburn R	0	0	**40**	**1**
1999–2000	Ipswich T	21	1		
2000–01	Ipswich T	8	0		
2001–02	Ipswich T	0	0	**29**	**1**
2001–02	*Wigan Ath*	7	0	**7**	**0**
2001–02	*Cardiff C*	6	1		
2002–03	Cardiff C	43	1		
2003–04	Cardiff C	27	1		
2004–05	Cardiff C	1	0	**77**	**3**

FISH, Nicky (M) **0 0**
H: 5 10 W: 11 02 b.Cardiff 15-9-84
Source: Scholar. *Honours:* Wales Youth, Under-21.

2001–02	Cardiff C	0	0		
2002–03	Cardiff C	0	0		
2003–04	Cardiff C	0	0		
2004–05	Cardiff C	0	0		

FLEETWOOD, Stuart (F) **8 0**
H: 5 10 W: 12 07 b.Gloucester 23-4-86
Source: Scholar. *Honours:* Wales Youth, Under-21.

2003–04	Cardiff C	2	0		
2004–05	Cardiff C	6	0	**8**	**0**

GABBIDON, Daniel (D) **217 10**
H: 6 0 W: 13 05 b.Cwmbran 8-8-79
Source: Trainee. *Honours:* Wales Youth, Under-21, 26 full caps.

1998–99	WBA	2	0		
1999–2000	WBA	18	0		
2000–01	WBA	0	0	**20**	**0**
2000–01	Cardiff C	43	3		
2001–02	Cardiff C	44	3		
2002–03	Cardiff C	24	0		
2003–04	Cardiff C	41	3		
2004–05	Cardiff C	45	1	**197**	**10**

HUGGINS, Kirk (D) **0 0**
H: 5 11 W: 11 12 b.Barry 4-6-85
Source: Scholar.

2002–03	Cardiff C	0	0		
2003–04	Cardiff C	0	0		
2004–05	Cardiff C	0	0		

INGRAM, Richard (F) **0 0**
H: 5 9 W: 10 08 b.Merthyr 15-2-85
Source: Scholar.

2001–02	Cardiff C	0	0		
2002–03	Cardiff C	0	0		
2003–04	Cardiff C	0	0		
2004–05	Cardiff C	0	0		

JEROME, Cameron (F) **29 6**
H: 6 1 W: 13 06 b.Huddersfield 14-8-86

2004–05	Cardiff C	29	6	**29**	**6**

KOSKELA, Toni (M) **2 0**
H: 6 2 W: 12 08 b.Finland 16-3-83
Source: KTP. *Honours:* Finland Youth, Under-21.

2004–05	Cardiff C	2	0	**2**	**0**

LANGLEY, Richard (M) **202 26**
H: 5 10 W: 12 08 b.Harlesden 27-12-79
Source: From Trainee. *Honours:* England Youth. Jamaica 17 full caps.

1996–97	QPR	0	0		
1997–98	QPR	0	0		
1998–99	QPR	8	1		
1999–2000	QPR	41	3		
2000–01	QPR	26	1		
2001–02	QPR	18	3		
2002–03	QPR	39	9		
2003–04	QPR	1	1	**133**	**18**
2003–04	Cardiff C	44	6		
2004–05	Cardiff C	25	2	**69**	**8**

LEDLEY, Joe (M) **28** **3**
H: 6 0 W: 11 07 b.Cardiff 23-1-87
Source: Scholar. *Honours:* Wales Youth, Under-21.

2004–05	Cardiff C	28	3	**28**	**3**

LEE-BARRETT, Arran (G) **0** **0**
H: 6 2 W: 14 01 b.Ipswich 28-2-84
Source: Norwich C Scholar.

2002–03	Cardiff C	0	0		
2003–04	Cardiff C	0	0		
2004–05	Cardiff C	0	0		

LEE, Alan (F) **205** **49**
H: 6 2 W: 15 04 b.Galway 21-8-78
Source: Trainee. *Honours:* Eire Under-21, 8 full caps.

1995–96	Aston Villa	0	0		
1996–97	Aston Villa	0	0		
1997–98	Aston Villa	0	0		
1998–99	Aston Villa	0	0		
1998–99	*Torquay U*	7	2	**7**	**2**
1998–99	*Port Vale*	11	2	**11**	**2**
1999–2000	Burnley	15	0		
2000–01	Burnley	0	0	**15**	**0**
2000–01	Rotherham U	31	13		
2001–02	Rotherham U	38	9		
2002–03	Rotherham U	41	15		
2003–04	Rotherham U	1	0	**111**	**37**
2003–04	Cardiff C	23	3		
2004–05	Cardiff C	38	5	**61**	**8**

MARGETSON, Martyn (G) **166** **0**
H: 6 0 W: 14 00 b.West Neath 8-9-71
Source: Trainee. *Honours:* Wales Schools, Youth, Under-21, B, 1 full cap.

1990–91	Manchester C	2	0		
1991–92	Manchester C	3	0		
1992–93	Manchester C	1	0		
1993–94	Manchester C	0	0		
1993–94	*Bristol R*	3	0	**3**	**0**
1993–94	*Bolton W*	0	0		
1994–95	Manchester C	0	0		
1994–95	*Luton T*	0	0		
1995–96	Manchester C	0	0		
1996–97	Manchester C	17	0		
1997–98	Manchester C	28	0	**51**	**0**
1998–99	Southend U	32	0	**32**	**0**
1999–2000	Huddersfield T	0	0		
2000–01	Huddersfield T	2	0		
2001–02	Huddersfield T	46	0	**48**	**0**
2002–03	Cardiff C	6	0		
2003–04	Cardiff C	22	0		
2004–05	Cardiff C	4	0	**32**	**0**

McANUFF, Jobi (M) **152** **16**
H: 5 11 W: 10 12 b.Edmonton 9-11-81
Source: Scholar. *Honours:* Jamaica 1 full cap.

2000–01	Wimbledon	0	0		
2001–02	Wimbledon	38	4		
2002–03	Wimbledon	31	4		
2003–04	Wimbledon	27	5	**96**	**13**
2003–04	West Ham U	12	1		
2004–05	West Ham U	1	0	**13**	**1**
2004–05	Cardiff C	43	2	**43**	**2**

PARKINS, Michael (M) **0** **0**
H: 5 8 W: 11 02 b.Cardiff 12-1-85
Source: Scholar.

2001–02	Cardiff C	0	0		
2002–03	Cardiff C	0	0		
2003–04	Cardiff C	0	0		
2004–05	Cardiff C	0	0		

PARRY, Paul (M) **41** **5**
H: 5 11 W: 12 12 b.Newport 19-8-80
Source: Hereford U. *Honours:* Wales 4 full caps, 1 goal.

2003–04	Cardiff C	17	1		
2004–05	Cardiff C	24	4	**41**	**5**

THOMAS, Danny (F) **1** **0**
H: 5 5 W: 10 10 b.Blackwood 13-5-85
Source: Scholar. *Honours:* Wales Youth.

2002–03	Cardiff C	0	0		
2003–04	Cardiff C	0	0		
2004–05	Cardiff C	1	0	**1**	**0**

THORNE, Peter (F) **372** **138**
H: 6 0 W: 14 00 b.Manchester 21-6-73
Source: Trainee.

1991–92	Blackburn R	0	0		
1992–93	Blackburn R	0	0		
1993–94	Blackburn R	0	0		
1993–94	*Wigan Ath*	11	0	**11**	**0**
1994–95	Blackburn R	0	0		
1994–95	Swindon T	20	9		
1995–96	Swindon T	26	10		
1996–97	Swindon T	31	8	**77**	**27**
1997–98	Stoke C	36	12		
1998–99	Stoke C	34	9		
1999–2000	Stoke C	45	24		
2000–01	Stoke C	38	16		
2001–02	Stoke C	5	4	**158**	**65**
2001–02	Cardiff C	26	8		
2002–03	Cardiff C	46	13		
2003–04	Cardiff C	23	13		
2004–05	Cardiff C	31	12	**126**	**46**

VIDMAR, Tony (D) **411** **30**
H: 6 1 W: 13 00 b.Adelaide 15-4-69
Honours: Australia Schools, Youth, Under-23, 69 full caps, 3 goals.

1989	Adelaide City	11	1		
1989–90	Adelaide City	27	4		
1990–91	Adelaide City	27	3		
1991–92	Adelaide City	24	1		
1992–93	Adelaide City	9	0		
1992–93	Ekeren	9	1	**9**	**1**
1993–94	Adelaide City	27	4		
1994–95	Adelaide City	24	1	**149**	**14**
1995–96	NAC	30	2		
1996–97	NAC	31	2	**61**	**4**
1997–98	Rangers	12	0		
1998–99	Rangers	28	1		
1999–2000	Rangers	27	6		
2000–01	Rangers	15	1		
2001–02	Rangers	25	1	**107**	**9**
2002–03	Middlesbrough	12	0	**12**	**0**
2003–04	Cardiff C	45	1		
2004–05	Cardiff C	28	1	**73**	**2**

WARNER, Tony (G) **237** **0**
H: 6 4 W: 15 06 b.Liverpool 11-5-74
Source: School.

1993–94	Liverpool	0	0		
1994–95	Liverpool	0	0		
1995–96	Liverpool	0	0		
1996–97	Liverpool	0	0		
1997–98	Liverpool	0	0		
1997–98	*Swindon T*	2	0	**2**	**0**
1998–99	Liverpool	0	0		
1998–99	*Celtic*	3	0	**3**	**0**
1998–99	*Aberdeen*	6	0	**6**	**0**
1999–2000	Millwall	45	0		
2000–01	Millwall	35	0		
2001–02	Millwall	46	0		
2002–03	Millwall	46	0		
2003–04	Millwall	28	0	**200**	**0**
2004–05	Cardiff C	26	0	**26**	**0**

WESTON, Rhys (D) **153** **2**
H: 6 1 W: 12 12 b.Kingston 27-10-80
Source: Trainee. *Honours:* England Schools, Youth. Wales Under-21, 7 full caps.

1999–2000	Arsenal	1	0		
2000–01	Arsenal	0	0	**1**	**0**
2000–01	Cardiff C	28	0		
2001–02	Cardiff C	37	0		
2002–03	Cardiff C	38	2		
2003–04	Cardiff C	24	0		
2004–05	Cardiff C	25	0	**152**	**2**

WILLIAMS, Darren (D) **239** **4**
H: 5 11 W: 12 06 b.Middlesbrough 28-4-77
Source: Trainee. *Honours:* England Under-21, B.

1994–95	York C	1	0		
1995–96	York C	18	0		
1996–97	York C	1	0	**20**	**0**
1996–97	Sunderland	11	2		
1997–98	Sunderland	36	2		
1998–99	Sunderland	25	0		
1999–2000	Sunderland	25	0		
2000–01	Sunderland	28	0		
2001–02	Sunderland	28	0		
2002–03	Sunderland	16	0		
2003–04	Sunderland	29	0		
2004–05	Sunderland	1	0	**199**	**4**
2004–05	Cardiff C	20	0	**20**	**0**

YOUNG, Scott (D) **277** **22**
H: 6 1 W: 12 00 b.Tonypandy 14-1-76
Source: Trainee. *Honours:* Wales Under-21, B.

1993–94	Cardiff C	6	0		
1994–95	Cardiff C	22	0		
1995–96	Cardiff C	41	0		
1996–97	Cardiff C	32	1		
1997–98	Cardiff C	31	3		
1998–99	Cardiff C	33	1		
1999–2000	Cardiff C	22	2		
2000–01	Cardiff C	45	10		
2001–02	Cardiff C	33	4		
2002–03	Cardiff C	12	1		
2003–04	Cardiff C	0	0		
2004–05	Cardiff C	0	0	**277**	**22**

CHARLTON ATH (19)

ANDERSEN, Stephan (G) **2** **0**
H: 6 2 W: 13 07 b.Copenhagen 26-11-81
Source: AB Copenhagen. *Honours:* Denmark Youth, Under-21, 1 full cap.

2004–05	Charlton Ath	2	0	**2**	**0**

ASHTON, Nathan (D) **0** **0**
H: 5 9 W: 11 08 b.Plaistow 30-1-87
Source: From Scholar. *Honours:* England Youth.

2004–05	Charlton Ath	0	0		

BARTLETT, Shaun (F) **241** **65**
H: 6 0 W: 12 06 b.Cape Town 31-10-72
Honours: Cape Town Spurs. South Africa 72 full caps, 28 goals.

1996	Colorado Rapids	26	8		
1996–97	Amazulu	0	0		
1997	New York/ New Jersey M	13	2	**13**	**2**
1997	Colorado Rapids	10	1	**36**	**9**
1998	Cape Town Spurs	18	8	**18**	**8**
1998–99	Zurich	27	13		
1999–2000	Zurich	20	2		
2000–01	Zurich	20	8	**67**	**23**
2000–01	Charlton Ath	18	7		
2001–02	Charlton Ath	14	1		
2002–03	Charlton Ath	31	4		
2003–04	Charlton Ath	19	5		
2004–05	Charlton Ath	25	6	**107**	**23**

EL KARKOURI, Talal (D) **88** **5**
H: 6 1 W: 12 03 b.Casablanca 8-7-76
Source: Casablanca School of Sportsmen. *Honours:* Morocco full caps.

1999–2000	Paris St Germain	10	0		
2000–01	Paris St Germain	11	0		
2000–01	Aris Salonika	11	0	**11**	**0**
2001–02	Paris St Germain	16	0	**37**	**0**
2002–03	Sunderland	8	0		
2003–04	Sunderland	0	0	**8**	**0**
2004–05	Charlton Ath	32	5	**32**	**5**

ELLIOT, Rob (G) **4** **0**
H: 6 3 W: 14 10 b.Chatham 30-4-86
Source: Scholar.

2004–05	Charlton Ath	0	0		
2004–05	*Notts Co*	4	0	**4**	**0**

EUELL, Jason (F) **270** **74**
H: 5 11 W: 11 13 b.Lambeth 6-2-77
Source: Trainee. *Honours:* England Youth, Under-21, Jamaica 1 full cap.

1995–96	Wimbledon	9	2		
1996–97	Wimbledon	7	2		
1997–98	Wimbledon	19	4		
1998–99	Wimbledon	33	10		
1999–2000	Wimbledon	37	4		
2000–01	Wimbledon	36	19	**141**	**41**
2001–02	Charlton Ath	36	11		
2002–03	Charlton Ath	36	10		
2003–04	Charlton Ath	31	10		
2004–05	Charlton Ath	26	2	**129**	**33**

FISH, Mark (D) **350** **14**
H: 6 4 W: 12 11 b.Cape Town 14-3-74
Source: Arcadia Shepherds. *Honours:* South Africa 62 full caps, 2 goals.

1992	Jomo Cosmos	14	1		
1993	Jomo Cosmos	41	1	**55**	**2**
1994	Orlando Pirates	37	5		

1995	Orlando Pirates	38	1	**75**	**6**
1996–97	Lazio	15	1	**15**	**1**
1997–98	Bolton W	22	2		
1998–99	Bolton W	36	1		
1999–2000	Bolton W	31	0		
2000–01	Bolton W	14	0	**103**	**3**
2000–01	Charlton Ath	24	1		
2001–02	Charlton Ath	25	0		
2002–03	Charlton Ath	23	1		
2003–04	Charlton Ath	23	0		
2004–05	Charlton Ath	7	0	**102**	**2**

FORTUNE, Jon (D) 122 5

H: 6 2 W: 12 12 b.Islington 23-8-80

Source: Trainee.

1998–99	Charlton Ath	0	0		
1999–2000	Charlton Ath	0	0		
1999–2000	*Mansfield T*	4	0		
2000–01	Charlton Ath	0	0		
2000–01	*Mansfield T*	14	0	**18**	**0**
2001–02	Charlton Ath	19	0		
2002–03	Charlton Ath	26	1		
2003–04	Charlton Ath	28	2		
2004–05	Charlton Ath	31	2	**104**	**5**

FULLER, Barry (M) 0 0

H: 5 10 W: 11 10 b.Ashford 25-9-84

Source: Scholar.

2004–05	Charlton Ath	0	0		

HOLLAND, Matt (M) 433 65

H: 5 10 W: 12 03 b.Bury 11-4-74

Source: From Trainee. *Honours:* Eire B, 46 full caps, 5 goals.

1992–93	West Ham U	0	0		
1993–94	West Ham U	0	0		
1994–95	West Ham U	0	0		
1994–95	Bournemouth	16	1		
1995–96	Bournemouth	43	10		
1996–97	Bournemouth	45	7	**104**	**18**
1997–98	Ipswich T	46	10		
1998–99	Ipswich T	46	5		
1999–2000	Ipswich T	46	10		
2000–01	Ipswich T	38	3		
2001–02	Ipswich T	38	3		
2002–03	Ipswich T	45	7	**259**	**38**
2003–04	Charlton Ath	38	6		
2004–05	Charlton Ath	32	3	**70**	**9**

HREIDARSSON, Hermann (D) 337 19

H: 6 3 W: 12 12 b.Reykjavik 11-7-74

Honours: Iceland Under-21, 61 full caps, 3 goals.

1993	IBV	2	0		
1994	IBV	18	2		
1995	IBV	18	1		
1996	IBV	17	2		
1997	IBV	11	0	**66**	**5**
1997–98	Crystal Palace	30	2		
1998–99	Crystal Palace	7	0	**37**	**2**
1998–99	Brentford	33	4		
1999–2000	Brentford	8	2	**41**	**6**
1999–2000	Wimbledon	24	1	**24**	**1**
2000–01	Ipswich T	36	1		
2001–02	Ipswich T	38	1		
2002–03	Ipswich T	28	0	**102**	**2**
2002–03	Charlton Ath	0	0		
2003–04	Charlton Ath	33	2		
2004–05	Charlton Ath	34	1	**67**	**3**

HUGHES, Bryan (M) 359 47

H: 5 10 W: 11 08 b.Liverpool 19-6-76

Source: Trainee.

1993–94	Wrexham	11	0		
1994–95	Wrexham	38	9		
1995–96	Wrexham	22	0		
1996–97	Wrexham	23	3	**94**	**12**
1996–97	Birmingham C	11	0		
1997–98	Birmingham C	40	5		
1998–99	Birmingham C	28	3		
1999–2000	Birmingham C	45	10		
2000–01	Birmingham C	45	4		
2001–02	Birmingham C	31	7		
2002–03	Birmingham C	22	2		
2003–04	Birmingham C	26	3	**248**	**34**
2004–05	Charlton Ath	17	1	**17**	**1**

JEFFERS, Francis (F) 109 25

H: 5 10 W: 11 02 b.Liverpool 25-1-81

Source: Trainee. *Honours:* England Schools, Youth, Under-21, 1 full cap, 1 goal.

1997–98	Everton	1	0		
1998–99	Everton	15	6		
1999–2000	Everton	21	6		
2000–01	Everton	12	6		
2001–02	Arsenal	6	2		
2002–03	Arsenal	16	2		
2003–04	Arsenal	0	0	**22**	**4**
2003–04	*Everton*	18	0	**67**	**18**
2004–05	Charlton Ath	20	3	**20**	**3**

JOHANSSON, Jonatan (F) 232 56

H: 6 2 W: 12 08 b.Stockholm 16-8-75

Source: Flora Tallinn. *Honours:* Finland 64 full caps, 11 goals.

1995	TPS Turku	9	0		
1996	TPS Turku	23	6	**32**	**6**
1996–97	Flora Tallinn	9	9	**9**	**9**
1997–98	Rangers	6	0		
1998–99	Rangers	25	8		
1999–2000	Rangers	16	6	**47**	**14**
2000–01	Charlton Ath	31	11		
2001–02	Charlton Ath	30	5		
2002–03	Charlton Ath	31	3		
2003–04	Charlton Ath	26	4		
2004–05	Charlton Ath	26	4	**144**	**27**

KEMENES, Szabolcs (G) 0 0

H: 6 2 W: 12 12 b.Budapest 18-5-86

2004–05	Charlton Ath	0	0		

KIELY, Dean (G) 566 0

H: 6 1 W: 13 10 b.Salford 10-10-70

Source: WBA School. *Honours:* England Schools, FA Schools, Youth, Eire 8 full caps.

1987–88	Coventry C	0	0		
1988–89	Coventry C	0	0		
1989–90	Coventry C	0	0		
1989–90	*Ipswich T*	0	0		
1989–90	*York C*	0	0		
1990–91	York C	17	0		
1991–92	York C	21	0		
1992–93	York C	40	0		
1993–94	York C	46	0		
1994–95	York C	46	0		
1995–96	York C	40	0	**210**	**0**
1996–97	Bury	46	0		
1997–98	Bury	46	0		
1998–99	Bury	45	0	**137**	**0**
1999–2000	Charlton Ath	45	0		
2000–01	Charlton Ath	25	0		
2001–02	Charlton Ath	38	0		
2002–03	Charlton Ath	38	0		
2003–04	Charlton Ath	37	0		
2004–05	Charlton Ath	36	0	**219**	**0**

KISHISHEV, Radostin (D) 321 19

H: 5 11 W: 12 03 b.Bourgas 30-7-74

Honours: Bulgaria 57 full caps.

1991–92	Chernomorets	6	1		
1992–93	Chernomorets	23	2		
1993–94	Chernomorets	23	1	**52**	**4**
1994–95	Neftochimik	14	0		
1995–96	Neftochimik	30	0		
1996–97	Neftochimik	30	6		
1997–98	Neftochimik	1	0	**75**	**6**
1997–98	Bursaspor	20	3	**20**	**3**
1997–98	Litets Lovech	5	0		
1998–99	Litets Lovech	26	2		
1999–2000	Litets Lovech	15	2	**46**	**4**
2000–01	Charlton Ath	27	0		
2001–02	Charlton Ath	3	0		
2002–03	Charlton Ath	34	2		
2003–04	Charlton Ath	33	0		
2004–05	Charlton Ath	31	0	**128**	**2**

KONCHESKY, Paul (D) 161 5

H: 5 10 W: 11 07 b.Barking 15-5-81

Source: Trainee. *Honours:* England Youth, Under-20, Under-21, 1 full cap.

1997–98	Charlton Ath	3	0		
1998–99	Charlton Ath	2	0		
1999–2000	Charlton Ath	8	0		
2000–01	Charlton Ath	23	0		
2001–02	Charlton Ath	34	1		
2002–03	Charlton Ath	30	3		
2003–04	Charlton Ath	21	0		
2003–04	*Tottenham H*	12	0	**12**	**0**
2004–05	Charlton Ath	28	1	**149**	**5**

LISBIE, Kevin (F) 152 20

H: 5 10 W: 11 06 b.Hackney 17-10-78

Source: Trainee. *Honours:* England Youth. Jamaica 6 full caps.

1996–97	Charlton Ath	25	1		
1997–98	Charlton Ath	17	1		
1998–99	Charlton Ath	1	0		
1998–99	*Gillingham*	7	4	**7**	**4**
1999–2000	Charlton Ath	0	0		
1999–2000	*Reading*	2	0	**2**	**0**
2000–01	Charlton Ath	18	0		
2000–01	*QPR*	2	0	**2**	**0**
2001–02	Charlton Ath	22	5		
2002–03	Charlton Ath	32	4		
2003–04	Charlton Ath	9	4		
2004–05	Charlton Ath	17	1	**141**	**16**

LONG, Stacy (F) 0 0

H: 5 8 W: 10 00 b.Bromley 11-1-85

Source: Scholar. *Honours:* England Under-20, Youth.

2001–02	Charlton Ath	0	0		
2002–03	Charlton Ath	0	0		
2003–04	Charlton Ath	0	0		
2004–05	Charlton Ath	0	0		

McCAFFERTY, Neil (M) 22 0

H: 5 7 W: 10 00 b.Derry 19-7-84

Source: Scholar.

2001–02	Charlton Ath	0	0		
2002–03	Charlton Ath	0	0		
2003–04	Charlton Ath	0	0		
2003–04	*Cambridge U*	6	0	**6**	**0**
2004–05	Charlton Ath	0	0		
2004–05	*Rushden & D*	16	0	**16**	**0**

MURPHY, Danny (M) 358 56

H: 5 10 W: 11 09 b.Chester 18-3-77

Source: Trainee. *Honours:* England Schools, Youth, Under-21, 9 full caps, 1 goal.

1993–94	Crewe Alex	12	2		
1994–95	Crewe Alex	35	5		
1995–96	Crewe Alex	42	10		
1996–97	Crewe Alex	45	10		
1997–98	Liverpool	16	0		
1998–99	Liverpool	1	0		
1998–99	*Crewe Alex*	16	1	**150**	**28**
1999–2000	Liverpool	23	3		
2000–01	Liverpool	27	4		
2001–02	Liverpool	36	6		
2002–03	Liverpool	36	7		
2003–04	Liverpool	31	5	**170**	**25**
2004–05	Charlton Ath	38	3	**38**	**3**

PERRY, Chris (D) 335 7

H: 5 8 W: 11 03 b.Carshalton 26-4-73

Source: Trainee.

1991–92	Wimbledon	0	0		
1992–93	Wimbledon	0	0		
1993–94	Wimbledon	2	0		
1994–95	Wimbledon	22	0		
1995–96	Wimbledon	37	0		
1996–97	Wimbledon	37	1		
1997–98	Wimbledon	35	1		
1998–99	Wimbledon	34	0	**167**	**2**
1999–2000	Tottenham H	37	1		
2000–01	Tottenham H	32	1		
2001–02	Tottenham H	33	0		
2002–03	Tottenham H	18	1		
2003–04	Tottenham H	0	0	**120**	**3**
2003–04	Charlton Ath	29	1		
2004–05	Charlton Ath	19	1	**48**	**2**

RANDOLPH, Darren (G) 0 0

H: 6 1 W: 12 03 b.Dublin 12-5-87

Source: Ardmore R. *Honours:* Scholar.

2004–05	Charlton Ath	0	0		

ROMMEDAHL, Dennis (F) 230 36

H: 5 9 W: 11 08 b.Copenhagen 22-7-78

Honours: Denmark Youth, Under-21, 53 full caps, 9 goals.

1995–96	Lyngby	9	0	**9**	**0**
1996–97	PSV Eindhoven	2	0		
1997–98	RKC	34	5	**34**	**5**
1998–99	PSV Eindhoven	19	2		
1999–2000	PSV Eindhoven	23	0		
2000–01	PSV Eindhoven	31	5		
2001–02	PSV Eindhoven	34	12		
2002–03	PSV Eindhoven	33	6		
2003–04	PSV Eindhoven	19	4	**161**	**29**
2004–05	Charlton Ath	26	2	**26**	**2**

ROWETT, Gary (D) 338 20
H: 6 0 W: 13 00 b.Bromsgrove 6-3-74
Source: Trainee.

1991–92	Cambridge U	13	2		
1992–93	Cambridge U	21	2		
1993–94	Cambridge U	29	5	**63**	**9**
1993–94	Everton	2	0		
1994–95	Everton	2	0	**4**	**0**
1994–95	*Blackpool*	17	0	**17**	**0**
1995–96	Derby Co	35	0		
1996–97	Derby Co	35	1		
1997–98	Derby Co	35	1		
1998–99	Derby Co	0	0	**105**	**2**
1998–99	Birmingham C	42	5		
1999–2000	Birmingham C	45	1	**87**	**6**
2000–01	Leicester C	38	2		
2001–02	Leicester C	11	0	**49**	**2**
2001–02	Charlton Ath	0	0		
2002–03	Charlton Ath	12	1		
2003–04	Charlton Ath	1	0		
2004–05	Charlton Ath	0	0	**13**	**1**

ROYCE, Simon (G) 214 0
H: 6 1 W: 13 09 b.Forest Gate 9-9-71
Source: Heybridge Swifts.

1991–92	Southend U	1	0		
1992–93	Southend U	3	0		
1993–94	Southend U	6	0		
1994–95	Southend U	13	0		
1995–96	Southend U	46	0		
1996–97	Southend U	43	0		
1997–98	Southend U	37	0	**149**	**0**
1998–99	Charlton Ath	8	0		
1999–2000	Charlton Ath	0	0		
2000–01	Leicester C	19	0		
2001–02	Leicester C	0	0		
2001–02	*Brighton & HA*	6	0	**6**	**0**
2001–02	*Manchester C*	0	0		
2002–03	Leicester C	0	0	**19**	**0**
2002–03	*QPR*	16	0		
2003–04	Charlton Ath	1	0		
2004–05	Charlton Ath	0	0	**9**	**0**
2004–05	*Luton T*	2	0	**2**	**0**
2004–05	*QPR*	13	0	**29**	**0**

RUFUS, Richard (D) 288 12
H: 6 1 W: 12 12 b.Lewisham 12-1-75
Source: Trainee. *Honours:* England Under-21.

1993–94	Charlton Ath	0	0		
1994–95	Charlton Ath	28	0		
1995–96	Charlton Ath	41	0		
1996–97	Charlton Ath	34	0		
1997–98	Charlton Ath	42	0		
1998–99	Charlton Ath	27	1		
1999–2000	Charlton Ath	44	6		
2000–01	Charlton Ath	32	2		
2001–02	Charlton Ath	10	1		
2002–03	Charlton Ath	30	2		
2003–04	Charlton Ath	0	0		
2004–05	Charlton Ath	0	0	**288**	**12**

SAM, Lloyd (F) 11 0
H: 5 8 W: 10 00 b.Leeds 27-9-84
Honours: England Youth, Under-20.

2002–03	Charlton Ath	0	0		
2003–04	Charlton Ath	0	0		
2003–04	*Leyton Orient*	10	0	**10**	**0**
2004–05	Charlton Ath	1	0	**1**	**0**

SANKOFA, Osei (D) 1 0
H: 6 0 W: 12 04 b.London 19-3-85
Source: Scholar. *Honours:* England Youth, Under-20.

2002–03	Charlton Ath	1	0		
2003–04	Charlton Ath	0	0		
2004–05	Charlton Ath	0	0	**1**	**0**

THOMAS, Jerome (M) 35 6
H: 5 9 W: 11 09 b.Brent 23-3-83
Source: Scholar. *Honours:* England Youth, Under-20.

2001–02	Arsenal	0	0		
2001–02	*QPR*	4	1		
2002–03	Arsenal	0	0		
2002–03	*QPR*	6	2	**10**	**3**
2003–04	Arsenal	0	0		
2003–04	Charlton Ath	1	0		
2004–05	Charlton Ath	24	3	**25**	**3**

VARNEY, Alex (F) 0 0
b.Farnborough 27-12-84
Source: Trainee.

2003–04	Charlton Ath	0	0		
2004–05	Charlton Ath	0	0		

WALKER, James (F) 0 0
H: 5 11 W: 11 13 b.Hackney 25-11-87
Source: Scholar. *Honours:* England Youth.

2004–05	Charlton Ath	0	0		

YOUNG, Luke (D) 184 2
H: 6 0 W: 12 04 b.Harlow 19-7-79
Source: Trainee. *Honours:* England Youth, Under-21, 2 full caps.

1997–98	Tottenham H	0	0		
1998–99	Tottenham H	15	0		
1999–2000	Tottenham H	20	0		
2000–01	Tottenham H	23	0	**58**	**0**
2001–02	Charlton Ath	34	0		
2002–03	Charlton Ath	32	0		
2003–04	Charlton Ath	24	0		
2004–05	Charlton Ath	36	2	**126**	**2**

Scholars
Burt, Paul; Carvill, Michael Desmond; Clifford, Jack Joseph; Cottrell, Adam Stuart; John, Alistair Alexandra; Kamara, Sheku; Mohamoud, Abdigani; Phillips, Daniel; Ricketts, Mark James; Sodje, Onome; Tanska, Jani; Weston, Myles Arthur; Wilson, Lawrie

CHELSEA (20)

AMBROSIO, Marco (G) 136 0
H: 6 1 W: 13 04 b.Brescia 30-5-73

1991–92	Lumezzane	2	0	**2**	**0**
1992–93	Atalanta	0	0		
1993–94	Pisa	9	0	**9**	**0**
1993–94	Atalanta	0	0		
1994–95	Prato	15	0		
1995–96	Atalanta	0	0		
1995–96	Ravenna	10	0	**10**	**0**
1996–97	Prato	34	0	**49**	**0**
1997–98	Sampdoria	3	0		
1998–99	Sampdoria	7	0		
1999–2000	Sampdoria	0	0	**10**	**0**
1999–2000	Lucchese	13	0		
2000–01	Lucchese	33	0	**46**	**0**
2001–02	Chievo	2	0	**2**	**0**
2003–04	Chelsea	8	0		
2004–05	Chelsea	0	0	**8**	**0**

BRIDGE, Wayne (D) 200 3
H: 5 10 W: 12 13 b.Southampton 5-8-80
Source: Trainee. *Honours:* England Youth, Under-21, 20 full caps, 1 goal.

1997–98	Southampton	0	0		
1998–99	Southampton	23	0		
1999–2000	Southampton	19	1		
2000–01	Southampton	38	0		
2001–02	Southampton	38	0		
2002–03	Southampton	34	1	**152**	**2**
2003–04	Chelsea	33	1		
2004–05	Chelsea	15	0	**48**	**1**

CECH, Petr (G) 163 0
H: 6 5 W: 14 03 b.Plzen 20-5-82
Honours: Czech Republic 32 full caps.

1998–99	Viktoria Plzen	0	0		
1999–2000	Chmel	1	0		
2000–01	Chmel	26	0	**27**	**0**
2001–02	Sparta Prague	26	0	**26**	**0**
2002–03	Rennes	37	0		
2003–04	Rennes	38	0	**75**	**0**
2004–05	Chelsea	35	0	**35**	**0**

COLE, Carlton (F) 71 12
H: 6 3 W: 13 10 b.Croydon 12-10-83
Source: Scholar. *Honours:* England Youth, Under-20, Under-21.

2000–01	Chelsea	0	0		
2001–02	Chelsea	3	1		
2002–03	Chelsea	13	3		
2002–03	*Wolverhampton W*	7	1	**7**	**1**
2003–04	Chelsea	0	0		
2003–04	*Charlton Ath*	21	4	**21**	**4**
2004–05	Chelsea	0	0	**16**	**4**
2004–05	*Aston Villa*	27	3	**27**	**3**

COLE, Joe (M) 189 19
H: 5 9 W: 11 07 b.Islington 8-11-81
Source: Trainee. *Honours:* England Schools, Youth, Under-21, 23 full caps, 3 goals.

1998–99	West Ham U	8	0		
1999–2000	West Ham U	22	1		
2000–01	West Ham U	30	5		
2001–02	West Ham U	30	0		
2002–03	West Ham U	36	4	**126**	**10**
2003–04	Chelsea	35	1		
2004–05	Chelsea	28	8	**63**	**9**

CRESPO, Hernan (F) 299 151
H: 6 0 W: 12 13 b.Florida 5-7-75
Honours: Argentina 51 full caps, 26 goals.

1993–94	River Plate	25	13		
1994–95	River Plate	18	5		
1995–96	River Plate	21	5	**64**	**23**
1996–97	Parma	27	12		
1997–98	Parma	25	12		
1998–99	Parma	30	16		
1999–2000	Parma	34	22	**116**	**62**
2000–01	Lazio	32	26		
2001–02	Lazio	22	13	**54**	**39**
2002–03	Internazionale	18	7	**18**	**7**
2003–04	Chelsea	19	10	**19**	**10**
2004–05	*AC Milan*	28	10	**28**	**10**

CUDICINI, Carlo (G) 201 0
H: 6 1 W: 12 06 b.Milan 6-9-73
Honours: Italy Under-21.

1991–92	AC Milan	0	0		
1992–93	AC Milan	0	0		
1993–94	Como	6	0	**6**	**0**
1994–95	AC Milan	0	0		
1995–96	AC Milan	0	0		
1995–96	Prato	30	0	**30**	**0**
1996–97	Lazio	1	0	**1**	**0**
1997–98	Castel di Sangro	14	0		
1998–99	Castel di Sangro	32	0	**46**	**0**
1999–2000	Chelsea	1	0		
2000–01	Chelsea	24	0		
2001–02	Chelsea	28	0		
2002–03	Chelsea	36	0		
2003–04	Chelsea	26	0		
2004–05	Chelsea	3	0	**118**	**0**

DI CESARE, Valerio (D) 0 0
H: 6 0 W: 12 11 b.Rome 23-5-83

2000–01	Chelsea	0	0		
2001–02	Chelsea	0	0		
2002–03	Chelsea	0	0		
2003–04	Chelsea	0	0		
2004–05	Chelsea	0	0		

DROGBA, Didier (F) 170 59
H: 6 2 W: 13 08 b.Abidjan 11-3-78
Honours: Ivory Coast full caps.

1998–99	Le Mans	2	0		
1999–2000	Le Mans	30	6		
2000–01	Le Mans	11	0		
2001–02	Le Mans	21	5	**64**	**11**
2001–02	Guingamp	11	3		
2002–03	Guingamp	34	17	**45**	**20**
2003–04	Marseille	35	18	**35**	**18**
2004–05	Chelsea	26	10	**26**	**10**

DUFF, Damien (M) 237 38
H: 5 9 W: 12 03 b.Ballyboden 2-3-79
Source: Lourdes Celtic. *Honours:* Eire Schools, Youth, B, 54 full caps, 6 goals.

1995–96	Blackburn R	0	0		
1996–97	Blackburn R	1	0		
1997–98	Blackburn R	26	4		
1998–99	Blackburn R	28	1		
1999–2000	Blackburn R	39	5		
2000–01	Blackburn R	32	1		
2001–02	Blackburn R	32	7		
2002–03	Blackburn R	26	9	**184**	**27**
2003–04	Chelsea	23	5		
2004–05	Chelsea	30	6	**53**	**11**

FORSSELL, Mikael (F) 154 46
H: 6 0 W: 13 08 b.Steinfurt 15-3-81
Honours: Finland Youth, Under-21, 32 full caps, 12 goals.

1997	HJK Helsinki	1	0		
1998	HJK Helsinki	16	1	**17**	**1**
1998–99	Chelsea	10	1		
1999–2000	Chelsea	0	0		
1999–2000	*Crystal Palace*	13	3		

2000–01	Chelsea	0	0		
2000–01	*Crystal Palace*	39	13	**52**	**16**
2001–02	Chelsea	22	4		
2002–03	*M'gladbach*	16	7	**16**	**7**
2002–03	Chelsea	0	0		
2003–04	Chelsea	0	0		
2003–04	*Birmingham C*	32	17		
2004–05	Chelsea	1	0	**33**	**5**
2004–05	*Birmingham C*	4	0	**36**	**17**

GALLACCIO, Michele (F) **0 0**
H: 5 9 W: 11 03 b.Rome 3-3-86
Source: Lazio.

2002–03	Chelsea	0	0		
2003–04	Chelsea	0	0		
2004–05	Chelsea	0	0		

GALLAS, William (D) **228 9**
H: 6 0 W: 11 13 b.Asnieres 17-8-77
Honours: France Under-21, 30 full caps.

1996–97	Caen	18	0	**18**	**0**
1997–98	Marseille	3	0		
1998–99	Marseille	30	0		
1999–2000	Marseille	22	0		
2000–01	Marseille	30	2	**85**	**2**
2001–02	Chelsea	30	1		
2002–03	Chelsea	38	4		
2003–04	Chelsea	29	0		
2004–05	Chelsea	28	2	**125**	**7**

GEREMI (M) **179 17**
H: 5 10 W: 13 05 b.Bafoussam 20-12-78
Source: Racing Bafousam. *Honours:* Cameroon 69 full caps, 1 goal.

1997	Cerro Porteno	6	0	**6**	**0**
1997–98	Genclerbirligi	28	4		
1998–99	Genclerbirligi	29	5	**57**	**9**
1999–2000	Real Madrid	20	0		
2000–01	Real Madrid	16	0		
2001–02	Real Madrid	9	0	**45**	**0**
2002–03	Middlesbrough	33	7	**33**	**7**
2003–04	Chelsea	25	1		
2004–05	Chelsea	13	0	**38**	**1**

GRANT, Anthony (M) **1 0**
H: 5 11 W: 11 03 b.Lambeth 4-6-87
Source: Scholar.

2004–05	Chelsea	1	0	**1**	**0**

GUDJOHNSEN, Eidur (F) **251 80**
H: 6 1 W: 14 02 b.Reykjavik 15-9-78
Honours: Iceland Youth, Under-21, 36 full caps, 15 goals.

1994–95	Valur	17	7	**17**	**7**
1995–96	PSV Eindhoven	13	3		
1996–97	PSV Eindhoven	0	0	**13**	**3**
1998	KR	6	0	**6**	**0**
1998–99	Bolton W	14	5		
1999–2000	Bolton W	41	13	**55**	**18**
2000–01	Chelsea	30	10		
2001–02	Chelsea	32	14		
2002–03	Chelsea	35	10		
2003–04	Chelsea	26	6		
2004–05	Chelsea	37	12	**160**	**52**

HOLLANDS, Danny (M) **0 0**
H: 6 0 W: 11 11 b.Ashford 6-11-85
Source: Trainee.

2003–04	Chelsea	0	0		
2004–05	Chelsea	0	0		

HUTH, Robert (D) **29 0**
H: 6 3 W: 14 01 b.Berlin 18-8-84
Source: From Scholar. *Honours:* Germany Youth, Under-21.

2001–02	Chelsea	1	0		
2002–03	Chelsea	2	0		
2003–04	Chelsea	16	0		
2004–05	Chelsea	10	0	**29**	**0**

JAROSIK, Jiri (M) **200 34**
H: 6 4 W: 13 03 b.Usti Nad Lebem 27-10-77
Source: Teplice, Sparta Prague. *Honours:* Czech Republic 22 full caps.

1997–98	Slovan Liberec	18	0		
1998–99	Slovan Liberec	21	2	**39**	**2**
1999–2000	Sparta Prague	21	3		
2000–01	Sparta Prague	28	8		
2001–02	Sparta Prague	27	6		
2002–03	Sparta Prague	15	3	**91**	**20**
2003	CSKA Moscow	27	7		
2004	CSKA Moscow	29	5	**56**	**12**
2004–05	Chelsea	14	0	**14**	**0**

JOHNSON, Glen (D) **59 3**
H: 6 0 W: 12 13 b.Greenwich 23-8-84
Source: Scholar. *Honours:* England Youth, Under-20, Under-21, 4 full caps.

2001–02	West Ham U	0	0		
2002–03	West Ham U	15	0	**15**	**0**
2002–03	*Millwall*	8	0	**8**	**0**
2003–04	Chelsea	19	3		
2004–05	Chelsea	17	0	**36**	**3**

KEENAN, Joe (M) **2 0**
H: 5 8 W: 10 03 b.Southampton 14-10-82
Source: Trainee. *Honours:* England Youth, Under-20.

1999–2000	Chelsea	0	0		
2000–01	Chelsea	0	0		
2001–02	Chelsea	1	0		
2002–03	Chelsea	1	0		
2003–04	Chelsea	0	0		
2004–05	Chelsea	0	0	**2**	**0**

KEZMAN, Mateja (F) **241 161**
H: 5 11 W: 11 09 b.Zemun 12-4-79
Source: Zemun, Radnicki Pirot.
Honours: Serbia & Montenegro 37 full caps, 12 goals.

1997–98	Loznica	17	9	**17**	**9**
1997–98	Sartid	17	9	**17**	**9**
1998–99	Partizan Belgrade	22	6		
1999–2000	Partizan Belgrade	38	28	**60**	**34**
2000–01	PSV Eindhoven	33	24		
2001–02	PSV Eindhoven	27	15		
2002–03	PSV Eindhoven	33	35		
2003–04	PSV Eindhoven	29	31	**122**	**105**
2004–05	Chelsea	25	4	**25**	**4**

KNEISSL, Sebastian (F) **11 1**
H: 6 0 W: 13 03 b.Lindelfels 13-1-83

2000–01	Chelsea	0	0		
2001–02	Chelsea	0	0		
2002–03	Chelsea	0	0		
2003–04	Chelsea	0	0		
2003–04	*Dundee*	11	1	**11**	**1**
2004–05	Chelsea	0	0		

LAMPARD, Frank (M) **308 58**
H: 6 0 W: 14 01 b.Romford 20-6-78
Source: Trainee. *Honours:* England Youth, Under-21, B, 32 full caps, 8 goals.

1994–95	West Ham U	0	0		
1995–96	West Ham U	2	0		
1995–96	*Swansea C*	9	1	**9**	**1**
1996–97	West Ham U	13	0		
1997–98	West Ham U	31	4		
1998–99	West Ham U	38	5		
1999–2000	West Ham U	34	7		
2000–01	West Ham U	30	7	**148**	**23**
2001–02	Chelsea	37	5		
2002–03	Chelsea	38	6		
2003–04	Chelsea	38	10		
2004–05	Chelsea	38	13	**151**	**34**

MA KALAMBAY, Yves (G) **0 0**
H: 6 5 W: 15 00 b.Brussels 31-1-86

2003–04	Chelsea	0	0		
2004–05	Chelsea	0	0		

MAKELELE, Claude (M) **432 17**
H: 5 7 W: 10 08 b.Kinshasa 18-2-73
Source: Brest. *Honours:* France Under-21, B, 35 full caps.

1992–93	Nantes	34	1		
1993–94	Nantes	30	0		
1994–95	Nantes	36	3		
1995–96	Nantes	33	0		
1996–97	Nantes	36	5	**169**	**9**
1997–98	Marseille	33	4	**33**	**4**
1998–99	Celta Vigo	36	2		
1999–2000	Celta Vigo	34	1	**70**	**3**
2000–01	Real Madrid	33	0		
2001–02	Real Madrid	32	0		
2002–03	Real Madrid	29	0	**94**	**0**
2003–04	Chelsea	30	0		
2004–05	Chelsea	36	1	**66**	**1**

McKINLAY, Kevin (M) **0 0**
H: 5 11 W: 11 01 b.Stirling 28-2-86
Source: Trainee.

2003–04	Chelsea	0	0		
2004–05	Chelsea	0	0		

MORAIS, Filipe (M) **0 0**
H: 5 9 W: 11 07 b.Lisbon 21-11-85
Source: Trainee.

2003–04	Chelsea	0	0		
2004–05	Chelsea	0	0		

MUTU, Adrian (F) **199 73**
H: 5 11 W: 11 13 b.Calinesti 8-1-79
Honours: Romania Youth, Under-21, 39 full caps, 13 goals.

1996–97	Arges	5	0		
1997–98	Arges	21	4		
1998–99	Arges	15	7	**41**	**11**
1998–99	Dinamo Bucharest	15	4		
1999–2000	Dinamo Bucharest	18	18	**33**	**22**
1999–2000	Internazionale	10	0	**10**	**0**
2000–01	Verona	25	4		
2001–02	Verona	32	12	**57**	**16**
2002–03	Parma	31	18	**31**	**18**
2003–04	Chelsea	25	6		
2004–05	Chelsea	2	0	**27**	**6**

NUNO MORAIS (D) **2 0**
H: 6 0 W: 12 05 b.Penafiel 29-1-84
Source: Penafiel.
Honours: Portugal Under-21.

2004–05	Chelsea	2	0	**2**	**0**

OLIVEIRA, Filipe (M) **10 0**
H: 5 11 W: 11 05 b.Braga 27-5-84
Source: From Porto. *Honours:* Portugal Youth, Under 21.

2001–02	Chelsea	0	0		
2002–03	Chelsea	3	0		
2003–04	Chelsea	1	0		
2004–05	Chelsea	1	0	**5**	**0**
2004–05	*Preston NE*	5	0	**5**	**0**

PARKER, Scott (M) **149 11**
H: 5 9 W: 11 10 b.Lambeth 13-10-80
Source: Trainee. *Honours:* England Schools, Youth, Under-21, 2 full caps.

1997–98	Charlton Ath	3	0		
1998–99	Charlton Ath	4	0		
1999–2000	Charlton Ath	15	1		
2000–01	Charlton Ath	20	1		
2000–01	*Norwich C*	6	1	**6**	**1**
2001–02	Charlton Ath	38	1		
2002–03	Charlton Ath	28	4		
2003–04	Charlton Ath	20	2	**128**	**9**
2003–04	Chelsea	11	1		
2004–05	Chelsea	4	0	**15**	**1**

PAULO FERREIRA (D) **194 4**
H: 6 0 W: 11 13 b.Cascais 18-1-79
Honours: Portugal 22 full caps.

1997–98	Estoril	1	0		
1998–99	Estoril	16	0		
1999–2000	Estoril	18	2	**35**	**2**
2000–01	Vitoria Setubal	34	2		
2001–02	Vitoria Setubal	34	0	**68**	**2**
2002–03	Porto	30	0		
2003–04	Porto	32	0	**62**	**0**
2004–05	Chelsea	29	0	**29**	**0**

PETTIGREW, Adrian (D) **0 0**
b.Hackney 12-11-86
Source: Scholar.

2004–05	Chelsea	0	0		

PIDGELEY, Lenny (G) **28 0**
H: 6 4 W: 14 07 b.Isleworth 7-2-84
Source: From Scholar. *Honours:* England Under-20.

2003–04	Chelsea	0	0		
2003–04	*Watford*	27	0	**27**	**0**
2004–05	Chelsea	1	0	**1**	**0**

RICARDO CARVALHO (D) **173 8**
H: 6 0 W: 12 06 b.Amarante 18-5-78
Honours: Portugal 16 full caps.

1996–97	Leca	0	0		
1997–98	Leca	22	1	**22**	**1**
1998–99	Porto	1	0		
1999–2000	Vitoria Setubal	25	2	**25**	**2**
2000–01	Alverca	29	1	**29**	**1**
2001–02	Porto	25	0		
2002–03	Porto	17	1		
2003–04	Porto	29	2	**72**	**3**
2004–05	Chelsea	25	1	**25**	**1**

ROBBEN, Arjen (M) **125 32**
H: 5 11 W: 12 08 b.Groningen 23-1-84
Honours: Holland 14 full caps, 4 goals.

2000–01	Groningen	18	2		
2001–02	Groningen	28	6	**46**	**8**
2002–03	PSV Eindhoven	33	12		
2003–04	PSV Eindhoven	28	5	**61**	**17**
2004–05	Chelsea	18	7	**18**	**7**

SMERTIN, Alexei (M) **389 27**
H: 5 9 W: 10 10 b.Barnaul 1-5-75
Honours: Russia 49 full caps.

1992	Dynamo Barnaul	18	2		
1993	Dynamo Barnaul	24	0	**42**	**2**
1994	Zarya	49	2		
1995	Zarya	37	7		
1996	Zarya	34	4		
1997	Zarya	13	0	**133**	**13**
1997	Uralan	23	0		
1998	Uralan	26	3	**49**	**3**
1999	Lokomotiv Moscow	29	6		
2000	Lokomotiv Moscow	10	1	**39**	**7**
2000–01	Bordeaux	23	0		
2001–02	Bordeaux	28	0		
2002–03	Bordeaux	33	2	**84**	**2**
2003–04	Chelsea	0	0		
2003–04	*Portsmouth*	26	0	**26**	**0**
2004–05	Chelsea	16	0	**16**	**0**

SMITH, Dean (D) **0 0**
H: 5 10 W: 10 05 b.Islington 13-8-86
Source: Trainee.

2003–04	Chelsea	0	0		
2004–05	Chelsea	0	0		

SMITH, Jimmy (M) **0 0**
b.Newham 7-1-87
Source: From Scholar. *Honours:* England Youth.

2004–05	Chelsea	0	0		

TERRY, John (D) **156 10**
H: 6 1 W: 13 08 b.Barking 7-12-80
Source: Trainee. *Honours:* England Under-21, 16 full caps.

1997–98	Chelsea	0	0		
1998–99	Chelsea	2	0		
1999–2000	Chelsea	4	0		
1999–2000	*Nottingham F*	6	0	**6**	**0**
2000–01	Chelsea	22	1		
2001–02	Chelsea	33	1		
2002–03	Chelsea	20	3		
2003–04	Chelsea	33	2		
2004–05	Chelsea	36	3	**150**	**10**

TIAGO (M) **184 26**
H: 6 0 W: 11 07 b.Viana do Costelo 2-5-81
Honours: Portugal 15 full caps.

1999–2000	Braga B	12	0		
1999–2000	Braga	18	1		
2000–01	Braga B	1	0	**13**	**0**
2000–01	Braga	27	0		
2001–02	Braga	17	2	**62**	**3**
2001–02	Benfica	15	1		
2002–03	Benfica	31	13		
2003–04	Benfica	29	5	**75**	**19**
2004–05	Chelsea	34	4	**34**	**4**

TILLEN, Joe (M) **0 0**
b.Reading 15-12-86
Source: Scholar.

2004–05	Chelsea	0	0		

TILLEN, Sam (D) **0 0**
H: 5 10 W: 11 09 b.Reading 16-4-85
Source: From Trainee. *Honours:* England Youth.

2002–03	Chelsea	0	0		
2003–04	Chelsea	0	0		
2004–05	Chelsea	0	0		

VERON, Juan Sebastian (F) **299 41**
H: 5 11 W: 12 04 b.La Plata 9-3-75
Honours: Argentina 58 full caps, 9 goals.

1993–94	Estudiantes	7	0		
1994–95	Estudiantes	38	5		
1995–96	Estudiantes	15	2	**60**	**7**
1995–96	Boca Juniors	17	4	**17**	**4**
1996–97	Sampdoria	32	5		
1997–98	Sampdoria	29	2	**61**	**7**
1998–99	Parma	26	1	**26**	**1**
1999–2000	Lazio	31	8		
2000–01	Lazio	22	3	**53**	**11**
2001–02	Manchester U	26	5		
2002–03	Manchester U	25	2	**51**	**7**
2003–04	Chelsea	7	1	**7**	**1**
2004–05	*Internazionale*	24	3	**24**	**3**

WATT, Steven (D) **1 0**
H: 6 3 W: 13 12 b.Aberdeen 1-5-85
Source: Trainee. *Honours:* Scotland Under-21, B.

2002–03	Chelsea	0	0		
2003–04	Chelsea	0	0		
2004–05	Chelsea	1	0	**1**	**0**

WOODARDS, Danny (M) **0 0**
H: 5 11 W: 11 01 b.Forest Gate 7-10-83
Source: Trainee.

2003–04	Chelsea	0	0		
2004–05	Chelsea	0	0		

YOUNGHUSBAND, Phil (F) **0 0**
b.Ashford 4-8-87
Source: Scholar.

2004–05	Chelsea	0	0		

Scholars
Furman, Dean; Hamann, Nick; Hudell, Ben John Clement; Mancienne, Michael Ian; Russell, James Peter; Simmonds, James-Robert; Watkins, Jack; Younghusband, James Joseph

CHELTENHAM T (21)

BIRD, David (M) **72 0**
H: 5 9 W: 12 00 b.Gloucester 26-12-84
Source: Cinderford T.

2001–02	Cheltenham T	0	0		
2002–03	Cheltenham T	14	0		
2003–04	Cheltenham T	24	0		
2004–05	Cheltenham T	34	0	**72**	**0**

BROUGH, John (D) **231 10**
H: 6 0 W: 12 10 b.Ilkeston 8-1-73

1991–92	Notts Co	0	0		
1992–93	Shrewsbury T	14	1		
1993–94	Shrewsbury T	2	0	**16**	**1**
From Telford U.					
1994–95	Hereford U	18	1		
1995–96	Hereford U	22	1		
1996–97	Hereford U	39	1	**79**	**3**
1999–2000	Cheltenham T	37	2		
2000–01	Cheltenham T	10	0		
2001–02	Cheltenham T	21	1		
2002–03	Cheltenham T	29	1		
2003–04	Cheltenham T	26	2		
2004–05	Cheltenham T	13	0	**136**	**6**

BROWN, Scott (G) **0 0**
H: 6 2 W: 13 01 b.Wolverhampton 26-4-85
Source: Wolverhampton W Trainee. From Welshpool T

2003–04	Bristol C	0	0		
2004–05	Cheltenham T	0	0		

CAINES, Gavin (D) **29 2**
H: 6 1 W: 12 00 b.Birmingham 20-9-83
Source: Scholar.

2003–04	Walsall	0	0		
2004–05	Cheltenham T	29	2	**29**	**2**

CONNOLLY, Adam (M) **4 0**
H: 5 9 W: 12 04 b.Manchester 10-4-86
Source: Scholar.

2004–05	Cheltenham T	4	0	**4**	**0**

CORBETT, Luke (F) **1 0**
H: 6 0 W: 11 06 b.Worcester 10-8-84
Source: Juniors.

2002–03	Cheltenham T	0	0		
2003–04	Cheltenham T	1	0		
2004–05	Cheltenham T	0	0	**1**	**0**

DEVANEY, Martin (F) **203 38**
H: 5 11 W: 12 00 b.Cheltenham 1-6-80
Source: Trainee.

1997–98	Coventry C	0	0		
1998–99	Coventry C	0	0		
1999–2000	Cheltenham T	26	6		
2000–01	Cheltenham T	34	10		
2001–02	Cheltenham T	25	1		
2002–03	Cheltenham T	40	6		
2003–04	Cheltenham T	40	5		
2004–05	Cheltenham T	38	10	**203**	**38**

DUFF, Shane (D) **78 2**
H: 6 1 W: 12 10 b.Wroughton 2-4-82
Source: Juniors. *Honours:* Northern Ireland Under-21.

2000–01	Cheltenham T	0	0		
2001–02	Cheltenham T	0	0		
2002–03	Cheltenham T	18	0		
2003–04	Cheltenham T	15	1		
2004–05	Cheltenham T	45	1	**78**	**2**

FINNIGAN, John (M) **257 10**
H: 5 8 W: 10 09 b.Wakefield 29-3-76
Source: Trainee.

1992–93	Nottingham F	0	0		
1993–94	Nottingham F	0	0		
1994–95	Nottingham F	0	0		
1995–96	Nottingham F	0	0		
1996–97	Nottingham F	0	0		
1997–98	Nottingham F	0	0		
1997–98	*Lincoln C*	6	0		
1998–99	Lincoln C	37	1		
1999–2000	Lincoln C	37	2		
2000–01	Lincoln C	40	0		
2001–02	Lincoln C	23	0	**143**	**3**
2001–02	Cheltenham T	12	2		
2002–03	Cheltenham T	37	1		
2003–04	Cheltenham T	33	1		
2004–05	Cheltenham T	32	3	**114**	**7**

FYFE, Graham (M) **35 1**
H: 5 6 W: 10 06 b.Dundee 7-12-82

2001–02	Celtic	0	0		
2002–03	Raith R	12	1	**12**	**1**
2003–04	Cheltenham T	20	0		
2004–05	Cheltenham T	3	0	**23**	**0**

GALLINAGH, Andy (D) **0 0**
H: 5 8 W: 11 08 b.Sutton Coldfield 16-3-85
Source: Stratford T.

2004–05	Cheltenham T	0	0		

GILL, Jeremy (D) **152 0**
H: 5 11 W: 12 00 b.Clevedon 8-9-70
Source: Yeovil T.

1997–98	Birmingham C	3	0		
1998–99	Birmingham C	3	0		
1999–2000	Birmingham C	11	0		
2000–01	Birmingham C	29	0		
2001–02	Birmingham C	14	0		
2002–03	Birmingham C	0	0	**60**	**0**
2002–03	Northampton T	41	0		
2003–04	Northampton T	0	0	**41**	**0**
2003–04	Cheltenham T	7	0		
2004–05	Cheltenham T	44	0	**51**	**0**

GUINAN, Stephen (F) **129 20**
H: 6 1 W: 13 02 b.Birmingham 24-12-75
Source: Trainee.

1992–93	Nottingham F	0	0		
1993–94	Nottingham F	0	0		
1994–95	Nottingham F	0	0		
1995–96	Nottingham F	2	0		
1995–96	*Darlington*	3	1	**3**	**1**
1996–97	Nottingham F	2	0		
1996–97	*Burnley*	6	0	**6**	**0**
1997–98	Nottingham F	2	0		
1997–98	*Crewe Alex*	3	0	**3**	**0**
1998–99	Nottingham F	0	0		
1998–99	*Halifax T*	12	2	**12**	**2**
1998–99	*Plymouth Arg*	11	7		
1999–2000	Nottingham F	1	0	**7**	**0**
1999–2000	*Scunthorpe U*	3	1	**3**	**1**
1999–2000	Cambridge U	6	0	**6**	**0**
1999–2000	Plymouth Arg	8	2		
2000–01	Plymouth Arg	22	1		
2001–02	Plymouth Arg	0	0	**41**	**10**
2001–02	Shrewsbury T	5	0		
2002–03	Shrewsbury T	0	0		
2003–04	Shrewsbury T	0	0	**5**	**0**
2004–05	Cheltenham T	43	6	**43**	**6**

HIGGS, Shane (G) **110 0**
H: 6 3 W: 14 06 b.Oxford 13-5-77
Source: Trainee.

1994–95	Bristol R	0	0		
1995–96	Bristol R	0	0		
1996–97	Bristol R	2	0		
1997–98	Bristol R	8	0	**10**	**0**
From Worcester C.					
1999–2000	Cheltenham T	0	0		
2000–01	Cheltenham T	1	0		

2001–02	Cheltenham T	1	0		
2002–03	Cheltenham T	10	0		
2003–04	Cheltenham T	42	0		
2004–05	Cheltenham T	46	0	**100**	**0**

McCANN, Grant (M) **145** **21**
H: 5 10 W: 11 00 b.Belfast 14-4-80
Source: Trainee. *Honours:* Northern Ireland Youth, Under-21, 9 full caps.

1998–99	West Ham U	0	0		
1999–2000	West Ham U	0	0		
2000–01	West Ham U	1	0		
2000–01	*Notts Co*	2	0	**2**	**0**
2000–01	*Cheltenham T*	30	3		
2001–02	West Ham U	3	0		
2002–03	West Ham U	0	0	**4**	**0**
2002–03	Cheltenham T	27	6		
2003–04	Cheltenham T	43	8		
2004–05	Cheltenham T	39	4	**139**	**21**

MELLIGAN, John (M) **94** **15**
H: 5 9 W: 11 02 b.Dublin 11-2-82
Source: Trainee. *Honours:* Eire Under-21.

2000–01	Wolverhampton W	0	0		
2001–02	Wolverhampton W	0	0		
2001–02	*Bournemouth*	8	0	**8**	**0**
2002–03	Wolverhampton W	2	0		
2002–03	*Kidderminster H*	29	10		
2003–04	Wolverhampton W	0	0	**2**	**0**
2003–04	*Kidderminster H*	5	1	**34**	**11**
2003–04	*Doncaster R*	21	2	**21**	**2**
2004–05	Cheltenham T	29	2	**29**	**2**

MURPHY, Chris (M) **12** **0**
H: 5 5 W: 9 06 b.Leamington Spa 8-3-83
Source: Scholar.

2000–01	Shrewsbury T	1	0		
2001–02	Shrewsbury T	4	0		
2002–03	Shrewsbury T	3	0		
2003–04	Shrewsbury T	0	0	**8**	**0**
2004–05	Cheltenham T	4	0	**4**	**0**

ODEJAYI, Kayode (F) **68** **6**
H: 6 2 W: 12 02 b.Ibadon 21-2-82
Source: Scholarship.

1999–2000	Bristol C	3	0		
2000–01	Bristol C	3	0		
2001–02	Bristol C	0	0		
2002–03	Bristol C	0	0	**6**	**0**
2003–04	Cheltenham T	30	5		
2004–05	Cheltenham T	32	1	**62**	**6**

SPENCER, Damien (F) **126** **24**
H: 6 1 W: 14 00 b.Ascot 19-9-81
Source: Scholarship.

1999–2000	Bristol C	9	1		
2000–01	Bristol C	4	0		
2000–01	*Exeter C*	6	0	**6**	**0**
2001–02	Bristol C	0	0	**13**	**1**
2002–03	Cheltenham T	30	6		
2003–04	Cheltenham T	36	9		
2004–05	Cheltenham T	41	8	**107**	**23**

TAYLOR, Michael (D) **25** **0**
H: 6 1 W: 13 08 b.Liverpool 21-11-82
Source: Scholarship.

1999–2000	Blackburn R	0	0		
2000–01	Blackburn R	0	0		
2001–02	Blackburn R	0	0		
2002–03	Blackburn R	0	0		
2002–03	*Carlisle U*	10	0	**10**	**0**
2002–03	*Rochdale*	2	0	**2**	**0**
2003–04	Blackburn R	0	0		
2004–05	Cheltenham T	13	0	**13**	**0**

TOWNSEND, Michael (D) **0** **0**
H: 6 1 W: 13 12 b.Walsall 17-5-86
Source: Wolverhampton W scholar.

2004–05	Cheltenham T	0	0		

VICTORY, Jamie (D) **242** **20**
H: 5 10 W: 12 13 b.Hackney 14-11-75
Source: Trainee.

1994–95	West Ham U	0	0		
1995–96	Bournemouth	16	1		
1996–97	Bournemouth	0	0	**16**	**1**
1999–2000	Cheltenham T	46	4		
2000–01	Cheltenham T	3	1		
2001–02	Cheltenham T	46	7		
2002–03	Cheltenham T	45	2		
2003–04	Cheltenham T	44	2		
2004–05	Cheltenham T	42	3	**226**	**19**

VINCENT, Ashley (F) **26** **1**
H: 5 10 W: 11 08 b.Oldbury 26-5-85
Source: Wolverhampton W Scholar.

2004–05	Cheltenham T	26	1	**26**	**1**

WARD, Graham (M) **23** **0**
H: 5 8 W: 11 09 b.Dublin 25-2-83
Source: Scholar. *Honours:* Eire Under-21.

2000–01	Wolverhampton W	0	0		
2001–02	Wolverhampton W	0	0		
2002–03	Wolverhampton W	0	0		
2003–04	Kidderminster H	21	0	**21**	**0**
2004–05	Cheltenham T	2	0	**2**	**0**

WILSON, Brian (D) **63** **3**
H: 5 10 W: 11 00 b.Manchester 9-5-83
Source: Scholar.

2001–02	Stoke C	1	0		
2002–03	Stoke C	3	0		
2003–04	Stoke C	2	0	**6**	**0**
2003–04	Cheltenham T	14	0		
2004–05	Cheltenham T	43	3	**57**	**3**

CHESTER C (22)

BELLE, Cortez (F) **22** **1**
H: 6 4 W: 14 08 b.Newport 27-8-83
Source: Merthyr T.

2004–05	Chester C	22	1	**22**	**1**

BOLLAND, Phil (D) **62** **2**
H: 6 4 W: 12 13 b.Liverpool 26-8-76

2001–02	Oxford U	20	1		
2002–03	Oxford U	0	0		
2003–04	Oxford U	0	0	**20**	**1**
2004–05	Chester C	42	1	**42**	**1**

BOOTH, Robbie (M) **11** **1**
H: 5 7 W: 11 08 b.Liverpool 30-12-85

2004–05	Chester C	11	1	**11**	**1**

BRANCH, Michael (F) **192** **33**
H: 5 10 W: 12 08 b.Liverpool 18-10-78
Source: Trainee. *Honours:* England Schools, Youth, Under-21.

1995–96	Everton	3	0		
1996–97	Everton	25	3		
1997–98	Everton	6	0		
1998–99	Everton	7	0		
1998–99	*Manchester C*	4	0	**4**	**0**
1999–2000	Everton	0	0	**41**	**3**
2000–01	Wolverhampton W	38	4		
1999–2000	Wolverhampton W	27	6		
2001–02	Wolverhampton W	7	0		
2001–02	*Reading*	2	0	**2**	**0**
2002–03	Wolverhampton W	0	0	**72**	**10**
2002–03	*Hull C*	7	3	**7**	**3**
2003–04	Bradford C	33	6	**33**	**6**
2004–05	Chester C	33	11	**33**	**11**

BROWN, Wayne (G) **108** **0**
H: 6 0 W: 13 11 b.Southampton 14-1-77
Source: Trainee.

1993–94	Bristol C	1	0		
1994–95	Bristol C	0	0		
1995–96	Bristol C	0	0	**1**	**0**
From Weston-S-Mare					
1996–97	Chester C	2	0		
1997–98	Chester C	13	0		
1998–99	Chester C	23	0		
1999–2000	Chester C	46	0		
2000–01	Chester C	0	0		
2001–02	Chester C	0	0		
2004–05	Chester C	23	0	**107**	**0**

CARDEN, Paul (M) **97** **0**
H: 5 8 W: 12 03 b.Liverpool 29-3-79
Source: Trainee.

1996–97	Blackpool	1	0		
1997–98	Blackpool	0	0	**1**	**0**
1997–98	Rochdale	7	0		
1998–99	Rochdale	25	0		
1999–2000	Rochdale	13	0	**45**	**0**
1999–2000	Chester C	11	0		
From Doncaster R.					
2004–05	Chester C	40	0	**51**	**0**

COOK, Matty (D) **0** **0**
H: 6 0 W: 11 02 b.Crewe 7-9-85
Source: Scholar.

2004–05	Chester C	0	0		

DAVIES, Ben (M) **56** **2**
H: 5 7 W: 11 09 b.Birmingham 27-5-81
Source: Walsall trainee.

2000–01	Kidderminster H	3	0		
2001–02	Kidderminster H	9	0	**12**	**0**
2004–05	Chester C	44	2	**44**	**2**

DRUMMOND, Stuart (M) **45** **6**
H: 6 2 W: 13 00 b.Preston 11-12-75
Source: Morecambe.

2004–05	Chester C	45	6	**45**	**6**

EDMONDSON, Darren (D) **413** **15**
H: 6 0 W: 12 12 b.Ulverston 4-11-71
Source: Trainee.

1990–91	Carlisle U	31	0		
1991–92	Carlisle U	27	2		
1992–93	Carlisle U	34	0		
1993–94	Carlisle U	22	3		
1994–95	Carlisle U	38	2		
1995–96	Carlisle U	42	1		
1996–97	Carlisle U	20	1	**214**	**9**
1996–97	Huddersfield T	10	0		
1997–98	Huddersfield T	19	0		
1998–99	Huddersfield T	3	0		
1998–99	*Plymouth Arg*	4	0	**4**	**0**
1999–2000	Huddersfield T	5	0	**37**	**0**
1999–2000	York C	7	0		
2000–01	York C	23	0		
2001–02	York C	36	0		
2002–03	York C	38	5		
2003–04	York C	27	1	**131**	**6**
2004–05	Chester C	27	0	**27**	**0**

HARRIS, Andy (D) **240** **2**
H: 5 10 W: 12 05 b.Springs 26-2-77
Source: Trainee.

1993–94	Liverpool	0	0		
1994–95	Liverpool	0	0		
1995–96	Liverpool	0	0		
1996–97	Southend U	44	0		
1997–98	Southend U	27	0		
1998–99	Southend U	1	0	**72**	**0**
1999–2000	Leyton Orient	15	0		
2000–01	Leyton Orient	44	0		
2001–02	Leyton Orient	45	1		
2002–03	Leyton Orient	45	1	**149**	**2**
2004–05	Chester C	19	0	**19**	**0**

HESSEY, Sean (D) **95** **2**
H: 6 1 W: 12 09 b.Liverpool 19-9-78
Source: Liverpool Trainee.

1997–98	Wigan Ath	0	0		
1997–98	Leeds U	0	0		
1997–98	Huddersfield T	1	0		
1998–99	Huddersfield T	10	0	**11**	**0**
1999–2000	Kilmarnock	11	0		
2000–01	Kilmarnock	6	0		
2001–02	Kilmarnock	15	0		
2002–03	Kilmarnock	5	0		
2003–04	Kilmarnock	7	1	**44**	**1**
2003–04	Blackpool	6	0	**6**	**0**
2004–05	Chester C	34	1	**34**	**1**

HOPE, Richard (D) **262** **10**
H: 6 3 W: 13 13 b.Middlesbrough 22-6-78
Source: Trainee.

1995–96	Blackburn R	0	0		
1996–97	Blackburn R	0	0		
1996–97	Darlington	20	0		
1997–98	Darlington	35	1		
1998–99	Darlington	8	0	**63**	**1**
1998–99	Northampton T	19	0		
1999–2000	Northampton T	17	0		
2000–01	Northampton T	33	0		
2001–02	Northampton T	43	6		
2002–03	Northampton T	23	1	**135**	**7**
2003–04	York C	36	2	**36**	**2**
2004–05	Chester C	28	0	**28**	**0**

LOWE, Ryan (M) **175** **30**
H: 5 11 W: 11 03 b.Liverpool 18-9-78
Source: Burscough.

2000–01	Shrewsbury T	30	4		
2001–02	Shrewsbury T	38	7		
2002–03	Shrewsbury T	39	9		
2003–04	Shrewsbury T	30	3		
2004–05	Shrewsbury T	30	3	**167**	**26**
2004–05	Chester C	8	4	**8**	**4**

LYNCH, Gavin (F) **1** **0**
H: 5 8 W: 10 10 b.Chester 7-9-85

2004–05	Chester C	1	0	**1**	**0**

MACKENZIE, Chris (G) **114** **1**
H: 6 0 W: 13 05 b.Northampton 14-5-72
Source: Corby T.

1994–95	Hereford U	22	0		
1995–96	Hereford U	38	1		
1996–97	Hereford U	0	0	**60**	**1**
1997–98	Leyton Orient	4	0		
1998–99	Leyton Orient	26	0	**30**	**0**
From Telford U					
2004–05	Chester C	24	0	**24**	**0**

RAPLEY, Kevin (F) **201** **33**
H: 5 10 W: 12 07 b.Reading 21-9-77
Source: Trainee.

1996–97	Brentford	2	0		
1997–98	Brentford	37	9		
1998–99	Brentford	12	3	**51**	**12**
1998–99	*Southend U*	9	4	**9**	**4**
1998–99	Notts Co	16	2		
1999–2000	Notts Co	29	2		
2000–01	Notts Co	7	0	**52**	**4**
2000–01	*Exeter C*	7	0	**7**	**0**
2000–01	*Scunthorpe U*	5	0	**5**	**0**
2001–02	Colchester U	35	9		
2002–03	Colchester U	21	2	**56**	**11**
2004–05	Chester C	21	2	**21**	**2**

REGAN, Carl (D) **81** **0**
H: 6 0 W: 11 03 b.Liverpool 14-1-80
Source: Trainee. *Honours:* England Youth.

1997–98	Everton	0	0		
1998–99	Everton	0	0		
1999–2000	Everton	0	0		
2000–01	Barnsley	27	0		
2001–02	Barnsley	10	0		
2002–03	Barnsley	0	0	**37**	**0**
2002–03	Hull C	38	0		
2003–04	Hull C	0	0		
2004–05	Hull C	0	0	**38**	**0**
2004–05	Chester C	6	0	**6**	**0**

SESTANOVICH, Ashley (M) **31** **2**
H: 6 3 W: 13 00 b.London 18-9-81
Source: Hampton & Richmond B.

2002–03	Sheffield U	0	0		
2003–04	Sheffield U	2	0		
2004–05	Sheffield U	0	0	**2**	**0**
2004–05	*Grimsby T*	22	2	**22**	**2**
2004–05	Chester C	7	0	**7**	**0**

STAMP, Darryn (F) **92** **11**
H: 6 3 W: 13 10 b.Beverley 21-9-78

1997–98	Scunthorpe U	10	1		
1998–99	Scunthorpe U	25	4		
1999–2000	Scunthorpe U	10	0		
1999–2000	*Halifax T*	5	0	**5**	**0**
2000–01	Scunthorpe U	12	1	**57**	**6**
From Scarborough.					
2002–03	Northampton T	22	4		
2003–04	Northampton T	0	0	**22**	**4**
2004–05	Chester C	4	0	**4**	**0**
2004–05	*Kidderminster H*	4	1	**4**	**1**

VAUGHAN, Stephen (D) **21** **0**
H: 5 6 W: 11 01 b.Liverpool 22-1-85
Source: Scholar.

2001–02	Liverpool	0	0		
2002–03	Liverpool	0	0		
2003–04	Liverpool	0	0		
2004–05	Chester C	21	0	**21**	**0**

WALSH, Mike (M) **5** **1**
H: 5 9 W: 10 05 b.Liverpool 30-5-86

2004–05	Chester C	5	1	**5**	**1**

WATSON, Andy (M) **0** **0**
H: 5 10 W: 11 00 b.Leeds 13-11-78

2004–05	Chester C	0	0		

WHALLEY, Shaun (F) **3** **0**
H: 5 9 W: 10 07 b.Prescot 7-8-87

2004–05	Chester C	3	0	**3**	**0**

CHESTERFIELD (23)

ALLISON, Wayne (F) **675** **156**
H: 6 0 W: 15 00 b.Huddersfield 16-10-68
Source: Trainee.

1986–87	Halifax T	8	4		
1987–88	Halifax T	35	4		
1988–89	Halifax T	41	15	**84**	**23**
1989–90	Watford	7	0	**7**	**0**
1990–91	Bristol C	37	6		
1991–92	Bristol C	43	10		
1992–93	Bristol C	39	4		
1993–94	Bristol C	39	15		
1994–95	Bristol C	37	13	**195**	**48**
1995–96	Swindon T	44	17		
1996–97	Swindon T	41	11		
1997–98	Swindon T	16	3	**101**	**31**
1997–98	Huddersfield T	27	6		
1998–99	Huddersfield T	44	9		
1999–2000	Huddersfield T	3	0	**74**	**15**
1999–2000	Tranmere R	40	16		
2000–01	Tranmere R	36	6		
2001–02	Tranmere R	27	4	**103**	**26**
2002–03	Sheffield U	34	6		
2003–04	Sheffield U	39	1	**73**	**7**
2004–05	Chesterfield	38	6	**38**	**6**

ALLOTT, Mark (M) **293** **39**
H: 6 0 W: 11 10 b.Manchester 3-10-77
Source: Trainee.

1995–96	Oldham Ath	0	0		
1996–97	Oldham Ath	5	1		
1997–98	Oldham Ath	22	2		
1998–99	Oldham Ath	41	7		
1999–2000	Oldham Ath	32	10		
2000–01	Oldham Ath	39	7		
2001–02	Oldham Ath	15	4	**154**	**31**
2001–02	Chesterfield	21	4		
2002–03	Chesterfield	33	0		
2003–04	Chesterfield	40	2		
2004–05	Chesterfield	45	2	**139**	**8**

BAILEY, Alex (D) **45** **1**
H: 5 9 W: 11 03 b.Newham 21-9-83
Source: Scholar. *Honours:* England Youth.

2001–02	Arsenal	0	0		
2002–03	Arsenal	0	0		
2003–04	Arsenal	0	0		
2004–05	Chesterfield	45	1	**45**	**1**

BLATHERWICK, Steve (D) **248** **9**
H: 6 2 W: 14 06 b.Nottingham 20-9-73
Source: Notts Co.

1992–93	Nottingham F	0	0		
1993–94	Nottingham F	3	0		
1993–94	*Wycombe W*	2	0	**2**	**0**
1994–95	Nottingham F	0	0		
1995–96	Nottingham F	0	0		
1995–96	*Hereford U*	10	1	**10**	**1**
1996–97	Nottingham F	7	0	**10**	**0**
1996–97	*Reading*	7	0	**7**	**0**
1997–98	Burnley	21	0		
1998–99	Burnley	3	0	**24**	**0**
1998–99	Chesterfield	14	1		
1999–2000	Chesterfield	36	0		
2000–01	Chesterfield	38	1		
2001–02	Chesterfield	5	0		
2002–03	Chesterfield	31	0		
2003–04	Chesterfield	36	2		
2004–05	Chesterfield	35	4	**195**	**8**

DAVIES, Gareth (M) **81** **2**
H: 6 0 W: 12 00 b.Chesterfield 4-2-83
Source: Trainee.

2001–02	Chesterfield	0	0		
2002–03	Chesterfield	34	1		
2003–04	Chesterfield	28	0		
2004–05	Chesterfield	19	1	**81**	**2**

DAWSON, Kevin (D) **67** **1**
H: 5 11 W: 13 10 b.Northallerton 18-6-81
Source: Trainee.

1998–99	Nottingham F	0	0		
1999–2000	Nottingham F	7	0		
2000–01	Nottingham F	1	0		
2000–01	*Barnet*	5	0	**5**	**0**
2001–02	Nottingham F	3	0	**11**	**0**
2002–03	Chesterfield	26	1		
2003–04	Chesterfield	24	0		
2004–05	Chesterfield	1	0	**51**	**1**

DE BOLLA, Mark (F) **36** **4**
H: 5 7 W: 12 00 b.Greenwich 1-1-83
Source: Trainee.

1999–2000	Aston Villa	0	0		
2000–01	Charlton Ath	0	0		
2001–02	Charlton Ath	0	0		
2002–03	Charlton Ath	0	0		
2003–04	Charlton Ath	0	0		
2003–04	Chesterfield	8	1		
2004–05	Chesterfield	28	3	**36**	**4**

DOWNES, Aaron (D) **9** **2**
H: 6 3 W: 13 00 b.Mudgee 15-5-85
Honours: Australia Youth, Under-20.

2004–05	Chesterfield	9	2	**9**	**2**

EVATT, Ian (D) **129** **9**
H: 6 3 W: 14 00 b.Coventry 19-11-81
Source: Trainee.

1998–99	Derby Co	0	0		
1999–2000	Derby Co	0	0		
2000–01	Derby Co	1	0		
2001–02	*Northampton T*	11	0	**11**	**0**
2001–02	Derby Co	3	0		
2002–03	Derby Co	30	0	**34**	**0**
2003–04	Chesterfield	43	5		
2004–05	Chesterfield	41	4	**84**	**9**

FOLAN, Caleb (F) **59** **7**
H: 6 2 W: 14 00 b.Leeds 26-10-82
Source: Trainee.

1999–2000	Leeds U	0	0		
2000–01	Leeds U	0	0		
2001–02	Leeds U	0	0		
2001–02	*Rushden & D*	6	0	**6**	**0**
2001–02	*Hull C*	1	0	**1**	**0**
2002–03	Leeds U	0	0		
2002–03	Chesterfield	13	1		
2003–04	Chesterfield	7	0		
2004–05	Chesterfield	32	6	**52**	**7**

FOX, Michael (M) **1** **0**
H: 5 11 W: 11 00 b.Mansfield 7-9-85
Source: Scholar.

2004–05	Chesterfield	1	0	**1**	**0**

HUDSON, Mark (M) **113** **10**
H: 5 11 W: 12 00 b.Bishop Auckland 24-10-80
Source: Trainee.

1999–2000	Middlesbrough	0	0		
2000–01	Middlesbrough	3	0		
2001–02	Middlesbrough	2	0		
2002–03	Middlesbrough	0	0	**5**	**0**
2002–03	*Carlisle U*	15	1	**15**	**1**
2002–03	Chesterfield	24	3		
2003–04	Chesterfield	35	2		
2004–05	Chesterfield	34	4	**93**	**9**

McMASTER, Jamie (M) **41** **3**
H: 5 11 W: 12 00 b.Sydney 29-11-82
Source: NSW Academy. *Honours:* England Youth, Under-20.

1999–2000	Leeds U	0	0		
2000–01	Leeds U	0	0		
2001–02	Leeds U	0	0		
2002–03	Leeds U	4	0		
2002–03	*Coventry C*	2	0	**2**	**0**
2003–04	Leeds U	7	0		
2003–04	*Chesterfield*	6	2		
2004–05	Leeds U	7	0	**18**	**0**
2004–05	*Swindon T*	4	1	**4**	**1**
2004–05	*Peterborough U*	3	0	**3**	**0**
2004–05	Chesterfield	8	0	**14**	**2**

MUGGLETON, Carl (G) **391** **0**
H: 6 2 W: 14 12 b.Leicester 13-9-68
Source: Apprentice. *Honours:* England Under-21.

1986–87	Leicester C	0	0		
1987–88	Leicester C	0	0		
1987–88	*Chesterfield*	17	0		
1987–88	*Blackpool*	2	0	**2**	**0**
1988–89	Leicester C	3	0		
1988–89	*Hartlepool U*	8	0	**8**	**0**
1989–90	Leicester C	0	0		
1989–90	*Stockport Co*	4	0	**4**	**0**
1990–91	Leicester C	22	0		
1990–91	*Liverpool*	0	0		
1991–92	Leicester C	4	0		
1992–93	Leicester C	17	0		
1993–94	Leicester C	0	0	**46**	**0**

1993–94 *Stoke C* 6 0
1993–94 *Sheffield U* 0 0
1993–94 Celtic 12 0 **12 0**
1994–95 Stoke C 24 0
1995–96 Stoke C 6 0
1995–96 *Rotherham U* 6 0 **6 0**
1995–96 *Sheffield U* 1 0 **1 0**
1996–97 Stoke C 33 0
1997–98 Stoke C 34 0
1998–99 Stoke C 40 0
1999–2000 Stoke C 0 0
1999–2000 *Mansfield T* 9 0 **9 0**
1999–2000 *Chesterfield* 5 0
2000–01 Stoke C 12 0 **155 0**
2000–01 *Cardiff C* 6 0 **6 0**
2001–02 Cheltenham T 7 0 **7 0**
2001–02 *Bradford C* 4 0 **4 0**
2002–03 Chesterfield 26 0
2003–04 Chesterfield 46 0
2004–05 Chesterfield 37 0 **131 0**

N'TOYA, Tcham (F) 44 8
H: 5 11 W: 12 11 b.Kinshasa 3-11-83
Source: Troyes.
2003–04 Chesterfield 6 0
2004–05 Chesterfield 38 8 **44 8**

NICHOLSON, Shane (D) 482 26
H: 5 11 W: 12 06 b.Newark 3-6-70
Source: Trainee.
1986–87 Lincoln C 7 0
1987–88 Lincoln C 0 0
1988–89 Lincoln C 34 1
1989–90 Lincoln C 23 0
1990–91 Lincoln C 40 4
1991–92 Lincoln C 29 1 **133 6**
1991–92 Derby Co 0 0
1992–93 Derby Co 17 0
1993–94 Derby Co 22 1
1994–95 Derby Co 15 0
1995–96 Derby Co 20 0 **74 1**
1995–96 WBA 18 0
1996–97 WBA 18 0
1997–98 WBA 16 0 **52 0**
1998–99 Chesterfield 24 0
1999–2000 Stockport Co 42 1
2000–01 Stockport Co 35 2 **77 3**
2001–02 Sheffield U 25 3 **25 3**
2002–03 Tranmere R 38 4
2003–04 Tranmere R 16 2 **54 6**
2004–05 Chesterfield 43 7 **67 7**

NIVEN, Derek (M) 61 2
H: 6 0 W: 12 02 b.Falkirk 12-12-83
Source: Stenhousemuir.
2000–01 Raith R 1 0 **1 0**
2001–02 Bolton W 0 0
2002–03 Bolton W 0 0
2003–04 Bolton W 0 0
2003–04 Chesterfield 22 1
2004–05 Chesterfield 38 1 **60 2**

O'HARE, Alan (D) 102 1
H: 6 2 W: 12 08 b.Drogheda 31-7-82
Source: Scholar.
2001–02 Bolton W 0 0
2001–02 *Chesterfield* 19 0
2002–03 Bolton W 0 0
2002–03 Chesterfield 22 0
2003–04 Chesterfield 40 1
2004–05 Chesterfield 21 0 **102 1**

RICHMOND, Andy (G) 8 0
H: 6 3 W: 14 05 b.Nottingham 9-1-83
Source: Scholar.
2002–03 Chesterfield 7 0
2003–04 Chesterfield 0 0
2004–05 Chesterfield 1 0 **8 0**

SMITH, Adam (M) 19 0
H: 5 11 W: 12 00 b.Huddersfield 20-2-85
Source: Scholar.
2003–04 Chesterfield 3 0
2004–05 Chesterfield 16 0 **19 0**

THOMPSON, Glyn (G) 37 0
H: 6 2 W: 13 01 b.Telford 24-2-81
Source: Trainee.
1998–99 Shrewsbury T 1 0
1999–2000 Shrewsbury T 0 0
1999–2000 Fulham 0 0
1999–2000 *Mansfield T* 16 0 **16 0**
2000–01 Fulham 0 0
2000–01 *Shrewsbury T* 0 0 **1 0**
2001–02 Fulham 0 0
2002–03 Fulham 0 0
2002–03 Northampton T 11 0
2003–04 Northampton T 8 0 **19 0**
2004–05 Walsall 0 0
2004–05 Chesterfield 1 0 **1 0**

WARNE, Stephen (M) 3 0
H: 5 10 W: 12 00 b.Sutton-in-Ashfield 27-2-84
Source: Scholar.
2002–03 Chesterfield 3 0
2003–04 Chesterfield 0 0
2004–05 Chesterfield 0 0 **3 0**

COLCHESTER U (24)

BALDWIN, Pat (D) 61 0
H: 6 3 W: 12 07 b.City of London 12-11-82
Source: Chelsea Academy.
2002–03 Colchester U 19 0
2003–04 Colchester U 4 0
2004–05 Colchester U 38 0 **61 0**

BOWDITCH, Ben (M) 5 0
H: 5 10 W: 12 00 b.Bishops Stortford 19-2-84
Source: Scholar. *Honours:* England Youth, Under-20.
2000–01 Tottenham H 0 0
2001–02 Tottenham H 0 0
2002–03 Tottenham H 0 0
2003–04 Tottenham H 0 0
2004–05 Colchester U 5 0 **5 0**

BOWRY, Bobby (M) 296 8
H: 5 9 W: 10 08 b.Hampstead 19-5-71
Honours: St. Kitts & Nevis full caps.
1990–91 QPR 0 0
From Carshalton Ath
1991–92 Crystal Palace 0 0
1992–93 Crystal Palace 11 1
1993–94 Crystal Palace 21 0
1994–95 Crystal Palace 18 0 **50 1**
1995–96 Millwall 38 2
1996–97 Millwall 28 1
1997–98 Millwall 43 2
1998–99 Millwall 25 0
1999–2000 Millwall 5 0
2000–01 Millwall 1 0 **140 5**
2001–02 Colchester U 36 1
2002–03 Colchester U 35 1
2003–04 Colchester U 24 0
2004–05 Colchester U 11 0 **106 2**

BROWN, Wayne (D) 157 7
H: 6 0 W: 12 06 b.Barking 20-8-77
Source: Trainee.
1995–96 Ipswich T 0 0
1996–97 Ipswich T 0 0
1997–98 Ipswich T 1 0
1997–98 *Colchester U* 2 0
1998–99 Ipswich T 1 0
1999–2000 Ipswich T 25 0
2000–01 Ipswich T 4 0
2000–01 *QPR* 2 0 **2 0**
2001–02 Ipswich T 0 0
2001–02 *Wimbledon* 17 1 **17 1**
2001–02 *Watford* 11 3
2002–03 Ipswich T 9 0 **40 0**
2002–03 Watford 13 1
2003–04 Watford 12 0 **36 4**
2003–04 *Gillingham* 4 1 **4 1**
2003–04 *Colchester U* 16 0
2004–05 Colchester U 40 1 **58 1**

CADE, Jamie (F) 34 2
H: 5 8 W: 10 10 b.Durham 15-1-84
Source: Scholar. *Honours:* England Youth.
2001–02 Middlesbrough 0 0
2002–03 Middlesbrough 0 0
2003–04 Middlesbrough 0 0
2003–04 *Chesterfield* 10 2 **10 2**
2003–04 Colchester U 15 0
2004–05 Colchester U 9 0 **24 0**

CHILVERS, Liam (D) 95 2
H: 6 2 W: 12 03 b.Chelmsford 6-11-81
Source: Scholar.
2000–01 Arsenal 0 0
2000–01 *Northampton T* 7 0 **7 0**
2001–02 Arsenal 0 0
2001–02 *Notts Co* 9 1 **9 1**
2002–03 Arsenal 0 0
2002–03 *Colchester U* 6 0
2003–04 Arsenal 0 0
2003–04 *Colchester U* 32 0
2004–05 Colchester U 41 1 **79 1**

CROUCH, Ross (D) 0 0
H: 6 0 W: 12 02 b.Colchester 26-3-85
Source: Scholar.
2004–05 Colchester U 0 0

DANNS, Neil (M) 56 14
H: 5 8 W: 10 12 b.Liverpool 23-11-82
Source: Scholar.
2000–01 Blackburn R 0 0
2001–02 Blackburn R 0 0
2002–03 Blackburn R 2 0
2003–04 Blackpool 12 2 **12 2**
2003–04 Blackburn R 1 0
2003–04 *Hartlepool U* 9 1 **9 1**
2004–05 Blackburn R 0 0 **3 0**
2004–05 Colchester U 32 11 **32 11**

DAVISON, Aidan (G) 286 0
H: 6 1 W: 13 12 b.Sedgefield 11-5-68
Source: Billingham Synthonia. *Honours:* Northern Ireland B, 3 full caps.
1987–88 Notts Co 0 0
1988–89 Notts Co 1 0
1989–90 Notts Co 0 0 **1 0**
1989–90 *Leyton Orient* 0 0
1989–90 Bury 0 0
1989–90 *Chester C* 0 0
1990–91 Bury 0 0
1990–91 *Blackpool* 0 0
1991–92 Millwall 33 0
1992–93 Millwall 1 0 **34 0**
1993–94 Bolton W 31 0
1994–95 Bolton W 4 0
1995–96 Bolton W 2 0
1996–97 Bolton W 0 0 **37 0**
1996–97 *Ipswich T* 0 0
1996–97 *Hull C* 9 0 **9 0**
1996–97 Bradford C 10 0
1997–98 Grimsby T 42 0
1998–99 Grimsby T 35 0
1999–2000 Grimsby T 0 0
1999–2000 Sheffield U 2 0 **2 0**
1999–2000 Bradford C 6 0
2000–01 Bradford C 2 0
2001–02 Bradford C 9 0
2002–03 Bradford C 34 0 **61 0**
2003–04 Grimsby T 32 0 **109 0**
2004–05 Colchester U 33 0 **33 0**

DUGUID, Karl (M) 270 37
H: 5 11 W: 11 06 b.Hitchin 21-3-78
Source: Trainee.
1995–96 Colchester U 16 1
1996–97 Colchester U 20 3
1997–98 Colchester U 21 3
1998–99 Colchester U 33 4
1999–2000 Colchester U 41 12
2000–01 Colchester U 41 5
2001–02 Colchester U 41 4
2002–03 Colchester U 27 3
2003–04 Colchester U 30 2
2004–05 Colchester U 0 0 **270 37**

ELOKOBI, George (D) 5 0
H: 6 0 W: 13 02 b.Cameroon 31-1-86
Source: Dulwich Hamlet.
2004–05 Colchester U 0 0
2004–05 *Chester C* 5 0 **5 0**

GARCIA, Richard (F) 58 8
H: 5 11 W: 12 01 b.Perth 4-9-81
Source: Trainee. *Honours:* Australia Under-23.
1998–99 West Ham U 0 0
1999–2000 West Ham U 0 0
2000–01 West Ham U 0 0
2000–01 *Leyton Orient* 18 4 **18 4**
2001–02 West Ham U 8 0
2002–03 West Ham U 0 0

2003–04 West Ham U 7 0
2004–05 West Ham U 1 0 **16 0**
2004–05 Colchester U 24 4 **24 4**

GERKEN, Dean (G) 14 0
H: 6 1 W: 12 08 b.Rochford 22-5-85
Source: Scholar.
2003–04 Colchester U 1 0
2004–05 Colchester U 13 0 **14 0**

GUY, Jamie (M) 2 0
H: 6 1 W: 13 00 b.Barking 1-8-87
Source: Scholar.
2004–05 Colchester U 2 0 **2 0**

HALFORD, Greg (D) 63 8
H: 6 4 W: 12 10 b.Chelmsford 8-12-84
Source: From Scholar. *Honours:* England Youth, Under-20.
2002–03 Colchester U 1 0
2003–04 Colchester U 18 4
2004–05 Colchester U 44 4 **63 8**

HUNT, Stephen (D) 20 1
H: 6 1 W: 13 00 b.Southampton 11-11-84
Source: Southampton Scholar.
2004–05 Colchester U 20 1 **20 1**

IZZET, Kem (M) 139 15
H: 5 7 W: 10 05 b.Mile End 29-9-80
Source: Trainee.
1998–99 Charlton Ath 0 0
1999–2000 Charlton Ath 0 0
2000–01 Charlton Ath 0 0
2000–01 Colchester U 6 1
2001–02 Colchester U 40 3
2002–03 Colchester U 45 8
2003–04 Colchester U 44 3
2004–05 Colchester U 4 0 **139 15**

JOHNSON, Gavin (M) 386 32
H: 5 11 W: 11 12 b.Stowmarket 10-10-70
Source: Trainee.
1988–89 Ipswich T 4 0
1989–90 Ipswich T 6 0
1990–91 Ipswich T 7 0
1991–92 Ipswich T 42 5
1992–93 Ipswich T 40 5
1993–94 Ipswich T 16 1
1994–95 Ipswich T 17 0 **132 11**
1995–96 Luton T 5 0 **5 0**
1995–96 Wigan Ath 27 3
1996–97 Wigan Ath 37 3
1997–98 Wigan Ath 20 2 **84 8**
1998–99 Dunfermline Ath 18 0 **18 0**
1999–2000 Colchester U 27 0
2000–01 Colchester U 37 2
2001–02 Colchester U 20 1
2002–03 Colchester U 8 0
2003–04 Colchester U 18 1
2004–05 Colchester U 37 9 **147 13**

KEITH, Joe (M) 211 23
H: 5 7 W: 10 06 b.Plaistow 1-10-78
Source: Trainee.
1997–98 West Ham U 0 0
1998–99 West Ham U 0 0
1999–2000 Colchester U 45 1
2000–01 Colchester U 27 3
2001–02 Colchester U 41 4
2002–03 Colchester U 36 9
2003–04 Colchester U 28 2
2004–05 Colchester U 31 4 **208 23**
2004–05 *Bristol C* 3 0 **3 0**

KEITH, Marino (F) 216 68
H: 5 10 W: 12 13 b.Peterhead 16-12-74
Source: Fraserburgh.
1995–96 Dundee U 4 0
1996–97 Dundee U 0 0 **4 0**
1997–98 Falkirk 32 10
1998–99 Falkirk 29 17 **61 27**
1999–2000 Livingston 9 4
2000–01 Livingston 13 3 **22 7**
2001–02 Plymouth Arg 23 9
2002–03 Plymouth Arg 37 11
2003–04 Plymouth Arg 40 9
2004–05 Plymouth Arg 17 1 **117 30**
2004–05 Colchester U 12 4 **12 4**

N'DUMBU NSUNGU, Guylain (F) 49 11
H: 6 1 W: 12 08 b.Kinshasa 26-12-82
Source: Amiens.
2003–04 Sheffield W 24 9
2004–05 Sheffield W 11 1 **35 10**
2004–05 *Preston NE* 6 0 **6 0**
2004–05 Colchester U 8 1 **8 1**

PARKINSON, Phil (M) 507 25
H: 6 0 W: 12 09 b.Chorley 1-12-67
Source: Apprentice.
1985–86 Southampton 0 0
1986–87 Southampton 0 0
1987–88 Southampton 0 0
1987–88 Bury 8 1
1988–89 Bury 39 0
1989–90 Bury 22 2
1990–91 Bury 44 2
1991–92 Bury 32 0 **145 5**
1992–93 Reading 39 4
1993–94 Reading 42 3
1994–95 Reading 31 0
1995–96 Reading 42 0
1996–97 Reading 24 1
1997–98 Reading 37 0
1998–99 Reading 42 5
1999–2000 Reading 22 1
2000–01 Reading 44 4
2001–02 Reading 33 2
2002–03 Reading 6 0 **362 20**
2003–04 Colchester U 0 0
2004–05 Colchester U 0 0

STOCKLEY, Sam (D) 337 4
H: 6 0 W: 12 08 b.Tiverton 5-9-77
Source: Trainee.
1996–97 Southampton 0 0
1996–97 Barnet 21 0
1997–98 Barnet 41 0
1998–99 Barnet 41 0
1999–2000 Barnet 34 1
2000–01 Barnet 45 1 **182 2**
2001–02 Oxford U 41 0
2002–03 Oxford U 0 0 **41 0**
2002–03 Colchester U 33 1
2003–04 Colchester U 44 0
2004–05 Colchester U 37 1 **114 2**

WATSON, Kevin (M) 305 12
H: 6 0 W: 12 06 b.Hackney 3-1-74
Source: Trainee.
1991–92 Tottenham H 0 0
1992–93 Tottenham H 5 0
1993–94 Tottenham H 0 0
1993–94 *Brentford* 3 0 **3 0**
1994–95 Tottenham H 0 0
1994–95 *Bristol C* 2 0 **2 0**
1994–95 *Barnet* 13 0 **13 0**
1995–96 Tottenham H 0 0 **5 0**
1996–97 Swindon T 27 1
1997–98 Swindon T 18 0
1998–99 Swindon T 18 0 **63 1**
1999–2000 Rotherham U 44 1
2000–01 Rotherham U 46 5
2001–02 Rotherham U 19 1 **109 7**
2001–02 Reading 12 1
2002–03 Reading 32 1
2003–04 Reading 22 0 **66 2**
2004–05 Colchester U 44 2 **44 2**

WHITE, John (M) 20 0
H: 5 10 W: 12 01 b.Maldon 26-7-86
Source: Scholar.
2004–05 Colchester U 20 0 **20 0**

WILLIAMS, Gareth (F) 54 12
H: 5 10 W: 11 13 b.Germiston 10-9-82
Source: From Scholar. *Honours:* Wales Under-21.
2002–03 Crystal Palace 5 0
2002–03 *Colchester U* 8 6
2003–04 Crystal Palace 0 0
2003–04 *Cambridge U* 4 1 **4 1**
2003–04 *Bournemouth* 1 0 **1 0**
2003–04 *Colchester U* 7 2
2004–05 Crystal Palace 0 0 **5 0**
2004–05 Colchester U 29 3 **44 11**

COVENTRY C (25)

ADEBOLA, Dele (F) 368 86
H: 6 3 W: 15 00 b.Lagos 23-6-75
Source: Trainee.
1992–93 Crewe Alex 6 0
1993–94 Crewe Alex 0 0
1994–95 Crewe Alex 30 8
1995–96 Crewe Alex 29 8
1996–97 Crewe Alex 32 16
1997–98 Crewe Alex 27 7 **124 39**
1997–98 Birmingham C 17 7
1998–99 Birmingham C 39 13
1999–2000 Birmingham C 42 5
2000–01 Birmingham C 31 6
2001–02 Birmingham C 0 0 **129 31**
2001–02 *Oldham Ath* 5 0 **5 0**
2002–03 Crystal Palace 39 5 **39 5**
2003–04 Coventry C 28 2
2003–04 *Burnley* 3 1 **3 1**
2004–05 Coventry C 25 5 **53 7**
2004–05 *Bradford C* 15 3 **15 3**

BARRETT, Graham (F) 117 12
H: 5 10 W: 11 07 b.Dublin 6-10-81
Source: Trainee. *Honours:* Eire Schools, Youth, Under-21, 6 full caps, 2 goals.
1998–99 Arsenal 0 0
1999–2000 Arsenal 2 0
2000–01 Arsenal 0 0
2000–01 *Bristol R* 1 0 **1 0**
2001–02 Arsenal 0 0
2001–02 *Crewe Alex* 3 0 **3 0**
2001–02 *Colchester U* 20 4 **20 4**
2002–03 Arsenal 0 0 **2 0**
2002–03 *Brighton & HA* 30 1 **30 1**
2003–04 Coventry C 31 2
2004–05 Coventry C 24 4 **55 6**
2004–05 *Sheffield W* 6 1 **6 1**

BARRY, Anthony (M) 0 0
H: 5 7 W: 10 00 b.Liverpool 29-5-86
Source: Everton.
2004–05 Coventry C 0 0

BATES, Tom (M) 1 0
H: 5 10 W: 12 00 b.Coventry 31-10-85
2002–03 Coventry C 1 0
2003–04 Coventry C 0 0
2004–05 Coventry C 0 0 **1 0**

BENJAMIN, Trevor (F) 256 58
H: 6 2 W: 14 08 b.Kettering 8-2-79
Source: Trainee. *Honours:* England Under-21, Jamaica 2 full caps.
1995–96 Cambridge U 5 0
1996–97 Cambridge U 7 1
1997–98 Cambridge U 25 4
1998–99 Cambridge U 42 10
1999–2000 Cambridge U 44 20 **123 35**
2000–01 Leicester C 21 1
2001–02 Leicester C 11 0
2001–02 *Crystal Palace* 6 1 **6 1**
2001–02 *Norwich C* 6 0 **6 0**
2001–02 *WBA* 3 1 **3 1**
2002–03 Leicester C 35 8
2003–04 Leicester C 4 0
2003–04 *Gillingham* 4 1 **4 1**
2003–04 *Rushden & D* 6 1 **6 1**
2003–04 *Brighton & HA* 10 5 **10 5**
2004–05 Leicester C 10 2 **81 11**
2004–05 *Northampton T* 5 2 **5 2**
2004–05 Coventry C 12 1 **12 1**

BRUSH, Richard (G) 0 0
H: 6 1 W: 12 00 b.Birmingham 26-11-84
Source: Scholar.
2002–03 Coventry C 0 0
2003–04 Coventry C 0 0
2004–05 Coventry C 0 0

COONEY, Sean (D) 1 0
H: 6 3 W: 13 00 b.Perth 31-10-83
Source: Scholar.
2002–03 Coventry C 1 0
2003–04 Coventry C 0 0
2004–05 Coventry C 0 0 **1 0**

DELOUMEAUX, Eric (M) 140 7
H: 5 10 W: 11 13 b.Montbeliard 12-5-73
1999–2000 Le Havre 28 0
2000–01 Le Havre 25 2 **53 2**
2001–02 Motherwell 23 0 **23 0**
2002–03 Aberdeen 32 2
2003–04 Aberdeen 11 2 **43 4**
2003–04 Coventry C 19 1
2004–05 Coventry C 2 0 **21 1**

DOYLE, Micky (M) 84 7
H: 5 8 W: 11 00 b.Dublin 8-7-81
Source: Celtic. *Honours:* Eire Under-21, 1 full cap.
2003–04 Coventry C 40 5
2004–05 Coventry C 44 2 **84 7**

GIDDINGS, Stuart (M) 13 0
H: 6 0 W: 11 08 b.Coventry 27-3-86
Source: Scholar. *Honours:* England Youth.
2003–04 Coventry C 1 0
2004–05 Coventry C 12 0 **13 0**

HALL, Marcus (D) 222 3
H: 6 1 W: 12 02 b.Coventry 24-3-76
Source: Trainee. *Honours:* England Under-21, B.
1994–95 Coventry C 5 0
1995–96 Coventry C 25 0
1996–97 Coventry C 13 0
1997–98 Coventry C 25 1
1998–99 Coventry C 5 0
1999–2000 Coventry C 9 0
2000–01 Coventry C 21 0
2001–02 Coventry C 29 1
2002–03 Nottingham F 1 0 **1 0**
2002–03 Stoke C 24 0
2003–04 Stoke C 35 0
2004–05 Stoke C 20 1 **79 1**
2004–05 Coventry C 10 0 **142 2**

HUGHES, Stephen (M) 136 9
H: 5 9 W: 12 12 b.Wokingham 18-9-76
Source: Trainee. *Honours:* England Schools, Youth, Under-21.
1994–95 Arsenal 1 0
1995–96 Arsenal 1 0
1996–97 Arsenal 14 1
1997–98 Arsenal 17 2
1998–99 Arsenal 14 1
1999–2000 Fulham 3 0 **3 0**
1999–2000 Arsenal 2 0 **49 4**
1999–2000 Everton 11 1
2000–01 Everton 18 0 **29 1**
2001–02 Watford 15 0
2002–03 Watford 0 0 **15 0**
2003–04 Charlton Ath 0 0
2004–05 Coventry C 40 4 **40 4**

JOHN, Stern (F) 234 89
H: 6 0 W: 12 11 b.Trinidad 30-10-76
Honours: Trinidad & Tobago 16 full caps, 8 goals.
1998 Columbus Crew 27 26
1999 Columbus Crew 28 18 **55 44**
1999–2000 Nottingham F 17 3
2000–01 Nottingham F 29 2
2001–02 Nottingham F 26 13 **72 18**
2001–02 Birmingham C 15 7
2002–03 Birmingham C 30 5
2003–04 Birmingham C 29 4
2004–05 Birmingham C 3 0 **77 16**
2004–05 Coventry C 30 11 **30 11**

JORGENSEN, Claus (M) 179 29
H: 5 11 W: 11 00 b.Holstebro 27-4-76
Source: Resen-Humlum, Struer BK, Holstebro, Aarhus, AC Horsens. *Honours:* Faroe Islands 5 full caps.
1999–2000 Bournemouth 44 6
2000–01 Bournemouth 43 8
2001–02 Bradford C 18 1
2002–03 Bradford C 32 11 **50 12**
2003–04 Coventry C 8 0
2003–04 *Bournemouth* 17 0 **104 14**
2004–05 Coventry C 17 3 **25 3**

MACKEY, Ben (M) 3 0
H: 5 8 W: 11 09 b.Leamington 27-10-86
2002–03 Coventry C 3 0
2003–04 Coventry C 0 0
2004–05 Coventry C 0 0 **3 0**

McCRINK, Paul (M) 0 0
H: 5 10 W: 11 05
2004–05 Coventry C 0 0

McSHEFFREY, Gary (F) 125 39
H: 5 8 W: 10 06 b.Coventry 13-8-82
Source: Trainee. *Honours:* England Youth, Under-20.
1998–99 Coventry C 1 0
1999–2000 Coventry C 3 0
2000–01 Coventry C 0 0
2001–02 *Stockport Co* 5 1 **5 1**
2001–02 Coventry C 8 1
2002–03 Coventry C 29 4
2003–04 Coventry C 19 11
2003–04 *Luton T* 18 9
2004–05 Coventry C 37 12 **97 28**
2004–05 *Luton T* 5 1 **23 10**

MORRELL, Andy (F) 174 55
H: 5 11 W: 11 06 b.Doncaster 28-9-74
Source: Newcastle Blue Star.
1998–99 Wrexham 7 0
1999–2000 Wrexham 13 1
2000–01 Wrexham 20 3
2001–02 Wrexham 25 2
2002–03 Wrexham 45 34 **110 40**
2003–04 Coventry C 30 9
2004–05 Coventry C 34 6 **64 15**

MUNN, Stephen (D) 0 0
H: 5 10 W: 12 00 b.Belfast 28-4-86
Source: Scholar.
2003–04 Coventry C 0 0
2004–05 Coventry C 0 0

O'DONOVAN, Roy (F) 0 0
H: 5 10 W: 11 07 b.Cork 10-8-85
Source: Scholar.
2002–03 Coventry C 0 0
2003–04 Coventry C 0 0
2004–05 Coventry C 0 0

OSBOURNE, Isaac (M) 11 0
H: 5 9 W: 11 11 b.Birmingham 22-6-86
Source: Scholar.
2002–03 Coventry C 2 0
2003–04 Coventry C 0 0
2004–05 Coventry C 9 0 **11 0**

PAGE, Robert (D) 341 3
H: 6 0 W: 13 10 b.Llwynpia 3-9-74
Source: Trainee. *Honours:* Wales Schools, Youth, Under-21, B, 38 full caps.
1992–93 Watford 0 0
1993–94 Watford 4 0
1994–95 Watford 5 0
1995–96 Watford 19 0
1996–97 Watford 36 0
1997–98 Watford 41 0
1998–99 Watford 39 0
1999–2000 Watford 36 1
2000–01 Watford 36 1
2001–02 Watford 0 0 **216 2**
2001–02 Sheffield U 43 0
2002–03 Sheffield U 34 0
2003–04 Sheffield U 30 1 **107 1**
2004–05 Cardiff C 9 0 **9 0**
2004–05 Coventry C 9 0 **9 0**

PEAD, Craig (M) 55 3
H: 5 9 W: 11 06 b.Bromsgrove 15-9-81
Source: Trainee. *Honours:* England Youth, Under-20.
1998–99 Coventry C 0 0
1999–2000 Coventry C 0 0
2000–01 Coventry C 0 0
2001–02 Coventry C 1 0
2002–03 Coventry C 24 2
2003–04 Coventry C 17 1
2004–05 Coventry C 0 0 **42 3**
2004–05 *Notts Co* 5 0 **5 0**
2004–05 *Walsall* 8 0 **8 0**

REID, Craig (F) 0 0
H: 5 10 W: 11 10 b.Coventry 17-12-85
Honours: Ipswich T Scholar.
2004–05 Coventry C 0 0

SHAW, Richard (D) 503 4
H: 5 9 W: 12 08 b.Brentford 11-9-68
Source: Apprentice.
1986–87 Crystal Palace 0 0
1987–88 Crystal Palace 3 0
1988–89 Crystal Palace 14 0
1989–90 Crystal Palace 21 0
1989–90 *Hull C* 4 0 **4 0**
1990–91 Crystal Palace 36 1
1991–92 Crystal Palace 10 0
1992–93 Crystal Palace 33 0
1993–94 Crystal Palace 34 2
1994–95 Crystal Palace 41 0
1995–96 Crystal Palace 15 0 **207 3**
1995–96 Coventry C 21 0
1996–97 Coventry C 35 0
1997–98 Coventry C 33 0
1998–99 Coventry C 37 0
1999–2000 Coventry C 29 0
2000–01 Coventry C 24 0
2001–02 Coventry C 32 0
2002–03 Coventry C 29 0
2003–04 Coventry C 19 1
2004–05 Coventry C 33 0 **292 1**

SHEARER, Scott (G) 100 0
H: 6 3 W: 14 08 b.Glasgow 15-2-81
Source: Tower Hearts. *Honours:* Scotland B.
2000–01 Albion R 3 0
2001–02 Albion R 10 0
2002–03 Albion R 36 0 **49 0**
2003–04 Coventry C 30 0
2004–05 Coventry C 8 0 **38 0**
2004–05 *Rushden & D* 13 0 **13 0**

SHERWOOD, Tim (M) 483 50
H: 6 0 W: 12 08 b.St Albans 2-2-69
Source: Trainee. *Honours:* England Under-21, B, 3 full caps.
1986–87 Watford 0 0
1987–88 Watford 13 0
1988–89 Watford 19 2 **32 2**
1989–90 Norwich C 27 3
1990–91 Norwich C 37 7
1991–92 Norwich C 7 0 **71 10**
1991–92 Blackburn R 11 0
1992–93 Blackburn R 39 3
1993–94 Blackburn R 38 2
1994–95 Blackburn R 38 6
1995–96 Blackburn R 33 3
1996–97 Blackburn R 37 3
1997–98 Blackburn R 31 5
1998–99 Blackburn R 19 3 **246 25**
1998–99 Tottenham H 14 2
1999–2000 Tottenham H 27 8
2000–01 Tottenham H 33 2
2001–02 Tottenham H 19 0
2002–03 Tottenham H 0 0 **93 12**
2002–03 Portsmouth 17 1
2003–04 Portsmouth 13 0 **30 1**
2004–05 Coventry C 11 0 **11 0**

STAUNTON, Steve (D) 474 21
H: 6 0 W: 12 12 b.Dundalk 19-1-69
Source: Dundalk. *Honours:* Eire Under-21, 102 full caps, 7 goals.
1986–87 Liverpool 0 0
1987–88 Liverpool 0 0
1987–88 *Bradford C* 8 0 **8 0**
1988–89 Liverpool 21 0
1989–90 Liverpool 20 0
1990–91 Liverpool 24 0
1991–92 Aston Villa 37 4
1992–93 Aston Villa 42 2
1993–94 Aston Villa 24 2
1994–95 Aston Villa 35 5
1995–96 Aston Villa 13 0
1996–97 Aston Villa 30 2
1997–98 Aston Villa 27 1
1998–99 Liverpool 31 0
1999–2000 Liverpool 12 0
2000–01 Liverpool 1 0 **109 0**
2000–01 *Crystal Palace* 6 1 **6 1**
2000–01 Aston Villa 14 0
2001–02 Aston Villa 33 0
2002–03 Aston Villa 26 0
2003–04 Aston Villa 0 0 **281 16**
2003–04 Coventry C 35 3
2004–05 Coventry C 35 1 **70 4**

SUFFO, Patrick (F) 114 19
H: 5 9 W: 13 05 b.Ebolowa 17-1-78
Source: Tonnerre Yaounde. *Honours:* Cameroon full caps.
1995–96 Nantes 0 0
1996–97 Barcelona 0 0
1997–98 Nantes 4 0
1998–99 Nantes 21 4
1999–2000 Nantes 5 0 **30 4**
2000–01 Sheffield U 16 1
2001–02 Sheffield U 20 4
2002–03 Sheffield U 0 0 **36 5**
2003–04 Coventry C 27 7
2004–05 Coventry C 21 3 **48 10**

THORNTON, Kevin (M) 0 0
H: 5 7 W: 11 00 b.Drogheda 9-7-86
Source: Scholar.
2003–04 Coventry C 0 0
2004–05 Coventry C 0 0

TUFFEY, Jonathan (G) 0 0
H: 6 0 W: 12 00 b.Newry 20-1-87
Source: Scholar.
2003–04 Coventry C 0 0
2004–05 Coventry C 0 0

WHING, Andrew (D) 58 2
H: 6 0 W: 12 00 b.Birmingham 20-9-84
Source: Scholar.
2002–03 Coventry C 14 0
2003–04 Coventry C 28 1
2004–05 Coventry C 16 1 **58 2**

WILLIAMS, Adrian (D) 381 20
H: 6 2 W: 13 02 b.Reading 16-8-71
Source: Trainee. *Honours:* Wales 13 full caps, 1 goal.
1988–89 Reading 8 0
1989–90 Reading 16 2
1990–91 Reading 7 0
1991–92 Reading 40 4
1992–93 Reading 31 4
1993–94 Reading 41 0
1994–95 Reading 22 1
1995–96 Reading 31 3
1996–97 Wolverhampton W 6 0
1997–98 Wolverhampton W 20 0
1998–99 Wolverhampton W 0 0
1999–2000 Wolverhampton W 1 0 **27 0**
1999–2000 *Reading* 15 1
2000–01 Reading 5 0
2001–02 Reading 35 1
2002–03 Reading 38 1
2003–04 Reading 33 1
2004–05 Reading 11 0 **333 18**
2004–05 Coventry C 21 2 **21 2**

WOOD, Neil (M) 26 2
H: 5 10 W: 13 02 b.Manchester 4-1-83
Source: Trainee. *Honours:* England Youth.
1999–2000 Manchester U 0 0
2000–01 Manchester U 0 0
2001–02 Manchester U 0 0
2002–03 Manchester U 0 0
2003–04 Manchester U 0 0
2003–04 *Peterborough U* 3 1 **3 1**
2003–04 *Burnley* 10 1 **10 1**
2004–05 Coventry C 13 0 **13 0**

CREWE ALEX (26)

AUSTIN, Ryan (D) 0 0
H: 6 2 W: 12 09 b.Stoke 15-11-84
Source: Scholar.
2004–05 Crewe Alex 0 0

BELL, Lee (M) 37 1
H: 5 11 W: 11 00 b.Crewe 26-1-83
Source: Scholar.
2000–01 Crewe Alex 0 0
2001–02 Crewe Alex 0 0
2002–03 Crewe Alex 17 1
2003–04 Crewe Alex 3 0
2004–05 Crewe Alex 17 0 **37 1**

BIGNOT, Paul (D) 5 0
H: 6 1 W: 12 03 b.Birmingham 14-2-86
Source: Scholar.
2004–05 Crewe Alex 5 0 **5 0**

COCHRANE, Justin (M) 69 0
H: 5 11 W: 11 07 b.Hackney 26-1-82
Source: Scholarship.
1999–2000 QPR 0 0
2000–01 QPR 1 0
2001–02 QPR 0 0
2002–03 QPR 0 0 **1 0**
From Hayes.
2003–04 Crewe Alex 39 0
2004–05 Crewe Alex 29 0 **68 0**

EDWARDS, Paul (F) 12 0
H: 6 0 W: 11 07 b.Derby 10-11-82
Source: Scholar.
2000–01 Crewe Alex 0 0
2001–02 Crewe Alex 0 0
2002–03 Crewe Alex 2 0
2003–04 Crewe Alex 10 0
2004–05 Crewe Alex 0 0 **12 0**

FOSTER, Stephen (D) 179 12
H: 6 0 W: 11 05 b.Warrington 10-9-80
Source: Trainee. *Honours:* England Schools.
1998–99 Crewe Alex 1 0
1999–2000 Crewe Alex 0 0
2000–01 Crewe Alex 30 0
2001–02 Crewe Alex 34 5
2002–03 Crewe Alex 35 4
2003–04 Crewe Alex 45 2
2004–05 Crewe Alex 34 1 **179 12**

HIGDON, Michael (M) 30 4
H: 6 2 W: 11 05 b.Liverpool 2-9-83
Source: School.
2000–01 Crewe Alex 0 0
2001–02 Crewe Alex 0 0
2002–03 Crewe Alex 0 0
2003–04 Crewe Alex 10 1
2004–05 Crewe Alex 20 3 **30 4**

INCE, Clayton (G) 123 0
H: 6 3 W: 13 00 b.Trinidad 13-7-72
Source: Defence Force. *Honours:* Trinidad & Tobago 34 full caps.
1999–2000 Crewe Alex 1 0
2000–01 Crewe Alex 1 0
2001–02 Crewe Alex 19 0
2002–03 Crewe Alex 43 0
2003–04 Crewe Alex 36 0
2004–05 Crewe Alex 23 0 **123 0**

JONES, Billy (D) 47 1
H: 5 11 W: 13 00 b.Shrewsbury 24-3-87
Source: Scholar. *Honours:* England Youth.
2003–04 Crewe Alex 27 1
2004–05 Crewe Alex 20 0 **47 1**

JONES, Steve (F) 127 35
H: 5 10 W: 10 05 b.Derry 25-10-76
Source: Leigh RMI. *Honours:* Northern Ireland 16 full caps, 2 goals.
2001–02 *Rochdale* 9 1 **9 1**
2001–02 Crewe Alex 6 0
2002–03 Crewe Alex 31 9
2003–04 Crewe Alex 45 15
2004–05 Crewe Alex 36 10 **118 34**

LUNT, Kenny (M) 330 31
H: 5 10 W: 10 05 b.Runcorn 20-11-79
Source: Trainee. *Honours:* England Schools, Youth.
1997–98 Crewe Alex 41 2
1998–99 Crewe Alex 18 1
1999–2000 Crewe Alex 43 3
2000–01 Crewe Alex 46 1
2001–02 Crewe Alex 45 5
2002–03 Crewe Alex 46 7
2003–04 Crewe Alex 45 7
2004–05 Crewe Alex 46 5 **330 31**

McCREADY, Chris (D) 51 0
H: 6 1 W: 12 05 b.Ellesmere Port 5-9-81
Source: Scholar.
2000–01 Crewe Alex 0 0
2001–02 Crewe Alex 1 0
2002–03 Crewe Alex 8 0
2003–04 Crewe Alex 22 0
2004–05 Crewe Alex 20 0 **51 0**

McGOWAN, Lloyd (M) 0 0
H: 6 0 W: 11 10 b.Telford 10-10-84
Source: Scholar.
2004–05 Crewe Alex 0 0

MORRIS, Alex (M) 0 0
H: 6 0 W: 11 08 b.Stoke 5-10-82
Source: Scholar.
2000–01 Crewe Alex 0 0
2001–02 Crewe Alex 0 0
2002–03 Crewe Alex 0 0
2003–04 Crewe Alex 0 0
2004–05 Crewe Alex 0 0

MOSES, Adi (D) 262 4
H: 5 11 W: 13 01 b.Doncaster 4-5-75
Source: School. *Honours:* England Under-21.
1993–94 Barnsley 0 0
1994–95 Barnsley 4 0
1995–96 Barnsley 24 1
1996–97 Barnsley 28 2
1997–98 Barnsley 35 0
1998–99 Barnsley 34 0
1999–2000 Barnsley 12 0
2000–01 Barnsley 14 0 **151 3**
2000–01 Huddersfield T 12 0
2001–02 Huddersfield T 17 0
2002–03 Huddersfield T 40 1 **69 1**
2003–04 Crewe Alex 21 0
2004–05 Crewe Alex 21 0 **42 0**

MOSS, Darren (D) 171 16
H: 5 10 W: 11 00 b.Wrexham 24-5-81
Source: Trainee. *Honours:* Wales Under-21.
1998–99 Chester C 7 0
1999–2000 Chester C 35 0
2000–01 Chester C 0 0 **42 0**
2001–02 Shrewsbury T 31 2
2002–03 Shrewsbury T 40 2
2003–04 Shrewsbury T 26 6
2004–05 Shrewsbury T 26 6 **123 16**
2004–05 Crewe Alex 6 0 **6 0**

MURDOCK, Colin (D) 230 9
H: 6 3 W: 13 05 b.Belfast 12-7-76
Source: Trainee. *Honours:* Northern Ireland Schools, Youth, B, 28 full caps, 1 goal.
1992–93 Manchester U 0 0
1993–94 Manchester U 0 0
1994–95 Manchester U 0 0
1995–96 Manchester U 0 0
1996–97 Manchester U 0 0
1997–98 Preston NE 27 1
1998–99 Preston NE 33 1
1999–2000 Preston NE 33 2
2000–01 Preston NE 37 0
2001–02 Preston NE 23 2
2002–03 Preston NE 24 0 **177 6**
2003–04 Hibernian 32 3
2004–05 Hibernian 5 0 **37 3**
2004–05 Crewe Alex 16 0 **16 0**

PLATT, Matthew (F) 1 0
H: 6 0 W: 11 03 b.Crewe 15-10-83
Source: Scholar.
2002–03 Crewe Alex 0 0
2003–04 Crewe Alex 0 0
2004–05 Crewe Alex 1 0 **1 0**

RIVERS, Mark (F) 311 60
H: 5 10 W: 11 04 b.Crewe 26-11-75
Source: Trainee.
1993–94 Crewe Alex 0 0
1994–95 Crewe Alex 0 0
1995–96 Crewe Alex 33 10
1996–97 Crewe Alex 27 6
1997–98 Crewe Alex 35 6
1998–99 Crewe Alex 43 7
1999–2000 Crewe Alex 32 7
2000–01 Crewe Alex 33 7
2001–02 Norwich C 32 2
2002–03 Norwich C 30 4
2003–04 Norwich C 12 4 **74 10**
2004–05 Crewe Alex 34 7 **237 50**

RIX, Ben (M) 70 2
H: 5 9 W: 11 05 b.Wolverhampton 11-12-82
Source: Scholar.
2000–01 Crewe Alex 0 0
2001–02 Crewe Alex 21 0
2002–03 Crewe Alex 23 0
2003–04 Crewe Alex 26 2
2004–05 Crewe Alex 0 0 **70 2**

ROBERTS, Gary (M) 4 0
H: 5 8 W: 10 05 b.Chester 4-2-87
Source: Scholar. *Honours:* England Youth.
2003–04 Crewe Alex 2 0
2004–05 Crewe Alex 2 0 **4 0**

ROBERTS, Mark (D) 8 0
H: 6 1 W: 12 00 b.Northwich 16-10-83
Source: Scholar.
2002–03 Crewe Alex 0 0
2003–04 Crewe Alex 2 0
2004–05 Crewe Alex 6 0 **8 0**

ROBINSON, James (M) 10 1
H: 5 10 W: 11 03 b.Whiston 18-9-82
Source: Scholar.
2001–02 Crewe Alex 0 0
2002–03 Crewe Alex 1 0
2003–04 Crewe Alex 9 1
2004–05 Crewe Alex 0 0 **10 1**

SORVEL, Neil (M) **345 20**
H: 6 0 W: 12 03 b.Widnes 2-3-73
Source: Trainee.

1991–92	Crewe Alex	9	0		
1992–93	Crewe Alex	0	0		
1997–98	Macclesfield T	45	3		
1998–99	Macclesfield T	41	4	**86**	**7**
1999–2000	Crewe Alex	46	6		
2000–01	Crewe Alex	46	1		
2001–02	Crewe Alex	38	0		
2002–03	Crewe Alex	43	3		
2003–04	Crewe Alex	31	0		
2004–05	Crewe Alex	46	3	**259**	**13**

TOMLINSON, Stuart (G) **2 0**
H: 6 1 W: 11 02 b.Chester 10-5-85
Source: Scholar.

2002–03	Crewe Alex	1	0		
2003–04	Crewe Alex	1	0		
2004–05	Crewe Alex	0	0	**2**	**0**

TONKIN, Anthony (D) **85 0**
H: 5 11 W: 12 02 b.Newlyn 19-1-80
Source: Yeovil T.

2002–03	Stockport Co	24	0		
2003–04	Stockport Co	0	0	**24**	**0**
2003–04	Crewe Alex	26	0		
2004–05	Crewe Alex	35	0	**61**	**0**

VARNEY, Luke (F) **34 5**
H: 5 11 W: 11 00 b.Leicester 28-9-82
Source: Quorn.

2002–03	Crewe Alex	0	0		
2003–04	Crewe Alex	8	1		
2004–05	Crewe Alex	26	4	**34**	**5**

VAUGHAN, David (M) **121 9**
H: 5 7 W: 11 00 b.Abergele 18-2-83
Source: Scholar. *Honours:* Wales Youth, Under-21, 2 full caps.

2000–01	Crewe Alex	1	0		
2001–02	Crewe Alex	13	0		
2002–03	Crewe Alex	32	3		
2003–04	Crewe Alex	31	0		
2004–05	Crewe Alex	44	6	**121**	**9**

WALKER, Richard (D) **82 5**
H: 6 2 W: 12 08 b.Bolton 17-9-80
Source: Brook House.

1999–2000	Crewe Alex	0	0		
2000–01	Crewe Alex	3	0		
2001–02	Crewe Alex	1	0		
2002–03	Crewe Alex	35	2		
2003–04	Crewe Alex	20	1		
2004–05	Crewe Alex	23	2	**82**	**5**

WHITE, Andy (F) **105 15**
H: 6 4 W: 14 03 b.Derby 6-11-81
Source: Hucknall T.

2000–01	Mansfield T	4	0		
2001–02	Mansfield T	22	4		
2002–03	Mansfield T	28	6		
2002–03	*Crewe Alex*	2	0		
2003–04	Mansfield T	14	0	**68**	**10**
2003–04	*Boston U*	6	0	**6**	**0**
2003–04	*Kidderminster H*	7	1	**7**	**1**
2004–05	Crewe Alex	22	4	**24**	**4**

WILLIAMS, Ben (G) **47 0**
H: 6 0 W: 13 01 b.Manchester 27-8-82
Source: Scholar. *Honours:* England Schools.

2001–02	Manchester U	0	0		
2002–03	Manchester U	0	0		
2002–03	*Coventry C*	0	0		
2002–03	*Chesterfield*	14	0	**14**	**0**
2003–04	Manchester U	0	0		
2003–04	*Crewe Alex*	10	0		
2004–05	Crewe Alex	23	0	**33**	**0**

WILLS, Karl (G) **0 0**
H: 6 2 W: 11 05 b.Warrington 31-8-87
Source: Juniors.

2004–05	Crewe Alex	0	0		

WILSON, Kyle (F) **0 0**
H: 5 10 W: 11 05 b.Wirrall 14-11-85
Source: From Scholar. *Honours:* England Youth.

2003–04	Crewe Alex	0	0		
2004–05	Crewe Alex	0	0		

CRYSTAL PALACE (27)

ANDREWS, Wayne (F) **132 34**
H: 5 10 W: 11 06 b.Paddington 25-11-77
Source: Trainee.

1995–96	Watford	1	0		
1996–97	Watford	25	4		
1997–98	Watford	2	0		
1998–99	Watford	0	0	**28**	**4**
1998–99	*Cambridge U*	2	0	**2**	**0**
1998–99	*Peterborough U*	10	5	**10**	**5**

From Aldershot T, Chesham U

2001–02	Oldham				
2002–03	Oldham Ath	37	11	**37**	**11**
2003–04	Colchester U	41	12		
2004–05	Colchester U	5	2	**46**	**14**
2004–05	Crystal Palace	9	0	**9**	**0**

BERRY, Tyrone (F) **0 0**
H: 5 8 W: 10 02 b.London 11-3-87
Source: Scholar.

2004–05	Crystal Palace	0	0		

BERTHELIN, Cedric (G) **35 0**
H: 6 4 W: 15 00 b.Courrieres 25-12-76

2002–03	Luton T	9	0	**9**	**0**
2002–03	Crystal Palace	9	0		
2003–04	Crystal Palace	17	0		
2004–05	Crystal Palace	0	0	**26**	**0**

BLACK, Tommy (M) **140 12**
H: 5 7 W: 11 10 b.Chigwell 26-11-79
Source: Trainee.

1998–99	Arsenal	0	0		
1999–2000	Arsenal	1	0	**1**	**0**
1999–2000	*Carlisle U*	5	1	**5**	**1**
1999–2000	*Bristol C*	4	0	**4**	**0**
2000–01	Crystal Palace	40	4		
2001–02	Crystal Palace	25	0		
2002–03	Crystal Palace	36	6		
2003–04	Crystal Palace	25	0		
2004–05	Crystal Palace	0	0	**126**	**10**
2004–05	*Sheffield U*	4	1	**4**	**1**

BORROWDALE, Gary (D) **43 0**
H: 6 0 W: 12 01 b.Sutton 16-7-85
Source: Scholar. *Honours:* England Youth, Under-20.

2002–03	Crystal Palace	13	0		
2003–04	Crystal Palace	23	0		
2004–05	Crystal Palace	7	0	**43**	**0**

BOYCE, Emmerson (D) **213 8**
H: 6 0 W: 12 03 b.Aylesbury 24-9-79
Source: Trainee.

1997–98	Luton T	0	0		
1998–99	Luton T	1	0		
1999–2000	Luton T	30	1		
2000–01	Luton T	42	3		
2001–02	Luton T	37	0		
2002–03	Luton T	34	0		
2003–04	Luton T	42	4	**186**	**8**
2004–05	Crystal Palace	27	0	**27**	**0**

BUTTERFIELD, Danny (D) **222 8**
H: 5 10 W: 11 06 b.Boston 21-11-79
Source: Trainee. *Honours:* England Youth.

1997–98	Grimsby T	7	0		
1998–99	Grimsby T	12	0		
1999–2000	Grimsby T	29	0		
2000–01	Grimsby T	30	1		
2001–02	Grimsby T	46	2	**124**	**3**
2002–03	Crystal Palace	46	1		
2003–04	Crystal Palace	45	4		
2004–05	Crystal Palace	7	0	**98**	**5**

CLARKE, Matt (G) **212 0**
H: 6 4 W: 13 08 b.Sheffield 3-11-73
Source: Trainee.

1992–93	Rotherham U	9	0		
1993–94	Rotherham U	30	0		
1994–95	Rotherham U	45	0		
1995–96	Rotherham U	40	0	**124**	**0**
1996–97	Sheffield W	1	0		
1997–98	Sheffield W	3	0		
1998–99	Sheffield W	0	0	**4**	**0**
1999–2000	Bradford C	21	0		
2000–01	Bradford C	17	0		
2000–01	*Bolton W*	8	0	**8**	**0**
2001–02	Bradford C	0	0	**38**	**0**
2001–02	*Fulham*	0	0		
2001–02	Crystal Palace	28	0		
2002–03	Crystal Palace	6	0		
2003–04	Crystal Palace	4	0		
2004–05	Crystal Palace	0	0	**38**	**0**

CRONIN, Lance (G) **1 0**
H: 6 1 W: 13 04 b.Brighton 11-9-85
Source: Scholar.

2002–03	Crystal Palace	0	0		
2003–04	Crystal Palace	0	0		
2004–05	Crystal Palace	0	0		
2004–05	*Wycombe W*	1	0	**1**	**0**

DANZE, Anthony (M) **13 0**
H: 6 0 W: 12 00 b.Perth 15-3-84
Honours: Australia Youth, Under-20, Under-23.

2002–03	Perth Glory	7	0		
2003–04	Perth Glory	4	0	**11**	**0**
2004–05	Crystal Palace	0	0		
2004–05	*Milton Keynes D*	2	0	**2**	**0**

FREEDMAN, Dougie (F) **386 140**
H: 5 9 W: 12 05 b.Glasgow 21-1-74
Source: Trainee. *Honours:* Scotland Schools, Under-21, B, 2 full caps, 1 goal.

1991–92	QPR	0	0		
1992–93	QPR	0	0		
1993–94	QPR	0	0		
1994–95	Barnet	42	24		
1995–96	Barnet	5	3	**47**	**27**
1995–96	Crystal Palace	39	20		
1996–97	Crystal Palace	44	11		
1997–98	Crystal Palace	7	0		
1997–98	Wolverhampton W	29	10	**29**	**10**
1998–99	Nottingham F	31	9		
1999–2000	Nottingham F	34	9		
2000–01	Nottingham F	5	0	**70**	**18**
2000–01	Crystal Palace	26	11		
2001–02	Crystal Palace	40	20		
2002–03	Crystal Palace	29	9		
2003–04	Crystal Palace	35	13		
2004–05	Crystal Palace	20	1	**240**	**85**

GRANVILLE, Danny (D) **309 19**
H: 6 0 W: 12 00 b.Islington 19-1-75
Source: Trainee. *Honours:* England Under-21.

1993–94	Cambridge U	11	5		
1994–95	Cambridge U	16	2		
1995–96	Cambridge U	35	0		
1996–97	Cambridge U	37	0	**99**	**7**
1996–97	Chelsea	5	0		
1997–98	Chelsea	13	0	**18**	**0**
1998–99	Leeds U	9	0		
1999–2000	Leeds U	0	0	**9**	**0**
1999–2000	Manchester C	35	2		
2000–01	Manchester C	19	0		
2000–01	*Norwich C*	6	0	**6**	**0**
2001–02	Manchester C	16	1	**70**	**3**
2001–02	Crystal Palace	16	0		
2002–03	Crystal Palace	35	3		
2003–04	Crystal Palace	21	3		
2004–05	Crystal Palace	35	3	**107**	**9**

HALL, Fitz (D) **91 7**
H: 6 3 W: 13 00 b.Leytonstone 20-12-80
Source: Barnet Trainee, Chesham U.

2001–02	Oldham Ath	4	1		
2002–03	Oldham Ath	40	4	**44**	**5**
2003–04	Southampton	11	0	**11**	**0**
2004–05	Crystal Palace	36	2	**36**	**2**

HUDSON, Mark (D) **36 1**
H: 6 1 W: 12 01 b.Guildford 30-3-82
Source: Trainee.

1998–99	Fulham	0	0		
1999–2000	Fulham	0	0		
2000–01	Fulham	0	0		
2001–02	Fulham	0	0		
2002–03	Fulham	0	0		
2003–04	Fulham	0	0		
2003–04	*Oldham Ath*	15	0	**15**	**0**
2003–04	*Crystal Palace*	14	0		
2004–05	Crystal Palace	7	1	**21**	**1**

HUGHES, Michael (M) **380 33**
H: 5 6 W: 10 08 b.Larne 2-8-71
Source: Carrick R. *Honours:* Northern Ireland Schools, Youth, Under-21, Under-23, 71 full caps, 5 goals.

1988–89	Manchester C	1	0		

1989–90	Manchester C	0	0		
1990–91	Manchester C	1	0		
1991–92	Manchester C	24	1	**26**	**1**
1992–93	Strasbourg	36	2		
1993–94	Strasbourg	34	7		
1994–95	Strasbourg	13	0	**83**	**9**
1994–95	*West Ham U*	17	2		
1995–96	*West Ham U*	28	0		
1996–97	West Ham U	33	3		
1997–98	West Ham U	5	0	**83**	**5**
1997–98	Wimbledon	29	4		
1998–99	Wimbledon	30	2		
1999–2000	Wimbledon	20	2		
2000–01	Wimbledon	10	1		
2001–02	Wimbledon	26	4		
2001–02	*Birmingham C*	3	0	**3**	**0**
2002–03	Wimbledon	0	0	**115**	**13**
2003–04	Crystal Palace	34	3		
2004–05	Crystal Palace	36	2	**70**	**5**

JOHNSON, Andy (F) **190** **67**
H: 5 7 W: 10 09 b.Bedford 10-2-81
Source: Trainee. *Honours:* England Youth, Under-20, 2 full caps.

1997–98	Birmingham C	0	0		
1998–99	Birmingham C	4	0		
1999–2000	Birmingham C	22	1		
2000–01	Birmingham C	34	4		
2001–02	Birmingham C	23	3	**83**	**8**
2002–03	Crystal Palace	28	11		
2003–04	Crystal Palace	42	27		
2004–05	Crystal Palace	37	21	**107**	**59**

KAVIEDES, Ivan (F) **148** **68**
H: 6 0 W: 11 09 b.Santo Domingo 24-10-77
Honours: Ecuador 40 full caps, 13 goals.

1995	Emelec	1	0		
1996	Emelec	6	1		
1997	Emelec	16	4		
1998	Emelec	41	43	**64**	**48**
1998–99	Perugia	14	4	**14**	**4**
1999–2000	Celta Vigo	5	0		
1999–2000	Puebla	13	4		
2000–01	Valladolid	23	6	**23**	**6**
2001–02	Celta Vigo	0	0		
2001–02	Porto	0	0		
2000	Barcelona (Ecu)	8	4	**8**	**4**
2002–03	Celta Vigo	1	0	**6**	**0**
2002–03	Puebla	6	0	**19**	**4**
2003	Dep Quito	10	2	**10**	**2**
From Barcelona (Ecu)					
2004–05	Crystal Palace	4	0	**4**	**0**

KIRALY, Gabor (G) **297** **0**
H: 6 3 W: 13 06 b.Szombathely 1-4-76
Honours: Hungary 57 full caps.

1993–94	Haladas	15	0		
1994–95	Haladas	0	0		
1995–96	Haladas	19	0		
1996–97	Haladas	33	0	**67**	**0**
1997–98	Hertha Berlin	27	0		
1998–99	Hertha Berlin	34	0		
1999–2000	Hertha Berlin	27	0		
2000–01	Hertha Berlin	34	0		
2001–02	Hertha Berlin	25	0		
2002–03	Hertha Berlin	33	0		
2003–04	Hertha Berlin	18	0	**198**	**0**
2004–05	Crystal Palace	32	0	**32**	**0**

KOLKKA, Joonas (M) **272** **48**
H: 5 9 W: 11 08 b.Lahti 28-9-74
Source: Reipas Lahti. *Honours:* Finland 65 full caps.

1994	MyPa	21	11		
1995	MyPa	22	6	**43**	**17**
1995–96	Willem II	7	0		
1996–97	Willem II	19	4		
1997–98	Willem II	29	9	**55**	**13**
1998–99	PSV Eindhoven	19	1		
1999–2000	PSV Eindhoven	32	5		
2000–01	PSV Eindhoven	27	4	**78**	**10**
2001–02	Panathinaikos	23	2		
2002–03	Panathinaikos	22	1	**45**	**3**
2003–04	M'gladbach	28	2	**28**	**2**
2004–05	Crystal Palace	23	3	**23**	**3**

LAKIS, Vassilis (M) **299** **51**
H: 5 9 W: 10 06 b.Salonika 10-9-76
Honours: Greece 34 full caps, 3 goals.

1992–93	Naousa	9	0		
1993–94	Naousa	17	2		
1994–95	Naousa	28	3		
1995–96	Naousa	13	2	**67**	**7**
1995–96	Paniliakos	13	0		
1996–97	Paniliakos	25	4		
1997–98	Paniliakos	31	3	**69**	**7**
1998–99	AEK Athens	24	2		
1999–2000	AEK Athens	17	3		
2000–01	AEK Athens	28	2		
2001–02	AEK Athens	26	8		
2002–03	AEK Athens	27	12		
2003–04	AEK Athens	23	10	**145**	**37**
2004–05	Crystal Palace	18	0	**18**	**0**

LEIGERTWOOD, Mikele (D) **96** **3**
H: 6 1 W: 11 04 b.Enfield 12-11-82
Source: Scholar.

2001–02	Wimbledon	1	0		
2001–02	*Leyton Orient*	8	0	**8**	**0**
2002–03	Wimbledon	28	0		
2003–04	Wimbledon	27	2	**56**	**2**
2003–04	Crystal Palace	12	0		
2004–05	Crystal Palace	20	1	**32**	**1**

POPOVIC, Tony (D) **362** **34**
H: 6 5 W: 13 01 b.Australia 7-4-73
Honours: Australia Youth, Under-20, Under-23, 49 full caps, 7 goals.

1989–90	Sydney U	13	0		
1990–91	Sydney U	17	1		
1991–92	Sydney U	20	1		
1992–93	Sydney U	24	2		
1993–94	Sydney U	27	2		
1994–95	Sydney U	25	3		
1995–96	Sydney U	29	4		
1995–96	Wolverhampton W	0	0		
1996–97	Wolverhampton W	0	0		
1996–97	Sydney U	7	2	**162**	**15**
1997	Sanfrecce	11	0		
1998	Sanfrecce	25	4		
1999	Sanfrecce	23	6		
2000	Sanfrecce	21	3		
2001	Sanfrecce	7	0	**87**	**13**
2001–02	Crystal Palace	20	2		
2002–03	Crystal Palace	36	3		
2003–04	Crystal Palace	34	1		
2004–05	Crystal Palace	23	0	**113**	**6**

POWELL, Darren (D) **188** **9**
H: 6 4 W: 13 03 b.Hammersmith 10-3-76
Source: Hampton.

1998–99	Brentford	33	2		
1999–2000	Brentford	36	2		
2000–01	Brentford	18	1		
2001–02	Brentford	41	1	**128**	**6**
2002–03	Crystal Palace	39	1		
2003–04	Crystal Palace	10	0		
2004–05	Crystal Palace	6	1	**55**	**2**
2004–05	*West Ham U*	5	1	**5**	**1**

RIIHILAHTI, Aki (M) **167** **16**
H: 5 11 W: 12 06 b.Helsinki 9-9-76
Honours: Finland Youth, Under-21, 59 full caps, 10 goals.

1999	Valerenga	25	5	**25**	**5**
2000–01	Crystal Palace	9	1		
2001–02	Crystal Palace	45	5		
2002–03	Crystal Palace	25	1		
2003–04	Crystal Palace	31	0		
2004–05	Crystal Palace	32	4	**142**	**11**

ROUTLEDGE, Wayne (F) **110** **10**
H: 5 6 W: 10 07 b.Eltham 7-1-85
Source: Scholar. *Honours:* England Youth, Under-20, Under-21.

2001–02	Crystal Palace	2	0		
2002–03	Crystal Palace	26	4		
2003–04	Crystal Palace	44	6		
2004–05	Crystal Palace	38	0	**110**	**10**

SHIPPERLEY, Neil (F) **396** **109**
H: 6 0 W: 13 00 b.Chatham 30-10-74
Source: Trainee. *Honours:* England Under-21.

1992–93	Chelsea	3	1		
1993–94	Chelsea	24	4		
1994–95	Chelsea	10	2	**37**	**7**
1994–95	*Watford*	6	1	**6**	**1**
1994–95	Southampton	19	4		
1995–96	Southampton	37	7		
1996–97	Southampton	10	1	**66**	**12**
1996–97	Crystal Palace	32	12		
1997–98	Crystal Palace	26	7		
1998–99	Crystal Palace	3	1		
1998–99	Nottingham F	20	1	**20**	**1**
1999–2000	Barnsley	39	13		
2000–01	Barnsley	39	14	**78**	**27**
2001–02	Wimbledon	41	12		
2002–03	Wimbledon	46	20	**87**	**32**
2003–04	Crystal Palace	40	9		
2004–05	Crystal Palace	1	0	**102**	**29**

SOARES, Tom (M) **25** **0**
H: 6 0 W: 11 04 b.Reading 10-7-86
Source: Scholar. *Honours:* England Youth, Under-20.

2003–04	Crystal Palace	3	0		
2004–05	Crystal Palace	22	0	**25**	**0**

SORONDO, Gonzalo (D) **114** **6**
H: 5 11 W: 12 08 b.Montevideo 9-10-79
Honours: Uruguay 26 full caps, 1 goal.

1998	Defensor	4	0		
1999	Defensor	12	0		
2000	Defensor	27	4		
2001	Defensor	17	0	**60**	**4**
2001–02	Internazionale	11	0		
2002–03	Internazionale	0	0		
2003–04	Internazionale	0	0	**11**	**0**
2003–04	Standard Liege	23	2	**23**	**2**
2004–05	Crystal Palace	20	0	**20**	**0**

SPERONI, Julian (G) **100** **0**
H: 6 0 W: 11 00 b.Buenos Aires 18-5-79

1999–2000	Platense	2	0		
2000–01	Platense	0	0	**2**	**0**
2001–02	Dundee	17	0		
2002–03	Dundee	38	0		
2003–04	Dundee	37	0	**92**	**0**
2004–05	Crystal Palace	6	0	**6**	**0**

SYMONS, Kit (D) **436** **27**
H: 6 1 W: 13 00 b.Basingstoke 8-3-71
Source: Trainee. *Honours:* Wales Youth, Under-21, B, 37 full caps, 2 goals.

1988–89	Portsmouth	2	0		
1989–90	Portsmouth	1	0		
1990–91	Portsmouth	1	0		
1991–92	Portsmouth	46	1		
1992–93	Portsmouth	41	2		
1993–94	Portsmouth	29	3		
1994–95	Portsmouth	40	4		
1995–96	Portsmouth	1	0	**161**	**10**
1995–96	Manchester C	38	2		
1996–97	Manchester C	44	0		
1997–98	Manchester C	42	2	**124**	**4**
1998–99	Fulham	45	11		
1999–2000	Fulham	29	2		
2000–01	Fulham	24	0		
2001–02	Fulham	4	0	**102**	**13**
2001–02	Crystal Palace	9	0		
2002–03	Crystal Palace	25	0		
2003–04	Crystal Palace	15	0		
2004–05	Crystal Palace	0	0	**49**	**0**

TOGWELL, Sam (D) **13** **0**
H: 5 11 W: 12 04 b.Beaconsfield 14-10-84
Source: Scholar.

2002–03	Crystal Palace	1	0		
2003–04	Crystal Palace	0	0		
2004–05	Crystal Palace	0	0	**1**	**0**
2004–05	*Oxford U*	4	0	**4**	**0**
2004–05	*Northampton T*	8	0	**8**	**0**

TORGHELLE, Sandor (F) **112** **24**
H: 6 1 W: 13 06 b.Budapest 5-5-82
Honours: Hungary 13 full caps, 4 goals.

1999–2000	Kispest Honved	7	0		
2000–01	Kispest Honved	25	1		
2001–02	Kispest Honved	19	4		
2002–03	Kispest Honved	27	10	**78**	**15**
2003–04	MTK	22	9	**22**	**9**
2004–05	Crystal Palace	12	0	**12**	**0**

VENTOLA, Nicola (F) **155** **37**
H: 6 3 W: 12 13 b.Bari 24-5-78
Honours: Italy Under-21.

1994–95	Bari	1	0		
1995–96	Bari	7	0		
1996–97	Bari	29	10		
1997–98	Bari	8	2	**45**	**12**
1998–99	Internazionale	21	6		
1999–2000	Bologna	14	0	**14**	**0**
2000–01	Atalanta	28	10	**28**	**10**
2001–02	Internazionale	16	4		

2002–03 Internazionale 0 0 **37 10**
2003–04 Siena 28 4 **28 4**
2004–05 Crystal Palace 3 1 **3 1**

WATSON, Ben (M) 42 1
H: 5 10 W: 10 11 b.Camberwell 9-7-85
Source: Scholar. *Honours:* England Under-21.
2002–03 Crystal Palace 5 0
2003–04 Crystal Palace 16 1
2004–05 Crystal Palace 21 0 **42 1**

Scholars
Banks, Rikki; Beckles, Wesley; Berry, Tyrone Michael; Fray, Arron; French, Mark; Grabban, Lewis James; Hall, Ryan; Hickie, Luke Oliver; Marshall, Scott John David; Simpson, Nathaniel; Spence, Lewwis; Starkey, Philip Gregory; Watanabe, Taku; Welch, Thomas Charles; Wiggins, Rhoys Barry; Wilkinson, David Michael; Wilson, Glenn Michael

DARLINGTON (28)

ALEXANDER, John (F) 4 0
H: 5 11 W: 12 00 b.Middlesbrough 24-9-85
2002–03 Darlington 1 0
2003–04 Darlington 3 0
2004–05 Darlington 0 0 **4 0**

APPLEBY, Matty (M) 321 17
H: 5 10 W: 11 04 b.Middlesbrough 16-4-72
Source: Trainee.
1989–90 Newcastle U 0 0
1990–91 Newcastle U 1 0
1991–92 Newcastle U 18 0
1992–93 Newcastle U 0 0
1993–94 Newcastle U 1 0 **20 0**
1993–94 *Darlington* 10 1
1994–95 Darlington 36 1
1995–96 Darlington 43 6
1996–97 Barnsley 35 0
1997–98 Barnsley 15 0
1998–99 Barnsley 34 0
1999–2000 Barnsley 36 5
2000–01 Barnsley 19 2
2001–02 Barnsley 0 0 **139 7**
2001–02 Oldham Ath 17 2
2002–03 Oldham Ath 12 0
2003–04 Oldham Ath 17 0
2004–05 Oldham Ath 17 0 **63 2**
2004–05 Darlington 10 0 **99 8**

ARMSTRONG, Alun (F) 311 81
H: 6 0 W: 13 08 b.Gateshead 22-2-75
Source: School.
1993–94 Newcastle U 0 0
1994–95 Stockport Co 45 14
1995–96 Stockport Co 46 13
1996–97 Stockport Co 39 9
1997–98 Stockport Co 29 12 **159 48**
1997–98 Middlesbrough 11 7
1998–99 Middlesbrough 6 1
1999–2000 Middlesbrough 12 1
1999–2000 *Huddersfield T* 6 0 **6 0**
2000–01 Middlesbrough 0 0 **29 9**
2000–01 Ipswich T 21 7
2001–02 Ipswich T 32 4
2002–03 Ipswich T 19 1
2003–04 Ipswich T 7 2
2003–04 *Bradford C* 6 1 **6 1**
2004–05 Ipswich T 0 0 **79 14**
2004–05 Darlington 32 9 **32 9**

CLARK, Ian (M) 302 46
H: 5 11 W: 11 07 b.Stockton 23-10-74
Source: Stockton.
1995–96 Doncaster R 23 1
1996–97 Doncaster R 20 2
1997–98 Doncaster R 2 0 **45 3**
1997–98 Hartlepool U 24 7
1998–99 Hartlepool U 39 2
1999–2000 Hartlepool U 44 6
2000–01 Hartlepool U 24 0
2001–02 Hartlepool U 7 2 **138 17**
2001–02 Darlington 28 13
2002–03 Darlington 33 7
2003–04 Darlington 34 4
2004–05 Darlington 24 2 **119 26**

CLARKE, Matthew (D) 195 12
H: 6 3 W: 13 00 b.Leeds 18-12-80
Source: Wolverhampton W Trainee.
1999–2000 Halifax T 19 0
2000–01 Halifax T 19 1
2001–02 Halifax T 31 1 **69 2**
2002–03 Darlington 38 3
2003–04 Darlington 45 4
2004–05 Darlington 43 3 **126 10**

CLOSE, Brian (D) 58 1
H: 5 10 W: 12 00 b.Belfast 27-1-82
Honours: Northern Ireland Under-21.
1999–2000 Middlesbrough 0 0
2000–01 Middlesbrough 0 0
2001–02 Middlesbrough 0 0
2002–03 Middlesbrough 0 0
2002–03 *Chesterfield* 8 1 **8 1**
2003–04 Middlesbrough 0 0
2003–04 Darlington 12 0
2004–05 Darlington 38 0 **50 0**

COGHLAN, Michael (M) 3 0
H: 5 10 W: 11 00 b.Sunderland 15-1-85
Source: Scholar.
2003–04 Darlington 3 0
2004–05 Darlington 0 0 **3 0**

CONVERY, Mark (M) 76 3
H: 5 6 W: 10 05 b.Newcastle 29-5-81
Source: Trainee.
1998–99 Sunderland 0 0
1999–2000 Sunderland 0 0
2000–01 Sunderland 0 0
2000–01 Darlington 11 0
2001–02 Darlington 17 1
2002–03 Darlington 0 0
2003–04 Darlington 25 2
2004–05 Darlington 23 0 **76 3**

DICKMAN, Jonjo (M) 11 1
H: 5 11 W: 11 12 b.Hexham 22-9-81
1998–99 Sunderland 0 0
1999–2000 Sunderland 0 0
2000–01 Sunderland 0 0
2001–02 Sunderland 0 0
2002–03 Sunderland 1 0
2003–04 Sunderland 0 0
2003–04 *York C* 2 0 **2 0**
2004–05 Sunderland 0 0 **1 0**
2004–05 Darlington 8 1 **8 1**

FLEMING, Curtis (D) 344 3
H: 5 10 W: 12 09 b.Manchester 8-10-68
Source: St Patrick's Ath. *Honours:* Eire Youth, Under-21, B, 10 full caps.
1991–92 Middlesbrough 28 0
1992–93 Middlesbrough 24 0
1993–94 Middlesbrough 40 0
1994–95 Middlesbrough 21 0
1995–96 Middlesbrough 13 1
1996–97 Middlesbrough 30 0
1997–98 Middlesbrough 31 1
1998–99 Middlesbrough 14 1
1999–2000 Middlesbrough 27 0
2000–01 Middlesbrough 30 0
2001–02 Middlesbrough 8 0 **266 3**
2001–02 *Birmingham C* 6 0 **6 0**
2001–02 Crystal Palace 17 0
2002–03 Crystal Palace 11 0
2003–04 Crystal Palace 17 0 **45 0**
2004–05 Darlington 27 0 **27 0**

GILROY, Keith (F) 2 0
H: 5 10 W: 11 04 b.Sligo 8-7-83
Honours: Eire Youth, Under-21.
2000–01 Middlesbrough 0 0
2001–02 Middlesbrough 0 0
2002–03 Middlesbrough 0 0
2003–04 Middlesbrough 0 0
2004–05 Middlesbrough 0 0
From Scarborough.
2004–05 Darlington 2 0 **2 0**

GREGORIO, Adolfo (M) 24 2
H: 5 9 W: 10 12 b.Hilmar 1-10-82
Source: ULCA.
2004–05 Darlington 24 2 **24 2**

HIGNETT, Craig (M) 464 125
H: 5 9 W: 12 06 b.Whiston 12-1-70
Source: Liverpool Trainee.
1987–88 Crewe Alex 0 0
1988–89 Crewe Alex 1 0
1989–90 Crewe Alex 35 8
1990–91 Crewe Alex 38 13
1991–92 Crewe Alex 33 13
1992–93 Crewe Alex 14 8
1992–93 Middlesbrough 21 4
1993–94 Middlesbrough 29 5
1994–95 Middlesbrough 26 8
1995–96 Middlesbrough 22 5
1996–97 Middlesbrough 22 4
1997–98 Middlesbrough 36 7 **156 33**
1998–99 Aberdeen 13 2 **13 2**
1998–99 Barnsley 24 9
1999–2000 Barnsley 42 19 **66 28**
2000–01 Blackburn R 30 3
2001–02 Blackburn R 20 4
2002–03 Blackburn R 3 1 **53 8**
2002–03 *Coventry C* 8 2 **8 2**
2003–04 Leicester C 13 1 **13 1**
2003–04 *Crewe Alex* 15 0 **136 42**
2004–05 Leeds U 0 0
2004–05 Darlington 19 9 **19 9**

HUGHES, Chris (M) 45 2
H: 5 11 W: 10 10 b.Sunderland 5-3-84
Source: Scholar.
2003–04 Darlington 30 2
2004–05 Darlington 15 0 **45 2**

HUTCHINSON, Jonathan (D) 51 0
H: 5 11 W: 11 11 b.Middlesbrough 2-4-82
Source: Scholar.
2000–01 Birmingham C 0 0
2001–02 Birmingham C 3 0
2002–03 Birmingham C 1 0 **4 0**
2003–04 Darlington 39 0
2004–05 Darlington 8 0 **47 0**

KELTIE, Clark (M) 83 4
H: 6 0 W: 11 08 b.Newcastle 31-8-83
Source: Shildon.
2001–02 Darlington 1 0
2002–03 Darlington 30 3
2003–04 Darlington 31 1
2004–05 Darlington 21 0 **83 4**

KENDRICK, Joseph (D) 31 1
H: 6 0 W: 11 05 b.Dublin 26-6-83
Source: Scholar. *Honours:* Eire Youth, Under-21.
2000–01 Newcastle U 0 0
2001–02 Newcastle U 0 0
2002–03 Newcastle U 0 0
2003–04 Munich 1860 0 0
2004–05 Darlington 31 1 **31 1**

LIDDLE, Craig (D) 310 17
H: 5 11 W: 12 03 b.Chester-le-Street 21-10-71
Source: Blyth Spartans.
1994–95 Middlesbrough 1 0
1995–96 Middlesbrough 13 0
1996–97 Middlesbrough 5 0
1997–98 Middlesbrough 6 0 **25 0**
1997–98 *Darlington* 15 0
1998–99 Darlington 44 3
1999–2000 Darlington 45 1
2000–01 Darlington 45 2
2001–02 Darlington 31 2
2002–03 Darlington 42 4
2003–04 Darlington 43 4
2004–05 Darlington 20 1 **285 17**

LOGAN, Richard (M) 1 0
H: 6 0 W: 11 12 b.Washington 18-2-88
2004–05 Darlington 1 0 **1 0**

MADDISON, Neil (M) 349 28
H: 5 10 W: 12 00 b.Darlington 2-10-69
Source: Trainee.
1987–88 Southampton 0 0
1988–89 Southampton 5 2
1989–90 Southampton 2 0
1990–91 Southampton 4 0
1991–92 Southampton 6 0
1992–93 Southampton 37 4
1993–94 Southampton 41 7
1994–95 Southampton 35 3
1995–96 Southampton 15 1
1996–97 Southampton 18 1
1997–98 Southampton 6 1 **169 19**
1997–98 Middlesbrough 22 4

1998–99	Middlesbrough	21	0		
1999–2000	Middlesbrough	13	0		
2000–01	Middlesbrough	0	0	**56**	**4**
2000–01	*Barnsley*	3	0	**3**	**0**
2000–01	*Bristol C*	7	1	**7**	**1**
2001–02	Darlington	30	1		
2002–03	Darlington	28	1		
2003–04	Darlington	32	1		
2004–05	Darlington	24	1	**114**	**4**

MASON, Chris (M) **1 0**
H: 6 0 W: 12 00 b.Newton Aycliffe 26-6-86
Source: Scholar.

2003–04	Darlington	1	0		
2004–05	Darlington	0	0	**1**	**0**

McGURK, David (D) **53 6**
H: 6 0 W: 11 10 b.Middlesbrough 30-9-82
Source: Scholar.

2001–02	Darlington	12	0		
2002–03	Darlington	4	0		
2003–04	Darlington	27	4		
2004–05	Darlington	10	2	**53**	**6**

PETTA, Bobby (M) **91 10**
H: 5 7 W: 11 05 b.Rotterdam 6-8-74

1996–97	Ipswich T	6	0		
1997–98	Ipswich T	32	7		
1998–99	Ipswich T	32	2	**70**	**9**
1999–2000	Celtic	0	0		
2000–01	Celtic	0	0		
2001–02	Celtic	0	0		
2003–04	Celtic	0	0		
2003–04	*Fulham*	9	0	**9**	**0**
2004–05	Celtic	0	0		
2004–05	Darlington	12	1	**12**	**1**

PRICE, Mike (G) **36 0**
H: 6 3 W: 13 10 b.Ashington 3-4-83
Source: Scholar.

2000–01	Leicester C	0	0		
2001–02	Leicester C	0	0		
2002–03	Leicester C	0	0		
2003–04	Darlington	36	0		
2004–05	Darlington	0	0	**36**	**0**

RUSSELL, Craig (F) **306 42**
H: 5 10 W: 12 06 b.Jarrow 4-2-74
Source: Trainee.

1991–92	Sunderland	4	0		
1992–93	Sunderland	0	0		
1993–94	Sunderland	35	9		
1994–95	Sunderland	38	5		
1995–96	Sunderland	41	13		
1996–97	Sunderland	29	4		
1997–98	Sunderland	3	0	**150**	**31**
1997–98	Manchester C	24	1		
1998–99	Manchester C	7	1		
1998–99	*Tranmere R*	4	0	**4**	**0**
1998–99	*Port Vale*	8	1	**8**	**1**
1999–2000	Manchester C	0	0	**31**	**2**
1999–2000	*Darlington*	12	2		
1999–2000	*Oxford U*	6	0	**6**	**0**
1999–2000	*St Johnstone*	1	1		
2000–01	St Johnstone	13	1		
2001–02	St Johnstone	14	1		
2002–03	St Johnstone	8	0	**36**	**3**
2002–03	Carlisle U	13	1		
2003–04	Carlisle U	6	0	**19**	**1**
2003–04	Darlington	12	1		
2004–05	Darlington	28	1	**52**	**4**

RUSSELL, Sam (G) **57 0**
H: 6 0 W: 11 00 b.Middlesbrough 4-10-82
Source: Scholar.

2000–01	Middlesbrough	0	0		
2001–02	Middlesbrough	0	0		
2002–03	Middlesbrough	0	0		
2002–03	*Darlington*	1	0		
2003–04	Middlesbrough	0	0		
2003–04	*Scunthorpe U*	10	0	**10**	**0**
2004–05	Darlington	46	0	**47**	**0**

SCARTISCINI, Leandro (M) **0 0**
H: 5 11 W: 12 02 b.Buenos Aires 30-1-85

2004–05	Darlington	0	0		

ST'JUSTE, Jason (M) **15 2**
H: 5 6 W: 10 05 b.Leeds 21-9-85

2004–05	Darlington	15	2	**15**	**2**

THOMAS, Steve (M) **127 7**
H: 5 10 W: 11 07 b.Hartlepool 23-6-79
Source: Trainee. *Honours:* Wales Youth, Under-21.

1997–98	Wrexham	0	0		
1998–99	Wrexham	4	0		
1999–2000	Wrexham	2	0		
2000–01	Wrexham	6	0		
2001–02	Wrexham	38	3		
2002–03	Wrexham	25	2		
2003–04	Wrexham	40	2	**115**	**7**
2004–05	Darlington	12	0	**12**	**0**

VALENTINE, Ryan (D) **119 4**
H: 5 10 W: 11 05 b.Wrexham 19-8-82
Source: Trainee. *Honours:* Wales Under-21.

1999–2000	Everton	0	0		
2000–01	Everton	0	0		
2001–02	Everton	0	0		
2002–03	Darlington	43	1		
2003–04	Darlington	40	2		
2004–05	Darlington	36	1	**119**	**4**

WAINWRIGHT, Neil (M) **184 23**
H: 6 0 W: 12 00 b.Warrington 4-11-77
Source: Trainee.

1996–97	Wrexham	0	0		
1997–98	Wrexham	11	3	**11**	**3**
1998–99	Sunderland	2	0		
1999–2000	Sunderland	0	0		
1999–2000	*Darlington*	17	4		
2000–01	Sunderland	0	0		
2000–01	*Halifax T*	13	0	**13**	**0**
2001–02	Sunderland	0	0	**2**	**0**
2001–02	Darlington	35	4		
2002–03	Darlington	33	1		
2003–04	Darlington	35	7		
2004–05	Darlington	38	4	**158**	**20**

WEBSTER, Adrian (M) **22 0**
H: 5 8 W: 10 09 b.Hawkes Bay 11-10-80
Source: Charlton Ath. *Honours:* New Zealand 1 full cap.

1999–2000	Colchester U	0	0		
2000–01	Colchester U	0	0		
2001–02	Colchester U	0	0		

From Margate, Maidstone U

2004–05	Darlington	22	0	**22**	**0**

WIJNHARD, Clyde (F) **277 92**
H: 5 11 W: 13 02 b.Paramaribo 1-11-73

1992–93	Ajax	4	2		
1993–94	Groningen	23	3	**23**	**3**
1994–95	Ajax	0	0	**4**	**2**
1995–96	RKC	33	8		
1996–97	RKC	17	10	**50**	**18**
1997–98	Willem II	29	14	**29**	**14**
1998–99	Leeds U	18	3	**18**	**3**
1999–2000	Huddersfield T	45	15		
2000–01	Huddersfield T	4	0		
2001–02	Huddersfield T	13	1	**62**	**16**
2001–02	Preston NE	6	3	**6**	**3**
2002–03	Oldham Ath	25	10	**25**	**10**
2003–04	Beira Mar	29	9	**29**	**9**
2004–05	Darlington	31	14	**31**	**14**

DERBY CO (29)

BISGAARD, Morten (M) **267 50**
H: 6 1 W: 12 04 b.Randers 25-6-74
Honours: Denmark Youth, Under-21, 8 full caps, 1 goal.

1993–94	Odense	7	1		
1994–95	Odense	27	4		
1995–96	Odense	25	6		
1996–97	Odense	33	16		
1997–98	Odense	29	8	**121**	**35**
1998–99	Udinese	3	0		
1999–2000	Udinese	20	1		
2000–01	Udinese	13	0	**36**	**1**
2001–02	FC Copenhagen	27	6		
2002–03	FC Copenhagen	27	1		
2003–04	FC Copenhagen	20	3	**74**	**10**
2004–05	Derby Co	36	4	**36**	**4**

BOERTIEN, Paul (D) **127 3**
H: 5 10 W: 11 02 b.Haltwhistle 21-1-79
Source: Trainee.

1996–97	Carlisle U	0	0		
1997–98	Carlisle U	9	0		
1998–99	Carlisle U	8	1	**17**	**1**
1998–99	Derby Co	1	0		
1999–2000	Derby Co	2	0		
1999–2000	*Crewe Alex*	2	0	**2**	**0**
2000–01	Derby Co	8	1		
2001–02	Derby Co	32	0		
2002–03	Derby Co	42	1		
2003–04	Derby Co	18	0		
2003–04	*Notts Co*	5	0	**5**	**0**
2004–05	Derby Co	0	0	**103**	**2**

BOLDER, Adam (M) **138 9**
H: 5 9 W: 10 08 b.Hull 25-10-80
Source: Trainee.

1998–99	Hull C	1	0		
1999–2000	Hull C	19	0	**20**	**0**
1999–2000	Derby Co	0	0		
2000–01	Derby Co	2	0		
2001–02	Derby Co	11	0		
2002–03	Derby Co	45	6		
2003–04	Derby Co	24	1		
2004–05	Derby Co	36	2	**118**	**9**

CAMP, Lee (G) **58 0**
H: 5 11 W: 11 11 b.Derby 22-8-84
Source: Scholar. *Honours:* England Youth, Under-20, Under-21.

2002–03	Derby Co	1	0		
2003–04	Derby Co	0	0		
2003–04	*QPR*	12	0	**12**	**0**
2004–05	Derby Co	45	0	**46**	**0**

CASSIDY, David (M) **0 0**
H: 5 7 W: 11 00 b.Dublin 23-5-85
Source: Scholar.

2004–05	Derby Co	0	0		

DOYLE, Nathan (M) **5 0**
H: 5 10 W: 12 06 b.Derby 12-1-87
Source: From Scholar. *Honours:* England Youth.

2003–04	Derby Co	2	0		
2004–05	Derby Co	3	0	**5**	**0**

GRANT, Lee (G) **67 0**
H: 6 3 W: 13 01 b.Hemel Hempstead 27-1-83
Source: Scholar. *Honours:* England Youth, Under-21.

2000–01	Derby Co	0	0		
2001–02	Derby Co	0	0		
2002–03	Derby Co	29	0		
2003–04	Derby Co	36	0		
2004–05	Derby Co	2	0	**67**	**0**

HOLMES, Lee (M) **43 3**
H: 5 8 W: 10 06 b.Sutton-in-Ashfield 2-4-87
Source: Scholar. *Honours:* FA Schools, England Youth.

2002–03	Derby Co	2	0		
2003–04	Derby Co	23	2		
2004–05	Derby Co	3	0	**28**	**2**
2004–05	*Swindon T*	15	1	**15**	**1**

HUDDLESTONE, Tom (M) **88 0**
H: 6 2 W: 11 02 b.Nottingham 28-12-86
Source: Scholar. *Honours:* England Youth, Under-20, Under-21.

2003–04	Derby Co	43	0		
2004–05	Derby Co	45	0	**88**	**0**

IDIAKEZ, Inigo (M) **360 64**
H: 6 0 W: 12 02 b.San Sebastian 8-11-73

1992–93	Real Sociedad	1	0		
1993–94	Real Sociedad B	25	13		
1993–94	Real Sociedad	2	0		
1994–95	Real Sociedad	26	4		
1995–96	Real Sociedad	33	4		
1996–97	Real Sociedad	31	4		
1997–98	Real Sociedad	16	1		
1998–99	Real Sociedad	29	7		
1999–2000	Real Sociedad	27	4		
2000–01	Real Sociedad	33	7		
2001–02	Real Sociedad	34	2	**232**	**33**
2002–03	Oviedo	33	4	**33**	**4**
2003–04	Rayo Vallecano	29	5	**29**	**5**
2004–05	Derby Co	41	9	**41**	**9**

JACKSON, Richard (D) **109 0**
H: 5 8 W: 12 10 b.Whitby 18-4-80
Source: Trainee.

1997–98	Scarborough	2	0		

1998–99 Scarborough 20 0 **22 0**
1998–99 Derby Co 0 0
1999–2000 Derby Co 2 0
2000–01 Derby Co 2 0
2001–02 Derby Co 7 0
2002–03 Derby Co 21 0
2003–04 Derby Co 36 0
2004–05 Derby Co 19 0 **87 0**

JOHNSON, Michael (D) 444 15
H: 5 11 W: 11 12 b.Nottingham 4-7-73
Source: Trainee. *Honours:* Jamaica 14 full caps.
1991–92 Notts Co 5 0
1992–93 Notts Co 37 0
1993–94 Notts Co 34 0
1994–95 Notts Co 31 0
1995–96 Notts Co 0 0 **107 0**
1995–96 Birmingham C 33 0
1996–97 Birmingham C 35 0
1997–98 Birmingham C 38 3
1998–99 Birmingham C 45 5
1999–2000 Birmingham C 34 2
2000–01 Birmingham C 39 2
2001–02 Birmingham C 32 1
2002–03 Birmingham C 6 0
2003–04 Birmingham C 0 0 **262 13**
2003–04 Derby Co 39 1
2004–05 Derby Co 36 1 **75 2**

JUNIOR (F) 78 21
H: 6 0 W: 13 00 b.Fortaleza 20-7-76
Source: Trezze.
2002–03 Walsall 36 15 **36 15**
2003–04 Derby Co 12 4
2004–05 Derby Co 18 0 **30 4**
2004–05 *Rotherham U* 12 2 **12 2**

KENNA, Jeff (D) 410 9
H: 5 11 W: 12 12 b.Dublin 27-8-70
Source: Trainee. *Honours:* Eire Youth, Under-21, B, 27 full caps.
1988–89 Southampton 0 0
1989–90 Southampton 0 0
1990–91 Southampton 2 0
1991–92 Southampton 14 0
1992–93 Southampton 29 2
1993–94 Southampton 41 2
1994–95 Southampton 28 0 **114 4**
1994–95 Blackburn R 9 1
1995–96 Blackburn R 32 0
1996–97 Blackburn R 37 0
1997–98 Blackburn R 37 0
1998–99 Blackburn R 23 0
1999–2000 Blackburn R 11 0
2000–01 Blackburn R 6 0
2000–01 *Tranmere R* 11 0 **11 0**
2001–02 Blackburn R 0 0 **155 1**
2001–02 *Wigan Ath* 6 1 **6 1**
2001–02 Birmingham C 21 0
2002–03 Birmingham C 37 1
2003–04 Birmingham C 17 2 **75 3**
2003–04 Derby Co 9 0
2004–05 Derby Co 40 0 **49 0**

KONJIC, Muhamed (D) 316 16
H: 6 3 W: 13 00 b.Bosnia 14-5-70
Honours: Bosnia 38 full caps, 3 goals.
1990–91 Tuzla 3 0
1991–92 Tuzla 5 0 **8 0**
1992–93 Belisce 18 0 **18 0**
1993–94 Zagreb 29 3
1994–95 Zagreb 19 1
1995–96 Zagreb 15 1 **63 5**
1996–97 Zurich 29 2
1997–98 Zurich 7 3 **36 5**
1997–98 Monaco 19 0
1998–99 Monaco 18 2 **37 2**
1998–99 Coventry C 4 0
1999–2000 Coventry C 4 0
2000–01 Coventry C 8 0
2001–02 Coventry C 38 2
2002–03 Coventry C 42 0
2003–04 Coventry C 42 2 **138 4**
2003–04 Derby Co 0 0
2004–05 Derby Co 16 0 **16 0**

LABARTHE, Gianfranco (F) 6 0
H: 5 9 W: 10 12 b.Lima 20-9-84
Source: Sport Boys.
2002–03 Huddersfield T 3 0 **3 0**
2003–04 Derby Co 3 0
2004–05 Derby Co 0 0 **3 0**

MARTIN, Daniel (D) 0 0
H: 6 1 W: 12 13 b.Derby 24-9-86
Source: Scholar.
2004–05 Derby Co 0 0

MILLS, Pablo (D) 57 0
H: 5 9 W: 11 04 b.Birmingham 27-5-84
Source: From Trainee. *Honours:* England Youth.
2002–03 Derby Co 16 0
2003–04 Derby Co 19 0
2004–05 Derby Co 22 0 **57 0**

NIX, Korey (M) 0 0
H: 5 8 W: 10 03 b.Sydney 28-9-87
Source: Scholar.
2004–05 Derby Co 0 0

PESCHISOLIDO, Paul (F) 395 110
H: 5 7 W: 10 12 b.Scarborough, Canada 25-5-71
Source: From Toronto Blizzard. *Honours:* Canada Youth, Under-21, 53 full caps, 10 goals.
1992–93 Birmingham C 19 7
1993–94 Birmingham C 24 9
1994–95 Stoke C 40 13
1995–96 Stoke C 26 6 **66 19**
1995–96 Birmingham C 9 1 **52 17**
1996–97 WBA 37 15
1997–98 WBA 8 3 **45 18**
1997–98 Fulham 32 13
1998–99 Fulham 33 7
1999–2000 Fulham 30 4
2000–01 Fulham 0 0 **95 24**
2000–01 *QPR* 5 1 **5 1**
2000–01 *Sheffield U* 5 2
2000–01 *Norwich C* 5 0 **5 0**
2001–02 Sheffield U 29 6
2002–03 Sheffield U 23 3
2003–04 Sheffield U 27 8 **84 19**
2003–04 Derby Co 11 4
2004–05 Derby Co 32 8 **43 12**

RASIAK, Grzegorz (F) 129 59
H: 6 3 W: 13 03 b.Szczecin 12-1-79
Honours: Poland 18 full caps, 3 goals.
2000–01 Odra 28 9 **28 9**
2001–02 Groclin 26 14
2002–03 Groclin 22 10
2003–04 Groclin 18 10 **66 34**
2003–04 Siena 0 0
2004–05 Derby Co 35 16 **35 16**

REICH, Marco (M) 193 15
H: 6 0 W: 12 00 b.Meisenheim 30-12-77
Honours: Germany 1 full cap.
1996–97 Kaiserslautern 0 0
1997–98 Kaiserslautern 31 1
1998–99 Kaiserslautern 27 3
1999–2000 Kaiserslautern 28 2
2000–01 Kaiserslautern 18 2 **104 8**
2001–02 Cologne 24 0 **24 0**
2002–03 Werder Bremen 15 0 **15 0**
2003–04 Derby Co 13 1
2004–05 Derby Co 37 6 **50 7**

SMITH, Tommy (F) 226 48
H: 5 8 W: 11 04 b.Hemel Hempstead 22-5-80
Source: Trainee. *Honours:* England Youth, Under-21.
1997–98 Watford 1 0
1998–99 Watford 8 2
1999–2000 Watford 22 2
2000–01 Watford 43 11
2001–02 Watford 40 11
2002–03 Watford 35 7
2003–04 Watford 0 0 **149 33**
2003–04 Sunderland 35 4 **35 4**
2004–05 Derby Co 42 11 **42 11**

TAYLOR, Ian (M) 411 71
H: 6 1 W: 12 04 b.Birmingham 4-6-68
Source: Moor Green.
1992–93 Port Vale 41 15
1993–94 Port Vale 42 13 **83 28**
1994–95 Sheffield W 14 1 **14 1**
1994–95 Aston Villa 22 1
1995–96 Aston Villa 25 3
1996–97 Aston Villa 34 2
1997–98 Aston Villa 32 6
1998–99 Aston Villa 33 4
1999–2000 Aston Villa 29 5
2000–01 Aston Villa 29 4
2001–02 Aston Villa 16 3
2002–03 Aston Villa 13 0 **233 28**
2003–04 Derby Co 42 11
2004–05 Derby Co 39 3 **81 14**

TUDGAY, Marcus (F) 71 15
H: 5 10 W: 12 04 b.Worthing 3-2-83
Source: Trainee.
2002–03 Derby Co 8 0
2003–04 Derby Co 29 6
2004–05 Derby Co 34 9 **71 15**

TURNER, Chris (D) 0 0
H: 5 9 W: 11 09 b.Ballymoney 3-1-87
Source: Scholar.
2004–05 Derby Co 0 0

TWIGG, Gary (F) 17 0
H: 6 0 W: 11 02 b.Glasgow 19-3-84
Source: Scholar.
2000–01 Derby Co 0 0
2001–02 Derby Co 1 0
2002–03 Derby Co 8 0
2003–04 Derby Co 0 0
2003–04 *Bristol R* 8 0 **8 0**
2004–05 Derby Co 0 0 **9 0**

VINCENT, Jamie (D) 279 10
H: 5 10 W: 11 08 b.Wimbledon 18-6-75
Source: Trainee.
1993–94 Crystal Palace 0 0
1994–95 Crystal Palace 0 0
1994–95 *Bournemouth* 8 0
1995–96 Crystal Palace 25 0
1996–97 Crystal Palace 0 0 **25 0**
1996–97 Bournemouth 29 0
1997–98 Bournemouth 44 3
1998–99 Bournemouth 32 2 **113 5**
1998–99 Huddersfield T 7 0
1999–2000 Huddersfield T 36 2
2000–01 Huddersfield T 16 0 **59 2**
2000–01 Portsmouth 14 0
2001–02 Portsmouth 34 1
2002–03 Portsmouth 0 0
2003–04 Portsmouth 0 0 **48 1**
2003–04 *Walsall* 12 0 **12 0**
2003–04 Derby Co 7 1
2004–05 Derby Co 15 1 **22 2**

WECKSTROM, Kristoffer (M) 0 0
H: 5 9 W: 11 04 b.Helsinki 26-5-83
Source: IFK Mariehamn.
2000–01 Derby Co 0 0
2001–02 Derby Co 0 0
2002–03 Derby Co 0 0
2003–04 Derby Co 0 0
2004–05 Derby Co 0 0

ZAVAGNO, Luciano (D) 113 4
H: 5 11 W: 11 07 b.Rosario 6-8-77
1997–98 Strasbourg 5 0
1998–99 Strasbourg 9 1 **14 1**
1999–2000 Troyes 26 0
2000–01 Troyes 13 0
2001–02 Troyes 8 0 **47 0**
2001–02 Derby Co 26 0
2002–03 Derby Co 9 2
2003–04 Derby Co 17 1
2004–05 Derby Co 0 0 **52 3**

DONCASTER R (30)

ALBRIGHTON, Mark (D) 45 4
H: 6 1 W: 12 07 b.Nuneaton 6-3-76
Source: Atherstone U, Nuneaton B, Telford U.
2003–04 Doncaster R 28 3
2004–05 Doncaster R 17 1 **45 4**

BEECH, Chris (D) 114 2
H: 5 10 W: 11 12 b.Congleton 5-11-75
Source: Trainee. *Honours:* England Schools, Youth.
1992–93 Manchester C 0 0
1993–94 Manchester C 0 0
1994–95 Manchester C 0 0
1995–96 Manchester C 0 0
1996–97 Manchester C 0 0
1997–98 Cardiff C 46 1 **46 1**

1998–99	Rotherham U	24	0		
1999–2000	Rotherham U	6	0		
2000–01	Rotherham U	15	0		
2001–02	Rotherham U	8	1		
2002–03	Rotherham U	2	0	**55**	**1**
2003–04	Doncaster R	11	0		
2004–05	Doncaster R	2	0	**13**	**0**

BLACK, Chris (M) 4 0

H: 6 0 W: 12 00 b.Ashington 7-9-82

Source: Scholar.

2000–01	Sunderland	0	0		
2001–02	Sunderland	0	0		
2002–03	Sunderland	2	0		
2003–04	Sunderland	1	0	**3**	**0**
2003–04	Doncaster R	1	0		
2004–05	Doncaster R	0	0	**1**	**0**

BLUNDELL, Greg (F) 85 27

H: 5 9 W: 12 12 b.Liverpool 3-10-77

Source: Tranmere R Trainee, Vauxhall M, Northwich Vic.

2003–04	Doncaster R	44	18		
2004–05	Doncaster R	41	9	**85**	**27**

BROWN, Adam (M) 3 1

H: 5 10 W: 10 07 b.Sunderland 17-12-87

Source: Scholar.

2004–05	Doncaster R	3	1	**3**	**1**

COPPINGER, James (F) 99 10

H: 5 7 W: 10 03 b.Middlesbrough 10-1-81

Source: Darlington Trainee. *Honours:* England Youth.

1997–98	Newcastle U	0	0		
1998–99	Newcastle U	0	0		
1999–2000	Newcastle U	0	0		
1999–2000	*Hartlepool U*	10	3		
2000–01	Newcastle U	1	0		
2001–02	Newcastle U	0	0	**1**	**0**
2001–02	*Hartlepool U*	14	2	**24**	**5**
2002–03	Exeter C	43	5		
2003–04	Exeter C	0	0	**43**	**5**
2004–05	Doncaster R	31	0	**31**	**0**

DOOLAN, John (M) 342 19

H: 6 1 W: 13 00 b.Liverpool 7-5-74

Source: Trainee.

1992–93	Everton	0	0		
1993–94	Everton	0	0		
1994–95	Mansfield T	24	1		
1995–96	Mansfield T	42	2		
1996–97	Mansfield T	41	6		
1997–98	Mansfield T	24	1	**131**	**10**
1997–98	Barnet	17	0		
1998–99	Barnet	42	2		
1999–2000	Barnet	44	2		
2000–01	Barnet	31	3		
2001–02	Barnet	0	0		
2002–03	Barnet	0	0	**134**	**7**
2003–04	Doncaster R	39	0		
2004–05	Doncaster R	38	2	**77**	**2**

FENTON, Nick (D) 234 11

H: 6 0 W: 12 02 b.Preston 23-11-79

Source: Trainee. *Honours:* England Youth.

1996–97	Manchester C	0	0		
1997–98	Manchester C	0	0		
1998–99	Manchester C	15	0		
1999–2000	Manchester C	0	0		
1999–2000	*Notts Co*	13	1		
1999–2000	*Bournemouth*	8	0		
2000–01	Manchester C	0	0	**15**	**0**
2000–01	*Bournemouth*	5	0	**13**	**0**
2000–01	Notts Co	30	2		
2001–02	Notts Co	42	3		
2002–03	Notts Co	40	3		
2003–04	Notts Co	43	1	**168**	**10**
2004–05	Doncaster R	38	1	**38**	**1**

FORTUNE-WEST, Leo (F) 311 89

H: 6 3 W: 13 10 b.Stratford 9-4-71

Source: Tiptree, Dagenham, Dartford, Bishops Stortford, Stevenage Bor.

1995–96	Gillingham	40	12		
1996–97	Gillingham	7	2		
1996–97	*Leyton Orient*	5	0	**5**	**0**
1997–98	Gillingham	20	4	**67**	**18**
1998–99	Lincoln C	9	1	**9**	**1**
1998–99	Brentford	11	0	**11**	**0**
1998–99	Rotherham U	20	12		
1999–2000	Rotherham U	39	17		
2000–01	Rotherham U	5	1	**64**	**30**
2000–01	Cardiff C	37	12		
2001–02	Cardiff C	36	9		
2002–03	Cardiff C	19	2	**92**	**23**
2003–04	Doncaster R	39	11		
2004–05	Doncaster R	24	6	**63**	**17**

FOSTER, Steve (D) 280 9

H: 6 1 W: 12 00 b.Mansfield 3-12-74

Source: Trainee.

1993–94	Mansfield T	5	0	**5**	**0**
From Telford U, Woking					
1997–98	Bristol R	34	0		
1998–99	Bristol R	43	1		
1999–2000	Bristol R	43	1		
2000–01	Bristol R	44	4		
2001–02	Bristol R	33	1		
2002–03	Bristol R	0	0	**197**	**7**
2003–04	Doncaster R	44	1		
2004–05	Doncaster R	34	1	**78**	**2**

GILL, Robert (F) 1 0

H: 5 11 W: 11 00 b.Nottingham 10-2-82

Source: Nottingham F Trainee.

2003–04	Doncaster R	1	0		
2004–05	Doncaster R	0	0	**1**	**0**

GREEN, Paul (M) 85 15

H: 5 10 W: 12 00 b.Pontefract 10-4-83

Source: Trainee.

2003–04	Doncaster R	43	8		
2004–05	Doncaster R	42	7	**85**	**15**

GUY, Lewis (F) 9 3

H: 5 10 W: 10 07 b.Penrith 27-8-85

Source: Trainee. *Honours:* England Youth, Under-20.

2002–03	Newcastle U	0	0		
2003–04	Newcastle U	0	0		
2004–05	Newcastle U	0	0		
2004–05	Doncaster R	9	3	**9**	**3**

IPOUA, Guy (F) 191 39

H: 6 0 W: 13 13 b.Douala 14-1-76

Source: Atletico Madrid, Novelda.

1998–99	Bristol R	24	3	**24**	**3**
1999–2000	Scunthorpe U	40	9		
2000–01	Scunthorpe U	25	14	**65**	**23**
2000–01	Gillingham	9	0		
2001–02	Gillingham	40	8		
2002–03	Gillingham	33	5		
2003–04	Gillingham	0	0	**82**	**13**
2004–05	Doncaster R	9	0	**9**	**0**
2004–05	*Mansfield T*	5	0	**5**	**0**
2004–05	*Lincoln C*	6	0	**6**	**0**

JACKSON, Ben (F) 1 0

H: 5 9 W: 11 07 b.Peterlee 20-10-85

Source: Scholar.

2003–04	Doncaster R	0	0		
2004–05	Doncaster R	1	0	**1**	**0**

JONES, Stuart (G) 39 0

H: 6 1 W: 14 00 b.Bristol 24-10-77

Source: Weston-Super-Mare.

1997–98	Sheffield W	0	0		
1998–99	Sheffield W	0	0		
1998–99	*Crewe Alex*	0	0		
1999–2000	Sheffield W	0	0		
1999–2000	Torquay U	16	0		
2000–01	Torquay U	16	0		
2001–02	Torquay U	0	0		
2002–03	Torquay U	0	0		
2003–04	Torquay U	0	0	**32**	**0**
Fr Weston Super Mare					
2003–04	Brighton & HA	3	0		
2004–05	Brighton & HA	0	0	**3**	**0**
2004–05	Doncaster R	4	0	**4**	**0**

MALONEY, Jon (M) 3 0

H: 6 0 W: 11 12 b.Leeds 3-3-85

Source: Trainee.

2003–04	Doncaster R	1	0		
2004–05	Doncaster R	2	0	**3**	**0**

MARPLES, Simon (D) 28 0

H: 5 10 W: 11 00 b.Sheffield 30-7-75

Source: Stocksbridge Park Steels.

2003–04	Doncaster R	16	0		
2004–05	Doncaster R	12	0	**28**	**0**

McINDOE, Michael (M) 128 20

H: 5 8 W: 11 00 b.Edinburgh 2-12-79

Source: Trainee. *Honours:* Scotland B.

1997–98	Luton T	0	0		
1998–99	Luton T	22	0		
1999–2000	Luton T	17	0	**39**	**0**
Fr Hereford, Yeovil					
2003–04	Doncaster R	45	10		
2004–05	Doncaster R	44	10	**89**	**20**

McSPORRAN, Jermaine (M) 190 31

H: 5 10 W: 10 12 b.Manchester 1-1-77

Source: Oxford C.

1998–99	Wycombe W	26	4		
1999–2000	Wycombe W	38	9		
2000–01	Wycombe W	20	2		
2001–02	Wycombe W	32	7		
2002–03	Wycombe W	9	1		
2003–04	Wycombe W	33	7	**158**	**30**
2003–04	Walsall	6	0	**6**	**0**
2004–05	Doncaster R	26	1	**26**	**1**

MULLIGAN, David (D) 110 3

H: 5 8 W: 9 13 b.Bootle 24-3-82

Source: Scholar. *Honours:* New Zealand Youth, Under-23, 6 full caps.

2000–01	Barnsley	0	0		
2001–02	Barnsley	28	0		
2002–03	Barnsley	33	1		
2003–04	Barnsley	4	0	**65**	**1**
2003–04	Doncaster R	14	1		
2004–05	Doncaster R	31	1	**45**	**2**

NELTHORPE, Craig (M) 1 0

H: 5 10 W: 11 00 b.Doncaster 10-6-87

Source: Scholar.

2004–05	Doncaster R	1	0	**1**	**0**

PRICE, Jamie (D) 25 0

H: 5 10 W: 11 00 b.Normanton 27-10-81

Source: Trainee.

2003–04	Doncaster R	19	0		
2004–05	Doncaster R	6	0	**25**	**0**

PRIET, Nicolas (D) 7 0

H: 6 4 W: 12 10 b.Lyon 31-1-83

2003–04	Leicester C	0	0		
2004–05	Doncaster R	7	0	**7**	**0**

RAVENHILL, Ricky (M) 71 6

H: 5 10 W: 11 03 b.Doncaster 16-1-81

Source: Barnsley Trainee.

2003–04	Doncaster R	36	3		
2004–05	Doncaster R	35	3	**71**	**6**

RIGOGLIOSO, Adriano (M) 29 0

H: 6 1 W: 12 07 b.Liverpool 28-5-79

Source: Morecambe.

2003–04	Doncaster R	17	0		
2004–05	Doncaster R	12	0	**29**	**0**

ROBERTS, Neil (F) 240 43

H: 5 10 W: 11 00 b.Wrexham 7-4-78

Source: Trainee. *Honours:* Wales Youth, Under-21, B, 3 full caps.

1996–97	Wrexham	0	0		
1997–98	Wrexham	34	8		
1998–99	Wrexham	22	3		
1999–2000	Wrexham	19	6	**75**	**17**
1999–2000	Wigan Ath	9	1		
2000–01	Wigan Ath	34	6		
2001–02	*Hull C*	6	0	**6**	**0**
2001–02	Wigan Ath	17	4		
2002–03	Wigan Ath	37	6		
2003–04	Wigan Ath	28	2		
2004–05	Wigan Ath	0	0	**125**	**19**
2004–05	*Bradford C*	3	1	**3**	**1**
2004–05	Doncaster R	31	6	**31**	**6**

RYAN, Tim (D) 111 6

H: 5 10 W: 11 00 b.Stockport 10-12-74

Source: Trainee.

1992–93	Scunthorpe U	1	0		
1993–94	Scunthorpe U	1	0		
1994–95	Scunthorpe U	0	0	**2**	**0**
From Buxton.					
1996–97	Doncaster R	28	0		
From Southport					
2003–04	Doncaster R	42	2		
2004–05	Doncaster R	39	4	**109**	**6**

TIERNEY, Fran (M) **140 18**
H: 5 10 W: 12 07 b.Liverpool 10-9-75
Source: Trainee.
1992–93 Crewe Alex 1 0
1993–94 Crewe Alex 8 1
1994–95 Crewe Alex 20 4
1995–96 Crewe Alex 22 2
1996–97 Crewe Alex 32 3
1997–98 Crewe Alex 4 0
1998–99 Crewe Alex 0 0 **87 10**
1998–99 Notts Co 20 3
1999–2000 Notts Co 13 1 **33 4**
From Witton Alb
2000–01 Exeter C 7 1 **7 1**
2003–04 Doncaster R 13 3
2004–05 Doncaster R 0 0 **13 3**

WARRINGTON, Andy (G) **141 0**
H: 6 3 W: 12 13 b.Sheffield 10-6-76
Source: Trainee.
1994–95 York C 0 0
1995–96 York C 6 0
1996–97 York C 27 0
1997–98 York C 17 0
1998–99 York C 11 0 **61 0**
2003–04 Doncaster R 46 0
2004–05 Doncaster R 34 0 **80 0**

EVERTON (31)

ARTETA, Mikel (M) **107 16**
H: 5 9 W: 10 01 b.San Sebastian 28-3-82
2000–01 Barcelona B 0 0
2000–01 Paris St Germain 6 1
2001–02 Paris St Germain 25 1 **31 2**
2002–03 Rangers 27 4
2003–04 Rangers 23 8 **50 12**
2004–05 Real Sociedad 14 1 **14 1**
2004–05 Everton 12 1 **12 1**

BEATTIE, James (F) **219 69**
H: 6 1 W: 13 06 b.Lancaster 27-2-78
Source: Trainee. *Honours:* England Under-21, 5 full caps.
1994–95 Blackburn R 0 0
1995–96 Blackburn R 0 0
1996–97 Blackburn R 1 0
1997–98 Blackburn R 3 0 **4 0**
1998–99 Southampton 35 5
1999–2000 Southampton 18 0
2000–01 Southampton 37 11
2001–02 Southampton 28 12
2002–03 Southampton 38 23
2003–04 Southampton 37 14
2004–05 Southampton 11 3 **204 68**
2004–05 Everton 11 1 **11 1**

BENT, Marcus (F) **337 78**
H: 6 2 W: 13 03 b.Hammersmith 19-5-78
Source: Trainee. *Honours:* England Under-21.
1995–96 Brentford 12 1
1996–97 Brentford 34 3
1997–98 Brentford 24 4 **70 8**
1997–98 Crystal Palace 16 5
1998–99 Crystal Palace 12 0 **28 5**
1998–99 Port Vale 15 0
1999–2000 Port Vale 8 1 **23 1**
1999–2000 Sheffield U 32 15
2000–01 Sheffield U 16 5 **48 20**
2000–01 Blackburn R 28 8
2001–02 Blackburn R 9 0 **37 8**
2001–02 Ipswich T 25 9
2002–03 Ipswich T 32 11
2003–04 Ipswich T 4 1 **61 21**
2003–04 *Leicester C* 33 9 **33 9**
2004–05 Everton 37 6 **37 6**

BOSNAR, Eddy (D) **119 3**
H: 6 3 W: 13 05 b.Sydney 29-4-80
Honours: Australia Youth, Under-20, Under-23.
1997–98 Newcastle Breackers 6 1 **6 1**
1998–99 Northern Spirit 13 0 **13 0**
1999–2000 Sydney U 27 1 **27 1**
2000–01 Dynamo Zagreb 20 0 **20 0**
2001–02 Sturm Graz 20 0
2002–03 Sturm Graz 19 1
2003–04 Sturm Graz 14 0 **53 1**
2004–05 Everton 0 0

CAHILL, Tim (M) **250 63**
H: 5 10 W: 10 12 b.Sydney 6-12-79
Source: Sydney U. *Honours:* Western Samoa Youth, Australia 10 full caps, 7 goals.
1997–98 Millwall 1 0
1998–99 Millwall 36 6
1999–2000 Millwall 45 12
2000–01 Millwall 41 9
2001–02 Millwall 43 13
2002–03 Millwall 11 3
2003–04 Millwall 40 9 **217 52**
2004–05 Everton 33 11 **33 11**

CARSLEY, Lee (M) **320 29**
H: 5 10 W: 12 04 b.Birmingham 28-2-74
Source: Trainee. *Honours:* Eire 29 full caps.
1992–93 Derby Co 0 0
1993–94 Derby Co 0 0
1994–95 Derby Co 23 2
1995–96 Derby Co 35 1
1996–97 Derby Co 24 0
1997–98 Derby Co 34 1
1998–99 Derby Co 22 1 **138 5**
1998–99 Blackburn R 8 0
1999–2000 Blackburn R 30 10
2000–01 Blackburn R 8 0 **46 10**
2000–01 Coventry C 21 2
2001–02 Coventry C 26 2 **47 4**
2001–02 Everton 8 1
2002–03 Everton 24 3
2003–04 Everton 21 2
2004–05 Everton 36 4 **89 10**

FERGUSON, Duncan (F) **333 97**
H: 6 4 W: 13 07 b.Stirling 27-12-71
Source: Carse T. *Honours:* Scotland Schools, Youth, Under-21, B, 7 full caps.
1990–91 Dundee U 9 1
1991–92 Dundee U 38 15
1992–93 Dundee U 30 12 **77 28**
1993–94 Rangers 10 1
1994–95 Rangers 4 1 **14 2**
1994–95 Everton 23 7
1995–96 Everton 18 5
1996–97 Everton 33 10
1997–98 Everton 29 11
1998–99 Everton 13 4
1998–99 Newcastle U 7 2
1999–2000 Newcastle U 23 6 **30 8**
2000–01 Everton 12 6
2001–02 Everton 22 6
2002–03 Everton 7 0
2003–04 Everton 20 5
2004–05 Everton 35 5 **212 59**

FOX, Daniel (D) **0 0**
H: 5 11 W: 12 06 b.Crewe 29-5-86
Source: Scholar.
2004–05 Everton 0 0

GERRARD, Anthony (D) **8 0**
H: 6 2 W: 13 07 b.Liverpool 6-2-86
Source: Scholar.
2004–05 Everton 0 0
2004–05 *Walsall* 8 0 **8 0**

GRAVESEN, Thomas (M) **273 27**
H: 5 9 W: 13 06 b.Vejle 11-3-76
Honours: Denmark Under-21, 56 full caps, 5 goals.
1995–96 Vejle 28 2
1996–97 Vejle 30 8 **58 10**
1997–98 Hamburg 26 2
1998–99 Hamburg 22 3
1999–2000 Hamburg 26 1 **74 6**
2000–01 Everton 32 2
2001–02 Everton 25 2
2002–03 Everton 33 1
2003–04 Everton 30 2
2004–05 Everton 21 4 **141 11**

HIBBERT, Tony (D) **98 0**
H: 5 9 W: 11 05 b.Liverpool 20-2-81
Source: Trainee.
1998–99 Everton 0 0
1999–2000 Everton 0 0
2000–01 Everton 3 0
2001–02 Everton 10 0
2002–03 Everton 24 0
2003–04 Everton 25 0
2004–05 Everton 36 0 **98 0**

HOPKINS, Paul (F) **0 0**
b.Liverpool 29-11-86
Source: Scholar.
2004–05 Everton 0 0

HUGHES, Mark (D) **0 0**
H: 6 2 W: 13 00 b.Liverpool 9-12-86
Source: Scholar.
2004–05 Everton 0 0

KILBANE, Kevin (M) **334 30**
H: 6 1 W: 13 05 b.Preston 1-2-77
Source: From Trainee. *Honours:* Eire Under-21, 64 full caps, 5 goals.
1993–94 Preston NE 0 0
1994–95 Preston NE 0 0
1995–96 Preston NE 11 1
1996–97 Preston NE 36 2 **47 3**
1997–98 WBA 43 4
1998–99 WBA 44 6
1999–2000 WBA 19 5 **106 15**
1999–2000 Sunderland 20 1
2000–01 Sunderland 30 4
2001–02 Sunderland 28 2
2002–03 Sunderland 30 1
2003–04 Sunderland 5 0 **113 8**
2003–04 Everton 30 3
2004–05 Everton 38 1 **68 4**

LI TIE (M) **34 0**
H: 6 0 W: 11 10 b.China 18-9-77
Source: Liaoning Bodao. *Honours:* China 79 full caps, 5 goals.
2002–03 Everton 29 0
2003–04 Everton 5 0
2004–05 Everton 0 0 **34 0**

MARTYN, Nigel (G) **646 0**
H: 6 1 W: 15 11 b.St Austell 11-8-66
Source: St Blazey. *Honours:* England Under-21, B, 23 full caps.
1987–88 Bristol R 39 0
1988–89 Bristol R 46 0
1989–90 Bristol R 16 0 **101 0**
1989–90 Crystal Palace 25 0
1990–91 Crystal Palace 38 0
1991–92 Crystal Palace 38 0
1992–93 Crystal Palace 42 0
1993–94 Crystal Palace 46 0
1994–95 Crystal Palace 37 0
1995–96 Crystal Palace 46 0 **272 0**
1996–97 Leeds U 37 0
1997–98 Leeds U 37 0
1998–99 Leeds U 34 0
1999–2000 Leeds U 38 0
2000–01 Leeds U 23 0
2001–02 Leeds U 38 0
2002–03 Leeds U 0 0
2003–04 Leeds U 0 0 **207 0**
2003–04 Everton 34 0
2004–05 Everton 32 0 **66 0**

McFADDEN, James (M) **109 27**
H: 6 0 W: 12 11 b.Glasgow 14-4-83
Honours: Scotland Under-21, B, 21 full caps, 2 goals.
2000–01 Motherwell 6 0
2001–02 Motherwell 24 10
2002–03 Motherwell 30 13
2003–04 Motherwell 3 3 **63 26**
2003–04 Everton 23 0
2004–05 Everton 23 1 **46 1**

NAYSMITH, Gary (D) **209 8**
H: 5 9 W: 12 01 b.Edinburgh 16-11-78
Source: Whitehill Welfare Colts. *Honours:* Scotland Schools, Under-21, B, 28 full caps, 1 goal.
1995–96 Hearts 1 0
1996–97 Hearts 10 0
1997–98 Hearts 16 2
1998–99 Hearts 26 0
1999–2000 Hearts 35 1
2000–01 Hearts 9 0 **97 3**
2000–01 Everton 20 2
2001–02 Everton 24 0
2002–03 Everton 28 1
2003–04 Everton 29 2
2004–05 Everton 11 0 **112 5**

NYARKO, Alex (M) 199 16
H: 6 0 W: 13 00 b.Accra 15-10-73
Source: Asanti Kotoko, Deawe Youngsters.
Honours: Ghana full caps.

1994–95	Sportul	0	0		
1995–96	Basle	26	3		
1996–97	Basle	29	5	**55**	**8**
1997–98	Karlsruhe	22	1	**22**	**1**
1998–99	Lens	24	3		
1999–2000	Lens	21	1	**45**	**4**
2000–01	Everton	22	1		
2001–02	Everton	0	0		
2001–02	Monaco	26	2	**26**	**2**
2002–03	Paris St Germain	18	0	**18**	**0**
2003–04	Everton	11	0		
2004–05	Everton	0	0	**33**	**1**

OSMAN, Leon (F) 64 11
H: 5 8 W: 10 09 b.Billinge 17-5-81
Source: Trainee. *Honours:* England Schools, Youth.

1998–99	Everton	0	0		
1999–2000	Everton	0	0		
2000–01	Everton	0	0		
2001–02	Everton	0	0		
2002–03	Everton	2	0		
2002–03	*Carlisle U*	12	1	**12**	**1**
2003–04	Everton	4	1		
2003–04	*Derby Co*	17	3	**17**	**3**
2004–05	Everton	29	6	**35**	**7**

PISTONE, Alessandro (D) 247 8
H: 5 11 W: 11 08 b.Milan 27-7-75

1992–93	Vicenza	0	0		
1993–94	Solbiatese	20	1	**20**	**1**
1994–95	Crevalcore	29	4	**29**	**4**
1995–96	Vicenza	6	0	**6**	**0**
1995–96	Internazionale	19	1		
1996–97	Internazionale	26	0	**45**	**1**
1997–98	Newcastle U	28	0		
1998–99	Newcastle U	3	0		
1999–2000	Newcastle U	15	1	**46**	**1**
2000–01	Everton	7	0		
2001–02	Everton	25	1		
2002–03	Everton	15	0		
2003–04	Everton	21	0		
2004–05	Everton	33	0	**101**	**1**

PLESSIS, Guillaume (M) 0 0
H: 6 2 W: 12 02 b.Saint Denis 16-1-85
Source: Lens.

2004–05	Everton	0	0		

STUBBS, Alan (D) 432 15
H: 6 2 W: 13 12 b.Kirkby 6-10-71
Source: Trainee.

1990–91	Bolton W	23	0		
1991–92	Bolton W	32	1		
1992–93	Bolton W	42	2		
1993–94	Bolton W	41	1		
1994–95	Bolton W	39	1		
1995–96	Bolton W	25	4	**202**	**9**
1996–97	Celtic	20	0		
1997–98	Celtic	29	1		
1998–99	Celtic	23	1		
1999–2000	Celtic	23	0		
2000–01	Celtic	11	1	**106**	**3**
2001–02	Everton	31	2		
2002–03	Everton	35	0		
2003–04	Everton	27	0		
2004–05	Everton	31	1	**124**	**3**

TURNER, Iain (G) 8 0
H: 6 3 W: 12 10 b.Stirling 26-1-84
Source: Trainee. *Honours:* Scotland Under-21.

2002–03	Everton	0	0		
2003–04	Everton	0	0		
2004–05	Everton	0	0		
2004–05	*Doncaster R*	8	0	**8**	**0**

VAUGHAN, James (F) 2 1
H: 5 11 W: 12 08 b.Birmingham 14-7-88
Source: Scholar. *Honours:* England Youth.

2004–05	Everton	2	1	**2**	**1**

WATSON, Steve (D) 375 26
H: 6 0 W: 12 07 b.North Shields 1-4-74
Source: Trainee. *Honours:* England Youth, Under-21, B.

1990–91	Newcastle U	24	0		
1991–92	Newcastle U	28	1		
1992–93	Newcastle U	2	0		
1993–94	Newcastle U	32	2		
1994–95	Newcastle U	27	4		
1995–96	Newcastle U	23	3		
1996–97	Newcastle U	36	1		
1997–98	Newcastle U	29	1		
1998–99	Newcastle U	7	0	**208**	**12**
1998–99	Aston Villa	27	0		
1999–2000	Aston Villa	14	0	**41**	**0**
2000–01	Everton	34	0		
2001–02	Everton	25	4		
2002–03	Everton	18	5		
2003–04	Everton	24	5		
2004–05	Everton	25	0	**126**	**14**

WEIR, David (D) 422 24
H: 6 5 W: 14 03 b.Falkirk 10-5-70
Source: Celtic BC. *Honours:* Scotland 40 full caps, 1 goal.

1992–93	Falkirk	30	1		
1993–94	Falkirk	37	3		
1994–95	Falkirk	32	1		
1995–96	Falkirk	34	3	**133**	**8**
1996–97	Hearts	34	6		
1997–98	Hearts	35	1		
1998–99	Hearts	23	1	**92**	**8**
1998–99	Everton	14	0		
1999–2000	Everton	35	2		
2000–01	Everton	37	1		
2001–02	Everton	36	4		
2002–03	Everton	31	0		
2003–04	Everton	10	0		
2004–05	Everton	34	1	**197**	**8**

WILSON, Laurence (M) 0 0
H: 5 10 W: 11 00 b.Liverpool 10-10-86
Source: Scholar. *Honours:* England Youth.

2004–05	Everton	0	0		

WRIGHT, Richard (G) 296 0
H: 6 2 W: 14 04 b.Ipswich 5-11-77
Source: Trainee. *Honours:* England Schools, Youth, Under-21, 2 full caps.

1994–95	Ipswich T	3	0		
1995–96	Ipswich T	23	0		
1996–97	Ipswich T	40	0		
1997–98	Ipswich T	46	0		
1998–99	Ipswich T	46	0		
1999–2000	Ipswich T	46	0		
2000–01	Ipswich T	36	0	**240**	**0**
2001–02	Arsenal	12	0	**12**	**0**
2002–03	Everton	33	0		
2003–04	Everton	4	0		
2004–05	Everton	7	0	**44**	**0**

YOBO, Joseph (D) 150 4
H: 6 1 W: 13 00 b.Kano 6-9-80
Source: Mechelen. *Honours:* Nigeria full caps.

1998–99	Standard Liege	0	0		
1999–2000	Standard Liege	18	0		
2000–01	Standard Liege	30	2	**48**	**2**
2001–02	Marseille	23	0	**23**	**0**
2002–03	Everton	24	0		
2003–04	Everton	28	2		
2004–05	Everton	27	0	**79**	**2**

Scholars
Anichebe, Victor Chinedu; Boyle, Patrick Joseph Gerard; Davidsen, Johann Troest; Harris, James William; Holt, Mathew John; Kearney, Alan; Lake, Sean; Phelan, Scott Richard; Seargeant, Christian Michael; Vaughan, James Oliver; Vidarsspm, Bjarni Thor; Wright, Sean Glenn; Wynne, Stephen

FULHAM (32)

BAKER, Nicholas (G) 0 0
b.London 18-12-84

2003–04	Fulham	0	0		
2004–05	Fulham	0	0		

BATISTA, Ricardo (G) 0 0
H: 6 3 W: 12 06 b.Portugal 19-11-86
Source: Vitoria Setubal.

2004–05	Fulham	0	0		

BEASANT, Dave (G) 773 0
H: 6 4 W: 14 04 b.Willesden 20-3-59
Source: From Edgware T. *Honours:* England B, 2 full caps.

1979–80	Wimbledon	2	0		
1980–81	Wimbledon	34	0		
1981–82	Wimbledon	46	0		
1982–83	Wimbledon	46	0		
1983–84	Wimbledon	46	0		
1984–85	Wimbledon	42	0		
1985–86	Wimbledon	42	0		
1986–87	Wimbledon	42	0		
1987–88	Wimbledon	40	0	**340**	**0**
1988–89	Newcastle U	20	0	**20**	**0**
1988–89	Chelsea	22	0		
1989–90	Chelsea	38	0		
1990–91	Chelsea	35	0		
1991–92	Chelsea	21	0		
1992–93	Chelsea	17	0		
1992–93	*Grimsby T*	6	0	**6**	**0**
1992–93	*Wolverhampton W*	4	0	**4**	**0**
1993–94	Chelsea	0	0	**133**	**0**
1993–94	Southampton	25	0		
1994–95	Southampton	13	0		
1995–96	Southampton	36	0		
1996–97	Southampton	14	0		
1997–98	Southampton	0	0	**88**	**0**
1997–98	Nottingham F	41	0		
1998–99	Nottingham F	26	0		
1999–2000	Nottingham F	27	0		
2000–01	Nottingham F	45	0	**139**	**0**
2001–02	Portsmouth	27	0	**27**	**0**
2002–03	Bradford C	0	0		
2002–03	Wigan Ath	0	0		
2002–03	Brighton & HA	16	0	**16**	**0**
2003–04	Fulham	0	0		
2004–05	Fulham	0	0		

BOA MORTE, Luis (F) 194 39
H: 5 9 W: 12 06 b.Lisbon 4-8-77
Source: Sporting Lisbon, Lourihanense (loan). *Honours:* Portugal Youth, Under-21, 21 full caps, 1 goal.

1997–98	Arsenal	15	0		
1998–99	Arsenal	8	0		
1999–2000	Arsenal	2	0	**25**	**0**
1999–2000	Southampton	14	1		
2000–01	Southampton	0	0	**14**	**1**
2000–01	*Fulham*	39	18		
2001–02	Fulham	23	1		
2002–03	Fulham	29	2		
2003–04	Fulham	33	9		
2004–05	Fulham	31	8	**155**	**38**

BOCANEGRA, Carlos (D) 130 6
H: 5 11 W: 12 07 b.Alta Loma 25-5-79
Honours: USA 36 full caps, 6 goals.

2000	Chicago Fire	27	1		
2001	Chicago Fire	15	1		
2002	Chicago Fire	26	2		
2003	Chicago Fire	19	1	**87**	**5**
2003–04	Fulham	15	0		
2004–05	Fulham	28	1	**43**	**1**

BONNISSEL, Jerome (D) 283 1
H: 5 9 W: 11 02 b.Montpellier 16-4-73
Honours: France B.

1992–93	Montpellier	18	0		
1993–94	Montpellier	32	1		
1994–95	Montpellier	37	0		
1995–96	Montpellier	32	0	**119**	**1**
1996–97	La Coruna	20	0		
1997–98	La Coruna	27	0		
1998–99	La Coruna	16	0	**63**	**0**
1999–2000	Bordeaux	26	0		
2000–01	Bordeaux	31	0		
2001–02	Bordeaux	13	0		
2002–03	Bordeaux	12	0	**82**	**0**
2002–03	Rangers	3	0	**3**	**0**
2003–04	Fulham	16	0		
2004–05	Fulham	0	0	**16**	**0**

BUARI, Malik (M) 3 0
H: 5 11 W: 11 13 b.Accra 21-1-84
Source: Trainee.

2003–04	Fulham	3	0		
2004–05	Fulham	0	0	**3**	**0**

CLARK, Lee (M) 417 59
H: 5 8 W: 11 07 b.Wallsend 27-10-72
Source: Trainee. *Honours:* England Schools, Youth, Under-21.

1989–90	Newcastle U	0	0		
1990–91	Newcastle U	19	2		
1991–92	Newcastle U	29	5		
1992–93	Newcastle U	46	9		

1993–94	Newcastle U	29	2		
1994–95	Newcastle U	19	1		
1995–96	Newcastle U	28	2		
1996–97	Newcastle U	25	2	**195**	**23**
1997–98	Sunderland	46	13		
1998–99	Sunderland	27	3	**73**	**16**
1999–2000	Fulham	42	8		
2000–01	Fulham	45	7		
2001–02	Fulham	9	0		
2002–03	Fulham	11	2		
2003–04	Fulham	25	2		
2004–05	Fulham	17	1	**149**	**20**

COLE, Andy (F) **434 210**
H: 5 10 W: 12 11 b.Nottingham 15-10-71
Source: Trainee. *Honours:* England Schools, Youth, Under-21, B, 15 full caps, 1 goal. Football League.

1989–90	Arsenal	0	0		
1990–91	Arsenal	1	0		
1991–92	Arsenal	0	0	**1**	**0**
1991–92	*Fulham*	13	3		
1991–92	*Bristol C*	12	8		
1992–93	Bristol C	29	12	**41**	**20**
1992–93	Newcastle U	12	12		
1993–94	Newcastle U	40	34		
1994–95	Newcastle U	18	9	**70**	**55**
1994–95	Manchester U	18	12		
1995–96	Manchester U	34	11		
1996–97	Manchester U	20	6		
1997–98	Manchester U	33	15		
1998–99	Manchester U	32	17		
1999–2000	Manchester U	28	19		
2000–01	Manchester U	19	9		
2001–02	Manchester U	11	4	**195**	**93**
2001–02	Blackburn R	15	9		
2002–03	Blackburn R	34	7		
2003–04	Blackburn R	34	11	**83**	**27**
2004–05	Fulham	31	12	**44**	**15**

COLLINS, Matthew (M) **0 0**
b.Merthyr 31-3-86
Source: Trainee.

2002–03	Fulham	0	0		
2003–04	Fulham	0	0		
2004–05	Fulham	0	0		

CROSSLEY, Mark (G) **358 0**
H: 6 3 W: 15 09 b.Barnsley 16-6-69
Source: Trainee. *Honours:* England Under-21, Wales B, 8 full caps.

1987–88	Nottingham F	0	0		
1988–89	Nottingham F	2	0		
1989–90	Nottingham F	8	0		
1989–90	*Manchester U*	0	0		
1990–91	Nottingham F	38	0		
1991–92	Nottingham F	36	0		
1992–93	Nottingham F	37	0		
1993–94	Nottingham F	37	0		
1994–95	Nottingham F	42	0		
1995–96	Nottingham F	38	0		
1996–97	Nottingham F	33	0		
1997–98	Nottingham F	0	0		
1997–98	*Millwall*	13	0	**13**	**0**
1998–99	Nottingham F	12	0		
1999–2000	Nottingham F	20	0	**303**	**0**
2000–01	Middlesbrough	5	0		
2001–02	Middlesbrough	18	0		
2002–03	Middlesbrough	0	0	**23**	**0**
2002–03	*Stoke C*	12	0	**12**	**0**
2003–04	Fulham	1	0		
2004–05	Fulham	6	0	**7**	**0**

DIOP, Papa Bouba (M) **123 21**
H: 6 4 W: 14 12 b.Dakar 28-1-78
Source: Espoir, Jaraaf, Vevey Sports.
Honours: Senegal full caps.

1999–2000	Neuchatel Xamax	0	0		
2000–01	Neuchatel Xamax	18	4	**18**	**4**
2000–01	Grasshoppers	11	1		
2001–02	Grasshoppers	18	4	**29**	**5**
2001–02	Lens	5	0		
2002–03	Lens	16	3		
2003–04	Lens	26	3	**47**	**6**
2004–05	Fulham	29	6	**29**	**6**

DOHERTY, Sean (M) **1 0**
H: 5 8 W: 10 08 b.Basingstoke 10-5-85
Source: Scholar. *Honours:* England Youth, Under-20.

2001–02	Fulham	0	0		
2002–03	Fulham	0	0		
2003–04	Fulham	0	0		
2003–04	*Blackpool*	1	0	**1**	**0**
2004–05	Fulham	0	0		

EHUI, Ismael (F) **0 0**
H: 5 7 W: 10 10 b.Lille 10-12-86
Source: Scholar.

2004–05	Fulham	0	0		

FLITNEY, Ross (G) **3 0**
H: 6 1 W: 11 11 b.Hitchin 1-6-84
Source: Scholar.

2003–04	Fulham	0	0		
2003–04	*Brighton & HA*	3	0	**3**	**0**
2004–05	Fulham	0	0		
2004–05	*Doncaster R*	0	0		

FONTAINE, Liam (D) **16 0**
H: 6 3 W: 12 02 b.Beckenham 7-1-86
Source: Trainee. *Honours:* England Under-20.

2003–04	Fulham	0	0		
2004–05	Fulham	1	0	**1**	**0**
2004–05	*Yeovil T*	15	0	**15**	**0**

GOMA, Alain (D) **333 5**
H: 6 0 W: 13 01 b.Sault 5-10-72
Honours: France 2 full caps.

1990–91	Auxerre	1	0		
1991–92	Auxerre	1	0		
1992–93	Auxerre	15	1		
1993–94	Auxerre	33	0		
1994–95	Auxerre	28	0		
1995–96	Auxerre	32	0		
1996–97	Auxerre	34	2		
1997–98	Auxerre	22	1	**166**	**4**
1998–99	Paris St Germain	30	0	**30**	**0**
1999–2000	Newcastle U	14	0		
2000–01	Newcastle U	19	1	**33**	**1**
2000–01	Fulham	3	0		
2001–02	Fulham	33	0		
2002–03	Fulham	29	0		
2003–04	Fulham	23	0		
2004–05	Fulham	16	0	**104**	**0**

GREEN, Adam (D) **14 0**
H: 5 9 W: 10 08 b.Hillingdon 12-1-84
Source: Scholar.

2003–04	Fulham	4	0		
2004–05	Fulham	4	0	**8**	**0**
2004–05	*Sheffield W*	3	0	**3**	**0**
2004–05	*Bournemouth*	3	0	**3**	**0**

HAMMOND, Elvis (F) **22 0**
H: 5 10 W: 11 02 b.Accra 6-10-80
Source: Trainee.

1999–2000	Fulham	0	0		
2000–01	Fulham	0	0		
2001–02	Fulham	0	0		
2001–02	*Bristol R*	7	0	**7**	**0**
2002–03	Fulham	10	0		
2003–04	Fulham	0	0		
2003–04	*Norwich C*	4	0	**4**	**0**
2004–05	Fulham	1	0	**11**	**0**

HERRERA, Martin (G) **135 0**
H: 6 0 W: 12 06 b.Argentina 13-9-70

1997–98	Toluca	5	0	**5**	**0**
1998–99	Ferro Carril	34	0	**34**	**0**
1999–2000	Alaves	38	0		
2000–01	Alaves	36	0		
2001–02	Alaves	20	0	**94**	**0**
2002–03	Fulham	2	0		
2003–04	Fulham	0	0		
2004–05	Fulham	0	0	**2**	**0**

JENSEN, Claus (M) **286 38**
H: 6 0 W: 13 01 b.Nykobing 29-4-77
Source: Stubbekobing, Nykobing. *Honours:* Denmark Under-21, 37 full caps, 6 goals.

1995–96	Naestved	4	0	**4**	**0**
1996–97	Lyngby	31	3		
1997–98	Lyngby	31	11	**62**	**14**
1998–99	Bolton W	44	2		
1999–2000	Bolton W	42	6	**86**	**8**
2000–01	Charlton Ath	38	5		
2001–02	Charlton Ath	18	1		
2002–03	Charlton Ath	35	6		
2003–04	Charlton Ath	31	4	**122**	**16**
2004–05	Fulham	12	0	**12**	**0**

JOHN, Collins (F) **70 19**
H: 5 11 W: 12 13 b.Zwandru 17-10-85
Honours: Holland Youth, Under-21.

2002–03	Twente	17	2		
2003–04	Twente	18	9	**35**	**11**
2003–04	Fulham	8	4		
2004–05	Fulham	27	4	**35**	**8**

KNIGHT, Zat (D) **101 1**
H: 6 6 W: 15 02 b.Solihull 2-5-80
Source: Rushall Olympic. *Honours:* England Under-21, 2 full caps.

1998–99	Fulham	0	0		
1999–2000	Fulham	0	0		
1999–2000	*Peterborough U*	8	0	**8**	**0**
2000–01	Fulham	0	0		
2001–02	Fulham	10	0		
2002–03	Fulham	17	0		
2003–04	Fulham	31	0		
2004–05	Fulham	35	1	**93**	**1**

LAWLESS, Alex (F) **0 0**
b.Llwynupion 26-3-85

2003–04	Fulham	0	0		
2004–05	Fulham	0	0		

LEACOCK, Dean (D) **17 0**
H: 6 2 W: 12 04 b.Croydon 10-6-84
Source: Trainee. *Honours:* England Youth, Under-20.

2002–03	Fulham	0	0		
2003–04	Fulham	4	0		
2004–05	Fulham	0	0	**4**	**0**
2004–05	*Coventry C*	13	0	**13**	**0**

LEGWINSKI, Sylvain (M) **289 23**
H: 6 1 W: 11 07 b.Clermont-Ferrand 6-10-73
Honours: France Under-21.

1992–93	Monaco	2	0		
1993–94	Monaco	0	0		
1994–95	Monaco	21	1		
1995–96	Monaco	29	2		
1996–97	Monaco	37	9		
1997–98	Monaco	22	0		
1998–99	Monaco	14	1	**125**	**13**
1999–2000	Bordeaux	13	1		
2000–01	Bordeaux	32	1		
2001–02	Bordeaux	4	0	**49**	**2**
2001–02	Fulham	33	3		
2002–03	Fulham	35	4		
2003–04	Fulham	32	0		
2004–05	Fulham	15	1	**115**	**8**

MALBRANQUE, Steed (M) **215 31**
H: 5 8 W: 11 07 b.Mouscron 6-1-80
Honours: France Under-21.

1997–98	Lyon	2	0		
1998–99	Lyon	21	0		
1999–2000	Lyon	28	3		
2000–01	Lyon	26	2	**77**	**5**
2001–02	Fulham	37	8		
2002–03	Fulham	37	6		
2003–04	Fulham	38	6		
2004–05	Fulham	26	6	**138**	**26**

MARLET, Steve (F) **247 64**
H: 5 11 W: 11 10 b.Pithiviers 10-1-74
Honours: France 23 full caps, 6 goals.

1996–97	Auxerre	24	3		
1997–98	Auxerre	18	6		
1998–99	Auxerre	32	7		
1999–2000	Auxerre	33	9	**107**	**25**
2000–01	Lyon	31	12	**31**	**12**
2001–02	Fulham	26	6		
2002–03	Fulham	28	4		
2003–04	Fulham	1	1	**55**	**11**
2003–04	*Marseille*	23	9		
2004–05	*Marseille*	31	7	**54**	**16**

McBRIDE, Brian (F) **237 78**
H: 6 0 W: 12 08 b.Chicago 19-6-72
Source: St Louis Univ. *Honours:* USA 88 full caps, 28 goals.

1994–95	Wolfsburg	12	1	**12**	**1**
1996	Columbus Crew	28	17		
1997	Columbus Crew	13	6		
1998	Columbus Crew	24	10		
1999	Columbus Crew	25	5		
2000	Columbus Crew	18	6		
2000–01	Preston NE	9	1	**9**	**1**
2001	Columbus Crew	15	1		

2002	Columbus Crew	14	5		
2002–03	Everton	8	4	**8**	**4**
2003	Columbus Crew	24	12	**161**	**62**
2003–04	Fulham	16	4		
2004–05	Fulham	31	6	**47**	**10**

McDERMOTT, Neale (M) 0 0
H: 5 9 W: 10 11 b.Newcastle 8-3-85
Source: Scholar. *Honours:* England Youth.

2001–02	Newcastle U	0	0		
2002–03	Newcastle U	0	0		
2002–03	Fulham	0	0		
2003–04	Fulham	0	0		
2004–05	Fulham	0	0		

McKINLAY, Billy (M) 390 27
H: 5 8 W: 10 12 b.Glasgow 22-4-69
Source: Hamilton Th. *Honours:* Scotland Under-21, B, 29 full caps, 4 goals.

1986–87	Dundee U	3	0		
1987–88	Dundee U	12	1		
1988–89	Dundee U	30	1		
1989–90	Dundee U	13	0		
1990–91	Dundee U	34	2		
1991–92	Dundee U	22	1		
1992–93	Dundee U	37	1		
1993–94	Dundee U	39	9		
1994–95	Dundee U	27	4		
1995–96	Dundee U	5	4	**222**	**23**
1995–96	Blackburn R	19	2		
1996–97	Blackburn R	25	1		
1997–98	Blackburn R	30	0		
1998–99	Blackburn R	16	0		
1999–2000	Blackburn R	0	0		
2000–01	Blackburn R	0	0	**90**	**3**
2000–01	*Leicester C*	0	0		
2000–01	Bradford C	11	0	**11**	**0**
2001–02	Preston NE	0	0		
2001–02	Clydebank	8	0	**8**	**0**
2002–03	Leicester C	37	1		
2003–04	Leicester C	16	0	**53**	**1**
2004–05	*Ross Co*	4	0	**4**	**0**
2004–05	Fulham	2	0	**2**	**0**

NOBLE, Stuart (F) 7 0
H: 6 0 W: 12 13 b.Edinburgh 14-10-83
Source: Trainee.

2002–03	Fulham	0	0		
2003–04	Fulham	0	0		
2004–05	Fulham	0	0		
2004–05	*Torquay U*	3	0	**3**	**0**
2004–05	*Northampton T*	4	0	**4**	**0**

OUADDOU, Abdes (D) 131 4
H: 6 4 W: 12 03 b.Ksar-Askour 1-11-78
Honours: Morocco full caps.

1999–2000	Nancy	16	0		
2000–01	Nancy	31	0	**47**	**0**
2001–02	Fulham	8	0		
2002–03	Fulham	13	0	**21**	**0**
2003–04	*Rennes*	29	2		
2004–05	*Rennes*	34	2	**63**	**4**

PEARCE, Ian (D) 232 11
H: 6 3 W: 15 06 b.Bury St Edmunds 7-5-74
Source: School. *Honours:* England Youth, Under-21.

1990–91	Chelsea	1	0		
1991–92	Chelsea	2	0		
1992–93	Chelsea	1	0		
1993–94	Chelsea	0	0	**4**	**0**
1993–94	Blackburn R	5	1		
1994–95	Blackburn R	28	0		
1995–96	Blackburn R	12	1		
1996–97	Blackburn R	12	0		
1997–98	Blackburn R	5	0	**62**	**2**
1997–98	West Ham U	30	1		
1998–99	West Ham U	33	2		
1999–2000	West Ham U	1	0		
2000–01	West Ham U	15	1		
2001–02	West Ham U	9	2		
2002–03	West Ham U	30	2		
2003–04	West Ham U	24	1	**142**	**9**
2003–04	Fulham	13	0		
2004–05	Fulham	11	0	**24**	**0**

PEMBRIDGE, Mark (M) 413 51
H: 5 9 W: 11 13 b.Merthyr 29-11-70
Source: Trainee. *Honours:* Wales Schools, Under-21, B, 54 full caps, 6 goals.

1989–90	Luton T	0	0		
1990–91	Luton T	18	1		
1991–92	Luton T	42	5	**60**	**6**
1992–93	Derby Co	42	8		
1993–94	Derby Co	41	11		
1994–95	Derby Co	27	9	**110**	**28**
1995–96	Sheffield W	25	1		
1996–97	Sheffield W	34	6		
1997–98	Sheffield W	34	4	**93**	**11**
1998–99	Benfica	19	1	**19**	**1**
1999–2000	Everton	31	2		
2000–01	Everton	21	0		
2001–02	Everton	14	1		
2002–03	Everton	21	1		
2003–04	Everton	4	0	**91**	**4**
2003–04	Fulham	12	1		
2004–05	Fulham	28	0	**40**	**1**

PRATLEY, Darren (M) 15 1
H: 6 1 W: 11 05 b.Barking 22-4-85
Source: Scholar.

2001–02	Fulham	0	0		
2002–03	Fulham	0	0		
2003–04	Fulham	1	0		
2004–05	Fulham	0	0	**1**	**0**
2004–05	*Brentford*	14	1	**14**	**1**

RADZINSKI, Tomasz (F) 308 125
H: 5 8 W: 11 11 b.Poznan 14-12-73
Source: Toronto Rockets, St Catherines Roma. *Honours:* Canada Under-23, 27 full caps, 7 goals.

1994–95	Ekeren	28	6		
1995–96	Ekeren	22	9		
1996–97	Ekeren	23	8		
1997–98	Ekeren	31	19	**104**	**42**
1998–99	Anderlecht	22	15		
1999–2000	Anderlecht	25	14		
2000–01	Anderlecht	31	23	**78**	**52**
2001–02	Everton	27	6		
2002–03	Everton	30	11		
2003–04	Everton	34	8	**91**	**25**
2004–05	Fulham	35	6	**35**	**6**

REHMAN, Zesh (M) 29 2
H: 6 2 W: 12 08 b.Birmingham 14-10-83
Source: Scholar. *Honours:* England Youth.

2001–02	Fulham	0	0		
2002–03	Fulham	0	0		
2003–04	Fulham	1	0		
2003–04	*Brighton & HA*	11	2	**11**	**2**
2004–05	Fulham	17	0	**18**	**0**

ROSENIOR, Liam (M) 49 2
H: 5 9 W: 11 05 b.Wandsworth 9-7-84
Source: Scholar. *Honours:* England Youth, Under-20, Under-21.

2001–02	Bristol C	1	0		
2002–03	Bristol C	21	2		
2003–04	Bristol C	0	0	**22**	**2**
2003–04	Fulham	0	0		
2003–04	*Torquay U*	10	0	**10**	**0**
2004–05	Fulham	17	0	**17**	**0**

SAVA, Facundo (F) 299 82
H: 6 0 W: 13 01 b.Ituzaingo 3-7-74

1993–94	Ferro Carril	27	3		
1994–95	Ferro Carril	18	0		
1995–96	Ferro Carril	34	4		
1996–97	Ferro Carril	1	0	**80**	**7**
1996–97	Boca Juniors	7	0	**7**	**0**
1997–98	Gimnasia	32	8		
1998–99	Gimnasia	28	10		
1999–2000	Gimnasia	35	12		
2000–01	Gimnasia	34	13		
2001–02	Gimnasia	34	23	**163**	**66**
2002–03	Fulham	20	5		
2003–04	Fulham	6	1	**26**	**6**
2004–05	*Celta Vigo*	23	3	**23**	**3**

TIMLIN, Michael (M) 0 0
H: 5 9 W: 11 10 b.Lambeth 19-3-85
Source: Trainee. *Honours:* Eire Youth, Under-21.

2002–03	Fulham	0	0		
2003–04	Fulham	0	0		
2004–05	Fulham	0	0		

VAN DER SAR, Edwin (G) 419 1
H: 6 5 W: 13 01 b.Voorhout 29-10-70
Honours: Holland 100 full caps.

1990–91	Ajax	9	0		
1991–92	Ajax	0	0		
1992–93	Ajax	19	0		
1993–94	Ajax	32	0		
1994–95	Ajax	33	0		
1995–96	Ajax	33	0		
1996–97	Ajax	33	0		
1997–98	Ajax	33	1	**192**	**1**
1998–99	Juventus	34	0		
1999–2000	Juventus	32	0		
2000–01	Juventus	34	0	**100**	**0**
2001–02	Fulham	37	0		
2002–03	Fulham	19	0		
2003–04	Fulham	37	0		
2004–05	Fulham	34	0	**127**	**0**

VOLZ, Moritz (D) 74 1
H: 5 8 W: 11 07 b.Siegen 21-1-83
Source: Schalke. *Honours:* Germany Youth, Under-21.

1999–2000	Arsenal	0	0		
2000–01	Arsenal	0	0		
2001–02	Arsenal	0	0		
2002–03	Arsenal	0	0		
2002–03	*Wimbledon*	10	1	**10**	**1**
2003–04	Arsenal	0	0		
2003–04	Fulham	33	0		
2004–05	Fulham	31	0	**64**	**0**

WATKINS, Robert (D) 0 0
b.Carshalton 14-10-85
Source: Trainee.

2003–04	Fulham	0	0		
2004–05	Fulham	0	0		

Scholars
Brooks-Meade, Corrin; Brown, Wayne Johnathon; Casal, Yinka; Davidson, Mark; Hall, Lee; James, Christopher; Mabbutt, Gary David; Miguil, Aouled; Milsom, Robert Steven; Moncur, Thomas James; Murtagh, Nicholas Richard; Ottley, Andrew Patrick; Sankoh, Saheed; Warrell, Sam; Watts, Adam

GILLINGHAM (33)

ASHBY, Barry (D) 508 14
H: 6 3 W: 14 06 b.Park Royal 2-11-70
Source: Trainee.

1988–89	Watford	0	0		
1989–90	Watford	18	1		
1990–91	Watford	23	0		
1991–92	Watford	21	0		
1992–93	Watford	35	0		
1993–94	Watford	17	2	**114**	**3**
1993–94	Brentford	8	1		
1994–95	Brentford	40	1		
1995–96	Brentford	33	1		
1996–97	Brentford	40	1	**121**	**4**
1997–98	Gillingham	43	0		
1998–99	Gillingham	38	1		
1999–2000	Gillingham	41	3		
2000–01	Gillingham	40	1		
2001–02	Gillingham	28	1		
2002–03	Gillingham	38	0		
2003–04	Gillingham	23	1		
2004–05	Gillingham	22	0	**273**	**7**

AWUAH, Jones (F) 4 0
H: 5 11 W: 12 00 b.Ghana 10-7-83
Source: Scholar.

2002–03	Gillingham	4	0		
2003–04	Gillingham	0	0		
2004–05	Gillingham	0	0	**4**	**0**

BANKS, Steve (G) 339 0
H: 6 0 W: 14 01 b.Hillingdon 9-2-72
Source: Trainee.

1991–92	West Ham U	0	0		
1992–93	West Ham U	0	0		
1993–94	Gillingham	29	0		
1994–95	Gillingham	38	0		
1995–96	Blackpool	24	0		
1996–97	Blackpool	46	0		
1997–98	Blackpool	45	0		
1998–99	Blackpool	35	0	**150**	**0**
1998–99	Bolton W	9	0		
1999–2000	Bolton W	2	0		
2000–01	Bolton W	9	0		
2001–02	Bolton W	1	0		
2001–02	*Rochdale*	15	0	**15**	**0**
2002–03	Bolton W	0	0	**21**	**0**
2002–03	*Bradford C*	9	0	**9**	**0**

2002–03 Stoke C 14 0 **14 0**
2003–04 Wimbledon 24 0 **24 0**
2003–04 Gillingham 13 0
2004–05 Gillingham 26 0 **106 0**

BECKWITH, Dean (D) 1 0
H: 6 3 W: 13 04 b.Southwark 18-9-83
Source: Scholar.
2003–04 Gillingham 0 0
2004–05 Gillingham 1 0 **1 0**

BODKIN, Matt (F) 2 0
H: 5 6 W: 11 05 b.Chatham 23-11-83
Source: Scholar.
2002–03 Nottingham F 0 0
2003–04 Nottingham F 0 0
2004–05 Gillingham 2 0 **2 0**

BOSSU, Bertrand (G) 8 0
H: 6 7 W: 14 13 b.Calais 14-10-80
1999–2000 Barnet 0 0
2000–01 Barnet 0 0
2001–02 Barnet 0 0
2002–03 Barnet 0 0
From Hayes.
2003–04 Gillingham 4 0
2004–05 Gillingham 2 0 **6 0**
2004–05 *Torquay U* 2 0 **2 0**
2004–05 *Oldham Ath* 0 0

BROWN, Jason (G) 87 0
H: 6 0 W: 16 01 b.Southwark 18-5-82
Source: Charlton Ath Scholar. *Honours:* Wales Under-21.
2000–01 Gillingham 0 0
2001–02 Gillingham 10 0
2002–03 Gillingham 39 0
2003–04 Gillingham 22 0
2004–05 Gillingham 16 0 **87 0**

BYFIELD, Darren (F) 225 48
H: 5 11 W: 12 07 b.Sutton Coldfield 29-9-76
Source: Trainee. *Honours:* Jamaica 7 full caps.
1993–94 Aston Villa 0 0
1994–95 Aston Villa 0 0
1995–96 Aston Villa 0 0
1996–97 Aston Villa 0 0
1997–98 Aston Villa 7 0
1998–99 Aston Villa 0 0
1998–99 *Preston NE* 5 1 **5 1**
1999–2000 Aston Villa 0 0 **7 0**
1999–2000 *Northampton T* 6 1 **6 1**
1999–2000 *Cambridge U* 4 0 **4 0**
1999–2000 *Blackpool* 3 0 **3 0**
2000–01 Walsall 40 9
2001–02 Walsall 37 4 **77 13**
2001–02 Rotherham U 3 2
2002–03 Rotherham U 37 13
2003–04 Rotherham U 28 7 **68 22**
2003–04 Sunderland 17 5 **17 5**
2004–05 Gillingham 38 6 **38 6**

COX, Ian (D) 366 23
H: 6 1 W: 12 05 b.Croydon 25-3-71
Source: Carshalton Ath. *Honours:* Trinidad & Tobago 12 full caps.
1993–94 Crystal Palace 0 0
1994–95 Crystal Palace 11 0
1995–96 Crystal Palace 4 0 **15 0**
1995–96 Bournemouth 8 0
1996–97 Bournemouth 44 8
1997–98 Bournemouth 46 3
1998–99 Bournemouth 46 5
1999–2000 Bournemouth 28 0 **172 16**
1999–2000 Burnley 17 1
2000–01 Burnley 38 1
2001–02 Burnley 34 2
2002–03 Burnley 26 1 **115 5**
2003–04 Gillingham 33 0
2004–05 Gillingham 31 2 **64 2**

CROFTS, Andrew (D) 36 2
H: 5 10 W: 11 13 b.Chatham 29-5-84
Source: Trainee. *Honours:* Wales Youth, Under-21.
2000–01 Gillingham 1 0
2001–02 Gillingham 0 0
2002–03 Gillingham 0 0
2003–04 Gillingham 8 0
2004–05 Gillingham 27 2 **36 2**

EDUSEI, Akwasi (M) 2 0
H: 5 9 W: 11 00 b.London 12-9-86
2002–03 Gillingham 2 0
2003–04 Gillingham 0 0
2004–05 Gillingham 0 0 **2 0**

FLYNN, Michael (M) 60 5
H: 5 10 W: 12 10 b.Newport 17-10-80
Source: Barry T.
2002–03 Wigan Ath 17 1
2003–04 Wigan Ath 8 0
2004–05 Wigan Ath 13 1 **38 2**
2004–05 *Blackpool* 6 0 **6 0**
2004–05 Gillingham 16 3 **16 3**

HENDERSON, Darius (F) 123 27
H: 6 2 W: 13 11 b.Doncaster 7-9-81
Source: Trainee.
1999–2000 Reading 6 0
2000–01 Reading 4 0
2001–02 Reading 38 7
2002–03 Reading 22 4
2003–04 Reading 1 0 **71 11**
2003–04 *Brighton & HA* 10 2 **10 2**
2003–04 Gillingham 4 0
2004–05 Gillingham 32 9 **36 9**
2004–05 *Swindon T* 6 5 **6 5**

HESSENTHALER, Andy (M) 492 30
H: 5 8 W: 11 06 b.Gravesend 17-6-65
Source: Dartford, Redbridge Forest.
1991–92 Watford 35 1
1992–93 Watford 45 3
1993–94 Watford 42 5
1994–95 Watford 43 2
1995–96 Watford 30 0 **195 11**
1996–97 Gillingham 38 2
1997–98 Gillingham 42 0
1998–99 Gillingham 39 7
1999–2000 Gillingham 42 5
2000–01 Gillingham 23 2
2001–02 Gillingham 17 0
2002–03 Gillingham 33 1
2003–04 Gillingham 36 2
2004–05 Gillingham 17 0 **287 19**
2004–05 *Hull C* 10 0 **10 0**

HILLS, John (D) 235 19
H: 5 8 W: 12 13 b.St Annes-on-Sea 21-4-78
Source: Trainee.
1995–96 Blackpool 0 0
1995–96 Everton 0 0
1996–97 Everton 3 0
1996–97 *Swansea C* 11 0
1997–98 Everton 0 0 **3 0**
1997–98 *Swansea C* 7 1 **18 1**
1997–98 Blackpool 19 1
1998–99 Blackpool 28 1
1999–2000 Blackpool 33 2
2000–01 Blackpool 18 2
2001–02 Blackpool 37 5
2002–03 Blackpool 27 5 **162 16**
2003–04 Gillingham 29 2
2004–05 Gillingham 23 0 **52 2**

HOPE, Chris (D) 499 31
H: 6 1 W: 13 01 b.Sheffield 14-11-72
Source: Darlington.
1991–92 Nottingham F 0 0
1992–93 Nottingham F 0 0
1993–94 Scunthorpe U 41 0
1994–95 Scunthorpe U 24 0
1995–96 Scunthorpe U 40 3
1996–97 Scunthorpe U 46 3
1997–98 Scunthorpe U 46 5
1998–99 Scunthorpe U 46 5
1999–2000 Scunthorpe U 44 3 **287 19**
2000–01 Gillingham 46 2
2001–02 Gillingham 46 4
2002–03 Gillingham 46 1
2003–04 Gillingham 37 3
2004–05 Gillingham 37 2 **212 12**

JARVIS, Matthew (M) 40 3
H: 5 7 W: 11 05 b.Middlesbrough 22-5-86
Source: Scholar.
2003–04 Gillingham 10 0
2004–05 Gillingham 30 3 **40 3**

JOHNSON, Leon (M) 94 3
H: 6 0 W: 12 08 b.London 10-5-81
Source: Scholarship.
1999–2000 Southend U 0 0
2000–01 Southend U 20 1
2001–02 Southend U 28 2 **48 3**
2002–03 Gillingham 18 0
2003–04 Gillingham 20 0
2004–05 Gillingham 8 0 **46 0**

NOSWORTHY, Nayron (D) 174 5
H: 6 0 W: 13 00 b.Brixton 11-10-80
Source: Trainee.
1998–99 Gillingham 3 0
1999–2000 Gillingham 29 1
2000–01 Gillingham 10 0
2001–02 Gillingham 29 0
2002–03 Gillingham 39 2
2003–04 Gillingham 27 2
2004–05 Gillingham 37 0 **174 5**

POUTON, Alan (M) 247 19
H: 6 1 W: 13 06 b.Newcastle 1-2-77
Source: Newcastle U Trainee.
1995–96 Oxford U 0 0
1995–96 York C 0 0
1996–97 York C 22 1
1997–98 York C 41 5
1998–99 York C 27 1
1999–2000 York C 0 0 **90 7**
1999–2000 Grimsby T 35 1
2000–01 Grimsby T 21 1
2001–02 Grimsby T 35 5
2002–03 Grimsby T 25 5
2003–04 Grimsby T 5 0 **121 12**
2003–04 Gillingham 19 0
2004–05 Gillingham 12 0 **31 0**
2004–05 *Hartlepool U* 5 0 **5 0**

ROBERTS, Iwan (F) 647 202
H: 6 4 W: 14 08 b.Bangor 26-6-68
Source: Trainee. *Honours:* Wales Schools, Youth, B, 15 full caps.
1985–86 Watford 4 0
1986–87 Watford 3 1
1987–88 Watford 25 2
1988–89 Watford 22 6
1989–90 Watford 9 0 **63 9**
1990–91 Huddersfield T 44 13
1991–92 Huddersfield T 46 24
1992–93 Huddersfield T 37 9
1993–94 Huddersfield T 15 4 **142 50**
1993–94 Leicester C 26 13
1994–95 Leicester C 37 9
1995–96 Leicester C 37 19 **100 41**
1996–97 Wolverhampton W 33 12 **33 12**
1997–98 Norwich C 31 5
1998–99 Norwich C 45 19
1999–2000 Norwich C 44 17
2000–01 Norwich C 44 15
2001–02 Norwich C 30 13
2002–03 Norwich C 43 7
2003–04 Norwich C 41 8 **278 84**
2004–05 Gillingham 20 3 **20 3**
2004–05 *Cambridge U* 11 3 **11 3**

ROBINSON, John (M) 440 44
H: 5 10 W: 11 07 b.Bulawayo 29-8-71
Source: Apprentice. *Honours:* Wales Under-21, 30 full caps, 3 goals.
1989–90 Brighton & HA 5 0
1990–91 Brighton & HA 15 0
1991–92 Brighton & HA 36 6
1992–93 Brighton & HA 6 0 **62 6**
1992–93 Charlton Ath 15 2
1993–94 Charlton Ath 27 1
1994–95 Charlton Ath 21 3
1995–96 Charlton Ath 44 6
1996–97 Charlton Ath 42 3
1997–98 Charlton Ath 38 8
1998–99 Charlton Ath 30 2
1999–2000 Charlton Ath 45 7
2000–01 Charlton Ath 29 2
2001–02 Charlton Ath 28 1
2002–03 Charlton Ath 13 0 **332 35**
2003–04 Cardiff C 34 2
2004–05 Cardiff C 8 1 **42 3**
2004–05 Gillingham 4 0 **4 0**

ROSE, Richard (D) 53 0
H: 5 10 W: 11 09 b.Tunbridge Wells 8-9-82
Source: Trainee.
2000–01 Gillingham 4 0
2001–02 Gillingham 3 0
2002–03 Gillingham 2 0
2002–03 *Bristol R* 9 0 **9 0**
2003–04 Gillingham 17 0
2004–05 Gillingham 18 0 **44 0**

SAUNDERS, Mark (M) **244** **26**
H: 5 11 W: 13 03 b.Reading 23-7-71
Source: Tiverton.

1995–96	Plymouth Arg	10	1		
1996–97	Plymouth Arg	25	3		
1997–98	Plymouth Arg	37	7	**72**	**11**
1998–99	Gillingham	34	4		
1999–2000	Gillingham	26	1		
2000–01	Gillingham	35	5		
2001–02	Gillingham	19	1		
2002–03	Gillingham	34	3		
2003–04	Gillingham	21	1		
2004–05	Gillingham	3	0	**172**	**15**

SIDIBE, Mamady (F) **137** **17**
H: 6 4 W: 13 10 b.Mali 18-12-79
Source: CA Paris. *Honours:* Mali 7 full caps.

2001–02	Swansea C	31	7	**31**	**7**
2002–03	Gillingham	30	3		
2003–04	Gillingham	41	5		
2004–05	Gillingham	35	2	**106**	**10**

SMITH, Paul (M) **521** **33**
H: 6 0 W: 14 06 b.East Ham 18-9-71
Source: Trainee.

1989–90	Southend U	10	1		
1990–91	Southend U	2	0		
1991–92	Southend U	0	0		
1992–93	Southend U	8	0	**20**	**1**
1993–94	Brentford	32	3		
1994–95	Brentford	35	3		
1995–96	Brentford	46	4		
1996–97	Brentford	46	1	**159**	**11**
1997–98	Gillingham	46	3		
1998–99	Gillingham	45	6		
1999–2000	Gillingham	44	1		
2000–01	Gillingham	42	3		
2001–02	Gillingham	46	2		
2002–03	Gillingham	45	3		
2003–04	Gillingham	33	0		
2004–05	Gillingham	41	3	**342**	**21**

SOUTHALL, Nicky (M) **483** **49**
H: 5 11 W: 12 04 b.Stockton 28-1-72
Source: Trainee.

1990–91	Hartlepool U	0	0		
1991–92	Hartlepool U	22	3		
1992–93	Hartlepool U	39	6		
1993–94	Hartlepool U	40	9		
1994–95	Hartlepool U	37	6	**138**	**24**
1995–96	Grimsby T	33	2		
1996–97	Grimsby T	34	3		
1997–98	Grimsby T	5	0	**72**	**5**
1997–98	Gillingham	23	2		
1998–99	Gillingham	42	4		
1999–2000	Gillingham	45	9		
2000–01	Gillingham	44	2		
2001–02	Bolton W	18	1		
2002–03	Bolton W	0	0	**18**	**1**
2002–03	*Norwich C*	9	0	**9**	**0**
2002–03	Gillingham	24	1		
2003–04	Gillingham	35	0		
2004–05	Gillingham	33	1	**246**	**19**

SPILLER, Danny (M) **72** **6**
H: 5 8 W: 10 12 b.Maidstone 10-10-81
Source: Trainee.

2000–01	Gillingham	0	0		
2001–02	Gillingham	1	0		
2002–03	Gillingham	10	0		
2003–04	Gillingham	39	6		
2004–05	Gillingham	22	0	**72**	**6**

GRIMSBY T (34)

ANDERSON, Iain (M) **247** **35**
H: 5 8 W: 9 07 b.Glasgow 23-7-77
Source: X-Form. *Honours:* Scotland Under-21.

1994–95	Dundee	10	1		
1995–96	Dundee	17	0		
1996–97	Dundee	35	5		
1997–98	Dundee	36	6		
1998–99	Dundee	28	3	**126**	**15**
1999–2000	Toulouse	3	0	**3**	**0**
1999–2000	Preston NE	12	2		
2000–01	Preston NE	31	6		
2001–02	Preston NE	31	5		
2002–03	Preston NE	8	0	**82**	**13**
2002–03	*Tranmere R*	7	2	**7**	**2**
2003–04	Grimsby T	29	5		
2004–05	Grimsby T	0	0	**29**	**5**

ANTOINE-CURIER, Mickael (F) **38** **7**
H: 6 0 W: 12 00 b.Orsay 5-3-83

2000–01	Preston NE	0	0		
2001–02	Nottingham F	0	0		
2002–03	Nottingham F	0	0		
2002–03	*Brentford*	11	3	**11**	**3**
2003–04	Burnley	0	0		
2003–04	Oldham Ath	8	2	**8**	**2**
2003–04	Kidderminster H	1	0	**1**	**0**
2003–04	Rochdale	8	1	**8**	**1**
2003–04	Sheffield W	1	0	**1**	**0**
2003–04	Notts Co	4	1	**4**	**1**
2003–04	Grimsby T	5	0		
2004–05	Grimsby T	0	0	**5**	**0**

ASHTON, Paul (G) **0** **0**
H: 6 2 W: 13 05 b.Maesteg 20-9-77
Source: Scholar.

2004–05	Grimsby T	0	0		

BULL, Ronnie (D) **104** **2**
H: 5 8 W: 11 04 b.Hackney 26-12-80
Source: Trainee.

1998–99	Millwall	1	0		
1999–2000	Millwall	9	0		
2000–01	Millwall	2	0		
2001–02	Millwall	26	0		
2002–03	Millwall	12	0		
2003–04	Millwall	0	0	**50**	**0**
2003–04	*Yeovil T*	7	0	**7**	**0**
2003–04	Brentford	20	0	**20**	**0**
2004–05	Grimsby T	27	2	**27**	**2**

CARCHEDI, Gio (M) **0** **0**
H: 5 7 W: 12 00 b.Lincoln 10-11-83
Source: Scholar.

2004–05	Grimsby T	0	0		

CHAMBERLAIN, Miles (D) **0** **0**
H: 6 0 W: 12 00 b.Boston 14-12-86
Source: Scholar.

2004–05	Grimsby T	0	0		

COLDICOTT, Stacy (M) **331** **7**
H: 5 8 W: 12 08 b.Worcester 29-4-74
Source: Trainee.

1991–92	WBA	0	0		
1992–93	WBA	14	0		
1993–94	WBA	5	0		
1994–95	WBA	11	0		
1995–96	WBA	33	0		
1996–97	WBA	19	3		
1996–97	*Cardiff C*	6	0	**6**	**0**
1997–98	WBA	22	0	**104**	**3**
1998–99	Grimsby T	37	0		
1999–2000	Grimsby T	44	2		
2000–01	Grimsby T	37	1		
2001–02	Grimsby T	26	0		
2002–03	Grimsby T	31	0		
2003–04	Grimsby T	14	0		
2004–05	Grimsby T	32	1	**221**	**4**

CRAMB, Colin (F) **281** **70**
H: 5 11 W: 12 04 b.Lanark 23-6-74
Source: Hamilton A BC.

1990–91	Hamilton A	3	2		
1991–92	Hamilton A	12	1		
1992–93	Hamilton A	33	7	**48**	**10**
1993–94	Southampton	1	0	**1**	**0**
1994–95	Falkirk	8	1	**8**	**1**
1994–95	Hearts	6	1	**6**	**1**
1995–96	Doncaster R	21	7		
1996–97	Doncaster R	41	18	**62**	**25**
1997–98	Bristol C	40	9		
1998–99	Bristol C	13	0		
1998–99	*Walsall*	4	4	**4**	**4**
1999–2000	Bristol C	0	0	**53**	**9**
1999–2000	Crewe Alex	37	6		
2000–01	Crewe Alex	13	4		
2000–01	*Notts Co*	3	0	**3**	**0**
2000–01	*Bury*	15	5		
2001–02	Crewe Alex	0	0		
2002–03	Crewe Alex	0	0	**50**	**10**
2002–03	Bury	18	3		
2003–04	Bury	0	0	**33**	**8**
2004–05	Shrewsbury T	2	0	**2**	**0**
2004–05	Grimsby T	11	2	**11**	**2**

CRANE, Tony (D) **89** **7**
H: 6 5 W: 12 05 b.Liverpool 8-9-82
Source: Trainee. *Honours:* England Youth.

1999–2000	Sheffield W	0	0		
2000–01	Sheffield W	15	2		
2001–02	Sheffield W	15	0		
2002–03	Sheffield W	19	2	**49**	**4**
2003–04	Grimsby T	37	3		
2004–05	Grimsby T	3	0	**40**	**3**

CROWE, Jason (D) **172** **9**
H: 5 9 W: 10 09 b.Sidcup 30-9-78
Source: Trainee. *Honours:* England Schools, Youth.

1995–96	Arsenal	0	0		
1996–97	Arsenal	0	0		
1997–98	Arsenal	0	0		
1998–99	Arsenal	0	0		
1998–99	*Crystal Palace*	8	0	**8**	**0**
1999–2000	Portsmouth	25	0		
2000–01	Portsmouth	23	0		
2000–01	*Brentford*	9	0	**9**	**0**
2001–02	Portsmouth	22	1		
2002–03	Portsmouth	16	4	**86**	**5**
2003–04	Grimsby T	32	0		
2004–05	Grimsby T	37	4	**69**	**4**

DOWNEY, Glen (D) **1** **0**
H: 6 1 W: 13 00 b.Sunderland 20-9-78

1997–98	Hartlepool U	0	0		
1998–99	Hartlepool U	0	0		
1999–2000	Hartlepool U	0	0		
2000–01	Hartlepool U	0	0		
2001–02	Hartlepool U	0	0		

From Scarborough.

2004–05	Grimsby T	1	0	**1**	**0**

FLEMING, Terry (M) **424** **17**
H: 5 8 W: 11 00 b.Marston Green 5-1-73
Source: Trainee.

1990–91	Coventry C	2	0		
1991–92	Coventry C	0	0		
1992–93	Coventry C	11	0	**13**	**0**
1993–94	Northampton T	31	1	**31**	**1**
1994–95	Preston NE	27	2		
1995–96	Preston NE	5	0	**32**	**2**
1995–96	Lincoln C	22	0		
1996–97	Lincoln C	37	0		
1997–98	Lincoln C	40	3		
1998–99	Lincoln C	43	0		
1999–2000	Lincoln C	41	5	**183**	**8**
2000–01	Plymouth Arg	17	0	**17**	**0**
2000–01	Cambridge U	10	1		
2001–02	Cambridge U	34	0		
2002–03	Cambridge U	43	2		
2003–04	Cambridge U	18	1	**105**	**4**
2004–05	Grimsby T	43	2	**43**	**2**

FORBES, Terrell (D) **150** **0**
H: 6 0 W: 12 05 b.Southwark 17-8-81
Source: Trainee.

1999–2000	West Ham U	0	0		
1999–2000	*Bournemouth*	3	0	**3**	**0**
2000–01	West Ham U	0	0		
2001–02	QPR	43	0		
2002–03	QPR	38	0		
2003–04	QPR	30	0		
2004–05	QPR	3	0	**114**	**0**
2004–05	Grimsby T	33	0	**33**	**0**

FRASER, Paul (G) **0** **0**
H: 6 1 W: 13 00 b.Cleethorpes 1-9-85
Source: Scholar.

2004–05	Grimsby T	0	0		

GORDON, Dean (D) **329** **29**
H: 5 11 W: 13 08 b.Thornton Heath 10-2-73
Source: From Trainee. *Honours:* England Under-21.

1991–92	Crystal Palace	4	0		
1992–93	Crystal Palace	10	0		
1993–94	Crystal Palace	45	5		
1994–95	Crystal Palace	41	2		
1995–96	Crystal Palace	34	8		
1996–97	Crystal Palace	30	3		
1997–98	Crystal Palace	37	2	**201**	**20**
1998–99	Middlesbrough	38	3		
1999–2000	Middlesbrough	4	0		
2000–01	Middlesbrough	20	1		
2001–02	Middlesbrough	1	0	**63**	**4**
2001–02	*Cardiff C*	7	2	**7**	**2**

2002–03 Coventry C 30 1
2003–04 Coventry C 5 0
2003–04 *Reading* 3 0 **3 0**
2004–05 Coventry C 0 0 **35 1**
2004–05 Grimsby T 20 2 **20 2**

GRITTON, Martin (F) 160 34
H: 6 3 W: 13 10 b.Glasgow 1-6-78
Source: Porthleven.
1998–99 Plymouth Arg 2 0
1999–2000 Plymouth Arg 30 6
2000–01 Plymouth Arg 10 1
2001–02 Plymouth Arg 2 0
2002–03 Plymouth Arg 0 0 **44 7**
2002–03 Torquay U 43 13
2003–04 Torquay U 31 4
2004–05 Torquay U 19 6 **93 23**
2004–05 Grimsby T 23 4 **23 4**

HEGARTY, Nick (M) 1 0
H: 5 10 W: 11 00 b.Hemsworth 25-6-86
Source: Scholar.
2004–05 Grimsby T 1 0 **1 0**

HIGGINS, Ben (M) 0 0
b.Grimsby 13-9-87
Source: Scholar.
2004–05 Grimsby T 0 0

HILDRED, Ashley (M) 0 0
H: 5 59 W: 9 04 b.Cleethorpes 19-9-83
Source: Scholar.
2004–05 Grimsby T 0 0

HOCKLESS, Graham (M) 20 2
H: 5 7 W: 11 00 b.Hull 20-10-82
Source: Juniors.
2001–02 Grimsby T 0 0
2002–03 Grimsby T 1 0
2003–04 Grimsby T 13 2
2004–05 Grimsby T 6 0 **20 2**

HOWARD, Ben (D) 0 0
H: 6 3 W: 13 00 b.Grimsby 24-10-86
Source: Scholar.
2004–05 Grimsby T 0 0

HYAM, Chris (M) 0 0
b.Kingston-upon-Hull 10-9-85
Source: Scholar.
2004–05 Grimsby T 0 0

JONES, Rob (D) 37 3
H: 6 7 W: 13 07 b.Stockton 30-11-79
Source: Gateshead.
2002–03 Stockport Co 0 0
2003–04 Stockport Co 16 2 **16 2**
2003–04 *Macclesfield T* 1 0 **1 0**
2004–05 Grimsby T 20 1 **20 1**

LAMB, Alan (M) 0 0
b.Grimsby 20-12-85
Source: Scholar.
2004–05 Grimsby T 0 0

LIGHTOWLER, Joseph (F) 0 0
H: 5 6 W: 11 00 b.Beverley 15-5-86
Source: Scholar.
2004–05 Grimsby T 0 0

MANSARAM, Darren (F) 73 6
H: 6 1 W: 11 02 b.Doncaster 25-6-84
Source: Scholar.
2002–03 Grimsby T 34 2
2003–04 Grimsby T 31 3
2004–05 Grimsby T 8 1 **73 6**

MARCELLE, Clint (M) 171 13
H: 5 5 W: 10 00 b.Port of Spain 9-11-68
Source: Vitoria Setubal, Rio Ave. *Honours:* Trinidad & Tobago full caps.
1994–95 Falgueiras 30 3
1995–96 Falgueiras 21 0 **51 3**
1996–97 Barnsley 40 8
1997–98 Barnsley 20 0
1998–99 Barnsley 9 0
1999–2000 Barnsley 0 0
1999–2000 *Scunthorpe U* 10 0 **10 0**
2000–01 Barnsley 0 0 **69 8**
2000–01 *Hull C* 23 2 **23 2**
2000–01 Darlington 12 0
2001–02 Darlington 3 0
2002–03 Darlington 0 0
2003–04 Darlington 0 0 **15 0**
2004–05 Grimsby T 3 0 **3 0**

McDERMOTT, John (D) 592 9
H: 5 7 W: 11 02 b.Middlesbrough 3-2-69
Source: Trainee.
1986–87 Grimsby T 13 0
1987–88 Grimsby T 28 0
1988–89 Grimsby T 38 1
1989–90 Grimsby T 39 0
1990–91 Grimsby T 43 0
1991–92 Grimsby T 39 1
1992–93 Grimsby T 38 2
1993–94 Grimsby T 26 0
1994–95 Grimsby T 12 0
1995–96 Grimsby T 28 1
1996–97 Grimsby T 29 1
1997–98 Grimsby T 41 1
1998–99 Grimsby T 37 0
1999–2000 Grimsby T 26 0
2000–01 Grimsby T 36 0
2001–02 Grimsby T 24 0
2002–03 Grimsby T 35 0
2003–04 Grimsby T 21 0
2004–05 Grimsby T 39 2 **592 9**

MURRAY, Robert (M) 0 0
b.Leamington Spa 11-7-88
Source: Scholar.
2004–05 Grimsby T 0 0

NIMMO, Liam (F) 2 0
H: 6 0 W: 11 05 b.Boston 28-12-84
Source: Scholar.
2003–04 Grimsby T 2 0
2004–05 Grimsby T 0 0 **2 0**

NORTH, Danny (F) 1 0
H: 5 9 W: 12 08 b.Grimsby 7-9-87
Source: Scholar.
2004–05 Grimsby T 1 0 **1 0**

PARKER, Liam (F) 0 0
H: 6 1 W: 11 05 b.Boston 22-2-86
Source: Scholar.
2004–05 Grimsby T 0 0

PARKER, Wesley (D) 9 0
H: 5 8 W: 10 05 b.Boston 7-12-83
Source: Scholar.
2002–03 Grimsby T 5 0
2003–04 Grimsby T 4 0
2004–05 Grimsby T 0 0 **9 0**

PARKINSON, Andy (F) 230 29
H: 5 7 W: 10 07 b.Liverpool 27-5-79
Source: Liverpool Trainee.
1996–97 Tranmere R 0 0
1997–98 Tranmere R 18 1
1998–99 Tranmere R 29 2
1999–2000 Tranmere R 37 7
2000–01 Tranmere R 39 6
2001–02 Tranmere R 31 2
2002–03 Tranmere R 10 0 **164 18**
2003–04 Sheffield U 7 0 **7 0**
2003–04 *Notts Co* 14 3 **14 3**
2004–05 Grimsby T 45 8 **45 8**

PINAULT, Thomas (M) 176 12
H: 5 10 W: 12 00 b.Grasse 4-12-81
Source: Cannes.
1999–2000 Colchester U 4 0
2000–01 Colchester U 5 1
2001–02 Colchester U 42 0
2002–03 Colchester U 42 4
2003–04 Colchester U 40 0 **133 5**
2004–05 Grimsby T 43 7 **43 7**

RAMSDEN, Simon (D) 57 0
H: 6 0 W: 13 00 b.Bishop Auckland 17-12-81
Source: Scholar.
2000–01 Sunderland 0 0
2001–02 Sunderland 0 0
2002–03 Sunderland 0 0
2002–03 *Notts Co* 32 0 **32 0**
2003–04 Sunderland 0 0
2004–05 Grimsby T 25 0 **25 0**

REDDY, Michael (F) 111 24
H: 6 1 W: 13 00 b.Kilkenny 24-3-80
Source: Kilkenny C. *Honours:* Eire Under-21.
1999–2000 Sunderland 8 1
2000–01 Sunderland 2 0
2000–01 *Swindon T* 18 4 **18 4**
2001–02 Sunderland 0 0
2001–02 *Hull C* 5 4 **5 4**
2001–02 *Barnsley* 0 0
2002–03 Sunderland 0 0
2002–03 *York C* 11 2 **11 2**
2002–03 *Sheffield W* 15 3
2003–04 Sunderland 0 0 **10 1**
2003–04 *Sheffield W* 12 1 **27 4**
2004–05 Grimsby T 40 9 **40 9**

RICHARDSON, Oliver (G) 0 0
H: 5 10 W: 12 00 b.Grimsby 12-2-87
Source: Scholar.
2004–05 Grimsby T 0 0

ROCK, Stephen (M) 0 0
b.Grimsby 30-11-87
Source: Scholar.
2004–05 Grimsby T 0 0

SMITH, Michael (D) 0 0
H: 5 10 W: 10 05 b.Grimsby 5-11-85
Source: Scholar.
2004–05 Grimsby T 0 0

SOAMES, David (F) 24 1
H: 5 5 W: 10 08 b.Grimsby 10-2-84
Source: Scholar.
2002–03 Grimsby T 10 1
2003–04 Grimsby T 10 0
2004–05 Grimsby T 4 0 **24 1**

WARD, Andrew (M) 0 0
H: 6 0 W: 10 12 b.Grimsby 10-9-86
Source: Scholar.
2004–05 Grimsby T 0 0

WHEELER, Kirk (D) 0 0
H: 6 0 W: 12 01 b.Grimsby 13-6-84
2002–03 Grimsby T 0 0
2003–04 Grimsby T 0 0
2004–05 Grimsby T 0 0

WHITTLE, Justin (D) 312 4
H: 6 1 W: 13 00 b.Derby 18-3-71
Source: Celtic.
1994–95 Stoke C 0 0
1995–96 Stoke C 8 0
1996–97 Stoke C 37 0
1997–98 Stoke C 20 0
1998–99 Stoke C 14 1 **79 1**
1998–99 Hull C 24 1
1999–2000 Hull C 38 0
2000–01 Hull C 38 0
2001–02 Hull C 36 0
2002–03 Hull C 39 1
2003–04 Hull C 18 0 **193 2**
2004–05 Grimsby T 40 1 **40 1**

WILLIAMS, Anthony (G) 218 0
H: 6 2 W: 13 07 b.Maesteg 20-9-77
Source: Trainee. *Honours:* Wales Youth, Under-21.
1996–97 Blackburn R 0 0
1997–98 Blackburn R 0 0
1997–98 *QPR* 0 0
1998–99 Blackburn R 0 0
1998–99 *Macclesfield T* 4 0
1998–99 *Huddersfield T* 0 0
1998–99 *Bristol R* 9 0 **9 0**
1999–2000 Blackburn R 0 0
1999–2000 *Gillingham* 2 0 **2 0**
1999–2000 *Macclesfield T* 11 0 **15 0**
2000–01 Hartlepool U 41 0
2001–02 Hartlepool U 43 0
2002–03 Hartlepool U 46 0
2003–04 Hartlepool U 1 0 **131 0**
2003–04 *Swansea C* 0 0
2003–04 *Stockport Co* 15 0 **15 0**
2004–05 Grimsby T 46 0 **46 0**

YOUNG, Greg (D) 24 0
H: 6 2 W: 13 03 b.Doncaster 25-4-83
2002–03 Grimsby T 1 0
2003–04 Grimsby T 17 0
2004–05 Grimsby T 6 0 **24 0**

HARTLEPOOL U (35)

APPLEBY, Andy (M) 15 2
H: 5 10 W: 11 01 b.Seaham 11-10-85
Source: Scholar.
2004–05 Hartlepool U 15 2 **15 2**

BARRON, Micky (D) **284 3**
H: 5 11 W: 11 10 b.Lumley 22-12-74
Source: Trainee.

1992–93	Middlesbrough	0	0		
1993–94	Middlesbrough	2	0		
1994–95	Middlesbrough	0	0		
1995–96	Middlesbrough	1	0		
1996–97	Middlesbrough	0	0	**3**	**0**
1996–97	*Hartlepool U*	16	0		
1997–98	Hartlepool U	33	0		
1998–99	Hartlepool U	38	1		
1999–2000	Hartlepool U	40	0		
2000–01	Hartlepool U	28	0		
2001–02	Hartlepool U	39	1		
2002–03	Hartlepool U	42	0		
2003–04	Hartlepool U	32	1		
2004–05	Hartlepool U	13	0	**281**	**3**

BOYD, Adam (F) **137 53**
H: 5 9 W: 10 12 b.Hartlepool 25-5-82
Source: Scholarship.

1999–2000	Hartlepool U	4	1		
2000–01	Hartlepool U	5	0		
2001–02	Hartlepool U	29	9		
2002–03	Hartlepool U	22	5		
2003–04	Hartlepool U	18	12		
2003–04	*Boston U*	14	4	**14**	**4**
2004–05	Hartlepool U	45	22	**123**	**49**

BRACKSTONE, John (D) **15 0**
H: 6 0 W: 11 06 b.Hartlepool 9-2-85
Source: Scholar.

2003–04	Hartlepool U	6	0		
2004–05	Hartlepool U	9	0	**15**	**0**

BROWN, James (M) **0 0**

2004–05	Hartlepool U	0	0		

BUTLER, Thomas (M) **60 1**
H: 5 7 W: 10 06 b.Dublin 25-4-81
Source: Trainee. *Honours:* Eire Under-21, 2 full caps.

1998–99	Sunderland	0	0		
1999–2000	Sunderland	1	0		
2000–01	Sunderland	4	0		
2000–01	*Darlington*	8	0	**8**	**0**
2001–02	Sunderland	7	0		
2002–03	Sunderland	7	0		
2003–04	Sunderland	12	0	**31**	**0**
2004–05	Dunfermline Ath	12	0	**12**	**0**
2004–05	Hartlepool U	9	1	**9**	**1**

CARSON, Stephen (M) **36 1**
H: 5 10 W: 12 00 b.Ballymoney 6-10-80

2000–01	Rangers	2	0	**2**	**0**
2001–02	Dundee U	13	0		
2002–03	Dundee U	7	0	**20**	**0**
2003–04	Barnsley	11	1	**11**	**1**
2003–04	Hartlepool U	3	0		
2004–05	Hartlepool U	0	0	**3**	**0**

CLARK, Ben (D) **33 0**
H: 6 1 W: 13 11 b.Shotley Bridge 24-1-83
Source: Manchester U Trainee. *Honours:* England Youth, Under-20.

2000–01	Sunderland	0	0		
2001–02	Sunderland	0	0		
2002–03	Sunderland	1	0		
2003–04	Sunderland	5	0		
2004–05	Sunderland	2	0	**8**	**0**
2004–05	Hartlepool U	25	0	**25**	**0**

CLARKE, Darrell (M) **273 43**
H: 5 10 W: 11 05 b.Mansfield 16-12-77
Source: Trainee.

1995–96	Mansfield T	3	0		
1996–97	Mansfield T	19	2		
1997–98	Mansfield T	35	4		
1998–99	Mansfield T	33	5		
1999–2000	Mansfield T	39	7		
2000–01	Mansfield T	32	6	**161**	**24**
2001–02	Hartlepool U	33	7		
2002–03	Hartlepool U	45	7		
2003–04	Hartlepool U	33	5		
2004–05	Hartlepool U	0	0	**111**	**19**
2004–05	*Stockport Co*	1	0	**1**	**0**

CRADDOCK, Darren (D) **20 0**
H: 6 0 W: 12 02 b.Bishop Auckland 23-2-85
Source: Scholar.

2003–04	Hartlepool U	10	0		
2004–05	Hartlepool U	10	0	**20**	**0**

DALY, Jon (F) **113 17**
H: 6 3 W: 12 00 b.Dublin 8-1-83
Source: Trainee. *Honours:* Eire Under-21.

1999–2000	Stockport Co	4	0		
2000–01	Stockport Co	0	0		
2001–02	Stockport Co	13	1		
2002–03	Stockport Co	35	7		
2003–04	Stockport Co	25	3		
2003–04	*Bury*	7	1	**7**	**1**
2004–05	Stockport Co	14	3	**91**	**14**
2004–05	*Grimsby T*	3	1	**3**	**1**
2004–05	Hartlepool U	12	1	**12**	**1**

FOLEY, David (F) **3 0**
H: 5 4 W: 8 09 b.South Shields 12-5-87
Source: Scholar.

2003–04	Hartlepool U	1	0		
2004–05	Hartlepool U	2	0	**3**	**0**

HOWEY, Steve (D) **302 18**
H: 6 2 W: 13 05 b.Sunderland 26-10-71
Source: Trainee. *Honours:* England 4 full caps.

1988–89	Newcastle U	1	0		
1989–90	Newcastle U	0	0		
1990–91	Newcastle U	11	0		
1991–92	Newcastle U	21	1		
1992–93	Newcastle U	41	2		
1993–94	Newcastle U	14	0		
1994–95	Newcastle U	30	1		
1995–96	Newcastle U	28	1		
1996–97	Newcastle U	8	1		
1997–98	Newcastle U	14	0		
1998–99	Newcastle U	14	0		
1999–2000	Newcastle U	9	0	**191**	**6**
2000–01	Manchester C	36	6		
2001–02	Manchester C	34	3		
2002–03	Manchester C	24	2	**94**	**11**
2003–04	Leicester C	13	1	**13**	**1**
2003–04	Bolton W	3	0		
2004–05	Bolton W	0	0	**3**	**0**
From New England R.					
2004–05	Hartlepool U	1	0	**1**	**0**

HUMPHREYS, Richie (M) **273 33**
H: 5 11 W: 12 07 b.Sheffield 30-11-77
Source: Trainee. *Honours:* England Youth, Under-21.

1995–96	Sheffield W	5	0		
1996–97	Sheffield W	29	3		
1997–98	Sheffield W	7	0		
1998–99	Sheffield W	19	1		
1999–2000	Sheffield W	0	0		
1999–2000	*Scunthorpe U*	6	2	**6**	**2**
1999–2000	*Cardiff C*	9	2	**9**	**2**
2000–01	Sheffield W	7	0	**67**	**4**
2000–01	Cambridge U	7	3	**7**	**3**
2001–02	Hartlepool U	46	5		
2002–03	Hartlepool U	46	11		
2003–04	Hartlepool U	46	3		
2004–05	Hartlepool U	46	3	**184**	**22**

ISTEAD, Steven (F) **54 1**
H: 5 8 W: 11 06 b.South Shields 23-4-86
Source: Scholar.

2002–03	Hartlepool U	6	0		
2003–04	Hartlepool U	31	1		
2004–05	Hartlepool U	17	0	**54**	**1**

JORDAN, Andy (D) **21 0**
H: 6 2 W: 13 05 b.Manchester 14-12-79
Source: Trainee. *Honours:* Scotland Under-21.

1997–98	Bristol C	0	0		
1998–99	Bristol C	1	0		
1999–2000	Bristol C	8	0		
2000–01	Bristol C	2	0	**11**	**0**
2000–01	Cardiff C	5	0		
2001–02	Cardiff C	0	0		
2002–03	Cardiff C	0	0	**5**	**0**
2003–04	Hartlepool U	5	0		
2004–05	Hartlepool U	0	0	**5**	**0**

KONSTANTOPOULOS, Dimitrios (G) **25 0**
H: 6 4 W: 14 02 b.Kalamata 29-11-78

2003–04	Hartlepool U	0	0		
2004–05	Hartlepool U	25	0	**25**	**0**

MAIDENS, Michael (M) **1 0**
H: 5 11 W: 11 04 b.Middlesbrough 7-5-87
Source: Scholar.

2004–05	Hartlepool U	1	0	**1**	**0**

McCANN, Ryan (M) **22 3**
H: 5 8 W: 11 03 b.Bellshill 15-9-82

1999–2000	Celtic	1	0		
2000–01	Celtic	0	0		
2001–02	Celtic	0	0		
2002–03	Celtic	0	0	**1**	**0**
2002–03	St Johnstone	17	3	**17**	**3**
2003–04	Hartlepool U	4	0		
2004–05	Hartlepool U	0	0	**4**	**0**

NELSON, Michael (D) **155 12**
H: 6 2 W: 13 03 b.Gateshead 15-3-82

2000–01	Bury	2	1		
2001–02	Bury	31	2		
2002–03	Bury	39	5	**72**	**8**
2003–04	Hartlepool U	40	3		
2004–05	Hartlepool U	43	1	**83**	**4**

PORTER, Joel (F) **174 52**
H: 5 9 W: 11 13 b.Adelaide 25-12-78
Honours: Australia 4 full caps, 5 goals.

1998–99	West Adelaide	20	3	**20**	**3**
2000–01	Melbrne Knights	30	12		
2001–02	Melbrne Knights	26	12	**56**	**24**
2002–03	Sydney Olympic	32	8	**32**	**8**
2003–04	Hartlepool U	27	3		
2004–05	Hartlepool U	39	14	**66**	**17**

PROVETT, Jim (G) **66 0**
H: 6 0 W: 13 04 b.Stockton 22-12-82
Source: Trainee.

1999–2000	Hartlepool U	0	0		
2000–01	Hartlepool U	0	0		
2001–02	Hartlepool U	0	0		
2002–03	Hartlepool U	0	0		
2003–04	Hartlepool U	45	0		
2004–05	Hartlepool U	21	0	**66**	**0**

ROBERTSON, Hugh (D) **216 24**
H: 5 9 W: 13 11 b.Aberdeen 19-3-75
Source: Lewis U. *Honours:* Scotland Under-21.

1993–94	Aberdeen	8	0		
1994–95	Aberdeen	3	2		
1995–96	Aberdeen	11	0		
1996–97	Aberdeen	0	0	**22**	**2**
1996–97	Dundee	15	1		
1997–98	Dundee	0	0		
1997–98	*Brechin C*	7	0	**7**	**0**
1998–99	Dundee	10	0		
1998–99	Inverness CT	12	1	**12**	**1**
1999–2000	Dundee	0	0		
2000–01	Dundee	0	0	**25**	**1**
2000–01	Ayr U	8	1	**8**	**1**
2000–01	Ross Co	16	1		
2001–02	Ross Co	36	6		
2002–03	Ross Co	32	4		
2003–04	Ross Co	20	2	**104**	**13**
2003–04	Hartlepool U	18	4		
2004–05	Hartlepool U	20	2	**38**	**6**

ROBSON, Matty (D) **50 3**
H: 5 10 W: 11 02 b.Durham 23-1-85
Source: Scholar.

2002–03	Hartlepool U	0	0		
2003–04	Hartlepool U	23	1		
2004–05	Hartlepool U	27	2	**50**	**3**

ROSS, Jack (D) **24 0**
H: 6 1 W: 11 05 b.Falkirk 5-6-76

2004–05	Hartlepool U	24	0	**24**	**0**

STRACHAN, Gavin (M) **96 6**
H: 5 10 W: 11 07 b.Aberdeen 23-12-78
Source: Trainee. *Honours:* Scotland Youth, Under-21.

1996–97	Coventry C	0	0		
1997–98	Coventry C	9	0		
1998–99	Coventry C	0	0		
1998–99	*Dundee*	6	0	**6**	**0**
1999–2000	Coventry C	3	0		
2000–01	Coventry C	2	0		
2001–02	Coventry C	1	0		
2002–03	Coventry C	1	0	**16**	**0**
2002–03	*Peterborough U*	2	0	**2**	**0**
2002–03	Southend U	7	0	**7**	**0**
2003–04	Hartlepool U	36	5		
2004–05	Hartlepool U	29	1	**65**	**6**

SWEENEY, Anthony (M) **61 14**
H: 6 0 W: 11 07 b.Stockton 5-9-83
Source: Scholar.

2001–02	Hartlepool U	2	0		

2002–03	Hartlepool U	4	0		
2003–04	Hartlepool U	11	1		
2004–05	Hartlepool U	44	13	61	14

TINKLER, Mark (M) **361 42**
H: 6 2 W: 12 00 b.Bishop Auckland 24-10-74
Source: Trainee. *Honours:* England Schools, Youth.

1991–92	Leeds U	0	0		
1992–93	Leeds U	7	0		
1993–94	Leeds U	3	0		
1994–95	Leeds U	3	0		
1995–96	Leeds U	9	0		
1996–97	Leeds U	3	0	25	0
1996–97	York C	9	1		
1997–98	York C	44	5		
1998–99	York C	37	2		
1999–2000	York C	0	0	90	8
1999–2000	Southend U	41	0		
2000–01	Southend U	15	1	56	1
2000–01	Hartlepool U	28	3		
2001–02	Hartlepool U	40	9		
2002–03	Hartlepool U	45	13		
2003–04	Hartlepool U	44	6		
2004–05	Hartlepool U	33	2	190	33

TURNBULL, Stephen (M) **2 0**
H: 5 10 W: 11 00 b.South Shields 7-1-87
Source: Scholar.

2004–05	Hartlepool U	2	0	2	0

WESTWOOD, Chris (D) **254 8**
H: 5 11 W: 12 10 b.Dudley 13-2-77
Source: Trainee.

1995–96	Wolverhampton W	0	0		
1996–97	Wolverhampton W	0	0		
1997–98	Wolverhampton W	4	1		
1998–99	Wolverhampton W	0	0	4	1
1998–99	Hartlepool U	4	0		
1999–2000	Hartlepool U	37	0		
2000–01	Hartlepool U	46	1		
2001–02	Hartlepool U	35	1		
2002–03	Hartlepool U	46	1		
2003–04	Hartlepool U	45	0		
2004–05	Hartlepool U	37	4	250	7

WILKINSON, Jack (M) **7 2**
H: 5 8 W: 10 08 b.Beverley 12-9-85
Source: Scholar.

2003–04	Hartlepool U	4	2		
2004–05	Hartlepool U	3	0	7	2

WILLIAMS, Eifion (F) **243 61**
H: 5 11 W: 11 02 b.Bangor 15-11-75
Source: Barry T. *Honours:* Wales B.

1998–99	Torquay U	7	5		
1999–2000	Torquay U	42	9		
2000–01	Torquay U	37	9		
2001–02	Torquay U	25	1	111	24
2001–02	Hartlepool U	8	4		
2002–03	Hartlepool U	45	15		
2003–04	Hartlepool U	41	13		
2004–05	Hartlepool U	38	5	132	37

HUDDERSFIELD T (36)

ABBOTT, Pawel (F) **99 43**
H: 5 7 W: 11 07 b.York 5-5-82
Source: LKS Lodz. *Honours:* Poland Under-21.

2000–01	Preston NE	0	0		
2001–02	Preston NE	0	0		
2002–03	Preston NE	16	4		
2002–03	*Bury*	17	6	17	6
2003–04	Preston NE	9	2	25	6
2003–04	Huddersfield T	13	5		
2004–05	Huddersfield T	44	26	57	31

ADAMS, Danny (D) **192 2**
H: 5 8 W: 13 05 b.Manchester 3-1-76
Source: Altrincham.

2000–01	Macclesfield T	37	0		
2001–02	Macclesfield T	39	0		
2002–03	Macclesfield T	45	1		
2003–04	Macclesfield T	27	0	148	1
2003–04	Stockport Co	12	0		
2004–05	Stockport Co	27	1	39	1
2004–05	Huddersfield T	5	0	5	0

AHMED, Adnan (M) **19 1**
H: 5 10 W: 11 12 b.Burnley 7-6-84
Source: Scholar.

2003–04	Huddersfield T	1	0		
2004–05	Huddersfield T	18	1	19	1

BOOTH, Andy (F) **403 125**
H: 6 1 W: 13 00 b.Huddersfield 6-12-73
Source: Trainee. *Honours:* England Under-21.

1991–92	Huddersfield T	3	0		
1992–93	Huddersfield T	5	2		
1993–94	Huddersfield T	26	10		
1994–95	Huddersfield T	46	26		
1995–96	Huddersfield T	43	16		
1996–97	Sheffield W	35	10		
1997–98	Sheffield W	23	7		
1998–99	Sheffield W	34	6		
1999–2000	Sheffield W	23	2		
2000–01	Sheffield W	18	3	133	28
2000–01	*Tottenham H*	4	0	4	0
2000–01	Huddersfield T	8	3		
2001–02	Huddersfield T	36	11		
2002–03	Huddersfield T	33	6		
2003–04	Huddersfield T	37	13		
2004–05	Huddersfield T	29	10	266	97

BRANDON, Chris (M) **194 25**
H: 5 8 W: 10 13 b.Bradford 7-4-76
Source: Bradford PA.

1999–2000	Torquay U	42	5		
2000–01	Torquay U	2	0		
2001–02	Torquay U	27	3	71	8
2002–03	Chesterfield	36	7		
2003–04	Chesterfield	43	4	79	11
2004–05	Huddersfield T	44	6	44	6

BROWN, Nat (F) **76 0**
H: 6 2 W: 12 05 b.Sheffield 15-6-81
Source: Trainee.

1999–2000	Huddersfield T	0	0		
2000–01	Huddersfield T	0	0		
2001–02	Huddersfield T	0	0		
2002–03	Huddersfield T	38	0		
2003–04	Huddersfield T	21	0		
2004–05	Huddersfield T	17	0	76	0

CARSS, Tony (M) **279 12**
H: 5 11 W: 11 13 b.Alnwick 31-3-76
Source: Bradford C Trainee.

1994–95	Blackburn R	0	0		
1995–96	Darlington	28	2		
1996–97	Darlington	29	0	57	2
1997–98	Cardiff C	42	1	42	1
1998–99	Chesterfield	4	0		
1999–2000	Chesterfield	31	1	35	1
2000–01	Carlisle U	7	0	7	0
2000–01	Oldham Ath	35	2		
2001–02	Oldham Ath	14	1		
2002–03	Oldham Ath	26	2	75	5
2003–04	Huddersfield T	36	2		
2004–05	Huddersfield T	27	1	63	3

CLARKE, Nathan (D) **102 2**
H: 6 2 W: 12 00 b.Halifax 30-11-83
Source: Scholar.

2001–02	Huddersfield T	36	1		
2002–03	Huddersfield T	3	0		
2003–04	Huddersfield T	26	1		
2004–05	Huddersfield T	37	0	102	2

CLARKE, Tom (D) **12 0**
H: 5 11 W: 12 02 b.Halifax 21-12-87
Source: Scholar. *Honours:* England Youth.

2004–05	Huddersfield T	12	0	12	0

COLLINS, Michael (M) **8 0**
H: 6 0 W: 10 12 b.Halifax 30-4-86
Source: Scholar. *Honours:* Eire Youth.

2004–05	Huddersfield T	8	0	8	0

EDWARDS, Rob (D) **428 68**
H: 5 8 W: 12 01 b.Manchester 23-2-70
Source: Trainee.

1987–88	Crewe Alex	6	1		
1988–89	Crewe Alex	4	0		
1989–90	Crewe Alex	4	0		
1990–91	Crewe Alex	29	11		
1991–92	Crewe Alex	28	6		
1992–93	Crewe Alex	23	7		
1993–94	Crewe Alex	12	2		
1994–95	Crewe Alex	17	2		
1995–96	Crewe Alex	32	15	155	44
1995–96	Huddersfield T	13	7		
1996–97	Huddersfield T	33	3		
1997–98	Huddersfield T	38	1		
1998–99	Huddersfield T	45	2		
1999–2000	Huddersfield T	9	1		
2000–01	Huddersfield T	0	0		
2000–01	Chesterfield	34	4		
2001–02	Chesterfield	31	1		
2002–03	Chesterfield	29	2	94	7
2003–04	Huddersfield T	17	1		
2004–05	Huddersfield T	24	2	179	17

FOWLER, Lee (M) **43 0**
H: 5 7 W: 10 00 b.Cardiff 10-6-83
Source: Scholar. *Honours:* Wales Youth, Under-21.

2000–01	Coventry C	0	0		
2001–02	Coventry C	13	0		
2002–03	Coventry C	1	0		
2003–04	Coventry C	0	0	14	0
2003–04	Huddersfield T	29	0		
2004–05	Huddersfield T	0	0	29	0

FOWLER, Lee (M) **63 0**
H: 5 7 W: 10 00 b.Cardiff 10-6-83
Source: Scholar. *Honours:* Wales Under-21.

2000–01	Coventry C	0	0		
2001–02	Coventry C	13	0		
2002–03	Coventry C	1	0		
2003–04	Coventry C	0	0	14	0
2003–04	Huddersfield T	29	0		
2004–05	Huddersfield T	20	0	49	0

GRAY, Ian (G) **163 0**
H: 6 2 W: 13 13 b.Manchester 25-2-75
Source: Trainee.

1993–94	Oldham Ath	0	0		
1994–95	Oldham Ath	0	0		
1994–95	*Rochdale*	12	0		
1995–96	Rochdale	20	0		
1996–97	Rochdale	46	0	78	0
1997–98	Stockport Co	3	0		
1998–99	Stockport Co	3	0		
1999–2000	Stockport Co	10	0	16	0
2000–01	Rotherham U	33	0		
2001–02	Rotherham U	1	0		
2002–03	Rotherham U	6	0	40	0
2003–04	Huddersfield T	17	0		
2004–05	Huddersfield T	12	0	29	0

HOLDSWORTH, Andy (D) **76 0**
H: 5 9 W: 11 02 b.Pontefract 29-1-84
Source: Scholar.

2003–04	Huddersfield T	36	0		
2004–05	Huddersfield T	40	0	76	0

LLOYD, Anthony (D) **42 3**
H: 5 7 W: 11 00 b.Taunton 14-3-84
Source: Scholar.

2003–04	Huddersfield T	31	3		
2004–05	Huddersfield T	11	0	42	3

McALISKEY, John (F) **26 6**
H: 6 5 W: 12 07 b.Huddersfield 2-9-84
Source: Scholar. *Honours:* Eire Under-21.

2003–04	Huddersfield T	8	4		
2004–05	Huddersfield T	18	2	26	6

McCOMBE, John (D) **6 0**
H: 6 1 W: 14 02 b.Pontefract 7-5-85
Source: Scholar.

2002–03	Huddersfield T	1	0		
2003–04	Huddersfield T	0	0		
2004–05	Huddersfield T	5	0	6	0

MENDES, Junior (F) **127 28**
H: 5 11 W: 12 05 b.Balham 15-9-76
Source: Trainee. *Honours:* Montserrat full caps.

1995–96	Chelsea	0	0		
1996–97	Chelsea	0	0		
1997–98	Chelsea	0	0		
1998–99	St Mirren	22	4		
1998–99	*Carlisle U*	6	1		
1999–2000	Carlisle U	0	0		
2000–01	Carlisle U	0	0	6	1
2001–02	Rushden & D	0	0		
2002–03	St Mirren	17	6	39	10
2002–03	Mansfield T	18	1		
2003–04	Mansfield T	39	11	57	12
2004–05	Huddersfield T	25	5	25	5

MIRFIN, David (M) **63 6**
H: 6 2 W: 14 05 b.Sheffield 18-4-85
Source: Scholar.

Season	Club				
2002–03	Huddersfield T	1	0		
2003–04	Huddersfield T	21	2		
2004–05	Huddersfield T	41	4	**63**	**6**

RACHUBKA, Paul (G) **73 0**
H: 6 1 W: 13 01 b.San Luis Opispo 21-5-81
Source: Trainee. *Honours:* England Youth.

Season	Club				
1999–2000	Manchester U	0	0		
2000–01	Manchester U	1	0		
2001–02	Manchester U	0	0	**1**	**0**
2001–02	*Oldham Ath*	16	0	**16**	**0**
2001–02	Charlton Ath	0	0		
2002–03	Charlton Ath	0	0		
2003–04	Charlton Ath	0	0		
2003–04	*Huddersfield T*	13	0		
2004–05	Charlton Ath	0	0		
2004–05	*Milton Keynes D*	4	0	**4**	**0**
2004–05	*Northampton T*	10	0	**10**	**0**
2004–05	Huddersfield T	29	0	**42**	**0**

SCHOFIELD, Danny (F) **147 23**
H: 5 11 W: 12 00 b.Doncaster 10-4-80
Source: Brodsworth.

Season	Club				
1998–99	Huddersfield T	1	0		
1999–2000	Huddersfield T	2	0		
2000–01	Huddersfield T	1	0		
2001–02	Huddersfield T	40	8		
2002–03	Huddersfield T	30	2		
2003–04	Huddersfield T	40	8		
2004–05	Huddersfield T	33	5	**147**	**23**

SENIOR, Philip (G) **40 0**
H: 5 11 W: 11 00 b.Huddersfield 30-10-82
Source: Trainee.

Season	Club				
1999–2000	Huddersfield T	0	0		
2000–01	Huddersfield T	0	0		
2001–02	Huddersfield T	0	0		
2002–03	Huddersfield T	18	0		
2003–04	Huddersfield T	16	0		
2004–05	Huddersfield T	6	0	**40**	**0**

SODJE, Akpo (F) **14 1**
H: 6 2 W: 12 08 b.Greenwich 31-1-81
Source: QPR, Stevenage B, Margate, Gravesend & N, Erith & Belvedere.

Season	Club				
2004–05	Huddersfield T	7	0	**7**	**0**
2004–05	*Darlington*	7	1	**7**	**1**

THOMPSON, Tyrone (F) **3 0**
H: 5 10 W: 11 00 b.Sheffield 8-5-82
Source: Scholar.

Season	Club				
2000–01	Sheffield U	0	0		
2001–02	Sheffield U	0	0		
2002–03	Sheffield U	0	0		
2002–03	*Lincoln C*	1	0	**1**	**0**
2003–04	Sheffield U	0	0		
2003–04	Huddersfield T	2	0		
2004–05	Huddersfield T	0	0	**2**	**0**

WALSH, Joe (M) **0 0**
H: 5 9 W: 10 08 b.Dewsbury 29-11-84
Source: Scholar.

Season	Club				
2004–05	Huddersfield T	0	0		

WORTHINGTON, Jon (M) **100 6**
H: 5 9 W: 11 05 b.Dewsbury 16-4-83
Source: Scholar.

Season	Club				
2001–02	Huddersfield T	0	0		
2002–03	Huddersfield T	22	0		
2003–04	Huddersfield T	39	3		
2004–05	Huddersfield T	39	3	**100**	**6**

YATES, Steve (D) **508 10**
H: 5 11 W: 12 00 b.Bristol 29-1-70
Source: Trainee.

Season	Club				
1986–87	Bristol R	2	0		
1987–88	Bristol R	0	0		
1988–89	Bristol R	35	0		
1989–90	Bristol R	42	0		
1990–91	Bristol R	34	0		
1991–92	Bristol R	39	0		
1992–93	Bristol R	44	0		
1993–94	Bristol R	1	0	**197**	**0**
1993–94	QPR	29	0		
1994–95	QPR	23	1		
1995–96	QPR	30	0		
1996–97	QPR	16	1		
1997–98	QPR	30	0		
1998–99	QPR	6	0	**134**	**2**
1999–2000	Tranmere R	33	2		
2000–01	Tranmere R	43	2		
2001–02	Tranmere R	37	3	**113**	**7**
2002–03	Sheffield U	12	0	**12**	**0**
2003–04	Huddersfield T	35	1		
2004–05	Huddersfield T	17	0	**52**	**1**

HULL C (37)

ALLSOPP, Danny (F) **246 78**
H: 6 1 W: 12 00 b.Melbourne 10-8-78
Honours: Australia Youth, Under-20, Under-23.

Season	Club				
1995–96	South Melbourne	14	1		
1996–97	South Melbourne	6	1	**20**	**2**
1997–98	Carlton	16	3	**16**	**3**
1998–99	Manchester C	24	4		
1999–2000	Manchester C	4	0		
1999–2000	*Notts Co*	3	1		
1999–2000	*Wrexham*	3	4	**3**	**4**
2000–01	Manchester C	1	0	**29**	**4**
2000–01	*Bristol R*	6	0	**6**	**0**
2000–01	Notts Co	29	13		
2001–02	Notts Co	43	19		
2002–03	Notts Co	33	10	**108**	**43**
2002–03	Hull C	0	0		
2003–04	Hull C	36	15		
2004–05	Hull C	28	7	**64**	**22**

ASHBEE, Ian (M) **314 15**
H: 6 1 W: 13 07 b.Birmingham 6-9-76
Source: Trainee. *Honours:* England Youth.

Season	Club				
1994–95	Derby Co	1	0		
1995–96	Derby Co	0	0		
1996–97	Derby Co	0	0	**1**	**0**
1996–97	Cambridge U	18	0		
1997–98	Cambridge U	27	1		
1998–99	Cambridge U	31	4		
1999–2000	Cambridge U	45	1		
2000–01	Cambridge U	44	3		
2001–02	Cambridge U	38	2	**203**	**11**
2002–03	Hull C	31	1		
2003–04	Hull C	39	2		
2004–05	Hull C	40	1	**110**	**4**

BARMBY, Nick (M) **347 62**
H: 5 7 W: 11 03 b.Hull 11-2-74
Source: Trainee. *Honours:* England Schools, Youth, Under-21, B, 23 full caps, 4 goals.

Season	Club				
1991–92	Tottenham H	0	0		
1992–93	Tottenham H	22	6		
1993–94	Tottenham H	27	5		
1994–95	Tottenham H	38	9	**87**	**20**
1995–96	Middlesbrough	32	7		
1996–97	Middlesbrough	10	1	**42**	**8**
1996–97	Everton	25	4		
1997–98	Everton	30	2		
1998–99	Everton	24	3		
1999–2000	Everton	37	9	**116**	**18**
2000–01	Liverpool	26	2		
2001–02	Liverpool	6	0	**32**	**2**
2002–03	Leeds U	19	4		
2003–04	*Nottingham F*	6	1	**6**	**1**
2003–04	Leeds U	6	0	**25**	**4**
2004–05	Hull C	39	9	**39**	**9**

BURGESS, Ben (F) **151 59**
H: 6 4 W: 14 04 b.Buxton 9-11-81
Source: Trainee. *Honours:* Eire Under-21.

Season	Club				
1998–99	Blackburn R	0	0		
1999–2000	Blackburn R	2	0		
2000–01	Blackburn R	0	0		
2000–01	Northern Spirit	27	16	**27**	**16**
2001–02	Blackburn R	0	0	**2**	**0**
2001–02	*Brentford*	43	17	**43**	**17**
2002–03	Stockport Co	19	4	**19**	**4**
2002–03	*Oldham Ath*	7	0	**7**	**0**
2002–03	Hull C	7	4		
2003–04	Hull C	44	18		
2004–05	Hull C	2	0	**53**	**22**

CORT, Leon (D) **181 17**
H: 6 3 W: 13 01 b.Bermondsey 11-9-79
Source: Dulwich H.

Season	Club				
1997–98	Millwall	0	0		
1998–99	Millwall	0	0		
1999–2000	Millwall	0	0		
2000–01	Millwall	0	0		
2001–02	Southend U	45	4		
2002–03	Southend U	46	6		
2003–04	Southend U	46	1	**137**	**11**
2004–05	Hull C	44	6	**44**	**6**

DAWSON, Andy (D) **262 11**
H: 5 10 W: 11 02 b.Northallerton 20-10-78
Source: Trainee.

Season	Club				
1995–96	Nottingham F	0	0		
1996–97	Nottingham F	0	0		
1997–98	Nottingham F	0	0		
1998–99	Nottingham F	0	0		
1998–99	Scunthorpe U	24	0		
1999–2000	Scunthorpe U	43	2		
2000–01	Scunthorpe U	41	4		
2001–02	Scunthorpe U	44	0		
2002–03	Scunthorpe U	43	2	**195**	**8**
2003–04	Hull C	33	3		
2004–05	Hull C	34	0	**67**	**3**

DELANEY, Damien (D) **148 5**
H: 6 3 W: 14 00 b.Cork 20-7-81
Source: Cork C.

Season	Club				
2000–01	Leicester C	5	0		
2001–02	Leicester C	3	0		
2001–02	*Stockport Co*	12	1	**12**	**1**
2001–02	*Huddersfield T*	2	0	**2**	**0**
2002–03	Leicester C	0	0	**8**	**0**
2002–03	*Mansfield T*	7	0	**7**	**0**
2002–03	Hull C	30	1		
2003–04	Hull C	46	2		
2004–05	Hull C	43	1	**119**	**4**

DONALDSON, Clayton (F) **2 0**
H: 6 1 W: 11 07 b.Bradford 7-2-84
Source: Scholar.

Season	Club				
2002–03	Hull C	2	0		
2003–04	Hull C	0	0		
2004–05	Hull C	0	0	**2**	**0**

DUKE, Matt (G) **2 0**
H: 6 5 W: 13 04 b.Sheffield 16-7-77
Source: Alfreton T.

Season	Club				
1999–2000	Sheffield U	0	0		
2000–01	Sheffield U	0	0		
2001–02	Sheffield U	0	0		
2004–05	Hull C	2	0	**2**	**0**

EDGE, Roland (D) **116 1**
H: 5 9 W: 11 07 b.Gillingham 25-11-78
Source: Trainee.

Season	Club				
1997–98	Gillingham	0	0		
1998–99	Gillingham	8	0		
1999–2000	Gillingham	26	1		
2000–01	Gillingham	20	0		
2001–02	Gillingham	14	0		
2002–03	Gillingham	34	0		
2003–04	Gillingham	0	0	**102**	**1**
2004–05	Hull C	14	0	**14**	**0**

ELLIOTT, Stuart (M) **280 102**
H: 5 10 W: 11 09 b.Belfast 23-7-78
Honours: Northern Ireland Under-21, 27 full caps, 3 goals.

Season	Club				
1994–95	Glentoran	0	0		
1995–96	Glentoran	1	0		
1996–97	Glentoran	8	1		
1997–98	Glentoran	22	5		
1998–99	Glentoran	31	7		
1999–2000	Glentoran	34	16	**96**	**29**
2000–01	Motherwell	33	10		
2001–02	Motherwell	37	10	**70**	**20**
2002–03	Hull C	36	12		
2003–04	Hull C	42	14		
2004–05	Hull C	36	27	**114**	**53**

ELLISON, Kevin (M) **100 12**
H: 6 2 W: 13 04 b.Liverpool 23-2-79
Source: Altrincham.

Season	Club				
2000–01	Leicester C	1	0		
2001–02	Leicester C	0	0	**1**	**0**
2001–02	Stockport Co	11	0		
2002–03	Stockport Co	23	1		
2003–04	Stockport Co	14	1	**48**	**2**
2003–04	*Lincoln C*	11	0	**11**	**0**
2004–05	Chester C	24	9	**24**	**9**
2004–05	Hull C	16	1	**16**	**1**

FACEY, Delroy (F) **145 26**
H: 6 0 W: 13 00 b.Huddersfield 22-4-80
Source: Trainee.

Season	Club				
1996–97	Huddersfield T	3	0		
1997–98	Huddersfield T	3	0		
1998–99	Huddersfield T	20	3		
1999–2000	Huddersfield T	2	0		

2000–01 Huddersfield T 34 10
2001–02 Huddersfield T 13 2
2002–03 Huddersfield T 0 0
2002–03 *Bradford C* 6 1 **6 1**
2002–03 Bolton W 9 1
2003–04 Bolton W 1 0 **10 1**
2003–04 *Burnley* 14 5 **14 5**
2003–04 WBA 9 0 **9 0**
2004–05 Hull C 21 4 **21 4**
2004–05 *Huddersfield T* 4 0 **79 15**
2004–05 *Oldham Ath* 6 0 **6 0**

FAGAN, Craig (F) 82 22
H: 5 11 W: 11 08 b.Birmingham 11-12-82
Source: Scholar.
2001–02 Birmingham C 0 0
2002–03 Birmingham C 1 0
2002–03 *Bristol C* 6 1 **6 1**
2003–04 Birmingham C 0 0 **1 0**
2003–04 Colchester U 37 9
2004–05 Colchester U 26 8 **63 17**
2004–05 Hull C 12 4 **12 4**

FRANCE, Ryan (M) 59 4
H: 5 11 W: 11 11 b.Sheffield 13-12-80
Source: Alfreton T.
2003–04 Hull C 28 2
2004–05 Hull C 31 2 **59 4**

FRY, Russell (M) 1 0
H: 6 0 W: 12 01 b.Hull 4-12-85
Source: Scholar.
2002–03 Hull C 0 0
2003–04 Hull C 0 0
2004–05 Hull C 1 0 **1 0**

GREEN, Stuart (M) 125 25
H: 5 10 W: 11 01 b.Whitehaven 15-6-81
Source: Trainee.
1999–2000 Newcastle U 0 0
2000–01 Newcastle U 0 0
2001–02 Newcastle U 0 0
2001–02 *Carlisle U* 16 3
2002–03 Newcastle U 0 0
2002–03 Hull C 28 6
2002–03 *Carlisle U* 10 2 **26 5**
2003–04 Hull C 42 6
2004–05 Hull C 29 8 **99 20**

HINDS, Richard (D) 107 1
H: 6 2 W: 12 04 b.Sheffield 22-8-80
Source: Schoolboy.
1998–99 Tranmere R 2 0
1999–2000 Tranmere R 6 0
2000–01 Tranmere R 29 0
2001–02 Tranmere R 10 0
2002–03 Tranmere R 8 0 **55 0**
2003–04 Hull C 39 1
2004–05 Hull C 6 0 **45 1**
2004–05 *Scunthorpe U* 7 0 **7 0**

JOSEPH, Marc (D) 298 3
H: 6 0 W: 12 05 b.Leicester 10-11-76
Source: Trainee.
1995–96 Cambridge U 12 0
1996–97 Cambridge U 8 0
1997–98 Cambridge U 41 0
1998–99 Cambridge U 29 0
1999–2000 Cambridge U 33 0
2000–01 Cambridge U 30 0 **153 0**
2001–02 Peterborough U 44 2
2002–03 Peterborough U 17 0 **61 2**
2002–03 Hull C 23 0
2003–04 Hull C 32 1
2004–05 Hull C 29 0 **84 1**

LEWIS, Junior (M) 175 15
H: 6 2 W: 13 00 b.Wembley 9-10-73
Source: Trainee.
1992–93 Fulham 6 0 **6 0**
From Dover, Hendon
1999–2000 Gillingham 42 6
2000–01 Gillingham 17 2 **59 8**
2000–01 Leicester C 15 0
2001–02 Leicester C 6 0
2001–02 *Brighton & HA* 15 3 **15 3**
2002–03 Leicester C 9 1
2002–03 *Swindon T* 9 0
2003–04 Leicester C 0 0 **30 1**
2003–04 *Swindon T* 4 0 **13 0**
2003–04 *Hull C* 13 1
2004–05 Hull C 39 2 **52 3**

MYHILL, Boaz (G) 87 0
H: 6 3 W: 14 06 b.Modesto 9-11-82
Source: Scholar. *Honours:* England Youth, Under-20.
2000–01 Aston Villa 0 0
2001–02 Aston Villa 0 0
2001–02 *Stoke C* 0 0
2002–03 Aston Villa 0 0
2002–03 *Bristol C* 0 0
2002–03 *Bradford C* 2 0 **2 0**
2003–04 Aston Villa 0 0
2003–04 *Macclesfield T* 15 0 **15 0**
2003–04 *Stockport Co* 2 0 **2 0**
2003–04 Hull C 23 0
2004–05 Hull C 45 0 **68 0**

PEAT, Nathan (M) 18 0
H: 5 9 W: 10 09 b.Hull 19-9-82
Source: Scholar.
2002–03 Hull C 1 0
2003–04 Hull C 1 0
2003–04 *Cambridge U* 6 0 **6 0**
2004–05 Hull C 0 0 **2 0**
2004–05 *Lincoln C* 10 0 **10 0**

PRICE, Jason (M) 268 40
H: 6 2 W: 11 05 b.Pontypridd 12-4-77
Source: Aberaman Ath. *Honours:* Wales Under-21.
1995–96 Swansea C 0 0
1996–97 Swansea C 2 0
1997–98 Swansea C 34 3
1998–99 Swansea C 28 4
1999–2000 Swansea C 39 6
2000–01 Swansea C 41 4 **144 17**
2001–02 Brentford 15 1 **15 1**
2001–02 Tranmere R 24 7
2002–03 Tranmere R 25 4 **49 11**
2003–04 Hull C 33 9
2004–05 Hull C 27 2 **60 11**

STOCKDALE, Robbie (D) 145 3
H: 5 11 W: 12 04 b.Middlesbrough 30-11-79
Source: Trainee. *Honours:* England Under-21, Scotland 5 full caps.
1997–98 Middlesbrough 1 0
1998–99 Middlesbrough 19 0
1999–2000 Middlesbrough 11 1
2000–01 Middlesbrough 0 0
2000–01 *Sheffield W* 6 0 **6 0**
2001–02 Middlesbrough 28 1
2002–03 Middlesbrough 14 0
2003–04 Middlesbrough 2 0 **75 2**
2003–04 *West Ham U* 7 0 **7 0**
2003–04 *Rotherham U* 16 1
2004–05 Rotherham U 27 0 **43 1**
2004–05 Hull C 14 0 **14 0**

THELWELL, Alton (D) 47 1
H: 6 0 W: 12 00 b.Islington 5-9-80
Source: Trainee.
1998–99 Tottenham H 0 0
1999–2000 Tottenham H 0 0
2000–01 Tottenham H 16 0
2001–02 Tottenham H 2 0
2002–03 Tottenham H 0 0 **18 0**
2003–04 Hull C 26 1
2004–05 Hull C 3 0 **29 1**

WALTERS, Jonathan (F) 63 7
H: 6 1 W: 12 00 b.Birkenhead 20-9-83
Source: Blackburn R Scholar. *Honours:* Eire Under-21.
2001–02 Bolton W 0 0
2002–03 Bolton W 4 0
2002–03 *Hull C* 11 5
2003–04 Bolton W 0 0 **4 0**
2003–04 Crewe Alex 0 0
2003–04 *Barnsley* 8 0 **8 0**
2003–04 Hull C 16 1
2004–05 Hull C 21 1 **48 7**
2004–05 *Scunthorpe U* 3 0 **3 0**

WILBRAHAM, Aaron (F) 195 39
H: 6 3 W: 12 04 b.Knutsford 21-10-79
Source: Trainee.
1997–98 Stockport Co 7 1
1998–99 Stockport Co 26 0
1999–2000 Stockport Co 26 4
2000–01 Stockport Co 36 12
2001–02 Stockport Co 21 3
2002–03 Stockport Co 15 7
2003–04 Stockport Co 41 8 **172 35**
2004–05 Hull C 19 2 **19 2**
2004–05 *Oldham Ath* 4 2 **4 2**

WISEMAN, Scott (D) 7 0
H: 6 0 W: 11 06 b.Hull 9-10-85
Source: Scholar. *Honours:* England Youth, Under-20.
2003–04 Hull C 2 0
2004–05 Hull C 3 0 **5 0**
2004–05 *Boston U* 2 0 **2 0**

IPSWICH T (38)

ATAY, Adem (D) 0 0
H: 5 9 W: 11 00 b.Cambridge 8-12-85
Source: From Academy.
2003–04 Ipswich T 0 0
2004–05 Ipswich T 0 0

BARRON, Scott (D) 0 0
H: 5 9 W: 9 08 b.Preston 2-9-85
Source: Scholar.
2003–04 Ipswich T 0 0
2004–05 Ipswich T 0 0

BENT, Darren (F) 122 49
H: 5 11 W: 11 07 b.Tooting 6-2-84
Source: Scholar. *Honours:* England Youth, Under-21.
2001–02 Ipswich T 5 1
2002–03 Ipswich T 35 12
2003–04 Ipswich T 37 16
2004–05 Ipswich T 45 20 **122 49**

BOWDITCH, Dean (F) 52 8
H: 5 11 W: 10 08 b.Bishops Stortford 15-6-86
Source: Trainee. *Honours:* FA Schools, England Youth.
2002–03 Ipswich T 5 0
2003–04 Ipswich T 16 4
2004–05 Ipswich T 21 3 **42 7**
2004–05 *Burnley* 10 1 **10 1**

CLARKE, Billy (F) 0 0
H: 5 8 W: 10 02 b.Cork 13-12-87
Source: Scholar.
2004–05 Ipswich T 0 0

COLLINS, Aidan (D) 1 0
H: 6 3 W: 13 09 b.Harlow 18-10-86
2002–03 Ipswich T 1 0
2003–04 Ipswich T 0 0
2004–05 Ipswich T 0 0 **1 0**

COUNAGO, Pablo (F) 148 36
H: 5 11 W: 11 06 b.Pontevedra 9-8-79
1998–99 Numancia 13 1 **13 1**
1998–99 Celta Vigo 1 0
1999–2000 Huelva 26 4 **26 4**
2000–01 Celta Vigo 8 0 **9 0**
2001–02 Ipswich T 13 0
2002–03 Ipswich T 39 17
2003–04 Ipswich T 29 11
2004–05 Ipswich T 19 3 **100 31**

CURRIE, Darren (M) 399 48
H: 5 10 W: 12 07 b.Hampstead 29-11-74
Source: Trainee.
1993–94 West Ham U 0 0
1994–95 West Ham U 0 0
1994–95 *Shrewsbury T* 17 2
1995–96 West Ham U 0 0
1995–96 *Leyton Orient* 10 0 **10 0**
1995–96 Shrewsbury T 13 2
1996–97 Shrewsbury T 37 2
1997–98 Shrewsbury T 16 4 **83 10**
1997–98 Plymouth Arg 7 0 **7 0**
1998–99 Barnet 38 4
1999–2000 Barnet 44 5
2000–01 Barnet 45 10 **127 19**
2001–02 Wycombe W 46 3
2002–03 Wycombe W 38 4
2003–04 Wycombe W 42 7 **126 14**
2004–05 Brighton & HA 22 2 **22 2**
2004–05 Ipswich T 24 3 **24 3**

DAVIS, Kelvin (G) **311 0**
H: 6 1 W: 14 00 b.Bedford 29-9-76
Source: Trainee. *Honours:* England Youth, Under-21.

1993–94	Luton T	1	0		
1994–95	Luton T	9	0		
1994–95	*Torquay U*	2	0	**2**	**0**
1995–96	Luton T	6	0		
1996–97	Luton T	0	0		
1997–98	Luton T	32	0		
1997–98	*Hartlepool U*	2	0	**2**	**0**
1998–99	Luton T	44	0	**92**	**0**
1999–2000	Wimbledon	0	0		
2000–01	Wimbledon	45	0		
2001–02	Wimbledon	40	0		
2002–03	Wimbledon	46	0	**131**	**0**
2003–04	Ipswich T	45	0		
2004–05	Ipswich T	39	0	**84**	**0**

DE VOS, Jason (D) **272 25**
H: 6 4 W: 13 07 b.London, Can 2-1-74
Source: Montreal Impact. *Honours:* Canada Youth, Under-23, 49 full caps, 4 goals.

1996–97	Darlington	8	0		
1997–98	Darlington	24	3		
1998–99	Darlington	12	2	**44**	**5**
1998–99	Dundee U	25	0		
1999–2000	Dundee U	35	2		
2000–01	Dundee U	33	0	**93**	**2**
2001–02	Wigan Ath	20	5		
2002–03	Wigan Ath	43	8		
2003–04	Wigan Ath	27	2	**90**	**15**
2004–05	Ipswich T	45	3	**45**	**3**

DIALLO, Drissa (D) **59 1**
H: 6 0 W: 11 08 b.Nouadhibou 4-1-73
Honours: Guinea full caps.

2002–03	Burnley	14	1	**14**	**1**
2003–04	Ipswich T	19	0		
2004–05	Ipswich T	26	0	**45**	**0**

HOGG, Chris (D) **10 0**
H: 6 0 W: 12 07 b.Middlesbrough 12-3-85
Source: Trainee. *Honours:* England Youth.

2002–03	Ipswich T	0	0		
2003–04	Ipswich T	0	0		
2003–04	*Boston U*	10	0	**10**	**0**
2004–05	Ipswich T	0	0		

HORLOCK, Kevin (M) **435 60**
H: 6 0 W: 12 00 b.Erith 1-11-72
Source: Trainee. *Honours:* Northern Ireland B, 32 full caps.

1991–92	West Ham U	0	0		
1992–93	West Ham U	0	0		
1992–93	Swindon T	14	1		
1993–94	Swindon T	38	0		
1994–95	Swindon T	38	1		
1995–96	Swindon T	45	12		
1996–97	Swindon T	28	8	**163**	**22**
1996–97	Manchester C	18	4		
1997–98	Manchester C	25	5		
1998–99	Manchester C	37	9		
1999–2000	Manchester C	38	10		
2000–01	Manchester C	14	2		
2001–02	Manchester C	42	7		
2002–03	Manchester C	30	0	**204**	**37**
2003–04	West Ham U	27	1	**27**	**1**
2004–05	Ipswich T	41	0	**41**	**0**

JUAN, Jimmy (M) **0 0**
H: 6 2 W: 12 06 b.Valence 10-6-83

2004–05	Ipswich T	0	0		

KNIGHTS, Darryl (F) **1 0**
H: 5 7 W: 10 01 b.Ipswich 1-5-88
Source: Scholar. *Honours:* England Youth.

2004–05	Ipswich T	1	0	**1**	**0**

KUQI, Shefki (F) **300 88**
H: 6 2 W: 13 10 b.Kosovo 10-11-76
Source: Trepka, Miki. *Honours:* Albania 8 full caps, 1 goal; Finland 38 full caps, 6 goals.

1995	MP	24	3		
1996	MP	26	7	**50**	**10**
1997	HJK Helsinki	25	6		
1998	HJK Helsinki	22	1		
1999	HJK Helsinki	25	11	**72**	**18**
From Jokerit					
2000–01	Stockport Co	17	6		
2001–02	Stockport Co	18	5	**35**	**11**
2001–02	Sheffield W	17	6		
2002–03	Sheffield W	40	8		
2003–04	Sheffield W	7	5	**64**	**19**
2003–04	Ipswich T	36	11		
2004–05	Ipswich T	43	19	**79**	**30**

MAGILTON, Jim (M) **546 63**
H: 6 0 W: 14 00 b.Belfast 6-5-69
Source: Apprentice. *Honours:* Northern Ireland Schools, Youth, Under-21, Under-23, 52 full caps, 5 goals. Football League.

1986–87	Liverpool	0	0		
1987–88	Liverpool	0	0		
1988–89	Liverpool	0	0		
1989–90	Liverpool	0	0		
1990–91	Liverpool	0	0		
1990–91	Oxford U	37	6		
1991–92	Oxford U	44	12		
1992–93	Oxford U	40	11		
1993–94	Oxford U	29	5	**150**	**34**
1993–94	Southampton	15	0		
1994–95	Southampton	42	6		
1995–96	Southampton	31	3		
1996–97	Southampton	37	4		
1997–98	Southampton	5	0	**130**	**13**
1997–98	Sheffield W	21	1		
1998–99	Sheffield W	6	0	**27**	**1**
1998–99	Ipswich T	19	3		
1999–2000	Ipswich T	38	4		
2000–01	Ipswich T	33	1		
2001–02	Ipswich T	24	0		
2002–03	Ipswich T	40	3		
2003–04	Ipswich T	46	1		
2004–05	Ipswich T	39	3	**239**	**15**

McDONALD, Dean (F) **0 0**
H: 5 8 W: 10 07 b.Lambeth 19-2-86

2004–05	Ipswich T	0	0		

MILLER, Tommy (M) **254 65**
H: 6 1 W: 11 12 b.Shotton Colliery 8-1-79
Source: Trainee.

1997–98	Hartlepool U	13	1		
1998–99	Hartlepool U	34	4		
1999–2000	Hartlepool U	44	14		
2000–01	Hartlepool U	46	16		
2001–02	Hartlepool U	0	0	**137**	**35**
2001–02	Ipswich T	8	0		
2002–03	Ipswich T	30	6		
2003–04	Ipswich T	34	11		
2004–05	Ipswich T	45	13	**117**	**30**

MITCHELL, Scott (M) **2 0**
H: 5 11 W: 12 00 b.Ely 2-9-85
Source: Scholar.

2003–04	Ipswich T	2	0		
2004–05	Ipswich T	0	0	**2**	**0**

MURRAY, Antonio (M) **1 0**
H: 5 9 W: 11 00 b.Cambridge 15-9-84
Source: Scholar.

2002–03	Ipswich T	1	0		
2003–04	Ipswich T	0	0		
2004–05	Ipswich T	0	0	**1**	**0**

NASH, Gerard (D) **1 0**
H: 6 1 W: 11 08 b.Dublin 11-7-86
Source: Scholar. *Honours:* Eire Youth.

2003–04	Ipswich T	1	0		
2004–05	Ipswich T	0	0	**1**	**0**

NAYLOR, Richard (D) **238 34**
H: 6 1 W: 13 07 b.Leeds 28-2-77
Source: Trainee.

1995–96	Ipswich T	0	0		
1996–97	Ipswich T	27	4		
1997–98	Ipswich T	5	2		
1998–99	Ipswich T	30	5		
1999–2000	Ipswich T	36	8		
2000–01	Ipswich T	13	1		
2001–02	Ipswich T	14	1		
2001–02	*Millwall*	3	0	**3**	**0**
2001–02	*Barnsley*	8	0	**8**	**0**
2002–03	Ipswich T	17	2		
2003–04	Ipswich T	39	5		
2004–05	Ipswich T	46	6	**227**	**34**

PATTEN, Ben (D) **0 0**
H: 6 1 W: 12 08 b.London 16-2-86
Source: Ford U.

2003–04	Ipswich T	0	0		
2004–05	Ipswich T	0	0		

PRICE, Lewis (G) **15 0**
H: 6 3 W: 13 06 b.Poole 19-7-84
Source: Southampton Academy. *Honours:* Wales Youth, Under-21.

2002–03	Ipswich T	0	0		
2003–04	Ipswich T	1	0		
2004–05	Ipswich T	8	0	**9**	**0**
2004–05	*Cambridge U*	6	0	**6**	**0**

REUSER, Martijn (M) **189 34**
H: 5 7 W: 12 10 b.Amsterdam 1-2-75
Honours: Holland 1 full cap.

1993–94	Ajax	2	0		
1994–95	Ajax	2	0		
1995–96	Ajax	18	3		
1996–97	Ajax	19	3		
1997–98	Ajax	1	0	**42**	**6**
1997–98	Vitesse	24	6		
1998–99	Vitesse	32	8	**56**	**14**
1999–2000	Ipswich T	8	2		
2000–01	Ipswich T	26	6		
2001–02	Ipswich T	24	1		
2002–03	Ipswich T	16	2		
2003–04	Ipswich T	17	3		
2004–05	Ipswich T	0	0	**91**	**14**

RICHARDS, Matt (D) **81 2**
H: 5 8 W: 10 10 b.Harlow 26-12-84
Source: Scholar. *Honours:* England Under-21.

2001–02	Ipswich T	0	0		
2002–03	Ipswich T	13	0		
2003–04	Ipswich T	44	1		
2004–05	Ipswich T	24	1	**81**	**2**

SOBERS, Jerome (D) **1 1**
H: 6 2 W: 13 05 b.London 18-4-86

2003–04	Ipswich T	0	0		
2004–05	Ipswich T	0	0		
2004–05	*Brentford*	1	1	**1**	**1**

SUPPLE, Shane (G) **0 0**
H: 5 11 W: 11 07 b.Dublin 4-5-87
Source: Scholar.

2004–05	Ipswich T	0	0		

WESTLAKE, Ian (M) **88 13**
H: 5 11 W: 11 00 b.Clacton 10-11-83
Source: Scholar.

2002–03	Ipswich T	4	0		
2003–04	Ipswich T	39	6		
2004–05	Ipswich T	45	7	**88**	**13**

WILNIS, Fabian (D) **454 9**
H: 5 8 W: 12 06 b.Paramaribo 23-8-70
Source: Het Noorden, NOC, De Zwervers, Sparta.

1990–91	NAC	7	3		
1991–92	NAC	30	0		
1992–93	NAC	32	0		
1993–94	NAC	34	0		
1994–95	NAC	31	0	**134**	**3**
1995–96	De Graafschap	32	0		
1996–97	De Graafschap	23	0		
1997–98	De Graafschap	33	1		
1998–99	De Graafschap	19	0	**107**	**1**
1998–99	Ipswich T	18	1		
1999–2000	Ipswich T	35	0		
2000–01	Ipswich T	29	2		
2001–02	Ipswich T	14	0		
2002–03	Ipswich T	35	2		
2003–04	Ipswich T	41	0		
2004–05	Ipswich T	41	0	**213**	**5**

KIDDERMINSTER H (39)

ADVICE-DESRUISSEAU, Fred (M) **9 0**
H: 5 9 W: 11 07 b.Paris 12-1-83

2004–05	Kidderminster H	9	0	**9**	**0**

APPLEBY, Ritchie (M) **157 16**
H: 5 9 W: 11 04 b.Stockton 18-9-75
Source: Trainee. *Honours:* England Youth.

1993–94	Newcastle U	0	0		
1994–95	Newcastle U	0	0		
1994–95	*Darlington*	0	0		
1995–96	Ipswich T	3	0	**3**	**0**
1996–97	Swansea C	11	1		
1997–98	Swansea C	35	3		
1998–99	Swansea C	39	3		
1999–2000	Swansea C	20	4		
2000–01	Swansea C	5	0		

2001–02 Swansea C 10 0 120 11
2001–02 Kidderminster H 19 4
2002–03 Kidderminster H 0 0
2002–03 Hull C 6 0
2003–04 Hull C 0 0 6 0
2004–05 Kidderminster H 9 1 28 5

BEARDSLEY, Chris (F) 49 6
H: 6 0 W: 12 00 b.Derby 28-2-84
Source: Scholar.
2002–03 Mansfield T 5 0
2003–04 Mansfield T 15 1 20 1
2004–05 Doncaster R 4 0 4 0
2004–05 Kidderminster H 25 5 25 5

BENNETT, Tom (M) 417 16
H: 5 11 W: 11 08 b.Falkirk 12-12-69
Source: Trainee.
1987–88 Aston Villa 0 0
1988–89 Wolverhampton W 2 0
1989–90 Wolverhampton W 30 0
1990–91 Wolverhampton W 26 0
1991–92 Wolverhampton W 38 2
1992–93 Wolverhampton W 1 0
1993–94 Wolverhampton W 10 0
1994–95 Wolverhampton W 8 0 115 2
1995–96 Stockport Co 24 1
1996–97 Stockport Co 43 3
1997–98 Stockport Co 27 1
1998–99 Stockport Co 7 0
1999–2000 Stockport Co 9 0 110 5
1999–2000 *Walsall* 11 3
2000–01 Walsall 38 5
2001–02 Walsall 40 0 89 8
2002–03 Boston U 33 0
2003–04 Boston U 35 1
2004–05 Boston U 11 0 79 1
2004–05 Kidderminster H 24 0 24 0

BESWETHERICK, John (D) 174 0
H: 6 0 W: 12 07 b.Liverpool 15-1-78
Source: Trainee.
1996–97 Plymouth Arg 0 0
1997–98 Plymouth Arg 2 0
1998–99 Plymouth Arg 22 0
1999–2000 Plymouth Arg 45 0
2000–01 Plymouth Arg 45 0
2001–02 Plymouth Arg 32 0 146 0
2002–03 Sheffield W 6 0
2002–03 *Swindon T* 3 0 3 0
2003–04 Sheffield W 5 0
2003–04 *Macclesfield T* 4 0 4 0
2004–05 Sheffield W 0 0 11 0
2004–05 Kidderminster H 10 0 10 0

BIRCH, Gary (F) 114 15
H: 6 0 W: 12 03 b.Birmingham 8-10-81
Source: Trainee.
1998–99 Walsall 0 0
1999–2000 Walsall 0 0
2000–01 Walsall 0 0
2000–01 *Exeter C* 9 2
2001–02 *Exeter C* 15 0 24 2
2001–02 Walsall 1 0
2002–03 Walsall 19 1
2003–04 Walsall 35 4
2003–04 *Barnsley* 8 2 8 2
2004–05 Walsall 13 2 68 7
2004–05 Kidderminster H 14 4 14 4

BURNS, Liam (D) 124 0
H: 6 2 W: 13 10 b.Belfast 30-10-78
Source: Trainee. *Honours:* Northern Ireland Youth, Under-21.
1997–98 Port Vale 1 0
1998–99 Port Vale 4 0
1999–2000 Port Vale 24 0
2000–01 Port Vale 13 0
2001–02 Port Vale 33 0
2002–03 Port Vale 16 0
2003–04 Port Vale 27 0 118 0
2004–05 Bristol R 3 0 3 0
2004–05 Shrewsbury T 2 0 2 0
2004–05 Kidderminster H 1 0 1 0

BURTON, Steven (D) 39 0
H: 6 1 W: 11 05 b.Hull 10-10-82
Source: Scholar.
2002–03 Hull C 11 0
2003–04 Hull C 0 0 11 0
2003–04 Kidderminster H 12 0
2004–05 Kidderminster H 16 0 28 0

CHAMBERS, Adam (D) 69 1
H: 5 10 W: 11 12 b.Sandwell 20-11-80
Source: Trainee. *Honours:* England Youth.
1998–99 WBA 0 0
1999–2000 WBA 0 0
2000–01 WBA 11 1
2001–02 WBA 32 0
2002–03 WBA 13 0
2003–04 WBA 0 0
2003–04 *Sheffield W* 11 0 11 0
2004–05 WBA 0 0 56 1
2004–05 Kidderminster H 2 0 2 0

CHRISTIANSEN, Jesper (F) 65 4
H: 6 3 W: 13 06 b.Denmark 18-6-80
2002–03 Odense 26 3
2003–04 Odense 1 0 27 3
2003–04 Kidderminster H 21 1
2004–05 Kidderminster H 17 0 38 1

CHRISTIE, Iyseden (F) 224 56
H: 5 10 W: 12 02 b.Coventry 14-11-76
Source: Trainee.
1994–95 Coventry C 0 0
1995–96 Coventry C 1 0
1996–97 Coventry C 0 0 1 0
1996–97 *Bournemouth* 4 0 4 0
1996–97 *Mansfield T* 8 0
1997–98 Mansfield T 39 10
1998–99 Mansfield T 42 8
1999–2000 Leyton Orient 36 7
2000–01 Leyton Orient 7 2
2001–02 Leyton Orient 15 3 58 12
2002–03 Mansfield T 37 18
2003–04 Mansfield T 27 8 153 44
2004–05 Kidderminster H 8 0 8 0

COZIC, Bertrand (M) 36 1
H: 5 10 W: 12 06 b.Quimper 18-5-78
Source: Team Bath.
2003–04 Cheltenham T 7 1 7 1
From Hereford U
2004–05 Northampton T 14 0 14 0
2004–05 Kidderminster H 15 0 15 0

DANBY, John (G) 48 0
H: 6 2 W: 14 06 b.Stoke 20-9-83
Source: Juniors.
2001–02 Kidderminster H 2 0
2002–03 Kidderminster H 0 0
2003–04 Kidderminster H 9 0
2004–05 Kidderminster H 37 0 48 0

DIOP, Youssou (F) 10 0
H: 6 1 W: 12 07 b.Zinguinchor 5-5-80
Source: Toulouse.
2004–05 Kidderminster H 10 0 10 0

FOSTER, Ian (F) 129 20
H: 5 7 W: 11 00 b.Merseyside 11-11-76
Source: Liverpool Schoolboy. *Honours:* England Schools.
1996–97 Hereford U 19 0 19 0
From Barrow
2000–01 Kidderminster H 10 2
2001–02 Kidderminster H 33 8
2002–03 Kidderminster H 29 1
2003–04 Chester C 0 0
2003–04 *Kidderminster H* 11 3
2004–05 Kidderminster H 27 6 110 20

GLEESON, Jamie (F) 7 0
H: 6 0 W: 12 03 b.Poole 15-1-85
Source: Trainee.
2002–03 Southampton 0 0
2003–04 Southampton 0 0
2004–05 Kidderminster H 7 0 7 0

HATSWELL, Wayne (D) 120 3
H: 6 0 W: 13 10 b.Swindon 8-2-75
Source: Forest Green R.
2000–01 Oxford U 27 0
2001–02 Oxford U 21 0
2002–03 Oxford U 0 0 48 0
From Chester C.
2003–04 Kidderminster H 32 2
2004–05 Kidderminster H 40 1 72 3

HOLLIS, Jermain (M) 1 0
H: 5 10 W: 11 00 b.Nottingham 7-10-86
Honours: Jamaica Youth.
2004–05 Kidderminster H 1 0 1 0

JACKSON, Mark (D) 174 4
H: 5 11 W: 12 00 b.Barnsley 30-9-77
Source: Trainee. *Honours:* England Youth.
1995–96 Leeds U 1 0
1996–97 Leeds U 17 0
1997–98 Leeds U 1 0
1998–99 Leeds U 0 0
1998–99 *Huddersfield T* 5 0 5 0
1999–2000 Leeds U 0 0 19 0
1999–2000 *Barnsley* 1 0 1 0
1999–2000 Scunthorpe U 6 0
2000–01 Scunthorpe U 32 1
2001–02 Scunthorpe U 45 3
2002–03 Scunthorpe U 33 0
2003–04 Scunthorpe U 17 0
2004–05 Scunthorpe U 3 0 136 4
2004–05 Kidderminster H 13 0 13 0

JENKINS, Lee (M) 208 3
H: 5 9 W: 11 00 b.Pontypool 28-6-79
Source: Trainee. *Honours:* Wales Schools, Youth, Under-21.
1996–97 Swansea C 23 2
1997–98 Swansea C 21 0
1998–99 Swansea C 12 0
1999–2000 Swansea C 16 0
2000–01 Swansea C 39 0
2001–02 Swansea C 15 1
2002–03 Swansea C 32 0
2003–04 Swansea C 11 0 169 3
2003–04 Kidderminster H 7 0
2004–05 Kidderminster H 32 0 39 0

JONES, Billy (D) 84 0
H: 6 1 W: 11 05 b.Chatham 26-3-83
Source: Trainee.
2000–01 Leyton Orient 1 0
2001–02 Leyton Orient 16 0
2002–03 Leyton Orient 24 0
2003–04 Leyton Orient 31 0
2004–05 Leyton Orient 0 0 72 0
2004–05 Kidderminster H 12 0 12 0

KEATES, Dean (M) 258 20
H: 5 6 W: 10 10 b.Walsall 30-6-78
Source: Trainee.
1996–97 Walsall 2 0
1997–98 Walsall 33 1
1998–99 Walsall 43 2
1999–2000 Walsall 35 1
2000–01 Walsall 33 4
2001–02 Walsall 13 1 159 9
2002–03 Hull C 36 4
2003–04 Hull C 14 0 50 4
2003–04 Kidderminster H 8 2
2004–05 Kidderminster H 41 5 49 7

LEWIS, Daniel (G) 1 0
H: 6 1 W: 14 00 b.Redditch 18-6-82
Source: Studley.
2004–05 Kidderminster H 1 0 1 0

MATIAS, Pedro (M) 191 28
H: 6 0 W: 12 00 b.Madrid 11-10-73
1998–99 Logrones 12 0 12 0
1998–99 Macclesfield T 22 2 22 2
1999–2000 Tranmere R 4 0 4 0
1999–2000 Walsall 33 6
2000–01 Walsall 40 9
2001–02 Walsall 30 5
2002–03 Walsall 23 3
2003–04 Walsall 15 1 141 24
2003–04 *Blackpool* 7 1 7 1
2004–05 Bristol R 0 0
2004–05 Kidderminster H 5 1 5 1

McGRATH, John (M) 41 0
H: 5 10 W: 10 04 b.Limerick 27-3-80
Source: Belvedere. *Honours:* Eire Under-21.
1999–2000 Aston Villa 0 0
2000–01 Aston Villa 3 0
2001–02 Aston Villa 0 0
2002–03 Aston Villa 0 0 3 0
2003–04 Doncaster R 11 0
2004–05 Doncaster R 0 0 11 0
2004–05 *Shrewsbury T* 8 0 8 0
2004–05 Kidderminster H 19 0 19 0

McHALE, Chris (D) 15 0
H: 6 0 W: 12 00 b.Birmingham 4-11-82
Source: Juniors.
2003–04 Kidderminster H 1 0
2004–05 Kidderminster H 14 0 15 0

MELLON, Micky (M) **469 32**
H: 5 10 W: 12 11 b.Paisley 18-3-72
Source: Trainee.
1989–90 Bristol C 9 0
1990–91 Bristol C 0 0
1991–92 Bristol C 16 0
1992–93 Bristol C 10 1 **35 1**
1992–93 WBA 17 3
1993–94 WBA 21 2
1994–95 WBA 7 1 **45 6**
1994–95 Blackpool 26 4
1995–96 Blackpool 45 6
1996–97 Blackpool 43 4
1997–98 Blackpool 10 0 **124 14**
1997–98 Tranmere R 33 2
1998–99 Tranmere R 24 1
1998–99 Burnley 20 2
1999–2000 Burnley 42 3
2000–01 Burnley 22 0 **84 5**
2000–01 Tranmere R 13 1
2001–02 Tranmere R 27 1
2002–03 Tranmere R 34 1
2003–04 Tranmere R 43 0 **174 6**
2004–05 Kidderminster H 7 0 **7 0**

RAWLE, Mark (F) **126 26**
H: 5 11 W: 12 11 b.Leicester 27-4-79
Source: Boston U.
2000–01 Southend U 14 1
2001–02 Southend U 30 5
2002–03 Southend U 34 9 **78 15**
2003–04 Oxford U 31 8
2004–05 Oxford U 6 0 **37 8**
2004–05 Kidderminster H 11 3 **11 3**

RICKARDS, Scott (F) **17 1**
H: 5 9 W: 12 00 b.Birmingham 3-11-81
Source: Tamworth.
2003–04 Kidderminster H 13 1
2004–05 Kidderminster H 4 0 **17 1**

ROBERTS, Stuart (F) **179 20**
H: 5 6 W: 9 08 b.Carmarthen 22-7-80
Source: Trainee. *Honours:* Wales Under-21.
1998–99 Swansea C 32 3
1999–2000 Swansea C 11 1
2000–01 Swansea C 36 5
2001–02 Swansea C 13 5
2001–02 Wycombe W 26 0
2002–03 Wycombe W 28 4
2003–04 Wycombe W 16 0 **70 4**
2003–04 Swansea C 12 1
2004–05 Swansea C 0 0 **104 15**
2004–05 Kidderminster H 5 1 **5 1**

RUSSELL, Simon (M) **29 2**
H: 5 7 W: 10 06 b.Beverley 19-3-85
Source: Hull C scholar.
2002–03 Hull C 1 0
2003–04 Hull C 0 0 **1 0**
2004–05 Kidderminster H 28 2 **28 2**

SALL, Abdou (D) **53 2**
H: 6 3 W: 14 00 b.Senegal 1-11-80
Source: Toulouse.
2001–02 Kidderminster H 27 2
2002–03 Kidderminster H 4 0
2002–03 *Oxford U* 1 0 **1 0**
2003–04 Kidderminster H 7 0
2004–05 Kidderminster H 14 0 **52 2**

STURROCK, Blair (F) **112 13**
H: 6 0 W: 11 01 b.Dundee 25-8-81
Source: Dundee U.
2000–01 Brechin C 27 6 **27 6**
2001–02 Plymouth Arg 19 1
2002–03 Plymouth Arg 20 1
2003–04 Plymouth Arg 24 0
2004–05 Plymouth Arg 0 0 **63 2**
2004–05 Kidderminster H 22 5 **22 5**

WEAVER, Simon (D) **120 3**
H: 6 1 W: 10 07 b.Doncaster 20-12-77
Source: Trainee.
1996–97 Sheffield W 0 0
1996–97 *Doncaster R* 2 0 **2 0**
1997–98 Sheffield W 0 0
From Ilkeston T, Nuneaton B
2002–03 Lincoln
2003–04 Lincoln C 39 0
2004–05 Lincoln C 5 0 **88 3**
2004–05 *Macclesfield T* 7 0 **7 0**
2004–05 Kidderminster H 23 0 **23 0**

WILLIAMS, John (F) **452 71**
H: 6 1 W: 13 12 b.Birmingham 11-5-68
Source: Cradley T.
1991–92 Swansea C 39 11
1992–93 Coventry C 41 8
1993–94 Coventry C 32 3
1994–95 Coventry C 7 0
1994–95 *Notts Co* 5 2 **5 2**
1994–95 *Stoke C* 4 0 **4 0**
1994–95 *Swansea C* 7 2
1995–96 Coventry C 0 0 **80 11**
1995–96 Wycombe W 29 8
1996–97 Wycombe W 19 1 **48 9**
1996–97 Hereford U 11 3 **11 3**
1997–98 Walsall 1 0 **1 0**
1997–98 Exeter C 36 4 **36 4**
1998–99 Cardiff C 43 12
1999–2000 Cardiff C 0 0 **43 12**
1999–2000 York C 36 3
2000–01 York C 6 0 **42 3**
2000–01 Darlington 24 5 **24 5**
2001–02 Swansea C 41 4
2002–03 Swansea C 27 1 **114 18**
2003–04 Kidderminster H 44 4
2004–05 Kidderminster H 0 0 **44 4**

LEEDS U (40)

BAKKE, Eirik (M) **206 25**
H: 6 2 W: 12 10 b.Sogndal 13-9-77
Honours: Norway 25 full caps.
1994 Sogndal 5 0
1995 Sogndal 0 0
1996 Sogndal 19 8
1997 Sogndal 25 4
1998 Sogndal 19 2
1999 Sogndal 8 3 **76 17**
1999–2000 Leeds U 29 2
2000–01 Leeds U 29 2
2001–02 Leeds U 27 2
2002–03 Leeds U 34 1
2003–04 Leeds U 10 1
2004–05 Leeds U 1 0 **130 8**

BOWLER, Justin (F) **0 0**
H: 5 8 W: 11 03 b.Leeds 26-6-86
Source: Trainee.
2003–04 Leeds U 0 0
2004–05 Leeds U 0 0

BUTLER, Paul (D) **484 20**
H: 6 2 W: 15 04 b.Manchester 2-11-72
Source: From Trainee. *Honours:* Eire 1 full cap.
1990–91 Rochdale 2 0
1991–92 Rochdale 25 0
1992–93 Rochdale 16 2
1993–94 Rochdale 38 2
1994–95 Rochdale 39 3
1995–96 Rochdale 38 3 **158 10**
1996–97 Bury 41 2
1997–98 Bury 43 2 **84 4**
1998–99 Sunderland 44 2
1999–2000 Sunderland 32 1
2000–01 Sunderland 3 0 **79 3**
2000–01 Wolverhampton W 12 0
2001–02 Wolverhampton W 43 1
2002–03 Wolverhampton W 32 1
2003–04 Wolverhampton W 37 1 **124 3**
2004–05 Leeds U 39 0 **39 0**

CARLISLE, Clarke (D) **224 17**
H: 6 3 W: 14 12 b.Preston 14-10-79
Source: Trainee. *Honours:* England Under-21.
1997–98 Blackpool 11 2
1998–99 Blackpool 39 1
1999–2000 Blackpool 43 4 **93 7**
2000–01 QPR 27 3
2001–02 QPR 0 0
2002–03 QPR 36 2
2003–04 QPR 33 1 **96 6**
2004–05 Leeds U 35 4 **35 4**

CONSTABLE, Robert (D) **0 0**
H: 6 0 W: 12 13 b.Pontefract 26-1-86
Source: Trainee.
2002–03 Leeds U 0 0
2003–04 Leeds U 0 0
2004–05 Leeds U 0 0

CORR, Barry (F) **0 0**
H: 6 4 W: 12 08 b.Co Wicklow 2-4-85
Source: Scholar.
2001–02 Leeds U 0 0
2002–03 Leeds U 0 0
2003–04 Leeds U 0 0
2004–05 Leeds U 0 0

COUSINS, Andrew (M) **0 0**
H: 5 8 W: 11 03 b.Dublin 30-1-85
Source: Scholar.
2001–02 Leeds U 0 0
2002–03 Leeds U 0 0
2003–04 Leeds U 0 0
2004–05 Leeds U 0 0

COYLES, William (G) **0 0**
H: 6 0 W: 12 01 b.Co Antrim 20-12-84
Source: Scholar.
2001–02 Leeds U 0 0
2002–03 Leeds U 0 0
2003–04 Leeds U 0 0
2004–05 Leeds U 0 0

CRAINEY, Stephen (D) **55 0**
H: 5 9 W: 12 05 b.Glasgow 22-6-81
Honours: Scotland 6 full caps.
1999–2000 Celtic 9 0
2000–01 Celtic 2 0
2001–02 Celtic 15 0
2002–03 Celtic 13 0
2003–04 Celtic 2 0 **41 0**
2003–04 Southampton 5 0 **5 0**
2004–05 Leeds U 9 0 **9 0**

CRONIN, Kevin (D) **0 0**
H: 6 0 W: 12 04 b.Dublin 18-5-85
Source: Scholar.
2001–02 Leeds U 0 0
2002–03 Leeds U 0 0
2003–04 Leeds U 0 0
2004–05 Leeds U 0 0

DERRY, Shaun (M) **297 10**
H: 5 10 W: 13 02 b.Nottingham 6-12-77
Source: Trainee.
1995–96 Notts Co 12 0
1996–97 Notts Co 39 2
1997–98 Notts Co 28 2 **79 4**
1997–98 Sheffield U 12 0
1998–99 Sheffield U 26 0
1999–2000 Sheffield U 34 0 **72 0**
1999–2000 Portsmouth 9 1
2000–01 Portsmouth 28 0
2001–02 Portsmouth 12 0 **49 1**
2002–03 Crystal Palace 39 1
2003–04 Crystal Palace 37 2
2004–05 Crystal Palace 7 0 **83 3**
2004–05 *Nottingham F* 7 0 **7 0**
2004–05 Leeds U 7 2 **7 2**

EDWARDS, Stewart (D) **0 0**
H: 6 0 W: 12 08 b.Swansea 1-10-84
Source: Scholar.
2001–02 Leeds U 0 0
2002–03 Leeds U 0 0
2003–04 Leeds U 0 0
2004–05 Leeds U 0 0

EINARSSON, Gylfi (M) **111 27**
H: 6 0 W: 12 08 b.Iceland 27-10-78
Honours: Iceland Youth, 15 full caps, 1 goal.
1996 Fylkir 2 0
1997 Fylkir 0 0
1998 Fylkir 0 0
1999 Fylkir 0 0
2000 Fylkir 18 10 **20 10**
2000–01 Lille 18 1
2001–02 Lille 22 1
2002–03 Lille 17 2
2003–04 Lille 26 12 **83 16**
2004–05 Leeds U 8 1 **8 1**

GRAY, Nicholas (M) **0 0**
H: 6 1 W: 11 01 b.Harrogate 17-10-85
Source: Trainee.
2002–03 Leeds U 0 0
2003–04 Leeds U 0 0
2004–05 Leeds U 0 0

GREGAN, Sean (M) 462 18
H: 6 2 W: 15 08 b.Guisborough 29-3-74
Source: Trainee.
1991–92 Darlington 17 0
1992–93 Darlington 17 1
1993–94 Darlington 23 1
1994–95 Darlington 25 2
1995–96 Darlington 38 0
1996–97 Darlington 16 0 **136 4**
1996–97 Preston NE 21 1
1997–98 Preston NE 35 2
1998–99 Preston NE 41 3
1999–2000 Preston NE 33 3
2000–01 Preston NE 41 2
2001–02 Preston NE 41 1 **212 12**
2002–03 WBA 36 1
2003–04 WBA 43 1
2004–05 WBA 0 0 **79 2**
2004–05 Leeds U 35 0 **35 0**

HARTE, Ian (D) 213 28
H: 5 11 W: 12 06 b.Drogheda 31-8-77
Source: Trainee. *Honours:* Eire 56 full caps, 9 goals.
1995–96 Leeds U 4 0
1996–97 Leeds U 14 2
1997–98 Leeds U 12 0
1998–99 Leeds U 35 4
1999–2000 Leeds U 33 6
2000–01 Leeds U 29 7
2001–02 Leeds U 36 5
2002–03 Leeds U 27 3
2003–04 Leeds U 23 1
2004–05 Leeds U 0 0 **213 28**

HEALY, David (F) 197 56
H: 5 8 W: 11 07 b.Downpatrick 5-8-79
Source: Trainee. *Honours:* Northern Ireland Schools, Youth, Under-21, B, 43 full caps, 17 goals.
1997–98 Manchester U 0 0
1998–99 Manchester U 0 0
1999–2000 Manchester U 0 0
1999–2000 *Port Vale* 16 3 **16 3**
2000–01 Manchester U 1 0 **1 0**
2000–01 Preston NE 22 9
2001–02 Preston NE 44 10
2002–03 Preston NE 24 5
2002–03 *Norwich C* 13 2 **13 2**
2003–04 Preston NE 38 15
2004–05 Preston NE 11 5 **139 44**
2004–05 Leeds U 28 7 **28 7**

ILIC, Sasa (G) 91 0
H: 6 4 W: 14 12 b.Melbourne 18-7-72
Source: Partizan Belgrade, Radnicki, Ringwood, Daewoo Royals, St Leonards Stamcroft. *Honours:* Yugoslavia 1 full cap.
1997–98 Charlton Ath 14 0
1998–99 Charlton Ath 23 0
1999–2000 Charlton Ath 1 0
1999–2000 *West Ham U* 1 0 **1 0**
2000–01 Charlton Ath 13 0
2001–02 Charlton Ath 0 0 **51 0**
2001–02 *Portsmouth* 7 0
2001–02 *Portsmouth* 0 0
2002–03 Portsmouth 0 0 **7 0**
2002–03 Zalaegerszeg 4 0 **4 0**
2003–04 Barnsley 25 0 **25 0**
2003–04 Sheffield U 0 0
2004–05 Blackpool 3 0 **3 0**
2004–05 Aberdeen 0 0
2004–05 Leeds U 0 0

JOACHIM, Julian (F) 331 83
H: 5 6 W: 12 05 b.Boston 20-9-74
Source: Trainee. *Honours:* England Youth, Under-21.
1992–93 Leicester C 26 10
1993–94 Leicester C 36 11
1994–95 Leicester C 15 3
1995–96 Leicester C 22 1 **99 25**
1995–96 Aston Villa 11 1
1996–97 Aston Villa 15 3
1997–98 Aston Villa 26 8
1998–99 Aston Villa 36 14
1999–2000 Aston Villa 33 6
2000–01 Aston Villa 20 7 **141 39**
2001–02 Coventry C 16 1
2002–03 Coventry C 11 2
2003–04 Coventry C 29 8 **56 11**
2004–05 Leeds U 27 2 **27 2**
2004–05 *Walsall* 8 6 **8 6**

JOHNSON, Seth (M) 220 12
H: 5 10 W: 13 03 b.Birmingham 12-3-79
Source: Trainee. *Honours:* England Youth, Under-21, 1 full cap.
1996–97 Crewe Alex 11 1
1997–98 Crewe Alex 40 1
1998–99 Crewe Alex 42 4 **93 6**
1999–2000 Derby Co 36 1
2000–01 Derby Co 30 1
2001–02 Derby Co 7 0 **73 2**
2001–02 Leeds U 14 0
2002–03 Leeds U 9 1
2003–04 Leeds U 25 2
2004–05 Leeds U 6 1 **54 4**

JOHNSON, Simon (F) 54 8
H: 5 10 W: 12 02 b.West Bromwich 9-3-83
Source: Scholar. *Honours:* England Youth, Under-20.
2000–01 Leeds U 0 0
2001–02 Leeds U 0 0
2002–03 Leeds U 4 0
2002–03 *Hull C* 12 2 **12 2**
2003–04 Leeds U 5 0
2003–04 *Blackpool* 4 1 **4 1**
2004–05 Leeds U 2 0 **11 0**
2004–05 *Sunderland* 5 0 **5 0**
2004–05 *Doncaster R* 11 3 **11 3**
2004–05 *Barnsley* 11 2 **11 2**

JONES, Chris (M) 0 0
H: 5 8 W: 9 0 b.Bangor 9-10-85
Source: Trainee.
2002–03 Leeds U 0 0
2003–04 Leeds U 0 0
2004–05 Leeds U 0 0

KEEGAN, Paul (M) 2 0
H: 5 11 W: 11 05 b.Dublin 5-7-84
Source: Scholar. *Honours:* Eire Under-21.
2000–01 Leeds U 0 0
2001–02 Leeds U 0 0
2002–03 Leeds U 0 0
2003–04 Leeds U 0 0
2003–04 *Scunthorpe U* 2 0 **2 0**
2004–05 Leeds U 0 0

KELLY, Gary (D) 370 2
H: 5 10 W: 11 02 b.Drogheda 9-7-74
Source: Home Farm. *Honours:* Eire Youth, 52 full caps, 2 goals.
1991–92 Leeds U 2 0
1992–93 Leeds U 0 0
1993–94 Leeds U 42 0
1994–95 Leeds U 42 0
1995–96 Leeds U 34 0
1996–97 Leeds U 36 2
1997–98 Leeds U 34 0
1998–99 Leeds U 0 0
1999–2000 Leeds U 31 0
2000–01 Leeds U 24 0
2001–02 Leeds U 20 0
2002–03 Leeds U 25 0
2003–04 Leeds U 37 0
2004–05 Leeds U 43 0 **370 2**

KEYES, Edward (D) 0 0
H: 5 9 W: 10 10 b.Dublin 2-5-85
Source: Scholar.
2001–02 Leeds U 0 0
2002–03 Leeds U 0 0
2003–04 Leeds U 0 0
2004–05 Leeds U 0 0

KILGALLON, Matthew (D) 39 2
H: 6 1 W: 12 07 b.York 8-1-84
Source: Scholar. *Honours:* England Youth, Under-20, Under-21.
2000–01 Leeds U 0 0
2001–02 Leeds U 0 0
2002–03 Leeds U 2 0
2003–04 Leeds U 8 2
2003–04 *West Ham U* 3 0 **3 0**
2004–05 Leeds U 26 0 **36 2**

LEISTER, Brenton (M) 0 0
H: 5 11 W: 12 01 b.Leeds 3-9-85
Source: Scholar.
2002–03 Leeds U 0 0
2003–04 Leeds U 0 0
2004–05 Leeds U 0 0

LENNON, Aaron (F) 38 1
H: 5 5 W: 10 06 b.Leeds 16-4-87
Source: Trainee. *Honours:* England Youth.
2003–04 Leeds U 11 0
2004–05 Leeds U 27 1 **38 1**

McDAID, Sean (D) 0 0
H: 5 8 W: 10 12 b.Harrogate 6-3-86
Source: Trainee.
2002–03 Leeds U 0 0
2003–04 Leeds U 0 0
2004–05 Leeds U 0 0

McKEOWN, Steven (D) 0 0
H: 5 10 W: 12 00 b.Paisley 3-6-87
Source: Livingston.
2003–04 Leeds U 0 0
2004–05 Leeds U 0 0

McSTAY, Henry (D) 0 0
H: 6 0 W: 11 11 b.Co Armagh 6-3-85
Source: From Scholar. *Honours:* Eire Under-21.
2001–02 Leeds U 0 0
2002–03 Leeds U 0 0
2003–04 Leeds U 0 0
2004–05 Leeds U 0 0

MOORE, Ian (F) 371 70
H: 5 11 W: 12 00 b.Birkenhead 26-8-76
Source: Trainee. *Honours:* England Youth, Under-21.
1994–95 Tranmere R 1 0
1995–96 Tranmere R 36 9
1996–97 Tranmere R 21 3 **58 12**
1996–97 *Bradford C* 6 0 **6 0**
1996–97 Nottingham F 5 0
1997–98 Nottingham F 10 1 **15 1**
1997–98 *West Ham U* 1 0 **1 0**
1998–99 Stockport Co 38 3
1999–2000 Stockport Co 38 10
2000–01 Stockport Co 17 7 **93 20**
2000–01 Burnley 27 5
2001–02 Burnley 46 11
2002–03 Burnley 44 8
2003–04 Burnley 40 9
2004–05 Burnley 35 4 **192 37**
2004–05 Leeds U 6 0 **6 0**

MORRIS, Ian (M) 0 0
H: 6 0 W: 11 05 b.Dublin 27-2-87
Source: Scholar.
2003–04 Leeds U 0 0
2004–05 Leeds U 0 0

PARKER, Ben (D) 0 0
b.Pontefract 8-11-87
Source: From Scholar. *Honours:* England Youth.
2004–05 Leeds U 0 0

PUGH, Danny (M) 39 5
H: 6 0 W: 11 11 b.Manchester 19-10-82
Source: Scholar.
2000–01 Manchester U 0 0
2001–02 Manchester U 0 0
2002–03 Manchester U 1 0
2003–04 Manchester U 0 0 **1 0**
2004–05 Leeds U 38 5 **38 5**

RADEBE, Lucas (D) 200 0
H: 6 0 W: 13 01 b.Johannesburg 12-4-69
Source: Kaizer Chiefs. *Honours:* South Africa 70 full caps, 2 goals.
1994–95 Leeds U 12 0
1995–96 Leeds U 13 0
1996–97 Leeds U 32 0
1997–98 Leeds U 27 0
1998–99 Leeds U 29 0
1999–2000 Leeds U 31 0
2000–01 Leeds U 20 0
2001–02 Leeds U 0 0
2002–03 Leeds U 19 0
2003–04 Leeds U 14 0
2004–05 Leeds U 3 0 **200 0**

REEVES, Damian (F) 0 0
H: 5 9 W: 11 10 b.Doncaster 18-12-85
Source: Trainee.
2002–03 Leeds U 0 0
2003–04 Leeds U 0 0
2004–05 Leeds U 0 0

RICHARDSON, Frazer (D)				**55**	**2**
H: 5 11 W: 12 04 b.Rotherham 29-10-82					
Source: Trainee. *Honours:* England Youth, Under-20.					
1999–2000	Leeds U	0	0		
2000–01	Leeds U	0	0		
2001–02	Leeds U	0	0		
2002–03	Leeds U	0	0		
2002–03	*Stoke C*	7	0		
2003–04	Leeds U	4	0		
2003–04	*Stoke C*	6	1	**13**	**1**
2004–05	Leeds U	38	1	**42**	**1**

RICKETTS, Michael (F)				**238**	**54**
H: 6 2 W: 15 10 b.Birmingham 4-12-78					
Source: Trainee. *Honours:* England 1 full cap.					
1995–96	Walsall	1	1		
1996–97	Walsall	11	1		
1997–98	Walsall	24	1		
1998–99	Walsall	8	0		
1999–2000	Walsall	32	11	**76**	**14**
2000–01	Bolton W	39	19		
2001–02	Bolton W	37	12		
2002–03	Bolton W	22	6	**98**	**37**
2002–03	Middlesbrough	9	1		
2003–04	Middlesbrough	23	2	**32**	**3**
2004–05	Leeds U	21	0	**21**	**0**
2004–05	*Stoke C*	11	0	**11**	**0**

SHIELDS, Robbie (M)				**0**	**0**
H: 5 6 W: 9 11 b.Dublin 1-5-84					
Source: Scholar.					
2000–01	Leeds U	0	0		
2001–02	Leeds U	0	0		
2002–03	Leeds U	0	0		
2003–04	Leeds U	0	0		
2004–05	Leeds U	0	0		

SINGH, Harpal (M)				**52**	**4**
H: 5 7 W: 10 02 b.Bradford 15-9-81					
Source: Trainee.					
1998–99	Leeds U	0	0		
1999–2000	Leeds U	0	0		
2000–01	Leeds U	0	0		
2001–02	Leeds U	0	0		
2001–02	*Bury*	12	2		
2001–02	*Bristol C*	3	0	**3**	**0**
2002–03	Leeds U	0	0		
2002–03	*Bradford C*	3	0	**3**	**0**
2003–04	Leeds U	0	0		
2003–04	*Bury*	28	2	**40**	**4**
2004–05	Leeds U	0	0		
2004–05	*Stockport Co*	6	0	**6**	**0**

SMITH, Kevin (F)				**0**	**0**
H: 5 11 W: 11 09 b.Edinburgh 20-3-87					
Source: Scholar.					
2003–04	Leeds U	0	0		
2004–05	Leeds U	0	0		

SPRING, Matthew (M)				**263**	**26**
H: 6 0 W: 12 08 b.Harlow 17-11-79					
Source: Trainee.					
1997–98	Luton T	12	0		
1998–99	Luton T	45	3		
1999–2000	Luton T	45	6		
2000–01	Luton T	41	4		
2001–02	Luton T	42	6		
2002–03	Luton T	41	5		
2003–04	Luton T	24	1	**250**	**25**
2004–05	Leeds U	13	1	**13**	**1**

SULLIVAN, Neil (G)				**296**	**0**
H: 6 3 W: 15 08 b.Sutton 24-2-70					
Source: Trainee. *Honours:* Scotland 28 full caps.					
1988–89	Wimbledon	0	0		
1989–90	Wimbledon	0	0		
1990–91	Wimbledon	1	0		
1991–92	Wimbledon	1	0		
1991–92	*Crystal Palace*	1	0	**1**	**0**
1992–93	Wimbledon	1	0		
1993–94	Wimbledon	2	0		
1994–95	Wimbledon	11	0		
1995–96	Wimbledon	16	0		
1996–97	Wimbledon	36	0		
1997–98	Wimbledon	38	0		
1998–99	Wimbledon	38	0		
1999–2000	Wimbledon	37	0	**181**	**0**
2000–01	Tottenham H	35	0		
2001–02	Tottenham H	29	0		
2002–03	Tottenham H	0	0	**64**	**0**
2003–04	Chelsea	4	0	**4**	**0**
2004–05	Leeds U	46	0	**46**	**0**

TYRRELL, Derek (D)				**0**	**0**
H: 6 1 W: 12 05 b.Dublin 14-4-85					
Source: Scholar.					
2001–02	Leeds U	0	0		
2002–03	Leeds U	0	0		
2003–04	Leeds U	0	0		
2004–05	Leeds U	0	0		

WALTON, Simon (D)				**30**	**3**
H: 6 1 W: 13 05 b.Sherburn-in-Elmet 13-9-87					
Source: Scholar.					
2004–05	Leeds U	30	3	**30**	**3**

WILBERFORCE, Mark (G)				**0**	**0**
H: 5 10 W: 11 06 b.Hull 30-1-87					
Source: Scholar.					
2003–04	Leeds U	0	0		
2004–05	Leeds U	0	0		

WINTER, Jamie (M)				**0**	**0**
H: 5 10 W: 13 10 b.Dundee 4-8-85					
Source: Scholar.					
2002–03	Leeds U	0	0		
2003–04	Leeds U	0	0		
2004–05	Leeds U	0	0		

WOODS, Martin (M)				**7**	**0**
H: 5 11 W: 11 05 b.Airdrie 1-1-86					
Source: Trainee. *Honours:* Scotland Youth.					
2002–03	Leeds U	0	0		
2003–04	Leeds U	0	0		
2004–05	Leeds U	1	0	**1**	**0**
2004–05	*Hartlepool U*	6	0	**6**	**0**

WRIGHT, Jermaine (M)				**301**	**18**
H: 5 10 W: 13 00 b.Greenwich 21-10-75					
Source: Trainee. *Honours:* England Youth.					
1992–93	Millwall	0	0		
1993–94	Millwall	0	0		
1994–95	Millwall	0	0		
1994–95	Wolverhampton W	6	0		
1995–96	Wolverhampton W	7	0		
1995–96	*Doncaster R*	13	0	**13**	**0**
1996–97	Wolverhampton W	3	0		
1997–98	Wolverhampton W	4	0	**20**	**0**
1997–98	Crewe Alex	5	0		
1998–99	Crewe Alex	44	5	**49**	**5**
1999–2000	Ipswich T	34	1		
2000–01	Ipswich T	37	2		
2001–02	Ipswich T	29	1		
2002–03	Ipswich T	39	1		
2003–04	Ipswich T	45	5	**184**	**10**
2004–05	Leeds U	35	3	**35**	**3**

LEICESTER C (41)

AKMAN, Peter (G)				**0**	**0**
2004–05	Leicester C	0	0		

BLAKE, Nathan (F)				**452**	**145**
H: 5 11 W: 14 00 b.Cardiff 27-1-72					
Source: Chelsea Trainee. *Honours:* Wales Youth, B, Under-21, 29 full caps, 4 goals.					
1989–90	Cardiff C	6	0		
1990–91	Cardiff C	40	4		
1991–92	Cardiff C	31	6		
1992–93	Cardiff C	34	11		
1993–94	Cardiff C	20	14	**131**	**35**
1993–94	Sheffield U	12	5		
1994–95	Sheffield U	35	17		
1995–96	Sheffield U	22	12	**69**	**34**
1995–96	Bolton W	18	1		
1996–97	Bolton W	42	19		
1997–98	Bolton W	35	12		
1998–99	Bolton W	12	6	**107**	**38**
1998–99	Blackburn R	11	3		
1999–2000	Blackburn R	28	3		
2000–01	Blackburn R	12	6		
2001–02	Blackburn R	3	1	**54**	**13**
2001–02	Wolverhampton W	39	11		
2002–03	Wolverhampton W	23	12		
2003–04	Wolverhampton W	13	1	**75**	**24**
2004–05	Leicester C	14	0	**14**	**0**
2004–05	*Leeds U*	2	1	**2**	**1**

CANERO, Peter (D)				**130**	**10**
H: 5 9 W: 12 06 b.Glasgow 18-1-81					
Honours: Scotland 1 full cap.					
1999–2000	Kilmarnock	11	0		
2000–01	Kilmarnock	28	1		
2001–02	Kilmarnock	32	1		
2002–03	Kilmarnock	33	6		
2003–04	Kilmarnock	13	2	**117**	**10**
2003–04	Leicester C	7	0		
2004–05	Leicester C	6	0	**13**	**0**

CONNOLLY, David (F)				**261**	**117**
H: 5 9 W: 11 00 b.Willesden 6-6-77					
Source: Trainee. *Honours:* Eire 40 full caps, 9 goals.					
1994–95	Watford	2	0		
1995–96	Watford	11	8		
1996–97	Watford	13	2	**26**	**10**
1997–98	Feyenoord	10	2		
1998–99	Wolverhampton W	32	6	**32**	**6**
1999–2000	Excelsior	32	29	**32**	**29**
2000–01	Feyenoord	15	5	**25**	**7**
2001–02	Wimbledon	35	18		
2002–03	Wimbledon	28	24	**63**	**42**
2003–04	West Ham U	39	10	**39**	**10**
2004–05	Leicester C	44	13	**44**	**13**

DABIZAS, Nikos (D)				**285**	**19**
H: 6 0 W: 12 11 b.Amindeo 3-8-73					
Honours: Greece 69 full caps.					
1994–95	Olympiakos	26	2		
1995–96	Olympiakos	27	1		
1996–97	Olympiakos	31	0		
1997–98	Olympiakos	20	5	**104**	**8**
1997–98	Newcastle U	11	1		
1998–99	Newcastle U	30	3		
1999–2000	Newcastle U	29	3		
2000–01	Newcastle U	9	0		
2001–02	Newcastle U	35	3		
2002–03	Newcastle U	16	0		
2003–04	Newcastle U	0	0	**130**	**10**
2003–04	Leicester C	18	0		
2004–05	Leicester C	33	1	**51**	**1**

DAWSON, Stephen (M)				**0**	**0**
H: 5 9 W: 11 09 b.Dublin 4-12-85					
Source: Scholar.					
2003–04	Leicester C	0	0		
2004–05	Leicester C	0	0		

DE VRIES, Mark (F)				**154**	**41**
H: 6 3 W: 12 01 b.Surinam 24-8-75					
1995–96	Volendam	4	0		
1996–97	Volendam	10	0		
1997–98	Volendam	14	1	**28**	**1**
1998–99	Niort	0	0		
1999–2000	Dordrecht	8	0		
2000–01	Dordrecht	30	11		
2001–02	Dordrecht	0	0	**38**	**11**
2002–03	Hearts	32	15		
2003–04	Hearts	31	12		
2004–05	Hearts	9	1	**72**	**28**
2004–05	Leicester C	16	1	**16**	**1**

DUBLIN, Dion (F)				**510**	**170**
H: 6 2 W: 15 00 b.Leicester 22-4-69					
Source: Oakham U. *Honours:* England 4 full caps.					
1987–88	Norwich C	0	0		
1988–89	Cambridge U	21	6		
1989–90	Cambridge U	46	15		
1990–91	Cambridge U	46	16		
1991–92	Cambridge U	43	15	**156**	**52**
1992–93	Manchester U	7	1		
1993–94	Manchester U	5	1	**12**	**2**
1994–95	Coventry C	31	13		
1995–96	Coventry C	34	14		
1996–97	Coventry C	34	13		
1997–98	Coventry C	36	18		
1998–99	Coventry C	10	3	**145**	**61**
1998–99	Aston Villa	24	11		
1999–2000	Aston Villa	26	12		
2000–01	Aston Villa	33	8		
2001–02	Aston Villa	21	4		
2001–02	*Millwall*	5	2	**5**	**2**
2002–03	Aston Villa	28	10		
2003–04	Aston Villa	23	3	**155**	**48**
2004–05	Leicester C	37	5	**37**	**5**

ELLIOTT, Matt (D) **588 70**
H: 6 3 W: 15 00 b.Wandsworth 1-11-68
Source: Epsom & Ewell. *Honours:* Scotland 18 full caps, 1 goal.

1988–89	Charlton Ath	0	0		
1988–89	Torquay U	13	2		
1989–90	Torquay U	33	2		
1990–91	Torquay U	45	6		
1991–92	Torquay U	33	5	**124**	**15**
1991–92	*Scunthorpe U*	8	1		
1992–93	Scunthorpe U	39	6		
1993–94	Scunthorpe U	14	1	**61**	**8**
1993–94	Oxford U	32	5		
1994–95	Oxford U	45	4		
1995–96	Oxford U	45	8		
1996–97	Oxford U	26	4	**148**	**21**
1996–97	Leicester C	16	4		
1997–98	Leicester C	37	7		
1998–99	Leicester C	37	2		
1999–2000	Leicester C	37	6		
2000–01	Leicester C	34	2		
2001–02	Leicester C	31	0		
2002–03	Leicester C	44	5		
2003–04	Leicester C	7	0		
2003–04	*Ipswich T*	10	0	**10**	**0**
2004–05	Leicester C	2	0	**245**	**26**

GEMMILL, Scot (M) **366 27**
H: 5 10 W: 11 08 b.Paisley 2-1-71
Source: School. *Honours:* Scotland Under-21, B, 26 full caps, 1 goal.

1989–90	Nottingham F	0	0		
1990–91	Nottingham F	4	0		
1991–92	Nottingham F	39	8		
1992–93	Nottingham F	33	1		
1993–94	Nottingham F	31	8		
1994–95	Nottingham F	19	1		
1995–96	Nottingham F	31	1		
1996–97	Nottingham F	24	0		
1997–98	Nottingham F	44	2		
1998–99	Nottingham F	20	0	**245**	**21**
1998–99	Everton	7	1		
1999–2000	Everton	14	1		
2000–01	Everton	28	2		
2001–02	Everton	32	1		
2002–03	Everton	16	0		
2003–04	Everton	0	0	**97**	**5**
2003–04	*Preston NE*	7	1	**7**	**1**
2004–05	Leicester C	17	0	**17**	**0**

GILLESPIE, Keith (M) **290 23**
H: 5 10 W: 11 01 b.Larne 18-2-75
Source: Trainee. *Honours:* Northern Ireland Schools, Youth, Under-21, 62 full caps, 1 goal.

1992–93	Manchester U	0	0		
1993–94	Manchester U	0	0		
1993–94	*Wigan Ath*	8	4		
1994–95	Manchester U	9	1	**9**	**1**
1994–95	Newcastle U	17	2		
1995–96	Newcastle U	28	4		
1996–97	Newcastle U	32	1		
1997–98	Newcastle U	29	4		
1998–99	Newcastle U	7	0	**113**	**11**
1998–99	Blackburn R	16	1		
1999–2000	Blackburn R	22	2		
2000–01	Blackburn R	18	0		
2000–01	*Wigan Ath*	5	0	**13**	**4**
2001–02	Blackburn R	32	2		
2002–03	Blackburn R	25	0	**113**	**5**
2003–04	Leicester C	12	0		
2004–05	Leicester C	30	2	**42**	**2**

GUDJONSSON, Joey (M) **123 13**
H: 5 9 W: 12 04 b.Akranes 25-5-80
Honours: Iceland Youth, Under-21, 23 full caps, 1 goal.

1998–99	Genk	5	0	**5**	**0**
1999–2000	MVV	19	5	**19**	**5**
2000–01	RKC	31	4	**31**	**4**
2001–02	Betis	11	0	**11**	**0**
2002–03	Aston Villa	11	2	**11**	**2**
2003–04	Wolverhampton W	11	0	**11**	**0**
2004–05	Leicester C	35	2	**35**	**2**

HEATH, Matthew (D) **59 6**
H: 6 4 W: 13 13 b.Leicester 1-11-81
Source: Scholar.

2000–01	Leicester C	0	0		
2001–02	Leicester C	5	0		
2002–03	Leicester C	11	3		
2003–04	Leicester C	13	0		
2003–04	*Stockport Co*	8	0	**8**	**0**
2004–05	Leicester C	22	3	**51**	**6**

HIRSCHFELD, Lars (G) **10 0**
H: 6 4 W: 13 08 b.Edmonton 17-10-78
Honours: Canada Under-23, 18 full caps.

2002–03	Tottenham H	0	0		
2002–03	*Luton T*	5	0	**5**	**0**
2003–04	Tottenham H	0	0		
2003–04	*Gillingham*	2	0	**2**	**0**
2004–05	Dundee U	2	0	**2**	**0**
2004–05	Tottenham H	0	0		
2004–05	Leicester C	1	0	**1**	**0**

HUGHES, Stephen (M) **79 8**
H: 5 11 W: 9 06 b.Motherwell 14-11-82

2000–01	Rangers	1	0		
2001–02	Rangers	17	1		
2002–03	Rangers	12	1		
2003–04	Rangers	22	3		
2004–05	Rangers	11	2	**63**	**7**
2004–05	Leicester C	16	1	**16**	**1**

JONES, Matthew (M) **50 1**
H: 5 11 W: 12 10 b.Llanelli 1-9-80
Source: Trainee. *Honours:* Wales Youth, Under-21, B, 13 full caps.

1997–98	Leeds U	0	0		
1998–99	Leeds U	8	0		
1999–2000	Leeds U	11	0		
2000–01	Leeds U	4	0	**23**	**0**
2000–01	Leicester C	11	0		
2001–02	Leicester C	10	1		
2002–03	Leicester C	6	0		
2003–04	Leicester C	0	0		
2004–05	Leicester C	0	0	**27**	**1**

LOGAN, Conrad (G) **0 0**
H: 6 0 W: 14 09 b.Letterkenny 18-4-86
Source: Scholar.

2003–04	Leicester C	0	0
2004–05	Leicester C	0	0

MAKIN, Chris (D) **370 7**
H: 5 11 W: 13 00 b.Manchester 8-5-73
Source: Trainee. *Honours:* England Schools, Under-21.

1991–92	Oldham Ath	0	0		
1992–93	Oldham Ath	0	0		
1992–93	*Wigan Ath*	15	2	**15**	**2**
1993–94	Oldham Ath	27	1		
1994–95	Oldham Ath	28	1		
1995–96	Oldham Ath	39	2	**94**	**4**
1996–97	Marseille	29	0	**29**	**0**
1997–98	Sunderland	25	0		
1998–99	Sunderland	38	0		
1999–2000	Sunderland	34	1		
2000–01	Sunderland	23	0	**120**	**1**
2000–01	Ipswich T	10	0		
2001–02	Ipswich T	30	0		
2002–03	Ipswich T	33	0		
2003–04	Ipswich T	5	0	**78**	**0**
2004–05	Leicester C	21	0	**21**	**0**
2004–05	*Derby Co*	13	0	**13**	**0**

MAYBURY, Alan (D) **155 6**
H: 5 8 W: 11 08 b.Dublin 8-8-78
Source: Trainee. *Honours:* Eire Youth, Under-21, 10 full caps.

1995–96	Leeds U	1	0		
1996–97	Leeds U	0	0		
1997–98	Leeds U	12	0		
1998–99	Leeds U	0	0		
1998–99	*Reading*	8	0	**8**	**0**
1999–2000	Leeds U	0	0		
2000–01	Leeds U	0	0		
2000–01	*Crewe Alex*	6	0	**6**	**0**
2001–02	Leeds U	1	0	**14**	**0**
2001–02	Hearts	27	0		
2002–03	Hearts	35	2		
2003–04	Hearts	33	2		
2004–05	Hearts	15	0	**110**	**4**
2004–05	Leicester C	17	2	**17**	**2**

McANALLEN, Conor (D) **0 0**
H: 5 11 W: 9 13 b.Craigavon 3-1-86
Source: Scholar.

2003–04	Leicester C	0	0
2004–05	Leicester C	0	0

McCARTHY, Patrick (D) **30 0**
H: 6 2 W: 13 07 b.Dublin 31-5-83
Source: Scholar. *Honours:* Eire Youth, Under-21.

2000–01	Manchester C	0	0		
2001–02	Manchester C	0	0		
2002–03	Manchester C	0	0		
2002–03	*Boston U*	12	0	**12**	**0**
2002–03	*Notts Co*	6	0	**6**	**0**
2003–04	Manchester C	0	0		
2004–05	Manchester C	0	0		
2004–05	Leicester C	12	0	**12**	**0**

McGAVIGAN, Ryan (M) **0 0**
H: 5 9 W: 11 02 b.County Donegal 31-3-86
Source: Scholar.

2003–04	Leicester C	0	0
2004–05	Leicester C	0	0

MORRIS, Lee (F) **132 24**
H: 5 10 W: 11 07 b.Driffield 30-4-80
Source: Trainee. *Honours:* England Youth.

1997–98	Sheffield U	5	0		
1998–99	Sheffield U	20	6		
1999–2000	Sheffield U	1	0	**26**	**6**
1999–2000	Derby Co	3	0		
2000–01	Derby Co	20	0		
2000–01	*Huddersfield T*	5	1	**5**	**1**
2001–02	Derby Co	15	4		
2002–03	Derby Co	30	8		
2003–04	Derby Co	23	5	**91**	**17**
2003–04	Leicester C	0	0		
2004–05	Leicester C	10	0	**10**	**0**

NALIS, Lilian (M) **307 25**
H: 6 1 W: 12 12 b.Nogent sur Marne 29-9-71

1992–93	Auxerre	0	0		
1993–94	Caen	16	0		
1994–95	Caen	4	0	**20**	**0**
1995–96	Laval	42	4		
1996–97	Laval	39	8	**81**	**12**
1997–98	Guingamp	30	0	**30**	**0**
1998–99	Le Havre	27	3	**27**	**3**
1999–2000	Bastia	28	1		
2000–01	Bastia	28	1		
2001–02	Bastia	26	2	**82**	**4**
2002–03	Chievo	8	0	**8**	**0**
2003–04	Leicester C	20	1		
2004–05	Leicester C	39	5	**59**	**6**

O'GRADY, Christopher (F) **10 0**
H: 6 1 W: 14 02 b.Nottingham 25-1-86
Source: Trainee. *Honours:* England Youth.

2002–03	Leicester C	1	0		
2003–04	Leicester C	0	0		
2004–05	Leicester C	0	0	**1**	**0**
2004–05	*Notts Co*	9	0	**9**	**0**

PEARMAIN, Dominic (F) **0 0**
H: 5 9 W: 10 03 b.Peterborough 2-9-84
Source: Scholar.

2003–04	Leicester C	0	0
2004–05	Leicester C	0	0

PETRESCU, Tomi (M) **1 0**
H: 5 9 W: 10 05 b.Jyvaskyla 24-7-86
Source: Scholar.

2002–03	Leicester C	1	0		
2003–04	Leicester C	0	0		
2004–05	Leicester C	0	0	**1**	**0**

POWELL, Liam (D) **0 0**
H: 5 10 W: 12 06 b.Cardiff 18-9-85
Source: Scholar. *Honours:* Wales Under-21.

2003–04	Leicester C	0	0
2004–05	Leicester C	0	0

PRESSMAN, Kevin (G) **421 0**
H: 6 1 W: 14 07 b.Fareham 6-11-67
Source: Apprentice. *Honours:* England Schools, Youth, Under-21, B.

1985–86	Sheffield W	0	0		
1986–87	Sheffield W	0	0		
1987–88	Sheffield W	11	0		
1988–89	Sheffield W	9	0		
1989–90	Sheffield W	15	0		
1990–91	Sheffield W	23	0		
1991–92	Sheffield W	1	0		
1991–92	*Stoke C*	4	0	**4**	**0**
1992–93	Sheffield W	3	0		
1993–94	Sheffield W	32	0		
1994–95	Sheffield W	34	0		

1995–96 Sheffield W 30 0
1996–97 Sheffield W 38 0
1997–98 Sheffield W 36 0
1998–99 Sheffield W 15 0
1999–2000 Sheffield W 19 0
2000–01 Sheffield W 39 0
2001–02 Sheffield W 40 0
2002–03 Sheffield W 38 0
2003–04 *WBA* 0 0
2003–04 Sheffield W 21 0 **404 0**
2004–05 Leicester C 13 0 **13 0**

SCOWCROFT, James (F) 344 71
H: 6 1 W: 14 07 b.Bury St Edmunds 15-11-75
Source: Trainee. *Honours:* England Under-21.
1994–95 Ipswich T 0 0
1995–96 Ipswich T 23 2
1996–97 Ipswich T 41 9
1997–98 Ipswich T 31 6
1998–99 Ipswich T 32 13
1999–2000 Ipswich T 41 13
2000–01 Ipswich T 34 4
2001–02 Leicester C 24 5
2002–03 Leicester C 43 10
2003–04 Leicester C 35 5
2004–05 Leicester C 31 4 **133 24**
2004–05 *Ipswich T* 9 0 **211 47**

SHEEHAN, Alan (D) 1 0
H: 5 11 W: 11 02 b.Athlone 14-9-86
Source: Scholar. *Honours:* Eire Youth, Under-21.
2004–05 Leicester C 1 0 **1 0**

STEARMAN, Richard (D) 8 1
H: 6 2 W: 10 08 b.Wolverhampton 19-8-87
Source: Scholar.
2004–05 Leicester C 8 1 **8 1**

STEWART, Jordan (D) 114 6
H: 5 11 W: 12 08 b.Birmingham 3-3-82
Source: From Trainee. *Honours:* England Youth, Under-21.
1999–2000 Leicester C 1 0
1999–2000 *Bristol R* 4 0 **4 0**
2000–01 Leicester C 0 0
2001–02 Leicester C 12 0
2002–03 Leicester C 37 4
2003–04 Leicester C 25 1
2004–05 Leicester C 35 1 **110 6**

TIATTO, Danny (D) 239 9
H: 5 8 W: 11 08 b.Melbourne 22-5-73
Honours: Australia Under-23, 23 full caps, 1 goal.
1994–95 Melbourne Knights 25 3
1995–96 Melbourne Knights 18 0 **43 3**
1996–97 Salernitana 11 1 **11 1**
1997–98 Stoke C 15 1 **15 1**
From Baden
1998–99 Manchester C 17 0
1999–2000 Manchester C 35 0
2000–01 Manchester C 33 2
2001–02 Manchester C 37 1
2002–03 Manchester C 13 0
2003–04 Manchester C 5 0 **140 3**
2004–05 Leicester C 30 1 **30 1**

WALKER, Ian (G) 401 0
H: 6 2 W: 13 07 b.Watford 31-10-71
Source: Trainee. *Honours:* England Youth, Under-21, B, 4 full caps.
1989–90 Tottenham H 0 0
1990–91 Tottenham H 1 0
1990–91 *Oxford U* 2 0 **2 0**
1990–91 *Ipswich T* 0 0
1991–92 Tottenham H 18 0
1992–93 Tottenham H 17 0
1993–94 Tottenham H 11 0
1994–95 Tottenham H 41 0
1995–96 Tottenham H 38 0
1996–97 Tottenham H 37 0
1997–98 Tottenham H 29 0
1998–99 Tottenham H 25 0
1999–2000 Tottenham H 38 0
2000–01 Tottenham H 4 0 **259 0**
2001–02 Leicester C 35 0
2002–03 Leicester C 46 0
2003–04 Leicester C 37 0
2004–05 Leicester C 22 0 **140 0**

WESOLOWSKI, James (D) 0 0
H: 5 8 W: 11 11 b.Sydney 25-8-87
Source: Scholar. *Honours:* Australia Under-20.
2004–05 Leicester C 0 0

WILCOX, Jason (M) 364 36
H: 5 11 W: 11 01 b.Bolton 15-7-71
Source: Trainee. *Honours:* England B, 3 full caps.
1989–90 Blackburn R 1 0
1990–91 Blackburn R 18 0
1991–92 Blackburn R 38 4
1992–93 Blackburn R 33 4
1993–94 Blackburn R 33 6
1994–95 Blackburn R 27 5
1995–96 Blackburn R 10 3
1996–97 Blackburn R 28 2
1997–98 Blackburn R 31 4
1998–99 Blackburn R 30 3
1999–2000 Blackburn R 20 0 **269 31**
1999–2000 Leeds U 20 3
2000–01 Leeds U 17 0
2001–02 Leeds U 13 0
2002–03 Leeds U 25 1
2003–04 Leeds U 6 0 **81 4**
2004–05 Leicester C 14 1 **14 1**

WILLIAMS, Gareth (M) 175 10
H: 6 1 W: 12 03 b.Glasgow 16-12-81
Source: Trainee. *Honours:* Scotland Youth, Under-21, 5 full caps.
1998–99 Nottingham F 0 0
1999–2000 Nottingham F 2 0
2000–01 Nottingham F 17 0
2001–02 Nottingham F 44 0
2002–03 Nottingham F 40 3
2003–04 Nottingham F 39 6 **142 9**
2004–05 Leicester C 33 1 **33 1**

WILLIAMSON, Tom (M) 1 0
H: 5 9 W: 10 04 b.Leicester 24-12-84
Source: Scholar.
2001–02 Leicester C 1 0
2002–03 Leicester C 0 0
2003–04 Leicester C 0 0
2004–05 Leicester C 0 0 **1 0**

WRIGHT, Tommy (F) 46 5
H: 6 0 W: 12 02 b.Leicester 28-9-84
Source: Scholar. *Honours:* England Youth, Under-20
2001–02 Leicester C 1 0
2002–03 Leicester C 13 2
2003–04 Leicester C 0 0
2003–04 *Brentford* 25 3 **25 3**
2004–05 Leicester C 7 0 **21 2**

LEYTON ORIENT (42)

ALEXANDER, Gary (F) 231 72
H: 6 0 W: 12 00 b.Lambeth 15-8-79
Source: Trainee.
1998–99 West Ham U 0 0
1999–2000 West Ham U 0 0
1999–2000 *Exeter C* 37 16 **37 16**
2000–01 Swindon T 37 7 **37 7**
2001–02 Hull C 43 17
2002–03 Hull C 25 6 **68 23**
2002–03 Leyton Orient 17 2
2003–04 Leyton Orient 44 15
2004–05 Leyton Orient 28 9 **89 26**

BARNARD, Donny (D) 95 1
H: 5 9 W: 10 10 b.Forest Gate 1-7-84
Source: Trainee.
2001–02 Leyton Orient 10 0
2002–03 Leyton Orient 29 0
2003–04 Leyton Orient 23 0
2004–05 Leyton Orient 33 1 **95 1**

CARLISLE, Wayne (M) 156 22
H: 5 10 W: 11 00 b.Lisburn 9-9-79
Source: Trainee. *Honours:* Northern Ireland Schools, Youth, Under-21.
1996–97 Crystal Palace 0 0
1997–98 Crystal Palace 0 0
1998–99 Crystal Palace 6 0
1999–2000 Crystal Palace 26 3
2000–01 Crystal Palace 14 0
2001–02 Crystal Palace 0 0 **46 3**
2001–02 *Swindon T* 11 2 **11 2**
2001–02 Bristol R 5 0
2002–03 Bristol R 41 7
2003–04 Bristol R 25 7 **71 14**
2004–05 Leyton Orient 28 3 **28 3**

DUNCAN, Derek (M) 16 0
H: 5 9 W: 10 12 b.Newham 23-4-87
Source: Scholar.
2003–04 Leyton Orient 1 0
2004–05 Leyton Orient 15 0 **16 0**

ECHANOMI, Efe (M) 18 5
H: 5 7 W: 11 07 b.Nigeria 27-9-86
2004–05 Leyton Orient 18 5 **18 5**

GOURGEL, Nuno (F) 0 0
b.Angola 28-10-87
Source: Scholar.
2004–05 Leyton Orient 0 0

HARRISON, Lee (G) 269 0
H: 6 3 W: 11 13 b.Billericay 12-9-71
Source: Trainee.
1990–91 Charlton Ath 0 0
1991–92 Charlton Ath 0 0
1991–92 *Fulham* 0 0
1991–92 *Gillingham* 2 0 **2 0**
1992–93 Charlton Ath 0 0
1992–93 *Fulham* 0 0
1993–94 Fulham 0 0
1994–95 Fulham 7 0
1995–96 Fulham 5 0 **12 0**
1996–97 Barnet 21 0
1997–98 Barnet 46 0
1998–99 Barnet 43 0
1999–2000 Barnet 43 0
2000–01 Barnet 30 0
2001–02 Barnet 0 0 **183 0**
2002–03 Peterborough U 12 0 **12 0**
2002–03 Leyton Orient 6 0
2003–04 Leyton Orient 20 0
2004–05 Leyton Orient 34 0 **60 0**

IBEHRE, Jabo (F) 115 17
H: 6 1 W: 12 10 b.Islington 28-1-83
Source: Trainee.
1999–2000 Leyton Orient 3 0
2000–01 Leyton Orient 5 2
2001–02 Leyton Orient 28 4
2002–03 Leyton Orient 25 5
2003–04 Leyton Orient 35 4
2004–05 Leyton Orient 19 2 **115 17**

LOCKWOOD, Matt (D) 308 32
H: 6 0 W: 11 06 b.Rochford 17-10-76
Source: Trainee.
1994–95 QPR 0 0
1995–96 QPR 0 0
1996–97 Bristol R 39 1
1997–98 Bristol R 24 0 **63 1**
1998–99 Leyton Orient 37 3
1999–2000 Leyton Orient 41 6
2000–01 Leyton Orient 32 7
2001–02 Leyton Orient 24 2
2002–03 Leyton Orient 43 5
2003–04 Leyton Orient 25 2
2004–05 Leyton Orient 43 6 **245 31**

MACKIE, John (D) 118 8
H: 6 1 W: 12 00 b.Enfield 5-7-76
Source: Sutton U.
1999–2000 Reading 0 0
2000–01 Reading 10 0
2001–02 Reading 27 2
2002–03 Reading 25 0
2003–04 Reading 9 1 **71 3**
2003–04 Leyton Orient 20 1
2004–05 Leyton Orient 27 4 **47 5**

McMAHON, Daryl (M) 30 3
H: 5 11 W: 12 02 b.Dublin 10-10-83
Honours: Eire Youth.
2000–01 West Ham U 0 0
2001–02 West Ham U 0 0
2002–03 West Ham U 0 0
2003–04 West Ham U 0 0
2003–04 *Torquay U* 1 0 **1 0**
2004–05 Port Vale 5 0 **5 0**
2004–05 Leyton Orient 24 3 **24 3**

MILLER, Justin (D) **96 2**
H: 6 1 W: 11 07 b.Johannesburg 16-12-80
Source: Academy.
1999–2000 Ipswich T 0 0
2000–01 Ipswich T 0 0
2001–02 Ipswich T 0 0
2002–03 Ipswich T 0 0
2002–03 Leyton Orient 19 0
2003–04 Leyton Orient 34 2
2004–05 Leyton Orient 43 0 **96 2**

MORRIS, Glenn (G) **64 0**
H: 5 11 W: 11 00 b.Woolwich 20-12-83
Source: Scholar.
2001–02 Leyton Orient 2 0
2002–03 Leyton Orient 23 0
2003–04 Leyton Orient 27 0
2004–05 Leyton Orient 12 0 **64 0**

NEWEY, Tom (D) **83 4**
H: 5 11 W: 10 02 b.Sheffield 31-10-82
Source: Scholar.
2000–01 Leeds U 0 0
2001–02 Leeds U 0 0
2002–03 Leeds U 0 0
2002–03 *Cambridge U* 6 0
2002–03 *Darlington* 7 1 **7 1**
2003–04 Leyton Orient 34 2
2004–05 Leyton Orient 20 1 **54 3**
2004–05 *Cambridge U* 16 0 **22 0**

PALMER, Aiden (M) **5 0**
H: 5 8 W: 10 04 b.Enfield 2-1-87
Source: Scholar.
2004–05 Leyton Orient 5 0 **5 0**

PETERS, Mark (D) **235 12**
H: 6 2 W: 13 00 b.St Asaph 6-7-72
Source: From Trainee. *Honours:* Wales Under-21.
1991–92 Manchester C 0 0
1992–93 Norwich C 0 0
1993–94 Peterborough U 19 0
1994–95 Peterborough U 0 0 **19 0**
1994–95 Mansfield T 26 4
1995–96 Mansfield T 21 2
1996–97 Mansfield T 0 0
1997–98 Mansfield T 24 2
1998–99 Mansfield T 37 1 **108 9**
2001–02 Rushden & D 40 0
2002–03 Rushden & D 27 1
2003–04 Rushden & D 0 0 **67 1**
2003–04 Leyton Orient 39 2
2004–05 Leyton Orient 2 0 **41 2**

RAYNOR, Paul (M) **481 54**
H: 5 11 W: 12 03 b.Nottingham 29-4-66
Source: Apprentice.
1983–84 Nottingham F 0 0
1984–85 Nottingham F 3 0 **3 0**
1984–85 *Bristol R* 8 0 **8 0**
1985–86 Huddersfield T 30 5
1986–87 Huddersfield T 20 4 **50 9**
1986–87 Swansea C 12 1
1987–88 Swansea C 44 8
1988–89 Swansea C 26 5
1988–89 *Wrexham* 6 0 **6 0**
1989–90 Swansea C 40 6
1990–91 Swansea C 43 5
1991–92 Swansea C 26 2 **191 27**
1991–92 Cambridge U 8 0
1992–93 Cambridge U 41 2
1993–94 Preston NE 39 6
1994–95 Preston NE 38 3
1995–96 Preston NE 3 0 **80 9**
1995–96 Cambridge U 35 3
1996–97 Cambridge U 44 4
1997–98 Cambridge U 0 0 **128 9**
From Guang Deong
1997–98 Leyton Orient 10 0
1998–99 Leyton Orient 5 0
1999–2000 Leyton Orient 0 0
2000–01 Leyton Orient 0 0
2001–02 Leyton Orient 0 0
2004–05 Leyton Orient 0 0 **15 0**

SAAH, Brian (M) **18 0**
H: 6 1 W: 11 05 b.Rush Green 16-12-86
Source: Scholar.
2003–04 Leyton Orient 6 0
2004–05 Leyton Orient 12 0 **18 0**

SCOTT, Andy (F) **348 71**
H: 6 2 W: 12 00 b.Epsom 2-8-72
Source: Sutton U.
1992–93 Sheffield U 2 1
1993–94 Sheffield U 15 0
1994–95 Sheffield U 37 4
1995–96 Sheffield U 7 0
1996–97 Sheffield U 8 1
1996–97 *Chesterfield* 5 3 **5 3**
1996–97 *Bury* 8 0 **8 0**
1997–98 Sheffield U 6 0 **75 6**
1997–98 Brentford 26 5
1998–99 Brentford 34 7
1999–2000 Brentford 36 3
2000–01 Brentford 22 13 **118 28**
2000–01 Oxford U 21 5
2001–02 Oxford U 30 8
2002–03 Oxford U 38 11
2003–04 Oxford U 6 0 **95 24**
2003–04 Leyton Orient 8 1
2004–05 Leyton Orient 39 9 **47 10**

SIMPSON, Michael (M) **391 21**
H: 5 7 W: 10 05 b.Nottingham 28-2-74
Source: Trainee.
1992–93 Notts Co 0 0
1993–94 Notts Co 6 1
1994–95 Notts Co 19 2
1995–96 Notts Co 23 0
1996–97 Notts Co 1 0 **49 3**
1996–97 *Plymouth Arg* 12 0 **12 0**
1996–97 Wycombe W 20 1
1997–98 Wycombe W 21 0
1998–99 Wycombe W 33 4
1999–2000 Wycombe W 43 0
2000–01 Wycombe W 45 3
2001–02 Wycombe W 43 1
2002–03 Wycombe W 42 5
2003–04 Wycombe W 38 2 **285 16**
2004–05 Leyton Orient 45 2 **45 2**

SMITH, Dean (D) **566 54**
H: 6 1 W: 13 10 b.West Bromwich 19-3-71
Source: Trainee.
1988–89 Walsall 15 0
1989–90 Walsall 7 0
1990–91 Walsall 33 0
1991–92 Walsall 9 0
1992–93 Walsall 42 1
1993–94 Walsall 36 1 **142 2**
1994–95 Hereford U 35 3
1995–96 Hereford U 40 8
1996–97 Hereford U 42 8 **117 19**
1997–98 Leyton Orient 43 9
1998–99 Leyton Orient 37 9
1999–2000 Leyton Orient 44 4
2000–01 Leyton Orient 43 5
2001–02 Leyton Orient 45 2
2002–03 Leyton Orient 27 3
2002–03 Sheffield W 14 0
2003–04 Sheffield W 41 1 **55 1**
2004–05 Port Vale 13 0 **13 0**
2004–05 Leyton Orient 0 0 **239 32**

STEELE, Lee (F) **238 68**
H: 5 8 W: 11 08 b.Liverpool 2-12-73
Source: Bootle, Northwich V.
1997–98 Shrewsbury T 38 13
1998–99 Shrewsbury T 38 13
1999–2000 Shrewsbury T 37 11 **113 37**
2000–01 Brighton & HA 23 2
2001–02 Brighton & HA 37 9 **60 11**
2002–03 Oxford U 10 3
2003–04 Oxford U 16 1 **26 4**
2004–05 Leyton Orient 39 16 **39 16**

WALLIS, Scott (M) **3 0**
H: 5 10 W: 10 10 b.Enfield 28-6-88
Source: Scholar.
2004–05 Leyton Orient 3 0 **3 0**

YOUNGS, Tom (F) **186 44**
H: 5 9 W: 11 13 b.Bury St Edmunds 31-8-79
Source: Trainee.
1997–98 Cambridge U 4 0
1998–99 Cambridge U 10 0
1999–2000 Cambridge U 21 8
2000–01 Cambridge U 38 14
2001–02 Cambridge U 42 11
2002–03 Cambridge U 35 10 **150 43**
2002–03 Northampton T 5 0
2003–04 Northampton T 12 0
2004–05 Northampton T 9 0 **26 0**
2004–05 Leyton Orient 10 1 **10 1**

ZAKUANI, Gaby (D) **44 2**
H: 6 0 W: 11 08 b.Zaire 31-5-86
Source: Scholar.
2002–03 Leyton Orient 1 0
2003–04 Leyton Orient 10 2
2004–05 Leyton Orient 33 0 **44 2**

LINCOLN C (43)

ASAMOAH, Derek (F) **153 15**
H: 5 6 W: 10 12 b.Ghana 1-5-81
Source: Slough T.
2001–02 Northampton T 40 3
2002–03 Northampton T 42 4
2003–04 Northampton T 31 3 **113 10**
2004–05 Mansfield T 30 5 **30 5**
2004–05 Lincoln C 10 0 **10 0**

BEEVERS, Lee (D) **80 3**
H: 6 1 W: 13 00 b.Doncaster 4-12-83
Source: Scholar. *Honours:* Wales Youth, Under-21.
2000–01 Ipswich T 0 0
2001–02 Ipswich T 0 0
2002–03 Ipswich T 0 0
2002–03 *Boston U* 1 0
2003–04 Boston U 40 2
2004–05 Boston U 31 1 **72 3**
2004–05 Lincoln C 8 0 **8 0**

BLACKWOOD, Michael (D) **64 4**
H: 5 11 W: 11 10 b.Birmingham 30-9-79
Source: Trainee.
1998–99 Aston Villa 0 0
1999–2000 Aston Villa 0 0
1999–2000 *Chester C* 9 2 **9 2**
2000–01 Wrexham 15 0
2001–02 Wrexham 31 2 **46 2**
From Telford U
2004–05 Lincoln C 9 0 **9 0**

BLOOMER, Matt (D) **97 3**
H: 6 0 W: 11 08 b.Cleethorpes 3-11-78
Source: Trainee.
1997–98 Grimsby T 0 0
1998–99 Grimsby T 4 0
1999–2000 Grimsby T 2 0
2000–01 Grimsby T 6 0
2001–02 Grimsby T 0 0 **12 0**
2001–02 Hull C 3 0
2001–02 *Lincoln C* 5 0
2002–03 Hull C 0 0 **3 0**
2002–03 Lincoln C 13 1
2003–04 Lincoln C 27 0
2004–05 Lincoln C 37 2 **82 3**

BUTCHER, Richard (M) **104 11**
H: 6 0 W: 13 00 b.Northampton 22-1-81
Source: Kettering T.
2002–03 Lincoln C 26 3
2003–04 Lincoln C 32 6
2004–05 Lincoln C 46 2 **104 11**

CARRUTHERS, Martin (F) **415 110**
H: 5 11 W: 11 10 b.Nottingham 7-8-72
Source: Trainee.
1990–91 Aston Villa 0 0
1991–92 Aston Villa 3 0
1992–93 Aston Villa 1 0 **4 0**
1992–93 *Hull C* 13 6 **13 6**
1993–94 Stoke C 34 5
1994–95 Stoke C 32 5
1995–96 Stoke C 24 3
1996–97 Stoke C 1 0 **91 13**
1996–97 Peterborough U 14 4
1997–98 Peterborough U 39 15
1998–99 Peterborough U 14 2 **67 21**
1998–99 *York C* 6 0 **6 0**
1998–99 Darlington 11 2
1999–2000 Darlington 6 0 **17 2**
1999–2000 Southend U 38 19
2000–01 Southend U 32 7 **70 26**
2000–01 Scunthorpe U 8 1
2001–02 Scunthorpe U 33 13
2002–03 Scunthorpe U 45 20 **86 34**

2003–04 Macclesfield T 39 8 **39 8**
2004–05 Boston U 6 0 **6 0**
2004–05 Lincoln C 11 0 **11 0**
2004–05 *Cambridge U* 5 0 **5 0**

CORNELLY, Chris (M) 16 0
H: 5 7 W: 11 07 b.Huddersfield 7-7-76
Source: Leigh RMI, Ashton U.
2002–03 Lincoln C 16 0
2003–04 Lincoln C 0 0
2004–05 Lincoln C 0 0 **16 0**

FRECKLINGTON, Lee (M) 3 0
H: 5 8 W: 11 00 b.Lincoln 8-9-85
Source: Scholar.
2003–04 Lincoln C 0 0
2004–05 Lincoln C 3 0 **3 0**

FUTCHER, Ben (D) 131 13
H: 6 7 W: 12 05 b.Bradford 20-2-81
Source: Trainee.
1999–2000 Oldham Ath 5 0
2000–01 Oldham Ath 5 0
2001–02 Oldham Ath 0 0 **10 0**
From Stalybridge C, Doncaster R
2002–03 Lincoln
2003–04 Lincoln C 43 2
2004–05 Lincoln C 35 3 **121 13**

GAIN, Peter (M) 227 21
H: 6 0 W: 11 07 b.Hammersmith 2-11-76
Source: Trainee.
1995–96 Tottenham H 0 0
1996–97 Tottenham H 0 0
1997–98 Tottenham H 0 0
1998–99 Tottenham H 0 0
1998–99 Lincoln C 4 0
1999–2000 Lincoln C 32 2
2000–01 Lincoln C 24 5
2001–02 Lincoln C 42 2
2002–03 Lincoln C 43 5
2003–04 Lincoln C 42 7
2004–05 Lincoln C 40 0 **227 21**

GREEN, Francis (F) 180 29
H: 5 9 W: 11 06 b.Derby 25-4-80
Source: Ilkeston T.
1997–98 Peterborough U 4 1
1998–99 Peterborough U 7 1
1999–2000 Peterborough U 20 1
2000–01 Peterborough U 32 6
2001–02 Peterborough U 23 3
2002–03 Peterborough U 19 2
2003–04 Peterborough U 3 0 **108 14**
2003–04 Lincoln C 35 7
2004–05 Lincoln C 37 8 **72 15**

HOBBS, Jack (D) 1 0
H: 6 0 W: 12 00 b.Portsmouth 18-8-88
Source: Scholar.
2004–05 Lincoln C 1 0 **1 0**

KERLEY, Adam (F) 1 0
H: 5 6 W: 11 07 b.Sutton-in-Ashfield 25-2-85
Source: Scholar.
2004–05 Lincoln C 1 0 **1 0**

LOGAN, Richard (D) 228 21
H: 6 0 W: 12 08 b.Barnsley 24-5-69
Source: Gainsborough T.
1993–94 Huddersfield T 16 0
1994–95 Huddersfield T 27 1
1995–96 Huddersfield T 2 0 **45 1**
1995–96 Plymouth Arg 31 4
1996–97 Plymouth Arg 28 4
1997–98 Plymouth Arg 27 4 **86 12**
1998–99 Scunthorpe U 41 6
1999–2000 Scunthorpe U 39 1 **80 7**
2000–01 Lincoln C 5 0
2001–02 Lincoln C 2 0
2002–03 Lincoln C 10 1
2003–04 Lincoln C 0 0
2004–05 Lincoln C 0 0 **17 1**

MARRIOTT, Alan (G) 228 0
H: 6 0 W: 12 04 b.Bedford 3-9-78
Source: Trainee.
1997–98 Tottenham H 0 0
1998–99 Tottenham H 0 0
1999–2000 Lincoln C 18 0
2000–01 Lincoln C 30 0
2001–02 Lincoln C 43 0
2002–03 Lincoln C 46 0
2003–04 Lincoln C 46 0
2004–05 Lincoln C 45 0 **228 0**

McAULEY, Gareth (D) 37 3
H: 6 3 W: 13 00 b.Larne 5-12-79
Source: Coleraine. *Honours:* Northern Ireland Schools, B, 1 full cap.
2004–05 Lincoln C 37 3 **37 3**

McCOMBE, Jamie (D) 112 4
H: 6 5 W: 12 03 b.Pontefract 1-1-83
Source: Scholar.
2001–02 Scunthorpe U 17 0
2002–03 Scunthorpe U 31 1
2003–04 Scunthorpe U 15 0 **63 1**
2003–04 Lincoln C 8 0
2004–05 Lincoln C 41 3 **49 3**

McNAMARA, Niall (M) 15 0
H: 6 1 W: 12 07 b.Limerick 26-1-82
Source: Trainee.
1998–99 Nottingham F 0 0
1999–2000 Nottingham F 0 0
2000–01 Nottingham F 0 0
2001–02 Notts Co 4 0
2002–03 Notts Co 0 0 **4 0**
From Belper T.
2003–04 Lincoln C 10 0
2004–05 Lincoln C 1 0 **11 0**

MORGAN, Paul (D) 159 1
H: 6 0 W: 11 03 b.Belfast 23-10-78
Source: Trainee. *Honours:* Northern Ireland Under-21.
1997–98 Preston NE 0 0
1998–99 Preston NE 0 0
1999–2000 Preston NE 0 0
2000–01 Preston NE 0 0
2001–02 Lincoln C 34 1
2002–03 Lincoln C 45 0
2003–04 Lincoln C 41 0
2004–05 Lincoln C 39 0 **159 1**

RAYNER, Simon (G) 1 0
H: 6 4 W: 15 00 b.Vancouver 8-7-83
Source: Bournemouth, Barry T, Port Talbot. *Honours:* Canada Under 23.
2004–05 Lincoln C 1 0 **1 0**

RYAN, Oliver (M) 6 0
H: 5 9 W: 11 00 b.Boston 26-9-85
Source: Scholar.
2004–05 Lincoln C 6 0 **6 0**

SANDWITH, Kevin (D) 43 2
H: 5 11 W: 12 05 b.Workington 30-4-78
Source: Trainee.
1996–97 Carlisle U 0 0
1997–98 Carlisle U 3 0
1998–99 Carlisle U 0 0 **3 0**
From Halifax T
2003–04 Lincoln C 3 0
2004–05 Lincoln C 37 2 **40 2**

TAYLOR-FLETCHER, Gary (F) 106 28
H: 6 0 W: 11 00 b.Liverpool 4-6-81
Source: Northwich Vic. *Honours:* England Schools.
2000–01 Hull C 5 0 **5 0**
2001–02 Leyton Orient 9 0
2002–03 Leyton Orient 12 1 **21 1**
2003–04 Lincoln C 42 16
2004–05 Lincoln C 38 11 **80 27**

TONER, Ciaran (M) 87 4
H: 6 0 W: 12 08 b.Craigavon 30-6-81
Source: Trainee. *Honours:* Northern Ireland Under-21, 2 full caps.
1999–2000 Tottenham H 0 0
2000–01 Tottenham H 0 0
2001–02 Tottenham H 0 0
2001–02 *Peterborough U* 6 0 **6 0**
2001–02 Bristol R 6 0 **6 0**
2001–02 Leyton Orient 0 0
2002–03 Leyton Orient 25 1
2003–04 Leyton Orient 27 1 **52 2**
2004–05 Lincoln C 15 2 **15 2**
2004–05 *Cambridge U* 8 0 **8 0**

YEO, Simon (F) 122 37
H: 5 10 W: 11 08 b.Stockport 20-10-73
Source: Hyde U.
2002–03 Lincoln C 37 5
2003–04 Lincoln C 41 11
2004–05 Lincoln C 44 21 **122 37**

LIVERPOOL (44)

ALONSO, Xabi (M) 153 11
H: 6 0 W: 12 02 b.Tolosa 25-11-81
Honours: Spain 17 full caps.
1999–2000 Real Sociedad 0 0
2000–01 Eibar 14 0 **14 0**
2000–01 Real Sociedad 18 0
2001–02 Real Sociedad 29 3
2002–03 Real Sociedad 33 3
2003–04 Real Sociedad 35 3 **115 9**
2004–05 Liverpool 24 2 **24 2**

BAROS, Milan (F) 127 30
H: 5 9 W: 12 05 b.Valasske Mezirici 28-10-81
Honours: Czech Republic Youth, Under-21, 39 full caps, 24 goals.
1998–99 Banik Ostrava 6 0
1999–2000 Banik Ostrava 29 6
2000–01 Banik Ostrava 26 5 **61 11**
2001–02 Liverpool 0 0
2002–03 Liverpool 27 9
2003–04 Liverpool 13 1
2004–05 Liverpool 26 9 **66 19**

BISCAN, Igor (M) 151 14
H: 6 2 W: 13 03 b.Zagreb 4-5-78
Honours: Croatia 15 full caps, 1 goal.
1997–98 Samobor 12 1 **12 1**
1997–98 Dynamo Zagreb 5 0
1998–99 Dynamo Zagreb 19 2
1998–99 Dynamo Zagreb 0 0
1999–2000 Dynamo Zagreb 29 6
2000–01 Dynamo Zagreb 14 3 **67 11**
2000–01 Liverpool 13 0
2001–02 Liverpool 5 0
2002–03 Liverpool 6 0
2003–04 Liverpool 29 0
2004–05 Liverpool 19 2 **72 2**

BUTLER, Chris (M) 0 0
Source: Scholar.
2004–05 Liverpool 0 0

CARRAGHER, Jamie (D) 254 2
H: 5 9 W: 12 01 b.Liverpool 28-1-78
Source: From Trainee. *Honours:* England Youth, Under-21, B, 17 full caps.
1995–96 Liverpool 0 0
1996–97 Liverpool 2 1
1997–98 Liverpool 20 0
1998–99 Liverpool 34 1
1999–2000 Liverpool 36 0
2000–01 Liverpool 34 0
2001–02 Liverpool 33 0
2002–03 Liverpool 35 0
2003–04 Liverpool 22 0
2004–05 Liverpool 38 0 **254 2**

CARSON, Scott (G) 7 0
H: 6 3 W: 13 12 b.Whitehaven 3-9-85
Source: Scholar. *Honours:* England Youth, Under-21.
2002–03 Leeds U 0 0
2003–04 Leeds U 3 0
2004–05 Leeds U 0 0 **3 0**
2004–05 Liverpool 4 0 **4 0**

CHEYROU, Bruno (M) 145 31
H: 6 1 W: 13 03 b.Suresnes 10-5-78
Source: Lens, Racing. *Honours:* France 2 full caps.
1998–99 Lille 20 6
1999–2000 Lille 21 5
2000–01 Lille 27 6
2001–02 Lille 27 11 **95 28**
2002–03 Liverpool 19 0
2003–04 Liverpool 12 2 **31 2**
2004–05 *Marseille* 19 1 **19 1**

CISSE, Djibril (F) 144 74
H: 6 0 W: 13 00 b.Arles 12-8-81
Honours: France 20 full caps, 5 goals.
1998–99 Auxerre 1 0
1999–2000 Auxerre 2 0
2000–01 Auxerre 25 8
2001–02 Auxerre 29 22
2002–03 Auxerre 33 14
2003–04 Auxerre 38 26 **128 70**
2004–05 Liverpool 16 4 **16 4**

DIAO, Salif (M) 116 1
H: 6 1 W: 12 08 b.Kedougou 10-2-77
Honours: Senegal 29 full caps, 3 goals.

1996–97	Epinal	2	0	**2**	**0**
1996–97	Monaco	0	0		
1997–98	Monaco	12	0		
1998–99	Monaco	14	0		
1999–2000	Monaco	1	0	**27**	**0**
2000–01	Sedan	26	0		
2001–02	Sedan	22	0	**48**	**0**
2002–03	Liverpool	26	1		
2003–04	Liverpool	3	0		
2004–05	Liverpool	8	0	**37**	**1**
2004–05	*Birmingham C*	2	0	**2**	**0**

DIARRA, Alou (M) 94 6
H: 6 1 W: 12 03 b.Villepinte 15-7-81
Source: Louhans, Bayern Munich.

2002–03	Le Havre	25	0	**25**	**0**
2003–04	Liverpool	0	0		
2003–04	*Bastia*	35	4	**35**	**4**
2004–05	*Lens*	34	2	**34**	**2**

DIOUF, El Hadji (F) 179 31
H: 5 8 W: 12 05 b.Dakar 15-1-81
Honours: Senegal 31 full caps, 15 goals.

1998–99	Sochaux	15	0	**15**	**0**
1999–2000	Rennes	28	1	**28**	**1**
2000–01	Lens	28	8		
2001–02	Lens	26	10	**54**	**18**
2002–03	Liverpool	29	3		
2003–04	Liverpool	26	0		
2004–05	Liverpool	0	0	**55**	**3**
2004–05	*Bolton W*	27	9	**27**	**9**

DUDEK, Jerzy (G) 270 0
H: 6 2 W: 12 08 b.Ribnek 23-3-73
Source: GKS Tychy. *Honours:* Poland 51 full caps.

1995–96	Sokol Tychy	15	0	**15**	**0**
1996–97	Feyenoord	0	0		
1997–98	Feyenoord	34	0		
1998–99	Feyenoord	34	0		
1999–2000	Feyenoord	34	0		
2000–01	Feyenoord	34	0	**136**	**0**
2001–02	Liverpool	35	0		
2002–03	Liverpool	30	0		
2003–04	Liverpool	30	0		
2004–05	Liverpool	24	0	**119**	**0**

FINNAN, Steve (M) 339 15
H: 6 0 W: 12 03 b.Limerick 24-4-76
Source: Welling U. *Honours:* Eire Under-21, B, 36 full caps, 1 goal.

1995–96	Birmingham C	12	1		
1995–96	*Notts Co*	17	2		
1996–97	Birmingham C	3	0	**15**	**1**
1996–97	Notts Co	23	0		
1997–98	Notts Co	44	5		
1998–99	Notts Co	13	0	**97**	**7**
1998–99	Fulham	22	2		
1999–2000	Fulham	35	2		
2000–01	Fulham	45	2		
2001–02	Fulham	38	0		
2002–03	Fulham	32	0	**172**	**6**
2003–04	Liverpool	22	0		
2004–05	Liverpool	33	1	**55**	**1**

FOY, Robbie (F) 13 0
H: 5 6 W: 9 09 b.Edinburgh 29-10-85
Source: Trainee. *Honours:* Scotland Under-21.

2002–03	Liverpool	0	0		
2003–04	Liverpool	0	0		
2004–05	Liverpool	0	0		
2004–05	*Chester C*	13	0	**13**	**0**

GERRARD, Steven (M) 200 27
H: 6 0 W: 12 05 b.Whiston 30-5-80
Source: Trainee. *Honours:* England Youth, Under-21, 34 full caps, 6 goals.

1997–98	Liverpool	0	0		
1998–99	Liverpool	12	0		
1999–2000	Liverpool	29	1		
2000–01	Liverpool	33	7		
2001–02	Liverpool	28	3		
2002–03	Liverpool	34	5		
2003–04	Liverpool	34	4		
2004–05	Liverpool	30	7	**200**	**27**

GUTHRIE, Danny (D) 0 0
b.Shrewsbury 19-4-87
Source: Scholar. *Honours:* England Schools.

2004–05	Liverpool	0	0		

HAMANN, Dietmar (M) 302 18
H: 6 2 W: 13 00 b.Waldasson 27-8-73
Source: Wacker Munich. *Honours:* Germany Youth, Under-21, 58 full caps, 5 goals.

1993–94	Bayern Munich	5	1		
1994–95	Bayern Munich	30	0		
1995–96	Bayern Munich	20	2		
1996–97	Bayern Munich	22	1		
1997–98	Bayern Munich	28	2	**105**	**6**
1998–99	Newcastle U	23	4	**23**	**4**
1999–2000	Liverpool	28	1		
2000–01	Liverpool	30	2		
2001–02	Liverpool	31	1		
2002–03	Liverpool	30	2		
2003–04	Liverpool	25	2		
2004–05	Liverpool	30	0	**174**	**8**

HARRISON, Paul (G) 0 0
H: 5 9 W: 13 04 b.Liverpool 18-12-84
Source: Scholar.

2003–04	Liverpool	0	0		
2004–05	Liverpool	0	0		
2004–05	*Leeds U*	0	0		

HENCHOZ, Stephane (D) 351 3
H: 6 2 W: 13 02 b.Billens 7-9-74
Source: Bulle. *Honours:* Switzerland 72 full caps.

1992–93	Neuchatel Xamax	35	0		
1993–94	Neuchatel Xamax	21	1		
1994–95	Neuchatel Xamax	35	0	**91**	**1**
1995–96	Hamburg	31	2		
1996–97	Hamburg	18	0	**49**	**2**
1997–98	Blackburn R	36	0		
1998–99	Blackburn R	34	0	**70**	**0**
1999–2000	Liverpool	29	0		
2000–01	Liverpool	32	0		
2001–02	Liverpool	37	0		
2002–03	Liverpool	19	0		
2003–04	Liverpool	18	0	**135**	**0**
2004–05	*Celtic*	6	0	**6**	**0**

HYYPIA, Sami (D) 379 23
H: 6 3 W: 13 09 b.Porvoo 7-10-73
Source: KuMu. *Honours:* Finland Youth, Under-21, 69 full caps, 4 goals.

1993	MyPa 47	12	0		
1994	MyPa 47	25	0		
1995	MyPa 47	26	3	**63**	**3**
1995–96	Willem II	14	0		
1996–97	Willem II	30	1		
1997–98	Willem II	30	0		
1998–99	Willem II	26	2	**100**	**3**
1999–2000	Liverpool	38	2		
2000–01	Liverpool	35	3		
2001–02	Liverpool	37	3		
2002–03	Liverpool	36	3		
2003–04	Liverpool	38	4		
2004–05	Liverpool	32	2	**216**	**17**

JOSEMI (D) 108 0
H: 5 9 W: 12 08 b.Malaga 15-11-79

2000–01	Malaga	1	0		
2001–02	Malaga	23	0		
2002–03	Malaga	32	0		
2003–04	Malaga	37	0	**93**	**0**
2004–05	Liverpool	15	0	**15**	**0**

KEWELL, Harry (M) 235 53
H: 5 9 W: 12 06 b.Sydney 22-9-78
Source: NSW Soccer Academy. *Honours:* Australia Youth, Under-20, 17 full caps, 6 goals.

1995–96	Leeds U	2	0		
1996–97	Leeds U	1	0		
1997–98	Leeds U	29	5		
1998–99	Leeds U	38	6		
1999–2000	Leeds U	36	10		
2000–01	Leeds U	17	2		
2001–02	Leeds U	27	8		
2002–03	Leeds U	31	14	**181**	**45**
2003–04	Liverpool	36	7		
2004–05	Liverpool	18	1	**54**	**8**

KIRKLAND, Christopher (G) 49 0
H: 6 5 W: 14 08 b.Leicester 2-5-81
Source: Trainee. *Honours:* England Youth, Under-21.

1997–98	Coventry C	0	0		
1998–99	Coventry C	0	0		
1999–2000	Coventry C	0	0		
2000–01	Coventry C	23	0		
2001–02	Coventry C	1	0	**24**	**0**
2001–02	Liverpool	1	0		
2002–03	Liverpool	8	0		
2003–04	Liverpool	6	0		
2004–05	Liverpool	10	0	**25**	**0**

LE TALLEC, Anthony (M) 78 8
H: 6 0 W: 12 00 b.Hennebont 3-10-84
Honours: France Under-21.

2001–02	Le Havre	24	5		
2002–03	Le Havre	30	2	**54**	**7**
2003–04	Liverpool	13	0		
2004–05	Liverpool	4	0	**17**	**0**
2004–05	*St Etienne*	7	1	**7**	**1**

LUIS GARCIA (M) 244 72
H: 5 6 W: 10 05 b.Barcelona 24-6-78
Honours: Spain 2 full caps.

1997–98	Barcelona B	36	15		
1998–99	Barcelona B	36	10	**72**	**25**
1999–2000	Valladolid	6	0		
1999–2000	Toledo	17	4	**17**	**4**
2000–01	Tenerife	40	16	**40**	**16**
2001–02	Valladolid	25	6	**31**	**6**
2002–03	Atletico Madrid	30	9	**30**	**9**
2003–04	Barcelona	25	4	**25**	**4**
2004–05	Liverpool	29	8	**29**	**8**

LUZI-BERNARDI, Patrice (G) 1 0
H: 6 2 W: 13 08 b.Ajaccio 8-7-80
Source: Monaco.

2002–03	Liverpool	0	0		
2003–04	Liverpool	1	0		
2004–05	Liverpool	0	0	**1**	**0**

MANNIX, David (M) 0 0
H: 5 8 W: 11 06 b.Crewe 24-9-85
Source: Trainee. *Honours:* England Under-20.

2003–04	Liverpool	0	0		
2004–05	Liverpool	0	0		

MASSIE, Jason (M) 0 0
b.Whiston 13-9-84
Honours: England Youth.

2001–02	Liverpool	0	0		
2002–03	Liverpool	0	0		
2003–04	Liverpool	0	0		
2004–05	Liverpool	0	0		

MEDJANI, Carl (D) 25 0
H: 6 0 W: 13 04 b.Lyon 15-5-85

2003–04	Liverpool	0	0		
2004–05	*Lorient*	25	0	**25**	**0**

MELLOR, Neil (F) 28 4
H: 6 0 W: 13 05 b.Manchester 4-11-82
Source: Scholar.

2001–02	Liverpool	0	0		
2002–03	Liverpool	3	0		
2003–04	Liverpool	0	0		
2003–04	*West Ham U*	16	2	**16**	**2**
2004–05	Liverpool	9	2	**12**	**2**

MORIENTES, Fernando (F) 307 118
H: 6 0 W: 12 04 b.Caceres 5-4-76
Honours: Spain 38 full caps, 24 goals.

1993–94	Albacete	2	0		
1994–95	Albacete	20	5	**22**	**5**
1995–96	Zaragoza	29	13		
1996–97	Zaragoza	37	15	**66**	**28**
1997–98	Real Madrid	33	12		
1998–99	Real Madrid	33	19		
1999–2000	Real Madrid	26	12		
2000–01	Real Madrid	22	6		
2001–02	Real Madrid	33	18		
2002–03	Real Madrid	19	5		
2003–04	*Monaco*	28	10	**28**	**10**
2004–05	Real Madrid	12	0	**178**	**72**
2004–05	Liverpool	13	3	**13**	**3**

NUNEZ, Antonio (M) 86 12
H: 6 0 W: 12 02 b.Madrid 15-1-79

2001–02	Real Madrid B	24	2		
2002–03	Real Madrid B	33	9	**57**	**11**
2003–04	Real Madrid	11	1	**11**	**1**
2004–05	Liverpool	18	0	**18**	**0**

O'DONNELL, Daniel (D) **0 0**
b.Livepool 10-3-86
Source: Scholar.
2004–05 Liverpool 0 0

OTSEMOBOR, John (D) **28 4**
H: 5 9 W: 12 08 b.Liverpool 23-3-83
Source: From Trainee. *Honours:* England Youth, Under-20.
1999–2000 Liverpool 0 0
2000–01 Liverpool 0 0
2001–02 Liverpool 0 0
2002–03 Liverpool 0 0
2002–03 *Hull C* 9 3 **9 3**
2003–04 Liverpool 4 0
2003–04 *Bolton W* 1 0 **1 0**
2004–05 Liverpool 0 0 **4 0**
2004–05 *Crewe Alex* 14 1 **14 1**

PARTRIDGE, Richie (M) **33 5**
H: 5 5 W: 10 06 b.Dublin 12-9-80
Source: Trainee. *Honours:* Eire Under-21.
1998–99 Liverpool 0 0
1999–2000 Liverpool 0 0
2000–01 Liverpool 0 0
2000–01 *Bristol R* 6 1 **6 1**
2001–02 Liverpool 0 0
2002–03 Liverpool 0 0
2002–03 *Coventry C* 27 4 **27 4**
2003–04 Liverpool 0 0
2004–05 Liverpool 0 0

PELLEGRINO, Mauricio (D) **349 15**
H: 6 4 W: 13 03 b.Leones 5-10-71
Honours: Argentina 3 full caps.
1992 Velez Sarsfield 27 3
1993 Velez Sarsfield 15 1
1994 Velez Sarsfield 24 2
1995 Velez Sarsfield 28 1
1996 Velez Sarsfield 30 1
1997 Velez Sarsfield 30 2
1998 Velez Sarsfield 18 0
1998–99 Barcelona 23 0 **23 0**
1999 Velez Sarsfield 3 0 **175 10**
1999–2000 Valencia 33 1
2000–01 Valencia 27 0
2001–02 Valencia 30 1
2002–03 Valencia 28 1
2003–04 Valencia 20 2
2004–05 Valencia 1 0 **139 5**
2004–05 Liverpool 12 0 **12 0**

PELTIER, Lee (F) **0 0**
b.Liverpool 11-12-86
Source: Scholar.
2004–05 Liverpool 0 0

POTTER, Darren (M) **2 0**
H: 6 0 W: 10 08 b.Liverpool 21-12-84
Source: From Scholar. *Honours:* Eire Youth, Under-21.
2001–02 Liverpool 0 0
2002–03 Liverpool 0 0
2003–04 Liverpool 0 0
2004–05 Liverpool 2 0 **2 0**

RAVEN, David (D) **1 0**
H: 6 0 W: 11 04 b.Birkenhead 10-3-85
Source: Scholar. *Honours:* England Youth, Under-20.
2001–02 Liverpool 0 0
2002–03 Liverpool 0 0
2003–04 Liverpool 0 0
2004–05 Liverpool 1 0 **1 0**

RIISE, John Arne (M) **184 23**
H: 6 1 W: 14 00 b.Molde 24-9-80
Honours: Norway Youth, Under-21, 45 full caps, 7 goals.
1998–99 Monaco 7 0
1999–2000 Monaco 21 1
2000–01 Monaco 16 3 **44 4**
2001–02 Liverpool 38 7
2002–03 Liverpool 37 6
2003–04 Liverpool 28 0
2004–05 Liverpool 37 6 **140 19**

SINAMA-PONGOLLE, Florent (F) **42 6**
H: 5 7 W: 11 05 b.Saint-Pierre 20-10-84
Honours: France Under-21.
2001–02 Le Havre 11 2
2002–03 Le Havre 0 0 **11 2**
2003–04 Liverpool 15 2
2004–05 Liverpool 16 2 **31 4**

SMICER, Vladimir (M) **293 52**
H: 5 9 W: 12 03 b.Degin 24-5-73
Honours: Czechoslovakia 1 full cap, Czech Republic Under-21, 74 full caps, 25 goals.
1992–93 Slavia Prague 21 8
1993–94 Slavia Prague 17 6
1994–95 Slavia Prague 15 3
1995–96 Slavia Prague 28 9 **81 26**
1996–97 Lens 33 5
1997–98 Lens 28 7
1998–99 Lens 30 4 **91 16**
1999–2000 Liverpool 21 1
2000–01 Liverpool 27 2
2001–02 Liverpool 22 4
2002–03 Liverpool 21 0
2003–04 Liverpool 20 3
2004–05 Liverpool 10 0 **121 10**

SMITH, James (M) **0 0**
b.Liverpool 17-10-85
2004–05 Liverpool 0 0

SMYTH, Mark (M) **0 0**
H: 5 8 W: 10 08 b.Liverpool 9-1-85
Source: Scholar. *Honours:* England Youth, Under-20.
2001–02 Liverpool 0 0
2002–03 Liverpool 0 0
2003–04 Liverpool 0 0
2004–05 Liverpool 0 0

TRAORE, Djimi (D) **92 0**
H: 6 2 W: 12 07 b.Saint-Ouen 1-3-80
Source: Laval. *Honours:* France Youth, Under-21. Mali full caps.
1998–99 Liverpool 0 0
1999–2000 Liverpool 0 0
2000–01 Liverpool 8 0
2001–02 Liverpool 0 0
2001–02 Lens 19 0 **19 0**
2002–03 Liverpool 32 0
2003–04 Liverpool 7 0
2004–05 Liverpool 26 0 **73 0**

VIGNAL, Gregory (D) **61 3**
H: 5 9 W: 11 06 b.Montpellier 19-7-81
2000–01 Liverpool 6 0
2001–02 Liverpool 4 0
2002–03 Liverpool 1 0 **11 0**
2002–03 Bastia 15 0 **15 0**
2003–04 *Rennes* 5 0 **5 0**
2004–05 *Rangers* 30 3 **30 3**

WARNOCK, Stephen (M) **75 4**
H: 5 7 W: 11 09 b.Ormskirk 12-12-81
Source: Trainee. *Honours:* England Schools, Youth.
1998–99 Liverpool 0 0
1999–2000 Liverpool 0 0
2000–01 Liverpool 0 0
2001–02 Liverpool 0 0
2002–03 Liverpool 0 0
2002–03 *Bradford C* 12 1 **12 1**
2003–04 Liverpool 0 0
2003–04 *Coventry C* 44 3 **44 3**
2004–05 Liverpool 19 0 **19 0**

WELSH, John (M) **4 0**
H: 5 7 W: 12 02 b.Liverpool 10-1-84
Source: Scholar. *Honours:* England Youth, Under-20, Under-21.
2000–01 Liverpool 0 0
2001–02 Liverpool 0 0
2002–03 Liverpool 0 0
2003–04 Liverpool 1 0
2004–05 Liverpool 3 0 **4 0**

WHITBREAD, Zak (D) **0 0**
H: 6 2 W: 12 07 b.Houston 4-3-84
Honours: USA Under-23.
2002–03 Liverpool 0 0
2003–04 Liverpool 0 0
2004–05 Liverpool 0 0

WILKIE, Ryan (M) **0 0**
b.Glasgow 11-12-85
Source: Trainee.
2002–03 Liverpool 0 0
2003–04 Liverpool 0 0
2004–05 Liverpool 0 0

WILLIS, Paul (M) **0 0**
Source: Trainee.
2003–04 Liverpool 0 0
2004–05 Liverpool 0 0

WRIGHT, Andrew (M) **0 0**
b.Southport 15-1-85
Source: Scholar.
2001–02 Liverpool 0 0
2002–03 Liverpool 0 0
2003–04 Liverpool 0 0
2004–05 Liverpool 0 0

Scholars
Barratt, Paul James; Frayne, James Alexander; Hammill, Adam; Holmes, Jordan; Lancaster, Paul; Platt, Conel James; Smith, Francis Leslie; Woods, Calum Jack

LUTON T (45)

ANDREW, Calvin (F) **8 0**
H: 6 0 W: 12 11 b.Luton 19-12-86
Source: Scholar.
2004–05 Luton T 8 0 **8 0**

BARNETT, Leon (D) **0 0**
H: 6 1 W: 11 03 b.Stevenage 30-11-85
Source: Scholar.
2003–04 Luton T 0 0
2004–05 Luton T 0 0

BAYLISS, Dave (D) **232 9**
H: 6 0 W: 12 11 b.Liverpool 8-6-76
Source: Trainee.
1994–95 Rochdale 1 0
1995–96 Rochdale 28 0
1996–97 Rochdale 24 0
1997–98 Rochdale 29 2
1998–99 Rochdale 25 1
1999–2000 Rochdale 29 3
2000–01 Rochdale 41 3
2001–02 Rochdale 9 0 **186 9**
2001–02 Luton T 18 0
2002–03 Luton T 13 0
2003–04 Luton T 6 0
2004–05 Luton T 0 0 **37 0**
2004–05 *Chester C* 9 0 **9 0**

BECKWITH, Rob (G) **17 0**
H: 6 2 W: 13 05 b.London 12-9-84
Source: Scholar.
2002–03 Luton T 4 0
2003–04 Luton T 13 0
2004–05 Luton T 0 0 **17 0**

BERESFORD, Marlon (G) **407 0**
H: 6 1 W: 13 05 b.Lincoln 2-9-69
Source: Trainee.
1987–88 Sheffield W 0 0
1988–89 Sheffield W 0 0
1989–90 Sheffield W 0 0
1989–90 *Bury* 1 0 **1 0**
1989–90 *Ipswich T* 0 0
1990–91 Sheffield W 0 0
1990–91 *Northampton T* 13 0
1990–91 *Crewe Alex* 3 0 **3 0**
1991–92 Sheffield W 0 0
1991–92 *Northampton T* 15 0 **28 0**
1992–93 Burnley 44 0
1993–94 Burnley 46 0
1994–95 Burnley 40 0
1995–96 Burnley 36 0
1996–97 Burnley 40 0
1997–98 Burnley 34 0
1997–98 Middlesbrough 3 0
1998–99 Middlesbrough 4 0
1999–2000 Middlesbrough 1 0
2000–01 Middlesbrough 1 0
2000–01 *Sheffield W* 4 0 **4 0**
2001–02 Middlesbrough 1 0 **10 0**
2001–02 *Wolverhampton W* 0 0
2001–02 *Burnley* 13 0
2002–03 *York C* 6 0 **6 0**
2002–03 Burnley 34 0
2003–04 Burnley 0 0 **287 0**
2003–04 Bradford C 5 0 **5 0**
2003–04 Luton T 11 0
2003–04 Barnsley 14 0 **14 0**
2004–05 Luton T 38 0 **49 0**

BRILL, Dean (G) 5 0
H: 6 2 W: 12 05 b.Luton 2-12-85
Source: Scholar.

2003–04	Luton T	5	0		
2004–05	Luton T	0	0	**5**	**0**

BRKOVIC, Ahmet (M) 200 28
H: 5 8 W: 11 11 b.Dubrovnik 23-9-74
Source: Dubrovnik.

1999–2000	Leyton Orient	29	5		
2000–01	Leyton Orient	40	3		
2001–02	Leyton Orient	0	0	**69**	**8**
2001–02	Luton T	21	1		
2002–03	Luton T	36	3		
2003–04	Luton T	32	1		
2004–05	Luton T	42	15	**131**	**20**

COYNE, Chris (D) 184 11
H: 6 2 W: 13 12 b.Brisbane 20-12-78
Source: Perth SC. *Honours:* Australia Youth, Under-23.

1995–96	West Ham U	0	0		
1996–97	West Ham U	0	0		
1997–98	West Ham U	0	0		
1998–99	West Ham U	1	0	**1**	**0**
1998–99	*Brentford*	7	0	**7**	**0**
1998–99	*Southend U*	1	0	**1**	**0**
1999–2000	Dundee	2	0		
2000–01	Dundee	18	0	**20**	**0**
2001–02	Luton T	31	3		
2002–03	Luton T	40	1		
2003–04	Luton T	44	2		
2004–05	Luton T	40	5	**155**	**11**

DAVIES, Curtis (D) 50 1
H: 6 2 W: 11 13 b.London 15-3-85
Source: Scholar.

2003–04	Luton T	6	0		
2004–05	Luton T	44	1	**50**	**1**

DAVIS, Sol (D) 232 2
H: 5 8 W: 11 13 b.Cheltenham 4-9-79
Source: Trainee.

1997–98	Swindon T	6	0		
1998–99	Swindon T	25	0		
1999–2000	Swindon T	29	0		
2000–01	Swindon T	36	0		
2001–02	Swindon T	21	0		
2002–03	Swindon T	0	0	**117**	**0**
2002–03	Luton T	34	0		
2003–04	Luton T	36	0		
2004–05	Luton T	45	2	**115**	**2**

DEENEY, David (D) 0 0
H: 5 9 W: 10 06 b.Bulawayo 12-1-87
Source: Scholar.

2003–04	Luton T	0	0		
2004–05	Luton T	0	0		

FEENEY, Warren (F) 145 51
H: 5 10 W: 11 03 b.Belfast 17-1-81
Source: From Trainee. *Honours:* Northern Ireland Schools, Youth, Under-21, 5 full caps.

1997–98	Leeds U	0	0		
1998–99	Leeds U	0	0		
1999–2000	Leeds U	0	0		
2000–01	Leeds U	0	0		
2000–01	*Bournemouth*	10	4		
2001–02	Bournemouth	37	13		
2002–03	Bournemouth	21	7		
2003–04	Bournemouth	40	12	**108**	**36**
2004–05	Stockport Co	31	15	**31**	**15**
2004–05	Luton T	6	0	**6**	**0**

FOLEY, Kevin (M) 74 3
H: 5 10 W: 11 02 b.London 1-11-84
Source: Scholar. *Honours:* Eire Under-21.

2002–03	Luton T	2	0		
2003–04	Luton T	33	1		
2004–05	Luton T	39	2	**74**	**3**

HILLIER, Ian (D) 64 1
H: 6 2 W: 11 13 b.Neath 26-12-79
Source: Trainee. *Honours:* Wales Schools, Youth, Under-21.

1998–99	Tottenham H	0	0		
1999–2000	Tottenham H	0	0		
2000–01	Tottenham H	0	0		
2001–02	Tottenham H	0	0		
2001–02	Luton T	23	1		
2002–03	Luton T	22	0		
2003–04	Luton T	11	0		
2004–05	Luton T	0	0	**56**	**1**
2004–05	*Chester C*	8	0	**8**	**0**

HOLMES, Peter (M) 77 9
H: 5 11 W: 11 09 b.Bishop Auckland 18-11-80
Source: Trainee. *Honours:* England Schools.

1997–98	Sheffield W	0	0		
1998–99	Sheffield W	0	0		
1999–2000	Sheffield W	0	0		
2000–01	Luton T	18	1		
2001–02	Luton T	7	1		
2002–03	Luton T	17	1		
2003–04	Luton T	16	3		
2004–05	Luton T	19	3	**77**	**9**

HOWARD, Steve (F) 397 126
H: 6 3 W: 15 00 b.Durham 10-5-76
Source: Tow Law T.

1995–96	Hartlepool U	39	7		
1996–97	Hartlepool U	32	8		
1997–98	Hartlepool U	43	7		
1998–99	Hartlepool U	28	5	**142**	**27**
1998–99	Northampton T	12	0		
1999–2000	Northampton T	41	10		
2000–01	Northampton T	33	8	**86**	**18**
2000–01	Luton T	12	3		
2001–02	Luton T	42	24		
2002–03	Luton T	41	22		
2003–04	Luton T	34	14		
2004–05	Luton T	40	18	**169**	**81**

JUDGE, Matthew (F) 2 0
H: 6 0 W: 11 07 b.Barking 18-1-85
Source: Scholar. *Honours:* Eire Youth.

2002–03	Luton T	1	0		
2003–04	Luton T	1	0		
2004–05	Luton T	0	0	**2**	**0**

KEANE, Keith (M) 32 1
H: 5 9 W: 11 02 b.Luton 20-11-86
Source: Scholar.

2003–04	Luton T	15	1		
2004–05	Luton T	17	0	**32**	**1**

LEARY, Michael (M) 22 2
H: 6 0 W: 11 11 b.Ealing 17-4-83
Source: Scholar.

2001–02	Luton T	0	0		
2002–03	Luton T	0	0		
2003–04	Luton T	14	2		
2004–05	Luton T	8	0	**22**	**2**

MANSELL, Lee (M) 47 8
H: 5 9 W: 11 00 b.Gloucester 28-10-82
Source: Scholar.

2000–01	Luton T	18	5		
2001–02	Luton T	11	1		
2002–03	Luton T	1	0		
2003–04	Luton T	16	2		
2004–05	Luton T	1	0	**47**	**8**

NEILSON, Alan (D) 193 4
H: 5 11 W: 12 13 b.Wegburg 26-9-72
Source: Trainee. *Honours:* Wales Under-21, B, 5 full caps.

1990–91	Newcastle U	3	0		
1991–92	Newcastle U	16	1		
1992–93	Newcastle U	3	0		
1993–94	Newcastle U	14	0		
1994–95	Newcastle U	6	0	**42**	**1**
1995–96	Southampton	18	0		
1996–97	Southampton	29	0		
1997–98	Southampton	8	0	**55**	**0**
1997–98	Fulham	17	0		
1998–99	Fulham	4	1		
1999–2000	Fulham	5	1		
2000–01	Fulham	3	0		
2001–02	Fulham	0	0	**29**	**2**
2001–02	*Grimsby T*	10	0	**10**	**0**
2001–02	Luton T	8	0		
2002–03	Luton T	26	0		
2003–04	Luton T	14	1		
2004–05	Luton T	9	0	**57**	**1**

NICHOLLS, Kevin (M) 187 28
H: 5 10 W: 12 04 b.Newham 2-1-79
Source: Trainee. *Honours:* England Youth.

1995–96	Charlton Ath	0	0		
1996–97	Charlton Ath	6	1		
1997–98	Charlton Ath	6	0		
1998–99	Charlton Ath	0	0	**12**	**1**
1998–99	*Brighton & HA*	4	1	**4**	**1**
1999–2000	Wigan Ath	8	0		
2000–01	Wigan Ath	20	0	**28**	**0**
2001–02	Luton T	42	7		
2002–03	Luton T	36	5		
2003–04	Luton T	21	2		
2004–05	Luton T	44	12	**143**	**26**

O'LEARY, Stephen (M) 22 2
H: 6 0 W: 11 09 b.Barnet 12-2-85
Source: Scholar. *Honours:* Eire Youth.

2003–04	Luton T	5	1		
2004–05	Luton T	17	1	**22**	**2**

OKAI, Parys (M) 0 0
H: 5 9 W: 11 05 b.London 23-11-84
Source: Scholar.

2003–04	Luton T	0	0		
2004–05	Luton T	0	0		

PERRETT, Russell (D) 179 11
H: 6 1 W: 12 06 b.Barton-on-Sea 18-6-73
Source: AFC Lymington.

1995–96	Portsmouth	9	0		
1996–97	Portsmouth	32	1		
1997–98	Portsmouth	16	1		
1998–99	Portsmouth	15	0	**72**	**2**
1999–2000	Cardiff C	27	1		
2000–01	Cardiff C	2	0	**29**	**1**
2001–02	Luton T	40	3		
2002–03	Luton T	20	2		
2003–04	Luton T	6	2		
2004–05	Luton T	12	1	**78**	**8**

ROBINSON, Steve (M) 366 60
H: 5 9 W: 11 02 b.Lisburn 10-12-74
Source: Trainee. *Honours:* Northern Ireland Schools, Youth, Under-21, B, 5 full caps.

1992–93	Tottenham H	0	0		
1993–94	Tottenham H	2	0		
1994–95	Tottenham H	0	0	**2**	**0**
1994–95	*Leyton Orient*	0	0		
1994–95	Bournemouth	32	5		
1995–96	Bournemouth	41	7		
1996–97	Bournemouth	40	7		
1997–98	Bournemouth	45	10		
1998–99	Bournemouth	42	13		
1999–2000	Bournemouth	40	9	**240**	**51**
2000–01	Preston NE	22	1		
2001–02	Preston NE	2	0	**24**	**1**
2001–02	*Bristol C*	6	1	**6**	**1**
2002–03	Luton T	29	1		
2003–04	Luton T	34	2		
2004–05	Luton T	31	4	**94**	**7**

SEREMET, Dino (G) 13 0
H: 6 4 W: 14 09 b.Slovenia 16-8-80

2002–03	Maribor	6	0	**6**	**0**
2004–05	Luton T	7	0	**7**	**0**

SHOWUNMI, Enoch (F) 61 13
H: 6 3 W: 14 10 b.Kilburn 21-4-82
Source: Willesden Constantine.

2003–04	Luton T	26	7		
2004–05	Luton T	35	6	**61**	**13**

STEVENS, Danny (F) 0 0
b.Enfield 26-11-86
Source: Tottenham H Scholar.

2004–05	Luton T	0	0		

UNDERWOOD, Paul (M) 148 6
H: 5 11 W: 12 11 b.Wimbledon 16-8-73
Source: Enfield.

2001–02	Rushden & D	40	0		
2002–03	Rushden & D	40	1		
2003–04	Rushden & D	30	0	**110**	**1**
2003–04	Luton T	1	0		
2004–05	Luton T	37	5	**38**	**5**

MACCLESFIELD T (46)

ASKEY, John (F) 181 31
H: 6 0 W: 12 01 b.Stoke 4-11-64
Source: Port Vale.

1997–98	Macclesfield T	39	6		
1998–99	Macclesfield T	38	4		
1999–2000	Macclesfield T	40	15		
2000–01	Macclesfield T	37	3		
2001–02	Macclesfield T	18	1		
2002–03	Macclesfield T	9	2		
2003–04	Macclesfield T	0	0		
2004–05	Macclesfield T	0	0	**181**	**31**

BAILEY, Mark (D) **186** **4**
H: 5 10 W: 12 00 b.Stoke 12-8-76
Source: Trainee.

1994–95	Stoke C	0	0		
1995–96	Stoke C	0	0		
1996–97	Stoke C	0	0		
1996–97	Rochdale	15	0		
1997–98	Rochdale	33	0		
1998–99	Rochdale	19	1		
1999–2000	Rochdale	0	0		
2000–01	Rochdale	0	0	**67**	**1**
From Northwich Vic.					
2001–02	Lincoln C	18	0		
2002–03	Lincoln C	45	0		
2003–04	Lincoln C	35	1	**98**	**1**
2004–05	Macclesfield T	21	2	**21**	**2**

BARRAS, Tony (D) **466** **30**
H: 6 3 W: 14 09 b.Billingham 29-3-71
Source: Trainee.

1988–89	Hartlepool U	3	0		
1989–90	Hartlepool U	9	0	**12**	**0**
1990–91	Stockport Co	40	0		
1991–92	Stockport Co	42	5		
1992–93	Stockport Co	14	0		
1993–94	Stockport Co	3	0	**99**	**5**
1993–94	*Rotherham U*	5	1	**5**	**1**
1994–95	York C	31	1		
1995–96	York C	32	3		
1996–97	York C	46	1		
1997–98	York C	38	6		
1998–99	York C	24	0	**171**	**11**
1998–99	Reading	6	1	**6**	**1**
1999–2000	Walsall	24	4		
2000–01	Walsall	36	1		
2001–02	Walsall	26	4		
2002–03	Walsall	19	0	**105**	**9**
2002–03	*Plymouth Arg*	4	0	**4**	**0**
2003–04	Notts Co	40	2	**40**	**2**
2004–05	Macclesfield T	24	1	**24**	**1**

BRACKENRIDGE, Steve (M) **9** **2**
H: 5 8 W: 10 07 b.Rochdale 31-7-84
Source: Scholar.

2002–03	Macclesfield T	2	0		
2003–04	Macclesfield T	7	2		
2004–05	Macclesfield T	0	0	**9**	**2**

BRIGHTWELL, Ian (D) **449** **18**
H: 5 10 W: 12 08 b.Lutterworth 9-4-68
Source: Congleton T. *Honours:* England Schools, Youth, Under-21.

1986–87	Manchester C	16	1		
1987–88	Manchester C	33	5		
1988–89	Manchester C	26	6		
1989–90	Manchester C	28	2		
1990–91	Manchester C	33	0		
1991–92	Manchester C	40	1		
1992–93	Manchester C	21	1		
1993–94	Manchester C	7	0		
1994–95	Manchester C	30	0		
1995–96	Manchester C	29	0		
1996–97	Manchester C	37	2		
1997–98	Manchester C	21	0	**321**	**18**
1998–99	Coventry C	0	0		
1999–2000	Coventry C	0	0		
1999–2000	Walsall	10	0		
2000–01	Walsall	44	0		
2001–02	Walsall	27	0	**81**	**0**
2001–02	Stoke C	4	0	**4**	**0**
2002–03	Port Vale	35	0		
2003–04	Port Vale	2	0	**37**	**0**
2004–05	Macclesfield T	6	0	**6**	**0**

BRISCOE, Michael (D) **14** **0**
H: 6 1 W: 11 07 b.Northampton 4-7-83

2002–03	Coventry C	0	0		
2003–04	Coventry C	0	0		
2004–05	Macclesfield T	14	0	**14**	**0**

CARR, Michael (D) **11** **0**
H: 5 11 W: 11 04 b.Crewe 6-12-83
Source: Scholar.

2002–03	Macclesfield T	4	0		
2003–04	Macclesfield T	7	0		
2004–05	Macclesfield T	0	0	**11**	**0**

CARRAGHER, Matt (D) **362** **1**
H: 5 9 W: 12 12 b.Liverpool 14-1-76
Source: Trainee.

1993–94	Wigan Ath	32	0		
1994–95	Wigan Ath	41	0		
1995–96	Wigan Ath	28	0		
1996–97	Wigan Ath	18	0	**119**	**0**
1997–98	Port Vale	26	0		
1998–99	Port Vale	10	0		
1999–2000	Port Vale	37	1		
2000–01	Port Vale	45	0		
2001–02	Port Vale	41	0		
2002–03	Port Vale	35	0		
2003–04	Port Vale	0	0	**194**	**1**
2003–04	Macclesfield T	18	0		
2004–05	Macclesfield T	31	0	**49**	**0**

DEASY, Tim (G) **0** **0**
H: 6 0 W: 12 06 b.Salford 1-10-85
Source: Scholar.

2004–05	Macclesfield T	0	0		

FETTIS, Alan (G) **340** **2**
H: 6 2 W: 13 10 b.Belfast 1-2-71
Source: From Ards. *Honours:* Northern Ireland Schools, Youth, B, 25 full caps.

1991–92	Hull C	43	0		
1992–93	Hull C	20	0		
1993–94	Hull C	37	0		
1994–95	Hull C	28	2		
1995–96	Hull C	7	0		
1995–96	*WBA*	3	0	**3**	**0**
1996–97	Nottingham F	4	0		
1997–98	Nottingham F	0	0	**4**	**0**
1997–98	Blackburn R	8	0		
1998–99	Blackburn R	2	0		
1999–2000	Blackburn R	1	0	**11**	**0**
1999–2000	*Leicester C*	0	0		
1999–2000	York C	13	0		
2000–01	York C	46	0		
2001–02	York C	45	0		
2002–03	York C	21	0	**125**	**0**
2002–03	Hull C	17	0		
2003–04	Hull C	3	0	**155**	**2**
2003–04	*Sheffield U*	3	0	**3**	**0**
2003–04	*Grimsby T*	11	0	**11**	**0**
2004–05	Macclesfield T	28	0	**28**	**0**

HARSLEY, Paul (M) **294** **23**
H: 5 9 W: 11 10 b.Scunthorpe 29-5-78
Source: Trainee.

1996–97	Grimsby T	0	0		
1997–98	Scunthorpe U	15	1		
1998–99	Scunthorpe U	34	0		
1999–2000	Scunthorpe U	46	3		
2000–01	Scunthorpe U	33	1	**128**	**5**
2001–02	Halifax T	45	11	**45**	**11**
2002–03	Northampton T	45	2		
2003–04	Northampton T	14	0	**59**	**2**
2003–04	Macclesfield T	16	2		
2004–05	Macclesfield T	46	3	**62**	**5**

JONES, Joey (F) **0** **0**
H: 6 0 W: 12 02 b.Liverpool 11-12-85
Source: Everton scholar.

2004–05	Macclesfield T	0	0		

MACKENZIE, Neil (M) **200** **10**
H: 6 2 W: 12 06 b.Birmingham 15-4-76
Source: WBA schoolboy.

1996–97	Stoke C	22	1		
1997–98	Stoke C	12	0		
1998–99	Stoke C	6	0		
1998–99	*Cambridge U*	4	1		
1999–2000	Stoke C	2	0	**42**	**1**
1999–2000	Cambridge U	22	0		
2000–01	Cambridge U	6	0	**32**	**1**
2000–01	Kidderminster H	23	3	**23**	**3**
2001–02	Blackpool	14	1	**14**	**1**
2002–03	Mansfield T	24	1		
2003–04	Mansfield T	32	2		
2004–05	Mansfield T	15	1	**71**	**4**
2004–05	Macclesfield T	18	0	**18**	**0**

McINTYRE, Kevin (M) **35** **0**
H: 5 11 W: 12 00 b.Liverpool 23-12-77
Source: Trainee.

1996–97	Tranmere R	0	0		
1997–98	Tranmere R	2	0		
1998–99	Tranmere R	0	0		
1999–2000	Tranmere R	0	0		
2000–01	Tranmere R	0	0		
2001–02	Tranmere R	0	0	**2**	**0**
2004–05	Chester C	10	0	**10**	**0**
2004–05	Macclesfield T	23	0	**23**	**0**

MILES, John (F) **73** **14**
H: 5 10 W: 12 09 b.Fazackerley 28-9-81
Source: Trainee.

1998–99	Liverpool	0	0		
1999–2000	Liverpool	0	0		
2000–01	Liverpool	0	0		
2001–02	Liverpool	0	0		
2001–02	Stoke C	1	0	**1**	**0**
2002–03	Crewe Alex	5	1	**5**	**1**
2002–03	Macclesfield T	8	4		
2003–04	Macclesfield T	29	6		
2004–05	Macclesfield T	30	3	**67**	**13**

MISKELLY, David (G) **20** **0**
H: 6 0 W: 12 02 b.Ards 3-9-79
Source: Trainee. *Honours:* Northern Ireland Youth, Under-21.

1997–98	Oldham Ath	0	0		
1998–99	Oldham Ath	1	0		
1999–2000	Oldham Ath	2	0		
2000–01	Oldham Ath	2	0		
2001–02	Oldham Ath	4	0		
2002–03	Oldham Ath	11	0	**20**	**0**
2003–04	Macclesfield T	0	0		
2004–05	Macclesfield T	0	0		

MORGAN, Neil (M) **0** **0**
H: 5 11 W: 10 10 b.Coventry 6-2-85
Source: Nottingham F scholar.

2004–05	Macclesfield T	0	0		

MORLEY, Dave (D) **191** **8**
H: 6 3 W: 13 08 b.St Helens 25-9-77
Source: Trainee.

1995–96	Manchester C	0	0		
1996–97	Manchester C	0	0		
1997–98	Manchester C	3	1		
1997–98	*Ayr U*	4	0	**4**	**0**
1998–99	Manchester C	0	0	**3**	**1**
1998–99	Southend U	27	0		
1999–2000	Southend U	32	0		
2000–01	Southend U	17	0	**76**	**0**
2000–01	Carlisle U	23	1		
2001–02	Carlisle U	18	0	**41**	**1**
2001–02	Oxford U	18	3	**18**	**3**
2003–04	Doncaster R	21	1		
2004–05	Doncaster R	9	0	**30**	**1**
2004–05	Macclesfield T	19	2	**19**	**2**

OLSEN, James (D) **6** **0**
H: 5 10 W: 12 00 b.Bootle 23-10-81
Source: Liverpool scholar.

2000–01	Tranmere R	1	0		
2001–02	Tranmere R	0	0		
2002–03	Tranmere R	3	0		
2003–04	Tranmere R	0	0	**4**	**0**
2003–04	Macclesfield T	2	0		
2004–05	Macclesfield T	0	0	**2**	**0**

PARKIN, Jonathan (F) **139** **37**
H: 6 4 W: 13 12 b.Barnsley 30-12-81
Source: Scholarship.

1998–99	Barnsley	2	0		
1999–2000	Barnsley	0	0		
2000–01	Barnsley	4	0		
2001–02	Barnsley	4	0	**10**	**0**
2001–02	*Hartlepool U*	1	0	**1**	**0**
2001–02	York C	18	2		
2002–03	York C	41	10		
2003–04	York C	15	2	**74**	**14**
2003–04	Macclesfield T	12	1		
2004–05	Macclesfield T	42	22	**54**	**23**

PAYNE, Steve (D) **241** **10**
H: 6 0 W: 13 03 b.Castleford 1-8-75
Source: Trainee.

1993–94	Huddersfield T	0	0		
1994–95	Huddersfield T	0	0		
1995–96	Huddersfield T	0	0		
1996–97	Huddersfield T	0	0		
1997–98	Macclesfield T	39	0		
1998–99	Macclesfield T	38	2		
1999–2000	Chesterfield	18	3		
2000–01	Chesterfield	35	1		
2001–02	Chesterfield	44	1		
2002–03	Chesterfield	34	2		
2003–04	Chesterfield	20	1	**151**	**8**
2003–04	Macclesfield T	13	0		
2004–05	Macclesfield T	0	0	**90**	**2**

POTTER, Graham (D) **315 16**
H: 6 1 W: 12 03 b.Solihull 20-5-75
Source: Trainee. *Honours:* England Youth, Under-21.
1992–93 Birmingham C 18 2
1993–94 Birmingham C 7 0 **25 2**
1993–94 *Wycombe W* 3 0 **3 0**
1993–94 Stoke C 3 0
1994–95 Stoke C 1 0
1995–96 Stoke C 41 1 **45 1**
1996–97 Southampton 8 0 **8 0**
1996–97 WBA 6 0
1997–98 WBA 5 0
1997–98 *Northampton T* 4 0 **4 0**
1998–99 WBA 22 0
1999–2000 WBA 10 0 **43 0**
1999–2000 *Reading* 4 0 **4 0**
2000–01 York C 38 2
2001–02 York C 37 2
2002–03 York C 39 1 **114 5**
2003–04 Boston U 12 0 **12 0**
2003–04 Macclesfield T 16 2
2004–05 Macclesfield T 41 6 **57 8**

ROONEY, Tommy (F) **1 0**
H: 6 0 W: 12 05 b.Liverpool 30-12-84
Source: Tranmere R.
2004–05 Macclesfield T 1 0 **1 0**

ROSS, Neil (F) **28 2**
H: 6 1 W: 12 02 b.West Bromwich 10-8-82
Source: Birmingham C Trainee, Leeds U Trainee.
1999–2000 Leeds U 0 0
1999–2000 Stockport Co 2 0
2000–01 Stockport Co 0 0
2001–02 *Bristol R* 5 0 **5 0**
2001–02 Stockport Co 3 1
2002–03 Stockport Co 4 1 **9 2**
2002–03 Macclesfield T 8 0
2003–04 Macclesfield T 6 0
2004–05 Macclesfield T 0 0 **14 0**

SMART, Andrew (D) **0 0**
H: 6 1 W: 14 00 b.Wythenshawe 17-3-86
Source: Scholar.
2004–05 Macclesfield T 0 0

SWADI-FAYADH, Jassim (M) **1 0**
H: 5 10 W: 11 02 b.Baghdad 1-7-75
Honours: Iraq full caps.
2004–05 Macclesfield T 1 0 **1 0**

SWAILES, Danny (D) **181 13**
H: 6 3 W: 13 07 b.Bolton 1-4-79
Source: Trainee.
1997–98 Bury 0 0
1998–99 Bury 0 0
1999–2000 Bury 24 3
2000–01 Bury 11 0
2001–02 Bury 28 1
2002–03 Bury 39 3
2003–04 Bury 42 5
2004–05 Bury 20 1 **164 13**
2004–05 Macclesfield T 17 0 **17 0**

TEAGUE, Andrew (D) **5 0**
H: 6 2 W: 12 00 b.Preston 5-2-86
Source: Scholar.
2004–05 Macclesfield T 5 0 **5 0**

TIPTON, Matt (F) **243 56**
H: 5 10 W: 11 02 b.Bangor 29-6-80
Source: From Trainee. *Honours:* Wales Youth, Under-21.
1997–98 Oldham Ath 3 0
1998–99 Oldham Ath 28 2
1999–2000 Oldham Ath 29 3
2000–01 Oldham Ath 30 5
2001–02 Oldham Ath 22 5 **112 15**
2001–02 Macclesfield T 13 3
2002–03 Macclesfield T 36 10
2003–04 Macclesfield T 38 16
2004–05 Macclesfield T 44 12 **131 41**

WELCH, Michael (D) **114 5**
H: 6 3 W: 11 12 b.Winsford 11-1-82
Source: Barnsley Scholar.
2001–02 Macclesfield T 6 0
2002–03 Macclesfield T 39 3
2003–04 Macclesfield T 38 0
2004–05 Macclesfield T 31 2 **114 5**

WHITAKER, Danny (M) **129 19**
H: 5 10 W: 11 02 b.Manchester 14-11-80
Source: Wilmslow Sports.
2000–01 Macclesfield T 0 0
2001–02 Macclesfield T 16 2
2002–03 Macclesfield T 41 10
2003–04 Macclesfield T 36 5
2004–05 Macclesfield T 36 2 **129 19**

WILSON, Steve (G) **315 0**
H: 6 0 W: 11 02 b.Hull 24-4-74
Source: Trainee.
1990–91 Hull C 2 0
1991–92 Hull C 3 0
1992–93 Hull C 26 0
1993–94 Hull C 9 0
1994–95 Hull C 20 0
1995–96 Hull C 19 0
1996–97 Hull C 15 0
1997–98 Hull C 37 0
1998–99 Hull C 23 0
1999–2000 Hull C 27 0
2000–01 Hull C 0 0 **181 0**
2000–01 *Macclesfield T* 1 0
2001–02 Macclesfield T 38 0
2002–03 Macclesfield T 44 0
2003–04 Macclesfield T 32 0
2004–05 Macclesfield T 19 0 **134 0**

MANCHESTER C (47)

ANELKA, Nicolas (F) **242 77**
H: 6 1 W: 13 03 b.Versailles 14-3-79
Honours: France Youth, Under-21, 28 full caps, 6 goals.
1995–96 Paris St Germain 2 0
1996–97 Paris St Germain 8 1
1996–97 Arsenal 4 0
1997–98 Arsenal 26 6
1998–99 Arsenal 35 17 **65 23**
1999–2000 Real Madrid 19 2 **19 2**
2000–01 Paris St Germain 27 8
2001–02 Paris St Germain 12 2 **49 11**
2001–02 Liverpool 20 4 **20 4**
2002–03 Manchester C 38 14
2003–04 Manchester C 32 16
2004–05 Manchester C 19 7 **89 37**

BARTON, Joey (M) **66 3**
H: 5 11 W: 11 09 b.Huyton 2-9-82
Source: Scholar. *Honours:* England Under-21.
2001–02 Manchester C 0 0
2002–03 Manchester C 7 1
2003–04 Manchester C 28 1
2004–05 Manchester C 31 1 **66 3**

BENNETT, Ian (M) **0 0**
b.Rochdale 24-2-86
Source: Trainee.
2003–04 Manchester C 0 0
2004–05 Manchester C 0 0

BERMINGHAM, Karl (M) **2 0**
H: 5 10 W: 12 07 b.Dublin 6-10-85
Source: Scholar. *Honours:* Eire Youth.
2002–03 Manchester C 0 0
2003–04 Manchester C 0 0
2004–05 Manchester C 0 0
2004–05 *Lincoln C* 2 0 **2 0**

BISCHOFF, Mikkel (D) **22 1**
H: 6 3 W: 13 11 b.Denmark 3-2-82
Honours: Denmark Under-21.
2001–02 AB Copenhagen 10 0 **10 0**
2002–03 Manchester C 1 0
2003–04 Manchester C 0 0
2004–05 Manchester C 0 0 **1 0**
2004–05 *Wolverhampton W* 11 1 **11 1**

BOSVELT, Paul (M) **434 81**
H: 6 0 W: 13 00 b.Doetinchem 26-3-70
Honours: Holland 24 full caps.
1989–90 Go Ahead 32 2
1990–91 Go Ahead 26 8
1991–92 Go Ahead 27 4
1992–93 Go Ahead 22 4
1993–94 Go Ahead 32 9 **139 27**
1994–95 Twente 33 7
1995–96 Twente 32 7
1996–97 Twente 31 7 **96 21**
1997–98 Feyenoord 30 4
1998–99 Feyenoord 33 4
1999–2000 Feyenoord 32 8
2000–01 Feyenoord 20 8
2001–02 Feyenoord 31 7 **146 31**
2003–04 Manchester C 25 0
2004–05 Manchester C 28 2 **53 2**

COLLINS, Paul (D) **0 0**
b.Droylsden
Source: Scholar.
2004–05 Manchester C 0 0

CROFT, Lee (F) **19 0**
H: 5 9 W: 13 01 b.Wigan 21-6-85
Source: From Scholar. *Honours:* England Youth, Under-20, Under-21.
2002–03 Manchester C 0 0
2003–04 Manchester C 0 0
2004–05 Manchester C 7 0 **7 0**
2004–05 *Oldham Ath* 12 0 **12 0**

D'LARYEA, Jonathan (M) **0 0**
H: 5 10 W: 12 02 b.Manchester 3-9-85
Source: Trainee.
2003–04 Manchester C 0 0
2004–05 Manchester C 0 0

D'LARYEA, Nathan (D) **0 0**
b.Manchester 3-9-85
Source: Trainee.
2003–04 Manchester C 0 0
2004–05 Manchester C 0 0

DE VLIEGER, Geert (G) **0 0**
H: 6 2 W: 14 00 b.Dendermonde 16-10-71
2004–05 Manchester C 0 0

DISTIN, Sylvain (D) **225 7**
H: 6 3 W: 14 08 b.Bagnolet 16-12-77
1998–99 Tours 26 3 **26 3**
1999–2000 Gueugnon 33 1 **33 1**
2000–01 Paris St Germain 28 0 **28 0**
2001–02 Newcastle U 28 0 **28 0**
2002–03 Manchester C 34 0
2003–04 Manchester C 38 2
2004–05 Manchester C 38 1 **110 3**

DUNNE, Richard (D) **217 3**
H: 6 2 W: 15 12 b.Dublin 21-9-79
Source: Trainee. *Honours:* Eire Schools, Youth, Under-21, B, 23 full caps, 4 goals.
1996–97 Everton 7 0
1997–98 Everton 3 0
1998–99 Everton 16 0
1999–2000 Everton 31 0
2000–01 Everton 3 0 **60 0**
2000–01 Manchester C 25 0
2001–02 Manchester C 43 1
2002–03 Manchester C 25 0
2003–04 Manchester C 29 0
2004–05 Manchester C 35 2 **157 3**

ELLEGAARD, Kevin Stuhr (G) **6 0**
H: 6 5 W: 14 06 b.Charlottenlund 23-5-83
Source: Farum. *Honours:* Denmark Youth, Under-21.
2001–02 Manchester C 0 0
2002–03 Manchester C 0 0
2003–04 Manchester C 4 0
2004–05 Manchester C 0 0 **4 0**
2004–05 *Blackpool* 2 0 **2 0**

FLOOD, Willo (M) **15 1**
H: 5 6 W: 9 11 b.Dublin 10-4-85
Source: Trainee. *Honours:* Eire Youth, Under-21.
2001–02 Manchester C 0 0
2002–03 Manchester C 0 0
2003–04 Manchester C 0 0
2003–04 *Rochdale* 6 0 **6 0**
2004–05 Manchester C 9 1 **9 1**

FOWLER, Robbie (F) **342 154**
H: 5 10 W: 12 05 b.Liverpool 9-4-75
Source: Trainee. *Honours:* England Youth, B, Under-21, 26 full caps, 7 goals.
1991–92 Liverpool 0 0
1992–93 Liverpool 0 0
1993–94 Liverpool 28 12
1994–95 Liverpool 42 25
1995–96 Liverpool 38 28
1996–97 Liverpool 32 18
1997–98 Liverpool 20 9

1998–99 Liverpool 25 14
1999–2000 Liverpool 14 3
2000–01 Liverpool 27 8
2001–02 Liverpool 10 3 **236 120**
2001–02 Leeds U 22 12
2002–03 Leeds U 8 2 **30 14**
2002–03 Manchester C 13 2
2003–04 Manchester C 31 7
2004–05 Manchester C 32 11 **76 20**

JAMES, David (G) 516 0
H: 6 5 W: 14 02 b.Welwyn 1-8-70
Source: Trainee. *Honours:* England Youth, Under-21, B, 32 full caps.
1988–89 Watford 0 0
1989–90 Watford 0 0
1990–91 Watford 46 0
1991–92 Watford 43 0 **89 0**
1992–93 Liverpool 29 0
1993–94 Liverpool 14 0
1994–95 Liverpool 42 0
1995–96 Liverpool 38 0
1996–97 Liverpool 38 0
1997–98 Liverpool 27 0
1998–99 Liverpool 26 0 **214 0**
1999–2000 Aston Villa 29 0
2000–01 Aston Villa 38 0 **67 0**
2001–02 West Ham U 26 0
2002–03 West Ham U 38 0
2003–04 West Ham U 27 0 **91 0**
2003–04 Manchester C 17 0
2004–05 Manchester C 38 0 **55 0**

JIHAI, Sun (D) 97 3
H: 5 9 W: 12 02 b.Dalian 30-9-77
Source: Dalian Wanda. *Honours:* China 62 full caps, 8 goals.
1998–99 Crystal Palace 23 0 **23 0**
From Dalian Wanda.
2001–02 Manchester C 7 0
2002–03 Manchester C 28 2
2003–04 Manchester C 33 1
2004–05 Manchester C 6 0 **74 3**

JORDAN, Stephen (D) 33 0
H: 6 1 W: 11 13 b.Warrington 6-3-82
Source: Scholarship.
1998–99 Manchester C 0 0
1999–2000 Manchester C 0 0
2000–01 Manchester C 0 0
2001–02 Manchester C 0 0
2002–03 Manchester C 1 0
2002–03 *Cambridge U* 11 0 **11 0**
2003–04 Manchester C 2 0
2004–05 Manchester C 19 0 **22 0**

LAIRD, Marc (M) 0 0
b.Edinburgh 23-1-86
Source: Trainee.
2003–04 Manchester C 0 0
2004–05 Manchester C 0 0

MACKEN, Jon (F) 235 70
H: 5 11 W: 13 13 b.Manchester 7-9-77
Source: Trainee. *Honours:* England Youth. Eire 1 full cap.
1996–97 Manchester U 0 0
1997–98 Preston NE 29 6
1998–99 Preston NE 42 8
1999–2000 Preston NE 44 22
2000–01 Preston NE 38 19
2001–02 Preston NE 31 8 **184 63**
2001–02 Manchester C 8 5
2002–03 Manchester C 5 0
2003–04 Manchester C 15 1
2004–05 Manchester C 23 1 **51 7**

MATTHEWS, James (M) 0 0
b.Dublin 2-2-85
Source: Scholar.
2002–03 Manchester C 0 0
2003–04 Manchester C 0 0
2004–05 Manchester C 0 0

McMANAMAN, Steve (M) 399 54
H: 6 1 W: 11 11 b.Liverpool 11-2-72
Source: School. *Honours:* England Youth, Under-21, 37 full caps, 3 goals.
1989–90 Liverpool 0 0
1990–91 Liverpool 2 0
1991–92 Liverpool 30 5
1992–93 Liverpool 31 4
1993–94 Liverpool 30 2
1994–95 Liverpool 40 7
1995–96 Liverpool 38 6
1996–97 Liverpool 37 7
1997–98 Liverpool 36 11
1998–99 Liverpool 28 4 **272 46**
1999–2000 Real Madrid 28 3
2000–01 Real Madrid 26 2
2001–02 Real Madrid 23 2
2002–03 Real Madrid 15 1 **92 8**
2003–04 Manchester C 22 0
2004–05 Manchester C 13 0 **35 0**

MILLS, Danny (D) 272 6
H: 5 11 W: 12 06 b.Norwich 18-5-77
Source: Trainee. *Honours:* England Youth, Under-21, 19 full caps.
1994–95 Norwich C 0 0
1995–96 Norwich C 14 0
1996–97 Norwich C 32 0
1997–98 Norwich C 20 0 **66 0**
1997–98 Charlton Ath 9 1
1998–99 Charlton Ath 36 2 **45 3**
1999–2000 Leeds U 17 1
2000–01 Leeds U 23 0
2001–02 Leeds U 28 1
2002–03 Leeds U 33 1
2003–04 Leeds U 0 0 **101 3**
2003–04 *Middlesbrough* 28 0 **28 0**
2004–05 Manchester C 32 0 **32 0**

MURPHY, Paul (D) 0 0
b.Wexford 12-4-85
Source: Scholar.
2002–03 Manchester C 0 0
2003–04 Manchester C 0 0
2004–05 Manchester C 0 0

MUSAMPA, Kiki (F) 218 38
H: 5 11 W: 12 00 b.Kinshasa 20-7-77
Honours: Holland Under-21.
1994–95 Ajax 1 0
1995–96 Ajax 17 1
1996–97 Ajax 24 5 **42 6**
1997–98 Bordeaux 16 4
1998–99 Bordeaux 17 1 **33 5**
1999–2000 Malaga 13 2
2000–01 Malaga 11 3
2001–02 Malaga 37 9
2002–03 Malaga 35 8 **96 22**
2003–04 Atletico Madrid 26 2
2004–05 Atletico Madrid 7 0 **33 2**
2004–05 Manchester C 14 3 **14 3**

NEGOUAI, Christian (M) 53 7
H: 6 4 W: 14 01 b.Fort-de-France 20-1-75
1999–2000 Charleroi 9 0
2000–01 Charleroi 26 4
2001–02 Charleroi 10 2 **45 6**
2001–02 Manchester C 5 1
2002–03 Manchester C 0 0
2003–04 Manchester C 1 0
2004–05 Manchester C 1 0 **7 1**
2004–05 *Coventry C* 1 0 **1 0**

ONUOHA, Nedum (D) 17 0
H: 6 2 W: 12 04 b.Warri 12-11-86
Source: Scholar. *Honours:* England Youth, Under-20.
2004–05 Manchester C 17 0 **17 0**

PEARSON, Sean (M) 0 0
b.Manchester 7-3-85
2002–03 Manchester C 0 0
2003–04 Manchester C 0 0
2004–05 Manchester C 0 0

REYNA, Claudio (M) 184 20
H: 5 9 W: 11 08 b.New Jersey 20-7-73
Source: Union County SC, Univ Virginia. *Honours:* USA 106 full caps, 8 goals.
1996–97 Leverkusen 5 0 **5 0**
1997–98 Wolfsburg 28 4
1998–99 Wolfsburg 20 2 **48 6**
1998–99 Rangers 6 0
1999–2000 Rangers 29 5
2000–01 Rangers 18 2
2001–02 Rangers 10 1 **63 8**
2001–02 Sunderland 17 3
2002–03 Sunderland 11 0
2003–04 Sunderland 0 0 **28 3**
2003–04 Manchester C 23 1
2004–05 Manchester C 17 2 **40 3**

SCHMEICHEL, Kasper (G) 0 0
H: 6 0 W: 12 00 b.Denmark 5-11-86
Source: Scholar.
2003–04 Manchester C 0 0
2004–05 Manchester C 0 0

SIBIERSKI, Antoine (M) 328 70
H: 6 2 W: 12 04 b.Lille 5-8-74
Honours: France Youth.
1992–93 Lille 6 0
1993–94 Lille 22 1
1994–95 Lille 36 7
1995–96 Lille 33 9 **97 17**
1996–97 Auxerre 30 7
1997–98 Auxerre 12 1 **42 8**
1998–99 Nantes 4 0
1999–2000 Nantes 28 13 **32 13**
2000–01 Lens 27 5
2001–02 Lens 25 6
2002–03 Lens 37 12 **89 23**
2003–04 Manchester C 33 5
2004–05 Manchester C 35 4 **68 9**

SINCLAIR, Trevor (M) 489 70
H: 5 9 W: 13 05 b.Dulwich 2-3-73
Source: Trainee. *Honours:* England Youth, Under-21, B, 12 full caps.
1989–90 Blackpool 9 0
1990–91 Blackpool 31 1
1991–92 Blackpool 27 3
1992–93 Blackpool 45 11 **112 15**
1993–94 QPR 32 4
1994–95 QPR 33 4
1995–96 QPR 37 2
1996–97 QPR 39 3
1997–98 QPR 26 3 **167 16**
1997–98 West Ham U 14 7
1998–99 West Ham U 36 7
1999–2000 West Ham U 36 7
2000–01 West Ham U 19 3
2001–02 West Ham U 34 5
2002–03 West Ham U 38 8 **177 37**
2003–04 Manchester C 29 1
2004–05 Manchester C 4 1 **33 2**

SOMMEIL, David (D) 311 5
H: 5 10 W: 12 12 b.Ponte-a-Pitre 10-8-74
Honours: France B.
1993–94 Caen 1 0
1994–95 Caen 25 0
1995–96 Caen 30 0
1996–97 Caen 25 0
1997–98 Caen 38 1 **119 1**
1998–99 Rennes 33 0
1999–2000 Rennes 30 1 **63 1**
2000–01 Bordeaux 29 0
2001–02 Bordeaux 31 0
2002–03 Bordeaux 17 1 **77 1**
2002–03 Manchester C 14 1
2003–04 Manchester C 18 1
2003–04 *Marseille* 19 0 **19 0**
2004–05 Manchester C 1 0 **33 2**

TANDY, Jamie (M) 0 0
b.Manchester 1-9-84
Source: Scholar.
2002–03 Manchester C 0 0
2003–04 Manchester C 0 0
2004–05 Manchester C 0 0

THATCHER, Ben (D) 259 2
H: 5 10 W: 12 07 b.Swindon 30-11-75
Source: Trainee. *Honours:* England Youth, Under-21, Wales 7 full caps.
1992–93 Millwall 0 0
1993–94 Millwall 8 0
1994–95 Millwall 40 1
1995–96 Millwall 42 0 **90 1**
1996–97 Wimbledon 9 0
1997–98 Wimbledon 26 0
1998–99 Wimbledon 31 0
1999–2000 Wimbledon 20 0 **86 0**
2000–01 Tottenham H 12 0
2001–02 Tottenham H 12 0
2002–03 Tottenham H 12 0 **36 0**
2003–04 Leicester C 29 1 **29 1**
2004–05 Manchester C 18 0 **18 0**

TIMMS, Ashley (M) **0 0**
b.Manchester 6-11-85
Source: Scholar.

2002–03	Manchester C	0	0		
2003–04	Manchester C	0	0		
2004–05	Manchester C	0	0		

VUOSO, Vicente (D) **65 8**
H: 5 9 W: 12 05 b.Mar del Plata 3-11-81

2000–01	Independiente	29	7		
2001–02	Independiente	36	1	**65**	**8**
2002–03	Manchester C	0	0		
2003–04	Manchester C	0	0		
2004–05	Manchester C	0	0		

WATERREUS, Ronald (G) **350 0**
H: 6 1 W: 13 04 b.Lemiers 25-8-70
Honours: Holland 7 full caps.

1992–93	Roda JC	31	0		
1993–94	Roda JC	34	0	**65**	**0**
1994–95	PSV Eindhoven	20	0		
1995–96	PSV Eindhoven	33	0		
1996–97	PSV Eindhoven	31	0		
1997–98	PSV Eindhoven	30	0		
1998–99	PSV Eindhoven	32	0		
1999–2000	PSV Eindhoven	30	0		
2000–01	PSV Eindhoven	31	0		
2001–02	PSV Eindhoven	18	0		
2002–03	PSV Eindhoven	27	0		
2003–04	PSV Eindhoven	33	0	**285**	**0**
2004–05	Manchester C	0	0		

WEAVER, Nick (G) **148 0**
H: 6 4 W: 14 07 b.Sheffield 2-3-79
Source: Trainee. *Honours:* England Under-21.

1995–96	Mansfield T	1	0		
1996–97	Mansfield T	0	0	**1**	**0**
1996–97	Manchester C	0	0		
1997–98	Manchester C	0	0		
1998–99	Manchester C	45	0		
1999–2000	Manchester C	45	0		
2000–01	Manchester C	31	0		
2001–02	Manchester C	25	0		
2002–03	Manchester C	0	0		
2003–04	Manchester C	0	0		
2004–05	Manchester C	1	0	**147**	**0**

WRIGHT-PHILLIPS, Bradley (M) **14 1**
H: 5 8 W: 11 00 b.Lewisham 12-3-85
Source: Scholar. *Honours:* England Youth, Under-20.

2002–03	Manchester C	0	0		
2003–04	Manchester C	0	0		
2004–05	Manchester C	14	1	**14**	**1**

WRIGHT-PHILLIPS, Shaun (M) **153 26**
H: 5 5 W: 9 12 b.Greenwich 25-10-81
Source: Scholar. *Honours:* England Under-21, 4 full caps, 1 goal.

1998–99	Manchester C	0	0		
1999–2000	Manchester C	4	0		
2000–01	Manchester C	15	0		
2001–02	Manchester C	35	8		
2002–03	Manchester C	31	1		
2003–04	Manchester C	34	7		
2004–05	Manchester C	34	10	**153**	**26**

Scholars
Etuhu, Calvin; Grimes, Ashley James; Johnson, Michael; Logan, Shaleum; Matthewson, Lawrence; McGinlay, Michael Liam; Richards, Micah; Russell, Matthew Bradley; Wallwork, Kyle David; Ward, Michael Vincent; Williams, Ashley David; Williamson, Samuel James

MANCHESTER U (48)

BARDSLEY, Phillip (D) **0 0**
H: 5 11 W: 11 08 b.Salford 28-6-85
Source: Trainee.

2003–04	Manchester U	0	0		
2004–05	Manchester U	0	0		

BELLION, David (F) **44 4**
H: 6 0 W: 11 09 b.Sevres 27-11-82
Source: Cannes. *Honours:* France Under-21.

2001–02	Sunderland	9	0		
2002–03	Sunderland	11	1	**20**	**1**
2003–04	Manchester U	14	2		
2004–05	Manchester U	10	1	**24**	**3**

BERNABEU, Gerard (M) **0 0**
Source: Scholar.

2004–05	Manchester U	0	0		

BROWN, Wes (D) **121 1**
H: 6 1 W: 13 11 b.Manchester 13-10-79
Source: From Trainee. *Honours:* England Schools, Youth, Under-21, 8 full caps.

1996–97	Manchester U	0	0		
1997–98	Manchester U	2	0		
1998–99	Manchester U	14	0		
1999–2000	Manchester U	0	0		
2000–01	Manchester U	28	0		
2001–02	Manchester U	17	0		
2002–03	Manchester U	22	0		
2003–04	Manchester U	17	0		
2004–05	Manchester U	21	1	**121**	**1**

CALLISTE, Ramon (F) **0 0**
H: 5 10 W: 11 06 b.Cardiff 16-12-85
Source: Trainee. *Honours:* Wales Under-21.

2003–04	Manchester U	0	0		
2004–05	Manchester U	0	0		

CARROLL, Roy (G) **230 0**
H: 6 2 W: 13 12 b.Enniskillen 30-9-77
Source: Trainee. *Honours:* Northern Ireland Youth, Under-21, 17 full caps.

1995–96	Hull C	23	0		
1996–97	Hull C	23	0	**46**	**0**
1996–97	Wigan Ath	0	0		
1997–98	Wigan Ath	29	0		
1998–99	Wigan Ath	43	0		
1999–2000	Wigan Ath	34	0		
2000–01	Wigan Ath	29	0	**135**	**0**
2001–02	Manchester U	7	0		
2002–03	Manchester U	10	0		
2003–04	Manchester U	6	0		
2004–05	Manchester U	26	0	**49**	**0**

COLLETT, Ben (D) **0 0**
H: 5 8 W: 10 00 b.Bury 11-9-84
Source: Trainee.

2003–04	Manchester U	0	0		
2004–05	Manchester U	0	0		

COOPER, Kenny (F) **7 3**
H: 6 3 W: 14 01 b.Baltimore 21-10-84

2003–04	Manchester U	0	0		
2004–05	Manchester U	0	0		
2004–05	*Oldham Ath*	7	3	**7**	**3**

DJORDJIC, Bojan (F) **25 0**
H: 5 10 W: 11 01 b.Belgrade 6-2-82

1998–99	Manchester U	0	0		
1999–2000	Manchester U	0	0		
2000–01	Manchester U	1	0		
2001–02	Manchester U	0	0		
2001–02	*Sheffield W*	5	0	**5**	**0**
2002–03	Manchester U	0	0		
2003–04	*Red Star Belgrade*	19	0	**19**	**0**
2004–05	Manchester U	0	0	**1**	**0**

EAGLES, Chris (M) **13 1**
H: 6 0 W: 10 08 b.Hemel Hempstead 19-11-85
Source: Trainee. *Honours:* England Youth.

2003–04	Manchester U	0	0		
2004–05	Manchester U	0	0		
2004–05	*Watford*	13	1	**13**	**1**

EBANKS-BLAKE, Sylvan (F) **0 0**
H: 5 10 W: 13 04 b.Cambridge 29-3-86
Source: Scholar.

2004–05	Manchester U	0	0		

ECKERSLEY, Adam (D) **0 0**
b.Manchester 7-12-85
Source: Scholar.

2004–05	Manchester U	0	0		

EVANS, Jonny (D) **0 0**
b.Belfast 3-1-87
Source: From Scholar. *Honours:* Northern Ireland Schools, Youth.

2004–05	Manchester U	0	0		

FERDINAND, Rio (D) **270 4**
H: 6 2 W: 13 12 b.Peckham 7-11-78
Source: Trainee. *Honours:* England Youth, Under-21, 38 full caps, 1 goal.

1995–96	West Ham U	1	0		
1996–97	West Ham U	15	2		
1996–97	*Bournemouth*	10	0	**10**	**0**
1997–98	West Ham U	35	0		
1998–99	West Ham U	31	0		
1999–2000	West Ham U	33	0		
2000–01	West Ham U	12	0	**127**	**2**
2000–01	Leeds U	23	2		
2001–02	Leeds U	31	0	**54**	**2**
2002–03	Manchester U	28	0		
2003–04	Manchester U	20	0		
2004–05	Manchester U	31	0	**79**	**0**

FLETCHER, Darren (M) **40 3**
H: 6 0 W: 13 01 b.Edinburgh 1-2-84
Source: Scholar. *Honours:* Scotland Under-21, B, 15 full caps, 2 goals.

2000–01	Manchester U	0	0		
2001–02	Manchester U	0	0		
2002–03	Manchester U	0	0		
2003–04	Manchester U	22	0		
2004–05	Manchester U	18	3	**40**	**3**

FORLAN, Diego (F) **140 46**
H: 5 8 W: 11 11 b.Montevideo 19-5-79
Honours: Uruguay 27 full caps, 10 goals.

1998–99	Independiente	2	0		
1999–2000	Independiente	24	7		
2000–01	Independiente	36	18		
2001–02	Independiente	15	11	**77**	**36**
2001–02	Manchester U	13	0		
2002–03	Manchester U	25	6		
2003–04	Manchester U	24	4		
2004–05	Manchester U	1	0	**63**	**10**

FORTUNE, Quinton (F) **172 13**
H: 5 9 W: 11 09 b.Cape Town 21-5-77
Source: Kaizer Chiefs, Tottenham H schoolboy. *Honours:* South Africa Under-23, 47 full caps, 2 goals.

1995–96	Mallorca	8	1	**8**	**1**
1995–96	Atletico Madrid	3	0		
1996–97	Atletico Madrid B	30	2		
1996–97	Atletico Madrid	2	0		
1997–98	Atletico Madrid B	31	1		
1997–98	Atletico Madrid	0	0		
1998–99	Atletico Madrid	2	0		
1998–99	Atletico Madrid B	20	4	**7**	**0**
1999–2000	Manchester U	6	2		
2000–01	Manchester U	7	2		
2001–02	Manchester U	14	1		
2002–03	Manchester U	9	0		
2003–04	Manchester U	23	0		
2004–05	Manchester U	17	0	**76**	**5**

FOX, David (M) **4 1**
H: 5 9 W: 12 02 b.Leek 13-12-83
Source: Scholar. *Honours:* England Youth, Under-20.

2000–01	Manchester U	0	0		
2001–02	Manchester U	0	0		
2002–03	Manchester U	0	0		
2003–04	Manchester U	0	0		
2004–05	Manchester U	0	0		
2004–05	*Shrewsbury T*	4	1	**4**	**1**

GIGGS, Ryan (F) **447 91**
H: 5 11 W: 11 00 b.Cardiff 29-11-73
Source: School. *Honours:* England Schools, Wales Youth, Under-21, 51 full caps, 8 goals.

1990–91	Manchester U	2	1		
1991–92	Manchester U	38	4		
1992–93	Manchester U	41	9		
1993–94	Manchester U	38	13		
1994–95	Manchester U	29	1		
1995–96	Manchester U	33	11		
1996–97	Manchester U	26	3		
1997–98	Manchester U	29	8		
1998–99	Manchester U	24	3		
1999–2000	Manchester U	30	6		
2000–01	Manchester U	31	5		
2001–02	Manchester U	25	7		
2002–03	Manchester U	36	8		
2003–04	Manchester U	33	7		
2004–05	Manchester U	32	5	**447**	**91**

HEATH, Colin (F) **6 0**
H: 6 0 W: 13 01 b.Matlock 31-12-83
Source: Scholar.

2000–01	Manchester U	0	0		
2001–02	Manchester U	0	0		
2002–03	Manchester U	0	0		
2003–04	Manchester U	0	0		
2004–05	Manchester U	0	0		
2004–05	*Cambridge U*	6	0	**6**	**0**

HEATON, Tom (G) **0 0**
H: 6 1 W: 13 06 b.Chester 15-4-86
Source: Trainee. *Honours:* England Youth.

2003–04	Manchester U	0	0		
2004–05	Manchester U	0	0		

HEINZE, Gabriel (D) **192 7**
H: 5 10 W: 12 04 b.Crespo 19-4-78
Source: Union de Crespo. *Honours:* Argentina 26 full caps.

1997–98	Newell's Old Boys	8	0	**8**	**0**
1997–98	Valladolid	0	0		
1998–99	Sporting Lisbon	5	1	**5**	**1**
1999–2000	Valladolid	18	0		
2000–01	Valladolid	36	1	**54**	**1**
2001–02	Paris St Germain	31	0		
2002–03	Paris St Germain	35	2		
2003–04	Paris St Germain	33	2	**99**	**4**
2004–05	Manchester U	26	1	**26**	**1**

HOWARD, Tim (G) **129 0**
H: 6 3 W: 14 12 b.New Brunswick 6-3-79
Honours: USA 12 full caps.

1998	NY/NJ MetrStars	1	0		
1999	NY/NJ MetrStars	9	0		
2000	NY/NJ MetrStars	9	0		
2001	NY/NJ MetrStars	26	0		
2002	NY/NJ MetrStars	27	0		
2003	NY/NJ MetrStars	13	0	**85**	**0**
2003–04	Manchester U	32	0		
2004–05	Manchester U	12	0	**44**	**0**

JOHNSON, Eddie (F) **26 5**
H: 5 10 W: 13 05 b.Chester 20-9-84
Source: Scholar. *Honours:* England Youth, Under-20.

2001–02	Manchester U	0	0		
2002–03	Manchester U	0	0		
2003–04	Manchester U	0	0		
2004–05	Manchester U	0	0		
2004–05	*Coventry C*	26	5	**26**	**5**

JONES, David (M) **0 0**
H: 5 11 W: 10 00 b.Southport 4-11-84
Source: Trainee. *Honours:* England Youth, Under-21.

2003–04	Manchester U	0	0		
2004–05	Manchester U	0	0		

JONES, Richie (M) **0 0**
b.Manchester 26-9-86
Source: Scholar. *Honours:* England Youth.

2004–05	Manchester U	0	0		

KEANE, Roy (M) **435 55**
H: 5 11 W: 11 10 b.Cork 10-8-71
Source: Cobh Ramb. *Honours:* Eire Schools, Youth, Under-21, 61 full caps, 9 goals.

1990–91	Nottingham F	35	8		
1991–92	Nottingham F	39	8		
1992–93	Nottingham F	40	6	**114**	**22**
1993–94	Manchester U	37	5		
1994–95	Manchester U	25	2		
1995–96	Manchester U	29	6		
1996–97	Manchester U	21	2		
1997–98	Manchester U	9	2		
1998–99	Manchester U	35	2		
1999–2000	Manchester U	29	5		
2000–01	Manchester U	28	2		
2001–02	Manchester U	28	3		
2002–03	Manchester U	21	0		
2003–04	Manchester U	28	3		
2004–05	Manchester U	31	1	**321**	**33**

KLEBERSON, Jose (M) **120 14**
H: 5 9 W: 10 00 b.Urai Paranaense 19-6-79
Honours: Brazil 27 full caps, 2 goals.

1999	Atletico PR	14	1		
2000	Atletico PR	24	4		
2001	Atletico PR	29	3		
2002	Atletico PR	21	4		
2003	Atletico PR	12	0	**100**	**12**
2003–04	Manchester U	12	2		
2004–05	Manchester U	8	0	**20**	**2**

LAWRENCE, Lee (D) **0 0**
H: 5 7 W: 9 02 b.Boston 1-12-84
Source: Trainee.

2002–03	Manchester U	0	0		
2003–04	Manchester U	0	0		
2004–05	Manchester U	0	0		

LOGAN, Carlos (M) **9 1**
H: 5 8 W: 10 05 b.Wythenshawe 7-11-85
Source: Scholar.

2004–05	Manchester U	0	0		
2004–05	*Chesterfield*	9	1	**9**	**1**

MARTIN, Lee (M) **0 0**
b.Taunton 9-2-87
Source: Scholar. *Honours:* England Youth.

2004–05	Manchester U	0	0		

McSHANE, Paul (D) **4 1**
H: 5 11 W: 11 05 b.Wicklow 6-1-86
Source: Trainee. *Honours:* Eire Youth, Under-21.

2002–03	Manchester U	0	0		
2003–04	Manchester U	0	0		
2004–05	Manchester U	0	0		
2004–05	*Walsall*	4	1	**4**	**1**

MILLER, Liam (M) **52 8**
H: 5 8 W: 10 06 b.Cork 13-2-81
Honours: Eire Under-21, 9 full caps.

1999–2000	Celtic	1	0		
2000–01	Celtic	0	0		
2001–02	Celtic	0	0		
2001–02	Aarhus	18	6	**18**	**6**
2002–03	Celtic	0	0		
2003–04	Celtic	25	2	**26**	**2**
2004–05	Manchester U	8	0	**8**	**0**

N'GALULA, Floribert (D) **0 0**
b.Brussels 7-3-87
Source: Scholar.

2004–05	Manchester U	0	0		

NARDIELLO, Daniel (F) **48 14**
H: 5 11 W: 11 06 b.Coventry 22-10-82
Source: Trainee.

1999–2000	Manchester U	0	0		
2000–01	Manchester U	0	0		
2001–02	Manchester U	0	0		
2002–03	Manchester U	0	0		
2003–04	Manchester U	0	0		
2003–04	*Swansea C*	4	0	**4**	**0**
2003–04	*Barnsley*	16	7		
2004–05	Manchester U	0	0		
2004–05	*Barnsley*	28	7	**44**	**14**

NEUMAYR, Marcus (M) **0 0**
H: 5 11 W: 11 05 b.Aschaffenburg 26-3-86
Source: Scholar.

2003–04	Manchester U	0	0		
2004–05	Manchester U	0	0		

NEVILLE, Gary (D) **315 5**
H: 5 11 W: 12 04 b.Bury 18-2-75
Source: Trainee. *Honours:* England Youth, 76 full caps.

1992–93	Manchester U	0	0		
1993–94	Manchester U	1	0		
1994–95	Manchester U	18	0		
1995–96	Manchester U	31	0		
1996–97	Manchester U	31	1		
1997–98	Manchester U	34	0		
1998–99	Manchester U	34	1		
1999–2000	Manchester U	22	0		
2000–01	Manchester U	32	1		
2001–02	Manchester U	34	0		
2002–03	Manchester U	26	0		
2003–04	Manchester U	30	2		
2004–05	Manchester U	22	0	**315**	**5**

NEVILLE, Phil (D) **263 5**
H: 5 11 W: 12 00 b.Bury 21-1-77
Source: Trainee. *Honours:* England Schools, Youth, Under-21, 52 full caps.

1994–95	Manchester U	2	0		
1995–96	Manchester U	24	0		
1996–97	Manchester U	18	0		
1997–98	Manchester U	30	1		
1998–99	Manchester U	28	0		
1999–2000	Manchester U	29	0		
2000–01	Manchester U	29	1		
2001–02	Manchester U	28	2		
2002–03	Manchester U	25	1		
2003–04	Manchester U	31	0		
2004–05	Manchester U	19	0	**263**	**5**

O'SHEA, John (D) **107 5**
H: 6 3 W: 12 10 b.Waterford 30-4-81
Source: Waterford. *Honours:* Eire Youth, Under-21, 24 full caps, 1 goal.

1998–99	Manchester U	0	0		
1999–2000	Manchester U	0	0		
1999–2000	*Bournemouth*	10	1	**10**	**1**
2000–01	Manchester U	0	0		
2001–02	Manchester U	9	0		
2002–03	Manchester U	32	0		
2003–04	Manchester U	33	2		
2004–05	Manchester U	23	2	**97**	**4**

PICKEN, Phil (D) **0 0**
b.Manchester 12-11-85
Source: Scholar.

2004–05	Manchester U	0	0		

PIQUE, Gerard (D) **0 0**
H: 6 3 W: 12 10 b.Barcelona 2-2-87
Source: Scholar. *Honours:* Spain Youth.

2004–05	Manchester U	0	0		

POOLE, David (F) **0 0**
H: 5 8 W: 12 00 b.Manchester 25-11-84
Source: Trainee.

2002–03	Manchester U	0	0		
2003–04	Manchester U	0	0		
2004–05	Manchester U	0	0		

PUUSTINEN, Jami (F) **0 0**
b.Espoo 9-1-87
Source: Scholar.

2004–05	Manchester U	0	0		

RICARDO (G) **154 0**
H: 6 2 W: 13 12 b.Madrid 31-12-71
Honours: Spain 1 full cap.

1994–95	Atletico Madrid B	29	0		
1995–96	Atletico Madrid	0	0		
1996–97	Atletico Madrid	1	0	**1**	**0**
1997–98	Atletico Madrid B	35	0	**64**	**0**
1998–99	Valladolid	0	0		
1999–2000	Valladolid	3	0		
2000–01	Valladolid	12	0		
2001–02	Valladolid	38	0	**53**	**0**
2002–03	Manchester U	1	0		
2003–04	*Santander*	35	0	**35**	**0**
2004–05	Manchester U	0	0	**1**	**0**

RICHARDSON, Kieran (M) **18 3**
H: 5 8 W: 11 00 b.Greenwich 21-10-84
Source: Scholar. *Honours:* England Under-21, 2 full caps, 2 goals.

2002–03	Manchester U	2	0		
2003–04	Manchester U	2	0		
2004–05	Manchester U	2	0	**6**	**0**
2004–05	*WBA*	12	3	**12**	**3**

RONALDO, Cristiano (M) **87 12**
H: 6 1 W: 12 04 b.Funchal 5-2-85
Honours: Portugal Youth, Under-21, 21 full caps, 9 goals.

2002–03	Sporting Lisbon	25	3	**25**	**3**
2003–04	Manchester U	29	4		
2004–05	Manchester U	33	5	**62**	**9**

ROONEY, Wayne (F) **96 26**
H: 5 10 W: 12 04 b.Liverpool 24-10-85
Source: Scholar. *Honours:* FA Schools, England Youth, 23 full caps, 9 goals.

2002–03	Everton	33	6		
2003–04	Everton	34	9	**67**	**15**
2004–05	Manchester U	29	11	**29**	**11**

ROSSI, Giuseppe (F) **0 0**
H: 5 9 W: 11 03 b.New Jersey 1-2-87
Honours: Italy Youth.

2004–05	Manchester U	0	0		

SAHA, Louis (F) **201 67**
H: 6 1 W: 12 06 b.Paris 8-8-78
Honours: France Youth, Under-21, 8 full caps, 2 goals.

1997–98	Metz	21	1		
1998–99	Metz	3	0		
1998–99	Newcastle U	11	1	**11**	**1**
1999–2000	Metz	23	4	**47**	**5**
2000–01	Fulham	43	27		
2001–02	Fulham	36	8		
2002–03	Fulham	17	5		
2003–04	Fulham	21	13	**117**	**53**
2003–04	Manchester U	12	7		
2004–05	Manchester U	14	1	**26**	**8**

SCHOLES, Paul (M) 321 87
H: 5 7 W: 11 00 b.Salford 16-11-74
Source: Trainee. *Honours:* England Youth, 66 full caps, 14 goals.
1992–93 Manchester U 0 0
1993–94 Manchester U 0 0
1994–95 Manchester U 17 5
1995–96 Manchester U 26 10
1996–97 Manchester U 24 3
1997–98 Manchester U 31 8
1998–99 Manchester U 31 6
1999–2000 Manchester U 31 9
2000–01 Manchester U 32 6
2001–02 Manchester U 35 8
2002–03 Manchester U 33 14
2003–04 Manchester U 28 9
2004–05 Manchester U 33 9 **321 87**

SILVESTRE, Mikael (D) 266 5
H: 6 0 W: 13 01 b.Chambray les Tours 9-8-77
Honours: France Youth, Under-21, 36 full caps, 2 goals.
1995–96 Rennes 1 0
1996–97 Rennes 16 0
1997–98 Rennes 32 0 **49 0**
1998–99 Internazionale 18 1 **18 1**
1999–2000 Manchester U 31 0
2000–01 Manchester U 30 1
2001–02 Manchester U 35 0
2002–03 Manchester U 34 1
2003–04 Manchester U 34 0
2004–05 Manchester U 35 2 **199 4**

SMITH, Alan (F) 203 44
H: 5 10 W: 12 01 b.Leeds 28-10-80
Source: Trainee. *Honours:* England Youth, Under-21, 15 full caps, 1 goal.
1997–98 Leeds U 0 0
1998–99 Leeds U 22 7
1999–2000 Leeds U 26 4
2000–01 Leeds U 33 11
2001–02 Leeds U 23 4
2002–03 Leeds U 33 3
2003–04 Leeds U 35 9 **172 38**
2004–05 Manchester U 31 6 **31 6**

SOLSKJAER, Ole Gunnar (F) 255 115
H: 5 10 W: 11 11 b.Kristiansund 26-2-73
Honours: Norway Under-21, 62 full caps, 21 goals.
1995 Molde 26 20
1996 Molde 16 11 **42 31**
1996–97 Manchester U 33 18
1997–98 Manchester U 22 6
1998–99 Manchester U 19 12
1999–2000 Manchester U 28 12
2000–01 Manchester U 31 10
2001–02 Manchester U 30 17
2002–03 Manchester U 37 9
2003–04 Manchester U 13 0
2004–05 Manchester U 0 0 **213 84**

SPECTOR, Jonathan (D) 3 0
H: 6 0 W: 12 08 b.Chicago 1-3-86
Honours: USA Youth.
2003–04 Manchester U 0 0
2004–05 Manchester U 3 0 **3 0**

STEELE, Luke (G) 34 0
H: 6 2 W: 12 00 b.Peterborough 24-9-84
Source: Scholar. *Honours:* England Youth, Under-20.
2001–02 Peterborough U 2 0 **2 0**
2001–02 Manchester U 0 0
2002–03 Manchester U 0 0
2003–04 Manchester U 0 0
2004–05 Manchester U 0 0
2004–05 *Coventry C* 32 0 **32 0**

STEWART, Michael (M) 20 0
H: 5 11 W: 11 11 b.Edinburgh 26-2-81
Source: Trainee. *Honours:* Scotland Schools, Under-21, 3 full caps.
1997–98 Manchester U 0 0
1998–99 Manchester U 0 0
1999–2000 Manchester U 0 0
2000–01 Manchester U 3 0
2001–02 Manchester U 3 0
2002–03 Manchester U 1 0
2003–04 Manchester U 0 0
2003–04 *Nottingham F* 13 0 **13 0**
2004–05 Manchester U 0 0 **7 0**

TIERNEY, Paul (D) 35 1
H: 5 10 W: 12 05 b.Salford 15-9-82
Source: Scholar. *Honours:* Eire Under-21.
2000–01 Manchester U 0 0
2001–02 Manchester U 0 0
2002–03 Manchester U 0 0
2002–03 *Crewe Alex* 17 1 **17 1**
2003–04 Manchester U 0 0
2003–04 *Colchester U* 2 0 **2 0**
2004–05 Manchester U 0 0
2004–05 *Bradford C* 16 0 **16 0**

TIMM, Mads (F) 0 0
H: 5 9 W: 12 10 b.Odense 31-10-84
Source: Scholar.
2001–02 Manchester U 0 0
2002–03 Manchester U 0 0
2003–04 Manchester U 0 0
2004–05 Manchester U 0 0

VAN NISTELROOY, Ruud (F) 282 166
H: 6 2 W: 12 13 b.Oss 1-7-76
Source: Nooit Gedacht, Margriet. *Honours:* Holland 44 full caps, 22 goals.
1993–94 Den Bosch 2 0
1994–95 Den Bosch 15 3
1995–96 Den Bosch 21 2
1996–97 Den Bosch 31 12 **69 17**
1997–98 Heerenveen 31 13 **31 13**
1998–99 PSV Eindhoven 34 31
1999–2000 PSV Eindhoven 23 29
2000–01 PSV Eindhoven 10 2 **67 62**
2001–02 Manchester U 32 23
2002–03 Manchester U 34 25
2003–04 Manchester U 32 20
2004–05 Manchester U 17 6 **115 74**

Scholars
Burns, Aaron Tyrone Stewart; Campbell, Fraizer Lee; Crockett, Lee Adam; Evans, Sean William; Gibson, Darron Thomas Daniel; Gray, David Peter; Howard, Mark James; Lea, Michael Robert; Lee, Kieran Christopher; Lee, Thomas Edward; Marsyh, Philip; Moran, Kyle Martin; Mullan, Jamie John; Rose, Daniel Stephen; Shawcross, Ryan James; Simpson, Daniel Peter

MANSFIELD T (49)

ARTELL, Dave (D) 110 10
H: 6 3 W: 14 07 b.Rotherham 22-11-80
Source: Trainee.
1999–2000 Rotherham U 1 0
2000–01 Rotherham U 36 4
2001–02 Rotherham U 0 0
2002–03 Rotherham U 0 0 **37 4**
2002–03 *Shrewsbury T* 28 1 **28 1**
2003–04 Mansfield T 26 3
2004–05 Mansfield T 19 2 **45 5**

BARKER, Richard (F) 292 57
H: 6 1 W: 14 06 b.Sheffield 30-5-75
Source: Trainee. *Honours:* England Schools.
1993–94 Sheffield W 0 0
1994–95 Sheffield W 0 0
1995–96 Sheffield W 0 0
1995–96 *Doncaster R* 6 0 **6 0**
1996–97 Sheffield W 0 0
From Linfield
1997–98 Brighton & HA 17 2
1998–99 Brighton & HA 43 10 **60 12**
1999–2000 Macclesfield T 35 16
2000–01 Macclesfield T 23 7 **58 23**
2000–01 Rotherham U 19 1
2001–02 Rotherham U 35 3
2002–03 Rotherham U 37 7
2003–04 Rotherham U 32 1
2004–05 Rotherham U 17 0 **140 12**
2004–05 Mansfield T 28 10 **28 10**

BARROWMAN, Andrew (F) 10 1
H: 5 11 W: 11 06 b.Wishaw 27-11-84
Source: Scholar. *Honours:* Scotland Youth.
2001–02 Birmingham C 0 0
2002–03 Birmingham C 0 0
2003–04 Birmingham C 1 0
2003–04 *Crewe Alex* 4 1 **4 1**
2004–05 Birmingham C 0 0 **1 0**
2004–05 *Blackpool* 2 0 **2 0**
2004–05 Mansfield T 3 0 **3 0**

BROWN, Simon (F) 42 4
H: 5 10 W: 11 05 b.West Bromwich 18-9-83
Source: Scholar.
2003–04 WBA 0 0
2003–04 *Kidderminster H* 8 2
2004–05 WBA 0 0
2004–05 *Kidderminster H* 13 0 **21 2**
2004–05 Mansfield T 21 2 **21 2**

BUXTON, Jake (D) 42 2
H: 6 1 W: 13 05 b.Sutton-in-Ashfield 4-3-85
Source: Scholar.
2002–03 Mansfield T 3 0
2003–04 Mansfield T 9 1
2004–05 Mansfield T 30 1 **42 2**

COKE, Gilles (M) 9 0
H: 6 0 W: 11 11 b.London 3-6-86
Source: Kingstonian.
2004–05 Mansfield T 9 0 **9 0**

CURLE, Thomas (M) 1 0
H: 5 10 W: 10 00 b.Bristol 3-3-86
Source: Scholar.
2003–04 Mansfield T 1 0
2004–05 Mansfield T 0 0 **1 0**

CURTIS, Tom (M) 358 12
H: 5 10 W: 11 13 b.Exeter 1-3-73
Source: School.
1991–92 Derby Co 0 0
1992–93 Derby Co 0 0
1993–94 Chesterfield 36 3
1994–95 Chesterfield 40 2
1995–96 Chesterfield 46 0
1996–97 Chesterfield 40 3
1997–98 Chesterfield 36 1
1998–99 Chesterfield 24 3
1999–2000 Chesterfield 18 0 **240 12**
2000–01 Portsmouth 4 0
2001–02 Portsmouth 9 0
2001–02 *Walsall* 4 0 **4 0**
2002–03 Portsmouth 0 0 **13 0**
2002–03 *Tranmere R* 8 0 **8 0**
2002–03 Mansfield T 23 0
2003–04 Mansfield T 38 0
2004–05 Mansfield T 32 0 **93 0**

DAY, Rhys (D) 91 10
H: 6 2 W: 13 12 b.Bridgend 31-8-82
Source: Scholarship. *Honours:* Wales Under-21.
1999–2000 Manchester C 0 0
2000–01 Manchester C 0 0
2001–02 Manchester C 0 0
2001–02 *Blackpool* 9 0 **9 0**
2002–03 Manchester C 0 0
2002–03 Mansfield T 23 1
2003–04 Mansfield T 41 6
2004–05 Mansfield T 18 3 **82 10**

DIMECH, Luke (M) 45 1
H: 5 11 W: 14 02 b.Malta 11-1-77
Source: Shamrock R. *Honours:* Malta 37 full caps.
2003–04 Mansfield T 20 1
2004–05 Mansfield T 25 0 **45 1**

EATON, Adam (D) 39 0
H: 5 11 W: 12 02 b.Wigan 2-5-80
Source: Trainee.
1997–98 Everton 0 0
1998–99 Everton 0 0
1999–2000 Preston NE 0 0
2000–01 Preston NE 1 0
2001–02 Preston NE 12 0
2002–03 Preston NE 1 0 **14 0**
2002–03 Mansfield T 20 0
2003–04 Mansfield T 3 0
2004–05 Mansfield T 2 0 **25 0**

HANKEY, Dean (M) 1 0
H: 5 8 W: 10 10 b.Sutton-in-Ashfield 23-8-86
Source: Scholar.
2002–03 Mansfield T 1 0
2003–04 Mansfield T 0 0
2004–05 Mansfield T 0 0 **1 0**

HERON, Daniel (M) 3 0
H: 5 11 W: 10 09 b.Cambridge 9-10-86
Source: Scholar.
2004–05 Mansfield T 3 0 **3 0**

HURST, Mark (D) 1 0
H: 5 11 W: 11 08 b.Mansfield 18-2-85
Source: Scholar.
2002–03 Mansfield T 1 0
2003–04 Mansfield T 0 0
2004–05 Mansfield T 0 0 **1 0**

JELLEYMAN, Gareth (D) 118 0
H: 5 10 W: 11 05 b.Holywell 14-11-80
Source: Trainee. *Honours:* Wales Youth, Under-21.
1998–99 Peterborough U 0 0
1999–2000 Peterborough U 20 0
2000–01 Peterborough U 8 0
2001–02 Peterborough U 10 0
2002–03 Peterborough U 32 0
2003–04 Peterborough U 17 0
2004–05 Peterborough U 14 0 **101 0**
2004–05 *Boston U* 3 0 **3 0**
2004–05 Mansfield T 14 0 **14 0**

JOHN-BAPTISTE, Alex (D) 62 1
H: 5 11 W: 11 11 b.Sutton-in-Ashfield 31-1-86
Source: Scholar.
2002–03 Mansfield T 4 0
2003–04 Mansfield T 17 0
2004–05 Mansfield T 41 1 **62 1**

JONES, Andy (M) 1 0
H: 5 8 W: 11 07 b.Sutton-in-Ashfield 12-2-86
Source: Scholar.
2002–03 Mansfield T 1 0
2003–04 Mansfield T 0 0
2004–05 Mansfield T 0 0 **1 0**

KITAMIRIKE, Joel (D) 24 0
H: 5 11 W: 12 11 b.Kampala 5-4-84
Source: Scholar. *Honours:* England Youth.
2000–01 Chelsea 0 0
2001–02 Chelsea 0 0
2002–03 Chelsea 0 0
2003–04 Chelsea 0 0
2003–04 *Brentford* 22 0 **22 0**
2004–05 Mansfield T 2 0 **2 0**

LAMBU, Goma (M) 1 0
H: 5 3 W: 9 8 b.Ghana 10-11-84
Source: Scholar. *Honours:* England Youth.
2001–02 Millwall 0 0
2002–03 Millwall 0 0
2003–04 Millwall 0 0
2004–05 Mansfield T 1 0 **1 0**

LARKIN, Colin (F) 128 31
H: 5 9 W: 11 07 b.Dundalk 27-4-82
Source: Trainee.
1998–99 Wolverhampton W 0 0
1999–2000 Wolverhampton W 1 0
2000–01 Wolverhampton W 2 0
2001–02 Wolverhampton W 0 0 **3 0**
2001–02 *Kidderminster H* 33 6 **33 6**
2002–03 Mansfield T 22 7
2003–04 Mansfield T 37 7
2004–05 Mansfield T 33 11 **92 25**

LLOYD, Callum (M) 10 4
H: 5 9 W: 11 04 b.Nottingham 1-1-86
Source: Scholar.
2004–05 Mansfield T 10 4 **10 4**

LONSDALE, Richard (M) 0 0
H: 5 9 W: 10 10 b.Burton 29-10-87
Source: Scholar.
2004–05 Mansfield T 0 0

MAXWELL, Leyton (M) 58 3
H: 5 8 W: 11 00 b.Rhyl 3-10-79
Source: From Trainee. *Honours:* Wales Youth, Under-21.
1997–98 Liverpool 0 0
1998–99 Liverpool 0 0
1999–2000 Liverpool 0 0
2000–01 Liverpool 0 0
2000–01 *Stockport Co* 20 2 **20 2**
2001–02 Cardiff C 17 1
2002–03 Cardiff C 16 0
2003–04 Cardiff C 1 0 **34 1**
2003–04 Swansea C 3 0 **3 0**
2004–05 Mansfield T 1 0 **1 0**

McINTOSH, Austin (M) 1 0
H: 5 11 W: 10 09 b.Newham 5-11-87
Source: Scholar.
2004–05 Mansfield T 1 0 **1 0**

McLACHLAN, Fraser (M) 74 4
H: 5 11 W: 12 04 b.Knutsford 9-11-82
Source: Scholar.
2001–02 Stockport Co 11 1
2002–03 Stockport Co 22 0
2003–04 Stockport Co 20 3
2004–05 Stockport Co 0 0 **53 4**
2004–05 Mansfield T 21 0 **21 0**

McNIVEN, Scott (D) 332 4
H: 5 10 W: 13 08 b.Leeds 27-5-78
Source: Trainee. *Honours:* Scotland Youth, Under-21.
1994–95 Oldham Ath 1 0
1995–96 Oldham Ath 15 0
1996–97 Oldham Ath 12 0
1997–98 Oldham Ath 32 1
1998–99 Oldham Ath 37 1
1999–2000 Oldham Ath 45 1
2000–01 Oldham Ath 45 0
2001–02 Oldham Ath 35 0 **222 3**
2002–03 Oxford U 44 1
2003–04 Oxford U 41 0 **85 1**
2004–05 Mansfield T 25 0 **25 0**

MURRAY, Adam (M) 126 15
H: 5 9 W: 11 11 b.Solihull 30-9-81
Source: Trainee. *Honours:* England Youth, Under-20.
1998–99 Derby Co 4 0
1999–2000 Derby Co 8 0
2000–01 Derby Co 14 0
2001–02 Derby Co 6 0
2001–02 *Mansfield T* 13 7
2002–03 Derby Co 24 0
2003–04 Derby Co 0 0 **56 0**
2003–04 Kidderminster H 22 3 **22 3**
From Burton Alb.
2003–04 Notts Co 3 0 **3 0**
2004–05 Mansfield T 32 5 **45 12**

NEIL, Alex (M) 178 10
H: 5 8 W: 11 00 b.Bellshill 9-6-81
Source: Dunfermline Ath.
1999–2000 Airdrieonians 16 5 **16 5**
2000–01 Barnsley 32 0
2001–02 Barnsley 25 2
2002–03 Barnsley 33 0
2003–04 Barnsley 31 2 **121 4**
2004–05 Mansfield T 41 1 **41 1**

PILKINGTON, Kevin (G) 219 0
H: 6 1 W: 13 03 b.Hitchin 8-3-74
Source: Trainee. *Honours:* England Schools.
1992–93 Manchester U 0 0
1993–94 Manchester U 0 0
1994–95 Manchester U 1 0
1995–96 Manchester U 3 0
1995–96 *Rochdale* 6 0 **6 0**
1996–97 Manchester U 0 0
1996–97 *Rotherham U* 17 0 **17 0**
1997–98 Manchester U 2 0
1998–99 Manchester U 0 0 **6 0**
1998–99 Port Vale 8 0
1999–2000 Port Vale 15 0 **23 0**
2000–01 Macclesfield T 0 0
2000–01 Wigan Ath 0 0
2000–01 Mansfield T 2 0
2001–02 Mansfield T 45 0
2002–03 Mansfield T 32 0
2003–04 Mansfield T 46 0
2004–05 Mansfield T 42 0 **167 0**

RUNDLE, Adam (F) 79 5
H: 5 8 W: 11 02 b.Durham 8-7-84
Source: Scholar.
2001–02 Darlington 12 0
2002–03 Darlington 5 0 **17 0**
2002–03 Carlisle U 21 1
2003–04 Carlisle U 23 0
2004–05 Carlisle U 0 0 **44 1**
2004–05 Mansfield T 18 4 **18 4**

SMELTZ, Shane (F) 5 0
H: 6 1 W: 12 06 b.Goppingen 20-9-80
Honours: New Zealand full caps.
2004–05 Mansfield T 5 0 **5 0**

TATE, Chris (F) 146 27
H: 6 0 W: 12 08 b.York 27-12-77
Source: York C Trainee.
1996–97 Sunderland 0 0
1997–98 Scarborough 24 1
1998–99 Scarborough 25 12 **49 13**
1999–2000 Halifax T 18 4 **18 4**
From Scarborough.
2000–01 Leyton Orient 22 3
2001–02 Leyton Orient 7 0
2002–03 Leyton Orient 23 6
2003–04 Leyton Orient 23 1 **75 10**
2004–05 Mansfield T 4 0 **4 0**

WHITE, Jason (G) 5 0
H: 6 2 W: 12 13 b.Mansfield 28-1-83
Source: Trainee.
2002–03 Mansfield T 1 0
2003–04 Mansfield T 0 0
2004–05 Mansfield T 4 0 **5 0**

WOOD, Chris (M) 1 0
H: 6 0 W: 10 11 b.Worksop 24-1-87
2004–05 Mansfield T 1 0 **1 0**

MIDDLESBROUGH (50)

BATES, Matthew (D) 8 0
H: 5 10 W: 12 03 b.Stockton 10-12-86
Source: Scholar. *Honours:* England Youth.
2003–04 Middlesbrough 2 0
2004–05 Middlesbrough 2 0 **4 0**
2004–05 *Darlington* 4 0 **4 0**

BOATENG, George (M) 315 13
H: 5 9 W: 12 06 b.Nkawkaw 5-9-75
Honours: Holland 2 full caps.
1994–95 Excelsior 9 0 **9 0**
1995–96 Feyenoord 24 1
1996–97 Feyenoord 26 0
1997–98 Feyenoord 18 0 **68 1**
1997–98 Coventry C 14 1
1998–99 Coventry C 33 4 **47 5**
1999–2000 Aston Villa 33 2
2000–01 Aston Villa 33 1
2001–02 Aston Villa 37 1 **103 4**
2002–03 Middlesbrough 28 0
2003–04 Middlesbrough 35 0
2004–05 Middlesbrough 25 3 **88 3**

CHRISTIE, Malcolm (F) 140 36
H: 6 0 W: 12 06 b.Peterborough 11-4-79
Source: Nuneaton B. *Honours:* England Under-21.
1998–99 Derby Co 2 0
1999–2000 Derby Co 21 5
2000–01 Derby Co 34 8
2001–02 Derby Co 35 9
2002–03 Derby Co 24 8 **116 30**
2002–03 Middlesbrough 12 4
2003–04 Middlesbrough 10 1
2004–05 Middlesbrough 2 1 **24 6**

COOPER, Colin (D) 605 37
H: 5 11 W: 11 11 b.Sedgefield 28-2-67
Honours: England Under-21, 2 full caps.
1984–85 Middlesbrough 0 0
1985–86 Middlesbrough 11 0
1986–87 Middlesbrough 46 0
1987–88 Middlesbrough 43 2
1988–89 Middlesbrough 35 2
1989–90 Middlesbrough 21 2
1990–91 Middlesbrough 32 0
1991–92 Millwall 36 2
1992–93 Millwall 41 4 **77 6**
1993–94 Nottingham F 37 7
1994–95 Nottingham F 35 1
1995–96 Nottingham F 37 5
1996–97 Nottingham F 36 2
1997–98 Nottingham F 35 5
1998–99 Nottingham F 0 0 **180 20**
1998–99 Middlesbrough 32 1
1999–2000 Middlesbrough 26 0
2000–01 Middlesbrough 27 2
2001–02 Middlesbrough 18 2

2002–03 Middlesbrough 20 0
2003–04 Middlesbrough 19 0
2003–04 *Sunderland* 3 0 **3 0**
2004–05 Middlesbrough 15 0 **345 11**

DAVIES, Andrew (D) 23 0
H: 6 3 W: 14 08 b.Stockton 17-12-84
Source: Scholar. *Honours:* England Youth, Under-20, Under-21.
2002–03 Middlesbrough 1 0
2003–04 Middlesbrough 10 0
2004–05 Middlesbrough 3 0 **14 0**
2004–05 *QPR* 9 0 **9 0**

DORIVA (M) 233 10
H: 5 7 W: 11 04 b.Mirasol 28-5-72
Honours: Brazil 12 full caps.
1993 Sao Paulo 12 0
1994 Sao Paulo 15 0 **27 0**
1995 Atletico Mineiro 11 1
1996 Atletico Mineiro 24 0
1997 Atletico Mineiro 24 0 **59 1**
1997–98 Porto 13 1
1998–99 Porto 17 4 **30 5**
1999–2000 Sampdoria 31 3 **31 3**
2000–01 Celta Vigo 17 1
2001–02 Celta Vigo 14 0
2002–03 Celta Vigo 3 0 **34 1**
2002–03 Middlesbrough 5 0
2003–04 Middlesbrough 21 0
2004–05 Middlesbrough 26 0 **52 0**

DOWNING, Stewart (M) 67 8
H: 5 11 W: 10 04 b.Middlesbrough 22-7-84
Source: Scholar. *Honours:* England Youth, Under-21, 1 full cap.
2001–02 Middlesbrough 3 0
2002–03 Middlesbrough 2 0
2003–04 Middlesbrough 20 0
2003–04 *Sunderland* 7 3 **7 3**
2004–05 Middlesbrough 35 5 **60 5**

EHIOGU, Ugo (D) 347 19
H: 6 2 W: 14 10 b.Hackney 3-11-72
Source: Trainee. *Honours:* England Under-21, B, 4 full caps, 1 goal.
1990–91 WBA 2 0 **2 0**
1991–92 Aston Villa 8 0
1992–93 Aston Villa 4 0
1993–94 Aston Villa 17 0
1994–95 Aston Villa 39 3
1995–96 Aston Villa 36 1
1996–97 Aston Villa 38 3
1997–98 Aston Villa 37 2
1998–99 Aston Villa 25 2
1999–2000 Aston Villa 31 1
2000–01 Aston Villa 2 0 **237 12**
2000–01 Middlesbrough 21 3
2001–02 Middlesbrough 29 1
2002–03 Middlesbrough 32 3
2003–04 Middlesbrough 16 0
2004–05 Middlesbrough 10 0 **108 7**

GRAHAM, Danny (F) 20 3
H: 5 11 W: 12 05 b.Gateshead 12-8-85
Source: Trainee. *Honours:* England Youth, Under-20.
2003–04 Middlesbrough 0 0
2003–04 *Darlington* 9 2 **9 2**
2004–05 Middlesbrough 11 1 **11 1**

HASSELBAINK, Jimmy Floyd (F) 335 172
H: 5 10 W: 13 10 b.Paramaribo 27-3-72
Honours: Holland 23 full caps, 9 goals.
1995–96 Campomairorense 31 12 **31 12**
1996–97 Boavista 29 20 **29 20**
1997–98 Leeds U 33 16
1998–99 Leeds U 36 18 **69 34**
1999–2000 Atletico Madrid 34 24 **34 24**
2000–01 Chelsea 35 23
2001–02 Chelsea 35 23
2002–03 Chelsea 36 11
2003–04 Chelsea 30 12 **136 69**
2004–05 Middlesbrough 36 13 **36 13**

JOB, Joseph-Desire (F) 156 31
H: 5 11 W: 11 00 b.Venissieux 1-12-77
Honours: Cameroon 48 full caps, 7 goals.
1997–98 Lyon 22 5
1998–99 Lyon 19 6 **41 11**
1999–2000 Lens 24 4 **24 4**
2000–01 Middlesbrough 12 3
2001–02 Middlesbrough 4 0
2002–03 Middlesbrough 28 4
2003–04 Middlesbrough 24 5
2004–05 Middlesbrough 23 4 **91 16**

JOHNSON, Adam (M) 0 0
H: 5 9 W: 9 11 b.Sunderland 14-7-87
Source: Scholar.
2004–05 Middlesbrough 0 0

JONES, Brad (G) 26 0
H: 6 3 W: 12 01 b.Armadale 19-3-82
Source: From Trainee. *Honours:* Australia Youth Under-20, Under-23.
1998–99 Middlesbrough 0 0
1999–2000 Middlesbrough 0 0
2000–01 Middlesbrough 0 0
2001–02 Middlesbrough 0 0
2002 Shelbourne 2 0 **2 0**
2002–03 Middlesbrough 0 0
2002–03 *Stockport Co* 1 0 **1 0**
2003–04 Middlesbrough 1 0
2003–04 *Blackpool* 5 0
2003–04 *Rotherham U* 0 0
2004–05 Middlesbrough 5 0 **6 0**
2004–05 *Blackpool* 12 0 **17 0**

KENNEDY, Jason (M) 1 0
H: 6 1 W: 11 10 b.Stockton 11-9-86
Source: Scholar.
2004–05 Middlesbrough 1 0 **1 0**

KNIGHT, David (G) 0 0
b.Sunderland 15-1-87
Source: From Scholar. *Honours:* England Youth.
2004–05 Middlesbrough 0 0

LIDDLE, Gary (D) 0 0
b.Middlesbrough 15-6-86
Source: Trainee. *Honours:* England Youth.
2003–04 Middlesbrough 0 0
2004–05 Middlesbrough 0 0

MACCARONE, Massimo (F) 92 31
H: 5 10 W: 12 05 b.Galliate 6-9-79
Honours: Italy 2 full caps.
2000–01 Empoli 35 16
2001–02 Empoli 0 0 **35 16**
2002–03 Middlesbrough 34 9
2003–04 Middlesbrough 23 6
2004–05 Middlesbrough 0 0 **57 15**

McMAHON, Anthony (D) 13 0
H: 5 10 W: 11 04 b.Bishop Auckland 24-3-86
Source: Scholar. *Honours:* England Youth.
2003–04 Middlesbrough 0 0
2004–05 Middlesbrough 13 0 **13 0**

MENDIETA, Gaizka (M) 385 50
H: 5 9 W: 11 02 b.Bilbao 27-3-74
Honours: Spain 40 full caps, 8 goals.
1991–92 Castellon 16 0 **16 0**
1992–93 Valencia B 31 2
1992–93 Valencia 2 0
1993–94 Valencia B 17 0 **48 2**
1993–94 Valencia 20 0
1994–95 Valencia 13 1
1995–96 Valencia 34 0
1996–97 Valencia 29 1
1997–98 Valencia 30 10
1998–99 Valencia 38 7
1999–2000 Valencia 33 13
2000–01 Valencia 31 10 **230 42**
2001–02 Lazio 20 0 **20 0**
2002–03 Barcelona 33 4 **33 4**
2003–04 Middlesbrough 31 2
2004–05 Middlesbrough 7 0 **38 2**

MORRISON, James (M) 15 0
H: 5 10 W: 10 06 b.Darlington 25-5-86
Source: Trainee. *Honours:* England Youth.
2003–04 Middlesbrough 1 0
2004–05 Middlesbrough 14 0 **15 0**

NEMETH, Szilard (F) 268 107
H: 5 11 W: 11 04 b.Komarno 8-8-77
Honours: Slovakia 52 full caps, 20 goals.
1994–95 Slovan Bratislava 3 0
1995–96 Slovan Bratislava 28 12
1996–97 Slovan Bratislava 30 13 **61 25**
1997–98 Kosice 18 12
1998–99 Kosice 19 8 **37 20**
1999–2000 Inter Bratislava 26 16
2000–01 Inter Bratislava 32 23 **58 39**
2001–02 Middlesbrough 21 3
2002–03 Middlesbrough 28 7
2003–04 Middlesbrough 32 9
2004–05 Middlesbrough 31 4 **112 23**

PARLOUR, Ray (M) 372 22
H: 5 10 W: 11 12 b.Romford 7-3-73
Source: Trainee. *Honours:* England Under-21, B, 10 full caps.
1990–91 Arsenal 0 0
1991–92 Arsenal 6 1
1992–93 Arsenal 21 1
1993–94 Arsenal 27 2
1994–95 Arsenal 30 0
1995–96 Arsenal 22 0
1996–97 Arsenal 30 2
1997–98 Arsenal 34 5
1998–99 Arsenal 35 6
1999–2000 Arsenal 30 1
2000–01 Arsenal 33 4
2001–02 Arsenal 27 0
2002–03 Arsenal 19 0
2003–04 Arsenal 25 0 **339 22**
2004–05 Middlesbrough 33 0 **33 0**

PARNABY, Stuart (M) 59 0
H: 5 11 W: 11 00 b.Durham City 19-7-82
Source: Trainee. *Honours:* England Youth, Under-20, Under-21.
1999–2000 Middlesbrough 0 0
2000–01 Middlesbrough 0 0
2000–01 *Halifax T* 6 0 **6 0**
2001–02 Middlesbrough 0 0
2002–03 Middlesbrough 21 0
2003–04 Middlesbrough 13 0
2004–05 Middlesbrough 19 0 **53 0**

PEACOCK, Anthony (M) 0 0
b.Middlesbrough 6-9-85
Source: Trainee.
2003–04 Middlesbrough 0 0
2004–05 Middlesbrough 0 0

QUEUDRUE, Franck (D) 163 10
H: 6 1 W: 12 01 b.Paris 27-8-78
Source: Meaux.
1999–2000 Lens 16 1
2000–01 Lens 24 1
2001–02 Lens 2 0 **42 2**
2001–02 Middlesbrough 28 2
2002–03 Middlesbrough 31 1
2003–04 Middlesbrough 31 0
2004–05 Middlesbrough 31 5 **121 8**

REIZIGER, Mikael (D) 309 9
H: 5 7 W: 11 07 b.Amsterdam 3-5-73
Honours: Holland 72 full caps, 1 goal.
1990–91 Ajax 1 0
1991–92 Ajax 1 0
1992–93 Ajax 1 0
1992–93 Volendam 10 2 **10 2**
1993–94 Groningen 34 5 **34 5**
1994–95 Ajax 34 0
1995–96 Ajax 26 1 **63 1**
1996–97 AC Milan 10 0 **10 0**
1997–98 Barcelona 29 0
1998–99 Barcelona 26 0
1999–2000 Barcelona 30 0
2000–01 Barcelona 25 0
2001–02 Barcelona 13 0
2002–03 Barcelona 21 0
2003–04 Barcelona 30 0 **174 0**
2004–05 Middlesbrough 18 1 **18 1**

RIGGOTT, Chris (D) 134 9
H: 6 2 W: 13 09 b.Derby 1-9-80
Source: Trainee. *Honours:* England Youth, Under-21.
1998–99 Derby Co 0 0
1999–2000 Derby Co 1 0
2000–01 Derby Co 31 3
2001–02 Derby Co 37 0
2002–03 Derby Co 22 2 **91 5**
2002–03 Middlesbrough 5 2
2003–04 Middlesbrough 17 0
2004–05 Middlesbrough 21 2 **43 4**

SCHWARZER, Mark (G) **347 0**
H: 6 4 W: 14 07 b.Sydney 6-10-72
Honours: Australia Youth, Under-20, 30 full caps.

1990–91	Marconi Stallions	1	0		
1991–92	Marconi Stallions	9	0		
1992–93	Marconi Stallions	23	0		
1993–94	Marconi Stallions	25	0	**58**	**0**
1994–95	Dynamo Dresden	2	0	**2**	**0**
1995–96	Kaiserslautern	4	0		
1996–97	Kaiserslautern	0	0	**4**	**0**
1996–97	Bradford C	13	0	**13**	**0**
1996–97	Middlesbrough	7	0		
1997–98	Middlesbrough	35	0		
1998–99	Middlesbrough	34	0		
1999–2000	Middlesbrough	37	0		
2000–01	Middlesbrough	31	0		
2001–02	Middlesbrough	21	0		
2002–03	Middlesbrough	38	0		
2003–04	Middlesbrough	36	0		
2004–05	Middlesbrough	31	0	**270**	**0**

SOUTHGATE, Gareth (D) **479 26**
H: 6 0 W: 12 03 b.Watford 3-9-70
Source: Trainee. *Honours:* England 57 full caps, 2 goals.

1988–89	Crystal Palace	0	0		
1989–90	Crystal Palace	0	0		
1990–91	Crystal Palace	1	0		
1991–92	Crystal Palace	30	0		
1992–93	Crystal Palace	33	3		
1993–94	Crystal Palace	46	9		
1994–95	Crystal Palace	42	3	**152**	**15**
1995–96	Aston Villa	31	1		
1996–97	Aston Villa	28	1		
1997–98	Aston Villa	32	0		
1998–99	Aston Villa	38	1		
1999–2000	Aston Villa	31	2		
2000–01	Aston Villa	31	2	**191**	**7**
2001–02	Middlesbrough	37	1		
2002–03	Middlesbrough	36	2		
2003–04	Middlesbrough	27	1		
2004–05	Middlesbrough	36	0	**136**	**4**

TAYLOR, Andrew (D) **0 0**
H: 5 10 W: 11 04 b.Hartlepool 1-8-86
Source: Trainee. *Honours:* England Youth, Under-20.

2003–04	Middlesbrough	0	0		
2004–05	Middlesbrough	0	0		

TURNBULL, Ross (G) **29 0**
H: 6 4 W: 15 00 b.Bishop Auckland 4-1-85
Source: Trainee. *Honours:* England Youth, Under-20.

2002–03	Middlesbrough	0	0		
2003–04	Middlesbrough	0	0		
2003–04	*Darlington*	1	0	**1**	**0**
2003–04	*Barnsley*	3	0		
2004–05	Middlesbrough	0	0		
2004–05	*Bradford C*	2	0	**2**	**0**
2004–05	*Barnsley*	23	0	**26**	**0**

VIDUKA, Mark (F) **315 174**
H: 6 2 W: 15 01 b.Melbourne 9-10-75
Honours: Australia Youth, Under-20, Under-23, 24 full caps, 3 goals.

1992–93	Melbourne Knights	4	2		
1993–94	Melbourne Knights	20	17		
1994–95	Melbourne Knights	24	21	**48**	**40**
1995–96	Croatia Zagreb	27	12		
1996–97	Croatia Zagreb	25	18		
1997–98	Croatia Zagreb	25	8		
1998–99	Croatia Zagreb	7	2	**84**	**40**
1998–99	Celtic	9	5		
1999–2000	Celtic	28	25	**37**	**30**
2000–01	Leeds U	34	17		
2001–02	Leeds U	33	11		
2002–03	Leeds U	33	20		
2003–04	Leeds U	30	11	**130**	**59**
2004–05	Middlesbrough	16	5	**16**	**5**

WHEATER, David (D) **0 0**
H: 6 4 W: 12 12 b.Redcar 14-2-87
Source: Scholar. *Honours:* England Youth.

2004–05	Middlesbrough	0	0		

WILSON, Mark (M) **54 6**
H: 5 10 W: 12 07 b.Scunthorpe 9-2-79
Source: Trainee. *Honours:* England Schools, Under-21.

1995–96	Manchester U	0	0		
1996–97	Manchester U	0	0		
1997–98	Manchester U	0	0		
1997–98	*Wrexham*	13	4	**13**	**4**
1998–99	Manchester U	0	0		
1999–2000	Manchester U	3	0		
2000–01	Manchester U	0	0	**3**	**0**
2001–02	Middlesbrough	10	0		
2002–03	Middlesbrough	6	0		
2002–03	*Stoke C*	4	0	**4**	**0**
2003–04	Middlesbrough	0	0		
2003–04	*Swansea C*	12	2	**12**	**2**
2003–04	*Sheffield W*	3	0	**3**	**0**
2004–05	Middlesbrough	0	0	**16**	**0**
2004–05	*Doncaster R*	3	0	**3**	**0**

ZENDEN, Boudewijn (M) **285 39**
H: 5 8 W: 11 11 b.Maastricht 15-8-76
Honours: Holland 54 full caps, 7 goals.

1994–95	PSV Eindhoven	27	5		
1995–96	PSV Eindhoven	25	7		
1996–97	PSV Eindhoven	34	8		
1997–98	PSV Eindhoven	25	3	**111**	**23**
1998–99	Barcelona	25	0		
1999–2000	Barcelona	29	2		
2000–01	Barcelona	10	1	**64**	**3**
2001–02	Chelsea	22	3		
2002–03	Chelsea	21	1		
2003–04	Chelsea	0	0	**43**	**4**
2003–04	*Middlesbrough*	31	4		
2004–05	Middlesbrough	36	5	**67**	**9**

Scholars
Burgess, Kevin; Cattermole, Lee Barry; Clough, Adam Paul; Craddock, Thomas; Grounds, Jonathan Martin; Hines, Sebastian; Lemaire, Christophe Philippe Olivier; Mulligan, Nathan Michael; Owens, Graeme Adams; Pennock, Christopher; Williams, Rhys

MILLWALL (51)

BRANIFF, Kevin (F) **45 4**
H: 5 11 W: 10 03 b.Belfast 4-3-83
Source: Scholarship. *Honours:* Northern Ireland Schools, Youth, Under-21, Under-23.

1999–2000	Millwall	0	0		
2000–01	Millwall	5	0		
2001–02	Millwall	1	0		
2002–03	Millwall	10	0		
2003–04	Millwall	16	1		
2004–05	Millwall	1	0	**33**	**1**
2004–05	*Rushden & D*	12	3	**12**	**3**

CLANCY, Tim (M) **0 0**
H: 5 11 W: 10 11 b.Trim 8-6-84

2002–03	Millwall	0	0		
2003–04	Millwall	0	0		
2004–05	Millwall	0	0		

COGAN, Barry (F) **10 0**
H: 5 9 W: 9 0 b.Sligo 4-11-84
Source: Scholar. *Honours:* Eire Under-21.

2001–02	Millwall	0	0		
2002–03	Millwall	0	0		
2003–04	Millwall	3	0		
2004–05	Millwall	7	0	**10**	**0**

CRAIG, Tony (D) **35 1**
H: 6 0 W: 10 03 b.Greenwich 20-4-85
Source: Scholar.

2002–03	Millwall	2	1		
2003–04	Millwall	9	0		
2004–05	Millwall	10	0	**21**	**1**
2004–05	*Wycombe W*	14	0	**14**	**0**

DICHIO, Danny (F) **282 66**
H: 6 6 W: 14 02 b.Hammersmith 19-10-74
Source: Trainee. *Honours:* England Schools, Under-21.

1993–94	QPR	0	0		
1993–94	*Barnet*	9	2	**9**	**2**
1994–95	QPR	9	3		
1995–96	QPR	29	10		
1996–97	QPR	37	7	**75**	**20**
1997–98	Sampdoria	0	0		
1997–98	Lecce	4	1	**4**	**1**
1997–98	Sunderland	13	0		
1998–99	Sunderland	36	10		
1999–2000	Sunderland	12	0		
2000–01	Sunderland	15	1		
2001–02	Sunderland	0	0	**76**	**11**
2001–02	WBA	27	9		
2002–03	WBA	28	5		
2003–04	WBA	11	0	**66**	**14**
2003–04	*Derby Co*	6	1	**6**	**1**
2003–04	Millwall	15	7		
2004–05	Millwall	31	10	**46**	**17**

DOLAN, Joe (D) **63 4**
H: 6 2 W: 12 03 b.Harrow 27-5-80
Source: Chelsea Trainee. *Honours:* Northern Ireland Youth, Under-21.

1998–99	Millwall	9	1		
1999–2000	Millwall	17	1		
2000–01	Millwall	20	1		
2001–02	Millwall	0	0		
2002–03	Millwall	2	0		
2003–04	Millwall	1	0		
2004–05	Millwall	0	0	**49**	**3**
2004–05	*Stockport Co*	11	1	**11**	**1**
2004–05	*Brighton & HA*	3	0	**3**	**0**

DONOVAN, James (M) **0 0**
H: 6 2 W: 13 12 b.Sidcup 11-9-84
Source: Scholar.

2003–04	Millwall	0	0		
2004–05	Millwall	0	0		

DUNNE, Alan (D) **32 3**
H: 5 10 W: 10 13 b.Dublin 23-8-82
Source: Trainee.

1999–2000	Millwall	0	0		
2000–01	Millwall	0	0		
2001–02	Millwall	1	0		
2002–03	Millwall	4	0		
2003–04	Millwall	8	0		
2004–05	Millwall	19	3	**32**	**3**

ELLIOTT, Marvin (M) **63 1**
H: 6 0 W: 12 02 b.Wandsworth 15-9-84
Source: Scholar.

2001–02	Millwall	0	0		
2002–03	Millwall	1	0		
2003–04	Millwall	21	0		
2004–05	Millwall	41	1	**63**	**1**

HAYLES, Barry (F) **273 88**
H: 5 10 W: 12 11 b.Lambeth 17-5-72
Source: Stevenage Bor. *Honours:* Jamaica 10 full caps.

1997–98	Bristol R	45	23		
1998–99	Bristol R	17	9	**62**	**32**
1998–99	Fulham	30	8		
1999–2000	Fulham	35	5		
2000–01	Fulham	35	18		
2001–02	Fulham	35	8		
2002–03	Fulham	14	1		
2003–04	Fulham	26	4	**175**	**44**
2004–05	Sheffield U	4	0	**4**	**0**
2004–05	Millwall	32	12	**32**	**12**

HEALY, Joe (F) **2 0**
H: 6 0 W: 12 04 b.Sidcup 26-12-86

2003–04	Millwall	0	0		
2004–05	Millwall	2	0	**2**	**0**

HEARN, Charley (M) **42 1**
H: 5 11 W: 11 13 b.Ashford 5-11-83
Source: School.

2000–01	Millwall	0	0		
2001–02	Millwall	2	0		
2002–03	Millwall	9	0		
2003–04	Millwall	7	0		
2004–05	Millwall	0	0	**18**	**0**
2004–05	*Northampton T*	24	1	**24**	**1**

IFILL, Paul (M) **230 40**
H: 6 0 W: 12 01 b.Brighton 20-10-79
Source: Trainee. *Honours:* England Youth, Barbados full caps.

1998–99	Millwall	15	1		
1999–2000	Millwall	44	11		
2000–01	Millwall	35	6		
2001–02	Millwall	40	4		
2002–03	Millwall	45	6		
2003–04	Millwall	33	8		
2004–05	Millwall	18	4	**230**	**40**

LAWRENCE, Matthew (D) 331 5
H: 6 1 W: 12 12 b.Northampton 19-6-74
Source: Grays Ath. *Honours:* England Schools.
1995–96 Wycombe W 3 0
1996–97 Wycombe W 13 1
1996–97 Fulham 15 0
1997–98 Fulham 43 0
1998–99 Fulham 1 0 **59 0**
1998–99 Wycombe W 34 2
1999–2000 Wycombe W 29 2 **79 5**
1999–2000 Millwall 9 0
2000–01 Millwall 45 0
2001–02 Millwall 26 0
2002–03 Millwall 33 0
2003–04 Millwall 36 0
2004–05 Millwall 44 0 **193 0**

LIVERMORE, David (M) 232 10
H: 5 11 W: 12 02 b.Edmonton 20-5-80
Source: Trainee.
1998–99 Arsenal 0 0
1999–2000 Millwall 32 2
2000–01 Millwall 39 3
2001–02 Millwall 43 0
2002–03 Millwall 41 2
2003–04 Millwall 36 1
2004–05 Millwall 41 2 **232 10**

MARSHALL, Andy (G) 302 0
H: 6 3 W: 14 08 b.Bury 14-4-75
Source: Trainee. *Honours:* England Under-21.
1993–94 Norwich C 0 0
1994–95 Norwich C 21 0
1995–96 Norwich C 3 0
1996–97 Norwich C 7 0
1996–97 *Bournemouth* 11 0 **11 0**
1996–97 *Gillingham* 5 0 **5 0**
1997–98 Norwich C 42 0
1998–99 Norwich C 37 0
1999–2000 Norwich C 44 0
2000–01 Norwich C 41 0 **195 0**
2001–02 Ipswich T 13 0
2002–03 Ipswich T 40 0
2003–04 Ipswich T 0 0 **53 0**
2003–04 Millwall 16 0
2004–05 Millwall 22 0 **38 0**

MASTERSON, Terence (G) 0 0
H: 6 2 W: 11 04 b.Dublin 5-6-86
Source: Scholar.
2003–04 Millwall 0 0
2004–05 Millwall 0 0

MAY, Ben (F) 89 11
H: 6 3 W: 12 12 b.Gravesend 10-3-84
Source: Juniors.
2000–01 Millwall 0 0
2001–02 Millwall 0 0
2002–03 Millwall 10 1
2002–03 *Colchester U* 6 0
2003–04 Millwall 0 0
2003–04 *Brentford* 41 7
2004–05 Millwall 8 1 **18 2**
2004–05 *Colchester U* 14 1 **20 1**
2004–05 Brentford 10 1 **51 8**

MORRIS, Jody (F) 183 11
H: 5 5 W: 10 03 b.Hammersmith 22-12-78
Source: Trainee. *Honours:* England Schools, Youth, Under-21.
1995–96 Chelsea 1 0
1996–97 Chelsea 12 0
1997–98 Chelsea 12 1
1998–99 Chelsea 18 1
1999–2000 Chelsea 30 3
2000–01 Chelsea 21 0
2001–02 Chelsea 5 0
2002–03 Chelsea 25 0 **124 5**
2003–04 Leeds U 12 0 **12 0**
2003–04 Rotherham U 10 1 **10 1**
2004–05 Millwall 37 5 **37 5**

MUSCAT, Kevin (D) 386 22
H: 5 11 W: 12 08 b.Crawley 7-8-73
Honours: Australia Youth, Under-20, Under-23, 45 full caps, 10 goals.
1989–90 Sunshine 9 0
1990–91 Sunshine 0 0 **9 0**
1991–92 Heidelberg 18 0 **18 0**
1992–93 South Melbourne 17 0
1993–94 South Melbourne 24 2
1994–95 South Melbourne 20 3
1995–96 South Melbourne 12 1 **73 6**
1996–97 Crystal Palace 44 2
1997–98 Crystal Palace 9 0 **53 2**
1997–98 Wolverhampton W 24 3
1998–99 Wolverhampton W 37 4
1999–2000 Wolverhampton W 45 4
2000–01 Wolverhampton W 37 3
2001–02 Wolverhampton W 37 0
2002–03 Wolverhampton W 0 0 **180 14**
2003–04 Millwall 27 0
2004–05 Millwall 26 0 **53 0**

PEETERS, Bob (F) 276 74
H: 6 5 W: 13 12 b.Lier 28-1-72
Source: Ternesse. *Honours:* Belgium 13 full caps, 4 goals.
1992–93 Lierse 12 0
1993–94 Lierse 17 0
1994–95 Lierse 26 8
1995–96 Lierse 29 7
1996–97 Lierse 34 7 **118 22**
1997–98 Roda 30 11
1998–99 Roda 33 13
1999–2000 Roda 30 15 **93 39**
2000–01 Vitesse 32 8
2001–02 Vitesse 10 2 **42 10**
2003–04 Millwall 20 3
2004–05 Millwall 3 0 **23 3**

PHILLIPS, Mark (D) 33 1
H: 6 2 W: 11 00 b.Lambeth 27-1-82
Source: Scholarship.
1999–2000 Millwall 0 0
2000–01 Millwall 0 0
2001–02 Millwall 1 0
2002–03 Millwall 7 0
2003–04 Millwall 0 0
2004–05 Millwall 25 1 **33 1**

QUIGLEY, Mark (M) 9 0
H: 5 10 W: 11 07 b.Dublin 27-10-85
Source: Scholar. *Honours:* Eire Youth, Under-21.
2002–03 Millwall 0 0
2003–04 Millwall 1 0
2004–05 Millwall 8 0 **9 0**

REES, Matt (D) 3 1
H: 6 2 W: 12 00 b.Swansea 2-9-82
Source: Trainee. *Honours:* Wales Under-21.
1999–2000 Millwall 0 0
2000–01 Millwall 0 0
2001–02 Millwall 0 0
2002–03 Millwall 0 0
2003–04 Millwall 0 0
2003–04 *Swansea C* 3 1 **3 1**
2004–05 Millwall 0 0

ROBERTS, Andy (M) 418 16
H: 5 11 W: 14 05 b.Dartford 20-3-74
Source: Trainee. *Honours:* England Under-21.
1991–92 Millwall 7 0
1992–93 Millwall 45 0
1993–94 Millwall 42 2
1994–95 Millwall 44 3
1995–96 Crystal Palace 38 0
1996–97 Crystal Palace 45 2
1997–98 Crystal Palace 25 0 **108 2**
1997–98 Wimbledon 12 1
1998–99 Wimbledon 28 2
1999–2000 Wimbledon 16 0
2000–01 Wimbledon 27 2
2001–02 Wimbledon 18 1 **101 6**
2001–02 *Norwich C* 5 0 **5 0**
2002–03 Millwall 33 2
2003–04 Millwall 33 1
2004–05 Millwall 0 0 **204 8**

ROBINSON, Anton (M) 0 0
H: 5 9 W: 10 03 b.Harrow 17-2-86
Source: Scholar.
2003–04 Millwall 0 0
2004–05 Millwall 0 0

ROBINSON, Paul (D) 35 0
H: 6 1 W: 11 09 b.Barnet 7-1-82
Source: Scholar.
2000–01 Millwall 0 0
2001–02 Millwall 0 0
2002–03 Millwall 14 0
2003–04 Millwall 9 0
2004–05 Millwall 0 0 **23 0**
2004–05 *Torquay U* 12 0 **12 0**

ROBINSON, Trevor (M) 10 1
H: 5 9 W: 12 11 b.Jamaica 20-9-84
Source: Scholar.
2003–04 Millwall 1 0
2004–05 Millwall 9 1 **10 1**

ROSE, Jason (D) 0 0
H: 6 1 W: 10 13 b.Sidcup 28-1-85
Source: Scholar.
2003–04 Millwall 0 0
2004–05 Millwall 0 0

SERIOUX, Adrian (D) 19 0
H: 6 0 W: 12 12 b.Scarborough, Canada 12-5-79
Source: Toronto Lynx. *Honours:* Canada 3 full caps.
2004–05 Millwall 19 0 **19 0**

SIMPSON, Josh (M) 30 1
H: 5 10 W: 12 02 b.Vancouver 15-5-83
Source: Univ of Portland. *Honours:* Canada 7 full caps.
2004–05 Millwall 30 1 **30 1**

SUTTON, John (F) 12 1
H: 6 2 W: 13 11 b.Norwich 26-12-83
Source: From Scholar. *Honours:* England Youth.
2001–02 Tottenham H 0 0
2002–03 Tottenham H 0 0
2002–03 *Carlisle U* 7 1 **7 1**
2002–03 Swindon T 1 0 **1 0**
2003–04 Millwall 4 0
2004–05 Millwall 0 0 **4 0**

SWEENEY, Peter (F) 59 5
H: 6 0 W: 12 01 b.Glasgow 25-9-84
Source: Scholar. *Honours:* Scotland Youth, Under-21, B.
2001–02 Millwall 1 0
2002–03 Millwall 5 1
2003–04 Millwall 29 2
2004–05 Millwall 24 2 **59 5**

WARD, Darren (D) 215 6
H: 6 3 W: 13 11 b.Kenton 13-9-78
Source: Trainee.
1995–96 Watford 1 0
1996–97 Watford 7 0
1997–98 Watford 0 0
1998–99 Watford 1 0
1999–2000 Watford 9 1
1999–2000 *QPR* 14 0 **14 0**
2000–01 Watford 40 1
2001–02 Watford 1 0 **59 2**
2001–02 Millwall 14 0
2002–03 Millwall 39 1
2003–04 Millwall 46 3
2004–05 Millwall 43 0 **142 4**

WESTON, Curtis (M) 4 0
H: 5 11 W: 11 09 b.Greenwich 24-1-87
Source: Scholar.
2003–04 Millwall 1 0
2004–05 Millwall 3 0 **4 0**

WISE, Dennis (M) 569 88
H: 5 6 W: 10 10 b.Kensington 16-12-66
Source: Southampton Apprentice. *Honours:* England Under-21, B, 21 full caps, 1 goal.
1984–85 Wimbledon 1 0
1985–86 Wimbledon 4 0
1986–87 Wimbledon 28 4
1987–88 Wimbledon 30 10
1988–89 Wimbledon 37 5
1989–90 Wimbledon 35 8 **135 27**
1990–91 Chelsea 33 10
1991–92 Chelsea 38 10
1992–93 Chelsea 27 3
1993–94 Chelsea 35 4
1994–95 Chelsea 19 6
1995–96 Chelsea 35 7
1996–97 Chelsea 31 3
1997–98 Chelsea 26 3
1998–99 Chelsea 22 0
1999–2000 Chelsea 30 4
2000–01 Chelsea 36 3 **332 53**
2001–02 Leicester C 17 1
2002–03 Leicester C 0 0 **17 1**

2002–03	Millwall	29	3		
2003–04	Millwall	31	1		
2004–05	Millwall	25	3	**85**	**7**

MILTON KEYNES D (52)

BAKER, Matt (G) **35** **0**
H: 6 0 W: 14 00 b.Harrogate 18-12-79
Source: Trainee.

1998–99	Hull C	0	0		
1999–2000	Hull C	2	0		
2000–01	Hull C	0	0		
2001–02	Hull C	0	0	**2**	**0**
From Hereford U.					
2004–05	Wrexham	13	0	**13**	**0**
2004–05	Milton Keynes D	20	0	**20**	**0**

BEVAN, Scott (G) **52** **0**
H: 6 6 W: 15 10 b.Southampton 16-9-79
Source: Trainee.

1997–98	Southampton	0	0		
1998–99	Southampton	0	0		
1999–2000	Southampton	0	0		
2000–01	Southampton	0	0		
2001–02	Southampton	0	0		
2001–02	*Stoke C*	0	0		
2002–03	Southampton	0	0		
2002–03	*Huddersfield T*	30	0	**30**	**0**
2003–04	Southampton	0	0		
2003–04	*Wycombe W*	5	0	**5**	**0**
2003–04	Wimbledon	10	0	**10**	**0**
2004–05	Milton Keynes D	7	0	**7**	**0**

CHORLEY, Ben (M) **88** **4**
H: 6 3 W: 13 02 b.Sidcup 30-9-82
Source: Scholar.

2001–02	Arsenal	0	0		
2002–03	Arsenal	0	0		
2002–03	*Brentford*	2	0	**2**	**0**
2002–03	Wimbledon	10	0		
2003–04	Wimbledon	35	2	**45**	**2**
2004–05	Milton Keynes D	41	2	**41**	**2**

CROOKS, Leon (M) **17** **0**
H: 6 0 W: 11 12 b.Greenwich 21-11-85
Source: Scholar.

2004–05	Milton Keynes D	17	0	**17**	**0**

EDDS, Gareth (D) **92** **6**
H: 5 11 W: 11 01 b.Sydney 3-2-81
Source: From Trainee. *Honours:* Australia Under-20, Under-23.

1997–98	Nottingham F	0	0		
1998–99	Nottingham F	0	0		
1999–2000	Nottingham F	2	0		
2000–01	Nottingham F	13	1		
2001–02	Nottingham F	1	0	**16**	**1**
2002–03	Swindon T	14	0	**14**	**0**
2003–04	Bradford C	23	0	**23**	**0**
2004–05	Milton Keynes D	39	5	**39**	**5**

HARDING, Ben (M) **41** **4**
H: 5 10 W: 11 02 b.Carshalton 6-9-84
Source: Scholar. *Honours:* England Youth.

2001–02	Wimbledon	0	0		
2002–03	Wimbledon	0	0		
2003–04	Wimbledon	15	0	**15**	**0**
2004–05	Milton Keynes D	26	4	**26**	**4**

HEALD, Paul (G) **223** **0**
H: 6 2 W: 14 00 b.Wath-on-Dearne 20-9-68
Source: Trainee.

1987–88	Sheffield U	0	0		
1988–89	Sheffield U	0	0		
1988–89	Leyton Orient	28	0		
1989–90	Leyton Orient	37	0		
1990–91	Leyton Orient	38	0		
1991–92	Leyton Orient	2	0		
1991–92	*Coventry C*	2	0	**2**	**0**
1992–93	Leyton Orient	26	0		
1992–93	*Crystal Palace*	0	0		
1993–94	Leyton Orient	0	0		
1993–94	*Swindon T*	2	0	**2**	**0**
1994–95	Leyton Orient	45	0	**176**	**0**
1995–96	Wimbledon	18	0		
1996–97	Wimbledon	2	0		
1997–98	Wimbledon	0	0		
1998–99	Wimbledon	0	0		
1999–2000	Wimbledon	1	0		
2000–01	Wimbledon	3	0		
2001–02	Wimbledon	4	0		
2001–02	*Sheffield W*	5	0	**5**	**0**
2002–03	Wimbledon	0	0		
2003–04	Wimbledon	10	0	**38**	**0**
2004–05	Milton Keynes D	0	0		

HERVE, Laurent (M) **96** **2**
H: 5 10 W: 11 07 b.Quimper 19-6-76

1995–96	Guingamp	3	0		
1996–97	Guingamp	4	0		
1997–98	Guingamp	4	0		
1998–99	Guingamp	12	0		
1999–2000	Guingamp	35	2		
2000–01	Guingamp	8	0		
2001–02	Guingamp	10	0		
2002–03	Guingamp	0	0	**76**	**2**
2003–04	Beauvais-Oise	0	0		
2004–05	Milton Keynes D	20	0	**20**	**0**

HERZIG, Nico (M) **19** **0**
H: 5 10 W: 11 00 b.Pobneck 10-12-83
Source: Carl Zeiss Jena.

2001–02	Wimbledon	0	0		
2002–03	Wimbledon	0	0		
2003–04	Wimbledon	19	0	**19**	**0**
2004–05	Milton Keynes D	0	0		

HORNUSS, Julien (F) **3** **0**
H: 5 10 W: 11 00 b.Paris 12-6-86
Source: Sedan.

2004–05	Milton Keynes D	3	0	**3**	**0**

KAMARA, Malvin (M) **54** **3**
H: 5 11 W: 13 00 b.London 17-11-83
Source: Scholar.

2002–03	Wimbledon	2	0		
2003–04	Wimbledon	27	2	**29**	**2**
2004–05	Milton Keynes D	25	1	**25**	**1**

KOO-BOOTHE, Nathan (D) **1** **0**
H: 6 4 W: 13 12 b.Westminster 18-7-84

2002–03	Watford	0	0		
2003–04	Watford	0	0		
2004–05	Milton Keynes D	1	0	**1**	**0**

LEWINGTON, Dean (D) **72** **3**
H: 5 11 W: 11 07 b.Kingston 18-5-84
Source: Scholar.

2002–03	Wimbledon	1	0		
2003–04	Wimbledon	28	1	**29**	**1**
2004–05	Milton Keynes D	43	2	**43**	**2**

MACKIE, Jamie (F) **16** **0**
H: 5 8 W: 11 00 b.Dorking 22-9-85
Source: Leatherhead.

2003–04	Wimbledon	13	0	**13**	**0**
2004–05	Milton Keynes D	3	0	**3**	**0**

MAKOFO, Serge (M) **1** **0**
H: 5 11 W: 12 06 b.Kinshasa 22-10-86
Source: Scholar.

2004–05	Milton Keynes D	1	0	**1**	**0**

MARTIN, David (G) **17** **0**
H: 6 1 W: 13 04 b.Romford 22-1-86
Source: From Scholar. *Honours:* England Youth.

2003–04	Wimbledon	2	0	**2**	**0**
2004–05	Milton Keynes D	15	0	**15**	**0**

McKOY, Nick (M) **3** **0**
H: 6 0 W: 12 06 b.Newham 3-9-86

2003–04	Wimbledon	3	0	**3**	**0**
2004–05	Milton Keynes D	0	0		

McLEOD, Izale (F) **89** **20**
H: 6 1 W: 11 02 b.Perry Bar 15-10-84
Source: Scholar.

2002–03	Derby Co	29	3		
2003–04	Derby Co	10	1	**39**	**4**
2003–04	*Sheffield U*	7	0	**7**	**0**
2004–05	Milton Keynes D	43	16	**43**	**16**

NTIMBAN-ZEH, Harry (D) **21** **0**
H: 6 1 W: 12 07 b.Aubervilliers 26-9-73
Source: SC Espinho.

2003–04	Wimbledon	10	0	**10**	**0**
2004–05	Milton Keynes D	11	0	**11**	**0**

OYEDELE, Shola (D) **34** **0**
H: 5 11 W: 12 07 b.Kano 14-9-84
Source: Scholar.

2003–04	Wimbledon	9	0	**9**	**0**
2004–05	Milton Keynes D	25	0	**25**	**0**

PALMER, Steve (D) **505** **20**
H: 6 1 W: 12 13 b.Brighton 31-3-68
Source: Cambridge Univ. *Honours:* England Schools.

1989–90	Ipswich T	5	0		
1990–91	Ipswich T	23	1		
1991–92	Ipswich T	23	0		
1992–93	Ipswich T	7	0		
1993–94	Ipswich T	36	1		
1994–95	Ipswich T	12	0		
1995–96	Ipswich T	5	0	**111**	**2**
1995–96	Watford	35	1		
1996–97	Watford	41	2		
1997–98	Watford	41	2		
1998–99	Watford	41	2		
1999–2000	Watford	38	0		
2000–01	Watford	39	1	**235**	**8**
2001–02	QPR	46	4		
2002–03	QPR	46	1		
2003–04	QPR	35	4	**127**	**9**
2004–05	Milton Keynes D	32	1	**32**	**1**

PENSEE-BILONG, Michel (D) **18** **1**
H: 6 4 W: 14 02 b.Cameroon 16-6-73
Source: Sanfrecce. *Honours:* Cameroon full caps.

2004–05	Milton Keynes D	18	1	**18**	**1**

PLATT, Clive (F) **277** **46**
H: 6 4 W: 12 07 b.Wolverhampton 27-10-77
Source: Trainee.

1995–96	Walsall	4	2		
1996–97	Walsall	1	0		
1997–98	Walsall	20	1		
1998–99	Walsall	7	1		
1999–2000	Walsall	0	0	**32**	**4**
1999–2000	Rochdale	41	9		
2000–01	Rochdale	43	8		
2001–02	Rochdale	43	7		
2002–03	Rochdale	42	6	**169**	**30**
2003–04	Notts Co	19	3	**19**	**3**
2003–04	Peterborough U	18	2		
2004–05	Peterborough U	19	4	**37**	**6**
2004–05	Milton Keynes D	20	3	**20**	**3**

PUNCHEON, Jason (M) **33** **1**
H: 5 9 W: 12 05 b.Croydon 26-6-86
Source: Scholar.

2003–04	Wimbledon	8	0	**8**	**0**
2004–05	Milton Keynes D	25	1	**25**	**1**

RIZZO, Nicky (M) **75** **5**
H: 5 10 W: 12 00 b.Sydney 9-6-79
Source: Sydney Olympic. *Honours:* Australia Youth, Under-20, Under-23, 1 full cap.

1996–97	Liverpool	0	0		
1997–98	Liverpool	0	0		
1998–99	Crystal Palace	19	1		
1999–2000	Crystal Palace	17	0	**36**	**1**
2000–01	Ternana	0	0		
2001–02	Ternana	1	0		
2002–03	Ternana	0	0	**1**	**0**
2003–04	Prato	20	2	**20**	**2**
2004–05	Milton Keynes D	18	2	**18**	**2**

SMALL, Wade (M) **71** **11**
H: 5 8 W: 11 05 b.Croydon 23-2-84
Source: Scholar.

2003–04	Wimbledon	27	1	**27**	**1**
2004–05	Milton Keynes D	44	10	**44**	**10**

SMART, Allan (F) **201** **45**
H: 6 2 W: 12 07 b.Perth 8-7-74

1994–95	Caledonian Th	4	0	**4**	**0**
1994–95	Preston NE	19	6		
1995–96	Preston NE	2	0		
1995–96	*Carlisle U*	4	0		
1996–97	Preston NE	0	0	**21**	**6**
1996–97	*Northampton T*	1	0	**1**	**0**
1996–97	Carlisle U	28	10		
1997–98	Carlisle U	16	6	**48**	**16**
1998–99	Watford	35	7		
1999–2000	Watford	14	5		
2000–01	Watford	8	0		
2001–02	Watford	0	0	**57**	**12**
2001–02	*Hibernian*	5	1	**5**	**1**
2001–02	*Stoke C*	2	0	**2**	**0**
2001–02	Oldham Ath	21	6	**21**	**6**
2002–03	Dundee U	18	0	**18**	**0**
2003–04	Crewe Alex	6	0	**6**	**0**
2004–05	Milton Keynes D	18	4	**18**	**4**

SMITH, Gary (M) **34** **4**
H: 5 8 W: 10 09 b.Middlesbrough 30-1-84
Source: Trainee.

2002–03	Middlesbrough	0	0		
2003–04	Middlesbrough	0	0		
2003–04	*Wimbledon*	11	3	**11**	**3**
2004–05	Milton Keynes D	23	1	**23**	**1**

TAPP, Alex (M) **50** **4**
H: 5 8 W: 10 13 b.Redhill 7-6-82
Source: Trainee.

1999–2000	Wimbledon	0	0		
2000–01	Wimbledon	0	0		
2001–02	Wimbledon	0	0		
2002–03	Wimbledon	24	2		
2003–04	Wimbledon	14	1	**38**	**3**
2004–05	Milton Keynes D	12	1	**12**	**1**

WILLIAMS, Mark (D) **404** **24**
H: 6 0 W: 13 00 b.Stalybridge 28-9-70
Source: Newtown. *Honours:* Northern Ireland B, 36 full caps, 1 goal.

1991–92	Shrewsbury T	3	0		
1992–93	Shrewsbury T	28	1		
1993–94	Shrewsbury T	36	1		
1994–95	Shrewsbury T	35	1	**102**	**3**
1995–96	Chesterfield	42	3		
1996–97	Chesterfield	42	3		
1997–98	Chesterfield	44	3		
1998–99	Chesterfield	40	3	**168**	**12**
1999–2000	Watford	22	1	**22**	**1**
2000–01	Wimbledon	42	6		
2001–02	Wimbledon	5	0		
2002–03	Wimbledon	23	1		
2002–03	Stoke C	6	0	**6**	**0**
2003	Columbus Crew	5	0	**5**	**0**
2003–04	Wimbledon	11	1	**81**	**8**
2004–05	Milton Keynes D	13	0	**13**	**0**
2004–05	*Rushden & D*	7	0	**7**	**0**

NEWCASTLE U (53)

AMBROSE, Darren (M) **67** **13**
H: 6 0 W: 11 00 b.Harlow 29-2-84
Source: Scholar. *Honours:* England Youth, Under-20, Under-21.

2001–02	Ipswich T	1	0		
2002–03	Ipswich T	29	8	**30**	**8**
2002–03	Newcastle U	1	0		
2003–04	Newcastle U	24	2		
2004–05	Newcastle U	12	3	**37**	**5**

AMEOBI, Foluwashola (F) **120** **16**
H: 6 3 W: 11 13 b.Zaria 12-10-81
Source: Trainee. *Honours:* England Under-21.

1998–99	Newcastle U	0	0		
1999–2000	Newcastle U	0	0		
2000–01	Newcastle U	20	2		
2001–02	Newcastle U	15	0		
2002–03	Newcastle U	28	5		
2003–04	Newcastle U	26	7		
2004–05	Newcastle U	31	2	**120**	**16**

BABAYARO, Celestine (D) **214** **13**
H: 5 9 W: 12 06 b.Kaduna 29-8-78
Source: Plateau U. *Honours:* Nigeria 26 full caps.

1994–95	Anderlecht	22	0		
1995–96	Anderlecht	28	5		
1996–97	Anderlecht	25	3	**75**	**8**
1997–98	Chelsea	8	0		
1998–99	Chelsea	28	3		
1999–2000	Chelsea	25	0		
2000–01	Chelsea	24	0		
2001–02	Chelsea	18	0		
2002–03	Chelsea	19	1		
2003–04	Chelsea	6	1		
2004–05	Chelsea	4	0	**132**	**5**
2004–05	Newcastle U	7	0	**7**	**0**

BELLAMY, Craig (F) **223** **72**
H: 5 8 W: 10 05 b.Cardiff 13-7-79
Source: Trainee. *Honours:* Wales Schools, Youth, Under-21, 33 full caps, 9 goals.

1996–97	Norwich C	3	0		
1997–98	Norwich C	36	13		
1998–99	Norwich C	40	17		
1999–2000	Norwich C	4	2		
2000–01	Norwich C	1	0	**84**	**32**
2000–01	Coventry C	34	6	**34**	**6**
2001–02	Newcastle U	27	9		
2002–03	Newcastle U	29	7		
2003–04	Newcastle U	16	4		
2004–05	Newcastle U	21	7	**93**	**27**
2004–05	*Celtic*	12	7	**12**	**7**

BOUMSONG, Jean-Alain (D) **205** **6**
H: 6 3 W: 13 03 b.Douala 14-12-79
Source: US Palaiseau. *Honours:* France, 11 full caps.

1997–98	Le Havre	1	0		
1998–99	Le Havre	18	1		
1999–2000	Le Havre	23	0	**42**	**1**
2000–01	Auxerre	32	0		
2001–02	Auxerre	34	1		
2002–03	Auxerre	33	1		
2003–04	Auxerre	32	1	**131**	**3**
2004–05	Rangers	18	2	**18**	**2**
2004–05	Newcastle U	14	0	**14**	**0**

BOWYER, Lee (M) **310** **51**
H: 5 9 W: 10 12 b.London 3-1-77
Source: Trainee. *Honours:* England Youth, Under-21, 1 full cap.

1993–94	Charlton Ath	0	0		
1994–95	Charlton Ath	5	0		
1995–96	Charlton Ath	41	8	**46**	**8**
1996–97	Leeds U	32	4		
1997–98	Leeds U	25	3		
1998–99	Leeds U	35	9		
1999–2000	Leeds U	33	5		
2000–01	Leeds U	38	9		
2001–02	Leeds U	25	5		
2002–03	Leeds U	15	3	**203**	**38**
2002–03	West Ham U	10	0	**10**	**0**
2003–04	Newcastle U	24	2		
2004–05	Newcastle U	27	3	**51**	**5**

BRAMBLE, Titus (D) **114** **2**
H: 6 2 W: 13 10 b.Ipswich 31-7-81
Source: Trainee. *Honours:* England Under-21.

1998–99	Ipswich T	4	0		
1999–2000	Ipswich T	0	0		
1999–2000	*Colchester U*	2	0	**2**	**0**
2000–01	Ipswich T	26	1		
2001–02	Ipswich T	18	0	**48**	**1**
2002–03	Newcastle U	16	0		
2003–04	Newcastle U	29	0		
2004–05	Newcastle U	19	1	**64**	**1**

BRENNAN, Stephen (D) **0** **0**
H: 5 8 W: 11 10 b.Dublin 26-3-83
Honours: Eire Under-21.

1999–2000	Newcastle U	0	0		
2000–01	Newcastle U	0	0		
2001–02	Newcastle U	0	0		
2002–03	Newcastle U	0	0		
2003–04	Newcastle U	0	0		
2004–05	Newcastle U	0	0		

BRITTAIN, Martin (M) **1** **0**
H: 5 8 W: 10 08 b.Newcastle 29-12-84
Source: Trainee.

2003–04	Newcastle U	1	0		
2004–05	Newcastle U	0	0	**1**	**0**

BUTT, Nicky (M) **288** **22**
H: 5 10 W: 11 05 b.Manchester 21-1-75
Source: Trainee. *Honours:* England Schools, Youth, Under-21, 39 full caps.

1992–93	Manchester U	1	0		
1993–94	Manchester U	1	0		
1994–95	Manchester U	22	1		
1995–96	Manchester U	32	2		
1996–97	Manchester U	26	5		
1997–98	Manchester U	33	3		
1998–99	Manchester U	31	2		
1999–2000	Manchester U	32	3		
2000–01	Manchester U	28	3		
2001–02	Manchester U	25	1		
2002–03	Manchester U	18	0		
2003–04	Manchester U	21	1	**270**	**21**
2004–05	Newcastle U	18	1	**18**	**1**

CAIG, Tony (G) **289** **0**
H: 6 0 W: 13 03 b.Whitehaven 11-4-74
Source: Trainee.

1992–93	Carlisle U	1	0		
1993–94	Carlisle U	20	0		
1994–95	Carlisle U	40	0		
1995–96	Carlisle U	33	0		
1996–97	Carlisle U	46	0		
1997–98	Carlisle U	46	0		
1998–99	Carlisle U	37	0	**223**	**0**
1998–99	Blackpool	10	0		
1999–2000	Blackpool	33	0		
2000–01	Blackpool	6	0	**49**	**0**
2000–01	Charlton Ath	1	0	**1**	**0**
2001–02	Hibernian	8	0		
2002–03	Hibernian	5	0	**13**	**0**
2002–03	Newcastle U	0	0		
2003–04	Newcastle U	0	0		
2003–04	*Barnsley*	3	0	**3**	**0**
2004–05	Newcastle U	0	0		

CARR, Stephen (D) **252** **8**
H: 5 9 W: 12 02 b.Dublin 29-8-76
Source: Trainee. *Honours:* Eire Schools, Youth, Under-21, 37 full caps.

1993–94	Tottenham H	1	0		
1994–95	Tottenham H	0	0		
1995–96	Tottenham H	0	0		
1996–97	Tottenham H	26	0		
1997–98	Tottenham H	38	0		
1998–99	Tottenham H	37	0		
1999–2000	Tottenham H	34	3		
2000–01	Tottenham H	28	3		
2001–02	Tottenham H	0	0		
2002–03	Tottenham H	30	0		
2003–04	Tottenham H	32	1	**226**	**7**
2004–05	Newcastle U	26	1	**26**	**1**

CHOPRA, Michael (F) **57** **22**
H: 5 9 W: 10 03 b.Newcastle 23-12-83
Source: Scholar. *Honours:* England Youth, Under-20, Under-21.

2000–01	Newcastle U	0	0		
2001–02	Newcastle U	0	0		
2002–03	Newcastle U	1	0		
2002–03	*Watford*	5	5	**5**	**5**
2003–04	Newcastle U	6	0		
2003–04	*Nottingham F*	5	0	**5**	**0**
2004–05	Newcastle U	1	0	**8**	**0**
2004–05	*Barnsley*	39	17	**39**	**17**

DYER, Kieron (M) **248** **27**
H: 5 8 W: 10 00 b.Ipswich 29-12-78
Source: Trainee. *Honours:* England Youth, Under-21, B, 28 full caps.

1996–97	Ipswich T	13	0		
1997–98	Ipswich T	41	4		
1998–99	Ipswich T	37	5	**91**	**9**
1999–2000	Newcastle U	30	3		
2000–01	Newcastle U	26	5		
2001–02	Newcastle U	18	3		
2002–03	Newcastle U	35	2		
2003–04	Newcastle U	25	1		
2004–05	Newcastle U	23	4	**157**	**18**

ELLIOTT, Robbie (D) **211** **16**
H: 5 10 W: 10 12 b.Gosforth 25-12-73
Source: Trainee. *Honours:* England Under-21.

1990–91	Newcastle U	6	0		
1991–92	Newcastle U	9	0		
1992–93	Newcastle U	0	0		
1993–94	Newcastle U	15	0		
1994–95	Newcastle U	14	2		
1995–96	Newcastle U	6	0		
1996–97	Newcastle U	29	7		
1997–98	Bolton W	4	0		
1998–99	Bolton W	22	0		
1999–2000	Bolton W	27	3		
2000–01	Bolton W	33	2	**86**	**5**
2001–02	Newcastle U	27	1		
2002–03	Newcastle U	2	0		
2003–04	Newcastle U	0	0		
2004–05	Newcastle U	17	1	**125**	**11**

FAYE, Amdy (M) **136** **2**
H: 6 1 W: 12 04 b.Dakar 12-3-77
Source: Frejus. *Honours:* Senegal full caps.

1998–99	Auxerre	0	0		
1999–2000	Auxerre	3	0		
2000–01	Auxerre	23	0		
2001–02	Auxerre	20	0		
2002–03	Auxerre	34	2	**80**	**2**
2003–04	Portsmouth	27	0		
2004–05	Portsmouth	20	0	**47**	**0**
2004–05	Newcastle U	9	0	**9**	**0**

GATE, Kris (D) **0 0**
H: 5 7 W: 10 03 b.Newcastle 1-1-85
Source: Trainee.

2003–04	Newcastle U	0	0		
2004–05	Newcastle U	0	0		

GIVEN, Shay (G) **277 0**
H: 6 0 W: 13 03 b.Lifford 20-4-76
Source: Celtic. *Honours:* Eire Youth, Under-21, 70 full caps.

1994–95	Blackburn R	0	0		
1994–95	*Swindon T*	0	0		
1995–96	Blackburn R	0	0		
1995–96	*Swindon T*	5	0	**5**	**0**
1995–96	*Sunderland*	17	0	**17**	**0**
1996–97	Blackburn R	2	0	**2**	**0**
1997–98	Newcastle U	24	0		
1998–99	Newcastle U	31	0		
1999–2000	Newcastle U	14	0		
2000–01	Newcastle U	34	0		
2001–02	Newcastle U	38	0		
2002–03	Newcastle U	38	0		
2003–04	Newcastle U	38	0		
2004–05	Newcastle U	36	0	**253**	**0**

HARPER, Steve (G) **73 0**
H: 6 2 W: 13 10 b.Easington 14-3-75
Source: Seaham Red Star.

1993–94	Newcastle U	0	0		
1994–95	Newcastle U	0	0		
1995–96	Newcastle U	0	0		
1995–96	*Bradford C*	1	0	**1**	**0**
1996–97	Newcastle U	0	0		
1996–97	*Stockport Co*	0	0		
1997–98	Newcastle U	0	0		
1997–98	*Hartlepool U*	15	0	**15**	**0**
1997–98	*Huddersfield T*	24	0	**24**	**0**
1998–99	Newcastle U	8	0		
1999–2000	Newcastle U	18	0		
2000–01	Newcastle U	5	0		
2001–02	Newcastle U	0	0		
2002–03	Newcastle U	0	0		
2003–04	Newcastle U	0	0		
2004–05	Newcastle U	2	0	**33**	**0**

HUGHES, Aaron (D) **205 4**
H: 6 1 W: 11 02 b.Cookstown 8-11-79
Source: Trainee. *Honours:* Northern Ireland Youth, B, 43 full caps.

1996–97	Newcastle U	0	0		
1997–98	Newcastle U	4	0		
1998–99	Newcastle U	14	0		
1999–2000	Newcastle U	27	2		
2000–01	Newcastle U	35	0		
2001–02	Newcastle U	34	0		
2002–03	Newcastle U	35	1		
2003–04	Newcastle U	34	0		
2004–05	Newcastle U	22	1	**205**	**4**

JENAS, Jermaine (M) **135 13**
H: 5 10 W: 11 13 b.Nottingham 18-2-83
Source: Scholar. *Honours:* England Youth, Under-21, 12 full caps.

1999–2000	Nottingham F	0	0		
2000–01	Nottingham F	1	0		
2001–02	Nottingham F	28	4	**29**	**4**
2001–02	Newcastle U	12	0		
2002–03	Newcastle U	32	6		
2003–04	Newcastle U	31	2		
2004–05	Newcastle U	31	1	**106**	**9**

JOHNSEN, Ronny (D) **227 20**
H: 6 2 W: 13 05 b.Sandefjord 10-6-69
Honours: Norway 61 full caps, 3 goals.

1992	Lyn	12	1		
1993	Lyn	19	6	**31**	**7**
1994	Lillestrom	10	3		
1995	Lillestrom	13	1	**23**	**4**
1995–96	Besiktas	22	1	**22**	**1**
1996–97	Manchester U	31	0		
1997–98	Manchester U	22	2		
1998–99	Manchester U	22	3		
1999–2000	Manchester U	3	0		
2000–01	Manchester U	11	1		
2001–02	Manchester U	10	1	**99**	**7**
2002–03	Aston Villa	26	0		
2003–04	Aston Villa	23	1	**49**	**1**
2004–05	Newcastle U	3	0	**3**	**0**

KLUIVERT, Patrick (F) **303 140**
H: 6 2 W: 13 03 b.Amsterdam 1-7-76
Honours: Holland 79 full caps, 41 goals.

1994–95	Ajax	25	18		
1995–96	Ajax	28	15		
1996–97	Ajax	17	6	**70**	**39**
1997–98	AC Milan	27	6	**27**	**6**
1998–99	Barcelona	34	15		
1999–2000	Barcelona	26	15		
2000–01	Barcelona	31	17		
2001–02	Barcelona	33	18		
2002–03	Barcelona	36	16		
2003–04	Barcelona	21	8	**181**	**89**
2004–05	Newcastle U	25	6	**25**	**6**

McCLEN, Jamie (M) **14 0**
H: 5 8 W: 10 12 b.Newcastle 13-5-79
Source: Trainee.

1997–98	Newcastle U	0	0		
1998–99	Newcastle U	1	0		
1999–2000	Newcastle U	9	0		
2000–01	Newcastle U	0	0		
2001–02	Newcastle U	3	0		
2002–03	Newcastle U	1	0		
2003–04	Newcastle U	0	0		
2004–05	Newcastle U	0	0	**14**	**0**

MILNER, James (M) **79 8**
H: 5 10 W: 11 00 b.Leeds 4-1-86
Source: Trainee. *Honours:* FA Schools, Youth, England Under-20, Under-21.

2002–03	Leeds U	18	2		
2003–04	Leeds U	30	3	**48**	**5**
2003–04	*Swindon T*	6	2	**6**	**2**
2004–05	Newcastle U	25	1	**25**	**1**

N'ZOGBIA, Charles (M) **14 0**
H: 5 9 W: 11 00 b.France 28-5-86

2004–05	Newcastle U	14	0	**14**	**0**

O'BRIEN, Alan (M) **0 0**
H: 5 9 W: 11 00 b.Dublin 20-2-85
Source: Scholar.

2001–02	Newcastle U	0	0		
2002–03	Newcastle U	0	0		
2003–04	Newcastle U	0	0		
2004–05	Newcastle U	0	0		

O'BRIEN, Andy (D) **253 9**
H: 6 2 W: 11 13 b.Harrogate 29-6-79
Source: Trainee. *Honours:* England Youth, Under-21, Eire Under-21, 21 full caps, 1 goal.

1996–97	Bradford C	22	2		
1997–98	Bradford C	26	0		
1998–99	Bradford C	31	0		
1999–2000	Bradford C	36	1		
2000–01	Bradford C	18	0	**133**	**3**
2000–01	Newcastle U	9	1		
2001–02	Newcastle U	34	2		
2002–03	Newcastle U	26	0		
2003–04	Newcastle U	28	1		
2004–05	Newcastle U	23	2	**120**	**6**

RAMAGE, Peter (D) **4 0**
H: 6 1 W: 11 03 b.Whitley Bay 22-11-83
Source: Trainee.

2003–04	Newcastle U	0	0		
2004–05	Newcastle U	4	0	**4**	**0**

ROBERT, Laurent (M) **314 64**
H: 5 8 W: 10 12 b.Saint-Benoit 21-5-75
Honours: France 9 full caps, 1 goal.

1994–95	Montpellier	7	0		
1995–96	Montpellier	21	5		
1996–97	Nancy	38	1	**38**	**1**
1997–98	Montpellier	26	2		
1998–99	Montpellier	32	11	**86**	**18**
1999–2000	Paris St Germain	28	9		
2000–01	Paris St Germain	32	14		
2001–02	Paris St Germain	1	0	**61**	**23**
2001–02	Newcastle U	36	8		
2002–03	Newcastle U	27	5		
2003–04	Newcastle U	35	6		
2004–05	Newcastle U	31	3	**129**	**22**

SHANKS, Chris (D) **0 0**
H: 6 0 W: 11 00 b.Ashington 16-10-86
Source: Scholar.

2004–05	Newcastle U	0	0		

SHEARER, Alan (F) **527 273**
H: 5 11 W: 12 06 b.Newcastle 13-8-70
Source: From Trainee. *Honours:* England Youth, Under-21, B, 63 full caps, 30 goals.

1987–88	Southampton	5	3		
1988–89	Southampton	10	0		
1989–90	Southampton	26	3		
1990–91	Southampton	36	4		
1991–92	Southampton	41	13	**118**	**23**
1992–93	Blackburn R	21	16		
1993–94	Blackburn R	40	31		
1994–95	Blackburn R	42	34		
1995–96	Blackburn R	35	31	**138**	**112**
1996–97	Newcastle U	31	25		
1997–98	Newcastle U	17	2		
1998–99	Newcastle U	30	14		
1999–2000	Newcastle U	37	23		
2000–01	Newcastle U	19	5		
2001–02	Newcastle U	37	23		
2002–03	Newcastle U	35	17		
2003–04	Newcastle U	37	22		
2004–05	Newcastle U	28	7	**271**	**138**

TAYLOR, Steven (D) **20 0**
H: 6 1 W: 13 01 b.Greenwich 23-1-86
Source: Trainee. *Honours:* FA Schools, Youth, England Under-20, Under-21.

2002–03	Newcastle U	0	0		
2003–04	Newcastle U	1	0		
2003–04	*Wycombe W*	6	0	**6**	**0**
2004–05	Newcastle U	13	0	**14**	**0**

VIANA, Hugo (M) **65 3**
H: 5 9 W: 11 09 b.Barcelos 15-1-83
Honours: Portugal 12 full caps.

2001–02	Sporting Lisbon	26	1	**26**	**1**
2002–03	Newcastle U	23	2		
2003–04	Newcastle U	16	0		
2004–05	Newcastle U	0	0	**39**	**2**

Scholars
Atkin, Liam; Baxter, Craig Michael; Cave, Philip Adam; Deverdics, Nicholas Ferenc; Edgar, David Edward; Farman, Christopher; Finnigan, Carl John; Huntington, Paul David; Marshall, Scott Anthony; Pattison, Matthew; Smith, Benjamin James; Smylie, Daryl; Terrell, Michael John; Troisi, James; Walton, Marc David; Webster, Benjamin Gordon

NORTHAMPTON T (54)

ALSOP, Julian (F) **281 61**
H: 6 4 W: 15 02 b.Nuneaton 28-5-73
Source: Nuneaton, VS Rugby, RC Warwick, Tamworth, Halesowen T.

1996–97	Bristol R	16	3		
1997–98	Bristol R	17	1	**33**	**4**
1997–98	Swansea C	12	3		
1998–99	Swansea C	41	10		
1999–2000	Swansea C	37	3	**90**	**16**
2000–01	Cheltenham T	39	5		
2001–02	Cheltenham T	41	20		
2002–03	Cheltenham T	37	10	**117**	**35**
2003–04	Oxford U	29	5		
2004–05	Oxford U	5	0	**34**	**5**
2004–05	Northampton T	7	1	**7**	**1**

AMOO, Ryan (M) **6 0**
H: 5 10 W: 9 12 b.Leicester 11-10-83
Source: Scholar.

2001–02	Aston Villa	0	0		
2002–03	Aston Villa	0	0		
2003–04	Aston Villa	0	0		
2003–04	Northampton T	1	0		
2004–05	Northampton T	5	0	**6**	**0**

BOJIC, Pedj (D) **36 0**
H: 5 11 W: 11 12 b.Sydney 9-4-84
Source: Sydney Olympic. *Honours:* Australia Youth.

2004–05	Northampton T	36	0	**36**	**0**

BUNN, Mark (G) **0 0**
H: 6 0 W: 12 02 b.Camden 16-11-84
Source: Scholar.

2004–05	Northampton T	0	0		

CARRUTHERS, Chris (D) 79 1
H: 5 10 W: 12 03 b.Kettering 19-8-83
Source: From Scholar. *Honours:* England Under-20.
2000–01 Northampton T 3 0
2001–02 Northampton T 13 1
2002–03 Northampton T 33 0
2003–04 Northampton T 24 0
2004–05 Northampton T 1 0 **74 1**
2004–05 *Bristol R* 5 0 **5 0**

CHAMBERS, Luke (D) 52 0
H: 6 1 W: 11 13 b.Kettering 29-8-85
Source: Scholar.
2002–03 Northampton T 1 0
2003–04 Northampton T 24 0
2004–05 Northampton T 27 0 **52 0**

CLARK, Peter (D) 160 4
H: 6 1 W: 12 01 b.Romford 10-12-79
Source: Arsenal Trainee.
1998–99 Carlisle U 36 0
1999–2000 Carlisle U 43 1 **79 1**
2000–01 Stockport Co 37 2
2001–02 Stockport Co 14 0
2002–03 Stockport Co 21 1 **72 3**
2002–03 *Mansfield T* 3 0 **3 0**
2003–04 Northampton T 6 0
2004–05 Northampton T 0 0 **6 0**

CROSS, Scott (M) 1 0
H: 5 10 W: 11 00 b.Northampton 30-10-87
Source: Scholar.
2004–05 Northampton T 1 0 **1 0**

GALBRAITH, David (M) 25 1
H: 5 8 W: 11 00 b.Luton 21-12-83
Source: Trainee.
2003–04 Tottenham H 0 0
2003–04 Northampton T 0 0
2004–05 Northampton T 25 1 **25 1**

GRAHAM, Luke (D) 0 0
b.Kettering 27-4-86
Source: Scholar.
2004–05 Northampton T 0 0

HARPER, Lee (G) 228 0
H: 6 1 W: 15 06 b.Chelsea 30-10-71
Source: Sittingbourne.
1994–95 Arsenal 0 0
1995–96 Arsenal 0 0
1996–97 Arsenal 1 0 **1 0**
1997–98 QPR 36 0
1998–99 QPR 15 0
1999–2000 QPR 38 0
2000–01 QPR 29 0 **118 0**
2001–02 Walsall 3 0 **3 0**
2002–03 Northampton T 31 0
2003–04 Northampton T 39 0
2004–05 Northampton T 36 0 **106 0**

HASLAM, Steven (M) 147 2
H: 5 11 W: 10 10 b.Sheffield 6-9-79
Source: Trainee. *Honours:* England Schools, Youth.
1996–97 Sheffield W 0 0
1997–98 Sheffield W 0 0
1998–99 Sheffield W 2 0
1999–2000 Sheffield W 23 0
2000–01 Sheffield W 27 1
2001–02 Sheffield W 41 0
2002–03 Sheffield W 26 1
2003–04 Sheffield W 25 0 **144 2**
2004–05 Northampton T 3 0 **3 0**

HICKS, David (M) 3 0
H: 5 10 W: 10 08 b.Enfield 13-11-85
Source: Tottenham H Scholar.
2003–04 Northampton T 0 0
2004–05 Northampton T 3 0 **3 0**

HUNT, David (D) 71 1
H: 5 10 W: 11 08 b.Dulwich 10-9-82
Source: Scholar.
2002–03 Crystal Palace 2 0 **2 0**
2003–04 Leyton Orient 38 1
2004–05 Leyton Orient 27 0 **65 1**
2004–05 Northampton T 4 0 **4 0**

JASZCZUN, Tommy (D) 154 0
H: 5 10 W: 10 10 b.Kettering 16-9-77
Source: Trainee.
1996–97 Aston Villa 0 0
1997–98 Aston Villa 0 0
1998–99 Aston Villa 0 0
1999–2000 Aston Villa 0 0
1999–2000 Blackpool 19 0
2000–01 Blackpool 35 0
2001–02 Blackpool 40 0
2002–03 Blackpool 21 0
2003–04 Blackpool 7 0 **122 0**
2004–05 Northampton T 32 0 **32 0**

KIRK, Andy (F) 89 44
H: 5 11 W: 11 07 b.Belfast 29-5-79
Honours: Northern Ireland Schools, Youth, Under-21, 8 full caps.
1995–96 Glentoran 1 1
1996–97 Glentoran 25 8
1997–98 Glentoran 25 9 **51 18**
1998–99 Hearts 5 0
1999–2000 Hearts 0 0
2000–01 Hearts 0 0
2001–02 Hearts 0 0 **5 0**
2004–05 Boston U 25 19 **25 19**
2004–05 Northampton T 8 7 **8 7**

LOW, Josh (F) 190 20
H: 6 2 W: 14 03 b.Bristol 15-2-79
Source: Trainee. *Honours:* Wales Youth, Under-21.
1995–96 Bristol R 1 0
1996–97 Bristol R 3 0
1997–98 Bristol R 10 0
1998–99 Bristol R 8 0 **22 0**
1999–2000 Leyton Orient 5 1 **5 1**
1999–2000 Cardiff C 17 2
2000–01 Cardiff C 36 4
2001–02 Cardiff C 22 0
2002–03 Cardiff C 0 0 **75 6**
2002–03 Oldham Ath 21 3 **21 3**
2003–04 Northampton T 33 3
2004–05 Northampton T 34 7 **67 10**

McGLEISH, Scott (F) 408 108
H: 5 9 W: 11 09 b.Barnet 10-2-74
Source: Edgware T.
1994–95 Charlton Ath 6 0 **6 0**
1994–95 *Leyton Orient* 6 1
1995–96 Peterborough U 12 0
1995–96 *Colchester U* 15 6
1996–97 Peterborough U 1 0 **13 0**
1996–97 *Cambridge U* 10 7 **10 7**
1996–97 Leyton Orient 28 7
1997–98 Leyton Orient 8 0 **42 8**
1997–98 Barnet 37 13
1998–99 Barnet 36 8
1999–2000 Barnet 42 10
2000–01 Barnet 19 5 **134 36**
2000–01 Colchester U 21 5
2001–02 Colchester U 46 15
2002–03 Colchester U 43 8
2003–04 Colchester U 34 10 **159 44**
2004–05 Northampton T 44 13 **44 13**

MORISON, Steven (F) 23 3
H: 6 2 W: 13 07 b.Enfield 29-8-83
Source: Scholar.
2001–02 Northampton T 1 0
2002–03 Northampton T 13 1
2003–04 Northampton T 5 1
2004–05 Northampton T 4 1 **23 3**

MURRAY, Fred (D) 126 0
H: 5 10 W: 11 12 b.Tipperary 22-5-82
Source: Trainee.
1998–99 Blackburn R 0 0
1999–2000 Blackburn R 0 0
2000–01 Blackburn R 0 0
2001–02 Blackburn R 0 0
2001–02 Cambridge U 21 0
2002–03 Cambridge U 29 0
2003–04 Cambridge U 38 0 **88 0**
2004–05 Northampton T 38 0 **38 0**

NGOYI, Greg (F) 0 0
b.Zaire 20-7-87
Source: Scholar.
2004–05 Northampton T 0 0

REEVES, Martin (M) 31 1
H: 6 0 W: 12 01 b.Birmingham 7-9-81
Source: Scholar.
2000–01 Leicester C 0 0
2001–02 Leicester C 5 0
2002–03 Leicester C 3 0 **8 0**
2002–03 *Hull C* 8 1 **8 1**
2003–04 Northampton T 14 0
2004–05 Northampton T 1 0 **15 0**

RICHARDS, Marc (F) 89 19
H: 6 0 W: 13 04 b.Wolverhampton 8-7-82
Source: Trainee. *Honours:* England Youth, Under-20.
1999–2000 Blackburn R 0 0
2000–01 Blackburn R 0 0
2001–02 Blackburn R 0 0
2001–02 *Crewe Alex* 4 0 **4 0**
2001–02 *Oldham Ath* 5 0 **5 0**
2001–02 *Halifax T* 5 0 **5 0**
2002–03 Blackburn R 0 0
2002–03 *Swansea C* 17 7 **17 7**
2003–04 Northampton T 41 8
2004–05 Northampton T 12 2 **53 10**
2004–05 *Rochdale* 5 2 **5 2**

ROWSON, David (M) 180 11
H: 5 10 W: 11 10 b.Aberdeen 14-9-76
Source: FC Stoneywood. *Honours:* Scotland Under-21.
1994–95 Aberdeen 0 0
1995–96 Aberdeen 9 0
1996–97 Aberdeen 34 2
1997–98 Aberdeen 30 5
1998–99 Aberdeen 22 0
1999–2000 Aberdeen 0 0
2000–01 Aberdeen 0 0 **95 7**
2001–02 Stoke C 13 0
2002–03 Stoke C 0 0 **13 0**
2003–04 Partick T 35 2 **35 2**
2004–05 Northampton T 37 2 **37 2**

SABIN, Eric (F) 164 26
H: 6 1 W: 12 04 b.Sarcelles 22-1-75
Source: Ajaccio, Nimes.
2000–01 Wasquehal 28 3 **28 3**
2001–02 Swindon T 34 5
2002–03 Swindon T 39 4 **73 9**
2003–04 QPR 10 1 **10 1**
2003–04 *Boston U* 2 0 **2 0**
2003–04 Northampton T 11 5
2004–05 Northampton T 40 8 **51 13**

SMITH, Martin (F) 303 85
H: 5 11 W: 12 07 b.Sunderland 13-11-74
Source: Trainee. *Honours:* England Schools, Under-21.
1992–93 Sunderland 0 0
1993–94 Sunderland 29 8
1994–95 Sunderland 35 10
1995–96 Sunderland 20 2
1996–97 Sunderland 11 0
1997–98 Sunderland 16 2
1998–99 Sunderland 8 3 **119 25**
1999–2000 Sheffield U 26 10 **26 10**
1999–2000 Huddersfield T 12 4
2000–01 Huddersfield T 30 8
2001–02 Huddersfield T 0 0
2002–03 Huddersfield T 38 17 **80 29**
2003–04 Northampton T 44 11
2004–05 Northampton T 34 10 **78 21**

TAYLOR, John (F) 524 152
H: 6 2 W: 13 12 b.Norwich 24-10-64
Source: Local.
1982–83 Colchester U 0 0
1983–84 Colchester U 0 0
1984–85 Colchester U 0 0
From Sudbury T
1988–89 Cambridge U 40 12
1989–90 Cambridge U 45 15
1990–91 Cambridge U 40 14
1991–92 Cambridge U 35 5
1991–92 Bristol R 8 7
1992–93 Bristol R 42 14
1993–94 Bristol R 45 23 **95 44**
1994–95 Bradford C 36 11 **36 11**
1994–95 Luton T 9 3
1995–96 Luton T 28 0
1996–97 Luton T 0 0 **37 3**
1996–97 *Lincoln C* 5 2 **5 2**
1996–97 *Colchester U* 8 5 **8 5**
1996–97 Cambridge U 21 4
1997–98 Cambridge U 34 10
1998–99 Cambridge U 40 17
1999–2000 Cambridge U 40 6

2000–01 Cambridge U 30 3
2001–02 Cambridge U 0 0
2002–03 Cambridge U 1 0
2003–04 Cambridge U 9 0 **335 86**
2003–04 Northampton T 8 1
2004–05 Northampton T 0 0 **8 1**

WESTWOOD, Ashley (D) 232 18
H: 6 0 W: 12 09 b.Bridgnorth 31-8-76
Source: Trainee. *Honours:* England Youth.
1994–95 Manchester U 0 0
1995–96 Crewe Alex 33 4
1996–97 Crewe Alex 44 2
1997–98 Crewe Alex 21 3 **98 9**
1998–99 Bradford C 19 2
1999–2000 Bradford C 5 0
2000–01 Bradford C 0 0 **24 2**
2000–01 Sheffield W 33 2
2001–02 Sheffield W 26 1
2002–03 Sheffield W 23 2 **82 5**
2003–04 Northampton T 9 0
2004–05 Northampton T 19 2 **28 2**

WILLIAMSON, Lee (M) 181 3
H: 5 10 W: 11 13 b.Derby 7-6-82
Source: Trainee.
1999–2000 Mansfield T 4 0
2000–01 Mansfield T 15 0
2001–02 Mansfield T 46 3
2002–03 Mansfield T 40 0
2003–04 Mansfield T 35 0
2004–05 Mansfield T 4 0 **144 3**
2004–05 Northampton T 37 0 **37 0**

WILLMOTT, Chris (D) 161 3
H: 6 2 W: 13 08 b.Bedford 30-9-77
Source: Trainee.
1995–96 Luton T 0 0
1996–97 Luton T 0 0
1997–98 Luton T 0 0
1998–99 Luton T 14 0
1999–2000 Wimbledon 7 0
2000–01 Wimbledon 14 1
2001–02 Wimbledon 27 1
2002–03 Wimbledon 5 0 **53 2**
2002–03 *Luton T* 13 0 **27 0**
2003–04 Northampton T 36 1
2004–05 Northampton T 45 0 **81 1**

NORWICH C (55)

ASHTON, Dean (F) 175 67
H: 6 2 W: 12 08 b.Swindon 24-11-83
Source: Schoolboy. *Honours:* England Youth, Under-20, Under-21.
2000–01 Crewe Alex 21 8
2001–02 Crewe Alex 31 7
2002–03 Crewe Alex 39 9
2003–04 Crewe Alex 44 19
2004–05 Crewe Alex 24 17 **159 60**
2004–05 Norwich C 16 7 **16 7**

BRENNAN, Jim (D) 205 5
H: 5 11 W: 12 12 b.Toronto 8-5-77
Source: Sora Lazio. *Honours:* Canada Under-23, 38 full caps, 5 goals.
1994–95 Bristol C 0 0
1995–96 Bristol C 0 0
1996–97 Bristol C 8 0
1997–98 Bristol C 6 0
1998–99 Bristol C 29 1
1999–2000 Bristol C 12 2 **55 3**
1999–2000 Nottingham F 25 0
2000–01 Nottingham F 12 0
2000–01 *Huddersfield T* 2 0 **2 0**
2001–02 Nottingham F 41 0
2002–03 Nottingham F 45 1 **123 1**
2003–04 Norwich C 15 1
2004–05 Norwich C 10 0 **25 1**

CHARLTON, Simon (D) 454 4
H: 5 8 W: 11 05 b.Huddersfield 25-10-71
Source: Trainee. *Honours:* FA Schools.
1989–90 Huddersfield T 3 0
1990–91 Huddersfield T 30 0
1991–92 Huddersfield T 45 0
1992–93 Huddersfield T 46 1 **124 1**
1993–94 Southampton 33 1
1994–95 Southampton 25 1
1995–96 Southampton 26 0
1996–97 Southampton 27 0
1997–98 Southampton 3 0 **114 2**
1998–99 Birmingham C 28 0
1997–98 Birmingham C 24 0
1999–2000 Birmingham C 20 0 **72 0**
2000–01 Bolton W 22 0
2001–02 Bolton W 36 0
2002–03 Bolton W 31 0
2003–04 Bolton W 31 0 **120 0**
2004–05 Norwich C 24 1 **24 1**

CROW, Danny (F) 13 2
H: 5 10 W: 11 00 b.Great Yarmouth 26-1-86
Source: Scholar.
2004–05 Norwich C 3 0 **3 0**
2004–05 *Northampton T* 10 2 **10 2**

DOHERTY, Gary (D) 154 18
H: 6 2 W: 13 04 b.Carndonagh 31-1-80
Source: Trainee. *Honours:* Eire Youth, Under-21, 31 full caps, 4 goals.
1997–98 Luton T 10 0
1998–99 Luton T 20 6
1999–2000 Luton T 40 6 **70 12**
1999–2000 Tottenham H 2 0
2000–01 Tottenham H 22 3
2001–02 Tottenham H 7 0
2002–03 Tottenham H 15 1
2003–04 Tottenham H 17 0
2004–05 Tottenham H 1 0 **64 4**
2004–05 Norwich C 20 2 **20 2**

DRURY, Adam (D) 309 5
H: 5 10 W: 11 08 b.Cottenham 29-8-78
Source: Trainee.
1995–96 Peterborough U 1 0
1996–97 Peterborough U 5 1
1997–98 Peterborough U 31 0
1998–99 Peterborough U 40 0
1999–2000 Peterborough U 42 1
2000–01 Peterborough U 29 0 **148 2**
2000–01 Norwich C 6 0
2001–02 Norwich C 35 0
2002–03 Norwich C 45 2
2003–04 Norwich C 42 0
2004–05 Norwich C 33 1 **161 3**

EDWORTHY, Marc (D) 364 2
H: 5 8 W: 10 05 b.Barnstaple 24-12-72
Source: Trainee.
1990–91 Plymouth Arg 0 0
1991–92 Plymouth Arg 15 0
1992–93 Plymouth Arg 15 0
1993–94 Plymouth Arg 12 0
1994–95 Plymouth Arg 27 1 **69 1**
1995–96 Crystal Palace 44 0
1996–97 Crystal Palace 45 0
1997–98 Crystal Palace 34 0
1998–99 Crystal Palace 3 0 **126 0**
1998–99 Coventry C 22 0
1999–2000 Coventry C 10 0
2000–01 Coventry C 24 1
2001–02 Coventry C 20 0 **76 1**
2002–03 Wolverhampton W 22 0 **22 0**
2003–04 Norwich C 43 0
2004–05 Norwich C 28 0 **71 0**

FLEMING, Craig (D) 518 12
H: 5 11 W: 12 05 b.Halifax 6-10-71
Source: Trainee.
1988–89 Halifax T 1 0
1989–90 Halifax T 10 0
1990–91 Halifax T 46 0 **57 0**
1991–92 Oldham Ath 32 1
1992–93 Oldham Ath 24 0
1993–94 Oldham Ath 37 0
1994–95 Oldham Ath 5 0
1995–96 Oldham Ath 22 0
1996–97 Oldham Ath 44 0 **164 1**
1997–98 Norwich C 22 1
1998–99 Norwich C 37 3
1999–2000 Norwich C 39 3
2000–01 Norwich C 39 0
2001–02 Norwich C 46 0
2002–03 Norwich C 30 0
2003–04 Norwich C 46 3
2004–05 Norwich C 38 1 **297 11**

FRANCIS, Damien (M) 170 29
H: 6 0 W: 11 10 b.Wandsworth 27-2-79
Source: Trainee. *Honours:* Jamaica 1 full cap.
1996–97 Wimbledon 0 0
1997–98 Wimbledon 2 0
1998–99 Wimbledon 0 0
1999–2000 Wimbledon 9 0
2000–01 Wimbledon 29 8
2001–02 Wimbledon 23 1
2002–03 Wimbledon 34 6 **97 15**
2003–04 Norwich C 41 7
2004–05 Norwich C 32 7 **73 14**

GALLACHER, Paul (G) 122 0
H: 6 0 W: 12 00 b.Glasgow 16-8-79
Honours: Scotland Under-21, 8 full caps.
1999–2000 Dundee U 1 0
2000–01 Dundee U 15 0
2001–02 Dundee U 38 0
2002–03 Dundee U 34 0
2003–04 Dundee U 23 0 **111 0**
2004–05 Norwich C 0 0
2004–05 *Gillingham* 3 0 **3 0**
2004–05 *Sheffield W* 8 0 **8 0**

GREEN, Robert (G) 181 0
H: 6 3 W: 13 01 b.Chertsey 18-1-80
Source: Trainee. *Honours:* England Youth, 1 full cap.
1997–98 Norwich C 0 0
1998–99 Norwich C 2 0
1999–2000 Norwich C 3 0
2000–01 Norwich C 5 0
2001–02 Norwich C 41 0
2002–03 Norwich C 46 0
2003–04 Norwich C 46 0
2004–05 Norwich C 38 0 **181 0**

HELVEG, Thomas (D) 398 10
H: 5 10 W: 12 04 b.Odense 24-6-71
Honours: Denmark Under-21, 95 full caps, 1 goal.
1988–89 Odense 2 1
1989–90 Odense 19 2
1990–91 Odense 17 0
1991–92 Odense 21 0
1992–93 Odense 31 1
1993–94 Odense 13 0 **103 4**
1993–94 Udinese 22 2
1994–95 Udinese 30 1
1995–96 Udinese 31 2
1996–97 Udinese 30 1
1997–98 Udinese 28 0 **141 6**
1998–99 AC Milan 27 0
1999–2000 AC Milan 27 0
2000–01 AC Milan 28 0
2001–02 AC Milan 15 0
2002–03 AC Milan 8 0 **105 0**
2003–04 Internazionale 29 0 **29 0**
2004–05 Norwich C 20 0 **20 0**

HENDERSON, Ian (F) 42 5
H: 5 9 W: 10 12 b.Thetford 24-1-85
Source: Scholar. *Honours:* England Youth, Under-20.
2002–03 Norwich C 20 1
2003–04 Norwich C 19 4
2004–05 Norwich C 3 0 **42 5**

HOLT, Gary (M) 320 12
H: 6 0 W: 12 00 b.Irvine 9-3-73
Source: Celtic. *Honours:* Scotland 10 full caps, 1 goal.
1994–95 Stoke C 0 0
1995–96 Kilmarnock 26 0
1996–97 Kilmarnock 12 1
1997–98 Kilmarnock 27 2
1998–99 Kilmarnock 33 3
1999–2000 Kilmarnock 35 0
2000–01 Kilmarnock 19 3 **152 9**
2000–01 Norwich C 4 0
2001–02 Norwich C 46 2
2002–03 Norwich C 45 0
2003–04 Norwich C 46 1
2004–05 Norwich C 27 0 **168 3**

HUCKERBY, Darren (F) 320 85
H: 5 10 W: 12 00 b.Nottingham 23-4-76
Source: Trainee. *Honours:* England Under-21, B.
1993–94 Lincoln C 6 1
1994–95 Lincoln C 6 2
1995–96 Lincoln C 16 2 **28 5**
1995–96 Newcastle U 1 0
1996–97 Newcastle U 0 0 **1 0**
1996–97 *Millwall* 6 3 **6 3**

1996–97 Coventry C 25 5
1997–98 Coventry C 34 14
1998–99 Coventry C 34 9
1999–2000 Coventry C 1 0 **94 28**
1999–2000 Leeds U 33 2
2000–01 Leeds U 7 0 **40 2**
2000–01 Manchester C 13 1
2001–02 Manchester C 40 20
2002–03 Manchester C 16 1
2002–03 *Nottingham F* 9 5 **9 5**
2003–04 Manchester C 0 0 **69 22**
2003–04 Norwich C 36 14
2004–05 Norwich C 37 6 **73 20**

JARVIS, Ryan (F) 25 2
H: 6 0 W: 11 05 b.Fakenham 11-7-86
Source: Scholar. *Honours:* FA Schools, England Youth.
2002–03 Norwich C 3 0
2003–04 Norwich C 12 1
2004–05 Norwich C 4 1 **19 2**
2004–05 *Colchester U* 6 0 **6 0**

JONSON, Mattias (M) 304 87
H: 5 10 W: 11 09 b.Orebro 16-1-74
Honours: Sweden 44 full caps, 8 goals.
1993 Orebro 15 1
1994 Orebro 26 14
1995 Orebro 20 9 **61 24**
1996 Helsingborg 21 3
1997 Helsingborg 19 11
1998 Helsingborg 20 4
1999 Helsingborg 24 5 **84 23**
1999–2000 Brondby 15 2
2000–01 Brondby 29 14
2001–02 Brondby 30 7
2002–03 Brondby 29 11
2003–04 Brondby 26 6
2004–05 Brondby 2 0 **131 40**
2004–05 Norwich C 28 0 **28 0**

LEWIS, Joe (G) 0 0
H: 6 5 W: 11 12 b.Bury St Edmunds 6-10-87
Source: Scholar. *Honours:* England Youth.
2004–05 Norwich C 0 0

McKENZIE, Leon (F) 247 76
H: 5 10 W: 10 06 b.Croydon 17-5-78
Source: Trainee.
1995–96 Crystal Palace 12 0
1996–97 Crystal Palace 21 2
1997–98 Crystal Palace 3 0
1997–98 *Fulham* 3 0 **3 0**
1998–99 Crystal Palace 16 1
1998–99 *Peterborough U* 14 8
1999–2000 Crystal Palace 25 4
2000–01 Crystal Palace 8 0 **85 7**
2000–01 Peterborough U 30 13
2001–02 Peterborough U 30 18
2002–03 Peterborough U 11 5
2003–04 Peterborough U 19 9 **104 53**
2003–04 Norwich C 18 9
2004–05 Norwich C 37 7 **55 16**

McVEIGH, Paul (F) 162 30
H: 5 6 W: 10 12 b.Belfast 6-12-77
Source: Trainee. *Honours:* Northern Ireland Schools, Youth, Under-21, 20 full caps.
1995–96 Tottenham H 0 0
1996–97 Tottenham H 3 1
1997–98 Tottenham H 0 0
1998–99 Tottenham H 0 0
1999–2000 Tottenham H 0 0 **3 1**
1999–2000 Norwich C 1 0
2000–01 Norwich C 11 1
2001–02 Norwich C 42 8
2002–03 Norwich C 44 14
2003–04 Norwich C 44 5
2004–05 Norwich C 17 1 **159 29**

MULRYNE, Phil (M) 162 18
H: 5 9 W: 11 03 b.Belfast 1-1-78
Source: Trainee. *Honours:* Northern Ireland Youth, Under-21, B, 26 full caps, 3 goals.
1994–95 Manchester U 0 0
1995–96 Manchester U 0 0
1996–97 Manchester U 0 0
1997–98 Manchester U 1 0
1998–99 Manchester U 0 0 **1 0**
1998–99 Norwich C 7 2
1999–2000 Norwich C 9 0
2000–01 Norwich C 28 1
2001–02 Norwich C 40 6
2002–03 Norwich C 33 6
2003–04 Norwich C 34 3
2004–05 Norwich C 10 0 **161 18**

SAFRI, Youseff (M) 109 2
H: 5 8 W: 11 00 b.Casablanca 13-1-77
Source: Raja. *Honours:* Morocco full caps.
2001–02 Coventry C 33 1
2002–03 Coventry C 27 0
2003–04 Coventry C 31 0 **91 1**
2004–05 Norwich C 18 1 **18 1**

SHACKELL, Jason (D) 19 0
H: 6 3 W: 12 09 b.Hitchin 27-9-83
Source: Scholar.
2002–03 Norwich C 2 0
2003–04 Norwich C 6 0
2004–05 Norwich C 11 0 **19 0**

STUART, Graham (M) 432 69
H: 5 9 W: 12 01 b.Tooting 24-10-70
Source: Trainee. *Honours:* FA Schools, England Under-21.
1989–90 Chelsea 2 1
1990–91 Chelsea 19 4
1991–92 Chelsea 27 0
1992–93 Chelsea 39 9 **87 14**
1993–94 Everton 30 3
1994–95 Everton 28 3
1995–96 Everton 29 9
1996–97 Everton 35 5
1997–98 Everton 14 2 **136 22**
1997–98 Sheffield U 28 5
1998–99 Sheffield U 25 6 **53 11**
1998–99 Charlton Ath 9 4
1999–2000 Charlton Ath 37 7
2000–01 Charlton Ath 35 5
2001–02 Charlton Ath 31 3
2002–03 Charlton Ath 4 0
2003–04 Charlton Ath 28 3
2004–05 Charlton Ath 4 0 **148 22**
2004–05 Norwich C 8 0 **8 0**

SVENSSON, Mathias (F) 227 57
H: 6 1 W: 12 07 b.Boras 24-9-74
Honours: Sweden 3 full caps.
1996 Elfsborg 22 15 **22 15**
1996–97 Portsmouth 19 6
1997–98 Portsmouth 26 4 **45 10**
1998–99 Innsbruck 6 1 **6 1**
1998–99 Crystal Palace 8 1
1999–2000 Crystal Palace 24 9 **32 10**
1999–2000 Charlton Ath 18 2
2000–01 Charlton Ath 22 5
2001–02 Charlton Ath 12 0
2002–03 Charlton Ath 15 0
2003–04 Charlton Ath 3 0 **70 7**
2003–04 *Derby Co* 10 3 **10 3**
2003–04 Norwich C 20 7
2004–05 Norwich C 22 4 **42 11**

WARD, Darren (G) 456 0
H: 6 0 W: 13 03 b.Worksop 11-5-74
Source: Trainee. *Honours:* Wales Under-21, B, 5 full caps.
1992–93 Mansfield T 13 0
1993–94 Mansfield T 33 0
1994–95 Mansfield T 35 0 **81 0**
1995–96 Notts Co 46 0
1996–97 Notts Co 38 0
1997–98 Notts Co 44 0
1998–99 Notts Co 43 0
1999–2000 Notts Co 45 0
2000–01 Notts Co 35 0 **251 0**
2000–01 Nottingham F 0 0
2001–02 Nottingham F 46 0
2002–03 Nottingham F 45 0
2003–04 Nottingham F 32 0
2004–05 Nottingham F 0 0 **123 0**
2004–05 Norwich C 1 0 **1 0**

Scholars
Cave-Brown, Andrew Robert; Clarke, Joshua Kieran; Eagle, Robert John; El Ouargui, Asmat; Fisk, Andrew; Gusterson, Adam; Halliday, Matthew Richard; Herbert, Shane Richard; Howlett, Lee Richard Kent; Jarvis, Rossi; Watts, Matthew Thomas

NOTTINGHAM F (56)

BEAUMONT, James (M) 0 0
H: 5 7 W: 10 10 b.Stockton 11-11-84
Source: Scholar.
2001–02 Newcastle U 0 0
2002–03 Newcastle U 0 0
2003–04 Nottingham F 0 0
2004–05 Nottingham F 0 0

BIGGINS, James (D) 0 0
H: 5 9 W: 11 13 b.Nottingham 6-6-85
Source: Scholar. *Honours:* England Youth.
2002–03 Nottingham F 0 0
2003–04 Nottingham F 0 0
2004–05 Nottingham F 0 0

BOPP, Eugene (M) 65 7
H: 5 11 W: 12 03 b.Kiev 5-9-83
Source: Bayern Munich.
2000–01 Nottingham F 0 0
2001–02 Nottingham F 19 1
2002–03 Nottingham F 13 2
2003–04 Nottingham F 15 1
2004–05 Nottingham F 18 3 **65 7**

COMMONS, Kris (M) 71 11
H: 5 6 W: 9 08 b.Nottingham 30-8-83
Source: Scholar.
2000–01 Stoke C 0 0
2001–02 Stoke C 0 0
2002–03 Stoke C 8 1
2003–04 Stoke C 33 4 **41 5**
2004–05 Nottingham F 30 6 **30 6**

CULLINGWORTH, James (D) 0 0
b.Nottingham 18-9-87
Source: Scholar.
2004–05 Nottingham F 0 0

CURTIS, John (D) 159 2
H: 5 10 W: 11 07 b.Nuneaton 3-9-78
Source: From Trainee. *Honours:* England Schools, Youth, Under-21, B.
1995–96 Manchester U 0 0
1996–97 Manchester U 0 0
1997–98 Manchester U 8 0
1998–99 Manchester U 4 0
1999–2000 Manchester U 1 0 **13 0**
1999–2000 *Barnsley* 28 2 **28 2**
2000–01 Blackburn R 46 0
2001–02 Blackburn R 10 0
2002–03 Blackburn R 5 0 **61 0**
2002–03 *Sheffield U* 12 0 **12 0**
2003–04 Leicester C 15 0 **15 0**
2003–04 Portsmouth 6 0
2004–05 Portsmouth 1 0 **7 0**
2004–05 *Preston NE* 12 0 **12 0**
2004–05 Nottingham F 11 0 **11 0**

DOBIE, Scott (F) 280 49
H: 6 1 W: 12 05 b.Workington 10-10-78
Source: Trainee. *Honours:* Scotland 6 full caps, 1 goal.
1996–97 Carlisle U 2 1
1997–98 Carlisle U 23 0
1998–99 Carlisle U 33 6
1998–99 *Clydebank* 6 0 **6 0**
1999–2000 Carlisle U 34 7
2000–01 Carlisle U 44 10 **136 24**
2001–02 WBA 43 10
2002–03 WBA 31 5
2003–04 WBA 31 5
2004–05 WBA 5 1 **110 21**
2004–05 Millwall 16 3 **16 3**
2004–05 Nottingham F 12 1 **12 1**

DOIG, Chris (D) 86 1
H: 6 2 W: 13 07 b.Dumfries 13-2-81
Source: Trainee. *Honours:* Scotland Schools, Youth, Under-21.
1997–98 Nottingham F 0 0
1998–99 Nottingham F 2 0
1999–2000 Nottingham F 11 0
2000–01 Nottingham F 15 0
2001–02 Nottingham F 8 1
2002–03 Nottingham F 10 0
2003–04 Nottingham F 10 0
2003–04 *Northampton T* 9 0 **9 0**
2004–05 Nottingham F 21 0 **77 1**

EVANS, Paul (M) **427 67**
H: 5 8 W: 12 06 b.Oswestry 1-9-74
Source: Trainee. *Honours:* Wales Youth, Under-21, 1 full cap.

1991–92	Shrewsbury T	2	0		
1992–93	Shrewsbury T	4	0		
1993–94	Shrewsbury T	13	0		
1994–95	Shrewsbury T	32	5		
1995–96	Shrewsbury T	34	3		
1996–97	Shrewsbury T	42	6		
1997–98	Shrewsbury T	39	6		
1998–99	Shrewsbury T	32	6	**198**	**26**
1998–99	Brentford	14	3		
1999–2000	Brentford	33	7		
2000–01	Brentford	43	7		
2001–02	Brentford	40	14	**130**	**31**
2002–03	Bradford C	19	2		
2002–03	*Blackpool*	10	1	**10**	**1**
2003–04	Bradford C	23	3	**42**	**5**
2003–04	Nottingham F	8	0		
2004–05	Nottingham F	39	4	**47**	**4**

FERNANDEZ, Vincent (D) **0 0**
b.France 19-9-86
Source: Scholar.

2004–05	Nottingham F	0	0		

FRIIO, David (M) **172 39**
H: 6 0 W: 11 05 b.Thionville 17-2-73
Source: Epinal, Nimes, ASOA Valence.

2000–01	Plymouth Arg	26	5		
2001–02	Plymouth Arg	41	8		
2002–03	Plymouth Arg	36	6		
2003–04	Plymouth Arg	36	14		
2004–05	Plymouth Arg	28	6	**167**	**39**
2004–05	Nottingham F	5	0	**5**	**0**

GARDNER, Ross (M) **16 0**
H: 5 8 W: 10 06 b.South Shields 15-12-85
Source: Scholar. *Honours:* England Youth, Under-20.

2001–02	Newcastle U	0	0		
2002–03	Newcastle U	0	0		
2003–04	Nottingham F	2	0		
2004–05	Nottingham F	14	0	**16**	**0**

GERRARD, Paul (G) **296 1**
H: 6 2 W: 13 11 b.Heywood 22-1-73
Source: Trainee. *Honours:* England Under-21.

1991–92	Oldham Ath	0	0		
1992–93	Oldham Ath	25	0		
1993–94	Oldham Ath	16	0		
1994–95	Oldham Ath	42	0		
1995–96	Oldham Ath	36	1	**119**	**1**
1996–97	Everton	5	0		
1997–98	Everton	4	0		
1998–99	Everton	0	0		
1998–99	*Oxford U*	16	0	**16**	**0**
1999–2000	Everton	34	0		
2000–01	Everton	32	0		
2001–02	Everton	13	0		
2002–03	Everton	2	0		
2002–03	*Ipswich T*	5	0	**5**	**0**
2003–04	Everton	0	0	**90**	**0**
2003–04	*Sheffield U*	16	0	**16**	**0**
2003–04	*Nottingham F*	8	0		
2004–05	Nottingham F	42	0	**50**	**0**

HAMILTON, Paul (D) **0 0**
b.Belfast 28-10-86
Source: Scholar.

2003–04	Nottingham F	0	0		
2004–05	Nottingham F	0	0		

HARRIS, Neil (F) **249 94**
H: 5 11 W: 12 00 b.Orsett 12-7-77
Source: Cambridge C.

1997–98	Millwall	3	0		
1998–99	Millwall	39	15		
1999–2000	Millwall	38	25		
2000–01	Millwall	42	27		
2001–02	Millwall	21	4		
2002–03	Millwall	40	12		
2003–04	Millwall	38	9		
2004–05	Millwall	12	1	**233**	**93**
2004–05	*Cardiff C*	3	1	**3**	**1**
2004–05	Nottingham F	13	0	**13**	**0**

HJELDE, Jon Olav (D) **198 5**
H: 6 3 W: 13 07 b.Levanger 30-7-72

1994	Rosenborg	1	0		
1995	Rosenborg	7	0		
1996	Rosenborg	16	1		
1997	Rosenborg	3	0	**27**	**1**
1997–98	Nottingham F	28	1		
1998–99	Nottingham F	17	1		
1999–2000	Nottingham F	33	0		
2000–01	Nottingham F	11	2		
2001–02	Nottingham F	42	0		
2002–03	Nottingham F	26	0		
2003–04	Nottingham F	0	0		
2004–05	Nottingham F	14	0	**171**	**4**

IMPEY, Andrew (M) **407 15**
H: 5 8 W: 11 11 b.Hammersmith 30-9-71
Source: Yeading. *Honours:* England Under-21.

1990–91	QPR	0	0		
1991–92	QPR	13	0		
1992–93	QPR	40	2		
1993–94	QPR	33	3		
1994–95	QPR	40	3		
1995–96	QPR	29	3		
1996–97	QPR	32	2	**187**	**13**
1997–98	West Ham U	19	0		
1998–99	West Ham U	8	0	**27**	**0**
1998–99	Leicester C	18	0		
1999–2000	Leicester C	29	1		
2000–01	Leicester C	33	0		
2001–02	Leicester C	27	0		
2002–03	Leicester C	32	0		
2003–04	Leicester C	13	0	**152**	**1**
2003–04	*Nottingham F*	16	1		
2004–05	Nottingham F	20	0	**36**	**1**
2004–05	*Millwall*	5	0	**5**	**0**

JAMES, Kevin (M) **62 4**
H: 5 7 W: 11 12 b.Southwark 3-1-80
Source: Trainee.

1998–99	Charlton Ath	0	0		
1999–2000	Charlton Ath	0	0		
2000–01	Gillingham	7	0		
2001–02	Gillingham	10	0		
2002–03	Gillingham	15	3		
2003–04	Gillingham	17	1	**49**	**4**
2004–05	Nottingham F	7	0	**7**	**0**
2004–05	*Boston U*	6	0	**6**	**0**

JESS, Eoin (M) **484 103**
H: 5 10 W: 11 09 b.Aberdeen 13-12-70
Source: Rangers 'S' Form. *Honours:* Scotland Under-21, B, 18 full caps, 2 goals.

1987–88	Aberdeen	0	0		
1988–89	Aberdeen	2	0		
1989–90	Aberdeen	11	3		
1990–91	Aberdeen	27	13		
1991–92	Aberdeen	39	12		
1992–93	Aberdeen	31	12		
1993–94	Aberdeen	41	6		
1994–95	Aberdeen	25	1		
1995–96	Aberdeen	25	3		
1995–96	Coventry C	12	1		
1996–97	Coventry C	27	0	**39**	**1**
1997–98	Aberdeen	34	9		
1998–99	Aberdeen	36	14		
1999–2000	Aberdeen	26	5		
2000–01	Aberdeen	0	0	**297**	**78**
2000–01	Bradford C	17	3		
2001–02	Bradford C	45	14	**62**	**17**
2002–03	Nottingham F	32	3		
2003–04	Nottingham F	34	2		
2004–05	Nottingham F	20	2	**86**	**7**

JOHNSON, David (F) **374 123**
H: 5 6 W: 12 00 b.Kingston, Jamaica 15-8-76
Source: Trainee. *Honours:* England Schools, B. Jamaica 4 full caps.

1994–95	Manchester U	0	0		
1995–96	Bury	36	5		
1996–97	Bury	44	8		
1997–98	Bury	17	5	**97**	**18**
1997–98	Ipswich T	31	20		
1998–99	Ipswich T	42	13		
1999–2000	Ipswich T	44	22		
2000–01	Ipswich T	14	0	**131**	**55**
2000–01	Nottingham F	19	2		
2001–02	Nottingham F	22	3		
2001–02	*Sheffield W*	7	2	**7**	**2**
2001–02	*Burnley*	8	5	**8**	**5**
2002–03	Nottingham F	42	25		
2003–04	Nottingham F	17	7		
2004–05	Nottingham F	31	6	**131**	**43**
2004–05	*Sheffield U*	0	0		

KING, Marlon (F) **213 64**
H: 6 0 W: 12 10 b.Dulwich 26-4-80
Source: Trainee. *Honours:* Jamaica 11 full caps.

1998–99	Barnet	22	6		
1999–2000	Barnet	31	8	**53**	**14**
2000–01	Gillingham	38	15		
2001–02	Gillingham	42	17		
2002–03	Gillingham	10	4		
2003–04	Gillingham	11	4	**101**	**40**
2003–04	Nottingham F	24	5		
2004–05	Nottingham F	26	5	**50**	**10**
2004–05	*Leeds U*	9	0	**9**	**0**

KUBILSKIS, Alexis (F) **0 0**
b.Berchem 10-12-86
Source: Scholar.

2003–04	Nottingham F	0	0		
2004–05	Nottingham F	0	0		

LESTER, Jack (F) **290 52**
H: 5 9 W: 12 08 b.Sheffield 8-10-75
Source: Trainee. *Honours:* England Schools.

1994–95	Grimsby T	7	0		
1995–96	Grimsby T	5	0		
1996–97	Grimsby T	22	5		
1996–97	*Doncaster R*	11	1	**11**	**1**
1997–98	Grimsby T	40	4		
1998–99	Grimsby T	33	4		
1999–2000	Grimsby T	26	4	**133**	**17**
1999–2000	Nottingham F	15	2		
2000–01	Nottingham F	19	7		
2001–02	Nottingham F	32	5		
2002–03	Nottingham F	33	7		
2003–04	Sheffield U	32	12		
2004–05	Sheffield U	12	0	**44**	**12**
2004–05	Nottingham F	3	1	**102**	**22**

LOUIS-JEAN, Mathieu (D) **276 3**
H: 5 9 W: 11 03 b.Mont-St-Aignan 22-2-76

1993–94	Le Havre	7	0		
1994–95	Le Havre	9	0		
1995–96	Le Havre	15	0		
1996–97	Le Havre	31	0		
1997–98	Le Havre	16	0	**78**	**0**
1998–99	Nottingham F	16	0		
1999–2000	Nottingham F	27	0		
2000–01	Nottingham F	13	0		
2001–02	Nottingham F	38	1		
2002–03	Nottingham F	41	1		
2003–04	Nottingham F	38	1		
2004–05	Nottingham F	25	0	**198**	**3**

LUKIC, John (G) **0 0**
b.Enfield 25-4-86
Source: Scholar.

2002–03	Nottingham F	0	0		
2003–04	Nottingham F	0	0		
2004–05	Nottingham F	0	0		

MORGAN, Wes (D) **80 4**
H: 6 2 W: 14 00 b.Nottingham 21-1-84
Source: Scholar.

2002–03	Nottingham F	0	0		
2002–03	*Kidderminster H*	5	1	**5**	**1**
2003–04	Nottingham F	32	2		
2004–05	Nottingham F	43	1	**75**	**3**

MULLARKEY, Sam (F) **0 0**
b.Lincoln 24-9-87
Source: Scholar.

2004–05	Nottingham F	0	0		

NOWLAND, Adam (M) **148 12**
H: 5 11 W: 11 06 b.Preston 6-7-81
Source: Trainee.

1997–98	Blackpool	1	0		
1998–99	Blackpool	37	2		
1999–2000	Blackpool	21	3		
2000–01	Blackpool	10	0	**69**	**5**
2001–02	Wimbledon	7	0		
2002–03	Wimbledon	24	2		
2003–04	Wimbledon	25	3	**56**	**5**
2003–04	West Ham U	11	0		
2004–05	West Ham U	4	1	**15**	**1**
2004–05	*Gillingham*	3	1	**3**	**1**
2004–05	Nottingham F	5	0	**5**	**0**

PERCH, James (D)				**22**	**0**
H: 5 11 W: 11 05 b.Mansfield 29-9-85					
Source: Scholar.					
2002–03	Nottingham F	0	0		
2003–04	Nottingham F	0	0		
2004–05	Nottingham F	22	0	**22**	**0**

POWELL, Darryl (M)				**369**	**26**
H: 6 1 W: 13 03 b.Lambeth 15-11-71					
Source: Trainee. *Honours:* Jamaica full caps.					
1988–89	Portsmouth	3	0		
1989–90	Portsmouth	0	0		
1990–91	Portsmouth	8	0		
1991–92	Portsmouth	36	6		
1992–93	Portsmouth	23	0		
1993–94	Portsmouth	28	5		
1994–95	Portsmouth	34	5	**132**	**16**
1995–96	Derby Co	37	5		
1996–97	Derby Co	33	1		
1997–98	Derby Co	23	0		
1998–99	Derby Co	33	0		
1999–2000	Derby Co	31	2		
2000–01	Derby Co	27	1		
2001–02	Derby Co	23	1		
2002–03	Derby Co	0	0	**207**	**10**
2002–03	Birmingham C	11	0	**11**	**0**
2002–03	Sheffield W	8	0		
2003–04	Sheffield W	0	0	**8**	**0**
2004–05	Nottingham F	11	0	**11**	**0**

RICHARDSON, Barry (G)				**307**	**0**
H: 6 1 W: 12 01 b.Willington Quay 5-8-69					
Source: Trainee.					
1987–88	Sunderland	0	0		
1988–89	Scunthorpe U	0	0		
1989–90	Scarborough	24	0		
1990–91	Scarborough	6	0	**30**	**0**
1991–92	Northampton T	27	0		
1992–93	Northampton T	42	0		
1993–94	Northampton T	27	0	**96**	**0**
1994–95	Preston NE	17	0		
1995–96	Preston NE	3	0	**20**	**0**
1995–96	Lincoln C	34	0		
1996–97	Lincoln C	36	0		
1997–98	Lincoln C	26	0		
1998–99	Lincoln C	13	0		
1999–2000	Lincoln C	22	0		
1999–2000	*Mansfield T*	6	0	**6**	**0**
1999–2000	*Sheffield W*	0	0		
2000–01	Lincoln C	0	0	**131**	**0**
From Doncaster R.					
2001–02	Halifax T	24	0	**24**	**0**
From Gainsborough T					
2003–04	Doncaster R	0	0		
2004–05	Nottingham F	0	0		

RIGBY, Andrew (M)				**0**	**0**
b.Nottingham 19-1-87					
2003–04	Nottingham F	0	0		
2004–05	Nottingham F	0	0		

ROBERTS, Justyn (D)				**0**	**0**
b.Lewisham 12-2-86					
Source: Scholar.					
2002–03	Nottingham F	0	0		
2003–04	Nottingham F	0	0		
2004–05	Nottingham F	0	0		

ROBERTSON, Gregor (D)				**36**	**0**
H: 6 0 W: 12 04 b.Edinburgh 19-1-84					
Honours: Scotland Under-21.					
2000–01	Nottingham F	0	0		
2001–02	Nottingham F	0	0		
2002–03	Nottingham F	0	0		
2003–04	Nottingham F	16	0		
2004–05	Nottingham F	20	0	**36**	**0**

ROCHE, Barry (G)				**13**	**0**
H: 6 5 W: 14 00 b.Dublin 6-4-82					
Source: Trainee.					
1999–2000	Nottingham F	0	0		
2000–01	Nottingham F	2	0		
2001–02	Nottingham F	0	0		
2002–03	Nottingham F	1	0		
2003–04	Nottingham F	8	0		
2004–05	Nottingham F	2	0	**13**	**0**

ROGERS, Alan (D)				**306**	**18**
H: 5 9 W: 12 10 b.Liverpool 3-1-77					
Source: Trainee.					
1995–96	Tranmere R	26	2		
1996–97	Tranmere R	31	0	**57**	**2**
1997–98	Nottingham F	46	1		
1998–99	Nottingham F	34	3		
1999–2000	Nottingham F	37	9		
2000–01	Nottingham F	17	3		
2001–02	Nottingham F	3	0		
2001–02	Leicester C	13	0		
2002–03	Leicester C	41	0		
2003–04	Leicester C	8	0	**62**	**0**
2003–04	*Wigan Ath*	5	0	**5**	**0**
2003–04	*Nottingham F*	12	0		
2004–05	Nottingham F	33	0	**182**	**16**

TARKA, David (D)				**45**	**1**
b.Perth 11-2-83					
Honours: Australia Schools, Under-20, Under-23, 2 full caps.					
2001–02	Perth Glory	17	0		
2002–03	Perth Glory	28	1	**45**	**1**
2003–04	Nottingham F	0	0		
2004–05	Nottingham F	0	0		

TAYLOR, Charlie (M)				**0**	**0**
b.Lewisham 28-12-85					
2002–03	Crystal Palace	0	0		
2003–04	Nottingham F	0	0		
2004–05	Nottingham F	0	0		

TAYLOR, Gareth (F)				**369**	**103**
H: 6 2 W: 13 07 b.Weston-Super-Mare 25-2-73					
Source: Southampton Trainee. *Honours:* Wales Under-21, 15 full caps, 1 goal.					
1991–92	Bristol R	1	0		
1992–93	Bristol R	0	0		
1993–94	Bristol R	0	0		
1994–95	Bristol R	39	12		
1995–96	Bristol R	7	4	**47**	**16**
1995–96	Crystal Palace	20	1	**20**	**1**
1995–96	Sheffield U	10	2		
1996–97	Sheffield U	34	12		
1997–98	Sheffield U	28	10		
1998–99	Sheffield U	12	1	**84**	**25**
1998–99	Manchester C	26	4		
1999–2000	Manchester C	17	5		
1999–2000	*Port Vale*	4	0	**4**	**0**
1999–2000	*QPR*	6	1	**6**	**1**
2000–01	Manchester C	0	0	**43**	**9**
2000–01	*Burnley*	15	4		
2001–02	Burnley	40	16		
2002–03	Burnley	40	16		
2003–04	Burnley	0	0	**95**	**36**
2003–04	Nottingham F	34	8		
2004–05	Nottingham F	36	7	**70**	**15**

THOMPSON, John (D)				**80**	**4**
H: 6 0 W: 12 01 b.Dublin 12-10-81					
Source: Home Farm. *Honours:* Eire Under-21, 1 full cap.					
1999–2000	Nottingham F	0	0		
2000–01	Nottingham F	0	0		
2001–02	Nottingham F	8	0		
2002–03	Nottingham F	20	3		
2003–04	Nottingham F	32	1		
2004–05	Nottingham F	20	0	**80**	**4**

WALKER, Des (D)				**658**	**1**
H: 5 11 W: 11 13 b.Enfield 26-11-65					
Source: Apprentice. *Honours:* England Under-21, 59 full caps.					
1983–84	Nottingham F	4	0		
1984–85	Nottingham F	3	0		
1985–86	Nottingham F	39	0		
1986–87	Nottingham F	41	0		
1987–88	Nottingham F	35	0		
1988–89	Nottingham F	34	0		
1989–90	Nottingham F	38	0		
1990–91	Nottingham F	37	0		
1991–92	Nottingham F	33	1		
1992–93	Sampdoria	30	0	**30**	**0**
1993–94	Sheffield W	42	0		
1994–95	Sheffield W	38	0		
1995–96	Sheffield W	36	0		
1996–97	Sheffield W	36	0		
1997–98	Sheffield W	38	0		
1998–99	Sheffield W	37	0		
1999–2000	Sheffield W	37	0		
2000–01	Sheffield W	43	0	**307**	**0**
2001–02	Nottingham F	0	0		
2002–03	Nottingham F	31	0		
2003–04	Nottingham F	25	0		
2004–05	Nottingham F	1	0	**321**	**1**

WEIR-DALEY, Spencer (F)				**0**	**0**
b.Leicester 5-9-85					
Source: Scholar.					
2003–04	Nottingham F	0	0		
2004–05	Nottingham F	0	0		

WESTCARR, Craig (F)				**33**	**2**
H: 5 11 W: 11 04 b.Nottingham 29-1-85					
Source: Scholar. *Honours:* England Youth.					
2001–02	Nottingham F	8	0		
2002–03	Nottingham F	11	1		
2003–04	Nottingham F	3	0		
2004–05	Nottingham F	1	0	**23**	**1**
2004–05	*Lincoln C*	6	1	**6**	**1**
2004–05	*Milton Keynes D*	4	0	**4**	**0**

WILMET, Jonathan (F)				**0**	**0**
b.Ottignies 7-1-86					
2003–04	Nottingham F	0	0		
2004–05	Nottingham F	0	0		

NOTTS CO (57)

BAUDET, Julien (D)				**94**	**8**
H: 6 3 W: 15 03 b.St Martin D'heres 13-1-79					
Source: Toulouse.					
2001–02	Oldham Ath	20	1		
2002–03	Oldham Ath	24	2	**44**	**3**
2003–04	Rotherham U	11	0	**11**	**0**
2004–05	Notts Co	39	5	**39**	**5**

BOLLAND, Paul (M)				**184**	**6**
H: 6 0 W: 12 05 b.Bradford 23-12-79					
Source: Trainee.					
1997–98	Bradford C	10	0		
1998–99	Bradford C	2	0	**12**	**0**
1998–99	Notts Co	13	0		
1999–2000	Notts Co	25	1		
2000–01	Notts Co	7	0		
2001–02	Notts Co	19	0		
2002–03	Notts Co	29	3		
2003–04	Notts Co	39	1		
2004–05	Notts Co	40	1	**172**	**6**

DEENEY, Saul (G)				**42**	**0**
H: 6 0 W: 12 13 b.Londonderry 12-3-83					
Source: Scholar. *Honours:* Eire Youth, Under-21.					
2000–01	Notts Co	0	0		
2001–02	Notts Co	0	0		
2002–03	Notts Co	7	0		
2003–04	Notts Co	3	0		
2004–05	Notts Co	32	0	**42**	**0**

EDWARDS, Mike (D)				**225**	**7**
H: 6 1 W: 13 01 b.North Ferriby 25-4-80					
Source: Trainee.					
1997–98	Hull C	21	0		
1998–99	Hull C	30	0		
1999–2000	Hull C	40	1		
2000–01	Hull C	42	4		
2001–02	Hull C	39	1		
2002–03	Hull C	6	0	**178**	**6**
2002–03	Colchester U	5	0	**5**	**0**
2003–04	Grimsby T	33	1	**33**	**1**
2004–05	Notts Co	9	0	**9**	**0**

FRANCIS, Willis (M)				**13**	**0**
H: 5 5 W: 10 10 b.Nottingham 26-7-85					
Source: Scholar.					
2002–03	Notts Co	10	0		
2003–04	Notts Co	3	0		
2004–05	Notts Co	0	0	**13**	**0**

FRIARS, Emmet (D)				**9**	**0**
H: 6 1 W: 11 06 b.Derry 14-9-85					
Honours: Northern Ireland Youth, Under-21.					
2003–04	Notts Co	0	0		
2004–05	Notts Co	9	0	**9**	**0**

GILL, Matthew (M)				**194**	**5**
H: 5 10 W: 11 05 b.Cambridge 8-11-80					
Source: Trainee.					
1997–98	Peterborough U	2	0		
1998–99	Peterborough U	26	0		
1999–2000	Peterborough U	20	1		
2000–01	Peterborough U	17	1		
2001–02	Peterborough U	12	2		
2002–03	Peterborough U	41	1		
2003–04	Peterborough U	33	0	**151**	**5**
2004–05	Notts Co	43	0	**43**	**0**

GORDON, Gavin (F) 220 48
H: 6 2 W: 13 01 b.Manchester 24-6-79
Source: Trainee.

1995–96	Hull C	13	3		
1996–97	Hull C	20	4		
1997–98	Hull C	5	2	**38**	**9**
1997–98	Lincoln C	13	3		
1998–99	Lincoln C	27	5		
1999–2000	Lincoln C	41	11		
2000–01	Lincoln C	18	9	**99**	**28**
2000–01	Cardiff C	10	1		
2001–02	Cardiff C	15	1		
2002–03	Cardiff C	10	2		
2002–03	*Oxford U*	6	1	**6**	**1**
2003–04	Cardiff C	15	1	**50**	**5**
2004–05	Notts Co	27	5	**27**	**5**

HACKWORTH, Tony (F) 54 1
H: 6 1 W: 13 03 b.Durham 19-5-80
Source: Trainee. *Honours:* England Youth.

1997–98	Leeds U	0	0		
1998–99	Leeds U	0	0		
1999–2000	Leeds U	0	0		
2000–01	Leeds U	0	0		
2001–02	Notts Co	33	1		
2002–03	Notts Co	9	0		
2003–04	Notts Co	12	0		
2004–05	Notts Co	0	0	**54**	**1**

HARRAD, Shaun (F) 29 1
H: 5 10 W: 12 04 b.Nottingham 11-12-84
Source: Scholar.

2002–03	Notts Co	5	0		
2003–04	Notts Co	8	0		
2004–05	Notts Co	16	1	**29**	**1**

HURST, Glynn (F) 226 80
H: 5 10 W: 11 11 b.Barnsley 17-1-76
Source: Tottenham H Trainee.

1994–95	Barnsley	2	0		
1995–96	Barnsley	5	0		
1995–96	*Swansea C*	2	1	**2**	**1**
1996–97	Barnsley	1	0	**8**	**0**
1996–97	*Mansfield T*	6	0	**6**	**0**
1998–99	Ayr U	34	18		
1999–2000	Ayr U	25	14	**59**	**32**
2000–01	Stockport Co	11	0		
2001–02	Stockport Co	15	4	**26**	**4**
2001–02	Chesterfield	23	9		
2002–03	Chesterfield	32	7		
2003–04	Chesterfield	29	13	**84**	**29**
2004–05	Notts Co	41	14	**41**	**14**

KUDUZOVIC, Fahrudin (M) 3 0
H: 6 3 W: 13 03 b.Bosnia 10-10-84

2004–05	Notts Co	3	0	**3**	**0**

McFAUL, Shane (M) 30 0
H: 6 1 W: 11 11 b.Dublin 23-5-86
Source: Scholar. *Honours:* Eire Youth.

2003–04	Notts Co	6	0		
2004–05	Notts Co	24	0	**30**	**0**

McHUGH, Frazer (M) 37 0
H: 5 9 W: 12 05 b.Nottingham 14-7-81
Source: Trainee.

1998–99	Swindon T	1	0		
1999–2000	Swindon T	14	0		
2000–01	Swindon T	4	0		
2001–02	Swindon T	0	0	**19**	**0**

From Tamworth, Gainsborough T

2002–03	Bradford				
2003–04	Bradford C	3	0	**5**	**0**
2003–04	Notts Co	13	0		
2004–05	Notts Co	0	0	**13**	**0**

McINTYRE, Eddie (D) 0 0
H: 5 7 W: 9 06 b.Derry 7-9-85
Source: Scholar.

2004–05	Notts Co	0	0		

OAKES, Stefan (M) 121 7
H: 6 1 W: 13 07 b.Leicester 6-9-78
Source: Trainee.

1997–98	Leicester C	0	0		
1998–99	Leicester C	3	0		
1999–2000	Leicester C	22	1		
2000–01	Leicester C	13	0		
2001–02	Leicester C	21	1		
2002–03	Leicester C	5	0	**64**	**2**
2002–03	*Crewe Alex*	7	0	**7**	**0**
2003–04	Walsall	5	0	**5**	**0**
2003–04	Notts Co	14	0		
2004–05	Notts Co	31	5	**45**	**5**

PALMER, Chris (M) 25 4
H: 5 7 W: 10 12 b.Derby 16-10-83
Source: Scholar.

2003–04	Derby Co	0	0		
2004–05	Notts Co	25	4	**25**	**4**

PIPE, David (M) 80 3
H: 5 10 W: 12 04 b.Caerphilly 5-11-83
Source: Scholar. *Honours:* Wales Youth, Under-21, 1 full cap.

2000–01	Coventry C	0	0		
2001–02	Coventry C	0	0		
2002–03	Coventry C	21	1		
2003–04	Coventry C	0	0	**21**	**1**
2003–04	Notts Co	18	0		
2004–05	Notts Co	41	2	**59**	**2**

RHODES, Chris (M) 1 0
H: 5 9 W: 10 12 b.Mansfield 9-1-87
Source: Scholar.

2003–04	Notts Co	1	0		
2004–05	Notts Co	0	0	**1**	**0**

RICHARDSON, Ian (D) 260 21
H: 5 11 W: 12 04 b.Barking 22-10-70
Source: Dagenham & Redbridge.

1995–96	Birmingham C	7	0	**7**	**0**
1995–96	Notts Co	15	0		
1996–97	Notts Co	19	1		
1997–98	Notts Co	30	2		
1998–99	Notts Co	23	7		
1999–2000	Notts Co	33	4		
2000–01	Notts Co	25	1		
2001–02	Notts Co	24	2		
2002–03	Notts Co	34	1		
2003–04	Notts Co	40	3		
2004–05	Notts Co	10	0	**253**	**21**

SCOFFHAM, Steve (F) 22 2
H: 5 11 W: 12 13 b.Germany 12-7-83
Source: Gedling.

2003–04	Notts Co	15	2		
2004–05	Notts Co	7	0	**22**	**2**

SCULLY, Tony (M) 166 9
H: 5 8 W: 11 11 b.Dublin 12-6-76
Source: Trainee. *Honours:* Eire Under-21.

1993–94	Crystal Palace	0	0		
1994–95	Crystal Palace	0	0		
1994–95	*Bournemouth*	10	0	**10**	**0**
1995–96	Crystal Palace	2	0		
1995–96	*Cardiff C*	14	0	**14**	**0**
1996–97	Crystal Palace	1	0		
1997–98	Crystal Palace	0	0	**3**	**0**
1997–98	Manchester C	9	0	**9**	**0**
1997–98	*Stoke C*	7	0	**7**	**0**
1997–98	QPR	7	0		
1998–99	QPR	23	2		
1999–2000	QPR	8	0		
2000–01	QPR	2	0	**40**	**2**
2001–02	Cambridge U	25	2		
2002–03	Cambridge U	6	0	**31**	**2**
2002–03	*Southend U*	8	0	**8**	**0**
2002–03	*Peterborough U*	3	0		
2003–04	Peterborough U	0	0	**3**	**0**

From Dagenham & R

2003–04	Notts Co	10	3		
2004–05	Notts Co	31	2	**41**	**5**

ULLATHORNE, Robert (D) 232 9
H: 5 7 W: 11 07 b.Wakefield 11-10-71
Source: Trainee.

1989–90	Norwich C	0	0		
1990–91	Norwich C	2	0		
1991–92	Norwich C	20	3		
1992–93	Norwich C	0	0		
1993–94	Norwich C	16	2		
1994–95	Norwich C	27	2		
1995–96	Norwich C	29	0	**94**	**7**
1996–97	Osasuna	18	0	**18**	**0**
1996–97	Leicester C	0	0		
1997–98	Leicester C	6	1		
1998–99	Leicester C	25	0		
1999–2000	Leicester C	0	0	**31**	**1**
2000–01	Sheffield U	14	0		
2001–02	Sheffield U	14	0		
2002–03	Sheffield U	12	0	**40**	**0**
2003–04	Northampton T	13	1	**13**	**1**
2004–05	Notts Co	36	0	**36**	**0**

WHITLOW, Mike (D) 397 15
H: 6 0 W: 13 03 b.Northwich 13-1-68
Source: Witton Alb.

1988–89	Leeds U	20	1		
1989–90	Leeds U	29	1		
1990–91	Leeds U	18	1		
1991–92	Leeds U	10	1	**77**	**4**
1991–92	Leicester C	5	0		
1992–93	Leicester C	24	1		
1993–94	Leicester C	31	2		
1994–95	Leicester C	28	2		
1995–96	Leicester C	42	3		
1996–97	Leicester C	17	0		
1997–98	Leicester C	0	0	**147**	**8**
1997–98	Bolton W	13	0		
1998–99	Bolton W	28	0		
1999–2000	Bolton W	37	1		
2000–01	Bolton W	8	1		
2001–02	Bolton W	29	0		
2002–03	Bolton W	17	0	**132**	**2**
2003–04	Sheffield U	17	1	**17**	**1**
2004–05	Notts Co	24	0	**24**	**0**

WILLIAMS, Matthew (F) 25 1
H: 5 8 W: 10 10 b.St Asaph 5-11-82
Honours: Wales Under-21.

1999–2000	Manchester U	0	0		
2000–01	Manchester U	0	0		
2001–02	Manchester U	0	0		
2002–03	Manchester U	0	0		
2003–04	Manchester U	0	0		
2003–04	Notts Co	7	0		
2004–05	Notts Co	18	1	**25**	**1**

WILSON, Kelvin (D) 44 2
H: 6 1 W: 11 13 b.Nottingham 3-9-85
Source: Scholar.

2003–04	Notts Co	3	0		
2004–05	Notts Co	41	2	**44**	**2**

ZADKOVICH, Ruben (M) 8 1
H: 5 10 W: 11 07 b.Australia 23-5-86
Honours: Australia Youth, Under-20.

2004–05	Notts Co	8	1	**8**	**1**

OLDHAM ATH (58)

BARLOW, Matty (F) 10 0
H: 5 11 W: 10 02 b.Oldham 25-6-87
Source: Scholar.

2003–04	Oldham Ath	1	0		
2004–05	Oldham Ath	9	0	**10**	**0**

BEHARALL, David (D) 80 3
H: 6 0 W: 11 06 b.Newcastle 8-3-79
Source: Trainee.

1997–98	Newcastle U	0	0		
1998–99	Newcastle U	4	0		
1999–2000	Newcastle U	2	0		
2000–01	Newcastle U	0	0	**6**	**0**
2001–02	Grimsby T	14	0	**14**	**0**
2001–02	Oldham Ath	18	1		
2002–03	Oldham Ath	32	0		
2003–04	Oldham Ath	7	2		
2004–05	Oldham Ath	3	0	**60**	**3**

BETSY, Kevin (M) 158 22
H: 6 1 W: 12 00 b.Seychelles 20-3-78
Source: Woking.

1998–99	Fulham	7	1		
1999–2000	Fulham	2	0		
1999–2000	*Bournemouth*	5	0	**5**	**0**
1999–2000	*Hull C*	2	0	**2**	**0**
2000–01	Fulham	5	0		
2001–02	Fulham	1	0	**15**	**1**
2001–02	Barnsley	10	0		
2002–03	Barnsley	39	5		
2003–04	Barnsley	45	10		
2004–05	Barnsley	0	0	**94**	**15**
2004–05	*Hartlepool U*	6	1	**6**	**1**
2004–05	Oldham Ath	36	5	**36**	**5**

BONNER, Mark (M) 348 17
H: 5 10 W: 11 00 b.Ormskirk 7-6-74
Source: Trainee.

1991–92	Blackpool	3	0		
1992–93	Blackpool	15	0		
1993–94	Blackpool	40	7		
1994–95	Blackpool	17	0		
1995–96	Blackpool	42	3		

1996–97 Blackpool 29 1
1997–98 Blackpool 32 3 **178 14**
1998–99 Cardiff C 25 1
1998–99 *Hull C* 1 1 **1 1**
1999–2000 Cardiff C 31 0
2000–01 Cardiff C 24 1
2001–02 Cardiff C 29 0
2002–03 Cardiff C 14 0
2003–04 Cardiff C 20 0 **143 2**
2003–04 Oldham Ath 7 0
2004–05 Oldham Ath 19 0 **26 0**

BOSHELL, Danny (M) 76 2
H: 5 11 W: 11 08 b.Bradford 30-5-81
Source: Trainee.
1998–99 Oldham Ath 0 0
1999–2000 Oldham Ath 8 0
2000–01 Oldham Ath 18 1
2001–02 Oldham Ath 4 0
2002–03 Oldham Ath 2 0
2003–04 Oldham Ath 22 0
2004–05 Oldham Ath 16 1 **70 2**
2004–05 *Bury* 6 0 **6 0**

BRANSTON, Guy (D) 173 17
H: 6 1 W: 15 03 b.Leicester 9-1-79
Source: Trainee.
1997–98 Leicester C 0 0
1997–98 *Colchester U* 12 1
1998–99 Leicester C 0 0
1998–99 *Colchester U* 1 0 **13 1**
1998–99 *Plymouth Arg* 7 1 **7 1**
1999–2000 Leicester C 0 0
1999–2000 *Lincoln C* 4 0 **4 0**
1999–2000 Rotherham U 30 4
2000–01 Rotherham U 41 6
2001–02 Rotherham U 10 1
2002–03 Rotherham U 15 2
2003–04 Rotherham U 8 0 **104 13**
2003–04 *Wycombe W* 9 0 **9 0**
2003–04 *Peterborough U* 14 0
2004–05 Sheffield W 11 0 **11 0**
2004–05 *Peterborough U* 4 1 **18 1**
2004–05 Oldham Ath 7 1 **7 1**

CLEGG, Michael (D) 64 0
H: 5 9 W: 11 07 b.Ashton-under-Lyne 3-7-77
Source: Trainee. *Honours:* England Under-21.
1995–96 Manchester U 0 0
1996–97 Manchester U 4 0
1997–98 Manchester U 3 0
1998–99 Manchester U 0 0
1999–2000 Manchester U 2 0
1999–2000 *Ipswich T* 3 0 **3 0**
1999–2000 *Wigan Ath* 6 0 **6 0**
2000–01 Manchester U 0 0
2001–02 Manchester U 0 0 **9 0**
2001–02 Oldham Ath 6 0
2002–03 Oldham Ath 8 0
2003–04 Oldham Ath 32 0
2004–05 Oldham Ath 0 0 **46 0**

EYRE, John (M) 353 79
H: 6 0 W: 11 05 b.Hull 9-10-74
Source: Trainee.
1993–94 Oldham Ath 2 0
1994–95 Oldham Ath 8 1
1994–95 *Scunthorpe U* 9 8
1995–96 Scunthorpe U 39 10
1996–97 Scunthorpe U 42 8
1997–98 Scunthorpe U 42 10
1998–99 Scunthorpe U 41 15 **173 51**
1999–2000 Hull C 24 8
2000–01 Hull C 28 5 **52 13**
2001–02 Oldham Ath 20 5
2002–03 Oldham Ath 31 2
2003–04 Oldham Ath 43 6
2004–05 Oldham Ath 24 1 **128 15**

EYRES, David (M) 627 126
H: 5 11 W: 11 06 b.Liverpool 26-2-64
Source: Rhyl.
1989–90 Blackpool 35 7
1990–91 Blackpool 36 6
1991–92 Blackpool 41 9
1992–93 Blackpool 46 16 **158 38**
1993–94 Burnley 45 19
1994–95 Burnley 39 8
1995–96 Burnley 42 6
1996–97 Burnley 36 3
1997–98 Burnley 13 1 **175 37**
1997–98 Preston NE 28 4
1998–99 Preston NE 34 8
1999–2000 Preston NE 41 7
2000–01 Preston NE 5 0 **108 19**
2000–01 Oldham Ath 30 3
2001–02 Oldham Ath 45 9
2002–03 Oldham Ath 40 13
2003–04 Oldham Ath 29 3
2004–05 Oldham Ath 42 4 **186 32**

FLEMING, Craig (M) 1 0
H: 5 10 W: 11 02 b.Stockport 1-12-84
Source: Scholar.
2003–04 Oldham Ath 1 0
2004–05 Oldham Ath 0 0 **1 0**

FORDE, Danny (D) 0 0
H: 5 10 W: 11 07 b.Salford 26-10-87
Source: Scholar.
2003–04 Oldham Ath 0 0
2004–05 Oldham Ath 0 0

GRIFFIN, Adam (D) 62 3
H: 5 7 W: 10 03 b.Manchester 26-8-84
Source: Scholar.
2001–02 Oldham Ath 1 0
2002–03 Oldham Ath 0 0
2003–04 Oldham Ath 26 1
2004–05 Oldham Ath 35 2 **62 3**

HAINING, Will (D) 96 9
H: 6 0 W: 11 00 b.Glasgow 2-10-82
Source: Scholar.
2001–02 Oldham Ath 4 0
2002–03 Oldham Ath 26 2
2003–04 Oldham Ath 31 2
2004–05 Oldham Ath 35 5 **96 9**

HALL, Chris (F) 7 0
H: 6 1 W: 11 04 b.Manchester 27-11-86
2003–04 Oldham Ath 1 0
2004–05 Oldham Ath 6 0 **7 0**

HALL, Danny (D) 54 1
H: 6 0 W: 12 01 b.Tameside 14-11-83
Source: Scholar.
2002–03 Oldham Ath 2 0
2003–04 Oldham Ath 31 1
2004–05 Oldham Ath 21 0 **54 1**

HOLDEN, Dean (D) 121 11
H: 6 1 W: 12 05 b.Salford 15-9-79
Source: Trainee. *Honours:* England Youth.
1997–98 Bolton W 0 0
1998–99 Bolton W 0 0
1999–2000 Bolton W 12 0
2000–01 Bolton W 1 1
2001–02 Bolton W 0 0 **13 1**
2001–02 *Oldham Ath* 23 2
2002–03 Oldham Ath 6 2
2003–04 Oldham Ath 39 4
2004–05 Oldham Ath 40 2 **108 10**

JACK, Rodney (F) 305 71
H: 5 7 W: 10 05 b.Kingston, Jamaica 28-9-72
Source: Lambada. *Honours:* St Vincent full caps.
1995–96 Torquay U 14 2
1996–97 Torquay U 33 10
1997–98 Torquay U 40 12 **87 24**
1998–99 Crewe Alex 39 9
1999–2000 Crewe Alex 23 4
2000–01 Crewe Alex 30 4
2001–02 Crewe Alex 33 7
2002–03 Crewe Alex 38 9 **163 33**
2003–04 Rushden & D 45 12 **45 12**
2004–05 Oldham Ath 10 2 **10 2**

JOHNSON, Jermaine (M) 51 9
H: 5 11 W: 11 05 b.Kingston, Jamaica 25-6-80
Source: Tivoli Gardens. *Honours:* Jamaica full caps.
2001–02 Bolton W 10 0
2002–03 Bolton W 2 0
2003–04 Bolton W 0 0 **12 0**
2003–04 Oldham Ath 20 5
2004–05 Oldham Ath 19 4 **39 9**

KILLEN, Chris (F) 90 24
H: 6 0 W: 11 05 b.Wellington 8-10-81
Source: Miramar R. *Honours:* New Zealand Under-20, Under-23, 16 full caps, 7 goals.
1998–99 Manchester C 0 0
1999–2000 Manchester C 0 0
2000–01 Manchester C 0 0
2000–01 *Wrexham* 12 3 **12 3**
2001–02 *Port Vale* 9 6 **9 6**
2001–02 Manchester C 3 0 **3 0**
2002–03 Oldham Ath 27 3
2003–04 Oldham Ath 13 2
2004–05 Oldham Ath 26 10 **66 15**

LEE, David (M) 71 9
H: 5 11 W: 12 12 b.Basildon 28-3-80
Source: Trainee.
1998–99 Tottenham H 0 0
1999–2000 Tottenham H 0 0
2000–01 Southend U 42 8 **42 8**
2001–02 Hull C 11 1 **11 1**
2001–02 Brighton & HA 2 0
2002–03 Brighton & HA 0 0
2002–03 *Bristol R* 5 0 **5 0**
2003–04 Brighton & HA 4 0 **6 0**
2004–05 Oldham Ath 7 0 **7 0**

LOMAX, Kelvin (D) 10 0
H: 5 11 W: 12 03 b.Bury 12-11-86
Source: Scholar.
2003–04 Oldham Ath 1 0
2004–05 Oldham Ath 9 0 **10 0**

MAWSON, Craig (G) 13 0
H: 6 2 W: 13 04 b.Keighley 16-5-79
Source: Trainee.
1997–98 Burnley 0 0
1998–99 Burnley 0 0
1999–2000 Burnley 0 0
2000–01 Burnley 0 0
2000–01 *Lincoln C* 0 0
2000–01 Halifax T 9 0
2001–02 Halifax T 0 0 **9 0**
From Morecambe.
2004–05 Oldham Ath 4 0 **4 0**

MILDENHALL, Steve (G) 115 0
H: 6 6 W: 15 06 b.Swindon 13-5-78
Source: Trainee.
1996–97 Swindon T 1 0
1997–98 Swindon T 4 0
1998–99 Swindon T 0 0
1999–2000 Swindon T 5 0
2000–01 Swindon T 23 0 **33 0**
2001–02 Notts Co 26 0
2002–03 Notts Co 21 0
2003–04 Notts Co 28 0
2004–05 Notts Co 1 0 **76 0**
2004–05 Oldham Ath 6 0 **6 0**

POGLIACOMI, Les (G) 225 0
H: 6 4 W: 13 02 b.Sydney 3-5-76
Honours: Australia Schools, Under-20.
1994–95 Marconi Stallions 11 0
1995–96 Marconi Stallions 1 0
1996–97 Marconi Stallions 10 0 **22 0**
1997–98 Adelaide City 0 0
1998–99 Wollongong Wolves 22 0
1999–2000 Wollongong Wolves 34 0 **56 0**
2000–01 Parramatta Power 8 0
2001–02 Parramatta Power 19 0 **27 0**
2002–03 Oldham Ath 37 0
2003–04 Oldham Ath 46 0
2004–05 Oldham Ath 37 0 **120 0**

ROCA, Carlos (F) 7 0
H: 5 4 W: 10 07 b.Manchester 4-9-84
Source: Scholar.
2003–04 Oldham Ath 7 0
2004–05 Oldham Ath 0 0 **7 0**

SANOKHO, Amadou (M) 4 0
H: 6 3 W: 12 06 b.Paris 1-9-79
2004–05 Burnley 3 0 **3 0**
2004–05 Oldham Ath 1 0 **1 0**

SHERIDAN, John (M) 606 88
H: 5 10 W: 11 12 b.Stretford 1-10-64
Source: Local. *Honours:* Eire Youth, Under-21, Under-23, B, 34 full caps, 5 goals.
1981–82 Leeds U 0 0
1982–83 Leeds U 27 2
1983–84 Leeds U 11 1

1984–85 Leeds U 42 6
1985–86 Leeds U 32 4
1986–87 Leeds U 40 15
1987–88 Leeds U 38 12
1988–89 Leeds U 40 7 **230 47**
1989–90 Nottingham F 0 0
1989–90 Sheffield W 27 2
1990–91 Sheffield W 46 10
1991–92 Sheffield W 24 6
1992–93 Sheffield W 25 3
1993–94 Sheffield W 20 3
1994–95 Sheffield W 36 1
1995–96 Sheffield W 17 0
1995–96 *Birmingham C* 2 0 **2 0**
1996–97 Sheffield W 2 0 **197 25**
1996–97 Bolton W 20 2
1997–98 Bolton W 12 0 **32 2**
From Doncaster R
1998–99 Oldham Ath 30 2
1999–2000 Oldham Ath 36 1
2000–01 Oldham Ath 25 4
2001–02 Oldham Ath 27 2
2002–03 Oldham Ath 5 0
2003–04 Oldham Ath 22 5
2004–05 Oldham Ath 0 0 **145 14**

STAM, Stefan (D) 13 0
H: 6 2 W: 13 00 b.Amersfoort 14-9-79
Honours: Holland Under-21.
2004–05 Oldham Ath 13 0 **13 0**

TIERNEY, Marc (D) 13 0
H: 5 11 W: 11 02 b.Manchester 7-9-86
Source: Trainee.
2003–04 Oldham Ath 2 0
2004–05 Oldham Ath 11 0 **13 0**

VERNON, Scott (F) 79 23
H: 6 0 W: 11 10 b.Manchester 8-7-84
Source: Scholar.
2002–03 Oldham Ath 8 1
2003–04 Oldham Ath 45 12
2004–05 Oldham Ath 22 7 **75 20**
2004–05 *Blackpool* 4 3 **4 3**

WALKER, Rob (M) 1 0
H: 5 9 W: 11 00 b.Bolton 20-9-85
Source: Scholar.
2003–04 Oldham Ath 1 0
2004–05 Oldham Ath 0 0 **1 0**

WILKINSON, Wes (F) 6 0
H: 5 10 W: 11 01 b.Wythenshawe 1-5-84
Source: Nantwich T.
2003–04 Oldham Ath 5 0
2004–05 Oldham Ath 1 0 **6 0**

WINN, Ashley (M) 2 0
H: 5 11 W: 11 02 b.Stockton 1-12-85
Source: Scholar.
2004–05 Oldham Ath 2 0 **2 0**

WOLFENDEN, Matthew (M) 2 0
H: 5 9 W: 11 01 b.Oldham 23-7-87
Source: Scholar.
2003–04 Oldham Ath 1 0
2004–05 Oldham Ath 1 0 **2 0**

OXFORD U (59)

ALEXIS, Michael (M) 0 0
H: 6 2 W: 12 01 b.Oxford 2-1-85
2001–02 Oxford U 0 0
2002–03 Oxford U 0 0
2003–04 Oxford U 0 0
2004–05 Oxford U 0 0

ASHTON, Jon (D) 75 0
H: 6 2 W: 13 12 b.Nuneaton 4-10-82
Source: Scholar.
2000–01 Leicester C 0 0
2001–02 Leicester C 7 0
2002–03 *Notts Co* 4 0 **4 0**
2003–04 Leicester C 0 0 **7 0**
2003–04 Oxford U 34 0
2004–05 Oxford U 30 0 **64 0**

BASHAM, Steve (F) 200 47
H: 5 11 W: 12 04 b.Southampton 2-12-77
Source: Trainee.
1996–97 Southampton 6 0
1997–98 Southampton 9 0
1997–98 *Wrexham* 5 0 **5 0**
1998–99 Southampton 4 1 **19 1**
1998–99 *Preston NE* 17 10
1999–2000 Preston NE 24 2
2000–01 Preston NE 11 2
2001–02 Preston NE 16 1 **68 15**
2002–03 Oxford U 31 8
2003–04 Oxford U 38 14
2004–05 Oxford U 39 9 **108 31**

BEECHERS, Billy (M) 3 0
H: 5 9 W: 11 10 b.Oxford 1-6-87
Source: Scholar.
2004–05 Oxford U 3 0 **3 0**

BRADBURY, Lee (F) 313 72
H: 6 0 W: 13 12 b.Isle of Wight 3-7-75
Source: From Cowes. *Honours:* England Under-21.
1995–96 Portsmouth 12 0
1995–96 *Exeter C* 14 5 **14 5**
1996–97 Portsmouth 42 15
1997–98 Manchester C 27 7
1998–99 Manchester C 13 3 **40 10**
1998–99 Crystal Palace 22 4
1998–99 *Birmingham C* 7 0 **7 0**
1999–2000 Crystal Palace 10 2 **32 6**
1999–2000 Portsmouth 35 10
2000–01 Portsmouth 39 10
2001–02 Portsmouth 22 7
2002–03 Portsmouth 3 1
2002–03 *Sheffield W* 11 3 **11 3**
2003–04 Portsmouth 0 0 **153 43**
2003–04 *Derby Co* 7 0 **7 0**
2003–04 Walsall 8 1 **8 1**
2004–05 Oxford U 41 4 **41 4**

BROOKS, Jamie (M) 41 13
H: 5 10 W: 11 05 b.Oxford 12-8-83
Source: Scholar.
2000–01 Oxford U 4 1
2001–02 Oxford U 25 10
2002–03 Oxford U 0 0
2003–04 Oxford U 0 0
2004–05 Oxford U 12 2 **41 13**

BROWN, Danny (M) 69 3
H: 6 0 W: 13 01 b.Bethnal Green 12-9-80
Source: Trainee.
1997–98 Leyton Orient 0 0
1998–99 Leyton Orient 0 0
1999–2000 Barnet 24 3
2000–01 Barnet 29 0
2001–02 Barnet 0 0
2002–03 Barnet 0 0 **53 3**
2003–04 Oxford U 12 0
2004–05 Oxford U 4 0 **16 0**

BURTON, Paul (M) 1 0
H: 6 0 W: 11 12 b.London 30-11-85
Source: Scholar.
2004–05 Oxford U 1 0 **1 0**

CLARKE, Bradie (G) 4 0
H: 6 2 W: 13 10 b.Cambridge 26-5-86
Source: Scholar.
2004–05 Oxford U 4 0 **4 0**

COMINELLI, Lucas (M) 16 1
H: 6 1 W: 12 06 b.Buenos Aires 25-12-76
Source: Granada.
1999–2000 Newcastle U 0 0
2000–01 Newcastle U 0 0
2001–02 Newcastle U 0 0
2004–05 Oxford U 16 1 **16 1**

CORBO, Mateo (M) 105 2
H: 5 9 W: 12 12 b.Montevideo 21-4-76
1996 River Plate (Uru) 16 0
1997 River Plate (Uru) 25 1
1998 River Plate (Uru) 16 0
1999 River Plate (Uru) 11 1 **68 2**
1999–2000 Oviedo 6 0 **6 0**
2000–01 Barnsley 17 0
2001–02 Barnsley 1 0
2002–03 Barnsley 0 0
2003–04 Barnsley 0 0
2004–05 Barnsley 0 0 **18 0**
2004–05 Oxford U 13 0 **13 0**

COX, Simon (G) 8 0
H: 6 0 W: 11 09 b.Clapham 23-3-84
Source: Scholar.
2003–04 Oxford U 5 0
2004–05 Oxford U 3 0 **8 0**

DAVIES, Craig (F) 28 6
H: 6 2 W: 13 05 b.Burton-on-Trent 9-1-86
Source: Manchester C. *Honours:* Wales Youth, Under-21.
2004–05 Oxford U 28 6 **28 6**

DIAZ, Emiliano (M) 7 0
H: 5 7 W: 10 02 b.Naples 22-6-83
2004–05 Oxford U 7 0 **7 0**

DOUDOU, Ebeli M'bombo (F) 47 3
H: 5 5 W: 9 11 b.Kinshasa 11-9-80
Source: Monaco.
2001–02 QPR 36 3
2002–03 QPR 10 0
2003–04 QPR 0 0 **46 3**
2004–05 Oxford U 1 0 **1 0**

E'BEYER, Mark (M) 10 2
H: 5 11 W: 11 05 b.Stevenage 21-9-84
Source: Milton Keynes Dons Scholar.
2004–05 Oxford U 10 2 **10 2**

GARNER, Adam (D) 0 0
H: 6 1 W: 13 11 b.Oxford 7-12-84
Source: Scholar.
2004–05 Oxford U 0 0

HACKETT, Chris (M) 104 7
H: 6 0 W: 12 08 b.Oxford 1-3-83
Source: Scholarship.
1999–2000 Oxford U 2 0
2000–01 Oxford U 16 2
2001–02 Oxford U 15 0
2002–03 Oxford U 12 0
2003–04 Oxford U 22 1
2004–05 Oxford U 37 4 **104 7**

JUDGE, Alan (G) 285 0
H: 5 11 W: 11 06 b.Kingsbury 14-5-60
Source: Amateur.
1977–78 Luton T 0 0
1978–79 Luton T 0 0
1979–80 Luton T 1 0
1980–81 Luton T 2 0
1981–82 Luton T 4 0
1982–83 Luton T 4 0 **11 0**
1982–83 *Reading* 33 0
1983–84 Reading 41 0
1984–85 Reading 3 0 **77 0**
1984–85 Oxford U 0 0
1985–86 Oxford U 19 0
1985–86 *Lincoln C* 2 0 **2 0**
1986–87 Oxford U 9 0
1987–88 Oxford U 9 0
1987–88 *Cardiff C* 8 0 **8 0**
1988–89 Oxford U 20 0
1989–90 Oxford U 17 0
1990–91 Oxford U 6 0
1991–92 Hereford U 24 0
1992–93 Hereford U 42 0
1993–94 Hereford U 39 0 **105 0**
1994–95 Chelsea 0 0
2002–03 Oxford U 1 0
From retirement
2002–03 Swindon T 0 0
2003–04 Oxford U 0 0
2004–05 Oxford U 1 0 **82 0**

KARAM, Amine (F) 2 0
H: 5 7 W: 10 08 b.Besancon 3-1-84
2004–05 Oxford U 2 0 **2 0**

MACKAY, David (D) 44 0
H: 6 0 W: 13 03 b.Rutherglen 2-5-81
2004–05 Oxford U 44 0 **44 0**

MOLYNEAUX, Lee (D) 16 0
H: 6 0 W: 12 08 b.Portsmouth 16-1-83
Source: Scholar.
2001–02 Portsmouth 0 0
2002–03 Portsmouth 0 0
2003–04 Portsmouth 0 0
2004–05 Oxford U 16 0 **16 0**

MOONEY, Tommy (F) 515 145
H: 5 10 W: 13 05 b.Billingham 11-8-71
Source: Trainee.
1989–90 Aston Villa 0 0
1990–91 Scarborough 27 13
1991–92 Scarborough 40 8
1992–93 Scarborough 40 9 **107 30**
1993–94 Southend U 14 5 **14 5**
1993–94 *Watford* 10 2

1994–95	Watford	29	3		
1995–96	Watford	42	6		
1996–97	Watford	37	13		
1997–98	Watford	45	6		
1998–99	Watford	36	9		
1999–2000	Watford	12	2		
2000–01	Watford	39	19	**250**	**60**
2001–02	Birmingham C	33	13		
2002–03	Birmingham C	1	0	**34**	**13**
2002–03	*Stoke C*	12	3	**12**	**3**
2002–03	*Sheffield U*	3	0	**3**	**0**
2002–03	*Derby Co*	8	0	**8**	**0**
2003–04	Swindon T	45	19	**45**	**19**
2004–05	Oxford U	42	15	**42**	**15**

MORGAN, Danny (F) **3** **0**
H: 6 0 W: 14 00 b.Stepney 4-11-84
Source: Milton Keynes D Scholar.

2004–05	Oxford U	3	0	**3**	**0**

PARKER, Terry (D) **8** **0**
H: 5 9 W: 11 11 b.Southampton 20-12-83
Source: Scholar.

2002–03	Portsmouth	0	0		
2003–04	Portsmouth	0	0		
2004–05	Oxford U	8	0	**8**	**0**

POWELL, Paul (D) **178** **17**
H: 5 8 W: 11 13 b.Wallingford 30-6-78
Source: Trainee.

1995–96	Oxford U	3	0		
1996–97	Oxford U	0	0		
1997–98	Oxford U	21	1		
1998–99	Oxford U	44	3		
1999–2000	Oxford U	40	6		
2000–01	Oxford U	20	1		
2001–02	Oxford U	36	4		
2002–03	Oxford U	14	2		
2003–04	Oxford U	0	0		
2004–05	Oxford U	0	0	**178**	**17**

QUINN, Barry (M) **129** **0**
H: 6 0 W: 13 01 b.Dublin 9-5-79
Source: Trainee. *Honours:* Eire Under-21, 4 full caps.

1996–97	Coventry C	0	0		
1997–98	Coventry C	0	0		
1998–99	Coventry C	7	0		
1999–2000	Coventry C	11	0		
2000–01	Coventry C	25	0		
2001–02	Coventry C	22	0		
2002–03	Coventry C	18	0		
2003–04	Coventry C	0	0	**83**	**0**
2003–04	*Rushden & D*	4	0	**4**	**0**
2003–04	*Oxford U*	6	0		
2004–05	Oxford U	36	0	**42**	**0**

RAPONI, Juan Pablo (M) **10** **0**
H: 5 11 W: 11 03 b.Santa Fe 7-5-80

2004–05	Oxford U	10	0	**10**	**0**

ROBINSON, Matt (D) **275** **5**
H: 5 11 W: 11 02 b.Exeter 23-12-74
Source: Trainee.

1993–94	Southampton	0	0		
1994–95	Southampton	1	0		
1995–96	Southampton	5	0		
1996–97	Southampton	7	0		
1997–98	Southampton	1	0	**14**	**0**
1997–98	Portsmouth	15	0		
1998–99	Portsmouth	29	1		
1999–2000	Portsmouth	25	0	**69**	**1**
1999–2000	Reading	19	0		
2000–01	Reading	32	0		
2001–02	Reading	14	0	**65**	**0**
2002–03	Oxford U	42	1		
2003–04	Oxford U	40	1		
2004–05	Oxford U	45	2	**127**	**4**

ROGET, Leo (D) **233** **10**
H: 6 2 W: 13 05 b.Ilford 1-8-77
Source: Trainee.

1995–96	Southend U	8	1		
1996–97	Southend U	25	0		
1997–98	Southend U	11	0		
1998–99	Southend U	14	0		
1999–2000	Southend U	36	2		
2000–01	Southend U	26	4	**120**	**7**
2000–01	Stockport Co	9	0		
2001–02	Stockport Co	22	1	**31**	**1**
2001–02	*Reading*	1	0	**1**	**0**
2002–03	Brentford	14	0		
2003–04	Brentford	15	0	**29**	**0**
2003–04	Rushden & D	17	0	**17**	**0**
2004–05	Oxford U	35	2	**35**	**2**

TARDIF, Chris (G) **54** **0**
H: 6 1 W: 13 03 b.Guernsey 19-9-79
Source: Trainee.

1998–99	Portsmouth	0	0		
1999–2000	Portsmouth	0	0		
2000–01	Portsmouth	4	0		
2001–02	Portsmouth	1	0		
2002–03	Portsmouth	0	0		
2002–03	*Bournemouth*	9	0	**9**	**0**
2003–04	Portsmouth	0	0	**5**	**0**
2004–05	Oxford U	40	0	**40**	**0**

WANLESS, Paul (M) **389** **50**
H: 6 0 W: 14 10 b.Banbury 14-12-73
Source: Trainee.

1991–92	Oxford U	6	0		
1992–93	Oxford U	7	0		
1993–94	Oxford U	9	0		
1994–95	Oxford U	10	0		
1995–96	Lincoln C	8	0	**8**	**0**
1995–96	*Cambridge U*	14	1		
1996–97	Cambridge U	30	3		
1997–98	Cambridge U	42	8		
1998–99	Cambridge U	45	8		
1999–2000	Cambridge U	42	3		
2000–01	Cambridge U	43	10		
2001–02	Cambridge U	29	6		
2002–03	Cambridge U	39	5	**284**	**44**
2003–04	Oxford U	38	5		
2004–05	Oxford U	27	1	**97**	**6**

WINTERS, Tom (M) **5** **0**
H: 5 9 W: 10 10 b.Banbury 11-12-85
Source: Scholar.

2003–04	Oxford U	1	0		
2004–05	Oxford U	4	0	**5**	**0**

WOLLEASTON, Robert (M) **52** **1**
H: 5 11 W: 13 01 b.Perivale 21-12-79
Source: Trainee.

1998–99	Chelsea	0	0		
1999–2000	Chelsea	1	0		
1999–2000	*Bristol R*	4	0	**4**	**0**
2000–01	Chelsea	0	0		
2000–01	*Portsmouth*	6	0	**6**	**0**
2001–02	Chelsea	0	0		
2001–02	*Northampton T*	7	0	**7**	**0**
2002–03	Chelsea	0	0	**1**	**0**
2003–04	Bradford C	14	1	**14**	**1**
2004–05	Oxford U	20	0	**20**	**0**

WOOZLEY, David (D) **122** **4**
H: 6 3 W: 15 00 b.Ascot 6-12-79
Source: Trainee.

1997–98	Crystal Palace	0	0		
1998–99	Crystal Palace	7	0		
1999–2000	Crystal Palace	23	0		
2000–01	Crystal Palace	0	0		
2000–01	*Bournemouth*	6	0	**6**	**0**
2001–02	Crystal Palace	0	0	**30**	**0**
2001–02	Torquay U	16	0		
2002–03	Torquay U	46	3		
2003–04	Torquay U	10	0	**72**	**3**
2004–05	Oxford U	13	1	**13**	**1**
2004–05	*Yeovil T*	1	0	**1**	**0**

PETERBOROUGH U (60)

ARBER, Mark (D) **229** **21**
H: 6 1 W: 12 11 b.Johannesburg 8-10-77
Source: Trainee.

1995–96	Tottenham H	0	0		
1996–97	Tottenham H	0	0		
1997–98	Tottenham H	0	0		
1998–99	Tottenham H	0	0		
1998–99	Barnet	35	2		
1999–2000	Barnet	45	6		
2000–01	Barnet	45	7		
2001–02	Barnet	0	0	**125**	**15**
2002–03	Peterborough U	25	2		
2003–04	Peterborough U	44	3		
2004–05	Oldham Ath	14	1	**14**	**1**
2004–05	Peterborough U	21	0	**90**	**5**

BOUCAUD, Andre (M) **36** **2**
H: 5 10 W: 11 04 b.Enfield 9-10-84
Source: Scholar. *Honours:* Trinidad & Tobago 6 full caps.

2001–02	Reading	0	0		
2002–03	Reading	0	0		
2002–03	*Peterborough U*	6	0		
2003–04	Reading	0	0		
2003–04	*Peterborough U*	8	1		
2004–05	Peterborough U	22	1	**36**	**2**

BURTON, Sagi (D) **198** **5**
H: 6 2 W: 13 06 b.Birmingham 25-11-77
Source: Trainee. *Honours:* St Kitts & Nevis full caps.

1995–96	Crystal Palace	0	0		
1996–97	Crystal Palace	0	0		
1997–98	Crystal Palace	2	0		
1998–99	Crystal Palace	23	1	**25**	**1**
1999–2000	Colchester U	9	0	**9**	**0**
1999–2000	Sheffield U	0	0		
1999–2000	Port Vale	20	2		
2000–01	Port Vale	29	0		
2001–02	Port Vale	37	0	**86**	**2**
2002–03	Crewe Alex	1	0	**1**	**0**
2002–03	Peterborough U	31	0		
2003–04	Peterborough U	30	1		
2004–05	Peterborough U	16	1	**77**	**2**

CASKEY, Darren (M) **358** **50**
H: 5 8 W: 12 04 b.Basildon 21-8-74
Source: Trainee. *Honours:* England Schools, Youth.

1991–92	Tottenham H	0	0		
1992–93	Tottenham H	0	0		
1993–94	Tottenham H	25	4		
1994–95	Tottenham H	4	0		
1995–96	Tottenham H	3	0	**32**	**4**
1995–96	*Watford*	6	1	**6**	**1**
1995–96	Reading	15	2		
1996–97	Reading	35	0		
1997–98	Reading	23	0		
1998–99	Reading	42	7		
1999–2000	Reading	44	17		
2000–01	Reading	43	9	**202**	**35**
2001–02	Notts Co	42	5		
2002–03	Notts Co	39	3		
2003–04	Notts Co	33	2	**114**	**10**
2003–04	Bristol C	0	0		
From Hornchurch					
2004–05	Peterborough U	4	0	**4**	**0**

CLARKE, Andy (F) **410** **74**
H: 5 10 W: 11 07 b.Islington 22-7-67
Source: Barnet.

1990–91	Wimbledon	12	3		
1991–92	Wimbledon	34	3		
1992–93	Wimbledon	33	5		
1993–94	Wimbledon	23	2		
1994–95	Wimbledon	25	1		
1995–96	Wimbledon	18	2		
1996–97	Wimbledon	11	1		
1997–98	Wimbledon	14	0		
1998–99	Wimbledon	0	0	**170**	**17**
1998–99	*Port Vale*	6	0	**6**	**0**
1998–99	*Northampton T*	4	0	**4**	**0**
1998–99	Peterborough U	0	0		
1999–2000	Peterborough U	37	15		
2000–01	Peterborough U	42	9		
2001–02	Peterborough U	28	5		
2002–03	Peterborough U	45	16		
2003–04	Peterborough U	45	9		
2004–05	Peterborough U	33	3	**230**	**57**

CLARKE, Lee (F) **2** **0**
H: 5 11 W: 10 08 b.Peterborough 28-7-83
Source: Yaxley. *Honours:* Northern Ireland Under-21.

2001–02	Peterborough U	1	0		
2002–03	Peterborough U	1	0		
2003–04	Peterborough U	0	0		
2004–05	Peterborough U	0	0	**2**	**0**

COULSON, Mark (M) **7** **0**
H: 5 8 W: 10 03 b.Huntingdon 11-2-86
Source: Scholar.

2002–03	Peterborough U	0	0		
2003–04	Peterborough U	0	0		
2004–05	Peterborough U	7	0	**7**	**0**

DAY, Jamie (M) **1 0**
H: 5 9 W: 10 06 b.Wycombe 7-5-86
Source: Scholar.
2003–04 Peterborough U 0 0
2004–05 Peterborough U 1 0 **1 0**

DEEN, Ahmed (M) **5 0**
H: 5 9 W: 11 05 b.Sierra Leone 30-6-85
Source: Leicester C Scholar.
2004–05 Peterborough U 5 0 **5 0**

FARRELL, Dave (M) **379 45**
H: 5 11 W: 11 08 b.Birmingham 11-11-71
Source: Redditch U.
1992–93 Aston Villa 2 0
1992–93 *Scunthorpe U* 5 1 **5 1**
1993–94 Aston Villa 4 0
1994–95 Aston Villa 0 0
1995–96 Aston Villa 0 0 **6 0**
1995–96 Wycombe W 33 7
1996–97 Wycombe W 27 1 **60 8**
1997–98 Peterborough U 42 6
1998–99 Peterborough U 37 4
1999–2000 Peterborough U 35 3
2000–01 Peterborough U 44 7
2001–02 Peterborough U 38 6
2002–03 Peterborough U 37 3
2003–04 Peterborough U 44 5
2004–05 Peterborough U 31 2 **308 36**

FOTIADIS, Andrew (F) **142 20**
H: 6 0 W: 12 13 b.Hitchin 6-9-77
Source: School. *Honours:* England Schools.
1996–97 Luton T 17 3
1997–98 Luton T 15 1
1998–99 Luton T 21 2
1999–2000 Luton T 23 2
2000–01 Luton T 22 3
2001–02 Luton T 8 1
2002–03 Luton T 17 6 **123 18**
2002–03 Peterborough U 11 2
2003–04 Peterborough U 8 0
2004–05 Peterborough U 0 0 **19 2**

FRY, Adam (M) **3 0**
H: 5 8 W: 10 07 b.Bedford 9-2-85
Source: Scholar.
2002–03 Peterborough U 0 0
2003–04 Peterborough U 0 0
2004–05 Peterborough U 3 0 **3 0**

HUKE, Shane (M) **8 0**
H: 5 11 W: 12 07 b.Reading 2-10-85
Source: Scholar.
2003–04 Peterborough U 0 0
2004–05 Peterborough U 8 0 **8 0**

IRELAND, Craig (D) **234 10**
H: 6 3 W: 13 09 b.Dundee 29-11-75
Source: Aberdeen Lads.
1994–95 Aberdeen 0 0
1995–96 Aberdeen 0 0
1995–96 Dunfermline Ath 10 0
1996–97 Dunfermline Ath 9 1
1997–98 Dunfermline Ath 12 1
1998–99 Dunfermline Ath 23 0
1999–2000 Dunfermline Ath 3 0 **57 2**
1999–2000 Dundee 14 1 **14 1**
2000–01 Airdrieonians 12 2 **12 2**
2000–01 *Notts Co* 16 0
2001–02 Notts Co 27 1
2002–03 Notts Co 37 1 **80 2**
2003–04 Barnsley 43 3 **43 3**
2004–05 Peterborough U 23 0 **23 0**
2004–05 *Bristol C* 5 0 **5 0**

KANU, Chris (D) **34 0**
H: 5 8 W: 11 04 b.Owerri 4-12-79
Source: TOP Oss. *Honours:* Nigeria full caps.
2003–04 Peterborough U 21 0
2004–05 Peterborough U 13 0 **34 0**

KENNEDY, Peter (D) **224 23**
H: 5 11 W: 11 11 b.Lisburn 10-9-73
Source: Portadown. *Honours:* Northern Ireland B, 20 full caps.
1996–97 Notts Co 22 0 **22 0**
1997–98 Watford 34 11
1998–99 Watford 46 6
1999–2000 Watford 18 1
2000–01 Watford 17 0 **115 18**
2001–02 Wigan Ath 31 0
2002–03 Wigan Ath 22 1
2003–04 Wigan Ath 12 1 **65 2**
2003–04 *Derby Co* 5 1 **5 1**
2004–05 Peterborough U 17 2 **17 2**

LEGG, Andy (M) **576 61**
H: 5 8 W: 10 07 b.Neath 28-7-66
Source: Briton Ferry. *Honours:* Wales 6 full caps.
1988–89 Swansea C 6 0
1989–90 Swansea C 26 3
1990–91 Swansea C 39 5
1991–92 Swansea C 46 9
1992–93 Swansea C 46 12 **163 29**
1993–94 Notts Co 30 2
1994–95 Notts Co 34 3
1995–96 Notts Co 25 4 **89 9**
1995–96 Birmingham C 12 1
1996–97 Birmingham C 33 4
1997–98 Birmingham C 0 0 **45 5**
1997–98 *Ipswich T* 6 1 **6 1**
1997–98 Reading 10 0
1998–99 Reading 2 0 **12 0**
1998–99 *Peterborough U* 5 0
1998–99 Cardiff C 24 2
1999–2000 Cardiff C 42 2
2000–01 Cardiff C 39 3
2001–02 Cardiff C 35 2
2002–03 Cardiff C 35 3 **175 12**
2003–04 Peterborough U 42 0
2004–05 Peterborough U 39 5 **86 5**

LOGAN, Richard (F) **119 27**
H: 6 0 W: 12 05 b.Bury St Edmunds 4-1-82
Source: Trainee. *Honours:* England Youth.
1998–99 Ipswich T 2 0
1999–2000 Ipswich T 1 0
2000–01 Ipswich T 0 0
2000–01 *Cambridge U* 5 1 **5 1**
2001–02 Ipswich T 0 0
2001–02 *Torquay U* 16 4 **16 4**
2002–03 Ipswich T 0 0 **3 0**
2002–03 Boston U 27 10
2003–04 Boston U 8 0 **35 10**
2003–04 Peterborough U 29 7
2004–05 Peterborough U 26 4 **55 11**
2004–05 *Shrewsbury T* 5 1 **5 1**

McSHANE, Luke (G) **0 0**
H: 6 1 W: 10 09 b.Peterborough 6-11-85
Source: Scholar.
2003–04 Peterborough U 0 0
2004–05 Peterborough U 0 0

NEWTON, Adam (M) **138 6**
H: 5 10 W: 11 00 b.Ascot 4-12-80
Source: West Ham U Trainee. *Honours:* England Under-21. St Kitts & Nevis full caps.
1999–2000 West Ham U 2 0
1999–2000 *Portsmouth* 3 0 **3 0**
2000–01 West Ham U 0 0
2000–01 *Notts Co* 20 1 **20 1**
2001–02 West Ham U 0 0 **2 0**
2001–02 *Leyton Orient* 10 1 **10 1**
2002–03 Peterborough U 36 2
2003–04 Peterborough U 37 2
2004–05 Peterborough U 30 0 **103 4**

NOLAN, Matt (F) **1 0**
H: 6 0 W: 12 00 b.Hitchin 25-2-82
Source: Hitchin T.
2003–04 Peterborough U 1 0
2004–05 Peterborough U 0 0 **1 0**

ONIBUJE, Fola (F) **7 0**
H: 6 7 W: 12 00 b.Lagos 25-9-84
2002–03 Preston NE 0 0
2003–04 Preston NE 0 0
2003–04 *Huddersfield T* 2 0 **2 0**
2004–05 Barnsley 3 0 **3 0**
2004–05 Peterborough U 2 0 **2 0**

PLUMMER, Chris (D) **85 2**
H: 6 2 W: 12 12 b.Isleworth 12-10-76
Source: Trainee. *Honours:* England Youth, Under-21.
1994–95 QPR 0 0
1995–96 QPR 1 0
1996–97 QPR 5 0
1997–98 QPR 0 0
1998–99 QPR 10 0
1999–2000 QPR 18 0
2000–01 QPR 25 2
2001–02 QPR 1 0
2002–03 QPR 2 0
2002–03 *Bristol R* 2 0 **2 0**
2003–04 QPR 0 0
2004–05 QPR 0 0 **62 2**
2004–05 Peterborough U 21 0 **21 0**

PULLEN, James (G) **20 0**
H: 6 2 W: 14 00 b.Chelmsford 18-3-82
Source: Heybridge S.
1999–2000 Ipswich T 0 0
2000–01 Ipswich T 0 0
2001–02 Ipswich T 0 0
2001–02 *Blackpool* 16 0 **16 0**
2002–03 Ipswich T 1 0
2003–04 Ipswich T 0 0 **1 0**
2003–04 Peterborough U 3 0
2004–05 Peterborough U 0 0 **3 0**

PURSER, Wayne (F) **94 18**
H: 5 8 W: 12 05 b.Basildon 13-4-80
Source: Trainee.
1996–97 QPR 0 0
1997–98 QPR 0 0
1998–99 QPR 0 0
1999–2000 QPR 0 0
2000–01 Barnet 18 3
2001–02 Barnet 0 0
2002–03 Barnet 0 0 **18 3**
2002–03 Leyton Orient 7 3
2003–04 Leyton Orient 41 5
2004–05 Leyton Orient 2 1 **50 9**
From Hornchurch.
2004–05 Peterborough U 26 6 **26 6**

REA, Simon (D) **164 8**
H: 6 1 W: 13 00 b.Coventry 20-9-76
Source: Trainee.
1994–95 Birmingham C 0 0
1995–96 Birmingham C 1 0
1996–97 Birmingham C 0 0
1997–98 Birmingham C 0 0
1998–99 Birmingham C 0 0
1999–2000 Birmingham C 0 0 **1 0**
1999–2000 Peterborough U 14 1
2000–01 Peterborough U 36 2
2001–02 Peterborough U 30 1
2002–03 Peterborough U 37 3
2003–04 Peterborough U 28 1
2004–05 Peterborough U 14 0 **159 8**
2004–05 *Cambridge U* 4 0 **4 0**

SCOTT, Richard (M) **214 26**
H: 5 11 W: 12 08 b.Dudley 29-9-74
Source: Trainee.
1992–93 Birmingham C 1 0
1993–94 Birmingham C 6 0
1994–95 Birmingham C 5 0 **12 0**
1994–95 Shrewsbury T 8 1
1995–96 Shrewsbury T 36 6
1996–97 Shrewsbury T 27 1
1997–98 Shrewsbury T 34 10 **105 18**
1998–99 Peterborough U 27 4
1999–2000 Peterborough U 34 3
2000–01 Peterborough U 20 0
From Telford U, Stevenage B
2002–03 Peterborough
2003–04 Peterborough U 0 0
2004–05 Peterborough U 0 0 **97 8**

SEMPLE, Ryan (M) **13 0**
H: 5 11 W: 10 11 b.Belfast 4-7-85
Source: Scholar.
2002–03 Peterborough U 3 0
2003–04 Peterborough U 2 0
2004–05 Peterborough U 8 0 **13 0**

SHOWLER, Paul (M) **186 33**
H: 5 10 W: 11 00 b.Doncaster 10-10-66
Source: Sheffield W, Sunderland, Colne Dynamoes, Altrincham.
1991–92 Barnet 39 7
1992–93 Barnet 32 5 **71 12**
1993–94 Bradford C 32 5
1994–95 Bradford C 23 2
1995–96 Bradford C 33 8 **88 15**
1996–97 Luton T 23 6
1997–98 Luton T 1 0
1998–99 Luton T 3 0 **27 6**
1999–2000 Peterborough U 0 0
2000–01 Peterborough U 0 0
2001–02 Peterborough U 0 0

2002–03 Peterborough U 0 0
2003–04 Peterborough U 0 0
2004–05 Peterborough U 0 0

SONNER, Danny (M) 241 15
H: 5 11 W: 12 08 b.Wigan 9-1-72
Source: Wigan Ath. *Honours:* Northern Ireland B, 13 full caps.
1990–91 Burnley 2 0
1991–92 Burnley 3 0
1992–93 Burnley 1 0 **6 0**
1992–93 *Bury* 5 3 **5 3**
From Erzgebirge Aue
1996–97 Ipswich T 29 2
1997–98 Ipswich T 23 1
1998–99 Ipswich T 4 0 **56 3**
1998–99 Sheffield W 26 3
1999–2000 Sheffield W 27 0 **53 3**
2000–01 Birmingham C 26 1
2001–02 Birmingham C 15 1 **41 2**
2002–03 Walsall 24 4 **24 4**
2003–04 Nottingham F 28 0
2004–05 Nottingham F 0 0 **28 0**
2004–05 Peterborough U 15 0 **15 0**
2004–05 *Port Vale* 13 0 **13 0**

ST LEDGER-HALL, Sean (D) 36 0
H: 6 0 W: 11 09 b.Solihull 28-12-84
Source: Scholar.
2002–03 Peterborough U 1 0
2003–04 Peterborough U 2 0
2004–05 Peterborough U 33 0 **36 0**

THOMAS, Bradley (D) 0 0
H: 6 2 W: 13 02 b.Forest Green 29-3-84
Source: Scholar.
2003–04 Peterborough U 0 0
2004–05 Peterborough U 0 0

THOMSON, Steve (M) 171 4
H: 5 8 W: 10 04 b.Glasgow 23-1-78
Source: Trainee. *Honours:* Scotland Youth.
1995–96 Crystal Palace 0 0
1996–97 Crystal Palace 0 0
1997–98 Crystal Palace 0 0
1998–99 Crystal Palace 16 0
1999–2000 Crystal Palace 21 0
2000–01 Crystal Palace 18 0
2001–02 Crystal Palace 23 0
2002–03 Crystal Palace 27 1 **105 1**
2003–04 Peterborough U 35 1
2004–05 Peterborough U 31 2 **66 3**

TYLER, Mark (G) 315 0
H: 5 11 W: 12 00 b.Norwich 2-4-77
Source: Trainee. *Honours:* England Youth.
1994–95 Peterborough U 5 0
1995–96 Peterborough U 0 0
1996–97 Peterborough U 3 0
1997–98 Peterborough U 46 0
1998–99 Peterborough U 27 0
1999–2000 Peterborough U 32 0
2000–01 Peterborough U 40 0
2001–02 Peterborough U 44 0
2002–03 Peterborough U 29 0
2003–04 Peterborough U 43 0
2004–05 Peterborough U 46 0 **315 0**

WILLOCK, Calum (F) 77 20
H: 6 0 W: 12 09 b.Lambeth 29-10-81
Source: Scholar. *Honours:* England Schools. St Kitts & Nevis full caps.
2000–01 Fulham 1 0
2001–02 Fulham 2 0
2002–03 Fulham 2 0
2002–03 *QPR* 3 0 **3 0**
2003–04 Fulham 0 0 **5 0**
2003–04 *Bristol R* 5 0 **5 0**
2003–04 Peterborough U 29 8
2004–05 Peterborough U 35 12 **64 20**

WOODHOUSE, Curtis (M) 224 19
H: 5 7 W: 12 02 b.Driffield 17-4-80
Source: Trainee. *Honours:* England Youth, Under-21
1997–98 Sheffield U 9 0
1998–99 Sheffield U 33 3
1999–2000 Sheffield U 37 3
2000–01 Sheffield U 25 0 **104 6**
2000–01 Birmingham C 17 2
2001–02 Birmingham C 28 0
2002–03 Birmingham C 3 0
2002–03 *Rotherham U* 11 0 **11 0**
2003–04 Birmingham C 0 0 **48 2**
2003–04 Peterborough U 27 7
2004–05 Peterborough U 34 4 **61 11**

PLYMOUTH ARG (61)

ALJOFREE, Hasney (D) 124 6
H: 6 0 W: 12 03 b.Manchester 11-7-78
Source: Trainee.
1996–97 Bolton W 0 0
1997–98 Bolton W 2 0
1998–98 Bolton W 4 0
1999–2000 Bolton W 8 0 **14 0**
2000–01 Dundee U 26 2
2001–02 Dundee U 27 2 **53 4**
2002–03 Plymouth Arg 19 1
2003–04 Plymouth Arg 24 0
2004–05 Plymouth Arg 12 1 **55 2**
2004–05 *Sheffield W* 2 0 **2 0**

BASTOW, Darren (M) 42 3
H: 5 11 W: 12 00 b.Torquay 22-12-81
Source: Trainee.
1998–99 Plymouth Arg 29 2
1999–2000 Plymouth Arg 13 1
2000–01 Plymouth Arg 0 0
2001–02 Plymouth Arg 0 0
2002–03 Plymouth Arg 0 0
2003–04 Plymouth Arg 0 0
2004–05 Plymouth Arg 0 0 **42 3**

BUZSAKY, Akos (M) 15 1
H: 5 11 W: 11 09 b.Hungary 7-5-82
2004–05 Plymouth Arg 15 1 **15 1**

CAPALDI, Tony (M) 69 9
H: 6 0 W: 12 00 b.Porsgrunn 12-8-81
Source: Trainee. *Honours:* Northern Ireland Youth, Under-21, 11 full caps.
1999–2000 Birmingham C 0 0
2000–01 Birmingham C 0 0
2001–02 Birmingham C 0 0
2002–03 Birmingham C 0 0
2002–03 Plymouth Arg 1 0
2003–04 Plymouth Arg 33 7
2004–05 Plymouth Arg 35 2 **69 9**

CHADWICK, Nick (F) 50 8
H: 5 11 W: 10 09 b.Stoke 26-10-82
1999–2000 Everton 0 0
2000–01 Everton 0 0
2001–02 Everton 9 3
2002–03 Everton 1 0
2002–03 *Derby Co* 6 0 **6 0**
2003–04 Everton 3 0
2003–04 *Millwall* 15 4 **15 4**
2004–05 Everton 1 0 **14 3**
2004–05 Plymouth Arg 15 1 **15 1**

CONNOLLY, Paul (D) 51 0
H: 6 0 W: 11 10 b.Liverpool 29-9-83
Source: Scholar.
2000–01 Plymouth Arg 1 0
2001–02 Plymouth Arg 0 0
2002–03 Plymouth Arg 2 0
2003–04 Plymouth Arg 29 0
2004–05 Plymouth Arg 19 0 **51 0**

COUGHLAN, Graham (D) 236 27
H: 6 2 W: 13 04 b.Dublin 18-11-74
Source: Bray Wanderers.
1995–96 Blackburn R 0 0
1996–97 Blackburn R 0 0
1996–97 *Swindon T* 3 0 **3 0**
1997–98 Blackburn R 0 0
1998–99 Livingston 6 0
1999–2000 Livingston 29 0
2000–01 Livingston 21 2 **56 2**
2001–02 Plymouth Arg 46 11
2002–03 Plymouth Arg 42 5
2003–04 Plymouth Arg 46 7
2004–05 Plymouth Arg 43 2 **177 25**

CRAWFORD, Steve (F) 422 124
H: 5 10 W: 10 07 b.Dunfermline 9-1-74
Source: Rosyth Recreation. *Honours:* Scotland Under-21, B, 25 full caps, 4 goals.
1992–93 Raith R 20 3
1993–94 Raith R 36 5
1994–95 Raith R 31 11
1995–96 Raith R 28 3 **115 22**
1996–97 Millwall 42 11 **42 11**
1997–98 Hibernian 35 9
1998–99 Hibernian 35 14 **70 23**
1999–2000 Dunfermline Ath 25 16
2000–01 Dunfermline Ath 37 9
2001–02 Dunfermline Ath 36 6
2002–03 Dunfermline Ath 37 18
2003–04 Dunfermline Ath 34 13 **169 62**
2004–05 Plymouth Arg 26 6 **26 6**

DICKSON, Ryan (M) 3 0
H: 5 10 W: 11 05 b.Saltash 14-12-86
Source: Scholar.
2004–05 Plymouth Arg 3 0 **3 0**

DOUMBE, Stephen (D) 71 4
H: 6 1 W: 12 05 b.Paris 28-10-79
Source: Paris St Germain.
2001–02 Hibernian 0 0
2002–03 Hibernian 12 0
2003–04 Hibernian 33 2 **45 2**
2004–05 Plymouth Arg 26 2 **26 2**

EVANS, Micky (F) 445 82
H: 6 0 W: 13 04 b.Plymouth 1-1-73
Source: Trainee. *Honours:* Eire 1 full cap.
1990–91 Plymouth Arg 4 0
1991–92 Plymouth Arg 13 0
1992–93 Plymouth Arg 23 1
1992–93 *Blackburn R* 0 0
1993–94 Plymouth Arg 22 9
1994–95 Plymouth Arg 23 4
1995–96 Plymouth Arg 45 12
1996–97 Plymouth Arg 33 12
1996–97 Southampton 12 4
1997–98 Southampton 10 0 **22 4**
1997–98 WBA 10 1
1998–99 WBA 20 2
1999–2000 WBA 33 3
2000–01 WBA 0 0 **63 6**
2000–01 Bristol R 21 4 **21 4**
2000–01 Plymouth Arg 10 4
2001–02 Plymouth Arg 38 7
2002–03 Plymouth Arg 42 4
2003–04 Plymouth Arg 44 11
2004–05 Plymouth Arg 42 4 **339 68**

GILBERT, Peter (D) 78 1
H: 5 11 W: 12 00 b.Newcastle 31-7-83
Source: Scholar. *Honours:* Wales Under-21.
2001–02 Birmingham C 0 0
2002–03 Birmingham C 0 0
2003–04 Birmingham C 0 0
2003–04 Plymouth Arg 40 1
2004–05 Plymouth Arg 38 0 **78 1**

GUDJONSSON, Bjarni (M) 214 29
H: 5 7 W: 11 02 b.Reykjavik 26-2-79
Honours: Iceland Youth, Under-21, 15 full caps, 1 goal.
1995 IA Akranes 2 0
1996 IA Akranes 17 13
1997 IA Akranes 6 2 **25 15**
1997–98 Newcastle U 0 0
1998–99 Newcastle U 0 0
1999–2000 Genk 14 0 **14 0**
1999–2000 Stoke C 8 1
2000–01 Stoke C 42 6
2001–02 Stoke C 46 3
2002–03 Stoke C 36 1 **132 11**
2003–04 Coventry C 18 3
2004–05 Coventry C 10 0 **28 3**
2004–05 Plymouth Arg 15 0 **15 0**

HODGES, Lee (M) 339 49
H: 6 0 W: 12 01 b.Epping 4-9-73
Source: Trainee.
1991–92 Tottenham H 0 0
1992–93 Tottenham H 4 0
1992–93 *Plymouth Arg* 7 2
1993–94 Tottenham H 0 0 **4 0**
1993–94 *Wycombe W* 4 0 **4 0**
1994–95 Barnet 34 4
1995–96 Barnet 40 17
1996–97 Barnet 31 5 **105 26**
1997–98 Reading 24 6
1998–99 Reading 1 0
1999–2000 Reading 25 2
2000–01 Reading 29 2
2001–02 Reading 0 0 **79 10**
2001–02 Plymouth Arg 45 6
2002–03 Plymouth Arg 39 2

2003–04 Plymouth Arg 37 3
2004–05 Plymouth Arg 19 0 **147 13**

LARRIEU, Romain (G) 132 0
H: 6 2 W: 13 00 b.Mont-de-Marsan 31-8-76
Source: Montpellier, ASOA Valence.
2000–01 Plymouth Arg 15 0
2001–02 Plymouth Arg 45 0
2002–03 Plymouth Arg 43 0
2003–04 Plymouth Arg 6 0
2004–05 Plymouth Arg 23 0 **132 0**

LASLEY, Keith (M) 121 9
H: 5 8 W: 10 07 b.Glasgow 21-9-79
2000–01 Motherwell 12 1
2001–02 Motherwell 28 2
2002–03 Motherwell 24 3
2003–04 Motherwell 33 3 **97 9**
2004–05 Plymouth Arg 24 0 **24 0**

MAKEL, Lee (M) 244 17
H: 5 11 W: 11 07 b.Sunderland 11-1-73
Source: Trainee.
1990–91 Newcastle U 3 0
1991–92 Newcastle U 9 1 **12 1**
1992–93 Blackburn R 1 0
1993–94 Blackburn R 2 0
1994–95 Blackburn R 0 0
1995–96 Blackburn R 3 0 **6 0**
1995–96 Huddersfield T 33 2
1996–97 Huddersfield T 19 3
1997–98 Huddersfield T 13 0 **65 5**
1997–98 Hearts 5 0
1998–99 Hearts 14 1
1999–2000 Hearts 17 0
2000–01 Hearts 13 0 **49 1**
2001–02 Bradford C 13 0 **13 0**
2001–02 Livingston 13 0
2002–03 Livingston 31 2
2003–04 Livingston 36 8 **80 10**
2004–05 Plymouth Arg 19 0 **19 0**

MARTIN, Marcus (M) 0 0
b.Torquay 9-2-85
Source: Scholar.
2004–05 Plymouth Arg 0 0

McCORMICK, Luke (G) 69 0
H: 6 0 W: 13 12 b.Coventry 15-8-83
Source: Scholar.
2000–01 Plymouth Arg 1 0
2001–02 Plymouth Arg 0 0
2002–03 Plymouth Arg 3 0
2003–04 Plymouth Arg 40 0
2004–05 Plymouth Arg 23 0 **67 0**
2004–05 *Boston U* 2 0 **2 0**

MILNE, Steven (F) 100 23
H: 5 7 W: 10 00 b.Dundee 5-5-80
Source: Downfield J.
1997–98 Dundee 2 0
1998–99 Dundee 0 0
1999–2000 Dundee 0 0
2000–01 Dundee 21 4
2001–02 Dundee 20 5
2002–03 Dundee 25 6
2003–04 Dundee 20 8 **88 23**
2004–05 Plymouth Arg 12 0 **12 0**

NORRIS, David (M) 119 15
H: 5 7 W: 11 06 b.Peterborough 22-2-81
Source: Boston U.
1999–2000 Bolton W 0 0
2000–01 Bolton W 0 0
2001–02 Bolton W 0 0
2001–02 *Hull C* 6 1 **6 1**
2002–03 Bolton W 0 0
2002–03 Plymouth Arg 33 6
2003–04 Plymouth Arg 45 5
2004–05 Plymouth Arg 35 3 **113 14**

SAWYER, Gary (D) 0 0
b.Bideford 5-7-85
Source: Scholar.
2004–05 Plymouth Arg 0 0

SUMMERFIELD, Luke (M) 1 0
H: 6 0 W: 11 00 b.Ivybridge 6-12-87
Source: Scholar.
2004–05 Plymouth Arg 1 0 **1 0**

TAYLOR, Scott (F) 323 72
H: 5 10 W: 11 04 b.Chertsey 5-5-76
Source: Staines T.
1994–95 Millwall 6 0
1995–96 Millwall 22 0 **28 0**
1995–96 Bolton W 1 0
1996–97 Bolton W 11 1
1997–98 Bolton W 0 0
1997–98 *Rotherham U* 10 3 **10 3**
1997–98 *Blackpool* 5 1
1998–99 Bolton W 0 0 **12 1**
1998–99 Tranmere R 36 9
1999–2000 Tranmere R 35 3
2000–01 Tranmere R 37 5 **108 17**
2001–02 Stockport Co 28 4 **28 4**
2001–02 Blackpool 17 2
2002–03 Blackpool 44 13
2003–04 Blackpool 31 16
2004–05 Blackpool 24 12 **121 44**
2004–05 Plymouth Arg 16 3 **16 3**

VILLIS, Matt (D) 22 0
H: 6 3 W: 12 07 b.Bridgwater 13-4-84
2002–03 Plymouth Arg 0 0
2003–04 Plymouth Arg 0 0
2004–05 Plymouth Arg 0 0
2004–05 *Torquay U* 22 0 **22 0**

WORRELL, David (D) 164 0
H: 5 11 W: 11 08 b.Dublin 12-1-78
Source: Trainee. *Honours:* Eire Youth, Under-21.
1994–95 Blackburn R 0 0
1995–96 Blackburn R 0 0
1996–97 Blackburn R 0 0
1997–98 Blackburn R 0 0
1998–99 Blackburn R 0 0
1998–99 Dundee U 4 0
1999–2000 Dundee U 13 0 **17 0**
2000–01 Plymouth Arg 14 0
2001–02 Plymouth Arg 42 0
2002–03 Plymouth Arg 43 0
2003–04 Plymouth Arg 18 0
2004–05 Plymouth Arg 30 0 **147 0**

WOTTON, Paul (D) 319 41
H: 5 11 W: 11 01 b.Plymouth 17-8-77
Source: Trainee.
1994–95 Plymouth Arg 7 0
1995–96 Plymouth Arg 1 0
1996–97 Plymouth Arg 9 1
1997–98 Plymouth Arg 34 1
1998–99 Plymouth Arg 36 1
1999–2000 Plymouth Arg 23 0
2000–01 Plymouth Arg 42 4
2001–02 Plymouth Arg 46 5
2002–03 Plymouth Arg 43 8
2003–04 Plymouth Arg 38 9
2004–05 Plymouth Arg 40 12 **319 41**

YETTON, Stuart (F) 3 0
H: 5 8 W: 10 03 b.Plymouth 27-7-85
Source: Scholar.
2002–03 Plymouth Arg 1 0
2003–04 Plymouth Arg 1 0
2004–05 Plymouth Arg 1 0 **3 0**

PORT VALE (62)

ABBEY, George (D) 118 1
H: 5 9 W: 10 08 b.Port Harcourt 20-10-78
Source: Sharks. *Honours:* Nigeria 16 full caps.
1999–2000 Macclesfield T 18 0
2000–01 Macclesfield T 18 0
2001–02 Macclesfield T 17 0
2002–03 Macclesfield T 22 1
2003–04 Macclesfield T 25 0
2004–05 Macclesfield T 0 0 **100 1**
2004–05 Port Vale 18 0 **18 0**

ARMSTRONG, Ian (F) 89 14
H: 5 8 W: 10 09 b.Liverpool 16-11-81
Source: Trainee. *Honours:* England Schools, Youth.
1998–99 Liverpool 0 0
1999–2000 Liverpool 0 0
2000–01 Liverpool 0 0
2001–02 Port Vale 31 3
2002–03 Port Vale 29 7
2003–04 Port Vale 20 1
2004–05 Port Vale 9 3 **89 14**

BIRCHALL, Chris (M) 47 6
H: 5 9 W: 13 02 b.Stafford 5-5-84
Source: Scholar. *Honours:* Trinidad & Tobago 4 full caps.
2001–02 Port Vale 1 0
2002–03 Port Vale 2 0
2003–04 Port Vale 10 0
2004–05 Port Vale 34 6 **47 6**

BRAIN, Jonny (G) 59 0
H: 6 3 W: 13 05 b.Carlisle 11-2-83
Source: Newcastle U Trainee.
2003–04 Port Vale 32 0
2004–05 Port Vale 27 0 **59 0**

BROWN, Ryan (D) 38 0
H: 5 9 W: 11 06 b.Stoke 15-3-85
Source: Scholar.
2002–03 Port Vale 1 0
2003–04 Port Vale 17 0
2004–05 Port Vale 20 0 **38 0**

COLLINS, Sam (D) 239 12
H: 6 3 W: 13 11 b.Pontefract 5-6-77
Source: Trainee.
1994–95 Huddersfield T 0 0
1995–96 Huddersfield T 0 0
1996–97 Huddersfield T 4 0
1997–98 Huddersfield T 10 0
1998–99 Huddersfield T 23 0 **37 0**
1999–2000 Bury 19 0
2000–01 Bury 34 2
2001–02 Bury 29 0 **82 2**
2002–03 Port Vale 44 5
2003–04 Port Vale 43 4
2004–05 Port Vale 33 1 **120 10**

CUMMINS, Michael (M) 216 21
H: 5 11 W: 13 10 b.Dublin 1-6-78
Source: Trainee. *Honours:* Eire Youth, Under-21.
1995–96 Middlesbrough 0 0
1996–97 Middlesbrough 0 0
1997–98 Middlesbrough 0 0
1998–99 Middlesbrough 1 0
1999–2000 Middlesbrough 1 0 **2 0**
1999–2000 Port Vale 12 1
2000–01 Port Vale 45 2
2001–02 Port Vale 46 8
2002–03 Port Vale 30 4
2003–04 Port Vale 42 4
2004–05 Port Vale 39 2 **214 21**

ELDERSHAW, Simon (F) 15 1
H: 5 11 W: 11 04 b.Stoke 2-12-83
Source: Scholar.
2002–03 Port Vale 2 0
2003–04 Port Vale 0 0
2004–05 Port Vale 13 1 **15 1**

GOODLAD, Mark (G) 144 0
H: 6 2 W: 14 00 b.Barnsley 9-9-79
Source: Trainee.
1996–97 Nottingham F 0 0
1997–98 Nottingham F 0 0
1998–99 Nottingham F 0 0
1998–99 *Scarborough* 3 0 **3 0**
1999–2000 Nottingham F 0 0
1999–2000 Port Vale 1 0
2000–01 Port Vale 40 0
2001–02 Port Vale 43 0
2002–03 Port Vale 37 0
2003–04 Port Vale 0 0
2004–05 Port Vale 20 0 **141 0**

HANSON, Christian (D) 19 0
H: 6 1 W: 12 11 b.Middlesbrough 3-8-81
Source: Trainee. *Honours:* England Schools, Youth.
1998–99 Middlesbrough 0 0
1999–2000 Middlesbrough 0 0
2000–01 Middlesbrough 0 0
2000–01 *Cambridge U* 8 0 **8 0**
2001–02 Middlesbrough 0 0
2001–02 *Torquay U* 6 0 **6 0**
2002–03 Middlesbrough 0 0
2003–04 Middlesbrough 0 0
From Havant & W
2004–05 Port Vale 5 0 **5 0**

HIBBERT, David (M) **9 2**
H: 6 2 W: 12 06 b.Eccleshall 28-1-86
Source: Scholar.

2004–05	Port Vale	9	2	**9**	**2**

HULBERT, Robin (M) **99 0**
H: 5 10 W: 11 10 b.Plymouth 14-3-80
Source: From Trainee. *Honours:* England Youth.

1997–98	Swindon T	1	0		
1997–98	*Newcastle U*	0	0		
1998–99	Swindon T	16	0		
1999–2000	Swindon T	12	0	**29**	**0**
1999–2000	Bristol C	2	0		
2000–01	Bristol C	19	0		
2001–02	Bristol C	11	0		
2002–03	Bristol C	7	0		
2002–03	*Shrewsbury T*	7	0	**7**	**0**
2003–04	Bristol C	0	0	**39**	**0**
2004–05	Port Vale	24	0	**24**	**0**

INNES, Mark (M) **154 3**
H: 5 11 W: 12 01 b.Bellshill 27-9-78
Source: Trainee.

1995–96	Oldham Ath	0	0		
1996–97	Oldham Ath	0	0		
1997–98	Oldham Ath	4	0		
1998–99	Oldham Ath	13	1		
1999–2000	Oldham Ath	21	0		
2000–01	Oldham Ath	30	0		
2001–02	Oldham Ath	5	0	**73**	**1**
2001–02	Chesterfield	23	2		
2002–03	Chesterfield	10	0		
2003–04	Chesterfield	22	0		
2004–05	Chesterfield	21	0	**76**	**2**
2004–05	Port Vale	5	0	**5**	**0**

JAMES, Craig (D) **49 2**
H: 6 2 W: 13 03 b.Middlesbrough 15-11-82
Source: Scholar.

2000–01	Sunderland	0	0		
2001–02	Sunderland	0	0		
2002–03	Sunderland	0	0		
2003–04	Sunderland	1	0	**1**	**0**
2003–04	*Darlington*	10	1	**10**	**1**
2003–04	Port Vale	8	0		
2004–05	Port Vale	30	1	**38**	**1**

LIPA, Andreas (M) **32 2**
H: 6 2 W: 12 09 b.Vienna 26-4-71
Source: Xanthi. *Honours:* Austria 1 full cap.

2003–04	Port Vale	30	2		
2004–05	Port Vale	2	0	**32**	**2**

LOWNDES, Nathan (F) **159 28**
H: 5 10 W: 12 06 b.Salford 2-6-77
Source: Trainee.

1994–95	Leeds U	0	0		
1995–96	Leeds U	0	0		
1995–96	Watford	0	0		
1996–97	Watford	3	0		
1997–98	Watford	4	0	**7**	**0**
1998–99	St Johnstone	29	2		
1999–2000	St Johnstone	25	10		
2000–01	St Johnstone	10	2	**64**	**14**
2001–02	Livingston	21	3	**21**	**3**
2001–02	*Rotherham U*	2	0	**2**	**0**
2002–03	Plymouth Arg	16	2		
2003–04	Plymouth Arg	33	8		
2004–05	Plymouth Arg	4	0	**53**	**10**
2004–05	Port Vale	12	1	**12**	**1**

MATTHEWS, Lee (F) **106 21**
H: 6 2 W: 14 00 b.Middlesbrough 16-1-79
Source: Trainee. *Honours:* England Youth.

1995–96	Leeds U	0	0		
1996–97	Leeds U	0	0		
1997–98	Leeds U	3	0		
1998–99	Leeds U	0	0		
1998–99	*Notts Co*	5	0	**5**	**0**
1999–2000	Leeds U	0	0		
1999–2000	*Gillingham*	5	0	**5**	**0**
2000–01	Leeds U	0	0	**3**	**0**
2000–01	Bristol C	6	3		
2001–02	Bristol C	22	3		
2002–03	Bristol C	7	1		
2003–04	Bristol C	8	2	**43**	**9**
2003–04	*Darlington*	6	1	**6**	**1**
2003–04	*Bristol R*	9	0	**9**	**0**
2003–04	*Yeovil T*	4	0	**4**	**0**
2004–05	Port Vale	31	11	**31**	**11**

McPHEE, Stephen (F) **130 39**
H: 5 8 W: 12 02 b.Glasgow 5-6-81
Honours: Scotland Under-21.

1998–99	Coventry C	0	0		
1999–2000	Coventry C	0	0		
2000–01	Coventry C	0	0		
2001–02	Port Vale	44	11		
2002–03	Port Vale	40	3		
2003–04	Port Vale	46	25		
2004–05	Port Vale	0	0	**130**	**39**

PAYNTER, Billy (F) **128 28**
H: 6 0 W: 13 08 b.Liverpool 13-7-84
Source: Schoolboy.

2000–01	Port Vale	1	0		
2001–02	Port Vale	7	0		
2002–03	Port Vale	31	5		
2003–04	Port Vale	44	13		
2004–05	Port Vale	45	10	**128**	**28**

PILKINGTON, George (D) **94 1**
H: 5 11 W: 12 00 b.Rugeley 7-11-81
Source: Trainee. *Honours:* England Youth.

1998–99	Everton	0	0		
1999–2000	Everton	0	0		
2000–01	Everton	0	0		
2001–02	Everton	0	0		
2002–03	Everton	0	0		
2002–03	*Exeter C*	7	0	**7**	**0**
2003–04	Port Vale	44	1		
2004–05	Port Vale	43	0	**87**	**1**

PORTER, Andy (F) **401 23**
H: 5 9 W: 12 03 b.Holmes Chapel 17-9-68
Source: Trainee.

1986–87	Port Vale	1	0		
1987–88	Port Vale	6	0		
1988–89	Port Vale	14	1		
1989–90	Port Vale	36	1		
1990–91	Port Vale	40	0		
1991–92	Port Vale	32	1		
1992–93	Port Vale	17	1		
1993–94	Port Vale	37	0		
1994–95	Port Vale	44	3		
1995–96	Port Vale	45	10		
1996–97	Port Vale	44	4		
1997–98	Port Vale	41	1		
1998–99	Wigan Ath	16	1		
1999–2000	Wigan Ath	5	0	**21**	**1**
1999–2000	*Mansfield T*	5	0	**5**	**0**
1999–2000	*Chester C*	16	0	**16**	**0**
From Northwich Vic, Kidsgrove					
2004–05	Port Vale	2	0	**359**	**22**

REID, Levi (M) **42 0**
H: 5 7 W: 11 12 b.Stafford 19-12-83
Source: Scholar.

2002–03	Port Vale	1	0		
2003–04	Port Vale	11	0		
2004–05	Port Vale	30	0	**42**	**0**

ROBINSON, Simon (D) **0 0**
H: 5 10 W: 11 12 b.Crewe 24-9-84
Source: Scholar.

2004–05	Port Vale	0	0

ROWLAND, Stephen (D) **103 1**
H: 5 10 W: 11 12 b.Wrexham 2-11-81
Source: Scholar.

2001–02	Port Vale	25	1		
2002–03	Port Vale	25	0		
2003–04	Port Vale	29	0		
2004–05	Port Vale	24	0	**103**	**1**

SMITH, Jeff (M) **54 3**
H: 5 11 W: 11 05 b.Middlesbrough 28-6-80
Source: Trainee.

1998–99	Hartlepool U	3	0		
1999–2000	Hartlepool U	0	0	**3**	**0**
From Bishop Auckland					
2000–01	Bolton W	1	0		
2001–02	*Macclesfield T*	8	2	**8**	**2**
2001–02	Bolton W	1	0		
2002–03	Bolton W	0	0		
2003–04	Bolton W	0	0	**2**	**0**
2003–04	*Scunthorpe U*	1	0	**1**	**0**
2003–04	*Rochdale*	1	0	**1**	**0**
2003–04	Preston NE	5	0	**5**	**0**
2004–05	Port Vale	34	1	**34**	**1**

WALSH, Michael (D) **254 5**
H: 6 0 W: 13 10 b.Rotherham 5-8-77
Source: Trainee.

1994–95	Scunthorpe U	3	0		
1995–96	Scunthorpe U	25	0		
1996–97	Scunthorpe U	36	0		
1997–98	Scunthorpe U	39	1	**103**	**1**
1998–99	Port Vale	19	1		
1999–2000	Port Vale	12	1		
2000–01	Port Vale	39	1		
2001–02	Port Vale	28	0		
2002–03	Port Vale	17	1		
2003–04	Port Vale	13	0		
2004–05	Port Vale	23	0	**151**	**4**

WIDDRINGTON, Tommy (M) **372 24**
H: 5 10 W: 12 07 b.Newcastle 1-10-71
Source: Trainee.

1989–90	Southampton	0	0		
1990–91	Southampton	0	0		
1991–92	Southampton	3	0		
1991–92	*Wigan Ath*	6	0	**6**	**0**
1992–93	Southampton	12	0		
1993–94	Southampton	11	1		
1994–95	Southampton	28	0		
1995–96	Southampton	21	2	**75**	**3**
1996–97	Grimsby T	42	4		
1997–98	Grimsby T	21	3		
1998–99	Grimsby T	26	1	**89**	**8**
1998–99	*Port Vale*	9	1		
1999–2000	Port Vale	38	5		
2000–01	Port Vale	35	2		
2001–02	Hartlepool U	24	2		
2002–03	Hartlepool U	32	3	**56**	**5**
2003–04	Macclesfield T	35	0		
2004–05	Macclesfield T	23	0	**58**	**0**
2004–05	Port Vale	6	0	**88**	**8**

PORTSMOUTH (63)

ASHDOWN, Jamie (G) **50 0**
H: 6 1 W: 13 05 b.Reading 30-11-80

1999–2000	Reading	0	0		
2000–01	Reading	1	0		
2001–02	Reading	1	0		
2001–02	*Arsenal*	0	0		
2002–03	Reading	1	0		
2002–03	*Bournemouth*	2	0	**2**	**0**
2003–04	Reading	10	0	**13**	**0**
2003–04	*Rushden & D*	19	0	**19**	**0**
2004–05	Portsmouth	16	0	**16**	**0**

BERGER, Patrik (M) **314 64**
H: 6 1 W: 13 00 b.Prague 10-11-73
Honours: Czechoslovakia 2 full caps.Czech Republic 44 full caps, 18 goals.

1991–92	Slavia Prague	20	3		
1992–93	Slavia Prague	29	10		
1993–94	Slavia Prague	12	4		
1994–95	Slavia Prague	28	7	**89**	**24**
1995–96	Borussia Dortmund	25	4	**25**	**4**
1996–97	Liverpool	23	6		
1997–98	Liverpool	22	3		
1998–99	Liverpool	32	7		
1999–2000	Liverpool	34	9		
2000–01	Liverpool	14	2		
2001–02	Liverpool	21	1		
2002–03	Liverpool	2	0	**148**	**28**
2003–04	Portsmouth	20	5		
2004–05	Portsmouth	32	3	**52**	**8**

BERKOVIC, Eyal (M) **342 60**
H: 5 9 W: 10 13 b.Haifa 2-4-72
Honours: Israel Under-21, 78 full caps, 9 goals.

1992–93	Maccabi Haifa	32	7		
1993–94	Maccabi Haifa	38	10		
1994–95	Maccabi Haifa	29	5		
1995–96	Maccabi Haifa	29	3	**128**	**25**
1996–97	Southampton	28	4	**28**	**4**
1997–98	West Ham U	35	7		
1998–99	West Ham U	30	3	**65**	**10**
1999–2000	Celtic	28	9		
2000–01	Celtic	4	1	**32**	**10**
2000–01	Blackburn R	11	2	**11**	**2**
2001–02	Manchester C	25	6		
2002–03	Manchester C	27	1		
2003–04	Manchester C	4	0	**56**	**7**

2003–04 Portsmouth 11 1
2004–05 Portsmouth 11 1 **22 2**

BURCHILL, Mark (F) 79 24
H: 5 8 W: 11 09 b.Broxburn 18-8-80
Source: Celtic BC. *Honours:* Scotland Schools, Under-21, 6 full caps.
1997–98 Celtic 0 0
1998–99 Celtic 21 9
1999–2000 Celtic 0 0
2000–01 Celtic 2 1 **23 10**
2000–01 *Birmingham C* 13 4 **13 4**
2000–01 *Ipswich T* 7 1
2001–02 Ipswich T 0 0 **7 1**
2001–02 Portsmouth 6 4
2002–03 Portsmouth 18 4
2003–04 Portsmouth 0 0
2003–04 *Wigan Ath* 4 0 **4 0**
2003–04 *Sheffield W* 5 0 **5 0**
2004–05 Portsmouth 0 0 **24 8**
2004–05 *Rotherham U* 3 1 **3 1**

CHALKIAS, Kostas (G) 161 0
H: 6 6 W: 15 03 b.Larisa 30-5-74
Honours: Greece 5 full caps.
1995–96 Panathinaikos 0 0
1996–97 Apollon 29 0
1997–98 Apollon 30 0
1998–99 Panathinaikos 0 0
1998–99 Apollon 16 0 **75 0**
1999–2000 Panathinaikos 6 0
2000–01 Panathinaikos 4 0
2001–02 Iraklis 25 0
2002–03 Iraklis 25 0 **50 0**
2003–04 Panathinaikos 11 0
2004–05 Panathinaikos 10 0 **31 0**
2004–05 Portsmouth 5 0 **5 0**

CISSE, Aliou (M) 122 2
H: 5 9 W: 12 02 b.Zinguichor 24-3-76
Honours: Senegal 23 full caps, 1 goal.
1994–95 Lille 6 0
1995–96 Lille 0 0
1996–97 Lille 0 0 **6 0**
From Sedan
1998–99 Paris St Germain 8 0
1999–2000 Paris St Germain 25 1
2000–01 Paris St Germain 10 0 **43 1**
2001–02 Montpellier 17 1 **17 1**
2002–03 Birmingham C 21 0
2003–04 Birmingham C 15 0 **36 0**
2004–05 Portsmouth 20 0 **20 0**

CLARK, Chris (M) 2 0
H: 6 0 W: 10 12 b.Shoreham 9-6-84
Source: Scholar.
2002–03 Portsmouth 0 0
2003–04 Portsmouth 0 0
2004–05 Portsmouth 0 0
2004–05 *Stoke C* 2 0 **2 0**

COOPER, Shaun (D) 26 0
H: 5 10 W: 10 07 b.Isle of Wight 5-10-83
Source: School.
2000–01 Portsmouth 0 0
2001–02 Portsmouth 7 0
2002–03 Portsmouth 0 0
2003–04 Portsmouth 0 0
2003–04 *Leyton Orient* 9 0 **9 0**
2004–05 Portsmouth 0 0 **7 0**
2004–05 *Kidderminster H* 10 0 **10 0**

DE ZEEUW, Arjan (D) 472 23
H: 6 0 W: 13 06 b.Castricum 16-4-70
Source: Vitesse 22.
1992–93 Telstar 30 1
1993–94 Telstar 31 2
1994–95 Telstar 29 1
1995–96 Telstar 12 1 **102 5**
1995–96 Barnsley 31 1
1996–97 Barnsley 43 2
1997–98 Barnsley 26 0
1998–99 Barnsley 38 4 **138 7**
1999–2000 Wigan Ath 39 3
2000–01 Wigan Ath 45 1
2001–02 Wigan Ath 42 2 **126 6**
2002–03 Portsmouth 38 1
2003–04 Portsmouth 36 1
2004–05 Portsmouth 32 3 **106 5**

DUFFY, Richard (D) 40 2
H: 5 10 W: 9 05 b.Swansea 30-8-85
Source: Scholar. *Honours:* Wales Youth, Under-21.
2002–03 Swansea C 0 0
2003–04 Swansea C 18 1 **18 1**
2003–04 Portsmouth 1 0
2004–05 Portsmouth 0 0 **1 0**
2004–05 *Burnley* 7 1 **7 1**
2004–05 *Coventry C* 14 0 **14 0**

FOXE, Hayden (D) 95 7
H: 6 3 W: 13 05 b.Sydney 23-6-77
Honours: Australia Youth, Under-20, Under-23, 11 full caps, 2 goals.
1997–98 Arminia Bielefeld 1 0 **1 0**
1998 Sanfrecce 15 3
1999 Sanfrecce 22 2 **37 5**
2000–01 Mechelen 4 0 **4 0**
2000–01 West Ham U 5 0
2001–02 West Ham U 6 0 **11 0**
2002–03 Portsmouth 32 1
2003–04 Portsmouth 10 1
2004–05 Portsmouth 0 0 **42 2**

FULLER, Ricardo (F) 124 36
H: 6 3 W: 13 13 b.Kingston, Jamaica 31-10-79
Source: Tivoli Gardens. *Honours:* Jamaica full caps.
2000–01 Crystal Palace 8 0 **8 0**
2001–02 Hearts 27 8 **27 8**
From Tivoli Gardens.
2002–03 Preston NE 18 9
2003–04 Preston NE 38 17
2004–05 Preston NE 2 1 **58 27**
2004–05 Portsmouth 31 1 **31 1**

GRIFFIN, Andy (D) 155 4
H: 5 9 W: 10 10 b.Billinge 7-3-79
Source: Trainee. *Honours:* England Youth, Under-21.
1996–97 Stoke C 34 1
1997–98 Stoke C 23 1 **57 2**
1997–98 Newcastle U 4 0
1998–99 Newcastle U 14 0
1999–2000 Newcastle U 3 1
2000–01 Newcastle U 19 0
2001–02 Newcastle U 4 0
2002–03 Newcastle U 27 1
2003–04 Newcastle U 5 0 **76 2**
2004–05 Portsmouth 22 0 **22 0**

GUATELLI, Andrea (G) 0 0
H: 6 0 W: 12 00 b.Parma 5-5-84
2004–05 Portsmouth 0 0

HARRIS, Scott (M) 0 0
b.Worthing 24-7-85
Source: Scholar.
2004–05 Portsmouth 0 0

HISLOP, Shaka (G) 355 0
H: 6 4 W: 14 04 b.Hackney 22-2-69
Source: From Howard Univ, USA. *Honours:* England Under-21. Trinidad & Tobago 21 full caps.
1992–93 Reading 12 0
1993–94 Reading 46 0
1994–95 Reading 46 0 **104 0**
1995–96 Newcastle U 24 0
1996–97 Newcastle U 16 0
1997–98 Newcastle U 13 0 **53 0**
1998–99 West Ham U 37 0
1999–2000 West Ham U 22 0
2000–01 West Ham U 34 0
2001–02 West Ham U 12 0 **105 0**
2002–03 Portsmouth 46 0
2003–04 Portsmouth 30 0
2004–05 Portsmouth 17 0 **93 0**

HORSTED, Liam (F) 0 0
b.Portsmouth 28-10-85
Source: Scholar.
2004–05 Portsmouth 0 0

HUGHES, Richard (M) 176 15
H: 6 0 W: 13 03 b.Glasgow 25-6-79
Source: From Atalanta. *Honours:* Scotland Youth, Under-21, 4 full caps.
1997–98 Arsenal 0 0
1998–99 Bournemouth 44 2
1999–2000 Bournemouth 21 2
2000–01 Bournemouth 44 8
2001–02 Bournemouth 22 2 **131 14**
2002–03 Portsmouth 6 0
2002–03 *Grimsby T* 12 1 **12 1**
2003–04 Portsmouth 11 0
2004–05 Portsmouth 16 0 **33 0**

KAMARA, Diomansy (F) 112 22
H: 6 0 W: 11 05 b.Paris 8-11-80
Honours: Senegal full caps.
1999–2000 Catanzaro 11 4
2000–01 Catanzaro 23 5 **34 9**
2001–02 Chievo 0 0
2001–02 Modena 24 4
2002–03 Modena 29 5 **53 9**
2004–05 Portsmouth 25 4 **25 4**

KEENE, James (M) 7 0
H: 5 11 W: 11 08 b.Wells 26-12-85
Source: Portsmouth Scholar.
2004–05 *Kidderminster H* 5 0 **5 0**
2004–05 Portsmouth 2 0 **2 0**

LUA-LUA, Lomano (F) 160 30
H: 5 8 W: 12 00 b.Kinshasa 28-12-80
Honours: DR Congo 4 full caps.
1998–99 Colchester U 13 1
1999–2000 Colchester U 41 12
2000–01 Colchester U 7 2 **61 15**
2000–01 Newcastle U 21 0
2001–02 Newcastle U 20 3
2002–03 Newcastle U 11 2
2003–04 Newcastle U 7 0 **59 5**
2003–04 *Portsmouth* 15 4
2004–05 Portsmouth 25 6 **40 10**

MEZAGUE, Valery (M) 55 7
H: 6 1 W: 13 00 b.Marseille 8-12-83
2001–02 Montpellier 5 0
2002–03 Montpellier 27 6
2003–04 Montpellier 12 1 **44 7**
2004–05 Portsmouth 11 0 **11 0**

MORNAR, Ivica (F) 251 67
H: 6 2 W: 13 01 b.Split 12-1-74
Honours: Croatia 20 full caps, 1 goal.
1992–93 Hajduk Split 21 7
1993–94 Hajduk Split 27 8
1994–95 Hajduk Split 9 3
1995–96 Hajduk Split 1 0 **58 18**
1995–96 Eintracht Frankfurt 19 1 **19 1**
1996–97 Sevilla 11 2 **11 2**
1997–98 Ourense 28 8 **28 8**
1998–99 Standard Liege 15 3
1999–2000 Standard Liege 24 8
2000–01 Standard Liege 30 12 **69 23**
2001–02 Anderlecht 23 8
2002–03 Anderlecht 20 6 **43 14**
2003–04 Portsmouth 8 1 **8 1**
2004–05 *Rennes* 15 0 **15 0**

O'NEIL, Gary (M) 118 10
H: 5 10 W: 11 00 b.Beckenham 18-5-83
Source: Scholar. *Honours:* England Youth, Under-20, Under-21.
1999–2000 Portsmouth 1 0
2000–01 Portsmouth 10 1
2001–02 Portsmouth 33 1
2002–03 Portsmouth 31 3
2003–04 Portsmouth 3 2
2003–04 *Walsall* 7 0 **7 0**
2004–05 Portsmouth 24 2 **102 9**
2004–05 *Cardiff C* 9 1 **9 1**

PERICARD, Vincent de Paul (F) 38 9
H: 6 1 W: 13 08 b.Efko 3-10-82
Source: Juventus.
2002–03 Portsmouth 32 9
2003–04 Portsmouth 6 0
2004–05 Portsmouth 0 0 **38 9**

PRIMUS, Linvoy (D) 367 11
H: 5 10 W: 12 04 b.Forest Gate 14-9-73
Source: Trainee.
1992–93 Charlton Ath 4 0
1993–94 Charlton Ath 0 0 **4 0**
1994–95 Barnet 39 0
1995–96 Barnet 42 4
1996–97 Barnet 46 3 **127 7**
1997–98 Reading 36 1
1998–99 Reading 31 0
1999–2000 Reading 28 0 **95 1**
2000–01 Portsmouth 23 0

2001–02 Portsmouth 22 2
2002–03 Portsmouth 40 0
2003–04 Portsmouth 21 0
2004–05 Portsmouth 35 1 **141 3**

RODIC, Alexsander (F) 63 17
H: 6 2 W: 12 11 b.Serbia 26-12-79
Honours: Slovenia 4 full caps, 1 goal.
2002–03 Gorica 16 1
2003–04 Gorica 29 8
2004–05 Gorica 14 8 **59 17**
2004–05 Portsmouth 4 0 **4 0**

SCHEMMEL, Sebastian (D) 283 4
H: 5 8 W: 11 13 b.Nancy 2-6-75
1993–94 Nancy 6 0
1994–95 Nancy 35 0
1995–96 Nancy 33 0
1996–97 Nancy 32 0
1997–98 Nancy 40 1 **146 1**
1998–99 Metz 20 1
1999–2000 Metz 21 1
2000–01 Metz 19 0 **60 2**
2000–01 West Ham U 12 0
2001–02 West Ham U 35 1
2002–03 West Ham U 16 0 **63 1**
2003–04 Portsmouth 14 0
2004–05 Portsmouth 0 0 **14 0**

SILK, Gary (M) 22 0
H: 5 9 W: 13 07 b.Newport (IW) 13-9-84
Source: Scholar.
2003–04 Portsmouth 0 0
2004–05 Portsmouth 0 0
2004–05 *Wycombe W* 22 0 **22 0**

SKOPELITIS, Giannis (M) 192 6
H: 5 11 W: 11 12 b.Greece 2-3-78
1996–97 Apollon 0 0
1996–97 Aigaleo 11 1
1997–98 Aigaleo 8 1
1998–99 Aigaleo 21 0
1999–2000 Aigaleo 23 2
2000–01 Aigaleo 28 0
2001–02 Aigaleo 23 0
2002–03 Aigaleo 25 0
2003–04 Aigaleo 25 2
2004–05 Aigaleo 15 0 **179 6**
2004–05 Portsmouth 13 0 **13 0**

STEFANOVIC, Dejan (D) 270 20
H: 6 2 W: 13 01 b.Belgrade 28-10-74
Honours: Serbia-Montenegro 23 full caps.
1992–93 Red Star Belgrade 14 0
1993–94 Red Star Belgrade 2 0
1994–95 Red Star Belgrade 30 9 **46 9**
1995–96 Sheffield W 6 0
1996–97 Sheffield W 29 2
1997–98 Sheffield W 20 2
1998–99 Sheffield W 11 0 **66 4**
1999–2000 Perugia 0 0
1999–2000 OFK Belgrade 0 0
1999–2000 Vitesse 14 0
2000–01 Vitesse 27 1
2001–02 Vitesse 25 3
2002–03 Vitesse 28 0 **94 4**
2003–04 Portsmouth 32 3
2004–05 Portsmouth 32 0 **64 3**

STONE, Steve (F) 356 36
H: 5 8 W: 12 07 b.Gateshead 20-8-71
Source: Trainee. *Honours:* England 9 full caps, 2 goals.
1989–90 Nottingham F 0 0
1990–91 Nottingham F 0 0
1991–92 Nottingham F 1 0
1992–93 Nottingham F 12 1
1993–94 Nottingham F 45 5
1994–95 Nottingham F 41 5
1995–96 Nottingham F 34 7
1996–97 Nottingham F 5 0
1997–98 Nottingham F 29 2
1998–99 Nottingham F 26 3 **193 23**
1998–99 Aston Villa 10 0
1999–2000 Aston Villa 24 1
2000–01 Aston Villa 34 2
2001–02 Aston Villa 22 1
2002–03 Aston Villa 0 0 **90 4**
2002–03 Portsmouth 18 4
2003–04 Portsmouth 32 2
2004–05 Portsmouth 23 3 **73 9**

TAYLOR, Matthew (D) 226 24
H: 5 11 W: 12 03 b.Oxford 27-11-81
Source: Trainee. *Honours:* England Under-21.
1998–99 Luton T 0 0
1999–2000 Luton T 41 4
2000–01 Luton T 45 1
2001–02 Luton T 43 11 **129 16**
2002–03 Portsmouth 35 7
2003–04 Portsmouth 30 0
2004–05 Portsmouth 32 1 **97 8**

TODOROV, Svetoslav (F) 146 67
H: 6 0 W: 12 02 b.Dobrich 30-8-78
Honours: Bulgaria 31 full caps, 4 goals.
1996–97 Dobrudzha 12 2 **12 2**
1997–98 Litets Lovech 19 9
1998–99 Litets Lovech 11 2
1999–2000 Litets Lovech 26 19
2000–01 Litets Lovech 15 7 **71 37**
2000–01 West Ham U 8 1
2001–02 West Ham U 6 0 **14 1**
2001–02 Portsmouth 3 1
2002–03 Portsmouth 45 26
2003–04 Portsmouth 1 0
2004–05 Portsmouth 0 0 **49 27**

UNSWORTH, Dave (D) 367 39
H: 6 1 W: 15 02 b.Chorley 16-10-73
Source: Trainee. *Honours:* England Youth, Under-21, 1 full cap.
1991–92 Everton 2 1
1992–93 Everton 3 0
1993–94 Everton 8 0
1994–95 Everton 38 3
1995–96 Everton 31 2
1996–97 Everton 34 5
1997–98 West Ham U 32 2 **32 2**
1998–99 Aston Villa 0 0
1998–99 Everton 34 1
1999–2000 Everton 33 6
2000–01 Everton 29 5
2001–02 Everton 33 3
2002–03 Everton 33 5
2003–04 Everton 26 3 **304 34**
2004–05 Portsmouth 15 2 **15 2**
2004–05 *Ipswich T* 16 1 **16 1**

VINE, Rowan (F) 135 25
H: 6 1 W: 11 12 b.Basingstoke 21-9-82
Source: Scholar.
2000–01 Portsmouth 2 0
2001–02 Portsmouth 11 0
2002–03 Portsmouth 0 0
2002–03 *Brentford* 42 10 **42 10**
2003–04 Portsmouth 0 0
2003–04 *Colchester U* 35 6 **35 6**
2004–05 Portsmouth 0 0 **13 0**
2004–05 *Luton T* 45 9 **45 9**

WAPENAAR, Harald (G) 243 0
H: 6 1 W: 13 07 b.Vlaardingen 10-4-70
1992–93 Feyenoord 0 0
1993–94 RBC 4 0 **4 0**
1994–95 Helmond Sp 20 0
1995–96 Helmond Sp 33 0
1996–97 Helmond Sp 28 0
1997–98 Helmond Sp 0 0 **81 0**
1997–98 Utrecht 21 0
1998–99 Udinese 2 0 **2 0**
1999–2000 Utrecht 33 0
2000–01 Utrecht 34 0
2001–02 Utrecht 33 0
2002–03 Utrecht 30 0 **151 0**
2003–04 Portsmouth 5 0
2004–05 Portsmouth 0 0 **5 0**

YAKUBU, Ayegbeni (F) 140 57
H: 6 0 W: 13 01 b.Nigeria 22-11-82
Source: Julius Berger. *Honours:* Nigeria full caps.
1999–2000 Gil Vicente 0 0
1999–2000 Hapoel Kfar-Sava 23 6 **23 6**
2000–01 Maccabi Haifa 14 3
2001–02 Maccabi Haifa 22 13 **36 16**
2002–03 Portsmouth 14 7
2003–04 Portsmouth 37 16
2004–05 Portsmouth 30 12 **81 35**

Scholars
Bye, Joseph; Carter-Harris, Joe; Cousins, Phillip; Day, Matthew James; Donaghey, Harry; Eyles, James Alexander; Fordyce, Daryl Thomas; Harris, Dean Gary; Pearce, Jason Daniel; Settle, Thomas David; Swayne, Kyle; Wilson, Marc David

PRESTON NE (64)

AGYEMANG, Patrick (F) 193 32
H: 6 1 W: 13 10 b.Walthamstow 29-9-80
Source: Trainee. *Honours:* Ghana 1 full cap.
1998–99 Wimbledon 0 0
1999–2000 Wimbledon 0 0
1999–2000 *Brentford* 12 0 **12 0**
2000–01 Wimbledon 29 4
2001–02 Wimbledon 33 4
2002–03 Wimbledon 33 5
2003–04 Wimbledon 26 7 **121 20**
2003–04 Gillingham 20 6
2004–05 Gillingham 13 2 **33 8**
2004–05 Preston NE 27 4 **27 4**

ALEXANDER, Graham (D) 576 76
H: 5 10 W: 12 02 b.Coventry 10-10-71
Source: Trainee. *Honours:* Scotland B, 16 full caps.
1989–90 Scunthorpe U 0 0
1990–91 Scunthorpe U 1 0
1991–92 Scunthorpe U 36 5
1992–93 Scunthorpe U 41 5
1993–94 Scunthorpe U 41 4
1994–95 Scunthorpe U 40 4 **159 18**
1995–96 Luton T 37 1
1996–97 Luton T 45 2
1997–98 Luton T 39 8
1998–99 Luton T 29 4 **150 15**
1998–99 Preston NE 10 0
1999–2000 Preston NE 46 6
2000–01 Preston NE 34 5
2001–02 Preston NE 45 6
2002–03 Preston NE 45 10
2003–04 Preston NE 45 9
2004–05 Preston NE 42 7 **267 43**

BROOMES, Marlon (D) 151 2
H: 6 1 W: 12 12 b.Meriden 28-11-77
Source: Trainee. *Honours:* England Schools, Youth, Under-21.
1994–95 Blackburn R 0 0
1995–96 Blackburn R 0 0
1996–97 Blackburn R 0 0
1996–97 *Swindon T* 12 1 **12 1**
1997–98 Blackburn R 4 0
1998–99 Blackburn R 13 0
1999–2000 Blackburn R 13 1
2000–01 Blackburn R 1 0
2000–01 *QPR* 5 0 **5 0**
2001–02 Blackburn R 0 0 **31 1**
2001–02 *Grimsby T* 15 0 **15 0**
2001–02 Sheffield W 19 0 **19 0**
2002–03 Preston NE 28 0
2003–04 Preston NE 30 0
2004–05 Preston NE 11 0 **69 0**

BROWN, Michael (M) 18 0
H: 5 11 W: 11 07 b.Preston 27-2-85
Source: Scholar.
2004–05 Preston NE 0 0
2004–05 *Chester C* 18 0 **18 0**

CRESSWELL, Richard (F) 323 73
H: 6 0 W: 11 05 b.Bridlington 20-9-77
Source: Trainee. *Honours:* England Under-21.
1995–96 York C 16 1
1996–97 York C 17 0
1996–97 *Mansfield T* 5 1 **5 1**
1997–98 York C 26 4
1998–99 York C 36 16 **95 21**
1998–99 Sheffield W 7 1
1999–2000 Sheffield W 20 1
2000–01 Sheffield W 4 0 **31 2**
2000–01 Leicester C 8 0 **8 0**
2000–01 *Preston NE* 11 2
2001–02 Preston NE 40 13
2002–03 Preston NE 42 16
2003–04 Preston NE 45 2
2004–05 Preston NE 46 16 **184 49**

DALEY, Omar (M)				**20**	**0**

H: 5 10 W: 11 03 b.Kingston, Jamaica 25-4-81
Source: Portmore U. *Honours:* Jamaica full caps.

2003–04	Reading	6	0	**6**	**0**
2004–05	Preston NE	14	0	**14**	**0**

DAVIDSON, Callum (D)				**229**	**8**

H: 5 10 W: 11 00 b.Stirling 25-6-76
Source: 'S' Form. *Honours:* Scotland Under-21, 17 full caps.

1994–95	St Johnstone	7	1		
1995–96	St Johnstone	2	0		
1996–97	St Johnstone	20	2		
1997–98	St Johnstone	15	1	**44**	**4**
1997–98	Blackburn R	1	0		
1998–99	Blackburn R	34	1		
1999–2000	Blackburn R	30	0	**65**	**1**
2000–01	Leicester C	28	1		
2001–02	Leicester C	30	0		
2002–03	Leicester C	30	1		
2003–04	Leicester C	13	0	**101**	**2**
2004–05	Preston NE	19	1	**19**	**1**

DAVIS, Claude (D)				**54**	**1**

H: 6 2 W: 13 09 b.Jamaica 6-3-79
Source: Portmore U. *Honours:* Jamaica full caps.

2003–04	Preston NE	22	1		
2004–05	Preston NE	32	0	**54**	**1**

ELEBERT, David (D)				**0**	**0**

b.Dublin 21-3-86
Source: Scholar.

2002–03	Preston NE	0	0		
2003–04	Preston NE	0	0		
2004–05	Preston NE	0	0		

ETUHU, Dixon (M)				**133**	**15**

H: 6 2 W: 13 00 b.Kano 8-6-82
Source: Scholarship.

1999–2000	Manchester C	0	0		
2000–01	Manchester C	0	0		
2001–02	Manchester C	12	0	**12**	**0**
2001–02	Preston NE	16	3		
2002–03	Preston NE	39	6		
2003–04	Preston NE	31	3		
2004–05	Preston NE	35	3	**121**	**15**

HILL, Matt (D)				**212**	**6**

H: 5 8 W: 11 13 b.Bristol 26-3-81
Source: Trainee.

1998–99	Bristol C	3	0		
1999–2000	Bristol C	14	0		
2000–01	Bristol C	34	0		
2001–02	Bristol C	40	1		
2002–03	Bristol C	42	3		
2003–04	Bristol C	42	2		
2004–05	Bristol C	23	0	**198**	**6**
2004–05	Preston NE	14	0	**14**	**0**

JACKSON, Mark (F)				**3**	**0**

H: 5 11 W: 10 09 b.Preston 3-2-86
Source: Scholar.

2003–04	Preston NE	1	0		
2004–05	Preston NE	2	0	**3**	**0**

KEMPSON, Darran (D)				**0**	**0**

H: 6 2 W: 13 00 b.Blackpool 6-12-84
Source: Scholar.

2004–05	Preston NE	0	0		

LEWIS, Eddie (M)				**242**	**24**

H: 5 10 W: 11 05 b.Cerritos 17-5-74
Honours: USA 64 full caps, 8 goals.

1996	San Jose Clash	25	0		
1997	San Jose Clash	29	2		
1998	San Jose Clash	32	3		
1999	San Jose Clash	29	4	**115**	**9**
1999–2000	Fulham	8	0		
2000–01	Fulham	7	0		
2001–02	Fulham	1	0	**16**	**0**
2002–03	Preston NE	38	5		
2003–04	Preston NE	33	6		
2004–05	Preston NE	40	4	**111**	**15**

LONERGAN, Andrew (G)				**34**	**1**

H: 6 2 W: 13 00 b.Preston 19-10-83
Source: Scholar. *Honours:* England Youth, Under-20.

2000–01	Preston NE	1	0		
2001–02	Preston NE	0	0		
2002–03	Preston NE	0	0		
2002–03	*Darlington*	2	0	**2**	**0**
2003–04	Preston NE	8	0		
2004–05	Preston NE	23	1	**32**	**1**

LUCKETTI, Chris (D)				**543**	**20**

H: 6 1 W: 13 00 b.Littleborough 28-9-71
Source: Trainee.

1988–89	Rochdale	1	0		
1989–90	Rochdale	0	0	**1**	**0**
1990–91	Stockport Co	0	0		
1991–92	Halifax T	36	0		
1992–93	Halifax T	42	2	**78**	**2**
1993–94	Bury	27	1		
1994–95	Bury	39	3		
1995–96	Bury	42	1		
1996–97	Bury	38	0		
1997–98	Bury	46	2		
1998–99	Bury	43	1	**235**	**8**
1999–2000	Huddersfield T	26	0		
2000–01	Huddersfield T	40	1		
2001–02	Huddersfield T	2	0	**68**	**1**
2001–02	Preston NE	40	2		
2002–03	Preston NE	43	2		
2003–04	Preston NE	37	1		
2004–05	Preston NE	41	4	**161**	**9**

LYNCH, Simon (F)				**65**	**8**

H: 5 10 W: 10 07 b.Montreal 19-5-82
Honours: Scotland Under-21, B.

1999–2000	Celtic	2	1		
2000–01	Celtic	0	0		
2001–02	Celtic	1	2		
2002–03	Celtic	1	0	**4**	**3**
2002–03	Preston NE	17	1		
2003–04	Preston NE	19	1		
2003–04	*Stockport Co*	9	3	**9**	**3**
2004–05	Preston NE	9	0	**45**	**2**
2004–05	*Blackpool*	7	0	**7**	**0**

MAWENE, Youl (D)				**107**	**3**

H: 6 1 W: 13 00 b.Caen 16-7-79

1999–2000	Lens	6	0	**6**	**0**
2000–01	Derby Co	8	0		
2001–02	Derby Co	17	1		
2002–03	Derby Co	0	0		
2003–04	Derby Co	30	0	**55**	**1**
2004–05	Preston NE	46	2	**46**	**2**

McKENNA, Paul (M)				**271**	**24**

H: 5 8 W: 11 00 b.Eccleston 20-10-77
Source: Trainee.

1995–96	Preston NE	0	0		
1996–97	Preston NE	5	1		
1997–98	Preston NE	5	0		
1998–99	Preston NE	36	0		
1999–2000	Preston NE	24	2		
2000–01	Preston NE	44	5		
2001–02	Preston NE	38	4		
2002–03	Preston NE	41	3		
2003–04	Preston NE	39	6		
2004–05	Preston NE	39	3	**271**	**24**

MEARS, Tyrone (D)				**39**	**2**

H: 6 1 W: 11 10 b.Stockport 18-2-83

2000–01	Manchester C	0	0		
2001–02	Manchester C	1	0	**1**	**0**
2002–03	Preston NE	22	1		
2003–04	Preston NE	12	1		
2004–05	Preston NE	4	0	**38**	**2**

NASH, Carlo (G)				**158**	**0**

H: 6 3 W: 15 03 b.Bolton 13-9-73
Source: Clitheroe.

1996–97	Crystal Palace	21	0		
1997–98	Crystal Palace	0	0	**21**	**0**
1998–99	Stockport Co	43	0		
1999–2000	Stockport Co	38	0		
2000–01	Stockport Co	8	0	**89**	**0**
2000–01	Manchester C	6	0		
2001–02	Manchester C	23	0		
2002–03	Manchester C	9	0	**38**	**0**
2003–04	Middlesbrough	1	0		
2004–05	Middlesbrough	2	0	**3**	**0**
2004–05	Preston NE	7	0	**7**	**0**

NEAL, Chris (G)				**1**	**0**

H: 6 2 W: 12 04 b.St Albans 23-10-85
Source: Scholar.

2004–05	Preston NE	1	0	**1**	**0**

NUGENT, Dave (F)				**106**	**26**

H: 5 11 W: 12 00 b.Liverpool 2-5-85
Source: From Scholar. *Honours:* England Youth, Under-20.

2001–02	Bury	5	0		
2002–03	Bury	31	4		
2003–04	Bury	26	3		
2004–05	Bury	26	11	**88**	**18**
2004–05	Preston NE	18	8	**18**	**8**

O'NEIL, Brian (M)				**308**	**16**

H: 6 1 W: 12 04 b.Paisley 6-9-72
Source: X Form. *Honours:* Scotland Schools, Youth, Under-21, 6 full caps.

1991–92	Celtic	28	1		
1992–93	Celtic	17	3		
1993–94	Celtic	28	2		
1994–95	Celtic	26	0		
1995–96	Celtic	5	0		
1996–97	Celtic	16	2	**120**	**8**
1996–97	*Nottingham F*	5	0	**5**	**0**
1997–98	Aberdeen	29	1	**29**	**1**
1998–99	Wolfsburg	26	2		
1999–2000	Wolfsburg	16	1		
2000–01	Wolfsburg	8	0	**50**	**3**
2000–01	Derby Co	4	0		
2001–02	Derby Co	10	0		
2002–03	Derby Co	3	0	**17**	**0**
2002–03	Preston NE	15	0		
2003–04	Preston NE	29	1		
2004–05	Preston NE	43	3	**87**	**4**

O'NEILL, Joe (F)				**53**	**4**

H: 6 0 W: 10 05 b.Blackburn 28-10-82
Source: Scholar.

2001–02	Preston NE	0	0		
2002–03	Preston NE	0	0		
2003–04	Preston NE	2	0		
2003–04	*Bury*	23	3	**23**	**3**
2004–05	Preston NE	2	0	**4**	**0**
2004–05	*Mansfield T*	15	0	**15**	**0**
2004–05	*Chester C*	11	1	**11**	**1**

SEDGWICK, Chris (M)				**267**	**20**

H: 6 0 W: 12 01 b.Sheffield 28-4-80
Source: Trainee.

1997–98	Rotherham U	4	0		
1998–99	Rotherham U	33	4		
1999–2000	Rotherham U	38	5		
2000–01	Rotherham U	21	2		
2001–02	Rotherham U	44	1		
2002–03	Rotherham U	43	1		
2003–04	Rotherham U	40	2		
2004–05	Rotherham U	20	2	**243**	**17**
2004–05	Preston NE	24	3	**24**	**3**

SKORA, Eric (M)				**68**	**2**

H: 5 11 W: 12 00 b.Metz 20-8-81
Source: Nancy.

2001–02	Preston NE	4	0		
2002–03	Preston NE	36	0		
2003–04	Preston NE	2	0		
2003–04	*Kilmarnock*	17	2	**17**	**2**
2004–05	Preston NE	9	0	**51**	**0**

SMITH, Andy (F)				**15**	**0**

H: 5 11 W: 11 10 b.Lisburn 25-9-80
Honours: Northern Ireland B, 11 full caps.

2004–05	Preston NE	14	0	**14**	**0**
2004–05	*Stockport Co*	1	0	**1**	**0**

WARD, Gavin (G)				**278**	**0**

H: 6 3 W: 14 00 b.Sutton Coldfield 30-6-70
Source: Aston Villa Trainee.

1988–89	Shrewsbury T	0	0		
1989–90	WBA	0	0		
1989–90	Cardiff C	2	0		
1990–91	Cardiff C	1	0		
1991–92	Cardiff C	24	0		
1992–93	Cardiff C	32	0	**59**	**0**
1993–94	Leicester C	32	0		
1994–95	Leicester C	6	0	**38**	**0**
1995–96	Bradford C	36	0	**36**	**0**
1995–96	Bolton W	5	0		
1996–97	Bolton W	11	0		
1997–98	Bolton W	6	0		
1998–99	Bolton W	0	0	**22**	**0**
1998–99	*Burnley*	17	0	**17**	**0**
1998–99	Stoke C	6	0		
1999–2000	Stoke C	46	0		
2000–01	Stoke C	17	0		

2001–02	Stoke C	10	0	**79**	**0**
2002–03	Walsall	7	0	**7**	**0**
2003–04	Coventry C	12	0	**12**	**0**
2003–04	*Barnsley*	1	0	**1**	**0**
2004–05	Preston NE	7	0	**7**	**0**

QPR (65)

AINSWORTH, Gareth (M) 335 76
H: 5 10 W: 12 05 b.Blackburn 10-5-73
Source: Blackburn R Trainee.

1991–92	Preston NE	5	0		
1992–93	Cambridge U	4	1	**4**	**1**
1992–93	Preston NE	26	0		
1993–94	Preston NE	38	11		
1994–95	Preston NE	16	1		
1995–96	Preston NE	2	0		
1995–96	Lincoln C	31	12		
1996–97	Lincoln C	46	22		
1997–98	Lincoln C	6	3	**83**	**37**
1997–98	Port Vale	40	5		
1998–99	Port Vale	15	5	**55**	**10**
1998–99	Wimbledon	8	0		
1999–2000	Wimbledon	2	2		
2000–01	Wimbledon	12	2		
2001–02	Wimbledon	2	0		
2001–02	*Preston NE*	5	1	**92**	**13**
2002–03	Wimbledon	12	2	**36**	**6**
2002–03	*Walsall*	5	1	**5**	**1**
2002–03	Cardiff C	9	0	**9**	**0**
2003–04	QPR	29	6		
2004–05	QPR	22	2	**51**	**8**

BAIDOO, Shabazz (M) 4 0
H: 5 8 W: 10 07 b.Hackney 13-4-88
Source: Scholar.

2004–05	QPR	4	0	**4**	**0**

BAILEY, Stefan (M) 2 0
H: 5 11 W: 12 08 b.London 10-11-87
Source: Scholar.

2004–05	QPR	2	0	**2**	**0**

BEAN, Marcus (M) 66 2
H: 5 11 W: 11 06 b.Hammersmith 2-11-84
Source: Scholar.

2002–03	QPR	7	0		
2003–04	QPR	31	1		
2004–05	QPR	20	1	**58**	**2**
2004–05	*Swansea C*	8	0	**8**	**0**

BIGNOT, Marcus (D) 292 4
H: 5 7 W: 11 04 b.Birmingham 22-8-74
Source: Kidderminster H.

1997–98	Crewe Alex	42	0		
1998–99	Crewe Alex	26	0		
1999–2000	Crewe Alex	27	0	**95**	**0**
2000–01	Bristol R	26	1	**26**	**1**
2000–01	QPR	9	1		
2001–02	QPR	45	0		
2002–03	Rushden & D	33	0		
2003–04	Rushden & D	35	2	**68**	**2**
2003–04	QPR	6	0		
2004–05	QPR	43	0	**103**	**1**

BIRCHAM, Marc (M) 213 8
H: 5 11 W: 11 06 b.Hammersmith 11-5-78
Source: Trainee. *Honours:* Canada 17 full caps, 1 goal.

1996–97	Millwall	6	0		
1997–98	Millwall	4	0		
1998–99	Millwall	28	0		
1999–2000	Millwall	22	1		
2000–01	Millwall	20	2		
2001–02	Millwall	24	0	**104**	**3**
2002–03	QPR	36	2		
2003–04	QPR	38	2		
2004–05	QPR	35	1	**109**	**5**

BRANCO, Serge (M) 7 0
H: 5 9 W: 11 11 b.Douala 11-10-80
Source: Unisport de Bafang, Braunschweig, Eintracht, Frankfurt. *Honours:* Cameroon Olympic.

2003–04	Stuttgart	0	0		
2004–05	QPR	7	0	**7**	**0**

BROWN, Aaron (M) 171 13
H: 5 11 W: 12 13 b.Bristol 14-3-80
Source: Trainee.England Schools.

1997–98	Bristol C	0	0		
1998–99	Bristol C	14	0		
1999–2000	Bristol C	13	2		
1999–2000	*Exeter C*	5	1	**5**	**1**
2000–01	Bristol C	35	2		
2001–02	Bristol C	36	1		
2002–03	Bristol C	32	2		
2003–04	Bristol C	30	5	**160**	**12**
2004–05	QPR	1	0	**1**	**0**
2004–05	*Torquay U*	5	0	**5**	**0**

COOK, Lee (M) 121 11
H: 5 8 W: 11 10 b.Hammersmith 3-8-82
Source: Aylesbury U.

1999–2000	Watford	0	0		
2000–01	Watford	4	0		
2001–02	Watford	10	0		
2002–03	Watford	4	0		
2002–03	*York C*	7	1	**7**	**1**
2002–03	*QPR*	13	1		
2003–04	Watford	41	7	**59**	**7**
2004–05	QPR	42	2	**55**	**3**

CULKIN, Nick (G) 93 0
H: 6 2 W: 13 07 b.York 6-7-78
Source: York C.

1995–96	Manchester U	0	0		
1996–97	Manchester U	0	0		
1997–98	Manchester U	0	0		
1998–99	Manchester U	0	0		
1999–2000	Manchester U	1	0		
1999–2000	*Hull C*	4	0	**4**	**0**
2000–01	Manchester U	0	0		
2000–01	*Bristol R*	45	0	**45**	**0**
2001–02	Manchester U	0	0	**1**	**0**
2001–02	*Livingston*	21	0	**21**	**0**
2002–03	QPR	17	0		
2003–04	QPR	5	0		
2004–05	QPR	0	0	**22**	**0**

CURETON, Jamie (F) 359 134
H: 5 8 W: 12 08 b.Bristol 28-8-75
Source: Trainee. *Honours:* England Youth.

1992–93	Norwich C	0	0		
1993–94	Norwich C	0	0		
1994–95	Norwich C	17	4		
1995–96	Norwich C	12	2		
1995–96	*Bournemouth*	5	0	**5**	**0**
1996–97	Norwich C	0	0	**29**	**6**
1996–97	Bristol R	38	11		
1997–98	Bristol R	43	13		
1998–99	Bristol R	46	25		
1999–2000	Bristol R	46	22		
2000–01	Bristol R	1	1	**174**	**72**
2000–01	Reading	43	26		
2001–02	Reading	38	15		
2002–03	Reading	27	9	**108**	**50**
From Busan Icons.					
2003–04	QPR	13	2		
2004–05	QPR	30	4	**43**	**6**

DALY, Wesley (M) 9 0
H: 5 9 W: 11 00 b.Hammersmith 7-3-84
Source: Scholar.

2001–02	QPR	1	0		
2002–03	QPR	6	0		
2003–04	QPR	2	0		
2004–05	QPR	0	0	**9**	**0**

DAY, Chris (G) 142 0
H: 6 2 W: 13 06 b.Whipps Cross 28-7-75
Source: Trainee. *Honours:* England Under-21.

1992–93	Tottenham H	0	0		
1993–94	Tottenham H	0	0		
1994–95	Tottenham H	0	0		
1995–96	Tottenham H	0	0		
1996–97	Crystal Palace	24	0	**24**	**0**
1997–98	Watford	0	0		
1998–99	Watford	0	0		
1999–2000	Watford	11	0		
2000–01	Watford	0	0	**11**	**0**
2000–01	*Lincoln C*	14	0	**14**	**0**
2001–02	QPR	16	0		
2002–03	QPR	12	0		
2003–04	QPR	29	0		
2004–05	QPR	30	0	**87**	**0**
2004–05	*Preston NE*	6	0	**6**	**0**

DONNELLY, Scott (M) 2 0
H: 5 8 W: 11 10 b.Hammersmith 25-12-87
Source: Scholar.

2004–05	QPR	2	0	**2**	**0**

EDGHILL, Richard (D) 225 1
H: 5 9 W: 12 01 b.Oldham 23-9-74
Source: From Trainee. *Honours:* England Under-21.

1992–93	Manchester C	0	0		
1993–94	Manchester C	22	0		
1994–95	Manchester C	14	0		
1995–96	Manchester C	13	0		
1996–97	Manchester C	0	0		
1997–98	Manchester C	36	0		
1998–99	Manchester C	38	0		
1999–2000	Manchester C	41	1		
2000–01	Manchester C	6	0		
2000–01	*Birmingham C*	3	0	**3**	**0**
2001–02	Manchester C	11	0	**181**	**1**
2002–03	Wigan Ath	0	0		
2002–03	Sheffield U	1	0	**1**	**0**
2003–04	QPR	20	0		
2004–05	QPR	20	0	**40**	**0**

FURLONG, Paul (F) 427 154
H: 6 0 W: 13 11 b.London 1-10-68
Source: Enfield.

1991–92	Coventry C	37	4	**37**	**4**
1992–93	Watford	41	19		
1993–94	Watford	38	18	**79**	**37**
1994–95	Chelsea	36	10		
1995–96	Chelsea	28	3	**64**	**13**
1996–97	Birmingham C	43	10		
1997–98	Birmingham C	25	15		
1998–99	Birmingham C	29	13		
1999–2000	Birmingham C	19	11		
2000–01	Birmingham C	4	0		
2000–01	*QPR*	3	1		
2001–02	Birmingham C	11	1		
2001–02	*Sheffield U*	4	2	**4**	**2**
2002–03	Birmingham C	0	0	**131**	**50**
2002–03	QPR	33	13		
2003–04	QPR	36	16		
2004–05	QPR	40	18	**112**	**48**

GALLEN, Kevin (F) 376 95
H: 5 11 W: 13 05 b.Hammersmith 21-9-75
Source: Trainee. *Honours:* England Schools, Youth, Under-21.

1992–93	QPR	0	0		
1993–94	QPR	0	0		
1994–95	QPR	37	10		
1995–96	QPR	30	8		
1996–97	QPR	2	3		
1997–98	QPR	27	3		
1998–99	QPR	44	8		
1999–2000	QPR	31	4		
2000–01	Huddersfield T	38	10	**38**	**10**
2001–02	Barnsley	9	2	**9**	**2**
2001–02	QPR	25	7		
2002–03	QPR	42	13		
2003–04	QPR	45	17		
2004–05	QPR	46	10	**329**	**83**

GNOHERE, Arthur (D) 130 8
H: 6 0 W: 13 00 b.Yamoussoukro 20-11-78

2000–01	Caen	28	2	**28**	**2**
2001–02	Burnley	34	3		
2002–03	Burnley	33	2		
2003–04	Burnley	14	1	**81**	**6**
2003–04	QPR	18	0		
2004–05	QPR	3	0	**21**	**0**

HAMILTON, Lewis (D) 1 0
H: 6 0 W: 11 08 b.Derby 21-11-84
Source: Derby Co Trainee.

2004–05	QPR	1	0	**1**	**0**

HISLOP, Matthew (D) 0 0
H: 5 11 W: 12 00 b.Wolverhampton 31-1-87
Source: Arsenal Scholar.

2004–05	QPR	0	0		

JOHNSON, Richard (M) 274 21
H: 5 10 W: 11 13 b.Kurri Kurri 27-4-74
Source: From Trainee. *Honours:* Australia 1 full cap.

1991–92	Watford	2	0		
1992–93	Watford	1	0		
1993–94	Watford	27	0		
1994–95	Watford	35	3		
1995–96	Watford	20	1		
1996–97	Watford	37	2		
1997–98	Watford	42	7		
1998–99	Watford	40	4		

1999–2000	Watford	23	3		
2000–01	Watford	3	0		
2001–02	Watford	0	0		
2002–03	Watford	12	0		
2002–03	*Northampton T*	6	1	**6**	**1**
2003–04	Watford	0	0	**242**	**20**
2003–04	Colchester U	0	0		
2003–04	Stoke C	7	0	**7**	**0**
2003–04	QPR	11	0		
2004–05	QPR	6	0	**17**	**0**
2004–05	*Milton Keynes D*	2	0	**2**	**0**

KANYUKA, Patrick (D) **1 0**
H: 6 0 W: 12 06 b.Kinshasa 19-7-87

2004–05	QPR	1	0	**1**	**0**

MILLER, Adam (M) **14 0**
H: 5 11 W: 11 06 b.Hemel Hempstead 19-2-82
From Aldershot T

2004–05	QPR	14	0	**14**	**0**

MULHOLLAND, Scott (M) **1 0**
H: 5 8 W: 10 05 b.Bexleyheath 7-9-86

2004–05	QPR	1	0	**1**	**0**

PADULA, Gino (D) **119 4**
H: 5 9 W: 12 11 b.Buenos Aires 11-7-76
Source: Xerex.

1999–2000	Bristol R	0	0		
1999–2000	Walsall	25	0	**25**	**0**
2000–01	Wigan Ath	4	0		
2001–02	Wigan Ath	0	0	**4**	**0**
2002–03	QPR	21	1		
2003–04	QPR	36	3		
2004–05	QPR	33	0	**90**	**4**

PERRY, Jack (M) **0 0**
b.Islington 26-10-84
Source: Juniors.

2003–04	QPR	0	0		
2004–05	QPR	0	0		

ROSE, Matthew (D) **221 8**
H: 5 11 W: 12 02 b.Dartford 24-9-75
Source: From Trainee. *Honours:* England Under-21.

1994–95	Arsenal	0	0		
1995–96	Arsenal	4	0		
1996–97	Arsenal	1	0	**5**	**0**
1997–98	QPR	16	0		
1998–99	QPR	29	0		
1999–2000	QPR	29	1		
2000–01	QPR	27	0		
2001–02	QPR	39	3		
2002–03	QPR	28	2		
2003–04	QPR	20	0		
2004–05	QPR	28	2	**216**	**8**

ROSSI, Generoso (G) **178 0**
H: 6 3 W: 13 05 b.Naples 3-1-79
Source: Bari.

1998–99	Savoia	32	0	**32**	**0**
1999–2000	Crotone	33	0	**33**	**0**
2000–01	Bari	6	0	**6**	**0**
2000–01	Venezia	15	0		
2001–02	Venezia	31	0		
2002–03	Venezia	0	0	**46**	**0**
2002–03	Lecce	37	0	**37**	**0**
2003–04	Siena	21	0	**21**	**0**
2004–05	QPR	3	0	**3**	**0**

ROWLANDS, Martin (M) **226 33**
H: 5 9 W: 10 10 b.Hammersmith 8-2-79
Source: Farnborough T. *Honours:* Eire Under-21, 3 full caps.

1998–99	Brentford	36	4		
1999–2000	Brentford	40	6		
2000–01	Brentford	32	2		
2001–02	Brentford	23	7		
2002–03	Brentford	18	1	**149**	**20**
2003–04	QPR	42	10		
2004–05	QPR	35	3	**77**	**13**

SANTOS, Georges (M) **219 15**
H: 6 3 W: 14 00 b.Marseille 15-8-70
Source: Toulon.

1998–99	Tranmere R	37	1		
1999–2000	Tranmere R	10	1	**47**	**2**
1999–2000	WBA	8	0	**8**	**0**
2000–01	Sheffield U	31	4		
2001–02	Sheffield U	30	2	**61**	**6**
2002–03	Grimsby T	26	1	**26**	**1**
2003–04	Ipswich T	34	1	**34**	**1**
2004–05	QPR	43	5	**43**	**5**

SHIMMIN, Dominic (D) **0 0**
H: 6 0 W: 12 06 b.Bermondsey 13-10-87
Source: Arsenal Scholar.

2004–05	QPR	0	0		

SHITTU, Dan (D) **141 15**
H: 6 2 W: 16 03 b.Lagos 2-9-80
Honours: Nigeria 1 full cap.

1999–2000	Charlton Ath	0	0		
2000–01	Charlton Ath	0	0		
2000–01	*Blackpool*	17	2	**17**	**2**
2001–02	Charlton Ath	0	0		
2001–02	QPR	27	2		
2002–03	QPR	43	7		
2003–04	QPR	20	0		
2004–05	QPR	34	4	**124**	**13**

STURRIDGE, Dean (F) **310 95**
H: 5 8 W: 12 02 b.Birmingham 27-7-73
Source: Trainee.

1991–92	Derby Co	1	0		
1992–93	Derby Co	10	0		
1993–94	Derby Co	0	0		
1994–95	Derby Co	12	1		
1994–95	*Torquay U*	10	5	**10**	**5**
1995–96	Derby Co	39	20		
1996–97	Derby Co	30	11		
1997–98	Derby Co	30	9		
1998–99	Derby Co	29	5		
1999–2000	Derby Co	25	6		
2000–01	Derby Co	14	1	**190**	**53**
2000–01	Leicester C	13	3		
2001–02	Leicester C	9	3	**22**	**6**
2001–02	Wolverhampton W	27	20		
2002–03	Wolverhampton W	39	10		
2003–04	Wolverhampton W	5	0		
2003–04	*Sheffield U*	4	0	**4**	**0**
2004–05	Wolverhampton W	11	1	**82**	**31**
2004–05	QPR	2	0	**2**	**0**

THORPE, Tony (F) **357 135**
H: 5 9 W: 12 01 b.Leicester 10-4-74
Source: Leicester C.

1992–93	Luton T	0	0		
1993–94	Luton T	14	1		
1994–95	Luton T	4	0		
1995–96	Luton T	33	7		
1996–97	Luton T	41	28		
1997–98	Luton T	28	14		
1997–98	Fulham	13	3	**13**	**3**
1998–99	Bristol C	16	2		
1998–99	*Reading*	6	1	**6**	**1**
1998–99	*Luton T*	8	4		
1999–2000	Bristol C	31	13		
1999–2000	*Luton T*	4	1		
2000–01	Bristol C	39	19		
2001–02	Bristol C	42	16	**128**	**50**
2002–03	Luton T	30	13		
2003–04	Luton T	2	2	**164**	**70**
2003–04	QPR	31	10		
2004–05	QPR	10	0	**41**	**10**
2004–05	*Rotherham U*	5	1	**5**	**1**

TOWNSEND, Luke (M) **2 0**
H: 6 0 W: 11 10 b.Guildford 28-9-86

2004–05	QPR	2	0	**2**	**0**

READING (66)

BROOKER, Paul (M) **235 19**
H: 5 8 W: 10 06 b.Hammersmith 25-11-76
Source: Trainee.

1995–96	Fulham	20	2		
1996–97	Fulham	26	2		
1997–98	Fulham	9	0		
1998–99	Fulham	1	0		
1999–2000	Fulham	0	0	**56**	**4**
1999–2000	*Brighton & HA*	15	2		
2000–01	Brighton & HA	41	3		
2001–02	Brighton & HA	41	4		
2002–03	Brighton & HA	37	6	**134**	**15**
2003–04	Leicester C	3	0	**3**	**0**
2003–04	*Reading*	11	0		
2004–05	Reading	31	0	**42**	**0**

BROWN, Steve (D) **282 10**
H: 6 1 W: 13 10 b.Brighton 13-5-72
Source: Trainee.

1990–91	Charlton Ath	0	0		
1991–92	Charlton Ath	1	0		
1992–93	Charlton Ath	0	0		
1993–94	Charlton Ath	19	0		
1994–95	Charlton Ath	42	3		
1995–96	Charlton Ath	19	0		
1996–97	Charlton Ath	27	0		
1997–98	Charlton Ath	34	2		
1998–99	Charlton Ath	18	0		
1999–2000	Charlton Ath	40	2		
2000–01	Charlton Ath	25	0		
2001–02	Charlton Ath	14	2		
2002–03	Charlton Ath	3	0	**242**	**9**
2002–03	Reading	21	1		
2003–04	Reading	19	0		
2004–05	Reading	0	0	**40**	**1**

CAMPBELL, Darren (M) **1 0**
H: 5 5 W: 10 00 b.Huntingdon 16-4-86
Source: Scholar. *Honours:* England Youth.

2002–03	Reading	1	0		
2003–04	Reading	0	0		
2004–05	Reading	0	0	**1**	**0**

CASTLE, Peter (D) **1 0**
H: 6 0 W: 12 02 b.Southampton 12-3-87
Source: Scholar. *Honours:* FA Schools.

2002–03	Reading	1	0		
2003–04	Reading	0	0		
2004–05	Reading	0	0	**1**	**0**

CONVEY, Bobby (M) **18 0**
H: 5 9 W: 11 04 b.Philadelphia 27-5-83
Source: DC United. *Honours:* USA, 31 full caps, 1 goal.

2004–05	Reading	18	0	**18**	**0**

FERDINAND, Les (F) **443 184**
H: 5 11 W: 13 05 b.Paddington 8-12-66
Source: From Hayes. *Honours:* England B, 17 full caps, 5 goals.

1986–87	QPR	2	0		
1987–88	QPR	1	0		
1987–88	*Brentford*	3	0	**3**	**0**
1988–89	QPR	0	0		
1988–89	*Besiktas*	24	14	**24**	**14**
1989–90	QPR	9	2		
1990–91	QPR	18	8		
1991–92	QPR	23	10		
1992–93	QPR	37	20		
1993–94	QPR	36	16		
1994–95	QPR	37	24	**163**	**80**
1995–96	Newcastle U	37	25		
1996–97	Newcastle U	31	16	**68**	**41**
1997–98	Tottenham H	21	5		
1998–99	Tottenham H	24	5		
1999–2000	Tottenham H	9	2		
2000–01	Tottenham H	28	10		
2001–02	Tottenham H	25	9		
2002–03	Tottenham H	11	2	**118**	**33**
2002–03	West Ham U	14	2	**14**	**2**
2003–04	Leicester C	29	12	**29**	**12**
2004–05	Bolton W	12	1	**12**	**1**
2004–05	Reading	12	1	**12**	**1**

FORSTER, Nicky (F) **431 134**
H: 5 8 W: 11 05 b.Caterham 8-9-73
Source: Horley T. *Honours:* England Under-21.

1992–93	Gillingham	26	6		
1993–94	Gillingham	41	18	**67**	**24**
1994–95	Brentford	46	24		
1995–96	Brentford	38	5		
1996–97	Brentford	25	10	**109**	**39**
1996–97	Birmingham C	7	3		
1997–98	Birmingham C	28	3		
1998–99	Birmingham C	33	5	**68**	**11**
1999–2000	Reading	36	10		
2000–01	Reading	9	1		
2001–02	Reading	42	19		
2002–03	Reading	40	16		
2003–04	Reading	30	7		
2004–05	Reading	30	7	**187**	**60**

GOATER, Shaun (F) **518 206**
H: 6 1 W: 11 10 b.Bermuda 25-2-70
Honours: Bermuda 19 full caps.

1988–89	Manchester U	0	0		
1989–90	Manchester U	0	0		
1989–90	Rotherham U	12	2		
1990–91	Rotherham U	22	2		
1991–92	Rotherham U	24	9		
1992–93	Rotherham U	23	7		

1993–94	Rotherham U	39	13		
1993–94	*Notts Co*	1	0	**1**	**0**
1994–95	Rotherham U	45	19		
1995–96	Rotherham U	44	18	**209**	**70**
1996–97	Bristol C	42	23		
1997–98	Bristol C	33	17	**75**	**40**
1997–98	Manchester C	7	3		
1998–99	Manchester C	43	17		
1999–2000	Manchester C	40	23		
2000–01	Manchester C	26	6		
2001–02	Manchester C	42	28		
2002–03	Manchester C	26	7	**184**	**84**
2003–04	Reading	34	12		
2004–05	Reading	9	0	**43**	**12**
2004–05	*Coventry C*	6	0	**6**	**0**

HAHNEMANN, Marcus (G) 202 0
H: 6 3 W: 16 04 b.Seattle 15-6-72
Honours: USA 4 full caps.

1997	Colorado Rapids	25	0		
1998	Colorado Rapids	28	0		
1999	Colorado Rapids	13	0	**66**	**0**
1999–2000	Fulham	0	0		
2000–01	Fulham	2	0		
2001–02	Fulham	0	0	**2**	**0**
2001–02	*Rochdale*	5	0	**5**	**0**
2001–02	*Reading*	6	0		
2002–03	Reading	41	0		
2003–04	Reading	36	0		
2004–05	Reading	46	0	**129**	**0**

HARPER, James (M) 157 8
H: 5 10 W: 11 02 b.Chelmsford 9-11-80
Source: Trainee.

1999–2000	Arsenal	0	0		
2000–01	Arsenal	0	0		
2000–01	*Cardiff C*	3	0	**3**	**0**
2000–01	Reading	12	1		
2001–02	Reading	26	1		
2002–03	Reading	36	2		
2003–04	Reading	39	1		
2004–05	Reading	41	3	**154**	**8**

HAYES, Jonathan (M) 0 0
H: 5 7 W: 11 00 b.Dublin 9-7-87
Source: Scholar.

2004–05	Reading	0	0

HOWELL, Simieon (M) 0 0
H: 5 11 W: 12 00 b.Reading 26-8-85
Source: Scholar.

2004–05	Reading	0	0

HUGHES, Andy (M) 309 36
H: 5 11 W: 12 01 b.Stockport 2-1-78
Source: Trainee.

1995–96	Oldham Ath	15	1		
1996–97	Oldham Ath	8	0		
1997–98	Oldham Ath	10	0	**33**	**1**
1997–98	Notts Co	15	2		
1998–99	Notts Co	30	3		
1999–2000	Notts Co	35	7		
2000–01	Notts Co	30	5	**110**	**17**
2001–02	Reading	39	6		
2002–03	Reading	43	9		
2003–04	Reading	43	3		
2004–05	Reading	41	0	**166**	**18**

INGIMARSSON, Ivar (D) 295 27
H: 6 0 W: 12 07 b.Reykjavik 20-8-77
Honours: Iceland Youth, Under-21, 16 full caps.

1995	Valur	12	0		
1996	Valur	17	2		
1997	Valur	16	3	**45**	**5**
1998	IBV	18	1		
1999	IBV	18	4	**36**	**5**
1999–2000	Torquay U	4	1	**4**	**1**
1999–2000	Brentford	25	1		
2000–01	Brentford	42	3		
2001–02	Brentford	46	6	**113**	**10**
2002–03	Wolverhampton W	13	2		
2002–03	*Brighton & HA*	15	0	**15**	**0**
2003–04	Wolverhampton W	0	0	**13**	**2**
2003–04	Reading	25	1		
2004–05	Reading	44	3	**69**	**4**

KEOWN, Martin (D) 585 8
H: 6 1 W: 13 09 b.Oxford 24-7-66
Source: Apprentice. *Honours:* England Youth, Under-21, B, 43 full caps, 2 goals.

1983–84	Arsenal	0	0		
1984–85	Arsenal	0	0		
1984–85	*Brighton & HA*	16	0		
1985–86	Arsenal	22	0		
1985–86	*Brighton & HA*	7	1	**23**	**1**
1986–87	Aston Villa	36	0		
1987–88	Aston Villa	42	3		
1988–89	Aston Villa	34	0	**112**	**3**
1989–90	Everton	20	0		
1990–91	Everton	24	0		
1991–92	Everton	39	0		
1992–93	Everton	13	0	**96**	**0**
1992–93	Arsenal	16	0		
1993–94	Arsenal	33	0		
1994–95	Arsenal	31	1		
1995–96	Arsenal	34	0		
1996–97	Arsenal	33	1		
1997–98	Arsenal	18	0		
1998–99	Arsenal	34	1		
1999–2000	Arsenal	27	1		
2000–01	Arsenal	28	0		
2001–02	Arsenal	22	0		
2002–03	Arsenal	24	0		
2003–04	Arsenal	10	0	**332**	**4**
2004–05	Leicester C	17	0	**17**	**0**
2004–05	Reading	5	0	**5**	**0**

KITSON, Dave (F) 156 64
H: 6 3 W: 13 00 b.Hitchin 21-1-80
Source: Arlesey.

2000–01	Cambridge U	8	1		
2001–02	Cambridge U	33	9		
2002–03	Cambridge U	44	20		
2003–04	Cambridge U	17	10	**102**	**40**
2003–04	Reading	17	5		
2004–05	Reading	37	19	**54**	**24**

LITTLE, Glen (M) 297 35
H: 6 3 W: 13 00 b.Wimbledon 15-10-75
Source: Trainee.

1994–95	Crystal Palace	0	0		
1995–96	Crystal Palace	0	0		
1996–97	Glentoran	6	2	**6**	**2**
1996–97	Burnley	9	0		
1997–98	Burnley	24	4		
1998–99	Burnley	34	5		
1999–2000	Burnley	41	3		
2000–01	Burnley	34	3		
2001–02	Burnley	37	9		
2002–03	Burnley	33	5		
2002–03	*Reading*	6	1		
2003–04	Burnley	34	3	**246**	**32**
2003–04	*Bolton W*	4	0	**4**	**0**
2004–05	Reading	35	0	**41**	**1**

MORGAN, Dean (F) 102 9
H: 6 0 W: 12 02 b.Enfield 3-10-83
Source: Scholar.

2000–01	Colchester U	4	0		
2001–02	Colchester U	30	0		
2002–03	Colchester U	37	6		
2003–04	Colchester U	0	0	**71**	**6**
2003–04	Reading	13	1		
2004–05	Reading	18	2	**31**	**3**

MULLINS, John (D) 21 2
H: 5 11 W: 12 07 b.Hampstead 6-11-85

2004–05	Reading	0	0		
2004–05	*Kidderminster H*	21	2	**21**	**2**

MURTY, Graeme (D) 332 8
H: 5 10 W: 11 10 b.Saltburn 13-11-74
Source: Trainee. *Honours:* Scotland B, 1 full cap.

1992–93	York C	0	0		
1993–94	York C	1	0		
1994–95	York C	20	2		
1995–96	York C	35	2		
1996–97	York C	27	2		
1997–98	York C	34	1	**117**	**7**
1998–99	Reading	9	0		
1999–2000	Reading	17	0		
2000–01	Reading	23	1		
2001–02	Reading	43	0		
2002–03	Reading	44	0		
2003–04	Reading	38	0		
2004–05	Reading	41	0	**215**	**1**

NEWMAN, Ricky (D) 329 10
H: 5 10 W: 12 06 b.Guildford 5-8-70
Source: Trainee.

1987–88	Crystal Palace	0	0		
1988–89	Crystal Palace	0	0		
1989–90	Crystal Palace	0	0		
1990–91	Crystal Palace	0	0		
1991–92	Crystal Palace	0	0		
1991–92	*Maidstone U*	10	1	**10**	**1**
1992–93	Crystal Palace	2	0		
1993–94	Crystal Palace	11	0		
1994–95	Crystal Palace	35	3	**48**	**3**
1995–96	Millwall	36	1		
1996–97	Millwall	41	3		
1997–98	Millwall	35	1		
1998–99	Millwall	24	0		
1999–2000	Millwall	14	0	**150**	**5**
1999–2000	*Reading*	7	1		
2000–01	Reading	39	0		
2001–02	Reading	0	0		
2002–03	Reading	28	0		
2003–04	Reading	30	0		
2004–05	Reading	17	0	**121**	**1**

OWUSU, Lloyd (F) 257 83
H: 6 1 W: 13 07 b.Slough 12-12-76
Source: Slough T.

1998–99	Brentford	46	22		
1999–2000	Brentford	41	12		
2000–01	Brentford	33	10		
2001–02	Brentford	44	20	**164**	**64**
2002–03	Sheffield W	32	4		
2003–04	Sheffield W	20	5	**52**	**9**
2003–04	Reading	16	4		
2004–05	Reading	25	6	**41**	**10**

RIFAT, Ahmet (D) 0 0
H: 6 3 W: 11 08 b.London 3-1-86
Source: Scholar. *Honours:* England Youth.

2002–03	Reading	0	0
2003–04	Reading	0	0
2004–05	Reading	0	0

SAVAGE, Bas (F) 25 0
H: 6 4 W: 13 08 b.London 7-1-82
Source: Walton & Hersham.

2001–02	Reading	1	0		
2002–03	Reading	0	0		
2003–04	Reading	15	0		
2004–05	Reading	0	0	**16**	**0**
2004–05	*Wycombe W*	4	0	**4**	**0**
2004–05	*Bury*	5	0	**5**	**0**

SHOREY, Nicky (D) 169 7
H: 5 9 W: 10 10 b.Romford 19-2-81
Source: Trainee.

1999–2000	Leyton Orient	7	0		
2000–01	Leyton Orient	8	0	**15**	**0**
2000–01	Reading	0	0		
2001–02	Reading	32	0		
2002–03	Reading	43	2		
2003–04	Reading	35	2		
2004–05	Reading	44	3	**154**	**7**

SIDWELL, Steven (M) 142 24
H: 5 10 W: 11 00 b.Wandsworth 14-12-82
Source: Scholar. *Honours:* England Under-20, Under-21.

2001–02	Arsenal	0	0		
2001–02	*Brentford*	30	4	**30**	**4**
2002–03	Arsenal	0	0		
2002–03	*Brighton & HA*	12	5	**12**	**5**
2002–03	Reading	13	2		
2003–04	Reading	43	8		
2004–05	Reading	44	5	**100**	**15**

SONKO, Ibrahima (D) 119 9
H: 6 3 W: 13 07 b.Bignola 22-1-81

2002–03	Brentford	37	5		
2003–04	Brentford	43	3	**80**	**8**
2004–05	Reading	39	1	**39**	**1**

YOUNG, Jamie (G) 1 0
H: 5 11 W: 13 01 b.Brisbane 25-8-85
Source: Scholar. *Honours:* England Youth, Under-20.

2003–04	Reading	1	0		
2004–05	Reading	0	0	**1**	**0**

ROCHDALE (67)

BERTOS, Leo (M) 94 14
H: 5 10 W: 12 07 b.Wellington 20-12-81
Honours: New Zealand Schools, Youth, Under-23, 7 full caps.

2000–01	Barnsley	2	0

2001–02 Barnsley 4 0
2002–03 Barnsley 6 1 **12** **1**
2003–04 Rochdale 40 9
2004–05 Rochdale 42 4 **82** **13**

BRISCO, Neil (M) **129** **2**
H: 5 11 W: 13 05 b.Billinge 26-1-78
Source: Trainee.
1996–97 Manchester C 0 0
1997–98 Manchester C 0 0
1998–99 Port Vale 1 0
1999–2000 Port Vale 12 0
2000–01 Port Vale 17 1
2001–02 Port Vale 37 0
2002–03 Port Vale 24 1
2003–04 Port Vale 27 0 **118** **2**
2004–05 Rochdale 11 0 **11** **0**

BROWN, Gary (D) **1** **0**
H: 5 6 W: 10 02 b.Darwem 29-10-85
Source: Scholar.
2004–05 Rochdale 1 0 **1** **0**

BURGESS, Daryl (D) **449** **12**
H: 6 0 W: 13 07 b.Birmingham 24-1-71
Source: Trainee.
1989–90 WBA 34 0
1990–91 WBA 25 0
1991–92 WBA 36 2
1992–93 WBA 18 1
1993–94 WBA 43 2
1994–95 WBA 22 0
1995–96 WBA 45 2
1996–97 WBA 33 1
1997–98 WBA 27 1
1998–99 WBA 20 0
1999–2000 WBA 26 1
2000–01 WBA 3 0 **332** **10**
2001–02 Northampton T 36 1
2002–03 Northampton T 25 1 **61** **2**
2003–04 Rochdale 35 0
2004–05 Rochdale 21 0 **56** **0**

CLARKE, Jamie (M) **75** **2**
H: 6 2 W: 13 02 b.Sunderland 18-9-82
Source: Scholar.
2001–02 Mansfield T 1 0
2002–03 Mansfield T 21 1
2003–04 Mansfield T 12 0 **34** **1**
2004–05 Rochdale 41 1 **41** **1**

COOKSEY, Ernie (M) **71** **9**
H: 5 9 W: 11 12 b.Bishops Stortford 17-9-78
Source: Crawley T.
2003–04 Oldham Ath 36 4
2004–05 Oldham Ath 1 0 **37** **4**
2004–05 Rochdale 34 5 **34** **5**

DOUGHTY, Matt (D) **141** **2**
H: 5 8 W: 11 00 b.Warrington 2-11-81
Source: Scholarship.
1999–2000 Chester C 33 1 **33** **1**
2001–02 Rochdale 36 1
2002–03 Rochdale 41 0
2003–04 Rochdale 31 0
2004–05 Rochdale 0 0 **108** **1**

EDWARDS, Neil (G) **403** **0**
H: 5 9 W: 12 11 b.Aberdare 5-12-70
Source: Trainee.
1988–89 Leeds U 0 0
1989–90 Leeds U 0 0
1990–91 Leeds U 0 0
1990–91 *Huddersfield T* 0 0
1991–92 Stockport Co 39 0
1992–93 Stockport Co 35 0
1993–94 Stockport Co 26 0
1994–95 Stockport Co 19 0
1995–96 Stockport Co 45 0
1996–97 Stockport Co 0 0
1997–98 Stockport Co 0 0 **164** **0**
1997–98 Rochdale 27 0
1998–99 Rochdale 45 0
1999–2000 Rochdale 40 0
2000–01 Rochdale 44 0
2001–02 Rochdale 7 0
2002–03 Rochdale 26 0
2003–04 Rochdale 34 0
2004–05 Rochdale 16 0 **239** **0**

EVANS, Wayne (D) **442** **4**
H: 5 11 W: 12 00 b.Abermule 25-8-71
Source: Welshpool.
1993–94 Walsall 41 0
1994–95 Walsall 36 0
1995–96 Walsall 24 0
1996–97 Walsall 28 0
1997–98 Walsall 43 1
1998–99 Walsall 11 0 **183** **1**
1999–2000 Rochdale 46 1
2000–01 Rochdale 45 2
2001–02 Rochdale 43 0
2002–03 Rochdale 40 0
2003–04 Rochdale 45 0
2004–05 Rochdale 40 0 **259** **3**

GALLIMORE, Tony (D) **478** **13**
H: 5 10 W: 13 02 b.Nantwich 21-2-72
Source: Trainee.
1989–90 Stoke C 1 0
1990–91 Stoke C 7 0
1991–92 Stoke C 3 0
1991–92 *Carlisle U* 16 0
1992–93 Stoke C 0 0 **11** **0**
1992–93 *Carlisle U* 8 1
1993–94 Carlisle U 40 1
1994–95 Carlisle U 40 5
1995–96 Carlisle U 36 2 **140** **9**
1995–96 Grimsby T 10 1
1996–97 Grimsby T 42 1
1997–98 Grimsby T 35 2
1998–99 Grimsby T 43 0
1999–2000 Grimsby T 39 0
2000–01 Grimsby T 28 0
2001–02 Grimsby T 38 0
2002–03 Grimsby T 38 0 **273** **4**
2003–04 Barnsley 20 0
2004–05 Barnsley 0 0 **20** **0**
2004–05 Rochdale 34 0 **34** **0**

GILKS, Matthew (G) **84** **0**
H: 6 3 W: 13 09 b.Rochdale 4-6-82
Source: Scholar.
2000–01 Rochdale 3 0
2001–02 Rochdale 19 0
2002–03 Rochdale 20 0
2003–04 Rochdale 12 0
2004–05 Rochdale 30 0 **84** **0**

GOODALL, Alan (D) **34** **2**
H: 5 9 W: 11 06 b.Birkenhead 2-12-81
Source: Bangor C.
2004–05 Rochdale 34 2 **34** **2**

GRIFFITHS, Gareth (D) **308** **18**
H: 6 4 W: 13 11 b.Winsford 10-4-70
Source: Rhyl.
1992–93 Port Vale 0 0
1993–94 Port Vale 4 2
1994–95 Port Vale 20 0
1995–96 Port Vale 41 2
1996–97 Port Vale 26 0
1997–98 Port Vale 3 0 **94** **4**
1997–98 *Shrewsbury T* 6 0 **6** **0**
1998–99 Wigan Ath 20 0
1999–2000 Wigan Ath 16 1
2000–01 Wigan Ath 17 1 **53** **2**
2001–02 Rochdale 41 4
2002–03 Rochdale 42 6
2003–04 Rochdale 33 1
2004–05 Rochdale 39 1 **155** **12**

HEALD, Greg (D) **294** **23**
H: 6 1 W: 12 07 b.Enfield 26-9-71
Source: Enfield. *Honours:* England Schools.
1994–95 Peterborough U 29 0
1995–96 Peterborough U 40 4
1996–97 Peterborough U 36 2 **105** **6**
1997–98 Barnet 43 3
1998–99 Barnet 19 2
1999–2000 Barnet 40 5
2000–01 Barnet 39 3
2001–02 Barnet 0 0
2002–03 Barnet 0 0 **141** **13**
2002–03 Leyton Orient 5 1
2003–04 Leyton Orient 4 0 **9** **1**
2003–04 Rochdale 10 1
2004–05 Rochdale 29 2 **39** **3**

HOLT, Grant (F) **84** **24**
H: 6 1 W: 13 09 b.Carlisle 12-4-81
Source: Workington.
1999–2000 Halifax T 4 0
2000–01 Halifax T 2 0 **6** **0**
From Sengkang, Barrow
2002–03 Sheffield W 7 1
2003–04 Sheffield W 17 2 **24** **3**
2003–04 Rochdale 14 4
2004–05 Rochdale 40 17 **54** **21**

JONES, Gary (M) **269** **36**
H: 5 10 W: 12 05 b.Birkenhead 3-6-77
1997–98 Swansea C 8 0 **8** **0**
1997–98 Rochdale 17 2
1998–99 Rochdale 20 0
1999–2000 Rochdale 39 7
2000–01 Rochdale 44 8
2001–02 Rochdale 20 5
2001–02 Barnsley 25 1
2002–03 Barnsley 31 1
2003–04 Barnsley 0 0 **56** **2**
2003–04 Rochdale 26 4
2004–05 Rochdale 39 8 **205** **34**

KITCHEN, Ben (M) **1** **0**
H: 5 9 W: 11 07 b.Bolton 19-8-86
Source: Scholar.
2004–05 Rochdale 1 0 **1** **0**

LAMBERT, Ricky (M) **160** **32**
H: 6 2 W: 12 01 b.Liverpool 16-2-82
Source: Trainee.
1999–2000 Blackpool 3 0
2000–01 Blackpool 0 0 **3** **0**
2000–01 Macclesfield T 9 0
2001–02 Macclesfield T 35 8 **44** **8**
2001–02 Stockport Co 0 0
2002–03 Stockport Co 29 2
2003–04 Stockport Co 40 12
2004–05 Stockport Co 29 4 **98** **18**
2004–05 Rochdale 15 6 **15** **6**

McCOURT, Patrick (F) **79** **8**
H: 6 0 W: 11 10 b.Derry 16-12-83
Source: Scholar. *Honours:* Northern Ireland Under-21, 1 full cap.
2001–02 Rochdale 23 4
2002–03 Rochdale 26 2
2003–04 Rochdale 24 2
2004–05 Rochdale 6 0 **79** **8**

McGIVERN, Leighton (M) **25** **1**
H: 5 8 W: 11 01 b.Liverpool 2-6-84
Honours: from Vauxhall Motors.
2004–05 Rochdale 25 1 **25** **1**

PATTERSON, Rory (M) **15** **0**
H: 5 10 W: 10 13 b.Derry 16-7-84
Source: Scholar.
2002–03 Rochdale 8 0
2003–04 Rochdale 7 0
2004–05 Rochdale 0 0 **15** **0**

PROBETS, Ashley (D) **9** **0**
H: 5 9 W: 10 11 b.Bexleyheath 13-12-84
2003–04 Arsenal 0 0
2004–05 Rochdale 9 0 **9** **0**

SIMPKINS, Mike (D) **77** **0**
H: 6 1 W: 13 03 b.Sheffield 28-11-78
Source: Trainee.
1997–98 Sheffield W 0 0
1997–98 Chesterfield 0 0
1998–99 Chesterfield 1 0
1999–2000 Chesterfield 9 0
2000–01 Chesterfield 16 0 **26** **0**
2001–02 Cardiff C 17 0
2002–03 Cardiff C 0 0 **17** **0**
2002–03 *Exeter C* 5 0 **5** **0**
2002–03 *Cheltenham T* 2 0 **2** **0**
2003–04 Rochdale 27 0
2004–05 Rochdale 0 0 **27** **0**

SMITH, Shaun (D) **454** **42**
H: 5 10 W: 11 00 b.Leeds 9-4-71
Source: Trainee.
1988–89 Halifax T 1 0
1989–90 Halifax T 6 0
1990–91 Halifax T 0 0 **7** **0**
1991–92 Crewe Alex 10 0
1992–93 Crewe Alex 36 4
1993–94 Crewe Alex 37 7

1994–95	Crewe Alex	45	8		
1995–96	Crewe Alex	29	1		
1996–97	Crewe Alex	38	4		
1997–98	Crewe Alex	43	6		
1998–99	Crewe Alex	46	4		
1999–2000	Crewe Alex	31	2		
2000–01	Crewe Alex	45	4		
2001–02	Crewe Alex	42	1	**402**	**41**
2002–03	Hull C	22	1		
2003–04	Hull C	0	0	**22**	**1**
2003–04	*Stockport Co*	6	0	**6**	**0**
2003–04	*Carlisle U*	4	0	**4**	**0**
2003–04	Rochdale	13	0		
2004–05	Rochdale	0	0	**13**	**0**

TAIT, Paul (F) **180 27**
H: 6 2 W: 12 00 b.Newcastle 24-10-74
Source: Trainee.

1993–94	Everton	0	0		
1994–95	Wigan Ath	5	0		
1995–96	Wigan Ath	0	0	**5**	**0**
From Northwich Vic.					
1999–2000	Crewe Alex	33	6		
2000–01	Crewe Alex	18	0		
2001–02	*Hull C*	2	0	**2**	**0**
2001–02	Crewe Alex	12	0	**63**	**6**
2002–03	Bristol R	41	7		
2003–04	Bristol R	33	12	**74**	**19**
2004–05	Rochdale	36	2	**36**	**2**

TOWNSON, Kevin (F) **108 25**
H: 5 8 W: 11 06 b.Kirby 19-4-83
Honours: England Youth.

2000–01	Rochdale	3	0		
2001–02	Rochdale	41	14		
2002–03	Rochdale	24	1		
2003–04	Rochdale	33	10		
2004–05	Rochdale	1	0	**102**	**25**
2004–05	*Macclesfield T*	6	0	**6**	**0**

WARNER, Scott (M) **49 1**
H: 5 11 W: 12 06 b.Rochdale 3-12-83
Source: Scholar.

2002–03	Rochdale	7	0		
2003–04	Rochdale	14	1		
2004–05	Rochdale	28	0	**49**	**1**

WELLER, Paul (M) **257 11**
H: 5 8 W: 11 02 b.Brighton 6-3-75
Source: Trainee.

1993–94	Burnley	0	0		
1994–95	Burnley	0	0		
1995–96	Burnley	25	1		
1996–97	Burnley	31	2		
1997–98	Burnley	39	2		
1998–99	Burnley	1	0		
1999–2000	Burnley	7	1		
2000–01	Burnley	44	3		
2001–02	Burnley	38	2		
2002–03	Burnley	34	0		
2003–04	Burnley	33	0		
2004–05	Burnley	0	0	**252**	**11**
2004–05	Rochdale	5	0	**5**	**0**

WILLIAMS, Matt (M) **1 0**
H: 5 11 W: 12 00 b.Bury 21-6-88
Source: Scholar.

2004–05	Rochdale	1	0	**1**	**0**

ROTHERHAM U (68)

BARKER, Shaun (D) **80 4**
H: 6 3 W: 12 09 b.Nottingham 19-9-82
Source: Scholar.

2002–03	Rotherham U	11	0		
2003–04	Rotherham U	36	2		
2004–05	Rotherham U	33	2	**80**	**4**

BUTLER, Martin (F) **338 102**
H: 5 11 W: 12 09 b.Wordsley 15-9-74
Source: Trainee.

1993–94	Walsall	15	3		
1994–95	Walsall	8	0		
1995–96	Walsall	28	4		
1996–97	Walsall	23	1	**74**	**8**
1997–98	Cambridge U	31	10		
1998–99	Cambridge U	46	17		
1999–2000	Cambridge U	26	14	**103**	**41**
1999–2000	Reading	17	4		
2000–01	Reading	45	24		
2001–02	Reading	17	2		
2002–03	Reading	21	2		
2003–04	Reading	3	0	**103**	**32**
2003–04	Rotherham U	37	15		
2004–05	Rotherham U	21	6	**58**	**21**

CAMPBELL-RYCE, Jamal (F) **62 2**
H: 5 7 W: 11 10 b.Lambeth 6-4-83
Source: Scholar. *Honours:* Jamaica 1 full cap.

2002–03	Charlton Ath	1	0		
2002–03	*Leyton Orient*	17	2	**17**	**2**
2003–04	Charlton Ath	2	0		
2003–04	*Wimbledon*	4	0	**4**	**0**
2004–05	Charlton Ath	0	0	**3**	**0**
2004–05	*Chesterfield*	14	0	**14**	**0**
2004–05	Rotherham U	24	0	**24**	**0**

DUNCUM, Sam (M) **2 0**
H: 5 9 W: 11 02 b.Sheffield 18-2-87
Source: Scholar.

2004–05	Rotherham U	2	0	**2**	**0**

GARNER, Darren (M) **300 24**
H: 5 10 W: 12 09 b.Plymouth 10-12-71
Source: Trainee.

1988–89	Plymouth Arg	1	0		
1989–90	Plymouth Arg	1	0		
1990–91	Plymouth Arg	5	1		
1991–92	Plymouth Arg	10	0		
1992–93	Plymouth Arg	10	0		
1993–94	Plymouth Arg	0	0	**27**	**1**
From Dorchester T.					
1995–96	Rotherham U	31	1		
1996–97	Rotherham U	30	2		
1997–98	Rotherham U	40	3		
1998–99	Rotherham U	40	4		
1999–2000	Rotherham U	35	9		
2000–01	Rotherham U	31	1		
2001–02	Rotherham U	0	0		
2002–03	Rotherham U	26	3		
2003–04	Rotherham U	13	0		
2004–05	Rotherham U	18	0	**264**	**23**
2004–05	*Torquay U*	9	0	**9**	**0**

GILCHRIST, Phil (D) **422 12**
H: 6 0 W: 14 07 b.Stockton 25-8-73
Source: Trainee.

1990–91	Nottingham F	0	0		
1991–92	Middlesbrough	0	0		
1992–93	Hartlepool U	24	0		
1993–94	Hartlepool U	35	0		
1994–95	Hartlepool U	23	0	**82**	**0**
1994–95	Oxford U	18	1		
1995–96	Oxford U	42	3		
1996–97	Oxford U	38	2		
1997–98	Oxford U	39	2		
1998–99	Oxford U	39	2		
1999–2000	Oxford U	1	0	**177**	**10**
1999–2000	Leicester C	27	1		
2000–01	Leicester C	12	0	**39**	**1**
2000–01	WBA	8	0		
2001–02	WBA	43	0		
2002–03	WBA	22	0		
2003–04	WBA	17	0	**90**	**0**
2003–04	*Rotherham U*	10	0		
2004–05	Rotherham U	24	1	**34**	**1**

HOSKINS, Will (F) **26 4**
H: 5 11 W: 11 08 b.Nottingham 6-5-86
Source: Scholar. *Honours:* England Youth.

2003–04	Rotherham U	4	2		
2004–05	Rotherham U	22	2	**26**	**4**

HURST, Paul (D) **379 13**
H: 5 5 W: 10 03 b.Sheffield 25-9-74
Source: Trainee.

1993–94	Rotherham U	4	0		
1994–95	Rotherham U	13	0		
1995–96	Rotherham U	40	1		
1996–97	Rotherham U	30	3		
1997–98	Rotherham U	30	0		
1998–99	Rotherham U	32	2		
1999–2000	Rotherham U	30	2		
2000–01	Rotherham U	44	3		
2001–02	Rotherham U	45	0		
2002–03	Rotherham U	44	1		
2003–04	Rotherham U	28	1		
2004–05	Rotherham U	39	0	**379**	**13**

KEANE, Michael (M) **94 8**
H: 5 7 W: 13 07 b.Dublin 29-12-82
Source: Scholar. *Honours:* Eire Under-21.

2000–01	Preston NE	2	0		
2001–02	Preston NE	20	2		
2002–03	Preston NE	5	0		
2002–03	*Grimsby T*	7	2	**7**	**2**
2003–04	Preston NE	30	1	**57**	**3**
2004–05	Hull C	20	3	**20**	**3**
2004–05	Rotherham U	10	0	**10**	**0**

McINTOSH, Martin (D) **398 43**
H: 6 2 W: 13 02 b.East Kilbride 19-3-71
Honours: Scotland B.

1988–89	St Mirren	2	0		
1989–90	St Mirren	2	0		
1990–91	St Mirren	0	0	**4**	**0**
1991–92	Clydebank	28	5		
1992–93	Clydebank	33	4		
1993–94	Clydebank	4	1	**65**	**10**
1993–94	Hamilton A	13	2		
1994–95	Hamilton A	30	2		
1995–96	Hamilton A	23	1		
1996–97	Hamilton A	33	7	**99**	**12**
1997–98	Stockport Co	38	2		
1998–99	Stockport Co	41	3		
1999–2000	Stockport Co	20	0	**99**	**5**
1999–2000	Hibernian	9	0		
2000–01	Hibernian	0	0		
2001–02	Hibernian	0	0	**9**	**0**
2001–02	Rotherham U	39	4		
2002–03	Rotherham U	42	5		
2003–04	Rotherham U	18	2		
2004–05	Rotherham U	23	5	**122**	**16**

McLAREN, Paul (M) **296 13**
H: 6 2 W: 12 12 b.High Wycombe 17-11-76
Source: Trainee.

1993–94	Luton T	1	0		
1994–95	Luton T	0	0		
1995–96	Luton T	12	1		
1996–97	Luton T	24	0		
1997–98	Luton T	43	0		
1998–99	Luton T	23	0		
1999–2000	Luton T	29	1		
2000–01	Luton T	35	2	**167**	**4**
2001–02	Sheffield W	35	2		
2002–03	Sheffield W	36	4		
2003–04	Sheffield W	25	2	**96**	**8**
2004–05	Rotherham U	33	1	**33**	**1**

MINTO, Scott (D) **362 11**
H: 5 10 W: 12 10 b.Bromborough 6-8-71
Source: Trainee. *Honours:* England Youth, Under-21.

1988–89	Charlton Ath	3	0		
1989–90	Charlton Ath	23	2		
1990–91	Charlton Ath	43	1		
1991–92	Charlton Ath	33	1		
1992–93	Charlton Ath	36	1		
1993–94	Charlton Ath	42	2	**180**	**7**
1994–95	Chelsea	19	0		
1995–96	Chelsea	10	0		
1996–97	Chelsea	25	4	**54**	**4**
1997–98	Benfica	21	0		
1998–99	Benfica	10	0	**31**	**0**
1998–99	West Ham U	15	0		
1999–2000	West Ham U	18	0		
2000–01	West Ham U	1	0		
2001–02	West Ham U	5	0		
2002–03	West Ham U	12	0	**51**	**0**
2003–04	Rotherham U	32	0		
2004–05	Rotherham U	14	0	**46**	**0**

MONKHOUSE, Andy (M) **116 8**
H: 6 2 W: 13 00 b.Leeds 23-10-80
Source: Trainee.

1998–99	Rotherham U	5	1		
1999–2000	Rotherham U	0	0		
2000–01	Rotherham U	12	0		
2001–02	Rotherham U	38	2		
2002–03	Rotherham U	20	0		
2003–04	Rotherham U	27	3		
2004–05	Rotherham U	14	2	**116**	**8**

MONTGOMERY, Gary (G) **15 0**
H: 6 2 W: 13 06 b.Leamington Spa 8-10-82
Source: Scholar.

2000–01	Coventry C	0	0		
2001–02	Coventry C	0	0		
2001–02	*Crewe Alex*	0	0		

2001–02	*Kidderminster H*	2	0	**2**	**0**
2002–03	Coventry C	8	0	**8**	**0**
2003–04	Rotherham U	4	0		
2004–05	Rotherham U	1	0	**5**	**0**

MULLIN, John (M) **280** **24**
H: 6 1 W: 12 09 b.Bury 11-8-75
Source: School.

1992–93	Burnley	0	0		
1993–94	Burnley	6	1		
1994–95	Burnley	12	1		
1995–96	Sunderland	10	1		
1996–97	Sunderland	10	1		
1997–98	Sunderland	6	0		
1997–98	*Preston NE*	7	0	**7**	**0**
1997–98	*Burnley*	6	0		
1998–99	Sunderland	9	2	**35**	**4**
1999–2000	Burnley	37	5		
2000–01	Burnley	36	3		
2001–02	Burnley	4	0	**101**	**10**
2001–02	Rotherham U	34	2		
2002–03	Rotherham U	34	3		
2003–04	Rotherham U	38	4		
2004–05	Rotherham U	31	1	**137**	**10**

NEWSHAM, Mark (M) **4** **0**
H: 5 10 W: 9 11 b.Hatfield 24-3-87
Source: Scholar.

2004–05	Rotherham U	4	0	**4**	**0**

POLLITT, Mike (G) **462** **0**
H: 6 4 W: 15 03 b.Farnworth 29-2-72
Source: Trainee.

1990–91	Manchester U	0	0		
1990–91	*Oldham Ath*	0	0		
1991–92	Bury	0	0		
1992–93	Lincoln C	27	0		
1993–94	Lincoln C	30	0	**57**	**0**
1994–95	Darlington	40	0		
1995–96	Darlington	15	0	**55**	**0**
1995–96	Notts Co	0	0		
1996–97	Notts Co	8	0		
1997–98	Notts Co	2	0	**10**	**0**
1997–98	*Oldham Ath*	16	0	**16**	**0**
1997–98	*Gillingham*	6	0	**6**	**0**
1997–98	*Brentford*	5	0	**5**	**0**
1997–98	Sunderland	0	0		
1998–99	Rotherham U	46	0		
1999–2000	Rotherham U	46	0		
2000–01	Chesterfield	46	0	**46**	**0**
2001–02	Rotherham U	46	0		
2002–03	Rotherham U	41	0		
2003–04	Rotherham U	43	0		
2004–05	Rotherham U	45	0	**267**	**0**

PROCTOR, Michael (F) **152** **34**
H: 6 0 W: 12 13 b.Sunderland 3-10-80
Source: Trainee.

1997–98	Sunderland	0	0		
1998–99	Sunderland	0	0		
1999–2000	Sunderland	0	0		
2000–01	Sunderland	0	0		
2000–01	*Halifax T*	12	4	**12**	**4**
2001–02	Sunderland	0	0		
2001–02	*York C*	41	14	**41**	**14**
2002–03	Sunderland	21	2		
2002–03	*Bradford C*	12	4	**12**	**4**
2003–04	Sunderland	17	1	**38**	**3**
2003–04	Rotherham U	17	6		
2004–05	Rotherham U	28	1	**45**	**7**
2004–05	*Swindon T*	4	2	**4**	**2**

SCOTT, Rob (D) **284** **33**
H: 6 0 W: 12 09 b.Epsom 15-8-73
Source: Sutton U.

1993–94	Sheffield U	0	0		
1994–95	Sheffield U	1	0		
1994–95	*Scarborough*	8	3	**8**	**3**
1995–96	Sheffield U	5	1	**6**	**1**
1995–96	*Northampton T*	5	0	**5**	**0**
1995–96	Fulham	21	5		
1996–97	Fulham	43	9		
1997–98	Fulham	17	3		
1998–99	Fulham	3	0	**84**	**17**
1998–99	*Carlisle U*	7	3	**7**	**3**
1998–99	Rotherham U	6	1		
1999–2000	Rotherham U	34	1		
2000–01	Rotherham U	39	2		
2001–02	Rotherham U	38	3		
2002–03	Rotherham U	23	0		
2003–04	Rotherham U	10	0		
2004–05	Rotherham U	24	2	**174**	**9**

SWAILES, Chris (D) **375** **25**
H: 6 2 W: 13 07 b.Gateshead 19-10-70
Source: Ipswich T Trainee, Peterborough U, Boston U, Birmingham C, Bridlington T.

1993–94	Doncaster R	17	0		
1994–95	Doncaster R	32	0	**49**	**0**
1995–96	Ipswich T	5	0		
1996–97	Ipswich T	23	1		
1997–98	Ipswich T	5	0	**33**	**1**
1997–98	Bury	13	1		
1998–99	Bury	43	3		
1999–2000	Bury	27	2		
2000–01	Bury	43	4	**126**	**10**
2001–02	Rotherham U	44	6		
2002–03	Rotherham U	43	3		
2003–04	Rotherham U	43	3		
2004–05	Rotherham U	37	2	**167**	**14**

VERNAZZA, Paulo (M) **137** **3**
H: 5 11 W: 12 03 b.Islington 1-11-79
Source: Trainee. *Honours:* England Youth, Under-21.

1997–98	Arsenal	1	0		
1998–99	Arsenal	0	0		
1998–99	*Ipswich T*	2	0	**2**	**0**
1999–2000	Arsenal	2	0		
1999–2000	*Portsmouth*	7	0	**7**	**0**
2000–01	Arsenal	2	1	**5**	**1**
2000–01	Watford	23	2		
2001–02	Watford	21	0		
2002–03	Watford	23	0		
2003–04	Watford	29	0	**96**	**2**
2004–05	Rotherham U	27	0	**27**	**0**

WARNE, Paul (M) **273** **32**
H: 5 10 W: 11 07 b.Norwich 8-5-73
Source: Wroxham.

1997–98	Wigan Ath	25	2		
1998–99	Wigan Ath	11	1	**36**	**3**
1998–99	Rotherham U	19	8		
1999–2000	Rotherham U	43	10		
2000–01	Rotherham U	44	7		
2001–02	Rotherham U	25	0		
2002–03	Rotherham U	40	1		
2003–04	Rotherham U	35	1		
2004–05	Rotherham U	24	1	**230**	**28**
2004–05	*Mansfield T*	7	1	**7**	**1**

RUSHDEN & D (69)

AFANDJYEV, Farhad (G) **0** **0**
Source: Hinckley U.

2004–05	Rushden & D	0	0		

ALLEN, Graham (D) **232** **11**
H: 6 1 W: 13 00 b.Bolton 8-4-77
Source: From Trainee. *Honours:* England Youth.

1994–95	Everton	0	0		
1995–96	Everton	0	0		
1996–97	Everton	1	0		
1997–98	Everton	5	0		
1998–99	Everton	0	0	**6**	**0**
1998–99	Tranmere R	41	5		
1999–2000	Tranmere R	24	0		
2000–01	Tranmere R	22	0		
2001–02	Tranmere R	31	1		
2002–03	Tranmere R	41	3		
2003–04	Tranmere R	41	1	**200**	**10**
2004–05	Rushden & D	26	1	**26**	**1**

BELL, David (M) **107** **7**
H: 5 10 W: 12 01 b.Kettering 21-1-84
Source: Trainee. *Honours:* Eire Youth, Under-21.

2001–02	Rushden & D	0	0		
2002–03	Rushden & D	30	3		
2003–04	Rushden & D	37	1		
2004–05	Rushden & D	40	3	**107**	**7**

BROUGHTON, Drewe (F) **211** **36**
H: 6 2 W: 13 06 b.Hitchin 25-10-78
Source: Trainee.

1996–97	Norwich C	8	1		
1997–98	Norwich C	1	0		
1997–98	*Wigan Ath*	4	0	**4**	**0**
1998–99	Norwich C	0	0	**9**	**1**
1998–99	Brentford	1	0	**1**	**0**
1998–99	Peterborough U	25	7		
1999–2000	Peterborough U	10	1		
2000–01	Peterborough U	0	0	**35**	**8**
2000–01	Kidderminster H	19	7		
2001–02	Kidderminster H	38	8		
2002–03	Kidderminster H	37	4	**94**	**19**
2003–04	Southend U	35	2		
2004–05	Southend U	9	0	**44**	**2**
2004–05	Rushden & D	21	6	**21**	**6**
2004–05	*Wycombe W*	3	0	**3**	**0**

BURGESS, Andy (M) **138** **10**
H: 6 2 W: 11 12 b.Bedford 10-8-81
Source: Juniors.

2001–02	Rushden & D	32	4		
2002–03	Rushden & D	27	1		
2003–04	Rushden & D	37	4		
2004–05	Rushden & D	42	1	**138**	**10**

CHALMER-STEVENS, Scott (G) **0** **0**

2004–05	Rushden & D	0	0		

CONNELLY, Sean (D) **428** **6**
H: 5 8 W: 11 08 b.Sheffield 26-6-70
Source: Hallam.

1991–92	Stockport Co	0	0		
1992–93	Stockport Co	7	0		
1993–94	Stockport Co	32	0		
1994–95	Stockport Co	39	0		
1995–96	Stockport Co	43	0		
1996–97	Stockport Co	45	0		
1997–98	Stockport Co	45	2		
1998–99	Stockport Co	35	1		
1999–2000	Stockport Co	43	3		
2000–01	Stockport Co	13	0	**302**	**6**
2000–01	Wolverhampton W	6	0		
2001–02	Wolverhampton W	8	0		
2002–03	Wolverhampton W	0	0	**14**	**0**
2002–03	Tranmere R	33	0		
2003–04	Tranmere R	37	0	**70**	**0**
2004–05	Rushden & D	42	0	**42**	**0**

DEMPSTER, John (D) **52** **1**
H: 6 0 W: 12 05 b.Kettering 1-4-83
Source: Trainee. *Honours:* Scotland Youth, Under-21.

2001–02	Rushden & D	2	0		
2002–03	Rushden & D	16	1		
2003–04	Rushden & D	19	0		
2004–05	Rushden & D	15	0	**52**	**1**

DOVE, Craig (F) **37** **6**
H: 5 8 W: 11 00 b.Hartlepool 16-8-83
Source: Scholar. *Honours:* England Youth, Under-20.

2000–01	Middlesbrough	0	0		
2001–02	Middlesbrough	0	0		
2002–03	Middlesbrough	0	0		
2003–04	Middlesbrough	0	0		
2003–04	*York C*	1	0	**1**	**0**
2004–05	Rushden & D	36	6	**36**	**6**

DUFFY, Robert (F) **29** **1**
H: 6 1 W: 13 01 b.Swansea 2-12-82
Source: Juniors. *Honours:* Wales Under-18.

2001–02	Rushden & D	8	1		
2002–03	Rushden & D	12	0		
2003–04	Rushden & D	8	0		
2004–05	Rushden & D	1	0	**29**	**1**

GIER, Rob (D) **103** **2**
H: 5 10 W: 11 00 b.Ascot 6-1-80
Source: Trainee.

1998–99	Wimbledon	0	0		
1999–2000	Wimbledon	0	0		
2000–01	Wimbledon	14	0		
2001–02	Wimbledon	3	0		
2002–03	Wimbledon	29	0		
2003–04	Wimbledon	25	0	**71**	**0**
2004–05	Rushden & D	32	2	**32**	**2**

GRAY, Stuart (M) **203** **16**
H: 5 10 W: 13 07 b.Harrogate 18-12-73
Source: Giffnock N. *Honours:* Scotland Under-21.

1992–93	Celtic	1	0		
1993–94	Celtic	0	0		
1994–95	Celtic	11	0		
1995–96	Celtic	5	1		
1996–97	Celtic	11	0		
1997–98	Celtic	0	0	**28**	**1**
1997–98	Reading	7	0		
1998–99	Reading	27	2		
1999–2000	Reading	15	0		

2000–01 Reading 3 0 **52 2**
2001–02 Rushden & D 12 0
2002–03 Rushden & D 38 7
2003–04 Rushden & D 35 5
2004–05 Rushden & D 38 1 **123 13**

GULLIVER, Phil (D) 54 0
H: 6 2 W: 14 09 b.Bishop Auckland 12-9-82
Source: Scholar.
2000–01 Middlesbrough 0 0
2001–02 Middlesbrough 0 0
2002–03 Middlesbrough 0 0
2002–03 *Blackpool* 3 0 **3 0**
2002–03 *Carlisle U* 1 0 **1 0**
2002–03 *Bournemouth* 6 0 **6 0**
2003–04 Middlesbrough 0 0
2003–04 *Bury* 10 0 **10 0**
2003–04 *Scunthorpe U* 2 0 **2 0**
2004–05 Rushden & D 32 0 **32 0**

HANLON, Ritchie (M) 123 11
H: 6 1 W: 13 09 b.Kenton 25-5-78
Source: Chelsea Trainee.
1996–97 Southend U 2 0
1997–98 Southend U 0 0 **2 0**
From Rushden & D.
1998–99 Peterborough U 4 1
From Welling U.
1999–2000 Peterborough U 16 1
2000–01 Peterborough U 26 1
2001–02 Peterborough U 1 0 **47 3**
2001–02 Rushden & D 35 6
2002–03 Rushden & D 0 0
2003–04 Rushden & D 27 1
From Stevenage B.
2004–05 Rushden & D 0 0 **62 7**
2004–05 *Lincoln C* 12 1 **12 1**

HAWKINS, Peter (D) 175 1
H: 6 0 W: 12 04 b.Maidstone 19-9-78
Source: Trainee.
1996–97 Wimbledon 0 0
1997–98 Wimbledon 0 0
1998–99 Wimbledon 0 0
1999–2000 Wimbledon 0 0
1999–2000 *York C* 14 0 **14 0**
2000–01 Wimbledon 30 0
2001–02 Wimbledon 29 0
2002–03 Wimbledon 43 0
2003–04 Wimbledon 18 0 **120 0**
2004–05 Rushden & D 41 1 **41 1**

HAY, Alex (F) 83 6
H: 6 0 W: 12 02 b.Birkenhead 14-10-81
Source: Scholarship.
1999–2000 Tranmere R 0 0
2000–01 Tranmere R 0 0
2001–02 Tranmere R 3 0
2002–03 Tranmere R 19 3
2003–04 Tranmere R 19 0 **41 3**
2004–05 Rushden & D 42 3 **42 3**

HUNTER, Barry (D) 287 16
H: 6 4 W: 12 06 b.Coleraine 18-11-68
Source: Crusaders. *Honours:* Northern Ireland Youth, B, 15 full caps, 1 goal.
1993–94 Wrexham 23 1
1994–95 Wrexham 37 0
1995–96 Wrexham 31 3 **91 4**
1996–97 Reading 27 2
1997–98 Reading 0 0
1998–99 Reading 3 0
1998–99 *Southend U* 5 2 **5 2**
1999–2000 Reading 31 1
2000–01 Reading 23 1
2001–02 Reading 0 0 **84 4**
2001–02 Rushden & D 23 1
2002–03 Rushden & D 40 1
2003–04 Rushden & D 43 4
2004–05 Rushden & D 1 0 **107 6**

JACKSON, Simeon (M) 3 0
H: 5 8 W: 11 00 b.Kingston, Jamaica 28-3-87
Source: Scholar.
2004–05 Rushden & D 3 0 **3 0**

KELLY, Marcus (M) 19 0
H: 5 7 W: 10 00 b.Ketteringham 16-3-86
Source: Juniors.
2003–04 Rushden & D 8 0
2004–05 Rushden & D 11 0 **19 0**

KENNEDY, Luke (M) 3 0
H: 6 1 W: 11 03 b.Peterborough 22-5-86
Source: Scholar.
2004–05 Rushden & D 3 0 **3 0**

LITTLEJOHN, Adrian (M) 418 71
H: 5 10 W: 11 05 b.Wolverhampton 26-9-71
Source: WBA Trainee.
1989–90 Walsall 11 0
1990–91 Walsall 33 1 **44 1**
1991–92 Sheffield U 7 0
1992–93 Sheffield U 27 8
1993–94 Sheffield U 19 3
1994–95 Sheffield U 16 1
1995–96 Plymouth Arg 42 17
1996–97 Plymouth Arg 37 6
1997–98 Plymouth Arg 31 6 **110 29**
1997–98 Oldham Ath 5 3
1998–99 Oldham Ath 16 2 **21 5**
1998–99 Bury 20 1
1999–2000 Bury 42 9
2000–01 Bury 37 4 **99 14**
2001–02 Sheffield U 3 0
2002–03 Sheffield U 0 0 **72 12**
2002–03 Port Vale 13 3
2003–04 Port Vale 36 7
2004–05 Port Vale 0 0 **49 10**
2004–05 Lincoln C 8 0 **8 0**
2004–05 Rushden & D 15 0 **15 0**

MANANGU, Eric (M) 1 0
b.DR Congo 9-9-85
Source: Scholar.
2003–04 Rushden & D 1 0
2004–05 Rushden & D 0 0 **1 0**

MILLS, Gary (M) 76 2
H: 5 9 W: 11 11 b.Sheppey 20-5-81
Source: Juniors.
2001–02 Rushden & D 9 0
2002–03 Rushden & D 30 0
2003–04 Rushden & D 30 1
2004–05 Rushden & D 7 1 **76 2**

NAYLOR, Stuart (G) 541 0
H: 6 4 W: 13 12 b.Wetherby 6-12-62
Source: Yorkshire Amateur. *Honours:* England Youth, B.
1980–81 Lincoln C 0 0
1981–82 Lincoln C 3 0
1982–83 Lincoln C 1 0
1982–83 *Peterborough U* 8 0 **8 0**
1983–84 Lincoln C 0 0
1983–84 *Crewe Alex* 38 0
1984–85 *Crewe Alex* 17 0 **55 0**
1984–85 Lincoln C 25 0
1985–86 Lincoln C 20 0 **49 0**
1985–86 WBA 12 0
1986–87 WBA 42 0
1987–88 WBA 35 0
1988–89 WBA 44 0
1989–90 WBA 39 0
1990–91 WBA 28 0
1991–92 WBA 34 0
1992–93 WBA 32 0
1993–94 WBA 20 0
1994–95 WBA 42 0
1995–96 WBA 27 0 **355 0**
1996–97 Bristol C 35 0
1997–98 Bristol C 2 0
1998–99 Bristol C 0 0 **37 0**
1998–99 *Mansfield T* 6 0 **6 0**
1998–99 Walsall 0 0
1999–2000 Exeter C 31 0
2000–01 Exeter C 0 0 **31 0**
2001–02 Rushden & D 0 0
2002–03 Rushden & D 0 0
2003–04 Rushden & D 0 0
2004–05 Rushden & D 0 0

OKUONGHAE, Magnus (F) 1 0
H: 6 3 W: 13 04 b.Nigeria 16-2-86
Source: Scholar.
2003–04 Rushden & D 1 0
2004–05 Rushden & D 0 0 **1 0**

SAMBROOK, Andrew (D) 70 0
H: 5 10 W: 11 09 b.Chatham 13-7-79
Source: Trainee.
1996–97 Gillingham 1 0
1997–98 Gillingham 0 0
1998–99 Gillingham 0 0 **1 0**
2001–02 Rushden & D 26 0
2002–03 Rushden & D 15 0
2003–04 Rushden & D 20 0
2004–05 Rushden & D 8 0 **69 0**

SEDDON, Gareth (F) 79 17
H: 5 11 W: 12 00 b.Burnley 23-5-80
Source: Atherstone U.
2001–02 Bury 35 6
2002–03 Bury 4 0
2003–04 Bury 40 11 **79 17**
2004–05 Rushden & D 0 0

TALBOT, Daniel (M) 23 1
H: 5 9 W: 11 00 b.Enfield 30-1-84
2001–02 Rushden & D 3 0
2002–03 Rushden & D 13 0
2003–04 Rushden & D 7 1
2004–05 Rushden & D 0 0 **23 1**

TAYLOR, Jason (M) 20 2
H: 6 2 W: 12 00 b.Burgess Hill 12-10-85
2004–05 Rushden & D 20 2 **20 2**

TURLEY, Billy (G) 176 0
H: 6 3 W: 15 11 b.Wolverhampton 15-7-73
Source: Evesham U.
1995–96 Northampton T 2 0
1996–97 Northampton T 1 0
1997–98 Northampton T 0 0
1997–98 *Leyton Orient* 14 0 **14 0**
1998–99 Northampton T 25 0 **28 0**
2001–02 Rushden & D 43 0
2002–03 Rushden & D 44 0
2003–04 Rushden & D 25 0
2004–05 Rushden & D 22 0 **134 0**

WARK, Scott (M) 1 0
H: 6 3 W: 13 04 b.Glasgow 9-6-87
Source: Scholar.
2004–05 Rushden & D 1 0 **1 0**

WORGAN, Lee (G) 12 0
H: 6 0 W: 11 02 b.Eastbourne 1-12-83
Source: From Scholar. *Honours:* Wales Youth, Under-21.
2003–04 Wimbledon 3 0 **3 0**
2003–04 *Wycombe W* 2 0 **2 0**
2004–05 Rushden & D 7 0 **7 0**

SCUNTHORPE U (70)

BARACLOUGH, Ian (M) 516 36
H: 6 1 W: 12 02 b.Leicester 4-12-70
Source: Trainee.
1988–89 Leicester C 0 0
1989–90 Leicester C 0 0
1989–90 *Wigan Ath* 9 2 **9 2**
1990–91 Leicester C 0 0
1990–91 *Grimsby T* 4 0
1991–92 Grimsby T 0 0
1992–93 Grimsby T 1 0 **5 0**
1992–93 Lincoln C 36 5
1993–94 Lincoln C 37 5 **73 10**
1994–95 Mansfield T 36 3
1995–96 Mansfield T 11 2 **47 5**
1995–96 Notts Co 35 2
1996–97 Notts Co 38 2
1997–98 Notts Co 38 6
1997–98 QPR 8 0
1998–99 QPR 43 1
1999–2000 QPR 45 0
2000–01 QPR 29 0 **125 1**
2001–02 Notts Co 33 3
2002–03 Notts Co 34 2
2003–04 Notts Co 34 0 **212 15**
2004–05 Scunthorpe U 45 3 **45 3**

BARWICK, Terry (M) 46 1
H: 5 11 W: 11 12 b.Doncaster 11-1-83
Source: Scholarship.
1999–2000 Scunthorpe U 1 0
2000–01 Scunthorpe U 0 0
2001–02 Scunthorpe U 10 0
2002–03 Scunthorpe U 5 0
2003–04 Scunthorpe U 30 1
2004–05 Scunthorpe U 0 0 **46 1**

BEAGRIE, Peter (M) 631 85
H: 5 8 W: 12 00 b.Middlesbrough 28-11-65
Source: Local. *Honours:* England Under-21, B.
1983–84 Middlesbrough 0 0
1984–85 Middlesbrough 7 1
1985–86 Middlesbrough 26 1 **33 2**
1986–87 Sheffield U 41 9
1987–88 Sheffield U 43 2 **84 11**
1988–89 Stoke C 41 7
1989–90 Stoke C 13 0 **54 7**
1989–90 Everton 19 0
1990–91 Everton 17 2
1991–92 Everton 27 3
1991–92 *Sunderland* 5 1 **5 1**
1992–93 Everton 22 3
1993–94 Everton 29 3
1993–94 Manchester C 9 1
1994–95 Manchester C 37 2
1995–96 Manchester C 5 0
1996–97 Manchester C 1 0 **52 3**
1997–98 Bradford C 34 0
1997–98 *Everton* 6 0 **120 11**
1998–99 Bradford C 43 12
1999–2000 Bradford C 35 7
2000–01 Bradford C 19 1 **131 20**
2000–01 Wigan Ath 10 1 **10 1**
2001–02 Scunthorpe U 40 11
2002–03 Scunthorpe U 34 5
2003–04 Scunthorpe U 32 11
2004–05 Scunthorpe U 36 2 **142 29**

BRIGHTON, Tom (M) 5 0
H: 5 10 W: 11 11 b.Irvine 28-3-84
Honours: Scotland Youth, Under-21.
2004–05 Scunthorpe U 5 0 **5 0**

BUTLER, Andy (D) 72 12
H: 6 2 W: 14 02 b.Doncaster 4-11-83
Source: Scholar.
2003–04 Scunthorpe U 35 2
2004–05 Scunthorpe U 37 10 **72 12**

BYRNE, Cliff (D) 81 2
H: 6 0 W: 12 11 b.Dublin 27-4-82
Honours: Eire Under-21.
1999–2000 Sunderland 0 0
2000–01 Sunderland 0 0
2001–02 Sunderland 0 0
2002–03 Sunderland 0 0
2002–03 *Scunthorpe U* 13 0
2003–04 Scunthorpe U 39 1
2004–05 Scunthorpe U 29 1 **81 2**

CAPP, Adam (G) 0 0
H: 6 4 W: 12 00 b.Scunthorpe 17-9-84
Source: Scholar.
2004–05 Scunthorpe U 0 0

CORDEN, Wayne (M) 266 36
H: 5 10 W: 12 04 b.Leek 1-11-75
Source: Trainee.
1994–95 Port Vale 1 0
1995–96 Port Vale 2 0
1996–97 Port Vale 12 0
1997–98 Port Vale 33 1
1998–99 Port Vale 16 0
1999–2000 Port Vale 2 0 **66 1**
2000–01 Mansfield T 34 3
2001–02 Mansfield T 46 8
2002–03 Mansfield T 44 13
2003–04 Mansfield T 44 8
2004–05 Mansfield T 24 3 **192 35**
2004–05 Scunthorpe U 8 0 **8 0**

CROSBY, Andy (D) 500 27
H: 6 2 W: 13 07 b.Rotherham 3-3-73
Source: Leeds U Trainee.
1991–92 Doncaster R 22 0
1992–93 Doncaster R 29 0
1993–94 Doncaster R 0 0 **51 0**
1993–94 Darlington 25 0
1994–95 Darlington 35 0
1995–96 Darlington 45 1
1996–97 Darlington 42 1
1997–98 Darlington 34 1 **181 3**
1998–99 Chester C 41 4 **41 4**
1999–2000 Brighton & HA 36 3
2000–01 Brighton & HA 34 2
2001–02 Brighton & HA 2 0 **72 5**
2001–02 Oxford U 23 1
2002–03 Oxford U 46 6
2003–04 Oxford U 42 5 **111 12**
2004–05 Scunthorpe U 44 3 **44 3**

EVANS, Tom (G) 227 0
H: 6 0 W: 13 02 b.Doncaster 31-12-76
Source: Trainee. *Honours:* Northern Ireland Youth.
1995–96 Sheffield U 0 0
1996–97 Crystal Palace 0 0
1996–97 *Coventry C* 0 0
1997–98 Scunthorpe U 5 0
1998–99 Scunthorpe U 24 0
1999–2000 Scunthorpe U 28 0
2000–01 Scunthorpe U 46 0
2001–02 Scunthorpe U 42 0
2002–03 Scunthorpe U 46 0
2003–04 Scunthorpe U 36 0
2004–05 Scunthorpe U 0 0 **227 0**

FEATHERSTONE, Lee (M) 32 0
H: 6 0 W: 12 08 b.Chesterfield 20-7-83
Source: Scholar.
2001–02 Sheffield U 0 0
2002–03 Sheffield U 0 0
2002–03 Scunthorpe U 20 0
2003–04 Scunthorpe U 11 0
2004–05 Scunthorpe U 1 0 **32 0**

GRAVES, Wayne (M) 135 6
H: 5 8 W: 11 07 b.Scunthorpe 18-9-80
Source: Trainee.
1997–98 Scunthorpe U 3 0
1998–99 Scunthorpe U 0 0
1999–2000 Scunthorpe U 19 0
2000–01 Scunthorpe U 34 2
2001–02 Scunthorpe U 17 3
2002–03 Scunthorpe U 41 1
2003–04 Scunthorpe U 21 0
2004–05 Scunthorpe U 0 0 **135 6**

GROVES, Paul (M) 627 101
H: 5 11 W: 13 04 b.Derby 28-2-66
Source: Burton Alb.
1987–88 Leicester C 1 1
1988–89 Leicester C 15 0
1989–90 Leicester C 0 0 **16 1**
1989–90 *Lincoln C* 8 1 **8 1**
1989–90 Blackpool 19 1
1990–91 Blackpool 46 11
1991–92 Blackpool 42 9 **107 21**
1992–93 Grimsby T 46 12
1993–94 Grimsby T 46 11
1994–95 Grimsby T 46 5
1995–96 Grimsby T 46 10
1996–97 WBA 29 4 **29 4**
1997–98 Grimsby T 46 7
1998–99 Grimsby T 46 14
1999–2000 Grimsby T 43 3
2000–01 Grimsby T 45 4
2001–02 Grimsby T 43 2
2002–03 Grimsby T 36 3
2003–04 Grimsby T 11 0 **454 71**
2003–04 Scunthorpe U 13 3
2004–05 Scunthorpe U 0 0 **13 3**

HAYES, Paul (F) 99 28
H: 6 0 W: 12 02 b.Dagenham 20-9-83
Source: Norwich C Scholar.
2002–03 Scunthorpe U 18 8
2003–04 Scunthorpe U 35 2
2004–05 Scunthorpe U 46 18 **99 28**

HUNT, Jon (D) 1 0
H: 5 10 W: 13 00 b.Leeds 11-9-84
Source: Scholar.
2003–04 Scunthorpe U 1 0
2004–05 Scunthorpe U 0 0 **1 0**

KELL, Richard (M) 98 11
H: 6 1 W: 12 00 b.Bishop Auckland 15-9-79
Source: Trainee.
1998–99 Middlesbrough 0 0
1999–2000 Middlesbrough 0 0
2000–01 Middlesbrough 0 0
2000–01 Torquay U 15 3
2001–02 Torquay U 0 0 **15 3**
2001–02 Scunthorpe U 16 1
2002–03 Scunthorpe U 0 0
2003–04 Scunthorpe U 24 2
2004–05 Scunthorpe U 43 5 **83 8**

KEOGH, Andrew (F) 29 5
H: 6 0 W: 11 06 b.Dublin 16-5-86
Source: Scholar. *Honours:* Eire Youth.
2003–04 Leeds U 0 0
2004–05 Leeds U 0 0
2004–05 *Bury* 4 2 **4 2**
2004–05 Scunthorpe U 25 3 **25 3**

MUSSELWHITE, Paul (G) 585 0
H: 6 2 W: 14 02 b.Portsmouth 22-12-68
Source: Apprentice.
1987–88 Portsmouth 0 0
1988–89 Scunthorpe U 41 0
1989–90 Scunthorpe U 29 0
1990–91 Scunthorpe U 38 0
1991–92 Scunthorpe U 24 0
1992–93 Port Vale 41 0
1993–94 Port Vale 46 0
1994–95 Port Vale 44 0
1995–96 Port Vale 39 0
1996–97 Port Vale 33 0
1997–98 Port Vale 41 0
1998–99 Port Vale 38 0
1999–2000 Port Vale 30 0 **312 0**
2000–01 Sheffield W 0 0
2000–01 Hull C 37 0
2001–02 Hull C 20 0
2002–03 Hull C 20 0
2003–04 Hull C 18 0 **95 0**
2004–05 Scunthorpe U 46 0 **178 0**

PARTON, Andy (F) 13 0
H: 5 10 W: 12 00 b.Doncaster 29-9-83
Source: Scholar.
2001–02 Scunthorpe U 1 0
2002–03 Scunthorpe U 8 0
2003–04 Scunthorpe U 3 0
2004–05 Scunthorpe U 1 0 **13 0**

PENN, Russell (M) 0 0
H: 5 11 W: 11 06 b.Dudley 8-11-85
Source: Scholar.
2004–05 Scunthorpe U 0 0

RANKINE, Michael (F) 21 1
H: 6 1 W: 14 12 b.Doncaster 15-1-85
2004–05 Scunthorpe U 21 1 **21 1**

RIDLEY, Lee (D) 79 1
H: 5 9 W: 11 09 b.Scunthorpe 5-12-81
Source: Scholar.
2000–01 Scunthorpe U 2 0
2001–02 Scunthorpe U 4 0
2002–03 Scunthorpe U 11 0
2003–04 Scunthorpe U 18 1
2004–05 Scunthorpe U 44 0 **79 1**

SHARP, Kevin (D) 295 12
H: 5 9 W: 11 01 b.Ontario 19-9-74
Source: Auxerre. *Honours:* England Schools, Youth.
1992–93 Leeds U 4 0
1993–94 Leeds U 10 0
1994–95 Leeds U 2 0
1995–96 Leeds U 1 0 **17 0**
1995–96 Wigan Ath 20 6
1996–97 Wigan Ath 35 2
1997–98 Wigan Ath 38 0
1998–99 Wigan Ath 31 2
1999–2000 Wigan Ath 21 0
2000–01 Wigan Ath 31 0
2001–02 Wigan Ath 2 0 **178 10**
2001–02 Wrexham 15 0 **15 0**
2002–03 Huddersfield T 39 0 **39 0**
2003–04 Scunthorpe U 40 2
2004–05 Scunthorpe U 6 0 **46 2**

SPARROW, Matt (M) 170 22
H: 5 11 W: 11 06 b.Wembley 3-10-81
Source: Scholarship.
1999–2000 Scunthorpe U 11 0
2000–01 Scunthorpe U 11 4
2001–02 Scunthorpe U 24 1
2002–03 Scunthorpe U 42 9
2003–04 Scunthorpe U 38 3
2004–05 Scunthorpe U 44 5 **170 22**

STANTON, Nathan (D) 215 0
H: 5 9 W: 11 03 b.Nottingham 6-5-81
Source: Trainee. *Honours:* England Youth.
1997–98 Scunthorpe U 1 0
1998–99 Scunthorpe U 4 0
1999–2000 Scunthorpe U 34 0

2000–01 Scunthorpe U 38 0
2001–02 Scunthorpe U 42 0
2002–03 Scunthorpe U 42 0
2003–04 Scunthorpe U 33 0
2004–05 Scunthorpe U 21 0 **215 0**

TAYLOR, Cleveland (M) 67 9
H: 5 8 W: 10 07 b.Leicester 9-9-83
Source: Scholar.
2001–02 Bolton W 0 0
2002–03 Bolton W 0 0
2002–03 *Exeter C* 3 0 **3 0**
2003–04 Bolton W 0 0
2003–04 Scunthorpe U 20 3
2004–05 Scunthorpe U 44 6 **64 9**

TORPEY, Steve (F) 540 137
H: 6 3 W: 14 13 b.Islington 8-12-70
Source: Trainee.
1988–89 Millwall 0 0
1989–90 Millwall 7 0
1990–91 Millwall 0 0 **7 0**
1990–91 Bradford C 29 7
1991–92 Bradford C 43 10
1992–93 Bradford C 24 5 **96 22**
1993–94 Swansea C 40 9
1994–95 Swansea C 41 11
1995–96 Swansea C 42 15
1996–97 Swansea C 39 9 **162 44**
1997–98 Bristol C 29 8
1998–99 Bristol C 21 4
1998–99 *Notts Co* 6 1 **6 1**
1999–2000 Bristol C 20 1 **70 13**
1999–2000 Scunthorpe U 15 1
2000–01 Scunthorpe U 40 10
2001–02 Scunthorpe U 39 13
2002–03 Scunthorpe U 28 10
2003–04 Scunthorpe U 43 11
2004–05 Scunthorpe U 34 12 **199 57**

WILLIAMS, Marcus (D) 5 0
H: 5 10 W: 10 07 b.Doncaster 8-4-86
Source: Scholar.
2003–04 Scunthorpe U 1 0
2004–05 Scunthorpe U 4 0 **5 0**

SHEFFIELD U (71)

ARMSTRONG, Chris (D) 110 3
H: 5 7 W: 11 08 b.Newcastle 5-8-82
Source: Scholar. *Honours:* England Under-20.
2000–01 Bury 22 1
2001–02 Bury 11 0 **33 1**
2001–02 Oldham Ath 32 0
2002–03 Oldham Ath 33 1 **65 1**
2003–04 Sheffield U 12 1
2004–05 Sheffield U 0 0 **12 1**

ASHMORE, James (M) 0 0
H: 5 8 W: 11 00 b.Sheffield 2-3-86
Source: Scholar.
2004–05 Sheffield U 0 0

BARNES, Phil (G) 149 0
H: 6 2 W: 15 04 b.Sheffield 2-3-79
Source: Trainee.
1996–97 Rotherham U 2 0 **2 0**
1997–98 Blackpool 1 0
1998–99 Blackpool 1 0
1999–2000 Blackpool 12 0
2000–01 Blackpool 34 0
2001–02 Blackpool 30 0
2002–03 Blackpool 44 0
2003–04 Blackpool 19 0 **141 0**
2004–05 Sheffield U 1 0 **1 0**
2004–05 *Torquay U* 5 0 **5 0**

BAXTER, Lee (G) 1 0
H: 6 1 W: 13 06 b.Helsingborg 17-7-76
Source: Malmo.
2003–04 Sheffield U 1 0
2004–05 Sheffield U 0 0 **1 0**

BECKETT, Luke (F) 241 104
H: 5 11 W: 11 02 b.Sheffield 25-11-76
Source: Trainee.
1995–96 Barnsley 0 0
1996–97 Barnsley 0 0
1997–98 Barnsley 0 0
1998–99 Chester C 28 11
1999–2000 Chester C 46 14 **74 25**
2000–01 Chesterfield 41 16
2001–02 Chesterfield 21 6 **62 22**
2001–02 Stockport Co 19 7
2002–03 Stockport Co 42 27
2003–04 Stockport Co 8 4
2004–05 Stockport Co 15 7 **84 45**
2004–05 Sheffield U 5 0 **5 0**
2004–05 *Huddersfield T* 7 6 **7 6**
2004–05 *Oldham Ath* 9 6 **9 6**

BRITTON, Andrew (G) 0 0
H: 6 1 W: 13 07 b.California 26-5-85
2003–04 Sheffield U 0 0
2004–05 Sheffield U 0 0

BROMBY, Leigh (D) 161 8
H: 6 0 W: 12 04 b.Dewsbury 2-6-80
Honours: England Schools.
1998–99 Sheffield W 0 0
1999–2000 Sheffield W 0 0
1999–2000 *Mansfield T* 10 1 **10 1**
2000–01 Sheffield W 18 0
2001–02 Sheffield W 26 1
2002–03 Sheffield W 27 0
2002–03 *Norwich C* 5 0 **5 0**
2003–04 Sheffield W 29 1 **100 2**
2004–05 Sheffield U 46 5 **46 5**

CADAMARTERI, Danny (F) 171 20
H: 5 7 W: 13 05 b.Bradford 12-10-79
Source: Trainee. *Honours:* England Youth, Under-21.
1996–97 Everton 1 0
1997–98 Everton 26 4
1998–99 Everton 30 4
1999–2000 Everton 17 1
1999–2000 *Fulham* 5 1 **5 1**
2000–01 Everton 16 4
2001–02 Everton 3 0 **93 13**
2001–02 Bradford C 14 2
2002–03 Bradford C 20 0
2003–04 Bradford C 18 3 **52 5**
2004–05 Leeds U 0 0
2004–05 Sheffield U 21 1 **21 1**

CULLIP, Danny (D) 297 9
H: 6 0 W: 12 12 b.Ascot 17-9-76
Source: Trainee.
1995–96 Oxford U 0 0
1996–97 Fulham 29 1
1997–98 Fulham 21 1 **50 2**
1997–98 Brentford 13 0
1998–99 Brentford 2 0
1999–2000 Brentford 0 0 **15 0**
1999–2000 Brighton & HA 33 2
2000–01 Brighton & HA 38 2
2001–02 Brighton & HA 44 0
2002–03 Brighton & HA 44 2
2003–04 Brighton & HA 40 1
2004–05 Brighton & HA 18 0 **217 7**
2004–05 Sheffield U 11 0 **11 0**
2004–05 *Watford* 4 0 **4 0**

FORTE, Jonathan (M) 29 1
H: 6 0 W: 12 06 b.Sheffield 25-7-86
Source: Scholar. *Honours:* England Youth.
2003–04 Sheffield U 7 0
2004–05 Sheffield U 22 1 **29 1**

FRANCIS, Simon (D) 66 1
H: 6 0 W: 14 09 b.Nottingham 16-2-85
Source: Scholar. *Honours:* England Youth, Under-20.
2002–03 Bradford C 25 1
2003–04 Bradford C 30 0 **55 1**
2003–04 Sheffield U 5 0
2004–05 Sheffield U 6 0 **11 0**

GABRIELI, Emanuele (D) 5 0
H: 5 11 W: 12 08 b.L'Aquila 31-12-80
2004–05 Sheffield U 1 0 **1 0**
2004–05 *Boston U* 4 0 **4 0**

GEARY, Derek (D) 136 1
H: 5 6 W: 10 08 b.Dublin 19-6-80
1997–98 Sheffield W 0 0
1998–99 Sheffield W 0 0
1999–2000 Sheffield W 0 0
2000–01 Sheffield W 5 0
2001–02 Sheffield W 32 0
2002–03 Sheffield W 26 0
2003–04 Sheffield W 41 0 **104 0**
2004–05 Stockport Co 13 0 **13 0**
2004–05 Sheffield U 19 1 **19 1**

GRAY, Andy (F) 235 46
H: 6 2 W: 14 02 b.Harrogate 15-11-77
Source: Trainee. *Honours:* Scotland Youth, 2 full caps.
1995–96 Leeds U 15 0
1996–97 Leeds U 7 0
1997–98 Leeds U 0 0
1997–98 *Bury* 6 1 **6 1**
1998–99 Leeds U 0 0 **22 0**
1998–99 Nottingham F 8 0
1998–99 *Preston NE* 5 0 **5 0**
1998–99 *Oldham Ath* 4 0 **4 0**
1999–2000 Nottingham F 22 0
2000–01 Nottingham F 18 0
2001–02 Nottingham F 16 1 **64 1**
2002–03 Bradford C 44 15
2003–04 Bradford C 33 5 **77 20**
2003–04 Sheffield U 14 9
2004–05 Sheffield U 43 15 **57 24**

HAIDONG, Hao (F) 0 0
H: 5 10 W: 11 00 b.Qingdao 9-5-70
Source: Dalian Shide.
2004–05 Sheffield U 0 0

HARLEY, Jon (D) 134 9
H: 5 8 W: 11 09 b.Maidstone 26-9-79
Source: From Trainee. *Honours:* England Under-21.
1996–97 Chelsea 0 0
1997–98 Chelsea 3 0
1998–99 Chelsea 0 0
1999–2000 Chelsea 17 2
2000–01 Chelsea 10 0 **30 2**
2000–01 *Wimbledon* 6 2 **6 2**
2001–02 Fulham 10 0
2002–03 Fulham 11 1
2002–03 *Sheffield U* 9 1
2003–04 Fulham 4 0 **25 1**
2003–04 *Sheffield U* 5 0
2003–04 *West Ham U* 15 1 **15 1**
2004–05 Sheffield U 44 2 **58 3**

HARPER, Adrian (M) 0 0
H: 5 9 W: 10 01 b.Dublin 4-5-85
Source: Scholar.
2004–05 Sheffield U 0 0

HAYSTEAD, Daniel (G) 0 0
H: 6 1 W: 11 09 b.Chesterfield 13-2-86
Source: Scholar.
2004–05 Sheffield U 0 0

HORWOOD, Evan (D) 10 0
H: 6 0 W: 10 06 b.Billingham 10-3-86
Source: Scholar.
2004–05 Sheffield U 0 0
2004–05 *Stockport Co* 10 0 **10 0**

HURST, Kevan (M) 22 2
H: 5 10 W: 11 07 b.Chesterfield 27-8-85
Source: Sheffield U Scholar.
2003–04 *Boston U* 7 1 **7 1**
2004–05 Sheffield U 1 0 **1 0**
2004–05 *Stockport Co* 14 1 **14 1**

JAGIELKA, Phil (D) 170 6
H: 5 11 W: 14 00 b.Manchester 17-8-82
Source: Scholar. *Honours:* England Youth, Under-20, Under-21.
1999–2000 Sheffield U 1 0
2000–01 Sheffield U 15 0
2001–02 Sheffield U 23 3
2002–03 Sheffield U 42 0
2003–04 Sheffield U 43 3
2004–05 Sheffield U 46 0 **170 6**

JOHNSON, Tommy (F) 357 113
H: 6 0 W: 12 11 b.Newcastle 15-1-71
Source: Trainee. *Honours:* England Under-21.
1988–89 Notts Co 10 4
1989–90 Notts Co 40 18
1990–91 Notts Co 37 16
1991–92 Notts Co 31 9 **118 47**
1991–92 Derby Co 12 2
1992–93 Derby Co 35 8
1993–94 Derby Co 37 13
1994–95 Derby Co 14 7 **98 30**
1994–95 Aston Villa 14 4
1995–96 Aston Villa 23 5
1996–97 Aston Villa 20 4 **57 13**
1996–97 Celtic 4 1

1997–98	Celtic	2	0		
1998–99	Celtic	3	3		
1999–2000	Celtic	10	9		
1999–2000	*Everton*	3	0	**3**	**0**
2000–01	Celtic	0	0		
2001–02	Celtic	0	0	**19**	**13**
2001–02	Sheffield W	8	3	**8**	**3**
2002–03	Gillingham	26	2		
2003–04	Gillingham	15	3		
2004–05	Gillingham	8	2	**49**	**7**
2004–05	Sheffield U	5	0	**5**	**0**

KABBA, Steven (F) **63 16**
H: 5 8 W: 12 06 b.Lambeth 7-3-81
Source: Trainee.

1999–2000	Crystal Palace	1	0		
2000–01	Crystal Palace	1	0		
2001–02	Crystal Palace	4	0		
2001–02	*Luton T*	3	0	**3**	**0**
2002–03	Crystal Palace	4	1	**10**	**1**
2002–03	*Grimsby T*	13	6	**13**	**6**
2002–03	Sheffield U	25	7		
2003–04	Sheffield U	1	0		
2004–05	Sheffield U	11	2	**37**	**9**

KENNY, Paddy (G) **245 0**
H: 6 0 W: 15 10 b.Halifax 17-5-78
Source: Bradford PA. *Honours:* Eire 5 full caps.

1998–99	Bury	0	0		
1999–2000	Bury	46	0		
2000–01	Bury	46	0		
2001–02	Bury	41	0		
2002–03	Bury	0	0	**133**	**0**
2002–03	Sheffield U	45	0		
2003–04	Sheffield U	27	0		
2004–05	Sheffield U	40	0	**112**	**0**

KOZLUK, Rob (D) **198 2**
H: 5 8 W: 11 07 b.Sutton-in-Ashfield 5-8-77
Source: Trainee. *Honours:* England Under-21.

1995–96	Derby Co	0	0		
1996–97	Derby Co	0	0		
1997–98	Derby Co	9	0		
1998–99	Derby Co	7	0	**16**	**0**
1998–99	Sheffield U	10	0		
1999–2000	Sheffield U	39	0		
2000–01	Sheffield U	27	0		
2000–01	*Huddersfield T*	14	0	**14**	**0**
2001–02	Sheffield U	8	0		
2002–03	Sheffield U	32	1		
2003–04	Sheffield U	42	1		
2004–05	Sheffield U	9	0	**167**	**2**
2004–05	*Preston NE*	1	0	**1**	**0**

LIDDELL, Andy (M) **448 107**
H: 5 7 W: 11 11 b.Leeds 28-6-73
Source: Trainee. *Honours:* Scotland Under-21.

1990–91	Barnsley	0	0		
1991–92	Barnsley	1	0		
1992–93	Barnsley	21	2		
1993–94	Barnsley	22	1		
1994–95	Barnsley	39	13		
1995–96	Barnsley	43	9		
1996–97	Barnsley	38	8		
1997–98	Barnsley	26	1		
1998–99	Barnsley	8	0	**198**	**34**
1998–99	Wigan Ath	28	10		
1999–2000	Wigan Ath	41	8		
2000–01	Wigan Ath	37	9		
2001–02	Wigan Ath	34	18		
2002–03	Wigan Ath	37	16		
2003–04	Wigan Ath	40	9	**217**	**70**
2004–05	Sheffield U	33	3	**33**	**3**

McCALL, Stuart (M) **763 67**
H: 5 8 W: 10 02 b.Leeds 10-6-64
Source: Apprentice. *Honours:* Scotland Under-21, 40 full caps, 1 goal.

1982–83	Bradford C	28	4		
1983–84	Bradford C	46	5		
1984–85	Bradford C	46	8		
1985–86	Bradford C	38	4		
1986–87	Bradford C	36	7		
1987–88	Bradford C	44	9		
1988–89	Everton	33	0		
1989–90	Everton	37	3		
1990–91	Everton	33	3	**103**	**6**
1991–92	Rangers	36	1		
1992–93	Rangers	36	5		
1993–94	Rangers	34	3		
1994–95	Rangers	30	2		
1995–96	Rangers	21	3		
1996–97	Rangers	7	0		
1997–98	Rangers	30	0	**194**	**14**
1998–99	Bradford C	43	3		
1999–2000	Bradford C	34	1		
2000–01	Bradford C	37	1		
2001–02	Bradford C	43	3	**395**	**45**
2002–03	Sheffield U	34	0		
2003–04	Sheffield U	37	2		
2004–05	Sheffield U	0	0	**71**	**2**

McFADZEAN, Kyle (D) **0 0**
H: 6 1 W: 13 04 b.Sheffield 20-2-87
Source: Scholar.

2004–05	Sheffield U	0	0		

MONTGOMERY, Nick (M) **142 6**
H: 5 8 W: 12 08 b.Leeds 28-10-81
Source: From Scholar. *Honours:* Scotland Under-21.

2000–01	Sheffield U	27	0		
2001–02	Sheffield U	31	2		
2002–03	Sheffield U	23	0		
2003–04	Sheffield U	36	3		
2004–05	Sheffield U	25	1	**142**	**6**

MORGAN, Chris (D) **258 10**
H: 6 0 W: 13 06 b.Barnsley 9-11-77
Source: Trainee.

1996–97	Barnsley	0	0		
1997–98	Barnsley	11	0		
1998–99	Barnsley	19	0		
1999–2000	Barnsley	37	0		
2000–01	Barnsley	40	1		
2001–02	Barnsley	42	4		
2002–03	Barnsley	36	2	**185**	**7**
2003–04	Sheffield U	32	1		
2004–05	Sheffield U	41	2	**73**	**3**

NDLOVU, Peter (F) **425 88**
H: 5 7 W: 10 02 b.Bulawayo 25-2-73
Source: Highlanders. *Honours:* Zimbabwe full caps.

1991–92	Coventry C	23	2		
1992–93	Coventry C	32	7		
1993–94	Coventry C	40	11		
1994–95	Coventry C	30	11		
1995–96	Coventry C	32	5		
1996–97	Coventry C	20	1	**177**	**37**
1997–98	Birmingham C	39	9		
1998–99	Birmingham C	43	10		
1999–2000	Birmingham C	13	1		
2000–01	Birmingham C	12	2	**107**	**22**
2000–01	*Huddersfield T*	6	4	**6**	**4**
2000–01	Sheffield U	15	4		
2001–02	Sheffield U	45	4		
2002–03	Sheffield U	39	8		
2003–04	Sheffield U	36	9		
2004–05	Sheffield U	0	0	**135**	**25**

QUINN, Alan (M) **206 23**
H: 5 9 W: 11 09 b.Dublin 13-6-79
Source: Cherry Orchard. *Honours:* Eire Youth, Under-21, 6 full caps.

1997–98	Sheffield W	1	0		
1998–99	Sheffield W	1	0		
1999–2000	Sheffield W	19	3		
2000–01	Sheffield W	37	2		
2001–02	Sheffield W	38	2		
2002–03	Sheffield W	37	5		
2003–04	Sheffield W	24	4	**157**	**16**
2003–04	*Sunderland*	6	0	**6**	**0**
2004–05	Sheffield U	43	7	**43**	**7**

ROMA, Dominic (D) **2 0**
H: 5 9 W: 12 04 b.Sheffield 29-11-85
Source: Scholar. *Honours:* England Youth.

2004–05	Sheffield U	0	0		
2004–05	*Boston U*	2	0	**2**	**0**

ROSS, Ian (M) **0 0**
H: 5 11 W: 11 07 b.Sheffield 23-1-86
Source: Scholar.

2004–05	Sheffield U	0	0		

SHARP, Billy (F) **18 9**
H: 5 8 W: 12 02 b.Sheffield 5-2-86
Source: Scholar.

2004–05	Sheffield U	2	0	**2**	**0**
2004–05	*Rushden & D*	16	9	**16**	**9**

SHAW, Paul (F) **326 73**
H: 5 10 W: 13 01 b.Burnham 4-9-73
Source: Trainee.

1991–92	Arsenal	0	0		
1992–93	Arsenal	0	0		
1993–94	Arsenal	0	0		
1994–95	Arsenal	1	0		
1994–95	*Burnley*	9	4	**9**	**4**
1995–96	Arsenal	3	0		
1995–96	*Cardiff C*	6	0	**6**	**0**
1995–96	*Peterborough U*	12	5	**12**	**5**
1996–97	Arsenal	8	2		
1997–98	Arsenal	0	0	**12**	**2**
1997–98	Millwall	40	11		
1998–99	Millwall	34	10		
1999–2000	Millwall	35	5	**109**	**26**
2000–01	Gillingham	33	1		
2001–02	Gillingham	37	7		
2002–03	Gillingham	44	12		
2003–04	Gillingham	21	6	**135**	**26**
2003–04	Sheffield U	13	1		
2004–05	Sheffield U	21	7	**34**	**8**
2004–05	*Rotherham U*	9	2	**9**	**2**

THIRLWELL, Paul (M) **119 1**
H: 6 2 W: 12 02 b.Springwell 13-2-79
Source: Trainee. *Honours:* England Under-21.

1996–97	Sunderland	0	0		
1997–98	Sunderland	0	0		
1998–99	Sunderland	2	0		
1999–2000	Sunderland	8	0		
1999–2000	*Swindon T*	12	0	**12**	**0**
2000–01	Sunderland	5	0		
2001–02	Sunderland	14	0		
2002–03	Sunderland	19	0		
2003–04	Sunderland	29	0	**77**	**0**
2004–05	Sheffield U	30	1	**30**	**1**

TONGE, Michael (M) **156 15**
H: 5 10 W: 12 06 b.Manchester 7-4-83
Source: Scholar. *Honours:* England Under-20, Under-21.

2000–01	Sheffield U	2	0		
2001–02	Sheffield U	30	3		
2002–03	Sheffield U	44	6		
2003–04	Sheffield U	46	4		
2004–05	Sheffield U	34	2	**156**	**15**

TRAVIS, Nicholas (M) **0 0**
H: 5 9 W: 10 10 b.Sheffield 12-3-87
Source: Scholar.

2004–05	Sheffield U	0	0		

WARD, Ashley (F) **388 110**
H: 6 0 W: 13 10 b.Manchester 24-11-70
Source: Trainee.

1989–90	Manchester C	1	0		
1990–91	Manchester C	0	0	**1**	**0**
1990–91	*Wrexham*	4	2	**4**	**2**
1991–92	Leicester C	10	0		
1992–93	Leicester C	0	0	**10**	**0**
1992–93	*Blackpool*	2	1	**2**	**1**
1992–93	Crewe Alex	20	4		
1993–94	Crewe Alex	25	13		
1994–95	Crewe Alex	16	8	**61**	**25**
1994–95	Norwich C	25	8		
1995–96	Norwich C	28	10	**53**	**18**
1995–96	Derby Co	7	1		
1996–97	Derby Co	30	8		
1997–98	Derby Co	3	0	**40**	**9**
1997–98	Barnsley	29	8		
1998–99	Barnsley	17	12	**46**	**20**
1998–99	Blackburn R	17	5		
1999–2000	Blackburn R	37	8	**54**	**13**
2000–01	Bradford C	33	4		
2001–02	Bradford C	27	10		
2002–03	Bradford C	24	3	**84**	**17**
2003–04	Sheffield U	23	4		
2004–05	Sheffield U	10	1	**33**	**5**

WRIGHT, Alan (D) **469 7**
H: 5 3 W: 9 13 b.Ashton-under-Lyne 28-9-71
Source: Trainee. *Honours:* England Schools, Youth, Under-21.

1987–88	Blackpool	1	0		
1988–89	Blackpool	16	0		
1989–90	Blackpool	24	0		
1990–91	Blackpool	45	0		
1991–92	Blackpool	12	0	**98**	**0**

1991–92 Blackburn R 33 1
1992–93 Blackburn R 24 0
1993–94 Blackburn R 12 0
1994–95 Blackburn R 5 0 **74** **1**
1994–95 Aston Villa 8 0
1995–96 Aston Villa 38 2
1996–97 Aston Villa 38 1
1997–98 Aston Villa 37 0
1998–99 Aston Villa 38 0
1999–2000 Aston Villa 32 1
2000–01 Aston Villa 36 1
2001–02 Aston Villa 23 0
2002–03 Aston Villa 10 0 **260** **5**
2003–04 Middlesbrough 2 0 **2** **0**
2003–04 Sheffield U 21 1
2004–05 Sheffield U 14 0 **35** **1**

SHEFFIELD W (72)

ADAMS, Steve (M) **166** **7**
H: 6 0 W: 12 01 b.Plymouth 25-9-80
Source: Trainee.
1999–2000 Plymouth Arg 1 0
2000–01 Plymouth Arg 17 0
2001–02 Plymouth Arg 46 2
2002–03 Plymouth Arg 37 2
2003–04 Plymouth Arg 36 2
2004–05 Plymouth Arg 20 1 **157** **7**
2004–05 Sheffield W 9 0 **9** **0**

ADAMSON, Chris (G) **24** **0**
H: 6 0 W: 11 07 b.Ashington 4-11-78
Source: Trainee.
1997–98 WBA 3 0
1998–99 WBA 0 0
1998–99 *Mansfield T* 2 0 **2** **0**
1999–2000 WBA 9 0
1999–2000 *Halifax T* 7 0 **7** **0**
2000–01 WBA 0 0
2001–02 WBA 0 0 **12** **0**
2001–02 *Plymouth Arg* 1 0 **1** **0**
From St Patrick's At
2004–05 Sheffield W 2 0 **2** **0**

ARANALDE, Zigor (D) **197** **5**
H: 6 1 W: 13 03 b.Ibarra 28-2-73
Source: Logrones.
2000–01 Walsall 45 0
2001–02 Walsall 45 2
2002–03 Walsall 39 3
2003–04 Walsall 36 0
2004–05 Walsall 30 0 **195** **5**
2004–05 Sheffield W 2 0 **2** **0**

BRUNT, Chris (M) **51** **6**
H: 6 1 W: 13 02 b.Belfast 14-12-84
Source: Trainee. *Honours:* Northern Ireland Under-21, Under-23, 2 full caps.
2002–03 Middlesbrough 0 0
2003–04 Middlesbrough 0 0
2003–04 Sheffield W 9 2
2004–05 Sheffield W 42 4 **51** **6**

BULLEN, Lee (D) **46** **7**
H: 6 1 W: 12 08 b.Edinburgh 29-3-71
2004–05 Sheffield W 46 7 **46** **7**

CARR, Chris (D) **2** **0**
H: 6 1 W: 12 07 b.Newcastle 14-12-84
Source: Trainee.
2003–04 Newcastle U 0 0
2003–04 Sheffield W 2 0
2004–05 Sheffield W 0 0 **2** **0**

COLLINS, Patrick (D) **28** **1**
H: 6 2 W: 12 07 b.Newcastle 4-2-85
Source: Scholar. *Honours:* England Youth, Under-20.
2001–02 Sunderland 0 0
2002–03 Sunderland 0 0
2003–04 Sunderland 0 0
2004–05 Sheffield W 28 1 **28** **1**

DRURY, Martin (D) **0** **0**
H: 5 9 W: 11 00 b.Huddersfield 10-4-86
Source: Trainee.
2003–04 Doncaster R 0 0
2004–05 Sheffield W 0 0

EVANS, Richard (M) **10** **1**
H: 5 10 W: 12 05 b.Cardiff 19-6-83
Source: Scholar.
2002–03 Birmingham C 0 0
2002–03 Sheffield W 4 1
2003–04 Sheffield W 6 0
2004–05 Sheffield W 0 0 **10** **1**

FOSTER, Luke (D) **0** **0**
H: 6 2 W: 12 08 b.Mexborough 8-9-85
Source: Scholar.
2004–05 Sheffield W 0 0

GREENWOOD, Ross (D) **2** **0**
H: 5 11 W: 11 02 b.York 1-11-85
2004–05 Sheffield W 2 0 **2** **0**

HAMSHAW, Matthew (M) **74** **2**
H: 5 9 W: 12 08 b.Rotherham 1-1-82
Source: Trainee. *Honours:* England Youth, Under-20.
1998–99 Sheffield W 0 0
1999–2000 Sheffield W 0 0
2000–01 Sheffield W 18 0
2001–02 Sheffield W 21 0
2002–03 Sheffield W 15 1
2003–04 Sheffield W 0 0
2004–05 Sheffield W 20 1 **74** **2**

HECKINGBOTTOM, Paul (D) **245** **10**
H: 6 0 W: 12 12 b.Barnsley 17-7-77
Source: Manchester U Trainee.
1995–96 Sunderland 0 0
1996–97 Sunderland 0 0
1997–98 Sunderland 0 0
1997–98 *Scarborough* 29 0 **29** **0**
1998–99 Sunderland 0 0
1998–99 *Hartlepool U* 5 1 **5** **1**
1998–99 *Darlington* 10 0
1999–2000 Darlington 45 1
2000–01 Darlington 18 1
2001–02 Darlington 42 3 **115** **5**
2002–03 Norwich C 15 0 **15** **0**
2003–04 Bradford C 43 0 **43** **0**
2004–05 Sheffield W 38 4 **38** **4**

LEE, Graeme (D) **271** **23**
H: 6 2 W: 13 07 b.Middlesbrough 31-5-78
Source: Trainee.
1995–96 Hartlepool U 6 0
1996–97 Hartlepool U 24 0
1997–98 Hartlepool U 37 3
1998–99 Hartlepool U 24 3
1999–2000 Hartlepool U 38 7
2000–01 Hartlepool U 6 0
2001–02 Hartlepool U 39 4
2002–03 Hartlepool U 45 2 **219** **19**
2003–04 Sheffield W 30 3
2004–05 Sheffield W 22 1 **52** **4**

LUCAS, David (G) **191** **0**
H: 6 1 W: 13 06 b.Preston 23-11-77
Source: Trainee. *Honours:* England Youth.
1995–96 Preston NE 1 0
1995–96 *Darlington* 6 0
1996–97 Preston NE 2 0
1996–97 *Darlington* 7 0 **13** **0**
1996–97 *Scunthorpe U* 6 0 **6** **0**
1997–98 Preston NE 6 0
1998–99 Preston NE 30 0
1999–2000 Preston NE 6 0
2000–01 Preston NE 29 0
2001–02 Preston NE 24 0
2002–03 Preston NE 21 0
2003–04 Preston NE 2 0 **121** **0**
2003–04 *Sheffield W* 17 0
2004–05 Sheffield W 34 0 **51** **0**

MACLEAN, Steve (F) **81** **41**
H: 5 10 W: 12 01 b.Edinburgh 23-8-82
Honours: Scotland Under-21.
2002–03 Rangers 3 0 **3** **0**
2003–04 Scunthorpe U 42 23 **42** **23**
2004–05 Sheffield W 36 18 **36** **18**

MARSDEN, Chris (M) **423** **22**
H: 6 0 W: 12 07 b.Sheffield 3-1-69
Source: Trainee.
1986–87 Sheffield U 0 0
1987–88 Sheffield U 16 1 **16** **1**
1988–89 Huddersfield T 14 1
1989–90 Huddersfield T 32 2
1990–91 Huddersfield T 43 5
1991–92 Huddersfield T 23 1
1992–93 Huddersfield T 7 0
1993–94 Huddersfield T 2 0 **121** **9**
1993–94 *Coventry C* 7 0 **7** **0**
1993–94 Wolverhampton W 8 0
1994–95 Wolverhampton W 0 0 **8** **0**
1994–95 Notts Co 7 0
1995–96 Notts Co 3 0 **10** **0**
1995–96 Stockport Co 20 1
1996–97 Stockport Co 35 2
1997–98 Stockport Co 10 0 **65** **3**
1997–98 Birmingham C 32 1
1998–99 Birmingham C 20 2 **52** **3**
1998–99 Southampton 14 2
1999–2000 Southampton 21 0
2000–01 Southampton 23 0
2001–02 Southampton 28 3
2002–03 Southampton 30 1
2003–04 Southampton 13 0 **129** **6**
2004–05 Sheffield W 15 0 **15** **0**

McARDLE, Rory (D) **0** **0**
H: 6 1 W: 11 11 b.Doncaster 1-5-87
Source: Scholar.
2004–05 Sheffield W 0 0

McGOVERN, John-Paul (M) **61** **7**
H: 5 8 W: 11 11 b.Glasgow 3-10-80
Source: Celtic BC.
2001–02 Celtic 0 0
2002–03 Celtic 0 0
2002–03 *Sheffield U* 15 1 **15** **1**
2003–04 Celtic 0 0
2004–05 Sheffield W 46 6 **46** **6**

McMAHON, Lewis (M) **25** **2**
H: 5 9 W: 11 06 b.Doncaster 2-5-85
Source: Scholar.
2003–04 Sheffield W 10 0
2004–05 Sheffield W 15 2 **25** **2**

NEEDHAM, Liam (M) **0** **0**
H: 5 11 W: 12 02 b.Sheffield 19-10-85
Source: Scholar.
2004–05 Sheffield W 0 0

NIXON, Eric (G) **524** **0**
H: 6 4 W: 15 07 b.Manchester 4-10-62
Source: Curzon Ashton.
1983–84 Manchester C 0 0
1984–85 Manchester C 0 0
1985–86 Manchester C 28 0
1986–87 Manchester C 5 0
1986–87 *Wolverhampton W* 16 0 **16** **0**
1986–87 *Bradford C* 3 0
1986–87 *Southampton* 4 0 **4** **0**
1986–87 *Carlisle U* 16 0 **16** **0**
1987–88 Manchester C 25 0 **58** **0**
1987–88 *Tranmere R* 8 0
1988–89 Tranmere R 45 0
1989–90 Tranmere R 46 0
1990–91 Tranmere R 43 0
1991–92 Tranmere R 46 0
1992–93 Tranmere R 45 0
1993–94 Tranmere R 42 0
1994–95 Tranmere R 41 0
1995–96 Tranmere R 0 0
1995–96 *Blackpool* 20 0 **20** **0**
1996–97 Tranmere R 25 0
1996–97 *Bradford C* 12 0 **15** **0**
1997–98 Stockport Co 43 0
1998–99 Stockport Co 0 0 **43** **0**
1998–99 Wigan Ath 3 0 **3** **0**
1999–2000 Tranmere R 2 0
2000–01 Tranmere R 0 0
2001–02 Kidderminster H 2 0 **2** **0**
2001–02 Tranmere R 1 0
2002–03 Tranmere R 2 0 **346** **0**
2003–04 Sheffield W 1 0
2004–05 Sheffield W 0 0 **1** **0**

OLSEN, Kim (F) **10** **0**
H: 6 4 W: 13 07 b.Herning 11-2-79
Source: Midtjylland.
2003–04 Sheffield W 10 0
2004–05 Sheffield W 0 0 **10** **0**

PEACOCK, Lee (F) **346** **98**
H: 6 0 W: 13 00 b.Paisley 9-10-76
Source: Trainee. *Honours:* Scotland Youth, Under-21.
1993–94 Carlisle U 1 0

1994–95	Carlisle U	7	0		
1995–96	Carlisle U	22	2		
1996–97	Carlisle U	44	9		
1997–98	Carlisle U	2	0	**76**	**11**
1997–98	Mansfield T	32	5		
1998–99	Mansfield T	45	17		
1999–2000	Mansfield T	12	7	**89**	**29**
1999–2000	Manchester C	8	0	**8**	**0**
2000–01	Bristol C	35	13		
2001–02	Bristol C	31	15		
2002–03	Bristol C	37	12		
2003–04	Bristol C	41	14	**144**	**54**
2004–05	Sheffield W	29	4	**29**	**4**

POULTER, Robert (G) **0** **0**
H: 5 11 W: 13 00 b.Sheffield 2-2-86
Source: Scholar.

2003–04	Sheffield W	0	0		
2004–05	Sheffield W	0	0		

PROUDLOCK, Adam (F) **132** **28**
H: 6 0 W: 13 12 b.Wellington 9-5-81
Source: Trainee.

1999–2000	Wolverhampton W	0	0		
2000–01	*Clyde*	4	4	**4**	**4**
2000–01	Wolverhampton W	35	8		
2001–02	Wolverhampton W	19	3		
2001–02	*Nottingham F*	3	0	**3**	**0**
2002–03	Wolverhampton W	17	2		
2002–03	*Tranmere R*	5	0	**5**	**0**
2002–03	*Sheffield W*	5	2		
2003–04	Wolverhampton W	0	0	**71**	**13**
2003–04	Sheffield W	30	3		
2004–05	Sheffield W	14	6	**49**	**11**

QUINN, James (M) **297** **52**
H: 6 1 W: 12 10 b.Coventry 15-12-74
Source: Trainee. *Honours:* Northern Ireland Youth, Under-21, B, 37 full caps, 4 goals.

1992–93	Birmingham C	4	0	**4**	**0**
1993–94	Blackpool	14	2		
1993–94	*Stockport Co*	1	0	**1**	**0**
1994–95	Blackpool	41	9		
1995–96	Blackpool	44	9		
1996–97	Blackpool	38	13		
1997–98	Blackpool	14	4	**151**	**37**
1997–98	WBA	13	2		
1998–99	WBA	43	6		
1999–2000	WBA	37	0		
2000–01	WBA	14	1		
2001–02	WBA	7	0		
2001–02	*Notts Co*	6	3	**6**	**3**
2001–02	*Bristol R*	6	1	**6**	**1**
2002–03	WBA	0	0		
2003–04	WBA	0	0	**114**	**9**
2004–05	Sheffield W	15	2	**15**	**2**

ROCASTLE, Craig (M) **18** **1**
H: 6 1 W: 12 13 b.Lewisham 17-8-81
Source: Kingstonian.

2003–04	Chelsea	0	0		
2003–04	*Barnsley*	5	0	**5**	**0**
2003–04	*Lincoln C*	2	0	**2**	**0**
2004–05	Chelsea	0	0		
2004–05	Sheffield W	11	1	**11**	**1**

SHAW, Jon (F) **26** **2**
H: 6 0 W: 13 01 b.Sheffield 10-11-83
Source: Scholar.

2002–03	Sheffield W	1	0		
2003–04	Sheffield W	14	2		
2003–04	*York C*	8	0	**8**	**0**
2004–05	Sheffield W	3	0	**18**	**2**

SMITH, Paul (M) **198** **11**
H: 6 1 W: 13 00 b.Easington 22-1-76
Source: Trainee.

1993–94	Burnley	1	0		
1994–95	Burnley	0	0		
1995–96	Burnley	10	0		
1996–97	Burnley	37	4		
1997–98	Burnley	14	0		
1998–99	Burnley	12	0		
1999–2000	Burnley	24	0		
2000–01	Burnley	14	1	**112**	**5**
2000–01	*Oldham Ath*	4	0	**4**	**0**
2001–02	Torquay U	0	0		
2001–02	Hartlepool U	31	4		
2002–03	Hartlepool U	24	0	**55**	**4**
2003–04	Sheffield W	19	2		
2004–05	Sheffield W	8	0	**27**	**2**

TALBOT, Drew (F) **21** **4**
H: 5 10 W: 11 00 b.Barnsley 19-7-86
Source: Trainee.

2003–04	Sheffield W	0	0		
2004–05	Sheffield W	21	4	**21**	**4**

TIDMAN, Ola (G) **59** **0**
H: 6 2 W: 12 07 b.Malmo 11-5-79
Honours: Sweden Under-21.

1998	Malmo	1	0		
1999	Malmo	14	0		
2000	Malmo	6	0	**21**	**0**
2000–01	Gent	0	0		
2001–02	La Louviere	6	0		
2002–03	La Louviere	1	0	**7**	**0**
2002–03	Stockport Co	18	0	**18**	**0**
2003–04	Sheffield W	9	0		
2004–05	Sheffield W	4	0	**13**	**0**

WHELAN, Glenn (M) **49** **2**
H: 5 11 W: 12 07 b.Dublin 13-1-84
Source: Scholar. *Honours:* Eire Youth, Under-21.

2000–01	Manchester C	0	0		
2001–02	Manchester C	0	0		
2002–03	Manchester C	0	0		
2003–04	Manchester C	0	0		
2003–04	*Bury*	13	0	**13**	**0**
2004–05	Sheffield W	36	2	**36**	**2**

WILSON, Laurie (M) **0** **0**
H: 5 10 W: 11 00 b.Brighton 5-12-84
Source: Scholar. *Honours:* Northern Ireland Youth.

2003–04	Sheffield W	0	0		
2004–05	Sheffield W	0	0		

WOOD, Richard (D) **49** **2**
H: 6 3 W: 12 03 b.Ossett 5-7-85
Source: Scholar.

2002–03	Sheffield W	3	1		
2003–04	Sheffield W	12	0		
2004–05	Sheffield W	34	1	**49**	**2**

SHREWSBURY T (73)

ADAGGIO, Marco (F) **5** **0**
H: 5 8 W: 12 04 b.Malaga 6-10-87

2004–05	Shrewsbury T	5	0	**5**	**0**

AISTON, Sam (M) **194** **7**
H: 6 1 W: 12 10 b.Newcastle 21-11-76
Source: Newcastle U Trainee. *Honours:* England Schools.

1995–96	Sunderland	14	0		
1996–97	Sunderland	2	0		
1996–97	*Chester C*	14	0		
1997–98	Sunderland	3	0		
1998–99	Sunderland	1	0		
1998–99	*Chester C*	11	0	**25**	**0**
1999–2000	Sunderland	0	0	**20**	**0**
1999–2000	*Stoke C*	6	0	**6**	**0**
1999–2000	*Shrewsbury T*	10	0		
2000–01	Shrewsbury T	42	2		
2001–02	Shrewsbury T	35	2		
2002–03	Shrewsbury T	21	2		
2003–04	Shrewsbury T	0	0		
2004–05	Shrewsbury T	35	1	**143**	**7**

BRIGGS, Mark (M) **0** **0**
H: 6 0 W: 11 07 b.Wolverhampton 16-2-82
Source: Scholar.

2000–01	WBA	0	0		
2001–02	WBA	0	0		
2002–03	WBA	0	0		
2003–04	Notts Co	0	0		
2004–05	Notts Co	0	0		
2004–05	Shrewsbury T	0	0		

CHALLIS, Trevor (D) **196** **1**
H: 5 8 W: 11 05 b.Paddington 23-10-75
Source: Trainee. *Honours:* England Youth, Under-21.

1994–95	QPR	0	0		
1995–96	QPR	11	0		
1996–97	QPR	2	0		
1997–98	QPR	0	0	**13**	**0**
1998–99	Bristol R	38	0		
1999–2000	Bristol R	40	1		
2000–01	Bristol R	22	0		
2001–02	Bristol R	29	0		
2002–03	Bristol R	16	0	**145**	**1**

From Telford U.

2004–05	Shrewsbury T	38	0	**38**	**0**

CLAMPITT, Carl (M) **0** **0**
H: 6 0 W: 12 07 b.Birkenhead 13-12-84
Source: Cammel Laird.

2004–05	Shrewsbury T	0	0		

COWAN, Gavin (D) **5** **0**
H: 6 4 W: 12 06 b.Hanover 24-5-81
Source: Braintree T, Canvey Island.

2004–05	Shrewsbury T	5	0	**5**	**0**

DARBY, Duane (F) **334** **86**
H: 5 11 W: 12 06 b.Birmingham 17-10-73
Source: Trainee.

1991–92	Torquay U	14	2		
1992–93	Torquay U	34	12		
1993–94	Torquay U	36	8		
1994–95	Torquay U	24	4	**108**	**26**
1995–96	Doncaster R	17	4	**17**	**4**
1995–96	Hull C	8	1		
1996–97	Hull C	41	13		
1997–98	Hull C	29	13		
1998–99	Notts Co	0	0		
1998–99	*Hull C*	8	0	**86**	**27**
1999–2000	Notts Co	28	5		
2000–01	Notts Co	0	0	**28**	**5**
2001–02	Rushden & D	30	7		
2002–03	Rushden & D	37	14		
2003–04	Rushden & D	12	2	**79**	**23**
2004–05	Shrewsbury T	16	1	**16**	**1**

EDWARDS, Dave (M) **28** **5**
H: 5 11 W: 11 05 b.Shrewsbury 3-2-86
Source: Scholar. *Honours:* Wales Youth.

2002–03	Shrewsbury T	1	0		
2003–04	Shrewsbury T	0	0		
2004–05	Shrewsbury T	27	5	**28**	**5**

GRANT, John (F) **26** **2**
H: 5 11 W: 10 08 b.Manchester 9-8-81
Source: Trainee.

1999–2000	Crewe Alex	4	0		
2000–01	Crewe Alex	2	0		
2001–02	Crewe Alex	1	0	**7**	**0**
2001–02	*Rushden & D*	0	0		

From Here U, Telfd U

2004–05	Shrewsbury T	19	2	**19**	**2**

HART, Joe (G) **6** **0**
H: 6 3 W: 13 03 b.Shrewsbury 19-4-87

2004–05	Shrewsbury T	6	0	**6**	**0**

HOWIE, Scott (G) **341** **0**
H: 6 2 W: 13 07 b.Motherwell 4-1-72
Source: Ferguslie U. *Honours:* Scotland Under-21.

1991–92	Clyde	15	0		
1992–93	Clyde	39	0		
1993–94	Clyde	1	0	**55**	**0**
1993–94	Norwich C	2	0	**2**	**0**
1994–95	Motherwell	3	0		
1995–96	Motherwell	36	0		
1996–97	Motherwell	30	0		
1997–98	Motherwell	0	0	**69**	**0**
1997–98	Reading	7	0		
1998–99	Reading	42	0		
1999–2000	Reading	36	0		
2000–01	Reading	0	0	**85**	**0**
2001–02	Bristol R	46	0		
2002–03	Bristol R	44	0	**90**	**0**
2003–04	Shrewsbury T	0	0		
2004–05	Shrewsbury T	40	0	**40**	**0**

LANGMEAD, Kelvin (F) **51** **5**
H: 6 1 W: 12 00 b.Coventry 23-3-85
Source: Scholar.

2003–04	Preston NE	1	0		
2003–04	*Carlisle U*	11	1	**11**	**1**
2004–05	Preston NE	1	0	**2**	**0**
2004–05	*Kidderminster H*	10	1	**10**	**1**
2004–05	Shrewsbury T	28	3	**28**	**3**

LYNG, Ciaran (M) **4** **0**
H: 5 11 W: 12 08 b.Wexford 24-7-85
Source: Scholar. *Honours:* Eire Youth.

2003–04	Preston NE	0	0		
2004–05	Preston NE	0	0		
2004–05	Shrewsbury T	4	0	**4**	**0**

O'CONNOR, Martin (M) **380 43**
H: 5 9 W: 11 08 b.Walsall 10-12-67
Source: Bromsgrove R. *Honours:* Cayman Islands 2 full caps.

1992–93	Crystal Palace	0	0		
1992–93	*Walsall*	10	1		
1993–94	Crystal Palace	2	0	**2**	**0**
1993–94	Walsall	14	2		
1994–95	Walsall	39	10		
1995–96	Walsall	41	9		
1996–97	Peterborough U	18	3	**18**	**3**
1996–97	Birmingham C	24	4		
1997–98	Birmingham C	33	1		
1998–99	Birmingham C	37	4		
1999–2000	Birmingham C	39	2		
2000–01	Birmingham C	30	5		
2001–02	Birmingham C	24	0	**187**	**16**
2001–02	Walsall	13	1		
2002–03	Walsall	35	1	**152**	**24**
2003–04	Shrewsbury T	0	0		
2004–05	Shrewsbury T	21	0	**21**	**0**

RIDLER, Dave (D) **181 1**
H: 6 1 W: 12 02 b.Liverpool 12-3-76
Source: Prescot T.

1996–97	Wrexham	11	0		
1997–98	Wrexham	20	0		
1998–99	Wrexham	36	1		
1999–2000	Wrexham	25	0		
2000–01	Wrexham	24	0	**116**	**1**
2001–02	Macclesfield T	39	0		
2002–03	Macclesfield T	17	0	**56**	**0**
From Scarborough.					
2004–05	Shrewsbury T	9	0	**9**	**0**

RODGERS, Luke (F) **142 52**
H: 5 7 W: 11 00 b.Birmingham 1-1-82
Source: Trainee.

1999–2000	Shrewsbury T	6	1		
2000–01	Shrewsbury T	26	7		
2001–02	Shrewsbury T	38	22		
2002–03	Shrewsbury T	36	16		
2003–04	Shrewsbury T	0	0		
2004–05	Shrewsbury T	36	6	**142**	**52**

SEDGEMORE, Jake (D) **31 5**
H: 6 1 W: 12 10 b.Wolverhampton 10-10-78
Source: WBA, Hednesford T, Hereford U, Northwich Vic.

2004–05	Shrewsbury T	31	5	**31**	**5**

SHERON, Mike (F) **488 126**
H: 5 10 W: 12 07 b.St Helens 11-1-72
Source: Trainee. *Honours:* England Under-21.

1990–91	Manchester C	0	0		
1990–91	*Bury*	5	1	**5**	**1**
1991–92	Manchester C	29	7		
1992–93	Manchester C	38	11		
1993–94	Manchester C	33	6	**100**	**24**
1994–95	Norwich C	21	1		
1995–96	Norwich C	7	1	**28**	**2**
1995–96	Stoke C	28	15		
1996–97	Stoke C	41	19	**69**	**34**
1997–98	QPR	40	11		
1998–99	QPR	23	8	**63**	**19**
1998–99	Barnsley	15	2		
1999–2000	Barnsley	36	9		
2000–01	Barnsley	34	1		
2001–02	Barnsley	33	12		
2002–03	Barnsley	34	9	**152**	**33**
2003–04	Blackpool	38	8	**38**	**8**
2004–05	Macclesfield T	26	3	**26**	**3**
2004–05	Shrewsbury T	7	2	**7**	**2**

SMITH, Ben (M) **13 3**
H: 5 10 W: 12 13 b.Chelmsford 23-11-78
Source: Yeovil T.

2001–02	Southend U	1	0	**1**	**0**
From Hereford U					
2004–05	Shrewsbury T	12	3	**12**	**3**

STEPHENS, Ross (M) **3 0**
H: 5 10 W: 10 09 b.Landiloes 28-5-85
Source: Scholar.

2002–03	Shrewsbury T	1	0		
2003–04	Shrewsbury T	0	0		
2004–05	Shrewsbury T	2	0	**3**	**0**

STREET, Kevin (M) **171 12**
H: 5 10 W: 10 08 b.Crewe 25-11-77
Source: Trainee.

1996–97	Crewe Alex	0	0		
1997–98	Crewe Alex	32	4		
1998–99	Crewe Alex	23	2		
1999–2000	Crewe Alex	28	1		
2000–01	Crewe Alex	23	1		
2001–02	*Luton T*	2	0	**2**	**0**
2001–02	Crewe Alex	9	1		
2002–03	Crewe Alex	0	0	**115**	**9**
From Northwich Vic.					
2002–03	Bristol R	20	1		
2003–04	Bristol R	13	1	**33**	**2**
2004–05	Shrewsbury T	21	1	**21**	**1**

TINSON, Darren (D) **306 5**
H: 6 0 W: 12 12 b.Birmingham 15-11-69
Source: Northwich V.

1997–98	Macclesfield T	44	0		
1998–99	Macclesfield T	37	0		
1999–2000	Macclesfield T	46	1		
2000–01	Macclesfield T	45	3		
2001–02	Macclesfield T	46	1		
2002–03	Macclesfield T	45	0	**263**	**5**
2003–04	Shrewsbury T	0	0		
2004–05	Shrewsbury T	43	0	**43**	**0**

TOLLEY, Jamie (M) **124 10**
H: 6 0 W: 11 03 b.Ludlow 12-5-83
Source: Scholarship. *Honours:* Wales Under-21.

1999–2000	Shrewsbury T	2	0		
2000–01	Shrewsbury T	24	2		
2001–02	Shrewsbury T	23	1		
2002–03	Shrewsbury T	39	3		
2003–04	Shrewsbury T	0	0		
2004–05	Shrewsbury T	36	4	**124**	**10**

WALTON, David (D) **317 15**
H: 6 2 W: 14 08 b.Bedlington 10-4-73
Source: Trainee.

1991–92	Sheffield U	0	0		
1992–93	Sheffield U	0	0		
1993–94	Sheffield U	0	0		
1993–94	Shrewsbury T	27	5		
1994–95	Shrewsbury T	36	3		
1995–96	Shrewsbury T	35	0		
1996–97	Shrewsbury T	24	1		
1997–98	Shrewsbury T	6	1		
1997–98	Crewe Alex	27	0		
1998–99	Crewe Alex	38	1		
1999–2000	Crewe Alex	11	0		
2000–01	Crewe Alex	20	0		
2001–02	Crewe Alex	31	1		
2002–03	Crewe Alex	28	1	**155**	**3**
2003–04	Derby Co	5	0	**5**	**0**
2003–04	*Stockport Co*	7	0	**7**	**0**
2004–05	Shrewsbury T	22	2	**150**	**12**

WHITEHEAD, Stuart (D) **215 2**
H: 6 0 W: 12 02 b.Bromsgrove 17-7-77
Source: Bromsgrove R.

1995–96	Bolton W	0	0		
1996–97	Bolton W	0	0		
1997–98	Bolton W	0	0		
1998–99	Carlisle U	37	0		
1999–2000	Carlisle U	29	0		
2000–01	Carlisle U	45	1		
2001–02	Carlisle U	32	1		
2002–03	Carlisle U	9	0	**152**	**2**
2002–03	Darlington	23	0	**23**	**0**
From Telford U					
2004–05	Shrewsbury T	40	0	**40**	**0**

SOUTHAMPTON (74)

ANACLET, Edward (F) **0 0**
H: 5 9 W: 10 00 b.Tanzania 31-8-85
Source: Scholar.

2004–05	Southampton	0	0		

BAIRD, Chris (D) **25 0**
H: 5 10 W: 11 11 b.Ballymoney 25-2-82
Source: From Scholar. *Honours:* Northern Ireland Under-21, 16 full caps.

2000–01	Southampton	0	0		
2001–02	Southampton	0	0		
2002–03	Southampton	3	0		
2003–04	Southampton	4	0		
2003–04	*Walsall*	10	0	**10**	**0**
2003–04	*Watford*	8	0	**8**	**0**
2004–05	Southampton	0	0	**7**	**0**

BERNARD, Olivier (D) **125 8**
H: 5 9 W: 10 10 b.Paris 14-10-79

2000–01	Newcastle U	0	0		
2000–01	*Darlington*	10	2	**10**	**2**
2001–02	Newcastle U	16	3		
2002–03	Newcastle U	30	2		
2003–04	Newcastle U	35	1		
2004–05	Newcastle U	21	0	**102**	**6**
2004–05	Southampton	13	0	**13**	**0**

BEST, Leon (F) **8 0**
H: 6 1 W: 13 03 b.Nottingham 19-9-86
Source: Scholar. *Honours:* Eire Youth.

2004–05	Southampton	3	0	**3**	**0**
2004–05	*QPR*	5	0	**5**	**0**

BLACKSTOCK, Dexter (F) **23 5**
H: 6 2 W: 13 00 b.Oxford 20-5-86
Source: Scholar. *Honours:* England Youth.

2004–05	Southampton	9	1	**9**	**1**
2004–05	*Plymouth Arg*	14	4	**14**	**4**

BLAYNEY, Alan (G) **18 0**
H: 6 2 W: 13 12 b.Belfast 9-10-81
Source: Scholar. *Honours:* Northern Ireland Under-21.

2001–02	Southampton	0	0		
2002–03	Southampton	0	0		
2002–03	*Stockport Co*	2	0	**2**	**0**
2002–03	*Bournemouth*	2	0	**2**	**0**
2003–04	Southampton	2	0		
2004–05	Southampton	1	0	**3**	**0**
2004–05	*Rushden & D*	4	0	**4**	**0**
2004–05	*Brighton & HA*	7	0	**7**	**0**

CRANIE, Martin (M) **7 0**
H: 6 1 W: 12 09 b.Yeovil 23-9-86
Source: Scholar. *Honours:* England Youth, Under-20.

2003–04	Southampton	1	0		
2004–05	Southampton	3	0	**4**	**0**
2004–05	*Bournemouth*	3	0	**3**	**0**

CROUCH, Peter (F) **158 50**
H: 6 7 W: 13 03 b.Macclesfield 30-1-81
Source: Trainee. *Honours:* England Youth, Under-20, Under-21, 1 full cap.

1998–99	Tottenham H	0	0		
1999–2000	Tottenham H	0	0		
2000–01	QPR	42	10	**42**	**10**
2001–02	Portsmouth	37	18	**37**	**18**
2001–02	Aston Villa	7	2		
2002–03	Aston Villa	14	0		
2003–04	Aston Villa	16	4	**37**	**6**
2003–04	*Norwich C*	15	4	**15**	**4**
2004–05	Southampton	27	12	**27**	**12**

DELAP, Rory (M) **284 23**
H: 6 3 W: 13 00 b.Sutton Coldfield 6-7-76
Source: Trainee. *Honours:* Eire 11 full caps.

1992–93	Carlisle U	1	0		
1993–94	Carlisle U	1	0		
1994–95	Carlisle U	3	0		
1995–96	Carlisle U	19	3		
1996–97	Carlisle U	32	4		
1997–98	Carlisle U	9	0	**65**	**7**
1997–98	Derby Co	13	0		
1998–99	Derby Co	23	0		
1999–2000	Derby Co	34	8		
2000–01	Derby Co	33	3	**103**	**11**
2001–02	Southampton	28	2		
2002–03	Southampton	24	0		
2003–04	Southampton	27	1		
2004–05	Southampton	37	2	**116**	**5**

DELGADO, Agustin (F) **165 73**
H: 6 3 W: 13 08 b.Ibarra 23-12-74
Honours: Ecuador 54 full caps, 22 goals.

1996	Nacional	30	18	**30**	**18**
1997	Barcelona	25	12		
1998	Barcelona	9	3	**34**	**15**
1998–99	Cruz Azul	8	2	**8**	**2**
1998–99	Necaxa	15	5		
1999–2000	Necaxa	33	25		
2000–01	Necaxa	34	8	**82**	**38**
2001–02	Southampton	1	0		
2002–03	Southampton	6	0		
2003–04	Southampton	4	0		
2004–05	Southampton	0	0	**11**	**0**

DODD, Jason (D) **402 9**
H: 5 10 W: 12 11 b.Bath 2-11-70
Source: Bath C. *Honours:* England Under-21.

1988–89	Southampton	0	0		
1989–90	Southampton	22	0		
1990–91	Southampton	19	0		
1991–92	Southampton	28	0		
1992–93	Southampton	30	1		
1993–94	Southampton	10	0		
1994–95	Southampton	26	2		
1995–96	Southampton	37	2		
1996–97	Southampton	23	1		
1997–98	Southampton	36	1		
1998–99	Southampton	28	1		
1999–2000	Southampton	31	0		
2000–01	Southampton	31	1		
2001–02	Southampton	29	0		
2002–03	Southampton	15	0		
2003–04	Southampton	28	0		
2004–05	Southampton	5	0	**398**	**9**
2004–05	*Plymouth Arg*	4	0	**4**	**0**

FERNANDES, Fabrice (M) **161 11**
H: 5 8 W: 10 07 b.Aubervilliers 29-10-79

1998–99	Rennes	15	2		
1999–2000	Rennes	17	1		
2000–01	Fulham	29	2	**29**	**2**
2000–01	Rangers	4	1	**4**	**1**
2001–02	Marseille	4	0	**4**	**0**
2001–02	Southampton	11	1		
2001–02	Rennes	1	0	**33**	**3**
2002–03	Southampton	37	3		
2003–04	Southampton	27	1		
2004–05	Southampton	16	0	**91**	**5**

FOLLY, Yoann (M) **15 0**
H: 5 9 W: 11 04 b.Togo 6-6-85
Source: St Etienne. *Honours:* France Youth.

2003–04	Southampton	9	0		
2004–05	Southampton	3	0	**12**	**0**
2004–05	*Nottingham F*	1	0	**1**	**0**
2004–05	*Preston NE*	2	0	**2**	**0**

GILLETT, Simon (M) **0 0**
H: 5 6 W: 11 07 b.London 6-11-85
Source: Trainee.

2003–04	Southampton	0	0		
2004–05	Southampton	0	0		

GRIFFIT, Leandre (M) **10 2**
H: 5 8 W: 11 04 b.Maubeuge 21-5-84
Source: Amiens.

2003–04	Southampton	5	2		
2003–04	Southampton	0	0		
2004–05	Southampton	2	0	**7**	**2**
2004–05	*Leeds U*	1	0	**1**	**0**
2004–05	*Rotherham U*	2	0	**2**	**0**

HIGGINBOTHAM, Danny (D) **147 4**
H: 6 2 W: 13 01 b.Manchester 29-12-78
Source: Trainee.

1997–98	Manchester U	1	0		
1998–99	Manchester U	0	0		
1999–2000	Manchester U	3	0	**4**	**0**
2000–01	Derby Co	26	0		
2001–02	Derby Co	37	1		
2002–03	Derby Co	23	2	**86**	**3**
2002–03	Southampton	9	0		
2003–04	Southampton	27	0		
2004–05	Southampton	21	1	**57**	**1**

JAKOBSSON, Andreas (D) **426 18**
H: 6 2 W: 13 00 b.Utanfor 6-10-72
Honours: Sweden 36 full caps, 2 goals.

1990	Landskrona	5	0		
1991	Landskrona	24	0		
1992	Landskrona	28	0		
1993	Landskrona	25	2		
1994	Landskrona	17	0	**99**	**2**
1995	Helsingborg	25	2		
1996	Helsingborg	26	0		
1997	Helsingborg	25	1		
1998	Helsingborg	26	1		
1999	Helsingborg	25	0		
2000	Helsingborg	8	1	**135**	**5**
2000–01	Hansa Rostock	34	1		
2000–01	Hansa Rostock	34	1		
2001–02	Hansa Rostock	32	2		
2002–03	Hansa Rostock	33	1	**133**	**5**
2003–04	Brondby	32	4	**32**	**4**
2004–05	Southampton	27	2	**27**	**2**

JONES, Kenwyne (F) **22 10**
H: 6 2 W: 13 06 b.Trinidad & Tobago 5-10-84
Source: W.Connection. *Honours:* Trinidad & Tobago 18 full caps.

2004–05	Southampton	2	0	**2**	**0**
2004–05	*Sheffield W*	7	7	**7**	**7**
2004–05	*Stoke C*	13	3	**13**	**3**

KENTON, Darren (D) **184 9**
H: 5 10 W: 12 06 b.Wandsworth 13-9-78
Source: Trainee.

1997–98	Norwich C	11	0		
1998–99	Norwich C	22	1		
1999–2000	Norwich C	26	1		
2000–01	Norwich C	29	2		
2001–02	Norwich C	33	4		
2002–03	Norwich C	37	1	**158**	**9**
2002–03	Southampton	0	0		
2003–04	Southampton	7	0		
2004–05	Southampton	9	0	**16**	**0**
2004–05	*Leicester C*	10	0	**10**	**0**

LE SAUX, Graeme (D) **403 20**
H: 5 10 W: 12 00 b.Jersey 17-10-68
Source: St Pauls. *Honours:* England Under-21, B, 36 full caps, 1 goal.

1987–88	Chelsea	0	0		
1988–89	Chelsea	1	0		
1989–90	Chelsea	7	1		
1990–91	Chelsea	28	4		
1991–92	Chelsea	40	3		
1992–93	Chelsea	14	0		
1992–93	Blackburn R	9	0		
1993–94	Blackburn R	41	2		
1994–95	Blackburn R	39	3		
1995–96	Blackburn R	14	1		
1996–97	Blackburn R	26	1	**129**	**7**
1997–98	Chelsea	26	1		
1998–99	Chelsea	31	0		
1999–2000	Chelsea	8	0		
2000–01	Chelsea	20	0		
2001–02	Chelsea	27	1		
2002–03	Chelsea	28	2	**230**	**12**
2003–04	Southampton	19	0		
2004–05	Southampton	25	1	**44**	**1**

LUNDEKVAM, Claus (D) **343 2**
H: 6 3 W: 13 05 b.Austevoll 22-2-73
Honours: Norway Under-21, 37 full caps, 1 goal.

1993	Brann	3	0		
1994	Brann	20	0		
1995	Brann	14	0		
1996	Brann	16	1	**53**	**1**
1996–97	Southampton	29	0		
1997–98	Southampton	31	0		
1998–99	Southampton	33	0		
1999–2000	Southampton	27	0		
2000–01	Southampton	38	0		
2001–02	Southampton	34	0		
2002–03	Southampton	33	0		
2003–04	Southampton	31	1		
2004–05	Southampton	34	0	**290**	**1**

MACDONALD, Chris (D) **0 0**
H: 6 1 W: 14 00 b.Wycombe 28-12-85
Source: Trainee.

2002–03	Southampton	0	0		
2003–04	Southampton	0	0		
2004–05	Southampton	0	0		

McCANN, Neil (M) **294 42**
H: 5 10 W: 11 00 b.Greenock 11-8-74
Source: Port Glasgow BC. *Honours:* Scotland Under-21, B, 23 full caps, 3 goals.

1992–93	Dundee	3	0		
1993–94	Dundee	22	1		
1994–95	Dundee	32	2		
1995–96	Dundee	22	2	**79**	**5**
1996–97	Hearts	30	5		
1997–98	Hearts	35	10		
1998–99	Hearts	8	3	**73**	**18**
1998–99	Rangers	19	5		
1999–2000	Rangers	30	3		
2000–01	Rangers	21	3		
2001–02	Rangers	25	7		
2002–03	Rangers	18	1	**113**	**19**
2003–04	Southampton	18	0		
2004–05	Southampton	11	0	**29**	**0**

McNEIL, Andrew (G) **0 0**
H: 5 11 W: 13 03 b.Edinburgh 19-1-87
Source: Scholar.

2004–05	Southampton	0	0		

MILLS, Matthew (D) **16 3**
H: 6 3 W: 12 12 b.Swindon 14-7-86
Source: From Scholar. *Honours:* England Youth.

2004–05	Southampton	0	0		
2004–05	*Coventry C*	4	0	**4**	**0**
2004–05	*Bournemouth*	12	3	**12**	**3**

NIEMI, Antti (G) **332 0**
H: 6 1 W: 12 04 b.Oulu 31-5-72
Honours: Finland Youth, Under-21, 66 full caps.

1991	HJK Helsinki	2	0		
1992	HJK Helsinki	28	0		
1993	HJK Helsinki	24	0		
1994	HJK Helsinki	24	0		
1995	HJK Helsinki	24	0	**102**	**0**
1995–96	FC Copenhagen	17	0		
1996–97	FC Copenhagen	30	0	**47**	**0**
1997–98	Rangers	5	0		
1998–99	Rangers	7	0		
1999–2000	Rangers	1	0	**13**	**0**
1999–2000	Hearts	17	0		
2000–01	Hearts	37	0		
2001–02	Hearts	32	0		
2002–03	Hearts	3	0	**89**	**0**
2002–03	Southampton	25	0		
2003–04	Southampton	28	0		
2004–05	Southampton	28	0	**81**	**0**

NILSSON, Mikael (M) **142 28**
H: 5 10 W: 12 00 b.Kristianstad 24-6-78
Source: Ovesholm. *Honours:* Sweden 25 full caps, 3 goals.

1999	Ahus Horna	22	11	**22**	**11**
2000	Halmstad	14	1		
2001	Halmstad	26	6		
2002	Halmstad	26	5		
2003	Halmstad	25	3		
2004	Halmstad	13	2	**104**	**17**
2004–05	Southampton	16	0	**16**	**0**

OAKLEY, Matthew (M) **232 12**
H: 5 10 W: 12 06 b.Peterborough 17-8-77
Source: Trainee. *Honours:* England Under-21.

1994–95	Southampton	1	0		
1995–96	Southampton	10	0		
1996–97	Southampton	28	3		
1997–98	Southampton	33	1		
1998–99	Southampton	22	2		
1999–2000	Southampton	31	3		
2000–01	Southampton	35	1		
2001–02	Southampton	27	1		
2002–03	Southampton	31	0		
2003–04	Southampton	7	0		
2004–05	Southampton	7	1	**232**	**12**

ORMEROD, Brett (F) **220 58**
H: 5 10 W: 11 12 b.Blackburn 18-10-76
Source: Blackburn R Trainee, Accrington S.

1996–97	Blackpool	4	0		
1997–98	Blackpool	9	2		
1998–99	Blackpool	40	8		
1999–2000	Blackpool	13	5		
2000–01	Blackpool	41	17		
2001–02	Blackpool	21	13	**128**	**45**
2001–02	Southampton	18	1		
2002–03	Southampton	31	5		
2003–04	Southampton	22	5		
2004–05	Southampton	9	0	**80**	**11**
2004–05	*Leeds U*	6	0	**6**	**0**
2004–05	*Wigan Ath*	6	2	**6**	**2**

PAHARS, Marian (F) **247 93**
H: 5 8 W: 10 08 b.Latvia 5-8-76
Honours: Latvia 63 full caps, 15 goals.

1994	Pardaugava Riga	17	3	**17**	**3**
1995	Skonto/Metals Riga	16	4	**16**	**4**
1995	Skonto Riga	9	8		
1996	Skonto Riga	28	12		
1997	Skonto Riga	22	5		
1998	Skonto Riga	26	19	**85**	**44**
1998–99	Southampton	6	3		
1999–2000	Southampton	33	13		
2000–01	Southampton	31	9		

2001–02	Southampton	36	14		
2002–03	Southampton	9	1		
2003–04	Southampton	14	2		
2004–05	Southampton	0	0	**129**	**42**

PHILLIPS, Kevin (F) **331 159**
H: 5 7 W: 12 00 b.Hitchin 25-7-73
Source: Baldock T. *Honours:* England B, 8 full caps.

1994–95	Watford	16	9		
1995–96	Watford	27	11		
1996–97	Watford	16	4	**59**	**24**
1997–98	Sunderland	43	29		
1998–99	Sunderland	26	23		
1999–2000	Sunderland	36	30		
2000–01	Sunderland	34	14		
2001–02	Sunderland	37	11		
2002–03	Sunderland	32	6	**208**	**113**
2003–04	Southampton	34	12		
2004–05	Southampton	30	10	**64**	**22**

POKE, Michael (G) **0 0**
H: 6 1 W: 13 12 b.Spelthorne 21-11-85
Source: Trainee.

2003–04	Southampton	0	0		
2004–05	Southampton	0	0		

PRUTTON, David (M) **205 9**
H: 5 10 W: 13 00 b.Hull 12-9-81
Source: Trainee. *Honours:* England Youth, Under-21.

1998–99	Nottingham F	0	0		
1999–2000	Nottingham F	34	2		
2000–01	Nottingham F	42	1		
2001–02	Nottingham F	43	3		
2002–03	Nottingham F	24	1	**143**	**7**
2002–03	Southampton	12	0		
2003–04	Southampton	27	1		
2004–05	Southampton	23	1	**62**	**2**

QUASHIE, Nigel (M) **262 19**
H: 5 9 W: 12 08 b.Nunhead 20-7-78
Source: Trainee. *Honours:* England Youth, Under-21, B, Scotland 7 full caps, 1 goal.

1995–96	QPR	11	0		
1996–97	QPR	13	0		
1997–98	QPR	33	3		
1998–99	QPR	0	0	**57**	**3**
1998–99	Nottingham F	16	0		
1999–2000	Nottingham F	28	2	**44**	**2**
2000–01	Portsmouth	31	5		
2001–02	Portsmouth	35	2		
2002–03	Portsmouth	42	5		
2003–04	Portsmouth	21	1		
2004–05	Portsmouth	19	0	**148**	**13**
2004–05	Southampton	13	1	**13**	**1**

REDKNAPP, Jamie (M) **314 34**
H: 6 0 W: 13 03 b.Barton-on-Sea 25-6-73
Source: Tottenham H Schoolboy, Bournemouth Trainee. *Honours:* England Schools, Youth, B, Under-21, 17 full caps, 1 goal.

1989–90	Bournemouth	4	0		
1990–91	Bournemouth	9	0	**13**	**0**
1990–91	Liverpool	0	0		
1991–92	Liverpool	6	1		
1992–93	Liverpool	29	2		
1993–94	Liverpool	35	4		
1994–95	Liverpool	41	3		
1995–96	Liverpool	23	3		
1996–97	Liverpool	23	2		
1997–98	Liverpool	20	3		
1998–99	Liverpool	34	8		
1999–2000	Liverpool	22	3		
2000–01	Liverpool	0	0		
2001–02	Liverpool	4	1	**237**	**30**
2001–02	Tottenham H	0	0		
2002–03	Tottenham H	17	3		
2003–04	Tottenham H	17	1		
2004–05	Tottenham H	14	0	**48**	**4**
2004–05	Southampton	16	0	**16**	**0**

SMITH, Paul (G) **93 0**
H: 6 3 W: 14 00 b.Epsom 17-12-79

1998–99	Charlton Ath	0	0		
1998–99	*Brentford*	0	0		
1999–2000	Charlton Ath	0	0		

From Carshalton Ath.

2000–01	Brentford	2	0		
2001–02	Brentford	18	0		
2002–03	Brentford	43	0		
2003–04	Brentford	24	0	**87**	**0**
2003–04	Southampton	0	0		
2004–05	Southampton	6	0	**6**	**0**

SPARV, Tim (M) **0 0**
H: 6 4 W: 12 05 b.Vasa 20-2-87
Source: Scholar.

2004–05	Southampton	0	0		

SURMAN, Andrew (M) **14 2**
H: 6 0 W: 11 09 b.Johannesburg 20-8-86
Source: Trainee.

2003–04	Southampton	0	0		
2004–05	Southampton	0	0		
2004–05	*Walsall*	14	2	**14**	**2**

SVENSSON, Anders (M) **284 47**
H: 5 10 W: 12 10 b.Gothenburg 17-7-76
Honours: Sweden 59 full caps, 11 goals.

1992	Hestrafors	2	0	**2**	**0**
1993	Elfsborg	0	0		
1994	Elfsborg	1	0		
1995	Elfsborg	26	3		
1996	Elfsborg	24	9		
1997	Elfsborg	26	3		
1998	Elfsborg	26	5		
1999	Elfsborg	20	3		
2000	Elfsborg	24	10		
2001	Elfsborg	8	5	**155**	**38**
2001–02	Southampton	34	4		
2002–03	Southampton	33	2		
2003–04	Southampton	30	0		
2004–05	Southampton	30	3	**127**	**9**

SVENSSON, Michael (D) **238 11**
H: 6 2 W: 12 02 b.Sweden 25-11-75
Honours: Sweden 25 full caps.

1992	Skillingaryds	21	0	**21**	**0**
1993	Varnamo	20	0		
1994	Varnamo	20	0		
1995	Varnamo	17	1		
1996	Varnamo	0	0	**57**	**1**
1997	Halmstad	0	0		
1998	Halmstad	14	2		
1999	Halmstad	20	0		
2000	Halmstad	25	2		
2001	Halmstad	18	1	**77**	**5**
2001–02	Troyes	23	1	**23**	**1**
2002–03	Southampton	34	2		
2003–04	Southampton	26	2		
2004–05	Southampton	0	0	**60**	**4**

TELFER, Paul (D) **463 26**
H: 5 10 W: 11 13 b.Edinburgh 21-10-71
Source: Trainee. *Honours:* Scotland Under-21, B, 1 full cap.

1988–89	Luton T	0	0		
1989–90	Luton T	0	0		
1990–91	Luton T	1	0		
1991–92	Luton T	20	1		
1992–93	Luton T	32	2		
1993–94	Luton T	45	7		
1994–95	Luton T	46	9	**144**	**19**
1995–96	Coventry C	31	1		
1996–97	Coventry C	34	0		
1997–98	Coventry C	33	3		
1998–99	Coventry C	32	2		
1999–2000	Coventry C	30	0		
2000–01	Coventry C	31	0		
2001–02	Coventry C	0	0	**191**	**6**
2001–02	Southampton	28	1		
2002–03	Southampton	33	0		
2003–04	Southampton	37	0		
2004–05	Southampton	30	0	**128**	**1**

TESSEM, Jo (M) **222 50**
H: 6 2 W: 13 01 b.Orlandet 28-2-72
Honours: Norway 9 full caps.

1996	Lyn	22	15		
1997	Lyn	26	8	**48**	**23**
1998	Molde	26	8		
1999	Molde	26	6	**52**	**14**
1999–2000	Southampton	25	4		
2000–01	Southampton	33	4		
2001–02	Southampton	22	2		
2002–03	Southampton	27	2		
2003–04	Southampton	3	0		
2004–05	Southampton	0	0	**110**	**12**
2004–05	*Millwall*	12	1	**12**	**1**

VAN DAMME, Jelle (D) **31 0**
H: 6 4 W: 13 01 b.Lokeren 10-10-83
Honours: Belgium 7 full caps.

2001–02	Beerschot	7	0	**7**	**0**
2001–02	Ajax	1	0		
2002–03	Ajax	11	0		
2003–04	Ajax	6	0	**18**	**0**
2004–05	Southampton	6	0	**6**	**0**

WILLIAMSON, Mike (D) **51 2**
H: 6 4 W: 13 03 b.Stoke 8-11-83
Source: Trainee.

2001–02	Torquay U	3	0		
2001–02	Southampton	0	0		
2002–03	Southampton	0	0		
2003–04	Southampton	0	0		
2003–04	*Torquay U*	11	0	**14**	**0**
2003–04	*Doncaster R*	0	0		
2004–05	Southampton	0	0		
2004–05	*Wycombe W*	37	2	**37**	**2**

YAHIA, Alaeddine (D) **46 1**
H: 6 1 W: 13 07 b.Courbevoie 6-9-81

2000–01	Louhans-Cuisseau	4	0	**4**	**0**
2001–02	Guingamp	3	0		
2002–03	Guingamp	18	0		
2003–04	Guingamp	14	1	**35**	**1**
2004–05	Southampton	0	0		
2004–05	*St Etienne*	7	0	**7**	**0**

Scholars
Critchell, Kyle Andrew Ross; Dutton-Black, Joshua Robert; Dyer, Nathan Antone Jonah; James, Lloyd Roger Stuart; Lallana, Adam David; McGoldrick, David James; Richards, Craig; Rudd, Sean Paul Robert

SOUTHEND U (75)

BARRETT, Adam (D) **222 20**
H: 6 1 W: 12 09 b.Dagenham 29-11-79
Source: Leyton Orient Trainee.

1998–99	Plymouth Arg	1	0		
1999–2000	Plymouth Arg	42	3		
2000–01	Plymouth Arg	9	0	**52**	**3**
2000–01	Mansfield T	8	1		
2001–02	Mansfield T	29	0	**37**	**1**
2002–03	Bristol R	45	1		
2003–04	Bristol R	45	4	**90**	**5**
2004–05	Southend U	43	11	**43**	**11**

BENTLEY, Mark (M) **60 7**
H: 6 2 W: 13 04 b.Hertford 7-1-78
Source: Enfield, Aldershot T, Gravesend & N, Dagenham & R.

2003–04	Southend U	21	2		
2004–05	Southend U	39	5	**60**	**7**

BRAMBLE, Tesfaye (F) **148 32**
H: 6 2 W: 13 13 b.Ipswich 20-7-80
Source: Cambridge C.

2000–01	Southend U	16	6		
2001–02	Southend U	35	9		
2002–03	Southend U	34	9		
2003–04	Southend U	34	4		
2004–05	Southend U	20	1	**139**	**29**
2004–05	*Cambridge U*	9	3	**9**	**3**

BYRNE, Paul (M) **125 11**
H: 5 11 W: 13 00 b.Dublin 30-6-72
Source: Trainee. *Honours:* Eire Youth.

1989–90	Oxford U	3	0		
1990–91	Oxford U	2	0		
1991–92	Oxford U	1	0	**6**	**0**

From Bangor

1993–94	Celtic	22	2		
1994–95	Celtic	6	2	**28**	**4**
1994–95	*Brighton & HA*	8	1	**8**	**1**
1995–96	Southend U	41	5		
1996–97	Southend U	32	1		
1997–98	Southend U	10	0		
1998–99	Southend U	0	0		
1999–2000	Southend U	0	0		
2000–01	Southend U	0	0		
2001–02	Southend U	0	0		
2002–03	Southend U	0	0		
2003–04	Southend U	0	0		
2004–05	Southend U	0	0	**83**	**6**

CLARK, Anthony (M) **2 0**
H: 5 10 W: 8 10 b.Camden 5-10-84
Source: Scholar.

2001–02	Southend U	2	0		
2002–03	Southend U	0	0		
2003–04	Southend U	0	0		
2004–05	Southend U	0	0	**2**	**0**

CORBETT, Jimmy (M) **49 6**
H: 5 9 W: 11 08 b.Hackney 6-7-80
Source: Trainee.

1997–98	Gillingham	16	2	**16**	**2**
1998–99	Blackburn R	0	0		
1999–2000	Blackburn R	0	0		
2000–01	Blackburn R	0	0		
2001–02	Blackburn R	0	0		
2002–03	Blackburn R	0	0		
2002–03	*Darlington*	10	2	**10**	**2**
2003–04	Southend U	17	1		
2004–05	Southend U	6	1	**23**	**2**

DUDFIELD, Lawrie (F) **156 29**
H: 6 1 W: 13 00 b.Southwark 7-5-80
Source: Kettering T.

1997–98	Leicester C	0	0		
1998–99	Leicester C	0	0		
1999–2000	Leicester C	2	0		
2000–01	Leicester C	0	0	**2**	**0**
2000–01	*Lincoln C*	3	0	**3**	**0**
2000–01	*Chesterfield*	14	3	**14**	**3**
2001–02	Hull C	38	12		
2002–03	Hull C	21	1	**59**	**13**
2002–03	Northampton T	10	1		
2003–04	Northampton T	19	3	**29**	**4**
2003–04	Southend U	13	5		
2004–05	Southend U	36	4	**49**	**9**

EASTWOOD, Freddy (F) **33 19**
H: 5 11 W: 12 00 b.Epsom 29-10-83
Source: West Ham U Trainee, Grays Ath.

2004–05	Southend U	33	19	**33**	**19**

EDWARDS, Andy (D) **506 21**
H: 6 4 W: 13 09 b.Epping 17-9-71
Source: Trainee.

1988–89	Southend U	1	0		
1989–90	Southend U	8	0		
1990–91	Southend U	2	1		
1991–92	Southend U	9	0		
1992–93	Southend U	41	0		
1993–94	Southend U	42	1		
1994–95	Southend U	44	3		
1995–96	Birmingham C	37	1		
1996–97	Birmingham C	3	0	**40**	**1**
1996–97	Peterborough U	25	0		
1997–98	Peterborough U	46	2		
1998–99	Peterborough U	41	2		
1999–2000	Peterborough U	44	2		
2000–01	Peterborough U	43	1		
2001–02	Peterborough U	44	2		
2002–03	Peterborough U	23	1	**266**	**10**
2002–03	Rushden & D	12	1		
2003–04	Rushden & D	29	3	**41**	**4**
2004–05	Southend U	12	1	**159**	**6**

FLAHAVAN, Darryl (G) **176 0**
H: 5 11 W: 12 06 b.Southampton 28-11-78
Source: Trainee.
From Woking.

2000–01	Southend U	29	0		
2001–02	Southend U	41	0		
2002–03	Southend U	41	0		
2003–04	Southend U	37	0		
2004–05	Southend U	28	0	**176**	**0**

GOWER, Mark (M) **101 14**
H: 5 8 W: 12 02 b.Edmonton 5-10-78
Source: Trainee. *Honours:* England Schools, Youth.

1996–97	Tottenham H	0	0		
1997–98	Tottenham H	0	0		
1998–99	Tottenham H	0	0		
1998–99	*Motherwell*	9	1	**9**	**1**
1999–2000	Tottenham H	0	0		
2000–01	Tottenham H	0	0		
2000–01	Barnet	14	1		
2001–02	Barnet	0	0		
2002–03	Barnet	0	0	**14**	**1**
2003–04	Southend U	40	6		
2004–05	Southend U	38	6	**78**	**12**

GRAY, Wayne (F) **153 25**
H: 5 10 W: 13 05 b.Dulwich 7-11-80
Source: Trainee.

1998–99	Wimbledon	0	0		
1999–2000	Wimbledon	1	0		
1999–2000	*Swindon T*	12	2	**12**	**2**
2000–01	Wimbledon	11	0		
2000–01	*Port Vale*	3	0	**3**	**0**
2001–02	Wimbledon	0	0		
2001–02	*Leyton Orient*	15	5	**15**	**5**
2001–02	*Brighton & HA*	4	1	**4**	**1**
2002–03	Wimbledon	30	2		
2003–04	Wimbledon	33	4	**75**	**6**
2004–05	Southend U	44	11	**44**	**11**

GRIEMINK, Bart (G) **221 0**
H: 6 3 W: 14 06 b.Holland 29-3-72
Source: WKE.

1995–96	Birmingham C	20	0		
1996–97	Birmingham C	0	0	**20**	**0**
1996–97	*Barnsley*	0	0		
1996–97	Peterborough U	27	0		
1997–98	Peterborough U	0	0		
1998–99	Peterborough U	17	0		
1999–2000	Peterborough U	14	0	**58**	**0**
1999–2000	*Swindon T*	4	0		
2000–01	Swindon T	25	0		
2001–02	Swindon T	45	0		
2002–03	Swindon T	44	0		
2003–04	Swindon T	6	0	**124**	**0**
2004–05	Southend U	19	0	**19**	**0**

GUTTRIDGE, Luke (M) **142 17**
H: 5 5 W: 8 06 b.Barnstaple 27-3-82
Source: Trainee.

1999–2000	Torquay U	1	0		
2000–01	Torquay U	0	0	**1**	**0**
2000–01	Cambridge U	1	1		
2001–02	Cambridge U	29	2		
2002–03	Cambridge U	43	3		
2003–04	Cambridge U	46	11		
2004–05	Cambridge U	17	0	**136**	**17**
2004–05	Southend U	5	0	**5**	**0**

HUNT, Lewis (D) **68 0**
H: 5 11 W: 12 09 b.Birmingham 25-8-82
Source: Scholar.

2000–01	Derby Co	0	0		
2001–02	Derby Co	0	0		
2002–03	Derby Co	10	0		
2003–04	Derby Co	1	0	**11**	**0**
2003–04	*Southend U*	26	0		
2004–05	Southend U	31	0	**57**	**0**

HUSBANDS, Michael (F) **11 0**
H: 5 8 W: 10 10 b.Birmingham 13-11-83
Source: Scholar.

2001–02	Aston Villa	0	0		
2002–03	Aston Villa	0	0		
2003–04	Southend U	9	0		
2004–05	Southend U	2	0	**11**	**0**

JUPP, Duncan (D) **219 2**
H: 6 1 W: 12 12 b.Guildford 25-1-75
Source: Trainee. *Honours:* Scotland Under-21.

1992–93	Fulham	3	0		
1993–94	Fulham	30	0		
1994–95	Fulham	36	2		
1995–96	Fulham	36	0	**105**	**2**
1996–97	Wimbledon	6	0		
1997–98	Wimbledon	3	0		
1998–99	Wimbledon	6	0		
1999–2000	Wimbledon	9	0		
2000–01	Wimbledon	4	0		
2001–02	Wimbledon	2	0		
2002–03	Wimbledon	0	0	**30**	**0**
2002–03	*Notts Co*	8	0	**8**	**0**
2002–03	Luton T	5	0	**5**	**0**
2003–04	Southend U	40	0		
2004–05	Southend U	31	0	**71**	**0**

KIGHTLY, Michael (F) **13 0**
H: 5 10 W: 10 10 b.Basildon 24-1-86
Source: Scholar.

2002–03	Southend U	1	0		
2003–04	Southend U	11	0		
2004–05	Southend U	1	0	**13**	**0**

LAWSON, James (M) **1 0**
H: 5 9 W: 10 03 b.Basildon 21-1-87
Source: Scholar.

2004–05	Southend U	1	0	**1**	**0**

MAHER, Kevin (M) **279 16**
H: 6 0 W: 12 00 b.Ilford 17-10-76
Source: Trainee.

1995–96	Tottenham H	0	0		
1996–97	Tottenham H	0	0		
1997–98	Tottenham H	0	0		
1997–98	Southend U	18	1		
1998–99	Southend U	34	4		
1999–2000	Southend U	24	0		
2000–01	Southend U	41	2		
2001–02	Southend U	36	5		
2002–03	Southend U	42	2		
2003–04	Southend U	42	1		
2004–05	Southend U	42	1	**279**	**16**

McCORMACK, Alan (M) **25 2**
H: 5 8 W: 11 00 b.Dublin 10-1-84

2002–03	Preston NE	0	0		
2003–04	Preston NE	5	0		
2003–04	*Leyton Orient*	10	0	**10**	**0**
2004–05	Preston NE	3	0	**8**	**0**
2004–05	Southend U	7	2	**7**	**2**

NICOLAU, Nicky (D) **31 1**
H: 5 7 W: 10 03 b.Camden 12-10-83
Source: Trainee.

2002–03	Arsenal	0	0		
2003–04	Arsenal	0	0		
2003–04	*Southend U*	9	0		
2004–05	Southend U	22	1	**31**	**1**

PETTEFER, Carl (M) **91 1**
H: 5 8 W: 10 06 b.Burnham 22-3-81
Source: Trainee.

1998–99	Portsmouth	0	0		
1999–2000	Portsmouth	0	0		
2000–01	Portsmouth	1	0		
2001–02	Portsmouth	2	0		
2002–03	Portsmouth	0	0		
2002–03	*Exeter C*	31	1	**31**	**1**
2003–04	Portsmouth	0	0	**3**	**0**
2003–04	*Southend U*	11	0		
2004–05	Southend U	46	0	**57**	**0**

PRIOR, Spencer (D) **479 13**
H: 6 3 W: 13 00 b.Rochford 22-4-71
Source: Trainee.

1988–89	Southend U	14	1		
1989–90	Southend U	15	1		
1990–91	Southend U	19	0		
1991–92	Southend U	42	1		
1992–93	Southend U	45	0		
1993–94	Norwich C	13	0		
1994–95	Norwich C	17	0		
1995–96	Norwich C	44	1	**74**	**1**
1996–97	Leicester C	34	0		
1997–98	Leicester C	30	0	**64**	**0**
1998–99	Derby Co	34	1		
1999–2000	Derby Co	20	0	**54**	**1**
1999–2000	Manchester C	9	3		
2000–01	Manchester C	21	1	**30**	**4**
2001–02	Cardiff C	37	2		
2002–03	Cardiff C	37	0		
2003–04	Cardiff C	7	0	**81**	**2**
2004–05	Southend U	41	2	**176**	**5**

SMITH, Jay (M) **49 6**
H: 5 7 W: 10 11 b.London 24-9-81
Source: Scholar.

2000–01	Aston Villa	0	0		
2001–02	Aston Villa	0	0		
2002–03	Aston Villa	0	0		
2002–03	Southend U	31	5		
2003–04	Southend U	18	1		
2004–05	Southend U	0	0	**49**	**6**

TILSON, Steve (M) **245 26**
H: 5 11 W: 13 00 b.Wickford 27-7-66
Source: Burnham Ramb.

1988–89	Southend U	16	2		
1989–90	Southend U	16	0		
1990–91	Southend U	38	8		
1991–92	Southend U	46	7		
1992–93	Southend U	31	3		
1993–94	Southend U	10	0		
1993–94	*Brentford*	2	0	**2**	**0**
1994–95	Southend U	26	2		

1995–96 Southend U 28 3
1996–97 Southend U 28 1
1997–98 Southend U 0 0
1998–99 Southend U 0 0
From Canvey Island
2002–03 Southend U 3 0
2003–04 Southend U 1 0
2004–05 Southend U 0 0 **243 26**

WILSON, Che (D) 151 0
H: 5 9 W: 12 01 b.Ely 17-1-79
Source: Trainee.
1997–98 Norwich C 0 0
1998–99 Norwich C 17 0
1999–2000 Norwich C 5 0 **22 0**
2000–01 Bristol R 37 0
2001–02 Bristol R 38 0
2002–03 Bristol R 0 0 **75 0**
From Cambridge C.
2003–04 Southend U 14 0
2004–05 Southend U 40 0 **54 0**

STOCKPORT CO (76)

ALLEN, Damien (M) 21 1
H: 5 11 W: 11 04 b.Cheadle 1-8-86
Source: Trainee.
2004–05 Stockport Co 21 1 **21 1**

ARMSTRONG, Chris (F) 17 1
H: 6 1 W: 13 07 b.Ripon 8-11-84
Source: Scholar.
2001–02 Leeds U 0 0
2002–03 Leeds U 0 0
2003–04 Leeds U 0 0
2004–05 Rochdale 0 0
2004–05 Queen of the South6 0 **6 0**
2004–05 Stockport Co 11 1 **11 1**

BAILEY, Matt (F) 5 0
H: 6 5 W: 11 06 b.Crewe 12-3-86
Source: Nantwich T.
2003–04 Stockport Co 0 0
2004–05 Stockport Co 1 0 **1 0**
2004–05 *Scunthorpe U* 4 0 **4 0**

BARLOW, Stuart (F) 402 111
H: 5 10 W: 11 05 b.Liverpool 16-7-68
Source: School.
1990–91 Everton 2 0
1991–92 Everton 7 0
1991–92 *Rotherham U* 0 0
1992–93 Everton 26 5
1993–94 Everton 22 3
1994–95 Everton 11 2
1995–96 Everton 3 0 **71 10**
1995–96 Oldham Ath 26 7
1996–97 Oldham Ath 35 12
1997–98 Oldham Ath 32 12 **93 31**
1997–98 Wigan Ath 9 3
1998–99 Wigan Ath 41 19
1999–2000 Wigan Ath 33 18 **83 40**
2000–01 Tranmere R 27 2
2001–02 Tranmere R 38 14
2002–03 Tranmere R 29 3 **94 19**
2003–04 Stockport Co 30 8
2004–05 Stockport Co 31 3 **61 11**

BRIDGE-WILKINSON, Marc (M) 166 36
H: 5 6 W: 11 00 b.Coventry 16-3-79
Source: Trainee.
1996–97 Derby Co 0 0
1997–98 Derby Co 0 0
1998–99 Derby Co 1 0
1998–99 *Carlisle U* 7 0 **7 0**
1999–2000 Derby Co 0 0 **1 0**
2000–01 Port Vale 42 9
2001–02 Port Vale 19 6
2002–03 Port Vale 31 9
2003–04 Port Vale 32 7 **124 31**
2004–05 Stockport Co 22 2 **22 2**
2004–05 *Bradford C* 12 3 **12 3**

BRIGGS, Keith (M) 82 4
H: 6 0 W: 11 05 b.Glossop 11-12-81
Source: Trainee.
1999–2000 Stockport Co 7 1
2000–01 Stockport Co 0 0
2001–02 Stockport Co 32 0
2002–03 Stockport Co 19 1
2002–03 Norwich C 2 0
2003–04 Norwich C 3 0
2004–05 Norwich C 0 0 **5 0**
2004–05 *Crewe Alex* 3 0 **3 0**
2004–05 Stockport Co 16 2 **74 4**

BROWNHILL, Liam (D) 0 0
b.Altrincham 28-11-86
Source: Scholar.
2004–05 Stockport Co 0 0

CARTWRIGHT, Lee (M) 431 23
H: 5 10 W: 11 00 b.Rawtenstall 19-9-72
Source: Trainee.
1990–91 Preston NE 14 1
1991–92 Preston NE 33 3
1992–93 Preston NE 34 3
1993–94 Preston NE 39 1
1994–95 Preston NE 36 1
1995–96 Preston NE 26 3
1996–97 Preston NE 14 1
1997–98 Preston NE 36 2
1998–99 Preston NE 27 4
1999–2000 Preston NE 30 1
2000–01 Preston NE 38 0
2001–02 Preston NE 36 1
2002–03 Preston NE 22 1
2003–04 Preston NE 12 0 **397 22**
2003–04 Stockport Co 15 0
2004–05 Stockport Co 19 1 **34 1**

COLLINS, Wayne (M) 228 24
H: 5 11 W: 12 02 b.Manchester 4-3-69
Source: Winsford U.
1993–94 Crewe Alex 35 2
1994–95 Crewe Alex 40 11
1995–96 Crewe Alex 42 1
1996–97 Sheffield W 12 1
1997–98 Sheffield W 19 5 **31 6**
1997–98 Fulham 13 1
1998–99 Fulham 21 2
1999–2000 Fulham 19 1
2000–01 Fulham 5 0 **58 4**
2001–02 Crewe Alex 20 0
2002–03 Crewe Alex 0 0 **137 14**
2003–04 Stockport Co 2 0
2004–05 Stockport Co 0 0 **2 0**

COPPINGER, Ben (G) 0 0
b. 17-9-85
2004–05 Stockport Co 0 0

CUTLER, Neil (G) 145 0
H: 6 4 W: 12 00 b.Birmingham 3-9-76
Source: Trainee. *Honours:* England Schools, Youth.
1993–94 WBA 0 0
1994–95 WBA 0 0
1995–96 WBA 0 0
1995–96 *Coventry C* 0 0
1995–96 *Chester C* 1 0
1996–97 Crewe Alex 0 0
1996–97 *Chester C* 5 0
1997–98 Crewe Alex 0 0
1998–99 Chester C 23 0
1999–2000 Chester C 0 0 **29 0**
1999–2000 Aston Villa 1 0
2000–01 Aston Villa 0 0
2000–01 *Oxford U* 11 0 **11 0**
2001–02 Aston Villa 0 0 **1 0**
2001–02 Stoke C 36 0
2002–03 Stoke C 20 0
2002–03 *Swansea C* 13 0 **13 0**
2003–04 Stoke C 13 0 **69 0**
2004–05 Stockport Co 22 0 **22 0**

DJE, Ludovic (M) 3 0
H: 6 4 W: 14 06 b.Paris 22-7-77
2004–05 Stockport Co 3 0 **3 0**

DOUGLAS, Paul (M) 0 0
2004–05 Stockport Co 0 0

GOODWIN, Jim (M) 103 7
H: 5 9 W: 12 01 b.Waterford 20-11-81
Source: Tramore. *Honours:* Eire Under-21, 1 full cap.
2001–02 Celtic 0 0
2002–03 Stockport Co 33 3
2003–04 Stockport Co 34 4
2004–05 Stockport Co 36 0 **103 7**

GRIFFIN, Danny (D) 185 6
H: 5 11 W: 12 05 b.Belfast 10-8-77
Source: St Andrews, Belfast. *Honours:* Northern Ireland Under-21, 29 full caps, 1 goal.
1993–94 St Johnstone 0 0
1994–95 St Johnstone 3 0
1995–96 St Johnstone 31 1
1996–97 St Johnstone 29 1
1997–98 St Johnstone 13 0
1998–99 St Johnstone 19 1
1999–2000 St Johnstone 29 1 **124 4**
2000–01 Dundee U 0 0
2001–02 Dundee U 0 0
2002–03 Dundee U 17 1
2003–04 Dundee U 13 0 **30 1**
2003–04 Stockport Co 15 1
2004–05 Stockport Co 16 0 **31 1**

HADFIELD, Jordan (M) 1 0
H: 5 10 W: 11 04 b.Swinton 12-8-87
Source: Trainee.
2004–05 Stockport Co 1 0 **1 0**

HARDIKER, John (M) 103 3
H: 5 11 W: 11 01 b.Preston 17-7-82
Source: Morecambe.
2001–02 Stockport Co 12 3
2002–03 Stockport Co 23 0
2003–04 Stockport Co 39 0
2004–05 Stockport Co 29 0 **103 3**

JACKMAN, Danny (D) 67 5
H: 5 4 W: 9 0 b.Worcester 3-1-83
Source: Scholar.
2000–01 Aston Villa 0 0
2001–02 Aston Villa 0 0
2001–02 *Cambridge U* 7 1 **7 1**
2002–03 Aston Villa 0 0
2003–04 Aston Villa 0 0
2003–04 Stockport Co 27 2
2004–05 Stockport Co 33 2 **60 4**

LE FONDRE, Adam (F) 20 4
H: 5 9 W: 11 04 b.Stockport 2-12-86
Source: Trainee.
2004–05 Stockport Co 20 4 **20 4**

MAIR, Lee (D) 111 4
H: 6 1 W: 12 03 b.Aberdeen 9-12-80
2000–01 Dundee 0 0
2000–01 East Fife 13 2 **13 2**
2001–02 Falkirk 20 0 **20 0**
2002–03 Dundee 28 1
2003–04 Dundee 36 1 **64 2**
2004–05 Stockport Co 14 0 **14 0**

McEVEN, Sam (G) 0 0
b.Manchester 14-7-87
2004–05 Stockport Co 0 0

PEMBERTON, Martin (M) 133 7
H: 5 11 W: 12 06 b.Bradford 1-2-76
Source: Trainee.
1994–95 Oldham Ath 0 0
1995–96 Oldham Ath 2 0
1996–97 Oldham Ath 3 0 **5 0**
1996–97 Doncaster R 9 1
1997–98 Doncaster R 26 1 **35 2**
1997–98 Scunthorpe U 6 0 **6 0**
1998–99 Hartlepool U 4 0
1999–2000 Hartlepool U 0 0 **4 0**
From Bradford PA.
2000–01 Mansfield T 18 1
2001–02 Mansfield T 38 4 **56 5**
2001–02 Stockport Co 0 0
2002–03 Stockport Co 20 0
2003–04 Stockport Co 6 0
2003–04 *Rochdale* 1 0 **1 0**
2004–05 Stockport Co 0 0 **26 0**

RAYNES, Michael (M) 19 0
H: 6 2 W: 12 02 b.Wythenshawe 15-10-87
2004–05 Stockport Co 19 0 **19 0**

REILLY, Philip (M) 0 0
2003–04 Stockport Co 0 0
2004–05 Stockport Co 0 0

ROBERTSON, Mark (M) 157 5
H: 5 9 W: 12 04 b.Sydney 6-4-77
Honours: Australia Schools, Under-20, Under-23, 1 full cap.
1994–95 Marconi Stallions 8 0

1996–97	Marconi Stallions	15	0	**23**	**0**
1997–98	Burnley	11	0		
1998–99	Burnley	24	1		
1999–2000	Burnley	1	0	**36**	**1**
1999–2000	Wollongong Wolves	12	0	**12**	**0**
2000–01	Dundee	4	0		
2000–01	Swindon T	10	1	**10**	**1**
2001–02	Dundee	16	0		
2002–03	Dundee	5	0	**25**	**0**
2002–03	St Johnstone	10	1		
2003–04	St Johnstone	9	1	**19**	**2**
2003–04	Stockport Co	12	1		
2004–05	Stockport Co	20	0	**32**	**1**

ROBINSON, Marvin (F) **70 13**
H: 6 0 W: 12 03 b.Crewe 11-4-80
Source: Trainee.

1998–99	Derby Co	1	0		
1999–2000	Derby Co	8	0		
2000–01	Derby Co	0	0		
2000–01	*Stoke C*	3	1	**3**	**1**
2001–02	Derby Co	2	1		
2002–03	Derby Co	1	0	**12**	**1**
2002–03	*Tranmere R*	6	1	**6**	**1**
2003–04	Chesterfield	32	6		
2004–05	Chesterfield	0	0	**32**	**6**
2004–05	Notts Co	2	0	**2**	**0**
2004–05	Rushden & D	2	0	**2**	**0**
2004–05	Walsall	10	4	**10**	**4**
2004–05	Stockport Co	3	0	**3**	**0**

SPENCER, James (G) **42 0**
H: 6 3 W: 15 04 b.Stockport 11-4-85
Source: Trainee.

2001–02	Stockport Co	2	0		
2002–03	Stockport Co	1	0		
2003–04	Stockport Co	15	0		
2004–05	Stockport Co	24	0	**42**	**0**

TOMLINSON, Ezekiel (M) **5 0**
H: 5 9 W: 11 02 b.Birmingham 9-11-85
Source: Scholar.

2004–05	WBA	0	0		
2004–05	Stockport Co	5	0	**5**	**0**

TURNBULL, Paul (F) **1 0**
H: 5 10 W: 11 07 b.Stockport 23-1-89
Source: Scholar.

2004–05	Stockport Co	1	0	**1**	**0**

WILLIAMS, Ashley (D) **54 1**
H: 6 0 W: 11 02 b.Wolverhampton 23-8-84
Source: Hednesford T.

2003–04	Stockport Co	10	0		
2004–05	Stockport Co	44	1	**54**	**1**

WILLIAMS, Chris (F) **34 3**
H: 5 7 W: 9 0 b.Manchester 2-2-85
Source: Scholar.

2001–02	Stockport Co	5	0		
2002–03	Stockport Co	1	0		
2003–04	Stockport Co	16	3		
2004–05	Stockport Co	9	0	**31**	**3**
2004–05	*Grimsby T*	3	0	**3**	**0**

STOKE C (77)

ASABA, Carl (F) **313 103**
H: 6 2 W: 13 00 b.London 28-1-73
Source: Dulwich Hamlet.

1994–95	Brentford	0	0		
1994–95	*Colchester U*	12	2	**12**	**2**
1995–96	Brentford	10	2		
1996–97	Brentford	44	23	**54**	**25**
1997–98	Reading	32	8		
1998–99	Reading	1	0	**33**	**8**
1998–99	Gillingham	41	20		
1999–2000	Gillingham	11	6		
2000–01	Gillingham	25	10	**77**	**36**
2000–01	Sheffield U	10	5		
2001–02	Sheffield U	29	7		
2002–03	Sheffield U	28	11	**67**	**23**
2003–04	Stoke C	37	8		
2004–05	Stoke C	33	1	**70**	**9**

BRAMMER, Dave (M) **340 20**
H: 5 10 W: 12 00 b.Bromborough 28-2-75
Source: Trainee.

1992–93	Wrexham	2	0		
1993–94	Wrexham	22	2		
1994–95	Wrexham	14	1		
1995–96	Wrexham	11	2		
1996–97	Wrexham	21	1		
1997–98	Wrexham	33	4		
1998–99	Wrexham	34	2	**137**	**12**
1998–99	Port Vale	9	0		
1999–2000	Port Vale	29	0		
2000–01	Port Vale	35	3	**73**	**3**
2001–02	Crewe Alex	30	2		
2002–03	Crewe Alex	41	1		
2003–04	Crewe Alex	16	1	**87**	**4**
2004–05	Stoke C	43	1	**43**	**1**

BUXTON, Lewis (D) **93 0**
H: 6 1 W: 13 10 b.Newport (IW) 10-12-83
Source: School.

2000–01	Portsmouth	0	0		
2001–02	Portsmouth	29	0		
2002–03	Portsmouth	1	0		
2002–03	*Exeter C*	4	0	**4**	**0**
2002–03	*Bournemouth*	17	0		
2003–04	Portsmouth	0	0		
2003–04	*Bournemouth*	26	0	**43**	**0**
2004–05	Portsmouth	0	0	**30**	**0**
2004–05	Stoke C	16	0	**16**	**0**

CLARKE, Clive (D) **223 9**
H: 5 11 W: 12 03 b.Dublin 14-1-80
Source: Trainee. *Honours:* Eire Under-21, 2 full caps.

1996–97	Stoke C	0	0		
1997–98	Stoke C	0	0		
1998–99	Stoke C	2	0		
1999–2000	Stoke C	42	1		
2000–01	Stoke C	21	0		
2001–02	Stoke C	43	1		
2002–03	Stoke C	31	3		
2003–04	Stoke C	42	3		
2004–05	Stoke C	42	1	**223**	**9**

DE GOEY, Ed (G) **523 0**
H: 6 6 W: 12 00 b.Gouda 20-12-66
Honours: Holland 31 full caps.

1985–86	Sparta	12	0		
1986–87	Sparta	34	0		
1987–88	Sparta	34	0		
1988–89	Sparta	31	0		
1989–90	Sparta	34	0	**145**	**0**
1990–91	Feyenoord	34	0		
1991–92	Feyenoord	34	0		
1992–93	Feyenoord	33	0		
1993–94	Feyenoord	34	0		
1994–95	Feyenoord	32	0		
1995–96	Feyenoord	34	0	**201**	**0**
1997–98	Chelsea	28	0		
1998–99	Chelsea	35	0		
1999–2000	Chelsea	37	0		
2000–01	Chelsea	15	0		
2001–02	Chelsea	6	0		
2002–03	Chelsea	2	0	**123**	**0**
2003–04	Stoke C	37	0		
2004–05	Stoke C	17	0	**54**	**0**

DENNY, Jay (M) **0 0**
H: 5 11 W: 12 00 b.Los Angeles 6-1-86
Source: Scholar.

2004–05	Stoke C	0	0		

DICKINSON, Carl (D) **1 0**
H: 6 0 W: 12 00 b.Swadlincote 31-3-87
Source: Scholar.

2004–05	Stoke C	1	0	**1**	**0**

DUBERRY, Michael (D) **176 5**
H: 6 1 W: 14 09 b.Enfield 14-10-75
Source: From Trainee. *Honours:* England Under-21.

1993–94	Chelsea	1	0		
1994–95	Chelsea	0	0		
1995–96	Chelsea	22	0		
1995–96	*Bournemouth*	7	0	**7**	**0**
1996–97	Chelsea	15	1		
1997–98	Chelsea	23	0		
1998–99	Chelsea	25	0	**86**	**1**
1999–2000	Leeds U	13	1		
2000–01	Leeds U	5	0		
2001–02	Leeds U	3	0		
2002–03	Leeds U	14	0		
2003–04	Leeds U	19	3		
2004–05	Leeds U	4	0	**58**	**4**
2004–05	Stoke C	25	0	**25**	**0**

EUSTACE, John (M) **131 13**
H: 5 11 W: 11 12 b.Solihull 3-11-79
Source: Trainee.

1996–97	Coventry C	0	0		
1997–98	Coventry C	0	0		
1998–99	Coventry C	0	0		
1998–99	Dundee U	11	1	**11**	**1**
1999–2000	Coventry C	16	1		
2000–01	Coventry C	32	2		
2001–02	Coventry C	6	0		
2002–03	Coventry C	32	4	**86**	**7**
2002–03	*Middlesbrough*	1	0	**1**	**0**
2003–04	Stoke C	26	5		
2004–05	Stoke C	7	0	**33**	**5**

FOSTER, Ben (G) **19 0**
H: 6 2 W: 12 08 b.Leamington Spa 3-4-83
Source: Racing Club Warwick.

2000–01	Stoke C	0	0		
2001–02	Stoke C	0	0		
2002–03	Stoke C	0	0		
2003–04	Stoke C	0	0		
2004–05	Stoke C	0	0		
2004–05	*Kidderminster H*	2	0	**2**	**0**
2004–05	*Wrexham*	17	0	**17**	**0**

GREENACRE, Chris (F) **231 61**
H: 5 11 W: 12 08 b.Halifax 23-12-77
Source: Trainee.

1995–96	Manchester C	0	0		
1996–97	Manchester C	4	0		
1997–98	Manchester C	3	1		
1997–98	*Cardiff C*	11	2	**11**	**2**
1997–98	*Blackpool*	4	0	**4**	**0**
1998–99	Manchester C	1	0		
1998–99	*Scarborough*	12	2	**12**	**2**
1999–2000	Manchester C	0	0	**8**	**1**
1999–2000	Mansfield T	31	9		
2000–01	Mansfield T	46	19		
2001–02	Mansfield T	44	21	**121**	**49**
2002–03	Stoke C	30	4		
2003–04	Stoke C	13	2		
2004–05	Stoke C	32	1	**75**	**7**

GUDJONSSON, Thordur (M) **263 68**
H: 5 10 W: 11 06 b.Reykjavik 23-1-73
Honours: Iceland Youth, Under-21, 58 full caps, 13 goals.

1990	KA	16	2	**16**	**2**
1991	IA Akranes	0	0		
1992	IA Akranes	18	6		
1993	IA Akranes	18	19	**36**	**25**
1994–95	Bochum	16	3		
1995–96	Bochum	28	3		
1996–97	Bochum	13	1		
1997–98	Genk	33	9		
1998–99	Genk	28	9		
1999–2000	Genk	33	10	**94**	**28**
2000–01	Las Palmas	9	1		
2000–01	Derby Co	10	1	**10**	**1**
2001–02	Las Palmas	0	0	**9**	**1**
2001–02	Preston NE	7	0	**7**	**0**
2002–03	Bochum	29	3		
2003–04	Bochum	3	1	**89**	**11**
2004–05	Stoke C	2	0	**2**	**0**

GUDMUNDSSON, Tryggvi (M) **209 115**
b.Iceland 30-7-74
Honours: Iceland 34 full caps, 9 goals.

1992	IBV	0	0		
1993	IBV	17	12		
1994	KR	13	3	**13**	**3**
1995	IBV	18	14		
1996	IBV	16	8		
1997	IBV	18	19	**69**	**53**
1998	Tromso	25	8		
1999	Tromso	26	14		
2000	Tromso	25	15	**76**	**37**
2001	Stabaek	26	7		
2002	Stabaek	25	15	**51**	**22**

From Orgryte, FH.

2004–05	Stoke C	0	0		

HALLS, John (M) **62 0**
H: 6 0 W: 11 00 b.Islington 14-2-82
Source: Scholar. *Honours:* England Youth, Under-20.

2000–01	Arsenal	0	0		
2001–02	Arsenal	0	0		
2001–02	*Colchester U*	6	0	**6**	**0**
2002–03	Arsenal	0	0		

2003–04 Arsenal 0 0
2003–04 Stoke C 34 0
2004–05 Stoke C 22 0 **56 0**

HARPER, Kevin (F) 276 26
H: 5 6 W: 12 00 b.Oldham 15-1-76
Source: Hutcheson Vale BC. *Honours:* Scotland Schools, Under-21, B.
1993–94 Hibernian 2 0
1994–95 Hibernian 23 5
1995–96 Hibernian 16 3
1996–97 Hibernian 26 5
1997–98 Hibernian 27 1
1998–99 Hibernian 2 1 **96 15**
1998–99 Derby Co 27 1
1999–2000 Derby Co 5 0 **32 1**
1999–2000 *Walsall* 9 1 **9 1**
1999–2000 Portsmouth 12 2
2000–01 Portsmouth 24 2
2001–02 Portsmouth 39 1
2002–03 Portsmouth 37 4
2003–04 Portsmouth 7 0
2003–04 *Norwich C* 9 0 **9 0**
2004–05 Portsmouth 0 0 **119 9**
2004–05 *Leicester C* 2 0 **2 0**
2004–05 Stoke C 9 0 **9 0**

HENRY, Karl (M) 105 2
H: 6 0 W: 12 00 b.Wolverhampton 26-11-82
Source: Trainee. *Honours:* England Youth, Under-20.
1999–2000 Stoke C 0 0
2000–01 Stoke C 0 0
2001–02 Stoke C 24 0
2002–03 Stoke C 18 1
2003–04 Stoke C 20 0
2003–04 *Cheltenham T* 9 1 **9 1**
2004–05 Stoke C 34 0 **96 1**

HILL, Clint (D) 201 18
H: 6 0 W: 11 06 b.Liverpool 19-10-78
Source: Trainee.
1997–98 Tranmere R 14 0
1998–99 Tranmere R 33 4
1999–2000 Tranmere R 29 5
2000–01 Tranmere R 34 5
2001–02 Tranmere R 30 2 **140 16**
2002–03 Oldham Ath 17 1 **17 1**
2003–04 Stoke C 12 0
2004–05 Stoke C 32 1 **44 1**

KEOGH, Richard (M) 0 0
H: 6 2 W: 12 00 b.Harlow 11-8-86
Source: Scholar.
2004–05 Stoke C 0 0

NEAL, Lewis (M) 70 2
H: 5 10 W: 10 11 b.Leicester 14-7-81
Source: Juniors.
1998–99 Stoke C 0 0
1999–2000 Stoke C 0 0
2000–01 Stoke C 1 0
2001–02 Stoke C 11 0
2002–03 Stoke C 16 0
2003–04 Stoke C 19 1
2004–05 Stoke C 23 1 **70 2**

NOEL-WILLIAMS, Gifton (F) 257 56
H: 6 1 W: 13 06 b.Islington 21-1-80
Source: Trainee. *Honours:* England Youth.
1996–97 Watford 25 2
1997–98 Watford 38 7
1998–99 Watford 26 10
1999–2000 Watford 3 0
2000–01 Watford 32 8
2001–02 Watford 29 6
2002–03 Watford 16 0 **169 33**
2003–04 Stoke C 42 10
2004–05 Stoke C 46 13 **88 23**

OWEN, Gareth (D) 34 1
H: 6 1 W: 11 07 b.Stoke 21-9-82
Source: Scholar. *Honours:* Wales Youth.
2001–02 Stoke C 0 0
2002–03 Stoke C 0 0
2003–04 Stoke C 3 0
2003–04 *Oldham Ath* 15 1
2004–05 Stoke C 2 0 **5 0**
2004–05 *Torquay U* 5 0 **5 0**
2004–05 *Oldham Ath* 9 0 **24 1**

PALMER, Jermaine (F) 4 0
H: 6 1 W: 11 03 b.Nottingham 28-8-86
Source: Scholar.
2003–04 Stoke C 3 0
2004–05 Stoke C 1 0 **4 0**

PATERSON, Mark (M) 3 0
H: 5 9 W: 11 05 b.Tunstall 13-5-87
Source: Scholar.
2004–05 Stoke C 3 0 **3 0**

PULIS, Anthony (M) 3 0
H: 5 10 W: 11 10 b.Bristol 21-7-84
Source: Scholar.
2002–03 Portsmouth 0 0
2003–04 Portsmouth 0 0
2004–05 Portsmouth 0 0
2004–05 Stoke C 0 0
2004–05 *Torquay U* 3 0 **3 0**

RUSSELL, Darel (M) 223 13
H: 6 0 W: 11 09 b.Mile End 22-10-80
Source: Trainee. *Honours:* England Youth.
1997–98 Norwich C 1 0
1998–99 Norwich C 13 1
1999–2000 Norwich C 33 4
2000–01 Norwich C 41 2
2001–02 Norwich C 23 0
2002–03 Norwich C 21 0 **132 7**
2003–04 Stoke C 46 4
2004–05 Stoke C 45 2 **91 6**

SIMONSEN, Steve (G) 96 0
H: 6 2 W: 12 08 b.South Shields 3-4-79
Source: Trainee. *Honours:* England Youth, Under-21.
1996–97 Tranmere R 0 0
1997–98 Tranmere R 30 0
1998–99 Tranmere R 5 0 **35 0**
1998–99 Everton 0 0
1999–2000 Everton 1 0
2000–01 Everton 1 0
2001–02 Everton 25 0
2002–03 Everton 2 0
2003–04 Everton 1 0 **30 0**
2004–05 Stoke C 31 0 **31 0**

TAGGART, Gerry (D) 462 34
H: 6 2 W: 14 00 b.Belfast 18-10-70
Source: Trainee. *Honours:* Northern Ireland Schools, Youth, Under-23, 51 full caps, 7 goals.
1988–89 Manchester C 11 1
1989–90 Manchester C 1 0 **12 1**
1989–90 Barnsley 21 2
1990–91 Barnsley 30 2
1991–92 Barnsley 38 3
1992–93 Barnsley 44 4
1993–94 Barnsley 38 2
1994–95 Barnsley 41 3 **212 16**
1995–96 Bolton W 11 1
1996–97 Bolton W 43 3
1997–98 Bolton W 15 0 **69 4**
1998–99 Leicester C 15 0
1999–2000 Leicester C 31 6
2000–01 Leicester C 24 2
2001–02 Leicester C 1 0
2002–03 Leicester C 37 1
2003–04 Leicester C 9 0 **117 9**
2003–04 Stoke C 21 2
2004–05 Stoke C 31 2 **52 4**

THOMAS, Wayne (D) 312 12
H: 5 11 W: 11 12 b.Gloucester 17-5-79
Source: Trainee.
1995–96 Torquay U 6 0
1996–97 Torquay U 12 0
1997–98 Torquay U 21 1
1998–99 Torquay U 44 1
1999–2000 Torquay U 40 3 **123 5**
2000–01 Stoke C 34 0
2001–02 Stoke C 40 2
2002–03 Stoke C 41 0
2003–04 Stoke C 39 3
2004–05 Stoke C 35 2 **189 7**

WILKINSON, Andy (D) 13 0
H: 5 11 W: 11 00 b.Stone 6-8-84
Source: Scholar.
2001–02 Stoke C 0 0
2002–03 Stoke C 0 0
2003–04 Stoke C 3 0
2004–05 Stoke C 1 0 **4 0**
2004–05 *Shrewsbury T* 9 0 **9 0**

WILLIAMS, Paul (D) 390 31
H: 6 0 W: 13 00 b.Burton 26-3-71
Source: Trainee. *Honours:* England Under-21.
1989–90 Derby Co 10 1
1989–90 *Lincoln C* 3 0 **3 0**
1990–91 Derby Co 19 4
1991–92 Derby Co 41 13
1992–93 Derby Co 19 4
1993–94 Derby Co 34 1
1994–95 Derby Co 37 3 **160 26**
1995–96 Coventry C 32 2
1996–97 Coventry C 32 2
1997–98 Coventry C 20 0
1998–99 Coventry C 22 0
1999–2000 Coventry C 28 1
2000–01 Coventry C 30 0
2001–02 Coventry C 5 0 **169 5**
2001–02 Southampton 28 0
2002–03 Southampton 11 0
2003–04 Southampton 0 0 **39 0**
2003–04 Stoke C 19 0
2004–05 Stoke C 0 0 **19 0**

SUNDERLAND (78)

ALNWICK, Ben (G) 3 0
H: 6 2 W: 13 12 b.Prudhoe 1-1-87
Source: Scholar. *Honours:* England Youth.
2003–04 Sunderland 0 0
2004–05 Sunderland 3 0 **3 0**

ARCA, Julio (M) 169 17
H: 5 9 W: 11 13 b.Quilmes 31-1-81
1999–2000 Argentinos Juniors 19 0
2000–01 Argentinos Juniors 17 1 **36 1**
2000–01 Sunderland 27 2
2001–02 Sunderland 22 1
2002–03 Sunderland 13 0
2003–04 Sunderland 31 4
2004–05 Sunderland 40 9 **133 16**

BELL, Ryan (D) 0 0
H: 6 1 W: 13 06 b.Ashington 30-3-86
Source: Trainee.
2003–04 Sunderland 0 0
2004–05 Sunderland 0 0

BREEN, Gary (D) 411 11
H: 6 3 W: 13 03 b.Hendon 12-12-73
Source: Charlton Ath. *Honours:* Eire Under-21, 62 full caps, 6 goals.
1991–92 Maidstone U 19 0 **19 0**
1992–93 Gillingham 29 0
1993–94 Gillingham 22 0 **51 0**
1994–95 Peterborough U 44 1
1995–96 Peterborough U 25 0 **69 1**
1995–96 Birmingham C 18 1
1996–97 Birmingham C 22 1 **40 2**
1996–97 Coventry C 9 0
1997–98 Coventry C 30 1
1998–99 Coventry C 25 0
1999–2000 Coventry C 21 0
2000–01 Coventry C 31 1
2001–02 Coventry C 30 0 **146 2**
2002–03 West Ham U 14 0 **14 0**
2003–04 Sunderland 32 4
2004–05 Sunderland 40 2 **72 6**

BRIDGES, Michael (F) 160 36
H: 6 0 W: 12 04 b.North Shields 5-8-78
Source: Trainee. *Honours:* England Schools, Youth, Under-21.
1995–96 Sunderland 15 4
1996–97 Sunderland 25 3
1997–98 Sunderland 9 1
1998–99 Sunderland 30 8
1999–2000 Leeds U 34 19
2000–01 Leeds U 7 0
2001–02 Leeds U 0 0
2002–03 Leeds U 5 0
2003–04 Leeds U 10 0 **56 19**
2003–04 *Newcastle U* 6 0 **6 0**
2004–05 Bolton W 0 0
2004–05 Sunderland 19 1 **98 17**

BROWN, Chris (F) **59 15**
H: 6 3 W: 13 08 b.Doncaster 11-12-84
Source: Trainee. *Honours:* England Youth.

2002–03	Sunderland	0	0		
2003–04	Sunderland	0	0		
2003–04	*Doncaster R*	22	10	**22**	**10**
2004–05	Sunderland	37	5	**37**	**5**

CALDWELL, Stephen (D) **97 6**
H: 6 2 W: 13 13 b.Stirling 12-9-80
Source: Trainee. *Honours:* Scotland Youth, Under-21, B, 5 full caps.

1997–98	Newcastle U	0	0		
1998–99	Newcastle U	0	0		
1999–2000	Newcastle U	0	0		
2000–01	Newcastle U	9	0		
2001–02	Newcastle U	0	0		
2001–02	*Blackpool*	6	0	**6**	**0**
2001–02	*Bradford C*	9	0	**9**	**0**
2002–03	Newcastle U	14	1		
2003–04	Newcastle U	5	0	**28**	**1**
2003–04	*Leeds U*	13	1	**13**	**1**
2004–05	Sunderland	41	4	**41**	**4**

COLLINS, Danny (D) **26 1**
H: 6 2 W: 12 00 b.Buckley 6-8-80
Source: Buckley T. *Honours:* Wales 1 full cap.

2004–05	Chester C	12	1	**12**	**1**
2004–05	Sunderland	14	0	**14**	**0**

COLLINS, Neil (D) **106 4**
H: 6 3 W: 13 00 b.Irvine 2-9-83
Honours: Scotland Under-21.

2000–01	Queen's Park	4	0		
2001–02	Queen's Park	28	0	**32**	**0**
2002–03	Dumbarton	33	2		
2003–04	Dumbarton	30	2	**63**	**4**
2004–05	Sunderland	11	0	**11**	**0**

DEANE, Brian (F) **643 193**
H: 6 3 W: 14 02 b.Leeds 7-2-68
Source: Apprentice. *Honours:* England B, 3 full caps.

1985–86	Doncaster R	3	0		
1986–87	Doncaster R	20	2		
1987–88	Doncaster R	43	10	**66**	**12**
1988–89	Sheffield U	43	22		
1989–90	Sheffield U	45	21		
1990–91	Sheffield U	38	13		
1991–92	Sheffield U	30	12		
1992–93	Sheffield U	41	14		
1993–94	Leeds U	41	11		
1994–95	Leeds U	35	9		
1995–96	Leeds U	34	7		
1996–97	Leeds U	28	5		
1997–98	Sheffield U	24	11	**221**	**93**
1997–98	Benfica	14	7		
1998–99	Benfica	4	0	**18**	**7**
1998–99	Middlesbrough	26	6		
1999–2000	Middlesbrough	29	9		
2000–01	Middlesbrough	25	2		
2001–02	Middlesbrough	7	1	**87**	**18**
2001–02	Leicester C	15	6		
2002–03	Leicester C	32	13		
2003–04	Leicester C	5	0	**52**	**19**
2003–04	West Ham U	26	6	**26**	**6**
2004–05	Leeds U	31	6	**169**	**38**
2004–05	Sunderland	4	0	**4**	**0**

DENNEHY, Billy (F) **0 0**

2004–05	Sunderland	0	0		

DODDS, Lewis (D) **0 0**
H: 5 8 W: 11 02 b.Spennymoor 14-12-85
Source: Trainee. *Honours:* England Youth.

2002–03	Sunderland	0	0		
2003–04	Sunderland	0	0		
2004–05	Sunderland	0	0		

ELLIOTT, Stephen (F) **44 15**
H: 5 8 W: 11 08 b.Dublin 6-1-84
Source: School. *Honours:* Eire Youth, Under-21, 3 full caps.

2000–01	Manchester C	0	0		
2001–02	Manchester C	0	0		
2002–03	Manchester C	0	0		
2003–04	Manchester C	2	0	**2**	**0**
2004–05	Sunderland	42	15	**42**	**15**

FLYNN, Niall (M) **0 0**
H: 5 7 W: 10 03 b.Dublin 22-1-86
Source: Trainee.

2002–03	Sunderland	0	0		
2003–04	Sunderland	0	0		
2004–05	Sunderland	0	0		

HEALY, Colin (M) **65 3**
H: 6 1 W: 12 13 b.Cork 14-3-80
Source: Wilton U. *Honours:* Eire 13 full caps, 1 goal.

1998–99	Celtic	3	0		
1999–2000	Celtic	10	1		
2000–01	Celtic	11	0		
2001–02	Celtic	4	0		
2001–02	*Coventry C*	17	2	**17**	**2**
2002–03	Celtic	0	0	**28**	**1**
2003–04	Sunderland	20	0		
2004–05	Sunderland	0	0	**20**	**0**

INGHAM, Michael (G) **59 0**
H: 6 4 W: 14 06 b.Preston 7-9-80
Source: Malachians. *Honours:* Northern Ireland Youth, Under-21, 1 full cap.

1998–99	Cliftonville	18	0	**18**	**0**
1999–2000	Sunderland	0	0		
1999–2000	*Carlisle U*	7	0	**7**	**0**
2000–01	Sunderland	0	0		
2001–02	Sunderland	0	0		
2001–02	*Stoke C*	0	0		
2002–03	Sunderland	0	0		
2002–03	*Darlington*	3	0	**3**	**0**
2002–03	*York C*	17	0	**17**	**0**
2003–04	Sunderland	0	0		
2003–04	*Wrexham*	11	0	**11**	**0**
2004–05	Sunderland	2	0	**2**	**0**
2004–05	*Doncaster R*	1	0	**1**	**0**

KINGSBERRY, Chris (M) **0 0**
H: 5 7 W: 9 02 b.Lisburn 10-9-85
Source: Trainee.

2002–03	Sunderland	0	0		
2003–04	Sunderland	0	0		
2004–05	Sunderland	0	0		

KYLE, Kevin (F) **91 11**
H: 6 3 W: 14 08 b.Stranraer 7-6-81
Source: Ayr Boswell. *Honours:* Scotland Under-21, B, 9 full caps, 1 goal.

1998–99	Sunderland	0	0		
1999–2000	Sunderland	0	0		
2000–01	Sunderland	3	0		
2000–01	*Huddersfield T*	4	0	**4**	**0**
2000–01	*Darlington*	5	1	**5**	**1**
2000–01	*Rochdale*	6	0	**6**	**0**
2001–02	Sunderland	6	0		
2002–03	Sunderland	17	0		
2003–04	Sunderland	44	10		
2004–05	Sunderland	6	0	**76**	**10**

LAWRENCE, Liam (M) **168 41**
H: 5 11 W: 12 06 b.Retford 14-12-81
Source: Trainee.

1999–2000	Mansfield T	2	0		
2000–01	Mansfield T	18	4		
2001–02	Mansfield T	32	2		
2002–03	Mansfield T	43	10		
2003–04	Mansfield T	41	18	**136**	**34**
2004–05	Sunderland	32	7	**32**	**7**

LEADBITTER, Grant (M) **0 0**
H: 5 9 W: 11 06 b.Sunderland 7-1-86
Source: Trainee. *Honours:* FA Schools, England Youth.

2002–03	Sunderland	0	0		
2003–04	Sunderland	0	0		
2004–05	Sunderland	0	0		

LYNCH, Mark (D) **31 0**
H: 5 11 W: 11 03 b.Manchester 2-9-81
Source: Trainee.

1999–2000	Manchester U	0	0		
2000–01	Manchester U	0	0		
2001–02	Manchester U	0	0		
2001–02	*St Johnstone*	20	0	**20**	**0**
2002–03	Manchester U	0	0		
2003–04	Manchester U	0	0		
2004–05	Sunderland	11	0	**11**	**0**

McCARTNEY, George (D) **121 0**
H: 5 11 W: 11 03 b.Belfast 29-4-81
Source: Trainee. *Honours:* Northern Ireland Schools, Youth, Under-21, 19 full caps, 1 goal.

1998–99	Sunderland	0	0		
1999–2000	Sunderland	0	0		
2000–01	Sunderland	2	0		
2001–02	Sunderland	18	0		
2002–03	Sunderland	24	0		
2003–04	Sunderland	41	0		
2004–05	Sunderland	36	0	**121**	**0**

McLEAN, Euan (G) **0 0**
H: 6 3 W: 13 07 b.Kilmarnock 9-1-86
Source: Trainee.

2003–04	Sunderland	0	0		
2004–05	Sunderland	0	0		

MEDINA, Nicolas (M) **47 1**
H: 5 9 W: 10 04 b.Buenos Aires 17-2-82

1999–2000	Argentinos Jun	26	0		
2000–01	Argentinos Jun	21	1	**47**	**1**
2001–02	Sunderland	0	0		
2002–03	Sunderland	0	0		
2003–04	Sunderland	0	0		
2004–05	Sunderland	0	0		

MYHRE, Thomas (G) **256 0**
H: 6 4 W: 14 02 b.Sarpsborg 16-10-73
Honours: Norway Youth, Under-21, 40 full caps.

1993	Viking	22	0		
1994	Viking	22	0		
1995	Viking	24	0		
1996	Viking	0	0		
1997	Viking	26	0	**94**	**0**
1997–98	Everton	22	0		
1998–99	Everton	38	0		
1999–2000	Everton	4	0		
1999–2000	*Rangers*	3	0	**3**	**0**
1999–2000	*Birmingham C*	7	0	**7**	**0**
2000–01	Everton	6	0		
2000–01	*Tranmere R*	3	0	**3**	**0**
2000–01	FC Copenhagen	14	0	**14**	**0**
2001–02	Everton	0	0	**70**	**0**
2001–02	Besiktas	13	0	**13**	**0**
2002–03	Sunderland	2	0		
2003–04	Sunderland	4	0		
2003–04	*Crystal Palace*	15	0	**15**	**0**
2004–05	Sunderland	31	0	**37**	**0**

PIPER, Matt (M) **48 2**
H: 6 1 W: 13 08 b.Leicester 29-9-81
Source: Trainee.

1999–2000	Leicester C	0	0		
2000–01	Leicester C	0	0		
2001–02	*Mansfield T*	8	1	**8**	**1**
2001–02	Leicester C	16	1		
2002–03	Leicester C	0	0	**16**	**1**
2002–03	Sunderland	13	0		
2003–04	Sunderland	9	0		
2004–05	Sunderland	2	0	**24**	**0**

POOM, Mart (G) **249 1**
H: 6 4 W: 13 13 b.Tallinn 3-2-72
Honours: Estonia 101 full caps.

1992–93	Flora Tallinn	11	0		
1993–94	Flora Tallinn	11	0		
1994–95	Portsmouth	0	0		
1995–96	Portsmouth	4	0		
1995–96	Flora Tallinn	7	0		
1996–97	Portsmouth	0	0	**4**	**0**
1996–97	Flora Tallinn	12	0	**41**	**0**
1996–97	Derby Co	4	0		
1997–98	Derby Co	36	0		
1998–99	Derby Co	17	0		
1999–2000	Derby Co	28	0		
2000–01	Derby Co	33	0		
2001–02	Derby Co	15	0		
2002–03	Derby Co	13	0	**146**	**0**
2002–03	Sunderland	4	0		
2003–04	Sunderland	43	1		
2004–05	Sunderland	11	0	**58**	**1**

ROBINSON, Carl (M) **265 26**
H: 5 11 W: 12 08 b.Llandrindod Wells 13-10-76
Source: Trainee. *Honours:* Wales Youth, Under-21, B, 21 full caps.

1995–96	Wolverhampton W	0	0		
1995–96	*Shrewsbury T*	4	0	**4**	**0**
1996–97	Wolverhampton W	2	0		

1997–98	Wolverhampton W	32	3		
1998–99	Wolverhampton W	34	8		
1999–2000	Wolverhampton W	33	3		
2000–01	Wolverhampton W	40	3		
2001–02	Wolverhampton W	23	2	**164**	**19**
2002–03	Portsmouth	15	0		
2002–03	*Sheffield W*	4	1	**4**	**1**
2002–03	*Walsall*	11	1	**11**	**1**
2003–04	Portsmouth	1	0	**16**	**0**
2003–04	*Rotherham U*	14	0	**14**	**0**
2003–04	*Sheffield U*	5	0	**5**	**0**
2003–04	*Sunderland*	7	1		
2004–05	Sunderland	40	4	**47**	**5**

RYAN, Richie (M) **2 0**
H: 5 10 W: 11 09 b.Kilkenny 6-1-85
Source: Scholar.

2001–02	Sunderland	0	0		
2002–03	Sunderland	2	0		
2003–04	Sunderland	0	0		
2004–05	Sunderland	0	0	**2**	**0**
2004–05	*Scunthorpe U*	0	0		

SMITH, Dan (D) **0 0**
H: 5 9 W: 10 10 b.Sunderland 5-10-86
Source: Scholar.

2003–04	Sunderland	0	0		
2004–05	Sunderland	0	0		

STEWART, Marcus (F) **481 173**
H: 5 11 W: 12 02 b.Bristol 7-11-72
Source: Trainee. *Honours:* England Schools, Football League.

1991–92	Bristol R	33	5		
1992–93	Bristol R	38	11		
1993–94	Bristol R	29	5		
1994–95	Bristol R	27	15		
1995–96	Bristol R	44	21	**171**	**57**
1996–97	Huddersfield T	20	7		
1997–98	Huddersfield T	41	15		
1998–99	Huddersfield T	43	22		
1999–2000	Huddersfield T	29	14	**133**	**58**
1999–2000	Ipswich T	10	2		
2000–01	Ipswich T	34	19		
2001–02	Ipswich T	28	6		
2002–03	Ipswich T	3	0	**75**	**27**
2002–03	Sunderland	19	1		
2003–04	Sunderland	40	14		
2004–05	Sunderland	43	16	**102**	**31**

TAYLOR, Sean (D) **0 0**
H: 5 7 W: 11 00 b.Amble 9-12-85
Source: Trainee.

2002–03	Sunderland	0	0		
2003–04	Sunderland	0	0		
2004–05	Sunderland	0	0		

TEGGART, Neil (F) **16 0**
H: 6 2 W: 12 06 b.Downpatrick 16-9-84
Source: Scholar. *Honours:* Northern Ireland Youth, Under-21.

2001–02	Sunderland	0	0		
2002–03	Sunderland	0	0		
2003–04	Sunderland	0	0		
2003–04	*Darlington*	15	0	**15**	**0**
2004–05	Sunderland	0	0		
2004–05	*Scunthorpe U*	1	0	**1**	**0**

THORNTON, Sean (M) **63 10**
H: 5 11 W: 13 11 b.Drogheda 18-5-83
Source: Scholar. *Honours:* Eire Youth, Under-21.

2001–02	Tranmere R	11	1	**11**	**1**
2002–03	Sunderland	11	1		
2002–03	*Blackpool*	3	0	**3**	**0**
2003–04	Sunderland	22	4		
2004–05	Sunderland	16	4	**49**	**9**

WANLESS, Jack (F) **0 0**
H: 5 7 W: 11 01 b.Hexham 23-11-85
Source: Scholar.

2004–05	Sunderland	0	0		

WELSH, Andy (F) **88 6**
H: 5 8 W: 9 06 b.Manchester 24-11-83
Source: Scholar.

2001–02	Stockport Co	15	0		
2002–03	Stockport Co	13	2		
2002–03	*Macclesfield T*	6	2	**6**	**2**
2003–04	Stockport Co	34	1		
2004–05	Stockport Co	13	0	**75**	**3**
2004–05	Sunderland	7	1	**7**	**1**

WHITEHEAD, Dean (M) **164 14**
H: 5 11 W: 12 06 b.Oxford 12-1-82
Source: Trainee.

1999–2000	Oxford U	0	0		
2000–01	Oxford U	20	0		
2001–02	Oxford U	40	1		
2002–03	Oxford U	18	1		
2003–04	Oxford U	44	7	**122**	**9**
2004–05	Sunderland	42	5	**42**	**5**

WHITLEY, Jeff (M) **218 12**
H: 5 8 W: 11 06 b.Zambia 28-1-79
Source: Trainee. *Honours:* Northern Ireland Under-21, B, 19 full caps, 2 goals.

1995–96	Manchester C	0	0		
1996–97	Manchester C	23	1		
1997–98	Manchester C	17	1		
1998–99	Manchester C	8	1		
1998–99	*Wrexham*	9	2	**9**	**2**
1999–2000	Manchester C	42	4		
2000–01	Manchester C	31	1		
2001–02	Manchester C	2	0		
2001–02	*Notts Co*	6	0		
2002–03	Manchester C	0	0	**123**	**8**
2002–03	*Notts Co*	12	0	**18**	**0**
2003–04	Sunderland	33	2		
2004–05	Sunderland	35	0	**68**	**2**

WRIGHT, Stephen (D) **124 2**
H: 6 0 W: 12 08 b.Liverpool 8-2-80
Source: Trainee. *Honours:* England Youth, Under-21.

1997–98	Liverpool	0	0		
1998–99	Liverpool	0	0		
1999–2000	Liverpool	0	0		
1999–2000	*Crewe Alex*	23	0	**23**	**0**
2000–01	Liverpool	2	0		
2001–02	Liverpool	12	0	**14**	**0**
2002–03	Sunderland	26	0		
2003–04	Sunderland	22	1		
2004–05	Sunderland	39	1	**87**	**2**

SWANSEA C (79)

ANDERSON, Ijah (D) **273 4**
H: 5 8 W: 10 06 b.Hackney 30-12-75
Source: Tottenham H Trainee.

1994–95	Southend U	0	0		
1995–96	Brentford	25	2		
1996–97	Brentford	46	1		
1997–98	Brentford	17	0		
1998–99	Brentford	38	1		
1999–2000	Brentford	31	0		
2000–01	Brentford	1	0		
2001–02	Brentford	35	0		
2002–03	Brentford	9	0	**202**	**4**
2002–03	*Wycombe W*	5	0	**5**	**0**
2002–03	Bristol R	14	0		
2003–04	Bristol R	39	0		
2004–05	Bristol R	0	0	**53**	**0**
2004–05	Swansea C	13	0	**13**	**0**

AUSTIN, Kevin (D) **348 5**
H: 6 2 W: 15 00 b.Hackney 12-2-73
Source: Saffron Walden. *Honours:* Trinidad & Tobago 1 full cap.

1993–94	Leyton Orient	30	0		
1994–95	Leyton Orient	39	2		
1995–96	Leyton Orient	40	1	**109**	**3**
1996–97	Lincoln C	44	1		
1997–98	Lincoln C	46	0		
1998–99	Lincoln C	39	1	**129**	**2**
1999–2000	Barnsley	3	0		
2000–01	Barnsley	0	0	**3**	**0**
2000–01	*Brentford*	3	0	**3**	**0**
2001–02	Cambridge U	6	0	**6**	**0**
2002–03	Bristol R	33	0		
2003–04	Bristol R	23	0	**56**	**0**
2004–05	Swansea C	42	0	**42**	**0**

BRITTON, Leon (M) **97 4**
H: 5 6 W: 10 00 b.Merton 16-9-82
Source: Trainee. *Honours:* England Youth.

1999–2000	West Ham U	0	0		
2000–01	West Ham U	0	0		
2001–02	West Ham U	0	0		
2002–03	West Ham U	0	0		
2002–03	*Swansea C*	25	0		
2003–04	Swansea C	42	3		
2004–05	Swansea C	30	1	**97**	**4**

CONNOR, Paul (F) **200 55**
H: 6 2 W: 11 08 b.Bishop Auckland 12-1-79
Source: Trainee.

1996–97	Middlesbrough	0	0		
1997–98	Middlesbrough	0	0		
1997–98	*Hartlepool U*	5	0	**5**	**0**
1998–99	Middlesbrough	0	0		
1998–99	*Stoke C*	3	2		
1999–2000	Stoke C	26	5		
2000–01	Stoke C	7	0	**36**	**7**
2000–01	*Cambridge U*	13	5	**13**	**5**
2000–01	Rochdale	14	10		
2001–02	Rochdale	17	1		
2002–03	Rochdale	39	12		
2003–04	Rochdale	24	5	**94**	**28**
2003–04	Swansea C	12	5		
2004–05	Swansea C	40	10	**52**	**15**

CORBISIERO, Antonio (M) **5 0**
H: 5 8 W: 11 04 b.Reading 17-11-84
Source: Scholar.

2003–04	Swansea C	5	0		
2004–05	Swansea C	0	0	**5**	**0**

FISKEN, Gary (M) **27 1**
H: 5 11 W: 12 10 b.Watford 27-10-81
Source: Scholarship.

1999–2000	Watford	0	0		
2000–01	Watford	0	0		
2001–02	Watford	17	1		
2002–03	Watford	4	0		
2003–04	Watford	1	0	**22**	**1**
2004–05	Swansea C	5	0	**5**	**0**

FORBES, Adrian (F) **224 29**
H: 5 9 W: 12 06 b.Greenford 23-1-79
Source: Trainee. *Honours:* England Youth.

1996–97	Norwich C	10	0		
1997–98	Norwich C	33	4		
1998–99	Norwich C	15	0		
1999–2000	Norwich C	25	1		
2000–01	Norwich C	29	3	**112**	**8**
2001–02	Luton T	40	4		
2002–03	Luton T	5	1		
2003–04	Luton T	27	9	**72**	**14**
2004–05	Swansea C	40	7	**40**	**7**

GUERET, Willy (G) **58 0**
H: 6 2 W: 14 01 b.Saint Claude 3-8-73
Source: Le Mans.

2000–01	Millwall	11	0		
2001–02	Millwall	1	0		
2002–03	Millwall	0	0		
2003–04	Millwall	2	0	**14**	**0**
2004–05	Swansea C	44	0	**44**	**0**

GURNEY, Andy (D) **399 43**
H: 6 0 W: 13 04 b.Bristol 25-1-74
Source: Trainee.

1992–93	Bristol R	0	0		
1993–94	Bristol R	3	0		
1994–95	Bristol R	38	1		
1995–96	Bristol R	43	6		
1996–97	Bristol R	24	2	**108**	**9**
1997–98	Torquay U	44	9		
1998–99	Torquay U	20	1	**64**	**10**
1998–99	Reading	8	0		
1999–2000	Reading	38	2		
2000–01	Reading	21	1	**67**	**3**
2001–02	Swindon T	43	6		
2002–03	Swindon T	41	8		
2003–04	Swindon T	42	6		
2004–05	Swindon T	6	0	**132**	**20**
2004–05	Swansea C	28	1	**28**	**1**

HYLTON, Leon (D) **19 0**
H: 5 9 W: 11 00 b.Birmingham 27-1-83
Honours: England Youth, Under-20.

1999–2000	Aston Villa	0	0		
2000–01	Aston Villa	0	0		
2001–02	Aston Villa	0	0		
2002–03	Aston Villa	0	0		
2002–03	*Swansea C*	8	0		
2003–04	Swansea C	11	0		
2004–05	Swansea C	0	0	**19**	**0**

IRIEKPEN, Ezomo (D) **81 5**
H: 6 1 W: 12 02 b.East London 14-5-82
Source: Trainee. *Honours:* England Youth.

1998–99	West Ham U	0	0		
1999–2000	West Ham U	0	0		

2000–01	West Ham U	0	0		
2001–02	West Ham U	0	0		
2002–03	West Ham U	0	0		
2002–03	*Leyton Orient*	5	1	**5**	**1**
2002–03	*Cambridge U*	13	1	**13**	**1**
2003–04	Swansea C	34	1		
2004–05	Swansea C	29	2	**63**	**3**

JONES, Stuart (D) **34 0**
H: 6 0 W: 11 08 b.Aberystwyth 14-3-84
Source: Scholar. *Honours:* Wales Youth, Under-21.

2002–03	Swansea C	6	0		
2003–04	Swansea C	24	0		
2004–05	Swansea C	4	0	**34**	**0**

MARTINEZ, Roberto (M) **293 19**
H: 5 9 W: 12 02 b.Balaguer 13-7-73
Source: Balaguer.

1995–96	Wigan Ath	42	9		
1996–97	Wigan Ath	43	4		
1997–98	Wigan Ath	33	1		
1998–99	Wigan Ath	10	0		
1999–2000	Wigan Ath	25	3		
2000–01	Wigan Ath	34	0	**187**	**17**
2001–02	Motherwell	17	0	**17**	**0**
2002–03	Walsall	6	0	**6**	**0**
2002–03	Swansea C	19	2		
2003–04	Swansea C	27	0		
2004–05	Swansea C	37	0	**83**	**2**

MAYLETT, Brad (M) **109 8**
H: 5 10 W: 10 04 b.Manchester 24-12-80
Source: Trainee.

1998–99	Burnley	17	0		
1999–2000	Burnley	0	0		
2000–01	Burnley	12	0		
2001–02	Burnley	10	0		
2002–03	Burnley	6	0	**45**	**0**
2002–03	*Swansea C*	6	0		
2003–04	Swansea C	33	5		
2004–05	Swansea C	16	0	**55**	**5**
2004–05	*Boston U*	9	3	**9**	**3**

McLEOD, Kevin (M) **83 6**
H: 5 11 W: 12 00 b.Liverpool 12-9-80
Source: Trainee.

1998–99	Everton	0	0		
1999–2000	Everton	0	0		
2000–01	Everton	5	0		
2001–02	Everton	0	0		
2002–03	Everton	0	0		
2002–03	*QPR*	8	2		
2003–04	Everton	0	0	**5**	**0**
2003–04	QPR	35	3		
2004–05	QPR	24	1	**67**	**6**
2004–05	Swansea C	11	0	**11**	**0**

MONK, Garry (D) **95 0**
H: 6 1 W: 13 00 b.Bedford 6-3-79
Source: Trainee.

1995–96	Torquay U	5	0		
1996–97	Southampton	0	0		
1997–98	Southampton	0	0		
1998–99	Southampton	4	0		
1998–99	*Torquay U*	6	0	**11**	**0**
1999–2000	Southampton	2	0		
1999–2000	*Stockport Co*	2	0	**2**	**0**
2000–01	Southampton	2	0		
2000–01	*Oxford U*	5	0	**5**	**0**
2001–02	Southampton	2	0		
2002–03	Southampton	1	0		
2002–03	*Sheffield W*	15	0	**15**	**0**
2003–04	Southampton	0	0	**11**	**0**
2003–04	Barnsley	17	0	**17**	**0**
2004–05	Swansea C	34	0	**34**	**0**

MURPHY, Brian (G) **14 0**
H: 6 0 W: 13 00 b.Waterford 7-5-83
Honours: Eire Youth, Under-21.

2000–01	Manchester C	0	0		
2001–02	Manchester C	0	0		
2002–03	Manchester C	0	0		
2002–03	*Oldham Ath*	0	0		
2002–03	*Peterborough U*	1	0	**1**	**0**
From Waterford					
2003–04	Swansea C	11	0		
2004–05	Swansea C	2	0	**13**	**0**

NUGENT, Kevin (F) **495 115**
H: 6 1 W: 13 03 b.Edmonton 10-4-69
Source: Trainee. *Honours:* Eire Youth.

1987–88	Leyton Orient	11	3		
1988–89	Leyton Orient	3	0		
1989–90	Leyton Orient	11	0		
1990–91	Leyton Orient	33	5		
1991–92	Leyton Orient	36	12		
1991–92	Plymouth Arg	4	0		
1992–93	Plymouth Arg	45	11		
1993–94	Plymouth Arg	39	14		
1994–95	Plymouth Arg	37	7		
1995–96	Plymouth Arg	6	0	**131**	**32**
1995–96	Bristol C	34	8		
1996–97	Bristol C	36	6	**70**	**14**
1997–98	Cardiff C	4	0		
1998–99	Cardiff C	41	15		
1999–2000	Cardiff C	39	10		
2000–01	Cardiff C	14	4		
2001–02	Cardiff C	1	0	**99**	**29**
2001–02	Leyton Orient	9	1		
2002–03	Leyton Orient	19	3	**122**	**24**
2002–03	Swansea C	15	5		
2003–04	Swansea C	39	8		
2004–05	Swansea C	19	3	**73**	**16**

O'LEARY, Kristian (M) **235 8**
H: 6 0 W: 12 09 b.Port Talbot 30-8-77
Source: Trainee. *Honours:* Wales Youth.

1995–96	Swansea C	1	0		
1996–97	Swansea C	12	1		
1997–98	Swansea C	29	0		
1998–99	Swansea C	19	2		
1999–2000	Swansea C	20	0		
2000–01	Swansea C	24	2		
2001–02	Swansea C	31	2		
2002–03	Swansea C	33	0		
2003–04	Swansea C	34	0		
2004–05	Swansea C	32	1	**235**	**8**

PRITCHARD, Mark (F) **4 0**
H: 5 10 W: 12 04 b.Tredegar 23-11-85
Source: Scholar.

2003–04	Swansea C	4	0		
2004–05	Swansea C	0	0	**4**	**0**

REWBURY, Jamie (D) **2 0**
H: 6 2 W: 12 01 b.Wattstown 15-2-86
Source: Scholar. *Honours:* Wales Youth.

2003–04	Swansea C	2	0		
2004–05	Swansea C	0	0	**2**	**0**

RICKETTS, Sam (D) **87 1**
H: 6 0 W: 12 11 b.Aylesbury 11-10-81
Source: Trainee. *Honours:* Wales 3 full caps.

1999–2000	Oxford U	0	0		
2000–01	Oxford U	14	0		
2001–02	Oxford U	29	1		
2002–03	Oxford U	2	0	**45**	**1**
From Telford U					
2004–05	Swansea C	42	0	**42**	**0**

ROBINSON, Andy (M) **74 16**
H: 5 8 W: 11 04 b.Birkenhead 3-11-79
Source: Cammell Laird.

2002–03	Tranmere R	0	0		
2003–04	Swansea C	37	8		
2004–05	Swansea C	37	8	**74**	**16**

TATE, Alan (D) **76 1**
H: 6 1 W: 13 05 b.Easington 2-9-82
Source: Scholar.

2000–01	Manchester U	0	0		
2001–02	Manchester U	0	0		
2002–03	Manchester U	0	0		
2002–03	*Swansea C*	27	0		
2003–04	Manchester U	0	0		
2003–04	Swansea C	26	1		
2004–05	Swansea C	23	0	**76**	**1**

THOMAS, James (F) **90 21**
H: 6 0 W: 13 05 b.Swansea 16-1-79
Source: Trainee. *Honours:* Wales Under-21.

1996–97	Blackburn R	0	0		
1997–98	Blackburn R	0	0		
1997–98	*WBA*	3	0	**3**	**0**
1998–99	Blackburn R	0	0		
1999–2000	Blackburn R	0	0		
1999–2000	*Blackpool*	9	2	**9**	**2**
2000–01	Blackburn R	4	1		
2000–01	*Sheffield U*	10	1	**10**	**1**
2001–02	Blackburn R	0	0	**4**	**1**
2001–02	*Bristol R*	7	1	**7**	**1**
2002–03	Swansea C	39	13		
2003–04	Swansea C	16	3		
2004–05	Swansea C	2	0	**57**	**16**

THORPE, Lee (F) **315 77**
H: 6 1 W: 12 07 b.Wolverhampton 14-12-75
Source: Trainee.

1993–94	Blackpool	1	0		
1994–95	Blackpool	1	0		
1995–96	Blackpool	1	0		
1996–97	Blackpool	9	0	**12**	**0**
1997–98	Lincoln C	44	14		
1998–99	Lincoln C	38	8		
1999–2000	Lincoln C	42	16		
2000–01	Lincoln C	31	7		
2001–02	Lincoln C	37	13	**192**	**58**
2001–02	Leyton Orient	0	0		
2002–03	Leyton Orient	38	8		
2003–04	Leyton Orient	17	4	**55**	**12**
2003–04	*Grimsby T*	6	0	**6**	**0**
2003–04	Bristol R	10	1		
2004–05	Bristol R	25	3	**35**	**4**
2004–05	Swansea C	15	3	**15**	**3**

TRUNDLE, Lee (F) **167 65**
H: 6 0 W: 13 03 b.Liverpool 10-10-76
Source: Rhyl.

2000–01	Wrexham	14	8		
2001–02	Wrexham	36	8		
2002–03	Wrexham	44	11	**94**	**27**
2003–04	Swansea C	31	16		
2004–05	Swansea C	42	22	**73**	**38**

SWINDON T (80)

BAMPTON, David (M) **3 0**
H: 5 8 W: 11 02 b.Swindon 5-5-85

2002–03	Swindon T	3	0		
2003–04	Swindon T	0	0		
2004–05	Swindon T	0	0	**3**	**0**

BOOK, Steve (G) **174 0**
H: 5 11 W: 11 01 b.Bournemouth 7-7-69

1997–98	Brighton & HA	0	0		
1998–99	Lincoln C	0	0		
From Forest Green R.					
1999–2000	Cheltenham T	46	0		
2000–01	Cheltenham T	46	0		
2001–02	Cheltenham T	39	0		
2002–03	Cheltenham T	36	0		
2003–04	Cheltenham T	5	0	**172**	**0**
2004–05	Swindon T	2	0	**2**	**0**

CATON, Andy (M) **8 1**
H: 6 0 W: 12 03 b.Oxford 3-12-87

2004–05	Swindon T	8	1	**8**	**1**

DUKE, David (M) **204 7**
H: 5 10 W: 11 03 b.Inverness 7-11-78
Source: Redby CA.

1997–98	Sunderland	0	0		
1998–99	Sunderland	0	0		
1999–2000	Sunderland	0	0		
2000–01	Swindon T	32	1		
2001–02	Swindon T	42	2		
2002–03	Swindon T	44	2		
2003–04	Swindon T	42	1		
2004–05	Swindon T	44	1	**204**	**7**

EVANS, Rhys (G) **108 0**
H: 6 1 W: 12 02 b.Swindon 27-1-82
Source: Trainee. *Honours:* England Schools, Youth, Under-20, Under-21.

1998–99	Chelsea	0	0		
1999–2000	Chelsea	0	0		
1999–2000	*Bristol R*	4	0	**4**	**0**
2000–01	Chelsea	0	0		
2001–02	Chelsea	0	0		
2001–02	*QPR*	11	0	**11**	**0**
2002–03	Chelsea	0	0		
2002–03	*Leyton Orient*	7	0	**7**	**0**
2003–04	Swindon T	41	0		
2004–05	Swindon T	45	0	**86**	**0**

FALLON, Rory (F) **119 21**
H: 6 2 W: 11 10 b.Gisbourne 20-3-82
Source: North Shore U. *Honours:* England Youth.

1998–99	Barnsley	0	0		

1999–2000	Barnsley	0	0		
2000–01	Barnsley	1	0		
2001–02	Barnsley	9	0		
2001–02	*Shrewsbury T*	11	0	**11**	**0**
2002–03	Barnsley	26	7		
2003–04	Barnsley	16	4	**52**	**11**
2003–04	Swindon T	19	6		
2004–05	Swindon T	31	3	**50**	**9**
2004–05	*Yeovil T*	6	1	**6**	**1**

GARRARD, Luke (M) **11** **0**

H: 5 10 W: 11 09 b.Barnet 22-9-85

2002–03	Swindon T	1	0		
2003–04	Swindon T	1	0		
2004–05	Swindon T	9	0	**11**	**0**

HEWLETT, Matt (M) **308** **15**

H: 6 2 W: 11 03 b.Bristol 25-2-76

Source: Trainee. *Honours:* England Youth.

1993–94	Bristol C	12	0		
1994–95	Bristol C	1	0		
1995–96	Bristol C	27	2		
1996–97	Bristol C	36	2		
1997–98	Bristol C	34	4		
1998–99	Bristol C	10	1		
1998–99	*Burnley*	2	0	**2**	**0**
1999–2000	Bristol C	7	0	**127**	**9**
2000–01	Swindon T	26	0		
2001–02	Swindon T	39	1		
2002–03	Swindon T	40	1		
2003–04	Swindon T	43	3		
2004–05	Swindon T	31	1	**179**	**6**

HEYWOOD, Matthew (D) **196** **8**

H: 6 2 W: 14 00 b.Chatham 26-8-79

Source: Trainee.

1998–99	Burnley	13	0		
1999–2000	Burnley	0	0		
2000–01	Burnley	0	0	**13**	**0**
2000–01	Swindon T	21	2		
2001–02	Swindon T	44	3		
2002–03	Swindon T	46	1		
2003–04	Swindon T	40	1		
2004–05	Swindon T	32	1	**183**	**8**

HOLGATE, Ashan (F) **2** **0**

H: 6 2 W: 12 00 b.Swindon 9-11-86

Source: Scholar.

2004–05	Swindon T	2	0	**2**	**0**

HOWARD, Brian (M) **70** **9**

H: 5 8 W: 11 05 b.Winchester 23-1-83

Source: From Trainee. *Honours:* England Youth, Under-20.

1999–2000	Southampton	0	0		
2000–01	Southampton	0	0		
2001–02	Southampton	0	0		
2002–03	Southampton	0	0		
2003–04	Swindon T	35	4		
2004–05	Swindon T	35	5	**70**	**9**

IFIL, Jerel (D) **73** **0**

H: 6 1 W: 12 11 b.Wembley 27-6-82

Source: Academy.

1999–2000	Watford	0	0		
2000–01	Watford	0	0		
2001–02	Watford	0	0		
2001–02	*Huddersfield T*	2	0	**2**	**0**
2002–03	Watford	1	0		
2002–03	*Swindon T*	9	0		
2003–04	Watford	10	0	**11**	**0**
2003–04	*Swindon T*	16	0		
2004–05	Swindon T	35	0	**60**	**0**

IGOE, Sammy (M) **328** **27**

H: 5 6 W: 10 00 b.Staines 30-9-75

Source: Trainee.

1993–94	Portsmouth	0	0		
1994–95	Portsmouth	1	0		
1995–96	Portsmouth	22	0		
1996–97	Portsmouth	40	2		
1997–98	Portsmouth	31	3		
1998–99	Portsmouth	40	5		
1999–2000	Portsmouth	26	1	**160**	**11**
1999–2000	Reading	6	0		
2000–01	Reading	31	6		
2001–02	Reading	35	1		
2002–03	Reading	15	0	**87**	**7**
2002–03	*Luton T*	2	0	**2**	**0**
2003–04	Swindon T	36	5		
2004–05	Swindon T	43	4	**79**	**9**

JENKINS, Steve (D) **485** **6**

H: 5 11 W: 12 12 b.Merthyr 16-7-72

Source: Trainee. *Honours:* Wales Youth, Under-21, 16 full caps.

1990–91	Swansea C	1	0		
1991–92	Swansea C	34	0		
1992–93	Swansea C	33	0		
1993–94	Swansea C	40	1		
1994–95	Swansea C	42	0		
1995–96	Swansea C	15	0	**165**	**1**
1995–96	Huddersfield T	31	1		
1996–97	Huddersfield T	33	0		
1997–98	Huddersfield T	29	1		
1998–99	Huddersfield T	36	1		
1999–2000	Huddersfield T	33	0		
2000–01	Huddersfield T	30	0		
2000–01	*Birmingham C*	3	0	**3**	**0**
2001–02	Huddersfield T	40	1		
2002–03	Huddersfield T	26	0	**258**	**4**
2002–03	Cardiff C	4	0	**4**	**0**
2003–04	Notts Co	17	0	**17**	**0**
2003–04	Peterborough U	8	0		
2004–05	Peterborough U	6	1	**14**	**1**
2004–05	Swindon T	24	0	**24**	**0**

LAPHAM, Kyle (D) **2** **0**

H: 5 11 W: 11 00 b.Swindon 5-1-86

Source: Scholar.

2004–05	Swindon T	2	0	**2**	**0**

MIGLIORANZI, Stefani (M) **132** **9**

H: 6 0 W: 11 12 b.Pacos de Caldas 20-9-77

Source: St Johns Univ.

1998–99	Portsmouth	7	0		
1999–2000	Portsmouth	13	2		
2000–01	Portsmouth	12	0		
2001–02	Portsmouth	3	0	**35**	**2**
2002–03	Swindon T	41	3		
2003–04	Swindon T	35	4		
2004–05	Swindon T	21	0	**97**	**7**

NICHOLAS, Andrew (D) **52** **1**

H: 6 0 W: 12 10 b.Liverpool 10-10-83

Honours: Liverpool Trainee.

2003–04	Swindon T	31	1		
2004–05	Swindon T	16	0	**47**	**1**
2004–05	*Chester C*	5	0	**5**	**0**

O'HANLON, Sean (D) **59** **5**

H: 6 1 W: 12 05 b.Southport 2-1-83

Honours: England Youth, Under-20.

1999–2000	Everton	0	0		
2000–01	Everton	0	0		
2001–02	Everton	0	0		
2002–03	Everton	0	0		
2003–04	Everton	0	0		
2003–04	Swindon T	19	2		
2004–05	Swindon T	40	3	**59**	**5**

OPARA, Lloyd (F) **16** **1**

H: 6 1 W: 12 08 b.Enfield 6-1-84

Source: Scholar.

2001–02	Colchester U	1	0		
2002–03	Colchester U	5	0	**6**	**0**
2002–03	Cambridge U	2	0		
2003–04	Cambridge U	8	1	**10**	**1**

From Grays Ath.

2004–05	Swindon T	0	0		

PARKIN, Sam (F) **186** **79**

H: 6 2 W: 13 00 b.Roehampton 14-3-81

Honours: England Schools.

1998–99	Chelsea	0	0		
1999–2000	Chelsea	0	0		
2000–01	Chelsea	0	0		
2000–01	*Millwall*	7	4	**7**	**4**
2000–01	*Wycombe W*	8	1	**8**	**1**
2000–01	*Oldham Ath*	7	3	**7**	**3**
2001–02	Chelsea	0	0		
2001–02	*Northampton T*	40	4	**40**	**4**
2002–03	Swindon T	43	25		
2003–04	Swindon T	40	19		
2004–05	Swindon T	41	23	**124**	**67**

POOK, Michael (M) **5** **0**

H: 5 11 W: 11 10 b.Swindon 22-10-85

Source: Scholar.

2003–04	Swindon T	0	0		
2004–05	Swindon T	5	0	**5**	**0**

REEVES, Alan (D) **443** **27**

H: 6 0 W: 12 00 b.Birkenhead 19-11-67

Source: Heswall.

1988–89	Norwich C	0	0		
1988–89	*Gillingham*	18	0	**18**	**0**
1989–90	Chester C	30	2		
1990–91	Chester C	10	0	**40**	**2**
1991–92	Rochdale	34	3		
1992–93	Rochdale	41	3		
1993–94	Rochdale	41	3		
1994–95	Rochdale	5	0	**121**	**9**
1994–95	Wimbledon	31	3		
1995–96	Wimbledon	24	1		
1996–97	Wimbledon	2	0		
1997–98	Wimbledon	0	0	**57**	**4**
1998–99	Swindon T	24	2		
1999–2000	Swindon T	43	1		
2000–01	Swindon T	44	3		
2001–02	Swindon T	25	2		
2002–03	Swindon T	36	3		
2003–04	Swindon T	27	0		
2004–05	Swindon T	8	1	**207**	**12**

ROBERTS, Chris (F) **217** **45**

H: 5 9 W: 13 02 b.Cardiff 22-10-79

Source: Trainee. *Honours:* Wales Youth, Under-21.

1997–98	Cardiff C	11	3		
1998–99	Cardiff C	4	0		
1999–2000	Cardiff C	8	0	**23**	**3**
2000–01	Exeter C	42	8		
2001–02	Exeter C	37	11	**79**	**19**
2001–02	Bristol C	4	0		
2002–03	Bristol C	44	13		
2003–04	Bristol C	38	6		
2004–05	Bristol C	8	1	**94**	**20**
2004–05	Swindon T	21	3	**21**	**3**

ROBINSON, Steve (M) **228** **5**

H: 5 9 W: 11 03 b.Nottingham 17-1-75

Source: Trainee.

1993–94	Birmingham C	0	0		
1994–95	Birmingham C	6	0		
1995–96	Birmingham C	0	0		
1995–96	*Peterborough U*	5	0	**5**	**0**
1996–97	Birmingham C	9	0		
1997–98	Birmingham C	25	0		
1998–99	Birmingham C	31	0		
1999–2000	Birmingham C	6	0		
2000–01	Birmingham C	4	0	**81**	**0**
2000–01	Swindon T	18	2		
2001–02	Swindon T	40	0		
2002–03	Swindon T	44	2		
2003–04	Swindon T	22	1		
2004–05	Swindon T	18	0	**142**	**5**

SMITH, Grant (M) **63** **11**

H: 6 1 W: 12 07 b.Irvine 5-5-80

1998–99	Reading	0	0		
1999–2000	Reading	0	0		
2000–01	Reading	0	0		
2001–02	*Halifax T*	11	0	**11**	**0**
2001–02	Sheffield U	7	0		
2002–03	Sheffield U	3	0	**10**	**0**
2002–03	*Plymouth Arg*	5	1	**5**	**1**
2003–04	Swindon T	7	0		
2004–05	Swindon T	30	10	**37**	**10**

TAYLOR, Chris (D) **4** **0**

H: 5 8 W: 10 05 b.Swindon 30-10-85

Source: Scholar.

2002–03	Swindon T	4	0		
2003–04	Swindon T	0	0		
2004–05	Swindon T	0	0	**4**	**0**

VIVEASH, Adrian (D) **372** **19**

H: 6 2 W: 12 13 b.Swindon 30-9-69

Source: Trainee.

1988–89	Swindon T	0	0		
1989–90	Swindon T	0	0		
1990–91	Swindon T	25	1		
1991–92	Swindon T	10	0		
1992–93	Swindon T	5	0		
1992–93	*Reading*	5	0		
1993–94	Swindon T	0	0		
1994–95	Swindon T	14	1		
1994–95	*Reading*	6	0		
1995–96	Swindon T	0	0		
1995–96	*Barnsley*	2	1	**2**	**1**
1995–96	Walsall	31	0		
1996–97	Walsall	46	9		

1997–98	Walsall	42	3		
1998–99	Walsall	40	0		
1999–2000	Walsall	43	1	**202**	**13**
2000–01	Reading	40	2		
2001–02	Reading	18	1		
2002–03	Reading	5	0	**74**	**3**
2002–03	*Oxford U*	11	0	**11**	**0**
2003–04	Swindon T	15	0		
2003–04	*Kidderminster H*	7	0		
2004–05	Swindon T	0	0	**69**	**2**
2004–05	*Kidderminster H*	7	0	**14**	**0**

WELLS, Ben (M) **1** **0**
H: 5 9 W: 10 07 b.Basingstoke 26-3-88
Source: Scholar.

2004–05	Swindon T	1	0	**1**	**0**

TORQUAY U (81)

ABBEY, Zema (F) **103** **15**
H: 6 1 W: 12 10 b.Luton 17-4-77
Source: Arlesey, Baldock T, Hitchin T.

1999–2000	Cambridge U	8	0		
2000–01	Cambridge U	14	5	**22**	**5**
2000–01	Norwich C	20	1		
2001–02	Norwich C	6	1		
2002–03	Norwich C	30	5		
2003–04	Norwich C	3	0		
2004–05	Norwich C	0	0	**59**	**7**
2004–05	*Boston U*	5	1	**5**	**1**
2004–05	Wycombe W	5	0	**5**	**0**
2004–05	Bradford C	6	1	**6**	**1**
2004–05	Torquay U	6	1	**6**	**1**

AKINFENWA, Adebayo (F) **73** **23**
H: 6 0 W: 15 04 b.Nigeria 10-5-82

2001	Atlantas	19	4		
2002	Atlantas	4	1	**23**	**5**
From Barry T					
2003–04	Boston U	3	0	**3**	**0**
2003–04	Leyton Orient	1	0	**1**	**0**
2003–04	Rushden & D	0	0		
2003–04	Doncaster R	9	4	**9**	**4**
2004–05	Torquay U	37	14	**37**	**14**

BEDEAU, Anthony (F) **277** **49**
H: 5 9 W: 12 00 b.Hammersmith 24-3-79
Source: Trainee. *Honours:* Grenada full caps.

1995–96	Torquay U	4	0		
1996–97	Torquay U	8	1		
1997–98	Torquay U	34	5		
1998–99	Torquay U	36	9		
1999–2000	Torquay U	38	16		
2000–01	Torquay U	34	5		
2001–02	Torquay U	21	4		
2001–02	*Barnsley*	3	0	**3**	**0**
2002–03	Torquay U	40	6		
2003–04	Torquay U	24	1		
2004–05	Torquay U	35	2	**274**	**49**

BOARDLEY, Stuart (M) **6** **0**
H: 5 10 W: 11 00 b.Ipswich 14-2-85
Source: Ipswich T Scholar.

2004–05	Torquay U	6	0	**6**	**0**

BOND, Kain (F) **3** **0**
H: 5 8 W: 11 03 b.Torquay 19-6-85
Source: Scholar.

2002–03	Torquay U	1	0		
2003–04	Torquay U	1	0		
2004–05	Torquay U	1	0	**3**	**0**

CANOVILLE, Lee (D) **114** **2**
H: 6 1 W: 12 08 b.Ealing 14-3-81
Source: Trainee. *Honours:* FA Schools, England Youth.

1998–99	Arsenal	0	0		
1999–2000	Arsenal	0	0		
2000–01	Arsenal	0	0		
2000–01	*Northampton T*	2	0	**2**	**0**
2001–02	Torquay U	12	1		
2002–03	Torquay U	36	0		
2003–04	Torquay U	33	1		
2004–05	Torquay U	31	0	**112**	**2**

CONSTANTINE, Leon (F) **111** **34**
H: 6 2 W: 11 10 b.Hackney 24-2-78
Source: Edgware T.

2000–01	Millwall	1	0		
2001–02	Millwall	0	0	**1**	**0**
2001–02	*Leyton Orient*	10	3	**10**	**3**
2001–02	*Partick T*	2	0	**2**	**0**
2002–03	Brentford	17	0	**17**	**0**
2003–04	Southend U	43	21	**43**	**21**
2004–05	Peterborough U	11	1	**11**	**1**
2004–05	Torquay U	27	9	**27**	**9**

DEARDEN, Kevin (G) **438** **0**
H: 5 11 W: 14 00 b.Luton 8-3-70
Source: Trainee.

1988–89	Tottenham H	0	0		
1988–89	*Cambridge U*	15	0	**15**	**0**
1989–90	Tottenham H	0	0		
1989–90	*Hartlepool U*	10	0	**10**	**0**
1989–90	*Oxford U*	0	0		
1989–90	*Swindon T*	1	0	**1**	**0**
1990–91	Tottenham H	0	0		
1990–91	*Peterborough U*	7	0	**7**	**0**
1990–91	*Hull C*	3	0	**3**	**0**
1991–92	Tottenham H	0	0		
1991–92	*Rochdale*	2	0	**2**	**0**
1991–92	*Birmingham C*	12	0	**12**	**0**
1992–93	Tottenham H	1	0		
1992–93	*Portsmouth*	0	0		
1993–94	Tottenham H	0	0	**1**	**0**
1993–94	Brentford	35	0		
1994–95	Brentford	43	0		
1995–96	Brentford	41	0		
1996–97	Brentford	44	0		
1997–98	Brentford	35	0		
1998–99	Brentford	7	0	**205**	**0**
1998–99	*Barnet*	1	0	**1**	**0**
1998–99	*Huddersfield T*	0	0		
1999–2000	Wrexham	45	0		
2000–01	Wrexham	36	0	**81**	**0**
2001–02	Torquay U	46	0		
2002–03	Torquay U	27	0		
2003–04	Torquay U	22	0		
2004–05	Torquay U	5	0	**100**	**0**

FOWLER, Jason (M) **267** **21**
H: 6 2 W: 13 05 b.Bristol 20-8-74
Source: Trainee.

1992–93	Bristol C	1	0		
1993–94	Bristol C	1	0		
1994–95	Bristol C	13	0		
1995–96	Bristol C	10	0	**25**	**0**
1996–97	Cardiff C	37	5		
1997–98	Cardiff C	38	5		
1998–99	Cardiff C	37	3		
1999–2000	Cardiff C	28	1		
2000–01	Cardiff C	5	0		
2001–02	Cardiff C	0	0	**145**	**14**
2001–02	Torquay U	14	1		
2002–03	Torquay U	40	4		
2003–04	Torquay U	31	2		
2004–05	Torquay U	12	0	**97**	**7**

GOSLING, Jamie (M) **19** **2**
H: 6 0 W: 10 06 b.Bath 21-3-82
Source: Bath C.

2003–04	Yeovil T	12	1		
From Aldershot T.					
2004–05	Yeovil T	0	0	**12**	**1**
From Weymouth					
2004–05	Torquay U	7	1	**7**	**1**

GOTTSKALKSSON, Olafur (G) **319** **0**
H: 6 3 W: 13 12 b.Keflavik 12-3-68
Honours: Iceland 9 full caps.

1988	IA Akranes	18	0		
1989	IA Akranes	15	0	**33**	**0**
1990	KR	18	0		
1991	KR	18	0		
1992	KR	18	0		
1993	KR	17	0	**71**	**0**
1994	Keflavik	18	0		
1995	Keflavik	17	0		
1996	Keflavik	18	0		
1997	Keflavik	10	0	**63**	**0**
1997–98	Hibernian	16	0		
1998–99	Hibernian	36	0		
1999–2000	Hibernian	0	0		
2000–01	Hibernian	12	0	**64**	**0**
2000–01	Brentford	45	0		
2001–02	Brentford	28	0		
2002–03	Brentford	0	0		
2003–04	Brentford	0	0	**73**	**0**
From Margate					
2004–05	Torquay U	15	0	**15**	**0**

HILL, Kevin (F) **326** **39**
H: 5 11 W: 11 00 b.Exeter 6-3-76
Source: Torrington.

1997–98	Torquay U	37	7		
1998–99	Torquay U	35	5		
1999–2000	Torquay U	43	2		
2000–01	Torquay U	44	9		
2001–02	Torquay U	44	2		
2002–03	Torquay U	39	4		
2003–04	Torquay U	45	5		
2004–05	Torquay U	39	5	**326**	**39**

HOCKLEY, Matthew (D) **137** **9**
H: 5 10 W: 12 07 b.Paignton 5-6-82
Source: Trainee.

2000–01	Torquay U	6	1		
2001–02	Torquay U	12	0		
2002–03	Torquay U	40	2		
2003–04	Torquay U	45	5		
2004–05	Torquay U	34	1	**137**	**9**

JARVIE, Paul (G) **2** **0**
H: 6 0 W: 12 03 b.Aberdeen 14-6-82
Source: Stoneywood BC.

2000–01	Dundee U	0	0		
2001–02	Dundee U	1	0		
2002–03	Dundee U	0	0		
2003–04	Dundee U	0	0	**1**	**0**
2004–05	Torquay U	1	0	**1**	**0**

KEANE, Ashley (M) **0** **0**
H: 6 0 W: 12 06 b.Camden 20-11-81

2004–05	Torquay U	0	0		

LOPES, Osvaldo (M) **10** **0**
H: 5 10 W: 11 07 b.France 6-4-80

2002–03	Plymouth Arg	9	0		
2003–04	Plymouth Arg	0	0		
2004–05	Plymouth Arg	0	0	**9**	**0**
From Cork C					
2004–05	Torquay U	1	0	**1**	**0**

MARRIOTT, Andy (G) **365** **0**
H: 6 0 W: 12 04 b.Sutton-in-Ashfield 11-10-70
Source: Trainee. *Honours:* England Schools, FA Schools, Youth, Under-21, Wales 5 full caps.

1988–89	Arsenal	0	0		
1989–90	Nottingham F	0	0		
1989–90	*WBA*	3	0	**3**	**0**
1989–90	*Blackburn R*	2	0	**2**	**0**
1989–90	*Colchester U*	10	0	**10**	**0**
1990–91	Nottingham F	0	0		
1991–92	Nottingham F	6	0		
1991–92	*Burnley*	15	0	**15**	**0**
1992–93	Nottingham F	5	0		
1993–94	Nottingham F	0	0	**11**	**0**
1993–94	Wrexham	36	0		
1994–95	Wrexham	46	0		
1995–96	Wrexham	46	0		
1996–97	Wrexham	43	0		
1997–98	Wrexham	42	0		
1998–99	Wrexham	0	0	**213**	**0**
1998–99	Sunderland	1	0		
1999–2000	Sunderland	1	0		
2000–01	Sunderland	0	0	**2**	**0**
2000–01	*Wigan Ath*	0	0		
2000–01	Barnsley	0	0		
2001–02	Barnsley	18	0		
2002–03	Barnsley	36	0	**54**	**0**
2002–03	Birmingham C	1	0	**1**	**0**
2003–04	Beira Mar	24	0	**24**	**0**
2004–05	Bury	19	0	**19**	**0**
2004–05	Torquay U	11	0	**11**	**0**

McGLINCHEY, Brian (D) **164** **4**
H: 5 9 W: 11 07 b.Derry 26-10-77
Source: Trainee. *Honours:* Northern Ireland Youth, Under-21, B.

1995–96	Manchester C	0	0		
1996–97	Manchester C	0	0		
1997–98	Manchester C	0	0		
1998–99	Port Vale	15	1	**15**	**1**
1999–2000	Gillingham	13	1		
2000–01	Gillingham	1	0	**14**	**1**
2000–01	Plymouth Arg	20	0		
2001–02	Plymouth Arg	29	1		
2002–03	Plymouth Arg	19	1		
2003–04	Plymouth Arg	0	0	**68**	**2**
2003–04	Torquay U	34	0		
2004–05	Torquay U	33	0	**67**	**0**

MEIRELLES, Bruno (M) **9 0**

H: 6 1 W: 13 00 b.Leiria 23-2-82

Source: Benfica.

2004–05	Torquay U	9	0	**9**	**0**

OGBODOT, Andrew (M) **0 0**

Source: Bury.

2004–05	Torquay U	0	0		

OSEI-KUFFOUR, Jo (F) **116 23**

H: 5 8 W: 12 00 b.Edmonton 17-11-81

Source: Scholar.

2000–01	Arsenal	0	0		
2001–02	Arsenal	0	0		
2001–02	*Swindon T*	11	2	**11**	**2**
2002–03	Torquay U	30	5		
2003–04	Torquay U	41	10		
2004–05	Torquay U	34	6	**105**	**21**

PHILLIPS, Martin (M) **248 18**

H: 5 8 W: 10 03 b.Exeter 13-3-76

Source: Trainee.

1992–93	Exeter C	6	0		
1993–94	Exeter C	9	0		
1994–95	Exeter C	24	2		
1995–96	Exeter C	13	3		
1995–96	Manchester C	11	0		
1996–97	Manchester C	4	0		
1997–98	Manchester C	0	0		
1997–98	*Scunthorpe U*	3	0	**3**	**0**
1997–98	*Exeter C*	8	0	**60**	**5**
1998–99	Manchester C	0	0	**15**	**0**
1998–99	Portsmouth	17	1		
1998–99	*Bristol R*	2	0	**2**	**0**
1999–2000	Portsmouth	7	0	**24**	**1**
2000–01	Plymouth Arg	42	1		
2001–02	Plymouth Arg	39	6		
2002–03	Plymouth Arg	24	2		
2003–04	Plymouth Arg	9	1	**114**	**10**
2004–05	Torquay U	30	2	**30**	**2**

RUSSELL, Alex (M) **336 43**

H: 5 10 W: 11 10 b.Crosby 17-3-73

Source: Burscough.

1994–95	Rochdale	7	1		
1995–96	Rochdale	25	0		
1996–97	Rochdale	39	9		
1997–98	Rochdale	31	4	**102**	**14**
1998–99	Cambridge U	37	6		
1999–2000	Cambridge U	15	0		
2000–01	Cambridge U	29	2	**81**	**8**
2001–02	Torquay U	33	7		
2002–03	Torquay U	39	9		
2003–04	Torquay U	43	2		
2004–05	Torquay U	38	3	**153**	**21**

SKINNER, Nicholas (M) **0 0**

H: 5 10 W: 11 07 b.Torquay 6-9-85

Source: Scholar.

2004–05	Torquay U	0	0		

SMALL, Michael (M) **0 0**

H: 5 8 W: 10 04 b.Plymouth 16-1-86

Source: Scholar.

2004–05	Torquay U	0	0		

STORY, Owen (M) **7 0**

H: 5 11 W: 10 10 b.Burton 3-8-84

Source: Scholar.

2003–04	Rushden & D	5	0		
2004–05	Rushden & D	0	0	**5**	**0**
From Team Bath					
2004–05	Torquay U	2	0	**2**	**0**

TAYLOR, Craig (D) **227 13**

H: 6 1 W: 13 00 b.Plymouth 24-1-74

Source: Dorchester T.

1996–97	Swindon T	0	0		
1997–98	Swindon T	32	2		
1998–99	Swindon T	21	0		
1998–99	*Plymouth Arg*	6	1		
1999–2000	Swindon T	2	0	**55**	**2**
1999–2000	Plymouth Arg	41	3		
2000–01	Plymouth Arg	39	3		
2001–02	Plymouth Arg	1	0		
2002–03	Plymouth Arg	1	0	**88**	**7**
2002–03	*Torquay U*	5	0		
2003–04	Torquay U	43	4		
2004–05	Torquay U	36	0	**84**	**4**

VAN HEUSDEN, Arjan (G) **206 0**

H: 6 3 W: 14 00 b.Alphen 11-12-72

Source: Noordwijk.

1994–95	Port Vale	2	0		
1995–96	Port Vale	7	0		
1996–97	Port Vale	13	0		
1997–98	Port Vale	5	0	**27**	**0**
1997–98	*Oxford U*	11	0	**11**	**0**
1998–99	Cambridge U	27	0		
1999–2000	Cambridge U	15	0	**42**	**0**
2000–01	Exeter C	41	0		
2001–02	Exeter C	33	0	**74**	**0**
2002–03	Mansfield T	5	0	**5**	**0**
2002–03	Torquay U	15	0		
2003–04	Torquay U	25	0		
2004–05	Torquay U	7	0	**47**	**0**

WOODS, Steve (D) **193 10**

H: 6 0 W: 12 05 b.Northwich 15-12-76

Source: Trainee.

1995–96	Stoke C	0	0		
1996–97	Stoke C	0	0		
1997–98	Stoke C	1	0		
1997–98	*Plymouth Arg*	5	0	**5**	**0**
1998–99	Stoke C	33	0	**34**	**0**
1999–2000	Chesterfield	25	0		
2000–01	Chesterfield	0	0	**25**	**0**
2001–02	Torquay U	38	2		
2002–03	Torquay U	9	0		
2003–04	Torquay U	46	6		
2004–05	Torquay U	36	2	**129**	**10**

TOTTENHAM H (82)

ACIMOVIC, Milenko (M) **169 47**

H: 6 2 W: 12 08 b.Ljubljana 15-2-77

Honours: Slovenia 52 full caps, 10 goals.

1996–97	Olimpija	18	3		
1997–98	Olimpija	16	4	**34**	**7**
1997–98	Red Star Belgrade	9	1		
1998–99	Red Star Belgrade	22	8		
1999–2000	Red Star Belgrade	21	4		
2000–01	Red Star Belgrade	28	14		
2001–02	Red Star Belgrade	22	7	**102**	**34**
2001–02	Tottenham H	0	0		
2002–03	Tottenham H	17	0		
2003–04	*Lille*	16	6	**16**	**6**
2004–05	Tottenham H	0	0	**17**	**0**

ATOUBA, Thimothee (M) **132 6**

H: 6 3 W: 12 06 b.Douala 17-2-82

Source: Union Douala. *Honours:* Cameroon 23 full caps.

2000–01	Neuchatel Xamax	26	1		
2001–02	Neuchatel Xamax	19	1	**45**	**2**
2001–02	Basle	14	1		
2002–03	Basle	26	0		
2003–04	Basle	29	2	**69**	**3**
2004–05	Tottenham H	18	1	**18**	**1**

BARNARD, Lee (F) **16 0**

H: 5 10 W: 10 10 b.Romford 18-7-84

Source: Trainee.

2002–03	Tottenham H	0	0		
2002–03	*Exeter C*	3	0	**3**	**0**
2003–04	Tottenham H	0	0		
2004–05	Tottenham H	0	0		
2004–05	*Leyton Orient*	8	0	**8**	**0**
2004–05	*Northampton T*	5	0	**5**	**0**

BARNARD, Lee (F) **0 0**

H: 5 10 W: 10 10 b.Romford 18-7-84

Source: Trainee.

2002–03	Tottenham H	0	0		
2003–04	Tottenham H	0	0		
2004–05	Tottenham H	0	0		

BROWN, Michael (M) **291 32**

H: 5 9 W: 12 04 b.Hartlepool 25-1-77

Source: Trainee. *Honours:* England Under-21.

1994–95	Manchester C	0	0		
1995–96	Manchester C	21	0		
1996–97	Manchester C	11	0		
1996–97	*Hartlepool U*	6	1	**6**	**1**
1997–98	Manchester C	26	0		
1998–99	Manchester C	31	2		
1999–2000	Manchester C	0	0	**89**	**2**
1999–2000	*Portsmouth*	4	0	**4**	**0**
1999–2000	Sheffield U	24	3		
2000–01	Sheffield U	36	1		
2001–02	Sheffield U	36	5		
2002–03	Sheffield U	40	16		
2003–04	Sheffield U	15	2	**151**	**27**
2003–04	Tottenham H	17	1		
2004–05	Tottenham H	24	1	**41**	**2**

BUNJEVCEVIC, Goran (D) **236 21**

H: 6 3 W: 12 02 b.Karlovac 17-2-73

Honours: Serbia-Montenegro 17 full caps.

1994–95	Rad	17	0		
1995–96	Rad	13	2		
1996–97	Rad	30	3	**60**	**5**
1997–98	Red Star Belgrade	30	5		
1998–99	Red Star Belgrade	22	4		
1999–2000	Red Star Belgrade	40	7		
2000–01	Red Star Belgrade	33	0	**125**	**16**
2001–02	Tottenham H	6	0		
2002–03	Tottenham H	35	0		
2003–04	Tottenham H	7	0		
2004–05	Tottenham H	3	0	**51**	**0**

BURCH, Rob (G) **0 0**

H: 6 2 W: 12 13 b.Yeovil 8-10-83

Source: Trainee. *Honours:* England Under-20.

2002–03	Tottenham H	0	0		
2003–04	Tottenham H	0	0		
2004–05	Tottenham H	0	0		
2004–05	*West Ham U*	0	0		

CARRICK, Michael (M) **173 8**

H: 6 1 W: 11 10 b.Wallsend 28-7-81

Source: Trainee. *Honours:* England Youth, Under-21, 3 full caps.

1998–99	West Ham U	0	0		
1999–2000	West Ham U	8	1		
1999–2000	*Swindon T*	6	2	**6**	**2**
1999–2000	*Birmingham C*	2	0	**2**	**0**
2000–01	West Ham U	33	1		
2001–02	West Ham U	30	2		
2002–03	West Ham U	30	1		
2003–04	West Ham U	35	1		
2004–05	West Ham U	0	0	**136**	**6**
2004–05	Tottenham H	29	0	**29**	**0**

CERNY, Radek (G) **3 0**

H: 6 1 W: 14 02 b.Prague 18-2-74

Source: Slavia Prague. *Honours:* Czech Republic, 3 full caps.

2004–05	Tottenham H	3	0	**3**	**0**

DAVENPORT, Calum (D) **93 3**

H: 6 4 W: 14 00 b.Bedford 1-1-83

Source: From Trainee. *Honours:* England Youth, Under-20, Under-21.

1999–2000	Coventry C	0	0		
2000–01	Coventry C	1	0		
2001–02	Coventry C	3	0		
2002–03	Coventry C	32	3		
2003–04	Coventry C	33	0		
2004–05	Coventry C	6	0	**75**	**3**
2004–05	*Southampton*	7	0	**7**	**0**
2004–05	Tottenham H	1	0	**1**	**0**
2004–05	*West Ham U*	10	0	**10**	**0**

DAVIES, Simon (M) **186 19**

H: 5 10 W: 11 07 b.Haverfordwest 23-10-79

Source: Trainee. *Honours:* Wales Youth, Under-21, B, 24 full caps, 4 goals.

1997–98	Peterborough U	6	0		
1998–99	Peterborough U	43	4		
1999–2000	Peterborough U	16	2	**65**	**6**
1999–2000	Tottenham H	3	0		
2000–01	Tottenham H	13	2		
2001–02	Tottenham H	31	4		
2002–03	Tottenham H	36	5		
2003–04	Tottenham H	17	2		
2004–05	Tottenham H	21	0	**121**	**13**

DAVIS, Sean (M) **170 14**

H: 5 10 W: 12 00 b.Clapham 20-9-79

Source: Trainee. *Honours:* England Under-21.

1996–97	Fulham	1	0		
1997–98	Fulham	0	0		
1998–99	Fulham	6	0		
1999–2000	Fulham	26	0		
2000–01	Fulham	40	6		
2001–02	Fulham	30	0		

2002–03	Fulham	28	3		
2003–04	Fulham	24	5	**155**	**14**
2004–05	Tottenham H	15	0	**15**	**0**

DAWSON, Michael (D) **88** **7**

H: 6 2 W: 12 02 b.Northallerton 18-11-83

Source: School. *Honours:* England Youth, Under-21.

2000–01	Nottingham F	0	0		
2001–02	Nottingham F	1	0		
2002–03	Nottingham F	38	5		
2003–04	Nottingham F	30	1		
2004–05	Nottingham F	14	1	**83**	**7**
2004–05	Tottenham H	5	0	**5**	**0**

DEFENDI, Rodrigo (D) **0** **0**

H: 6 2 W: 13 01 b.Ribeirao Preto 16-6-86

Source: Cruzeiro.

2004–05	Tottenham H	0	0		

DEFOE, Jermain (F) **172** **67**

H: 5 7 W: 10 04 b.Beckton 7-10-82

Source: From Charlton Ath. *Honours:* England Youth, Under-21, 12 full caps, 1 goal.

1999–2000	West Ham U	0	0		
2000–01	West Ham U	1	0		
2000–01	*Bournemouth*	29	18	**29**	**18**
2001–02	West Ham U	35	10		
2002–03	West Ham U	38	8		
2003–04	West Ham U	19	11	**93**	**29**
2003–04	Tottenham H	15	7		
2004–05	Tottenham H	35	13	**50**	**20**

EDMAN, Erik (D) **181** **3**

H: 5 10 W: 12 04 b.Huskvarna 11-11-78

Source: Habo. *Honours:* Sweden 30 full caps, 1 goal.

1997	Helsingborg	24	0		
1998	Helsingborg	25	0		
1999	Helsingborg	12	1	**61**	**1**
1999–2000	Torino	0	0		
1999–2000	Karlsruher	8	0	**8**	**0**
2000	AIK Stockholm	8	0		
2001	AIK Stockholm	13	0	**21**	**0**
2001–02	Heerenveen	33	1		
2002–03	Heerenveen	30	0	**63**	**1**
2004–05	Tottenham H	28	1	**28**	**1**

EL HAMDAOUI, Mounir (F) **74** **32**

H: 6 0 W: 13 05 b.Rotterdam 14-7-84

2001–02	Excelsior	6	2		
2002–03	Excelsior	21	2		
2003–04	Excelsior	33	17		
2004–05	Excelsior	14	11	**74**	**32**
2004–05	Tottenham H	0	0		

EYRE, Nicky (G) **0** **0**

b.Braintree 7-9-85

Source: Trainee.

2002–03	Tottenham H	0	0		
2003–04	Tottenham H	0	0		
2004–05	Tottenham H	0	0		

FULOP, Marton (G) **7** **0**

H: 6 3 W: 12 08 b.Budapest 3-5-83

Honours: Hungary Under-21, 1 full cap.

2004–05	Tottenham H	0	0		
2004–05	*Chesterfield*	7	0	**7**	**0**

GARDNER, Anthony (D) **126** **5**

H: 6 3 W: 14 00 b.Stafford 19-9-80

Source: Trainee. *Honours:* England Under-21, 1 full cap.

1998–99	Port Vale	15	1		
1999–2000	Port Vale	26	3	**41**	**4**
1999–2000	Tottenham H	0	0		
2000–01	Tottenham H	8	0		
2001–02	Tottenham H	15	0		
2002–03	Tottenham H	12	1		
2003–04	Tottenham H	33	0		
2004–05	Tottenham H	17	0	**85**	**1**

HALLFREDSSON, Emil (M) **0** **0**

H: 6 1 W: 13 01 b.Iceland 29-6-84

2004–05	Tottenham H	0	0		

HUGHES, Mark (M) **30** **0**

H: 5 10 W: 12 04 b.Dungannon 16-9-83

Source: Scholar. *Honours:* Northern Ireland Schools, Youth, Under-21, Under-23.

2001–02	Tottenham H	0	0		
2002–03	Tottenham H	0	0		
2003–04	Tottenham H	0	0		
2004–05	Tottenham H	0	0		
2004–05	*Northampton T*	3	0	**3**	**0**
2004–05	*Oldham Ath*	27	0	**27**	**0**

IFIL, Phil (D) **2** **0**

H: 5 9 W: 10 08 b.Willesden 18-11-86

Honours: England Youth.

2004–05	Tottenham H	2	0	**2**	**0**

JACKSON, Johnnie (M) **60** **4**

H: 6 1 W: 12 00 b.Camden 15-8-82

Source: Trainee. *Honours:* England Youth, Under-20.

1999–2000	Tottenham H	0	0		
2000–01	Tottenham H	0	0		
2001–02	Tottenham H	0	0		
2002–03	Tottenham H	0	0		
2002–03	*Swindon T*	13	1	**13**	**1**
2002–03	*Colchester U*	8	0	**8**	**0**
2003–04	Tottenham H	11	1		
2003–04	*Coventry C*	5	2	**5**	**2**
2004–05	Tottenham H	8	0	**19**	**1**
2004–05	*Watford*	15	0	**15**	**0**

KANOUTE, Frederic (F) **183** **52**

H: 6 3 W: 13 08 b.Ste. Foy-Les-Lyon 2-9-77

Honours: France Under-21. Mali 5 full caps, 4 goals.

1997–98	Lyon	18	6		
1998–99	Lyon	9	2		
1999–2000	Lyon	13	1	**40**	**9**
1999–2000	West Ham U	8	2		
2000–01	West Ham U	32	11		
2001–02	West Ham U	27	11		
2002–03	West Ham U	17	5	**84**	**29**
2003–04	Tottenham H	27	7		
2004–05	Tottenham H	32	7	**59**	**14**

KEANE, Robbie (F) **254** **87**

H: 5 9 W: 12 06 b.Dublin 8-7-80

Source: Trainee. *Honours:* Eire Youth, B, 61 full caps, 25 goals.

1997–98	Wolverhampton W	38	11		
1998–99	Wolverhampton W	33	11		
1999–2000	Wolverhampton W	2	2	**73**	**24**
1999–2000	Coventry C	31	12	**31**	**12**
2000–01	Internazionale	6	0	**6**	**0**
2000–01	Leeds U	18	9		
2001–02	Leeds U	25	3		
2002–03	Leeds U	3	1	**46**	**13**
2002–03	Tottenham H	29	13		
2003–04	Tottenham H	34	14		
2004–05	Tottenham H	35	11	**98**	**38**

KELLER, Kasey (G) **415** **0**

H: 6 1 W: 13 08 b.Washington 27-11-69

Source: Portland Univ. *Honours:* USA 81 full caps.

1991–92	Millwall	1	0		
1992–93	Millwall	45	0		
1993–94	Millwall	44	0		
1994–95	Millwall	44	0		
1995–96	Millwall	42	0	**176**	**0**
1996–97	Leicester C	31	0		
1997–98	Leicester C	32	0		
1998–99	Leicester C	36	0	**99**	**0**
1999–2000	Rayo Vallecano	28	0		
2000–01	Rayo Vallecano	23	0	**51**	**0**
2001–02	Tottenham H	9	0		
2002–03	Tottenham H	38	0		
2003–04	Tottenham H	38	0		
2004–05	Tottenham H	0	0	**85**	**0**
2004–05	*Southampton*	4	0	**4**	**0**

KELLY, Stephen (D) **58** **2**

H: 6 1 W: 12 01 b.Dublin 6-9-83

Source: Juniors. *Honours:* Eire Youth, Under-21.

2000–01	Tottenham H	0	0		
2001–02	Tottenham H	0	0		
2002–03	Tottenham H	0	0		
2002–03	*Southend U*	10	0	**10**	**0**
2002–03	*QPR*	7	0	**7**	**0**
2003–04	Tottenham H	11	0		
2003–04	*Watford*	13	0	**13**	**0**
2004–05	Tottenham H	17	2	**28**	**2**

KING, Ledley (D) **146** **4**

H: 6 2 W: 14 05 b.Bow 12-10-80

Source: Trainee. *Honours:* England Youth, Under-21, 12 full caps, 1 goal.

1998–99	Tottenham H	1	0		
1999–2000	Tottenham H	3	0		
2000–01	Tottenham H	18	1		
2001–02	Tottenham H	32	0		
2002–03	Tottenham H	25	0		
2003–04	Tottenham H	29	1		
2004–05	Tottenham H	38	2	**146**	**4**

LIMBERSKY, David (M) **26** **1**

H: 5 11 W: 12 08 b.Plzen 6-10-83

2003–04	Viktoria Plzen	12	0		
2003–04	Modena	4	0	**4**	**0**
2004–05	Viktoria Plzen	10	1	**22**	**1**
2004–05	Tottenham H	0	0		

MABIZELA, Mbulelo (D) **68** **8**

H: 5 11 W: 13 01 b.Pietermaritzburg 16-9-80

Source: Mamelodi Sundowns, Maritzburg City. *Honours:* South Africa 37 full caps.

2001–02	Orlando Pirates	26	4		
2002–03	Orlando Pirates	35	3	**61**	**7**
2003–04	Tottenham H	6	1		
2004–05	Tottenham H	1	0	**7**	**1**

MALCOLM, Michael (F) **0** **0**

b.Harrow 13-10-85

Source: Trainee. *Honours:* England Youth.

2002–03	Tottenham H	0	0		
2003–04	Tottenham H	0	0		
2004–05	Tottenham H	0	0		

MARNEY, Dean (D) **22** **2**

H: 5 9 W: 11 04 b.Barking 31-1-84

Source: Scholar. *Honours:* England Under-21.

2002–03	Tottenham H	0	0		
2002–03	*Swindon T*	9	0	**9**	**0**
2003–04	Tottenham H	3	0		
2003–04	*QPR*	2	0	**2**	**0**
2004–05	Tottenham H	5	2	**8**	**2**
2004–05	*Gillingham*	3	0	**3**	**0**

McKENNA, Kieran (M) **0** **0**

b.London 14-5-86

Source: Academy.

2003–04	Tottenham H	0	0		
2004–05	Tottenham H	0	0		

McKIE, Marcel (D) **0** **0**

b.Edmonton 22-9-84

Source: From Scholar. *Honours:* England Youth.

2001–02	Tottenham H	0	0		
2002–03	Tottenham H	0	0		
2003–04	Tottenham H	0	0		
2004–05	Tottenham H	0	0		

MIDO (F) **112** **48**

H: 6 3 W: 12 11 b.Cairo 23-2-83

Honours: Egypt 36 full caps, 24 goals.

1999–2000	Zamalek	4	3	**4**	**3**
2000–01	Gent	21	11	**21**	**11**
2001–02	Ajax	24	12		
2002–03	Ajax	16	9	**40**	**21**
2002–03	Celta Vigo	8	4	**8**	**4**
2003–04	Marseille	22	7	**22**	**7**
2004–05	Roma	8	0	**8**	**0**
2004–05	Tottenham H	9	2	**9**	**2**

NAYBET, Nourredine (D) **327** **17**

H: 6 0 W: 11 11 b.Casablanca 10-2-70

Source: WAC. *Honours:* Morocco 105 full caps.

1993–94	Nantes	34	1	**34**	**1**
1994–95	Sporting Lisbon	26	2		
1995–96	Sporting Lisbon	28	3	**54**	**5**
1996–97	La Coruna	34	1		
1997–98	La Coruna	31	4		
1998–99	La Coruna	30	0		
1999–2000	La Coruna	25	0		
2000–01	La Coruna	26	1		
2001–02	La Coruna	24	2		
2002–03	La Coruna	25	1		
2003–04	La Coruna	17	1	**212**	**10**
2004–05	Tottenham H	27	1	**27**	**1**

O'DONOGHUE, Paul (D) **0** **0**

H: 6 1 W: 13 10 b.Lewisham 14-12-83

Source: Scholar.

2001–02	Tottenham H	0	0		

2002–03 Tottenham H 0 0
2003–04 Tottenham H 0 0
2004–05 Tottenham H 0 0

O'HARA, Jamie (M) 0 0
H: 5 11 W: 12 04 b.South London 25-9-86
2004–05 Tottenham H 0 0

PAMAROT, Noe (D) 172 9
H: 5 11 W: 13 08 b.Fontenay-sous-Bois 14-4-79
Source: Martigues, Nice.
1997–98 Martigues 25 2
1998–99 Martigues 0 0 **25 2**
1999–2000 Nice 0 0
1999–2000 Portsmouth 2 0 **2 0**
2000–01 Nice 23 0
2001–02 Nice 33 3
2002–03 Nice 33 1
2003–04 Nice 33 2 **122 6**
2004–05 Tottenham H 23 1 **23 1**

PEDRO MENDES (M) 164 10
H: 5 10 W: 12 02 b.Guimaraes 26-2-79
Honours: Portugal 2 full caps.
1998–99 Felgueiras 31 2 **31 2**
1999–2000 Guimaraes 13 1
2000–01 Guimaraes 12 0
2001–02 Guimaraes 26 0
2002–03 Guimaraes 32 6 **83 7**
2003–04 Porto 26 0 **26 0**
2004–05 Tottenham H 24 1 **24 1**

PRICE, Owen (F) 0 0
b.London 20-10-85
2003–04 Tottenham H 0 0
2004–05 Tottenham H 0 0

REID, Andy (F) 157 22
H: 5 8 W: 11 02 b.Dublin 29-7-82
Source: Trainee. *Honours:* Eire Youth, Under-21, 16 full caps, 2 goals.
1999–2000 Nottingham F 0 0
2000–01 Nottingham F 14 2
2001–02 Nottingham F 29 0
2002–03 Nottingham F 30 1
2003–04 Nottingham F 46 13
2004–05 Nottingham F 25 5 **144 21**
2004–05 Tottenham H 13 1 **13 1**

RICHARDS, Dean (D) 348 18
H: 6 2 W: 13 01 b.Bradford 9-6-74
Source: Trainee. *Honours:* England Under-21.
1991–92 Bradford C 7 1
1992–93 Bradford C 3 0
1993–94 Bradford C 46 2
1994–95 Bradford C 30 1 **86 4**
1994–95 *Wolverhampton W* 10 2
1995–96 Wolverhampton W 37 1
1996–97 Wolverhampton W 21 1
1997–98 Wolverhampton W 13 0
1998–99 Wolverhampton W 41 3 **122 7**
1999–2000 Southampton 35 2
2000–01 Southampton 28 1
2001–02 Southampton 4 0 **67 3**
2001–02 Tottenham H 24 2
2002–03 Tottenham H 26 2
2003–04 Tottenham H 23 0
2004–05 Tottenham H 0 0 **73 4**

RICKETTS, Rohan (M) 43 2
H: 5 8 W: 11 05 b.Clapham 22-12-82
Source: Scholar. *Honours:* England Youth, Under-20.
2001–02 Arsenal 0 0
2002–03 Tottenham H 0 0
2003–04 Tottenham H 24 1
2004–05 Tottenham H 6 0 **30 1**
2004–05 *Coventry C* 6 0 **6 0**
2004–05 *Wolverhampton W* 7 1 **7 1**

ROBINSON, Paul (G) 131 0
H: 6 4 W: 15 07 b.Beverley 15-10-79
Source: Trainee. *Honours:* England Under-21, 12 full caps.
1996–97 Leeds U 0 0
1997–98 Leeds U 0 0
1998–99 Leeds U 5 0
1999–2000 Leeds U 0 0
2000–01 Leeds U 16 0
2001–02 Leeds U 0 0
2002–03 Leeds U 38 0
2003–04 Leeds U 36 0 **95 0**
2003–04 Tottenham H 0 0
2004–05 Tottenham H 36 0 **36 0**

SILVA, Edson (F) 35 4
H: 6 2 W: 13 00 b.Sao Vicente 3-9-83
Source: Batoque, Estoril, Benfica.
1999–2000 Baden 25 4 **25 4**
2000–01 Solothun 8 0 **8 0**
2001–02 Lucerne 1 0
2002–03 Lucerne 0 0 **1 0**
2003–04 PSV Eindhoven 1 0 **1 0**
2004–05 Tottenham H 0 0

SLABBER, Jamie (F) 10 0
H: 6 2 W: 11 10 b.Enfield 31-12-84
Source: Scholar. *Honours:* England Youth.
2001–02 Tottenham H 0 0
2002–03 Tottenham H 1 0
2003–04 Tottenham H 0 0
2004–05 Tottenham H 0 0 **1 0**
2004–05 *Swindon T* 9 0 **9 0**

YEATES, Mark (F) 16 0
H: 5 9 W: 10 07 b.Dublin 11-1-85
Source: Trainee. *Honours:* Eire Youth, Under-21.
2002–03 Tottenham H 0 0
2003–04 Tottenham H 1 0
2003–04 *Brighton & HA* 9 0 **9 0**
2004–05 Tottenham H 2 0 **3 0**
2004–05 *Swindon T* 4 0 **4 0**

ZIEGLER, Reto (M) 61 1
H: 6 0 W: 12 06 b.Nyon 16-1-86
Source: FC Gland, Servette, Terre-Sainte, Lausanne. *Honours:* Switzerland Under-21, 3 full caps.
2002–03 Grasshoppers 10 0
2003–04 Grasshoppers 28 0 **38 0**
2004–05 Tottenham H 23 1 **23 1**

Scholars
Barcham, Andrew; Daniels, Charlie; Dawkins, Simon; Forecast, Tommy Stephen; Heller, Richard Nathaniel; Kyriacou, John William; Lee, Charlie; Lewis, Stuart Allan; Maghoma, Jacques Ilonda; Mills, Leigh; Peprah-Annan, Nathaniel; Riley, Christopher Daniel; Seanla, Claude Stephane

TRANMERE R (83)

ACHTERBERG, John (G) 263 0
H: 6 1 W: 13 00 b.Utrecht 8-7-71
Source: VV RUC, Utrecht.
1993–94 NAC 1 0
1994–95 NAC 2 0
1995–96 NAC 6 0 **9 0**
1996–97 Eindhoven 32 0 **32 0**
From Utrecht.
1998–99 Tranmere R 24 0
1999–2000 Tranmere R 26 0
2000–01 Tranmere R 25 0
2001–02 Tranmere R 25 0
2002–03 Tranmere R 38 0
2003–04 Tranmere R 45 0
2004–05 Tranmere R 39 0 **222 0**

ASHTON, Neil (M) 25 0
H: 5 7 W: 12 03 b.Liverpool 15-1-85
Source: Scholar.
2002–03 Tranmere R 0 0
2003–04 Tranmere R 1 0
2004–05 Tranmere R 0 0 **1 0**
2004–05 *Shrewsbury T* 24 0 **24 0**

BERESFORD, David (M) 220 9
H: 5 8 W: 10 09 b.Middleton 11-11-76
Source: Trainee. *Honours:* England Schools, Youth.
1993–94 Oldham Ath 1 0
1994–95 Oldham Ath 2 0
1995–96 Oldham Ath 28 2
1995–96 *Swansea C* 6 0 **6 0**
1996–97 Oldham Ath 33 0 **64 2**
1996–97 Huddersfield T 6 1
1997–98 Huddersfield T 8 0
1998–99 Huddersfield T 19 2
1999–2000 Huddersfield T 0 0
1999–2000 *Preston NE* 4 0 **4 0**
2000–01 Huddersfield T 2 0 **35 3**
2000–01 *Port Vale* 4 0 **4 0**
2001–02 Hull C 41 1 **41 1**
2002–03 Plymouth Arg 16 0
2003–04 Plymouth Arg 1 0 **17 0**
2003–04 *Macclesfield T* 5 0 **5 0**
2003–04 Tranmere R 25 1
2004–05 Tranmere R 19 2 **44 3**

BROWN, Paul (M) 4 0
H: 5 8 W: 12 02 b.Liverpool 10-9-84
Source: Scholar.
2004–05 Tranmere R 4 0 **4 0**

DADI, Eugene (F) 175 42
H: 6 2 W: 12 11 b.Abidjan 20-8-73
1997–98 Linz 19 4
1998–99 Linz 20 3
1999–2000 Linz 13 3 **52 10**
2000–01 Toulouse 3 0 **3 0**
2001–02 Aberdeen 28 4 **28 4**
2002–03 Livingston 23 3 **23 3**
2003–04 Tranmere R 38 16
2004–05 Tranmere R 31 9 **69 25**

DAGNALL, Chris (F) 33 7
H: 5 8 W: 11 11 b.Liverpool 15-4-86
Source: Scholar.
2003–04 Tranmere R 10 1
2004–05 Tranmere R 23 6 **33 7**

GOODISON, Ian (D) 126 2
H: 6 1 W: 12 06 b.St James, Jamaica 21-11-72
Source: Olympic Gardens. *Honours:* Jamaica full caps.
1999–2000 Hull C 18 0
2000–01 Hull C 36 1
2001–02 Hull C 16 0
2002–03 Hull C 0 0 **70 1**
From Seba U.
2003–04 Tranmere R 12 0
2004–05 Tranmere R 44 1 **56 1**

HALL, Paul (M) 525 88
H: 5 9 W: 10 04 b.Manchester 3-7-72
Source: Trainee. *Honours:* Jamaica 41 full caps, 9 goals.
1989–90 Torquay U 10 0
1990–91 Torquay U 17 0
1991–92 Torquay U 38 1
1992–93 Torquay U 28 0 **93 1**
1992–93 Portsmouth 0 0
1993–94 Portsmouth 28 4
1994–95 Portsmouth 43 5
1995–96 Portsmouth 46 10
1996–97 Portsmouth 42 13
1997–98 Portsmouth 29 5 **188 37**
1998–99 Coventry C 9 0
1998–99 *Bury* 7 0 **7 0**
1999–2000 Coventry C 1 0 **10 0**
1999–2000 *Sheffield U* 4 1 **4 1**
1999–2000 *WBA* 4 0 **4 0**
1999–2000 Walsall 10 4
2000–01 Walsall 42 6
2001–02 Walsall 0 0 **52 10**
2001–02 Rushden & D 34 8
2002–03 Rushden & D 45 16
2003–04 Rushden & D 33 2 **112 26**
2003–04 Tranmere R 9 2
2004–05 Tranmere R 46 11 **55 13**

HARRISON, Danny (M) 77 2
H: 5 11 W: 12 04 b.Liverpool 4-11-82
Source: Scholar.
2001–02 Tranmere R 1 0
2002–03 Tranmere R 12 0
2003–04 Tranmere R 32 2
2004–05 Tranmere R 32 0 **77 2**

HAWORTH, Simon (F) 244 84
H: 6 1 W: 13 08 b.Cardiff 30-3-77
Source: Trainee. *Honours:* Wales Youth, Under-21, B, 5 full caps.
1995–96 Cardiff C 13 0
1996–97 Cardiff C 24 9 **37 9**
1997–98 Coventry C 10 0
1998–99 Coventry C 1 0 **11 0**
1998–99 Wigan Ath 20 10
1999–2000 Wigan Ath 40 13
2000–01 Wigan Ath 30 11
2001–02 Wigan Ath 27 10 **117 44**

2001–02 Tranmere R 12 5
2002–03 Tranmere R 42 20
2003–04 Tranmere R 22 6
2004–05 Tranmere R 3 0 **79 31**

HOWARTH, Russell (G) 20 0
H: 6 2 W: 14 05 b.York 27-3-82
Source: Scholar. *Honours:* England Youth, Under-20.
1999–2000 York C 6 0
2000–01 York C 0 0
2001–02 York C 2 0
2002–03 York C 0 0 **8 0**
2002–03 Tranmere R 3 0
2003–04 Tranmere R 1 0
2004–05 Tranmere R 8 0 **12 0**

HUME, Iain (F) 144 31
H: 5 7 W: 11 02 b.Brampton 31-10-83
Source: Juniors. *Honours:* Canada Youth, 11 full caps.
1999–2000 Tranmere R 3 0
2000–01 Tranmere R 10 0
2001–02 Tranmere R 14 0
2002–03 Tranmere R 35 6
2003–04 Tranmere R 40 10
2004–05 Tranmere R 42 15 **144 31**

JACKSON, Michael (D) 424 31
H: 6 0 W: 13 08 b.Runcorn 4-12-73
Source: Trainee.
1991–92 Crewe Alex 1 0
1992–93 Crewe Alex 4 0 **5 0**
1993–94 Bury 39 0
1994–95 Bury 24 2
1995–96 Bury 31 4
1996–97 Bury 31 3 **125 9**
1996–97 Preston NE 7 0
1997–98 Preston NE 40 2
1998–99 Preston NE 44 8
1999–2000 Preston NE 46 5
2000–01 Preston NE 30 1
2001–02 Preston NE 13 0
2002–03 Preston NE 22 1
2002–03 *Tranmere R* 6 0
2003–04 Preston NE 43 0 **245 17**
2004–05 Tranmere R 43 5 **49 5**

JAMES, Oliver (D) 0 0
H: 6 0 W: 11 10 b.Birkenhead 13-1-87
Source: Scholar.
2004–05 Tranmere R 0 0

JENNINGS, Steven (M) 15 0
H: 5 7 W: 11 07 b.Liverpool 28-10-84
Source: Scholar.
2002–03 Tranmere R 0 0
2003–04 Tranmere R 4 0
2004–05 Tranmere R 11 0 **15 0**

JONES, Gary (M) 306 46
H: 6 3 W: 15 02 b.Chester 10-5-75
Source: Trainee.
1993–94 Tranmere R 6 2
1994–95 Tranmere R 19 3
1995–96 Tranmere R 23 1
1996–97 Tranmere R 30 6
1997–98 Tranmere R 43 8
1998–99 Tranmere R 26 5
1999–2000 Tranmere R 31 3
2000–01 Nottingham F 31 1
2001–02 Nottingham F 5 1
2002–03 Nottingham F 0 0 **36 2**
2002–03 Tranmere R 40 6
2003–04 Tranmere R 42 9
2004–05 Tranmere R 10 1 **270 44**

LINWOOD, Paul (D) 30 0
H: 6 2 W: 13 04 b.Birkenhead 24-10-83
Source: Scholar.
2001–02 Tranmere R 0 0
2002–03 Tranmere R 0 0
2003–04 Tranmere R 20 0
2004–05 Tranmere R 10 0 **30 0**

LORAN, Tyrone (D) 53 0
H: 6 1 W: 13 08 b.Amsterdam 29-6-81
2002–03 Manchester C 0 0
2002–03 Tranmere R 17 0
2003–04 Tranmere R 28 0
2004–05 Tranmere R 2 0 **47 0**
2004–05 *Port Vale* 6 0 **6 0**

McATEER, Jason (M) 373 24
H: 5 9 W: 11 05 b.Birkenhead 18-6-71
Source: Marine. *Honours:* Eire B, 52 full caps, 3 goals.
1991–92 Bolton W 0 0
1992–93 Bolton W 21 0
1993–94 Bolton W 46 3
1994–95 Bolton W 43 5
1995–96 Bolton W 4 0 **114 8**
1995–96 Liverpool 29 0
1996–97 Liverpool 37 1
1997–98 Liverpool 21 2
1998–99 Liverpool 13 0 **100 3**
1998–99 Blackburn R 13 1
1999–2000 Blackburn R 28 2
2000–01 Blackburn R 27 1
2001–02 Blackburn R 4 0 **72 4**
2001–02 Sunderland 26 2
2002–03 Sunderland 9 1
2003–04 Sunderland 18 2 **53 5**
2004–05 Tranmere R 34 4 **34 4**

NAVARRO, Alan (M) 74 3
H: 5 10 W: 11 07 b.Liverpool 31-5-81
Source: Trainee.
1998–99 Liverpool 0 0
1999–2000 Liverpool 0 0
2000–01 Liverpool 0 0
2000–01 *Crewe Alex* 8 1
2001–02 Liverpool 0 0
2001–02 *Crewe Alex* 7 0 **15 1**
2001–02 Tranmere R 21 1
2002–03 Tranmere R 5 0
2003–04 Tranmere R 19 0
2004–05 Tranmere R 0 0 **45 1**
2004–05 *Chester C* 3 0 **3 0**
2004–05 *Macclesfield T* 11 1 **11 1**

PALETHORPE, Philip (G) 0 0
H: 6 2 W: 11 08 b.Wallasey 17-9-86
Source: Scholar.
2003–04 Tranmere R 0 0
2004–05 Tranmere R 0 0

RANKINE, Mark (M) 589 33
H: 5 10 W: 11 01 b.Doncaster 30-9-69
Source: Trainee.
1987–88 Doncaster R 18 2
1988–89 Doncaster R 46 11
1989–90 Doncaster R 36 2
1990–91 Doncaster R 40 2
1991–92 Doncaster R 24 3 **164 20**
1991–92 Wolverhampton W 15 1
1992–93 Wolverhampton W 27 0
1993–94 Wolverhampton W 31 0
1994–95 Wolverhampton W 27 0
1995–96 Wolverhampton W 32 0
1996–97 Wolverhampton W 0 0 **132 1**
1996–97 Preston NE 23 0
1997–98 Preston NE 35 1
1998–99 Preston NE 42 3
1999–2000 Preston NE 44 0
2000–01 Preston NE 44 4
2001–02 Preston NE 26 4
2002–03 Preston NE 19 0 **233 12**
2002–03 *Sheffield U* 6 0
2003–04 Sheffield U 13 0 **19 0**
2004–05 Tranmere R 41 0 **41 0**

ROBERTS, Gareth (D) 237 11
H: 5 8 W: 11 00 b.Wrexham 6-2-78
Source: Trainee. *Honours:* Wales Under-21, B, 8 full caps.
1995–96 Liverpool 0 0
1996–97 Liverpool 0 0
1997–98 Liverpool 0 0
1998–99 Liverpool 0 0
1999–2000 Tranmere R 37 1
2000–01 Tranmere R 34 0
2001–02 Tranmere R 45 2
2002–03 Tranmere R 37 4
2003–04 Tranmere R 44 1
2004–05 Tranmere R 40 3 **237 11**

ROBINSON, Paul (F) 2 0
H: 6 0 W: 12 00 b.Seaton Delaval 25-5-83
Source: Scholar.
2002–03 Tranmere R 0 0
2003–04 Tranmere R 0 0
2004–05 Tranmere R 0 0
2004–05 *Grimsby T* 2 0 **2 0**

SCOTT, Ged (M) 0 0
H: 5 9 W: 12 06 b.Liverpool 27-4-86
Source: Scholar.
2004–05 Tranmere R 0 0

SHARPS, Ian (D) 131 5
H: 6 3 W: 13 05 b.Warrington 23-10-80
Source: Trainee.
1998–99 Tranmere R 1 0
1999–2000 Tranmere R 0 0
2000–01 Tranmere R 0 0
2001–02 Tranmere R 29 0
2002–03 Tranmere R 30 3
2003–04 Tranmere R 27 1
2004–05 Tranmere R 44 1 **131 5**

TAYLOR, Ryan (D) 98 14
H: 5 8 W: 10 04 b.Liverpool 19-8-84
Source: Scholar. *Honours:* England Youth.
2001–02 Tranmere R 0 0
2002–03 Tranmere R 25 1
2003–04 Tranmere R 30 5
2004–05 Tranmere R 43 8 **98 14**

TREMARCO, Carl (D) 3 0
H: 5 10 W: 12 02 b.Liverpool 11-10-85
Source: Scholar.
2003–04 Tranmere R 0 0
2004–05 Tranmere R 3 0 **3 0**

VAUGHAN, James (D) 0 0
H: 5 10 W: 12 09 b.Liverpool 6-12-86
Source: Scholar.
2004–05 Tranmere R 0 0

WHITMORE, Theo (M) 113 14
H: 6 2 W: 12 10 b.Montego Bay 5-8-72
Source: From Seba U. *Honours:* Jamaica full caps.
1999–2000 Hull C 17 2
2000–01 Hull C 26 5
2001–02 Hull C 34 2 **77 9**
From Seba U
2003–04 Livingston 3 0 **3 0**
2004–05 Tranmere R 33 5 **33 5**

ZOLA MAKONGO, Calvin (F) 40 7
H: 6 3 W: 13 07 b.Kinshasa 31-12-84
Source: Scholar.
2001–02 Newcastle U 0 0
2002–03 Newcastle U 0 0
2003–04 Newcastle U 0 0
2003–04 *Oldham Ath* 25 5 **25 5**
2004–05 Tranmere R 15 2 **15 2**

WALSALL (84)

ATIENO, Taiwo (F) 20 3
H: 6 2 W: 12 13 b.Brixton 6-8-85
Source: Scholar.
2004–05 Walsall 3 0 **3 0**
2004–05 *Rochdale* 13 2 **13 2**
2004–05 *Chester C* 4 1 **4 1**

BAZELEY, Darren (D) 399 25
H: 5 10 W: 11 02 b.Northampton 5-10-72
Source: Trainee. *Honours:* England Under-21.
1989–90 Watford 1 0
1990–91 Watford 7 0
1991–92 Watford 34 6
1992–93 Watford 22 1
1993–94 Watford 10 1
1994–95 Watford 28 4
1995–96 Watford 41 1
1996–97 Watford 41 3
1997–98 Watford 16 3
1998–99 Watford 40 2 **240 21**
1999–2000 Wolverhampton W 46 3
2000–01 Wolverhampton W 24 1
2001–02 Wolverhampton W 0 0 **70 4**
2002–03 Walsall 43 0
2003–04 Walsall 39 0
2004–05 Walsall 7 0 **89 0**

BENNETT, Julian (D) 32 2
H: 6 1 W: 13 00 b.Nottingham 17-12-84
Source: Scholar.
2003–04 Walsall 1 0
2004–05 Walsall 31 2 **32 2**

BEWERS, Jon (D) **5 0**
H: 5 8 W: 9 13 b.Kettering 10-9-82
Source: Trainee. *Honours:* England Youth, Under-20.

1999–2000	Aston Villa	1	0		
2000–01	Aston Villa	0	0		
2001–02	Aston Villa	0	0		
2002–03	Aston Villa	0	0		
2003–04	Aston Villa	0	0	**1**	**0**
2003–04	Notts Co	3	0		
2004–05	Notts Co	0	0	**3**	**0**
2004–05	Walsall	1	0	**1**	**0**

BRADLEY, Mark (D) **1 0**
H: 6 0 W: 11 05 b.Dudley 14-1-88

2004–05	Walsall	1	0	**1**	**0**

BROAD, Joseph (M) **36 0**
H: 5 11 W: 12 07 b.Bristol 24-8-82
Source: Trainee.

2000–01	Plymouth Arg	0	0		
2001–02	Plymouth Arg	7	0		
2002–03	Plymouth Arg	5	0		
2003–04	Plymouth Arg	0	0	**12**	**0**
2003–04	Torquay U	14	0	**14**	**0**
2004–05	Walsall	10	0	**10**	**0**

BURLEY, Craig (M) **251 36**
H: 6 1 W: 13 03 b.Ayr 24-9-71
Source: Trainee. *Honours:* Scotland Schools, Youth, Under-21, 46 full caps, 3 goals.

1989–90	Chelsea	0	0		
1990–91	Chelsea	1	0		
1991–92	Chelsea	8	0		
1992–93	Chelsea	3	0		
1993–94	Chelsea	23	3		
1994–95	Chelsea	25	2		
1995–96	Chelsea	22	0		
1996–97	Chelsea	31	2	**113**	**7**
1997–98	Celtic	35	10		
1998–99	Celtic	21	9		
1999–2000	Celtic	0	0	**56**	**19**
1999–2000	Derby Co	18	5		
2000–01	Derby Co	24	2		
2001–02	Derby Co	11	0		
2002–03	Derby Co	20	3		
2003–04	Derby Co	0	0	**73**	**10**
2003–04	Preston NE	4	0	**4**	**0**
2003–04	Walsall	5	0		
2004–05	Walsall	0	0	**5**	**0**

COLEMAN, Dean (G) **2 0**
H: 6 1 W: 14 03 b.Dudley 18-9-85

2004–05	Walsall	2	0	**2**	**0**

CORICA, Steve (M) **335 44**
H: 5 8 W: 10 10 b.Cairns 24-3-73
Honours: Australia Youth, Under-20, Under-23, 31 full caps, 5 goals.

1990–91	Marconi Stallions	17	0		
1991–92	Marconi Stallions	17	2		
1992–93	Marconi Stallions	27	4		
1993–94	Marconi Stallions	24	5		
1994–95	Marconi Stallions	18	3	**103**	**14**
1995–96	Leicester C	16	2	**16**	**2**
1995–96	Wolverhampton W	17	0		
1996–97	Wolverhampton W	36	2		
1997–98	Wolverhampton W	1	0		
1998–99	Wolverhampton W	31	2		
1999–2000	Wolverhampton W	15	1	**100**	**5**
2000	Sanfrecce	21	3		
2001	Sanfrecce	22	11	**43**	**14**
2001–02	Walsall	13	3		
2002–03	Walsall	41	4		
2003–04	Walsall	19	2		
2004–05	Walsall	0	0	**73**	**9**

DAKINAH, Kofi (D) **1 0**
H: 6 3 W: 12 11 b.Copenhagen 1-2-80
Source: Herfolge. *Honours:* Denmark Youth.

2004–05	Walsall	1	0	**1**	**0**

DANN, Scott (D) **1 0**
H: 6 2 W: 12 00 b.Liverpool 14-2-87
Source: Scholar.

2004–05	Walsall	1	0	**1**	**0**

EMBLEN, Neil (D) **321 23**
H: 6 1 W: 13 11 b.Bromley 19-6-71
Source: Tonbridge, Sittingbourne.

1993–94	Millwall	12	0	**12**	**0**
1994–95	Wolverhampton W	27	7		
1995–96	Wolverhampton W	33	2		
1996–97	Wolverhampton W	28	0		
1997–98	Wolverhampton W	7	0		
1997–98	Crystal Palace	13	0	**13**	**0**
1998–99	Wolverhampton W	33	2		
1999–2000	Wolverhampton W	46	5		
2000–01	Wolverhampton W	28	0	**202**	**16**
2001–02	Norwich C	2	0		
2002–03	Norwich C	12	0	**14**	**0**
2002–03	Walsall	5	0		
2003–04	Walsall	39	5		
2004–05	Walsall	36	2	**80**	**7**

FRYATT, Matty (F) **57 17**
H: 5 10 W: 11 00 b.Nuneaton 5-3-86
Source: Scholar. *Honours:* England Youth.

2002–03	Walsall	0	0		
2003–04	Walsall	11	1		
2003–04	*Carlisle U*	10	1	**10**	**1**
2004–05	Walsall	36	15	**47**	**16**

HARKNESS, Jon (M) **1 0**
H: 5 11 W: 11 12 b.Co Antrim 18-11-85
Source: Scholar.

2004–05	Walsall	1	0	**1**	**0**

HERIVELTO, Harry (M) **29 5**
H: 5 10 W: 11 06 b.Brazil 23-8-75
Source: Flamengo, Maritimo, Cruzeiro.

2001–02	Walsall	24	4		
2002–03	Walsall	4	1		
2003–04	Walsall	0	0		
2004–05	Walsall	1	0	**29**	**5**

JAMIESON, Nathan (M) **0 0**
H: 5 11 W: 12 03 b.Middlesbrough 20-3-85
Source: Scholar.

2004–05	Walsall	0	0		

KINSELLA, Mark (M) **449 47**
H: 5 8 W: 11 04 b.Dublin 12-8-72
Source: From Home Farm. *Honours:* Eire 48 full caps, 3 goals.

1989–90	Colchester U	6	0		
1990–91	Colchester U	0	0		
1991–92	Colchester U	0	0		
1992–93	Colchester U	38	6		
1993–94	Colchester U	42	8		
1994–95	Colchester U	42	6		
1995–96	Colchester U	45	5		
1996–97	Colchester U	7	2	**180**	**27**
1996–97	Charlton Ath	37	6		
1997–98	Charlton Ath	46	6		
1998–99	Charlton Ath	38	2		
1999–2000	Charlton Ath	38	3		
2000–01	Charlton Ath	32	2		
2001–02	Charlton Ath	17	0		
2002–03	Charlton Ath	0	0	**208**	**19**
2002–03	Aston Villa	19	0		
2003–04	Aston Villa	2	0	**21**	**0**
2003–04	WBA	18	1	**18**	**1**
2004–05	Walsall	22	0	**22**	**0**

LEITAO, Jorge (F) **207 52**
H: 5 11 W: 13 04 b.Oporto 14-1-74
Source: Feirense.

2000–01	Walsall	44	18		
2001–02	Walsall	38	8		
2002–03	Walsall	44	11		
2003–04	Walsall	39	7		
2004–05	Walsall	42	8	**207**	**52**

McDERMOTT, David (M) **0 0**
H: 5 5 W: 10 00 b.Stourbridge 6-2-88
Source: Scholar.

2004–05	Walsall	0	0		

McKINNEY, Richard (G) **30 0**
H: 6 2 W: 13 06 b.Ballymoney 18-5-79
Source: Ballymena U.

1999–2000	Manchester C	0	0		
2000–01	Manchester C	0	0		
2001–02	Swindon T	1	0	**1**	**0**
2002–03	Colchester U	21	0		
2003–04	Colchester U	5	0	**26**	**0**
2004–05	Walsall	3	0	**3**	**0**

MERSON, Paul (M) **614 125**
H: 6 0 W: 13 02 b.Harlesden 20-3-68
Source: Apprentice. *Honours:* England Youth, Under-21, B, 21 full caps, 3 goals.

1985–86	Arsenal	0	0		
1986–87	Arsenal	7	3		
1986–87	*Brentford*	7	0	**7**	**0**
1987–88	Arsenal	15	5		
1988–89	Arsenal	37	10		
1989–90	Arsenal	29	7		
1990–91	Arsenal	37	13		
1991–92	Arsenal	42	12		
1992–93	Arsenal	33	6		
1993–94	Arsenal	33	7		
1994–95	Arsenal	24	4		
1995–96	Arsenal	38	5		
1996–97	Arsenal	32	6	**327**	**78**
1997–98	Middlesbrough	45	11		
1998–99	Middlesbrough	3	0	**48**	**11**
1998–99	Aston Villa	26	5		
1999–2000	Aston Villa	32	5		
2000–01	Aston Villa	38	6		
2001–02	Aston Villa	21	2	**117**	**18**
2002–03	Portsmouth	45	12	**45**	**12**
2003–04	Walsall	34	4		
2004–05	Walsall	36	2	**70**	**6**

OAKES, Andy (G) **72 0**
H: 6 3 W: 12 04 b.Crewe 11-1-77

1995–96	Bury	0	0		
1996–97	Bury	0	0		
1997–98	Bury	0	0		
From Winsford U.					
1998–99	Hull C	19	0	**19**	**0**
1999–2000	Derby Co	0	0		
1999–2000	*Port Vale*	0	0		
2000–01	Derby Co	6	0		
2001–02	Derby Co	20	0		
2002–03	Derby Co	7	0		
2003–04	Derby Co	10	0		
2004–05	Derby Co	0	0	**43**	**0**
2004–05	*Bolton W*	1	0	**1**	**0**
2004–05	Walsall	9	0	**9**	**0**

ONUORA, Iffy (F) **452 116**
H: 6 1 W: 13 10 b.Glasgow 28-7-67
Source: British Univ.

1989–90	Huddersfield T	20	3		
1990–91	Huddersfield T	43	7		
1991–92	Huddersfield T	41	8		
1992–93	Huddersfield T	39	6		
1993–94	Huddersfield T	22	6		
1994–95	Mansfield T	14	7		
1995–96	Mansfield T	14	1	**28**	**8**
1996–97	Gillingham	40	21		
1997–98	Gillingham	22	2		
1997–98	Swindon T	6	1		
1998–99	Swindon T	43	20		
1999–2000	Swindon T	24	4	**73**	**25**
1999–2000	Gillingham	22	6		
2000–01	Gillingham	31	9		
2001–02	Gillingham	33	11	**148**	**49**
2002–03	Sheffield U	7	1		
2003–04	Sheffield U	0	0	**7**	**1**
2003–04	*Wycombe W*	6	0	**6**	**0**
2003–04	*Grimsby T*	19	3	**19**	**3**
2003–04	Tranmere R	3	0	**3**	**0**
2003–04	Huddersfield T	3	0	**168**	**30**
2004–05	Walsall	0	0		

OSBORN, Simon (M) **401 31**
H: 5 9 W: 11 04 b.New Addington 19-1-72
Source: Apprentice.

1989–90	Crystal Palace	0	0		
1990–91	Crystal Palace	4	0		
1991–92	Crystal Palace	14	2		
1992–93	Crystal Palace	31	2		
1993–94	Crystal Palace	6	1	**55**	**5**
1994–95	Reading	32	5	**32**	**5**
1995–96	QPR	9	1	**9**	**1**
1995–96	Wolverhampton W	21	2		
1996–97	Wolverhampton W	35	5		
1997–98	Wolverhampton W	24	2		
1998–99	Wolverhampton W	37	2		
1999–2000	Wolverhampton W	25	0		
2000–01	Wolverhampton W	20	0	**162**	**11**
2000–01	Tranmere R	9	1	**9**	**1**
2001–02	Port Vale	7	0	**7**	**0**
2001–02	Gillingham	28	4		
2002–03	Gillingham	18	1	**46**	**5**
2003–04	Walsall	43	3		
2004–05	Walsall	38	0	**81**	**3**

PASTON, Mark (G) **22 0**
H: 6 5 W: 14 03 b.Hastings, NZ 13-12-76
Source: Napier City R. *Honours:* New Zealand 7 full caps.

2003–04	Bradford C	13	0	**13**	**0**
2004–05	Walsall	9	0	**9**	**0**

PETTERSON, Andy (G) 156 0
H: 6 2 W: 15 02 b.Fremantle 29-9-69

1988–89	Luton T	0	0		
1988–89	*Swindon T*	0	0		
1989–90	Luton T	0	0		
1990–91	Luton T	0	0		
1991–92	Luton T	0	0		
1991–92	*Ipswich T*	0	0		
1992–93	Luton T	14	0		
1992–93	*Ipswich T*	1	0		
1993–94	Luton T	5	0	**19**	**0**
1994–95	Charlton Ath	9	0		
1994–95	*Bradford C*	3	0	**3**	**0**
1995–96	Charlton Ath	9	0		
1995–96	*Ipswich T*	1	0	**2**	**0**
1995–96	*Plymouth Arg*	6	0	**6**	**0**
1995–96	*Colchester U*	5	0	**5**	**0**
1996–97	Charlton Ath	21	0		
1997–98	Charlton Ath	23	0		
1998–99	Charlton Ath	10	0	**72**	**0**
1998–99	Portsmouth	13	0		
1999–2000	Portsmouth	17	0		
1999–2000	*Wolverhampton W*	0	0		
2000–01	Portsmouth	2	0		
2000–01	*Torquay U*	6	0	**6**	**0**
2001–02	Portsmouth	0	0	**32**	**0**
2001–02	WBA	0	0		
2002–03	Bournemouth	0	0		
2002–03	Brighton & HA	7	0	**7**	**0**
2002–03	Bournemouth	0	0		
2003–04	Rushden & D	0	0		
2003–04	Southend U	1	0	**1**	**0**
2003–04	Walsall	3	0		
2004–05	Walsall	0	0	**3**	**0**

ROPER, Ian (D) 254 2
H: 6 3 W: 14 00 b.Nuneaton 20-6-77
Source: Trainee.

1994–95	Walsall	0	0		
1995–96	Walsall	5	0		
1996–97	Walsall	11	0		
1997–98	Walsall	21	0		
1998–99	Walsall	32	1		
1999–2000	Walsall	34	1		
2000–01	Walsall	25	0		
2001–02	Walsall	27	0		
2002–03	Walsall	40	0		
2003–04	Walsall	33	0		
2004–05	Walsall	26	0	**254**	**2**

STANDING, Michael (M) 62 6
H: 5 10 W: 10 07 b.Shoreham 20-3-81
Source: Trainee. *Honours:* England Schools.

1997–98	Aston Villa	0	0		
1998–99	Aston Villa	0	0		
1999–2000	Aston Villa	0	0		
2000–01	Aston Villa	0	0		
2001–02	Aston Villa	0	0		
2001–02	Bradford C	0	0		
2002–03	Bradford C	24	2		
2003–04	Bradford C	6	0	**30**	**2**
2004–05	Walsall	32	4	**32**	**4**

TAYLOR, Daryl (F) 19 3
H: 5 10 W: 11 03 b.Birmingham 14-11-84
Source: Scholar.

2004–05	Walsall	19	3	**19**	**3**

TAYLOR, Kris (M) 23 3
H: 5 9 W: 11 05 b.Stafford 12-1-84
Source: From Scholar. *Honours:* England Youth.

2000–01	Manchester U	0	0		
2001–02	Manchester U	0	0		
2002–03	Manchester U	0	0		
2002–03	Walsall	0	0		
2003–04	Walsall	11	1		
2004–05	Walsall	12	2	**23**	**3**

WILLETTS, Ryan (D) 0 0
H: 5 9 W: 12 00 b.Coventry 3-11-84
Source: Scholar.

2004–05	Walsall	0	0		

WILLIAMS, Leroy (F) 7 1
H: 5 7 W: 11 00 b.Birmingham 22-10-86
Source: Scholar.

2004–05	Walsall	7	1	**7**	**1**

WRACK, Darren (M) 317 46
H: 5 9 W: 12 02 b.Cleethorpes 5-5-76
Source: Trainee.

1994–95	Derby Co	16	1		
1995–96	Derby Co	10	0	**26**	**1**
1996–97	Grimsby T	12	1		
1996–97	*Shrewsbury T*	4	0	**4**	**0**
1997–98	Grimsby T	1	0	**13**	**1**
1998–99	Walsall	46	13		
1999–2000	Walsall	44	4		
2000–01	Walsall	28	4		
2001–02	Walsall	43	4		
2002–03	Walsall	43	6		
2003–04	Walsall	27	6		
2004–05	Walsall	43	7	**274**	**44**

WRIGHT, Mark (M) 57 4
H: 5 11 W: 11 00 b.Wolverhampton 24-2-82
Source: Scholar.

2000–01	Walsall	4	0		
2001–02	Walsall	0	0		
2002–03	Walsall	5	0		
2003–04	Walsall	11	2		
2004–05	Walsall	37	2	**57**	**4**

WATFORD (85)

BANGURA, Alhassan (M) 2 0
H: 5 8 W: 10 07 b.Sierra Leone 24-1-88
Source: Scholar.

2004–05	Watford	2	0	**2**	**0**

BLIZZARD, Dominic (M) 19 2
H: 6 2 W: 13 05 b.High Wycombe 2-9-83
Source: Scholar.

2001–02	Watford	0	0		
2002–03	Watford	0	0		
2003–04	Watford	2	1		
2004–05	Watford	17	1	**19**	**2**

BOUAZZA, Hameur (F) 37 2
H: 5 11 W: 12 01 b.Evry 22-2-85
Source: Scholar.

2003–04	Watford	9	1		
2004–05	Watford	28	1	**37**	**2**

CHAMBERLAIN, Alec (G) 675 0
H: 6 2 W: 14 00 b.March 20-6-64
Source: Ramsey T.

1981–82	Ipswich T	0	0		
1982–83	Colchester U	4	0		
1983–84	Colchester U	46	0		
1984–85	Colchester U	46	0		
1985–86	Colchester U	46	0		
1986–87	Colchester U	46	0	**188**	**0**
1987–88	Everton	0	0		
1987–88	*Tranmere R*	15	0	**15**	**0**
1988–89	Luton T	6	0		
1989–90	Luton T	38	0		
1990–91	Luton T	38	0		
1991–92	Luton T	24	0		
1992–93	Luton T	32	0	**138**	**0**
1992–93	*Chelsea*	0	0		
1993–94	Sunderland	43	0		
1994–95	Sunderland	18	0		
1994–95	*Liverpool*	0	0		
1995–96	Sunderland	29	0	**90**	**0**
1996–97	Watford	4	0		
1997–98	Watford	46	0		
1998–99	Watford	46	0		
1999–2000	Watford	27	0		
2000–01	Watford	21	0		
2001–02	Watford	32	0		
2002–03	Watford	42	0		
2003–04	Watford	21	0		
2004–05	Watford	5	0	**244**	**0**

CHAMBERS, James (D) 113 0
H: 5 10 W: 12 05 b.Sandwell 20-11-80
Source: Trainee. *Honours:* England Youth.

1998–99	WBA	0	0		
1999–2000	WBA	12	0		
2000–01	WBA	31	0		
2001–02	WBA	5	0		
2002–03	WBA	8	0		
2003–04	WBA	17	0		
2004–05	WBA	0	0	**73**	**0**
2004–05	Watford	40	0	**40**	**0**

COLEMAN, Omari (F) 0 0
H: 5 10 W: 12 05 b.Birmingham 23-11-81
Source: Dulwich Hamlet.

2004–05	Watford	0	0		

COLLINS, Jamie (M) 0 0
H: 6 3 W: 12 00 b.Barking 28-9-84
Source: Scholar.

2004–05	Watford	0	0		

COX, Neil (D) 464 34
H: 5 11 W: 13 08 b.Scunthorpe 8-10-71
Source: From Trainee. *Honours:* England Under-21.

1989–90	Scunthorpe U	0	0		
1990–91	Scunthorpe U	17	1	**17**	**1**
1990–91	Aston Villa	0	0		
1991–92	Aston Villa	7	0		
1992–93	Aston Villa	15	1		
1993–94	Aston Villa	20	2	**42**	**3**
1994–95	Middlesbrough	40	1		
1995–96	Middlesbrough	35	2		
1996–97	Middlesbrough	31	0	**106**	**3**
1997–98	Bolton W	21	1		
1998–99	Bolton W	44	4		
1999–2000	Bolton W	15	2	**80**	**7**
1999–2000	Watford	21	0		
2000–01	Watford	44	5		
2001–02	Watford	40	2		
2002–03	Watford	40	9		
2003–04	Watford	35	4		
2004–05	Watford	39	0	**219**	**20**

DARLINGTON, Jermaine (D) 202 5
H: 5 8 W: 11 05 b.Hackney 11-4-74
Source: Aylesbury U.

1998–99	QPR	4	0		
1999–2000	QPR	34	2		
2000–01	QPR	33	0	**71**	**2**
2001–02	Wimbledon	29	0		
2002–03	Wimbledon	35	2		
2003–04	Wimbledon	41	1	**105**	**3**
2004–05	Watford	26	0	**26**	**0**

DE MERIT, Jay (D) 24 3
H: 6 1 W: 13 05 b.Wisconsin 4-12-79

2004–05	Watford	24	3	**24**	**3**

DEVLIN, Paul (M) 472 85
H: 5 7 W: 11 13 b.Birmingham 14-4-72
Source: Stafford R. *Honours:* Scotland 10 full caps.

1991–92	Notts Co	2	0		
1992–93	Notts Co	32	3		
1993–94	Notts Co	41	7		
1994–95	Notts Co	40	9		
1995–96	Notts Co	26	6		
1995–96	Birmingham C	16	7		
1996–97	Birmingham C	38	16		
1997–98	Birmingham C	22	5		
1997–98	Sheffield U	10	1		
1998–99	Sheffield U	33	5		
1998–99	*Notts Co*	5	0	**146**	**25**
1999–2000	Sheffield U	44	11		
2000–01	Sheffield U	41	5		
2001–02	Sheffield U	19	2	**147**	**24**
2001–02	Birmingham C	13	1		
2002–03	Birmingham C	32	3		
2003–04	Birmingham C	2	0	**123**	**32**
2003–04	Watford	39	3		
2004–05	Watford	17	1	**56**	**4**

DIAGOURAGA, Toumani (M) 0 0
H: 6 1 W: 12 00 b.Corbeil-Essones 10-6-87
Source: Scholar.

2004–05	Watford	0	0		

DOYLEY, Lloyd (D) 80 0
H: 5 10 W: 12 05 b.Whitechapel 1-12-82
Source: Scholar.

2000–01	Watford	0	0		
2001–02	Watford	20	0		
2002–03	Watford	22	0		
2003–04	Watford	9	0		
2004–05	Watford	29	0	**80**	**0**

DYCHE, Sean (D) 403 12
H: 6 1 W: 13 12 b.Kettering 28-6-71
Source: Trainee.

1988–89	Nottingham F	0	0		
1989–90	Nottingham F	0	0		
1989–90	Chesterfield	22	2		
1990–91	Chesterfield	28	2		

1991–92	Chesterfield	42	3		
1992–93	Chesterfield	20	1		
1993–94	Chesterfield	20	0		
1994–95	Chesterfield	22	0		
1995–96	Chesterfield	41	0		
1996–97	Chesterfield	36	0	**231**	**8**
1997–98	Bristol C	11	0		
1998–99	Bristol C	6	0	**17**	**0**
1998–99	*Luton T*	14	1	**14**	**1**
1999–2000	Millwall	1	0		
2000–01	Millwall	33	0		
2001–02	Millwall	35	3	**69**	**3**
2002–03	Watford	24	0		
2003–04	Watford	25	0		
2004–05	Watford	23	0	**72**	**0**

DYER, Bruce (F) 416 114
H: 5 11 W: 12 11 b.Ilford 13-4-75
Source: Trainee. *Honours:* England Under-21.

1992–93	Watford	2	0		
1993–94	Watford	29	6		
1993–94	Crystal Palace	11	0		
1994–95	Crystal Palace	16	1		
1995–96	Crystal Palace	35	13		
1996–97	Crystal Palace	43	17		
1997–98	Crystal Palace	24	4		
1998–99	Crystal Palace	6	2	**135**	**37**
1998–99	Barnsley	28	7		
1999–2000	Barnsley	32	6		
2000–01	Barnsley	38	15		
2001–02	Barnsley	44	14		
2002–03	Barnsley	40	17	**182**	**59**
2003–04	Watford	32	3		
2004–05	Watford	36	9	**99**	**18**

FERRELL, Andrew (M) 0 0
H: 5 9 W: 11 13 b.Newcastle 9-1-84
Source: Trainee.

2002–03	Newcastle U	0	0		
2003–04	Newcastle U	0	0		
2004–05	Watford	0	0		

GUNNARSSON, Brynjar (M) 238 22
H: 6 2 W: 12 12 b.Reykjavik 16-10-75
Honours: Iceland Youth, Under-21, 50 full caps, 3 goals.

1995	KR	16	1		
1996	KR	18	0		
1997	KR	16	0	**50**	**1**
1998	Moss	5	2	**5**	**2**
1999–2000	Stoke C	22	1		
2000–01	Stoke C	46	5		
2001–02	Stoke C	23	5		
2002–03	Stoke C	40	5		
2003–04	Nottingham F	13	0	**13**	**0**
2003–04	*Stoke C*	3	0	**134**	**16**
2004–05	Watford	36	3	**36**	**3**

HAND, Jamie (M) 66 0
H: 5 10 W: 12 13 b.Uxbridge 7-2-84
Source: Scholar. *Honours:* England Youth.

2001–02	Watford	10	0		
2002–03	Watford	23	0		
2003–04	Watford	22	0		
2004–05	Watford	0	0	**55**	**0**
2004–05	*Oxford U*	11	0	**11**	**0**

HELGUSON, Heidar (F) 218 73
H: 5 10 W: 12 09 b.Akureyri 22-8-77
Source: Throttur. *Honours:* Iceland Youth, Under-21, 34 full caps, 5 goals.

1998	Lillestrom	19	2		
1999	Lillestrom	25	16	**44**	**18**
1999–2000	Watford	16	6		
2000–01	Watford	33	8		
2001–02	Watford	34	6		
2002–03	Watford	30	11		
2003–04	Watford	22	8		
2004–05	Watford	39	16	**174**	**55**

HERD, Ben (D) 0 0
H: 5 9 W: 10 12 b.Welwyn 21-6-85
Source: Scholar.

2002–03	Watford	0	0		
2003–04	Watford	0	0		
2004–05	Watford	0	0		

LEE, Richard (G) 37 0
H: 6 0 W: 13 03 b.Oxford 5-10-82
Source: Scholar. *Honours:* England Under-20.

2000–01	Watford	0	0		
2001–02	Watford	0	0		
2002–03	Watford	4	0		
2003–04	Watford	0	0		
2004–05	Watford	33	0	**37**	**0**

MAHON, Gavin (M) 250 11
H: 6 0 W: 13 00 b.Birmingham 2-1-77
Source: Trainee.

1995–96	Wolverhampton W	0	0		
1996–97	Hereford U	11	1		
1997–98	Hereford U	0	0		
1998–99	Hereford U	0	0	**11**	**1**
1998–99	Brentford	29	4		
1999–2000	Brentford	37	3		
2000–01	Brentford	40	1		
2001–02	Brentford	35	0	**141**	**8**
2001–02	Watford	6	0		
2002–03	Watford	17	0		
2003–04	Watford	32	2		
2004–05	Watford	43	0	**98**	**2**

MAYO, Paul (D) 131 6
H: 6 0 W: 12 11 b.Lincoln 13-10-81
Source: Scholarship.

1999–2000	Lincoln C	19	0		
2000–01	Lincoln C	27	0		
2001–02	Lincoln C	14	0		
2002–03	Lincoln C	15	0		
2003–04	Lincoln C	31	6	**106**	**6**
2003–04	Watford	12	0		
2004–05	Watford	13	0	**25**	**0**

McNAMEE, Anthony (M) 46 1
H: 5 6 W: 9 11 b.Lambeth 13-7-84
Source: Scholar. *Honours:* England Youth, Under-20.

2001–02	Watford	7	1		
2002–03	Watford	23	0		
2003–04	Watford	2	0		
2004–05	Watford	14	0	**46**	**1**

NORVILLE, Jason (F) 14 1
H: 6 0 W: 11 07 b.Trinidad & Tobago 9-9-83
Source: Scholar.

2001–02	Watford	2	0		
2002–03	Watford	12	1		
2003–04	Watford	0	0		
2004–05	Watford	0	0	**14**	**1**

OSBORNE, Junior (M) 1 0
H: 5 10 W: 12 03 b.Watford 12-2-88
Source: Scholar.

2004–05	Watford	1	0	**1**	**0**

SMITH, Jack (D) 25 2
H: 5 10 W: 11 05 b.Hemel Hempstead 14-11-83
Source: Scholar.

2001–02	Watford	0	0		
2002–03	Watford	1	0		
2003–04	Watford	17	2		
2004–05	Watford	7	0	**25**	**2**

WEBBER, Danny (F) 83 24
H: 5 8 W: 11 00 b.Manchester 28-12-81
Source: Trainee. *Honours:* England Youth, Under-20.

1998–99	Manchester U	0	0		
1999–2000	Manchester U	0	0		
2000–01	Manchester U	0	0		
2001–02	Manchester U	0	0		
2001–02	*Port Vale*	4	0	**4**	**0**
2001–02	*Watford*	5	2		
2002–03	Manchester U	0	0		
2002–03	*Watford*	12	2		
2003–04	Watford	27	5		
2004–05	Watford	28	12	**72**	**21**
2004–05	*Sheffield U*	7	3	**7**	**3**

YOUNG, Ashley (M) 39 3
H: 5 9 W: 9 13 b.Stevenage 9-7-85
Source: Juniors.

2002–03	Watford	0	0		
2003–04	Watford	5	3		
2004–05	Watford	34	0	**39**	**3**

WBA (86)

ALBRECHTSEN, Martin (D) 185 3
H: 6 1 W: 12 13 b.Copenhagen 30-3-80
Source: Denmark Youth, Under-21, 3 full caps.

1998–99	Aalborg	9	1		
1999–2000	Aalborg	31	1		
2000–01	Aalborg	30	0		
2001–02	Aalborg	19	1	**89**	**3**
2001–02	FC Copenhagen	14	0		
2002–03	FC Copenhagen	27	0		
2003–04	FC Copenhagen	31	0	**72**	**0**
2004–05	WBA	24	0	**24**	**0**

BERTHE, Sekou (D) 23 0
H: 6 4 W: 13 02 b.Bamako 7-10-77
Source: Monaco. *Honours:* Mali full caps.

1999–2000	Troyes	10	0		
2000–01	Troyes	6	0		
2001–02	Troyes	4	0		
2002–03	Troyes	0	0	**20**	**0**
2003–04	WBA	3	0		
2004–05	WBA	0	0	**3**	**0**

CAMPBELL, Kevin (F) 451 145
H: 6 0 W: 13 08 b.Lambeth 4-2-70
Source: Trainee. *Honours:* England Under-21, B.

1987–88	Arsenal	1	0		
1988–89	Arsenal	0	0		
1988–89	*Leyton Orient*	16	9	**16**	**9**
1989–90	Arsenal	15	2		
1989–90	*Leicester C*	11	5	**11**	**5**
1990–91	Arsenal	22	9		
1991–92	Arsenal	31	13		
1992–93	Arsenal	37	4		
1993–94	Arsenal	37	14		
1994–95	Arsenal	23	4	**166**	**46**
1995–96	Nottingham F	21	3		
1996–97	Nottingham F	17	6		
1997–98	Nottingham F	42	23	**80**	**32**
1998–99	Trabzonspor	17	5	**17**	**5**
1998–99	Everton	8	9		
1999–2000	Everton	26	12		
2000–01	Everton	29	9		
2001–02	Everton	23	4		
2002–03	Everton	36	10		
2003–04	Everton	17	1		
2004–05	Everton	6	0	**145**	**45**
2004–05	WBA	16	3	**16**	**3**

CHAPLOW, Richard (M) 69 7
H: 5 9 W: 9 03 b.Accrington 2-2-85
Source: Scholar. *Honours:* England Youth, Under-20, Under-21.

2002–03	Burnley	5	0		
2003–04	Burnley	39	5		
2004–05	Burnley	21	2	**65**	**7**
2004–05	WBA	4	0	**4**	**0**

CLEMENT, Neil (D) 228 20
H: 6 0 W: 12 03 b.Reading 3-10-78
Source: Trainee. *Honours:* England Schools, Youth.

1995–96	Chelsea	0	0		
1996–97	Chelsea	1	0		
1997–98	Chelsea	0	0		
1998–99	Chelsea	0	0		
1998–99	*Reading*	11	1	**11**	**1**
1998–99	*Preston NE*	4	0	**4**	**0**
1999–2000	Chelsea	0	0	**1**	**0**
1999–2000	*Brentford*	8	0	**8**	**0**
1999–2000	*WBA*	8	0		
2000–01	WBA	45	5		
2001–02	WBA	45	6		
2002–03	WBA	36	3		
2003–04	WBA	35	2		
2004–05	WBA	35	3	**204**	**19**

CONTRA, Cosmin (D) 235 17
H: 5 11 W: 11 09 b.Timisoara 15-12-75
Honours: Romania, 46 full caps, 5 goals.

1995–96	Dinamo Bucharest	12	1		
1996–97	Dinamo Bucharest	32	2		
1997–98	Dinamo Bucharest	28	3		
1998–99	Dinamo Bucharest	29	2	**101**	**8**
1999–2000	Alaves	33	2		
2000–01	Alaves	33	4	**66**	**6**
2001–02	AC Milan	29	3	**29**	**3**

2002–03	Atletico Madrid	31	0		
2003–04	Atletico Madrid	3	0	**34**	**0**
2004–05	WBA	5	0	**5**	**0**

DYER, Lloyd (M) **34 3**
H: 5 10 W: 11 04 b.Aston 13-9-82
Source: Aston Villa Juniors.

2001–02	WBA	0	0		
2002–03	WBA	0	0		
2003–04	WBA	17	2		
2003–04	*Kidderminster H*	7	1	**7**	**1**
2004–05	WBA	4	0	**21**	**2**
2004–05	*Coventry C*	6	0	**6**	**0**

EARNSHAW, Robert (F) **212 98**
H: 5 6 W: 9 09 b.Mulfulira 6-4-81
Source: Trainee. *Honours:* Wales Youth, Under-21, 19 full caps, 9 goals.

1997–98	Cardiff C	5	0		
1998–99	Cardiff C	5	1		
1998–99	*Middlesbrough*	0	0		
1999–2000	Cardiff C	6	1		
1999–2000	*Morton*	3	2	**3**	**2**
2000–01	Cardiff C	36	19		
2001–02	Cardiff C	30	11		
2002–03	Cardiff C	46	31		
2003–04	Cardiff C	46	21		
2004–05	Cardiff C	4	1	**178**	**85**
2004–05	WBA	31	11	**31**	**11**

GAARDSOE, Thomas (D) **177 14**
H: 6 2 W: 12 08 b.Randers 23-11-79
Honours: Denmark Under-23, 2 full caps, 1 goal.

1996–97	Aalborg	1	0		
1997–98	Aalborg	6	1		
1998–99	Aalborg	17	2		
1999–2000	Aalborg	18	2		
2000–01	Aalborg	20	0	**62**	**5**
2001–02	Ipswich T	4	1		
2002–03	Ipswich T	37	4	**41**	**5**
2003–04	WBA	45	4		
2004–05	WBA	29	0	**74**	**4**

GERA, Zoltan (M) **168 42**
H: 6 0 W: 11 11 b.Pecs 22-4-79
Source: Hakarny.
Honours: Hungary 30 full caps, 9 goals.

1999–2000	Pecsi	15	4	**15**	**4**
2000–01	Ferencvaros	32	7		
2001–02	Ferencvaros	27	8		
2002–03	Ferencvaros	26	6		
2003–04	Ferencvaros	30	11	**115**	**32**
2004–05	WBA	38	6	**38**	**6**

GREENING, Jonathan (M) **172 6**
H: 5 11 W: 11 00 b.Scarborough 2-1-79
Source: Trainee. *Honours:* England Youth, Under-21.

1996–97	York C	5	0		
1997–98	York C	20	2	**25**	**2**
1997–98	Manchester U	0	0		
1998–99	Manchester U	3	0		
1999–2000	Manchester U	4	0		
2000–01	Manchester U	7	0	**14**	**0**
2001–02	Middlesbrough	36	1		
2002–03	Middlesbrough	38	2		
2003–04	Middlesbrough	25	1	**99**	**4**
2004–05	WBA	34	0	**34**	**0**

HAAS, Bernt (D) **233 7**
H: 6 1 W: 12 08 b.Vienna 8-4-78
Honours: Switzerland 36 full caps, 3 goals.

1994–95	Grasshoppers	2	0		
1995–96	Grasshoppers	20	0		
1996–97	Grasshoppers	29	1		
1997–98	Grasshoppers	27	2		
1998–99	Grasshoppers	28	1		
1999–2000	Grasshoppers	29	1		
2000–01	Grasshoppers	25	1	**160**	**6**
2001–02	Sunderland	27	0		
2002–03	Sunderland	0	0	**27**	**0**
2003–04	WBA	36	1		
2004–05	WBA	10	0	**46**	**1**

HORSFIELD, Geoff (F) **254 70**
H: 5 10 W: 11 02 b.Barnsley 1-11-73

1992–93	Scarborough	6	1		
1993–94	Scarborough	6	0	**12**	**1**
From Witton Alb					
1998–99	Halifax T	10	7	**10**	**7**
1998–99	Fulham	28	15		
1999–2000	Fulham	31	7	**59**	**22**
2000–01	Birmingham C	34	7		
2001–02	Birmingham C	40	11		
2002–03	Birmingham C	31	5		
2003–04	Birmingham C	3	0	**108**	**23**
2003–04	Wigan Ath	16	7	**16**	**7**
2003–04	WBA	20	7		
2004–05	WBA	29	3	**49**	**10**

HOULT, Russell (G) **369 0**
H: 6 3 W: 14 09 b.Ashby 22-11-72
Source: Trainee.

1990–91	Leicester C	0	0		
1991–92	Leicester C	0	0		
1991–92	*Lincoln C*	2	0		
1991–92	*Blackpool*	0	0		
1992–93	Leicester C	10	0		
1993–94	Leicester C	0	0		
1993–94	*Bolton W*	4	0	**4**	**0**
1994–95	Leicester C	0	0	**10**	**0**
1994–95	*Lincoln C*	15	0	**17**	**0**
1994–95	*Derby Co*	15	0		
1995–96	Derby Co	41	0		
1996–97	Derby Co	32	0		
1997–98	Derby Co	2	0		
1998–99	Derby Co	23	0		
1999–2000	Derby Co	10	0	**123**	**0**
1999–2000	Portsmouth	18	0		
2000–01	Portsmouth	22	0	**40**	**0**
2000–01	WBA	13	0		
2001–02	WBA	45	0		
2002–03	WBA	37	0		
2003–04	WBA	44	0		
2004–05	WBA	36	0	**175**	**0**

HULSE, Rob (F) **167 62**
H: 6 1 W: 11 04 b.Crewe 25-10-79
Source: Trainee.

1998–99	Crewe Alex	0	0		
1999–2000	Crewe Alex	4	1		
2000–01	Crewe Alex	33	11		
2001–02	Crewe Alex	41	12		
2002–03	Crewe Alex	38	22	**116**	**46**
2003–04	WBA	33	10		
2004–05	WBA	5	0	**38**	**10**
2004–05	*Leeds U*	13	6	**13**	**6**

INAMOTO, Junichi (M) **176 20**
H: 6 0 W: 11 11 b.Kagoshima 18-9-79
Honours: Japan 57 full caps, 4 goals.

1997	Gamba Osaka	27	3		
1998	Gamba Osaka	28	6		
1999	Gamba Osaka	22	1		
2000	Gamba Osaka	28	4		
2001	Gamba Osaka	13	2	**118**	**16**
2001–02	Arsenal	0	0		
2002–03	Fulham	19	2		
2003–04	Fulham	22	2	**41**	**4**
2004–05	WBA	3	0	**3**	**0**
2004–05	*Cardiff C*	14	0	**14**	**0**

JOHNSON, Andy (M) **309 29**
H: 6 0 W: 13 00 b.Bristol 2-5-74
Source: Trainee. *Honours:* England Youth, Wales 15 full caps.

1991–92	Norwich C	2	0		
1992–93	Norwich C	2	1		
1993–94	Norwich C	2	0		
1994–95	Norwich C	7	0		
1995–96	Norwich C	26	7		
1996–97	Norwich C	27	5	**66**	**13**
1997–98	Nottingham F	34	4		
1998–99	Nottingham F	28	0		
1999–2000	Nottingham F	25	2		
2000–01	Nottingham F	31	3		
2001–02	Nottingham F	1	0	**119**	**9**
2001–02	WBA	32	4		
2002–03	WBA	32	1		
2003–04	WBA	38	2		
2004–05	WBA	22	0	**124**	**7**

KANU, Nwankwo (F) **273 73**
H: 6 5 W: 12 08 b.Owerri 1-8-76
Honours: Nigeria 39 full caps, 6 goals.

1991–92	Federation Works	30	9	**30**	**9**
1992–93	Iwanyanwu	30	6	**30**	**6**
1993–94	Ajax	6	2		
1994–95	Ajax	18	10		
1995–96	Ajax	30	13	**54**	**25**
1996–97	Internazionale	0	0		
1997–98	Internazionale	11	1		
1998–99	Internazionale	1	0	**12**	**1**
1998–99	Arsenal	12	6		
1999–2000	Arsenal	31	12		
2000–01	Arsenal	27	3		
2001–02	Arsenal	23	3		
2002–03	Arsenal	16	5		
2003–04	Arsenal	10	1	**119**	**30**
2004–05	WBA	28	2	**28**	**2**

KOUMAS, Jason (M) **211 39**
H: 5 10 W: 11 02 b.Wrexham 25-9-79
Source: Trainee. *Honours:* Wales 14 full caps, 1 goal.

1997–98	Tranmere R	0	0		
1998–99	Tranmere R	23	3		
1999–2000	Tranmere R	23	2		
2000–01	Tranmere R	39	10		
2001–02	Tranmere R	38	8		
2002–03	Tranmere R	4	2	**127**	**25**
2002–03	WBA	32	4		
2003–04	WBA	42	10		
2004–05	WBA	10	0	**84**	**14**

KUSZCZAK, Tomasz (G) **3 0**
H: 6 3 W: 13 03 b.Krosno Odrzansia 20-3-82
Source: Uerdingen. *Honours:* Poland 2 full caps.

2001–02	Hertha Berlin	0	0		
2002–03	Hertha Berlin	0	0		
2003–04	Hertha Berlin	0	0		
2004–05	WBA	3	0	**3**	**0**

MARSHALL, Lee (M) **182 12**
H: 6 0 W: 11 10 b.Islington 21-1-79
Source: Enfield. *Honours:* England Under-21.

1996–97	Norwich C	0	0		
1997–98	Norwich C	4	0		
1998–99	Norwich C	44	3		
1999–2000	Norwich C	33	5		
2000–01	Norwich C	36	3	**117**	**11**
2000–01	Leicester C	9	0		
2001–02	Leicester C	35	0		
2002–03	Leicester C	1	0	**45**	**0**
2002–03	WBA	9	1		
2003–04	WBA	0	0		
2003–04	*Hull C*	11	0	**11**	**0**
2004–05	WBA	0	0	**9**	**1**

MIDWORTH, Phil (M) **0 0**
H: 6 0 W: 12 00 b.Birmingham 17-5-85
Source: Scholar.

2004–05	WBA	0	0		

MIOTTO, Simon (G) **14 0**
H: 6 1 W: 13 03 b.Tasmania 5-9-69
Source: Riverside Olympic.

1994–95	Blackpool	0	0		
1995–96	Blackpool	0	0		
1996–97	Blackpool	0	0		
1997–98	Blackpool	0	0		
1998–99	Hartlepool U	5	0		
1999–2000	Hartlepool U	0	0	**5**	**0**
2000–01	Raith R	0	0		
2001–02	Raith R	9	0	**9**	**0**
2002–03	St Johnstone	0	0		
2003–04	WBA	0	0		
2004–05	WBA	0	0		

MOORE, Darren (D) **399 26**
H: 6 2 W: 15 07 b.Birmingham 22-4-74
Source: Trainee. *Honours:* Jamaica 3 full caps.

1991–92	Torquay U	5	1		
1992–93	Torquay U	31	2		
1993–94	Torquay U	37	2		
1994–95	Torquay U	30	3	**103**	**8**
1995–96	Doncaster R	35	2		
1996–97	Doncaster R	41	5	**76**	**7**
1997–98	Bradford C	18	0		
1998–99	Bradford C	44	3		
1999–2000	Bradford C	0	0	**62**	**3**
1999–2000	Portsmouth	25	1		
2000–01	Portsmouth	32	1		
2001–02	Portsmouth	2	0	**59**	**2**
2001–02	WBA	32	2		
2002–03	WBA	29	2		
2003–04	WBA	22	2		
2004–05	WBA	16	0	**99**	**6**

MURPHY, Joe (G) **93 0**
H: 6 2 W: 13 06 b.Dublin 21-8-81
Source: Trainee. *Honours:* Eire Under-21, 1 full cap.
1999–2000 Tranmere R 21 0
2000–01 Tranmere R 20 0
2001–02 Tranmere R 22 0 **63 0**
2002–03 WBA 2 0
2003–04 WBA 3 0
2004–05 WBA 0 0 **5 0**
2004–05 *Walsall* 25 0 **25 0**

PURSE, Darren (D) **304 17**
H: 6 2 W: 12 08 b.Stepney 14-2-77
Source: Trainee. *Honours:* England Under-21.
1993–94 Leyton Orient 5 0
1994–95 Leyton Orient 38 3
1995–96 Leyton Orient 12 0 **55 3**
1996–97 Oxford U 31 1
1997–98 Oxford U 28 4 **59 5**
1997–98 Birmingham C 8 0
1998–99 Birmingham C 20 0
1999–2000 Birmingham C 38 2
2000–01 Birmingham C 37 3
2001–02 Birmingham C 36 3
2002–03 Birmingham C 20 1
2003–04 Birmingham C 9 0 **168 9**
2004–05 WBA 22 0 **22 0**

ROBINSON, Paul (D) **280 9**
H: 5 9 W: 11 12 b.Watford 14-12-78
Source: Trainee. *Honours:* England Under-21.
1996–97 Watford 12 0
1997–98 Watford 22 2
1998–99 Watford 29 0
1999–2000 Watford 32 0
2000–01 Watford 39 0
2001–02 Watford 38 3
2002–03 Watford 37 3
2003–04 Watford 10 0 **219 8**
2003–04 WBA 31 0
2004–05 WBA 30 1 **61 1**

SAKIRI, Artim (M) **28 1**
H: 5 11 W: 12 00 b.Struga 23-9-73
Source: CSKA Sofia. *Honours:* Macedonia 67 full caps, 15 goals.
2003–04 WBA 25 1
2004–05 WBA 3 0 **28 1**

SCIMECA, Riccardo (D) **286 10**
H: 6 1 W: 12 09 b.Leamington Spa 13-6-75
Source: Trainee. *Honours:* England Under-21, B.
1993–94 Aston Villa 0 0
1994–95 Aston Villa 0 0
1995–96 Aston Villa 17 0
1996–97 Aston Villa 17 0
1997–98 Aston Villa 21 0
1998–99 Aston Villa 18 2 **73 2**
1999–2000 Nottingham F 38 0
2000–01 Nottingham F 36 4
2001–02 Nottingham F 37 0
2002–03 Nottingham F 40 3 **151 7**
2003–04 Leicester C 29 1 **29 1**
2004–05 WBA 33 0 **33 0**

SIGURDSSON, Larus (M) **316 8**
H: 6 0 W: 11 06 b.Akureyri 4-6-73
Source: Thor. *Honours:* Iceland 42 full caps, 2 goals.
1994–95 Stoke C 23 1
1995–96 Stoke C 46 0
1996–97 Stoke C 45 0
1997–98 Stoke C 43 1
1998–99 Stoke C 38 4
1999–2000 Stoke C 5 1 **200 7**
1999–2000 WBA 27 0
2000–01 WBA 12 0
2001–02 WBA 43 1
2002–03 WBA 29 0
2003–04 WBA 5 0
2004–05 WBA 0 0 **116 1**

WALLWORK, Ronnie (M) **95 6**
H: 5 10 W: 12 09 b.Manchester 10-9-77
Source: Trainee. *Honours:* England Youth.
1994–95 Manchester U 0 0
1995–96 Manchester U 0 0
1996–97 Manchester U 0 0
1997–98 Manchester U 1 0
1997–98 *Carlisle U* 10 1 **10 1**
1997–98 *Stockport Co* 7 0 **7 0**
1998–99 Manchester U 0 0
1999–2000 Manchester U 5 0
2000–01 Manchester U 12 0
2001–02 Manchester U 1 0 **19 0**
2002–03 WBA 27 0
2003–04 WBA 5 0
2003–04 *Bradford C* 7 4 **7 4**
2004–05 WBA 20 1 **52 1**

Scholars
Daniels, Luke Matthew; Davies, Robert John; Elvins, Robert Mark; Forsyth, Jeffrey James; Hodgkiss, Jared; Humphrey, Christopher Charles; Kelleher, Seamus Joshua; Nicholson, Stuart Ian; Pringle, Ben Philip; Smikle, Brian Junior

WEST HAM U (87)

ASHIKODI, Moses (M) **5 0**
H: 6 0 W: 11 09 b.Lagos 27-6-87
Honours: FA Schools, England Youth.
2002–03 Millwall 5 0
2003–04 Millwall 0 0 **5 0**
2004–05 West Ham U 0 0

BLEWITT, Darren (M) **1 0**
H: 6 2 W: 13 00 b.Newham 3-9-85
Source: Scholar.
2004–05 West Ham U 0 0
2004–05 *Southend U* 1 0 **1 0**

BREVETT, Rufus (D) **459 6**
H: 5 9 W: 11 13 b.Derby 24-9-69
Source: Trainee.
1987–88 Doncaster R 17 0
1988–89 Doncaster R 23 0
1989–90 Doncaster R 42 0
1990–91 Doncaster R 27 3 **109 3**
1990–91 QPR 10 0
1991–92 QPR 7 0
1992–93 QPR 15 0
1993–94 QPR 7 0
1994–95 QPR 19 0
1995–96 QPR 27 1
1996–97 QPR 44 0
1997–98 QPR 23 0 **152 1**
1997–98 Fulham 11 0
1998–99 Fulham 45 1
1999–2000 Fulham 23 0
2000–01 Fulham 39 0
2001–02 Fulham 35 0
2002–03 Fulham 20 0 **173 1**
2002–03 West Ham U 13 0
2003–04 West Ham U 2 0
2004–05 West Ham U 10 1 **25 1**

BYWATER, Steve (G) **64 0**
H: 6 2 W: 12 00 b.Manchester 7-6-81
Source: Trainee. *Honours:* England Youth, Under-20, Under-21.
1997–98 Rochdale 0 0
1998–99 West Ham U 0 0
1999–2000 West Ham U 4 0
1999–2000 *Wycombe W* 2 0 **2 0**
1999–2000 *Hull C* 4 0 **4 0**
2000–01 West Ham U 1 0
2001–02 West Ham U 0 0
2001–02 *Wolverhampton W* 0 0
2001–02 *Cardiff C* 0 0
2002–03 West Ham U 0 0
2003–04 West Ham U 17 0
2004–05 West Ham U 36 0 **58 0**

CARRICK, Graeme (M) **0 0**
H: 6 0 W: 12 00 b.Wallsend 3-4-85
Source: Scholar.
2004–05 West Ham U 0 0

CHADWICK, Luke (M) **108 9**
H: 5 11 W: 11 08 b.Cambridge 18-11-80
Source: From Trainee. *Honours:* England Youth, Under-21.
1998–99 Manchester U 0 0
1999–2000 Manchester U 0 0
2000–01 Manchester U 16 2
2001–02 Manchester U 8 0
2002–03 Manchester U 1 0
2002–03 *Reading* 15 1 **15 1**
2003–04 Manchester U 0 0 **25 2**
2003–04 *Burnley* 36 5 **36 5**
2004–05 West Ham U 32 1 **32 1**

COHEN, Chris (M) **18 0**
H: 5 11 W: 10 11 b.Norwich 5-3-87
Source: Scholar. *Honours:* England Youth.
2003–04 West Ham U 7 0
2004–05 West Ham U 11 0 **18 0**

COLE, Mitchell (M) **0 0**
b.London 6-10-85
Source: Trainee. *Honours:* England Youth.
2002–03 West Ham U 0 0
2003–04 West Ham U 0 0
2004–05 West Ham U 0 0

DAILLY, Christian (D) **400 28**
H: 6 1 W: 12 10 b.Dundee 23-10-73
Source: 'S' Form. *Honours:* Scotland Schools, Youth, B, Under-21, 55 full caps, 5 goals.
1990–91 Dundee U 18 5
1991–92 Dundee U 8 0
1992–93 Dundee U 14 4
1993–94 Dundee U 38 4
1994–95 Dundee U 33 4
1995–96 Dundee U 30 1 **141 18**
1996–97 Derby Co 36 3
1997–98 Derby Co 30 1
1998–99 Derby Co 1 0 **67 4**
1998–99 Blackburn R 17 0
1999–2000 Blackburn R 43 4
2000–01 Blackburn R 10 0 **70 4**
2000–01 West Ham U 12 0
2001–02 West Ham U 38 0
2002–03 West Ham U 26 0
2003–04 West Ham U 43 2
2004–05 West Ham U 3 0 **122 2**

EPHRAIM, Hogan (F) **0 0**
H: 5 9 W: 10 06 b.Islington 31-3-88
Source: Scholar. *Honours:* England Youth.
2004–05 West Ham U 0 0

ETHERINGTON, Matthew (M) **183 17**
H: 5 10 W: 10 12 b.Truro 14-8-81
Source: School. *Honours:* England Youth, Under-21.
1996–97 Peterborough U 1 0
1997–98 Peterborough U 2 0
1998–99 Peterborough U 29 3
1999–2000 Peterborough U 19 3 **51 6**
1999–2000 Tottenham H 5 0
2000–01 Tottenham H 6 0
2001–02 *Bradford C* 13 1 **13 1**
2001–02 Tottenham H 11 0
2002–03 Tottenham H 23 1 **45 1**
2003–04 West Ham U 35 5
2004–05 West Ham U 39 4 **74 9**

FERDINAND, Anton (D) **49 1**
H: 6 2 W: 11 00 b.Peckham 18-2-85
Source: Trainee. *Honours:* England Youth, Under-20, Under-21.
2002–03 West Ham U 0 0
2003–04 West Ham U 20 0
2004–05 West Ham U 29 1 **49 1**

FLETCHER, Carl (M) **225 21**
H: 5 10 W: 11 07 b.Camberley 7-4-80
Source: Trainee. *Honours:* Wales 8 full caps.
1997–98 Bournemouth 1 0
1998–99 Bournemouth 1 0
1999–2000 Bournemouth 25 3
2000–01 Bournemouth 43 6
2001–02 Bournemouth 35 5
2002–03 Bournemouth 42 1
2003–04 Bournemouth 40 2
2004–05 Bournemouth 6 2 **193 19**
2004–05 West Ham U 32 2 **32 2**

HAREWOOD, Marlon (F) **261 82**
H: 6 1 W: 13 07 b.Hampstead 25-8-79
Source: Trainee.
1996–97 Nottingham F 0 0
1997–98 Nottingham F 1 0
1998–99 Nottingham F 23 1
1998–99 *Ipswich T* 6 1 **6 1**
1999–2000 Nottingham F 34 4
2000–01 Nottingham F 33 3
2001–02 Nottingham F 28 11
2002–03 Nottingham F 44 20

2003–04	Nottingham F	19	12	**182**	**51**
2003–04	West Ham U	28	13		
2004–05	West Ham U	45	17	**73**	**30**

HUTCHISON, Don (M) **354** **48**
H: 6 2 W: 11 08 b.Gateshead 9-5-71
Source: Trainee. *Honours:* Scotland B, 26 full caps, 6 goals.

1989–90	Hartlepool U	13	2		
1990–91	Hartlepool U	11	0	**24**	**2**
1990–91	Liverpool	0	0		
1991–92	Liverpool	3	0		
1992–93	Liverpool	31	7		
1993–94	Liverpool	11	0	**45**	**7**
1994–95	West Ham U	23	9		
1995–96	West Ham U	12	2		
1995–96	Sheffield U	19	2		
1996–97	Sheffield U	41	3		
1997–98	Sheffield U	18	0	**78**	**5**
1997–98	Everton	11	1		
1998–99	Everton	33	3		
1999–2000	Everton	31	6	**75**	**10**
2000–01	Sunderland	32	8		
2001–02	Sunderland	2	0	**34**	**8**
2001–02	West Ham U	24	1		
2002–03	West Ham U	10	0		
2003–04	West Ham U	24	4		
2004–05	West Ham U	5	0	**98**	**16**

KUCIAK, Dusan (G) **0** **0**
H: 6 4 W: 14 00 b.Slovakia 21-5-87
Source: Zilina.

2004–05	West Ham U	0	0		

LAWS, Tommy (D) **0** **0**
b.Barking 27-11-85
Source: Scholar.

2004–05	West Ham U	0	0		

LOMAS, Steve (M) **298** **18**
H: 6 0 W: 12 08 b.Hanover 18-1-74
Source: From Trainee. *Honours:* Northern Ireland Schools, Youth, B, 45 full caps, 3 goals.

1991–92	Manchester C	0	0		
1992–93	Manchester C	0	0		
1993–94	Manchester C	23	0		
1994–95	Manchester C	20	2		
1995–96	Manchester C	33	3		
1996–97	Manchester C	35	3	**111**	**8**
1996–97	West Ham U	7	0		
1997–98	West Ham U	33	2		
1998–99	West Ham U	30	1		
1999–2000	West Ham U	25	1		
2000–01	West Ham U	20	1		
2001–02	West Ham U	15	4		
2002–03	West Ham U	29	0		
2003–04	West Ham U	5	0		
2004–05	West Ham U	23	1	**187**	**10**

MACKAY, Malky (D) **337** **27**
H: 6 3 W: 13 02 b.Bellshill 19-2-72
Source: Queen's Park Youth. *Honours:* Scotland 5 full caps.

1990–91	Queen's Park	10	0		
1991–92	Queen's Park	27	3		
1992–93	Queen's Park	33	3	**70**	**6**
1993–94	Celtic	0	0		
1994–95	Celtic	1	0		
1995–96	Celtic	11	1		
1996–97	Celtic	20	1		
1997–98	Celtic	4	1		
1998–99	Celtic	1	1	**37**	**4**
1998–99	Norwich C	27	1		
1999–2000	Norwich C	21	0		
2000–01	Norwich C	38	1		
2001–02	Norwich C	44	3		
2002–03	Norwich C	37	6		
2003–04	Norwich C	45	4		
2004–05	Norwich C	0	0	**212**	**15**
2004–05	West Ham U	18	2	**18**	**2**

McCLENAHAN, Trent (D) **10** **0**
H: 5 11 W: 12 00 b.Australia 4-2-85
Source: Scholar. *Honours:* Australia Youth, Under-20.

2004–05	West Ham U	2	0	**2**	**0**
2004–05	*Milton Keynes D*	8	0	**8**	**0**

MELVILLE, Andy (D) **703** **54**
H: 6 2 W: 12 13 b.Swansea 29-11-68
Source: School. *Honours:* Wales Under-21, B, 64 full caps, 3 goals.

1985–86	Swansea C	5	0		
1986–87	Swansea C	42	3		
1987–88	Swansea C	37	4		
1988–89	Swansea C	45	10		
1989–90	Swansea C	46	5	**175**	**22**
1990–91	Oxford U	46	3		
1991–92	Oxford U	45	4		
1992–93	Oxford U	44	6	**135**	**13**
1993–94	Sunderland	44	2		
1994–95	Sunderland	36	3		
1995–96	Sunderland	40	4		
1996–97	Sunderland	30	2		
1997–98	Sunderland	10	1		
1997–98	*Bradford C*	6	1	**6**	**1**
1998–99	Sunderland	44	2	**204**	**14**
1999–2000	Fulham	40	3		
2000–01	Fulham	43	1		
2001–02	Fulham	35	0		
2002–03	Fulham	26	0		
2003–04	Fulham	9	0	**153**	**4**
2003–04	West Ham U	14	0		
2004–05	West Ham U	3	0	**17**	**0**
2004–05	*Nottingham F*	13	0	**13**	**0**

MULLINS, Hayden (D) **286** **19**
H: 5 11 W: 11 12 b.Reading 27-3-79
Source: Trainee. *Honours:* England Under-21.

1996–97	Crystal Palace	0	0		
1997–98	Crystal Palace	0	0		
1998–99	Crystal Palace	40	5		
1999–2000	Crystal Palace	45	10		
2000–01	Crystal Palace	41	1		
2001–02	Crystal Palace	43	0		
2002–03	Crystal Palace	43	2		
2003–04	Crystal Palace	10	0	**222**	**18**
2003–04	West Ham U	27	0		
2004–05	West Ham U	37	1	**64**	**1**

NEWTON, Shaun (M) **381** **32**
H: 5 8 W: 11 00 b.Camberwell 20-8-75
Source: Trainee. *Honours:* England Under-21.

1992–93	Charlton Ath	2	0		
1993–94	Charlton Ath	19	2		
1994–95	Charlton Ath	26	0		
1995–96	Charlton Ath	41	5		
1996–97	Charlton Ath	43	3		
1997–98	Charlton Ath	41	5		
1998–99	Charlton Ath	16	0		
1999–2000	Charlton Ath	42	5		
2000–01	Charlton Ath	10	0	**240**	**20**
2001–02	Wolverhampton W	45	8		
2002–03	Wolverhampton W	33	3		
2003–04	Wolverhampton W	28	0		
2004–05	Wolverhampton W	24	1	**130**	**12**
2004–05	West Ham U	11	0	**11**	**0**

NOBLE, Mark (M) **13** **0**
H: 5 11 W: 12 00 b.West Ham 8-5-87
Source: Scholar. *Honours:* England Youth.

2004–05	West Ham U	13	0	**13**	**0**

PEARSON, Greg (F) **3** **0**
H: 5 11 W: 12 00 b.Birmingham 3-4-85
Source: Trainee.

2003–04	West Ham U	0	0		
2004–05	West Ham U	0	0		
2004–05	*Lincoln C*	3	0	**3**	**0**

POWELL, Chris (D) **589** **5**
H: 5 11 W: 11 12 b.Lambeth 8-9-69
Source: Trainee. *Honours:* England 5 full caps.

1987–88	Crystal Palace	0	0		
1988–89	Crystal Palace	3	0		
1989–90	Crystal Palace	0	0	**3**	**0**
1989–90	*Aldershot*	11	0	**11**	**0**
1990–91	Southend U	45	1		
1991–92	Southend U	44	0		
1992–93	Southend U	42	2		
1993–94	Southend U	46	0		
1994–95	Southend U	44	0		
1995–96	Southend U	27	0	**248**	**3**
1995–96	Derby Co	19	0		
1996–97	Derby Co	35	0		
1997–98	Derby Co	37	1	**91**	**1**
1998–99	Charlton Ath	38	0		
1999–2000	Charlton Ath	40	0		
2000–01	Charlton Ath	33	0		
2001–02	Charlton Ath	36	1		
2002–03	Charlton Ath	37	0		
2003–04	Charlton Ath	16	0		
2004–05	Charlton Ath	0	0	**200**	**1**
2004–05	West Ham U	36	0	**36**	**0**

REBROV, Sergei (F) **314** **118**
H: 5 8 W: 11 00 b.Gorlovka 3-6-74
Honours: Ukraine 65 full caps, 13 goals.

1991	Shakhtor Donetsk	7	2		
1991–92	Shakhtor Donetsk	19	10	**26**	**12**
1992–93	Dynamo Kiev	23	5		
1993–94	Dynamo Kiev	10	2		
1994–95	Dynamo Kiev	25	8		
1995–96	Dynamo Kiev	31	9		
1996–97	Dynamo Kiev	30	20		
1997–98	Dynamo Kiev	29	22		
1998–99	Dynamo Kiev	22	9		
1999–2000	Dynamo Kiev	20	18	**190**	**93**
2000–01	Tottenham H	29	9		
2001–02	Tottenham H	30	1		
2002–03	*Fenerbahce*	13	2	**13**	**2**
2003–04	Tottenham H	0	0	**59**	**10**
2004–05	West Ham U	26	1	**26**	**1**

REID, Kyle (M) **0** **0**
H: 5 10 W: 12 05 b.South London 26-11-87
Source: Scholar. *Honours:* England Youth.

2004–05	West Ham U	0	0		

REO-COKER, Nigel (M) **112** **11**
H: 5 8 W: 12 03 b.Southwark 14-5-84
Source: Scholar. *Honours:* England Youth, Under-20, Under-21.

2001–02	Wimbledon	1	0		
2002–03	Wimbledon	32	2		
2003–04	Wimbledon	25	4	**58**	**6**
2003–04	West Ham U	15	2		
2004–05	West Ham U	39	3	**54**	**5**

REPKA, Tomas (D) **392** **9**
H: 6 0 W: 12 04 b.Slavicin Zlin 2-1-74
Honours: Czechoslovakia 1 full cap.Czech Republic 46 full caps, 1 goal.

1991–92	Banik Ostrava	16	1		
1992–93	Banik Ostrava	19	0		
1993–94	Banik Ostrava	26	2		
1994–95	Banik Ostrava	16	0	**77**	**3**
1995–96	Sparta Prague	29	3		
1996–97	Sparta Prague	25	1		
1997–98	Sparta Prague	28	2	**82**	**6**
1998–99	Fiorentina	31	0		
1999–2000	Fiorentina	29	0		
2000–01	Fiorentina	28	0	**88**	**0**
2001–02	West Ham U	31	0		
2002–03	West Ham U	32	0		
2003–04	West Ham U	40	0		
2004–05	West Ham U	42	0	**145**	**0**

SHERINGHAM, Teddy (F) **672** **264**
H: 6 0 W: 12 05 b.Highams Park 2-4-66
Source: Apprentice. *Honours:* England Youth, 51 full caps, 11 goals.

1983–84	Millwall	7	1		
1984–85	Millwall	0	0		
1984–85	*Aldershot*	5	0	**5**	**0**
1985–86	Millwall	18	4		
1986–87	Millwall	42	13		
1987–88	Millwall	43	22		
1988–89	Millwall	33	11		
1989–90	Millwall	31	9		
1990–91	Millwall	46	33	**220**	**93**
1991–92	Nottingham F	39	13		
1992–93	Nottingham F	3	1	**42**	**14**
1992–93	Tottenham H	38	21		
1993–94	Tottenham H	19	13		
1994–95	Tottenham H	42	18		
1995–96	Tottenham H	38	16		
1996–97	Tottenham H	29	7		
1997–98	Manchester U	31	9		
1998–99	Manchester U	17	2		
1999–2000	Manchester U	27	5		
2000–01	Manchester U	29	15	**104**	**31**
2001–02	Tottenham H	34	10		
2002–03	Tottenham H	36	12	**236**	**97**
2003–04	Portsmouth	32	9	**32**	**9**
2004–05	West Ham U	33	20	**33**	**20**

SOFIANE, Youssef (F) **5** **0**
H: 5 8 W: 11 00 b.Lyon 8-7-84
Honours: France Youth.

2001–02	Auxerre	0	0		
2002–03	West Ham U	0	0		
2003–04	West Ham U	1	0		

2004–05 West Ham U 0 0 **1 0**
2004–05 *Notts Co* 4 0 **4 0**

TARICCO, Mauricio (D) **289 6**
H: 5 8 W: 11 07 b.Buenos Aires 10-3-73
Honours: Argentina Under-23.
1993–94 Argentinos Juniors 21 0 **21 0**
1994–95 Ipswich T 0 0
1995–96 Ipswich T 39 0
1996–97 Ipswich T 41 3
1997–98 Ipswich T 41 0
1998–99 Ipswich T 16 1 **137 4**
1998–99 Tottenham H 13 0
1999–2000 Tottenham H 29 0
2000–01 Tottenham H 5 0
2001–02 Tottenham H 30 0
2002–03 Tottenham H 21 1
2003–04 Tottenham H 32 1
2004–05 Tottenham H 0 0 **130 2**
2004–05 West Ham U 1 0 **1 0**

WALKER, Jim (G) **413 0**
H: 5 11 W: 13 04 b.Sutton-in-Ashfield 9-7-73
Source: Trainee.
1991–92 Notts Co 0 0
1992–93 Notts Co 0 0
1993–94 Walsall 31 0
1994–95 Walsall 4 0
1995–96 Walsall 26 0
1996–97 Walsall 36 0
1997–98 Walsall 46 0
1998–99 Walsall 46 0
1999–2000 Walsall 43 0
2000–01 Walsall 44 0
2001–02 Walsall 43 0
2002–03 Walsall 41 0
2003–04 Walsall 43 0 **403 0**
2004–05 West Ham U 10 0 **10 0**

WARD, Elliot (D) **14 0**
H: 6 2 W: 13 00 b.Harrow 19-1-85
Source: Scholar.
2001–02 West Ham U 0 0
2002–03 West Ham U 0 0
2003–04 West Ham U 0 0
2004–05 West Ham U 11 0 **11 0**
2004–05 *Bristol R* 3 0 **3 0**

WILLIAMS, Gavin (M) **65 12**
H: 5 10 W: 11 05 b.Merthyr 20-6-80
Source: Hereford U.
2003–04 Yeovil T 42 9
2004–05 Yeovil T 13 2 **55 11**
2004–05 West Ham U 10 1 **10 1**

ZAMORA, Bobby (F) **196 88**
H: 6 1 W: 11 11 b.Barking 16-1-81
Source: Trainee. *Honours:* England Under-21.
1999–2000 Bristol R 4 0 **4 0**
1999–2000 *Brighton & HA* 6 6
2000–01 Brighton & HA 43 28
2001–02 Brighton & HA 41 28
2002–03 Brighton & HA 35 14 **125 76**
2003–04 Tottenham H 16 0 **16 0**
2003–04 West Ham U 17 5
2004–05 West Ham U 34 7 **51 12**

WIGAN ATH (88)

BAINES, Leighton (D) **73 1**
H: 5 8 W: 11 10 b.Liverpool 11-12-84
Source: Trainee. *Honours:* England Under-21.
2002–03 Wigan Ath 6 0
2003–04 Wigan Ath 26 0
2004–05 Wigan Ath 41 1 **73 1**

BRECKIN, Ian (D) **440 14**
H: 6 2 W: 13 05 b.Rotherham 24-2-75
Source: Trainee.
1993–94 Rotherham U 10 0
1994–95 Rotherham U 41 2
1995–96 Rotherham U 39 1
1996–97 Rotherham U 42 3 **132 6**
1997–98 Chesterfield 43 1
1998–99 Chesterfield 44 2
1999–2000 Chesterfield 38 1
2000–01 Chesterfield 45 3
2001–02 Chesterfield 42 1 **212 8**
2002–03 Wigan Ath 9 0
2003–04 Wigan Ath 45 0
2004–05 Wigan Ath 42 0 **96 0**

BULLARD, Jimmy (M) **175 17**
H: 5 10 W: 11 07 b.Newham 23-10-78
Source: Corinthian, Dartford, Gravesend & N.
1998–99 West Ham U 0 0
1999–2000 West Ham U 0 0
2000–01 West Ham U 0 0
2001–02 Peterborough U 40 8
2002–03 Peterborough U 26 3 **66 11**
2002–03 Wigan Ath 17 1
2003–04 Wigan Ath 46 2
2004–05 Wigan Ath 46 3 **109 6**

DINNING, Tony (M) **363 49**
H: 6 0 W: 13 00 b.Wallsend 12-4-75
Source: Trainee.
1993–94 Newcastle U 0 0
1994–95 Stockport Co 40 1
1995–96 Stockport Co 10 1
1996–97 Stockport Co 20 2
1997–98 Stockport Co 30 4
1998–99 Stockport Co 41 5
1999–2000 Stockport Co 44 12
2000–01 Stockport Co 6 0 **191 25**
2000–01 Wolverhampton W 31 6
2001–02 Wolverhampton W 4 0 **35 6**
2001–02 Wigan Ath 33 5
2001–02 *Stoke C* 5 0 **5 0**
2002–03 Wigan Ath 38 7
2003–04 Wigan Ath 13 0
2003–04 *Walsall* 5 0 **5 0**
2003–04 *Blackpool* 10 3 **10 3**
2004–05 Wigan Ath 0 0 **84 12**
2004–05 *Ipswich T* 7 0 **7 0**
2004–05 *Bristol C* 19 0 **19 0**
2004–05 *Port Vale* 7 3 **7 3**

EADEN, Nicky (D) **489 13**
H: 5 9 W: 12 02 b.Sheffield 12-12-72
Source: Trainee.
1991–92 Barnsley 0 0
1992–93 Barnsley 2 0
1993–94 Barnsley 37 2
1994–95 Barnsley 45 1
1995–96 Barnsley 46 2
1996–97 Barnsley 46 3
1997–98 Barnsley 35 0
1998–99 Barnsley 40 1
1999–2000 Barnsley 42 1 **293 10**
2000–01 Birmingham C 45 2
2001–02 Birmingham C 29 1
2002–03 Birmingham C 0 0 **74 3**
2002–03 Wigan Ath 37 0
2003–04 Wigan Ath 46 0
2004–05 Wigan Ath 39 0 **122 0**

ELLINGTON, Nathan (F) **250 94**
H: 5 10 W: 13 01 b.Bradford 2-7-81
Source: Walton & Hersham.
1998–99 Bristol R 10 1
1999–2000 Bristol R 37 4
2000–01 Bristol R 42 15
2001–02 Bristol R 27 15 **116 35**
2001–02 Wigan Ath 3 2
2002–03 Wigan Ath 42 15
2003–04 Wigan Ath 44 18
2004–05 Wigan Ath 45 24 **134 59**

EMERSON (D) **167 3**
H: 6 2 W: 13 04 b.Porto Alegre 30-3-72
Source: Benfica.
1997–98 Sheffield W 6 0
1998–99 Sheffield W 38 1
1999–2000 Sheffield W 17 0 **61 1**
1999–2000 Chelsea 20 0
2000–01 Chelsea 1 0 **21 0**
2000–01 Sunderland 31 1
2001–02 Sunderland 12 1
2002–03 Sunderland 1 0
2003–04 Sunderland 0 0 **44 2**
2003–04 Bolton W 26 0 **26 0**
2004–05 Wigan Ath 15 0 **15 0**

FILAN, John (G) **389 0**
H: 6 2 W: 14 06 b.Sydney 8-2-70
Honours: Australia Under-20, Under-23, 2 full caps.
1989–90 St George 26 0
1990–91 St George 26 0 **52 0**
1991–92 Wollongong Wolves 23 0
1992–93 Wollongong Wolves 6 0 **29 0**
1992–93 Cambridge U 6 0
1993–94 Cambridge U 46 0
1994–95 Cambridge U 16 0 **68 0**
1994–95 *Nottingham F* 0 0
1994–95 Coventry C 2 0
1995–96 Coventry C 13 0
1996–97 Coventry C 1 0 **16 0**
1997–98 Blackburn R 7 0
1998–99 Blackburn R 26 0
1999–2000 Blackburn R 16 0
2000–01 Blackburn R 13 0
2001–02 Blackburn R 0 0 **62 0**
2001–02 Wigan Ath 25 0
2002–03 Wigan Ath 46 0
2003–04 Wigan Ath 45 0
2004–05 Wigan Ath 46 0 **162 0**

FRANDSEN, Per (M) **494 89**
H: 6 1 W: 12 06 b.Copenhagen 6-2-70
Honours: Denmark 23 full caps.
1990 B 1903 25 15 **25 15**
1990–91 Lille 19 4
1991–92 Lille 27 8
1992–93 Lille 32 3
1993–94 Lille 31 4 **109 19**
1994–95 FC Copenhagen 29 12
1995–96 FC Copenhagen 26 7 **55 19**
1996–97 Bolton W 41 5
1997–98 Bolton W 38 2
1998–99 Bolton W 44 8
1999–2000 Bolton W 7 2
1999–2000 Blackburn R 31 5 **31 5**
2000–01 Bolton W 39 7
2001–02 Bolton W 29 3
2002–03 Bolton W 34 2
2003–04 Bolton W 33 1 **265 30**
2004–05 Wigan Ath 9 1 **9 1**

GRAHAM, David (F) **193 52**
H: 5 11 W: 12 01 b.Edinburgh 6-10-78
Source: Rangers SABC. *Honours:* Scotland Under-21.
1995–96 Rangers 0 0
1996–97 Rangers 0 0
1997–98 Rangers 0 0
1998–99 Rangers 3 0 **3 0**
1998–99 Dunfermline Ath 21 2
1999–2000 Dunfermline Ath 15 2
2000–01 Dunfermline Ath 4 0 **40 4**
2000–01 Torquay U 5 2
2001–02 Torquay U 36 8
2002–03 Torquay U 34 15
2003–04 Torquay U 45 22 **120 47**
2004–05 Wigan Ath 30 1 **30 1**

JACKSON, Matt (D) **468 13**
H: 6 1 W: 14 00 b.Leeds 19-10-71
Source: School. *Honours:* England Schools, Under-21.
1990–91 Luton T 0 0
1990–91 *Preston NE* 4 0 **4 0**
1991–92 Luton T 9 0 **9 0**
1991–92 Everton 30 1
1992–93 Everton 27 3
1993–94 Everton 38 0
1994–95 Everton 29 0
1995–96 Everton 14 0
1995–96 *Charlton Ath* 8 0 **8 0**
1996–97 Everton 0 0 **138 4**
1996–97 *QPR* 7 0 **7 0**
1996–97 *Birmingham C* 10 0 **10 0**
1996–97 Norwich C 19 2
1997–98 Norwich C 41 3
1998–99 Norwich C 37 1
1999–2000 Norwich C 38 0
2000–01 Norwich C 26 0
2001–02 Norwich C 0 0 **161 6**
2001–02 Wigan Ath 26 0
2002–03 Wigan Ath 45 1
2003–04 Wigan Ath 24 1
2004–05 Wigan Ath 36 1 **131 3**

JARRETT, Jason (M) **162 5**
H: 6 1 W: 13 01 b.Bury 14-9-79
Source: Trainee.
1998–99 Blackpool 2 0
1999–2000 Blackpool 0 0 **2 0**

1999–2000 Wrexham 1 0 **1 0**
2000–01 Bury 25 2
2001–02 Bury 37 2 **62 4**
2001–02 Wigan Ath 5 0
2002–03 Wigan Ath 35 0
2003–04 Wigan Ath 41 1
2004–05 Wigan Ath 14 0 **95 1**
2004–05 *Stoke C* 2 0 **2 0**

JOHANSSON, Andreas (M) 231 67
H: 5 11 W: 12 05 b.Vanersborg 5-7-78
Honours: Sweden 12 full caps.
1993 Melleruds 2 0
1994 Melleruds 15 1
1995 Melleruds 21 10 **38 11**
1996 Degerfors 10 1
1997 Degerfors 23 4
1998 Degerfors 23 5 **56 10**
1999 AIK 12 1 **12 1**
2000 Djurgaarden 24 7
2001 Djurgaarden 25 5
2002 Djurgaarden 26 10
2003 Djurgaarden 26 12
2004 Djurgaarden 23 11 **124 45**
2004–05 Wigan Ath 1 0 **1 0**

KAVANAGH, Graham (M) 399 66
H: 5 10 W: 13 02 b.Dublin 2-12-73
Source: Home Farm. *Honours:* Eire Schools, Youth, Under-21, B, 12 full caps, 1 goal.
1991–92 Middlesbrough 0 0
1992–93 Middlesbrough 10 0
1993–94 Middlesbrough 11 2
1993–94 *Darlington* 5 0 **5 0**
1994–95 Middlesbrough 7 0
1995–96 Middlesbrough 7 1
1996–97 Middlesbrough 0 0 **35 3**
1996–97 Stoke C 38 4
1997–98 Stoke C 44 5
1998–99 Stoke C 36 11
1999–2000 Stoke C 45 7
2000–01 Stoke C 43 8 **206 35**
2001–02 Cardiff C 43 13
2002–03 Cardiff C 44 5
2003–04 Cardiff C 27 7
2004–05 Cardiff C 28 3 **142 28**
2004–05 Wigan Ath 11 0 **11 0**

MAHON, Alan (M) 224 25
H: 5 8 W: 11 10 b.Dublin 4-4-78
Source: Crumplin U. *Honours:* Eire Under-21, 2 full caps.
1994–95 Tranmere R 0 0
1995–96 Tranmere R 2 0
1996–97 Tranmere R 25 2
1997–98 Tranmere R 18 1
1998–99 Tranmere R 39 6
1999–2000 Tranmere R 36 4 **120 13**
2000–01 Sporting Lisbon 1 0 **1 0**
2000–01 Blackburn R 18 0
2001–02 Blackburn R 13 1
2002–03 Blackburn R 2 0
2002–03 *Cardiff C* 15 2 **15 2**
2003–04 Blackburn R 3 0 **36 1**
2003–04 *Ipswich T* 11 1 **11 1**
2003–04 Wigan Ath 14 1
2004–05 Wigan Ath 27 7 **41 8**

McCULLOCH, Lee (F) 287 57
H: 6 1 W: 13 00 b.Bellshill 14-5-78
Source: Cumbernauld U. *Honours:* Scotland Under-18, Under-21, B, 4 full caps.
1995–96 Motherwell 1 0
1996–97 Motherwell 15 0
1997–98 Motherwell 25 2
1998–99 Motherwell 26 3
1999–2000 Motherwell 29 9
2000–01 Motherwell 26 8 **122 22**
2000–01 Wigan Ath 10 3
2001–02 Wigan Ath 34 6
2002–03 Wigan Ath 38 6
2003–04 Wigan Ath 41 6
2004–05 Wigan Ath 42 14 **165 35**

McMILLAN, Steve (D) 242 6
H: 5 9 W: 11 12 b.Edinburgh 19-1-76
Source: Troon Juniors. *Honours:* Scotland Under-21.
1993–94 Motherwell 1 0
1994–95 Motherwell 3 0
1995–96 Motherwell 12 0
1996–97 Motherwell 16 0
1997–98 Motherwell 34 1
1998–99 Motherwell 30 2
1999–2000 Motherwell 31 3
2000–01 Motherwell 25 0 **152 6**
2000–01 Wigan Ath 6 0
2001–02 Wigan Ath 29 0
2002–03 Wigan Ath 32 0
2003–04 Wigan Ath 15 0
2004–05 Wigan Ath 8 0 **90 0**

MITCHELL, Paul (D) 95 0
H: 5 9 W: 11 12 b.Manchester 26-8-81
Source: Trainee.
2000–01 Wigan Ath 1 0
2000–01 *Halifax T* 11 0 **11 0**
2001–02 Wigan Ath 23 0
2002–03 Wigan Ath 27 0
2003–04 Wigan Ath 12 0
2004–05 Wigan Ath 1 0 **64 0**
2004–05 *Swindon T* 7 0 **7 0**
2004–05 *Milton Keynes D* 13 0 **13 0**

MOORE, David (F) 3 0
H: 5 10 W: 12 13 b.Worsley 4-4-85
Source: Scholar.
2004–05 Wigan Ath 0 0
2004–05 *Bury* 3 0 **3 0**

ROBERTS, Jason (F) 253 99
H: 6 0 W: 12 06 b.Park Royal 25-1-78
Source: Hayes. *Honours:* Grenada 6 full caps.
1997–98 Wolverhampton W 0 0
1997–98 *Torquay U* 14 6 **14 6**
1997–98 *Bristol C* 3 1 **3 1**
1998–99 Bristol R 37 16
1999–2000 Bristol R 41 22 **78 38**
2000–01 WBA 43 14
2001–02 WBA 14 7
2002–03 WBA 32 3
2003–04 WBA 0 0 **89 24**
2003–04 *Portsmouth* 10 1 **10 1**
2003–04 Wigan Ath 14 8
2004–05 Wigan Ath 45 21 **59 29**

SALISBURY, James (G) 0 0
H: 6 1 W: 14 01 b.Preston 10-3-84
Source: Burnley Scholar.
2003–04 Wigan Ath 0 0
2004–05 Wigan Ath 0 0

TEALE, Gary (F) 296 35
H: 5 11 W: 12 00 b.Glasgow 21-7-78
Honours: Scotland Under-21.
1996–97 Clydebank 33 6
1997–98 Clydebank 27 6
1998–99 Clydebank 8 2 **68 14**
1998–99 Ayr U 23 4
1999–2000 Ayr U 32 0
2000–01 Ayr U 29 5
2001–02 Ayr U 18 4 **102 13**
2001–02 Wigan Ath 23 1
2002–03 Wigan Ath 38 2
2003–04 Wigan Ath 28 2
2004–05 Wigan Ath 37 3 **126 8**

TRAYNOR, Greg (M) 1 0
H: 5 10 W: 11 00 b.Salford 17-10-84
Source: Scholar.
2001–02 Wigan Ath 1 0
2002–03 Wigan Ath 0 0
2003–04 Wigan Ath 0 0
2004–05 Wigan Ath 0 0 **1 0**

VIEIRA, Magno (F) 10 2
H: 5 9 W: 11 00 b.Brazil 13-2-85
Source: Juniors.
2003–04 Wigan Ath 0 0
2003–04 *Northampton T* 10 2 **10 2**
2004–05 Wigan Ath 0 0

WALSH, Gary (G) 241 0
H: 6 3 W: 14 13 b.Wigan 21-3-68
Source: Apprentice. *Honours:* England Under-21.
1984–85 Manchester U 0 0
1985–86 Manchester U 0 0
1986–87 Manchester U 14 0
1987–88 Manchester U 16 0
1988–89 Manchester U 0 0
1988–89 *Airdrieonians* 3 0 **3 0**
1989–90 Manchester U 0 0
1990–91 Manchester U 5 0
1991–92 Manchester U 2 0
1992–93 Manchester U 0 0
1993–94 Manchester U 3 0
1993–94 *Oldham Ath* 6 0 **6 0**
1994–95 Manchester U 10 0 **50 0**
1995–96 Middlesbrough 32 0
1996–97 Middlesbrough 12 0
1997–98 Middlesbrough 0 0
1997–98 Bradford C 35 0
1998–99 Bradford C 46 0
1999–2000 Bradford C 11 0
2000–01 Bradford C 19 0
2000–01 *Middlesbrough* 3 0 **47 0**
2001–02 Bradford C 18 0
2002–03 Bradford C 3 0 **132 0**
2003–04 Wigan Ath 3 0
2004–05 Wigan Ath 0 0 **3 0**

WHALLEY, Gareth (M) 339 14
H: 5 10 W: 11 00 b.Manchester 19-12-73
Source: Trainee.
1992–93 Crewe Alex 25 1
1993–94 Crewe Alex 15 1
1994–95 Crewe Alex 40 1
1995–96 Crewe Alex 44 2
1996–97 Crewe Alex 38 3
1997–98 Crewe Alex 18 1
1998–99 Bradford C 45 2
1999–2000 Bradford C 16 1
2000–01 Bradford C 19 0
2001–02 Bradford C 23 0 **103 3**
2001–02 *Crewe Alex* 7 0 **187 9**
2002–03 Cardiff C 19 0
2003–04 Cardiff C 22 2
2004–05 Cardiff C 0 0 **41 2**
2004–05 Wigan Ath 8 0 **8 0**

WRIGHT, David (D) 242 3
H: 5 11 W: 11 00 b.Warrington 1-5-80
Source: Trainee. *Honours:* England Youth.
1997–98 Crewe Alex 3 0
1998–99 Crewe Alex 20 1
1999–2000 Crewe Alex 45 0
2000–01 Crewe Alex 42 0
2001–02 Crewe Alex 30 0
2002–03 Crewe Alex 31 1
2003–04 Crewe Alex 40 1 **211 3**
2004–05 Wigan Ath 31 0 **31 0**

WOLVERHAMPTON W (89)

ANDREWS, Keith (M) 95 3
H: 6 0 W: 13 05 b.Dublin 13-9-80
Source: Trainee.
1997–98 Wolverhampton W 0 0
1998–99 Wolverhampton W 0 0
1999–2000 Wolverhampton W 2 0
2000–01 Wolverhampton W 22 0
2000–01 *Oxford U* 4 1 **4 1**
2001–02 Wolverhampton W 11 0
2002–03 Wolverhampton W 9 0
2003–04 Wolverhampton W 1 0
2003–04 *Stoke C* 16 0 **16 0**
2003–04 *Walsall* 10 2 **10 2**
2004–05 Wolverhampton W 20 0 **65 0**

BJORKLUND, Joachim (D) 335 1
H: 5 11 W: 12 08 b.Vaxjo 15-3-71
Honours: Sweden 75 full caps.
1988 Osters 6 0
1989 Osters 0 0 **6 0**
1990 Brann 21 0
1991 Brann 22 0
1992 Brann 13 0 **56 0**
1993 IFK Gothenburg 19 0
1994 IFK Gothenburg 16 0
1995 IFK Gothenburg 11 0 **46 0**
1995–96 Vicenza 33 0 **33 0**
1996–97 Rangers 28 0
1997–98 Rangers 31 0 **59 0**
1998–99 Valencia 24 1
1999–2000 Valencia 23 0
2000–01 Valencia 10 0 **57 1**
2001–02 Venezia 18 0 **18 0**
2001–02 Sunderland 12 0
2002–03 Sunderland 20 0
2003–04 Sunderland 25 0 **57 0**
2004–05 Wolverhampton W 3 0 **3 0**

BONNAR, Thomas (M) 0 0
b.Letterkenny 20-10-85
Source: Scholar.
2003–04 Wolverhampton W 0 0
2004–05 Wolverhampton W 0 0

CAMARA, Henri (F) 163 61
H: 5 9 W: 10 08 b.Dakar 10-5-77
Honours: Senegal full caps.
1999–2000 Neuchatel Xamax 20 12
2000–01 Neuchatel Xamax 12 5 **32 17**
2000–01 Grasshoppers 11 3 **11 3**
2001–02 Sedan 25 8
2002–03 Sedan 34 14 **59 22**
2003–04 Wolverhampton W 30 7
2004–05 Wolverhampton W 0 0 **30 7**
2004–05 *Celtic* 18 8 **18 8**
2004–05 *Southampton* 13 4 **13 4**

CAMERON, Colin (M) 418 87
H: 5 8 W: 11 00 b.Kirkcaldy 23-10-72
Source: Lochore Welfare. *Honours:* Scotland B, 29 full caps, 2 goals.
1990–91 Raith R 0 0
1991–92 *Sligo R* 0 0
1992–93 Raith R 16 1
1993–94 Raith R 41 6
1994–95 Raith R 35 7
1995–96 Raith R 30 9 **122 23**
1995–96 Hearts 4 2
1996–97 Hearts 36 7
1997–98 Hearts 31 8
1998–99 Hearts 11 6
1999–2000 Hearts 32 8
2000–01 Hearts 37 12
2001–02 Hearts 4 3 **155 46**
2001–02 Wolverhampton W 41 4
2002–03 Wolverhampton W 33 7
2003–04 Wolverhampton W 30 4
2004–05 Wolverhampton W 37 3 **141 18**

CLARKE, Leon (F) 32 7
H: 6 2 W: 14 02 b.Birmingham 10-2-85
Source: Scholar.
2003–04 Wolverhampton W 0 0
2003–04 *Kidderminster H* 4 0 **4 0**
2004–05 Wolverhampton W 28 7 **28 7**

CLINGAN, Sammy (M) 15 2
H: 5 11 W: 11 06 b.Belfast 13-1-84
Source: Scholar. *Honours:* Northern Ireland Schools, Youth, Under-21, Under-23.
2001–02 Wolverhampton W 0 0
2002–03 Wolverhampton W 0 0
2003–04 Wolverhampton W 0 0
2004–05 Wolverhampton W 0 0
2004–05 *Chesterfield* 15 2 **15 2**

CLYDE, Mark (D) 48 0
H: 6 2 W: 12 04 b.Limavady 27-12-82
Source: Scholar. *Honours:* Northern Ireland Under-21, 3 full caps.
2001–02 Wolverhampton W 0 0
2002–03 Wolverhampton W 17 0
2002–03 *Kidderminster H* 4 0 **4 0**
2003–04 Wolverhampton W 9 0
2004–05 Wolverhampton W 18 0 **44 0**

COOPER, Kevin (M) 294 43
H: 5 8 W: 10 04 b.Derby 8-2-75
Source: Trainee.
1993–94 Derby Co 0 0
1994–95 Derby Co 1 0
1995–96 Derby Co 1 0
1996–97 Derby Co 0 0 **2 0**
1996–97 *Stockport Co* 12 3
1997–98 Stockport Co 38 8
1998–99 Stockport Co 38 1
1999–2000 Stockport Co 46 4
2000–01 Stockport Co 34 5 **168 21**
2000–01 Wimbledon 11 3
2001–02 Wimbledon 40 10 **51 13**
2001–02 Wolverhampton W 5 0
2002–03 Wolverhampton W 26 3
2003–04 Wolverhampton W 1 0
2003–04 *Sunderland* 1 0 **1 0**
2003–04 *Norwich C* 10 0 **10 0**
2004–05 Wolverhampton W 30 6 **62 9**

CORNES, Christopher (M) 0 0
b.Worcester 20-12-86
Source: Scholar.
2004–05 Wolverhampton W 0 0

CORT, Carl (F) 154 44
H: 6 4 W: 12 07 b.Southwark 1-11-77
Source: From Trainee. *Honours:* England Under-21.
1996–97 Wimbledon 1 0
1996–97 *Lincoln C* 6 1 **6 1**
1997–98 Wimbledon 22 4
1998–99 Wimbledon 16 3
1999–2000 Wimbledon 34 9 **73 16**
2000–01 Newcastle U 13 6
2001–02 Newcastle U 8 1
2002–03 Newcastle U 1 0
2003–04 Newcastle U 0 0 **22 7**
2003–04 Wolverhampton W 16 5
2004–05 Wolverhampton W 37 15 **53 20**

CRADDOCK, Jody (D) 375 8
H: 6 2 W: 12 00 b.Bromsgrove 25-7-75
Source: Christchurch.
1993–94 Cambridge U 20 0
1994–95 Cambridge U 38 0
1995–96 Cambridge U 46 3
1996–97 Cambridge U 41 1 **145 4**
1997–98 Sunderland 32 0
1998–99 Sunderland 6 0
1999–2000 Sunderland 19 0
1999–2000 *Sheffield U* 10 0 **10 0**
2000–01 Sunderland 34 0
2001–02 Sunderland 30 1
2002–03 Sunderland 25 1 **146 2**
2003–04 Wolverhampton W 32 1
2004–05 Wolverhampton W 42 1 **74 2**

DAVIES, Mark (M) 0 0
b.Wolverhampton 18-12-88
Source: Scholar.
2004–05 Wolverhampton W 0 0

EDWARDS, Rob (D) 43 2
H: 6 1 W: 11 10 b.Telford 25-12-82
Source: From Trainee. *Honours:* Wales Youth, 7 full caps.
1999–2000 Aston Villa 0 0
2000–01 Aston Villa 0 0
2001–02 Aston Villa 0 0
2002–03 Aston Villa 8 0
2003–04 Aston Villa 0 0 **8 0**
2003–04 *Crystal Palace* 7 1 **7 1**
2003–04 *Derby Co* 11 1 **11 1**
2004–05 Wolverhampton W 17 0 **17 0**

FLYNN, Patrick (M) 0 0
b.Dublin 13-1-85
Source: Scholar.
2002–03 Wolverhampton W 0 0
2003–04 Wolverhampton W 0 0
2004–05 Wolverhampton W 0 0

GANEA, Viorel (F) 267 79
H: 5 10 W: 12 06 b.Fagaras 10-8-73
Honours: Romania 44 full caps, 19 goals.
1994–95 Brasov 30 0
1995–96 Brasov 20 4 **50 4**
1995–96 Uni Craiova 17 5
1996–97 Uni Craiova 19 6
1997–98 Uni Craiova 26 11 **62 22**
1998–99 Rapid Bucharest 16 11 **16 11**
1999–2000 Stuttgart 29 7
2000–01 Stuttgart 32 8
2001–02 Stuttgart 23 10
2002–03 Stuttgart 23 9 **107 34**
2003–04 Bursa 16 5 **16 5**
2003–04 Wolverhampton W 16 3
2004–05 Wolverhampton W 0 0 **16 3**

GOBERN, Lewis (M) 1 0
H: 5 10 W: 11 07 b.Birmingham 28-1-85
Source: Scholar.
2003–04 Wolverhampton W 0 0
2004–05 Wolverhampton W 0 0
2004–05 *Hartlepool U* 1 0 **1 0**

HENNESSEY, Wayne (G) 0 0
b.Anglesey 24-1-87
Source: Scholar. *Honours:* Wales Schools, Youth.
2004–05 Wolverhampton W 0 0

INCE, Paul (M) 587 68
H: 5 10 W: 12 04 b.Ilford 21-10-67
Source: Trainee. *Honours:* England Youth, Under-21, B, 53 full caps, 2 goals.
1985–86 West Ham U 0 0
1986–87 West Ham U 10 1
1987–88 West Ham U 28 3
1988–89 West Ham U 33 3
1989–90 West Ham U 1 0 **72 7**
1989–90 Manchester U 26 0
1990–91 Manchester U 31 3
1991–92 Manchester U 33 3
1992–93 Manchester U 41 5
1993–94 Manchester U 39 8
1994–95 Manchester U 36 5 **206 24**
1995–96 Internazionale 30 3
1996–97 Internazionale 24 6 **54 9**
1997–98 Liverpool 31 8
1998–99 Liverpool 34 6 **65 14**
1999–2000 Middlesbrough 32 3
2000–01 Middlesbrough 30 2
2001–02 Middlesbrough 31 2 **93 7**
2002–03 Wolverhampton W 37 2
2003–04 Wolverhampton W 32 2
2004–05 Wolverhampton W 28 3 **97 7**

JONES, Paul (G) 309 0
H: 6 3 W: 15 02 b.Chirk 18-4-67
Source: Bridgnorth, Kidderminster H. *Honours:* Wales 43 full caps.
1991–92 Wolverhampton W 0 0
1992–93 Wolverhampton W 16 0
1993–94 Wolverhampton W 0 0
1994–95 Wolverhampton W 9 0
1995–96 Wolverhampton W 8 0
1996–97 Stockport Co 46 0 **46 0**
1997–98 Southampton 38 0
1998–99 Southampton 31 0
1999–2000 Southampton 31 0
2000–01 Southampton 35 0
2001–02 Southampton 36 0
2002–03 Southampton 14 0
2003–04 Southampton 8 0 **193 0**
2003–04 *Liverpool* 2 0 **2 0**
2003–04 Wolverhampton W 16 0
2004–05 Wolverhampton W 10 0 **59 0**
2004–05 *Watford* 9 0 **9 0**

KENNEDY, Mark (M) 281 29
H: 5 11 W: 11 09 b.Dublin 15-5-76
Source: Belvedere, Trainee. *Honours:* Eire Under-21, 34 full caps, 3 goals.
1992–93 Millwall 1 0
1993–94 Millwall 12 4
1994–95 Millwall 30 5 **43 9**
1994–95 Liverpool 6 0
1995–96 Liverpool 4 0
1996–97 Liverpool 5 0
1997–98 Liverpool 1 0 **16 0**
1997–98 *QPR* 8 2 **8 2**
1997–98 Wimbledon 4 0
1998–99 Wimbledon 17 0 **21 0**
1999–2000 Manchester C 41 8
2000–01 Manchester C 25 0 **66 8**
2001–02 Wolverhampton W 35 5
2002–03 Wolverhampton W 31 3
2003–04 Wolverhampton W 31 2
2004–05 Wolverhampton W 30 0 **127 10**

LESCOTT, Jolean (D) 166 12
H: 6 2 W: 14 00 b.Birmingham 16-8-82
Source: Trainee. *Honours:* England Youth, Under-20, Under-21.
1999–2000 Wolverhampton W 0 0
2000–01 Wolverhampton W 37 2
2001–02 Wolverhampton W 44 5
2002–03 Wolverhampton W 44 1
2003–04 Wolverhampton W 0 0
2004–05 Wolverhampton W 41 4 **166 12**

LOWE, Keith (D) 11 0
H: 6 2 W: 13 03 b.Wolverhampton 13-9-85
Source: Scholar.
2004–05 Wolverhampton W 11 0 **11 0**

MILLER, Kenny (F) 207 62
H: 5 10 W: 11 04 b.Edinburgh 23-12-79
Source: Hutchison Vale. *Honours:* Scotland Under-21, B, 19 full caps, 2 goals.
1996–97 Hibernian 0 0
1997–98 Hibernian 7 0

1998–99	Hibernian	7	1		
1999–2000	Hibernian	31	11	**45**	**12**
2000–01	Rangers	27	8		
2001–02	Rangers	3	0	**30**	**8**
2001–02	Wolverhampton W	20	2		
2002–03	Wolverhampton W	43	19		
2003–04	Wolverhampton W	25	2		
2004–05	Wolverhampton W	44	19	**132**	**42**

MULLIGAN, Gary (M) **14** **3**
H: 6 1 W: 12 03 b.Dublin 23-4-85
Source: Scholar.

2002–03	Wolverhampton W	0	0		
2003–04	Wolverhampton W	0	0		
2004–05	Wolverhampton W	1	0	**1**	**0**
2004–05	*Rushden & D*	13	3	**13**	**3**

MURRAY, Matt (G) **42** **0**
H: 6 4 W: 13 10 b.Solihull 2-5-81
Source: Trainee. *Honours:* England Youth, Under-21.

1997–98	Wolverhampton W	0	0		
1998–99	Wolverhampton W	0	0		
1999–2000	Wolverhampton W	0	0		
2000–01	Wolverhampton W	0	0		
2001–02	Wolverhampton W	0	0		
2002–03	Wolverhampton W	40	0		
2003–04	Wolverhampton W	1	0		
2004–05	Wolverhampton W	1	0	**42**	**0**

NAYLOR, Lee (D) **250** **6**
H: 5 10 W: 12 00 b.Bloxwich 19-3-80
Source: Trainee. *Honours:* England Youth, Under-21.

1997–98	Wolverhampton W	16	0		
1998–99	Wolverhampton W	23	1		
1999–2000	Wolverhampton W	30	2		
2000–01	Wolverhampton W	46	1		
2001–02	Wolverhampton W	27	0		
2002–03	Wolverhampton W	32	1		
2003–04	Wolverhampton W	38	0		
2004–05	Wolverhampton W	38	1	**250**	**6**

NDAH, George (F) **234** **38**
H: 6 1 W: 12 06 b.Dulwich 23-12-74
Source: Trainee.

1992–93	Crystal Palace	13	0		
1993–94	Crystal Palace	1	0		
1994–95	Crystal Palace	12	1		
1995–96	Crystal Palace	23	4		
1995–96	*Bournemouth*	12	2	**12**	**2**
1996–97	Crystal Palace	26	3		
1997–98	Crystal Palace	3	0	**78**	**8**
1997–98	*Gillingham*	4	0	**4**	**0**
1997–98	Swindon T	14	2		
1998–99	Swindon T	41	11		
1999–2000	Swindon T	12	1	**67**	**14**
1999–2000	Wolverhampton W	4	0		
2000–01	Wolverhampton W	29	6		
2001–02	Wolverhampton W	15	1		
2002–03	Wolverhampton W	25	7		
2003–04	Wolverhampton W	0	0		
2004–05	Wolverhampton W	0	0	**73**	**14**

O'CONNOR, Kevin (M) **0** **0**
b.Dublin 19-10-85
Source: Scholar. *Honours:* Eire Under-21.

2003–04	Wolverhampton W	0	0		
2004–05	Wolverhampton W	0	0		

OAKES, Michael (G) **234** **0**
H: 6 2 W: 14 00 b.Northwich 30-10-73
Source: Trainee. *Honours:* England Under-21.

1991–92	Aston Villa	0	0		
1992–93	Aston Villa	0	0		
1993–94	Aston Villa	0	0		
1993–94	*Scarborough*	1	0	**1**	**0**
1993–94	*Tranmere R*	0	0		
1994–95	Aston Villa	0	0		
1995–96	Aston Villa	0	0		
1996–97	Aston Villa	20	0		
1997–98	Aston Villa	8	0		
1998–99	Aston Villa	23	0		
1999–2000	Aston Villa	0	0	**51**	**0**
1999–2000	Wolverhampton W	28	0		
2000–01	Wolverhampton W	46	0		
2001–02	Wolverhampton W	46	0		
2002–03	Wolverhampton W	6	0		
2003–04	Wolverhampton W	21	0		
2004–05	Wolverhampton W	35	0	**182**	**0**

OLOFINJANA, Seyi (M) **76** **16**
H: 6 2 W: 13 05 b.Lagos 30-6-80
Source: Kwara United Ilorin. *Honours:* Nigeria full caps.

2003	Brann	25	9		
2004	Brann	9	2	**34**	**11**
2004–05	Wolverhampton W	42	5	**42**	**5**

RAFFERTY, Conor (D) **0** **0**
b.Dundalk 3-2-87
Source: Scholar. *Honours:* Eire Schools, Youth.

2004–05	Wolverhampton W	0	0		

RILEY, Martin (D) **0** **0**
b.Wolverhampton 5-12-86
Source: Scholar.

2004–05	Wolverhampton W	0	0		

SEOL, Ki-Hyun (F) **133** **32**
H: 6 2 W: 12 08 b.South Korea 18-1-79
Honours: South Korea full caps.

2000–01	Antwerp	25	10	**25**	**10**
2001–02	Anderlecht	20	3		
2002–03	Anderlecht	32	12		
2003–04	Anderlecht	19	3	**71**	**18**
2004–05	Wolverhampton W	37	4	**37**	**4**

SILAS, Jorge (M) **73** **13**
H: 5 9 W: 11 03 b.Lisbon 1-9-76
Honours: Portugal 3 full caps.

2001–02	Uniao Leiria	32	5		
2002–03	Uniao Leiria	32	8	**64**	**13**
2003–04	Wolverhampton W	9	0		
2004–05	Wolverhampton W	0	0	**9**	**0**

STEWART, Thomas (F) **0** **0**
b.Craigavon 12-11-86
Source: Portadown. *Honours:* Northern Ireland Schools, Youth.

2004–05	Wolverhampton W	0	0		

WREXHAM (90)

ARMSTRONG, Chris (F) **406** **124**
H: 6 0 W: 13 03 b.Newcastle 19-6-71
Source: Llay Welfare. *Honours:* England B.

1988–89	Wrexham	0	0		
1989–90	Wrexham	22	3		
1990–91	Wrexham	38	10		
1991–92	Millwall	25	4		
1992–93	Millwall	3	1	**28**	**5**
1992–93	Crystal Palace	35	15		
1993–94	Crystal Palace	43	22		
1994–95	Crystal Palace	40	8	**118**	**45**
1995–96	Tottenham H	36	15		
1996–97	Tottenham H	12	5		
1997–98	Tottenham H	19	5		
1998–99	Tottenham H	34	7		
1999–2000	Tottenham H	31	14		
2000–01	Tottenham H	9	2		
2001–02	Tottenham H	0	0	**141**	**48**
2002–03	Bolton W	0	0		
2003–04	Wrexham	26	5		
2004–05	Wrexham	33	8	**119**	**26**

BENNETT, Dean (M) **187** **16**
H: 5 11 W: 11 00 b.Wolverhampton 13-12-77

1996–97	WBA	1	0		
1997–98	WBA	0	0	**1**	**0**
2000–01	Kidderminster H	42	4		
2001–02	Kidderminster H	42	8		
2002–03	Kidderminster H	32	1		
2003–04	Kidderminster H	38	3	**154**	**16**
2002–03	Wrexham	18	0		
2003–04	Wrexham	0	0		
2004–05	Wrexham	14	0	**32**	**0**

CAREY, Brian (D) **362** **17**
H: 6 3 W: 13 02 b.Cork 31-5-68
Source: Cork C. *Honours:* Eire 3 full caps.

1989–90	Manchester U	0	0		
1990–91	Manchester U	0	0		
1990–91	*Wrexham*	3	0		
1991–92	Manchester U	0	0		
1991–92	*Wrexham*	13	1		
1992–93	Manchester U	0	0		
1993–94	Leicester C	27	0		
1994–95	Leicester C	12	0		
1995–96	Leicester C	19	1	**58**	**1**
1996–97	Wrexham	38	0		
1997–98	Wrexham	43	1		
1998–99	Wrexham	36	2		
1999–2000	Wrexham	43	1		
2000–01	Wrexham	33	3		
2001–02	Wrexham	18	2		
2002–03	Wrexham	33	4		
2003–04	Wrexham	34	2		
2004–05	Wrexham	10	0	**304**	**16**

CROWELL, Matt (M) **43** **1**
H: 5 11 W: 10 10 b.Bridgend 3-7-84
Source: Scholar. *Honours:* Wales Youth, Under-21.

2001–02	Southampton	0	0		
2002–03	Southampton	0	0		
2003–04	Wrexham	15	1		
2004–05	Wrexham	28	0	**43**	**1**

DIBBLE, Andy (G) **395** **0**
H: 6 4 W: 13 07 b.Cwmbran 8-5-65
Source: Apprentice. *Honours:* Wales Schools, Youth, Under-21, 3 full caps.

1981–82	Cardiff C	1	0		
1982–83	Cardiff C	20	0		
1983–84	Cardiff C	41	0	**62**	**0**
1984–85	Luton T	13	0		
1985–86	Luton T	7	0		
1985–86	*Sunderland*	12	0	**12**	**0**
1986–87	Luton T	1	0		
1986–87	*Huddersfield T*	5	0	**5**	**0**
1987–88	Luton T	9	0		
1988–89	Manchester C	38	0		
1989–90	Manchester C	31	0		
1990–91	Manchester C	3	0		
1990–91	*Aberdeen*	5	0	**5**	**0**
1990–91	*Middlesbrough*	19	0		
1991–92	Manchester C	2	0		
1991–92	*Bolton W*	13	0	**13**	**0**
1991–92	*WBA*	9	0	**9**	**0**
1992–93	Manchester C	2	0		
1992–93	*Oldham Ath*	0	0		
1993–94	Manchester C	11	0		
1994–95	Manchester C	16	0		
1995–96	Manchester C	0	0		
1996–97	Manchester C	13	0	**116**	**0**
1996–97	Rangers	7	0	**7**	**0**
1997–98	Luton T	1	0	**31**	**0**
1997–98	Middlesbrough	2	0		
1998–99	Middlesbrough	0	0	**21**	**0**
From Altrincham					
1998–99	Hartlepool U	0	0		
1999–2000	Hartlepool U	6	0	**6**	**0**
1999–2000	*Carlisle U*	2	0	**2**	**0**
2000–01	Stockport Co	10	0		
2001–02	Stockport Co	13	0	**23**	**0**
2002–03	Wrexham	33	0		
2003–04	Wrexham	35	0		
2004–05	Wrexham	15	0	**83**	**0**

EDWARDS, Carlos (M) **166** **23**
H: 5 11 W: 11 01 b.Trinidad 24-10-78
Source: Defence Force. *Honours:* Trinidad & Tobago 38 full caps.

2000–01	Wrexham	36	4		
2001–02	Wrexham	26	5		
2002–03	Wrexham	44	8		
2003–04	Wrexham	42	5		
2004–05	Wrexham	18	1	**166**	**23**

EVANS, Danny (G) **0** **0**
H: 6 0 W: 13 00 b.Wrexham 11-3-86
Source: Scholar.

2004–05	Wrexham	0	0		

FERGUSON, Darren (M) **382** **26**
H: 6 0 W: 11 10 b.Glasgow 9-2-72
Source: From Trainee. *Honours:* Scotland Youth, Under-21.

1990–91	Manchester U	5	0		
1991–92	Manchester U	4	0		
1992–93	Manchester U	15	0		
1993–94	Manchester U	3	0	**27**	**0**
1993–94	Wolverhampton W	14	0		
1994–95	Wolverhampton W	24	0		
1995–96	Wolverhampton W	33	1		
1996–97	Wolverhampton W	16	3		
1997–98	Wolverhampton W	26	0		
1998–99	Wolverhampton W	4	0		
1999–2000	Wolverhampton W	0	0	**117**	**4**
1999–2000	Wrexham	37	4		

2000–01	Wrexham	43	9		
2001–02	Wrexham	38	3		
2002–03	Wrexham	41	2		
2003–04	Wrexham	39	1		
2004–05	Wrexham	40	3	**238**	**22**

GREEN, Scott (D) 446 38
H: 5 10 W: 12 05 b.Walsall 15-1-70
Source: Trainee.

1988–89	Derby Co	0	0		
1989–90	Derby Co	0	0		
1989–90	Bolton W	5	2		
1990–91	Bolton W	41	6		
1991–92	Bolton W	37	2		
1992–93	Bolton W	41	6		
1993–94	Bolton W	22	4		
1994–95	Bolton W	31	1		
1995–96	Bolton W	31	3		
1996–97	Bolton W	12	1	**220**	**25**
1997–98	Wigan Ath	38	1		
1998–99	Wigan Ath	37	0		
1999–2000	Wigan Ath	33	2		
2000–01	Wigan Ath	35	2		
2001–02	Wigan Ath	39	3		
2002–03	Wigan Ath	17	2	**199**	**10**
2002–03	Wrexham	15	3		
2003–04	Wrexham	0	0		
2004–05	Wrexham	12	0	**27**	**3**

HARRISON, Ryan (G) 0 0
b. 6-12-86
Source: Swansea C Scholar.

2004–05	Wrexham	0	0		

HOLT, Andy (M) 256 19
H: 6 1 W: 12 07 b.Stockport 21-5-78
Source: Trainee.

1996–97	Oldham Ath	1	0		
1997–98	Oldham Ath	14	1		
1998–99	Oldham Ath	43	5		
1999–2000	Oldham Ath	46	3		
2000–01	Oldham Ath	20	1	**124**	**10**
2000–01	*Hull C*	10	2		
2001–02	Hull C	30	0		
2002–03	Hull C	6	0		
2002–03	*Barnsley*	7	0	**7**	**0**
2002–03	*Shrewsbury T*	9	0	**9**	**0**
2003–04	Hull C	25	1	**71**	**3**
2004–05	Wrexham	45	6	**45**	**6**

JONES, Mark (M) 40 4
H: 5 11 W: 10 12 b.Wrexham 15-8-83
Source: Scholar. *Honours:* Wales Under-21.

2002–03	Wrexham	1	0		
2003–04	Wrexham	13	1		
2004–05	Wrexham	26	3	**40**	**4**

JONES, Michael (M) 1 0
H: 6 3 W: 13 00 b.Liverpool 3-12-87
Source: Scholar.

2004–05	Wrexham	1	0	**1**	**0**

LAWRENCE, Dennis (D) 156 12
H: 6 7 W: 11 13 b.Trinidad 1-8-74
Source: From Defence Force. *Honours:* Trinidad & Tobago 55 full caps.

2000–01	Wrexham	3	0		
2001–02	Wrexham	32	2		
2002–03	Wrexham	32	1		
2003–04	Wrexham	45	5		
2004–05	Wrexham	44	4	**156**	**12**

LLEWELLYN, Chris (F) 247 35
H: 6 0 W: 11 06 b.Merthyr 29-8-79
Source: Trainee. *Honours:* Wales Youth, Under-21, B, 4 full caps.

1996–97	Norwich C	0	0		
1997–98	Norwich C	15	4		
1998–99	Norwich C	31	2		
1999–2000	Norwich C	36	3		
2000–01	Norwich C	42	8		
2001–02	Norwich C	13	0		
2002–03	Norwich C	5	0	**142**	**17**
2002–03	*Bristol R*	14	3	**14**	**3**
2003–04	Wrexham	46	8		
2004–05	Wrexham	45	7	**91**	**15**

MACKIN, Levi (M) 11 0
H: 6 1 W: 12 00 b.Chester 4-4-86
Source: Scholar.

2003–04	Wrexham	1	0		
2004–05	Wrexham	10	0	**11**	**0**

McNULTY, Jim (D) 0 0
H: 6 1 W: 12 00 b.Liverpool 13-2-85
Source: Scholar.

2003–04	Wrexham	0	0		
2004–05	Wrexham	0	0		

MORGAN, Craig (D) 52 1
H: 6 0 W: 11 12 b.St Asaph 18-6-85
Source: From Scholar. *Honours:* Wales Youth, Under-21.

2001–02	Wrexham	2	0		
2002–03	Wrexham	6	1		
2003–04	Wrexham	18	0		
2004–05	Wrexham	26	0	**52**	**1**

PEJIC, Shaun (D) 96 0
H: 6 0 W: 11 07 b.Hereford 16-11-82
Source: Trainee. *Honours:* Wales Under-21.

2000–01	Wrexham	1	0		
2001–02	Wrexham	12	0		
2002–03	Wrexham	27	0		
2003–04	Wrexham	21	0		
2004–05	Wrexham	35	0	**96**	**0**

QUINN, Kieran (M) 0 0
H: 5 10 W: 10 00 b.Liverpool 20-3-86
Source: Scholar.

2004–05	Wrexham	0	0		

ROBERTS, Steve (D) 150 6
H: 6 2 W: 11 06 b.Wrexham 24-2-80
Source: From Trainee. *Honours:* Wales Youth, Under-21, 1 full cap.

1997–98	Wrexham	0	0		
1998–99	Wrexham	0	0		
1999–2000	Wrexham	19	0		
2000–01	Wrexham	7	0		
2001–02	Wrexham	24	1		
2002–03	Wrexham	39	2		
2003–04	Wrexham	27	0		
2004–05	Wrexham	34	3	**150**	**6**

SAM, Hector (F) 150 35
H: 5 9 W: 11 05 b.Trinidad 25-2-78
Source: San Juan Jabloteh. *Honours:* Trinidad & Tobago 20 full caps, 2 goals.

2000–01	Wrexham	20	6		
2001–02	Wrexham	29	5		
2002–03	Wrexham	26	5		
2003–04	Wrexham	37	10		
2004–05	Wrexham	38	9	**150**	**35**

SMITH, Alex (M) 178 7
H: 5 8 W: 10 09 b.Liverpool 15-2-76
Source: Trainee.

1994–95	Everton	0	0		
1995–96	Everton	0	0		
1995–96	Swindon T	8	0		
1996–97	Swindon T	18	1		
1997–98	Swindon T	5	0	**31**	**1**
1997–98	Huddersfield T	6	0	**6**	**0**
1998–99	Chester C	32	2	**32**	**2**
1998–99	Port Vale	8	0		
1999–2000	Port Vale	13	0		
2000–01	Port Vale	37	2	**58**	**2**
2001–02	Reading	13	2		
2002–03	Reading	1	0		
2002–03	*Shrewsbury T*	13	0	**13**	**0**
2003–04	Reading	0	0	**14**	**2**
2004–05	Wrexham	24	0	**24**	**0**

SPENDER, Simon (D) 19 0
H: 5 11 W: 11 00 b.Mold 15-11-85
Source: Scholar. *Honours:* Wales Youth, Under-21.

2003–04	Wrexham	6	0		
2004–05	Wrexham	13	0	**19**	**0**

UGARTE, Juan (F) 31 17
H: 5 10 W: 11 11 b.San Sebastian 7-11-80

2001–02	Real Sociedad	1	0		
2002–03	Real Sociedad	0	0		
2003–04	Real Sociedad	0	0	**1**	**0**
From Dorchester T					
2004–05	Wrexham	30	17	**30**	**17**

VALERO, Vicente (G) 3 0
H: 6 5 W: 14 02 b.Castellon 28-2-73

2004–05	Wrexham	3	0	**3**	**0**

WHITLEY, Jim (M) 199 2
H: 5 9 W: 10 12 b.Zambia 14-4-75
Source: Trainee. *Honours:* Northern Ireland B, 3 full caps.

1993–94	Manchester C	0	0		
1994–95	Manchester C	0	0		
1995–96	Manchester C	0	0		
1996–97	Manchester C	0	0		
1997–98	Manchester C	19	0		
1998–99	Manchester C	18	0		
1999–2000	Manchester C	1	0		
1999–2000	*Blackpool*	8	0	**8**	**0**
2000–01	Manchester C	0	0	**38**	**0**
2000–01	*Norwich C*	8	1	**8**	**1**
2000–01	*Swindon T*	2	0	**2**	**0**
2000–01	*Northampton T*	13	0	**13**	**0**
2000–01	*Nottingham F*	0	0		
2001–02	Wrexham	34	0		
2002–03	Wrexham	44	1		
2003–04	Wrexham	36	0		
2004–05	Wrexham	16	0	**130**	**1**

WILLIAMS, Danny (M) 177 12
H: 6 1 W: 13 00 b.Wrexham 12-7-79
Source: Trainee. *Honours:* Wales Under-21.

1996–97	Liverpool	0	0		
1997–98	Liverpool	0	0		
1998–99	Liverpool	0	0		
1998–99	Wrexham	0	0		
1999–2000	Wrexham	24	1		
2000–01	Wrexham	15	2		
2001–02	Kidderminster H	38	1		
2002–03	Kidderminster H	45	2		
2003–04	Kidderminster H	28	5	**111**	**8**
2003–04	Bristol R	6	1	**6**	**1**
2004–05	Wrexham	21	0	**60**	**3**

WYCOMBE W (91)

AHMED, Shahed (M) 4 1
H: 5 10 W: 11 02 b.East Ham 13-9-85
Source: Milton Keynes D.

2004–05	Wycombe W	4	1	**4**	**1**

ANYA, Ikechi (M) 3 0
H: 5 5 W: 11 04 b.Glasgow 3-1-88
Source: Scholar.

2004–05	Wycombe W	3	0	**3**	**0**

BLOOMFIELD, Matt (M) 38 3
H: 5 9 W: 11 00 b.Ipswich 8-2-84
Source: From Scholar. *Honours:* England Youth, Under-20.

2001–02	Ipswich T	0	0		
2002–03	Ipswich T	0	0		
2003–04	Ipswich T	0	0		
2003–04	Wycombe W	12	1		
2004–05	Wycombe W	26	2	**38**	**3**

BURNELL, Joe (M) 155 1
H: 5 8 W: 12 00 b.Bristol 10-10-80
Source: Trainee.

1999–2000	Bristol C	17	0		
2000–01	Bristol C	23	0		
2001–02	Bristol C	30	0		
2002–03	Bristol C	44	0		
2003–04	Bristol C	17	1	**131**	**1**
2004–05	Wycombe W	24	0	**24**	**0**

CACERES, Adrian (F) 76 11
H: 5 10 W: 12 04 b.Buenos Aires 10-1-82
Source: Perth SC.

2000–01	Southampton	0	0		
2001–02	Southampton	0	0		
2001–02	*Brentford*	5	0	**5**	**0**
2001–02	Hull C	4	0	**4**	**0**
2002–03	Perth Glory	18	4		
2003–04	Perth Glory	25	4	**43**	**8**
2004–05	Yeovil T	21	3	**21**	**3**
From Aldershot T.					
2004–05	Wycombe W	3	0	**3**	**0**

DIXON, Jonny (F) 46 6
H: 5 9 W: 11 01 b.Murcia 16-1-84
Source: Scholar.

2002–03	Wycombe W	22	5		
2003–04	Wycombe W	8	0		
2004–05	Wycombe W	16	1	**46**	**6**

EASTON, Clint (M) **147** **7**
H: 5 11 W: 11 00 b.Barking 1-10-77
Source: Trainee. *Honours:* England Youth.

1996–97	Watford	17	1		
1997–98	Watford	12	0		
1998–99	Watford	7	0		
1999–2000	Watford	17	0		
2000–01	Watford	11	0	**64**	**1**
2001–02	Norwich C	14	1		
2002–03	Norwich C	26	2		
2003–04	Norwich C	10	2	**50**	**5**
2004–05	Wycombe W	33	1	**33**	**1**

FAULCONBRIDGE, Craig (F) **192** **40**
H: 6 1 W: 13 00 b.Nuneaton 20-4-78
Source: Trainee.

1996–97	Coventry C	0	0		
1997–98	Coventry C	0	0		
1997–98	Dunfermline Ath	7	1		
1998–99	Dunfermline Ath	6	0	**13**	**1**
1998–99	*Hull C*	10	0	**10**	**0**
1999–2000	Wrexham	35	8		
2000–01	Wrexham	39	10		
2001–02	Wrexham	37	13	**111**	**31**
2002–03	Wycombe W	34	6		
2003–04	Wycombe W	16	2		
2004–05	Wycombe W	8	0	**58**	**8**

GUPPY, Steve (M) **328** **31**
H: 5 11 W: 11 11 b.Winchester 29-3-69
Source: Southampton. *Honours:* England Under-21, B, 1 full cap.

1993–94	Wycombe W	41	8		
1994–95	Newcastle U	0	0		
1994–95	Port Vale	27	2		
1995–96	Port Vale	44	4		
1996–97	Port Vale	34	6	**105**	**12**
1996–97	Leicester C	13	0		
1997–98	Leicester C	37	2		
1998–99	Leicester C	38	4		
1999–2000	Leicester C	30	2		
2000–01	Leicester C	28	1		
2001–02	Leicester C	0	0		
2003–04	Leicester C	15	0	**161**	**9**
2004–05	Leeds U	3	1	**3**	**1**
2004–05	Stoke C	4	0	**4**	**0**
2004–05	Wycombe W	14	1	**55**	**9**

HARDING, Billy (F) **2** **0**
H: 6 0 W: 12 07 b.Carshalton 20-1-85
Source: Scholar.

2003–04	Wycombe W	2	0		
2004–05	Wycombe W	0	0	**2**	**0**

HOLE, Stuart (D) **1** **0**
H: 6 0 W: 11 11 b.Oxford 17-7-85
Source: Scholar.

2003–04	Wycombe W	1	0		
2004–05	Wycombe W	0	0	**1**	**0**

JOHNSON, Roger (D) **112** **12**
H: 6 3 W: 11 00 b.Ashford 28-4-83
Source: Trainee.

1999–2000	Wycombe W	1	0		
2000–01	Wycombe W	1	0		
2001–02	Wycombe W	7	1		
2002–03	Wycombe W	33	3		
2003–04	Wycombe W	28	2		
2004–05	Wycombe W	42	6	**112**	**12**

LEE, Robert (M) **672** **105**
H: 5 10 W: 11 10 b.Plaistow 1-2-66
Source: Hornchurch. *Honours:* England Under-21, 21 full caps, 2 goals.

1983–84	Charlton Ath	11	4		
1984–85	Charlton Ath	39	10		
1985–86	Charlton Ath	35	8		
1986–87	Charlton Ath	33	3		
1987–88	Charlton Ath	23	2		
1988–89	Charlton Ath	31	5		
1989–90	Charlton Ath	37	1		
1990–91	Charlton Ath	43	13		
1991–92	Charlton Ath	39	12		
1992–93	Charlton Ath	7	1	**298**	**59**
1992–93	Newcastle U	36	10		
1993–94	Newcastle U	41	7		
1994–95	Newcastle U	35	9		
1995–96	Newcastle U	36	8		
1996–97	Newcastle U	33	5		
1997–98	Newcastle U	28	4		
1998–99	Newcastle U	26	0		
1999–2000	Newcastle U	30	0		
2000–01	Newcastle U	22	0		
2001–02	Newcastle U	16	1	**303**	**44**
2001–02	Derby Co	13	0		
2002–03	Derby Co	35	2	**48**	**2**
2003–04	West Ham U	16	0		
2004–05	West Ham U	0	0	**16**	**0**
2004–05	Oldham Ath	0	0		
2004–05	Wycombe W	7	0	**7**	**0**

MARTIN, Russell (M) **7** **0**
H: 6 0 W: 11 08 b.Brighton 4-1-86

2004–05	Wycombe W	7	0	**7**	**0**

NETHERCOTT, Stuart (D) **336** **12**
H: 6 0 W: 13 01 b.Ilford 21-3-73
Source: Trainee. *Honours:* England Under-21.

1991–92	Tottenham H	0	0		
1991–92	*Maidstone U*	13	1	**13**	**1**
1991–92	*Barnet*	3	0	**3**	**0**
1992–93	Tottenham H	5	0		
1993–94	Tottenham H	10	0		
1994–95	Tottenham H	17	0		
1995–96	Tottenham H	13	0		
1996–97	Tottenham H	9	0		
1997–98	Tottenham H	0	0	**54**	**0**
1997–98	Millwall	10	0		
1998–99	Millwall	37	2		
1999–2000	Millwall	37	0		
2000–01	Millwall	35	2		
2001–02	Millwall	46	3		
2002–03	Millwall	36	2		
2003–04	Millwall	14	1	**215**	**10**
2003–04	Wycombe W	22	1		
2004–05	Wycombe W	29	0	**51**	**1**

PERPETUINI, David (M) **114** **6**
H: 5 9 W: 12 01 b.Hitchin 26-9-79
Source: Trainee.

1997–98	Watford	0	0		
1998–99	Watford	1	0		
1999–2000	Watford	13	1		
2000–01	Watford	5	0	**19**	**1**
2001–02	Gillingham	34	1		
2002–03	Gillingham	29	2		
2003–04	Gillingham	20	2		
2004–05	Gillingham	3	0	**86**	**5**
2004–05	Wycombe W	2	0	**2**	**0**
2004–05	*Walsall*	7	0	**7**	**0**

PHILO, Mark (M) **17** **0**
H: 5 11 W: 11 05 b.Bracknell 5-10-84
Source: Scholar.

2003–04	Wycombe W	12	0		
2004–05	Wycombe W	5	0	**17**	**0**

REILLY, Andy (D) **5** **0**
H: 5 10 W: 12 08 b.Luton 26-10-85
Source: Scholar. *Honours:* Scotland Youth, Under-21.

2003–04	Wycombe W	5	0		
2004–05	Wycombe W	0	0	**5**	**0**

RYAN, Keith (M) **351** **29**
H: 5 10 W: 12 06 b.Northampton 25-6-70
Source: Berkhamsted T.

1993–94	Wycombe W	42	1		
1994–95	Wycombe W	24	4		
1995–96	Wycombe W	23	4		
1996–97	Wycombe W	0	0		
1997–98	Wycombe W	40	3		
1998–99	Wycombe W	28	1		
1999–2000	Wycombe W	38	6		
2000–01	Wycombe W	30	4		
2001–02	Wycombe W	35	1		
2002–03	Wycombe W	36	2		
2003–04	Wycombe W	17	1		
2004–05	Wycombe W	38	2	**351**	**29**

SENDA, Danny (M) **232** **9**
H: 5 10 W: 10 02 b.Harrow 17-4-81
Source: Southampton Trainee. *Honours:* England Youth.

1998–99	Wycombe W	6	0		
1999–2000	Wycombe W	27	1		
2000–01	Wycombe W	31	2		
2001–02	Wycombe W	43	0		
2002–03	Wycombe W	41	2		
2003–04	Wycombe W	40	0		
2004–05	Wycombe W	44	4	**232**	**9**

SIMPEMBA, Ian (M) **20** **2**
H: 6 2 W: 12 08 b.Dublin 28-3-83
Source: Scholar.

2001–02	Wycombe W	0	0		
2002–03	Wycombe W	1	0		
2003–04	Wycombe W	19	2		
2004–05	Wycombe W	0	0	**20**	**2**

STONEBRIDGE, Ian (F) **209** **42**
H: 6 0 W: 11 04 b.Lewisham 30-8-81
Source: Tottenham H Trainee. *Honours:* England Youth.

1999–2000	Plymouth Arg	31	9		
2000–01	Plymouth Arg	31	11		
2001–02	Plymouth Arg	42	8		
2002–03	Plymouth Arg	37	5		
2003–04	Plymouth Arg	30	5	**171**	**38**
2004–05	Wycombe W	38	4	**38**	**4**

TALIA, Frank (G) **238** **0**
H: 6 1 W: 13 06 b.Melbourne 20-7-72
Honours: Australia Schools, Under-20.

1990–91	Sunshine	11	0		
1991–92	Sunshine	0	0	**11**	**0**
1992–93	Blackburn R	0	0		
1992–93	*Hartlepool U*	14	0	**14**	**0**
1993–94	Blackburn R	0	0		
1994–95	Blackburn R	0	0		
1995–96	Blackburn R	0	0		
1995–96	Swindon T	16	0		
1996–97	Swindon T	15	0		
1997–98	Swindon T	2	0		
1998–99	Swindon T	43	0		
1999–2000	Swindon T	31	0	**107**	**0**
2000–01	Wolverhampton W	0	0		
2000–01	Sheffield U	6	0	**6**	**0**
2001–02	Antwerp	3	0	**3**	**0**
2001–02	Reading	0	0		
2002–03	Wycombe W	35	0		
2003–04	Wycombe W	17	0		
2004–05	Wycombe W	45	0	**97**	**0**

TYSON, Nathan (F) **115** **34**
H: 5 10 W: 10 02 b.Reading 4-5-82
Source: Trainee. *Honours:* England Under-20.

1999–2000	Reading	1	0		
2000–01	Reading	0	0		
2001–02	Reading	1	0		
2001–02	*Swansea C*	11	1	**11**	**1**
2001–02	*Cheltenham T*	8	1	**8**	**1**
2002–03	Reading	23	1		
2003–04	Reading	8	0	**33**	**1**
2003–04	Wycombe W	21	9		
2004–05	Wycombe W	42	22	**63**	**31**

UHLENBEEK, Gus (D) **368** **13**
H: 5 10 W: 12 00 b.Paramaribo 20-8-70

1990–91	Ajax	2	0		
1991–92	Ajax	0	0	**2**	**0**
1992–93	Cambuur	24	0		
1993–94	Cambuur	15	0	**39**	**0**
1994–95	TOPS SV	22	3	**22**	**3**
1995–96	Ipswich T	40	4		
1996–97	Ipswich T	38	0		
1997–98	Ipswich T	11	0	**89**	**4**
1998–99	Fulham	23	1		
1999–2000	Fulham	16	0	**39**	**1**
2000–01	Sheffield U	31	0		
2001–02	Sheffield U	20	0	**51**	**0**
2001–02	*Walsall*	5	0	**5**	**0**
2002–03	Bradford C	42	1	**42**	**1**
2003–04	Chesterfield	37	0	**37**	**0**
2004–05	Wycombe W	42	4	**42**	**4**

WILLIAMS, Steve (G) **20** **0**
H: 6 6 W: 13 10 b.Oxford 21-4-83
Source: Scholar.

2001–02	Wycombe W	0	0		
2002–03	Wycombe W	0	0		
2003–04	Wycombe W	19	0		
2004–05	Wycombe W	1	0	**20**	**0**

YEOVIL T (92)

AMANKWAAH, Kevin (D) **87** **1**
H: 6 1 W: 12 12 b.Harrow 19-5-82
Source: Scholar. *Honours:* England Youth.

1999–2000	Bristol C	5	0		
2000–01	Bristol C	14	0		
2001–02	Bristol C	24	1		

2002–03 Bristol C 1 0
2002–03 *Torquay U* 6 0 **6 0**
2003–04 Bristol C 5 0
2003–04 *Cheltenham T* 12 0 **12 0**
2004–05 Bristol C 5 0 **54 1**
2004–05 Yeovil T 15 0 **15 0**

BROWN, Marvin (F) 40 2
H: 5 9 W: 11 12 b.Bristol 6-7-83
Honours: England Youth.
1999–2000 Bristol C 2 0
2000–01 Bristol C 5 0
2001–02 Bristol C 10 0
2002–03 Bristol C 0 0
2002–03 *Torquay U* 4 0 **4 0**
2002–03 *Cheltenham T* 15 2 **15 2**
2003–04 Bristol C 2 0 **19 0**
From Tamworth.
2004–05 Yeovil T 2 0 **2 0**

COLLIS, Steve (G) 20 0
H: 6 3 W: 12 05 b.Harrow 18-3-81
1999–2000 Barnet 0 0
2000–01 Nottingham F 0 0
2001–02 Nottingham F 0 0
2003–04 Yeovil T 11 0
2004–05 Yeovil T 9 0 **20 0**

DAVIES, Arron (M) 27 8
H: 5 9 W: 11 00 b.Cardiff 22-6-84
Source: Trainee. *Honours:* Wales Under-21.
2002–03 Southampton 0 0
2003–04 Southampton 0 0
2003–04 *Barnsley* 4 0 **4 0**
2004–05 Southampton 0 0
2004–05 Yeovil T 23 8 **23 8**

ELAM, Lee (M) 12 1
H: 5 8 W: 10 12 b.Bradford 24-9-76
Source: Halifax T.
2003–04 Yeovil T 12 1
2004–05 Yeovil T 0 0 **12 1**

GALL, Kevin (F) 136 16
H: 5 9 W: 10 08 b.Merthyr 4-2-82
Source: Trainee. *Honours:* Wales Schools, Youth, Under-21.
1998–99 Newcastle U 0 0
1999–2000 Newcastle U 0 0
2000–01 Newcastle U 0 0
2000–01 Bristol R 10 2
2001–02 Bristol R 31 3
2002–03 Bristol R 9 0 **50 5**
2003–04 Yeovil T 43 8
2004–05 Yeovil T 43 3 **86 11**

GUYETT, Scott (D) 40 2
H: 6 2 W: 13 06 b.Ascot 20-1-76
Source: Brisbane C, Gresley R, Southport.
2001–02 Oxford U 22 0 **22 0**
From Chester C.
2004–05 Yeovil T 18 2 **18 2**

IBE, Kesie (F) 3 0
H: 5 10 W: 12 00 b.London 6-12-82
Source: Staines T.
2004–05 Yeovil T 3 0 **3 0**

JEVONS, Phil (F) 141 48
H: 5 11 W: 12 00 b.Liverpool 1-8-79
Source: Trainee.
1996–97 Everton 0 0
1997–98 Everton 0 0
1998–99 Everton 1 0
1999–2000 Everton 3 0
2000–01 Everton 4 0 **8 0**
2001–02 Grimsby T 31 6
2002–03 Grimsby T 3 0
2002–03 *Hull C* 24 3 **24 3**
2003–04 Grimsby T 29 12 **63 18**
2004–05 Yeovil T 46 27 **46 27**

JOHNSON, Lee (M) 89 12
H: 5 6 W: 10 07 b.Newmarket 7-6-81
Source: Trainee.
1998–99 Watford 0 0
1999–2000 Watford 0 0
2000–01 Brighton & HA 0 0
2000–01 Brentford 0 0
2001–02 Brentford 0 0
2003–04 Yeovil T 45 5
2004–05 Yeovil T 44 7 **89 12**

LINDEGAARD, Andy (F) 52 3
H: 5 8 W: 11 04 b.Taunton 10-9-80
Source: Westland Sp.
2003–04 Yeovil T 23 2
2004–05 Yeovil T 29 1 **52 3**

LOCKWOOD, Adam (D) 53 4
H: 6 0 W: 12 07 b.Wakefield 26-10-81
Source: Reading Trainee.
2003–04 Yeovil T 43 4
2004–05 Yeovil T 10 0 **53 4**

MILES, Colin (D) 62 4
H: 6 0 W: 13 10 b.Edmonton 6-9-78
Source: Trainee.
1996–97 Watford 0 0
1997–98 Watford 1 0
1998–99 Watford 0 0 **1 0**
1999–2000 Morton 4 0 **4 0**
From Dover Ath
2003–04 Yeovil T 36 4
2004–05 Yeovil T 21 0 **57 4**

MIRZA, Nicolas (M) 3 0
H: 6 2 W: 12 08 b.Paris 21-7-85
Source: Paris St. *Honours:* Germain.
2004–05 Yeovil T 3 0 **3 0**

O'BRIEN, Roy (D) 28 0
H: 6 0 W: 12 02 b.Cork 27-11-74
Source: Trainee.
1993–94 Arsenal 0 0
1994–95 Arsenal 0 0
1995–96 Arsenal 0 0
1996–97 Wigan Ath 0 0
1996–97 Bournemouth 1 0 **1 0**
From Dorchester T
2003–04 Yeovil T 13 0
2004–05 Yeovil T 14 0 **27 0**

ODUBADE, Yemi (F) 4 0
H: 5 7 W: 11 07 b.Lagos 4-7-84
Source: Eastbourne B.
2004–05 Yeovil T 4 0 **4 0**

REED, Steve (D) 8 0
H: 5 8 W: 12 02 b.Barnstaple 18-6-85
Source: Juniors.
2003–04 Yeovil T 5 0
2004–05 Yeovil T 3 0 **8 0**

RICHARDSON, Marcus (F) 140 29
H: 6 3 W: 12 05 b.Reading 31-8-77
Source: Harrow B.
2000–01 Cambridge U 10 2
2001–02 Cambridge U 6 0 **16 2**
2001–02 Torquay U 30 6
2002–03 Torquay U 9 2 **39 8**
2002–03 Hartlepool U 24 5
2003–04 Hartlepool U 3 0 **27 5**
2003–04 Lincoln C 38 10
2004–05 Lincoln C 14 4 **52 14**
2004–05 *Rochdale* 2 0 **2 0**
2004–05 Yeovil T 4 0 **4 0**

ROSE, Michael (D) 40 1
H: 5 10 W: 11 02 b.Salford 28-7-82
Source: Trainee.
1999–2000 Manchester U 0 0
2000–01 Manchester U 0 0
2001–02 Manchester U 0 0
From Hereford U
2004–05 Yeovil T 40 1 **40 1**

SKIVERTON, Terry (D) 84 7
H: 6 1 W: 13 06 b.Mile End 26-6-75
Source: Trainee.
1993–94 Chelsea 0 0
1994–95 Chelsea 0 0
1994–95 *Wycombe W* 10 0
1995–96 Chelsea 0 0
1995–96 Wycombe W 4 1
1996–97 Wycombe W 6 0 **20 1**
From Welling U
2003–04 Yeovil T 26 2
2004–05 Yeovil T 38 4 **64 6**

SODJE, Efe (D) 266 16
H: 6 1 W: 12 00 b.Greenwich 5-10-72
Source: Delta Steel Pioneer, Stevenage Bor.
Honours: Nigeria 10 full caps, 1 goal.
1997–98 Macclesfield T 41 3
1998–99 Macclesfield T 42 3 **83 6**
1999–2000 Luton T 9 0 **9 0**
1999–2000 Colchester U 3 0 **3 0**
2000–01 Crewe Alex 32 0
2001–02 Crewe Alex 36 2
2002–03 Crewe Alex 30 1 **98 3**
2003–04 Huddersfield T 39 4
2004–05 Huddersfield T 28 1 **67 5**
2004–05 Yeovil T 6 2 **6 2**

STOLCERS, Andrejs (F) 171 41
H: 5 8 W: 11 02 b.Riga 8-7-74
Honours: Latvia 79 full caps, 7 goals.
1996 Skonto Riga 26 6
1997 Skonto Riga 23 9 **49 15**
1997–98 Shakhtar Donetsk 13 4
1998–99 Shakhtar Donetsk 21 6
1999–2000 Shakhtar Donetsk 15 4 **49 14**
2000 Spartak Moscow 12 5 **12 5**
2000–01 Fulham 15 2
2001–02 Fulham 5 0
2002–03 Fulham 5 0
2003–04 Fulham 0 0 **25 2**
2004–05 Yeovil T 36 5 **36 5**

TARACHULSKI, Bartosz (F) 234 48
H: 6 3 W: 13 06 b.Gliwice 14-5-75
1994–95 Gornik Zabrze 8 3 **8 3**
1995–96 Polonia 0 0
1996–97 Polonia 15 6
1997–98 Polonia 25 5
1998–99 Polonia 25 4
1999–2000 Beveren 25 3 **25 3**
2000–01 Ruch 10 1 **10 1**
2000–01 Widzew 13 4 **13 4**
2001–02 Polonia 26 4
2002–03 Hapoel Beer Sheva 23 5 **23 5**
2003–04 Polonia 22 3 **113 22**
2004–05 Yeovil T 42 10 **42 10**

TERRY, Paul (M) 73 7
H: 5 10 W: 12 06 b.Barking 3-4-79
Source: Dagenham & R.
2003–04 Yeovil T 34 1
2004–05 Yeovil T 39 6 **73 7**

WAY, Darren (M) 84 12
H: 5 6 W: 10 00 b.Plymouth 21-11-79
Source: Norwich C Trainee.
2003–04 Yeovil T 39 5
2004–05 Yeovil T 45 7 **84 12**

WEALE, Chris (G) 73 0
H: 6 2 W: 13 03 b.Yeovil 9-2-82
Source: Juniors.
2003–04 Yeovil T 35 0
2004–05 Yeovil T 38 0 **73 0**

WEATHERSTONE, Simon (D) 135 14
H: 5 10 W: 12 00 b.Reading 26-1-80
Source: Trainee.
1996–97 Oxford U 1 0
1997–98 Oxford U 11 1
1998–99 Oxford U 12 1
1999–2000 Oxford U 21 1
2000–01 Oxford U 7 0 **52 3**
2002–03 Boston U 45 6
2003–04 Boston U 17 4 **62 10**
2003–04 Yeovil T 15 1
2004–05 Yeovil T 6 0 **21 1**

WILLIAMS, Dale (M) 0 0
H: 6 0 W: 11 04 b.Swansea 26-3-87
Source: Scholar.
2004–05 Yeovil T 0 0

ENGLISH LEAGUE PLAYERS – INDEX

TRANSFERS 2004–05

JUNE 2004	From	To	Fee in £
30 Branch, Paul M.	Bradford City	Chester City	undisclosed
16 Dickov, Paul	Leicester City	Blackburn Rovers	150,000
2 Keane, Michael	Preston North End	Hull City	50,000
14 Lucas, David A.	Preston North End	Sheffield Wednesday	100,000
14 Paston, Mark	Bradford City	Walsall	undisclosed
18 Purse, Darren J.	Birmingham City	West Bromwich Albion	500,000
30 Thatcher, Benjamin D.	Leicester City	Manchester City	100,000
29 Wright, David	Crewe Alexandra	Wigan Athletic	500,000
TEMPORARY TRANSFERS			
28 Bentley, David M.	Arsenal	Norwich City	
JULY 2004			
19 Asamoah, Derek	Northampton Town	Mansfield Town	Free
8 Bent, Marcus N.	Ipswich Town	Everton	400,000
8 Beresford, Marlon	Barnsley	Luton Town	Free
2 Brooker, Paul	Leicester City	Reading	Free
7 Burnell, Joseph M.	Bristol City	Wycombe Wanderers	Free
30 Butt, Nicholas	Manchester United	Newcastle United	2,500,000
29 Cahill, Timothy	Millwall	Everton	2,000,000
13 Charton, Simon T.	Bolton Wanderers	Norwich City	250,000
2 Commons, Kristian A.	Stoke City	Nottingham Forest	300,000
22 Connolly, David J.	West Ham United	Leicester City	500,000
7 Cook, Lee	Watford	Queens Park Rangers	undisclosed
9 Coppinger, James	Exeter City	Doncaster Rovers	Free
24 Coyne, Daniel	Leicester City	Burnley	25,000
14 Crouch, Peter J.	Aston Villa	Southampton	2,000,000
10 Davis, Sean	Fulham	Tottenham Hotspur	3,000,000
8 Duff, Michael J.	Cheltenham Town	Burnley	30,000
23 Duke, Matthew	Burton Albion	Hull City	20,000
29 Edds, Gareth J.	Bradford City	Milton Keynes Dons	Free
26 Edwards, Robert O.	Aston Villa	Wolverhampton Wanderers	125,000
29 Feeney, Warren J.	AFC Bournemouth	Stockport County	45,000
26 Graham, David	Torquay United	Wigan Athletic	215,000
30 Greening, Jonathan	Middlesbrough	West Bromwich Albion	1,250,000
30 Gronkjaer, Jesper	Chelsea	Birmingham City	2,200,000
2 Heskey, Emile W.	Liverpool	Birmingham City	3,500,000
12 Hudson, Mark A.	Fulham	Crystal Palace	550,000
14 Ifil, Jerel C.	Watford	Swindon Town	70,000
27 Jensen, Claus W.	Charlton Athletic	Fulham	1,250,000
13 Lua-Lua, Lomano T.	Newcastle United	Portsmouth	1,750,000
26 Lynch, Mark J.	Manchester United	Sunderland	undisclosed
27 MacLean, Steven	Rangers	Sheffield Wednesday	Free
5 McGovern, Jon P.	Livingston	Sheffield Wednesday	Free
21 Melligan, John J.	Wolverhampton Wanderers	Cheltenham Town	25,000
7 Milner, James P.	Leeds United	Newcastle United	3,600,000
31 Murray, Adam D.	Kidderminster Harriers	Mansfield Town	undisclosed
20 Murray, Frederick A.	Cambridge United	Northampton Town	Free
14 Opara, Lloyd	Grays Athletic	Swindon Town	undisclosed
30 Parlour, Raymond	Arsenal	Middlesbrough	Free
20 Pugh, Daniel A.	Manchester United	Leeds United	exch.
19 Reid, Paul M.	Northampton Town	Barnsley	undisclosed
8 Ricketts, Michael B.	Middlesbrough	Leeds United	Free
8 Robinson, Carl P.	Portsmouth	Sunderland	Free
13 Safri, Youssef	Coventry City	Norwich City	500,000
21 Speed, Gary A.	Newcastle United	Bolton Wanderers	750,000
19 Stockdale, Robert K.	Middlesbrough	Rotherham United	Free
8 Viduka, Mark A.	Leeds United	Middlesbrough	4,500,000
19 Wilbraham, Aaron T.	Stockport County	Hull City	100,000
12 Wolleaston, Robert A.	Bradford City	Oxford United	Free
TEMPORARY TRANSFERS			
30 Blinkhorn, Matthew D.	Blackpool	Luton Town	
30 Braniff, Kevin	Millwall	Rushden & Diamonds	
13 Cole, Carlton	Chelsea	Aston Villa	
2 Forssell, Mikael K.	Chelsea	Birmingham City	
16 Johnson, Edward W.	Manchester United	Coventry City	
16 Nardiello, Daniel A.	Manchester United	Barnsley	
15 Owen, Gareth J.	Stoke City	Torquay United	
26 Peat, Nathan N.M.	Hull City	Lincoln City	
1 Sestanovich, Ashley	Sheffield United	Grimsby Town	
6 Silk, Gary L.	Portsmouth	Wycombe Wanderers	
9 Stack, Graham	Arsenal	Millwall	
15 Villis, Matthew	Plymouth Argyle	Torquay United	
27 Ward, Elliott L.	West Ham United	Peterborough United	
8 Williamson, Michael J.	Southampton	Wycombe Wanderers	
AUGUST 2004			
24 Carrick, Michael	West Ham United	Tottenham Hotspur	3,000,000
12 Carr, Stephen	Tottenham Hotspur	Newcastle United	2,000,000
6 Cisse, Aliou	Birmingham City	Portsmouth	300,000
13 Crainey, Stephen	Southampton	Leeds United	200,000
31 Davenport, Calum R.P.	Coventry City	Tottenham Hotspur	1,100,000
20 Doherty, Gary M.T.	Tottenham Hotspur	Norwich City	undisclosed
6 Elliott, Stephen W.	Manchester City	Sunderland	125,000
6 Fisken, Gary S.	Watford	Swansea City	Free
31 Fletcher, Carl N.	AFC Bournemouth	West Ham United	250,000
27 Fuller, Ricardo	Preston North End	Portsmouth	200,000
12 Hall, Fitz	Southampton	Crystal Palace	1,000,000
31 Hayles, Barry	Sheffield United	Millwall	undisclosed

12 Jeffers, Francis	Arsenal	Charlton Athletic	2,600,000
5 Lawrence, Liam	Mansfield Town	Sunderland	175,000
13 McAnuff, Joel J.F.M.	West Ham United	Cardiff City	250,000
5 McAuley, Gareth	Coleraine	Lincoln City	10,000
4 McLeod, Izale M.	Derby County	Milton Keynes Dons	Free
12 Murphy, Daniel B.	Liverpool	Charlton Athletic	2,500,000
11 Radzinski, Tomasz	Everton	Fulham	175,000
31 Rooney, Wayne	Everton	Manchester United	27,000,000
6 Smith, Gary S.	Middlesbrough	Milton Keynes Dons	undisclosed
5 Stonebridge, Ian R.	Plymouth Argyle	Wycombe Wanderers	nominal
6 Ward, Darren	Nottingham Forest	Norwich City	undisclosed
2 Whitehead, Dean	Oxford United	Sunderland	150,000
31 Yorke, Dwight E.	Blackburn Rovers	Birmingham City	undisclosed

TEMPORARY TRANSFERS

26 Abbey, Zema	Norwich City	Boston United
13 Adebola, Bamberdele O.	Coventry City	Bradford City
6 Bailey, Matthew J.	Stockport County	Scunthorpe United
13 Banim, Jody	Shrewsbury Town	Accrington Stanley
6 Barker, Christopher A.	Cardiff City	Stoke City
3 Barrowman, Andrew	Birmingham City	Blackpool
13 Beck, Daniel G.	Brighton & Hove Albion	Bognor Regis Town
6 Betsy, Kevin	Barnsley	Hartlepool United
12 Bimson, Stuart J.	Cambridge United	Accrington Stanley
20 Birchall, Adam S.	Arsenal	Wycombe Wanderers
3 Bossu, Bertrand	Gillingham	Torquay United
6 Braniff, Kevin R.	Millwall	Rushden & Diamonds
5 Briggs, Keith	Norwich City	Crewe Alexandra
31 Brighton, Tom	Rangers	Scunthorpe United
6 Brown, Simon	West Bromwich Albion	Kidderminster Harriers
13 Budd, Darren L.	Brighton & Hove Albion	Bognor Regis Town
16 Burch, Robert K.	Tottenham Hotspur	Stevenage Borough
20 Campbell-Ryce, Jamal J.	Charlton Athletic	Chesterfield
20 Cash, Brian D.	Nottingham Forest	Rochdale
9 Chambers, James A.	West Bromwich Albion	Watford
27 Chopra, Rocky M.	Newcastle United	Barnsley
20 Commons, Spencer J.	Notts County	Grantham Town
6 Crainey, Stephen	Southampton	Leeds United
19 Daly, Wesley J.P.	Queens Park Rangers	Raith Rovers
9 Dinning, Tony	Wigan Athletic	Ipswich Town
20 Diouf, El Hadji O.	Liverpool	Bolton Wanderers
20 Flynn, Michael J.	Wigan Athletic	Blackpool
4 Folkes, Peter A.	Bradford City	Lincoln City
13 Fontaine, Liam V.H.	Fulham	Yeovil Town
13 Gould, Jonathan A.	Preston North End	Hereford United
27 Hand, Jamie	Watford	Oxford United
27 Hawkins, Darren M.	Bristol City	Bath City
20 Henderson, Darius A.	Gillingham	Swindon Town
9 Henderson, Wayne	Aston Villa	Notts County
6 Howe, Edward J.F.	Portsmouth	AFC Bournemouth
27 Hughes, Mark A.	Tottenham Hotspur	Northampton Town
6 Jelleyman, Gareth A.	Peterborough United	Boston United
6 Keogh, Andrew D.	Leeds United	Scunthorpe United
5 Livesey, Daniel	Bolton Wanderers	Blackpool
27 Louis, Jefferson L.	Oxford United	Gravesend & Northfleet
13 Martin, Marcus A.P.	Plymouth Argyle	Exeter City
13 Maxwell, Marcus A.	Plymouth Argyle	Exeter City
6 May, Ben S.	Millwall	Colchester United
31 McGrath, John M.	Doncaster Rovers	Shrewsbury Town
18 McGurk, David	Darlington	Bishop Auckland
27 McLachlan, Fraser M.	Stockport County	Northwich Victoria
31 McManus, Thomas K.	Hibernian	Boston United
6 Moore, Stefan	Aston Villa	Millwall
20 Navarro, Alan E.	Tranmere Rovers	Chester City
6 Nicolas, Alexis P.	Chelsea	Brighton & Hove Albion
24 Noble, Stuart W.	Fulham	Torquay United
31 Oakes, Andrew M.	Derby County	Bolton Wanderers
6 O'Neill, Joseph	Preston North End	Mansfield Town
20 Pearson, Gregory	West Ham United	Lincoln City
17 Perry, Jack J.	Queens Park Rangers	Raith Rovers
6 Rachubka, Paul S.	Charlton Athletic	Milton Keynes Dons
13 Ross, Neil J.	Macclesfield Town	Tamworth
13 Sawyer, Gary D.	Plymouth Argyle	Exeter City
6 Shaw, Paul	Sheffield United	Rotherham United
2 Silk, Gary L.	Portsmouth	Wycombe Wanderers
6 Smith, Jonathan	Accrington Stanley	Barrow
13 Thomas, Bradley M.	Peterborough United	Sutton United
6 Turnbull, Ross	Middlesbrough	Bradford City
6 Turner, Michael T.	Charlton Athletic	Brentford
19 Vieira, Magno S.	Wigan Athletic	Carlisle United
6 Vine, Rowan L.	Portsmouth	Luton Town
6 Viveash, Adrian L.	Swindon Town	Kidderminster Harriers
27 Yeates, Mark S.	Tottenham Hotspur	Swindon Town

SEPTEMBER 2004

9 Andrews, Wayne M.H.	Colchester United	Crystal Palace	undisclosed
30 Brooker, Stephen M.L.	Port Vale	Bristol City	150,000
30 Cadamarteri, Daniel L.	Leeds United	Sheffield United	50,000
21 Carruthers, Martin G.	Boston United	Lincoln City	exch.
28 Chambers, James	West Bromwich Albion	Watford	75,000
17 Regan, Sean M.	West Bromwich Albion	Leeds United	500,000
1 Gurney, Andrew R.	Swindon Town	Swansea City	undisclosed
14 John, Stern	Birmingham City	Coventry City	200,000
24 Louis, Jefferson	Oxford United	Forest Green Rovers	undisclosed
10 Mackay, Malcolm	Norwich City	West Ham United	300,000

3 Plummer, Christopher S.	Barnet	Peterborough United	30,000
14 Weatherstone, Simon	Yeovil Town	Hornchurch	Free
21 West, Dean	Lincoln City	Boston United	exch.
3 Williams, Gareth A.	Crystal Palace	Colchester United	exch.
9 Williamson, Lee T.	Mansfield Town	Northampton Town	undisclosed

TEMPORARY TRANSFERS

12 Adebola, Bamidele O.	Coventry City	Bradford City
23 Aljofree, Hasney	Plymouth Argyle	Sheffield Wednesday
17 Beck, Daniel G.	Brighton & Hove Albion	Bognor Regis Town
10 Beckwith, Dean	Gillingham	Margate
21 Birchall, Adam S.	Arsenal	Wycombe Wanderers
30 Bischoff, Mikkel	Manchester City	Wolverhampton Wanderers
17 Black, Thomas R.	Crystal Palace	Sheffield United
24 Bridges, Michael	Bolton Wanderers	Sunderland
10 Brown, Simon	West Bromwich Albion	Kidderminster Harriers
24 Burchill, Mark J.	Portsmouth	Rotherham United
3 Byrne, Michael T.	Stockport County	Leigh RMI
17 Campbell-Ryce, Jamal	Charlton Athletic	Chesterfield
17 Carter, Darren A.	Birmingham City	Sunderland
24 Chambers, James A.	West Bromwich Albion	Watford
9 Clancy, Timothy	Millwall	Walton & Hersham
18 Clarke, Peter M.	Everton	Blackpool
18 Comyn-Platt, Charlie	Bolton Wanderers	Wycombe Wanderers
24 Cooper, Shaun D.	Portsmouth	Kidderminster Harriers
24 Crouch, Ross A.	Colchester United	Wivenhoe Town
10 Curtis, John C.K.	Portsmouth	Preston North End
9 Danns, Neil A.	Blackburn Rovers	Colchester United
9 Davenport, Calum R.P.	Tottenham Hotspur	West Ham United
20 Day, Jamie R.	Peterborough United	Crawley Town
9 Dolan, Joseph	Millwall	Walton & Hersham
17 Donaldson, Clayton A.	Hull City	Harrogate Town
24 Duffy, Richard M.	Portsmouth	Burnley
23 Edwards, Paul	Crewe Alexandra	Redditch United
28 Fitzgerald, Scott P.	Watford	Swansea City
17 Flynn, Michael J.	Wigan Athletic	Blackpool
12 Fontaine, Liam V.H.	Fulham	Yeovil Town
9 Gerrard, Anthony	Everton	Accrington Stanley
12 Gould, Jonathan A.	Preston North End	Hereford United
26 Hand, Jamie	Watford	Oxford United
9 Harper, Kevin P.	Portsmouth	Leicester City
24 Harrad, Shaun N.	Notts County	Tamworth
29 Hawkins, Darren M.	Bristol City	Bath City
7 Howe, Edward J.	Portsmouth	AFC Bournemouth
10 Huke, Shane	Peterborough United	Cambridge City
10 Johnson, Simon A.	Leeds United	Sunderland
5 Keogh, Andrew D.	Leeds United	Scunthorpe United
4 Langmead, Kelvin S.	Preston North End	Kidderminster Harriers
10 Leacock, Dean	Fulham	Coventry City
17 Logan, Richard J.	Peterborough United	Shrewsbury Town
20 MacNamara, Niall A.	Lincoln City	Eastwood Town
13 Mansaram, Darren	Grimsby Town	Halifax Town
13 Masterson, Terence P.	Millwall	Weymouth
17 McGurk, David	Darlington	York City
4 McMahon, Stephen J.	Blackpool	Kidderminster Harriers
28 McMaster, Jamie	Leeds United	Swindon Town
18 McSheffrey, Gary	Coventry City	Luton Town
24 McStay, Henry M.P.	Leeds United	Halifax Town
18 Mills, Matthew C.	Southampton	Coventry City
3 Mitchell, Paul A.	Wigan Athletic	Swindon Town
10 Moore, David L.	Wigan Athletic	Stalybridge Celtic
28 Ndumbu-Nsungu, Guylain	Sheffield Wednesday	Preston North End
29 Nowland, Adam C.	West Ham United	Gillingham
3 O'Connor, James F.E.	Aston Villa	Port Vale
24 O'Grady, Christopher J.	Leicester City	Notts County
24 O'Neil, Gary P.	Portsmouth	Cardiff City
23 Ormerod, Brett R.	Southampton	Leeds United
30 Otsemobor, Jon	Liverpool	Crewe Alexandra
10 Pead, Craig G.	Coventry City	Notts County
10 Pouton, Alan	Gillingham	Hartlepool United
10 Powell, Christopher G.	Charlton Athletic	West Ham United
11 Price, Jamie B.	Doncaster Rovers	Burton Albion
10 Pullen, James D.C.	Peterborough United	Hornchurch
3 Rachubka, Paul S.	Charlton Athletic	Northampton Town
22 Reilly, Philip B.	Stockport County	Bradford Park Avenue
4 Rickards, Scott	Kidderminster Harriers	Redditch United
17 Roberts, Neil W.	Wigan Athletic	Bradford City
4 Robinson, Paul	Tranmere Rovers	Grimsby Town
2 Savage, Basir M.	Reading	Wycombe Wanderers
30 Simpson, Sekani	Bristol City	Tamworth
10 Sofiane, Youssef	West Ham United	Notts County
10 Spicer, John W.	Arsenal	AFC Bournemouth
11 Steele, Luke D.	Manchester United	Coventry City
17 Symes, Michael	Bradford City	Darlington
25 Talbot, Jason C.	Bolton Wanderers	Derby County
30 Townson, Kevin	Rochdale	Scarborough
7 Turner, Michael T.	Charlton Athletic	Brentford
10 Vernon, Scott M.	Oldham Athletic	Blackpool
20 Vieira, Magno S.	Wigan Athletic	Carlisle United
7 Vine, Rowan	Portsmouth	Luton Town
13 Wheeler, Kirk	Grimsby Town	Barrow
4 Williams, Christopher J.	Stockport County	Grimsby Town
23 Williams, Darren	Sunderland	Cardiff City
2 Wilson, Mark A.	Middlesbrough	Doncaster Rovers

25 Woodman, Craig A.	Bristol City	Mansfield Town	
10 Woods, Martin P.	Leeds United	Hartlepool United	
OCTOBER 2004			
22 Clark, Benjamin	Sunderland	Hartlepool United	undisclosed
12 Collins, Daniel L.	Chester City	Sunderland	140,000
22 Geary, Derek P.	Stockport County	Sheffield United	25,000
29 Healy, David J.	Preston North End	Leeds United	undisclosed
28 Hodgson, Richard J.	Crawley Town	Cambridge United	Free
22 Morison, Steve	Northampton Town	Bishop's Stortford	nominal
22 Nicolas, Alexis	Chelsea	Brighton & Hove Albion	undisclosed
15 Roberts, Christian J.	Bristol City	Swindon Town	20,000
7 Roberts, Neil W.	Wigan Athletic	Doncaster Rovers	undisclosed
TEMPORARY TRANSFERS			
13 Adebola, Bamidele O.	Coventry City	Bradford City	
22 Atieno, Taiwo L.	Walsall	Rochdale	
25 Birchall, Adam S.	Arsenal	Wycombe Wanderers	
29 Bossu, Bertrand	Gillingham	Oldham Athletic	
20 Brock, Stuart A.	AFC Telford United	Hull City	
14 Broughton, Drewe O.	Southend United	Rushden & Diamonds	
29 Brown, Simon	West Bromwich Albion	Kidderminster Harriers	
25 Campbell-Ryce, Jamal	Charlton Athletic	Chesterfield	
25 Chopra, Rocky M.	Newcastle United	Barnsley	
14 Clarke, Ryan A.	Boston United	King's Lynn	
14 Clarke, Ryan J.	Bristol Rovers	Southend United	
8 Clingan, Samuel G.	Wolverhampton Wanderers	Chesterfield	
29 Constantine, Leon	Peterborough United	Torquay United	
29 Cooper, Shaun D.	Portsmouth	Kidderminster Harriers	
22 Craig, Tony A.	Millwall	Wycombe Wanderers	
29 Cranie, Martin J.	Southampton	AFC Bournemouth	
22 Curtis, John C.K.	Portsmouth	Preston North End	
22 Daly, Jonathan M.	Stockport County	Grimsby Town	
11 Danns, Neil A.	Blackburn Rovers	Colchester United	
28 Dinning, Tony	Wigan Athletic	Bristol City	
15 Dolan, Joseph	Millwall	Crawley Town	
14 Donaldson, Clayton A.	Hull City	Harrogate Town	
22 Doyle, Colin	Birmingham City	Chester City	
15 Duberry, Michael W.	Leeds United	Stoke City	
25 Duffy, Richard	Portsmouth	Burnley	
4 Eastwood, Freddy	Grays Athletic	Southend United	
7 Eyre, Nicholas	Tottenham Hotspur	Grays Athletic	
11 Featherstone, Lee	Scunthorpe United	Barrow	
17 Fontaine, Liam V.H.	Fulham	Yeovil Town	
29 Foster, Benjamin	Stoke City	Kidderminster Harriers	
7 Fox, David L.	Manchester United	Shrewsbury Town	
7 Gleeson, Jamie	Kidderminster Harriers	Eastleigh	
6 Goodfellow, Marc D.	Bristol City	Port Vale	
12 Gould, Jonathan A.	Preston North End	Hereford United	
25 Guimaraes, Sanabio J.L.	Derby County	Rotherham United	
12 Harper, Kevin P.	Portsmouth	Leicester City	
29 Hildred, Ashley	Grimsby Town	Northwich Victoria	
15 Hockless, Graham	Grimsby Town	Leigh RMI	
14 Howe, Edward J.	Portsmouth	AFC Bournemouth	
29 Hunt, Jonathan	Scunthorpe United	Guiseley	
14 Ibe, Kezie	Yeovil Town	Tiverton Town	
15 Ikeme, Carl	Wolverhampton Wanderers	Accrington Stanley	
16 Ipoua, Guy	Doncaster Rovers	Mansfield Town	
29 Jenkins, Stephen R.	Peterborough United	Swindon Town	
27 Johnson, Richard M.	Queens Park Rangers	Milton Keynes Dons	
8 Johnson, Simon A.	Leeds United	Sunderland	
4 Keogh, Andrew D.	Leeds United	Scunthorpe United	
22 Kightly, Michael J.	Southend United	Farnborough Town	
8 Langmead, Kelvin S.	Preston North End	Kidderminster Harriers	
29 Laville, Florent	Bolton Wanderers	Coventry City	
11 Leacock, Dean	Fulham	Coventry City	
2 Loxton, Craig A.	Bristol City	Forest Green Rovers	
6 Mansaram, Darren	Grimsby Town	Halifax Town	
6 May, Ben S.	Millwall	Colchester United	
22 McCormick, Luke M.	Plymouth Argyle	Boston United	
6 McMahon, Stephen J.	Blackpool	Kidderminster Harriers	
22 McStay, Henry M.P.	Leeds United	Halifax Town	
1 Meadowcroft, Daniel B.	Stockport County	Mossley	
4 Mitchell, Paul A.	Wigan Athletic	Swindon Town	
22 Moore, David L.	Wigan Athletic	Bradford Park Avenue	
13 Mulligan, Gary	Wolverhampton Wanderers	Rushden & Diamonds	
8 Murphy, Joseph	West Bromwich Albion	Walsall	
1 Murphy, Paul	Manchester City	Mossley	
4 O'Connor, James F.E.	Aston Villa	Port Vale	
28 O'Connor, James	West Bromwich Albion	Burnley	
25 O'Grady, Christopher	Leicester City	Notts County	
22 Otsemobor, John	Liverpool	Crewe Alexandra	
13 Peat, Nathan N.M.	Hull City	Lincoln City	
7 Powell, Christopher G.	Charlton Athletic	West Ham United	
21 Pullen, James	Peterborough United	Welling United	
9 Rachubka, Paul S.	Charlton Athletic	Northampton Town	
15 Reed, Steven	Yeovil Town	Forest Green Rovers	
15 Ricketts, Rohan A.	Tottenham Hotspur	Coventry City	
1 Rifat, Ahmet	Reading	Kingstonian	
30 Royce, Simon E.	Charlton Athletic	Luton Town	
19 Simek, Franklin M.	Arsenal	Queens Park Rangers	
31 Simpson, Sekani	Bristol City	Tamworth	
1 Spicer, John W.	Arsenal	AFC Bournemouth	
14 Staff, David S.	Boston United	King's Lynn	
1 Stallard, Mark	Barnsley	Chesterfield	

Player	From	To	Fee
22 Talbot, Daniel	Rushden & Diamonds	Cambridge City	
1 Tessem, Jo	Southampton	Millwall	
22 Thomas, Bradley M.	Peterborough United	Welling United	
22 Togwell, Samuel J.	Crystal Palace	Oxford United	
22 Traynor, Greg	Wigan Athletic	Bradford Park Avenue	
6 Turnbull, Ross	Middlesbrough	Barnsley	
5 Turner, Michael T.	Charlton Athletic	Brentford	
25 Veira, Magno S.	Wigan Athletic	Carlisle United	
15 Weaver, Simon D.	Lincoln City	Macclesfield Town	
22 Wheeler, Kirk	Grimsby Town	Ossett Town	
29 Wilbraham, Aaron	Hull City	Oldham Athletic	
24 Woodman, Craig A.	Bristol City	Mansfield Town	
13 Woods, Martin P.	Leeds United	Hartlepool United	
7 Young, Gregory J.	Grimsby Town	Northwich Victoria	

NOVEMBER 2004

Player	From	To	Fee
17 Agyemang, Patrick	Gillingham	Preston North End	350,000
26 Barker, Richard I.	Rotherham United	Mansfield Town	Free
15 Beckett, Luke J.	Stockport County	Sheffield United	50,000
30 Campbell-Ryce, Jamal	Charlton Athletic	Rotherham United	nominal
19 Clare, Daryl A.	Chester City	Boston United	undisclosed
9 Dobie, Scott	West Bromwich Albion	Millwall	500,000
4 Eastwood, Freddie	Grays Athletic	Southend United	undisclosed
26 Lester, Jack	Sheffield United	Nottingham Forest	50,000
5 Lowndes, Nathan P.	Plymouth Argyle	Port Vale	Free
15 Miller, Adam E.	Aldershot Town	Queens Park Rangers	50,000
5 Nowland, Adam C.	West Ham United	Nottingham Forest	250,000
12 Purser, Wayne M.	Hornchurch	Peterborough United	Free
24 Sedgwick, Christopher E.	Rotherham United	Preston North End	300,000
4 Turner, Michael T.	Charlton Athletic	Brentford	nominal
23 Welsh, Andrew	Stockport County	Sunderland	15,000

TEMPORARY TRANSFERS

Player	From	To
5 Barnard, Lee J.	Tottenham Hotspur	Leyton Orient
20 Barnett, Leon P.	Luton Town	Aylesbury United
3 Bischoff, Mikkel	Manchester City	Wolverhampton Wanderers
18 Brisco, Neil A.	Rochdale	Northwich Victoria
11 Broughton, Drewe O.	Southend United	Rushden & Diamonds
8 Cahill, Gary J.	Aston Villa	Burnley
28 Campbell-Ryce, Jamal	Charlton Athletic	Rotherham United
19 Carruthers, Christopher P.	Northampton Town	Hornchurch
29 Chopra, Rocky M.	Newcastle United	Barnsley
12 Clarke, Ryan J.	Bristol Rovers	Kidderminster Harriers
8 Clingan, Samuel G.	Wolverhampton Wanderers	Chesterfield
20 Coghlan, Michael	Darlington	Bishop Auckland
4 Corbett, Luke J.	Cheltenham Town	Weston-Super-Mare
19 Craig, Tony A.	Millwall	Wycombe Wanderers
11 Croft, Lee	Manchester City	Oldham Athletic
5 Dixon, Jonathan J.	Wycombe Wanderers	Aldershot Town
15 Dolan, Joseph	Millwall	Crawley Town
12 Forde, Daniel	Oldham Athletic	Mossley
1 Gobern, Lewis T.	Wolverhampton Wanderers	Hartlepool United
5 Grant, Lee	Aston Villa	York City
23 Guimaraes, Sanabio J.L.	Derby County	Rotherham United
25 Haystead, Daniel	Sheffield United	Scarborough
19 Hicks, David	Northampton Town	Hornchurch
19 Hughes, Mark A.	Tottenham Hotspur	Oldham Athletic
15 Ibe, Kezie	Yeovil Town	Tiverton Town
1 Ingham, Michael	Sunderland	Doncaster Rovers
4 Jones, Bradley	Middlesbrough	Blackpool
26 Kaku, Blessing	Bolton Wanderers	Derby County
12 Keller, Kasey C.	Tottenham Hotspur	Southampton
18 Kerley, Adam	Lincoln City	Lincoln United
23 Kightly, Michael J.	Southend United	Farnborough Town
19 Kilkenny, Neil M.	Birmingham City	Oldham Athletic
26 Langmead, Kelvin S.	Preston North End	Shrewsbury Town
30 Laville, Florent	Bolton Wanderers	Coventry City
26 MacKenzie, Neil	Mansfield Town	Macclesfield Town
5 Marney, Dean E.	Tottenham Hotspur	Gillingham
11 McLachlan, Fraser	Stockport County	Mansfield Town
11 Mulligan, Gary	Wolverhampton Wanderers	Rushden & Diamonds
12 Nolan, Matthew L.	Peterborough United	St Albans City
11 Oakes, Andrew M.	Derby County	Bolton Wanderers
3 O'Connor, James F.E.	Aston Villa	Port Vale
29 O'Connor, James	West Bromwich Albion	Burnley
5 Oster, John	Sunderland	Leeds United
23 Otsemobor, John	Liverpool	Crewe Alexandra
12 Peters, Mark	Leyton Orient	Aldershot Town
4 Powell, Christopher G.	Charlton Athletic	West Ham United
19 Powell, Darren	Crystal Palace	West Ham United
19 Price, Lewis P.	Ipswich Town	Cambridge United
5 Rachubka, Paul S.	Charlton Athletic	Huddersfield Town
15 Reed, Steven	Yeovil Town	Forest Green Rovers
1 Rifat, Ahmet	Reading	Kingstonian
29 Simpson, Sekani	Bristol City	Tamworth
12 Smith, Andrew W.	Preston North End	Stockport County
11 Spicer, John W.	Arsenal	AFC Bournemouth
15 Staff, David S.	Boston United	King's Lynn
7 Stallard, Mark	Barnsley	Chesterfield
5 Stamp, Darryn	Chester City	Kidderminster Harriers
19 Talbot, Jason C.	Bolton Wanderers	Mansfield Town
18 Taylor, Stuart J.	Arsenal	Leicester City
1 Tessem, Jo	Southampton	Millwall
8 Turnbull, Ross	Middlesbrough	Barnsley
11 Vieira, Magno S.	Wigan Athletic	Carlisle United

26 Warne, Paul	Rotherham United	Mansfield Town	
5 Watson, Andrew	Chester City	Forest Green Rovers	
11 Weaver, Simon D.	Lincoln City	Macclesfield Town	
22 Wheeler, Kirk	Grimsby Town	Ossett Town	
3 Yetton, Stewart D.	Plymouth Argyle	Weymouth	

DECEMBER 2004

17 Anderson, Stuart	Southampton	Blackpool	undisclosed
10 Beardsley, Christopher K.	Doncaster Rovers	Kidderminster Harriers	Free
14 Birch, Gary S.	Walsall	Kidderminster Harriers	Free
6 Brown, Simon	West Bromwich Albion	Mansfield Town	50,000
24 Buxton, Lewis E.	Portsmouth	Stoke City	Free
10 Constantine, Leon	Peterborough United	Torquay United	75,000
17 Cullip, Daniel	Brighton & Hove Albion	Sheffield United	250,000
10 Currie, Darren	Brighton & Hove Albion	Ipswich Town	250,000
24 Danns, Neil A.	Blackburn Rovers	Colchester United	nominal
16 Davies, Arron R.	Southampton	Yeovil Town	undisclosed
24 Gritton, Martin	Torquay United	Grimsby Town	undisclosed
30 Langmead, Kelvin S.	Preston North End	Shrewsbury Town	nominal
23 Lyng, Ciaran	Preston North End	Shrewsbury Town	undisclosed
24 McIntyre, Kevin	Chester City	Macclesfield Town	undisclosed
20 Morrison, John O.	Stockport County	Bradford City	undisclosed
17 Powell, Christopher G.	Charlton Athletic	West Ham United	Free
24 Pulis, Anthony J.	Portsmouth	Stoke City	Free
6 Rachubka, Paul S.	Charlton Athletic	Huddersfield Town	Free
17 Spicer, John W.	Arsenal	AFC Bournemouth	10,000
30 Taylor, Scott J.	Blackpool	Plymouth Argyle	100,000
9 Weaver, Simon D.	Lincoln City	Kidderminster Harriers	Free
9 Williams, Gavin J.	Yeovil Town	West Ham United	250,000

TEMPORARY TRANSFERS

16 Angus, Stevland D.	Cambridge United	Hull City
21 Arber, Mark A.	Oldham Athletic	Peterborough United
9 Ashton, Neil J.	Tranmere Rovers	Shrewsbury Town
10 Awuah, Jones	Gillingham	Worthing
8 Barnard, Lee J.	Tottenham Hotspur	Leyton Orient
16 Bayliss, David A.	Luton Town	Chester City
31 Benjamin, Trevor J.	Leicester City	Northampton Town
10 Bennett, Ian M.	Birmingham City	Sheffield United
17 Best, Leon J.	Southampton	Queens Park Rangers
31 Blake, Nathan A.	Leicester City	Leeds United
3 Braniff, Kevin	Millwall	Canvey Island
30 Branston, Guy	Sheffield Wednesday	Peterborough United
31 Brisco, Neil A.	Rochdale	Northwich Victoria
17 Broughton, Drewe O	Southend United	Wycombe Wanderers
24 Brown, Michael	Preston North End	Chester City
23 Bruce, Alex	Blackburn Rovers	Oldham Athletic
9 Burch, Robert K.	Tottenham Hotspur	West Ham United
2 Cahill, Gary J.	Aston Villa	Burnley
6 Chillingworth, Daniel T.	Cambridge United	Leyton Orient
3 Clarke, Ryan A.	Boston United	Leigh RMI
16 Clarke, Ryan J.	Bristol Rovers	Kidderminster Harriers
21 Coghlan, Michael	Darlington	Bishop Auckland
10 Cooke, Stephen L.	Aston Villa	Wycombe Wanderers
31 Corbett, Luke J.	Cheltenham Town	Bath City
20 Craig, Tony A.	Millwall	Wycombe Wanderers
12 Croft, Lee	Manchester City	Oldham Athletic
23 Danze, Anthony	Crystal Palace	Milton Keynes Dons
16 De Oliveira, Filipe V.	Chelsea	Preston North End
24 Derry, Shaun	Crystal Palace	Nottingham Forest
17 Dixon, Jonathan J.	Wycombe Wanderers	Aldershot Town
20 Dolan, Joseph	Millwall	Crawley Town
24 Doyle, Colin	Birmingham City	Nottingham Forest
31 Ellegaard, Kevin S.	Manchester City	Blackpool
10 Gallacher, Paul	Norwich City	Gillingham
22 Graham, Luke	Northampton Town	Aylesbury United
5 Grant, Lee	Aston Villa	York City
27 Hamilton, Lewis E.	Queens Park Rangers	Kingstonian
17 Hanlon, Ritchie K.	Stevenage Borough	Lincoln City
18 Harrold, Matthew	Brentford	Dagenham & Redbridge
22 Haystead, Daniel	Sheffield United	Scarborough
26 Hearn, Charles R.	Millwall	Northampton Town
6 Heath, Colin	Manchester United	Cambridge United
3 Henderson, Wayne	Aston Villa	Notts County
16 Hillier, Ian M.	Luton Town	Chester City
22 Holmes, Lee D.	Derby County	Swindon Town
18 Hughes, Mark A.	Tottenham Hotspur	Oldham Athletic
24 Ibe, Kezie	Yeovil Town	Exeter City
23 Jackson, Johnnie	Tottenham Hotspur	Watford
30 James, Kevin E.	Nottingham Forest	Boston United
6 Johnson, Simon A.	Leeds United	Doncaster Rovers
17 Jones, Kenwyne J.	Southampton	Sheffield Wednesday
24 Jones, Paul S.	Wolverhampton Wanderers	Watford
21 Karbassiyon, Daniel	Arsenal	Ipswich Town
31 Kempson, Darren	Preston North End	Morecambe
24 Kightly, Michael J.	Southend United	Farnborough Town
30 Kilkenny, Neil M.	Birmingham City	Oldham Athletic
24 Livesey, Daniel	Bolton Wanderers	Carlisle United
3 Loran, Tyrone	Tranmere Rovers	Port Vale
16 Lynch, Simon	Preston North End	Blackpool
31 Maloney, Jonathan	Doncaster Rovers	York City
3 May, Ben S.	Millwall	Brentford
16 McCammon, Mark J.	Millwall	Brighton & Hove Albion
12 McLachlan, Fraser	Stockport County	Mansfield Town
23 McShane, Paul D.	Manchester United	Walsall

9 Mitchell, Paul A.	Wigan Athletic	Milton Keynes Dons	
10 Morrison, John O.	Stockport County	Bradford City	
13 Mulligan, Gary	Wolverhampton Wanderers	Rushden & Diamonds	
17 Mullins, John	Reading	Kidderminster Harriers	
31 Murphy, Joseph	West Bromwich Albion	Walsall	
21 Nacca, Francesco	Cambridge United	Histon	
17 Navarro, Alan E.	Tranmere Rovers	Macclesfield Town	
3 O'Brien, Joseph M.	Bolton Wanderers	Sheffield Wednesday	
3 O'Brien, Roy	Yeovil Town	Weymouth	
31 O'Donoghue, Paul M.	Tottenham Hotspur	Hornchurch	
6 Oster, John	Sunderland	Leeds United	
10 Pearson, Gregory	West Ham United	Canvey Island	
19 Price, Lewis P.	Ipswich Town	Cambridge United	
24 Pulis, Anthony J.	Stoke City	Torquay United	
23 Robinson, Paul M.J.	Millwall	Torquay United	
31 Slabber, Jamie	Tottenham Hotspur	Swindon Town	
3 Somner, Matthew J.	Brentford	Cambridge United	
13 Steele, Luke	Manchester United	Coventry City	
10 Strong, Greg	Boston United	Macclesfield Town	
17 Taylor, Kris	Walsall	Burton Albion	
18 Taylor, Stuart J.	Arsenal	Leicester City	
31 Teggart, Neil	Sunderland	Scunthorpe United	
10 Tierney, Marc	Oldham Athletic	Carlisle United	
21 Tierney, Paul T.	Manchester United	Bradford City	
3 Tomlinson, Stuart C.	Crewe Alexandra	Stafford Rangers	
29 Ward, Elliott L.	West Ham United	Bristol Rovers	
23 Warne, Paul	Rotherham United	Mansfield Town	
6 Watson, Andrew	Chester City	Forest Green Rovers	
31 Westcarr, Craig N.	Nottingham Forest	Lincoln City	
22 Wheeler, Kirk	Grimsby Town	Ossett Town	
10 Williams, Ryan N.	Bristol Rovers	Forest Green Rovers	
6 Woodman, Craig A.	Bristol City	Torquay United	
2 Young, Gregory J.	Grimsby Town	Northwich Victoria	

JANUARY 2005

11 Ashton, Dean	Crewe Alexandra	Norwich City	3,000,000
1 Babayaro, Celestine	Chelsea	Newcastle United	1,000,000
5 Beattie, James S.	Southampton	Everton	6,000,000
5 Blake, Robert J.	Burnley	Birmingham City	1,250,000
26 Bruce, Alex	Blackburn Rovers	Birmingham City	Free
21 Carson, Scott P.	Leeds United	Liverpool	750,000
31 Chaplow, Richard D.	Burnley	West Bromwich Albion	1,500,000
31 Dawson, Michael R.	Nottingham Forest	Tottenham Hotspur	8,000,000 combined
31 Djemba-Djemba, Eric D.	Manchester United	Aston Villa	1,350,000
12 Ellison, Kevin	Chester City	Hull City	100,000
25 Faye, Amdy M.	Portsmouth	Newcastle United	2,000,000
10 Hill, Matthew C.	Bristol City	Preston North End	100,000
25 Jelleyman, Gareth A.	Peterborough United	Mansfield Town	undisclosed
25 Livesey, Daniel	Bolton Wanderers	Carlisle United	Free
21 Mansaram, Darren	Grimsby Town	Halifax Town	5000
14 McGrath, John M.	Doncaster Rovers	Kidderminster Harriers	Free
7 McLachlan, Fraser	Stockport County	Mansfield Town	undisclosed
13 Morley, David T.	Doncaster Rovers	Macclesfield Town	15,000
11 Nugent, David J.	Bury	Preston North End	undisclosed
13 Platt, Clive L.	Peterborough United	Milton Keynes Dons	undisclosed
20 Quashie, Nigel F.	Portsmouth	Southampton	2,100,000
4 Redknapp, Jamie F.	Tottenham Hotspur	Southampton	Free
31 Reid, Andrew M.	Nottingham Forest	Tottenham Hotspur	8,000,000 combined
19 Savage, Robert W.	Birmingham City	Blackburn Rovers	3,100,000
31 Stockdale, Robert K.	Rotherham United	Hull City	Free
31 Stuart, Graham C.	Charlton Athletic	Norwich City	undisclosed
13 Swailes, Daniel	Bury	Macclesfield Town	40,000

TEMPORARY TRANSFERS

15 Angus, Stevland D.	Cambridge United	Hull City
13 Anyinsah, Joseph G.	Bristol City	Hereford United
14 Bayliss, David A.	Luton Town	Chester City
14 Beckett, Luke J.	Sheffield United	Huddersfield Town
7 Blayney, Alan	Southampton	Rushden & Diamonds
26 Brisco, Neil A.	Rochdale	Northwich Victoria
27 Bruce, Alex	Birmingham City	Oldham Athletic
7 Burch, Robert K.	Tottenham Hotspur	Stevenage Borough
31 Camara, Henri	Wolverhampton Wanderers	Southampton
26 Carruthers, Christopher P.	Northampton Town	Kettering Town
28 Carruthers, Martin G.	Lincoln City	Cambridge United
13 Claridge, Stephen E.	Brentford	Wycombe Wanderers
13 Clarke, Darrell J.	Hartlepool United	Stockport County
7 Clarke, Ryan A.	Boston United	Leigh RMI
20 Constable, Robert A.	Leeds United	York City
28 Cooper, Kenneth S.	Manchester United	Oldham Athletic
17 Croft, Lee	Manchester City	Oldham Athletic
17 Crouch, Ross A.	Colchester United	Redbridge
4 Davenport, Calum R.P.	Tottenham Hotspur	Southampton
12 Davies, Andrew	Middlesbrough	Queens Park Rangers
24 Derry, Shaun	Crystal Palace	Nottingham Forest
18 Diao, Salif	Liverpool	Birmingham City
21 Dolan, Joseph	Millwall	Stockport County
14 Doughty, Philip M.	Blackpool	Leigh RMI
26 Duffy, Richard	Portsmouth	Coventry City
13 Duffy, Robert J.	Rushden & Diamonds	Stamford AFC
21 Eagles, Christopher M.	Manchester United	Watford
28 Elliot, Robert	Charlton Athletic	Notts County
27 Elokobi, George N.	Colchester United	Chester City
7 Featherstone, Lee	Scunthorpe United	Harrogate Town
21 Fitzgerald, John	Blackburn Rovers	Bury

14 Fitzgerald, Scott	Watford	Leyton Orient	
28 Flitney, Ross	Fulham	Doncaster Rovers	
28 Flynn, Liam D.	Bradford City	Guiseley	
7 Folly, Yoann	Southampton	Nottingham Forest	
24 Fowler, Jordan	Arsenal	Chesterfield	
11 Gillespie, Steven	Bristol City	Cheltenham Town	
5 Grant, Lee	Aston Villa	York City	
25 Green, Adam	Fulham	Sheffield Wednesday	
6 Griffit, Leandre	Southampton	Leeds United	
21 Harrison, Paul A.	Liverpool	Leeds United	
14 Hillier, Ian M.	Luton Town	Chester City	
21 Holloway, Craig D.	Farnborough Town	Southend United	
24 Holmes, Lee D.	Derby County	Swindon Town	
24 Hughes, Mark A.	Tottenham Hotspur	Oldham Athletic	
10 Ireland, Craig	Peterborough United	Bristol City	
7 Jarrett, Jason L.	Wigan Athletic	Stoke City	
21 Jelleyman, Gareth A.	Peterborough United	Mansfield Town	
5 Johnson, Simon A.	Leeds United	Doncaster Rovers	
26 Jones, Paul S.	Wolverhampton Wanderers	Watford	
23 Karbassiyon, Daniel	Arsenal	Ipswich Town	
14 Keogh, Andrew D.	Leeds United	Bury	
6 Kozluk, Robert	Sheffield United	Preston North End	
17 Lynch, Simon	Preston North End	Blackpool	
10 Maloney, Jonathan	Doncaster Rovers	York City	
13 Marshall, Shaun A.	Cambridge United	Stevenage Borough	
5 May, Ben S.	Millwall	Brentford	
27 McCafferty, Neil	Charlton Athletic	Rushden & Diamonds	
28 McCammon, Mark J.	Millwall	Brighton & Hove Albion	
21 McMaster, Jamie	Leeds United	Peterborough United	
20 Mirza, Nicolas	Yeovil Town	Weymouth	
9 Mitchell, Paul A.	Wigan Athletic	Milton Keynes Dons	
21 Moore, David L.	Wigan Athletic	Bury	
17 Navarro, Alan E.	Tranmere Rovers	Macclesfield Town	
7 Neal, Christopher M.	Preston North End	Tamworth	
28 Negouai, Christian	Manchester City	Coventry City	
21 Newey, Thomas	Leyton Orient	Cambridge United	
4 O'Brien, Joseph M.	Bolton Wanderers	Sheffield Wednesday	
4 O'Brien, Roy	Yeovil Town	Weymouth	
27 O'Neill, Joseph	Preston North End	Chester City	
31 Pennant, Jermaine	Arsenal	Birmingham City	
28 Rapley, Kevin J.	Chester City	Forest Green Rovers	
21 Rawle, Mark A.	Oxford United	Tamworth	
7 Rea, Simon	Peterborough United	Cambridge United	
31 Richardson, Kieran E.	Manchester United	West Bromwich Albion	
23 Robinson, Paul M.J.	Millwall	Torquay United	
13 Royce, Simon E.	Charlton Athletic	Queens Park Rangers	
21 Sharp, William	Sheffield United	Rushden & Diamonds	
5 Somner, Matthew J.	Brentford	Cambridge United	
28 Surman, Andrew R.	Southampton	Walsall	
14 Taylor, Kris	Walsall	Burton Albion	
5 Thomas, Bradley M.	Peterborough United	Weymouth	
5 Tierney, Marc	Oldham Athletic	Carlisle United	
4 Tomlinson, Stuart C.	Crewe Alexandra	Stafford Rangers	
21 Watkins, Robert J.	Fulham	Crawley Town	
11 Williams, Ryan N.	Bristol Rovers	Forest Green Rovers	
28 Yelldell, David R.	Blackburn Rovers	Brighton & Hove Albion	
2 Young, Gregory J.	Grimsby Town	Northwich Victoria	
FEBRUARY 2005			
24 Akinbiyi, Adeola P.	Stoke City	Burnley	600,000
23 Beevers, Lee J.	Boston United	Lincoln City	50,000
16 Benjamin, Trevor J.	Northampton Town	Coventry City	undisclosed
18 Branston, Guy	Sheffield Wednesday	Oldham Athletic	Free
9 Chadwick, Nicholas E.	Everton	Plymouth Argyle	250,000
10 Claridge, Stephen E.	Brentford	Wycombe Wanderers	Free
11 Daly, Jonathan M.	Stockport County	Hartlepool United	undisclosed
18 Derry, Shaun	Crystal Palace	Leeds United	250,000
25 Dobie, Scott	Millwall	Nottingham Forest	525,000
28 Fagan, Craig	Colchester United	Hull City	150,000
3 Flynn, Michael J.	Wigan Athletic	Gillingham	Free
14 Friio, David	Plymouth Argyle	Nottingham Forest	100,000
21 Hall, Marcus T.J.	Stoke City	Coventry City	Free
2 Harper, Kevin P.	Portsmouth	Stoke City	undisclosed
23 Holmes, Derek	AFC Bournemouth	Carlisle United	undisclosed
15 Hughes, Mark A.	Tottenham Hotspur	Oldham Athletic	Free
18 Jackson, Mark G.	Scunthorpe United	Kidderminster Harriers	Free
14 Keogh, Andrew D.	Leeds United	Scunthorpe United	50,000
17 Lambert, Rickie L.	Stockport County	Rochdale	25,000
1 MacKenzie, Neil	Mansfield Town	Macclesfield Town	undisclosed
16 Makin, Christopher	Leicester City	Derby County	undisclosed
4 McCammon, Mark J.	Millwall	Brighton & Hove Albion	Free
3 Rocastle, Craig A.	Chelsea	Sheffield Wednesday	Free
2 Thomas, Bradley M.	Peterborough United	Weymouth	Free
TEMPORARY TRANSFERS			
3 Amankwaah, Kevin	Bristol City	Yeovil Town	
1 Angus, Stevland D.	Cambridge United	Scunthorpe United	
1 Atieno, Taiwo L.	Walsall	Chester City	
3 Barnes, Philip K.	Sheffield United	Torquay United	
14 Beckett, Luke J.	Sheffield United	Huddersfield Town	
21 Beevers, Lee J.	Boston United	Lincoln City	
17 Bennett, Ian M.	Birmingham City	Coventry City	
11 Bermingham, Karl	Manchester City	Lincoln City	
1 Blackstock, Dexter A.T.	Southampton	Plymouth Argyle	
25 Bridge-Wilkinson, Marc	Stockport County	Bradford City	

2 Clark, Christopher J.	Portsmouth	Stoke City	
4 Clarke, Ryan A.	Boston United	Leigh RMI	
4 Coulson, Mark D.	Peterborough United	Dunstable Town	
15 Crow, Daniel	Norwich City	Northampton Town	
21 Day, Christopher N.	Queens Park Rangers	Preston North End	
20 Dolan, Joseph	Millwall	Stockport County	
26 Facey, Delroy M.	Hull City	Huddersfield Town	
22 Fallon, Rory	Swindon Town	Yeovil Town	
22 Fitzgerald, John	Blackburn Rovers	Bury	
24 Folkes, Peter A.	Lincoln City	Stamford AFC	
27 Fowler, Jordan	Arsenal	Chesterfield	
18 Foy, Robert A.	Liverpool	Chester City	
26 Gillespie, Steven	Bristol City	Cheltenham Town	
25 Graham, Luke	Northampton Town	Kettering Town	
3 Gray, Michael	Blackburn Rovers	Leeds United	
8 Harkins, Gary	Blackburn Rovers	Bury	
18 Harris, Andrew D.D.	Chester City	Forest Green Rovers	
15 Healy, Joe B.	Millwall	Crawley Town	
1 Hessenthaler, Andrew	Gillingham	Hull City	
24 Holmes, Lee D.	Derby County	Swindon Town	
8 Hulse, Robert W.	West Bromwich Albion	Leeds United	
18 Hurst, Kevan	Sheffield United	Stockport County	
25 Ibe, Kezi	Yeovil Town	Weymouth	
11 Ipoua, Guy	Doncaster Rovers	Lincoln City	
7 Ireland, Craig	Peterborough United	Bristol City	
1 Jackson, Johnnie	Tottenham Hotspur	Watford	
4 Jackson, Nathan	Walsall	Bromsgrove Rovers	
24 Johnson, Simon A.	Leeds United	Barnsley	
14 Jones, Kenwyne J.	Southampton	Stoke City	
3 Kempson, Darren	Preston North End	Morecambe	
19 Kerley, Adam	Lincoln City	Spalding United	
21 Lynch, Simon	Preston North End	Blackpool	
24 Mackie, James	Milton Keynes Dons	Havant & Waterlooville	
28 Maloney, Jonathan	Doncaster Rovers	York City	
8 May, Ben S.	Millwall	Brentford	
28 McCafferty, Neil	Charlton Athletic	Rushden & Diamonds	
25 McHale, Christopher M.J.	Kidderminster Harriers	Redditch United	
9 Melville, Andrew R.	West Ham United	Nottingham Forest	
21 Mills, Matthew C.	Southampton	AFC Bournemouth	
21 Mirza, Nicolas	Yeovil Town	Weymouth	
10 Mitchell, Paul A.	Wigan Athletic	Milton Keynes Dons	
21 Moore, David L.	Wigan Athletic	Bury	
7 Neal, Christopher M.	Preston North End	Tamworth	
24 Newey, Thomas	Leyton Orient	Cambridge United	
3 Noble, Stuart W.	Fulham	Northampton Town	
11 O'Brien, Joseph M.	Bolton Wanderers	Sheffield Wednesday	
18 O'Connor, James F.E.	Aston Villa	AFC Bournemouth	
21 O'Neill, Matthew	Burnley	Accrington Stanley	
7 Paxton, Andrew	Scunthorpe United	Stalybridge Celtic	
22 Pratley, Darren	Fulham	Brentford	
21 Proctor, Michael A.	Rotherham United	Swindon Town	
17 Richardson, Marcus G.	Lincoln City	Rochdale	
22 Ricketts, Michael B.	Leeds United	Stoke City	
24 Robinson, Jake D.	Brighton & Hove Albion	Aldershot Town	
18 Roma, Dominic	Sheffield United	Boston United	
14 Royce, Simon E.	Charlton Athletic	Queens Park Rangers	
11 Savage, Basir M.	Reading	Bury	
15 Scowcroft, James B.	Leicester City	Ipswich Town	
19 Shakes, Ricky U.	Bolton Wanderers	Bristol Rovers	
20 Sharp, William	Sheffield United	Rushden & Diamonds	
18 Shearer, Scott	Coventry City	Rushden & Diamonds	
18 Singh, Harpal	Leeds United	Stockport County	
28 Soares, Louie P.	Reading	Tamworth	
22 Sonner, Daniel J.	Peterborough United	Port Vale	
4 Stallard, Mark	Barnsley	Notts County	
3 Tierney, Marc	Oldham Athletic	Carlisle United	
18 Tomlinson, Stuart C.	Crewe Alexandra	Stafford Rangers	
3 Unsworth, David G.	Portsmouth	Ipswich Town	
1 Walters, Jonathan R.	Hull City	Scunthorpe United	
14 Whittingham, Peter	Aston Villa	Burnley	
18 Wiseman, Scott N.K.	Hull City	Boston United	
MARCH 2005			
9 Adams, Stephen	Plymouth Argyle	Sheffield Wednesday	Free
24 Amankwaah, Kevin	Bristol City	Yeovil Town	undisclosed
11 Asamoah, Derek	Mansfield Town	Lincoln City	undisclosed
24 Deane, Brian C.	Leeds United	Sunderland	Free
3 Duberry, Michael W.	Leeds United	Stoke City	undisclosed
15 Easter, Jermaine	Cambridge United	Boston United	undisclosed
24 Feeney, Warren J.	Stockport County	Luton Town	175,000
29 Fitzgerald, Scott	Watford	Brentford	undisclosed
18 Guttridge, Luke	Cambridge United	Southend United	undisclosed
23 Hunt, David	Leyton Orient	Northampton Town	undisclosed
24 Keane, Michael	Hull City	Rotherham United	Free
2 Keith, Marino	Plymouth Argyle	Colchester United	undisclosed
11 Kirk, Andrew R.	Boston United	Northampton Town	undisclosed
3 McCarthy, Patrick	Manchester City	Leicester City	undisclosed
11 McMaster, Jamie	Leeds United	Chesterfield	undisclosed
24 Moore, Ian R.	Burnley	Leeds United	50,000
2 Moss, Darren M.	Shrewsbury Town	Crewe Alexandra	undisclosed
23 Murray, Adam D.	Mansfield Town	Carlisle United	nominal
23 Nash, Carlo J.	Middlesbrough	Preston North End	undisclosed
11 Newey, Thomas	Leyton Orient	Cambridge United	undisclosed
11 Newton, Shaun O.	Wolverhampton Wanderers	West Ham United	undisclosed

24 O'Connor, James	West Bromwich Albion	Burnley	175,000
24 O'Connor, James F.E.	Aston Villa	AFC Bournemouth	Free
24 Perpetuini, David P.	Wycombe Wanderers	Walsall	undisclosed
24 Robinson, Marvin L. St.C	Walsall	Stockport County	undisclosed
29 Singh, Harpal	Leeds United	Stockport County	undisclosed
23 Sodje, Efteobore	Huddersfield Town	Yeovil Town	Free
18 Sturridge, Dean	Wolverhampton Wanderers	Queens Park Rangers	undisclosed
18 Zadkovich, Ruben A.	Queens Park Rangers	Notts County	undisclosed

TEMPORARY TRANSFERS

6 Amankwaah, Kevin	Bristol City	Yeovil Town
6 Angus, Stevland D.	Cambridge United	Scunthorpe United
4 Barnard, Lee J.	Tottenham Hotspur	Northampton Town
24 Barrett, Graham	Coventry City	Sheffield Wednesday
4 Barrowman, Andrew	Birmingham City	Mansfield Town
24 Bates, Matthew D.	Middlesbrough	Darlington
18 Beckett, Luke J.	Sheffield United	Oldham Athletic
4 Beckwith, Robert	Luton Town	Rugby United
24 Bischoff, Mikkel	Manchester City	Wolverhampton Wanderers
6 Blackstock, Dexter A.T.	Southampton	Plymouth Argyle
24 Blayney, Alan	Southampton	Brighton & Hove Albion
16 Blewitt, Darren L.	West Ham United	Southend United
24 Boshell, Daniel	Oldham Athletic	Bury
9 Bowditch, Dean	Ipswich Town	Burnley
11 Bramble, Tesfaye	Southend United	Cambridge United
8 Briscoe, Michael J.	Macclesfield Town	Burton Albion
22 Brown, Aaron	Queens Park Rangers	Torquay United
10 Bruce, Alex	Birmingham City	Sheffield Wednesday
24 Carruthers, Christopher P.	Northampton Town	Bristol Rovers
7 Cooper, Kenneth S.	Manchester United	Oldham Athletic
24 Cornelly, Christopher	Lincoln City	Spalding United
2 Coulson, Mark D.	Peterborough United	Dunstable Town
31 Coyles, William A.	Leeds United	Carlisle United
18 Cronin, Lance	Crystal Palace	Wycombe Wanderers
22 Crow, Daniel	Norwich City	Northampton Town
24 Cullip, Daniel	Sheffield United	Watford
14 Davies, Andrew	Middlesbrough	Queens Park Rangers
23 Dinning, Tony	Bristol City	Port Vale
24 Dodd, Jason R.	Southampton	Plymouth Argyle
24 Dolan, Joseph	Millwall	Brighton & Hove Albion
27 Dolan, Joseph	Millwall	Stockport County
10 Dougals, Jonathan	Blackburn Rovers	Gillingham
22 Dyer, Lloyd	West Bromwich Albion	Coventry City
31 Elliot, Robert	Charlton Athletic	Notts County
22 Fitzgerald, John	Blackburn Rovers	Bury
4 Fitzgerald, Scott	Watford	Brentford
24 Flitney, Ross	Fulham	Yeading
14 Folly, Yoann	Southampton	Preston North End
21 Foy, Robert A.	Liverpool	Chester City
11 Fulop, Marton	Tottenham Hotspur	Chesterfield
18 Gallacher, Paul	Norwich City	Sheffield Wednesday
14 Garner, Darren	Rotherham United	Torquay United
24 Gerrard, Anthony	Everton	Walsall
23 Goater, Leonard S.	Reading	Coventry City
17 Goodfellow, Marc D.	Bristol City	Colchester United
28 Graham, Luke	Northampton Town	Kettering Town
11 Green, Adam	Fulham	AFC Bournemouth
11 Griffit, Leandre	Southampton	Rotherham United
31 Haldane, Lewis O.	Bristol Rovers	Forest Green Rovers
5 Hamilton, Lewis E.	Queens Park Rangers	AFC Wimbledon
22 Harris, Andrew D.D.	Chester City	Forest Green Rovers
4 Harrold, Matthew	Brentford	Grimsby Town
4 Hessenthaler, Andrew	Gillingham	Hull City
17 Hinds, Richard	Hull City	Scunthorpe United
24 Holloway, Craig D.	Farnborough Town	Southend United
18 Hurst, Kevan	Sheffield United	Stockport County
30 Ibe, Kezie	Yeovil Town	St Albans City
11 Impey, Andrew R.	Nottingham Forest	Millwall
4 Jackson, Ben	Doncaster Rovers	York City
6 Jackson, Johnnie	Tottenham Hotspur	Watford
24 Jarrett, Albert O.	Brighton & Hove Albion	Stevenage Borough
24 Jarvis, Ryan	Norwich City	Colchester United
24 Joachim, Julian K.	Leeds United	Walsall
10 Johnson, David A.	Nottingham Forest	Sheffield United
20 Jones, Kenwyne J.	Southampton	Stoke City
11 Keane, Michael	Hull City	Rotherham United
27 Keith, Joseph R.	Colchester United	Bristol City
3 Kenton, Darren E.	Southampton	Leicester City
24 Kerley, Adam	Lincoln City	Spalding United
4 King, Marlon F.	Nottingham Forest	Leeds United
3 Logan, Carlos S.	Manchester City	Chesterfield
30 McCafferty, Neil	Charlton Athletic	Rushden & Diamonds
24 McClenahan, Trent	West Ham United	Milton Keynes Dons
17 McCormack, Alan	Preston North End	Southend United
10 McEveley, James	Blackburn Rovers	Gillingham
28 McHale, Christopher M.J.	Kidderminster Harriers	Redditch United
4 McMaster, Jamie	Leeds United	Chesterfield
24 Miller, Kevin	Bristol Rovers	Derby County
21 Mills, Matthew C.	Southampton	AFC Bournemouth
11 Moore, Stefan	Aston Villa	Leicester City
24 Morgan, Alan	Blackburn Rovers	Cheltenham Town
18 Morgan, Daniel F.	Oxford United	Brackley Town
18 Nicholas, Andrew P.	Swindon Town	Chester City
20 O'Neill, Matthew	Burnley	Accrington Stanley

18 Ormerod, Brett R.	Southampton	Wigan Athletic	
19 Owen, Gareth J.	Stoke City	Oldham Athletic	
4 Parker, Terry J.	Oxford United	Farnborough Town	
3 Parton, Andrew	Scunthorpe United	Stalybridge Celtic	
23 Pead, Craig G.	Coventry City	Walsall	
24 Perpetuini, David P.	Wycombe Wanderers	Walsall	
25 Pratley, Darren	Fulham	Brentford	
31 Rapley, Kevin J.	Chester City	Droylsden	
24 Richards, Marc J.	Northampton Town	Rochdale	
22 Ricketts, Michael B.	Leeds United	Stoke City	
15 Ricketts, Rohan A.	Tottenham Hotspur	Wolverhampton Wanderers	
1 Roberts, Iwan W.	Gillingham	Cambridge United	
14 Royce, Simon E.	Charlton Athletic	Queens Park Rangers	
24 Ryan, Richard	Sunderland	Scunthorpe United	
11 Salisbury, James A.	Wigan Athletic	Halifax Town	
24 Shakes, Ricky U.	Bolton Wanderers	Bury	
21 Sharp, William	Sheffield United	Rushden & Diamonds	
11 Shearer, Scott	Coventry City	Rushden & Diamonds	
24 Simek, Franklin M.	Arsenal	AFC Bournemouth	
24 Sobers, Jerome	Ipswich Town	Brentford	
24 Sodje, Akpo	Huddersfield Town	Darlington	
23 Sonner, Daniel J.	Peterborough United	Port Vale	
4 Surman, Andrew R.	Southampton	Walsall	
24 Taylor, Daryl S.	Walsall	Hereford United	
14 Thorpe, Anthony L.	Queens Park Rangers	Rotherham United	
24 Togwell, Samuel J.	Crystal Palace	Northampton Town	
19 Toner, Ciaran	Lincoln City	Cambridge United	
24 Townson, Kevin	Rochdale	Macclesfield Town	
18 Turner, Iain R.	Everton	Doncaster Rovers	
24 Ward, Graham W.	Cheltenham Town	Burton Albion	
24 Webber, Daniel V.	Watford	Sheffield United	
24 Westcarr, Craig N.	Nottingham Forest	Milton Keynes Dons	
8 Wilkinson, Andrew G.	Stoke City	Shrewsbury Town	
24 Williams, Leroy D.	Walsall	Hereford United	
3 Williams, Mark S.	Milton Keynes Dons	Rushden & Diamonds	
21 Woozley, David J.	Oxford United	Yeovil Town	
APRIL 2005			
27 Pennant, Jermaine	Arsenal	Birmingham City	undisclosed
TEMPORARY TRANSFERS			
1 Beckwith, Robert	Luton Town	Rugby United	
10 Bowditch, Dean	Ipswich Town	Burnley	
5 Cooney, Sean P.	Coventry City	Woking	
10 Douglas, Jonathan	Blackburn Rovers	Gillingham	
24 Flitney, Ross	Fulham	Yeading	
18 Foy, Robert A.	Liverpool	Chester City	
10 Fulop, Marton	Tottenham Hotspur	Chesterfield	
14 Gallacher, Paul	Norwich City	Sheffield Wednesday	
12 Garner, Darren	Rotherham United	Torquay United	
13 Hinds, Richard	Hull City	Scunthorpe United	
11 Horwood, Evan D.	Sheffield United	Stockport County	
17 Hurst, Kevan	Sheffield United	Stockport County	
4 Jackson, Ben	Doncaster Rovers	York City	
25 Jarrett, Albert O.	Brighton & Hove Albion	Stevenage Borough	
6 Kenton, Darren E.	Southampton	Leicester City	
3 Logan, Carlos S.	Manchester City	Chesterfield	
17 McCormack, Alan	Preston North End	Southend United	
10 McEveley, James	Blackburn Rovers	Gillingham	
26 Mills, Matthew C.	Southampton	AFC Bournemouth	
21 Morgan, Alan W.	Blackburn Rovers	Cheltenham Town	
1 O'Donoghue, Paul M.	Tottenham Hotspur	Heybridge Swifts	
17 Ormerod, Brett R.	Southampton	Wigan Athletic	
27 Owen, Gareth J.	Stoke City	Oldham Athletic	
12 Ricketts, Rohan A.	Tottenham Hotspur	Wolverhampton Wanderers	
3 Robinson, Jake D.	Brighton & Hove Albion	Aldershot Town	
22 Ryan, Richard	Sunderland	Scunthorpe United	
26 Simek, Franklin M.	Arsenal	AFC Bournemouth	
21 Togwell, Samuel J.	Crystal Palace	Northampton Town	
24 Vieira, Magno S.	Wigan Athletic	Carlisle United	
5 Williams, Mark S.	Milton Keynes Dons	Rushden & Diamonds	
24 Woozley, David J.	Oxford United	Yeovil Town	
MAY 2005			
11 Bailey, Matthew	Northwich Victoria	Crewe Alexandra	undisclosed
26 Davies, Simon	Tottenham Hotspur	Everton	3,500,000
24 Ifill, Paul E.	Millwall	Sheffield United	800,000
20 Ruddy, John T.G.	Cambridge United	Everton	250,000
31 Ward, Darren P.	Millwall	Crystal Palace	1,100,000
28 Woodhouse, Curtis	Peterborough United	Hull City	25,000
TEMPORARY TRANSFERS			
11 Blewitt, Darren L.	West Ham United	Southend United	
5 Graham, Luke	Northampton Town	Kettering Town	

THE NEW FOREIGN LEGION 2004–05

JUNE 2004	*From*	*To*	*Fee in £*
30 Albrechtsen, Martin	FC Copenhagen	West Bromwich Albion	2,700,000
8 Fulop, Marton	MTK	Tottenham Hotspur	undisclosed
JULY 2004			
19 Almunia, Manuel	Celta Vigo	Arsenal	500,000
6 Andersen, Stephan	AB Copenhagen	Charlton Athletic	721,000
30 Ben Haim, Tal	Maccabi Tel Aviv	Bolton Wanderers	undisclosed
9 Bisgaard, Morten	FC Copenhagen	Derby County	undisclosed
19 Cech, Petr	Rennes	Chelsea	9,000,000
16 Cisse, Djibril	Auxerre	Liverpool	14,000,000
16 Pedro Mendes	Porto	Tottenham Hotspur	2,000,000
16 De Pedro, Javi	Real Sociedad	Blackburn Rovers	undisclosed
13 De Vlieger, Geert	Willem II	Manchester City	undisclosed
30 Diop, Papa Bouba	Lens	Fulham	undisclosed
23 Drogba, Didier	Marseille	Chelsea	24,000,000
20 Paulo Ferreira	Porto	Chelsea	13,200,000
29 Josemi	Malaga	Liverpool	2,000,000
7 Heinze, Gabriel	Paris St Germain	Manchester United	6,900,000
28 Idiakez, Inigo	Rayo Vallecano	Derby County	Free
14 Jaidi, Radhi	Esperance	Bolton Wanderers	undisclosed
20 Reiziger, Michael	Barcelona	Middlesbrough	undisclosed
22 Robben, Arjen	PSV Eindhoven	Chelsea	13,000,000
23 Rommedahl, Dennis	PSV Eindhoven	Charlton Athletic	2,000,000
30 Ricardo Carvalho	Porto	Chelsea	16,500,000
14 Speroni, Julian	Dundee	Crystal Palace	750,000
30 Tarachulski, Bartosz	Gornik Zabrze	Yeovil Town	undisclosed
5 Van Damme, Jelle	Ajax	Southampton	2,500,000
AUGUST 2004			
27 Xabi Alonso	Real Sociedad	Liverpool	undisclosed
13 Atouba, Timothee	Basle	Tottenham Hotspur	undisclosed
31 Nuno Morais	Penafiel	Chelsea	undisclosed
11 Berson, Mathieu	Nantes	Aston Villa	1,600,000
4 Bosnar, Eddy	Sturm Graz	Everton	undisclosed
31 Contra, Cosmin	Atletico Madrid	West Bromwich Albion	Loan
25 Defendi, Rodrigo	Cruzeiro	Tottenham Hotspur	600,000
11 Drobny, Vaclav	Strasbourg	Aston Villa	undisclosed
5 Edman, Erik	Heerenveen	Tottenham Hotspur	1,300,000
11 Flamini, Mathieu	Marseille	Arsenal	undisclosed
27 Luis Garcia	Barcelona	Liverpool	6,000,000
9 Gera, Zoltan	Ferencvaros	West Bromwich Albion	1,500,000
11 Guatelli, Andrea	Parma	Portsmouth	undisclosed
3 Helveg, Thomas	Internazionale	Norwich City	undisclosed
9 Hierro, Fernando	Al Rayyan	Bolton Wanderers	undisclosed
31 Jakobsson, Andreas	Brondby	Southampton	1,000,000
10 Jonson, Mattias	Brondby	Norwich City	undisclosed
13 Julio Cesar	Real Madrid	Bolton Wanderers	undisclosed
25 Kaku, Blessing	MS Ashdod	Bolton Wanderers	Free
17 Kaviedes, Ivan	Barcelona (Guayaquil)	Crystal Palace	2,000,000
12 Kiraly, Gabor	Hertha Berlin	Crystal Palace	undisclosed
2 Kuszczak, Tomasz	Hertha Berlin	West Bromwich Albion	undisclosed
13 Naybet, Nourredine	La Coruna	Tottenham Hotspur	undisclosed
4 Nilsson, Mikael	Halmstad	Southampton	500,000
18 Nunez, Antonio	Real Madrid	Liverpool	exch.
14 Olofinjana, Seyi	Brann	Wolverhampton Wanderers	1,700,000
24 Pamarot, Noe	Nice	Tottenham Hotspur	1,700,000
27 Pedersen, Morten	Tromso	Blackburn Rovers	1,500,000
13 Silva, Edson	PSV Eindhoven	Tottenham Hotspur	Free
10 Tiago	Benfica	Chelsea	10,000,000
6 Torghelle, Sandor	MTK	Crystal Palace	undisclosed
26 Waterreus, Ronald	PSV Eindhoven	Manchester City	Free
31 Yahia, Alaeddine	Guingamp	Southampton	300,000
31 Ziegler, Reto	Grasshoppers	Tottenham Hotspur	undisclosed
SEPTEMBER 2004			
1 Kamara, Diomansy	Modena	Portsmouth	2,000,000
1 Seol, Ki-Hyeon	Anderlecht	Wolverhampton Wanderers	1,200,000
JANUARY 2005			
28 Mido	Roma	Tottenham Hotspur	Loan
31 Arteta, Mikel	Real Sociedad	Everton	Loan
4 Boumsong, Jean Alain	Rangers	Newcastle United	8,000,000
21 Buzsaky, Akos	Porto	Plymouth Argyle	Loan
31 Candela, Vincent	Roma	Bolton Wanderers	Free
28 Cerny, Radek	Slavia Prague	Tottenham Hotspur	Loan
28 Chalkias, Konstantinos	Panathinaikos	Portsmouth	100,000
7 Eboue, Emmanuel	Beveren	Arsenal	1,540,000
1 Einarsson, Gylfi	Lillestrom	Leeds United	Free
28 El Hamdaoui, Mounir	Excelsior	Tottenham Hotspur	undisclosed
28 Gudmundsson, Tryggvi	Hafnarfjordur	Stoke City	Free
28 Haidong, Hao	Dalian Shide	Sheffield United	Free
6 Hallfredsson, Emil	Hafnarfjordur	Tottenham Hotspur	undisclosed
6 Jarosik, Jiri	CSKA Moscow	Chelsea	3,000,000
13 Johansson, Andreas	Djurgaarden	Wigan Athletic	undisclosed
4 Kuqi, Njazi	Lahti	Birmingham City	400,000
6 Limbersky, David	Viktoria Plzen	Tottenham Hotspur	Loan
5 Mokoena, Aaron	Genk	Blackburn Rovers	300,000
13 Morientes, Fernando	Real Madrid	Liverpool	6,300,000
31 Musampa, Kiki	Atletico Madrid	Manchester City	Loan
31 Nafti, Mehdi	Santander	Birmingham City	Loan
10 Nelsen, Ryan	DC United	Blackburn Rovers	Free
10 Pellegrino, Mauricio	Valencia	Liverpool	Free
31 Plessis, Guillaume	Lens	Everton	Free
31 Rodic, Aleksander	Gorica	Portsmouth	1,000,000
28 Skopelitis, Ioannis	Egaleo	Portsmouth	1,000,000

REFEREEING AND THE LAWS OF THE GAME

The thrust of the Law changes for this forthcoming season relate to substitutes, further clarification of Law 11 relating to offside, fouls and misconduct including penalties and at long last a vital change regarding the taking of throw-ins.

Perhaps the offside Law causes more controversy than any other. Problems have manifested themselves for years as to when a player is level with an opponent either under the old provisions or the new, particularly if a player had some part of his body beyond an opponent, but not all of it. We now have a clear definition which takes in that part of the Law which has always been there namely being "nearer to his opponents' goal line". Now any part of a player's body head or feet being nearer to that line than both the ball and a second last opponent will make the attacker offside. Arms are not included in the definition. Even more problems have come in interpreting when a player is "active". Based on experiences over the last 2 seasons the International Board have decreed –

(a) Interfering with the play means the involvement of a player at least touching a ball projected by his team-mate.
(b) Interfering means preventing an opponent playing or being able to play the ball by obstructing his vision, movements, or making gestures that in the opinion of the referee deceive or distract him.
(c) Gaining an advantage is being initially in an offside position but not interfering with the ball but subsequently playing it when it rebounds from posts, bar or an opponent. Although not referred to in the Laws this is frequently termed a "secondary offside".

On substitutions it is confirmed that in National A team games there is now a maximum of 6 substitutes allowed. In all other matches or dependent on the rules of the competition the teams agree the number prior to the start and inform the referee, who if he is not informed can only allow six. This overcomes the total confusion that occurred in pre-season games last year. There has been some tightening up where a substitute enters the field of play without notifying the referee. After a caution the player goes off and play is restarted with an indirect free kick rather than a drop ball, as before, in order to show the seriousness of the offence.

In regard to fouls and misconduct there are several alterations. The first of these being that a tackle that endangers an opponent MUST be sanctioned as serious foul play which is a dismissal offence. Next another neat clarification confirms that Referees only show red and yellow cards from when they enter the field to when they leave it after the final whistle. Anyone committing an offence thereafter in the technical area or tunnel after the Referee has left the field will be reported for misconduct. There is a tidying up exercise at penalties where encroachment occurs. The Law now explains which it failed to do before what should happen if at a penalty the ball does not enter the goal. Hereafter the game must restart with an indirect free kick to the defending side. This definition relates to (a) the offending player stopping in his run up although it does not apply to feinting and (b) where there is encroachment but the ball rebounds not to the encroacher but to another player who had not previously encroached as this is deemed against the spirit of the Law and is not to be allowed.

Finally, at the throw-in, the Law has been amended to include for the first time the minimum distance an opponent should stand from the thrower. This will mean that the nasty habit of a defender standing almost in front of the thrower to stop him taking a legitimate throw will be stopped. The tactic was actually dangerous because it could have caused injury to the thrower who could have damaged hands or arms or to the opponent who could have received a blow to the face. Furthermore it could have caused argument between the two players. The change also helps those of us who were awarding an indirect free kick for "obstructing the thrower" when not entitled to do so to overcome the problem. The measurement in football distances is unique and the position is that "all opponents must stand no less than two metres from the point from which the throw in is taken". It is presumed that failure to retreat this distance will result in a caution for delaying a restart. Perhaps the distance has been culled from the five- and six-a-side games.

An opportunity has again been missed to change the unfortunate situation at the drop ball where last season – an act of sportsmanship resulted in an unsporting goal but thanks to their opponents the opposition was allowed to run through unimpeded to equalise. A similar problem has occurred in the past in relation to throw-ins. However there is a great reluctance to legislate against perceived sportsmanship but which allows chaos to run wild in these circumstances. Nonetheless there is an experiment to take place (which is arguably unworkable) that relates to the defending side when the Referee has stopped the match to award a free kick. Any such defender who deliberately touches the ball will be considered as delaying the restart of play and will be cautioned. It also applies to a player who touches the ball at a throw-in or corner against his team or takes the ball from the goal net after his team has scored. This will lead to sanctions against players who sportingly attempt to return the ball to their opponents as well as those who cunningly touch the ball away to waste time. A report on this experiment will take place at the next FIFA AGM. More interestingly goal line technology will be the subject of an experiment at the FIFA U-17 World Championship in Peru and at the FIFA Club World Championship in Japan.

From the start of the season commencing 2006 all active registered Referees must have a Child Protection Certificate. This was intended to come in from the start of this campaign but its administration has proved so onerous that the deadline for obtaining clearance of the CRB checks has been extended to 31 December 2005 with re-registration for 2006 dependent on obtaining such clearance. The FA publishes a booklet entitled "Child Protection and Best Practice – A Guide", and has both generously and rightly agreed to pay for all CRB checks for Referees outside of the professional level of the game. These checks are done through the Referee's Local County FA.

The Football Association Match Officials Association (FAMOA) continues its expansion with development days organised around the country and they are now in their fourth series. Produced annually are two News Letters and a Journal whilst the FAOMA's section of the FA's website provide details on such things as fitness and diet advice, and up to date information on the Laws and how to apply them.

Some of the more important Refereeing "plums" fell to the following:

Graham Poll:	Who refereed the UEFA Cup Final between Sporting Lisbon and CSKA Moscow along with Fourth Official Steve Bennett and Assistant Referees Mike Tingay and Glen Turner.
Rob Styles:	Who took charge of the FA Cup Final between Arsenal and Manchester United with Fourth Official Neale Barry and Assistants John Devine and Paul Caradine.
Steve Bennett:	Who Refereed the Carling Cup Final between Chelsea and Manchester United.
Alexandra Ihringova (SVK):	Who Refereed the Women's EURO 2005 Final between Germany and Norway.

KEN GOLDMAN

NATIONAL LIST OF REFEREES FOR SEASON 2005–06

Armstrong, P (Paul) – Berkshire
Atkinson, M (Martin) – Yorkshire
Barry, NS (Neale) – Lincolnshire
Bates, A (Tony) – Staffordshire
Beeby, RJ (Richard) – Northamptonshire
Bennett, SG (Steve) – Kent
Booth, RJ (Russell) – Nottinghamshire
Boyeson, C (Carl) – Yorkshire
Clattenburg, M (Mark) – Tyne & Wear
Cowburn, MG (Mark) – Lancashire
Crossley, PT (Phil) – Kent
Curson, B (Brian) – Leicestershire
Deadman, D (Darren) – Cambridgeshire
Dean, ML (Mike) – Wirral
Dorr, SJ (Steve) – Worcestershire
Dowd, P (Phil) – Staffordshire
Drysdale, D (Darren) – Lincolnshire
Dunn, SW (Steve) – Gloucestershire
D'Urso, AP (Andy) – Essex
Fletcher, M (Mick) – Worcestershire
Foy, CJ (Chris) – Merseyside
Friend, KA (Kevin) – Leicestershire
Gallagher, DJ (Dermot) – Oxfordshire
Hall, AR (Andy) – West Midlands
Halsey, MR (Mark) – Lancashire
Hegley, GK (Grant) – Hertfordshire
Hill, KD (Keith) – Hertfordshire
Ilderton, EL – Tyne & Wear
Jones, MJ (Michael) – Cheshire
Joslin, PJ (Phil) – Nottinghamshire
Kettle, TM (Trevor) – Rutland
Knight, B (Barry) – Kent
Laws, G (Graham) – Tyne & Wear
Leake, AR (Tony) – Lancashire
Lewis, GJ (Gary) – Cambridgeshire
Marriner, AM (Andre) – West Midlands
Mason, LS (Lee) – Lancashire
Mathieson, SW (Scott) – Cheshire
Mellin, PW (Paul) – Surrey
Messias, MD (Matt) – Yorkshire
Miller, NS (Nigel) – Durham
Miller, P (Patrick) – Bedfordshire
Moss, J (Jonathan) – Yorkshire
Oliver, CW (Clive) – Northumberland
Olivier, RJ (Ray) – West Midlands
Parkes, TA (Trevor) – West Midlands
Penn, AM (Andy) – West Midlands
Penton, C (Clive) – Sussex
Pike, MS (Mike) – Cumbria
Poll, G (Graham) – Hertfordshire
Probert, LW (Lee) – Gloucestershire
Prosser, PJ (Phil) – Yorkshire
Rennie, UD (Uriah) – Yorkshire
Riley, MA (Mike) – Yorkshire
Robinson, JP (Paul) – Yorkshire
Russell, MP (Mike) – Hertfordshire
Ryan, M (Michael) – Lancashire
Salisbury, G (Graham) – Lancashire
Singh, J (Jarnail) – Middlesex
Stroud, KP (Keith) – Hampshire
Styles, R (Rob) – Hampshire
Sutton, GJ (Gary) – Lincolnshire
Swarbrick, ND (Neil) – Lancashire
Tanner, SJ, (Steve) – Somerset
Taylor, P (Paul) – Hertfordshire
Thorpe, M (Mike) – Suffolk
Walton, P (Peter) – Northamptonshire
Webb, HM (Howard) – Yorkshire
Webster, CH (Colin) – Tyne & Wear
Wiley, AG (Alan) – Staffordshire
Williamson, IG, (Iain) – Berkshire
Woolmer, KA (Andy) – Northamptonshire
Wright, KK (Kevin) – Cambridgeshire

ASSISTANT REFEREES

No changes announced from last season at time of going to press.

Ansell, I (Ian) – Devon; Appleby, ND (Norman) – Hertfordshire; Artis, SG (Stephen) – Norfolk; Astley, MA (Mark) – Greater Manchester; Aston, GA (Glenn) – W. Midlands; Atkins, G (Graeme) – W. Yorkshire; Babski, DS (Dave) – Lincolnshire; Baker, BD (Bernard) – Hampshire; Bannister, N (Nigel) – E. Yorkshire; Barker, CA (Craig) – W. Yorkshire; Barnes, K G (Kevin) – Wiltshire; Barnes, PW (Paul) – Cambridgeshire; Bassindale, C (Carl) – S. Yorkshire; Beadle, J (Jon) – Kent; Beale, GA (Guy) – Somerset; Beck, SP (Simon) – Essex; Beevor, R (Richard) – Norfolk; Bentley, I F (Ian) – Kent; Benton, DK (David) – S. Yorkshire; Birkett, DJ (Dave) – Lincolnshire; Bone, R (Ralph) – Kent; Bramley, P (Philip) – W. Yorkshire; Bratt, SJ (Steve) – W. Midlands; Brittain, GM (Gary) – S. Yorkshire; Brown, M (Mark) – E. Yorkshire; Brumwell, CA (Chris) – Cumbria; Bryan, DS (Dave) – Lincolnshire; Bull, M (Michael) – Essex; Buller, KR (Keith) – Somerset; Burton, R (Roy) – Staffordshire; Butler, AN (Andrew) – Lancashire; Cairns, MJ (Mike) – Northamptonshire; Canadine, P (Paul) – S. Yorkshire; Cann, DJ (Darren) – Norfolk; Carter, JE (John) – Tyne & Wear; Cassidy, MT (Martin) – Somerset; Castle, S (Steve) – W. Midlands; Chapman, A (Alison) – Berkshire; Chapman, GJ (Gary) – Gloucestershire; Chittenden, S (Steve) – Hertfordshire, ; Clyde, AL (Alec) – S. Yorkshire; Cook, SJ (Steve) – Derbyshire; Cooke, SG (Stephen) – Nottinghamshire; Cooper MA (Mark) – West Midlands, ; Cordy, JN (Jon) – S. Gloucestershire; Coulson, DH (Des) – N. Yorkshire; Creighton, SW (Steve) – Berkshire; Curry, PE (Paul) – Northumberland; Darlow, M (Martin) – Bedfordshire; Deadman, D (Darren) – Cambridgeshire; Desmond, RP (Bob) – Wiltshire; Devine, JP (Jim) – Cleveland; Dewfield, A (Adam) – Leicestershire; Dexter, MC (Martin) – Leicestershire; Dorr, SJ (Steve) – Worcestershire; Drew, S (Steve) – Tyne & Wear; Duncan, SAJ (Scott) – Tyne & Wear; Dunn, C (Carl) – Staffordshire; East, R (Roger) – Wiltshire; Eastwood, P (Peter) – Greater Manchester; Ebbage, M (Martin) – Hampshire; Evans, C (Craig) – Lincolnshire; Evans, IA (Ian) – W. Midlands; Evans, KG (Karl) – Greater Manchester; Evetts, GS (Gary) – Hertfordshire; Farries, J (John) – Oxfordshire; Faulkner, IL (Ian) – Merseyside; Flynn, J (John) – Wiltshire; Foster, D (Dave) – Tyne & Wear; Foulkes, GW (Gary) – Merseyside; Francis, CJ (Chris) – Cambridgeshire; Ganfield, RS (Ron) – Somerset; Garratt, AM (Andy) – W. Midlands; Gate, S (Stan) – Tyne & Wear; Gibbs, PN (Phil) – W. Midlands; Gosling, IJ (Ian) – Kent; Gould, R (Ray) – Staffordshire; Greaves, AJ (Alan) – S. Yorkshire; Green, AJ (Tony) – Leicestershire; Green, RC (Russell) – Gloucestershire; Grove, PJ (Peter) – W. Midlands; Haines, A (Andy) – Tyne & Wear; Halliday, A (Andy) – N. Yorkshire; Hambling, GS (Glenn) – Norfolk; Hancox, N (Neil) – W. Midlands; Harris, IR (Ian) – Cornwall; Harris, MA (Martin) – Lincolnshire; Harwood, CN (Colin) – Greater Manchester; Hawken, MA (Mike) – Cornwall; Hawkes, KJ (Kevin) – Gloucestershire; Hayto, JM (John) – Essex; Haywood, M (Mark) – W. Yorkshire; Hendley, AR (Andy) – W. Midlands; Hewitt, RT (Richard) – N. Yorkshire; Hilton, G (Gary) – Lancashire; Hine, DJ (David) – Worcestershire; Hogg, AS (Andy) – S. Yorkshire; Holbrook, JH (John) – Worcestershire; Holdsworth, RJ (Richard) – W. Yorkshire; Hollick, S (Simon) – Devon; Horton, AJ (Tony) – W. Midlands; Horwood, GD (Graham) – Bedfordshire; Howes, TP (Tim) – Norfolk; Hubbard, JR (Jim) – Leicestershire; Hutchinson, AD (Andrew) – Cheshire; Hutchinson, SM (Mark) – Nottinghamshire; Ingram, KR (Kevin) – W. Midlands; Ives, GL (Gary) – Essex; Ives, M (Mark) – Bedfordshire; James, RG (Ron) – Buckinghamshire; John, MA (Mark) – Surrey; Keane, PJ (Patrick) – W. Midlands; Kellett, DG (Gary) – W. Yorkshire; Kinseley, N (Nick) – Essex; Kirkup, PJ (Peter) – Northamptonshire; Knight, MT (Matthew) – Sussex; Law, GC (Geoff) – Leicestershire; Lee, R (Ray) – Essex; Lewis, RL (Robert) – Shropshire; Linington, JJ (James) – Isle of Wight; Lockhart, R (Bob) – Tyne & Wear; Lodge, JR (John) – Essex; Lomas, WD (Wayne) – S. Yorkshire; McCallum, DA (Dave) – Tyne & Wear; McCoy, MT (Michael) – Kent; McDermid, DS (Danny) – Hampshire; McDonough, M (Mick) – Tyne & Wear; McGee, A (Tony) – Merseyside; McIntosh, WA (Wayne) – Lincolnshire; McPherson, MW (Michael) – Cambridgeshire; Mackrell, EB (Eric) – Hampshire; Malone, B (Brendan) – Wiltshire; Martin, AJ (Andy) – Staffordshire; Martin, EAC (Edward) – Somerset; Martin, PC (Paul) – Northamptonshire; Martin, RW (Rob) – S. Yorkshire; Mason, T (Tony) – Kent; Massey, T (Trevor) – Cheshire; Matadar, M (Mo) – Lancashire; Mattocks, KJ (Kevin) – Lancashire; Mellor, G (Glyn) – Derbyshire; Mellor, GS (Gary) – S. Yorkshire; Merchant, K (Kevin) – Surrey; Miller, P (Patrick) – Bedfordshire; Morrison, DP (Des) – Derbyshire; Moss, J (Jonathon) – W. Yorkshire; Mullarkey, M (Mike) – Devon; Murphy, ME (Michael) – W. Midlands; Murphy, N (Nigel) – Nottinghamshire; Naylor, D (Dave) – Nottinghamshire; Nicholson, AR (Andy) – W. Yorkshire; Nicholson, PW (Paul) – Co. Durham; Nolan, I (Ian) – Lancashire; Norman, PV (Paul) – Dorset; Oliver, M (Michael) – Northumberland; Page, A (Andy) – Derbyshire; Palmer, R (Richard) – Somerset; Parker, AR (Alan) – Derbyshire; Parry, B (Brian) – Co. Durham; Pearce, JE (John) – Essex; Perlejewski, AJ (Andy) – Dorset; Phillips, D (David) – Sussex; Pickavance, SD (Stephen) – S. Yorkshire; Pike, K (Kevin) – Dorset; Pollard, TJ (Trevor) – Suffolk; Pollock, RM (Bob) – Merseyside; Powell, K (Ken) – Co. Durham; Procter-Green, SRM (Shaun) – Lincolnshire; Pryme, GD (Greg) – Essex; Ramsay, W (William) – W. Midlands; Rawcliffe, A (Allan) – Greater Manchester; Rayner, AE (Amy) – Leicestershire; Reeves, CL (Christopher) – E. Yorkshire; Richards, DC (Ceri) – Carmarthenshire; Richardson, D (David) – W. Yorkshire; Roberts, DJ (Danny) – Greater Manchester; Roberts, B (Bob) – Lancashire; Robinson, MG (Martin) – Co. Durham; Rubery, SP (Steve) – Essex; Russell, GR (Geoff) – Northamptonshire; Sainsbury, A (Andrew) – Wiltshire; Sarginson, CD (Christopher) – Staffordshire; Scarr, IK (Ian) – W. Midlands; Scholes, MS (Mark) – Buckinghamshire; Searle, IR (Ian) – Hertfordshire; Sharp, PR (Phil) – Hertfordshire; Sheffield, JA (Alan) – W. Midlands; Shoebridge, RL (Robert) – Derbyshire; Short, M (Michael) – S. Yorkshire; Short, ML (Martyn) – Lincolnshire; Sim, TJ (Tom) – Staffordshire; Simpson, GH (George) – N. Yorkshire; Simpson, P (Paul) – Co. Durham; Smallwood, W (William) – Cheshire; Smith, AN (Andrew) – W. Yorkshire; Smith, RH (Richard) – W. Midlands; Snartt, SP (Simon) – S. Gloucestershire; Steans, RJ (Rob) – Leicestershire; Stewart, M (Matt) – Essex; Stokes, JD (John) – Merseyside; Storrie, D (David) – W. Yorkshire; Stott, GT (Gary) – Greater Manchester; Stretton, GS (Guy) – Leicestershire; Sutton, GJ (Gary) – Lincolnshire; Swarbrick, ND (Neil) – Lancashire; Sygmuta, BC (Barry) – N. Yorkshire; Tarry, EJ (Eddie) – Greater Manchester; Tattan, JF (James) – Merseyside; Taylor, JT (Joe) – Lancashire; Thiarra, SS (Sukhdev) – Bedfordshire; Tiffin, R (Russell) – Co. Durham; Tilling, MR (Mark) – Cleveland; Tincknell, SW (Steve) – Hertfordshire; Tingey, M (Mike) – Buckinghamshire; Tomlinson, SD (Stephen) – Hampshire; Toms, WA (Wendy) – Dorset; Turner, A (Andrew) – Devon; Turner, GB (Glenn) – Derbyshire; Unsworth, D (David) – Lancashire; Varley, PC (Paul) – W. Yorkshire; Vaughan, RG (Roger) – Somerset; Wallace, G (Gary) – Tyne & Wear; Ward, GL (Gavin) – Kent; Waring, J (Jim) – Lancashire; Weaver, M (Mark) – W. Midlands; West, MG (Malcolm) – Cornwall; West, RJ (Richard) – E. Yorkshire; Whitby, D (Dave) – Merseyside; Whitestone, D (Dean) – Northamptonshire; Wilkinson, K (Keith) – Northumberland; Williams, MA (Andy) – Herefordshire; Wilson, SM (Stuart) – W. Yorkshire; Wood, PM (Paul) – Lancashire; Woodward, IJ (Irvine) – E. Sussex; Yates, NA (Neil) – Lancashire; Yeo, KG (Keith) – Essex; Yerby, MS (Martin) – Kent; Young, GR (Gary) – Bedfordshire

THE THINGS THEY SAID . . .

Talking about Alan Shearer, Newcastle United chairman Freddy Shepherd:
"As far as I'm concerned, Geordies don't grow old, they just get better."

Gary Lineker revealing perfect timing as usual:
"England scored three goals just after the second half ended."

September time and Graeme Souness at one with Craig Bellamy at Newcastle:
"Craig's preferred position is through the middle but we had a chat last week and he understood. He is fully committed to the club."

Craig Bellamy self assessment:
"My image is not the greatest, I imagine."

David Beckham showing his improvement in Spanish (translating it back to English):
"It's erm . . . the match against Atletico er, er, er, was much better for all of us."

Before Ken Bates left Chelsea and were about to sign Claude Makelele:
"Who does he play for? I've only heard of his brother, Ukelele."

Stuart Pearce on unintentionally snubbing Liverpool manager Rafael Benitez after City's 1-0 win:
"Anyone who has followed my career as a player knows I never shook hands as a player – I was straight off the pitch, win, lose or draw."

Paul Elliott on the European Player of the Year:
"Shevchenko is without doubt probably one of the best strikers in the world."

Chris Coleman, Fulham manager on his neighbours:
"Chelsea have the best players, they are well organised, they have a real sense of togetherness and play for each other. They are worthy champions."

Arsene Wenger on the same subject:
"Basically there is only one player in the world who could strengthen Chelsea and that is Thierry Henry."

Jose Mourinho on the way Champions League fixtures unfold, giving Chelsea five away Premier fixtures, Arsenal five at home following the first Euro matches:
"It is always Chelsea who get the worst games, the worst fixtures to play while Arsenal always have the best ones."

Lennart Johansson, UEFA President on women's football:
"There are so many companies that could make use of the fact that you can see the girl playing on the ground, sweaty, in the rainy weather and coming out of the dressing room, lovely-looking. That would sell."

Racing's Jenny Pitman on the King of Sports:
"The Grand National is like the FA Cup final – everyone in Britain can tell you who's won. Although I couldn't tell you who won the FA Cup final."

Michael Owen on reaching 29 goals for England:
"I need 20 goals to catch Bobby Charlton and that does seem miles away. But I've got time on my hands."

Guy Roux legendary French coach on whether the lack of goalscoring in France made it inferior to England:
"For me a high-scoring match is sometimes like an easy girl. I prefer a good 0-0. It resembles a girl full of charm and virtue and harder to catch."

Harry Redknapp after Southampton were summarily knocked out of the FA Cup by Manchester United:
"It was always going to be difficult for us from the first kick. I don't make excuses but out of the 11 players only three or four were from my first team."

Sir Alex Ferguson talking in the aftermath of the same game:
"I see this as the start of a long road to European success – we are not far away and I think this team will get there."

Arsene Wenger analysing Chelsea:
"They are a bit like in a corridor where they wait until the bull gets weak. They have the patience to wait and when the bull has lost enough blood, they just kill him off."

Kevin Keegan on Michael Owen's move from Liverpool to Real Madrid:
"You can't say Michael's left Liverpool and gone down, or even sideways – Real Madrid is a step up."

Shaun Wright-Phillips on his goalscoring debut for England against Ukraine:
"I just dreamt about playing well but the goal was a bonus and hopefully I can do it again."

Alan Green proving even the most observant of individuals does occasionally have an identity block:
"Surely Chelsea will bring on Geremi. I'm positive they will – in fact I think that's Geremi waiting to come on. No, it's Kezman."

Assistant referee (linesman to us) Rob Lewis on failing to arrive on time to see Roy Carroll throw Pedro Mendes lob into his own goal:
"There was nothing I could have done differently apart from run faster than Linford Christie."

Everton Manager David Moyes on being lured elsewhere:
"Another Premiership club – and I'm not saying which one or even in which country – did ask me to be their manager, so I could have left if I'd wanted to."

Tony Cottee explaining the simplicity of the game:
"If Villa got another now it would change the scoreline completely."

Harry Redknapp on events at the FA before the start of the season:
"Sven's a lot livelier than he looks. Obviously there's a bit of a lad in there somewhere . . . Fair play to him."

Players just want to be fit and and turn out without making a pain of the process, as Clinton Morrison of Birmingham City explained:
"I'd been ill and hadn't trained for a week and I'd been out of the team for three weeks before that, so I wasn't sharp. I got cramp before half-time as well. But I'm not one to make excuses."

Steven Gerrard looking ahead to the 2005–06 season:
"My form has been hot and cold but I'm going to put that to bed. You'll see a different player next season."

Sir Bobby Robson wiping away the mystique behind Brazilians:
"Don't ask me what a typical Brazilian is because I don't know what a typical Brazilian is, but Romario was a typical Brazilian."

Sir Alex Ferguson on the events which unfolded in the FA Cup Final:
"I think the fact that we missed so many chances encouraged Arsenal to go for penalty kicks."

One-time referee David Elleray:
"Gary Neville is a serial moaner on the field and his voluble comments when Rio Ferdinand was stopped from playing for England shows he is the same off it as well."

Bryan Robson even before his rescue act in charge of West Bromwich Albion:
"Where I want to go is with championships and European Cups. That may sound a bit silly, looking at where we are now, but that's what I want."

Berti Vogts when he was still Scotland's manager and they had just lost 3-0 to Hungary and he must have lost sight of the scoreboard:
"I just cannot understand what happened after half-time."

Steve Bruce on an unnamed man in the middle and possibly thinking of a change of sport:
"The standard of refereeing was pathetic. Some officials are spoiling things, particularly this one. These days you might as well play netball."

Another Champions League accolade for Liverpool:
"Not even the great Brazil of 1970 would have come back from three down v AC Milan."

Wayne Rooney's former Everton club colleague Leon Osman:
"The bigger the game, the better he plays. That is probably the best quality you can have as a player and he's got it in abundance."

Oldham Athletic's David Eyres, 41, preparing to mark Shaun Wright-Phillips of Manchester City:
"I will have to turbo charge my Zimmer frame."

Sven-Goran Eriksson musing about a leading marksman in the game:
"I would have loved the opportunity to have worked with Alan Shearer but have always respected his decision to retire from international football when he did."

When Robbie Fowler missed the penalty which would have put Manchester City in Europe, his manager and a 1990 World Cup spot kick sinner Stuart Pearce offered these words of comfort:
"Join the club, Robbie."

Tummy trouble can cause all kinds of confusion as Arsene Wenger found out:
"My gut reaction is that Edu will stay – but my guts have let me down many times in the past."

Former Chelsea player Marcel Desailly on the eve of the crunch Arsenal–Chelsea match:
"You can't criticise Arsenal. For the last five years they have tried to do crazy, beautiful things."

Glenn Hoddle on parts of the body which can be difficult to fathom out:
"Groins have got to be 100% or not at all."

Shane Nicholson, one-time bad boy, now rejuvenated at Chesterfield and Player of the Season there:
"I was popping pills like Smarties and boozing night and day. The way I abused my body I should be surprised I'm alive."

After survival Sunday for the four threatened Premiership clubs – Delia Smith for Norwich City:
"We are the poor kids on the block, the Cinderella. We are poor in a rich man's world but we have plenty of spirit."

Iain Dowie for Crystal Palace:
"I can't fault the lads. I'm proud to be their manager. They deserve better than that. The performance was full of pride and passion."

Harry Redknapp of Southampton:
"We all think we are clever and take the chance and think 'I can do it' and we tried, but in the end we weren't good enough."

And the survivor Bryan Robson at West Bromwich Albion:
"I told them. Let's go and make history by staying in this division after being bottom at Christmas. The lads have taken that on board."

A before Christmas view at Newcastle United by Graeme Souness:
"The fact is we are in the performance business and if you don't perform, then you're shown the door. We will make a decision at the end of the season."

Dennis Wise when he was still manager of Millwall and at a peak of fitness:
"I'm knackered. I've got a sore neck, sore calf, sore back and a cold coming."

Steve Coppell after the 4-1 defeat against Wolverhampton Wanderers in December:
"I'm a man of few words but most of the ones I said to the players began with F."

Rick Parry at Liverpool showing pre-Christmas determination to hang on to Steven Gerrard come what may:
"There is no chance of Stevie going in January. That just won't happen. Our intention is that we will never let him go."

The then Millwall chairman Theo Paphitis describing the violence and hostility in the UEFA Cup trip to Ferencvaros:
"It was like going back into the dismal time of football that we all try to forget."

Football pundit Mark Lawrenson with a firm grip on gravity:
"Fulham have been slowly sinking to the bottom and very, very quickly."

Five-goal Juan Ugarte after his nap hand for Wrexham at Hartlepool United:
"I'm delighted but the most important thing is that the team won. We need more results like this and if I can keep up this form then who knows what might happen."

Patrick Vieira shortly after his proposed move to Real Madrid collapsed in August 2004. Could it be taken two ways?
"I'm still in love with the club."

After the referee at a village game in South Africa shot dead the coach of one team, injured two players then ran off:
"I am the master of the universe."

West Ham United manager Alan Pardew on an unhappy return to Reading:
"But I said to the players after the game that they had not let me down, they had let themselves and the fans down – and the badge that is West Ham United."

Alan Smith proving the onlooker can invariably cut to the chase with simple language:
"In a word that was over the line."

After the tsunami fund-raising match, Thierry Henry put everything in perspective;
"I have always realised football is pretty irrelevant – I didn't need this to make me see that."

Just saying sorry could be the beginning of wisdom perhaps for El Hadji Diouf:
"I apologised to everyone for spitting. It was wrong and I let the team down. Now I want to have a good year and take Bolton to the top four or five."

Andy Gray who can put everything right just like Zebedee:
"At the end of the day, it's been a great night."

THE FA CHARITY SHIELD WINNERS 1908–2004

1908	Manchester U v QPR	4-0 after 1-1 draw
1909	Newcastle U v Northampton T	2-0
1910	Brighton v Aston Villa	1-0
1911	Manchester U v Swindon T	8-4
1912	Blackburn R v QPR	2-1
1913	Professionals v Amateurs	7-2
1920	WBA v Tottenham H	2-0
1921	Tottenham H v Burnley	2-0
1922	Huddersfield T v Liverpool	1-0
1923	Professionals v Amateurs	2-0
1924	Professionals v Amateurs	3-1
1925	Amateurs v Professionals	6-1
1926	Amateurs v Professionals	6-3
1927	Cardiff C v Corinthians	2-1
1928	Everton v Blackburn R	2-1
1929	Professionals v Amateurs	3-0
1930	Arsenal v Sheffield W	2-1
1931	Arsenal v WBA	1-0
1932	Everton v Newcastle U	5-3
1933	Arsenal v Everton	3-0
1934	Arsenal v Manchester C	4-0
1935	Sheffield W v Arsenal	1-0
1936	Sunderland v Arsenal	2-1
1937	Manchester C v Sunderland	2-0
1938	Arsenal v Preston NE	2-1
1948	Arsenal v Manchester U	4-3
1949	Portsmouth v Wolverhampton W	1-1*
1950	World Cup Team v Canadian Touring Team	4-2
1951	Tottenham H v Newcastle U	2-1
1952	Manchester U v Newcastle U	4-2
1953	Arsenal v Blackpool	3-1
1954	Wolverhampton W v WBA	4-4*
1955	Chelsea v Newcastle U	3-0
1956	Manchester U v Manchester C	1-0
1957	Manchester U v Aston Villa	4-0
1958	Bolton W v Wolverhampton W	4-1
1959	Wolverhampton W v Nottingham F	3-1
1960	Burnley v Wolverhampton W	2-2*
1961	Tottenham H v FA XI	3-2
1962	Tottenham H v Ipswich T	5-1
1963	Everton v Manchester U	4-0
1964	Liverpool v West Ham U	2-2*
1965	Manchester U v Liverpool	2-2*
1966	Liverpool v Everton	1-0
1967	Manchester U v Tottenham H	3-3*
1968	Manchester C v WBA	6-1
1969	Leeds U v Manchester C	2-1
1970	Everton v Chelsea	2-1
1971	Leicester C v Liverpool	1-0
1972	Manchester C v Aston Villa	1-0
1973	Burnley v Manchester C	1-0
1974	Liverpool† v Leeds U	1-1
1975	Derby Co v West Ham U	2-0
1976	Liverpool v Southampton	1-0
1977	Liverpool v Manchester U	0-0*
1978	Nottingham F v Ipswich T	5-0
1979	Liverpool v Arsenal	3-1
1980	Liverpool v West Ham U	1-0
1981	Aston Villa v Tottenham H	2-2*
1982	Liverpool v Tottenham H	1-0
1983	Manchester U v Liverpool	2-0
1984	Everton v Liverpool	1-0
1985	Everton v Manchester U	2-0
1986	Everton v Liverpool	1-1*
1987	Everton v Coventry C	1-0
1988	Liverpool v Wimbledon	2-1
1989	Liverpool v Arsenal	1-0
1990	Liverpool v Manchester U	1-1*
1991	Arsenal v Tottenham H	0-0*
1992	Leeds U v Liverpool	4-3
1993	Manchester U† v Arsenal	1-1
1994	Manchester U v Blackburn R	2-0
1995	Everton v Blackburn R	1-0
1996	Manchester U v Newcastle U	4-0
1997	Manchester U† v Chelsea	1-1
1998	Arsenal v Manchester U	3-0
1999	Arsenal v Manchester U	2-1
2000	Chelsea v Manchester U	2-0
2001	Liverpool v Manchester U	2-1
2002	Arsenal v Liverpool	1-0
2003	Manchester U† v Arsenal	1-1
2004	Arsenal v Manchester U	3-1

** Each club retained shield for six months. † Won on penalties.*

THE FA COMMUNITY SHIELD 2004

Arsenal (0) 3, Manchester U (0) 1

At Millennium Stadium, 8 August 2004, attendance 63,317

Arsenal: Lehmann; Lauren, Cole, Silva, Toure, Cygan, Pennant, Fabregas (Svard), Henry (Van Persie), Bergkamp (Aliadiere) (Clichy), Reyes (Hoyte).

Scorers: Silva 49, Reyes 59, Silvestre 79 (og).

Manchester U: Howard; Neville G, Fortune (Neville P), O'Shea (Spector), Keane (Fletcher), Silvestre, Bellion, Djemba-Djemba, Smith (Eagles), Scholes (Richardson), Giggs (Forlan).

Scorer: Smith 55.

Referee: M. Dean (Wirral).

ENGLISH LEAGUE HONOURS 1888 TO 2005

FA PREMIER LEAGUE

MAXIMUM POINTS: *a* 126; *b* 114.
**Won or placed on goal average (ratio), goal difference or most goals scored. ††Not promoted after play-offs.*

	First	*Pts*	*Second*	*Pts*	*Third*	*Pts*
1992–93*a*	Manchester U	84	Aston Villa	74	Norwich C	72
1993–94*a*	Manchester U	92	Blackburn R	84	Newcastle U	77
1994–95*a*	Blackburn R	89	Manchester U	88	Nottingham F	77
1995–96*a*	Manchester U	82	Newcastle U	78	Liverpool	71
1996–97*b*	Manchester U	75	Newcastle U*	68	Arsenal*	68
1997–98*b*	Arsenal	78	Manchester U	77	Liverpool	65
1998–99*b*	Manchester U	79	Arsenal	78	Chelsea	75
1999–2000*b*	Manchester U	91	Arsenal	73	Leeds U	69
2000–01	Manchester U	80	Arsenal	70	Liverpool	69
2001–02	Arsenal	87	Liverpool	80	Manchester U	77
2002–03	Manchester U	83	Arsenal	78	Newcastle U	69
2003–04	Arsenal	90	Chelsea	79	Manchester U	75
2004–05	Chelsea	95	Arsenal	83	Manchester U	77

FOOTBALL LEAGUE CHAMPIONSHIP

MAXIMUM POINTS: 138

2004–05	Sunderland	94	Wigan Ath	87	Ipswich T††	85

FIRST DIVISION

MAXIMUM POINTS: 138

1992–93	Newcastle U	96	West Ham U*	88	Portsmouth††	88
1993–94	Crystal Palace	90	Nottingham F	83	Millwall††	74
1994–95	Middlesbrough	82	Reading††	79	Bolton W	77
1995–96	Sunderland	83	Derby Co	79	Crystal Palace††	75
1996–97	Bolton W	98	Barnsley	80	Wolverhampton W††	76
1997–98	Nottingham F	94	Middlesbrough	91	Sunderland††	90
1998–99	Sunderland	105	Bradford C	87	Ipswich T††	86
1999–2000	Charlton Ath	91	Manchester C	89	Ipswich T	87
2000–01	Fulham	101	Blackburn R	91	Bolton W	87
2001–02	Manchester C	99	WBA	89	Wolverhampton W††	86
2002–03	Portsmouth	98	Leicester C	92	Sheffield U††	80
2003–04	Norwich C	94	WBA	86	Sunderland††	79

FOOTBALL LEAGUE CHAMPIONSHIP 1

MAXIMUM POINTS: 138

2004–05	Luton T	98	Hull C	86	Tranmere R††	79

SECOND DIVISION

MAXIMUM POINTS: 138

1992–93	Stoke C	93	Bolton W	90	Port Vale††	89
1993–94	Reading	89	Port Vale	88	Plymouth Arg*††	85
1994–95	Birmingham C	89	Brentford††	85	Crewe Alex††	83
1995–96	Swindon T	92	Oxford U	83	Blackpool††	82
1996–97	Bury	84	Stockport Co	82	Luton T††	78
1997–98	Watford	88	Bristol C	85	Grimsby T	72
1998–99	Fulham	101	Walsall	87	Manchester C	82
1999–2000	Preston NE	95	Burnley	88	Gillingham	85
2000–01	Millwall	93	Rotherham U	91	Reading††	86
2001–02	Brighton & HA	90	Reading	84	Brentford*††	83
2002–03	Wigan Ath	100	Crewe Alex	86	Bristol C††	83
2003–04	Plymouth Arg	90	QPR	83	Bristol C††	82

FOOTBALL LEAGUE CHAMPIONSHIP 2

MAXIMUM POINTS: 138

2004–05	Yeovil T	83	Scunthorpe U*	80	Swansea C	80

THIRD DIVISION

MAXIMUM POINTS: *a* 126; *b* 138.

1992–93*a*	Cardiff C	83	Wrexham	80	Barnet	79
1993–94*a*	Shrewsbury T	79	Chester C	74	Crewe Alex	73
1994–95*a*	Carlisle U	91	Walsall	83	Chesterfield	81
1995–96*b*	Preston NE	86	Gillingham	83	Bury	79
1996–97*b*	Wigan Ath*	87	Fulham	87	Carlisle U	84
1997–98*b*	Notts Co	99	Macclesfield T	82	Lincoln C	72
1998–99*b*	Brentford	85	Cambridge U	81	Cardiff C	80
1999–2000*b*	Swansea C	85	Rotherham U	84	Northampton T	82
2000–01	Brighton & HA	92	Cardiff C	82	Chesterfield¶	80
2001–02	Plymouth Arg	102	Luton T	97	Mansfield T	79
2002–03	Rushden & D	87	Hartlepool U	85	Wrexham	84
2003–04	Doncaster R	92	Hull C	88	Torquay U*	81

¶9pts deducted for irregularities.

FOOTBALL LEAGUE

MAXIMUM POINTS: *a* 44; *b* 60

	First	*Pts*	*Second*	*Pts*	*Third*	*Pts*
1888–89*a*	Preston NE	40	Aston Villa	29	Wolverhampton W	28
1889–90*a*	Preston NE	33	Everton	31	Blackburn R	27
1890–91*a*	Everton	29	Preston NE	27	Notts Co	26
1891–92*b*	Sunderland	42	Preston NE	37	Bolton W	36

FIRST DIVISION to 1991–92

MAXIMUM POINTS: ***a*** **44;** ***b*** **52;** ***c*** **60;** ***d*** **68;** ***e*** **76;** ***f*** **84;** ***g*** **126;** ***h*** **120;** ***k*** **114.**

	First	*Pts*	*Second*	*Pts*	*Third*	*Pts*
1892–93*c*	Sunderland	48	Preston NE	37	Everton	36
1893–94*c*	Aston Villa	44	Sunderland	38	Derby Co	36
1894–95*c*	Sunderland	47	Everton	42	Aston Villa	39
1895–96*c*	Aston Villa	45	Derby Co	41	Everton	39
1896–97*c*	Aston Villa	47	Sheffield U*	36	Derby Co	36
1897–98*c*	Sheffield U	42	Sunderland	37	Wolverhampton W*	35
1898–99*d*	Aston Villa	45	Liverpool	43	Burnley	39
1899–1900*d*	Aston Villa	50	Sheffield U	48	Sunderland	41
1900–01*d*	Liverpool	45	Sunderland	43	Notts Co	40
1901–02*d*	Sunderland	44	Everton	41	Newcastle U	37
1902–03*d*	The Wednesday	42	Aston Villa*	41	Sunderland	41
1903–04*d*	The Wednesday	47	Manchester C	44	Everton	43
1904–05*d*	Newcastle U	48	Everton	47	Manchester C	46
1905–06*e*	Liverpool	51	Preston NE	47	The Wednesday	44
1906–07*e*	Newcastle U	51	Bristol C	48	Everton*	45
1907–08*e*	Manchester U	52	Aston Villa*	43	Manchester C	43
1908–09*e*	Newcastle U	53	Everton	46	Sunderland	44
1909–10*e*	Aston Villa	53	Liverpool	48	Blackburn R*	45
1910–11*e*	Manchester U	52	Aston Villa	51	Sunderland*	45
1911–12*e*	Blackburn R	49	Everton	46	Newcastle U	44
1912–13*e*	Sunderland	54	Aston Villa	50	Sheffield W	49
1913–14*e*	Blackburn R	51	Aston Villa	44	Middlesbrough*	43
1914–15*e*	Everton	46	Oldham Ath	45	Blackburn R*	43
1919–20*f*	WBA	60	Burnley	51	Chelsea	49
1920–21*f*	Burnley	59	Manchester C	54	Bolton W	52
1921–22*f*	Liverpool	57	Tottenham H	51	Burnley	49
1922–23*f*	Liverpool	60	Sunderland	54	Huddersfield T	53
1923–24*f*	Huddersfield T*	57	Cardiff C	57	Sunderland	53
1924–25*f*	Huddersfield T	58	WBA	56	Bolton W	55
1925–26*f*	Huddersfield T	57	Arsenal	52	Sunderland	48
1926–27*f*	Newcastle U	56	Huddersfield T	51	Sunderland	49
1927–28*f*	Everton	53	Huddersfield T	51	Leicester C	48
1928–29*f*	Sheffield W	52	Leicester C	51	Aston Villa	50
1929–30*f*	Sheffield W	60	Derby Co	50	Manchester C*	47
1930–31*f*	Arsenal	66	Aston Villa	59	Sheffield W	52
1931–32*f*	Everton	56	Arsenal	54	Sheffield W	50
1932–33*f*	Arsenal	58	Aston Villa	54	Sheffield W	51
1933–34*f*	Arsenal	59	Huddersfield T	56	Tottenham H	49
1934–35*f*	Arsenal	58	Sunderland	54	Sheffield W	49
1935–36*f*	Sunderland	56	Derby Co*	48	Huddersfield T	48
1936–37*f*	Manchester C	57	Charlton Ath	54	Arsenal	52
1937–38*f*	Arsenal	52	Wolverhampton W	51	Preston NE	49
1938–39*f*	Everton	59	Wolverhampton W	55	Charlton Ath	50
1946–47*f*	Liverpool	57	Manchester U*	56	Wolverhampton W	56
1947–48*f*	Arsenal	59	Manchester U*	52	Burnley	52
1948–49*f*	Portsmouth	58	Manchester U*	53	Derby Co	53
1949–50*f*	Portsmouth*	53	Wolverhampton W	53	Sunderland	52
1950–51*f*	Tottenham H	60	Manchester U	56	Blackpool	50
1951–52*f*	Manchester U	57	Tottenham H*	53	Arsenal	53
1952–53*f*	Arsenal*	54	Preston NE	54	Wolverhampton W	51
1953–54*f*	Wolverhampton W	57	WBA	53	Huddersfield T	51
1954–55*f*	Chelsea	52	Wolverhampton W*	48	Portsmouth*	48
1955–56*f*	Manchester U	60	Blackpool*	49	Wolverhampton W	49
1956–57*f*	Manchester U	64	Tottenham H*	56	Preston NE	56
1957–58*f*	Wolverhampton W	64	Preston NE	59	Tottenham H	51
1958–59*f*	Wolverhampton W	61	Manchester U	55	Arsenal*	50
1959–60*f*	Burnley	55	Wolverhampton W	54	Tottenham H	53
1960–61*f*	Tottenham H	66	Sheffield W	58	Wolverhampton W	57
1961–62*f*	Ipswich T	56	Burnley	53	Tottenham H	52
1962–63*f*	Everton	61	Tottenham H	55	Burnley	54
1963–64*f*	Liverpool	57	Manchester U	53	Everton	52
1964–65*f*	Manchester U*	61	Leeds U	61	Chelsea	56
1965–66*f*	Liverpool	61	Leeds U*	55	Burnley	55
1966–67*f*	Manchester U	60	Nottingham F*	56	Tottenham H	56
1967–68*f*	Manchester C	58	Manchester U	56	Liverpool	55
1968–69*f*	Leeds U	67	Liverpool	61	Everton	57
1969–70*f*	Everton	66	Leeds U	57	Chelsea	55
1970–71*f*	Arsenal	65	Leeds U	64	Tottenham H*	52
1971–72*f*	Derby Co	58	Leeds U*	57	Liverpool*	57
1972–73*f*	Liverpool	60	Arsenal	57	Leeds U	53
1973–74*f*	Leeds U	62	Liverpool	57	Derby Co	48
1974–75*f*	Derby Co	53	Liverpool*	51	Ipswich T	51
1975–76*f*	Liverpool	60	QPR	59	Manchester U	56
1976–77*f*	Liverpool	57	Manchester C	56	Ipswich T	52
1977–78*f*	Nottingham F	64	Liverpool	57	Everton	55
1978–79*f*	Liverpool	68	Nottingham F	60	WBA	59
1979–80*f*	Liverpool	60	Manchester U	58	Ipswich T	52
1980–81*f*	Aston Villa	60	Ipswich T	56	Arsenal	53
1981–82*g*	Liverpool	87	Ipswich T	83	Manchester U	78
1982–83*g*	Liverpool	82	Watford	71	Manchester U	70
1983–84*g*	Liverpool	80	Southampton	77	Nottingham F*	74
1984–85*g*	Everton	90	Liverpool*	77	Tottenham H	77
1985–86*g*	Liverpool	88	Everton	86	West Ham U	84

	First	Pts	Second	Pts	Third	Pts
1986–87*g*	Everton	86	Liverpool	77	Tottenham H	71
1987–88*h*	Liverpool	90	Manchester U	81	Nottingham F	73
1988–89*k*	Arsenal*	76	Liverpool	76	Nottingham F	64
1989–90*k*	Liverpool	79	Aston Villa	70	Tottenham H	63
1990–91*k*	Arsenal†	83	Liverpool	76	Crystal Palace	69
1991–92*g*	Leeds U	82	Manchester U	78	Sheffield W	75

No official competition during 1915–19 and 1939–46; Regional Leagues operated. †2 pts deducted.

SECOND DIVISION to 1991–92

MAXIMUM POINTS: ***a*** **44;** ***b*** **56;** ***c*** **60;** ***d*** **68;** ***e*** **76;** ***f*** **84;** ***g*** **126;** ***h*** **132;** ***k*** **138.**

	First	Pts	Second	Pts	Third	Pts
1892–93*a*	Small Heath	36	Sheffield U	35	Darwen	30
1893–94*b*	Liverpool	50	Small Heath	42	Notts Co	39
1894–95*c*	Bury	48	Notts Co	39	Newton Heath*	38
1895–96*c*	Liverpool*	46	Manchester C	46	Grimsby T*	42
1896–97*c*	Notts Co	42	Newton Heath	39	Grimsby T	38
1897–98*c*	Burnley	48	Newcastle U	45	Manchester C	39
1898–99*d*	Manchester C	52	Glossop NE	46	Leicester Fosse	45
1899–1900*d*	The Wednesday	54	Bolton W	52	Small Heath	46
1900–01*d*	Grimsby T	49	Small Heath	48	Burnley	44
1901–02*d*	WBA	55	Middlesbrough	51	Preston NE*	42
1902–03*d*	Manchester C	54	Small Heath	51	Woolwich A	48
1903–04*d*	Preston NE	50	Woolwich A	49	Manchester U	48
1904–05*d*	Liverpool	58	Bolton W	56	Manchester U	53
1905–06*e*	Bristol C	66	Manchester U	62	Chelsea	53
1906–07*e*	Nottingham F	60	Chelsea	57	Leicester Fosse	48
1907–08*e*	Bradford C	54	Leicester Fosse	52	Oldham Ath	50
1908–09*e*	Bolton W	52	Tottenham H*	51	WBA	51
1909–10*e*	Manchester C	54	Oldham Ath*	53	Hull C*	53
1910–11*e*	WBA	53	Bolton W	51	Chelsea	49
1911–12*e*	Derby Co*	54	Chelsea	54	Burnley	52
1912–13*e*	Preston NE	53	Burnley	50	Birmingham	46
1913–14*e*	Notts Co	53	Bradford PA*	49	Woolwich A	49
1914–15*e*	Derby Co	53	Preston NE	50	Barnsley	47
1919–20*f*	Tottenham H	70	Huddersfield T	64	Birmingham	56
1920–21*f*	Birmingham*	58	Cardiff C	58	Bristol C	51
1921–22*f*	Nottingham F	56	Stoke C*	52	Barnsley	52
1922–23*f*	Notts Co	53	West Ham U*	51	Leicester C	51
1923–24*f*	Leeds U	54	Bury*	51	Derby Co	51
1924–25*f*	Leicester C	59	Manchester U	57	Derby Co	55
1925–26*f*	Sheffield W	60	Derby Co	57	Chelsea	52
1926–27*f*	Middlesbrough	62	Portsmouth*	54	Manchester C	54
1927–28*f*	Manchester C	59	Leeds U	57	Chelsea	54
1928–29*f*	Middlesbrough	55	Grimsby T	53	Bradford PA*	48
1929–30*f*	Blackpool	58	Chelsea	55	Oldham Ath	53
1930–31*f*	Everton	61	WBA	54	Tottenham H	51
1931–32*f*	Wolverhampton W	56	Leeds U	54	Stoke C	52
1932–33*f*	Stoke C	56	Tottenham H	55	Fulham	50
1933–34*f*	Grimsby T	59	Preston NE	52	Bolton W*	51
1934–35*f*	Brentford	61	Bolton W*	56	West Ham U	56
1935–36*f*	Manchester U	56	Charlton Ath	55	Sheffield U*	52
1936–37*f*	Leicester C	56	Blackpool	55	Bury	52
1937–38*f*	Aston Villa	57	Manchester U*	53	Sheffield U	53
1938–39*f*	Blackburn R	55	Sheffield U	54	Sheffield W	53
1946–47*f*	Manchester C	62	Burnley	58	Birmingham C	55
1947–48*f*	Birmingham C	59	Newcastle U	56	Southampton	52
1948–49*f*	Fulham	57	WBA	56	Southampton	55
1949–50*f*	Tottenham H	61	Sheffield W*	52	Sheffield U*	52
1950–51*f*	Preston NE	57	Manchester C	52	Cardiff C	50
1951–52*f*	Sheffield W	53	Cardiff C*	51	Birmingham C	51
1952–53*f*	Sheffield U	60	Huddersfield T	58	Luton T	52
1953–54*f*	Leicester C*	56	Everton	56	Blackburn R	55
1954–55*f*	Birmingham C*	54	Luton T*	54	Rotherham U	54
1955–56*f*	Sheffield W	55	Leeds U	52	Liverpool*	48
1956–57*f*	Leicester C	61	Nottingham F	54	Liverpool	53
1957–58*f*	West Ham U	57	Blackburn R	56	Charlton Ath	55
1958–59*f*	Sheffield W	62	Fulham	60	Sheffield U*	53
1959–60*f*	Aston Villa	59	Cardiff C	58	Liverpool*	50
1960–61*f*	Ipswich T	59	Sheffield U	58	Liverpool	52
1961–62*f*	Liverpool	62	Leyton Orient	54	Sunderland	53
1962–63*f*	Stoke C	53	Chelsea*	52	Sunderland	52
1963–64*f*	Leeds U	63	Sunderland	61	Preston NE	56
1964–65*f*	Newcastle U	57	Northampton T	56	Bolton W	50
1965–66*f*	Manchester C	59	Southampton	54	Coventry C	53
1966–67*f*	Coventry C	59	Wolverhampton W	58	Carlisle U	52
1967–68*f*	Ipswich T	59	QPR*	58	Blackpool	58
1968–69*f*	Derby Co	63	Crystal Palace	56	Charlton Ath	50
1969–70*f*	Huddersfield T	60	Blackpool	53	Leicester C	51
1970–71*f*	Leicester C	59	Sheffield U	56	Cardiff C*	53
1971–72*f*	Norwich C	57	Birmingham C	56	Millwall	55
1972–73*f*	Burnley	62	QPR	61	Aston Villa	50
1973–74*f*	Middlesbrough	65	Luton T	50	Carlisle U	49
1974–75*f*	Manchester U	61	Aston Villa	58	Norwich C	53
1975–76*f*	Sunderland	56	Bristol C*	53	WBA	53
1976–77*f*	Wolverhampton W	57	Chelsea	55	Nottingham F	52

	First	Pts	Second	Pts	Third	Pts
1977–78*f*	Bolton W	58	Southampton	57	Tottenham H*	56
1978–79*f*	Crystal Palace	57	Brighton & HA*	56	Stoke C	56
1979–80*f*	Leicester C	55	Sunderland	54	Birmingham C*	53
1980–81*f*	West Ham U	66	Notts Co	53	Swansea C*	50
1981–82*g*	Luton T	88	Watford	80	Norwich C	71
1982–83*g*	QPR	85	Wolverhampton W	75	Leicester C	70
1983–84*g*	Chelsea*	88	Sheffield W	88	Newcastle U	80
1984–85*g*	Oxford U	84	Birmingham C	82	Manchester C	74
1985–86*g*	Norwich C	84	Charlton Ath	77	Wimbledon	76
1986–87*g*	Derby Co	84	Portsmouth	78	Oldham Ath††	75
1987–88*h*	Millwall	82	Aston Villa*	78	Middlesbrough	78
1988–89*k*	Chelsea	99	Manchester C	82	Crystal Palace	81
1989–90*k*	Leeds U*	85	Sheffield U	85	Newcastle U††	80
1990–91*k*	Oldham Ath	88	West Ham U	87	Sheffield W	82
1991–92*k*	Ipswich T	84	Middlesbrough	80	Derby Co	78

No official competition during 1915–19 and 1939–46; Regional Leagues operated.

THIRD DIVISION to 1991–92

MAXIMUM POINTS: 92; 138 FROM 1981–82.

	First	Pts	Second	Pts	Third	Pts
1958–59	Plymouth Arg	62	Hull C	61	Brentford*	57
1959–60	Southampton	61	Norwich C	59	Shrewsbury T*	52
1960–61	Bury	68	Walsall	62	QPR	60
1961–62	Portsmouth	65	Grimsby T	62	Bournemouth*	59
1962–63	Northampton T	62	Swindon T	58	Port Vale	54
1963–64	Coventry C*	60	Crystal Palace	60	Watford	58
1964–65	Carlisle U	60	Bristol C*	59	Mansfield T	59
1965–66	Hull C	69	Millwall	65	QPR	57
1966–67	QPR	67	Middlesbrough	55	Watford	54
1967–68	Oxford U	57	Bury	56	Shrewsbury T	55
1968–69	Watford*	64	Swindon T	64	Luton T	61
1969–70	Orient	62	Luton T	60	Bristol R	56
1970–71	Preston NE	61	Fulham	60	Halifax T	56
1971–72	Aston Villa	70	Brighton & HA	65	Bournemouth*	62
1972–73	Bolton W	61	Notts Co	57	Blackburn R	55
1973–74	Oldham Ath	62	Bristol R*	61	York C	61
1974–75	Blackburn R	60	Plymouth Arg	59	Charlton Ath	55
1975–76	Hereford U	63	Cardiff C	57	Millwall	56
1976–77	Mansfield T	64	Brighton & HA	61	Crystal Palace*	59
1977–78	Wrexham	61	Cambridge U	58	Preston NE*	56
1978–79	Shrewsbury T	61	Watford*	60	Swansea C	60
1979–80	Grimsby T	62	Blackburn R	59	Sheffield W	58
1980–81	Rotherham U	61	Barnsley*	59	Charlton Ath	59
1981–82	Burnley*	80	Carlisle U	80	Fulham	78
1982–83	Portsmouth	91	Cardiff C	86	Huddersfield T	82
1983–84	Oxford U	95	Wimbledon	87	Sheffield U*	83
1984–85	Bradford C	94	Millwall	90	Hull C	87
1985–86	Reading	94	Plymouth Arg	87	Derby Co	84
1986–87	Bournemouth	97	Middlesbrough	94	Swindon T	87
1987–88	Sunderland	93	Brighton & HA	84	Walsall	82
1988–89	Wolverhampton W	92	Sheffield U*	84	Port Vale	84
1989–90	Bristol R	93	Bristol C	91	Notts Co	87
1990–91	Cambridge U	86	Southend U	85	Grimsby T*	83
1991–92	Brentford	82	Birmingham C	81	Huddersfield T	78

FOURTH DIVISION (1958–1992)

MAXIMUM POINTS: 92; 138 FROM 1981–82.

	First	Pts	Second	Pts	Third	Pts	Fourth	Pts
1958–59	Port Vale	64	Coventry C*	60	York C	60	Shrewsbury T	58
1959–60	Walsall	65	Notts Co*	60	Torquay U	60	Watford	57
1960–61	Peterborough U	66	Crystal Palace	64	Northampton T*	60	Bradford PA	60
1961–62†	Millwall	56	Colchester U	55	Wrexham	53	Carlisle U	52
1962–63	Brentford	62	Oldham Ath*	59	Crewe Alex	59	Mansfield T*	57
1963–64	Gillingham*	60	Carlisle U	60	Workington	59	Exeter C	58
1964–65	Brighton & HA	63	Millwall*	62	York C	62	Oxford U	61
1965–66	Doncaster R*	59	Darlington	59	Torquay U	58	Colchester U*	56
1966–67	Stockport Co	64	Southport*	59	Barrow	59	Tranmere R	58
1967–68	Luton T	66	Barnsley	61	Hartlepools U	60	Crewe Alex	58
1968–69	Doncaster R	59	Halifax T	57	Rochdale*	56	Bradford C	56
1969–70	Chesterfield	64	Wrexham	61	Swansea C	60	Port Vale	59
1970–71	Notts Co	69	Bournemouth	60	Oldham Ath	59	York C	56
1971–72	Grimsby T	63	Southend U	60	Brentford	59	Scunthorpe U	57
1972–73	Southport	62	Hereford U	58	Cambridge U	57	Aldershot*	56
1973–74	Peterborough U	65	Gillingham	62	Colchester U	60	Bury	59
1974–75	Mansfield T	68	Shrewsbury T	62	Rotherham U	59	Chester*	57
1975–76	Lincoln C	74	Northampton T	68	Reading	60	Tranmere R	58
1976–77	Cambridge U	65	Exeter C	62	Colchester U*	59	Bradford C	59
1977–78	Watford	71	Southend U	60	Swansea C*	56	Brentford	56
1978–79	Reading	65	Grimsby T*	61	Wimbledon*	61	Barnsley	61
1979–80	Huddersfield T	66	Walsall	64	Newport Co	61	Portsmouth*	60
1980–81	Southend U	67	Lincoln C	65	Doncaster R	56	Wimbledon	55
1981–82	Sheffield U	96	Bradford C*	91	Wigan Ath	91	Bournemouth	88
1982–83	Wimbledon	98	Hull C	90	Port Vale	88	Scunthorpe U	83

	First	Pts	Second	Pts	Third	Pts	Fourth	Pts
1983–84	York C	101	Doncaster R	85	Reading*	82	Bristol C	82
1984–85	Chesterfield	91	Blackpool	86	Darlington	85	Bury	84
1985–86	Swindon T	102	Chester C	84	Mansfield T	81	Port Vale	79
1986–87	Northampton T	99	Preston NE	90	Southend U	80	Wolverhampton W††	79
1987–88	Wolverhampton W	90	Cardiff C	85	Bolton W	78	Scunthorpe U††	77
1988–89	Rotherham U	82	Tranmere R	80	Crewe Alex	78	Scunthorpe U††	77
1989–90	Exeter C	89	Grimsby T	79	Southend U	75	Stockport Co††	74
1990–91	Darlington	83	Stockport Co*	82	Hartlepool U	82	Peterborough U	80
1991–92†*	Burnley	83	Rotherham U*	77	Mansfield T	77	Blackpool	76

†*Maximum points:* 88 owing to Accrington Stanley's resignation.
†*Maximum points:* 126 owing to Aldershot being expelled (and only 23 teams started the competition).

THIRD DIVISION—SOUTH (1920–1958)

1920–21 SEASON AS THIRD DIVISION. MAXIMUM POINTS: *a* 84; *b* 92.

	First	Pts	Second	Pts	Third	Pts
1920–21*a*	Crystal Palace	59	Southampton	54	QPR	53
1921–22*a*	Southampton*	61	Plymouth Arg	61	Portsmouth	53
1922–23*a*	Bristol C	59	Plymouth Arg*	53	Swansea T	53
1923–24*a*	Portsmouth	59	Plymouth Arg	55	Millwall	54
1924–25*a*	Swansea T	57	Plymouth Arg	56	Bristol C	53
1925–26*a*	Reading	57	Plymouth Arg	56	Millwall	53
1926–27*a*	Bristol C	62	Plymouth Arg	60	Millwall	56
1927–28*a*	Millwall	65	Northampton T	55	Plymouth Arg	53
1928–29*a*	Charlton Ath*	54	Crystal Palace	54	Northampton T*	52
1929–30*a*	Plymouth Arg	68	Brentford	61	QPR	51
1930–31*a*	Notts Co	59	Crystal Palace	51	Brentford	50
1931–32*a*	Fulham	57	Reading	55	Southend U	53
1932–33*a*	Brentford	62	Exeter C	58	Norwich C	57
1933–34*a*	Norwich C	61	Coventry C*	54	Reading*	54
1934–35*a*	Charlton Ath	61	Reading	53	Coventry C	51
1935–36*a*	Coventry C	57	Luton T	56	Reading	54
1936–37*a*	Luton T	58	Notts Co	56	Brighton & HA	53
1937–38*a*	Millwall	56	Bristol C	55	QPR*	53
1938–39*a*	Newport Co	55	Crystal Palace	52	Brighton & HA	49
1939–46	Competition cancelled owing to war. Regional Leagues operated.					
1946–47*a*	Cardiff C	66	QPR	57	Bristol C	51
1947–48*a*	QPR	61	Bournemouth	57	Walsall	51
1948–49*a*	Swansea T	62	Reading	55	Bournemouth	52
1949–50*a*	Notts Co	58	Northampton T*	51	Southend U	51
1950–51*b*	Nottingham F	70	Norwich C	64	Reading*	57
1951–52*b*	Plymouth Arg	66	Reading*	61	Norwich C	61
1952–53*b*	Bristol R	64	Millwall*	62	Northampton T	62
1953–54*b*	Ipswich T	64	Brighton & HA	61	Bristol C	56
1954–55*b*	Bristol C	70	Leyton Orient	61	Southampton	59
1955–56*b*	Leyton Orient	66	Brighton & HA	65	Ipswich T	64
1956–57*b*	Ipswich T*	59	Torquay U	59	Colchester U	58
1957–58*b*	Brighton & HA	60	Brentford*	58	Plymouth Arg	58

THIRD DIVISION—NORTH (1921–1958)

MAXIMUM POINTS: *a* 76; *b* 84; *c* 80; *d* 92.

	First	Pts	Second	Pts	Third	Pts
1921–22*a*	Stockport Co	56	Darlington*	50	Grimsby T	50
1922–23*a*	Nelson	51	Bradford PA	47	Walsall	46
1923–24*b*	Wolverhampton W	63	Rochdale	62	Chesterfield	54
1924–25*b*	Darlington	58	Nelson*	53	New Brighton	53
1925–26*b*	Grimsby T	61	Bradford PA	60	Rochdale	59
1926–27*b*	Stoke C	63	Rochdale	58	Bradford PA	55
1927–28*b*	Bradford PA	63	Lincoln C	55	Stockport Co	54
1928–29*b*	Bradford C	63	Stockport Co	62	Wrexham	52
1929–30*b*	Port Vale	67	Stockport Co	63	Darlington*	50
1930–31*b*	Chesterfield	58	Lincoln C	57	Wrexham*	54
1931–32*c*	Lincoln C*	57	Gateshead	57	Chester	50
1932–33*b*	Hull C	59	Wrexham	57	Stockport Co	54
1933–34*b*	Barnsley	62	Chesterfield	61	Stockport Co	59
1934–35*b*	Doncaster R	57	Halifax T	55	Chester	54
1935–36*b*	Chesterfield	60	Chester*	55	Tranmere R	55
1936–37*b*	Stockport Co	60	Lincoln C	57	Chester	53
1937–38*b*	Tranmere R	56	Doncaster R	54	Hull C	53
1938–39*b*	Barnsley	67	Doncaster R	56	Bradford C	52
1939–46	Competition cancelled owing to war. Regional Leagues operated.					
1946–47*b*	Doncaster R	72	Rotherham U	60	Chester	56
1947–48*b*	Lincoln C	60	Rotherham U	59	Wrexham	50
1948–49*b*	Hull C	65	Rotherham U	62	Doncaster R	50
1949–50*b*	Doncaster R	55	Gateshead	53	Rochdale*	51
1950–51*d*	Rotherham U	71	Mansfield T	64	Carlisle U	62
1951–52*d*	Lincoln C	69	Grimsby T	66	Stockport Co	59
1952–53*d*	Oldham Ath	59	Port Vale	58	Wrexham	56
1953–54*d*	Port Vale	69	Barnsley	58	Scunthorpe U	57
1954–55*d*	Barnsley	65	Accrington S	61	Scunthorpe U*	58
1955–56*d*	Grimsby T	68	Derby Co	63	Accrington S	59
1956–57*d*	Derby Co	63	Hartlepools U	59	Accrington S*	58
1957–58*d*	Scunthorpe U	66	Accrington S	59	Bradford C	57

PROMOTED AFTER PLAY-OFFS

(NOT ACCOUNTED FOR IN PREVIOUS SECTION)

1986–87	Aldershot to Division 3.
1987–88	Swansea C to Division 3.
1988–89	Leyton Orient to Division 3.
1989–90	Sunderland to Division 1; Notts Co to Division 2; Cambridge U to Division 3.
1990–91	Notts Co to Division 1; Tranmere R to Division 2; Torquay U to Division 3.
1991–92	Blackburn R to Premier League; Peterborough U to Division 1.
1992–93	Swindon T to Premier League; WBA to Division 1; York C to Division 2.
1993–94	Leicester C to Premier League; Burnley to Division 1; Wycombe W to Division 2.
1994–95	Huddersfield T to Division 1.
1995–96	Leicester C to Premier League; Bradford C to Division 1; Plymouth Arg to Division 2.
1996–97	Crystal Palace to Premier League; Crewe Alex to Division 1; Northampton T to Division 2.
1997–98	Charlton Ath to Premier League; Colchester U to Division 2.
1998–99	Watford to Premier League; Scunthorpe U to Division 2.
1999–2000	Peterborough U to Division 2
2000–01	Walsall to Division 1; Blackpool to Division 2
2001–02	Birmingham C to Premier League; Stoke C to Division 1; Cheltenham T to Division 2
2002–03	Wolverhampton W to Premier League; Cardiff C to Division 1; Bournemouth to Division 2
2003–04	Crystal Palace to Premier League; Brighton & HA to Division 1; Huddersfield T to Division 2
2004–05	West Ham U to Premier League; Sheffield W to Championship; Southend U to Championship 1

LEAGUE TITLE WINS

FA PREMIER LEAGUE – Manchester U 8, Arsenal 3, Blackburn R 1, Chelsea 1.

FOOTBALL LEAGUE CHAMPIONSHIP – Sunderland 1.

LEAGUE DIVISION 1 – Liverpool 18, Arsenal 10, Everton 9, Sunderland 8, Aston Villa 7, Manchester U 7, Newcastle U 5, Sheffield W 4, Huddersfield T 3, Leeds U 3, Manchester C 3, Portsmouth 3, Wolverhampton W 3, Blackburn R 2, Burnley 2, Derby Co 2, Nottingham F 2, Preston NE 2, Tottenham H 2; Bolton W, Charlton Ath, Chelsea, Crystal Palace, Fulham, Ipswich T, Middlesbrough, Norwich C, Sheffield U, WBA 1 each.

FOOTBALL LEAGUE CHAMPIONSHIP 1 – Luton T 1.

LEAGUE DIVISION 2 – Leicester C 6, Manchester C 6, Birmingham C (one as Small Heath) 5, Sheffield W 5, Derby Co 4, Liverpool 4, Preston NE 4, Ipswich T 3, Leeds U 3, Middlesbrough 3, Notts Co 3, Stoke C 3, Aston Villa 2, Bolton W 2, Burnley 2, Bury 2, Chelsea 2, Fulham 2, Grimsby T 2, Manchester U 2, Millwall 2, Norwich C 2, Nottingham F 2, Tottenham H 2, WBA 2, West Ham U 2, Wolverhampton W 2; Blackburn R, Blackpool, Bradford C, Brentford, Brighton & HA, Bristol C, Coventry C, Crystal Palace, Everton, Huddersfield T, Luton T, Newcastle U, QPR, Oldham Ath, Oxford U, Plymouth Arg, Reading, Sheffield U, Sunderland, Swindon T, Watford, Wigan Ath 1 each.

FOOTBALL LEAGUE CHAMPIONSHIP 2– Yeovil T 1.

LEAGUE DIVISION 3 – Brentford 2, Carlisle U 2, Oxford U 2, Plymouth Arg 2, Portsmouth 2, Preston NE 2, Shrewsbury T 2; Aston Villa, Blackburn R, Bolton W, Bournemouth, Bradford C, Brighton & HA, Bristol R, Burnley, Bury, Cambridge U, Cardiff C, Coventry C, Doncaster R. Grimsby T, Hereford U, Hull C, Leyton Orient, Mansfield T, Northampton T, Notts Co, Oldham Ath, QPR, Reading, Rotherham U, Rushden & D Southampton, Sunderland, Swansea C, Watford, Wigan Ath, Wolverhampton W, Wrexham 1 each.

LEAGUE DIVISION 4 – Chesterfield 2, Doncaster R 2, Peterborough U 2; Brentford, Brighton & HA, Burnley, Cambridge U, Darlington, Exeter C, Gillingham, Grimsby T, Huddersfield T, Lincoln C, Luton T, Mansfield T, Millwall, Northampton T, Notts Co, Port Vale, Reading, Rotherham U, Sheffield U, Southend U, Southport, Stockport Co, Swindon T, Walsall, Watford, Wimbledon, Wolverhampton W, York C 1 each.

TO 1957–58

DIVISION 3 (South) – Bristol C 3, Charlton Ath 2, Ipswich T 2, Millwall 2, Notts Co 2, Plymouth Arg 2, Swansea T 2; Brentford, Brighton & HA, Bristol R, Cardiff C, Coventry C, Crystal Palace, Fulham, Leyton Orient, Luton T, Newport Co, Norwich C, Nottingham F, Portsmouth, QPR, Reading, Southampton 1 each.

DIVISION 3 (North) – Barnsley 3, Doncaster R 3, Lincoln C 3, Chesterfield 2, Grimsby T 2, Hull C 2, Port Vale 2, Stockport Co 2; Bradford C, Bradford PA, Darlington, Derby Co, Nelson, Oldham Ath, Rotherham U, Scunthorpe U, Stoke C, Tranmere R, Wolverhampton W 1 each.

RELEGATED CLUBS

1891–92 League extended. Newton Heath, Sheffield W and Nottingham F admitted. *Second Division formed* including Darwen.
1892–93 In Test matches, Sheffield U and Darwen won promotion in place of Notts Co and Accrington S.
1893–94 In Tests, Liverpool and Small Heath won promotion. Newton Heath and Darwen relegated.
1894–95 After Tests, Bury promoted, Liverpool relegated.
1895–96 After Tests, Liverpool promoted, Small Heath relegated.
1896–97 After Tests, Notts Co promoted, Burnley relegated.
1897–98 Test system abolished after success of Stoke C and Burnley. League extended. Blackburn R and Newcastle U elected to First Division. *Automatic promotion and relegation introduced.*

FA PREMIER LEAGUE TO DIVISION 1

1992–93 Crystal Palace, Middlesbrough, Nottingham F
1993–94 Sheffield U, Oldham Ath, Swindon T
1994–95 Crystal Palace, Norwich C, Leicester C, Ipswich T
1995–96 Manchester C, QPR, Bolton W
1996–97 Sunderland, Middlesbrough, Nottingham F
1997–98 Bolton W, Barnsley, Crystal Palace
1998–99 Charlton Ath, Blackburn R, Nottingham F
1999–2000 Wimbledon, Sheffield W, Watford
2000–01 Manchester C, Coventry C, Bradford C
2001–02 Ipswich T, Derby Co, Leicester C
2002–03 West Ham U, WBA, Sunderland
2003–04 Leicester C, Leeds U, Wolverhampton W.

FA PREMIER LEAGUE TO CHAMPIONSHIP

2004–05 Crystal Palace, Norwich C, Southampton

DIVISION 1 TO DIVISION 2

1898–99 Bolton W and Sheffield W
1899–1900 Burnley and Glossop
1900–01 Preston NE and WBA
1901–02 Small Heath and Manchester C
1902–03 Grimsby T and Bolton W
1903–04 Liverpool and WBA
1904–05 League extended. Bury and Notts Co, two bottom clubs in First Division, re-elected.
1905–06 Nottingham F and Wolverhampton W
1906–07 Derby Co and Stoke C
1907–08 Bolton W and Birmingham C
1908–09 Manchester C and Leicester Fosse
1909–10 Bolton W and Chelsea
1910–11 Bristol C and Nottingham F
1911–12 Preston NE and Bury
1912–13 Notts Co and Woolwich Arsenal
1913–14 Preston NE and Derby Co
1914–15 Tottenham H and Chelsea*
1919–20 Notts Co and Sheffield W
1920–21 Derby Co and Bradford PA
1921–22 Bradford C and Manchester U
1922–23 Stoke C and Oldham Ath
1923–24 Chelsea and Middlesbrough
1924–25 Preston NE and Nottingham F
1925–26 Manchester C and Notts Co
1926–27 Leeds U and WBA
1927–28 Tottenham H and Middlesbrough
1928–29 Bury and Cardiff C
1929–30 Burnley and Everton
1930–31 Leeds U and Manchester U
1931–32 Grimsby T and West Ham U
1932–33 Bolton W and Blackpool
1933–34 Newcastle U and Sheffield U
1934–35 Leicester C and Tottenham H
1935–36 Aston Villa and Blackburn R
1936–37 Manchester U and Sheffield W
1937–38 Manchester C and WBA
1938–39 Birmingham C and Leicester C
1946–47 Brentford and Leeds U
1947–48 Blackburn R and Grimsby T
1948–49 Preston NE and Sheffield U
1949–50 Manchester C and Birmingham C
1950–51 Sheffield W and Everton
1951–52 Huddersfield T and Fulham
1952–53 Stoke C and Derby Co
1953–54 Middlesbrough and Liverpool
1954–55 Leicester C and Sheffield W
1955–56 Huddersfield T and Sheffield U
1956–57 Charlton Ath and Cardiff C
1957–58 Sheffield W and Sunderland
1958–59 Portsmouth and Aston Villa
1959–60 Luton T and Leeds U
1960–61 Preston NE and Newcastle U
1961–62 Chelsea and Cardiff C
1962–63 Manchester C and Leyton Orient
1963–64 Bolton W and Ipswich T
1964–65 Wolverhampton W and Birmingham C
1965–66 Northampton T and Blackburn R
1966–67 Aston Villa and Blackpool
1967–68 Fulham and Sheffield U
1968–69 Leicester C and QPR
1969–70 Sunderland and Sheffield W
1970–71 Burnley and Blackpool
1971–72 Huddersfield T and Nottingham F
1972–73 Crystal Palace and WBA
1973–74 Southampton, Manchester U, Norwich C
1974–75 Luton T, Chelsea, Carlisle U
1975–76 Wolverhampton W, Burnley, Sheffield U
1976–77 Sunderland, Stoke C, Tottenham H
1977–78 West Ham U, Newcastle U, Leicester C
1978–79 QPR, Birmingham C, Chelsea
1979–80 Bristol C, Derby Co, Bolton W
1980–81 Norwich C, Leicester C, Crystal Palace
1981–82 Leeds U, Wolverhampton W, Middlesbrough
1982–83 Manchester C, Swansea C, Brighton & HA
1983–84 Birmingham C, Notts Co, Wolverhampton W
1984–85 Norwich C, Sunderland, Stoke C
1985–86 Ipswich T, Birmingham C, WBA
1986–87 Leicester C, Manchester C, Aston Villa
1987–88 Chelsea**, Portsmouth, Watford, Oxford U
1988–89 Middlesbrough, West Ham U, Newcastle U
1989–90 Sheffield W, Charlton Ath, Millwall
1990–91 Sunderland and Derby Co
1991–92 Luton T, Notts Co, West Ham U
1992–93 Brentford, Cambridge U, Bristol R
1993–94 Birmingham C, Oxford U, Peterborough U
1994–95 Swindon T, Burnley, Bristol C, Notts Co
1995–96 Millwall, Watford, Luton T
1996–97 Grimsby T, Oldham Ath, Southend U
1997–98 Manchester C, Stoke C, Reading
1998–99 Bury, Oxford U, Bristol C
1999–2000 Walsall, Port Vale, Swindon T
2000–01 Huddersfield T, QPR, Tranmere R
2001–02 Crewe Alex, Barnsley, Stockport Co
2002–03 Sheffield W, Brighton & HA, Grimsby T
2003–04 Walsall, Bradford C, Wimbledon

***Relegated after play-offs.*
**Subsequently re-elected to Division 1 when League was extended after the War.*

FOOTBALL LEAGUE CHAMPIONSHIP TO FOOTBALL LEAGUE CHAMPIONSHIP 1

2004–05 Gillingham, Nottingham F, Rotherham U

DIVISION 2 TO DIVISION 3

1920–21 Stockport Co
1921–22 Bradford PA and Bristol C
1922–23 Rotherham Co and Wolverhampton W
1923–24 Nelson and Bristol C
1924–25 Crystal Palace and Coventry C
1925–26 Stoke C and Stockport Co
1926–27 Darlington and Bradford C
1927–28 Fulham and South Shields
1928–29 Port Vale and Clapton Orient
1929–30 Hull C and Notts Co
1930–31 Reading and Cardiff C
1931–32 Barnsley and Bristol C
1932–33 Chesterfield and Charlton Ath
1933–34 Millwall and Lincoln C
1934–35 Oldham Ath and Notts Co
1935–36 Port Vale and Hull C
1936–37 Doncaster R and Bradford C
1937–38 Barnsley and Stockport Co
1938–39 Norwich C and Tranmere R
1946–47 Swansea T and Newport Co
1947–48 Doncaster R and Millwall
1948–49 Nottingham F and Lincoln C
1949–50 Plymouth Arg and Bradford PA
1950–51 Grimsby T and Chesterfield
1951–52 Coventry C and QPR
1952–53 Southampton and Barnsley
1953–54 Brentford and Oldham Ath
1954–55 Ipswich T and Derby Co
1955–56 Plymouth Arg and Hull C
1956–57 Port Vale and Bury
1957–58 Doncaster R and Notts Co
1958–59 Barnsley and Grimsby T
1959–60 Bristol C and Hull C
1960–61 Lincoln C and Portsmouth
1961–62 Brighton & HA and Bristol R
1962–63 Walsall and Luton T
1963–64 Grimsby T and Scunthorpe U
1964–65 Swindon T and Swansea T
1965–66 Middlesbrough and Leyton Orient
1966–67 Northampton T and Bury
1967–68 Plymouth Arg and Rotherham U
1968–69 Fulham and Bury
1969–70 Preston NE and Aston Villa
1970–71 Blackburn R and Bolton W
1971–72 Charlton Ath and Watford
1972–73 Huddersfield T and Brighton & HA
1973–74 Crystal Palace, Preston NE, Swindon T
1974–75 Millwall, Cardiff C, Sheffield W
1975–76 Oxford U, York C, Portsmouth
1976–77 Carlisle U, Plymouth Arg, Hereford U
1977–78 Blackpool, Mansfield T, Hull C
1978–79 Sheffield U, Millwall, Blackburn R
1979–80 Fulham, Burnley, Charlton Ath
1980–81 Preston NE, Bristol C, Bristol R
1981–82 Cardiff C, Wrexham, Orient
1982–83 Rotherham U, Burnley, Bolton W

1983–84 Derby Co, Swansea C, Cambridge U
1984–85 Notts Co, Cardiff C, Wolverhampton W
1985–86 Carlisle U, Middlesbrough, Fulham
1986–87 Sunderland**, Grimsby T, Brighton & HA
1987–88 Huddersfield T, Reading, Sheffield U**
1988–89 Shrewsbury T, Birmingham C, Walsall
1989–90 Bournemouth, Bradford C, Stoke C
1990–91 WBA and Hull C
1991–92 Plymouth Arg, Brighton & HA, Port Vale
1992–93 Preston NE, Mansfield T, Wigan Ath, Chester C
1993–94 Fulham, Exeter C, Hartlepool U, Barnet
1994–95 Cambridge U, Plymouth Arg, Cardiff C, Chester C, Leyton Orient
1995–96 Carlisle U, Swansea C, Brighton & HA, Hull C
1996–97 Peterborough U, Shrewsbury T, Rotherham U, Notts Co
1997–98 Brentford, Plymouth Arg, Carlisle U, Southend U
1998–99 York C, Northampton T, Lincoln C, Macclesfield T
1999–2000 Cardiff C, Blackpool, Scunthorpe U, Chesterfield
2000–01 Bristol R, Luton T, Swansea C, Oxford U
2001–02 Bournemouth, Bury, Wrexham, Cambridge U
2002–03 Cheltenham T, Huddersfield T, Mansfield T Northampton T
2003–04 Grimsby T, Rushden & D, Notts Co, Wycombe W

FOOTBALL LEAGUE CHAMPIONSHIP 1 TO FOOTBALL LEAGUE CHAMPIONSHIP 2

2004–05 Torquay U, Wrexham, Peterborough U, Stockport Co

DIVISION 3 TO DIVISION 4

1958–59 Stockport Co, Doncaster R, Notts Co, Rochdale
1959–60 York C, Mansfield T, Wrexham, Accrington S
1960–61 Tranmere R, Bradford C, Colchester U, Chesterfield
1961–62 Torquay U, Lincoln C, Brentford, Newport Co
1962–63 Bradford PA, Brighton & HA, Carlisle U, Halifax T
1963–64 Millwall, Crewe Alex, Wrexham, Notts Co
1964–65 Luton T, Port Vale, Colchester U, Barnsley
1965–66 Southend U, Exeter C, Brentford, York C
1966–67 Swansea T, Darlington, Doncaster R, Workington
1967–68 Grimsby T, Colchester U, Scunthorpe U, Peterborough U (demoted)
1968–69 Northampton T, Hartlepool, Crewe Alex, Oldham Ath
1969–70 Bournemouth, Southport, Barrow, Stockport Co
1970–71 Reading, Bury, Doncaster R, Gillingham
1971–72 Mansfield T, Barnsley, Torquay U, Bradford C
1972–73 Rotherham U, Brentford, Swansea C, Scunthorpe U
1973–74 Cambridge U, Shrewsbury T, Southport, Rochdale
1974–75 Bournemouth, Tranmere R, Watford, Huddersfield T
1975–76 Aldershot, Colchester U, Southend U, Halifax T
1976–77 Reading, Northampton T, Grimsby T, York C
1977–78 Port Vale, Bradford C, Hereford U, Portsmouth
1978–79 Peterborough U, Walsall, Tranmere R, Lincoln C
1979–80 Bury, Southend U, Mansfield T, Wimbledon
1980–81 Sheffield U, Colchester U, Blackpool, Hull C
1981–82 Wimbledon, Swindon T, Bristol C, Chester
1982–83 Reading, Wrexham, Doncaster R, Chesterfield
1983–84 Scunthorpe U, Southend U, Port Vale, Exeter C
1984–85 Burnley, Orient, Preston NE, Cambridge U
1985–86 Lincoln C, Cardiff C, Wolverhampton W, Swansea C
1986–87 Bolton W**, Carlisle U, Darlington, Newport Co
1987–88 Rotherham U**, Grimsby T, York C, Doncaster R
1988–89 Southend U, Chesterfield, Gillingham, Aldershot
1989–90 Cardiff C, Northampton T, Blackpool, Walsall
1990–91 Crewe Alex, Rotherham U, Mansfield T
1991–92 Bury, Shrewsbury T, Torquay U, Darlington

** *Relegated after play-offs.*

APPLICATIONS FOR RE-ELECTION

FOURTH DIVISION
Eleven: Hartlepool U.
Seven: Crewe Alex.
Six: Barrow (lost League place to Hereford U 1972), Halifax T, Rochdale, Southport (lost League place to Wigan Ath 1978), York C.
Five: Chester C, Darlington, Lincoln C, Stockport Co, Workington (lost League place to Wimbledon 1977).
Four: Bradford PA (lost League place to Cambridge U 1970), Newport Co, Northampton T.
Three: Doncaster R, Hereford U.
Two: Bradford C, Exeter C, Oldham Ath, Scunthorpe U, Torquay U.
One: Aldershot, Colchester U, Gateshead (lost League place to Peterborough U 1960), Grimsby T, Swansea C, Tranmere R, Wrexham, Blackpool, Cambridge U, Preston NE.
Accrington S resigned and Oxford U were elected 1962.
Port Vale were forced to re-apply following expulsion in 1968.
Aldershot expelled March 1992. Maidstone U resigned August 1992.

THIRD DIVISIONS NORTH & SOUTH
Seven: Walsall.
Six: Exeter C, Halifax T, Newport Co.
Five: Accrington S, Barrow, Gillingham, New Brighton, Southport.
Four: Rochdale, Norwich C.
Three: Crystal Palace, Crewe Alex, Darlington, Hartlepool U, Merthyr T, Swindon T.
Two: Aberdare Ath, Aldershot, Ashington, Bournemouth, Brentford, Chester, Colchester U, Durham C, Millwall, Nelson, QPR, Rotherham U, Southend U, Tranmere R, Watford, Workington.
One: Bradford C, Bradford PA, Brighton & HA, Bristol R, Cardiff C, Carlisle U, Charlton Ath, Gateshead, Grimsby T, Mansfield T, Shrewsbury T, Torquay U, York C.

LEAGUE STATUS FROM 1986–87

RELEGATED FROM LEAGUE
1986–87 Lincoln C
1987–88 Newport Co;
1988–89 Darlington
1989–90 Colchester U
1990–91 —
1991–92 —
1992–93 Halifax T
1993–94 —
1994–95 —
1995–96 —
1996–97 Hereford U
1997–98 Doncaster R
1998–99 Scarborough
1999–2000 Chester C
2000–01 Barnet
2001–02 Halifax T
2002–03 Shrewsbury T, Exeter C
2003–04 Carlisle U, York C
2004–05 Kidderminster H, Cambridge U

PROMOTED TO LEAGUE
1986–87 Scarborough
1987–88 Lincoln C
1988–89 Maidstone U
1989–90 Darlington
1990–91 Barnet
1991–92 Colchester U
1992–93 Wycombe W
1993–94 —
1994–95 —
1995–96 —
1996–97 Macclesfield T
1997–98 Halifax T
1998–99 Cheltenham T
1999–2000 Kidderminster H
2000–01 Rushden & D
2001–02 Boston U
2002–03 Yeovil T, Doncaster R
2003–04 Chester C, Shrewsbury T
2004–05 Barnet, Carlisle U

FOOTBALL AWARDS 2005

FOOTBALLER OF THE YEAR

The Football Writers' Association Sir Stanley Matthews Trophy for the Footballer of the Year went to Frank Lampard of Chelsea and England.

Past Winners

1947–48 Stanley Matthews (Blackpool), 1948–49 Johnny Carey (Manchester U), 1949–50 Joe Mercer (Arsenal), 1950–51 Harry Johnston (Blackpool), 1951–52 Billy Wright (Wolverhampton W), 1952–53 Nat Lofthouse (Bolton W), 1953–54 Tom Finney (Preston NE), 1954–55 Don Revie (Manchester C), 1955–56 Bert Trautmann (Manchester C), 1956–57 Tom Finney (Preston NE), 1957–58 Danny Blanchflower (Tottenham H), 1958–59 Syd Owen (Luton T), 1959–60 Bill Slater (Wolverhampton W), 1960–61 Danny Blanchflower (Tottenham H), 1961–62 Jimmy Adamson (Burnley), 1962–63 Stanley Matthews (Stoke C), 1963–64 Bobby Moore (West Ham U), 1964–65 Bobby Collins (Leeds U), 1965–66 Bobby Charlton (Manchester U), 1966–67 Jackie Charlton (Leeds U), 1967–68 George Best (Manchester U), 1968–69 Dave Mackay (Derby Co) shared with Tony Book (Manchester C), 1969–70 Billy Bremner (Leeds U), 1970–71 Frank McLintock (Arsenal), 1971–72 Gordon Banks (Stoke C), 1972–73 Pat Jennings (Tottenham H), 1973–74 Ian Callaghan (Liverpool), 1974–75 Alan Mullery (Fulham), 1975–76 Kevin Keegan (Liverpool), 1976–77 Emlyn Hughes (Liverpool), 1977–78 Kenny Burns (Nottingham F), 1978–79 Kenny Dalglish (Liverpool), 1979–80 Terry McDermott (Liverpool), 1980–81 Frans Thijssen (Ipswich T), 1981–82 Steve Perryman (Tottenham H), 1982–83 Kenny Dalglish (Liverpool), 1983–84 Ian Rush (Liverpool), 1984–85 Neville Southall (Everton), 1985–86 Gary Lineker (Everton), 1986–87 Clive Allen (Tottenham H), 1987–88 John Barnes (Liverpool), 1988–89 Steve Nicol (Liverpool), 1989–90 John Barnes (Liverpool), 1990–91 Gordon Strachan (Leeds U), 1991–92 Gary Lineker (Tottenham H), 1992–93 Chris Waddle (Sheffield W), 1993–94 Alan Shearer (Blackburn R), 1994–95 Jurgen Klinsmann (Tottenham H), 1995–96 Eric Cantana (Manchester U), 1996–97 Gianfranco Zola (Chelsea), 1997–98 Dennis Bergkamp (Arsenal), 1998–99 David Ginola (Tottenham H), 1999–2000 Roy Keane (Manchester U), 2000–01 Teddy Sheringham (Manchester U), 2001–02 Robert Pires (Arsenal), 2002–03 Thierry Henry (Arsenal), 2003–04 Thierry Henry (Arsenal).

THE PFA AWARDS 2005

Player of the Year: John Terry, Chelsea and England.
Young Player of the Year: Wayne Rooney, Manchester U and England.
Merit Award: Shaka Hislop (Portsmouth).

SCOTTISH FOOTBALL WRITERS ASSOCIATION 2005

Player of the Year: John Hartson (Celtic).

SCOTTISH PFA 'PLAYER OF THE YEAR' AWARDS 2005

Player of the Year: John Hartson (Celtic) and Fernando Ricksen (Rangers).
First Division: Russell Latapy (Falkirk).
Second Division: Steven Hampshire (Brechin C).
Third Division: David Bingham (Gretna).
Young Player of the Year: Derek Riordan (Hibernian).

EUROPEAN FOOTBALLER OF THE YEAR 2004

Andriy Shevchenko, AC Milan and Ukraine.

WORLD PLAYER OF THE YEAR 2004

Ronaldinho, Barcelona and Brazil.

WOMEN'S PLAYER OF THE YEAR 2004

Birgit Prinz, Germany.

LEAGUE ATTENDANCES SINCE 1946–47

Season	*Matches*	*Total*	*Div. 1*	*Div. 2*	*Div. 3 (S)*	*Div. 3 (N)*
1946–47	1848	35,604,606	15,005,316	11,071,572	5,664,004	3,863,714
1947–48	1848	40,259,130	16,732,341	12,286,350	6,653,610	4,586,829
1948–49	1848	41,271,414	17,914,667	11,353,237	6,998,429	5,005,081
1949–50	1848	40,517,865	17,278,625	11,694,158	7,104,155	4,440,927
1950–51	2028	39,584,967	16,679,454	10,780,580	7,367,884	4,757,109
1951–52	2028	39,015,866	16,110,322	11,066,189	6,958,927	4,880,428
1952–53	2028	37,149,966	16,050,278	9,686,654	6,704,299	4,708,735
1953–54	2028	36,174,590	16,154,915	9,510,053	6,311,508	4,198,114
1954–55	2028	34,133,103	15,087,221	8,988,794	5,996,017	4,051,071
1955–56	2028	33,150,809	14,108,961	9,080,002	5,692,479	4,269,367
1956–57	2028	32,744,405	13,803,037	8,718,162	5,622,189	4,601,017
1957–58	2028	33,562,208	14,468,652	8,663,712	6,097,183	4,332,661
					Div. 3	*Div. 4*
1958–59	2028	33,610,985	14,727,691	8,641,997	5,946,600	4,276,697
1959–60	2028	32,538,611	14,391,227	8,399,627	5,739,707	4,008,050
1960–61	2028	28,619,754	12,926,948	7,033,936	4,784,256	3,874,614
1961–62	2015	27,979,902	12,061,194	7,453,089	5,199,106	3,266,513
1962–63	2028	28,885,852	12,490,239	7,792,770	5,341,362	3,261,481
1963–64	2028	28,535,022	12,486,626	7,594,158	5,419,157	3,035,081
1964–65	2028	27,641,168	12,708,752	6,984,104	4,436,245	3,512,067
1965–66	2028	27,206,980	12,480,644	6,914,757	4,779,150	3,032,429
1966–67	2028	28,902,596	14,242,957	7,253,819	4,421,172	2,984,648
1967–68	2028	30,107,298	15,289,410	7,450,410	4,013,087	3,354,391
1968–69	2028	29,382,172	14,584,851	7,382,390	4,339,656	3,075,275
1969–70	2028	29,600,972	14,868,754	7,581,728	4,223,761	2,926,729
1970–71	2028	28,194,146	13,954,337	7,098,265	4,377,213	2,764,331
1971–72	2028	28,700,729	14,484,603	6,769,308	4,697,392	2,749,426
1972–73	2028	25,448,642	13,998,154	5,631,730	3,737,252	2,081,506
1973–74	2027	24,982,203	13,070,991	6,326,108	3,421,624	2,163,480
1974–75	2028	25,577,977	12,613,178	6,955,970	4,086,145	1,992,684
1975–76	2028	24,896,053	13,089,861	5,798,405	3,948,449	2,059,338
1976–77	2028	26,182,800	13,647,585	6,250,597	4,152,218	2,132,400
1977–78	2028	25,392,872	13,255,677	6,474,763	3,332,042	2,330,390
1978–79	2028	24,540,627	12,704,549	6,153,223	3,374,558	2,308,297
1979–80	2028	24,623,975	12,163,002	6,112,025	3,999,328	2,349,620
1980–81	2028	21,907,569	11,392,894	5,175,442	3,637,854	1,701,379
1981–82	2028	20,006,961	10,420,793	4,750,463	2,836,915	1,998,790
1982–83	2028	18,766,158	9,295,613	4,974,937	2,943,568	1,552,040
1983–84	2028	18,358,631	8,711,448	5,359,757	2,729,942	1,557,484
1984–85	2028	17,849,835	9,761,404	4,030,823	2,667,008	1,390,600
1985–86	2028	16,488,577	9,037,854	3,551,968	2,490,481	1,408,274
1986–87	2028	17,379,218	9,144,676	4,168,131	2,350,970	1,715,441
1987–88	2030	17,959,732	8,094,571	5,341,599	2,751,275	1,772,287
1988–89	2036	18,464,192	7,809,993	5,887,805	3,035,327	1,791,067
1989–90	2036	19,445,442	7,883,039	6,867,674	2,803,551	1,891,178
1990–91	2036	19,508,202	8,618,709	6,285,068	2,835,759	1,768,666
1991–92	2064*	20,487,273	9,989,160	5,809,787	2,993,352	1,694,974
		Total	*FA Premier*	*Div. 1*	*Div. 2*	*Div. 3*
1992–93	2028	20,657,327	9,759,809	5,874,017	3,483,073	1,540,428
1993–94	2028	21,683,381	10,644,551	6,487,104	2,972,702	1,579,024
1994–95	2028	21,856,020	11,213,168	6,044,293	3,037,752	1,560,807
1995–96	2036	21,844,416	10,469,107	6,566,349	2,843,652	1,965,308
1996–97	2036	22,783,163	10,804,762	6,931,539	3,195,223	1,851,639
1997–98	2036	24,692,608	11,092,106	8,330,018	3,503,264	1,767,220
1998–99	2036	25,435,542	11,620,326	7,543,369	4,169,697	2,102,150
1999-2000	2036	25,341,090	11,668,497	7,810,208	3,700,433	2,161,952
2000–01	2036	26,030,167	12,472,094	7,909,512	3,488,166	2,160,395
2001–02	2036	27,756,977	13,043,118	8,352,128	3,963,153	2,398,578
2002–03	2036	28,343,386	13,468,965	8,521,017	3,892,469	2,460,935
2003–04	2036	29,197,510	13,303,136	8,772,780	4,146,495	2,975,099
2004–05	2036	29,245,870	12,878,791	9,612,761	4,270,674	2,483,644

**Figures include matches played by Aldershot.*
Football League official total for their three divisions in 2001–02 was 14,716,162.
The official Premiership total was 12,881,768 for 2004–05.

ENGLISH LEAGUE ATTENDANCES 2004–05

FA BARCLAYCARD PREMIERSHIP ATTENDANCES

	Average Gate			Season 2004/05	
	2003/04	2004/05	+/–%	Highest	Lowest
Arsenal	38,079	37,978	–0.27	38,164	37,010
Aston Villa	36,622	37,354	+2.00	42,593	31,312
Birmingham City	29,078	28,760	–1.09	29,382	27,177
Blackburn Rovers	24,376	22,314	–8.46	29,271	18,006
Bolton Wanderers	26,718	26,006	–2.66	27,880	23,692
Charlton Athletic	26,278	26,403	+0.48	27,104	24,263
Chelsea	41,272	41,870	+1.45	42,328	40,864
Crystal Palace	17,344	24,108	+39.00	26,193	20,705
Everton	38,837	36,834	–5.16	40,552	32,406
Fulham	16,240	19,838	+22.16	21,940	16,180
Liverpool	42,677	42,587	–0.21	44,224	35,064
Manchester City	46,830	45,192	–3.50	47,221	42,453
Manchester United	67,641	67,871	+0.34	67,989	67,704
Middlesbrough	30,395	31,965	+5.17	34,836	29,603
Newcastle United	51,966	51,844	–0.23	52,326	50,430
Norwich City	19,074	24,354	+27.68	25,522	23,549
Portsmouth	20,054	20,072	+0.09	20,210	19,620
Southampton	31,717	30,610	–3.49	32,066	27,343
Tottenham Hotspur	34,872	35,883	+2.90	36,254	35,105
West Bromwich Albion	24,765	25,987	+4.93	27,751	23,849

TOTAL ATTENDANCES: 12,878,791 (380 games)
Average 33,892 (–3.19%)
HIGHEST: 67,989 Manchester United v Portsmouth
LOWEST: 16,180 Fulham v West Bromwich Albion
HIGHEST AVERAGE: 67,871 Manchester United
LOWEST AVERAGE: 19,838 Fulham

FOOTBALL LEAGUE: CHAMPIONSHIP ATTENDANCES

	Average Gate			Season 2004/05	
	2003/04	2004/05	+/–%	Highest	Lowest
Brighton & Hove Albion	6,248	6,434	+3.0	6,848	5,996
Burnley	12,541	12,466	–0.6	17,789	7,200
Cardiff City	15,569	12,976	–16.7	17,006	10,007
Coventry City	14,816	16,048	+8.3	22,728	11,966
Crewe Alexandra	7,741	7,403	–4.4	9,269	5,409
Derby County	22,200	25,219	+13.6	31,237	22,096
Gillingham	8,517	8,528	+0.1	10,810	6,089
Ipswich Town	24,520	25,651	+4.6	30,003	21,246
Leeds United	36,666	29,207	–20.3	34,496	24,585
Leicester City	30,983	24,137	–22.1	30,231	21,249
Millwall	10,497	11,699	+11.5	15,603	8,835
Nottingham Forest	24,759	23,608	–4.6	28,887	19,209
Plymouth Argyle	12,654	16,428	+29.8	20,555	13,508
Preston North End	14,150	13,889	–1.8	20,221	10,339
Queens Park Rangers	14,785	16,056	+8.6	18,363	13,559
Reading	15,095	17,169	+13.7	23,203	11,404
Rotherham United	7,138	6,272	–12.1	9,050	3,804
Sheffield United	21,646	19,594	–9.5	22,959	16,079
Stoke City	14,425	16,456	+14.1	23,029	12,785
Sunderland	27,119	28,821	+6.3	47,350	22,267
Watford	14,856	14,290	–3.8	19,673	11,084
West Ham United	31,167	27,403	–12.1	33,482	22,031
Wigan Athletic	9,505	11,571	+21.7	20,745	7,547
Wolverhampton Wanderers	28,864	26,620	–7.8	28,516	24,336

TOTAL ATTENDANCES: 9,612,761 (552 games)
Average 17,414 (+9.6%)
HIGHEST: 47,350 Sunderland v Stoke City
LOWEST: 3,804 Rotherham United v Reading
HIGHEST AVERAGE: 29,207 Leeds United
LOWEST AVERAGE: 6,272 Rotherham United

Premiership and Football League attendance averages and highest crowd figures for 2004–05 are unofficial. The official Premiership total was 12,881,768.

FOOTBALL LEAGUE: CHAMPIONSHIP 1 ATTENDANCES

	Average Gate			*Season 2004/05*	
	2003/04	2004/05	+/–%	Highest	Lowest
Barnsley	9,620	9,779	+1.7	19,659	7,466
Blackpool	6,326	6,032	–4.6	8,774	4,179
AFC Bournemouth	6,913	7,123	+3.0	9,058	5,390
Bradford City	11,377	8,839	–22.3	15,417	6,409
Brentford	5,542	6,082	+9.7	9,604	4,643
Bristol City	12,879	11,391	–11.6	14,852	8,267
Chesterfield	4,331	4,961	+14.5	7,831	3,715
Colchester United	3,536	3,534	–0.1	4,834	2,616
Doncaster Rovers	6,939	6,886	–0.8	10,131	5,209
Hartlepool United	5,419	5,182	–4.4	6,520	4,206
Huddersfield Town	10,528	11,905	+13.1	17,292	9,194
Hull City	16,847	18,027	+7.0	24,277	14,317
Luton Town	6,339	7,940	+25.3	9,500	6,603
Milton Keynes Dons	4,751	4,896	+3.1	7,620	3,015
Oldham Athletic	6,566	6,462	–1.6	9,645	4,291
Peterborough United	5,274	4,341	–17.7	7,662	3,048
Port Vale	5,810	4,973	–14.4	8,671	3,496
Sheffield Wednesday	22,336	23,100	+3.4	28,798	18,465
Stockport County	5,315	5,000	–5.9	7,473	3,850
Swindon Town	7,925	5,835	–26.4	8,275	4,484
Torquay United	3,460	3,511	+1.5	5,347	2,384
Tranmere Rovers	7,606	9,044	+18.9	12,684	7,613
Walsall	7,853	6,085	–22.5	8,225	4,966
Wrexham	4,440	4,751	+7.0	7,833	2,391

TOTAL ATTENDANCES: 4,270,674 (552 games)
Average 7,737 (+3.0%)
HIGHEST: 28,798 Sheffield Wednesday v Bristol City
LOWEST: 2,384 Torquay United v Wrexham
HIGHEST AVERAGE: 23,100 Sheffield Wednesday
LOWEST AVERAGE: 3,511 Torquay United

FOOTBALL LEAGUE: CHAMPIONSHIP 2 ATTENDANCES

	Average Gate			*Season 2004/05*	
	2003/04	2004/05	+/–%	Highest	Lowest
Boston United	2,964	2,932	–1.1	6,445	2,053
Bristol Rovers	7,142	7,077	–0.9	9,295	5,294
Bury	2,892	3,032	+4.8	7,575	1,866
Cambridge United	3,919	3,616	–7.7	6,715	2,021
Cheltenham Town	4,116	3,648	–11.4	5,511	2,706
Chester City	3,065	2,812	–8.3	3,847	1,643
Darlington	5,023	4,245	–15.5	7,028	2,709
Grimsby Town	4,730	4,943	+4.5	7,941	3,144
Kidderminster Harriers	2,980	2,785	–6.5	4,288	2,082
Leyton Orient	4,157	3,712	–10.7	4,753	2,436
Lincoln City	4,910	4,927	+0.3	8,056	3,274
Macclesfield Town	2,385	2,272	–4.7	3,076	1,436
Mansfield Town	5,207	4,092	–21.4	7,682	2,497
Northampton Town	5,306	5,927	+11.7	7,107	4,373
Notts County	5,940	5,384	–9.4	10,005	3,586
Oxford United	6,296	5,347	–15.1	7,830	4,089
Rochdale	3,277	2,690	–17.9	3,912	2,107
Rushden & Diamonds	4,457	3,321	–25.5	5,520	1,803
Scunthorpe United	3,840	5,178	+34.8	8,054	3,402
Shrewsbury Town	4,007	4,251	+6.1	6,285	2,956
Southend United	4,535	6,077	+34.0	11,735	3,753
Swansea City	6,853	8,458	+23.4	11,469	6,462
Wycombe Wanderers	5,291	4,937	–6.7	8,124	3,844
Yeovil Town	6,197	6,320	+2.0	9,153	4,639

TOTAL ATTENDANCES: 2,483,644 (552 games)
Average 4,499 (–16.5%)
HIGHEST: 11,735 Southend United v Yeovil Town
LOWEST: 1,436 Macclesfield Town v Cambridge United
HIGHEST AVERAGE: 8,458 Swansea City
LOWEST AVERAGE: 2,272 Macclesfield Town

LEAGUE CUP FINALISTS 1961–2005

Played as a two-leg final until 1966. All subsequent finals at Wembley until 2000, then at Millennium Stadium, Cardiff.

Year	*Winners*	*Runners-up*	*Score*
1961	Aston Villa	Rotherham U	0-2, 3-0 (aet)
1962	Norwich C	Rochdale	3-0, 1-0
1963	Birmingham C	Aston Villa	3-1, 0-0
1964	Leicester C	Stoke C	1-1, 3-2
1965	Chelsea	Leicester C	3-2, 0-0
1966	WBA	West Ham U	1-2, 4-1
1967	QPR	WBA	3-2
1968	Leeds U	Arsenal	1-0
1969	Swindon T	Arsenal	3-1 (aet)
1970	Manchester C	WBA	2-1 (aet)
1971	Tottenham H	Aston Villa	2-0
1972	Stoke C	Chelsea	2-1
1973	Tottenham H	Norwich C	1-0
1974	Wolverhampton W	Manchester C	2-1
1975	Aston Villa	Norwich C	1-0
1976	Manchester C	Newcastle U	2-1
1977	Aston Villa	Everton	0-0, 1-1 (aet), 3-2 (aet)
1978	Nottingham F	Liverpool	0-0 (aet), 1-0
1979	Nottingham F	Southampton	3-2
1980	Wolverhampton W	Nottingham F	1-0
1981	Liverpool	West Ham U	1-1 (aet), 2-1

MILK CUP

1982	Liverpool	Tottenham H	3-1 (aet)
1983	Liverpool	Manchester U	2-1 (aet)
1984	Liverpool	Everton	0-0 (aet), 1-0
1985	Norwich C	Sunderland	1-0
1986	Oxford U	QPR	3-0

LITTLEWOODS CUP

1987	Arsenal	Liverpool	2-1
1988	Luton T	Arsenal	3-2
1989	Nottingham F	Luton T	3-1
1990	Nottingham F	Oldham Ath	1-0

RUMBELOWS LEAGUE CUP

1991	Sheffield W	Manchester U	1-0
1992	Manchester U	Nottingham F	1-0

COCA-COLA CUP

1993	Arsenal	Sheffield W	2-1
1994	Aston Villa	Manchester U	3-1
1995	Liverpool	Bolton W	2-1
1996	Aston Villa	Leeds U	3-0
1997	Leicester C	Middlesbrough	1-1 (aet), 1-0 (aet)
1998	Chelsea	Middlesbrough	2-0 (aet)

WORTHINGTON CUP

1999	Tottenham H	Leicester C	1-0
2000	Leicester C	Tranmere R	2-1
2001	Liverpool	Birmingham C	1-1 (aet)
Liverpool won 5-4 on penalties			
2002	Blackburn R	Tottenham H	2-1
2003	Liverpool	Manchester U	2-0

CARLING CUP

2004	Middlesbrough	Bolton W	2-1
2005	Chelsea	Liverpool	3-2 (aet)

LEAGUE CUP WINS

Liverpool 7, Aston Villa 5, Nottingham F 4, Chelsea 3, Leicester C 3, Tottenham H 3, Arsenal 2, Manchester C 2, Norwich C 2, Wolverhampton W 2, Birmingham C 1, Blackburn R 1, Leeds U 1, Luton T 1, Manchester U 1, Middlesbrough 1, Oxford U 1, QPR 1, Sheffield W 1, Stoke C 1, Swindon T 1, WBA 1.

APPEARANCES IN FINALS

Liverpool 10, Aston Villa 7, Nottingham F 6, Arsenal 5, Leicester C 5, Manchester U 5, Tottenham H 5, Chelsea 4, Norwich C 4, Manchester C 3, Middlesbrough 3, WBA 3, Birmingham C 2, Bolton W 2, Everton 2, Leeds U 2, Luton T 2, QPR 2, Sheffield W 2, Stoke C 2, West Ham U 2, Wolverhampton W 2, Blackburn R 1, Newcastle U 1, Oldham Ath 1, Oxford U 1, Rochdale 1, Rotherham U 1, Southampton 1, Sunderland 1, Swindon T 1, Tranmere R 1.

APPEARANCES IN SEMI-FINALS

Liverpool 13, Aston Villa 12, Arsenal 10, Tottenham H 10, Manchester U 9, Chelsea 8, West Ham U 7, Nottingham F 6, Leeds U 5, Leicester C 5, Manchester C 5, Middlesbrough 5, Norwich C 5, Birmingham C 4, Blackburn R 4, Bolton W 4, Sheffield W 4, WBA 4, Burnley 3, Crystal Palace 3, Everton 3, Ipswich T 3, QPR 3, Sunderland 3, Swindon T 3, Wolverhampton W 3, Bristol C 2, Coventry C 2, Luton T 2, Oxford U 2, Plymouth Arg 2, Southampton 2, Stoke C 2, Tranmere R 2, Watford 2, Wimbledon 2, Blackpool 1, Bury 1, Cardiff C 1, Carlisle U 1, Chester C 1, Derby Co 1, Huddersfield T 1, Newcastle U 1, Oldham Ath 1, Peterborough U 1, Rochdale 1, Rotherham U 1, Sheffield U 1, Shrewsbury T 1, Stockport Co 1, Walsall 1.

CARLING CUP 2004–05

▪ *Denotes player sent off.*

FIRST ROUND

Monday, 23 August 2004

Rochdale (2) 2 *(Holt 4, Tait 26)*
Wolverhampton W (1) 4 *(Ince 42, Clarke 53, Miller 60, Andrews 78)* 3292
Rochdale: Edwards; Evans, Gallimore, Heald, Burgess, Jones, Cash, Clarke, Tait, Holt (McGivern), Probets (McCourt).
Wolverhampton W: Oakes; Lowe, Clyde, Ince (Olofinjana), Edwards, Craddock, Newton, Andrews, Clarke, Miller, Cooper.

Tuesday, 24 August 2004

Brighton & HA (1) 1 *(Butters 11)*
Bristol R (2) 2 *(Thorpe 25, Walker 30)* 4217
Brighton & HA: Kuipers; Virgo, Harding, Cullip, Butters, Hinshelwood, Currie, Nicolas, Knight, Molango (Robinson), Jarrett (Jones).
Bristol R: Miller; Hinton, Ryan, Edwards, Campbell, Elliott, Trollope, Hunt, Walker (Agogo), Thorpe (Savage), Gibb.

Bury (2) 2 *(Mattis 12, Challinor 18)*
Burnley (2) 3 *(Mattis 17 (og), Blake 33 (pen), 52)* 3648
Bury: Garner; Whaley (Newby), Barry-Murphy (Dunfield), Challinor, Unsworth, Scott, Flitcroft, Mattis, Porter, Nugent, Kennedy.
Burnley: Coyne; Camara, Branch, McGreal, Duff, Sinclair, Moore, Chaplow, Blake, Hyde (Roche), Grant.

Colchester U (1) 2 *(Fagan 12, Johnson 61)*
Cheltenham T (0) 1 *(Devaney 70)* 2144
Colchester U: Davison; Stockley, Keith, Brown, Chilvers, Halford (White), Johnson (May), Cade (Bowditch), Andrews, Fagan, Watson.
Cheltenham T: Higgs; Wilson, Victory, Gill, Duff, Taylor, Melligan, Devaney (Vincent), Bird (Odejayi), Guinan (Spencer), McCann.

Crewe Alex (4) 4 *(Jones S 3, 44, Rivers 9, Ashton 12)*
Blackpool (0) 1 *(Taylor 75)* 2994
Crewe Alex: Williams; Jones B, Tonkin, Lunt, Foster, Moses, Vaughan, Rivers, Ashton, Jones S, Sorvel (Cochrane).
Blackpool: Jones L; Richardson, Edwards R, Grayson, McGregor, Clare, Bullock, Michael Flynn, Parker, Taylor, Coid.

Darlington (0) 0
Barnsley (1) 2 *(Shuker 14, Reid 75 (pen))* 2789
Darlington: Russell S; Hughes (Convery), Kendrick, Keltie (Maddison), Fleming, Hutchinson, Wainwright, Close, Clarke (Scartiscini), Russell C, Clark.
Barnsley: Colgan; Hassell, Williams T, Reid, Carbon, Vaughan, Kay, Wroe, Boulding (Nardiello), Conlon (Stallard), Shuker.

Doncaster R (1) 3 *(Fortune-West 36, Doolan 53, McIndoe 56)*
Port Vale (1) 1 *(Smith D 25)* 3943
Doncaster R: Warrington; Marples, Ryan, Foster, Fenton, Green (Ravenhill), Coppinger (Mulligan), Doolan, Blundell, Fortune-West, McIndoe.
Port Vale: Brain; Brown, James, Collins, Smith D (Smith J), Pilkington, Armstrong (Birchall), Paynter, Brooker, Matthews, Reid.

Gillingham (0) 1 *(Sidibe 56)*
Northampton T (2) 2 *(Sabin 32, McGleish 41)* 3108
Gillingham: Brown; Rose, Johnson L, Smith, Ashby, Cox, Jarvis, Pouton (Spiller), Sidibe, Agyemang, Perpetuini (Roberts).
Northampton T: Harper; Chambers, Jaszczun, Bojic, Willmott, Galbraith (Reeves), Low, Richards (Youngs), Sabin, McGleish (Morison), Hicks.

Grimsby T (1) 1 *(Parkinson 17)*
Wigan Ath (0) 0 3005
Grimsby T: Williams A; McDermott, Crowe, Whittle, Ramsden, Gordon, Fleming, Pinault, Parkinson, Sestanovich (Marcelle), Reddy.
Wigan Ath: Walsh; Eaden, Baines, Mahon, Breckin, Emerson, Mitchell, Bullard, Graham, Roberts N (Teale), McCulloch.

Hartlepool U (0) 2 *(Boyd 79, Sweeney 87)*
Macclesfield T (0) 1 *(Parkin 48)* 2883
Hartlepool U: Konstantopoulos; Craddock (Williams), Robson, Nelson, Westwood, Tinkler, Strachan, Sweeney, Boyd, Betsy (Porter), Humphreys.
Macclesfield T: Wilson; Bailey, Potter, Welch, Barras, Briscoe, Widdrington, Harsley, Tipton (Sheron), Parkin, Whitaker.

Hull C (1) 2 *(Keane 22, France 66)*
Wrexham (2) 2 *(Sam 14, Ferguson 35)* 6079
Hull C: Duke; Joseph, Edge (Dawson), Ashbee, Cort, Delaney, Price (Green), Keane, Facey (Elliott), Walters, France.
Wrexham: Dibble; Bennett, Holt, Carey, Pejic, Roberts (Mackin), Smith (Spender), Ferguson, Armstrong, Sam (Llewellyn), Williams.
aet; Wrexham won 3-1 on penalties.

Ipswich T (0) 2 *(Miller 73, Westlake 90)*
Brentford (0) 0 10,190
Ipswich T: Price; Mitchell (Horlock), Barron, Dinning, Diallo, Naylor, Magilton (Miller), Bowditch, Counago (Kuqi), Bent, Westlake.
Brentford: Nelson; Dobson, Frampton, Rhodes (Rankin), Fitzgerald SB, Myers, Smith (Talbot), O'Connor, Peters (Tabb), Burton, Hargreaves.

Kidderminster H (1) 1 *(Brown 32)*
Cardiff C (1) 1 *(Earnshaw 28)* 1897
Kidderminster H: Danby; Jenkins, Burton, Advice-Desruisseaux, Hatswell, McHale, Mellon (Appleby), Keates, Christiansen, Brown (Foster I), Roberts (Gleeson).
Cardiff C: Warner; Weston, Vidmar▪, Boland, Gabbidon, Collins, McAnuff, Bullock (Kavanagh), Earnshaw, Campbell (Fleetwood), Parry (Robinson).
aet; Cardiff C won 5-4 on penalties.

Leeds U (1) 1 *(Pugh 23)*
Huddersfield T (0) 0 30,115
Leeds U: Sullivan; Kelly, Crainey, Wright, Butler, Carlisle, Richardson, Pugh, Ricketts, Joachim, Guppy (McMaster).
Huddersfield T: Gray; Holdsworth, Edwards (McAliskey), Mirfin, Clarke N, Sodje E, Worthington, Brandon, Abbott, Booth (Mendes), Carss.

Leyton Orient (1) 1 *(Steele 12)*
Bournemouth (1) 3 *(Browning 33, Cummings 64, Hayter 71)* 1705
Leyton Orient: Morris; Lockwood, Scott (Newey), Miller, White, Zakuani, Carlisle (Alexander), Hunt (Saah), Steele, Ibehre, Simpson.
Bournemouth: Moss N; Young, Cummings, Broadhurst, Fletcher C, Maher, Stock (O'Connor G), Browning, Hayter, Holmes (Connell), Elliott.

Lincoln C (0) 3 *(Taylor-Fletcher 79 (pen), Yeo 80, McCombe 90)*
Derby Co (1) 1 *(Idiakez 28)* 4982
Lincoln C: Marriott; Bloomer, McAuley, McCombe, Weaver (Green), Futcher, Butcher, Blackwood, Taylor-Fletcher, Yeo, Gain (Peat).
Derby Co: Camp; Jackson (Kenna), Vincent, Bolder (Junior), Johnson, Huddlestone, Holmes (Taylor), Idiakez, Tudgay, Peschisolido, Reich.

Oldham Ath (0) 2 *(Eyres 72, Eyre 76 (pen))*
Stoke C (1) 1 *(Asaba 25)* 2861
Oldham Ath: Pogliacomi; Holden, Griffin, Bonner, Haining (Beharall), Arber, Eyre, Boshell, Killen (Barlow), Johnson, Eyres.
Stoke C: Simonsen; Thomas■, Clarke, Henry, Halls, Hill, Russell, Asaba, Greenacre (Brammer), Neal (Noel-Williams), Hall.

Peterborough U (0) 0
Milton Keynes D (0) 3 *(McLeod 63, Smart 80, Kamara 90)* 2886
Peterborough U: Tyler; Kanu, Legg (Semple), Kennedy, Rea, Ireland, Farrell (Sonner), Thomson (Nolan), Clarke, Platt, Woodhouse.
Milton Keynes D: Martin; Edds, Palmer, Chorley, Ntimban-Zeh, Crooks, Herve (Kamara), Small, Smart, McLeod, Koo-Boothe (Puncheon).

QPR (1) 3 *(Cureton 39, Rowlands 77, Gallen 90)*
Swansea C (0) 0 4882
QPR: Day; Bignot, Padula, Santos, Shittu (Bean), Forbes, Rowlands, Gallen, Furlong (McLeod), Cureton (Bircham), Cook.
Swansea C: Gueret; Tate, Ricketts, Austin, Monk, O'Leary, Forbes, Nugent (Maylett), Trundle, Britton, Robinson (Fisken).

Rotherham U (1) 2 *(Proctor 33, Barker R 83)*
Chesterfield (1) 1 *(Allott 15)* 3845
Rotherham U: Pollitt; Stockdale, Minto, Vernazza, Swailes, Barker S, Sedgwick, Mullin, Proctor, Barker R, Garner.
Chesterfield: Muggleton; Bailey, Nicholson, Campbell-Ryce (Smith), O'Hare (Blatherwick), Evatt, Niven, Innes, De Bolla, Allott, N'Toya.

Rushden & D (0) 0
Swindon T (0) 1 *(Hewlett 90)* 1672
Rushden & D: Turley; Connelly, Hawkins, Gulliver, Gier, Gray, Bell (Dove), Mills, Braniff, Hay (Kelly), Burgess.
Swindon T: Book; Garrard (O'Hanlon), Nicolas, Smith (Igoe), Reeves, Ifil, Robinson, Howard, Fallon, Opara (Parkin), Hewlett.

Sheffield U (1) 4 *(Morgan 36, Cutler 108 (og), Tonge 112, Lester 116)*
Stockport Co (1) 1 *(Harley 2 (og))* 5399
Sheffield U: Kenny; Jagielka, Harley, Forte (McCall), Bromby, Morgan, Montgomery (Tonge), Thirlwell, Ward, Hayles (Lester), Quinn.
Stockport Co: Cutler; Geary, Adams, Hardiker, Williams A, Goodwin, Cartwright, Jackman (Morrison), Daly, Beckett (Williams C), Bridge-Wilkinson (Welsh).
aet.

Sunderland (1) 3 *(Hessey 41 (og), Kyle 55, Caldwell 69)*
Chester C (0) 0 11,450
Sunderland: Myhre (Poom); Caldwell, Arca (Lawrence), Robinson, Breen, Whitehead, Lynch, Thornton, Kyle, Stewart (Elliott), Oster.
Chester C: Brown W; Vaughan, McIntyre, Collins, Hessey, Bolland, Drummond, Navarro, Branch (Davies), Belle (Carden), Ellison.

Tranmere R (0) 2 *(Zola 49, McAteer 80)*
Shrewsbury T (0) 1 *(Rodgers 67)* 4489
Tranmere R: Achterberg; Taylor, Roberts, McAteer, Jackson, Sharps, Hall, Rankine (Harrison), Hume, Zola (Dadi), Beresford (Jennings).
Shrewsbury T: Howie; Moss, Lowe, Walton, Tinson, Ridler (Cramb), Smith, Edwards (Tolley), Rodgers, Grant, Aiston.

Watford (0) 1 *(Ferrell 82)*
Cambridge U (0) 0 6558
Watford: Lee; Darlington, Mayo, Mahon, Cox, Demerit, Ardley, Young, Webber (Dyer), Helguson (Bouazza), Devlin (Ferrell).
Cambridge U: Ruddy; Gleeson, El Kholti, Tann, Angus (Duncan), Walker, Tudor (Guttridge), Quinton, Easter, Turner (Chillingworth), Nicholls.

West Ham U (1) 2 *(Harewood 11, 90)*
Southend U (0) 0 16,910
West Ham U: Walker; McClenahan, Brevett, Reo-Coker, Repka, Ward, Chadwick (Noble), Nowland, Rebrov (Sheringham), Harewood, Cohen.
Southend U: Griemink; Jupp, Nicolau, Maher, Barrett, Edwards, Gower, Bentley, Broughton (Bramble), Dudfield (Gray), Pettefer.

Wycombe W (0) 0
Bristol C (0) 1 *(Lita 70)* 1778
Wycombe W: Talia; Uhlenbeek, Silk, Burnell, Nethercott, Johnson, Senda, Tyson, Stonebridge, Birchall, Easton.
Bristol C: Phillips; Smith, Woodman, Doherty, Fortune, Hill, Murray (Gillespie), Orr, Lita, Miller, Roberts (Tinnion).

Yeovil T (1) 3 *(Johnson 28, 69, 102)*
Plymouth Arg (2) 2 *(Crawford 30, Wotton 42 (pen))* 6217
Yeovil T: Weale; Rose, Lockwood (Terry), Skiverton, Fontaine, Gall, Way, Tarachulski (Weatherstone), Jevons, Johnson, Caceres (O'Brien).
Plymouth Arg: McCormick; Worrell, Gilbert, Adams, Wotton, Coughlan (Doumbe), Lasley, Hodges (Friio), Crawford (Milne), Keith, Capaldi.
aet.

Wednesday, 25 August 2004

Bradford C (1) 1 *(Windass 6 (pen))*
Notts Co (0) 2 *(Richardson 64, Ullathorne 105)* 3517
Bradford C: Henderson; Holloway, Emanuel, Crooks (Penford), Gavin (Colbeck), Bower, Summerbee, Schumacher, Windass, Symes (Sanasy), Muirhead.
Notts Co: Deeney; Gill, Ullathorne, Baudet, Edwards, Richardson, Pipe, Bolland, Scully (Wilson), Hurst, Williams.
aet.

Coventry C (0) 4 *(Hughes 51, Suffo 63, 66, Morrell 82)*
Torquay U (0) 1 *(Osei-Kuffour 74)* 6180
Coventry C: Shearer; Carey, Staunton (Whing), Wood (Barrett), Shaw, Davenport, Gudjonsson, Hughes, Morrell, McSheffrey (Suffo), Doyle.
Torquay U: Van Heusden; Meirelles, McGlinchey, Hockley (Wardley), Owen, Woods, Bedeau, Fowler (Phillips), Noble, Gritton (Akinfenwa), Osei-Kuffour.

Nottingham F (1) 2 *(Taylor 36, King 78)*
Scunthorpe U (0) 0 7344
Nottingham F: Gerrard; Louis-Jean, Rogers, Hjelde, Morgan, Evans, Impey, King, Johnson, Taylor, Jess (Commons).
Scunthorpe U: Musselwhite; Stanton, Ridley, Kell, Crosby, Butler, Baraclough, Taylor (Sparrow), Hayes, Bailey (Parton), Beagrie.

Oxford U (0) 0
Reading (0) 2 *(Goater 62, Hughes 77)* 5919
Oxford U: Tardif; Mackay, Robinson, Brown (Parker), Roget, Ashton, Wolleaston, Wanless (Burton), Mooney, Basham (Morgan), Bradbury.
Reading: Hahnemann; Murty, Shorey, Ingimarsson, Williams, Harper, Little (Convey), Hughes, Owusu, Goater, Brooker (Forster).

Sheffield W (1) 1 *(Peacock 20)*
Walsall (0) 0 8959
Sheffield W: Lucas; Bullen, Heckingbottom, Collins, Branston, Whelan, Marsden, McGovern (Proudlock), MacLean, Peacock (McMahon), Brunt (Ndumbu-Nsungu).
Walsall: Paston; Aranalde, Willetts, Wright (McDermott), Dakinah, Taylor K, Standing, Merson, Atieno, Birch (Williams), Broad.

Tuesday, 7 September 2004

Boston U (1) 4 *(Pitt 23, Lee 57, Thompson 90, 94)*

Luton T (0) 3 *(Lee 52 (og), Nicholls 77 (pen), Showunmi 90)* 2631

Boston U: Abbey N; Beevers, McCann, Bennett, Greaves, Ellender, Rusk (Carruthers), Holland, McManus (Thompson), Lee, Pitt (Thomas).
Luton T: Beresford; Mansell (Showunmi), Davis (Blinkhorn), Robinson, Davies, Coyne, Underwood, Nicholls, Howard, Vine, Brkovic.
aet.

Tuesday, 21 September 2004

Mansfield T (0) 0

Preston NE (3) 4 *(Cresswell 3, Alexander 9, Daley 31, Lynch 84)* 3208

Mansfield T: Pilkington; Day, Dimech, Curtis (Tate) (Heron), Artell, John-Baptiste, Murray, MacKenzie, Larkin, Neil, Corden.
Preston NE: Lonergan; Alexander, Etuhu, Davis, Davidson, Mawene, Daley (Jackson), O'Neil (McCormack), Cresswell, Smith (Lynch), Lewis■.

SECOND ROUND

Tuesday, 21 September 2004

Birmingham C (0) 3 *(Gronkjaer 64, Morrison 77, Savage 80 (pen))*

Lincoln C (0) 1 *(Yeo 84 (pen))* 14,500

Birmingham C: Maik Taylor; Melchiot (Dunn), Gray, Savage (Clapham), Upson, Martin Taylor, Anderton, Clemence, Heskey (Morrison), Yorke, Gronkjaer.
Lincoln C: Marriott; Bloomer, Peat (Taylor-Fletcher), McAuley, Morgan, Futcher, Butcher, Green (Toner), McCombe (Richardson), Yeo, Gain.

Burnley (0) 1 *(Blake 50)*

Wolverhampton W (1) 1 *(Seol 45)* 5013

Burnley: Jensen; Duff, Camara, Grant, McGreal (Sinclair), Branch, Hyde, Chaplow, Moore, Blake, Valois.
Wolverhampton W: Oakes; Clyde, Naylor, Andrews, Craddock, Bjorklund (Lowe), Newton, Olofinjana, Cort, Seol, Cameron (Clarke).
aet; Burnley won 4-2 on penalties.

Colchester U (1) 2 *(Fagan 29, May 118)*

WBA (0) 1 *(Horsfield 50)* 4591

Colchester U: Davison; Baldwin, Hunt, Brown, Chilvers (Halford), Watson, Garcia, Danns, Williams (Bowry), Fagan (May), Keith.
WBA: Kuszczak; Scimeca, Contra (O'Connor), Gera (Greening), Gaardsoe, Moore, Albrechtsen, Dyer, Dobie (Hulse), Horsfield, Koumas.
aet.

Crewe Alex (1) 3 *(Jones S 19, Ashton 64, Foster 119)*

Sunderland (1) 3 *(Brown 37, 83, Elliott 103)* 3804

Crewe Alex: Williams; Moses (Bignot), Roberts M (Higdon), Lunt, Walker, Foster, Sorvel, Cochrane (Rivers), Ashton, Jones S, Vaughan.
Sunderland: Myhre; Lynch, Williams, Leadbitter (Whitehead), Collins N, Caldwell, Oster, Clark (Elliott), Brown, Lawrence (Wright), Thornton.
aet; Crewe Alex won 4-2 on penalties.

Crystal Palace (0) 2 *(Freedman 80, Soares 110)*

Hartlepool U (0) 1 *(Williams 70)* 4233

Crystal Palace: Kiraly; Boyce, Granville, Derry (Soares), Sorondo (Borrowdale), Powell, Routledge, Watson, Freedman, Torghelle (Kaviedes), Kolkka.
Hartlepool U: Provett; Woods (Istead), Robson, Nelson, Westwood, Tinkler, Sweeney, Strachan (Maidens), Porter (Williams), Boyd, Humphreys.
aet.

Doncaster R (1) 2 *(Ravenhill 6, McSporran 46)*

Ipswich T (0) 0 6020

Doncaster R: Warrington; Priet, Albrighton, Foster, Fenton, Ravenhill (Green), McSporran (Mulligan), Doolan, Ipoua (Coppinger), Fortune-West, McIndoe.
Ipswich T: Price; Diallo, Richards, Dinning, De Vos, Naylor, Bowditch (Miller), Magilton, Bent, Counago (Kuqi), Westlake.

Grimsby T (0) 0

Charlton Ath (1) 2 *(Murphy 8, Jeffers 79)* 5735

Grimsby T: Williams A; Crowe (Bull), McDermott, Gordon, Young, Whittle, Fleming, Pinault (Coldicott), Parkinson, Sestanovich (Hockless), Reddy.
Charlton Ath: Kiely; Young (Kishishev), Hreidarsson, El Karkouri, Fortune (Euell), Perry, Stuart, Murphy, Jeffers, Johansson (Lisbie), Hughes.

Leeds U (1) 1 *(Ricketts 9)*

Swindon T (0) 0 18,476

Leeds U: Sullivan; Kelly, Kilgallon, Spring, Butler, Carlisle, Gregan, Pugh, Ricketts (Deane), Joachim (Cadamarteri), McMaster (Walton).
Swindon T: Evans; Smith (Heywood), Duke, Ifil, O'Hanlon, Hewlett (Fallon), Igoe, Miglioranzi (Pook), Robinson, Parkin, Howard.

Manchester C (5) 7 *(Barton 21, Macken 28, 44, Flood 33, Wright-Phillips S 36, Sibierski 56, 84)*

Barnsley (0) 1 *(Conlon 47)* 19,578

Manchester C: Waterreus; Mills, Jihai, Thatcher (Jordan), Distin (Sommeil), Barton, Flood, Bosvelt, Macken (Wright-Phillips B), Wright-Phillips S, Sibierski.
Barnsley: Colgan; Hassell, Williams R (Boulding), Burns, Kay, Williams T, Wroe, Conlon, Chopra, Shuker (Nardiello), McPhail.

Milton Keynes D (0) 1 *(McLeod 85)*

Cardiff C (3) 4 *(Thorne 14, 21, Bullock 19, Anthony 72)* 2266

Milton Keynes D: Bevan; Edds, Lewington, Chorley, Williams, Ntimban-Zeh■, Small, Herve (Smith), Smart (Oyedele), McLeod, Puncheon (Hornuss).
Cardiff C: Alexander; Anthony, Barker, Boland, Collins, Vidmar, McAnuff (Ledley), Bullock, Lee, Thorne (Campbell), Parry.

Norwich C (1) 1 *(Safri 45)*

Bristol R (0) 0 18,658

Norwich C: Green; Helveg, Drury, Fleming, Charlton, Holt, McVeigh (Bentley), Safri (Edworthy), Huckerby, Doherty (Svensson), Francis.
Bristol R: Miller; Gibb, Beswetherick (Disley), Edwards, Anderson, Hinton, Trollope (Lescott), Hunt, Campbell (Walker), Agogo, Elliott■.

Reading (0) 0

Watford (1) 3 *(Cox 14 (pen), Bouazza 89, Ingimarsson 90 (og))* 8429

Reading: Hahnemann; Murty, Hughes (Harper), Ingimarsson, Williams, Newman (Owusu), Brooker (Morgan), Sidwell, Kitson, Goater, Convey.
Watford: Lee; Doyley, Mayo, Cox, Demerit, Blizzard, Darlington (Ferrell), Gunnarsson, Bouazza, Dyer (Fitzgerald), Young (Ardley).

Tranmere R (0) 0

Portsmouth (0) 1 *(Kamara 65)* 6966

Tranmere R: Achterberg; Taylor, Roberts, McAteer, Goodison, Sharps, Hall, Rankine, Hume, Dadi (Zola), Whitmore (Beresford).
Portsmouth: Ashdown; Griffin, Taylor, O'Neil, Primus, Unsworth, Cisse, Mezague, Kamara, Fuller (Yakubu), Berger (Stefanovic).

West Ham U (1) 3 *(Zamora 1, 54, Rebrov 62)*

Notts Co (1) 2 *(Wilson 13, Richardson 57)* 11,111

West Ham U: Walker; Repka (Melville), Brevett, Lomas, Mackay, Mullins, Rebrov, Reo-Coker, Harewood, Zamora, Etherington (Cohen).
Notts Co: Deeney; Wilson, Ullathorne (Oakes), Richardson, Whitlow, Edwards (Williams), Pipe, Bolland, Scully, Hurst, Gill.

Wrexham (2) 2 *(Morgan 6, Llewellyn 45)*
Sheffield U (1) 3 *(Gray 21, 69, Jagielka 54)* 3423
Wrexham: Baker; Bennett, Holt, Carey (Spender), Morgan, Pejic, Williams, Ferguson, Smith (Mark Jones), Sam (Whitley), Llewellyn.
Sheffield U: Kenny; Jagielka, Harley, McCall (Thirlwell), Bromby, Morgan, Quinn, Montgomery, Forte (Hurst), Gray, Black (Shaw).

Yeovil T (0) 0
Bolton W (0) 2 *(Julio Cesar 80, Pedersen 87)* 8047
Yeovil T: Weale; Rose, O'Brien, Way (Gall), Skiverton, Fontaine, Caceres (Williams), Johnson, Jevons, Stolcers (Tarachulski), Terry.
Bolton W: Poole; Ben-Haim, Shakes, Hierro (O'Brien), Barness, Julio Cesar, Nolan, Kaku, Diouf, Ferdinand (Davies), Giannakopoulos (Pedersen).

Wednesday, 22 September 2004

Aston Villa (2) 3 *(Vassell 29, Angel 38, Solano 78)*
QPR (0) 1 *(McLeod 48)* 26,975
Aston Villa: Sorensen; De la Cruz, Samuel, McCann, Mellberg, Barry (Berson), Solano, Whittingham, Angel, Vassell (Cole), Hendrie (Hitzlsperger).
QPR: Day; Bignot, Edghill, Johnson (Furlong), Shittu, Gnohere (Santos), Rowlands (Cook), Branco, Cureton, Gallen, McLeod.

Blackburn R (1) 3 *(Emerton 8, Pedersen 90, Gallagher 91)*
Bournemouth (1) 3 *(O'Connor G 13, Broadhurst 82, Spicer 115)* 7226
Blackburn R: Enckelman; Neill, Gresko (Gallagher), Johansson, Amoruso, Tugay, Emerton, De Pedro (Pedersen), Bothroyd (Stead), Jansen, Douglas.
Bournemouth: Moss N; O'Connor G, Cummings, Broadhurst, Howe, Maher, Elliott, Stock (Andrade), Hayter (Connell), Rodgrigues (Holmes), Spicer.
aet; Bournemouth won 7-6 on penalties.

Boston U (0) 1 *(Beevers 56)*
Fulham (3) 4 *(Radzinski 9, 70, Malbranque 28, McBride 34)* 5373
Boston U: Abbey N; West, McCann, Bennett, Beevers, Ellender, Noble, Gascoigne (Rusk), Lee, Kirk (McManus), Pitt (Thompson).
Fulham: Crossley; Buari, Green, McKinlay, Goma, Rehman, Rosenior■, Boa Morte (John), McBride, Radzinski, Malbranque (Timlin).

Bristol C (0) 2 *(Stubbs 50 (og), Lita 53)*
Everton (2) 2 *(Ferguson 30 (pen), Chadwick 45)* 15,264
Bristol C: Phillips; Smith (Miller), Hill, Doherty, Coles, Butler, Murray, Orr, Lita, Roberts (Fortune), Wilkshire (Heffernan).
Everton: Wright; Hibbert, Naysmith (Pistone), Stubbs, Yobo, Carsley, Osman (Chadwick), Watson, Ferguson (Campbell), Cahill, McFadden.
aet; Everton won 4-3 on penalties.

Coventry C (1) 1 *(Doyle 36)*
Sheffield W (0) 0 8362
Coventry C: Steele; Carey, Giddings (Whing), Wood, Shaw, Mills, Doyle, Gudjonsson, Suffo (Johnson), John, Barrett (Jorgensen).
Sheffield W: Lucas; Bullen, Greenwood, Whelan■, Collins, McMahon (Shaw), Marsden, McGovern, MacLean, Proudlock (Brunt), Smith.

Northampton T (0) 0
Southampton (2) 3 *(Phillips 32, Prutton 35, McCann 65)* 6343
Northampton T: Rachubka; Low, Galbraith, Bojic (Chambers), Willmott, Williamson, Cozic, Youngs (Morison), McGleish (Carruthers), Sabin, Jaszczun.
Southampton: Niemi; Nilsson, Van Damme, Delap, Lundekvam, Jakobsson, Fernandes (Folly), Prutton (Cranie), Crouch, Phillips (Best), McCann.

Nottingham F (1) 2 *(Taylor 17, 94)*
Rotherham U (1) 1 *(Sedgwick 9)* 11,168
Nottingham F: Gerrard; Impey (Bopp), Robertson, Perch, Morgan, Doig, Evans, Jess, Johnson, Taylor, Rogers.
Rotherham U: Pollitt; Stockdale, Minto (Hurst), Garner (Vernazza), Swailes, Gilchrist, Sedgwick, Mullin, Proctor (Hoskins), Barker R, Warne.
aet.

Oldham Ath (0) 0
Tottenham H (1) 6 *(Kanoute 37, 90, Keane 64, Defoe 71, Bunjevcevic 87, Gardner 89)* 8548
Oldham Ath: Mawson; Holden, Griffin, Boshell, Haining, Arber, Eyre (Barlow), Appleby, Killen (Jack), Johnson, Eyres.
Tottenham H: Keller; Mabizela, Bunjevcevic, Brown, Gardner, King, Davies (Ricketts), Redknapp (Pedro Mendes), Keane (Defoe), Kanoute, Jackson.

Monday, 4 October 2004

Leicester C (0) 2 *(Gudjonsson 68 (pen), Blake 75)*
Preston NE (1) 3 *(Cresswell 34, 90 (pen), 113)* 6751
Leicester C: Pressman; Makin, Stewart, Williams, Heath, Dabizas (Elliott), Scowcroft, Gudjonsson, Blake, Wright (Gillespie), Tiatto (Wilcox).
Preston NE: Lonergan; Alexander (Daley), Broomes, O'Neil, Davis■, Mawene, Etuhu, McKenna, Cresswell, Jackson (Smith), Lewis (Davidson).
aet.

THIRD ROUND

Tuesday, 26 October 2004

Bournemouth (1) 3 *(Hayter 8, 90, Stock 118)*
Cardiff C (1) 3 *(Lee 24, Bullock 49, Jerome 108)* 8598
Bournemouth: Moss N; Young (Holmes), O'Connor G (Connell), Broadhurst, Howe, Maher (Browning), Elliott, Stock, Hayter, Fletcher S, Spicer.
Cardiff C: Alexander; Weston (Anthony), Barker, Kavanagh, Collins, Vidmar■, Fish (Parry), Bullock, Lee, Thorne (Jerome), Ledley.
aet; Cardiff C won 5-4 on penalties.

Burnley (1) 3 *(Branch 9, Camara 65, Valois 86)*
Aston Villa (0) 1 *(Angel 81)* 11,184
Burnley: Coyne; Roche, Camara, Grant, McGreal, Duff, Duffy, Hyde, Blake, Branch, Valois.
Aston Villa: Sorensen; Delaney, Samuel (Hitzlsperger), McCann, Mellberg, Ridgewell, Solano (Moore L), Hendrie, Angel, Cole, Whittingham.

Crewe Alex (0) 0
Manchester U (1) 3 *(Smith 10, Miller 57, Foster 59 (og))* 10,103
Crewe Alex: Williams; Otsemobor, Tonkin, Lunt, Jones B (Walker), Foster, Sorvel (Rivers), Cochrane, Ashton, Jones S (White), Vaughan.
Manchester U: Howard; Richardson, O'Shea (Pique), Miller, Brown, Kleberson, Fletcher (Eagles), Djemba-Djemba, Smith, Saha, Bellion (Ebanks-Blake).

Doncaster R (0) 0
Nottingham F (1) 2 *(King 33, Perch 63)* 9261
Doncaster R: Warrington; Price (Beardsley), Ryan, Morley, Fenton, Green, McSporran, Doolan (Rigoglioso), Blundell (Coppinger), Fortune-West, McIndoe.
Nottingham F: Gerrard; Louis-Jean, Perch, Jess, Dawson, Morgan, Impey, Commons (Robertson), Johnson, King, Rogers.

Millwall (0) 0
Liverpool (1) 3 *(Diao 18, Baros 70, 90)* 17,655
Millwall: Stack; Muscat, Livermore, Dunne (Healy), Lawrence, Ward, Elliott, Morris, Harris, Tessem, Serioux (McCammon).
Liverpool: Dudek; Josemi, Traore, Biscan, Henchoz, Whitbread, Potter, Diao, Mellor (Finnan), Sinama-Pongolle (Baros), Warnock (Riise).

Portsmouth (2) 2 *(Kamara 14, Berkovic 32 (pen))*
Leeds U (1) 1 *(Deane 40)* 15,215
Portsmouth: Ashdown; Griffin, Taylor, Hughes, Primus, De Zeeuw, Mezague, Cisse, Kamara (Berger), Fuller, Berkovic (Yakubu).
Leeds U: Sullivan; Kelly, Walton, Gregan (Keogh), Carlisle, Spring, Richardson, Pugh, Deane, Joachim (Lennon), Simon Johnson (Ricketts).

Sheffield U (0) 0
Watford (0) 0 7689
Sheffield U: Kenny; Jagielka, Harley, Thirlwell, Bromby, Morgan, Liddell, Tonge (Hurst), Gray, Lester (Forte), Montgomery (Shaw).
Watford: Lee; Darlington, Chambers, Doyley, Dyche, Mahon, Blizzard, Demerit, Bouazza, Dyer, Young (Smith).
aet; Watford won 4-2 on penalties.

Wednesday, 27 October 2004

Birmingham C (0) 0
Fulham (0) 1 *(Pembridge 76)* 26,371
Birmingham C: Maik Taylor; Melchiot, Clapham, Clemence, Upson, Cunningham (Johnson), Gronkjaer, Anderton, Heskey, Yorke (Lazaridis), Gray.
Fulham: Crossley; Volz, Bocanegra, Diop, Knight, Rehman, Malbranque, Jensen (John), Cole (McBride), Boa Morte, Pembridge.

Bolton W (1) 3 *(King 27 (og), Okocha 75 (pen), Ferdinand 105)*
Tottenham H (1) 4 *(Defoe 44, 103, Bunjevcevic 84, Brown 95)* 18,037
Bolton W: Poole; Hunt, Gardner, Hierro (Kaku), Ben-Haim, Julio Cesar, Nolan (Giannakopoulos), Diouf, Pedersen, Davies (Ferdinand), Okocha.
Tottenham H: Keller; Pamarot, Bunjevcevic, Davis (Carrick), Naybet, King, Pedro Mendes, Davies (Brown), Kanoute (Keane), Defoe, Ziegler.
aet.

Charlton Ath (1) 1 *(Hreidarsson 5)*
Crystal Palace (1) 2 *(Freedman 41, Torghelle 54)* 19,030
Charlton Ath: Kiely; Young (Hughes), Hreidarsson, Holland, Fortune, Perry, Stuart (Johansson), Murphy (Euell), Jeffers, Lisbie, Thomas.
Crystal Palace: Speroni; Butterfield, Borrowdale, Hudson, Sorondo, Leigertwood, Soares, Derry, Freedman, Torghelle■, Watson (Powell).

Chelsea (0) 1 *(Kezman 57)*
West Ham U (0) 0 41,774
Chelsea: Cudicini; Paulo Ferreira, Babayaro, Parker (Lampard), Gallas, Ricardo Carvalho, Tiago, Kezman, Cole (Duff), Robben (Gudjohnsen), Geremi.
West Ham U: Walker; Repka, Brevett, Mullins, Ferdinand, Lomas, Nowland (Noble), Reo-Coker, Harewood, Zamora (Hutchison), Etherington (Rebrov).

Everton (0) 2 *(Carsley 52, Bent 89)*
Preston NE (0) 0 33,932
Everton: Wright; Hibbert, Pistone, Carsley■, Weir, Yobo, Watson, McFadden (Cahill), Ferguson (Bent), Osman, Kilbane.
Preston NE: Ward; Alexander (Jackson), Etuhu, Davis (Skora), Lucketti, Mawene, McKenna, O'Neil, Cresswell, Healy, Smith (Daley).

Manchester C (0) 1 *(Fowler 90)*
Arsenal (0) 2 *(Van Persie 78, Karbassiyoon 89)* 21,708
Manchester C: Waterreus; Thatcher, Onuoha, D'Laryea J (Wright-Phillips B), Mills, Distin, Flood, Sibierski, Wright-Phillips S, Fowler, Sinclair (Negouai) (Jordan).
Arsenal: Almunia; Hoyte, Larsson, Flamini, Senderos, Cygan, Pennant (Djourou), Fabregas, Lupoli (Karbassiyoon), Van Persie, Smith (Owusu-Abeyie).

Middlesbrough (2) 3 *(Nemeth 4, Morrison 25, Graham 70)*
Coventry C (0) 0 11,833
Middlesbrough: Nash; Davies, Cooper, Riggott, Ehiogu, Doriva, Morrison, Wilson, Nemeth, Job (McMahon), Downing (Graham).
Coventry C: Steele; Carey, Giddings, Hughes, Shaw (Whing), Leacock, Doyle, Deloumeaux, Morrell, Johnson (McSheffrey), Gudjonsson (Suffo).

Newcastle U (2) 2 *(Jenas 2, Ameobi 42 (pen))*
Norwich C (0) 1 *(Huckerby 56 (pen))* 42,153
Newcastle U: Harper; Hughes, Bernard, Ambrose, Johnsen, Bramble, Milner, Jenas, Kluivert, Ameobi (Bowyer), Robert (Bellamy).
Norwich C: Green; Edworthy, Drury (Helveg), Fleming, Shackell, Holt (Safri), Francis, Svensson, Huckerby, Doherty (Henderson), Jonson.

Southampton (0) 3 *(Blackstock 50, 54, 80)*
Colchester U (1) 2 *(Danns 7, Halford 64)* 20,588
Southampton: Niemi; Kenton, Van Damme, Prutton, Lundekvam, Jakobsson, Nilsson, Svensson A (Fernandes), Best (Blackstock), Ormerod, McCann (Telfer).
Colchester U: Gerken; Stockley, Hunt, Brown, Baldwin, Watson, Johnson (Garcia), Danns, Fagan, Halford, Keith.

FOURTH ROUND

Tuesday, 9 November 2004

Arsenal (1) 3 *(Owusu-Abeyie 25, Lupoli 52, 85)*
Everton (1) 1 *(Gravesen 8)* 27,791
Arsenal: Almunia; Hoyte, Karbassiyoon, Flamini, Djourou, Senderos, Pennant, Edu (Larsson), Van Persie, Lupoli (Cregg), Smith (Owusu-Abeyie).
Everton: Wright; Hibbert, Pistone, Stubbs, Yobo, Gravesen, Watson (Osman), McFadden, Bent (Chadwick), Cahill, Kilbane.

Burnley (0) 0
Tottenham H (1) 3 *(Keane 31, 52, Defoe 58)* 10,639
Burnley: Jensen; Roche, Camara, Duff, Cahill, Sanokho, Hyde, Grant, Blake, Branch (Valois) (Pilkington), Duffy.
Tottenham H: Robinson; Kelly, Pamarot (Ifil), Brown, Naybet, King, Pedro Mendes (Davies), Carrick, Keane (Kanoute), Defoe, Ziegler.

Cardiff C (0) 0
Portsmouth (0) 2 *(Yakubu 47, 55 (pen))* 13,555
Cardiff C: Warner; Vidmar, Barker, Kavanagh (Bullock), Gabbidon, Collins, McAnuff (Jerome), Boland, Lee, Parry (Fleetwood), Ledley.
Portsmouth: Ashdown; Griffin, Unsworth, Faye (Hughes), Stefanovic, De Zeeuw, Mezague, Cisse (Pulis), Yakubu (Fuller), Lua-Lua, Taylor.

Watford (1) 5 *(Dyer 39, Chambers 52, 62, Helguson 66, Bouazza 84)*
Southampton (0) 2 *(Blackstock 84, Ormerod 88)* 13,008
Watford: Lee; Darlington, Chambers (Young), Doyley, Dyche, Cox (Demerit), Ardley, Gunnarsson, Dyer (Bouazza), Helguson, Mahon.
Southampton: Blayney; Kenton (Van Damme), Higginbotham, Delap, Lundekvam, Jakobsson, Telfer, Svensson A, Ormerod, Phillips (Blackstock), Nilsson (Griffit).

Wednesday, 10 November 2004

Liverpool (0) 2 *(Mellor 83, 89)*
Middlesbrough (0) 0 28,176
Liverpool: Dudek; Finnan, Traore, Diao (Welsh), Henchoz, Whitbread, Potter, Biscan, Mellor, Sinama-Pongolle (Partridge), Warnock (Riise).
Middlesbrough: Nash; Davies, Queudrue, Riggott, Cooper, Doriva, Morrison (Graham), Downing, Job, Viduka, Zenden.

Manchester U (2) 2 *(Saha 22, Richardson 39)*
Crystal Palace (0) 0 48,891
Manchester U: Howard; Neville P, Fortune, Brown, Kleberson (Spector), O'Shea, Fletcher, Djemba-Djemba, Bellion (Rossi), Saha, Richardson (Eagles).
Crystal Palace: Speroni; Butterfield (Shipperley), Borrowdale, Hudson, Powell, Leigertwood, Soares, Danze (Lakis), Derry, Freedman, Torghelle (Kaviedes).

Newcastle U (0) 0
Chelsea (0) 2 *(Gudjohnsen 100, Robben 112)* 38,055
Newcastle U: Given; O'Brien, Bernard (Hughes), Butt (Dyer), Johnsen, Bramble, Bellamy, Jenas, Shearer, Kluivert (Ameobi), Robert.
Chelsea: Cudicini; Johnson, Bridge, Parker (Gudjohnsen), Terry, Gallas, Paulo Ferreira, Tiago, Kezman, Cole (Lampard), Duff (Robben).
aet.

Nottingham F (0) 2 *(King 71, Reid 104)*
Fulham (0) 4 *(Radzinski 86, 93, McBride 101, Cole 119)* 9252
Nottingham F: Gerrard; Louis-Jean (Perch) (Jess), Rogers, Evans, Dawson, Morgan, Thompson, Commons (Taylor), Johnson, King, Reid.
Fulham: Crossley; Volz, Bocanegra, Diop (McBride), Knight, Rehman, Malbranque (Legwinski), Radzinski (Rosenior), Cole, Boa Morte, Pembridge.
aet.

FIFTH ROUND

Tuesday, 30 November 2004

Fulham (0) 1 *(McBride 74)*
Chelsea (0) 2 *(Duff 55, Lampard 88)* 14,531
Fulham: Van der Sar; Volz, Bocanegra, Diop, Pearce, Rehman, Malbranque, Legwinski, Cole (Hammond), McBride, Pembridge.
Chelsea: Cudicini; Johnson, Bridge, Makelele, Terry, Ricardo Carvalho, Smertin, Parker, Robben (Cole), Drogba (Gudjohnsen), Duff (Lampard).

Watford (1) 3 *(Helguson 24, 57, Dyer 61)*
Portsmouth (0) 0 18,877
Watford: Lee; Doyley, Darlington, Cox, Dyche, Mahon, Ardley, Gunnarsson (Blizzard), Dyer (Devlin), Helguson (Fitzgerald), Chambers.
Portsmouth: Ashdown; Unsworth (Griffin), Taylor, O'Neil (Cisse), Primus, De Zeeuw, Stone, Berkovic (Harper), Quashie, Fuller, Berger.

Wednesday, 1 December 2004

Manchester United (1) 1 *(Bellion 1)*
Arsenal (0) 0 67,103
Manchester United: Howard; Neville P, Fortune, Brown, Miller, O'Shea, Eagles (Rossi), Djemba-Djemba, Bellion, Kleberson (Jones), Richardson.
Arsenal: Almunia; Hoyte, Clichy (Karbassiyoon), Flamini, Senderos, Djourou, Pennant, Larsson (Cregg), Van Persie, Lupoli (Smith), Owusu-Abeyie.

Tottenham H (0) 1 *(Defoe 108)*
Liverpool (0) 1 *(Sinama-Pongolle 117 (pen))* 36,100
Tottenham H: Robinson; Pamarot, Atouba, Brown, Gardner, King, Ricketts (Defoe), Carrick, Keane (Pedro Mendes), Kanoute, Ziegler.
Liverpool: Dudek; Raven, Warnock, Diao (Partridge), Henchoz, Whitbread, Nunez (Smyth), Biscan, Mellor (Welsh), Sinama-Pongolle, Potter.
aet; Liverpool won 4-3 on penalties.

SEMI-FINAL FIRST LEG

Tuesday, 11 January 2005

Liverpool (0) 1 *(Gerrard 56)*
Watford (0) 0 35,739
Liverpool: Dudek; Finnan, Riise, Hamann (Biscan), Carragher, Traore, Nunez, Gerrard, Mellor (Baros), Sinama-Pongolle (Warnock), Luis Garcia.
Watford: Jones; Chambers, Darlington, Cox, Demerit, Mahon, Ardley (Blizzard), Gunnarsson, Bouazza, Helguson, Devlin.

Wednesday, 12 January 2005

Chelsea (0) 0
Manchester U (0) 0 41,492
Chelsea: Cudicini; Paulo Ferreira, Bridge, Makelele, Terry, Gallas, Tiago (Kezman), Lampard, Cole (Jarosik), Gudjohnsen (Drogba), Duff.
Manchester U: Howard; Neville P, Heinze, O'Shea, Fortune, Silvestre, Ronaldo (Smith), Djemba-Djemba (Scholes), Saha, Rooney, Fletcher.

SEMI-FINAL SECOND LEG

Tuesday, 25 January 2005

Watford (0) 0
Liverpool (0) 1 *(Gerrard 77)* 19,797
Watford: Jones; Darlington, Chambers, Cox, Demerit, Mahon, Ardley, Gunnarsson (Dyer), Bouazza (Webber), Helguson, Devlin (McNamee).
Liverpool: Dudek; Carragher, Riise, Hamann, Pellegrino, Traore, Finnan, Gerrard (Potter), Baros (Sinama-Pongolle) (Luis Garcia), Morientes, Biscan.

Wednesday, 26 January 2005

Manchester U (0) 1 *(Giggs 67)*
Chelsea (1) 2 *(Lampard 29, Duff 85)* 67,000
Manchester U: Howard; Neville G, Heinze, Ferdinand, Keane, Silvestre, Ronaldo, Fortune (Rooney), Saha, Scholes, Giggs.
Chelsea: Cech; Paulo Ferreira, Bridge, Makelele, Terry, Gallas, Tiago, Lampard, Robben (Cole), Drogba (Gudjohnsen), Duff (Jarosik).

FINAL (AT MILLENNIUM STADIUM)

Sunday, 27 February 2005

Liverpool (1) 2 *(Riise 1, Nunez 113)*
Chelsea (0) 3 *(Gerrard 79 (og), Drogba 107, Kezman 112)* 78,000
Liverpool: Dudek; Finnan, Traore (Biscan), Hamann, Carragher, Hyypia, Kewell (Nunez), Gerrard, Luis Garcia, Morientes (Baros), Riise.
Chelsea: Cech; Paulo Ferreira, Gallas (Kezman), Makelele, Terry, Ricardo Carvalho, Jarosik (Gudjohnsen), Lampard, Drogba, Cole (Johnson), Duff.
aet.
Referee: S. Bennett (Orpington).

FOOTBALL LEAGUE COMPETITION ATTENDANCES

LEAGUE CUP ATTENDANCES

Season	*Attendances*	*Games*	*Average*
1960–61	1,204,580	112	10,755
1961–62	1,030,534	104	9,909
1962–63	1,029,893	102	10,097
1963–64	945,265	104	9,089
1964–65	962,802	98	9,825
1965–66	1,205,876	106	11,376
1966–67	1,394,553	118	11,818
1967–68	1,671,326	110	15,194
1968–69	2,064,647	118	17,497
1969–70	2,299,819	122	18,851
1970–71	2,035,315	116	17,546
1971–72	2,397,154	123	19,489
1972–73	1,935,474	120	16,129
1973–74	1,722,629	132	13,050
1974–75	1,901,094	127	14,969
1975–76	1,841,735	140	13,155
1976–77	2,236,636	147	15,215
1977–78	2,038,295	148	13,772
1978–79	1,825,643	139	13,134
1979–80	2,322,866	169	13,745
1980–81	2,051,576	161	12,743
1981–82	1,880,682	161	11,681
1982–83	1,679,756	160	10,498
1983–84	1,900,491	168	11,312
1984–85	1,876,429	167	11,236
1985–86	1,579,916	163	9,693
1986–87	1,531,498	157	9,755
1987–88	1,539,253	158	9,742
1988–89	1,552,780	162	9,585
1989–90	1,836,916	168	10,934
1990–91	1,675,496	159	10,538
1991–92	1,622,337	164	9,892
1992–93	1,558,031	161	9,677
1993–94	1,744,120	163	10,700
1994–95	1,530,478	157	9,748
1995–96	1,776,060	162	10,963
1996–97	1,529,321	163	9,382
1997–98	1,484,297	153	9,701
1998–99	1,555,856	153	10,169
1999–2000	1,354,233	153	8,851
2000–01	1,501,304	154	9,749
2001–02	1,076,390	93	11,574
2002-03	1,242,478	92	13,505
2003-04	1,267,729	93	13,631

CARLING CUP 2004–05

Round	*Aggregate*	*Games*	*Average*
One	193,696	35	5,534
Two	236,860	25	9,474
Three	315,131	16	19,696
Four	189,367	8	23,671
Five	136,611	4	34,153
Semi-finals	164,028	4	41,007
Final	78,000	1	78,000
Total	1,313,693	93	14,216

LDV VANS TROPHY 2004–05

Round	*Aggregate*	*Games*	*Average*
One	59,330	28	2,119
Two	37,496	16	2,344
Area Quarter-finals	27,623	8	3,453
Area Semi-finals	12,895	4	3,224
Area finals	23,950	4	5,988
Final	36,216	1	36,216
Total	197,510	61	3,238

FA CUP ATTENDANCES 1968–2005

	1st Round	*2nd Round*	*3rd Round*	*4th Round*	*5th Round*	*6th Round*	*Semi-finals & Final*	*Total*	*No. of matches*	*Average per match*
2004–05	161,197	98,702	602,152	477,472	339,082	127,914	193,233	1,999,752	146	13,697
2003–04	162,738	117,967	624,732	347,964	292,521	156,780	167,401	1,870,103	149	12,551
2002–03	189,905	104,103	577,494	404,599	242,483	156,244	175,498	1,850,326	150	12,336
2001–02	198,369	119,781	566,284	330,434	249,190	173,757	171,278	1,809,093	148	12,224
2000–01	171,689	122,061	577,204	398,241	256,899	100,663	177,778	1,804,535	151	11,951
1999–2000	181,485	127,728	514,030	374,795	182,511	105,443	214,921	1,700,913	158	10,765
1998–99	191,954	132,341	609,486	431,613	359,398	181,005	202,150	2,107,947	155	13,599
1997–98	204,803	130,261	629,127	455,557	341,290	192,651	172,007	2,125,696	165	12,883
1996–97	209,521	122,324	651,139	402,293	199,873	67,035	191,813	1,843,998	151	12,211
1995–96	185,538	115,669	748,997	391,218	274,055	174,142	156,500	2,046,199	167	12,252
1994–95	219,511	125,629	640,017	438,596	257,650	159,787	174,059	2,015,249	161	12,517
1993–94	190,683	118,031	691,064	430,234	172,196	134,705	228,233	1,965,146	159	12,359
1992–93	241,968	174,702	612,494	377,211	198,379	149,675	293,241	2,047,670	161	12,718
1991–92	231,940	117,078	586,014	372,576	270,537	155,603	201,592	1,935,340	160	12,095
1990–91	194,195	121,450	594,592	530,279	276,112	124,826	196,434	2,038,518	162	12,583
1989–90	209,542	133,483	683,047	412,483	351,423	123,065	277,420	2,190,463	170	12,885
1988–89	212,775	121,326	690,199	421,255	206,781	176,629	167,353	1,966,318	164	12,173
1987–88	204,411	104,561	720,121	443,133	281,461	119,313	177,585	2,050,585	155	13,229
1986–87	209,290	146,761	593,520	349,342	263,550	119,396	195,533	1,877,400	165	11,378
1985–86	171,142	130,034	486,838	495,526	311,833	184,262	192,316	1,971,951	168	11,738
1984–85	174,604	137,078	616,229	320,772	269,232	148,690	242,754	1,909,359	157	12,162
1983–84	192,276	151,647	625,965	417,298	181,832	185,382	187,000	1,941,400	166	11,695
1982–83	191,312	150,046	670,503	452,688	260,069	193,845	291,162	2,209,625	154	14,348
1981–82	236,220	127,300	513,185	356,987	203,334	124,308	279,621	1,840,955	160	11,506
1980–81	246,824	194,502	832,578	534,402	320,530	288,714	339,250	2,756,800	169	16,312
1979–80	267,121	204,759	804,701	507,725	364,039	157,530	355,541	2,661,416	163	16,328
1978–79	243,773	185,343	880,345	537,748	243,683	263,213	249,897	2,604,002	166	15,687
1977–78	258,248	178,930	881,406	540,164	400,751	137,059	198,020	2,594,578	160	16,216
1976–77	379,230	192,159	942,523	631,265	373,330	205,379	258,216	2,982,102	174	17,139
1975–76	255,533	178,099	867,880	573,843	471,925	206,851	205,810	2,759,941	161	17,142
1974–75	283,956	170,466	914,994	646,434	393,323	268,361	291,369	2,968,903	172	17,261
1973–74	214,236	125,295	840,142	747,909	346,012	233,307	273,051	2,779,952	167	16,646
1972–73	259,432	169,114	938,741	735,825	357,386	241,934	226,543	2,928,975	160	18,306
1971–72	277,726	236,127	986,094	711,399	486,378	230,292	248,546	3,158,562	160	19,741
1970–71	329,687	230,942	956,683	757,852	360,687	304,937	279,644	3,220,432	162	19,879
1969–70	345,229	195,102	925,930	651,374	319,893	198,537	390,700	3,026,765	170	17,805
1968–69	331,858	252,710	1,094,043	883,675	464,915	188,121	216,232	3,431,554	157	21,857

LDV VANS TROPHY 2004–05

■ *Denotes player sent off.*

NORTHERN SECTION FIRST ROUND

Tuesday, 28 September 2004

Carlisle U (1) 2 *(Henderson 4, Grand 70)*

Grimsby T (1) 1 *(Cramb 45)* 2580

Carlisle U: Westwood; Andrews, Cowan (Murphy), Billy (McDonagh■), Gray, Grand, Arnison, Lumsdon, Henderson, Farrell, McGill.
Grimsby T: Williams A; Young, Bull, Jones, Forbes, Coldicott, Marcelle, Pinault (Fleming), Robinson (Reddy), Cramb, Hockless.

Hartlepool U (0) 3 *(Strachan 55 (pen), Pouton 60, Porter 114)*

Hull C (1) 3 *(Price 12, Green 46, Elliott 107)* 1535

Hartlepool U: Konstantopoulos; Barron (Craddock), Robson, Nelson, Brackstone, Istead (Boyd), Pouton (Humphreys), Strachan, Williams, Porter, Woods.
Hull C: Myhill■; Thelwell (Wiseman), Hinds, Ashbee, Edge, Keane (Duke), Green, Price, Facey (Elliott), Walters, Lewis.
aet; Hartlepool U won 4-1 on penalties.

Hereford U (1) 1 *(Stanley 35)*

Scunthorpe U (0) 1 *(Torpey 58)* 1414

Hereford U: Gould; Travis, Smith, Tretton, Mkandawire, Hyde, Stanley, Robinson, Stansfield (Mills), Brown (Carey-Bertram), Williams D.
Scunthorpe U: Evans; Stanton, Byrne, Barwick, Jackson, Brighton, Sparrow (Graves), Featherstone (Williams), Rankine, Torpey (Hayes), Taylor.
aet; Hereford U won 4-3 on penalties.

Huddersfield T (0) 3 *(Mirfin 47, Mendes 84 (pen), Fowler 90)*

Morecambe (0) 0 3831

Huddersfield T: Senior; McCombe, Lloyd, Mirfin, Clarke N, Fowler, Worthington, Schofield■, Mendes (Ahmed), Sodje A (McAliskey), Brown.
Morecambe: Sollitt; Howard, Heard (Stringfellow), Perkins, Bentley, Swan (Thompson), Curtis, Blackburn, Walmsley, Hunter, Twiss (Carlton).

Lincoln C (0) 0

Doncaster R (0) 1 *(Beardsley 77)* 1875

Lincoln C: Rayner; Folkes, Sandwith, McAuley, McCombe, Futcher, Butcher, Toner (Yeo), Taylor-Fletcher (Green), Carruthers (Kerley), Gain.
Doncaster R: Jones; Priet, Albrighton, Foster (Mulligan), Fenton, Ravenhill, Coppinger, Wilson, Beardsley, Fortune-West (Jackson), McIndoe.

Macclesfield T (1) 2 *(Tipton 23, Whitaker 63)*

Chesterfield (0) 1 *(Campbell-Ryce 58)* 813

Macclesfield T: Fettis; Bailey (Potter), Miles, Welch, Barras, Briscoe, Whitaker, Widdrington (Carragher), Tipton (Sheron), Parkin, Harsley.
Chesterfield: Muggleton; Bailey, O'Hare, Downes, Blatherwick, Davies, Smith, Hudson, Allott, Allison, Campbell-Ryce (De Bolla).

Mansfield T (0) 0

Darlington (0) 0 1651

Mansfield T: Pilkington; McNiven, Dimech, Curle T (Lonsdale), Day, John-Baptiste, Murray, MacKenzie, Larkin, O'Neill, Lloyd.
Darlington: Russell S; Valentine, Kendrick, Hughes (Clark), Clarke, Close (Convery), Gregorio, Maddison (Keltie), Thomas, Russell C, Wainwright.
aet; Mansfield T won 4-3 on penalties.

Notts Co (1) 2 *(Sofiane 24, Hurst 71)*

Wrexham (1) 3 *(Pejic 20, Llewellyn 79, Sam 87)* 1359

Notts Co: Henderson; Wilson, Pead, Friars, Whitlow, Baudet (Scully), Pipe, Sofiane (Gordon), O'Grady, Hurst, Gill.
Wrexham: Baker; Smith, Holt, Morgan, Roberts, Pejic, Mark Jones (Crowell), Whitley, Bennett (Sam), Llewellyn, Williams.

Port Vale (1) 1 *(Paynter 45 (pen))*

Barnsley (0) 0 1970

Port Vale: Brain; O'Connor, James, Reid, Pilkington, Collins, Brown, Cummins, Brooker (Smith J), Paynter, Hibbert (Birchall).
Barnsley: Colgan; Hassell, Williams T (Williams R), Kay, Reid, Vaughan, Wroe (Burns), Conlon, Chopra, Nardiello (Boulding), McPhail.

Rochdale (1) 4 *(Griffiths 3, 77, 90 (pen), Holt 75)*

Scarborough (1) 1 *(Gilroy 45)* 837

Rochdale: Gilks; Evans, Gallimore, Jones, Burgess (Clarke), Griffiths, McCourt, Warner (Probets), Tait (McGivern), Holt, Cooksey.
Scarborough: Walker■; Foster, Nicholson, Kerr (Lyth), Hotte, Cryan, Thompson, Pounder (Gill), Senior, Hackworth (Burton), Gilroy.

Stockport Co (1) 3 *(Daly 15, Barlow 93, Le Fondre 116)*

Bury (1) 1 *(Scott 25)* 1416

Stockport Co: Cutler; Geary, Griffin, Robertson (Le Fondre), Williams A, Adams, Cartwright, Goodwin, Lambert, Daly (Barlow), Jackman.
Bury: Garner; Barrass (Dunfield), Kennedy, Scott■, Challinor, Woodthorpe (Swailes), Flitcroft (Whaley), Kazim-Richards, Porter■, Newby, Barry-Murphy.
aet.

SOUTHERN SECTION FIRST ROUND

Tuesday, 28 September 2004

Aldershot T (0) 0

Wycombe W (0) 1 *(Dixon 66)* 1632

Aldershot T: Barnard R; Warner (Short), Barnard D, Antwi, Johnson, Giles, Smith (McLean), McAuley, Sills, Barnes-Homer (Miller), Challinor.
Wycombe W: Williams; Uhlenbeek, Silk (Martin), Johnson, Reilly, Comyn-Platt, Senda (Anya), Savage, Stonebridge, Birchall (Dixon), Easton.

Barnet (0) 3 *(Bailey 55 (pen), 83, Roache 90)*

Stevenage B (0) 1 *(Elding 57)* 1337

Barnet: Tynan; Batt, Valdaz (Samuels), Champion, Maddix, Dobson, Lopez, Bailey, McBean (Garness), Roache, Elmes.
Stevenage B: Croudson; Schillaci, Shadrack, Lamapraft, Stewart, Williams, Hodgson, Quinn, Elding, Hunter, Black.

Brentford (0) 0

Milton Keynes D (3) 3 *(Pacquette 7, Lewington 22, Small 27)* 1679

Brentford: Julian (Lennie); Hillier, Myers, Lawrence, Fitzgerald SB, Palmer, Tabb, Rhodes, Harrold, Peters (Weight), Hunt (Muldowney).
Milton Keynes D: Martin; Edds, Lewington, Chorley (Herve), Williams, Palmer (Ntimban-Zeh), Oyedele (Hornuss), Smith, Small, Pacquette, Puncheon.

Bristol R (0) 1 *(Agogo 80)*

Kidderminster H (0) 0 3281

Bristol R: Miller; Hinton, Ryan, Edwards, Anderson, Elliott, Trollope (Agogo), Disley (Campbell), Walker (Forrester), Thorpe, Lescott.
Kidderminster H: Danby; Cooper, Burton, Keates, Hatswell, McHale, Foster I (Diop), Brown, Langmead, Christiansen, McMahon (Jenkins).

Cheltenham T (1) 5 *(Vincent 11, 50, McCann 58 (pen), Finnigan 80, Spencer 86)*

Dagenham & R (0) 1 *(Moore 52)* 1048

Cheltenham T: Higgs; Wilson, Victory, Duff, Brough, McCann (Fyfe), Melligan (Bird), Finnigan, Vincent (Spencer), Guinan, Devaney.
Dagenham & R: Roberts; Goodwin, Flynn, Cole, Uddin, Leberl, Janney, Griffiths (Bruce), Moore, Boot, Hill.

Shrewsbury T (1) 3 *(Rodgers 41, Young 46 (og), Logan 66)*

Bournemouth (0) 2 *(Stock 72, Whitehead 90 (og))* 1278

Shrewsbury T: Howie; Moss, Stephens, Whitehead, Tinson, Ridler (Lowe), Sedgemore, Tolley, Rodgers, Logan, Smith (Street).
Bournemouth: Stewart; Young, Cummings, Broadhurst, Holmes, Browning (Connell), Elliott, Stock, Hayter, Rodrigues (Andrade), O'Connor.

Swansea C (0) 2 *(Nugent 89, Ricketts 90)*

Luton T (0) 0 3559

Swansea C: Gueret; Gurney, Ricketts, O'Leary, Austin, Monk, Forbes, Martinez, Fitzgerald (Nugent), Robinson, Maylett.
Luton T: Seremet; Keane, Neilson, Mansell, Barnett■, Bayliss (Perrett), O'Leary, Holmes, Showunmi, Andrew, Hughes.

Torquay U (1) 4 *(Osei-Kuffour 17, Taylor 53, Akinfenwa 59, 116)*

Yeovil T (1) 3 *(Stolcers 42, Caceres 67, Tarachulski 84)* 1610

Torquay U: Van Heusden (Dearden); Canoville (Bedeau), McGlinchey, Hockley, Taylor, Villis, Boardley, Fowler, Akinfenwa■, Osei-Kuffour (Bond), Phillips.
Yeovil T: Collis; Reed (Rose), O'Brien, Mirza (Johnson), Lindegaard, Fontaine, Caceres, Gall, Tarachulski, Stolcers (Odubade), Terry.
aet.

Walsall (0) 1 *(Leitao 75)*

Rushden & D (0) 0 2987

Walsall: Paston; Taylor K, Bennett, Osborn, Roper, Wright, Broad, Merson, Leitao (Birch), Fryatt, Wrack.
Rushden & D: Turley; Connelly, Hawkins, Sambrook (Kennedy), Allen, Gulliver, Bell, Dove, Braniff, Hay, Burgess.

Woking (0) 0

Leyton Orient (1) 3 *(Ibehre 33, Saah 61, Miller 76)* 1166

Woking: Basso; Jackson, MacDonald, Boardman, Oliver, Smith, Johnson (Selley), Canham, Foyewa, Tiesse (Nade), Ferguson (Richards).
Leyton Orient: Morris; Barnard D, Lockwood, Miller, Peters, Saah, Carlisle (Duncan), Simpson (Hunt), Ibehre, Steele (Alexander), Newey.

NORTHERN SECTION FIRST ROUND

Wednesday, 29 September 2004

Bradford C (1) 1 *(Adebola 29)*

Accrington S (1) 2 *(Flynn 27, McEvilly 88)* 1868

Bradford C: Henderson; Denton, Emanuel, Schumacher, Gavin, Bower, Roberts, Crooks (Penford), Windass, Adebola (Symes), Muirhead.
Accrington S: Kennedy; Cavanagh, Gerrard, Cook (Williams), Flynn, Howarth (Smith), Jagielka, Brannan, McEvilly, Mullin, Craney.

Sheffield W (1) 1 *(MacLean 29)*

Chester C (0) 2 *(Hope 66, Ellison 68)* 7640

Sheffield W: Lucas; Bullen, Aljofree, Smith, Collins, McMahon (Greenwood), Marsden, McGovern, MacLean, Proudlock, Brunt (Needham).
Chester C: MacKenzie; Vaughan, McIntyre, Hope, Bolland, Harris, Booth (Drummond), Carden (Davies), Rapley (Whalley), Stamp, Ellison.

York C (0) 0

Blackpool (1) 2 *(Murphy 10, Parker 66 (pen))* 1072

York C: Stockdale; Law, Merris, Groves (Harrison), McGurk, Pearson, Nogan (Yalcin), Dunning, Robinson, Bishop, Stewart.
Blackpool: Ilic; Richardson, Edwards R (Wiles), Burns, Grayson, Clare, Doughty, Parker, Murphy, Coid (Whittaker), Edwards P (Evans).

SOUTHERN SECTION FIRST ROUND

Wednesday, 29 September 2004

Boston U (0) 0

Cambridge U (0) 1 *(Easter 66)* 1489

Boston U: Abbey N; Beevers, Thompson, Bennett, Clarke, Strong, Holland (O'Halloran), Rusk, McManus, Thomas (Kirk), Staff.
Cambridge U: Ruddy; Gleeson, Goodhind (Robinson), Tann, Angus (Davies), Walker, Quinton, Nicholls, Oli (Chillingworth), Easter, El Kholti.

Bristol C (1) 1 *(Heffernan 7)*

Peterborough U (0) 0 3092

Bristol C: Phillips; Amankwaah (Hill), Fortune (Bell), Orr, Coles, Butler, Murray, Tinnion, Lita, Heffernan, Wilkshire (Brown).
Peterborough U: Tyler; Jenkins, Legg, Woodhouse (Fry), Ireland (Kanu), St Ledger-Hall, Sonner, Boucaud (Semple), Clarke, Constantine, Jelleyman.

Colchester U (0) 1 *(Garcia 63)*

Southend U (1) 1 *(Bramble 40)* 3469

Colchester U: Davison; Hunt, Halford, Brown, Baldwin, Watson, Bowry (Johnson), Danns, Williams (Cade), Garcia, Keith J.
Southend U: Flahavan; Jupp (Hunt), Wilson, Maher, Barrett, Edwards, Gower (Corbett), Bentley■, Gray, Bramble (Broughton), Pettefer.
aet; Southend U won 5-3 on penalties.

Oxford U (1) 2 *(Winters 3, Hand 90)*

Exeter C (1) 2 *(Edwards 12, Jeannin 64)* 1842

Oxford U: Tardif; Mackay, Robinson, Winters, Molyneaux, Woozley, Basham, Hand, Mooney (Hackett), Bradbury (Davies), Wolleaston (Wanless).
Exeter C: Bittner; Hiley (Afful), Jeannin, Martin, Sawyer, Todd, McConnell, Clay, Edwards (Flack), Canham, O'Sullivan (Taylor).
aet; Exeter C won 3-1 on penalties.

NORTHERN SECTION SECOND ROUND

Tuesday, 2 November 2004

Blackpool (1) 6 *(Blinkhorn 37, 61, Parker 97, Burns 100, 110, Coid 105)*

Huddersfield T (0) 3 *(McAliskey 47, Schofield 53, Ahmed 105)* 3533

Blackpool: Ilic; Coid, Edwards R, Warhurst (Wellens), Clare, Doughty, Wiles (Richardson), Southern, Blinkhorn, Parker, Edwards P (Burns).
Huddersfield T: Senior; Holdsworth, Lloyd, McCombe, Yates, Sodje E■, Schofield, Fowler (Ahmed), Booth (Abbott), McAliskey (Sodje A), Carss.
aet.

Carlisle U (0) 0

Hartlepool U (0) 1 *(Sweeney 66)* 2871

Carlisle U: Westwood; Shelley, Cowan, Billy, Gray, Andrews, Arnison, Lumsdon, Vieira (Henderson), Preece, Farrell.
Hartlepool U: Konstantopoulos; Ross (Craddock), Robson, Clark, Westwood, Tinkler, Williams, Nelson, Porter (Gobern), Sweeney, Humphreys (Foley).

Chester C (0) 1 *(Hessey 54)*

Rochdale (0) 0 1419

Chester C: Doyle; Vaughan, McIntyre, Hessey, Bolland (Hope), Harris, Watson (Branch), Carden (Drummond), Rapley, Clare, Booth.
Rochdale: Gilks; Goodall (Probets), Gallimore, Clarke, Burgess, Griffiths, Bertos, Warner (McGivern), Tait, Atieno, Cooksey (Brisco).

Hereford U (0) 1 *(Williams D 72)*

Doncaster R (0) 1 *(Rigoglioso 59)* 1375

Hereford U: Mawson; Travis, Robinson, Hyde (Pitman), Mkandawire, James, Stanley, Purdie (Mills), Stansfield (Green), Brown, Williams D.
Doncaster R: Ingham; Mulligan, Priet (Ryan), Morley, Fenton, Ravenhill (Price), Tierney (Jackson), Rigoglioso, Coppinger, Beardsley, McIndoe.
aet; Hereford U won 3-1 on penalties.

Macclesfield T (3) 4 *(Barras 10, Parkin 30, 63, Tipton 37)*
Mansfield T (0) 0 1027
Macclesfield T: Fettis; Harsley, Potter, Weaver, Barras, Carragher, Whitaker, Widdrington, Tipton (Swadi Fayadh), Parkin (Briscoe), Sheron (Miles).
Mansfield T: White; Buxton, Woodman, Dimech, Artell (John-Baptiste), Murray, Lloyd (Larkin), MacKenzie, Curle T (Asamoah), O'Neill, Corden.

Oldham Ath (1) 3 *(Appleby 25 (pen), Griffin 72, Holden 82)*
Accrington S (1) 2 *(McEvilly 42, Craney 47)* 2812
Oldham Ath: Pogliacomi; Holden, Lomax (Griffin), Appleby, Arber, Hall D, Lee D, Johnson (Vernon), Wilbraham, Betsy■, Eyres (Beharall).
Accrington S: Ikeme; Cavanagh, Butler (Cook), Brannan, Williams, Flynn, Proctor (Smith), Flitcroft, McEvilly, Mullin, Craney.

Tranmere R (2) 2 *(Zola 6, Hume 40)*
Port Vale (0) 1 *(Birchall 68)* 3735
Tranmere R: Achterberg; Taylor, Roberts, Jennings, Jackson, Goodison, Hall, Harrison, Hume, Zola (Beresford), Sharps (Jones).
Port Vale: Brain; O'Connor, James, Collins, Smith D (Smith J), Hulbert (McMahon), Brown (Armstrong), Cummins, Paynter, Birchall, Pilkington.

Wrexham (1) 2 *(Lawrence 19, Williams 83)*
Stockport Co (0) 0 2130
Wrexham: Baker; Spender, Holt, Lawrence, Roberts, Pejic, Crowell (Smith), Ferguson, Sam (Ugarte), Llewellyn (Mark Jones), Williams.
Stockport Co: Cutler; Hardiker, Jackman, Cartwright, Griffin, Mair, Allen (Lambert), Goodwin, Le Fondre (Bailey), Barlow, Welsh.

SOUTHERN SECTION SECOND ROUND

Tuesday, 2 November 2004

Bristol C (1) 2 *(Lita 45, 52)*
Milton Keynes D (0) 1 *(Makofo 66)* 3367
Bristol C: Phillips; Amankwaah, Bell, Hill, Coles, Fortune, Murray (Anyinsah), Doherty (Harley), Lita (Cotterill), Gillespie, Dinning.
Milton Keynes D: Bevan; Oyedele, Puncheon, Chorley, Crooks, Ntimban-Zeh, Kamara (Makofo), Herve (McKoy), Mackie, Pacquette, Tapp (Johnson).

Cambridge U (0) 0
Leyton Orient (0) 2 *(Ibehre 51, Carlisle 74)* 1812
Cambridge U: Ruddy; Gleeson, El Kholti (Quinton), Tann, Latte-Yedo, Walker, Tudor, Mbome, Easter (Webb), Turner, Robinson (Daniels).
Leyton Orient: Morris; Barnard D, Lockwood, Hunt, Mackie, Zakuani, Carlisle (Duncan), Saah, Ibehre, Newey, Scott (Wardley).

Cheltenham T (1) 2 *(Guinan 23, Brough 111)*
Walsall (0) 2 *(Leitao 56, 114)* 2042
Cheltenham T: Higgs; Gill, Victory, Duff, Brough, McCann, Melligan, Bird, Wilson (Vincent), Guinan (Spencer), Devaney.
Walsall: Murphy; Bazeley, Aranalde, Taylor K (Taylor D), Emblen, Bennett, Standing, Merson, Birch (Williams), Leitao, Wrack.
aet; Walsall won 4-3 on penalties.

Exeter C (0) 1 *(Gaia 82)*
Swindon T (1) 2 *(Nicolas 19, Fallon 54)* 1898
Exeter C: Bittner; Sawyer, Moxey, Taylor, Todd (Gaia), Cronin, Clay, O'Sullivan (Ampadu), Edwards, Martin (Flack), Afful.
Swindon T: Book; Garrard, Nicolas, Ifil, Reeves, Hewlett, Smith, Caton (Parkin), Fallon, Heywood, Pook (Igoe).

Southend U (3) 4 *(Eastwood 13, 38, Gray 35 (pen), Bentley 84)*
Shrewsbury T (1) 1 *(Tolley 28)* 2599
Southend U: Flahavan; Hunt (Edwards), Nicolau, Maher, Barrett, Prior, Gower, Bentley, Gray (Dudfield), Eastwood (Corbett), Pettefer.
Shrewsbury T: Howie; Sedgemore, Challis, Whitehead, Ridler, Fox (Lowe), Street (Edwards), Tolley, Rodgers, Darby (Grant), Aiston.

Torquay U (0) 1 *(Bedeau 54)*
Northampton T (1) 3 *(Alsop 6, Williamson 70, McGleish 76)* 1395
Torquay U: Gottskalksson; Canoville, McGlinchey, Hockley, Villis, Woods, Phillips, Meirelles (Hill), Gritton, Keane (Bedeau), Boardley (Akinfenwa).
Northampton T: Harper; Chambers, Galbraith (Carruthers), Bojic, Willmott, Murray, Cozic, Youngs, McGleish (Sabin), Alsop, Williamson (Hicks).

Wycombe W (1) 1 *(Birchall 4)*
Swansea C (0) 0 1021
Wycombe W: Talia; Craig, Silk, Martin, Johnson, Williamson, Senda, Birchall, Stonebridge, Abbey (Tyson), Bloomfield.
Swansea C: Gueret; Austin, Ricketts, O'Leary, Tate (Iriekpen), Monk, Maylett (Britton), Martinez, Connor (Nugent), Trundle, Forbes.

Wednesday, 3 November 2004

Bristol R (1) 2 *(Forrester 43, Thorpe 56)*
Barnet (0) 0 4460
Bristol R: Miller; Hinton, Ryan, Edwards, Anderson (Burns), Disley, Trollope (Williams), Campbell, Forrester (Haldane), Thorpe, Lescott.
Barnet: Millard; Batt, Champion, Clist, Maddix, Graham (Ming), Lee (Bailey), Sinclair (Elmes), Roache, McBean, Lopez.

NORTHERN QUARTER-FINALS

Tuesday, 30 November 2004

Chester C (0) 0
Wrexham (1) 1 *(Ugarte 19)* 5028
Chester C: Brown W; Vaughan, McIntyre (Hope), Bolland, Hessey, Davies (Booth), Drummond (Whalley), Carden, Rapley, Harris, Ellison.
Wrexham: Baker; Spender, Holt, Lawrence, Morgan, Pejic, Green, Ferguson, Llewellyn, Ugarte (Sam), Mark Jones (Armstrong).

Hereford U (1) 2 *(Pitman 15, Mills 87)*
Blackpool (0) 1 *(Blinkhorn 58)* 2181
Hereford U: Mawson; Travis, Robinson, Pitman (Hyde), Mkandawire, Smith, Stanley, Brown (Carey-Bertram), Stansfield (Mills), Purdie, Williams D.
Blackpool: Jones L; Richardson, Edwards R, Grayson (Wellens), McGregor, Wiles (Taylor), Doughty (Clarke), Southern, Blinkhorn, Parker, Burns.

Macclesfield T (0) 0
Tranmere R (1) 1 *(Roberts 18)* 1609
Macclesfield T: Wilson; Harsley (Tipton), Potter, Welch, Weaver, Carragher, Whitaker, Widdrington, Parkin, Sheron, Miles.
Tranmere R: Achterberg; Taylor, Roberts, Harrison, Jackson, Goodison (Dadi), Hall, Rankine, Hume, Whitmore, Sharps.

Oldham Ath (2) 3 *(Kilkenny 14, Killen 17 (pen), Croft 79)*
Hartlepool U (1) 1 *(Boyd 32)* 2835
Oldham Ath: Pogliacomi; Croft, Griffin, Holden, Haining, Hall D, Lee R (Hughes), Kilkenny, Killen (Vernon), Betsy, Eyres.
Hartlepool U: Konstantopoulos; Barron (Craddock), Brackstone, Nelson, Westwood, Tinkler, Strachan (Istead), Sweeney, Porter (Appleby), Boyd, Humphreys.

SOUTHERN QUARTER-FINALS

Tuesday, 30 November 2004

Bristol R (0) 1 *(Forrester 49)*
Wycombe W (0) 0 3667
Bristol R: Miller; Hinton, Campbell, Edwards, Elliott, Lescott, Savage (Trollope), Hunt, Forrester (Agogo), Thorpe, Disley.
Wycombe W: Talia; Craig, Silk, Senda (Ahmed), Nethercott (Johnson), Williamson, Martin, Bloomfield, Stonebridge, Faulconbridge, Guppy (Tyson).

Leyton Orient (0) 1 *(Wright 48 (og))*
Walsall (0) 0 1452
Leyton Orient: Morris; Barnard D (Duncan), Lockwood, Saah, White, Mackie, Carlisle, Simpson, Ibehre (Scott), Barnard L (Wardley), Newey.
Walsall: Murphy; Wright, Aranalde, Kinsella (Taylor D), Emblen, Bennett, Standing, Osborn, Birch (Fryatt), Leitao, Wrack.

Northampton T (0) 0
Southend U (2) 2 *(Dudfield 14, Pettefer 21)* 3280
Northampton T: Harper; Galbraith, Jaszczun, Bojic (Chambers), Willmott, Murray, Rowson, Williamson (Cozic), McGleish, Alsop (Sabin), Smith.
Southend U: Griemink; Hunt, Nicolau, Maher, Barrett, Edwards, Gower, Bentley, Bramble (Gray), Dudfield (Eastwood), Pettefer.

Swindon T (0) 1 *(Parkin 64)*
Bristol C (0) 0 7571
Swindon T: Book; Garrard, Nicolas, Ifil, Reeves (O'Hanlon), Heywood, Igoe, Robinson, Fallon (Smith), Parkin, Howard.
Bristol C: Phillips; Amankwaah, Bell (Anyinsah), Doherty, Butler, Hill (Gillespie), Murray, Tinnion, Lita, Heffernan, Wilkshire (Brown).

NORTHERN SEMI-FINALS

Tuesday, 25 January 2005

Hereford U (1) 1 *(Carey-Bertram 20)*
Wrexham (1) 2 *(Ugarte 21, Llewellyn 74)* 2710
Hereford U: Mawson; Travis, Smith (Williams), Pitman, Mkandawire, James, Stanley, Purdie, Stansfield (Brown), Carey-Bertram, Robinson.
Wrexham: Foster; Whitley, Holt, Lawrence, Morgan, Roberts, Crowell (Ferguson), Mark Jones, Ugarte, Llewellyn, Williams (Green).

Oldham Ath (1) 1 *(Eyres 35)*
Tranmere R (1) 1 *(Hall 3)* 4069
Oldham Ath: Pogliacomi; Bruce, Griffin, Hughes, Haining, Hall D (Lomax), Croft, Kilkenny, Vernon (Eyre), Betsy, Eyres (Hall C).
Tranmere R: Howarth; Taylor, Roberts, Linwood, Jackson, Goodison, Hall (Whitmore), Rankine (Jennings), Hume, Dagnall (Dadi), Harrison.
aet; Oldham Ath won 5-4 on penalties.

SOUTHERN SEMI-FINALS

Tuesday, 25 January 2005

Leyton Orient (1) 1 *(Alexander 43)*
Bristol R (0) 2 *(Disley 47, Haldane 90)* 1846
Leyton Orient: Morris; Barnard D, Lockwood, Miller, White, Mackie, Hunt, Simpson, Alexander, Steele, Scott.
Bristol R: Clarke; Hinton, Ryan, Campbell, Anderson, Elliott, Trollope, Hunt, Forrester (Haldane), Thorpe, Disley.

Southend U (1) 2 *(Dudfield 36, Nicolau 73)*
Swindon T (0) 0 4270
Southend U: Flahavan; Hunt, Wilson, Maher, Barrett, Prior, Pettefer, Bentley, Gray (Eastwood), Dudfield, Nicolau.
Swindon T: Evans; O'Hanlon, Duke (Howard), Ifil, Heywood, Hewlett, Miglioranzi, Smith, Fallon, Parkin, Holmes (Slabber).

NORTHERN FINAL FIRST LEG

Tuesday, 15 February 2005

Oldham Ath (1) 3 *(Vernon 35, 83 (pen), Eyres 76)*
Wrexham (2) 5 *(Ugarte 29, 55, 62, Mark Jones 32, Ferguson 58)* 2881
Oldham Ath: Pogliacomi; Bruce, Griffin, Bonner (Hughes), Haining, Hall D, Holden (Hall C), Kilkenny, Vernon, Betsy, Eyre (Eyres).
Wrexham: Foster; Edwards, Smith, Lawrence, Pejic, Morgan, Crowell, Ferguson (Whitley), Ugarte (Sam), Llewellyn, Mark Jones.

SOUTHERN FINAL FIRST LEG

Tuesday, 15 February 2005

Bristol R (0) 1 *(Walker 56)*
Southend U (1) 2 *(Dudfield 8, Gower 67)* 7110
Bristol R: Clarke; Lescott, Ryan, Elliott, Hinton, Campbell, Trollope (Walker), Hunt, Williams, Agogo, Disley.
Southend U: Flahavan; Hunt, Wilson, Maher, Barrett, Prior, Gower (Nicolau), Bentley, Bramble (Gray), Dudfield, Pettefer.

NORTHERN FINAL SECOND LEG

Tuesday, 8 March 2005

Wrexham (0) 1 *(Llewellyn 65)*
Oldham Ath (0) 0 5814
Wrexham: Foster; Edwards (Green), Holt, Lawrence, Roberts, Morgan, Crowell, Ferguson, Ugarte, Llewellyn (Sam), Mark Jones.
Oldham Ath: Pogliacomi; Holden, Griffin, Bonner (Hughes), Haining, Branston■, Appleby, Kilkenny, Cooper (Wilkinson), Betsy, Eyres (Stam).

SOUTHERN FINAL SECOND LEG

Tuesday, 8 March 2005

Southend U (1) 2 *(Gray 30, Eastwood 61)*
Bristol R (1) 2 *(Walker 44, Agogo 73)* 8145
Southend U: Flahavan; Jupp, Wilson, Maher, Barrett, Prior, Pettefer, Bentley, Gray (Dudfield), Eastwood, Gower (Nicolau).
Bristol R: Miller; Hinton, Ryan, Edwards (Shakes), Anderson, Elliott, Trollope (Williams), Hunt, Walker, Agogo, Lescott.

FINAL (AT MILLENNIUM STADIUM)

Sunday, 10 April 2005

Southend U (0) 0
Wrexham (0) 2 *(Ugarte 99, Ferguson 118)* 36,216
Southend U: Flahavan; Jupp, Wilson, Maher, Barrett, Prior, Pettefer (Guttridge), Bentley, Gray, Eastwood (Dudfield), Gower (McCormack).
Wrexham: Foster; Edwards, Holt, Lawrence, Roberts (Pejic), Morgan, Crowell (Bennett), Ferguson, Ugarte, Llewellyn, Mark Jones (Williams).
aet.
Referee: B. Carson (Leicestershire).

FA CUP FINALS 1872–2005

1872 and 1874–92	Kennington Oval	1910	Replay at Everton
1873	Lillie Bridge	1911	Replay at Old Trafford
1886	Replay at Derby (Racecourse Ground)	1912	Replay at Bramall Lane
		1915	Old Trafford, Manchester
1893	Fallowfield, Manchester	1920–22	Stamford Bridge
1894	Everton	1923 to 2000	Wembley
1895–1914	Crystal Palace	1970	Replay at Old Trafford
1901	Replay at Bolton	2001 to date	Millennium Stadium, Cardiff

Year	*Winners*	*Runners-up*	*Score*
1872	Wanderers	Royal Engineers	1-0
1873	Wanderers	Oxford University	2-0
1874	Oxford University	Royal Engineers	2-0
1875	Royal Engineers	Old Etonians	2-0 (after 1-1 draw aet)
1876	Wanderers	Old Etonians	3-0 (after 1-1 draw aet)
1877	Wanderers	Oxford University	2-1 (aet)
1878	Wanderers*	Royal Engineers	3-1
1879	Old Etonians	Clapham R	1-0
1880	Clapham R	Oxford University	1-0
1881	Old Carthusians	Old Etonians	3-0
1882	Old Etonians	Blackburn R	1-0
1883	Blackburn Olympic	Old Etonians	2-1 (aet)
1884	Blackburn R	Queen's Park, Glasgow	2-1
1885	Blackburn R	Queen's Park, Glasgow	2-0
1886	Blackburn R†	WBA	2-0 (after 0-0 draw)
1887	Aston Villa	WBA	2-0
1888	WBA	Preston NE	2-1
1889	Preston NE	Wolverhampton W	3-0
1890	Blackburn R	The Wednesday	6-1
1891	Blackburn R	Notts Co	3-1
1892	WBA	Aston Villa	3-0
1893	Wolverhampton W	Everton	1-0
1894	Notts Co	Bolton W	4-1
1895	Aston Villa	WBA	1-0
1896	The Wednesday	Wolverhampton W	2-1
1897	Aston Villa	Everton	3-2
1898	Nottingham F	Derby Co	3-1
1899	Sheffield U	Derby Co	4-1
1900	Bury	Southampton	4-0
1901	Tottenham H	Sheffield U	3-1 (after 2-2 draw)
1902	Sheffield U	Southampton	2-1 (after 1-1 draw)
1903	Bury	Derby Co	6-0
1904	Manchester C	Bolton W	1-0
1905	Aston Villa	Newcastle U	2-0
1906	Everton	Newcastle U	1-0
1907	The Wednesday	Everton	2-1
1908	Wolverhampton W	Newcastle U	3-1
1909	Manchester U	Bristol C	1-0
1910	Newcastle U	Barnsley	2-0 (after 1-1 draw)
1911	Bradford C	Newcastle U	1-0 (after 0-0 draw)
1912	Barnsley	WBA	1-0 (aet, after 0-0 draw)
1913	Aston Villa	Sunderland	1-0
1914	Burnley	Liverpool	1-0
1915	Sheffield U	Chelsea	3-0
1920	Aston Villa	Huddersfield T	1-0 (aet)
1921	Tottenham H	Wolverhampton W	1-0
1922	Huddersfield T	Preston NE	1-0
1923	Bolton W	West Ham U	2-0
1924	Newcastle U	Aston Villa	2-0
1925	Sheffield U	Cardiff C	1-0
1926	Bolton W	Manchester C	1-0
1927	Cardiff C	Arsenal	1-0
1928	Blackburn R	Huddersfield T	3-1
1929	Bolton W	Portsmouth	2-0
1930	Arsenal	Huddersfield T	2-0
1931	WBA	Birmingham	2-1
1932	Newcastle U	Arsenal	2-1
1933	Everton	Manchester C	3-0
1934	Manchester C	Portsmouth	2-1
1935	Sheffield W	WBA	4-2
1936	Arsenal	Sheffield U	1-0
1937	Sunderland	Preston NE	3-1
1938	Preston NE	Huddersfield T	1-0 (aet)
1939	Portsmouth	Wolverhampton W	4-1
1946	Derby Co	Charlton Ath	4-1 (aet)
1947	Charlton Ath	Burnley	1-0 (aet)
1948	Manchester U	Blackpool	4-2
1949	Wolverhampton W	Leicester C	3-1
1950	Arsenal	Liverpool	2-0
1951	Newcastle U	Blackpool	2-0
1952	Newcastle U	Arsenal	1-0
1953	Blackpool	Bolton W	4-3
1954	WBA	Preston NE	3-2
1955	Newcastle U	Manchester C	3-1
1956	Manchester C	Birmingham C	3-1

Year	Winners	Runners-up	Score
1957	Aston Villa	Manchester U	2-1
1958	Bolton W	Manchester U	2-0
1959	Nottingham F	Luton T	2-1
1960	Wolverhampton W	Blackburn R	3-0
1961	Tottenham H	Leicester C	2-0
1962	Tottenham H	Burnley	3-1
1963	Manchester U	Leicester C	3-1
1964	West Ham U	Preston NE	3-2
1965	Liverpool	Leeds U	2-1 (aet)
1966	Everton	Sheffield W	3-2
1967	Tottenham H	Chelsea	2-1
1968	WBA	Everton	1-0 (aet)
1969	Manchester C	Leicester C	1-0
1970	Chelsea	Leeds U	2-1 (aet)
	(after 2-2 draw,	*after extra time)*	
1971	Arsenal	Liverpool	2-1 (aet)
1972	Leeds U	Arsenal	1-0
1973	Sunderland	Leeds U	1-0
1974	Liverpool	Newcastle U	3-0
1975	West Ham U	Fulham	2-0
1976	Southampton	Manchester U	1-0
1977	Manchester U	Liverpool	2-1
1978	Ipswich T	Arsenal	1-0
1979	Arsenal	Manchester U	3-2
1980	West Ham U	Arsenal	1-0
1981	Tottenham H	Manchester C	3-2
	(after 1-1 draw,	*after extra time)*	
1982	Tottenham H	QPR	1-0
	(after 1-1 draw,	*after extra time)*	
1983	Manchester U	Brighton & HA	4-0
	(after 2-2 draw,	*after extra time)*	
1984	Everton	Watford	2-0
1985	Manchester U	Everton	1-0 (aet)
1986	Liverpool	Everton	3-1
1987	Coventry C	Tottenham H	3-2 (aet)
1988	Wimbledon	Liverpool	1-0
1989	Liverpool	Everton	3-2 (aet)
1990	Manchester U	Crystal Palace	1-0
	(after 3-3 draw,	*after extra time)*	
1991	Tottenham H	Nottingham F	2-1 (aet)
1992	Liverpool	Sunderland	2-0
1993	Arsenal	Sheffield W	2-1 (aet)
	(after 1-1 draw,	*after extra time)*	
1994	Manchester U	Chelsea	4-0
1995	Everton	Manchester U	1-0
1996	Manchester U	Liverpool	1-0
1997	Chelsea	Middlesbrough	2-0
1998	Arsenal	Newcastle U	2-0
1999	Manchester U	Newcastle U	2-0
2000	Chelsea	Aston Villa	1-0
2001	Liverpool	Arsenal	2-1
2002	Arsenal	Chelsea	2-0
2003	Arsenal	Southampton	1-0
2004	Manchester U	Millwall	3-0
2005	Arsenal	Manchester U	0-0 (aet)
	(Arsenal won	*5-4 on penalties)*	

* *Won outright, but restored to the Football Association.*
† *A special trophy was awarded for third consecutive win.*

FA CUP WINS

Manchester U 11, Arsenal 10, Tottenham H 8, Aston Villa 7, Blackburn R 6, Liverpool 6, Newcastle U 6, Everton 5, The Wanderers 5, WBA 5, Bolton W 4, Manchester C 4, Sheffield U 4, Wolverhampton W 4, Chelsea 3, Sheffield W 3, West Ham U 3, Bury 2, Nottingham F 2, Old Etonians 2, Preston NE 2, Sunderland 2, Barnsley 1, Blackburn Olympic 1, Blackpool 1, Bradford C 1, Burnley 1, Cardiff C 1, Charlton Ath 1, Clapham R 1, Coventry C 1, Derby Co 1, Huddersfield T 1, Ipswich T 1, Leeds U 1, Notts Co 1, Old Carthusians 1, Oxford University 1, Portsmouth 1, Royal Engineers 1, Southampton 1, Wimbledon 1.

APPEARANCES IN FINALS

Arsenal 17, Manchester U 17, Newcastle U 13, Everton 12, Liverpool 12, Newcastle U 12, Aston Villa 10, WBA 10, Tottenham H 9, Blackburn R 8, Manchester C 8, Wolverhampton W 8, Bolton W 7, Chelsea 7, Preston NE 7, Old Etonians 6, Sheffield U 6, Sheffield W 6, Huddersfield T 5, *The Wanderers 5, Derby Co 4, Leeds U 4, Leicester C 4, Oxford University 4, Royal Engineers 4, Southampton 4, Sunderland 4, West Ham U 4, Blackpool 3, Burnley 3, Nottingham F 3, Portsmouth 3, Barnsley 2, Birmingham C 2, *Bury 2, Cardiff C 2, Charlton Ath 2, Clapham R 2, Notts Co 2, Queen's Park (Glasgow) 2, *Blackburn Olympic 1, *Bradford C 1, Brighton & HA 1, Bristol C 1, *Coventry C 1, Crystal Palace 1, Fulham 1, *Ipswich T 1, Luton T 4, Middlesbrough 1, Millwall 1, *Old Carthusians 1, QPR 1, Watford 1, *Wimbledon 1.
* *Denotes undefeated.*

APPEARANCES IN SEMI-FINALS

Arsenal 25, Manchester U 24, Everton 23, Liverpool 21, Aston Villa 19, WBA 19, Blackburn R 17, Newcastle U 17, Tottenham H 17, Sheffield W 16, Chelsea 15, Wolverhampton W 14, Bolton W 13, Derby Co 13, Sheffield U 13, Nottingham F 12, Sunderland 12, Southampton 11, Manchester C 10, Preston NE 10, Birmingham C 9, Burnley 8, Leeds U 8, Leicester C 8, Huddersfield T 7, Old Etonians 6, Fulham 6, Oxford University 6, West Ham U 6, Notts Co 5, Portsmouth 5, The Wanderers 5, Luton T 4, Millwall 4, Queen's Park (Glasgow) 4, Royal Engineers 4, Watford 4, Blackpool 3, Cardiff C 3, Clapham R 3, Crystal Palace (professional club) 3, Ipswich T 3, Norwich C 3, Old Carthusians 3, Oldham Ath 3, Stoke C 3, The Swifts 3, Barnsley 2, Blackburn Olympic 2, Bristol C 2, Bury 2, Charlton Ath 2, Grimsby T 2, Middlesbrough 2, Swansea T 2, Swindon T 2, Wimbledon 2, Bradford C 1, Brighton & HA 1, Cambridge University 1, Chesterfield 1, Coventry C 1, Crewe Alex 1, Crystal Palace (amateur club) 1, Darwen 1, Derby Junction 1, Glasgow R 1, Hull C 1, Marlow 1, Old Harrovians 1, Orient 1, Plymouth Arg 1, Port Vale 1, QPR 1, Reading 1, Shropshire W 1, Wycombe W 1, York C 1.

THE FA CUP 2004–05

PRELIMINARY AND QUALIFYING ROUNDS

EXTRA PRELIMINARY ROUND

Hebburn Town v Silsden 1-4
Maine Road v Durham City 3-2
Skelmersdale United v Brodsworth MW 3-1
Newcastle Blue Star v Liversedge 1-4
Winterton Rangers v Goole 1-1, 0-1
Curzon Ashton v Morpeth Town 1-3
Norton & Stockton Ancients v Yorkshire Amateur 1-0
Tadcaster Albion v Fleetwood Town 2-5
Rossington Main v Washington Nissan 1-2
Nelson v Chester-Le-Street Town 0-1
St Helens Town v Newcastle Benfield Saints 4-3
Peterlee Newtown v Colne 1-1, 0-2
Parkgate v Kennek Ryhope CA 3-1
Holbeach United v Alvechurch 0-1
Barwell v Oldbury United 1-0
Cradley Town v Chasetown 0-4
Biddulph Victoria v Staveley MW 3-1
Causeway United v Leek CSOB 4-3
Boldmere St Michaels v Norton United 1-3
Coalville Town v Daventry Town 3-0
Lowestoft Town v AFC Wallingford 8-0
Woodbridge Town v Ware 2-0
Concord Rangers v Ilford 1-3
Norwich United v Harefield United 2-0
North Greenford United v Clapton 3-3, 1-0
Chalfont St Peter v Wroxham 2-10
Great Yarmouth Town v Long Melford 1-1, 1-2
Bury Town v Hullbridge Sports 6-0
Tiptree United v Ruislip Manor 2-2, 2-6
Witham Town v Dereham Town 0-1
Enfield Town v Leverstock Green 0-0, 3-1
Wembley v Edgware Town 0-2
Hanwell Town v Hadleigh United 6-1
Royston Town v Harpenden Town 3-0
Bowers Pitsea v London Colney 0-0, 5-7
AFC Sudbury v Harringey Borough 5-1
Ely City v Brook House 1-2
Felixstowe & Walton United v Leiston 1-1, 1-4
Wisbech Town v Sawbridgeworth Town 0-1
Enfield v March Town United 5-3
Buckingham Town v Kingsbury Town 4-2
Ipswich Wanderers v St Neots Town 6-1
Haverhill Rovers v Needham Market 5-0
Potters Bar Town v Clacton Town 0-0, 1-0
Newmarket Town v Ford Sports Daventry 1-1, 1-2
Cove v Fareham Town 0-2
VCD Athletic v Godalming & Guildford 2-0
Camberley Town v Thatcham Town 1-0
Lordswood v Winchester City 1-4
Chessington United v Chichester City United 3-3, 0-5
Walton Casuals v Three Bridges 2-0
Hythe Town v Littlehampton Town 1-1, 2-3
Wick v Saltdean United 2-0
Broadbridge Heath v Brockenhurst 0-2
Selsey v Merstham 1-2
Moneyfields v Redhill 4-1
Arundel v Whitstable Town 1-3
Greenwich Borough v Eastbourne United 6-3
Whitehawk v AFC Totton 1-1, 4-4
AFC Totton won 5-4 on penalties.
Slade Green v Reading Town 0-0, 1-2
Bishop Sutton v Frome Town 1-1, 0-1
Hamworthy United v Liskeard Athletic 1-0
Willand Rovers v St Blazey 1-4
Highworth Town v Falmouth Town 2-1
Devizes Town v Exmouth Town 1-4
Street v Welton Rovers 4-2
Bristol Manor Farm v Bridport 2-3
Bishop's Cleeve v Minehead 7-0
Tuffley Rovers v Barnstaple Town 0-3
Portland United v Bridgwater Town 0-3
Keynsham Town v Saltash United 0-1
Downton v Porthleven 0-1
Backwell United v Odd Down 3-2

PRELIMINARY ROUND

Warrington Town v Pontefract Collieries 3-0
South Shields v Blackpool Mechanics 3-5
Flixton v Parkgate 5-2
Willington v Woodleigh Sports 0-9
Maltby Main v Penrith 7-1
Abbey Hey v Squires Gate 0-1
North Shields v Ashington 0-1
Consett v Crook Town 1-1, 1-3
Atherton Collieries v Alsager Town 1-2
Jarrow Roofing Boldon CA v Wretford United 1-1, 0-1
Prudhoe Town v Sheffield 0-1
Chadderton v Norton & Stockton Ancients 2-1
Northallerton Town v Billingham Town 1-1, 0-1
Marske United v Colwyn Bay 0-1
Harrogate Railway v Esh Winning 1-1, 3-7
Pickering Town v Bedlington Terriers 1-0
Padiham v Billingham Synthonia 1-5
Silsden v Hallam 1-1, 3-1
Clitheroe v Tow Law Town 6-1
St Helens Town v West Auckland Town 0-3
Kendal Town v Eccleshill United 4-1
Bacup Borough v Chorley 0-3
Cheadle Town v Maine Road 0-3
Horden CW v AFC Telford United 1-0
Armthorpe Welfare v Thackley 1-1, 4-1
Ossett Albion v Washington 0-0, 1-0
Great Harwood Town v Glasshoughton Welfare 0-2
Seaham Red Star v Whickham 3-3, 4-0
(first replay abandoned half time (0-0); floodlight failure)
Guisborough Town v Brigg Town 1-3
Cammell Laird v Goole 2-0
Mossley v Selby Town 3-0
Thornaby v Easington Colliery 2-1
Fleetwood Town v Alnwick Town 6-0
Chester-le-Street Town v Colne 0-2
Ramsbottom United v Evenwood Town 3-0
Darwen v Brandon United 0-0, 1-4
Washington Nissan v Dunston FB 1-1, 1-4
Shildon v Garforth Town 2-0
Oldham Town v Atherton LR 0-0, 0-1
Trafford v North Ferriby United 4-2
Whitley Bay v Salford City 3-1
Rossendale United v Liversedge 1-4
Winsford United v Morpeth Town 2-1
Skelmersdale United v Stocksbridge Park Steels 1-1, 2-0
Shepshed Dynamo v Racing Club Warwick 3-2
Congleton Town v Carlton Town 0-1
Causeway United v Lincoln Moorlands 1-1, 3-0
Eastwood Town v Willenhall Town 1-2
Gedling Town v Coalville Town 0-3
Stourbridge v Norton United 1-3
Glossop North End v Ludlow Town 2-3
Stratford Town v Mickleover Sports 2-1
Bedworth United v Quorn 2-0
Long Eaton United v Spalding United 0-3
Boston Town v Stone Dominoes 1-2
Chasetown v Belper Town 2-2, 0-2
Borrowash Victoria v Biddulph Victoria 1-0
Arnold Town v Rocester 1-4
Kidsgrove Athletic v Newcastle Town 1-4
Rushall Olympic v Bourne Town 3-0
Blackstones v Barwell 1-2
Sutton Coldfield Town v Nantwich Town 1-0
Buxton v Stourport Swifts 1-1, 1-1
Stourport Swifts won 8-7 on penalties.
Sutton Town v Oadby Town 2-1
Shirebrook Town v Bromsgrove Rovers 3-1
Alvechurch v Ilkeston Town 1-3
Gresley Rovers v Studley 1-0
Corby Town v Westfields 1-2
Deeping Rangers v Glapwell 2-0
Cogenhoe United v Woodford United 7-0
Soham Town Rangers v Leighton Town 1-0
Sawbridgeworth Town v Haverhill Rovers 0-3
Rothwell Town v Berkhamsted Town 2-3
Royston Town v Barkingside 0-5
Brackley Town v Stowmarket Town 5-2
Fakenham Town v Gorleston 2-3
Enfield v Long Buckby 1-0
Great Wakering Rovers v Maldon Town 1-1, 1-3
London Colney v St Margaretsbury 2-2, 1-2
East Thurrock United v Halstead Town 3-3, 0-1
Bedford United & Valerio v Potton United 0-3
Ford Sports Daventry v Southend Manor 1-1, 1-3
Long Melford v Woodbridge Town 1-0
Stanway Rovers v Boreham Wood 0-3
Desborough Town v North Greenford United 1-4
Potters Bar Town v Uxbridge 1-7
Flackwell Heath v Hanwell Town 2-2, 3-2
Brook House v Romford 4-0
Norwich United v Thame United 0-1
Wroxham v Beaconsfield SYCOB 0-1
Holmer Green v Newport Pagnell Town 2-1
Diss Town v Barking & East Ham United 0-2
Burnham Ramblers v Waltham Forest 0-3
Harlow Town v Buckingham Town 3-1
Harwich & Parkeston v Stansted 3-2
Arlesey Town v Godmanchester Rovers 3-0
Yaxley v Stotfold 1-2
Raunds Town v Hertford Town 1-1, 0-1
Hoddesdon Town v Barton Rovers 1-10

Ruislip Manor v Henley Town 1-1, 1-0
Lowestoft Town v Northampton Spencer 7-1
Leiston v Tilbury 0-2
Wingate & Finchley v Fleet Town 4-1
Dereham Town v Marlow 0-2
Eton Manor v Cornard United 1-3
Ilford v Wivenhoe Town 0-1
Mildenhall Town v Aveley 1-1, 0-3
Wootton Blue Cross v Broxbourne Borough V&E 1-0
Edgware Town v Ipswich Wanderers 1-0
Bury Town v Brentwood Town 2-1
Hungerford Town v Dorking 1-2
Frimley Green v Raynes Park Vale 1-2
Lymington & New Milton v Sittingbourne 1-1, 2-1
Molesey v Westfield 5-0
Walton & Hersham v Leatherhead 1-2
Hastings United v Croydon 3-1
Pagham v Tunbridge Wells 1-2
Ramsgate v Lancing 7-0
Newport (IW) v Walton Casuals 0-0, 1-1
Walton Casuals won 4-1 on penalties.
Horsham v Chipstead 3-0
Hillingdon Borough v Ashford Town (Middlesex) 0-1
Moneyfields v Tooting & Mitcham United 0-5
Metropolitan Police v Alton Town 4-3
Bedfont v Bracknell Town 0-3
Herne Bay v Gosport Borough 1-2
Oxford City v Abingdon Town 7-0
Rye & Iden United v East Preston 0-0, 1-3
Cobham v Hailsham Town 0-3
North Leigh v Deal Town 3-1
Sandhurst Town v Southwick 4-2
Cray Wanderers v Epsom & Ewell 4-0
Whyteleafe v Erith & Belvedere 2-4
AFC Wimbledon v Ashford Town 3-0
Hartley Wintney v Ash United 1-2
Croydon Athletic v Farnham Town 5-0
Burgess Hill Town v Brockenhurst 1-2
Wantage Town v Carterton 1-2
Peacehaven & Telscombe v AFC Totton 1-3
Abingdon United v Cowes Sports 2-1
Whitstable Town v Wick 6-0
Bashley v Camberley Town 2-1
Hassocks v Merstham 1-3
Sidlesham v Didcot Town 0-5
Maidstone United v Chichester City United 3-1
Thamesmead Town v Eastbourne United 1-0
Eastbourne United reinstated after Greenwich Borough were removed.
Chatham Town v Reading Town 1-1, 3-2
Banstead Athletic v Littlehampton Town 3-1
Corinthian Casuals v Winchester City 0-3
BAT Sports v Egham Town 3-0
Ringmer v Andover 3-2
Erith Town v Steyning Town 5-3
AFC Newbury v East Grinstead Town 3-0
Dulwich Hamlet v Burnham 2-1
Chessington & Hook United v Bromley 0-1
Mile Oak v Fareham Town 1-0
VCD Athletic v Chertsey Town 5-1
Evesham United v Saltash United 3-1
Bournemouth v Shepton Mallet 3-2
Backwell United v Bridgwater Town 2-1
Wimborne Town v Yate Town 1-2
Swindon Supermarine v Calne Town 1-0
Paulton Rovers v St Blazey 0-1
Bitton v Hamworthy United 2-0
Exmouth Town v Wootton Bassett Town 3-2
Torrington v Barnstaple Town 0-3
Dawlish Town v Corsham Town 0-2
Bridport v Chard Town 1-1, 1-0
Hallen v Melksham Town 2-0
Bodmin Town v Clevedon United 4-0
Bemerton Heath Harlequins v Westbury United 3-1
Brislington v Bishop's Cleeve 0-1
Taunton Town v Frome Town 2-3
Christchurch v Clevedon Town 1-2
Highworth Town v Elmore 6-0
Porthleven v Bideford 1-6
Mangotsfield United v Shortwood United 3-2
Cinderford Town v Street 1-1, 1-2
Fairford Town v Almondsbury Town 4-0
Holker Old Boys v Hall Road Rangers 2-0
Enfield Town v AFC Sudbury 2-1
Fisher Athletic v Eastbourne Town 5-0
Dartford v Horsham YMCA 5-0

FIRST QUALIFYING ROUND

Frickley Athletic v Chadderton Town 4-1
Billingham Synthonia v Whitby Town 1-3
Clitheroe v Wakefield & Emley 2-2, 0-0
Clitheroe won 4-2 on penalties.
Billingham Town v Ossett Town 1-0
Marine v Farsley Celtic 1-1, 0-4
Bridlington Town v Cammell Laird 1-5
Flixton v Dunston FB 1-6
Hyde United v Maine Road 3-0
West Auckland Town v Ashington 0-2
Thornaby v Esh Winning 1-2
Colne v Sheffield 2-1
Guiseley v Chorley 0-0, 1-2
Witton Albion v Winsford United 0-1
Burscough v Wretford United 1-0
Alsager Town v Radcliffe Borough 0-1
Atherton LR v Whickham 3-0
Gateshead v Pickering Town 2-0
Ramsbottom United v Colwyn Bay 2-1
Brigg Town v Whitley Bay 3-1
Brandon United v Liversedge 1-4
Bishop Auckland v Workington 1-2
Kendal Town v Prescot Cables 1-1, 2-5
Crook Town v Glasshoughton Welfare 1-3
Spennymoor United v Fleetwood Town 1-1, 2-3
Horden CW v Warrington Town 1-1, 2-1
Mossley v Ossett Albion 3-2
Armthorpe Welfare v Maltby Main 1-2
Bamber Bridge v Blackpool Mechanics 6-0
Shildon v Woodleigh Sports 1-1, 2-0
Blyth Spartans v Skelmersdale United 0-2
Holker Old Boys v Silsden 2-2, 2-1
Trafford v Squires Gate 1-2
Westfields v Carlton Town 1-2
Ludlow Town v Newcastle Town 5-1
Matlock Town v Shirebrook Town 2-1
Grantham Town v Shepshed Dynamo 2-4
Rugby United v Hednesford Town 2-2, 1-2
Ilkeston Town v Gresley Rovers 0-3
Spalding United v Causeway United 4-0
Solihull Borough v Leek Town 0-1
Sutton Town v Stone Dominoes 1-1, 0-3
Stamford v Bedworth United 1-0
Borrowash Victoria v Halesowen Town 0-5
Norton United v Lincoln United 0-1
Deeping Rangers v Coalville Town 2-2, 1-3
Sutton Coldfield Town v Stratford Town 2-1
Tie awarded to Stratford Town; Sutton Coldfield Town fielded an ineligible player.
Willenhall Town v Barwell 1-0
Belper Town v Rocester 2-0
Stourport Swifts v Rushall Olympic 1-2
Harrow Borough v Potton United 2-0
Uxbridge v Staines Town 4-3
Brook House v Northwood 1-1, 0-3
Southend Manor v Billericay Town 0-3
Histon v Hampton & Richmond Borough 2-0
Cheshunt v Barton Rovers 2-2, 4-3
Haverhill Rovers v Wivenhoe Town 0-1
Heybridge Swifts v Barking & East Ham United 1-0
Thame United v Gorleston 3-3, 5-3
(first replay abandoned 34 mins (1-1); floodlight failure)
Lowestoft Town v Boreham Wood 0-1
Wingate & Finchley v Halstead Town 2-3
Hendon v Holmer Green 1-0
Wealdstone v Banbury United 2-1
Dunstable Town v St Margaretsbury 5-0
Maldon Town v King's Lynn 2-3
Wootton Blue Cross v Stotfold 1-2
Hemel Hempstead Town v North Greenford United 5-1
Marlow v Long Melford 1-2
Hertford Town v Bury Town 0-0, 1-1
Hertford Town won 4-3 on penalties.
Cornard United v Aylesbury United 0-6
Chelmsford City v Yeading 0-1
Beaconsfield SYCOB v Hitchin Town 5-3
Enfield v Arlesey Town 1-4
Leyton v Tilbury 1-0
Waltham Forest v Cogenhoe United 2-1
Ruislip Manor v Harwich & Parkeston 1-1, 0-2
Harlow Town v Enfield Town 0-1
Braintree Town v Soham Town Rangers 2-0
Aveley v Berkhamsted Town 2-1
Chesham United v Bedford Town 1-1, 1-4
Brackley Town v Flackwell Heath 2-2, 0-2
Edgware Town v Barkingside 4-1
Gosport Borough v Eastleigh 1-2
Didcot Town v Tooting & Mitcham United 2-2, 0-2
Whitstable Town v Hailsham Town 4-0
Leatherhead v Cray Wanderers 1-0
East Preston v Merstham 1-0
Ash United v Maidstone United 2-2, 0-2
Dartford v Dorking 0-1
Banstead Athletic v Oxford City 2-3
VCD Athletic v Brockenhurst 0-0, 0-1
Chatham Town v Windsor & Eton 1-1, 0-3
Thamesmead Town v Worthing 2-1
Ringmer v Erith Town 1-1, 0-3
Tonbridge Angels v Winchester City 2-1
Bracknell Town v Sandhurst Town 0-2
AFC Newbury v BAT Sports 4-0
Croydon Athletic v Slough Town 0-1
Metropolitan Police v Dulwich Hamlet 3-4
AFC Totton v Tunbridge Wells 2-1
Ashford Town (Middlesex) v Bashley 3-1

Horsham v Abingdon United	4-3
Fisher Athletic v Bromley	2-2, 0-1
Dover Athletic v AFC Wimbledon	0-1
Raynes Park Vale v Folkestone Invicta	0-6
Kingstonian v Ramsgate	0-2
Carterton v Erith & Belvedere	1-1, 3-4
Molesey v Lymington & New Milton	0-2
Hastings United v Mile Oak	2-0
North Leigh v Walton Casuals	1-0
Chippenham Town v Bitton	4-0
Hallen v Bemerton Heath Harlequins	2-0
Bridport v Bath City	1-4
Fairford Town v Bideford	0-0, 0-2
Highworth Town v Bishop's Cleeve	3-5
Street v Gloucester City	3-2
Clevedon Town v Merthyr Tydfil	1-2
St Blazey v Evesham United	1-2
Swindon Supermarine v Corsham Town	0-1
Exmouth Town v Salisbury City	1-2
Bodmin Town v Cirencester Town	0-3
Frome Town v Backwell United	2-2, 3-1
Tiverton Town v Mangotsfield United	3-2
Barnstaple Town v Bournemouth	3-1
Yate Town v Team Bath	0-1

SECOND QUALIFYING ROUND

Holker Old Boys v Harrogate Town	0-3
Horden CW v Frickley Athletic	3-0
Bradford Park Avenue v Squires Gate	2-1
Maltby Main v Ashton United	1-3
Whitby Town v Mossley	0-2
Glasshoughton Welfare v Clitheroe	2-1
Barrow v Stalybridge Celtic	3-3, 2-3
Gateshead v Chorley	4-1
Brigg Town v Colne	1-0
Lancaster City v Esh Winning	3-2
Altrincham v Farsley Celtic	4-1
Ramsbottom United v Southport	0-2
Fleetwood Town v Runcorn FC Halton	1-1, 1-2
Atherton LR v Hyde United	2-3
Dunston FB v Cammell Laird	2-2, 0-2
Billingham Town v Vauxhall Motors	1-3
Liversedge v Prescot Cables	3-0
Skelmersdale United v Burscough	2-3
Bamber Bridge v Workington	1-5
Ashington v Droylsden	1-3
Radcliffe Borough v Shildon	3-3, 2-0
Willenhall Town v Shepshed Dynamo	0-0, 3-3
Willenhall Town won 4-3 on penalties.	
Matlock Town v Alfreton Town	0-5
Spalding United v Belper Town	5-4
Gainsborough Trinity v Halesowen Town	2-3
Redditch United v Histon	2-3
King's Lynn v Ludlow Town	1-0
Leek Town v Nuneaton Borough	1-1, 2-1
Worcester City v Cambridge City	1-3
Coalville Town v Rushall Olympic	2-1
Gresley Rovers v Hucknall Town	2-2, 1-3
Hinckley United v Stamford	3-1
Moor Green v Carlton Town	5-0
Stafford Rangers v Kettering Town	2-2, 1-0
Worksop Town v Stone Dominoes	3-0
Stratford Town v Hednesford Town	1-0
Lincoln United v Winsford United	5-0
Bishop's Stortford v Hayes	3-4
Lewes v Brockenhurst	1-2
Slough Town v Welling United	4-1
Bromley v Thamesmead Town	3-0
Oxford City v Leyton	0-1
Dorking v Billericay Town	0-1
Whitstable Town v Maidenhead United	0-0, 1-1
Maidenhead United won 3-2 on penalties.	
Dunstable Town v AFC Wimbledon	0-3
Ramsgate v Dulwich Hamlet	3-6
Halstead Town v Thurrock	0-3
Cheshunt v Northwood	3-0
Edgware Town v North Leigh	0-1
Wealdstone v Grays Athletic	3-1
Eastbourne Borough v Sutton United	3-4
Tooting & Mitcham United v Hemel Hempstead Town	2-2, 3-0
Harwich & Parkeston v Hornchurch	0-3
Margate v Waltham Forest	2-1
Carshalton Athletic v Hastings United	1-3
Erith & Belvedere v Flackwell Heath	0-1
Harrow Borough v Folkestone Invicta	2-2, 1-1
Harrow Borough won 5-4 on penalties.	
Yeading v Long Melford	2-0
Tonbridge Angels v Braintree Town	1-1, 0-2
Sandhurst Town v Leatherhead	0-2
Erith Town v Horsham	2-3
Heybridge Swifts v St Albans City	0-2
Tie awarded to Heybridge Swifts; St Albans City fielded an ineligible player.	
Maidstone United v Redbridge	2-1
Boreham Wood v Aveley	2-1
Beaconsfield SYCOB v Windsor & Eton	1-2
Arlesey Town v Wivenhoe Town	2-3
Ashford Town (Middlesex) v Hertford Town	3-1
Enfield Town v Thame United	0-1
East Preston v Uxbridge	1-0
Bedford Town v Hendon	1-3
Stotfold v Aylesbury United	1-1, 2-4
Dorchester Town v Weymouth	0-1
Corsham Town v Newport County	0-2
Basingstoke Town v AFC Newbury	2-4
Eastleigh v Barnstaple Town	5-0
Street v Merthyr Tydfil	1-2
Bishop's Cleeve v AFC Totton	4-1
Salisbury City v Frome Town	1-1, 3-0
Havant & Waterlooville v Bath City	0-2
Team Bath v Hallen	0-0, 0-0
Hallen won 5-4 on penalties.	
Tiverton Town v Bideford	0-0, 3-1
Bognor Regis Town v Cirencester Town	4-3
Evesham United v Weston-Super-Mare	1-3
Lymington & New Milton v Chippenham Town	3-2

THIRD QUALIFYING ROUND

AFC Wimbledon v Thurrock	0-2
Altrincham v Hucknall Town	3-3, 0-1
Ashton United v Burscough	0-3
Aylesbury United v Ashford Town (Middlesex)	0-1
Bognor Regis Town v AFC Newbury	2-0
Bradford Park Avenue v Brigg Town	1-2
Braintree Town v Margate	3-1
Brockenhurst v Bath City	0-3
Cammell Laird v Alfreton Town	2-3
East Preston v Billericay Town	0-2
Halesowen Town v Glasshoughton Welfare	4-1
Hallen v Bishop's Cleeve	3-2
Harrow Borough v Flackwell Heath	0-1
Hayes v Wivenhoe Town	2-0
Heybridge Swifts v Yeading	2-3
Hinckley United v Mossley	6-1
Histon v Horsham	5-0
Horden CW v Gateshead	2-3
Hornchurch v Dulwich Hamlet	9-0
Lancaster City v King's Lynn	1-0
Leatherhead v Maidstone United	2-1
Leek Town v Stalybridge Celtic	2-1
Leyton v Hendon	1-1, 1-3
Lincoln United v Hyde United	1-2
Liversedge v Harrogate Town	3-2
Maidenhead United v Windsor & Eton	2-1
Merthyr Tydfil v Lymington & New Milton	0-1
North Leigh v Newport County	0-0, 2-6
Radcliffe Borough v Moor Green	1-0
Runcorn FC Halton v Stafford Rangers	0-1
Slough Town v Cheshunt	4-0
Spalding United v Hastings United	1-0
Stratford Town v Southport	0-3
Sutton United v Bromley	2-2, 1-2
Tiverton Town v Eastleigh	3-3, 1-0
Tooting & Mitcham United v Cambridge City	2-4
Vauxhall Motors v Workington	1-0
Wealdstone v Boreham Wood	5-1
Weston-Super-Mare v Salisbury City	1-3
Weymouth v Thame United	1-1, 1-2
Willenhall Town v Coalville Town	1-2
Worksop Town v Droylsden	3-2

FOURTH QUALIFYING ROUND

Accrington Stanley v Leigh RMI	0-2
Aldershot Town v Maidenhead United	2-1
Barnet v Farnborough Town	2-1
Bath City v Leatherhead	1-0
Billericay Town v Flackwell Heath	3-0
Bognor Regis Town v Yeading	0-2
Brigg Town v Halesowen Town	1-4
Bromley v Cambridge City	0-3
Canvey Island v Hallen	4-1
Carlisle United v York City	3-1
Dagenham & Redbridge v Crawley Town	2-1
Exeter City v Braintree Town	2-0
Halifax Town v Leek Town	2-2, 1-0
Hayes v Ashford Town (Middlesex)	4-0
Hereford United v Radcliffe Borough	2-1
Hinckley United v Burton Albion	0-0, 1-1
Hinckley United won 4-1 on penalties.	
Hornchurch v Gravesend & Northfleet	3-2
Lancaster City v Scarborough	1-1, 1-0
Liversedge v Coalville Town	0-0, 0-2
Lymington & New Milton v Woking	1-1, 2-4
Morecambe v Hucknall Town	5-1
Northwich Victoria v Vauxhall Motors	1-2
Slough Town v Salisbury City	3-2
Southport v Hyde United	3-1
Stafford Rangers v Gateshead	2-1
Stevenage Borough v Hendon	5-0
Tamworth v Burscough	2-1
Thame United v Forest Green Rovers	0-5
Thurrock v Spalding United	6-0
Tiverton Town v Newport County	4-1
Wealdstone v Histon	0-2
Worksop Town v Alfreton Town	1-1, 1-2

THE FA CUP 2004–05

COMPETITION PROPER

▪ *Denotes player sent off.*

FIRST ROUND

Friday, 12 November 2004

Bristol C (0) 1 *(Lita 89)*
Brentford (1) 1 *(Salako 7)* 10,000
Bristol C: Phillips; Coles, Bell (Gillespie), Doherty, Butler (Smith), Hill, Murray, Orr (Tinnion), Lita, Brooker, Wilkshire.
Brentford: Nelson; O'Connor, Frampton, Talbot, Sodje, Turner, Tabb, Hargreaves, Rankin, Burton (Rhodes), Salako (Lawrence).

Port Vale (0) 3 *(Paynter 53, 65, Reid 59)*
Kidderminster H (1) 1 *(Hatswell 4)* 4141
Port Vale: Brain; Walsh (Rowland), Brown, Collins, Pilkington, Birchall, Reid (Hulbert), Cummins, Paynter, Lowndes, Smith J.
Kidderminster H: Clarke; Bennett, Beswetherick, Burton, Hatswell, Sall, Keates, Russell, Stamp (Foster I) (Jenkins), Cooper, Keene (Christiansen).

Southend U (0) 0
Luton T (3) 3 *(Howard 12, 15, Brkovic 33)* 6683
Southend U: Griemink; Jupp, Wilson, Maher, Barrett, Prior (Edwards), Gower (Bramble), Hunt, Gray, Eastwood, Pettefer (Bentley).
Luton T: Seremet; Foley, Davis, Robinson (Bayliss), Davies, Coyne, O'Leary, Brkovic, Howard, Vine (Showunmi), Underwood.

Saturday, 13 November 2004

Aldershot T (0) 4 *(Dixon 46, 79, McLean 65, 90)*
Canvey Island (0) 0 2600
Aldershot T: Bull; Giles, Barnard D, McAuley (Clarke), Peters (Antwi), Johnson, Crittenden N, Watson, McLean, Dixon (Sills), Challinor.
Canvey Island: Potter; Joseph, Duffy, Cowan, Smith (Chenery), Sterling, Keeling, Minton, Gregory, Berquez (Hallett), Sedgemore (Goodwin).

Alfreton T (0) 1 *(Sale 90)*
Macclesfield T (0) 1 *(Whitaker 86)* 2251
Alfreton T: Butler; Bradshaw, Chapman, Ward, Blount, Brown, Bettney (Robinson), Fisher, Duffield, Godber (Sale), Nwadike (Goddard).
Macclesfield T: Fettis; Harsley, Potter (Brightwell), Welch, Barras, Carragher, Whitaker, Widdrington, Tipton (Miles), Parkin, Sheron.

Barnet (0) 1 *(Hatch 48)*
Bath C (0) 2 *(Partridge 65, 90)* 2147
Barnet: Tynan; Hendon, King, Clist, Yakubu, Graham, Lopez, Sinclair, Grazioli (Roache), Hatch, Strevens.
Bath C: Perrin; Rollo, Power, Ford (Coupe), Bailey, Jones, Owers, Benefield, Williams, Partridge, Sykes.

Billericay T (0) 0
Stevenage B (0) 1 *(Hanlon 72)* 1804
Billericay T: Gothard; McSweeney, Kerrigan (Henty), Forbes, Sappleton, Trott, Dormer, Hunter, Brayley (Stowe), Cousins, Gallagher (Wareham).
Stevenage B: Woodman; Hocking, Gregory (Rogers), Hanlon, Laker, Goodliffe▪, Bulman (Brough), Boyd, Elding, Brady, Quinn (McAllister).

Blackpool (1) 3 *(Wellens 9, 76, Parker 46)*
Tamworth (0) 0 4796
Blackpool: Jones L; Clare, Evans (Edwards R), Grayson (Blinkhorn), McGregor, Clarke, Coid (Southern), Wellens, Parker, Taylor, Edwards P.
Tamworth: Price; Stamps, Smith A, Colkin (Francis), Redmile, Turner (Sheppard), Cooper, Simpson, Taylor, Whitman (Curtis), Ebdon.

Boston U (0) 5 *(Thompson 48, McManus 49, 67, Noble 81, Ellender 89)*
Hornchurch (1) 2 *(Castle 4, Everett 78)* 2437
Boston U: Abbey N; West, McCann, Greaves, Beevers, Ellender, Thompson, Noble (Rusk), Lee (Norris), Kirk (McManus), Thomas.
Hornchurch: Baruwa; Clancy, Deen, Castle (Locke), Popovic, Downer▪, Shipp, Penn, Huke (Peters), Sigere, Douglas (Everett).

Bradford C (0) 0
Rushden & D (0) 1 *(Robinson 87)* 4171
Bradford C: Henderson; Holloway, Emanuel, Schumacher, Wetherall, Bower, Summerbee, Kearney, Windass, Symes (Forrest), Muirhead.
Rushden & D: Turley; Connelly, Hawkins, Gray, Allen, Gulliver, Hay, Dove, Robinson, Taylor, Burgess.

Bristol R (0) 1 *(Walker 77)*
Carlisle U (0) 1 *(McGill 79)* 5658
Bristol R: Miller; Hinton, Ryan, Edwards, Burns, Campbell (Haldane), Trollope, Hunt, Walker, Agogo, Disley.
Carlisle U: Glennon; Shelley, Cowan, Billy, Gray, Grand, McGill, Lumsdon, Vieira (Farrell), Preece (Henderson), Hawley.

Bury (4) 5 *(Mattis 8, 26, Porter 19, Challinor 39, Nugent 74)*
Vauxhall M (0) 2 *(McDermott 61, O'Donnell 73)* 2566
Bury: Marriott; Unsworth, Kennedy, Swailes, Challinor (Scott), Woodthorpe, Flitcroft (Whaley), Mattis, Porter, Nugent (Newby), Barry-Murphy.
Vauxhall M: Dittmar; Spellman (O'Brien), Woodyatt, Nesbitt, Glendenning, Brazier, Lawton, Olsen, Cumiskey (O'Donnell), McDermott (Flood), Wright D.

Cambridge C (0) 2 *(Sadler 58, Stevenson 90)*
Leigh RMI (1) 1 *(Simms 14)* 930
Cambridge C: Roberts; Pope, Chaffey (Summerscales), Scott, Langston, Fuff, Williams, Fiddes (Miller), Simpson, Sadler (Stevenson), Binns.
Leigh RMI: Crichton; Stoker, Lane, Connell (Shilton), Gaunt, Miller, Rose, Starbuck, Simms, Williams, Roscoe.

Darlington (1) 3 *(Armstrong 19, 73, Keltie 86)*
Yeovil T (0) 3 *(Miles 46, Tarachulski 55, 90)* 3698
Darlington: Russell S; Valentine, Kendrick (Wainwright), Close▪, Clarke, Liddle, Webster (Keltie), Maddison, Armstrong, Wijnhard, Clark (Convery).
Yeovil T: Weale; Rose, Guyett, Way, Terry, Miles, Gall, Johnson, Tarachulski, Stolcers (Lindegaard), Williams.

Exeter C (1) 1 *(Gaia 6)*
Grimsby T (0) 0 3378
Exeter C: Rice; Hiley, Jeannin, Taylor, Gaia, Sawyer, Afful (Moxey), Ampadu, Flack, Devine, Clay.
Grimsby T: Williams A; Crowe, McDermott (Cramb), Jones, Gordon, Whittle, Fleming, Pinault, Parkinson, Sestanovich, Reddy▪.

Forest Green R (0) 1 *(Louis 56)*
Bournemouth (1) 1 *(Fletcher 24)* 1837
Forest Green R: Williams; Lyttle, Davies, Gadsby, Richardson (Louis), Garner, Watson, Rogers, Griffin, Roberts, Reed.
Bournemouth: Moss N; Young, Cummings, Stock, Howe, Broadhurst, Elliott, O'Connor (Browning), Hayter (Connell), Fletcher, Spicer.

Halifax T (1) 3 *(Foster 6, Midgley 69, Ross 84)*
Cambridge U (1) 1 *(Tudor 35)* 2368
Halifax T: Dunbavin; Haslam, Doughty, Quinn, Stoneman, Bushell, Foster, Toulson (Howell), Killeen (Mallon), Sugden (Ross), Midgley.
Cambridge U: Ruddy; Goodhind, Bimson, Duncan, Tann, Nicholls (Hodgson), Tudor, Mbome, Webb, Turner, Easter (El Kholti).

Hartlepool U (3) 3 *(Williams 23, Robson 27, Porter 43)*
Lincoln C (0) 0 4533
Hartlepool U: Konstantopoulos; Ross, Robson, Nelson, Westwood, Clark (Istead), Williams, Sweeney, Porter, Boyd (Foley), Humphreys (Strachan).
Lincoln C: Marriott; Bloomer, Sandwith, McAuley, McCombe, Futcher, Butcher, Richardson (Folkes), Taylor-Fletcher, Yeo (Ryan), Peat (Littlejohn).

Hayes (0) 0
Wrexham (3) 4 *(Holt 17, Lawrence 30, Sam 37, Llewellyn 82)* 1751
Hayes: Davies; Collins (Goodall), Gray, Williams, Everitt, Yeboah, Case, Molesley, Warner K (Scott), Knight, Warner D (Dean).
Wrexham: Baker; Spender, Holt, Lawrence, Roberts, Pejic, Crowell (Smith), Ferguson, Armstrong (Mark Jones), Sam (Ugarte), Llewellyn.

Hinckley U (1) 2 *(Lavery 38, Cartwright 79)*
Torquay U (0) 0 2129
Hinckley U: Whittle; Cartwright, Stone, Lavery, Willis, Storer, Lenton, Dyer, Lewis (Smith), Barnes, Burns (McMahon).
Torquay U: Gottskalksson; Canoville, McGlinchey, Fowler (Gritton), Hockley, Taylor, Bedeau, Russell, Akinfenwa (Boardley), Constantine, Hill.

Histon (1) 2 *(Cambridge I 4, Liban 90)*
Shrewsbury T (0) 0 1538
Histon: Key; Farrington, Vowden, Nightingale (Okay), Goddard, Hipperson, Cambridge A, Andrews, Kennedy, Cambridge I (Liban), Barker.
Shrewsbury T: Howie; Sedgemore (Walton), Challis, Whitehead, Tinson, O'Connor, Street, Edwards, Rodgers, Lowe, Aiston.

Hull C (1) 3 *(Green 30, Keane 66, Walters 86)*
Morecambe (1) 2 *(Bentley 12, Twiss 60)* 10,129
Hull C: Myhill; Joseph (France), Dawson, Ashbee, Cort, Delaney, Green, Barmby, Allsopp (Walters), Elliott, Keane.
Morecambe: Sollitt; Heard (Rogan), Blackburn, Perkins, Bentley, Swan (McFlynn), Hunter, Twiss, Curtis, Walmsley, Thompson (Carlton).

Leyton Orient (2) 3 *(Lockwood 11, Hunt 37, Carlisle 58)*
Dagenham & R (0) 1 *(Moore 83 (pen))* 4155
Leyton Orient: Harrison; Miller (Barnard D), Lockwood (Newey), Hunt, White, Zakuani, Carlisle, Simpson, Ibehre, Steele (Wardley), Scott.
Dagenham & R: Roberts; Cole, Vickers, Goodwin, Uddin, Leberl, Janney, Southam, Douglas (Moore), Mackail-Smith, Flynn (Boot).

Mansfield T (1) 1 *(John-Baptiste 28)*
Colchester U (1) 1 *(Halford 25)* 3202
Mansfield T: Pilkington; Buxton, Curtis, Dimech, Artell, John-Baptiste, McLachlan, Mackenzie, Larkin (Day), Asamoah■, Corden (Murray).
Colchester U: Gerken; Stockley, Baldwin, White (Cade), Chilvers, Watson, Johnson, Garcia, Fagan, Halford, Keith.

Milton Keynes D (0) 1 *(Small 48)*
Lancaster C (0) 0 2065
Milton Keynes D: Martin; Edds, Lewington, Herve, Palmer, Ntimban-Zeh, Kamara, Smith, Small, McLeod, Puncheon.
Lancaster C: Speare; Clarke (Elderton), Scott, Bauress, Sparrow, McMahon, Hollis (Sullivan), Black, Jones, Thomson, Prince (Dawes).

Northampton T (1) 1 *(McGleish 5)*
Barnsley (0) 0 4876
Northampton T: Harper; Low (Cozic), Jaszczun, Bojic, Willmott, Murray, Rowson, Sabin (Alsop), McGleish, Smith (Galbraith), Williamson.
Barnsley: Turnbull; Hassell, Williams R (Tonge), Kay (Burns), Carbon, Reid, Wroe, Conlon (Onibuje), Chopra, Shuker, Williams T.

Notts Co (1) 2 *(Baudet 35 (pen), Gordon 90)*
Woking (0) 0 4700
Notts Co: Deeney; Wilson, McFaul (Gill), Palmer, Whitlow, Baudet, Oakes, Bolland, Gordon, Hurst, Pipe (Scully).
Woking: Jalal; Oliver, Jackson, Murray, Boardman■, MacDonald, Smith (Canham), Richards, Foweya, Nade, Evans (Johnson).

Peterborough U (1) 2 *(Kennedy 10, Woodhouse 89)*
Tranmere R (1) 1 *(Taylor 42)* 2940
Peterborough U: Tyler; Newton, Legg, Woodhouse, St Ledger-Hall, Burton■, Farrell (Semple), Clarke (Logan), Platt, Kennedy (Plummer), Jelleyman.
Tranmere R: Achterberg; Taylor, Roberts, McAteer, Jackson, Goodison, Hall, Rankine, Hume, Zola■, Sharps.

Rochdale (1) 2 *(Holt 36, 90)*
Oxford U (1) 1 *(Bradbury 20)* 2333
Rochdale: Gilks; Evans, Goodall, Clarke, Griffiths, Gallimore, Atieno (McGivern), Jones, Tait (Bertos), Holt, Cooksey.
Oxford U: Tardif; Mackay, Robinson, Quinn, Woozley, Togwell, Basham, Wanless, Mooney (Brooks), Bradbury, E'Beyer (Hackett).

Scunthorpe U (1) 2 *(Hayes 13, Baraclough 76)*
Chesterfield (0) 0 4869
Scunthorpe U: Musselwhite; Byrne, Ridley, Crosby, Butler, Baraclough, Sparrow (Taylor), Kell, Hayes, Torpey (Sharp), Beagrie (Rankine).
Chesterfield: Muggleton; Bailey, Nicholson, Niven, Blatherwick, Evatt, Allott, Hudson (Davies), Stallard (N'Toya), Folan, Smith (De Bolla).

Slough T (1) 2 *(Hodges 24, Harris 73)*
Walsall (1) 1 *(Wrack 32)* 2023
Slough T: Allaway; Carbon, Murphy, Metcalfe, Daly, Saulisdury, Haddow, Harris (Steer), Hodges, Spencer (Seedell), Wilkinson.
Walsall: Paston; Wright (Taylor D), Aranalde, Osborn, Emblen, Bennett■, Standing, Merson, Fryatt (Williams), Leitao, Wrack.

Southport (0) 1 *(Fearns 75)*
Hereford U (1) 3 *(Mills 26, Stansfield 58, Purdie 63)* 2045
Southport: Dickinson; Williams, Mortimer (Baker), Morley, Kilbane, Davis, Lynch (Mulvaney), Price, Daly (Fitzgerald), Fearns, Robinson.
Hereford U: Mawson; Travis, Robinson, Hyde, Mkandawire, James, Stanley, Brown (Purdie), Stansfield (Pitman), Mills (Carey-Bertram), Williams D.

Stafford R (0) 0
Chester C (1) 2 *(Belle 32, Rapley 71)* 2492
Stafford R: Dormand; Brown, Daniel, Lovatt, Talbott, McAughtrie, Gibson, Downes, Danks (Jackson), Wilding, Heath (Grayson).
Chester C: MacKenzie; Edmondson, Hessey (McIntyre), Hope, Bolland, Davies (Harris), Drummond, Carden, Belle, Clare (Rapley), Ellison.

Stockport Co (3) 3 *(Williams A 8, Feeney 19, 45)*
Huddersfield T (0) 1 *(Abbott 90)* 3479
Stockport Co: Spencer; Hardiker, Adams, Griffin, Williams A, Robertson (Mair), Cartwright (Lambert), Goodwin, Feeney, Smith (Barlow), Williams C.
Huddersfield T: Rachubka; Holdsworth, Lloyd, Mirfin, Yates (Fowler), Clarke N, Worthington, Schofield, Mendes, Abbott, Brandon.

Swindon T (1) 4 *(Howard 43, Jenkins 48, Duke 83, Roberts 86)*
Sheffield W (0) 1 *(Whelan 63)* 6160
Swindon T: Evans; Jenkins, Duke, Ifil, O'Hanlon, Heywood, Igoe, Hewlett, Roberts (Fallon), Parkin, Howard.
Sheffield W: Lucas; Collins, Wood, Branston, Lee, McMahon, Whelan, McGovern, MacLean, Talbot (Hamshaw), Brunt.

Tiverton T (0) 1 *(Winter 90 (pen))*
Doncaster R (2) 3 *(McIndoe 18, Fenton 26, Blundell 84)* 1618
Tiverton T: Ovendale; Rudge, Winter, Booth (Goff), Cousins, Stocco (Milson), Wills, Harvey (Steele), Ibe, Mudge, Vinnicombe.
Doncaster R: Warrington; Price, Ryan, Morley, Fenton, Green, Coppinger (McSporran), Ravenhill, Blundell, Roberts (Beardsley), McIndoe (Rigoglioso).

Wycombe W (0) 1 *(Johnson 71)*
Coalville T (0) 0 2816
Wycombe W: Talia; Uhlenbeek, Silk, Johnson, Williamson, Craig, Senda (Bloomfield), Martin, Stonebridge, Tyson, Ryan.
Coalville T: Bowles; Garner, Brown (Peake), Woodhall (Russell), Tonge, Wilkes, Stevens, Pollard (Chapman), Warner, McGlinchey, Geary.

Yeading (2) 2 *(Haywood 5 (og), Campbell 45 (pen))*
Halesowen T (1) 1 *(Cowley 9)* 524
Yeading: Preddie; Barima (Behzadi), Protain, Clarke, Saroya, Leach, Stanley, Brown, Campbell (Woodruffe), Quamina, Haule.
Halesowen T: Taylor; Preston, Cowley, Baker, Pope, Jones, Cooper (Strachan), Forsdick, Haarhoff (Burgess), Moore, Haywood (Steane).

Sunday, 14 November 2004

Cheltenham T (0) 1 *(Spencer 71)*
Swansea C (1) 3 *(O'Leary 19, Trundle 46, Connor 90)* 4551
Cheltenham T: Higgs; Gill (Spencer), Victory, Duff, Brough (Vincent), Caines, Melligan, Bird, Devaney, Guinan, Wilson.
Swansea C: Gueret; Tate, Ricketts, O'Leary, Austin, Monk, Forbes (Britton), Martinez, Connor, Trundle (Nugent), Robinson (Fisken).

Thurrock (0) 0
Oldham Ath (0) 1 *(Killen 48 (pen))* 1156
Thurrock: McMahon; Goddard, Collis, Heffer (Lee), Purdie (Buffong), McFarlane, Hodges, Kirby, Akurang, Kandol, Goodfellow.
Oldham Ath: Pogliacomi; Holden, Griffin, Beharall, Hall D, Lee D, Croft, Appleby (Boshell), Killen, Vernon, Eyres.

FIRST ROUND REPLAYS

Tuesday, 23 November 2004

Carlisle U (0) 1 *(Vieira 109)*
Bristol R (0) 0 4813
Carlisle U: Glennon; Shelley, Cowan, Billy, Andrews, Grand, McGill, Lumsdon, Preece (Henderson), Hawley (Vieira), Murphy.
Bristol R: Miller; Hinton, Ryan, Edwards, Campbell (Gibb), Elliott, Trollope (Haldane), Hunt, Lescott, Agogo, Savage (Thorpe).
aet.

Colchester U (2) 4 *(Garcia 10, Curtis 14 (og), Fagan 67 (pen), Williams 90 (pen))*
Mansfield T (0) 1 *(Neil 87)* 2492
Colchester U: Davison; Stockley, Keith (Bowry), Baldwin, White, Chilvers, Johnson (Williams), Garcia, Fagan (Hunt), Halford, Watson.
Mansfield T: Pilkington; Buxton, Lloyd (Heron), Dimech, Artell, John-Baptiste■, Neil, MacKenzie, Larkin, Murray (Wood), Curtis (McIntosh).

Macclesfield T (0) 2 *(Parkin 54, Sheron 78)*
Alfreton T (0) 0 1783
Macclesfield T: Wilson; Harsley, Potter, Weaver, Barras, Carragher, Whitaker, Brightwell (Briscoe), Parkin, Sheron, Miles.
Alfreton T: Butler; Bradshaw, Blount, Fisher, Chapman, Brown, Ward, Robinson, Duffield (Sale), Godber, Nwadike (Goddard).

Yeovil T (0) 1 *(Way 56)*
Darlington (0) 0 5365
Yeovil T: Weale; Rose, Terry, Way, Miles, Guyett, Stolcers (Gall), Johnson, Jevons, Tarachulski, Williams.
Darlington: Russell S; Valentine (Kendrick), Clark, Close, Clarke, Liddle, Wainwright, Maddison, Armstrong, Wijnhard, Webster.

Wednesday, 24 November 2004

Bournemouth (1) 3 *(Connell 10, Spicer 79, Rodrigues 90)*
Forest Green R (0) 1 *(Lyttle 88)* 5489
Bournemouth: Moss N; Young, Cummings (Maher), Broadhurst, Howe (Browning), Stock, Elliott, O'Connor, Holmes, Connell (Rodrigues), Spicer.
Forest Green R: Williams; Lyttle, Davies, Rogers, Garner, Gadsby, Watson, Appleby (Beesley), Roberts (Louis), Griffin, Reed (Cleverley).

Thursday, 25 November 2004

Brentford (1) 1 *(Frampton 44)*
Bristol C (0) 1 *(Heffernan 77)* 3706
Brentford: Nelson; O'Connor, Frampton, Talbot, Sodje, Turner, Lawrence, Hargreaves, Rankin (Rhodes), Harrold (Tabb), Salako.
Bristol C: Phillips; Smith, Fortune, Doherty (Lita), Butler, Hill (Coles), Murray (Brown), Orr, Miller, Heffernan, Tinnion.
aet; Brentford won 4-3 on penalties.

SECOND ROUND

Friday, 3 December 2004

Cambridge C (0) 0
Milton Keynes D (1) 1 *(Smart 6)* 2000
Cambridge C: Roberts; Pope, Summerscales (Simpson), Scott, Fuff, Langston, Williams, Miller (Fiddes), Stevenson, Sadler, Binns.
Milton Keynes D: Martin; Oyedele, Lewington, Rizzo (Tapp), Palmer, Chorley, Kamara, Smith, Small, Smart (McLeod), Herve.

Scunthorpe U (1) 2 *(Ridley 14, Sparrow 54)*
Wrexham (0) 0 5698
Scunthorpe U: Musselwhite; Byrne, Ridley, Crosby, Butler, Baraclough, Sparrow, Kell (Taylor), Hayes, Torpey, Beagrie.
Wrexham: Baker; Spender, Holt, Lawrence, Morgan (Roberts), Pejic, Green (Armstrong), Ferguson, Llewellyn, Ugarte, Mark Jones (Sam).

Saturday, 4 December 2004

Blackpool (0) 1 *(Taylor 76)*
Port Vale (0) 0 4669
Blackpool: Jones L; Clare, Edwards R (Evans), Grayson, McGregor, Clarke, Coid, Wellens, Blinkhorn (Parker), Taylor, Burns.
Port Vale: Brain; Loran, Brown (Armstrong), Pilkington, Walsh (Rowlands), Hulbert (Birchall), Reid, Cummins, Paynter, Lowndes, Smith J.

Bournemouth (0) 2 *(Holmes 48, Connell 64)*
Carlisle U (0) 1 *(Farrell 89)* 5815
Bournemouth: Moss N; Young, Broadhurst, Maher, Howe (Cummings), Stock, Elliott, O'Connor, Holmes (Browning), Connell (Rodrigues), Spicer.
Carlisle U: Glennon; Shelley, Arnison, Billy, Andrews, Grand, McGill (Farrell), Lumsdon, Vieira (Roca), Hawley, Preece (Henderson).

Exeter C (1) 2 *(Flack 25, Moxey 49)*
Doncaster R (0) 1 *(Blundell 86)* 4797
Exeter C: Rice; Hiley, Jeannin, Taylor, Gaia, Sawyer, Afful (Sheldon), Ampadu (Moxey), Flack (Edwards), Devine, Clay.
Doncaster R: Warrington; Price (Ipoua), Ryan, Morley, Fenton, Green, McSporran (Coppinger), Ravenhill (Rigoglioso), Blundell, Roberts, McIndoe.

Halifax T (0) 1 *(Ross 66)*
Chester C (1) 3 *(Branch 41, 50 (pen), Rapley 74)* 4497
Halifax T: Dunbavin; Doughty, Haslam, Bushell, Quinn, Ingram (Clarke), Howell, Foster (Blunt), Killeen, Sugden (Ross), Midgley.
Chester C: Brown W; Edmondson (Rapley), Vaughan, Hope, Hessey, Harris, Booth (Anaclet), Carden, Branch (Lynch), Ellison, McIntyre.

Hartlepool U (2) 5 *(Westwood 13, 30, Boyd 63, 68, Tinkler 75)*
Aldershot T (1) 1 *(Sills 36)* 4556
Hartlepool U: Provett; Barron (Ross), Brackstone, Clark, Westwood, Tinkler, Strachan (Istead), Sweeney, Porter, Boyd, Humphreys (Robson).
Aldershot T: Bull; Warner, Barnard D, Watson (McAuley), Viveash (McLean), Giles, Crittenden N, Challinor, Sills (Jinadu), Dixon, Clarke.

Hereford U (1) 2 *(Mkandawire 9, Stanley 89)*
Boston U (1) 3 *(Lee 30, Kirk 71, 78)* 3601
Hereford U: Mawson; Travis, Robinson, Hyde, Mkandawire, Smith, Stanley, Purdie (Brown), Stansfield, Mills, Williams D.
Boston U: Abbey N; West, McCann, Greaves, Beevers, Ellender, Rusk (O'Halloran), Holland, Lee, Kirk (Thompson), Thomas.

Histon (0) 1 *(Kennedy 71)*
Yeovil T (0) 3 *(Jevons 52 (pen), Johnson 57, Odubade 90)* 2564
Histon: Key; Okay, Goddard (Liban) (Manns), Cambridge A, Vowden, Hipperson (Coburn), Nightingale, Andrews, Cambridge I, Kennedy, Barker.
Yeovil T: Weale; Lindegaard, Miles, Guyett, Skiverton, Way, Gall (Odubade), Johnson, Jevons, Tarachulski (Stolcers), Rose.

Hull C (3) 4 *(France 28, Facey 35, 46, Elliott 39)*
Macclesfield T (0) 0 9831
Hull C: Myhill; Joseph, Dawson, Ashbee (Lewis), Cort, Delaney, France, Barmby (Walters), Facey (Price), Elliott, Keane.
Macclesfield T: Wilson; Harsley, Potter, Welch, Weaver, Carragher, Whitaker, Widdrington, Parkin (Rooney), Sheron, Miles (Tipton).

Northampton T (1) 1 *(McGleish 23)*
Bury (0) 0 4415
Northampton T: Harper; Hearn, Jaszczun (Chambers), Bojic, Willmott, Murray, Rowson, Sabin, McGleish, Smith (Westwood), Cozic (Low).
Bury: Marriott; Unsworth, Kennedy (Whaley), Swailes, Barrass, Woodthorpe, Flitcroft (Newby), Mattis, Porter (Kazim-Richards), Nugent, Barry-Murphy.

Oldham Ath (2) 4 *(Killen 26 (pen), 39, 65, Croft 85)*
Leyton Orient (0) 0 4657
Oldham Ath: Pogliacomi; Croft, Griffin, Holden, Haining, Hall D, Hughes, Kilkenny (Boshell), Killen (Vernon), Betsy, Eyres (Wolfenden).
Leyton Orient: Harrison; Barnard D, Lockwood, Saah (McMahon), White, Mackie, Carlisle (Duncan), Simpson, Ibehre (Newey), Barnard L, Scott.

Peterborough U (2) 2 *(Willock 36, 41)*
Bath C (0) 0 4187
Peterborough U: Tyler; Newton, Legg, Woodhouse, St Ledger-Hall, Burton (Plummer), Farrell (Kennedy), Boucaud (Semple), Clarke, Willock, Jelleyman.
Bath C: Perrin; Rollo, Power, Ford, Jones, Bailey, Benefield (Moor), Owers, Partridge, Williams, Sykes.

Rushden & D (0) 2 *(Broughton 82, Gray 86)*
Colchester U (3) 5 *(Halford 4, 47, 90, Fagan 25, 35)* 3077
Rushden & D: Turley; Connelly, Hawkins, Gray, Allen (Gier), Gulliver, Hay (Bell), Dove (Kelly), Broughton, Robinson, Burgess.
Colchester U: Davison; Stockley, Baldwin, Chilvers, White (Brown), Watson, Garcia (Cade), Bowry (Bowditch), Fagan, Halford, Keith.

Slough T (1) 1 *(Harris 3 (pen))*
Yeading (1) 3 *(Campbell 27, 52, Haule 62)* 2418
Slough T: Allaway; Murphy, Carbon, Haddow, Daly, Saulisdury, Wilkinson, Metcalfe, Hodges, Spencer (Moller), Hodges.
Yeading: Preddie; Barima (Behazdi), Saroya, Haule, Stanley, Leach, Protain, Brown, Campbell (Woodruffe), Telemaque (Newby), Clarke.

Stevenage B (0) 0
Rochdale (0) 2 *(Holt 70, 90)* 2700
Stevenage B: Woodman■; Hocking, Laker, Hanlon (Boyd), Rogers, Quinn (Flack), Gregory, Bulman, Quailey, McAllister (Brady), Brough.
Rochdale: Gilks; Evans, Gallimore, Clarke, Heald, Griffiths, Bertos, Jones (Warner), Tait, Holt, Cooksey.

Stockport Co (0) 0
Swansea C (0) 0 2680
Stockport Co: Spencer (Cutler); Goodwin, Adams, Griffin, Williams A, Robertson, Allen (Williams C), Hardiker, Daly, Feeney (Barlow), Bridge-Wilkinson.
Swansea C: Gueret; Gurney, Ricketts, O'Leary, Austin, Tate, Forbes, Martinez, Connor, Trundle, Goodfellow.

Swindon T (1) 1 *(O'Hanlon 19)*
Notts Co (0) 1 *(Oakes 90)* 5768
Swindon T: Evans; Jenkins, Duke, Ifil, O'Hanlon, Heywood, Igoe (Garrard), Robinson, Fallon (Smith), Parkin, Howard.
Notts Co: Deeney; McFaul, Wilson, Palmer, Whitlow, Baudet (O'Grady), Pipe, Gill, Williams (Scully), Gordon, Oakes.

Wycombe W (0) 0
Luton T (1) 3 *(Howard 20, 80, Nicholls 70)* 4767
Wycombe W: Talia; Uhlenbeek, Silk (Nethercott), Johnson, Williamson, Craig, Senda, Ryan, Stonebridge (Faulconbridge), Tyson, Guppy (Bloomfield).
Luton T: Beresford; Keane, Davis, O'Leary, Davies, Coyne, Underwood, Nicholls, Howard, Vine (Andrew), Brkovic (Showunmi).

Sunday, 5 December 2004

Hinckley U (0) 0
Brentford (0) 0 2661
Hinckley U: Whittle; Willis, Cartwright, Dyer (Jackson), Storer, Stone, Lavery, Lewis (Morrison), Barnes, Burns (McMahon), Lenton.
Brentford: Nelson; O'Connor, Frampton, Talbot, Sodje, Turner, Lawrence (Rhodes), Hargreaves, Rankin (Tabb), May, Salako (Harrold).

SECOND ROUND REPLAYS

Tuesday, 14 December 2004

Brentford (0) 2 *(Rhodes 52 (pen), Talbot 59)*
Hinckley U (0) 1 *(Lavery 57)* 4002
Brentford: Nelson; O'Connor, Myers, Talbot (Hutchinson), Sodje, Rhodes, Tabb, Hargreaves, May (Harrold), Burton (Rankin), Salako.
Hinckley U: Whittle; Willis, Cartwright, Dyer, Storer (Goodwin), Piercewright■, Lavery, Burns (McMahon), Lewis, Barnes (Marrison), Lenton.

Swansea C (0) 2 *(Connor 47, Goodfellow 88)*
Stockport Co (0) 1 *(Griffin 72)* 5572
Swansea C: Gueret; Gurney, Ricketts, O'Leary, Austin, Monk, Forbes (Goodfellow), Martinez, Connor, Trundle, Robinson (Tate).
Stockport Co: Cutler; Hardiker, Jackman (Williams C), Griffin, Williams A, Mair (Raynes), Robertson (Barlow), Lambert, Daly, Goodwin, Bridge-Wilkinson.

Wednesday, 15 December 2004

Notts Co (1) 2 *(Gordon 31, 47)*
Swindon T (0) 0 3770
Notts Co: Deeney; Pipe (McFaul), Gill, Palmer, Whitlow, Wilson, Scully, Bolland, Gordon, Harrad (Hurst), Williams.
Swindon T: Evans; Garrard, Duke (Smith■), Reeves (Fallon), O'Hanlon, Heywood, Igoe, Hewlett, Roberts (Robinson), Parkin, Howard.

THIRD ROUND

Saturday, 8 January 2005

Birmingham C (2) 3 *(Heskey 11, Carter 21, 65)*
Leeds U (0) 0 25,159
Birmingham C: Maik Taylor; Melchiot, Lazaridis (Clapham), Clemence, Upson, Cunningham, Anderton (Tebily), Carter, Morrison, Heskey (Blake), Gray.
Leeds U: Sullivan; Kelly, Richardson, Gregan, Duberry (Pugh), Kilgallon, Walton, Lennon, Blake (Joachim), Healy, Wright.

Bournemouth (1) 2 *(Maher 33, Elliott 56)*
Chester C (0) 1 *(Ellison 69)* 7653
Bournemouth: Moss N; Young, Cummings (Purches), Broadhurst, Maher, Browning, Elliott, O'Connor (Holmes), Connell (Hayter), Fletcher, Spicer.
Chester C: MacKenzie; Vaughan (Booth), Hessey (Walsh), Bolland, Bayliss, Davies, Drummond, Carden, Rapley (Belle), Brown M, Ellison.

Cardiff C (1) 1 *(Lee 35)*
Blackburn R (1) 1 *(Pedersen 5)* 14,145
Cardiff C: Warner; Weston, Barker, Kavanagh, Gabbidon, Collins, McAnuff, Inamoto, Jerome, Lee (Thorne), Langley (Bullock).
Blackburn R: Friedel; Neill, Matteo, Ferguson (Mokoena), Johansson, Todd, Flitcroft, Pedersen, Stead (Gallagher), Dickov (Johnson), Thompson.

Charlton Ath (2) 4 *(Hughes 19, 56, Fortune 44, Murphy 64)*
Rochdale (0) 1 *(Holt 51)* 13,955
Charlton Ath: Kiely; Young, Hreidarsson, Holland, Fortune (Fish), El Karkouri, Hughes, Euell (Murphy), Jeffers, Johansson (Konchesky), Thomas.
Rochdale: Gilks; Evans, Goodall, Clarke (Warner), Burgess, Heald, Bertos, Jones, Tait (Atieno), Holt, Cooksey (McGivern).

Chelsea (1) 3 *(Kezman 26, Gudjohnsen 86, Crosby 58 (og))*
Scunthorpe U (1) 1 *(Hayes 8)* 40,019
Chelsea: Cudicini; Geremi (Paulo Ferreira), Johnson, Nuno Morais, Watt, Cole, Smertin, Kezman (Robben), Drogba (Jarosik), Gudjohnsen, Tiago.
Scunthorpe U: Musselwhite; Byrne, Ridley, Crosby, Butler, Baraclough, Sparrow, Kell, Hayes, Rankine (Taylor), Beagrie (Williams).

Coventry C (2) 3 *(McSheffrey 25, 69, John 45)*
Crewe Alex (0) 0 7629
Coventry C: Steele; Carey (Leacock), Staunton, Hughes, Williams, Shaw, Doyle, John (Suffo), Morrell (Jorgensen), McSheffrey, Wood.
Crewe Alex: Ince; Moses, Jones S (McCready), Lunt, Walker, Foster, Sorvel, Bell, Varney (White), Rivers, Vaughan.

Derby Co (0) 2 *(Idiakez 71, Junior 79)*
Wigan Ath (1) 1 *(Mahon 30)* 14,457
Derby Co: Camp; Boertien, Jackson, Huddlestone, Mills, Idiakez, Bisgaard, Taylor, Tudgay (Junior), Smith (Bolder), Reich.
Wigan Ath: Filan; Wright, McMillan, Flynn, Jackson (Breckin), Emerson, Teale, Whalley (Bullard), Graham, Roberts J, Mahon.

Hartlepool U (0) 0
Boston U (0) 0 5342
Hartlepool U: Konstantopoulos; Ross, Robertson, Nelson, Westwood, Tinkler (Clark), Williams (Istead), Sweeney, Porter (Appleby), Boyd, Humphreys.
Boston U: Abbey N; James, McCann, Greaves, Beevers, Ellender, Rusk (Noble), Holland, Lee, Kirk (Thompson), Thomas.

Hull C (0) 0
Colchester U (2) 2 *(Williams 27, Fagan 29)* 14,027
Hull C: Myhill; Angus (Wiseman), Dawson, Green, Cort, Delaney, Price, Keane (Allsopp), Facey, Wilbraham (Fry), Lewis.
Colchester U: Gerken; Stockley, Keith, Chilvers, Brown, Baldwin, Johnson, Watson, Fagan, Williams (Cade), Halford.

Ipswich T (0) 1 *(Miller 70)*
Bolton W (0) 3 *(Giannakopoulos 60, Pedersen 65, 68)* 20,080
Ipswich T: Davis; Mitchell, Karbassiyoon (Richards), Horlock, De Vos, Wilnis, Currie (Counago), Magilton (Miller), Bent, Kuqi, Westlake.
Bolton W: Jaaskelainen; Ben Haim, Gardner, Campo, N'Gotty, Hierro (Hunt), Fadiga, Vaz Te (Nolan), Pedersen, Davies (Diouf), Giannakopoulos.

Leicester C (1) 2 *(Williams 82, Edwards R 35 (og))*
Blackpool (1) 2 *(Clarke 52, Southern 77)* 16,750
Leicester C: Pressman; Keown (De Vries), Makin (Maybury), Williams, Dublin, Dabizas, Gemmill (Nalis), Gudjonsson, Scowcroft, Connolly, Stewart.
Blackpool: Ellegaard; Edwards R, Clare, Grayson (Wellens), McGregor, Clarke, Parker, Southern, Murphy, Lynch (Burns), Coid.

Luton T (0) 0
Brentford (0) 2 *(Hargreaves 71, Tabb 89)* 6861
Luton T: Beresford; Foley, Davis, Robinson (Showunmi), Davies, Coyne, Underwood, Nicholls, Howard, Vine, Brkovic (Andrew).
Brentford: Nelson; Lawrence (Tabb), Frampton, Talbot, Fitzgerald SB, Turner, Hutchinson, Hargreaves, May, Burton, Rankin (Salako).

Manchester U (0) 0
Exeter C (0) 0 67,551
Manchester U: Howard; Neville P, Spector, Jones, Brown, Pique, Eagles (Ronaldo), Djemba-Djemba, Bellion (Smith), Richardson, Miller (Scholes).
Exeter C: Jones; Hiley, Jeannin, Taylor (Edwards), Gaia, Sawyer, Clay (Ampadu), Martin, Flack (Afful), Devine, Moxey.

Milton Keynes D (0) 0

Peterborough U (1) 2 *(Logan 45, Arber 57)* 4407

Milton Keynes D: Martin; Edds, Lewington, Chorley, Oyedele (Palmer), Rizzo (Puncheon), Mitchell, Smith, Smart (Tapp), McLeod, Small.
Peterborough U: McShane; Newton, Legg, Arber, St Ledger-Hall, Ireland, Farrell, Plummer, Logan, Willock, Thomson.

Northampton T (1) 1 *(Williamson 30)*

Southampton (2) 3 *(Phillips 29, Crouch 41, Redknapp 53)* 7383

Northampton T: Harper; Low (Bojic), Jaszczun (Sabin), Chambers, Willmott, Westwood, Rowson, Smith, McGleish, Benjamin, Williamson (Hearn).
Southampton: Niemi; Telfer, Higginbotham, Delap, Lundekvam, Davenport, Prutton, Redknapp (Oakley), Crouch (Ormerod), Phillips, McCann (Cranie).

Notts Co (1) 1 *(Scully 2)*

Middlesbrough (0) 2 *(Doriva 54, Job 76)* 13,671

Notts Co: Deeney; Wilson, Ullathorne, Palmer (Williams), Whitlow, Gill (Oakes), Pipe, Bolland, Gordon (Harrad), Hurst, Scully.
Middlesbrough: Schwarzer; Reiziger, Queudrue, Riggott, Ehiogu, Doriva, Morrison (Graham), Parlour, Hasselbaink, Job (Zenden), Downing.

Oldham Ath (1) 1 *(Vernon 14)*

Manchester C (0) 0 13,171

Oldham Ath: Pogliacomi; Bruce, Griffin, Hughes, Haining, Hall D, Eyre, Kilkenny, Vernon, Betsy, Eyres.
Manchester C: James; Mills, Thatcher, Dunne, Distin, Barton, Wright-Phillips S, Bosvelt, Macken, Wright-Phillips B (McManaman), Sibierski (Flood).

Plymouth Arg (1) 1 *(Gudjonsson 34)*

Everton (2) 3 *(Osman 16, McFadden 18, Chadwick 84)* 20,112

Plymouth Arg: Larrieu; Connolly, Gilbert, Friio, Doumbe, Coughlan, Hodges (Keith), Wotton, Evans, Gudjonsson, Capaldi.
Everton: Wright; Pistone, Naysmith, Stubbs, Yobo, Carsley, Osman, McFadden (Chadwick), Bent (Gravesen), Beattie (Cahill), Kilbane.

Portsmouth (0) 1 *(Yakubu 49)*

Gillingham (0) 0 14,252

Portsmouth: Ashdown; Griffin (Quashie), Unsworth, O'Neil (Stone), Stefanovic, De Zeeuw, Hughes, Kamara, Yakubu, Fuller (Primus), Berger.
Gillingham: Banks; Southall, Rose (Beckwith), Smith, Ashby (Hope), Cox, Bodkin (Roberts), Hessenthaler, Henderson, Byfield, Crofts.

Preston NE (0) 0

WBA (0) 2 *(Earnshaw 76, 83)* 13,005

Preston NE: Lonergan; Alexander, Kozluk, Etuhu, Lucketti, Mawene, Sedgwick (Mears), McKenna, O'Neill (Jackson), Agyemang, Lewis.
WBA: Hoult; Albrechtsen, Robinson, Wallwork, Purse, Clement, Gera, Johnson, Earnshaw, Horsfield (Hulse), Greening (Koumas).

QPR (0) 0

Nottingham F (2) 3 *(Reid 24, Commons 25, Folly 82)* 11,140

QPR: Day; Branco (Thorpe), Edghill, Rowlands, Shittu, Bean, Ainsworth, Cureton, Gallen, McLeod, Cook (Padula).
Nottingham F: Gerrard; Louis-Jean, Doig, Folly, Dawson, Morgan, Bopp (Perch), Commons, Reid, Taylor, Robertson.

Reading (0) 1 *(Ingimarsson 88)*

Swansea C (1) 1 *(Connor 32)* 13,642

Reading: Hahnemann; Hughes, Shorey, Ingimarsson, Sonko, Harper (Morgan), Little, Sidwell, Ferdinand (Owusu), Forster, Convey.
Swansea C: Gueret; Gurney, Ricketts, Austin, Monk, Iriekpen, Forbes, Britton, Connor (Anderson), Trundle, Robinson.

Rotherham U (0) 0

Yeovil T (0) 3 *(Jevons 61 (pen), Way 87, Stolcers 90)* 5397

Rotherham U: Pollitt; Scott (Gilchrist), Hurst, Vernazza, Swailes, McIntosh, Monkhouse, McLaren, Butler, Proctor (Hoskins), Campbell-Ryce.
Yeovil T: Weale; Skiverton, Terry, Way, Guyett, Lindegaard, Gall (Caceres), Johnson, Jevons (Davies), Tarachulski (O'Brien), Stolcers.

Sheffield U (0) 3 *(Cullip 55, Liddell 82, 83)*

Aston Villa (0) 1 *(Barry 47)* 14,003

Sheffield U: Kenny; Geary (Montgomery), Wright, Cullip, Bromby, Jagielka, Tonge (Cadamarteri), Quinn (Thirlwell), Gray, Liddell, Harley.
Aston Villa: Sorensen; Delaney, Samuel, McCann (Berson), Mellberg, Ridgewell, Solano (Davis), Hendrie, Angel, Cole (Moore L), Barry.

Sunderland (1) 2 *(Welsh 44, Stewart 60 (pen))*

Crystal Palace (1) 1 *(Collins N 41 (og))* 17,536

Sunderland: Myhre; Wright, McCartney, Robinson, Caldwell, Collins N, Thornton, Whitehead, Elliott (Bridges), Stewart (Brown), Welsh (Piper).
Crystal Palace: Kiraly; Butterfield, Granville, Leigertwood, Powell, Hall, Routledge, Hughes, Johnson, Lakis (Soares), Watson (Shipperley).

Tottenham H (1) 2 *(King 40, Keane 83)*

Brighton & HA (0) 1 *(Carpenter 48)* 36,094

Tottenham H: Robinson; Kelly (Marney), Edman, Brown, Gardner, King, Pedro Mendes (Yeates), Carrick, Keane, Defoe, Ziegler.
Brighton & HA: Kuipers; Hinshelwood, Mayo, Virgo, Butters, Carpenter, Reid, Oatway, Knight, Hart, Harding.

Watford (1) 1 *(Helguson 42 (pen))*

Fulham (1) 1 *(Knight 17)* 14,896

Watford: Chamberlain; Chambers, Darlington, Cox, Demerit, Mahon, Ardley (Webber), Gunnarsson, Bouazza (McNamee), Helguson, Devlin (Dyer).
Fulham: Van der Sar; Rosenior, Bocanegra, Pembridge, Knight, Fontaine, John, Legwinski (Clark), Cole, Boa Morte, Malbranque.

West Ham U (0) 1 *(Harewood 81)*

Norwich C (0) 0 23,389

West Ham U: Walker; Ferdinand, Powell C, Fletcher, Mackay, Repka, Chadwick (Cohen), Mullins, Harewood, Rebrov, Noble.
Norwich C: Green; Edworthy, Charlton, Fleming, Doherty, Brennan, Jonson (Crow), Helveg (Jarvis), Huckerby, Francis, Bentley (Mulryne).

Wolverhampton W (2) 2 *(Seol 8, Cort 11)*

Millwall (0) 0 12,566

Wolverhampton W: Murray; Clyde, Naylor, Ince, Craddock, Lescott, Seol, Olofinjana (Cameron), Cort, Miller (Newton), Kennedy.
Millwall: Stack; Simpson, Elliott, Dunne, Lawrence, Phillips, Robinson (Weston), Sweeney (Healy), Morris, Braniff, Hayles.

Sunday, 9 January 2005

Arsenal (0) 2 *(Reyes 52, Van Persie 70)*

Stoke C (1) 1 *(Thomas 45)* 36,579

Arsenal: Lehmann; Eboue (Hoyte), Clichy, Vieira, Toure, Senderos, Pennant, Fabregas, Reyes, Van Persie, Pires.
Stoke C: Simonsen; Buxton, Clarke (Eustace), Thomas, Taggart, Halls (Henry), Russell, Greenacre (Asaba), Akinbiyi, Jarrett, Hall.

Yeading (0) 0

Newcastle U (0) 2 *(Bowyer 52, Ameobi 60)* 10,824

Yeading: Preddie; Saroya, Barima (Behzadi), Brown, Leach, Stanley, Haule, Clarke, Telemaque (Quarima), Campbell, Pontain (Woodruffe).
Newcastle U: Harper; Taylor, Babayaro, Jenas, Boumsong, Bramble (O'Brien), N'Zogbia (Ambrose), Bowyer, Ameobi, Bellamy, Robert (Milner).
at Loftus Road.

Tuesday, 18 January 2005

Burnley (0) 1 *(Traore 51 (og))*

Liverpool (0) 0 19,033

Burnley: Jensen; Roche, Camara, Grant, Cahill, Sinclair, McGreal, Hyde, Moore, Chaplow, Valois.
Liverpool: Dudek; Raven, Traore (Baros), Biscan, Whitbread, Hyypia, Nunez■, Welsh (Mellor), Sinama-Pongolle, Potter, Warnock.

THIRD ROUND REPLAYS

Monday, 17 January 2005

Swansea C (0) 0

Reading (0) 1 *(Forster 95)* 7354

Swansea C: Gueret; Gurney, Ricketts, Austin, Monk, Iriekpen, Forbes (Maylett), Britton, Connor, Trundle, Anderson (Robinson).
Reading: Hahnemann; Murty, Shorey, Ingimarsson, Sonko, Harper, Little (Brooker), Sidwell, Convey (Owusu), Forster, Hughes.
aet.

Tuesday, 18 January 2005

Blackpool (0) 0

Leicester C (1) 1 *(Gudjonsson 16)* 6938

Blackpool: Edge; Clare, Edwards R, Grayson (Wellens), McGregor, Clarke, Bullock (Shaw), Southern, Parker, Lynch (Warhurst), Coid.
Leicester C: Walker; Maybury, Stewart, Williams, Heath, Dabizas, Gillespie, Scowcroft, Dublin (Nalis), Connolly (Wright), Gudjonsson.

Wednesday, 19 January 2005

Blackburn R (2) 3 *(Thompson 9, 32, Pedersen 47)*

Cardiff C (1) 2 *(McAnuff 24, Collins 54)* 9140

Blackburn R: Friedel; Neill, Matteo, Tugay (Johansson), Todd, Mokoena, Emerton, Pedersen, Gallagher (Reid), Dickov, Thompson.
Cardiff C: Warner; Weston (Vidmar), Barker, Kavanagh, Gabbidon, Collins, McAnuff, Inamoto (Ledley), Lee, Thorne (Campbell), Langley.

Boston U (0) 0

Hartlepool U (0) 1 *(Boyd 72)* 3653

Boston U: Abbey N; Beevers, McCann, Greaves (Rusk), James (Thompson), Ellender, Holland, Noble (Lee), Strong, Kirk, Thomas.
Hartlepool U: Konstantopoulos; Ross, Robertson, Nelson, Westwood, Tinkler, Clark, Sweeney, Appleby (Istead), Boyd, Humphreys.

Exeter C (0) 0

Manchester U (1) 2 *(Ronaldo 9, Rooney 87)* 9033

Exeter C: Jones; Hiley, Jeannin, Taylor (Martin), Gaia, Sawyer, Clay, Ampadu (Afful), Flack (Edwards), Devine, Moxey.
Manchester U: Howard; Neville P, Fortune, Miller (Fletcher), Neville G, O'Shea, Ronaldo, Djemba-Djemba (Silvestre), Scholes, Rooney, Giggs (Saha).

Fulham (1) 2 *(Volz 13, Radzinski 65)*

Watford (0) 0 11,306

Fulham: Van der Sar; Volz, Bocanegra, Diop, Knight, Rehmann, Clark (Pembridge), Radzinski, Cole (McBride), Boa Morte (John), Legwinski.
Watford: Chamberlain; Chambers, Darlington, Cox, Demerit, Mahon, Bouazza (Ardley), Blizzard (Dyer), Webber, Helguson, Devlin (Gunnarsson).

FOURTH ROUND

Saturday, 29 January 2005

Arsenal (0) 2 *(Vieira 53 (pen), Ljungberg 82)*

Wolverhampton W (0) 0 37,153

Arsenal: Lehmann; Eboue, Clichy, Vieira, Campbell, Cygan, Ljungberg (Owusu-Abeyie), Flamini, Henry, Van Persie (Fabregas), Reyes (Pires).
Wolverhampton W: Oakes; Newton, Kennedy, Bjorklund (Miller), Craddock, Lescott, Ince (Cameron), Olofinjana (Clarke), Seol, Cort, Naylor.

Blackburn R (2) 3 *(Watson 21 (og), Johnson 27, Matteo 51)*

Colchester U (0) 0 10,634

Blackburn R: Friedel; Neill, Matteo, Savage, Mokoena (Nelsen), Todd, Emerton (Reid), Tugay, Pedersen (Stead), Johnson, Thompson.
Colchester U: Davison; Stockley, Hunt (Chilvers), Brown, Baldwin, Watson, Johnson (Keith), Danns, Williams (Ndumbu-Nsungu), Fagan, Halford.

Brentford (0) 0

Hartlepool U (0) 0 8967

Brentford: Nelson; Dobson, Salako, Talbot (Hunt), Sodje, Turner, Tabb, Rankin, May, Burton, Hutchinson (Frampton).
Hartlepool U: Konstantopoulos; Ross, Robertson, Nelson, Westwood, Tinkler, Clark (Istead), Sweeney, Porter (Appleby), Boyd, Humphreys.

Burnley (1) 2 *(Moore 17, 90)*

Bournemouth (0) 0 9944

Burnley: Jensen; Sinclair, Camara, Grant, McGreal, Cahill, Oster (Roche), Hyde, Moore (Pilkington), Branch, Chaplow (Valois).
Bournemouth: Moss N; Purches (Holmes), Cummings, Broadhurst, Maher, Browning (Fletcher), O'Connor, Stock, Elliott, Hayter (Connell), Spicer.

Charlton Ath (1) 3 *(Hughes 37, Jeffers 51, Bartlett 57)*

Yeovil T (1) 2 *(Terry 44, Davies 66)* 22,873

Charlton Ath: Kiely; Young, Hreidarsson, Holland, Fortune, El Karkouri, Murphy (Euell), Hughes (Konchesky), Bartlett, Jeffers (Johansson), Thomas.
Yeovil T: Weale; Terry (Rose), Lindegaard, Way, Skiverton, Guyett, Gall, Johnson, Jevons, Tarachulski (Davies), Stolcers (Caceres).

Derby Co (0) 1 *(Tudgay 56)*

Fulham (0) 1 *(John 71)* 22,040

Derby Co: Camp; Kenna, Idiakez, Huddlestone, Mills, Johnson, Bisgaard, Taylor, Rasiak, Smith, Reich (Tudgay).
Fulham: Van der Sar; Volz, Rosenior, Clark, Knight, Goma, Legwinski, Radzinski (John), Cole, Boa Morte, Pembridge.

Everton (2) 3 *(McFadden 9, Beattie 27, Cahill 80)*

Sunderland (0) 0 33,186

Everton: Wright; Pistone, Naysmith, Stubbs (Weir), Yobo, Carsley, Osman, McFadden, Beattie (Chadwick), Cahill, Kilbane (Bent).
Sunderland: Myhre; Wright (Brown), McCartney, Robinson, Collins N, Collins D, Whitehead, Thornton, Elliott (Bridges), Stewart, Arca.

Manchester U (1) 3 *(O'Shea 10, Rooney 67, 82)*

Middlesbrough (0) 0 67,251

Manchester U: Carroll; Neville G, Heinze (Silvestre), Ferdinand, Neville P, Brown, Ronaldo (Miller), O'Shea, Rooney, Giggs (Saha), Fortune.
Middlesbrough: Schwarzer; Reiziger, Queudrue, Cooper (McMahon), Southgate, Doriva (Job), Downing, Parlour, Hasselbaink (Graham), Morrison, Zenden.

Newcastle U (2) 3 *(Shearer 37, Ameobi 42, Babayaro 52)*

Coventry C (1) 1 *(Adebola 45)* 44,044

Newcastle U: Harper; Carr, Babayaro, Faye (Hughes), O'Brien, Bramble, Dyer, Jenas, Shearer, Ameobi, Kluivert.
Coventry C: Steele; Duffy, Giddings, Negouai, Williams, Leacock, Doyle, Hughes, Morrell (Adebola), McSheffrey (Jorgensen), John (Johnson).

Nottingham F (1) 1 *(King 10)*

Peterborough U (0) 0 16,774

Nottingham F: Gerrard; Thompson, Rogers, Evans, Doig, Morgan, Reid (Harris), Derry, King, Taylor, Commons (Nowland) (Johnson).
Peterborough U: Tyler; Woodhouse, Semple (Kanu), Arber, St Ledger-Hall, Burton, Farrell, Thomson, Logan (Clarke), Willock, McMaster.

Reading (1) 1 *(Forster 10)*

Leicester C (1) 2 *(Williams 32, Scowcroft 90)* 14,825

Reading: Hahnemann; Murty, Shorey, Ingimarsson, Sonko, Harper, Little, Newman■, Ferdinand (Owusu), Forster, Hughes.
Leicester C: Walker; Maybury, Stewart, Williams, Heath, Dabizas, Gillespie (Dublin), Gudjonsson (Nalis), Scowcroft, Connolly (De Vries), Tiatto.

Southampton (0) 2 *(Oakley 54, Crouch 90 (pen))*

Portsmouth (0) 1 *(Yakubu 57 (pen))* 29,453

Southampton: Niemi; Telfer, Higginbotham, Delap, Lundekvam, Davenport, Prutton, Oakley (Jakobsson), Crouch, Svensson A, Nilsson (Jones).
Portsmouth: Chalkias; Primus, Kamara■, O'Neil, Stefanovic, De Zeeuw, Berger, Hughes, Yakubu (Fuller), Cisse, Taylor.

WBA (1) 1 *(Earnshaw 17)*

Tottenham H (1) 1 *(Defoe 31 (pen))* 22,441

WBA: Hoult; Albrechtsen, Robinson, Wallwork, Purse, Clement, Gera, Scimeca, Kanu (Horsfield), Earnshaw (Campbell), Greening.
Tottenham H: Robinson; Kelly, Edman, Brown, King, Gardner, Davies (Marney), Carrick, Kanoute, Defoe (Keane), Atouba.

West Ham U (1) 1 *(Harewood 39)*

Sheffield U (0) 1 *(Jagielka 57)* 19,444

West Ham U: Bywater; Repka, Powell C, Mullins (Rebrov), Mackay, Ferdinand, Noble, Fletcher, Harewood, Sheringham, Chadwick (Reo-Coker).
Sheffield U: Kenny; Geary, Jagielka, Cullip, Bromby, Morgan, Montgomery, Tonge, Gray, Liddell (Forte), Harley.

Sunday, 30 January 2005

Chelsea (1) 2 *(Huth 6, Terry 80)*

Birmingham C (0) 0 40,379

Chelsea: Cudicini; Johnson, Bridge, Huth, Terry, Smertin, Jarosik, Cole, Kezman (Lampard), Gudjohnsen (Drogba), Duff (Robben).
Birmingham C: Maik Taylor; Melchiot, Clapham, Martin Taylor (Tebily), Upson, Clemence, Anderton (Yorke), Carter, Blake, Heskey (Morrison), Gray.

Oldham Ath (0) 0

Bolton W (1) 1 *(Vaz Te 9)* 12,029

Oldham Ath: Pogliacomi; Bruce, Griffin, Hughes, Haining (Lomax), Hall D, Croft, Kilkenny, Eyre (Cooper), Betsy, Eyres.
Bolton W: Jaaskelainen; Hunt (Barness), Gardner, Hierro, N'Gotty, Ben Haim, Vaz Te (Campo), Nolan, Pedersen, Davies, Fadiga (Diouf).

FOURTH ROUND REPLAYS

Saturday, 12 February 2005

Fulham (1) 4 *(Diop 45 (pen), Boa Morte 50, John 94, Jensen 105)*

Derby Co (1) 2 *(Rasiak 4, Peschisolido 86)* 15,528

Fulham: Van der Sar; Rosenior, Bocanegra, Diop, Knight, Rehman (Goma), Clark, Radzinski, Cole (John), Boa Morte, Legwinski (Jensen).
Derby Co: Camp; Kenna, Boertien, Bolder (Peschisolido), Mills, Johnson, Bisgaard, Tudgay, Rasiak, Smith (Junior) (Doyle), Idiakez.
aet.

Hartlepool U (0) 0

Brentford (0) 1 *(Rankin 48)* 7580

Hartlepool U: Konstantopoulos; Ross■, Robertson, Nelson, Westwood, Tinkler (Williams), Clark, Sweeney, Porter (Istead), Boyd, Humphreys.
Brentford: Nelson; Dobson, Salako, Talbot, Sodje, Turner, Hutchinson, Hargreaves, Rankin, Burton (May), Hunt (Tabb).

Tottenham H (1) 3 *(Keane 45 (pen), Defoe 50, 55)*

WBA (1) 1 *(Kanu 12)* 27,860

Tottenham H: Robinson; Kelly, Atouba, Brown, Gardner, King, Carrick, Kanoute, Keane (Davies), Defoe, Ziegler.
WBA: Hoult (Kuszczak); Albrechtsen, Robinson, Wallwork, Gaardsoe, Clement, Koumas, Scimeca (O'Connor), Kanu (Earnshaw), Campbell, Gera.

Sunday, 13 February 2005

Sheffield U (1) 1 *(Liddell 8)*

West Ham U (0) 1 *(Sheringham 63 (pen))* 15,067

Sheffield U: Kenny; Jagielka, Harley, Cullip, Bromby, Morgan■, Montgomery, Tonge, Gray, Shaw (Geary), Liddell.
West Ham U: Bywater; Repka, Powell C, Fletcher, Mackay, Ferdinand, Chadwick (Mullins), Reo-Coker, Harewood, Sheringham, Noble.
aet; Sheffield U won 3-1 on penalties.

FIFTH ROUND

Saturday, 19 February 2005

Arsenal (0) 1 *(Pires 78)*

Sheffield U (0) 1 *(Gray 90 (pen))* 36,891

Arsenal: Almunia; Eboue, Clichy, Flamini, Toure, Senderos, Ljungberg, Fabregas, Van Persie (Pires), Bergkamp■, Reyes (Cygan).
Sheffield U: Kenny; Geary, Harley, Cullip, Bromby, Jagielka, Montgomery (Forte), Thirlwell (Shaw), Gray, Liddell (Francis), Tonge.

Bolton W (1) 1 *(Davies 12)*

Fulham (0) 0 16,151

Bolton W: Jaaskelainen; Hunt, Candela, Hierro, N'Gotty, Ben Haim, Okocha (Barness), Fadiga (Gardner), Pedersen (Nolan), Davies, Speed.
Fulham: Van der Sar; Rosenior, Bocanegra, Diop, Knight, Goma, Clark, Radzinski, Cole (McBride), Boa Morte (John), Legwinski (Jensen).

Charlton Ath (1) 1 *(Bartlett 45)*

Leicester C (1) 2 *(Dabizas 38, Dublin 90)* 23,719

Charlton Ath: Kiely; Young, Hreidarsson, Holland, Fortune (Johansson), El Karkouri, Murphy, Hughes (Euell), Bartlett, Rommedahl (Thomas), Konchesky.
Leicester C: Walker; Maybury, Stewart, Williams, Dublin, Dabizas, Gillespie, Hughes (Nalis), De Vries (Connolly), Gudjonsson, Tiatto.

Everton (0) 0

Manchester U (1) 2 *(Fortune 23, Ronaldo 58)* 38,664

Everton: Martyn; Hibbert, Naysmith, Stubbs, Yobo, Carsley, Osman, Arteta (Pistone), Bent, McFadden (Weir), Kilbane.

Manchester U: Carroll; Neville G, Heinze, Ferdinand, Keane (Miller), Brown, Ronaldo, Neville P, Scholes, Rooney, Fortune.

Southampton (2) 2 *(Camara 4, 36)*

Brentford (1) 2 *(Rankin 40, Sodje 58)* 24,741

Southampton: Smith; Bernard, Le Saux (McCann), Delap, Lundekvam, Davenport, Prutton, Oakley, Crouch, Phillips, Camara.
Brentford: Nelson; Dobson, Frampton, Talbot, Sodje, Turner, Tabb (Harrold), Hutchinson, Rankin (May), Burton (Hunt), Salako.

Sunday, 20 February 2005

Burnley (0) 0

Blackburn R (0) 0 21,468

Burnley: Jensen; Duff, Camara, Grant, McGreal (Roche), Sinclair (Oster), Hyde, Cahill, Moore (Branch), Whittingham, Valois.
Blackburn R: Friedel; Neill, Johansson, Tugay (Reid), Nelsen, Todd, Emerton, Savage, Gallagher (Thompson), Dickov (Johnson), Pedersen.

Newcastle U (1) 1 *(Kluivert 4)*

Chelsea (0) 0 45,740

Newcastle U: Given; Carr, Babayaro, Butt, Boumsong, Bramble, Dyer (Milner), Jenas, Shearer (Ameobi), Kluivert, Robert.
Chelsea: Cudicini■; Johnson, Bridge, Jarosik, Ricardo Carvalho, Gallas, Tiago (Gudjohnsen), Cole (Duff), Kezman, Geremi (Lampard), Smertin.

Tottenham H (1) 1 *(Defoe 45)*

Nottingham F (0) 1 *(Taylor 56)* 35,640

Tottenham H: Robinson; Kelly, Atouba, Brown, Naybet, King, Davies, Carrick, Kanoute (Mido), Defoe, Ziegler (Keane).
Nottingham F: Doyle; Curtis, Rogers, Melville, Doig, Morgan, Perch, Powell, Taylor, Commons (King), Evans (Thompson).

FIFTH ROUND REPLAYS

Tuesday, 1 March 2005

Blackburn R (1) 2 *(Tugay 31, Pedersen 86)*

Burnley (1) 1 *(Hyde 42)* 28,691

Blackburn R: Friedel; Neill, Johansson, Tugay, Mokoena, Nelsen, Emerton, Savage (Flitcroft), Gallagher (Bothroyd) (Reid), Dickov, Pedersen.
Burnley: Jensen; Duff, Camara, Grant (Branch), Cahill, Sinclair, Oster, Hyde (Roche), Moore, Whittingham, Valois.

Brentford (1) 1 *(Hutchinson 4)*

Southampton (1) 3 *(Crouch 11, 90, Phillips 67)* 11,720

Brentford: Nelson; Dobson (Peters), Frampton (Hunt), Talbot, Sodje, Turner, Tabb, Hutchinson (O'Connor), Rankin, Burton, Salako.
Southampton: Smith; Telfer, Higginbotham, Delap, Jakobsson, Davenport, Nilsson, Oakley, Crouch, Phillips (Camara), Bernard (McCann).

Sheffield U (0) 0

Arsenal (0) 0 27,595

Sheffield U: Kenny; Geary, Harley, Thirlwell, Bromby, Morgan, Montgomery, Jagielka, Gray, Liddell, Tonge (Quinn).
Arsenal: Almunia; Lauren, Cole, Vieira, Senderos, Cygan, Flamini (Aliadiere), Fabregas (Toure), Ljungberg, Lupoli (Owusu-Abeyie), Clichy.
aet; Arsenal won 4-2 on penalties.

Wednesday, 2 March 2005

Nottingham F (0) 0

Tottenham H (0) 3 *(Pamarot 60, Keane 72, Mido 90)* 28,062

Nottingham F: Gerrard; Curtis, Doig, Evans (Thompson), Morgan, Melville, Perch, Powell, Johnson (Harris), Taylor, Robertson.
Tottenham H: Robinson; Pamarot, Atouba (Edman), Brown, Gardner, Kelly, Davies, Pedro Mendes (Carrick), Keane, Kanoute (Mido), Ziegler.

SIXTH ROUND

Saturday, 12 March 2005

Bolton W (0) 0

Arsenal (1) 1 *(Ljungberg 3)* 23,523

Bolton W: Jaaskelainen; Hunt (Jaidi), Gardner, Hierro (Candela), N'Gotty, Ben Haim (Pedersen), Nolan, Speed, Diouf■, Davies, Giannakopoulos.
Arsenal: Lehmann; Lauren, Clichy, Vieira, Toure, Senderos, Ljungberg, Flamini, Reyes, Bergkamp, Pires.

Southampton (0) 0

Manchester U (2) 4 *(Keane 2, Ronaldo 45, Scholes 48, 87)* 30,971

Southampton: Smith; Cranie, Higginbotham, Oakley, Lundekvam (Davenport), Jakobsson, Telfer, Svensson A, Crouch, Camara (Phillips), Bernard (McCann).
Manchester U: Howard; Brown, Heinze (O'Shea), Ferdinand, Keane (Neville P), Silvestre, Ronaldo (Smith), Scholes, Van Nistelrooy, Rooney, Fortune.

Sunday, 13 March 2005

Blackburn R (0) 1 *(Dickov 83 (pen))*

Leicester C (0) 0 22,113

Blackburn R: Friedel; Neill, Johansson, Mokoena (Stead), Todd, Nelsen, Reid (Emerton), Flitcroft, Pedersen, Dickov, Thompson.
Leicester C: Walker; Kenton, Maybury, Williams (Hughes), Dublin, Dabizas, Gillespie, Gudjonsson, De Vries, Nalis (McCarthy), Tiatto (Connolly).

Newcastle U (1) 1 *(Kluivert 5)*

Tottenham H (0) 0 51,307

Newcastle U: Given; Carr, Hughes, Faye, Bramble (Jenas), Boumsong, Dyer, Bowyer, Shearer, Kluivert (Ameobi), Robert (Milner).
Tottenham H: Robinson; Pamarot (Marney), Atouba (Keane), Brown, Naybet (Gardner), King, Davies, Carrick, Kanoute, Defoe, Ziegler.

SEMI-FINALS (AT MILLENNIUM STADIUM)

Saturday, 16 April 2005

Arsenal (1) 3 *(Pires 42, Van Persie 86, 90)*

Blackburn R (0) 0 52,077

Arsenal: Lehmann; Lauren, Cole, Vieira, Toure, Senderos, Ljungberg (Fabregas), Silva, Reyes (Aliadiere), Bergkamp (Van Persie), Pires.
Blackburn R: Friedel; Neill, Matteo (Stead), Mokoena, Todd, Nelsen, Thompson (Savage), Flitcroft (Emerton), Dickov, Pedersen, Reid.

Sunday, 17 April 2005

Newcastle U (0) 1 *(Ameobi 59)*

Manchester U (2) 4 *(Van Nistelrooy 19, 58, Scholes 45, Ronaldo 76)* 69,280

Newcastle U: Given; Carr, Babayaro (O'Brien), Faye (N'Zogbia), Taylor, Boumsong, Milner (Kluivert), Butt, Shearer, Ameobi, Robert.
Manchester U: Howard; Neville G, Heinze, Brown, Keane, Ferdinand, Ronaldo (Smith), Scholes (Fletcher), Van Nistelrooy, Rooney (Giggs), Fortune.

THE FA CUP FINAL

Saturday, 21 May 2005

(at Millennium Stadium, Cardiff, attendance 71,896)

Arsenal (0) 0 Manchester U (0) 0

Arsenal: Lehmann; Lauren, Cole, Vieira, Toure, Senderos, Fabregas (Van Persie), Silva, Reyes■, Bergkamp (Ljungberg), Pires (Edu).

Manchester U: Carroll; Brown, O'Shea (Fortune), Ferdinand, Keane, Silvestre, Fletcher (Giggs), Scholes, Van Nistelrooy, Rooney, Ronaldo.

aet; Arsenal won 5-4 on penalties: Van Nistelrooy scored; Lauren scored; Scholes saved; Ljungberg scored; Ronaldo scored; Van Persie scored; Rooney scored; Cole scored; Keane scored; Vieira scored.

Referee: R. Styles (Waterlooville).

Patrick Vieira's penalty is too good for Manchester United goalkeeper Roy Carroll as Arsenal win the FA Cup Final in Cardiff. (Actionimages)

CONFERENCE NATIONAL 2004–05

The value of being able to field a settled team from the outset was underlined by Barnet in winning the Conference in some style. Indeed but for a lapse of concentration when it seemed the title was well within their grasp, they might well have established records which would have been difficult to overhaul in later years.

Nine of the players who took part in the opening game were in action in the last one. Barnet lost just once in the opening half of the season, 3-2 at home to Burton Albion on 21 September. At the time their lead at the top was a massive 13 points. Interestingly enough the team in second place was Carlisle United who were to join them in promotion via the play-offs, both ex-Football League clubs returning upstairs.

Barnet failed to score in only five matches but had two wobbles of five games with just one victory squeezed in which did not alter the inevitable march to the championship.

The race for the remaining elevation place was well contested again. In fact on the last day of the season there were still chances for several clubs. Carlisle, who had actually gone 13 matches before their first defeat at home to Barnet, had virtually booked a spot along with Hereford United, but two slots remained and Aldershot Town, Morecambe, Woking, Stevenage Borough and Exeter City were in the frame for them.

On paper at least Exeter and Woking had uphill tasks away to Carlisle and Halifax respectively. Stevenage were at home to long-since doomed Leigh RMI with Aldershot hosting Scarborough. Morecambe were at Tamworth.

Exeter needed a win and hope others faltered. They won 3-0 but it was not enough. Morecambe, too, could only draw goalless while Woking were beaten 3-1. Aldershot beat Scarborough 2-0 and Stevenage recorded a similar score in their success to clinch the places on offer.

In the play-offs, Aldershot took a slender 1-0 lead over Carlisle at the Recreation Ground, while Stevenage were held by Hereford. In the return matches Aldershot forced extra time at Carlisle but lost on penalties, and a single goal was enough for Stevenage.

Carlisle, who had suffered through the floods in their area and had had to play home games elsewhere, triumphed at Stoke in the final again by the minimum.

Arguably the most disappointed teams of the season might have been Accrington Stanley and Halfiax. Accrington were third early in January, but finished with only one win in the last seven, while Halifax won only one of the last five and that when they had no chance at all.

With an unbeaten last stretch of nine games, it seemed Hereford had hit form at the right time, but again failed in the play-offs for a second season as did Aldershot who lying eighth by the end of February had seemed out of it completely.

Thirteenth at Christmas, Exeter revived and with encouraging displays against Manchester United slowly improved but even three wins at the death were not enough. Yet Stevenage's last trio of victories was enough to propel them into the play-offs after they had been as low as 11th in February.

Again Morecambe missed out despite an unbeaten run of nine games at the end after a poor opening spell. Woking, too, following a 12 match unbeaten run before crashing 4-0 at Aldershot, were also denied. Dagenham & Redbridge, 11th in December were 11th at the finish after a stronger finale.

Newcomers Crawley Town had excelled themselves climbing to second place in February, but won only one more fixture while fellow travellers Canvey Island struggled and a late slump with no wins in 13 was a concern.

Scarborough disappointed after mid-season as did Gravesend & Northfleet with 14 without a win at one stage. Tamworth disposed of any relegation fears with an eleven match unbeaten sequence and Burton Albion's highlight was that win at Barnet.

York City, expected to be among the promotion seekers, were largely ineffective and though Northwich Victoria gallantly fought off a ten-point deduction for administration, found themselves bounced out when their new ground did not come up to the requirements. This reprieved Forest Green Rovers for the second time. Farnborough Town with problems off the field and Leigh RMI with more on it were relegated. Grays Athletic, conquerors of Burton in the Trophy semi-final, Southport plus Altrincham the play-off victors emerged from the Conference North and South, while Cambridge United and Kidderminster Harriers came down from the Football League.

CONFERENCE NATIONAL PLAY-OFFS 2004–05

CONFERENCE FIRST LEG

Monday, 2 May 2005

Aldershot T (0) 1 *(Crittenden N 48)*

Carlisle U (0) 0 6617

Aldershot T: Bull; Mustafa, Barnard D, Lee, Antwi, Johnson, Crittenden N, Holloway (Challinor), Sills (Slabber), Watson, Clarke.
Carlisle U: Glennon; Arnison, Beharall, Billy, Gray, Cowan, Lumsdon, Murray A (McGill), Vieira (Hawley), Holmes (Murray G), Murphy.

Stevenage B (0) 1 *(Maamria 87)*

Hereford U (0) 1 *(Carey-Bertram 74)* 6520

Stevenage B: Julian; Warner, Gregory, Bulman, Henry, Goodliffe, Brady, Stamp, Maamria, Elding, Nurse (Boyd).
Hereford U: Mawson; Green, Robinson, Pitman, Mkandawire, Tretton, Stanley, Purdie, Stansfield (James), Mills (Carey-Bertram), Travis (Williams D).

CONFERENCE SECOND LEG

Friday, 6 May 2005

Carlisle U (2) 2 *(Livesey 13, Billy 35)*

Aldershot T (0) 1 *(Slabber 90)* 10,803

Carlisle U: Glennon; Beharall, Cowan, Billy, Gray, Livesey, McGill, Lumsdon, Murray G, Holmes (Vieira), Murphy.
Aldershot T: Bull; Mustafa, Barnard D (Giles), Lee, Antwi, Johnson, Crittenden N, Watson, Sills (Slabber), Holloway, Clarke (Challinor).
aet; Carlisle U won 5-4 on penalties:- Antwi (scored), Lumsdon (scored), Lee (scored), McGill (saved), Slabber (scored), Murray G (saved), Giles (saved), Vieira (scored), Crittenden N (saved), Murphy (scored), Holloway (scored), Billy (scored), Challinor (saved), Livesey (scored).

Hereford U (0) 0

Stevenage B (0) 1 *(Maamria 69)* 6862

Hereford U: Mawson; Green, Robinson, Hyde (Travis), Mkandawire, Tretton, Stanley, Purdie, Stansfield, Carey-Bertram, Williams D (Williams L).
Stevenage B: Julian; Warner, Gregory, Bulman, Henry, Goodliffe, Brady, Stamp (Nurse), Maamria, Elding, Laker (Boyd).

CONFERENCE FINAL (at Britannia Stadium)

Saturday, 14 May 2005

Stevenage B (0) 0

Carlisle U (1) 1 *(Murphy 23)* 13,422

Stevenage B: Julian; Warner, Gregory, Bulman, Henry, Goodliffe (Weatherstone), Brady, Stamp (Nurse), Maamria, Elding, Laker (Boyd).
Carlisle U: Glennon; Beharall, Cowan, Billy, Gray, Livesey, McGill, Lumsdon, Murray G (Vieira), Holmes (Hawley), Murphy.
Referee: J. Moss (West Yorkshire).

CONFERENCE NATIONAL 2004–05 FINAL LEAGUE TABLE

			Home					Away					Total						
		P	W	D	L	F	A	W	D	L	F	A	W	D	L	F	A	GD	Pts
1	Barnet	42	16	2	3	56	20	10	6	5	34	24	26	8	8	90	44	46	86
2	Hereford U	42	10	7	4	28	14	11	4	6	40	27	21	11	10	68	41	27	74
3	Carlisle U	42	12	5	4	39	18	8	8	5	35	19	20	13	9	74	37	37	73
4	Aldershot T	42	13	3	5	38	22	8	7	6	30	30	21	10	11	68	52	16	73
5	Stevenage B	42	13	2	6	35	21	9	4	8	30	31	22	6	14	65	52	13	72
6	Exeter C	42	11	5	5	39	22	9	6	6	32	28	20	11	11	71	50	21	71
7	Morecambe	42	12	5	4	38	23	7	9	5	31	27	19	14	9	69	50	19	71
8	Woking	42	11	6	4	29	19	7	8	6	29	26	18	14	10	58	45	13	68
9	Halifax T	42	13	4	4	45	24	6	5	10	29	32	19	9	14	73	56	18	66
10	Accrington S	42	11	6	4	43	26	7	5	9	29	32	18	11	13	72	58	14	65
11	Dagenham & R	42	12	4	5	39	27	7	4	10	29	33	19	8	15	68	60	8	65
12	Crawley T	42	13	4	4	35	18	3	5	13	15	32	16	9	17	50	50	0	57
13	Scarborough	42	9	12	0	42	17	5	2	14	18	29	14	14	14	60	46	14	56
14	Gravesend & N	42	7	7	7	34	31	6	4	11	24	33	13	11	18	58	64	–6	50
15	Tamworth*	42	10	3	8	22	22	4	8	9	31	41	14	11	17	53	63	–10	50
16	Burton Alb	42	6	7	8	25	29	7	4	10	25	37	13	11	18	50	66	–16	50
17	York C	42	7	6	8	22	23	4	4	13	17	43	11	10	21	39	65	–27	43
18	Canvey Is	42	6	10	5	34	31	3	5	13	19	34	9	15	18	53	65	–12	42
19	Northwich Vic†	42	9	5	7	37	29	5	5	11	21	43	14	10	18	58	72	–14	42
20	Forest Green R	42	2	9	10	19	40	4	6	11	22	41	6	15	21	41	81	–40	33
21	Farnborough T	42	4	5	12	20	40	2	6	13	15	49	6	11	25	35	89	–54	29
22	Leigh RMI	42	2	2	17	18	52	2	4	15	13	46	4	6	32	31	98	–67	18

**Tamworth deducted 3 points – breach of league rules.*
†Northwich Victoria deducted 10 points – entered administration.

CONFERENCE NATIONAL LEADING GOALSCORERS 2004–05

	League	P-offs	FA Cup	LDV	Trophy	Total
Guiliano Grazioli *(Barnet)*	29	0	0	0	0	29
Michael Twiss *(Morecambe)*	22	0	3	0	0	25
Paul Mullin *(Accrington S)*	20	0	0	0	0	20
Anthony Elding *(Stevenage B)*	19	0	1	1	0	21
Chris Moore *(Dagenham & R)*	19	0	1	1	0	21
Adam Stansfield *(Hereford U)*	19	0	1	0	1	20
Bob Taylor *(Tamworth)*	19	0	0	0	0	19
Charlie Griffin *(Forest Green R)*	17	0	1	0	0	18
Lee McEvilly *(Accrington S)*	15	0	0	2	0	17
John Allan *(Northwich Vic)*	15	0	0	0	1	16
Lee Boylan *(Canvey Island)*	14	0	0	0	3	17
Tim Sills *(Aldershot T)*	14	0	2	0	0	16
Justin Richards *(Woking)*	14	0	1	0	1	16
Neil Redfearn *(Scarborough)*	14	0	0	0	0	14
Karl Hawley *(Carlisle U)*	13	0	1	0	1	15
Paul Brayson *(Northwich Vic)*	13	0	0	0	0	13

ATTENDANCES BY CLUB 2004–05

	Aggregate 2004–05	Average 2004–05	Highest Attendance 2004–05
Carlisle United	115,772	5,513	9,215 v Barnet
Exeter City	71,166	3,389	4,529 v Scarborough
Hereford United	64,429	3,068	3,978 v Exeter City
Aldershot Town	63,904	3,043	4,458 v Woking
Barnet	52,753	2,512	3,924 v Halifax Town
York City	48,941	2,331	4,439 v Scarborough
Woking	47,940	2,283	3,718 v Aldershot Town
Stevenage Borough	43,985	2,095	4,307 v Barnet
Crawley Town	42,368	2,018	2,949 v Barnet
Scarborough	37,423	1,782	4,586 v York City
Morecambe	36,783	1,752	4,660 v Carlisle United
Halifax Town	36,099	1,719	2,696 v Carlisle United
Accrington Stanley	32,278	1,537	3,024 v Carlisle United
Dagenham & Redbridge	28,938	1,378	1,923 v Barnet
Burton Albion	28,738	1,368	1,914 v Carlisle United
Gravesend & Northfleet	28,061	1,336	2,030 v Carlisle United
Tamworth	27,219	1,296	2,443 v Burton Albion
Farnborough Town	19,029	906	2,369 v Aldershot Town
Northwich Victoria	18,134	864	1,803 v Carlisle United
Forest Green Rovers	17,956	855	2,142 v Hereford United
Canvey Island	16,879	804	1,309 v Dagenham & Redbridge
Leigh RMI	9,129	435	1,540 v Carlisle United

BARNET ROLL CALL 2004–05

Player	Position	Height	Weight	Birthplace	Birthdate	Source
Nicky Bailey	M	5 10	12 08	Hammersmith	10 06 84	Sutton U
Damien Batt	D			Welwyn	16 09 84	Norwich C
Tom Champion	D			Barnet	15 05 86	Enfield
Anthony Charles	D			Isleworth	11 03 81	Farnborough T
Simon Clist	D	5 10	11 05	Bournemouth	13 06 81	Bristol C
James Elmes	M			Harlow	08 06 86	Broxbourne B
Shane Gore	G	6 1	12 01	Ashford	28 10 81	Wimbledon
Richard Graham	F	5 10	12 03	London	20 03 75	Bristol R
Liam Hatch	F	6 4	13 01	Hitchin	03 04 82	Gravesend & Northfleet
Ian Hendon	D	6 1	13 05	Ilford	05 12 71	Peterborough U
Simon King	D	6 0	13 00	Oxford	11 04 83	Oxford U
Dwane Lee	M			Hillingdon	26 11 79	Exeter C
Guy Lopez	M			Senegal	19 05 79	
Danny Maddix	D	5 11	12 07	Ashford	11 10 67	Sheffield W
Warren McBean	F			London	13 02 86	Broxbourne B
Ricky Millard	G	6 3	13 07	Dagenham	03 05 84	
Andy Reilly	D	5 10	12 08	Luton	26 10 85	Wycombe W
Lee Roache	F	5 8	11 00	Leytonstone	30 04 84	
Dean Sinclair	M	5 10	11 00	St Albans	17 12 84	Norwich C
Ben Strevens	M	6 2	12 00	Edgware	24 05 80	Wingate & Finchley
Scott Tynan	G			Liverpool	27 11 83	Nottingham F
Ishmail Yakubu	D	6 1	12 09	Nigeria	08 04 85	

CARLISLE UNITED ROLL CALL 2004–05

Player	Position	Height	Weight	Birthplace	Birthdate	Source
Lee Andrews	D	5 11	11 00	Carlisle	23 04 83	Scholar
Paul Arnison	D	5 10	10 12	Hartlepool	18 09 77	Hartlepool U
Chris Beech	D	5 10	11 12	Congleton	05 11 75	Doncaster R
David Beharall	D	6 0	11 06	Newcastle	08 03 79	Oldham Ath
Chris Billy	M	5 11	11 08	Huddersfield	02 01 73	Bury
Tom Cowan	D	5 8	11 08	Bellshill	28 08 69	York C
Craig Farrell	F	6 0	12 06	Middlesbrough	05 12 82	Leeds U
Matt Glennon	G	6 2	13 11	Stockport	08 10 78	Hull C
Simon Grand	D	6 0	10 03	Chorley	23 02 84	Rochdale
Kevin Gray	D	6 0	14 00	Sheffield	07 01 72	Tranmere R
Simon Hackney	M			Manchester	05 02 84	Woodley Sports
Karl Hawley	F	5 8	12 02	Walsall	06 12 81	Walsall
Kevin Henderson	F	5 11	13 02	Ashington	08 06 74	Hartlepool U
Derek Holmes	F	6 2	13 00	Lanark	18 10 78	Bournemouth
Danny Livesey	D	6 3	12 10	Salford	31 12 84	Bolton W
Chris Lumsdon	M	5 11	10 06	Newcastle	15 12 79	Barnsley
Brendan McGill	M	5 8	9 02	Dublin	22 03 81	Sunderland
Peter Murphy	M	5 10	12 10	Dublin	27 10 80	Blackburn R
Adam Murray	M	5 8	10 12	Solihull	30 09 81	Mansfield T
Glen Murray	F			Maryport	25 09 83	
Carlos Roca	F	5 4	10 07	Manchester	04 09 84	Oldham Ath
Brian Shelley	D	6 0	13 00	Dublin	15 11 81	Bohemians
Paul Simpson	M	5 8	11 11	Carlisle	26 07 66	Rochdale
Keiren Westwood	G			Manchester	23 10 84	

ACCRINGTON STANLEY Conference

Ground: The Crown Ground, Livingstone Road, Accrington, Lancashire.
Tel: 01254 397 869.
Year Formed: 1968 (formerly 1893).
Record Gate: 2,270 (1992 v Gateshead FA Cup First Round) (in Football League 17,634).
Nickname: Stanley.
Manager: John Coleman.
Secretary: Philip Terry.
Colours: Red shirts, white shorts, red stockings.

ACCRINGTON STANLEY 2004–05 LEAGUE RECORD

Match No.	*Date*	*Venue*	*Opponents*	*Result*		*H/T Score*	*Lg. Pos.*	*Goalscorers*	*Attendance*
1	Aug 14	H	Burton Alb	W	3-1	1-0	—	Mullin [40], Cavanagh [53], James [71]	1705
2	17	A	Morecambe	W	2-1	2-0	—	Craney [8], Williams [35]	2393
3	21	A	Stevenage Bor	L	0-5	0-2	7		1521
4	28	H	Crawley T	W	4-0	2-0	4	James (pen) [19], Mullin 2 [35, 64], Craney [57]	1270
5	31	A	York C	W	1-0	0-0	—	Mullin [55]	2272
6	Sept 4	H	Woking	D	0-0	0-0	4		2004
7	11	A	Dagenham & R	W	5-0	1-0	2	Brannan 3 (2 pens) [44 (p), 71 (p), 90], Craney [63], Mullin [75]	1165
8	18	H	Leigh RMI	W	2-1	1-0	3	McEvilly 2 [17, 61]	1507
9	21	A	Northwich Vic	D	3-3	1-1	—	Craney 2 [20, 50], McEvilly [54]	729
10	25	H	Gravesend & N	L	1-2	0-1	5	Smith [70]	1426
11	Oct 2	A	Farnborough T	L	1-2	0-1	6	Brannan (pen) [51]	706
12	5	H	Tamworth	L	2-3	1-1	—	Mullin [33], Smith [63]	1201
13	11	H	Hereford U	W	2-1	1-1	—	Mullin 2 [1, 87]	1481
14	16	A	Aldershot T	D	0-0	0-0	6		2834
15	23	A	Scarborough	L	0-4	0-3	8		1704
16	Nov 6	H	Exeter C	D	0-0	0-0	8		1464
17	13	H	Northwich Vic	W	5-0	2-0	3	Flitcroft [2], McEvilly 3 [36, 55, 79], Brannan [68]	1203
18	20	A	Barnet	L	0-3	0-1	6		1990
19	27	H	Canvey Is	W	1-0	0-0	5	Mullin [47]	1249
20	Dec 4	A	Forest Green R	L	0-1	0-0	5		691
21	7	H	Carlisle U	L	1-2	1-0	—	Prendergast [40]	3024
22	11	A	Leigh RMI	W	6-0	4-0	5	Craney 2 [26, 75], Mullin [43], Prendergast 2 [44, 64], Howarth [45]	402
23	18	H	Dagenham & R	L	0-3	0-0	6		1131
24	28	A	Gravesend & N	D	2-2	2-1	9	Mullin [3], Jagielka [37]	1372
25	Jan 3	A	Halifax T	W	2-1	1-1	—	Jagielka [43], Brannan [51]	2472
26	8	H	Farnborough T	W	2-1	1-1	3	McEvilly 2 [11, 56]	1115
27	22	A	Tamworth	L	0-1	0-0	6		1064
28	Feb 5	H	Scarborough	W	2-1	1-0	6	Prendergast [16], Mullin [63]	1315
29	12	A	Exeter C	W	2-1	1-1	7	McEvilly 2 [8, 57]	4031
30	19	H	Barnet	W	4-1	1-0	2	McEvilly [12], Prendergast [55], Mullin [83], Craney [84]	1841
31	22	H	Halifax T	D	1-1	0-0	—	Craney [89]	1402
32	Mar 5	H	Forest Green R	D	2-2	0-0	6	Cavanagh [56], Mullin [86]	1412
33	12	A	Carlisle U	L	0-2	0-1	8		4861
34	19	H	Morecambe	W	2-1	1-1	7	McEvilly [36], Mullin [71]	1804
35	22	A	Canvey Is	W	2-0	1-0	—	Mullin 2 [7, 65]	525
36	25	A	Burton Alb	D	2-2	1-0	5	Williams [4], Craney [52]	1508
37	28	H	York C	D	2-2	0-0	5	Mullin [68], Roberts [70]	2201
38	Apr 2	A	Crawley T	L	0-2	0-1	7		1646
39	9	H	Stevenage Bor	W	4-1	3-0	6	Mullin [20], McEvilly [23], Brown [38], Jagielka [86]	1251
40	16	A	Woking	L	1-2	1-1	10	Mullin [13]	2557
41	19	H	Aldershot T	D	3-3	1-1	—	Roberts [4], McEvilly 2 [62, 78]	1272
42	23	A	Hereford U	D	0-0	0-0	10		3738

Final League Position: 10

GOALSCORERS

League (72): Mullin 20, McEvilly 15, Craney 10, Brannan 6 (3 pens), Prendergast 5, Jagielka 3, Cavanagh 2, James 2 (1 pen), Roberts 2, Smith 2, Williams 2, Brown 1, Flitcroft 1, Howarth 1.
FA Cup (0).
LDV Vans Trophy (4): McEvilly 2, Craney 1, Flynn 1.
Trophy (0).

Kennedy 15	Cavanagh 34	Bimson 6	Brannan 26 + 3	Williams 38	Halford 4	James 6 + 7	Jagielka 35 + 4	McEvilly 36 + 3	Mullin 42	Craney 30 + 8	Howson 5 + 3	Cook 4 + 21	Banim — + 3	Prendergast 20 + 12	Howarth 11 + 6	Smith 8 + 17	Gerrard 5	Flynn 31	Tuck — + 1	Butler 27	Alcock 5	Ikeme 3	Proctor 24 + 2	Flitcroft 11 + 2	Crichton 19	O'Neill 2 + 2	Roberts 6 + 2	Brown 9	*Match No.*
1	2	3	4^{1}	5	6	7	8	9	10	11^{2}	12	13																	1
1	2	3	4	5	6	7^{2}	8	9^{1}	10	11	12	13																	2
1	2	3	4	5	6	7^{3}	8^{1}	9^{2}	10	11		12	14	13															3
1	2^{1}	3	4	5	6^{2}	7^{3}	8	9	10	11	13		12	14															4
1	2	3	4	5		12	8	9	10	11^{1}	6	13		7^{2}															5
1	2	3	4	5^{1}		7^{2}	8	9	10	11^{3}	6		14	13	12														6
1	2^{1}		4				8	9	10	11	6			7	12	5	3												7
1	2		4	5		12	8	9	10	11^{2}	6	13		7^{1}			3												8
1	2		4	5■			8	9^{2}	10	11	6	7^{1}		12		13	3												9
1	2		4			12	8	9	10	11		7^{1}				5	3	6											10
1	2		4	5^{2}			8	9	10	11		12			7^{3}	13	3^{1}	6	14										11
1	2		4	5^{1}		13	8	9	10	11				7^{2}		12		6		3									12
	2		4^{3}			7	8	9^{1}	10	11		14		12	13	5		6		3^{2}	1								13
	2		4	5		12	8^{1}	9	10	11^{2}		13				3		6				1	7						14
	2		4	5			8	9	10	11		12				3		6				1	7^{1}						15
	2		4	5		12		9	10^{1}	11						13		6		3^{2}		1	7	8					16
	2		4	5		12	13	9	10	11^{2}		14						6		3	1		7^{3}	8^{1}					17
	2		4	5			12	9	10	11						13		6		3^{2}			7^{1}	8	1				18
	2		4^{1}	5			12	9	10	11				13				6		3			7	8^{2}	1				19
	2			5			8	9^{3}	10	11		13		12		14		6		3			7^{2}	4^{1}	1				20
				5			8	9	10	11		12		7	2^{1}	13		6^{2}		3	1		4						21
				5			8	9^{1}	10	11				7	2	6				3			4	12	1				22
	2		12	5			8	9	10	11				7		13		6		3^{2}			4^{1}		1				23
	2		4	5			8	14	10^{3}	11^{2}		13		9		12■		6		3^{1}			7		1				24
	2		4^{2}	5			8	12	10	11^{1}		13		9	3			6					7		1				25
	2		4	5			8	9^{2}	10	11^{1}				7	3			6					13	12	1				26
	2			5				9	10	12		11^{1}		8		6				3			7	4	1				27
	2			5			8^{2}	9^{1}	10	12				11	14	13		6		3			7	4^{3}	1				28
	2			5			8	9	10					11	12	13		6		3^{1}			7	4^{2}	1				29
	2		4^{2}	5			8	9^{3}	10	13		12		11	14			6		3				7^{1}	1				30
	2		4^{3}	5			8	9	10	14		13		11		12		6		3^{1}				7^{2}	1				31
	2			5			8	9	10	13		14		11		12		6		3^{1}			7^{3}		1	4^{2}			32
	2		4^{2}	5			8	9^{3}	10	14				11		13		6		3				7^{1}	1	12			33
	2		4^{2}	5			8	9■	10	14				12				6		3			13		1		7^{1}	11^{3}	34
	2			5			8		10	11				9		12		6		3			7		1			4^{1}	35
	2^{1}			5			8		10	11^{2}		14		9^{3}		12		6		3			7		1		13	4	36
				5			8^{1}		10	11^{2}		13		9^{3}	2			6		3			7		1	12	14	4	37
				5			14	13	10			11^{3}		12	2			6^{1}		3	1		7			4^{2}	9	8	38
1			13	5			8^{3}	9	10			14			2	12		6^{1}		3			11				7	4^{2}	39
1			12■	5			8^{1}	9	10					13	2			6		3			7				11^{2}	4	40
1				5			8^{1}	9	10	12				13	2			6		3			7				11^{2}	4	41
								9	10	11^{2}		13		12	2	5		6		3^{1}	1		7				8	4	42

FA Cup

Fourth Qual	Leigh RMI	(h)	0-2

LDV Vans Trophy

First Round	Bradford C	(a)	2-1
Second Round	Oldham Ath	(a)	2-3

FA Trophy

Third Round	Hereford U	(h)	0-0
		(a)	0-4

ALDERSHOT TOWN — Conference

Ground: Recreation Ground, High Street, Aldershot, Hampshire GU11 1TW.
Tel: (01252) 320 211.
Year Formed: 1992 (formerly 1926).
Record Gate: 7,500 (2000 v Brighton & Hove Albion FA Cup First Round) (in Football League 19,138).
Nickname: Shots.
Manager: Terry Brown.
Secretary: Andy Morgan.
Colours: Red shirts with blue trim, red shorts, red stockings with blue trim.

ALDERSHOT TOWN 2004–05 LEAGUE RECORD

Match No.	Date	Venue	Opponents	Result		H/T Score	Lg. Pos.	Goalscorers	Attendance
1	Aug 14	H	York C	W	2-0	0-0	—	Challinor [65], Watson [72]	3368
2	17	A	Stevenage Bor	W	1-0	0-0	—	D'Sane (pen) [53]	2287
3	21	A	Crawley T	L	0-1	0-0	6		2508
4	28	H	Burton Alb	W	3-0	1-0	3	Simpkins (og) [39], Challinor [61], Miller [90]	2506
5	30	A	Woking	W	2-1	0-1	2	Sills [61], Barnard D [90]	3718
6	Sept 4	H	Northwich Vic	W	2-1	1-1	2	D'Sane 2 [25, 62]	2644
7	11	A	Leigh RMI	D	3-3	0-1	3	Giles [65], Challinor [89], McLean [90]	464
8	18	H	Dagenham & R	W	4-0	3-0	2	Sills [12], Challinor [25], McLean [26], Crittenden [73]	2748
9	21	A	Hereford U	L	0-2	0-1	—		3647
10	25	H	Carlisle U	L	0-5	0-1	6		3482
11	Oct 2	A	Tamworth	W	2-1	0-1	5	Miller [54], Challinor [65]	1621
12	5	H	Gravesend & N	W	1-0	0-0	—	Sills [90]	2486
13	9	A	Scarborough	D	2-2	2-0	3	Barnard D [2], Miller [34]	1622
14	16	H	Accrington S	D	0-0	0-0	3		2834
15	23	A	Exeter C	L	1-3	0-2	3	Sills [69]	3224
16	Nov 6	H	Morecambe	D	3-3	1-0	3	Challinor [17], Crittenden N [52], Miller (pen) [54]	2382
17	20	A	Halifax T	L	0-2	0-1	7		1724
18	27	H	Barnet	L	2-3	1-1	8	Dixon 2 [35, 76]	3494
19	Dec 7	H	Canvey Is	W	2-0	1-0	—	Crittenden N [2], Challinor [85]	1923
20	11	A	Dagenham & R	L	0-3	0-2	10		1407
21	18	H	Leigh RMI	W	2-0	1-0	7	Smith [45], Dixon (pen) [50]	2312
22	26	H	Forest Green R	L	1-2	0-0	11	Sills [52]	2740
23	28	A	Carlisle U	D	1-1	1-0	12	Watson [43]	6712
24	Jan 1	A	Forest Green R	D	0-0	0-0	11		1240
25	8	H	Tamworth	W	4-3	2-2	10	Sills [9], Crittenden N [14], Challinor [61], Smith [82]	2373
26	18	A	Farnborough T	W	2-1	1-0	—	Dixon [27], Sills [49]	2369
27	22	A	Gravesend & N	W	3-1	1-0	3	Dixon 3 [10, 56, 64]	1491
28	30	H	Hereford U	L	0-2	0-0	4		3799
29	Feb 6	A	York C	W	2-0	2-0	2	Sills [15], Watson [41]	2133
30	19	H	Halifax T	D	0-0	0-0	5		2903
31	26	A	Barnet	L	1-2	0-1	8	Robinson [61]	2839
32	Mar 1	H	Exeter C	W	2-1	1-0	—	Robinson [31], Lee (pen) [85]	2579
33	5	H	Farnborough T	W	3-1	1-0	2	Johnson [2], Crittenden N [54], Robinson [69]	4181
34	8	A	Morecambe	D	0-0	0-0	—		1108
35	11	A	Canvey Is	D	2-2	2-2	—	Sills [5], Robinson [39]	904
36	19	H	Stevenage Bor	L	0-1	0-1	4		3150
37	22	A	Burton Alb	W	3-1	3-1	—	Sills [22], Barnard D [33], Johnson [43]	1148
38	27	H	Woking	W	4-0	3-0	2	Clarke [17], Sills [27], Barnard D [31], Challinor [88]	4458
39	Apr 9	H	Crawley T	W	1-0	0-0	4	Barnard D [78]	3105
40	16	A	Northwich Vic	W	2-1	1-1	4	Crittenden N [24], Watson [52]	1234
41	19	A	Accrington S	D	3-3	1-1	—	Barnard D 2 (1 pen) [20, 56 (p)], Sills [71]	1272
42	23	H	Scarborough	W	2-0	1-0	4	Sills 2 [33, 85]	4437

Final League Position: 4

GOALSCORERS

League (68): Sills 14, Challinor 9, Barnard D 7 (1 pen), Dixon 7 (1 pen), Crittenden N 6, Miller 4 (1 pen), Robinson 4, Watson 4, D'Sane 3 (1 pen), Johnson 2, McLean 2, Smith 2, Clarke 1, Giles 1, Lee 1 (pen), own goal 1.
FA Cup (7): Dixon 2, McLean 2, Sills 2, Crittenden N 1.
LDV Vans Trophy (0).
Trophy (0).
Play-offs (2): Crittenden N 1, Slabber 1.

Bull 42	Warner 18 + 1	Barnard D 35	McAuley 24 + 2	Warburton 22 + 3	Giles 28 + 5	Crittenden N 29 + 12	Watson 31	McLean 19 + 6	D'Sane 7 + 3	Miller 15	Johnson 25 + 4	Challinor 30 + 7	Antwi 23 + 9	Sills 30 + 8	Smith 3 + 9	Barnes-Homer — + 2	Jinadu 5 + 6	Crittenden A — + 2	Dixon 10	Clarke 13 + 10	Viveash 6	Eribenne 1 + 2	Mustafa 10 + 2	Reeves 1	Rendell 1 + 6	Lee 10 + 1	Robinson 8	Caceres 6	Holloway 9	Slabber 1 + 1	*Match No.*
1	2	3	4	5^{1}	6	7^{2}	8	9	10^{3}	11	12	13	14																		1
1	2	3	4^{2}	5	6	12	8	9	10	11^{1}		7	13																		2
1	2^{1}	3	14	5	6^{2}	12	8	9	10	11^{3}		7	4	13																	3
1		3	4^{1}	5	6	12	8	9^{3}	10^{2}	11		7	2	13	14																4
1		3	4	5	6	13	8	9	10	11		7^{2}	2^{1}	12																	5
1	2	3	4	5	6	13	8	9	10^{3}	11^{1}	12	7^{2}		14																	6
1	2	3	4	5	6	7^{1}	8■	9	10^{2}			11		13	12																7
1	2	3	4	5^{3}	6	7		10^{1}	12	11^{2}		8	14	9	13																8
1	2^{3}	3	4	5^{2}	6	7^{1}		10	12	11		8	13	9		14															9
1	2^{3}	3	4	5^{1}	6	7^{2}		10		11		8	12	9	13	14															10
1		3	4		6	7		10		11	5	8	2^{1}	9			12														11
1	2^{2}	3	7	5^{3}	6	12	8^{1}	9		11	4	10		13			14														12
1	2	3^{3}	7	5	6	13	8	9	12	11^{1}	4	10^{2}					14														13
1	2^{1}	3	7^{2}	5^{3}	6	12	8	9		11	4	10	14	13																	14
1	2^{1}	3	4^{2}		6^{3}	12	8	10■		11	5	7	13	9			14														15
1		3	4		6	7		9		11^{1}	5	8	2				12	13	10^{2}												16
1		3	4		2	7		9			6	8	5	12					10^{1}	11											17
1	2^{1}	3			6	7	8	12				4		9			5		10	11											18
1	2	3			6	7	8	10^{1}				4		9				12		11	5										19
1		3	13		6^{1}	7	8				14	4^{2}	2	9			12			11	5	10^{3}									20
1			4			7	8				3			9^{1}	2		6		10	11	5	12									21
1	2^{3}				6^{2}	7	8	12			3		13	9^{1}	4				10	11	5	14									22
1	2		4^{1}			7	8	13			3		12	9	11		6		10^{2}		5										23
1	2■		4^{1}		13		8	14			3		7	9	12		6		10^{3}	11^{2}	5										24
1		3^{2}	4		12	7	8^{3}				6	11	2	9	14		5^{1}		10	13											25
1	2	3	4			7^{1}	8				6	12	5	9	13				10	11^{2}											26
1		3	4		2	7^{1}	8	13			6	12	5	9					10^{2}	11											27
1		3	4	13	12	7^{3}	8	10			6^{2}	11	5	9	14								2^{1}								28
1	12	3	4^{1}	5	2	7	8	13				11	6	9^{3}										10^{2}	14						29
1		3		5	13	7	8					4	6	9	12					11^{1}			2		10^{2}						30
1				5^{1}		7^{2}	8^{3}				3	4	6	9						13			2		14	12	10	11			31
1				5^{1}	12	7					3	4	6	9^{3}						13			2		14	8	10	11^{2}			32
1				5	6	7					3	4		9						12			2		13	8	10^{2}	11^{1}			33
1		3		5		12					6	7^{1}		9						13			2			4	10	11^{2}	8		34
1		3		5		7					6			9						12			2			4■	10	11^{1}	8		35
1		3		5		7^{3}	4					14	6	9						13			2^{1}		12		10	11^{2}	8		36
1		3		5^{2}		14	8^{3}				12	11	6	9						13			2^{1}			4	10		7		37
1		3			2	12	8^{1}				6	13	5	9^{3}						11^{2}					14	4	10		7		38
1		3			2	7^{1}					6	11	5	9						13			12			4			8	10^{2}	39
1		3			2	7	8				6	13	5	9						11^{2}			12			4			10^{1}		40
1		3		12	2■	7^{2}	8				6	11^{1}	5	9						13						4			10		41
1		3		12		7^{2}	8				6^{1}	14	5	9						11^{3}			2			4			10	13	42

FA Cup

Fourth Qual	Maidenhead U	(h)	2-1
First Round	Canvey Island	(h)	4-0
Second Round	Hartlepool U	(a)	1-5

LDV Vans Trophy

First Round	Wycombe W	(h)	0-1

FA Trophy

Third Round	Thurrock	(a)	0-1

Play-offs

Semi-Final	Carlisle U	(h)	1-0
		(a)	1-2

BARNET

FL Championship 2

Ground: Underhill Stadium, Barnet Lane, Barnet, Hertfordshire EN5 2BE.
Tel: (0208) 441 6932.
Year Formed: 1888.
Record Gate: 11,026 (1952 v Wycombe Wanderers FA Amateur Cup Fourth Round).
Nickname: The Bees.
Manager: Paul Fairclough.
Secretary: Andrew Adie.
Colours: Amber shirts with black trim, amber shorts, amber stockings.

BARNET 2004–05 LEAGUE RECORD

Match No.	*Date*	*Venue*	*Opponents*	*Result*		*H/T Score*	*Lg. Pos.*	*Goalscorers*	*Attendance*
1	Aug 14	H	Forest Green R	W	3-1	0-1	—	Graham [50], Grazioli 2 [58, 69]	1321
2	17	A	Farnborough T	D	0-0	0-0	—		1069
3	21	A	Halifax T	W	3-2	0-2	3	Haslam (og) [50], Hatch [68], Grazioli [69]	1382
4	28	H	Northwich Vic	W	4-0	2-0	2	Hendon (pen) [38], Sinclair [40], Hatch [52], Grazioli [66]	1422
5	30	A	Canvey Is	W	1-0	1-0	1	Sinclair [27]	1230
6	Sept 4	H	Morecambe	W	5-1	0-0	1	King [61], Hendon (pen) [71], Grazioli 2 [74, 76], Bailey [90]	1787
7	11	A	Tamworth	W	2-0	2-0	1	Sinclair [13], Grazioli [45]	1199
8	18	H	Gravesend & N	W	4-1	3-0	1	Hatch 2 [36, 45], Grazioli [44], Sinclair [80]	2235
9	21	H	Burton Alb	L	2-3	2-1	—	Sinclair [14], Hatch [43]	1919
10	25	A	Scarborough	D	1-1	1-0	1	Grazioli [19]	1542
11	Oct 2	H	Woking	D	2-2	1-0	1	Grazioli 2 [42, 70]	2106
12	5	A	Exeter C	W	3-0	0-0	—	Lee [63], Graham [75], Sinclair [76]	3589
13	9	H	Dagenham & R	W	5-0	2-0	1	Hendon 2 (1 pen) [2, 76 (p)], Strevens [6], Roache [69], Bailey [73]	1894
14	16	A	Carlisle U	W	3-1	2-1	1	Hendon (pen) [3], Gray (og) [30], Lee [78]	9215
15	23	H	York C	W	4-0	2-0	1	Bailey [16], Lee [36], Yakubu [65], Sinclair [74]	2501
16	Nov 6	A	Hereford U	D	1-1	1-1	1	Grazioli [5]	3645
17	20	H	Accrington S	W	3-0	1-0	1	King [21], Graham [58], Flynn (og) [88]	1990
18	27	A	Aldershot T	W	3-2	1-1	1	Grazioli [7], Graham [67], King [83]	3494
19	Dec 4	H	Leigh RMI	W	3-2	1-2	1	Grazioli [2], Bailey [58], Roache [90]	1961
20	7	A	Crawley T	W	3-1	1-0	—	Grazioli 2 [30, 48], Sinclair [90]	2949
21	11	A	Gravesend & N	W	3-1	0-1	1	Hatch [61], Bailey [65], Sinclair [73]	1707
22	18	H	Tamworth	L	0-3	0-2	1		2507
23	26	A	Stevenage Bor	L	1-2	0-0	1	Grazioli [61]	4307
24	28	H	Scarborough	W	1-0	0-0	1	Roache [77]	2504
25	Jan 2	H	Stevenage Bor	W	2-1	1-0	1	Grazioli [33], Yakubu [87]	3520
26	8	A	Woking	D	1-1	1-0	1	Roache [10]	2832
27	22	H	Exeter C	W	1-0	1-0	1	Grazioli [15]	3489
28	29	A	Burton Alb	D	1-1	1-0	1	Roache [40]	1685
29	Feb 12	H	Hereford U	L	0-2	0-1	1		2668
30	19	A	Accrington S	L	1-4	0-1	1	Grazioli [85]	1841
31	26	H	Aldershot T	W	2-1	1-0	1	Strevens [19], Grazioli [58]	2839
32	Mar 1	A	York C	L	1-2	0-1	—	Grazioli [58]	1926
33	5	A	Leigh RMI	W	3-0	1-0	1	Grazioli 2 [37, 77], Hatch [56]	402
34	12	H	Crawley T	W	3-0	1-0	1	Sinclair [1], Hatch [49], Lee [71]	2302
35	19	H	Farnborough T	W	7-1	4-1	1	Grazioli 3 [14, 21, 40], Strevens [34], Batt [75], Roache [82], Sinclair [90]	2418
36	25	A	Forest Green R	W	2-0	0-0	1	Strevens [55], Hatch [67]	1655
37	28	H	Canvey Is	W	1-0	0-0	1	Strevens [58]	3759
38	Apr 2	A	Northwich Vic	L	0-2	0-0	1		1552
39	9	H	Halifax T	W	3-1	1-1	1	Strevens [35], King [48], Grazioli [77]	3924
40	16	A	Morecambe	D	1-1	1-0	1	Hatch [27]	2385
41	19	H	Carlisle U	D	1-1	0-1	—	Grazioli [90]	3687
42	23	A	Dagenham & R	L	0-2	0-1	1		1923

Final League Position: 1

GOALSCORERS

League (90): Grazioli 29, Sinclair 11, Hatch 10, Roache 6, Strevens 6, Bailey 5, Hendon 5 (4 pens), Graham 4, King 4, Lee 4, Yakubu 2, Batt 1, own goals 3.
FA Cup (3): Graham 1, Hatch 1, Yakubu 1.
LDV Vans Trophy (3): Bailey 2 (1 pen), Roache 1.
Trophy (2): Bailey 2.

Gore 7	Hendon 37	King 40	Clist 40	Yakubu 35	Graham 38 + 1	Lee 35 + 2	Sinclair 39	Grazioli 37	Hatch 32 + 4	Stevens 35 + 4	Champion — + 2	Plummer 3	Bailey 23 + 13	Roache 8 + 20	Lopez 2 + 11	Millard 8	Dobson — + 3	Batt 8 + 7	Tynan 27 + 1	Elmes — + 2	McBean — + 4	Charles 8 + 1	Ada — + 2	*Match No.*
1	2	3	4	5^1	6	7	8	9	10	11	12													1
1	2	3	4		6	7^1	8	9	10^2	11		5	12	13										2
1	2	3	4		6	7	8^2	9	10	11^1		5	13		12									3
	2	3	4		6	7	8^1	9^2	10^3	11		5	12	13		1	14							4
	2	3	4	5	6	7	8^1	9	10	11					12	1								5
	2	3	4	5	6	7^1	8^2	9	10^3	11			13	14	12	1								6
	2	3	4	5	6	7■	8	9^2	10	11^1			12		13	1								7
	2	3	4	5	6		8	9^1	10	11^3			13	12	7^2	1	14							8
	2	3	4^1	5	6	7^3	8	9	10	11^2			14	12		1	13							9
	2	3	4	5	6	7	8	9	10	11						1								10
	2^3	3	4	5	6	7	8	9^1	10^2	11			13	12		1		14						11
		3	4	5	6	7	8^1		10	9			11					2	1	12				12
	2	3	4	5^2	6	7	8		10^1	9			11	12				13	1					13
	2	3	4	5	6	7	8			10			11	9					1					14
	2	3	4	5	6	7^1	8^2			10			11	9^3	12			13	1		14			15
	2	3	4	5	6	7	8	9^1	12	10			11						1					16
	2	3	4	5	6	7	8	9^1	10	11									1		12			17
	2	3	4	5	6	7	8^1	9	10	11					12				1					18
		3	4	5	6	7		9	10^1	11			8^2	12	13			2	1					19
	2	3	4	5	6	7	8	9^1	10	12			11						1					20
	2	3	4	5	6	7	8	9^1	10^2	13			11	12					1					21
	2	3■	4	5	6^1	7^3	8	9		10^2			11	12				13	1	14				22
	2		4	5		7■	8	9	10	11			6					3	1					23
	2	3	4	5		7	8^2	9	10				11	12	13			6^1	1					24
		3^1	4	5	13		8	9		11	12		7	10^3	6^2			2	1		14			25
	2		4	5			8	9^3	13	11			7	10^2	12			3^1	1		14	6		26
	2	3	4	5^2	6	7	8	9^1	10				11	12					1			13		27
	2	3	4		6		8			11			7	9				10	1			5		28
	2	3	4		6^1	7	8	9	10^2	13			11		12				1			5		29
	2	3	4^1	5	6	7	8	9	10				11	12					1					30
	2	3	4	5	6	13	8■	9^1	12	11			7	10^2					1					31
1	2	3	4	5	6	7		9	12	11			8	10^1										32
1		3	4	2	6		8	9	10	11			7									5		33
	2	3	4		6	7	8^1	9^2	10	11				13	12				1			5		34
	2	3	4		6	7^2	8	9^3	10	11^1			13	14				12	1			5		35
	2	3	4	5	6	7^1	8	9^2	10	11			12	13					1					36
	2	3	4	5	6	7^1	8	9^2	10	11			12	13					1					37
	2	3	4^1	5	6^2	14	8	9	10^3	11			7	12				13	1					38
	2	3	4	5	6	7	8	9^1	10	11			12						1					39
1■		3		5	6^1	7		9^6	10	11^2			8	12				2	15			4	13	40
	2	3	4^1	5	6	7	8	9	10	11^2			12	13					1					41
1	2^1	3		5	6	7^2	8	9^3		14			11	10				13				4	12	42

FA Cup

Fourth Qual	Farnborough T	(h)	2-1
First Round	Bath C	(h)	1-2

LDV Vans Trophy

First Round	Stevenage B	(h)	3-1
Second Round	Bristol R	(a)	0-2

FA Trophy

Third Round	Farnborough	(h)	1-0
Fourth Round	Carlisle U	(a)	1-4

BURTON ALBION — Conference

Ground: Eton Park, Princess Way, Burton-on-Trent DE14 2RU.
Tel: (01283) 565 938.
Year Formed: 1950.
Record Gate: 5,806 (1964 v Weymouth Southern League Cup Final).
Nickname: Brewers.
Manager: Nigel Clough.
Secretary: Tony Kirkland.
Colours: All yellow with black trim.

BURTON ALBION 2004–05 LEAGUE RECORD

Match No.	Date	Venue	Opponents	Result		H/T Score	Lg. Pos.	Goalscorers	Attendance
1	Aug 14	A	Accrington S	L	1-3	0-1	—	Ducros [70]	1705
2	17	H	Leigh RMI	D	0-0	0-0	—		1305
3	21	H	Dagenham & R	L	1-3	0-1	21	Clough [61]	1221
4	28	A	Aldershot T	L	0-3	0-1	20		2506
5	30	H	Scarborough	L	2-3	0-3	21	Talbot [50], Dudley (pen) [88]	1302
6	Sept 4	A	Carlisle U	D	0-0	0-0	20		4582
7	11	A	Stevenage Bor	W	1-0	1-0	20	Dudley (pen) [41]	1788
8	18	H	Crawley T	W	1-0	1-0	15	Ducros [30]	1207
9	21	A	Barnet	W	3-2	1-2	—	Talbot 2 [29, 55], Anderson [57]	1919
10	25	H	York C	L	0-2	0-0	17		1789
11	Oct 2	A	Hereford U	D	0-0	0-0	17		3320
12	9	H	Gravesend & N	W	3-2	2-1	17	Dudley [5], Talbot [37], Ducros [63]	943
13	12	H	Halifax T	D	2-2	1-2	—	Dudley [39], Talbot [82]	1194
14	16	A	Northwich Vic	L	0-4	0-1	17		857
15	23	A	Woking	L	0-1	0-1	18		1710
16	Nov 6	H	Farnborough T	D	0-0	0-0	17		1238
17	20	A	Forest Green R	L	2-3	1-0	17	Shaw [14], Dudley [53]	622
18	27	H	Exeter C	W	1-0	1-0	17	Shaw [42]	1582
19	Dec 4	A	Canvey Is	D	2-2	1-0	17	Robins [18], Anderson [83]	685
20	7	H	Morecambe	L	1-3	0-3	—	Ducros [65]	1257
21	11	A	Crawley T	L	0-4	0-2	18		1360
22	18	H	Stevenage Bor	L	0-3	0-2	19		1221
23	29	A	York C	W	2-1	1-0	19	Shaw [27], Taylor K [64]	2184
24	Jan 1	A	Tamworth	W	2-0	2-0	17	Shaw [35], Taylor K [45]	2443
25	8	H	Hereford U	W	3-0	1-0	15	Taylor K [19], Dudley (pen) [49], Shaw (pen) [73]	1589
26	25	A	Halifax T	L	0-2	0-0	—		1256
27	29	H	Barnet	D	1-1	0-1	17	Stride [90]	1685
28	Feb 1	H	Tamworth	D	1-1	1-0	—	Hall [4]	1673
29	12	A	Farnborough T	W	3-1	2-0	14	Shilton [7], Shaw 2 [29, 84]	698
30	19	H	Forest Green R	W	4-1	3-1	14	Dudley 2 [6, 45], Anderson [34], Shaw [80]	1241
31	Mar 5	H	Canvey Is	D	1-1	0-0	15	Anderson [73]	1098
32	8	H	Woking	L	0-1	0-0	—		910
33	15	A	Exeter C	L	1-3	1-0	—	Simpkins [2]	2418
34	19	A	Leigh RMI	W	4-1	1-1	16	Shaw [37], Miller [50], Hall [53], Corbett [73]	325
35	22	H	Aldershot T	L	1-3	1-3	—	Wilson [15]	1148
36	25	H	Accrington S	D	2-2	0-1	16	Shaw [67], Miller [84]	1508
37	28	A	Scarborough	D	1-1	1-1	16	Hall [21]	1675
38	Apr 5	A	Dagenham & R	L	1-3	1-0	—	Ward [40]	1136
39	12	A	Morecambe	L	0-3	0-2	—		1596
40	16	H	Carlisle U	L	0-1	0-1	16		1914
41	19	H	Northwich Vic	W	1-0	1-0	—	Shaw [37]	1713
42	23	A	Gravesend & N	W	2-0	0-0	16	Hall [49], Ducros [55]	1169

Final League Position: 16

GOALSCORERS

League (50): Shaw 11 (1 pen), Dudley 8 (3 pens), Ducros 5, Talbot 5, Anderson 4, Hall 4, Taylor K 3, Miller 2, Clough 1, Corbett 1, Robins 1, Shilton 1, Simpkins 1, Stride 1, Ward 1, Wilson 1.
FA Cup (1): Ayres 1.
Trophy (7): Anderson 1, Miller 1, Shaw 1, Stride 1, Talbot 1, Taylor 1, Webster 1 (pen).

Taylor M 5	Henshaw 3 + 2	Simpkins 14 + 6	Ayers 23 + 3	Kirkwood 12 + 15	Webster 36 + 2	Hall 29 + 10	Stride 25	Anderson 14 + 15	Dudley 33 + 2	Wilson 13 + 7	Ducros 32 + 5	Corbett 30 + 7	Wright 1 + 1	Shilton 28 + 3	Clough 21 + 4	Austin 26 + 5	Talbo t9 + 5	Crane 36	Price 3	Crosby — + 1	Wassall — + 1	Elam 1	Robins 8 + 2	Shaw 18 + 1	Miller 17 + 2	Taylor K 5	Britton — + 1	Midworth 4 + 3	Briscoe 10	Ward 3 + 1	Jones 1	Coates 1 + 1	Alexis 1	Garner — + 1	*Match No.*
1	2	3	4	5[1]	6	7	8	9	10[2]	11[3]	12	13	14																						1
1	2	3	4[2]		6	7	8	9		11	10[3]	14	5[1]	12	13																				2
1	2[1]		12	5[2]	6	7	8	13	10	14	11[3]	9		3	4																				3
1		5[2]	4		6[1]	7	8		10[3]	13	11	9		3	2	12	14																		4
1		13	4[1]	5[2]		7	8[3]	12	10	14	11			3	6	2	9																		5
		3			6	7		9[1]	10	8				11	4	5	12	1	2																6
		3	4		6			9[3]	10[2]	7	14	12		11	8[1]	5	13	1	2																7
		3	4	12	6		8	13	10	11■	9[2]			7	2[1]	5		1																	8
		3	4	2	6	12		9[3]	7		8			11[2]	14	5	10[1]	1		13															9
		3	12	4[2]	6	7			10[3]	11	8				13	5[1]	9	1	2		14														10
		3	4	5[1]	6	7	8		10	12	2	11			13		9[2]	1																	11
		3	4	13	6	12		14	7[1]	5	8	10		11	2[2]		9[3]	1																	12
		3[1]	4	14	6	13			10[3]	5[2]	8	2		11	7	12	9	1																	13
		3[1]	4	10[3]	6	14		13		5	8[2]	2		11	7	12	9	1																	14
			4		6	12	8	14	10	13	7[2]	3		11	2[1]	5	9[3]	1																	15
			4	10[3]	6	12		13		11	8	2		3		5	9[2]	1				7[1]	14												16
			4	12		7	8		10[2]	11[1]	6	2		3	5		13	1					14	9[3]											17
		12[2]	4	13	6	7			10		8	2		3[1]	5			1					11	9											18
			4	13	6	7		12	11		8	2		3	5			1					9[1]	10[2]											19
			4		6	7		13	11[1]		8	2		3	5		12	1					9[2]	10											20
				12	6	7		14	8	13	4	2		3	11[2]	5[1]		1					9[3]	10											21
			4[1]		6	12		14	7		8	13		3		5[2]		1					9	10[3]	2	11									22
		12			6	11	8	13	7			2			4[1]	5		1						10[2]	3	9									23
		12		14	6	7	8	13	4[1]			2				5		1					9[2]	10[3]	3	11									24
		13			6	7[2]	8		4[1]		12	2				5		1					9	10	3	11									25
				12	6	7[2]	8	9[3]	10		13	2		11[1]		5		1						14	3	4									26
				12	6	7	8	13	4		11[1]	2				5		1					9[2]	10	3										27
					6	7	8	9	11		4	2				5		1						10	3										28
			4	12	6	7[1]	8		9		11[3]	2		3				1						10[2]	5		13	14							29
			4	13	6	14	8[2]	9[3]	7[1]		11	2		3				1						10	5			12							30
		12		13	6[1]	7[2]	8	9	11[3]		4	2		3		5		1							10			14							31
		3		10		11	8[2]		7[1]		12	9		13	4	5		1							6			2							32
		3[1]		10	12	7					8	9		11	4[2]	5		1							13			2	6						33
				13	6	12	8	9[2]	7		4[1]	14		11		5		1						10[3]	3				2						34
			4[1]	9		7				6		10		3	8	12		1■										2	5			13	11[2]		35
					6		8[1]	9[2]	7		4	13		3		5								10	2				11	12		1			36
			4[1]	9	14	7			13	11[2]		2			8	12		1										3	5	6	10[3]				37
				12	6	14			7[1]	13	8[3]	9		11[2]		5		1						10	4				2	3					38
	12		13		6	7	8	14			9	10			4	5[1]		1							3[2]				2	11[3]					39
			4[1]		6	7	8	9	3		11	10				5		1							12				2						40
					6	7	8	9	12		11	13		3[1]		5		1						10[2]	4				2						41
	12				6	7	8	9[2]			11[1]	4		13		5		1						10[3]	3				2					14	42

FA Cup

Fourth Qual	Hinckley U	(a)	0-0
		(h)	1-1

FA Trophy

Third Round	York C	(h)	3-0
Fourth Round	Hednesford T	(h)	2-0
Fifth Round	Morecambe	(h)	1-0
Sixth Round	Woking	(h)	1-0
Semi-Final	Grays Ath	(a)	0-5
		(h)	0-2

CANVEY ISLAND

Conference

Ground: Park Lane, Canvey Island, Essex SS8 7PX.
Tel: (01268) 511 888.
Year Formed: 1950.
Record Gate: 3,553 (2002 v Aldershot T Ryman Premier League).
Nickname: Gulls.
Manager: Jeff King.
Secretary: Wayne Purser.
Colours: Yellow and blue.

CANVEY ISLAND 2004–05 LEAGUE RECORD

Match No.	Date	Venue	Opponents	Result		H/T Score	Lg. Pos.	Goalscorers	Attendance
1	Aug 14	A	Carlisle U	D	0-0	0-0	—		7234
2	17	H	Gravesend & N	D	1-1	0-1	—	Boylan 57	1223
3	21	H	Tamworth	D	3-3	1-2	14	Keeling 44, Boylan 2 (1 pen) 55 (p), 65	686
4	28	A	Exeter C	W	1-0	1-0	13	Sawyer (og) 22	2827
5	30	H	Barnet	L	0-1	0-1	13		1230
6	Sept 4	A	Scarborough	D	1-1	0-1	13	McDougald 76	1732
7	11	A	Farnborough T	W	3-1	2-1	10	Boylan 3 6, 9, 87	748
8	18	H	Halifax T	L	0-1	0-1	11		789
9	21	H	Crawley T	D	2-2	0-1	—	Berquez 49, Duffy 90	737
10	25	A	Woking	L	0-1	0-1	15		1845
11	Oct 2	H	Morecambe	D	0-0	0-0	16		692
12	5	A	Stevenage Bor	W	4-1	2-1	—	Berquez 5, Boylan 13, Gregory (pen) 60, Midgley 77	1513
13	9	H	Forest Green R	W	2-1	1-1	11	Gregory (pen) 6, Keeling 50	356
14	16	A	York C	D	0-0	0-0	13		2207
15	23	H	Leigh RMI	W	3-0	1-0	11	Berquez 31, Keeling 47, McDougald 87	532
16	Nov 5	A	Northwich Vic	L	1-3	0-2	—	Duffy 64	504
17	20	H	Hereford U	L	0-4	0-2	15		921
18	27	A	Accrington S	L	0-1	0-0	16		1249
19	Dec 4	H	Burton Alb	D	2-2	0-1	15	Gregory 64, Braniff 73	685
20	7	A	Aldershot T	L	0-2	0-1	—		1923
21	11	A	Halifax T	L	1-4	0-3	16	Sedgemore 76	1522
22	18	H	Farnborough T	D	1-1	1-1	16	Pearson 40	509
23	28	H	Woking	D	2-2	1-1	16	Berquez 2 38, 75	912
24	Jan 1	H	Dagenham & R	W	4-2	2-0	16	Gregory 6, Berquez 8, Midgley 56, McDougald 80	1309
25	8	A	Morecambe	L	0-4	0-0	17		1279
26	22	H	Stevenage Bor	W	3-0	2-0	16	Duffy 6, Berquez 16, McDougald 85	814
27	29	A	Crawley T	L	1-2	1-0	15	Boylan 8	1941
28	31	A	Dagenham & R	L	1-3	0-0	—	Midgley 78	1542
29	Feb 12	H	Northwich Vic	D	2-2	1-2	17	Duffy 41, Boylan 90	624
30	19	A	Hereford U	L	0-1	0-1	17		2656
31	Mar 5	A	Burton Alb	D	1-1	0-0	18	Boylan 86	1098
32	11	H	Aldershot T	D	2-2	2-2	—	Burton 16, Boylan 45	904
33	19	A	Gravesend & N	L	2-3	1-2	18	Theobald 13, Boylan 90	1224
34	22	H	Accrington S	L	0-2	0-1	—		525
35	25	H	Carlisle U	L	0-3	0-3	18		1183
36	28	A	Barnet	L	0-1	0-0	18		3759
37	Apr 2	H	Exeter C	D	2-2	1-0	18	McDougald 2, McGhee 90	921
38	5	A	Leigh RMI	L	1-2	1-2	—	McDougald (pen) 18	201
39	9	A	Tamworth	L	0-1	0-0	19		1046
40	16	H	Scarborough	W	1-0	1-0	19	Boylan 4	510
41	19	H	York C	W	4-0	3-0	—	Boylan 5, Berquez 2 15, 42, Midgley 77	817
42	23	A	Forest Green R	D	2-2	1-1	18	Minton 22, Noto 90	589

Final League Position: 18

GOALSCORERS

League (53): Boylan 14 (1 pen), Berquez 9, McDougald 6 (1 pen), Duffy 4, Gregory 4 (2 pens), Midgley 4, Keeling 3, Braniff 1, Burton 1, McGhee 1, Minton 1, Noto 1, Pearson 1, Sedgemore 1, Theobald 1, own goal 1.
FA Cup (4): Berquez 1, Gregory 1 (pen), McDougald 1, Midgley 1.
Trophy (7): Boylan 3, Berquez 2, Minton 1, Sedgemore 1.

Potter 40	Joseph 11 + 4	Duffy 36 + 3	Smith 16 + 7	Chenery 14 + 1	McGhee 22	Kennedy 21 + 4	Minton 18 + 1	Gregory 29 + 5	Boylan 24 + 4	Sedgemore 36 + 1	Midgley 20 + 6	Keeling 24 + 9	Gooden 2 + 2	McDougald 10 + 24	Cowan 8 + 3	Berquez 26 + 6	Sterling 34	Ward 23	Goodwin — + 4	Hallett 3 + 4	Williamson 9 + 3	Braniff 3 + 1	Pearson 5	Theobald 15 + 2	Noto 5 + 4	Burton 5 + 3	Mapes 1 + 1	Harrison 2 + 1	*Match No.*
1	2^{1}	3^{2}	4	5	6	7^{3}	8	9	10	11	12	13	14																1
1	2^{1}	3	4	5	6	7	8	9^{2}	10	11		12		13															2
1	12	3^{1}	4	5	6	7	8^{2}	9^{3}	10	11		2■	13	14															3
1	2^{2}	3	4	5	6	7		9	10^{3}	11	13		8^{1}	14	12														4
1	2	3	4^{1}	5	6	7		9	10^{3}	11			8^{2}	13	12	14													5
1	2^{1}	3^{2}		5	6	7		9	10	11	13			8		12	4												6
1	2		4	5		7		9^{1}	10	11	8			12		3	6												7
1	2^{1}	3	4	5		7		9	10^{2}	11		12		13		8	6												8
1	2	3		5^{1}	6	7		9^{2}	10	11		14		13	12	8^{3}	4												9
1		3	4^{1}			7		13	10^{2}	11		12		9	2	8	6	5■											10
1		3				7^{1}		9	10^{2}	11	4	12		13	2	8	6	5											11
1		3				13		9	10^{3}	11	7	2^{2}		14	4	8	6^{1}	5	12										12
1	12	3				13		9		11^{2}	7	2^{1}		10	4	8^{3}	6	5	14										13
1		3				7		9^{2}		11		2^{1}		10	4	8	6	5	13	12									14
1		3^{1}				7		9^{2}		11	12	2		10	4	8^{3}	6	5	13	14									15
1		12				2^{1}	13	9		11	3^{2}	7		10	4	8	6	5											16
1	12	3	13			2	8	9				14			4	11^{1}	6	5^{2}		10^{3}	7								17
1	2	11^{3}		4	3	12	8^{2}	13			9	7^{1}				14	6	5			10								18
1	12			4	3^{2}	2^{1}		9		13	11					7	6	5			8	10							19
1	2		12	4				9^{2}		11	3			13		8	6	5^{1}			7	10							20
1	2^{2}	3	12	5■	6	7				11		13					4				8^{1}	10	9						21
1		3						9		11	7	2				8	6	5				12	10^{1}	4					22
1		3		12	6			9	13	11	2	7				8		5^{1}					10^{2}	4					23
1		3	12		6			9^{2}	14	11	2^{1}	7		13		8	4						10^{3}	5					24
1		3	12		6			9^{2}	14	11	7	2		13		8	4^{1}						10^{3}	5					25
1		3	4			12		9^{2}	10	11		2		13		8	6				7^{1}			5					26
1		3				2		9	10^{1}	11		7		12		8	6	4■						5					27
1		3	4			7		9^{1}	10	11^{3}	13	2		12		8^{2}	6							5	14				28
1		3		5^{2}		7^{3}	8	9	10			2				14	6	4^{1}						13	11	12			29
1		3			6	7^{1}	8^{2}		10^{3}	11		2		13		12		4						5	9	14			30
1		3			6^{1}		8		10			2		14		13	4	5			11			12		9^{3}	7^{2}		31
1		3					8		10	11	2^{1}	12		14		6■	4	5			7^{2}				13	9^{3}			32
1		3					8^{1}		10	11		2		13			4	5						6	7^{2}	9	12		33
1		3^{3}	12				8		10	11	13	2^{2}		14		6	4^{1}							5	7	9			34
1■		12			6		8		10^{2}		7	2^{1}		13		11■	4	5						3		9^{6}		15	35
		3	9^{2}		6^{1}		8	13		11	7	2		10			4	5								12		1	36
		3	9^{1}		6		8	12		11^{2}	7	2		10			4	5							13			1	37
1		3	9		6		8	13		11		2		10			4	5^{1}		12					7^{2}				38
1		13	3		6		8	9		11	7	2^{2}		10^{3}			4^{1}			14	12			5					39
1		3	2		6			9	10^{2}	11	7			13		8^{1}	4				12			5					40
1		3	12		6^{1}		8		10	11^{2}	2			14		7	4			9^{3}	13			5					41
1		3	4				8	9^{2}	13	11	2			14		7				10^{3}	6^{1}			5	12				42

FA Cup

Fourth Qual	Hallen	(h)	4-1
First Round	Aldershot T	(a)	0-4

FA Trophy

Third Round	Bath C	(a)	3-0
Fourth Round	Aylesbury U	(a)	1-0
Fifth Round	Bishop's Stortford	(h)	2-2
		(a)	1-2

CARLISLE UNITED

Conference

Ground: Brunton Park, Warwick Road, Carlisle CA1 1LL.
Tel: (01228) 526 237.
Year Formed: 1903.
Record Gate: 27,500 (v Birmingham C, FA Cup 3rd rd, 5 January 1957 and v Middlesbrough, FA Cup 5th rd, 7 February 1970).
Nicknames: 'Cumbrians' or 'The Blues'.
Manager: Paul Simpson.
Secretary: Sarah McKnight.
Colours: Blue shirts, white shorts, blue stockings.

CARLISLE UNITED 2004–05 LEAGUE RECORD

Match No.	Date	Venue	Opponents	Result		H/T Score	Lg. Pos.	Goalscorers	Attendance
1	Aug 14	H	Canvey Is	D	0-0	0-0	—		7234
2	17	A	Northwich Vic	D	2-2	1-0	—	Hawley [44], Gray [56]	1803
3	21	A	Forest Green R	W	3-0	1-0	8	Preece [20], Vieira [74], Murphy [84]	1074
4	28	H	Farnborough T	W	7-0	5-0	5	Hawley 3 [7, 19, 28], Preece 2 (1 pen) [16 (p), 36], Vieira [58], McGill [90]	5505
5	31	A	Halifax T	D	2-2	0-0	9	Hawley [83], Preece [85]	2696
6	Sept 4	H	Burton Alb	D	0-0	0-0	6		4582
7	11	A	Woking	D	1-1	0-0	9	Hawley [57]	2581
8	18	H	Tamworth	W	2-1	0-0	6	Hawley [46], Grand [75]	5007
9	21	H	Scarborough	W	2-1	0-1	—	Henderson [69], Gray [86]	5111
10	25	A	Aldershot T	W	5-0	1-0	3	Lumsdon [28], Vieira 3 [46, 68, 78], Billy [65]	3482
11	Oct 2	H	Crawley T	W	1-0	0-0	2	Farrell [84]	5850
12	5	A	Leigh RMI	W	6-1	1-1	—	McGill 2 [13, 48], Cowan [67], Billy [78], Murphy [89], Farrell [90]	1540
13	9	A	Exeter C	D	0-0	0-0	2		2532
14	16	H	Barnet	L	1-3	1-2	2	McGill [45]	9215
15	23	H	Hereford U	W	3-1	2-1	2	Vieira 2 [41, 42], Murphy [47]	6772
16	Nov 6	A	Gravesend & N	W	3-1	2-1	2	Hawley 2 [5, 54], Murphy [41]	2030
17	20	H	Dagenham & R	W	1-0	0-0	2	Hawley [88]	5962
18	27	A	York C	L	1-2	0-1	2	Henderson [87]	3842
19	Dec 7	A	Accrington S	W	2-1	0-1	—	Preece 2 [49, 61]	3024
20	11	A	Tamworth	L	0-1	0-0	2		1555
21	18	H	Woking	W	2-1	0-0	2	Lumsdon [86], Grand [88]	5159
22	26	A	Morecambe	D	1-1	1-0	2	Hawley [15]	4660
23	28	H	Aldershot T	D	1-1	0-1	2	Murray G [89]	6712
24	Jan 2	H	Morecambe	D	3-3	3-1	2	Murray G [4], Preece [9], Vieira [39]	6751
25	8	A	Crawley T	L	0-1	0-0	2		2457
26	29	A	Scarborough	D	1-1	0-1	2	Lumsdon [87]	2828
27	Feb 12	H	Gravesend & N	D	2-2	2-0	3	Cowan [40], Livesey [42]	5284
28	19	A	Dagenham & R	L	0-1	0-0	8		1684
29	22	H	Stevenage Bor	L	1-2	0-2	—	Lumsdon (pen) [80]	3146
30	Mar 5	A	Stevenage Bor	L	1-2	1-0	10	Murphy [20]	2217
31	8	H	Leigh RMI	W	3-0	1-0	—	Hawley [43], Lumsdon [69], Murphy [75]	3047
32	12	H	Accrington S	W	2-0	1-0	5	Holmes [7], Hawley [53]	4861
33	19	H	Northwich Vic	W	1-0	0-0	5	Holmes [48]	5062
34	25	A	Canvey Is	W	3-0	3-0	4	Lumsdon 2 (1 pen) [10, 45 (p)], Holmes [34]	1183
35	28	H	Halifax T	W	1-0	0-0	2	Vieira [89]	5474
36	Apr 2	A	Farnborough T	W	2-1	1-0	2	Beharall [40], Murphy [57]	1061
37	5	A	Hereford U	D	0-0	0-0	—		3819
38	9	H	Forest Green R	L	0-1	0-0	2		4640
39	12	H	York C	W	6-0	2-0	—	Livesey [11], Lumsdon 2 (1 pen) [26 (p), 87], Murray A [63], Holmes [70], Merris (og) [79]	3810
40	16	A	Burton Alb	W	1-0	1-0	2	Holmes [28]	1914
41	19	A	Barnet	D	1-1	1-0	—	Vieira [31]	3687
42	23	H	Exeter C	L	0-2	0-0	3		6588

Final League Position: 3

GOALSCORERS

League (74): Hawley 13, Vieira 10, Lumsdon 9 (3 pens), Murphy 7, Preece 7 (1 pen), Holmes 5, McGill 4, Billy 2, Cowan 2, Farrell 2, Grand 2, Gray 2, Henderson 2, Livesey 2, Murray G 2, Beharall 1, Murray A 1, own goal 1.
FA Cup (6): Farrell 1, Gray 1, Hawley 1, McGill 1, Preece 1, Vieira 1.
LDV Vans Trophy (2): Grand 1, Henderson 1.
Trophy (7): Farrell 2, Vieira 2, Hawley 1, Livesey 1, Preece 1.
Play-offs (3): Billy 1, Livesey 1, Murphy 1.

Glennon 38	Shelley 20 + 1	Murphy 38	Billy 37 + 1	Andrews 12 + 2	Cowan 29	McGill 26 + 2	Lumsdon 38	Henderson 2 + 11	Hawley 36 + 4	Roca 4 + 7	Farrell 3 + 15	Gray 30	Preece 10 + 5	Vieira 26 + 10	Arnison 15 + 10	Grand 23	Tierney 10	Simpson — + 2	Murray G 5 + 15	Livesey 20	Beharall 13 + 1	Westwood 4	Holmes 13	Beech 2	Murray A 8	Hackney — + 2	*Match No.*
1	2	3	4	5	6	7	8	9¹	10	11	12																1
1	2	3	4		6	7	8		10	11	12	5	9¹														2
1	2	3	4		6	7	8		10	11¹	12	5	9²	13													3
1	2	3	4		6	7	8²		10	12	14	5	9³	11¹	13												4
1	2	3	4		6	7	8		10	12		5	9	11¹													5
1	2	3	4		6	7	8		10	12	13	5	9²	11¹													6
1	2	3	4		6	7	8		10		12	5		9¹		11											7
1	2	3	4		6	7¹	8		10		13	5		9²	12	11											8
1	2	3	4		6	7¹	8	12	10			5		9		11											9
1	7¹	3	4	12	6		8	14	10²		13	5		9³	2	11											10
1		3	4	2¹	6²	7		12	10		13	5		9	8	11											11
1		3	4	2	6	7		12	10¹		13	5		9²	8	11											12
1		3	4	2	6¹	7		13	10		12	5		9²	8	11											13
1		3	4	2	6¹	7	8	13³	10		12	5		9²	14	11											14
1	12	3¹	4	2		7	8		10²		13	5	14	9³	6	11											15
1	2	3²	4		6	7	8		10	12		5	13	9¹		11											16
1	2		4		3³	7	8	12	10	13		5	11¹	9²	14	6											17
1	2¹	11■	4	5	3²	7	8	14	10	12				9³	13	6											18
1	2		4	5		7	8	9¹	10		11		12		3	6											19
1	2¹		4	5		7	8		10		11³		9²	14	12	6	3	13									20
1	2	11	4	12		7²	8		10			5¹	13	9³		6	3		14								21
1	2	11	4			7	8		10					9¹		6	3		12	5							22
1	2	3²	4			14	8		10	11¹			13	9³		6	7		12	5							23
1		3	4				8				12		7	9¹	2	6	11		10	5							24
1		3		2		12	8		10		13		7		4¹	6	11		9²	5							25
1		3²	4	2¹		7³	8		10	13			9		12	6	11		14	5							26
1				2	3		8	12	10¹					9²	7	6	11		13	5	4						27
1	2	3			6		8		12		11²			9	7¹	4			13	5	10						28
1	2¹	3	13			7²	8		10					9		6	11		12	5	4						29
		3	4		6¹	7			10			5		9	12					2	8	1	11				30
		11	4			7	8		10¹			5		12	2		3		13	6		1	9²				31
		11	4			7¹	8	13	10			5		12	2					6		1	9²	3			32
		11	4■				8		10¹			5		7	2				13	6	12	1	9²	3			33
1		11			3		8¹	13	10³			5		14	4				7	6	2		9²			12	34
1		11	4		3¹		8		10²			5		13					12	6	2		9		7		35
1		11	4		3		8		10³			5		14	12				13	6¹	2		9²		7		36
1		11	4		3		8		10			5							12	6	2		9¹		7		37
1		11	4		3¹		8		10²			5		13					14	6	2		9³		7	12	38
1		11	4		3		8		13			5		12²					10¹	6	2		9		7		39
1		11	4		3		8		12			5		13					10²	6	2		9¹		7		40
1		11	4		3■		8					5		9²	13				12	6■	2		10¹		7		41
1		11	4¹		3		8		13			5		9²	2			12	14		6		10³		7		42

FA Cup

Fourth Qual	York C	(h)	3-1
First Round	Bristol R	(a)	1-1
		(h)	1-0
Second Round	Bournemouth	(a)	1-2

LDV Vans Trophy

First Round	Grimsby T	(a)	2-1
Second Round	Hartlepool U	(h)	0-1

FA Trophy

Third Round	Redditch U	(h)	3-1
Fourth Round	Barnet	(h)	4-1
Fifth Round	Woking	(a)	0-1

Play-offs

Semi-Final	Aldershot T	(a)	0-1
		(h)	2-1
Final	Stevenage B		1-0

(at Britannia Stadium)

CRAWLEY TOWN — Conference

Ground: Broadfield Ground, Broadfield Stadium, Brighton Road, West Sussex RH11 9RX.
Tel: (01293) 410 000.
Year Formed: 1896.
Record Gate: 4,522 (2004 v Weymouth Dr Martens League).
Nickname: The Reds.
Manager: Francis Vines.
Secretary: Barry Munn.
Colours: All red.

CRAWLEY TOWN 2004–05 LEAGUE RECORD

Match No.	Date	Venue	Opponents	Result		H/T Score	Lg. Pos.	Goalscorers	Attendance
1	Aug 14	A	Leigh RMI	W	2-1	0-1	—	MacDonald 2 (1 pen) [54 (p), 80]	401
2	17	H	Hereford U	D	1-1	0-1	—	Mapes [86]	2570
3	21	H	Aldershot T	W	1-0	0-0	4	MacDonald [67]	2508
4	28	A	Accrington S	L	0-4	0-2	10		1270
5	30	H	Dagenham & R	W	2-0	0-0	8	MacDonald [48], Palmer [61]	2177
6	Sept 4	A	Exeter C	L	2-3	2-1	10	Todd (og) [11], MacDonald (pen) [23]	2574
7	11	H	York C	W	1-0	1-0	7	Davidson [11]	2134
8	18	A	Burton Alb	L	0-1	0-1	8		1207
9	21	A	Canvey Is	D	2-2	1-0	—	Tait 2 [25, 67]	737
10	25	H	Forest Green R	W	4-2	2-2	7	Tait [13], MacDonald 2 (1 pen) [33 (p), 55], Manuella [54]	1943
11	Oct 2	A	Carlisle U	L	0-1	0-0	8		5850
12	5	H	Farnborough T	W	2-0	1-0	—	Marney [23], Deane [49]	2036
13	9	H	Northwich Vic	D	0-0	0-0	6		1696
14	16	A	Stevenage Bor	L	0-1	0-1	10		1747
15	23	A	Tamworth	L	0-1	0-1	14		859
16	Nov 6	H	Woking	W	2-1	1-0	11	Tait [1], Dolan [89]	2341
17	20	A	Morecambe	W	2-1	1-1	9	Davidson [35], Marney [55]	1405
18	27	H	Scarborough	W	2-1	1-0	6	Nicholson (og) [38], Tait [50]	1804
19	Dec 7	H	Barnet	L	1-3	0-1	—	Davidson [68]	2949
20	11	H	Burton Alb	W	4-0	2-0	6	Jenkins [18], Wormull [38], Tait [53], Marney [69]	1360
21	18	A	York C	L	1-3	0-1	8	Marney [51]	1848
22	26	H	Gravesend & N	D	1-1	1-1	10	Jenkins [7]	1863
23	28	A	Forest Green R	D	1-1	0-0	11	Harkin [84]	956
24	Jan 1	A	Gravesend & N	D	0-0	0-0	10		1496
25	8	H	Carlisle U	W	1-0	0-0	9	Armstrong [67]	2457
26	11	A	Halifax T	L	0-1	0-1	—		1267
27	22	A	Farnborough T	W	3-2	0-0	4	Armstrong [62], Tait [65], Hankin [76]	1020
28	29	H	Canvey Is	W	2-1	0-1	3	Opinel [85], Harkin (pen) [90]	1941
29	Feb 12	A	Woking	L	0-2	0-0	8		2611
30	15	H	Tamworth	W	3-0	1-0	—	Watkins [20], Jenkins [72], Tait [74]	1237
31	21	H	Morecambe	W	2-1	2-0	—	Robinson [26], Jenkins [31]	2516
32	26	A	Scarborough	D	2-2	1-1	2	Tait [37], Armstrong [58]	1451
33	Mar 5	H	Halifax T	L	1-2	0-1	7	Robinson [51]	1957
34	12	A	Barnet	L	0-3	0-1	9		2302
35	19	A	Hereford U	D	0-0	0-0	10		2211
36	25	H	Leigh RMI	D	2-2	1-0	11	Tait [16], MacDonald [68]	1831
37	28	A	Dagenham & R	L	0-1	0-0	11		1393
38	Apr 2	H	Accrington S	W	2-0	1-0	11	Burton N [34], Marney [53]	1646
39	9	A	Aldershot T	L	0-1	0-0	12		3105
40	16	H	Exeter C	L	0-1	0-1	12		1989
41	19	H	Stevenage Bor	L	1-2	0-1	—	Burton S [76]	1413
42	23	A	Northwich Vic	L	0-1	0-0	12		806

Final League Position: 12

GOALSCORERS

League (50): Tait 10, MacDonald 8 (3 pens), Marney 5, Jenkins 4, Armstrong 3, Davidson 3, Harkin 2 (1 pen), Robinson 2, Burton N 1, Burton S 1, Deane 1, Dolan 1, Hankin 1, Manuella 1, Mapes 1, Opinel 1, Palmer 1, Watkins 1, Wormull 1, own goals 2.
FA Cup (1): Tait 1.
Trophy (7): MacDonald 2, Davidson 1, Harkin 1 (pen), Opinel 1, Tait 1, Wormull 1 (pen).

Little 7	Judge 29 + 2	Simpemba 39	Kember 22 + 4	Jenkins 40 + 1	Hemsley 4 + 3	Mapes 20 + 7	Hankin 24 + 2	MacDonald 26 + 3	Deane 6 + 5	Davidson 16 + 12	Marney 17 + 12	Traynor 9 + 5	Tait 23 + 11	Palmer 19 + 4	Rees 4 + 1	Manuella 4 + 2	Smith 35	Day 1	Armstrong 25 + 5	Dolan 12	Harkin 16 + 5	Platel 1 + 1	Wormull 19 + 1	Opinel 7 + 1	Watkins 5	El-Abd — + 1	Keehan — + 2	Robinson 8	Healy 1 + 3	Burton N 7	Gooding 6 + 1	Donovan 6	Burton S 4	*Match No.*
1	2	3	4	5	6	7		9	10[1]	11	12										8													1
1	2	3	4	5	6[1]	7	12	9	10[2]		8[3]	11	13	14																				2
1	2[1]	3	4	5	12	7	6	9		11		10		8																				3
1		3	4	5	6[1]	7[3]	2	9		11		8[2]	14	10	12	13																		4
		3	4	5		7	2	9	10[1]	11[2]	12		13	8	6		1																	5
		3	4[1]	5		7[2]	2	9[3]	10	11	13	12	14	8	6		1																	6
	2	3		5[1]		7	4	9		11[2]	13	8	12	10	6		1																	7
	2	3		5[3]		7		9	12	11[2]	13	8	14	4[1]	6	10	1																	8
	2	3		5		7		9[1]		12		8	11	6		4	1	10																9
	2	3		5[1]		7	6	9[2]	12		13	8	10	4		11	1																	10
	2	3		5		7	6	9[3]	12	14		4[1]	10[2]	8		11■	1		13															11
	2[1]	3		12		7[2]	6	9[3]	10	14	8	13	11	5			1		4															12
		3		5		7	6		10[1]	11	8	12	9[2]	4		13	1		2															13
		3	14	5[2]		7	4	9	13	11[3]		6[1]		8			1		10	2	12													14
		3	4	5[1]	13	7[2]		9[3]	12		14		10	2			1		11	8	6													15
		3	4[1]			7	6				11	13	9	2			1		12	5	8	10[2]												16
	2	3	4	7[3]		13	6[1]			11	8			12			1		14	5	10[2]		9											17
	2	3		5		12				13	10[2]		9	4			1		8	6	7[1]		11											18
	2[1]	3	4	5		13	6			9[2]	14		10[3]				1		12	7	8		11											19
	2	3		5[3]		12				11[2]	7	14	13	4			1		8[1]	6	9		10											20
	2	3	13	5[2]		12		14			11		9[3]	4[1]			1		7	6	8		10											21
	2	3	12	5			6	14		11[3]	8[2]		13				1		4	7	9		10[1]											22
	2	3	4	5		7		12		11[1]	8						1		9	6	10													23
	2	3	4	6				9		11	10						1		7	5	8													24
	2[1]	3	4[2]	5		13		9			7		10	12			1		11	6	8													25
		3		11		7	6[1]	9		13	8		10[3]	2			1		4		5[2]	14					12							26
	2		4	5			6	9					10				1		7		8[1]		12	3	11									27
	2	3	4[1]	5				9[2]		13			10				1		8		12		7	6	11									28
	2	3	14	5[1]	13		6■				10[3]		9	12			1		7[2]				8	11■	4									29
	2[1]	3		5[2]	6	7		9					10				1		11				8		4	13	12							30
	2	3		5			6	9					10[2]				1		11		12		8[1]		4			7	13					31
	2	3	4	5			6	9[2]			12		10				1		11				8					7[1]	13					32
		3	4	5									9	2			1				12		8	11[1]				7	10	6				33
	2[1]	3	4	11			6	9[3]			13		10[2]				1		12				8■					7	14	5				34
	2	3		11			6	9[2]		13	12						1		10		8[1]			4■							7	5		35
	2	3		11				9		12			10[1]				1		4		6		8					7				5		36
		3		11			6	9		12			10[1]				1		2		13		8					7[2]		5	4			37
1			4	11			6			12	8[1]		13						7				10	3						9[2]	2	5		38
1	12		4	11			6			14	8[3]		13						7				10[2]							5[1]	2	3	9	39
1	12	3	4	11							10[2]		13						6				8					7[1]			2	5	9	40
	2	3	4	11		12				14			10[3]				1						8[2]	13				7		5	6[1]		9	41
	2[2]	3		11		7	12			10[3]	14						1		8					4						5	13	6[1]	9	42

FA Cup

Fourth Qual	Dagenham & R	(a)	1-2

FA Trophy

Third Round	Worthing	(h)	3-2
Fourth Round	Cambridge C	(a)	3-3
		(h)	1-2

DAGENHAM & REDBRIDGE Conference

Ground: Victoria Road, Dagenham, Essex RM10 7XL.
Tel: (0208) 592 7194.
Year Formed: 1992.
Record Gate: 5,500 (1992 v Leyton Orient FA Cup First Round).
Nickname: Daggers.
Manager: John Still.
Secretary: Derek Almond.
Colours: Red shirts, white shorts, red stockings.

DAGENHAM & REDBRIDGE 2004–05 LEAGUE RECORD

Match No.	*Date*	*Venue*	*Opponents*	*Result*		*H/T Score*	*Lg. Pos.*	*Goalscorers*	*Attendance*
1	Aug 14	H	Stevenage Bor	W	3-1	0-0	—	Moore [55], Southam [76], Janney [85]	1706
2	17	A	Forest Green R	W	4-1	1-1	—	Moore 2 [30, 61], Flynn [49], Southam [80]	676
3	21	A	Burton Alb	W	3-1	1-0	1	Taylor [5], Janney [54], Mackail-Smith [76]	1221
4	28	H	Woking	D	1-1	1-0	1	Moore [24]	1512
5	30	A	Crawley T	L	0-2	0-0	6		2177
6	Sept 4	H	York C	L	0-3	0-1	9		1475
7	11	H	Accrington S	L	0-5	0-1	11		1165
8	18	A	Aldershot T	L	0-4	0-3	12		2748
9	21	A	Gravesend & N	L	1-2	0-1	—	Moore [66]	1545
10	25	H	Halifax T	W	4-2	0-1	14	Boot 2 [49, 90], Mackail-Smith [55], Bruce [69]	1122
11	Oct 2	A	Northwich Vic	D	2-2	1-1	15	Southam 2 [28, 61]	581
12	5	H	Hereford U	W	3-1	0-0	—	Mackail-Smith 2 [57, 90], Moore [64]	1417
13	9	A	Barnet	L	0-5	0-2	15		1894
14	16	H	Leigh RMI	W	2-0	0-0	12	Mackail-Smith 2 [47, 75]	1157
15	23	A	Farnborough T	L	1-2	0-1	15	Midson [79]	784
16	Nov 6	H	Scarborough	L	0-3	0-2	16		1186
17	20	A	Carlisle U	L	0-1	0-0	16		5962
18	27	H	Morecambe	W	2-1	1-1	15	Vickers [30], Mackail-Smith [53]	1101
19	Dec 4	A	Tamworth	W	4-0	0-0	11	Mackail-Smith [51], Smith A (og) [55], Cole [66], Southam [90]	1017
20	7	H	Exeter C	L	2-3	1-2	—	Mackail-Smith [22], Moore (pen) [59]	1234
21	11	H	Aldershot T	W	3-0	2-0	11	Flynn (pen) [28], Uddin [39], Moore [69]	1407
22	18	A	Accrington S	W	3-0	0-0	11	Goodwin [47], Moore [58], Harrold [65]	1131
23	28	A	Halifax T	D	2-2	2-0	13	Moore 2 [15, 36]	1934
24	Jan 1	A	Canvey Is	L	2-4	0-2	13	Sterling (og) [77], Leberl [78]	1309
25	8	H	Northwich Vic	L	2-3	1-1	13	Bruce [39], Moore (pen) [72]	1753
26	22	A	Hereford U	W	1-0	1-0	13	Uddin [35]	2510
27	29	H	Gravesend & N	W	5-0	2-0	13	Boot 2 [28, 83], Clark [45], Moore [66], Leberl [78]	1268
28	31	H	Canvey Is	W	3-1	0-0	—	Boot [49], Moore [61], Mackail-Smith [89]	1542
29	Feb 5	H	Farnborough T	D	0-0	0-0	11		1281
30	12	A	Scarborough	L	0-2	0-2	12		1358
31	19	H	Carlisle U	W	1-0	0-0	11	Bruce [68]	1684
32	Mar 5	H	Tamworth	D	0-0	0-0	11		1238
33	12	A	Morecambe	L	0-1	0-1	13		1253
34	19	H	Forest Green R	D	2-2	2-2	13	Southam [15], Moore (pen) [45]	1238
35	25	A	Stevenage Bor	L	0-1	0-1	13		2604
36	28	H	Crawley T	W	1-0	0-0	13	Moore [83]	1393
37	Apr 2	A	Woking	W	4-2	2-1	12	Moore 2 [6, 87], Southam 2 [27, 56]	2351
38	5	H	Burton Alb	W	3-1	0-1	—	Mackail-Smith [54], Leberl [58], Southam [64]	1136
39	12	A	Exeter C	D	1-1	0-1	—	Boot [90]	2730
40	16	A	York C	D	0-0	0-0	11		1933
41	19	A	Leigh RMI	W	1-0	1-0	—	Moore [29]	245
42	23	H	Barnet	W	2-0	1-0	11	Mackail-Smith [45], Southam [51]	1923

Final League Position: 11

GOALSCORERS

League (68): Moore 19 (3 pens), Mackail-Smith 12, Southam 10, Boot 6, Bruce 3, Leberl 3, Flynn 2 (1 pen), Janney 2, Uddin 2, Clark 1, Cole 1, Goodwin 1, Harrold 1, Midson 1, Taylor 1, Vickers 1, own goals 2.
FA Cup (3): Boot 1, Janney 1, Moore 1 (pen).
LDV Vans Trophy (1): Moore 1.
Trophy (1): Uddin 1.

Roberts 38	Goodwin 32 + 1	Vickers 27 + 3	Cole 20	Uddin 41 + 1	Leberl 35 + 1	Janney 21 + 4	Southam 41	Moore 38	Taylor 4 + 1	Flynn2 4 + 2	Mackail-Smith 30 + 10	Griffiths 17 + 1	Blackett 12 + 13	Hill 1 + 5	Boot 13 + 14	Midson 2 + 8	Baruwa — + 1	O'Reilly 3	Barton — + 2	Bruce 30 + 2	Foster 19	Brennan — + 1	Bastock 1	Douglas — + 5	Harrold 2 + 2	Clark 11 + 1	McGowen — + 1	Lettejallon — + 2	Baimass — + 1	Vaughan — + 1	Francis — + 1	Match No.
1	2	3	4	5	6	7	8	9^{1}	10	11	12																					1
1	2	3	4	5	6	7	8	9	10^{2}	11^{1}	13	12																				2
1	2	3■	4	5	6	7^{1}	8	9	10^{3}	11^{2}	14		12	13																		3
1	2		4■	5	6	7	8	9	10^{2}	11^{1}	13		3		12																	4
1	2^{1}	4		5	6^{2}	7	8	9	14	11^{3}	10		3	12	13																	5
1	2	4		5	6^{2}	7	8^{1}	9		11^{3}	13		3	14	12	10																6
1■	2	3		5	6	7	8	9					4^{G}	11	10		15															7
	2	3■	4	5	6	7	8	9		11	12					10^{1}		1														8
	2^{1}		4	5	6	7^{2}	8	9		11^{3}	14		3		10			1	12	13												9
	2		4	5	6	13	8	9		3	10^{1}			12	7			1		11^{2}												10
1			4	5	6	14	8^{1}	9^{3}		3	10		13	12	7					11^{2}	2											11
1		3	4^{1}	5		7	8	9		6	10								12	11	2											12
1		6	4	5		7	8	9		3	10									11	2											13
1		4	2	5	6	7	8	9^{1}		3	10				12					11												14
1■		4	2	5	6	7^{1}	8			3	10				9^{2}	12				11		13										15
	12	4	2	5	6	7	8			3	10		11^{1}		9^{2}								1	13								16
1	2	3	4	5	6■	7^{1}	8	9		11	10													12								17
1	2	3	4	5		7	8	9^{3}		6	10^{1}		14		12					11^{2}				13								18
1	2		4	5	6	7	8	9^{3}		3	10^{2}		12		13					11^{1}				14								19
1	2		4	5	6	7	8	9^{2}		3	10				12					11^{1}				13								20
1	2	5^{1}	4	12	6	7	8	9		3	10		13							11^{2}												21
1	2		4	5	6	7	8	9^{1}		3	10^{2}		12							11					13							22
1	2	4		5	6	13	8	9		3^{1}	10^{2}		12							11					7							23
1	2	3	4^{1}	5	6	14	8	9			10		12							11^{2}					7^{3}	13						24
1	2	4		5	6	7^{1}		9			10	3			13					11^{2}					12	8						25
1	2^{1}	3		5			8	9			10^{3}	4^{2}	14		12					11	6					7	13					26
1		4		5	6^{1}		8^{2}	9				3	12		10					11	2					7		13				27
1		4		5	6		8	9			12	3	13		10^{1}					11^{2}	2					7						28
1		4		5	6		8				10	3	12		9					11^{1}	2					7						29
1	6	4		5			8	9			10^{2}	3	13							11	2					7^{1}			12			30
1	2			5			8	9			12	3	6		10^{1}					11	4					7						31
1	4	6■		5	13		8	9			10	3			12					11^{2}	2					7^{1}						32
1	4^{1}			5	6		8				10	3			9^{2}	13				11	2					7				12		33
1	4			5	6		8	9			10	3			12	13				11^{2}	2					7^{1}						34
1				5	6		8	9			10	3	4		12					11	2					7^{1}						35
1	2			5	6^{1}		8	9			10	4	3		7^{2}	12				11								13				36
1	2	12		5	6		8	9			10^{2}	3^{1}	4			13				11	7											37
1	2	12		5	6		8	9^{2}		14	10	3	4^{3}		13					11^{1}	7											38
1	2	12		5	6		8	9			10^{2}	3	4^{1}		13	14				11^{3}	7											39
1	2	3		5	6		8	9		11^{2}	14	4			10^{3}	13				12	7^{1}											40
1	2	3		5	6		8	9		4	10									11	7											41
1	2^{3}	3		5	6		8^{2}	9		14	10	4^{1}				12				11	7										13	42

FA Cup

Fourth Qual	Crawley T	(h)	2-1
First Round	Leyton Orient	(a)	1-3

LDV Vans Trophy

First Round	Cheltenham T	(a)	1-5

FA Trophy

Third Round	Bishop's Stortford	(h)	1-2

EXETER CITY — Conference

Ground: St James Park, Exeter EX4 6PX.
Tel: (01392) 411 243.
Year Formed: 1904.
Record Gate: 20,984 v Sunderland, FA Cup 6th rd (replay), 4 March 1931.
Nickname: The Grecians.
Manager: Alex Inglethorpe.
Secretary: Sally Cooke.
Colours: Red and white shirts, white shorts, white stockings.

EXETER CITY 2004–05 LEAGUE RECORD

Match No.	Date	Venue	Opponents	Result		H/T Score	Lg. Pos.	Goalscorers	Attendance
1	Aug 14	H	Morecambe	D	1-1	1-0	—	Devine 6	3449
2	17	A	Woking	D	3-3	1-0	—	Gaia 6, Edwards 55, Flack 90	2523
3	21	A	Northwich Vic	W	2-1	1-1	10	Gaia 43, Hiley 54	607
4	28	H	Canvey Is	L	0-1	0-1	14		2827
5	30	A	Farnborough T	L	1-2	1-1	14	Sheldon 17	1301
6	Sept 4	H	Crawley T	W	3-2	1-2	12	Sheldon 29, Smith (og) 70, Martin 73	2574
7	11	A	Scarborough	D	1-1	1-1	13	McConnell (pen) 39	1715
8	18	H	Stevenage Bor	W	2-0	1-0	9	Gaia 14, Flack 63	2716
9	21	A	Forest Green R	W	3-2	2-1	—	Gaia 19, Devine 23, McConnell 61	1191
10	25	H	Tamworth	D	2-2	1-1	9	Devine 28, McConnell (pen) 67	2664
11	Oct 2	A	Halifax T	L	1-2	0-0	9	Todd 48	1438
12	5	H	Barnet	L	0-3	0-0	—		3589
13	9	H	Carlisle U	D	0-0	0-0	14		2532
14	16	A	Gravesend & N	D	1-1	1-0	15	Gaia 22	1721
15	23	H	Aldershot T	W	3-1	2-0	12	Devine 17, Taylor 43, Gaia 48	3224
16	Nov 6	A	Accrington S	D	0-0	0-0	13		1464
17	20	H	Leigh RMI	W	5-1	1-0	10	Flack 17, Devine 54, Sawyer 80, Taylor 84, Edwards 90	3544
18	27	A	Burton Alb	L	0-1	0-1	11		1582
19	Dec 7	A	Dagenham & R	W	3-2	2-1	—	Gaia 9, Sheldon 14, O'Sullivan 81	1234
20	11	A	Stevenage Bor	L	2-3	2-1	13	Flack 2 44, 45	1907
21	18	H	Scarborough	W	3-1	0-1	13	Moxey 51, Flack 64, Devine (pen) 89	4529
22	26	H	Hereford U	W	4-0	2-0	8	Mawson (og) 12, Moxey 45, Devine 50, James (og) 60	4280
23	28	A	Tamworth	W	2-1	1-0	6	Ibe 22, Edwards 89	1808
24	Jan 1	A	Hereford U	W	2-1	1-0	4	Stansfield (og) 21, Taylor 71	3978
25	22	A	Barnet	L	0-1	0-1	9		3489
26	29	H	Forest Green R	W	2-0	1-0	8	Edwards 20, Moxey 49	3860
27	Feb 12	H	Accrington S	L	1-2	1-1	10	Edwards 24	4031
28	19	A	Leigh RMI	W	1-0	1-0	9	Devine 32	451
29	22	H	York C	L	0-1	0-0	—		2762
30	Mar 1	A	Aldershot T	L	1-2	0-1	—	Sawyer 90	2579
31	5	A	York C	W	2-1	1-1	9	Edwards 45, Phillips 63	2272
32	15	H	Burton Alb	W	3-1	0-1	—	Taylor 51, Flack 82, Devine 90	2418
33	19	H	Woking	D	0-0	0-0	8		3929
34	25	A	Morecambe	D	2-2	1-1	9	Phillips 40, Jeannin 53	2189
35	28	H	Farnborough T	W	2-1	1-1	9	Devine 20, Flack 77	4043
36	Apr 2	A	Canvey Is	D	2-2	0-1	9	Flack 66, Sterling (og) 81	921
37	5	H	Halifax T	W	2-1	2-1	—	Buckle 15, Taylor 35	3568
38	9	H	Northwich Vic	L	2-3	1-3	9	Devine 13, Flack 90	3950
39	12	H	Dagenham & R	D	1-1	1-0	—	Ampadu 11	2730
40	16	A	Crawley T	W	1-0	1-0	8	Sheldon 45	1989
41	19	H	Gravesend & N	W	3-0	0-0	—	Jeannin 47, Phillips 50, Flack 79	3947
42	23	A	Carlisle U	W	2-0	0-0	6	Flack 53, Phillips 64	6588

Final League Position: 6

GOALSCORERS

League (71): Flack 12, Devine 11 (1 pen), Gaia 7, Edwards 6, Taylor 5, Phillips 4, Sheldon 4, McConnell 3 (2 pens), Moxey 3, Jeannin 2, Sawyer 2, Ampadu 1, Buckle 1, Hiley 1, Ibe 1, Martin 1, O'Sullivan 1, Todd 1, own goals 5.
FA Cup (3): Edwards 1, Devine 1, Gaia 1.
LDV Vans Trophy (3): Edwards 1, Gaia 1, Jeannin 1.
Trophy (9): Devine 3 (1 pen), Edwards 2, Ampadu 1, Clay 1, Sheldon 1, Taylor 1.

Rice 15	Hiley 42	Jeannin 33	Taylor 39 + 2	Gaia 33	Todd 27	Sheldon 18 + 10	Ampadu 29 + 1	Edwards 22 + 12	Devine 25 + 12	Afful 33 + 6	Moxey 22 + 8	Flack 20 + 16	O'Sullivan 1 + 8	Bittner 5	Sawyer 27 + 5	Cronin 3 + 1	McConnell 5 + 5	Martin 9 + 12	Canham 1 + 1	Clay 9 + 4	Jones 22 + 1	Buckle 9 + 2	Ibe 2 + 2	Phillips 11 + 3	Tully — + 2	*Match No.*
1	2	3	4	5	6	7^{1}	8	9^{2}	10	11^{3}	12	13	14													1
	2^{1}		4	5	6	7^{2}		9^{3}	10	11	3	14		1	12	8	13									2
	2	3		5	6^{1}		8	9^{3}	10	7^{2}	11	14		1	12	4		13								3
	2	3	4	5		7	8^{2}	9^{3}	10	11	12	14		1	6^{1}			13								4
1	2	3	4^{2}	5^{1}		7	8	9^{3}	10	11	6	14					12	13								5
1	2^{1}		4	5	6	7	8	9^{3}	14	11^{2}	3	13					10	12								6
1	2		4^{2}	5^{1}	6	11^{3}	8	9	14	10	3				12		7	13								7
1	2		4	5	6	11^{1}	8	9^{3}	13	10^{2}	3	14					7	12								8
1	2		4	5	6		8	13	10^{2}	11^{1}	3	9					7	12								9
1	2		4	5^{1}	6				10	11	3	9	13		12		7^{2}	8								10
1	2		4	5	6		8		10^{3}	11	3^{1}	9	7^{2}		12				13	14						11
1	2		4^{1}	5	6		8	9^{2}	13	11	3	14	12						10^{3}	7						12
1	2	3	4	5	6		8	9^{2}	13	11^{1}		10^{3}					12	14		7						13
1	2	3	4	5	6		8	9^{1}	12	11^{2}	13	10					14			7^{3}						14
1	2	3	4	5	6		8^{2}	12	10^{1}	11^{3}		9				13	14			7						15
1	2^{1}	3	4	5			8		10	12	11	9			6	7^{2}				13						16
	2	3	4			12	8	13	10	11^{3}	6	9^{2}		1	5			14		7^{1}						17
	2^{2}	3	4^{3}	5		7	8	12	10	11^{1}	13	9		1	6					14						18
1■	2	3	12	5^{1}		7		8^{6}	10	11^{2}	6		13		4			9			15					19
	2^{1}	3	13			7		14	10^{3}	11^{2}	4	9	12		5			6		8	1					20
	2	3	4	5^{1}		7		13	10	12	11	9^{2}			6						1	8				21
	2	3	4^{1}	5		14		9^{2}	10	7	11^{3}		12		6						1	8	13			22
	2	3	4	5				12		11^{1}	13	9			6			7			1	8	10^{2}			23
1	2	3	4	5				13	10^{1}		11	9^{2}			6			7				8	12			24
	2	3	4	5				9^{1}	12	13	11^{2}	14			6			8		7	1		10^{3}			25
	2	3	4	5		13	8	9^{2}	10	7^{1}	11		12		6						1					26
	2	3	4	5			8^{2}	9	10	7	11^{1}	12			6			13			1					27
	2	3	4		5	12		9^{2}	10	7^{1}	11	13			6					8	1					28
	2	3	4		5	7	8^{1}		10	13	11^{2}	9^{3}			6			12			1			14		29
	2	3	4	5		12		13	10	11^{3}			14		6			8		7^{1}	1			9^{2}		30
	2	3	4		5	12	8	9^{2}	13	11^{1}		14			6			7			1			10^{3}		31
	2	3	4	5	6	12	8	9^{3}	14	7^{1}		13			11						1			10^{2}		32
	2	3	4	5	6	12	8	9^{2}	13	7^{1}		14			11						1			10^{3}		33
	2	3	4	5	6	12	8	9	13	11^{1}					7						1			10^{2}		34
	2	3	4	5	6	7^{1}	8	14	10^{3}	11		13									1			9^{2}	12	35
	2		4	5	6	7^{2}	8	10^{1}	14	11		12			3						1	13		9^{3}		36
	2	3^{2}	4	5	6		13		10^{3}	11^{1}		9			7			12			1	8		14		37
	2	3	4	5^{1}	6	12		13■	10^{3}	7^{2}		9			11						1	8		14		38
	2	3	4		6	7	8			12		9			5						1	11		10^{1}		39
	2	3	4		6	7^{1}	8^{2}				12	9^{3}			5			11■			1	13		10	14	40
	2	3	4		6	7^{2}	8^{1}			14	13	9^{3}			5					12	1	11		10		41
	2	3	4		6	7^{1}	8	13			12	9			5						1	11		10^{2}		42

FA Cup

Fourth Qual	Braintree T	(h)	2-0
First Round	Grimsby T	(h)	1-0
Second Round	Doncaster R	(h)	2-1
Third Round	Manchester U	(a)	0-0
		(h)	0-2

LDV Vans Trophy

First Round	Oxford U	(a)	2-2
Second Round	Swindon T	(h)	1-2

FA Trophy

Third Round	Billericay T	(a)	2-2
		(h)	2-0
Fourth Round	Tamworth	(a)	3-0
Fifth Round	Stamford	(a)	1-0
Sixth Round	Grays Ath	(a)	1-4

FARNBOROUGH TOWN Conference South

Ground: Cherrywood Road, Farnborough, Hampshire GU14 8UD.
Tel: (01252) 541 469.
Year Formed: 1967.
Record Gate: 3,581 (1995 v Brentford FA Cup First Round).
Nickname: The Boro.
Manager: Frank Gray.
Secretary: Vince Williams.
Colours: All red and white.

FARNBOROUGH TOWN 2004–05 LEAGUE RECORD

Match No.	Date	Venue	Opponents	Result		H/T Score	Lg. Pos.	Goalscorers	Attendance
1	Aug 14	A	Hereford U	L	1-3	0-0	—	Blackman 90	3644
2	17	H	Barnet	D	0-0	0-0	—		1069
3	21	H	Scarborough	L	0-1	0-1	20		633
4	28	A	Carlisle U	L	0-7	0-5	21		5505
5	30	H	Exeter C	W	2-1	1-1	17	Harkness 45, Townsend 90	1301
6	Sept 4	A	Tamworth	W	2-0	1-0	15	Blackman 8, Opinel 77	1150
7	11	H	Canvey Is	L	1-3	1-2	16	Blackman 18	748
8	18	A	Forest Green R	D	1-1	1-1	16	Blackman 14	665
9	21	H	Stevenage Bor	L	0-3	0-1	—		901
10	25	A	Morecambe	D	1-1	0-1	18	Hughes S 51	1287
11	Oct 2	H	Accrington S	W	2-1	1-0	18	Allen-Page 26, Taggart (pen) 55	706
12	5	A	Crawley T	L	0-2	0-1	—		2036
13	9	H	York C	D	1-1	1-0	18	Holloway G 14	724
14	16	A	Halifax T	L	0-2	0-0	19		1285
15	23	H	Dagenham & R	W	2-1	1-0	19	Taggart 2 (1 pen) 33, 90 (p)	784
16	Nov 6	A	Burton Alb	D	0-0	0-0	18		1238
17	20	H	Northwich Vic	L	0-2	0-1	18		884
18	27	A	Leigh RMI	W	2-1	1-0	18	Hughes S 32, Harkness 88	225
19	Dec 7	A	Gravesend & N	D	2-2	2-1	—	Harkness 2 7, 18	810
20	11	H	Forest Green R	D	1-1	1-1	17	Hughes S 27	647
21	18	A	Canvey Is	D	1-1	1-1	18	Opinel 8	509
22	26	A	Woking	L	0-2	0-2	18		3004
23	28	H	Morecambe	L	1-2	0-2	18	Pacquette 80	790
24	Jan 1	H	Woking	D	0-0	0-0	18		1730
25	8	A	Accrington S	L	1-2	1-1	19	Holloway G 22	1115
26	18	H	Aldershot T	L	1-2	0-1	—	Charles M 87	2369
27	22	H	Crawley T	L	2-3	0-0	19	Charles M 89, Eribenne (pen) 90	1020
28	29	A	Stevenage Bor	L	1-3	0-2	19	Traynor 72	1715
29	Feb 5	A	Dagenham & R	D	0-0	0-0	19		1281
30	12	H	Burton Alb	L	1-3	0-2	19	Charles M 82	698
31	19	A	Northwich Vic	L	0-2	0-0	20		628
32	26	H	Leigh RMI	L	0-1	0-0	20		501
33	Mar 5	A	Aldershot T	L	1-3	0-1	21	Taggart 64	4181
34	19	A	Barnet	L	1-7	1-4	21	Smith 6	2418
35	25	H	Hereford U	L	0-6	0-1	21		1059
36	28	A	Exeter C	L	1-2	1-1	21	Gibbs 11	4043
37	Apr 2	H	Carlisle U	L	1-2	0-1	21	Taggart (pen) 85	1061
38	9	A	Scarborough	L	0-4	0-2	21		1451
39	12	H	Gravesend & N	L	0-3	0-1	—		425
40	16	H	Tamworth	D	2-2	1-2	21	Blackman 16, Gibbs 74	510
41	19	H	Halifax T	W	3-2	1-2	—	Taggart 5, Johnson 2 50, 53	469
42	23	A	York C	L	0-4	0-1	21		2055

Final League Position: 21

GOALSCORERS

League (35): Taggart 6 (3 pens), Blackman 5, Harkness 4, Charles M 3, Hughes S 3, Gibbs 2, Holloway G 2, Johnson 2, Opinel 2, Allen-Page 1, Eribenne 1 (pen), Pacquette 1, Smith 1, Townsend 1, Traynor 1.
FA Cup (1): Hughes S 1.
Trophy (0).

Holloway C 30	Rooney 21 + 1	Townsend 12 + 2 Howe — + 2	Harkness 15 + 4	Charles A 15 + 2 Petterson 4	Theo 24 + 6	Mulhern 4 + 17	Holloway G 28	Hughes R 10 + 1 Fenton 8	Blackman 24 + 2	Taggart 38 + 3	Miles 22 + 7	Chabaan 5 + 9 Heeroo 2 + 4	Allen-Page 27 + 2	Belaid — + 1 Ashwood — + 1	Opinel 20 + 1	Hamilton 3 + 4	Riddell — + 3	Burton 21 + 1	Hughes S 18 + 3	Smith 26	Kightly 10 + 1	Deane 5 + 7	Pacquette 2 + 3	Osborn 7	Traynor 9 + 4	Charles M — + 11	Eribenne 4	Turner 9	Bernard 4	Canham 7 + 2	Braley 4	Johnson 8 + 4	Williams 1	Gibbs 9	Parker 3	Hemsley 2	Cole 1	*Match No.*
1	2	3	4[2]	5	6[1]	7	8	9	10	11	12	13																										1
1	2	3	13	5	6	7[1]	8	4	10	11		9[2]	12																									2
1	2	3	14	5	6[1]	13	8	4	10	11	12	9[3]	7[2]																									3
1	2	3	4[1]	5		13		6[3]	10	11	8	14	7[2]	12	9																							4
1	2	3	4	5		12		9	10	11[2]	6		7[1]		8	13																						5
1		3		5			8	4	10	11	6		7		2	9[1]	12																					6
1		2		5			8	6	10	11	4		7		3	9[1]	12																					7
1		2		5		12	8	6[2]	10[3]	11	4	14	7[1]		3	9		13																				8
1		2		5▮	12	13	8▮	4[2]	10	11	14	9[3]	7		3			6[1]																				9
1		2			6	13		4	9	11	8	14	7[2]		3		12	5[1]	10[3]																			10
1	12	3			6		8		9[1]	11	4		7		2			5▮	10																			11
1	2[1]	3	14		6		8	12	9[3]	11	5		7		4	13			10[2]																			12
1	2			5	6[1]		8		9	11	12		7		3			4	10																			13
1	2	12		5			8		9[2]	11	6	14	7[1]		3	13		4	10[3]																			14
1	2	12	13				8		9	11	5				3			6	10[2]	4	7[1]																	15
1	2				12		8		9[2]	11[3]	5[1]	13			3	14		6		7	10	4																16
1	2				13		8		14	11	5	10[3]			3[1]			4[2]	9	6	7	12																17
1	2		4	5[1]	12	13	8			11	6								9	7	10[2]	3																18
1			4[3]	5		12	8			11[1]	6		7		13			2	9[2]	10	3		14▮															19
1			4	12		13	8			11[3]	6		2		3			5	9[1]	7	10[2]	14																20
1			11	5			8			14	6		13		3			4[2]	9[3]	7	12	2[1]	10															21
1			10[3]		6	12	8			11		14	2		3			5	13	4	7[1]		9[2]															22
1			10[3]	5		12	8[2]			11		13	2		3			6	9	4	7[1]		14															23
1			10	12	6[1]	13	8			11			2		3			5	9[3]	4		7[2]	14															24
1			10		6		8			11	12	14	2[1]		3			5	9[3]	4	7[2]	13																25
1			4		6		8			11	12	9[3]	2[1]					5		3	7[2]	13			10	14												26
			4[2]		6	12	8			11			2					5		3		7[1]		1	10	13	9											27
			4[1]				8			11	6							5		7				1	10	12	9	2▮	3									28
			4[1]		6	12	8			11	5							2		10		13		1	7[2]				3	9								29
					6[1]	7				13	4									10		12		1	11	14			5[2]	9	2	8[3]	3					30
	2				12		8			11	6							5[1]		7[2]				1		14		3		4	10	13		9[3]				31
	2				6	14	8				4[1]							5				12		1	9			3	7	11[2]	10[3]	13						32
	2				6[1]	13				11[2]	12													1	7		9	3		8	10[3]	14			5	4		33
	8	12			13	7[1]			14	11[2]	6									4					10[3]		9	2							3▮	5▮	1	34
		12		1	6			5	10[2]	3		8							13	4					7	14		2[1]				11		9[3]				35
				1	6[1]			5	10	14		8	7						13	4						12		2				11[3]		9	3[2]			36
				1	6			5	10[3]	3		13	7							4					12	14		2[1]		8[2]		11		9				37
	2				6			5	10	3		12[2]	7	15						4					13					8[1]		11		9				38
1	2			1[G]	6			5	10[2]	11			7						8[3]	4[1]					12	14		3▮				13		9				39
1	2				6	13		5	11	3			7						10[2]	4					12							8[1]		9				40
1	2				6[1]			5	10[3]	3		14	7						8	4						13				12		11[2]		9				41
1	2[2]				6			5	10	3		13	7						8[3]	4						14				12		11[1]		9				42

FA Cup
Fourth Qual Barnet (a) 1-2

FA Trophy
Third Round Barnet (a) 0-1

FOREST GREEN ROVERS Conference

Ground: The Lawn, Nympsfield Road, Forest Green, Nailsworth GL6 0ET.
Tel: (01453) 834 860.
Year Formed: 1890.
Record Gate: 3,002 (1999 v St Albans City FA Umbro Trophy).
Nickname: Rovers.
Manager: Gary Owers.
Secretary: David Honeybill.
Colours: Black and white striped shirts, black shorts, red stockings.

FOREST GREEN ROVERS 2004–05 LEAGUE RECORD

Match No.	Date	Venue	Opponents	Result		H/T Score	Lg. Pos.	Goalscorers	Attendance
1	Aug 14	A	Barnet	L	1-3	1-0	—	Griffin [29]	1321
2	17	H	Dagenham & R	L	1-4	1-1	—	Griffin [3]	676
3	21	H	Carlisle U	L	0-3	0-1	22		1074
4	28	A	Tamworth	L	0-4	0-1	22		1101
5	30	H	Gravesend & N	L	1-5	0-2	22	Beesley [51]	517
6	Sept 4	A	Leigh RMI	L	0-2	0-1	22		305
7	11	A	Halifax T	L	0-4	0-1	22		1418
8	18	H	Farnborough T	D	1-1	1-1	22	Griffin [39]	665
9	21	H	Exeter C	L	2-3	1-2	—	Hodgson [14], Griffin (pen) [59]	1191
10	25	A	Crawley T	L	2-4	2-2	22	Griffin 2 [8, 26]	1943
11	Oct 2	H	Scarborough	L	0-1	0-0	21		686
12	5	A	Woking	W	1-0	1-0	—	Cleverley [44]	1643
13	9	A	Canvey Is	L	1-2	1-1	21	Gadsby [39]	356
14	16	H	Morecambe	L	0-3	0-1	21		614
15	23	H	Northwich Vic	L	1-3	0-3	21	Louis [62]	521
16	Nov 6	A	York C	W	3-1	2-0	20	Griffin 3 [2, 24, 62]	2132
17	20	H	Burton Alb	W	3-2	0-1	20	Gadsby [79], Griffin [83], Rogers [90]	622
18	27	A	Stevenage Bor	D	2-2	1-0	20	Beesley 2 [18, 49]	1804
19	Dec 4	H	Accrington S	W	1-0	0-0	20	Beesley [64]	691
20	7	A	Hereford U	L	1-2	1-2	—	Rogers [29]	2166
21	11	A	Farnborough T	D	1-1	1-1	20	Griffin [13]	647
22	18	H	Halifax T	D	0-0	0-0	20		613
23	26	A	Aldershot T	W	2-1	0-0	20	Alsop [60], Beesley [74]	2740
24	28	H	Crawley T	D	1-1	0-0	20	Williams (pen) [86]	956
25	Jan 1	H	Aldershot T	D	0-0	0-0	20		1240
26	8	A	Scarborough	D	0-0	0-0	20		1420
27	22	H	Woking	L	1-3	1-2	20	Griffin [34]	719
28	29	A	Exeter C	L	0-2	0-1	20		3860
29	Feb 5	H	Leigh RMI	D	1-1	0-0	20	Beesley [56]	449
30	12	H	York C	D	1-1	0-1	20	Griffin (pen) [73]	870
31	19	A	Burton Alb	L	1-4	1-3	21	Beesley [15]	1241
32	26	H	Stevenage Bor	D	1-1	0-1	21	Griffin (pen) [89]	622
33	Mar 5	A	Accrington S	D	2-2	0-0	20	Griffin [65], Beesley [73]	1412
34	19	A	Dagenham & R	D	2-2	2-2	20	Gadsby [4], Beesley [27]	1238
35	25	H	Barnet	L	0-2	0-0	20		1655
36	28	A	Gravesend & N	D	0-0	0-0	19		1196
37	Apr 2	H	Tamworth	D	1-1	0-1	22	Griffin (pen) [90]	844
38	5	A	Northwich Vic	L	1-2	1-2	—	Warhurst [24]	882
39	9	A	Carlisle U	W	1-0	0-0	20	Searle [63]	4640
40	12	H	Hereford U	L	1-3	0-1	—	Warhurst [62]	2142
41	19	A	Morecambe	L	1-3	0-1	—	Griffin [79]	2096
42	23	H	Canvey Is	D	2-2	1-1	20	Searle [34], Harris [89]	589

Final League Position: 20

GOALSCORERS

League (41): Griffin 17 (4 pens), Beesley 9, Gadsby 3, Rogers 2, Searle 2, Warhurst 2, Alsop 1, Cleverley 1, Harris 1, Hodgson 1, Louis 1, Williams 1 (pen).
FA Cup (7): Beesley 2, Louis 2, Griffin 1, Lyttle 1, Richardson 1.
Trophy (1): own goal 1.

Perrin 19	Green 7 + 6	Gadsby 36 + 2	Sykes6	Davies 27 + 2	Gould 4	Rogers 28 + 9	Cowe 5 + 1	Griffin 33 + 6	Beesley 25 + 7	Holloway 9 + 1	Danks 3 + 15	Cleverley 8 + 8	Brown, Marvin — + 4	Turner 1 / Harkin 5 + 1	Richardson 28 + 2	Brown, Matt — + 1	Betts 3	Hodgson 5 + 2 / Warhurst 6	Rushbury 2 + 1	Greaves 2 / Gill 2 + 4	Lyttle3 6	Roberts 16 + 3	Garner 24 + 2	Louis 7 + 1	Williams 27	Loxton 3	Reed 7	Appleby 4 + 3 / Haldane 6	Watson 4 + 3	Searle 26	Alsop 3	Alexis — + 2 / Davis — + 4	Beswetherick 8 + 2	Burns 2 + 1	Rapley 5	McAuley 8 + 2	Harris 12	*Match No.*
1	2^{1}	3	4	5	6	7^{2}	8^{3}	9	10	11	12	13	14																									1
1	2^{1}	3	4	5		7^{2}	8	9	10^{3}	11	14	13	12	6																								2
1		3	4^{3}		6	7	8^{1}	9	10	11^{2}	13	5	12		2	14																						3
1	12	3	4		6^{1}	13	8	9^{3}	10		14				5		2	7	11^{2}																			4
	2	3	4			7			10	11^{1}	9^{3}	12	14		5		6	8^{2}	13	1																		5
	2	3				13	12		10	11^{3}	9	8			5		6^{2}	14	7^{1}	1	4																	6
1	9	3	4		6^{2}	7^{1}	8		10^{3}	11	14	13			5			12			2																	7
1		3		5		7		9^{2}	10	11	13	12			6			8^{1}			2	4																8
1		3		5		7		9	10	11^{1}	12				4			8			2	6																9
1		3		5^{1}		7		9	12	11^{2}		14			4			8^{3}			2	6	13	10														10
		3		5		12		9^{2}	13			11			6						2	4	8	10	1	7^{1}												11
		3		5				9^{1}	12			11			6						2	7	4	10	1	8												12
		3		5^{1}		13		9	12			11			6						2	7	4	10	1	8^{2}												13
		3				12		9^{2}	13			11^{1}			5						2	7	4	10	1		6	8										14
						7		12	10			11^{1}			5						2	6	4	9	1		3	8										15
		3		14		7^{2}		9	10^{3}	12		13			5^{1}						2	8	4		1		6		11									16
		3				7		12	13												2	9	5	10	1		11	8^{2}	6^{1}	4								17
		3		5				9	10												2	7	4	12	1		11		8^{1}	6								18
		3		5		13		9	10^{3}		14										2	11^{2}	6		1		7	12	8^{1}	4								19
		3		5		7^{2}		9	10		14				13						2	8^{1}	4		1		11^{3}	12		6								20
1		3		5		7^{2}		9^{3}	10						13						2	8^{1}	4		11			14■	12	6								21
1		3		5		7		9^{1}	10						6						2	13	8		4				12^{2}	11								22
1		3^{1}		5		7		13	10^{2}						4						2		6		11				12	8	9							23
1		4				7		8^{1}	10		12				5						2		6		11					3	9							24
1				6		7		9^{2}			13				5						2	8^{1}	4		11					3	10■	12						25
1		3				7		9^{2}			13				5						2				11			8^{1}		10		12	6	4				26
1		3		5		7		9			10				4						2	12								6			11^{1}	8				27
1		3^{3}		5^{2}		7		9	14		13				6						2		4^{1}							8			11	12	10			28
1		12		5		7		9^{1}	10		13				6						2		4							3			11^{2}		8			29
1		3^{1}		5		7		9	10		12				6						2		4							11					8			30
		13		5		7^{1}		14	10						6						2	12^{2}			1					3			11^{3}		9	4	8	31
	12	3		14				9	10			13			5						2^{1}		4		1					11					8^{3}	6^{2}	7	32
		7		5^{1}				9	10						6						2		8		1					3			12			4	11	33
	12	3		5^{2}		14		9	10						4						2^{1}		6		1					11			13			8^{3}	7	34
	12	4^{2}		5^{3}		13		9	10						6						2^{1}		7		1					3		14				8	11	35
	11			10		7		9				5									2^{1}		4		1					3						8	6	36
	13			11^{3}		7^{2}		9						12				5		14	2		4^{1}		1			10		3						8	6	37
		4^{2}		5^{1}		12		9						11				7		13	2				1			10		3						8	6	38
	12	4		6		7^{1}		9						11				5		13	2				1			10^{2}		3							8	39
		4^{2}				7		9						11				5		12	2^{1}				1			10^{3}		6		14	3			13	8	40
		4				7^{2}		14						11				5		9	2^{1}				1			10^{3}		6		12	3			13	8	41
1	2	4						12						11^{2}				5		9		7^{1}	13					10^{3}		6		14	3				8	42

FA Cup

Fourth Qual	Thame U	(a)	5-0
First Round	Bournemouth	(h)	1-1
		(a)	1-3

FA Trophy

Third Round	Aylesbury U	(h)	1-2

GRAVESEND & NORTHFLEET Conference

Ground: Stonebridge Road, Northfleet, Kent DA11 9BA.
Tel: (01474) 533 796.
Year Formed: 1946.
Record Gate: 12,036 (1963 v Sunderland FA Cup Fourth Round).
Nickname: The Fleet.
Manager: Liam Daish.
Secretary: Roly Edwards.
Colours: Red shirts, white shorts, red stockings.

GRAVESEND & NORTHFLEET 2004–05 LEAGUE RECORD

Match No.	Date	Venue	Opponents	Result	H/T Score	Lg. Pos.	Goalscorers	Attendance
1	Aug 14	H	Northwich Vic	D 2-2	1-0	—	Jackson [12], Moore [86]	1064
2	17	A	Canvey Is	D 1-1	1-0	—	Essandoh [14]	1223
3	21	A	Morecambe	W 3-1	1-0	9	Saunders 2 [31, 77], Omoyinmi [61]	1473
4	28	H	York C	W 4-0	2-0	6	Omoyinmi [29], Louis [44], Skinner (pen) [54], Davis (og) [77]	1350
5	30	A	Forest Green R	W 5-1	2-0	4	Drury 2 [28, 66], Skinner (pen) [34], Essandoh [61], Louis [90]	517
6	Sept 4	H	Stevenage Bor	W 2-1	0-1	3	Sidibe 2 [75, 88]	1756
7	11	H	Hereford U	L 1-2	1-0	4	Lovell [44]	1678
8	18	A	Barnet	L 1-4	0-3	7	Omoyinmi [88]	2235
9	21	H	Dagenham & R	W 2-1	1-0	—	McKimm [27], Omoyinmi [49]	1545
10	25	A	Accrington S	W 2-1	1-0	4	Essandoh [45], Omoyinmi [51]	1426
11	Oct 2	H	Leigh RMI	W 4-1	0-0	3	Protheroe [53], Essandoh 2 [55, 65], McKimm [75]	1340
12	5	A	Aldershot T	L 0-1	0-0	—		2486
13	9	A	Burton Alb	L 2-3	1-2	4	Drury [45], Protheroe [78]	943
14	16	H	Exeter C	D 1-1	0-1	4	Essandoh [71]	1721
15	23	A	Halifax T	L 0-1	0-0	5		1410
16	Nov 6	H	Carlisle U	L 1-3	1-2	9	Pinnock [35]	2030
17	20	A	Tamworth	L 1-2	0-1	11	Saunders [90]	1984
18	27	H	Woking	D 1-1	0-0	10	Skinner (pen) [69]	1189
19	Dec 4	A	Scarborough	L 0-1	0-0	12		1634
20	7	H	Farnborough T	D 2-2	1-2	—	Moore [41], Omoyinmi [77]	810
21	11	H	Barnet	L 1-3	1-0	15	Yakubu (og) [15]	1707
22	18	A	Hereford U	L 0-1	0-0	15		2416
23	26	A	Crawley T	D 1-1	1-1	15	McAllister [2]	1863
24	28	H	Accrington S	D 2-2	1-2	15	Saunders [33], McAllister (pen) [82]	1372
25	Jan 1	H	Crawley T	D 0-0	0-0	14		1496
26	8	A	Leigh RMI	W 1-0	1-0	14	Drury [38]	251
27	22	H	Aldershot T	L 1-3	0-1	14	Saunders [59]	1491
28	29	A	Dagenham & R	L 0-5	0-2	14		1268
29	Feb 12	A	Carlisle U	D 2-2	0-2	15	Lovell [66], Saunders [75]	5284
30	19	H	Tamworth	W 2-0	1-0	15	McCarthy [43], Essandoh [55]	1042
31	Mar 5	H	Scarborough	W 4-0	2-0	14	Sigere [24], Saunders [27], Pinnock [57], Jackson [76]	1178
32	8	H	Halifax T	L 0-3	0-2	—		716
33	19	H	Canvey Is	W 3-2	2-1	14	Drury [2], Skinner (pen) [33], Bunce [70]	1224
34	25	A	Northwich Vic	W 2-1	1-1	14	Skinner (pen) [36], McCarthy (og) [55]	919
35	28	H	Forest Green R	D 0-0	0-0	14		1196
36	Apr 2	A	York C	D 0-0	0-0	14		2090
37	9	H	Morecambe	L 1-2	1-2	15	Protheroe [39]	987
38	12	A	Farnborough T	W 3-0	1-0	—	Drury [3], Essandoh 2 [60, 88]	425
39	14	A	Woking	L 0-2	0-2	—		1557
40	16	A	Stevenage Bor	L 0-2	0-0	14		2008
41	19	A	Exeter C	L 0-3	0-0	—		3947
42	23	H	Burton Alb	L 0-2	0-0	14		1169

Final League Position: 14

GOALSCORERS

League (58): Essandoh 9, Saunders 7, Drury 6, Omoyinmi 6, Skinner 5 (5 pens), Protheroe 3, Jackson 2, Louis 2, Lovell 2, McAllister 2 (1 pen), McKimm 2, Moore 2, Pinnock 2, Sidibe 2, Bunce 1, McCarthy 1, Sigere 1, own goals 3.
FA Cup (2): Saunders 1, Skinner 1 (pen).
Trophy (9): Omoyinmi 4, Jackson 2, Saunders 2, McCarthy 1.

Wilkerson 24	Gledhill 21 + 2	Jackson 19 + 9	Surey 28 + 3	Moore 19 + 4	Porter 20 + 1	Drury 35 + 3	McKimm 34 + 1	Omoyinmi 21 + 2	Essandoh 31 + 5	Rouse —	Sidibe 10 + 16	Pinnock 14 + 17	Saunders 36	Skinner 33	Protheroe 28 + 3	Louis 3 + 2	Shearer 4 + 1	Lovell 15 + 8	Mitten 1	Bouadji 2	Davis — + 2	Popovic 5	McCarthy 13	Pullen 17	Peters — + 1	McAllister 5	Bunce 10	Harrhy — + 1	Sigere 11	Anselin — + 1	Deane 3 + 2	Groombridge — + 1	*Match No.*
1	2	3	4	5	6	7^1	8	9	10		12■							11															1
1	2	12	4	5	6	7^2	8	9^1	10			13	3					11■															2
1	2		4	5	6	7^1	8	9^2	10		12	13	11	3																			3
1	2^1		4	5	6	7^2	8	9	14		12		11	3	13	10^3																	4
1	12		4	5	6^1	7	8	9^2	10				11	3	2	13																	5
1			4^3	5		7	8	9^2	12		14	13	11	3	2	10^1	6																6
1			4^1	5		7^2	8	9^3	10		13	12	3		2	14	6	11															7
		12^2	4	5■		7	8	14	10^3		13		11		2	9	6^1	3	1														8
1		11	4				8	9	10		7		6	3	2					5													9
1		12	4	5		13	8	9	10		7^2		11	3	2					6^1													10
1		11	4	5		12	8	9	10^2		7^1	13	6	3	2																		11
1		11	4	5		12	8	9	10^2		7^1		6■	3	2		13																12
1		11^1	4^2	5	6	7		9	10		8	13		3	2						12												13
1			4^3		6	7^2	8	9	10		14	12	11	3	2^1		5	13															14
1			4^3	5	6^1		8	9	10		7	14	11	3^2	2			13			12												15
1	2		4	5		7		12	10		13	9	6	3^1	8			11^2															16
1				5		7	8		10^1		12	9	4	3	2			11				6											17
1						7	8		10		11	9	4	3	2							5	6										18
1	12		4^3	13		7	8	9				10	11	3	2^1			14				5^2	6										19
	2			5		7	8^1	9			11	10	4	3	12								6	1									20
	2			5		7	8	9^1	10		11	13	4	3									6	1	12^2								21
	2	6^1		5		7	8		10		12		4					11					3	1		9							22
	2^1	3		5		7	8	9^2	13				4		12			11					6	1		10							23
		11^3		12		7	8		10		13	14	4	3^2	2							5	6^1	1		9							24
						7	8		10		11	12	4	3	2							5		1		9^1	6						25
		11				7	8		10			12	4	3	2								6	1		9^1	5						26
	2	12	4					9	10^3		13	11^2	8	3	7^1								6	1			5	14					27
		11	4		5		8^1		10		12	9	7	3	2								6	1									28
		11^2			5	7^1	8	9	10		12		4	3	2			13					6	1									29
		12			5	7^1	8	9	10		13		4	3	2			11^2					6	1									30
	5	13	12			7	8^1				14	9	4	3	2			11^2					6	1					10^3				31
	5	11	4			7^1						9	8	3	2			12						1			6		10				32
	2	11	4		5^1	7	8		10^2			12		3										1			6		9	13			33
1	2	11	4		6	7	8		12			9^1		3													5		10				34
1	2	12	4		6	7	8		13			9^2		3				11^1									5		10				35
1	2	13	12		6	7	8		9^3			14	4^1	3				11^2									5		10				36
1		11	13		6	7	8		9^3			14	4	3^1	2			12^2									5		10				37
1	6	3^1	4		13	7^3	12		10			9	8		2			11									5^2				14		38
1	6	3^1	4		5	7	8^2		9			12			2			11											10		13		39
	6	3^1	4		5	7						9	8		2■			12						1					10		11		40
	2	13	4	14	6	7^2			9^3			12	8	3				11^1						1					10		5		41
	2^1	11^2	4	14	6	7						9^3	8	3				13						1					10		5	12	42

FA Cup

Fourth Qual	Hornchurch	(a)	2-3

FA Trophy

Third Round	Eastbourne Borough	(h)	0-0
		(a)	1-0
Fourth Round	Histon	(h)	2-1
Fifth Round	Sutton U	(h)	3-2
Sixth Round	Bishop's Stortford	(a)	1-1
		(h)	2-3

HALIFAX TOWN Conference

Ground: The Shay Stadium, Shay Syke, Halifax, West Yorkshire HX1 2YS.
Tel: (01422) 341 222.
Year Formed: 1911.
Record Gate: 36,885 (1953 v Tottenham Hotspur FA Cup Fifth Round).
Nickname: The Shaymen.
Manager: Chris Wilder
Secretary: Jenna Helliwell.
Colours: All blue.

HALIFAX TOWN 2004–05 LEAGUE RECORD

Match No.	Date	Venue	Opponents	Result	H/T Score	Lg. Pos.	Goalscorers	Attendance
1	Aug 14	A	Tamworth	L 1-2	1-2	—	Foster 6	1325
2	17	H	Scarborough	W 2-1	1-0	—	Monington 11, Midgley (pen) 82	1887
3	21	H	Barnet	L 2-3	2-0	15	Howell 25, Monington 35	1382
4	28	A	Leigh RMI	W 3-0	1-0	12	Monington 23, Killeen 74, Midgley 88	575
5	31	H	Carlisle U	D 2-2	0-0	—	Monington 72, Bushell 86	2696
6	Sept 4	A	Hereford U	W 3-2	3-1	8	Killeen 3, Sugden 35, Bushell 40	3022
7	11	H	Forest Green R	W 4-0	1-0	5	Mansaram 9, Sugden 2 50, 62, Killeen 75	1418
8	18	A	Canvey Is	W 1-0	1-0	4	Mansaram 45	789
9	21	H	Morecambe	L 1-3	1-2	—	Stoneman 28	1667
10	25	A	Dagenham & R	L 2-4	1-0	8	Killeen 2 32, 53	1122
11	Oct 2	H	Exeter C	W 2-1	0-0	7	Mansaram 47, Howell (pen) 72	1438
12	8	A	Woking	L 1-2	1-0	—	Quinn 8	1864
13	12	A	Burton Alb	D 2-2	2-1	—	Howell 10, Mallon 19	1194
14	16	H	Farnborough T	W 2-0	0-0	7	Quinn 59, Mansaram 68	1285
15	23	H	Gravesend & N	W 1-0	0-0	4	Mallon 46	1410
16	Nov 6	A	Stevenage Bor	L 1-2	0-1	6	Sugden 58	1820
17	20	H	Aldershot T	W 2-0	1-0	3	Sugden 5, Killeen 71	1724
18	27	A	Northwich Vic	W 2-1	0-0	3	Quinn 70, Killeen 83	1272
19	Dec 7	A	York C	D 1-1	0-0	—	Killeen 85	2394
20	11	H	Canvey Is	W 4-1	3-0	3	Midgley 2 23, 88, Ross 27, Foster 35	1522
21	18	A	Forest Green R	D 0-0	0-0	4		613
22	28	H	Dagenham & R	D 2-2	0-2	5	Midgley (pen) 78, Ross 83	1934
23	Jan 3	H	Accrington S	L 1-2	1-1	—	Howell 37	2472
24	11	H	Crawley T	W 1-0	1-0	—	Ross (pen) 38	1267
25	25	H	Burton Alb	W 2-0	0-0	—	Mansaram 71, Sugden 80	1256
26	29	A	Morecambe	L 1-2	0-0	5	Midgley (pen) 89	1910
27	Feb 12	H	Stevenage Bor	W 2-1	1-0	4	Midgley (pen) 22, Howell 52	1497
28	19	A	Aldershot T	D 0-0	0-0	6		2903
29	22	A	Accrington S	D 1-1	0-0	—	Sugden 60	1402
30	26	H	Northwich Vic	D 2-2	1-1	4	Midgley 11, Mansaram 72	1636
31	Mar 5	A	Crawley T	W 2-1	1-0	3	Foster 15, Midgley (pen) 82	1957
32	8	A	Gravesend & N	W 3-0	2-0	—	Foster 4, Howell 36, Killeen 89	716
33	14	H	York C	W 2-0	0-0	—	Groves (og) 57, Meechan 84	2165
34	19	A	Scarborough	L 1-3	0-0	2	Ross (pen) 89	2109
35	25	H	Tamworth	D 3-3	2-2	3	Young 39, Sugden 45, Midgley 56	1998
36	28	A	Carlisle U	L 0-1	0-0	4		5474
37	Apr 2	H	Leigh RMI	W 5-1	0-1	3	Sugden 49, Midgley 70, Killeen 71, Chin 88, Ingram 90	1704
38	5	A	Exeter C	L 1-2	1-2	—	Killeen 20	3568
39	9	A	Barnet	L 1-3	1-1	5	Killeen 11	3924
40	16	H	Hereford U	L 0-1	0-0	9		2343
41	19	A	Farnborough T	L 2-3	2-1	—	Young 4, Grant 40	469
42	23	H	Woking	W 3-1	0-0	9	Blunt 63, Sugden 2 74, 76	1398

Final League Position: 9

GOALSCORERS

League (74): Killeen 12, Midgley 11 (5 pens), Sugden 11, Howell 6 (1 pen), Mansaram 6, Foster 4, Monington 4, Ross 4 (2 pens), Quinn 3, Bushell 2, Mallon 2, Young 2, Blunt 1, Chin 1, Grant 1, Ingram 1, Meechan 1, Stoneman 1, own goal 1.
FA Cup (6): Midgley 3 (1 pen), Ross 2, Bushell 1, Foster 1.
Trophy (0).

Dunbavin 39	Ingram 37	Hockenhul 15 + 2	Bushell 24	Quinn 37 + 2	Munroe 5 + 1	Doughty 28	Foster 33 + 2	Killeen 28 + 11	Sugden 38 + 1	Haslam 32	Monington 5 + 4	Howell 26 + 8	Mallon 4 + 10	Willis 2	Midgley 30 + 9	Toulson — + 1	Mansaram 12 + 6	Stoneman 10 + 6	Senior 3 + 1	Sanasy — + 2	McStay 7 + 1	Blunt 22 + 4	Farrell — + 1	Meechan 4 + 5	Ross 4 + 9	Chin 2 + 7	Clarke 3 + 1	McClare 1	Naylor — + 1	Young1 2 + 1	Parry 1 + 1	Salisbury 2	Grant 6 + 2	*Match No.*
1	2	3^1	4	5	6^2	7	8	9^3	10	11▮	12	13	14																					1
1	2	3^1	4^2	5	13	7	8	14	10^3		6	12		9	11																			2
1	2	12			6	7	8	13	10^2	4	5	3		11^1	9^3	14																		3
1	2		4		6	7	8	9	10		5	3			11																			4
1	2	3^1	4	12	6	7		9	10^2		5	8	13		11																			5
1	2	13	4	12	6^1	7	8^2	9	10		5	3^3			11		14																	6
1	2^1	3	4^3	5		7	8	9^2	10				13		11		6	12	14															7
1	2	3^1		5		7	8	9	10			13			11^2		6	12	4															8
1	2			5▮		7	8	9^2	10			13	12		11		6	4	3^1															9
1	2					7	8	9	10			6^1	13				11^2	4		12	5	3												10
1	2			5		7		9^1	10	11		6	12		13		8^2				4	3												11
1	2			5		7		9▮	10^3	11		6^2	8^1		13		14	12	4			3												12
1	2			5		7			10	11		6^1	9		13		8^2			12	4	3												13
1	2			5		7^1		12	10	11		6	9^2		13		8				4	3												14
1	2			5		7		13	10^1	11		6	9		12		8^2				4	3												15
1	2▮		4	5		7	14	9	10	6		8^3			11^1			12				3^2	13											16
1			4	5		7	8	9^3	10^2	11		3	12		2^1			6						14	13									17
1				5		7	8	9	10^2	11			12		13			6				3		4		2^1								18
1	2		4	5		7	13	14		11		8	12		3							6^1		10^3	9^2									19
1	2^1		4	5		7	8			11			13		3			12				6^2		10	9^3	14								20
1	2			5		7	8	9		11		12			3			6^1				4		10^2		13								21
1	2		4	5		7	8	13	10^2	9		6			11							3^1			12									22
1	2		4	5		7	3	9	13	11		8			10^1									12	6^2									23
1	2		4	5		7	8	9	10	11												3		12	6^1									24
1	2		4^1	5		7	8	9	10^3	11		12			14		6^2					3			13									25
1	2			5		7^2	8	9	10			13			12		6^3					3			14	11^1	4							26
1	2			5		7		9	10	11	13	8^2			3			6								12		4^1						27
1			4	5		7^1	8	9	10	2	13	6^2			11			3											12					28
1	2		4	5			8	9^2	10	11		7			3^1		13	6				12												29
1	2		4	5			8	9	10^3	11		7^2			3		12	6^1				13								14				30
1	2		4	5			8	12	10^1	11		7			3		9^2								13					6				31
	2		4	5			8	14	10	11		7^2			6^1		9^3					12			13					3	1			32
	2		4	5			8	9^2	10	11		7			3^1									13		12				6		1		33
	2▮		4	5			8	9^2	10	11		7			3^1							12			13					6	15	1^{G}		34
1			4	5			8	12	10	11		7			3			9^2							13					2			6^1	35
1				5			8		10^2	11		7			2^1							4			13	12	6			3			9	36
1	2			5			8	14	10	11		7^2			4						12	6				13				3^1			9^3	37
1	2		4	5			8	9^2	10						7		13				3	6^1								11			12	38
1	2		4^1	5			8	9^2	10^3	11					7		14					6					12			3			13▮	39
1	2			5			8	9	10	11^1	13	12			7^2							3								4			6	40
1	2			5			8	12	10	11^2					13						4^1	3					6			9			7	41
1	2^1			5			8	9	10^3	11					6			12				3		13		14				7			4^2	42

FA Cup

Fourth Qual	Leek T	(h)	2-2
		(a)	1-0
First Round	Cambridge U	(h)	3-1
Second Round	Chester C	(h)	1-3

FA Trophy

Third Round	Northwich Vic	(h)	0-1

HEREFORD UNITED — Conference

Ground: Edgar Street, Hereford, Herefordshire HR4 9JU.
Tel: (01432) 276 666.
Year Formed: 1924.
Record Gate: 18,114 (1958 v Sheffield Wednesday FA Cup Third Round).
Nickname: The Bulls.
Manager: Graham Turner.
Secretary: Joan Fennessy.
Colours: White and black shirts, black shorts, white stockings.

HEREFORD UNITED 2004–05 LEAGUE RECORD

Match No.	Date	Venue	Opponents	Result		H/T Score	Lg. Pos.	Goalscorers	Attendance
1	Aug 14	H	Farnborough T	W	3-1	0-0	0	James (pen) [48], Travis [51], Mills [84]	3644
2	17	A	Crawley T	D	1-1	1-0	—	Stansfield [42]	2570
3	21	A	York C	W	3-0	2-0	2	Williams D [13], Brown 2 [31, 49]	2602
4	28	H	Stevenage Bor	L	0-1	0-0	7		3616
5	30	A	Northwich Vic	W	4-1	2-1	5	Stansfield 2 [14, 17], Green [59], Brown [71]	1132
6	Sept 4	H	Halifax T	L	2-3	1-3	7	Stansfield [28], Ingram (og) [90]	3022
7	11	A	Gravesend & N	W	2-1	0-1	6	Tretton [53], Stanley [78]	1678
8	18	H	Scarborough	W	1-0	1-0	5	Brown [27]	2874
9	21	H	Aldershot T	W	2-0	1-0	—	Williams D [4], Mills [90]	3647
10	25	A	Leigh RMI	W	4-3	1-0	2	Mills 2 [7, 59], Stansfield 2 [82, 90]	585
11	Oct 2	H	Burton Alb	D	0-0	0-0	4		3320
12	5	A	Dagenham & R	L	1-3	0-0	—	Mills [47]	1417
13	11	A	Accrington S	L	1-2	1-1	—	Brown [28]	1481
14	16	H	Woking	D	2-2	2-0	5	Williams D [1], Stansfield [35]	2878
15	23	A	Carlisle U	L	1-3	1-2	6	Andrews (og) [23]	6772
16	Nov 6	H	Barnet	D	1-1	1-1	7	Brown [8]	3645
17	20	A	Canvey Is	W	4-0	2-0	4	Mills [13], Williams D [29], Stansfield 2 [79, 85]	921
18	27	H	Tamworth	W	2-1	2-1	4	Mkandawire [5], Mills [31]	2714
19	Dec 7	H	Forest Green R	W	2-1	2-1	—	Stanley [12], Stansfield [20]	2166
20	11	A	Scarborough	D	0-0	0-0	4		1608
21	18	H	Gravesend & N	W	1-0	0-0	3	Pitman [73]	2416
22	26	A	Exeter C	L	0-4	0-2	4		4280
23	28	H	Leigh RMI	W	3-0	2-0	3	Stanley [25], Pitman [40], Brown [50]	3014
24	Jan 1	H	Exeter C	L	1-2	0-1	3	Stansfield [66]	3978
25	8	A	Burton Alb	L	0-3	0-1	4		1589
26	22	H	Dagenham & R	L	0-1	0-1	8		2510
27	30	A	Aldershot T	W	2-0	0-0	6	Johnson (og) [62], Brown [90]	3799
28	Feb 12	A	Barnet	W	2-0	1-0	5	Carey-Bertram [33], Stansfield [90]	2668
29	19	H	Canvey Is	W	1-0	1-0	4	Williams D [38]	2656
30	Mar 5	H	Morecambe	D	1-1	1-1	8	Mkandawire [42]	2657
31	8	A	Tamworth	D	2-2	1-1	—	Williams D [33], Mkandawire [51]	1012
32	19	H	Crawley T	D	0-0	0-0	9		2211
33	22	A	Morecambe	L	1-2	0-0	—	Williams D [61]	1465
34	25	A	Farnborough T	W	6-0	1-0	8	Williams L [18], Carey-Bertram 2 (1 pen) [48 (p), 54], Stansfield 2 [80, 90], Purdie [87]	1059
35	28	H	Northwich Vic	W	4-0	3-0	7	Stansfield 2 [31, 41], Carey-Bertram [35], Mills [77]	2931
36	Apr 2	A	Stevenage Bor	W	1-0	0-0	5	Stansfield [55]	2614
37	5	H	Carlisle U	D	0-0	0-0	—		3819
38	9	H	York C	W	2-0	2-0	3	Purdie (pen) [3], Smith (og) [40]	2973
39	12	A	Forest Green R	W	3-1	1-0	—	Stansfield 2 [19, 49], Carey-Bertram [80]	2142
40	16	A	Halifax T	W	1-0	0-0	3	Mkandawire [52]	2343
41	19	A	Woking	D	1-1	0-0	—	Carey-Bertram [82]	3298
42	23	H	Accrington S	D	0-0	0-0	2		3738

Final League Position: 2

GOALSCORERS

League (68): Stansfield 19, Brown 8, Mills 8, Williams D 7, Carey-Bertram 6 (1 pen), Mkandawire 4, Stanley 3, Pitman 2, Purdie 2 (1 pen), Green 1, James 1 (pen), Travis 1, Tretton 1, Williams L 1, own goals 4.
FA Cup (7): Mills 2, Mkandawire 1, Purdie 1, Stanley 1, Stansfield 1, Travis 1.
LDV Vans Trophy (5): Carey-Bertram 1, Mills 1, Pitman 1, Stanley 1, Williams D 1.
Trophy (14): Carey-Bertram 4, James 2 (1 pen), Mkandawire 1, Purdie 1, Robinson 1, Smikie 1, Smith 1, Stanley 1, Stansfield 1, Williams D 1.
Play-offs (1): Carey-Bertram 1.

Gould 14	Travis 33 + 2	Robinson 34 + 2	Tretton 26 + 1	Mkandawire 33 + 1	James 29 + 1	Stanley 41	Pitman 30 + 2	Stansfield 30 + 9	Brown 23 + 6	Williams D 30 + 6	Smith 8 + 3	Mills 16 + 15	Purdie 22 + 9	Hyde 21 + 11	Green 20 + 6	Carey-Bertram 12 + 9	Scott 1	Mawson 27	Anyinsah 3	Smikle 3	Taylor 5	Williams L 1 + 4	Match No.
1	2	3	4	5	6	7	8^1	9^2	10	11^3	12	13	14										1
1	2	3	4	5	6	7^1	8	9^2	10^3	11		12	14	13									2
1	2	3	4	5	6	7	8	9	10^2	11^1		13		12									3
1		3	4	5	6	7	8^2	9^3	10	11^1		14	12	13	2								4
1	2		4	5	6	7	8	9	10	11					3								5
1	2		4	5^1	6	7	8^2	9	10	11		12		13	3								6
1	2		4		6	7	8	9^1	10	11	5	12			3								7
1	2	3	4		6	7	8^1	13	10^2	11	5	9		12									8
1	2	3	4		6	7	8^1		10	11	5	9		12									9
1	2	3	4	13	6	7		12	10^2	11^1	5	9		8									10
1	2	3	4	5■	13	7		9^2	14	11^1	6	10^3	12	8									11
1	2	3	4		6	7		12	10	11^1	5	9^2	13	8									12
1	2		4		6	7		12	10	11^1		9	8^2	3	5	13							13
1	2		4		6	7		9	10	11^1		12	8	3	5								14
	2	3	4	5		7	8	9	10	12			11		6^1		1						15
	2	3		5	6	7		9^2	10	11			8^1	4	12	13		1					16
	2	3		5	6	7^1	12	9	10	11		8		4				1					17
	2	3		5	6■	7		9^2	10^1	11	12	8	13	4				1					18
	2	3		5	6	7	8	9^3	10^1	11^2		12	4	13		14		1					19
	2	3		5	6	7	8	9	12			10^1	4	11				1					20
	2	3		5	6	7	8	9	10^2				4^1	11	12	13		1					21
	2	3		5	6	7	8	9^1	12				13	11^2	4	10		1					22
	2	3	12	5	6^1	7	8^2	9	10				4	11^3	13	14		1					23
	2	3		5	6	7^2	8	9	10				4^1	11	12	13		1					24
	2	3^1		5	6	7	8	9	10^3	13		14		11^2	4	12		1					25
	2	13			6	7	8	9^3	10	11^2	5	12	14		3^1			1	4				26
	2	3		5	6	7	8		12	11	13		4^1			9^2		1	10				27
	2	3		5	6	7	8	14	12	11^1			10^3		13	9^2		1	4				28
	2	3		5	6	7	8^1	9^2	13	11			4	12		10		1					29
	2	3		5	6	7				11^1		12	8	4		10		1		9			30
	2^1	3		5	6	7		13		11		9		4	12	10		1		8^2			31
	2		4	5		7	8^1	12		11		13	10	6^2	3	9		1					32
	2	12	4			7	8	13		11	3	10^2		6	5^1	9		1					33
	2	3	4	5		7	8	13		11^1			12			9^2		1			6	10■	34
		3	4	5		7^2	8^1	9^3		13		14	11	12	2	10■		1			6		35
		3	4	5		7	8	9		12		10	11		2			1			6^1		36
		3	4	5		7	8	9		12		10	11		2			1			6^1		37
		3	4	5		7	8^2	9		12		10^3	11	13	2			1			6^1	14	38
		3	4	5		7	8^1	9^3		11		10^2	6	12	2	13		1				14	39
	12	3	4	5		7		9		11^1		10^2	8	6	2	13		1					40
	12	3	4	5			8	9^3				14	6	7	2	10^2		1		11^1		13	41
		3	4	5		7	12	9^2		11		14	8	6^1	2	10^3		1				13	42

FA Cup

Fourth Qual	Radcliffe B	(h)	2-1
First Round	Southport	(a)	3-1
Second Round	Boston U	(h)	2-3

LDV Vans Trophy

First Round	Scunthorpe U	(h)	1-1
Second Round	Doncaster R	(h)	1-1
Quarter-Final	Blackpool	(h)	2-1
Semi-Final	Wrexham	(h)	1-2

FA Trophy

Third Round	Accrington S	(a)	0-0
		(h)	4-0
Fourth Round	Hyde U	(h)	3-0
Fifth Round	Eastwood T	(a)	1-1
		(h)	4-2
Sixth Round	Hucknall T	(h)	2-2
		(a)	0-1

Play-offs

Semi-Final	Stevenage B	(a)	1-1
		(h)	0-1

LEIGH RMI Conference North

Ground: Hilton Park, Kirkhall Lane, Leigh, Lancashire WN7 1RN.
Tel: (01942) 743 743.
Year Formed: 1896.
Record Gate: 7,125 (1999 v Fulham FA Cup Third Round) (at Horwich 8,500 1954 v Wigan Athletic).
Nickname: Railwaymen.
Secretary: Alan Robinson.
Colours: Red and white shirts, black shorts, white stockings.

LEIGH RMI 2004–05 LEAGUE RECORD

Match No.	Date	Venue	Opponents	Result		H/T Score	Lg. Pos.	Goalscorers	Attendance
1	Aug 14	H	Crawley T	L	1-2	1-0	—	Gaunt 15	401
2	17	A	Burton Alb	D	0-0	0-0	—		1305
3	21	A	Woking	L	0-1	0-0	18		1499
4	28	H	Halifax T	L	0-3	0-1	19		575
5	30	A	Morecambe	L	1-2	0-1	20	Meechan 51	1382
6	Sept 4	H	Forest Green R	W	2-0	1-0	19	Simms 3, Fitzpatrick 68	305
7	11	H	Aldershot T	D	3-3	1-0	19	Byrne 2 32, 68, Rose 82	464
8	18	A	Accrington S	L	1-2	0-1	20	Byrne 90	1507
9	21	A	York C	D	1-1	0-0	—	Miller 90	1708
10	25	H	Hereford U	L	3-4	0-1	20	Peyton 54, Stoker 61, Smith S 89	585
11	Oct 2	A	Gravesend & N	L	1-4	0-0	20	Williams 86	1340
12	5	H	Carlisle U	L	1-6	1-1	—	Stoker 34	1540
13	9	H	Stevenage Bor	L	1-2	0-1	20	Stoker 59	235
14	16	A	Dagenham & R	L	0-2	0-0	20		1157
15	23	A	Canvey Is	L	0-3	0-1	20		532
16	Nov 6	H	Tamworth	L	2-3	2-0	22	Connell 8, Williams 26	338
17	20	A	Exeter C	L	1-5	0-1	22	Simms 75	3544
18	27	H	Farnborough T	L	1-2	0-1	22	Stoker 57	225
19	Dec 4	A	Barnet	L	2-3	2-1	22	Rose 15, Stoker 21	1961
20	7	H	Scarborough	D	1-1	0-1	—	Williams 90	325
21	11	H	Accrington S	L	0-6	0-4	22		402
22	18	A	Aldershot T	L	0-2	0-1	22		2312
23	28	A	Hereford U	L	0-3	0-2	22		3014
24	Jan 8	H	Gravesend & N	L	0-1	0-1	22		251
25	29	H	York C	L	0-3	0-0	22		701
26	Feb 5	A	Forest Green R	D	1-1	0-0	22	Taylor 85	449
27	15	H	Northwich Vic	L	0-1	0-0	—		402
28	19	H	Exeter C	L	0-1	0-1	22		451
29	22	A	Tamworth	W	1-0	0-0	—	Peers 90	902
30	26	A	Farnborough T	W	1-0	0-0	22	Williams 60	501
31	Mar 5	H	Barnet	L	0-3	0-1	22		402
32	8	A	Carlisle U	L	0-3	0-1	—		3047
33	12	A	Scarborough	L	0-3	0-1	22		1219
34	19	H	Burton Alb	L	1-4	1-1	22	Lane 8	325
35	25	A	Crawley T	D	2-2	0-1	22	Williams 70, Mulvaney 77	1831
36	28	H	Morecambe	L	0-2	0-1	22		541
37	Apr 2	A	Halifax T	L	1-5	1-0	22	Allen 43	1704
38	5	H	Canvey Is	W	2-1	2-1	—	Mulvaney 9, Jones 28	201
39	9	H	Woking	L	0-3	0-1	22		215
40	12	A	Northwich Vic	L	0-2	0-0	—		734
41	19	H	Dagenham & R	L	0-1	0-1	—		245
42	23	A	Stevenage Bor	L	0-2	0-1	22		3516

Final League Position: 22

GOALSCORERS

League (31): Stoker 5, Williams 5, Byrne 3, Mulvaney 2, Rose 2, Simms 2, Allen 1, Connell 1, Fitzpatrick 1, Gaunt 1, Jones 1, Lane 1, Meechan 1, Miller 1, Peers 1, Peyton 1, Smith S 1, Taylor 1.
FA Cup (3): Simms 2, Rose 1 (pen).
LDV Vans Trophy (0).
Trophy (1): Reed 1.

Martin 17	Lane 39	Miller 18 / Taylor 2 + 6	Holmes 10 + 1 / Reed 2 + 1	Moran 7 / Ridler 6	Stoker 22	Gaunt 16 / Walsh 3	Meechan 12 + 2 / Turner 4 + 1	Adams 3 + 2 / Houlickin 2	Peyton 30 + 4	Mitchell 5 + 7	Rose 20 + 1 / Murray 6	Roscoe 27 + 3	Smith S 8 + 13	Simms 15 + 10	Rioch 2 / Simpkins 6	Tench 1 + 3 / Clarke C 4	Smith N 1 + 1	Byrne 7 / Jones 7 + 5	Fitzpatrick 6	Williams 20 + 2	Ashmole 3 + 8	McGuire — + 1 / Warsnop 15	Robertson 5 / Douglas-Pringle 1	Crichton 4 / Farrer — + 1	Hockless 2 / Ryder 3	Shilton 1 + 2 / Gibson 12	Howarth 1 / Peers 3 + 4	Starbuck — + 2 / Allen 2 + 7	Burton 2 / Smith C 6	Connell 3	Drew 10 + 8	Shillito 15 + 2	Clarke R 21 + 1	Mann 6 / Marrison 1 + 1	Coyne 6 + 3	Warrick 1 / Sanasy 1	Rezai 1 / Mulvaney 9	*Match No.*
1	2	3	4	5	6^{1}	7	8	9^{2}	10	11	12	13																										1
1	2	3	4		6■	7	8^{2}	12	10	11^{1}	9^{3}		13	14	5																							2
1	2	3	4^{3}	5		7	8	9	10	12^{2}	6			13	11^{1}	14																						3
1	2	3		5	6	7	8	9^{3}	10^{2}	11^{1}	4		12	14			13																					4
1	2	3	4	5	6	7	13		12		9^{2}		14	10^{3}		11^{1}	8																					5
1	2	3		5	6	7	8^{3}	14		13	9		12	10^{2}				4^{1}	11																			6
1	2	3		5^{1}	6	7	8^{2}			14	9	12		4				10	11^{3}	13																		7
1	2	3			6	7	8^{1}			13	9	11	14	4^{3}				10	5^{2}		12																	8
1	2	3			6	7	13		14	11^{3}	9	8	12	4^{2}				10	5^{1}																			9
1	2	3			6	7	8^{1}		11	14	9	4^{3}	13					10	5^{2}			12																10
1	2	3			6	7	8^{1}		4		9	11	14	12				10^{3}	5^{2}	13																		11
1	2		4^{3}	5^{1}	6	7	8^{2}				9	12	14	13				10		11			3															12
	2	3	4^{1}		6	7	8^{2}		12	13	9	11								10			5	1														13
	2	3	12		6^{2}	7	8^{3}				9	11	13							4^{1}			5	1	10	14												14
		3				7					9		4	14		12				10^{3}			5	1	11^{2}	8	6^{1}	13	2									15
	2	3				7					9	6	12	4						5			10^{3}	1		14		13	11^{2}	8^{1}								16
1	2	3^{1}							10		9	4	8	5						6^{2}	13									7	12	11						17
1	2	3	4		6				11			7		8						10										9	5■							18
1		3■	4		6						9	11	7	8^{1}		13				10	12											5^{2}	2					19
1	2		4		6				10		9	3	7							11	12										8	5^{1}						20
1	2		4		6				12		9^{1}	3	5	10						11											7		8					21
	2				6				11^{1}			3	7	8						5	4										9■		10	1	12			22
	2				6				10		9	3	4	11						8													5	1		7		23
	2	9			6				11	7■		3	12■							10													5	1	4		8^{1}	24
	2		8				11	9	6			3		7									10								5		4	1				25
	2	13	9^{3}				4	8^{2}	11	12		3	6^{1}											14							7	10	5	1				26
	2	13	14				3		8^{2}			11		9^{3}				10								4^{1}	12				5	7	6	1				27
	2	13							8			11		14		6		10^{3}				1			9^{2}	3	12				5^{1}	7	4					28
	2	13				9^{3}			11			7				5		6^{1}		10^{2}	14	1				4	12					3	8					29
	2	14			6^{1}	9^{2}			11			7		13		5				10^{3}	12	1					4					3	8					30
					4^{2}	9^{3}	12		11			3		14		5^{1}				8		1				7	10				13	2	6■					31
	6	7^{2}							11			3		10				13		9^{3}	14	1				4	12				5^{1}	2			8			32
	7	14							11			3■		12				13				1					8^{2}				5^{1}	2	4	9	6	10^{3}		33
	6						2^{1}		11^{2}									14		9^{3}		1			3	4		13				7	5	12	8		10	34
	3								11		6		12							10^{3}	4^{1}	1			8^{2}			13			14	7	5		2		9	35
	2								11		3									9^{1}	10^{2}	1				4		13			12	8	5		6		7	36
	2			5					11		10				6			3^{2}			12	1				8		13	4^{1}				7				9	37
	3			2					11		8				6			9^{2}				1				7		13	4^{1}		12	14	5				10^{3}	38
	3			5					11^{2}		2				6			10				1				8		12	4			13	7^{1}				9	39
	2			5					8		6^{2}	11			3^{1}			14				1				7		9^{3}	4		13		12				10	40
	2			5					8^{1}			11			3			10^{2}				1				7		13	4		12		6		14		9^{3}	41
	2			5					8			11			3			12				1						7^{1}	4^{2}		13	10	6		14		9^{3}	42

FA Cup			
Fourth Qual	Accrington S	(a)	2-0
First Round	Cambridge C	(a)	1-2

FA Trophy			
Third Round	Altrincham	(h)	1-2

MORECAMBE — Conference

Ground: Christie Park, Lancaster Road, Morecambe, Lancashire LA4 5TJ.
Tel: (01524) 411 797.
Year Formed: 1920.
Record Gate: 9,326 (1962 v Weymouth FA Cup Third Round).
Nickname: The Shrimps.
Manager: Jim Harvey.
Secretary: Neil Marsdin.
Colours: Red shirts, white shorts, black stockings.

MORECAMBE 2004–05 LEAGUE RECORD

Match No.	Date	Venue	Opponents	Result		H/T Score	Lg. Pos.	Goalscorers	Attendance
1	Aug 14	A	Exeter C	D	1-1	0-1	—	Stringfellow [83]	3449
2	17	H	Accrington S	L	1-2	0-2	—	Bentley [78]	2393
3	21	H	Gravesend & N	L	1-3	0-1	19	Curtis [82]	1473
4	28	A	Scarborough	D	1-1	1-0	17	Walmsley [32]	1742
5	30	H	Leigh RMI	W	2-1	1-0	15	Hunter [32], Curtis [50]	1382
6	Sept 4	A	Barnet	L	1-5	0-0	18	McFlynn [59]	1787
7	11	A	Northwich Vic	D	2-2	2-1	17	Twiss [11], Carlton [35]	723
8	18	H	Woking	W	2-1	1-1	14	Twiss [24], Carlton [67]	1295
9	21	A	Halifax T	W	3-1	2-1	—	Carlton [12], Bentley [26], Twiss [79]	1667
10	25	H	Farnborough T	D	1-1	1-0	13	Twiss [45]	1287
11	Oct 2	A	Canvey Is	D	0-0	0-0	14		692
12	5	H	York C	W	2-1	1-0	—	Twiss [11], Thompson [87]	1734
13	9	H	Tamworth	W	3-0	0-0	9	Twiss [49], Walmsley [61], Thompson [83]	1410
14	16	A	Forest Green R	W	3-0	1-0	8	Bentley [14], Carlton [59], Curtis [90]	614
15	23	H	Stevenage Bor	L	1-3	1-0	10	Walmsley [1]	1565
16	Nov 6	A	Aldershot T	D	3-3	0-1	10	Bentley [61], Carlton [69], Twiss [85]	2382
17	20	H	Crawley T	L	1-2	1-1	12	Curtis [38]	1405
18	27	A	Dagenham & R	L	1-2	1-1	13	Twiss [20]	1101
19	Dec 7	A	Burton Alb	W	3-1	3-0	—	Elam [13], Carlton 2 [26, 27]	1257
20	11	A	Woking	D	0-0	0-0	14		1810
21	18	H	Northwich Vic	W	3-1	1-0	14	Curtis 2 [18, 90], Twiss [79]	1266
22	26	H	Carlisle U	D	1-1	0-1	12	Twiss [49]	4660
23	28	A	Farnborough T	W	2-1	2-0	10	Carlton [12], Curtis [45]	790
24	Jan 2	A	Carlisle U	D	3-3	1-3	9	Curtis [20], Hunter [62], Thompson [77]	6751
25	8	H	Canvey Is	W	4-0	0-0	8	Carlton [47], Hunter (pen) [61], Thompson [69], Elam [77]	1279
26	22	A	York C	L	0-1	0-0	12		2270
27	29	H	Halifax T	W	2-1	0-0	10	Twiss 2 (1 pen) [73, 90 (p)]	1910
28	Feb 21	A	Crawley T	L	1-2	0-2	—	Twiss [78]	2516
29	Mar 1	A	Stevenage Bor	W	1-0	1-0	—	Walmsley [16]	1250
30	5	A	Hereford U	D	1-1	1-1	12	Kempson [2]	2657
31	8	H	Aldershot T	D	0-0	0-0	—		1108
32	12	H	Dagenham & R	W	1-0	1-0	10	Twiss [29]	1253
33	19	A	Accrington S	L	1-2	1-1	12	Curtis [13]	1804
34	22	H	Hereford U	W	2-1	0-0	—	Twiss 2 (1 pen) [66, 86 (p)]	1465
35	25	H	Exeter C	D	2-2	1-1	10	Carlton [45], Twiss (pen) [87]	2189
36	28	A	Leigh RMI	W	2-0	1-0	10	Twiss 2 [44, 66]	541
37	Apr 2	H	Scarborough	W	2-1	0-1	6	Carlton [53], Twiss [55]	1632
38	9	A	Gravesend & N	W	2-1	2-1	7	Curtis [3], Kempson [23]	987
39	12	H	Burton Alb	W	3-0	2-0	—	Twiss (pen) [18], Carlton [27], Curtis [90]	1596
40	16	H	Barnet	D	1-1	0-1	5	Elam [58]	2385
41	19	H	Forest Green R	W	3-1	1-0	—	Twiss [26], Curtis [69], Thompson [90]	2096
42	23	A	Tamworth	D	0-0	0-0	7		1846

Final League Position: 7

GOALSCORERS

League (69): Twiss 22 (4 pens), Carlton 12, Curtis 12, Thompson 5, Bentley 4, Walmsley 4, Elam 3, Hunter 3 (1 pen), Kempson 2, McFlynn 1, Stringfellow 1.
FA Cup (7): Twiss 3, Curtis 2, Bentley 1, Hunter 1.
LDV Vans Trophy (0).
Trophy (4): Carlton 1, Curtis 1, Hunter 1, McFlynn 1.

Sollitt 27	Howard 30 + 2	O'Connor 2	Swan 30 + 4	Bentley 38	Curtis 36 + 4	Thompson 15 + 20	Twiss 40	Walmsley 28 + 9	Blackburn 39	McFlynn 8 + 5	Hunter 28 + 7	Rogan 1 + 8	Stringfellow 5 + 9	Carlton 21 + 17	Perkins 35	Dodgson — + 4	Edwards — + 1	Heard 20 + 7	Elam 18 + 6	Robinson 15 + 1	Kempson 19	Osborne 1	Kelly 6 + 1	*Match No.*
1	2	3[1]	4	5	6	7	8[2]	9	10	11[3]	12	13	14											1
1	2	3[3]	4	5	6	7	8[2]	9	10	11[1]	13		12	14										2
1	2		4[1]	5	6	13	8[2]	9	10			12	7	11	3									3
1	2		4[1]	5	6[2]		8	9	10	11	7	13		12	3									4
1	2		4	5	6[2]		8	9[1]	10	11	7	12		13[3]	3	14								5
1	2[1]		4	5	6		8	9■	10	11	7			12	3									6
1			4	5	6	7[2]	8		10		11[3]	13	3	9	2[1]	14	12							7
1			4[1]	5	6	7[2]	8	9	10	12	13		3	11[3]	2	14								8
1			4	5	6	7	8	9	10	13	12		3[1]	11[2]	2									9
1			4[1]	5	6	7	8	9	10	12			3[2]	11[3]	2	14		13						10
1	2		4[1]	5	6[2]	13	8[3]	9	10		11		12	14	3			7						11
1			4[1]	5	9[3]	13	8	7	2	11[2]	10		12	14	3			6						12
1			4	5	10[3]	14	8	9	2	11[2]	7		12	13	6			3[1]						13
1			4	5	6	12	8[2]	9	11		7	13		10[1]	3			2						14
1	13		4	5[1]	6	7		9	2	14	11	12		10[3]	3			8[2]						15
1			4	5	13	7[1]	8	9	10	11[2]	6			12	2			3						16
1	13		4[1]	5	9[3]	7	8	2	10		11		12	14	3			6[2]						17
1	2		4	5	6		8	9	10					11	3				7					18
1	2		4	5	10[1]		8	9	3				12	11[2]	6			13	7					19
1	2		4	5	6		8	9	10					11	3				7					20
1	2		4	5	10		8	9			12	6[1]			3			7	11					21
1[G]	2		4	5[1]	10	13	8	9	3					11[2]	6			12	7	15				22
	2		4		10	7[1]		8	6■	13	14	12[2]		9[3]	3			5	11	1				23
1	2[1]		4		10	14	8				11		12	13	3			6	7[2]		5	9[3]		24
1	2		4		10[2]	13	8[3]	14			6		12	9	3[1]			11	7		5			25
1	2			5	10	12	8		6		13			9[2]	4			3[1]	7		11			26
1				5	3	14	8	9	6		11[2]			10[3]	2			12	7[1]		4		13	27
1				5		7	8		10		11			9[1]	4			12	2		6		3	28
	2		4	5		12[2]	8	9[1]	10		11			13				3		1	6		7	29
	2		4[1]	5	13	14	8	9	10		11							3	12[2]	1	6		7[3]	30
	2			5	13	7[3]	8	9	10[1]		11			14				3	12	1	4		6[2]	31
	2		13	5[2]	6	7[3]	8	9	10		11			12				3[1]	14	1	4			32
	2		4[1]	5	9	7[2]	8	14	10		11			12					13	1	3		6[3]	33
	2			5	9[3]	13	8	7[2]	10		11			12	3			4[1]	14	1	6			34
	2			5	9	7[2]	8	14	4[1]		11			10	6[3]			12	13	1	3			35
	2		12	5	13	14	8		10					9[3]	11			3	7[2]	1	6[1]		4	36
	2		14		6[2]	13	8	12	10		11			9[3]	3			4	7[1]	1	5			37
	2		4[1]	5	9	13	8	12	10		11				3				7[2]	1	6			38
	2		14	5	10	13	8[3]	12	3[1]		11			9	4				7[2]	1	6			39
	2		4[2]	5	9	14	8	12	10[1]		11			13	3				7[3]	1	6			40
	2			5	10[2]	12	8	13	3		11			9[3]	6			14	7[1]	1	4			41
	2			5	10	14	8	13	9[2]		11			12	3			4[1]	7[3]	1	6			42

FA Cup

Fourth Qual	Hucknall T	(h)	5-1
First Round	Hull C	(a)	2-3

LDV Vans Trophy

First Round	Huddersfield T	(a)	0-3

FA Trophy

Third Round	Sutton Coldfield T	(h)	2-1
Fourth Round	Lancaster C	(a)	2-1
Fifth Round	Burton Alb	(a)	0-1

NORTHWICH VICTORIA Conference North

Ground: Victoria Stadium, Northwich, Cheshire.
Tel: (01606) 43008.
Year Formed: 1874.
Record Gate: 12,000 (1977 v Watford FA Cup Fourth Round).
Nickname: The Vics.
Manager: Steve Burr.
Secretary: Derek Nuttall.
Colours: Green shirts with white trim, white shorts, black stockings.

NORTHWICH VICTORIA 2004–05 LEAGUE RECORD

Match No.	*Date*	*Venue*	*Opponents*	*Result*		*H/T Score*	*Lg. Pos.*	*Goalscorers*	*Attendance*
1	Aug 14	A	Gravesend & N	D	2-2	0-1	—	Allan [60], Devlin [90]	1064
2	17	H	Carlisle U	D	2-2	0-1	—	Devlin [57], Allan [64]	1803
3	21	H	Exeter C	L	1-2	1-1	17	Brayson [20]	607
4	28	A	Barnet	L	0-4	0-2	18		1422
5	30	H	Hereford U	L	1-4	1-2	19	Brayson [18]	1132
6	Sept 4	A	Aldershot T	L	1-2	1-1	21	Giles (og) [45]	2644
7	11	H	Morecambe	D	2-2	1-2	21	Brayson (pen) [45], Thompson [84]	723
8	18	A	York C	D	0-0	0-0	21		2087
9	21	H	Accrington S	D	3-3	1-1	—	Devlin [32], Quayle 2 (2 pens) [76, 85]	729
10	25	A	Stevenage Bor	L	1-4	0-2	21	Devlin [72]	1901
11	Oct 2	H	Dagenham & R	D	2-2	1-1	22	Allan 2 [42, 77]	581
12	5	A	Scarborough	L	0-3	0-1	—		1598
13	9	A	Crawley T	D	0-0	0-0	22		1696
14	16	H	Burton Alb	W	4-0	1-0	22	Garvey [23], Devlin [46], Allan [50], Quayle [74]	857
15	23	A	Forest Green R	W	3-1	3-0	22	Quayle [14], Foran [29], Young [41]	521
16	Nov 5	H	Canvey Is	W	3-1	2-0	—	Allan [20], Hughes [28], Brayson (pen) [90]	504
17	13	A	Accrington S	L	0-5	0-2	21		1203
18	20	A	Farnborough T	W	2-0	1-0	21	Hughes [45], Garvey [64]	884
19	27	H	Halifax T	L	1-2	0-0	21	Brayson [90]	1272
20	Dec 4	A	Woking	L	0-2	0-1	21		1833
21	8	H	Tamworth	L	1-2	1-0	—	Brayson (pen) [44]	460
22	11	H	York C	W	3-0	3-0	21	Allan [11], Devlin [26], Brisco [43]	673
23	18	A	Morecambe	L	1-3	0-1	21	Quayle [72]	1266
24	28	H	Stevenage Bor	D	1-1	1-0	21	Brayson (pen) [42]	620
25	Jan 8	A	Dagenham & R	W	3-2	1-1	21	Quayle 2 [8, 61], Mayman [64]	1753
26	22	H	Scarborough	W	1-0	0-0	21	Quayle [56]	638
27	Feb 12	A	Canvey Is	D	2-2	2-1	21	Allan [6], Carr [13]	624
28	15	A	Leigh RMI	W	1-0	0-0	—	Quayle [69]	402
29	19	H	Farnborough T	W	2-0	0-0	19	Allan 2 [64, 72]	628
30	26	A	Halifax T	D	2-2	1-1	19	Allan 2 [31, 90]	1636
31	Mar 5	H	Woking	L	1-3	0-1	19	Carr [72]	780
32	12	A	Tamworth	L	0-3	0-2	19		1059
33	19	A	Carlisle U	L	0-1	0-0	19		5062
34	25	H	Gravesend & N	L	1-2	1-1	19	Bunce (og) [37]	919
35	28	A	Hereford U	L	0-4	0-3	20		2931
36	Apr 2	H	Barnet	W	2-0	0-0	19	Brayson 2 [50, 72]	1552
37	5	H	Forest Green R	W	2-1	2-1	—	Brayson [13], Allan [22]	882
38	9	A	Exeter C	W	3-2	3-1	18	Allan [8], Brayson [16], Taylor (og) [28]	3950
39	12	H	Leigh RMI	W	2-0	0-0	—	Band [72], Brayson [78]	734
40	16	H	Aldershot T	L	1-2	1-1	18	Brayson (pen) [11]	1234
41	19	A	Burton Alb	L	0-1	0-1	—		1713
42	23	H	Crawley T	W	1-0	0-0	19	Allan [65]	806

Final League Position: 19

GOALSCORERS

League (58): Allan 15, Brayson 13 (5 pens), Quayle 9 (2 pens), Devlin 6, Carr 2, Garvey 2, Hughes 2, Band 1, Brisco 1, Foran 1, Mayman 1, Thompson 1, Young 1, own goals 3.
FA Cup (1): Quayle 1.
Trophy (1): Allan 1.

Connett 14 + 2	Royle 8 + 5	Garvey 29 + 5	Forsyth 3	Foran 10 + 1	Handyside 30	Hadland 4 + 9	Burke 8	Allan 36	Quayle 27 + 5	Hunter 4 + 1	Brayson 26 + 4	Devlin 38 + 1	Norris 1 + 4	Ralph 21	O'Neill 1	Came 1 + 1 / Roca 3 + 1	Charnock 39	McLachlan 3 / Byrne 1 + 7	McCarthy 34 + 1	Thompson — + 2	Pearce 7 + 1	Lancaster 5 / Munroe 7 + 3	Clegg 1 + 1	Kuduzovic 1 / Bailey 2 + 3	Harrison 7	Young 6 / Rogers 7	Fitzpatrick — + 2	Hildred 2 + 2 / Tierney 1 + 2	Hughes 6 + 2	Brisco 10	Carratt — + 4	Band1 7 + 2	Gaghan 1 + 6	Mayman 19 + 1	Garner 6 + 2	Briggs — + 1	Carr 16	*Match No.*
1	2	3^{1}	4	5	6	7^{2}	8	9	10	11	12	13																										1
1	2	3	4^{1}	5	6	12	8	9^{3}	10	11^{2}	13	7	14																									2
15	2	3	4	5			8		10^{G}	11	9	7		1■	6^{1}	12																						3
1	2	3		5^{1}	6■	14	8		10	13	9^{3}	7	12				4	11^{2}																				4
	2	3				11^{1}	8		10^{3}	6^{2}	9	7	13	1		5	4		12	14																		5
	2				6	13	8^{1}	9	10^{2}		11	7	12	1			4	3	5																			6
	2	12		5	6	7^{2}		9			10	8		1			3	4^{1}	11	13																		7
	12	3^{2}			6	13		8	10		9	11		1			4		7^{1}		2	5																8
		3			6	7		9	10			8		1			2		11^{1}		4	5	12															9
	12	13			6^{1}	14		7	10^{2}		9	8		1			3		11		4	5		2^{3}														10
		14		5		12	8^{1}	10	13		9	11		1			3		7^{2}			6	4^{3}		2													11
				5		12	8^{1}	7	10		9	11		1			6		3			2			4													12
		3		5		12		8	10^{1}		9	11		1			4		7						6	2												13
		3		5				9	10		8	11		1			6		2						7^{1}	4	12											14
		3		5				9	10^{2}		7	11		1			6		2		12				8^{1}	4	13											15
		3^{1}			6	13		9			10	11		1			5		2		4				8			12	7^{2}									16
		3^{1}			5			9	13		10	11		1			6		2		4				7			12	8^{2}									17
		3			6			9^{1}	12			7		1			4		2		5							11	10■	8								18
		3		12	6^{1}			9	10^{3}		13	7		1			5		2		4							11^{2}		8	14							19
		3						9			8	7		1			6		2							4			10^{1}	5	12	11						20
		3^{1}						9	14		10^{2}	7		1			6		2							4			11^{3}	8	13	5	12					21
1	13	3						9	14		10	7					6		2^{1}							8^{2}			12	4		5		11^{3}				22
1	12	3			6				10		9^{3}	7	8^{2}				4		2^{1}										14			5	13	11				23
1		3			6			9	10		8	7					4		2										11^{1}		12	5						24
1	13	3			6			9	10			7					4													8		5^{2}		11	2^{1}	12		25
1		3			6			9	10			7					4		2											5				11	8			26
1					6^{1}			9	10^{2}		13	11					3		2											8		5		7	12		4	27
1		12						9	10			11					6		2											8		5		7^{1}	4		3	28
1					4			9	10			11				13	6		2											8^{2}		5^{1}		7	12		3	29
1	2				6			9	10			11				8	4	12	3															7^{1}			5	30
1					6			9	10^{2}							11^{1}	4	13	2													5	12	7	3		8	31
1					6			9	10^{3}			7				8^{2}	4	13	2			12										5^{1}	14	11			3	32
		12			6			9	10			7		1			4	13	2			8^{1}		14								5		11^{3}			3^{2}	33
					6			9	10^{3}			11■		1			4	14	2^{1}			3^{2}		12								5	13	7			8	34
15		3			6			9	10					1^{G}			4		7^{1}			12										5^{2}	11	13	8		2	35
		3			6			9			10	7					4		5			8				1								11			2	36
		3^{1}			6			9			10	7					4		2			5				1		12						8			11	37
		3			6^{1}			9			10	7					4		2			5				1						12		8			11	38
		6									9	11					4	10	2			12		3^{1}		1						5		7			8	39
		3			6						9	11^{2}					4	12				2		10		1		13				5^{1}		7			8	40
		3			6			9			10	11■					4	13				2^{1}		12		1						5		7			8^{2}	41
		3			6			9			10						4		2							1		11^{2}				13	12	7^{1}	5		8	42

FA Cup
Fourth Qual Vauxhall M (h) 1-2

FA Trophy
Third Round Halifax T (a) 1-0
Fourth Round Hucknall T (h) 0-1

SCARBOROUGH — Conference

Ground: McCain Stadium, Seamer Road, Scarborough, Yorkshire YO12 4HF.
Tel: (01723) 375 094.
Year Formed: 1879.
Record Gate: 11,130 (1987 v Luton Town FA Cup Third Round).
Nickname: The Boro.
Manager: Nick Henry.
Secretary: Kevin Philliskirk.
Colours: All red.

SCARBOROUGH 2004–05 LEAGUE RECORD

Match No.	*Date*	*Venue*	*Opponents*	*Result*		*H/T Score*	*Lg. Pos.*	*Goalscorers*	*Attendance*
1	Aug 14	H	Woking	W	2-0	2-0	—	Hackworth [38], Redfearn (pen) [45]	1602
2	17	A	Halifax T	L	1-2	0-1	—	Redfearn [48]	1887
3	21	A	Farnborough T	W	1-0	1-0	5	Redfearn [45]	633
4	28	H	Morecambe	D	1-1	0-1	9	Senior [59]	1742
5	30	A	Burton Alb	W	3-2	3-0	7	Redfearn [5], Austin (og) [10], Gill [12]	1302
6	Sept 4	H	Canvey Is	D	1-1	1-0	5	Burton [38]	1732
7	11	H	Exeter C	D	1-1	1-1	8	Redfearn [26]	1715
8	18	A	Hereford U	L	0-1	0-1	10		2874
9	21	A	Carlisle U	L	1-2	1-0	—	Redfearn [12]	5111
10	25	H	Barnet	D	1-1	0-1	11	Thompson [52]	1542
11	Oct 2	A	Forest Green R	W	1-0	0-0	10	Gilroy [90]	686
12	5	H	Northwich Vic	W	3-0	1-0	—	Redfearn (pen) [37], Senior 2 [75, 77]	1598
13	9	H	Aldershot T	D	2-2	0-2	6	Senior 2 [51, 52]	1622
14	16	A	Tamworth	L	0-1	0-0	11		1027
15	23	H	Accrington S	W	4-0	3-0	9	Hackworth [3], Redfearn [9], Nicholson [15], Senior [69]	1704
16	Nov 6	A	Dagenham & R	W	3-0	2-0	5	Senior [18], Redfearn [35], Cryan [85]	1186
17	20	H	Stevenage Bor	D	3-3	3-1	8	Senior 2 [1, 9], Nicholson [5]	1669
18	27	A	Crawley T	L	1-2	0-1	9	Burton [88]	1804
19	Dec 4	H	Gravesend & N	W	1-0	0-0	6	Hackworth [72]	1634
20	7	A	Leigh RMI	D	1-1	1-0	—	Gill [10]	325
21	11	H	Hereford U	D	0-0	0-0	7		1608
22	18	A	Exeter C	L	1-3	1-0	9	Redfearn [21]	4529
23	26	H	York C	W	5-1	3-0	6	Thompson [25], Redfearn 2 (1 pen) [28, 41 (p)], Hackworth [81], Lyth [90]	4586
24	28	A	Barnet	L	0-1	0-0	8		2504
25	Jan 2	A	York C	W	2-0	0-0	6	Senior [89], Hackworth [90]	4439
26	8	H	Forest Green R	D	0-0	0-0	7		1420
27	22	A	Northwich Vic	L	0-1	0-0	11		638
28	29	H	Carlisle U	D	1-1	1-0	12	Hotte [37]	2828
29	Feb 5	A	Accrington S	L	1-2	0-1	13	Hackworth [83]	1315
30	12	H	Dagenham & R	W	2-0	2-0	9	Cryan 2 [11, 45]	1358
31	19	A	Stevenage Bor	L	0-1	0-0	12		1728
32	26	H	Crawley T	D	2-2	1-1	12	Hackworth [44], Pounder [64]	1451
33	Mar 5	A	Gravesend & N	L	0-4	0-2	13		1178
34	12	H	Leigh RMI	W	3-0	1-0	12	Senior [43], Cryan [69], Hotte [79]	1219
35	15	H	Tamworth	D	2-2	1-2	—	Hackworth [28], Coulson [80]	1158
36	19	H	Halifax T	W	3-1	0-0	11	Bishop [64], Senior [76], Reeves (pen) [90]	2109
37	23	A	Woking	D	1-1	0-0	—	Coulson [90]	2567
38	28	H	Burton Alb	D	1-1	1-1	12	Redfearn [23]	1675
39	Apr 2	A	Morecambe	L	1-2	1-0	13	Redfearn (pen) [36]	1632
40	9	H	Farnborough T	W	4-0	2-0	13	Reeves 3 [41, 45, 67], Kerr [86]	1451
41	16	A	Canvey Is	L	0-1	0-1	13		510
42	23	A	Aldershot T	L	0-2	0-1	13		4437

Final League Position: 13

GOALSCORERS

League (60): Redfearn 14 (4 pens), Senior 12, Hackworth 8, Cryan 4, Reeves 4 (1 pen), Burton 2, Coulson 2, Gill 2, Hotte 2, Nicholson 2, Thompson 2, Bishop 1, Gilroy 1, Kerr 1, Lyth 1, Pounder 1, own goal 1.
FA Cup (1): Hotte 1.
LDV Vans Trophy (1): Gilroy 1.
Trophy (1): Senior 1.

Walker 39	Lyth 10 + 15	Nicholson 42	Kerr 35 + 3	Hotte 34 + 1	Cryan 42	Thompson 42	Redfearn 36 + 3	Gill 14 + 6	Hackworth 28 + 9	Gilroy 19 + 4	Senior 24 + 18	Burton 5 + 10	Foot 23 + 3	Baker 30	Pounder 8 + 10	Foster 4 + 3	Keen 3	Townson 4	Horrigan — + 1	Coulson — + 11	Grant — + 1	Reeves1 0	Jones — + 2	Bishop 10	Beadle — + 1	*Match No.*
1	2	3	4	5	6	7	8	9^{1}	10^{2}	11	12	13														1
1	2	3^{1}	4	5	6	7^{2}	8	9^{3}	10	11	12	14	13													2
1	2	3^{1}	4	5	6	7	8	9^{2}	10^{3}	11	13	14	12													3
1	2^{1}	3	4	5	6	7	8	9	10^{2}	11	12	13														4
1	12	3	4	5	6	7	8^{1}	9^{2}	10^{3}		13	11		2	14											5
1		3	4	5	6	7	8	9^{1}	10	12	13	11^{2}		2												6
1		3	4^{1}	5	6	7	8	9^{3}	10	14	13	11^{2}		2	12											7
1		3^{1}	4	5▮	6	7	8	12	10	13	11			2^{3}	9^{2}	14										8
1	2	3	4		6	7	8	12	10	11^{1}	9^{2}		13			5										9
1		3	4	2	6	7	8		10	11	9					5										10
		3		5	6	7	8	13^{3}		11	12	9^{1}	4	2		14	1	10^{2}								11
		3^{1}	4		6	7	8		12	11^{2}	14	9	5	2	13		1	10^{3}								12
		11	4	2	6	7	8		10		12	13	5	3^{1}			1^{G}	9^{2}	15							13
1		3	4	5	6	7	8		10		12	13		2^{2}	11			9^{1}								14
1	2	11^{1}	4	3	6	7	8		10		9^{2}		5		12					13						15
1		11	4	5	6	7^{2}	8	9			10^{3}		3^{1}	2	13	12				14						16
1	12	3	4		6	7	8	9^{2}	13		10		5	2		11^{1}										17
1		3	4		6	7	8^{2}	9^{3}	14	12	10	13	5	2		11^{1}										18
1	12	3	4		6	7	8^{1}	9^{2}	13	11	10		5	2												19
1	13	3	4^{2}	12	6	7	8	9^{3}	14	11	10		5^{1}	2												20
1		3	4^{1}	5	6	7	12	13	10^{2}	11	9^{3}	14	8	2												21
1		3		5	6	7	8		10	11^{1}	9	12	4	2												22
1	12	3		5	6	7	8^{1}	13	10^{2}	11	9^{3}	14	4	2												23
1		3	12	5	6	7	8		10	11^{1}	9		4	2												24
1	12	3	13	5	6	7^{2}	8		10	11^{1}	9		4	2												25
1	12	3	13	5	6	7^{2}	8		10	11	9^{3}		4	2^{1}							14					26
1		3^{1}	4	5	6	7	8		10	11	13		9^{2}	2	12											27
1		3	4	5	6	7	8		13	11	10^{2}			2^{1}	12							9				28
1	12	3	4	5	6	7	8		13	11^{1}	10^{2}			2								9				29
1		3	4	5	6	7	8		10^{1}		12		11	2								9				30
1	14	3	4	5	6^{1}	9	8^{2}	11^{3}	10		12		7	2	13											31
1		3	4	5	6	7		9^{1}	10		12		2	8	11											32
1	13	3		5	6	7			10^{2}		12		4	2	11^{1}							9^{3}	14	8		33
1	12	3	4^{1}	5	6	7		14	10^{3}		9^{2}			2	11					13				8		34
1	12	3	4	5^{2}	6	7^{1}	13		10		9			2	11^{3}					14				8		35
1	12	3	4	5	6	7	8^{1}				10^{2}			2						13		9		11		36
1	12	3	4		6	7^{2}	8				14		5	2^{1}	10^{3}					13		9		11		37
1	2	3	4		6	7	8^{1}				10^{2}		5							12		9	13	11		38
1	2	3	4	5	6^{1}	7	8		14		12				11					13		9^{3}		10^{2}		39
1	2	3	4	5	6	7	8^{1}		14		10^{2}									13		9^{3}		11	12	40
1	2	3^{1}	4	5	6	7^{2}	14		10		9				13					12		8^{3}		11		41
1	12	3	4	5	6	7^{2}	8		10		9^{3}		2^{1}		13					14				11		42

FA Cup
Fourth Qual Lancaster C (a) 1-1
(h) 0-1

LDV Vans Trophy
First Round Rochdale (a) 1-4

FA Trophy
Third Round Barrow (a) 1-2

STEVENAGE BOROUGH — Conference

Ground: Broadhall Way Stadium, Broadhall Way, Stevenage, Hertfordshire SG2 8RH.
Tel: (01438) 223 223.
Year Formed: 1976.
Record Gate: 6,489 (1997 v Kidderminster Harriers Conference).
Nickname: The Boro.
Manager: Graham Westley.
Secretary: Roger Austin.
Colours: Red and white shirts, black shorts, white stockings.

STEVENAGE BOROUGH 2004–05 LEAGUE RECORD

Match No.	Date	Venue	Opponents	Result		H/T Score	Lg. Pos.	Goalscorers	Attendance
1	Aug 14	A	Dagenham & R	L	1-3	0-0	—	Brady [90]	1706
2	17	H	Aldershot T	L	0-1	0-0	—		2287
3	21	H	Accrington S	W	5-0	2-0	13	Quailey [6], Hanlon [10], Goodliffe 2 [59, 61], Flack [80]	1521
4	28	A	Hereford U	W	1-0	0-0	11	Brough [90]	3616
5	30	H	Tamworth	W	2-0	0-0	10	Brady [69], Goodliffe [79]	1878
6	Sept 4	A	Gravesend & N	L	1-2	1-0	11	Bulman [20]	1756
7	11	H	Burton Alb	L	0-1	0-1	12		1788
8	18	A	Exeter C	L	0-2	0-1	13		2716
9	21	A	Farnborough T	W	3-0	1-0	—	Elding 2 [30, 58], Nurse [49]	901
10	25	H	Northwich Vic	W	4-1	2-0	10	Hunter 2 [16, 58], Boyd [45], Elding [83]	1901
11	Oct 2	A	York C	L	1-3	0-2	11	Flack [72]	2043
12	5	H	Canvey Is	L	1-4	1-2	—	Hanlon [15]	1513
13	9	A	Leigh RMI	W	2-1	1-0	12	Elding [32], Maamria [77]	235
14	16	H	Crawley T	W	1-0	1-0	9	Elding [29]	1747
15	23	A	Morecambe	W	3-1	0-1	7	Goodliffe [58], Hocking [59], Brady [90]	1565
16	Nov 6	H	Halifax T	W	2-1	1-0	4	Quailey [19], Elding [64]	1820
17	20	A	Scarborough	D	3-3	1-3	5	Elding 2 [34, 68], Quinn [54]	1669
18	27	H	Forest Green R	D	2-2	0-1	7	Maamria 2 [89, 90]	1804
19	Dec 7	H	Woking	L	0-2	0-0	—		1816
20	11	H	Exeter C	W	3-2	1-2	8	Elding [33], Maamria 2 [60, 84]	1907
21	18	A	Burton Alb	W	3-0	2-0	5	Weatherstone [36], Maamria [45], Elding [74]	1221
22	26	H	Barnet	W	2-1	0-0	3	Elding [59], Maamria (pen) [65]	4307
23	28	A	Northwich Vic	D	1-1	0-1	4	Maamria [62]	620
24	Jan 2	A	Barnet	L	1-2	0-1	5	Weatherstone [49]	3520
25	8	H	York C	D	2-2	1-2	6	Elding 2 [27, 79]	2044
26	22	A	Canvey Is	L	0-3	0-2	10		814
27	29	H	Farnborough T	W	3-1	2-0	9	Stamp 2 [12, 34], Bulman [50]	1715
28	Feb 12	A	Halifax T	L	1-2	0-1	11	Maamria [73]	1497
29	19	H	Scarborough	W	1-0	0-0	10	Stamp [48]	1728
30	22	A	Carlisle U	W	2-1	2-0	—	Stamp 2 [35, 36]	3146
31	26	A	Forest Green R	D	1-1	1-0	7	Elding [26]	622
32	Mar 1	H	Morecambe	L	0-1	0-1	—		1250
33	5	H	Carlisle U	W	2-1	0-1	5	Boyd [85], Brady [90]	2217
34	19	A	Aldershot T	W	1-0	1-0	6	Maamria [16]	3150
35	25	H	Dagenham & R	W	1-0	1-0	6	Elding [45]	2604
36	28	A	Tamworth	D	0-0	0-0	6		1251
37	Apr 2	H	Hereford U	L	0-1	0-0	8		2614
38	5	A	Woking	W	2-1	1-0	—	Stamp [4], Elding [48]	1951
39	9	A	Accrington S	L	1-4	0-3	8	Laker [88]	1251
40	16	H	Gravesend & N	W	2-0	0-0	7	Stamp [74], Elding [89]	2008
41	19	A	Crawley T	W	2-1	1-0	—	Elding [10], Goodliffe [56]	1413
42	23	H	Leigh RMI	W	2-0	1-0	5	Elding [6], Stamp [90]	3516

Final League Position: 5

GOALSCORERS

League (65): Elding 19, Maamria 10 (1 pen), Stamp 8, Goodliffe 5, Brady 4, Boyd 2, Bulman 2, Flack 2, Hanlon 2, Hunter 2, Quailey 2, Weatherstone 2, Brough 1, Hocking 1, Laker 1, Nurse 1, Quinn 1.
FA Cup (6): Boyd 1, Brough 1, Elding 1, Hanlon 1, McAlister 1, Quinn 1.
LDV Vans Trophy (1): Elding 1.
Trophy (0).
Play-offs (2): Maamria 2.

Woodman 21	Brady 23 + 11	Boyd 20 + 12	Gregory 36 + 1	Rogers 16	Hocking 34 + 3	Brough 12 + 10	Bulman 39 + 1	Nurse 8 + 9	Quailey 8 + 2	Quinn 28 + 2	Hanlon 14 + 4	Elding 39 + 2	Warner 12 + 2	Burch 3	Flack 1 + 17	Goodliffe 37	Laker 30 + 1	Maamria 23 + 6	Hunter 2 + 5	Stewart — + 1	Schillaci — + 1	McAllister 2 + 4	Weatherstone1 3 + 8	Croudson 1	Sullivan — + 1	Farrow 1 + 1	Marshall 2	Pacquette 1	Henry 6 + 5	Stamp 15 + 1	Julian 14	Lee — + 1	Jarrett 1 + 3	Match No.
1^{6}	2	3	4	5	6	7	8	9	10^{1}	11^{2}	15	12	13																					1
	11^{2}	3	4	5	6^{1}	7	8	14	10^{3}		12	9	2	1	13																			2
	13	12	4	5	6	7	8		10^{3}		11^{1}	9		1	14	2	3^{2}																	3
1	12	13	4	5	6	7	8^{1}				11	9^{3}			14	2	3	10^{2}																4
1	12	13	10^{3}	5^{1}	6	7	8	14			11	9			4^{2}	2	3																	5
1	14	12	4	5	6	7	8			13■	11^{2}	9^{3}				2	3^{1}	10																6
1	12	13	4	5	6	7^{2}	8	14			11	9				2	3^{1}	10^{3}																7
1	2	3	4^{2}	5^{1}	6	7	8	9			14				12	11		10^{3}	13															8
1	2^{2}	13	4		6	7	8	9^{3}		11	3	10			14	5^{1}		12																9
1		3	4		6		8			11	2	9^{2}			14	5	7^{1}		10^{3}	12	13													10
1			4^{1}		6	13	8	9		11	7^{2}	10			14	5	3	12	2^{3}															11
1		3	4^{2}		6	7^{3}	8	9		11	12	10			13	5^{1}	2	14																12
1		3	4		6		8		11	7	5	9					2	10																13
1		3^{1}	4		6		8	12	10^{3}	11	5	9			14		2	7^{2}				13												14
1	13	3	4		6	12	8		10^{2}	11	7^{1}	9^{3}				5	2					14												15
1	2^{1}	3^{2}	4		6	12			10^{3}	11	7	9				5	8		14			13												16
1	2^{2}	3	4	5^{1}	6	13	8			11	7	9			14							10^{3}	12											17
1	14	3	4		6	7	8			11^{1}	5^{2}	9				2		12				10^{3}	13											18
	13	3	4^{1}		6	7	8		10^{2}			9				2	5					12	11	1										19
1	2	3^{1}	12	5			8			11		9				4	6	10					7											20
1	2		4^{1}	5			8	13		11		9^{3}				3	6	10^{2}	12				7		14									21
1	2^{1}	3^{2}		5	12		8	14	13	11		9				4	6	10^{3}					7											22
1	2	13	4^{2}	5^{1}	12		8	14		11		9^{3}				3	6	10					7											23
1	2	3	4	5			8		12	11^{2}		9				6		10^{1}	13				7											24
	2	3		5	6^{1}	12	8			11^{2}		9		1^{6}	13	10	4						7			15								25
	2	3■		5^{1}		14	8					9	11^{2}		13	4	6		12				7■				1	10^{3}						26
	2^{2}		4		6	13	8			11		9	3^{1}		14	5							12			1			7	10^{3}				27
	2	14	4		6^{2}		8			11		9	3			5^{1}		12					13				1		7^{3}	10				28
	2	3^{2}	4		6							9	8		13	11	5^{1}						7							10	1	12		29
		13	4		6	12	8			11		9^{2}	7			2	5	10^{1}												3	1			30
		13	4		6^{1}	14	8			11		9	2		12	3	5	10^{3}												7^{2}	1			31
	12	3^{3}	4		6^{1}		8			11^{2}		9			14	2	5	13					7							10	1			32
	2	14	4		6	12	8			11^{1}		9				3	5^{2}	10					13							7^{3}	1			33
	2		4^{2}		6		8			11		9^{3}			14	3	5	10^{1}					12						13	7	1			34
	3^{2}		4^{1}		6		8					9^{3}	14			2	5	10					7						12	11	1		13	35
			4		6		8	12				9^{2}	2^{1}			3	5	10^{3}					11						14	7	1		13	36
	2	14	4		6^{1}		8	12		11^{2}		9				3	5	10											13	7^{3}	1			37
	13	3^{3}	4		6		8			11		9^{1}				2	5	10^{2}					12						14	7	1			38
	13				6		8^{2}			11^{1}		9	3			2	5	10^{3}					12						4	7	1		14	39
	2				6^{1}		13	9		11^{3}		14	3			5		10					7^{2}						4	12	1		8■	40
	2		4		12		8	11^{1}		13		9	3			6		10^{2}											5	7	1			41
	2		4				8	11^{1}				9	3			6	12	10											5	7	1			42

FA Cup

Fourth Qual	Hendon	(h)	5-0
First Round	Billericay T	(a)	1-0
Second Round	Rochdale	(h)	0-2

LDV Vans Trophy

First Round	Barnet	(a)	1-3

FA Trophy

Third Round	Woking	(a)	0-1

Play-offs

Semi-Final	Hereford U	(h)	1-1
		(a)	1-0
Final	Carlisle U		0-1
(at Britannia Stadium)			

TAMWORTH Conference

Ground: The Lamb Ground, Kettlebrook, Tamworth, Staffordshire B77 1AA.
Tel: (01827) 65798.
Year Formed: 1933.
Record Gate: 4,920 (1948 v Atherstone Town Birmingham Combination).
Nickname: Lambs.
Manager: Mark Cooper.
Secretary: Russell Moore.
Colours: Red shirts with white sleeves, black shorts, red stockings.

TAMWORTH 2004–05 LEAGUE RECORD

Match No.	Date	Venue	Opponents	Result	H/T Score	Lg. Pos.	Goalscorers	Attendance
1	Aug 14	H	Halifax T	W 2-1	2-1	—	Brown A [18], Whitman [29]	1325
2	17	A	York C	L 0-2	0-1	—		2466
3	21	A	Canvey Is	D 3-3	2-1	11	Ross [23], Colkin [35], Whitman [71]	686
4	28	H	Forest Green R	W 4-0	1-0	8	Whitman 2 [19, 73], Ebdon [46], Ross [52]	1101
5	30	A	Stevenage Bor	L 0-2	0-0	12		1878
6	Sept 4	H	Farnborough T	L 0-2	0-1	14		1150
7	11	H	Barnet	L 0-2	0-2	15		1199
8	18	A	Carlisle U	L 1-2	0-0	18	Taylor [90]	5007
9	21	H	Woking	L 1-3	1-3	—	May [27]	814
10	25	A	Exeter C	D 2-2	1-1	19	Taylor [19], Harrad (pen) [47]	2664
11	Oct 2	H	Aldershot T	L 1-2	1-0	19	Harrad [10]	1621
12	5	A	Accrington S	W 3-2	1-1	—	Taylor [18], Harrad [48], Brown M [55]	1201
13	9	A	Morecambe	L 0-3	0-0	19		1410
14	16	H	Scarborough	W 1-0	0-0	18	Whitman [90]	1027
15	23	H	Crawley T	W 1-0	1-0	16	Ebdon [4]	859
16	Nov 6	A	Leigh RMI	W 3-2	0-2	15	Taylor 3 [67, 70, 77]	338
17	20	H	Gravesend & N	W 2-1	1-0	14	Ebdon (pen) [45], Taylor [82]	1984
18	27	A	Hereford U	L 1-2	1-2	14	Taylor [38]	2714
19	Dec 4	H	Dagenham & R	L 0-4	0-0	16		1017
20	8	A	Northwich Vic	W 2-1	0-1	—	Ebdon (pen) [47], Whitman [65]	460
21	11	H	Carlisle U	W 1-0	0-0	12	Redmile [68]	1555
22	18	A	Barnet	W 3-0	2-0	12	Whitman [23], Taylor 2 [30, 53]	2507
23	28	H	Exeter C	L 1-2	0-1	14	Taylor [87]	1808
24	Jan 1	H	Burton Alb	L 0-2	0-2	15		2443
25	8	A	Aldershot T	L 3-4	2-2	18	Storer [7], Taylor 2 [30, 90]	2373
26	22	H	Accrington S	W 1-0	0-0	15	Rawle [48]	1064
27	29	A	Woking	L 1-2	0-0	15	Bampton [90]	2114
28	Feb 1	A	Burton Alb	D 1-1	0-1	—	Taylor [62]	1673
29	15	A	Crawley T	L 0-3	0-1	—		1237
30	19	A	Gravesend & N	L 0-2	0-1	16		1042
31	22	H	Leigh RMI	L 0-1	0-0	—		902
32	Mar 5	A	Dagenham & R	D 0-0	0-0	17		1238
33	8	H	Hereford U	D 2-2	1-1	—	Taylor [5], Cooper [82]	1012
34	12	H	Northwich Vic	W 3-0	2-0	16	Redmile [3], Soares [26], Taylor [57]	1059
35	15	A	Scarborough	D 2-2	2-1	—	Whitman [8], Smith A [45]	1158
36	19	H	York C	W 1-0	1-0	15	Taylor [31]	1136
37	25	A	Halifax T	D 3-3	2-2	15	Redmile [5], Taylor [13], Smith A [70]	1998
38	28	H	Stevenage Bor	D 0-0	0-0	15		1251
39	Apr 2	A	Forest Green R	D 1-1	1-0	15	Taylor [29]	844
40	9	H	Canvey Is	W 1-0	0-0	14	Whitman [60]	1046
41	16	A	Farnborough T	D 2-2	2-1	15	Whitman 2 [11, 15]	510
42	23	H	Morecambe	D 0-0	0-0	15		1846

Final League Position: 15

GOALSCORERS

League (53): Taylor 19, Whitman 11, Ebdon 4 (2 pens), Harrad 3 (1 pen), Redmile 3, Ross 2, Smith A 2, Bampton 1, Brown A 1, Brown M 1, Colkin 1, Cooper 1, May 1, Rawle 1, Soares 1, Storer 1.
FA Cup (2): Cooper 2.
Trophy (5): Ebdon 3 (1 pen), Cooper 1, Smith 1.

Price 35	Smith A 34	Brown A 18 + 6	Sheppard 10 + 12	Redmile 38	Stamps 29 + 1	Blunt 7	Cooper 22 + 3	Ross 7	Whitman 27 + 7	Ebdon 31	May 2 + 6	Shaw 1 + 5	Johnson 2 + 2	Bampton 17 + 5	Colkin 17 + 2	Smith N 1 + 4	Taylor 31 + 4	Storer 17 + 12	Sylla 1	Brown M 5	Robinson 20 + 1	Harrad 6	Simpson 27 + 2	Turner 12 + 1	Francis — + 11	Curtis 3 + 3	Hawkins 1 + 1	Neal 5	Rawle 3	Douglas — + 1	McIntyre 2 + 1	Rose 6	Millard 2	Soares 6 + 1	Marcelle 6 + 4	Stirling 5	Morrison 6	*Match No.*
1	2	3	4	5	6	7	8	9^1	10^2	11	12	13																										1
1	2	3	4^2		6	7	8	9	10	11	13	12	5^1																									2
1	2	3	12	5	6	7^1	8	9^3	10	11^2	14			13	4																							3
1	2	3	4	5	6		8	9^3	10	11^1	14	13		12	7^2																							4
1	2	3^1	4	5	6		13	9^3	10		14	7^2		8	11	12																						5
1	2^1	3		5	6	7^2	8	9	10			13		4	11		12																					6
1	2	3	4	5	6	7^1	8^2	9^3	10		14		13		11		12																					7
1	2^1	3^2	12	5	6	7					9	14	13	8		11^3	10	4																				8
1		13	12	5	6	7^1	8				9^2		3	2			10	4	11																			9
1		12	13	5	6^2		8							2^1	11		9	7		10	3	4																10
1		12	13	5	6		8								7		10	4^1		11^2	3	9	2															11
1		3	4	5	6					11^1				12	8		10	13		7		9^2	2															12
1	8	13	4^2		6^1				14	11					7		10	12		3	5	9^3	2															13
1	2^1	12		5	6		8		14	7							10	13		4^2	3	9^3	11															14
1	2			5	6		8		13	11^1					7		10	12			4	9^2	3															15
1				5	6		8		10^1	11					7		9				3		2	4	12													16
1	2		12	5	6^1					11				7^2	4		9	13			3			8		10												17
1	2			5	6					11					4	12	10				3		8	7^1	13	9^2												18
1	2				6		8		10					4	3^1		9	13			5			7	12	11^2												19
1	2			5	6				10^2	11					12		9	4			3		8	7^1	13													20
1	2			5	6^1				10^2	11					12		9	7			3		8	4		13												21
1	2			5					10^3	11				12	3		8^2	7^1			6		4	9	13	14												22
1	2			5	12				10	11					3^1		9	7			6		8^2	4			13											23
1	2^1		13	5			14		10	11				12			9	7^2			3		8	4			6^3											24
	2		13	5	6		14		10	11^1							9	7^2			8		3	4^3		12		1										25
			4^1	5	6		8		13	11				3	2	12	10						7					1	9^2									26
	2^1			5	6		8^2		14	11				7			10^3	12			3		4		13			1	9									27
	2		13	5	6		8							4^1		12	10	7^2			3		11					1	9									28
	2^1		4	5					10^3	7				6■			9^2	13			8			14				1		12	3	11						29
	2		4^2	5	6				14	7							9				3		13	8^1	12						11	10^3	1					30
	2			5	6^1				10	11				4			9^3	14			7^2		13	3							12	8	1					31
1	2			5	6		8		10^3	11				4■			13	12					3									9^2		7^1	14			32
1	2■	12		5	6^1		8		10^2	11							9						3									7		4	13			33
1		3	12	5			8		10	11^1							9^3	13					4									7^2		6	14	2		34
1	2^1	3	12	5			8		10									7					6		13									4^2	9	11		35
1		3	13	5			8		10^2								9	7					2		12									6^1	11	4		36
1	2	3		5					10^1	11							9	7					4											12		6	8	37
1	2	3		5					12	11							10	8^1					6											7^2	13	4	9	38
1	2	3					8■		7	11				5			10						6												9		4	39
1	2	3		5					10	7				6^1				8^2			12		4		13										9		11	40
1	2	3		5					10	11				6			12	8					7												9^1		4	41
1	2	3		5					10	7				4			9	12					8		13										11^1		6^2	42

FA Cup

Fourth Qual	Burscough	(h)	2-1
First Round	Blackpool	(a)	0-3

FA Trophy

Third Round	Gresley R	(h)	5-0
Fourth Round	Exeter C	(h)	0-3

WOKING

Conference

Ground: Kingfield Sports Ground, Kingfield, Woking, Surrey GU22 9AA.
Tel: (01483) 772 470.
Year Formed: 1889.
Record Gate: 6,084 (1997 v Coventry City, FA Cup Third Round).
Nickname: The Cards.
Manager: Glenn Cockerill.
Secretary: Phil Ledger.
Colours: Red and white shirts, black shorts, red stockings.

WOKING 2004–05 LEAGUE RECORD

Match No.	Date	Venue	Opponents	Result		H/T Score	Lg. Pos.	Goalscorers	Attendance
1	Aug 14	A	Scarborough	L	0-2	0-2	—		1602
2	17	H	Exeter C	D	3-3	0-1	—	Selley 2 (1 pen) 52 (p), 84, Ferguson 69	2523
3	21	H	Leigh RMI	W	1-0	0-0	12	Richards 54	1499
4	28	A	Dagenham & R	D	1-1	0-1	15	Evans 80	1512
5	30	H	Aldershot T	L	1-2	1-0	16	Ferguson 10	3718
6	Sept 4	A	Accrington S	D	0-0	0-0	16		2004
7	11	H	Carlisle U	D	1-1	0-0	14	Richards 50	2581
8	18	A	Morecambe	L	1-2	1-1	17	Canham 39	1295
9	21	A	Tamworth	W	3-1	3-1	—	Nade 3, Richards 13, Evans 37	814
10	25	H	Canvey Is	W	1-0	1-0	12	Richards 17	1845
11	Oct 2	A	Barnet	D	2-2	0-1	12	Nade 49, Selley 84	2106
12	5	H	Forest Green R	L	0-1	0-1	—		1643
13	8	H	Halifax T	W	2-1	0-1	—	Evans 64, Selley (pen) 90	1864
14	16	A	Hereford U	D	2-2	0-2	14	Richards 50, Murray 53	2878
15	23	H	Burton Alb	W	1-0	1-0	13	Oliver 2	1710
16	Nov 6	A	Crawley T	L	1-2	0-1	14	Foyewa 85	2341
17	20	H	York C	W	1-0	0-0	13	Canham 72	2072
18	27	A	Gravesend & N	D	1-1	0-0	12	Nade 65	1189
19	Dec 4	H	Northwich Vic	W	2-0	1-0	9	MacDonald 8, Murray 77	1833
20	7	A	Stevenage Bor	W	2-0	0-0	—	Louis 53, Oliver 70	1816
21	11	H	Morecambe	D	0-0	0-0	9		1810
22	18	A	Carlisle U	L	1-2	0-0	10	Richards 47	5159
23	26	H	Farnborough T	W	2-0	2-0	7	Selley 35, Louis 45	3004
24	28	A	Canvey Is	D	2-2	1-1	7	Nade 45, Selley (pen) 85	912
25	Jan 1	A	Farnborough T	D	0-0	0-0	8		1730
26	8	H	Barnet	D	1-1	0-1	12	Oliver 68	2832
27	22	A	Forest Green R	W	3-1	2-1	7	Murray 21, Richards 23, Oliver 54	719
28	29	H	Tamworth	W	2-1	0-0	7	Oliver 51, Richards 56	2114
29	Feb 12	H	Crawley T	W	2-0	0-0	6	Selley (pen) 55, Evans 58	2611
30	19	A	York C	W	2-0	1-0	3	Richards 2 41, 89	2038
31	Mar 5	A	Northwich Vic	W	3-1	1-0	4	Sharpling 29, Murray 64, Nade 88	780
32	8	A	Burton Alb	W	1-0	0-0	—	Evans 55	910
33	19	A	Exeter C	D	0-0	0-0	3		3929
34	23	H	Scarborough	D	1-1	0-0	—	Nade 64	2567
35	27	A	Aldershot T	L	0-4	0-3	7		4458
36	Apr 2	H	Dagenham & R	L	2-4	1-2	10	Louis 18, Richards 90	2351
37	5	H	Stevenage Bor	L	1-2	0-1	—	Goodliffe (og) 56	1951
38	9	A	Leigh RMI	W	3-0	1-0	10	Nade 2 35, 78, Richards 80	215
39	14	H	Gravesend & N	W	2-0	2-0	—	Richards 16, Nade 32	1557
40	16	H	Accrington S	W	2-1	1-1	6	Sharpling 45, MacDonald 90	2557
41	19	H	Hereford U	D	1-1	0-0	—	Boardman 88	3298
42	23	A	Halifax T	L	1-3	0-0	8	Richards 90	1398

Final League Position: 8

GOALSCORERS

League (58): Richards 14, Nade 9, Selley 7 (4 pens), Evans 5, Oliver 5, Murray 4, Louis 3, Canham 2, Ferguson 2, MacDonald 2, Sharpling 2, Boardman 1, Foyewa 1, own goal 1.
FA Cup (5): Murray 2, Richards 1, Selley 1, Tiesse 1.
LDV Vans Trophy (0).
Trophy (5): Louis 2, Evans 1, Murray 1, Richards 1.

Basso 22	Murray 38 + 1	Cockerill 10 + 3	Boardman 40	MacDonald 33 + 1	Oliver 38 + 1	Selley 39	Canham 11 + 4	Richards 34 + 7	Nade 33 + 7	Smith 27 + 5	Johnson 9 + 6	Ferguson 6 + 11	Foyewa 11 + 24	Evans 28 + 1	Jackson 20 + 5	Tiesse 1 + 2	Jalal 20 + 1	Sharpling 18 + 5	Louis 21 + 2	Gosling 2 + 6	Cooney1	Match No.
1	2	3	4	5	6	7	8	9	10	11												1
1	2	3	4	5		7		9	10	6	8[1]	12	11[2]	13								2
1	2	3■	4	5	12	7	14	9	10	6[1]	13	8[2]	11[3]									3
1	2		4		6■	7	8	9	10	3		12	11[1]	5								4
1	2		4			7	8■	9■	10	3[1]	12	6		5	11							5
1	2		4		6	7			10		5	8	9[1]	11	3	12						6
1	2	12	4		6	7		9	10		8	11[2]	13	3[1]	5							7
1	2[1]	3[3]	4	14	6	7	12[2]	9	10		11		13	5	8							8
			4	5	6	7	8	9	10	12	11[1]			3	2		1					9
			4	5	6	7	8	9	10		11[1]		12	3	2		1					10
			4	5	6	7	8	9■	10	12	11[2]	13		3	2[1]		1					11
	12		4	5	6	7	8	9	10		13	11[3]	14	3[2]	2[1]		1					12
	11		4	5	6	7	8	9	10		13[3]	14	12	3[2]	2[1]		1					13
	3		4	5	6	7	8[1]	9	10	13			12	11	2[2]		1					14
	2	12	4	5	6	7		9	8			13	10[2]	3[1]	11		1					15
	2		4	5	6	7		9	10	11	13		12			3[1]	1	8[2]				16
1	2			5	6	7	13	9	12	11[1]	8[3]		10	4[2]	3			14				17
1	2		4		6	7	12	9	10	5		13	11[2]	8	3[1]							18
1	2		4	5	6	7		9	10[1]	3			12	11					8			19
1	2		4	5	6	7		9[2]	10	11[1]			13	3	12			14	8[3]			20
1	2		4	5	6	7		9[3]	10[1]	3		14	13	11[2]				12	8			21
1	2		4	5	6	7	8	9[2]	10	3[1]		12	13						11			22
1	2		4	5	6	7		9[2]	13	11	3	14	12					8[1]	10[3]			23
1	2		4	5	6	7	8[1]	9	10[2]	3			13					12	11			24
1	2		4	5	6	7		13	10	3[1]			11[2]		12			8	9			25
	2		4	5	6	7		9		3		8	10[1]			12	1		11			26
	2	3[1]	4	5	6	7		9					10		11		1	12	8			27
	2		4	5	6	7		9[2]	13		12		11[1]		3		1	8	10			28
	2		4	5	6	7		9[3]	13	12			14	11	3[1]		1	8[2]	10			29
	2		4	5	6	7		9[2]	14	12			13	11	3[1]		1	8	10[3]			30
	2	13	4	5	6	7		14	10	3			12	11[2]			1	8[1]	9[3]			31
	2		4	5	6	7		12	10	3			13	11			1	8[1]	9[2]			32
	2	3	4[1]	5[2]	6	7[3]		14	10	11					13		1	8	9	12		33
	2	3	4		6■			9	10	5		12	13■				1	8[1]	7[2]	11		34
	2	3	4■			7[1]		9	10	5		13			6		1	8	11[2]	12		35
	2	3			6			14	10[3]	11			13	7[2]	4[1]		1	8	9	12	5	36
1	2		4	5	6			9	13	3			12	11[2]				8	10	7[1]		37
1	2		4	5	6	7		14	10	3			13	11[2]				8[1]	9[3]	12		38
1	2		4	5	6	7		9[3]	10[2]	3			13	11[1]				8	14	12		39
1	2		4	5	6	7		9	10	3[1]			14	11[3]	12			8[2]	13			40
1[6]	2		4	5	6	7		9	10[2]	3[1]			13	11	12		15	8				41
	2	3[1]	4	5	6	7		14	13					11	8		1	10[2]	9[3]	12		42

FA Cup

Fourth Qual	Lymington & New M	(a)	1-1
		(h)	4-2
First Round	Notts Co	(a)	0-2

LDV Vans Trophy

First Round	Leyton Orient	(h)	0-3

FA Trophy

Third Round	Stevenage B	(h)	1-0
Fourth Round	Alfreton T	(a)	3-0
Fifth Round	Carlisle U	(h)	1-0
Sixth Round	Burton Alb	(a)	0-1

YORK CITY — Conference

Ground: KitKat Crescent, York YO30 7AQ.
Tel: (01904) 624 447.
Year Formed: 1922.
Record Gate: 28,123 (1938 v Huddersfield T, FA Cup Sixth Round).
Nickname: Minster Men.
Manager: Billy McEwan.
Colours: Red shirts, navy shorts, navy stockings.

YORK CITY 2004–05 LEAGUE RECORD

Match No.	Date	Venue	Opponents	Result		H/T Score	Lg. Pos.	Goalscorers	Attendance
1	Aug 14	A	Aldershot T	L	0-2	0-0	—		3368
2	17	H	Tamworth	W	2-0	1-0	—	Groves 15, Robinson PD 60	2466
3	21	H	Hereford U	L	0-3	0-2	16		2602
4	28	A	Gravesend & N	L	0-4	0-2	16		1350
5	31	H	Accrington S	L	0-1	0-0	—		2272
6	Sept 4	A	Dagenham & R	W	3-0	1-0	17	Groves 23, Dunning 2 86, 89	1475
7	11	A	Crawley T	L	0-1	0-1	18		2134
8	18	H	Northwich Vic	D	0-0	0-0	19		2087
9	21	H	Leigh RMI	D	1-1	0-0	—	Dunning (pen) 49	1708
10	25	A	Burton Alb	W	2-0	0-0	16	Groves 74, Bishop 90	1789
11	Oct 2	H	Stevenage Bor	W	3-1	2-0	13	Bishop 27, Nogan 30, Brass 87	2043
12	5	A	Morecambe	L	1-2	0-1	—	Yalcin 90	1734
13	9	A	Farnborough T	D	1-1	0-1	16	Bishop 81	724
14	16	H	Canvey Is	D	0-0	0-0	16		2207
15	23	A	Barnet	L	0-4	0-2	17		2501
16	Nov 6	H	Forest Green R	L	1-3	0-2	19	Bishop 90	2132
17	20	A	Woking	L	0-1	0-0	19		2072
18	27	H	Carlisle U	W	2-1	1-0	19	Nogan 44, Merris 69	3842
19	Dec 7	H	Halifax T	D	1-1	0-0	—	Donovan 89	2394
20	11	A	Northwich Vic	L	0-3	0-3	19		673
21	18	H	Crawley T	W	3-1	1-0	17	Grant 40, Robinson P 69, Bishop 85	1848
22	26	A	Scarborough	L	1-5	0-3	17	Grant 65	4586
23	29	H	Burton Alb	L	1-2	0-1	—	Robinson P 74	2184
24	Jan 2	H	Scarborough	L	0-2	0-0	19		4439
25	8	A	Stevenage Bor	D	2-2	2-1	18	Maloney 24, Webster 34	2044
26	22	H	Morecambe	W	1-0	0-0	18	Bishop (pen) 88	2270
27	29	A	Leigh RMI	W	3-0	0-0	18	Bishop 2 65, 90, Nogan 67	701
28	Feb 6	H	Aldershot T	L	0-2	0-2	18		2133
29	12	A	Forest Green R	D	1-1	1-0	18	Bishop 35	870
30	19	H	Woking	L	0-2	0-1	18		2038
31	22	A	Exeter C	W	1-0	0-0	—	Merris 62	2762
32	Mar 1	H	Barnet	W	2-1	1-0	—	Donovan 45, Maloney 68	1926
33	5	H	Exeter C	L	1-2	1-1	16	Maloney 38	2272
34	14	A	Halifax T	L	0-2	0-0	—		2165
35	19	A	Tamworth	L	0-1	0-1	17		1136
36	28	A	Accrington S	D	2-2	0-0	17	Maloney 51, Bishop 65	2201
37	Apr 2	H	Gravesend & N	D	0-0	0-0	17		2090
38	9	A	Hereford U	L	0-2	0-2	17		2973
39	12	A	Carlisle U	L	0-6	0-2	—		3810
40	16	H	Dagenham & R	D	0-0	0-0	17		1933
41	19	A	Canvey Is	L	0-4	0-3	—		817
42	23	H	Farnborough T	W	4-0	1-0	17	Bishop 9, Stewart 53, Yalcin 60, Robinson PD 90	2055

Final League Position: 17

GOALSCORERS

League (39): Bishop 11 (1 pen), Maloney 4, Robinson P 4, Dunning 3 (1 pen), Groves 3, Nogan 3, Donovan 2, Grant 2, Merris 2, Robinson P 2, Robinson PD 2, Yalcin 2, Brass 1, Stewart 1, Webster 1.
FA Cup (1): Dunning 1.
LDV Vans Trophy (0).
Trophy (0).

Crichton 4	Brass 20 + 2	Smith 16 + 3	Groves 38 + 4	Clarke 5	Davies 16	Pearson 12	Dunning 37 + 1	Robinson PD 18 + 11	Bishop 37 + 1	Stewart 15 + 3	Law 24 + 7	Yalcin 10 + 21	Arthur — + 1	Merris 38 + 2	Donovan 30 + 1	Nogan 18 + 4	Porter 18	Stockdale 20 + 1	Harrison — + 3	McGurk 5 + 1	Coad 1 + 1	Haw — + 2	Staley 10 + 2	Grant 7 + 1	Ashcroft 2	Robinson P 9 + 8	Webster 13 + 2	Maloney 13	Constable 2	Jackson 7 + 3	Davis 14 + 1	Armstrong 3 + 2	*Match No.*
1	2	3	4	5^{1}		$7^{\blacksquare}$	8	9^{2}	10	11	12	13																			6		1
1	7^{1}	3	4	5			8	9	10^{2}	11	2	13	12																		6		2
1	7	3^{1}	4	5			8	9	10	11^{2}	2	13		12																	6		3
1	2	3^{2}	4	5			8	9^{1}	10	11^{3}	13			14	7	12															6		4
	5		4				8	14	10^{3}	11^{1}	2	13		3	7	9^{2}	$1^{\blacksquare}$	12													6		5
	5		4			7^{1}	8	14	10^{3}		2	13		3	11	9^{2}		1	12												6		6
	6		4	5		7	8	14	10^{3}		2	13		3	11^{1}	9^{2}		1	12														7
	6		4			7	8	9	10		2	12		3		11^{1}		1		5													8
	6^{1}		4			7	8	9	10	12	2	13		3		11^{2}		1		5													9
			4			6	8	9^{1}	10	11	2			3		7		1	12	5													10
	13		4			6	8	9^{1}	10	11	2	12		3		7^{2}		1		5													11
	12		4			6	8	9	10	11	2^{1}	14		3		7^{3}		1		5^{2}	13												12
	2	12	4		5	6	8	9	10	11^{1}		13		3		7^{2}		1															13
	2		4		6	5	8	9		11		10^{2}		3		7^{1}		1		12		13											14
	2	12	4		6	5^{1}	8	9^{2}	10	11		13		3				1			7^{3}	14											15
	2		4^{1}		5	6	8		10	11		9		3	13	7^{2}		1					12										16
	5		4		3		8		10			12		11	7^{1}	9		1					2	6									17
	5		4		6				10^{2}		12	13		3	7^{1}	9		1					2	11	8								18
	5^{1}		4		6		13	14			12	9^{3}		11	7	10		1					2	3	8^{2}								19
	3		4^{1}		6		8	12	10					11	7	9^{2}		1					2	5		13							20
	2	3	4		6		8	9^{1}	10			12		11	7			1						5									21
	2	$3^{\blacksquare}$	4		6		8	9^{1}	10					11	7			1						5		12							22
	2^{1}		4		6		8	9	10^{3}					11	7	13	1						3	5^{2}		14	12						23
		3	4				8	9^{2}	10^{3}		12			11	7	13	1						2			14	6	5^{1}					24
		3^{1}	4				8	9	10^{2}					11	7	13	1						2	12			6	5					25
			4		6		8	13	10		12			3	7	9^{2}	1						2^{1}					5	11				26
			4		6		$8^{\blacksquare}$	13	10			12		11	7	9^{2}	1						2				3^{1}	5					27
			4		6			14	10		12	13		11	7	9^{3}	1						2^{1}				3	5	8^{2}				28
			4		6		8	9^{1}	10		2	12		11	7		1										3	5					29
		3	4				8		10		2^{1}	13		11	7		1						12			9	6^{2}	5					30
			4		6		8		10		2			11	7		1									9	3	5					31
		3	4				8		10		2			11	7		1									9	6	5					32
		3	4				8^{1}	12	10^{2}		2			11	7		1									9	6	5		13			33
		3^{1}	4				8^{2}		10		2	13		11	7		1									14	6	5		9^{3}	12		34
		3^{1}	12				8	14			2	13		11	7		1									9^{3}	6^{2}	5		10	4		35
		3^{1}	12				8		10		2	6^{2}		11	7		1									14	13	5		9^{3}	4		36
		3^{1}	12				8	13	10^{3}		2	6		11	7		1									14				9^{2}	4	5	37
		3^{1}	12				8			13	2	4		11	7		1									9				10^{2}	6	5	38
			4^{2}				8^{1}		13	12	2	6		11	7		1									9				10	5	3	39
			4				8		10	11	2	6		3	7			1								9^{1}				12	5		40
			4						10	11	2^{1}	6		3	7			1								9^{2}	8			13	5	12	41
		13	4						10	11	2^{1}	6		3^{2}	7			1								14	8^{3}			9	5	12	42

FA Cup
Fourth Qual   Carlisle U   (a)   1-3

LDV Vans Trophy
First Round   Blackpool   (h)   0-2

FA Trophy
Third Round   Burton Alb   (a)   0-3

CONFERENCE SECOND DIVISION 2004–05

CONFERENCE NORTH FINAL LEAGUE TABLE

			Home					*Away*					*Total*						
		P	*W*	*D*	*L*	*F*	*A*	*W*	*D*	*L*	*F*	*A*	*W*	*D*	*L*	*F*	*A*	*GD*	*Pts*
1	Southport	42	12	6	3	35	20	13	3	5	48	25	25	9	8	83	45	38	84
2	Nuneaton Borough	42	13	3	5	29	17	12	3	6	39	28	25	6	11	68	45	23	81
3	Droylsden	42	13	3	5	46	26	11	4	6	36	26	24	7	11	82	52	30	79
4	Kettering Town	42	10	4	7	22	21	11	3	7	34	29	21	7	14	56	50	6	70
5	Altrincham	42	12	6	3	45	21	7	6	8	21	25	19	12	11	66	46	20	69
6	Harrogate Town	42	13	5	3	40	22	6	6	9	22	27	19	11	12	62	49	13	68
7	Worcester City	42	10	5	6	32	25	6	7	8	27	28	16	12	14	59	53	6	60
8	Stafford Rangers	42	8	10	3	33	20	6	7	8	19	24	14	17	11	52	44	8	59
9	Redditch United*	42	11	3	7	36	32	7	5	9	29	27	18	8	16	65	59	6	59
10	Hucknall Town	42	7	8	6	31	32	8	6	7	28	25	15	14	13	59	57	2	59
11	Gainsborough Trinity	42	7	8	6	27	22	9	1	11	28	33	16	9	17	55	55	0	57
12	Hinckley United	42	8	5	8	29	31	7	6	8	26	31	15	11	16	55	62	–7	56
13	Lancaster City	42	9	4	8	23	22	5	8	8	28	37	14	12	16	51	59	–8	54
14	Alfreton Town	42	7	5	9	24	23	8	3	10	29	32	15	8	19	53	55	–2	53
15	Vauxhall Motors	42	7	7	7	20	22	7	4	10	28	35	14	11	17	48	57	–9	53
16	Barrow	42	8	5	8	32	39	6	5	10	18	25	14	10	18	50	64	–14	52
17	Worksop Town†	42	11	4	6	36	29	5	8	8	23	30	16	12	14	59	59	0	50
18	Moor Green	42	8	4	9	26	28	5	6	10	29	36	13	10	19	55	64	–9	49
19	Stalybridge Celtic	42	7	6	8	30	36	5	6	10	22	34	12	12	18	52	70	–18	48
20	Runcorn FC Halton	42	7	6	8	24	26	3	6	12	20	37	10	12	20	44	63	–19	42
21	Ashton United	42	6	2	13	27	39	2	7	12	19	40	8	9	25	46	79	–33	33
22	Bradford Park Avenue	42	3	5	13	20	37	2	4	15	17	33	5	9	28	37	70	–33	24

**Redditch United deducted 3 points.*
†Worksop Town deducted 10 points.

CONFERENCE NORTH LEADING GOALSCORERS

Terry Fearns *(Southport)*	28
Colin Little *(Altrincham)*	24
Norman Sylla *(Redditch United)*	22
Adam Webster *(Worcester City)*	22
Peter Duffield *(Alfreton Town)*	20

CONFERENCE SOUTH FINAL LEAGUE TABLE

			Home					*Away*					*Total*						
		P	*W*	*D*	*L*	*F*	*A*	*W*	*D*	*L*	*F*	*A*	*W*	*D*	*L*	*F*	*A*	*GD*	*Pts*
1	Grays Athletic	42	15	4	2	60	13	15	4	2	58	18	30	8	4	118	31	87	98
2	Cambridge City	42	10	3	8	29	25	13	3	5	31	19	23	6	13	60	44	16	75
3	Thurrock	42	9	3	9	29	32	12	3	6	32	24	21	6	15	61	56	5	69
4	Lewes	42	11	6	4	42	29	7	5	9	31	35	18	11	13	73	64	9	65
5	Eastbourne Borough	42	10	5	6	38	26	8	5	8	27	21	18	10	14	65	47	18	64
6	Basingstoke Town	42	12	3	6	37	20	7	3	11	20	32	19	6	17	57	52	5	63
7	Weymouth	42	8	8	5	32	28	9	3	9	30	31	17	11	14	62	59	3	62
8	Dorchester Town	42	11	5	5	40	33	6	6	9	37	48	17	11	14	77	81	–4	62
9	Bognor Regis Town	42	11	4	6	46	31	6	5	10	24	34	17	9	16	70	65	5	60
10	Bishop's Stortford	42	13	3	5	39	25	4	5	12	31	41	17	8	17	70	66	4	59
11	Weston-Super-Mare	42	12	5	4	33	23	3	8	10	22	37	15	13	14	55	60	–5	58
12	Hayes	42	9	4	8	29	30	6	7	8	26	27	15	11	16	55	57	–2	56
13	Havant and Waterlooville	42	12	3	6	38	26	4	4	13	26	43	16	7	19	64	69	–5	55
14	St Albans City	42	8	3	10	34	37	8	3	10	30	39	16	6	20	64	76	–12	54
15	Sutton United	42	5	6	10	25	38	9	5	7	35	33	14	11	17	60	71	–11	53
16	Welling United	42	5	5	11	23	30	10	2	9	41	38	15	7	20	64	68	–4	52
17	Hornchurch*	42	11	5	5	44	24	6	5	10	27	39	17	10	15	71	63	8	51
18	Newport County	42	8	5	8	36	34	5	6	10	20	27	13	11	18	56	61	–5	50
19	Carshalton Athletic	42	7	3	11	19	31	6	6	9	25	41	13	9	20	44	72	–28	48
20	Maidenhead United	42	5	7	9	31	41	7	3	11	23	40	12	10	20	54	81	–27	46
21	Margate*	42	9	3	9	30	29	3	5	13	24	46	12	8	22	54	75	–21	34
22	Redbridge†	42	6	3	12	25	40	5	0	16	25	46	11	3	28	50	86	–36	33

**Hornchurch and Margate deducted 10 points.*
†Redbridge deducted 3 points.

CONFERENCE SOUTH LEADING GOALSCORERS

Luke Nightingale *(Bognor Regis Town)*	32
Lee Clarke *(St Albans City)*	25
Matt Groves *(Dorchester Town)*	24
Dean Holdsworth *(Havant & Waterlooville)*	23
Paul Booth *(Welling United)*	20

CONFERENCE SECOND DIVISION NORTH RESULTS 2004–05

	Alfreton T	Altrincham	Ashton U	Barrow	Bradford PA	Droylsden	Gainsborough T	Harrogate T	Hinckley U	Hucknall T	Kettering T	Lancaster C	Moor Green	Nuneaton B	Redditch U	Runcorn	Southport	Stafford R	Stalybridge C	Vauxhall M	Worcester C	Worksop T
Alfreton T	—	0-2	1-1	1-1	2-1	0-1	0-1	2-0	0-2	0-2	1-2	2-3	2-2	2-0	1-2	4-0	2-1	0-1	1-0	3-1	0-0	0-0
Altrincham	1-2	—	1-2	2-0	0-0	2-2	4-1	3-0	4-1	1-1	3-3	4-0	0-2	1-0	0-0	3-3	2-1	1-0	4-1	3-1	2-0	4-1
Ashton U	3-1	0-1	—	1-2	0-0	1-0	1-3	3-2	0-2	0-0	0-2	2-0	1-3	2-3	2-3	5-4	0-3	1-2	2-3	0-2	1-0	2-3
Barrow	0-3	2-0	1-1	—	3-2	1-3	2-0	1-0	3-0	0-3	2-1	2-2	3-4	1-3	1-6	1-1	0-2	2-2	2-1	1-2	2-2	2-1
Bradford PA	0-4	1-2	3-3	0-1	—	2-0	0-3	1-2	1-1	2-4	1-2	1-0	1-1	2-2	0-3	0-1	3-1	3-1	0-1	0-1	0-1	1-1
Droylsden	3-2	2-0	4-0	2-0	3-3	—	2-1	2-1	1-0	3-1	2-3	3-4	2-2	1-0	1-0	3-0	1-3	4-0	0-0	4-0	2-3	1-3
Gainsborough T	1-2	0-1	1-0	1-0	2-0	1-1	—	0-0	1-1	0-1	1-1	4-2	1-1	1-2	2-1	2-3	1-0	1-1	2-2	1-2	3-0	1-1
Harrogate T	2-1	1-1	5-1	2-1	2-1	2-1	5-1	—	1-1	0-0	2-1	1-1	1-2	3-1	4-2	1-0	2-5	0-1	2-0	2-1	2-0	0-0
Hinckley U	1-0	2-1	3-1	1-0	4-0	3-3	3-1	0-1	—	0-3	0-1	2-2	2-1	2-3	1-2	0-0	0-0	0-2	1-1	1-4	0-4	3-1
Hucknall T	4-0	4-2	2-1	1-2	0-0	0-4	2-5	1-1	1-1	—	2-1	0-2	1-1	1-3	2-1	0-0	2-4	2-1	3-0	1-1	2-2	0-0
Kettering T	1-1	0-1	0-0	2-0	1-0	0-2	0-1	0-0	3-1	3-1	—	0-2	1-2	1-0	1-0	2-1	0-5	0-1	2-0	1-1	2-1	2-1
Lancaster C	0-1	1-1	2-0	2-1	0-1	0-1	2-0	0-3	2-3	2-2	1-0	—	3-1	0-2	0-0	2-1	1-1	1-0	0-1	3-1	0-2	1-0
Moor Green	0-1	2-2	2-0	1-1	1-0	1-2	2-1	2-1	2-1	1-1	1-2	0-2	—	1-3	1-0	2-1	2-3	0-1	2-2	0-2	1-2	2-0
Nuneaton B	1-1	0-0	1-0	1-1	2-1	3-2	1-0	2-0	0-1	1-3	2-0	2-0	1-0	—	0-1	3-0	0-1	4-3	1-0	2-1	2-0	0-2
Redditch U	1-3	0-1	3-2	2-0	3-1	1-1	0-1	2-1	3-0	1-1	2-3	0-0	3-1	1-5	—	1-0	3-2	1-0	2-3	4-1	0-4	3-2
Runcorn	1-0	2-1	2-0	1-0	2-1	1-3	0-1	0-0	1-2	1-2	2-0	2-2	2-1	0-0	0-1	—	0-2	3-3	1-1	1-1	2-2	0-1
Southport	3-1	2-1	1-2	0-0	1-0	3-0	2-1	2-3	3-2	1-0	1-3	0-0	2-1	3-0	1-1	3-1	—	0-0	2-0	2-1	2-2	1-1
Stafford R	3-1	0-1	1-1	2-2	1-0	2-0	2-0	1-1	1-1	1-2	3-0	2-2	2-1	2-3	1-1	0-0	1-1	—	3-2	1-1	0-0	4-0
Stalybridge C	2-3	1-1	2-1	1-2	1-4	1-3	2-2	1-3	0-2	2-0	1-2	2-2	2-2	1-1	1-0	1-0	3-5	1-0	—	2-1	1-0	2-2
Vauxhall M	2-0	2-0	0-0	0-2	1-0	1-2	1-0	1-1	0-2	1-0	0-2	3-1	1-0	1-1	1-1	1-2	0-3	0-0	1-2	—	2-2	1-1
Worcester C	0-0	2-1	2-2	0-1	2-1	3-1	1-2	1-2	1-1	3-0	2-2	3-1	4-1	0-2	2-1	2-1	1-3	0-0	2-1	1-0	—	0-2
Worksop T	3-2	1-1	3-1	2-1	2-1	0-2	1-3	2-0	3-1	2-1	0-3	2-0	1-0	2-3	5-3	1-1	1-2	0-0	1-1	2-3	2-0	—

CONFERENCE SECOND DIVISION SOUTH RESULTS 2004–05

	Basingstoke T	Bishop's Stortford	Bognor Regis T	Cambridge C	Carshalton Ath	Dorchester T	Eastbourne B	Grays Ath	Havant & W	Hayes	Hornchurch	Lewes	Maidenhead U	Margate	Newport Co	Redbridge	St Albans C	Sutton U	Thurrock	Welling U	Weston-S-Mare	Weymouth
Basingstoke T	—	2-3	2-1	2-1	0-1	2-2	0-2	0-3	3-2	2-0	2-0	0-0	0-1	2-1	3-0	3-0	5-1	1-0	3-0	4-0	1-1	0-1
Bishop's Stortford	1-3	—	2-3	3-0	2-0	2-1	2-0	1-2	1-1	0-4	3-1	1-0	2-1	3-0	3-0	2-1	2-0	3-2	0-0	4-2	2-2	0-2
Bognor Regis T	2-1	3-1	—	1-2	1-0	7-2	1-0	0-0	1-1	1-2	3-1	1-3	1-2	2-2	0-2	4-1	4-1	0-1	3-2	6-5	3-0	2-2
Cambridge C	2-1	3-2	1-0	—	3-0	2-2	2-2	0-2	2-0	1-0	0-3	2-3	0-1	2-1	2-0	2-1	2-0	0-1	0-0	0-1	1-2	4-1
Carshalton Ath	2-0	0-3	0-0	0-2	—	4-3	1-4	0-2	2-1	3-2	0-2	1-0	1-1	0-1	1-0	1-0	1-3	1-2	0-2	0-1	1-1	0-1
Dorchester T	0-1	4-3	1-0	0-0	1-1	—	3-1	0-7	2-1	1-1	3-1	1-1	4-2	2-0	1-0	4-1	2-3	2-2	0-2	3-2	2-3	4-1
Eastbourne B	2-0	1-1	4-1	1-2	1-4	3-2	—	2-2	1-2	1-0	4-2	1-2	0-0	1-1	1-0	1-2	1-0	2-2	4-0	0-1	3-0	4-2
Grays Ath	0-1	3-0	6-0	1-2	4-0	2-2	1-1	—	3-0	1-0	5-1	4-0	4-0	5-0	0-0	4-1	2-0	5-1	2-1	4-2	2-0	2-0
Havant & W	5-1	0-4	0-0	0-2	4-1	4-0	2-1	1-2	—	0-0	4-1	2-1	2-1	3-1	1-0	1-0	1-1	2-3	0-2	2-3	3-2	1-0
Hayes	0-1	2-3	0-1	4-0	1-3	0-1	1-1	1-1	1-5	—	1-1	3-2	2-1	1-0	3-1	1-0	3-2	1-0	1-3	1-1	1-0	1-3
Hornchurch	6-0	3-1	1-1	0-1	2-2	2-3	2-0	1-2	4-0	1-1	—	3-2	6-0	1-0	1-1	2-0	1-1	3-0	0-1	0-5	3-2	2-1
Lewes	0-0	2-1	2-1	2-2	1-1	3-1	1-0	3-2	3-1	3-2	1-2	—	0-1	7-3	2-2	5-4	1-2	0-1	1-1	2-1	3-1	0-0
Maidenhead U	1-1	2-2	2-3	1-5	4-0	0-1	1-2	0-3	1-0	1-1	2-2	1-0	—	2-4	0-2	4-3	3-3	2-2	0-3	2-1	0-0	2-3
Margate	2-1	1-0	2-3	0-2	0-1	1-2	2-1	0-6	5-1	3-1	0-1	1-1	2-0	—	1-1	2-0	2-3	1-1	2-1	1-2	2-0	0-1
Newport Co	0-1	6-3	1-0	0-1	0-1	3-2	1-3	1-4	1-1	1-1	2-2	2-2	2-1	2-0	—	2-3	1-0	2-4	1-2	4-1	2-2	2-0
Redbridge	0-3	1-1	1-2	0-0	1-3	4-1	0-3	1-3	3-1	0-1	0-1	0-1	4-1	2-1	0-5	—	2-1	0-5	1-2	1-2	1-1	3-2
St Albans C	2-1	2-0	4-0	1-0	3-1	1-1	0-0	1-4	3-1	0-1	4-3	2-3	1-2	3-3	0-1	2-3	—	1-2	1-3	2-5	1-0	0-3
Sutton U	1-0	0-0	0-0	0-3	4-1	3-2	0-0	0-6	1-1	2-4	1-2	3-5	2-2	2-0	0-0	2-3	1-2	—	1-2	1-0	1-2	0-3
Thurrock	3-1	1-0	0-5	0-1	2-2	1-2	1-0	2-4	1-3	2-1	1-0	2-0	1-2	1-2	2-2	1-0	1-2	1-2	—	1-1	3-1	2-1
Welling U	0-1	0-0	1-1	0-2	4-0	1-4	0-3	1-2	0-1	1-1	1-1	1-0	1-2	1-0	3-1	1-2	2-3	3-2	1-2	—	1-1	0-1
Weston-S-Mare	2-1	2-1	2-1	2-1	1-1	2-2	0-2	2-0	2-1	0-1	0-0	1-2	2-1	2-2	3-1	1-0	3-0	2-1	2-1	0-2	—	2-2
Weymouth	1-1	3-2	2-1	1-2	2-2	1-1	0-1	1-1	3-2	3-1	2-0	3-3	3-1	2-2	0-1	1-0	1-0	1-1	1-2	0-3	1-1	—

CONFERENCE CUP 2004–05

PRELIMINARY ROUND NORTH
Ashton United 6, Altrincham 2
Moor Green 1, Redditch United 2

PRELIMINARY ROUND SOUTH
Redbridge 0, Grays Athletic 3
Basingstoke Town 2, Lewes 1

FIRST ROUND NORTH
Droylsden 1, Ashton United 0
Worcester City 2, Stafford Rangers 1
Hucknall Town 1, Gainsborough Trinity 4
Nuneaton Borough 4, Redditch United 3
Vauxhall Motors 1, Runcorn FC Halton 2
Barrow 4, Southport 1
Kettering Town 4, Hinckley United 2
Alfreton Town 0, Worksop Town 1
Harrogate Town 0, Bradford Park Avenue 1
Stalybridge Celtic 4, Lancaster City 2

FIRST ROUND SOUTH
Bishops Stortford 5, Cambridge City 0
Bognor Regis Town 2, Eastbourne Borough 1
Hayes 1, Maidstone United 2
Hornchurch 1, Thurrock 2
St Albans City 2, Grays Athletic 6
Welling United 0, Margate 2
Dorchester Town 2, Weston-Super-Mare 1
Sutton United 3, Carshalton Athletic 2
Weymouth 0, Newport County 2
Havant & Waterlooville 2, Basingstoke Town 1

SECOND ROUND NORTH
Droylsden 1, Worcester City 2
Kettering Town 4, Nuneaton Borough 2
Barrow 0, Runcorn FC Halton 1
Worksop Town 4, Gainsborough Trinity 1
Stalybridge Celtic 1, Bradford Park Avenue 0

SECOND ROUND SOUTH
Thurrock 1, Margate 2
Dorchester Town 0, Newport County 1
Grays Athletic w.o. v Bishops Stortford withdrew
Maidstone United 2, Sutton United 4
Havant & Waterlooville 5, Bognor Regis Town 1

THIRD ROUND NORTH
Burton Albion 2, Hereford United 4
Kettering Town 1, Worksop Town 2
Tamworth 3, Worcester City 1
Morecambe 2, Scarborough 1
Northwich Victoria 1, Leigh RMI 0
Runcorn FC Halton 2, Carlisle United 6
Accrington Stanley 2, York City 1
Stalybridge Celtic 7, Halifax Town 3

THIRD ROUND SOUTH
Barnet 0, Grays Athletic 3
Forest Green Rovers 4, Newport County 2
Margate 2, Dagenham & Redbridge 1
Gravesend & Northfleet 0, Stevenage Borough 1
Sutton United 0, Woking 3
Havant & Waterlooville 2, Farnborough Town 0
Aldershot Town 1, Exeter City 0
Canvey Island 0, Crawley Town 0
Crawley Town won 6-4 on penalties.

FOURTH ROUND NORTH
Accrington Stanley 6, Tamworth 0
Morecambe 1, Carlisle United 1
Morecambe won 3-1 on penalties.
Hereford United 0, Northwich Victoria 1
Worksop Town 0, Stalybridge Celtic 1

FOURTH ROUND SOUTH
Stevenage Borough 1, Grays Athletic 1
Stevenage Borough won 3-1 on penalties.
Forest Green Rovers 5, Aldershot Town 1
Woking 2, Havant & Waterlooville 2
Woking won 4-3 on penalties.
Crawley Town 2, Margate 1

FIFTH ROUND NORTH
Accrington Stanley 4, Northwich Victoria 3
Morecambe 1, Stalybridge Celtic 2

FIFTH ROUND SOUTH
Stevenage Borough 2, Crawley Town 1
Woking 3, Forest Green Rovers 1

SEMI-FINAL NORTH
Stalybridge Celtic 0, Accrington Stanley 0
Stalybridge Celtic won 5-4 on penalties.

SEMI-FINAL SOUTH
Woking 4, Stevenage Borough 2

FINAL
Stalybridge Celtic 0, Woking 1
Stalybridge Celtic had won the toss for choice of ground.

CONFERENCE SECOND DIVISION PLAY-OFFS

NORTH PLAY-OFFS
SEMI-FINALS

Droylsden 1, Kettering Town 2
Nuneaton Borough 1, Altrincham 1
(Altrincham won 4-2 on penalties.)

FINAL

Kettering Town 2, Altrincham 3

SOUTH PLAY-OFFS
SEMI-FINALS

(Lewes declined place)
Thurrock 2, Eastbourne Borough 4

FINAL

Cambridge C 0, Eastbourne Borough 3

CONFERENCE SECOND DIVISION NORTH/SOUTH PLAY-OFF

FINAL

Cambridge C 0, Eastbourne Borough 3

REVIEW OF THE SCOTTISH SEASON 2004–05

In the Scottish League, pretty well everything was cut and dried with time to spare. On the last day there were no palpitations, no frenzied crowds, no despair, no exultation. No, everything had been fully settled and everyone knew exactly where he was for the new (and not very far distant) season. All the excitement was reserved this year for the SPL: there were intriguing situations across the board, and only a handful of the top-echelon clubs could rest easy: it did look straightforward at the top, where Celtic were about to come out above Rangers for the umpteenth time; there had been a fair bit of cut and thrust during the last months, but now an easy win for the Bhoys would leave Rangers once again in second place. This is a position which neither of the clubs enjoys. Rangers duly won their final match against Hibs, who were determined to hold on to their third place in the table and so qualify for European football. This they would do unless they lost heavily and allowed Aberdeen to make up the necessary ground on goal difference. Celtic cruised gently towards their win – until, in the last two minutes, they lost two startling goals and the match. And the league. Even Rangers were dumbfounded at this most unexpected result.

Now to the other end: Kilmarnock had moved above Inverness, and both were nicely clear of any trouble in 7th and 8th places. For the rest, turmoil and doubt. Thanks to some timely and refreshingly unlikely encouragement from Jim Leishman (doubtless with a poem or two thrown in), Dunfermline were all but clear of bottom spot, though even they could still go down if they lost by a bucketful and the other teams had the appropriate results. However, it did seem that one of Livingston, Dundee and Dundee United would finish in the relegation spot. In a fascinating set of games, with all looking over their shoulders at the others' scores, Dundee came out the losers; and that was that.

Well, actually it was not. Before the dust had time to settle, there were further storms on the horizon. There never does seem to be a clear-cut end to the SPL season, and the fixture makers must always be unsure, at least for a while, which team is going to be playing where next season.

Hibs did well during the season, and deserved their 3rd place. Inverness Caley Thistle, too, need a mention. They were many people's choice for a quick return to the First Division: they had to play their home games in Aberdeen, a difficult winter drive for home fans, until the SPL relaxed some conditions, and a frantic building effort allowed them into their newly furbished stadium in late January. The team showed a great deal of determination in maintaining their position in this league.

Falkirk won the First Division in style. At last they can ascend – and they certainly deserve to after the various bunkers that have attended their previous attempts after winning the Division. Clyde for a while looked to be serious competitors, but they fell away. St Mirren finished well, but a long way behind.

Raith Rovers were soon candidates for relegation from the First Division. They started badly, and got worse. Subsequently the arrival of Gordon Dalziel restored some pride, but he had an insurmountable problem, and must now address himself to a quick return from the Second Division. Going down with them are Partick Thistle. If the Jags did not quite emulate these basement proceedings, they did not show enough confidence, and they could not be salvaged by Dick Campbell. The Second Division also had a very clear winner, and Brechin go up again – this time with the brothers Campbell passing each other on the way up and down. Stranraer played Morton in their penultimate match. This was a vital result: with the draw, Stranraer went up (having also achieved promotion last year) and Morton were again left to rue one or two untidy earlier results. Berwick and Arbroath went down. This pair were not that far away from safety, and the final placings here were left till late on in the season. So to the Third Division, where Gretna and Peterhead soon forged ahead of the rest. Peterhead finished well above third-placed Cowdenbeath, and Gretna were twenty points ahead of Peterhead! They scored 130 League goals in the season – how often is that done? Gretna have solid backing, and intend to move on upwards. They may well do so. Peterhead have hovered near promotion in the last few seasons: this time they surprised themselves in achieving the move with some ease, and with a relatively small squad.

There were few surprises in the Bell's League Challenge Cup, though perhaps a sign or two of things to come in the League. Forfar reached the semi-final, where they lost to Ross County. In the other semi-final, Falkirk defeated St Johnstone, and then went on to win a close final. The CIS League Cup was won by Rangers. In the early stages, Forfar took five goals off St Mirren at Love Street; while Albion Rovers beat Queen of the South, then Brechin City, before losing to Hibs; Falkirk were seen off by Celtic, who subsequently lost to Rangers; Motherwell disposed of Morton, Inverness, Livingston and Hearts before losing easily to Rangers in the final.

Those two contests are largely for the early part of the season. The Tennent's Scottish Cup does not start until everyone has had a chance to settle down. Forfar, who had been in rampant form early in the season, now had a taste of their own medicine, losing heavily at home to Montrose; Gretna had an exciting tie with Dundee United, who scored three times in the first twenty minutes, and then were happy to win 4–3 as the home side came back with great gusto, and showed something of their goal-scoring skills which were so striking in the Third Division. The semi-finals promised a possible all-Edinburgh final: however, it was not to be as both teams lost, and the final was between Dundee United and Celtic. United had long faced the threat of relegation from the SPL, but by the time of the cup final that particular cloud had evaporated. In an interesting final, Celtic scored in eleven minutes, and that proved to be the only goal. Many had hoped for a Celtic victory as a fitting tribute to their manager. Martin O'Neill was leaving after a most successful incumbency. He achieved much with the club, and made its name one to be reckoned with in Europe again. All are sad to see him go, and wish him and his family good fortune.

Once again, though, little impact was made in Europe. Our teams made a reasonable-enough showing, but we are not yet sufficiently good to achieve the extra mile.

The same may be said of the (men's) international teams. Coming on. Nearly, at times. But not quite. With Walter Smith now at the helm, there must be hope. True, there is little chance of qualifying in our group, but a first victory was a step forward, followed by a difficult away-from-home draw. There always seem to be plenty of promising youngsters; a major difficulty seems to be to keep them playing in top teams; too often, they are gathered in to the bigger teams and then, after a game or two, they are cast aside into the lesser games; that may soon lead to a route south, where they so often lapse into obscurity. Strenuous efforts are now being made by the SFA with young players, and perhaps we may look forward to more Scottish teams full of Scots. The women's teams have been having a considerable success: we could not yet cope with Germany in the European competition, but at least held our own and more with the other members of our qualifying group, finishing just a point behind the second-placed Czechs. At Under-19 level, it all looks very promising, with some enormous wins. The final matches are still to come, so let's keep our fingers well crossed.

A sad closing note was the recent death of 'Tiny' Tom Wharton. A large man, and a larger-than-life referee, who continued to give great service to the game even after retiring from the field, he was very widely known and well trusted. Referees are often forgotten – this dedicated body who, for modest reward, do their best to maintain fair play, and often have to put up with a good deal from the fans. This year, a number of our Class 1 referees are retiring, amongst the best kent, John Rowbotham, who was given the Scottish Cup Final to referee on his last appearance, and who controlled it extremely well and unobtrusively; Willie Young, who at one time or another has refereed all three finals of the cups; and Hugh Dallas, who has distinguished himself greatly all over the world scene. All have given dedicated service to the Scottish game, as do their colleagues, week-in, week-out.

Now, and as usual, we are almost into next season: Hope springs Eternal.

ALAN ELLIOTT

ABERDEEN Premier League

Year Formed: 1903. *Ground & Address:* Pittodrie Stadium, Pittodrie St, Aberdeen AB24 5QH. *Telephone:* 01224 650400. *Fax:* 01224 644173.
Ground Capacity: all seated: 21,467. *Size of Pitch:* 115yd × 72yd.
Executive Director: Duncan Fraser. *Director of Football:* Willie Miller. *Secretary:* David Johnston. *Operations Manager:* John Morgan.
Manager: Jim Calderwood. *Assistant Manager:* Jimmy Nichol. *U-19 Manager:* Neil Cooper. *Physios:* David Wylie, John Sharp. *Reserve Team Coach:* Sandy Clark.
Managers since 1975: Ally MacLeod, Billy McNeill, Alex Ferguson, Ian Porterfield, Alex Smith and Jocky Scott, Willie Miller, Roy Aitken, Alex Miller, Paul Hegarty, Ebbe Skovdahl, Steve Paterson. *Club Nicknames(s):* The Dons. *Previous Grounds:* None.
Record Attendance: 45,061 v Hearts, Scottish Cup 4th rd, 13 Mar 1954.
Record Transfer Fee received: £1.75 million for Eoin Jess to Coventry City (February 1996).
Record Transfer Fee paid: £1m+ for Paul Bernard from Oldham Athletic (September 1995).
Record Victory: 13-0 v Peterhead, Scottish Cup, 9 Feb 1923.
Record Defeat: 0-8 v Celtic, Division 1, 30 Jan 1965.
Most Capped Players: Jim Leighton, 91 (Scotland); Alex McLeish, 77 (Scotland); Willie Miller, 65 (Scotland); Gordon Strachan, 50 (Scotland).
Most League Appearances: 556: Willie Miller, 1973-90.
Most League Goals in Season (Individual): 38: Benny Yorston, Division I, 1929-30.
Most Goals Overall (Individual): 199: Joe Harper.

ABERDEEN 2004–05 LEAGUE RECORD

Match No.	Date	Venue	Opponents	Result		H/T Score	Lg. Pos.	Goalscorers	Attendance
1	Aug 7	H	Rangers	D	0-0	0-0	—		19,028
2	14	A	Hearts	D	0-0	0-0	9		13,864
3	21	A	Dunfermline Ath	W	1-0	1-0	4	Whelan 23	8533
4	28	H	Livingston	W	2-0	0-0	2	Craig 2 (1 pen) 64 (p), 69	13,888
5	Sept 11	A	Dundee U	D	1-1	1-0	2	Mackie 6	11,595
6	18	A	Kilmarnock	W	1-0	0-0	2	Fowler (og) 54	6686
7	25	H	Hibernian	L	0-1	0-0	4		12,137
8	Oct 2	H	Dundee	D	1-1	1-1	4	Heikkinen 42	11,217
9	16	A	Inverness CT	W	3-1	1-1	3	Adams 2 (1 pen) 27, 63 (p), Mackie (pen) 87	9830
10	23	H	Motherwell	W	2-1	0-1	3	Adams 77, Severin 88	10,737
11	27	A	Celtic	W	3-2	2-1	—	Mackie 4, Pasquinelli 5, Stewart 90	57,060
12	31	A	Rangers	L	0-5	0-1	3		48,918
13	Nov 7	H	Hearts	L	0-1	0-0	4		13,055
14	13	H	Dunfermline Ath	W	2-1	1-0	3	Tod (og) 34, Mackie 49	10,398
15	20	A	Livingston	W	2-0	2-0	3	Foster 1, Mackie 20	4270
16	27	H	Dundee U	W	1-0	1-0	3	Tosh 26	12,038
17	Dec 4	H	Kilmarnock	W	3-2	2-2	3	Pasquinelli 2 8, 31, Clark 71	11,139
18	11	A	Hibernian	L	1-2	1-1	3	Mackie 37	13,503
19	18	A	Dundee	L	0-1	0-0	3		7310
20	27	H	Inverness CT	D	0-0	0-0	4		18,250
21	Jan 3	A	Motherwell	D	0-0	0-0	4		6948
22	16	H	Celtic	L	0-1	0-1	4		17,051
23	23	H	Rangers	L	1-2	1-2	4	Mackie 19	17,495
24	29	A	Hearts	L	0-1	0-0	5		12,269
25	Feb 12	A	Dunfermline Ath	L	1-2	0-0	5	Diamond 71	5609
26	19	H	Livingston	W	2-0	1-0	5	McNaughton 45, Whelan 58	9214
27	Mar 2	A	Dundee U	W	2-1	2-0	—	Diamond 5, Stewart 44	6688
28	5	A	Kilmarnock	W	1-0	0-0	4	McNaughton 79	5181
29	12	H	Hibernian	W	3-0	2-0	3	Anderson 12, Foster 13, Mackie (pen) 83	14,465
30	19	H	Dundee	D	1-1	0-0	4	Whelan 62	10,474
31	Apr 2	A	Inverness CT	W	1-0	1-0	4	Whelan 38	7026
32	9	H	Motherwell	L	1-3	1-2	4	Heikkinen 36	10,443
33	16	A	Celtic	L	2-3	2-1	4	Diamond 10, Mackie 13	59,984
34	23	A	Motherwell	W	1-0	1-0	4	Mackie 33	5063
35	May 1	H	Rangers	L	1-3	1-2	4	Clark 32	17,198
36	8	A	Celtic	L	0-2	0-0	4		59,516
37	14	A	Hibernian	W	2-1	1-0	4	Mackie 2 28, 70	15,288
38	22	H	Hearts	W	2-0	1-0	4	Byrne 45, Adams 47	16,155

Final League Position: 4

Honours
League Champions: Division I 1954-55. Premier Division 1979-80, 1983-84, 1984-85; *Runners-up:* Division I 1910-11, 1936-37, 1955-56, 1970-71, 1971-72. Premier Division 1977-78, 1980-81, 1981-82, 1988-89, 1989-90, 1990-91, 1992-93, 1993-94.
Scottish Cup Winners: 1947, 1970, 1982, 1983, 1984, 1986, 1990; *Runners-up:* 1937, 1953, 1954, 1959, 1967, 1978, 1993, 2000.
League Cup Winners: 1955-56, 1976-77, 1985-86, 1989-90, (Coca Cola cup) 1995-96; *Runners-up:* 1946-47, 1978-79, 1979-80, 1987-88, 1988-89, 1992-93, 1999-2000.
Drybrough Cup Winners: 1971, 1980.

European: *European Cup:* 12 matches (1980-81, 1984-85, 1985-86); *Cup Winners' Cup:* 39 matches (1967-68, 1970-71, 1978-79, 1982-83 winners, 1983-84 semi-finals, 1986-87, 1990-91, 1993-94); *UEFA Cup:* 48 matches (*Fairs Cup:* 1968-69. *UEFA Cup:* 1971-72, 1972-73, 1973-74, 1977-78, 1979-80, 1981-82, 1987-88, 1988-89, 1989-90, 1991-92, 1994-95, 1996-97, 2000-01, 2002-03).

Club colours: Shirt, Shorts, Stockings: Red with white trim.

Goalscorers: *League* (44): Mackie 12 (2 pens), Adams 4 (1 pen), Whelan 4, Diamond 3, Pasquinelli 3, Clark 2, Craig 2 (1 pen), Foster 2, Heikkinen 2, McNaughton 2, Stewart 2, Anderson 1, Byrne 1, Severin 1, Tosh 1, own goals 2.
Scottish Cup (5): Mackie 3, Byrne 1, Heikkinen 1.
CIS Cup (3): Adams 1, Craig 1, Diamond 1.

Preece D 17	McGuire P 22 + 8	McNaughton K 35	Anderson R 31	Diamond A 29	Severin S 31	Heikkinen M 29 + 1	Adams D 16 + 4	Hart M 28 + 4	Clark C 30 + 1	Whelan N 18 + 2	Craig S 6 + 7	Tosh S 14 + 3	Morrison S 6 + 5	Foster R 11 + 14	Stewart J 6 + 18	Pasquinelli F 5 + 5	Muirhead S 6 + 8	Mackie D 33 + 1	Esson R 21 + 2	Winter J 9 + 3	Kristjansson T 1 + 2	Byrne R 11 + 2	Blaha L 2 + 6	Dempsey G — + 4	Considine A 1	*Match No.*
1	2[3]	3[2]	4	5	6	7	8	9	10	11[1]	12	13	14													1
1	2	3	4	5	6	7	12		10[1]	11	9[2]	8		13												2
1	2	3	4	5	6[3]	7	9[2]	13		11[1]	10	8		14	12											3
1	2	3	4	5	6	7	9	12			10[3]	8[1]			11[2]	13	14									4
1	2	3	4	5	6	7	9[1]	8			10[3]	12		14	13			11[2]								5
1	2	3	4		6		9	5			10[1]	8		7			12	11								6
1	2	3	4		6	12	9	5[2]				8	13	7	10[1]	14		11[3]								7
1	2	3	4		6	7	9	5[2]			10[3]	8		11[1]		13	14	12								8
1	2	3			6	4	9[3]	5	10[1]		12	8		7[2]	14	13		11								9
1	2[1]	3	4		6	7	9	5	10	12		8			13			11[2]								10
1[G]	2	3[2]	4		6		7	5	10			8		12	13	9[1]		11	15							11
	2	3	4		6		7[3]	5	10	14		8[2]		13	12	9[1]		11	1							12
1	2	3■	4	5	6		7		10	9		8						11								13
1	12		4	3	6	5[2]	7		10	9[3]		8[1]	2	13	14			11								14
1	12	3[1]	4	5	6	7			10	9[2]			2	8		13		11								15
1	2	3		5	6	7	13			10[2]	12	8[1]	4	9				11								16
1	2[1]	3	4	5	6	7		12	9			8[2]		13	14	10[3]		11								17
1■	2[1]	3[2]	4	5	6	7		8	9					12	13	10[6]		11	15							18
		3	4	5[2]	6	7		2	9		12■			8[3]	14	10[1]	13	11	1							19
	13	3	4	5	6	7		2	10[1]					8	9[2]		12	11	1							20
	2[3]	3	4	5		7	13	6	10		12		8	9[1]			14	11[2]	1							21
	2[1]	3	4	5		7	8[2]	6	9[3]	10		12						11	1	13	14					22
		3	4	5		7		2	9	10[1]				8[3]	14		13	11	1	6[2]	12					23
		3	4	5		7		2	9	10				13	12			11	1	6[2]	8[1]					24
	12[3]	3		5		7	10	2[1]	9		14		13		8			11	1	6[2]		4				25
		3	4	5		7		6	13	10[3]			2[1]	14	9			11	1	8[2]		12				26
	2	3	4	5■				7	10	9[1]			13		12[2]			11	1	8		6				27
		3	4		6			7	10		12		2	13	9[1]		14	11[3]	1	8[2]		5				28
	12	3[1]	4	5	6			7	10	9[2]				8	13			11	1			2				29
	2[1]	3	4		6	7		5	10	9				12	13			11	1	8[2]						30
	12		4[1]	5	6	7		3	10	9[3]				13				11	1	8[2]		2	14			31
	2	3		5	6	7		8[3]	10	9			14		13			11[2]	1			4[1]	12			32
	13	3[3]		5	6	7		4	10					12			9	11	1	14		2[2]	8[1]			33
		3	4	5[1]	6	7		2	10	9[2]					14		8	11[3]	1			12	13			34
		3	4	5	6	7		12	10	9[2]							8[3]	11	1			2[1]	13	14		35
		3[1]	4	5	6			7	10								8	11	1	14		2[3]	12	13	9[2]	36
	13			5	6	7[2]	12	3	10								8[3]	11	1	4		2	9[1]	14		37
	2[1]	3		5	6	7[2]	9[3]		10						14		8	11	1			4	12	13		38

AIRDRIE UNITED — First Division

Year Formed: 2002. *Ground & Address:* Shyberry Excelsior Stadium, Broomfield Park, Craigneuk Avenue, Airdrie ML6 8QZ. *E-mail:* enquiries@airdrieunitedfc.com
Ground Capacity: all seated: 10,000. *Size of Pitch:* 112yd × 76yd.
Chairman: James Ballantyne. *Secretary:* Ann Marie Ballantyne. *Commercial Manager:* Les Jones.
Manager: Sandy Stewart.
Record Attendance: 5704 v Morton, Second Division, 15 May 2004.
Record Victory: 6-0 v Berwick R, Second Division, 3 Apr 2004.
Record Defeat: 1-6 v Morton, Second Division, 1 Nov 2003.
Most League Appearances: 101, Mark McGeown, 2002-05.
Most League Goals in Season (Individual): 18, Jerome Vareille, 2002-03.
Most Goals Overall (Individual): 28, Jerome Vareille, 2002-04.

AIRDRIE UNITED 2004–05 LEAGUE RECORD

Match No.	Date	Venue	Opponents	Result		H/T Score	Lg. Pos.	Goalscorers	Attendance
1	Aug 7	H	St Johnstone	W	1-0	0-0	—	Vareille [82]	2365
2	14	A	Partick Th	L	2-3	1-1	7	Coyle 2 [18, 67]	4011
3	21	H	Raith R	D	1-1	0-1	5	McKeown [61]	2009
4	28	A	Falkirk	L	0-5	0-2	7		3790
5	Sept 4	H	Queen of the S	L	0-1	0-1	9		1652
6	11	A	Clyde	W	2-1	1-1	8	Barkey [40], Coyle [70]	1680
7	18	H	Ross Co	L	1-2	1-1	8	McKeown (pen) [41]	1486
8	25	A	St Mirren	D	1-1	0-1	8	Roberts [90]	3569
9	Oct 2	H	Hamilton A	L	0-2	0-0	9		1900
10	16	H	Partick Th	W	4-2	2-1	8	Wilson M [20], Coyle 2 [34, 83], McLaren [84]	2548
11	23	A	St Johnstone	D	1-1	0-0	8	Coyle [88]	2447
12	30	H	Falkirk	L	1-3	0-2	8	Coyle [75]	3247
13	Nov 6	A	Queen of the S	L	0-1	0-0	8		2022
14	13	H	Clyde	W	3-1	2-0	8	Coyle [13], Roberts [15], Gow [61]	1862
15	20	A	Ross Co	W	2-1	1-1	6	Hardie [17], Lovering [86]	2173
16	27	A	Hamilton A	W	3-1	2-1	6	Coyle [24], Gow 2 [43, 77]	2295
17	Dec 4	H	St Mirren	W	3-2	1-1	6	Coyle 2 [32, 83], Hardie [68]	2514
18	11	H	St Johnstone	D	0-0	0-0	6		1865
19	18	A	Raith R	W	2-0	0-0	6	Hardie [67], Wilson M [88]	1795
20	26	A	Falkirk	L	0-1	0-1	6		4133
21	29	H	Queen of the S	W	2-0	1-0	—	Coyle [31], Gow [74]	1781
22	Jan 1	A	Clyde	L	0-1	0-0	5		1513
23	15	H	Ross Co	W	2-1	1-0	4	McLaren [42], Coyle [90]	1512
24	22	A	St Mirren	L	0-1	0-0	5		3047
25	Feb 12	A	Partick Th	D	1-1	1-1	5	McManus [24]	3791
26	19	H	Raith R	W	2-1	1-1	3	Roberts [28], McKeown [86]	1599
27	Mar 5	A	Queen of the S	D	0-0	0-0	4		1683
28	8	H	Hamilton A	W	1-0	0-0	—	Gow [89]	xxx
29	12	H	Falkirk	D	2-2	0-1	4	Gow (pen) [52], McKeown [60]	3111
30	19	H	Clyde	L	2-4	2-3	4	Hardie [17], Coyle [25]	1641
31	Apr 2	A	Ross Co	L	1-3	1-1	5	Gow [3]	2024
32	9	A	Hamilton A	D	1-1	1-1	4	Christie [45]	2030
33	16	H	St Mirren	L	0-2	0-0	6		1989
34	23	A	St Johnstone	W	2-1	1-0	4	McLaren [21], Gow [90]	2239
35	30	H	Partick Th	L	0-1	0-1	5		1747
36	May 7	A	Raith R	W	1-0	1-0	5	Gow (pen) [40]	1296

Final League Position: 5

Honours
League Champions: Second Division 2003-04.
Bell's League Challenge Cup runners-up: 2003-04.

Club colours: Shirt: White with red diamond. Shorts: White with two red horizontal stripes. Stockings: White with red hoops.

Goalscorers: *League* (44): Coyle 14, Gow 9 (2 pens), Hardie 4, McKeown 4 (1 pen), McLaren 3, Roberts 3, Wilson M 2, Barkey 1, Christie 1, Lovering 1, McManus 1, Vareille 1.
Scottish Cup (1): Hardie 1.
CIS Cup (3): Coyle 1, Roberts 1, Vareille 1.
Challenge Cup (0).

McGeown M 30	Wilson W 10 + 9	Lovering P 29	McGowan N 30 + 2	McManus A 27 + 3	Dunn D 12 + 12	Vareille J 12 + 16	Wilson M 36	Coyle O 33	Gow A 23 + 3	Roberts M 20 + 11	Wilson S 1 + 1	Docherty S 24 + 4	McKeown S 18 + 4	Christie K 17 + 1	Hoey T — + 2	Barkey K 10 + 8	McGroarty C 2	Hardie M 23 + 2	McLaren W 22 + 5	Hollis L 6	McKenna S 8	Stewart A 2	McDougall S 1	Match No.
1	2	3	4^{1}	5	6	7^{3}	8	9	10^{2}	11	12	13	14											1
1	2	3		4	6^{2}	7	8	9		11	5^{1}	13	10^{3}	12	14									2
1	2^{1}	3	4	5	6^{2}	7	8	9		11		12	10			13								3
1	2	3		4	10	7	8	9		11		6		5										4
1	12	3^{1}	4^{2}	2		7	8	9		11		6	10	5		13								5
1	2			4	6^{3}	12	8	9^{1}		11			10^{2}	5	14	7	3	13						6
1	2		12	4	6^{2}	11^{1}	8^{3}	9				14	10	5		7	3	13						7
1			3	4	13		8	9^{1}		12		2	10	5		7		6^{2}	11					8
1			3	4	14	13	8	9^{1}		12		2	10^{2}	5		7		6^{3}	11					9
1	14	3	4				8	9	13	12		2^{3}	10^{1}	5		7		6	11^{2}					10
1		3	4^{2}	13			8	9	14	12		2	10^{1}	5		7		6^{3}	11					11
1		3	4	12			8	9	13	14		2^{1}	10^{2}	5		7		6	11^{3}					12
			3	4		13	8	9		12		2	10^{1}	5		7^{2}		6	11	1				13
		3	4	5	13	12	8^{3}	9	10	7^{1}		2				14		6	11^{2}	1				14
	12	3	4	5^{1}	13		8	9^{2}	10	7		2						6	11	1				15
		3	4			12	8	9	10	7^{1}		2		5				6	11	1				16
		3	4	12	13	14	8	9	10^{3}	7		2^{1}		5				6^{2}	11	1				17
1		3	4		6^{1}	7	8	9		10		2		5		12			11					18
1	2	3	4			12	8^{3}	9	10^{2}	7			13	5		14		6	11^{1}					19
1		3	4	5		12	8	9	10	7^{1}		2						6	11					20
1	13	3	4	5	14	12	8	9	10^{3}	7^{1}		2^{2}						6	11					21
1		3	4	5			8	9	10	7		2						6	11					22
1		3	4	5		12	8	9	10	7^{1}		2						6	11					23
1	2	3	4	5	12	13	8	9^{2}	10	7^{1}								6	11					24
1		3	4	5	11^{2}	13	8	9	10	7^{1}								6	12		2			25
1		3	4	5	12	13	8	9^{3}	10	7^{2}			14					6^{1}	11		2			26
1	12	3	4^{1}	5	6	7^{2}	8	9	10	13			11								2			27
1		3		5	6^{1}	7^{3}	8	9^{2}	10	13		4	11			14			12		2			28
1		3	12	5^{1}	13	7^{3}	8	9	10	14		4^{2}	11					6			2			29
1		3	4			7^{1}	8	9^{2}	10	13			11	5				6	12		2			30
1	14		3		6^{2}	11^{3}	8	9	10	12		4	7	5					13		2^{3}			31
1	12	3	6^{1}	5			8	9^{2}	10			2	7	4				11	13					32
1	2		3	4	12	13	8	9^{2}	10			6^{3}	7^{1}			14			11		5			33
1	12	3	6^{1}	5	13		8		9			2				7		10	11^{2}			4		34
1	2	3	6	5	13	14	8		9				12			7^{1}		10^{3}	11			4^{2}		35
	14	3	4	5	6	12	8		10	9^{2}		2				13			11^{3}	1			7^{1}	36

ALBION ROVERS — Third Division

Year Formed: 1882. *Ground & Address:* Cliftonhill Stadium, Main St, Coatbridge ML5 3RB. *Telephone/Fax:* 01236 606334.
Ground capacity: total: 2496, seated: 538. *Size of Pitch:* 110yd × 72yd.
Chairman: Andrew Dick, *Company Secretary:* David Shanks BSc. *General Manager:* John Reynolds.
Manager: Jim Chapman. *Assistant Manager:* Graham Diamond. *Youth Development:* Jimmy Lindsay. *Physio:* Derek Kelly.
Managers since 1975: G. Caldwell, S. Goodwin, H. Hood, J. Baker, D. Whiteford, M. Ferguson, W. Wilson, B. Rooney, A. Ritchie, T. Gemmell, D. Provan, M. Oliver, B. McLaren, T. Gemmell, T Spence, J. Crease, V. Moore, B. McLaren, J. McVeigh, P. Hetherston, K. McAllister.
Club Nickname(s): The Wee Rovers. *Previous Grounds:* Cowheath Park, Meadow Park, Whifflet.
Record Attendance: 27,381 v Rangers, Scottish Cup 2nd rd, 8 Feb 1936.
Record Transfer Fee received: £40,000 from Motherwell for Bruce Cleland.
Record Transfer Fee paid: £7000 for Gerry McTeague to Stirling Albion, September 1989.
Record Victory: 12-0 v Airdriehill, Scottish Cup, 3 Sept 1887.
Record Defeat: 1-11 v Partick T, League Cup, 11 Aug 1993.
Most Capped Player: Jock White, 1 (2), Scotland.
Most League Appearances: 399, Murdy Walls, 1921-36.
Most League Goals in Season (Individual): 41: Jim Renwick, Division II, 1932-33.
Most Goals Overall (Individual): 105: Bunty Weir, 1928-31.

ALBION ROVERS 2004–05 LEAGUE RECORD

Match No.	*Date*	*Venue*	*Opponents*	*Result*		*H/T Score*	*Lg. Pos.*	*Goalscorers*	*Attendance*
1	Aug 7	A	Gretna	L	0-6	0-2	—		646
2	14	H	East Fife	W	2-0	0-0	7	McManus 2 [85, 87]	384
3	21	A	Queen's Park	D	1-1	0-1	7	Stirling [90]	505
4	28	H	Peterhead	L	0-1	0-1	7		351
5	Sept 4	A	Montrose	D	1-1	1-0	7	Connolly [28]	330
6	11	H	Stenhousemuir	W	1-0	1-0	7	McManus [30]	339
7	18	A	Elgin C	L	0-1	0-0	7		450
8	25	H	East Stirling	D	3-3	3-3	7	Stirling 2 [13, 27], McManus [33]	225
9	Oct 2	A	Cowdenbeath	L	0-2	0-1	8		243
10	16	A	East Fife	L	0-1	0-0	9		396
11	23	H	Gretna	L	2-6	0-1	9	Bradford 2 [74, 81]	326
12	30	A	Peterhead	L	1-4	0-2	9	Bradford (pen) [48]	729
13	Nov 6	H	Montrose	L	1-2	1-0	9	Stirling [21]	245
14	13	A	Stenhousemuir	L	0-3	0-3	9		318
15	20	A	Gretna	L	2-6	1-2	9	Aitken (og) [45], McManus [62]	627
16	27	H	Elgin C	D	2-2	0-1	9	Crabbe [58], McLaughlin [78]	262
17	Dec 4	A	East Stirling	D	1-1	1-0	9	Mercer [24]	262
18	18	H	Cowdenbeath	L	2-3	1-1	9	McManus (pen) [34], Mercer [52]	303
19	Jan 3	H	Peterhead	L	0-4	0-1	—		306
20	15	A	Montrose	W	1-0	1-0	9	Mercer [37]	269
21	29	A	Elgin C	D	1-1	0-0	9	Bradford [61]	380
22	Feb 5	H	East Stirling	D	1-1	0-0	9	Bradford [51]	350
23	12	A	Cowdenbeath	W	2-1	0-1	9	Potter [47], Gordon [71]	254
24	19	A	Queen's Park	W	3-0	3-0	9	Bradford [32], Mercer 2 [33, 35]	497
25	Mar 1	H	Queen's Park	L	0-4	0-0	—		355
26	5	H	Montrose	L	1-2	0-1	9	Wilson [58]	307
27	8	H	Stenhousemuir	D	1-1	1-0	—	Wilson [8]	222
28	12	A	Peterhead	W	3-2	0-0	9	Gordon [46], McCaul [78], Fleming [84]	532
29	19	A	Stenhousemuir	D	1-1	0-0	9	Wilson [46]	370
30	22	H	East Fife	L	0-6	0-4	—		316
31	Apr 2	H	Elgin C	W	2-0	0-0	9	Bradford (pen) [62], McKenzie [90]	246
32	9	H	Cowdenbeath	L	1-4	0-2	9	Wilson (pen) [80]	323
33	16	A	East Stirling	W	2-0	1-0	9	Wilson 2 [12, 80]	285
34	23	H	Queen's Park	L	1-2	0-2	9	Patrick [67]	353
35	30	A	East Fife	D	1-1	1-1	9	Douglas [1]	568
36	May 7	H	Gretna	L	0-5	0-2	9		519

Final League Position: 9

Honours
League Champions: Division II 1933-34, Second Division 1988-89; *Runners-up:* Division II 1913-14, 1937-38, 1947-48.
Scottish Cup Runners-up: 1920.

Club colours: Shirt: Scarlet and yellow. Shorts: Scarlet. Stockings: Yellow.

Goalscorers: *League* (40): Bradford 7 (2 pens), McManus 6 (1 pen), Wilson 6 (1 pen), Mercer 5, Stirling 4, Gordon 2, Connolly 1, Crabbe 1, Douglas 1, Fleming 1, McCaul 1, McKenzie 1, McLaughlin 1, Patrick 1, Potter 1, own goal 1.
Scottish Cup (0).
CIS Cup (4): Bradford 1, McKenzie 1, McLaren 1, Mercer 1.
Challenge Cup (3): Bradford 2, McCaul 1.

Peat M 8 + 1	Paterson A 12 + 2	Stirling J 35	Black D 30	McGowan J 8	McLaren G 17	McKenzie M 28 + 5	Boyle J 5 + 5	Yardley M 8 + 2	Bradford J 20 + 6	Mercer J 25	Patrick R 19 + 7	McManus P 15 + 2	Silvestro C 27	Fahey C 28	Crabbe S 7 + 3	McCaul G 8 + 5	Smith J 2	Connolly C 7 + 3	Selkirk A 6 + 6	McLaughlin P 3 + 1	Potter K 16 + 1	Fleming G 4 + 6	Friel S 16	Wallace N 5 + 1	McInulty S 11 + 1	Wilson L 11 + 1	Gordon W 10 + 5	Richardson G — + 5	Thomson D 3	Douglas I 2 + 2	Preston F — + 1	*Match No.*
1	2	3	4	5	6	7^{1}	8^{2}	9	10	11	12	13																				1
1		3	4	5	6	7	8	9	10^{1}	11		12	2																			2
		3	4	5	6	7		9	10^{1}	11	8^{2}		2	1	12	13																3
	12	3	2	5	6^{2}	7		9^{3}	10	11	13		8	1	14		4^{1}															4
		3	4		5	7		9	12		6	10	8	1		11^{1}		2														5
		3	4		5	7			9	11	6	10	8	1				2														6
		3	4		5	7		12	9	11	6^{2}	10^{1}	8	1		13		2														7
		3	4	5	6^{1}	7		9		11	14	10	2^{3}	1	12	8^{2}		13														8
	2	3	4	5	6	7^{1}	13			11	8^{2}	10		1	9	12																9
1	2	3	4		5	7	6				8	10			9	11^{1}			12													10
1	12	3	4	5	6^{1}	7	11^{3}		14		8^{2}	10	2		9				13													11
1	2	3	4	5	6^{1}	7^{2}	14	12	11		13	10	8		9^{3}																	12
	2^{1}	3	4		5	7	13	9	12		6	10	8	1	11^{2}																	13
	2^{3}	3	4		6	7	14	9^{2}	13			10	8	1	11^{1}			5	12													14
	2	3	4		6	7			9	11		10	8	1						5												15
	2^{2}	3				7			13	11		10	8	1	9	6	4^{1}			5	12											16
	2	3				7			9	11		10	8	1		6				5	4											17
		3	4		6	7	8			11		10	2^{1}	1				12	9		5											18
		3^{1}	4		5	7	13		9^{3}	11		10	8	1				2	6^{2}	12		14										19
	3					7			10	11	13		8	1				2	12		6	9^{1}	4	5^{2}								20
	2	3				7			10	11	13		8	1				12			6	9^{1}	4	5^{2}								21
	2	4				13			10	11			8	1							6	7^{2}		5^{1}	3	9	12					22
		8	4^{1}						10	11	7			1		14					6	9^{3}	2	5^{2}	3	12	13					23
		8	4			14			10^{1}	11^{2}	5		7	1							6		2		3	9^{3}	12	13				24
		8	4^{1}			13			9	11	5^{2}		7	1							6	14	2		3^{3}	10	12					25
15		8	4						9^{1}	11^{2}			7	1^{6}		13			12		6		2		3	5	10					26
1		8	4			7^{2}							5			11					6	13	2	12	3^{1}	9	10					27
1		8	4			14					7		5^{2}			11					6	12	2			9^{1}	10^{3}	13	3			28
1		6				7				11	8					5^{1}					4		2			9	10	12	3			29
		8	4			7				11	5^{1}			1								12	2		3	9	10		6			30
		3	6			7			9	11	5			1							4		2			10	8					31
		3	6			7			9^{1}	11^{2}	5			1					12		4		2		13	10	8					32
		6	4			7					5		8	1					11				2		3	10	9^{1}			12		33
		8	4								11		7	1					9		6^{1}	12	5	2^{3}	3		10^{2}	14		13		34
		6	4			12			10^{3}	11^{1}	14		7	1				2^{2}	8				5		3		13			9^{1}		35
		8	4			7			13		11^{1}			1					5		6		2		3		10^{3}	12		9^{2}	14	36

ALLOA ATHLETIC Second Division

Year Formed: 1878. *Ground & Address:* Recreation Park, Clackmannan Rd, Alloa FK10 1RY. *Telephone:* 01259 722695. *Website:* www.alloaathletic.co.uk
Ground Capacity: total: 3100, seated: 400. *Size of Pitch:* 110yd × 75yd.
Chairman: Ian Henderson. *Secretary:* Ewen G. Cameron.
Manager: Tom Hendrie. *First Team Coach:* Gareth Evans. *Physios:* Vanessa Smith & Stuart Murphy.
Managers since 1975: H. Wilson, A. Totten, W. Garner, J. Thomson, D. Sullivan, G. Abel, B. Little, H. McCann, W. Lamont, P. McAuley, T. Hendrie, T. Christie.
Club Nickname(s): The Wasps. *Previous Grounds:* None.
Record Attendance: 13,000 v Dunfermline Athletic, Scottish Cup 3rd rd replay, 26 Feb 1939.
Record Transfer Fee received: £100,000 for Martin Cameron to Bristol Rovers.
Record Transfer Fee paid: £26,000 for Ross Hamilton from Stenhousemuir.
Record Victory: 9-2 v Forfar Ath, Division II, 18 Mar 1933.
Record Defeat: 0-10 v Dundee, Division II, 8 Mar 1947 v Third Lanark, League Cup, 8 Aug 1953.
Most Capped Player: Jock Hepburn, 1, Scotland.
Most League Goals in Season (Individual): 49: 'Wee' Willie Crilley, Division II, 1921-22.

ALLOA ATHLETIC 2004–05 LEAGUE RECORD

Match No.	Date	Venue	Opponents	Result	H/T Score	Lg. Pos.	Goalscorers	Attendance
1	Aug 7	A	Stranraer	L 0-3	0-0	—		479
2	14	H	Forfar Ath	L 2-3	0-0	8	Brown A 60, Ferguson (pen) 79	446
3	21	A	Stirling A	L 0-2	0-0	9		1069
4	28	A	Brechin C	L 0-4	0-3	9		428
5	Sept 4	H	Ayr U	L 1-3	1-2	9	Nicolson 15	585
6	11	A	Berwick R	W 3-2	2-1	9	Callaghan 7, Nicolson 29, Hamilton 51	295
7	18	H	Dumbarton	W 3-2	0-1	8	McMillan 75, Bolochoweckyj 80, Walker R 89	505
8	25	H	Morton	L 1-6	0-1	8	Hill 75	1056
9	Oct 2	A	Arbroath	W 3-0	1-0	8	Callaghan 3 35, 52, 84	227
10	16	A	Forfar Ath	L 1-3	0-2	8	Brown A 60	411
11	23	H	Stranraer	L 1-2	0-2	9	Daly 88	492
12	30	H	Brechin C	D 2-2	1-1	9	Brown A 18, Callaghan 90	474
13	Nov 6	A	Ayr U	L 3-4	1-1	8	Townsley 15, Ovenstone 43, Brown A 73	1218
14	13	H	Berwick R	D 2-2	1-1	8	Brown A 26, Daly 60	462
15	30	A	Dumbarton	W 1-0	0-0	—	Hill 75	522
16	Dec 4	A	Morton	D 2-2	1-2	8	Brown A 32, Bolochoweckyj 81	2357
17	18	H	Arbroath	W 4-2	0-1	7	Townsley 67, Bolochoweckyj 2 71, 82, Ferguson 75	435
18	27	A	Stranraer	W 1-0	0-0	6	Stevenson 51	596
19	Jan 3	A	Brechin C	W 3-2	0-1	—	Ferguson (pen) 47, Hamilton 70, Bolochoweckyj 87	604
20	15	H	Ayr U	W 5-1	2-1	6	Bolochoweckyj 25, Nicolson 44, McLaughlin (og) 53, Brown A 58, Ross 63	647
21	29	H	Dumbarton	W 4-2	4-0	6	Ross 7, Quitongo 11, Brown A 23, Ferguson 24	608
22	Feb 12	A	Arbroath	L 1-2	1-0	6	Nicolson 21	525
23	19	A	Stirling A	W 4-0	1-0	6	Nicolson 35, Quitongo 2 60, 75, Ovenstone 82	1135
24	26	H	Forfar Ath	L 0-2	0-1	6		516
25	Mar 5	A	Ayr U	D 1-1	0-1	6	Hamilton 79	1003
26	8	H	Stirling A	D 1-1	0-1	—	Townsley 56	626
27	12	H	Brechin C	D 1-1	0-1	5	Ferguson 81	522
28	19	H	Berwick R	D 2-2	0-1	6	Brown G 48, Ross 55	452
29	23	H	Morton	D 2-2	2-1	—	Ovenstone 9, Quitongo 42	959
30	26	A	Berwick R	L 1-2	1-0	6	Stevenson 5	306
31	Apr 2	A	Dumbarton	L 2-3	1-1	7	Brown G 1, Hamilton 76	787
32	9	H	Arbroath	D 2-2	0-2	7	Ross 53, Stevenson 65	502
33	16	A	Morton	L 0-2	0-0	7		2721
34	23	H	Stirling A	W 3-0	1-0	6	Hamilton 44, Quitongo 60, Bolochoweckyj 70	921
35	30	A	Forfar Ath	D 1-1	1-1	6	Calderon 27	453
36	May 7	H	Stranraer	W 3-0	1-0	6	Nicolson 18, Ferguson 68, Ross 85	606

Final League Position: 6

Honours
League Champions: Division II 1921-22; Third Division 1997-98. *Runners-up:* Division II 1938-39. Second Division 1976-77, 1981-82, 1984-85, 1988-89, 1999-2000, 2001-02.
Bell's League Challenge Winners: 1999-2000; *Runners-up:* 2001-02.

Club colours: Shirt: Gold with black trim. Shorts: Black with gold stripe. Stockings: Gold with black hoop on top.

Goalscorers: *League* (66): Brown A 8, Bolochoweckyj 7, Ferguson 6 (2 pens), Nicolson 6, Callaghan 5, Hamilton 5, Quitongo 5, Ross 5, Ovenstone 3, Stevenson 3, Townsley 3, Brown G 2, Daly 2, Hill 2, Calderon 1, McMillan 1, Walker R 1, own goal 1.
Scottish Cup (4): Brown A 1, Ferguson 1 (pen), Ovenstone 1, Webster 1.
CIS Cup (3): Callaghan 1, Ferguson 1, Hamilton 1.
Challenge Cup (3): Callaghan 1, Ferguson 1, Hamilton 1.

McGlynn G 16	Walker R 32 + 1	Hill D 13 + 2	Mortimer P 13 + 6	Bolochoweckyj M 34	Townsley C 34 + 1	Nicholas S 5 + 2	Ferguson B 26 + 3	Brown A 25 + 1	Hamilton R 25 + 3	Daly M 16 + 10	McLeod R 1 + 3	McMillan A 2 + 9	McLaughlin P 4 + 5	McDermott M 1 + 4	Nicolson I 26 + 3	Callaghan S 16	Stevenson J 24 + 7	Ovenstone J 26	Evans J 20 + 1	Calderon J 1 + 3	Ross I 9 + 1	Quitongo J 16 + 1	Mackie S — + 1	Ebanda H — + 1	Brown G 8 + 2	Thomson D 3	Learmonth S — + 1	*Match No.*
1	2	3	4	5	6^{2}	7^{1}	8	9	10	11^{3}	12	13	14															1
1	2	3^{1}	4	5	6	13	7	9	10	11	12		8^{2}															2
1	2	3	4	5	6	7^{2}	8	9	10				11^{1}	12	13													3
1	2	3^{2}		5	4	12	8	9^{3}	10	7^{1}	6	14		13		11												4
1	2	13^{3}		5	6	9			10	8	14	7^{2}	12	3^{1}	4	11												5
1	2		4	5	6	7^{1}		9	10	8^{2}			13		3	11	12											6
1	2		4^{1}	5	6	7^{2}			10^{3}	8		14	12	13	3	11	9											7
1	9	3^{2}	4^{1}	5	6					8		7	12	13	2	11	10											8
1	10^{2}	3	8	5	6			9		7^{1}		13	4		2	11	12											9
1	10	3	8	5	6			9		7^{1}			4		2	11	12											10
1	10^{2}	3^{1}	8	4	5^{3}		12	9		7		14			2	11	13	6										11
1	10		8^{1}	4	5		3	9		2		12				11	7	6										12
1^{6}	10		8^{1}	4	5		3	9		13		12			2^{2}	11	7	6	15									13
	8			4	5		3	9	10^{1}	12		13			2	11	7^{2}	6	1									14
	7	3^{1}	12	4	5			9		8		13			2	11	10^{2}	6	1									15
	7	3^{2}	14	4^{3}	5		12	9		8					2	11	10^{1}	6	1	13								16
	7	3^{1}		4	5		10	9^{3}	13	8^{2}					2	11	12	6	1	14								17
	7^{1}			4	5		3	9	12	8					2	11	10	6	1									18
	7			4	5		3	9	10^{1}	12					2	11	8	6	1									19
	7^{1}			4	5		8^{2}	9^{3}	10	14					2		11	6	1	13	3	12						20
	2		12	4			8	9	10	14					5^{1}		11	6	1		3	7^{2}	13^{3}					21
	2			4	5		8	9	10						3		11	6	1			7						22
	2	12		4	5		8	9	10	13					3^{1}		11^{2}	6	1			7						23
		3		4	5^{2}		8	9^{1}	10	13					2		11	6	1			7		12				24
	2			4	5		8	9	10						3		11	6	1			7						25
	2			4	5		8	9	10						3		11	6	1			7						26
	2			4	5		8	9^{1}	10						3		11	6	1			7			12			27
	2			4	5		8^{3}	9^{1}	10	14					13		11	6	1		3^{2}	7			12			28
			12	4	5		8	13	10^{3}	14					2		11	6^{1}	1		3	7			9^{2}			29
	2			4	5		8		12						10		11	6	1		13	7^{1}			9	3^{2}		30
	2			4	5		8		10	12							11	6	1		3	7			9^{1}			31
	2		12	4	5		8		10								11	6	1		3	7			9^{1}			32
1	2		12	4	5		8		10								11	6			3	7			9^{1}			33
1	2^{1}			4	5		8		10						12		11	6			3	7			9			34
1		5	4		13		12		10	8^{1}					2		14	6^{2}		11^{1}		7			9	3		35
	12		4		5		8		10^{1}						2		13	6	1		11	7^{3}			9	3^{2}	14	36

ARBROATH — Third Division

Year Formed: 1878. *Ground & Address:* Gayfield Park, Arbroath DD11 1QB. *Telephone:* 01241 872157. *Fax:* 01241 431125. *E-mail:* AFCwebmaster@arbroathfc.co.uk. *Website:* www.arbroathfc.co.uk.
Ground Capacity: 4020, seated: 715. *Size of Pitch:* 115yd × 71yd.
President: John D. Christison. *Secretary:* Dr Gary Callon. *Administrator:* Mike Cargill. *Commercial Manager:* M. Fairweather.
Manager: Harry Cairney. *Assistant Manager:* Stuart Sorbie. *Physio:* Jim Crosby.
Managers since 1975: A. Henderson, I. J. Stewart, G. Fleming, J. Bone, J. Young, W. Borthwick, M. Lawson, D. McGrain MBE, J. Scott, J. Brogan, T. Campbell, G. Mackie, D. Baikie, J. Brownlie, S. Kirk.
Club Nickname(s): The Red Lichties. *Previous Grounds:* None.
Record Attendance: 13,510 v Rangers, Scottish Cup 3rd rd, 23 Feb 1952.
Record Transfer Fee received: £120,000 for Paul Tosh to Dundee (Aug 1993).
Record Transfer Fee paid: £20,000 for Douglas Robb from Montrose (1981).
Record Victory: 36-0 v Bon Accord, Scottish Cup 1st rd, 12 Sept 1885.
Record Defeat: 1-9 v Celtic, League Cup 3rd rd, 25 Aug 1993.
Most Capped Player: Ned Doig, 2 (5), Scotland.
Most League Appearances: 445: Tom Cargill, 1966-81.
Most League Goals in Season (Individual): 45: Dave Easson, Division II, 1958-59.
Most Goals Overall (Individual): 120: Jimmy Jack, 1966-71.

ARBROATH 2004–05 LEAGUE RECORD

Match No.	Date	Venue	Opponents	Result		H/T Score	Lg. Pos.	Goalscorers	Attendance
1	Aug 7	A	Stirling A	L	2-5	0-2	—	McLean 53, Henslee 56	706
2	14	H	Dumbarton	L	0-2	0-1	10		505
3	21	A	Forfar Ath	L	0-5	0-1	10		696
4	28	H	Stranraer	L	0-1	0-0	10		405
5	Sept 4	A	Morton	L	1-2	0-1	10	Henslee 78	2360
6	11	A	Brechin C	L	1-4	1-1	10	Farquharson 16	559
7	18	H	Ayr U	D	0-0	0-0	10		481
8	25	A	Berwick R	W	3-0	0-0	9	Henslee 58, McLean 2 74, 89	335
9	Oct 2	H	Alloa Ath	L	0-3	0-1	10		227
10	16	A	Dumbarton	W	3-1	2-0	9	Swankie 2 29, 66, McMullan 42	716
11	23	H	Stirling A	W	2-1	1-0	8	Cusick (pen) 29, Brazil 69	620
12	30	A	Stranraer	L	1-2	1-1	8	McLean 44	503
13	Nov 6	H	Morton	L	0-3	0-0	9		857
14	13	H	Brechin C	D	2-2	0-1	9	McMullan 65, McLean 87	682
15	27	A	Ayr U	D	1-1	0-1	8	Bishop 59	1189
16	Dec 4	H	Berwick R	D	1-1	0-1	9	Bishop 50	450
17	18	A	Alloa Ath	L	2-4	1-0	10	Brazil 34, Henslee 52	435
18	27	A	Stirling A	W	3-0	1-0	9	Brazil 2 36, 60, McMullan 56	755
19	Jan 1	H	Forfar Ath	L	0-2	0-1	9		825
20	3	H	Stranraer	L	0-4	0-2	—		432
21	15	A	Morton	L	0-2	0-1	9		2689
22	29	H	Ayr U	W	2-0	0-0	9	Henslee 57, Brazil 70	426
23	Feb 5	A	Berwick R	W	3-2	3-1	9	McGlashan 2, Brazil 6, Diack 18	309
24	9	A	Brechin C	L	3-4	2-2	—	Henslee 25, Swankie 42, Rennie 87	651
25	12	H	Alloa Ath	W	2-1	0-1	8	Bishop 73, McMullan 80	525
26	19	A	Forfar Ath	D	1-1	0-1	8	McGlashan 83	758
27	26	H	Dumbarton	W	2-1	1-0	8	Swankie 29, Henslee 72	502
28	Mar 5	H	Morton	L	0-1	0-0	8		832
29	12	A	Stranraer	D	3-3	1-1	9	Miller G 32, Henslee 66, McLeod 88	357
30	19	H	Brechin C	L	1-4	1-2	9	Henslee (pen) 9	775
31	Apr 2	A	Ayr U	D	2-2	1-1	9	Diack 3, McLeod 49	1115
32	9	A	Alloa Ath	D	2-2	2-0	9	McLeod 24, Diack 31	502
33	16	H	Berwick R	W	2-0	2-0	9	Henslee 31, McLeod 44	460
34	23	H	Forfar Ath	L	1-2	1-2	9	Brazil 7	697
35	30	A	Dumbarton	L	0-3	0-0	9		1192
36	May 7	H	Stirling A	W	3-2	3-2	9	McMullan 32, Cook 68, Henslee 75	535

Final League Position: 9

Honours
League Runners-up: Division II 1934-35, 1958-59, 1967-68, 1971-72; Second Division 2000-01; Third Division 1997-98.
Scottish Cup: Quarter-finals 1993.

Club colours: Shirt: Maroon with white trim. Shorts: White. Stockings: Maroon.

Goalscorers: *League* (49): Henslee 11 (1 pen), Brazil 7, McLean 5, McMullan 5, McLeod 4, Swankie 4, Bishop 3, Diack 3, McGlashan 2, Cook 1, Cusick 1 (pen), Farquharson 1, Miller G 1, Rennie 1.
Scottish Cup (1): Brazil 1.
CIS Cup (1): Cusick 1.
Challenge Cup (2): Cusick 1, McLean 1.

Inglis N 27 + 1	McMullan K 29 + 5	Beith G 4 + 2	Renwick M 1	Bishop J 25 + 6	Cusick J 18 + 8	Miller G 21 + 3	MacDonald S 21 + 6	McLean D 9 + 6	Brazil A 28 + 3	Swankie G 34	Henslee G 34 + 1	McAulay J — + 3	Farquharson P 5 + 8	Cook S 1 + 11	McLeod C 34	Collier J — + 5	Woodcock T 4	Rennie S 28	Donaldson E 24 + 3	Millar M 8 + 1	Fraser S 2	McGlashan J 11	Diack I 11 + 2	McCulloch M 11 + 1	Coyle C 5	Watson P 1	*Match No.*
1	2	3	4^{1}	5	6	7	8	9	10^{2}	11^{3}	12	13	14														1
1	2			5	6^{1}	7	8	9	10^{2}	11			12	3	4	13											2
	2	3^{3}		4		7	8	9^{1}		11	10^{2}		12	13	5	14	1	6									3
	2^{1}	3		5		7^{2}	8^{3}	9	13	11	10		14	12	6		1	4									4
	2	3^{2}		5			8^{3}	9	7	11	10^{1}		12	14	6		1	4	13								5
	2	12		5	7^{1}		8	13		11^{3}	10		9	14	6		1	4^{2}	3								6
1	2			6	7		8			11	10		9		5			4	3								7
1	2			6	7^{1}		8	9	12	11	10				5			4	3								8
1	2	13		6	7^{1}		8	9	12	11^{3}	10				5	14		4	3^{2}								9
1	2			6	7		8	13	9^{2}	11^{3}	10	12		14	5			4^{1}	3								10
1	2			6	7		8		9	11	10				5			4	3								11
1	2			6	7		8	9		11	10				5			4	3								12
1	2			6	7		8	9^{1}		11	10				5			4	3	12							13
1	2			6	7^{2}		8	13	9	11	10				5			4	12	3^{1}							14
1	2			6	7^{1}		8		9	11^{2}	10		13		5			4	12	3							15
1	2			6		12	8^{1}	13	9		10		11^{2}		5			4	3	7							16
1	2			6^{1}		12	8		9	11	10				5				3	7	4						17
1	2			6	12	4	8^{2}		9	11	10		13		5				3	7^{1}							18
1	2			6		4	8^{1}	13	9	11^{2}	10		12		5				3	7							19
1	2			6	12	13	8		9	11	10				5^{1}				3	7^{2}	4						20
1	2			6	12		8	13	9		10		11^{2}		5			4	3	7^{1}							21
1					7^{2}	2	13		9	11	10		8^{1}	12	5			4	3			6					22
1	12				7^{3}	2	14		9	11^{1}	10				5			4	3^{2}			6	8	13			23
1	13			5		2			9^{2}	11	10					12		4	3			6	8^{1}	7			24
1	13			12	14	2			9	11	10				5^{1}			4	3			6	8^{2}	7^{3}			25
1	13			12	14	2			9	11	10				5			4^{1}	3^{3}			6	8^{2}	7			26
1	12				13	2			9^{1}	11	10^{2}				5			4	3			6	8	7			27
1				4		2			9	11	10			12	5				3			6	8^{1}	7			28
1	4^{1}				8	2			9	11	10				5				3			6	12	7			29
1	8			13	12	2			9^{3}	11	10				5			4^{2}	3^{1}			6	14	7			30
	3			13	7^{1}	2^{2}	12		9	11	10				5			4				6	8		1		31
15	3			7	12	2			9	11	10			13	5			4				6^{1}	8^{2}		1^{G}		32
	3				7^{1}	2	12		9	11	10			13	5			4					8	6^{2}	1		33
	3			13	7^{1}	2			9	11	10			12	5			4					8^{2}	6	1		34
	3			13		2^{2}	12		9	11	10				5	14		4	6^{1}				8^{3}	7	1		35
1	7^{1}			6		2	13		9^{3}	11	10	14		12	5			4^{2}						8		3	36

AYR UNITED Second Division

Year Formed: 1910. *Ground & Address:* Somerset Park, Tryfield Place, Ayr KA8 9NB. *Telephone:* 01292 263435. *E-mail:* info@aufc.co.uk. *Website:* ayrunitedfc.co.uk.
Ground Capacity: 10,185, seated: 1549. *Size of Pitch:* 110yd × 72yd.
Chairman (acting): Donald Cameron. *Managing Director:* Hugh Cameron. *General Manager:* Lachlan Cameron. *Administrator:* Brian Caldwell. *Lottery Manager:* Andrew Downie.
Manager: Robert Connor. *Assistant Manager:* Robert Reilly. *Physio:* John Kerr.
Managers since 1975: Alex Stuart, Ally MacLeod, Willie McLean, George Caldwell, Ally MacLeod, George Burley, Simon Stainrod, Gordon Dalziel. *Club Nickname(s):* The Honest Men. *Previous Grounds:* None.
Record Attendance: 25,225 v Rangers, Division I, 13 Sept 1969.
Record Transfer Fee received: £300,000 for Steven Nicol to Liverpool (Oct 1981).
Record Transfer Fee paid: £90,000 for Mark Campbell from Stranraer (March 1999).
Record Victory: 11-1 v Dumbarton, League Cup, 13 Aug 1952.
Record Defeat: 0-9 in Division I v Rangers (1929); v Hearts (1931); B Division v Third Lanark (1954).
Most Capped Player: Jim Nisbet, 3, Scotland.
Most League Appearances: 459, John Murphy, 1963-78.
Most League League and Cup Goals in Season (Individual): 66, Jimmy Smith, 1927-28.
Most League and Cup Goals Overall (Individual): 213, Peter Price, 1955-61.

AYR UNITED 2004–05 LEAGUE RECORD

Match No.	Date	Venue	Opponents	Result		H/T Score	Lg. Pos.	Goalscorers	Attendance
1	Aug 7	A	Dumbarton	L	0-1	0-1	—		1016
2	14	H	Berwick R	W	2-1	2-0	7	Burgess 10, Connolly 40	1342
3	21	A	Stranraer	L	1-2	1-0	6	Kean 23	885
4	28	H	Morton	W	2-0	0-0	6	Kean 2 57, 72	2264
5	Sept 4	A	Alloa Ath	W	3-1	2-1	5	Conway 2 18, 76, Kean 24	585
6	11	H	Forfar Ath	D	3-3	2-2	4	Conway 6, Kean 2 23, 63	1386
7	18	A	Arbroath	D	0-0	0-0	5		481
8	25	H	Brechin C	L	0-1	0-0	6		1399
9	Oct 2	A	Stirling A	D	1-1	0-0	6	Ferguson A 80	1022
10	16	A	Berwick R	W	1-0	0-0	6	Kean 89	403
11	23	H	Dumbarton	L	0-1	0-0	6		1468
12	30	A	Morton	W	1-0	0-0	5	Henderson 81	3232
13	Nov 6	H	Alloa Ath	W	4-3	1-1	5	Smyth 21, Kean 2 55, 65, Connolly 61	1218
14	13	A	Forfar Ath	W	3-2	1-2	5	Kean (pen) 45, Connolly 59, Smyth 70	518
15	27	H	Arbroath	D	1-1	1-0	5	McCulloch 19	1189
16	Dec 4	A	Brechin C	L	0-5	0-4	5		576
17	18	H	Stirling A	W	3-2	1-0	4	Ferguson A 3, Wardlaw 2 79, 84	1288
18	27	A	Dumbarton	D	1-1	1-1	4	Connolly 7	1118
19	Jan 1	H	Stranraer	L	0-1	0-0	5		1467
20	3	H	Morton	W	2-1	1-0	—	Connolly 45, Ferguson A 76	2455
21	15	A	Alloa Ath	L	1-5	1-2	4	Evans J (og) 5	647
22	29	A	Arbroath	L	0-2	0-0	5		426
23	Feb 12	A	Stirling A	L	0-2	0-2	5		711
24	19	A	Stranraer	W	3-1	1-1	5	McCulloch 41, Wardlaw 77, Lyle (pen) 89	619
25	26	H	Berwick R	L	0-1	0-1	5		1017
26	Mar 5	H	Alloa Ath	D	1-1	1-0	5	Connolly 22	1003
27	12	A	Morton	L	1-2	0-2	6	McGrady 54	2448
28	15	H	Brechin C	L	0-1	0-0	—		737
29	19	A	Forfar Ath	L	0-1	0-0	7		490
30	26	H	Forfar Ath	W	1-0	1-0	5	Chaplain 9	1076
31	Apr 2	H	Arbroath	D	2-2	1-1	5	Boyd 25, Chaplain 58	1115
32	9	H	Stirling A	L	0-3	0-0	5		1046
33	16	A	Brechin C	L	0-3	0-1	6		624
34	23	H	Stranraer	D	0-0	0-0	7		1367
35	30	A	Berwick R	L	1-2	1-1	8	Connolly 8	425
36	May 7	H	Dumbarton	D	1-1	0-1	8	Smyth 76	1236

Final League Position: 8

Honours
League Champions: Division II 1911-12, 1912-13, 1927-28, 1936-37, 1958-59, 1965-66. Second Division 1987-88, 1996-97;
Runners-up: Division II 1910-11, 1955-56, 1968-69.
Scottish Cup: Semi-finals 2002.
League Cup: Runners-up: 2001-02.
B&Q Cup Runners-up: 1990-91, 1991-92.

Club colours: Shirt: White with black trim. Shorts: Black. Stockings: White with black.

Goalscorers: *League* (39): Kean 10 (1 pen), Connolly 7, Conway 3, Ferguson A 3, Smyth 3, Wardlaw 3, Chaplain 2, McCulloch 2, Boyd 1, Burgess 1, Henderson 1, Lyle 1 (pen), McGrady 1, own goal 1.
Scottish Cup (6): Ferguson A 2, Henderson 2, Conway 1, Lyle 1.
CIS Cup (1): Ferguson A 1.
Challenge Cup (0).

Roy L 22	Lyle W 29 + 4	McGrady S 19 + 7	Chaplain S 16 + 7	McLaughlin B 34	Smyth M 33	Connolly P 27 + 7	Dunning A 3 + 1	Kean S 14	Henderson D 29	Conway C 22 + 1	Dunlop M 24 + 4	Ferguson A 10 + 16	Ramsay D 14 + 5	Burgess R 1 + 3	Cargill A — + 2	O'Neill M — + 2	Ferguson S 2 + 5	Craig D 1	Brown G 5 + 6	McKay G — + 1	Hillcoat J 9 + 2	Doyle J 7 + 4	Cherrie P 5 + 1	McCulloch S 10 + 1	Gilmour N 3 + 1	Tait T 22 + 3	Wardlaw G 11 + 4	Nesovic A 1	Reid A 3 + 5	Buckley R 9 + 2	Boyd S 10	Johnston D — + 1	Crawford S — + 1	Templeton P 1	*Match No.*
1	2	3	4	5	6	7[2]	8[1]	9	10	11[3]	12	13	14																						1
1	2[1]	3	4[3]		7	10		9	11[2]		6		8	5	12	13	14																		2
1	2		4[1]	5	7	10		9	11		3[3]	14	13			12	8[2]	6																	3
1	2		13	5	4	12		10	11[2]	7	3	14	8				6[1]		9[3]																4
1	2	13	6	5	4			10	11	7[3]	3[2]	12	8						9[1]	14															5
1	2	13	6	5	4			10	11	7	3		8[2]						9[1]		12														6
	2	13	6	5	4	12		10	11	7[3]	3[2]		8	14					9[1]		1														7
1		2	6	5	4	12		10	11	7[1]	3	9[3]	8[2]		13				14																8
1	2[3]		13	5	4	10	14		11	7[1]	3	9	6[2]	12								8													9
1	2	8	6	5	4	10[1]	7[2]	9	11		3		13						12																10
1	2	8	6	5	4	10[3]	7[2]	9[1]	11		3	12	13						14																11
	2			5		10			11		3	9[2]	8						13			6	1	4[1]	7	12									12
	2			5	4	10[3]		9			3	14	7[2]									8[1]	1	6	11	12	13								13
	2		12	5	4	10[3]		9[2]			3	13	7[1]										1	6	11	8	14								14
	2			5	4	10[1]		9	11	7	3												1	6		8	12								15
	2			5	4	10		9	11[1]	7	3												1	6	12	8									16
1	2	12		5	4	10[1]			11	7		9[3]					14							3		6	13	8[2]							17
1[6]	2	6		5	4	10			11	7	12												15	3[1]		8	9								18
	12	6	13	5[2]	4	8			11	7	3	9									1					2	10[1]								19
	14	6	12	5	4	8[1]			11[3]	7	3	9					13				1					2[2]	10								20
	2	6		5		12			11	7	4	9[1]					13				1	14		3[2]		8[3]	10								21
1	4	6		5		8			11	7		9[1]	14				13					2[2]				3	10[3]		12						22
1	2	3	10	5	4	8[3]			11	7[2]		14							13					12		6[1]	9								23
1	2	13	7	5	4	10[3]			11[1]		3[2]											12		6		8	9		14						24
1	2[3]	12	11	5	4[2]	10				7	3[1]								13					6		8	9		14						25
1		3		5	4	8						12	11						10			13				6[2]	9[1]		7	2					26
1[6]		3		5	4	8			6			13	7								15					12	9[2]		11[1]	2	10				27
	2	14		5	4	13			3[3]	11[2]		12	8								1					6	9[1]			7	10				28
1[6]	2		12	5	4	9			3[2]	11		13	8[1]													6				7	10	15			29
	12	11	10	5	4	9			3[3]	7[1]		13									1	14				6				2	8[2]				30
	13	11[2]	10	5	4	9			3	7	12										1					6[1]				2	8				31
	2	11[1]	10	5	4	9			3[3]	7	13	14									1					6[2]				12	8				32
	2		10	5	4	12					3[2]	9									1	11				6				7	8[1]		13		33
1	2	7			4	13			11[1]		3	9[3]		12								10				6			14	5	8[2]				34
1	2	11	12	5	4	9[3]					3	14										10				6			13	7[1]	8[2]				35
1	2	11[1]		5	4	7				12	3	14														6[2]			9	13	8[3]			10	36

BERWICK RANGERS Third Division

Year Formed: 1881. *Ground & Address:* Shielfield Park, Tweedmouth, Berwick-upon-Tweed TD15 2EF. *Telephone:* 01289 307424. *Fax:* 01289 309424. Club 24 hour hotline 09068 800697. *Ground Capacity:* 4131, seated: 1366. *Size of Pitch:* 110yd × 70yd.
Chairman: Robert L. Wilson. *Vice-chairman:* Moray McLaren. *Company Secretary:* Ross Hood. *Club Secretary:* Dennis McCleary. *Treasurer:* J. N. Simpson.
Manager: John Coughlin. *Assistant Manager:* Neil Oliver. *Coach:* Ian Smith. *Physios:* Kerry Sneddon & Jamie Dougal. *Ground/Kit:* Ian Oliver.
Managers since 1975: H. Melrose, G. Haig, W. Galbraith, D. Smith, F. Connor, J. McSherry, E. Tait, J. Thomson, J. Jefferies, R. Callachan, J. Anderson, J. Crease, T. Hendrie, I. Ross, J. Thomson, P. Smith, S. Clark.
Club Nickname(s): The Borderers. *Previous Grounds:* Bull Stob Close, Pier Field, Meadow Field, Union Park, Old Shielfield.
Record Attendance: 13,365 v Rangers, Scottish Cup 1st rd, 28 Jan 1967.
Record Victory: 8-1 v Forfar Ath, Division II, 25 Dec 1965; v Vale of Leithen, Scottish Cup, Dec 1966.
Record Defeat: 1-9 v Hamilton A, First Division, 9 Aug 1980.
Most League Appearances: 435: Eric Tait, 1970-87.
Most League Goals in Season (Individual): 33: Ken Bowron, Division II, 1963-64.
Most Goals Overall (Individual): 115: Eric Tait, 1970-87.

BERWICK RANGERS 2004–05 LEAGUE RECORD

Match No.	Date	Venue	Opponents	Result		H/T Score	Lg. Pos.	Goalscorers	Attendance
1	Aug 7	H	Morton	W	2-1	2-0	—	Hutchison [32], Forrest [44]	907
2	14	A	Ayr U	L	1-2	0-2	6	Hutchison [87]	1342
3	21	H	Brechin C	L	0-2	0-0	7		429
4	28	A	Stirling A	L	1-3	0-2	8	Hutchison [65]	695
5	Sept 4	H	Dumbarton	L	0-4	0-2	8		412
6	11	H	Alloa Ath	L	2-3	1-2	8	Seaton [18], Smith D [64]	295
7	18	A	Forfar Ath	D	1-1	0-1	9	Hutchison [68]	435
8	25	H	Arbroath	L	0-3	0-0	10		335
9	Oct 2	A	Stranraer	D	2-2	2-1	9	Connelly [21], Little [29]	521
10	16	H	Ayr U	L	0-1	0-0	10		403
11	23	A	Morton	L	0-2	0-1	10		2720
12	30	H	Stirling A	L	0-1	0-0	10		453
13	Nov 6	A	Dumbarton	L	1-3	0-2	10	Gordon [56]	790
14	13	A	Alloa Ath	D	2-2	1-1	10	Smith D 2 [9, 68]	462
15	20	A	Stirling A	W	1-0	1-0	10	Smith D [9]	551
16	30	H	Forfar Ath	W	1-0	0-0	—	McGarty [63]	294
17	Dec 4	A	Arbroath	D	1-1	1-0	10	McGarty (pen) [45]	450
18	27	H	Morton	D	2-2	1-1	10	Clarke [11], Little [90]	968
19	Jan 1	A	Brechin C	L	1-4	0-1	10	McGarty [68]	515
20	15	H	Dumbarton	L	0-3	0-1	10		322
21	29	A	Forfar Ath	W	2-0	2-0	10	McKeown [9], Seaton [43]	435
22	Feb 5	H	Arbroath	L	2-3	1-3	10	Hutchison [31], Little [59]	309
23	12	A	Stranraer	L	0-1	0-0	10		351
24	19	H	Brechin C	W	2-1	1-0	10	Gordon [5], Smith D [69]	323
25	26	A	Ayr U	W	1-0	1-0	10	Connelly [34]	1017
26	Mar 1	H	Stranraer	L	1-2	1-1	—	Smith D [4]	296
27	5	A	Dumbarton	D	1-1	1-0	10	Connelly [32]	690
28	12	H	Stirling A	D	2-2	1-1	10	Connelly [2], Seaton (pen) [90]	366
29	19	A	Alloa Ath	D	2-2	1-0	10	Hutchison [15], Little [72]	452
30	26	H	Alloa Ath	W	2-1	0-1	10	Smith D [73], Gordon [84]	306
31	Apr 2	H	Forfar Ath	D	1-1	0-1	10	Hutchison [49]	369
32	9	H	Stranraer	L	1-2	0-1	10	McLeish [85]	363
33	16	A	Arbroath	L	0-2	0-2	10		460
34	23	A	Brechin C	D	1-1	1-0	10	Gordon [42]	630
35	30	H	Ayr U	W	2-1	1-1	10	Smith D [10], Gordon [49]	425
36	May 7	A	Morton	L	2-4	0-1	10	Gordon [79], Hutchison [86]	2475

Final League Position: 10

Honours
League Champions: Second Division 1978-79; *Runners-up:* Second Division 1993-94. Third Division 1999-2000.
Scottish Cup: Quarter-finals 1953-54, 1979-80.
League Cup: Semi-finals 1963-64.
Bell's League Challenge: Quarter-finals 2004-05

Club colours: Shirt: Black with broad gold vertical stripes. Shorts: Black with white trim. Stockings: Gold with black and white trim.

Goalscorers: *League* (40): Hutchison 8, Smith D 8, Gordon 6, Connelly 4, Little 4, McGarty 3 (1 pen), Seaton 3 (1 pen), Clarke 1, Forrest 1, McKeown 1, Mcleish 1.
Scottish Cup (4): Clarke 1, Connelly 1, Hutchison 1, McNicoll 1.
CIS Cup (3): Hampshire 1, McNicoll 1, Smith D 1.
Challenge Cup (4): Forrest 1, Gordon 1, Neil 1, Seaton 1 (pen).

O'Connor G 35	Murie D 34	Seaton A 30 + 1	Cowan M 33	Horn R 16 + 1	Connell G 31	Connelly G 20 + 5	Forrest G 9 + 3	Hutchison G 21 + 9	Gordon K 25 + 5	Hampshire P 13 + 6	Little I 24 + 7	Smith D 26 + 5	McNicoll G 17 + 3	Neil M 9 + 1	Smith E 3 + 3	Clarke P 10	McGarty M 14 + 3	McKeown C 4	MacSween I 1 + 6	Greenhill G 4 + 5	McLeish K 16	Brittain G — + 1	McCann G 1	*Match No.*
1	2	3	4	5	6	7	8	9	10^{1}	11	12													1
1	2	3	4^{1}	5	6^{2}		8	9	10	11^{3}	14	7	12	13										2
1	2	3		5	6		8	9	10^{1}	11^{2}	12	13	4^{3}	7	14									3
1		3	4	5			7	9	6	11^{1}	10	12		8	2									4
1	2	3^{3}	5	4^{1}	6		7	9	10^{2}	11	13	14	12	8										5
1	2	3	5	4		7^{1}	6	9	12		10	11		8										6
1	2	3	5			7	6	9		10	12	11^{1}		8	4									7
1	2	3	5		6^{1}	7		9		10	12	11		8	4									8
1	2	3	5	4	6	7	13	9		12	10^{2}	11^{1}		8										9
1	2	3	5	4	6	7^{1}	14	9	13	12	10^{2}	11^{2}		8										10
1	2		5	4	6	7^{1}	11	9	13	3	10^{2}	12		8										11
1	2		5	4	6	12	8	9^{1}	7	3		11^{2}			13	10								12
1	2	13	5	4^{1}	6^{3}		14		10	3^{2}	7	11	12			9	8							13
1	2	3	5		6	12		13	10^{1}		7	11	4			9^{2}	8							14
1	2	3	5		6	12		13	10^{2}		7	11^{1}	4			9	8							15
1	2	3	5		6	12		13	10^{1}		7	11	4			9^{2}	8							16
1		3	5		6	2		12	7^{1}		10	11	4			9	8							17
1	2	3	5		6	7^{1}		9			12	11				10	8	4						18
1	2	3	5		6			9	7^{2}	12		11			13	10^{1}	8	4						19
1	2	3	5					9^{1}	12		6	11				10^{2}	8	4	7	13				20
1	2	3	5		6	7		12			10^{1}					9^{2}	8	4	13	14	11^{3}			21
1	2	3	5		6^{1}	7		9			10	12	4				8				11			22
1	2	3	5	4	6^{2}	12		9^{3}	14		10	11					8^{1}			13	7			23
1	2	3	5		6	7			9		10	11	4								8			24
1	2	3	5		6	7			9^{1}		10	11	4						12		8			25
1	2	3	5		6	7			9^{1}		10	11	4						12		8			26
1	2	3		5	6	7			9		10	11	4								8			27
1	2	3	5		6	7^{1}		12	9	11	10		4								8			28
1	2	3	5		6^{2}			7	9^{1}	11	10^{3}		4				14			13	8	12		29
1	2	3	5	4	6^{1}			7	9^{3}	13	10	11^{2}					14			12	8			30
1	2	3	5	4				7	9	13	10	11^{2}							12	6^{1}	8			31
1	2	3		5	6			7	9	11^{1}			4				13		12	10^{2}	8			32
1	2	3	5		6	7		12	9		10	11^{1}	4								8			33
1	2		5		6	7			9^{1}		10	11	4				3		12		8			34
1	2		5		6	7		12	9			11	4				3			10^{1}	8			35
	2		5^{1}	12	6	7		14	9	13		11	4^{2}				3			10^{3}	8		1	36

BRECHIN CITY — First Division

Year Formed: 1906. *Ground & Address:* Glebe Park, Trinity Rd, Brechin, Angus DD9 6BJ. *Telephone:* 01356 622856. *Fax (to Secretary):* 01356 625524.
Ground Capacity: total: 3060, seated: 1518. *Size of Pitch:* 110yd × 67yd.
Chairman: David Birse. *Vice-Chairman:* Hugh Campbell Adamson. *Secretary:* Ken Ferguson.
Manager: Ian Campbell. *Assistant Manager:* Bert Paton. *Youth Coach:* Paul Martin. *Physio:* Tom Gilmartin.
Managers since 1975: C. Dunn, I. Stewart, D. Houston, I. Fleming, J. Ritchie, I. Redford, J. Young, R. Campbell.
Club Nickname(s): The City. *Previous Grounds:* Nursery Park.
Record Attendance: 8122 v Aberdeen, Scottish Cup 3rd rd, 3 Feb 1973.
Record Transfer Fee received: £100,000 for Scott Thomson to Aberdeen (1991).
Record Transfer Fee paid: £16,000 for Sandy Ross from Berwick Rangers (1991).
Record Victory: 12-1 v Thornhill, Scottish Cup 1st rd, 28 Jan 1926.
Record Defeat: 0-10 v Airdrieonians, Albion R and Cowdenbeath, all in Division II, 1937-38.
Most League Appearances: 459: David Watt, 1975-89.
Most League Goals in Season (Individual): 26: W. McIntosh, Division II, 1959-60.
Most Goals Overall (Individual): 131: Ian Campbell.

BRECHIN CITY 2004–05 LEAGUE RECORD

Match No.	Date	Venue	Opponents	Result		H/T Score	Lg. Pos.	Goalscorers	Attendance
1	Aug 7	A	Forfar Ath	L	0-1	0-1	—		766
2	14	H	Stirling A	L	0-3	0-2	9		491
3	21	A	Berwick R	W	2-0	0-0	8	Templeman 2 [79, 85]	429
4	28	H	Alloa Ath	W	4-0	3-0	5	Ritchie [8], Gibson [18], McLeish [45], Hampshire [80]	428
5	Sept 4	A	Stranraer	L	2-4	0-2	7	Gibson (pen) [63], Ritchie [69]	436
6	11	H	Arbroath	W	4-1	1-1	6	Gibson 2 [43, 47], King [71], Templeman [89]	559
7	18	A	Morton	W	3-0	1-0	4	Gibson [45], Hampshire [60], Templeman [79]	2432
8	25	A	Ayr U	W	1-0	0-0	3	Ritchie [48]	1399
9	Oct 2	H	Dumbarton	W	4-0	0-0	3	White [51], Ritchie 3 [69, 81, 85]	503
10	16	A	Stirling A	W	5-1	1-0	2	Templeman 4 [34, 50, 56, 85], Byers [69]	736
11	23	H	Forfar Ath	W	2-0	1-0	2	Winter [36], Smith [72]	869
12	30	A	Alloa Ath	D	2-2	1-1	2	Ritchie [45], Templeman [71]	474
13	Nov 6	H	Stranraer	W	4-1	2-1	2	Templeman 2 [28, 84], Winter [30], Walker [48]	620
14	13	A	Arbroath	D	2-2	1-0	2	Ritchie [6], Gibson [71]	682
15	27	H	Morton	W	2-1	1-0	2	Gibson [18], Templeman [60]	989
16	Dec 4	H	Ayr U	W	5-0	4-0	2	Walker 2 [1, 49], Templeman 2 [19, 43], White [28]	576
17	27	A	Forfar Ath	W	3-1	1-1	2	Hampshire [6], Ritchie 2 (1 pen) [53 (p), 89]	901
18	Jan 1	H	Berwick R	W	4-1	1-0	1	Hampshire 3 (1 pen) [30, 53, 79 (p)], King [77]	515
19	3	H	Alloa Ath	L	2-3	1-0	—	Ritchie [17], Gibson [69]	604
20	15	A	Stranraer	W	1-0	0-0	1	Callaghan [62]	552
21	29	A	Morton	W	2-0	0-0	1	Hampshire 2 [57, 85]	3004
22	Feb 9	H	Arbroath	W	4-3	2-2	—	Hampshire 2 [39, 90], White [42], Callaghan [89]	651
23	12	H	Dumbarton	L	0-2	0-2	1		589
24	19	A	Berwick R	L	1-2	0-1	1	King [51]	323
25	26	H	Stirling A	W	5-3	3-1	1	Hampshire 2 [4, 23], White [15], King [56], Gibson [59]	515
26	Mar 1	A	Dumbarton	D	1-1	1-1	—	Callaghan [2]	548
27	5	H	Stranraer	W	2-1	0-1	1	Hampshire 2 [51, 62]	606
28	12	A	Alloa Ath	D	1-1	1-0	1	Ritchie [42]	522
29	15	A	Ayr U	W	1-0	0-0	—	Gibson [84]	737
30	19	A	Arbroath	W	4-1	2-1	1	King [16], Hampshire 2 [19, 83], Panther [50]	775
31	Apr 2	H	Morton	L	1-2	0-0	1	Ritchie [80]	1340
32	9	A	Dumbarton	D	1-1	0-0	1	Sharp [71]	777
33	16	H	Ayr U	W	3-0	1-0	1	Ritchie (pen) [43], Gibson [47], Hampshire [90]	624
34	23	H	Berwick R	D	1-1	0-1	1	White [75]	630
35	30	A	Stirling A	W	2-1	2-1	1	Walker [2], King [41]	667
36	May 7	H	Forfar Ath	L	0-3	0-0	1		1074

Final League Position: 1

Honours
League Champions: C Division 1953-54. Second Division 1982-83, 1989-90. Third Division 2001-02. *Runners-up:* Second Division 1992-93, 2002-03. Third Division 1995-96. Second Division 2004-05.
Bell's League Challenge: Runners-up 2002-03. Semi-finals 2001-02.

Club colours: Shirt, Shorts, Stockings: Red with white trimmings.

Goalscorers: *League* (81): Hampshire 17 (1 pen), Ritchie 14 (2 pens), Templeman 14, Gibson 11 (1 pen), King 6, White 5, Walker 4, Callaghan 3, Winter 2, Byers 1, McLeish 1, Panther 1, Sharp 1, Smith 1.
Scottish Cup (7): Hampshire 3, Templeman 2, Ritchie 1, Winter 1.
CIS Cup (6): Gibson 2, Ritchie 2, Templeman 2.
Challenge Cup (0).

Hay D 2	Smith J 7 + 4	Deas P 33	Johnson G 10 + 14	Dennis S 4 + 1	Walker S 33 + 2	King C 24 + 9	Byers K 17 + 8	Ritchie P 29 + 6	Templeman C 11 + 5	Mitchell A 8 + 11	MacNicol S 1 + 2	Gibson G 28 + 8	Black R 1 + 6	Winter C 24 + 3	Jackson C 3 + 7	McLeish K 7 + 4	Nelson C 34	White D 27 + 3	Hampshire S 32 + 2	McCulloch S 1 + 1	Hamilton S 22 + 2	Callaghan S 11 + 2	Ferguson S 11	Sharp J 13	Panther E 3 + 5	*Match No.*
1	2	3	4	5	6	7^{1}	8^{3}	9	10^{2}	11	12	13	14													1
1^{1}		3^{2}		4^{3}	6	7	8	9	10		2	11	14	5	12	13										2
	2^{2}	3	8	5	6			9	13			12		14	11	7^{3}	1	4	10^{1}							3
	2	3	8		4	7		9^{1}	14			11		13	6^{2}	10^{3}	1	5	12							4
	2	3^{2}	10^{1}	5	6	12		9	14			11			8	7^{3}	1	4	13							5
		3		14	6^{3}	11	4	9	12	13		10^{2}		8		2	1	5	7^{1}							6
					6	7^{1}	8	9	12			11	13	4	14	2^{3}	1	5	10	3^{2}						7
		3			6		8^{2}	9^{3}	10^{1}			7	12	4	13	14	1	5	11		2					8
		3	12		6^{3}		8^{2}	9	10			7	13	4^{1}			1	5	11	14	2					9
		3	12		6	13	8	9	10			7		4^{3}	14		1	5	11^{2}		2^{1}					10
	2	3	12		6	13	8^{1}	9	10			7^{3}		4	14		1	5	11^{2}							11
	2	3			6	12	8	9^{1}	10			7^{2}	13	4			1	5	11							12
		3			6	12	8^{3}	9	10			7^{1}		4^{2}	13	14	1	5	11		2					13
		3			6	12	8	9	10			7		4			1	5	11^{1}		2					14
		3	12		6	14	8^{2}	9^{3}	10	13		7		4^{1}			1	5	11		2					15
	12	3	13		6	14	8	9	10			7^{3}		4^{2}			1	5	11		2^{1}					16
		3	12		6	7^{3}	8^{1}	9		14		10		4		13	1	5	11		2^{2}					17
		3	12		6	7	8^{1}	9		13		10^{2}		4^{3}	14	2	1	5	11							18
		3	8		6	7	13	9^{1}		12	14	10		4^{2}		2^{3}	1	5	11							19
	12	3			5	11^{2}	14	9^{1}		13		7		8			1	4	10^{3}		2	6				20
	12	3			5	7	13	9^{2}		14		11		8			1	4	10		2^{1}	6^{3}				21
	2^{3}	3	8		5	7		13		11^{2}		12					1	4	9		14	10	6^{1}			22
	14				5	7	13	9		11^{3}		12	3^{2}	8^{1}			1	4	10		2	6				23
		3	13		5	7^{1}		9				11		8^{2}			1	14	10		2^{3}	6		4	12	24
		3	8			7^{2}		14				9^{3}		12			1	4	10		2	6	11^{1}	5	13	25
		3	8		14	7^{2}		12				11					1	4	9^{1}		2^{3}	6	10	5	13	26
		3	14		13	7^{3}		9				12		8^{1}			1	4	10		2	6	11^{2}	5		27
		3			6	13	14	9^{2}		12		11^{3}					1		10		2	8	4	5	7^{1}	28
			8^{3}		5	7	11^{2}	9		13		12					1	4	10^{1}		2	6		3	14	29
		3	12		5	7				13		11		4^{1}			1		9^{3}		2	14	8	6^{2}	10	30
		3			5	7		13		14		10		4			1		9		2^{2}	12	8	6^{3}	11^{1}	31
		3	14		5	7	13	9^{1}		11		12		4^{2}			1		10		2		8^{3}	6		32
		3	14		5	7	12	9		8		11^{3}		4^{1}			1	13	10		2			6^{2}		33
		3	12		5	7	11^{1}	9^{2}		8^{3}		13					1	14	10		2		4	6		34
		3	8		6	7^{2}	12	14		10^{1}		11^{3}					1	2	9				4	5	13	35
		4	13		3	7		14		8^{2}		10					1	2	9		12	11^{3}	6	5^{1}		36

CELTIC Premier League

Year Formed: 1888. *Ground & Address:* Celtic Park, Glasgow G40 3RE. *Telephone:* 0845 671 1888. *Fax:* 0141 551 8106.
Ground Capacity: all seated: 60,554. *Size of Pitch:* 105m × 68m.
Chairman: Brian Quinn. *Chief Executive:* Peter Lawwell. *Secretary:* Robert Howat.
Manager: Gordon Strachan. *Assistant Manager:* Gary Pendry. *Youth Development Manager:* Tommy Burns. *Head Youth Coach:* Willie McStay. *Physio:* Tim Williamson. *Club Doctor:* Dr Roddy Macdonald. *Kit Manager:* John Clark.
Managers since 1975: Jock Stein, Billy McNeill, David Hay, Billy McNeill, Liam Brady, Lou Macari, Tommy Burns, Wim Jansen, Dr Jozef Venglos, John Barnes, Martin O'Neill. *Club Nickname(s):* The Bhoys. *Previous Grounds:* None.
Record Attendance: 92,000 v Rangers, Division I, 1 Jan 1938.
Record Transfer Fee received: £4,700,000 for Paolo Di Canio to Sheffield W (August 1997).
Record Transfer Fee paid: £6,000,000 for Chris Sutton from Chelsea (July 2000).
Record Victory: 11-0 Dundee, Division I, 26 Oct 1895.
Record Defeat: 0-8 v Motherwell, Division I, 30 Apr 1937.
Most Capped Player: Pat Bonner 80, Republic of Ireland.
Most League Appearances: 486: Billy McNeill, 1957-75.
Most League Goals in Season (Individual): 50: James McGrory, Division I, 1935-36.
Most Goals Overall (Individual): 397: James McGrory, 1922-39.

Honours
League Champions: (39 times) Division I 1892-93, 1893-94, 1895-96, 1897-98, 1904-05, 1905-06, 1906-07, 1907-08, 1908-09, 1909-10, 1913-14, 1914-15, 1915-16, 1916-17, 1918-19, 1921-22, 1925-26, 1935-36, 1937-38, 1953-54, 1965-66, 1966-67, 1967-68, 1968-69, 1969-70, 1970-71, 1971-72, 1972-73, 1973-74. Premier Division 1976-77, 1978-79, 1980-81, 1981-82, 1985-86, 1987-88, 1997-98, 2000-01, 2001-02, 2003–04. *Runners-up:* 27 times.

CELTIC 2004–05 LEAGUE RECORD

Match No.	*Date*	*Venue*	*Opponents*	*Result*	*H/T Score*	*Lg. Pos.*	*Goalscorers*	*Attendance*
1	Aug 8	H	Motherwell	W 2-0	1-0	—	McNamara [8], Sutton [56]	56,957
2	14	A	Kilmarnock	W 4-2	3-2	1	Hartson 2 [14, 69], Thompson 2 [36, 42]	10,526
3	22	A	Inverness CT	W 3-1	1-1	1	Hartson 2 [25, 76], Petrov [68]	8788
4	29	H	Rangers	W 1-0	0-0	1	Thompson [85]	58,763
5	Sept 11	H	Dundee	W 3-0	2-0	1	Camara 2 [21, 85], Hartson [36]	56,840
6	19	A	Hibernian	D 2-2	2-2	1	Camara [33], Sutton [44]	13,573
7	25	H	Dunfermline Ath	W 3-0	2-0	1	Varga [19], Camara 2 [38, 54]	56,873
8	Oct 3	A	Dundee U	W 3-0	3-0	1	Sutton 2 (1 pen) [9, 37 (p)], Petrov [17]	10,329
9	16	H	Hearts	W 3-0	1-0	1	Camara [41], Juninho [56], Petrov [85]	59,242
10	24	A	Livingston	W 4-2	4-1	1	Petrov [2], Camara [14], Hartson [19], Sutton [31]	6695
11	27	H	Aberdeen	L 2-3	1-2	—	Hartson 2 [45, 68]	57,060
12	30	A	Motherwell	W 3-2	1-0	1	McGeady [41], Thompson (pen) [65], Beattie [78]	10,592
13	Nov 6	H	Kilmarnock	W 2-1	1-0	1	McGeady [44], Thompson (pen) [63]	57,268
14	13	H	Inverness CT	W 3-0	1-0	1	Sutton [3], Hartson 2 [52, 77]	56,965
15	20	A	Rangers	L 0-2	0-2	1		50,043
16	28	A	Dundee	D 2-2	0-1	2	Camara [53], Hartson [62]	9539
17	Dec 4	H	Hibernian	W 2-1	1-0	1	Hartson 2 [17, 83]	58,399
18	12	A	Dunfermline Ath	W 2-0	2-0	1	Sutton [15], Petrov [30]	7650
19	18	H	Dundee U	W 1-0	1-0	1	Sutton [17]	56,281
20	26	A	Hearts	W 2-0	1-0	1	McGeady [9], Petrov [69]	16,163
21	Jan 2	H	Livingston	W 2-1	1-1	1	Hartson [15], Sutton (pen) [51]	57,564
22	16	A	Aberdeen	W 1-0	1-0	1	Sutton [24]	17,051
23	22	H	Motherwell	W 2-0	1-0	1	Petrov [31], Sutton [57]	58,244
24	30	A	Kilmarnock	W 1-0	1-0	1	Sutton (pen) [37]	9723
25	Feb 20	H	Rangers	L 0-2	0-0	2		58,993
26	Mar 2	H	Dundee	W 3-0	0-0	—	Petrov [49], Balde 2 [59, 86]	56,077
27	6	A	Hibernian	W 3-1	2-0	2	Petrov [4], Hartson [30], Bellamy [69]	15,787
28	12	H	Dunfermline Ath	W 6-0	1-0	2	Hartson 2 [8, 68], McGeady (pen) [62], Petrov 2 [71, 74], Beattie [88]	58,593
29	16	A	Inverness CT	W 2-0	0-0	—	Bellamy [62], Thompson [83]	7047
30	19	A	Dundee U	W 3-2	2-1	1	Bellamy 3 [5, 33, 80]	10,428
31	Apr 2	H	Hearts	L 0-2	0-2	2		59,551
32	13	A	Livingston	W 4-0	1-0	—	Hartson 3 [42, 74, 85], Varga [90]	7750
33	16	H	Aberdeen	W 3-2	1-2	1	Varga [26], Hartson [50], Bellamy [56]	59,984
34	24	A	Rangers	W 2-1	2-0	1	Petrov [21], Bellamy [34]	49,593
35	30	H	Hibernian	L 1-3	0-1	1	Beattie [59]	58,289
36	May 8	H	Aberdeen	W 2-0	0-0	1	Hartson 2 [47, 70]	59,516
37	15	A	Hearts	W 2-1	1-0	1	Thompson [25], Beattie [77]	16,163
38	22	A	Motherwell	L 1-2	1-0	2	Sutton [29]	12,944

Final League Position: 2

Scottish Cup Winners: (33 times) 1892, 1899, 1900, 1904, 1907, 1908, 1911, 1912, 1914, 1923, 1925, 1927, 1931, 1933, 1937, 1951, 1954, 1965, 1967, 1969, 1971, 1972, 1974, 1975, 1977, 1980, 1985, 1988, 1989, 1995, 2001, 2004, 2005. *Runners-up:* 18 times.
League Cup Winners: (12 times) 1956-57, 1957-58, 1965-66, 1966-67, 1967-68, 1968-69, 1969-70, 1974-75, 1982-83, 1997-98, 1999-2000, 2000-01. *Runners-up:* 13 times.

European: *European Cup:* 102 matches (1966-67 winners, 1967-68, 1968-69, 1969-70 runners-up, 1970-71, 1971-72 semi-finals, 1972-73, 1973-74 semi-finals, 1974-75, 1977-78, 1979-80, 1981-82, 1982-83, 1986-87, 1988-89, 1998-99, 2001-02, 2002-03, 2003-04). *Cup Winners' Cup:* 39 matches (1963-64 semi-finals, 1965-66 semi-finals, 1975-76, 1980-81, 1984-85, 1985-86, 1989-90, 1995-96). *UEFA Cup:* 73 matches (*Fairs Cup:* 1962-63, 1964-65. *UEFA Cup:* 1976-77, 1983-84, 1987-88, 1991-92, 1992-93, 1993-94, 1996-97, 1997-98, 1998-99, 1999-2000, 2000-01, 2001-02, 2002-03 runners-up, 2003-04 quarter-finals.

Club colours: Shirt: Emerald green and white hoops. Shorts: White with emerald trim. Stockings: White.

Goalscorers: *League* (85): Hartson 23, Sutton 13 (3 pens), Petrov 12, Camara 8, Bellamy 7, Thompson 7 (2 pens), Beattie 4, McGeady 4 (1 pen), Varga 3, Balde 2, Juninho 1, McNamara 1.
Scottish Cup (13): Hartson 3, Sutton 3, Bellamy 2, Thompson 2, Varga 2, Petrov 1.
CIS Cup (9): Wallace 3, Balde 1, Hartson 1, Lambert 1, McGeady 1, McManus 1, Sylla 1.

Marshall D 18	Varga S 34	Valgaeren J 18 + 1	McNamara J 34	Thompson A 32	Petrov S 37	Agathe D 14 + 2	Lennon N 38	Sutton C 25 + 2	Hartson J 38	McGeady A 20 + 7	Camara H 12 + 6	Pearson S 1 + 7	Sylla M 1 + 5	Laursen U 12 + 5	Beattie C — + 11	Balde D 34	Wallace R 4 + 12	Lambert P — + 4	Juninho9 + 5	McManus S 2	Hedman M 6	Douglas R 14	Bellamy C 12	Fernandez D — + 1	Henchoz S 2 + 4	Maloney S 1 + 1	*Match No.*
1	2	3	4	5	6^{3}	7	8	9	10^{1}	11^{2}	12	13	14														1
1	2	3	4^{2}	5	6^{3}	7	8	9	10	11^{1}	12			13	14												2
1	2	3		5	6^{1}	7	8		10		9	13				4	11^{2}	12									3
1	2	14	3	5	6	7	8		10^{2}		9^{1}		13			4	12		11^{3}								4
1	2^{1}	3	5	7	6		8		10^{3}		9	14	13	12		4			11^{2}								5
1	2	3		5	6	12	8	7^{1}	10		9	13				4			11^{2}								6
1	2	3		5	6^{1}		8		10^{3}	14	9		7	13		4	12		11^{2}								7
1	2	3^{1}			6	5	8	7	10^{2}		9^{3}			12		4	13	14	11								8
1	2		5		6^{3}	3	8	4	10^{2}	14	9		12				7	13	11^{1}								9
1	2^{3}		3		6		8	7	10		9^{2}	12				4	11	14	13	5^{1}							10
1	2		3		6	7	8	5^{2}	10	12			13			4	11		9^{1}								11
1		3	2	5	6	7	8		10	11^{2}					12	4	13		9^{1}								12
1	2	3	4	5	6	7	8		10	11^{2}	9^{1}				12		13										13
	2	3	5	6			8	7^{1}	10	11	9^{2}	13				4			12		1						14
	2	3	5	7■	6^{2}		8	11■	10	13	9^{1}	12				4					1						15
		3	2		6	7	8		10	11	9	5				4					1						16
	2	3	5	7	6^{1}		8	9	10	11	12					4					1						17
	2	3	5	7	6		8	9	10	11						4					1						18
	2	3^{2}	5	7^{1}	6		8	9	10	11^{3}				13		4	14		12		1						19
	2		5	7	6		8	9	10	11				3		4						1					20
	2		5	7	6		8	9	10	11^{1}				3		4			12			1					21
			5		6		8	7	10	11^{2}	12			3		4	13		9^{1}	2		1					22
	2		5	7	6		8	9	10^{1}	11^{2}	13			3		4			12			1					23
	2		5	7	6		8	9	10	11^{1}	12			3		4						1					24
	2		5^{1}	7	6		8	9	10	12				3		4						1	11				25
	2		5	7	6		8	9	10					3		4						1	11				26
	2		5	7^{3}	6		8	9^{1}	10^{2}	12				3	13	4						1	11	14			27
	2		5^{2}	7	6		8		10	9^{3}				3^{1}	13	4	14					1	11		12		28
			5	7	6		8		10^{1}	9				3	12	4						1	11		2		29
	2		5	7	6		8	12	10^{1}	9^{3}				3^{2}		4	13					1	11		14		30
1	2		5	7	6		8		10	9^{2}						4	12						11		3^{1}	13	31
1	2	3	5	7	6		8	9^{1}	10	13						4^{2}							11		12		32
1	2	3^{1}	5	7	6	12^{2}	8	14	10	9^{3}						4							11		13		33
1	2		5	7	6	3	8	9	10						12^{2}	4	13						11^{1}				34
1	2	3	5	7	6		8		10	9^{2}					12	4	13									11^{1}	35
	2		5	7	6	9	8	11	10					3^{1}	12	4						1					36
	2		5	7	6	3	8	9	10^{1}						12	4						1	11				37
	2		5	7	6	3	8	9	10^{1}						12	4						1	11				38

CLYDE

First Division

Year Formed: 1877. *Ground & Address:* Broadwood Stadium, Cumbernauld, G68 9NE. *Telephone:* 01236 451511.
Ground Capacity: all seated: 8200. *Size of Pitch:* 112yd × 76yd.
Chairman: Len McGuire. *Secretary:* John D. Taylor.
Manager: Graham Roberts. *Assistant Manager:* Joe Miller. *Physio:* Ian McKinlay.
Managers since 1975: S. Anderson, C. Brown, J. Clark, A. Smith, G. Speirs, A. Maitland, A. Kernaghan, B. Reid.
Club Nickname(s): The Bully Wee. *Previous Grounds:* Barrowfield Park 1877-97, Shawfield Stadium 1897-1994.
Record Attendance: 52,000 v Rangers, Division I, 21 Nov 1908.
Record Transfer Fee received: £175,000 for Scott Howie to Norwich City (Aug 1993).
Record Transfer Fee paid: £14,000 for Harry Hood from Sunderland (1966).
Record Victory: 11-1 v Cowdenbeath, Division II, 6 Oct 1951.
Record Defeat: 0-11 v Dumbarton, Scottish Cup 4th rd, 22 Nov, 1879; v Rangers, Scottish Cup 4th rd, 13 Nov 1880.
Most Capped Player: Tommy Ring, 12, Scotland.
Most League Appearances: 428: Brian Ahern.
Most League Goals in Season (Individual): 32: Bill Boyd, 1932-33.

CLYDE 2004–05 LEAGUE RECORD

Match No.	Date	Venue	Opponents	Result	H/T Score	Lg. Pos.	Goalscorers	Attendance
1	Aug 7	H	Partick Th	W 2-1	2-0	—	Harty [22], Gibson [44]	3352
2	14	A	Raith R	W 3-2	2-0	1	Bryson [4], Harty [22], Potter [56]	1784
3	21	H	Ross Co	W 1-0	0-0	1	Wilford [56]	1307
4	28	A	Queen of the S	W 1-0	1-0	1	Harty [20]	1639
5	Sept 4	H	St Mirren	D 0-0	0-0	1		2472
6	11	H	Airdrie U	L 1-2	1-1	3	Wilford [25]	1680
7	18	A	Hamilton A	W 1-0	1-0	3	Harty [22]	2017
8	25	A	Falkirk	D 1-1	0-1	3	Harty [77]	3813
9	Oct 2	H	St Johnstone	W 1-0	1-0	2	Sheridan [17]	1456
10	16	H	Raith R	W 2-0	2-0	2	Conway [11], Wilson [36]	1196
11	23	A	Partick Th	D 0-0	0-0	2		4026
12	30	H	Queen of the S	W 2-0	2-0	2	Harty 2 (1 pen) [9 (p), 38]	1284
13	Nov 6	A	St Mirren	D 0-0	0-0	1		3788
14	13	A	Airdrie U	L 1-3	0-2	2	Walker [84]	1862
15	20	H	Hamilton A	W 2-1	1-1	2	Sheridan [34], Potter [90]	1408
16	27	A	St Johnstone	L 0-3	0-0	3		2026
17	Dec 4	H	Falkirk	L 0-2	0-2	3		2859
18	11	H	Partick Th	D 1-1	1-1	2	Bollan [29]	1938
19	18	A	Ross Co	W 1-0	0-0	2	Harty [70]	1939
20	Jan 1	H	Airdrie U	W 1-0	0-0	2	Jones [78]	1513
21	15	A	Hamilton A	W 1-0	0-0	2	Arbuckle [58]	1873
22	Feb 12	A	Raith R	D 3-3	1-1	2	Harty 3 (2 pens) [39, 56 (p), 73 (p)]	1394
23	19	H	Ross Co	W 1-0	0-0	2	Harty [68]	1076
24	Mar 2	A	Queen of the S	W 1-0	1-0	—	Bollan [28]	1448
25	5	A	St Mirren	D 0-0	0-0	2		2730
26	8	H	St Mirren	D 0-0	0-0	—		1008
27	12	H	Queen of the S	L 0-1	0-0	2		1033
28	15	A	Falkirk	D 0-0	0-0	—		3834
29	19	A	Airdrie U	W 4-2	3-2	2	Harty 3 (1 pen) [2 (p), 34, 56], Jones [29]	1641
30	22	H	St Johnstone	D 1-1	0-0	—	Burns [68]	862
31	Apr 2	H	Hamilton A	L 1-3	0-0	2	Bryson [83]	1240
32	9	A	St Johnstone	D 0-0	0-0	2		1770
33	16	H	Falkirk	L 0-1	0-1	2		2090
34	23	A	Partick Th	L 0-1	0-1	3		2757
35	30	H	Raith R	W 1-0	1-0	3	Gilhaney [28]	1122
36	May 7	A	Ross Co	D 1-1	1-0	3	Bryson [23]	2130

Final League Position: 3

Honours
League Champions: Division II 1904-05, 1951-52, 1956-57, 1961-62, 1972-73. Second Division 1977-78, 1981-82, 1992-93, 1999-2000.
Runners-up: Division II 1903-04, 1905-06, 1925-26, 1963-64. Second Division 2003-04.
Scottish Cup Winners: 1939, 1955, 1958; *Runners-up:* 1910, 1912, 1949.
Bell's League Challenge: Quarter-finals 2004-05.

Club colours: Shirt: White with red and black trim. Shorts: Black. Stockings: white.

Goalscorers: *League* (35): Harty 15 (4 pens), Bryson 3, Bollan 2, Jones 2, Potter 2, Sheridan 2, Wilford 2, Arbuckle 1, Burns 1, Conway 1, Gibson 1, Gilhaney 1, Walker 1, Wilson 1.
Scottish Cup (5): Harty 2, Arbuckle 1, Bollan 1, Bryson 1.
CIS Cup (1): Wilford 1.
Challenge Cup (2): Harty 1, Valois 1.

Halliwell B 36	Mensing S 30	Bollan G 25	Balmer S 12 + 1	Potter J 36	Sheridan D 28 + 1	Arbuckle G 12 + 14	Gibson J 29	Wilford A 12 + 6	Fotheringham K 3	Harty I 33	Gilhaney M 18 + 16	Bryson C 23 + 5	Doyle P — + 1	Greenhill D 2 + 3	Kerkar K 2	Walker A 8 + 6	Conway A 5 + 6	Malone E 27 + 1	Wilson S 17 + 2	Bradley K 2 + 12	Marsigua M 1	McKeever J — + 3	Jones G 11 + 2	Burns A 15	Gardiner C 2 + 5	Espinola M 6	Harris R 1	Morrison A — + 1	Match No.
1	2	3	4	5	6	7	8	9^{1}	10	11	12																		1
1	2	3		5	6	7^{2}		9^{1}	10	11	8	4	12	13															2
1	2	3		5	6	12	8	9^{3}	10	11^{1}	14	7			4^{2}	13													3
1	2	3		5	6	13	8	9^{2}		11	14	7			10^{1}	4^{3}	12												4
1	2			5	6	12	8	9		11	13	7^{1}					10^{3}	3	4^{2}	14									5
1	2			5		12	8	9^{2}		11^{3}	10	7				6^{1}	13	3	4	14									6
1	2			5	6	10	8	9^{2}		11	13					12		3	4		7^{1}								7
1	2	3		5	6	10		13		11^{2}		7				9^{1}		8	4	12									8
1	2	3		5	6	7^{2}	8	9^{1}		11	13	12						10	4										9
1	2			5	6^{3}	13	8^{1}	14		11	10	7				12	9^{2}	3	4										10
1	2	3		5	6	7^{2}	8	12		11						13	9^{1}	10	4										11
1	2	3		5	6		8	9^{1}		11	10	7^{3}				4^{2}	12			13		14							12
1	2	3		5	6	12^{3}	8	13		11	9^{2}	7^{1}				14		10	4										13
1	2	3^{1}		5	6		8^{2}	14		11	12	7				13	9^{3}	10	4										14
1	2	3	12	5	6		8^{2}	9^{3}		11	7	13				10	14		4^{1}										15
1	2	3		5	6			9		11	12	7				8^{3}	13	10^{2}	4^{1}	14									16
1	2	3		5	6	13	8^{1}	14		11^{2}	9^{3}	7				10		12	4										17
1	2	3	4	5		6	8	9^{2}		11^{1}	12	7					13	10											18
1	2	3	4	5		6^{2}	8			11	13					7	9^{1}	10		12									19
1	2	3		5	6	7	8			11	12	4^{1}						10	13				9^{2}						20
1	2			5	6	7	8				11^{1}							10	4				9	3	12				21
1	2	3		5	6^{2}		8			11	13	12						10	4				9^{1}	7					22
1	2	3	4	5^{2}	6	12	8			11	13	9						10						7^{1}					23
1	2	3	4	5		12	8^{1}			11^{3}	14	7						10	13				9^{2}	6					24
1	2	3	4	5^{1}	13	7^{3}	8			11	12	9^{2}						10					14	6					25
1	2	3	4	5		13				11^{2}	7	9^{1}						10	8	12				6^{3}	14				26
1	2	3	4^{1}	5	6	13	8^{3}			11	9	14						10					12	7^{2}					27
1	2	3	4	5	6	11^{2}					12							10	8	13			9^{1}	7					28
1	2	3	4	5	6	12				11^{2}	8							10		13			9^{1}	7					29
1	2	3	4	5	6	12				11^{2}	8							10					9^{1}	7	13				30
1				5	6	13	8^{1}			11	3	12						10	4^{2}				9	7		2			31
1			4	5			8			11^{1}	3	10		6						12			9	7		2			32
1				5			8			11	3	10		4^{1}						6			9	7	12	2			33
1				5	6^{2}		8			11	3	4						10		12			9^{1}	7	13	2			34
1				5	6^{2}		8			11	3^{3}	4		13				10		12		14		7	9^{1}	2			35
1^{6}				5	6^{2}		8				3	4^{1}		13				10		7		12			9	2	11	15	36

COWDENBEATH Third Division

Year Formed: 1881. *Ground & Address:* Central Park, Cowdenbeath KY4 9EY. *Telephone:* 01383 610166. *Fax:* 01383 512132.
E-mail: bluebrazil@cowdenbeathfc.com. *Website:* www.cowdenbeathfc.com
Ground Capacity: total: 5268, seated: 1622. *Size of Pitch:* 107yd × 66yd.
Chairman: Gordon McDougall. *Secretary:* Tom Ogilvie. *Commercial Manager:* Joe McNamara.
Manager: David Baikie. *Assistant Manager:* Graeme Irons. *Physio:* Neil Bryson.
Managers since 1975: D. McLindon, F. Connor, P. Wilson, A. Rolland, H. Wilson, W. McCulloch, J. Clark, J. Craig, R. Campbell, J. Blackley, J. Brownlie, A. Harrow, J. Reilly, P. Dolan, T. Steven, S. Conn, C. Levein, G. Kirk, K. Wright.
Previous Grounds: North End Park, Cowdenbeath.
Record Attendance: 25,586 v Rangers, League Cup quarter-final, 21 Sept 1949.
Record Transfer Fee received: £30,000 for Nicky Henderson to Falkirk (March 1994).
Record Victory: 12-0 v Johnstone, Scottish Cup 1st rd, 21 Jan 1928.
Record Defeat: 1-11 v Clyde, Division II, 6 Oct 1951.
Most Capped Player: Jim Paterson, 3, Scotland.
Most League and Cup Appearances: 491 Ray Allan 1972-75, 1979-89.
Most League Goals in Season (Individual): 54, Rab Walls, Division II, 1938-39.
Most Goals Overall (Individual): 127, Willie Devlin, 1922-26, 1929-30.

COWDENBEATH 2004–05 LEAGUE RECORD

Match No.	Date	Venue	Opponents	Result		H/T Score	Lg. Pos.	Goalscorers	Attendance
1	Aug 7	A	Queen's Park	L	2-3	1-1	—	Reilly (og) 26, Gilfillan 62	490
2	14	H	Stenhousemuir	L	0-6	0-4	10		233
3	21	A	East Fife	D	1-1	1-0	8	Shields 15	555
4	28	H	East Stirling	W	2-1	0-1	8	Buchanan 46, Williams 54	232
5	Sept 4	A	Gretna	L	1-2	0-1	9	McHale 55	568
6	11	H	Elgin C	W	3-1	1-1	9	Mowat 6, McKeown 66, Shields 90	275
7	18	A	Montrose	L	1-3	1-1	9	Mauchlen 33	351
8	25	A	Peterhead	L	1-3	1-2	9	Gribben 40	582
9	Oct 2	H	Albion R	W	2-0	1-0	7	Gribben 30, Buchanan 89	243
10	16	A	Stenhousemuir	D	2-2	1-2	7	Shields 11, McHale 46	300
11	23	H	Queen's Park	W	2-1	2-1	6	Shields 33, Gribben 35	280
12	30	A	East Stirling	W	2-0	1-0	5	McKeown 37, Gribben 55	637
13	Nov 6	H	Gretna	L	0-8	0-6	6		322
14	13	A	Elgin C	W	4-0	1-0	5	Gribben 3 44, 55, 72, Shields 67	336
15	30	H	Montrose	D	0-0	0-0	—		145
16	Dec 4	H	Peterhead	L	0-4	0-0	5		201
17	18	A	Albion R	W	3-2	1-1	3	Williams 2 22, 56, Ritchie 90	303
18	27	A	Queen's Park	W	3-2	2-0	3	Buchanan 12, Gribben 2 35, 65	568
19	Jan 1	H	East Fife	D	1-1	0-0	3	Buchanan 61	454
20	8	H	East Stirling	W	3-2	1-2	3	Shields 3 30, 72, 73	212
21	15	A	Gretna	L	0-2	0-2	3		738
22	29	A	Montrose	W	2-1	1-1	3	McCallum 26, Gribben 59	292
23	Feb 5	A	Peterhead	D	1-1	0-1	3	Fusco 84	563
24	12	H	Albion R	L	1-2	1-0	3	Black (og) 22	254
25	19	A	East Fife	D	1-1	1-1	3	McHale 7	671
26	Mar 5	H	Gretna	L	0-1	0-1	3		339
27	12	A	East Stirling	L	1-2	1-0	3	Gribben 27	204
28	15	H	Elgin C	D	1-1	1-0	—	Buchanan 2	149
29	19	A	Elgin C	L	0-2	0-1	4		338
30	22	H	Stenhousemuir	L	0-2	0-1	—		173
31	Apr 2	H	Montrose	D	0-0	0-0	6		199
32	9	A	Albion R	W	4-1	2-0	4	Fusco 14, Buchanan 26, Gribben 77, Kelly JP 90	323
33	16	H	Peterhead	W	4-0	2-0	4	Buchanan 6, Ritchie 18, McHale 63, McGregor 67	153
34	23	H	East Fife	W	4-2	2-0	3	Fusco 2 10, 38, McHale 55, McCallum 87	348
35	30	A	Stenhousemuir	D	1-1	1-0	4	Williams 17	360
36	May 7	H	Queen's Park	W	1-0	1-0	3	Millar M 7	346

Final League Position: 3

Honours
League Champions: Division II 1913-14, 1914-15, 1938-39; *Runners-up:* Division II 1921-22, 1923-24, 1969-70. Second Division 1991-92. *Runners-up:* Third Division 2000-01.
Scottish Cup: Quarter-finals 1931.
League Cup: Semi-finals 1959-60, 1970-71.

Club colours: Shirt: Royal blue with white cuffs and collar. Shorts: White. Stockings: White.

Goalscorers: *League* (54): Gribben 12, Shields 8, Buchanan 7, McHale 5, Fusco 4, Williams 4, McCallum 2, McKeown 2, Ritchie 2, Gilfillan 1, Kelly JP 1, McGregor 1, Mauchlen 1, Millar M 1, Mowat 1, own goals 2.
Scottish Cup (2): Buchanan 1, Gribben 1.
CIS Cup (2): Gilfillan 1, Mauchlen 1.
Challenge Cup (0).

Carlin A 29	Shand C 25+1	Campbell A 21	Gilfillan B 1	McKeown J 33+1	Ritchie I 30	Mauchlen I 19+7	McHale P 28+1	Scott C 1+2	Mowat D 12+1	Burns J 2	Kelly JP 5+19	Buchanan L 18+13	McCallum R 13+7	Gollasch S 1	Fusco G 33+1	McGregor D 13+3	Shields D 18	Gray C 2+2	Fleming A 5+3	Miller D 3+5	Findlay S 1	Williams D 22+5	Bathgate S —+4	Gibson N —+2	Gribben D 26+5	McEwen M —+1	Cargill A 2+1	Newall C 7	Fraser S 1	Baird S 2+1	Bain J 9+2	Kelly P 2	Millar M 10	Howitt K —+1	Carruth J 1	Mallan S 1	*Match No.*
1	2	3	4	5	6	7	8	9[2]	10[3]	11[1]	12	13	14																								1
	2			12	6		8[3]	14	3		7[2]	10	13	1	4	5	9	11[1]																			2
	2			5		11	12		3	7		10[2]			8	4	9	13	1	6[1]																	3
	2			5	6		7		3		13	10			8		9	11[1]	15	4[2]	1[G]	12															4
	2			5	6		7		8[3]				10[2]		11	4	9	12	1			3[1]	13	14													5
1	2	3		5	6	7[1]	8		4						11		9					12	13		10[2]												6
1	2[2]	3		5		11[3]	7		13		6				8	4	9					14	12		10[1]												7
1	2	3		5			11		6		7[1]		12		8		9			4[2]				14	10[3]	13											8
		3		5	6	11	7		2		12	14			8	4[1]	9[3]		1				13		10[2]												9
1	2	3		5	6		7		4			13			10		8			12		11[1]			9[2]												10
1		2		5	6	11			4		7[2]	12			8	13	9					3			10[1]												11
1		2		5	6	11	8[2]		7		13	10			4							3[1]			9		12										12
1		2		5	6		10		11						7		9					3			12		8[1]	4									13
1	2	3		5	6		8	14				13					9			12		11[2]			10[3]		7[1]	4									14
1		3		5	6	11	8				12	7			2		9			13					10[2]			4[1]									15
1	13	3		5	6	11	8				4[1]	7			2		9			12					10[2]												16
1		3		5	6	14	8				13	7[1]			2		9		12			11[2]			10[3]			4									17
		3		5[1]								7[2]			2	6	9		1	12		11			10			4	8	13							18
1		3		5	6	12						7[2]	13		8	2	9					11			10			4[1]									19
1				5	6	13	8					7	14		12	3	9					11			10[3]			4[2]		2[1]							20
1	2	3			6	4	8				12	13	9[2]		7[1]	5						11[3]			10						14						21
1	2			5	6	7	8				12	13	9[2]		4	14						3			10[3]						11[1]						22
1	2			5	6	7	8				12	13	9[2]		4							3			10						11[1]						23
1■	2			5	6	7	8				13	12	9		4				14			3[3]			10[1]						11[2]						24
	2	3		5		13	8				14	12	9[1]		4				1						10[3]					6	11	7[2]					25
1	2			5	6	12	8				14	13	9[3]		7							11[1]			10[2]						3		4				26
1	2			5	6	13	8[3]				14	12	9[1]		7							11[2]			10						3		4				27
1	2			5	6	7					13	9			8	3						12			10						11[1]		4[2]				28
1	2				6						12	8	9		7	5						3			10[2]						11[1]		4	13			29
1	3			5	6	11	8					9[1]			7										12								4		2	10	30
1	2	3		5	6	11					13	14	9[3]		8							12			10							7[1]	4[2]				31
1	2	3		5	6	7					13	10	9[1]		8							11			12								4[2]				32
1	2	3		5	6[1]		8				13	9[3]	14		7	12						11[2]			10								4				33
1	2	3[3]		5	6	13	8					9[1]	10[2]		7							11			12						14		4				34
1	2■			5	6	7[1]	8					9	10		4	3						11			12												35
1				5		2	8				13	9[2]	12		7	6						11			10[1]						3		4				36

DUMBARTON — Second Division

Year Formed: 1872. *Ground:* Strathclyde Homes Stadium, Dumbarton G82 1JJ. *Telephone:* 01389 762569/767864.
E-mail: dumbarton.footballclub@btopenworld.com. *Fax:* 01389 762629
Ground Capacity: total: 2050. *Size of Pitch:* 110yd × 75yd.
Chairman: Neil Rankine. *Club Secretary:* David Prophet. *Company Secretary:* Gilbert Lawrie.
Manager: Paul Martin. *Assistant Manager:* John Gallagher. *Physio:* Jackie West.
Managers since 1975: A. Wright, D. Wilson, S. Fallon, W. Lamont, D. Wilson, D. Whiteford, A. Totten, M. Clougherty, R. Auld, J. George, W. Lamont, M. MacLeod, J. Fallon, I. Wallace, T. Carson, D. Winnie, B. Fairley.
Club Nickname(s): The Sons. *Previous Grounds:* Broadmeadow, Ropework Lane, Townend Ground, Boghead Park.
Record Attendance: 18,000 v Raith Rovers, Scottish Cup, 2 Mar 1957.
Record Transfer Fee received: £125,000 for Graeme Sharp to Everton (March 1982).
Record Transfer Fee paid: £50,000 for Charlie Gibson from Stirling Albion (1989).
Record Victory: 13-1 v Kirkintilloch Central. 1st rd, 1 Sept 1888.
Record Defeat: 1-11 v Albion Rovers, Division II; 30 Jan, 1926: v Ayr United, League Cup, 13 Aug 1952.
Most Capped Player: James McAulay, 9, Scotland.
Most League Appearances: 297: Andy Jardine, 1957-67.
Most Goals in Season (Individual): 38: Kenny Wilson, Division II, 1971-72. *(League and Cup):* 46 Hughie Gallacher, 1955-56.
Most Goals Overall (Individual): 169: Hughie Gallacher, 1954-62 (including C Division 1954-55). *(League and Cup):* 202 Hughie Gallacher, 1954-62

DUMBARTON 2004–05 LEAGUE RECORD

Match No.	Date	Venue	Opponents	Result	H/T Score	Lg. Pos.	Goalscorers	Attendance
1	Aug 7	H	Ayr U	W 1-0	1-0	—	Dillon [18]	1016
2	14	A	Arbroath	W 2-0	1-0	2	Russell 2 [8, 84]	505
3	21	H	Morton	L 0-3	0-1	5		1670
4	28	H	Forfar Ath	L 0-1	0-0	7		723
5	Sept 4	A	Berwick R	W 4-0	2-0	6	Annand 3 [30, 45, 49], Donald [72]	412
6	11	H	Stranraer	L 1-3	0-1	7	Annand [47]	841
7	18	A	Alloa Ath	L 2-3	1-0	7	Rodgers [10], Russell [57]	505
8	25	H	Stirling A	D 1-1	1-0	7	Russell [30]	990
9	Oct 2	A	Brechin C	L 0-4	0-0	7		503
10	16	H	Arbroath	L 1-3	0-2	7	McEwan (pen) [78]	716
11	23	A	Ayr U	W 1-0	0-0	7	Rodgers [87]	1468
12	30	A	Forfar Ath	W 2-0	0-0	7	Dunn 2 [58, 71]	486
13	Nov 6	H	Berwick R	W 3-1	2-0	6	Boyle [22], Rodgers [33], Holmes [67]	790
14	13	A	Stranraer	L 0-1	0-0	6		532
15	30	H	Alloa Ath	L 0-1	0-0	—		522
16	Dec 4	A	Stirling A	L 0-1	0-0	6		688
17	27	H	Ayr U	D 1-1	1-1	7	Russell [11]	1118
18	Jan 1	A	Morton	L 0-3	0-1	8		2764
19	3	H	Forfar Ath	D 1-1	0-0	—	Rodgers [66]	714
20	15	A	Berwick R	W 3-0	1-0	8	Dillon [38], Rodgers [58], Annand [68]	322
21	29	A	Alloa Ath	L 2-4	0-4	8	McKinstry [58], Rodgers [82]	608
22	Feb 5	H	Stirling A	L 0-2	0-2	8		981
23	12	A	Brechin C	W 2-0	2-0	7	Annand [20], McKinstry [36]	589
24	19	H	Morton	W 3-0	2-0	7	Ronald [14], Russell 2 [41, 67]	1508
25	26	A	Arbroath	L 1-2	0-1	7	Annand [78]	502
26	Mar 1	H	Brechin C	D 1-1	1-1	—	McEwan [21]	548
27	5	H	Berwick R	D 1-1	0-1	7	McEwan (pen) [88]	690
28	12	A	Forfar Ath	L 0-6	0-2	8		443
29	19	A	Stranraer	L 1-2	0-2	8	McEwan (pen) [89]	436
30	26	H	Stranraer	D 1-1	1-0	8	Russell [40]	848
31	Apr 2	H	Alloa Ath	W 3-2	1-1	8	Russell 3 [35, 62, 88]	787
32	9	H	Brechin C	D 1-1	0-0	8	Dillon [64]	777
33	16	A	Stirling A	L 0-3	0-2	8		705
34	23	A	Morton	D 0-0	0-0	8		3229
35	30	H	Arbroath	W 3-0	0-0	7	Boyle [68], Dillon [77], Gemmell [83]	1192
36	May 7	A	Ayr U	D 1-1	1-0	7	Gemmell [20]	1236

Final League Position: 7

Honours
League Champions: Division I 1890-91 (shared with Rangers), 1891-92. Division II 1910-11, 1971-72. Second Division 1991-92; *Runners-up:* First Division 1983-84. Division II 1907-08. Third Division 2001-02.
Scottish Cup Winners: 1883; *Runners-up:* 1881, 1882, 1887, 1891, 1897.

Club colours: Shirt: Yellow with black facing. Shorts: Yellow with black stripe. Stockings: Yellow.

Goalscorers: *League* (43): Russell 11, Annand 7, Rodgers 6, Dillon 4, McEwan 4 (3 pens), Boyle 2, Dunn 2, Gemmell 2, McKinstry 2, Donald 1, Holmes 1, Ronald 1.
Scottish Cup (5): Annand 1, Dillon 1, Dunn 1, McEwan 1 (pen), Russell 1.
CIS Cup (1): Russell 1.
Challenge Cup (1): Bonar 1.

Grindlay S 30	McEwan C 31	Brittain C 32 + 1	McKinstry J 28 + 4	Dobbins I 24 + 2	Donald B 19 + 4	Dunn R 8 + 6	Ronald P 18 + 5	Herd G 2 + 1	Rodgers A 17 + 14	Dillon J 26 + 5	Bradley M 3 + 11	Borris R 7 + 9	Boyle C 18 + 4	Bonar S 15 + 2	Russell I 25 + 7	Annand E 22 + 6	Holmes G 8 + 4	Allan D 5 + 2	McGroarty C 4 + 2	Wight J 6	Walker R 16	Gemmell J 8 + 8	Dempsie M 14	Allan J 9 + 1	Anderson K 1	Match No.
1	2	3	4	5	6^{1}	7^{3}	8	9^{2}	10	11	12	13	14													1
1	2	3	4	5	6	8^{2}	13	12	9^{1}	11		14		7	10^{3}											2
1	2	3	4	5	6	7^{3}	12	9^{2}	10	11	14	13		8^{1}												3
1	2	3	4	5	6^{2}	14	8		12	11^{3}				7^{1}	10	9	13									4
1	2	3	4	5	14	13	6^{3}		10	11				12	8^{1}	9^{2}	7									5
1	2	3	4	5	6^{1}	13			10^{3}	11	12			7	14	9^{2}	8									6
1	2^{3}	3		5		13	6		10^{2}	11			14	12	7^{1}	9	8	4								7
1		3	4		12	13			10				6^{1}	2	7	9^{2}	8	5	11							8
1		3	4	13	8	14			10				6^{1}	2	7	9^{2}	12	5	11^{3}							9
1	2	3	4	5					13	11		14	6^{1}	7	10^{3}	9^{2}	8		12							10
1	2	3	4	5		9^{2}			14	12			6	7	10^{3}	13	8		11^{1}							11
1	2	3	4	6		9			10^{1}				11^{2}	7	12		8	5	13							12
1	2	3	4	5		9^{1}	13		10^{3}	11			6	7	14	12	8^{2}									13
1	2		4	5	6	9	8^{2}		10^{1}				11	7	13	12			3							14
1	2	3	4	5	8	9^{1}	14		12	11^{3}			6	7^{2}	10		13									15
1		3	4	5	6^{1}		8		9	11^{3}	14	7	12	2	10^{2}	13										16
	2	3	4	5	6		8		12	11		13		7	10^{1}	9^{2}				1						17
	2	3	4	5	6		8		14	11		13		7^{1}	10^{3}	9^{2}	12			1						18
	2	3	4	5^{1}	6				13	10^{3}	14	11^{2}	8		7	9		12		1						19
	2	3	4	5	6				10	11		12	8		7	9^{1}				1						20
	2		4	5					11	3	13	8	10^{2}		7^{1}	9^{3}		12		1	6	14				21
1	2	13	4	5			6			8	12	7^{1}			14	9^{3}		11^{2}			3	10				22
1	2	3	8				6			10					7	9^{1}					4	12	5	11		23
1	2	3	8^{3}		13		6			10	14	12			7						4	9^{1}	5	11^{2}		24
1		3	8^{2}		2		6		12	10					7^{1}	9					4	13	5	11		25
1	2	3	13		8^{2}		6		9^{1}	10^{3}	14				7						4	12	5	11		26
1	2	3	8		12		6^{1}		7^{3}	10					13	9					4	14	5	11^{2}		27
1	2	3	8		6				7^{1}	10^{2}	13				12	9^{3}					4	14	5	11		28
1	2	3					6		14	12	8		10^{2}		7^{3}	13					4	9	5	11^{1}		29
1	2	3	12				6		13		8		10^{1}		7	9					4	11^{2}	5			30
1	2	3	12				6			13	8^{1}		11		7	9^{3}					4	10^{2}	5	14		31
1	2	3		6	8^{1}				14	12			10		7	13					4	9^{2}	5	11^{3}		32
1	2	3		6	8^{1}				13	14		12	10			11					4	9^{3}	5	7^{2}		33
1	2	3	10^{2}	6					13	11	14	7^{3}	8			9^{1}					4	12	5			34
1	2	3	14	6			8^{3}			11		7	13		10^{2}	9^{1}					4	12	5			35
			9	12	7^{2}		13		14	6		3	4		10^{3}					1	11	8	5		2^{1}	36

DUNDEE — First Division

Year Formed: 1893. *Ground & Address:* Dens Park Stadium, Sandeman St, Dundee DD3 7JY. *Telephone:* 01382 889966. *Fax:* 01382 832284.
Ground Capacity: all seated: 11,760. *Size of Pitch:* 101m × 66m.
Chairman: Jim Marr. *Chief Executive:* Peter Marr.
Manager: Jim Duffy. *Goalkeeping Coach:* Paul Mathers. *Under 21 Coach:* Ray Farningham. *Under 18 Coach:* Steve Campbell. *Youth Development Coach:* Kenny Cameron. *Community Coach:* Kevin Lee. *Physio:* Jim Law.
Managers since 1975: David White, Tommy Gemmell, Donald Mackay, Archie Knox, Jocky Scott, Dave Smith, Gordon Wallace, Iain Munro, Simon Stainrod, Jim Duffy, John McCormack, John Scott, Ivano Bonetti.
Club Nickname(s): The Dark Blues or The Dee. *Previous Grounds:* Carolina Port 1893-98.
Record Attendance: 43,024 v Rangers, Scottish Cup, 1953.
Record Transfer Fee received: £500,000 for Tommy Coyne to Celtic (March 1989).
Record Transfer Fee paid: £200,000 for Jim Leighton (Feb 1992).
Record Victory: 10-0 Division II v Alloa, 9 Mar 1947 and v Dunfermline Ath, 22 Mar 1947.
Record Defeat: 0-11 v Celtic, Division I, 26 Oct 1895.
Most Capped Player: Alex Hamilton, 24, Scotland. *Most League Appearances:* 341: Doug Cowie, 1945-61.
Most League Goals in Season (Individual): 52: Alan Gilzean, 1963-64.
Most Goals Overall (Individual): 113: Alan Gilzean.

DUNDEE 2004–05 LEAGUE RECORD

Match No.	Date	Venue	Opponents	Result		H/T Score	Lg. Pos.	Goalscorers	Attendance
1	Aug 7	H	Hearts	L	0-1	0-0	—		7770
2	15	A	Dundee U	W	2-1	1-0	4	Lovell (pen) 16, Sutton 46	11,118
3	21	H	Motherwell	L	1-2	0-1	6	Lovell 78	4849
4	28	A	Hibernian	D	4-4	1-2	8	Sutton 6, Brady 65, Larsen 77, Hernandez 81	9344
5	Sept 11	A	Celtic	L	0-3	0-2	9		56,840
6	18	H	Livingston	D	0-0	0-0	10		4387
7	26	H	Rangers	L	0-2	0-0	9		9404
8	Oct 2	A	Aberdeen	D	1-1	1-1	8	Sutton 1	11,217
9	16	H	Kilmarnock	W	3-1	1-1	8	Robb 29, Sutton 62, Anderson 86	4637
10	23	H	Dunfermline Ath	L	1-2	0-1	9	Anderson 52	5456
11	27	A	Inverness CT	L	1-2	0-1	—	Lovell 72	1282
12	30	A	Hearts	L	0-3	0-1	10		10,172
13	Nov 6	H	Dundee U	W	1-0	0-0	10	Sutton 86	9845
14	13	A	Motherwell	L	0-3	0-1	10		4406
15	20	H	Hibernian	L	1-4	0-2	10	Lovell 67	5274
16	28	H	Celtic	D	2-2	1-0	10	Lovell 2 34, 76	9539
17	Dec 4	A	Livingston	L	0-1	0-1	11		4009
18	11	A	Rangers	L	0-3	0-2	12		48,114
19	18	H	Aberdeen	W	1-0	0-0	10	Barrett 57	7310
20	27	A	Kilmarnock	L	1-3	1-2	11	Sutton 38	5468
21	Jan 1	A	Dunfermline Ath	L	1-3	1-2	12	Barrett 39	4426
22	15	H	Inverness CT	W	3-1	1-0	10	Robb 27, McManus 47, Sutton (pen) 55	5567
23	22	H	Hearts	D	1-1	0-0	10	Caballero 54	5780
24	29	A	Dundee U	D	2-2	0-1	10	McManus 70, Lovell 82	12,719
25	Feb 12	H	Motherwell	W	2-1	1-1	10	Lovell 2 44, 54	5746
26	19	A	Hibernian	L	0-4	0-1	10		10,938
27	Mar 2	A	Celtic	L	0-3	0-0	—		56,077
28	5	H	Livingston	L	0-1	0-0	10		5830
29	13	H	Rangers	L	0-2	0-0	10		9876
30	19	A	Aberdeen	D	1-1	0-0	10	McManus 72	10,474
31	Apr 2	H	Kilmarnock	W	1-0	0-0	9	Lovell (pen) 62	5494
32	9	H	Dunfermline Ath	W	2-1	0-1	9	Lovell (pen) 55, Sancho 61	5995
33	16	A	Inverness CT	L	2-3	0-2	9	McManus 74, Sutton 80	4786
34	23	A	Kilmarnock	L	0-1	0-0	9		3485
35	30	H	Dundee U	L	1-2	0-0	11	Lovell (pen) 63	11,263
36	May 7	A	Dunfermline Ath	L	0-5	0-4	12		8313
37	14	H	Inverness CT	D	1-1	0-0	12	Sancho 48	6691
38	21	A	Livingston	D	1-1	1-1	12	MacDonald 17	7468

Final League Position: 12

Honours
League Champions: Division I 1961-62. First Division 1978-79, 1991-92, 1997-98. Division II 1946-47; *Runners-up:* Division I 1902-03, 1906-07, 1908-09, 1948-49, 1980-81.
Scottish Cup Winners: 1910; *Runners-up:* 1925, 1952, 1964, 2003.
League Cup Winners: 1951-52, 1952-53, 1973-74; *Runners-up:* 1967-68, 1980-81. *(Coca-Cola Cup):* 1995-96.
B&Q (Centenary) Cup Winners: 1990-91; *Runners-up:* 1994-95.

European: *European Cup:* 8 matches (1962-63 semi-finals). *Cup Winners' Cup:* 2 matches: (1964-65). *UEFA Cup:* 22 matches: (*Fairs Cup:* 1967-68 semi-finals. *UEFA Cup:* 1971-72, 1973-74, 1974-75, 2003-04).

Club colours: Shirt: Navy with white and red shoulder and sleeve flashes. Shorts: White with navy/red piping. Stockings: Navy, top with two white hoops.

Goalscorers: *League* (37): Lovell 12 (4 pens), Sutton 8 (1 pen), McManus 4, Anderson 2, Barrett 2, Robb 2, Sancho 2, Brady 1, Caballero 1, Hernandez 1, Larsen 1, MacDonald 1.
Scottish Cup (0).
CIS Cup (2): Lovell 1, Anderson 1.

Soutar D 36 + 1	MacDonald C 32	Sancho B 24 + 3	Mann R 28 + 2	Hernandez J 13 + 1	Smith B 37	Jablonski N 2 + 4	Robb S 32 + 1	Brady G 20 + 6	Lovell S 33	Sutton J 20 + 12	Anderson I 18 + 2	Fotheringham M 20 + 7	Barrett N 25 + 5	McNally S 17 + 4	Larsen G 2 + 14	Jack K 2	Caballero F 19 + 9	Hutchinson T 3 + 1	Cerdeira A 1 + 5	Reilly A — + 2	Wilkie L 12	McManus T 14	Robertson S 1 + 8	Kitamarike J 7	Conway A — + 2	*Match No.*
1	2	3	4	5	6	7^{1}	8^{2}	9	10	11	12	13														1
1	2	3	4	5	6	13	8^{1}	7	10^{2}	11	9^{3}	14	12													2
1	2		4	5	3	13	8^{1}	7^{2}	10	11	9	6^{3}		12	14											3
	7	3	4	5	6			12	10	11	9	8^{2}	2^{1}		13	1										4
1	7	3	4	5	6		13	8^{2}	10	11	9	12	2^{1}													5
1	2	3	4		6		7	8^{2}	10■	11	9	12	5^{1}		13											6
1	7	3	4	5	6			12		11	10	8	2^{1}		9											7
1		3	4	12	6		7	14	10^{3}	11^{2}	9^{1}	8■	2	5			13									8
1		3	4		6	12	7	8^{1}	10^{3}	11	9		2^{2}	5	13			14								9
1		3	4		6		7	8^{1}	10^{3}	11^{2}	9		2	5	14		12		13							10
1		3	4		6		7	8	10	11		13	2^{2}	5	9^{1}		12									11
1	9		4	5■	6		7^{1}		10	12		8		2	13		11^{2}	3								12
15	2	3			6		7^{1}	12	10	13	9	8		5		1^{6}	11^{2}	4								13
1		3		5	6				10^{2}	11	9	7		2	12		8^{1}	4		13						14
1		3^{1}	4	5	6	9^{2}		8	10	14		7		2			11^{3}		12	13						15
1	3		4	5	6		9	12	10		11^{2}	7	13	2					8^{1}							16
1	2^{3}	3	4	5	6		8		10	11^{2}	9^{1}	7		12			13		14							17
1	7	3		5	6		9	8	10^{2}				4	2	12		11^{1}		13							18
1	5	3			6	12	7	8	10	11			4	2			9^{1}									19
1	7	3		5	6		9^{1}	8	10	11		13	4^{2}	2					12							20
1	7		4		6		9			11		8	3	2	12		10^{1}				5					21
1	4		14		6		7			11		8	3^{3}	2	13		10^{2}				5	9^{1}	12			22
1	4				6		7			11		8	3	2			10				5	9^{1}	12			23
1	4	2	12		6		7		10^{3}	13		8	3				11				5^{1}	9^{2}	14			24
1	4	2			6		7		10			8	3				11				5	9				25
1	2				6		7		10^{1}	13		8	3		12		11^{3}				5	9^{2}		4	14	26
1	7	2	4		6		9	12	10^{2}	13		8^{1}	3				11				5					27
1	2		4		6		7		10	9		8^{2}	3^{1}		12		11				5		13			28
1	3		4		6			8	10^{3}	13			2^{2}				11				5	9^{1}	12	7	14	29
1	3	13	4		6		9	8		12			2^{1}				11^{2}				5	10		7		30
1	3	13	4		6		9	8	10				2^{2}				12				5	11		7^{1}		31
1	3	13	4		6		7	8	10	9^{3}		12	2^{1}				14				5^{2}	11				32
1	3	5	4				7		10^{1}	14	12	8^{2}	2^{3}				11					9	13	6		33
1	3	2^{1}	4		6		7	8	10^{2}	13	9		12				14					11^{3}		5		34
1	2		4		6^{3}		5	7	10	12	8			13	14		11^{1}					9■		3^{2}		35
1	2		4		6		5	8	10^{3}		9	7^{1}	14	3^{2}	13		11						12			36
1	3	2	4		6		5	8^{2}	10^{3}		9		14	12			13					11	7^{1}			37
1	3	2	4		6		8^{1}		10	12	9^{3}		7^{2}	5			13					11	14			38

DUNDEE UNITED Premier League

Year Formed: 1909 (1923). *Ground & Address:* Tannadice Park, Tannadice St, Dundee DD3 7JW. *Telephone:* 01382 833166. *Fax:* 01382 889398. *Ground Capacity:* total: 14,223 all seated: stands: east 2868, west 2096, south 2201, Fair Play 1601, George Fox 5151, executive boxes 292.
Size of Pitch: 110yd × 72yd.
Chairman: Eddie Thompson, OBE. *Secretary:* Spence Anderson. *General Manager:* Bill Campbell. *Community Development Officer:* Gordon Grady.
Manager: Gordon Chisholm. *Assistant Manager:* Billy Dodds. *First Team Coach:* Tony Docherty. *Coaches:* Dave Bowman, Graeme Liveston. *Physio:* Jeff Clarke. *Stadium Manager:* Ron West.
Managers since 1975: J. McLean, I. Golac, W. Kirkwood, T. McLean, P. Sturrock, A. Smith, I. McCall.
Club Nickname(s): The Terrors. *Previous Grounds:* None.
Record Attendance: 28,000 v Barcelona, Fairs Cup, 16 Nov 1966.
Record Transfer Fee received: £4,000,000 for Duncan Ferguson from Rangers (July 1993).
Record Transfer Fee paid: £750,000 for Steven Pressley from Coventry C (July 1995).
Record Victory: 14-0 v Nithsdale Wanderers, Scottish Cup 1st rd, 17 Jan 1931.
Record Defeat: 1-12 v Motherwell, Division II, 23 Jan 1954.
Most Capped Player: Maurice Malpas, 55, Scotland.
Most League Appearances: 612, Dave Narey, 1973-94.
Most Appearances in European Matches: 76, Dave Narey (record for Scottish player).
Most League Goals in Season (Individual): 41: John Coyle, Division II, 1955-56.
Most Goals Overall (Individual): 158: Peter McKay.

DUNDEE UNITED 2004–05 LEAGUE RECORD

Match No.	Date	Venue	Opponents	Result	H/T Score	Lg. Pos.	Goalscorers	Attendance
1	Aug 7	A	Dunfermline Ath	D 1-1	0-0	—	McIntyre 76	6474
2	15	H	Dundee	L 1-2	0-1	10	Archibald 90	11,118
3	21	A	Livingston	D 1-1	0-0	11	Dodds (pen) 60	3159
4	28	H	Inverness CT	W 2-1	0-0	7	Innes 70, McIntyre 85	6017
5	Sept 11	H	Aberdeen	D 1-1	0-1	8	Wilson (pen) 82	11,595
6	18	A	Motherwell	L 2-4	1-0	8	Grady 45, McIntyre 67	5091
7	25	A	Kilmarnock	L 2-5	1-4	8	Archibald 29, Dodds 78	4711
8	Oct 3	H	Celtic	L 0-3	0-3	11		10,329
9	16	A	Hibernian	L 0-2	0-1	11		9850
10	24	A	Rangers	D 1-1	0-0	11	Robson 87	46,796
11	27	H	Hearts	D 1-1	0-1	—	Wilson 46	5723
12	30	H	Dunfermline Ath	L 1-2	1-1	12	Wilson (pen) 7	6297
13	Nov 6	A	Dundee	L 0-1	0-0	12		9845
14	13	H	Livingston	W 1-0	0-0	11	McCracken 75	5507
15	23	A	Inverness CT	D 1-1	0-0	—	McIntyre 62	1125
16	27	A	Aberdeen	L 0-1	0-1	11		12,038
17	Dec 4	H	Motherwell	L 0-1	0-1	12		5394
18	11	H	Kilmarnock	W 3-0	2-0	11	McIntyre 2 16, 46, Robson 21	5097
19	18	A	Celtic	L 0-1	0-1	11		56,281
20	27	H	Hibernian	L 1-4	1-2	12	Scotland 8	10,152
21	Jan 1	H	Rangers	D 1-1	1-0	10	McCracken 10	10,461
22	15	A	Hearts	L 2-3	1-1	10	Robson 19, Archibald 52	10,305
23	22	A	Dunfermline Ath	D 1-1	0-1	11	Crawford 72	6578
24	29	H	Dundee	D 2-2	1-0	11	Duff 11, McIntyre 78	12,719
25	Feb 12	A	Livingston	W 2-0	2-0	11	Crawford 13, Grady 41	4658
26	19	H	Inverness CT	D 1-1	1-1	11	Munro (og) 29	6110
27	Mar 2	H	Aberdeen	L 1-2	0-2	—	Scotland 59	6688
28	5	A	Motherwell	L 0-2	0-1	11		5110
29	12	A	Kilmarnock	L 0-3	0-1	12		4353
30	19	H	Celtic	L 2-3	1-2	12	McIntyre 23, Robson 70	10,428
31	Apr 2	A	Hibernian	L 2-3	0-1	12	McIntyre 23, Scotland 70	11,058
32	12	A	Rangers	W 1-0	1-0	—	Duff 7	49,302
33	16	H	Hearts	W 2-1	1-1	10	Robson 37, Brebner 90	7704
34	23	H	Livingston	D 1-1	1-0	10	Crawford 38	7687
35	30	A	Dundee	W 2-1	0-0	9	Wilson 51, McIntyre 69	11,263
36	May 7	H	Kilmarnock	D 1-1	1-0	10	McIntyre 16	6576
37	15	H	Dunfermline Ath	L 0-1	0-0	11		10,763
38	21	A	Inverness CT	W 1-0	0-0	9	Robson (pen) 83	5479

Final League Position: 9

Honours
League Champions: Premier Division 1982-83. Division II 1924-25, 1928-29; *Runners-up:* Division II 1930-31, 1959-60. First Division Runners-up 1995-96.
Scottish Cup Winners: 1994; *Runners-up:* 1974, 1981, 1985, 1987, 1988, 1991, 2005.
League Cup Winners: 1979-80, 1980-81; *Runners-up:* 1981-82, 1984-85, 1997-98.
Summer Cup Runners-up: 1964-65. *Scottish War Cup Runners-up:* 1939-40.

European: *European Cup:* 8 matches (1983-84, semi-finals). *Cup Winners' Cup:* 10 matches (1974-75, 1988-89, 1994-95). *UEFA Cup:* 84 matches (*Fairs Cup:* 1966-67, 1969-70, 1970-71. *UEFA Cup:* 1975-76, 1977-78, 1978-79, 1979-80, 1980-81, 1981-82, 1982-83, 1984-85, 1985-86, 1986-87 runners-up, 1987-88, 1989-90, 1990-91, 1993-94, 1997-98).

Club colours: Shirts: Tangerine. Shorts: Tangerine. Stockings: Tangerine.

Goalscorers: *League* (41): McIntyre 11, Robson 6 (1 pen), Wilson 4 (2 pens), Archibald 3, Crawford 3, Scotland 3, Dodds 2 (1 pen), Duff 2, Grady 2, McCracken 2, Brebner 1, Innes 1, own goal 1.
Scottish Cup (13): Crawford 2, Grady 2, McIntyre 2, Wilson 2, Archibald 1, Duff 1, Kerr 1, Robson 1, Scotland 1.
CIS Cup (10): McIntyre 3, Brebner 1, Grady 1, Innes 1, Kerr 1, Robson 1, Scotland 1, Wilson 1.

Bullock A 26	McCracken D 19 + 5	Archibald A 38	Innes C 16	Wilson M 37	McInnes D 21 + 6	Kerr M 28 + 2	Robson B 34 + 2	Dodds W 11 + 10	Grady J 19 + 10	Scotland J 11 + 18	Samuel C 5 + 13	McIntyre J 32 + 3	Duff S 21 + 4	Ritchie P 24	McLaren A 1 + 5	Brebner G 31 + 3	Hirschfeld L 1	Jarvie P 10	Kerkar K 4 + 6	Robertson D — + 1	Cameron G — + 2	Crawford S 15 + 2	Mair L 3 + 1	Colgan N 1	Callaghan B — + 1	Kenneth G 10 + 1	Match No.
1	2	3	4	5	6	7	8^{2}	9^{1}	10	11^{3}	12	13	14														1
1	2	3	4	5	6^{2}	7^{3}	8	9	10^{1}	12	14	11	13														2
1	12	3	4	5	14	7	8^{2}	9^{3}		11		10	6	2^{1}	13												3
1	2	3	4	5		7	8	9^{2}	12	11^{1}		10			13	6											4
1	2	3	4	5	12	7^{1}	8	9^{2}	11^{3}		14	10			13	6											5
1	2	3	4	5	6^{1}	7	8		11^{2}	13		10			12	9											6
	2	3	4	5^{3}	6	12	8	14		13		10	7		11^{2}	9^{1}	1										7
	2^{1}	3	4	5	12	13	8	9^{3}	11			10	7			6^{2}		1	14								8
		3	4	5	6	7^{2}	8		11^{1}	12		10^{3}	9			2		1	14	13							9
	2	3	4	5	6		8	9	11^{2}		10^{1}	12				7		1	13								10
	2	3	4	5	6		8	9^{2}	11^{3}	12	10^{1}	13				7		1	14								11
	2	3	4	5	6		8^{2}	12	13	11		10				7		1	9^{1}								12
	12	3	4■	5■	6		8		14	11^{3}	10^{2}		13	2		7		1	9^{1}								13
	4	3			6	7^{1}	8	14	11^{2}	12		10	5	2		13		1	9^{3}								14
	4	3		5	6		8^{3}	9^{1}	14	11^{2}	13	10		2		7		1	12								15
	4	3		5^{3}	6		8^{1}		11^{2}	13	14	10	7	2		9		1	12								16
	4	3		5			8	14	11^{2}	13	12	10	6^{3}	2		7		1	9^{1}								17
1		3	4	5	6	9	8	14		11^{1}	12	10^{3}		2		7^{2}					13						18
1		3	4	5	6	9^{2}	8	13	14	12	11^{1}	10^{3}		2		7											19
1	12	3	4	5	6	9^{1}	8			11	13	10		2		7^{2}											20
1	4	3		5	6	9	8		11			10		2		7											21
1	4	3		5	6	9	8			13		10		2		7^{1}						11^{2}	12				22
1	12	3		5	6^{2}	9	8		13			10		2		7^{1}						11	4				23
	4	3		5	6^{1}	8		13	9^{3}	14		10	7^{2}	2		12						11		1			24
1		3		5		7^{1}		8	9			10	4		12	6						11	2				25
1		3		5		7^{3}	12	8^{2}	9^{1}	13		10	6	2		14						11	4				26
1		3		5		7^{1}	8	12	9	10^{2}	13		4	2■		6^{3}						11			14		27
1	2^{1}	3		5		7	8	14	9^{3}	10^{2}	13		4			6						11				12	28
1		3		5	6^{2}		12	13	9^{3}	14		10^{1}	8	2		7						11				4	29
1		3		5	12	6^{1}	9		13	14		10	8^{3}	2		7						11^{2}				4	30
1		3		5		6	8		9^{1}	13		10	7	2							12	11^{2}				4	31
1		3		5		6	9		13		11^{1}	10^{2}	8	2		7						12				4	32
1		3		5		6	9			11^{1}	13	10	8^{2}	2		7						12				4	33
1		3		5		6	9			13	12	10	8^{1}	2		7						11^{2}				4	34
1		3		5	13	6	9		14	12		10^{3}	8	2		7^{2}						11^{1}				4	35
1		3		5		6	9				12	10	8^{1}	2		7						11				4	36
1	13	3		5	12	6	9					10	8^{1}	2^{2}		7						11				4	37
1	2	3		5	6	8	9■		14	12		10^{3}	13			7^{2}						11^{1}				4	38

DUNFERMLINE ATHLETIC Premier League

Year Formed: 1885. *Ground & Address:* East End Park, Halbeath Rd, Dunfermline KY12 7RB. *Telephone:* 01383 724295. *Fax:* 01383 723468. *Ticket office telephone:* 0870 300 1201. *e-mail:* pars@dunfermline-ath.com
Ground Capacity: all seated: 12,500. *Size of Pitch:* 115yd × 71yd.
Chairman: John Yorkston. *Club Secretary:* Murray Falconer. *Commercial Manager:* Karen Brown.
Manager: Jim Leishman. *Assistant Manager:* Craig Robertson. *Physio:* Paul Atkinson.
Assistant Coaches: Hamish French & Scott Thomson.
Managers since 1975: G. Miller, H. Melrose, P. Stanton, T. Forsyth, J. Leishman, I. Munro, J. Scott, B. Paton, R. Campbell, J. Calderwood, D. Hay.
Club Nickname(s): The Pars. *Previous Grounds:* None.
Record Attendance: 27,816 v Celtic, Division I, 30 Apr 1968.
Record Transfer Fee received: £650,000 for Jackie McNamara to Celtic (Oct 1995).
Record Transfer Fee paid: £540,000 for Istvan Kozma from Bordeaux (Sept 1989).
Record Victory: 11-2 v Stenhousemuir, Division II, 27 Sept 1930.
Record Defeat: 1-11 v Hibernian, Scottish Cup, 3rd rd replay, 26 Oct 1889.
Most Capped Player: Colin Miller 16 (61), Canada.
Most League Appearances: 497: Norrie McCathie, 1981-96.
Most League Goals in Season (Individual): 53: Bobby Skinner, Division II, 1925-26.
Most Goals Overall (Individual): 154: Charles Dickson.

DUNFERMLINE ATHLETIC 2004–05 LEAGUE RECORD

Match No.	Date	Venue	Opponents	Result		H/T Score	Lg. Pos.	Goalscorers	Attendance
1	Aug 7	H	Dundee U	D	1-1	0-0	—	Tod 48	6474
2	15	A	Inverness CT	L	0-2	0-1	11		2583
3	21	H	Aberdeen	L	0-1	0-1	12		8533
4	29	A	Kilmarnock	L	0-1	0-1	12		4854
5	Sept 11	H	Motherwell	D	1-1	1-0	12	Brewster 8	4438
6	19	H	Hearts	W	1-0	0-0	9	Nicholson 64	5883
7	25	A	Celtic	L	0-3	0-2	11		56,873
8	Oct 2	H	Hibernian	D	1-1	0-1	10	Donnelly 85	7295
9	16	A	Livingston	L	0-2	0-2	10		2815
10	23	A	Dundee	W	2-1	1-0	10	Thomson 34, Young Derek 48	5456
11	27	H	Rangers	L	1-2	1-0	—	Brewster 21	8555
12	30	A	Dundee U	W	2-1	1-1	8	Tod 8, Young Darren 89	6297
13	Nov 6	H	Inverness CT	D	1-1	1-0	8	Young Darren 28	4921
14	13	A	Aberdeen	L	1-2	0-1	8	Donnelly 70	10,398
15	20	H	Kilmarnock	W	4-1	2-0	8	Nicholson 27, Mehmet 37, Wilson S 59, Brewster 88	4344
16	27	A	Motherwell	L	1-2	0-1	8	Tod 65	5084
17	Dec 4	A	Hearts	L	0-3	0-1	8		10,084
18	12	H	Celtic	L	0-2	0-2	10		7650
19	18	A	Hibernian	L	1-2	0-0	9	Tod 67	9859
20	27	H	Livingston	D	0-0	0-0	9		5092
21	Jan 1	H	Dundee	W	3-1	2-1	8	Tod 2 13, 54, McNally (og) 28	4426
22	15	A	Rangers	L	0-3	0-2	8		48,055
23	22	H	Dundee U	D	1-1	1-0	9	Christiansen 22	6578
24	29	A	Inverness CT	L	0-2	0-1	9		5449
25	Feb 12	H	Aberdeen	W	2-1	0-0	9	Mehmet 52, Donnelly 82	5609
26	19	A	Kilmarnock	L	1-2	1-2	9	Christiansen 20	4701
27	Mar 2	H	Motherwell	D	0-0	0-0	—		3427
28	5	H	Hearts	D	1-1	1-0	9	Wilson S 31	5935
29	12	A	Celtic	L	0-6	0-1	9		58,593
30	19	H	Hibernian	L	1-4	1-0	9	Nicholson 42	7204
31	Apr 2	A	Livingston	D	1-1	0-0	10	Hunt 79	4036
32	9	A	Dundee	L	1-2	1-0	10	Young Darren 8	5995
33	17	H	Rangers	L	0-1	0-1	11		8261
34	23	H	Inverness CT	D	0-0	0-0	11		4471
35	30	A	Livingston	L	0-2	0-1	12		5102
36	May 7	H	Dundee	W	5-0	4-0	11	Young Derek 3 3, 30, 64, MacDonald (og) 33, Skerla 39	8313
37	15	A	Dundee U	W	1-0	0-0	9	Kerr (og) 89	10,763
38	21	A	Kilmarnock	L	0-4	0-1	11		5100

Final League Position: 11

Honours
League Champions: First Division 1988-89, 1995-96. Division II 1925-26. Second Division 1985-86; *Runners-up:* First Division 1986-87, 1993-94, 1994-95, 1999-2000. Division II 1912-13, 1933-34, 1954-55, 1957-58, 1972-73. Second Division 1978-79.
Scottish Cup Winners: 1961, 1968; *Runners-up:* 1965, 2004.
League Cup Runners-up: 1949-50, 1991-92.

European: *Cup Winners' Cup:* 14 matches (1961-62, 1968-69 semi-finals). *UEFA Cup:* 30 matches (*Fairs Cup:* 1962-63, 1964-65, 1965-66, 1966-67, 1969-70. *UEFA Cup:* 2004-05).

Club colours: Shirt: Black and white vertical stripes. Shorts: White. Stockings: White.

Goalscorers: *League* (34): Tod 6, Derek Young 4, Brewster 3, Donnelly 3, Nicholson 3, Darren Young 3, Christiansen 2, Mehmet 2, Wilson S 2, Hunt 1, Skerla 1, Thomson 1, own goals 3.
Scottish Cup (3): Dempsey 1, Hunt 1, Tod 1.
CIS Cup (4): Brewster 1, Hunt 1, Mehmet 1, Thomson 1.

Stillie D 38	Shields G 13	Wilson S 31	Skerla A 30	Byrne R 5+1	Thomson S 35	Nicholson B 26+1	Mason G 34+1	Dempsey G 16+1	Hunt N 13+10	Tod A 24+7	Young Darren 29+6	Brewster C 13+1	Mehmet W 16+15	Donnelly S 18+8	Young Derek 10+7	Labonte A 9+6	Butler T 6+6	Ross G 11+3	Bradley S 1+1	Scullion P —+1	Campbell I 11+2	Makel L 11	Christiansen J 10+3	Hristov G 4+4	Wilson C 4	McKeown C —+1	McGlinchey S —+1	*Match No.*
1	2	3	4	5	6^{1}	7	8	9	10^{2}	11^{3}	12	13	14															1
1	2	3	4	5^{1}	6	7	8	9	10^{2}		12	11^{3}	14	13														2
1	2	3	4		5		8	7^{3}	10	14	6	11^{2}	13	9^{1}	12													3
1	2		4	3	5		8^{3}	7	10^{1}	14	6	11	9^{2}		12	13												4
1	2	3	4		5	7^{2}	8	9	12		6	11	10^{1}	13														5
1	2	3	4		5	7	8	9			6	11^{1}	10				12											6
1	2	3	4		5	7	8^{1}	9	13^{3}		6^{2}	11	10			12	14											7
1	2	3	4		5	7		8		13	6^{3}	11	10^{1}	14	12		9^{2}											8
1	2	3	4		5	7	12	8^{1}		14	6^{2}	11		10^{3}	13		9											9
1	2	3	4		5	7	6			13	14	11^{2}	12	10^{3}	9		8^{1}											10
1	2	3	4		5	7	6^{2}			13		11	12	10^{1}	9		8											11
1		3	4	2^{2}	5	7	8			9	6	11	12	10^{1}		13												12
1	2	3	4^{1}	12	5	7	8			9^{2}	6	11	10^{3}	14	13													13
1		3		4	5	7	8			9			11	10		2	6											14
1		3			5	7	8				6^{1}	11	9	10		2		4	12									15
1	2	3			5	7	8			11	6		9	10^{1}		4	12											16
1		3			5	7	8	4	12	11	6						9	2	10^{1}									17
1		3			5	7	8	4	12	11	6		9	10^{1}		2^{2}		13										18
1		3	4		5^{3}	7^{2}	8	9	10^{1}	11	6						14	2		12	13							19
1		3	4			7	8	9^{1}	13	11	6^{2}		10			5	12	2										20
1		3	4		5	7	8	13	12	11	6^{2}		10^{1}			9	14	2^{3}										21
1			4		5	7	8	9	12	11	6^{1}							2				3	10					22
1			4		5	7	8	6	10^{1}	11			12			2						3	9					23
1			4		5	7	8	6	10^{2}	11	14		13			2^{1}		12				3	9^{3}					24
1					5	7	8		10^{3}	4	14		11^{1}	12				2			3	6	9^{2}	13				25
1			4		5	7	8		10^{1}	3	12		11^{2}	13				2				6	9^{3}	14				26
1		3			5^{1}		8			4	6^{3}		13	10	14			2			12	7	9	11^{2}				27
1		3				13	8			4	6			10	12			2			5	7^{2}	9	11^{1}				28
1		3	4			7				8	6			10^{2}				2			5		9		11^{1}	12	13	29
1			4		5	7			13	3	6		8	10	11^{2}	2^{1}		12					9					30
1		3	4		5		8		12	7	6		13	10	11^{2}						2		9^{1}					31
1		3	4		5		8		9^{1}	7^{3}	6		12	10^{2}	11						2		13	14				32
1		3	4		5		8		9		6		12	10^{1}	11						2		13	7^{2}				33
1		3	4		5		8		9^{2}	14	6		13	10^{3}	11						2		12	7^{1}				34
1		3	4		5		8		9^{1}		6		11	10^{2}		12					2	7		13				35
1		3	4		5^{2}		8		14	10^{1}	6		12		11^{3}	13					2	7			9			36
1		3	4		5		8			10	6			12	11^{1}						2	7			9			37
1		3	4		5		8			10^{1}	6		12	13	11^{2}	14					2	7			9^{3}			38

EAST FIFE

Third Division

Year Formed: 1903. *Ground & Address:* Bayview Stadium, Harbour View, Methil, Fife KY8 3RW. *Telephone:* 01333 426323. *Fax:* 01333 426376. *E-mail:* secretary@eastfife.org. *Website:* www.eastfife.org.
Ground Capacity: all seated: 2000. *Size of Pitch:* 115yd × 75yd.
Chairman and Secretary: Derrick Brown.
Manager: James Moffat. *Assistant Manager:* Greig Shaw. *Physio:* Ian Barrett.
Managers since 1975: Frank Christie, Roy Barry, David Clarke, Gavin Murray, Alex Totten, Steve Archibald, James Bone, Steve Kirk, Rab Shannon, David Clarke.
Club Nickname(s): The Fifers. *Previous Ground:* Bayview Park.
Record Attendance: 22,515 v Raith Rovers, Division I, 2 Jan 1950.
Record Transfer Fee received: £150,000 for Paul Hunter from Hull C (March 1990).
Record Transfer Fee paid: £70,000 for John Sludden from Kilmarnock (July 1991).
Record Victory: 13-2 v Edinburgh City, Division II, 11 Dec 1937.
Record Defeat: 0-9 v Hearts, Division I, 5 Oct 1957.
Most Capped Player: George Aitken, 5 (8), Scotland.
Most League Appearances: 517: David Clarke, 1968-86.
Most League Goals in Season (Individual): 41: Jock Wood, Division II; 1926-27 and Henry Morris, Division II, 1947-48.
Most Goals Overall (Individual): 225: Phil Weir (215 in League).

EAST FIFE 2004–05 LEAGUE RECORD

Match No.	Date	Venue	Opponents	Result		H/T Score	Lg. Pos.	Goalscorers	Attendance
1	Aug 7	H	Montrose	W	1-0	0-0	—	Tarditi [88]	437
2	14	A	Albion R	L	0-2	0-0	6		384
3	21	H	Cowdenbeath	D	1-1	0-1	6	Fairbairn [82]	555
4	28	H	Stenhousemuir	D	0-0	0-0	6		468
5	Sept 4	A	Peterhead	L	0-2	0-2	6		507
6	11	H	East Stirling	W	1-0	1-0	6	Colquhoun [34]	425
7	18	A	Gretna	L	1-5	1-1	8	Fairbairn [34]	457
8	25	H	Queen's Park	L	1-4	0-1	8	Tarditi [90]	445
9	Oct 2	A	Elgin C	L	1-2	1-2	9	Herkes [44]	404
10	16	H	Albion R	W	1-0	0-0	8	Colquhoun [84]	396
11	23	A	Montrose	L	1-2	0-1	8	Duncan [90]	435
12	30	A	Stenhousemuir	L	2-5	1-1	8	Nicholas [35], Colquhoun [53]	382
13	Nov 6	H	Peterhead	L	0-2	0-0	8		410
14	13	A	East Stirling	D	1-1	1-1	8	Nicholas [12]	364
15	27	H	Gretna	L	1-3	1-2	8	Nicholas [44]	551
16	Dec 4	A	Queen's Park	W	2-1	2-0	8	Fairbairn [26], McDonald G [43]	575
17	27	H	Montrose	W	1-0	0-0	8	Fairbairn [69]	784
18	Jan 1	A	Cowdenbeath	D	1-1	0-0	8	Paliczka [64]	454
19	3	H	Stenhousemuir	W	2-0	0-0	—	Lumsden [78], Fairbairn (pen) [88]	491
20	15	A	Peterhead	D	0-0	0-0	8		587
21	29	A	Gretna	L	0-4	0-2	8		828
22	Feb 5	H	Queen's Park	L	0-1	0-0	8		601
23	12	A	Elgin C	L	1-2	0-1	8	Nicholas (pen) [68]	379
24	15	H	East Stirling	W	2-0	1-0	—	Nicholas [32], McDonald G [86]	441
25	19	H	Cowdenbeath	D	1-1	1-1	7	Mitchell [28]	671
26	Mar 5	H	Peterhead	L	1-2	0-1	8	Nicholas [82]	495
27	12	A	Stenhousemuir	W	2-1	2-0	8	McDonald G [3], Nicholas [37]	334
28	19	A	East Stirling	L	0-1	0-1	8		315
29	22	A	Albion R	W	6-0	4-0	—	Paliczka 3 [2, 21, 59], Beith [14], Fairbairn [28], McDonald G [54]	316
30	26	H	Elgin C	W	2-0	0-0	7	McDonald G [75], Mitchell [87]	456
31	Apr 2	H	Gretna	L	0-2	0-1	8		723
32	9	H	Elgin C	L	1-2	1-1	8	Nicholas (pen) [37]	466
33	16	A	Queen's Park	L	1-2	1-2	8	Mitchell [26]	451
34	23	A	Cowdenbeath	L	2-4	0-2	8	Nicholas [47], Lumsden [64]	348
35	30	H	Albion R	D	1-1	1-1	8	Mitchell [7]	568
36	May 7	A	Montrose	D	2-2	0-0	8	Mitchell [54], Byle [59]	496

Final League Position: 8

Honours
League Champions: Division II 1947-48; *Runners-up:* Division II 1929-30, 1970-71. Second Division 1983-84, 1995-96. Third Division 2002-03
Scottish Cup Winners: 1938; *Runners-up:* 1927, 1950.
League Cup Winners: 1947-48, 1949-50, 1953-54.

Club colours: Shirt: Gold and black. Shorts: White. Stockings: Black.

Goalscorers: *League* (40): Nicholas 9 (2 pens), Fairbairn 6 (1 pen), McDonald G 5, Mitchell 5, Paliczka 4, Colquhoun 3, Lumsden 2, Tarditi 2, Beith 1, Byle 1, Duncan 1, Herkes 1.
Scottish Cup (7): McDonald G 2, Mitchell 2, Byle 1, Lumsden 1, Nicholas 1.
CIS Cup (0).
Challenge Cup (0).

Dodds J 8	Lumsden C 32	McDonald I 3	Bain K 16+2	Hall M 5	Kelly G 34	Herkes J 14+1	McDonald G 22+3	Fairbairn B 25+3	Tarditi S 9+9	Brash K 25+5	Paliczka S 14+8	Mitchell J 20+7	Byle L 18+4	Renwick M 32	Mathie G 17+1	Steele K 9+5	Morrison S 23	Colquhoun D 7+1	Duncan F 10+1	Linton S 2	Crawford R —+2	Gaughan P 4	Nicholas S 25	Ferguson J 1+3	Boyle J 6+4	Beith G 10+2	McCafferty J 5+1	Match No.
1	2	3	4	5	6	7	8	9[1]	10	11[2]	12	13																1
1	2	3	4	5	6[2]	11	8	9	10		12	7[1]	13															2
1		3	4	5	6	7	8	9	10[1]	11[2]	12	13		2														3
1	4			5	8	7			10	12	9		6	2	3	11[1]												4
	4			5[1]	6	7		14	10[2]	12	9[3]		8	2	3	11	1	13										5
	4				8	7		9	12	3			6	2	5	11[1]	1	10										6
	4		5		8	7		9[2]	13	3			6	2		11[1]	1	10	12									7
	4				8	7		9	12	3			6	2		11[2]	1	10[1]		5	13							8
	4		12		6	7		10		3			8	2		11	1	9		5[1]								9
					6	7		11	12	3			8	2			1	10[1]	5			4	9					10
					6	7		11[1]	13	3[2]		12	8	2			1	10	5			4	9					11
			12		6[1]	7		11[2]		3		13	8	2			1	10	5			4	9					12
	4		5		8	7	12	11	10[2]		13		6[1]	2			1		3				9					13
	4				8	7	12	11[3]	10[2]		13		6[1]	2		14	1		3			5	9					14
	4		6		8		5	11		12		7		2		10[1]	1		3				9					15
	4		5		6		8	11	13	3	7[1]	10		2		12	1						9[2]					16
	4		5		6	13	8[1]	11	14	3	7[2]	10[3]	12	2			1						9					17
	4		5		8			11	12	3	7	10	6	2			1						9[1]					18
	4		5		8		12	11	9[2]	3	7[3]	10	6[1]	2		14	1							13				19
	4		5		6		8	11		3	7	10		2			1						9					20
	4		5		6		8	11[3]		3[1]	7[2]	10	14	2	12	13	1						9					21
	4		5				8			12	13	10	6[3]	2	3	7[2]	1						9		11[1]	14		22
	4		5[1]				8			12	7[3]	10	6	2	3	13	1						9	14	11[2]			23
	4				8		5			11		7	6	2	3		1						9		10			24
	4				8		5			11		7	6[1]	2	3		1						9		10	12		25
	4				6		8	12				7[2]		2	5	11[1]	1		3				9		13	10		26
	4				6		8				12	7		2	5		1[G]		3				9		11[1]	10	15	27
	4				6[2]		8	12	13			7		2	5				3				9		11[1]	10	1	28
	4				6		8	11		3	7[1]	12		2	5								9			10	1	29
	4				6		8	11	9[1]	3	7	12		2	5											10	1	30
	4				6		8[2]	11[1]		3	7	12		2	5								9		13	10	1	31
	4				6		8	11		3		7[1]		2	5								9		12	10	1	32
1	4				6		8	7		3	12	10		2	5								9			11[1]		33
1	4				6		8	11		3	7[1]	10		2[*]	5								9		12			34
1	2		4		8		6[1]			3		10	12		5								9	7		11		35
1	4		5		6[1]					3	7[2]	10	8						2		12		9	13		11		36

EAST STIRLINGSHIRE Third Division

Year Formed: 1880. *Ground & Address:* Firs Park, Firs St, Falkirk FK2 7AY. *Telephone:* 01324 623583. *Fax:* 01324 637 862.
Ground Capacity: total: 1880, seated: 200. *Size of Pitch:* 112yd × 72yd.
Chairman: A. Mackin. *Vice Chairman:* Douglas Morrison. *Chief Executive/Secretary:* Leslie G. Thomson.
Head Coach: Dennis Newall. *Assistant Coach:* Gordon Wylde. *Physio:* David Jenkins.
Managers since 1975: I. Ure, D. McLinden, W. P. Lamont, A. Ferguson, W. Little, D. Whiteford, D. Lawson, J. D. Connell, A. Mackin, D. Sullivan, B. McCulley, B. Little, J. Brownlie, H. McCann, G. Fairley, B. Ross, D. Diver.
Club Nickname(s): The Shire. *Previous Grounds:* Burnhouse, Randyford Park, Merchiston Park, New Kilbowie Park.
Record Attendance: 12,000 v Partick T, Scottish Cup 3rd rd, 21 Feb 1921.
Record Transfer Fee received: £35,000 for Jim Docherty to Chelsea (1978).
Record Transfer Fee paid: £6,000 for Colin McKinnon from Falkirk (March 1991).
Record Victory: 11-2 v Vale of Bannock, Scottish Cup 2nd rd, 22 Sept 1888.
Record Defeat: 1-12 v Dundee United, Division II, 13 Apr 1936.
Most Capped Player: Humphrey Jones, 5 (14), Wales.
Most League Appearances: 415: Gordon Russell, 1983-2001.
Most League Goals in Season (Individual): 36: Malcolm Morrison, Division II, 1938-39.

EAST STIRLINGSHIRE 2004–05 LEAGUE RECORD

Match No.	Date	Venue	Opponents	Result		H/T Score	Lg. Pos.	Goalscorers	Attendance
1	Aug 7	A	Peterhead	L	0-5	0-2	—		561
2	14	H	Gretna	L	1-2	1-2	9	Miller 37	276
3	21	A	Stenhousemuir	L	0-6	0-1	10		465
4	28	A	Cowdenbeath	L	1-2	1-0	10	Robertson 12	232
5	Sept 4	H	Elgin C	L	0-1	0-0	10		617
6	11	A	East Fife	L	0-1	0-1	10		425
7	18	H	Queen's Park	L	0-5	0-2	10		335
8	25	A	Albion R	D	3-3	3-3	10	Ure 14, Robertson 17, Thywissen 30	225
9	Oct 2	H	Montrose	D	1-1	1-0	10	Robertson 17	247
10	16	A	Gretna	L	1-8	1-4	10	Ure 9	468
11	23	H	Peterhead	L	1-2	0-1	10	Robertson (pen) 78	281
12	30	H	Cowdenbeath	L	0-2	0-1	10		637
13	Nov 6	A	Elgin C	W	3-1	0-0	10	Thywissen 2 65, 73, Robertson 80	502
14	13	H	East Fife	D	1-1	1-1	10	Oates 34	364
15	27	A	Queen's Park	D	0-0	0-0	10		457
16	Dec 4	H	Albion R	D	1-1	0-1	10	Robertson (pen) 85	262
17	27	A	Peterhead	L	0-3	0-2	10		647
18	Jan 8	A	Cowdenbeath	L	2-3	2-1	10	Mackay 38, Robertson 44	212
19	15	H	Elgin C	L	0-3	0-1	10		191
20	29	H	Queen's Park	W	3-1	3-1	10	McGroarty 2 4, 15, Diack (pen) 36	317
21	Feb 5	A	Albion R	D	1-1	0-0	10	Oates 48	350
22	12	H	Montrose	L	1-2	0-0	10	Ure 58	198
23	15	A	East Fife	L	0-2	0-1	—		441
24	19	A	Stenhousemuir	L	2-3	0-1	10	Livingstone 48, Donaldson 75	422
25	Mar 1	A	Montrose	L	1-4	1-1	—	McGroarty 11	270
26	5	A	Elgin C	D	0-0	0-0	10		394
27	8	H	Gretna	L	0-4	0-2	—		185
28	12	H	Cowdenbeath	W	2-1	0-1	10	McGroarty 48, Tyrrell M 60	204
29	15	H	Stenhousemuir	W	3-2	2-0	—	Donaldson 3, McGroarty 20, Ross 68	211
30	19	H	East Fife	W	1-0	1-0	10	Ure 24	315
31	Apr 2	A	Queen's Park	L	0-2	0-1	10		486
32	9	A	Montrose	L	1-4	1-1	10	Donaldson 19	329
33	16	H	Albion R	L	0-2	0-1	10		285
34	23	H	Stenhousemuir	L	1-4	1-3	10	Oates 43	242
35	30	A	Gretna	L	0-1	0-1	10		1585
36	May 7	H	Peterhead	L	1-5	0-3	10	Ure 81	192

Final League Position: 10

Honours
League Champions: Division II 1931-32; C Division 1947-48. *Runners-up:* Division II 1962-63. Second Division 1979-80. Division Three 1923-24.

Club colours: Shirt: Black with white. Shorts: Black with white. Stockings: Black with white hoops.

Goalscorers: *League* (32): Robertson 7 (2 pens), McGroarty 5, Ure 5, Donaldson 3, Oates 3, Thywissen 3, Diack 1 (pen), Livingstone 1, Mackay 1, Miller 1, Ross 1, Tyrrell M 1.
Scottish Cup (1): Livingstone 1.
CIS Cup (2): Parks 1, Ure 1.
Challenge Cup (1): Donaldson 1.

Mitchell A 12+1	Harvey D 29	McGhee G 27+3	Mackay J 16+5	Newall C 8+1	McAuley S 5+6	Ross P 21+10	Moffat A 4+2	Donaldson R 29	Dunbar J 11+4	Miller C 2	Ure D 26+8	Baldwin C 7+2	Leishman J —+3	Gilpin R 9	Parks G —+9	Denham G 16	Livingstone S 30	Robertson J 15+1	Stuart W —+1	Findlay G 3+8	Thywissen C 19+2	Oates S 20	Peutherer S —+3	Walker J 19+2	Diack I 5	McGroarty C 16	Rae D 2+6	Jackson D 15	Tyrrell P 15	Gerrard D 1	Walker N 1	Tyrrell M 13	*Match No.*
1	2	3	4^{1}	5	6	7^{2}	8^{3}	9	10	11	12	13	14																				1
	2	5	13	4		6^{1}	8^{2}	10	7	3^{3}	9	11	12	1	14																		2
1	2	3	5	4	7^{1}	12	8^{3}	9^{2}	6		10	11	14		13																		3
	2	3	4		8^{1}	7^{3}	12	9	10		14	13		1		5	6	11^{2}															4
	2	3	4	8		7		9^{1}	11^{3}		10			1	12	5^{2}	6		13	14													5
	2	3	5	4		7		9^{2}	10		12			1			6	11^{1}		13	8												6
	2	3	4	5		7^{1}	12	9^{2}	10		14			1			6	11^{3}		13	8												7
	2	3	5			12	6^{1}	9^{3}			10^{2}			1	14		11	7			8	4	13										8
	2	3				6		9^{1}	12		10			1		5	11	7			8	4											9
	2	3		12		6^{1}			10^{3}		9^{2}			1	14	5	7	11		13	8	4											10
1	2	3		8				9^{2}	12		10					5^{1}	6	11			7	4	13										11
1	2	3		8		14			10^{3}		11^{2}				13	5^{1}	6	9			7	4	12										12
1	2	3	4			6		9^{1}	10^{2}		12						11	8			7	5		13									13
1	2^{3}	3	4		14	6^{1}		9	10^{2}		13						11	8			7	5		12									14
1	2	6	5		13	14		9^{1}	12		10						3	11^{2}			8	4		7^{3}									15
1	2	6	4		12			9									3	11			8^{1}	5		7	10								16
1	2^{2}	3	5		8	13		9			12	11									7	4		6	10^{1}								17
1	2		4		12	13		10^{3}				11^{2}			14		3	8			7	5		6^{1}	9								18
		6^{1}	5		7^{2}				12		10			1			2	11			8	4			9	3	13						19
	2				12	7^{1}		9^{2}			13					5	3					4		6	10	11		1	8				20
	2					7		9^{2}			10					5	3^{1}	12			13	4		6		11^{3}	14	1	8				21
	2^{1}		4		12	7^{2}		9			10^{3}					5	3	11		14				6			13	1	8				22
	2^{2}	3				12		10			11					5				13				6			7^{1}	1	8	4	9		23
15						2		9			10					5	3							4		11	7	1^{6}	8			6	24
1		3				6^{1}		9			10	11^{2}				5				13		4				8	12		7			2	25
	4					12		9^{2}			10	3^{1}			13	5	2					6				11		1	8			7	26
	2	12				7^{1}		9			10					5	3							4		11		1	8			6	27
	2	12				7^{1}		9			10					5	3							4		11		1	8			6	28
	2	13				7		9^{3}			10				14	5^{2}	3				12			4		11		1	8^{1}			6	29
	4	3				7		9			10	8					2							6		11		1				5	30
	2	3	12			7^{1}		9^{3}			10						11			14	6^{2}			4		8	13	1				5	31
	2^{1}	3	12					9[illegible]			10						6				7			4		11		1	8			5	32
		6	4			7^{1}					9						3					5		8		11	12	1	10			2	33
		3	12								9						11			10^{1}	6	5		4		8		1	7			2	34
		3				12					9						2			10	7	4		6^{1}		11		1	8			5	35
1		3^{1}	12			13					9						2			10^{2}	7	4		6[illegible]		11			8			5	36

ELGIN CITY — Third Division

Year Formed: 1893. *Ground and Address:* Borough Briggs, Borough Briggs Road, Elgin IV30 1AP.
Telephone: 01343 551114. *Fax:* 01343 547921.
Ground Capacity: 3927, seated 478, standing 3449. *Size of pitch:* 111yd × 72yd.
Chairman: Denis J. Miller. *Secretary:* John A. Milton. *Commercial:* Audrey Fanning & Kevin Cruikshank. *Commercial Manager:* Michael Teasdale.
Manager: David Robertson. *Assistant Manager:* Kenny Black. *Physio:* Leigh Thomas.
Managers since 1975: McHardy, Wilson, McHardy, Dickson, Shewan, Tedcastle, Grant, Cochran, Cumming, Cowie, Paterson, Winton, Black, Teasdale, Fleming, McHardy, Tatters, Caldwell.
Previous names: 1893-1900 Elgin City, 1900-03 Elgin City United, 1903- Elgin City.
Club Nickname(s): City or Black & Whites. *Previous Grounds:* Association Park 1893-95; Milnfield Park 1895-1909; Station Park 1909-19; Cooper Park 1919-21.
Record Attendance: 12,608 v Arbroath, Scottish Cup, 17 Feb 1968.
Record Transfer Fee received: £32,000 for Michael Teasdale to Dundee (Jan 1994).
Record Transfer Fee paid: £10,000 to Fraserburgh for Russell McBride (July 2001).
Record Victory: 18-1 v Brora Rangers, North of Scotland Cup, 6 Feb 1960.
Record Defeat: 1-14 v Hearts, Scottish Cup, 4 Feb 1939.
Most League Appearances: 124: Martin Pirie, 2000-04.
Most League Goals in Season (Individual): A. Bone, 18, 2003-04.
Most Goals Overall (Individual): A. Bone, 18, 2003-05.

ELGIN CITY 2004–05 LEAGUE RECORD

Match No.	Date	Venue	Opponents	Result		H/T Score	Lg. Pos.	Goalscorers	Attendance
1	Aug 7	A	Stenhousemuir	W	2-0	1-0	—	Bone 2 (1 pen) 29, 59 (p)	267
2	14	H	Queen's Park	W	1-0	1-0	3	Roddie 29	523
3	21	A	Peterhead	L	1-2	0-2	4	Dickson 55	688
4	28	H	Montrose	L	1-3	1-0	5	Bone 23	555
5	Sept 4	A	East Stirling	W	1-0	0-0	3	Dempsie 68	617
6	11	A	Cowdenbeath	L	1-3	1-1	3	Kaczan 8	275
7	18	H	Albion R	W	1-0	0-0	3	Nelson 72	450
8	25	A	Gretna	L	0-3	0-2	4		574
9	Oct 2	H	East Fife	W	2-1	2-1	3	Martin 4, McKenzie J 19	404
10	16	A	Queen's Park	W	1-0	1-0	3	Harty 31	507
11	23	H	Stenhousemuir	D	1-1	0-0	3	Reid 60	622
12	30	A	Montrose	L	0-2	0-1	3		447
13	Nov 6	H	East Stirling	L	1-3	0-0	4	Martin 49	502
14	13	H	Cowdenbeath	L	0-4	0-1	7		336
15	27	A	Albion R	D	2-2	1-0	6	Dickson 37, Martin 58	262
16	Dec 4	H	Gretna	L	1-3	0-2	7	Dickson 77	505
17	27	A	Stenhousemuir	L	0-4	0-1	7		329
18	Jan 3	H	Montrose	D	2-2	1-1	—	Dickson 33, Martin 83	446
19	15	A	East Stirling	W	3-0	1-0	6	Martin 29, Donnachie 47, Kaczan 86	191
20	29	H	Albion R	D	1-1	0-0	6	Roddie 66	380
21	Feb 5	A	Gretna	L	1-2	1-1	6	Roddie 32	809
22	12	H	East Fife	W	2-1	1-0	6	Harty 44, McKenzie J (pen) 86	379
23	Mar 1	A	Peterhead	L	0-3	0-2	—		611
24	5	H	East Stirling	D	0-0	0-0	7		394
25	8	H	Peterhead	D	2-2	1-1	—	Cumming 25, Kaczan 75	383
26	12	A	Montrose	L	0-2	0-0	7		308
27	15	A	Cowdenbeath	D	1-1	0-1	—	Harty 65	149
28	19	H	Cowdenbeath	W	2-0	1-0	7	Higgins 15, Martin 81	338
29	22	H	Queen's Park	W	1-0	1-0	—	Molloy (og) 1	354
30	26	A	East Fife	L	0-2	0-0	5		456
31	Apr 2	A	Albion R	L	0-2	0-0	7		246
32	9	A	East Fife	W	2-1	1-1	5	Martin 6, Harty 80	466
33	16	H	Gretna	L	2-6	1-3	6	Martin 2 11, 56	503
34	23	H	Peterhead	L	0-2	0-1	7		507
35	30	A	Queen's Park	L	0-1	0-0	7		581
36	May 7	H	Stenhousemuir	W	4-2	0-2	6	McKenzie J 60, Donnachie 2 67, 68, Napier 83	314

Final League Position: 6

Honours
Scottish Cup: Quarter-finals 1968.
Highland League Champions: winners 15 times.
Scottish Qualifying Cup (North): winners 7 times.
North of Scotland Cup: winners 17 times.
Highland League Cup: winners 5 times.
Inverness Cup: winners twice.

Club colours: Shirt: Black and white vertical stripes. Shorts: Black. Stockings: Red.

Goalscorers: *League* (39): Martin 9, Harty 4, Dickson 4, Bone 3 (1 pen), Donnachie 3, Kaczan 3, McKenzie J 3 (1 pen), Roddie 3, Cumming 1, Dempsie 1, Higgins 1, Napier 1, Nelson 1, Reid 1, own goal 1.
Scottish Cup (0).
CIS Cup (2): Bone 1, Martin 1.
Challenge Cup (0).

Renton K 36	Cumming S 33	Dempsie A 24	Kaczan P 25 + 1	Dickson H 30 + 1	Black S 4	Martin W 33	Nelson A 34	Bone A 4	Reid P 13 + 10	Roddie A 24 + 2	Napier P 4 + 22	Bremner F 23 + 3	Harty M 31 + 1	Vigurs I 8 + 5	McKenzie J 28	McDonald J — + 3	McKendrick K 2 + 1	Higgins C 18	Wood G 2 + 9	Lennox A — + 2	Melrose G — + 5	Vigurs P 4 + 7	Allison J 3 + 3	Donnachie S 10 + 1	Thomson D 3	Huckins M — + 1	Match No.
1	2	3	4	5	6	7	8	9	10[1]	11	12																1
1	2	3	4	5	6	7	8	9	10[1]	11		12															2
1	2	3	4	5		7	8	9	10[1]	11		12	6														3
1	2	3	4	5		7	8	9		11		6[1]	10	12													4
1	5	2	4			10	8			11[1]	12	7	9[2]	3	6	13											5
1	5	2	4	12		10[1]	8			11	13	7[2]	9	3	6												6
1	2	3	4	5		10	8			11[1]	12	7	9		6												7
1	2	3	4	5		10	8[2]				12	7	9[3]	11[1]	6	14	13										8
1	2	3[2]	4	5[1]		10	8		9[3]		13	7	11	12	6	14											9
1	2		5				8		9[3]	11[2]	10	7	3	12	6[1]			4	13	14							10
1	2		4				8		9	11	5[1]	7	10	3	6				12								11
1	2		4				8[1]		9	11[2]	3	7	10	13	6			5			12						12
1			4			10[3]	8		9[2]	11	13	6	7	3[1]			2	5		14	12						13
1	5		4	6		10[3]			9	11	12	7	8	3[2]			2[1]		14		13						14
1	2		4	6		10[2]	8			11	12	7■	3					5			13	9[1]					15
1	2		4	6		10	8		7[3]	11[1]	12		3[2]	13				5	14			9					16
1	2		4	5		10	8				7[2]		11[3]	3	6				13		12	9[1]	14				17
1	2		4	5	7	10	8				12		11	3[1]	6				13			9[2]					18
1		3	4	5	11	10	8						7		6			2						9			19
1	7	3■	4	5[1]		10	8			12			11		6			2						9			20
1	2		4	3		10[2]	8			11■	13		7		6			5[1]				12		9			21
1	2	4		5		10	8		12			7[2]	11		6							13		9[1]	3		22
1	2	3		5[2]		10	8■		12		14				6			7	13				4[3]	9[1]	11		23
1	4	3	13	8		10			12		14	7[1]			6			5	9				2[2]		11[3]		24
1	2	3	4	6		10	7		12	11			9		8			5[1]									25
1	2■	3	4[2]	5		10	8		13	11[3]		12	7		6				14					9[1]			26
1		3		5		10	8			11		6	7		4				9				2[1]	12			27
1	2	3		5		10	8		12	11[2]	13	6[3]	9[1]		4			7					14				28
1	2	3		5		10[2]	8		11		14	6	9		4			7[1]				13	12[3]				29
1	2		5	3		10	8		9[1]	11	13		7[2]		4			6	12								30
1	2		5[3]	3		10	8		9[1]	11■	14	6[2]	12		4			7								13	31
1	2	3		5		10	8		12			6	11		4			7						9[1]			32
1	2	3		5		10	8			12	14	7[1]	11[2]		4			6				13		9[3]			33
1	2	3		5		10[3]	8		12	11[2]	13	6	7		4							14		9[1]			34
1	2	3		5[3]		10	8		12	11[1]	13	7	9		4[2]			6				14					35
1	2	3		5		10	8		13	11[1]	12	6[2]	7[3]		4							14		9			36

FALKIRK — Premier League

Year Formed: 1876. *Ground & Address:* The Falkirk Stadium, Westfield, Falkirk FK2 9DX. *Telephone:* 01324 624121. *Fax:* 01324 612418. *Website:* www.falkirkfc.co.uk.
Ground Capacity: seated: 6123. *Size of Pitch:* 110yd × 72yd.
Chairman: Campbell Christie. *Managing Director:* George Craig. *Head of Development:* Eddie May. *Secretary:* Alex Blackwood. *General Manager:* Crawford Baptie.
Head Coach: John Hughes. *Assistant Coach:* Brian Rice. *Director of Football:* Alex Totten. *Youth Co-ordinator:* Ian McIntyre.
Managers since 1975: J. Prentice, G. Miller, W. Little, J. Hagart, A. Totten, G. Abel, W. Lamont, D. Clarke, J. Duffy, W. Lamont, J. Jefferies, J. Lambie E. Bannon, A. Totten, I. McCall. *Club Nickname(s):* The Bairns. *Previous Grounds:* Randyford 1876-81; Blinkbonny Grounds 1881-83; Brockville Park 1883-2003.
Record Attendance: 23,100 v Celtic, Scottish Cup 3rd rd, 21 Feb 1953.
Record Transfer Fee received: £380,000 for John Hughes to Celtic (Aug 1995).
Record Transfer Fee paid: £225,000 to Chelsea for Kevin McAllister (Aug 1991).
Record Victory: 12-1 v Laurieston, Scottish Cup 2nd rd, 23 Sept 1893.
Record Defeat: 1-11 v Airdrieonians, Division I, 28 Apr 1951.
Most Capped Player: Alex Parker, 14 (15), Scotland.
Most League Appearances: (post-war): 353, George Watson, 1975-87.
Most League Goals in Season (Individual): 43: Evelyn Morrison, Division I, 1928-29.
Most Goals Overall (Individual): Dougie Moran, 86, 1957-61 and 1964-67.

FALKIRK 2004–05 LEAGUE RECORD

Match No.	Date	Venue	Opponents	Result	H/T Score	Lg. Pos.	Goalscorers	Attendance
1	Aug 7	A	St Mirren	L 0-2	0-0	—		3817
2	14	H	Hamilton A	D 1-1	0-1	8	Duffy (pen) [70]	3423
3	21	A	Queen of the S	W 3-1	1-1	6	Nicholls [9], Duffy [48], McAnespie [85]	2521
4	28	H	Airdrie U	W 5-0	2-0	4	Thomson 2 [9, 78], Nicholls [25], Lawrie [54], Latapy [62]	3790
5	Sept 4	A	Partick Th	W 4-1	2-0	3	Duffy 2 [13, 24], Campbell [50], Scally [86]	5157
6	11	H	Raith R	W 4-2	0-1	2	Duffy 2 [54, 59], Thomson 2 [67, 81]	3449
7	18	A	St Johnstone	W 2-1	2-0	2	O'Neil [8], Nicholls [10]	3835
8	25	H	Clyde	D 1-1	1-0	2	Thomson [19]	3813
9	Oct 2	A	Ross Co	W 1-0	1-0	1	Thomson (pen) [39]	3062
10	16	A	Hamilton A	W 1-0	0-0	1	Moutinho [52]	2870
11	23	H	St Mirren	D 0-0	0-0	1		4611
12	30	A	Airdrie U	W 3-1	2-0	1	Latapy [7], Thomson [44], Lawrie [76]	3247
13	Nov 13	A	Raith R	W 2-0	1-0	1	McBreen [45], Duffy (pen) [59]	3050
14	20	H	St Johnstone	W 3-1	1-1	1	McBreen 2 [33, 76], Latapy [68]	3439
15	23	H	Partick Th	W 3-0	0-0	—	Duffy [53], McBreen 2 [73, 87]	3335
16	27	H	Ross Co	D 2-2	0-1	1	McBreen [56], Thomson [67]	3182
17	Dec 4	A	Clyde	W 2-0	2-0	1	Hughes [12], Mackenzie [18]	2859
18	11	A	St Mirren	W 1-0	0-0	1	Moutinho [55]	4676
19	18	H	Queen of the S	W 4-2	3-2	1	Moutinho [17], McBreen 3 [25, 42, 73]	3370
20	26	H	Airdrie U	W 1-0	1-0	1	Duffy [34]	4133
21	29	A	Partick Th	L 1-2	1-1	—	Duffy [6]	4120
22	Jan 1	H	Raith R	W 2-0	2-0	1	Latapy [6], Thomson [27]	3379
23	15	A	St Johnstone	W 3-0	1-0	1	Latapy [23], Moutinho [52], Duffy (pen) [81]	3395
24	29	A	Ross Co	W 1-0	1-0	1	Duffy (pen) [45]	3151
25	Feb 12	H	Hamilton A	D 1-1	1-1	1	Hughes [11]	3535
26	19	A	Queen of the S	D 1-1	0-1	1	Lawrie [55]	2551
27	Mar 5	H	Partick Th	W 2-1	2-1	1	McBreen [17], Duffy [27]	4157
28	12	A	Airdrie U	D 2-2	1-0	1	Duffy [2], James (pen) [84]	3111
29	15	H	Clyde	D 0-0	0-0	—		3834
30	19	A	Raith R	D 3-3	2-1	1	McBreen 2 [12, 69], Duffy [34]	2369
31	Apr 2	H	St Johnstone	W 3-0	1-0	1	McBreen [36], Latapy [51], Duffy [65]	3748
32	9	H	Ross Co	W 1-0	0-0	1	McStay [67]	5272
33	16	A	Clyde	W 1-0	1-0	1	Latapy (pen) [6]	2090
34	23	H	St Mirren	L 1-2	1-1	1	Duffy [41]	4342
35	30	A	Hamilton A	L 0-1	0-1	1		2300
36	May 7	H	Queen of the S	L 1-2	1-0	1	Lawrie [17]	5067

Final League Position: 1

Honours

League Champions: Division II 1935-36, 1969-70, 1974-75. First Division 1990-91, 1993-94, 2002-03, 2004-05. Second Division 1979-80; *Runners-up:* Division I 1907-08, 1909-10. First Division 1985-86, 1988-89. Division II 1904-05, 1951-52, 1960-61.
Scottish Cup Winners: 1913, 1957; *Runners-up:* 1997. *League Cup Runners-up:* 1947-48. *B&Q Cup Winners:* 1993-94. *League Challenge Cup Winners:* 1997-98, 2004-05.

Club colours: Shirt: Navy blue with white seams. Shorts: Navy. Stockings: Navy with two white hoops.

Goalscorers: *League* (66): Duffy 17 (4 pens), McBreen 13, Thomson 9 (1 pen), Latapy 7 (1 pen), Lawrie 4, Moutinho 4, Nicholls 3, Hughes 2, Campbell 1, James 1 (pen), McAnespie 1, Mackenzie 1, McStay 1, O'Neil 1, Scally 1.
Scottish Cup (0).
CIS Cup (11): Duffy 4, Thomson 4, Latapy 1, Mackenzie 1, O'Neil 1.
Challenge Cup (15): Duffy 6, Latapy 3, Lawrie 2, Nicholls 1, O'Neil 1, Scally 1, Thomson 1.

Hill D 10	Lawrie A 27 + 4	McPherson C 33	Mackenzie S 34	Campbell M 25 + 6	Sharp J 3 + 1	O'Neil J 30 + 2	Scally N 19 + 14	Thomson A 13 + 11	McStay R 10 + 5	Duffy D 35	McAnespie K — + 8	Moutinho P 12 + 7	Hughes J 17 + 2	James K 29	Nicholls D 12 + 6	Latapy R 31 + 1	Ferguson A 26	Rahim B — + 3	Marshall C — + 12	McBreen D 21 + 2	Kernaghan A 9	Barr D — + 2	Scobbie T — + 1	Henry J — + 1	Ramsay M — + 1	Match No.
1	2^{1}	3^{2}	4	5	6	7	8	9	10	11	12	13														1
1	2	3	7	4			13	9		11	12		5^{1}	6^{2}	8	10										2
1	2	3	4	5		7^{1}	12	9^{3}		11	13	14		6	8^{2}	10										3
1	2	3	4^{3}	5		7	14	9		11	12	13		6	8^{1}	10^{2}										4
1	2	3	4	5		7	12	9^{3}		11^{2}		13	14	6	8	10^{1}										5
1	2	3	4^{2}	5		7	13	9		11	12	14		6	8^{1}	10^{3}										6
1	2	3	4^{1}	5		7	12	9		11	13		14	6	8^{2}	10^{3}										7
	2	3	4	5		7^{1}	12	9		11	13			6	8^{2}	10	1									8
	2	3	4			7	12	9		11		10^{1}	5	6	8^{2}		1	13								9
	2	3	4			7				11		9	5	6	8	10	1									10
	2	3	4	5		7^{1}		9^{2}		11		12		6	8	10	1		13							11
	2	3	4	5		7^{1}	12	9^{2}		11				6	8	10	1			13						12
	2	3	4	5		7^{2}	6^{3}		12	11	14	8				10	1		13	9^{1}						13
	2	3	4^{3}	5		7^{2}	14			11^{1}		8	6		12	10	1		13	9						14
	2	3^{1}	4	5		7	12			11^{2}		8	6		13	10^{3}	1		14	9						15
	2		4	5^{1}		7	12	13		11^{2}		8^{3}	6		3	10	1		14	9						16
	2		4^{3}		3	7	10	12		11		8^{1}	5	6	14	13	1			9^{2}						17
	2			12	3	7	4	13		11		8^{3}	5^{1}	6	14	10	1			9^{2}						18
	2	3	4^{3}	5		7		12		11		8^{1}		6	13	10	1		14	9^{2}						19
	2	3	4	5		7	13	12		11^{2}		8^{1}		6		10	1			9						20
	2	3	4^{2}	5	13	7	12	8^{1}		11				6		10	1			9						21
	2	3	4^{2}	5		7^{1}	8	9^{3}		11		14		6	12	10	1		13							22
	2	3	4				8		7	11		9	5	6		10^{1}	1		12							23
1	2	3	4	13			7		14	11		9^{1}	5	6		10^{3}				12	8^{2}					24
1	2^{1}	3	4	6		12	7			11			5			10				9	8					25
1	2	3^{1}	4	6		12	7		13	11			5			10				9	8^{2}					26
		3	4	14		7	8	12	13	11^{3}			5	6		10^{2}	1			9^{1}	2					27
		3	4^{2}	12		7	8		2	11				6		10^{3}	1	14	13	9	5^{1}					28
		3	4^{1}			7^{3}	8	13	12	11			5	6		10	1		14	9^{2}	2					29
		3		4		7^{1}	8	13	2	11^{2}			5	6		10	1		12	9						30
		3	4	13		7^{1}	2		8^{3}	11			5^{2}	6		10	1		12	9		14				31
	13	3	4	12		7^{2}	2	14	8	11			5^{1}	6		10	1			9^{3}						32
	12	3	4	5		11^{1}	2	13	8					6		10	1			9^{2}	7					33
	13	3	4	5		7^{1}	2	12	8^{2}	11				6		10	1			9						34
	12	3	4^{2}	5^{3}		7^{1}	10		8	11				6			1	13		9	2		14			35
	2	3	4^{1}	5^{2}			10		8	11^{3}				6			1			9	7	13		12	14	36

FORFAR ATHLETIC Second Division

Year Formed: 1885. *Ground & Address:* Station Park, Carseview Road, Forfar. *Telephone:* 01307 463576/462259. *Fax:* 01307 466956. *E-mail:* pat@ramsayladders.co.uk. *Website:* www.forfarathletic.co.uk.
Ground Capacity: total: 5177, seated: 739. *Size of Pitch:* 115yd × 69yd.
Chairman and Secretary: David McGregor.
Manager: Brian Fairley. *Assistant Manager:* Allan McGonigal. *Coach:* Allan Fraser. *Physio:* Brian McNeil.
Managers since 1975: Jerry Kerr, Archie Knox, Alex Rae, Doug Houston, Henry Hall, Bobby Glennie, Paul Hegarty, Tommy Campbell, Ian McPhee, Neil Cooper, R. Stewart.
Club Nickname(s): Loons. *Previous Grounds:* None.
Record Attendance: 10,780 v Rangers, Scottish Cup 2nd rd, 2 Feb 1970.
Record Transfer Fee received: £65,000 for David Bingham to Dunfermline Ath (September 1995).
Record Transfer Fee paid: £50,000 for Ian McPhee from Airdrieonians (1991).
Record Victory: 14-1 v Lindertis, Scottish Cup 1st rd, 1 Sept 1988.
Record Defeat: 2-12 v King's Park, Division II, 2 Jan 1930.
Most League Appearances: 484: Ian McPhee, 1978-88 and 1991-98.
Most League Goals in Season (Individual): 45: Dave Kilgour, Division II, 1929-30.
Most Goals Overall (Individual): 124, John Clark.

FORFAR ATHLETIC 2004–05 LEAGUE RECORD

Match No.	*Date*	*Venue*	*Opponents*	*Result*		*H/T Score*	*Lg. Pos.*	*Goalscorers*	*Attendance*
1	Aug 7	H	Brechin C	W	1-0	1-0	—	Sellars [43]	766
2	14	A	Alloa Ath	W	3-2	0-0	3	Tosh 2 (1 pen) [48 (p), 81], Stein [84]	446
3	21	H	Arbroath	W	5-0	1-0	2	Shields 2 [33, 47], Stein [61], Tosh [67], King D [77]	696
4	28	A	Dumbarton	W	1-0	0-0	2	Tosh [54]	723
5	Sept 4	H	Stirling A	L	0-2	0-0	2		841
6	11	A	Ayr U	D	3-3	2-2	3	Tosh 2 [24, 25], Sellars [54]	1386
7	18	H	Berwick R	D	1-1	1-0	3	Shields [3]	435
8	25	H	Stranraer	L	0-1	0-0	4		524
9	Oct 2	A	Morton	L	1-2	1-0	5	Shields [41]	2736
10	16	H	Alloa Ath	W	3-1	2-0	4	McClune [26], Shields [44], Tosh [50]	411
11	23	A	Brechin C	L	0-2	0-1	5		869
12	30	H	Dumbarton	L	0-2	0-0	6		486
13	Nov 6	A	Stirling A	L	1-3	0-1	7	Tosh [89]	756
14	13	H	Ayr U	L	2-3	2-1	7	Rattray [10], King M [25]	518
15	30	A	Berwick R	L	0-1	0-0	—		294
16	Dec 4	A	Stranraer	L	0-1	0-0	7		411
17	27	H	Brechin C	L	1-3	1-1	8	Tosh [40]	901
18	Jan 1	A	Arbroath	W	2-0	1-0	7	Stein [27], Shields [61]	825
19	3	A	Dumbarton	D	1-1	0-0	—	Tosh [57]	714
20	15	H	Stirling A	W	4-1	2-0	7	Shields 3 [25, 32, 50], Tosh [64]	501
21	29	H	Berwick R	L	0-2	0-2	7		435
22	Feb 5	H	Stranraer	L	1-2	0-2	7	Sellars [57]	453
23	12	A	Morton	L	0-4	0-3	9		2244
24	19	H	Arbroath	D	1-1	1-0	9	Shields [19]	758
25	26	A	Alloa Ath	W	2-0	1-0	9	McClune 2 [44, 56]	516
26	Mar 5	A	Stirling A	L	2-3	1-2	9	Tosh [16], Shields [84]	537
27	8	H	Morton	W	2-0	1-0	—	Waddell [12], Shields [58]	555
28	12	H	Dumbarton	W	6-0	2-0	7	Shields 3 [41, 53, 57], King M [51], McClune [64], Tosh [72]	443
29	19	H	Ayr U	W	1-0	0-0	5	Shields (pen) [69]	490
30	26	A	Ayr U	L	0-1	0-1	7		1076
31	Apr 2	A	Berwick R	D	1-1	1-0	6	Shields [13]	369
32	9	H	Morton	D	0-0	0-0	6		1064
33	16	A	Stranraer	D	0-0	0-0	5		456
34	23	A	Arbroath	W	2-1	2-1	5	Shields 2 [33, 44]	697
35	30	H	Alloa Ath	D	1-1	1-1	5	Stein [45]	453
36	May 7	A	Brechin C	W	3-0	0-0	5	King M [55], McClune [58], Shields [66]	1074

Final League Position: 5

Honours
League Champions: Second Division 1983-84. Third Division 1994-95; *Runners-up:* 1996-97. C Division 1948-49.
Scottish Cup: Semi-finals 1982.
League Cup: Semi-finals 1977-78.
Bell's League Challenge: Semi-finals 2004-05.

Club colours: Shirt: Navy with sky blue side panels. Shorts: Sky blue with navy side panels. Stockings: Sky blue with navy tops.

Goalscorers: *League* (51): Shields 20 (1 pen), Tosh 13 (1 pen), McClune 5, Stein 4, King M 3, Sellars 3, King D 1, Rattray 1, Waddell 1.
Scottish Cup (1): Tosh 1.
CIS Cup (4): Tosh 2, McClune 1, Sellars 1, own goal 1.
Challenge Cup (9): Shields 4, Tosh 3, Booth 1, McClune 1.

Brown M 27	Rattray A 17	Lowing D 31	Forrest E 34	King D 16	McClune D 34 + 1	Sellars B 25	Lunan P 33 + 3	Tosh P 28 + 2	Shields P 33 + 3	Stein J 23 + 8	Booth M 11 + 7	King M 9 + 17	Maher M — + 11	Cameron D 1 + 4	Clark N — + 5	Ferrie N 4	Creer A 5	Davidson H 11 + 7	Florence S 7 + 5	Dunn D 17 + 1	Bonar S 14	Waddell R 14 + 1	McAlpine J 1 + 1	McKenzie D 1 + 1	*Match No.*
1	2	3	4	5	6	7	8	9	10	11															1
1[2]	2	3	4	5	6	7	8	9	10	12	11[1]	13													2
1	2	3	4	5	6	7[3]	8[1]	9[2]	10	11	12	13	14												3
1	2	3	4	5	6	7[1]	8	9	10[2]	11	12	13													4
1	2	3	4	5	6		8[2]	9	10	11[3]	7[1]	13		12	14										5
1	2[1]	3	4	5	6	7[2]	12	9	10	11	8	13													6
	2	3	4	5	6		8	9	10[1]	11	7[2]			12	13	1									7
	2	3[2]	4	5	6		7[3]	9	10	11	14		12	8[1]	13	1									8
	2	3	4	5	8	7	12	9	10[2]	11	6[1]	13				1									9
	2	3	4	5	6[1]		7	9[3]	10	11	12		13		14		1	8[2]							10
	2	3	4	5	6		7	9	10	11			12				1	8[1]							11
	2[3]		4	5	6		7	9	10[2]	11	12	13	14				1	8[1]	3						12
	2	5[2]	4		6[1]	7	8	9	13	11			12	14			1	10[3]	3						13
	2	3	4				7	9	10	11	5	8	12				1	6[1]							14
1	2[2]	3	4	5	6	7	8		10	9	11[1]			13	12										15
1	2	3	5		4	7	8	9	12	11	6	10[1]													16
1	2[1]	3	4		8	6	13	9	10	11[3]		14						7[2]	12	5					17
1		3	4		8[1]	6	7	9[2]	10	11	2	12	13							5					18
1		3	4		8[3]	6	7	9	10[2]	11[1]	2	13	14					12		5					19
1		3	4		12	6	7[1]	9	10	11			13					8[2]		5	2				20
1		3	4	5	8	6	2	9[3]	10	11[2]		14	12					7[1]		13					21
1		3	4	5	8[2]	6	7[1]	9	10									13	12		2	11[3]	14		22
1		3	4	5	8	6	2	9	10[2]			12							13			11	7[1]		23
1		3	4		8	6	2	9	10		7									5		11			24
1		3	4		8	6	7[1]	9[2]	10			13							12	5	2	11			25
1			4		8	6	7	9	10	12		13							3[1]	5	2	11[2]			26
1		3	4		8	6	7[2]		10	12		9[1]						13		5	2	11			27
1			4		8[3]	6	7	12	10[1]	13		9						14	3	5	2	11[2]			28
1		4			8		7		10	13	12	9[2]						6[1]	3	5	2	11			29
1		3	4		8[3]	6	7[2]		10	12	13	9[1]						14		5	2	11			30
1		3	4		8	6[1]	7	9[2]	10			13							12	5	2	11			31
1		3	4		8		7	9	10	6[1]		12								5	2	11			32
1		3	4		8		7	12	10	6[1]		9[2]						13		5	2	11			33
1		3	4		8		7	9[1]	10[2]	13		12						6		5	2	11			34
					8[1]	6	7		12	11[2]		9				1		10	3	5	2	13		4	35
1			4		8	6[1]	7[3]		10	13		9[2]						12	3	5	2	11		14	36

GRETNA — Second Division

Year Formed: 1946. *Ground & Address:* Raydale Park, Dominion Rd, Gretna DG16 5AP. *Telephone:* 01461 337602. *Fax:* 01461 338047. *E-mail:* info@gretnafootballclub.co.uk.
Ground Capacity: 2200.
Club Shop: Alan Watson, 01387 251550.
President: Brian Fulton. *Chairman:* Ron MacGregor. *Secretary:* Helen MacGregor. *Managing Director:* Brookes Mileson. *General Manager:* Colin Carter.
Manager: Rowan Alexander. *Assistant Manager:* David Irons. *Coaches:* Danny Lennon, Leigh Manson. *Physios:* William Bentley & Gael Moffat.
Record Attendance: 3000 v Dundee U, Scottish Cup, 17 Jan 2005.
Record Victory: 20-0 v Silloth, 1962.
Record Defeat: 0-6 v Worksop Town, 1994-95 and 0-6 v Bradford (Park Avenue) 1999-2000.
Most League Appearances: 88, David Irons, 2002-05.
Most League Goals in Season (Individual): 17, M. Cameron, 2003-04.
Most Goals Overall (Individual): 17, M. Cameron, 2003-04.

GRETNA 2004–05 LEAGUE RECORD

Match No.	Date	Venue	Opponents	Result	H/T Score	Lg. Pos.	Goalscorers	Attendance
1	Aug 7	H	Albion R	W 6-0	2-0	—	Bingham 2 [22, 25], Galloway [60], Smith [72], Cosgrove [86], Deuchar [90]	646
2	14	A	East Stirling	W 2-1	2-1	1	Aitken [34], Townsley [41]	276
3	21	H	Montrose	W 1-0	0-0	1	Skelton [46]	501
4	28	A	Queen's Park	L 2-3	0-0	2	Baldacchino [48], Bingham [82]	496
5	Sept 4	H	Cowdenbeath	W 2-1	1-0	2	Smith [41], Bingham [63]	568
6	11	A	Peterhead	D 1-1	0-1	2	Gilfillan [90]	861
7	18	H	East Fife	W 5-1	1-1	2	Bingham [2], Deuchar 3 [51, 68, 71], Lumsden (og) [63]	457
8	25	H	Elgin C	W 3-0	2-0	2	Bingham 2 [21, 40], Deuchar [52]	574
9	Oct 2	A	Stenhousemuir	W 3-0	1-0	2	Deuchar [23], Bingham 2 [53, 82]	343
10	16	H	East Stirling	W 8-1	4-1	2	Birch [28], Gilfillan [30], Deuchar 3 [39, 41, 61], Skelton [54], Wake [82], Baldacchino [90]	468
11	23	A	Albion R	W 6-2	1-0	2	Bingham 2 [32, 71], McQuilken [51], Birch [59], Skelton [67], Wake [83]	326
12	30	H	Queen's Park	W 4-1	3-0	2	McGuffie [22], Deuchar [27], Skelton [32], Wake [88]	706
13	Nov 6	A	Cowdenbeath	W 8-0	6-0	2	McGuffie [12], Birch 3 (1 pen) [20, 24 (p), 28], Baldacchino [30], Bingham 2 [36, 53], Deuchar [86]	322
14	13	H	Peterhead	W 2-1	1-1	1	Bingham 2 [17, 87]	2200
15	20	H	Albion R	W 6-2	2-1	1	Gilfillan [17], Deuchar 5 [21, 47, 53, 82, 87]	627
16	27	A	East Fife	W 3-1	2-1	1	Deuchar [18], Baldacchino [35], Gilfillan [83]	551
17	Dec 4	A	Elgin C	W 3-1	2-0	1	Bingham [1], Deuchar 2 [32, 52]	505
18	18	H	Stenhousemuir	W 3-0	2-0	1	Bingham [4], McGuffie [36], Gilfillan [73]	1078
19	Jan 1	A	Montrose	W 3-2	3-2	1	Deuchar 2 [19, 24], Baldacchino [32]	592
20	3	A	Queen's Park	D 1-1	1-1	—	Bingham [22]	803
21	15	H	Cowdenbeath	W 2-0	2-0	1	Deuchar [3], Skelton [25]	738
22	22	A	Peterhead	L 2-4	0-0	1	Birch (pen) [46], McGuffie [90]	1207
23	29	H	East Fife	W 4-0	2-0	1	Deuchar 3 [2, 9, 85], Innes [78]	828
24	Feb 5	H	Elgin C	W 2-1	1-1	1	Bingham [34], Townsley [90]	809
25	12	A	Stenhousemuir	W 4-1	1-1	1	Townsley [11], Deuchar 3 [61, 79, 80]	416
26	19	H	Montrose	W 4-1	1-1	1	Skelton [45], Deuchar 2 [56, 72], Birch (pen) [59]	913
27	Mar 5	A	Cowdenbeath	W 1-0	1-0	1	Tosh [30]	339
28	8	A	East Stirling	W 4-0	2-0	—	Bingham [9], McQuilken [11], Nicholls [68], Baldacchino [71]	185
29	12	H	Queen's Park	W 4-0	3-0	1	Skelton 2 [13, 46], Bingham 2 [24, 26]	978
30	19	H	Peterhead	W 6-1	1-0	1	Deuchar 3 [3, 87, 90], McGuffie 2 [61, 67], Bingham [62]	1538
31	Apr 2	A	East Fife	W 2-0	1-0	1	Innes [24], Skelton [60]	723
32	9	H	Stenhousemuir	W 7-0	3-0	1	Aitken [30], Skelton [34], Deuchar 2 [39, 59], Bingham [61], Gilfillan [66], Smith [82]	908
33	16	A	Elgin C	W 6-2	3-1	1	Deuchar [5], Bingham 3 [24, 46, 50], Skelton [45], Townsley [75]	503
34	23	A	Montrose	W 4-0	1-0	1	Townsley [33], Nicholls [55], Deuchar 2 [83, 88]	462
35	30	H	East Stirling	W 1-0	1-0	1	Baldacchino [15]	1585
36	May 7	A	Albion R	W 5-0	2-0	1	McGuffie 2 [23, 75], Skelton [39], Baldacchino 2 [55, 63]	519

Final League Position: 1

Honours
League Champions: Third Division 2004–05.
Bell's League Challenge: Quarter-finals 2004-05.

Club colours: Shirt: White with black detail. Shorts: White. Stockings: White topped with black hoops.

Goalscorers: *League* (130): Deuchar 38, Bingham 27, Skelton 12, Baldacchino 9, McGuffie 8, Birch 7 (3 pens), Gilfillan 6, Townsley 5, Smith 3, Wake 3, Aitken 2, Innes 2, McQuilken 2, Nicholls 2, Cosgrove 1, Galloway 1, Tosh 1, own goal 1.
Scottish Cup (6): Deuchar 3, Birch 1 (1 pen), Skelton 1, own goal 1.
CIS Cup (0).
Challenge Cup (4): Smith 2, Baldacchino 1, Bingham 1.

Mathieson D 32	Birch M 29 + 1	Skelton G 35	Prokas R 5 + 1	Aitken A 34	Holdsworth D 4 + 1	Baldacchino R 29	Galloway M 4 + 2	Smith A 6 + 6	Bingham D 36	Townsley D 9 + 11	Deuchar K 30 + 6	McGuffie R 30 + 6	Cosgrove S — + 6	Gilfillan B 21 + 5	Boyd M 1 + 1	McQuilken J 29 + 3	Lennon D 2 + 1	Irons D 19 + 1	Gordon W 1	Wake B — + 6	Nicholls D 3 + 9	Tosh S 13	Innes C 11	Graham D — + 11	Collins D 7	Shields D — + 3	Main A 4	Grainger D 2 + 1	Match No.
1	2	3	4^{2}	5	6	7	8	9^{1}	10	11^{3}	12	13	14																1
1	2	3	4	5	6	7	8	9^{2}	10	11^{1}	13	12																	2
1	2	3	4	5	6	7	8	9^{2}	10^{3}	11^{1}	13	12		14															3
1	2	3	4^{3}	5	6^{2}	7	8	9	10		14	13			11^{1}	12													4
1	2		14	5		7	13	9^{1}	10		12	8				3	4^{2}	6	11^{3}										5
1	2	11^{1}		5		7	13	9^{3}	10		12	8		14		3	4^{2}	6											6
1	2	11		5		7			10		9^{1}	8^{3}	14	4^{2}	13	3		6		12									7
1	2	11^{1}		5		7			10		9	8	13	4^{2}		3		6		12									8
1	2	11		5		7			10^{1}		9	8		4		3		6		12									9
1	2	11		5^{3}		7			10	14	9^{1}	8	13	4^{2}		3		6		12									10
1	2	11		5		7			10^{2}		9	8		4^{1}		3	12	6		13									11
1	2	11		5		7^{2}			10^{1}	13	9	8		4		3		6		12									12
1	2	11		5		7^{1}			10	12	9	8		4		3		6											13
1	2	11		5		7			10	12	9	8		4^{1}		3		6											14
1	2	11		5		7			10	12	9	8^{1}		4		3		6											15
1	2	11		5		7			10		9	8		4		3		6											16
1	2	11		5	12	7^{2}		14	10^{3}		9	8	13	4		3^{1}		6											17
1	2^{1}	11		5		7			10	12	9	8		4		3		6											18
1	2	11		5		7^{1}			10	12	9	8		4		3		6											19
1	2	11		5					10	7^{1}	9	8	12	4		3		6											20
1	2	11		5				12	10		9^{1}	8		4		3		6			7								21
1	2^{1}	11		5				12	10		9	8		4^{2}		3		6			13	7							22
1	2^{1}	11		5					10	14	9^{2}	8		4		3					13	7	6^{3}	12					23
1		11	4^{1}	5					10	6	9^{2}	8				3						7		12	2	13			24
1	2	11		5				14	10^{2}	6	9^{3}	8		4^{1}		3					12	7		13					25
1	2	11		5					10	6	9^{3}	8^{2}		4		3					12	7^{1}		13		14			26
1	2	11		5		7^{1}			10		9^{3}	8^{2}		13		3						4	6	14		12			27
1		11		5		7			10^{3}		9^{2}	14		8^{1}		3					12	4	6	13	2				28
1		11				7			10		9^{1}	8^{2}				3		6			13	4	5	12	2				29
1		11		5		7			10^{1}		9	8^{2}		14		3					13	4^{3}	6	12	2				30
1		11		5		7			10^{1}	14	9	8				3^{2}					13	4	6	12	2^{3}				31
1	12	11		5		7		14	10		9	8		13		3^{3}						4^{2}	6		2^{1}				32
	2	11		5^{2}		7			10	13	9^{1}	14									8^{3}	4	6	12			1	3	33
	2	11		5^{1}		7^{3}			10	12	9	8				3^{2}					4		6	14			1	13	34
	2	11		3^{2}		7			10	5	9	8				13					12	4^{1}	6				1		35
		11				7		13	10	5	9^{2}	8		4^{1}		14		12					6		2		1	3^{3}	36

HAMILTON ACADEMICAL First Division

Year Formed: 1874. *Ground:* New Douglas Park, Cadzow Avenue, Hamilton ML3 0FT. *Telephone:* 01698 368650. *Fax:* 01698 285422. *Ground Capacity:* 5396. *Size of Pitch:* 115yd × 75yd.
Chairman: Ronnie MacDonald. *Chief Executive:* George W. Fairley. *Secretary:* Scott A. Struthers BA. *Commercial Director:* Arthur Lynch.
Manager: Allan Maitland. *Assistant Manager:* Denis McDaid. *First Team Coach:* Jimmy McQuade. *Coach:* James Ward. *Physio:* Michael Valentine.
Managers since 1975: J. Eric Smith, Dave McParland, John Blackley, Bertie Auld, John Lambie, Jim Dempsey, John Lambie, Billy McLaren, Iain Munro, Sandy Clark, Colin Miller, Ally Dawson, Chris Hillcoat.
Club Nickname(s): The Accies. *Previous Grounds:* Bent Farm, South Avenue, South Haugh, Douglas Park, Cliftonhill Stadium, Firhill Stadium.
Record Attendance: 28,690 v Hearts, Scottish Cup 3rd rd, 3 Mar 1937.
Record Transfer Fee received: £380,000 for Paul Hartley to Millwall (July 1996).
Record Transfer Fee paid: £60,000 for Paul Martin from Kilmarnock (Oct 1988) and for John McQuade from Dumbarton (Aug 1993).
Record Victory: 11-1 v Chryston, Lanarkshire Cup, 28 Nov 1885.
Record Defeat: 1-11 v Hibernian, Division I, 6 Nov 1965.
Most Capped Player: Colin Miller, 29, Canada, 1988-94.

HAMILTON ACADEMICAL 2004–05 LEAGUE RECORD

Match No.	Date	Venue	Opponents	Result		H/T Score	Lg. Pos.	Goalscorers	Attendance
1	Aug 7	H	Raith R	W	2-0	0-0	80	McLaughlin [77], Smart (og) [80]	2176
2	14	A	Falkirk	D	1-1	1-0	2	Carrigan (pen) [37]	3423
3	21	H	Partick Th	L	0-1	0-1	4		3543
4	28	A	St Mirren	L	0-1	0-1	5		2987
5	Sept 4	H	St Johnstone	D	1-1	0-0	7	Corcoran [46]	1904
6	11	A	Queen of the S	D	1-1	1-0	9	Lumsden [17]	1708
7	18	H	Clyde	L	0-1	0-1	9		2017
8	25	H	Ross Co	L	1-2	1-1	9	Tunbridge [9]	1522
9	Oct 2	A	Airdrie U	W	2-0	0-0	8	McLaughlin [69], Tunbridge [90]	1900
10	16	H	Falkirk	L	0-1	0-0	9		2870
11	23	A	Raith R	D	2-2	1-1	9	Carrigan 2 [6, 50]	1943
12	30	H	St Mirren	D	2-2	1-1	9	Carrigan [15], Tunbridge [57]	2529
13	Nov 6	A	St Johnstone	L	0-3	0-1	9		1869
14	13	H	Queen of the S	W	1-0	0-0	9	Thomson [88]	1592
15	20	A	Clyde	L	1-2	1-1	9	Tunbridge [29]	1408
16	27	H	Airdrie U	L	1-3	1-2	9	McPhee [11]	2295
17	Dec 4	A	Ross Co	D	1-1	0-0	9	Tunbridge [62]	2034
18	11	H	Raith R	W	1-0	0-0	8	McPhee [86]	1371
19	18	A	Partick Th	W	1-0	1-0	7	McPhee [13]	3051
20	26	A	St Mirren	W	1-0	0-0	7	Van Zanten (og) [68]	2888
21	29	H	St Johnstone	L	0-3	0-2	—		1718
22	Jan 1	A	Queen of the S	W	2-1	1-0	7	Corcoran [31], McLeod [48]	1790
23	15	H	Clyde	L	0-1	0-0	8		1873
24	22	H	Ross Co	L	0-1	0-0	8		1476
25	Feb 12	A	Falkirk	D	1-1	1-1	9	Javary [1]	3535
26	19	H	Partick Th	W	1-0	0-0	8	Keogh [70]	3128
27	Mar 5	A	St Johnstone	W	2-0	1-0	8	Corcoran [44], Cramb [72]	1772
28	8	A	Airdrie U	L	0-1	0-0	—		xxx
29	12	H	St Mirren	D	0-0	0-0	8		1950
30	19	H	Queen of the S	D	1-1	0-1	8	Cramb (pen) [80]	1560
31	Apr 2	A	Clyde	W	3-1	0-0	8	Keogh 2 [53, 68], Hardy [55]	1240
32	9	H	Airdrie U	D	1-1	1-1	8	Hardy (pen) [41]	2030
33	16	A	Ross Co	L	1-2	0-1	8	Convery [89]	2107
34	23	A	Raith R	W	2-0	2-0	8	Keogh [3], Hamilton [23]	1474
35	30	H	Falkirk	W	1-0	1-0	7	Convery [31]	2300
36	May 7	A	Partick Th	D	1-1	0-1	7	Hardy [60]	2845

Final League Position: 7

Most League Appearances: 452: Rikki Ferguson, 1974-88.
Most League Goals in Season (Individual): 35: David Wilson, Division I; 1936-37.
Most Goals Overall (Individual): 246: David Wilson, 1928-39.

Honours
League Champions: First Division 1985-86, 1987-88; Third Division 2000-01. *Runners-up:* Division II 1903-04, 1952-53, 1964-65; Second Division 1996-97, 2003-04.
Scottish Cup Runners-up: 1911, 1935. *League Cup:* Semi-finalists three times.
B&Q Cup Winners: 1991-92, 1992-93.

Club colours: Shirt: Red and white hoops. Shorts: White. Stockings: White.

Goalscorers: *League* (35): Tunbridge 5, Carrigan 4 (1 pen), Keogh 4, Corcoran 3, Hardy 3 (1 pen), McPhee 3, Convery 2, Cramb 2 (1 pen), McLaughlin 2, Hamilton 1, Javary 1, Lumsden 1, McLeod 1, Thomson 1, own goals 2.
Scottish Cup (0).
CIS Cup (4): Convery 3, Thomson 1.
Challenge Cup (0).

McEwan D 35	Walker R 6+1	Waddell R 16+3	Thomson S 30+1	McLaughlin M 29	Tunbridge S 18+2	Carrigan B 16+11	Aitken C 9+8	Blackadder R 7+4	McPhee B 18+10	Corcoran M 30+4	Hamilton D 15+10	Keogh P 23+3	Convery S 4+8	Hodge A 30+2	Ferguson D 16+1	Fyfe I 13+5	Lumsden T 11+3	Arbuckle A 3+5	Halliday R 1	McGlinchey K —+1	Carney D 6+2	Irons S —+2	McLeod P —+2	Javary J 11+2	Cramb C 7+3	Hardy L 12+1	McArthur J 5+1	Ortiz F 12	MahouvÇ M 12	Jellema R 1	*Match No.*
1	2	3	4	5	6	7^{3}	8	9^{1}	10	11^{2}	12	13	14																		1
1	2	11	4	5	6	7^{2}	8^{1}			13	12	9	14	3	10^{3}																2
1	2	3	4	5	6^{1}	7^{2}	8	12		11	10	9	13																		3
1	2^{1}	3	4	5		7^{3}	13	8^{2}	10	11	6	9	12			14															4
1		12	4	5	3^{1}		14	8	10	11	6^{2}	9^{3}			7	13	2														5
1		3	4		14	12	13	8	10^{1}	11	6^{3}	9		5	7^{2}		2														6
1		3	4		12	13	14	8	10	11	6^{1}	9		5	7^{3}		2^{2}														7
1		14	4		2	7	13	6^{2}	10	11		9		3	5^{1}	8^{3}		12													8
1		8	4	5	2			13	10	11		9	12	3		6^{2}			7^{1}												9
1		9	4	5	2	7	8		12	11^{1}	6^{3}			3		10^{2}	14	13													10
1		9	4	5	2^{2}	7	8	14	13	11	6			12		10^{3}	3^{1}														11
1		3	4	5	9	7	8^{2}	13	10	11				12		6	2^{1}														12
1		6	4	5	9	7	14	8^{3}	10^{2}	11				3		2^{1}		12		13											13
1	14	8	4	5	9	7			11^{3}	13			10^{2}	3		12		2			6^{1}										14
1		8	4	5	9	7			11	12			10^{1}	3		13		2			6^{2}										15
1		10	4	5	6	7			9	11				3		12		2^{1}			8										16
1		10	4	5	7		8		9^{2}	11				3	6^{1}	2		12				13									17
1		6	4	5	7	13	8^{2}		9	11	14	12		3	10^{3}	2^{1}															18
1			4	5	10^{1}	12			8	11	6	9		3	7	2															19
1			4	5	10	12	14		8^{2}	11^{3}	6^{1}	9		3	7	2					13										20
1			4	5^{1}	10	8	13			11	6	9		3^{2}	7^{3}	2	12				14										21
1	5	14	4				8^{2}			11	6	9	7^{1}	3		2		13			10		12^{3}								22
1	5		4			12			8^{2}	11		10		3		2					7^{1}	13		6	9						23
1			4			7^{2}			13	11	6^{1}	2		5			14				3			8^{3}	9	10	12				24
1			4	5		7^{1}			12	11	13	9^{2}		3										6		8		2	10		25
1			4	5		7^{1}				12		13		3	8									6	9^{2}	11		2	10		26
1			4	5		13				11	14	9^{1}		3	7^{3}									6	12	8^{2}		2	10		27
1			4	5		13			14	11	12			3	7									6^{1}	9^{2}	8^{3}		2	10		28
1			4	5		13				11^{2}	14	9^{1}		3	7									6^{3}	12	8		2	10		29
1			4^{1}	5					13	11	14	9		3	7^{3}									6^{2}	8	12		2	10		30
1				5		13			14	11^{3}	12	9^{2}		3			4							6^{1}		8	7	2	10		31
1				5					12	11^{2}		9	13	3			4^{1}							6		8	7	2	10		32
1				5						11	12	9	13	3	14		4							6^{2}		8^{1}	7	2	10^{3}		33
1									12	11	6	9^{1}	14	5	7		4							13	8^{3}	3		2	10^{2}		34
1				5		13			12		6		9^{2}	3			4							14	8^{1}	11	7^{3}	2	10		35
			12	5					8^{3}		6	9		3			4^{2}						14		13	11	7	2^{1}	10	1	36

HEART OF MIDLOTHIAN Premier League

Year Formed: 1874. *Ground & Address:* Tynecastle Stadium, Gorgie Rd, Edinburgh EH11 2NL. *Telephone:* 0131 200 7200. *Fax:* 0131 200 7222. *Website:* www.heartsfc.co.uk
Ground Capacity: 17,412. *Size of Pitch:* 100m × 64m.
Chairman: Lord George Foulkes. *Chief Executive:* Phil Anderton.
Head Coach: George Burley. *Assistant Head Coach:* John McGlynn. *Physio:* Alan Rae.
Managers since 1975: J. Hagart, W. Ormond, R. Moncur, T. Ford, A. MacDonald, A. MacDonald & W. Jardine, A. MacDonald, J. Jordan, S. Clark, T. McLean, J. Jefferies, C. Levein, J. Robertson.
Club Nickname(s): Hearts, Jambo's. *Previous Grounds:* The Meadows 1874, Powderhall 1878, Old Tynecastle 1881, (Tynecastle Park, 1886).
Record Attendance: 53,396 v Rangers, Scottish Cup 3rd rd, 13 Feb 1932.
Record Transfer Fee received: £2,100,000 for Alan McLaren from Rangers (October 1994).
Record of Transfer paid: £750,000 for Derek Ferguson to Rangers (July 1990).
Record Victory: 21-0 v Anchor, EFA Cup, 30 Oct 1880.
Record Defeat: 1-8 v Vale of Leven, Scottish Cup, 1888.
Most Capped Player: Bobby Walker, 29, Scotland.
Most League Appearances: 515: Gary Mackay, 1980-97.
Most League Goals in Season (Individual): 44: Barney Battles.
Most Goals Overall (Individual): 214: John Robertson, 1983-98.

HEART OF MIDLOTHIAN 2004–05 LEAGUE RECORD

Match No.	Date	Venue	Opponents	Result		H/T Score	Lg. Pos.	Goalscorers	Attendance
1	Aug 7	A	Dundee	W	1-0	0-0	—	Pressley (pen) 83	7770
2	14	H	Aberdeen	D	0-0	0-0	3		13,864
3	21	H	Kilmarnock	W	3-0	1-0	3	Weir 18, Pereira 57, Pressley (pen) 69	11,403
4	28	A	Motherwell	L	0-2	0-0	4		7095
5	Sept 12	H	Rangers	D	0-0	0-0	5		14,601
6	19	A	Dunfermline Ath	L	0-1	0-0	6		5883
7	25	H	Inverness CT	W	1-0	1-0	6	Hartley 16	10,340
8	Oct 3	H	Livingston	D	0-0	0-0	5		10,646
9	16	A	Celtic	L	0-3	0-1	6		59,242
10	24	H	Hibernian	W	2-1	1-0	5	Kisnorbo 14, Hamill 76	16,720
11	27	A	Dundee U	D	1-1	1-0	—	McKenna 5	5723
12	30	H	Dundee	W	3-0	1-0	4	McKenna 34, Hartley 81, Wyness 90	10,172
13	Nov 7	A	Aberdeen	W	1-0	0-0	3	Hartley (pen) 62	13,055
14	13	A	Kilmarnock	D	1-1	0-1	4	Wyness 68	6129
15	20	H	Motherwell	L	0-1	0-1	5		10,598
16	28	A	Rangers	L	2-3	1-1	6	Hartley (pen) 15, De Vries 66	48,494
17	Dec 4	H	Dunfermline Ath	W	3-0	1-0	5	Wyness 11, Pereira 47, Hartley (pen) 50	10,084
18	11	A	Inverness CT	D	1-1	0-0	5	Hartley (pen) 62	2011
19	26	H	Celtic	L	0-2	0-1	6		16,163
20	Jan 2	A	Hibernian	D	1-1	0-1	6	Hartley 54	17,259
21	15	H	Dundee U	W	3-2	1-1	5	Pressley 44, Miller 48, Hartley 85	10,305
22	22	A	Dundee	D	1-1	0-0	5	Hamill 60	5780
23	25	A	Livingston	W	2-1	0-0	—	Hartley 84, Miller 86	3816
24	29	H	Aberdeen	W	1-0	0-0	4	Wyness (pen) 63	12,269
25	Feb 12	H	Kilmarnock	W	3-0	2-0	4	Mikoliunas 14, Combee (og) 24, Miller 66	9220
26	19	A	Motherwell	L	0-2	0-2	4		7390
27	Mar 2	H	Rangers	L	1-2	0-0	—	Burchill 86	13,842
28	5	A	Dunfermline Ath	D	1-1	0-1	5	Hartley (pen) 60	5935
29	12	H	Inverness CT	L	0-2	0-0	5		9822
30	19	H	Livingston	W	3-1	1-1	5	Miller 22, Burchill 66, Neilson 68	9187
31	Apr 2	A	Celtic	W	2-0	2-0	5	Miller 8, Burchill 19	59,551
32	13	H	Hibernian	L	1-2	1-0	—	Miller 39	17,673
33	16	A	Dundee U	L	1-2	1-1	5	Miller 38	7704
34	23	A	Hibernian	D	2-2	1-1	5	Miller 23, Webster 88	16,620
35	30	H	Motherwell	D	0-0	0-0	5		9337
36	May 7	A	Rangers	L	1-2	0-2	5	Andrews (og) 81	49,342
37	15	H	Celtic	L	1-2	0-1	5	Hartley 71	16,163
38	22	A	Aberdeen	L	0-2	0-1	5		16,155

Final League Position: 5

Honours
League Champions: Division I 1894-95, 1896-97, 1957-58, 1959-60. First Division 1979-80; *Runners-up:* Division I 1893-94, 1898-99, 1903-04, 1905-06, 1914-15, 1937-38, 1953-54, 1956-57, 1958-59, 1964-65. Premier Division 1985-86, 1987-88, 1991-92. First Division 1977-78, 1982-83.
Scottish Cup Winners: 1891, 1896, 1901, 1906, 1956, 1998; *Runners-up:* 1903, 1907, 1968, 1976, 1986, 1996.
League Cup Winners: 1954-55, 1958-59, 1959-60, 1962-63; *Runners-up:* 1961-62, 1996-97.

European: *European Cup:* 4 matches (1958-59, 1960-61). *Cup Winners' Cup:* 10 matches (1976-77, 1996-97, 1998-99). *UEFA Cup:* 45 matches (*Fairs Cup:* 1961-62, 1963-64, 1965-66. *UEFA Cup:* 1984-85, 1986-87, 1988-89, 1990-91, 1992-93, 1993-94, 2000-01, 2003-04, 2004-05).

Club colours: Shirt: Maroon. Shorts: White. Stockings: Maroon.

Goalscorers: *League* (43): Hartley 11 (5 pens), Miller 8, Wyness 4 (1 pen), Burchill 3, Pereira 2, Hamill 2, McKenna 2, Pressley 3 (2 pens), De Vries 1, Kisnorbo 1, Mikoliunas 1, Neilson 1, Webster 1, Weir 1, own goals 2.
Scottish Cup (10): Miller 3, Cesnauskis 2, Wyness 2, McAllister 1, MacFarlane 1, Wallace 1.
CIS Cup (7): Hartley 3, Burchill 1, Hamill 1, Thosarinsson 1, Webster 1.

Gordon C 38	Maybury A 16 + 1	Kisnorbo P 17	Pressley S 32	Webster A 35	Hamill J 25 + 7	Neilson R 35	Stamp P 15 + 1	Hartley P 32 + 1	Pereira R 12 + 4	Weir G 11 + 9	Stewart M 5 + 12	Wyness D 19 + 10	Sloan R — + 2	McAllister J 23 + 7	De Vries M 7 + 2	Janczyk N 2 + 4	MacFarlane N 16 + 4	Sives C 2	Berra C 7 + 5	Elliot C — + 4	McKenna K 7 + 6	Miller L 17 + 1	Simmons S 5 + 6	Mikoliunas S 10 + 1	Thorradisson H — + 4	Burchill M 5 + 7	Wallace L 13	Kizys M 2 + 5	Cesnauskis D 7 + 1	Thomson J 3	McGeown D — + 2	Tierney G — + 1	Match No.
1	2	3	4	5	6	7	8^1	9	10^3	11^2	12	13	14																				1
1	2	3	4	5	6^2	7	8	9	10	11^1	13	12																					2
1	2	3	4	5	6^1	7	8	9^2	10^3	11	13	14		12																			3
1	2	3	4	5	6	7^2	8^1	9	10	11^3	12	14		13																			4
1	2	3^3	4	5	6^2	7	8	9		11				13	10^1	12	14																5
1	13			5	12	7	8^1	14			10^3	11		3		6	9	2^2	4														6
1	2	3	4	5	9	7	8^2	10				11^1	13	6^3		14				12													7
1	2	3	4	5	13	7	8^3	10			9^2	11^1		6	12						14												8
1	2	3	4	5	14	7	8^3	10		11^1	9^2	13		6							12												9
1	2	3	4	5	6	7	8^1	10	13	11^2		12		14							9^3												10
1	2	3	4	5	6	7		9^3	12	11^1	14	10^2		13							8												11
1	2	3^1	4	5	8^2	7		10	11^3	12		14		6		13					9												12
1	2	3	4	5	13	7	8^3	10	11^1	12				6^2			14				9												13
1	2	3		5	9^2	7		10	13			11		8	12				4		6^1												14
1	2■	3^3	4	5		7		9	8^2	13		11^1		6	10	12					14												15
1		3	4^1	5	6	7		9	8^3	13	14	11^2		2	10				12														16
1		3	4	5	6^1	7^2	12	9	8	14	13	11^3		2	10																		17
1		3	4	5■	6^3	7		9	8^2	12	13	11^1		2	10				14														18
1	2		4^3		13	7	6	9		14	8^1	11^2		3	10		12				5												19
1	2		4^3	5	6	7	3^1	9		11				12	10^2		8		14		13												20
1			4	5	8^1	7	6	10	11			13		2			9^3				3^2	12	14										21
1			4	5	12	7	3	9	8^1	13		11^2		2			6^3					10	14										22
1			4	5^3	6	7		9				11^1		2			8				14	10	3^2	12	13								23
1			4	5	6	7					13	11^1		2			8		14			10	3^3	9^2		12							24
1			4			7		9				11^1		2					3			10^3	6^2	8	14	12	5	13					25
1			4			7		9				11^1		13					3			10	6^3	8		12	2	14	5^2				26
1				5	14	7		9						2^2			8^1		3			10		11■		13	4	12	6^3				27
1				5	6^2	7^1		9				11		2			12		3			10				13	4		8				28
1				5	6				12	9		11				2^2			3	14		10^3			13.		7		8^1	4			29
1			4	5		7				14	13			2			8^2					10	6^1			11^3	3	12	9				30
1			4	5	6	7					13			2^3			8			12		10	14			11^1	3	9^2					31
1			4	5				9^1						2			8		14		13	10				11	6^3	12	7	3^2			32
1			4	5	6						12	11^2		2			8					10		9		13		7^1		3			33
1			4	2	6	7		9									5^2					10	13	8^1		11	3		12				34
1			4	2		7		9				12					5					10		8		11^1	3		6				35
1			4	2	6^2	7		11			8	12					5					10^1	14	9^3		13	3						36
1			4■	2	6	7		9		11^3							5^1					10	12	8^2	14		3				13		37
1				2	6	7		9				11					5	4^3		13		10^1		8^2			3				12	14	38

HIBERNIAN — Premier League

Year Formed: 1875. *Ground & Address:* Easter Road Stadium, Albion Rd, Edinburgh EH7 5QG. *Telephone:* 0131 661 2159. *Fax:* 0131 659 6488.
Ground Capacity: total: 17,400. *Size of Pitch:* 112yd × 74yd.
Managing Director: Rod Petrie. *Club Secretary:* Garry O'Hagan. *Marketing & Communications Manager:* Colin McNeill.
Manager: Tony Mowbray. *Assistant Manager:* Mark Venus.
Managers since 1975: Eddie Turnbull, Willie Ormond, Bertie Auld, Pat Stanton, John Blackley, Alex Miller, Jim Duffy, Alex McLeish, Frank Sauzee, B. Williamson.
Club Nickname(s): Hibees. *Previous Grounds:* Meadows 1875-78, Powderhall 1878-79, Mayfield 1879-80, First Easter Road 1880-92, Second Easter Road 1892-.
Record Attendance: 65,860 v Hearts, Division I, 2 Jan 1950.
Record Victory: 22-1 v 42nd Highlanders, 3 Sept 1881.
Record Defeat: 0-10 v Rangers, 24 Dec 1898.
Most Capped Player: Lawrie Reilly, 38, Scotland.
Most League Appearances: 446: Arthur Duncan.
Most League Goals in Season (Individual): 42: Joe Baker.
Most Goals Overall (Individual): 364: Gordon Smith.

HIBERNIAN 2004–05 LEAGUE RECORD

Match No.	Date	Venue	Opponents	Result		H/T Score	Lg. Pos.	Goalscorers	Attendance
1	Aug 7	H	Kilmarnock	L	0-1	0-0	—		10,933
2	14	A	Motherwell	W	2-1	1-1	4	O'Connor 2 [2, 78]	5859
3	21	A	Rangers	L	1-4	1-2	9	Caldwell [34]	48,702
4	28	H	Dundee	D	4-4	2-1	9	Shiels [22], Riordan [40], O'Connor 2 [46, 49]	9344
5	Sept 11	A	Inverness CT	W	2-1	1-1	7	Riordan 2 [10, 59]	2011
6	19	H	Celtic	D	2-2	2-2	7	Balde (og) [8], Murphy [35]	13,573
7	25	A	Aberdeen	W	1-0	0-0	7	Riordan [61]	12,137
8	Oct 2	A	Dunfermline Ath	D	1-1	1-0	6	O'Connor [38]	7295
9	16	H	Dundee U	W	2-0	1-0	4	O'Connor [10], Fletcher [55]	9850
10	24	A	Hearts	L	1-2	0-1	4	Riordan [86]	16,720
11	27	H	Livingston	W	2-1	2-0	—	Beuzelin [8], Fletcher [23]	9087
12	30	A	Kilmarnock	L	1-3	0-3	6	Shiels [66]	5959
13	Nov 6	H	Motherwell	W	1-0	0-0	5	Murray I [78]	9931
14	14	H	Rangers	L	0-1	0-0	5		13,825
15	20	A	Dundee	W	4-1	2-0	4	Beuzelin [17], Riordan [43], Orman [73], Shiels [85]	5274
16	27	H	Inverness CT	W	2-1	1-1	4	Beuzelin [39], Riordan [47]	9739
17	Dec 4	A	Celtic	L	1-2	0-1	4	Caldwell [75]	58,399
18	11	H	Aberdeen	W	2-1	1-1	4	Riordan [24], Glass [54]	13,503
19	18	H	Dunfermline Ath	W	2-1	0-0	4	Glass [65], Riordan [89]	9859
20	27	A	Dundee U	W	4-1	2-1	3	Riordan [12], O'Connor [22], Orman [58], Morrow [81]	10,152
21	Jan 2	H	Hearts	D	1-1	1-0	3	Riordan [24]	17,259
22	15	A	Livingston	W	2-0	0-0	3	O'Connor [52], Morrow [75]	6188
23	22	H	Kilmarnock	W	3-0	2-0	3	Riordan 3 [30, 33, 52]	12,660
24	Feb 12	A	Rangers	L	0-3	0-1	3		50,143
25	15	A	Motherwell	D	1-1	0-1	—	Riordan [67]	7453
26	19	H	Dundee	W	4-0	1-0	3	O'Connor 2 [26, 78], Whittaker [47], Fletcher [76]	10,938
27	Mar 2	A	Inverness CT	L	0-3	0-1	—		4443
28	6	H	Celtic	L	1-3	0-2	3	Beuzelin [89]	15,787
29	12	A	Aberdeen	L	0-3	0-2	4		14,465
30	19	A	Dunfermline Ath	W	4-1	0-1	3	Riordan 2 [66, 81], Fletcher 2 [69, 75]	7204
31	Apr 2	H	Dundee U	W	3-2	1-0	3	Shiels [34], O'Connor [68], Smith [89]	11,058
32	13	A	Hearts	W	2-1	0-1	—	O'Connor [68], Shiels [73]	17,673
33	16	H	Livingston	L	0-3	0-0	3		10,637
34	23	H	Hearts	D	2-2	1-1	3	O'Connor [8], Riordan [62]	16,620
35	30	A	Celtic	W	3-1	1-0	3	O'Connor [6], Sproule [79], Scott Brown [84]	58,289
36	May 7	A	Motherwell	D	2-2	0-1	3	Caldwell [81], Konte [90]	8903
37	14	H	Aberdeen	L	1-2	0-1	3	Riordan [51]	15,288
38	22	H	Rangers	L	0-1	0-0	3		16,604

Final League Position: 3

Honours
League Champions: Division I 1902-03, 1947-48, 1950-51, 1951-52. First Division 1980-81, 1998-99. Division II 1893-94, 1894-95, 1932-33; *Runners-up:* Division I 1896-97, 1946-47, 1949-50, 1952-53, 1973-74, 1974-75.
Scottish Cup Winners: 1887, 1902; *Runners-up:* 1896, 1914, 1923, 1924, 1947, 1958, 1972, 1979, 2001.
League Cup Winners: 1972-73, 1991-92; *Runners-up:* 1950-51, 1968-69, 1974-75, 1993-94, 2003-04.

European: *European Cup:* 6 matches (1955-56 semi-finals). *Cup Winners' Cup:* 6 matches (1972-73). *UEFA Cup:* 61 matches (*Fairs Cup:* 1960-61 semi-finals, 1961-62, 1962-63, 1965-66, 1967-68, 1968-69, 1970-71. *UEFA Cup:* 1973-74, 1974-75, 1975-76, 1976-77, 1978-79, 1989-90, 1992-93, 2001-02).

Club colours: Shirt: Green with white sleeves and collar. Shorts: White with green stripe. Stockings: White with green trim.

Goalscorers: *League* (64): Riordan 20, O'Connor 14, Fletcher 5, Shiels 5, Beuzelin 4, Caldwell 3, Glass 2, Orman 2, Scott Brown 1, Konte 1, Morrow 1, Murphy 1, Murray I 1, Smith 1, Sproule 1, Whittaker 1, own goal 1.
Scottish Cup (9): O'Connor 3, Morrow 2, Scott Brown 1, Caldwell 1, Riordan 1 (pen), Whittaker 1.
CIS Cup (8): Riordan 2, Dobbie 1, Glass 1, Murdock 1, O'Connor 1, Orman 1, Shiels 1.

Brown Simon 38	Murdock C 5	Caldwell G 37	Murphy D 27	Whittaker S 37	Glass S 34+2	Beuzelin G 21+5	Brebner G 2	Brown Scott 18+2	McManus T 2	O'Connor G 34+2	Morrow S 5+17	Riordan D 36+1	Shiels D 28+9	Shields J —+6	Smith G 19+1	Dobbie S —+7	Nicol K —+1	Baillie J —+1	Murray I 29	Rocastle C 11+2	Fletcher S 11+9	Orman A 10+2	McCluskey J —+10	McDonald K —+3	Brown A —+1	Murray A 10+2	Konte A 3+9	Sproule I 1+6	Thomson K —+3	*Match No.*
1	2	3	4	5	6	7	8^{3}	9	10^{1}	11^{2}	12	13	14																	1
1	2■	3	4^{1}	5	6	7	8■	9	10^{2}	11^{3}	12		13	14																2
1		2	4	5	6^{2}	7		9		11^{3}	12	10	8^{1}	14	3	13														3
1	2	3^{2}	4	5	6^{1}	7		9		11^{3}	14	10	8				12	13												4
1		2	4	5	7^{1}	3		9		11		10^{2}	8^{3}	14		13			6	12										5
1		2	4	5	7	3		9^{1}		11		10	8^{3}	14		12^{2}			6		13									6
1		2	4	5	7	3				11		10^{1}	8	12		13			6		9^{2}									7
1		2	4	5	7	3				11		10	8	12					6		9^{1}									8
1		2		5	7	3				11^{2}		10	8			14			6	12	9^{3}	4^{1}	13							9
1		2	4	5	7	3				11		10	8			12			6		9^{1}									10
1		2	4	5	7^{2}	3				11^{1}		10	13						6	8	12	9^{3}	14							11
1		2	4	5	7^{2}	3						10	13			12			6	8	11^{3}	9^{1}	14							12
1	2	4		5	7	3					12	10	9						6	8	11^{1}									13
1	2^{3}	4		5	7	3				11^{1}	12	10	9		13				6	8^{2}			14							14
1			4	2	7^{1}	8				13	11^{2}	10	12		3				5	9		6								15
1		2	4	3	14	7				13	11^{2}	10	9^{1}						5	8		6^{3}	12							16
1		2	4	3	7^{2}	6				11^{1}	12	10	9						5	8^{3}			13	14						17
1		2	4	3	7^{3}	6				11^{1}	12	10	9^{2}						5	8	14	13								18
1^{6}		2	4	3	7^{2}	6^{1}				11	13	10	9						5	8		12			15					19
1		2	4	3	7					11^{1}	12	10	9						5	8	13	6^{2}								20
1		2	4	3	7					11	12	10	9						5	8		6^{1}								21
1		2		5	7	12				11^{2}	13	10	9^{3}		3						8	4^{1}	14			6				22
1		2		4	7	12				11^{2}	13	10	9		3				5		8^{1}		14			6^{3}				23
1		2	4^{3}	5	7					11	8^{1}	10^{2}	9		3				6		14					13	12			24
1		2	4	5	7			12		11^{3}	8^{1}	10	9^{2}		3						13					6	14			25
1		2	4	5	7^{2}			13		11^{3}	9^{1}	10			3						8		14			6	12			26
1		2	4	5				9		11		10	14		3				6^{2}			8^{3}		12		7^{1}		13		27
1		2	4	5		12		8		11^{2}		10^{3}	9		3				6			7^{1}					13	14		28
1		2	4	5	12	7^{1}		8		11		10^{2}	9^{3}		3				6					13				14		29
1		2^{2}	4	5	7			8^{1}		11^{3}		10	9		3				6		12		13				14			30
1		2	4		7			8		11	12	10^{1}	9		3				6		5^{2}								13	31
1		2		5	7			8		11		10^{2}	9^{3}		3				6^{1}		14					4	13		12	32
1		2	4	5	7^{3}			8		11	13	10	9^{1}		3						6^{2}						14		12	33
1		2		5	7			8		11^{1}	12	10	9		3						13					4	6^{2}			34
1		2		5	7			9		11^{3}	14	10^{1}	13		3				6							4^{2}	8	12		35
1		2		5	7	12		8		11		10^{2}	9		3^{1}				6							4^{3}	13	14		36
1		2		5	7	12		9		11^{1}		10^{2}	14		3				6							4^{3}	8	13		37
1		2		5	7	4^{3}		9		11^{2}		10	12		3				6							14	13	8^{1}		38

INVERNESS CALEDONIAN THISTLE

Premier League

Year Formed: 1994. *Ground & Address:* Tulloch Caledonian Stadium, East Longman, Inverness IV1 1FF. *Telephone:* 01463 222880. *Fax:* 01463 715816.
Ground Capacity: seated: 7400. *Size of Pitch:* 115yd × 75yd.
Chairman: Kenneth Mackie. *President:* John MacDonald. *Secretary:* Jim Falconer. *Commercial Manager:* Morven Reid.
Youth Administrator: Charlie Christie. *Football and Community Development Manager:* Danny MacDonald.
Manager: Craig Brewster. *Assistant Manager:* Malcolm Thomson. *First Team Coach:* John Docherty. *Physio:* David Brandie.
Managers since 1994: S. Baltacha, S. Paterson, J. Robertson.
Record Attendance: 7100 v Celtic, SPL, 16 March 2005.
Record Victory: 8-1, v Annan Ath, Scottish Cup 3rd rd, 24 January 1998.
Record Defeat: 1-5, v Morton, First Division, 12 November 1999 and v Airdrieonians, First Division, 15 April 2000.
Most League Appearances: 308, Charlie Christie, 1995-2003.
Most League Goals in Season: 27, Iain Stewart, 1996-97; Denis Wyness 2002-03.
Most Goals Overall (Individual): 82, Iain Stewart, 1995-2001.

INVERNESS CALEDONIAN TH 2004–05 LEAGUE RECORD

Match No.	*Date*	*Venue*	*Opponents*	*Result*		*H/T Score*	*Lg. Pos.*	*Goalscorers*	*Attendance*
1	Aug 7	A	Livingston	L	0-3	0-1	—		3315
2	15	H	Dunfermline Ath	W	2-0	1-0	8	Golabek 12, Juanjo 70	2583
3	22	H	Celtic	L	1-3	1-1	8	Wilson 43	8788
4	28	A	Dundee U	L	1-2	0-0	11	Wilson (pen) 59	6017
5	Sept 11	H	Hibernian	L	1-2	1-1	11	Wilson (pen) 26	2011
6	19	A	Rangers	L	0-1	0-1	12		47,063
7	25	A	Hearts	L	0-1	0-1	12		10,340
8	Oct 3	H	Motherwell	D	1-1	0-1	12	McCaffrey 89	1438
9	16	H	Aberdeen	L	1-3	1-1	12	McBain 34	9830
10	23	A	Kilmarnock	D	2-2	1-2	12	Wilson 15, Fox 82	4721
11	27	H	Dundee	W	2-1	1-0	—	Bayne 41, Hart 52	1282
12	30	H	Livingston	W	2-0	1-0	9	Bayne 38, Wilson 86	1284
13	Nov 6	A	Dunfermline Ath	D	1-1	0-1	9	Tokely 79	4921
14	13	A	Celtic	L	0-3	0-1	9		56,965
15	23	H	Dundee U	D	1-1	0-0	—	Juanjo 49	1125
16	27	A	Hibernian	L	1-2	1-1	9	Juanjo 33	9739
17	Dec 5	H	Rangers	D	1-1	1-0	10	Bayne 3	6543
18	11	H	Hearts	D	1-1	0-0	10	Juanjo (pen) 67	2011
19	18	A	Motherwell	W	2-1	2-0	8	Hart 16, Bayne 42	4267
20	27	A	Aberdeen	D	0-0	0-0	8		18,250
21	Jan 3	H	Kilmarnock	L	0-2	0-0	9		1359
22	15	A	Dundee	L	1-3	0-1	9	Brewster 89	5567
23	22	A	Livingston	W	4-1	2-1	8	Hart 8, Duncan 37, Bayne 50, Juanjo 71	3606
24	29	H	Dunfermline Ath	W	2-0	1-0	8	Wilson 35, Brewster 74	5449
25	Feb 19	A	Dundee U	D	1-1	1-1	8	Wilson (pen) 36	6110
26	Mar 2	H	Hibernian	W	3-0	1-0	—	Juanjo 39, Brewster 52, Wilson 77	4443
27	5	A	Rangers	D	1-1	0-0	8	Prunty 90	49,945
28	12	A	Hearts	W	2-0	0-0	8	Dods 55, Wilson (pen) 72	9822
29	16	H	Celtic	L	0-2	0-0	—		7047
30	Apr 2	H	Aberdeen	L	0-1	0-1	8		7026
31	9	A	Kilmarnock	W	1-0	1-0	7	Wilson 32	4862
32	12	H	Motherwell	W	1-0	1-0	—	Bayne 21	3746
33	16	H	Dundee	W	3-2	2-0	7	McBain 17, Wilson 38, Brewster 64	4786
34	23	A	Dunfermline Ath	D	0-0	0-0	7		4471
35	30	H	Kilmarnock	L	1-2	1-1	7	Tokely 28	3108
36	May 7	H	Livingston	L	0-1	0-1	7		3021
37	14	A	Dundee	D	1-1	0-0	8	Fox 87	6691
38	21	H	Dundee U	L	0-1	0-0	8		5479

Final League Position: 8

Honours
Scottish Cup: Semi-finals 2003, 2004; Quarter-finals 1996.
League Champions: First Division 2003-04. Third Division 1996-97; *Runners-up:* Second Division 1998-99.
Bell's League Challenge Cup Winners: 2003-04. *Runners-up:* 1999-2000.

Club colours: Shirts: Royal blue with red stripes. Shorts: Royal blue. Stockings: Royal blue.

Goalscorers: *League* (41): Wilson 11 (4 pens), Bayne 6, Juanjo 6 (1 pen), Brewster 4, Hart 3, Fox 2, McBain 2, Tokely 2, Dods 1, Duncan 1, Golabek 1, McCaffrey 1, Prunty 1.
Scottish Cup (2): Brewster 1, Golabek 1.
CIS Cup (2): Tokely 2.

Brown M 38	Tokely R 34	Golabek S 37	Munro G 36	McCaffrey S 14 + 2	Duncan R 27 + 2	Keogh L 16 + 5	McBain R 31 + 3	Wilson B 30 + 6	Hislop S 2 + 5	Bayne G 32 + 6	Hart R 34 + 3	Juanjo26 + 3	Black I 7 + 6	Prunty B 8 + 19	Hastings R 5 + 6	Fox L 1 + 8	Dods D 28	Fraser M — + 1	Thomson D — + 1	Brewster C 11 + 2	Fetai B — + 8	Proctor D 1 + 3	McAllister R — + 4	*Match No.*
1	2	3	4	5	6	7^{1}	8^{3}	9	10^{2}	11	12	13	14											1
1	2	3	4	5		7	8	12	10^{1}	11	6	9^{2}		13										2
1	2	3	4	5		7	8^{3}	9^{2}	12	11^{1}	6	10	14	13										3
1	2	3	4	5		7	8^{2}	9	13	11	6	10^{1}		12										4
1	2	3	4	5		7	8^{1}	9^{2}	12	11	6	10^{3}	13	14										5
1	2	3	4■	5		7	8	9	12	11^{1}	6	10^{2}		13										6
1	2	3		5	8	7	12	9	13^{3}	11	6^{1}	10^{2}		14	4									7
1	2	3	4	5	8	7^{2}	13	9		11	6^{3}	10^{1}		12		14								8
1	2	3	4	5^{3}	7^{2}	14	8	9		11	6	12	13	10^{1}										9
1	2	3	4	5■	7	13	8^{2}	9		11	6^{3}	10^{1}			12	14								10
1^{G}	2	3	4		7	12	8	9		11^{2}	6^{1}	10		13			5	15						11
1	2	3	4		7	12	8	9		11	6^{1}	10^{2}					5		13					12
1	2	3	4		7^{2}	14	8	9^{3}		11	6^{1}	10	13			12	5							13
1		3	4	5	7	8		9^{1}		11	6	10^{2}		13		12	2							14
1	2■	3	4	13	7		8	9^{1}		11	6^{2}	10				12	5							15
1		3	4	5	7	8		9^{1}		11	6	10^{2}		13		12	2							16
1	2	3	4		7	9	8^{1}	13		11	6^{2}	10^{3}		14	12		5							17
1	2^{3}	3	4^{1}	14	7	9	8	13		11	6^{2}	10			12		5							18
1	2	3	4		7	9	8^{2}	12		11^{1}	6	10			13		5							19
1	2	3	4		7	9	8			11	6	10^{1}		12			5							20
1	2■	3	4^{1}		7	9	8^{3}	13		11	6^{2}	10		14	12		5							21
1		3	4	2	7	9^{2}	6^{1}	8		11	12	13					5			10				22
1		3	4	2	7			8		11^{1}	6	9^{2}		13			5			10	12			23
1	2	3	4		7		14	8^{3}		11^{2}	6	9^{1}		13			5			10	12			24
1	2	3	4		7		8	9		11	6						5			10				25
1	2	3	4		7		8	9		12	6^{3}	11^{1}					5			10^{2}	13	14		26
1	2	3	4		7		8	9^{1}		11^{2}	6	10		13			5				12			27
1	2	3	4		7		8	9^{3}		12	6	11^{1}		13		14	5			10^{2}				28
1	2	3	4		7^{3}		8	9		11^{2}	6	10^{1}	14	12			5				13			29
1	2	3	4		7		8^{3}	9		14	6^{1}	11^{2}		13			5			10	12			30
1	2	3	4				8	9		11	6		7				5			10				31
1	2	3	4		12		8^{1}	9^{3}		11^{2}	6		7	10			5				13	14		32
1	2		4		13		8	9		14	6^{1}		7^{2}	11	3		5			10^{3}		12		33
1	2	3	4				8	9		13	6^{1}		7	11^{2}			5			10	12			34
1	2	3					8	9		12			7	11^{2}	4		5			10		6^{1}	13	35
1	2	3	4		6		8^{2}	9^{1}		10	12		7	11^{3}	13		5						14	36
1	2	3	4		7		8^{2}			10^{3}	9			11^{1}	6	13	5			12			14	37
1	2	3	4					13		10^{1}	8^{3}		7	11^{2}	6	9	5			12			14	38

KILMARNOCK Premier League

Year Formed: 1869. *Ground & Address:* Rugby Park, Kilmarnock KA1 2DP. *Telephone:* 01563 545300. *Fax:* 01563 522181. *Website:* www.kilmarnockfc.co.uk
Ground Capacity: all seated: 18,128. *Size of Pitch:* 114yd × 72yd.
Chairman: Michael Johnston. *Secretary:* Angela Burnett. *General Manager:* David MacKinnon.
Manager: Jim Jefferies. *Assistant Manager:* Billy Brown. *Physio:* A. MacQueen.
Managers since 1975: W. Fernie, D. Sneddon, J. Clunie, E. Morrison, J. Fleeting, T. Burns, A. Totten, B. Brown.
Club Nickname(s): Killie. *Previous Grounds:* Rugby Park (Dundonald Road); The Grange; Holm Quarry; Present ground since 1899.
Record Attendance: 35,995 v Rangers, Scottish Cup, 10 Mar 1962.
Record Transfer Fee received: £300,000 for Shaun McSkimming to Motherwell (1995).
Record Transfer Fee paid: £300,000 for Paul Wright from St Johnstone (1995).
Record Victory: 11-1 v Paisley Academical, Scottish Cup, 18 Jan 1930 (15-0 v Lanemark, Ayrshire Cup, 15 Nov 1890).
Record Defeat: 1-9 v Celtic, Division I, 13 Aug 1938.
Most Capped Player: Joe Nibloe, 11, Scotland.
Most League Appearances: 481: Alan Robertson, 1972-88.
Most League Goals in Season (Individual): 34: Harry 'Peerie' Cunningham 1927-28 and Andy Kerr 1960-61.
Most Goals Overall (Individual): 148: W. Culley, 1912-23.

KILMARNOCK 2004–05 LEAGUE RECORD

Match No.	Date	Venue	Opponents	Result		H/T Score	Lg. Pos.	Goalscorers	Attendance
1	Aug 7	A	Hibernian	W	1-0	0-0	—	Boyd [72]	10,933
2	14	H	Celtic	L	2-4	2-3	6	McDonald [14], Wales [28]	10,526
3	21	A	Hearts	L	0-3	0-1	10		11,403
4	29	H	Dunfermline Ath	W	1-0	1-0	6	Invincibile [10]	4854
5	Sept 11	A	Livingston	W	2-0	0-0	3	Lilley [59], Invincibile [71]	2776
6	18	H	Aberdeen	L	0-1	0-0	5		6686
7	25	H	Dundee U	W	5-2	4-1	5	Boyd 5 (1 pen) [1, 17, 33, 37 (p), 87]	4711
8	Oct 3	A	Rangers	L	0-2	0-1	7		46,278
9	16	A	Dundee	L	1-3	1-1	7	Boyd [4]	4637
10	23	H	Inverness CT	D	2-2	2-1	7	Murray [4], Greer [26]	4721
11	27	A	Motherwell	W	1-0	0-0	—	Nish [57]	4605
12	30	H	Hibernian	W	3-1	3-0	5	Nish 2 [20, 42], Dargo [40]	5959
13	Nov 6	A	Celtic	L	1-2	0-1	6	Nish [88]	57,268
14	13	H	Hearts	D	1-1	1-0	6	Leven [30]	6129
15	20	A	Dunfermline Ath	L	1-4	0-2	7	Wales [80]	4344
16	27	H	Livingston	L	1-3	1-2	7	Johnston A [4]	5389
17	Dec 4	A	Aberdeen	L	2-3	2-2	7	Invincibile [7], Leven [18]	11,139
18	11	A	Dundee U	L	0-3	0-2	7		5097
19	19	H	Rangers	L	0-1	0-1	7		11,156
20	27	H	Dundee	W	3-1	2-1	7	Invincibile [16], Ford [38], Boyd [82]	5468
21	Jan 3	A	Inverness CT	W	2-0	0-0	7	Invincibile 2 [77, 89]	1359
22	15	H	Motherwell	W	2-0	2-0	7	Boyd 2 [1, 44]	5225
23	22	A	Hibernian	L	0-3	0-2	7		12,660
24	30	H	Celtic	L	0-1	0-1	7		9723
25	Feb 12	A	Hearts	L	0-3	0-2	7		9220
26	19	H	Dunfermline Ath	W	2-1	2-1	7	Naismith [12], Boyd [43]	4701
27	26	A	Rangers	L	1-2	0-2	7	Boyd [76]	48,575
28	Mar 2	A	Livingston	L	1-3	1-1	—	Johnston A [12]	1931
29	5	H	Aberdeen	L	0-1	0-0	7		5181
30	12	H	Dundee U	W	3-0	1-0	7	Boyd 2 (1 pen) [26, 77 (p)], Invincibile [88]	4353
31	Apr 2	A	Dundee	L	0-1	0-0	7		5494
32	9	H	Inverness CT	L	0-1	0-1	8		4862
33	16	A	Motherwell	D	1-1	1-0	8	Leven [33]	4999
34	23	H	Dundee	W	1-0	0-0	8	Dargo [84]	3485
35	30	A	Inverness CT	W	2-1	1-1	8	McDonald [21], Leven (pen) [72]	3108
36	May 7	A	Dundee U	D	1-1	0-1	8	Boyd [53]	6576
37	14	H	Livingston	W	2-0	0-0	7	Boyd [75], Johnston A [84]	4184
38	21	H	Dunfermline Ath	W	4-0	1-0	7	Locke [25], Dodds [46], Boyd [54], McDonald [63]	5100

Final League Position: 7

Honours
League Champions: Division I 1964-65. Division II 1897-98, 1898-99; *Runners-up:* Division I 1959-60, 1960-61, 1962-63, 1963-64. First Division 1975-76, 1978-79, 1981-82, 1992-93. Division II 1953-54, 1973-74. Second Division 1989-90.
Scottish Cup Winners: 1920, 1929, 1997; *Runners-up:* 1898, 1932, 1938, 1957, 1960.
League Cup Runners-up: 1952-53, 1960-61, 1962-63, 2000-01.

European: *European Cup:* 4 matches (1965-66). *Cup Winners' Cup:* 4 matches (1997-98). *UEFA Cup:* 24 matches (*Fairs Cup:* 1964-65, 1966-67, 1969-70, 1970-71, *UEFA Cup:* 1998-99, 1999-2000, 2001-02).

Club colours: Shirt: Blue and white vertical stripes. Shorts: White. Stockings: White.

Goalscorers: *League* (49): Boyd 17 (2 pens), Invincibile 7, Leven 4 (1 pen), Nish 4, Johnston A 3, McDonald 3, Dargo 2, Wales 2, Dodds 1, Ford 1, Greer 1, Lilley 1, Locke 1, Murray 1, Naismith 1.
Scottish Cup (5): Boyd 2, McDonald 1, Naismith 1, Nish 1.
CIS Cup (4): Invincibile 2, Leven 1, McDonald 1.

Combe A 32	Lilley D 33	Dindeleux F 27 + 2	Fowler J 24 + 5	Hay G 22 + 3	McDonald G 38	Murray S 8 + 13	Locke G 22 + 3	Invincibile D 28 + 3	Boyd K 29 + 1	Wales G 12 + 12	Joly E — + 6	Leven P 29 + 3	Dargo C 10 + 10	Dodds R 4 + 4	Greer G 19 + 3	Dillon S 4 + 2	Naismith S 16 + 8	Johnston A 19 + 10	Nish C 16 + 10	Ford S 17 + 1	Smith G 6	Fontaine L 3	*Match No.*
1	2	3	4	5	6	7^2	8^1	9	10	11^3	12	13	14										1
1	2	3	4	5^2	6	7^1	8		10	11^3				9	12	13	14						2
1		3	4	5	6	13	8	9	10^3	11^1	14		12		2			7^2					3
1	2^3	3	4		6^2	7	8	10		11^1	13		12		14	5		9					4
1	2	3	4		6		8	11	10			12		9		5		7^1					5
1	2	3	4^2		6	12	8^1	11	10^3	14			13	9		5		7					6
1	2	3	12		6^1			11	10	13		8	9^2	14	4	5		7^3					7
1	2	3	4		6		8	11	10			5	9^1					7	12				8
1	2	3	4		6	7^2	8	11	10		14	5^1	9^3			12			13				9
1	2	3		13	6	7^2	8^1	11	10		12	5	9^3		4		14						10
1	2	3	13		6	12		11				5	10^2		4			7^1	9	8			11
1	2	3		13	6	7^2		11				5	10^1		4		12		9	8			12
	2	3	12		6		13	11^1				5	10^2		4		14	7^3	9	8	1		13
1	2	3^1	14		6		12	11		13		5	10^2		4			7^3	9	8			14
1	2	12			6	14	8	11		13		5	10^1		4			7^2	9^3	3			15
1	2	3	5		6	13		10^3		11^2	12				4^1		14	7	9	8			16
1	2	3			7			11	10^1	13		6			4		12	8^2	9	5			17
1	2	3			7	12		11^2	10^3	14		6	13		4		9	8^1		5			18
		3		2	7^1	13		11	10	12		6		14	4		8^2		9^3	5	1		19
		3		2	7			11	10			6			4		8^1	12	9	5	1		20
			14	2	7		8	11	10^3	13		5			4		6^2	12	9^1	3	1		21
1	2	3		4	7		12	11	10			6^1					8^2	13	9	5			22
1	2^1		3	4	7	13	8	11	10					14			6^3	12	9^2	5			23
1	2			4	7		8	11^3	10^1	14		6					9^2	13	12	3		5	24
1	2	12	3^3	13	7	6^2	8		10	14		4					11	9				5^1	25
1	2		3	4	7	13		11	10			6					9	8^2		12		5^1	26
1	2		3	4^1	7		8	11	10^2			12	13				9^3	6	14	5			27
1	2		3	4	7	14	8^3	13	10^1			6^2					11	9	12	5			28
	2		3	4	7			11	10^1			6	12				13	8	9^2	5	1		29
	2	3	4	5	7			12	10^2	14		6	13				11	8^1	9^3		1		30
1	2	3	4	5	7	14		9	10	13		6^2	12				11^3		8^1				31
1	2	3	4	5	7	8			10	9^1		6					11^2	13	12				32
1	2	3	6	5	9		8		10^1	11		7			4				12				33
1	2	3	6	5	9		8	12	10^2	11^3		7	13		4^1				14				34
1	2	3	4	5	7		8	10^2		11^3		6	9^1		13			14	12				35
1	2	3	6	5	9		8		12	10^3		7			4^2		13	14	11^1				36
1	2		3	5	7^1	13	8		10	11		6^2		12	4		9^3	14					37
1			3	2	7	13	8		10	11^3		6^1		5	4		9^2	12	14				38

LIVINGSTON Premier League

Year Formed: 1974. *Ground:* Almondvale Stadium, Alderton Road, Livingston EH54 7DN. *Telephone:* 01506 417000. *Fax:* 01506 418888. *Email:* info@livingstonfc.co.uk
Ground Capacity: 10,024 (all seated). *Size of Pitch:* 105yd × 72yd.
Chairman: Pearse Flynn. *Chief Executive:* Vivien Kyles. *General Manager:* David Hay. *Secretary:* M. Kaplan.
Team Manager: Paul Lambert. *Assistant Manager:* Norrie McWhirter. *Physios:* Arthur Duncan, Marie McPhail.
Managers since 1975: M. Lawson, T. Christie, W. MacFarlane, A. Ness, J. Bain, J. Leishman, R. Stewart, H. Leishman, M. Barcellos, D. Hay, A. Preston.
Club Nickname: Livi Lions. *Previous Grounds:* None.
Record Attendance: 10,024 v Celtic, Premier League, 18 Aug 2001.
Record Transfer Fee received: £1,000,000 for D. Fernandez to Celtic (June 2002).
Record Transfer Fee paid: £60,000 for Barry Wilson from Inverness CT (May 2000).
Record Victory: 7-0 v Queen of the South, Scottish Cup, 29 Jan 2000.
Record Defeat: 0-8 v Hamilton A. Division II, 14 Dec 1974.
Most Capped Player (under 18): I. Little.
Most League Appearances: 446: Walter Boyd, 1979-89.
Most League Goals in Season (Individual): 21: John McGachie, 1986-87. *(Team):* 69; Second Division, 1986-87.
Most Goals Overall (Individual): 64: David Roseburgh, 1986-93.

LIVINGSTON 2004–05 LEAGUE RECORD

Match No.	Date	Venue	Opponents	Result		H/T Score	Lg. Pos.	Goalscorers	Attendance
1	Aug 7	H	Inverness CT	W	3-0	1-0	—	O'Brien 43, Easton 58, Lovell 66	3315
2	14	A	Rangers	L	0-4	0-2	6		48,102
3	21	H	Dundee U	D	1-1	0-0	5	McMenamin 83	3159
4	28	A	Aberdeen	L	0-2	0-0	10		13,888
5	Sept 11	H	Kilmarnock	L	0-2	0-0	10		2776
6	18	A	Dundee	D	0-0	0-0	11		4387
7	25	H	Motherwell	L	2-3	2-1	10	O'Brien 37, Hamilton 45	3950
8	Oct 3	A	Hearts	D	0-0	0-0	9		10,646
9	16	H	Dunfermline Ath	W	2-0	2-0	9	Wilson (og) 5, Snodgrass 42	2815
10	24	H	Celtic	L	2-4	1-4	8	O'Brien 2 45, 53	6695
11	27	A	Hibernian	L	1-2	0-2	—	Lilley 65	9087
12	30	A	Inverness CT	L	0-2	0-1	11		1284
13	Nov 7	H	Rangers	L	1-4	0-1	11	Easton 60	7800
14	13	A	Dundee U	L	0-1	0-0	12		5507
15	20	H	Aberdeen	L	0-2	0-2	12		4270
16	27	A	Kilmarnock	W	3-1	2-1	12	Hamilton 2 7, 34, O'Brien 59	5389
17	Dec 4	H	Dundee	W	1-0	1-0	9	McPake 24	4009
18	11	A	Motherwell	L	0-2	0-1	8		4363
19	27	A	Dunfermline Ath	D	0-0	0-0	10		5092
20	Jan 2	A	Celtic	L	1-2	1-1	11	Hamilton 37	57,564
21	15	H	Hibernian	L	0-2	0-0	12		6188
22	22	H	Inverness CT	L	1-4	1-2	12	Horvath 42	3606
23	25	H	Hearts	L	1-2	0-0	—	Lilley 74	3816
24	29	A	Rangers	L	0-3	0-1	12		48,579
25	Feb 12	H	Dundee U	L	0-2	0-2	12		4658
26	19	A	Aberdeen	L	0-2	0-1	12		9214
27	Mar 2	H	Kilmarnock	W	3-1	1-1	—	Horvath 35, McNamee 65, Snodgrass 82	1931
28	5	A	Dundee	W	1-0	0-0	12	O'Brien 48	5830
29	12	H	Motherwell	D	1-1	0-1	11	McMenamin 80	4049
30	19	A	Hearts	L	1-3	1-1	11	Dair 44	9187
31	Apr 2	H	Dunfermline Ath	D	1-1	0-0	11	Kashloul 78	4036
32	13	H	Celtic	L	0-4	0-1	—		7750
33	16	A	Hibernian	W	3-0	0-0	12	Lilley 48, Kashloul 60, O'Brien 86	10,637
34	23	A	Dundee U	D	1-1	0-1	12	Deloumeaux 62	7687
35	30	H	Dunfermline Ath	W	2-0	1-0	10	O'Brien 33, McPake 75	5102
36	May 7	A	Inverness CT	W	1-0	1-0	9	Dair 29	3021
37	14	A	Kilmarnock	L	0-2	0-0	10		4184
38	21	H	Dundee	D	1-1	1-1	10	Easton 25	7468

Final League Position: 10

Honours
League Champions: First Division: Champions: 2000-01. Second Division 1986-87, 1998-99. Third Division 1995-96;
Runners-up: Second Division 1982-83. First Division 1987-88.
Scottish Cup: Semi-finals 2004.
League Cup Winners: 2003-04. Semi-finals 1984-85. *B&Q Cup:* Semi-finals 1992-93, 1993-94, 2001.
Bell's League Challenge Runners-up: 2000-01.

European: *UEFA Cup:* 4 matches (2002-03).

Club colours: Shirt: Gold with black sleeves and side panels. Shorts: Black. Stockings: Gold with black trim.

Goalscorers: *League* (34): O'Brien 8, Hamilton 4, Easton 3, Lilley 3, Dair 2, Horvath 2, Kashloul 2, McMenamin 2, McPake 2, Snodgrass 2, Deloumeaux 1, Lovell 1, McNamee 1, own goal 1.
Scottish Cup (4): Easton 1, McMenamin 1, Rubio 1, Snodgrass 1.
CIS Cup (4): Easton 3 (1 pen), Hamilton 1.

McKenzie R 33	McNamee D 29	Dorado E 30 + 1	Rubio O 24 + 3	McLaughlin S 7 + 3	Easton C 24 + 7	Boyack S 4 + 2	O'Brien B 38	Lovell S 19 + 1	Libbra M 2 + 9	Lilley D 23 + 8	Hamilton C 17 + 4	Bahoken S 17 + 1	McMenamin C 13 + 9	Stanic G 18 + 2	Dair J 22 + 2	Snodgrass R 8 + 9	Kernaghan A 4	Brittain R 8 + 5	Snowdon W 1 + 2	McPake J 7 + 8	Harding G 3	Adam S 4 + 3	Meldrum C 5	Hand J 5 + 2	Kriston A 3 + 2	Horvath F 6 + 2	Vincze G 14	Wilson M 4 + 1	Deloumeaux E 13	Strong G 6 + 3	Nouma P — + 2	Kashloul H 7 + 1	Dorrans G — + 1	*Match No.*
1	2	3	4	5	6	7	8	9	10^1	11	12																							1
1	2	3	4	5^1	6	7	8	9	10^2	11^3	14	12	13																					2
1	2	3	4		6	7^1	8	9^2		11	10		12	5	13																			3
1	2	3	4	13	6	7^2	8	9		11	10^1	5	12																					4
1		3	4		6		8	7	13	11	10^2	5	9^1	2		12																		5
1	2	3	4		6		8	9		11			10	5			7																	6
1		3	4	12	6^1		8	9^2	14	13	10		11	2	5		7^3																	7
1	2	3	4		6		8	9		13	10^2		12	5	7	11^1																		8
1	2	3	4		6		8	9		12	10			5	7	11^1																		9
1	2	3	4	7	6		8	9	14	13	10^2			5^3		11^1		12																10
1		3	4	7^3	6	14	8	9	13	12	10^2	5		2				11^1																11
1	2	3	4		6		8	7^1	13	11^2	10			5		12		9																12
1	2	3	4	7	9	12	8		13	14	10^3			5^1				11	6^2															13
1	2	3		5	6^2		8	9	14	11^3	12		10^1				4	7		13														14
1	2	3	12	5^1	6^2		8	9		11^3	13		10			14	4	7																15
1	2		4		6		8			11	10				7	12		13		9^1	3	5^2												16
1			4		6^2		8	14		11	10			2	7			12	13	9^1	3	5^3												17
1		3	4		6^2		8	9^3		11	10			2	7			14	13	12		5^1												18
	2	3	4	13	12		8	9	14		10	5			7^1					11^3		6^2	1											19
	2	3	4				8	11	12		10	6		5^3	13	9^1		7^2				14	1											20
	2	3					8	9			10	5			7	14				11^2	4^1		1	6^3	12	13								21
		3					8	9		13	10^2	5		2^1		12							1	6	4	11	7							22
1		3	4		13		8			11		2^1		12	7					10^3				6	5^2	14		9						23
1		3	4		12		8			11		2			7			13						6^2	5^1		10	9						24
1	2		4				8			11^3		3	10					7^1		14		13			12			9^2	6	5				25
	2						8			11		3^2	14	13				7^1				12	1	6^3		10		9	4	5				26
1	2				6		8						12	3	7^1	13				11^2				14		10^3	9		4	5				27
1	2				6		8						12	3	7^2	11								13		10^1	9		4	5				28
1	2^3	14	4		6		8						12	3	7^1	11				13						10^2	9			5				29
1	2				6		8			14			12	3	7^3	11^2				13						10^1	9		4	5				30
1	2	3			6		8						10^2		5	11^3				9^1							7	14	4		12	13		31
1	2	3	4^2				8			11		5^1			7					13							10		6		12	9		32
1	2	3			13		8			11^2		5	10		7					12							6		4			9^1		33
1	2	3^1	12				8			11		5	10		7												6		4			9		34
1	2	3			12		8^3			11		5	10		7^1	14				13							6		4			9^2		35
1	2	3			12		8			11		5	10		7^1												6		4	13		9^2		36
1	2^1	3	4		13		8			11			10^3		7												6		5	12		9^2	14	37
1		3	12		6		8			11^2		2^1	10		5	14											7		4	13		9^3		38

MONTROSE Third Division

Year Formed: 1879. *Ground & Address:* Links Park, Wellington St, Montrose DD10 8QD. *Telephone:* 01674 673200. *Fax:* 01674 677311. *E-mail:* montrosefootballclub@tesco.net. *Website:* www.montrosefc.co.uk.
Ground Capacity: total: 3292, seated: 1338. *Size of Pitch:* 113yd × 70yd.
Chairman: John F. Paton. *Secretary:* John Crawford. *Assistant Secretary:* Andrew Stephen.
Manager: Henry Hall. *Coach:* Ian Gilzean. *Physio:* Fiona Fairlie.
Managers since 1975: A. Stuart, K. Cameron, R. Livingstone, S. Murray, D. D'Arcy, I. Stewart, C. McLelland, D. Rougvie, J. Leishman, J Holt, A. Dornan, D. Smith, T. Campbell, K. Drinkell.
Club Nickname(s): The Gable Endies. *Previous Grounds:* None.
Record Attendance: 8983 v Dundee, Scottish Cup 3rd rd, 17 Mar 1973.
Record Transfer Fee received: £50,000 for Gary Murray to Hibernian (Dec 1980).
Record Transfer Fee paid: £17,500 for Jim Smith from Airdrieonians (Feb 1992).
Record Victory: 12-0 v Vale of Leithen, Scottish Cup 2nd rd, 4 Jan 1975.
Record Defeat: 0-13 v Aberdeen, 17 Mar 1951.
Most Capped Player: Alexander Keillor, 2 (6), Scotland.
Most League Appearances: 432: David Larter, 1987-98.
Most League Goals in Season (Individual): 28: Brian Third, Division II, 1972-73.

MONTROSE 2004–05 LEAGUE RECORD

Match No.	*Date*	*Venue*	*Opponents*	*Result*		*H/T Score*	*Lg. Pos.*	*Goalscorers*	*Attendance*
1	Aug 7	A	East Fife	L	0-1	0-0	—		437
2	14	H	Peterhead	L	0-1	0-1	8		379
3	21	A	Gretna	L	0-1	0-0	9		501
4	28	A	Elgin C	W	3-1	0-1	9	Smart [59], Sharp 2 [76, 90]	555
5	Sept 4	H	Albion R	D	1-1	0-1	8	Stirling (og) [52]	330
6	11	A	Queen's Park	W	2-1	1-1	8	Watson [39], Smart [90]	406
7	18	H	Cowdenbeath	W	3-1	1-1	5	Smart 3 (1 pen) [23 (p), 62, 75]	351
8	25	H	Stenhousemuir	L	0-2	0-0	6		360
9	Oct 2	A	East Stirling	D	1-1	0-1	6	Webster [83]	247
10	16	A	Peterhead	L	2-3	1-2	6	Greenhill [41], Sharp [73]	626
11	23	H	East Fife	W	2-1	1-0	5	Doyle [10], Webster [83]	435
12	30	H	Elgin C	W	2-0	1-0	4	Smart [16], Wood [70]	447
13	Nov 6	A	Albion R	W	2-1	0-1	3	Smart (pen) [62], Wood [71]	245
14	13	H	Queen's Park	L	2-4	0-3	4	Webster 2 [62, 89]	410
15	30	A	Cowdenbeath	D	0-0	0-0	—		145
16	Dec 4	A	Stenhousemuir	D	1-1	1-0	3	Smart [26]	309
17	27	A	East Fife	L	0-1	0-0	6		784
18	Jan 1	H	Gretna	L	2-3	2-3	6	Sharp [17], Hall [30]	592
19	3	A	Elgin C	D	2-2	1-1	—	Kerrigan [30], Smart [55]	446
20	15	H	Albion R	L	0-1	0-1	7		269
21	22	A	Queen's Park	L	0-1	0-0	7		575
22	29	H	Cowdenbeath	L	1-2	1-1	7	Doyle [5]	292
23	Feb 5	H	Stenhousemuir	L	0-3	0-2	7		305
24	12	A	East Stirling	W	2-1	0-0	7	Smart [48], Watson [89]	198
25	19	A	Gretna	L	1-4	1-1	8	Wood [27]	913
26	26	H	Peterhead	L	0-2	0-0	8		467
27	Mar 1	H	East Stirling	W	4-1	1-1	—	McLean 2 [27, 70], Webster 2 [53, 60]	270
28	5	A	Albion R	W	2-1	1-0	6	Stephen [12], McLean [90]	307
29	12	H	Elgin C	W	2-0	0-0	5	Stephen [62], Smart (pen) [67]	308
30	19	H	Queen's Park	W	2-0	0-0	3	Wood [50], Smart (pen) [59]	377
31	Apr 2	A	Cowdenbeath	D	0-0	0-0	3		199
32	9	H	East Stirling	W	4-1	1-1	3	Wood [45], Sharp [54], Ferguson [62], McLean [84]	329
33	16	A	Stenhousemuir	W	1-0	0-0	3	Smart (pen) [48]	263
34	23	H	Gretna	L	0-4	0-1	5		462
35	30	A	Peterhead	L	1-4	0-1	5	Smart [64]	702
36	May 7	H	East Fife	D	2-2	0-0	5	Sharp 2 [84, 90]	496

Final League Position: 5

Honours
League Champions: Second Division 1984-85; *Runners-up:* 1990-91. Third Division, *Runners-up:* 1994-95.
Scottish Cup: Quarter-finals 1973, 1976.
League Cup: Semi-finals 1975-76.
B&Q Cup: Semi-finals 1992-93.
League Challenge Cup: Semi-finals 1996-97.

Club colours: Shirt: Royal blue. Shorts: Royal blue. Stockings: White.

Goalscorers: *League* (47): Smart 14 (5 pens), Sharp 7, Webster 6, Wood 5, McLean 4, Doyle 2, Stephen 2, Watson 2, Ferguson 1, Greenhill 1, Hall 1, Kerrigan 1, own goal 1.
Scottish Cup (7): Sharp 2, Smart 2, Dodds 1, Webster 1, Wood 1.
CIS Cup (1): Jones 1.
Challenge Cup (0).

Hankinson M 12	Donachie B 33+1	Budd A 6+2	Stephen N 33+1	Smith G 1	Kerrigan S 21	Webster K 28+3	Smart C 31+1	Watson C 10+16	Spink D 7+9	Sharp G 27+6	Smith D 1+10	Hall E 19+6	Bremner K —+3	Jones D —+2	Morrice K —+1	O'Reilly C 4+6	Doyle P 28	Wood M 29+1	Dodds K 19+7	Greenhill D 8+4	Ferguson s 25+1	Butter J 24	Slater M 4+4	Graham R —+7	McLean D 8+2	Fraser S 7+1	Smith E 11	*Match No.*
1	2	3	4	5^{2}	6	7	8	9^{3}	10	11^{1}	12	13	14															1
1	2	3	5		4		10	9^{2}	6	11^{3}	7^{1}	8	13	12	14													2
1	2	3	5^{2}		4	7	10	9^{1}	6			8	12	13		11												3
1	2	3	5		6	7^{2}	10			12		8				11^{1}	4	9	13									4
1	2		5		6	12	10	14		7^{3}		8				11^{1}	3	9	13	4^{2}								5
1	2^{2}	13	5		6	12	10	9^{1}	14	11		7					4		3	8^{3}								6
1	2		5		6	7	9		12	11		10^{2}				13	4		3	8^{1}								7
1	2		5		6	7^{1}	9		14	11		10				12	4		3^{2}	8^{3}	13							8
1	2		5		6	7		11^{2}	8^{3}	12		10^{1}				13	4	9		14	3							9
1	2		12		6^{1}	7^{3}		14		11		10^{2}				13	5	9	4	8	3							10
	12		5		6	7	10	13		11							4	9	2	8^{2}	3^{1}	1						11
	2		5		6	7	10	13		11^{3}		14				12	4	9^{2}		8^{1}	3	1						12
	2		5		6	7	8	12	13	11^{3}		10^{1}					4	9^{2}	14		3	1						13
	2^{1}		5		6^{2}	7	8	14		11^{3}		10					4	9	12		3	1	13					14
	2	13	5			7	8		14			12				11^{1}	4	9	6^{2}		3	1	10^{3}					15
	2	11^{1}	5		6	7^{2}	8				13	10				12	4	9			3	1						16
	2		5		6	7^{2}	8	13		12		10^{3}					4	9	11^{1}	14	3	1						17
	2	10^{1}	5		6	12	14	13		11		8^{3}					4	9	7^{2}		3	1						18
	2		5		6	7	8			11							4	9	10		3	1						19
	2		5		6	7	8	12		11^{3}		10^{2}					4	9^{1}		13	3	1	14					20
			5^{2}		6		8	14		12		10					4	9	2	7	3	1	11^{1}	13^{3}				21
	2		5		6^{1}		8	10^{2}		11							4	9	7	13	3	1	12					22
	2		5				8	10^{1}	13	11	14						4	12	7^{3}		3	1	6^{2}		9			23
1	2		5			7^{1}	8^{3}	14	13	11	12						4	9	6		3				10^{2}			24
	2^{1}		5			7^{2}		14		11	13						4	9	6		3	1	12		10^{3}	8		25
	2					7^{2}		12	14	11	13						5	9			3	1	8^{1}		10^{3}	6	4	26
	2					7^{1}	8	13		11^{3}	14						5	9	12		3	1			10^{2}	6	4	27
	2		6			7^{2}	8		14	12							5^{3}	9	13		3	1			10	11^{1}	4	28
	2		5			7	8	14		11^{2}							6^{1}	9^{3}	13		3	1			12	10	4	29
	2		5			7^{2}	8	10^{1}		13								9	11		3	1			12	6	4	30
	2		5			7^{3}	8	10^{1}		11^{2}	14	13					6	9			3	1		12			4	31
			5			7^{2}	8			11		13					6^{1}	9	2		3	1		12	10		4	32
	2		5				8	12		11		7^{2}						9	6		3	1		13	10^{1}		4	33
	2		5			7	8		4	11		10^{1}						9	6			1		12			3	34
1	2		5			7	8		4	11^{3}	14	10^{2}						9	6^{1}					13		12	3	35
	2		5			7	8	10^{3}	4	11	14	12						9^{2}				1		13		6^{1}	3	36

MORTON Second Division

Year Formed: 1874. *Ground & Address:* Cappielow Park, Sinclair St, Greenock. *Telephone:* 01475 723571. *Fax:* 01475 781084.
Ground Capacity: total: 11,612, seated: 6062. *Size of Pitch:* 110yd × 71yd.
Chairman: Douglas Rae. *Chief Executive:* Gillian Donaldson. *Company Secretary:* Mary Davidson. *Commercial Manager:* Susan Gregory.
Manager: John McInally. *Assistant Manager:* Martin Clark. *Physios:* Paul Kelly, Bruce Coyle. *Managers since 1975:* Joe Gilroy, Benny Rooney, Alex Miller, Tommy McLean, Willie McLean, Allan McGraw, Billy Stark, Ian McCall, Allan Evans, Peter Cormack, Dave McPherson, J. McCormack.
Club Nickname(s): The Ton. *Previous Grounds:* Grant Street 1874, Garvel Park 1875, Cappielow Park 1879, Ladyburn Park 1882, (Cappielow Park 1883).
Record Attendance: 23,500 v Celtic, 29 April 1922.
Record Transfer Fee received: £350,000 for Neil Orr to West Ham U.
Record Transfer Fee paid: £150,000 for Allan Mahood from Nottingham Forest.
Record Victory: 11-0 v Carfin Shamrock, Scottish Cup 1st rd, 13 Nov 1886.
Record Defeat: 1-10 v Port Glasgow Ath, Division II, 5 May, 1894 and v St Bernards, Division II, 14 Oct 1933.
Most Capped Player: Jimmy Cowan, 25, Scotland.
Most League Appearances: 358: David Hayes, 1969-84.
Most League Goals in Season (Individual): 58: Allan McGraw, Division II, 1963-64.

MORTON 2004–05 LEAGUE RECORD

Match No.	Date	Venue	Opponents	Result		H/T Score	Lg. Pos.	Goalscorers	Attendance
1	Aug 7	A	Berwick R	L	1-2	0-2	—	Walker J 72	907
2	14	H	Stranraer	W	3-1	2-0	4	McAlister 8, Wright (og) 41, Williams (pen) 54	2653
3	21	A	Dumbarton	W	3-0	1-0	3	Walker J 32, Weatherson 67, Greacen 84	1670
4	28	A	Ayr U	L	0-2	0-0	4		2264
5	Sept 4	H	Arbroath	W	2-1	1-0	4	Weatherson 2 7, 65	2360
6	11	A	Stirling A	D	1-1	1-1	5	Millar 43	1831
7	18	H	Brechin C	L	0-3	0-1	6		2432
8	25	A	Alloa Ath	W	6-1	1-0	5	Weatherson 2 28, 52, Millar 49, Walker J 2 68, 76, Maisano J 89	1056
9	Oct 2	H	Forfar Ath	W	2-1	0-1	4	Weatherson 69, Millar 74	2736
10	16	A	Stranraer	L	0-1	0-0	5		918
11	23	H	Berwick R	W	2-0	1-0	3	Walker J 36, Maisano J (pen) 88	2720
12	30	H	Ayr U	L	0-1	0-0	4		3232
13	Nov 6	A	Arbroath	W	3-0	0-0	4	Weatherson 49, Rennie (og) 62, Walker P 71	857
14	13	H	Stirling A	W	3-0	1-0	3	Walker P 9, Walker J 83, Millar 84	3020
15	27	A	Brechin C	L	1-2	0-1	4	Deas (og) 76	989
16	Dec 4	H	Alloa Ath	D	2-2	2-1	4	Walker P 3, Maisano J 42	2357
17	27	A	Berwick R	D	2-2	1-1	5	Maisano M 34, Millar 75	968
18	Jan 1	H	Dumbarton	W	3-0	1-0	3	Weatherson (pen) 24, McCluskey 54, Millar 63	2764
19	3	A	Ayr U	L	1-2	0-1	—	Walker P 47	2455
20	15	H	Arbroath	W	2-0	1-0	3	Millar 37, Templeman 54	2689
21	26	A	Stirling A	D	1-1	1-0	—	Greacen 2	1075
22	29	H	Brechin C	L	0-2	0-0	3		3004
23	Feb 12	H	Forfar Ath	W	4-0	3-0	4	Templeman 3 34, 41, 42, Weatherson (pen) 71	2244
24	19	A	Dumbarton	L	0-3	0-2	4		1508
25	26	H	Stranraer	W	2-0	1-0	3	McLaren 2 7, 57	2592
26	Mar 5	A	Arbroath	W	1-0	0-0	3	Millar 90	832
27	8	A	Forfar Ath	L	0-2	0-1	—		555
28	12	H	Ayr U	W	2-1	2-0	3	Millar 11, Maisano J 12	2448
29	19	H	Stirling A	W	2-0	1-0	3	Harding 16, Templeman 83	2764
30	23	A	Alloa Ath	D	2-2	1-2	—	Weatherson 42, Millar 68	959
31	Apr 2	A	Brechin C	W	2-1	0-0	3	McAlister 46, McLaren 66	1340
32	9	A	Forfar Ath	D	0-0	0-0	3		1064
33	16	H	Alloa Ath	W	2-0	0-0	3	Walker P 63, Millar 72	2721
34	23	H	Dumbarton	D	0-0	0-0	3		3229
35	30	A	Stranraer	D	1-1	1-1	3	Weatherson 40	2778
36	May 7	H	Berwick R	W	4-2	1-0	3	Templeman 40, Dillon 72, Maisano J 2 81, 90	2475

Final League Position: 3

Honours
League Champions: First Division 1977-78, 1983-84, 1986-87. Division II 1949-50, 1963-64, 1966-67. Second Division 1994-95. Third Division 2002-03. *Runners-up:* Division 1 1916-17, Division II 1899-1900, 1928-29, 1936-37.
Scottish Cup Winners: 1922; *Runners-up:* 1948. *League Cup Runners-up:* 1963-64.
B&Q Cup Runners-up: 1992-93.

European: *UEFA Cup:* 2 matches (*Fairs Cup:* 1968-69).

Club colours: Shirt: Royal blue with 3½ inch white hoops. Shorts: White with royal blue panel down side. Stockings: Royal blue with white tops.

Goalscorers: *League* (60): Millar 11, Weatherson 11 (2 pens), Maisano J 6 (1 pen), Templeman 6, Walker J 6, Walker P 5, McLaren 3, Greacen 2, McAlister 2, Dillon 1, Harding 1, Maisano M 1, McCluskey 1, Williams 1 (pen), own goals 3.
Scottish Cup (11): Millar 3, Weatherson 3, Walker J 2, Adam 1, Hawke 1, Williams 1.
CIS Cup (1): Walker P 1.
Challenge Cup (1): Walker J 1.

Coyle C 14	Collins D 21	McCulloch M 8 + 3	McCluskey S 22	Greacen S 32	Maisano M 9 + 1	Millar C 34	Maisano J 19 + 11	Williams A 12 + 5	Diack I 1 + 3	Walker P 20 + 11	Weatherson P 26 + 6	Walker J 11 + 16	McAlister J 35 + 1	Hawke W 4 + 2	Bannerman S 6 + 10	Keenan D 15 + 5	McLean K 1	McGurn D 22 + 1	Adam J 6 + 9	Mahood A 8 + 3	Templeman C 18 + 1	Dillon S 17	McLaughlin S 14 + 1	McLaren A 12	Harding R 9	*Match No.*
1	2	3	4	5	6	7	8	9^{2}	10^{1}	11^{3}	12	13	14													1
1	2	3	4	5		7	8^{3}	9		13	14	11^{2}	6^{1}	10	12											2
1	2	3	4^{3}	5		7	8	9^{1}		13	12	11	6	10^{2}		14										3
1	2	3	4^{3}	5		7	8	13		12	10	11^{2}	6	9^{1}	14											4
1	2	3		5		7	8	9^{2}	13	12	10		6			4	11^{1}									5
1	2	3		5	6	7	8	12			9		11	10^{1}		4										6
1	2	3		5	6	7	8^{2}	10		13	9^{1}	12	11			4										7
1	2	14	3	5	6	7	8	10^{1}			9	12	11^{3}		13	4^{2}										8
1	2	14	3	5	6	7	8	10^{1}			9	12	11^{3}		13	4^{2}										9
1	2	12	4	5	6	11	8	13		14	9	10^{2}	3^{1}		7^{3}											10
	2	3	4	5	6	7	8	9^{1}	14	13		10^{3}	11^{2}			12		1								11
	2^{1}		4	5	6	7		9		13	10	8	11		12	3^{2}		1								12
	2		4^{3}	5		7		9^{1}	13	8^{2}	10	12	11		14	3		1	6							13
	2		4	5	14	7	12	9^{2}		8^{1}	10	13	11			3		1	6^{3}							14
	2		4	5^{2}		7	14	9^{1}		11^{2}	10	12	8			3		1	6	13						15
1	2			5		7	10^{1}	13		8	12	9	11			3			6^{2}	4						16
1	2				5	7		13		8		10^{2}	11		12	3			6^{1}	4	9					17
1^{6}	2		4			7				8^{2}	5	10	11		13			15	12	6^{1}	9	3				18
1	2		4			7				8	5	10^{2}	11^{1}	13	14				12	6^{3}	9	3				19
	2		4	5		7^{3}				8^{2}	10^{1}	13	11			12		1	14	6	9	3				20
	2		4	5		7	14			8	10^{1}	13	11			12		1		6^{3}	9^{2}	3				21
			4	5		7	14			8	12	10^{1}	11^{3}			2^{2}		1	6		9	3	13			22
			4^{2}	5		7	12			8^{1}	3	14	11		2^{3}	13		1		6	9		10			23
			4	5		7	14			8^{3}	3	12	11		2			1	13	6^{2}	9^{1}		10			24
			4			7	10			8	5		11		2			1				3	6	9		25
			4	5		7	8^{2}				6^{1}	13	11		2			1	14		12	3	10^{3}	9		26
			4	5		7	6^{3}				12	13	11		2			1	14		8	3^{2}	10^{1}	9		27
				5		7	6^{1}			12	2		11					1			8	3	10	9	4	28
				5^{2}		7	14			6^{1}	2	12	11					1	13		8^{3}	3	10	9	4	29
				5		7	12			6^{1}	2		11					1			8	3	10	9	4	30
				5		7	6^{1}			13	2		11					1		12	9^{2}	3	10	8	4	31
				5		7	6^{1}			12			11			2		1			9	3	10	8	4	32
				5		7^{3}	13			6^{2}			11^{1}			2		1	12	14	9	3	10	8	4	33
				5			7^{1}			6	2	12	11					1	13		9	3^{2}	10	8	4	34
				5		7^{1}	13			6	2	12	11					1			9	3^{2}	10	8	4	35
				5			13			6	2		11^{1}	14	12	7^{2}		1			9^{3}	3	10	8	4	36

MOTHERWELL — Premier League

Year Formed: 1886. *Ground & Address:* Fir Park Stadium, Motherwell ML1 2QN. *Telephone:* 01698 333333. *Fax:* 01698 338001.
Ground Capacity: all seated: 13,742. *Size of Pitch:* 110yd × 75yd.
Chairman: Willian H. Dickie. *Secretary:* Stewart Robertson.
First Team Coach: Terry Butcher. *Coach:* Maurice Malpas. *Physios:* John Porteous, Peter Salila.
Managers since 1975: Ian St. John, Willie McLean, Rodger Hynd, Ally MacLeod, David Hay, Jock Wallace, Bobby Watson, Tommy McLean, Alex McLeish, Harri Kampman, Billy Davies, Eric Black.
Club Nickname(s): The Well. *Previous Grounds:* Roman Road, Dalziel Park.
Record Attendance: 35,632 v Rangers, Scottish Cup 4th rd replay, 12 Mar 1952.
Record Transfer Fee received: £1,750,000 for Phil O'Donnell to Celtic (September 1994).
Record Transfer Fee paid: £500,000 for John Spencer from Everton (Jan 1999).
Record Victory: 12-1 v Dundee U, Division II, 23 Jan 1954.
Record Defeat: 0-8 v Aberdeen, Premier Division, 26 Mar 1979.
Most Capped Player: Tommy Coyne, 13, Republic of Ireland.
Most League Appearances: 626: Bobby Ferrier, 1918-37.
Most League Goals in Season (Individual): 52: Willie McFadyen, Division I, 1931-32.
Most Goals Overall (Individual): 283: Hugh Ferguson, 1916-25.

MOTHERWELL 2004–05 LEAGUE RECORD

Match No.	Date	Venue	Opponents	Result		H/T Score	Lg. Pos.	Goalscorers	Attendance
1	Aug 8	A	Celtic	L	0-2	0-1	—		56,957
2	14	H	Hibernian	L	1-2	1-1	12	O'Donnell [21]	5859
3	21	A	Dundee	W	2-1	1-0	7	McDonald 2 [28, 62]	4849
4	28	H	Hearts	W	2-0	0-0	5	McBride (pen) [58], O'Donnell [66]	7095
5	Sept 11	A	Dunfermline Ath	D	1-1	0-1	6	McDonald [87]	4438
6	18	H	Dundee U	W	4-2	0-1	4	McDonald 2 [53, 68], Clarkson [57], Burns [90]	5091
7	25	A	Livingston	W	3-2	1-2	3	McBride [11], McDonald [50], Foran [71]	3950
8	Oct 3	A	Inverness CT	D	1-1	1-0	3	McDonald [38]	1438
9	17	H	Rangers	L	0-2	0-1	5		10,946
10	23	A	Aberdeen	L	1-2	1-0	6	McBride (pen) [28]	10,737
11	27	H	Kilmarnock	L	0-1	0-0	—		4605
12	30	H	Celtic	L	2-3	0-1	7	Corrigan [68], Foran (pen) [71]	10,592
13	Nov 6	A	Hibernian	L	0-1	0-0	7		9931
14	13	H	Dundee	W	3-0	1-0	7	Clarkson [44], Paterson 2 [52, 63]	4406
15	20	A	Hearts	W	1-0	1-0	6	Foran (pen) [27]	10,598
16	27	H	Dunfermline Ath	W	2-1	1-0	5	Tod (og) [26], Foran [61]	5084
17	Dec 4	A	Dundee U	W	1-0	1-0	5	Paterson [16]	5394
18	11	H	Livingston	W	2-0	1-0	4	O'Donnell [17], Foran [46]	4363
19	18	H	Inverness CT	L	1-2	0-2	5	Clarkson [64]	4267
20	27	A	Rangers	L	1-4	0-2	5	McDonald [49]	49,909
21	Jan 3	H	Aberdeen	D	0-0	0-0	5		6948
22	15	A	Kilmarnock	L	0-2	0-2	6		5225
23	22	A	Celtic	L	0-2	0-1	6		58,244
24	Feb 12	A	Dundee	L	1-2	1-1	6	McDonald [40]	5746
25	15	H	Hibernian	D	1-1	1-0	—	Craigan [26]	7453
26	19	H	Hearts	W	2-0	2-0	6	McDonald [25], Fitzpatrick [38]	7390
27	Mar 2	A	Dunfermline Ath	D	0-0	0-0	—		3427
28	5	H	Dundee U	W	2-0	1-0	6	Partridge [4], McDonald [47]	5110
29	12	A	Livingston	D	1-1	1-0	6	McDonald [18]	4049
30	Apr 3	H	Rangers	L	2-3	0-2	6	McBride [70], Corrigan [83]	10,210
31	9	A	Aberdeen	W	3-1	2-1	6	McBride (pen) [21], Hamilton [31], McDonald [72]	10,443
32	12	A	Inverness CT	L	0-1	0-1	—		3746
33	16	H	Kilmarnock	D	1-1	0-1	6	Combe (og) [86]	4999
34	23	H	Aberdeen	L	0-1	0-1	6		5063
35	30	A	Hearts	D	0-0	0-0	6		9337
36	May 7	H	Hibernian	D	2-2	1-0	6	Craigan 2 [15, 48]	8903
37	14	A	Rangers	L	1-4	0-2	6	Andrews (og) [88]	49,495
38	22	H	Celtic	W	2-1	0-1	6	McDonald 2 [87, 90]	12,944

Final League Position: 6

Honours
League Champions: Division I 1931-32. First Division 1981-82, 1984-85. Division II 1953-54, 1968-69; *Runners-up:* Premier Division 1994-95. Division I 1926-27, 1929-30, 1932-33, 1933-34. Division II 1894-95, 1902-03. *Scottish Cup:* 1952, 1991; *Runners-up:* 1931, 1933, 1939, 1951.
League Cup Winners: 1950-51. *Runners-up:* 1954-55, 2004-05. *Scottish Summer Cup:* 1944, 1965.

Club colours: Shirt: Amber with claret hoop and trimmings. Shorts: Amber. Stockings: Amber with claret trim.

European: *Cup Winners' Cup:* 2 matches (1991-92). *UEFA Cup:* 6 matches (1994-95, 1995-96).

Goalscorers: *League* (46): McDonald 15, Foran 5 (2 pens), McBride 5 (3 pens), Clarkson 3, Craigan 3, O'Donnell 3, Paterson 3, Corrigan 2, Burns 1, Fitzpatrick 1, Hamilton 1, Partridge 1, own goals 3.
Scottish Cup (0).
CIS Cup (15): Foran 4, McBride 2, O'Donnell 2, Partridge 2, Craigan 1, Clarkson 1, Fitzpatrick 1, Paterson 1, Wright 1.

Marshall G 33	Corrigan M 31	Kinniburgh W 10 + 3	Hammell S 32	Craigan S 37	Paterson J 27 + 8	O'Donnell P 18	Leitch S 28 + 1	Fagan S 11 + 12	Burns A 4 + 7	Clarkson D 25 + 10	McDonald S 26 + 1	Foran R 25 + 10	Fitzpatrick M 14 + 11	McBride K 24 + 1	Partridge D 29	Smith D — + 1	Quinn P 20 + 3	Wright K — + 6	Corr B 5 + 1	Hamilton J 13 + 1	Britton G — + 3	Kerr B 6 + 2	Keogh D — + 3	*Match No.*
1	2	3	4	5	6	7	8	9^3	10^1	11^2	12	13	14											1
1	2	3	4	5	6^3	7	8	9^1	10^2	13	11	14		12										2
1	2	3	4	5	6^1	7	8	13		11	10^2		12	9										3
1	2	3	4	5		7	8	13		11	10	9^1	12	6^2										4
1	2	3	4	5	12	7^1	8	13		11	10	9^2		6										5
1	2	3	4	5	14	7	8^1	12	13	11	10^2	9^3		6										6
1	2	3	4	5	13	7^1	8	12^3		11^2	10	9	14	6										7
1	2		4	5	12		8	7	13	11^1	10^2	9^3		6	3	14								8
1	2		4	5	12	7^1	8			11	10	9		6	3									9
1	2		4	5	12	7	8	13	14	11	10^3	9^2		6^1	3									10
1	2		4	5	6		8^1	12	13	11	10^2	9			3		7							11
1	2		4	5	6	8			10	11		9			3		7							12
1	2		4	5	6^1	8		13	10^2	11		9	12		3		7							13
1	2		4	5	6	8^1	12		13	11		10^3	9^2		3		7	14						14
1	2		4	5	6		8		12	11^2		10	9^1		3		7	13						15
1	2		4	5	6	7	8			11^1		10	9		3		12							16
1	2		4	5	9		8^1	14		11^2		10^3	6	7	3		12	13						17
1	2			5	9	7	8			11		10^1	4	6	3			12						18
1	2			5	9	7^1	8			11■		10	4	6	3		12							19
	2		4	5	9			12	13		11^1	10	6^2	8	3		7		1					20
	2	13	4	5	7^1		8			11	9	10	12	6	3^2				1					21
1	2		4	5			8^2	13		11^3	9	10^1	12	6	3		7	14						22
1	2		4	5	8^2			12		11^1	9	10^3	13	6	3		7	14						23
1			4	5	9^1	7	8			13	11	12		6	3		2			10^2				24
1			4	5	9^3	7^1	8			14	11^2	13	12	6	3		2			10				25
1			4	5	9^2		8			12	11^1	13	7	6	3		2			10				26
1		12	4	5^1	9		8				11	13	7	6^2	3		2			10				27
1	2		4	5	9	7^3	8			13	11^2	12	14	6^1	3					10				28
	2		4	5	9^1					13	11^2	12	8	7	3		6		1	10				29
1	2		4	5	9^1		8			11^2	10	12		7	3		6				13			30
1			4	5	9		8^1	7		13	11^2			6	3		2			10		12		31
1■			4	5	9		8	7^2		12	11^1			6^3	3		2		13	10		14		32
			4	5	9^1		8^2	7		11		12	13		3		2		1	10	14	6^3		33
	2	6	4	5			8^1	7				11			3				1	10		9	12	34
1	2			5	12			8^1		11		9^2	7		3		4			10		6	13	35
1	2	12		5	13			8		14	11^3	9^2	7		3^1		4			10		6		36
1	2	4			8			7		11	10	9^2	6				3^1			13		5	12	37
1	2	4		5	8			7		13	11	9	6^2							10^1	12	3		38

PARTICK THISTLE — Second Division

Year Formed: 1876. *Ground & Address:* Firhill Stadium, 80 Firhill Rd, Glasgow G20 7AL. *Telephone:* 0141 579 1971. *Fax:* 0141 945 1525. *E-mail:* mail@ptfc.co.uk. *Website:* www.ptfc.co.uk.
Ground Capacity: total: 13,141, seated: 10,921. *Size of Pitch:* 110yd × 75yd.
Chairman: Brown McMaster. *Secretary:* Antonia Kerr. *Commercial Manager:* Michael Max.
Manager: Dick Campbell. *Coach:* Jimmy Bone. *Physio:* George Hannah.
Managers since 1975: R. Auld, P. Cormack, B. Rooney, R. Auld, D. Johnstone, W. Lamont, S. Clark, J. Lambie, M. MacLeod, J. McVeigh, T. Bryce, J. Lambie, G. Collins, G. Britton & D. Whyte.
Club Nickname(s): The Jags. *Previous Grounds:* Jordanvale Park; Muirpark; Inchview; Meadowside Park.
Record Attendance: 49,838 v Rangers, Division I, 18 Feb 1922. *Ground Record:* 54,728, Scotland v Ireland, 25 Feb 1928.
Record Transfer Fee received: £200,000 for Mo Johnston to Watford.
Record Transfer Fee paid: £85,000 for Andy Murdoch from Celtic (Feb 1991).
Record Victory: 16-0 v Royal Albert, Scottish Cup 1st rd, 17 Jan 1931.
Record Defeat: 0-10 v Queen's Park, Scottish Cup, 3 Dec 1881.
Most Capped Player: Alan Rough, 51 (53), Scotland.
Most League Appearances: 410: Alan Rough, 1969-82.
Most League Goals in Season (Individual): 41: Alex Hair, Division I, 1926-27.

PARTICK THISTLE 2004–05 LEAGUE RECORD

Match No.	Date	Venue	Opponents	Result	H/T Score	Lg. Pos.	Goalscorers	Attendance
1	Aug 7	A	Clyde	L 1-2	0-2	—	Escalas [79]	3352
2	14	H	Airdrie U	W 3-2	1-1	6	Escalas [34], Hinds [54], Mitchell [69]	4011
3	21	A	Hamilton A	W 1-0	1-0	3	Escalas [31]	3543
4	28	A	Ross Co	W 1-0	0-0	3	Hinds [54]	2781
5	Sept 4	H	Falkirk	L 1-4	0-2	4	Panther [65]	5157
6	11	A	St Mirren	L 1-2	1-0	4	Escalas [16]	4711
7	18	H	Queen of the S	L 1-2	1-0	6	Escalas [9]	3233
8	25	A	St Johnstone	L 1-2	0-0	7	Milne [66]	2763
9	Oct 2	H	Raith R	W 2-0	2-0	6	Panther [2], Oné [21]	3059
10	16	A	Airdrie U	L 2-4	1-2	7	Madaschi [44], Escalas [66]	2548
11	23	H	Clyde	D 0-0	0-0	7		4026
12	30	H	Ross Co	W 4-0	2-0	4	Escalas 2 [13, 17], Madaschi [53], Oné [88]	2898
13	Nov 13	H	St Mirren	L 0-3	0-0	7		1949
14	20	A	Queen of the S	L 0-1	0-0	8		2221
15	23	A	Falkirk	L 0-3	0-0	—		3335
16	27	A	Raith R	D 0-0	0-0	8		2452
17	Dec 4	H	St Johnstone	L 0-4	0-2	8		2945
18	11	A	Clyde	D 1-1	1-1	9	Wilkinson [39]	1938
19	18	H	Hamilton A	L 0-1	0-1	9		3051
20	27	A	Ross Co	L 1-2	0-1	9	Escalas [76]	2844
21	29	H	Falkirk	W 2-1	1-1	—	Oné 2 [9, 61]	4120
22	Jan 1	A	St Mirren	D 1-1	1-0	9	Fleming [41]	3779
23	15	H	Queen of the S	W 3-1	2-1	9	Oné [20], Craig (og) [37], Paton (og) [69]	3257
24	22	A	St Johnstone	D 1-1	0-0	9	Hinds [66]	2814
25	29	H	Raith R	W 4-1	1-1	8	Ross A [41], Oné [63], McConalogue 2 [80, 86]	3181
26	Feb 12	H	Airdrie U	D 1-1	1-1	8	Fleming [14]	3791
27	19	A	Hamilton A	L 0-1	0-0	9		3128
28	Mar 5	A	Falkirk	L 1-2	1-2	9	Murray (pen) [29]	4157
29	12	H	Ross Co	D 0-0	0-0	9		2939
30	19	H	St Mirren	D 0-0	0-0	9		3730
31	Apr 2	A	Queen of the S	L 1-3	0-2	9	McConalogue [57]	2589
32	9	A	Raith R	L 1-2	0-1	9	Escalas [87]	1403
33	16	H	St Johnstone	L 0-4	0-3	9		2310
34	23	H	Clyde	W 1-0	1-0	9	McConalogue [43]	2757
35	30	A	Airdrie U	W 1-0	1-0	9	Hinds [7]	1747
36	May 7	H	Hamilton A	D 1-1	1-0	9	Lumsden (og) [21]	2845

Final League Position: 9

Honours
League Champions: First Division 1975-76, 2001-02. Division II 1896-97, 1899-1900, 1970-71; Second Division 2000-01; *Runners-up:* First Division 1991-92. Division II 1901-02.
Scottish Cup Winners: 1921; *Runners-up:* 1930; *Semi-finals:* 2002.
League Cup Winners: 1971-72; *Runners-up:* 1953-54, 1956-57, 1958-59.
Bell's League Challenge: Quarter-finals 2004-05.

European: *Fairs Cup:* 4 matches (1963-64). *UEFA Cup:* 2 matches (1972-73). *Intertoto Cup:* 4 matches 1995-96.

Club colours: Shirt: Red and yellow halves with black sleeves. Shorts: Black. Stockings: Black.

Goalscorers: *League* (38): Escalas 10, Oné 6, Hinds 4, McConalogue 4, Fleming 2, Madaschi 2, Panther 2, Milne 1, Mitchell 1, Murray 1 (pen), Ross A 1, Wilkinson 1, own goals 3.
Scottish Cup (1): Oné 1.
CIS Cup (6): Hinds 2, Dowie 1, Escalas 1, Fleming 1, Gibson W 1.
Challenge Cup (6): Gibson W 2, Panther 2, Escalas 1, Hinds 1.

Arthur K 35	Gibson W 22 + 6	Howie W 4 + 3	Murray G 31 + 1	Dowie A 26 + 1	Fulton S 16 + 3	Mitchell J 17 + 4	Fleming D 32 + 3	Escalas J 27 + 3	Hinds L 24 + 11	Anis J 14 + 2	Oné A 15 + 12	Wilkinson A 9 + 2	Panther E 6 + 8	Milne K 26 + 4	Madaschi A 26 + 1	Strachan A 6 + 7	Britton G — + 1	Ross A 11 + 3	McLaren A 5 + 4	Ross I 6 + 1	Gibson A 11 + 2	McConalogue S 8 + 4	Brady D 10 + 1	Snowdon W 7 + 1	Bennett N 1	Paterson S 1	Stewart M — + 2	Cameron I — + 2	*Match No.*
1	2	3[3]	4	5	6	7	8[1]	9	10[2]	11	12	13	14																1
1	2	13	4		6[2]	7	8	9	10	11		5	12	3[1]															2
1	2		4	5	6	7	8	9	10[1]	11	12		13	3[2]															3
1	2	12	4	5	6	7	8		10	11[1]	9		13	3[2]															4
1	2	11	4		6	7	8[2]	9	10		13		12	3[1]	5														5
1	2	11	4	5	6	7	8[2]	9	10		13		3[1]	12															6
1		7	4	5	6[2]		8[3]	9	11	12	10[1]		2	14	3	13													7
1		13	4	5			8	9	7[1]	12	10[3]	2[2]	6	11	3		14												8
1			4	5		13	8	9[1]	12	7[2]	10	2	6	11	3														9
1	12		4	5[1]		13	8	9	14	7[2]	10[3]	2	6	11	3														10
1	2			3	6	7	8	9	10[1]		12		4	11	5														11
1	2[1]		4	3	6	7	8	9	10[2]		13		12	11[3]	5					14									12
1	2		4	3	6	7[2]	8	9[3]	10		13		14	11[1]	5				12										13
1	2		4	3	6		8[3]	9	10[2]	7[1]	14		12		5				13	11									14
1	8		4	3	6[2]		13	9[1]	10		12	2[3]			5	14			7	11									15
1	7		4	5[1]	6		8	9	10			2			12	13			11[2]	3									16
1	2		4	3	6		8[1]	9	10			7		13	5[2]				12	11									17
1			4	3		12	8	9[1]	10			2		11	5				7	6									18
1	2[2]		4	3		14	8	9[3]	10		13			11	5	12			7	6[1]									19
1	8		2	5[3]	12	7[2]	6	9	10		14	4[1]		11	3				13										20
1	14		4			7[3]	6	9	13	2	8[2]	12		3	5	11[1]			10										21
1	12		4			7	6	9[1]		2	8			3	5	11					10								22
1				4	13	7[1]	6	9[2]	14	2	8[3]			3	5	10		12			11								23
1	14		4	6[3]	13			9	12	2	8[1]			3	5	11[2]		10			7								24
1	2		4	14	6[3]		11	13	8[2]		9[1]			3	5			10			7	12							25
1	2		4	5	6[3]		11	12	8[2]		9[1]			3				10			7	13	14						26
1			2	4			3	11	12		9[1]				5	13		10			7[2]	8	6						27
1	12		2	4		7	6		14		9[3]			3	5[1]	13		8				10[2]	11						28
1			5	6		10	13	9[3]	12					3		11[1]		8			7[2]	14	4	2					29
1			5	4		7[1]	11	9[2]	14		13			3				8			12	10[3]	6	2					30
1	12		4	5		7[3]	11		13		9[2]			3[1]	6			10				14	8	2					31
	7		4				14	13	8					3	5	11[1]		10[3]			12	9[2]	6	2	1				32
1	7[3]		2				6	9	14					3	5			13			11	10	8[2]	12		4[1]			33
1	8						3		7	2	9[1]			6				12			11	10[2]	4	5			13		34
1	8		13				3		9	2					5[3]	12		11[2]			7	10	6[1]	4				14	35
1	4						3		10[2]	2				12	6			11			7[3]	9[1]	8	5			13	14	36

PETERHEAD — Second Division

Year Formed: 1891. *Ground and Address:* Balmoor Stadium, Lord Catto Park, Peterhead AB42 1EU.
Telephone: 01779 478256. *Fax:* 01779 490682. *E-mail:* shona@peterheadfc.org.uk. *Website:* www.peterheadfc.org.uk.
Ground Capacity: 3250, seated 1000.
Chairman: Roger Taylor. *General Manager:* Dave Watson. *Secretary:* George Moore.
Manager: Iain Stewart. *Assistant Manager:* Paul Mathers. *Coach:* Shaun McSkimming. *Physio:* Sandy Rennie.
Managers since 1975: C. Grant, D. Darcy, I. Taylor, J. Harper, D. Smith, J. Hamilton, G. Adams, J. Guyan, I. Wilson, D. Watson, R. Brown, D. Watson, I. Wilson.
Club Nickname(s): Blue Toon. *Previous Ground:* Recreation Park.
Record Attendance: 6310 friendly v Celtic, 1948.
Record Victory: 17-0 v Fort William, 1998-99 (in Highland League).
Record Defeat: 0-13 v Aberdeen, Scottish Cup, 1923-24.
Most League Appearances: 135, Martin Johnston, 2000-05.
Most League Goals in Season (Individual): 21, Iain Stewart, 2002-03.
Most Goals Overall (Individual): 58, Iain Stewart, 2000-05.

PETERHEAD 2004–05 LEAGUE RECORD

Match No.	Date	Venue	Opponents	Result	H/T Score	Lg. Pos.	Goalscorers	Attendance
1	Aug 7	H	East Stirling	W 5-0	2-0	—	Tully 2 [12, 30], Buchan [52], Hagen [60], Johnston [89]	561
2	14	A	Montrose	W 1-0	1-0	2	Michie [36]	379
3	21	H	Elgin C	W 2-1	2-0	2	Bavidge [23], Michie [35]	688
4	28	A	Albion R	W 1-0	1-0	1	Robertson S [34]	351
5	Sept 4	H	East Fife	W 2-0	2-0	1	Michie 2 (1 pen) [5 (p), 25]	507
6	11	H	Gretna	D 1-1	1-0	1	Buchan [43]	861
7	18	A	Stenhousemuir	W 2-1	0-1	1	Michie 2 [68, 77]	307
8	25	H	Cowdenbeath	W 3-1	2-1	1	Raeside [10], Michie 2 [37, 73]	582
9	Oct 2	A	Queen's Park	W 2-1	1-1	1	Michie [8], Buchan [75]	625
10	16	H	Montrose	W 3-2	2-1	1	Campbell [23], Tully [37], Linn [70]	626
11	23	A	East Stirling	W 2-1	1-0	1	Michie 2 (1 pen) [30, 61 (p)]	281
12	30	H	Albion R	W 4-1	2-0	1	Raeside [35], Michie 2 [45, 52], McGowan (og) [67]	729
13	Nov 6	A	East Fife	W 2-0	0-0	1	Raeside [52], Hagen [83]	410
14	13	A	Gretna	L 1-2	1-1	2	Hagen (pen) [32]	2200
15	30	H	Stenhousemuir	W 5-0	2-0	—	Bavidge 4 (1 pen) [22, 34, 77 (p), 80], Stewart G [67]	499
16	Dec 4	A	Cowdenbeath	W 4-0	0-0	2	Michie 3 (1 pen) [52, 65, 82 (p)], Linn [77]	201
17	18	H	Queen's Park	D 2-2	1-0	2	Bavidge [27], Tully [79]	569
18	27	H	East Stirling	W 3-0	2-0	2	Stewart G [13], Tully [37], Bavidge [79]	647
19	Jan 3	A	Albion R	W 4-0	1-0	—	Buchan 2 [25, 76], Linn [46], Bavidge [61]	306
20	15	H	East Fife	D 0-0	0-0	2		587
21	22	H	Gretna	W 4-2	0-0	2	Bavidge [61], Stewart G [70], Tully [73], Michie [83]	1207
22	29	A	Stenhousemuir	D 1-1	0-0	2	Michie [67]	394
23	Feb 5	H	Cowdenbeath	D 1-1	1-0	2	Cameron [3]	563
24	12	A	Queen's Park	D 1-1	0-0	2	Michie [90]	454
25	26	A	Montrose	W 2-0	0-0	2	Michie 2 (1 pen) [56, 80 (p)]	467
26	Mar 1	H	Elgin C	W 3-0	2-0	—	Cameron [2], Linn [30], Buchan [60]	611
27	5	A	East Fife	W 2-1	1-0	2	Linn [23], Youngson [52]	495
28	8	A	Elgin C	D 2-2	1-1	—	Linn [28], Nelson (og) [47]	383
29	12	H	Albion R	L 2-3	0-0	2	Raeside [64], Stewart G [89]	532
30	19	A	Gretna	L 1-6	0-1	2	Bavidge (pen) [70]	1538
31	Apr 2	H	Stenhousemuir	D 1-1	1-1	2	Bavidge [3]	523
32	9	H	Queen's Park	D 1-1	0-1	2	Buchan [61]	479
33	16	A	Cowdenbeath	L 0-4	0-2	2		153
34	23	A	Elgin C	W 2-0	1-0	2	Hegarty [31], Buchan [87]	507
35	30	H	Montrose	W 4-1	1-0	2	Stewart G 2 [5, 89], Tully [67], Cameron [76]	702
36	May 7	A	East Stirling	W 5-1	3-0	2	Cameron [3], Bavidge 2 [14, 42], Stewart I [64], Youngson [79]	192

Final League Position: 2

Honours
Third Division Runners up: 2004-05.
Scottish Cup: Quarter-finals 2001.
Highland League Champions: winners 5 times.
Scottish Qualifying Cup (North): winners 6 times.
North of Scotland Cup: winners 5 times.
Aberdeenshire Cup: winners: 20 times.

Club colours: Shirt: Royal blue with white; Shorts: Royal blue; Stockings: Royal blue tops with white hoops.

Goalscorers: *League* (81): Michie 21 (4 pens), Bavidge 13 (2 pens), Buchan 8, Tully 7, Linn 6, Stewart G 6, Cameron 4, Raeside 4, Hagen 3 (1 pen), Youngson 2, Campbell 1, Hegarty 1, Johnston 1, Robertson S 1, Stewart I 1, own goals 2.
Scottish Cup (1): Bavidge 1.
CIS Cup (4): Bavidge 2, Michie 2 (1 pen).
Challenge Cup (5): Bavidge 3, Buchan 1, Gibson 1.

Mathers P 33	Tully C 34	Good I 31 + 1	Raeside R 32 + 1	Perry M 34	Gibson K 27 + 5	Campbell C 12 + 11	Buchan J 35 + 1	Michie S 30 + 6	Bavidge M 31 + 5	Hagen D 25 + 1	Youngson A 14 + 17	Johnston M — + 5	Tindal K — + 2	Robertson S 10 + 3	Milne D — + 1	Stewart G 13 + 8	Linn R 14 + 13	McSkimming S — + 3	Shand R — + 1	Cameron D 13 + 3	Thompson B 3	Hegarty C 4 + 1	Stewart I — + 2	Robertson C 1	Duncan R — + 1	*Match No.*
1	2	3	4^{1}	5	6	7^{2}	8	9^{3}	10	11	12	13	14													1
1	2	4		5	6	7	8	9^{2}	10	11	3^{1}	12	13													2
1	2	4		5	6	7	8	9^{1}	10	11	3	12														3
1	2	4		5	6	7	8	9^{1}	10	11	12			3												4
1	2	3	4	5	6	13	8	9^{3}	10^{1}		11^{2}	12		7	14											5
1	2	3	4	5	6		8	9^{1}	10	11		12		7												6
1	2	3	4	5	6^{1}	14	8	9	10	11^{2}	13			7^{3}		12										7
1	2	3	4	5	6	12	8	9	10^{3}	11^{2}	13			7^{1}		14										8
1	2	3	4	5	6	12	8	9^{2}	10	11	13			7^{1}												9
1	2	3	4	5	6^{2}	7^{1}	8	9	10	11^{3}	14			13			12									10
1	2	3^{1}	4	5	6	7	8	9^{3}	10^{2}	11	12			14			13									11
1	2		4	5	6		8	9	10	11^{2}	3			7^{1}		12	13									12
1	2	14	4	5	6	13	8	9^{1}	10	11	3^{3}			7^{2}			12									13
1	2	3	4	5	6	7	8	12	10	11							9^{1}									14
1	2	3	4	5	6		8	9^{1}	10		11^{3}			13		7^{2}	12	14								15
1	2	3	4^{3}	5	6		8	9	10^{1}					7		11^{2}	12	14	13							16
1	2	3	4	5	6		8	9^{2}	10		12			7		11^{1}	13									17
1	2	3	4	5	14	13	8	9^{2}	10	11^{1}	12					6^{3}	7									18
1	2	3	4	5	12	7	8	14	10	11^{2}	13					6^{1}	9^{3}									19
1	2	3	4	5	12		8	13	10	11	7^{1}					6	9^{2}									20
1	2	3	4	5	12	7	8	9^{2}	10							6	13			11^{1}						21
1	2	3	4	5	12	7	8	9^{2}	10							6	13			11^{1}						22
1	2^{2}	3	4^{3}	5	6	13	8	9	10		14					7^{1}	12			11						23
1	2	3^{1}	4	5	6	7	8	9	10^{2}		12						13	14		11^{3}						24
1	2	3	4	5	6^{2}		8	9	14	11^{1}	12					13	10^{3}			7						25
1	2	3	4	5	6	12	8^{3}	9^{2}	13		11^{1}					14	10			7						26
1	2	3	4	5	6	13	8	9^{3}	12		11^{2}					14	10^{1}			7						27
1	2	3^{1}	4	5	6		8	9^{2}	13	12	11^{3}					14	10			7						28
1	2		4	5	6	7^{1}	8	12	9	11^{3}	3^{2}					13	10			14						29
1	2	3	4	5	6	12	8	13	10	11^{3}	14						9^{2}			7^{1}						30
	2		4	5	6	13	12	9^{2}	10	11^{1}	7^{3}					8■	14			3	1					31
	2■	4	12	5	6		8	9	13	11^{3}	3^{1}						10^{2}			14	1	7				32
		3	4	5			8	13	10	11^{2}	12					6	9			2^{1}	1	7				33
1		3	4	5			8	9^{1}	10	11	13					6	12			2^{2}		7				34
1	2	3^{1}	4				8	9	10	11	5^{2}					6	7^{3}			13		12	14			35
1	2		4				8	9^{1}	10	11	13						7			6^{3}		3	12	5^{2}	14	36

QUEEN OF THE SOUTH First Division

Year Formed: 1919. *Ground & Address:* Palmerston Park, Dumfries DG2 9BA. *Telephone and Fax:* 01387 254853.
Ground Capacity: total: 8352, seated: 3549. *Size of Pitch:* 112yd × 73yd.
Chairman: David Rae. *Vice-Chairman:* Thomas Harkness. *Commercial Manager:* Margaret Heuchan. *Physio/Business Development Manager:* Kenny Crichton.
Manager: Ian Scott. *Assistant Manager:* Warren Pearson. *First Team Coach:* Brian Reid.
Managers since 1975: M. Jackson, W. Hunter, B. Little, G. Herd, H. Hood, A. Busby, R. Clark, M. Jackson, D. Wilson, W. McLaren, F. McGarvey, A. MacLeod, D. Frye, W. McLaren, M. Shanks, R. Alexander, J. Connolly.
Club Nickname(s): The Doonhamers. *Previous Grounds:* None.
Record Attendance: 26,552 v Hearts, Scottish Cup 3rd rd, 23 Feb 1952.
Record Transfer Fee received: £250,000 for Andy Thomson to Southend U (1994).
Record Transfer Fee paid: £30,000 for Jim Butter from Alloa Athletic (1995).
Record Victory: 11-1 v Stranraer, Scottish Cup 1st rd, 16 Jan 1932.
Record Defeat: 2-10 v Dundee, Division I, 1 Dec 1962.
Most Capped Player: Billy Houliston, 3, Scotland.
Most League Appearances: 731: Allan Ball, 1963-82.
Most League Goals in Season (Individual): 37: Jimmy Gray, Division II, 1927-28.
Most Goals in Season: 41: Jimmy Rutherford, 1931-32.
Most Goals Overall (Individual): 250: Jim Patterson, 1949-63.

QUEEN OF THE SOUTH 2004–05 LEAGUE RECORD

Match No.	Date	Venue	Opponents	Result		H/T Score	Lg. Pos.	Goalscorers	Attendance
1	Aug 7	H	Ross Co	L	0-1	0-1	—		1910
2	14	A	St Johnstone	W	3-1	2-0	5	Wood 4, McNiven 2 34, 73	2384
3	21	H	Falkirk	L	1-3	1-1	8	McNiven (pen) 25	2521
4	28	H	Clyde	L	0-1	0-1	8		1639
5	Sept 4	A	Airdrie U	W	1-0	1-0	6	McLaughlin 40	1652
6	11	H	Hamilton A	D	1-1	0-1	5	McNiven 57	1708
7	18	A	Partick Th	W	2-1	0-1	4	McNiven 64, Payne 90	3233
8	25	A	Raith R	W	2-1	1-1	4	English 45, Bowey 70	1491
9	Oct 2	H	St Mirren	W	2-1	2-0	4	Burns 5, McNiven 13	2734
10	16	H	St Johnstone	L	0-1	0-0	4		2059
11	23	A	Ross Co	L	0-1	0-0	4		2354
12	30	A	Clyde	L	0-2	0-2	5		1284
13	Nov 6	H	Airdrie U	W	1-0	0-0	4	Bowey 53	2022
14	13	A	Hamilton A	L	0-1	0-0	4		1592
15	20	H	Partick Th	W	1-0	0-0	4	Craig 80	2221
16	27	A	St Mirren	D	2-2	0-0	4	Lyle 52, Bowey 55	2850
17	Dec 4	H	Raith R	W	2-0	1-0	4	Lyle 26, Paton 65	1646
18	11	H	Ross Co	W	1-0	1-0	4	Lyle 28	1588
19	18	A	Falkirk	L	2-4	2-3	4	Lyle 12, McLaughlin 14	3370
20	29	A	Airdrie U	L	0-2	0-1	—		1781
21	Jan 1	H	Hamilton A	L	1-2	0-1	6	Paton 54	1790
22	15	A	Partick Th	L	1-3	1-2	7	Lyle 4	3257
23	22	A	Raith R	W	1-0	0-0	7	Lyle 87	1534
24	29	H	St Mirren	D	0-0	0-0	6		2016
25	Feb 12	A	St Johnstone	D	0-0	0-0	6		1782
26	19	H	Falkirk	D	1-1	1-0	6	Lyle 35	2551
27	Mar 2	H	Clyde	L	0-1	0-1	—		1448
28	5	H	Airdrie U	D	0-0	0-0	6		1683
29	12	A	Clyde	W	1-0	0-0	6	McNiven 69	1033
30	19	A	Hamilton A	D	1-1	1-0	6	McNiven 1	1560
31	Apr 2	H	Partick Th	W	3-1	2-0	4	McNiven 2 29, 50, Paton 35	2589
32	9	A	St Mirren	L	0-3	0-2	5		2331
33	16	H	Raith R	D	1-1	1-1	7	McNiven 25	1361
34	23	A	Ross Co	D	1-1	1-1	7	Paton 21	2403
35	30	H	St Johnstone	W	2-0	2-0	4	Wood 2 20, 24	1784
36	May 7	A	Falkirk	W	2-1	0-1	4	Kernaghan (og) 79, McNiven 87	5067

Final League Position: 4

Honours
League Champions: Division II 1950-51. Second Division 2001-02. *Runners-up:* Division II 1932-33, 1961-62, 1974-75. Second Division 1980-81, 1985-86.
Scottish Cup: semi-finals 1949-50.
League Cup: semi-finals 1950-51, 1960-61.
B&Q Cup: semi-finals 1991-92. *League Challenge Cup Winners:* 2002-03; *Runners-up:* 1997-98.

Club colours: Shirt: Royal blue with white sleeves. Shorts: White with blue piping. Stockings: Royal blue.

Goalscorers: *League* (36): McNiven 12 (1 pen), Lyle 7, Paton 4, Bowey 3, Wood 3, McLaughlin 2, Burns 1, Craig 1, English 1, Payne 1, own goal 1.
Scottish Cup (2): Gibson 1, Lyle 1.
CIS Cup (1): McNiven 1.
Challenge Cup (2): English 1, Wood 1.

Scott Colin 23 + 1	Scott Christopher 1	English T 29 + 1	McColligan B 27 + 5	Reid B 21	Thomson J 34	Bagan D 17 + 4	Bowey S 34	McNiven D 22 + 8	Armstrong C 2 + 5	McLaughlin B 25 + 5	Burns P 18 + 5	Gibson W 13 + 8	Payne S 10 + 7	Paton E 28 + 2	Wood G 20 + 8	Craig D 18	Jaconelli E 3 + 12	George L — + 2	Lyle D 22 + 1	Bernard R 13	Bell S 1 + 1	Williams A 1 + 4	Lovell S 12	Carr C 2 + 1	Match No.
1	2	3	4^1	5	6	7	8	9^2	10	11^3	12	13	14												1
1		3	4	5	6	7	8	9	12	11				2	10^1										2
1		3	4	5	6	7^2	8	9	13	11	12			2^1	10										3
1		3	4	5	6	7^1	8	9	10	11	2		12												4
1		3	4		6	7	8	9		11	2		10		5										5
1		8^2	4		6	7		9^3	14	11	2		10^1	12	5	3	13								6
1		8^1	4	5	6	12		9		11^2	10		14	7	2	3^3		13							7
1		3	12	5	6	7	8	9^2		11	10			4^1	2		13								8
1		3	4	5	6	7	8	9^3		11^2	10^1			12	2		13	14							9
1		3^2	4	5	6	7^1	8	9		11		12		10	2		13								10
1		3	4	5	6	7^2	8	9		11^3		12	14	10^1	2		13								11
1		3^1	12	5^2	6	4	8	9^3	14		7	11			2		13		10						12
1		3	4		6		8	9^1		12	7	11		2	5				10						13
1		14	4		6		8	9^2	13	12	7	11^1		2	5	3			10^3						14
1		3	4		6	13	8^2			9^3	7^1	11	12	2	14	5			10						15
1		3	4		6	7	8	12		9^3		11^2	13	2		5	14		10^1						16
1		3	12		6	7	8^1	13		9^3	4	11^2		2		5	14		10						17
1		3	12		6	7^1	8			9	4	11		2	13	5			10^2						18
1		3	4		6	7^1	8	14		9^2	11	12		2		5	13		10^3						19
					6	7	8	12		9	4	11^1		2	5	3	13		10^2	1					20
1		3^3			6	7^1	8	13		9^2	4	11		2	12	5	14		10						21
1			3		6	12	8	13		9^2	7	11		2		5			10		4^1				22
1		3	4		6	13	8			7^2		11		2		5	9^1		10			12			23
1			4	5	6		8				7	11		2		3	12		10			9^1			24
			4	5	6		8			11				2	9	3			10	1			7		25
			4	5	6		8			11^1				2	9	3			10	1		12	7		26
				5	6		8	14		11^2	4^3	13		2	9	3^1	10			1		12	7		27
		3		5	6		8	13		11^1	12		14	2	4		9		10^2	1			7^3		28
		3	4	5	6		8^2	9				13	11	2^1	12				10	1			7		29
		3	4	5	6		8	9					11^1	2	12				10^2	1		13	7		30
		3	4	5			8^2	9^3		14		13	11	2	12	6			10^1	1			7		31
15^1		3	4	5			8	9					11	2	12	6			10	1^6			7		32
		3	4^1	5	6		8^3	9		14			11	2	13				10^2	1	12		7		33
		3	12		6		8^1	9^2				11	4	2	10				13	1			7	5	34
		3	4^3	6	5		8	9		13	14		11		2^1				10^2	1			7	12	35
		3	4^1		6		8	9		10^2	13	12	11		2					1			7	5	36

QUEEN'S PARK — Third Division

Year Formed: 1867. *Ground & Address:* Hampden Park, Mount Florida, Glasgow G42 9BA. *Telephone:* 0141 632 1275. *Fax:* 0141 636 1612.
Ground Capacity: all seated: 52,000. *Size of Pitch:* 115yd × 75yd.
President: Garry Templeman. *Secretary:* Alistair Mackay. *Treasurer:* David Gordon.
Coach: Billy Stark. *Physio:* R. C. Findlay.
Coaches since 1975: D. McParland, J. Gilroy, E. Hunter, H. McCann, J. McCormack, K. Brannigan.
Club Nickname(s): The Spiders. *Previous Grounds:* 1st Hampden (Recreation Ground); (Titwood Park was used as an interim measure between 1st & 2nd Hampdens); 2nd Hampden (Cathkin); 3rd Hampden.
Record Attendance: 95,772 v Rangers, Scottish Cup, 18 Jan 1930.
Record for Ground: 149,547 Scotland v England, 1937.
Record Transfer Fee received: Not applicable due to amateur status.
Record Transfer Fee paid: Not applicable due to amateur status.
Record Victory: 16-0 v St. Peters, Scottish Cup 1st rd, 29 Aug 1885.
Record Defeat: 0-9 v Motherwell, Division I, 26 Apr 1930.
Most Capped Player: Walter Arnott, 14, Scotland.
Most League Appearances: 532: Ross Caven.
Most League Goals in Season (Individual): 30: William Martin, Division I, 1937-38.
Most Goals Overall (Individual): 163: J. B. McAlpine.

QUEEN'S PARK 2004–05 LEAGUE RECORD

Match No.	Date	Venue	Opponents	Result		H/T Score	Lg. Pos.	Goalscorers	Attendance
1	Aug 7	H	Cowdenbeath	W	3-2	1-1	—	Carroll 2 [8, 88], McCallum [86]	490
2	14	A	Elgin C	L	0-1	0-1	5		523
3	21	H	Albion R	D	1-1	1-0	5	Clark R [19]	505
4	28	H	Gretna	W	3-2	0-0	4	Felvus [80], Carroll [84], Kettlewell [88]	496
5	Sept 4	A	Stenhousemuir	D	1-1	0-1	5	Felvus [61]	410
6	11	H	Montrose	L	1-2	1-1	5	Trouten [45]	406
7	18	A	East Stirling	W	5-0	2-0	4	Carroll 2 [15, 49], Harvey (2 og) [27, 73], Graham [46]	335
8	25	A	East Fife	W	4-1	1-0	3	Clark R [34], Graham 3 [47, 58, 68]	445
9	Oct 2	H	Peterhead	L	1-2	1-1	4	Carroll [12]	625
10	16	H	Elgin C	L	0-1	0-1	4		507
11	23	A	Cowdenbeath	L	1-2	1-2	4	Carroll [2]	280
12	30	A	Gretna	L	1-4	0-3	7	Clark R (pen) [62]	706
13	Nov 6	H	Stenhousemuir	W	4-3	0-2	5	Clark R 2 (1 pen) [54, 70 (p)], Ferry D [60], Murphy (og) [81]	491
14	13	A	Montrose	W	4-2	3-0	3	Carroll [1], Ferry D 2 [14, 73], Harvey [23]	410
15	27	H	East Stirling	D	0-0	0-0	3		457
16	Dec 4	H	East Fife	L	1-2	0-2	4	Ferry D [75]	575
17	18	A	Peterhead	D	2-2	0-1	4	Carroll [79], Reilly (pen) [90]	569
18	27	H	Cowdenbeath	L	2-3	0-2	5	Trouten 2 [8, 46]	568
19	Jan 3	H	Gretna	D	1-1	1-1	—	Kettlewell [44]	803
20	15	A	Stenhousemuir	D	0-0	0-0	5		356
21	22	H	Montrose	W	1-0	0-0	4	Carroll [72]	575
22	29	A	East Stirling	L	1-3	1-3	4	Graham [26]	317
23	Feb 5	A	East Fife	W	1-0	0-0	4	Ferry M [82]	601
24	12	H	Peterhead	D	1-1	0-0	4	Carroll [90]	454
25	19	H	Albion R	L	0-3	0-3	5		497
26	Mar 1	A	Albion R	W	4-0	0-0	—	Ferry M [56], Carroll 2 [70, 72], Harvey [79]	355
27	5	H	Stenhousemuir	D	0-0	0-0	4		512
28	12	A	Gretna	L	0-4	0-3	4		978
29	19	A	Montrose	L	0-2	0-0	5		377
30	22	A	Elgin C	L	0-1	0-1	—		354
31	Apr 2	H	East Stirling	W	2-0	1-0	5	Quinn [21], Bowers [47]	486
32	9	A	Peterhead	D	1-1	1-0	6	Ferry M [21]	479
33	16	H	East Fife	W	2-1	2-1	5	Clark R [2], Bowers [31]	451
34	23	A	Albion R	W	2-1	2-0	4	McNulty (og) [27], Wallace (og) [36]	353
35	30	H	Elgin C	W	1-0	0-0	3	Carroll [69]	581
36	May 7	A	Cowdenbeath	L	0-1	0-1	4		346

Final League Position: 4

Honours
League Champions: Division II 1922-23. B Division 1955-56. Second Division 1980-81. Third Division 1999-2000.
Scottish Cup Winners: 1874, 1875, 1876, 1880, 1881, 1882, 1884, 1886, 1890, 1893; *Runners-up:* 1892, 1900.
League Cup: —.
FA Cup runners-up: 1884, 1885.

Club colours: Shirt: White and black hoops. Shorts: White. Stockings: Black with white tops.

Goalscorers: *League* (51): Carroll 14, Clark R 6 (2 pens), Graham 5, Ferry D 4, Ferry M 3, Trouten 3, Bowers 2, Felvus 2, Harvey 2, Kettlewell 2, McCallum 1, Quinn 1, Reilly 1 (pen), own goals 5.
Scottish Cup (0).
CIS Cup (2): Carroll 1, Clark R 1.
Challenge Cup (3): Carroll 1, Graham 1, Reilly 1.

McCue B 1	Blair B 16+3	McCallum D 7	Rushford G 24+3	Reilly S 13+1	Molloy S 26+2	Clark R 33	Harvey P 27+3	Graham A 20+7	Carroll F 33	Clarke D 2	Sloan T —+1	Trouten A 31+2	McGovern S 1	Agostini D 10+3	Weatherston D 2+5	Felvus B 4+16	Bonnar M —+3	Crawford D 34	Kettlewell S 23+4	Sinclair R 24+1	Weir J 1	Ferry M 18+1	Whelan J 3+5	Livingston A —+7	McGinty A 4+2	Ferry D 25+2	Quinn A 10	Bowers R 4	Canning S —+2	*Match No.*
1	2	3	4	5	6	7^{2}	8	9	10	11^{1}	12	13																		1
	2		4	5	6	7	8	9		11^{1}			1	3	10^{2}	12	13													2
	11	3^{1}	4	5	6	7	8^{3}	9	10^{2}			2		12		13		1	14											3
	11^{2}	3	4	5	6	7	8^{1}	9^{3}	10			2		14		13		1	12											4
	11		4		6	10		9^{2}				2		3	13	12		1	8	5	7^{1}									5
	11		4		6	8	13	9^{3}	10^{1}			2		3	14	12		1	7^{2}	5										6
	11^{2}		4		6^{1}	8	13	9^{3}	10			2		3		14		1	7	5		12								7
	11	6^{3}	4		13	8	14	9	10			2		3				1	7^{1}	5^{2}						12				8
	11^{1}	6	4		5	8^{2}		9	10			2		3		13		1	7											9
		3	4			8	6	9	10			2		5				1	7							11				10
		3	4			8	6	12	10			2		5■		9^{1}		1	7■							11				11
	7^{1}		4		3	8	6	9	10			2					12	1		5						11				12
	13		4^{1}	12	3	8	6^{2}	9^{3}	10			2				14		1	7	5						11				13
	13			4	3	8^{2}	6	9^{1}	10			2				12		1	7	5						11				14
			13	4	3	8	6^{3}	9	10			2				14	12^{2}	1	7^{1}	5						11				15
	6			4	3	8^{1}		9^{2}	10			2		13		12		1	7	5						11				16
	10^{1}		5	4	3^{3}	8	6		9			2						1	7^{2}				12	13	14	11				17
			5	4^{2}		8^{3}	6	9^{1}	10			2			14			1	7	3		11	12			13				18
	9^{1}		4			8	6	12	10			2						1	7	5		11				3				19
	6^{1}		4			8		9	10			2				12		1	7	5		11				3				20
	6^{1}		4		3	8		13	10			2				12		1	7	5		11				9^{2}				21
	6^{1}		4		3	8		9^{2}	10							13		1	7^{3}	5		11	12	14		2				22
			4		3	8	6		10			2				7^{1}		1		5		11	12			9				23
					3	8	6		10			2			12	7^{1}		1		5		11			4	9				24
					3^{2}	8	6		10			2			13	7		1		5		11^{1}		12	4	9				25
	12		4		3^{2}		6		10			2						1	7^{1}			11	5	13		9	8			26
			4		3^{1}		6	13	10			2						1	7	12		11^{2}	5			9	8			27
			12		14	9	6	13	10			2^{1}						1	7	4		11^{2}	5			3^{3}	8			28
			4		3	8	6	9^{1}	10			2				12		1	7	5		11								29
			4^{2}		3	8^{1}	6		10			2				12		1	7	5			14	13		9	11^{3}			30
				4	3^{1}	7^{2}	6	14	10			12						1		5		9		13		2	8	11^{3}		31
				4		7^{2}	6		10			3						1		5		9		12		2	8	11^{1}	13	32
				4		7	6	10^{2}				3						1	13	5^{1}		9			12	2	8	11^{3}	14	33
				4	3	7	6		10			2						1				9			5	11	8			34
			13		3^{1}	7	6		10					4	11^{2}			1	12			9			5■	2	8			35
							6	12	10			2		4				1	7^{1}	5		9				3	8	11		36

RAITH ROVERS Second Division

Year Formed: 1883. *Ground & Address:* Stark's Park, Pratt St, Kirkcaldy KY1 1SA. *Telephone:* 01592 263514. *Fax:* 01592 642833. *E-mail:* office@raithroversfc.com. *Website:* www.raithroversfc.com.
Ground Capacity: all seated: 10,104. *Size of Pitch:* 113yd × 70yd.
Chairman: none at present. *Office Manager:* Bob Mullen. *Club Secretary:* Bob Mullen.
Manager: Gordon Dalziel. *Assistant Manager:* Francisco Ortez Rivas. *Coach:* Shaun Dennis.
Managers since 1975: R. Paton, A. Matthew, W. McLean, G. Wallace, R. Wilson, F. Connor, J. Nicholl, J. Thomson, T. McLean, I. Munro, J. Nicholl, J. McVeigh, P. Hetherston, J. Scott, A. Calderon, C. Anelka.
Club Nickname: Rovers. *Previous Grounds:* Robbie's Park.
Record Attendance: 31,306 v Hearts, Scottish Cup 2nd rd, 7 Feb 1953.
Record Transfer Fee received: £900,000 for S. McAnespie to Bolton Wanderers (Sept 1995).
Record Transfer Fee paid: £225,000 for Paul Harvey from Airdrieonians (1996).
Record Victory: 10-1 v Coldstream, Scottish Cup 2nd rd, 13 Feb 1954.
Record Defeat: 2-11 v Morton, Division II, 18 Mar 1936.
Most Capped Player: David Morris, 6, Scotland.
Most League Appearances: 430: Willie McNaught.
Most League Goals in Season (Individual): 38: Norman Haywood, Division II, 1937-38.
Most Goals Overall (Individual): 154: Gordon Dalziel (League), 1987-94.

RAITH ROVERS 2004–05 LEAGUE RECORD

Match No.	Date	Venue	Opponents	Result		H/T Score	Lg. Pos.	Goalscorers	Attendance
1	Aug 7	A	Hamilton A	L	0-2	0-0	—		2176
2	14	H	Clyde	L	2-3	0-2	9	Sacko 79, Potter (og) 85	1784
3	21	A	Airdrie U	D	1-1	1-0	9	Sacko 6	2009
4	28	A	St Johnstone	L	0-1	0-0	10		2574
5	Sept 4	H	Ross Co	L	1-2	0-1	10	Ebanda 68	1540
6	11	A	Falkirk	L	2-4	1-0	10	Sacko 12, Young 89	3449
7	18	H	St Mirren	L	0-3	0-1	10		2111
8	25	H	Queen of the S	L	1-2	1-1	10	Ebanda 5	1491
9	Oct 2	A	Partick Th	L	0-2	0-2	10		3059
10	16	A	Clyde	L	0-2	0-2	10		1196
11	23	H	Hamilton A	D	2-2	1-1	10	Sacko 4, Daly (pen) 64	1943
12	30	H	St Johnstone	W	1-0	1-0	10	Martin 36	2089
13	Nov 13	H	Falkirk	L	0-2	0-1	10		3050
14	20	A	St Mirren	L	0-1	0-0	10		3002
15	23	A	Ross Co	D	1-1	0-1	—	Ouattara 71	1183
16	27	H	Partick Th	D	0-0	0-0	10		2452
17	Dec 4	A	Queen of the S	L	0-2	0-1	10		1646
18	11	A	Hamilton A	L	0-1	0-0	10		1371
19	18	H	Airdrie U	L	0-2	0-0	10		1795
20	26	A	St Johnstone	L	0-2	0-2	10		2579
21	29	H	Ross Co	L	1-4	1-0	—	Malcolm 14	1127
22	Jan 1	A	Falkirk	L	0-2	0-2	10		3379
23	15	H	St Mirren	W	2-0	0-0	10	Brady 60, Martin 63	1393
24	22	H	Queen of the S	L	0-1	0-0	10		1534
25	29	A	Partick Th	L	1-4	1-1	10	Murtagh 9	3181
26	Feb 12	H	Clyde	D	3-3	1-1	10	Tulloch 16, Clarke 2 70, 80	1394
27	19	A	Airdrie U	L	1-2	1-1	10	Tulloch 38	1599
28	Mar 5	A	Ross Co	L	0-2	0-0	10		2086
29	12	H	St Johnstone	L	1-2	1-1	10	Clarke 21	1350
30	19	H	Falkirk	D	3-3	1-2	10	Martin 2 44, 58, McMullan 71	2369
31	Apr 2	A	St Mirren	L	0-3	0-3	10		2193
32	9	H	Partick Th	W	2-1	1-0	10	Jablowski 12, Clarke 72	1403
33	16	A	Queen of the S	D	1-1	1-1	10	Jablowski 35	1361
34	23	H	Hamilton A	L	0-2	0-2	10		1474
35	30	A	Clyde	L	0-1	0-1	10		1122
36	May 7	H	Airdrie U	L	0-1	0-1	10		1296

Final League Position: 10

Honours
League Champions: First Division: 1992-93, 1994-95. Division II 1907-08, 1909-10 (shared), 1937-38, 1948-49; *Runners-up:* Division II 1908-09, 1926-27, 1966-67. Second Division 1975-76, 1977-78, 1986-87.
Scottish Cup Runners-up: 1913. *League Cup Winners: (Coca-Cola Cup):* 1994-95. *Runners-up:* 1948-49.

European: *UEFA Cup:* 6 matches (1995-96).

Club colours: Shirt: Navy blue with white sleeves. Shorts: White with navy and red trim. Stockings: Navy blue with white turnover.

Goalscorers: *League* (26): Clarke 4, Martin 4, Sacko 4, Ebanda 2, Jablowski 2, Tulloch 2, Brady 1, Daly 1 (pen), McMullan 1, Malcolm 1, Murtagh 1, Ouattara 1, Young 1, own goal 1.
Scottish Cup (0).
CIS Cup (1): Ortiz 1.
Challenge Cup (0).

Pounoussamy R 9+2	Rivas Ortiz F 14	McAlpine J 6+5	Hajovsky T 6	Davidson I 25+1	Brady D 19	Young L 6+9	Sacko H 19+3	Hagan P 1	Ebanda H 13+4	Lusamba N 1	Boyle J —+5	Smart J 29+1	Ouattara M 29+1	Bartholome A 26	O'Reilly C 5+4	Tagro B 4+1	Malcolm C 1+10	Berthelot D 26	Perry J 6	Daly W 9+1	Martin J 19+14	Maxwell D 2+2	Millar P 19+1	Dennis S 12	Raffell B 8+3	Mendy M 8+1	Leiper C 5+1	McMullan P 10	Tulloch S 10+3	Murtagh C 10+1	Jablowski N 12	Crabbe S 12	Fullerton E 4+7	McGowan M —+1	Clarke P 10+1	Hall S 1	Gilfillan J —+1	*Match No.*
1	2	3	4	5^{3}	6	7	8	9^{1}	10	11^{2}	12	13	14																									1
1	8	3	4		6	7	9				13		2	5	10^{1}	11^{2}	12																					2
	8	11	4		6		10		9^{1}			5	3					1	2	7	12																	3
	8	11^{2}	4		6	12	10				13	5	3					1	2^{1}	7	9																	4
1	8^{2}	11	4^{3}		6		10		12			5	3			14			2	7	9^{1}	13																5
			4	8^{2}		13	11		10			5	3	6		9^{3}		1	2^{1}	7	14		12															6
		12		4			11		10			8	6^{2}	5		9^{1}		1	2	7		13	3															7
	8	14			4	12	10		9^{2}			5		6^{3}				1	7^{1}	11	13	2	3															8
		12		6	4		10		9			5	2	8^{1}				1		11	13	7^{2}	3															9
	2	11^{2}		8	4		10		9				7^{1}	6				1		12	13		3	5														10
	8	12^{3}			4	7	10		9^{1}			2^{2}		6				1		11	14		3	5	13													11
15	2	12			8	7	10				13	4^{1}		6				1^{G}			9		3	5	11^{2}													12
1	2			5		8	10		12				7	6						11^{1}	9		3		4^{1}													13
	2^{1}			4		7^{2}	10		13				11	6				1			9		3	5	8	12												14
				7		12	13		9			4	11	6				1			10^{2}		3	5	8^{1}	2												15
	8			12	7^{1}		10^{2}		9			4	11	6				1			13		3	5		2												16
15	8			2^{1}	7	13	10		9			4^{2}	11	6				1^{G}			12		3	5														17
1				7	11	13	12		9			4	8	6							10^{2}		3	5		2^{1}												18
1					8		7		9^{1}			4	11^{2}	6			12				10		3	5	13	2												19
1					7		10					4^{2}	3	6			12				9		11	5	8	2^{1}	13											20
1	2			8	7	14	13				12	4					10^{3}				9		3	5	11^{2}		6^{1}											21
1				4	8		10^{3}		13				7	6	9^{1}	11^{2}	14				12		3	5		2												22
				4	7	12						5	2	6	9^{2}		13	1			10		11		8^{1}			3^{3}	14									23
				4	7							5		6	9		13	1			10		11^{2}		8^{1}	2		3		12								24
				4								5		6	14			1			9		3^{2}			2^{1}			13	8	7	10	11^{3}	12				25
				4		12						5	2					1			9								6	7	8	10^{1}	3		11			26
				4								5	2	6				1			12								3^{1}	7	8	9	11		10			27
				4								5	2	6^{1}	14			1			13							3	11	7^{2}	8	9^{3}	12		10			28
				4								5	2	6			12	1			9^{1}							3^{2}	8		7	11	13		10			29
				4								5^{1}	2	6	13			1			12							3	11^{3}	7	8	10	14		9^{2}			30
				5									2^{1}	6			12	1			7^{2}				14			11	3	8	4	10	13		9^{3}			31
				4								5	2	6				1			7							11	3^{1}		8	10	12		9			32
				4								5	2					1			12						6	11	3	7	8	10			9^{1}			33
												5	2		12		14	1			7^{3}						6	11	3^{2}	8^{1}	4	10	13		9			34
				4								5	2		9^{3}			1			12						6^{1}	11	3^{2}	7	8	10	13		14			35
				4								5	2				13				11						6		12	7^{2}	8	10	3^{1}		9^{3}	1	14	36

RANGERS Premier League

Year Formed: 1873. *Ground & Address:* Ibrox Stadium, 150 Edmiston Drive, Glasgow G51 2XD.
Telephone: 0870 600 1972. *Fax:* 0870 600 1978. *Website:* www.rangers.co.uk
Ground Capacity: all seated: 50,444. *Size of Pitch:* 114.5m × 81.5m.
Chairman: David Murray. *Chief Executive:* Martin Bain.
Manager: Alex McLeish. *Assistant Manager:* Andy Watson. *First Team Coach:* Jan Wouters. *Physio:* David Henderson.
Reserve team coach: John Brown.
Managers since 1975: Jock Wallace, John Greig, Jock Wallace, Graeme Souness, Walter Smith, Dick Advocaat.
Club Nickname(s): The Gers. *Previous Grounds:* Flesher's Haugh, Burnbank, Kinning Park, Old Ibrox.
Record Attendance: 118,567 v Celtic, Division I, 2 Jan 1939.
Record Transfer Fee received: £8,500,000 for G. Van Bronckhorst to Arsenal (2001).
Record Transfer Fee paid: £12 million for Tore Andre Flo from Chelsea (November 2000).
Record Victory: 14-2 v Blairgowrie, Scottish Cup 1st rd, 20 Jan, 1934. *Record Defeat:* 2-10 v Airdrieonians; 1886.
Most Capped Player: Ally McCoist, 60, Scotland. *Most League Appearances:* 496: John Greig, 1962-78.
Most League Goals in Season (Individual): 44: Sam English, Division I, 1931-32.
Most Goals Overall (Individual): 355: Ally McCoist; 1985-98.

Honours
League Champions: (51 times) Division I 1890-91 (shared), 1898-99, 1899-1900, 1900-01, 1901-02, 1910-11, 1911-12, 1912-13, 1917-18, 1919-20, 1920-21, 1922-23, 1923-24, 1924-25, 1926-27, 1927-28, 1928-29, 1929-30, 1930-31, 1932-33, 1933-34, 1934-35, 1936-37, 1938-39, 1946-47, 1948-49, 1949-50, 1952-53, 1955-56, 1956-57, 1958-59, 1960-61, 1962-63, 1963-64, 1974-75. Premier Division: 1975-76, 1977-78, 1986-87, 1988-89, 1989-90, 1990-91, 1991-92, 1992-93, 1993-94, 1994-95, 1995-96, 1996-97, 1998-99, 1999-2000, 2002-03, 2004-05; *Runners-up:* 25 times.

RANGERS 2004–05 LEAGUE RECORD

Match No.	Date	Venue	Opponents	Result		H/T Score	Lg. Pos.	Goalscorers	Attendance
1	Aug 7	A	Aberdeen	D	0-0	0-0	—		19,028
2	14	H	Livingston	W	4-0	2-0	2	Hughes 2 21, 78, Prso 24, Arveladze 87	48,102
3	21	H	Hibernian	W	4-1	2-1	2	Arveladze 10, Prso 14, Boumsong 58, Lovenkrands 83	48,702
4	29	A	Celtic	L	0-1	0-0	3		58,763
5	Sept 12	A	Hearts	D	0-0	0-0	4		14,601
6	19	H	Inverness CT	W	1-0	1-0	3	Prso 16	47,063
7	26	A	Dundee	W	2-0	0-0	2	Novo 2 77, 80	9404
8	Oct 3	H	Kilmarnock	W	2-0	1-0	2	Andrews 10, Novo 81	46,278
9	17	A	Motherwell	W	2-0	1-0	2	Prso 2 6, 83	10,946
10	24	H	Dundee U	D	1-1	0-0	2	Novo 65	46,796
11	27	A	Dunfermline Ath	W	2-1	0-1	—	Boumsong 46, Novo 56	8555
12	31	H	Aberdeen	W	5-0	1-0	2	Thompson 38, Novo 2 (1 pen) 75, 88 (p), Lovenkrands 78, Ricksen 86	48,918
13	Nov 7	A	Livingston	W	4-1	1-0	2	Lovenkrands 26, Novo 54, Thompson 66, Namouchi 83	7800
14	14	A	Hibernian	W	1-0	0-0	2	Prso (pen) 63	13,825
15	20	H	Celtic	W	2-0	2-0	2	Novo (pen) 14, Prso 35	50,043
16	28	H	Hearts	W	3-2	1-1	1	McAllister (og) 45, Novo 2 56, 80	48,494
17	Dec 5	A	Inverness CT	D	1-1	0-1	2	Prso 50	6543
18	11	H	Dundee	W	3-0	2-0	2	Novo (pen) 2, Prso 4, Malcolm 49	48,114
19	19	A	Kilmarnock	W	1-0	1-0	2	Arveladze 16	11,156
20	27	H	Motherwell	W	4-1	2-0	2	Novo 2 2, 14, Arveladze 52, Thompson 86	49,909
21	Jan 1	A	Dundee U	D	1-1	0-1	2	Namouchi 89	10,461
22	15	H	Dunfermline Ath	W	3-0	2-0	2	Thompson 5, Andrews 37, Rae A 63	48,055
23	23	A	Aberdeen	W	2-1	2-1	2	Prso 8, Ricksen 15	17,495
24	29	H	Livingston	W	3-0	1-0	2	Prso 14, Ricksen 62, Novo 68	48,579
25	Feb 12	H	Hibernian	W	3-0	1-0	1	Prso 2 35, 49, Buffel 60	50,143
26	20	A	Celtic	W	2-0	0-0	1	Vignal 70, Novo 81	58,993
27	26	H	Kilmarnock	W	2-1	2-0	—	Prso 29, Novo 41	48,575
28	Mar 2	A	Hearts	W	2-1	0-0	—	Novo 49, Ricksen 90	13,842
29	5	H	Inverness CT	D	1-1	0-0	1	Ferguson 57	49,945
30	13	A	Dundee	W	2-0	0-0	1	Andrews 81, Ricksen 83	9876
31	Apr 3	A	Motherwell	W	3-2	2-0	1	Vignal 2 3, 31, Prso 50	10,210
32	12	H	Dundee U	L	0-1	0-1	—		49,302
33	17	A	Dunfermline Ath	W	1-0	1-0	2	Prso 7	8261
34	24	H	Celtic	L	1-2	0-2	2	Thompson 87	49,593
35	May 1	A	Aberdeen	W	3-1	2-1	2	Ferguson 9, Prso 2 43, 58	17,198
36	7	H	Hearts	W	2-1	2-0	2	Buffel 8, Andrews 42	49,342
37	14	H	Motherwell	W	4-1	2-0	2	Buffel 2 12, 56, Arveladze 2 17, 54	49,495
38	22	A	Hibernian	W	1-0	0-0	1	Novo 58	16,604

Final League Position: 1

Scottish Cup Winners: (31 times) 1894, 1897, 1898, 1903, 1928, 1930, 1932, 1934, 1935, 1936, 1948, 1949, 1950, 1953, 1960, 1962, 1963, 1964, 1966, 1973, 1976, 1978, 1979, 1981, 1992, 1993, 1996, 1999, 2000, 2002, 2003; *Runners-up:* 17 times.
League Cup Winners: (24 times) 1946-47, 1948-49, 1960-61, 1961-62, 1963-64, 1964-65, 1970-71, 1975-76, 1977-78, 1978-79, 1981-82, 1983-84, 1984-85, 1986-87, 1987-88, 1988-89, 1990-91, 1992-93, 1993-94, 1996-97, 1998-99, 2001-02, 2002-03, 2004-05; *Runners-up:* 6 times.

European: *European Cup:* 119 matches (1956-57, 1957-58, 1959-60 semi-finals, 1961-62, 1963-64, 1964-65, 1975-76, 1976-77, 1978-79, 1987-88, 1989-90, 1990-91, 1991-92, 1992-93 final pool, 1993-94, 1994-95, 1995-96; 1996-97, 1997-98, 1999-2000, 2000-01, 2003-04).
Cup Winners' Cup: 54 matches (1960-61 runners-up, 1962-63, 1966-67 runners-up, 1969-70, 1971-72 winners, 1973-74, 1977-78, 1979-80, 1981-82, 1983-84). *UEFA Cup:* 58 matches (*Fairs Cup:* 1967-68, 1968-69 semi-finals, 1970-71.
UEFA Cup: 1982-83, 1984-85, 1985-86, 1986-87, 1988-89, 1997-98, 1998-99, 1999-2000, 2000-01, 2002-03, 2004-05).

Club colours: Shirt: Royal blue with red and white trim. Shorts: White with red and blue trim. Stockings: Black with red tops.

Goalscorers: *League* (78): Novo 19 (3 pens), Prso 18 (1 pen), Arveladze 6, Ricksen 5, Thompson 5, Andrews 4, Buffel 4, Lovenkrands 3, Vignal 3, Boumsong 2, Ferguson 2, Hughes 2, Namouchi 2, Malcolm 1, Rae A 1, own goal 1.
Scottish Cup (1): Ricksen 1.
CIS Cup (16): Novo 3, Ricksen 3, Thompson 3, Kyrgiakos 2, Prso 2, Arveladze 1, Buffel 1, Ross 1.

Klos S 23	Ricksen F 38	Khizanishvili Z 14 + 2	Boumsong J 18	Vignal G 29 + 1	Hughes S 6 + 5	Rae A 17 + 8	Burke C 7 + 5	Prso D 33 + 1	Novo I 34 + 1	Lovenkrands P 12 + 5	Arveladze S 11 + 13	Andrews M 30	Vanoli P 3 + 2	Thompson S 7 + 17	Adam C — + 1	Mladenovic D 6 + 1	Moore C 3	Hutton A 8 + 2	Malcolm R 19 + 3	Ross M 13	Namouchi H 13 + 7	Ball M 12 + 2	Smith S 2 + 2	Davidson R — + 1	Djordjic B 4	Buffel T 13 + 2	McGregor A 2	Kyrgiakos S 15	Waterreus R 13	Ferguson B 13	McCormack R — + 1	*Match No.*
1	2	3	4	5	6	7	8^{1}	9	10	11	12																					1
1	2		4	5^{1}	6	7		9^{2}	10	11^{3}	8	3	12	13	14																	2
1	2	3	4	5	6^{1}	7		9^{2}	10	11^{3}	8		14	13		12																3
1	6		4	5		7		11	10	12	9^{1}			13		8^{2}	3	2														4
1	2		4	5			9	11^{2}	10^{1}	14	12		7^{3}	13		8	3		6													5
1	2	13	4		12		7	9	10^{3}	11	14		6			8^{1}	3		5^{2}													6
1	2	5	4	12	7^{2}		9		14	13	10^{3}	3	8^{1}	11						6												7
1	2		4	5	7			12	10^{2}	11	13	3		9^{1}					6	8												8
1	7	5	4	2			8^{2}	11	10		12	3		9^{1}					6		13											9
1	7	5	4	2			8^{2}	11	10		9^{1}	3		12					6		13											10
1	7	5	4	2	12		9	11	10			3							6		8^{1}											11
1	7	5	4^{2}	2				9^{1}	10	11		3		12				13	6		8											12
1	7^{1}		4	5		12			10^{2}	11	13	3		9				2	6		8											13
1	2	5^{2}	4			12		9	10	11^{1}		3						13	6		8	7										14
1	6	5^{3}	4	2^{2}		8		9	10	11^{1}	12	3							14		7	13										15
1	2	5	4		13	8		9	10	11		3								6^{1}	7^{2}		12									16
1	2	5	4^{1}		8	12		11	10			3							7		9^{2}		6	13								17
1	2	5		4^{2}		12		11	10		9^{1}	3				6			7		8		13									18
1	6		4	5		9	13	11^{2}			10	3		12		7		2			8^{1}											19
1	6	4		5		12		11^{2}	10		9	3		13		8^{1}		2	7													20
1	6	4		5		8		11			9^{1}	3		10				2	7		12											21
1	2			5	14	8	12					3		11					7	4	9^{1}	13			6^{2}	10^{3}						22
1	2			5	13	8		11^{3}	10			3		12					7	4	14				6^{1}	9^{2}						23
	6					8		11^{2}	10			3		13						5	12	2			7^{1}	9	1	4				24
	6			8		14		11^{1}	10^{2}		13	3		12				2				5				9		4	1	7^{3}		25
	6			8		12		11	10			3						2				5^{1}				9		4	1	7		26
	6			8		12	14	11^{2}	10			3		13				2^{1}					5			9^{3}	1	4		7		27
	6			8				11	10			3								2	12	5				9^{1}		4	1	7		28
	6			8					10			3		11					12	2					5^{1}	9		4	1	7		29
	6			8				11	10^{3}			3^{2}		13					9^{1}	2		5				12		4	1	7	14	30
	2	14		3^{1}		8		11	10	12	13								6		9^{2}	5						4^{3}	1	7^{1}		31
	6			3^{2}		8		11	10	13	12			14					7^{3}	2	9^{1}	5						4	1			32
	6			3				11	10^{1}		12								8	2	13	5				9^{2}		4	1	7		33
	6			8^{2}				11	10			3^{3}		13					14	2^{1}	9	5				12		4	1	7		34
	6					5		11^{2}	10	8^{1}	12	3		13						2						9		4	1	7		35
	2			5		6	14	11^{2}	10	8^{1}	12	3		13												9^{3}		4	1	7		36
	2					6	12	11	10^{1}		9	3										5				8		4	1	7		37
	2					6		11	10		9	3										5				8		4	1	7		38

ROSS COUNTY First Division

Year Formed: 1929. *Ground & Address:* Victoria Park, Dingwall IV15 9QW. *Telephone:* 01349 860860. *Fax:* 01349 866277.
E-mail: donnie@rosscountyfootballclub.co.uk. *Website:* www.rosscountyfootballclub.co.uk
Ground Capacity: 6700. *Size of Ground:* 105×68m.
Chairman: Peter Swanson. *Secretary:* Donnie MacBean.
Manager: John Robertson. *Assistant Manager:* Donald Park. *Physio:* Douglas Sim.
Managers since 1975: N. Cooper, A. Smith.
Club Nickname(s): The Staggies.
Record Attendance: 6600, benefit match v Celtic, 31 August 1970.
Record Transfer Fee Received: £200,000 for Neil Tarrant to Aston Villa (April 1999).
Record Transfer Fee Paid: £25,000 for Barry Wilson from Southampton (Oct. 1992).
Record Victory: 11-0 v St Cuthbert Wanderers, Scottish Cup, 11 Dec 1993.
Record Defeat: 1-10 v Inverness Thistle, Highland League.
Most League Appearances: 157: David Mackay, 1995-2001.
Most League Goals in Season: 22: D. Adams, 1996-97.
Most League Goals (Overall): 44: Steven Ferguson, 1996-2002.

ROSS COUNTY 2004–05 LEAGUE RECORD

Match No.	*Date*	*Venue*	*Opponents*	*Result*		*H/T Score*	*Lg. Pos.*	*Goalscorers*	*Attendance*
1	Aug 7	A	Queen of the S	W	1-0	1-0	—	Burke [39]	1910
2	14	H	St Mirren	D	1-1	1-0	4	Burke [3]	2666
3	21	A	Clyde	L	0-1	0-0	7		1307
4	28	H	Partick Th	L	0-1	0-0	6		2781
5	Sept 4	A	Raith R	W	2-1	1-0	5	Lauchlan [35], Adam [48]	1540
6	11	H	St Johnstone	L	0-1	0-1	6		2486
7	18	A	Airdrie U	W	2-1	1-1	5	Canning [6], Winters [54]	1486
8	25	A	Hamilton A	W	2-1	1-1	5	Lauchlan [28], Higgins [74]	1522
9	Oct 2	H	Falkirk	L	0-1	0-1	5		3062
10	16	A	St Mirren	L	2-3	1-1	5	Gillies (og) [21], Adam [67]	2538
11	23	H	Queen of the S	W	1-0	0-0	5	Cowie [46]	2354
12	30	A	Partick Th	L	0-4	0-2	6		2898
13	Nov 13	A	St Johnstone	D	1-1	0-1	6	Higgins [46]	2018
14	20	H	Airdrie U	L	1-2	1-1	7	Docherty (og) [42]	2173
15	23	H	Raith R	D	1-1	1-0	—	Burke [16]	1183
16	27	A	Falkirk	D	2-2	1-0	7	McGarry [21], Malcolm [89]	3182
17	Dec 4	H	Hamilton A	D	1-1	0-0	7	McGarry [58]	2034
18	11	A	Queen of the S	L	0-1	0-1	7		1588
19	18	H	Clyde	L	0-1	0-0	8		1939
20	27	H	Partick Th	W	2-1	1-0	8	Cowie [11], Canning [53]	2844
21	29	A	Raith R	W	4-1	0-1	—	Cowie [53], Lauchlan [60], Winters [73], Burke [78]	1127
22	Jan 3	H	St Johnstone	W	4-0	3-0	—	Winters 2 [15, 17], Canning [34], Lauchlan [81]	3105
23	15	A	Airdrie U	L	1-2	0-1	6	Winters [60]	1512
24	22	A	Hamilton A	W	1-0	0-0	6	Winters [77]	1476
25	29	H	Falkirk	L	0-1	0-1	7		3151
26	Feb 19	A	Clyde	L	0-1	0-0	7		1076
27	Mar 1	H	St Mirren	L	0-1	0-1	—		1302
28	5	H	Raith R	W	2-0	0-0	7	Burke [67], Higgins [87]	2086
29	12	A	Partick Th	D	0-0	0-0	7		2939
30	19	A	St Johnstone	W	2-0	0-0	7	Canning [47], McGarry [55]	1828
31	Apr 2	H	Airdrie U	W	3-1	1-1	6	Cowie [44], Higgins 2 [57, 78]	2024
32	9	A	Falkirk	L	0-1	0-0	6		5272
33	16	H	Hamilton A	W	2-1	1-0	4	Cowie [20], Kilgannon [60]	2107
34	23	H	Queen of the S	D	1-1	1-1	5	McGarry [13]	2403
35	30	A	St Mirren	L	0-1	0-1	6		3942
36	May 7	H	Clyde	D	1-1	0-1	6	Burke [70]	2130

Final League Position: 6

Honours
League Champions: Third Division: 1998-99. *Bell's League Challenge Cup: Runners up:* 2004-05.

Club colours: Shirt: Navy blue with white trim. Shorts: White with navy side panels. Stockings: Navy blue with two white hoops.

Goalscorers: *League* (40): Burke 6, Winters 6, Cowie 5, Higgins 5, Canning 4, Lauchlan 4, McGarry 4, Adam 2, Kilgannon 1, Malcolm 1, own goals 2.
Scottish Cup (5): Winters 2, Burke 1 (pen), Rankin 1, own goal 1.
CIS Cup (3): Burke 3.
Challenge Cup (11): Winters 5, Burke 4, Canning 1, Cowie 1.

Garden S 15 + 1	Robertson J 25 + 1	McCulloch M 36	McCunnie J 24 + 3	Canning M 33	Lauchlan J 28	Rankin J 28 + 2	Cowie D 33 + 1	McSwegan G 10 + 7	McGarry S 19 + 14	Burke A 28 + 4	Mackay S 3 + 9	Winters D 18 + 14	Higgins S 13 + 13	Malcolm S 10 + 3	Mahood A — + 1	Kilgannon S 20 + 9	Adam C 8 + 2	McKinlay K 1 + 3	Gunn C — + 1	Stewart C 21	Tiernan F 16	Macdonald N 2 + 6	Taylor S 5	Moffat A — + 2	Kerr S — + 3	*Match No.*
1	2	3	4	5	6	7	8^{1}	9^{2}	10	11^{3}	12	13	14													1
1^{3}	2	3	4	5	6	7	8		10^{1}	11	12	9^{2}	13	14												2
1	2	3	4^{3}	5	6	7	8	9^{2}	10^{1}	11	14	13			12											3
1	2	3	4	5	6	7		14	10^{3}	11	12	13	9^{2}			8^{1}										4
1	2	3		5	6	7^{1}	12	9^{2}	13	11	14			4		10	8^{3}									5
1	2	3		5	6		7	9	13	11	10	12		4^{1}			8^{2}									6
1		3	2	5	6		7	14	10	11	12	9^{3}	13			4^{2}	8^{1}									7
1	12	3	2		6		7	10^{1}		11		9^{3}	13	5		4	8^{2}	14								8
1	4	3	2		6		7	13	10^{1}			9	12	5		11^{2}	8^{3}		14							9
1	2	3	4	5	6		7	12	10^{2}			9^{1}	13			11	8									10
1	2^{1}	3	4	5	6	14	7	9				13	10^{2}	12		11^{3}	8									11
1		3	2	5	6	12	7	9^{3}	14		4^{1}	13	10			11^{2}	8									12
1	2	3	13	5	6^{1}	7	4		14	8^{2}		10	9^{3}	12		11										13
1	2	3	4	5		7^{1}	8		14	10		11^{2}	9^{3}	6		13	12									14
1	2^{1}	3	12	5	6	7^{2}	8		14	10	11		9^{3}	4			13									15
		3		2	6	7	4	14	8^{2}	10	12	13	9^{3}	5		11^{1}				1						16
		3		2	6	7	4	14	8^{3}	10	13	12	9^{1}	5		11^{2}				1						17
		3	12	2	6	4	7	13	8^{1}	11	14	9^{2}		5		10^{3}				1						18
		3	2		6	7	8	9^{2}	13	11		10^{1}		5		12				1	4					19
	2	3	4^{2}	5	6	7	8	9^{1}	14	11^{3}		12				13				1	10					20
	2	3	4^{1}	5	6	7	8	9^{2}	14	11^{3}		13				12				1	10					21
	2	3		5	6	7	8		13	11^{2}		9^{3}	14			10^{1}				1	4	12				22
	2	3		5	6	7	8		12	11^{1}		9^{2}	13			10				1	4					23
	2	3	10	5	6	7	8			11		9								1	4					24
	2	3	10^{2}	5	6	7^{1}	8		14	11^{3}		9	13			12				1	4					25
	2	3		5	6	7	8		13	12		9^{1}	14			11^{2}				1	4		10^{3}			26
	2	3		5	6^{1}	7	8		14	11		9				13				1	4^{2}	12	10^{3}			27
		6	2	5		7	8		10	11		9^{1}	12							1		3	4^{2}	13		28
		3	2	5	6	7	4		10^{2}	11		13	9^{1}			12				1			8			29
		3	2	5	6	7^{3}			10	11^{2}		12	9^{1}			13				1	8	14	4			30
	6	3	2	5		7	8		10^{2}	11^{1}			9			12				1	4^{3}	14			13	31
	6	3	2	5			8		10^{2}	12		7^{1}	9^{3}			11				1	4	13			14	32
	6	3	2	5		7	8		10^{3}	12		9^{1}				11^{2}		13		1	4				14	33
	6	3	2	5		7	8		10	9^{2}		12	13			11^{1}		14		1	4^{3}					34
	6	3	2^{3}	5		7	8		10	9^{1}		12	13			11^{2}				1	4	14				35
15		6		5		7	8		10	13			9			3^{1}		11		1[illegible]	4^{2}	2		12		36

ST JOHNSTONE — First Division

Year Formed: 1884. *Ground & Address:* McDiarmid Park, Crieff Road, Perth PH1 2SJ. *Telephone:* 01738 459090. *Fax:* 01738 625 771. *Clubcall:* 0898 121559. *E-mail:* angome@saints.sol.co.uk. *Website:* www.stjohnstonefc.co.uk
Ground Capacity: all seated: 10,673. *Size of Pitch:* 115yd × 75yd.
Chairman: G.S. Brown. *Secretary and Managing Director:* Stewart Duff. *Sales Executive:* Susan Weir.
Manager: Owen Coyle. *Coach:* Jin Weir. *Physio:* Nick Summersgill. *Youth Coach:* Tommy Campbell.
Managers since 1975: J. Stewart, J. Storrie, A. Stuart, A. Rennie, I. Gibson, A. Totten, J. McClelland, P. Sturrock, S. Clark, B. Stark, J. Connolly.
Club Nickname(s): Saints. *Previous Grounds:* Recreation Grounds, Muirton Park.
Record Attendance: (McDiarmid Park): 10,545 v Dundee, Premier Division, 23 May 1999.
Record Transfer Fee received: £1,750,000 for Calum Davidson to Blackburn R (March 1998).
Record Transfer Fee paid: £400,000 for Billy Dodds from Dundee (1994).
Record Victory: 9-0 v Albion R, League Cup, 9 Mar 1946.
Record Defeat: 1-10 v Third Lanark, Scottish Cup, 24 Jan 1903.
Most Capped Player: Nick Dasovic, 26, Canada.
Most League Appearances: 298: Drew Rutherford.
Most League Goals in Season (Individual): 36: Jimmy Benson, Division II, 1931-32.
Most Goals Overall (Individual): 140: John Brogan, 1977-83.

ST JOHNSTONE 2004–05 LEAGUE RECORD

Match No.	Date	Venue	Opponents	Result	H/T Score	Lg. Pos.	Goalscorers	Attendance
1	Aug 7	A	Airdrie U	L 0-1	0-0	—		2365
2	14	H	Queen of the S	L 1-3	0-2	10	Fotheringham M [79]	2384
3	21	A	St Mirren	L 1-2	1-0	10	Moore [7]	3079
4	28	H	Raith R	W 1-0	0-0	9	Fotheringham K [73]	2574
5	Sept 4	A	Hamilton A	D 1-1	0-0	8	Baxter [47]	1904
6	11	A	Ross Co	W 1-0	1-0	7	Hannah (pen) [31]	2486
7	18	H	Falkirk	L 1-2	0-2	7	Baxter [82]	3835
8	25	H	Partick Th	W 2-1	0-0	6	Macdonald 2 [83, 90]	2763
9	Oct 2	A	Clyde	L 0-1	0-1	7		1456
10	16	A	Queen of the S	W 1-0	0-0	6	Hay [60]	2059
11	23	H	Airdrie U	D 1-1	0-0	6	Christie (og) [70]	2447
12	30	A	Raith R	L 0-1	0-1	7		2089
13	Nov 6	H	Hamilton A	W 3-0	1-0	5	Macdonald [32], Moore [79], Hay [82]	1869
14	13	H	Ross Co	D 1-1	1-0	5	Macdonald [8]	2018
15	20	A	Falkirk	L 1-3	1-1	5	Hannah (pen) [6]	3439
16	27	H	Clyde	W 3-0	0-0	5	Sheerin [51], Moore 2 [80, 85]	2026
17	Dec 4	A	Partick Th	W 4-0	2-0	5	McCann [13], Anderson [33], Macdonald [73], Hay [82]	2945
18	11	A	Airdrie U	D 0-0	0-0	5		1865
19	18	H	St Mirren	W 1-0	1-0	5	McCann [40]	2233
20	26	H	Raith R	W 2-0	2-0	4	Maxwell [12], Macdonald [44]	2579
21	29	A	Hamilton A	W 3-0	2-0	—	Hay [17], Sheerin [39], McCann [70]	1718
22	Jan 3	A	Ross Co	L 0-4	0-3	—		3105
23	15	H	Falkirk	L 0-3	0-1	3		3395
24	22	H	Partick Th	D 1-1	0-0	4	Macdonald [65]	2814
25	Feb 12	H	Queen of the S	D 0-0	0-0	4		1782
26	19	A	St Mirren	D 1-1	1-0	5	Macdonald [12]	2716
27	Mar 5	H	Hamilton A	L 0-2	0-1	5		1772
28	12	A	Raith R	W 2-1	1-1	5	Anderson [33], McAnespie [77]	1350
29	19	H	Ross Co	L 0-2	0-0	5		1828
30	22	A	Clyde	D 1-1	0-0	—	McManus [51]	862
31	Apr 2	A	Falkirk	L 0-3	0-1	7		3748
32	9	H	Clyde	D 0-0	0-0	7		1770
33	16	A	Partick Th	W 4-0	3-0	5	Macdonald 3 [10, 44, 84], Dobbie [14]	2310
34	23	H	Airdrie U	L 1-2	0-1	6	Dobbie [57]	2239
35	30	A	Queen of the S	L 0-2	0-2	8		1784
36	May 7	H	St Mirren	D 0-0	0-0	8		2920

Final League Position: 8

Honours
League Champions: First Division 1982-83, 1989-90, 1996-97. Division II 1923-24, 1959-60, 1962-63; *Runners-up:* Division II 1931-32. Second Division 1987-88.
Scottish Cup: Semi-finals 1934, 1968, 1989, 1991.
League Cup: Runners-up: 1969-70, 1998-99.
League Challenge Cup: Runners-up: 1996-97.

European: *UEFA Cup:* 10 matches (1971-72, 1999-2000).

Club colours: Shirt: Royal blue with white trim. Shorts: White. Stockings: Royal blue with white hoops.

Goalscorers: *League* (38): Macdonald 11, Hay 4, Moore 4, McCann 3, Anderson 2, Baxter 2, Dobbie 2, Hannah 2 (2 pens), Sheerin 2, Fotheringham K 1, Fotheringham M 1, McAnespie 1, McManus 1, Maxwell 1, own goal 1.
Scottish Cup (0).
CIS Cup (2): Hannah 1, Hay 1.
Challenge Cup (7): Moore 2, Rutkiewicz 2, Fotheringham K 1, Hannah 1, Maxwell 1.

Cuthbert K 5	Tait J 13+1	Malone E 3	Hannah D 28+1	Rutkiewicz K 16+4	Maxwell I 33	Stevenson R 7+3	Bernard P 1+1	Hardy L 11+2	Moore M 19+5	Sheerin P 34	Hay C 13+16	Marshall C 1+1	McGregor A 20	Baxter M 12+3	Fraser S 1+1	Fotheringham M —+5	Jackson A —+6	Anderson S 19+1	Weir J 2	Webb S 15+4	Fotheringham K 8	McManus S 4+3	McConalogue S 4+5	McCann R 24+2	Mahood A 4+3	Macdonald P 26+1	Forsyth R 15+1	Linn R —+1	McAnespie K 13+4	Samson C 11+1	Cowan D 10	Sloan R 8	Bagan D 4+2	Dyer W 7	Dobbie S 5+3	*Match No.*
1	2	3	4	5	6	7¹	8	9	10	11²	12	13																								1
		11	4²	5	6	12			10	8	9³	7	1	2¹	3	13	14																			2
	3	11	4	12		7²			10	8	9¹		1			13		2	5	6																3
			4	13	6	10¹		11		8	9²		1					2	5		3	7	12													4
	12		4	5	6				10	11	14		1	7¹				2			3	13	9³	8²												5
			4	5	6			11¹	10	8			1					2			3		9	7	12											6
			4	5	6	13		11¹	10	8²			1	14				2³			3			7	12	9										7
				5		7¹			10	11²			1	12	13			2			6	8	9³	4		14	3									8
	2¹			5	6			11	13	8	9²		1	7³							3			14	4	10		12								9
	2			5²	6			11	12	8	9¹		1	7						13					4	10	3									10
	2		14	5				11²	12	8	9¹		1	7³						6			13		4	10	3									11
				5	6			13	9¹	8	11		1	7				2					12		4	10	3²									12
			4	5	6			11	9	8	12		1	2										7		10¹	3									13
			4	5	6			11³	9	8	12		1	2²						13			14	7		10¹	3									14
	2		4	5	6			11¹	9²	8³	13		1							12				7	14	10	3									15
	3		4		6			11¹	10	8	13		1	2						5				7		9²			12							16
	3		4		6			13	10	8	12		1					2		5				7		9¹			11²							17
	3		4		6				10	8	12		1					2		5				7		9¹			11							18
	3		4		6				10¹	8	12		1					2		5				7		9			11							19
	3		4		6				10¹	8	12		1					2		5				7		9			11							20
	3		4	12	6					8	10²		1					2		5			13	7		9	11¹									21
1	3²		4	13	6				12	8	10¹			2³		14				5				7		9			11							22
1G			4		6				10¹	8	12			2		13				5	3			7²		9			11	15						23
			4	5	6					8	12										3		10¹	7		9			13	1	2	11²				24
			4		6				10²	8¹							13			5				7		9	3		11	1	2		12			25
			4		6				13	8	10²									5				7¹		9	3		11	1	2		12			26
			4		6				10	8	9¹						14	12		5				13			3		11³	1	2		7²			27
			4	5	6					8							12	2				13				9	3		14	1		10¹	7²	11³		28
			4	5	6					8	13							2								9	3		14	1		10¹	7²	11	12³	29
			4		6	13												5				8		7		9²			11	1	2	10¹		3	12	30
			4		6									13				5				8²		7		9	14		11³	1	2	10¹		3	12	31
			4		6					8	12							5						7		9			11	1	2			3	10¹	32
					6	7				8	12							5						4		9				1	2	11		3	10¹	33
					6	7				8	13							5¹		12				4		9				1	2	11		3	10²	34
1					6					8	9²					12	13			5				4			3				2	11	7¹		10	35
1			8		5	7²	13			11³	9¹			2			12			4		14					6								10	36

ST MIRREN First Division

Year Formed: 1877. *Ground & Address:* St Mirren Park, Love St, Paisley PA3 2EJ. *Telephone:* 0141 889 2558/0141 840 1337. *Fax:* 0141 848 6444.
Ground Capacity: 10,866 (all seated). *Size of Pitch:* 112yd × 73yd.
Chairman: Stewart Gilmour. *Vice-Chairman:* George Campbell. *Secretary:* Allan Marshall.
Manager: Gus MacPherson. *Assistant Manager:* Andy Millen. *Commercial Manager:* Campbell Kennedy. *Youth Development Officer:* David Longwell.
Managers since 1975: Alex Ferguson, Jim Clunie, Rikki MacFarlane, Alex Miller, Alex Smith, Tony Fitzpatrick, David Hay, Jimmy Bone, Tony Fitzpatrick, Tom Hendrie, John Coughlin. *Club Nickname(s):* The Buddies. *Previous Grounds:* Short Roods 1877-79, Thistle Park Greenhill 1879-83, Westmarch 1883-94.
Record Attendance: 47,438 v Celtic, League Cup, 20 Aug 1949.
Record Transfer Fee received: £850,000 for Ian Ferguson to Rangers (1988).
Record Transfer Fee paid: £400,000 for Thomas Stickroth from Bayer Uerdingen (1990).
Record Victory: 15-0 v Glasgow University, Scottish Cup 1st rd, 30 Jan 1960.
Record Defeat: 0-9 v Rangers, Division I, 4 Dec 1897.
Most Capped Player: Godmundor Torfason, 29, Iceland.
Most League Appearances: 351: Tony Fitzpatrick, 1973-88.
Most League Goals in Season (Individual): 45: Dunky Walker, Division I, 1921-22.
Most Goals Overall (Individual): 221: David McCrae, 1923-34.

ST MIRREN 2004–05 LEAGUE RECORD

Match No.	Date	Venue	Opponents	Result		H/T Score	Lg. Pos.	Goalscorers	Attendance
1	Aug 7	H	Falkirk	W	2-0	0-0	—	Paatelainen 66, Russell 81	3817
2	14	A	Ross Co	D	1-1	0-1	3	O'Neil 90	2666
3	21	H	St Johnstone	W	2-1	0-1	2	O'Neil 47, Baird 86	3079
4	28	H	Hamilton A	W	1-0	1-0	2	Paatelainen 37	2987
5	Sept 4	A	Clyde	D	0-0	0-0	2		2472
6	11	H	Partick Th	W	2-1	0-1	1	O'Neil 56, Paatelainen 70	4711
7	18	A	Raith R	W	3-0	1-0	1	Lappin 25, Paatelainen 55, McGinty (pen) 58	2111
8	25	H	Airdrie U	D	1-1	1-0	1	McGinty 16	3569
9	Oct 2	A	Queen of the S	L	1-2	0-2	3	Baird 78	2734
10	16	H	Ross Co	W	3-2	1-1	3	Ellis 16, Cowie (og) 69, O'Neil 83	2538
11	23	A	Falkirk	D	0-0	0-0	3		4611
12	30	A	Hamilton A	D	2-2	1-1	3	O'Neil (pen) 35, Russell 75	2529
13	Nov 6	H	Clyde	D	0-0	0-0	3		3788
14	13	A	Partick Th	W	3-0	0-0	3	McGinty (pen) 51, Russell 66, O'Neil 85	1949
15	20	H	Raith R	W	1-0	0-0	3	McGinty (pen) 57	3002
16	27	H	Queen of the S	D	2-2	0-0	2	Broadfoot 2 57, 75	2850
17	Dec 4	A	Airdrie U	L	2-3	1-1	2	Gillies 45, O'Neil 66	2514
18	11	H	Falkirk	L	0-1	0-0	3		4676
19	18	A	St Johnstone	L	0-1	0-1	3		2233
20	26	H	Hamilton A	L	0-1	0-0	3		2888
21	Jan 1	H	Partick Th	D	1-1	0-1	4	Broadfoot 51	3779
22	15	A	Raith R	L	0-2	0-0	5		1393
23	22	H	Airdrie U	W	1-0	0-0	3	Kean 81	3047
24	29	A	Queen of the S	D	0-0	0-0	3		2016
25	Feb 19	H	St Johnstone	D	1-1	0-1	4	Broadfoot 50	2716
26	Mar 1	A	Ross Co	W	1-0	1-0	—	Kean 28	1302
27	5	H	Clyde	D	0-0	0-0	3		2730
28	8	A	Clyde	D	0-0	0-0	—		1008
29	12	A	Hamilton A	D	0-0	0-0	3		1950
30	19	A	Partick Th	D	0-0	0-0	3		3730
31	Apr 2	H	Raith R	W	3-0	3-0	3	Ellis 14, Russell 16, Kean 20	2193
32	9	H	Queen of the S	W	3-0	2-0	3	Baird 17, Murray 20, Reilly 90	2331
33	16	A	Airdrie U	W	2-0	0-0	3	Kean 2 65, 76	1989
34	23	A	Falkirk	W	2-1	1-1	2	Broadfoot 30, Russell 68	4342
35	30	H	Ross Co	W	1-0	1-0	2	Van Zanten 32	3942
36	May 7	A	St Johnstone	D	0-0	0-0	2		2920

Final League Position: 2

Honours
League Champions: First Division 1976-77, 1999-2000; *Runners-up:* 2004-05. Division II 1967-68; *Runners-up:* 1935-36.
Scottish Cup Winners: 1926, 1959, 1987. *Runners-up:* 1908, 1934, 1962.
League Cup Runners-up: 1955-56.
B&Q Cup Runners-up: 1993-94. *Anglo-Scottish Cup:* 1979-80.

European: *Cup Winners' Cup:* 4 matches (1987-88). *UEFA Cup:* 10 matches (1980-81, 1983-84, 1985-86).

Club colours: Shirt: Black and white vertical stripes. Shorts: White with black trim. Stockings: White with 2 black hoops. Change colours: Predominantly red.

Goalscorers: *League* (41): O'Neil 7 (1 pen), Broadfoot 5, Kean 5, Russell 5, McGinty 4 (3 pens), Paatelainen 4, Baird 3, Ellis 2, Gillies 1, Lappin 1, Murray 1, Reilly 1, Van Zanten 1, own goal 1.
Scottish Cup (5): Kean 3, Murray 1, Russell 1.
CIS Cup (2): O'Neil 1, Paatelainen 1.
Challenge Cup (1): Gillies 1.

Hinchcliffe C 34	Van Zanten D 33	Broadfoot K 36	Millen A 36	McGowne K 31	Reilly M 35	Gillies R 11 + 13	Murray H 30 + 2	Paatelainen M 12 + 4	Annand E 1	Lappin S 29 + 5	Russell A 12 + 13	Ellis L 14 + 8	O'Neil J 19 + 11	McGinty B 24 + 8	McCay R 6 + 5	Baird J 3 + 18	Crilly M 4 + 5	Kean S 14 + 1	Dempsie M 1	Reid A 8	McKenna D — + 3	Molloy C 1	Woods S — + 1	Smith C 2	*Match No.*
1	2	3	4	5	6	7	8^{3}	9	10^{1}	11^{2}	12	13	14												1
1	2	3	4	5	6^{2}	7	8^{1}	9		11			12	10^{3}	13	14									2
1	2	3	4	5	6	7^{1}		9		11^{2}			8	10	13	12									3
1	2	3	4	5	6		7	9		11^{2}			8	10^{1}	13	12									4
1	2	3	4	5	6	7^{2}	8				14	11^{1}	10	9^{3}	12	13									5
1	2	3	4	5	6		7	9		11^{1}		12	8	10^{2}		13									6
1	2	3	4	5	6	13	7	9		11^{3}	12	14	8^{2}	10^{1}											7
1	2	3	4	5	6	12	7	9		11^{2}	13		8^{1}	10											8
1	2^{2}	3	4	5	6	13	7	9		11^{1}		12	8^{3}	10		14									9
1	2	3	4	5	6^{3}	7	8	9^{1}		13		11^{2}	12	10		14									10
1	2^{2}	3	4	5	6	7	8			12		11^{1}	10^{3}	9		14	13								11
1	2	3	4	5	6^{2}	7^{3}	8			12	14	11^{1}	10	9			13								12
1	2	3	4	5	6	7^{1}	8			11^{3}	12	14	10^{2}	9		13									13
1	2	3	4	5	6		7			11^{3}	9^{2}	14	13	10^{1}		12	8								14
1	2	3	4	5	6		7	12		11^{2}	9^{3}	13	14	10			8^{1}								15
1	2	3	4	5	6		7	12		11^{2}	9^{1}	13	14	10			8^{3}								16
1	2	3	4	5	6^{3}	7^{2}	8	13			9^{1}	11	12	10			14								17
1	2	3	4	5^{1}	6		7^{2}	9		12	14	11	8	10^{3}				13							18
1	2^{3}	3	4		6	13	7	9		11		5^{1}	8^{2}	14	12			10							19
1	2	3	4		6^{3}	7^{1}		9		11^{2}	14			12	8		13	10	5						20
1	2	3	4	5	6		7^{2}	14		8	12		13	10^{1}	11			9^{3}							21
1	2^{2}	3	4	5	6		13			8^{3}	12			10^{1}	11	14	7	9							22
1	2	3	4	5	6	12	7			8^{1}			10^{2}	13	11			9							23
1	2	3	4	5	6	12	7			8^{1}	14		10^{2}	13	11			9^{3}							24
1	2	3	4	5	6	13	7			14	12		8^{2}	10^{1}	11^{3}			9							25
1	2	3	4	5		7	6			8	13	11	10^{2}	12				9^{1}							26
1	2^{1}	3	4	5	6	13	7			8	9^{2}		11^{3}	10		14	12								27
1		3	4	5	6	13				7	9	11	8	10^{2}		12				2^{1}					28
1		3	4	5	6^{1}	13	12			8	9^{3}	11	7	10^{2}		14				2					29
1		3	4	5	6		7			8	9^{2}	11	13	10^{1}		12				2					30
1	5	3	4		6^{1}	12	7			8^{2}	10	11		14		13		9^{3}		2					31
1	2	3	4		6	12	7			8^{2}	10	5		13		11^{1}		9^{3}			14				32
1	5	3	4		6		7			8	10	11^{1}				12		9		2					33
1^{6}	2	3	4	5	6					8	10		13			12		9^{2}		11		7^{1}	15		34
	2	3	4	5	6	13	7			8						10^{1}		9^{2}		11	12			1	35
	2	3	4	5	6		7			8^{2}			13	12		10^{1}		9^{3}		11	14			1	36

STENHOUSEMUIR — Third Division

Year Formed: 1884. *Ground & Address:* Ochilview Park, Gladstone Rd, Stenhousemuir FK5 5QL. *Telephone:* 01324 562992. *Fax:* 01324 562980.
Ground Capacity: total: 2374, seated: 626. *Size of Pitch:* 110yd × 72yd.
Chairman: David O. Reid. *Secretary:* Margaret Kilpatrick. *Commercial Manager:* Brian McGinlay.
Manager: Des McKeown. *Assistant Manager:* John McCormack. *Physio:* Alain Davidson.
Managers since 1975: H. Glasgow, J. Black, A. Rose, W. Henderson, A. Rennie, J. Meakin, D. Lawson, T. Christie, G. Armstrong, B. Fairley, J. McVeigh, T. Smith.
Club Nickname(s): The Warriors. *Previous Grounds:* Tryst Ground 1884-86, Goschen Park 1886-90.
Record Attendance: 12,500 v East Fife, Scottish Cup 4th rd, 11 Mar 1950.
Record Transfer Fee received: £70,000 for Euan Donaldson to St Johnstone (May 1995).
Record Transfer Fee paid: £20,000 to Livingston for Ian Little (June 1995).
Record Victory: 9-2 v Dundee U, Division II, 19 Apr 1937.
Record Defeat: 2-11 v Dunfermline Ath. Division II, 27 Sept 1930.
Most League Appearances: 360: Archie Rose.
Most League Goals in Season (Individual): 32: Robert Taylor, Division II, 1925-26.

STENHOUSEMUIR 2004–05 LEAGUE RECORD

Match No.	*Date*	*Venue*	*Opponents*	*Result*		*H/T Score*	*Lg. Pos.*	*Goalscorers*	*Attendance*
1	Aug 7	H	Elgin C	L	0-2	0-1	—		267
2	14	A	Cowdenbeath	W	6-0	4-0	3	McGrillen 3 (1 pen) [19 (p), 21, 30], McBride [33], Collins [67], Davidson [82]	233
3	21	H	East Stirling	W	6-0	1-0	3	Lauchlan [10], Savage 3 [48, 67, 87], McBride [71], McGrillen [86]	465
4	28	A	East Fife	D	0-0	0-0	3		468
5	Sept 4	H	Queen's Park	D	1-1	1-0	4	Collins [44]	410
6	11	A	Albion R	L	0-1	0-1	4		339
7	18	H	Peterhead	L	1-2	1-0	6	McInally [28]	307
8	25	A	Montrose	W	2-0	0-0	5	McBride [65], Stephen (og) [71]	360
9	Oct 2	H	Gretna	L	0-3	0-1	5		343
10	16	H	Cowdenbeath	D	2-2	2-1	5	McInally [11], Lauchlan [25]	300
11	23	A	Elgin C	D	1-1	0-0	7	Collins [76]	622
12	30	H	East Fife	W	5-2	1-1	6	McGrillen 2 [24, 57], Lauchlan [46], Davidson 2 [67, 78]	382
13	Nov 6	A	Queen's Park	L	3-4	2-0	7	McGrillen (pen) [13], Lauchlan [37], Davidson [55]	491
14	13	H	Albion R	W	3-0	3-0	6	Davidson [2], Collins [37], Savage [42]	318
15	30	A	Peterhead	L	0-5	0-2	—		499
16	Dec 4	H	Montrose	D	1-1	0-1	6	McGrillen (pen) [84]	309
17	18	A	Gretna	L	0-3	0-2	6		1078
18	27	H	Elgin C	W	4-0	1-0	4	Savage 2 [32, 55], McBride [52], Knox [74]	329
19	Jan 3	A	East Fife	L	0-2	0-0	—		491
20	15	H	Queen's Park	D	0-0	0-0	4		356
21	29	H	Peterhead	D	1-1	0-0	5	Murphy [84]	394
22	Feb 5	A	Montrose	W	3-0	2-0	5	McGrillen 2 [2, 54], Savage [14]	305
23	12	H	Gretna	L	1-4	1-1	5	McGrillen [3]	416
24	19	H	East Stirling	W	3-2	1-0	4	McGrillen 3 [31, 60, 87]	422
25	Mar 5	A	Queen's Park	D	0-0	0-0	5		512
26	8	A	Albion R	D	1-1	0-1	—	Savage [55]	222
27	12	H	East Fife	L	1-2	0-2	6	Sinclair [50]	334
28	15	A	East Stirling	L	2-3	0-2	—	McGrillen [58], McGregor [90]	211
29	19	H	Albion R	D	1-1	0-0	6	McBride [90]	370
30	22	A	Cowdenbeath	W	2-0	1-0	—	McKeown (og) [5], McInally [18]	173
31	Apr 2	A	Peterhead	D	1-1	1-1	4	McGrillen [45]	523
32	9	A	Gretna	L	0-7	0-3	7		908
33	16	H	Montrose	L	0-1	0-0	7		263
34	23	A	East Stirling	W	4-1	3-1	6	Murphy [20], Sinclair [36], Morrison D [42], McGrillen [61]	242
35	30	H	Cowdenbeath	D	1-1	0-1	6	McGrillen [53]	360
36	May 7	A	Elgin C	L	2-4	2-0	7	McInally [19], Savage [25]	314

Final League Position: 7

Honours
League Champions: Third Division runners-up: 1998-99.
Scottish Cup: Semi-finals 1902-03. Quarter-finals 1948-49, 1949-50, 1994-95.
League Cup: Quarter-finals 1947-48, 1960-61, 1975-76.
League Challenge Cup: Winners: 1995-96.

Club colours: Shirt: Maroon. Shorts: White. Stockings: Maroon.

Goalscorers: *League* (58): McGrillen 18 (3 pens), Savage 9, Davidson 5, McBride 5, Collins 4, Lauchlan 4, McInally 4, Murphy 2, Sinclair 2, Knox 1, McGregor 1, Morrison D 1, own goals 2.
Scottish Cup (1): Savage 1.
CIS Cup (4): Collins 1, McBride 1, McGrillen 1, Savage 1.
Challenge Cup (1): McGrillen 1.

McCulloch W 34	Fallon S 23 + 1	McInally D 27 + 3	Murphy P 29 + 3	Henderson R 25 + 1	McBride J 32 + 1	Lauchlan M 23 + 3	Morrison D 7 + 4	Kerrigan S 10	Davidson R 8 + 6	McGrillen P 32 + 2	Knox K 19 + 3	Savage J 24 + 6	Collins L 22	McGregor S 16 + 3	Sinclair T 12 + 9	Smith A 16 + 4	Gardiner M — + 3	Ogunmade D — + 1	Easton S 14 + 2	McCulloch G 11 + 1	Struthers K 4 + 3	Menzies C 5 + 4	Kirkham J 1 + 1	Orr D 1 + 1	Morrison M 1	Miles C — + 1	*Match No.*
1	2^{1}	3	4	5	6	7^{2}	8	9	10	11	12	13															1
1		3	4	5	6	7		10^{1}	12	11^{3}	2	9	8^{2}	13	14												2
1		3	4	5	6	7		10^{1}		11	2	9	8^{2}	13	12												3
1	2	3		5	6	7			10^{1}	11	4	9	8			12											4
1	2	3		5	6	7^{2}			10^{1}	11	4	9	8			12	13										5
1	2	3	12	5^{1}	10	7^{2}			14	11	4	9^{3}	8			6	13										6
1	7	3^{1}	4	6	10			9^{2}		11	2	13	8		12	5											7
1	2	3	10	6	13	7^{2}			12	11	4	9^{1}	8			5											8
1	2	3^{2}	7^{1}	6	10	13			9	11	4		8			5		12									9
1		3	4	6	10	7^{2}		9^{1}		11	2	12	8	13		5											10
1	12	3^{1}	4	6	10	7		9		11	2		8			5											11
1	2	3	6		10	7		9	12	11	4		8			5^{1}											12
1	2	3^{1}	6		10	7		9^{2}	4	11^{3}	5		8		13	12	14										13
1	2^{1}		4	3	6	7^{2}			10	11	12	9	8		13	5											14
1	2	14	4^{2}	3	6	7		9^{1}	10^{3}	11	13	12	8			5											15
1	2	3			6	7^{1}	12		10	11	4	9	8						5								16
1	2	11	12	3	6	8	7^{2}			13	4	10		9^{3}		5^{1}			14								17
1	11	3	10		6	7	12				2^{2}	9	8	5^{1}	13				4								18
1	11	3	5		6	7^{1}				12	2	10	8	9					4								19
1	3		6		10	7			12	11	2	9^{1}	8	5					4								20
1	3		6		10	7				11	2^{1}	9	8	5		12			4								21
1	2	3	6		10	7^{2}			12	11		9^{1}	8	5	13				4								22
1	2	3	6^{2}		10	7^{1}				11		9	8	5	12				4	13							23
1	2	3	6	13	10	7				11		9^{1}	8	5	12				4^{2}								24
1	2	12	6	3	10	7^{2}						9^{3}		5	8	11^{1}				4	13	14					25
1	2	9	6^{1}	3	10					11		12		5	8					4	7						26
1	2^{1}	9	6	3	10					11		13		5	8^{2}					4	7	12					27
1^{6}		9		3■	10		12			11				6	8	5				4^{1}	7	2	15				28
		3	13		10	12		9^{2}		11				6^{3}	8	5			14	4	7^{1}	2	1				29
1		3	8	6	10					11		9			7	5			4	2							30
1		3^{2}	8	6^{1}	10	13	12			11		9			7	5			4	2							31
1			5	3	10		6			11		9			8^{1}				4	2	12	7					32
1			6	3			7			11^{2}	2	9		4	10	5				8^{1}	13	12					33
1■			6	3	10^{1}		7			11		9^{2}		5	8				4	2		12		13			34
		12	6	3			8			11		9		5■	10				4^{1}	2		7		1			35
1		10	6	5			8			11		9			7				4			2			3^{1}	12	36

STIRLING ALBION Second Division

Year Formed: 1945. *Ground & Address:* Forthbank Stadium, Springkerse Industrial Estate, Stirling FK7 7UJ. *Telephone:* 01786 450399. *Fax:* 01786 448400.
Ground Capacity: 3808, seated: 2508. *Size of Pitch:* 110yd × 74yd.
Chairman: Peter McKenzie. *Secretary:* Mrs Marlyn Hallam.
Player/Coach: Allan Moore. *Physio:* Eddie Gilmartin.
Managers since 1975: A. Smith, G. Peebles, J. Fleeting, J. Brogan, K. Drinkell, J. Philliben, R. Stewart.
Club Nickname(s): The Binos. *Previous Grounds:* Annfield 1945-92.
Record Attendance: 26,400 (at Annfield) v Celtic, Scottish Cup 4th rd, 14 Mar 1959; 3808 v Aberdeen, Scottish Cup 4th rd, 15 February 1996 (Forthbank).
Record Transfer Fee received: £90,000 for Stephen Nicholas to Motherwell (Mar 1999).
Record Transfer Fee paid: £25,000 for Craig Taggart from Falkirk (Aug 1994).
Record Victory: 20-0 v Selkirk, Scottish Cup 1st rd, 8 Dec 1984.
Record Defeat: 0-9 v Dundee U, Division I, 30 Dec 1967.
Most League Appearances: 504: Matt McPhee, 1967-81.
Most League Goals in Season (Individual): 27: Joe Hughes, Division II, 1969-70.
Most Goals Overall (Individual): 129: Billy Steele, 1971-83.

STIRLING ALBION 2004–05 LEAGUE RECORD

Match No.	Date	Venue	Opponents	Result		H/T Score	Lg. Pos.	Goalscorers	Attendance
1	Aug 7	H	Arbroath	W	5-2	2-0	—	O'Brien 5, Hay 40, Devine 2 47, 70, McLean 89	706
2	14	A	Brechin C	W	3-0	2-0	1	Glancy 2 12, 60, McLean (pen) 31	491
3	21	H	Alloa Ath	W	2-0	0-0	1	McLean (pen) 72, Glancy 77	1069
4	28	H	Berwick R	W	3-1	2-0	1	McLean 2 7, 14, Gethins (pen) 74	695
5	Sept 4	A	Forfar Ath	W	2-0	0-0	1	Glancy 49, O'Brien 65	841
6	11	H	Morton	D	1-1	1-1	1	Devine 31	1831
7	18	A	Stranraer	D	0-0	0-0	1		645
8	25	A	Dumbarton	D	1-1	0-1	2	Glancy 46	990
9	Oct 2	H	Ayr U	D	1-1	0-0	2	Glancy 61	1022
10	16	H	Brechin C	L	1-5	0-1	3	O'Brien 67	736
11	23	A	Arbroath	L	1-2	0-1	4	McLean 51	620
12	30	A	Berwick R	W	1-0	0-0	3	McLean (pen) 78	453
13	Nov 6	H	Forfar Ath	W	3-1	1-0	3	Hay 20, McLean 47, Rowe 59	756
14	13	A	Morton	L	0-3	0-1	4		3020
15	20	H	Berwick R	L	0-1	0-1	4		551
16	27	H	Stranraer	D	1-1	0-0	3	Hay 79	678
17	Dec 4	H	Dumbarton	W	1-0	0-0	3	Gethins 51	688
18	18	A	Ayr U	L	2-3	0-1	3	McLean 67, O'Brien 90	1288
19	27	H	Arbroath	L	0-3	0-1	3		755
20	Jan 15	A	Forfar Ath	L	1-4	0-2	5	O'Brien 86	501
21	26	H	Morton	D	1-1	0-1	—	Di Giacomo 83	1075
22	29	A	Stranraer	W	3-0	1-0	4	O'Brien 41, Di Giacomo 2 46, 63	495
23	Feb 5	A	Dumbarton	W	2-0	2-0	3	Dunn 2 16, 41	981
24	12	H	Ayr U	W	2-0	2-0	3	Dunn 30, Hay 32	711
25	19	H	Alloa Ath	L	0-4	0-1	3		1135
26	26	A	Brechin C	L	3-5	1-3	4	Di Giacomo 31, Aitken 52, Dunn (pen) 69	515
27	Mar 5	H	Forfar Ath	W	3-2	2-1	4	Aitken 28, Devine 33, Di Giacomo 59	537
28	8	A	Alloa Ath	D	1-1	1-0	—	Nugent 21	626
29	12	A	Berwick R	D	2-2	1-1	4	Dunn (pen) 13, Wilson 88	366
30	19	A	Morton	L	0-2	0-1	4		2764
31	Apr 2	H	Stranraer	D	1-1	0-1	4	Aitken 53	658
32	9	A	Ayr U	W	3-0	0-0	4	Glancy 46, Devine 72, Dunn 83	1046
33	16	H	Dumbarton	W	3-0	2-0	4	Wilson 19, MacDonald 45, Nugent 90	705
34	23	A	Alloa Ath	L	0-3	0-1	4		921
35	30	H	Brechin C	L	1-2	1-2	4	Dunn 30	667
36	May 7	A	Arbroath	L	2-3	2-3	4	Di Giacomo 51, Wilson 75	535

Final League Position: 4

Honours
League Champions: Division II 1952-53, 1957-58, 1960-61, 1964-65. Second Division 1976-77, 1990-91, 1995-96;
Runners-up: Division II 1948-49, 1950-51. Third Division 2003-04.
League Cup: Semi-finals 1961-62.

Club colours: Shirt: Red with white side panels and trim. Shorts: Red with white side design. Stockings: White with red front stripe.

Goalscorers: *League* (56): McLean 9 (3 pens), Dunn 7 (2 pens), Glancy 7, Di Giacomo 6, O'Brien 6, Devine 5, Hay 4, Aitken 3, Wilson 3, Gethins 2 (1 pen), Nugent 2, MacDonald 1, Rowe 1.
Scottish Cup (0).
CIS Cup (3): McLean 2, Glancy 1.
Challenge Cup (5): McLean 2, Cummings 1, Gethins 1, Rowe 1.

Hogarth M 35	Nugent P 35	Devine S 26 + 2	McNally M 21	Rowe G 14	MacDonald K 27 + 4	Hay P 33 + 1	Ferguson C 17 + 7	McLean S 18	Glancy M 18 + 10	O'Brien D 33 + 1	Neville B 5 + 2	Allan J 3 + 6	Scotland C 21 + 4	Cummings D 1 + 5	Gethins C 3 + 9	Hutchison S 4 + 12	Prentice M — + 1	Wilson D 11 + 12	Galloway M 8 + 1	Gibson A 5 + 2	Roycroft S 3	Canning M 12 + 5	Di Giacomo P 16	Dunn R 16	Aitken C 8 + 5	Ferguson W — + 2	Forbes D 2	Christie S 1	Taggart N — + 1	*Match No.*
1	2^{1}	3	4	5	6	7	8	9	10	11^{2}	12^{3}	13	14																	1
1	2		4	5	6	7	8	9	10^{1}	11			3	12																2
1	2^{1}		4	5	6	7	8	9^{3}	10^{2}	11			3	14	12	13														3
1	2		4	5	6^{2}	7	8	9^{1}	10	11^{3}		14	3		12	13														4
1	2	3^{2}		5	6	7	8	9	10^{1}	11			4	12		13														5
1	2	8	4	5	6	7		9	10^{2}	11			3^{1}	13		12														6
1	2	3		5	6	7^{3}	8	9^{1}	10^{2}	11			4	12	13		14													7
1	2	3		5	6	7^{1}	8		10	11^{3}		14	4	9^{2}	13			12												8
1	2	3		5	14	7^{1}	8	9	10	11			4^{3}		13	6		12^{2}												9
1	2^{1}	14	4	5	6^{2}		8	9	10	11			3^{3}		12	7			13											10
1	2	3	4				8	10	7	11^{3}		14	5^{1}		9^{2}	12		13	6											11
1	2	3		5	6	7		9	10^{1}	11	4				12				8											12
1	2	3^{1}		5	6	7		9^{2}	10		4	11^{3}			13			12	8	14										13
1	2	3		5	6	7		9	10	13	4^{1}	11^{2}							8	12										14
1	2				6	3	8^{1}	9	10^{3}	11	4^{2}		12		14	5		13		7										15
1	2		4			6	8^{3}	9	12	11^{2}		14			10^{1}			13	5	7	3									16
1	2		4			5	8^{1}	9	13	11		12			10^{2}			14	6	7^{3}	3									17
1	2	3	4^{2}		14	13	8^{3}	9	10	11^{1}								12	6	7	5									18
1	2	3	4		13	6		9^{2}	12	11		10	5					14	8^{1}	7^{3}										19
1		12	4	5	7	3	8^{2}			11	2^{1}					13		9				6	10							20
1	4	3			8	2	13		12	11			5					7				6^{2}	9	10^{1}						21
1	5	3			8	2^{3}			13	11			4			14		7^{1}				6	9	10^{2}	12					22
1	5	3			8	2			13	11			4^{3}			14		7^{1}				6	9	10^{2}	12					23
1	5	3			8	2			13	11			4					7^{1}				6^{3}	9	10^{2}	12	14				24
1	5	3			8	2			12	11			4^{1}					7^{2}				6	9	10	13					25
1	5		4		7	2	8^{1}		13		14					12						11^{2}	9	10	6		3^{3}			26
1	5	3	4^{1}		7	2				11^{2}			12			13						8	9	10	6					27
1	2	3	5			7				11			4									6	9	10	8					28
1	2	3	5		6	7^{3}	13		9^{1}	11^{2}			4					12				8		10		14				29
1	2	3	5		8	7	13			11^{2}			4					12				6^{1}	9	10						30
1	5	3	4		6	2			12	11								7^{1}				13	9	10	8^{2}					31
1	5	3	4		6^{3}	2	14		10^{1}	11								12				13	9	7	8^{2}					32
1	5	3	4^{3}		6^{1}	2	12			11			14					7				13	9	10	8^{2}					33
1	5	3	4		6	2	13			11^{2}						14		7^{1}				12	9	10	8^{3}					34
	5	3				2	6^{1}			11			4			12		7^{2}				14	9	10	8^{3}			1	13	35
1	5				14	2	13			11^{2}			4			8^{3}		7				6^{1}	9	10	12		3			36

STRANRAER First Division

Year Formed: 1870. *Ground & Address:* Stair Park, London Rd, Stranraer DG9 8BS. *Telephone:* 01776 703271. *Website:* www.stranraerfc.org.
Ground Capacity: 5600, seated: 1830. *Size of Pitch:* 110yd × 70yd.
Chairman: James Bark. *Secretary:* Graham Rodgers. *Commercial Manager:* B. Reilly.
Manager: Neil Watt. *Assistant Manager:* Stuart Millar. *Physio:* Walter Cannon.
Managers since 1975: J. Hughes, N. Hood, G. Hamilton, D. Sneddon, J. Clark, R. Clark, A. McAnespie, C. Money, W. McLaren.
Club Nickname(s): The Blues. *Previous Grounds:* None.
Record Attendance: 6500 v Rangers, Scottish Cup 1st rd, 24 Jan 1948.
Record Transfer Fee received: £90,000 for Mark Campbell to Ayr Utd, 1999.
Record Transfer Fee paid: £15,000 for Colin Harkness from Kilmarnock (Aug 1989).
Record Victory: 7-0 v Brechin C, Division II, 6 Feb 1965.
Record Defeat: 1-11 v Queen of the South, Scottish Cup 1st rd, 16 Jan 1932.
Most League Appearances: 301, Keith Knox, 1986-90; 1999-2001.
Most League Goals in Season (Individual): 59, Tommy Sloan.

STRANRAER 2004–05 LEAGUE RECORD

Match No.	*Date*	*Venue*	*Opponents*	*Result*		*H/T Score*	*Lg. Pos.*	*Goalscorers*	*Attendance*
1	Aug 7	H	Alloa Ath	W	3-0	0-0	—	Graham 2 56, 79, Swift 86	479
2	14	A	Morton	L	1-3	0-2	5	Henderson 52	2653
3	21	H	Ayr U	W	2-1	0-1	4	Graham 2 52, 82	885
4	28	A	Arbroath	W	1-0	0-0	3	Sharp 77	405
5	Sept 4	H	Brechin C	W	4-2	2-0	3	Graham 2 19, 54, Wright 29, Finlayson 51	436
6	11	A	Dumbarton	W	3-1	1-0	2	Finlayson 2, Guy (pen) 79, Graham 85	841
7	18	H	Stirling A	D	0-0	0-0	2		645
8	25	A	Forfar Ath	W	1-0	0-0	1	Fraser 50	524
9	Oct 2	H	Berwick R	D	2-2	1-2	1	Gaughan K 2 28, 86	521
10	16	H	Morton	W	1-0	0-0	1	Graham 64	918
11	23	A	Alloa Ath	W	2-1	2-0	1	Graham 2 5, 39	492
12	30	H	Arbroath	W	2-1	1-1	1	Finlayson 29, Graham 84	503
13	Nov 6	A	Brechin C	L	1-4	1-2	1	Henderson 14	620
14	13	H	Dumbarton	W	1-0	0-0	1	Guy (pen) 52	532
15	27	A	Stirling A	D	1-1	0-0	1	Graham 59	678
16	Dec 4	H	Forfar Ath	W	1-0	0-0	1	Graham 65	411
17	27	H	Alloa Ath	L	0-1	0-0	1		596
18	Jan 1	A	Ayr U	W	1-0	0-0	2	Dunlop (og) 69	1467
19	3	A	Arbroath	W	4-0	2-0	—	Graham 5, Henderson 13, Finlayson 71, Jenkins 85	432
20	15	H	Brechin C	L	0-1	0-0	2		552
21	29	H	Stirling A	L	0-3	0-1	2		495
22	Feb 5	A	Forfar Ath	W	2-1	2-0	2	Jenkins 40, Henderson 42	453
23	12	H	Berwick R	W	1-0	0-0	2	Jenkins 51	351
24	19	H	Ayr U	L	1-3	1-1	2	Jenkins 30	619
25	26	A	Morton	L	0-2	0-1	2		2592
26	Mar 1	A	Berwick R	W	2-1	1-1	—	Fox 5, McManus 63	296
27	5	A	Brechin C	L	1-2	1-0	2	McManus 29	606
28	12	H	Arbroath	D	3-3	1-1	2	Gaughan K 13, Wright 56, Moore 71	357
29	19	H	Dumbarton	W	2-1	2-0	2	Moore 21, McManus 28	436
30	26	A	Dumbarton	D	1-1	0-1	2	Swift 87	848
31	Apr 2	A	Stirling A	D	1-1	1-0	2	Sharp 28	658
32	9	A	Berwick R	W	2-1	1-0	2	Gaughan K 11, Finlayson 49	363
33	16	H	Forfar Ath	D	0-0	0-0	2		456
34	23	A	Ayr U	D	0-0	0-0	2		1367
35	30	H	Morton	D	1-1	1-1	2	Jenkins 42	2778
36	May 7	A	Alloa Ath	L	0-3	0-1	2		606

Final League Position: 2

Honours
League Champions: Second Division 1993-94, 1997-98; *Runners-up:* 2004-05. Third Division 2003-04.
Qualifying Cup Winners: 1937.
Scottish Cup: Quarter-finals 2003
League Challenge Cup Winners: 1996-97.

Club colours: Shirt: Blue with white side panels. Shorts: Blue with white side panels. Stockings: Blue with two white hoops.

Goalscorers: *League* (48): Graham 14, Finlayson 5, Jenkins 5, Gaughan K 4, Henderson 4, McManus 3, Guy 2 (2 pens), Moore 2, Sharp 2, Swift 2, Wright 2, Fox 1, Fraser 1, own goal 1.
Scottish Cup (4): Gaughan K 1, McCutcheon 1, Swift 1, Wingate 1.
CIS Cup (3): Henderson 1, Sharp 1, Turnbull 1.
Challenge Cup (0).

Meechan K 3	Swift S 31	Wright F 35	Wingate D 23 + 2	Henderson M 36	Fraser J 15 + 5	Finlayson K 36	Gaughan K 23 + 6	Turnbull D 4 + 7	Graham D 20	Sharp L 23 + 7	McCutcheon G 4 + 13	Gaughan P — + 1	Jenkins A 35	Aitken S 12 + 3	Crawford B 3 + 8	McCondichie A 14	Donnachie S — + 2	Guy G 10 + 8	McPhee G 16 + 9	Cruickshank C 2 + 2	McCaulay M — + 1	McGovern M 19	McManus P 15 + 1	Fox D 10 + 1	Moore M 7	*Match No.*
1	2	3	4	5	6^{2}	7	8	9^{1}	10	11	12	13														1
1	2	3	4	5	12	7^{3}		9^{2}	10	11	13		6	8^{1}	14											2
1	2	3	4	5	8	7^{2}	12		10	11	9^{1}		6		13											3
	2	3	4	5	8	7	9^{2}		10^{3}	11	14		6^{1}	13		1	12									4
	2^{1}	3	4	5	9	7	12	14	10^{3}	11			6	8^{2}		1	13									5
		3	4	5	9^{2}	7	13		10	11			6	8^{1}		1		2	12							6
	2	3	4^{1}	5	9^{3}	7	12		10	11	14		6	8^{2}		1			13							7
	2	3		5	9	7	4	8^{1}	10	11			6			1			12							8
	2	3		5	9^{1}	7^{3}	4	8^{2}	10	11	13		6		14	1			12							9
	2	3		5	9	7	4		10	11			6			1		8^{1}	12							10
	2	3		5	9^{1}	7		13	10^{2}	11			6			1		8	12	4						11
	2	3		5	9^{1}	7			10	11	12		6	8		1				4						12
	2^{1}	3		5	9^{3}	7	4		10	11^{2}	14		6	8		1		13		12						13
	2	3^{3}		5	12	7	4		10	13			6	8^{2}	9^{1}	1		11		14						14
	2	3		5	9^{2}	7^{3}	4	14	10				6	8^{1}	13	1		11	12							15
	2	3	4	5		7	8^{2}	13	10				6		9^{1}	1		11	12							16
	2		4	5		7	8	12	10	11^{2}			6		9^{1}	1^{6}		13	3		15					17
	2	3	4	5	9^{1}	7	8		10	11			6						12			1				18
	2^{1}	3	4	5	14	7^{3}	8		10^{2}	11	13		6					12	9			1				19
	2	3	4	5		7^{2}	8		10	11^{1}	13		6						9			1	12			20
		3	4	5		7^{2}	8			11^{1}	13		6		12			2	9			1	10			21
		3	4	5		7^{2}	13				9^{1}		6		12			2	8			1	10	11		22
		3	4	5		7^{2}	13			14	9^{1}		6		12			2	8			1	10^{3}	11		23
		3	4	5		7							6	9^{1}	12			2	8			1	10	11		24
	2	3	4	5		7		12			9^{1}		6					13	8^{2}			1	10	11		25
	2	3	4	5		7^{1}	8			14	12		6					13	9			1	10^{2}	11^{3}		26
	2	3	4	5		7	8			13			6					12	9^{1}			1	10	11^{2}		27
	2	3	4	5		7	8						6									1	10	11	9	28
	2	3	4	5		7				12			6						8			1	10	11^{1}	9	29
	2	3	4^{2}	5		7				12			6	13					8			1	10	11^{1}	9	30
	2	3		5	12	7	4			11			6						8			1	10^{1}		9	31
	2^{1}	3	13	5		7	4			11			6					12	8			1	10^{2}		9	32
	2	3		5	9^{1}	7	4	12		11			6^{2}	8				13				1	10			33
	2	3		5	12	7	4			11	13		6^{1}	8					9			1	10^{2}			34
	2	3	13	5		7^{2}	4			11			6	8^{1}					10			1		12	9	35
	2	3	4	5		7	8^{1}			14	13		6	12								1	10^{2}	11^{3}	9	36

SCOTTISH LEAGUE TABLES 2004–05

PREMIER DIVISION

			Home					Away					Total						
		P	*W*	*D*	*L*	*F*	*A*	*W*	*D*	*L*	*F*	*A*	*W*	*D*	*L*	*F*	*A*	*GD*	*Pts*
1	Rangers	38	15	2	2	48	12	14	4	1	30	10	29	6	3	78	22	56	93
2	Celtic	38	15	0	4	41	15	15	2	2	44	20	30	2	6	85	35	50	92
3	Hibernian	38	9	4	6	32	26	9	3	7	32	31	18	7	13	64	57	7	61
4	Aberdeen	38	8	4	6	22	17	10	3	7	22	22	18	7	13	44	39	5	61
5	Hearts	38	9	4	6	25	15	4	7	8	18	26	13	11	14	43	41	2	50
6	Kilmarnock	38	10	2	7	32	20	5	2	12	17	35	15	4	19	49	55	–6	49
7	Motherwell	38	8	4	7	29	22	5	5	9	17	27	13	9	16	46	49	–3	48
8	Inverness CT	38	7	4	9	23	24	4	7	7	18	23	11	11	16	41	47	–6	44
9	Dundee U	38	4	7	8	22	28	4	5	10	19	31	8	12	18	41	59	–18	36
10	Livingston	38	5	4	10	22	34	4	4	11	12	27	9	8	21	34	61	–27	35
11	Dunfermline Ath	38	5	9	5	23	19	3	1	15	11	41	8	10	20	34	60	–26	34
12	Dundee	38	7	4	8	21	24	1	5	13	16	47	8	9	21	37	71	–34	33

FIRST DIVISION

			Home					Away					Total						
		P	*W*	*D*	*L*	*F*	*A*	*W*	*D*	*L*	*F*	*A*	*W*	*D*	*L*	*F*	*A*	*GD*	*Pts*
1	Falkirk	36	10	6	2	35	15	12	3	3	31	15	22	9	5	66	30	36	75
2	St Mirren	36	10	6	2	24	11	5	9	4	17	12	15	15	6	41	23	18	60
3	Clyde	36	9	4	5	17	13	7	8	3	18	16	16	12	8	35	29	6	60
4	Queen of the S	36	7	5	6	17	14	7	4	7	19	24	14	9	13	36	38	–2	51
5	Airdrie U	36	8	3	7	25	25	6	5	7	19	23	14	8	14	44	48	–4	50
6	Ross Co	36	6	5	7	20	16	7	3	8	20	21	13	8	15	40	37	3	47
7	Hamilton A	36	5	5	8	13	18	7	6	5	22	18	12	11	13	35	36	–1	47
8	St Johnstone	36	6	6	6	18	18	6	4	8	20	21	12	10	14	38	39	–1	46
9	Partick Th	36	7	5	6	23	25	3	4	11	15	27	10	9	17	38	52	–14	39
10	Raith R	36	3	4	11	19	33	0	3	15	7	34	3	7	26	26	67	–41	16

SECOND DIVISION

			Home					Away					Total						
		P	*W*	*D*	*L*	*F*	*A*	*W*	*D*	*L*	*F*	*A*	*W*	*D*	*L*	*F*	*A*	*GD*	*Pts*
1	Brechin C	36	12	1	5	47	25	10	5	3	34	18	22	6	8	81	43	38	72
2	Stranraer	36	9	5	4	24	19	9	4	5	24	22	18	9	9	48	41	7	63
3	Morton	36	13	2	3	35	14	5	6	7	25	23	18	8	10	60	37	23	62
4	Stirling Alb	36	8	5	5	29	26	6	4	8	27	29	14	9	13	56	55	1	51
5	Forfar Ath	36	7	4	7	29	20	6	4	8	22	25	13	8	15	51	45	6	47
6	Alloa Ath	36	6	7	5	39	35	6	3	9	27	33	12	10	14	66	68	–2	46
7	Dumbarton	36	5	7	6	22	23	6	2	10	21	30	11	9	16	43	53	–10	42
8	Ayr U	36	6	6	6	22	23	5	3	10	17	31	11	9	16	39	54	–15	42
9	Arbroath	36	6	3	9	18	30	4	5	9	31	43	10	8	18	49	73	–24	38
10	Berwick R	36	5	3	10	20	33	3	7	8	20	31	8	10	18	40	64	–24	34

THIRD DIVISION

			Home					Away					Total						
		P	*W*	*D*	*L*	*F*	*A*	*W*	*D*	*L*	*F*	*A*	*W*	*D*	*L*	*F*	*A*	*GD*	*Pts*
1	Gretna	36	18	0	0	70	10	14	2	2	60	19	32	2	2	130	29	101	98
2	Peterhead	36	11	6	1	46	17	12	3	3	35	21	23	9	4	81	38	43	78
3	Cowdenbeath	36	8	4	6	24	32	6	5	7	30	29	14	9	13	54	61	–7	51
4	Queen's Park	36	7	5	6	24	24	6	4	8	27	26	13	9	14	51	50	1	48
5	Montrose	36	7	2	9	27	29	6	5	7	20	24	13	7	16	47	53	–6	46
6	Elgin C	36	7	5	6	24	31	5	2	11	15	30	12	7	17	39	61	–22	43
7	Stenhousemuir	36	5	7	6	31	25	5	5	8	27	33	10	12	14	58	58	0	42
8	East Fife	36	7	4	7	17	19	3	4	11	23	37	10	8	18	40	56	–16	38
9	Albion R	36	3	4	11	20	46	5	6	7	20	32	8	10	18	40	78	–38	34
10	East Stirlingshire	36	4	3	11	17	39	1	4	13	15	49	5	7	24	32	88	–56	22

SCOTTISH LEAGUE ATTENDANCES 2004–05

PREMIER LEAGUE

	Average	Highest	Lowest
Aberdeen	13,577	19,028	9214
Celtic	57,972	59,984	56,077
Dundee	6880	11,263	4387
Dundee U	8230	12,719	5097
Dunfermline Ath	6179	8555	3427
Hearts	12,232	17,673	9187
Hibernian	12,447	17,259	9087
Inverness CT	4118	9830	1125
Kilmarnock	5916	11,156	3485
Livingston	4600	7800	1931
Motherwell	6912	12,944	4267
Rangers	48,708	50,143	46,278

FIRST DIVISION

	Average	Highest	Lowest
Airdrie U	2014	3247	1430
Clyde	1605	3352	862
Falkirk	3882	5272	3182
Hamilton A	2103	3543	1371
Partick Th	3292	5157	1949
Queen of the S	1959	2734	1361
Raith R	1755	3050	1127
Ross Co	2324	3151	1183
St Johnstone	2403	3835	1770
St Mirren	3258	4711	2193

SECOND DIVISION

	Average	Highest	Lowest
Alloa Ath	601	1056	435
Arbroath	569	857	227
Ayr U	1337	2455	737
Berwick R	421	968	294
Brechin C	677	1340	428
Dumbarton	913	1670	522
Forfar Ath	596	1064	411
Morton	2691	3232	2244
Stirling A	832	1831	537
Stranraer	665	2778	351

THIRD DIVISION

	Average	Highest	Lowest
Albion R	318	519	222
Cowdenbeath	253	454	145
East Fife	521	784	396
East Stirlingshire	298	637	185
Elgin C	439	622	314
Gretna	896	2200	457
Montrose	382	592	269
Peterhead	637	1207	479
Queen's Park	527	803	406
Stenhousemuir	353	465	263

Rangers' manager Alex McLeish jubilant after CIS Cup Final win. (PA/Empics)

SCOTTISH LEAGUE HONOURS 1890 to 2005

*On goal average (ratio)/difference. †Held jointly after indecisive play-off. ‡Won on deciding match. ††Held jointly. ¶Two points deducted for fielding ineligible player.
Competition suspended 1940–45 during war; Regional Leagues operating. ‡‡Two points deducted for registration irregularities.

PREMIER LEAGUE

Maximum points: 108

	First	*Pts*	*Second*	*Pts*	*Third*	*Pts*
1998–99	Rangers	77	Celtic	71	St Johnstone	57
1999–2000	Rangers	90	Celtic	69	Hearts	54
			Maximum points: 114			
2000–01	Celtic	97	Rangers	82	Hibernian	66
2001–02	Celtic	103	Rangers	85	Livingston	58
2002–03	Rangers*	97	Celtic	97	Hearts	63
2003–04	Celtic	98	Rangers	81	Hearts	68
2004–05	Rangers	93	Celtic	92	Hibernian*	61

PREMIER DIVISION

Maximum points: 72

1975–76	Rangers	54	Celtic	48	Hibernian	43
1976–77	Celtic	55	Rangers	46	Aberdeen	43
1977–78	Rangers	55	Aberdeen	53	Dundee U	40
1978–79	Celtic	48	Rangers	45	Dundee U	44
1979–80	Aberdeen	48	Celtic	47	St Mirren	42
1980–81	Celtic	56	Aberdeen	49	Rangers*	44
1981–82	Celtic	55	Aberdeen	53	Rangers	43
1982–83	Dundee U	56	Celtic*	55	Aberdeen	55
1983–84	Aberdeen	57	Celtic	50	Dundee U	47
1984–85	Aberdeen	59	Celtic	52	Dundee U	47
1985–86	Celtic*	50	Hearts	50	Dundee U	47
			Maximum points: 88			
1986–87	Rangers	69	Celtic	63	Dundee U	60
1987–88	Celtic	72	Hearts	62	Rangers	60
			Maximum points: 72			
1988–89	Rangers	56	Aberdeen	50	Celtic	46
1989–90	Rangers	51	Aberdeen*	44	Hearts	44
1990–91	Rangers	55	Aberdeen	53	Celtic*	41
			Maximum points: 88			
1991–92	Rangers	72	Hearts	63	Celtic	62
1992–93	Rangers	73	Aberdeen	64	Celtic	60
1993–94	Rangers	58	Aberdeen	55	Motherwell	54
			Maximum points: 108			
1994–95	Rangers	69	Motherwell	54	Hibernian	53
1995–96	Rangers	87	Celtic	83	Aberdeen*	55
1996–97	Rangers	80	Celtic	75	Dundee U	60
1997–98	Celtic	74	Rangers	72	Hearts	67

FIRST DIVISION

Maximum points: 52

1975–76	Partick Th	41	Kilmarnock	35	Montrose	30
			Maximum points: 78			
1976–77	St Mirren	62	Clydebank	58	Dundee	51
1977–78	Morton*	58	Hearts	58	Dundee	57
1978–79	Dundee	55	Kilmarnock*	54	Clydebank	54
1979–80	Hearts	53	Airdrieonians	51	Ayr U*	44
1980–81	Hibernian	57	Dundee	52	St Johnstone	51
1981–82	Motherwell	61	Kilmarnock	51	Hearts	50
1982–83	St Johnstone	55	Hearts	54	Clydebank	50
1983–84	Morton	54	Dumbarton	51	Partick Th	46
1984–85	Motherwell	50	Clydebank	48	Falkirk	45
1985–86	Hamilton A	56	Falkirk	45	Kilmarnock	44
			Maximum points: 88			
1986–87	Morton	57	Dunfermline Ath	56	Dumbarton	53
1987–88	Hamilton A	56	Meadowbank T	52	Clydebank	49
			Maximum points: 78			
1988–89	Dunfermline Ath	54	Falkirk	52	Clydebank	48
1989–90	St Johnstone	58	Airdrieonians	54	Clydebank	44
1990–91	Falkirk	54	Airdrieonians	53	Dundee	52
			Maximum points: 88			
1991–92	Dundee	58	Partick Th*	57	Hamilton A	57
1992–93	Raith R	65	Kilmarnock	54	Dunfermline Ath	52
1993–94	Falkirk	66	Dunfermline Ath	65	Airdrieonians	54
			Maximum points: 108			
1994–95	Raith R	69	Dunfermline Ath*	68	Dundee	68
1995–96	Dunfermline Ath	71	Dundee U*	67	Morton	67
1996–97	St Johnstone	80	Airdieonians	60	Dundee*	58
1997–98	Dundee	70	Falkirk	65	Raith R*	60
1998–99	Hibernian	89	Falkirk	66	Ayr U	62
1999–2000	St Mirren	76	Dunfermline Ath	71	Falkirk	68
2000–01	Livingston	76	Ayr U	69	Falkirk	56
2001–02	Partick Th	66	Airdrieonians	56	Ayr U	52
2002–03	Falkirk	81	Clyde	72	St Johnstone	67
2003–04	Inverness CT	70	Clyde	69	St Johnstone	57
2004–05	Falkirk	75	St Mirren*	60	Clyde	60

SECOND DIVISION

Maximum points: 52

	First	*Pts*	*Second*	*Pts*	*Third*	*Pts*
1975–76	Clydebank*	40	Raith R	40	Alloa	35
			Maximum points: 78			
1976–77	Stirling A	55	Alloa	51	Dunfermline Ath	50
1977–78	Clyde*	53	Raith R	53	Dunfermline Ath	48
1978–79	Berwick R	54	Dunfermline Ath	52	Falkirk	50
1979–80	Falkirk	50	East Stirling	49	Forfar Ath	46
1980–81	Queen's Park	50	Queen of the S	46	Cowdenbeath	45
1981–82	Clyde	59	Alloa*	50	Arbroath	50
1982–83	Brechin C	55	Meadowbank Th	54	Arbroath	49
1983–84	Forfar Ath	63	East Fife	47	Berwick R	43
1984–85	Montrose	53	Alloa	50	Dunfermline Ath	49
1985–86	Dunfermline Ath	57	Queen of the S	55	Meadowbank Th	49
1986–87	Meadowbank Th	55	Raith R*	52	Stirling A*	52
1987–88	Ayr U	61	St Johnstone	59	Queen's Park	51
1988–89	Albion R	50	Alloa	45	Brechin C	43
1989–90	Brechin C	49	Kilmarnock	48	Stirling A	47
1990–91	Stirling A	54	Montrose	46	Cowdenbeath	45
1991–92	Dumbarton	52	Cowdenbeath	51	Alloa	50
1992–93	Clyde	54	Brechin C*	53	Stranraer	53
1993–94	Stranraer	56	Berwick R	48	Stenhousemuir*	47
			Maximum points: 108			
1994–95	Morton	64	Dumbarton	60	Stirling A	58
1995–96	Stirling A	81	East Fife	67	Berwick R	60
1996–97	Ayr U	77	Hamilton A	74	Livingston	64
1997–98	Stranraer	61	Clydebank	60	Livingston	59
1998–99	Livingston	77	Inverness CT	72	Clyde	53
1999–2000	Clyde	65	Alloa Ath	64	Ross Co	62
2000–01	Partick Th	75	Arbroath	58	Berwick R*	54
2001–02	Queen of the S	67	Alloa	59	Forfar Ath	53
2002–03	Raith R	59	Brechin C	55	Airdrie U	54
2003–04	Airdrie U	70	Hamilton A	62	Dumbarton	60
2004–05	Brechin C	72	Stranraer	63	Morton	62

THIRD DIVISION

Maximum points: 108

	First	Pts	Second	Pts	Third	Pts
1994–95	Forfar Ath	80	Montrose	67	Ross Co	60
1995–96	Livingston	72	Brechin C	63	Inverness CT	57
1996–97	Inverness CT	76	Forfar Ath*	67	Ross Co	67
1997–98	Alloa Ath	76	Arbroath	68	Ross Co*	67
1998–99	Ross Co	77	Stenhousemuir	64	Brechin C	59
1999–2000	Queen's Park	69	Berwick R	66	Forfar Ath	61
2000–01	Hamilton A*	76	Cowdenbeath	76	Brechin C	72
2001–02	Brechin C	73	Dumbarton	61	Albion R	59
2002–03	Morton	72	East Fife	71	Albion R	70
2003–04	Stranraer	79	Stirling A	77	Gretna	68
2004–05	Gretna	98	Peterhead	78	Cowdenbeath	51

FIRST DIVISION to 1974–75

Maximum points: a 36; *b* 44; *c* 40; *d* 52; *e* 60; *f* 68; g 76; *h* 84.

	First	Pts	Second	Pts	Third	Pts
1890–91*a*	Dumbarton††	29	Rangers††	29	Celtic	21
1891–92*b*	Dumbarton	37	Celtic	35	Hearts	34
1892–93*a*	Celtic	29	Rangers	28	St Mirren	20
1893–94*a*	Celtic	29	Hearts	26	St Bernard's	23
1894–95*a*	Hearts	31	Celtic	26	Rangers	22
1895–96*a*	Celtic	30	Rangers	26	Hibernian	24
1896–97*a*	Hearts	28	Hibernian	26	Rangers	25
1897–98*a*	Celtic	33	Rangers	29	Hibernian	22
1898–99*a*	Rangers	36	Hearts	26	Celtic	24
1899–1900*a*	Rangers	32	Celtic	25	Hibernian	24
1900–01*c*	Rangers	35	Celtic	29	Hibernian	25
1901–02*a*	Rangers	28	Celtic	26	Hearts	22
1902–03*b*	Hibernian	37	Dundee	31	Rangers	29
1903–04*d*	Third Lanark	43	Hearts	39	Celtic*	38
1904–05*d*	Celtic‡	41	Rangers	41	Third Lanark	35
1905–06*e*	Celtic	49	Hearts	43	Airdrieonians	38
1906–07*f*	Celtic	55	Dundee	48	Rangers	45
1907–08*f*	Celtic	55	Falkirk	51	Rangers	50
1908–09*f*	Celtic	51	Dundee	50	Clyde	48
1909–10*f*	Celtic	54	Falkirk	52	Rangers	46
1910–11*f*	Rangers	52	Aberdeen	48	Falkirk	44
1911–12*f*	Rangers	51	Celtic	45	Clyde	42
1912–13*f*	Rangers	53	Celtic	49	Hearts*	41
1913–14*g*	Celtic	65	Rangers	59	Hearts*	54
1914–15*g*	Celtic	65	Hearts	61	Rangers	50
1915–16*g*	Celtic	67	Rangers	56	Morton	51
1916–17*g*	Celtic	64	Morton	54	Rangers	53
1917–18*f*	Rangers	56	Celtic	55	Kilmarnock*	43
1918–19*f*	Celtic	58	Rangers	57	Morton	47

	First	*Pts*	*Second*	*Pts*	*Third*	*Pts*
1919–20*h*	Rangers	71	Celtic	68	Motherwell	57
1920–21*h*	Rangers	76	Celtic	66	Hearts	50
1921–22*h*	Celtic	67	Rangers	66	Raith R	51
1922–23*g*	Rangers	55	Airdrieonians	50	Celtic	46
1923–24*g*	Rangers	59	Airdrieonians	50	Celtic	46
1924–25*g*	Rangers	60	Airdrieonians	57	Hibernian	52
1925–26*g*	Celtic	58	Airdrieonians*	50	Hearts	50
1926–27*g*	Rangers	56	Motherwell	51	Celtic	49
1927–28*g*	Rangers	60	Celtic*	55	Motherwell	55
1928–29*g*	Rangers	67	Celtic	51	Motherwell	50
1929–30*g*	Rangers	60	Motherwell	55	Aberdeen	53
1930–31*g*	Rangers	60	Celtic	58	Motherwell	56
1931–32*g*	Motherwell	66	Rangers	61	Celtic	48
1932–33*g*	Rangers	62	Motherwell	59	Hearts	50
1933–34*g*	Rangers	66	Motherwell	62	Celtic	47
1934–35*g*	Rangers	55	Celtic	52	Hearts	50
1935–36*g*	Celtic	66	Rangers*	61	Aberdeen	61
1936–37*g*	Rangers	61	Aberdeen	54	Celtic	52
1937–38*g*	Celtic	61	Hearts	58	Rangers	49
1938–39*g*	Rangers	59	Celtic	48	Aberdeen	46
1946–47*e*	Rangers	46	Hibernian	44	Aberdeen	39
1947–48*e*	Hibernian	48	Rangers	46	Partick Th	36
1948–49*e*	Rangers	46	Dundee	45	Hibernian	39
1949–50*e*	Rangers	50	Hibernian	49	Hearts	43
1950–51*e*	Hibernian	48	Rangers*	38	Dundee	38
1951–52*e*	Hibernian	45	Rangers	41	East Fife	37
1952–53*e*	Rangers*	43	Hibernian	43	East Fife	39
1953–54*e*	Celtic	43	Hearts	38	Partick Th	35
1954–55*e*	Aberdeen	49	Celtic	46	Rangers	41
1955–56*f*	Rangers	52	Aberdeen	46	Hearts*	45
1956–57*f*	Rangers	55	Hearts	53	Kilmarnock	42
1957–58*f*	Hearts	62	Rangers	49	Celtic	46
1958–59*f*	Rangers	50	Hearts	48	Motherwell	44
1959–60*f*	Hearts	54	Kilmarnock	50	Rangers*	42
1960–61*f*	Rangers	51	Kilmarnock	50	Third Lanark	42
1961–62*f*	Dundee	54	Rangers	51	Celtic	46
1962–63*f*	Rangers	57	Kilmarnock	48	Partick Th	46
1963–64*f*	Rangers	55	Kilmarnock	49	Celtic*	47
1964–65*f*	Kilmarnock*	50	Hearts	50	Dunfermline Ath	49
1965–66*f*	Celtic	57	Rangers	55	Kilmarnock	45
1966–67*f*	Celtic	58	Rangers	55	Clyde	46
1967–68*f*	Celtic	63	Rangers	61	Hibernian	45
1968–69*f*	Celtic	54	Rangers	49	Dunfermline Ath	45
1969–70*f*	Celtic	57	Rangers	45	Hibernian	44
1970–71*f*	Celtic	56	Aberdeen	54	St Johnstone	44
1971–72*f*	Celtic	60	Aberdeen	50	Rangers	44
1972–73*f*	Celtic	57	Rangers	56	Hibernian	45
1973–74*f*	Celtic	53	Hibernian	49	Rangers	48
1974–75*f*	Rangers	56	Hibernian	49	Celtic	45

SECOND DIVISION to 1974–75

Maximum points: a 76; *b* 72; *c* 68; *d* 52; *e* 60; *f* 36; *g* 44.

1893–94*f*	Hibernian	29	Cowlairs	27	Clyde	24
1894–95*f*	Hibernian	30	Motherwell	22	Port Glasgow	20
1895–96*f*	Abercorn	27	Leith Ath	23	Renton	21
1896–97*f*	Partick Th	31	Leith Ath	27	Kilmarnock*	21
1897–98*f*	Kilmarnock	29	Port Glasgow	25	Morton	22
1898–99*f*	Kilmarnock	32	Leith Ath	27	Port Glasgow	25
1899–1900*f*	Partick Th	29	Morton	28	Port Glasgow	20
1900–01*f*	St Bernard's	25	Airdrieonians	23	Abercorn	21
1901–02*g*	Port Glasgow	32	Partick Th	31	Motherwell	26
1902–03*g*	Airdrieonians	35	Motherwell	28	Ayr U*	27
1903–04*g*	Hamilton A	37	Clyde	29	Ayr U	28
1904–05*g*	Clyde	32	Falkirk	28	Hamilton A	27
1905–06*g*	Leith Ath	34	Clyde	31	Albion R	27
1906–07*g*	St Bernard's	32	Vale of Leven*	27	Arthurlie	27
1907–08*g*	Raith R	30	Dumbarton*‡‡	27	Ayr U	27
1908–09*g*	Abercorn	31	Raith R*	28	Vale of Leven	28
1909–10*g*	Leith Ath‡	33	Raith R	33	St Bernard's	27
1910–11*g*	Dumbarton	31	Ayr U	27	Albion R	25
1911–12*g*	Ayr U	35	Abercorn	30	Dumbarton	27
1912–13*d*	Ayr U	34	Dunfermline Ath	33	East Stirling	32
1913–14*g*	Cowdenbeath	31	Albion R	27	Dunfermline Ath*	26
1914–15*d*	Cowdenbeath*	37	St Bernard's*	37	Leith Ath	37
1921–22*a*	Alloa	60	Cowdenbeath	47	Armadale	45
1922–23*a*	Queen's Park	57	Clydebank¶	50	St Johnstone¶	45
1923–24*a*	St Johnstone	56	Cowdenbeath	55	Bathgate	44
1924–25*a*	Dundee U	50	Clydebank	48	Clyde	47
1925–26*a*	Dunfermline Ath	59	Clyde	53	Ayr U	52
1926–27*a*	Bo'ness	56	Raith R	49	Clydebank	45
1927–28*a*	Ayr U	54	Third Lanark	45	King's Park	44

	First	*Pts*	*Second*	*Pts*	*Third*	*Pts*
1928–29*b*	Dundee U	51	Morton	50	Arbroath	47
1929–30*a*	Leith Ath*	57	East Fife	57	Albion R	54
1930–31*a*	Third Lanark	61	Dundee U	50	Dunfermline Ath	47
1931–32*a*	East Stirling*	55	St Johnstone	55	Raith R*	46
1932–33*c*	Hibernian	54	Queen of the S	49	Dunfermline Ath	47
1933–34*c*	Albion R	45	Dunfermline Ath*	44	Arbroath	44
1934–35*c*	Third Lanark	52	Arbroath	50	St Bernard's	47
1935–36*c*	Falkirk	59	St Mirren	52	Morton	48
1936–37*c*	Ayr U	54	Morton	51	St Bernard's	48
1937–38*c*	Raith R	59	Albion R	48	Airdrieonians	47
1938–39*c*	Cowdenbeath	60	Alloa*	48	East Fife	48
1946–47*d*	Dundee	45	Airdrieonians	42	East Fife	31
1947–48*e*	East Fife	53	Albion R	42	Hamilton A	40
1948–49*e*	Raith R*	42	Stirling A	42	Airdrieonians*	41
1949–50*e*	Morton	47	Airdrieonians	44	Dunfermline Ath*	36
1950–51*e*	Queen of the S*	45	Stirling A	45	Ayr U*	36
1951–52*e*	Clyde	44	Falkirk	43	Ayr U	39
1952–53*e*	Stirling A	44	Hamilton A	43	Queen's Park	37
1953–54*e*	Motherwell	45	Kilmarnock	42	Third Lanark*	36
1954–55*e*	Airdrieonians	46	Dunfermline Ath	42	Hamilton A	39
1955–56*b*	Queen's Park	54	Ayr U	51	St Johnstone	49
1956–57*b*	Clyde	64	Third Lanark	51	Cowdenbeath	45
1957–58*b*	Stirling A	55	Dunfermline Ath	53	Arbroath	47
1958–59*b*	Ayr U	60	Arbroath	51	Stenhousemuir	46
1959–60*b*	St Johnstone	53	Dundee U	50	Queen of the S	49
1960–61*b*	Stirling A	55	Falkirk	54	Stenhousemuir	50
1961–62*b*	Clyde	54	Queen of the S	53	Morton	44
1962–63*b*	St Johnstone	55	East Stirling	49	Morton	48
1963–64*b*	Morton	67	Clyde	53	Arbroath	46
1964–65*b*	Stirling A	59	Hamilton A	50	Queen of the S	45
1965–66*b*	Ayr U	53	Airdrieonians	50	Queen of the S	47
1966–67*a*	Morton	69	Raith R	58	Arbroath	57
1967–68*b*	St Mirren	62	Arbroath	53	East Fife	49
1968–69*b*	Motherwell	64	Ayr U	53	East Fife*	48
1969–70*b*	Falkirk	56	Cowdenbeath	55	Queen of the S	50
1970–71*b*	Partick Th	56	East Fife	51	Arbroath	46
1971–72*b*	Dumbarton*	52	Arbroath	52	Stirling A	50
1972–73*b*	Clyde	56	Dumfermline Ath	52	Raith R*	47
1973–74*b*	Airdrieonians	60	Kilmarnock	58	Hamilton A	55
1974–75*a*	Falkirk	54	Queen of the S*	53	Montrose	53

Elected to First Division: 1894 Clyde; 1895 Hibernian; 1896 Abercorn; 1897 Partick Th; 1899 Kilmarnock; 1900 Morton and Partick Th; 1902 Port Glasgow and Partick Th; 1903 Airdrieonians and Motherwell; 1905 Falkirk and Aberdeen; 1906 Clyde and Hamilton A; 1910 Raith R; 1913 Ayr U and Dumbarton.

RELEGATED FROM PREMIER LEAGUE

1998–99 Dunfermline Ath
1999–2000 *No relegation due to League reorganization*
2000–01 St Mirren
2001–02 St Johnstone
2002–03 *No relegated team*
2003–04 Partick Th
2004–05 Dundee

RELEGATED FROM PREMIER DIVISION

1974–75 *No relegation due to League reorganization*
1975–76 Dundee, St Johnstone
1976–77 Hearts, Kilmarnock
1977–78 Ayr U, Clydebank
1978–79 Hearts, Motherwell
1979–80 Dundee, Hibernian
1980–81 Kilmarnock, Hearts
1981–82 Partick Th, Airdrieonians
1982–83 Morton, Kilmarnock
1983–84 St Johnstone, Motherwell
1984–85 Dumbarton, Morton
1985–86 *No relegation due to League reorganization*
1986–87 Clydebank, Hamilton A
1987–88 Falkirk, Dunfermline Ath, Morton
1988–89 Hamilton A
1989–90 Dundee
1990–91 *None*
1991–92 St Mirren, Dunfermline Ath
1992–93 Falkirk, Airdrieonians
1993–94 *See footnote*
1994–95 Dundee U
1995–96 Partick Th, Falkirk
1996–97 Raith R
1997–98 Hibernian

RELEGATED FROM DIVISION 1

1974–75 *No relegation due to League reorganization*
1975–76 Dunfermline Ath, Clyde
1976–77 Raith R, Falkirk
1977–78 Alloa Ath, East Fife
1978–79 Montrose, Queen of the S
1979–80 Arbroath, Clyde
1980–81 Stirling A, Berwick R
1981–82 East Stirling, Queen of the S
1982–83 Dunfermline Ath, Queen's Park
1983–84 Raith R, Alloa
1984–85 Meadowbank Th, St Johnstone
1985–86 Ayr U, Alloa
1986–87 Brechin C, Montrose
1987–88 East Fife, Dumbarton
1988–89 Kilmarnock, Queen of the S
1989–90 Albion R, Alloa
1990–91 Clyde, Brechin C
1991–92 Montrose, Forfar Ath
1992–93 Meadowbank Th, Cowdenbeath
1993–94 *See footnote*
1994–95 Ayr U, Stranraer
1995–96 Hamilton A, Dumbarton
1996–97 Clydebank, East Fife
1997–98 Partick Th, Stirling A
1998–99 Hamilton A, Stranraer
1999–2000 Clydebank
2000–01 Morton, Alloa
2001–02 Raith R
2002–03 Alloa, Arbroath
2003–04 Ayr U, Brechin C
2004–05 Partick Th, Raith R

RELEGATED FROM DIVISION 2

1994–95 Meadowbank Th, Brechin C
1995–96 Forfar Ath, Montrose
1996–97 Dumbarton, Berwick R
1997–98 Stenhousemuir, Brechin C
1998–99 East Fife, Forfar Ath
1999–2000 Hamilton A**
2000–01 Queen's Park, Stirling A
2001–02 Morton
2002–03 Stranraer, Cowdenbeath
2003–04 East Fife, Stenhousemuir
2004–05 Arbroath, Berwick R

RELEGATED FROM DIVISION 1 (TO 1973–74)

1921–22 *Queen's Park, Dumbarton, Clydebank
1922–23 Albion R, Alloa Ath
1923–24 Clyde, Clydebank
1924–25 Third Lanark, Ayr U
1925–26 Raith R, Clydebank
1926–27 Morton, Dundee U
1927–28 Dunfermline Ath, Bo'ness
1928–29 Third Lanark, Raith R
1929–30 St Johnstone, Dundee U
1930–31 Hibernian, East Fife
1931–32 Dundee U, Leith Ath
1932–33 Morton, East Stirling
1933–34 Third Lanark, Cowdenbeath
1934–35 St Mirren, Falkirk
1935–36 Airdrieonians, Ayr U
1936–37 Dunfermline Ath, Albion R
1937–38 Dundee, Morton
1938–39 Queen's Park, Raith R
1946–47 Kilmarnock, Hamilton A
1947–48 Airdrieonians, Queen's Park
1948–49 Morton, Albion R
1949–50 Queen of the S, Stirling A
1950–51 Clyde, Falkirk
1951–52 Morton, Stirling A
1952–53 Motherwell, Third Lanark
1953–54 Airdrieonians, Hamilton A
1954–55 *No clubs relegated*
1955–56 Stirling A, Clyde
1956–57 Dunfermline Ath, Ayr U
1957–58 East Fife, Queen's Park
1958–59 Queen of the S, Falkirk
1959–60 Arbroath, Stirling A
1960–61 Ayr U, Clyde
1961–62 St Johnstone, Stirling A
1962–63 Clyde, Raith R
1963–64 Queen of the S, East Stirling
1964–65 Airdrieonians, Third Lanark
1965–66 Morton, Hamilton A
1966–67 St Mirren, Ayr U
1967–68 Motherwell, Stirling A
1968–69 Falkirk, Arbroath
1969–70 Raith R, Partick Th
1970–71 St Mirren, Cowdenbeath
1971–72 Clyde, Dunfermline Ath
1972–73 Kilmarnock, Airdrieonians
1973–74 East Fife, Falkirk

*Season 1921–22 – only 1 club promoted, 3 clubs relegated. ***15pts deducted for failing to field a team.*

Scottish League championship wins: Rangers 51, Celtic 39, Aberdeen 4, Hearts 4, Hibernian 4, Dumbarton 2, Dundee 1, Dundee U 1, Kilmarnock 1, Motherwell 1, Third Lanark 1.

At the end of the 1993–94 season four divisions were created assisted by the admission of two new clubs Ross County and Caledonian Thistle. Only one club was promoted from Division 1 and Division 2. The three relegated from the Premier joined with teams finishing second to seventh in Division 1 to form the new Division 1. Five relegated from Division 1 combined with those who finished second to sixth to form a new Division 2 and the bottom eight in Division 2 linked with the two newcomers to form a new Division 3. At the end of the 1997–98 season the nine clubs remaining in the Premier Division plus the promoted team from Division 1 formed a breakaway Premier League. At the end of the 1999–2000 season two teams were added to the Scottish League. There was no relegation from the Premier League but two promoted from the First Division and three from each of the Second and Third Divisions. One team was relegated from the First Division and one from the Second Division, leaving 12 teams in each division. In season 2002–03, Falkirk were not promoted to the Premier League due to the failure of their ground to meet League Standards. Inverness CT were promoted after a previous refusal in 2003–04 because of ground sharing.

Motherwell's Scott McDonald's shot flies past Celtic goalkeeper Rab Douglas. (PA/Empics)

SCOTTISH LEAGUE CUP FINALS 1946–2005

Season	*Winners*	*Runners-up*	*Score*
1946–47	Rangers	Aberdeen	4-0
1947–48	East Fife	Falkirk	4-1 after 0-0 draw
1948–49	Rangers	Raith R	2-0
1949–50	East Fife	Dunfermline Ath	3-0
1950–51	Motherwell	Hibernian	3-0
1951–52	Dundee	Rangers	3-2
1952–53	Dundee	Kilmarnock	2-0
1953–54	East Fife	Partick Th	3-2
1954–55	Hearts	Motherwell	4-2
1955–56	Aberdeen	St Mirren	2-1
1956–57	Celtic	Partick Th	3-0 after 0-0 draw
1957–58	Celtic	Rangers	7-1
1958–59	Hearts	Partick Th	5-1
1959–60	Hearts	Third Lanark	2-1
1960–61	Rangers	Kilmarnock	2-0
1961–62	Rangers	Hearts	3-1 after 1-1 draw
1962–63	Hearts	Kilmarnock	1-0
1963–64	Rangers	Morton	5-0
1964–65	Rangers	Celtic	2-1
1965–66	Celtic	Rangers	2-1
1966–67	Celtic	Rangers	1-0
1967–68	Celtic	Dundee	5-3
1968–69	Celtic	Hibernian	6-2
1969–70	Celtic	St Johnstone	1-0
1970–71	Rangers	Celtic	1-0
1971–72	Partick Th	Celtic	4-1
1972–73	Hibernian	Celtic	2-1
1973–74	Dundee	Celtic	1-0
1974–75	Celtic	Hibernian	6-3
1975–76	Rangers	Celtic	1-0
1976–77	Aberdeen	Celtic	2-1
1977–78	Rangers	Celtic	2-1
1978–79	Rangers	Aberdeen	2-1
1979–80	Dundee U	Aberdeen	3-0 after 0-0 draw
1980–81	Dundee U	Dundee	3-0
1981–82	Rangers	Dundee U	2-1
1982–83	Celtic	Rangers	2-1
1983–84	Rangers	Celtic	3-2
1984–85	Rangers	Dundee U	1-0
1985–86	Aberdeen	Hibernian	3-0
1986–87	Rangers	Celtic	2-1
1987–88	Rangers	Aberdeen	3-3
		(Rangers won 5-3 on penalties)	
1988–89	Rangers	Aberdeen	3-2
1989–90	Aberdeen	Rangers	2-1
1990–91	Rangers	Celtic	2-1
1991–92	Hibernian	Dunfermline Ath	2-0
1992–93	Rangers	Aberdeen	2-1
1993–94	Rangers	Hibernian	2-1
1994–95	Raith R	Celtic	2-2
		(Raith R won 6-5 on penalties)	
1995–96	Aberdeen	Dundee	2-0
1996–97	Rangers	Hearts	4-3
1997–98	Celtic	Dundee U	3-0
1998–99	Rangers	St Johnstone	2-1
1999–2000	Celtic	Aberdeen	2-0
2000–01	Celtic	Kilmarnock	3-0
2001–02	Rangers	Ayr U	4-0
2002–03	Rangers	Celtic	2-1
2003–04	Livingston	Hibernian	2-0
2004–05	Rangers	Motherwell	5-1

SCOTTISH LEAGUE CUP WINS

Rangers 24, Celtic 12, Aberdeen 5, Hearts 4, Dundee 3, East Fife 3, Dundee U 2, Hibernian 2, Livingston 1, Motherwell 1, Partick Th 1, Raith R 1.

APPEARANCES IN FINALS

Rangers 30, Celtic 25, Aberdeen 12, Hibernian 8, Dundee 6, Hearts 6, Dundee U 5, Kilmarnock 4, Partick Th 4, East Fife 3, Motherwell 3, Dunfermline Ath 2, Raith R 2, St Johnstone 2, Ayr U 1, Falkirk 1, Livingston 1, Morton 1, St Mirren 1, Third Lanark 1.

CIS SCOTTISH LEAGUE CUP 2004–05

■ *Denotes player sent off.*

FIRST ROUND

Tuesday, 10 August 2004

Airdrie U (2) 3 *(Vareille 9, Coyle 45, Roberts 60)*
East Fife (0) 0 1054

Airdrie U: McGeown; Wilson W, Lovering, McManus, Wilson S, Dunn, Vareille (Barkey), Wilson M (Docherty), Coyle, Gow (McKeown), Roberts.
East Fife: Dodds; Condie, McDonald I, Lumsden (Linton), Hall, Byle, Herkes, Kelly, Fairbairn, Tarditi, Brash (Mitchell).

Berwick R (0) 3 *(McNicoll 78, Smith D 80, Hampshire 84)*
Elgin C (1) 2 *(Bone 14, Martin 69)* 283

Berwick R: O'Connor; Murie, Smith E (Seaton), Cowan (Horn), McNicoll, Connell (Hampshire), Neil, Forrest, Hutchison, Little, Smith D.
Elgin C: Renton; Cumming, Dempsie, Kaczan, Dickson, Black (McKenzie J), Martin, Nelson, Bone, Reid (Harty), Roddie.

Brechin C (1) 5 *(Templeman 41, 119, Ritchie 73, Gibson 94, 96)*
Cowdenbeath (1) 2 *(Carlin 1, 46)* 304

Brechin C: Hay; Smith (McLeish), Walker, Johnson, Dennis, White, McNicoll (Gibson), Winter (Byers), Ritchie, Templeman, King.
Cowdenbeath: Carlin; Shand, Campbell (McHale), Gilfillan, McGregor, Ritchie, Mauchlen (Scott), Fusco, Shields, Buchanan (Gray), Mowat.
aet.

Dumbarton (1) 1 *(Russell 39)*
Ross Co (2) 3 *(Burke 26, 40, 85)* 437

Dumbarton: Grindlay; McEwan■, Brittain, McKinstry, Dobbins, Donald, Bonar, Ronald (Herd), Rodgers, Russell, Dillon (Boyle).
Ross Co: Garden; Robertson, McCulloch, McCunnie (Mackay), Canning, Lauchlan, Rankin, Cowie, McSwegan (Winters), McGarry (Higgins), Burke.

Falkirk (2) 4 *(Duffy 15, 31, Latapy 58, Mackenzie 88)*
Montrose (0) 1 *(Hankinson 46)* 1379

Falkirk: Hill; Lawrie (McAnespie), McPherson, Campbell (McStay), Hughes, James, Mackenzie, Nicholls, Thomson, Latapy, Duffy (Moutinho).
Montrose: Hankinson; Donachie, Budd, Kerrigan, Stephen, Spink, Webster (Lindsay), Hall, Watson (Bremner), Smart, Lannen (Jones).

Peterhead (1) 3 *(Bavidge 4, Michie 75 (pen), 78)*
East Stirling (0) 2 *(Ure 60, Parks 84)* 482

Peterhead: Mathers; Tully, McSkimming (Youngson), Good, Perry, Gibson, Campbell (Johnston), Buchan, Michie, Bavidge, Hagen.
East Stirling: Gilpin; Harvey (Leishman), Miller, Newall, McGhee, Ross, Dunbar, Moffat, Ure (Parks), Donaldson (Findlay), Baldwin.

St Johnstone (0) 2 *(Hannah 84, Hay 85)*
Alloa Ath (1) 3 *(Hamilton 38, Callaghan 55, Ferguson 60)* 1500

St Johnstone: McGregor; Baxter, Fraser, Hannah, Rutkiewicz, Sheerin, Marshall, Bernard, Stevenson (Hay), Moore, Hardy (Malone).
Alloa Ath: McGlynn; Walker, Hill (McLeod), Mortimer, Bolochoweckyj, Townsley, Stevenson (Daly), Ferguson■, Brown, Hamilton, Callaghan.

St Mirren (1) 2 *(Paatelainen 6, O'Neil 76)*
Forfar Ath (2) 5 *(Tosh 23, 51, Millen (og) 43, Sellars 49, McClune 70)* 1104

St Mirren: Hinchcliffe; Van Zanten, Broadfoot, Millen, McGowne, Reilly, Gillies, Murray, Paatelainen, Annand (McGinty), Lappin (Ellis).
Forfar Ath: Brown; Rattray, Forrest, King D, Lowing, Sellars (Maher), Lunan, Booth, McClune, Tosh (King M), Shields.

Stenhousemuir (0) 2 *(McBride 75, Collins 87)*
Arbroath (1) 1 *(Cusick 38)* 145

Stenhousemuir: McCulloch W; Knox, McInally, Murphy, Smith A (Armit) (Savage), Henderson, Lauchlan, Collins, Kerrigan, McBride, McGrillen.
Arbroath: Inglis; McMullen, Henslee, Rennie (Cook), Bishop, Cusick, Miller G, MacDonald, McLean, Brazil (Collier), Swankie.

Stranraer (0) 2 *(Sharp 52, Turnbull 71)*
Raith R (0) 1 *(Ortiz 52)* 393

Stranraer: Meechan; Swift, Wright, Wingate, Henderson, Jenkins, Finlayson, Aitken, Turnbull, Graham, Sharp.
Raith R: Berthelot; Ouattara (Leiper), Benaissa (Boyle), Hajovsky, Smart, Ortiz, Brady, McAlpine, Young (Hagan), Sacko, O'Reilly.

Wednesday, 11 August 2004

Stirling Albion (2) 3 *(Glancy 11, McLean 25, 75)*
Queen's Park (0) 2 *(Carroll 46, Clark R 47)* 669

Stirling Albion: Hogarth; Nugent, Devine (Scotland), McNally, Rowe, McDonald, Hay, Ferguson, McLean, Glancy (Cummings), O'Brien.
Queen's Park: McCue; Kettlewell (Agostini), McCallum (Bonnar), Rushford, Reilly, Molloy, Clark R, Harvey, Graham, Carroll, Blair.

Tuesday, 17 August 2004

Hamilton A (2) 4 *(Thomson 22, Convery 34, 51, 58)*
Ayr U (0) 1 *(Ferguson 87)* 1017

Hamilton A: McEwan; Lumsden, Hodge, Thomson, Ferguson (Fyfe), Tunbridge (Hamilton), Convery, Aitken (Sim), Keogh, Corcoran, Waddell.
Ayr U: Roy; Lyle, McGrady, Chaplain, Burgess (Conway), Dunlop, McLaughlin, Ramsay, Kean, Connolly (Ferguson), Henderson (O'Neill).

Morton (0) 1 *(Walker P 73)*
Gretna (0) 0 2106

Morton: Coyle; Collins, McCulloch, McCluskey, Greacen, McAlister, Millar, Maisano J, Williams (Bannerman), Hawke (Weatherson), Walker J (Walker P).
Gretna: Mathieson; Birch, Skelton (McGuffie), Prokas (Deuchar), Aitken, Holdsworth, Baldacchino, Galloway, Smith, Bingham, Townsley.

Queen of the S (1) 1 *(McNiven 28)*
Albion R (0) 2 *(Mercer 83, McKenzie 87)* 1240

Queen of the S: Colin Scott; Paton (Chris Scott), English, McColligan, Hilland, Thomson, Bagan, Bowey (Burns), McNiven (Armstrong), Wood, McLaughlin.
Albion R: Fahey; Silvestro, Stirling, Black, McGowan, McLaren, McKenzie, Patrick (Bradford), Yardley, McManus, Mercer (McCaul).

SECOND ROUND

Tuesday, 24 August 2004

Aberdeen (2) 3 *(Diamond 5, Adams 36, Craig 46)*
Berwick R (0) 0 4549

Aberdeen: Preece; McNaughton (McGuire), Anderson, Diamond, Severin, Tosh (Tiernan), Heikkinen, Craig (Stewart), Adams, Hart, Morrison.
Berwick R: O'Connor; Murie (Smith E), Seaton, Cowan, Horn, Connell (Gordon), Forrest, Neil, Hutchison, Little, Smith D (Hampshire).

Airdrie U (0) 0
Clyde (0) 1 *(Wilford 73)* 1595

Airdrie U: McGeown; Wilson W (Hoey), Lovering, McManus, Christie, Docherty (Barkey), Vareille (Gow), Wilson M, Coyle, McKeown■, Roberts.
Clyde: Halliwell; Mensing, Bollan, Walker (Arbuckle), Potter, Sheridan, Bryson (Doyle), Gibson, Wilford, Kerkar, Harty (Gilhaney).

Albion R (0) 1 *(Bradford 53)*
Brechin C (0) 1 *(Ritchie 74)* 167
Albion R: Fahey; Paterson A (Black), Stirling, Smith, McGowan, Silvestro, McKenzie, Patrick (McLaren), Yardley (Crabbe), Bradford, Mercer.
Brechin C: Nelson; Smith, Deas, McNicoll (Gibson), White, Walker, Johnson, Jackson (King), Ritchie, Templeman (Hampshire), McLeish.
aet; Albion R won 4-3 on penalties.

Dundee (0) 4 *(Lovell 62, 84, 88, Anderson 86)*
Forfar A (0) 0 3047
Dundee: Soutar (Jack); MacDonald, Sancho, Mann, Hernandez, Smith, Brady, Jablonski (Fotheringham), Anderson, Lovell, Sutton (Larsen).
Forfar A: Brown; Rattray, Lowing (King M), Forrest, King D, McClune (Booth), Sellars, Lunan (Maher), Tosh, Shields, Stein.

Hibernian (1) 4 *(Glass 20, Orman 48, Murdock 51, Riordan 53)*
Alloa Ath (0) 0 5156
Hibernian: Simon Brown; Caldwell, Smith (Baillie), Murphy, Murdock, Beuzelin (Nicol), Glass, Orman, Morrow, Riordan, Shiels (Dobbie).
Alloa Ath: McGlynn; Walker, Hill (McDermott), Mortimer (MacLeod), Bolochoweckyj, Townsley, Nicholas, Daly, Brown (Nicolson), Hamilton, Callaghan.

Kilmarnock (0) 3 *(Invincibile 61, 84, McDonald 70)*
Hamilton A (0) 0 3375
Kilmarnock: Combe; Fowler, Hay, McDonald, Lilley, Dindeleux, Invincibile, Locke (Joly), Boyd, Dargo (Murray), Johnston A (Dodds).
Hamilton A: McEwan; Walker, Waddell (McPhee), Thomson, McLaughlin, Hamilton, Carrigan (Hodge), Aitken, Keogh (Convery), Tunbridge, Corcoran.

Morton (0) 0
Motherwell (1) 3 *(Paterson 40, McBride 65, Clarkson 70)* 3767
Morton: Coyle; Collins■, McCulloch, McCluskey, Greacen, McAlister, Millar, Maisano J (Bannerman), Williams (Walker P), Weatherson, Walker J.
Motherwell: Marshall; Corrigan, Hammell, Kinniburgh, Craigan, McBride, McDonald (Burns), Leitch (Fagan), Paterson (Foran), O'Donnell, Clarkson.

Peterhead (1) 1 *(Bavidge 24)*
Falkirk (2) 6 *(O'Neil 4, Duffy 34, 47, Thomson 58, 83, 89)* 622
Peterhead: Mathers; Tully, Youngson, Good, Perry■, Gibson (Stewart G), Tindal (Campbell), Buchan, Hagen, Michie (Milne), Bavidge.
Falkirk: Hill; Lawrie, McPherson, Mackenzie, Campbell, James, O'Neil (Scally), Nicholls (McAnespie), Thomson, Latapy, Duffy (Moutinho).

Ross Co (0) 0
Inverness CT (0) 1 *(Tokely 64)* 3323
Ross Co: Garden; Robertson, McCulloch, Mackay, Canning, Lauchlan, Rankin, Cowie, McSwegan (Winters), Kilgannon (Higgins), Burke (McGarry).
Inverness CT: Brown; Tokely, Golabek, McCaffrey, Wilson, Munro, Duncan, Hislop, Bayne, Keogh, Juanjo (McBain).

Stenhousemuir (0) 2 *(McGrillen 51, Savage 64)*
Partick Th (3) 5 *(Gibson W 13, Escalas 20, Fleming 38, Hinds 84, 86)* 1019
Stenhousemuir: McCulloch W; Knox, McInally, Murphy (Fallon), Henderson, McBride, Lauchlan, Collins, Savage, Kerrigan (Davidson), McGrillen.
Partick Th: Arthur; Gibson W (Fulton), Milne (Anis), Murray, Dowie, Wilkinson, Howie, Fleming, Escalas (Oné), Hinds, Panther.

Wednesday, 25 August 2004

Dundee U (1) 3 *(Grady 43, Kerr 63, Innes 73)*
Stranraer (1) 1 *(Henderson 39)* 2511
Dundee U: Bullock; McCracken, Archibald, Innes, Wilson, Duff, Kerr, Robson (Dodds), Grady, Scotland (McIntyre), McLaren (Samuel).
Stranraer: McCondichie; Swift, Wright, Wingate, Henderson, Jenkins, Finlayson, Fraser, Gaughan K (Aitken), Graham (Donnachie), Sharp.

Stirling Albion (0) 0
Livingston (1) 2 *(Easton 31, Hamilton 90)* 1094
Stirling Albion: Hogarth; Nugent (Hutchison), Scotland, McNally, Rowe, McDonald, Hay (Gethins), Ferguson, McLean, Glancy, O'Brien (Allen).
Livingston: McKenzie; McNamee, Stanic, Rubio, Bahoken, Easton, Boyack (McLaughlin), O'Brien, Dair (Lovell), Hamilton, Lilley.

THIRD ROUND

Tuesday, 21 September 2004

Celtic (4) 8 *(Sylla 2, Wallace 5, 57, 80, Balde 39, Lambert 45, McManus 48, McGeady 90)*
Falkirk (0) 1 *(Thomson 67)* 24,345
Celtic: Douglas; Laursen, Valgaeren, Balde, Sylla, Wallace, Pearson, Lambert, McManus (Thompson), Juninho, McGeady.
Falkirk: Hill; Lawrie, McPherson, Mackenzie, Campbell (Hughes), James, O'Neil, Nicholls (McAnespie), Thomson, Latapy (Moutinho), Duffy.

Dundee U (2) 4 *(McIntyre 34, Robson 44, Brebner 55, Wilson 62)*
Clyde (0) 0 2336
Dundee U: Hirschfeld; McCracken, Archibald, Innes, Wilson (Dodds), McInnes, Brebner, Duff, Robson, McIntyre (Samuel), McLaren (Scotland).
Clyde: Halliwell; Mensing, Walker, Balmer, Potter, Sheridan, Arbuckle, Gibson (Bryson), Wilford, Marsiglia (McCracken), Harty.

Livingston (0) 2 *(Easton 90 (pen), 111)*
Dundee (0) 1 *(Lovell 69)* 1736
Livingston: McKenzie; McNamee, Stanic, Rubio, Dorado, Kernaghan, Easton (Hamilton), O'Brien, McMenamin (Dair), Lovell, Lilley (Libbra).
Dundee: Soutar; McDonald, Sancho, Mann, Barrett (Hutchinson), Smith, Robb (Hegarty), Fotheringham M (Brady), Lovell, Sutton, Anderson.
aet.

Wednesday, 22 September 2004

Aberdeen (0) 0
Rangers (1) 2 *(Ricksen 45, Thompson 88)* 14,876
Aberdeen: Preece; McGuire, McNaughton, Anderson, Hart, Severin, Tosh, Foster, Adams, Craig (Muirhead), Mackie.
Rangers: Klos; Khizanishvili, Moore, Boumsong, Vignal, Ricksen, Malcolm■, Arveladze (Novo), Vanoli, Burke, Thompson.

Albion R (1) 1 *(McLaren 7)*
Hibernian (2) 3 *(Dobbie 42, Shiels 43, O'Connor 70)* 1576
Albion R: Fahey; Silvestro, Stirling, Black, McGowan, McLaren, McKenzie, McCaul (Patrick), Bradford (Selkirk), McManus, Mercer.
Hibernian: Brown A; Caldwell, Venus, Murphy, Whittaker, Murray I, Glass, McCluskey (Orman), Dobbie (Fletcher), Riordan (O'Connor), Shiels.

Dunfermline Ath (1) 3 *(Brewster 30, Thomson 51, Hunt 76)*
Partick Th (1) 1 *(Dowie 38)* 2349
Dunfermline Ath: Stillie; Thomson, Wilson S, Skerla, Butler (Hunt), Darren Young, Nicholson, Shields, Dempsey, Brewster (Labonte), Mehmet (Tod).
Partick Th: Arthur; Wilkinson, Madaschi, Murray, Dowie, Fulton (One), Hinds (Anis), Fleming (Howie), Escalas, Panther, Milne.

Hearts (1) 2 *(Hartley 14, 51)*
Kilmarnock (0) 1 *(Leven 56)* 5944
Hearts: Gordon; McAllister, Kisnorbo, Maybury, Webster, Berra, Neilson, Hamill, Hartley, De Vries (Sloan), Wyness.
Kilmarnock: Combe; Lilley, Dindeleux, Greer, Fowler, Leven, Joly, McDonald (Dargo), Johnston A, Boyd, Invincibile (Wales).

Inverness CT (0) 1 *(Tokely 58)*
Motherwell (0) 3 *(Foran 52, O'Donnell 55, McBride 84)* 1464

Inverness CT: Brown; Tokely, Golabek, McCaffrey, Munro, McBain, Wilson, Hislop (Bayne), Prunty (Juanjo), Hart, Keogh (Duncan).
Motherwell: Marshall; Corrigan, Hammell, Kinniburgh, Craigan, McBride (Fagan), McDonald, Leitch, Foran, O'Donnell, Clarkson (Paterson).

QUARTER-FINALS

Tuesday, 9 November 2004

Dundee U (0) 2 *(McIntyre 87, 107)*
Hibernian (1) 1 *(Riordan 30)* 4865

Dundee U: Jarvie; Ritchie, Archibald, Wilson, Innes, McInnes, Brebner (McCracken), Robson, Samuel (Dodds), McIntyre, Scotland (Grady).
Hibernian: Simon Brown; Caldwell, Murdock, Beuzelin, Whittaker, Murray I, Glass, Rocastle, Morrow (Fletcher), Riordan (Dobbie), Shiels (Shields).
aet.

Livingston (0) 0
Motherwell (2) 5 *(Partridge 3, Foran 35, 59, O'Donnell 56, Wright 90)* 2887

Livingston: McKenzie; McNamee, Dorado■, Rubio, Snowdon, Easton, Brittain, O'Brien, Lovell (Lilley), Hamilton (McLaughlin), Snodgrass (McMenamin).
Motherwell: Marshall; Corrigan, Partridge, Quinn P, Craigan, Hammell, O'Donnell (Wright), Fitzpatrick, Paterson, Foran (Fagan), Clarkson.

Wednesday, 10 November 2004

Dunfermline Ath (0) 1 *(Mehmet 58)*
Hearts (1) 3 *(Webster 36, Hartley 66, Hamill 84)* 4405

Dunfermline Ath: Stillie; Tod, Wilson, Butler, Byrne, Thomson, Nicholson, Mason, Labonte, Brewster (Mehmet), Derek Young (Donnelly).
Hearts: Gordon; Maybury, Kisnorbo, Pressley, Webster, McAllister, Neilson, Stamp (Hamill), McKenna, Hartley, Wyness (Weir).

Rangers (0) 2 *(Prso 84, Arveladze 100)*
Celtic (0) 1 *(Hartson 66)* 47,298

Rangers: Klos; Khizanishvili, Andrews, Boumsong, Vignal, Ricksen, Namouchi, Rae A (Hughes), Lovenkrands (Arveladze), Novo, Thompson (Prso).
Celtic: Marshall; Varga, Valgaeren, Balde, McNamara, Petrov (Beattie) (McGeady), Lennon, Thompson, Agathe, Hartson, Juninho (Camara).
aet.

SEMI-FINALS (at Hampden Park)

Tuesday, 1 February 2005

Motherwell (1) 3 *(Craigan 19, Foran 78, Fitzpatrick 119)*
Hearts (0) 2 *(Burchill 85, Thorarisson 90)* 14,069

Motherwell: Marshall; Corrigan, Partridge, Hammell, Craigan, McBride (Clarkson), O'Donnell, Leitch, Paterson (Fitzpatrick), Foran (Quinn), McDonald.
Hearts: Gordon; McAllister, Hamill (Thorarisson), Pressley, Webster, MacFarlane (Simmons), Neilson, Mikoliunas, Hartley, Miller, Wyness (Burchill).
aet.

Wednesday, 2 February 2005

Rangers (2) 7 *(Novo 7, 85, Prso 18, Buffel 67, Ricksen 77, Thompson 80, 88)*
Dundee U (0) 1 *(Scotland 50)* 25,622

Rangers: Waterreus; Ross, Andrews, Kyrgiakos, Ball, Ricksen, Vignal, Rae A (Ferguson), Buffel, Novo, Prso (Thompson).
Dundee U: Colgan; Ritchie, Archibald (Duff), Wilson, McCracken, McInnes (Scotland), Mair (Dodds), Kerr, Robson, McIntyre, Crawford.

FINAL (at Hampden Park)

Sunday, 20 March 2005

Motherwell (1) 1 *(Partridge 12)*
Rangers (3) 5 *(Ross 5, Kyrgiakos 9, 86, Ricksen 33, Novo 48)* 50,182

Motherwell: Marshall; Corrigan, Partridge, Hammell, Craigan, McBride (Quinn P), O'Donnell, Leitch, Paterson (Fitzpatrick), Foran (Clarkson), McDonald.
Rangers: Waterreus; Ross, Malcolm, Kyrgiakos, Ball, Ricksen, Ferguson, Vignal (Rae A), Buffel, Novo (Thompson), Prso.
Referee: Mike McCurry.

Barry Ferguson (left) in the heat of battle with Motherwell's Marc Fitzpatrick during Rangers' 5-1 success in the CIS Scottish League Cup final at Hampden Park. (PA/Empics)

BELL'S LEAGUE CHALLENGE 2004–05

▪ *Denotes player sent off.*

FIRST ROUND

Saturday, 31 July 2004

Airdrie U (0) 0

Queen of the S (0) 2 *(Wood 59, English 80)* 1488

Airdrie U: McGeown; Christie, Lovering, McGowan (McKeown), McManus, Dunn, Vareille, Wilson M, Coyle, Gow, Roberts.
Queen of the S: Colin Scott; Chris Scott, English, McColligan, Reid, Thomson, Bagan (Burns), Bowey, McNiven (Jaconelli) (Gibson), Wood, McLaughlin.

Alloa Ath (2) 2 *(Ferguson 12, Hamilton 42)*

Elgin C (0) 0 301

Alloa Ath: McGlynn; Walker, Hill, McLaughlin (Mortimer), Bolochoweckyj, Townsley, Stevenson, Ferguson (Nicholas), Brown, Hamilton, Callaghan (Daly).
Elgin C: Renton; Cumming, Black (Martin), Kaczan, Dickson, McKenzie J, Dempsie, Nelson, Bone (Reid), Harty (Bremner), Roddie.

Arbroath (1) 2 *(Cusick 3, McLean 75)*

Peterhead (1) 4 *(Bavidge 35, 48, Gibson 54, Buchan 60)* 448

Arbroath: Woodcock; McMullan (Cook), Beith (Rennie), McAulay, Bishop, Cusick (Henslee), Miller G, MacDonald, McLean, Brazil, Swankie.
Peterhead: Mathers; Tully, Good, Raeside, Perry, Gibson, Campbell (Tindal), Buchan, Michie (Johnston), Bavidge, Hagen (Youngson).

Ayr U (0) 0

Falkirk (0) 3 *(Lawrie 50, O'Neil 87, Duffy 89)* 1797

Ayr U: Roy; Smyth, McGrady, Chaplain, McLaughlin, Craig (Lyle), Brown (Ferguson), Ramsay (Connolly), Kean, Henderson, Conway.
Falkirk: Hill; Lawrie, McPherson, Mackenzie, Campbell, Sharp, O'Neil (Nicholls), McStay (Scally), Thomson, Latapy (Moutinho), Duffy.

Dumbarton (1) 1 *(Bonar 6)*

Stirling Albion (0) 2 *(McLean 46, 49)* 709

Dumbarton: Grindlay; McEwan, Brittain, McKinstry, Allan, Donald (Bradley), Bonar, Ronald, Rodgers (Dunn), Russell (Herd), Dillon.
Stirling Albion: Hogarth; Nugent, Devine, McNally, Rowe, McDonald (Hutchison), Hay, Ferguson, McLean, Gethins (Allan), O'Brien.

East Fife (0) 0

Cowdenbeath (0) 0 468

East Fife: Dodds; Lumsden, McDonald I, Bain, Hall, Byle (Kelly), Mitchell, McDonald G (Crawford), Fairbairn, Tarditi, Brash (Herkes).
Cowdenbeath: Carlin; Shand, Campbell, Gilfillan, McKeown, Ritchie, Mauchlen (Buchanan), McHale (Fusco), Shields, Mowat, Burns (Kelly JP).
aet; Cowdenbeath won 4-3 on penalties.

East Stirling (0) 1 *(Donaldson 59)*

Berwick R (1) 2 *(Gordon 11, Forrest 70)* 264

East Stirling: Mitchell; Harvey, McGhee, Mackay, Newall, McAuley (Findlay), Ross, Moffat (Leishman), Donaldson (Parks), Dunbar, Miller.
Berwick R: O'Connor; Smith E, Seaton, Cowan, Horn, Connell, Forrest (McNicoll), Neil (Connelly), Hutchison, Gordon, Hampshire.

Forfar Ath (1) 3 *(Shields 2, 48, Tosh 52)*

Morton (1) 1 *(Walker J 24)* 742

Forfar Ath: Brown; Rattray, Lowing (Dunn), Forrest, King D, McClune, Sellars, Lunan, Tosh (King M), Shields▪, Stein.
Morton: Coyle; Bannerman, McCulloch, McCluskey, Greacen, Maisano M (Williams), Millar, McAlister (Maisano J▪), Walker J, Weatherson, Walker P (Hawke).

Gretna (2) 3 *(Bingham 7, Smith 26, Baldacchino 83)*

Montrose (0) 0 454

Gretna: Mathieson; Birch, Skelton, Prokas, Aitken, Holdsworth, Baldacchino, Galloway (McGuffie), Smith (Deuchar), Bingham, Townsley (Boyd).
Montrose: Butter; Donachie, Budd (Jones), Stephen, Smith G, Kerrigan, Smith D (Webster), Spink, Smart, Hall, Sharp (Morrice).

Partick Th (2) 3 *(Gibson W 15, Escalas 44, 61)*

Brechin C (0) 0 1803

Partick Th: Arthur; Gibson W, Howie (Ross A), Murray, Dowie, Fulton, Mitchell, Fleming, Escalas, Gibson A (Panther), Anis (Wilkinson).
Brechin C: Hay; McNicol, Deas, Johnson, Dennis (Smith), Walker, King (Templeman), Winter, Ritchie, Hampshire (Gibson), Mitchell.

Queen's Park (0) 1 *(Reilly (pen) 106)*

Stenhousemuir (0) 1 *(McGrillen 94)* 461

Queen's Park: McCue; Kettlewell (Trouten), McCallum, Rushford▪, Reilly, Molloy, Clark R▪, Blair, Graham, Carroll (Sloan), Clarke D (Harvey).
Stenhousemuir: McCulloch W; Fallon, McInally, Murphy, Smith A (Davidson), Henderson, Lauchlan (Morrison), Collins▪, Kerrigan (Savage), McBride, McGrillen.
aet; Queen's Park won 4-2 on penalties.

Raith R (0) 0

Albion R (0) 2 *(Bradford 46, 64)* 1206

Raith R: Berthelot; Smart (Malcolm), McAlpine, Hajovsky, Davidson, Brady, Outtara (Boyle), Ortiz, Sacko, Young, Hagan (Eloujdi).
Albion R: Peat; Silvestro, Stirling, Black, McGowan, McLaren, McKenzie, Boyle, Yardley, Bradford, Mercer.

Ross Co (0) 2 *(Garden 46, 48)*

St Mirren (0) 1 *(Hinchcliffe 47)* 992

Ross Co: Garden; Robertson, McCulloch, McCunnie (Kilgannon), Canning, Lauchlan, Rankin, Cowie, McSwegan (Winters), McGarry (Mackay), Burke.
St Mirren: Hinchcliffe; Van Zanten, Broadfoot, Millen, McGowne, Reilly, Gillies, Crilly (Baird), Paatelainen, McGinty (Annand), Lappin (O'Neil).

St Johnstone (1) 2 *(Hannah 6, Moore 66)*

Hamilton A (0) 0 1850

St Johnstone: Cuthbert; Tait, Fraser, Hannah, Rutkiewicz, Maxwell, Stevenson, Sheerin, Hay (McConalogue), Moore, Malone.
Hamilton A: McEwan; Walker, Waddell, Thomson, McLaughlin, Tunbridge, Carrigan, Aitken, Blackadder (Fyfe), McPhee, Corcoran (Convery).

SECOND ROUND

Tuesday, 31 August 2004

Albion R (0) 1 *(McCaul 62)*

Partick Th (2) 2 *(Panther 16, Hinds 41)* 1093

Albion R: Fahey; Paterson A, Stirling, Black, McGowan (McCaul (Richardson)), Patrick, McKenzie, Silvestro, Crabbe (Mercer), Selkirk, McLaren.
Partick Th: Pinkowski; Gibson W (Anis), Wilkinson, Murray, Madaschi, Ross A, Howie, Fleming, Oné (Mitchell), Hinds, Panther.

Alloa Ath (1) 1 *(Callaghan 27)*

Berwick R (1) 2 *(Seaton 44 (pen), Neil 60)* 268

Alloa Ath: McGlynn; Walker, McDermott (Hill), Nicolson, Bolochoweckyj, Townsley, McMillan, Ferguson (Daly), Brown▪, Hamilton▪, Callaghan.
Berwick R: O'Connor; Murie, Seaton, Cowan, Horn, Connell, Forrest (Gordon), Neil, Hutchison, Little (Hampshire), Smith D.

Clyde (0) 1 *(Valois 75)*
Stranraer (0) 0 752
Clyde: Morrison; Mensing, Bollan (McKeever), Wilson, Potter, McCracken, Bryson, Arbuckle, Conway, Valois (Bradley), Gilhaney.
Stranraer: McCondichie; Swift, Wright, Wingate, Henderson, Jenkins, Finlayson, Aitken, Donnachie (McCutcheon), Graham (Crawford), Sharp.

Falkirk (2) 5 *(Nicholls 34, Duffy 38, 79, Latapy 48, 68)*
Stirling Albion (1) 3 *(Gethins 27, Cummings 74, Rowe 87)* 2695
Falkirk: Hill; Lawrie, McPherson, Mackenzie (Scally), Campbell, James (Sharp), O'Neil, Nicholls, Thomson, Latapy (Moutinho), Duffy.
Stirling Albion: Hogarth; Nugent, Scotland, McNally, Rowe, McDonald, Hay (Hutchison), Ferguson, Gethins (Cummings), Glancy, O'Brien.

Forfar Ath (1) 2 *(Booth 6, Tosh 100)*
Queen's Park (1) 2 *(Carroll 20, Graham 119)* 421
Forfar Ath: Brown; Rattray, Lowing, Forrest, King D, McClune, Booth, Lunan, Tosh, King M (Clark), Stein (Maher).
Queen's Park: Crawford; Trouten, McCallum, Agostini, Reilly (Sinclair), Molloy, Bonnar (Felvus), Kettlewell, Graham, Carroll, Blair.
aet; Forfar Ath won 4-3 on penalties.

Gretna (1) 1 *(Smith 40)*
Cowdenbeath (0) 0 551
Gretna: Mathieson; Birch, McQuilken, Lennon, Aitken, Irons, Baldacchino, McGuffie, Smith, Bingham, Skelton (Gordon).
Cowdenbeath: Fleming; Shand, Williams (Kelly JP), Miller, McKeown, Ritchie, Mauchlen, McHale, Shields (Gibson), Buchanan (McCallum), Fusco.

Peterhead (0) 1 *(Bavidge 88)*
Ross Co (2) 2 *(Burke 30, Canning 44)* 617
Peterhead: Mathers; Tully, Good, Raeside, Perry, Gibson (Stewart G), Robertson (Campbell), Buchan, Michie (Johnston), Bavidge, Youngson.
Ross Co: Garden; Robertson, McCulloch, Malcolm, Canning, Lauchlan, Rankin, Adam (Mackay), McSwegan, Kilgannon (Winters), Burke (McGarry).

St Johnstone (2) 3 *(Maxwell 29, Fotheringham K 31, Rutkiewicz 60)*
Queen of the S (0) 0 1201
St Johnstone: McGregor; Anderson, Fotheringham K, McManus, Webb (Rutkiewicz), Maxwell, Baxter, Sheerin, McConalogue, Moore (Hay), Hardy (Tait).
Queen of the S: Samson; Chris Scott (Bagan), English, McColligan (Beattie), Wood, Thomson, Burns, Bowey, McNiven, Armstrong (Payne), McLaughlin.

QUARTER-FINALS

Tuesday, 14 September 2004

Berwick R (0) 0
St Johnstone (1) 1 *(Moore 2)* 279
Berwick R: O'Connor; Murie, Seaton, Smith E, Cowan, Forrest, Connelly, Neil, Hutchison, Connell (Little), Smith D (Hampshire).
St Johnstone: McGregor; Anderson, Fotheringham K, Hannah, Rutkiewicz, Maxwell, McCann, Sheerin (Baxter), McConalogue (Hay), Moore, Hardy.

Falkirk (1) 3 *(Latapy 39, Thomson 62, Duffy 72)*
Gretna (0) 0 1416
Falkirk: Ferguson; Lawrie, McPherson, Scally, Campbell, James, McStay, Nicholls (McAnespie), Thomson (McBreen), Latapy, Duffy (Moutinho).
Gretna: Mathieson; Birch, McQuilken, Lennon (Galloway), Aitken, Irons, Baldacchino, McGuffie, Smith (Deuchar), Bingham, Skelton (Wake).

Wednesday, 15 September 2004

Clyde (1) 1 *(Harty 11)*
Forfar Ath (1) 2 *(Tosh 34, McClune 72)* 532
Clyde: Halliwell; Mensing■, Wilson, Balmer (Arbuckle), Potter, Walker, Bryson (Conway), Gibson, Wilford, Gilhaney, Harty.
Forfar Ath: Brown (Ferrie); Rattray, Lowing, Forrest, King D, McClune, Booth, Lunan, Tosh, Shields (Cameron), Stein.

Ross Co (0) 1 *(Winters 55)*
Partick Th (0) 1 *(Panther 72)* 708
Ross Co: Garden; McCunnie, McCulloch, Malcolm (Gunn), Canning, Lauchlan, Cowie, Adam (Mackay), Winters (Higgins), McGarry, Burke.
Partick Th: Arthur; Gibson W (Wilkinson), Milne■, Murray, Dowie, Fulton (Howie), Hinds, Fleming, Escalas, Oné (Strachan), Panther.
aet; Ross Co won 5-3 on penalties.

SEMI-FINALS

Tuesday, 28 September 2004

St Johnstone (1) 1 *(Rutkiewicz 5)*
Falkirk (1) 2 *(Duffy 9, Lawrie 62)* 2328
St Johnstone: McGregor; Anderson, Forsyth (McManus), Hannah, Rutkiewicz, Maxwell, McCann (Sheerin), Fotheringham K, MacDonald (Fraser), Moore, McConalogue.
Falkirk: Ferguson; Lawrie, McPherson, Mackenzie, Hughes, James, O'Neil, Nicholls, Moutinho, Latapy, Duffy.

Ross Co (2) 5 *(Winters 19, 23, 66, Burke 47, Cowie 89)*
Forfar Ath (2) 2 *(Shields 7, 30)* 911
Ross Co: Garden; McCunnie, McCulloch, Kilgannon (Mackay), Malcolm, Lauchlan, Cowie, Adam, Winters, McGarry (Robertson), Burke (Higgins).
Forfar Ath: Ferrie; Rattray, Lowing, Forrest, King D, McClune (Cameron), Lunan (Clark), Booth, Tosh, Shields, Stein.

FINAL (at MacDiarmid Park)

Sunday, 7 November 2004

Falkirk (0) 2 *(Scally 70, Duffy 75)*
Ross Co (0) 1 *(Winters 57)* 7471
Falkirk: Ferguson; Lawrie, McPherson, Mackenzie, Campbell, James, O'Neil (Scally), Nicholls (Moutinho), Thomson (McBreen), Latapy, Duffy.
Ross Co: Garden; Robertson, McCulloch, McCunnie, Canning, Lauchlan, Cowie, Adam (Kilgannon), Higgins (McGarry), Rankin, Winters (Malcolm).
Referee: Kenny Clark.

LEAGUE CHALLENGE FINALS 1991–2005

Year	*Winners*	*Runners-up*	*Score*
1991	Dundee	Ayr U	3-2
1992	Hamilton A	Ayr U	1-0
1993	Hamilton A	Morton	3-2
1994	St Mirren	Falkirk	9-3
1995	Airdrieonians	Dundee	3-2
1996	Stenhousemuir	Dundee U	0-0
	(Stenhousemuir won 5-4 on penalties)		
1997	Stranraer	St Johnstone	1-0
1998	Falkirk 1 Qeeen of the South 0		
1999	no competition		
2000	Alloa	Inverness CT	4-4
	(Alloa won 5-4 on penalties)		
2001	Airdrieonians	Livingston	2-2
	(Airdrieonians won 3-2 on penalties)		
2002	Airdrieonians	Alloa	2-1
2003	Queen of the S	Brechin C	2-0
2004	Inverness CT	Airdrie U	2-0
2005	Falkirk	Ross Co	2-1

SCOTTISH CUP FINALS 1874–2005

Year	*Winners*	*Runners-up*	*Score*
1874	Queen's Park	Clydesdale	2-0
1875	Queen's Park	Renton	3-0
1876	Queen's Park	Third Lanark	2-0 after 1-1 draw
1877	Vale of Leven	Rangers	3-2 after 0-0 and 1-1 draws
1878	Vale of Leven	Third Lanark	1-0
1879	Vale of Leven*	Rangers	
1880	Queen's Park	Thornlibank	3-0
1881	Queen's Park†	Dumbarton	3-1
1882	Queen's Park	Dumbarton	4-1 after 2-2 draw
1883	Dumbarton	Vale of Leven	2-1 after 2-2 draw
1884	Queen's Park‡	Vale of Leven	
1885	Renton	Vale of Leven	3-1 after 0-0 draw
1886	Queen's Park	Renton	3-1
1887	Hibernian	Dumbarton	2-1
1888	Renton	Cambuslang	6-1
1889	Third Lanark§	Celtic	2-1
1890	Queen's Park	Vale of Leven	2-1 after 1-1 draw
1891	Hearts	Dumbarton	1-0
1892	Celtic¶	Queen's Park	5-1
1893	Queen's Park	Celtic	2-1
1894	Rangers	Celtic	3-1
1895	St Bernard's	Renton	2-1
1896	Hearts	Hibernian	3-1
1897	Rangers	Dumbarton	5-1
1898	Rangers	Kilmarnock	2-0
1899	Celtic	Rangers	2-0
1900	Celtic	Queen's Park	4-3
1901	Hearts	Celtic	4-3
1902	Hibernian	Celtic	1-0
1903	Rangers	Hearts	2-0 after 1-1 and 0-0 draws
1904	Celtic	Rangers	3-2
1905	Third Lanark	Rangers	3-1 after 0-0 draw
1906	Hearts	Third Lanark	1-0
1907	Celtic	Hearts	3-0
1908	Celtic	St Mirren	5-1
1909	••		
1910	Dundee	Clyde	2-1 after 2-2 and 0-0 draws
1911	Celtic	Hamilton A	2-0 after 0-0 draw
1912	Celtic	Clyde	2-0
1913	Falkirk	Raith R	2-0
1914	Celtic	Hibernian	4-1 after 0-0 draw
1920	Kilmarnock	Albion R	3-2
1921	Partick Th	Rangers	1-0
1922	Morton	Rangers	1-0
1923	Celtic	Hibernian	1-0
1924	Airdrieonians	Hibernian	2-0
1925	Celtic	Dundee	2-1
1926	St Mirren	Celtic	2-0
1927	Celtic	East Fife	3-1
1928	Rangers	Celtic	4-0
1929	Kilmarnock	Rangers	2-0
1930	Rangers	Partick Th	2-1 after 0-0 draw
1931	Celtic	Motherwell	4-2 after 2-2 draw
1932	Rangers	Kilmarnock	3-0 after 1-1 draw
1933	Celtic	Motherwell	1-0
1934	Rangers	St Mirren	5-0
1935	Rangers	Hamilton A	2-1
1936	Rangers	Third Lanark	1-0
1937	Celtic	Aberdeen	2-1
1938	East Fife	Kilmarnock	4-2 after 1-1 draw
1939	Clyde	Motherwell	4-0
1947	Aberdeen	Hibernian	2-1
1948	Rangers	Morton	1-0 after 1-1 draw
1949	Rangers	Clyde	4-1
1950	Rangers	East Fife	3-0
1951	Celtic	Motherwell	1-0
1952	Motherwell	Dundee	4-0
1953	Rangers	Aberdeen	1-0 after 1-1 draw
1954	Celtic	Aberdeen	2-1
1955	Clyde	Celtic	1-0 after 1-1 draw
1956	Hearts	Celtic	3-1
1957	Falkirk	Kilmarnock	2-1 after 1-1 draw
1958	Clyde	Hibernian	1-0
1959	St Mirren	Aberdeen	3-1
1960	Rangers	Kilmarnock	2-0
1961	Dunfermline Ath	Celtic	2-0 after 0-0 draw
1962	Rangers	St Mirren	2-0
1963	Rangers	Celtic	3-0 after 1-1 draw
1964	Rangers	Dundee	3-1
1965	Celtic	Dunfermline Ath	3-2
1966	Rangers	Celtic	1-0 after 0-0 draw
1967	Celtic	Aberdeen	2-0
1968	Dunfermline Ath	Hearts	3-1
1969	Celtic	Rangers	4-0
1970	Aberdeen	Celtic	3-1

Year	*Winners*	*Runners-up*	*Score*
1971	Celtic	Rangers	2-1 after 1-1 draw
1972	Celtic	Hibernian	6-1
1973	Rangers	Celtic	3-2
1974	Celtic	Dundee U	3-0
1975	Celtic	Airdrieonians	3-1
1976	Rangers	Hearts	3-1
1977	Celtic	Rangers	1-0
1978	Rangers	Aberdeen	2-1
1979	Rangers	Hibernian	3-2 after 0-0 and 0-0 draws
1980	Celtic	Rangers	1-0
1981	Rangers	Dundee U	4-1 after 0-0 draw
1982	Aberdeen	Rangers	4-1 (aet)
1983	Aberdeen	Rangers	1-0 (aet)
1984	Aberdeen	Celtic	2-1 (aet)
1985	Celtic	Dundee U	2-1
1986	Aberdeen	Hearts	3-0
1987	St Mirren	Dundee U	1-0 (aet)
1988	Celtic	Dundee U	2-1
1989	Celtic	Rangers	1-0
1990	Aberdeen	Celtic	0-0 (aet)
		(Aberdeen won 9-8 on penalties)	
1991	Motherwell	Dundee U	4-3 (aet)
1992	Rangers	Airdrieonians	2-1
1993	Rangers	Aberdeen	2-1
1994	Dundee U	Rangers	1-0
1995	Celtic	Airdrieonians	1-0
1996	Rangers	Hearts	5-1
1997	Kilmarnock	Falkirk	1-0
1998	Hearts	Rangers	2-1
1999	Rangers	Celtic	1-0
2000	Rangers	Aberdeen	4-0
2001	Celtic	Hibernian	3-0
2002	Rangers	Celtic	3-2
2003	Rangers	Dundee	1-0
2004	Celtic	Dunfermline Ath	3-1
2005	Celtic	Dundee U	1-0

*Vale of Leven awarded cup, Rangers failing to appear for replay after 1-1 draw.
†After Dumbarton protested the first game, which Queen's Park won 2-1.
‡Queen's Park awarded cup, Vale of Leven failing to appear.
§Replay by order of Scottish FA because of playing conditions in first match, won 3-0 by Third Lanark.
¶After mutually protested game which Celtic won 1-0.
••Owing to riot, the cup was withheld after two drawn games – between Celtic and Rangers 2-2 and 1-1.

SCOTTISH CUP WINS

Celtic 33, Rangers 31, Queen's Park 10, Aberdeen 7, Hearts 6, Clyde 3, Kilmarnock 3, St Mirren 3, Vale of Leven 3, Dunfermline Ath 2, Falkirk 2, Hibernian 2, Motherwell 2, Renton 2, Third Lanark 2, Airdrieonians 1, Dumbarton 1, Dundee 1, Dundee U 1, East Fife 1, Morton 1, Partick Th 1, St Bernard's 1.

APPEARANCES IN FINAL

Celtic 52, Rangers 48, Aberdeen 15, Queen's Park 12, Hearts 12, Hibernian 11, Dundee U 8, Kilmarnock 8, Vale of Leven 7, Clyde 6, Dumbarton 6, Motherwell 6, St Mirren 6, Third Lanark 6, Dundee 5, Renton 5, Airdrieonians 4, Dunfermline Ath 4, East Fife 3, Falkirk 3, Hamilton A 2, Morton 2, Partick Th 2, Albion R 1, Cambuslang 1, Clydesdale 1, Raith R 1, St Bernard's 1, Thornlibank 1.

TENNENT'S SCOTTISH CUP 2004–05

▪ *Denotes player sent off.*

FIRST ROUND

Saturday, 20 November 2004

East Fife (1) 3 *(Mitchell 35, 78, Nicholas 64)*

Whitehill Welfare (0) 0 355

East Fife: Morrison; Lumsden, Renwick, Bain, Duncan, Kelly, Herkes, McDonald G, Nicholas, Mitchell, Steele (Fairbairn).
Whitehill Welfare: McGyrk; Jamieson, Lee, Clyde, Hunter, Johnston▪, Young, Shanks (Baigrie), McDonald C, Hogg, Forrester (White).

Inverurie Locos (1) 1 *(McLean 29)*

Keith (1) 2 *(Donaldson 30, McKenzie 81)* 732

Inverurie Locos: Coull M; Young, Buchan, Wilson, Simpson, Park, Singer (Low), Walker, Coull K, Ross, McLean (McKay).
Keith: Shearer; Watt (Lonie), Simmers, Robertson (Mackay), McKenzie, Niddrie, Still, Brown, Donaldson, Nicol, Stephen (Walker).

Tuesday, 23 November 2004

Glasgow University (0) 0

Brechin C (2) 3 *(Hampshire 8, Templeman 30, 47)* 451

Glasgow University: King; McColl, Steele, Hawkins, Checketts, Brogan (Phillips), Riou, Barr, Connelly (Buckley), O'Donnell (Macdonald), Scott.
Brechin C: Hay; Hamilton, Mitchell, Johnstone, Smith, Walker, King, Gibson (Winter), Ritchie, Templeman, Hampshire (McNicoll).

Morton (3) 3 *(Williams 14, Weatherson 32, Millar 34)*

East Stirling (1) 1 *(Livingstone 9)* 1902

Morton: McGurn; Collins, Keenan, Gilbride (Maisano J), Greacen, Adam, Millar, Walker P (Walker J), Williams (McLean), Weatherson, McAllister.
East Stirling: Mitchell; Harvey (Denham), Baldwin, Walker, Livingstone, McGhee, Ross, McAuley, Donaldson (Findlay), Dunbar, Ure.

Saturday, 27 November 2004

Cove R (3) 4 *(Robertson 12, 30, Milne 18, 54)*

Dalbeattie (0) 1 *(Cook 59)* 140

Cove R: Thain; McHattie, McCraw, Hendry, Tindal, Morrison, Clark (Flaws), Johnston, Milne (Devine), Robertson (Steel), Brown.
Dalbeattie: Wilson F; True (Tennant), Proudfoot, Lawrie, McMinn, Harkness (Docherty), Cook, Wilson C, Dick (Prentice), Parker, Tuchewicz.

Cowdenbeath (1) 2 *(Gribben 32, Buchanan 90)*

Dumbarton (1) 3 *(McEwan 37, Dunn 50, Russell 79)* 279

Cowdenbeath: Carlin; Fusco, Campbell, Newall, McKeown, Ritchie, Mauchlen, McHale, Shields, Gribben (Kelly JP), Williams (Buchanan).
Dumbarton: Grindlay; McEwan, Brittain, McKinstry, Dobbins, Boyle, Bonar, Donald, Annand (Russell), Dunn (Rodgers), Dillon (McGroarty).

Forfar Ath (0) 1 *(Tosh 83)*

Montrose (2) 5 *(Webster 19, Smart 22, Sharp 54, 55, Dodds 70)* 535

Forfar Ath: Creer; Rattray, Lowing, Forrest, King D, Lunan (Clark), Sellars, McClune, Tosh, King M (Shields), Stein (Booth).
Montrose: Butter; Donachie, Ferguson, Doyle, Stephen (Doyle), Dodds, Webster (Smith D), Smart, Wood, Hall, Sharp (Watson).

Huntly (2) 3 *(Taylor 11, 56, Guild 34)*

Peterhead (0) 1 *(Bavidge 76)* 530

Huntly: Bowman; Gray, Scott, Anderson, Campbell, McGinlay, Stephen, Guild, O'Driscoll, Taylor (Stainer) (Stewart), McGowan (Reid).
Peterhead: Mathers; Campbell, Good, Raeside, Perry, Gibson, Michie, Buchan, Linn, Bavidge, Youngson (Stewart I).

SECOND ROUND

Saturday, 11 December 2004

Albion R (0) 0

Arbroath (1) 1 *(Brazil 33)* 202

Albion R: Fahey; Paterson A (Boyle), Stirling, Potter, McLaughlin (Bradford), McCaul (McLaren), McKenzie, Silvestro, Crabbe, McManus, Mercer.
Arbroath: Inglis; McMullan, Donaldson, Rennie, McLeod, Bishop, Millar M, MacDonald, Brazil (Farquharson), Henslee, Swankie (McLean).

Alloa Ath (1) 2 *(Brown 23, Walker 67)*

Stenhousemuir (0) 1 *(Savage 83)* 370

Alloa Ath: Evans J; Nicolson, Hill, Bolochoweckyj, Townsley, Ovenstone, Walker, Daly, Brown, Ferguson, Callaghan.
Stenhousemuir: McCulloch W; Fallon, McInally, Knox (Savage), Henderson, McBride, Morrison, Collins, McGregor, Davidson, McGrillen.

Ayr U (1) 3 *(Ferguson 23, Henderson 68, Lyle 72)*

Edinburgh C (0) 0 1183

Ayr U: Cherrie; Lyle, McCulloch, Smyth, McLaughlin, Henderson, Conway, Tait (Ramsay), Ferguson, Connolly (Wardlaw), Gilmour (Nesovic).
Edinburgh C: Mackintosh; Morrison, Seeley (Noon), Moriarty, Macnamara, Hunter, Elola, Doherty (Johnston), Young, Carnie (Gair), Cole.

Brechin C (1) 1 *(Ritchie 29)*

Stirling Albion (0) 0 516

Brechin C: Nelson; Hamilton, Deas, Winter (Smith), White, Walker, King (Johnson), Byers (McNicoll), Ritchie, Gibson, Hampshire.
Stirling Albion: Hogarth; Nugent, Devine (Wilson), McNally, Roycroft, Galloway, Hay (O'Brien), McDonald, McLean, Glancy (Gethins), Ferguson.

Cove R (1) 1 *(Johnston 45)*

Morton (3) 7 *(Weatherson 6, Walker J 9, 44, Adam 52, Hawke 67, Millar 70, 83)* 697

Cove R: Thain; McHattie, McCrow, Hendry, Tindal, Morrison, Clark (Flaws), Johnston, Milne (Devine), Robertson, Brown.
Morton: Coyle; Collins, Weatherson, McCluskey, Greacen (Hawke), Adam (Keenan), Millar, Walker P, Walker J (Bannerman), Mahood, McAllister.

Dumbarton (1) 1 *(Dillon 37)*

Berwick R (1) 1 *(McNicoll 6)* 692

Dumbarton: Grindlay; Bonar, Brittain, McKinstry, Dobbins, Ronald, McEwan (Boyle), Donald, Borris (Annand), Russell (Rodgers), Dillon.
Berwick R: O'Connor; Murie, Seaton, McNicoll, Cowan, Connell, Connelly (Clarke), McGarty, Hutchison (Hampshire), Little▪, Smith D (Gordon).

Gretna (0) 3 *(Deuchar 46, 59, Kaczan (og) 56)*

Elgin C (0) 0 661

Gretna: Mathieson; Birch, McQuilken, Gilfillan, Aitken, Irons, Baldacchino, McGuffie (Prokas), Deuchar, Bingham, Skelton (Smith).
Elgin C: Renton; Cumming, Harty (Vigurs I), Kaczan, Higgins, Dickson, Bremner, Nelson, Vigurs P (Napier), Martin, Reid (Melrose).

Huntly (0) 0

East Fife (0) 0 545

Huntly: Bowman; Reid N, Scott, Anderson, Campbell, Gray, Stephen, Guild, O'Driscoll (Stewart), Taylor, McGowan (De Barros).
East Fife: Morrison; Lumsden, Renwick, Bain, Paliczka, Kelly, Brash, McDonald G, Nicholas, Mitchell, Fairbairn (Herkes).

Keith (0) 0
Montrose (1) 1 *(Wood 34)* 293
Keith: Shearer; Brown, Simmers, Mackay (Robertson), McKenzie, Niddrie, Still, Donaldson, Nicol, Stephen, Lonie (Walker).
Montrose: Butter; Donachie, Ferguson, Doyle, Stephen, Kerrigan, Webster (Dodds), Smart, Wood, Hall, Sharp (Watson).

Stranraer (0) 1 *(Swift 83)*
Queen's Park (0) 0 391
Stranraer: McCondichie; Swift, McGhee, Wingate, Henderson, Jenkins, Finlayson, Gaughan K, Crawford (Turnbull), Graham, Guy.
Queen's Park: Crawford; Trouten, Molloy, Reilly, Sinclair (Clark R), Agostini, Kettlewell, Harvey, Graham (Felvus), Carroll, Ferry M.

SECOND ROUND REPLAYS

Saturday, 18 December 2004

Berwick R (1) 3 *(Clark 30, Connelly 73, Hutchison 89)*
Dumbarton (1) 1 *(Annand 24)* 318
Berwick R: O'Connor; Murie, Seaton, McNicoll, Cowan, Connell, Connelly, McGarty, Hutchison, Clarke, Smith D.
Dumbarton: Grindlay; Bonar (Bradley), Brittain, McKinstry, Dobbins, Ronald (Boyle), McEwan, Donald, Annand, Russell (Rodgers), Dillon.

East Fife (1) 3 *(Lumsden 21, McDonald G 70, 112)*
Huntly (2) 3 *(O'Driscoll 33, De Barros 43, Guild 107)* 575
East Fife: Morrison; Lumsden, Renwick, Bain, Paliczka (Herkes), Kelly (Byle), Brash (Tarditi), McDonald G, Nicholas, Mitchell, Fairbairn.
Huntly: Bowman; Reid N, McGowan (Stainer), Anderson, Campbell, Gray, Stephen, Guild, O'Driscoll, Taylor (Green), De Barros (Reid A).
aet; East Fife won 4-3 on penalties.

THIRD ROUND

Saturday, 8 January 2005

Arbroath (0) 0
Aberdeen (1) 2 *(Heikkinen 11, Mackie 66)* 3996
Arbroath: Inglis; McMullan, Donaldson, Rennie, McLeod, Bishop, Millar M (Cusick), MacDonald, Brazil, Henslee (McLean), Swankie (Farquharson).
Aberdeen: Esson; McGuire, McNaughton, Anderson, Hart, Tosh (Morrison), Heikkinen, Stewart (Whelan), Adams, Clark, Mackie.

Ayr U (2) 3 *(Conway 30, Ferguson 42, Henderson 45)*
Stranraer (2) 3 *(Gaughan K 40, McCutcheon 44, Wingate 71)* 1905
Ayr U: Hillcoat; Tait, Dunlop, Smyth, McLaughlin, McGrady, Conway, Connolly, Ferguson, Wardlaw (Lyle), Henderson.
Stranraer: McCaulay; Guy, Cruickshank (Graham), Wingate, McPhee, Jenkins, Finlayson, Gaughan K, McCutcheon (Crawford), Turnbull (Henderson), Sharp.

Berwick R (0) 0
Brechin C (0) 3 *(Hampshire 47, 74, Winter 57)* 386
Berwick R: O'Connor; Murie, Seaton (Hampshire), McKeown, Horn, Connell, Connelly (Gordon), McGarty, Hutchison, MacSween, Smith D.
Brechin C: Nelson; Hamilton (McNicoll), Deas, White, Walker, Byers (Mitchell), King, Johnson, Ritchie (Gibson), Winter, Hampshire.

Clyde (1) 3 *(Harty 35, 72, Bollan 68)*
Falkirk (0) 0 3565
Clyde: Halliwell; Mensing, Bollan, Balmer, Potter, Sheridan (Gibson), Burns, Wilson, Jones, Malone, Harty.
Falkirk: Ferguson; Lawrie, McPherson, Mackenzie, Campbell, James (Sharp), O'Neil (McBreen), Scally, Thomson, Latapy, Duffy.

East Fife (0) 0
Dunfermline Ath (0) 0 1722
East Fife: Morrison; Lumsden, Renwick, Bain, Paliczka, Kelly, Brash, McDonald G, Nicholas, Mitchell, Fairbairn.
Dunfermline Ath: Stillie; Ross, Labonte, Skerla, Thomson (Campbell), Darren Young (Dempsey), Makel, Nicholson, Mason, Tod, Christiansen (Hunt).

Hibernian (0) 2 *(Whittaker 75, Morrow 87)*
Dundee (0) 0 9706
Hibernian: Simon Brown; Caldwell, Smith, Murphy (McCluskey), Whittaker, Murray I, Glass, Orman (Morrow) (Fletcher), Shiels, Riordan, O'Connor.
Dundee: Soutar; Sancho, Barrett (Sutton), McDonald, Wilkie, Smith, Robb, Fotheringham M, Robertson (Larsen), Lovell, Caballero.

Kilmarnock (2) 2 *(McDonald 42, Boyd 45)*
Motherwell (0) 0 6093
Kilmarnock: Combe; Lilley, Dindeleux (Locke), Hay, Greer, Leven, McDonald, Nish, Naismith (Johnston A), Boyd (Wales), Invincibile.
Motherwell: Marshall; Corrigan, Kinniburgh, Hammell, Craigan, McBride, Fitzpatrick, Leitch, Foran, McDonald, Clarkson (Fagan).

Montrose (1) 1 *(Smart 44)*
Queen of the S (1) 2 *(Lyle 43, Gibson 49)* 717
Montrose: Butter; Donachie, Dodds, Doyle, Stephen, Kerrigan (Slater), Webster (Smith D), Smart, Wood, Hall (Watson), Sharp.
Queen of the S: Colin Scott; Paton, Wood, McColligan, Craig (Hill), Thomson, Burns, Bowey, Jaconelli, Lyle, Gibson.

Partick Th (0) 0
Hearts (0) 0 5666
Partick Th: Arthur; Anis, Milne, Murray, Madaschi, Fleming, Mitchell (Dowie), Oné, Escalas, Strachan (Fulton), Gibson A (Gibson W).
Hearts: Gordon; McAllister, McKenna, Pressley, Webster, Hamill (Simmons), Neilson, MacFarlane, Stamp, Weir (Pereira), Wyness (Kisnorbo).

Raith R (0) 0
Alloa Ath (1) 2 *(Ovenstone 44, Ferguson 88)* 1545
Raith R: Pounoussamy; Mendy, McMullan, Raffell (Martin), Smart, Bartholome, Ouattara, Sacko (O'Reilly), Ebanda (Malcolm), Brady, Millar.
Alloa Ath: Evans J; Nicolson (Quitongo), Ross, Bolochoweckyj (Mortimer), Townsley, Ovenstone, Walker, Ferguson, Brown, Hamilton, Stevenson (Calderon).

St Mirren (1) 3 *(Kean 18, 79, Russell 76)*
Hamilton A (0) 0 2907
St Mirren: Hinchcliffe; Van Zanten, Broadfoot, Millen, McGowne, Reilly, Murray (Crilly), Lappin, Kean (Baird), McGinty (Russell), McCay.
Hamilton A: McEwan; Fyfe (McLeod), Hodge, Thomson, Walker, Arbuckle (Carrigan), Ferguson (Aitken), McPhee, Keogh, Carney, Corcoran.

Sunday, 9 January 2005

Celtic (1) 2 *(Sutton 38, Hartson 77)*
Rangers (0) 1 *(Ricksen 47)* 58,559
Celtic: Douglas; Varga, Laursen, Balde, McNamara, Petrov, Agathe, Thompson, Sutton, Hartson, McGeady (Camara).
Rangers: Klos; Hutton, Andrews, Khizanishvili, Vignal, Ricksen, Djordjic (Buffel), Rae A, Namouchi (Thompson), Novo, Prso.

Inverness CT (0) 1 *(Golabek 73)*
St Johnstone (0) 0 1821
Inverness CT: Brown; Tokely, Golabek, Dods, Munro, McBain (Hart), Wilson, Duncan, Brewster (Bayne), Keogh, Prunty (Juanjo).
St Johnstone: Cuthbert; Baxter, Fotheringham K (Forsyth), Hannah, Webb, Maxwell, McCann (McAnespie), Rutkiewicz (Hay), MacDonald, Moore, Sheerin.

Tuesday, 11 January 2005

Livingston (1) 2 *(Rubio 35, Snodgrass 80)*
Morton (1) 1 *(Weatherson 37)* 2764
Livingston: Meldrum; McNamee, Rubio, Bahoken, Stanic (Snodgrass), Harding, Brittain (Hand), O'Brien, Lovell, Hamilton, McPake (Dair).
Morton: McGurn; Collins, Dillon (Bannerman), McCluskey, Greacen, Mahood (Hawke), Millar, Walker P (Walker J), Weatherson, Keenan, McAllister.

Monday, 17 January 2005

Gretna (1) 3 *(Deuchar 40, Birch 48 (pen), Skelton 63)*
Dundee U (3) 4 *(Robson 3, Kerr 7, Wilson 20, Crawford 55)* 3000
Gretna: Mathieson; Birch (Smith), McQuilken, Gilfillan, Aitken, Irons, Baldacchino (Prokas), McGuffie, Deuchar, Bingham, Skelton.
Dundee U: Bullock; Ritchie, Archibald, McCracken, Wilson, McInnes, Kerr, Robson (Mair), Grady, McIntyre, Crawford.

Monday, 24 January 2005

Ross Co (2) 4 *(Stewart 1, 2, 46, 47)*
Airdrie U (1) 1 *(McGeown 3)* 1302
Ross Co: Stewart; Robertson, McCulloch, Tiernan, Canning, Lauchlan, Rankin (Kilgannon), Cowie, Winters, McCunnie (McGarry), Burke (Higgins).
Airdrie U: McGeown; Wilson W (McKenna), Lovering, McGowan, McManus, Hardie, Dunn, Wilson M, Coyle (Vareille), Roberts (McKeown), McLaren.

THIRD ROUND REPLAYS

Tuesday, 18 January 2005

Dunfermline Ath (1) 3 *(Tod 1, Hunt 56, Dempsey 69)*
East Fife (0) 1 *(Byle 89)* 3542
Dunfermline Ath: Stillie; Ross, Tod, Skerla, Thomson, Darren Young (Campbell), Nicholson, Mason, Dempsey, Hunt, Christiansen (Dunn).
East Fife: Morrison; Lumsden, Renwick, Bain, Paliczka (Tarditi), Kelly (Byle), Brash, McDonald, Nicholas, Mitchell (Steele), Fairbairn.

Wednesday, 19 January 2005

Hearts (1) 2 *(MacFarlane 33, Wyness 89)*
Partick Th (1) 1 *(Oné 8)* 7375
Hearts: Gordon; McAllister, McKenna, Pressley, Webster, Stamp, Neilson, Macfarlane (Simmons), Hartley, Pereira (Hamill), Wyness.
Partick Th: Arthur; Anis (Gibson A), Milne, Murray, Madaschi, Dowie (Fulton), Gibson W (Strachan), Oné, Escalas, Ross A, Fleming.

Tuesday, 25 January 2005

Stranraer (0) 0
Ayr U (2) 2 *(Conway 27, Wardlaw 42)* 1044
Stranraer: McCaulay; Swift (Guy), Wright, Wingate, Henderson, Jenkins, Finlayson (McCutcheon), Gaughan K, McPhee (Fraser), Graham, Sharp.
Ayr U: Roy; Tait, Dunlop, Smyth, McLaughlin, McGrady (Lyle), Conway, Connolly (Ramsay), Ferguson (Reid), Wardlaw, Henderson.

FOURTH ROUND

Saturday, 5 February 2005

Aberdeen (2) 2 *(Mackie 16, 34)*
Inverness CT (1) 1 *(Brewster 24)* 10,595
Aberdeen: Esson; Byrne, McNaughton, Anderson, Hart, Heikkinen, Winter, Clark (Stewart), Whelan (Adams), Craig, Mackie (McGuire).
Inverness CT: Brown; Tokely, Golabek, Munro, Dodds, Hart (McBain), Duncan, Wilson, Juanjo (Fetai), Brewster, Bayne.

Alloa Ath (0) 0
Livingston (0) 1 *(McMenamin 88)* 2127
Alloa Ath: Evans J; Walker, Ross, Bolochoweckyj, Townsley, Ovenstone, Nicolson (Quitongo), Ferguson, Brown, Hamilton, Stevenson.
Livingston: McKenzie; Strong, Deloumeaux, Rubio (Dair), Behoken, Vincze, Easton, O'Brien, Hand (Kriston), McPake (McMenamin), Lilley.

Ayr U (0) 0
St Mirren (1) 2 *(Kean 44, Murray 81)* 4796
Ayr U: Roy; Tait, Dunlop (Lyle), Smyth, McLaughlin, McGrady, Conway, Connolly, Ferguson (Ramsay), Reid (Brown), Henderson.
St Mirren: Hinchcliffe; Van Zanten, Broadfoot, Millen, McGowne, Reilly, Murray (Crilly), O'Neil (Gillies), Kean, McGinty (Russell), McCay.

Hearts (2) 2 *(Wyness 16, Miller 45)*
Kilmarnock (1) 2 *(Nish 25, Naismith 88)* 10,483
Hearts: Gordon; McAllister, Wallace, Pressley, Webster, Simmons (MacFarlane), Neilson, Mikoliunus (Hamill), Hartley, Miller, Wyness (Burchill).
Kilmarnock: Combe; Lilley, Hay, Fontaine, Ford, Leven, Johnston A, Locke (Naismith), McDonald, Nish (Boyd), Invincibile (Murray).

Hibernian (2) 4 *(Morrow 24, O'Connor 32, 57, Caldwell 63)*
Brechin C (0) 0 13,563
Hibernian: Simon Brown; Caldwell, Smith, Beuzelin (Murray A), Whittaker, Murray I, Glass, Morrow (McCluskey), Shiels (Fletcher), Riordan, O'Connor.
Brechin C: Nelson; Hamilton (Smith), Deas, White, Walker, Byers, King (Strachan), Winter, Ritchie, Hampshire, Gibson (Johnson).

Queen of the S (0) 0
Dundee U (3) 3 *(McIntyre 13, Wilson 24, Duff 38)* 5532
Queen of the S: Colin Scott; Paton, Craig, McColligan, Reid, Thomson, Burns (Payne), Bowey, McNiven (Jaconelli), Lyle, Gibson (McLaughlin).
Dundee U: Bullock; Ritchie, Archibald, McCracken (Kenneth), Wilson, Mair, Kerr (Brebner), Robson (Scotland), Duff, McIntyre, Crawford.

Ross Co (0) 0
Clyde (0) 0 1629
Ross Co: Stewart; Robertson, McCulloch, Tiernan, Canning, Lauchlan, Rankin (Kilgannon), Cowie, Winters, McCunnie, Burke.
Clyde: Halliwell; Mensing, Bollan, Balmer, Potter, Sheridan (Arbuckle), Burns, Gibson, Jones (Bryson), Malone, Harty.

Sunday, 6 February 2005

Dunfermline Ath (0) 0
Celtic (3) 3 *(Hartson 5, 44, Sutton 10)* 8504
Dunfermline Ath: Stillie; Ross, Wilson S (Hristov), Skerla, Thomson, Darren Young, Nicholson, Mason, Makel, Christiansen, Tod.
Celtic: Douglas; Varga, Laursen, Balde, Henchoz, Petrov (Lambert), Thompson (Juninho), Lennon, Sutton, Hartson (Wallace), McGeady.

FOURTH ROUND REPLAY

Tuesday, 15 February 2005

Clyde (1) 2 *(Bryson 35, Arbuckle 91)*
Ross Co (1) 1 *(Rankin 16)* 1566
Clyde: Halliwell; Mensing, Bollan, Balmer (Gilhaney), Potter, Sheridan, Burns (Arbuckle), Gibson, Bryson (Wilson), Malone, Harty.
Ross Co: Stewart; Robertson (Higgins), McCulloch, Tiernan, Canning, Laughlan, Rankin, Cowie, Winters, Burke (McCunnie), Kilgannon (McGarry).
aet.

FOURTH ROUND REPLAYS

Wednesday, 16 February 2005

Kilmarnock (0) 1 *(Boyd 90)*
Hearts (2) 3 *(Wallace 6, Miller 13, Cesnauskis 57)* 6366
Kilmarnock: Combe; Lilley, Hay, Fontaine, Ford, Leven, McDonald, Johnston A, Naismith (Murray), Boyd, Invincibile.
Hearts: Gordon; Cesnauskis, Wallace, Pressley, Webster, Simmons (MacFarlane), Neilson, Mikoliunas, Hartley, Miller (Thorarinsson), Wyness (Burchill).

QUARTER-FINALS

Saturday, 26 February 2005

Hibernian (1) 2 *(Scott Brown 45, O'Connor 72)*
St Mirren (0) 0 15,195
Hibernian: Simon Brown; Caldwell, Smith, Murphy, Whittaker, Murray I, Murray A, Fletcher (Orman), Scott Brown (McDonald), Riordan, O'Connor.
St Mirren: Hinchcliffe; Van Zanten, Broadfoot, Millen, McGowne, Reilly, Murray, Lappin (Gillies), Kean, Russell (O'Neil), McCay (McGinty).

Sunday, 27 February 2005

Clyde (0) 0
Celtic (1) 5 *(Varga 39, 67, Thompson 47, Petrov 60, Bellamy 72)* 6862
Clyde: Halliwell; Mensing, Bollan, Balmer, Potter, Sheridan (Burns), Arbuckle (Gilhaney), Gibson, Bryson (Jones), Malone, Harty.
Celtic: Douglas; Varga, Henchoz, Balde, McNamara, Petrov (McGeady), Thompson, Lennon (Lambert), Sutton (Maloney), Bellamy, Juninho.

Dundee U (3) 4 *(Archibald 19, Grady 28, 46, Crawford 41)*
Aberdeen (1) 1 *(Byrne 32)* 8661
Dundee U: Bullock; Ritchie, Archibald, Duff, Wilson, Brebner, Kerr (Cameron), Robson, Scotland (Samuel), Grady, Crawford.
Aberdeen: Esson; Byrne (Morrison), McNaughton, Anderson, Diamond, Heikkinen (Foster), Hart, Winter, Clark (Stewart), Whelan, Mackie.

Hearts (2) 2 *(Miller 1, McAllister 9)*
Livingston (0) 1 *(Easton 60)* 10,923
Hearts: Gordon; McAllister, Wallace, Berra, Webster, Simmons (MacFarlane), Neilson, Mikoliunas (Cesnauskis), Hartley, Miller, Burchill (Wyness).
Livingston: Meldrum; McNamee, Deloumeaux, Strong, Bahoken (Stanic), Dair, Easton, O'Brien, Wilson (Vincze), McPake, Lilley (Horvath).

SEMI-FINALS (at Hampden Park)

Saturday, 9 April 2005

Dundee U (0) 2 *(McIntyre 73, Scotland 76)*
Hibernian (0) 1 *(Riordan 57)* 27271
Dundee U: Bullock; Ritchie, Archibald, Duff (Scotland), Wilson, McInnes (Kerr), Brebner, Kenneth, Robson, McIntyre, Crawford.
Hibernian: Simon Brown; Caldwell, Smith, Murphy (Thomson), Whittaker, Fletcher, Glass, Shiels (Sproule), Scott Brown, Riordan (Morrow), O'Connor.

Sunday, 10 April 2005

Hearts (0) 1 *(Cesnauskis 59)*
Celtic (1) 2 *(Sutton 2, Bellamy 48)* 38,505
Hearts: Gordon; McAllister, Wallace, Pressley, Webster, Hamill (Kizys), Neilson (Cesnauskis), MacFarlane (Wyness), Hartley, Miller, Burchill.
Celtic: Marshall; Varga, Valgaeren, Balde, McNamara, Petrov, Lennon, Thompson, Sutton, Hartson (McGeady), Bellamy.

FINAL (at Hampden Park)

Saturday, 28 May 2005

Celtic (1) 1 *(Thompson 10)*
Dundee U (0) 0 50,635
Celtic: Douglas; Agathe, Varga, Balde, McNamara, Petrov, Lennon, Thompson (McGeady), Sutton, Hartson (Valgaeren), Bellamy.
Dundee U: Bullock; Ritchie, Archibald, Wilson, Kenneth, McInnes (Samuel), Brebner (Duff), Kerr, Robson, Crawford (Grady), Scotland.
Referee: John Rowbotham.

Stevie Crawford of Dundee United in action against Stilian Petrov of Celtic during the Bell's Scottish Cup Final at Hampden Park. (Actionimages)

WELSH FOOTBALL 2004–05

"*Gosh it's Tosh!*" wasn't only the title of John Toshack's first and – to date – only published book of poems, it also summed up the general reaction to his inevitable appointment as Welsh manager in November 2004.

It came as no surprise that when Mark Hughes decided to jump ship and move to Blackburn, the Welsh FA turned to the former Swansea manager. Despite an apparently strong challenge from Dean Saunders and Phillippe Troussier, Toshack was the only person with the right credentials to reinvigorate the national team. Without a competitive win for 10 games and with just two points from three World Cup qualifiers, Hughes had taken the struggling side as far as he could and it was patently time for a change.

Aided and abetted by an often embarrassingly sycophantic but unnecessary campaign by the *Western Mail* newspaper, the Welsh FA predictably gave the former Cardiff and Liverpool striker the opportunity to make use of his 26 years' experience of club management in Spain, Portugal, Turkey, Italy and France on the international stage.

Not suprisingly, Toshack's outspoken views as a media pundit had ruffled a few feathers. His appointment hastened the retirement of a handful of ageing players and provoked the petulant Robbie Savage to join them after throwing his toys out of the pram when he was dropped from Toshack's first World Cup squad.

After a creditable 2-0 friendly win over Hungary in Toshack's first match, reality kicked in with successive World Cup defeats against Austria – although the away game provided evidence that, under the captaincy of Ryan Giggs, a mixture of youth and experience could turn around Welsh fortunes in time for the 2008 European Championship.

The Coca-Cola League clubs provided very little fizz for Welsh football. Swansea marked their move to a new stadium in Morfa by clinching promotion to League One with a last-day win at Bury but Cardiff and Wrexham both lurched from crisis to crisis on and off the pitch. The Bluebirds struggled for most of the season before finally securing safety in their penultimate match after debts of £30m had been revealed. The arrival of former Leeds chairman, Peter Ridsdale, as executive deputy chairman led to key departures – local businessmen Kim Walker and Michael Isaac left the board and manager Lennie Lawrence was shamefully treated after two years of hard work by being sacked while on a coaching course in Norway. His replacement, Dave Jones, will do well to keep Cardiff in the Championship as uncertainty over the club's new stadium continues and high-earning players – following in the footsteps of Robert Earnshaw, Graham Kavanagh, Danny Gabbidon and Jobi McAnuff – have to be sold to keep the club afloat.

Wrexham's financial crisis came to a head when the club slithered into administration and the resultant 10-point penalty in December cost them their place in League One. To their credit, the Dragons kept going right to the end and beat Southend in the LDV Vans Trophy Final at the Millennium Stadium. The Spaniard, Juan Ugarte, capped an incredible season with his 22nd goal in 29 starts in the 2-0 extra-time win but Wrexham's future – and in particular their future at the Racecourse ground – is still in grave doubt.

There was little to cheer about in the English non-league pyramid with Merthyr losing in a Southern Premier Division semi-final penalty shoot-out, Newport just avoiding relegation from the Conference South with a last-day win and Colwyn Bay finishing just below halfway in the First Division of the Unibond League.

TNS won the Welsh Premier League title before completing the 'double' by beating Carmarthen in the Welsh Cup Final while Swansea bade a fond farewell to the Vetch Field by overcoming Wrexham to lift the FAW Premier Cup. In Europe, Rhyl, TNS, Haverfordwest and Aberystwyth all went out at the first hurdle to Skonto Riga (Latvia), Osters IF Vaxio (Sweden), FH Hafnarfjordur (Iceland) and FC Dinaburg (Latvia) respectively. As well as TNS in the Champions League, Wales will be represented by Rhyl and Carmarthen in the UEFA Cup and Bangor in the Intertoto Cup in the 2005–06 season.

Congratulations must go to Grange Quins who won promotion to the Welsh Premier League under former Cardiff winger Paul Giles – thus becoming the first capital-based club in the top tier since the now defunct Inter Cabletel.

Welsh chances of reaching the 2006 World Cup in Germany may have disappeared but there's nothing like a fixture against the Old Enemy to concentrate the mind. September's qualifier with England at the Millennium Stadium in Cardiff will rekindle memories of the games John Toshack used to be involved in as a player before the demise of the Home International Championship. The first poem in *Gosh it's Tosh!* recalls one such encounter when the Welsh manager penned these lines:

"Wales come out in brand new kit
But I don't play 'cos I'm not fit."

The new man at the top may not be the greatest poet in the world but as a football coach, he talks anything but tosh. He knows that actions speak louder than words and I'm sure his tactical nous and, more importantly, his flexibility will stand him and Wales in good stead. As the pop song lyric, as opposed to the poem, goes, *"things can only get better"* and under him, I believe they will.

GRAHAME LLOYD

VAUXHALL MASTERFIT WELSH PREMIER LEAGUE RESULTS 2004–05

	Aberystwyth Town	Afan Lido	Airbus UK	Bangor City	Caernarfon Town	Caersws	Carmarthen Town	Connah's Quay Nomads	Cwmbran Town	Haverfordwest County	Llanelli	Newi Cefn Druids	Newtown	Porthmadog	Port Talbot Town	Rhyl	Total Network Solutions	Welshpool Town
Aberystwyth Town	—	1-1	1-0	1-2	5-0	1-0	0-0	1-0	0-1	4-0	2-0	2-1	1-1	0-0	0-0	1-2	1-1	0-0
Afan Lido	0-0	—	4-0	2-3	1-0	1-0	0-2	0-1	0-2	0-1	1-1	1-0	1-3	1-1	0-1	1-2	0-2	0-1
Airbus UK	1-2	1-4	—	0-0	1-1	0-3	0-1	3-3	0-1	1-2	0-3	1-2	2-2	0-1	3-1	1-0	0-6	0-2
Bangor City	4-2	1-0	5-0	—	2-0	1-0	0-1	2-0	0-3	1-1	6-0	2-0	2-3	0-2	3-2	2-1	1-0	4-2
Caernarfon Town	0-2	0-0	0-3	2-1	—	0-1	0-5	1-1	1-1	0-2	1-3	2-0	1-2	3-1	3-1	1-4	0-7	1-3
Caersws	4-1	4-1	3-0	2-2	3-1	—	1-2	1-2	5-2	1-0	2-0	7-0	2-0	0-1	2-2	1-4	0-0	2-1
Carmarthen Town	4-1	1-1	3-0	3-3	1-2	1-1	—	2-2	1-1	4-2	5-1	1-1	3-2	2-1	2-0	0-1	0-1	1-1
Connah's Quay Nomads	0-2	4-2	1-2	3-4	1-2	2-1	1-2	—	1-2	2-2	1-3	4-0	0-3	3-1	0-2	1-1	0-7	1-1
Cwmbran Town	2-3	1-0	4-4	0-3	2-1	1-4	0-2	1-0	—	0-2	2-0	3-3	1-2	2-1	3-1	0-1	2-2	2-3
Haverfordwest County	4-1	2-1	6-1	1-1	1-1	0-0	0-0	0-0	1-0	—	3-0	1-1	2-1	0-0	3-1	2-1	0-0	3-0
Llanelli	2-4	3-1	2-2	5-1	2-1	2-4	0-3	0-2	0-4	0-3	—	1-4	2-2	1-1	1-2	2-1	0-4	1-2
Newi Cefn Druids	0-1	3-0	2-2	0-4	0-1	0-5	0-1	0-5	1-3	0-2	2-3	—	0-2	1-2	1-0	0-3	1-3	2-1
Newtown	2-3	1-0	0-1	0-0	2-1	1-3	0-4	2-1	1-2	3-0	4-0	2-2	—	1-1	3-2	0-1	0-3	1-6
Porthmadog	2-0	2-0	3-3	3-0	2-0	0-1	3-2	0-0	1-1	0-2	1-1	0-0	0-2	—	1-0	0-3	1-2	1-1
Port Talbot Town	0-1	1-2	3-2	1-4	0-0	0-1	0-0	2-2	1-1	0-1	4-0	1-1	0-0	1-2	—	1-3	2-2	3-0
Rhyl	1-0	3-1	2-0	2-3	5-1	3-0	3-1	4-2	0-0	0-0	2-0	3-2	3-0	3-1	1-0	—	1-2	2-2
Total Network Solutions	3-1	2-1	1-1	1-1	5-0	5-0	2-0	2-1	2-0	2-0	4-2	1-0	3-0	2-1	1-1	2-2	—	1-0
Welshpool Town	2-0	2-1	2-1	1-5	1-1	2-3	3-0	0-1	0-2	1-1	4-0	2-0	2-1	1-1	0-0	1-2	5-2	—

VAUXHALL MASTERFIT RETAILERS WELSH PREMIER LEAGUE

			Home					Away						
		P	W	D	L	F	A	W	D	L	F	A	GD	Pts
1	Total Network Solutions	34	13	4	0	39	11	10	5	2	44	14	58	78
2	Rhyl	34	12	3	2	38	15	11	2	4	32	16	39	74
3	Bangor City	34	12	1	4	36	17	8	6	3	37	27	29	67
4	Haverfordwest County	34	9	8	0	29	9	8	4	5	21	19	22	63
5	Caersws	34	10	3	4	40	19	9	2	6	27	20	28	62
6	Carmarthen Town	34	7	7	3	34	21	10	3	4	26	13	26	61
7	Cwmbran Town	34	6	3	8	26	32	9	5	3	26	15	5	53
8	Aberystwyth Town	34	7	7	3	21	9	8	1	8	24	31	5	53
9	Welshpool Town	34	8	4	5	29	21	6	5	6	26	25	9	51
10	Newtown	34	6	3	8	23	30	7	4	6	26	25	–6	46
11	CPD Porthmadog	34	6	6	5	20	18	5	6	6	18	21	–1	45
12	Connah's Quay Nomads	34	4	3	10	25	37	5	6	6	23	21	–10	36
13	Port Talbot Town	34	3	7	7	20	22	3	4	10	16	27	–13	29
14	Llanelli	34	4	3	10	24	41	4	2	11	18	44	–43	29
15	Caernarfon Town	34	4	3	10	16	38	3	4	10	13	34	–43	28
16	Airbus UK	34	2	4	11	14	34	3	5	9	22	42	–40	24
17	Newi Cefn Druids	34	3	1	13	13	38	2	6	9	17	34	–42	22
18	Afan Lido*	34	4	3	10	13	20	2	3	12	16	32	23	21

** Deducted three points for fielding an ineligible player.*

PREVIOUS WELSH LEAGUE WINNERS

1993 Cwmbran Town
1994 Bangor City
1995 Bangor City
1996 Barry Town
1997 Barry Town
1998 Barry Town
1999 Barry Town
2000 TNS
2001 Barry Town
2002 Barry Town
2003 Barry Town
2004 Rhyl
2005 TNS

WELSH CUP 2004–05

THIRD ROUND

AFC Llwycoed v Welshpool Town 1-2
Airbus UK v Afan Lido 0-2
Bala Town v Ton Pentre 5-3 *(aet)*
Barry Town v Garden Village 2-1
Caernarfon Town v Grange Harlequins 2-1 *(aet)*
Dinas Powys v Bangor City 2-3
Gresford Athletic v Carmarthen Town 3-6 *(aet)*
Haverfordwest County v CPD Glantraeth 3-0
Holywell Town v Aberystwyth Town
bye: Aberystyth Town
Lex XI v Caersws 0-1
Llangefni Town v Bodedern 1-0
Porthmadog v Cwmbran Town 1-3 *(aet)*
Port Talbot Town v Halkyn United 0-1
Rhyl v Holyhead Hotspur 9-0
Total Network Solutions v Penrhiwfer 11-0
UWIC Inter Cardiff v Caerleon 3-1

FOURTH ROUND

Aberystwyth Town v Caernarfon Town 3-2
Barry Town v Afan Lido 2-5
Carmarthen Town v Cwmbran Town 1-0
Halkyn United v Caersws 0-5
Rhyl v Llangefni Town 4-0
Total Network Solutions v Bangor City 2-1
UWIC Inter Cardiff v Haverfordwest County 1-4
Welshpool Town v Bala Town 1-2

FIFTH ROUND

Aberystwyth Town v Haverfordwest County 0-2
Caersws v Carmarthen Town 0-1
Rhyl v Bala Town 4-0
Total Network Solutions v Afan Lido 4-1

SEMI-FINALS

Carmarthen Town v Haverfordwest County 1-0
(at Llanelli)
Total Network Solutions v Rhyl 3-1
(at Wrexham)

WELSH CUP FINAL

(at Llanelli)

8 May 2005

Carmarthen Town (0) 0 Total Network Solutions (0) 1

Carmarthen Town: Pennock; Hardy, Lloyd, Giles, Carter, Jones, Smothers (Coerall 77), Kennedy (Abdullahi 77), Burke (James 90), Dodds, Aherne-Evans.
Total Network Solutions: Doherty; Naylor, Holmes, Leah, Evans, Taylor, Ruscoe, Lloyd-Williams (King 83), Wilde, Wood, Lawless (Toner 90).

Scorer: Lawless 75.

Referee: S. Jones (Swansea).

Attendance: 1126.

PREVIOUS WELSH CUP WINNERS

1878	Wrexham Town	1908	Chester	1948	Lovell's Athletic	1978	Wrexham
1879	White Star Newtown	1909	Wrexham	1949	Merthyr Tydfil	1979	Shrewsbury Town
1880	Druids	1910	Wrexham	1950	Swansea Town	1980	Newport County
1881	Druids	1911	Wrexham	1951	Merthyr Tydfil	1981	Swansea City
1882	Druids	1912	Cardiff City	1952	Rhyl	1982	Swansea City
1883	Wrexham	1913	Swansea Town	1953	Rhyl	1983	Swansea City
1884	Oswestry United	1914	Wrexham	1954	Flint Town United	1984	Shrewsbury Town
1885	Druids	1915	Wrexham	1955	Barry Town	1985	Shrewsbury Town
1886	Druids	1920	Cardiff City	1956	Cardiff City	1986	Wrexham
1887	Chirk	1921	Wrexham	1957	Wrexham	1987	Merthyr Tydfil
1888	Chirk	1922	Cardiff City	1958	Wrexham	1988	Cardiff City
1889	Bangor	1923	Cardiff City	1959	Cardiff City	1989	Swansea City
1890	Druids	1924	Wrexham	1960	Wrexham	1990	Hereford United
1891	Shrewsbury Town	1925	Wrexham	1961	Swansea Town	1991	Swansea City
1892	Chirk	1926	Ebbw Vale	1962	Bangor City	1992	Cardiff City
1893	Wrexham	1927	Cardiff City	1963	Borough United	1993	Cardiff City
1894	Chirk	1928	Cardiff City	1964	Cardiff City	1994	Barry Town
1895	Newtown	1929	Connah's Quay	1965	Cardiff City	1995	Wrexham
1896	Bangor	1930	Cardiff City	1966	Swansea Town	1996	TNS
1897	Wrexham	1931	Wrexham	1967	Cardiff City	1997	Barry Town
1898	Druids	1932	Swansea Town	1968	Cardiff City	1998	Bangor City
1899	Druids	1933	Chester	1969	Cardiff City	1999	Inter Cable-Tel
1900	Aberystwyth	1934	Bristol City	1970	Cardiff City	2000	Bangor City
1901	Oswestry United	1935	Tranmere Rovers	1971	Cardiff City	2001	Barry Town
1902	Wellington Town	1936	Crewe Alexandra	1972	Wrexham	2002	Barry Town
1903	Wrexham	1937	Crewe Alexandra	1973	Cardiff City	2003	Barry Town
1904	Druids	1938	Shrewsbury Town	1974	Cardiff City	2004	Rhyl
1905	Wrexham	1939	South Liverpool	1975	Wrexham	2005	TNS
1906	Wellington Town	1940	Wellington Town	1976	Cardiff City		
1907	Oswestry United	1947	Chester	1977	Shrewsbury Town		

FAW PREMIER CUP

FIRST ROUND

Port Talbot Town v Cwmbran Town	3-2
Caernarfon Town v Caersws	1-0
Connah's Quay Nomads v Merthyr Tydfil	2-1
Newtown v Bangor City	0-4

SECOND ROUND

Bangor City v Connah's Quay Nomads	3-0
Port Talbot Town v Haverfordwest County	1-2
Caernarfon Town v Newport County	1-0
Total Network Solutions v Aberystwyth Town	2-1

byes: Cardiff City, Rhyl, Wrexham and Swansea City.

QUARTER-FINALS

Haverfordwest County v Wrexham	1-2
Bangor City v Cardiff City	1-0
Total Network Solutions v Rhyl	2-1
Caernarfon Town v Swansea City	0-5

SEMI-FINALS

Total Network Solutions v Swansea City	1-1
(aet; Swansea City won 4-2 on penalties.)	
Bangor City v Wrexham	1-2

FAW CUP FINAL

(at The Vetch)

11 May 2005

Swansea City (0) 2 Wrexham (0) 1

Swansea City: Gueret; Anderson, Austin, O'Leary, Tate, Martinez, Britton (Robinson 46), Iriekpen, Connor (Thorpe 86), Trundle, Forbes.
Scorers: Pejic (og) 68, Robinson 76.

Wrexham: Foster; Holt, Pejic, Morgan, Crowell, Lawrence, Edwards, Williams, Jones (Sam 67), Ugarte, Llewellyn.
Scorer: Ugarte 60.

Referee: B. Lawlor (Holyhead).

Attendance: 9324.

THE MOTAQUOTE INSURANCE WELSH LEAGUE

DIVISION ONE	*P*	*W*	*D*	*L*	*F*	*A*	*GD*	*Pts*
Ton Pentre	34	24	7	3	91	33	58	79
Grange Harlequins	34	23	4	7	76	23	53	73
AFC Llwydcoed	34	20	6	8	65	35	30	66
Skewen Athletic	34	17	8	9	56	32	24	59
Goytre United	34	17	7	10	63	48	15	58
Maesteg Park	34	18	3	13	58	47	11	57
Bridgend Town	34	16	8	10	60	43	17	56
Taffs Well	34	15	6	13	71	48	23	51
UWIC	34	15	6	13	65	49	16	51
Briton Ferry	34	15	4	15	61	55	6	49
Barry Town	34	14	5	15	45	44	1	47
Bettws	34	14	5	15	47	51	–4	47
Caerleon	34	11	11	12	44	47	–3	44
Ely Rangers	34	11	5	18	54	62	–8	38
Dinas Powys	34	10	8	16	43	51	–8	38
Neath	34	10	4	20	38	71	–33	31
Gwynfi United	34	2	4	28	25	124	–99	7
Garw	34	3	1	30	12	111	–99	7

HUWS GRAY-FITLOCK CYMRU ALLIANCE LEAGUE

	P	*W*	*D*	*L*	*F*	*A*	*GD*	*Pts*
Buckley Town	34	23	8	3	77	36	41	77
Glantraeth	34	21	7	6	84	33	51	70
Llangefni Town	34	21	5	8	69	33	36	68
Bala Town	34	18	6	10	60	41	19	60
Lex XI	34	16	8	10	86	60	26	56
Llandyrnog United	34	16	4	14	71	58	13	52
Guilsfield	34	14	8	12	78	66	12	50
Gresford Athletic	34	15	5	14	70	62	8	50
Holywell Town	34	13	7	14	77	64	13	46
Halkyn United	34	13	6	15	71	74	–3	45
Holyhead Hotspur	34	12	6	16	46	63	–17	42
Llanfairpwll	34	11	9	14	55	73	–18	42
Ruthin Town	34	11	7	16	57	70	–13	40
Penrhyncoch	34	9	12	13	62	71	–9	39
Flint Town United	34	9	11	14	50	57	–7	38
Llandudno*	34	12	10	12	66	61	5	37
Mold Alexandra	34	7	7	20	51	78	–27	28
Cemaes Bay†	34	1	2	31	31	161	–130	2

**Deducted 9 points for fielding ineligible players.*
†Deducted 3 points for non-fulfilment of fixture.

NORTHERN IRISH FOOTBALL 2004–05

Northern Ireland football, or to be more precise, the Irish FA, in its 125th anniversary year, has undergone a massive restructuring over the last 18 months as envisaged in the Government's Soccer Strategy Report and as a stipulation for the proposed £8m funding over three years covering all areas of the game.

The administration of the national association and the Irish Football League has been amalgamated with a 17-member executive committee, including two independents, and subsidiary committees taking over the powers of the Council which, while still in existence and meeting quarterly, has become an irrelevance. A Premier League was established with its own committee; the lower leagues are to be revamped at the end of next season and strict new club licence regulations introduced. Howard J.C. Wells was appointed as the new Chief Executive and several other senior posts established in what is a new era for Irish football.

Internationally, manager Lawrie Sanchez, whose contract was extended until 2008 covering the European Championship qualifiers, brought a feel good factor to the squad with some wins and promising performances in friendlies and on the Caribbean tour; attendances have improved while the support from the public was phenomenal, both at home and abroad, and their impeccable conduct favourably commented upon by the authorities.

Unfortunately, and significantly, the squad has yet to obtain a win in the World Cup Group Six so far collecting only three points from six matches, scoring five goals and conceding 13. They stand a point above Wales and Azerbaijan as England and Poland battle it out for top place and automatic finals qualification with England remaining favourites.

Sanchez, however, still believes the squad, young and inexperienced, possesses potential to make an impact. "We must restore a belief in ourselves, must eliminate that irritating habit of scoring a goal and then giving one away almost instantly", said Sanchez.

Domestically, it appeared as if Linfield would miss out on major trophies with Glentoran pipping them at the post to win the Irish Premier Division, and Portadown lifting the Irish Cup. Then, on an incredible May night at Tolka Park, Dublin, they defeated Shelbourne to win the inaugural Setanta All-Ireland Cup with its 150,000 Euro first prize.

This series between the top three Irish League and Eircom League teams, an outstanding success, will probably be increased numerically next season to eight clubs with the priority finding a suitable slot in the fixture schedules. The prospect of an all-Ireland League can be forgotten as travel expenses and compensation for loss of wages by part-time professionals, rules it out financially.

A highlight of the centenary celebrations was the staging of the prestigious UEFA Under-19 championship finals during July in Northern Ireland thanks to the efforts of Irish FA President, Jim Boyce, who played a major role along with retired general secretary David Bowen in Germany agreeing to open the celebrations with a game at Windsor Park on June 4. There is the possibility they will close with a match against Italy at Windsor Park just before the World Cup finals in Germany.

The harsh reality of a financial crisis hitting the Northern Ireland game was Omagh Town's decision to withdraw from football. They had finished bottom of the Premiership, were relegated to the First and, according to a club statement, they could not generate sufficient revenue to meet escalating overheads, existing debts and other expenditure. A sad occasion, but there are indications others may be forced down that route, too.

DR MALCOLM BRODIE

DAILY MIRROR IRISH PREMIER LEAGUE

	P	*W*	*D*	*L*	*F*	*A*	*GD*	*Pts*
Glentoran	30	24	2	4	73	22	51	74
Linfield	30	22	6	2	78	23	55	72
Portadown	30	18	4	8	64	29	35	58
Dungannon Swifts	30	15	5	10	57	40	17	50
Limavady United	30	13	9	8	52	36	16	48
Coleraine	30	14	5	11	62	47	15	47
Lisburn Distillery	30	13	8	9	49	42	7	47
Ballymena United	30	11	12	7	40	37	3	45
Institute	30	11	3	16	36	50	–14	36
Newry City	30	10	5	15	38	63	–25	35
Cliftonville	30	9	7	14	29	44	–15	34
Loughgall	30	8	6	16	34	53	–19	30
Larne	30	7	7	16	31	60	–29	28
Ards	30	6	8	16	33	54	–21	26
Crusaders†	30	5	9	16	27	48	–21	24
Omagh Town*	30	5	2	23	33	85	–55	17

**relegated; †play-off.*

PROMOTION/RELEGATION PLAY-OFF

First Leg

Glenavon 1, Crusaders 1 (*at Mourneview Park, Lurgan*)

Second Leg

Crusaders 1, Glenavon 2 (*at Seaview, Belfast*)

DAILY MIRROR IRISH INTERMEDIATE LEAGUE

FIRST DIVISION

	P	*W*	*D*	*L*	*F*	*A*	*GD*	*Pts*
Armagh C (P)	22	15	7	0	35	11	24	52
Glenavon†	22	14	4	4	43	17	26	46
Donegal Celtic	22	10	6	6	34	19	15	36
HW Welders	22	10	6	6	35	29	6	36
Bangor	22	9	6	7	33	29	4	33
Coagh United	22	8	5	9	39	42	–3	29
Ballyclare Com	22	7	7	8	22	24	–2	28
Dundela	22	7	6	9	28	33	–5	27
Moyola Park	22	6	5	11	18	29	–11	23
Carrick Rangers	22	6	4	12	25	37	–12	22
Ballymoney U (R)	22	6	2	14	29	45	–16	20
Ballinamallard U (R)	22	3	4	15	14	40	–26	13

INTERMEDIATE SECOND DIVISION

	P	*W*	*D*	*L*	*F*	*A*	*GD*	*Pts*
Tobermore U (C)	22	15	1	6	47	26	21	46
Banbridge Town (P)	22	13	5	4	48	22	26	44
Lurgan Celtic	22	9	7	6	45	34	11	34
Wakehurst	22	8	9	5	34	26	8	33
Annagh United	22	9	6	7	32	32	0	33
Portstewart	22	8	6	8	26	25	1	30
PSNI	22	8	6	8	27	29	–2	30
Chimney Corner	22	7	8	7	31	36	–5	29
Dergview	22	7	5	10	39	45	–6	26
Oxford United Stars	22	6	6	10	25	36	–11	24
Brantwood	22	4	7	11	30	46	–16	19
Queens University	22	1	8	13	25	52	–27	11

IRISH RESERVE LEAGUE

	P	*W*	*D*	*L*	*F*	*A*	*GD*	*Pts*
Linfield Swifts	28	21	5	2	89	20	69	68
Glentoran II	28	20	4	4	69	25	44	64
Dungannon Swifts Res	28	19	4	5	83	32	51	61
Limavady United Res	28	14	7	7	70	28	42	49
Coleraine Res	28	14	6	8	67	49	18	48
Cliftonville Olympic	28	12	7	9	60	49	11	43
Crusaders Res	28	11	7	10	60	40	20	40
Portadown Res	28	11	2	15	64	65	–1	35
Loughall United	28	10	4	14	55	74	–19	34
Lisburn Distillery II	28	8	9	11	54	66	–12	33
Institute II	28	7	9	12	47	52	–5	30
Larne Olympic	28	6	6	16	30	95	–65	24
Ards II	28	5	7	16	29	83	–54	22
Newry City Res	28	4	6	18	38	104	–66	18
Ballymena United Res	28	4	5	19	27	60	–33	17

IRISH YOUTH LEAGUE NORTH

	P	W	D	L	F	A	GD	Pts
Linfield Rangers	14	9	5	0	37	11	26	32
Crusaders Colts	14	10	1	3	35	20	15	31
Cliftonville Strollers	14	6	3	5	32	24	8	21
Ballyclare Comrades Colts	14	5	4	5	26	23	3	19
Ballymena United III	14	4	5	5	22	23	–1	17
Limavady United Youth	14	5	2	7	27	31	–4	17
Donegal Celtic Youth	14	4	4	6	21	21	0	16
Carrick Rangers Colts	14	0	2	12	12	59	–47	2

IRISH YOUTH LEAGUE SOUTH

	P	W	D	L	F	A	GD	Pts
Glentoran Colts	16	14	2	0	55	15	40	44
Glenavon III	16	11	3	2	50	18	32	36
Dungannon Swifts Colts	16	9	1	6	48	27	21	28
Ballinamallard United III	16	7	3	6	30	32	–2	24
Portadown III	16	6	3	7	32	34	–2	21
Lisburn Distillery III	16	6	3	7	28	36	–8	21
Ards II	16	4	1	11	30	40	–10	13
Newry City Wanderers	16	3	3	10	17	49	–32	12
Armagh City Youth	16	1	3	12	23	62	–39	6

IRISH LEAGUE CHAMPIONSHIP WINNERS

1891 Linfield
1892 Linfield
1893 Linfield
1894 Glentoran
1895 Linfield
1896 Distillery
1897 Glentoran
1898 Linfield
1899 Distillery
1900 Belfast Celtic
1901 Distillery
1902 Linfield
1903 Distillery
1904 Linfield
1905 Glentoran
1906 Cliftonville
Distillery
1907 Linfield
1908 Linfield
1909 Linfield
1910 Cliftonville
1911 Linfield
1912 Glentoran
1913 Glentoran
1914 Linfield
1915 Belfast Celtic
1920 Belfast Celtic
1921 Glentoran
1922 Linfield
1923 Linfield
1924 Queen's Island
1925 Glentoran
1926 Belfast Celtic
1927 Belfast Celtic
1928 Belfast Celtic
1929 Belfast Celtic
1930 Linfield
1931 Glentoran
1932 Linfield
1933 Belfast Celtic
1934 Linfield
1935 Linfield
1936 Belfast Celtic
1937 Belfast Celtic
1938 Belfast Celtic
1939 Belfast Celtic
1940 Belfast Celtic
1948 Belfast Celtic
1949 Linfield
1950 Linfield
1951 Glentoran
1952 Glenavon
1953 Glentoran
1954 Linfield
1955 Linfield
1956 Linfield
1957 Glentoran
1958 Ards
1959 Linfield
1960 Glenavon
1961 Linfield
1962 Linfield
1963 Distillery
1964 Glentoran
1965 Derry City
1966 Linfield
1967 Glentoran
1968 Glentoran
1969 Linfield
1970 Glentoran
1971 Linfield
1972 Glentoran
1973 Crusaders
1974 Coleraine
1975 Linfield
1976 Crusaders
1977 Glentoran
1978 Linfield
1979 Linfield
1980 Linfield
1981 Glentoran
1982 Linfield
1983 Linfield
1984 Linfield
1985 Linfield
1986 Linfield
1987 Linfield
1988 Glentoran
1989 Linfield
1990 Portadown
1991 Portadown
1992 Glentoran
1993 Linfield
1994 Linfield
1995 Crusaders
1996 Portadown
1997 Crusaders
1998 Cliftonville
1999 Glentoran
2000 Linfield
2001 Linfield
2002 Portadown
2003 Glentoran
2004 Linfield
2005 Glentoran

FIRST DIVISION

1996 Coleraine
1997 Ballymena United
1998 Newry Town
1999 Distillery
2000 Omagh Town
2001 Ards
2002 Lisburn Distillery
2003 Dungannon Swifts
2004 Loughgall
2005 Armagh City

SETANTA CUP

GROUP 1

Glentoran 2, Longford Town 1
Longford Town 2, Linfield 1
Linfield 3, Glentoran 2
Longford Town 1, Glentoran 0
Linfield 1, Longford Town 0
Glentoran 2, Linfield 4

	P	W	D	L	F	A	Pts
Linfield	4	3	0	1	9	6	9
Longford Town	4	2	0	2	4	4	6
Glentoran	4	1	0	3	6	9	3

GROUP 2

Shelbourne 3, Portadown 3
Cork City 1, Shelbourne 0
Portadown 1, Cork City 1
Portadown 0, Shelbourne 1
Shelbourne 1, Cork City 0
Cork City 0, Portadown 1

	P	W	D	L	F	A	Pts
Shelbourne	4	2	1	1	5	4	7
Portadown	4	1	2	1	5	5	5
Cork City	4	1	1	2	2	3	4

SETANTA CUP FINAL

(at Tolka Park, Dublin, 21 May 2005)

Shelbourne (0) 0
Linfield (2) 2 *(Ferguson 27, Thompson 37)*

Shelbourne: Williams; Brennan (Moore 58), Hawkins, Rogers, Crawley, Baker (Ryan 25), Byrne S, Crawford (Ndo 58), Cahill, Hoolahan, Byrne J.

Linfield: Mannus; Douglas, O'Kane, Gault, Murphy W, Murphy D, Thompson (Larmour 77), Mouncey (McCann 73), Ferguson, McAreavey, Bailie.
Referee: M. Courtney (Dungannon).

ULSTER CUP WINNERS

1949 Linfield
1950 Larne
1951 Glentoran
1952
1953 Glentoran
1954 Crusaders
1955 Glenavon
1956 Linfield
1957 Linfield
1958 Distillery
1959 Glenavon
1960 Linfield
1961 Ballymena U
1962 Linfield
1963 Crusaders
1964 Linfield
1965 Coleraine
1966 Glentoran
1967 Linfield
1968 Coleraine
1969 Coleraine
1970 Linfield
1971 Linfield
1972 Coleraine
1973 Ards
1974 Linfield
1975 Coleraine
1976 Glentoran
1977 Linfield
1978 Linfield
1979 Linfield
1980 Ballymena U
1981 Glentoran
1982 Glentoran
1983 Glentoran
1984 Linfield
1985 Coleraine
1986 Coleraine
1987 Larne
1988 Glentoran
1989 Glentoran
1990 Portadown
1991 Bangor
1992 Linfield
1993 Crusaders
1994 Bangor
1995 Portadown
1996 Portadown
1997 Coleraine
1998 Ballyclare Comrades
1999 Distillery
2000 *No competition*
2001 *No competition*
2002 *No competition*
2003 Dungannon Swifts *(Confined to First Division clubs)*
2004 *No competition*
2005 *No competition*

NATIONWIDE IRISH CUP 2004–05

FIFTH ROUND

Cliftonville v Banbridge Town	2-3
Armagh City v Dungannon Swifts	1-2
Carrick Rangers v Coleraine	1-5
Larne v East Belfast	3-0
Ballymoney United v Institute	0-4
HW Welders v Tobermore United	2-0
Glenavon v Portadown	0-2
Lisburn Distillery v Ballinamallard United	4-1
Donegal Celtic v Loughgall	1-5
Omagh Town v Crusaders	0-1
Linfield v Limavady United	1-1, 2-1
Lisburn Rangers v Glentoran	0-6
Ards v Ballyclare Comrades	1-1, 1-0
Bangor v Newry City	1-5
(Tie award to Bangor; Newry City field ineligible player.)	
Ballymena United v Coagh United	1-0
Kilmore Rec v Ballynure OB	1-0

SIXTH ROUND

Lisburn Distillery v HW Welders	1-1, 1-2
Dungannon Swifts v Larne	1-2
Glentoran v Linfield	1-1, 0-3
Institute v Ards	1-2
Crusaders v Coleraine	0-1
Loughgall v Banbridge Town	0-0, 2-0
Portadown v Bangor	2-1
Ballymena United v Kilmore Rec	4-1

QUARTER-FINALS

Coleraine v Glentoran	1-2
Ards v Portadown	0-1
Loughgall v Larne	1-1, 0-3
HW Welders v Ballymena United	0-0, 0-4

SEMI-FINALS

Portadown v Glentoran	0-0, 1-0
(at Windsor Park, Belfast)	
Ballymena United v Larne	0-1
(at The Oval, Belfast)	

NATIONWIDE IRISH CUP FINAL 2004–05

(at Windsor Park, 7 May 2005)

Portadown (3) 5 Larne (1) 1

Portadown: Murphy; Feeney (Quinn 80), O'Hara, Clarke, Convery, Kelly, Boyle, Collins, Neill (McCann P 49), Arkins, McCann M (Hamilton 47).
Scorers: Arkins 15, 58, Convery 34, McCann 36, Kelly 48.

Larne: Spackman; Small, Hughes, Curran, Murphy, Bonnar (Parker 52), Ogden, Weir (Crossley 53), Hamlin, Dickson, Rodgers (Tumilty 72).
Scorer: Ogden 3.

Referee: David Malcolm (Bangor).

IRISH CUP FINALS (from 1946–47)

1946–47 Belfast Celtic 1, Glentoran 0
1947–48 Linfield 3, Coleraine 0
1948–49 Derry City 3, Glentoran 1
1949–50 Linfield 2, Distillery 1
1950–51 Glentoran 3, Ballymena U 1
1951–52 Ards 1, Glentoran 0
1952–53 Linfield 5, Coleraine 0
1953–54 Derry City 1, Glentoran 0
1954–55 Dundela 3, Glenavon 0
1955–56 Distillery 1, Glentoran 0
1956–57 Glenavon 2, Derry City 0
1957–58 Ballymena U 2, Linfield 0
1958–59 Glenavon 2, Ballymena U 0
1959–60 Linfield 5, Ards 1
1960–61 Glenavon 5, Linfield 1
1961–62 Linfield 4, Portadown 0
1962–63 Linfield 2, Distillery 1
1963–64 Derry City 2, Glentoran 0
1964–65 Coleraine 2, Glenavon 1
1965–66 Glentoran 2, Linfield 0
1966–67 Crusaders 3, Glentoran 1
1967–68 Crusaders 2, Linfield 0
1968–69 Ards 4, Distillery 2
1969–70 Linfield 2, Ballymena U 1
1970–71 Distillery 3, Derry City
1971–72 Coleraine 2, Portadown 1
1972–73 Glentoran 3, Linfield 2
1973–74 Ards 2, Ballymena U 1
1974–75 Coleraine 1:0:1, Linfield 1:0:0
1975–76 Carrick Rangers 2, Linfield 1
1976–77 Coleraine 4, Linfield 1
1977–78 Linfield 3, Ballymena U 1
1978–79 Cliftonville 3, Portadown 2
1979–80 Linfield 2, Crusaders 0
1980–81 Ballymena U 1, Glenavon 0
1981–82 Linfield 2, Coleraine 1
1982–83 Glentoran 1:2, Linfield 1:1
1983–84 Ballymena U 4, Carrick Rangers 1
1984–85 Glentoran 1:1, Linfield 1:0
1985–86 Glentoran 2, Coleraine 1
1986–87 Glentoran 1, Larne 0
1987–88 Glentoran 1, Glenavon 0
1988–89 Ballymena U 1, Larne 0
1989–90 Glentoran 3, Portadown 0
1990–91 Portadown 2, Glenavon 1
1991–92 Glenavon 2, Linfield 1
1992–93 Bangor 1:1:1, Ards 1:1:0
1993–94 Linfield 2, Bangor 0
1994–95 Linfield 3, Carrick Rangers 1
1995–96 Glentoran 1, Glenavon 0
1996–97 Glenavon 1, Cliftonville 0
1997–98 Glentoran 1, Glenavon 0
1998–99 *Portadown awarded trophy after Cliftonville were eliminated for using an ineligible player in semi-final.*
1999–2000 Glentoran 1, Portadown 0
2000–01 Glentoran 1, Linfield 0
2001–02 Linfield 2, Portadown 1
2002–03 Coleraine 1 Glentoran 0
2003–04 Glentoran 1 Coleraine 0
2004–05 Portadown 5 Larne 1

DAILY MIRROR TROPHY

SEMI-FINALS

Carrick Rangers v Bangor	0-3
(at Dixon Park, Ballyclare, 5 October 2004)	
Glenavon v Brantwood	3-0
(at Taylor's Avenue, Carrickfergus, 12 October 2004)	

DAILY MIRROR TROPHY FINAL

(at Dixon Park, Ballyclare, 2 November 2004)

Bangor 3 Glenavon 1

Bangor: Brown R; Holland J, Harbinson, Strain, Massey, Officer (Johnston 88), Brown R, Martin, Morrow, Verner, Holland B.

Scorers: McAlinden 11 (og), Officer 27, Morrow 43.

Glenavon: McDonald; Reid, Hyndes, McAlinden (McMahon 67), Candlish, Murray, McShane (McAlorum 53), Topley (McCloskey 33), Walsh, Batey, Devine.

Scorer: Devine 37.

Referee: B. Turkington (Belfast).

COUNTY ANTRIM SHIELD

FIRST ROUND

Ballymena United v Kilmore Rec	0-1
Linfield v Malachians	5-0
Glentoran v Glebe Rangers	11-0
Ards v Dundela	2-1
Crusaders v Ballymena United	3-1
Cliftonville v Larne Tech OB	2-1
Lisburn Distillery v Newington YC	2-0
Larne v Bangor	2-3

QUARTER-FINALS

Lisburn Distillery v Kilmore Rec	3-4
Bangor v Linfield	1-3
Crusaders v Ards	3-0
Cliftonville v Glentoran	2-1

SEMI-FINALS

Linfield v Kilmore Rec *(at Seaview, Belfast)*	2-0
Cliftonville v Crusaders *(at The Oval)*	0-1

COUNTY ANTRIM SHIELD FINAL

(at The Oval)

Linfield 2 Crusaders 1 (aet.)

Linfield: Mannus; Bailie, Hunter (King 14), Murphy D■, Picking, McCann, Gault, O'Kane (Mouncey 95), Thompson (Campbell 100), Ferguson.

Scorer: Thompson 37, 96.

Crusaders: Armstrong N; Shaw (Livingstone 88), Coates, Spiers, McBride (Stirling 67), Armstrong D, Munster, Magill, Morrow, Russell, McDowell (Magowan 82).

Scorer: Munster 74.

Referee: A. McCourt (Bangor).

Attendance: 2000.

CIS INSURANCE IRISH LEAGUE CUP

FINAL SECTION TABLES

Section A	P	W	D	L	F	A	Pts
Linfield	6	5	1	0	15	3	16
Ards	6	2	1	3	6	7	7
Crusaders	6	2	1	3	7	10	7
Loughgall	6	1	1	4	4	12	4
Section B	P	W	D	L	F	A	Pts
Cliftonville	6	3	2	1	8	5	11
Dungannon	6	3	2	1	8	6	11
Portadown	6	3	1	2	11	7	10
Limavady	6	0	1	5	6	15	1
Section C	P	W	D	L	F	A	Pts
Lisburn Distillery	6	3	2	1	13	4	11
Ballymena	6	2	3	1	9	7	9
Institute	6	2	1	3	8	10	7
Larne	6	2	0	4	5	14	6
Section D	P	W	D	L	F	A	Pts
Glentoran	6	5	1	0	20	5	16
Coleraine	6	3	1	2	8	7	10
Newry City	6	3	0	3	12	12	9
Omagh T	6	0	0	6	5	21	0

QUARTER-FINALS

Linfield v Dungannon Swifts	3-1
Cliftonville v Ards	2-1
Lisburn Distillery v Coleraine	1-0
Glentoran v Ballymena United	1-0

SEMI-FINALS

Linfield 2 *(Thompson 90, 93)* **Cliftonville 1** *(Scannell 31)* *aet.*
(at The Oval, 19 October 2004).

Glentoran 2 *(Morgan 17, 56)* **Lisburn Distillery 0**
(at Windsor Park, 20 October 2004).

CIS INSURANCE IRISH LEAGUE CUP FINAL

(at Windsor Park)

Glentoran 2 Linfield 1 (aet.)

Glentoran: Morris; Melaugh, Nixon, Leeman, Glendinning, Keegan (McLaughlin 76), Lockhart, Kilmartin (McCann 91), Holmes, Morgan (McGibbon 106), Halliday.

Scorers: Lockhart 5, Morgan 105.

Linfield: Mannus; Douglas, McShane, Bailie, Hunter, Gault, Simpson (King 45), Murphy M (Picking 62), O'Kane (Crawford 90), Larmour, Thompson.

Scorer: Picking 81.

Referee: D. Malcolm (Bangor).

Attendance: 6000.

SUNDAY LIFE TROPHY FOR LEADING GOALSCORERS

Michael Halliday *(Glentoran)*	30
Chris Morgan *(Glentoran)*	28
Peter Thompson *(Linfield)*	25
Darren Armour *(L Distillery)*	23
Mark Dickson *(Larne)*	21
Vinny Arkins *(Portadown)*	20
Kevin Ramsey *(Limavady)*	20
Jody Tolan *(Coleraine)*	18
Darren Lockhart *(Glentoran)*	17
Glenn Ferguson *(Linfield)*	17
Gary Hamilton *(Portadown)*	16
Sean Armstrong *(Coleraine)*	16
Gary Kennedy *(Ards)*	16
Aiden O'Kane *(Linfield)*	15
Paul Brown *(Limavady)*	14
Gary Bownes *(Dungannon Sw)*	14
Vincent Sweeney *(Limavady Utd)*	14
David Larmour *(Linfield)*	13
James Willis *(L Distillery)*	13
Darren Fitzgerald *(Ballymena Utd)*	12
Mark Glendinning *(Glentoran)*	11
Barry Meehan *(Newry City)*	11
Damien Whitehead *(Institute)*	11

FIRST DIVISION

Marty Verner *(Bangor)*	29

ROLL OF HONOUR SEASON 2004-05

Competition	*Winner*	*Runner-up*
Setanta Cup (all Ireland)	Linfield	Shelbourne
Daily Mirror Irish Premier	Glentoran	Linfield
Daily Mirror First Division	Armagh City	Glenavon
Irish League Intermediate Second Division	Tobermore United	Banbridge Town
Irish Youth League (South)	Glentoran Colts	Glenavon III
Irish Youth League (North)	Linfield Rangers	Crusaders Colts
CIS Insurance League Cup	Glentoran	Linfield
Irish League Youth Cup	Dungannon Swifts Colts	Crusaders Colts
Daily Mirror Trophy Final	Bangor	Glenavon
Irish Reserve League	Linfield Swifts	Glentoran II
Nationwide Irish Cup	Portadown	Larne
County Antrim Shield	Linfield	Crusaders
Steel & Sons Cup	Bangor	Glentoran II
County Antrim Junior Shield	H&W Sports	Malachians II
Belfast Telegraph Intermediate Cup	Glenavon	Donegal Celtic
Irish Junior Cup	Hill Street	Ardoyne WMC
Rushmere Shopping Mid Ulster Cup	Glenavon	Loughgall
Village Windows North West Senior Cup	Limavady United	Institute
Harry Cavan Youth Cup	Glentoran Colts	Linfield Rangers
George Wilson Memorial Cup	Glentoran II	Linfield Swifts

CHAMPIONS LEAGUE REVIEW 2004–05

Any fictional account of a Champions League final would scarcely have dreamed up the events of 2005 in Istanbul on 25 May. No team in the last stage of the European Cup has had to retrieve a three-goal deficit, level the scores and go on to win the match albeit on the continuingly unsatisfactory method of penalty kicks. Liverpool achieved this feat against AC Milan.

A goal down in the first minute to Paolo Maldini, two more in a five minute spell just before the interval from Hernan Crespo the Chelsea loanee, talk of damage limitation was a serious half-time consideration for the Anfield contingent.

But in the 54th minute Steven Gerrard reduced the arrears and sparked an incredible five minute revival which produced goals from Vladimir Smicer and Xabi Alonso and turned the game on its head. This combined with a subsequent double reflex save from Jerzy Dudek in the Liverpool goal from Andriy Shevchenko the European Footballer of the Year ensured a penalty shoot-out after extra time.

Here the hyped up Dudek stole the show, more of a whirling Dervish than a dancing Pole but presenting a frightening sight to Milan penalty takers. The ploy succeeded and he was not censured for coming off his line. Who is? Thus Liverpool erased the awful memory of Heysel 20 years earlier.

Liverpool undoubtedly reserved their best performances of the season for the Champions League. They had also held favourites Chelsea at Stamford Bridge in the semi-final and completed the task with a Luis Garcia goal early in the return at Anfield. AC Milan meanwhile had had a tougher time with PSV Eindhoven.

Having taken what appeared to be a commanding 2-0 lead from the home leg, the Italian side were being well beaten 3-0 when they scrambled an injury time goal to win the tie on away goals.

With the second year of streamlining of the Champions League and dispensing with a second group stage in favour of a knock-out system, both Arsenal and Manchester United succeeded in reaching it. But United lost both legs 1-0 to AC Milan and losing 3-1 in Munich to Bayern was too big a hurdle for Arsenal and a Thierry Henry goal insufficent.

Mid-July starts are the accepted for the Champions League of course and while Linfield went out to HJK Helsinki and Rhyl to Skonto Riga, Shelbourne made a useful start against KR Reykjavik, then accounted for Hajduk Split. Rangers came in at the third qualifying stage only to be ousted by CSKA Moscow. Liverpool did better initially against Graz as did Manchester United with Dinamo Bucharest.

Shelbourne found themselves drawn against Deportivo La Coruna and at least held them before conceding three late goals in Spain. Liverpool embarrassed themselves when they lost the Graz home leg, but survived on aggregate.

Celtic kept their best performance for the last group game with a 1-1 draw in Barcelona when they had already packed their bags out of the tournament. However, Chelsea did even better against the Spaniards in the knock-out round though favoured with an own goal in the 2-1 away defeat, then surviving a comeback by Barca when three goals ahead to squeak in 4-2 on the night.

Sadly and frequently there seems to be a match which transcends acceptable behaviour. It happened in Rome where Roma were playing Dynamo Kiev who were leading 1-0 at half-time when Swedish referee Anders Frisk received injury from a missile thrown from the crowd. The game was abandoned and the score remained; Roma having to play their next home games behind closed doors.

Liverpool goalkeeper Jerzy Dudek makes a double save to deny AC Milan's Andriy Shevchenko (right) as Jon Dahl Tomasson closes in. (Empics)

EUROPEAN CUP

EUROPEAN CUP FINALS 1956–1992

Year	Winners	Runners-up	Venue	Attendance	Referee
1956	Real Madrid 4	Reims 3	Paris	38,000	Ellis (E)
1957	Real Madrid 2	Fiorentina 0	Madrid	124,000	Horn (Ho)
1958	Real Madrid 3	AC Milan 2 *(aet)*	Brussels	67,000	Alsteen (Bel)
1959	Real Madrid 2	Reims 0	Stuttgart	80,000	Dutsch (WG)
1960	Real Madrid 7	Eintracht Frankfurt 3	Glasgow	135,000	Mowat (S)
1961	Benfica 3	Barcelona 2	Berne	28,000	Dienst (Sw)
1962	Benfica 5	Real Madrid 3	Amsterdam	65,000	Horn (Ho)
1963	AC Milan 2	Benfica 1	Wembley	45,000	Holland (E)
1964	Internazionale 3	Real Madrid 1	Vienna	74,000	Stoll (A)
1965	Internazionale 1	Benfica 0	Milan	80,000	Dienst (Sw)
1966	Real Madrid 2	Partizan Belgrade 1	Brussels	55,000	Kreitlein (WG)
1967	Celtic 2	Internazionale 1	Lisbon	56,000	Tschenscher (WG)
1968	Manchester U 4	Benfica 1 *(aet)*	Wembley	100,000	Lo Bello (I)
1969	AC Milan 4	Ajax 1	Madrid	50,000	Ortiz (Sp)
1970	Feyenoord 2	Celtic 1 *(aet)*	Milan	50,000	Lo Bello (I)
1971	Ajax 2	Panathinaikos 0	Wembley	90,000	Taylor (E)
1972	Ajax 2	Internazionale 0	Rotterdam	67,000	Helies (F)
1973	Ajax 1	Juventus 0	Belgrade	93,500	Guglovic (Y)
1974	Bayern Munich 1	Atletico Madrid 1	Brussels	49,000	Loraux (Bel)
Replay	Bayern Munich 4	Atletico Madrid 0	Brussels	23,000	Delcourt (Bel)
1975	Bayern Munich 2	Leeds U 0	Paris	50,000	Kitabdjian (F)
1976	Bayern Munich 1	St Etienne 0	Glasgow	54,864	Palotai (H)
1977	Liverpool 3	Moenchengladbach 1	Rome	57,000	Wurtz (F)
1978	Liverpool 1	FC Brugge 0	Wembley	92,000	Corver (Ho)
1979	Nottingham F 1	Malmo 0	Munich	57,500	Linemayr (A)
1980	Nottingham F 1	Hamburg 0	Madrid	50,000	Garrido (P)
1981	Liverpool 1	Real Madrid 0	Paris	48,360	Palotai (H)
1982	Aston Villa 1	Bayern Munich 0	Rotterdam	46,000	Konrath (F)
1983	Hamburg 1	Juventus 0	Athens	80,000	Rainea (R)
1984	Liverpool 1	Roma 1	Rome	69,693	Fredriksson (Se)
	(aet; Liverpool won 4-2 on penalties)				
1985	Juventus 1	Liverpool 0	Brussels	58,000	Daina (Sw)
1986	Steaua Bucharest 0	Barcelona 0	Seville	70,000	Vautrot (F)
	(aet; Steaua won 2-0 on penalties)				
1987	Porto 2	Bayern Munich 1	Vienna	59,000	Ponnet (Bel)
1988	PSV Eindhoven 0	Benfica 0	Stuttgart	70,000	Agnolin (I)
	(aet; PSV won 6-5 on penalties)				
1989	AC Milan 4	Steaua Bucharest 0	Barcelona	97,000	Tritschler (WG)
1990	AC Milan 1	Benfica 0	Vienna	57,500	Kohl (A)
1991	Red Star Belgrade 0	Marseille 0	Bari	56,000	Lanese (I)
	(aet; Red Star won 5-3 on penalties)				
1992	Barcelona 1	Sampdoria 0 *(aet)*	Wembley	70,827	Schmidhuber (G)

UEFA CHAMPIONS LEAGUE FINALS 1993–2005

Year	Winners	Runners-up	Venue	Attendance	Referee
1993	Marseille* 1	AC Milan 0	Munich	64,400	Rothlisberger (Sw)
1994	AC Milan 4	Barcelona 0	Athens	70,000	Don (E)
1995	Ajax 1	AC Milan 0	Vienna	49,730	Craciunescu (Ro)
1996	Juventus 1	Ajax 1	Rome	67,000	Vega (Sp)
	(aet; Juventus won 4-2 on penalties)				
1997	Borussia Dortmund 3	Juventus 1	Munich	59,000	Puhl (H)
1998	Real Madrid 1	Juventus 0	Amsterdam	47,500	Krug (G)
1999	Manchester U 2	Bayern Munich 1	Barcelona	90,000	Collina (I)
2000	Real Madrid 3	Valencia 0	Paris	78,759	Braschi (I)
2001	Bayern Munich 1	Valencia 1	Milan	71,500	Jol (Ho)
	(aet; Bayern Munich won 5-4 on penalties)				
2002	Real Madrid 2	Leverkusen 1	Glasgow	52,000	Meier (Sw)
2003	AC Milan 0	Juventus 0	Manchester	63,215	Merk (G)
	(aet; AC Milan won 3-2 on penalties)				
2004	Porto 3	Monaco 0	Gelsenkirchen	52,000	Nielsen (Den)
2005	Liverpool 3	AC Milan 3	Istanbul	65,000	González (Sp)
	(aet; Liverpool won 3-2 on penalties)				

**Subsequently stripped of title.*

UEFA CHAMPIONS LEAGUE 2004–05

■ *Denotes player sent off.*

FIRST QUALIFYING ROUND FIRST LEG

Tuesday, 13 July 2004

Pobeda (0) 1 *(Gesoski 80)*

Pyunik (3) 3 *(Manucharian 15, 41, Hovhannisian 26)* 1500

Pobeda: Pandev; Kapinkovski, Nacev, Georgiev (Krstevski 71), Zdravevski, Dzokic, Georgioski, Zdraveski (Manevski 46), Dimitrovski D (Dimitrovski 18), Da Silva, Gesoski.
Pyunik: Bete; Hovsepian, Nazarian, Tadevosian, Lombe, Art Mkrtchyan (Balep Ba 77), Aleksanyan■, Ag Mkrtchyan, Pachayan, Hovhannisian (Petrosian 87), Manucharian (Antonian 90).

Siroki (0) 2 *(Tabi 67, Juricic 75)*

Neftchi (0) 1 *(Tagizade 90)* 2500

Siroki: Melher; Kozul, Medvid, Bajkusa, Duricic, Tabi, Silic (Lajtman 60), Abramovic (Coric 83), Rezic, Dujmovic (Juricic 53), Erceg.
Neftchi: Mahammedov; Getman, Sadikhov, Abbasov, Yadullayev (Alakbarov 80), Guliyev E, Rakhmanov (Isiani 85), Rzajev, Gurbonov M, Aslanov (Sadygov 88), Tagizade.

Sliema Wanderers (0) 0

Kaunas (0) 2 *(Zutautas 55, Sanajevas 77)* 445

Sliema Wanderers: Akanji; Laferla, Said, Chetcuti, Anonam, Giglio (Farrugia 86), Turner (Muscat 83), Mamo, Mangion (Sammut 60), Doncic, Miguel Mifsud.
Kaunas: Kurskis; Sanajevas, Zaliukas (Pacevicius 60), Zutautas (Baguzis 73), Kancelskis, Bezykornovas, Petrenko, Papeckys, Barevicius, Velicka (Mozgovoj 86), Mikoliunas.

Wednesday, 14 July 2004

Flora Tallinn (0) 2 *(Zahovaiko 81, Post 90)*

Gorica (1) 4 *(Srebrnic 30, Krsic 73, Rodic 75, Panic 90)* 700

Flora Tallinn: Kaalma; Allas, Jaager, Piiroja, Klavan, Reim, Haavistu, Lindpere, Viikmae, Zahovaiko, Saharov (Post 83).
Gorica: Pirih; Mavric, Kokot, Srebrnic, Sabec, Pus, Panic, Rodic (Burgic 89), Krsic, Zivec (Suler 82), Sturm (Komac 10).

Gomel (0) 0

SK Tirana (0) 2 *(Mukaj 75, Fortuzi 89)* 7500

Gomel: Afanasenko; Shahoyko, Popel, Charapniou, Pankovets, Lukashenko (Danilov 75), Bliznyuk, Razumov, Zinovev (Vusau 46), Karsakov, Khusyainov (Harautsou 46).
SK Tirana: Hidi; Sina, Dabulla, Dede, Bulku, Mukaj (Pinari 90), Agolli (Lici 63), Hajdari, Xhafa (Fortuzi 75), Patushi, Merkoci.

KR Reykjavik (0) 2 *(Sigurgeirsson 47, Olafsson 54)*

Shelbourne (0) 2 *(Moore 83, Sigurdsson 86 (og))* 1238

KR Reykjavik: Finnbogason KF; Thorsteinsson, Sigurdsson, Gylfason, Olafsson, Einarsson, Sigurgeirsson, Podzemsky, Kristjansson (Finnbogason KH 46), Elisabetarson, Gunnlaugsson (Bjarnason 70).
Shelbourne: Williams; Heary, Crawley, Rogers, Harris, Moore (Morgan 85), Cahill, Byrne S, McCarthy (Cawley 76), Byrne J, Hoolihan.

Linfield (0) 0

HJK Helsinki (0) 1 *(Kottila 76)* 2130

Linfield: Mannus; Douglas (O'Kane 75), McShane, Murphy D (McCann 46), Murphy W, Hunter, Larmour, Gault, Crawford (Thompson 66), King, Bailie.
HJK Helsinki: Vilnrotter; Turpeinen (Santala 90), Nylund, Jensen, Aalto, Gronlund, Zeneli (Oravainen 68), Eremenko Jr, Kallio, Savolainen, Kottila.

Serif (1) 2 *(Prigoniuc 32, Kuznetsov 67)*

Jeunesse Esch (0) 0 5300

Serif: Hutan; Dos Santos, Gumeniuk, Prigoniuc, Florescu, Burnadze, Kuznetsov, De Lima (Blanco 54), Barisev (Bychkov 77), Cocis, Lacusta.
Jeunesse Esch: Flick; Heinz, Pellegrino, Schauls, Wagner J, Schaaf, Wagner K-P, Mariani, Cardoni, Braun, Wagner S (Amodio 61).

Skonto Riga (1) 4 *(Miholaps 10, 56, Dedura 65, Visnakovs 78)*

Rhyl (0) 0 1950

Skonto Riga: Piedels; Zakresevskis, Isakovs (Nguimbat 81), Zemlinskis, Blagonadezdins (Blanks 46), Buitkus (Visnakovs 67), Mentesashvili, Miholaps, Semjonovs, Kalnins, Dedura.
Rhyl: Smith; Powell M, Brewerton (Stones 79), Jackson (Keegan 82), Edwards, Wood (Graves 69), Wilson, Limbert, Powell G, Atherton, Adamson.

WIT (3) 5 *(Gochashvili 20, Martsvaladze 32, Digmelashvili 43, Intskirveli 47, Ebanoidze 57)*

HB Torshavn (0) 0 2000

WIT: Mamardashvili; Datunaishvili, Kobiashvili, Intskirveli, Imedashvili, Gvelesiani, Nozadze (Kvaratskhelia 46), Digmelashvili, Merebashvili (Ebanoidze 46), Gochashvili (Kupreishvili 69), Martsvaladze.
HB Torshavn: Rasmussen; Joensen J, Nolsoe, Borg, Fernandez, Leivsson (Joensen P 46), Nielsen, Eliasen, Danielsen (Thorsteinsson 46), Mortensen, Lakjuni (Jespersen 75).

FIRST QUALIFYING ROUND SECOND LEG

Wednesday, 21 July 2004

Gorica (1) 3 *(Kokot 17 (pen), Sturm 50, 52)*

Flora Tallinn (0) 1 *(Zahovaiko 68)* 1138

Gorica: Pirih; Srebrnic, Mavric, Kokot, Krsic, Zivec, Komac (Panic 81), Pus, Ranic (Sabec 51), Sturm, Rodic (Burgic 61).
Flora Tallinn: Kaalma; Allas, Piiroja, Jaager, Reim, Lember (Saviauk 60), Haavistu, Lindpere, Viikmae (Jaager 79), Zahovaiko, Saharov (Kristal 60).

HB Torshavn (0) 3 *(Thorsteinsson 66, Jespersen 69, Eliasen 88)*

WIT (0) 0 752

HB Torshavn: Rasmussen; Joensen J, Leirsso, Borg (Jespersen 46), Nielsen, Eliasen, Danielsen (Nolsoe R 65), Mortensen, Lakjuni, Rubeksen (Thorsteinsson 61), Joensen P.
WIT: Mamardashvili; Datunaishvili, Kobiashvili, Intskirveli, Imedashvili, Martsvaladze■, Nozadze, Digmelashvili, Gvelesiani, Gochashvili (Malichava 89), Ebanoidze (Sakhokia 52).

HJK Helsinki (1) 1 *(Kottila 27)*

Linfield (0) 0 3125

HJK Helsinki: Vilnrotter; Turpeinen, Nylund, Jensen, Aalto, Gronlund, Eremenko Jr (Santala 84), Kallio, Savolainen, Kottila (Makela 69), Oravainen (Zeneli 72).
Linfield: Mannus; Douglas, McShane, Murphy D (McCann 67), Murphy W, Hunter (O'Kane 60), Larmour, Gault, Crawford (Thompson 74), King, Bailie.

Jeunesse Esch (0) 1 *(Cardoni 61)*

Serif (0) 0 1021

Jeunesse Esch: Flick; Heinz (Codello 86), Pellegrino, Schauls (Schaaf 77), Wagner K-P, Sabotic (Wagner S 81), Wagner J, Amodio, Cardoni, Schneider, Braun.
Serif: Hutan; Gumeniuk, Prigoniuc, Tarkhnishvili, Florescu, Burnadze, Blanco (Shiman 59), Kuznetsov, Barisev, Cocis, Lacusta.

Kaunas (2) 4 *(Gedgaudas 28, Sanajevas 43, Mikoliunas 53, Zaliukas 90)*

Sliema Wanderers (0) 1 *(Miguel Mifsud 71)* 3454

Kaunas: Kurskis; Sanajevas, Zaliukas, Kancelskis, Bezykornovas (Ivaskevicius 58), Petrenko, Papeckys, Gedgaudas, Velicka (Zvingilas 62), Mikoliunas (Baguzis 80), Pacevicius.
Sliema Wanderers: Akanji; Laferla, Said, Chetcuti (Lombardi 10), Anonam, Giglio (Mangion 46), Brincat, Doncic, Miguel Mifsud (Grima 89), Sammut, Muscat.

Neftchi (0) 1 *(Guliev E 80)*

Siroki (0) 0 20,000

Neftchi: Mahammedov; Getman, Sadikhov, Abbasov, Guliev E, Alakbarov (Gambarov 60), Rzajev (Yadullayev 83), Gurbonov M, Aslanov (Sadygov 66), Gurbanov G, Tagizade.
Siroki: Melher; Kozul (Coric 75), Medvid, Bajkusa, Duricic, Tabi, Silic (Juricic 85), Abramovic, Dujmovic (Lajtman 62), Erceg, Petrovic.

Pyunik (0) 1 *(Petrosian 77)*

Pobeda (1) 1 *(Dimitrovski D 21)* 4500

Pyunik: Bete; Hovsepian, Lombe, Tadevosian, Art Mkrtchyan (Davitian 90), Nazarian, Pachayan, Ag Mkrtchyan (Grigorian 79), Balep Ba (Petrosian 46), Hovhannisian, Manucharian.
Pobeda: Pandev; Kapinkovski, Nacev, Georgiev, Zdravevski, Dzokic, Dimitrovski, Georgioski, Manevski■, Dimitrovski D, Gesoski.

Rhyl (0) 1 *(Powell G 50)*

Skonto Riga (1) 3 *(Dedura 45, Miholaps 80, 88)* 1812

Rhyl: Smith; Powell M, Brewerton, Jackson (Stones 82), Edwards, Wood (Keegan 64), Wilson, Limbert, Powell G (McGinn 85), Atherton, Adamson.
Skonto Riga: Piedels; Zakresevskis, Isakovs, Zemlinskis, Nguimbat, Mentesashvili (Kipiani 55), Miholaps, Visnakovs, Semjonovs (Blanks 46), Kalnins (Starkovs 69), Dedura.

SK Tirana (0) 0

Gomel (1) 1 *(Bliznuk 38)* 1000

SK Tirana: Hidi; Sina, Dabulla, Dede, Bulku, Mukaj, Agolli, Hajdari, Xhafa, Patushi, Merkoci.
Gomel: Afanasenko; Shahoyko, Popel, Charapniou, Pankovets, Lukashenko, Bliznuk, Razumov, Karsakov, Harautsou, Khusyainov.

Shelbourne (0) 0

KR Reykjavik (0) 0 3674

Shelbourne: Williams; Heary, Crawley, Rogers, Harris, Morgan, Cahill, Byrne S, Moore (McCarthy 82), Byrne J (Rowe 90), Hoolihan (Cawley 87).
KR Reykjavik: Finnbogason KF; Sigurdsson, Gylfason, Davidsson, Olafsson, Einarsson (Magnusson 62), Podzemsky, Finnbogason KH, Kristjansson (Bjarnason 53), Elisabetarson, Gunnlaugsson (Benediktsson 53).

SECOND QUALIFYING ROUND FIRST LEG

Tuesday, 27 July 2004

Gorica (0) 1 *(Rodic 57)*

FC Copenhagen (1) 2 *(Santos 44, Moller 77)* 1214

Gorica: Pirih; Srebrnic, Mavric, Kokot, Zivec, Komac, Krsic, Pus, Ranic (Sabec 72), Rodic, Sturm (Burgic 72).
FC Copenhagen: Kihlstedt; Jacobsen, Svensson, Saarinen (Thomassen 46), Santos (Jonsson 89), Silberbauer, Tobiasen, Traore (Bergvold 21), Norregaard, Bech, Moller.

HJK Helsinki (0) 0

Maccabi Tel Aviv (0) 0 4035

HJK Helsinki: Vilnrotter; Nylund, Jensen, Aalto, Gronlund (Makela 64), Zeneli (Sorsa 82), De Gregorio (Santala 86), Kallio, Savolainen, Kottila, Oravainen.
Maccabi Tel Aviv: Strauber; Strool, Abu-Siam, Addo, Bruno Reis, Mesika, Pantsil, Cohen T, Oved (Dego 71), Giovanini, Biton (Mishaelof 90).

Neftchi (0) 0

CSKA Moscow (0) 0 25,000

Neftchi: Mahammedov; Getman, Sadikhov, Abbasov, Guliev E, Tebloiev (Gambarov 56), Rzayev (Rakhmanov 81), Gurbonov M, Sadygov (Aslanov 84), Gurbanov G, Tagizade.
CSKA Moscow: Akinfeev; Semberas, Semak (Kirichenko 46) (Shershun 89), Berezutski A, Gusev, Olic, Odiah, Krasic (Laizans 33), Zhirkov, Jarosik, Rahimic.

Pyunik (0) 1 *(Nazarian 49)*

Shakhtjor Donetsk (1) 3 *(Marica 30, 74, Aghahowa 86)* 3524

Pyunik: Bete; Hovsepian, Lombe, Tadevosian, Art Mkrtchyan (Petrosian 86), Aleksanyan (Grigorian 61), Pachayan, Ag Mkrtchyan, Nazarian, Hovhannisian, Manucharian.
Shakhtjor Donetsk: Shutkov; Tymoschuk (Joao Batista 60), Lalatovic, Aghahowa, Rat, Florea (Bakharev 73), Hubschman, Duljaj, Stoican, Marica, Vukic (Vorobei 60).

SK Tirana (0) 2 *(Mukaj 58, 68)*

Ferencvaros (1) 3 *(Huszti 41 (pen), 90, Hajdari 88 (og))* 3000

SK Tirana: Hidi; Sina, Dabulla, Dede, Bulku, Mukaj (Pinari 87), Hajdari, Lici, Xhafa (Fortuzi 65), Patushi, Merkoci (Halili 50).
Ferencvaros: Szucs; Balog, Lipcsei, Gyepes, Zavadszky, Kapic (Zovath 78), Rosa, Huszti, Gera (Nogradi 86), Penksa (Leandro 72), Sasu.

WIT (1) 2 *(Kobiashvili 13, Adamia 51)*

Wisla (4) 8 *(Frankowski 4, 5, 26, 51, Gorawski 24, Zurawski 58, 67, 76)* 2000

WIT: Mamardashvili; Imedashvili, Kobiashvili, Intskirveli, Datunaishvili, Gvelesiani, Digmelashvili, Nozadze, Gochashvili (Kvaratskhelia 66), Adamia (Merebashvili 75), Ebanoidze (Sakhokia 32).
Wisla: Majdan; Baszczynski, Glowacki, Klos, Mijailovic (Stolarczyk 46), Gorawski (Szymkowiak 46), Cantoro, Kukielka, Zienczuk, Zurawski, Frankowski (Kuzba 71).

Wednesday, 28 July 2004

Apoel (1) 2 *(Alexandrou N 6, Charalambides 47)*

Sparta Prague (0) 2 *(Pacanda 82, Sivok 89)* 11,006

Apoel: Morphis; Stojanoski, Okkarides, Germanos, Vakouftsis (Makridis 73), Alexandrou N, Georgiou, Satsias, Daskalakis, Charalambides (Neophytou 88), Michael.
Sparta Prague: Blazek; Hochmeister, Pergl, Poborsky, Meduna (Jun 55), Michalik, Vorisek (Zelenka 61), Cech (Sivok 82), Kovac, Pacanda, Koubsky.

Djurgaarden (0) 0

Kaunas (0) 0 6679

Djurgaarden: Tourray; Concha, Storm, Kuivasto, Arneng (Bapupa-Ngabu 67), Hysen, Den Ouden, Johansson A, Karlsson, Johannesson M (Barsom 85), Amoah (Dovicovic 70).
Kaunas: Kurskis; Sanajevas, Zaliukas (Ivaskevicius 67), Kancelskis, Bezykornovas, Petrenko (Baguzis 46), Papeckys, Gedgaudas, Velicka (Beniusis 78), Mikoliunas, Pacevicius.

FC Brugge (0) 2 *(Balaban 71, 88)*

Lokomotiv Plovdiv (0) 0 12,767

FC Brugge: Butina; Simons, Van der Heyden, Clement, Verheyen (Victor Simoes 90), Englebert (Stoica 81), Ceh, Balaban, Spilar, Lange (Saeternes 75), Maertens.
Lokomotiv Plovdiv: Kolev I; Kotev, Tunchev, Ivanov, Petrov, Iliev, Krizmanic (Michailov 58), Dimitrov, Kamburov, Jayeoba (Kostadinov 88), Stoynev (Yancevski 67).

Hajduk Split (1) 3 *(Blatnjak 18, 85, Suto 48)*

Shelbourne (1) 2 *(Fitzpatrick 5, Moore 89)* 9780

Hajduk Split: Balic; Suto, Cacic (Damjanovic 78), Turkovic (Munoz 61), Vejic, Blatnjak, Carevic, Racki (Mesic 70), Pralija, Neretljak, Rukavina.
Shelbourne: Williams; Heary, Crawley, Rogers, Harris, Moore, Cahill, Byrne S, Fitzpatrick, Byrne J (Crawford 78), Hoolihan (McCarthy 87).

Rosenborg (1) 2 *(Johnsen F 24, George 85)*
Serif (1) 1 *(Cocis 34)* 10,909
Rosenborg: Johnsen E; Hoftun, Winsnes (Olsen 78), Basma, Strand (George 66), Berg, Johnsen F, Riseth, Storflor, Stensaas, Brattbakk (Solli 66).
Serif: Hutan; Gumeniuk, Prigoniuc, Tarkhnishvili, Florescu (Dos Santos 88), Burnadze, Blanco (Shiman 86), Kuznetsov (Goginashvili 78), Barisev, Cocis, Lacusta.

Skonto Riga (0) 1 *(Kalnins 67)*
Trabzonspor (0) 1 *(Mehmet Y 86)* 5045
Skonto Riga: Piedels; Isakovs, Zemlinskis, Nguimbat, Blagonadezdins, Buitkus, Mentesashvili (Blanks 61), Miholaps, Semjonovs, Kalnins, Dedura.
Trabzonspor: Petkovic; Emrah, D'haene, Seyhan, Hasan (Ibrahima 82), Celaleddin, Huseyin, Adem K, Gokdeniz, Ahinful (Mehmet Y 60), Fatih.

Young Boys (1) 2 *(Chapuisat 6, Eugster 65)*
Red Star Belgrade (0) 2 *(Zigic 79, 88)* 10,350
Young Boys: Wolfli; Eugster, Knez, Valmeri Souza, Chapuisat, Urdaneta (Melunovic 81), Carreno, Magnin (De Napoli 76), Haberli (Coubageat 86), Rochat, Aziawonou.
Red Star Belgrade: Disljenkovic; Djordjevic, Popov, Dudic M, Miladinovic, Basta, Jankovic (Bisevac 89), Perovic (Tintor 69), Stancic■, Pantelic (Milovanovic 62), Zigic.

Zilina (0) 0
Dinamo Bucharest (0) 1 *(Danciulescu 89)* 4268
Zilina: Mucha; Dolezaj, Vomacka, Durica (Minarcik 80), Strba, Labant, Sestak, Barcik, Bartos (Kiska 83), Cisovsky, Sninsky (Pecalka 88).
Dinamo Bucharest: Munteanu; Ciobotariu, Alistar, Petre, Niculescu, Danciulescu, Iordache, Grigorie (Semeghin 59), Tames (Burca 82), Margaritescu, Balan (Irimia 65).

SECOND QUALIFYING ROUND SECOND LEG

Wednesday, 4 August 2004

CSKA Moscow (0) 2 *(Gusev 68, Silva De Souza 72)*
Neftchi (0) 0 10,000
CSKA Moscow: Akinfeev; Semberas, Semak (Silva De Souza 46), Berezutski A, Gusev, Olic, Zhirkov, Jarosik (Odiah 87), Aldonin (Laizans 54), Berezutski V, Rahimic.
Neftchi: Mahammedov; Getman, Sadikhov, Abbasov, Guliev E, Tebloyev (Yadullayev 76), Rzayev (Gambarov 73), Sadygov, Gurbonov M, Gurbanov G, Tagizade.

Dinamo Bucharest (1) 1 *(Danciulescu 19)*
Zilina (0) 0 11,000
Dinamo Bucharest: Munteanu■; Semeghin (Hayeu 42), Burca, Alistar, Petre, Niculescu (Ciobotariu 83), Danciulescu, Irimia, Iordache, Tames (Grigorie 67), Margaritescu.
Zilina: Trabalik; Dolezaj, Vomacka, Durica (Minarcik 46), Strba, Labant, Sestak, Barcik, Bartos, Cisovsky (Bazik 62), Sninsky (Simcek 69).

FC Copenhagen (0) 0
Gorica (3) 5 *(Rodic 28, 52, Sturm 39, 77, Srebrnic 45)* 13,601
FC Copenhagen: Kihlstedt; Jacobsen, Svensson, Saarinen, Santos (Jonsson 63), Silberbauer (Van Heerden 69), Tobiasen, Norregaard, Bech (Fredgaard 55), Bergvold, Moller.
Gorica: Pirih; Mavric, Kokot, Zivec, Srebrnic, Krsic (Sabec 69), Pus, Komac, Rodic (Panic 90), Ranic, Sturm (Burgic 85).

Ferencvaros (0) 0
SK Tirana (1) 1 *(Mukaj 13)* 5015
Ferencvaros: Szucs; Botis, Lipcsei, Gyepes, Rosa (Zovath 77), Kapic, Huszti, Zavadszky, Vukmir, Sasu (Sowunmi 85), Leandro (Penksa 79).
SK Tirana: Hidi; Dabulla, Dede, Bulku, Halili (Fortuzi 81), Hajdari, Lici, Xhafa, Patushi, Merkoci (Behari 77), Mukaj.

Kaunas (0) 0
Djurgaarden (1) 2 *(Johansson A 25, Barsom 68)* 5500
Kaunas: Kurskis; Sanajevas, Zaliukas (Mozgovoj 46), Zutautas, Kancelskis, Beniusis (Zvingilas 46) (Ivaskevicius 75), Bezykornovas, Petrenko, Papeckys, Gedgaudas, Pacevicius.
Djurgaarden: Concha; Stenman, Storm, Kuivasto, Arneng, Hysen (Amoah 66), Den Ouden (Bapupa-Ngabu 72), Johansson A, Tourray, Johannesson M, Barsom (Makondele 88).

Lokomotiv Plovdiv (0) 0
FC Brugge (2) 4 *(Balaban 14, 44, Saeternes 74, Ceh 84)* 7300
Lokomotiv Plovdiv: Kolev I; Kotev (Kolev II 50), Tunchev■, Kostadinov, Petrov (Hristev 26), Iliev, Krizmanic, Dimitrov, Kamburov, Stoynev, Jayeoba (Vandev 67).
FC Brugge: Butina; Simons, Van der Heyden, Clement, Verheyen, Englebert, Ceh, Balaban (Victor Simoes 76), Spilar, Lange (Saeternes 67), Maertens (Rozehnal 35).

Maccabi Tel Aviv (0) 1 *(Cohen L 88)*
HJK Helsinki (0) 0 5740
Maccabi Tel Aviv: Strauber; Strool, Abu-Siam, Addo, Bruno Reis, Mesika, Pantsil, Cohen T, Oved (Dego 60), Giovanini, Biton (Cohen L 64).
HJK Helsinki: Vilnrotter; Nylund (Peltola 41), Jensen, Aalto, Gronlund, Zeneli, De Gregorio (Makela 89), Kallio, Savolainen, Kottila, Oravainen (Santala 76).

Red Star Belgrade (1) 3 *(Miladinovic 39, Dudic M 49, Zigic 69)*
Young Boys (0) 0 35,000
Red Star Belgrade: Disljenkovic; Djordjevic, Bisevac, Miladinovic, Dudic M, Lukovic (Popov 89), Basta, Jankovic, Milovanovic (Perovic 67), Zigic (Tintor 83), Pantelic.
Young Boys: Wolfli; Eugster (Maksimovic 67), Knez, Valmeri Souza (De Napoli 18), Chapuisat, Urdaneta, Carreno, Magnin, Haberli (Melunovic 58), Rochat, Aziawonou.

Serif (0) 0
Rosenborg (2) 2 *(Berg 36, Brattbakk 40)* 9000
Serif: Hutan; Gumeniuk■, Prigoniuc, Florescu, Burnadze, Blanco (Shiman 60), Kuznetsov (Alexeev 53), Barisev (Yaraslauski 69), Cocis, Lacusta, Pascenco.
Rosenborg: Johnsen E; Hoftun, Winsnes (Olsen 82), Basma, Strand (George 76), Berg, Johnsen F, Riseth, Solli, Dorsin, Brattbakk.

Shakhtjor Donetsk (1) 1 *(Hubschman 31)*
Pyunik (0) 0 17,623
Shakhtjor Donetsk: Shutkov; Lalatovic, Hubschman, Florea (Aghahowa 74), Srna, Duljaj, Vukic, Bakharev, Bielik (Vorobei 71), Joao Batista, Brandao (Marica 73).
Pyunik: Bete; Hovsepian, Lombe, Tadevosian, Art Mkrtchyan, Aleksanyan, Pachayan, Ag Mkrtchyan, Nazarian, Hovhannisian (Petrosian 84), Manucharian.

Shelbourne (0) 2 *(Rogers 78, Moore 90)*
Hajduk Split (0) 0 8317
Shelbourne: Williams; Heary, Crawley, Rogers, Harris, Moore, Cahill, Byrne S, Fitzpatrick (McCarthy 72), Byrne J (Ndo 90), Hoolihan (Crawford 86).
Hajduk Split: Kale; Suto (Damjanovic 82), Vejic, Blatnjak, Carevic, Racki (Dragicevic 56), Pralija, Zilic, Filekovic, Neretljak, Rukavina (Mesic 80).

Sparta Prague (1) 2 *(Poborsky 31, Pacanda 55)*
Apoel (0) 1 *(Charalambides 52)* 14,408
Sparta Prague: Blazek; Sivok, Poborsky, Michalik (Vorisek 64), Cech, Kovac, Pacanda (Meduna 87), Petras, Jun (Rezek 72), Homola, Koubsky.
Apoel: Morphis; Stojanoski, Okkarides, Vakouftsis, Alexandrou N, Georgiou, Satsias, Daskalakis, Charalambides, Elia (Makridis 46), Michael (Neophytou 46).

Trabzonspor (0) 3 *(Ibrahima 57, Mehmet Y 65, Fatih 83)*
Skonto Riga (0) 0 12,060
Trabzonspor: Petkovic; Emrah, D'haene, Seyhan (Tayfun 69), Adem K, Ibrahima, Celaleddin, Huseyin, Gokdeniz, Mehmet Y (Ahinful 89), Fatih (Bayraktar 89).
Skonto Riga: Piedels; Isakovs, Zemlinskis, Nguimbat, Blagonadezdins, Buitkus, Mentesashvili (Visnakovs 79), Miholaps (Pereplyotkin 85), Semjonovs, Kalnins (Blanks 79), Dedura.

Wisla (2) 3 *(Kuzba 23, Omeonu 35, Gorawski 63)*
WIT (0) 0 4800
Wisla: Piekutowski; Mysiak, Kowalczyk, Glowacki, Stolarczyk, Gorawski (Fechner 71), Szymkowiak (Kwiek 57), Kukielka, Ekwueme, Omeonu, Kuzba.
WIT: Bediashvili; Datunaishvili, Kobiashvili, Intskirveli, Kvakhadze, Imedashvili (Kupreishvili 67), Digmelashvili, Nozadze (Ebanoidze 64), Gochashvili, Gvelesiani (Malichava 76), Sakhokia.

THIRD QUALIFYING ROUND FIRST LEG

Tuesday, 10 August 2004

Benfica (1) 1 *(Zahovic 13)*
Anderlecht (0) 0 62,077
Benfica: Quesnel; Miguel, Argel, Ricardo Rocha, Paulo Almeida, Petit, Joao Pereira, Dos Santos, Simao Sabrosa, Sokota (Karadas 72), Zahovic (Fernando Aguiar 60).
Anderlecht: Zitka; Hasi, Deschacht, Dindane, Kompany, Zewlakow (Vanden Borre 83), Lovre, Mpenza M (Iachtchouk 77), Baseggio, Wilhelmsson, Traore.

CSKA Moscow (1) 2 *(Silva De Souza 4, Jarosik 46)*
Rangers (1) 1 *(Novo 37)* 19,000
CSKA Moscow: Akinfeev; Odiah, Zhirkov, Berezutski V (Semak 46), Semberas, Berezutski A, Gusev (Aldonin 76), Rahimic, Silva De Souza (Dadu 70), Olic, Jarosik.
Rangers: Klos; Ross, Khizanishvili, Lovenkrands (Thompson 82), Rae, Boumsong, Vignal, Ricksen, Arveladze, Novo, Prso.

Dynamo Kiev (1) 1 *(Verpakovskis 21)*
Trabzonspor (1) 2 *(Gokdeniz 34, Ibrahima 65)* 16,863
Dynamo Kiev: Shovkovskyi; Nesmachni, Fedorov, Gusin (Rodolfo 54), Diogo Rincon, Gavrancic, Verpakovskis (Cernat 65), Belkevich, Leko, Shatskikh (Nanni 64), Gusev.
Trabzonspor: Petkovic; Emrah, D'haene, Tayfun, Kocak, Huseyin, Hasan, Celaleddin (Thijs 51), Gokdeniz, Ibrahima (Ahinful 69), Fatih.

Graz (0) 0
Liverpool (1) 2 *(Gerrard 23, 79)* 14,617
Graz: Schranz; Tokic, Ehmann, Ramusch, Standfest, Muratovic, Skoro (Bazina 62), Amerhauser (Dollinger 85), Pogatetz, Aufhauser (Sick 73), Kollmann.
Liverpool: Dudek; Josemi, Riise, Hamann, Carragher, Hyypia, Finnan (Potter 85), Gerrard (Warnock 79), Baros (Diao 73), Cisse, Kewell.

Juventus (0) 2 *(Trezeguet 50, Emerson 59)*
Djurgaarden (1) 2 *(Johansson A 45, Hysen 49)* 26,146
Juventus: Buffon; Blasi, Tacchinardi (Olivera 52), Montero, Zambrotta, Legrottaglie, Thuram (Birindelli 82), Emerson, Miccoli, Del Piero (Zalayeta 79), Trezeguet.
Djurgaarden: Tourray; Concha, Stenman (Bapupa-Ngabu 82), Storm, Karlsson, Kuivasto, Arneng, Hysen (Larsen 90), Johannesson M, Johansson A, Barsom (Dovicovic 68).

PAOK Salonika (0) 1 *(Yasemakis 50)*
Maccabi Tel Aviv (2) 2 *(Addo 12, Mesika 42)* 20,655
PAOK Salonika: Atmatzidis; Foucini, Karadimos, Vokolos, Udeze, Koutsis (Louka 67), Engomitis, Maladenis (Skarmoutsos 58), Yasemakis, Hagan (Spasic 46), Salpigidis.
Maccabi Tel Aviv: Strauber; Strool, Abu-Siam, Addo (Moosa 77), Bruno Reis, Mesika (Biton 90), Cohen L, Pantsil, Mishaelof, Cohen T (Dego 44), Giovanini.
result changed to 0-3 by UEFA.

Wednesday, 11 August 2004

Basle (1) 1 *(Huggel 25)*
Internazionale (1) 1 *(Adriano 19)* 29,500
Basle: Zuberbuhler; Huggel, Chipperfield, Gimenez (Carignano 69), Yakin M, Cantaluppi, Kleber, Delgado (Petric 60), Degen P, Smiljanic, Rossi.
Internazionale: Toldo; Cordoba, Materazzi, Zanetti J, Stankovic, Ze Maria, Cambiasso (Emre B 76), Veron, Favalli, Adriano, Recoba (Ventola 63).

Dinamo Bucharest (1) 1 *(Danciulescu 9)*
Manchester United (1) 2 *(Giggs 38, Alistar 72 (og))* 50,000
Dinamo Bucharest: Gaev; Ciobotariu (Galamaz 30), Balan (Baltoi 79), Semeghin, Alistar, Iordache, Margaritescu (Goian 52), Tames, Niculescu, Danciulescu, Petre.
Manchester United: Howard; Neville G, Fortune, Keane, O'Shea, Silvestre, Fletcher (Miller 87), Djemba-Djemba, Smith, Scholes (Forlan 90), Giggs (Neville P 81).

Ferencvaros (1) 1 *(Vagner 26)*
Sparta Prague (0) 0 8165
Ferencvaros: Szucs; Vukmir, Lipcsei, Gyepes, Balog, Leandro (Tozser 60), Kapic, Huszti, Rosa, Zavadszky (Penksa 77), Vagner (Bajevski 66).
Sparta Prague: Blazek; Sivok, Zelenka (Simak 71), Poborsky, Michalik (Rezek 84), Cech, Kovac, Pacanda, Petras, Jun (Meduna 57), Homola.

Gorica (0) 0
Monaco (0) 3 *(Kallon 9, 82, Chevanton 77)* 3066
Gorica: Pirih; Kokot, Mavric, Srebrnic, Komac, Krsic, Pus, Zivec (Sabec 65), Ranic, Sturm (Burgic 81), Rodic.
Monaco: Roma; Evra■, Givet, Modesto, Zikos, Adebayor (Perez 56), Squillaci, Maicon, Chevanton (Camara 90), Bernardi (Farnerud 79), Kallon.

Leverkusen (1) 5 *(Franca 11, 67, 88, Juan 74, Berbatov 82)*
Banik Ostrava (0) 0 19,500
Leverkusen: Butt; Ramelow, Roque Junior, Juan (Callsen Bracker 86), Nowotny, Franca, Ponte (Balitsch 62), Babic, Berbatov, Freier (Krzynowek 64), Schneider.
Banik Ostrava: Konig; Latal, Pospech, Kotrys, Dvornik (Velkoborsky 71), Bystron (Licka 83), Cizek, Besta, Zubek, Matusovic (Papadopoulos 76), Heinz.

Red Star Belgrade (2) 3 *(Dudic M 20, Jankovic 39, Pantelic 59)*
PSV Eindhoven (1) 2 *(Park 6, De Jong 65)* 44,288
Red Star Belgrade: Disljenkovic; Stancic, Lukovic, Miladinovic, Dudic M, Bisevac, Jankovic (Stojanovic 90), Pantelic (Krivokapic 77), Perovic (Tintor 89), Zigic, Basta.
PSV Eindhoven: Gomes; Bogelund (Cocu 46), Alex, Bouma, Lee, Ooijer, Van Bommel, De Jong, Park, Vennegoor of Hesselink, Beasley.

Rosenborg (2) 2 *(Brattbakk 1, Solli 8)*
Maccabi Haifa (1) 1 *(Roso 45)* 18,482
Rosenborg: Johnsen E; Hoftun, Winsnes, Basma, Strand (Storflor 69), Berg, Johnsen F, Riseth, Solli (George 87), Brattbakk (Braaten 80), Dorsin.
Maccabi Haifa: Davidovich; Benado, Badir, Goncalves, Bokoli, Colautti, Tal, Roso (Keinan 90), Grayev (Harazi 78), Gazal, Uzan.

Shakhtjor Donetsk (1) 4 *(Aghahowa 15, Marica 70, Vorobei 77, Brandao 90)*
FC Brugge (0) 1 *(Balaban 50)* 25,093
Shakhtjor Donetsk: Lastuvka; Stoican, Rat, Vukic (Duljaj 78), Marica (Brandao 86), Vorobei, Aghahowa (Srna 78), Tymoschuk, Matuzalem, Lewandowski, Barcauan.
FC Brugge: Butina; Simons, Rozehnal, Van der Heyden, Clement, Verheyen (Saeternes 80), Englebert, Ceh (Stoica 80), Balaban, Spilar, Lange (Victor Simoes 36).

Shelbourne (0) 0

La Coruna (0) 0 23,320

Shelbourne: Williams; Heary, Crawley, Moore, Rogers, Harris, Byrne J, Cahill, Fitzpatrick (Ndo 62), Byrne S, Hoolihan.
La Coruna: Molina (Munua 41); Manuel Pablo, Romero, Jorge Andrade, Cesar, Mauro Silva, Pandiani, Sergio (Duscher 67), Valeron, Victor, Luque (Munitis 80).

Wisla (0) 0

Real Madrid (0) 2 *(Morientes 72, 90)* 10,000

Wisla: Majdan; Baszczynski, Klos, Glowacki, Mijailovic, Uche (Gorawski 63), Szymkowiak, Zienczuk (Kukielka 82), Cantoro, Zurawski, Frankowski (Kuzba 76).
Real Madrid: Casillas; Michel Salgado, Roberto Carlos, Samuel, Helguera, Pavon (Celades 85), Beckham, Figo, Raul, Ronaldo (Morientes 68), Zidane (Guti 68).

THIRD QUALIFYING ROUND SECOND LEG

Tuesday, 24 August 2004

Anderlecht (1) 3 *(Mpenza M 34, 59, Jestrovic 73 (pen))*

Benfica (0) 0 20,107

Anderlecht: Zitka; Hasi, Deschacht, Dindane (Seol 90), Kompany, Zewlakow, Baseggio, Jestrovic (Iachtchouk 80), Mpenza M (Vanden Borre 90), Wilhelmsson, Traore.
Benfica: Quim; Argel■, Miguel, Sokota, Paulo Almeida (Ricardo Rocha 76), Petit, Carlitos (Geovanni 60), Da Silva, Simao Sabrosa, Dos Santos, Manuel Fernandes (Zahovic 66).

Internazionale (2) 4 *(Adriano 1, 52, Stankovic 12, Recoba 59)*

Basle (0) 1 *(Sterjovski 49)* 50,506

Internazionale: Toldo; Cordoba, Stankovic, Zanetti J, Materazzi, Favalli, Ze Maria (Cambiasso 80), Davids, Recoba (Cruz 66), Adriano (Vieri 85), Veron.
Basle: Zuberbuhler; Huggel, Sterjovski, Chipperfield (Delgado 66), Gimenez (Carignano 85), Yakin M, Cantaluppi, Kleber, Degen P, Smiljanic, Rossi (Petric 58).

La Coruna (0) 3 *(Victor 59, 65, Pandiani 88)*

Shelbourne (0) 0 20,224

La Coruna: Molina; Manuel Pablo (Scaloni 69), Romero, Victor, Cesar, Jorge Andrade, Mauro Silva (Duscher 46), Sergio, Valeron, Pandiani, Luque (Munitis 76).
Shelbourne: Williams; Heary, Crawley, Rogers, Harris, Moore■, Cahill, Byrne S, Ndo, Byrne J, Hoolihan (Crawford 69).

Liverpool (0) 0

Graz (0) 1 *(Tokic 55)* 42,350

Liverpool: Dudek; Carragher, Riise, Diao, Henchoz, Hyypia, Potter, Gerrard, Baros (Hamann 90), Cisse (Sinama-Pongolle 75), Kewell (Warnock 59).
Graz: Schranz; Standfest, Majstrovic (Dollinger 78), Sick, Tokic, Pogatetz, Plassnegger (Muratovic 69), Aufhauser, Bazina, Kollmann, Amerhauser.

Maccabi Haifa (2) 2 *(Badir 31, Bokoli 38)*

Rosenborg (0) 3 *(Brattbakk 90, Braaten 94, Berg 120)* 26,000

Maccabi Haifa: Davidovich; Benado, Badir (Zandberg 98), Goncalves, Bokoli (Gazal 72), Colautti (Keinan 47), Tal, Roso, Grayev■, Katan, Uzan.
Rosenborg: Johnsen E; Hoftun, Winsnes (Braaten 46), Basma (Storflor 81), Strand, Berg, Johnsen F, Riseth, Solli, Brattbakk, Dorsin (Stensaas 63).
aet.

Monaco (3) 6 *(Chevanton 18, Bernardi 32, El Fakiri 42, Kallon 47, Farnerud 66, Adebayor 84 (pen))*

Gorica (0) 0 9839

Monaco: Roma; Modesto, Perez, Bernardi (Oshadogan 57), Givet, El Fakiri, Maicon, Adebayor, Squillaci (Farnerud 46), Chevanton (Camara 57), Kallon.
Gorica: Pirih; Kokot, Suler■, Srebrnic, Komac (Panic 61), Sabec, Pus, Zivec, Ranic, Sturm (Nikolic 46), Rodic (Krsic 75).

Wednesday, 25 August 2004

Banik Ostrava (1) 2 *(Papadopoulos 38, Zurek 82)*

Leverkusen (0) 1 *(Berbatov 76)* 5396

Banik Ostrava: Raska; Bystron, Besta, Sloncik (Cizek 46), Zavadil (Zurek 71), Papadopoulos (Varadi 78), Hoffmann, Pospech, Matusovic, Licka, Velkoborsky.
Leverkusen: Butt; Ramelow (Balitsch 77), Roque Junior, Juan, Placente, Lucic, Ponte (Freier 60), Krzynowek, Berbatov, Franca (Voronin 72), Schneider.

Djurgaarden (1) 1 *(Arneng 19)*

Juventus (2) 4 *(Del Piero 10, Trezeguet 35, 67, Nedved 54)* 32,058

Djurgaarden: Tourray; Concha, Stenman (Makondele 77), Storm, Kuivasto, Arneng, Hysen, Johansson A, Karlsson, Johannesson M (Dovicovic 61), Bapupa-Ngabu (Barsom 46).
Juventus: Buffon; Thuram, Blasi, Montero, Zambrotta, Olivera, Birindelli, Emerson, Trezeguet, Del Piero (Zalayeta 81), Nedved (Kapo 87).

FC Brugge (2) 2 *(Ceh 14, 35 (pen))*

Shakhtjor Donetsk (1) 2 *(Vukic 6, 52)* 15,900

FC Brugge: Butina; Simons, Stoica, Cornelis, Van der Heyden, Clement, Verheyen, Victor Simoes (Blondel 85), Balaban, Ceh, Spilar (Lange 65).
Shakhtjor Donetsk: Lastuvka; Stoican■, Lewandowski, Rat, Tymoschuk, Matuzalem (Joao Batista 65), Vorobei, Marica (Brandao 71), Vukic, Aghahowa (Duljaj 46), Hubschman.

Maccabi Tel Aviv (1) 1 *(Cohen L 8)*

PAOK Salonika (0) 0 8450

Maccabi Tel Aviv: Strauber; Strool, Abu-Siam, Addo (Dego 80), Bruno Reis, Mesika, Pantsil, Mishaelof (Moosa 76), Cohen T, Giovanini, Cohen L (Biton 85).
PAOK Salonika: Atmatzidis; Karadimos, Chasiotis (Amafule 74), Udeze, Foucini, Markos (Spasic 46), Engomitis (Vagelis 46), Koutsis, Theodoridis, Skarmoutsos, Salpigidis.

Manchester United (0) 3 *(Smith 47, 50, Bellion 70)*

Dinamo Bucharest (0) 0 61,041

Manchester United: Howard; Neville G (Neville P 65), Spector, O'Shea, Eagles, Silvestre, Fletcher, Djemba-Djemba, Smith (Bellion 64), Kleberson, Ronaldo (Richardson 64).
Dinamo Bucharest: Munteanu; Irimia, Semeghin, Naidin, Galamaz, Iordache, Petre (Balan 67), Margaritescu, Niculescu (Serban 80), Danciulescu, Grigorie (Pacurar 46).

PSV Eindhoven (2) 5 *(Van Bommel 9 (pen), 56, Beasley 32, De Jong 57, Vennegoor of Hesselink 80)*

Red Star Belgrade (0) 0 29,794

PSV Eindhoven: Zoetebier; Bogelund, Alex, Ooijer (Farfan 73), Lee, Van Bommel, Vogel (Bouma 65), De Jong, Park, Vennegoor of Hesselink, Beasley (Leandro 60).
Red Star Belgrade: Disljenkovic; Lukovic (Milovanovic 46), Miladinovic, Dudic M, Bisevac■, Jankovic, Pantelic, Perovic (Tintor 76), Stancic, Popov, Basta (Krivokapic 86).

Rangers (0) 1 *(Thompson 87)*

CSKA Moscow (0) 1 *(Silva De Souza 60)* 49,010

Rangers: Klos; Ricksen, Moore, Boumsong, Vignal, Lovenkrands (Thompson 64), Mladenovic (Andrews 81), Hughes, Arveladze, Novo, Prso.
CSKA Moscow: Akinfeev; Semberas, Ignashevich, Berezutski A, Olic (Semak 76), Silva De Souza, Odiah, Zhirkov, Jarosik, Aldonin, Rahimic.

Real Madrid (2) 3 *(Ronaldo 3, 31, Pavon 85)*

Wisla (0) 1 *(Gorawski 89)* 67,500

Real Madrid: Casillas; Michel Salgado, Roberto Carlos, Samuel, Helguera, Pavon, Beckham, Figo (Solari 81), Zidane, Ronaldo (Morientes 65), Raul (Guti 65).
Wisla: Majdan; Baszczynski, Glowacki, Klos, Mijailovic (Stolarczyk 46), Cantoro, Kukielka (Kwiek 85), Zienczuk, Gorawski, Zurawski, Frankowski (Kuzba 59).

Sparta Prague (1) 2 *(Zelenka 45, Homola 114)*
Ferencvaros (0) 0 18,010
Sparta Prague: Blazek; Pergl, Sivok, Zelenka (Baranek 94), Poborsky, Cech, Pacanda, Petras (Michalik 29), Jun, Homola, Koubsky (Vorisek 64).
Ferencvaros: Szucs; Vukmir, Gyepes (Kiss 68), Botis, Rosa, Kapic (Zovath 90), Huszti, Leandro, Balog, Penksa, Vagner (Bajevski 57).
aet.

Trabzonspor (0) 0
Dynamo Kiev (2) 2 *(Gavrancic 6, Diogo Rincon 28)* 15,081
Trabzonspor: Petkovic; Emrah, Tayfun, D'haene, Kocak, Hasan (Ibrahima 30) (Yavuz 46), Huseyin, Thijs, Lee (Ahinful 63), Gokdeniz, Fatih.
Dynamo Kiev: Shovkovskyi; Rodolfo■, Leko, Peev (Gusev 62), Sablic, Diogo Rincon (Kleber 66), Shatskikh (Gusin 51), Ghioane, Verpakovskis, El Kaddouri, Gavrancic.

GROUP STAGE

GROUP A

Wednesday, 15 September 2004

La Coruna (0) 0
Olympiakos (0) 0 31,000
La Coruna: Molina; Manuel Pablo, Romero, Cesar, Pandiani, Sergio, Munitis (Hector 84), Scaloni, Jorge Andrade, Luque (Fran 70), Valeron.
Olympiakos: Nikopolidis; Kafes, Venetidis, Pantos (Kostoulas 88), Anatolakis, Schurrer, Giovanni (Mavrogenidis 77), Stoltidis, Georgatos (Georgiadis 86), Rivaldo, Okkas.

Liverpool (1) 2 *(Cisse 22, Baros 84)*
Monaco (0) 0 33,517
Liverpool: Dudek; Josemi, Riise, Finnan, Carragher, Hyypia, Xabi Alonso, Gerrard, Cisse (Baros 70), Luis Garcia (Biscan 87), Kewell (Warnock 77).
Monaco: Roma; Maicon, Evra (Camara 46), Zikos, Squilliaci, Rodriguez, Givet (El Fakiri 80), Perez (Juan 89), Kallon, Adebayor, Farnerud.

Tuesday, 28 September 2004

Monaco (2) 2 *(Kallon 5, Saviola 10)*
La Coruna (0) 0 13,673
Monaco: Roma; Evra (Modesto 85), Maicon, Squillaci, Kallon, Saviola, Zikos (Perez 58), Farnerud, Rodriguez, Givet, Adebayor (Chevanton 78).
La Coruna: Molina; Manuel Pablo, Jorge Andrade, Duscher, Pandiani (Luque 56), Capdevila, Sergio (Scaloni 46), Fran (Munitis 63), Pablo Amo, Victor, Valeron.

Olympiakos (1) 1 *(Stoltidis 17)*
Liverpool (0) 0 31,300
Olympiakos: Nikopolidis; Pantos■, Kafes, Anatolakis, Schurrer, Mavrogenidis (Venetidis 72), Stoltidis, Rivaldo, Georgatos (Vallas 85), Okkas, Giovanni (Georgiadis 72).
Liverpool: Dudek; Josemi (Cisse 74), Riise, Hamann (Diao 82), Carragher, Hyypia, Finnan, Xabi Alonso, Baros, Luis Garcia, Warnock (Kewell 46).

Tuesday, 19 October 2004

Liverpool (0) 0
La Coruna (0) 0 40,236
Liverpool: Kirkland; Josemi, Traore, Hamann, Carragher, Hyypia, Luis Garcia (Sinama-Pongolle 84), Xabi Alonso, Baros, Cisse (Finnan 76), Riise (Kewell 65).
La Coruna: Molina; Manuel Pablo, Capdevila, Mauro Silva (Scaloni 59), Cesar, Jorge Andrade, Duscher, Victor, Pandiani (Romero 82), Valeron (Fran 86), Luque.

Monaco (2) 2 *(Saviola 3, Chevanton 10)*
Olympiakos (0) 1 *(Okkas 60)* 16,624
Monaco: Roma; Zikos, Evra, Maicon, Squillaci, Rodriguez, Bernardi (Farnerud 79), Kallon, Saviola (Plasil 74), Chevanton (Ruso 53), Adebayor.
Olympiakos: Nikopolidis; Kafes (Castillo 77), Venetidis, Giovanni (Georgiadis 58), Schurrer, Stoltidis, Mavrogenidis, Georgatos (Maric 46), Rivaldo, Okkas, Anatolakis.

Wednesday, 3 November 2004

La Coruna (0) 0
Liverpool (1) 1 *(Jorge Andrade 14 (og))* 32,000
La Coruna: Molina; Hector (Scaloni 24), Romero, Duscher, Cesar (Pablo Amo 46), Jorge Andrade, Sergio, Victor, Pandiani (Diego Tristan 60), Valeron, Luque.
Liverpool: Kirkland; Josemi, Traore, Hamann, Carragher, Hyypia, Luis Garcia (Xabi Alonso 90), Biscan, Baros (Sinama-Pongolle 85), Kewell (Finnan 58), Riise.

Olympiakos (0) 1 *(Schurrer 84)*
Monaco (0) 0 33,500
Olympiakos: Nikopolidis; Kafes, Mavrogenidis (Georgatos 70), Djordjevic (Castillo 65), Giovanni (Maric 65), Okkas, Pantos, Anatolakis, Stoltidis, Schurrer, Rivaldo.
Monaco: Roma; Rodriguez, Evra, Givet, Squillaci, Plasil, Bernardi (Ruso 81), Kallon (Farnerud 61), Saviola, Adebayor (Chevanton 73), Zikos.

Tuesday, 23 November 2004

Monaco (0) 1 *(Saviola 54)*
Liverpool (0) 0 18,500
Monaco: Roma; Maicon, Evra, Zikos, Squillaci, Givet, Farnerud (Modesto 79), Nonda, Saviola (Adebayor 75, Chevanton (Perez 68), Plasil.
Liverpool: Kirkland; Finnan, Traore (Kewell 60), Hamann, Carragher, Hyypia, Biscan, Gerrard, Mellor, Luis Garcia (Josemi 5) (Warnock 65), Riise.

Olympiakos (0) 1 *(Djordjevic 68)*
La Coruna (0) 0 33,000
Olympiakos: Nikopolidis; Anatolakis, Schurrer, Pantos, Venetidis, Kafes (Georgatos 86), Stoltidis, Djordjevic, Okkas (Georgiadis 57), Giovanni, Rivaldo (Maric 86).
La Coruna: Molina; Manuel Pablo, Romero, Pablo Amo, Cesar, Fran (Changui 86), Duscher (Pandiani 72), Scaloni (Mauro Silva 79), Valeron, Luque, Munitis.

Wednesday, 8 December 2004

La Coruna (0) 0
Monaco (3) 5 *(Chevanton 21, Givet 35, Saviola 38, Maicon 54, Adebayor 75)* 12,000
La Coruna: Munua; Scaloni, Andrade, Capdevila, Pablo Amo, Hector, Duscher (Changui 80), Fran (Valeron 62), Victor (Luque 62), Pandiani, Munitis.
Monaco: Roma; Evra (Perez 60), Modesto, Maicon, Squillaci, Givet, Bernardi, Zikos, Kallon, Saviola (Adebayor 69), Chevanton (Farnerud 82).

Liverpool (0) 3 *(Sinama-Pongolle 47, Mellor 81, Gerrard 86)*
Olympiakos (1) 1 *(Rivaldo 26)* 42,045
Liverpool: Kirkland; Finnan (Josemi 85), Traore (Sinama-Pongolle 46), Gerrard, Carragher, Hyypia, Nunez, Xabi Alonso, Baros (Mellor 78), Kewell, Riise.
Olympiakos: Nikopolidis; Pantos, Anatolakis, Schurrer, Venetidis (Maric 84), Georgiadis (Rezic 70), Kafes, Stoltidis, Djordjevic, Rivaldo, Giovanini (Okkas 87).

Group A Final Table	*P*	*W*	*D*	*L*	*F*	*A*	*Pts*
Monaco	6	4	0	2	10	4	12
Liverpool	6	3	1	2	6	3	10
Olympiakos	6	3	1	2	5	5	10
La Coruna	6	0	2	4	0	9	2

GROUP B

Wednesday, 15 September 2004

Leverkusen (1) 3 *(Krzynowek 39, Franca 50, Berbatov 55)*

Real Madrid (0) 0 22,500

Leverkusen: Butt; Schneider, Krzynowek, Roque Junior, Juan, Placente, Freier (Bierofka 83), Ponte (Balitsch 80), Franca (Babic 69), Berbatov, Ramelow.
Real Madrid: Casillas; Michel Salgado, Roberto Carlos, Helguera, Samuel, Pavon, Figo (Celades 58), Beckham, Raul, Ronaldo (Solari 58), Zidane (Morientes 46).

Roma (0) 0

Dynamo Kiev (0) 1 *(Gavrancic 29)* 30,000

Roma: Pelizzoli; Panucci, Cufre, De Rossi, Ferrari, Mexes■, Mancini, Dacourt, Totti, Montella, Aquilani.
Dynamo Kiev: Shovkovskyi; Sablic, Gavrancic, Leko, Diogo Rincon, Ghioane, Gusev, El Kaddouri, Yussuf, Kleber, Verpakovskis.
abandoned at half-time; injury to referee Frisk.

Tuesday, 28 September 2004

Dynamo Kiev (1) 4 *(Diogo Rincon 30, 67, Cernat 74, 90)*

Leverkusen (0) 2 *(Voronin 58, Nowotny 66)* 82,893

Dynamo Kiev: Shovkovskyi; Sablic, Leko (Cernat 71), Rodolfo, Gavrancic, Yussuf, Diogo Rincon, Ghioane (Gusev 55), El Kaddouri, Verpakovskis (Shatskikh 60), Kleber.
Leverkusen: Butt; Juan, Krzynowek, Freier (Jones 77), Placente (Babic 79), Nowotny, Ponte, Schneider, Berbatov, Franca (Voronin■ 53), Ramelow.

Real Madrid (1) 4 *(Raul 38, 71, Figo 53 (pen), Roberto Carlos 79)*

Roma (2) 2 *(De Rossi 3, Cassano 21)* 60,000

Real Madrid: Casillas; Michel Salgado, Roberto Carlos, Helguera, Samuel, Celades (Guti 64), Figo, Beckham, Raul (Pavon 82), Ronaldo (Raul Bravo 84), Zidane.
Roma: Pelizzoli; Mancini, Dellas, De Rossi (Mido 75), Candela (Sartor 60), Cufre, Panucci, Dacourt, Cassano, Totti, Perrotta.

Tuesday, 19 October 2004

Leverkusen (0) 3 *(Roque Junior 48, Krzynowek 59, Franca 90)*

Roma (1) 1 *(Berbatov 26 (og))* 22,500

Leverkusen: Butt; Placente, Krzynowek, Roque Junior, Juan, Nowotny, Ponte (Balitsch 90), Jones (Freier 67), Berbatov, Schneider, Ramelow (Franca 46).
Roma: Zotti; Perrotta (Mido 73), Panucci■, De Rossi■, Mancini (Sartor 67), Cufre, Ferrari, Cassano, Montella (Aquilani 50), Totti, Scurto.

Real Madrid (0) 1 *(Owen 35)*

Dynamo Kiev (0) 0 45,000

Real Madrid: Casillas; Michel Salgado, Roberto Carlos, Pavon, Helguera, Guti, Figo (Solari 29), Owen (Celades 66), Raul, Ronaldo (Morientes 81), Zidane.
Dynamo Kiev: Shovkovskyi; Ghioane (Peev 87), El Kaddouri, Yussuf, Rodolfo, Diogo Rincon (Belkevich 75), Shatskikh, Gusev (Cernat 64), Kleber, Sablic, Gavrancic.

Wednesday, 3 November 2004

Dynamo Kiev (2) 2 *(Yussuf 13, Verpakovskis 23)*

Real Madrid (2) 2 *(Raul 37, Figo 44 (pen))* 78,000

Dynamo Kiev: Shovkovskyi; Yussuf, El Kaddouri (Nesmachni 65), Rodolfo, Ghioane, Gusev (Leko 85), Sablic, Gavrancic, Kleber, Diogo Rincon, Verpakovskis (Cernat 75).
Real Madrid: Casillas; Michel Salgado, Roberto Carlos, Pavon, Helguera, Guti, Owen (Celades 59), Zidane, Ronaldo (Morientes 87), Raul, Figo (Solari 90).

Roma (0) 1 *(Montella 90)*

Leverkusen (0) 1 *(Berbatov 82)*

Roma: Zotti; Cufre, D'Agostino (Mido 63), Mancini, Dellas, Mexes, Sartor (Chivu 63), Aquilani, Montella (Corvia 90), Totti, De Martino.
Leverkusen: Butt; Ramelow, Roque Junior, Juan (Nowotny 49), Placente, Ponte (Callsen-Bracker 90), Balitsch, Schneider (Freier 86), Berbatov, Babic, Krzynowek.
behind closed doors.

Tuesday, 23 November 2004

Dynamo Kiev (0) 2 *(Dellas 73 (og), Shatskikh 82)*

Roma (0) 0 40,000

Dynamo Kiev: Shovkovskyi; Ghioane, Gavrancic, El Kaddouri, Sablic, Gusin, Gusev (Leko 65), Yussuf, Diogo Rincon, Verpakovskis (Shatskikh 77), Kleber.
Roma: Pelizzoli; Scurto■, Dellas, Ferrari, Sartor (Cufre 78), Aquilani, Perrotta, Candela, Mido (D'Agostino 54), Cassano, Corvia.

Real Madrid (0) 1 *(Raul 69)*

Leverkusen (1) 1 *(Berbatov 36)* 65,000

Real Madrid: Casillas; Michel Salgado, Roberto Carlos, Samuel, Helguera, Guti, Beckham (Morientes 53), Zidane, Ronaldo, Raul, Figo.
Leverkusen: Butt; Roque Junior, Juan, Nowotny, Placente, Krzynowek (Freier 75), Babic, Schneider, Ramelow, Berbatov, Voronin (Balitsch 82).

Wednesday, 8 December 2004

Leverkusen (0) 3 *(Juan 51, Voronin 77, Babic 86)*

Dynamo Kiev (0) 0 22,500

Leverkusen: Butt; Roque Junior, Juan, Nowotny, Ponte, Berbatov, Freier (Bierofka 82), Voronin, Babic, Schneider, Ramelow.
Dynamo Kiev: Shovkovskyi; Rodolfo, Kleber, Sablic, Gusin (Fedorov 62), Diogo Rincon, Ghioane, Gusev (Cernat 75), Verpakovskis (Shatskikh 67), El Kaddouri, Gavrancic.

Roma (0) 0

Real Madrid (1) 3 *(Ronaldo 9, Figo 61 (pen), 82)*

Roma: Pelizzoli; Mexes, Ferrari, Dellas, Cufre, Perrotta (De Martino 82), Aquilani, Candela, Mancini, Delvecchio, Corvia.
Real Madrid: Casillas; Michel Salgado, Carlos Roberto, Guti, Helguera, Samuel, Beckham, Zidane (Celades 85), Ronaldo (Owen 84), Raul, Figo (Pavon 82).
behind closed doors.

Group B Final Table	P	W	D	L	F	A	Pts
Leverkusen	6	3	2	1	13	7	11
Real Madrid	6	3	2	1	11	8	11
Dynamo Kiev	6	3	1	2	11	8	10
Roma	6	0	1	5	4	16	1

GROUP C

Wednesday, 15 September 2004

Ajax (0) 0

Juventus (1) 1 *(Nedved 42)* 49,375

Ajax: Stekelenburg; Grygera (Escude 76), Maxwell, Sneijder (De Mul 68), Heitinga, De Jong, Obodai (Anastasiou 72), Van der Vaart, Sonck, Mitea, Pienaar.
Juventus: Buffon; Birindelli (Pessotto 66), Zambrotta, Emerson, Thuram, Cannavaro, Camoranesi, Blasi, Del Piero (Appiah 77), Ibrahimovic, Nedved (Olivera 66).

Maccabi Tel Aviv (0) 0

Bayern Munich (0) 1 *(Makaay 64 (pen))* 25,000

Maccabi Tel Aviv: Strauber; Pantsil, Nagar, Mishaelof (Zitoni 61), Strool, Giovanini, Bruno Reis (Dego 83), Cohen T, Addo, Mesika, Cohen L (Mbamba 73).
Bayern Munich: Kahn; Salihamidzic, Rau, Frings, Linke, Lucio, Deisler (Schweinsteiger 46), Hargreaves (Gorlitz 82), Makaay, Ballack (Kovac 90), Ze Roberto.

Tuesday, 28 September 2004

Bayern Munich (2) 4 *(Makaay 28, 44, 51 (pen), Ze Roberto 55)*

Ajax (0) 0 50,000

Bayern Munich: Kahn; Salihamidzic, Linke, Lucio, Kuffour, Frings (Hashemian 80), Hargreaves (Jeremies 80), Pizarro (Deisler 59), Makaay, Ballack, Ze Roberto.
Ajax: Lobont; Heitinga (Escude 63), Grygera, Maxwell, Galasek, Rosales (De Ridder 69), Obodai, De Jong (Mitea 52), Van der Vaart, Sneijder, Sonck.

Juventus (1) 1 *(Camoranesi 37)*

Maccabi Tel Aviv (0) 0 6494

Juventus: Buffon; Zambrotta, Zebina, Tacchinardi, Emerson, Tudor, Camoranesi, Thuram, Ibrahimovic (Olivera 79), Trezeguet, Nedved.
Maccabi Tel Aviv: Strauber; Strool, Mishaelof (Mbamba 76), Bruno Reis, Mesika, Pantsil, Addo, Cohen T, Nagar, Giovanini, Biton (Bounfeld 69).

Tuesday, 19 October 2004

Ajax (3) 3 *(Sonck 4, De Jong 21, Van der Vaart 33)*

Maccabi Tel Aviv (0) 0 49,500

Ajax: Lobont; Trabelsi, Heitinga, Obodai, Maxwell, Mitea (Boukhari 60), Sneijder, De Jong, Pienaar, Sonck (De Ridder 75), Van der Vaart (Aborah 71).
Maccabi Tel Aviv: Strauber; Strool, Cohen T, Mbamba (Mesika 46), Mishaelof (Zitoni 46), Pantsil, Addo, Bruno Reis, Nagar, Giovanini, Cohen L (Bounfeld 85).

Juventus (0) 1 *(Nedved 75)*

Bayern Munich (0) 0 18,089

Juventus: Buffon; Zambrotta, Blasi, Emerson, Cannavaro, Thuram, Camoranesi, Ibrahimovic, Del Piero (Zalayeta 60), Nedved, Zebina.
Bayern Munich: Kahn; Sagnol, Lucio, Kuffour (Hashemian 80), Salihamidzic, Linke, Schweinsteiger, Frings (Demichelis 86), Ballack, Ze Roberto, Makaay.

Wednesday, 3 November 2004

Bayern Munich (0) 0

Juventus (0) 1 *(Del Piero 90)* 59,000

Bayern Munich: Kahn; Sagnol (Gorlitz 46) (Scholl 69), Lucio, Salihamidzic (Guerrero 90), Kovac, Schweinsteiger, Pizarro, Frings, Ballack, Makaay, Hargreaves.
Juventus: Buffon; Zambrotta, Blasi, Thuram, Cannavaro, Camoranesi, Pessotto, Emerson, Ibrahimovic, Del Piero, Nedved.

Maccabi Tel Aviv (0) 2 *(Dego 49, 57)*

Ajax (0) 1 *(De Ridder 87)* 35,000

Maccabi Tel Aviv: Strauber; Strool (Bruno Reis 71), Abo Siam, Moosa, Mishaelof, Cohen L (Pantsil 77), Addo (Zitoni 86), Cohen T, Giovanini, Dego, Mesika.
Ajax: Stekelenburg; Trabelsi, Heitinga, Obodai (Sonck 57), Grygera, Mitea (Boukhari 54), Rosales, Pienaar (De Ridder 70), De Jong, Van der Vaart, Sneijder.

Tuesday, 23 November 2004

Bayern Munich (3) 5 *(Pizarro 12, Salihamidzic 37, Frings 44, Makaay 71, 80)*

Maccabi Tel Aviv (0) 1 *(Dego 55 (pen))* 45,000

Bayern Munich: Kahn; Sagnol (Deisler 46), Lucio, Kovac, Frings, Pizarro, Salihamidzic, Schweinsteiger (Scholl 27), Ballack, Makaay, Hargreaves (Kuffour 35).
Maccabi Tel Aviv: Strauber; Strool, Abo Siam, Mishaelof, Pantsil, Giovanini, Cohen L (Biton 72), Mesika (Bruno Reis 46), Dego, Cohen T, Addo (Mbamba 78).

Juventus (1) 1 *(Zalayeta 14)*

Ajax (0) 0 6885

Juventus: Buffon; Birindelli (Cannavaro 85), Zambrotta, Emerson, Thuram, Montero, Camoranesi (Olivera 70), Tacchinardi, Zalayeta, Ibrahimovic, Nedved.
Ajax: Vonk; Trabelsi, Maxwell, Galasek, Grygera, Escude, De Jong (Sneijder 70), Van der Vaart, Babel (Anastasiou 79), Rosales, Boukhari (Mitea 59).

Wednesday, 8 December 2004

Ajax (1) 2 *(Galasek 39, Mitea 64)*

Bayern Munich (1) 2 *(Makaay 9, Ballack 78)* 50,019

Ajax: Vonk; Trabelsi, Escude, De Jong, Grygera (Obodai 75), Maxwell, Galasek, Sneijder (Van der Vaart 75), Rosales, Mitea (Boukhari 72), Babel.
Bayern Munich: Kahn; Kuffour, Kovac, Demichelis, Rau, Frings (Ze Roberto 46), Pizarro (Guerrero 46), Deisler, Ballack, Makaay, Hargreaves.

Maccabi Tel Aviv (1) 1 *(Dego 30 (pen))*

Juventus (0) 1 *(Del Piero 71)* 18,500

Maccabi Tel Aviv: Nir; Strool, Abo Siam, Moosa, Mishaelov (Bruno Reis 75), Giovanini, Zitoni (Mesika 82), Cohen L, Cohen T, Dego, Mbamba (Addo 75).
Juventus: Chimenti; Montero, Pessotto (Zambrotta 69), Zebina, Cannavaro, Tacchinardi, Nedved, Blasi (Appiah 46), Kapo, Del Piero (Ibrahimovic 74), Zalayeta.

Group C Final Table	*P*	*W*	*D*	*L*	*F*	*A*	*Pts*
Juventus	6	5	1	0	6	1	16
Bayern Munich	6	3	1	2	12	5	10
Ajax	6	1	1	4	6	10	4
Maccabi Tel Aviv	6	1	1	4	4	12	4

GROUP D

Wednesday, 15 September 2004

Fenerbahce (1) 1 *(Van Hooijdonk 16)*

Sparta Prague (0) 0 41,000

Fenerbahce: Rustu; Deniz, Umit O, Marco Aurelio, Servet, Fabio Luciano, Serhat■, Fabiano, Van Hooijdonk, Alex (Serkan 90), Tuncay (Onder 78).
Sparta Prague: Blazek; Pergl, Cech (Meduna 75), Zelenka (Simak 46), Kovac, Homola, Baranek (Jun 60), Vorisek, Pacanda, Sivok, Urbanek.

Lyon (2) 2 *(Cris 35, Frau 44)*

Manchester United (0) 2 *(Van Nistelrooy 56, 61)* 36,000

Lyon: Coupet; Reveillere, Abidal, Essien, Cacapa, Cris (Nilmar 64), Wiltord (Clement 87), Juninho Pernambucano, Govou (Benarfa 75), Frau, Malouda.
Manchester United: Howard; O'Shea (Neville P 83), Heinze, Brown, Keane, Silvestre, Ronaldo, Djemba-Djemba, Van Nistelrooy (Smith 80), Scholes, Giggs.

Tuesday, 28 September 2004

Manchester United (3) 6 *(Giggs 7, Rooney 17, 28, 54, Van Nistelrooy 78, Bellion 81)*

Fenerbahce (0) 2 *(Nobre 47, Tuncay 60)* 67,128

Manchester United: Carroll; Neville G, Heinze (Neville P 81), Ferdinand, Kleberson, Silvestre, Bellion, Djemba-Djemba, Van Nistelrooy (Miller 81), Rooney, Giggs (Fletcher 62).
Fenerbahce: Rustu; Deniz, Fatih (Serhat 61), Nobre, Fabio Luciano, Umit O, Marco Aurelio, Serkan, Van Hooijdonk, Alex, Tuncay.

Sparta Prague (1) 1 *(Jun 7)*

Lyon (1) 2 *(Essien 25, Wiltord 58)* 12,050

Sparta Prague: Blazek; Pergl, Urbanek, Kovac, Sivok, Zelenka (Baranek 82), Cech (Vorisek 46), Pacanda (Strihavka 61), Jun, Homola, Poborsky.
Lyon: Coupet; Cris, Diarra, Malouda, Cacapa, Govou (Nilmar 85), Berthod, Wiltord (Frau 73), Essien, Juninho Pernambucano (Diatta 82), Reveillere.

Tuesday, 19 October 2004

Fenerbahce (0) 1 *(Nobre 68)*

Lyon (0) 3 *(Juninho Pernambucano 55, Cris 66, Frau 87)* 42,000

Fenerbahce: Rustu; Luciano, Servet, Umit O, Tuncay, Nobre, Marco Aurelio, Deniz (Mehmet 46), Serkan, Van Hooijdonk, Alex.
Lyon: Coupet; Abidal, Cris, Essien, Cacapa, Govou (Frau 85), Diarra, Juninho Pernambucano (Diatta 79), Wiltord (Nilmar 90), Malouda, Reveillere.

Sparta Prague (0) 0
Manchester United (0) 0 20,564
Sparta Prague: Blazek; Pergl, Petras (Cech 81), Sivok, Homola, Kovac, Poborsky, Zelenka (Simak 81), Jun (Meduna 75), Vorisek, Urbanek.
Manchester United: Carroll; Neville G, Heinze, Brown, O'Shea, Silvestre, Miller, Scholes, Van Nistelrooy, Rooney (Saha 78), Giggs (Ronaldo 78).

Wednesday, 3 November 2004

Lyon (1) 4 *(Essien 22, Malouda 53, Nilmar 89, 90)*
Fenerbahce (1) 2 *(Selcuk 14, Tuncay 73)* 36,000
Lyon: Coupet (Puydebois 73); Diatta, Cris, Essien, Govou (Nilmar 70), Abidal, Diarra, Juninho Pernambucano, Frau (Benarfa 83), Malouda, Reveillere.
Fenerbahce: Rustu; Fabio Luciano, Servet■, Deniz, Umit O, Serkan, Selcuk, Marco Aurelio, Serhat (Mehmet 86), Alex (Van Hooijdonk 89), Tuncay (Fabiano 90).

Manchester United (2) 4 *(Van Nistelrooy 14, 25 (pen), 60, 90)*
Sparta Prague (0) 1 *(Zelenka 53)* 66,706
Manchester United: Carroll; Neville G, Heinze, Ferdinand, Keane, Brown, Ronaldo (Kleberson 68), Miller, Van Nistelrooy, Rooney, Scholes (Neville P 68).
Sparta Prague: Blazek; Pergl, Petras, Zelenka, Homola, Kovak, Sivok, Vorisek (Meduna 71), Urbanek (Simak 81), Jun (Pacanda 80), Poborsky■.

Tuesday, 23 November 2004

Manchester United (1) 2 *(Neville G 19, Van Nistelrooy 53)*
Lyon (1) 1 *(Diarra 40)* 66,398
Manchester United: Carroll; Neville G (Brown 46), Heinze, Ferdinand, Keane (Fortune 90), Silvestre, Ronaldo, Scholes, Van Nistelrooy (Fletcher 70), Rooney, Smith.
Lyon: Puydebois; Reveillere, Diatta, Cris, Berthod, Diarra, Essien, Juninho Pernambucano, Govou (Wiltord 60), Frau (Bergougnoux 72), Nilmar (Malouda 72).

Sparta Prague (0) 0
Fenerbahce (1) 1 *(Kovac 20 (og))* 11,507
Sparta Prague: Blazek; Labant (Meduna 68), Petras, Rezek (Pacanda 46), Sivok, Vorisek, Urbanek, Kovac, Simak (Baranek 76), Zelenka, Jun.
Fenerbahce: Rustu (Volkan 46); Fabio Luciano, Umit O (Fabiano 86), Onder, Kemal, Selcuk, Marco Aurelio, Mehmet, Tuncay, Nobre, Alex.

Wednesday, 8 December 2004

Fenerbahce (0) 3 *(Tuncay 47, 62, 90)*
Manchester United (0) 0 35,000
Fenerbahce: Rustu; Onder, Servet, Fabio Luciano, Umit O, Serkan (Mehmet 72), Marco Aurelio, Selcuk, Tuncay (Fabiano 90), Nobre (Serhat 90), Alex.
Manchester United: Howard; Neville P, Fortune, Brown (Pique 63), Miller (Eagles 77), O'Shea, Fletcher, Djemba-Djemba, Bellion, Richardson (Spector 69), Ronaldo.

Lyon (2) 5 *(Essien 7, Nilmar 19, 51, Idangar 83, Bergougnoux 90)*
Sparta Prague (0) 0 38,571
Lyon: Puydebois; Reveillere, Bertod (Truchet 81), Clement, Diatta, Essien, Diarra (Gomez 58), Malouda (Idangar 67), Frau, Nilmar, Bergougnoux.
Sparta Prague: Blazek; Petras, Labant (Urbanek 28), Vorisek, Kovac, Homola, Poborsky, Sivok, Zelenka, Simak (Meduna 63), Jun (Pacanda 79).

Group D Final Table	*P*	*W*	*D*	*L*	*F*	*A*	*Pts*
Lyon	6	4	1	1	17	8	13
Manchester United	6	3	2	1	14	9	11
Fenerbahce	6	3	0	3	10	13	9
Sparta Prague	6	0	1	5	2	13	1

GROUP E

Tuesday, 14 September 2004

Arsenal (1) 1 *(Alex 42 (og))*
PSV Eindhoven (0) 0 34,068
Arsenal: Lehmann; Lauren, Cole, Vieira, Toure, Cygan, Reyes (Edu 78), Silva, Henry, Bergkamp, Pires.
PSV Eindhoven: Zoetebier; Ooijer, Lee, Park, Alex, Bouma, Cocu (De Jong 83), Van Bommel, Sibon (Vennegoor of Hesselink 66), Beasley (Farfan 59), Vogel.

Panathinaikos (1) 2 *(Gonzalez 43, 79)*
Rosenborg (0) 1 *(Johnsen F 90)* 13,204
Panathinaikos: Galinovic; Morris, Munch, Goumas, Gonzalez, Papadopoulos, Kirgiakos, Konstantinidis (Andric 57), Basinas, Mitu (Maric 72), Skacel (Konstantinou 88).
Rosenborg: Johnsen E; Hoftun, Winsnes, Basma (Russell 23), Strand (Braaten 74), Berg, Johnsen F, Riseth, Solli (Brattbakk 85), Storflor, Dorsin.

Wednesday, 29 September 2004

PSV Eindhoven (0) 1 *(Vennegoor of Hesselink 80)*
Panathinaikos (0) 0 26,500
PSV Eindhoven: Gomes; Lee, Lucius, Bouma, Park (Vogel 88), Cocu, Farfan (Sibon 64), De Jong, Van Bommel, Vennegoor of Hesselink, Alex.
Panathinaikos: Chalkias; Goumas, Andric, Munch, Gonzalez, Kirgiakos, Konstantinou, Basinas, Vyntra (Sapanis 84), Papadopoulos (Morris 70), Skacel (Epalle 59).

Rosenborg (0) 1 *(Strand 52)*
Arsenal (1) 1 *(Ljungberg 6)* 21,100
Rosenborg: Johnsen E; Basma (Russell 74), Dorsin, Solli, Riseth, Hoftun, Strand (George 64), Johnsen F, Brattbakk (Braaten 82), Storflor, Winsnes.
Arsenal: Lehmann; Lauren, Cole, Vieira, Toure, Campell, Ljungberg, Edu, Reyes, Henry, Pires (Van Persie 82).

Wednesday, 20 October 2004

Panathinaikos (0) 2 *(Gonzalez 65, Olisadebe 81)*
Arsenal (1) 2 *(Ljungberg 17, Henry 74)* 12,346
Panathinaikos: Chalkias; Vyntra, Konstantinidis, Basinas, Morris, Goumas, Kirgiakos, Mitu (Epalle 77), Gonzalez (Sapanis 90), Konstantinou (Olisadebe 64), Skacel.
Arsenal: Lehmann; Lauren, Cole, Edu, Toure, Campbell, Ljungberg, Fabregas, Reyes, Henry, Pires.

Rosenborg (1) 1 *(Storflor 42)*
PSV Eindhoven (1) 2 *(Farfan 26, De Jong 86)* 20,950
Rosenborg: Johnsen E; Helstad (Braaten 66), Hoftun, Winsnes, Stensaas, Strand, Storflor, Russell, Johnsen F (Brattbakk 83), Riseth, Solli.
PSV Eindhoven: Gomes; Lucius, Lee, Vogel, Bouma, Van Bommel, Park■, Cocu, Vennegoor of Hesselink (Sibon 90), Farfan (Beasley 82), De Jong.

Tuesday, 2 November 2004

Arsenal (1) 1 *(Henry 16 (pen))*
Panathinaikos (0) 1 *(Cygan 74 (og))* 35,137
Arsenal: Lehmann; Lauren, Cole, Vieira, Toure, Cygan, Ljungberg (Van Persie 83), Fabregas, Henry, Bergkamp (Reyes 72), Pires.
Panathinaikos: Chalkias; Vyntra, Konstantinidis, Kirgiakos, Henriksen, Kotsios, Maric (Morris 88), Basinas, Papadopoulos (Mitu 62), Gonzalez (Kostantinidis 60), Skacel.

PSV Eindhoven (1) 1 *(Beasley 10)*
Rosenborg (0) 0 26,250
PSV Eindhoven: Zoetebier; Vogel, Lee, Alex, Bouma (Feher 89), Van Bommel, Cocu, Lucius, Vennegoor of Hesselink (Sibon 76), Farfan, Beasley (Vonlanthen 82).
Rosenborg: Johnsen E; Hansen, Hoftun, Winsnes, Dorsin, Strand (George 30), Storflor (Helstad 85), Russell, Johnsen F, Stensaas (Braaten 66), Solli.

Wednesday, 24 November 2004

PSV Eindhoven (1) 1 *(Ooijer 8)*

Arsenal (1) 1 *(Henry 31)* 35,200

PSV Eindhoven: Gomes; Ooijer, Lee, Vogel (Beasley 65), Alex, Bouma, Van Bommel, Park, Sibon, Farfan, Cocu.
Arsenal: Lehmann; Lauren■, Cole, Vieira■, Toure, Campbell, Ljungberg, Fabregas, Reyes (Van Persie 63) (Flamini 81), Henry, Pires (Hoyte 69).

Rosenborg (0) 2 *(Helstad 68, 76)*

Panathinaikos (1) 2 *(Konstantinou 17, Skacel 70)* 18,000

Rosenborg: Johnsen E; Hoftun, Solli, Storflor (Helstad 55), Johnsen F, Strand, Hansen, Stensaas, Braaten (George 88), Dorsin, Brattbakk.
Panathinaikos: Chalkias; Henriksen, Kotsios, Maric (Mitu 77), Gonzalez, Kirgiakos, Konstantinou, Basinas, Vyntra, Skacel (Sapanis 82), Konstantinidis (Olisadebe 87).

Tuesday, 7 December 2004

Arsenal (4) 5 *(Reyes 3, Henry 24, Fabregas 29, Pires 41 (pen), Van Persie 84)*

Rosenborg (1) 1 *(Hoftun 38)* 35,421

Arsenal: Almunia; Hoyte, Cole (Van Persie 75), Flamini, Toure, Campbell, Pires (Owusu-Abeyie 88), Fabregas, Henry, Bergkamp (Clichy 71), Reyes.
Rosenborg: Johnsen E; Winsnes (Olsen 88), Stensaas, Strand (George 62), Hansen, Hoftun, Solli, Braaten, Johnsen F, Helstad (Storflor 78), Brattbakk.

Panathinaikos (2) 4 *(Papadopoulos 30, Munch 45 (pen), 57, Sanmartean 81)*

PSV Eindhoven (1) 1 *(Beasley 37)* 10,196

Panathinaikos: Galinovic; Morris, Munch, Kirgiakos, Vyntra, Maric (Mitu 85), Gonzalez (Goumas 78), Basinas, Konstantinidis, Papadopoulos, Olisadebe (Sanmartean 73).
PSV Eindhoven: Gomes; Lee, Alex (Lamey 76), Bouma, Feher (Vonlanthen 64), Van Bommel, Park, Cocu, Vogel, Beasley, Farfan.

Group E Final Table	*P*	*W*	*D*	*L*	*F*	*A*	*Pts*
Arsenal	6	2	4	0	11	6	10
PSV Eindhoven	6	3	1	2	6	7	10
Panathinaikos	6	2	3	1	11	8	9
Rosenborg	6	0	2	4	6	13	2

GROUP F

Tuesday, 14 September 2004

Celtic (0) 1 *(Sutton 59)*

Barcelona (1) 3 *(Deco 20, Giuly 78, Larsson 82)* 58,589

Celtic: Marshall; Agathe, McNamara (Sylla 80), Lennon, Varga, Balde, Petrov, Juninho (Sutton 46), Hartson (Valgaeren 62), Camara, Thompson.
Barcelona: Valdes; Belletti, Van Bronckhorst, Gerard, Puyol, Marquez (Oleguer 62), Giuly, Deco, Eto'o (Iniesta 74), Xavi, Ronaldinho (Larsson 62).

Shakhtjor Donetsk (0) 0

AC Milan (0) 1 *(Seedorf 84)* 30,000

Shakhtjor Donetsk: Lastuvka; Barcauan, Tymoschuk, Rat, Duljaj (Aghahowa 86), Matuzalem, Vukic, Lewandowski, Srna■, Vorobei (Joao Batista 76), Marica.
AC Milan: Dida; Cafu, Maldini, Nesta, Stam, Gattuso (Dhorasoo 71), Seedorf, Pirlo (Rui Costa 76), Shevchenko, Kaka, Tomasson (Crespo 63).

Wednesday, 29 September 2004

AC Milan (1) 3 *(Shevchenko 8, Inzaghi 89, Pirlo 90)*

Celtic (0) 1 *(Varga 74)* 52,648

AC Milan: Dida; Cafu, Pancaro, Pirlo, Nesta, Maldini, Gattuso (Rui Costa 86), Kaka, Shevchenko, Tomasson (Inzaghi 77), Seedorf (Ambrosini 73).
Celtic: Marshall; Agathe, Valgaeren, Lennon, Varga, Balde, Petrov, Sutton, Hartson (Sylla 86), Camara, Thompson (Juninho 59).

Barcelona (1) 3 *(Deco 14, Ronaldinho 63, Eto'o 89)*

Shakhtjor Donetsk (0) 0 64,148

Barcelona: Valdes; Belletti, Van Bronckhorst, Edmilson, Puyol, Oleguer (Fernando 89), Xavi, Giuly (Larsson 75), Eto'o, Ronaldinho, Deco (Iniesta 81).
Shakhtjor Donetsk: Lastuvka; Barcauan, Tymoschuk, Duljaj, Matuzalem, Vukic (Bakharev 75), Stoican, Lewandowski, Brandao (Vorobei 46), Rat, Marica.

Wednesday, 20 October 2004

AC Milan (1) 1 *(Shevchenko 31)*

Barcelona (0) 0 76,502

AC Milan: Dida; Cafu, Maldini, Nesta, Stam, Pirlo, Gattuso, Kaka (Serginho 83), Shevchenko (Crespo 89), Inzaghi (Ambrosini 76), Seedorf.
Barcelona: Valdes; Belletti, Van Bronckhorst, Marquez, Puyol, Xavi, Oleguer, Eto'o (Iniesta 69), Ronaldinho, Larsson, Deco.

Shakhtjor Donetsk (0) 3 *(Matuzalem 57, 62, Brandao 78)*

Celtic (0) 0 30,000

Shakhtjor Donetsk: Lastuvka; Stoican, Rat, Tymoschuk, Barcauan, Lewandowski, Matuzalem, Vorobei (Brandao 75), Vukic, Aghahowa (Srna 82), Marica (Duljaj 46).
Celtic: Marshall; Agathe, McNamara (McManus 30), Lennon, Varga, Balde, Petrov, Sutton (Wallace 46), Hartson, Camara, Juninho (McGeady 70).

Tuesday, 2 November 2004

Barcelona (1) 2 *(Eto'o 37, Ronaldinho 88)*

AC Milan (1) 1 *(Shevchenko 17)* 94,682

Barcelona: Valdes; Belletti, Van Bronckhorst, Marquez (Larsson 80), Puyol, Xavi, Deco, Giuly (Iniesta 67), Eto'o, Ronaldinho, Oleguer.
AC Milan: Dida; Cafu, Maldini, Kaladze, Nesta, Pirlo, Shevchenko (Tomasson 87), Gattuso, Kaka (Rui Costa 76), Serginho (Seedorf 74), Ambrosini.

Celtic (1) 1 *(Thompson 25)*

Shakhtjor Donetsk (0) 0 58,347

Celtic: Marshall; Agathe, McNamara, Lennon, Varga, Valgaeren, McGeady (Wallace 78), Petrov, Hartson, Camara (Beattie 80), Thompson.
Shakhtjor Donetsk: Lastuvka; Stoican, Srna, Tymoschuk■, Barcauan■, Lewandowski, Duljaj, Vukic (Hubschman 58), Aghahowa (Marica 66), Vorobei (Joao Batista 73), Matuzalem.

Wednesday, 24 November 2004

AC Milan (0) 4 *(Kaka 52, 90, Crespo 53, 85)*

Shakhtjor Donetsk (0) 0 38,841

AC Milan: Dida; Cafu, Nesta, Maldini, Costacurta, Gattuso (Brocchi 84), Pirlo (Ambrosini 72), Rui Costa (Dhorasoo 79), Crespo, Kaka, Seedorf.
Shakhtjor Donetsk: Lastuvka; Stoican, Hubschman, Lewandowski, Srna, Joao Batista (Vorobei 63), Duljaj, Matuzalem, Vukic (Pukanych 81), Brandao, Aghahowa (Marica 63).

Barcelona (1) 1 *(Eto'o 25)*

Celtic (1) 1 *(Hartson 45)* 74,119

Barcelona: Valdes; Belletti, Silvinho (Van Bronckhorst 65), Marquez, Puyol, Oleguer, Xavi, Deco, Eto'o, Ronaldinho, Giuly (Iniesta 60).
Celtic: Hedman; Agathe, McNamara, Balde, Valgaeren, Varga (Camara 65), Petrov, Lennon, Hartson, Sutton, Thompson (Wallace 86).

Tuesday, 7 December 2004

Celtic (0) 0

AC Milan (0) 0 59,228

Celtic: Hedman; McNamara, Valgaeren (Camara 66), Lennon, Varga, Balde, Petrov (Juninho 77), Hartson, Sutton, McGeady, Thompson.
AC Milan: Dida; Coloccini, Maldini, Nesta, Costacurta, Brocchi, Ambrosini, Dhorasoo (Kaka 86), Serginho, Rui Costa (Seedorf 80), Shevchenko (Crespo 63).

Shakhtjor Donetsk (2) 2 *(Aghahowa 14, 22)*

Barcelona (0) 0 20,000

Shakhtjor Donetsk: Lastuvka; Stoican (Chigrinski 90), Srna (Lalatovic 83), Vukic, Lewandowski, Hubschman, Duljaj, Barcauan, Aghahowa, Brandao (Vorobei 46), Matuzalem.
Barcelona: Valdes; Belletti (Marquez 59), Puyol (Oleguer 46), Fernando, Silvinho, Verdu, Xavi, Van Bronckhorst, Peral (Rodri 46), Iniesta, Messi.

Group F Final Table	P	W	D	L	F	A	Pts
AC Milan	6	4	1	1	10	3	13
Barcelona	6	3	1	2	9	6	10
Shakhtjor Donetsk	6	2	0	4	5	9	6
Celtic	6	1	2	3	4	10	5

GROUP G

Tuesday, 14 September 2004

Internazionale (1) 2 *(Adriano 33 (pen), 88)*

Werder Bremen (0) 0 45,000

Internazionale: Toldo; Cordoba, Zanetti J (Ze Maria 52), Emre B, Van der Meyde, Adriano, Veron, Favalli, Materazzi, Stankovic (Cambiasso 81), Vieri (Recoba 77).
Werder Bremen: Reinke; Fahrenhorst, Pasanen, Ernst, Baumann (Magnin 36), Stalteri, Micoud, Klasnic (Charisteas 60), Borowski, Ismael■, Valdez (Klose 81).

Valencia (2) 2 *(Vicente 17, Baraja 45)*

Anderlecht (0) 0 45,000

Valencia: Canizares; Curro Torres, Marchena, Navarro, Carboni, Baraja, Albelda (Sissoko 71), Vicente, Rufete (Corradi 57), Aimar (Fiore 76), Angulo.
Anderlecht: Zitka; Deschacht, De Boeck, Vanden Borre, Zewlakow (Lovre 79), Kompany, Traore, Baseggio, Hasi (Zetterberg 55), Mpenza M, Dindane.

Wednesday, 29 September 2004

Anderlecht (0) 1 *(Baseggio 90)*

Internazionale (1) 3 *(Martins 8, Adriano 51, Stankovic 54)* 22,500

Anderlecht: Peersman; Traore, Vanden Borre, Kompany, Dindane, Zetterberg, Wilhelmsson, Hasi (Baseggio 63), Deschacht, Jestrovic (Iachtchouck 70), Mpenza M.
Internazionale: Toldo; Cordoba, Burdisso, Emre B, Adriano (Cruz 67), Ze Maria, Veron, Favalli (Zanetti J 52), Cambiasso, Stankovic (Davids 68), Martins.

Werder Bremen (0) 2 *(Klose 60, Charisteas 84)*

Valencia (1) 1 *(Vicente 2)* 36,034

Werder Bremen: Reinke; Fahrenhorst, Micoud, Magnin, Ernst, Stalteri, Borowski, Klasnic, Schulz (Charisteas 61), Klose, Valdez.
Valencia: Canizares; Angulo, Curro Torres, Albelda, Corradi, Marchena■, Baraja (Sissoko 74), Di Vaio (Pellegrino 57), Carboni, Vicente (Moretti 79), Navarro.

Wednesday, 20 October 2004

Anderlecht (1) 1 *(Wilhelmsson 26)*

Werder Bremen (1) 2 *(Klasnic 36, 59)* 22,000

Anderlecht: Zitka; Hasi (Iachtchouk 67), Deschacht, Kompany, De Boeck, Wilhelmsson, Ehret (Lovre 64), Zetterberg, Mpenza M, Baseggio, Aruna.
Werder Bremen: Reinke; Ismael, Pasanen, Ernst, Magnin, Baumann, Stalteri, Micoud, Klasnic (Lagerblom 86) (Banecki 90), Klose (Valdez 77), Schulz.

Valencia (0) 1 *(Aimar 73)*

Internazionale (0) 5 *(Stankovic 47, Vieri 49, Van der Meyde 76, Adriano 81, Cruz 90)* 40,000

Valencia: Canizares; Caneira (Corradi 65), Angulo, Albelda, Carboni, Curro Torres, Rufete (Fiore 82), Aimar, Di Vaio, Baraja, Navarro.
Internazionale: Fontana; Cordoba, Burdisso (Zanetti J 46), Materazzi, Emre B, Stankovic, Vieri (Van der Meyde 75), Cambiasso, Veron, Adriano (Cruz 83), Favalli.

Tuesday, 2 November 2004

Internazionale (0) 0

Valencia (0) 0 40,000

Internazionale: Fontana; Cordoba, Martins (Recoba 78), Zanetti J, Materazzi, Stankovic (Pasquale 89), Ze Maria, Davids, Cambiasso, Adriano■, Veron (Zanetti C 79).
Valencia: Canizares; Mista (Moretti 84), Curro Torres, Carboni, Marchena, Albelda, Caneira, Baraja (Sissoko 74), Rufete, Angulo, Di Vaio (Corradi 71).

Werder Bremen (3) 5 *(Klasnic 2, 16, 79, Klose 33, Jensen 90)*

Anderlecht (1) 1 *(Iachtchouk 30)* 37,579

Werder Bremen: Reinke; Ismael, Magnin, Ernst, Klasnic (Charisteas 83), Baumann, Stalteri, Jensen, Schulz (Davala 66), Micoud, Klose (Valdez 71).
Anderlecht: Peersmann; Ehret (Vanden Borre 64), Deschacht, Iachtchouk, De Boeck, Zewlakow, Aruna, Traore, Baseggio, Wilhelmsson, Hasi (Zetterberg 67).

Wednesday, 24 November 2004

Anderlecht (1) 1 *(Wilhelmsson 23)*

Valencia (1) 2 *(Corradi 19, Di Vaio 47)* 30,000

Anderlecht: Zitka; Deschacht, Vanderhaeghe, De Boeck (Mpenza M 72), Zewlakow, Baseggio, Wilhelmsson, Zetterberg, Iachtchouck, Dindane, Kompany.
Valencia: Canizares; Baraja, Corradi, Caneira, Sissoko, Navarro, Xisco (Carboni 82), Rufete (Fiore 70), Di Vaio (Mista 86), Curro Torres, Moretti.

Werder Bremen (0) 1 *(Ismael 49 (pen))*

Internazionale (0) 1 *(Martins 55)* 37,000

Werder Bremen: Reinke; Pasanen, Baumann, Ismael, Stalteri (Charisteas 83), Micoud, Ernst, Magnin, Borowski (Jensen 67), Klasnic (Valdez 46), Klose.
Internazionale: Toldo; Cordoba, Zanetti J, Mihajlovic, Favalli, Davids (Zanetti C 81), Cambiasso, Stankovic (Karagounis 64), Van der Meyde, Cruz (Martins 53), Vieri.

Tuesday, 7 December 2004

Internazionale (1) 3 *(Cruz 33, Martins 60, 63)*

Anderlecht (0) 0 21,851

Internazionale: Carini; Ze Maria, Pasquale, Zanetti C (Emre B 59), Materazzi, Burdisso, Karagounis, Davids, Cruz, Martins (Dellafiore 70), Recoba.
Anderlecht: Van Steenberghe; Zewlakow, Deschacht (Vanden Borre 31), Hasi (Gerk 81), Kompany, Traore, Wilhelmsson (Lovre 75), Baseggio, Legear, Dindane, Vanderhaeghe.

Valencia (0) 0

Werder Bremen (0) 2 *(Valdez 83, 90)* 39,000

Valencia: Canizares; Marchena, Caneira, Navarro, Curro Torres, Moretti, Baraja (Vicente 60), Aimar (Di Vaio 60), Angulo■, Xisco, Mista (Corradi 60).
Werder Bremen: Reinke; Pasanen, Stalteri, Ismael, Ernst, Baumann, Micoud, Jensen (Magnin 44), Borowski, Charisteas (Valdez 80), Klose (Klasnic 88).

Group G Final Table	P	W	D	L	F	A	Pts
Internazionale	6	4	2	0	14	3	14
Werder Bremen	6	4	1	1	12	6	13
Valencia	6	2	1	3	6	10	7
Anderlecht	6	0	0	6	4	17	0

GROUP H

Tuesday, 14 September 2004

Paris St Germain (0) 0

Chelsea (2) 3 *(Terry 29, Drogba 45, 75)* 40,263

Paris St Germain: Letizi; Mendy, Armand, Cana, Helder, Pierre-Fanfan, Ogbeche (Pancrate 72), M'Bami, Coridon (Ljuboja 66), Pauleta, Rothen (Ateba 84).
Chelsea: Cech; Paulo Ferreira, Bridge, Makelele, Terry, Gallas, Tiago, Lampard, Drogba (Duff 80), Gudjohnsen (Kezman 12), Cole (Geremi 70).

Porto (0) 0
CSKA Moscow (0) 0 39,309
Porto: Vitor Baia; Jorge Costa, Pepe, Areias, Seitaridis, Costinha, Diego, Maniche, Quaresma (Leal 71), Carlos Alberto (Luis Fabiano 64), Helder Postiga (McCarthy 80).
CSKA Moscow: Akinfeev; Semberas, Ignashevich, Berezutski A, Odiah, Zhirkov, Jarosik, Aldonin (Semak 87), Rahimic, Olic, Vagner Love (Berezutski V 87).

Wednesday, 29 September 2004

CSKA Moscow (0) 2 *(Semak 64, Vagner Love 77)*
Paris St Germain (0) 0 28,000
CSKA Moscow: Akinfeev; Semberas, Ignashevich, Berezutski A, Gusev (Kirichenko 69), Olic (Semak 57), Vagner Love (Berezutski V 89), Zhirkov, Jarosik, Aldonin, Rahimic.
Paris St Germain: Letizi; Pierre-Fanfan, Cana, Helder, Badiane, Mendy, Cisse (M'Bami 23), Coridon (Pancrate 75), Pauleta, Ljuboja (Reinaldo 81), Armand.

Chelsea (1) 3 *(Smertin 7, Drogba 50, Terry 70)*
Porto (0) 1 *(McCarthy 68)* 39,237
Chelsea: Cech; Paulo Ferreira, Gallas, Makelele, Terry, Ricardo Carvalho, Smertin, Lampard, Drogba (Geremi 88), Gudjohnsen (Kezman 80), Duff (Tiago 66).
Porto: Vitor Baia; Bosingwa, Ricardo Costa, Costinha, Jorge Costa, Pepe, Maniche, Quaresma (Carlos Alberto 58), Luis Fabiano (McCarthy 58), Derlei (Helder Postiga 80), Diego.

Wednesday, 20 October 2004

Chelsea (2) 2 *(Terry 9, Gudjohnsen 45)*
CSKA Moscow (0) 0 33,945
Chelsea: Cech; Paulo Ferreira, Bridge, Makelele, Terry, Gallas, Smertin (Parker 84), Lampard, Kezman (Tiago 63), Gudjohnsen, Duff (Cole 77).
CSKA Moscow: Akinfeev; Ignashevich, Berezutski A, Aldonin, Semberas, Rahimic, Odiah, Carvalho (Laizans 25), Semak (Krasic 72), Zhirkov, Vagner Love (Dadu 60).

Paris St Germain (2) 2 *(Coridon 30, Pauleta 31)*
Porto (0) 0 41,000
Paris St Germain: Letizi; Pichot, Coridon, Cana, M'Bami, Pierre-Fanfan, Rothen (Boskovic 49), Armand, Pauleta (Ljuboja 82), Yepes, Reinaldo (Cisse 73).
Porto: Vitor Baia; Jorge Costa (Bosingwa 76), Carlos Alberto, Seitaridis, Ricardo Costa, Costinha (Quaresma 52), Pepe, Diego, Maniche, McCarthy, Derlei (Helder Postiga 69).

Tuesday, 2 November 2004

CSKA Moscow (0) 0
Chelsea (1) 1 *(Robben 24)* 28,000
CSKA Moscow: Akinfeev; Ignashevich, Semak (Olic 70), Zhirkov, Semberas, Berezutski A, Jarosik, Gusev, Krasic (Aldonin 46), Vagner Love (Kirichenko 81), Rahimic.
Chelsea: Cech; Johnson, Gallas (Paulo Ferreira 54), Makelele, Terry, Ricardo Carvalho, Parker (Tiago 65), Lampard, Robben, Gudjohnsen (Kezman 68), Duff.

Porto (0) 0
Paris St Germain (0) 0 30,210
Porto: Vitor Baia; Jorge Costa, Pedro Emanuel, Seitaridis, Ricardo Costa, Bosingwa, Maniche, Diego (Carlos Alberto 65), McCarthy (Hugo Almeida 65), Quaresma (Helder Postiga 78), Derlei.
Paris St Germain: Letizi; Pichot, Coridon (Mendy 74), Armand, M'Bami, Yepes, Pancrate, Pierre-Fanfan, Pauleta (Ljuboja 89), Cisse (Boskovic 86), Cana.

Wednesday, 24 November 2004

CSKA Moscow (0) 0
Porto (1) 1 *(McCarthy 28)* 20,000
CSKA Moscow: Akinfeev; Semberas, Ignashevich, Semak, Berezutski A, Krasic (Gusev 69), Zhirkov, Jarosik (Ferreyra 67), Aldonin, Rahimic, Vagner Love.
Porto: Nuno; Jorge Costa, Pedro Emanuel, Ricardo Costa, Costinha, Quaresma (Cesar Peixoto 58), Derlei (Pepe 90), Bosingwa, Maniche, Seitaridis, McCarthy (Hugo Almeida 77).

Chelsea (0) 0
Paris St Germain (0) 0 39,626
Chelsea: Cudicini; Johnson, Bridge, Parker, Gallas, Ricardo Carvalho, Smertin, Lampard (Gudjohnsen 63), Robben (Duff 46), Kezman (Drogba 62), Cole.
Paris St Germain: Letizi; Pichot, Armand, Cana, Pierre-Fanfan, Yepes, Mendy, M'Bami, Pauleta (Pancrate 89), Cisse (Boskovic 83), Reinaldo (Coridon 77).

Tuesday, 7 December 2004

Paris St Germain (1) 1 *(Pancrate 37)*
CSKA Moscow (1) 3 *(Semak 29, 64, 70)* 41,987
Paris St Germain: Letizi; Pichot (Ljuboja 73), Yepes, Pancrate, Pauleta, Cisse, Cana, Armand, M'Bami (Mendy■ 7), Pierre-Fanfan, Coridon (Boskovic 63).
CSKA Moscow: Akinfeev; Semberas■, Ignashevich, Semak, Berezutski A, Gusev, Vagner Love, Zhirkov, Jarosik (Laizans 90), Aldonin (Berezutski V 58), Rahimic.

Porto (0) 2 *(Diego 60, McCarthy 85)*
Chelsea (1) 1 *(Duff 33)* 42,409
Porto: Nuno; Jorge Costa, Pedro Emanuel, Costinha, Luis Fabiano (Helder Postiga 75), Seitaridis, Diego (Cesar Peixoto 77), Areias, McCarthy, Derlei (Quaresma 59), Maniche.
Chelsea: Cech; Paulo Ferreira, Gallas, Parker, Terry, Ricardo Carvalho, Smertin (Tiago 65), Lampard, Drogba (Kezman 77), Duff (Robben 54), Bridge.

Group H Final Table	*P*	*W*	*D*	*L*	*F*	*A*	*Pts*
Chelsea	6	4	1	1	10	3	13
Porto	6	2	2	2	4	6	8
CSKA Moscow	6	2	1	3	5	5	7
Paris St Germain	6	1	2	3	3	8	5

KNOCK-OUT STAGE

KNOCK-OUT ROUND FIRST LEG

Tuesday, 22 February 2005

Bayern Munich (1) 3 *(Pizarro 3, 58, Salihamidzic 65)*
Arsenal (0) 1 *(Toure 88)* 59,000
Bayern Munich: Kahn; Sagnol, Kovac, Lucio, Lizarazu, Demichelis, Salihamidzic (Hargreaves 74), Frings, Ze Roberto (Scholl 57), Makaay, Pizarro (Guerrero 68).
Arsenal: Lehmann; Lauren, Clichy (Cole 83), Vieira, Toure, Cygan, Ljungberg (Van Persie 76), Edu (Flamini 36), Reyes, Henry, Pires.

Liverpool (2) 3 *(Luis Garcia 15, Riise 35, Hamann 89)*
Leverkusen (0) 1 *(Franca 90)* 40,942
Liverpool: Dudek; Finnan, Traore, Hamann, Carragher, Hyypia, Luis Garcia, Biscan, Baros (Potter 85), Kewell (Le Tallec 77), Riise (Smicer 89).
Leverkusen: Butt; Schneider, Callsen-Bracker, Piacente, Juan, Ramelow, Ponte (Donovan 89), Freier (Bierofka 83), Kryznowek, Berbatov, Voronin (Franca 68).

PSV Eindhoven (1) 1 *(Alex 8)*
Monaco (0) 0 32,000
PSV Eindhoven: Gomes; Ooijer, Lee, Alex, Bouma, Van Bommel, Park, Cocu, Vogel, Vennegoor of Hesselink, Farfan (Beasley 52).
Monaco: Roma; Evra, Maicon, Rodriguez, Givet, Plasil, Bernardi, Zikos, Kallon, Saviola, Adebayor (Nonda 82).

Real Madrid (1) 1 *(Helguera 31)*
Juventus (0) 0 78,000
Real Madrid: Casillas; Michel Salgado (Bravo 9), Helguera, Samuel, Roberto Carlos, Beckham, Gravesen, Ronaldo (Owen 75), Raul, Figo, Zidane.
Juventus: Buffon; Zambrotta, Thuram, Blasi (Tacchinardi 68), Zebina, Cannavaro, Emerson, Nedved (Olivera 37), Ibrahimovic, Del Piero (Zalayeta 81), Camoranesi.

Wednesday, 23 February 2005

Barcelona (0) 2 *(Maxi Lopez 66, Eto'o 73)*
Chelsea (1) 1 *(Belletti 33 (og))* 89,000
Barcelona: Valdes; Belletti (Gerard 85), Van Bronckhorst, Xavi, Marquez, Puyol, Albertini (Iniesta 57), Deco, Eto'o, Ronaldinho, Giuly (Maxi Lopez 64).
Chelsea: Cech; Paulo Ferreira, Gallas, Makelele, Terry, Ricardo Carvalho, Tiago (Smertin 90), Lampard, Cole (Johnson 70), Drogba■, Duff (Gudjohnsen 76).

Manchester United (0) 0
AC Milan (0) 1 *(Crespo 78)* 67,162
Manchester United: Carroll; Neville G (Silvestre 80), Heinze, Ferdinand, Keane, Brown, Ronaldo (Van Nistelrooy 62), Scholes, Giggs, Rooney, Fortune (Saha 80).
AC Milan: Dida; Cafu (Costacurta 86), Kaladze, Pirlo (Ambrosini 84), Nesta, Maldini, Gattuso, Seedorf, Crespo, Kaka (Serginho 90), Rui Costa.

Porto (0) 1 *(Ricardo Costa 61)*
Internazionale (1) 1 *(Martins 23)* 38,177
Porto: Vitor Baia; Pedro Emanuel, Nuno Valente, Bosingwa (Luis Fabiano 28), Ricardo Costa, Costinha, Quaresma (Helder Postiga 83), Maniche, McCarthy, Seitaridis, Raul Meireles.
Internazionale: Toldo; Cordoba, Adriano (Vieri 80), Zanetti J, Zanetti C, Favalli, Veron (Emre B 70), Cambiasso, Materazzi, Martins, Stankovic.

Werder Bremen (0) 0
Lyon (1) 3 *(Wiltord 9, Diarra 77, Juninho Pernambucano 80)* 36,923
Werder Bremen: Reinke; Pasanen, Ernst, Stalteri, Ismael, Jensen, Magnin, Micoud, Klose, Valdez, Borowski (Hunt 61).
Lyon: Coupet; Abidal, Diatta, Cris, Essien, Govou (Benarfa 68), Diarra, Juninho Pernambucano, Malouda, Frau (Nilmar 83), Wiltord (Clement 77).

KNOCK-OUT ROUND SECOND LEG

Tuesday, 8 March 2005

AC Milan (0) 1 *(Crespo 61)*
Manchester United (0) 0 79,103
AC Milan: Dida; Cafu, Nesta, Maldini, Pirlo, Stam, Gattuso (Costacurta 89), Rui Costa (Dhorasoo 83), Seedorf, Crespo (Ambrosini 78), Kaka.
Manchester United: Howard; Brown (Smith 85), Heinze, Ferdinand, Keane, Silvestre, Ronaldo, Scholes, Van Nistelrooy, Rooney, Giggs (Fortune 57).

Chelsea (3) 4 *(Gudjohnsen 8, Lampard 17, Duff 19, Terry 76)*
Barcelona (2) 2 *(Ronaldinho 27 (pen), 38)* 41,315
Chelsea: Cech; Paulo Ferreira (Johnson 51), Gallas, Makelele, Terry, Ricardo Carvalho, Cole, Lampard, Kezman, Gudjohnsen (Tiago 78), Duff (Huth 81).
Barcelona: Valdes; Belletti (Giuly 84), Van Bronckhorst (Silvinho 46), Puyol, Oleguer, Gerard, Deco, Eto'o, Xavi, Ronaldinho, Iniesta (Maxi Lopez 85).

Lyon (3) 7 *(Wiltord 8, 54, 63, Essien 17, 29, Malouda 60, Bertod 78)*
Werder Bremen (1) 2 *(Micoud 31, Ismael 57 (pen))* 38,922
Lyon: Coupet; Cris (Clement 62), Bertod, Abidal, Diatta, Diarra, Essien, Juninho Pernambucano, Malouda, Wiltord (Nilmar 67), Govou (Frau 74).
Werder Bremen: Reinke; Ismael, Pasanen, Baumann, Ernst, Stalteri (Umit D 73), Micoud, Magnin, Klose (Borowski 46), Klasnic (Fahrenhorst 65), Valdez.

Wednesday, 9 March 2005

Arsenal (0) 1 *(Henry 66)*
Bayern Munich (0) 0 35,463
Arsenal: Lehmann; Lauren, Cole, Vieira, Toure, Senderos, Ljungberg (Van Persie 80), Flamini (Fabregas 63), Henry, Bergkamp, Reyes (Pires 63).
Bayern Munich: Kahn; Sagnol, Lucio, Kovac, Lizarazu, Demichelis, Salihamadzic (Hargreaves 90), Deisler (Ze Roberto 72), Ballack, Guerrero (Linke 85), Pizarro.

Juventus (0) 2 *(Trezeguet 75, Zalayeta 117)*
Real Madrid (0) 0 37,698
Juventus: Buffon; Pessotto (Tacchinardi■ 66), Thuram, Zebina, Cannavaro, Emerson, Camoranesi, Zambrotta, Zalayeta (Olivera 119), Ibrahimovic, Del Piero (Trezeguet 57).
Real Madrid: Casillas; Figo, Roberto Carlos, Samuel, Bravo, Helguera, Gravesen, Beckham (Solari 77), Raul (Owen 96), Ronaldo■, Zidane (Guti 74).
aet.

Leverkusen (0) 1 *(Krzynowek 88)*
Liverpool (2) 3 *(Luis Garcia 28, 32, Baros 67)* 23,000
Leverkusen: Butt; Schneider, Callsen-Bracker, Ramelow (Castro 70), Piacente, Babic, Bierofka, Krzynowek, Donovan (Fritz 52), Franca, Berbatov (Voronin 32).
Liverpool: Dudek; Finnan (Nunes 73), Warnock, Hamann (Smicer 62), Carragher (Welsh 70), Hyypia, Luis Garcia, Biscan, Baros, Gerrard, Riise.

Monaco (0) 0
PSV Eindhoven (1) 2 *(Vennegoor of Hesselink 27, Beasley 69)* 15,323
Monaco: Roma; Evra, Plasil (Adebayor 61), Bernardi, Kallon, Saviola (Nonda 72), Chevanton, Maicon, Zikos, Rodriguez, Givet■.
PSV Eindhoven: Gomes; Ooijer, Lee, Alex, Bouma, Van Bommel, Park, Cocu, Vennegoor of Hesselink (Beasley 67), Vogel, Farfan (Robert 75).

Tuesday, 15 March 2005

Internazionale (1) 3 *(Adriano 5, 63, 87)*

Porto (0) 1 *(Jorge Costa 69)* 71,000

Internazionale: Toldo; Zanetti J, Ze Maria, Zanetti C, Materazzi, Mihajlovic, Cambiasso, Stankovic (Kily Gonzalez 83), Veron (Van der Meyde 89), Adriano, Cruz (Martins 76).
Porto: Vitor Baia; Jorge Costa, Pedro Emanuel (Pepe 81), Ricardo Costa (Postiga 66), Costinha, Nuno Valente, Maniche, Diego, Seitaridis, Claudio (Quaresma 46), McCarthy.

QUARTER-FINALS FIRST LEG

Tuesday, 5 April 2005

Liverpool (2) 2 *(Hyypia 10, Luis Garcia 25)*

Juventus (0) 1 *(Cannavaro 63)* 41,216

Liverpool: Carson; Finnan, Traore, Biscan, Carragher, Hyypia, Luis Garcia, Gerrard, Le Tallec (Smicer 73), Baros (Nunes 66), Riise.
Juventus: Buffon; Zebina (Montero 81), Zambrotta, Emerson, Cannavaro, Thuram, Blasi (Pessotto 46), Camoranesi, Del Piero (Trezeguet 61), Ibrahimovic, Nedved.

Lyon (1) 1 *(Malouda 12)*

PSV Eindhoven (0) 1 *(Cocu 79)* 39,178

Lyon: Coupet; Cris, Reveillere, Juninho Pernambucano, Essien, Cacapa, Abidal, Diarra, Wiltord, Govou, Malouda.
PSV Eindhoven: Gomes; Ooijer, Bouma, Lee, Alex, Van Bommel, Park, Cocu, Farfan (Beasley 71), Vennegoor of Hesselink, Vogel.

Wednesday, 6 April 2005

AC Milan (1) 2 *(Stam 45, Shevchenko 74)*

Internazionale (0) 0 80,000

AC Milan: Dida; Cafu (Costacurta 90), Maldini, Nesta (Kaladze 71), Stam, Gattuso, Pirlo, Kaka, Crespo (Ambrosini 83), Shevchenko, Seedorf.
Internazionale: Toldo; Cordoba, Cruz (Vieri 55), Zanetti J, Zanetti C (Van der Meyde 80), Mihajlovic, Favalli, Stankovic, Martins, Cambiasso, Veron (Karagounis 70).

Chelsea (1) 4 *(Lucio 5 (og), Lampard 59, 70, Drogba 81)*

Bayern Munich (0) 2 *(Schweinsteiger 53, Ballack 90 (pen))* 40,253

Chelsea: Cech; Johnson (Huth 65), Gallas, Makelele, Terry, Ricardo Carvalho, Cole (Tiago 82), Lampard, Drogba (Forssell 89), Gudjohnsen, Duff.
Bayern Munich: Kahn; Sagnol, Lizarazu, Frings, Lucio, Kovac, Salihamidzic (Schweinsteiger 46), Ballack, Guerrero, Ze Roberto (Scholl 73), Hargreaves.

QUARTER-FINALS SECOND LEG

Tuesday, 12 April 2005

Bayern Munich (0) 3 *(Pizarro 65, Guerrero 89, Scholl 90)*

Chelsea (1) 2 *(Lampard 30, Drogba 80)* 59,000

Bayern Munich: Kahn; Sagnol, Lizarazu (Salihamidzic 78), Demichelis (Scholl 52), Lucio, Kovac, Schweinsteiger, Ballack, Makaay (Guerrero 73), Pizarro, Ze Roberto.
Chelsea: Cech; Huth, Gallas, Makelele, Terry, Ricardo Carvalho, Cole (Nuno Morais), Lampard, Drogba, Gudjohnsen (Geremi), Duff (Tiago).

Internazionale (0) 0

AC Milan (0) 1 *(Shevchenko 30)* 79,000

Internazionale: Toldo; Cordoba, Materazzi, Zanetti J, Zanetti C (Cruz 46), Favalli, Van der Meyde, Veron, Adriano (Martins 50), Cambiasso, Kily Gonzalez (Mihajlovic 46).
AC Milan: Dida (Abbiati 73); Cafu, Maldini, Ambrosini, Nesta, Stam, Pirlo, Kaka, Crespo (Rui Costa 68), Shevchenko, Seedorf.
match abandoned 71 minutes; crowd trouble.

Wednesday, 13 April 2005

Juventus (0) 0

Liverpool (0) 0 55,464

Juventus: Buffon; Thuram, Camoranesi (Appiah 84), Olivera (Zalayeta 46), Montero (Pessotto 83), Cannavaro, Emerson, Zambrotta, Ibrahimovic, Del Piero, Nedved.
Liverpool: Dudek; Finnan, Traore, Biscan, Carragher, Hyypia, Nunes (Smicer 58), Xabi Alonso, Baros (Cisse 75), Luis Garcia (Le Tallec 85), Riise.

PSV Eindhoven (0) 1 *(Alex 50)*

Lyon (1) 1 *(Wiltord 10)* 35,000

PSV Eindhoven: Gomes; Ooijer, Park, Lee, Alex, Bouma, Van Bommel, Cocu, Farfan (Robert 85), Vennegoor of Hesselink (Beasley 57), Vogel.
Lyon: Coupet; Cris, Cacapa, Abidal, Reveillere, Diarra, Essien, Malouda, Juninho Pernambucano, Wiltord (Nilmar 95), Govou (Benarfa 87).
aet; PSV Eindhoven won 4-2 on penalties.

SEMI-FINAL FIRST LEG

Tuesday, 26 April 2005

AC Milan (1) 2 *(Shevchenko 42, Tomasson 90)*

PSV Eindhoven (0) 0 74,655

AC Milan: Dida; Cafu, Maldini, Kaladze, Gattuso, Pirlo (Ambrosini 72), Stam, Crespo (Tomasson 64), Kaka, Shevchenko, Seedorf (Serginho 81).
PSV Eindhoven: Gomes; Ooijer, Lee, Alex, Bouma (Lucius 46), Van Bommel, Park, Cocu, Beasley (Vennegoor of Hesselink 61), Vogel, Farfan.

Wednesday, 27 April 2005

Chelsea (0) 0

Liverpool (0) 0 40,497

Chelsea: Cech; Johnson, Gallas, Makelele, Terry, Ricardo Carvalho, Tiago (Robben 59), Lampard, Drogba, Gudjohnsen, Cole (Kezman 78).
Liverpool: Dudek; Finnan, Carragher, Biscan (Kewell 86), Traore, Hyypia, Xabi Alonso, Gerrard, Baros (Cisse 65), Luis Garcia (Smicer 90), Riise.

SEMI-FINAL SECOND LEG

Tuesday, 3 May 2005

Liverpool (1) 1 *(Luis Garcia 4)*

Chelsea (0) 0 42,529

Liverpool: Dudek; Finnan, Traore, Hamann (Kewell 72), Carragher, Hyypia, Biscan, Gerrard, Baros (Cisse 59), Luis Garcia (Nunez 84), Riise.
Chelsea: Cech; Geremi (Huth 76), Gallas, Makelele, Terry, Ricardo Carvalho, Tiago (Kezman 68), Lampard, Drogba, Gudjohnsen, Cole (Robben 68).

Wednesday, 4 May 2005

PSV Eindhoven (1) 3 *(Park 9, Cocu 65, 89)*

AC Milan (0) 1 *(Ambrosini 90)* 35,000

PSV Eindhoven: Gomes; Lee, Alex, Bouma (Robert 70), Van Bommel, Park, Cocu, Vogel, Lucius, Vennegoor of Hesselink, Farfan.
AC Milan: Dida; Cafu, Maldini (Kaladze 46), Nesta, Stam, Gattuso, Seedorf (Tomasson 69), Pirlo, Ambrosini, Shevchenko, Kaka.

UEFA CHAMPIONS LEAGUE FINAL 2005

Wednesday, 25 May 2005

Liverpool (0) 3 *(Gerrard 54, Smicer 56, Xabi Alonso 59)* **AC Milan (3) 3** *(Maldini 1, Crespo 39, 44)*

(at Atatürk Olimpiyat, Istanbul, Turkey, 65,000)

Liverpool: Dudek; Finnan (Hamann 46), Traore, Xabi Alonso, Carragher, Hyypia, Luis Garcia, Gerrard, Baros (Cisse 85), Kewell (Smicer 23), Riise.

AC Milan: Dida; Cafu, Maldini, Pirlo, Nesta, Stam, Gattuso (Rui Costa 111), Kaka, Crespo (Tomasson 85), Shevchenko, Seedorf (Serginho 85).

aet; Liverpool won 3-2 on penalties: Serginho missed, Hamann scored, Pirlo saved, Cisse scored, Tomasson scored, Riise saved, Kaka scored, Smicer scored, Shevchenko saved.

Referee: M. González (Spain).

Liverpool captain Steven Gerrard lifts the Champions League trophy surrounded by his ecstatic teammates after their amazing cup final comeback win against AC Milan in the Ataturk Olympic Stadium, Istanbul. (Actionimages)

UEFA CHAMPIONS LEAGUE 2005–06

(Early results)

FIRST QUALIFYING ROUND, FIRST LEG

Levadia Tallinn	1	Dinamo Tbilisi	0
Kairat Almaty	2	Artmedia Bratislava	0
Neftchi	2	Hafnarfjördur	0
Rabotnicki	6	Skonto	0
Dinamo Minsk	1	Anorthosis Famagusta	1
Sliema Wanderers	1	Sheriff	4
HB Tórshavn	2	Kaunas	4
Liverpool	3	Total Network Solutions	0
Haka	1	Pyunik	0
Gorica	2	Tirana	0
Glentoran	1	Shelbourne	2
Dudelange	0	Zrinjski	1

EUROPEAN CUP-WINNERS' CUP FINALS 1961–99

Year	Winners	Runners-up	Venue	Attendance	Referee
1961	Fiorentina 2	Rangers 0 *(1st Leg)*	Glasgow	80,000	Steiner (A)
	Fiorentina 2	Rangers 1 *(2nd Leg)*	Florence	50,000	Hernadi (H)
1962	Atletico Madrid 1	Fiorentina 1	Glasgow	27,389	Wharton (S)
Replay	Atletico Madrid 3	Fiorentina 0	Stuttgart	38,000	Tschenscher (WG)
1963	Tottenham Hotspur 5	Atletico Madrid 1	Rotterdam	49,000	Van Leuwen (Ho)
1964	Sporting Lisbon 3	MTK Budapest 3 *(aet)*	Brussels	3000	Van Nuffel (Bel)
Replay	Sporting Lisbon 1	MTK Budapest 0	Antwerp	19,000	Versyp (Bel)
1965	West Ham U 2	Munich 1860 0	Wembley	100,000	Szolt (H)
1966	Borussia Dortmund 2	Liverpool 1 *(aet)*	Glasgow	41,657	Schwinte (F)
1967	Bayern Munich 1	Rangers 0 *(aet)*	Nuremberg	69,480	Lo Bello (I)
1968	AC Milan 2	Hamburg 0	Rotterdam	53,000	Ortiz (Sp)
1969	Slovan Bratislava 3	Barcelona 2	Basle	19,000	Van Ravens (Ho)
1970	Manchester C 2	Gornik Zabrze 1	Vienna	8,000	Schiller (A)
1971	Chelsea 1	Real Madrid 1 *(aet)*	Athens	42,000	Scheurer (Sw)
Replay	Chelsea 2	Real Madrid 1 *(aet)*	Athens	35,000	Bucheli (Sw)
1972	Rangers 3	Moscow Dynamo 2	Barcelona	24,000	Ortiz (Sp)
1973	AC Milan 1	Leeds U 0	Salonika	45,000	Mihas (Gr)
1974	Magdeburg 2	AC Milan 0	Rotterdam	4000	Van Gemert (Ho)
1975	Dynamo Kiev 3	Ferencvaros 0	Basle	13,000	Davidson (S)
1976	Anderlecht 4	West Ham U 2	Brussels	58,000	Wurtz (F)
1977	Hamburg 2	Anderlecht 0	Amsterdam	65,000	Partridge (E)
1978	Anderlecht 4	Austria/WAC 0	Paris	48,679	Adlinger (WG)
1979	Barcelona 4	Fortuna Dusseldorf 3 *(aet)*	Basle	58,000	Palotai (H)
1980	Valencia 0 *(aet; Valencia won 5-4 on penalties)*	Arsenal 0	Brussels	36,000	Christov (Cz)
1981	Dynamo Tbilisi 2	Carl Zeiss Jena 1	Dusseldorf	9000	Lattanzi (I)
1982	Barcelona 2	Standard Liege 1	Barcelona	100,000	Eschweiler (WG)
1983	Aberdeen 2	Real Madrid 1 *(aet)*	Gothenburg	17,804	Menegali (I)
1984	Juventus 2	Porto 1	Basle	60,000	Prokop (EG)
1985	Everton 3	Rapid Vienna 1	Rotterdam	50,000	Casarin (I)
1986	Dynamo Kiev 3	Atletico Madrid 0	Lyon	39,300	Wohrer (A)
1987	Ajax 1	Lokomotiv Leipzig 0	Athens	35,000	Agnolin (I)
1988	Mechelen 1	Ajax 0	Strasbourg	39,446	Pauly (WG)
1989	Barcelona 2	Sampdoria 0	Berne	45,000	Courtney (E)
1990	Sampdoria 2	Anderlecht 0	Gothenburg	20,103	Galler (Sw)
1991	Manchester U 2	Barcelona 1	Rotterdam	42,000	Karlsson (Se)
1992	Werder Bremen 2	Monaco 0	Lisbon	16,000	D'Elia (I)
1993	Parma 3	Antwerp 1	Wembley	37,393	Assenmacher (G)
1994	Arsenal 1	Parma 0	Copenhagen	33,765	Krondl (Czr)
1995	Zaragoza 2	Arsenal 1	Paris	42,424	Ceccarini (I)
1996	Paris St Germain 1	Rapid Vienna 0	Brussels	37,500	Pairetto (I)
1997	Barcelona 1	Paris St Germain 0	Rotterdam	45,000	Merk (G)
1998	Chelsea 1	Stuttgart 0	Stockholm	30,216	Braschi (I)
1999	Lazio 2	Mallorca 1	Villa Park	33,021	Benko (A)

INTER-CITIES FAIRS CUP FINALS 1958–71

(Winners in italics)

Year	First Leg	Attendance	Second Leg	Attendance
1958	London 2 Barcelona 2	45,466	*Barcelona* 6 London 0	62,000
1960	Birmingham C 0 Barcelona 0	40,500	*Barcelona* 4 Birmingham C 1	70,000
1961	Birmingham C 2 Roma 2	21,005	*Roma* 2 Birmingham C 0	60,000
1962	Valencia 6 Barcelona 2	65,000	Barcelona 1 *Valencia* 1	60,000
1963	Dynamo Zagreb 1 Valencia 2	40,000	*Valencia* 2 Dynamo Zagreb 0	55,000
1964	*Zaragoza* 2 Valencia 1	50,000	(in Barcelona)	
1965	*Ferencvaros* 1 Juventus 0	25,000	(in Turin)	
1966	Barcelona 0 Zaragoza 1	70,000	Zaragoza 2 *Barcelona* 4	70,000
1967	Dynamo Zagreb 2 Leeds U 0	40,000	Leeds U 0 *Dynamo Zagreb* 0	35,604
1968	Leeds U 1 Ferencvaros 0	25,368	Ferencvaros 0 *Leeds U* 0	70,000
1969	Newcastle U 3 Ujpest Dozsa 0	60,000	Ujpest Dozsa 2 *Newcastle U* 3	37,000
1970	Anderlecht 3 Arsenal 1	37,000	*Arsenal* 3 Anderlecht 0	51,612
1971	Juventus 0 Leeds U 0 *(abandoned 51 minutes)*	42,000		
	Juventus 2 Leeds U 2	42,000	*Leeds U* 1* Juventus 1	42,483

UEFA CUP FINALS 1972–97

(Winners in italics)

Year	First Leg	Attendance	Second Leg	Attendance
1972	Wolverhampton W 1 Tottenham H 2	45,000	*Tottenham H* 1 Wolverhampton W 1	48,000
1973	Liverpool 0 Moenchengladbach 0 *(abandoned 27 minutes)*	44,967		
	Liverpool 3 Moenchengladbach 0	41,169	Moenchengladbach 2 *Liverpool* 0	35,000
1974	Tottenham H 2 Feyenoord 2	46,281	*Feyenoord* 2 Tottenham H 0	68,000
1975	Moenchengladbach 0 Twente 0	45,000	Twente 1 *Moenchengladbach* 5	24,500
1976	Liverpool 3 FC Brugge 2	56,000	FC Brugge 1 *Liverpool* 1	32,000
1977	Juventus 1 Athletic Bilbao 0	75,000	Athletic Bilbao 2 *Juventus* 1*	43,000
1978	Bastia 0 PSV Eindhoven 0	15,000	*PSV Eindhoven* 3 Bastia 0	27,000
1979	Red Star Belgrade 1 Moenchengladbach 1	87,500	*Moenchengladbach* 1 Red Star Belgrade 0	45,000
1980	Moenchengladbach 3 Eintracht Frankfurt 2	25,000	*Eintracht Frankfurt* 1* Moenchengladbach 0	60,000
1981	Ipswich T 3 AZ 67 Alkmaar 0	27,532	AZ 67 Alkmaar 4 *Ipswich T* 2	28,500
1982	Gothenburg 1 Hamburg 0	42,548	Hamburg 0 *Gothenburg* 3	60,000
1983	Anderlecht 1 Benfica 0	45,000	Benfica 1 *Anderlecht* 1	80,000
1984	Anderlecht 1 Tottenham H 1	40,000	*Tottenham H* 1[1] Anderlecht 1	46,258
1985	Videoton 0 Real Madrid 3	30,000	*Real Madrid* 0 Videoton 1	98,300
1986	Real Madrid 5 Cologne 1	80,000	Cologne 2 *Real Madrid* 0	15,000
1987	Gothenburg 1 Dundee U 0	50,023	Dundee U 1 *Gothenburg* 1	20,911
1988	Espanol 3 Bayer Leverkusen 0	42,000	*Bayer Leverkusen* 3[2] Espanol 0	22,000
1989	Napoli 2 Stuttgart 1	83,000	Stuttgart 3 *Napoli* 3	67,000
1990	Juventus 3 Fiorentina 1	45,000	Fiorentina 0 *Juventus* 0	32,000
1991	Internazionale 2 Roma 0	68,887	Roma 1 *Internazionale* 0	70,901
1992	Torino 2 Ajax 2	65,377	*Ajax* 0* Torino 0	40,000
1993	Borussia Dortmund 1 Juventus 3	37,000	*Juventus* 3 Borussia Dortmund 0	62,781
1994	Salzburg 0 Internazionale 1	47,500	*Internazionale* 1 Salzburg 0	80,326
1995	Parma 1 Juventus 0	23,000	Juventus 1 *Parma* 1	80,750
1996	Bayern Munich 2 Bordeaux 0	62,000	Bordeaux 1 *Bayern Munich* 3	36,000
1997	Schalke 1 Internazionale 0	56,824	Internazionale 1 *Schalke* 0[3]	81,670

**won on away goals* [1]*aet; Tottenham H won 4-3 on penalties* [2]*aet; Bayer Leverkusen won 3-2 on penalties*
[3]*aet; Schalke won 4-1 on penalties*

UEFA CUP FINALS 1998–2005

Year	Winners	Runners-up	Venue	Attendance	Referee
1998	Internazionale 3	Lazio 0	Paris	42,938	Nieto (Sp)
1999	Parma 3	Marseille 0	Moscow	61,000	Dallas (S)
2000	Galatasaray 0	Arsenal 0	Copenhagen	38,919	Nieto (Sp)
	(aet; Galatasaray won 4-1 on penalties).				
2001	Liverpool 5	Alaves 4	Dortmund	65,000	Veissiere (F)
	(aet; Liverpool won on sudden death).				
2002	Feyenoord 3	Borussia Dortmund 2	Rotterdam	45,000	Pereira (P)
2003	Porto 3	Celtic 2	Seville	52,972	Michel (Slv)
	(aet).				
2004	Valencia 2	Marseille 0	Gothenburg	40,000	Collina (I)
2005	CSKA Moscow 3	Sporting Lisbon 1	Lisbon	48,000	Poll (E)

UEFA CUP 2004–05

▪ *Denotes player sent off.*

FIRST QUALIFYING ROUND, FIRST LEG

B36 (1) 1 *(Midjord 45)*, Metalurgs (2) 3 *(Solonitsin 1, Dobrecovs 4, 63)* 250
B68 (0) 0, Ventspils (2) 3 *(Rimkus 15, 24, 65)* 350
BATE (2) 2 *(Zhaunov 15, Strakhanovich 19)*, Dynamo Tbilisi (1) 3 *(Kakaladze 45, Gancharov 56, Romero 90)* 5000
Bystrica (0) 3 *(Semenik 50, Svintek 64, Pecovsky 77)*, Karabakh (0) 0 6050
Ekranas (1) 1 *(Gardzuauskas 38)*, Dudelange (0) 0 3500
Haka (2) 2 *(Nenonen 2, 19)*, Etzella (1) 1 *(Grettnich 25 (pen))* 2500
IA Akranes (2) 4 *(Leosson 6, Thordarson 36, Bjornsson 52, Jonsson 90)*, VMK (0) 2 *(Malov 48, Smirnov 58)* 2000
Mariupol (0) 2 *(Zakarliuka 53, 84)*, Banants (0) 0 1000
Marsaxlokk (0) 0, Primorje (1) 1 *(Jolic 41)* 350
Mika (0) 0, Kispest Honved (0) 1 *(Csobanki 90)* 2000
Omonia (1) 4 *(Charalambous 40, Kozlej 47, Makris 83, 90)*, Sloga (0) 0 9000
Otaci (0) 1 *(Groshev 73)*, Shakhtjor Donetsk (0) 1 *(Bespanski 47)* 7000
Otelul (4) 4 *(Negru 10, Nanu 19, Iacob 27, Apostol 42)*, Dinamo Tirana (0) 0 4500
Partizani (2) 4 *(Bulku 23, Bylykbashi 27 (pen), Alcani 51, Bejzade 69)*, Birkirkara (1) 2 *(Brachini 34 (og), Mallia 82)* 2500
Pennarossa (0) 1 *(Zatoul 86)*, Zeljeznicar (4) 5 *(Gredic 1, Rascic 6, 11, Karic 31, Vrsajevic 60)* 500
Santa Coloma (0) 0, Modrica (0) 1 *(Vasic 55)* 450
Shirak (0) 1 *(Davtyan 70)*, Tiraspol (2) 2 *(Josan 6, Barburos 40)* 2500
Sileks (0) 0, Maribor (1) 1 *(Kvas 45)* 3000
Tbilisi (1) 1 *(Tchelideze 34)*, Shamkir (0) 0 2000

Thursday, 15 July, 2004

Glentoran (1) 2 *(Parkhouse 22, Lockhart 88)*
Allianssi (0) 2 *(Solehmainen 52, Munoz 68)* 2500
Glentoran: Morris; Nixon, McCann, Holmes (Hill 87), McGibbon, Leeman, Keegan, Melaugh, Parkhouse, Morgan (McLoughlin 77), Lockhart.
Allianssi: Sillanpaa; Solehmainen, Haara, Simula, Mariamaa, Vajanne, Sampo (Vuorinen 21), Sarajarvi, Stafsula (Ojanen 78), Munoz, Rantanen.

Haverfordwest (0) 0
Hafnarfjordur (0) 1 *(Borgvardt 74)* 612
(at Ninian Park).
Haverfordwest: Kendall; Barnhouse, Jones R (Hudgell 46), Rossiter, Thomas, Jones W, Blain, Twynham (Heal 60), Griffiths (Algieri 74), Loss, Hicks.
Hafnarfjordur: Larusson; Saevarsson, Gardarsson S, Nielsen, Bjarnason, Bjornsson, Gardarsson J (Asgeirsson 75), Bett, Borgvardt, Gudjonsson (Karkov 87), Hallfredsson (Stefansson 68).

Levadia (0) 0
Bohemians (0) 0 3000
Levadia: Kotenko; Cepauskas, Leitan, Sisov, Nahk, Dmitrijev, Voskoboinikov (Ratnikov 85), Kruglov, Purje (Arbeiter 66), Dovydenas (Tselnokov 66), Hohlov-Simson.
Bohemians: Kelly; Lynch, Webb, Hunt, Heary, Caffrey, Morrison, Harkin, Grant A, Crowe, Oman.

Oster (0) 2 *(Cederqvist 77, 83)*
TNS (0) 0 1153
Oster: Kennfors; Jonsson (Ottossen 66), Petterssen, Thor, Gustafson, Velic, Goorks, Svensson, Cederqvist, Karlsson, Nouri (Wibran 52).
TNS: Doherty; Holmes, Alcide (Connelly 59), Hogan, Taylor, Aggrey, Ruscoe, Leah, Wood, Davies (Beck 81), Ward.

Portadown (2) 2 *(McCann P 12, 16)*
Zalgiris (0) 2 *(Maksimovic 66, Stesko A 80)* 528
Portadown: Miskelly; Feeney, O'Hara, Lindsay, Neill, Clarke (McCann M 46), McCann P, Boyle, Hamilton, Arkins, Alerdice.
Zalgiris: Malinauskas; Grazulis, Graziunas, Zekonis, Kilikevicius, Sorokinas (Stesko I 64), Lemezis, Jasaitis (Stesko A 77), Joksas (Maksimovic 46), Cepas, Kauspadas.

Vaduz (0) 1 *(Polverino 73)*
Longford Town (0) 0 1300
Vaduz: Silva; Hasler D, Martin Stocklasa, Weller (Ekye 64), Dos Santos, Perez (Polverino 46), Burgmeier, Zarn, Telser, Fischer (Gerster 82), Gohouri.
Longford Town: O'Brien; Murphy, Dillon, Perth (Martin 79), Ferguson, Keogh (Fitzgerald 28), Kirby, Lavine, Paisley, Barrett (Francis 85), Prunty.

FIRST QUALIFYING ROUND, SECOND LEG

Banants (0) 0, Mariupol (1) 2 *(Esin 30, Platonov 77)* 2500
Birkirkara (0) 2 *(Zahra 56, Dronca 84)*, Partizani (1) 1 *(Bylykbashi 45)* 2500
Dinamo Tirana (1) 1 *(Qosa 24)*, Otelul (2) 4 *(Danciu 22 (pen), 80, Rohat 37, Aldea 70)* 1750
Dudelange (0) 1 *(Mouny 86)*, Ekranas (1) 2 *(Savenas 6, Majus 50)* 1500
Dynamo Tbilisi (0) 1 *(Kvirkvelia 86)*, BATE (0) 0 15,000
Etzella (1) 1 *(Mischo 1)*, Haka (1) 3 *(Ristila 10, Terehhov 47, Innanen 64)* 1500
Karabakh (0) 0, Bystrica (0) 1 *(Jabbarov 61 (og))* 4500
Kispest Honved (0) 1 *(Babik 59)*, Mika (1) 1 *(Shahgeldyan 42)* 7500
Maribor (1) 1 *(Jelic 7)*, Sileks (0) 1 *(Ristic 78)* 8000
Metalurgs (6) 8 *(Dobrecovs 2, Katasonov 18, 30, 34, 42, Solonitsin 29 (pen), Lukosevicius 77, Grebis 78)*, B36 (0) 1 *(Joensen J 73)* 2000
Modrica (1) 3 *(Ljubicic 35, Novakovic 66, Pavic 88)*, Santa Coloma (0) 0 300
Primorje (2) 2 *(Jolic 12, Milos 15)*, Marsaxlokk (0) 0 1000
Shakhtjor Donetsk (1) 1 *(Slesarcuks 6)*, Otaci (1) 2 *(Belavusau 25 (og), Pogreban 88)* 8000
Shamkir (0) 1 *(Aliyev 90)*, Tbilisi (2) 4 *(Tchelideze 26, Mikuchadze 40, 78, Kvaratskhelia 83)* 4000
Sloga (0) 1 *(Nuhiji 84)*, Omonia (1) 4 *(Georgiou 10, Michailovic 50, Kaiafas 69, Kekic 90)* 1750
Tiraspol (1) 2 *(Corneencov 9, Nesteruk 56)*, Shirak (0) 0 1200
Ventspils (3) 8 *(Bicka 17, Stukalinas 33, Rimkus 43, Rekhviashvili 47, Smirnovs 56, Butriks 71, Krohmer 85, Agafonov 88)*, B68 (0) 0 750
VMK (0) 1 *(Borissov 89)*, IA Akranes (1) 2 *(Bjornsson 44, 51)* 2500
Zeljeznicar (2) 4 *(Kajtaz 21, Kurt 32, Rascic 40, 58)*, Pennarossa (0) 0 5000

Tuesday, 27 July, 2004

Bohemians (0) 1 *(Crowe 55)*
Levadia (1) 3 *(Cepauskas 10, Tselnokov 69, Dovydenas 78)* 4500
Bohemians: Kelly; Lynch (Keddy 71), Webb (Ward 78), Hunt, Hawkins, Caffrey (Ryan 46), Morrison, Harkin, Heary, Crowe, Grant A.
Levadia: Kotenko; Cepauskas, Leitan (Ratnikov 85), Arbeiter (Tselnokov 46), Sisov, Nahk, Dmitrijev, Voskoboinikov (Vassiljev 73), Kruglov, Dovydenas, Hohlov-Simson.

Thursday, 29 July, 2004

Allianssi (1) 1 *(Munoz 39)*

Glentoran (0) 2 *(McCallion 70, Nixon 81)* 1089

Allianssi: Sillanpaa; Solehmainen, Haara, Simula, Marjamaa, Vajanne, Sampo (Vuorinen 13) (Stafsula 74), Sarajarvi, Cleaver (Ahlberg 84), Munoz, Rantanen.
Glentoran: Morris; Nixon, McCann, Holmes, Leeman, McGibbon, Keegan, McCallion, Parkhouse, Morgan (Halliday 46), Lockhart.

Hafnarfjordur (1) 3 *(Thomas 20 (og), Hallfredsson 63, Bett 65)*

Haverfordwest (1) 1 *(Hicks 19)* 800

Hafnarfjordur: Larusson; Saevarsson, Gardarsson S, Nielsen, Bjarnason, Bjornsson, Gardarsson J (Asgeirsson 64), Bett, Borgvardt (Stefansson 65), Gudjonsson, Hallfredsson (Karkov 72).
Haverfordwest: Kendall; Blain, Jones, Rossiter, Thomas, Barnhouse, Heal, Twynham, Hicks, Loss, Hudgell.

Longford Town (0) 2 *(Fitzgerald 86, Ferguson 88)*

Vaduz (1) 3 *(Zarn 5, Burgmeier 49, Weller 54)* 2550

Longford Town: O'Brien; Murphy, Dillon, Sheridan (Fitzgerald 30), Ferguson, Baker D, Kirby (Perth 60), Paisley (Keegan 46), Lavine, Barrett, Prunty.
Vaduz: Silva; Michael Stocklasa, Hasler D, Martin Stocklasa (Gerster 63), Dos Santos, Perez, Burgmeier (Obhafuoso 86), Zarn, Telser, Gohouri, Polverino (Weller 53).

TNS (0) 1 *(Wilde 79)*

Oster (1) 2 *(Cederqvist 11, Soderberg 88)* 654

(at Wrexham).

TNS: Doherty; Holmes, McGuire (Davies 60), Hogan, Taylor (Alcide 78), Aggrey, Ruscoe, Leah, Wood, Wilde, Ward (Toner 46).
Oster: Green; Jonsson, Peterssen (Nouri 88), Thor, Wibran, Gustafson (Mattson 77), Soderberg, Goorks, Svensson, Karlsson, Cederqvist (Ottossen 75).

Zalgiris (2) 2 *(Mikuckis 7, Kauspadas 20)*

Portadown (0) 0 2000

Zalgiris: Malinauskas; Graziunas, Zekonis, Sorokinas, Mikuckis, Lemezis, Shyla, Naumovas, Maksimovic (Stesko A 61), Cepas (Stesko I 56), Kauspadas (Kilikevicius 83).
Portadown: Miskelly; Feeney (Craig 19), O'Hara, Lindsay, Neill (Clarke 46), Collins■, McCann P, Boyle, Hamilton, Arkins, Alerdice (Convery 46).

SECOND QUALIFYING ROUND, FIRST LEG

AEK Larnaca (3) 3 *(Isailovic 18, 31, 45)*, Maccabi Petah Tikva (0) 0 12,000
Amica (1) 1 *(Kryszalowicz 23)*, Kispest Honved (0) 0 2500
Beveren (2) 3 *(Tokpa 22, N'Dri 26, Ne 65)*, Vaduz (0) 1 *(Zarn 56)* 3000
Bodo Glimt (1) 2 *(Johansen 1 (pen), Berg 77 (pen))*, Levadia (1) 1 *(Voskoboinikov 9)* 3250
Buducnost (1) 1 *(Milosevic 22 (pen))*, Maribor (1) 2 *(Bersnjak 37, Teinovic 76)* 3700
Bystrica (0) 3 *(Semenik 75, 79 (pen), Jakubko 90)*, Wil (0) 1 *(Nushi 71)* 4500
Dynamo Zagreb (3) 4 *(Kranjcar 4, Bosnjak 19, Pranjic 28, Zahora 69)*, Primorje (0) 0 5000
Genclerbirligi (1) 1 *(Nas 45)*, Rijeka (0) 0 5000
Hammarby (1) 2 *(Runstrom 7, Ostlund 84)*, IA Akranes (0) 0 6000
Hapoel Bnei (2) 3 *(Sowan 16, Agoye 32, 54)*, Partizani (0) 0 2000
Levski (2) 5 *(Vasic 5 (og), Chilikov 13, 77, 79, Angelov 88)*, Modrica (0) 0 4500
Mariupol (0) 0, FK Austria (0) 0 1500
Metalurg Donetsk (1) 3 *(Ture 30, Stolica 74, 90)*, Tiraspol (0) 0 10,000
Odd (0) 3 *(Occean 46, 78, Rambekk 66)*, Ekranas (1) 1 *(Luksys 38)* 2000
Omonia (0) 1 *(Kozlej 57)*, CSKA Sofia (0) 1 *(Mujiri 77)* 7500
Oster (1) 2 *(Cederqvist 23, 85)*, Metalurgs (1) 2 *(Katasonov 36, Dobrecovs 90)* 2500
Otaci (0) 1 *(Bursuc 51 (pen))*, Sigma Olomouc (0) 2 *(Hudec 54, Babnic 84)* 7500
Otelul (0) 0, Partizan Belgrade (0) 0 5000
Pasching (2) 3 *(Glieder 16 (pen), 85 (pen), Mayrleb 35)*, Zenit (1) 1 *(Kafkas 10 (og))* 3000
Petrzalka (0) 0, Dnepr (0) 3 *(Semochko 61, Nazarenko 78, Mikhailenko 88)* 2500
Rapid Vienna (0) 0, Rubin (0) 2 *(Ronieliton 50, Boyarintsev 64)* 17,500
Slavia Prague (0) 3 *(Da Silva 60 (pen), Pitak 64, Kalivoda 77)*, Dynamo Tbilisi (1) 1 *(Melkadze 12)* 3500
Stabaek (0) 3 *(Gunnarsson 50, Markegard 53, Olsen 90)*, Haka (0) 1 *(Popovich 49)* 450
Tbilisi (0) 0, Legia (0) 1 *(Sokolowski 77)* 5000
Terek (0) 1 *(Khomukha 90)*, Lech (0) 0 2500
Ujpest (1) 3 *(Polonkai 42, Rajczi 56, Toth 63)*, Servette (0) 1 *(Alicarte 58 (pen))* 7500
Ventspils (0) 0, Brondby (0) 0 750
Zalgiris (1) 1 *(Kauspadas 34 (pen))*, Aalborg (0) 3 *(Nielsen 46, 49, Lundberg 74)* 4500
Zeleznik (0) 2 *(Drinic 66, Goulart 86)*, Steaua (3) 4 *(Oprita 18, Neaga 24, 49, Paraschiv 34)* 3000
Zeljeznicar (0) 1 *(Avdija 60)*, Litets (0) 2 *(Hidiouad 67, Neto 73)* 5500

Thursday, 12 August, 2004

Glentoran (0) 0

Elfsborg (0) 1 *(Alexandersson J 88)* 4700

Glentoran: Morris; Nixon, McCann, Holmes, Leeman, McGibbon, Keegan (Melaugh 81), McCallion, Parkhouse (McLoughlin 81), Halliday, Lockhart.
Elfsborg: Wiland; Sjoberg■, Karlsson, Holmen, Nilsson L, Berggren (Stromberg 90), Alexandersson J, Klarstrom (Alexandersson D 90), Samuelsson, Arvhage, Drugge (Andersson 46).

Hafnarfjordur (2) 2 *(Gardarsson J 19, Borgvardt 22)*

Dunfermline Athletic (0) 2 *(Brewster 72, Skerla 88)* 1500

Hafnarfjordur: Larusson; Saevarsson, Gardarsson S, Nielsen, Bjarnason, Bjornsson, Gardarsson J (Karkov 83), Bett (Vidarsson 73), Borgvardt (Stefansson 46), Gudjonsson, Hallfredsson.
Dunfermline Athletic: Stillie; Shields, Wilson S, Byrne, Skerla, Thomson (Donnelly 72), Nicholson, Mason, Hunt, Tod (Brewster 46), Dempsey (Derek Young 46).

SECOND QUALIFYING ROUND, SECOND LEG

Aalborg (0) 0, Zalgiris (0) 0 5000
Brondby (1) 1 *(Johansen 33 (pen))*, Ventspils (1) 1 *(Agafonov 5)* 4000
CSKA Sofia (0) 3 *(Mujiri 90, Sakaliev 110, Hazurov 116)*, Omonia (0) 1 *(Stjepanovic 78)* 5000
Dynamo Tbilisi (1) 2 *(Melkadze 44, Kankava 66)*, Slavia Prague (0) 0 7500
Dnepr (1) 1 *(Kostyshyn 43)*, Petrzalka (1) 1 *(Borbely 45)* 15,000
Ekranas (2) 2 *(Kavaliauskas 9, Paulauskas 30)*, Odd (0) 1 *(Knutsen 90)* 4000
FK Austria (1) 3 *(Sionko 31, Vastic 53 (pen), 61 (pen))*, Mariupol (0) 0 7500
Haka (1) 1 *(Ristila 31 (pen))*, Stabaek (2) 3 *(Wowoah 2, 36, Stenersen 61)* 2500
IA Akranes (1) 1 *(Sveinsson 38)*, Hammarby (2) 2 *(Brewah 18, Andersson 45)* 1250
Kispest Honved (0) 1 *(Takacs 46)*, Amica (0) 0 7000
(Amica won 5-4 on penalties).
Lech (0) 0, Terek (0) 1 *(Fedkov 81)* 2500
Legia (3) 6 *(Wlodarczyk 5 (pen), 44, 51, Magiera 23, Saganowski 80, Sokolowski 84)*, Tbilisi (0) 0 9000
Levadia (2) 2 *(Voskoboinikov 17, Vassiljev 45)*, Bodo Glimt (0) 1 *(Ludvigsen 90)* 2500
(Bodo Glimt won 8-7 on penalties).
Litets (5) 7 *(Neto 1, 9, 36, Tiago Silva 13, Hidiouad 42, Beliakov 73, 78)*, Zeljeznicar (0) 0 1250
Maccabi Petah Tikva (4) 4 *(Golan 1, Aristocleous 24 (og), Mashiach 40, 45 (pen))*, AEK Larnaca (0) 0 2500
Maribor (0) 0, Buducnost (0) 1 *(Novakovic 66)* 7500

Metalurgs (0) 1 *(Danilovs 53)*, Oster (1) 1 *(Cederqvist 29)* 3000
Modrica (0) 0, Levski (1) 3 *(Telkiyski 48, Lucio Wagner 82, 90)* 350
Partizan Belgrade (1) 1 *(Radonjic 29)*, Otelul (0) 0 9000
Partizani (0) 1 *(Bylykbashi 56)*, Hapoel Bnei (2) 3 *(Agoye 21, 45, Hamlid 72)* 2570
Primorje (0) 2 *(Mlakar 70, Gregoric 88)*, Dynamo Zagreb (0) 0 1500
Rijeka (1) 2 *(Erceg 13, 53)*, Genclerbirligi (0) 1 *(Ugur 90)* 3000
Rubin (0) 0, Rapid Vienna (2) 3 *(Hofmann 17, 70, Kincl 29)* 2000
Servette (0) 0, Ujpest (0) 2 *(Bukszegi 82, Feczesin 90)* 5500
Sigma Olomouc (2) 4 *(Vyskocil 31, 58, Kucera 36, Bednar 66)*, Otaci (0) 0 5000
Steaua (0) 1 *(Dica 79)*, Zeleznik (1) 2 *(Drinic 10, Goulart 73)* 15,000
Tiraspol (1) 1 *(Corneencov 29)*, Metalurg Donetsk (0) 2 *(Checher 53, Mendoza 88)* 1500
Vaduz (0) 1 *(Zarn 78)*, Beveren (1) 2 *(Djire 32, N'Dri 56)* 500
Wil (0) 1 *(Zverotic 67)*, Bystrica (0) 1 *(Semenik 61)* 1000
Zenit (2) 2 *(Vjestica 10, Kerzhakov 18)*, Pasching (0) 0 17,500

Thursday, 26 August, 2004

Dunfermline Athletic (0) 1 *(Dempsey 72)*

Hafnarfjordur (0) 2 *(Bjornsson 82, Nielsen 90)* 7189

Dunfermline Athletic: Stillie; Shields, Wilson S, Darren Young, Skerla, Thomson (Byrne 85), Mason (Tod 90), Hunt, Brewster, Derek Young (Donnelly 84), Dempsey.
Hafnarfjordur: Larusson; Saevarsson, Gardarsson S, Nielsen, Bjarnason, Hallfredsson, Gardarsson J (Asgeirsson 65), Bett, Borgvardt, Gudjonsson (Vidarsson 80), Stefansson (Bjornsson 75).

Elfsborg (1) 2 *(Klarstrom 45, Alexandersson J 78)*

Glentoran (1) 1 *(Halliday 28)* 1515

Elfsborg: Wiland; Karlsson, Andersson, Ilola, Holmen (Stromberg 81), Nilsson L, Berggren (Samuelsson 70), Alexandersson J, Klarstrom, Arvhage, Drugge (Alexandersson D 59).
Glentoran: Morris; Nixon, McCann (Glendinning 57), Holmes (Kilmartin 89), Leeman, McGibbon, Keegan (Hill 80), McCallion, Parkhouse, Halliday, Lockhart.

FIRST ROUND, FIRST LEG

Aalborg (1) 1 *(Borgersen 43)*, Auxerre (1) 1 *(Benjani 38)* 6084
Aigaleo (1) 1 *(Barkoglou 14 (pen))*, Genclerbirligi (0) 0 4500
FK Austria (0) 1 *(Kiesenebner 83)*, Legia (0) 0 16,000
Bodo Glimt (1) 1 *(Berg R 20)*, Besiktas (0) 1 *(Hassan 86)* 4196
FC Brugge (2) 4 *(Clement 17, Simons 42 (pen), Verheyen 80, Stoica 88)*, Chateauroux (0) 0 Ferreira■ 10,481
Bystrica (0) 0, Benfica (1) 3 *(Simao Sabrosa 38, 63, Joao Pereira 72)* 6500
Dynamo Zagreb (1) 2 *(Karic 6, Bosnjak 78)* Mijatovic■, Elfsborg (0) 0 10,000
Gorica (1) 1 *(Rodic 1)*, AEK Athens (1) 1 *(Katsouranis 40)* 1500
Graz (3) 5 *(Bazina 14, 51, Kollmann 39, 44, Pogatetz 85)*, Litets (0) 0 Zagorcic■ 7000
Hafnarfjordur (0) 1 *(Bjornsson 87)*, Aachen (3) 5 *(Michalke 12, 14, Meijer 44, Klitzpera 89, Plasshenrich 90)* 3000
Hammarby (1) 1 *(Runstrom 24)*, Villarreal (2) 2 *(Guayre 12, Gonzalo Rodriguez 23)* 11,122
Levski (0) 1 *(Telkiyski 62)*, Beveren (0) 1 *(Sanogo 64)* 20,000
Maccabi Haifa (1) 1 *(Solautti 31)*, Dnepr (0) 0 4500
Maccabi Petah Tikva v Heerenveen; match cancelled due to general strike in Israel; First Leg cancelled.
Metalurg Donetsk (0) 0, Lazio (0) 3 *(Rocchi 73, Cesar 75, Pandev 85)* 12,000
Odd (0) 0, Feyenoord (0) 1 *(Ono 74)* 4125
PAOK Salonika (2) 2 *(Salpigidis 25, Vokolos 31)*, AZ (2) 3 *(Van Galen 18, Landzaat 35, Meerdink 49)* 9000
Panionios (2) 3 *(Dodd 27, Giannopoulos 45, 59)* Tziolis■, Udinese (1) 1 *(Pinzi 28)* 7500
Parma (2) 3 *(Maccarone 8, 25, 67)*, Maribor (1) 2 *(Kvas 16 (pen), Golob 87)* 9000
Partizan Belgrade (0) 3 *(Tomic 53, Boya 54, Brnovic 85)*, Dynamo Bucharest (1) 1 *(Danciulescu 23)* 10,500
Schalke (1) 5 *(Sand 20, 52, 60, Kobiashvili 67, Asamoah 90)*, Metalurgs (1) 1 *(Katasonovs 34)* 50,304
Sevilla (1) 2 *(Baptista 31, Sergio 79)*, Nacional (0) 0 35,000
Sochaux (1) 4 *(Oruma 25, Zairi 60, Ilan 69, Isabey 84)*, Stabaek (0) 0 12,000
Sporting Lisbon (0) 2 *(Tinga 61, Liedson 85)* Polga■, Rapid Vienna (0) 0 19,861
Standard Liege (0) 0, Bochum (0) 0 9800
Steaua (1) 2 (Neaga 9, Dica 78), CSKA Sofia (1) 1 *(Yanev 28)* 17,000
Terek (1) 1 *(Fedkov 38)*, Basle (0) 1 *(Gimenez 57)* 3500
Trabzonspor (2) 3 *(Javi Gonzalez 26 (og), Yilmaz 27, Karadeniz 69)*, Athletic Bilbao (0) 2 *(Gurpegui 74, 80)* 18,000
Ujpest (0) 1 *(Nagy 63)*, Stuttgart (2) 3 *(Cacau 25, 90, Kuranyi 30)* 11,000
Utrecht (2) 4 *(Van der Haar 3, Tanghe 37, 89, Van den Bergh 75)*, Djurgaarden (0) 0 20,000
Ventspils (0) 1 *(Rimkus 72)*, Amica (1) 1 *(Gregorek 26)* 800
Wisla (0) 4 *(Gorawski 60, Zurawski 62, Frankowski 64, 76)*, Dinamo Tbilisi (2) 3 *(Kankava 18, Aladashvili 26, Klos 84 (og))* 6000
Zaragoza (0) 1 *(Generelo 83)*, Sigma Olomouc (0) 0 25,000
Zenit (3) 4 *(Arshavin 26, 45, Gorshkov 32, Kerzhakov 53)*, Red Star Belgrade (0) 0 22,000

Thursday, 16 September, 2004

Hearts (0) 3 *(Webster 52, Hartley 62, Kisnorbo 90)*

Braga (0) 1 *(Paulo Sergio 65)* 18,203

Hearts: Gordon; Neilson, Maybury, Kisnorbo, Pressley, Webster, Hamill (MacFarlane 81), Hartley, McAllister, De Vries, Stamp (Wyness 79).
Braga: Paulo Santos; Abel, Jorge Luiz, Vandinho, Paulo Jorge, Nunes, Luis Loureiro, Paulo Sergio (Cesinha 75), Baha (Jaime 37), Wender, Kenedy.

Maritimo (1) 1 *(Manduca 27)*

Rangers (0) 0 5000

Maritimo: Marcos; Ferreira, Briguel, Wenio, Tonel, Van der Gaag, Leo Lima (Zeca 84), Luis Filipe, Chainho, Alan, Manduca (Zumbi 73).
Rangers: Klos; Ross, Vignal, Ricksen, Moore, Boumsong, Burke, Mladenovic, Arveladze, Novo (Lovenkrands 83), Prso.

Middlesbrough (0) 3 *(Hasselbaink 57, Viduka 63, 80)*

Banik Ostrava (0) 0 29,746

Middlesbrough: Schwarzer; Parnaby, Queudrue, Riggott, Southgate, Boateng, Nemeth, Parlour, Hasselbaink, Viduka, Zenden.
Banik Ostrava: Raska; Pospech, Drozd, Bystron, Besta, Dvornik (Velkoborsky 15), Latal, Zubek, Matusovic (Papadopoulos 87), Licka (Lukes 65), Cizek.

Millwall (0) 1 *(Wise 66)*

Ferencvaros (0) 1 *(Lipcsei 78)* 15,000

Millwall: Stack; Elliott, Muscat, Livermore, Lawrence, Ward, Wise, Morris (Cogan 36), Moore (Ifill 77), Harris (Dichio 80), Simpson.
Ferencvaros: Szucs; Balog (Zavadszky 90), Tozser, Vukmir, Gyepes, Botis, Kapic, Rosa, Vagner (Penksa 71), Bajevszki (Sowunmi 80), Lipcsei.

Newcastle United (2) 2 *(Kluivert 4, 42)*

Hapoel Bnei (0) 0 30,221

Newcastle United: Given; Carr, Hughes (Bernard 15), Jenas, O'Brien, Elliott, Dyer (Butt■ 58), Bowyer, Kluivert, Ameobi (Milner 69), Robert.
Hapoel Bnei: Marambadoro; Rabah, Ghnaim (Salameh 80), Suan■, Etchi, Danan, Kassom (Edri 84), Eliyahu, Hamud (Rodrigues 54), Olumide, Masudi.

Shelbourne (0) 2 *(Fitzpatrick 80, 83)*

Lille (2) 2 *(Bodmer 20, Landrin 45)* 7463

Shelbourne: Williams; Heary, Byrne J, Rogers, Crawley, Harris, Crawford, Hoolihan (McCarthy 85), Morgan (Fitzpatrick 65), Ndo (Cawley 46), Cahill.
Lille: Sylva; Tavlaridis, Bodmer (Audel 70), Makoun, Moussilou (Raynier 75), Brunel (Chalme 85), Tafforeau, Vitakic, Angbwa, Dumont, Landrin.

FIRST ROUND, SECOND LEG

Aachen (0) 0, Hafnarfjordur (0) 0 21,704
(in Cologne).
AEK Athens (0) 1 *(Soares 90)*, Gorica (0) 0 14,000
Amica (1) 1 *(Dembinski 45)*, Ventspils (0) 0 2000
Athletic Bilbao (1) 2 *(Ezquerro 5, Yeste 61)*, Trabzonspor (0) 0 20,000
Auxerre (1) 2 *(Kalou 4, Mwaruwari 72)*, Aalborg (0) 0 5336
AZ (1) 2 *(Buskermolen 10, Mathijsen 72)*, PAOK Salonika (1) 1 *(Salpigidis 9)* 7923
Basle (1) 2 *(Rossi 11, Kleber 89)*, Terek (0) 0 15,895
Benfica (2) 2 *(Zahovic 14, Nuno Gomes 18)*, Bystrica (0) 0 3000
Besiktas (1) 1 *(Uzulmez 45)*, Bodo Glimt (0) 0 27,000
Beveren (1) 1 *(Ne 45)*, Levski (0) 0 5500
Bochum (1) 1 (Maltritz 45), Standard Liege (1) 1 *(Wiston 90)* 23,536
Chateauroux (1) 1 *(Chafni 25)*, FC Brugge (2) 2 *(Lange 15, Gvozdenovic 31)* 8170
CSKA Sofia (1) 2 *(Sakaliev 45, Gargarov 75)*, Steaua (2) 2 *(Oprita 14, Paraschiv 34)* 20,000
Dinamo Bucharest (0) 0, Partizan Belgrade (0) 0 20,000
Dynamo Tbilisi (0) 2 *(Nemsadze 60 (pen), Kakaladze 64)*, Wisla (0) 1 *(Frankowski 79)* Baszczynski■ 20,000
Djurgaarden (2) 3 *(Johansson 3, Hysen 39, 80)*, Utrecht (0) 0 4449
Dnepr (1) 2 *(Mikhailenko 34, Rusol 81)*, Maccabi Haifa (0) 0 25,000
Elfsborg (0) 0, Dynamo Zagreb (0) 0 1016
Feyenoord (2) 4 *(Bosschaart 2, Kuijt 45, Goor 73, Kalou 90)*, Odd (0) 1 (Occean 49) 18,500
Genclerbirligi (0) 1 *(Friesenbichler 54 (og))*, Aigaleo (1) 1 *(Barkoglou 42)* 8500
Heerenveen (2) 5 *(Bruggink 15, Vayrynen 16, Hansson 56, Sikora 71, Selakovic 80)*, Maccabi Petah Tikva (0) 0 14,000
Lazio (3) 3 *(Liverani 10, 27, Muzzi 23)*, Metalurg Donetsk (0) 0 5000
Legia (0) 1 *(Smolinski 85)*, FK Austria (2) 3 *(Vachousek 32, Poledica 42 (og), Sionko 90)* 13,000
Litets (0) 1 *(Joaozinho 67)*, Graz (0) 0 1500
Maribor (0) 0, Parma (0) 0 5500
Metalurgs (0) 0, Schalke (1) 4 *(Sand 44, Hanke 63, 78, 90)* 2000
Nacional (0) 1 *(Adriano 75)*, Sevilla (1) 2 *(Jesuli 35, Renato 83)* 4100
Rapid Vienna (0) 0, Sporting Lisbon (0) 0 17,500
Red Star Belgrade (1) 1 *(Pantelic 17)*, Zenit (0) 2 *(Spivak 58 (pen), Makarov 84)* 18,000
Sigma Olomouc (1) 2 *(Hudec 10, Kobylik 52 (pen))*, Zaragoza (0) 3 *(Soriano 77, Hudec 80 (og), Javi Moreno 86)* 8764
Stabaek (0) 0, Sochaux (2) 5 *(Santos 25, Zairi 35, Ilan 76, 90, Mathieu 81)* 503
Stuttgart (4) 4 *(Hinkel 14, Cacau 55, 61, Heldt 57 (pen))*, Ujpest (0) 0 23,000
Udinese (0) 1 *(Mauri 82)* Jankulovski■, Panionios (0) 0 21,000
Villarreal (1) 3 *(Guayre 10, Hector Font 57, Cazorla 84)*, Hammarby (0) 0 Covic■ 14,000

Thursday, 30 September, 2004

Banik Ostrava (1) 1 *(Bystron 19)*

Middlesbrough (0) 1 *(Morrison 90)* 15,351

Banik Ostrava: Raska; Pospech, Licka, Zubek (Zurek 69), Besta, Dvornik, Latal, Bystron, Matusovic, Papadopoulos (Velkovorsky 81), Cizek.
Middlesbrough: Schwarzer; Parnaby, Queudrue■, Cooper, Southgate, Doriva, Morrison, Boateng, Nemeth (Christie 84), Downing, Zenden.

Braga (1) 2 *(Joao Tomas 12, Jaime 77)*

Hearts (1) 2 *(De Vries 27, 47)* 13,007

Braga: Paulo Santos; Paulo Jorge, Nem, Jorge Luiz, Paulo Sergio, Joao Tomas, Jaime, Kenedy (Castanheira 44), Wender (Cesinha 68), Abel (Baha 60), Vandinho.
Hearts: Gordon; Maybury, Webster, Pressley, Kisnorbo, McAllister, Neilson, Stamp (Pereira 84), Hartley, MacFarlane, De Vries (McKenna 78).

Ferencvaros (3) 3 *(Rosa 26, Botis 31, Vagner 40)*

Millwall (1) 1 *(Wise 45)* 15,229

Ferencvaros: Szucs; Vukmir, Balog, Tozser (De Almeida 63), Gyepes, Botis, Rosa, Zovath, Vagner (Sowunmi 88), Penksa (Bajevszki 72), Lipcsei.
Millwall: Stack; Muscat, Simpson (Sweeney 61), Elliott (McCammon 46), Lawrence, Ward, Wise, Morris, Harris (Cogan 70), Ifill, Livermore.

Hapoel Bnei (1) 1 *(Masudi 13)*

Newcastle United (3) 5 *(Kluivert 9, 42, Shearer 38, 52 (pen), 90)* 1200

Hapoel Bnei: Marambadoro■; Rabah (Vieira 79), Ghnaim, Arshid (Edri 46), Etchi, Danan, Kassom, Khalaila, Eliyahu, Agoye (Abu Salah 71), Masudi.
Newcastle United: Given (Harper 46); Carr, Bernard, Jenas, O'Brien, Hughes, Bowyer, Bellamy, Shearer, Kluivert (Milner 61), Robert (Ambrose 61).

Lille (2) 2 *(Acimovic 17, Moussilou 27)*

Shelbourne (0) 0 10,787

Lille: Sylva; Acimovic (Chalme 83), Angbwa, Bodmer, Landrin, Makoun, Moussilou (Brunel 67), Schmitz, Tafforeau, Tavlaridis, Audel (Maralas 90).
Shelbourne: Williams; Heary, Crawley, Rogers, Harris, Crawford, Cahill, Byrne S (Cawley 88), Moore, Byrne J (Fitzpatrick 65), Hoolihan (McCarthy 80).

Rangers (0) 1 *(Prso 71)*

Maritimo (0) 0 47,360

Rangers: Klos; Ross, Khizanishvili, Boumsong, Vanoli (Vignal 66), Burke (Arveladze 96), Malcolm (Hughes 80), Ricksen, Prso, Thompson, Novo.
Maritimo: Marcos; Ferreira, Van der Gaag, Tonel, Briguel, Alan (Silas 67), Wenio, Chainho, Bino (Luis Filipe 72), Manduca (Souza 84), Leo Lima.
aet; Rangers won 4-2 on penalties.

GROUP STAGE

GROUP A

Thursday, 21 October 2004

Feyenoord (1) 3 *(Kuijt 22, 83, Goor 57)*
Hearts (0) 0 28,000
Feyenoord: Babos; Saidi, Bosschaart, Kuijt, Ono, Goor, Paauwe, Kalou (Buffel 67), Basto (Mtiliga 64), Castelen (Lazovic 81), Zuiverloon.
Hearts: Gordon; Maybury, Kisnorbo (Stewart 82), Pressley, McKenna, Webster, Neilson, McAllister (Wyness 71), Hamill, Hartley, MacFarlane (Weir 41).

Schalke (1) 1 *(Kobiashvili 8)*
Basle (0) 1 *(Delgado 82)* 52,870
Schalke: Rost; Poulsen, Kobiashvili, Oude Kamphuis, Bordon, Altintop (Varela 68), Asamoah, Krstajic, Pander, Lincoln (Ailton 87), Sand (Hanke 87).
Basle: Zuberbuhler; Zwyssig, Huggel, Petric, Chipperfield (Sterjovski 64), Gimenez (Carignano 83), Kleber, Degen D, Degen P, Smiljanic, Rossi (Delgado 64).

Thursday, 4 November 2004

Ferencvaros (1) 1 *(Tozser 27)*
Feyenoord (0) 1 *(Kalou 62)* 24,000
Ferencvaros: Szucs; Vukmir, Botis, Gyepes, Balog, Lipcsei, Kapic, Huszti, Tozser (Penksa 20), Sowunmi (Vagner 32), Bajevszki.
Feyenoord: Babos; Song, Saidi (Loovens 85), Mtiliga, Bosschaart, Castelen (Buffel 54), Kuijt, Ono, Kalou, Paauwe, Goor.

Hearts (0) 0
Schalke (0) 1 *(Lincoln 73)* 27,272
Hearts: Gordon; Maybury, Kisnorbo■, Pressley, McKenna (De Vries 67), Webster, Pereira (MacFarlane 52), Hamill (Weir 78), McAllister, Hartley, Neilsen.
Schalke: Rost; Poulsen, Bordon, Altintop (Kobiashvili 62), Ailton, Lincoln, Sand (Hanke 89), Asamoah (Varela 61), Waldoch, Oude Kamphuis, Pander.

Thursday, 25 November 2004

Basle (0) 1 *(Carignano 76)*
Hearts (1) 2 *(Wyness 31, Neilson 89)* 25,000
Basle: Zuberbuhler; Zwyssig, Huggel, Sterjovski (Degen D 71), Chipperfield, Gimenez, Kleber, Delgado (Barberis 84), Degen P, Smiljanic, Rossi (Carignano 62).
Hearts: Gordon; Neilson, Maybury, Stewart (MacFarlane 69), Pressley, Webster, Hamill, McAllister, De Vries (Weir 85), Pereira (Stamp 66), Wyness.

Schalke (2) 2 *(Gyepes 15 (og), Kobiashvili 40)*
Ferencvaros (0) 0 51,127
Schalke: Rost; Klasener (Poulsen 46), Bordon (Waldoch 40), Krstajic, Kobiashvili, Lincoln, Vermant, Pander, Ailton, Sand (Altintop 46), Asamoah.
Ferencvaros: Szucs; Gyepes, Zavadszky, Leandro, Rosa, Kapic, Huszti (Tozser 61), Lipcsei, Bajevszki (Sowunmi 83), Vukmir, Penksa (Vagner 72).

Wednesday, 1 December 2004

Ferencvaros (1) 1 *(Rosa 22)*
Basle (0) 2 *(Rossi 59, Huggel 79)* 17,000
Ferencvaros: Szucs; Vukmir, Gyepes, Huszti (Sowunmi 84), Rosa, Zovath, Lipcsei, Zavadszky, Kapic (Tozser 76), Bajevszki, Vagner (Penksa 58).
Basle: Zuberbuhler; Zwyssig, Kleber, Degen P, Smiljanic (Quennoz 46), Huggel, Chipperfield, Barberis (Degen D 57), Carignano, Gimenez (Delgado 77), Rossi.

Feyenoord (2) 2 *(Kalou 32, 41)*
Schalke (1) 1 *(Hanke 7)* 37,520
Feyenoord: Lodewijks; Saidi, Bosschaart, Ghali, Kuijt, Goor, Mtiglia (Ono 29), Paauwe, Gyan, Kalou (Buffel 71), Castelen (Smolarek 90).
Schalke: Rost; Poulsen, Kobiashvili, Altintop, Ailton (Sand 64), Waldoch, Vermant, Oude Kamphuis (Delura 64), Krstajic, Pander (Asamoah 46), Hanke.

Thursday, 16 December 2004

Basle (0) 1 *(Carignano 53)*
Feyenoord (0) 0 25,660
Basle: Zuberbuhler; Quennoz, Sterjovski (Degen D 79), Chipperfield, Zwyssig, Huggel, Carignano, Gimenez, Degen P, Rossi, Delgado (Barberis 90).
Feyenoord: Lodewijks; Song, Mtiglia, Kalou (Lazovic 64), Loovens, Paauwe (Artz 70), Bosschaart, Smolarek, Magrao, Buffel, Kuijt.

Hearts (0) 0
Ferencvaros (1) 1 *(Rosa 30)* 26,182
Hearts: Gordon; Neilson, Maybury, Kisnorbo (Wyness 71), Pressley, Webster, Stewart, Hartley, De Vries, Weir (McKenna 79), McAllister (Pereira 62).
Ferencvaros: Szucs; Vukmir, Rosa, Zavadszky, Gyepes, Balog, Lipcsei, Leandro, Bajevszki (Takacs 87), Penksa (Sowunmi 65), Tozser (Huszti 50).

Group A Final Table	P	W	D	L	F	A	Pts
Feyenoord	4	2	1	1	6	3	7
Schalke	4	2	1	1	5	3	7
Basle	4	2	1	1	5	4	7
Ferencvaros	4	1	1	2	3	5	4
Hearts	4	1	0	3	2	6	3

GROUP B

Thursday, 21 October 2004

Athletic Bilbao (1) 2 *(Gurpegui 6, Del Horno 49)*
Parma (0) 0 32,000
Athletic Bilbao: Lafuente; Prieto, Del Horno, Karanka, Iraola, Orbaiz, Etxeberria (Angulo 64), Gurpegui, Urzaiz, Yeste (Guerrero 74), Arriaga (Murillo 74).
Parma: Berti; Contini, Ruopolo (Gilardino 69), Pisanu (Morfeo 69), Bonera, Bolano, Rosina, Budel, Grieco (Marchionni 69), Cannavaro, Potenza.

Steaua (0) 2 *(Dragutinovic 68 (og), Neaga 81)*
Standard Liege (0) 0 20,000
Steaua: Tudor; Dumitru (Lovin 77), Neaga (Falemi 87), Ghionea, Paraschiv, Ogararu, Oprita (Ciocoiu 84), Baciu, Munteanu D, Dica, Marin.
Standard Liege: Runje; Deflandre, Dragutinovic, Leonard, Onyewu, Bangoura (Niemi 61), Mumlek, Geraerts, Tchite (Colin 76), Curbelo J, Vandooren.

Thursday, 4 November 2004

Besiktas (1) 3 *(Ali Gunes 26, Carew 63, Ibrahim A 89)*
Athletic Bilbao (0) 1 *(Ezquerro 49)* 30,000
Besiktas: Ramazan; Emre, Cagdas, Okan, Sergen (Ibrahim A 61), Juanfran, Ibrahim U, Ibrahim T, Ahmet (Tayfun 84), Ali Gunes, Carew (Pancu 90).
Athletic Bilbao: Lafuente; Casas (Del Horno 62), Karanka, Prieto, Iraola, Orbaiz (Tiko 72), Etxeberria (Azkorra 87), Urzaiz, Gurpegui, Ezquerro, Yeste.

Parma (0) 1 *(Budel 60)*
Steaua (0) 0 3949
Parma: Berti; Bovo, Zicu (Bresciano 46), Budel, Rosina, Cannavaro, Camara (Ruopolo 74), Grella, Maccarone, Contini, Pisanu (Marchionni 61).
Steaua: Tudor; Dumitru (Bostina 68), Marin, Oprita, Ogararu, Ghionea, Munteanu D (Lovin 73), Radoi, Dica, Paraschiv, Neaga (Cristea 61).

Thursday, 25 November 2004

Standard Liege (0) 2 *(Geraerts 54, Garbini 90)*
Parma (1) 1 *(Pisanu 44)* 21,000
Standard Liege: Runje; Deflandre, Dragutinovic, Onyewu, Leonard, Mutavdzic (Garbini 55), Curbelo J, Geraerts, Sergio Conceicao, Bangoura (Vandorren 62), Tchite.
Parma: Berti; Bovo, Contini, Ferronetti, Cannavaro, Budel (Fabio Simplicio 65), Rosina, Maccarone (Bresciano 58), Ruopolo, Pisanu (Marchionni 46), Grella.

Steaua (2) 2 *(Neaga 3, Ciocoiu 18)*
Besiktas (0) 1 *(Akin 87)* 20,000
Steaua: Khomutovsky; Radoi, Munteanu D, Bostina, Baciu (Lovin 88), Marin, Oprita■, Ogararu, Ghionea, Neaga, Ciocoiu (Dinita 62).
Besiktas: Kursunlu; Asik, Yildirim, Buruk, Juanfran, Uzulmez (Pancu 37), Carew (Metin 48), Sonkaya, Dogan, Gunes (Hassan 70), Akin.

Wednesday, 1 December 2004

Athletic Bilbao (1) 1 *(Etxeberria 45)*
Steaua (0) 0 35,000
Athletic Bilbao: Aranzubia; Del Horno, Prieto, Murillo, Orbaiz, Gurpegui, Yeste (Tiko 70), Iraola, Etxeberria, Ezquerro, Urzaiz (Azkorra 80).
Steaua: Khomutovsky; Radoi, Baciu, Ogararu, Ghionea, Munteanu D, Nesu, Cristea (Dinita 87), Bostina (Lovin 90), Dica, Neaga.

Besiktas (1) 1 *(Buruk 30)*
Standard Liege (0) 1 *(Bangoura 81)* 14,000
Besiktas: Kursunlu; Asik, Yildirim, Sonkaya, Dogan, Ali Gunes (Hassan 84), Buruk, Yalcin (Pancu 79), Metin, Uzulmez, Akin (Juanfran 69).
Standard Liege: Runje; Deflandre, Dragutinovic, Onyewu, Leonard, Curbelo J (Wiston 89), Garbini, Geraerts, Sergio Conceicao (Niemi 90), Bangoura, Tchite (Walasiak 57).

Thursday, 16 December 2004

Parma (2) 3 *(Gilardino 16, Cardone 35, Degano 59)*
Besiktas (1) 2 *(Buruk 5, Metin 88)* 3155
Parma: Berti; Cardone, Degano (Sorrentino 74), Pisanu, Bolano (Grella 46), Gilardino, Contini, Rosina (Budel 54), Cannavaro, Fabio Simplicio, Ferronetti.
Besiktas: Kursunlu; Uzulmez, Sonkaya, Buruk, Asik, Dogan, Yildirim (Havutcu 46), Hassan (Goktan 65), Yalcin, Metin, Juanfran (Akin 30).

Standard Liege (1) 1 *(Onyewu 14)*
Athletic Bilbao (3) 7 *(Ezquerro 5, 8, 54, Yeste 34, Iraola 57 (pen), Del Horno 63, Etxeberria 70)* 27,000
Standard Liege: Runje; Deflandre, Onyewu, Sergio Conceicao, Dragutinovic, Garbini, Mutavdzic (Niemi 15), Walasiak (De Almeida Jr 56), Tchite (Mumlek 83), Bangoura, Geraerts.
Athletic Bilbao: Aranzubia; Murillo, Del Horno, Gurpegui (Karanka 77), Prieto, Orbaiz, Iraola, Tiko, Yeste, Ezquerro (Urzaiz 68), Etxeberria (Guerrero 72).

Group B Final Table	*P*	*W*	*D*	*L*	*F*	*A*	*Pts*
Athletic Bilbao	4	3	0	1	11	4	9
Steaua	4	2	0	2	4	3	6
Parma	4	2	0	2	5	6	6
Besiktas	4	1	1	2	7	7	4
Standard Liege	4	1	1	2	4	11	4

GROUP C

Thursday, 21 October 2004

Dnepr (0) 3 *(Venhlynsky 14, 62, Rykun 45)*
FC Brugge (0) 2 *(Ceh 37, Balaban 43)* 25,000
Dnepr: Kernozenko; Yezersky, Radchenko, Rusol, Grytsay, Shelayev, Mikhailenko, Rykun, Nazarenko (Semochko 64), Kostyshyn, Venhlynsky.
FC Brugge: Butina; Gvozdenovic (Lange 46), Simons, Cornelis, Van der Heyden, Clement, Verheyen, Englebert, Balaban, Ceh (Stoica 77), Maertens (De Oliveira 70).

Zaragoza (0) 2 *(Villa 77, 82)*
Utrecht (0) 0 22,000
Zaragoza: Luis Garcia; Ponzio, Alvaro, Milito, Aranzabal, Galletti (Cani 80), Movilla, Zapater, Savio (Oscar 82), Javi Moreno, Villa (Generelo 85).
Utrecht: Terol (Ponk 78); Cornelisse, Schut, Di Tommaso, Zuidam (Van de Haar 67), De Jong, Tanghe, Somers, Douglas, Braafheid, Van den Bergh (Broerse 65).

Thursday, 4 November 2004

FK Austria (0) 1 *(Gilewicz 70)*
Zaragoza (0) 0 18,800
FK Austria: Didulica; Afolabi, Antonsson, Papac, Dospel, Sionko, Vastic, Vachousek (Janocko 67), Blanchard, Gilewicz (Dosunmu 74), Kiesenebner.
Zaragoza: Luis Garcia; Toledo, Ponzio, Movilla (Cani 75), Alvaro, Milito, Galletti, Villa (Generelo 66), Savio, Javi Moreno, Zapater (Oscar 66).

Utrecht (0) 1 *(Douglas 88)*
Dnepr (1) 2 *(Rotan 12, Semochko 83)* 14,150
Utrecht: Ponk; Cornelisse, El Gaaouiri (Shew-Atjon 46), Di Tommaso, Somers, De Jong, Douglas, Schut (Keller 46), Van de Haar, Tanghe, Braafheid (Rajcomar 66).
Dnepr: Kernozenko; Rusol, Grytsay, Rykun, Yezersky, Mikhailenko, Rotan (Semochko 30), Matyukhin (Sjelaje 60), Nazarenko (Lisitski 87), Kostyshyn, Venhlynsky.

Thursday, 25 November 2004

Dnepr (1) 1 *(Nazarenko 19)*
FK Austria (0) 0 18,000
Dnepr: Kernozenko; Rusol, Radchenko, Matyukhin, Yezersky, Mikhailenko, Kostyshyn (Melaschenko 67), Nazarenko, Rykun, Grytsay, Venhlynsky (Rotan 46) (Semochko 81).
FK Austria: Didulica; Afolabi, Troyanski, Antonsson, Papac, Metz (Janocko 69), Sionko, Vachousek, Blanchard, Vastic, Gilewicz (Dosunmu 65).

FC Brugge (0) 1 *(Lange 63)*
Utrecht (0) 0 21,561
FC Brugge: Butina; De Cock, Simons, Rozehnal, Van der Heyden, Clement, Englebert, Ceh■, Verheyen (Roelandts 90), Balaban (Gvozdenovic 46), Lange (Van Tornhout 90).
Utrecht: Ponk; Cornelisse■, Di Tommaso (Keller 40), Shew-Atjon (Broerse 68), Schut, De Jong, Douglas, Van den Bergh, Somers, Van der Haar (Rajcomar 65), Tanghe.

Wednesday, 1 December 2004

FK Austria (0) 1 *(Gilewicz 50)*
FC Brugge (0) 1 *(Balaban 90)* 20,000
FK Austria: Didulica (Safar 67); Afolabi, Antonsson, Papac■, Dospel, Sionko, Vastic (Dosunmu 78), Vachousek, Blanchard, Gilewicz (Janocko 88), Kiesenebner.
FC Brugge: Butina; De Cock, Simons, Rozehnal (Blondel 87), Van der Heyden, Englebert, Gvozdenovic (Van Tornhout 87), Lange, De Oliveira■, Balaban, Maertens (Serebrennikov 87).

Zaragoza (1) 2 *(Savio 9, Generelo 74)*
Dnepr (1) 1 *(Yezersky 2)* 10,000
Zaragoza: Luis Garcia; Alvaro, Milito, Cuartero, Toledo, Movilla (Generelo 59), Zapater, Savio, Galletti (Cani 46), Villa (Soriano 43), Javi Moreno.
Dnepr: Kernozenko; Lisitski (Poklonsky 62), Yezersky, Matyukhin■, Rusol, Grytsay, Shelayev, Andrenko, Rykun, Motuz (Kravchenko 77), Melaschenko.

Thursday, 16 December 2004

FC Brugge (0) 1 *(Ceh 67)*

Zaragoza (1) 1 *(Savio 49)* 23,000

FC Brugge: Butina; De Cock, Clement, Englebert, Simons, Van der Heyden, Verheyen (Van Tornhout 86), Ceh (Blondel 86), Gvozdenovic (Roelandts 46), Lange, Spilar■.
Zaragoza: Luis Garcia; Alvaro, Villa, Toledo, Milito, Cani, Savio (Galletti 63), Ponzio, Movilla, Zapater (Soriano 65), Oscar.

Utrecht (0) 1 *(Douglas 54)*

FK Austria (1) 2 *(Sionko 14, Rushfeldt 78)* 13,500

Utrecht: Ponk; Di Tommaso (Kruys 37), Keller, Braafheid, Schut, Zuidam (Leitoe 88), Douglas, Tanghe, Rajcomar (El Gaaouriri 46), Van den Bergh, Somers.
FK Austria: Safar; Afolabi, Dheedene, Vachousek (Janocko 71), Antonsson, Dospel, Sionko, Blanchard, Gilewicz (Metz 82), Rushfeldt, Vastic (Santos 90).

Group C Final Table	*P*	*W*	*D*	*L*	*F*	*A*	*Pts*
Dnepr	4	3	0	1	7	5	9
Zaragoza	4	2	1	1	5	3	7
FK Austria	4	2	1	1	4	3	7
FC Brugge	4	1	2	1	5	5	5
Utrecht	4	0	0	4	2	7	0

GROUP D

Thursday, 21 October 2004

Dynamo Tbilisi (0) 0

Sochaux (2) 2 *(Ilan 18, 37)* 30,000

Dynamo Tbilisi: Mamaladze; Chichiveishvili, Kandelaki, Salukvadze, Shashiashvili, Kashia (Aladashvili 72), Nemsadze, Melkadze, Akhalaia, Kakaladze, Romero (Dvali 82).
Sochaux: Richert; Pitau, Paisley, Lonfat, Diawara, Mathieu, Menez (De Carvalho 58), Daf, Ilan (N'Daw 46), Oruma, Isabey.

Panionios (0) 0

Newcastle United (0) 1 *(Shearer 87 (pen))* 8000

Panionios: Colceag; Dimoraud, Spiropoulos, Vicek, Giannopoulos, Makos, Dodd, Zimonjic (Goundoulakis 75), Tziolis, Breska, Parodi (Lagonikakis 75).
Newcastle United: Given; Carr, Bernard, Jenas, O'Brien, Elliott, Milner (Ameobi 67), Bowyer, Shearer, Bellamy, Robert.

Thursday, 4 November 2004

Newcastle United (1) 2 *(Shearer 38, Bellamy 56)*

Dynamo Tbilisi (0) 0 27,218

Newcastle United: Given; Hughes, Bernard, Jenas, O'Brien, Elliott (Bramble 69), Bowyer (Ambrose 64), Kluivert, Shearer (Milner 74), Bellamy, Robert.
Dynamo Tbilisi: Mamaladze; Kashia (Silagadze 62), Kvirkvelia, Kankava, Salukvadze, Shashiashvili, Aladashvili (Akhalaia 62), Nemsadze, Melkadze (Gancharov 81), Kandelaki, Kakaladze.

Sporting Lisbon (2) 4 *(Custodio 5, Douala 38, Liedson 79, Hugo Viana 80)*

Panionios (1) 1 *(Marcora 35)* 19,176

Sporting Lisbon: Ricardo; Rui Jorge, Custodio, Liedson, Anderson Polga, Carlos Martins (Pedro Barbosa 64), Enakarhire, Douala (Danny 71), Rochemback (Miguel Garcia 84), Rogerio, Hugo Viana.
Panionios: Colceag; Lagonikakis, Dimoraud, Marcora (Mitrou 74), Spiropoulos, Exouzidis (Makos 61), Breska, Vicek, Giannopoulos, Goundoulakis (Dodd 76), Parodi.

Thursday, 25 November 2004

Dynamo Tbilisi (0) 0

Sporting Lisbon (2) 4 *(Leidson 5, 28, 59, Chichiveishvili 89 (og))* 28,000

Dynamo Tbilisi: Zoidze; Chichiveishvili, Kandelaki, Shashiashvili, Silagadze, Salukvadze (Dvali 74), Kvirkvelia, Kankava (Makharadze 86), Romero, Kakaladze (Kutsura 74), Melkadze.
Sporting Lisbon: Ricardo; Anderson Polga, Enakahire, Miguel Garcia, Rui Jorge, Carlos Martins, Rochemback (Tinga 68), Custodio (Beto 68), Hugo Viana, Douala (Paulo Sergio 64), Leidson.

Sochaux (0) 0

Newcastle United (1) 4 *(Bowyer 29, Ameobi 46, Bellamy 75, Robert 90)* 15,173

Sochaux: Richert; Mathieu, Daf, Pitau, Paisley, Diawara, Lonfat (Boudarene 17), Oruma, Menez (Santos 57), Isabey (Diarra 84), Ilan.
Newcastle United: Given; Hughes, Bernard, Butt, Bramble, Elliott, Ambrose (Taylor 90), Bowyer (Dyer 61), Ameobi, Bellamy, Milner (Robert 80).

Wednesday, 1 December 2004

Panionios (0) 5 *(Mantzios 56, 67, 77, Breska 89, Marcora 90)*

Dynamo Tbilisi (1) 2 *(Kakaladze 38, Akhalaia 60)* 3000

Panionios: Drobny; Dodd (Breska 54), Giannopoulos, Makos, Goundoulakis, Lagonikakis (Dimoraud 70), Tziolis, Marcora, Tsiolis, Meszaros (Exouzidis 84), Mantzios.
Dynamo Tbilisi: Zoidze; Chichiveishvili, Kandelaki (Dvali 85), Shashiashvili, Silagadze, Kvirkvelia, Kankava, Romero (Khmaladze 80), Akhalaia (Kutsurua 78), Melkadze, Kakaladze.

Sporting Lisbon (0) 0

Sochaux (1) 1 *(Lonfat 2)* 21,349

Sporting Lisbon: Ricardo; Anderson Polga, Enakahire, Beto, Rui Jorge, Pedro Barbosa (Danny 66), Rochemback, Hugo Viana, Douala, Liedson, Rogerio (Tello 77).
Sochaux: Richert; Tall, Paisley, Diawara (Lavie 90), Daf, Isabey, Lonfat, Pitau, Mathieu, Santos (Ilan 73), Zairi (Menez 66).

Thursday, 16 December 2004

Newcastle United (1) 1 *(Bellamy 5)*

Sporting Lisbon (1) 1 *(Custodio 40)* 28,017

Newcastle United: Given; Taylor (O'Brien 78), Hughes, Jenas, Bramble, Elliott, Milner, Ambrose, Ameobi, Bellamy (Guy 79), Bernard.
Sporting Lisbon: Ricardo; Beto (Tello 83), Paito, Rochemback, Anderson Polga, Enakahire, Rogerio, Custodio, Pinilla (Douala 66), Liedson, Tinga.

Sochaux (0) 1 *(Isabey 86)*

Panionios (0) 0 10,479

Sochaux: Richert; Paisley, Isabey, Pitau, Diawara, Daf, Lonfat, Mathieu, Ilan, Zaira (Menez 75), Santos (Boudarene 82).
Panionios: Drobny; Vicek, Goundoulakis, Lagonikakis, Spiropoulos, Exouzidis, Parodi (Meszaros 52), Dimoraud, Mantzios, Breska (Xidis 72), Tziolis (Marcora 82).

Group D Final Table	*P*	*W*	*D*	*L*	*F*	*A*	*Pts*
Newcastle United	4	3	1	0	8	1	10
Sochaux	4	3	0	1	4	4	9
Sporting Lisbon	4	2	1	1	9	3	7
Panionios	4	1	0	3	6	8	3
Dinamo Tbilisi	4	0	0	4	2	13	0

GROUP E

Thursday, 21 October 2004

Aigaleo (0) 0

Middlesbrough (0) 1 *(Downing 78)* 4000

Aigaleo: Sidibe; Papoutsis, Edusei, Fotakis, Alexopoulos, Psomas, Chloros, Skopelitis, Manousakis, Nikolopoulos (Makris 77), Barkoglou (Christou 90).
Middlesbrough: Schwarzer; McMahon, Cooper, Riggott, Southgate, Doriva, Morrison (Mendieta 46), Parlour, Nemeth, Viduka (Hasselbaink 70), Zenden (Downing 70).

Lazio (0) 1 *(Rocchi 85)*

Villarreal (1) 1 *(Jose Mari 4)* 12,195

Lazio: Sereni; Oddo, Negro, Siviglia, Zauri, Manfredini (Rocchi 46), Dabo (Giannichedda 58), Liverani, Seric (Di Canio 67), Inzaghi, Pandev.
Villarreal: Reina; Javi Venta, Gonzalo Rodriguez, Quique Alvarez, Alcantara, Arzo (Armando Sa 87), Battaglia, Roger (Hector Font 73), Roman, Cazorla (Josico 77), Jose Mari■.

Thursday, 4 November 2004

Middlesbrough (1) 2 *(Zenden 16, 71)*

Lazio (0) 0 33,991

Middlesbrough: Schwarzer; McMahon, Queudrue, Riggott, Southgate, Boateng, Downing, Parlour, Hasselbaink (Job 80), Viduka, Zenden.
Lazio: Casazza; Oddo, Couto, Filippini A, Lopez, Seric, Giannichedda (Melara 13), Dabo, Delgado (Rocchi 50), Di Canio, Cesar (Manfredini 64).

Partizan Belgrade (1) 4 *(Christou 22 (og), Ilic 55, 60, Vukcevic 68)*

Aigaleo (0) 0 20,000

Partizan Belgrade: Kralj; Vukcevic, Mirkovic (Milovic 84), Brnovic, Boya, Ciric (Radovic 73), Djordjevic, Emeghara, Tomic, Ilic (Babovic 76), Rnic.
Aigaleo: Sidibe; Alexopoulos, Chatzis, Christou, Edusei (Nikolopoulos 65), Liapakis, Skopelitis, Tsatsos, Barkoglou (Fotakis 46), Chloros, Friesenbichler (Manousakis 65).

Thursday, 25 November 2004

Lazio (0) 2 *(Di Canio 51, Inzaghi 73)*

Partizan Belgrade (2) 2 *(Boya 6, 24)* 12,000

Lazio: Sereni; Oddo, Negro, Fernando Couto, Seric (Pandev 89), Dabo, Filippini E, Manfredini (Muzzi 52), Rocchi (Cesar 46), Inzaghi, Di Canio.
Partizan Belgrade: Kralj; Rnic, Mirkovic, Djordjevic, Emeghara, Tomic, Brnovic, Ilic (Bajic 89), Ciric (Petrovic 65), Vukcevic (Radoncic 77), Boya.

Villarreal (1) 2 *(Guayre 36, Javi Venta 74)*

Middlesbrough (0) 0 14,250

Villarreal: Reina; Javi Venta, Gonzalo Rodriguez, Quique Alvarez, Arruabarrena, Josico, Arzo, Hector Font, Riquelme (Pena 87), Cazorla, Guayre (Xisco 87).
Middlesbrough: Schwarzer; McMahon (Reiziger 72), Queudrue, Riggott, Southgate, Boateng, Downing, Doriva (Viduka 46), Nemeth, Job (Hasselbaink 46), Zenden.

Thursday, 2 December 2004

Aigaleo (1) 2 *(Chloros 8, Agritis 55)*

Lazio (2) 2 *(Muzzi 12, 36)* 1000

Aigaleo: Kljajevic; Papoutsis, Tsatsos, Psomas, Liapakis, Skopelitis (Barkoglou 46), Fotakis (Chatzis 76), Christou, Chloros, Makris, Manousakis (Agritis 46).
Lazio: Peruzzi; Lopez, Dabo, Cesar, Manfredini (Inzaghi 66), Muzzi, Liverani (Filippini A 73), Fernando Couto, Seric, Di Canio (Pandev 68), Oddo.

Partizan Belgrade (0) 1 *(Tomic 65 (pen))*

Villarreal (1) 1 *(Cazorla 17)* 26,000

Partizan Belgrade: Kralj; Rnic, Mirkovic, Djordjevic, Emeghara, Vukcevic, Ciric (Grubjesic 46), Tomic, Ilic (Nadj 62), Brnovic, Boya.
Villarreal: Reina; Arruabarrena, Quique Alvarez, Pena, Armando Sa, Cazorla (Javi Venta 85), Josico, Hector Font, Arzo, Guayre, Xisco (Garcia 84).

Wednesday, 15 December 2004

Middlesbrough (2) 3 *(Nemeth 10, Job 22, Morrison 90)*

Partizan Belgrade (0) 0 20,856

Middlesbrough: Schwarzer; Reiziger, Queudrue, Cooper, Southgate, Doriva, Downing, Parlour (Morrison), Nemeth, Job, Zenden.
Partizan Belgrade: Kralj (Pantic 40); Mirkovic, Ciric (Vukcevic 46), Emeghara, Brnovic, Boya, Djordjevic, Tomic, Rnic, Nadj, Ilic (Grubjesic 70).

Villarreal (2) 4 *(Hector Font 12, Guayre 39, Javi Venta 51, Cazorla 63)*

Aigaleo (0) 0 10,000

Villarreal: Lopez Vallejo; Gonzalo Rodriguez, Quique Alvarez (Garcia 53), Javi Venta, Pena, Armando Sa, Cazorla, Hector Font, Arzo, Jose Mari (Cases 63), Guayre (Verza 73).
Aigaleo: Sidibe; Papoutsis, Christou, Chatzis, Edusei (Psomas 24), Fotakis (Agritis 46), Barkoglou (Aggos 63), Skopelitis, Tsatsos, Chloros, Makris.

Group E Final Table	P	W	D	L	F	A	Pts
Middlesbrough	4	3	0	1	6	2	9
Villarreal	4	2	2	0	8	2	8
Partizan Belgrade	4	1	2	1	7	6	5
Lazio	4	0	3	1	5	7	3
Aigaleo	4	0	1	3	2	11	1

GROUP F

Thursday, 21 October 2004

Amica (0) 0

Rangers (1) 5 *(Lovenkrands 18, Novo 58, Ricksen 70, Arveladze 73 (pen), Thompson 88)* 3100

Amica: Malarz; Bieniuk, Dudka, Kucharski (Sobocinski 46), Skrzypek, Stasiak, Dembinski, Gregorek (Kikut 58), Kryszalowicz, Bartczak, Burkhardt M (Kowalczyk 66).
Rangers: Klos; Khizanishvili, Andrews, Boumsong, Vignal, Ricksen, Malcolm, Arveladze (Namouchi 78), Lovenkrands (Novo 54), Prso (Thompson 71), Burke.

Auxerre (0) 0

Graz (0) 0 5000

Auxerre: Cool; Grichting, Bolf, Kaboul, Sagna, Cheyrou, Lachuer, Tainio, Akale (Mathis 76), Kalou, Benjani (Pieroni 76).
Graz: Schranz; Tokic, Ehmann, Standfest (Ramusch 90), Pogatetz, Majstorovic, Muratovic (Aufhauser 76), Bazina, Sick, Plassnegger, Kollmann (Skoro 89).

Thursday, 4 November 2004

AZ (2) 2 *(Huysegems 2, 18)*

Auxerre (0) 0 8123

AZ: Timmer; Kromkamp, Mathijsen, Opdam (Jaliens 61), De Cler, Landzaat, Buskermolen, Meerdink, Huysegems, Van Galen (Ramzi 75), Perez (Elkhattabi 87).
Auxerre: Cool; Mwaruwari (Violeau 61), Bolf, Grichting, Kalou (Pieroni 84), Kaboul, Cheyrou, Lachuer, Sagna, Tainio, Mathis (Akale 81).

Graz (1) 3 *(Kollmann 32, 61 (pen), 71)*

Amica (1) 1 *(Dembinski 27)* 8000

Graz: Schranz; Plassnegger, Ehmann, Tokic, Pogatetz, Standfest, Sick, Aufhauser, Amerhauser, Bazina (Hassler 86), Kollmann (Skoro 74).
Amica: Malarz; Skrzypek, Dziewicki (Burkhardt F 68), Bieniuk, Dudka, Kikut, Bartczak, Dembinski, Burkhardt M (Kucharski 46), Grzybowski (Gregorek 62), Kryszalowicz.

Thursday, 25 November 2004

Amica (0) 1 *(Dembinski 59 (pen))*

AZ (3) 3 *(Van Galen 13, Meerdink 37, Huysegems 39)* 1000

Amica: Malarz; Dudka, Bieniuk, Dziewicki, Kucharski, Grzybowski (Gregorek 77), Kowalczyk (Burkhardt M 46), Bartczak, Kikut (Burkhardt F 66), Dembinski, Kryszalowicz.
AZ: Timmer; Kromkamp, Mathijsen, Opdam, De Cler, Landzaat, Van Galen (Elkhattabi 67), Buskermolen (Lindenbergh 67), Meerdink, Huysegems (Nelisse 67), Perez.

Rangers (0) 3 *(Novo 58, Arveladze 86, Namouchi 90)*

Graz (0) 0 46,453

Rangers: Klos; Khizanishvili, Vignal (Ball 30), Ricksen, Boumsong, Andrews, Namouchi, Malcolm, Novo, Prso, Lovenkrands (Arveladze 77).
Graz: Schranz; Plassnegger, Ehmann (Skoro 81), Tokic, Pogatetz, Standfest (Dollinger 72), Sick, Aufhauser (Muratovic 70), Amerhauser, Kollmann, Bazina.

Thursday, 2 December 2004

AZ (1) 1 *(Landzaat 7)*

Rangers (0) 0 8000

AZ: Timmer; Kromkamp, Mathijsen, Opdam, De Cler, Buskermolen (Lindenbergh 19), Landzaat, Meerdink, Huysegems (Nelisse 88), Van Galen (Ramzi 83), Perez.
Rangers: Klos; Khizanishvili, Andrews, Rae, Ball, Boumsong, Malcolm (Hughes 72), Ricksen, Novo, Prso, Lovenkrands (Namouchi 46).

Auxerre (4) 5 *(Mignot 1, Pieroni 5, 23, 26, Kalou 56)*

Amica (1) 1 *(Kryszalowicz 17)* 7000

Auxerre: Cool; Grichting, Violeau (Vandenbosshe 39), Cheyrou, Lachuer, Pieroni, Akale, Mignot (Recorbet 86), Kalou (Gonzales 70), Bolf, Sagna.
Amica: Malarz (Cierzniak■ 37); Bieniuk (Jacek 46), Dudka, Dziewicki, Kucharski (Stasiak 57), Dembinski, Kryszalowicz, Bartczak, Burkhardt M, Grzybowski, Kikut.

Wednesday, 15 December 2004

Graz (1) 2 *(Aufhauser 41, Kollmann 54 (pen))*

AZ (0) 0 13,000

Graz: Schranz; Potscher (Dollinger 86), Tokic, Ehmann, Pogatetz, Standfest, Muratovic, Amerhauser, Aufhauser, Bazina (Sick 80), Kollmann (Skoro 71).
AZ: Timmer; De Cler, Opdam (Jaliens 63), Mathijsen, Kromkamp, Landzaat, Buskermolen, Van Galen (Nelisse 46), Sektioui, Huysegems, Perez (Elkhattabi 73).

Rangers (0) 0

Auxerre (1) 2 *(Kalou 10, 47)* 48,847

Rangers: Klos; Khizanishvili (Hutton 54), Andrews, Boumsong, Vignal, Namouchi (Rae 79), Ricksen, Malcolm, Arveladze, Novo, Prso.
Auxerre: Cool; Sagna (Juares 81), Bolf, Mignot, Grichting, Violeau, Cheyrou, Tainio (Gonzalez 79), Kalou, Akale, Mwaruwari.

Group F Final Table	*P*	*W*	*D*	*L*	*F*	*A*	*Pts*
AZ	4	3	0	1	6	3	9
Auxerre	4	2	1	1	7	3	7
Graz	4	2	1	1	5	4	7
Rangers	4	2	0	2	8	3	6
Amica	4	0	0	4	3	16	0

GROUP G

Thursday, 21 October 2004

Benfica (2) 4 *(Dos Santos 14, Nuno Gomes 32, 78, Karadas 73)*

Heerenveen (0) 2 *(Yildirim 49, Huntelaar 53 (pen))* 7000

Benfica: Moreira; Luisao, Paulo Almeida, Petit (Manuel Fernandes 84), Miguel, Ricardo Rocha, Joao Pereira (Amoreirinha 78), Dos Santos, Simao Sabrosa, Nuno Gomes, Zahovic (Karadas 68).
Heerenveen: Vandenbussche; Huntelaar, Hansson, Yildirim, Seip, Radomski, Bruggink (Rose 77), Vayrynen, Sikora (Selakovic 63), Rzasa, Haarala.

Beveren (0) 1 *(N'Dri 86)*

Stuttgart (2) 5 *(Cacau 9, 52, Kuranyi 49, Lahm 76, Szabics 90)* 7000

Beveren: Copa; Lardenoit, Diawara, Kante, Seka (Tokpa 66), Ne, Eboue, Diallo, Sanogo (Vleminckx 86), N'Dri, Djire.
Stuttgart: Hildebrand; Hinkel, Babbel, Meissner (Vranjes 46), Hleb, Heldt (Tiffert 74), Delpierre, Cacau, Soldo, Lahm, Kuranyi (Szabics 59).

Thursday, 4 November 2004

Dynamo Zagreb (4) 6 *(Da Silva 16, Mijatovic 21, Zahora 35, 41, Kranjcar 55, Mujcin 87)*

Beveren (0) 1 *(Vleminckx 82)* 10,000

Dynamo Zagreb: Vasilj; Buljat, Milinovic, Mijatovic, Agic (Mujcin 62), Zahora (Ljubojevic 69), Bosnjak, Poldrugac, Kranjcar, Pranjic, Da Silva.
Beveren: Copa; Mahan, Lardenoit, Koudou (Vleminckx 75), Diallo, N'Dri, Djire, Eboue, Ne (Seka 74), Kante, Sanogo (Tokpa 46).

Stuttgart (1) 3 *(Cacau 31, Meissner 53, Kuranyi 72)*

Benfica (0) 0 46,000

Stuttgart: Hildebrand; Hinkel, Stranzl, Cacau, Babbel, Soldo, Meissner, Heldt (Tiffert 73), Hleb (Vranjes 87), Lahm, Kuranyi (Szabics 77).
Benfica: Moreira; Amoreirinha, Luisao, Paulo Almeida, Geovanni, Dos Santos, Simao Sabrosa, Nuno Gomes (Bruno Aguiar 64), Ricardo Rocha (Argel 44), Manuel Fernandes, Joao Pereira (Karadas 55).

Thursday, 25 November 2004

Benfica (2) 2 *(Sokota 11, Simao Sabrosa 29 (pen))*

Dynamo Zagreb (0) 0 12,000

Benfica: Moreira; Luisao, Fyssas, Ricardo Rocha, Joao Pereira, Petit (Paulo Almeida 15), Manuel Fernandes, Geovanni (Dos Santos 82), Simao Sabrosa, Karadas, Sokota (Bruno Aguiar 75).
Dynamo Zagreb: Vasilj; Buljat (Strok 63), Milinovic, Mijatovic, Agic, Mujcin, Bosnjak (Lucic 46), Poldrugac, Kranjcar (Karic 46), Pranjic, Da Silva.

Heerenveen (0) 1 *(Yildirim 65)*

Stuttgart (0) 0 17,500

Heerenveen: Vandenbussche; Hansson, Seip, Rzasa (Bakkati 56), Radomski, Hestad, Yildirim, Bruggink (Rose 16), Haarala, Huntelaar, Selakovic (Sikora 81).
Stuttgart: Hildebrand; Stranzl, Zivkovic (Gomez 87), Lahm, Babbel, Meissner, Hleb (Szabics 73), Heldt (Tiffert 68), Soldo, Cacau, Kuranyi.

Thursday, 2 December 2004

Beveren (0) 0

Benfica (2) 3 *(Simao Sabrosa 4 (pen), Zahovic 19, 59)* 8200

Beveren: Copa■; Mahan, Lardenoit, Badjan, Ne, Eboue, Koudou (Verhulst 4), Diallo (Seka 60), Sanogo, N'Dri, Djire (Bou-Sfia 90).
Benfica: Moreira; Luisao, Paulo Almeida (Geovanni 25), Bruno Aguiar, Zahovic (Everson 77), Dos Santos, Simao Sabrosa, Karadas (Sokota 73), Ricardo Rocha, Manuel Fernandes, Joao Pereira.

Dynamo Zagreb (1) 2 *(Bosnjak 15, Pranjic 57)*

Heerenveen (0) 2 *(Yildirim 86, Huntelaar 89 (pen))* 12,000

Dynamo Zagreb: Vasilj; Buljat, Milinovic, Jese, Agic, Mujcin (Tomic 46), Bosnjak (Strok 72), Lucic, Karic (Zahora 85), Pranjic, Da Silva.
Heerenveen: Vandenbussche; Bakkati (Samaras 46), Hansson, Breuer, Seip, Hestad, Selakovic (Sikora 67), Rose (Vayrynen 76), Rzasa, Huntelaar, Yildirim.

Wednesday, 15 December 2004

Heerenveen (1) 1 *(Bruggink 26)*
Beveren (0) 0 17,800
Heerenveen: Vandenbussche; Hansson, Seip (Samaras 69), Rzasa, Haarala, Radomski, Hestad, Vayrynen, Huntelaar, Yildirim (Selakovic 79), Bruggink (Sikora 31).
Beveren: Volders; Mahan, Lardenoit (Vleminckx 89), Badjan, Ouattara■, Tokpa (Bou-Sfia 56), Ne, Djire, Seka (Diallo 70), Sanogo, Romaric.

Stuttgart (1) 2 *(Tiffert 15, Meira 75)*
Dynamo Zagreb (0) 1 *(Bosnjak 66)* 41,000
Stuttgart: Hildebrand; Hinkel, Stranzl, Babbel (Delpierre 75), Meira (Vranjes 85), Lahm, Meissner, Hleb, Tiffert, Cacau, Kuranyi (Streller 83).
Dynamo Zagreb: Vasilj; Buljat, Mijatovic, Lucic, Mujcin (Hrman 78), Bosnjak, Poldrugac, Tomic (Saric 82), Pranjic, Karic (Zahora 82), Da Silva.

Group G Final Table	*P*	*W*	*D*	*L*	*F*	*A*	*Pts*
Stuttgart	4	3	0	1	10	3	9
Benfica	4	3	0	1	9	5	9
Heerenveen	4	2	1	1	6	6	7
Dynamo Zagreb	4	1	1	2	9	7	4
Beveren	4	0	0	4	2	15	0

GROUP H

Thursday, 21 October 2004

Aachen (0) 1 *(Meijer 67)*
Lille (0) 0 20,352
Aachen: Straub; Klitzpera, Landgraf, Plasshenrich, Rolfes, Meijer, Sichone, Pinto (Paulus 88), Fiel (Bruns 65), Michalke (Brinkmann 84), Blank.
Lille: Sylva; Acimovic (Audel 77), Angbwa, Brunel, Bodmer, Landrin (Dernis 77), Makoun, Moussilou, Rafael, Tafforeau (Vitakic 17), Tavlaridis.
in Cologne.

Zenit (1) 5 *(Arshavin 44, Kerzhakov 48, 54, 68, Denisov 86)*
AEK Athens (1) 1 *(Krassas 3)* 22,000
Zenit: Malafeev; Flachbart, Sumulikoski, Skrtel (Gorak 46), Mares, Bystrov (Vlasov 81), Radimov (Denisov 74), Gorshkov, Spivak, Arshavin, Kerzhakov.
AEK Athens: Michailidis; Kontis, Amponsah (Kampantais 56), Kostenoglou, Bruno Alves, Petkov M (Rusev 70), Katsouranis, Krassas, Konstantinidis (Giorgiopoulos 56), Liberopoulos, Soares.

Thursday, 4 November 2004

Lille (2) 2 *(Tafforeau 35, Moussilou 42)*
Zenit (1) 1 *(Kerzhakov 39)* 9109
Lille: Sylva; Acimovic (Brunel 54), Angbwa, Bodmer (Debuchy 82), Dumont, Landrin, Makoun, Moussilou (Audel 90), Rafael, Tafforeau, Tavlaridis.
Zenit: Chontofalsky; Chirita, Sumulikoski, Skrtel (Vieshtica 57), Spivak, Bystrov, Radimov (Makarov 79), Gorshkov (Denisov 46), Mares, Arshavin, Kerzhakov.

Sevilla (1) 2 *(Aranda 7, Baptista 77 (pen))*
Aachen (0) 0 25,000
Sevilla: Esteban; Javi Navarro, David, Marti, Aranda (Carlitos 87), Pablo Alfaro, Jesus Navas, Fernando Sales (Daniel Alves 66), Baptista (Jordi Lopez 84), Sergio Ramos, Renato.
Aachen: Straub; Klitzpera, Brinkmann, Landgraf (Iwelumo 78), Plasshenrich, Meijer, Sichone, Pinto (Bruns 66), Fiel (Scharping 78), Michalke, Blank.

Thursday, 25 November 2004

AEK Athens (0) 1 *(Amponsah 72)*
Lille (1) 2 *(Vitakic 26, Debuchy 63)* 15,000
AEK Athens: Michailidis; Bruno Alves, Kostenoglou, Tziortziopoulos, Amponsah, Konstantinidis (Kampantais 61), Katsouranis, Krassas, Paulo Assuncao, Soares, Liberopoulos.
Lille: Sylva; Tafforeau, Vitakic, Plestan, Angbwa, Debuchy (Dernis 79), Brunel (Audel 68), Acimovic (Bodmer 54), Makoun, Dumont, Moussilou.

Zenit (1) 1 *(Arshavin 35)*
Sevilla (0) 1 *(Baptista 72)* 20,000
Zenit: Malafeev; Vieshtica, Mares, Chirita, Radimov (Gorshkov 73), Spivak, Sumulikoski, Denisov, Bystrov (Hartig 77), Arshavin, Kerzhakov.
Sevilla: Esteban; Javi Navarro, David, Aitor Ocio, Sergio Ramos (Daniel Alves 46), Baptista, Renato, Marti, Dario Silva (Carlitos 57), Fernando Sales (Jordi Lopez 83), Jesuli.

Thursday, 2 December 2004

Aachen (1) 2 *(Meijer 85, Blank 89 (pen))*
Zenit (1) 2 *(Radimov 38 (pen), Gorshkov 76)* 25,300
Aachen: Straub; Klitzpera, Sichone, Blank, Brinkmann (Gomez 79), Plasshenrich (Landgraf 66), Rolfes, Fiel, Michalke, Meijer (Iwelumo 73), Pinto■.
Zenit: Malafeev; Chirita, Vieshtica, Skrtel, Mares, Bystrov, Denisov (Gorshkov 46), Radimov, Shirl (Flachbart 84), Arshavin, Kerzhakov.

Sevilla (2) 3 *(Baptista 18, 89 (pen), Antonito 28)*
AEK Athens (1) 2 *(Liberopoulos 9, Tziortziopoulos 47)* 29,000
Sevilla: Esteban; Javi Navarro, Aitor Ocio, Daniel Alves, David, Jesuli (Antonio Lopez 63), Renato, Marti, Fernando Sales (Navas 63), Baptista, Antonito (Blanco 76).
AEK Athens: Chiotis; Kostenoglou (Toskas 25), Moras, Amponsah (Georgeas 22), Tziortziopoulos, Katsouranis, Krassas, Paulo Assuncao, Konstantinidis (Petkov M 52), Bourbos, Liberopoulos.

Wednesday, 15 December 2004

AEK Athens (0) 0
Aachen (0) 2 *(Meijer 56, Gomez 84)* 5000
AEK Athens: Chiotis; Bruno Alves, Georgeas, Moras, Kontis, Toskas, Katsouranis, Krassas (Rusev 68), Paulo Assuncao (Soares 46), Kampantais (Liberopoulos 46), Bourbos.
Aachen: Straub; Klitzpera, Landgraf (Paulas 86), Sichone, Blank, Plasshenrich, Rolfes, Fiel (Stehle 66), Michalke, Meijer, Scharping (Gomez 76).

Lille (0) 1 *(Moussilou 77)*
Sevilla (0) 0 9000
Lille: Sylva; Schmitz■, Tafforeau, Plestan, Angbwa, Debuchy (Dernis 73), Cabaye, Brunel, Acimovic (Bodmer 78), Dumont, Audel (Moussilou 62).
Sevilla: Notario; David, Daniel Alves, Aitor Ocio, Pablo Alfaro (Antonito 89), Pablo (Jesuli 60), Sergio Ramos, Antonio Lopez (Kepa 83), Casquero, Jordi Lopez, Dario Silva.

Group H Final Table	*P*	*W*	*D*	*L*	*F*	*A*	*Pts*
Lille	4	3	0	1	5	3	9
Sevilla	4	2	1	1	6	4	7
Aachen	4	2	1	1	5	4	7
Zenit	4	1	2	1	9	6	5
AEK Athens	4	0	0	4	4	12	0

KNOCK-OUT STAGE

THIRD ROUND FIRST LEG

Wednesday, 16 February 2005

Ajax (1) 1 *(Maxwell 36)*
Auxerre (0) 0 42,319
Ajax: Stekelenburg; Trabelsi, De Jong, Pienaar (Obodai 46), Heitinga, Escude, Maxwell, Van der Vaart (Lindgren 77), Boukhari, Babel, Rosales (De Ridder 71).
Auxerre: Cool; Jaures, Sagna, Cheyrou, Mignot, Bolf, Mathis, Violeau, Akale, Mwaruwari (Pieroni 90), Kalou.

Panathinaikos (0) 1 *(Vyntra 75)*
Sevilla (0) 0 10,000
Panathinaikos: Galinovic; Kotsios, Morris, Vyntra, Munch, Goumas (Andric 56), Gonzalez, Basinas, Skacel (Konstantinidis 52), Gekas, Konstantinou (Maric 86).
Sevilla: Esteban; David, Aitor Ocio, Marti, Daniel Alves, Renato, Adriano Correia, Jordi Lopez (Fernando Sales 46), Makulula (Antonito 63), Baptista, Pablo Alfaro.

Parma (0) 0
Stuttgart (0) 0 5486
Parma: Bucci; Bettarini (Contini 46), Cardone, Bonera, Bolano, Ruopolo (Gilardino 65), Pisanu, Sorrentino, Cannavaro, Grella (Fabio Simplicio 70), Vignaroli.
Stuttgart: Hildebrand; Stranzl, Zivkovic, Babbel, Meira, Meissner, Hleb (Tiffert 75), Gerber, Cacau, Szabics (Heldt 75), Soldo.

Partizan Belgrade (2) 2 *(Odita 12, 45)*
Dnepr (1) 2 *(Nazarenko 28, Rusol 57)* 15,000
Partizan Belgrade: Kralj; Kirkovic (Radovic 79), Mirkovic, Djordjevic, Emeghara, Vukcevic, Brnovic, Tomic (Grubjesic 59), Ilic (Petrovic 80), Nadj, Odita.
Dnepr: Kernozenko; Yezersky, Shevchuk, Rusol, Grytsay, Shelayev (Rotan 46), Rykun (Mikhailenko 62), Bidenko, Nazarenko, Kostyshyn, Karnilenka (Radchenko 77).

Shakhtjor Donetsk (0) 1 *(Brandao 86)*
Schalke (1) 1 *(Ailton 7)* 24,500
Shakhtjor Donetsk: Lastuvka; Hubschman, Tymoschuk, Rat, Duljaj (Elano 46), Matuzalem, Vukic (Jadson 72), Lewandowski, Srna, Aghahowa, Brandao.
Schalke: Rost; Waldoch, Rodriguez, Krstaljic, Poulsen, Kobiashvili, Altintop (Asamoah 75), Vermant, Oude Kanphuis, Ailton, Sand (Hanke 80).

Sporting Lisbon (2) 2 *(Rogerio 22, Liedson 37)*
Feyenoord (1) 1 *(Goor 7)* 19,091
Sporting Lisbon: Ricardo; Anderson Polga, Rui Jorge, Rogerio, Carlos Martins, Rochemback, Sa Pinto, Enakahire, Custodio, Hugo Viana, Liedson.
Feyenoord: Ludewijks; Gibbs, Saidi, Basto, Zuiverloon, Castelen, Hofs, Paauwe, Goor, Kuijt, Lazovic (Kalou 46).

Valencia (1) 2 *(Di Vaio 38, Aimar 54)*
Steaua (0) 0 30,000
Valencia: Palop; Marchena, Caneira, Navarro, Moretti, Fiore, Baraja (Albelda 87), Sissoko (Rufete 75), Di Vaio, Mista (Corradi 83), Aimar.
Steaua: Khomutovsky; Radoi, Baciu, Marin, Ogararu, Ghionea, Munteanu D, Dica, Paraschiv, Oprita, Ciocoiu (Cristea 55).

Thursday, 17 February 2005

Aachen (0) 0
AZ (0) 0 38,000
Aachen: Straub; Brinkmann, Plasshenrich (Paulus 61), Gomez (Schlaudaff 75), Meijer, Stehle, Pinto, Michalke (Reghecampf 75), Klitzpera, Rolfes, Noll.
AZ: Timmer; Kronkamp, Mathijsen, Opdam, De Cler, Buskermolen (Nelisse 62), Landzaat, Ramzi (Lindenbergh 71), Meerdink, Huysegems (Van Galen 75), Sektioui.

Basle (0) 0
Lille (0) 0 19,092
Basle: Zuberbuhler; Zwyssig, Muller, Kleber, Degen P, Zanni (Sterjovski 71), Huggel, Chipperfield, Carignano, Gimenez (Petric 83), Rossi.
Lille: Sylva; Tavlaridis, Tafforeau, Vitakic, Angbwa, Debuchy (Cabaye 76), Brunel, Bodmer, Chalme, Dumont, Moussilou (Odemwingie 76).

CSKA Moscow (1) 2 *(Berezutski V 12, Vagner Love 60)*
Benfica (0) 0 28,000
CSKA Moscow: Akinfeev; Ignashevich, Berezutski A, Daniel Carvalho, Odiah, Berezutski V, Klasic (Laizans 81), Rahimic, Gusev (Shershun 79), Aldonin, Vagner Love (Samodin 90).
Benfica: Quim; Luisao, Petit, Alcides, Dos Santos, Simao Sabrosa, Geovanni (Bruno Aguiar 75), Nuno Gomes (Mantorras 73), Nuno Assis (Karadas 59), Joao Pereira, Manuel Fernandes.

Dynamo Kiev (0) 0
Villarreal (0) 0 11,000
Dynamo Kiev: Shovkovskyi; Rodolfo, Sablic, Nesmachny, Leko, Cernat (Ninkovic 70), Diogo Rincon, Gusev, Yussuf, Kleber, Shatskikh (Verpakovski 54).
Villarreal: Reina; Gonzalo Rodriguez, Arruabarrena, Sorin, Quique Alvarez, Pena, Armando Sa (Javi Venta 89), Cazorla (Hector Font 83), Senna, Figueroa (Riquelme 72), Jose Mari.

Fenerbahce (0) 0
Zaragoza (0) 1 *(Alvaro 72)* 49,000
Fenerbahce: Rustu; Fabio Luciano, Servet, Umit O, Alex, Onder, Serkan (Mehmet 46), Tuncay, Nobre, Selcuk, Anelka.
Zaragoza: Luis Garcia; Milito, Toledo, Savio, Alvaro, Poncio (Cuartero 90), Generelo (Oscar 87), Soriano, Zapater, Galletti (Cani 90), Villa.

Graz (0) 2 *(Bazina 64, Kollmann 79)*
Middlesbrough (0) 2 *(Zenden 51, Hasselbaink 66)* 13,000
Graz: Schranz; Plassnegger, Ehmann, Tokic, Pogatetz, Bleidelis (Standfest 70), Muratovic, Aufhauser (Sick 90), Dollinger (Amerhauser 72), Bazina, Kollmann■.
Middlesbrough: Schwarzer; Reiziger, Queudrue, Riggott, Southgate, Doriva, Downing, Parlour, Hasselbaink, Morrison, Zenden.

Heerenveen (1) 1 *(Huntelaar 24)*
Newcastle U (1) 2 *(Shearer 69, Bowyer 82)* 19,500
Heerenveen: Vandenbussche; Bakkati, Vayrynen, Hestad, Huntelaar (Samaras 79), Rzasa, Bruggink (Sikora 79), Yildirim, Prager (Rose 89), Breuer, Hansson.
Newcastle U: Given; Carr, Babayaro (Hughes 52), Faye, O'Brien, Bramble, Bowyer■, Jenas, Shearer (Taylor 89), Ameobi (Robert 62), Kluivert.

Olympiakos (1) 1 *(Okkas 29)*
Sochaux (0) 0 33,000
Olympiakos: Nikopolidis; Mavrogenidis, Kafes, Kostoulas, Vallas, Maric, Djordjevic (Pantos 73), Georgatos (Taralidis 85), Seitidis, Rivaldo, Okkas (Castillo 68).
Sochaux: Richert; Diawara, Isabey, Monsoreau, Potillon, Mathieu, Santos (Regnier 82), Pitau, Zairi, Menez, Boudarene.

Thursday, 24 February 2005

FK Austria (0) 0
Athletic Bilbao (0) 0 15,000
FK Austria: Didulica; Afolabi, Antonsson, Papac, Dospel, Sionko, Vastic (Mila 76), Vachousek, Blanchard, Kiesenebner (Wagner 85), Rushfeldt (Gilewicz 66).
Athletic Bilbao: Lafuente; Casas, Ezquerro (Urzaiz 83), Yeste (Bordas 90), Lacruz, Prieto, Iraola (Del Horno 72), Orbaiz, Etxeberria, Gurpegui, Murillo.

THIRD ROUND SECOND LEG

Thursday, 24 February 2005

AZ (0) 2 *(Van Galen 62, Mathijsen 80)*
Aachen (1) 1 *(Meijer 31)* 8006
AZ: Timmer; Kromkamp, Opdam, Mathijsen, De Cler, Lindenbergh, Ramzi (Nelisse 58), Van Galen (Jaliens 86), Huysegems (Sektioui 58), Meerdink, Perez.
Aachen: Straub; Paulus (Brinkmann 74), Klitzpera, Sichone (Iwelumo 86), Stehle■, Plasshenrich, Rolfes, Noll, Gomez (Michalke 77), Meijer, Pinto.

Auxerre (1) 3 *(Kalou 31, Cheyrou 55, Mathis 88)*
Ajax (1) 1 *(Babel 37)* 15,000
Auxerre: Cool; Jaures, Mignot, Bolf, Sagna, Violeau, Cheyrou, Tainio (Mathis 77), Akale (Gonzalez 90), Mwaruwari, Kalou.
Ajax: Stekelenburg; Trabelsi, Heitinga, Escude, De Jong, Maxwell, Obodai (Maduro 87), Sneijder (Emanuelson 80), Rosales (De Ridder 82), Boukhari, Babel.

Benfica (0) 1 *(Karadas 64)*
CSKA Moscow (0) 1 *(Ignashevich 49)* 25,000
Benfica: Quim; Luisao, Petit, Geovanni (Miguel 64), Alcides, Fyssas, Nuno Assis (Karadas 54), Simao Sabrosa, Nuno Gomes (Mantorras 61), Manuel Fernandes, Joao Pereira.
CSKA Moscow: Akinfeev; Ignashevich, Berezutski A, Daniel Carvalho (Gusev 90), Odiah (Shershun 78), Vagner Love (Olic 84), Krasic, Zhirkov, Aldonin, Berezutski V, Rahimic.

Dnepr (0) 0
Partizan Belgrade (0) 1 *(Djordjevic 87)* 20,000
Dnepr: Kernozenko; Yezersky, Shevchuk, Radchenko, Rusol, Mikhailenko, Rykun (Grytsay 88), Bidnenko (Kostyshyn 61), Nazerenko, Rotan, Karnilenka (Venhlynsky 56).
Partizan Belgrade: Kralj; Mirkovic, Djordjevic, Emeghara, Rnic (Cirkovic 64), Vukcevic, Tomic (Grubjesic 72), Ilic■, Nadj, Boya (Radovic 46), Odita.

Feyenoord (0) 1 *(Hofs 88)*
Sporting Lisbon (0) 2 *(Liedson 62, Rochemback 83)* 33,000
Feyenoord: Lodewijks; Saidi, Basto (Ono 46), Paauwe, Zuiverloon (Lazovic 72), Goor, Gibbs, Kalou, Kuijt, Castelen, Hofs.
Sporting Lisbon: Ricardo; Carlos Martins (Douala 75), Hugo (Miguel Garcia 74), Pedro Barbosa, Enakahire, Rui Jorge, Rochemback, Joao Moutinho, Liedson, Rogerio, Sa Pinto (Hugo Viana 87).

Lille (1) 2 *(Moussilou 37, Acimovic 78 (pen))*
Basle (0) 0 13,000
Lille: Sylva; Acimovic, Bodmer, Chalme, Debuchy (Cabaye 76), Dumont, Landrin, Moussilou (Odemwingie 68), Tafforeau, Tavlaridis, Vitakic.
Basle: Zuberbuhler; Zwyssig, Huggel, Sterjovski (Zanni 55), Carignano, Chipperfield, Gimenez, Muller, Kleber (Delgado 66), Degen P, Rossi.

Middlesbrough (1) 2 *(Morrison 19, Hasselbaink 61)*
Graz (1) 1 *(Bazina 9)* 20,371
Middlesbrough: Schwarzer; Reiziger, Queudrue, Riggott, Southgate, Parlour, Downing (Nemeth 86), Morrison (Parnaby 46), Hasselbaink, Job (Doriva 46), Zenden.
Graz: Schranz; Plassnegger, Tokic, Ehmann, Pogatetz, Bleidelis (Standfest 64), Muratovic, Aufhauser, Majstorovic (Dollinger 74), Skoro, Bazina.

Newcastle United (2) 2 *(Breuer 10 (og), Shearer 25)*
Heerenveen (0) 1 *(Bruggink 80 (pen))* 26,156
Newcastle United: Given; Carr, Hughes, Faye, O'Brien (Taylor 78), Bramble, Dyer (Jenas 46), Butt, Shearer (Milner 65), Ameobi, Robert.
Heerenveen: Vandenbussche; Bakkati, Hansson, Breuer (Seip 74), Rzasa, Yildirim, Vayrynen, Radomski, Hestad, Bruggink (Sikora 80), Huntelaar (Samaras 68).

Schalke (0) 0
Shakhtjor Donetsk (1) 1 *(Aghahowa 21)* 51,179
Schalke: Rost; Poulsen (Vermant 61), Kobiashvili, Ailton, Lincoln, Sand (Hanke 70), Asamoah, Rodriguez, Oude Kamphuis (Altintop 75), Krstajic, Pander.
Shakhtjor Donetsk: Lastuvka; Tymoschuk, Matuzalem, Aghahowa (Vorobei 76), Lewandowski, Brandao, Rat, Srna, Hubschman, Duljaj (Batista 55), Vukic (Elano 61).

Sevilla (0) 2 *(Makukula 80, Adriano Correia 90)*
Panathinaikos (0) 0 45,000
Sevilla: Esteban; David, Aitor Ocio, Pablo Alfaro (Adriano Correia 65), Daniel Alves, Baptista, Renato, Jesuli (Dario Silva 72), Marti (Makukula 78), Antonito, Aranda.
Panathinaikos: Galinovic; Kotsios, Morris, Munch, Goumas, Vyntra, Gonzalez■, Andric, Basinas, Papadopoulos (Sapanis 76), Konstantinou (Gekas 62).

Sochaux (0) 0
Olympiakos (0) 1 *(Stoltidis 67)* 10,962
Sochaux: Richert; Monsoreau, Potillon (Daf 61), Diawara, Isabey, Pitau, Mathieu, Santos, Boudarene (Lonfat 88), Menez, Zairi (Regnier 74).
Olympiakos: Nikopolidis; Schurrer, Mavrogenidis, Kostoulas, Anatolakis, Rivaldo (Giovanni 86), Stoltidis, Maric (Kafes 90), Djordjevic, Georgatos, Okkas (Castillo 80).

Steaua (0) 2 *(Cristea 50, 70)*
Valencia (0) 0 20,000
Steaua: Khomutovsky; Radoi, Marin, Ogaruru, Ghionea, Munteanu D, Dica, Paraschiv, Dinita (Bostina 85), Oprita (Lovin 112), Cristea (Baciu 95).
Valencia: Palop; Caneira, Aurelio, Carboni, Navarro, Moretti (Aimar 104), Albelda, Baraja, Rufete, Corradi (Mista 76), Xisco (Di Vaio 76).
aet; Steaua won 4-3 on penalties.

Stuttgart (0) 0
Parma (0) 2 *(Marchionni 97, Pisanu 116)* 37,000
Stuttgart: Hildebrand; Hinkel, Stranzl, Babbel (Gentner 106), Meira, Vranjes (Heidt 70), Tiffert (Szabics 86), Soldo, Hleb, Cacau, Kuranyi.
Parma: Bucci; Bettarini (Bovo 58), Cannavaro■, Bonera, Contini, Ruopolo, Bolano, Dessena (Marchionni 50), Fabio Simplicio, Gilardino, Pisanu.
aet.

Villarreal (2) 2 *(Figueroa 20, Cazorla 32)*
Dynamo Kiev (0) 0 8000
Villarreal: Reina; Gonzalo Rodriguez, Arruabarrena, Sorin (Hector Font 82), Quique Alvarez, Javi Venta, Cazorla, Riquelme■, Senna, Figueroa (Josico 60), Jose Mari (Guayre 75).
Dynamo Kiev: Shovkovskyi; Rodolfo, Sablic, Nesmachny (El Kaddouri 57), Gavrancic, Leko (Cernat 51), Diogo Rincon, Gusev, Yussuf, Kleber, Verpakovskis (Shatskikh 46).

Zaragoza (1) 2 *(Galletti 11, Savio 71)*
Fenerbahce (0) 1 *(Alex 87)* 21,000
Zaragoza: Luis Garcia; Aranzabal, Alvaro, Milito, Savio, Ponzio, Generelo (Cuartero 83), Soriano, Zapater (Movilla 74), Galletti (Cani 74), Villa.
Fenerbahce: Rustu; Fabio Luciano, Servet, Onder (Van Hooijdonk 60), Umit O, Marco Aurelio, Alex, Selcuk (Tuncay 38), Serkan, Nobre, Anelka.

Sunday, 27 February 2005

Athletic Bilbao (1) 1 *(Yeste 19 (pen))*
FK Austria (1) 2 *(Sionko 35, 69)* 35,000
Athletic Bilbao: Lafuente; Prieto (Lacruz 46), Iraola, Orbaiz, Murillo, Del Horno, Yeste, Gurpegui (Tiko 72), Ezquerro (Liorente 72), Etxeberria, Urzaiz.
FK Austria: Didulica; Afolabi, Antonsson, Papac, Dospel, Sionko, Vachousek (Metz 87), Blanchard, Kiesenebner, Vastic (Gilewicz 73), Dosunmu (Rushfeldt 84).

FOURTH ROUND FIRST LEG

Thursday, 10 March 2005

FK Austria (1) 1 *(Rushfeldt 32)*

Zaragoza (0) 1 *(Savio 74)* 21,000

FK Austria: Didulica; Antonsson, Afolabi, Papac, Dospel, Sionko, Kiesenebner, Blanchard, Vachousek, Rushfeldt (Dosunmu 81), Vastic (Gilewicz 72).
Zaragoza: Luis Garcia; Aranzabal, Alvaro, Milito, Ponzio, Generelo, Soriano, Zapater (Movilla 88), Savio, Galletti (Cani 46), Villa (Oscar 86).

Lille (0) 0

Auxerre (1) 1 *(Akale 45)* 8080

Lille: Sylva; Tavlaridis, Vitakic, Angbwa, Tafforeau (Fauvergue 77), Brunel, Bodmer, Acimovic (Odemwingie 56), Landrin (Debuchy 46), Dumont, Moussilou.
Auxerre: Cool; Jaures, Mignot, Bolf, Sagna, Violeau, Mathis, Gonzalez (Diaby 79), Akale (Vandenbosshe 88), Kalou, Mwaruwari.

Middlesbrough (0) 2 *(Job 79, Riggott 86)*

Sporting Lisbon (0) 3 *(Pedro Barbosa 49, Leidson 53, Douala 65)* 23,739

Middlesbrough: Schwarzer; Reiziger (Nemeth 46), Queudrue, Riggott, Southgate, Doriva, Downing, Parnaby, Hasselbaink, Graham (Job 53), Zenden.
Sporting Lisbon: Ricardo; Rogerio, Enakahire, Hugo, Rui Jorge, Pedro Barbosa (Sa Pinto 77), Rochemback, Joao Moutinho, Hugo Viana, Leidson (Tello 77), Douala (Beto 90).

Olympiakos (1) 1 *(Djordjevic 16 (pen))*

Newcastle United (2) 3 *(Shearer 12 (pen), Robert 34, Kluivert 69)* 33,000

Olympiakos: Nikopolidis; Mavrogenidis, Schurrer, Kostoulas■, Anatolakis, Maric, Stoltidis, Djordjevic (Kafes 76), Georgatos■, Rivaldo (Giovanni 65), Okkas (Pantos 65).
Newcastle United: Given; Carr, Hughes, Faye (N'Zogbia 84), O'Brien, Bramble, Dyer (Jenas 60), Butt, Shearer, Kluivert, Robert (Milner 60).

Partizan Belgrade (0) 1 *(Tomic 83 (pen))*

CSKA Moscow (1) 1 *(Aldonin 17)* 18,000

Partizan Belgrade: Kralj; Mirkovic, Djordjevic, Emeghara, Rnic, Vukcevic, Ciric (Grubjesic 76), Tomic, Brnovic, Boya (Radovic 12), Odita.
CSKA Moscow: Akinfeev; Ignashevich, Berezutski A, Odiah, Krasic, Zhirkov, Berezutski V, Aldonin (Olic 76), Rahimic, Daniel Carvalho, Vagner Love (Shershun 89).

Sevilla (0) 0

Parma (0) 0 40,000

Sevilla: Esteban; Javi Navarro, David, Daniel Alves, Pablo Alfaro, Baptista (Dario Silva 77), Marti, Jordi Lopez, Antonito (Makulula 70), Jesuli (Adriano Correia 65), Jesus Navas.
Parma: Frey; Cardone, Bovo, Contini, Camara, Marchionni, Dessena (Bonera 46), Vignaroli, Ruopolo, Grella (Fabio Simplicio 59), Pisanu.

Shakhtjor Donetsk (1) 1 *(Matuzalem 45)*

AZ (1) 3 *(Nelisse 27, Mathijsen 50, Perez 90 (pen))* 19,000

Shakhtjor Donetsk: Lastuvka; Tymoschuk, Hubschman, Rat, Batista (Elano 34), Matuzalem, Vukic (Jadson 46), Lewandowski, Srna, Aghahowa (Vorobei 66), Brandao.
AZ: Timmer; Kromkamp, Opdam, Mathijsen, De Cler, Landzaat (Jaliens 84), Lindenbergh, Sektioui (Ramzi 84), Meerdink, Nelisse (Huysegems 76), Perez.

Wednesday, 16 March 2005

Steaua (0) 0

Villarreal (0) 0 30,000

Steaua: Khomutovsky; Ogararu, Radoi, Ghionea, Marin, Oprita, Paraschiv, Munteanu, Dica (Ciocoiu 89), Dinita (Dumitru 75), Cristea (Bostina 72).
Villarreal: Reina; Javi Venta, Pena, Quique Alvarez (Arzo 89), Arruabarrena, Cazorla (Hector Font 87), Senna, Josico, Sorin, Jose Mari (Guayre 89), Figueroa.

FOURTH ROUND SECOND LEG

Wednesday, 16 March 2005

AZ (1) 2 *(Van Galen 9, Meerdink 65)*

Shakhtjor Donetsk (0) 1 *(Elano 66)* 8200

AZ: Timmer; Mathijsen, Opdam, De Cler, Landzaat, Kromkamp, Lindenbergh, Meerdink, Van Galen (Huysegems 76), Perez (Ramzi 85), Nelisse (Sektioui 76).
Shakhtjor Donetsk: Lastuvka; Rat, Hubschman, Lewandowski, Srna (Kulakov 60), Duljaj (Jadson 58), Elano, Matuzalem, Aghahowa, Bielik (Vorobei 72), Barcauan.

Newcastle United (2) 4 *(Dyer 18, Shearer 45, 69, Bowyer 54)*

Olympiakos (0) 0 32,163

Newcastle United: Given; Carr (Ramage 67), Hughes, Butt, O'Brien, Taylor, Bowyer, Jenas, Shearer, Dyer (Milner 58), Robert (N'Zogbia 58).
Olympiakos: Nikopolidis; Mavrogenidis, Vallas, Anatolakis, Pantos, Maric, Stoltidis (Taralidis 79), Kafes, Djordjevic (Okkas 60), Giovanni (Filipakos 67), Castillo.

Thursday, 17 March 2005

Auxerre (0) 0

Lille (0) 0 9000

Auxerre: Cool; Jaures, Violeau, Pieroni (Diaby 79), Akale (Vandenbosshe 88), Mignot, Kalou, Mathis, Gonzalez, Bolf, Sagna.
Lille: Sylva; Bodmer (Makoun 76), Brunel, Chalme, Landrin, Moussilou (Acimovic 76), Schmitz, Dumont, Tavlaridis, Cabaye (Odemwingie 70), Vitakic■.

CSKA Moscow (0) 2 *(Daniel Carvalho 69, Vagner Love 85 (pen))*

Partizan Belgrade (0) 0 28,500

CSKA Moscow: Akinfeev; Semberas (Aldonin 76), Ignashevich, Berezutski A, Odiah, Daniel Carvalho (Gusev 90), Berezutski V, Zhirkov, Rahimic, Olic (Krasic 46), Vagner Love.
Partizan Belgrade: Kralj; Cirkovic (Bajic 86), Mirkovic, Djordjevic■, Emeghara, Vukcevic, Brnovic, Ciric (Grubjesic 75), Tomic■, Nadj (Radovic 46), Odita.

Parma (1) 1 *(Cardone 18)*

Sevilla (0) 0 7654

Parma: Bucci; Cardone, Bonera, Contini, Bresciano (Pisanu 57), Gibbs (Gilardino 46), Camara, Fabio Simplicio, Grella, Dessena (Morfeo 67), Vignaroli.
Sevilla: Esteban; David, Baptista, Renato, Antonito, Adriano Correia (Kepa 78), Marti, Aitor Ocio, Pablo Alfaro (Dario Silva 73), Jesus Navas, Sergio Ramos (Daniel Alves 56).

Sporting Lisbon (0) 1 *(Pedro Barbosa 90)*

Middlesbrough (0) 0 21,217

Sporting Lisbon: Ricardo; Rogerio, Enakahire, Hugo (Douala 35), Rui Jorge, Beto, Hugo Viana, Joao Moutinho, Pedro Barbosa (Carlos Martins 90), Sa Pinto, Leidson (Niculae 88).
Middlesbrough: Schwarzer; McMahon (Graham 68), Queudrue, Riggott, Southgate, Doriva (Johnson 79), Downing (Wheater 90), Parnaby, Nemeth, Job, Zenden.

Zaragoza (0) 2 *(Villa 58, Galletti 62)*
FK Austria (2) 2 *(Papac 5, Dosunmu 10)* 27,000
Zaragoza: Luis Garcia; Aranzabal, Alvaro, Milito, Zapater (Javi Moreno 70), Savio, Ponzio (Cuartero 46), Movilla, Soriano (Oscar 32), Galletti, Villa.
FK Austria: Didulica■; Afolabi, Antonsson, Papac, Dospel, Sionko, Wagner, Blanchard, Kiesenebner (Metz 74), Rushfeldt (Safar 32), Dosunmu (Vastic 58).

Sunday, 20 March 2005

Villarreal (1) 2 *(Riquelme 5, 61 (pen))*
Steaua (0) 0 12,500
Villarreal: Reina; Gonzalo Rodriguez, Arruabarrena, Javi Venta, Pena, Josico, Riquelme (Arzo 90), Sorin (Cazorla 52), Senna, Figueroa, Jose Mari (Hector Font 85).
Steaua: Khomutovsky; Radoi, Marin, Ogararu, Ghionea, Munteanu D (Nicolita 75), Bostina, Dica, Lovin, Oprita (Dinita 76), Cristea (Ciociou 75).

QUARTER-FINALS FIRST LEG

Thursday, 7 April 2005

CSKA Moscow (1) 4 *(Odiah 21, Ignashevich 63 (pen), Vagner Love 71, Gusev 77)*
Auxerre (0) 0 26,000
CSKA Moscow: Akinfeev; Semberas, Ignashevich, Berezutski A, Daniel Carvalho, Olic (Krasic 59), Odiah (Gusev 77), Aldonin (Laizans 87), Zhirkov, Berezutski V, Vagner Love.
Auxerre: Cool; Jaures, Violeau, Tainio, Akale (Coulibaly 84), Mignot■, Kalou, Mathis, Mwaruwari (Pieroni 77), Recorbet, Kaboul.

FK Austria (0) 1 *(Mila 61)*
Parma (1) 1 *(Pisanu 34)* 39,000
FK Austria: Safar; Afolabi, Antonsson, Papac, Dospel, Vastic (Wagner 76), Vachousek (Kitzbichler 90), Blanchard, Kiesenebner (Dosunmu 59), Mila, Rushfeldt.
Parma: Bucci; Bovo, Cannavaro, Bonera, Bolano, Fabio Simplicio, Dessena (Morfeo 56), Gibbs, Pisanu (Bresciano 56), Camara, Vignaroli (Cardone 65).

Newcastle United (1) 1 *(Shearer 37)*
Sporting Lisbon (0) 0 36,753
Newcastle United: Given (Harper 46); Carr, Hughes, Faye, O'Brien, Taylor, Dyer (Bowyer 63), Jenas, Shearer, Ameobi, Robert (Milner 57).
Sporting Lisbon: Ricardo; Rogerio, Beto, Anderson Polga, Rui Jorge, Rochemback, Carlos Martins (Mota 67), Pedro Barbosa (Tello 82), Joao Moutinho, Liedson, Sa Pinto.

Villarreal (1) 1 *(Riquelme 14)*
AZ (1) 2 *(Landzaat 12, Nelisse 74)* 10,000
Villarreal: Reina; Gonzalo Rodriguez, Arruabarrena, Sorin (Cazorla 59), Armando Sa, Josico (Hector Font 73), Arzo, Senna, Riquelme, Jose Mari (Guayre 79), Figueroa.
AZ: Timmer; Jaliens, Opdam, Landzaat, Kromkamp, Lindenbergh, Buskermolen (De Cler 63), Sektioui, Nelisse (Huysegems 83), Van Galen (Ramzi 79), Perez.

QUARTER-FINALS SECOND LEG

Thursday, 14 April 2005

AZ (1) 1 *(Perez 8)*
Villarreal (0) 1 *(Figueroa 72)* 8678
AZ: Timmer; Kromkamp, Opdam, Mathijsen (Jaliens 17), De Cler, Landzaat, Lindenbergh, Van Galen (Huysegems 46), Sektioui, Nelisse (Buskermolen 67), Perez.
Villarreal: Reina; Gonzalo Rodriguez (Quique Alvarez 46), Arruabarrena, Pena, Armando Sa, Josico (Guayre 30), Riquelme, Sorin, Senna, Figueroa, Jose Mari.

Auxerre (1) 2 *(Lachuer 8, Kalou 80 (pen))*
CSKA Moscow (0) 0 13,000
Auxerre: Cool; Radet, Jaures, Grichting, Recorbet, Violeau, Lachuer (Tainio 55), Mathis, Akale, Kalou, Mwaruwari (Pieroni 76).
CSKA Moscow: Akinfeev; Semberas, Ignashevich, Odiah, Krasic, Zhirkov, Laizans (Daniel Carvalho 27), Rahimic, Olic (Aldonin 27), Vagner Love (Samodin 46), Berezutski V.

Parma (0) 0
FK Austria (0) 0 11,476
Parma: Bucci; Cardone, Bonera, Contini, Savi (Bolano 49), Bresciano, Gibbs (Gilardino 46), Cannavaro, Camara, Fabio Simplicio, Vignaroli (Morfeo 72).
FK Austria: Safar; Afolabi, Antonsson, Papac, Dospel, Sionko (Vastic 56), Vachousek (Dosunmu 71), Blanchard, Kiesenebner, Rushfeldt, Mila (Wagner 83).

Sporting Lisbon (1) 4 *(Niculae 49, Sa Pinto 71, Beto 77, Rochemback 90)*
Newcastle United (1) 1 *(Dyer 20)* 45,000
Sporting Lisbon: Ricardo; Anderson Polga, Rogerio, Rui Jorge, Beto, Carlos Martins (Pedro Barbosa 67), Rochemback, Joao Moutinho, Sa Pinto (Custodio 89), Niculae (Pinilla 75), Douala.
Newcastle United: Given; Carr, Babayaro, Faye, Bramble (O'Brien 57), Taylor, Bowyer, Jenas (Milner 46), Shearer, Dyer (Kluivert 60), N'Zogbia.

SEMI-FINAL FIRST LEG

Thursday, 28 April 2005

Parma (0) 0
CSKA Moscow (0) 0 7298
Parma: Bucci; Cardone (Bonera 58), Bovo, Savi, Ruopolo, Sorrentino (Bolano 78), Cannavaro, Camara, Dessena, Furlan (Pisanu 66), Vignaroli.
CSKA Moscow: Akinfeev; Semberas, Ignashevich, Berezutski A, Daniel Carvalho, Olic (Laizans 83), Odiah, Krasic (Vagner Love 57), Zhirkov, Berezutski V, Rahimic.

Sporting Lisbon (1) 2 *(Douala 36, Pinilla 80)*
AZ (1) 1 *(Landzaat 36)* 34,776
Sporting Lisbon: Ricardo; Rui Jorge, Anderson Polga, Enakahire, Rogerio (Pinilla 68), Rochemback (Hugo Viana 60), Custodio, Sa Pinto, Liedson, Douala, Pedro Barbosa (Joao Moutinho 46).
AZ: Timmer; Vlaar, De Cler, Buskermolen, Jaliens, Landzaat, Lindenbergh, Perez, Nelisse (Huysegems 71), Van Galen (Sektioui 77), Ramzi.

SEMI-FINAL SECOND LEG

Thursday, 5 May 2005

AZ (1) 3 *(Perez 6, Huysegens 79, Jaliens 109)*
Sporting Lisbon (1) 2 *(Liedson 45, Miguel Garcia 120)* 8603
AZ: Timmer; Vlaar, De Cler, Opdam, Jaliens, Landzaat, Sektioui (Janga 120), Perez, Nelisse (Huysegens 72), Van Galen, Ramzi (Elkhattabi 64).
Sporting Lisbon: Ricardo; Rui Jorge (Niculae 110), Anderson Polga, Miguel Garcia, Beto, Rochemback (Pedro Barbosa 86), Custodio, Sa Pinto, Liedson, Douala (Tello 75), Joao Moutinho.
aet.

CSKA Moscow (1) 3 *(Daniel Carvalho 11, 54, Berezutski V 61)*
Parma (0) 0 30,000
CSKA Moscow: Akinfeev; Ignashevich, Berezutski A, Daniel Carvalho (Semberas 76), Olic (Krasic 58), Vagner Love (Salougin 88), Odiah, Zhirkov, Aldonin, Rahimic, Berezutski V.
Parma: Bucci (Frey 20); Bovo, Bonera■, Savi, Ruopolo, Bresciano, Cannavaro, Camara, Grella (Simplicio 60), Dessena, Furlan (Gilardino 50).

UEFA CUP FINAL 2005

Wednesday, 18 May 2005
(in Lisbon, 48,000)

Sporting Lisbon (1) 1 *(Rogerio 28)* **CSKA Moscow (0) 3** *(Berezutski A 57, Zhirkov 66, Vagner Love 75)*

Sporting Lisbon: Ricardo; Miguel Garcia, Beto, Enakahire, Tello, Rogerio (Douala 79), Rochemback, Joao Moutinho (Viana 87), Pedro Barbosa, Leidson, Sa Pinto (Niculae 72).

CSKA Moscow: Akinfeev; Berezutski A, Ignashevich, Zhirkov, Odiah, Aldonin (Gusev 86), Berezutski V, Daniel Carvalho (Semberas 82), Rahimic, Olic (Krasic 67), Vagner Love.

Referee: G. Poll (England).

CSKA Moscow players celebrate with the UEFA Cup after defeating Sporting Lisbon in the final played in Lisbon. (ASP)

UEFA CHAMPIONS LEAGUE 2005–06

Champions League 2005–06 participating clubs

IOC	*Stage*	*Club*
ENG	Q1	Liverpool FC*
ESP	Grp	FC Barcelona
ESP	Grp	Real Madrid CF**
ESP	Q3	Villarreal CF***
ESP	Q3	Real Betis Balompié****
ENG	Grp	Chelsea FC
ENG	Grp	Arsenal FC**
ENG	Q3	Manchester United FC***
ENG	Q3	Everton FC****
ITA	Grp	Juventus FC
ITA	Grp	AC Milan**
ITA	Q3	FC Internazionale Milano***
ITA	Q3	Udinese Calcio****
GER	Grp	FC Bayern München
GER	Grp	FC Schalke 04**
GER	Q3	Werder Bremen***
FRA	Grp	Olympique Lyonnais
FRA	Grp	LOSC Lille Métropole**
FRA	Q3	AS Monaco FC***
POR	Grp	SL Benfica
POR	Grp	FC Porto**
POR	Q3	Sporting Clube de Portugal***
GRE	Grp	Olympiacos CFP
GRE	Q3	Panathinaikos FC**
NED	Grp	PSV Eindhoven
NED	Q3	AFC Ajax**
CZE	Grp	AC Sparta Praha
CZE	Q3	SK Slavia Praha**
TUR	Grp	Fenerbahçe SK
TUR	Q2	Trabzonspor**
SCO	Q3	Rangers FC
SCO	Q2	Celtic FC**
BEL	Q3	Club Brugge KV
BEL	Q2	RSC Anderlecht**
SUI	Q3	FC Basel 1893
SUI	Q2	FC Thun**
UKR	Q3	FC Shakhtar Donetsk
UKR	Q2	FC Dynamo Kyiv**
NOR	Q3	Rosenborg BK
NOR	Q2	Vålerenga IF**
POL	Q3	Wisla Kraków
ISR	Q2	Maccabi Haifa FC
AUT	Q2	SK Rapid Wien
SCG	Q2	FK Partizan
BUL	Q2	PFC CSKA Sofia
RUS	Q2	FC Lokomotiv Moskva
DEN	Q2	Brøndby IF
CRO	Q2	HNK Hajduk Split
SWE	Q2	Malmö FF
HUN	Q2	Debreceni VSC
ROU	Q2	FC Steaua Bucuresti
SVK	Q1	FC Artmedia Bratislava
SLO	Q1	NK Gorica
CYP	Q1	Anorthosis Famagusta FC
MOL	Q1	FC Sheriff
LAT	Q1	Skonto FC
FIN	Q1	FC Haka
BIH	Q1	NK Zrinjski
GEO	Q1	FC Dinamo Tbilisi
MKD	Q1	FK Rabotnicki
LIT	Q1	FBK Kaunas
BLS	Q1	FC Dinamo Minsk
ISL	Q1	FH Hafnarfjördur
MLT	Q1	Sliema Wanderers FC
IRL	Q1	Shelbourne FC
ARM	Q1	FC Pyunik
WAL	Q1	Total Network Solutions FC
ALB	Q1	KF Tirana
NIR	Q1	Glentoran FC
EST	Q1	FC Levadia Tallinn
LUX	Q1	F91 Dudelange
AZE	Q1	PFC Neftchi
FAR	Q1	HB Tórshavn
KAZ	Q1	FC Kairat Almaty

* Holders, ** domestic runners-up, *** domestic third-placed team, **** domestic fourth-placed team

UEFA CUP 2005–06

UEFA Cup 2005–06 participating clubs

IOC	*Round*	*Club*
UIC	1st	tbc
UIC	1st	tbc
UIC	1st	tbc
RUS	1st	PFC CSKA Moskva*****
ESP	1st	RCD Espanyol
ESP	1st	Sevilla FC
ESP	1st	CA Osasuna**
ENG	1st	Bolton Wanderers FC
ENG	1st	Middlesbrough FC
ITA	1st	UC Sampdoria
ITA	1st	US Città di Palermo
ITA	1st	AS Roma**
GER	1st	Hertha BSC Berlin
GER	1st	VfB Stuttgart
GER	1st	Bayer 04 Leverkusen
FRA	1st	AJ Auxerre*
FRA	1st	Stade Rennais FC
FRA	1st	RC Strasbourg****
POR	1st	Vitória FC*
POR	1st	SC Braga
POR	1st	Vitória SC
GRE	1st	AEK Athens FC
GRE	1st	Xanthi FC
GRE	1st	PAOK FC
GRE	1st	Aris Thessaloniki FC**
NED	1st	AZ Alkmaar
NED	1st	Feyenoord
NED	1st	SC Heerenveen
NED	1st	Willem II**
CZE	1st	FC Baník Ostrava*
TUR	1st	Galatasaray SK*
SCO	1st	Hibernian FC
BEL	1st	KFC Germinal Beerschot Antwerpen FC*
CZE	Q2	FK Teplice
TUR	Q2	Besiktas JK
SCO	Q2	Dundee United FC**
BEL	Q2	KRC Genk
SUI	Q2	FC Zürich*
SUI	Q2	Grasshopper-Club
UKR	Q2	FC Metalurh Donetsk
UKR	Q2	FC Dnipro Dnipropetrovsk
NOR	Q2	SK Brann*
NOR	Q2	Tromsø IL
POL	Q2	Groclin Grodzisk Wielkopolski*
POL	Q2	Legia Warszawa
POL	Q2	Wisla Plock
ISR	Q2	Maccabi Tel-Aviv FC*
ISR	Q2	Maccabi Petach-Tikva FC
ISR	Q2	FC Ashdod
AUT	Q2	FK Austria Wien*
AUT	Q2	Grazer AK
AUT	Q2	SV Pasching
SCG	Q2	FK Crvena Zvezda
SCG	Q2	FK Zeta
SCG	Q2	OFK Beograd
BUL	Q2	PFC Levski Sofia*
BUL	Q2	PFC Lokomotiv Plovdiv
BUL	Q2	PFC Litex Lovech
RUS	Q2	FC Krylya Sovetov Samara
RUS	Q2	FC Zenit St. Petersburg
DEN	Q2	FC København
DEN	Q2	FC Midtjylland**
CRO	Q2	HNK Rijeka*
CRO	Q2	NK Inter Zaprešic
SWE	Q2	Djurgårdens IF*
SWE	Q2	Halmstads BK
HUN	Q2	Matáv Football Club Sopron*
ROM	Q2	FC Dinamo Bucuresti*
SVK	Q2	FK Dukla Banská Bystrica*
SLO	Q2	NK Publikum*
NOR	Q1	Viking FK****
GER	Q1	1. FSV Mainz 05****
DEN	Q1	Esbjerg fB****
HUN	Q1	Ferencvárosi TC
ROU	Q1	AFC Rapid Bucuresti
SVK	Q1	MŠK Žilina
SLO	Q1	NK Domzale
CYP	Q1	AC Omonia*
CYP	Q1	APOEL FC
MDA	Q1	FC Nistru Otaci*
MDA	Q1	FC Dacia Chisinau
LAT	Q1	FK Ventspils*
LAT	Q1	FHK Liepajas Metalurgs
FIN	Q1	Myllykosken Pallo-47*
FIN	Q1	AC Allianssi
BIH	Q1	NK Široki Brijeg
BIH	Q1	NK Zepce
GEO	Q1	FC Lokomotiv Tbilisi*
GEO	Q1	FC Torpedo Kutaisi
MKD	Q1	FK Baskimi*
MKD	Q1	FK Vardar
LIT	Q1	FK Ekranas
LIT	Q1	FK Atlantas**
BLS	Q1	FC MTZ-RIPO Minsk*
BLS	Q1	FC BATE Borisov
ISL	Q1	Keflavík*
ISL	Q1	ÍBV Vestmannaeyjar
MLT	Q1	Birkirkara FC*
MLT	Q1	Hibernians FC
IRL	Q1	Longford Town FC*
IRL	Q1	Cork City FC
ARM	Q1	FC MIKA*
ARM	Q1	FC Banants
WAL	Q1	Rhyl FC
WAL	Q1	Carmarthen Town AFC**
LIE	Q1	FC Vaduz*
ALB	Q1	KS Teuta*
ALB	Q1	KS Elbasani
NIR	Q1	Portadown FC*
NIR	Q1	Linfield FC
EST	Q1	FC TVMK Tallinn
EST	Q1	FC Flora
LUX	Q1	CS Pétange*
LUX	Q1	FC Etzella Ettelbrück
AZE	Q1	FK Baku*
AZE	Q1	FK Khazar Lenkoran
FAR	Q1	B36 Tórshavn
FAR	Q1	NSÍ Runavík**
AND	Q1	UE Sant Julià***
SMR	Q1	SP Domagnano***

* domestic cup winners, ** losing cup finalists, *** national domestic championship winners, **** fair play winners, ***** UEFA Cup holders, UIC Intertoto cup winners.

SUMMARY OF APPEARANCES

EUROPEAN CUP AND CHAMPIONS LEAGUE (1955–2005)

ENGLISH CLUBS
16 Manchester U
15 Liverpool
9 Arsenal
4 Leeds U
3 Newcastle U, Nottingham F
3 Chelsea, Derby Co, Wolverhampton W, Everton, Aston Villa
1 Burnley, Tottenham H, Ipswich T, Manchester C, Blackburn R

SCOTTISH CLUBS
24 Rangers
20 Celtic
3 Aberdeen
2 Hearts
1 Dundee, Dundee U, Kilmarnock, Hibernian

WELSH CLUBS
6 Barry T
1 Cwmbran T, TNS, Rhyl

NORTHERN IRELAND CLUBS
21 Linfield
10 Glentoran
3 Crusaders, Portadown
1 Glenavon, Ards, Distillery, Derry C, Coleraine, Cliftonville

EIRE CLUBS
7 Shamrock R, Dundalk
6 Waterford
5 Shelbourne
4 Bohemians
3 Drumcondra, St Patrick's Ath,
2 Sligo R, Limerick, Athlone T, Derry C*
1 Cork Hibs, Cork Celtic, Cork City

Winners: Celtic 1966–67; Manchester U 1967–68, 1998–99; Liverpool 1976–77, 1977–78, 1980–81, 1983–84, 2004–05; Nottingham F 1978–79, 1979–80; Aston Villa 1981–82

Finalists: Celtic 1969–70; Leeds U 1974–75; Liverpool 1984–85

EUROPEAN CUP-WINNERS' CUP (1960–99)

ENGLISH CLUBS
6 Tottenham H
5 Manchester U, Liverpool, Chelsea
4 West Ham U
3 Arsenal, Everton
2 Manchester C
1 Wolverhampton W, Leicester C, WBA, Leeds U, Sunderland, Southampton, Ipswich T, Newcastle U

SCOTTISH CLUBS
10 Rangers
8 Aberdeen, Celtic
3 Hearts
2 Dunfermline Ath, Dundee U
1 Dundee, Hibernian, St Mirren, Motherwell, Airdrieonians, Kilmarnock

WELSH CLUBS
14 Cardiff C
8 Wrexham
7 Swansea C
3 Bangor C
1 Borough U, Newport Co, Merthyr Tydfil, Barry T, Llansantfraid, Cwmbran T

NORTHERN IRELAND CLUBS
9 Glentoran
5 Glenavon
4 Ballymena U, Coleraine
3 Crusaders, Linfield
2 Ards, Bangor
1 Derry C, Distillery, Portadown, Carrick Rangers, Cliftonville

EIRE CLUBS
6 Shamrock R
4 Shelbourne
3 Limerick, Waterford, Dundalk, Bohemians
2 Cork Hibs, Galway U, Derry C*, Cork City
1 Cork Celtic, St Patrick's Ath, Finn Harps, Home Farm, University College Dublin, Bray W, Sligo R

Winners: Tottenham H 1962–63; West Ham U 1964–65; Manchester C 1969–70; Chelsea 1970–71, 1997–98; Rangers 1971–72; Aberdeen 1982–83; Everton 1984–85; Manchester U 1990–91; Arsenal 1993–94

Finalists: Rangers 1960–61, 1966–67; Liverpool 1965–66; Leeds U 1972–73; West Ham U 1975–76; Arsenal 1979–80, 1994–95

EUROPEAN FAIRS CUP & UEFA CUP (1955–2005)

ENGLISH CLUBS
13 Leeds U
12 Liverpool
10 Aston Villa, Ipswich T
9 Arsenal, Newcastle U
7 Manchester U
6 Everton, Southampton, Tottenham H, Chelsea
5 Nottingham F, Manchester C
4 Birmingham C, Wolverhampton W, WBA, Blackburn R
3 Sheffield W
2 Stoke C, Derby Co, QPR, Leicester C
1 Burnley, Coventry C, Middlesbrough, Millwall, Norwich C, London Rep XI, Watford, West Ham U, Fulham

SCOTTISH CLUBS
18 Dundee U
15 Hibernian, Aberdeen, Celtic
14 Rangers
12 Hearts
7 Kilmarnock
6 Dunfermline Ath
5 Dundee
3 St Mirren
2 Partick T, Motherwell, St Johnstone
1 Morton, Raith R, Livingston

WELSH CLUBS
4 Bangor C, TNS
3 Inter Cardiff (formerly Inter Cable-Tel), Cwmbran T
2 Newtown, Barry T
1 Afan Lido, Haverfordwest

NORTHERN IRELAND CLUBS
15 Glentoran
8 Coleraine, Linfield
6 Portadown
7 Glenavon
3 Crusaders
1 Ards, Ballymena U, Bangor

EIRE CLUBS
12 Bohemians
7 Shelbourne
6 Dundalk
5 Shamrock R
4 Cork City
3 Finn Harps, St Patrick's Ath, Derry C*
2 Drumcondra, Longford T
1 Cork Hibs, Athlone T, Limerick, Drogheda U, Galway U, Bray Wanderers

Winners: Leeds U 1967–68, 1970–71; Newcastle U 1968–69; Arsenal 1969–70; Tottenham H 1971–72, 1983–84; Liverpool 1972–73, 1975–76, 2000–01; Ipswich T 1980–81

Finalists: London 1955–58, Birmingham C 1958–60, 1960–61; Leeds U 1966–67; Wolverhampton W 1971–72; Tottenham H 1973–74; Dundee U 1986–87

** Now play in League of Ireland*

INTERTOTO CUP 2004

FIRST ROUND

Home Team First Leg	*Aggregate Score*	*Away Team First Leg*	*1st Leg Score*	*2nd Leg Score*
Hibernians	2-4	Slaven	2-1	0-3
Aberystwyth	0-4	Dinaburg	0-0	0-4
EfB	7-1	NSÍ	3-1	4-0
Achnas	2-10	Vardar	1-5	1-5
Sopron	2-3	Teplice	1-0	1-3
Spartak Trnava	4-4	Debrecen	3-0	1-4
Spartak Trnava won on away goals.				
Publikum	2-2	Sloboda	2-1	0-1
Sloboda won on away goals.				
Cork	4-1	Malmö	3-1	1-0
Vetra	4-0	Trans	3-0	1-0
OB	7-0	Ballymena	0-0	7-0
Vllaznia	4-2	Hapoel Beer-Sheva	1-2	3-0*
**Hapoel Beer-Sheva forfeited match.*				
Sant Julià	0-11	Sartid	0-8	0-3
Bregenz	1-5	Khazar	0-3*	1-2
**Bregenz Sheva forfeited match.*				
AA Gent	3-1	Fylkir	2-1	1-0
Odra	1-2	Dinamo Minsk	1-0	0-2
Teuta	0-4	Dubnica	0-0	0-4
MyPa	3-4	Zlín	1-1	2-3
Marek	2-0	Dila	0-0	2-0
Spartak Moskva	2-1	Atlantas	2-0	0-1
Thun	2-0	Gloria	2-0	0-0
Grevenmacher	1-1	Tampere	1-1	0-0
Tampere won on away goals.				

SECOND ROUND

OB	0-5	Villarreal	0-3	0-2
Teplice	1-4	Shinnik	1-2	0-2
Dubnica	1-7	Liberec	1-2	0-5
Westerlo	0-3	Zlín	0-0	0-3
Hibernian	1-2	Vetra	1-1	0-1
Spartak Moskva	5-1	Kamen Ingrad	4-1	1-0
Spartak Trnava	3-1	Sloboda	2-1	1-0
Vardar	1-1	AA Gent	1-0	0-1
Vardar won 4-3 on penalties.				
Slaven	2-1	Vllaznia	2-0	0-1
NEC	0-1	Cork	0-0	0-1
EfB	2-1	Nice	1-0	1-1
Wolfsburg	3-7	Thun	2-3	1-4
OFK	5-1	Dinaburg	3-1	2-0
Genk	2-1	Marek	2-1	0-0
Tampere	3-1	Khazar	3-0	0-1
Dinamo Minsk	4-3	Sartid	1-2	3-1
Dinamo Minsk won on Silver Goal.				

THIRD ROUND

Genk	2-2	Borussia Dortmund	0-1	2-1
Lille	4-3	Dinamo Minsk	2-1	2-2
Nantes	4-2	Cork City	3-1	1-1
Schalke	7-1	Vardar	5-0	2-1
Shinnik	2-6	Uniao Leiria	1-4	1-2
Slaven	2-2	Spartak Trnava	0-0	2-2
Slovan Liberec	2-1	Roda JC	1-0	1-1
Tampere	0-1	OFK Belgrade	0-0	0-1
Thun	3-5	Hamburg	2-2	1-3
Vetra	1-5	Esbjerg	1-1	0-4
Villarreal	3-2	Spartak Moscow	1-0	2-2
Zlin	4-4	Atletico Madrid	2-4	2-0

SEMI-FINALS

Esbjerg	1-6	Schalke	1-3	0-3
Genk	0-2	Uniao Leiria	0-0	0-2
Lille	4-1	Slaven	3-0	1-1
OFK Belgrade	1-5	Atletico Madrid	1-3	0-2
Slovan Liberec	2-2	Nantes	1-0	1-2
Villarreal	2-0	Hamburg	1-0	1-0

FINALS

Lille	2-0	Uniao Leiria	0-0	2-0
Schalke	3-1	Slovan Liberec	2-1	1-0
Villarreal	2-2	Atletico Madrid	2-0	0-2
Villarreal won 3-1 on penalties.				

Lille, Schalke and Villarreal qualified for the UEFA Cup.

WORLD CLUB CHAMPIONSHIP

Played annually up to 1974 and intermittently since then between the winners of the European Cup and the winners of the South American Champions Cup — known as the Copa Libertadores. In 1980 the winners were decided by one match arranged in Tokyo in February 1981 and the venue has been the same since. AC Milan replaced Marseille who had been stripped of their European Cup title in 1993.

1960 Real Madrid beat Penarol 0-0, 5-1
1961 Penarol beat Benfica 0-1, 5-0, 2-1
1962 Santos beat Benfica 3-2, 5-2
1963 Santos beat AC Milan 2-4, 4-2, 1-0
1964 Inter-Milan beat Independiente 0-1, 2-0, 1-0
1965 Inter-Milan beat Independiente 3-0, 0-0
1966 Penarol beat Real Madrid 2-0, 2-0
1967 Racing Club beat Celtic 0-1, 2-1, 1-0
1968 Estudiantes beat Manchester United 1-0, 1-1
1969 AC Milan beat Estudiantes 3-0, 1-2
1970 Feyenoord beat Estudiantes 2-2, 1-0
1971 Nacional beat Panathinaikos* 1-1, 2-1
1972 Ajax beat Independiente 1-1, 3-0
1973 Independiente beat Juventus* 1-0
1974 Atlético Madrid* beat Independiente 0-1, 2-0
1975 Independiente and Bayern Munich could not agree dates; no matches.
1976 Bayern Munich beat Cruzeiro 2-0, 0-0
1977 Boca Juniors beat Borussia Moenchengladbach* 2-2, 3-0
1978 Not contested
1979 Olimpia beat Malmö* 1-0, 2-1
1980 Nacional beat Nottingham Forest 1-0
1981 Flamengo beat Liverpool 3-0
1982 Penarol beat Aston Villa 2-0
1983 Gremio Porto Alegre beat SV Hamburg 2-1
1984 Independiente beat Liverpool 1-0
1985 Juventus beat Argentinos Juniors 4-2 on penalties after a 2-2 draw
1986 River Plate beat Steaua Bucharest 1-0
1987 FC Porto beat Penarol 2-1 after extra time
1988 Nacional (Uru) beat PSV Eindhoven 7-6 on penalties after 1-1 draw
1989 AC Milan beat Atletico Nacional (Col) 1-0 after extra time
1990 AC Milan beat Olimpia 3-0
1991 Red Star Belgrade beat Colo Colo 3-0
1992 Sao Paulo beat Barcelona 2-1
1993 Sao Paulo beat AC Milan 3-2
1994 Velez Sarsfield beat AC Milan 2-0
1995 Ajax beat Gremio Porto Alegre 4-3 on penalties after 0-0 draw
1996 Juventus beat River Plate 1-0
1997 Borussia Dortmund beat Cruzeiro 2-0
1998 Real Madrid beat Vasco da Gama 2-1
1999 Manchester U beat Palmeiras 1-0
2000 Boca Juniors beat Real Madrid 2-1
2001 Bayern Munich beat Boca Juniors 1-0 after extra time
2002 Real Madrid beat Olimpia 2-0
2003 Boca Juniors beat AC Milan 3-1 on penalties after 1-1 draw

*European Cup runners-up; winners declined to take part.

2004

12 December 2004, in Yokohama

Porto (0) 0 Once Caldas (0) 0 45,748

aet; Porto won 8-7 on penalties: Venegas scored for Once Caldas; Diego scored for Porto and was sent off; Alcazar scored for Once Caldas; Carlos Alberto scored for Porto; Rojas scored for Once Caldas; Ricardo Quaresma scored for Porto; De Nigris scored for Once Caldas; Maniche hit the bar for Porto; Fabbro hit a post for Once Caldas; McCarthy scored for Porto.

sudden death: Velasquez scored for Once Caldas; Costinha scored for Porto; Diaz scored for Once Caldas; Jorge Costa scored for Porto; Catano scored for Once Caldas; Ricardo Costa scored for Porto; Garcia shot over for Once Caldas and Pedro Emanuel scored for Porto.

Porto: Vitor Baia (Nuno 105); Seitaridis, Jorge Costa, Pedro Emanuel, Ricardo Costa, Costinha, Maniche, Diego, Derlei (Carlos Alberto 78), McCarthy, Luis Fabbiano (Ricardo Quaresma 88).

Once Caldas: Henao; Rojas, Venegas, Cambindo (Catano 46), Garcia, Viafara, Velasquez, Arango (Diaz 61), Fabbro, Soto (Alcazar 97), De Nigris.

Referee: Larrionda (Uruguay).

EUROPEAN SUPER CUP

Played annually between the winners of the European Champions' Cup and the European Cup-Winners' Cup (UEFA Cup from 2000). AC Milan replaced Marseille in 1993–94.

1972 Ajax beat Rangers 3-1, 3-2
1973 Ajax beat AC Milan 0-1, 6-0
1974 Not contested
1975 Dynamo Kiev beat Bayern Munich 1-0, 2-0
1976 Anderlecht beat Bayern Munich 4-1, 1-2
1977 Liverpool beat Hamburg 1-1, 6-0
1978 Anderlecht beat Liverpool 3-1, 1-2
1979 Nottingham F beat Barcelona 1-0, 1-1
1980 Valencia beat Nottingham F 1-0, 1-2
1981 Not contested
1982 Aston Villa beat Barcelona 0-1, 3-0
1983 Aberdeen beat Hamburg 0-0, 2-0
1984 Juventus beat Liverpool 2-0
1985 Juventus v Everton not contested due to UEFA ban on English clubs
1986 Steaua Bucharest beat Dynamo Kiev 1-0
1987 FC Porto beat Ajax 1-0, 1-0
1988 KV Mechelen beat PSV Eindhoven 3-0, 0-1
1989 AC Milan beat Barcelona 1-1, 1-0
1990 AC Milan beat Sampdoria 1-1, 2-0
1991 Manchester U beat Red Star Belgrade 1-0
1992 Barcelona beat Werder Bremen 1-1, 2-1
1993 Parma beat AC Milan 0-1, 2-0
1994 AC Milan beat Arsenal 0-0, 2-0
1995 Ajax beat Zaragoza 1-1, 4-0
1996 Juventus beat Paris St Germain 6-1, 3-1
1997 Barcelona beat Borussia Dortmund 2-0, 1-1
1998 Chelsea beat Real Madrid 1-0
1999 Lazio beat Manchester U 1-0
2000 Galatasaray beat Real Madrid 2-1
2001 Liverpool beat Bayern Munich 3-2
2002 Real Madrid beat Feyenoord 3-1
2003 AC Milan beat Porto 1-0
2004 Valencia beat Porto 2-1

2004–05

27 August 2004, in Monaco

Porto (0) 1 *(Ricardo Quaresma 78)* **Valencia (1) 2** *(Baraja 33, Di Vaio 67)* 18,500

Porto: Vitor Baia; Seitaridis, Jorge Costa, Pepe, Nuno Valente, Hugo Leal (Ricardo Quaresma 61), Costinha, Maniche, Carlos Alberto, Helder Postiga, McCarthy (Cesar Peixanto 72).

Valencia: Canizares; Curro Torres, Navarro, Marchena, Carboni, Vicente, Baraja, Albelda, Rufete, Corradi (Aimar 67), Di Vaio (Mista 77).

Referee: Hauge (Norway).

INTERNATIONAL DIRECTORY

The latest available information has been given regarding numbers of clubs and players registered with FIFA, the world governing body. Where known, official colours are listed. With European countries, League tables show a number of signs. * indicates relegated teams, + play-offs, *+ relegated after play-offs, ++ promoted.

There are 197 member associations and one provisional member, Palestine. The four home countries, England, Scotland, Northern Ireland and Wales, are dealt with elsewhere in the Yearbook; but basic details appear in this directory.

Club names are anglicized wherever possible, i.e. Prague for Praha, Kiev for Kyiv, etc.

EUROPE

ALBANIA

The Football Association of Albania, Rruga Labinoti, Pallati Perballe Shkolles 'Gjuhet e Huaja'.
Founded: 1930; *Number of Clubs:* 49; *Number of Players:* 5,192; *National Colours:* Red shirts, black shorts, red stockings.
Telephone: 00-355-43/46 601; *Fax:* 00-355-43/46 609.

International matches 2004

Sweden (h) 2-1, Iceland (h) 2-1, Estonia (a) 1-1, Cyprus (a) 1-2, Greece (h) 2-1, Georgia (a) 0-2, Denmark (h) 0-2, Kazakhstan (a) 1-0.

League Championship wins (1930–37; 1945–2005)

SK Tirana 22 (including 17 Nentori 8); Dinamo Tirana 16; Partizani Tirana 15; Vllaznia 9; Flamurtari 1; Elbasan 2 (including Labinoti 1); Skenderbeu 1; Teuta 1.

Cup wins (1948–2005)

Partizani Tirana 15; Dinamo Tirana 13; SK Tirana 11 (including 17 Nentori 6); Vllaznia 5; Teuta 4; Elbasan 3 (including Labintoti 1); Flamurtari 2; Apolonia 1.

Final League Table 2004–05

	P	*W*	*D*	*L*	*F*	*A*	*Pts*
SK Tirana	36	26	6	4	82	32	84
Elbasan	36	24	7	5	59	27	79
Dinamo Tirana	36	18	8	10	51	30	62
Vllaznia	36	19	4	13	80	47	61
Teuta	36	16	4	16	47	49	52
Shkumbini	36	14	6	16	49	47	48
Lushnja	36	13	9	14	43	47	48
Partizani	36	13	7	16	59	58	46
Rrogozhine*	36	7	7	22	26	48	28
Laci*	36	0	2	34	13	124	2

Top scorer: Sinani (Vllazinia) 36.
Cup Final: Teuta 0, SK Tirana 0.
Teuta won 6-5 on penalties.

ANDORRA

Federacio Andorrana de Futbol, Avinguda Carlemany 67, 3er Pis, Apartado postal 65, Escaldes-Engordany, Principat D'Andorra.
Founded: 1994; *Number of Clubs:* 12; *Number of Players:* 300; *National Colours:* Yellow shirts, red shorts, blue stockings.
Telephone: 00376/805 830; *Fax:* 00376/862 006.

International matches 2004

China (h) 0-0, France (a) 0-4, Spain (a) 0-4, Finland (a) 0-3, Romania (h) 1-5, Macedonia (h) 1-0, Holland (h) 0-3.

League Championship wins (1996–2005)

Principat 3; Santa Coloma 2; St Julia 2; Dicoansa 1; Constelacio 1; Encamp 1.

Cup wins (1996–2005)

Principat 4; Santa Coloma 4; Constelacio 1; Lusitanos 1.

Qualifying League Table 2004–05

	P	*W*	*D*	*L*	*F*	*A*	*Pts*
St Julia	14	13	0	1	42	8	39
Rangers	14	12	0	2	46	13	36
Santa Coloma	14	11	0	3	43	15	33
Principat	14	6	1	7	19	21	19
Inter	14	5	2	7	27	37	17
Encamp	14	2	2	10	11	32	8
Lusitanos	14	2	1	11	13	37	7
Atletic	14	2	0	12	11	49	6

Championship Play-Offs

	P	*W*	*D*	*L*	*F*	*A*	*Pts*
St Julia	20	18	0	2	61	14	54
Rangers	20	17	0	3	59	15	51
Santa Coloma	20	12	1	7	50	26	37
Principat	20	6	2	12	23	45	20

Relegation Play-Offs

	P	W	D	L	F	A	Pts
Inter	20	7	4	9	36	44	25
Lusitanos	20	5	2	13	24	48	17
Encamp*	20	4	3	13	19	41	15
Atletic	20	5	0	15	19	58	15

Cup Final: St Julia 1, Santa Coloma 2.

ARMENIA

Football Federation of Armenia, Saryan 38, Yerevan, 375 010, Armenia.
Founded: 1992; *Number of Clubs:* 32; *Number of Players:* 15,000; *National Colours:* Red shirts, blue shorts, orange stockings.
Telephone: 00374-1/535 084; *Fax:* 00374-1/539517.

International matches 2004

Hungary (n) 0-2, Kazakhstan (n) 3-3, Georgia (n) 2-0, Turkmenistan (h) 1-0, Macedonia (a) 0-3, Finland (h) 0-2, Finland (a) 1-3, Czech Republic (h) 0-3, Romania (h) 1-1.

League Championship wins (1992–2004)

Pyunik 6; Shirak Gyumri 4*; Ararat Yerevan 2*; Homenmen 1; FC Yerevan 1; Tsement 1; Araks 1.
*Includes one unofficial title.

Cup wins (1992–2005)

Ararat Erevan 5; Mika 3; Pyunik 3; Tsement 2; Banants 1.

Final League Table 2004

	P	*W*	*D*	*L*	*F*	*A*	*Pts*
Pyunik	28	22	5	1	89	25	71
Mika	28	16	7	5	41	23	55
Banants	28	12	7	9	40	39	43
Ararat	28	12	7	9	40	33	43
Dinamo-Zenit	28	7	6	15	23	51	27
Kilikia	28	7	5	16	32	49	26
Kotiak	28	6	6	16	31	54	24
Shirak	28	4	9	15	27	49	21

No relegation; Dinamo renamed Dinamo-Zenit. Ararat absorbed Lernagorts.
Top scorers: Manucharian (Pyunik) 21, Petrosian (Pyunik) 21.
Cup Final: Mika 2, Kilikia 0.

AUSTRIA

Oesterreichischer Fussball-Bund, Ernst-Happel Stadion – Sektor A/F, Postfach 340, Meierestrasse 7, Wien 1021.
Founded: 1904; *Number of Clubs:* 2,081; *Number of Players:* 253,576; *National Colours:* White shirts, black shorts, white stockings.
Telephone: 0043-1/727 180; *Fax:* 0043-1/ 728 1632.

International matches 2004

Slovakia (a) 1-1, Luxembourg (h) 4-1, Russia (h) 0-0, Germany (h) 1-3, England (h) 2-2, Azerbaijan (h) 2-0, Poland (h) 1-3, Northern Ireland (a) 3-3.

League Championship wins (1912–2005)

Rapid Vienna 31; FK Austria 23; Tirol-Svarowski-Innsbruck 10; Admira-Energie-Wacker 9; First Vienna 6; Wiener Sportklub 3; Austria Salzburg 3; Sturm Graz 2; FAC 1; Hakoah 1; Linz ASK 1; WAF 1; Voest Linz 1; Graz 1.

Cup wins (1919–2005)
FK Austria 27; Rapid Vienna 14; TS Innsbruck (formerly Wacker Innsbruck) 7; Admira-Energie-Wacker (formerly Sportklub Admira & Admira-Energie) 5; Graz 4; First Vienna 3; Sturm Graz 3; Linz ASK 1; Wacker Vienna 1; WAF 1; Wiener Sportklub 1; Stockerau 1; Ried 1; Karnten 1.

Final League Table 2004–05

	P	*W*	*D*	*L*	*F*	*A*	*Pts*
Rapid	36	21	8	7	67	31	71
Graz	36	21	7	8	58	28	70
FK Austria	36	19	12	5	64	24	69
Pasching	36	17	9	10	53	48	60
Mattersburg	36	12	9	15	48	58	45
Tirol	36	11	11	14	48	48	44
Sturm Graz	36	10	10	16	37	47	40
Admira Modling	36	10	8	18	36	63	38
Salzburg	36	9	9	18	37	51	36
Bregenz*	36	4	9	23	30	80	21

Top scorer: Mayrleb (Pasching) 21.
Cup Final: Rapid 1, FK Austria 3.

AZERBAIJAN

Association of Football Federations of Azerbaijan, 42 Gussi Gadjiev Street, Baku 370 009.
Founded: 1992; *Number of Clubs:* 1,500;. *Number of Players:* 95,000; *National Colours:* White shirts, blue shorts, white stockings.
Telephone: 00994-12/944 916; *Fax:* 00994-12/ 989 393.

International matches 2004
Israel (a) 0-6, Moldova (a) 1-2, Kazakhstan (a) 3-2, Uzbekistan (h) 3-1, Latvia (a) 2-2, Jordan (a) 1-1, Wales (h) 1-1, Austria (a) 0-2, Northern Ireland (h) 0-0, England (h) 0-1, Bulgaria (h) 0-0.

League Championship wins (1992–2005)
Neftchi 4; Kopaz 3; Shamkir 3; Karabakh 2; Turan 1.
Includes one unofficial title for Shamkir in 2002.

Cup wins (1992–2005)
Kopaz 4; Neftchi 4; Karabakh 1; Inshatchi 1; Shafa 1; Baku 1.

Final League Table 2004–05

	P	*W*	*D*	*L*	*F*	*A*	*Pts*
Xazar	34	24	6	4	68	15	78
Neftchi	34	24	6	4	52	18	78
Karvan	34	23	7	4	66	18	76
Turan	34	22	7	5	64	21	73
Baku	34	21	10	3	60	14	73
Karabakh	34	22	5	7	61	31	71
Inter	34	19	9	6	44	24	66
MKT Araz	34	16	9	9	35	23	57
Ganca	34	11	9	14	37	37	42
Karat	34	12	4	18	40	62	40
Geyazan	34	9	6	19	30	52	33
Ganclarbirliyi	34	9	6	19	32	58	33
Shamkir	34	9	5	20	34	48	32
Shahdagh	34	8	8	18	39	51	32
MOIK*	34	7	9	18	24	34	30
Adliyya*	34	7	4	23	24	66	25
Bakili*	34	3	5	26	22	71	14
Safa*	34	2	1	31	16	95	7

Safa withdrew for financial reasons; remaining matches awarded 0-3 against them.
Baku formerly Dinamo Baku.
Inter formerly Xazar Uni.
Ganca formerly Kopaz.
Championship play-off: Neftchi 2, Xazar 1.
Top scorer: Ramazanov (Karvan) 21.
Cup Final: Inter 1, Baku 2.

BELARUS

Belarus Football Federation, Kirova Street 8/2, Minsk 220 600, Belarus.
Founded: 1992; *Number of Clubs:* 455; *Number of Players:* 120,000; *National Colours:* Red shirts, green shorts, red stockings.
Telephone: 00375-17/227 2920; *Fax:* 00375-17/227 2920.

International matches 2004
Cyprus (n) 2-0, Romania (n) 0-2, Latvia (n) 4-1, Lithuania (h) 1-0, Turkey (a) 2-1, Norway (a) 1-1, Moldova (h) 4-0, Italy (a) 3-4, UAE (a) 3-2.

League Championship wins (1992–2004)
Dynamo Minsk 7; Slavia Mozyr (formerly MPKC Mozyr) 2; BATE Borisov 2; Dnepr Mogilev 1; Belshina 1; Gomel 1.

Cup wins (1992–2005)
Belshina 3; Dynamo Minsk 3; Slavia Mozyr (formerly MPKC Mozyr) 2; Neman 1; Dynamo 93 Minsk 1; Lokomotiv 96 1; Gomel 1; Shakhter 1; MTZ-RIPA 1.

Final League Table 2004

	P	*W*	*D*	*L*	*F*	*A*	*Pts*
Dynamo Minsk	30	24	3	3	64	18	75
BATE Borisov	30	22	4	4	59	25	70
Shakhter	30	19	8	3	55	21	65
Torpedo Zhodino	30	19	2	9	57	28	59
Gomel	30	13	7	10	42	41	46
Torpedo Minsk	30	13	7	10	37	31	46
Neman	30	11	7	12	37	33	40
Dynamo Brest	30	10	9	11	39	41	39
Dnepr	30	11	4	15	29	37	37
Naftan	30	10	5	15	45	50	35
Daryda	30	9	8	13	38	48	35
Slavia	30	9	4	17	32	51	31
Zvezda	30	7	8	15	31	56	29
Lakamatyu+	30	8	3	19	34	54	27
MTZ-RIPA+	30	6	9	15	32	56	27
Belshina*	30	2	6	22	21	62	12

Play-off Lakamatyu 1, MTZ-RIPA 4; Lakamatyu relegated.
Top scorer: Stripeikis (Naftan) 18.
Cup Final: MTZ-RIPA 2, BATE Borisov 1.

BELGIUM

Union Royale Belge Des Societes De Football Association, 145 Avenue Houba de Strooper, B-1020 Bruxelles.
Founded: 1895; *Number of Clubs:* 2,120; *Number of Players:* 390,468; *National Colours:* All red.
Telephone: 0032-2/477 1211; *Fax:* 0032-2/ 478 2391.

International matches 2004
France (h) 0-2, Germany (a) 0-3, Turkey (h) 2-3, Holland (a) 1-0, Norway (a) 2-2, Lithuania (h) 1-1, Spain (a) 0-2, Serbia-Montenegro (h) 0-2.

League Championship wins (1896–2005)
Anderlecht 27; FC Brugge 13; Union St Gilloise 11; Standard Liege 8; Beerschot 7; RC Brussels 6; FC Liege 5; Daring Brussels 5; Antwerp 4; Mechelen 4; Lierse SK 4; Cercle Brugge 3; Beveren 2; Genk 2; RWD Molenbeek 1.

Cup wins (1954–2005)
FC Brugge 9; Anderlecht 8; Standard Liege 5; Beerschot 3; Waterschei 2; Beveren 2; Gent 2; Antwerp 2; Cercle Brugge 2; Lierse SK 2; Genk 2; Racing Doornik 1; Waregem 1; Mechelen 1; FC Liege 1; Ekeren 1; Westerlo 1; La Louviere 1.

Final League Table 2004–05

	P	*W*	*D*	*L*	*F*	*A*	*Pts*
FC Brugge	34	24	7	3	83	25	79
Anderlecht	34	23	7	4	75	34	76
Standard Liege	34	21	7	6	64	30	70
Genk	34	21	7	6	59	37	70
Charleroi	34	19	7	8	47	34	64
Gent	34	18	5	11	46	36	59
La Louviere	34	12	8	14	43	43	44
Lokeren	34	11	11	12	36	38	44
Beerschot	34	12	6	16	36	45	42
Lierse	34	12	5	17	56	60	41
Cercle Brugge	34	12	5	17	45	74	41
Westerlo	34	11	6	17	34	54	39
Mouscron	34	10	6	18	40	43	36
St Truiden	34	10	6	18	40	58	36
FC Brussels	34	10	3	21	32	60	33
Beveren	34	8	8	18	43	58	32
Ostend*	34	6	9	19	31	62	27
AEC Mons*	34	7	5	22	39	58	26

Top scorer: Jestrovic (Anderlecht) 18.
Cup Final: Beerschot 2, FC Brugge 1.

BOSNIA-HERZEGOVINA

Football Federation of Bosnia & Herzegovina, Ferhadija 30, Sarajevo 71000.
Founded: 1992; *National Colours:* White shirts, blue shorts, white stockings.
Telephone: 00387-33/276 660; *Fax:* 00387-33/444 332.

International matches 2004
Macedonia (a) 0-1, Luxembourg (a) 2-1, Finland (h) 1-0, France (a) 1-1, Spain (h) 1-1, Serbia-Montenegro (h) 0-0.

League Championship wins (1996–2005)
Zeljeznicar 3; Brotnjo 1; Leotar 1; Siroki 1; Zrinjski 1.

Cup wins (1996–2005)
Sarajevo 3; Zeljeznicar 3; Bosna 1; Celik 1; Modrica 1.

Final League Table 2004–05

	P	*W*	*D*	*L*	*F*	*A*	*Pts*
Zrinjski	30	19	4	7	56	30	61
Zeljeznicar	30	15	6	9	31	22	51
Siroki	30	12	9	9	42	33	45
Sarajevo	30	13	6	11	39	37	45
Travnik	30	14	2	14	42	47	44
Modrica	30	11	9	10	38	32	42
Orasje	30	13	3	14	45	43	42
Buducnost	30	13	3	14	37	40	42
Posusje	30	13	3	14	34	43	42
Istocno	30	12	5	13	36	34	41
Sloboda	30	11	8	11	30	28	41
Zepce	30	13	2	15	33	36	41
Celik	30	13	2	15	29	37	41
Leotar	30	13	2	15	35	45	41
Borac*	30	13	2	15	36	39	40
Rudar*	30	7	4	19	26	43	25

Borac deducted one point failing to appear in match 11.
Top scorer: Rajovic (Zrinjski) 17.
Cup Final: Siroki 0, 1, Sarajevo 1, 1.

BULGARIA

Bulgarian Football Union, Karnigradska Street 19, BG-1000 Sofia.
Founded: 1923; *Number of Clubs:* 376; *Number of Players:* 48,240; *National Colours:* White shirts, green shorts, white stockings.
Telephone: 00359-2/987 7490; *Fax:* 00359-2/986 2538.

International matches 2004
Greece (a) 0-2, Russia (h) 2-2, Cameroon (h) 3-0, Czech Republic (a) 1-3, Sweden (n) 0-5, Denmark (n) 0-2, Italy (n) 1-2, Republic of Ireland (a) 1-1, Iceland (a) 3-1, Croatia (a) 2-2, Malta (h) 4-1, Azerbaijan (a) 0-0, Egypt (a) 1-1.

League Championship wins (1925–2005)
CSKA Sofia 30; Levski Sofia 23; Slavia Sofia 7; Cherno More Varna 4 (formerly Vladislav Varna); Lokomotiv Sofia 4; Liteks 2; Trakia Plovdiv 2; AC 23 Sofia 1; Botev Plovdiv 1; SC Sofia 1; Spartak Varna 1; Spartak Plovdiv 1; Tichka Varna 1; JSZ Sofia 1; Beroe Stara Zagora 1; Etur 1; Lokomotiv Plovdiv 1.

Cup wins (1923–2005)
Levski Sofia 25; CSKA Sofia 19; Slavia Sofia 7; Lokomotiv Sofia 4; Liteks 2; Botev Plovdiv 2; Spartak Plovdiv 1; Spartak Sofia 1; Marek Stanke 1; Trakia Plovdiv 1; Spartak Varna 1; Sliven 1.

Final League Table 2004-05

	P	*W*	*D*	*L*	*F*	*A*	*Pts*
CSKA Sofia	30	25	4	1	81	16	79
Levski Sofia	30	24	4	2	76	19	76
Lokomotiv Plovdiv	30	18	4	8	65	34	58
Liteks	30	16	4	10	45	27	52
Slavia Sofia	30	13	9	8	43	33	48
Lokomotiv Sofia	30	14	7	9	43	35	46
Beroe	30	9	8	13	32	36	35
Cherno More Varna	30	10	5	15	30	38	35
Marek	30	9	8	13	34	44	35
Naftex	30	10	5	15	24	38	35
Belasitsa	30	9	7	14	25	47	34
Pirin	30	7	12	11	31	40	33
Rodopa	30	9	6	15	33	43	33
Vidima*	30	9	5	16	32	51	32
Neseber*	30	5	5	20	25	63	20
Spartak Varna*	30	5	3	22	18	73	18

Top scorer: Kambourov (Lokomotiv Plovdiv) 27.
Cup Final: Levski Sofia 2, CSKA Sofia 1.

CROATIA

Croatian Football Federation, Rusanova 13, Zagreb, 10 3000, Croatia.
Founded: 1912; *Number of Clubs:* 1,221; *Number of Players:* 78,127; *National Colours:* Red & white shirts, white shorts, blue stockings.
Telephone: 00385-1/236 1555; *Fax:* 00385-1/244 1501.

International matches 2004
Germany (h) 1-2, Turkey (h) 2-2, Macedonia (a) 1-0, Slovakia (h) 1-0, Denmark (a) 2-1, Switzerland (n) 0-0, France (n) 2-2, England (n) 2-4, Israel (h) 1-0, Hungary (h) 3-0, Sweden (a) 1-0, Bulgaria (h) 2-2, Republic of Ireland (a) 0-1.

League Championship wins (1941–44; 1992–2005)
Dynamo Zagreb (formerly Croatia Zagreb) 7; Hajduk Split 6; Gradanski 3; Concordia 1; Zagreb 1.

Cup wins (1993–2005)
Dynamo Zagreb (formerly Croatia Zagreb) 7; Hajduk Split 4; Osijek 1; Rijeka 1.

Qualifying Table 2004–05

	P	*W*	*D*	*L*	*F*	*A*	*Pts*
Hajduk Split	22	13	3	6	39	23	42
Rijeka	22	10	8	4	37	23	38
Slaven	22	11	4	7	29	25	37
Inter	22	10	5	7	25	22	35
Varteks	22	11	1	10	39	30	34
Dynamo Zagreb	22	9	6	7	38	30	33
Zagreb	22	10	3	9	27	24	33
Kamen	22	10	2	10	30	28	32
Osijek	22	7	9	6	29	32	30
Pula	22	6	8	8	21	23	26
Zadar	22	5	1	16	25	55	16
Medimurje	22	3	4	15	18	42	13

Championship Play-Off Table 2004-05

	P	*W*	*D*	*L*	*F*	*A*	*Pts*
Hajduk Split	32	16	8	8	58	56	56
Inter	32	15	9	8	44	54	54
Zagreb	32	15	5	12	50	50	50
Rijeka	32	11	4	7	52	47	47
Varteks	32	14	3	15	53	45	45
Slaven	32	12	9	11	37	45	45

Relegation Table 2004-05

	P	*W*	*D*	*L*	*F*	*A*	*Pts*
Dynamo Zagreb	32	12	11	9	55	37	47
Kamen	32	12	5	15	36	39	41
Osijek	32	9	14	9	41	45	41
Pula	32	7	14	11	28	31	35
Medimurje	32	9	6	17	29	52	33
Zadar*	32	10	2	20	36	70	32

Top scorer: Erceg (Rijeka) 17.
Cup Final: Rijeka 2, 1, Hajduk Split 1, 0.

CYPRUS

Cyprus Football Association, 1 Stasinos Str., Engomi, P.O. Box 25071, Nicosia 2404.
Founded: 1934; *Number of Clubs:* 85; *Number of Players:* 6,000; *National Colours:* Blue shirts, white shorts, blue stockings.
Telephone: 00357-22/590 960; *Fax:* 00357-22/590 544.

International matches 2004
Belarus (h) 0-2, Georgia (h) 3-1, Kazakhstan (h) 2-1, Jordan (h) 0-0, Albania (h) 2-1, Republic of Ireland (a) 0-3, Israel (a) 1-2, Faeroes (h) 2-2, France (h) 0-2, Israel (h) 1-2.

League Championship wins (1935–2005)
Omonia 19; Apoel 18; Anorthosis 12; AEL 5; EPA 3; Olympiakos 3; Apollon 2; Pezoporikos 2; Chetin Kayal 1; Trast 1.

Cup wins (1935–2005)
Apoel 17; Omonia 12; Anorthosis 7; AEL 6; EPA 5; Apollon 5; Trast 3; Chetin Kayal 2; Olympiakos 1; Pezoporikos 1; Salamina 1; AEK 1.

Final League Table 2004–05

	P	W	D	L	F	A	Pts
Anorthosis	25	19	5	1	64	23	62
Apoel	26	17	7	2	56	21	58
Omonia	26	13	8	5	47	29	47
Olympiakos	26	11	6	9	36	38	39
Digenis	26	10	6	10	36	31	36
NEA Salamina	26	11	3	12	36	40	36
Apollon	25	10	5	10	43	35	35
ENP	26	7	11	8	38	39	32
AEK	26	7	11	8	26	34	32
AEL	26	8	7	11	36	38	31
Ethnikos Achnas	26	8	6	12	31	40	30
AEP*	26	8	5	13	38	52	29
Alki*	26	8	5	13	39	55	29
Aris*	26	1	1	24	22	73	4

Anorthosis v Apollon match abandoned; not replayed.
Top scorer: Sosin (Apollon) 21.
Cup Final: Omonia 2, Digenis 0.

CZECH REPUBLIC

Football Association of Czech Republic, Diskarska 100, Prague 6 16017 - Strahov, Czech Republic.
Founded: 1901; *Number of Clubs:* 3,836; *Number of Players:* 319,500; *National Colours:* Red shirts, white shorts, blue stockings.
Telephone: 00420-2/3302 9111; *Fax:* 00420-2/3335 3107.

International matches 2004
Italy (a) 2-2, Republic of Ireland (a) 1-2, Japan (h) 0-1, Bulgaria (h) 3-1, Estonia (h) 2-0, Latvia (n) 2-1, Holland (n) 3-2, Germany (n) 2-1, Denmark (n) 3-0, Greece (n) 0-1, Greece (h) 0-0, Holland (a) 0-2, Romania (h) 1-0, Armenia (a) 3-0, Macedonia (a) 2-0.

League Championship wins (1926–93)
Sparta Prague 19; Slavia Prague 12; Dukla Prague (prev. UDA, now known as Marila Pribram) 11; Slovan Bratislava 7; Spartak Trnava 5; Banik Ostrava 3; Inter-Bratislava 1; Spartak Hradec Kralove 1; Viktoria Zizkov 1; Zbrojovka Brno 1; Bohemians 1; Vitkovice 1.

Cup wins (1961–93)
Dukla Prague 8; Sparta Prague 8; Slovan Bratislava 5; Spartak Trnava 4; Banik Ostrava 3; Lokomotiv Kosice 3; TJ Gottwaldov 1; Dunajska Streda 1.
From 1993–94, there were two separate countries: the Czech Republic and Slovakia.

League Championship wins (1994–2005)
Sparta Prague 9; Slavia Prague 1; Slovan Liberec 1; Banik Ostrava 1.

Cup wins (1994–2005)
Slavia Prague 4; Viktoria Zizkov 2; Sparta Prague 2; Spartak Hradec Kralove 1; Jablonec 1; Slovan Liberec 1; Teplice 1; Banik Osrava 1.

Final League Table 2004–05

	P	W	D	L	F	A	Pts
Sparta Prague	30	20	4	6	53	28	64
Slavia Prague	30	15	8	7	39	25	53
Teplice	30	14	11	5	36	27	53
Sigma Olomouc	30	15	6	9	39	34	51
Slovan Liberec	30	14	10	6	45	26	46
Jablonec	30	12	9	9	33	27	45
Banik Ostrava	30	9	10	11	33	36	37
Drnovic	30	9	8	13	30	34	35
Marila Pribram	30	9	8	13	30	41	35
Zlin	30	7	12	11	29	35	33
Brno	30	9	6	15	30	42	33
Slovacko	30	10	14	6	30	22	32
Chmel Blsany	30	7	11	12	25	38	32
Mada	30	6	13	11	26	35	31
Budejovice*	30	6	7	17	28	39	25
Opava*	30	5	9	16	25	42	18

Top scorer: Jun (Sparta Prague) 14.
Cup Final: Banik Ostrava 2, Slovacko 1.

DENMARK

Danish Football Association, Idraettens Hus, Brondby Stadion 20, DK-2605, Brondby.
Founded: 1889; *Number of Clubs:* 1,555; *Number of Players:* 268,517; *National Colours:* Red shirts, white shorts, red stockings.
Telephone: 0045-43/262 222; *Fax:* 0045-43/262 245.

International matches 2004
USA (a) 1-1, Turkey (a) 1-0, Spain (a) 0-2, Scotland (h) 1-0, Estonia (a) 2-2, Croatia (h) 1-2, Italy (n) 0-0, Bulgaria (n) 2-0, Sweden (n) 2-2, Czech Republic (n) 0-3, Poland (a) 5-1, Ukraine (h) 1-1, Albania (a) 2-0, Turkey (n) 1-1, Georgia (a) 2-2.

League Championship wins (1913–2005)
KB Copenhagen 15; Brondby 10; AB (Akademisk) 9; B 93 Copenhagen 9; B 1903 Copenhagen 7; Frem 6; Esbjerg BK 5; Vejle BK 5; AGF Aarhus 5; FC Copenhagen 4; Hvidovre 3; Odense BK 3; AaB Aalborg 2; B 1909 Odense 2; Koge BK 2; Lyngby 2; Silkeborg 1; Herfolge 1.

Cup wins (1955–2005)
Aarhus GF 9; Vejle BK 6; Brondby 5; OB Odense 4; Randers Freja 3; Lyngby 3; FC Copenhagen 3; B 1909 Odense 2; Aalborg BK 2; Esbjerg BK 2; Frem 2; B 1903 Copenhagen 2; B 93 Copenhagen 1; KB Copenhagen 1; Vanlose 1; Hvidovre 1; B1913 Odense 1, AB Copenhagen 1, Viborg 1; Silkeborg 1.

Final League Table 2004–05

	P	W	D	L	F	A	Pts
Brondby	33	20	9	4	61	23	69
FC Copenhagen	33	16	9	8	53	39	57
Midtjylland	33	17	6	10	49	40	57
Aalborg	33	15	8	10	59	45	53
Esbjerg	33	13	10	10	61	47	49
Odense	33	13	9	11	61	41	48
Viborg	33	13	9	11	43	45	48
Silkeborg	33	13	8	12	50	52	47
Aarhus	33	11	6	16	47	53	39
Nordsjaelland	33	8	6	19	36	59	30
Herfolge*	33	6	7	20	29	71	25
Randers*	33	5	9	19	30	64	24

Top scorer: Hojer (Odense) 20.
Cup Final: Brondby 3, Midtjylland 2.

ENGLAND

The Football Association, 25 Soho Square, London W1D 4FA.
Founded: 1863; *Number of Clubs:* 42,000; *Number of Players:* 2,250,000; *National Colours:* White shirts with navy blue collar, navy shorts, white stockings.
Telephone: 020 7745 4545, 020 7402 7151; *Fax:* 020 7745 4546; *Website:* www.the-fa.org

ESTONIA

Estonian Football Association, Rapia 8/10, Tallinn 11312.
Founded: 1921; *Number of Clubs:* 40; *Number of Players:* 12,000; *National Colours:* Blue shirts, black shorts, white stockings.
Telephone: 00372-6/512 720; *Fax:* 00372-6/512 729.

International matches 2004
Malta (n) 2-5, Moldova (n) 1-0, Northern Ireland (h) 0-1, Albania (h) 1-1, Scotland (h) 0-1, Denmark (h) 2-2, Czech Republic (a) 0-2, Macedonia (h) 2-4, Liechtenstein (a) 2-1, Luxembourg (h) 4-0, Portugal (a) 0-4, Latvia (a) 2-2, Russia (a) 0-4, Thailand (n) 0-0, Hungary (n) 0-5.

League Championship wins (1922–40; 1992–2004)
Sport 8; Flora Tallinn 7; Estonia 5; Levadia Maardu 2; Norma Tallinn 2; Tallinn JK 2; Kalev 2; LFLS 1; Olimpia 1; Lantana 1.

Cup wins (1992–2005)
Levadia Tallinn 3; Levadia Maardu 2; VMV Tallinn 1; Nikol Tallinn 1; Norma Tallinn 1; Lantana 1; Flora Tallinn 1; Trans 1.

Final League Table 2004

	P	W	D	L	F	A	Pts
Levadia Tallinn	28	21	6	1	82	14	69
VMK	28	19	6	3	89	29	63
Flora	28	18	4	6	63	25	58
Trans	28	15	2	11	43	39	47
Merkuur	28	10	5	13	47	58	35
Viijandi	28	6	7	15	30	53	25
Valga	28	5	2	21	30	80	17
Lootus+	28	1	2	25	11	117	5

Top scorer: Zanhovaiko (Flora) 28.
Cup Final: Levadia Tallinn 1, VMK 0.

FAEROE ISLANDS

Fotboltssamband Foroya, The Faeroes' Football Assn., Gundalur, P.O. Box 3028, FR-110, Torshavn.
Founded: 1979; *Number of Clubs:* 16; *Number of Players:* 1,014; *National Colours:* White shirts, blue shorts, white stockings.
Telephone: 00298/316 707; *Fax:* 00298/319 079.

International matches 2004
Poland (a) 0-6, Holland (a) 0-3, Malta (h) 3-2, Switzerland (a) 0-6, France (h) 0-2, Cyprus (a) 2-2, Republic of Ireland (a) 0-2.

League Championship wins (1942–2004)
HB Torshavn 18; KI Klaksvik 16; TB Tvoroyri 7; GI Gotu 7; B36 Torshavn 7; B68 Toftir 3; SI Sorvag 1; IF Fuglafjordur 1; B71 Sandur 1; VB 1.

Cup wins (1955–2004)
HB Torshavn 26; KI Klaksvik 5; GI Gotu 5; TB Tvoroyri 4; B36 Torshavn 3; NSI Runavik 2; VB Vagur 1; B71 Sandur 1.

Final League Table 2004

	P	*W*	*D*	*L*	*F*	*A*	*Pts*
HB	18	12	5	1	47	18	41
B36	18	10	4	4	37	21	34
Skala	18	9	3	6	32	23	30
KI	18	6	8	4	25	24	26
EB/Streymur	18	7	4	7	30	25	25
NSI	18	7	4	7	28	25	25
VB	18	7	4	7	27	24	25
GI	18	6	5	7	31	35	23
IF+	18	3	3	12	25	51	12
B68*	18	2	2	14	19	55	8

B71 1, IF 0, IF 5, B71 1. IF remain.
Top scorer: Petersen SL (EB/Streymur) 13.
Cup Final: HB 3, NSI 1.

FINLAND

Suomen Palloliitto Finlands Bollfoerbund, Urheilukatu 5, P.O. Box 191, Helsinki 00251.
Founded: 1907; *Number of Clubs:* 1,135; *Number of Players:* 66,100; *National Colours:* White shirts, blue shorts, white stockings.
Telephone: 00358-9/7421 51; *Fax:* 00358-9/7421 4200.

International matches 2004
China (a) 1-2, China (a) 1-2, Malta (a) 2-1, Bosnia (a) 0-1, Sweden (h) 1-3, Romania (a) 1-2, Andorra (h) 3-0, Armenia (a) 2-0, Armenia (h) 3-1, Holland (a) 1-3, Italy (a) 0-1, Bahrain (n) 2-1, Oman (n) 0-0.

League Championship wins (1949–2004)
HJK Helsinki 12; Valkeakosken Haka 9; Turun Palloseura 5; Kuopion Palloseura 5; Kuusysi 4; Lahden Reipas 3; IF Kamraterna 3; Ilves-Kissat 2; Jazz Pori 2; Kotkan TP 2; OPS Oulu 2; Torun Pyrkiva 1; IF Kronohagens 1; Helsinki PS 1; Kokkolan PV 1; Vasa 1; TPV Tampere 1; Tampere U 1.

Cup wins (1955–2004)
Valkeakosken Haka 11; HJK Helsinki 8; Lahden Reipas 7; Kotkan TP 4; MyPa 3; Mikkeli 2; Kuusysi 2; Kuopion Palloseura 2; Ilves Tampere 2; TPS Turku 2; IFK Abo 1; Drott 1; Helsinki PS 1; Pallo-Peikot 1; Rovaniemi PS 1; Jokerit 1 (formerly PK-35); Atlantis 1.

Final League Table 2004

	P	*W*	*D*	*L*	*F*	*A*	*Pts*
Haka	26	18	5	3	54	20	59
Allianssi	26	14	6	6	36	28	48
Tampere U	26	14	5	7	39	24	47
Inter	26	13	5	8	42	34	44
TPS Turku	26	12	6	8	36	31	42
HJK Helsinki	26	9	12	5	42	31	39
Lahti	26	9	11	6	37	33	38
MyPa	26	9	8	9	33	31	35
KooTeePee	26	8	8	10	28	28	32
TP 47	26	8	4	14	34	44	28
Jaro	26	8	4	14	31	43	28
RoPS	26	7	4	15	28	45	25
Jazz Pori+	26	4	7	15	28	53	19
Hameenlinna*	26	3	7	16	28	51	16

Jokerit withdrew to Division Two; KooTeePee replaced them.
Top scorer: Pohja (Tampere U) 16.
Cup Final: MyPa 2, Hameenlinna 1.

FRANCE

Federation Francaise De Football, 60 Bis Avenue d'Iena, Paris 75116.
Founded: 1919; *Number of Clubs:* 21,629; *Number of Players:* 1,692,205; *National Colours:* Blue shirts, white shorts, red stockings.
Telephone: 0033-1/ 4431 7300; *Fax:* 0033-1/4720 8296.

International matches 2004
Belgium (a) 2-0, Holland (a) 0-0, Brazil (n) 0-0, Andorra (h) 4-0, Ukraine (h) 1-0, England (n) 2-1, Croatia (n) 2-2, Switzerland (n) 3-1, Greece (n) 0-1, Bosnia (h) 1-1, Israel (h) 0-0, Faeroes (a) 2-0, Republic of Ireland (h) 0-0, Cyprus (a) 2-0, Poland (h) 0-0.

League Championship wins (1933–2005)
Saint Etienne 10; Olympique Marseille 8; Nantes 8; AS Monaco 7; Stade de Reims 6; Girondins Bordeaux 5; Lyon 4; OGC Nice 4; Lille OSC 3; Paris St Germain 2; FC Sete 2; Sochaux 2; Racing Club Paris 1; Roubaix-Tourcoing 1; Strasbourg 1; Auxerre 1; Lens 1.

Cup wins (1918–2005)
Olympique Marseille 10; Saint Etienne 6; AS Monaco 6; Lille OSC 5; Racing Club Paris 5; Red Star 5; Paris St Germain 5; Auxerre 4; Olympique Lyon 3; Girondins Bordeaux 3; OGC Nice 3; Nantes 3; Racing Club Strasbourg 3; CAS Genereaux 2; Nancy 2; Sedan 2; FC Sete 2; Stade de Reims 2; SO Montpellier 2; Stade Rennes 2; AS Cannes 1; Club Français 1; Excelsior Roubaix 1; Le Havre 1; Olympique de Pantin 1; CA Paris 1; Sochaux 1; Toulouse 1; Bastia 1; Metz 1; Lorient 1.

Final League Table 2004–05

	P	*W*	*D*	*L*	*F*	*A*	*Pts*
Lyon	38	22	13	3	56	22	79
Lille	38	18	13	7	52	29	67
Monaco	38	15	18	5	52	35	63
Rennes	38	15	10	13	49	42	55
Marseille	38	15	10	13	47	42	55
St Etienne	38	12	17	9	47	34	53
Lens	38	13	13	12	45	39	52
Auxerre	38	14	10	14	48	47	52
Paris St Germain	38	12	15	11	40	41	51
Sochaux	38	13	11	14	42	41	50
Strasbourg	38	12	12	14	42	43	48
Nice	38	10	16	12	38	45	46
Toulouse	38	12	10	16	36	43	46
Ajaccio	38	10	15	13	36	40	45
Bordeaux	38	8	20	10	37	41	44
Metz	38	10	14	14	33	45	44
Nantes	38	10	13	15	33	38	43
Caen*	38	10	12	16	36	60	42
Bastia*	38	11	8	19	32	48	41
Istres*	38	6	14	18	25	51	32

Top scorer: Frei (Rennes) 20.
Cup Final: Auxerre 2, Sedan 1.

GEORGIA

Georgian Football Federation, 76a Tchavtchavadze Avenue, Tbilisi 380062.
Founded: 1990; *Number of Clubs:* 4050. *Number of Players:* 115,000; *National Colours:* All white.
Telephone: 00995-32/912 610; *Fax:* 00995-32/001 128.

International matches 2004
Romania (n) 0-3, Cyprus (n) 1-3, Armenia (n) 0-2, Israel (h) 0-1, Moldova (a) 0-1, Turkey (a) 1-1, Albania (h) 2-0, Ukraine (a) 0-2, Denmark (h) 2-2.

League Championship wins (1990–2005)
Dynamo Tbilisi 12; Torpedo Kutaisi 3; WIT 1.

Cup wins (1990–2005)
Dynamo Tbilisi 8; Lokomotivi 3; Torpedo Kutaisi 2; Dynamo Batumi 1; Guria 1.

Final League Table 2004–05

	P	W	D	L	F	A	Pts
Dynamo Tbilisi	36	23	6	7	73	27	75
Torpedo Kutaisi	36	21	10	5	57	28	73
Tbilisi	36	21	6	9	60	36	69
Lokomotivi	36	16	15	5	42	24	63
Zestafoni	36	16	5	15	38	48	53
Georgia Tbilisi	36	13	9	14	54	41	48
Sioni	36	12	4	20	35	56	40
Dynamo Batumi	36	9	12	15	35	33	39
Kolkheti*	36	9	5	22	32	63	32
Dila Gori*	36	2	4	30	20	88	10

Top scorer: Melkadze (Dynamo Tbilisi) 27.
Cup Final: Lokomotivi 2, Zestafoni 0.

GERMANY

Deutscher Fussball-Bund, Otto-Fleck-Schneise 6, Postfach 710265, Frankfurt Am Main 60492.
Founded: 1900; *Number of Clubs:* 26,760; *Number of Players:* 5,260,320; *National Colours:* White shirts, black shorts, white stockings.
Telephone: 0049-69/678 80; *Fax:* 0049-69/678 8266.

International matches 2004
Croatia (a) 2-1, Belgium (h) 3-0, Romania (a) 1-5, Malta (h) 7-0, Switzerland (a) 2-0, Hungary (h) 0-2, Holland (n) 1-1, Latvia (n) 0-0, Czech Republic (n) 1-2, Austria (a) 3-1, Brazil (h) 1-1, Iran (a) 2-0, Cameroon (h) 3-0, Japan (a) 3-0, South Korea (a) 1-3, Thailand (a) 5-1.

League Championship wins (1903–2005)
Bayern Munich 19; IFC Nuremberg 9; Schalke 04 7; Borussia Dortmund 6; SV Hamburg 6; Borussia Moenchengladbach 5; VfB Stuttgart 4; IFC Kaiserslautern 4; Werder Bremen 4; VfB Leipzig 3; SpVgg Furth 3; IFC Cologne 3; Viktoria Berlin 2; Hertha Berlin 2; Hannover 96 2; Dresden SC 2; Munich 1860 1; Union Berlin 1; FC Freiburg 1; Phoenix Karlsruhe 1; Karlsruher FV 1; Holstein Kiel 1; Fortuna Dusseldorf 1; Rapid Vienna 1; VfR Mannheim 1; Rot-Weiss Essen 1; Eintracht Frankfurt 1; Eintracht Brunswick 1.

Cup wins (1935–2005)
Bayern Munich 12; Werder Bremen 5; IFC Cologne 4; Eintracht Frankfurt 4; Schalke 04 4; IFC Nuremberg 3; SV Hamburg 3; Moenchengladbach 3; VfB Stuttgart 3; Dresden SC 2; Fortuna Dusseldorf 2; Karlsruhe SC 2; Munich 1860 2; Borussia Dortmund 2; Kaiserslautern 2; First Vienna 1; VfB Leipzig 1; Kickers Offenbach 1; Rapid Vienna 1; Rot-Weiss Essen 1; SW Essen 1; Bayer Uerdingen 1; Hannover 96 1; Leverkusen 1.

Final League Table 2004–05

	P	W	D	L	F	A	Pts
Bayern Munich	34	24	5	5	75	33	77
Schalke	34	20	3	11	56	46	63
Werder Bremen	34	18	5	11	68	37	59
Hertha	34	15	13	6	59	31	58
Stuttgart	34	17	7	10	54	40	58
Leverkusen	34	16	9	9	65	44	57
Borussia Dortmund	34	15	10	9	47	44	55
Hamburg	34	16	3	15	55	50	51
Wolfsburg	34	15	3	16	49	51	48
Hannover	34	13	6	15	34	36	45
Mainz	34	12	7	15	50	55	43
Kaiserslautern	34	12	6	16	43	52	42
Arminia	34	11	7	16	37	49	40
Nuremberg	34	10	8	16	55	63	38
Moenchengladbach	34	8	12	14	35	51	36
Bochum*	34	9	8	17	47	68	35
Hansa Rostock*	34	7	9	18	31	65	30
Freiburg*	34	3	9	22	30	75	18

Top scorer: Mintal (Nuremberg) 24.
Cup Final: Bayern Munich 2, Schalke 1.

GREECE

Hellenic Football Federation, Singrou Avenue 137, Nea Smirni, 17121 Athens.
Founded: 1926; *Number of Clubs:* 4,050; *Number of Players:* 180,000; *National Colours:* Blue shirts, white shorts, blue stockings.
Telephone: 0030-210/930 6000; *Fax:* 0030-210/935 9666.

International matches 2004
Bulgaria (h) 2-0, Switzerland (h) 1-0, Holland (a) 0-4, Poland (a) 0-1, Liechtenstein (a) 2-0, Portugal (n) 2-1, Spain (n) 0-1, Russia (n) 1-2, France (n) 1-0, Czech Republic (n) 1-0, Portugal (n) 1-0, Czech Republic (a) 0-0, Albania (a) 1-2, Turkey (h) 0-0, Ukraine (a) 1-1, Kazakhstan (h) 3-1.

League Championship wins (1928–2005)
Olympiakos 33; Panathinaikos 19; AEK Athens 11; Aris Salonika 3; PAOK Salonika 2; Larissa 1.

Cup wins (1932–2005)
Olympiakos 22 Panathinaikos 17; AEK Athens 13; PAOK Salonika 4; Panionios 2; Aris Salonika 1; Ethnikos 1; Iraklis 1; Kastoria 1; Larissa 1; OFI Crete 1.

Final League Table 2004–05

	P	W	D	L	F	A	Pts
Olympiakos	30	19	8	3	54	18	65
Panathinaikos	30	19	7	4	51	18	64
AEK Athens	30	17	11	2	46	22	62
Xanthi	30	14	8	8	43	29	50
PAOK Salonika	30	13	7	10	43	39	46
Aigaleo	30	11	12	7	31	26	45
Iraklis	30	12	5	13	36	30	41
Halkidona	30	10	8	12	34	38	38
Kalithea	30	9	10	11	39	44	37
Ionikos	30	8	12	10	22	32	36
Panionios	30	8	11	11	25	32	35
Apollon	30	8	9	13	31	49	33
OFI Crete	30	8	8	14	36	44	32
Aris Salonika*	30	5	13	12	26	37	25
Ergotelis*	30	5	5	20	19	50	20
Kerkyra*	30	3	8	19	21	49	17

Top scorer: Gekas (Kalithea) 18.
Cup Final: Olympiakos 3, Aris Salonika 0.

HOLLAND

Koninklijke Nederlandsche Voetbalbond, Woudenbergseweg 56–58, Postbus 515, NL-3700 AM, Zeist.
Founded: 1889; *Number of Clubs:* 3,097; *Number of Players:* 962,397; *National Colours:* Orange shirts, black shorts, orange stockings.
Telephone: 0031-343/499 201; *Fax:* 0031-343/499 189.

International matches 2004
USA (h) 1-0, France (h) 0-0, Greece (h) 4-0, Belgium (h) 0-1, Faeroes (h) 3-0, Republic of Ireland (h) 0-1, Germany (n) 1-1, Czech Republic (n) 2-3, Latvia (n) 3-0, Sweden (n) 0-0, Portugal (n) 1-2, Sweden (a) 2-2, Liechtenstein (h) 3-0, Czech Republic (h) 2-0, Macedonia (a) 2-2, Finland (h) 3-1, Andorra (a) 3-0.

League Championship wins (1898–2005)
Ajax Amsterdam 29; PSV Eindhoven 18; Feyenoord 14; HVV The Hague 8; Sparta Rotterdam 6; Go Ahead Deventer 4; HBS The Hague 3; Willem II Tilburg 3; RAP 2; Heracles 2; ADO The Hague 2; Quick The Hague 1; BVV Den Bosch 2; NAC Breda 1; Eindhoven 1; Enschede 1; Volewijckers Amsterdam 1; Limburgia 1; Rapid JC Heerlen 3; DOS Utrecht 1; DWS Amsterdam 1; Haarlem 1; Be Quick Groningen 1; AZ 67 Alkmaar 1.

Cup wins (1899–2005)
Ajax Amsterdam 15; Feyenoord 10; PSV Eindhoven 8; Quick The Hague 4; AZ 67 Alkmaar 3; Rotterdam 3; Utrecht 3; DFC 2; Fortuna Geleen 2; Haarlem 2; HBS The Hague 2; RCH Haarlem 2; Roda 2; VOC 2; Wageningen 2; Willem II Tilburg 2; FC Den Haag 2; Twente Enschede 2; Concordia Rotterdam 1; CVV 1; Eindhoven 1; HVV The Hague 1; Longa 1; Quick Nijmegen 1; RAP 1; Roermond 1; Schoten 1; Velocitas Breda 1; Velocitas Groningen 1; VSV 1; VUC 1; VVV Groningen 1; ZFC 1; NAC Breda 1.

Final League Table 2004–05

	P	W	D	L	F	A	Pts
PSV Eindhoven	34	27	6	1	89	18	87
Ajax	34	24	5	5	74	33	77
AZ	34	19	7	8	71	41	64
Feyenoord	34	19	5	10	90	51	62
Heerenveen	34	18	6	10	64	52	60
Twente	34	15	9	10	48	38	54
Vitesse	34	16	6	12	53	49	54

Roda JC	34	13	8	13	60	55	42
RKC Waalwijk	34	13	8	13	44	51	47
Willem II	34	13	6	15	44	56	45
Utrecht	34	12	8	14	40	43	44
Groningen	34	11	7	16	50	58	40
NEC Nijmegen	34	9	10	15	41	47	37
Den Haag	34	10	6	18	44	59	36
NAC Breda	34	9	8	17	43	67	35
Roosendaal+	34	10	2	22	38	77	32
De Graafscha+	34	4	7	23	32	78	19
Den Bosch*	34	5	4	25	23	75	19

Top scorer: Kuijt (Feyenoord) 29.
Cup Final: PSV Eindhoven 4, Willem II 0.

HUNGARY

Hungarian Football Federation, Robert Karoly krt 61-65, Robert Haz Budapest 1134.
Founded: 1901; *Number of Clubs:* 1944; *Number of Players:* 95,986; *National Colours:* Red shirts, white shorts, green stockings.
Telephone: 0036-1/412 3340; *Fax:* 0036-1/452 0360.

International matches 2004
Armenia (n) 2-0, Latvia (n) 2-1, Romania (n) 0-3, Wales (h) 1-2, Japan (h) 3-2, Brazil (h) 1-4, China (a) 1-2, Germany (a) 2-0, Scotland (a) 3-0, Croatia (a) 0-3, Iceland (h) 3-2, Sweden (a) 0-3, Malta (a) 2-0, Slovakia (n) 0-1, Estonia (n) 5-0.

League Championship wins (1901–2005)
Ferencvaros 28; MTK-VM Budapest 21; Ujpest Dozsa 20; Kispest Honved 13; Vasas Budapest 6; Csepel 4; Raba Gyor 3; BTC 2; Nagyvarad 1; Vac 1; Dunaferr 1; Zalaegerszeg 1; Debrecen 1.

Cup wins (1910–2005)
Ferencvaros 19; MTK-VM Budapest 12; Ujpest Dozsa 9; Raba Gyor 4; Kispest Honved 5; Vasas Budapest 4; Diösgyör 2; Debrecen 2; Bocskai 1; III Ker 1; Kispesti AC 1; Soroksar 1; Szolnoki MAV 1; Siofok Banyasz 1; Bekescsaba 1; Pecsi 1; Matav 1.
Cup not regularly held until 1964.

Final League Table 2004–05

	P	W	D	L	F	A	Pts
Debrecen	30	19	5	6	57	25	62
Ferencvaros	30	17	5	8	56	31	56
MTK	30	16	9	5	47	26	56
Ujpest	30	15	10	5	60	34	55
Gyor	30	16	6	8	44	32	54
Zalaegerszeg	30	13	5	12	48	45	44
Matav	30	11	9	10	44	44	42
Fehervar	30	11	10	9	44	36	40
Diasgyor	30	11	4	15	39	45	37
Pecsi	30	9	9	12	33	35	36
Kispest Honved	30	10	5	15	37	58	35
Kaposvar	30	8	10	12	34	47	34
Vasas	30	10	3	17	34	48	33
Lombard	30	8	6	16	40	47	30
Myiregyhaza*	30	5	11	14	38	63	26
Bekescsaba*	30	4	7	19	26	65	15

Top scorer: Medved (Lombard) 18.
Cup Final: Matav 5, Ferencvaros 1.

ICELAND

Knattspyrnusamband Island, Laugardal, 104 Reykjavik.
Founded: 1929; *Number of Clubs:* 73; *Number of Players:* 23,673; *National Colours;* All blue.
Telephone: 00354/510 2900; *Fax:* 00354/568 9793.

International matches 2004
Albania (a) 1-2, Latvia (a) 0-0, Japan (n) 2-3, England (n) 1-6, Italy (h) 2-0, Bulgaria (h) 1-3, Hungary (a) 2-3, Malta (a) 0-0, Sweden (h) 1-4.

League Championship wins (1912–2004)
KR 24; Valur 19; Fram 18; IA Akranes 18; Vikingur 5; IBV Vestmann 4; IBK Keflavik 3; KA Akureyri 1; FH Hafnarfjordur 1.

Cup wins (1960–2004)
KR 10; Valur 8; Fram 7; IA Akranes 8; IBV Vestmann 4; IBK Keflavik 3; Fylkir 2; IBA Akureyri 1; Vikingur 1.

Final League Table 2004

	P	W	D	L	F	A	Pts
FH	18	10	7	1	33	16	37
IBV	18	9	4	5	35	20	31
IA	18	8	7	3	28	19	31
Fylkir	18	8	5	5	26	20	29
Keflavik	18	7	3	8	31	33	24
KR	18	5	7	6	21	22	22
Grindavik	18	5	7	6	24	31	22
Fram	18	4	5	9	19	28	17
Vikingur*	18	4	4	10	19	30	16
KA*	18	4	3	11	13	30	15

Top scorer: Thorvaldsson (IBV) 12.
Cup Final: Keflavik 3, KA 0.

REPUBLIC OF IRELAND

The Football Association of Ireland (Cumann Peile Na H-Eireann), 80 Merrion Square, South Dublin 2.
Founded: 1921; *Number of Clubs:* 3,190; *Number of Players:* 124,615; *National Colours:* Green shirts, white shorts, green and white stockings.
Telephone: 00353-1/676 6864; *Fax:* 00353-1/661 0931.

League Championship wins (1922–2004)
Shamrock Rovers 15; Shelbourne 12; Dundalk 9; Bohemians 9; St Patrick's Athletic 8; Waterford 6; Cork United 5; Drumcondra 5; St James's Gate 2; Cork Athletic 2; Sligo Rovers 2; Limerick 2; Athlone Town 2; Derry City 2; Dolphin 1; Cork Hibernians 1; Cork Celtic 1; Cork City 1.

Cup wins (1922–2004)
Shamrock Rovers 24; Dundalk 9; Shelbourne 6; Bohemians 6; Drumcondra 5; Derry City 3; Cork Athletic 2; Cork United 2; St James's Gate 2; St Patrick's Athletic 2; Cork Hibernians 2; Limerick 2; Waterford 2; Athlone Town 2; Sligo 2; Bray Wanderers 2; Longford Town 2; Alton United 1; Cork 1; Fordsons 1; Transport 1; Finn Harps 1; Home Farm 1; UCD 1; Galway United 1; Cork City 1.

Final League Table 2004

	P	W	D	L	F	A	Pts
Shelbourne	36	19	11	6	57	37	68
Cork City	36	18	11	7	52	32	65
Bohemians	36	15	15	6	51	30	60
Drogheda United	36	15	7	14	45	43	52
Waterford United	36	14	8	14	44	49	50
Longford Town	36	11	13	12	32	34	46
Derry City	36	11	11	14	23	32	44
St Patrick's Ath	36	11	9	16	38	49	42
Shamrock Rovers	36	10	8	18	41	47	38
Dublin City*	36	6	7	23	39	69	25

Top scorer: Byrne J (Shelbourne) 25.
Cup Final: Longford Town 2, Waterford United 1.

ISRAEL

Israel Football Association, Ramat-Gan Stadium, 299 Aba Hilell Street, Ramat-Gan 52134.
Founded: 1948; *Number of Clubs:* 544; *Number of Players:* 30,449; *National Colours:* Blue shirts, white shorts, blue stockings.
Telephone: 00972-3/617 1503; *Fax:* 00972-3/ 570 2044.

International matches 2004
Azerbaijan (h) 6-0, Lithuania (h) 2-1, Moldova (h) 1-1, Georgia (a) 1-0, Croatia (a) 0-1, France (a) 0-0, Cyprus (h) 2-1, Switzerland (h) 2-2, Cyprus (a) 2-1.

League Championship wins (1932–2005)
Maccabi Tel Aviv 19; Hapoel Tel Aviv 13; Maccabi Haifa 9; Hapoel Petach Tikva 6; Maccabi Netanya 5; Beitar Jerusalem 4; Hakoah Ramat Gan 2; Hapoel Beersheba 2; Bnei Yehouda 1; British Police 1; Hapoel Kfar Sava 1; Hapoel Ramat Gan 1; Hapoel Haifa 1.

Cup wins (1928–2005)
Maccabi Tel Aviv 22; Hapoel Tel Aviv 11; Beitar Jerusalem 5; Maccabi Haifa 5; Hapoel Haifa 3; Hapoel Kfar Sava 3; Beitar Tel Aviv 2; Bnei Yehouda 2; Hakoah Ramat Gan 2; Hapoel Petah Tikva 2; Maccabi Petach Tikva 2; British Police 1; Hapoel Jerusalem 1; Hapoel Lod 1; Maccabi Netanya 1; Hapoel Beersheba 1; Hapoel Ramat Gan 1; Hapoel Bnei Sakhnin 1.

Final League Table 2004-05

	P	W	D	L	F	A	Pts
Maccabi Haifa	33	21	8	4	66	27	71
Maccabi Petah Tikva	33	16	12	5	47	24	60
Ashdod	33	15	5	13	48	44	50
Beitar Jerusalem	33	13	8	12	46	44	47
Hapoel Nazrat Liit	33	12	10	11	46	46	46
Bnei Yehouda	33	12	8	13	40	46	44
Hapoel Petah Tikva	33	11	9	13	41	46	42
Maccabi Tel Aviv	33	10	10	13	32	42	40
Hapoel Tel Aviv	33	11	9	14	30	34	39
Hapoel Bnei Sakhnin	33	10	6	17	40	51	36
Hapoel Haifa*	33	9	8	16	36	44	35
Hapoel Beersheba*	33	7	11	15	33	57	32

Top scorer: Colautti (Maccabi Haifa) 13.
Cup Final: Maccabi Tel Aviv 2, Maccabi Herzliya 2.
Maccabi Tel Aviv won 5-3 on penalties.

ITALY

Federazione Italiana Giuoco Calcio, Via Gregorio Allegri 14, Roma 00198.
Founded: 1898; *Number of Clubs:* 20,961; *Number of Players:* 1,420,160; *National Colours:* Blue shirts, white shorts, blue stockings.
Telephone: 0039-06/84 911; *Fax:* 0039-06/84 912 526.

International matches 2004
Czech Republic (h) 2-2, Portugal (a) 2-1, Spain (h) 1-1, Tunisia (a) 4-0, Denmark (n) 0-0, Sweden (n) 1-1, Bulgaria (n) 2-1, Iceland (a) 0-2, Norway (h) 2-1, Moldova (a) 1-0, Slovenia (a) 0-1, Belarus (h) 4-3, Finland (h) 1-0.

League Championship wins (1898–2005)
Juventus 28; AC Milan 17; Inter-Milan 13; Genoa 9; Torino 8; Pro Vercelli 7; Bologna 7; AS Roma 3; Fiorentina 2; Lazio 2; Napoli 2; Casale 1; Novese 1; Cagliari 1; Verona 1; Sampdoria 1.

Cup wins (1922–2005)
Juventus 9; AS Roma 8; Fiorentina 6; AC Milan 5; Torino 4; Sampdoria 4; Lazio 4; Inter-Milan 4; Napoli 3; Parma 3; Bologna 2; Atalanta 1; Genoa 1; Vado 1; Venezia 1; Vicenza 1.

Final League Table 2004–05

	P	W	D	L	F	A	Pts
Juventus	38	26	8	4	67	27	86
AC Milan	38	23	10	5	63	28	79
Internazionale	38	18	18	2	65	37	72
Udinese	38	17	11	10	56	40	62
Sampdoria	38	17	10	11	42	29	61
Palermo	38	12	17	9	48	44	53
Messina	38	12	12	14	44	52	48
Roma	38	11	12	15	55	58	45
Livorno	38	11	12	15	49	60	45
Lazio	38	11	11	16	48	53	44
Lecce	38	10	14	14	66	73	44
Cagliari	38	10	14	14	51	60	44
Reggina	38	10	14	14	36	45	44
Siena	38	9	16	13	44	55	43
Chievo	38	11	10	17	32	49	43
Bologna+	38	9	15	14	33	36	42
Fiorentina	38	9	15	14	42	50	42
Parma+	38	10	12	16	48	65	42
Brescia*	38	11	8	19	37	54	41
Atalanta*	38	8	11	19	34	45	35

Fiorentina remain in Serie A because of better results against the three teams on 42 points.
Top scorer: Lucarelli (Livorno) 24.
Cup Final: Internazionale 2, 1, Roma 0, 0.

KAZAKHSTAN

The Football Union of Kazakhstan, Satpayev Street, 29/3 Almaty 480 072, Kazakhstan.
Founded: 1914; *Number of Clubs:* 5,793; *Number of Players:* 260,000; *National Colours:* Blue shirts, blue shorts, yellow stockings.
Telephone: 007-3272/920 444; *Fax:* 007-3272/921 885.

International matches 2004
Latvia (n) 1-3, Armenia (n) 3-3, Cyprus (n) 1-2, Azerbaijan (h) 2-3, Ukraine (h) 1-2, Turkey (a) 0-4, Albania (h) 0-1, Greece (a) 1-3.

League Championship wins (1992-2004)
Irtysh 5; Yelimai 3; Zhenis 2; Kairat 2; Taraz 1.

Cup wins (1992–2004)
Kairat 5; Zhenis 2; Dostyk 1; Vostok 1; Yelimai 1; Irtysh 1; Kaisar 1; Taraz 1.

Final League Table 2004

	P	W	D	L	F	A	Pts
Kairat	36	25	8	3	70	21	83
Irtysh	36	24	7	5	56	16	79
Tobol	36	22	11	3	87	27	77
Aqtobe	36	22	8	6	52	19	74
Atyrau	36	20	11	5	49	31	71
Yesil Bogatyr	36	18	5	13	53	40	59
Taraz	36	16	11	9	35	23	59
Yekibastuzets	36	17	7	12	42	27	58
Shakhter	36	16	9	11	44	28	57
Jenis	36	15	6	15	45	44	48
Oqjetpes	36	10	13	13	26	39	43
Vostok	36	11	7	18	42	54	40
Ordabasy	36	11	7	18	37	43	40
Jetisu	36	11	7	18	34	55	40
Yassy	36	9	8	19	30	49	35
Almaty+	36	4	8	24	22	53	20
Semey*	36	4	1	31	25	84	13
Qaysar#	36	9	4	23	24	61	31
Aq Jayiq#	36	7	4	25	24	83	25

Jenis deducted three points for unpaid transfer; Qaysar expelled after round 30 for attempting to strike the referee. All remaining matches awarded 3-0 against them. Aq Jayiq expelled for various infringements of regulations. Aq Jayiq formerly Batys; Yelimai now Semey.
Top scorers: Bakayev (Tobol) 22, Tiehugov (Qayrat) 22.
Cup Final: Taraz 1, Kairat 0.

LATVIA

Latvian Football Federation, Augsiela 1, LV-1009, Riga.
Founded: 1921; *Number of Clubs:* 50; *Number of Players:* 12,000; *National Colours:* Carmine red shirts, white shorts, carmine red stockings.
Telephone: 00371/729 2988; *Fax:* 00371/ 731 5604.

International matches 2004
Kazakhstan (n) 3-1, Hungary (n) 1-2, Belarus (n) 1-4, Slovenia (a) 1-0, Iceland (h) 0-0, Azerbaijan (h) 2-2, Czech Republic (n) 1-2, Germany (n) 0-0, Holland (n) 0-3, Wales (h) 0-2, Portugal (h) 0-2, Luxembourg (a) 4-3, Slovakia (a) 1-4, Estonia (h) 2-2, Liechtenstein (a) 3-1, Oman (n) 2-3, Bahrain (n) 2-2.

League Championship wins (1922–2004)
Skonto Riga 14; ASK Riga 9; RFK Riga 8; Olympia Liepaya 7; Sarkanais Metalurgs Liepaya 7; VEF Riga 6; Energija Riga 4; Elektrons Riga 3; Torpedo Riga 3; Daugava Liepaya 2; ODO Riga 2; Khimikis Daugavpils 2; RAF Yelgava 2; Keisermezhs Riga 2; Dinamo Riga 1; Zhmilyeva Team 1; Darba Rezervi 1; REZ Riga 1; Start Brotseni 1; Venta Ventspils 1; Yurnieks Riga 1; Alfa Riga 1; Gauya Valmiera 1.

Cup wins (1937–2004)
Elektrons Riga 7; Skonto Riga 7; Sarkanais Metalurgs Liepaya 5; ODO Riga 3; VEF Riga 3; ASK Riga 3; Tseltnieks Riga 3; RAF Yelgava 3; RFK Riga 2; Daugava Liepaya 2; Start Brotseni 2; Selmash Liepaya 2; Yurnieks Riga 2; Khimikis Daugavpils 2; FK Ventspils 2; Rigas Vilki 1; Dinamo Liepaya 1; Dinamo Riga 1; REZ Riga 1; Voulkan Kouldiga 1; Baltija Liepaya 1; Venta Ventspils 1; Pilot Riga 1; Lielupe Yurmala 1; Energija Riga 1; Torpedo Riga 1; Daugava SKIF Riga 1; Tseltnieks Daugavpils 1; Olympia Riga 1; FK Riga 1.

Final League Table 2004

	P	W	D	L	F	A	Pts
Skonto Riga	28	22	3	3	65	18	69
Metalurgs Liepaya	28	21	3	4	85	27	66
FK Ventspils	28	16	7	5	64	28	55
Dinaburg	28	10	6	12	35	36	36
Jurmala	28	8	10	10	30	33	34
FK Riga	28	6	9	13	32	43	27
Ditton Daugavpils+	28	7	5	16	20	62	26
Auda Riga*	28	0	1	27	13	97	1

Gauja Valmiera withdrew for financial reasons; place given to Ditton Daugavpils.

Top scorer: Katasonov (Metalurgs Liepaya) 21.
Cup Final: FK Ventspils 2, Skonto Riga 1.

LIECHTENSTEIN

Liechtensteiner Fussball-Verband, Malbuner Huus Altenbach 11, Postfach 165, 9490 Vaduz.
Founded: 1934; *Number of Clubs:* 7; *Number of Players:* 1,247; *National Colours:* Blue shirts, red shorts, blue stockings.
Telephone: 00423/237 4747; *Fax:* 00423/237 4748.

International matches 2004
San Marino (a) 0-1, Greece (h) 0-2, Switzerland (a) 0-1, Estonia (h) 1-2, Holland (a) 0-3, Slovakia (a) 0-7, Portugal (h) 2-2, Luxembourg (a) 4-0, Latvia (h) 1-3.
Liechtenstein has no national league. Teams compete in Swiss regional leagues.

Cup wins (1946–2005)
Vaduz 34; Balzers 11; Triesen 8; Eschen/Mauren 4; Schaan 3.
Cup Final: Vaduz 4, Eschen/Mauren 1.

LITHUANIA

Lithuanian Football Federation, Seimyniskiu str. 15, 2005 Vilnius.
Founded: 1922; *Number of Clubs:* 152; *Number of Players:* 16,600; *National Colours:* Yellow shirts, green shorts, yellow stockings.
Telephone: 00370/5263 8741; *Fax:* 00370/5263 8740.

International matches 2004
Israel (a) 1-2, Belarus (a) 0-1, Portugal (a) 1-4, Russia (a) 3-4, Belgium (a) 1-1, San Marino (h) 4-0, Spain (h) 0-0, San Marino (a) 1-0.

League Championship wins (1922–2004)
Kovas Kaunas 6; KSS Klaipeda 6; FBK Kaunas 6; LFLS Kaunas 4; Zalgiris Vilnius 4; LGSF Kaunas 2; Kareda 2; MSK Kaunas 1; Ekranas Panevezys 1; Romar Mazeikiai 1; Inkaras Grifas 1.

Cup wins (1992–2004)
Zalgiris Vilnius 4; Kareda 2; Ekranas 2; Atlantas 2; FBK Kaunas 2; Inkaras 1.

Final League Table 2004

	P	*W*	*D*	*L*	*F*	*A*	*Pts*
FBK Kaunas	28	20	5	3	49	19	65
Ekranas	28	20	2	6	59	22	62
Atlantas	28	15	5	8	36	29	50
Zalgiris	28	10	7	11	32	38	37
Vetra	28	9	8	11	29	33	35
Silute	28	6	7	15	34	44	25
Suduva	28	5	7	16	31	55	22
Vilnius	28	4	5	19	19	49	17

Vilnius formerly Sviesa.
On 5 November Ekranas were expelled for alleged match fixing but reinstated by the Lithuanian FA.
Cup Final: FBK Kaunas 0, Atlantas 0
FBK Kaunas won 2-1 on penalties.

LUXEMBOURG

Federation Luxembourgeoise De Football (F.L.F.), 68 Rue De Gasperich, Luxembourg 1617.
Founded: 1908; *Number of Clubs:* 126; *Number of Players:* 21,684; *National Colours:* All red.
Telephone: 00352/488 665 1; *Fax:* 00352/488 665 82.

International matches 2004
Bosnia (h) 1-2, Austria (a) 1-4, Portugal (a) 0-3, Slovakia (a) 1-3, Estonia (a) 0-4, Latvia (h) 3-4, Russia (h) 0-4, Liechtenstein (h) 0-4, Portugal (h) 0-5.

League Championship wins (1910–2005)
Jeunesse Esch 27; Spora Luxembourg 11; Stade Dudelange 10; Avenir Beggen 7; Red Boys Differdange 6; US Hollerich-Bonnevoie 5; Fola Esch 5; US Luxembourg 5; F91 Dudelange 4; Aris Bonnevoie 3; Progres Niedercorn 3; Grevenmacher 1.

Cup wins (1922–2005)
Red Boys Differdange 16; Jeunesse Esch 12; US Luxembourg 10; Spora Luxembourg 8; Avenir Beggen 7; Stade Dudelange 4; Progres Niedercorn 4; Fola Esch 3; Grevenmacher 3; Alliance Dudelange 2; US Rumelange 2; Aris Bonnevoie 1; US Dudelange 1; Jeunesse Hautcharage 1; National Schiffige 1; Racing Luxembourg 1; SC Tetange 1; Hesperange 1; Etzella 1; F91 Dudelange 1; Petange 1.

Qualifying Table 2004–05

	P	*W*	*D*	*L*	*F*	*A*	*Pts*
F91 Dudelange	22	18	2	2	56	13	56
Etzella	22	17	1	4	57	23	52
Jeunesse Esch	22	12	5	5	50	28	41
Victoria Rosport	22	12	5	5	43	33	41
Grevenmacher	22	9	5	8	40	27	32
Hesperange	22	8	5	9	28	34	29
Alliance	22	8	4	10	31	47	28
Petange	22	8	3	11	38	34	27
FC Wiltz 71	22	8	1	13	25	37	25
Spora	22	5	3	14	24	54	18
Union Luxembourg	22	3	5	14	14	44	14
Avenir Beggen	22	2	5	15	20	52	11

Championship Table 2004–05

	P	*W*	*D*	*L*	*F*	*A*	*Pts*
F91 Dudelange	28	22	4	2	74	15	70
Etzella	28	20	4	4	68	29	64
Jeunesse Esch	28	13	6	9	58	45	45
Victoria Rosport	28	13	5	10	45	47	44

Promotion/Relegation Table 2004–05

Group A	*P*	*W*	*D*	*L*	*F*	*A*	*Pts*
Alliance	28	12	5	11	45	54	41
Grevenmacher	28	11	7	10	57	40	40
FC Wiltz 71	28	8	2	18	30	56	26
Union Luxembourg*	28	6	7	15	26	53	25

Group B	*P*	*W*	*D*	*L*	*F*	*A*	*Pts*
Hesperange	28	11	6	11	39	46	39
Petange	28	10	5	13	50	45	35
Avenir Beggen	28	6	6	16	37	60	24
Spora*	28	5	5	18	29	68	20

Alliance, Spora and Union have now merged to form Racing Luxembourg.
Top scorer: Pupovac (Alliance) 24.
Cup Final: Petange 5, Cebra 0.

MACEDONIA

Football Association of Macedonia, VIII-ma Udarna Brigada 31-A, Skopje 1000.
Founded: 1948; *Number of Clubs:* 598; *Number of Players:* 15,165; *National Colours:* All red.
Telephone: 00389-2/3129 291; *Fax:* 00389-2/3165 448.

International matches 2004
China (a) 0-0, China (a) 0-1, Bosnia (h) 1-0, Ukraine (h) 1-0, Croatia (h) 0-1, Estonia (a) 4-2, Armenia (h) 3-0, Romania (a) 1-2, Holland (h) 2-2, Andorra (a) 0-1, Czech Republic (h) 0-2.

League Championship wins (1993–2005)
Vardar 5; Sileks 3; Sloga 3; Pobeda 1; Rabotnicki 1.

Cup wins (1993–2005)
Vardar 4; Sloga 2; Sileks 1; Pellister 1; Pobeda 1; Cement 1; Baskimi 1.

Final League Table 2004–05

	P	*W*	*D*	*L*	*F*	*A*	*Pts*
Rabotnicki	33	25	3	5	66	23	78
Vardar	33	22	6	5	68	34	72
Pobeda	33	16	7	10	59	49	55
Sileks	33	15	6	12	56	37	51
Shkendija	33	15	5	13	59	40	50
Baskimi	33	14	7	12	53	47	49
Belasica	33	14	6	13	53	47	48
Bregalnica	33	14	6	13	55	60	48
Cement+	33	13	7	13	54	50	43
Madzari+	33	12	5	16	35	46	41
Sloga*	33	5	2	26	37	80	17
Napredok*	33	1	4	28	17	99	7

Top scorer: Stevica (Sileks) 25.
Cup Final: Baskimi 2, Madzari 1.

MALTA

Malta Football Association, 280 St Paul Street, Valletta VLT07.
Founded: 1900; *Number of Clubs:* 252; *Number of Players:* 5,544; *National Colours:* Red shirts, white shorts, red stockings.
Telephone: 00356-21/232 581; *Fax:* 00356-21/245 136.

International matches 2004
Moldova (h) 0-0, Estonia (h) 5-2, Finland (h) 1-2, Germany (a) 0-7, Faeroes (a) 2-3, Sweden (h) 0-7, Iceland (h) 0-0, Bulgaria (a) 1-4, Hungary (h) 0-2.

League Championship wins (1910–2005)
Sliema Wanderers 26; Floriana 25; Valletta 18; Hibernians 9; Hamrun Spartans 7; Rabat Ajax 2; St George's 1; KOMR 1; Birkirkara 1.

Cup wins (1935–2005)
Sliema Wanderers 19; Floriana 18; Valletta 10; Hamrun Spartans 6; Hibernians 6; Birkirkara 3; Gzira United 1; Melita 1; Zurrieq 1; Rabat Ajax 1.

Qualifying League Table 2004–05

	P	W	D	L	F	A	Pts
Sliema Wanderers	18	13	3	2	33	15	42
Hibernians	18	10	6	2	34	22	36
Valletta	18	11	3	4	42	26	36
Birkirkara	18	9	5	4	44	25	32
Marsaxlokk	18	7	5	6	32	23	26
Floriana	18	6	6	6	21	22	24
Pieta Hotspurs	18	5	4	9	34	33	19
Msida St Joseph	18	4	6	8	27	34	16
St Patrick	18	2	3	13	17	45	9
Lija Athletic	18	2	1	15	10	49	7

Championship Table 2004–05

	P	W	D	L	F	A	Pts
Sliema Wanderers	28	18	7	3	47	23	40
Birkirkara	28	15	9	4	69	36	38
Hibernians	28	14	11	3	49	32	35
Valletta	28	16	4	8	57	41	34
Marsaxlokk	28	8	6	14	41	47	17
Floriana	28	7	7	14	28	39	16

Promotion/Relegation Table 2004–05

	P	W	D	L	F	A	Pts
Pieta Hospurs	24	8	5	11	44	38	20
Msida St Joseph	24	7	8	9	38	41	19
St Patrick*	24	5	3	16	27	56	14
Lija Athletic*	24	3	2	19	13	60	8

Top scorer: Cohen (Hibernians) 21.
Cup Final: Birkirkara 2, Msida St Joseph 1.

MOLDOVA

Football Association of Moldova, 39 Tricolorului Str, 2012, Chisinau.
Founded: 1990; *Number of Clubs:* 143; *Number of Players:* 75,000; *National Colours:* Red shirts, blue shorts, red stockings.
Telephone: 00373-22/210 413; *Fax:* 00373-22/210 432.

International matches 2004
Malta (n) 0-0, Estonia (n) 0-1, Azerbaijan (h) 2-1, Israel (a) 1-1, Georgia (h) 1-0, Slovenia (a) 0-3, Italy (h) 0-1, Belarus (a) 0-4, Scotland (h) 1-1.

League Championship wins (1992–2005)
Zimbru Chisinau 8; Serif 4; Constructorul 1.

Cup wins (1992–2005)
Tiligul 4; Zimbru Chisinau 4; Serif 3; Combat 1; Constructorul 1; Otaci 1.

Final League Table 2004-05

	P	W	D	L	F	A	Pts
Serif	28	22	4	2	54	12	70
Otaci	28	17	3	8	51	27	54
Dacia	28	14	3	11	38	31	45
Tiraspol	28	12	8	8	41	23	44
Zimbru Chisinau	28	12	7	9	29	15	43
Tiligul	28	11	8	9	32	27	41
Unisport+	28	3	5	20	16	51	14
Steaua*	28	0	4	24	8	83	4

Play-off: Unisport 0, Politehnica 4.
Top scorer: Lichioiu (Otaci) 16.
Cup Final: Otaci 1, Dacia 0.

NORTHERN IRELAND

Irish Football Association Ltd, 20 Windsor Avenue, Belfast BT9 6EE.
Founded: 1880; *Number of Clubs:* 1,555; *Number of Players:* 24,558; *National Colours:* Green shirts, white shorts, green stockings.
Telephone: 0044-28/9066 9458; *Fax:* 0044-28/9066 7620.

NORWAY

Norges Fotballforbund, Ullevaal Stadion, Sognsveien 75J, Serviceboks 1, Oslo 0855.
Founded: 1902; *Number of Clubs:* 1,810; *Number of Players:* 300,000; *National Colours:* Red shirts, white shorts, blue stockings.
Telephone: 0047/2102 9300; *Fax:* 0047/2102 9301.

International matches 2004
Sweden (n) 3-0, Honduras (n) 3-1, Singapore (a) 5-2, Northern Ireland (a) 4-1, Serbia-Montenegro (a) 1-0, Russia (h) 3-2, Wales (h) 0-0, Belgium (h) 2-2, Italy (a) 1-2, Belarus (h) 1-1, Scotland (a) 1-0, Slovenia (h) 3-0, Australia (a) 2-2.

League Championship wins (1938–2004)
Rosenborg Trondheim 18; Fredrikstad 9; Viking Stavanger 8; Lillestroem 6; Valerengen 4; Larvik Turn 3; Brann Bergen 2; Lyn Oslo 2; IK Start 2; Friedig 1; Skeid Oslo 1; Strömsgodset Drammen 1; Moss 1.

Cup wins (1902–2004)
Odds Bk Skien 11; Fredrikstad 10; Lyn Oslo 8; Skeid Oslo 8; Rosenborg Trondheim 8; Sarpsborg FK 6; Brann Bergen 6; Viking Stavanger 5; Orn F Horten 4; Lillestroem 4; Strömsgodset Drammen 4; Frigg 3; Mjondalens F 3; Valerenga 3; Bodo-Glimt 2; Mercantile 2; Tromso 2; Grane Nordstrand 1; Kvik Halden 1; Sparta 1; Gjovik 1; Moss 1; Byrne 1; Molde 1; Stabaek 1; Odd Grenland 1.
(Known as the Norwegian Championship for HM The King's Trophy).

Final League Table 2004

	P	W	D	L	F	A	Pts
Rosenborg	26	14	6	6	52	34	48
Valerenga	26	13	9	4	40	22	48
Brann	26	12	4	10	46	40	40
Tromso	26	12	4	10	38	32	40
Hamark	26	10	8	8	34	33	38
Lyn	26	9	10	7	30	31	37
Lillestrom	26	8	11	7	45	33	35
Odd	26	9	8	9	47	44	35
Viking	26	7	12	7	31	33	33
Fredrikstad	26	9	5	12	42	54	32
Molde	26	7	10	9	34	37	31
Bodo-Glimt+	26	7	6	13	28	41	27
Stabaek*	26	7	6	13	25	40	27
Sogndal*	26	5	7	14	39	57	22

Play-offs: Kongsvinger 1, Bodo-Glimt 0, Bodo-Glimt 4, Kongsvinger 0; Bodo-Glimt remain.
Top scorer: Johnsen F (Rosenborg) 19.
Cup Final: Brann 4, Lyn 1.

POLAND

Polish Football Association, Polski Zwiazek Pilki Noznej, Miodowa 1, Warsaw 00-080.
Founded: 1919; *Number of Clubs:* 5,881; *Number of Players:* 317,442; *National Colours:* White shirts, red shorts, white stockings.
Telephone: 0048-22/827 0914; *Fax:* 0048-22/827 0704.

International matches 2004
Slovenia (h) 2-0, Faeroes (h) 6-0, USA (h) 0-1, Republic of Ireland (h) 0-0, Greece (h) 1-0, Sweden (a) 1-3, USA (a) 1-1, Denmark (h) 1-5, Northern Ireland (a) 3-0, England (h) 1-2, Austria (a) 3-1, Wales (a) 3-2, France (a) 0-0.

League Championship wins (1921–2005)
Gornik Zabrze 14; Ruch Chorzow 13; Wisla Krakow 11;

Legia Warsaw 7; Widzew Lodz 6; Lech Poznan 5; Pogon Lwow 4; Cracovia 3; Warta Poznan 2; Polonia Bytom 2; Stal Mielec 2; LKS Lodz 2; Polonia Warsaw 2; Garbarnia Krakow 1; Slask Wroclaw 1; Szombierki Bytom 1; Zaglebie Lubin 1.

Cup wins (1951–2005)
Legia Warsaw 12; Gornik Zabrze 6; Zaglebie Sosnowiec 4; Lech Poznan 4; GKS Katowice 3; Ruch Chorzow 3; Amica Wronki 3; Wisla Krakow 3; Slask Wroclaw 2; Polonia Warsaw 2; Gwardia Warsaw 1; LKS Lodz 1; Stal Rzeszow 1; Arka Gdynia 1; Lechia Gdansk 1; Widzew Lodz 1; Miedz Legnica 1; Groclin 1.

Final League Table 2004–05

	P	*W*	*D*	*L*	*F*	*A*	*Pts*
Wisla	26	19	5	2	70	23	62
Groclin	26	16	3	7	46	28	51
Legia	26	13	8	5	42	19	47
Wisla Plock	26	12	5	9	35	30	41
Cracovia	26	12	4	10	37	29	40
Amica	26	10	8	8	29	28	38
Leczna	26	10	6	10	36	36	36
Lech	26	10	4	12	34	40	34
Pogon	26	7	10	9	34	43	31
Polonia	26	8	5	13	27	52	29
Gornik Zabrze	26	7	7	12	27	30	26
Zaglebie	26	6	10	10	31	41	28
Odra+	26	7	3	16	27	41	24
Katowice*	26	4	4	18	23	56	16

Top scorer: Frankowski (Wisla) 25.
Promotion/Relegation Play-off: Widzew 1, 1, Odra 3, 0.
Cup Final: Groclin 2, 0, Zaglebie 0, 1.

PORTUGAL

Federacao Portuguesa De Futebol, Praca De Alegria N.25, Apartado 21.100, P-1127, Lisboa 1250-004.
Founded: 1914; *Number of Clubs:* 204; *Number of Players:* 79,235; *National Colours:* Red shirts, green shorts, red stockings.
Telephone: 00351-21/325 2700; *Fax:* 00351-21/325 2780.

International matches 2004
England (h) 1-1, Italy (h) 1-2, Sweden (h) 2-2, Luxembourg (h) 3-0, Lithuania (h) 4-1, Greece (h) 1-2, Russia (h) 2-0, Spain (h) 1-0, England (h) 2-2, Holland (h) 2-1, Greece (h) 0-1, Latvia (a) 2-0, Estonia (h) 4-0, Liechtenstein (a) 2-2, Russia (h) 7-1, Luxembourg (a) 5-0.

League Championship wins (1935–2005)
Benfica 31; FC Porto 20; Sporting Lisbon 18; Belenenses 1; Boavista 1.

Cup wins (1939–2005)
Benfica 24; Sporting Lisbon 13; FC Porto 12; Boavista 5; Belenenses 3; Vitoria Setubal 3; Academica Coimbra 1; Leixoes Porto 1; Sporting Braga 1; Amadora 1; Beira Mar 1.

Final League Table 2004–05

	P	*W*	*D*	*L*	*F*	*A*	*Pts*
Benfica	34	19	8	7	51	31	65
Porto	34	17	11	6	39	26	62
Sporting Lisbon	34	18	7	9	66	36	61
Braga	34	16	10	8	45	28	58
Guimaraes	34	15	9	10	38	29	54
Boavista	34	13	11	10	39	43	50
Maritimo	34	12	13	9	39	32	49
Rio Ave	34	10	17	7	35	35	47
Belenenses	34	13	7	14	38	34	46
Setubal	34	11	11	12	46	45	44
Penafiel	34	13	4	17	39	53	53
Nacional	34	12	5	17	46	48	41
Gil Vicente	34	11	7	16	34	40	40
Uniao Leiria	34	8	14	12	29	36	38
Academica	34	9	11	14	29	41	38
Moreirense*	34	7	13	14	30	43	34
Estoril*	34	8	6	20	38	55	30
Beira Mar*	34	6	12	16	30	56	30

Top scorer: Liedson (Sporting Lisbon) 25.
Cup Final: Setubal 2, Benfica 1.

ROMANIA

Federatia Romana De Fotbal, House of Football, Str. Serg. Serbanica Vasile 12, Bucharest 73412.
Founded: 1909; *Number of Clubs:* 414; *Number of Players:* 22,920; *National Colours:* All yellow.
Telephone: 0040-21/325 0678; *Fax:* 0040-21/325 0679.

International matches 2004
Georgia (n) 3-0, Belarus (n) 2-0, Hungary (n) 3-0, Scotland (a) 2-1, Germany (h) 5-1, Republic of Ireland (a) 0-1, Finland (h) 2-1, Macedonia (h) 2-1, Andorra (a) 5-1, Czech Republic (a) 0-1, Armenia (a) 1-1.

League Championship wins (1910–2005)
Steaua Bucharest 22; Dinamo Bucharest 17; Venus Bucharest 8; Chinezul Timisoara 6; UT Arad 6; Ripensia Temesvar 4; Uni Craiova 4; Petrolul Ploesti 3; Rapid Bucharest 3; Olimpia Bucharest 2; Colentina Bucharest 2; Arges Pitesti 2; ICO Oradea 2; Soc RA Bucharest 1; Prahova Ploesti 1; Coltea Brasov 1; Juventus Bucharest 1; Metalochimia Resita 1; Ploesti United 1; Unirea Tricolor 1.

Cup wins (1934–2005)
Steaua Bucharest 20; Dinamo Bucharest 12; Rapid Bucharest 11; Uni Craiova 6; UT Arad 2; Ripensia Temesvar 2; Politehnica Timisoara 2; Petrolul Ploesti 2; ICO Oradeo 1; Metalochimia Resita 1; Stinta Cluj 1; CFR Turnu Severin 1; Chimia Ramnicu Vilcea 1; Jiul Petroseni 1; Progresul Bucharest 1; Progresul Oradea 1; Gloria Bistrita 1.

Final League Table 2004–05

	P	*W*	*D*	*L*	*F*	*A*	*Pts*
Steaua	30	19	6	5	47	18	63
Dinamo Bucharest	30	20	2	8	60	30	62
Rapid	30	16	9	5	51	27	57
National	30	17	6	7	50	33	57
Farul	30	15	7	8	42	28	52
Timisoara	30	13	6	11	37	34	45
Sportul	30	12	9	9	37	27	45
Otelul	30	12	4	14	31	32	40
Poli	30	10	8	12	26	41	38
Arges	30	8	12	10	32	37	36
Ecomax	30	9	9	12	33	44	36
Bacau	30	8	9	13	20	28	33
Gloria	30	9	5	16	38	46	32
Apulum*	30	6	8	16	28	62	26
Brasov*	30	5	6	19	28	45	21
Uni Craiova*	30	4	8	18	24	54	20

Top scorers: Bucur (Sportul), Niculescu (Dinamo Bucharest) 21.
Cup Final: Dinamo Bucharest 1, Farul 0.

RUSSIA

Football Union of Russia; Luzhnetskaya Naberezyhnaja 8, Moscow 119 992.
Founded: 1912; *Number of Clubs:* 43,700; *Number of Players:* 785,000; *National Colours:* All white.
Telephone: 007-095/201 1637; *Fax:* 007-502/220 2037.

International matches 2004
Bulgaria (a) 2-2, Norway (a) 2-3, Austria (a) 0-0, Spain (n) 0-1, Portugal (n) 0-2, Greece (n) 2-1, Lithuania (h) 4-3, Slovakia (h) 1-1, Luxembourg (a) 4-0, Portugal (a) 1-7, Estonia (h) 4-0.

League Championship wins (1945–2004)
Spartak Moscow 20; Dynamo Kiev 13; Dynamo Moscow 11; CSKA Moscow 8; Torpedo Moscow 3; Dynamo Tbilisi 2; Dnepr Dnepropetrovsk 2; Lokomotiv Moscow 2; Saria Voroshilovgrad 1; Ararat Erevan 1; Dynamo Minsk 1; Zenit Leningrad 1; Spartak Vladikavkaz 1.

Cup wins (1936–2005)
Spartak Moscow 13; Dynamo Kiev 10; Torpedo Moscow 7; Dynamo Moscow 7; CSKA Moscow 7; Lokomotiv Moscow 6; Shakhtjor Donetsk 4; Dynamo Tbilisi 2; Ararat Erevan 2; Zenit Leningrad 2; Karpaty Lvov 1; SKA Rostov 1; Metallist Kharkov 1; Dnepr 1; Terek 1.

Final League Table 2004

	P	W	D	L	F	A	Pts
Lokomotiv Moscow	30	18	7	5	44	19	61
CSKA Moscow	30	17	9	4	53	22	60
Krylia Sovekov	30	17	5	8	50	41	56
Zenit	30	17	5	8	55	37	56
Torpedo Moscow	30	16	6	8	53	37	54
Shinnik	30	12	8	10	29	29	44
Saturn	30	10	11	9	37	30	41
Spartak Moscow	30	11	7	12	43	44	40
FK Moscow	30	10	10	10	38	39	40
Rubin	30	7	12	11	32	31	33
Amkar	30	6	12	12	27	42	30
Rostov	30	7	8	15	28	42	29
Dynamo Moscow	30	6	11	13	27	38	29
Alania	30	7	7	16	28	52	28
Kuban*	30	6	10	14	26	42	28
Volgograd*	30	4	10	16	28	53	22

FK Moscow formerly Torpedo Metallurg.
Top scorer: Kerzhakov (Zenit) 18.
Cup Final: CSKA Moscow 1, Khimki 0.

SAN MARINO

Federazione Sammarinese Giuoco Calcio, Viale Campo dei Giudei, 14; Rep. San Marino 47890.
Founded: 1931; *Number of Clubs:* 17; *Number of Players:* 1,033; *National Colours:* All light blue.
Telephone: 00378-054/999 0515; *Fax:* 00378-054/999 2348.

International matches 2004
Liechtenstein (h) 1-0, Serbia-Montenegro (h) 0-3, Lithuania (a) 0-4, Serbia-Montenegro (a) 0-5, Lithuania (h) 0-1.

League Championship wins (1986–2005)
Tre Fiori 4; Domagnano 4; Faetano 3; Folgore 3; Fiorita 2; Montevito 1; Libertas 1; Cosmos 1; Pennarossa 1.

Cup wins (1986–2004)
Domagnano 7; Libertas 3; Faetano 3; Cosmos 2; Fiorita 1; Tre Penne 1; Murata 1; Pennarossa 1.

Qualifying League Table 2004–05

Group A	P	W	D	L	F	A	Pts
Tre Penne	20	14	2	4	43	23	44
Murata	20	11	6	3	39	23	39
Tre Fiore	20	10	4	6	38	24	34
Pennarossa	20	9	7	4	40	26	34
La Fiorita	20	6	7	7	27	28	25
Cailungo	20	4	5	11	27	42	17
Cosmos	20	1	2	17	16	71	5

Group B	P	W	D	L	F	A	Pts
Libertas	21	15	3	3	46	22	48
Domagnano	21	11	7	3	50	25	40
Virtus	21	11	4	6	37	22	37
Faetano	21	9	6	6	42	27	33
Juvenes/Dogana	21	9	6	6	35	22	33
Folgore/Falciano	21	4	6	11	26	40	18
Montevito	21	3	6	12	22	40	15
San Giovanni	21	1	1	19	16	69	4

Play-offs: Murata 1, Virtus 2; Domagnano 3, Tre Fiore 2; Tre Penne 1, Domagnano 1 (*Domagnano won 5-4 on penalties*); Libertas 1, Virtus 0; Tre Penne 1, Murata 7; Virtus 2, Tre Fiore 0; Domagnano 3, Libertas 0; Virtus 0, Murata 1; Libertas 1, Murata 1 (*Murata won 3-2 on penalties*).
Final: Domagnano 2, Murata 1.
Top scorer: Passaglia (Montevito) 19.

SCOTLAND

The Scottish Football Association Ltd, Hampden Park, Glasgow G42 9AY.
Founded: 1873; *Number of Clubs:* 6,148; *Number of Players:* 135,474; *National Colours:* Dark blue shirts, white shorts, dark blue stockings.
Telephone: 0044-141/616 6000; *Fax:* 0044-141/616 6001.

SERBIA-MONTENEGRO

Football Association of Serbia and Montenegro, Terazije 35, P.O. Box 263, 11000 Beograd.
Founded: 1919; *Number of Clubs:* 6,532; *Number of Players:* 229,024; *National Colours:* Blue shirts, white shorts, red stockings.
Telephone: 00381-11/ 323 4253; *Fax:* 00381-11/323 3433.

International matches 2004
Norway (h) 0-1, Northern Ireland (a) 1-1, Slovakia (n) 2-0, Japan (n) 0-1, Slovenia (a) 1-1, San Marino (a) 3-0, Bosnia (a) 0-0, San Marino (h) 5-0, Belgium (a) 2-0.

League Championship wins (1923–2005)
Red Star Belgrade 23; Partizan Belgrade 19; Hajduk Split 9; Gradjanski Zagreb 5; BSK Belgrade 5; Dynamo Zagreb 4; Jugoslavija Belgrade 2; Concordia Zagreb 2; FC Sarajevo 2; Vojvodina Novi Sad 2; HASK Zagreb 1; Zeljeznicar 1; Obilic 1.

Cup wins (1947–2005)
Red Star Belgrade 20; Hajduk Split 9; Partizan Belgrade 9; Dynamo Zagreb 8; BSK Belgrade 2; OFK Belgrade 2; Rijeka 2; Velez Mostar 2; Vardar Skopje 1; Borac Banjaluka 1; Sartid 1; Zeleznik 1.

Final League Table 2004–05

	P	W	D	L	F	A	Pts
Partizan Belgrade	30	25	5	0	81	20	80
Red Star Belgrade	30	23	5	2	66	18	74
Golubovci	30	18	5	7	52	30	59
OFK Belgrade	30	16	2	12	51	36	50
Zemun	30	12	7	11	31	34	43
Buducnost	30	12	5	13	37	37	41
Hajduk Kula	30	10	9	11	34	37	39
Vojvodina	30	10	8	12	31	37	38
Zeleznik	30	11	5	14	38	45	38
Sartid	30	9	10	11	28	36	37
Obilic	30	10	6	14	35	47	36
Radnicki	30	10	5	15	33	38	25
Borac*	30	9	7	14	34	44	34
Cukaricki*	30	8	8	14	32	41	32
Sutjeska*	30	5	7	18	21	48	22
Hajduk Belgrade*	30	2	6	22	20	76	12

Top scorer: Pantelic (Red Star Belgrade) 21.
Cup Final: Zeleznik 1, Red Star Belgrade 0.

SLOVAKIA

Slovak Football Association, Junacka 6, 83280 Bratislava, Slovakia.
Founded: 1993; *Number of Clubs:* 2,140; *Number of Players:* 141,000; *National Colours:* All blue and white.
Telephone: 00421-2/4924 9151; *Fax:* 00421-2/4924 9595.

International matches 2004
Austria (h) 1-1, Ukraine (a) 1-1, Croatia (a) 0-1, Japan (n) 1-3, Serbia-Montenegro (n) 0-2, Luxembourg (h) 3-1, Russia (a) 1-1, Liechtenstein (h) 7-0, Latvia (h) 4-1, Slovenia (h) 0-0, Hungary (n) 1-0, Thailand (n) 1-1.

League Championship wins (1939–44; 1994–2005)
Slovan Bratislava 8; Zilina 3; Kosice 2; Inter 2; Bystrica 1; OAP Bratislava 1; Artmedia Petrzalka 1.

Cup wins (1994–2005)
Inter 3; Slovan Bratislava 2; Tatran Presov 1; Humenne 1; Spartak Trnava 1; Koba 1; Matador 1; Petrzalka 1; Banska Bystrica 1.

Final League Table 2004-05

	P	W	D	L	F	A	Pts
Artmedia Petrzalka	36	20	12	4	64	28	72
Zilina	36	19	8	9	73	34	65
Banska Bystrica	36	13	13	10	45	38	52
Dubnica	36	13	12	11	42	43	51
Spartak Trnava	36	12	10	14	39	37	46
Matador	36	12	10	14	31	43	46
Ruzomberok	36	11	10	15	50	57	43
Trencin	36	12	7	17	36	50	43
Inter	36	9	11	16	37	60	38
Rimavska*	36	7	11	18	30	57	32

Top scorer: Sebo (Petrzalka) 22.
Cup Final: Bystrica 2, Petrzalka 1.

SLOVENIA

Football Association of Slovenia, Nogometna zveza Slovenije, Cerinova 4, P.P. 3986, 1001 Ljubljana, Slovenia.
Founded: 1920; *Number of Clubs:* 375; *Number of Players:* 20,117; *National Colours:* White shirts with green sleeves, white shorts, white stockings.
Telephone: 00386-1/530 0400; *Fax:* 00386-1/530 0410.

International matches 2004
Poland (a) 0-2, Latvia (h) 0-1, Switzerland (a) 1-2, Serbia-Montenegro (h) 1-1, Moldova (h) 3-0, Scotland (a) 0-0, Italy (h) 1-0, Norway (a) 0-3, Slovakia (a) 0-0.

League Championship wins (1992–2005)
Maribor 7; SCT Olimpija 4; Gorica 3.

Cup wins (1992–2005)
Maribor 5; SCT Olimpija 4; Gorica 2; Mura 1; Rudar 1; Publikum 1.

Qualifying League Table 2004–05

	P	*W*	*D*	*L*	*F*	*A*	*Pts*
Gorica	22	14	5	3	39	20	47
Publikum	22	11	4	7	33	18	37
Primorje	22	10	5	7	28	20	35
Olimpija	22	10	5	7	28	26	35
Domzale	22	9	6	7	33	27	33
Maribor	22	9	5	8	30	27	32
Drava	22	9	5	8	27	27	32
Ljubljana	22	7	8	7	30	32	29
Mura	22	7	7	8	31	28	28
Bela Krajina	22	5	6	11	20	39	21
Koper	22	4	7	11	20	30	19
Zagorje	22	2	7	13	11	36	13

Championship Play-off

	P	*W*	*D*	*L*	*F*	*A*	*Pts*
Gorica	32	18	11	3	49	23	65
Domzale	32	14	10	8	48	36	52
Publikum	32	16	4	12	47	28	52
Primorje	32	12	10	10	37	30	46
Drava	32	12	10	10	40	36	46
Olimpija*	32	10	7	15	34	52	37

Relegation Play-off

	P	*W*	*D*	*L*	*F*	*A*	*Pts*
Maribor	32	15	6	11	47	36	51
Mura	32	11	11	10	43	38	44
Ljubljana	32	10	12	10	38	43	42
Bela Krajina	32	9	10	13	31	44	37
Koper+	32	9	9	14	38	41	36
Zagorje*	32	2	8	22	17	62	14

Top scorer: Bozgo (Maribor) 18.
Cup Final: Publikum 1, Gorica 0.

SPAIN

Real Federacion Espanola De Futbol, Ramon y Cajal, s/n, Apartado Postale 385, Madrid 28230.
Founded: 1913; *Number of Clubs:* 10,240; *Number of Players:* 408,135; *National Colours:* Red shirts, blue shorts, blue stockings with red, blue and yellow border.
Telephone: 0034-91/495 9800; *Fax:* 0034-91/495 9801.

International matches 2004
Peru (h) 2-1, Denmark (h) 2-0, Italy (a) 1-1, Andorra (h) 4-0, Russia (n) 1-0, Greece (n) 1-1, Portugal (n) 0-1, Venezuela (h) 3-2, Scotland (h) 1-1, Bosnia (a) 1-1, Belgium (h) 2-0, Lithuania (a) 0-0, England (h) 1-0.

League Championship wins (1929–36; 1940–2005)
Real Madrid 29; Barcelona 17; Atletico Madrid 9; Athletic Bilbao 8; Valencia 6; Real Sociedad 2; Real Betis 1; Seville 1; La Coruna 1.

Cup wins (1902–2005)
Barcelona 24; Athletic Bilbao 23; Real Madrid 17; Atletico Madrid 9; Valencia 6; Real Zaragoza 6; Real Union de Irun 3; Seville 3; Espanyol 3; La Coruna 2; Real Betis 2; Arenas 1; Ciclista Sebastian 1; Racing de Irun 1; Vizcaya Bilbao 1; Real Sociedad 1; Mallorca 1.

Final League Table 2004–05

	P	*W*	*D*	*L*	*F*	*A*	*Pts*
Barcelona	38	25	9	4	73	29	84
Real Madrid	38	25	5	8	71	32	80
Villarreal	38	18	11	9	69	37	65
Betis	38	16	14	8	62	50	62
Espanyol	38	17	10	11	54	46	61
Sevilla	38	17	9	12	44	41	60
Valencia	38	14	16	8	54	39	58
La Coruna	38	12	15	11	46	50	51
Athletic Bilbao	38	14	9	15	59	54	51
Malaga	38	15	6	17	40	48	51
Atletico Madrid	38	13	11	14	40	34	50
Zaragoza	38	14	8	16	52	57	50
Getafe	38	12	11	15	38	46	47
Real Sociedad	38	13	8	17	47	56	47
Osasuna	38	12	10	16	46	65	46
Santander	38	12	8	18	41	58	44
Mallorca	38	10	9	19	42	63	39
Levante*	38	9	10	19	39	58	37
Numancia*	38	6	11	21	30	61	29
Albacete*	38	6	10	22	33	56	28

Top scorer: Forlan (Villarreal) 25.
Cup Final: Betis 2, Osasuna 1.

SWEDEN

Svenska Fotbollfoerbundet, Box 1216, S-17123 Solna.
Founded: 1904; *Number of Clubs:* 3,250; *Number of Players:* 485,000; *National Colours:* Yellow shirts, blue shorts, yellow stockings.
Telephone: 0046-8/735 0900; *Fax:* 0046-8/735 0901.

International matches 2004
Norway (n) 0-3, Albania (a) 1-2, England (h) 1-0, Portugal (a) 2-2, Finland (a) 3-1, Poland (h) 3-1, Bulgaria (n) 5-0, Italy (n) 1-1, Denmark (n) 2-2, Holland (n) 0-0, Holland (h) 2-2, Malta (a) 7-0, Croatia (h) 0-1, Hungary (h) 3-0, Iceland (a) 4-1, Scotland (a) 4-1.

League Championship wins (1896–2004)
IFK Gothenburg 17; Malmo FF 15; Oergryte IS Gothenburg 14; IFK Norrköping 12; AIK Stockholm 10; Djurgaarden 10; IF Helsingborg 6; GAIS Gothenburg 4; Boras IF Elfsborg 4; Oster Vaxjo 4; Halmstad 4; Atvidaberg 2; IFK Ekilstune 1; IF Gavic Brynas 1; IF Gothenburg 1; Fassbergs 1; Norrköping IK Sleipner 1; Hammarby 1.

Cup wins (1941–2004)
Malmo FF 14; AIK Stockholm 8; IFK Norrköping 6; IFK Gothenburg 4; Djurgaarden 3; Atvidaberg 2; Kalmar 2; Helsingborg 2; Elfsborg 2; GAIS Gothenburg 1; IF Raa 1; Landskrona 1; Oster Vaxjo 1; Degerfors 1; Halmstad 1; Orgryte 1.

Final League Table 2004

	P	*W*	*D*	*L*	*F*	*A*	*Pts*
Malmo	26	15	7	4	44	21	52
Halmstad	26	14	8	4	53	27	50
IFK Gothenburg	26	14	5	7	33	20	47
Djurgaarden	26	11	8	7	38	32	41
Kalmar	26	10	10	6	27	18	40
Hammarby	26	10	7	9	28	28	37
Orebro	26	9	6	11	32	45	33
Sundsvall	26	8	8	10	28	30	32
Elfsborg	26	8	8	10	25	32	32
Helsingborg	26	7	9	10	41	33	30
Landskrona	26	7	9	10	27	33	30
Orgryte+	26	6	10	10	25	33	28
AIK*	26	5	10	11	23	35	25
Trelleborg*	26	2	7	17	18	55	13

Play-offs: Assyriska 2, Orgryte 1; Orgryte 1, Assyriska 0.
Orgryte remain but Orebro refused a licence and replaced by Assyriska.
Top scorer: Rosenberg (Halmstad) 14.
Cup Final: Djurgaarden 3, IFK Gothenburg 1.

SWITZERLAND

Schweizerisher Fussballverband, Postfach 3000, Berne 15.
Founded: 1895; *Number of Clubs:* 1,473; *Number of Players:* 185,286; *National Colours:* Red shirts, white shorts, red stockings.
Telephone: 0041-31/950 8111; *Fax:* 0041-31/950 8181.

International matches 2004
Morocco (a) 1-2, Greece (a) 0-1, Slovenia (h) 2-1, Germany (h) 0-2, Liechtenstein (h) 1-0, Croatia (n) 0-0, England (n) 0-3, France (n) 1-3, Northern Ireland (h) 0-0, Faeroes (h) 6-0, Republic of Ireland (h) 1-1, Israel (a) 2-2.

League Championship wins (1898–2005)
Grasshoppers 26; Servette 17; Young Boys Berne 11; FC Basle 11; FC Zurich 9; Lausanne 7; La Chaux-de-Fonds

3; FC Lugano 3; Winterthur 3; FX Aarau 3; Neuchatel Xamax 3; Sion 2; St Gallen 2; FC Anglo-American 1; FC Brühl 1; Cantonal-Neuchatel 1; Biel 1; Bellinzona 1; FC Etoile La Chaux-de-Fonds 1; Lucerne 1.

Cup wins (1926–2005)
Grasshoppers 18; FC Sion 9; Lausanne 9; Servette 7; FC Basle 7; FC Zurich 7; La Chaux-de-Fonds 6; Young Boys Berne 6; Lucerne 2; FC Lugano 2; FC Granges 1; St Gallen 1; Urania Geneva 1; Young Fellows Zurich 1; Aarau 1; Wil 1.

Final League Table 2004–05

	P	*W*	*D*	*L*	*F*	*A*	*Pts*
Basle	34	21	7	6	81	45	70
Thun	34	18	6	10	69	42	60
Grasshoppers	34	12	14	8	51	50	50
Young Boys	34	12	13	9	60	52	49
Zurich	34	13	9	12	55	57	48
Neuchatel Xamax	34	10	8	16	36	48	38
St Gallen	34	8	12	14	51	60	36
Aarau	34	7	11	16	42	64	32
Schaffhausen	34	7	11	16	36	59	32
Servette*	18	6	5	7	24	28	20

Servette excluded in second half of the season for financial reasons.
Top scorer: Gimenez (Basle) 27.
Cup Final: Zurich 3, Lucerne 1.

TURKEY

Turkiye Futbol Federasyonu, Konaklar Mah. Ihlamurlu Sok. 9, 4 Levent, Istanbul 80620.
Founded: 1923; *Number of Clubs:* 230; *Number of Players:* 64,521; *National Colours:* All white.
Telephone: 0090-212/282 7020; *Fax:* 0090-212/282 7015.

International matches 2004
Denmark (h) 0-1, Croatia (a) 2-2, Belgium (a) 3-2, Australia (a) 3-1, Australia (a) 1-0, South Korea (a) 1-0, South Korea (a) 1-2, Belarus (h) 1-2, Georgia (h) 1-1, Greece (a) 0-0, Kazakhstan (h) 4-0, Denmark (a) 1-1, Ukraine (h) 0-3.

League Championship wins (1960–2005)
Fenerbahce 16; Galatasaray 15; Besiktas 11; Trabzonspor 6.

Cup wins (1963–2005)
Galatasaray 14; Trabzonspor 7; Besiktas 6; Fenerbahce 4; Goztepe Izmir 2; Altay Izmir 2; Ankaragucu 2; Genclerbirligi 2; Kocaeli 2; Eskisehirspor 1; Bursapor 1; Sakaryaspor 1.

Final League Table 2004–05

	P	*W*	*D*	*L*	*F*	*A*	*Pts*
Fenerbahce	34	26	2	6	77	24	80
Trabzonspor	34	24	5	5	73	29	77
Galatasaray	34	24	4	6	64	25	76
Besiktas	34	20	9	5	70	39	69
Genclerbirligi	34	14	9	11	52	41	51
Denizli	34	13	10	11	46	45	49
Ankara	34	13	9	12	52	48	48
Konya	34	11	12	11	62	62	45
Gaziantep	34	13	5	16	49	55	44
Rize	34	11	10	13	36	37	43
Malatya	34	12	7	15	47	53	43
Samsun	34	10	8	16	40	55	38
Ankaragucu	34	10	8	16	37	61	38
Diyarbakir	34	9	7	18	31	53	34
Kayseri	34	8	10	16	42	65	34
Sakaray*	34	9	5	20	51	72	32
Istanbul*	34	5	12	17	32	59	27
Sebat*	34	3	10	21	40	78	19

Top scorer: Fatih (Trabzonspor) 30.
Cup Final: Galatasaray 5, Fenerbahce 1.

UKRAINE

Football Federation of Ukraine, Laboratorna Str. 1, P.O. Box 293, Kiev 03150.
Founded: 1991; *Number of Clubs:* 1500; *Number of Players:* 759,500; *National Colours:* All yellow and blue.
Telephone: 00380-44/252 8498; *Fax:* 00380-44/252 8513.

International matches 2004
Libya (a) 1-1, Macedonia (a) 0-1, Slovakia (h) 1-1, France (a) 0-1, England (a) 0-3, Denmark (a) 1-1, Kazakhstan (a) 2-1, Greece (h) 1-1, Georgia (h) 2-0, Turkey (a) 3-0.

League Championship wins (1992–2005)
Dynamo Kiev 10; Shakhtjor Donetsk 2; Tavriya Simferopol 1.

Cup wins (1992–2005)
Dynamo Kiev 7; Shakhtjor Donetsk 5; Chernomorets 2.

Final League Table 2004–05

	P	*W*	*D*	*L*	*F*	*A*	*Pts*
Shakhtjor Donetsk	30	26	2	2	63	19	80
Dynamo Kiev	30	23	4	3	58	14	73
Metalurg Donetsk	30	14	7	9	38	35	49
Dnepr	30	13	9	8	38	34	48
Mariupol	30	12	8	10	38	34	44
Chernomorets	30	12	6	12	29	29	42
Tavriya	30	11	9	10	34	28	42
Volyn	30	11	7	12	35	37	40
Arsenal	30	9	10	11	30	33	37
Metalurg Zapor	30	8	11	11	25	32	35
Metalist	30	9	7	14	25	37	34
Zakarpattja	30	7	10	13	21	30	31
Krivbas	30	7	10	13	24	38	31
Vorskla	30	8	6	16	18	35	30
Obolon*	30	4	9	17	18	43	21
Borysfen*	30	3	11	16	15	31	20

Top scorer: Kosyrin (Chernomorets) 14.
Cup Final: Shakhtjor Donetsk 0, Dynamo Kiev 1.

WALES

The Football Association of Wales Limited, Plymouth Chambers, 3 Westgate Street, Cardiff, CF10 1DP.
Founded: 1876; *Number of Clubs:* 2,326; *Number of Players:* 53,926; *National Colours:* All red.
Telephone: 0044-29/2037 2325; *Fax:* 0044-29/2034 3961.

SOUTH AMERICA

ARGENTINA

Asociacion Del Futbol Argentina, Viamonte 1366/76, 1053 Buenos Aires.
Founded: 1893; *Number of Clubs:* 3,035; *Number of Players:* 306,365; *National Colours:* Light blue and white vertical striped shirts, dark blue shorts, white stockings.
Telephone: 0054-11/4372 7900; *Fax:* 0054-11/4375 4410.
International matches 2004
Ecuador (h) 1-0, Morocco (a) 1-0, Brazil (a) 1-3, Paraguay (h) 0-0, Colombia (n) 0-2, Peru (n) 2-1, Ecuador (n) 6-1, Mexico (n) 0-1, Uruguay (n) 4-2, Peru (n) 1-0, Colombia (n) 3-0, Brazil (n) 2-2, Japan (a) 2-1, Peru (a) 3-1, Uruguay (h) 4-2, Chile (a) 0-0, Venezuela (h) 3-2.

BOLIVIA

Federacion Boliviana De Futbol, Av. Libertador Bolivar No. 1168, Casilla de Correo 484, Cochabamba, Bolivia.
Founded: 1925; *Number of Clubs:* 305; *Number of Players:* 15,290; *National Colours:* Green shirts, white shorts, green stockings.
Telephone: 00591-4/424 4982; *Fax:* 00591-4/428 2132.
International matches 2004
Chile (h) 0-2, Paraguay (h) 2-1, Ecuador (a) 2-3, Peru (n) 2-2, Colombia (n) 0-1, Venezuela (n) 1-1, Brazil (a) 1-3, Peru (h) 1-0, Uruguay (h) 0-0, Guatemala (n) 0-1, Colombia (a) 0-1.

BRAZIL

Confederacao Brasileira De Futebol, Rua Victor Civita 66, Bloco 1-Edificio 5-5 Andar, Barra da Tijuca, Rio De Janeiro 22775-040.
Founded: 1914; *Number of Clubs:* 12,987; *Number of Players:* 551,358; *National Colours:* Yellow shirts with green collar and cuffs, blue shorts, white stockings with green and yellow border.
Telephone: 0055-21/3870 3610; *Fax:* 0055-21/3870 3612.

International matches 2004
Republic of Ireland (a) 0-0, Paraguay (a) 0-0, Hungary (a) 4-1, France (a) 0-0, Argentina (h) 3-1, Chile (a) 1-1, Chile (n) 1-0, Costa Rica (n) 4-1, Paraguay (n) 1-2, Mexico (n) 4-0, Uruguay (n) 1-1, Argentina (n) 2-2, Haiti (a) 6-0, Bolivia (h) 3-1, Germany (a) 1-1, Venezuela (a) 5-2, Colombia (h) 0-0, Ecuador (a) 0-1.

CHILE

Federacion De Futbol De Chile, Avda. Quillin No. 5635, Casilla postal 3733, Correo Central, Santiago de Chile.
Founded: 1895; *Number of Clubs:* 4,598; *Number of Players:* 609,724; *National Colours:* Red shirts with blue collar and cuffs, blue shorts, white stockings.
Telephone: 0056-2/284 9000; *Fax:* 0056-2/284 3510.
International matches 2004
Mexico (a) 1-1, Bolivia (a) 2-0, Peru (h) 1-1, Venezuela (a) 1-0, Brazil (h) 1-1, Brazil (n) 0-1, Paraguay (n) 1-1, Costa Rica (n) 1-2, Colombia (h) 0-0, Ecuador (a) 0-2, Argentina (h) 0-0, Peru (a) 1-2.

COLOMBIA

Federacion Colombiana De Futbol, Avenida 32, No. 16–22 piso 4o. Apartado Aereo 17602, Santafe de Bogota.
Founded: 1924; *Number of Clubs:* 3,685; *Number of Players:* 188,050; *National Colours:* Yellow shirts, blue shorts, red stockings.
Telephone: 0057-1/288 9740; *Fax:* 0057-1/288 9559.
International matches 2004
Honduras (a) 1-1, Peru (a) 2-0, El Salvador (a) 2-0, Ecuador (a) 1-2, Uruguay (h) 5-0, Argentina (n) 2-0, Venezuela (n) 1-0, Bolivia (n) 1-0, Peru (n) 2-2, Costa Rica (n) 2-0, Argentina (n) 0-3, Uruguay (n) 1-2, Chile (a) 0-0, Paraguay (h) 1-1, Brazil (a) 0-0, Bolivia (h) 1-0.

ECUADOR

Federacion Ecuatoriana del Futbol, km 4 1/2 via a la Costa (Avda. del Bombero), PO Box 09-01-7447 Guayaquil.
Founded: 1925; *Number of Clubs:* 170; *Number of Players:* 15,700; *National Colours:* Yellow shirts, blue shorts, red stockings.
Telephone: 00593-4/235 2372; *Fax:* 00593-4/235 2116.
International matches 2004
Mexico (a) 1-2, Argentina (a) 0-1, Honduras (a) 1-1, Colombia (h) 2-1, Bolivia (h) 3-2, Argentina (n) 1-6, Uruguay (n) 1-2, Mexico (n) 1-2, Uruguay (a) 0-1, Chile (h) 2-0, Venezuela (a) 1-3, Mexico (a) 1-2, Brazil (h) 1-0.

PARAGUAY

Asociacion Paraguaya de Futbol, Estadio De Los Defensores del Chaco, Calles Mayor Martinez 1393, Asuncion.
Founded: 1906; *Number of Clubs:* 1,500; *Number of Players:* 140,000; *National Colours:* Red and white shirts, blue shorts, blue stockings.
Telephone: 00595-21/480 120; *Fax:* 00595-21/480 124.
International matches 2004
Brazil (h) 0-0, South Korea (a) 0-0, Bolivia (a) 1-2, Argentina (a) 0-0, Costa Rica (n) 1-0, Chile (n) 1-1, Brazil (n) 2-1, Uruguay (n) 1-3, Venezuela (h) 1-0, Colombia (a) 1-1, Peru (h) 1-1, Uruguay (a) 0-1.

PERU

Federacion Peruana De Futbol, Av. Aviacion 2085, San Luis, Lima 30.
Founded: 1922; *Number of Clubs:* 10,000; *Number of Players:* 325,650; *National Colours:* White shirts with red stripe, white shorts with red lines, white stockings with red line.
Telephone: 0051-1/225 8236; *Fax:* 0051-1/225 8240.
International matches 2004
Spain (a) 1-2, Colombia (h) 0-2, Chile (a) 1-1, Uruguay (a) 3-1, Venezuela (h) 0-0, Argentina (n) 1-2, Bolivia (h) 2-2, Venezuela (h) 3-1, Colombia (h) 2-2, Argentina (h) 0-1, Argentina (h) 1-3, Bolivia (a) 0-1, Paraguay (a) 1-1, Chile (h) 2-1.

URUGUAY

Asociacion Uruguaya De Futbol, Guayabo 1531, 11200 Montevideo.
Founded: 1900; *Number of Clubs:* 1,091; *Number of Players:* 134,310; *National Colours:* Sky blue shirts with white collar/cuffs, black shorts and stockings with sky blue borders.
Telephone: 0059-82/400 4814; *Fax:* 0059-82/409 0550.
International matches 2004
Jamaica (a) 0-2, Venezuela (h) 0-3, Peru (h) 1-3, Colombia (a) 0-5, Mexico (n) 2-2, Ecuador (n) 2-1, Argentina (n) 2-4, Paraguay (n) 3-1, Brazil (n) 1-1, Colombia (n) 2-1, Ecuador (h) 1-0, Argentina (a) 2-4, Bolivia (a) 0-0, Paraguay (h) 1-0.

VENEZUELA

Federacion Venezolana De Futbol, Avda. Santos Erminy Ira, Calle las Delicias Torre Mega II, P.H. Sabana Grande, Caracas 1050.
Founded: 1926; *Number of Clubs:* 1,753; *Number of Players:* 63,175; *National Colours:* Burgundy shirts, white shorts and stockings.
Telephone: 0058-212/762 4472; *Fax:* 0058-212/762 0596.
International matches 2004
Australia (h) 1-1, Honduras (h) 2-1, Uruguay (a) 3-0, Jamaica (a) 1-2, Chile (h) 0-1, Peru (a) 0-0, Colombia (n) 0-1, Peru (n) 1-3, Bolivia (n) 1-1, Spain (a) 2-3, Paraguay (a) 0-1, Brazil (h) 2-5, Ecuador (h) 3-1, Argentina (a) 2-3, Guatemala (h) 0-1.

ASIA

AFGHANISTAN

Afghanistan Football Federation, PO Box 5099, Kabul.
Founded: 1933; *Number of Clubs*: 30; *Number of Players*: 3,300; *National Colours*: All white with red lines.
Telephone: 0093-20/210 2417; *Fax:* 0093-20/210 2417

BAHRAIN

Bahrain Football Association, P.O. Box 5464, Manama.
Founded: 1957; *Number of Clubs:* 25; *Number of Players:* 2,030; *National Colours:* All red.
Telephone: 00973/689 569; *Fax:* 00973/781 188.

BANGLADESH

Bangladesh Football Federation, Bangabandhu National Stadium-1, Dhaka 1000.
Founded: 1972; *Number of Clubs:* 1,265; *Number of Players:* 30,385; *National Colours:* Orange shirts, white shorts, green stockings.
Telephone: 00880-2/955 6072; *Fax:* 00880-2/956 3419.

BHUTAN

Bhutan Football Federation, P.O. Box 365, Thimphu.
National Colours: All yellow and red.
Telephone: 00975-2/322 350; *Fax:* 00975-2/321 131.

BRUNEI DARUSSALAM

The Football Association of Brunei Darussalam, P.O. Box 2010, 1920 Bandar Seri Begawan BS 8674.
Founded: 1959; *Number of Clubs:* 22; *Number of Players:* 830; *National Colours:* Yellow shirts, black shorts, black and white stockings.
Telephone: 00673-2/382 761; *Fax:* 00673-2/382 760.

CAMBODIA

Cambodian Football Federation, Chaeng Maeng Village, Rd. Kab Srov, Sangkat Samrong Krom, Khan Dangkor, Phnom-Penh .
Founded: 1933; *Number of Clubs:* 30; *Number of Players:* 650; *National Colours:* All blue.
Telephone: 00855-23/364 889; *Fax:* 00855-23/220 780.

CHINA PR

Football Association of The People's Republic of China, 9 Tiyuguan Road, Beijing 100763.
Founded: 1924; *Number of Clubs:* 1,045; *Number of Players:* 2,250,000; *National Colours:* All white.
Telephone: 0086-10/6711 7019; *Fax:* 0086-10/6714 2533.

CHINA TAIPEI

Chinese Taipei Football Association, 2F No. Yu Men St., Taipei, Taiwan 104.
Founded: 1936; *Number of Players:* 17,000; *National Colours:* Blue shirts and shorts, white stockings.
Telephone: 00886-2/2596 1185; *Fax:* 00886-2/2595 1594.

GUAM

Guam Football Association, P.O.Box 5093, Agana, Guam 96932.
Founded: 1975; *National Colours:* Blue shirts, white shorts, blue stockings.
Telephone: 001-671/477 5423; *Fax:* 001-671/477 5424.

HONG KONG

The Hong Kong Football Association Ltd, 55 Fat Kwong Street, Homantin, Kowloon, Hong Kong.
Founded: 1914; *Number of Clubs:* 69; *Number of Players:* 3,274; *National Colours:* All red.
Telephone: 00852/2712 9122; *Fax:* 00852/2760 4303.

INDIA

All India Football Federation, Nehru Stadium (West Stand), Fatorda Margao-Goa 403 602.
Founded: 1937; *Number of Clubs:* 2,000; *Number of Players:* 56,000; *National Colours:* Sky blue shirts, navy blue shorts, sky and navy blue stockings.
Telephone: 0091-832/2742 603; *Fax:* 0091-832/2741 172.

INDONESIA

Football Association of Indonesia, Gelora Bung Karno, Pintu X-XI, Jakarta 10270.
Founded: 1930; *Number of Clubs:* 2,880; *Number of Players:* 97,000; *National Colours:* Red shirts, white shorts, red stockings.
Telephone: 0062-21/570 4762; *Fax:* 0062-21/573 4386.

IRAN

IR Iran Football Federation, No. 16-4th deadend, Pakistan Street, PO Box 15316-6967 Shahid Beheshti Avenue, Tehran 15316.
Founded: 1920; *Number of Clubs:* 6,326; *Number of Players:* 306,000; *National Colours:* All white.
Telephone: 0098-21/873 2754; *Fax:* 0098-21/873 0305.

IRAQ

Iraqi Football Association, Olympic Committee Building, Palestine Street, PO Box 484, Baghdad.
Founded: 1948; *Number of Clubs:* 155; *Number of Players:* 4,400; *National Colours:* All black.
Telephone: 00964-1/772 9990; *Fax:* 00964-1/885 4321.

JAPAN

Japan Football Association, JFA House, 3-10-15, Hongo, Bunkyo-ku, Tokyo 113-0033.
Founded: 1921; *Number of Clubs:* 13,047; *Number of Players:* 358,989; *National Colours:* Blue shirts, white shorts, blue stockings.
Telephone: 0081-3/3830 2004; *Fax:* 0081-3/3830 2005.

JORDAN

Jordan Football Association, P.O. Box 962024 Al Hussein Sports City, 11196 Amman.
Founded: 1949; *Number of Clubs:* 98; *Number of Players:* 4,305; *National Colours:* All white and red.
Telephone: 00962-6/565 7662; *Fax:* 00962-6/565 7660.

KOREA, NORTH

Football Association of The Democratic People's Rep. of Korea, Kumsong-dong, Kwangbok Street, Mangyongdae Distr, PO Box 56, Pyongyang FNJ-PRK.
Founded: 1945; *Number of Clubs:* 90; *Number of Players:* 3,420; *National Colours:* All white.
Telephone: 00850-2/18 222; *Fax:* 00850-2/381 4403.

KOREA, SOUTH

Korea Football Association, 1-131 Sinmunno, 2-ga, Jongno-Gu, Seoul 110-062.
Founded: 1928; *Number of Clubs:* 476; *Number of Players:* 2,047; *National Colours:* Red shirts, blue shorts, red stockings.
Telephone: 0082-2/733 6764; *Fax:* 0082-2/735 2755.

KUWAIT

Kuwait Football Association, P.O. Box 2029, Udiliya, Block 4 Al-Ittihad Street, Safat 13021.
Founded: 1952; *Number of Clubs:* 14 (senior); *Number of Players:* 1,526; *National Colours:* All blue.
Telephone: 00965/255 5851; *Fax:* 00965/254 9955.

KYRGYZSTAN

Football Federation of Kyrgyz Republic, PO Box 1484, Kurenkeeva Street 195, Bishkek 720040, Kyrgyzstan.
Founded: 1992; *Number of Players:* 20,000; *National Colours:* Red shirts, white shorts, red stockings.
Telephone: 00996-312/670 573; *Fax:* 00996-312/670 573.

LAOS

Federation Lao de Football, National Stadium, Kounboulo Street, PO Box 3777, Vientiane 856-21, Laos.
Founded: 1951; *Number of Clubs:* 76; *Number of Players:* 2,060; *National Colours:* All red.
Telephone: 00856-21/251 593; *Fax:* 00856-21/213 460.

LEBANON

Federation Libanaise De Football-Association, P.O. Box 4732, Verdun Street, Bristol, Radwan Centre Building, Beirut.
Founded: 1933; *Number of Clubs:* 105; *Number of Players:* 8,125; *National Colours:* Red shirts, white shorts, red stockings.
Telephone: 00961-1/745 745; *Fax:* 00961-1/349 529.

MACAO

Associacao De Futebol De Macau (AFM), Ave. da Amizade 405, Seng Vo Kok, 13 Andar "A", Macau.
Founded: 1939; *Number of Clubs:* 52; *Number of Players:* 800; *National Colours:* All green.
Telephone: 00853/781 883; *Fax:* 00853/782 383.

MALAYSIA

Football Association of Malaysia, 3rd Floor, Wisma Fam, Jalan, SSA/9, Kelana Jaya Selangor Darul Ehsan 47301.
Founded: 1933; *Number of Clubs:* 450; *Number of Players:* 11,250; *National Colours:* All yellow and black.
Telephone: 0060-3/7876 3766; *Fax:* 0060-3/7875 7984.

MALDIVES REPUBLIC

Football Association of Maldives, National Stadium G. Banafsaa Magu 20-04, Male.
Founded: 1982; *Number of Clubs: Number of Players: National Colours:* Red shirts, Green shorts, white stockings.
Telephone: 00960/317 006; *Fax:* 00960/317 005.

MONGOLIA

Mongolia Football Federation, PO Box 259 Ulaan-Baatar 210646.
National Colours: White shirts, red shorts, white stockings.
Telephone: 00976-11/312 145; *Fax:* 00976-11/312 145.

MYANMAR

Myanmar Football Federation, Youth Training Centre, Thingankyun Township, Yangon.
Founded: 1947; *Number of Clubs:* 600; *Number of Players:* 21,000; *National Colours:* Red shirts, white shorts, red stockings.
Telephone: 00951/577 366; *Fax:* 00951/570 000.

NEPAL

All-Nepal Football Association, AMFA House, Ward No. 4, Bishalnagar, PO Box 12582, Kathmandu.
Founded: 1951; *Number of Clubs:* 85; *Number of Players:* 2,550; *National Colours:* All red.
Telephone: 00977-1/5539 059; *Fax:* 00977-1/442 4314.

OMAN

Oman Football Association, P.O. Box 3462, Ruwi Postal Code 112.
Founded: 1978; *Number of Clubs:* 47; *Number of Players:* 2,340; *National Colours:* All white.
Telephone: 00968/787 635; *Fax:* 00968/787 632.

PAKISTAN

Pakistan Football Federation, 6 National Hockey Stadium, Feroze Pure Road, Lahore, Pakistan.
Founded: 1948; *Number of Clubs:* 882; *Number of Players:* 21,000; *National Colours:* All green and white.
Telephone: 0092-42/923 0821; *Fax:* 0092-42/923 0823.

PALESTINE

Palestinian Football Federation, Al-Yarmouk, Gaza.
National Colours: White shirts, black shorts, white stockings.
Telephone: 00972-8/283 4339; *Fax:* 00972-8/282 5208.

PHILIPPINES

Philippine Football Federation, Room 405, Building V, Philsports Complex, Meralco Avenue, Pasig City, Metro Manila.
Founded: 1907; *Number of Clubs:* 650; *Number of Players:* 45,000; *National Colours:* All blue.
Telephone: 0063-2/687 1594; *Fax:* 0063-2/687 1598.

QATAR

Qatar Football Association, 7th Floor, QNOC Building, Cornich, P.O. Box 5333, Doha.
Founded: 1960; *Number of Clubs:* 8 (senior); *Number of Players:* 1,380; *National Colours:* All white.
Telephone: 00974/494 4411; *Fax:* 00974/494 4414.

SAUDI ARABIA

Saudi Arabian Football Federation, Al Mather Quarter (Olympic Complex), Prince Faisal Bin Fahad Street, P.O. Box 5844, Riyadh 11432.
Founded: 1959; *Number of Clubs:* 120; *Number of Players:* 9,600; *National Colours:* White shirts, green shorts, white stockings.
Telephone: 00966-1/482 2240; *Fax:* 00966-1/482 1215.

SINGAPORE

Football Association of Singapore, Jalan Besar Stadium, 100 Tyrwhitt Road, Singapore 207542.
Founded: 1892; *Number of Clubs:* 250; *Number of Players:* 8,000; *National Colours:* All red.
Telephone: 0065/6348 3477; *Fax:* 0065/6293 3728.

SRI LANKA

Football Federation of Sri Lanka, 100/9, Independence Avenue, Colombo 07.
Founded: 1939; *Number of Clubs:* 600; *Number of Players:* 18,825; *National Colours:* All white.
Telephone: 0094-11/268 6120; *Fax:* 0094-11/2682 471.

SYRIA

Syrian Football Federation, PO Box 421, Maysaloon Street, Damascus.
Founded: 1936; *Number of Clubs:* 102; *Number of Players:* 30,600; *National Colours:* All red.
Telephone: 00963-11/333 5866; *Fax:* 00963-11/333 1511.

TAJIKISTAN

Tajikistan Football Federation, 22 Shotemur Ave., Dushanbe 734 025.
Founded: 1991; *Number of Clubs:* 1,804; *Number of Players:* 71,400; *National Colours:* All white.
Telephone: 00992-372/210 265; *Fax:* 00992-372/510 157.

THAILAND

The Football Association of Thailand, Gate 3, Rama I Road, Patumwan, Bangkok 10330.
Founded: 1916; *Number of Clubs:* 168; *Number of Players:* 15,000; *National Colours:* All red.
Telephone: 0066-2/216 4691; *Fax:* 0066-2/215 4494.

TURKMENISTAN

Football Association of Turkmenistan, 32 Belinskiy Street, Stadium Kopetdag, Ashgabat 744 001.
Founded: 1992; *Number of Players:* 75,000; *National Colours:* Green shirts, white shorts, green stockings.
Telephone: 00993-12/362 392; *Fax:* 00993-12/362 355.

UNITED ARAB EMIRATES

United Arab Emirates Football Association, P.O. Box 916, Abu Dhabi.
Founded: 1971; *Number of Clubs:* 23 (senior); *Number of Players:* 1,787; *National Colours:* All white.
Telephone: 00971-2/444 5600; *Fax:* 00971-2/444 8558.

UZBEKISTAN

Uzbekistan Football Federation, Massiv Almazar Furkat Street 15/1, 700003 Tashkent, Uzbekistan.
Founded: 1946; *Number of Clubs:* 15,000; *Number of Players:* 217,000; *National Colours:* All white.
Telephone: 00998-71/144 1684; *Fax:* 00998-71/144 1683.

VIETNAM

Vietnam Football Federation, 18 Ly van Phuc, Dong Da District, Hanoi 844.
Founded: 1962; *Number of Clubs:* 55 (senior); *Number of Players:* 16,000; *National Colours:* All red.
Telephone: 0084-4/845 2480; *Fax:* 0084-4/823 3119.

YEMEN

Yemen Football Association, Quarter of Sport - Al Jeraf, Behind the Stadium of Ali Mushsen, Al Moreissy in the Sport, Al-Thawra City.
Founded: 1962; *Number of Clubs:* 26; *Number of Players:* 1750; *National Colours:* All green.
Telephone: 00967-1/310 927. *Fax:* 00967-1/310 921.

CONCACAF

ANGUILLA

Anguilla Football Association, P.O. Box 1318, The Valley, Anguilla, BWI.
National Colours: Turquoise, white, orange and blue shirts and shorts, turquoise and orange stockings.
Telephone: 001-264/497 7323; *Fax:* 001-264/497 7324.

ANTIGUA & BARBUDA

The Antigua/Barbuda Football Association, Newgate Street, P.O. Box 773, St John's.
Founded: 1928; *Number of Clubs:* 60; *Number of Players:* 1,008; *National Colours:* Red, black, yellow and blue shirts, black shorts and stockings.
Telephone: 001-268/727 8869; *Fax:* 001-268/562 1681.

ARUBA

Arubaanse Voetbal Bond, Ferguson Street, Z/N P.O. Box 376, Oranjestad, Aruba.
Founded: 1932; *Number of Clubs:* 50; *Number of Players:* 1,000; *National Colours:* Yellow shirts, blue shorts, yellow and blue stockings.
Telephone: 00297/829 550; *Fax:* 00297/829 550.

BAHAMAS

Bahamas Football Association, Plaza on the Way, West Bay Street, P.O. Box N 8434, Nassau, NP.
Founded: 1967; *Number of Clubs:* 14; *Number of Players:* 700; *National Colours:* Yellow shirts, black shorts, yellow stockings.
Telephone: 001-242/322 5897; *Fax:* 001-242/322 5898.

BARBADOS

Barbados Football Association, Hildor No. 4, 10th Avenue, P.O. Box 1362, Belleville-St. Michael, Barbados.
Founded: 1910; *Number of Clubs:* 92; *Number of Players:* 1,100; *National Colours:* Royal blue and gold shirts, gold shorts, white, gold and blue stockings.
Telephone:: 001-246/228 1707; *Fax:* 001-246/228 6484.

BELIZE

Belize National Football Association, 26 Hummingbird Highway, Belmopan, P.O. Box 1742, Belize City.
Founded: 1980; *National Colours:* Red, white and black shirts, black shorts, red and black stockings.
Telephone: 00501-822/3410; *Fax:* 00501-822/3377.

BERMUDA

The Bermuda Football Association, 48 Cedar Avenue, Hamilton HM12.
Founded: 1928; *Number of Clubs:* 30; *Number of Players:* 1,947; *National Colours:* All blue.
Telephone: 001-441/295 2199; *Fax:* 001-441/295 0773.

BRITISH VIRGIN ISLANDS

British Virgin Islands Football Association, P.O. Box 29, Road Town, Tortola, BVI.
National Colours: Gold and green shirts, green shorts, and stockings.
Telephone: 001-284/494 5655; *Fax:* 001-284/494 8968.

US VIRGIN ISLANDS

USVI Soccer Federation Inc., 54, Castle Coakley, PO Box 2346, Kingshill, St Croix 00851.
National Colours: Royal blue and gold shirts, royal blue shorts and stockings.
Telephone: 001-340/711 9676; *Fax:* 00-340/711 9707.

CANADA

The Canadian Soccer Association, Place Soccer Canada, 237 Metcalfe Street, Ottawa, ONT K2P 1R2.
Founded: 1912; *Number of Clubs:* 1,600; *Number of Players:* 224,290; *National Colours:* All red.
Telephone: 001-613/237 7678; *Fax:* 001-613/237 1516.

CAYMAN ISLANDS

Cayman Islands Football Association, PO Box 178 GT, Truman Bodden Sports Complex, Olympic Way Off Walkers Rd, George Town, Grand Cayman, Cayman Islands WI.
Founded: 1966; *Number of Clubs:* 25; *Number of Players:* 875; *National Colours:* Red and white shirts, blue and white shorts, white and red stockings.
Telephone: 001-345/949 5775. *Fax:* 001-345/945 7673.

COSTA RICA

Federacion Costarricense De Futbol, Costado Norte Estatua Leon Cortes, San Jose 670-1000.
Founded: 1921; *Number of Clubs:* 431; *Number of Players:* 12,429; *National Colours:* Red shirts, blue shorts, white stockings.
Telephone: 00506/222 1544; *Fax:* 00506/255 2674.

CUBA

Asociacion de Futbol de Cuba, Calle 13 No. 661, Esq. C. Vedado, ZP 4, La Habana.
Founded: 1924; *Number of Clubs:* 70; *Number of Players:* 12,900; *National Colours:* All red, white and blue.
Telephone: 0053-7/545 024; *Fax:* 0053-7/335 310.

DOMINICA

Dominica Football Association, 33 Great Marlborough Street, Roseau.
Founded: 1970; *Number of Clubs:* 30; *Number of Players:* 500; *National Colours:* Emerald green shirts, black shorts, green stockings.
Telephone: 001-767/448 7577; *Fax:* 001-767/448 7587.

DOMINICAN REPUBLIC

Federacion Dominicana De Futbol, Centro Olimpico Juan Pablo Duarte, Ensanche Miraflores, Apartado De Correos No. 1953, Santo Domingo.
Founded: 1953; *Number of Clubs:* 128; *Number of Players:* 10,706; *National Colours:* Navy blue shirts, white shorts, red stockings.
Telephone: 001-809/542 6923; *Fax:* 001-809/547 5363.

EL SALVADOR

Federacion Salvadorena De Futbol, Primera Calle Poniente No. 2025, San Salvador CA1029.
Founded: 1935; *Number of Clubs:* 944; *Number of Players:* 21,294; *National Colours:* All blue.
Telephone: 00503/263 7525; *Fax:* 00503/260 3129.

GRENADA

Grenada Football Association, P.O. Box 326, National Stadium, Queens Park, St George's, Grenada, W.I.
Founded: 1924; *Number of Clubs:* 15; *Number of Players:* 200; *National Colours:* Green and yellow striped shirts, red shorts, yellow stockings.
Telephone: 001-473/440 9903; *Fax:* 001-473/440 9973.

GUATEMALA

Federacion Nacional de Futbol de Guatemala, 2a Calle 15-57, Zona 15, Boulevard Vista Hermosa, Guatemala City 01009.
Founded: 1946; *Number of Clubs:* 1,611; *Number of Players:* 43,516; *National Colours:* Blue shirts, white shorts, blue stockings.
Telephone: 00502/279 1746; *Fax:* 00502/379 8345.

GUYANA

Guyana Football Federation, 159 Rupununi Street, Bel Air Park, P.O. Box 10727, Georgetown.
Founded: 1902; *Number of Clubs:* 103; *Number of Players:* 1,665; *National Colours:* Green shirts and shorts, yellow stockings.
Telephone: 00592-2/278 758; *Fax:* 00592-2/262 641.

HAITI

Federation Haitienne De Football, 128 Avenue Christiophe, P.O. Box 2258, Port-Au-Prince.
Founded: 1904; *Number of Clubs:* 40; *Number of Players:* 4,000; *National Colours:* Blue shirts, red shorts, blue stockings.
Telephone: 00509/244 0115; *Fax:* 00509/244 0117.

HONDURAS

Federacion Nacional Autonoma De Futbol De Honduras, Colonia Florencia Norte, Ave Roble, Edificio Plaza America, Ave. Roble 1 y 2 Nivel, Tegucigalpa, D.C.
Founded: 1951; *Number of Clubs:* 1,050; *Number of Players:* 15,300; *National Colours:* All white.
Telephone: 00504/232 0572; *Fax:* 00504/239 8826.

JAMAICA

Jamaica Football Federation Ltd, 20 St Lucia Crescent, Kingston 5.
Founded: 1910; *Number of Clubs:* 266; *Number of Players:* 45,200; *National Colours:* Gold shirts, black shorts, gold stockings.
Telephone: 001-876/929 8036; *Fax:* 001-876/929 0483.

MEXICO

Federacion Mexicana De Futbol Asociacion, A.C., Colima No. 373, Colonia Roma Mexico DF 06700.
Founded: 1927; *Number of Clubs:* 77 (senior); *Number of Players:* 1,402,270; *National Colours:* Green shirts with white collar, white shorts, red stockings.
Telephone: 0052-55/5241 0190; *Fax:* 0052-55/5241 0191.

MONSERRAT

Monserrat Football Association Inc., P.O. Box 505, Woodlands, Monserrat.
National Colours: Green shirts with black and white stripes, green shorts with white stripes, green stockings with black and white stripes.
Telephone: 001-664/491 8744; *Fax:* 001-664/491 8801.

NETHERLANDS ANTILLES

Nederlands Antiliaanse Voetbal Unie, Bonamweg 49, Curacao, NA.
Founded: 1921; *Number of Clubs:* 85; *Number of Players:* 4,500; *National Colours:* White shirts with red and blue stripes, red shorts with blue and white stripes, white stockings with red stripes.
Telephone: 00599-9736 5040; *Fax:* 00599/9736 5047.

NICARAGUA

Federacion Nicaraguense De Futbol, Hospital Pautista 1, Cuadra avajo, 1 cuada al Sur y 1/2, Cuadra Abajo, Managua 976.
Founded: 1931; *Number of Clubs:* 31; *Number of Players:* 160 (senior); *National Colours:* Blue shirts, white shorts, blue stockings.
Telephone: 00505/222 7035; *Fax:* 00505/222 7885.

PANAMA

Federacion Panamena De Futbol, Estadio Rommel Fernandez, Puerta 24, Ave. Jose Aeustin Araneo, Apartado Postal 8-391, Zona 8, Panama.
Founded: 1937; *Number of Clubs:* 65; *Number of Players:* 4,225; *National Colours:* All red.
Telephone: 00507/233 3896; *Fax:* 00507/233 0582.

PUERTO RICO

Federacion Puertorriquena De Futbol, P.O. Box 193590 San Juan 00919.
Founded: 1940; *Number of Clubs:* 175; *Number of Players:* 4,200; *National Colours:* Red, blue and white shirts and shorts, red and blue stockings.
Telephone: 001-787/759 7544; *Fax:* 001-787/759 7544.

SAINT KITTS & NEVIS

St Kitts & Nevis Football Association, P.O. Box 465, Warner Park, Basseterre, St Kitts, W.I.
Founded: 1932; *Number of Clubs:* 36; *Number of Players:* 600; *National Colours:* Green and yellow shirts, red shorts, yellow stockings.
Telephone: 001-869/466 8502; *Fax:* 001-869/465 9033.

SAINT LUCIA

St Lucia National Football Association, PO Box 255, Sans Souci, Castries, St Lucia.
Founded: 1979; *Number of Clubs:* 100; *Number of Players:* 4,000; *National Colours:* White shirts and shorts with yellow, blue and black stripes, white, blue and yellow stockings.
Telephone: 001-758/453 0687; *Fax:* 001-758/456 0510.

SAINT VINCENT & THE GRENADINES

St Vincent & The Grenadines Football Federation, Sharpe Street, PO Box 1278, Saint George.
Founded: 1979; *Number of Clubs:* 500; *Number of Players:* 5,000; *National Colours:* Green shirts with yellow border, blue shorts, yellow stockings.
Telephone: 001-784/456 1092; *Fax:* 001-784/457 2193.

SURINAM

Surinaamse Voetbal Bond, Letitia Vriesde Laan 7, P.O. Box 1223, Paramaribo.
Founded: 1920; *Number of Clubs:* 168; *Number of Players:* 4,430; *National Colours:* White, green and red shirts, green and white shirts and stockings.
Telephone: 00597/473 112; *Fax:* 00597/479 718.

TRINIDAD & TOBAGO

Trinidad & Tobago Football Federation, 24–26 Dundonald Street, PO Box 400, Port of Spain.
Founded: 1908; *Number of Clubs:* 124; *Number of Players:* 5,050; *National Colours:* Red shirts, black shorts, white stockings.
Telephone: 001-868/623 7312; *Fax:* 001-868/623 8109.

TURKS & CAICOS

Turks & Caicos Islands Football Association, P.O. Box 626, Tropicana Plaza, Leeward Highway, Providenciales.
National Colours: All white.
Telephone: 001-649/941 5532; *Fax:* 001-649/941 5554.

USA

US Soccer Federation, US Soccer House, 1801–1811 S. Prairie Avenue, Chicago, Illinois 60616.
Founded: 1913; *Number of Clubs:* 7,000; *Number of Players:* 1,411,500; *National Colours:* White shirts, blue shorts, white stockings.
Telephone: 001-312/808 1300; *Fax:* 001-312/808 1301.

OCEANIA

AMERICAN SAMOA

American Samoa Football Association, P.O. Box 282, Pago Pago AS 96799.
National Colours: Navy blue shirts, white shorts, red stockings.
Telephone: 00684/699 7380; *Fax:* 00684/699 7381.

AUSTRALIA

Soccer Australia Ltd, Level 3, East Stand, Stadium Australia, Edwin Flack Avenue, Homebush, NSW 2127.
Founded: 1961; *Number of Clubs:* 6,816; *Number of Players:* 433,957; *National Colours:* All green with gold trim.
Telephone: 0061-2/9739 5555; *Fax:* 0061-2/9739 5590.

COOK ISLANDS

Cook Islands Football Association, Victoria Road, Tupapa, P.O. Box 29, Avarua, Rarotonga, Cook Islands.
Founded: 1971; *Number of Clubs:* 9; *National Colours:* Green shirts with white sleeves, green shorts, white stockings.
Telephone: 00682/28 980; *Fax:* 00682/28 981.

FIJI

Fiji Football Association, PO Box 2514, Government Buildings, Suva.
Founded: 1938; *Number of Clubs;* 140: *Number of Players:* 21,300; *National Colours:* White shirts, blue shorts and stockings.
Telephone: 00679/330 0453; *Fax:* 00679/330 4642.

NEW ZEALAND

New Zealand Soccer Inc., PO Box 301 043, Albany, Auckland, New Zealand.
Founded: 1891; *Number of Clubs:* 312; *Number of Players:* 52,969; *National Colours:* All white.
Telephone: 0064-9/414 0175; *Fax:* 0064-9/414 0176.

PAPUA NEW GUINEA

Papua New Guinea Football Association, PO Box 957, Room II Level I, Haus Tisa, Lae.
Founded: 1962; *Number of Clubs:* 350; *Number of Players:* 8,250; *National Colours:* Red and yellow shirts, black shorts, yellow stockings.
Telephone: 00675/479 1998; *Fax:* 00675/479 1999.

SAMOA

The Samoa Football Soccer Federation, P.O. Box 960, Apia.
Founded: 1968; *National Colours:* Blue, white and red shirts, blue and white shorts, red and blue stockings.
Telephone: 00685/26 504; *Fax:* 00685/20 341.

SOLOMON ISLANDS

Solomon Islands Football Federation, PO Box 854, Honiara, Solomon Islands.
Founded: 1978; *Number of Players:* 4,000; *National Colours:* Gold and blue shirts, blue and white shorts, white and blue stockings.
Telephone: 00677/26 496; *Fax:* 00677/26 497.

TAHITI

Federation Tahitienne de Football, Rue Coppenrath Stade de Fautana, PO Box 50858 Pirae 98716.
Founded: 1989; *National Colours:* Red shirts, white shorts, red stockings.
Telephone: 00689/540 954; *Fax:* 00689/419 629.

TONGA

Tonga Football Association, Tungi Arcade, Taufa'Ahau Road, P.O. Box 852, Nuku'Alofa, Tonga.
Founded: 1965; *Number of Clubs:* 23; *Number of Players:* 350; *National Colours:* Red shirts, white shorts, red stockings.
Telephone: 00676/24 442; *Fax:* 00676/23 340.

VANUATU

Vanuatu Football Federation, P.O. Box 266, Port Vila, Vanuatu.
Founded: 1934; *National Colours:* Gold and black shirts, black shorts, gold and black stockings.
Telephone: 00678/25 236; *Fax:* 00678/25 236.

AFRICA

ALGERIA

Federation Algerienne De Foot-ball, Chemin Ahmed Ouaked, Boite Postale No. 39, Dely-Ibrahim-Alger.
Founded: 1962; *Number of Clubs:* 780; *Number of Players:* 58,567; *National Colours:* Green shirts, white shorts, green stockings.
Telephone: 00213-21/372 929; *Fax:* 00213-21/367 266.

ANGOLA

Federation Angolaise De Football, Compl. da Cidadela Desportiva, B.P. 3449, Luanda.
Founded: 1979; *Number of Clubs:* 276; *Number of Players:* 4,269; *National Colours:* Red shirts, black shorts, red stockings.
Telephone: 00244-2/264 948; *Fax:* 00244-2/260 566.

BENIN

Federation Beninoise De Football, Stade Rene Pleven d'Akpakpa, B.P. 965, Cotonou 01.
Founded: 1962; *Number of Clubs:* 117; *Number of Players:* 6,700; *National Colours:* Green shirts, Yellow shorts, red stockings.
Telephone: 00229/330 537; *Fax:* 00229/330 537

BOTSWANA

Botswana Football Association, P.O. Box 1396, Gabarone.
Founded: 1970; *National Colours:* Blue, white and black striped shirts, blue, white and black shorts and stockings.
Telephone: 00267/390 0279; *Fax:* 00267/ 390 0280.

BURKINA FASO

Federation Burkinabe De Foot-Ball, 01 B.P. 57, Ouagadougou 01.
Founded: 1960; *Number of Clubs:* 57; *Number of Players:* 4,672; *National Colours:* All green, red and white.
Telephone: 00226/318 815; *Fax:* 00226/318 843.

BURUNDI

Federation De Football Du Burundi, Bulding Nyogozi, Boulevard de l'Uprona, B.P. 3426, Bujumbura.
Founded: 1948; *Number of Clubs:* 132; *Number of Players:* 3,930; *National Colours:* Red and white shirts, white and red shorts, green stockings.
Telephone : 00257/921 105; *Fax:* 00257/242 892.

CAMEROON

Federation Camerounaise De Football, B.P. 1116, Yaounde.
Founded: 1959; *Number of Clubs:* 200; *Number of Players:* 9,328; *National Colours:* Green shirts, red shorts, yellow stockings.
Telephone: 00237/221 0012; *Fax:* 00237/221 6662.

CAPE VERDE ISLANDS

Federacao Cabo-Verdiana De Futebol, Praia Cabo Verde, FCF CX, P.O. Box 234, Praia.
Founded: 1982; *National Colours:* Blue and white shirts and shorts, blue and red stockings.
Telephone : 00238/611 362; *Fax:* 00238/611 362.

CENTRAL AFRICAN REPUBLIC

Federation Centrafricaine De Football, Immeuble Soca Constructa, B.P. 344, Bangui.
Founded: 1937; *Number of Clubs:* 256; *Number of Players:* 7,200; *National Colours:* Blue and white shirts, white shorts, blue stockings.
Telephone: 00236/619 545; *Fax:* 00236/615 660.

CHAD

Federation Tchadienne de Football, B.P. 886, N'Djamena.
Founded: 1962; *National Colours:* Blue shirts, yellow shorts, red stockings.
Telephone: 00235/515 982; *Fax:* 00235/525 538.

CONGO

Federation Congolaise De Football, 80 Rue Eugene-Etienne, Centre Ville, PO Box 11, Brazzaville.
Founded: 1962; *Number of Clubs:* 250; *Number of Players:* 5,940; *National Colours:* Green shirts, yellow shorts, red stockings.
Telephone: 00242/811 563; *Fax:* 00242/812 524.

CONGO DR

Federation Congolaise De Football-Association, Av. de l'Enseignemt 210, C/Kasa-Vubu, Kinshasa 1.
Founded: 1919; *Number of Clubs:* 3,800; *Number of Players:* 64,627; *National Colours:* Blue and yellow shirts, yellow and blue shorts, white and blue stockings.
Telephone: 00243/993 9635; *Fax:* 00243/139 8426.

DJIBOUTI

Federation Djiboutienne de Football, Stade el Haoj Hassan Gouled, B.P. 2694, Djibouti.
Founded: 1977; *Number of Players:* 2,000; *National Colours:* Green shirts, white shorts, blue stockings.
Telephone: 00253/341 964; *Fax:* 00253/341 963.

EGYPT

Egyptian Football Association, 5 Gabalaya Street, Guezira, El Borg Post Office, Cairo.
Founded: 1921; *Number of Clubs:* 247; *Number of Players:* 19,735; *National Colours:* Red shirts, white shorts, black stockings.
Telephone: 0020-2/735 1793; *Fax:* 0020-2/736 7817.

ERITREA

The Eritrean National Football Federation, Sematat Avenue 29–31, P.O. Box 3665, Asmara.
National Colours: Blue shirts, red shorts, green stockings.
Telephone: 00291-1/120 335; *Fax:* 00291-1/126 821.

ETHIOPIA

Ethiopia Football Federation, Addis Ababa Stadium, P.O. Box 1080, Addis Ababa.
Founded: 1943; *Number of Clubs:* 767; *Number of Players:* 20,594; *National Colours:* Green shirts, yellow shorts, red stockings.
Telephone: 00251-1/514 453; *Fax:* 00251-1/515 899.

GABON

Federation Gabonaise De Football, B.P. 181, Libreville.
Founded: 1962; *Number of Clubs:* 320; *Number of Players:* 10,000; *National Colours:* Green, yellow and blue shirts, blue and yellow shorts, white stockings with tri-colour trims.
Telephone: 00241/730 460; *Fax:* 00241/730 460.

GAMBIA

Gambia Football Association, Independence Stadium, Bakau, P.O. Box 523, Banjul.
Founded: 1952; *Number of Clubs:* 30; *Number of Players:* 860; *National Colours:* All red, blue and white.
Telephone: 00220/494 509; *Fax:* 00220/494 509.

GHANA

Ghana Football Association, National Sports Council, P.O. Box 1272, Accra.
Founded: 1957; *Number of Clubs:* 347; *Number of Players:* 11,275; *National Colours:* All yellow.
Telephone: 00233-21/671 501; *Fax:* 00233-21/668 590.

GUINEA

Federation Guineenne De Football, P.O. Box 3645, Conakry.
Founded: 1959; *Number of Clubs:* 351; *Number of Players:* 10,000; *National Colours:* Red shirts, yellow shorts, green stockings.
Telephone: 00224/455 878; *Fax:* 00224/455 879.

GUINEA-BISSAU

Federacao De Football Da Guinea-Bissau, Alto Bandim (Nova Sede), PO Box 375 Bissau 1035.
Founded: 1974; *National Colours:* Red, green and yellow shirts, green and yellow shorts, red, green and yellow stockings.
Telephone: 00245/201 918; *Fax:* 00245/211 414.

GUINEA, EQUATORIAL

Federacion Ecuatoguineana De Futbol, c/P Patricio Lumumba (Estadio La Paz), Malabo 1071.
Founded: 1986; *National Colours:* All red.
Telephone: 00240-9/74 049; *Fax:* 00240-9/2257.

IVORY COAST

Federation Ivoirienne De Football, 01 PO Box 1202, Abidjan 01.
Founded: 1960; *Number of Clubs:* 84 (senior); *Number of Players:* 3,655; *National Colours:* Orange shirts, black shorts, green stockings.
Telephone: 00225/2124 0027; *Fax:* 00225/2125 9352.

KENYA

Kenya Football Federation, Nyayo National Stadium, P.O. Box 40234, Nairobi.
Founded: 1960; *Number of Clubs:* 351; *Number of Players:* 8,880; *National Colours:* All red.
Telephone: 00254-2/608 422; *Fax:* 00254-2/249 855.

LESOTHO

Lesotho Football Association, P.O. Box 1879, Maseru-100, Lesotho.
Founded: 1932; *Number of Clubs:* 88; *Number of Players:* 2,076; *National Colours:* Blue shirts, green shorts, white stockings.
Telephone: 00266/2231 1879; *Fax:* 00266/2231 0586.

LIBERIA

Liberia Football Association, Broad and Center Streets, PO Box 10-1066, Monrovia 1000.
Founded: 1936; *National Colours:* Blue shirts, white shorts, red stockings.
Telephone: 00231/226 385; *Fax:* 00231/226 092.

LIBYA

Libyan Football Federation, Asayadi Street, Near Janat Al-Areet, P.O. Box 5137, Tripoli.
Founded: 1963; *Number of Clubs:* 89; *Number of Players:* 2,941; *National Colours:* Green and black shirts, black shorts and stockings.
Telephone: 00218-21/334 3600; *Fax:* 00218-21/444 1274.

MADAGASCAR

Federation Malagasy de Football, Immeuble Preservatrice Vie-Lot IBF-9B, Rue Rabearivelo-Antsahavola, PO Box 4409, Antananarivo 101.
Founded: 1961; *Number of Clubs:* 775; *Number of Players:* 23,536; *National Colours:* Red and green shirts, white and green shorts, green and white stockings.
Telephone: 00261-20/226 8374; *Fax:* 00261-20/226 8373.

MALAWI

Football Association of Malawi, Mpira House, Old Chileka Road, P.O. Box 865, Blantyre.
Founded: 1966; *Number of Clubs:* 465; *Number of Players:* 12,500; *National Colours:* Red shirts, white shorts, red and black stockings.
Telephone: 00265-1/623 197; *Fax:* 00265-1/623 204.

MALI

Federation Malienne De Football, Avenue du Mali, Hamdallaye ACI 2000, PO Box 1020, Bamako 12582.
Founded: 1960; *Number of Clubs:* 128; *Number of Players:* 5,480; *National Colours:* Green shirts, yellow shorts, red stockings.
Telephone: 00223/223 8844; *Fax:* 00223/222 4254.

MAURITANIA

Federation De Foot-Ball De La Rep. Islamique. De Mauritanie, B.P. 566, Nouakchott.
Founded: 1961; *Number of Clubs:* 59; *Number of Players:* 1,930; *National Colours:* Green and yellow shirts, yellow shorts, green stockings.
Telephone: 00222-5/241 860; *Fax:* 00222-5/241 861.

MAURITIUS

Mauritius Football Association, Chancery House, 2nd Floor Nos. 303–305, 14 Lislet Geoffroy Street, Port Louis.
Founded: 1952; *Number of Clubs:* 397; *Number of Players:* 29,375; *National Colours:* All red.
Telephone: 00230/212 1418; *Fax:* 00230/208 4100.

MOROCCO

Federation Royale Marocaine De Football, 51 Bis Av. Ibn Sina, PO Box 51, Agdal, Rabat 10 000.
Founded: 1955; *Number of Clubs:* 350; *Number of Players:* 19,768; *National Colours:* All green white and red.
Telephone: 00212-37/672 706; *Fax:* 00212-37/671 070.

MOZAMBIQUE

Federacao Mocambicana De Futebol, Av. Samora Machel 11-2, Caixa Postal 1467, Maputo.
Founded: 1978; *Number of Clubs:* 144; *National Colours:* Red shirts, black shorts, red and black stockings.
Telephone: 00258-1/300 366; *Fax:* 00258-1/300 367.

NAMIBIA

Namibia Football Association, Abraham Mashego Street 8521, Katurua Council of Churches in Namibia, P.O. Box 1345, Windhoek 9000, Namibia.
Founded: 1990; *Number of Clubs:* 244; *Number of Players:* 7320; *National Colours:* All red.
Telephone: 00264-61/265 691; Fax: 00264-61/265 693.

NIGER

Federation Nigerienne De Football, Rue de la Tapoa, PO Box 10299, Niamey.
Founded: 1967; *Number of Clubs:* 64; *Number of Players:* 1,525; *National Colours:* Orange shirts, white shorts, green stockings.
Telephone: 00227/725 127; *Fax:* 00227/725 127.

NIGERIA

Nigeria Football Association, Plot 2033, Olusegun, Obasanjo Way, Zone 7, Wuse Abuja, PO Box 5101 Garki, Abuja, Nigeria.
Founded: 1945; *Number of Clubs:* 326; *Number of Players:* 80,190; *National Colours:* All green and white.
Telephone: 00234-9/523 7326; *Fax:* 00234-9/523 7327.

RWANDA

Federation Rwandaise De Football Amateur, B.P. 2000, Kigali.
Founded: 1972; *Number of Clubs:* 167; *National Colours:* Red, green and yellow shirts, green shorts, red stockings.
Telephone: 00250/571 596; *Fax:* 00250/571 597.

SENEGAL

Federation Senegalaise De Football, Stade Leopold Sedar Senghor, Route De L'Aeroport De Yoff, B.P. 130 21, Dakar.
Founded: 1960; *Number of Clubs:* 75 (senior); *Number of Players:* 3,977; *National Colours:* All white and green.
Telephone: 00221/827 2935; *Fax:* 00221/827 3524.

SEYCHELLES

Seychelles Football Federation, P.O. Box 843, People's Stadium, Victoria-Mahe, Seychelles.
Founded: 1979; *National Colours:* Red and green shirts and shorts, red stockings.
Telephone: 00248/324 632; *Fax:* 00248/225 468.

ST THOMAS AND PRINCIPE

Federation Santomense De Futebol, Rua Ex-Joao de Deus No. QXXIII-426/26, PO Box 440, Sao Tome.
Founded: 1975; *National Colours:* Green and red shirts, yellow shorts, green stockings.
Telephone: 00239-2/22 4231; *Fax:* 00239-2/21 333.

SIERRA LEONE

Sierra Leone Football Association, 21 Battery Street, Kingtorn, P.O. Box 672, National Stadium, Brookfields, Freetown.
Founded: 1967; *Number of Clubs:* 104; *Number of Players:* 8,120; *National Colours:* Green and blue shirts, green, blue and white shorts and stockings.
Telephone: 00232-22/241 872; *Fax:* 00232-22/227 771.

SOMALIA

Somali Football Federation, PO Box 222, Mogadishu BN 03040.
Founded: 1951; *Number of Clubs:* 46 (senior); *Number of Players:* 1,150; *National Colours:* Sky blue and white shirts and shorts, white and sky blue stockings.
Telephone: 00252-1/229 843; *Fax:* 00252-1/215 513.

SOUTH AFRICA

South African Football Association, First National Bank Stadium, PO Box 910, Johannesburg 2000, South Africa.
Founded: 1991; *Number of Teams:* 51,944; *Number of Players:* 1,039,880; *National Colours:* White shirts with yellow striped sleeves, white shorts with yellow stripes, white stockings.
Telephone: 0027-11/494 3522; *Fax*: 0027-11/494 3013.

SUDAN

Sudan Football Association, Bladia Street, Khartoum.
Founded: 1936; *Number of Clubs:* 750; *Number of Players:* 42,200; *National Colours:* Red shirts, white shorts, black stockings.
Telephone: 00249-11/773 495; *Fax:* 00249-11/776 633.

SWAZILAND

National Football Association of Swaziland, Sigwaca House, Plot 582, Sheffield Road, PO Box 641, Mbabane H100.
Founded: 1968; *Number of Clubs:* 136; *National Colours:* Blue shirts, gold shorts, red stockings.
Telephone: 00268/404 6852; *Fax:* 00268/404 6206.

TANZANIA

Football Association of Tanzania, Uhuru/Shaurimoyo Road, Karume Memorial Stadium, P.O. Box 1574, Ilala/Dar Es Salaam.
Founded: 1930; *Number of Clubs:* 51; *National Colours:* Green, yellow and blue shirts, black shorts, green stockings with horizontal stripe.
Telephone: 00255-22/286 1815; *Fax:* 00255-22/286 1815.

TOGO

Federation Togolaise De Football, C.P. 5, Lome.
Founded: 1960; *Number of Clubs:* 144; *Number of Players:* 4,346; *National Colours:* White shirts, green shorts, red stockings with yellow and green stripes.
Telephone: 00228/221 2698; *Fax:* 00228/222 1413.

TUNISIA

Federation Tunisienne De Football, Maison des Federations Sportives, Cite Olympique, Tunis 1003.
Founded: 1956; *Number of Clubs:* 215; *Number of Players:* 18,300; *National Colours:* Red shirts, white shorts, red stockings.
Telephone: 00216-71/233 303; *Fax:* 00216-71/767 929.

UGANDA

Federation of Uganda Football Associations, Plot No. 879, Kyadondo Block 8, Mengo Wakaliga Road, P.O. Box 22518, Kampala.
Founded: 1924; *Number of Clubs:* 400; *Number of Players:* 1,518; *National Colours:* All yellow, red and white.
Telephone: 00256-41/272 702; *Fax:* 00256-41/272 702.

ZAMBIA

Football Association of Zambia, Football House, Alick Nkhata Road, P.O. Box 34751, Lusaka.
Founded: 1929; *Number of Clubs:* 20 (senior); *Number of Players:* 4,100; *National Colours:* White and green shirts, green and white shorts, white and green stockings.
Telephone: 00260-1/250 946; *Fax:* 00260-1/250 946.

ZIMBABWE

Zimbabwe Football Association, P.O. Box CY 114, Causeway, Harare.
Founded: 1965; *National Colours:* All green and gold.
Telephone: 00263-4/721 026; *Fax:* 00263-4/721 045.

THE WORLD CUP 2006

QUALIFYING RESULTS – EUROPE

▪ *Denotes player sent off.*

GROUP 1

Skopje, 18 August 2004, 10,000

Macedonia (2) 3 *(Pandev 5, Sakiri 38, Sumolikoski 90)*

Armenia (0) 0

Macedonia: Milosevski; Stavrevski, Krstev M, Mitreski I, Mitreski A, Trajanov V (Vasoski 67), Sumulikoski, Pandev, Sakiri (Toleski G 85), Dimitrovski, Sedloski.
Armenia: Ambartsumian; Melikian, Hovsepian, Vardanian▪, Dokhoyan, Khachatrian (Aleksanian K 46), Petrossian, Nazarian, Sargsian A, Art Karamian, Movsesian.
Referee: Genov (Bulgaria).

Bucharest, 18 August 2004, 15,000

Romania (0) 2 *(Mutu 50, Petre 89)*

Finland (0) 1 *(Eremenko Jr 90 (pen))*

Romania: Lobont; Stoican (Iencsi 84), Rat, Barcauan▪, Ghioane, Radoi, Dica (Soava 75), Petre, Caramarin (Cernat 46), Mutu, Danciulescu.
Finland: Niemi; Pasanen (Koppinen 60), Saarinen, Hyypia, Vayrynen▪, Nurmela (Kopteff 84), Litmanen (Eremenko Jr 57), Kolkka, Quivasto, Riihilahti, Johansson.
Referee: Gilewski (Poland).

Tampere, 4 September 2004, 7437

Finland (1) 3 *(Eremenko Jr 41, 63, Riihilahti 57)*

Andorra (0) 0

Finland: Niemi; Pasanen, Hyypia, Nurmela, Litmanen (Johansson 70), Kolkka (Heikkinen 81), Quivasto, Pohja (Kopteff 58), Riihilahti, Forssell, Eremenko Jr.
Andorra: Koldo; Ayala, Txema, Juli, Lima A, Sonejee, Pujol, Juli Sanchez (Silva 74), Sivera, Moreno, Ruiz (Jimenez 70).
Referee: Siric (Croatia).

Craiova, 4 September 2004, 26,000

Romania (1) 2 *(Pancu 15, Mutu 87)*

Macedonia (0) 1 *(Vasovski 75)*

Romania: Lobont; Stoican, Rat, Iencsi, Moldovan, Soava, Dica (Neaga 80), Petre, Pancu (Marica 62), Mutu, Danciulescu (Cernat 46).
Macedonia: Milosevski; Jancevski (Trajanov V 88), Krstev M (Bozinovski 46), Stojanovski, Mitreski I, Mitreski A, Vasoski, Sumulikoski▪, Popov, Sakiri (Toleski G 83), Pandev.
Referee: Plautz (Austria).

La Valle, 8 September 2004, 900

Andorra (1) 1 *(Pujol 30 (pen))*

Romania (3) 5 *(Cernat 2, Pancu 5, 85, Niculae 16, 72)*

Andorra: Koldo; Txema, Lima I▪, Fernandez (Sonejee 73), Lima A, Sivera, Ruiz, Bernaus, Juli Sanchez (Jimenez 13), Ayala, Pujol.
Romania: Lobont; Cernat, Pancu, Niculae (Dica 85), Barcauan, Rat, Stoican, Iencsi, Soava, Caramarin (Paraschiv 75), Neaga (Marica 60).
Referee: Kircher (Germany).

Erevan, 8 September 2004, 10,000

Armenia (0) 0

Finland (1) 2 *(Forssell 24, Eremenko Jr 67)*

Armenia: Ambartsumian; Melikian, Dokhoyan, Hovsepian, Mkrtchian, Khachatrian, Art Petrossian, Nazarian (Aleksanian K 73), Sarkissian (Manucharian 54), Arman Karamian (Gregorian 79), Movsesian.
Finland: Niemi; Nurmela, Quivasto, Hyypia, Pasanen, Riihilahti, Litmanen (Lagerblom 46), Eremenko Jr (Kopteff 73), Vayrynen, Kolkka (Pohja 85), Forssell.
Referee: Malzinskas (Lithuania).

Amsterdam, 8 September 2004, 48,000

Holland (1) 2 *(Van Hooijdonk 33, 84)*

Czech Republic (0) 0

Holland: Van der Sar; De Jong, Heitinga, Ooijer, Sneijder, Van der Vaart (Boulahrouz 64), Van Bommel, Davids, Castelen (Makaay 74), Van Hooijdonk (Van Bronckhorst 86), Kuijt.
Czech Republic: Cech; Ujfalusi, Bolf, Jiranek (Grygera 58), Jankulovski, Rosicky, Hubschman (Vachousek 62), Tyce (Lokvenc 76), Heinz, Baros, Koller.
Referee: Merk (Germany).

Prague, 9 October 2004, 16,028

Czech Republic (1) 1 *(Koller 36 (pen))*

Romania (0) 0

Czech Republic: Cech; Ujfalusi, Jankulovski, Galasek, Bolf, Jiranek, Rosicky (Kovak 90), Vachousek, Baros (Jarosik 84), Koller, Heinz (Sionko 69).
Romania: Lobont; Stoican, Rat, Petre (Sernat 58), Iencsi, Barcauan (Moldovan 46), Soava, Codrea, Marica, Mutu, Pancu (Dica 75).
Referee: Rosetti (Italy).

Tampere, 9 October 2004, 16,000

Finland (2) 3 *(Kuqi 8, 87, Eremenko Jr 28)*

Armenia (1) 1 *(Shakhgeldian 32)*

Finland: Niemi; Nurmela, Pasanen, Saarinen (Kallio 68), Kuivasto (Tainio 46), Hyypia, Riihilahti, Eremenko Jr, Kolkka (Johansson 83), Kuqi, Vayrynen.
Armenia: Ambartsumian; Dokhoyan, Hovsepian, Vardanian, Khachatrian (Aleksanian K 37), Nazarian, Mkhitarian, Shakhgeldian, Movsesian, Gregorian (Manucharian 61), Tadevosian.
Referee: Fandel (Germany).

Skopje, 9 October 2004, 20,000

Macedonia (1) 2 *(Pandev 45, Stoikov 70)*

Holland (1) 2 *(Bouma 43, Kuijt 65)*

Macedonia: Nikoloski; Bozinovski, Sedloski, Mitreski I, Vasoski, Krstev M, Mitreski A, Jancevski (Trajanov V 71), Sakiri, Pandev (Grozdanovski 87), Stoikov (Bajevski 75).
Holland: Van der Sar; Boulahrouz, De Jong, Cocu (Van der Vaart 60), Bouma (Landzaat 81), Van Bommel, Sneijder, Davids, Van Hooijdonk (Makaay 60), Kuijt, Castelen.
Referee: Frojdpeldt (Sweden).

La Valle, 13 October 2004, 200

Andorra (0) 1 *(Bernaus 60)*

Macedonia (0) 0

Andorra: Koldo; Escura, Lima A, Fernandez, Txema, Sonejee, Pujol (Garcia 78), Silva (Sanchez 85), Bernaus, Ruiz (Jonas 90), Sivera.
Macedonia: Nikoloski; Mitreski I, Mitreski A (Bozinovski 78), Stavrevski, Trajanov V (Bajevski 46), Jancevski, Grozdanovski, Stojanovski, Sakiri, Pandev, Stoikov.
Referee: Podeschi (San Marino).

Erevan, 13 October 2004, 8000

Armenia (0) 0

Czech Republic (2) 3 *(Koller 3, 78, Rosicky 30)*

Armenia: Bete; Dokhoyan (Mkrtchian 46), Hovsepian, Vardanian, Melikian, Nazarian, Mkhitarian, Shahgeldian (Movsesian 83), Aleksanian K (Sarkissian 73), Petrossian, Manucharian.
Czech Republic: Cech; Grygera, Bolf, Ujfalusi, Jankulovski, Galasek (Kovac 60), Sionko, Rosicky, Vachousek, Koller (Lokvenc 82), Heinz.
Referee: Granat (Poland).

Amsterdam, 13 October 2004, 49,000

Holland (2) 3 *(Sneijder 39, Van Nistelrooy 41, 63)*

Finland (1) 1 *(Tainio 14)*

Holland: Van der Sar; De Jong, Landzaat, Van der Vaart (Van Bronkhorst 72), Heitinga, Cocu, Sneijder (Van Bommel 83), Castelen (Makaay 77), Van Nistelrooy, Kuijt, Davids.
Finland: Niemi; Pasanen, Nurmela, Riihilahti (Johansson 60), Quivasto, Hyypia, Vayrynen (Pohja 85), Tainio, Kolkka, Kuqi, Eremenko Jr (Saarinen 72).
Referee: Bennett (England).

Barcelona, 17 November 2004, 2000

Andorra (0) 0

Holland (2) 3 *(Cocu 21, Robben 31, Sneijder 78)*

Andorra: Koldo; Escura, Fernandez, Lima A, Lima I, Sivera (Garcia 86), Txema, Jimenez (Ayala 78), Ruiz, Sonejee, Silva (Juli Sanchez 71).
Holland: Van der Sar; Ooijer, Van Bronckhorst, Cocu (Mathijsen 82), Melchiot, Sneijder, Van Galen (Van Hooijdonk 67), Landzaat, Kuijt, Van Nistelrooy (Makaay 35), Robben.
Referee: Yefet (Israel).

Erevan, 17 November 2004, 2500

Armenia (0) 1 *(Dokhoyan 62)*

Romania (1) 1 *(Marica 29)*

Armenia: Bete; Dokhoyan, Tadevosian, Hovsepian, Vardanian, Nazarian, Shahgeldian (Aleksanian K 87), Mikitarian, Gregorian (Mkrtchian A 73), Manucharian, Voskanian (Arman Karamian 74).
Romania: Lobont; Stoican, Barcauan, Moldovan, Dancia, Paraschiv (Bratu 74), Caramarian (Dica 46), Tararache, Cernat, Marica, Neaga.
Referee: De Bleeckere (Belgium).

Skopje, 17 November 2004, 12,000

Macedonia (0) 0

Czech Republic (0) 2 *(Lokvenc 88, Koller 90)*

Macedonia: Milosevski; Noveski, Sedloski, Mitreski I, Mitreski A, Krstev M (Jancevski 46), Pandev, Sakiri (Ignatov 77), Cadikovski (Stoikov 64), Bozinovski, Vasoski.
Czech Republic: Cech; Grygera (Lokvenc 77), Galasek, Bolf, Jankulovski, Poborsky, Koller, Rosicky, Vachousek (Jun 59), Baros (Heinz 17), Ujfalusi.
Referee: Meier (Switzerland).

Skopje, 9 February 2005, 1000

Macedonia (0) 0

Andorra (0) 0

Macedonia: Milosevski; Sedloski, Novevski, Mitreski A, Vasoski (Stavrevski 46), Krstev, Stoikov (Rajevski 68), Bozinovski (Popov G 75), Pandev, Sakiri, Cadikovski.
Andorra: Koldo; Txema, Escura, Lima A, Lima I, Pujol (Jonas 90), Sonejee, Silva (Juli Sanchez 62), Ruiz (Garcia 85), Sivera, Bernaus.
Referee: Verlist (Belgium).

Erevan, 26 March 2005, 9566

Armenia (1) 2 *(Hakobian 32, Khachatrian 73)*

Andorra (0) 1 *(Silva 57)*

Armenia: Berezovski; Aleksanian K, Arzumanian, Dokhoyan, Melikian, Khachatrian, Hakobian (Voskanian 90), Art Karamian (Mkrtchian 72), Nazarian (Jenebian 73), Shahgeldian, Michitarian.
Andorra: Koldo; Ayala, Escura, Fernandez, Txema, Sonejee, Pujol, Sivera (Juli Sanchez 89), Silva (Javi Sanchez 90), Jimenez (Genis Garcia 79), Ruiz.
Referee: Attard (Malta).

Teplice, 26 March 2005, 16,200

Czech Republic (2) 4 *(Baros 8, Rosicky 34, Polak 58, Lokvenc 87)*

Finland (0) 3 *(Litmanen 46, Riihilahti 73, Johansson 79)*

Czech Republic: Cech; Jirasek, Bolf, Ujfalusi, Jankulovski, Poborsky, Rosicky, Polak (Jun 82), Sionko (Jarosik 72), Lokvenc, Baros (Plasil 53).
Finland: Jaaskelainen; Pasanen, Kopteff, Nurmela, Tihinen, Hyypia, Litmanen (Johansson 78), Riihilahti, Kolkka (Eremenko Jr 60), Ilola, Kuqi.
Referee: Bo Larsen (Denmark).

Bucharest, 26 March 2005, 19,000

Romania (0) 0

Holland (1) 2 *(Cocu 1, Babel 85)*

Romania: Lobont; Ogararu, Radoi, Chiu, Marin, Petre, Ghioane (Plesan 46), Pancu, Munteanu, Moldovan (Cristea 69), Ilie (Bucur 86).
Holland: Van der Sar; Kromkamp, Boulahrouz, Mathijsen, Van Bronckhorst, Van Bommel (Maduro 73), Landzaat, Cocu, Kuijt (Kastelen 90), Van Nistelrooy, Robben (Babel 24).
Referee: Cantalejo (Spain).

La Valle, 30 March 2005, 1000

Andorra (0) 0

Czech Republic (2) 4 *(Jankulovski 31 (pen), Baros 40, Lokvenc 53, Rosicky 90 (pen))*

Andorra: Koldo; Escura, Txema (Ayala 59), Lima I, Sonejee, Pujol, Sivera, Silva (Juli Sanchez 65), Bernaus, Lima A, Ruiz (Fernandez 67).
Czech Republic: Cech; Jiranek (Plasil 75), Rozehnal, Ujfalusi, Jankulovski, Poborsky, Tyce (Polak 46), Rosicky, Vachousek, Lokvenc, Baros (Jun 60).
Referee: Messner (Austria).

Eindhoven, 30 March 2005, 34,000

Holland (2) 2 *(Castelen 3, Van Nistelrooy 34)*

Armenia (0) 0

Holland: Van der Sar; Kromkamp, Van Bronckhorst, Mathijsen, Bouma, Van Bommel, Landzaat (Van der Vaart 50), Cocu, Castelen (Babel 50), Van Nistelrooy, Kujit (Vennegoor of Hesselink 80).
Armenia: Berezovski; Hovsepian, Dokhoyan, Arzumanian (Tadevosian 85), Melikan, Mkhitarian, Shahgeldian, Khachatrian, Gregorian (Art Karamian 60), Voskanian, Hakobian (Nazarian 46).
Referee: Trefoloni (Italy).

Skopje, 30 March 2005, 12,000

Macedonia (1) 1 *(Maznov 31)*

Romania (1) 2 *(Mitea 18, 58)*

Macedonia: Milosevski; Popov R, Petrov (Bozinovski 46), Sedloski, Vasoski, Grozdanovski, Mitreski A, Krstev M, Sumulikoski (Ignatov 72), Jancevski (Bajevski 81), Maznov.
Romania: Lobont; Contra, Radoi, Chivu (Ghionea 46), Rat, Petre, Dica, Pancu, Munteanu, Moldovan (Cristea 78), Mitea (Ghioane 70).
Referee: Ovrebo (Norway).

Erevan, 4 June 2005, 8000

Armenia (0) 1 *(Manucharyan 55)*

Macedonia (1) 2 *(Pandev 29 (pen), 46)*

Armenia: Berezovski; Hovsepian, Dokhoyan, Tadevosian, Khachatrian, Sarkissian, Mkrtchian, Mkhitarian (Manucharyan 52), Aleksanian K (Dzenebian 78), Voskanian (Hakobian 67), Shahgeldian.
Macedonia: Madzovski; Petrov, Popov G (Krstev M 57), Sedloski, Vasoski, Grozdanovski, Mitreski A, Sumulikoski (Kralevski 83), Lazarevski, Pandev, Maznov (Ismaili 66).
Referee: Mikulski (Poland).

Liberec, 4 June 2005, 9520

Czech Republic (3) 8 *(Lokvenc 13, 90, Koller 29, Smicer 38, Galasek 52 (pen), Baros 80, Rosicky 85 (pen), Polak 87)*

Andorra (1) 1 *(Riera 35)*

Czech Republic: Cech; Ujfalusi, Grygera, Rozehnal (Polak 46), Galasek, Poborsky, Rosicky, Smicer (Plasil 46), Lokvenc, Koller (Jun 64), Baros.
Andorra: Koldo; Txema, Fernandez, Sonejee, Lima A, Escura, Ayala, Ruiz■, Jimenez (Moreno 88), Riera (Andorra 70), Sivera (Garcia 80).
Referee: Selcuk (Turkey).

Rotterdam, 4 June 2005, 50,000

Holland (1) 2 *(Robben 26, Kuijt 46)*

Romania (0) 0

Holland: Van der Sar; Lucius, Heitinga, Opdam, Van Bronkhorst, Landzaat, Van Bommel (De Jong 49), Van der Vaart (Maduro 80), Kuijt, Van Nistelrooy (Van Persie 62), Robben.
Romania: Lobont; Contra, Tamas, Chivu, Stoica, Petre, Munteanu, Mitea (Niculae 65), Mutu (Coman 83), Niculesci, Pancu.
Referee: De Santis (Italy).

Teplice, 8 June 2005, 14,150

Czech Republic (2) 6 *(Koller 42, 45, 49, 53, Rosicky 74 (pen), Baros 88)*

Macedonia (1) 1 *(Pandev 14)*

Czech Republic: Cech; Grygera, Hubschman, Ujfalusi, Poborsky (Zelenka 78), Galasek, Rosicky, Smicer (Plasil 61), Baros, Koller, Lokvenc (Polak 46).
Macedonia: Madzovski; Lazarevski, Petrov, Popov G, Sedloski, Vasoski, Krstev M (Banduliev 74), Mitreski A, Sumulikoski (Kralevski 70), Maznov, Pandev (Grozdanovski 67).
Referee: Ibanez (Spain).

Helsinki, 8 June 2005, 37,000

Finland (0) 0

Holland (2) 4 *(Van Nistelrooy 36, Kuijt 77, Cocu 84, Van Persie 87)*

Finland: Jaaskelainen; Nurmela, Tihinen, Hyypia, Saarinen, Tainio (Forssell 74), Riihilahti, Vayrynen, Litmanen (Johansson 29), Eremenko Jr (Kopteff 81), Kuqi.
Holland: Van der Sar; Lucius (Melchiot 27), Heitinga, Opdam, Van Bronckhorst, De Jong (Maduro 67), Landzaat, Cocu, Kuijt, Van Nistelrooy (Van Persie 74), Robben.
Referee: Hamer (Luxembourg).

Constanta, 8 June 2005, 15,000

Romania (2) 3 *(Petre 29, Bucur 40, 80)*

Armenia (0) 0

Romania: Lobont; Contra (Stoican 68), Tamas, Chivu, Rat, Petre, Piesan, Munteanu (Mazilu 87), Coman (Mitea 79), Niculae, Bucur.
Armenia: Berezovski; Melikian, Dokhoyan, Hovsepian, Khachatrian, Mkhitarian (Grigorian 82), Hakobian, Voskanian (Arzumanian 46), Tadevosian, Manucharian (Arman Karamian 50), Shahgeldian.
Referee: Briakos (Greece).

Group 1 Table

	P	*W*	*D*	*L*	*F*	*A*	*Pts*
Holland	8	7	1	0	20	3	22
Czech Republic	8	7	0	1	28	7	21
Romania	9	5	1	3	15	10	16
Finland	7	3	0	4	13	14	9
Macedonia	9	2	2	5	10	16	8
Armenia	9	1	1	7	5	20	4
Andorra	8	1	1	6	4	25	4

GROUP 2

Tirana, 4 September 2004, 19,000

Albania (2) 2 *(Murati 2, Aliaj 11)*

Greece (1) 1 *(Giannakopoulos 38)*

Albania: Strakosha; Beqiri E, Hasi, Aliaj, Cana, Lala, Skela, Duro (Beqiri A 86), Murati, Myrtaj (Dragusha 76), Tare.
Greece: Nikopolidis; Seitaridis, Fyssas (Tsartas 32), Dabizas (Giannakopoulos 27), Kapsis, Basinas, Zagorakis, Katsouranis, Charisteas, Karagounis, Vryzas (Papadopoulos 66).
Referee: Gonzalez (Spain).

Copenhagen, 4 September 2004, 36,335

Denmark (1) 1 *(Jorgensen 9)*

Ukraine (0) 1 *(Gusin 56)*

Denmark: Sorensen; Bogelund (Priske 43), Poulsen (Jensen C 65), Kroldrup, Jensen N, Helveg, Gravesen, Gronkjaer, Tomasson, Jorgensen, Madsen (Pedersen 79).
Ukraine: Shovkovskyi; Nesmachni, Rusol, Tymoschuk, Yezerski, Shelayev, Shevchenko, Gusin (Matykhin 67), Gusev (Zakarliuka 75), Starostiak, Vorobei (Radchenko 83).
Referee: Meier (Switzerland).

Trabzon, 4 September 2004, 15,000

Turkey (0) 1 *(Fatih 49)*

Georgia (0) 1 *(Astiani M 85)*

Turkey: Rustu; Serkan, Umit O, Deniz, Ibrahim, Okan B, Emre B, Tuncay (Huseyin 72), Hasan Sas■, Hakan Sukur (Nihat 79), Fatih (Gokdeniz 72).
Georgia: Devadze; Mzhavanadze, Khizanishvili, Khizaneishvili, Kaladze, Tskitshvili, Kvirkevlia, Rekhviashvili (Asatiani M 80), Jamarauli, Arveladze S, Demetradze (Jakobia 75).
Referee: Medina (Spain).

Tbilisi, 8 September 2004, 22,000

Georgia (1) 2 *(Iashvili 15, Demetradze 90)*

Albania (0) 0

Georgia: Devadze; Mzhavanadze, Kaladze, Khizanieshvili, Salukvadze, Tskitishvili, Jamarauli (Kvirkvelia 78), Asatiani M (Kankava 60), Kobiashvili, Iashvili, Arveladze S (Demetradze 89).
Albania: Strakosha; Beqiri A■, Cana, Aliaj, Hasi, Duro (Dragusha 59), Lala, Skela, Murati (Shkembi 81), Tare, Myrtaj (Bushi 63).
Referee: Courtney (Northern Ireland).

Piraeus, 8 September 2004, 33,000

Greece (0) 0

Turkey (0) 0

Greece: Nikopolidis; Seitaridis, Katsouranis, Kapsis, Fyssas (Papadopoulos 80), Karagounis, Giannakopoulos (Tsartas 80), Zagorakis, Basinas, Vryzas, Charisteas.
Turkey: Rustu; Serkan, Deniz, Servet, Umit O, Ibrahim, Okan B (Huseyin 73), Emre B, Gokdeniz, Fatih (Hamit 89), Nihat (Serhat 90).
Referee: Frisk (Sweden).

Almaty, 8 September 2004, 24,500

Kazakhstan (1) 1 *(Karpovich 35)*

Ukraine (1) 2 *(Bielik 15, Rotan 90)*

Kazakhstan: Novikov; Familtsev, Avdeyev, Irismetov, Dubinsky, Smakov (Musin 72), Baltiev, Chichulin (Urazbakhtin 53), Nizovtsev, Tieshev (Radionov 63), Karpovich.
Ukraine: Shovkovskyi; Rusol, Yezersky, Tymoschuk, Nesmachni, Gusin (Rotan 67), Bielik (Chelayev 90), Gusev, Zakarliouka, Starostiak (Voronin 51), Vorobei.
Referee: Garcia (Portugal).

Tirana, 9 October 2004, 20,000

Albania (0) 0

Denmark (0) 2 *(Jorgensen 52, Tomasson 72)*

Albania: Strakosha; Beqiri A, Murati, Haxhi, Cana, Hasi, Skela, Lala, Muka (Bushaj 78), Duro, Tare.
Denmark: Skov-Jensen; Priske, Helveg, Kroldrup, Jensen N, Poulsen, Gravesen, Tomasson, Gronkjaer (Kahlenberg 77), Jorgensen (Kristiansen 82), Pedersen (Rommedahl 46).
Referee: Baskalov (Russia).

Istanbul, 9 October 2004, 45,000

Turkey (1) 4 *(Gokdeniz 17, Nihat 50, Fatih 89, 90)*

Kazakhstan (0) 0

Turkey: Rustu; Umit O, Tolga, Servet, Deniz, Huseyin, Serkan (Hasan Sas 64), Gokdeniz (Tuncay 69), Necati, Nihat (Altintop 84), Fatih.
Kazakhstan: Novikov (Morev 52); Avdeyev, Chichulin (Baltiev 33), Dubinski, Lyapkin, Smakov (Kozulin 59), Irismetov, Karpovich, Nizovtsev, Buleshev, Familtsev.
Referee: Hrinak (Slovakia).

Kiev, 9 October 2004, 62,000

Ukraine (0) 1 *(Shevchenko 48)*

Greece (0) 1 *(Tsartas 81)*

Ukraine: Shovkovskyi; Nesmachni, Fedorov, Tymoschuk, Yezerski, Rusol, Shevchenko, Shelayev (Zakarliuka 85), Gusev, Voronin (Belik 90), Vorobei (Gusin 65).
Greece: Nikopolidis; Dellas, Seitaridis, Kapsis, Fyssas, Basinas (Georgiadis 78), Karagounis, Zagorakis, Giannakopoulos (Charisteas 61), Katsouranis, Vryzas (Tsartas 69).
Referee: Gonzalez (Spain).

Copenhagen, 13 October 2004, 41,331

Denmark (1) 1 *(Tomasson 27 (pen))*

Turkey (0) 1 *(Nihat 70)*

Denmark: Skov-Jensen; Priske, Jensen N, Gravesen, Poulsen, Kroldrup, Helveg, Tomasson, Perez (Rommedahl 62), Jorgensen (Kristiansen 77), Gronkjaer■.
Turkey: Rustu; Umit O, Ibrahim (Tuncay 46), Okan B, Tolga, Servet (Necati 67), Huseyin, Gokdeniz (Serkan 83), Fatih, Nihat, Emre B.
Referee: De Santis (Italy).

Almaty, 13 October 2004, 26,000

Kazakhstan (0) 0

Albania (0) 1 *(Bushaj 60)*

Kazakhstan: Morev; Lyapkin, Avdeyev, Smakov (Kamelov 53), Dubinski, Familtsev, Baltiev, Karpovitch (Shevchenko 62), Irismetov, Nizovtsev, Ourazbakhtin (Boulechev 56).
Albania: Strakosha; Beqiri A, Dragusha (Shkembi 90), Cana, Hasi, Lala, Skela, Bushaj (Rraklli 85), Haxhi, Luka (Lici 53), Tare.
Referee: Stuchlik (Austria).

Lvov, 13 October 2004, 28,000

Ukraine (1) 2 *(Bielik 9, Shevchenko 80)*

Georgia (0) 0

Ukraine: Shovkovskyi; Yezerski (Checher 46), Fedorov, Rusol, Nesmachni, Gusev, Tymoshchuk, Gusin, Bielik, Shevchenko, Vorinin (Shelayev 39) (Zakarliouka 64).
Georgia: Devadze; Saluquaze, Khizaneishvili, Khizanishvili, Mjavanadze (Burduli 46), Asatiani M, Jamarauli (Demetradze 85), Tskitishvili, Kobiashvili, Arveladze S, Iashvili.
Referee: Stark (Germany).

Tbilisi, 17 November 2004, 30,000

Georgia (1) 2 *(Demetradze 33, Asatiani 74)*

Denmark (1) 2 *(Tomasson 9, 64)*

Georgia: Devadze; Khizaneishvili, Khizanishvili, Kaladze, Mzhavanadze, Kobiashvili, Tskitishvili, Jikia (Kvirkvelia 72), Asatiani M, Iashvili (Arveladze S 73), Demetradze.
Denmark: Sorensen; Poulsen, Priske, Kroldrup, Jensen N, Lustu, Gravesen, Jensen D (Skoubo 84), Tomasson, Jorgensen (Lovenkrands 84), Perez (Rommedahl 46).
Referee: Ceferin (Slovenia).

Athens, 17 November 2004, 35,000

Greece (2) 3 *(Charisteas 24, 45, Katsouranis 86)*

Kazakhstan (0) 1 *(Baltiev 88 (pen))*

Greece: Nikopolidis; Dellas, Fyssas, Kapsis (Katsouranis 60), Zagorakis (Kaves 71), Seitaridis, Basinas, Karagounis, Tsartas (Georgiadis 72), Charisteas, Vryzas.
Kazakhstan: Novikov; Chichulin, Dubinsky, Lyapkin, Smakov, Irismetov, Karpovich, Urazbakhtin (Rodionov 53), Baltiev, Buleshev (Shevchenko 66), Zhalmagambetov (Kamelov 68).
Referee: Kostadinov (Bulgaria).

Istanbul, 17 November 2004, 52,000

Turkey (0) 0

Ukraine (2) 3 *(Gusev 9, Shevchenko 17, 90)*

Turkey: Rustu; Deniz, Servet (Tuncay 28), Umit O, Seyhan, Okan B, Huseyin (Necati 66), Emre B, Gokdeniz (Basturk 54), Nihat, Fatih.
Ukraine: Shovkovskyi; Gusev, Fedorov, Nesmachni, Rusol, Yezerski, Gusin, Shelayev, Vorobei (Dmitrulin 75), Shevchenko (Nazarenko 90), Voronin (Rykun 61).
Referee: Baptista (Portugal).

Tirana, 9 February 2005, 14,000

Albania (0) 0

Ukraine (1) 2 *(Rusol 39, Gusin 59)*

Albania: Strakosha; Duro, Cana, Haxhi, Cipi (Osmani 58), Lala, Aliaj, Skela, Tare (Bogdani 65), Bushi (Myrtaj 76), Dullku.
Ukraine: Shovkovskyi; Tymoschuk, Nesmachni, Yerzersky, Rusol, Shelayev, Gusev, Shevchenko, Voronin (Rykun 80), Rotan (Vorobei 66), Gusin.
Referee: Bennett (England).

Piraeus, 9 February 2005, 32,430

Greece (2) 2 *(Zakorakis 25, Basinas 31 (pen))*

Denmark (1) 1 *(Rommedahl 45)*

Greece: Nikopolidis; Seitaridis, Fyssas, Katsouranis, Dellas, Zakorakis (Kyrgiakos 46), Basinas, Giannakopoulos, Karagounis (Kafes 61), Charisteas, Vryzas (Amantidis 83).
Denmark: Sorensen; Poulsen, Kroldrup, Lustu (Nielsen P 64), Jensen N (Madsen 64), Priske, Gravesen, Rommedahl, Tomasson, Jensen D, Perez (Jorgensen 46).
Referee: Collina (Italy).

Copenhagen, 26 March 2005, 20,980

Denmark (2) 3 *(Moller 10, 48, Poulsen 33)*

Kazakhstan (0) 0

Denmark: Sorensen; Priske, Laursen, Helveg, Jensen N, Poulsen, Tomasson (Perez 46), Jensen D (Jensen C 46), Gronkjaer (Silberbauer 74), Moller, Jorgensen.
Kazakhstan: Novikov; Familtsev, Avdejev, Smakov, Lyapin, Chichulin (Larim 46), Travin (Baizhanov 56), Baltiev, Karpovich, Utabajev (Baizjanov 78), Rodionov.
Referee: Gilewski (Poland).

Tbilisi, 26 March 2005, 25,000

Georgia (1) 1 *(Asatiani 23)*

Greece (2) 3 *(Kapsis 44, Vryzas 45, Giannakopoulos 54)*

Georgia: Lomaia; Mzhavanadze, Khizanishvili, Khizaneishvili, Kaladze, Kvirkvelia, Gogua (Tskitishvili 46), Asatiani M, Kobiashvili, Demetradze, Arveladze S (Iashvili 62).
Greece: Nikopolidis; Seitaridis, Goumas, Kapsis, Katsouranis, Zagorakis, Basinas, Karagounis, Giannakopoulos, Charisteas, Vryzas.
Referee: Rosetti (Italy).

Istanbul, 26 March 2005, 30,000

Turkey (2) 2 *(Necati 3 (pen), Beqiri E 5 (og))*

Albania (0) 0

Turkey: Rustu; Avci, Seyhan, Balci, Umit O, Ibrahim, Emre B (Bulent K 84), Basturk, Altintop (Gokdeniz 76), Necati, Fatih (Ayhan 63).
Albania: Lika; Beqiri E, Dalku, Haxhi, Lala, Duro (Bushi 79), Cana, Bogdani, Aliaj, Skela, Tare.
Referee: Plautz (Austria).

Tbilisi, 30 March 2005, 20,000

Georgia (2) 2 *(Amisulashvili 13, Iashvili 41)*

Turkey (3) 5 *(Seyhan 12, Fatih 19, 35, Koray 74, Tuncay 85)*

Georgia: Asatiani M; Mzhavanadze, Khizaneishvili (Salukvadze 17), Kaladze, Devadze (Lomaia 20), Gogua■, Tskitishvili (Burduli 71), Iashvili, Kobiashvili, Amisulashvili, Ashvetia.
Turkey: Rustu; Seyhan, Ibrahim, Umit O, Koray, Basturk (Huseyin 46), Emre B, Gokdeniz, Altintop, Fatih, Necati (Tuncay 64).
Referee: Hauge (Norway).

Athens, 30 March 2005, 38,000

Greece (1) 2 *(Charisteas 35, Karagounis 85)*

Albania (0) 0

Greece: Nikopolidis; Seitaridis, Goumas, Kyrgiakos, Katsouranis, Zagorakis, Basinas, Karagounis, Giannakopoulos (Amanatidis 87), Charisteas, Vryzas (Gekas 89).
Albania: Lika; Beqiri E, Haxhi, Lici, Lala, Duro (Dalku 84), Cana, Osmani, Mukaj (Rraklli 46), Skela, Bogdani (Tare 65).
Referee: Layec (France).

Kiev, 30 March 2005, 55,000

Ukraine (0) 1 *(Voronin 67)*

Denmark (0) 0

Ukraine: Shovkoskyi; Sviderski, Yezersky, Rusol, Nesmachni, Gusev, Tymoschuk, Vorobei, Gusin, Voronin (Matyshin 90), Kosyrin (Bielik 59) (Radchenko 80).
Denmark: Sorensen; Priske, Helveg, Kroldrup, Jensen N (Moller 70), Gravesen, Jorgensen (Jensen C 84), Poulsen, Rommedahl (Silberbauer 75), Tomasson, Gronkjaer.
Referee: Michel (Slovakia).

Tirana, 4 June 2005

Albania (2) 3 *(Tare 6, 55, Skela 33)*

Georgia (0) 2 *(Burduli 85, Kobiashvili 90)*

Albania: Lika; Hasi, Beqiri E, Osmani (Cipi 27), Aliaj, Haxhi, Duro, Skela (Shkembi 85), Jupi, Tare, Bogdani (Myrtaj 64).
Georgia: Sturua; Khizanishvili, Kaladze, Salukvadze, Rekhviashvili, Kobiashvili, Asatiani M (Daraselia 58), Kvirkvelia, Magradze (Burduli 64), Demetradze (Bobokhidze 76), Jakobia.
Behind closed doors.
Referee: Tudor (Romania).

Istanbul, 4 June 2005, 32,000

Turkey (0) 0

Greece (0) 0

Turkey: Rustu; Tolga, Ibrahim, Umit O, Mustafa (Tuncay 46), Altintop, Emre B (Serkan 78), Basturk■, Huseyin, Gokdeniz (Necati 60), Fatih.
Greece: Nikopolidis; Seitaridis, Goumas, Kapsis, Fyssas, Karagounis, Basinas, Katsouranis, Giannakopoulos (Lakis 66), Charisteas, Vryzas.
Referee: Merk (Germany).

Kiev, 4 June 2005, 40,000

Ukraine (1) 2 *(Shevchenko 18, Avdeyev 83 (og))*

Kazakhstan (0) 0

Ukraine: Shovkovskyi; Yezersky, Nesmachni, Rusol, Radchenko (Fedorov 86), Tymoschuk, Rotan, Gusev (Gusin 46), Shevchenko, Vorobei, Voronin (Bielik 69).
Kazakhstan: Novikov; Lyapkin, Familtsev (Travin 78), Avdeyev, Dubinsky, Smakov (Nizovtsev 55), Karpovich, Baizhanov, Rodionov (Chichulin 30), Baltiev, Krokhmal.
Referee: Lehner (Austria).

Copenhagen, 8 June 2005, 26,366

Denmark (1) 3 *(Larsen S 4, 46, Jorgensen 54)*

Albania (0) 1 *(Bogdani 72)*

Denmark: Sorensen; Helveg, Nielsen P, Kroldrup, Jensen N, Poulsen, Gravesen (Jensen D 60), Tomasson (Perez 87), Rommedahl (Silberbauer 71), Larsen S, Jorgensen.
Albania: Lika; Beqiri E, Osmani, Hasi, Allaj, Cana, Lala, Jupi (Sina 90), Skela (Duro 67), Tare (Myrtaj 81), Bogdani.
Referee: Frojdfeldt (Sweden).

Piraeus, 8 June 2005, 33,000

Greece (0) 0

Ukraine (0) 1 *(Gusin 82)*

Greece: Nikopolidis; Seitaridis, Kapsis (Vyntra 58), Goumas (Papadopoulos 86), Fyssas, Basinas, Zagorakis, Karagounis (Tsartas 35), Giannakopoulos, Charisteas, Vryzas.
Ukraine: Shovkovskyi; Fedorov, Rusol, Yezersky, Nesmachni, Gusev, Gusin, Tymoshchuk, Vorobei (Rotan 55), Shevchenko (Bielik 80), Voronin (Shelayev 90).
Referee: Temmink (Holland).

Almaty, 8 June 2005, 20,000

Kazakhstan (0) 0

Turkey (3) 6 *(Fatih 13, 80, Ibrahim 15, Tuncay 38, 90, Hamit Altintop 88)*

Kazakhstan: Novikov; Lyapkin, Avdejev, Baizhanov (Chichulin 46), Baltiev, Karpovich, Familtsev (Smakov 62), Nizovtsev, Rodionov (Larin 73), Krokhmal, Dubinsky.
Turkey: Omer; Hamit Altintop, Tolga, Ibrahim, Umit O, Gokdeniz (Serhat 68), Huseyin, Emre B (Serkan 66), Necati (Halil Altintop 46), Tuncay, Fatih.
Referee: Kassai (Hungary).

Group 2 Table

	P	W	D	L	F	A	Pts
Ukraine	9	7	2	0	15	3	23
Turkey	9	4	4	1	19	7	16
Greece	9	4	3	2	12	7	15
Denmark	8	3	3	2	13	8	12
Albania	9	3	0	6	7	16	9
Georgia	7	1	2	4	10	16	5
Kazakhstan	7	0	0	7	2	21	0

GROUP 3

Vaduz, 18 August 2004, 1000

Liechtenstein (0) 1 *(D'Elia 48)*

Estonia (1) 2 *(Viikmae 31, Lindpere 80)*

Liechtenstein: Heeb; Hasler D, Ritter■, Michael Stocklasa, Telser, Gerster■, Martin Stocklasa, Beck R (Rohrer 65), Beck T (Vogt 80), Frick M, D'Elia.
Estonia: Kojenko; Allas, Jaager, Piiroja, Rooba U, Rahn, Smirnov (Haavistu 66), Reim, Viikmae, Zahhovaiko, Terehhov (Lindpere 60).
Referee: Bozinovski (Macedonia).

Bratislava, 18 August 2004, 4500

Slovakia (1) 3 *(Vittek 26, Gresko 48, Demo 89)*

Luxembourg (1) 1 *(Strasser 2)*

Slovakia: Konig; Kratochvil, Varga, Zabavnik, Gresko, Janocko (Demo 68), Karhan, Michalik (Sech 46), Mintal, Nemeth (Sestak 84), Vittek.
Luxembourg: Besic; Braun G (Molitor 61), Cardoni, Hoffmann, Huss (Leweck C 73), Leweck A (Mannon 61), Peters, Reiter, Remy, Schauls, Strasser.
Referee: Kassai (Hungary).

Tallinn, 4 September 2004, 4200

Estonia (2) 4 *(Teever 7, Schauls 41 (og), Oper 61, Viikmae 67)*

Luxembourg (0) 0

Estonia: Poom; Allas, Jaager, Piiroja, Rooba U, Rahn, Teever, Reim (Leetmae 75), Viikmae, Zahhovaiko (Oper 46), Lindpere (Klavan 64).
Luxembourg: Besic; Peters, Reiter (Hellenbrand 88), Hoffmann, Strasser, Remy, Schauls, Cardoni (Di Domenico 81), Huss■, Leweck A, Braun G (Leweck C 68).
Referee: Kelly (Republic of Ireland).

Riga, 4 September 2004, 9500

Latvia (0) 0

Portugal (0) 2 *(Ronaldo 58, Pauleta 59)*

Latvia: Kolinko; Isakov, Zemlinsky, Stepanovs, Laizans, Bleidelis, Lobanov, Astafjevs, Rubins, Prohorenkovs (Rimkus 77), Verpakovskis.
Portugal: Ricardo; Paulo Ferreira, Ricardo Carvalho, Jorge Andrade, Nuno Valente (Caneira 74), Costinha, Maniche, Simao Sabrosa (Boa Morte 68), Deco, Ronaldo (Petit 82), Pauleta.
Referee: Poll (England).

Moscow, 4 September 2004, 14,000

Russia (1) 1 *(Bulykin 14)*

Slovakia (0) 1 *(Vittek 87)*

Russia: Malafeev; Aniukov, Sharonov, Kolodin, Evseev (Sennikov 46), Smertin, Alenichev, Khokhlov (Boyarintsev 66), Bulykin, Karayaka, Kerzahkov.
Slovakia: Contofalsky; Zabavnik, Kratochvil, Varga, Gresko, Karhan, Hanek (Reiter 84), Mintal, Vittek, Michalik (Cech 76), Nemeth (Breska 76).
Referee: Mejuto (Spain).

Luxembourg, 8 September 2004, 2000

Luxembourg (1) 3 *(Braun G 11, Leweck A 55, Cardoni 62)*

Latvia (2) 4 *(Verpakovskis 4, Zemlinsky 40 (pen), Hoffmann 65 (og), Prohorenkovs 67)*

Luxembourg: Besic; Peters (Di Domenico 90), Hellenbrand, Hoffmann, Strasser, Remy, Schauls, Leweck A (Colette 87), Braun G (Leweck C 77), Cardoni, Molitor.
Latvia: Kolinko; Stepanovs, Astafjevs, Zemlinsky, Laizans, Lobanov, Isakov, Bleidelis (Prohorenkovs 32), Verpakovskis, Rubins, Rimkus (Semyonovs 64).
Referee: Kasnaferis (Greece).

Leiria, 8 September 2004, 27,214

Portugal (0) 4 *(Ronaldo 75, Helder Postiga 84, 90, Pauleta 87)*

Estonia (0) 0

Portugal: Ricardo; Paulo Ferreira, Ricardo Carvalho, Jorge Andrade, Rui Jorge (Miguel 56), Costinha, Maniche (Helder Postiga 46), Simao Sabrosa (Boa Morte 70), Deco, Ronaldo, Pauleta.
Estonia: Poom; Allas, Piroja, Rooba U (Klavan 46), Jaager, Leetma, Reim, Teever (Viikmae 62), Lindpere, Oper, Terehhov (Zahovaiko 70).
Referee: Demirlek (Turkey).

Bratislava, 8 September 2004, 5620

Slovakia (2) 7 *(Vitek 15, 59, 81 (pen), Karhan 41, Nemeth 84, Mintal 85, Zabavnik 90)*

Liechtenstein (0) 0

Slovakia: Contofalsky; Zabavnik, Kratochvil (Petrus 46), Gresko (Breska 67), Karhan, Demo (Janocko 46), Mintal, Vitek, Nemeth, Hanek, Cech.
Liechtenstein: Heeb; Telser, Vogt, D'Elia, Martin Stocklasa, Rohrer (Frick C 70), Buchel R (Alabor 76), Burgmeier, Frick M, Beck R, Beck T.
Referee: Delevic (Serbia-Montenegro).

Vaduz, 9 October 2004, 3518

Liechtenstein (0) 2 *(Burgmeier 48, Beck T 76)*

Portugal (2) 2 *(Pauleta 23, Hasler 39 (og))*

Liechtenstein: Jehle; Telser, Michael Stocklasa, Martin Stocklasa, Hasler, Ritter, Rohrer (Beck R 46), Frick M (Frick D 90), Gerster, Burgmeier, Beck T (Buchel 89).
Portugal: Ricardo; Paulo Ferreira, Jorge Ribeiro, Maniche, Ricardo Carvalho, Jorge Andrade, Costinha (Tiago 46), Simao Sabrosa (Petit 57), Pauleta, Deco, Ronaldo (Helder Postiga 61).
Referee: Panic (Bosnia).

Luxembourg, 9 October 2004, 4000

Luxembourg (0) 0

Russia (0) 4 *(Sychev 56, 69, 86, Arshavin 62)*

Luxembourg: Besic; Federspiel, Hoffmann, Schauls (Schnell 58), Strasser, Cardoni (Leweck C 77), Leweck A, Molitor (Mannon 77), Peters, Remy, Braun G.
Russia: Malafeev; Aniukov, Bugaev, Evseev, Ignachevitch, Gusev (Aldonin 75), Kantonistov (Boyarintsev 46), Smertin, Arshavin, Bulykin (Kirichenko 67), Sychev.
Referee: Braamhaar (Holland).

Bratislava, 9 October 2004, 13,025

Slovakia (0) 4 *(Nemeth 47, Reiter 50, Karhan 55, 87)*

Latvia (1) 1 *(Verpakovskis 3)*

Slovakia: Contofalsky; Zabavnik, Gresko, Hanek, Kratochvl (Reiter 46), Varga, Karhan, Mintal (Janocko 46), Michalik (Cech 75), Vittek, Nemeth.
Latvia: Kolinko; Isakov, Koravlovs, Smirnovs, Zirnis, Astafjevs (Kolesnicenko 90), Bleidelis (Semyonovs 87), Lobanov, Laizans, Rimkus (Mikholap 76), Verpakovskis.
Referee: Farina (Italy).

Riga, 13 October 2004, 8200

Latvia (0) 2 *(Astafjevs 65, Laizans 82)*

Estonia (0) 2 *(Oper 72, Teever 79)*

Latvia: Kolinko; Isakov, Zemlinksy, Zirinis, Laizans, Bleidelis (Rimkus 81), Lobanov, Astafjevs, Stepanovs (Rubins 46), Verpakovskis, Prohorenkovs.
Estonia: Poom; Allas, Jaager, Piroja, Rooba U, Rhan, Teever (Leetma 85), Oper, Lindpere, Viikmae, Terehhov (Kruglov 85).
Referee: Meier (Germany).

Luxembourg, 13 October 2004, 3500

Luxembourg (0) 0

Liechtenstein (2) 4 *(Martin Stocklasa 41, Burgmeier 44, 85, Frick M 57 (pen))*

Luxembourg: Besic; Federspiel, Hoffmann, Strasser, Hellenbrand, Leweck C, Molitor (Colette 46), Cardoni, Remy, Braun G, Leweck A (Di Domenico 74).
Liechtenstein: Jehle; Telser, Hasler D, Ritter, Michael Stocklasa, Beck R (D'Elia 57), Martin Stocklasa, Frick M (Rohrer 81), Gerster, Burgmeier, Beck T (Buchel 87).
Referee: Jara (Czech Republic).

Lisbon, 13 October 2004, 27,578

Portugal (3) 7 *(Ronaldo 39, 69, Pauleta 26, Deco 45, Simao Sabrosa 82, Petit 89, 90)*

Russia (0) 1 *(Arshavin 79)*

Portugal: Ricardo; Miguel, Paulo Ferreira, Maniche (Petit 73), Ricardo Carvalho, Jorge Andrade, Costinha, Simao Sabrosa, Pauleta (Nuno Gomes 67), Deco, Ronaldo (Boa Morte 84).
Russia: Malafeev; Aniukov, Bougayev, Ignachevitch, Sennikov (Gusev 46), Arshavin, Smertin, Aldonin (Boyarintsev 71), Evseev, Bulykin, Sychev (Kiritchenko 46).
Referee: Vassaras (Greece).

Vaduz, 17 November 2004, 1500

Liechtenstein (1) 1 *(Frick M 31)*

Latvia (1) 3 *(Verpakovsky 7, Zemlinsky 57 (pen), Prohorenkovs 89)*

Liechtenstein: Jehle; Hasler D, Ritter, Michael Stocklasa, Vogt (Buchel R 88), Burgmeier, Gerster (Frick D 82), Martin Stocklasa, Beck R (Rohrer 65), Beck T, Frick M.
Latvia: Kolinko; Isakovs, Stepanovs, Zemlinsky, Zirnis, Astafjevs, Bleidelis, Laizans (Lobanov 90), Rubins (Zakresevski 90), Rimkus (Prohorenkovs 59), Verpakovskis.
Referee: Szabo (Hungary).

Luxembourg, 17 November 2004, 8300

Luxembourg (0) 0

Portugal (2) 5 *(Federspiel 11 (og), Ronaldo 28, Maniche 51, Pauleta 67, 83 (pen))*

Luxembourg: Besic; Federspiel, Hoffmann, Peters, Reiter, Schauls, Leweck A, Mannon (Di Domenico 78), Remy, Huss (Colette 78), Leweck C.
Portugal: Ricardo; Jorge Andrade, Ribeiro, Paulo Ferreira, Ricardo Carvalho, Costinha (Petit 59), Deco (Tiago 73), Maniche, Boa Morte (Quaresma 46), Ronaldo, Pauleta.
Referee: Godulyan (Ukraine).

Krasnodar, 17 November 2004, 28,000

Russia (3) 4 *(Karayaka 25, Izmailov 27, Sychev 34, Lozkov 69 (pen))*

Estonia (0) 0

Russia: Malafeev; Evseev, Bugaev, Smertin, Berezutski A, Izmailov, Khokhlov (Gusev 87), Lozkov (Shemshov 82), Karayaka, Kerzhakov, Sychev.
Estonia: Kaalma; Allas, Jaager, Piroja, Rooba U, Rahn, Teever (Kruglov 90), Lindpere, Viikmae, Oper, Terehhov (Klavan 82).
Referee: Busacca (Switzerland).

Tallinn, 26 March 2005, 4000

Estonia (0) 1 *(Oper 58)*

Slovakia (0) 2 *(Mintal 59, Reiter 66)*

Estonia: Kotenka; Allas, Stepanov, Jaager, Rooba U (Klavan 79), Reim, Lindpere (Zahovaiko 86), Oper, Terehhov (Teever 79), Viikmae, Kruglov.
Slovakia: Contofalsky; Zabavnik, Valachovic, Varga, Petras, Kisel (Jakubko 54), Hlinka, Karhan, Mintal, Michalik (Reiter 46), Nemeth (Cech 90).
Referee: Frojdfeldt (Sweden).

Vaduz, 26 March 2005, 2500

Liechtenstein (1) 1 *(Beck T 40)*

Russia (2) 2 *(Kerzhakov 23, Karayaka 37)*

Liechtenstein: Jehle; Telser, Ritter, Hasler D, Michael Stocklasa, Beck R (Vogt 60), D'Elia (Buchel R 53), Gerster, Burgmeier, Frick M, Beck T.
Russia: Malafeev; Berezutski A, Berezutski V, Evseev, Ignachevitch, Arshavin (Sychev 55), Bystrov (Izmailov 67), Karayaka, Khokhlov (Aldonin 78), Lozkov, Kerzhakov.
Referee: Berntsen (Norway).

Tallinn, 30 March 2005, 9300

Estonia (0) 1 *(Terehhov 63)*

Russia (1) 1 *(Arshavin 18)*

Estonia: Kotenko; Allas, Stepanov, Jaager, Kruglov, Rahn, Reim, Oper, Terehhov (Smirnov 83), Lindpere (Klavan 24), Viikmae (Teever 90).
Russia: Akinfeev; Smertin, Ignachevitch, Berezutski V, Berezutski A, Bystrov, Khokhlov (Kolodin 63), Loskov, Zhirkov (Kariaka 72), Arshavin (Sychev 67), Kerzhakov.
Referee: Paparesta (Italy).

Riga, 30 March 2005, 3000

Latvia (2) 4 *(Bleidelis 33, Laizans 38 (pen), Verpakovskis 73, 90)*

Luxembourg (0) 0

Latvia: Kolinko; Zirnis, Smirnovs, Stepanovs, Bleidelis (Miholaps 68), Astafjevs, Laizans, Rubins (Zavoronkovs 39), Morozs, Verpakovskis, Prohorekovs (Rimkus 82).
Luxembourg: Oberweis; Schauls (Lang 82), Hoffmann, Strasser, Heinz, Capela, Pace (Mannon 89), Remy, Peters (Leweck C 50), Durrer, Collette.
Referee: Kovacic (Croatia).

Bratislava, 30 March 2005, 30,000

Slovakia (1) 1 *(Karhan 7 (pen))*

Portugal (0) 1 *(Helder Postiga 62)*

Slovakia: Contofalsky; Zabavnik, Varga, Hanek (Kisel 80), Petras, Hlinka, Karhan, Mintel, Michalik (Had 35), Jakubko (Reiter 64), Nemeth.
Portugal: Ricardo; Paulo Ferreira (Miguel 63), Ricardo Carvalho, Jorge Andrade, Nuno Valente, Costinha, Maniche, Ronaldo, Deco, Pauleta (Helder Postiga 56), Simao Sabrosa (Viana 90).
Referee: Sars (France).

Tallinn, 4 June 2005, 5000

Estonia (1) 2 *(Stepanov 27, Oper 57)*

Liechtenstein (0) 0

Estonia: Kotenko; Allas, Stepanov, Jaager, Kruglov, Reim, Lindpere, Oper, Terehhov (Smirnov 89), Viikmae (Teever 71), Klavan (Saharov 87).
Liechtenstein: Jehle; Telser, D'Elia (Alabor 84), Hasler D, Ritter, Martin Stocklasa, Beck R (Buchel R 56), Gerster, Beck T, Frick M, Burgmeier.
Referee: Whitby (Wales).

Lisbon, 4 June 2005, 60,000

Portugal (2) 2 *(Fernando Meira 21, Ronaldo 41)*

Slovakia (0) 0

Portugal: Ricardo; Alex, Fernando Meira, Jorge Andrade, Caneira, Petit, Maniche, Figo, Deco (Tiago 88), Ronaldo (Ricardo Quaresma 76), Pauleta (Helder Postiga 78).
Slovakia: Contofalsky; Zabavnik, Varga, Petras, Had, Hanek (Kisel 64), Karhan, Hlinka, Mintal, Jakubko (Vittek 59), Nemeth (Slovak 59).
Referee: Collina (Italy).

St Petersburg, 4 June 2005, 8400

Russia (0) 2 *(Arshavin 57, Loskov 78 (pen))*

Latvia (0) 0

Russia: Akinfeev; Berezutski A, Smertin, Berezutski V, Aldonin (Bistrov 56), Semchov (Sennikov 67), Anukov, Arshavin (Izmailov 82), Loskov, Jirkov, Kerzhakov.
Latvia: Piedels; Stepanovs, Astafjevs, Smirnovs, Laizans, Zirnis, Isakovs (Zavoronkovs 84), Bleidelis, Rubins, Prohorenkovs (Rimkus 78), Verpakovskis.
Referee: Poulat (France).

Tallinn, 8 June 2005, 7000

Estonia (0) 0

Portugal (1) 1 *(Ronaldo 33)*

Estonia: Kotenko; Allas, Stepanov, Jaager, Rooba U, Terehhov (Saharov 79), Reim, Rahn, Kruglov (Klavan 80), Oper, Viikmae (Zahovaiko 55).
Portugal: Ricardo; Alex, Fernando Meira, Jorge Andrade, Caneira, Costinha, Deco, Maniche (Petit 73), Figo, Pauleta (Helder Postiga 66), Ronaldo (Tiago 90).
Referee: Riley (England).

Riga, 8 June 2005, 8000

Latvia (1) 1 *(Bleidelis 16)*

Liechtenstein (0) 0

Latvia: Piedels; Astafjevs, Stepanovs, Laizans, Smirnovs, Bleidelis, Korablovs, Zavoronkovs, Rubins, Verpakovskis, Prohorenkovs (Rimkus 60).
Liechtenstein: Jehle; Telser, Hasler D, Ritter, D'Elia (Vogt 56), Beck R (Rohrer 77), Buchel R (Buchel M 90), Martin Stocklasa, Burgmeier, Frick M, Beck T.
Referee: Eriksson (Sweden).

Luxembourg, 8 June 2005, 4000

Luxembourg (0) 0

Slovakia (2) 4 *(Nemeth 5, Mintal 15, Kisel 54, Reiter 60)*

Luxembourg: Oberweis; Federspiel (Sabotic 62), Heinz, Hoffmann, Reiter, Lang (Durrer 90), Strasser, Leweck A, Collette, Leweck C, Remy.
Slovakia: Contofalsky; Had (Slovak 46), Varga, Petras (Reiter 59), Kisel, Hanek, Karhan, Hlinka (Sninsky 46), Nemeth, Mintal, Vittek.
Referee: Styles (England).

Group 3 Table

	P	W	D	L	F	A	Pts
Portugal	8	6	2	0	24	4	20
Slovakia	8	5	2	1	22	7	17
Russia	7	4	2	1	15	10	14
Latvia	8	4	1	3	15	14	13
Estonia	9	3	2	4	12	15	11
Liechtenstein	8	1	1	6	9	19	4
Luxembourg	8	0	0	8	4	32	0

GROUP 4

Saint-Denis, 4 September 2004, 43,526

France (0) 0

Israel (0) 0

France: Coupet; Gallas, Squillaci, Givet, Mendy (Giuly 57), Makelele, Vieira, Rothen (Pires 66), Evra, Henry, Saha.
Israel: Davidovitch; Ben-Haim, Saban, Antebi (Keisi 12), Benado, Afek (Gazal 71), Badir, Katan, Benayoun (Nimni 80), Goian, Tal.
Referee: Temmink (Holland).

Dublin, 4 September 2004, 35,900

Republic of Ireland (2) 3 *(Morrison 33, Reid A 38, Robbie Keane 55 (pen))*

Cyprus (0) 0

Republic of Ireland: Given; Carr (Finnan 70), O'Shea (Maybury 83), Kavanagh, O'Brien, Cunningham, Reid A, Kilbane, Robbie Keane, Morrison (Lee 81), Duff.
Cyprus: Panayiotou N; Theodotou, Kakoyiannis, Okkarides, Lambrou, Charalambous (Ilia 65), Makirdis, Satsias, Okkas (Krassas 77), Charalambides (Michael 70), Konstantinou.
Referee: Paniashvili (Georgia).

Basle, 4 September 2004, 13,013

Switzerland (4) 6 *(Vonlanthen 10, 14, 57, Rey 29, 44, 55)*

Faeroes (0) 0

Switzerland: Zuberbuhler; Haas, Yakin M, Muller, Spycher (Magnin 46), Cabanas (Huggel 63), Vogel, Wicky, Yakin H, Rey (Haberli 75), Vonlanthen.
Faeroes: Knudsen; Thorsteinsson, Johannesen O, Jacobsen JR, Olsen, Borg (Danielsen 64), Johnsson J, Benjaminsen, Jorgensen (Hansen 70), Frederiksberg, Petersen J (Jacobsen R 57).
Referee: Tudor (Romania).

Torshavn, 8 September 2004, 6000

Faeroes (0) 0

France (1) 2 *(Giuly 37, Cisse 73)*

Faeroes: Mikkelsen; Thorsteinsson, Olsen, Johannesen O, Jacobsen JR, Jacobsen R (Flotum 75), Borg, Benjaminsen, Johnsson J, Jorgensen (Danielsen A 83), Frederiksberg (Petersen J 68).
France: Coupet; Gallas, Evra, Vieira■, Squillaci, Givet, Giuly, Pedretti, Saha (Cisse 9), Henry (Dhorasoo 64), Pires.
Referee: Thompson (Scotland).

Tel Aviv, 8 September 2004, 17,000

Israel (0) 2 *(Benayoun 64, Badir 74)*

Cyprus (0) 1 *(Konstantinou 58)*

Israel: Davidovich; Saban, Ben-Haim, Benado, Keissi, Nimny (Balili 57), Badir, Benayoun, Tal (Afek 71), Katan (Gazal 84), Goian.
Cyprus: Panayiotou N; Okkarides, Kakoyiannis, Nikolaou, Theodotou (Georgiou 30), Makirdis, Satsias, Ilia, Charalambides (Michail 72), Okkas (Yiasoumi 79), Konstantinou.
Referee: Shmolik (Belarus).

Basle, 8 September 2004, 28,000

Switzerland (1) 1 *(Yakin H 17)*

Republic of Ireland (1) 1 *(Morrison 8)*

Switzerland: Zuberbuhler; Vogel, Barnetta, Yakin M, Muller, Magnin, Haas, Cabanas, Yakin H, Vonlanthen (Lonfat 73), Rey.
Republic of Ireland: Given; Carr, Finnan, Roy Keane, O'Brien, Cunningham, Reid A (Kavanagh 73), Kilbane, Robbie Keane, Morrison (Doherty 84), Duff.
Referee: Vassaras (Greece).

Nicosia, 9 October 2004, 3000

Cyprus (1) 2 *(Konstantinou 14 (pen), Okkas 82)*

Faeroes (2) 2 *(Jorgensen 22, Jacobsen R 43)*

Cyprus: Panayiotou N; Nikolaou, Okkarides (Kaiafas 51), Makridis, Okkas (Kakoyiannis 69), Charalambides, Konstantinou, Charalambous, Georgiou, Elia, Krassias (Satsias 46).
Faeroes: Mikkelsen; Thorsteinsson, Johannesen O, Jacobsen JR (Petersen J 76), Olsen, Johnsson J, Benjaminsen, Borg, Jorgensen (Danielsen A 46), Jacobsen R, Frederiksberg (Flotum 69).
Referee: Gadiev (Azerbaijan).

Saint-Denis, 9 October 2004, 78,863

France (0) 0

Republic of Ireland (0) 0

France: Barthez; Gallas, Silvestre, Mavuba, Squillaci, Givet, Wiltord, Dacourt (Diarra 64), Cisse (Gouvou 83), Henry, Pires.
Republic of Ireland: Given; Carr, O'Shea, Roy Keane, O'Brien, Cunningham, Finnan, Kilbane, Robbie Keane, Morrison (Reid A 41), Duff.
Referee: Ibanez (Spain).

Tel Aviv, 9 October 2004, 37,981

Israel (1) 2 *(Benayoun 9, 48)*

Switzerland (2) 2 *(Frei 26, Vonlanthen 34)*

Israel: Davidovich; Benado, Ben-Haim, Gershon (Saban 78), Gazal (Nimny 46), Badir, Tal, Keissi, Afek, Benayoun, Balili (Golan 58).
Switzerland: Zuberbuhler; Haas, Magnin, Vogel, Yakin M (Henchoz 63), Muller, Cabanas, Barnetta (Gygax 33), Frei, Vonlanthen, Yakin H (Lonfat 80).
Referee: Shield (Australia).

Nicosia, 13 October 2004, 4000

Cyprus (0) 0

France (1) 2 *(Wiltord 38, Henry 72)*

Cyprus: Panayiotou N; Ilia, Charalambous, Okkarides, Nikolaou (Lambrou 77), Kakoyiannis, Georgiou (Yiasoumi 83), Satsias, Charalambides (Makridis 56), Okkas, Konstantinou.
France: Barthez; Gallas, Silvestre, Vieira, Squillaci, Givet, Wiltord, Dacourt (Diarra 90), Luyindula (Evra 66), Henry, Pires (Moreira 46).
Referee: Larsen (Denmark).

Dublin, 13 October 2004, 36,000

Republic of Ireland (2) 2 *(Robbie Keane 14 (pen), 32)*

Faeroes (0) 0

Republic of Ireland: Given; Carr, O'Shea (Miller 57), Roy Keane, O'Brien, Cunningham, Finnan, Kilbane, Robbie Keane, Duff, Reid A.
Faeroes: Mikkelsen; Thorsteinsson, Olsen, Johnsson J, Johannesen O, Jacobsen JR, Borg (Danielsen 85), Benjaminsen, Petersen J, Frederiksberg (Flotum 82), Jacobsen R (Lakjuni 58).
Referee: Lajuks (Latvia).

Nicosia, 17 November 2004, 3500

Cyprus (1) 1 *(Okkas 45)*

Israel (1) 2 *(Keissi 17, Nimny 86)*

Cyprus: Panayiotou N; Kaiafas, Kakoyannis, Okkarides, Makrides, Okkas (Yiasoumi 55), Charalambides (Nikolaou 85), Konstantinou, Charalambous, Georgiou (Goumenos 70), Ilia.
Israel: Davidovich; Benado, Ben-Haim, Keissi, Balili (Goian 53), Nimny, Badir, Benayoun, Afek (Revivo 79), Kafan, Saban.
Referee: Kaldma (Estonia).

Paris, 26 March 2005, 79,373

France (0) 0

Switzerland (0) 0

France: Barthez; Sagnol, Boumsong, Givet, Gallas, Giuly, Pedretti, Vieira, Dhorasoo (Meriem 59), Trezeguet, Wiltord (Govou 82).
Switzerland: Zuberbuhler; Degen P, Senderos, Muller, Spycher, Gygax (Henchoz 90), Lonfat (Huggel 29), Cabanas, Vogel, Ziegler (Magnin 69), Frei.
Referee: De Santis (Italy).

Tel Aviv, 26 March 2005, 44,000

Israel (0) 1 *(Swan 90)*

Republic of Ireland (1) 1 *(Morrison 4)*

Israel: Awat; Afek (Nimny 65), Ben-Haim, Gershon, Benado, Keissi, Badir, Benayoun, Tal (Balili 65), Katan, Golan (Swan 73).
Republic of Ireland: Given; Carr, O'Shea, Finnan, O'Brien, Cunningham, Duff, Roy Keane, Robbie Keane, Morrison (Holland 85), Kilbane.
Referee: Ivanov (Russia).

Tel Aviv, 30 March 2005, 43,000

Israel (0) 1 *(Badir 83)*

France (0) 1 *(Trezeguet 50)*

Israel: Awat; Sabas, Gershon, Ben-Haim, Keissi, Badir, Nimny, Tal (Afek 67), Katan, Benayoun, Balili.
France: Barthez; Sagnol, Boumsong, Givet, Gallas, Vieira, Pedreti, Diarra, Wiltord (Dhorasoo 90), Trezeguet■, Malouda.
Referee: Merk (Germany).

Zurich, 30 March 2005, 16,066

Switzerland (0) 1 *(Frei 88)*

Cyprus (0) 0

Switzerland: Zuberbuhler; Degen P, Muller, Senderos, Spycher (Magnin 82), Gygax, Lonfat (Yakin H 62), Vogel, Cabanas, Ziegler (Vonlanthen 41), Frei.
Cyprus: Panayiotou■; Elia, Louka, Lambrou, Garpozis (Aloneftis 90), Charalambides, Makridis (Michael 65), Satsias, Krassas (Yiasoumi 80), Okkas, Konstantinou.
Referee: Dougal (Scotland).

Toftir, 4 June 2005, 2043

Faeroes (0) 1 *(Jacobsen R 70)*

Switzerland (1) 3 *(Wicky 25, Frei 73, 86)*

Faeroes: Mikkelsen; Hansen, Johannesen Y, Jacobsen JR, Olsen, Danielsen A, Borg (Frederiksberg 66), Benjaminsen, Jacobsen R, Jorgensen (Lakjuni 75), Flotum (Jacobsen C 63).
Switzerland: Zuberbuhler; Degen P, Muller, Rochat, Magnin, Gygas, Vogel, Wicky (Lonfat 90), Barnetta (Margairaz 68), Frei, Vonlanthen (Ziegler 77).
Referee: Gumienny (Belgium).

Dublin, 4 June 2005, 36,000

Republic of Ireland (2) 2 *(Harte 6, Robbie Keane 11)*

Israel (2) 2 *(Yehiel 39, Nimni 45 (pen))*

Republic of Ireland: Given; O'Shea, O'Brien■, Cunningham, Harte, Holland, Kilbane, Duff, Robbie Keane (Kavanagh 27), Morrison, Reid A (Doherty 64).
Israel: Awat; Yehiel, Gershon, Benado, Saban, Suan, Tal, Nimni (Goian 79), Keissi, Benayoun, Katan (Balili 66).
Referee: Vassaras (Greece).

Torshavn, 8 June 2005, 10,000

Faeroes (0) 0

Republic of Ireland (0) 2 *(Harte 51 (pen), Kilbane 58)*

Faeroes: Mikkelsen; Hansen, Johannesen O, Danielsen A, Olsen, Johnsson J, Benjaminsen (Borg 79), Jorgensen (Akselsen 79), Jacobsen R, Lakjuni, Flotum (Jacobsen C 59).
Republic of Ireland: Given; Carr, Harte, Roy Keane, O'Shea, Cunningham, Reid, Kilbane, Morrison (Doherty 79), Elliott, Duff.
Referee: Genov (Bulgaria).

Group 4 Table

	P	*W*	*D*	*L*	*F*	*A*	*Pts*
Republic of Ireland	7	3	4	0	11	4	13
Switzerland	6	3	3	0	13	4	12
Israel	7	2	5	0	10	8	11
France	6	2	4	0	5	1	10
Cyprus	6	0	1	5	4	12	1
Faeroes	6	0	1	5	3	17	1

GROUP 5

Palermo, 4 September 2004, 21,463

Italy (1) 2 *(De Rossi 4, Toni 79)*

Norway (1) 1 *(Carew 1)*

Italy: Buffon; Bonera, Nesta, Materazzi, Favalli (Diana 67), Fiore, Gattuso, De Rossi, Zambrotta, Gilardino (Corradi 59), Miccoli (Toni 68).
Norway: Johnsen E; Basma, Riseth, Lundekvam, Riise, Hoseth (Solli 90), Andresen, Sorensen (Pedersen M 85), Johnsen F, Rudi, Carew (Rushfeldt 72).
Referee: Sars (France).

Celje, 4 September 2004, 4000

Slovenia (2) 3 *(Acimovic 6, 28, 49)*

Moldova (0) 0

Slovenia: Mavric B; Karic, Pokore (Sukalo 81), Mavric M, Knavs, Seslar, Komac (Tanjic 74), Ceh (Koren 89), Acimovic, Dedic, Siljak.
Moldova: Hmaruc; Covalenco (Ivanov 71), Lascencov, Olexici (Lungu 46), Catinsus, Priganiuc, Covalciuc, Savinov, Rogaciov (Dadu 82), Cebotari, Miterev.
Referee: Hyytia (Finland).

Chisinau, 8 September 2004, 8500

Moldova (0) 0

Italy (1) 1 *(Del Piero 33)*

Moldova: Hmaruc; Lungu, Olexici, Catinsus, Lascencov, Priganiuc, Covalciuc, Ivanov, Rogaciov (Cebotari 81), Bursuc, Mitere (Dadu 62).
Italy: Buffon; Bonera (Blasi 84), Nesta, Materazzi, Zambrotta, Gattuso, Pirlo, Ambrosini (Oddo 74), Diana, Del Piero, Gilardino (Toni 80).
Referee: Benes (Czech Republic).

Oslo, 8 September 2004, 25,272

Norway (1) 1 *(Riseth 39)*

Belarus (0) 1 *(Kutuzov 77)*

Norway: Myhre; Hoiland, Riseth, Lundekvam, Riise, Andresen, Hoseth, Johnsen F, Rudi (Sorensen 46), Pedersen M, Rushfeldt (Carew 81).
Belarus: Khomutovski; Kulchi, Omelyunchuk, Shtanyuk, Yaskovich, Lavrik, Gurenko, Bulyga (Sashcheka 63), Romashchenko, Hleb V (Blizuk 44) (Suchkov 90), Kutuzov.
Referee: Costa (Portugal).

Glasgow, 8 September 2004, 38,278

Scotland (0) 0

Slovenia (0) 0

Scotland: Gordon; Caldwell G, Naysmith (Holt 59), Ferguson B, Webster, Mackay, McNamara, Fletcher, Dickov (Crawford 79), Quashie, McFadden.
Slovenia: Mavric B; Pokorn, Mavric M, Knavs, Karic, Ceh, Seslar, Komac, Acimovic, Siljak (Lavric 64), Dedic (Sukalo 79).
Referee: Larsen (Denmark).

Minsk, 9 October 2004, 20,000

Belarus (1) 4 *(Omelianchuk 44, Kutuzov 65, Bulyga 76, Romashchenko 90)*

Moldova (0) 0

Belarus: Khomutovski; Kulchi (Kovba 79), Yaskovich, Omelianchuk, Shtanyuk, Gurenko, Lavrik, Belkevich (Koval 83), Romashchenko, Korytko, Kutuzov (Bulyga 66).
Moldova: Hmaruc; Savinov, Lascencov, Olexici, Catinsus, Barisev (Pobreban 79), Covalciuc (Epureanu 84), Ivanov, Rogaciov, Bursuc, Miterev (Golban 77).
Referee: Selcuk (Turkey).

Glasgow, 9 October 2004, 48,882

Scotland (0) 0

Norway (0) 1 *(Iversen 55 (pen))*

Scotland: Gordon; Caldwell G, Naysmith, Ferguson B, Anderson, Webster, Fletcher, Holt (Thompson 80), Dickov (Miller 75), McFadden■, Hughes (Pearson 63).
Norway: Myhre; Bergdolmo, Hagen, Lundekvam, Riise, Sorensen (Andresen 74), Solli, Hoseth (Pedersen M 58), Carew, Iversen (Johnsen F 89), Larsen.
Referee: Allaerts (Belgium).

Celje, 9 October 2004, 9000

Slovenia (0) 1 *(Cesar 82)*

Italy (0) 0

Slovenia: Mavric B; Pokorn, Mavric M, Mitrakovic (Cesar 76), Karic (Dedic 65), Sukalo, Komac, Ceh (Lazic 88), Acimovic, Siljak, Seslar.
Italy: Buffon; Bonera, Zambrotta, De Rossi, Cannavaro, Nesta, Gattuso, Camoranesi (Di Vaio 83), Gilardino (Toni 69), Totti, Esposito (Fiore 69).
Referee: De Bleeckere (Belgium).

Parma, 13 October 2004, 16,510

Italy (2) 4 *(Totti 26 (pen), 73, De Rossi 33, Gilardino 86)*

Belarus (0) 3 *(Romashchenko 52, 90, Bulyga 77)*

Italy: Buffon; Oddo (Cannavaro 68), Pancaro, De Rossi (Blasi 75), Nesta, Materazzi, Diana (Perrotta 65), Gattuso, Gilardino, Totti, Zambrotta.
Belarus: Khomutovski; Kulchi (Koval 84), Shtanyuk, Yaskovich■, Gurenko, Lavrik (Kovba 76), Tarlovski, Korytko (Bulyga 35), Belkevich, Kutuzov, Romashchenko.
Referee: Davila (Spain).

Chisinau, 13 October 2004, 4500

Moldova (1) 1 *(Dadu 27)*

Scotland (1) 1 *(Thompson 30)*

Moldova: Hmaruc; Lascencov, Savinov, Ivanov, Catinsus, Priganiuc, Olexici (Cebotari 38), Bursuc, Dadu, Rogaciov, Covalciuc.
Scotland: Gordon; Caldwell G, Naysmith (Murray 46), Ferguson B, Caldwell S, Webster, Fletcher (Miller 66), Holt, Crawford, Thompson (McCulloch 86), Cameron.
Referee: Jacobsson (Iceland).

Oslo, 13 October 2004, 24,907

Norway (1) 3 *(Carew 7, Pedersen 60, Odegaard 90)*

Slovenia (0) 0

Norway: Myhre; Bergdolmo, Riise, Andresen, Hagen, Lundekvam, Solli, Larsen, Carew (Rushfeldt 77), Iversen (Johnsen F 88), Pedersen M (Odegaard 80).
Slovenia: Mavric B; Pokorn, Mitrakovic, Seslar (Komac 66), Mavric M, Cesar, Sukalo, Ceh, Lavric (Dedic 78), Siljak, Acimovic.
Referee: Ivanov (Russia).

Milan, 26 March 2005, 40,745

Italy (1) 2 *(Pirlo 35, 85)*

Scotland (0) 0

Italy: Buffon; Bonera, Cannavaro, Materazzi, Chiellini, Camoranesi, Pirlo, Totti (De Rossi 72), Gattuso, Gilardino, Cassano (Toni 83).
Scotland: Douglas (Gordon 38); McNamara, Naysmith, Caldwell G, Weir, Pressley, Hartley (Crawford 76), Ferguson, Miller (O'Connor 86), McCulloch, Quashie.
Referee: Vassaras (Greece).

Chisinau, 30 March 2005, 6000

Moldova (0) 0

Norway (0) 0

Moldova: Hmaruc; Savinov, Lascencov (Bursuc 85), Olexic, Epureanu (Barisev 80), Catinsus, Priganiuc, Boret, Ivanov, Dadu, Rogaciov (Frunza 89).
Norway: Myhre; Bergdolmo, Riise, Larsen F, Hagen, Lundekvam, Solli, Hoset (Carew 59), Pedersen M, Iversen, Rushfeldt (Karadas 81).
Referee: Meyer (Germany).

Celje, 30 March 2005, 6000

Slovenia (1) 1 *(Rodic 44)*

Belarus (0) 1 *(Kulchi 49)*

Slovenia: Handanovic; Ilic, Mavric M (Rodic 29), Knavs, Filekovic (Siljak 54), Komac, Cipot (Koren 71), Ceh, Seslar, Acimovic, Lazic.
Belarus: Zhevnov; Belkevich, Gurenko, Hleb, Katskevich (Ostrovski 85), Kovba, Kulchi, Kutuzov (Bulyga 64), Omelyunchuk, Romashchenko (Kalatzov 76), Lavrik.
Referee: Al Ghamdi (Saudi Arabia).

Minsk, 4 June 2005, 20,000

Belarus (1) 1 *(Belkevich 19)*

Slovenia (1) 1 *(Ceh 16)*

Belarus: Zhevnov; Gurenko, Yaskovich (Lavrik 76), Omelyunchuk (Tarlovsky 85), Shtanyuk, Kulchi, Kovba, Belkevich, Hleb A, Bulyga, Kutuzov (Kornilenko 72).
Slovenia: Handanovic; Cipot, Mavric M, Cesar, Ilic (Sukalo 68), Filekovic, Pokorn, Komac (Zlogar 90), Ceh, Lavrik K, Rodic Cimirotic 58).
Referee: Hansson (Sweden).

Oslo, 4 June 2005, 24,829

Norway (0) 0

Italy (0) 0

Norway: Myhre; Bergdolmo, Hagen, Lundekvam, Riise, Solli (Karadas 71), Andresen, Hestad, Pedersen M, Iversen (Johnsen F 84), Carew.
Italy: Buffon; Bonera (Diana 81), Cannavaro, Materazzi, Grosso, Camoranesi, Pirlo, De Rossi, Zambrotta, Vieri (Toni 57), Cassano (Iaquinta 68).
Referee: Gonzalez (Spain).

Glasgow, 4 June 2005, 45,317

Scotland (0) 2 *(Dailly 53, McFadden 89)*

Moldova (0) 0

Scotland: Gordon; Pressley, Webster (Dailly 26), Ferguson B, Weir, Alexander, McNamara, Hartley, Fletcher, Miller, McCulloch (McFadden 74).
Moldova: Hmaruc; Olexici, Priganiuc, Lascencov (Covalenko 46), Catinsus, Epureanu, Boret, Ivanov, Dadu, Savinov (Covalciuc 60), Rogaciov (Frunza 82).
Referee: Braamhaar (Holland).

Minsk, 8 June 2005, 20,000

Belarus (0) 0

Scotland (0) 0

Belarus: Zhevnov; Omelyunchuk, Kalachev (Hleb V 61), Gurenko, Shtanyuk, Jaskovic, Kovba, Hleb A, Bulyga (Kulchi 86), Belkevich, Kornichenko.
Scotland: Gordon; Weir, Webster, Caldwell G, Pressley, Dailly, Fletcher, Ferguson B, Miller (McFadden 76), Alexander, McCulloch.
Referee: Benquerenca (Portugal).

Group 5 Table

	P	*W*	*D*	*L*	*F*	*A*	*Pts*
Italy	6	4	1	1	9	5	13
Norway	6	2	3	1	6	3	9
Slovenia	6	2	3	1	6	5	9
Belarus	6	1	4	1	10	7	7
Scotland	6	1	3	2	3	4	6
Moldova	6	0	2	4	1	11	2

GROUP 6

Vienna, 4 September 2004, 48,500

Austria (0) 2 *(Kollmann 71, Ivanschitz 73)*

England (1) 2 *(Lampard 24, Gerrard 64)*

Austria: Manninger; Standfest, Stranzl, Martin Hiden, Pogatetz, Sick, Kuhbauer, Aufhauser (Kiesenebner 74), Ivanschitz, Glieder (Kollmann 68), Haas (Hleblinger 89).
England: James; Neville G, Cole A, Gerrard (Carragher 82), Terry, King, Beckham, Lampard, Smith (Defoe 74), Owen, Bridge (Cole J 84).
Referee: Michel (Slovakia).

Baku, 4 September 2004, 15,000

Azerbaijan (0) 1 *(Sadykhov 56)*

Wales (0) 1 *(Speed 48)*

Azerbaijan: Kramarenko; Shukurov, Hajiev, Agayev, Sadykhov, Kurbanov M, Huseynov (Mamedov A 73), Ponomarev (Kurbanov I 84), Kurbanov G, Aliyev (Noybiyev 71), Kerimov.
Wales: Jones P; Delaney, Gabbidon, Savage, Melville, Page, Koumas (Earnshaw 87), Speed, Hartson, Bellamy, Pembridge (Oster 46).
Referee: Trivkovic (Croatia).

Belfast, 4 September 2004, 14,000

Northern Ireland (0) 0

Poland (2) 3 *(Zurawski 4, Wlodarczyk 37, Krzynowek 57)*

Northern Ireland: Taylor; Hughes A, Capaldi, Whitley, Williams, Craigan, Johnson, Hughes M (Jones S 53), Quinn (Smith 73), Healy, Elliott (McVeigh 62).
Poland: Dudek; Michal Zewlakow, Bak, Glowacki, Rzasa, Krzynowek (Gorawski 67), Lewandowski M, Mila (Radomski 75), Zienczuk, Wlodarczyk■, Zurawski (Kryszalowicz 84).
Referee: Wegereef (Holland).

Vienna, 8 September 2004, 26,400

Austria (2) 2 *(Stranzl 23, Kollmann 44)*

Azerbaijan (0) 0

Austria: Manninger; Standfest, Stranzl, Martin Hiden, Pogatetz, Schopp (Dollinger 57), Kuhbauer, Aufhauser, Ivanschitz, Haas (Glieder 72), Kollmann (Linz 79).
Azerbaijan: Kramarenko; Agayev, Hajiev, Sadykhov, Shukurov, Guseynov, Kurbanov M (Mamedov I 46), Kerimov, Ponomarev (Nabiyev 46), Kurbanov G, Aliyev (Kurbanov I 46).
Referee: Sammut (Malta).

Chorzow, 8 September 2004, 38,000

Poland (0) 1 *(Zurawski 48)*

England (1) 2 *(Defoe 37, Glowacki 58 (og))*

Poland: Dudek; Michal Zewlakow, Bak, Glowacki, Krzynowek, Rzasa, Lewandowski M, Mila (Kukielka 63), Kosowski (Gorawski 80), Zurawski, Rasiak (Niedzielan 69).
England: Robinson; Neville G (Carragher 32), Cole A, Gerrard, Terry, King, Beckham (Hargreaves 90), Lampard, Defoe (Dyer 87), Owen, Bridge.
Referee: Farina (Italy).

Cardiff, 8 September 2004, 63,500

Wales (1) 2 *(Hartson 32, Earnshaw 75)*

Northern Ireland (2) 2 *(Whitley 11, Healy 21)*

Wales: Jones P; Delaney (Earnshaw 28), Thatcher (Parry 63), Savage■, Collins, Gabbidon, Oster, Speed, Hartson, Bellamy, Koumas.
Northern Ireland: Taylor; Clyde, Capaldi (McCartney 90), Murdock, Hughes A, Williams, Johnson, Whitley, Quinn (Smith 58) (McVeigh 89), Healy■, Hughes M■.
Referee: Messina (Italy).

Vienna, 9 October 2004, 46,100

Austria (1) 1 *(Schopp 30)*

Poland (1) 3 *(Kaluzny 9, Krzynowek 79, Frankowski 90)*

Austria: Manninger; Standfest, Pogatetz, Schopp, Stranzl, Martin Hiden, Kuhbauer, Aufhauser (Kiesenebner 46), Ivanschitz, Haas (Kollmann 38), Vastic (Mayrleb 80).
Poland: Dudek; Baszczynski, Rzasa, Hajto, Bak, Mila, Krzynowek, Zajac (Kosowski 46), Kaluzny (Radomski 72), Zurawski, Rasiak (Frankowski 67).
Referee: Batista (Portugal).

Baku, 9 October 2004, 20,000

Azerbaijan (0) 0

Northern Ireland (0) 0

Azerbaijan: Hasanzade; Amirbekov, Hajiev, Kuliyev E, Kuliyev K, Kurbanov M (Ponomarev 58), Nabiyev, Sadykhov, Mamedov I (Kurbanov I 55), Aliyev (Kurbanov G), Shukurov.
Northern Ireland: Taylor; Clyde, Hughes A, Doherty, Williams, Murdock, Johnson, Whitley, Quinn (Smith 76), Elliott, Baird (Gillespie 9).
Referee: Hanaczek (Hungary).

Old Trafford, 9 October 2004, 65,224

England (1) 2 *(Lampard 4, Beckham 76)*

Wales (0) 0

England: Robinson; Neville G, Cole A, Butt, Campbell, Ferdinand, Beckham (Hargreaves 85), Rooney (King 86), Owen, Defoe (Smith 70), Lampard.
Wales: Jones P; Delaney, Thatcher, Pembridge (Robinson 59), Gabbidon, Speed, Koumas (Earnshaw 73), Bellamy, Hartson, Giggs, Davies.
Referee: Haughe (Norway).

Baku, 13 October 2004, 20,000

Azerbaijan (0) 0

England (1) 1 *(Owen 22)*

Azerbaijan: Hasanzade; Hajiev, Shukurov, Kuliyev E (Kurbanov I 75), Sadykhov, Amirbekov, Kerimov, Ponomarev, Kuliyev K, Nabiyev (Abdullayev 79), Aliyev (Kurbanov G 59).
England: Robinson; Neville G, Cole A, Butt, Campbell, Ferdinand, Jenas (Wright-Phillips 72), Rooney (Cole J 85), Owen, Defoe (Smith 55), Lampard.
Referee: Hamer (Luxembourg).

Belfast, 13 October 2004, 11,830

Northern Ireland (1) 3 *(Healy 36, Murdock 60, Elliott 90)*

Austria (1) 3 *(Schopp 14, 72, Mayrleb 61)*

Northern Ireland: Carroll; Hughes A, McCarthy, Doherty (Jones S 86), Williams, Murdock (Elliott 78), Gillespie, Whitley (McVeigh 89), Quinn, Healy, Johnson.
Austria: Manninger; Ibertsberger, Pogatetz, Kuhbauer, Martin Hiden, Feldhofer, Schopp (Sick 81), Kiesenebner, Kirchler (Ivanschitz 64), Vastic, Mayrleb (Kollmann 81).
Referee: Shield (Australia).

Cardiff, 13 October 2004, 74,000

Wales (0) 2 *(Earnshaw 56, Hartson 90)*

Poland (0) 3 *(Frankowski 72, Zurawski 81, Krzynowek 85)*

Wales: Jones P; Delaney, Thatcher, Savage, Gabbidon, Collins, Davies, Speed (Hartson 79), Earnshaw, Bellamy, Koumas (Parry 86).
Poland: Dudek; Baszczynski, Krzynowek, Szymkowiak, Hajto, Bak (Klos 46), Kosowski, Kaluzny (Mila 71), Zurawski, Wlodarczyk (Frankowski 60), Rzasa.
Referee: Sars (France).

Old Trafford, 26 March 2005, 65,239

England (0) 4 *(Cole J 47, Owen 52, Baird 54 (og), Lampard 67)*

Northern Ireland (0) 0

England: Robinson; Neville G, Cole A, Gerrard (Hargreaves 72), Ferdinand, Terry, Beckham (Dyer 72), Lampard, Owen, Rooney (Defoe 80), Cole J.
Northern Ireland: Taylor; Baird, Capaldi, Doherty (Davis 59), Hughes A, Murdock, Gillespie, Johnson, Healy (Kirk 88), Elliott, Whitley (Jones S 80).
Referee: Stark (Germany).

Warsaw, 26 March 2005, 12,500

Poland (3) 8 *(Frankowski 12, 62, 65, Hajiev 16 (og), Kosowski 40, Krzynowek 71, Saganowski 83, 90)*

Azerbaijan (0) 0

Poland: Dudek; Baszczynski, Bak, Klos, Rzasa, Kosowski (Smolarek 46), Szymkowiak, Sobolewski, Krzynowek, Frankowski (Niedzielan 66), Zurawski (Saganowski 73).
Azerbaijan: Kramarenko; Hajiev, Sadykhov, Amirbekov, Kuliyev E (Malikov 20), Sjoeboerov, Kerimov (Actianov 46), Kuliyev V, Nadyov (Kurbanov I 46), Kurbanov G, Nabiev.
Referee: Vollquartz (Denmark).

Cardiff, 26 March 2005, 47,760

Wales (0) 0

Austria (0) 2 *(Vastic 82, Stranzl 86)*

Wales: Coyne; Delaney, Ricketts, Robinson, Gabbidon, Page, Davies (Earnshaw 75), Fletcher, Hartson, Bellamy, Giggs.
Austria: Payer; Dospel, Pogatetz, Ehmann, Katzer, Kirchler, Stranzl, Aufhauser, Ivanschitz (Hleblinger 90), Mayrleb (Mair 87), Haas (Vastic 78).
Referee: Allaerts (Belgium).

Vienna, 30 March 2005, 29,500

Austria (0) 1 *(Aufhauser 87)*

Wales (0) 0

Austria: Payer; Stranzl, Dospel (Kiesenebner 84), Ehmann, Katzer, Kirchler (Mair 77), Kuhbauer, Aufhauser, Ivanschitz, Mayrleb, Haas (Vastic 55).
Wales: Coyne; Delaney, Ricketts, Robinson, Gabbidon, Collins (Page 58), Partridge, Fletcher, Davies, Bellamy, Giggs.
Referee: Gonzalez (Spain).

Newcastle, 30 March 2005, 49,046

England (0) 2 *(Gerrard 51, Beckham 62)*

Azerbaijan (0) 0

England: Robinson; Neville G, Cole A, Ferdinand (King 77), Terry, Gerrard, Beckham (Defoe 84), Lampard, Owen, Rooney (Dyer 77), Cole J.
Azerbaijan: Kramarenko; Abdurahmanov, Amirbekov (Kuliyev V 46), Sadykhov, Hajiev, Hashimov, Bakhshiev, Malikov, Kerimov, Kurbanov G (Actiamov 74), Nabiev (Ponomarev 74).
Referee: Gomes Costa (Portugal).

Warsaw, 30 March 2005, 25,000

Poland (0) 1 *(Zurawski 86)*

Northern Ireland (0) 0

Poland: Dudek; Baszczynski, Bak, Klos, Rzasa (Kielbowicz 46), Karwan (Rasiak 74), Kaluzny (Mila 67), Symkowiak, Krzynowek, Frankowski, Zurawski.
Northern Ireland: Taylor; Baird, Capaldi, Williams (Elliott 88), Hughes A, Murdock, Gillespie, Davis, Quinn (Feeney 35), Healy (Smith 81), Whitley.
Referee: Frojdfeldt (Sweden).

Baku, 4 June 2005, 8000

Azerbaijan (0) 0

Poland (1) 3 *(Frankowski 27, Klos 56, Zurawski 77)*

Azerbaijan: Gasanzade; Kuliyev K, Sadykhov, Hajiev (Ismailov 75), Chukurov, Abdurahmanov (Kurbanov I 75), Kuliyev E, Abdullayev, Malikov (Ramazanov 59), Karimov, Kurbanov G.
Poland: Dudek; Baszczynski, Bak, Klos, Rzasa, Kosowski, Sobolewski, Szymkowiak (Radomski 89), Mila (Zienczuk 84), Frankowski (Niedzielan 55), Zurawski.
Referee: Mallenco (Spain).

Group 6 Table

	P	*W*	*D*	*L*	*F*	*A*	*Pts*
Poland	7	6	0	1	22	5	18
England	6	5	1	0	13	3	16
Austria	6	3	2	1	11	8	11
Northern Ireland	6	0	3	3	5	13	3
Wales	6	0	2	4	5	11	2
Azerbaijan	7	0	2	5	1	17	2

GROUP 7

Charleroi, 4 September 2004, 20,000

Belgium (0) 1 *(Sonck 61)*

Lithuania (0) 1 *(Jankauskas 72)*

Belgium: Peersman; Deflandre (Kompany 46), Dheedene, Simons, Van Buyten, Clement, Goor, Mpenza M (Dufer 22), Vernant (Pieroni 73), Buffel, Sonck.
Lithuania: Karcemarskas; Dziaukstas, Skarbalius (Morinas 8), Skerla, Stankevicius, Barasa, Cesnauskis, Vencevicius (Razanauskas 57), Danelevicius (Mikoliunas 66), Jankauskas, Poskus.
Referee: Loizou (Cyprus).

Serravalle, 4 September 2004, 500

San Marino (0) 0

Serbia-Montenegro (2) 3 *(Vukic 5, Jestrovic 15, 82)*

San Marino: Gasperoni F; Valentini C, Morani, Bacciocchi, Della Valle, Crescentini (Moretti M 46), Domenicioni, Gasperoni A (Maiani 85), Ciacci, Vannucci, Ugolini (Montagna 23).
Serbia-Montenegro: Jevric; Dragutinovic, Mladenovic (Duljaj 82), Vidic, Gavrancic, Koroman, Milosevic (Kezman 68), Stankovic, Jestrovic, Vukic (Brnovic 86), Krstajic.
Referee: Kholmatov (Kazakhstan).

Zenica, 8 September 2004, 15,000

Bosnia (0) 1 *(Bolic 74)*

Spain (0) 1 *(Vicente 66)*

Bosnia: Hasagic; Salihamidzic, Bajic, Spahic, Music, Grujic, Barbarez, Beslija, Baljic (Blatnjak 63), Misimovic, Bolic (Hililovic 83).
Spain: Casillas; Michel Salgado, Romero, Albelda (Xabi Alonso 71), Puyol, Helguera, Victor (Morientes 50), Baraja (Valeron 58), Reyes, Raul, Vicente.
Referee: De Santis (Italy).

Kaunas, 8 September 2004, 5000

Lithuania (1) 4 *(Jankauskas 18, 50, Danilevicius 65, Gedgaudas 90)*

San Marino (0) 0

Lithuania: Karcemarskas; Stankevicius, Dziaukstas, Skerla, Barasa, Vencevicius, Mikoliunas (Gedgaudas 74), Cesnauskis (Morinas 46), Danilevicius, Poskus, Jankauskas (Radzinevicius 68).
San Marino: Gasperoni F; Valentini C, Bacciocchi, Della Valle, Marani, Albani (Maiani 87), Domeniconi, Gasperoni A, Giacci, Vannucci (Nanni 82), Montagna (Moretti M 65).
Referee: Jareci (Albania).

Sarajevo, 9 October 2004, 32,000

Bosnia (0) 0

Serbia-Montenegro (0) 0

Bosnia: Tolja; Blatnjak, Spahic, Bajic (Hrgovic 62), Papac (Crnogorac 79), Grlic, Misimovic, Bolic, Barbarez, Baljic (Baiano 80), Beslija.
Serbia-Montenegro: Jevric; Gavrancic, Krstajic, Djordjevic (Markovic 57), Duljaj, Dragutinovic, Stankovic, Koroman (Brnovic 90), Vukic, Milosevic (Pantelic 77), Ljuboja.
Referee: Veissiere (France).

Santander, 9 October 2004, 20,000

Spain (0) 2 *(Luque 59, Raul 63)*

Belgium (0) 0

Spain: Casillas; Michel Salgado, Del Horno, Albelda (Xabi Alonso 58), Marchena, Puyol, Joachim, Xavi (Baraja 73), Raul, Fernando Torres (Luque 53), Reyes.
Belgium: Peersman; Deflandre■, Deschacht, Clement, Kompany, Van Buyten, Buffel (Dufer 79), Bisconti (Doll 60), Mpenza M (Huysegems 73), Sonck, Goor■.
Referee: Nielsen (Denmark).

Vilnius, 13 October 2004, 6000

Lithuania (0) 0

Spain (0) 0

Lithuania: Karcemarskas; Stankevicius, Dziaukstas, Skerla, Skarbalius, Gedgaudas (Mikoliunas 75), Vencevcius, Barasa, Cesnauskas, Jankauskas, Danilevicius (Radzinevicius 82).
Spain: Casillas; Michel Salgado, Capdevila (Torres 79), Albelda, Puyol, Marchena, Victor (Tamudo 53), Baraja (Reyes 65), Xavi, Raul, Luque.
Referee: Poulat (France).

Belgrade, 13 October 2004, 3000

Serbia-Montenegro (2) 5 *(Milosevic 35, Stankovic 45, 50, Koroman 52, Vukic 69)*

San Marino (0) 0

Serbia-Montenegro: Jevric; Markovic, Gavrancic, Dragutinovic (Vitakic 62), Koroman, Krstajic, Duljaj, Vukic, Stankovic, Milosevic, Ljuboja (Pantelic 70).
San Marino: Gasperoni F; Valentini C, Marani, Bacciocchi, Della Valle, Albani, Domeniconi (Moretti L 90), Vannucci, Ciacci (De Luigi 77), Gasperoni A, Moretti M (Gasperoni B 65).
Referee: Isaksen (Faeroes).

Brussels, 17 November 2004, 32,000

Belgium (0) 0

Serbia-Montenegro (1) 2 *(Vukic 7, Kezman 59)*

Belgium: Proto; De Cock, Kompany, Simons, Deschacht (Daerden 27), Van der Heyden, Bisconti (Pieroni 58), Baseggio, Clement, Buffel, Sonck (Huysegems 65).
Serbia-Montenegro: Jevric; Markovic, Mladenovic (Djordjevic N 77), Gavrancic, Dragutinovic, Stankovic, Djordjevic P, Koroman (Duljaj 55), Vukic, Milosevic (Kezman 29), Vidic.
Referee: Frojdfeldt (Sweden).

Serravalle, 17 November 2004, 1457

San Marino (0) 0

Lithuania (1) 1 *(Cesnauskis D 41)*

San Marino: Gasperoni F; Valentini C, Marani, Bacciocchi, Della Valle, Albani, Muccioli (Domeniconi 67), Gasperoni A, De Luigi (Bonifazi 82), Selva A, Vannucci.
Lithuania: Karcemarkas; Semberas, Dziaukstas, Stankevicius, Gedgaudas (Vencevicius 85), Zvirgzdauskas, Skarbalius, Cesnauskis E, Danilevicius, Cesnauskis D (Mikoliunas 76), Radzinevicius (Morinas 46).
Referee: Nalbandyan (Armenia).

Almeria, 9 February 2005, 15,000

Spain (3) 5 *(Joaquin 14, Torres 32, Raul 42, Guti 65, Del Horno 79)*

San Marino (0) 0

Spain: Casillas; Marchena, Puyol, Michel Salgado, De la Pena (Guayre 76), Del Horno, Joaquin, Xavi, Luque (Guti 46), Raul (Villa 46), Torres.
San Marino: Gasperoni F; Albani, Andreini (Gasperoni B 58), Bacciocchi, Domeniconi (Moretti 75), Vannucci, Della Valle, Gasperoni A, Marani, Valentini C, Selva A.
Referee: Clark (Scotland).

Brussels, 26 March 2005, 35,000

Belgium (2) 4 *(Mpenza E 15, 54, Daerden 44, Buffel 76)*

Bosnia (1) 1 *(Bajramovic 1)*

Belgium: Proto; Doll, Kompany, Van Buyten, Vanderheyden, Buffel (Bisconti 90), Vanderheyghe, Simons, Daerden, Mpenza E (Clement 90), Pieroni (Vandenbergh 86).
Bosnia: Hasagic; Spahic, Bajic, Milenkovic, Papac (Misimovic 58), Beslija, Grlic (Grujic 72), Barbarez, Bolic, Baljic (Halimovic 58), Bajramovic.
Referee: Hrinak (Slovakia).

Sarajevo, 30 March 2005, 15,000

Bosnia (1) 1 *(Bolic 21)*

Lithuania (0) 1 *(Stankevicius 64)*

Bosnia: Hasagic; Spahic, Bajic (Halilovic 73), Milenkovic, Vidic, Bajramovic, Grlic, Beslija (Baljic 46), Misimovic (Grujic 64), Barbarez, Bolic.
Lithuania: Karcemarskas; Stankevicius■, Skerla, Zutartas, Dziaukstas, Cesnauskis D (Barasa 54), Semberas, Cesnauskis E, Poskus, Danilevicius (Vencevicius 90), Jankauskas.
Referee: Baskakov (Russia).

Serravalle, 30 March 2005, 3000

San Marino (1) 1 *(Selva A 40)*

Belgium (1) 2 *(Simons 19 (pen), Van Buyten 65)*

San Marino: Gasperoni F; Albani, Della Valle, Bacciocchi, Marani, Valentini C, Vannucci, Domeniconi (Montagna 89), Gasperoni A, Ciacci (Gasperoni B 61), Selva A.
Belgium: Proto; Doll (Vandenbergh 58), Kompany, Van Buyten, Van der Heyden, Buffel (Chatelle 38), Simons, Vanderhaeghe, Daerden, Pieroni (Bisconti 83), Mpenza E.
Referee: Kasnaferis (Greece).

Belgrade, 30 March 2005, 56,000

Serbia-Montenegro (0) 0

Spain (0) 0

Serbia-Montenegro: Jevric; Vidic, Gavrancic, Krstajic, Dragutinovic, Koroman (Basta 77), Duljaj, Stankovic, Djordjevic, Kezman (Jestrovic 80), Milosevic (Ilic 65).
Spain: Casillas; Sergio Ramos, Pablo, Puyol (Juanito 46), Del Horno, Xavi, Albelda, De La Pena (Raul 46), Joaquin, Fernando Torres, Reyes (Antonio Lopez 62).
Referee: Busacca (Switzerland).

Serravalle, 4 June 2005, 747

San Marino (1) 1 *(Selva A 40)*

Bosnia (2) 3 *(Salihamidzic 17, 39, Barbarez 75)*

San Marino: Ceccoli; Valentini C (Gasperoni B 65), Crescentini, Della Valle, Bacciocchi, Marani, Gasperoni D, Domeniconi, Vannucci, De Luigi (Andreini 72), Selva A (Montagna 85).
Bosnia: Tolja; Berberovic, Vidic, Papac, Milenkovic, Beslija (Bartolovic 56), Grlic, Bajramovic (Kerkez 82), Misimovic (Halilovic 59), Barbarez, Salihamidzic.
Referee: Demirlek (Turkey).

Belgrade, 4 June 2005, 45,000

Serbia-Montenegro (0) 0

Belgium (0) 0

Serbia-Montenegro: Jevric; Dragutinovic, Krstajic, Gavrancic, Vidic, Vukic, Duljaj, Koroman (Vukcevic 81), Stankovic (Mladenovic 82), Ljuboja, Jestrovic (Vucinic 53).
Belgium: Proto; Clement, Van Buyten, Deschacht, Borre, Vanderhaeghe, Bisconti, Daerden (Leonard 79), Buffel (Pieroni 88), Mpenza E, Mpenza M (Vandenbergh 83).
Referee: Ivanov (Russia).

Valencia, 4 June 2005, 25,000

Spain (0) 1 *(Luque 68)*

Lithuania (0) 0

Spain: Casillas; Michel Salgado, Marchena, Puyol, Del Horno (Luis Garcia 61), Joaquim, Xavi, Albelda, Vicente, Fernando Torres (Luque 59), Raul (Sergio 79).
Lithuania: Karcemarskas; Skerla, Dziaukstas, Zvirgzdauskas, Paulauskas, Barasa, Kucys (Preksaitis 46), Cesnauskis D (Mikoliunas 73), Danilevicius, Poskus, Morinas (Cesnauskis E 77).
Referee: Farina (Italy).

Valencia, 8 June 2005, 36,400

Spain (0) 1 *(Marchena 90)*

Bosnia (1) 1 *(Misimovic 38)*

Spain: Casillas; Michel Salgado, Marchena, Puyol (Juanito 8), Antonio Lopez (Xabi Alonso 62), Joaquin, Xavi, Albelda, Vicente, Raul, Fernando Torres (Luque 35).
Bosnia: Tolja; Spahic, Bajic, Vidic (Milenkovic 76), Music, Grlic, Bajramovic, Grujic (Damjanovic 74), Barbarez, Misimovic (Halilovic■ 65), Beslija■.
Referee: Bennett (England).

Group 7 Table

	P	W	D	L	F	A	Pts
Spain	7	3	4	0	10	2	13
Serbia-Montenegro	6	3	3	0	10	0	12
Lithuania	6	2	3	1	7	3	9
Belgium	6	2	2	2	7	7	8
Bosnia	6	1	4	1	7	8	7
San Marino	7	0	0	7	2	23	0

GROUP 8

Zagreb, 4 September 2004, 25,000

Croatia (1) 3 *(Prso 32, Klasnic 57, Gyepes 80 (og))*

Hungary (0) 0

Croatia: Butina; Srna (Mornar 84), Simunic, Kovac R, Tudor, Vranjes, Kranjcar (Leko I 77), Babic, Prso (Olic 75), Kovac N, Klasnic.
Hungary: Kiraly; Bodnar, Huszti■, Stark (Gyepes 59), Toth A (Kovacs 81), Molnar, Rosa, Szabics, Gera, Simek (Low 18), Juhasz.
Referee: Riley (England).

Reykjavik, 4 September 2004, 5000

Iceland (0) 1 *(Gudjohnsen E 51 (pen))*

Bulgaria (1) 3 *(Berbatov 35, 49, Yanev 62)*

Iceland: Arason; Bjarnason, Sigurdsson K, Gunnarsson B■, Sigurdsson I (Helgason 65), Gretarsson (Gudjonsson J 57), Hreidarsson, Einarsson, Gudjohnsen E, Gudjonsson T, Helguson (Sigurdsson H 70).
Bulgaria: Ivankov; Kishishev, Kirilov, Petkov I, Yankov (Kamburov 80), Berbatov, Lazarov (Yanev 42), Hristov, Petrov S, Bojinov (Bukarev 72), Stoyanov.
Referee: Hamer (Luxembourg).

Ta'Qali, 4 September 2004, 4000

Malta (0) 0

Sweden (3) 7 *(Ibrahimovic 4, 11, 14, 71, Ljungberg 46, 74, Larsson 76)*

Malta: Muscat; Briffa, Pullicino, Said, Azzopardi, Dimech, Giglio, Woods (Mallia 79), Zahra (Agius G 57), Mifsud M, Galea.
Sweden: Isaksson; Lucic, Mellberg (Nilsson 61), Hansson (Ostlund 49), Edman, Linderoth, Wilhelmsson (Jonson 76), Svensson, Ljungberg, Ibrahimovic, Larsson.
Referee: Jakov (Israel).

Budapest, 8 September 2004, 8000

Hungary (0) 3 *(Gera 62, Torghelle 76, Szabics 80)*

Iceland (1) 2 *(Gudjohnsen E 40, Sigurdsson I 78)*

Hungary: Kiraly; Juhasz, Gyepes, Toth A, Szelesi (Szabics 46), Molnar, Rosa, Bodnar, Simek (Low 18), Gera, Kovacs (Torghelle 66).
Iceland: Arason; Sigurdsson K, Bjarnason, Hreidarsson, Gudjonsson T (Einarsson 75), Gretarsson (Gunnarsson V 85), Vidarsson, Gudjonsson J, Sigurdsson I, Helguson, Gudjohnsen E (Sigurdsson H 86).
Referee: Ovrebo (Norway).

Gothenburg, 8 September 2004, 40,023

Sweden (0) 0

Croatia (0) 1 *(Srna 64)*

Sweden: Isaksson; Ostlund, Mellberg, Lucic (Allback 80), Edman, Linderoth, Wilhelmsson, Anders Svensson (Jonson 73), Ljungberg, Larsson, Ibrahimovic.
Croatia: Butina; Kovac R, Tudor, Simunic, Srna, Kovac N, Kranjcar (Leko J 63), Vranjes, Babic, Prso (Tokic 90), Klasnic (Olic 46).
Referee: Ibanez (Spain).

Zagreb, 9 October 2004, 30,000

Croatia (2) 2 *(Srna 15, 32 (pen))*

Bulgaria (0) 2 *(Petrov M 77, Berbatov 86)*

Croatia: Butina; Srna, Simunic, Kovac N, Kovac R (Banovic 77), Tokic, Babic, Vranjes, Kranjcar (Balaban 69), Prso, Klasnic (Leko J 57).
Bulgaria: Ivankov; Kishishev (Manchev 55), Markov, Petkov I, Stoyanov, Petrov S, Yankov, Berbatov, Bojinov (Yanev 55), Petrov M, Georgiev (Paskov 90).
Referee: Collina (Italy).

Valletta, 9 October 2004, 6000

Malta (0) 0

Iceland (0) 0

Malta: Haber; Azzopardi, Briffa, Ciantar, Dimech, Said, Agius G (Mallia 65), Giglio, Mattocks, Woods (Galea 78), Mifsud M.
Iceland: Arason; Bjarnason, Hreidarsson, Gunnarsson B (Gretarsson 78), Sigurdsson K, Einarsson, Gudjonsson T (Gunnarsson V 68), Sigurdsson I (Sigurdsson H 59), Helguson, Gudjohnsen E, Vidarsson.
Referee: Corpodean (Romania).

Stockholm, 9 October 2004, 32,228

Sweden (1) 3 *(Ljungberg 26, Larsson 50, Svensson 67)*

Hungary (0) 0

Sweden: Isaksson; Ostlund, Lucic, Linderoth, Mellberg, Mjallby (Nilsson 46), Wilhelmsson (Alexandersson N 74), Ljungberg, Allback, Larsson, Svensson (Kallstrom 80).
Hungary: Kiraly; Gyepes, Bodnar (Feher C 80), Dardai, Stark, Toth A, Molnar (Hajnal 55), Gera, Szabics, Torghelle (Kovacs 70), Bodor.
Referee: Dougal (Scotland).

Sofia, 13 October 2004, 17,700

Bulgaria (1) 4 *(Berbatov 43, 66, Yanev 47, Yankov 87)*

Malta (1) 1 *(Mifsud M 12)*

Bulgaria: Ivankov; Stoyanov, Petkov I, Georgiev, Petrov S, Yankov, Yanev (Kirilov 71), Bojinov (Sakaliev 67), Manchev (Gargorov 64), Berbatov, Petrov M.
Malta: Haber; Briffa (Zahra 46), Said, Azzopardi, Ciantar, Dimech, Woods (Pulicino 75), Giglio, Agius G, Mattocks, Mifsud M.
Referee: Richards (Wales).

Reykjavik, 13 October 2004, 7035

Iceland (0) 1 *(Gudjohnsen E 66)*

Sweden (4) 4 *(Larsson 24, 39, Allback 27, Wilhelmsson 44)*

Iceland: Arason; Bjarnason (Gudjonsson T 57), Sigurdsson L (Jonsson 25), Gunnarsson B, Sigurdsson K, Einarsson, Marteinsson, Hreidarsson, Helguson (Sigurdsson H 81), Gudjohnsen E, Gudjonsson J.
Sweden: Isaksson (Hedman 31); Ostlund, Lucic, Linderoth, Mellberg, Nilsson, Wilhelmsson, Ljungberg (Alexandersson N 57), Allback, Larsson (Ibrahimovic 53), Anders Svensson.
Referee: Busacca (Switzerland).

Ta'Qali, 17 November 2004, 2000

Malta (0) 0

Hungary (1) 2 *(Gera 39, Kovacs 90)*

Malta: Haber; Ciantar, Azzopardi, Briffa, Said, Dimech, Agius G (Barbara 86), Giglio, Mifsud M, Woods (Cohen 73), Mattocks (Galea 60).
Hungary: Kiraly; Rosa (Gyepes 90), Huszti, Juhasz, Stark, Hajnal, Feher C, Dardai, Torghelle (Kovacs 66), Gera, Wallner (Lipcsei 79).
Referee: Asumaa (Finland).

Sofia, 26 March 2005, 42,563

Bulgaria (0) 0

Sweden (1) 3 *(Ljungberg 17, 90, Edman 74)*

Bulgaria: Ivankov; Markov■, Stoyanov, Petkov I, Kishishev (Kirilov 74), Borimirov (Janev 76), Yankov, Georgiev, Berbatov, Ivanov G, Lazarov (Topuzakov 60).
Sweden: Isaksson; Ostlund, Mellberg, Lucic, Edman, Alexandersson N (Wilhelmsson 61), Linderoth, Anders Svensson, Ljungberg, Ibrahimovic, Jonson (Allback 80).
Referee: Fandel (Germany).

Zagreb, 26 March 2005, 25,000

Croatia (1) 4 *(Kovac N 39, 76, Simunic 71, Prso 90)*

Iceland (0) 0

Croatia: Butina; Tomas, Tudor, Simunic, Seric (Bosnjak 86), Srna, Kovac N, Leko I (Leko J 79), Kranjcar, Klasnic (Olic 73), Prso.
Iceland: Arason; Bjarnason, Sigurdsson K, Gunnarsson B, Sigurdsson I, Sigurdsson H (Steinsson 50), Vidarsson, Helguson (Gislason 73), Einarsson, Gudjonsson I (Gudjonsson B 60), Marteinsson.
Referee: Damon (South Africa).

Zagreb, 30 March 2005, 10,000

Croatia (2) 3 *(Prso 24, 35, Tudor 80)*

Malta (0) 0

Croatia: Butina; Tomas, Kovac R (Olic 46), Tudor, Bosnjak (Tokic 68), Kovac N (Vranjes 77), Leko I, Kranjcar, Babic, Prso, Klasnic.
Malta: Haber; Pollicino, Said (Mallia 59), Dimech, Azzopardi, Agius G, Sammut, Grima (Woods 46), Giglio, Mattocks, Mifsud M (Barbara 68).
Referee: Kapitanis (Cyprus).

Budapest, 30 March 2005, 12,000

Hungary (0) 1 *(Rajczi 90)*

Bulgaria (0) 1 *(Petrov S 52)*

Hungary: Kiraly; Juhasz, Stark, Komlosi, Bodnar, Boor, Vincze (Rajczi 79), Korsos G (Kerekes 74), Huszti, Szabics, Torghelle.
Bulgaria: Ivankov; Kirilov, Stojanov, Petkov I, Georgiev, Lazarov (Borimirov 75), Petrov S, Yankov (Manchev 64), Petrov M (Ivanov 79), Berbatov, Topuzakov.
Referee: Wegereef (Holland).

Sofia, 4 June 2005, 30,738

Bulgaria (0) 1 *(Petrov M 73)*

Croatia (1) 3 *(Babic 18, Tudor 58, Kranjcar 80)*

Bulgaria: Ivankov; Kirilov, Stoyanov, Iliev, Kishishev (Lazarov 54), Yankov, Petrov S, Georgiev, Berbatov, Ivanov G (Bojinov 46), Petrov M.
Croatia: Butina; Tomas, Kovac R, Tudor, Simunic, Srna, Kovac N, Babic, Kranjcar (Leko J 82), Olic (Balaban 90), Prso.
Referee: Nielsen (Denmark).

Reykjavik, 4 June 2005, 4613

Iceland (1) 2 *(Gudjohnsen E 18, Sigurdsson K 69)*

Hungary (1) 3 *(Gera 45 (pen), 56 (pen), Huszti 73)*

Iceland: Arason; Sigurdsson K, Bjarnasson■, Gislason, Sigurdsson I, Gunnarsson B, Marteinsson (Gudmundsson H 25), Steinsson (Arnason 46), Einarsson (Thorvaldsson 57), Vidarsson, Gujohnsen E.
Hungary: Kiraly; Bodnar, Stark, Huszti, Vanczak (Balog Z 14), Takacs, Hajnal, Baranyos (Szabics 75), Toth N (Rajczi 90), Gera, Kerekes.
Referee: Batista (Portugal).

Gothenburg, 4 June 2005, 40,000

Sweden (4) 6 *(Jonson 6, Anders Svensson 18, Wilhelmsson 30, Ibrahimovic 40, Ljungberg 57, Elmander 81)*

Malta (0) 0

Sweden: Isaksson; Alexandersson N (Elmander 77), Mellberg, Lucic, Edman, Linderoth, Wilhelmsson, Anders Svensson (Kallstrom 62), Ljungberg, Ibrahimovic, Jonson (Allback 62).
Malta: Haber; Pullicino, Dimech, Said, Pulis, Sammut, Giglio, Agius (Mallia 73), Pace (Briffa 46), Woods, Mifsud M.
Referee: Ivanov (Russia).

Reykjavik, 8 June 2005, 4884

Iceland (2) 4 *(Thorvaldsson 28, Gudjohnsen E 34, Gudmundsson T 75, Gunnarsson V 86)*

Malta (0) 1 *(Said 59)*

Iceland: Arason; Vidarsson, Helgason, Gunnarsson B, Steinsson, Gislason, Gunnarsson V, Arnason (Hardarson 63), Thorvaldsson (Sigurdsson H 84), Gudmundsson T, Gudjohnsen E (Danielsson 81).
Malta: Gauci; Said, Dimech, Briffa, Pulis, Agius G, Sammut, Pullicino, Mattocks (Cohen 59), Mallia, Mifsud M.
Referee: Skomina (Slovenia).

Group 8 Table

	P	*W*	*D*	*L*	*F*	*A*	*Pts*
Croatia	6	5	1	0	16	3	16
Sweden	6	5	0	1	23	2	15
Hungray	6	3	1	2	9	11	10
Bulgaria	6	2	2	2	11	11	8
Iceland	7	1	1	5	10	18	4
Malta	7	0	1	6	2	26	1

QUALIFYING RESULTS – SOUTH AMERICA

Buenos Aires, 6 September 2003, 35,372

Argentina (2) 2 *(Kily Gonzalez 32, Aimar 36)*

Chile (0) 2 *(Mirosevic 60, Navia 77)*

Argentina: Cavallero; Vivas, Ayala, Samuel▪, Zanetti, Veron (Almeyda 65), Kily Gonzalez, Aimar, D'Alessandro, Delgado, Crespo (Saviola 71).
Chile: Tapia N; Alvarez▪, Contreras, Olarra, Perez, Martel, Marcos Gonzalez, Melendez (Mirosevic 38), Mark Gonzalez (Acuna 57), Tapia H (Pinilla 57), Navia▪.
Referee: Aquino (Paraguay).

Quito, 6 September 2003, 30,000

Ecuador (1) 2 *(Espinoza G 6, Tenorio C 67)*

Venezuela (0) 0

Ecuador: Cevallos; De la Cruz, Espinoza G, Hurtado I, Reasco, Ayovi M, Obregon, Mendez, Chala, Aguinaga (Tenorio O 43), Tenorio C.
Venezuela: Angelucci; Vallenilla, Rey, Alvarado, Rojas, Mea Vitali, Jimenez, Arango, Paez (Noriega 60), Urdaneta (Gonzalez H 60), Moran (Casseres 67).
Referee: Selman (Chile).

Lima, 6 September 2003, 43,000

Peru (2) 4 *(Solano 34, Mendoza 42, Jorge Soto 83, Farfan 90)*

Paraguay (1) 1 *(Gamarra 24)*

Peru: Delgado; Jorge Soto, Rebosio, Galliquio, Hidalgo, Jayo, Zegarra, Solano (Jose Soto 89), Palacios (Ciurlizza 76), Mendoza (Farfan 70), Pizarro.
Paraguay: Tavarelli; Arce, Gamarra, Da Silva, Caceres J, Toledo (Alvarenga 60), Enciso, Paredes, Bonet (Cuevas 81), Santa Cruz, Cardozo.
Referee: Baldassi (Argentina).

Barranquilla, 7 September 2003, 55,000

Colombia (1) 1 *(Angel 38)*

Brazil (1) 2 *(Ronaldo 25, Kaka 60)*

Colombia: Cordoba O; Martinez, Cordoba I, Yepes, Bedoya (Perea 35), Caballero, Restrepo (Becerra 63), Grisales, Patino (Molina 75), Hernandez, Angel.
Brazil: Dida; Cafu, Lucio, Roque Junior, Roberto Carlos, Emerson (Renato 59), Gilberto Silva, Ze Roberto, Alex (Kaka 59), Ronaldo, Rivaldo (Diego 87).
Referee: Elizondo (Argentina).

Montevideo, 7 September 2003, 42,000

Uruguay (2) 5 *(Forlan 17, Chevanton 38, 60, Abeijon 82, Bueno 87)*

Bolivia (0) 0

Uruguay: Munua; Gonzalez, Lopez, Lago, Sosa (Abeijon 69), Liguera (Oliveira 77), Nunez, Recoba, Bueno, Chevanton, Forlan (Sanchez 76).
Bolivia: Fernandez L; Hoyos, Sanchez O, Pena, Gatti Ribeiro (Baldivieso 46), Rojas, Cristaldo, Ricardi▪, Morejon (Botero 46), Castillo, Mendez.
Referee: Hidalgo (Peru).

Santiago, 9 September 2003, 55,000

Chile (1) 2 *(Pinilla 35, Norambuena 70)*

Peru (0) 1 *(Mendoza 57)*

Chile: Tapia N; Rojas R, Contreras, Olarra, Martel (Mark Gonzalez 46), Acuna, Marcos Gonzalez (Pizarro 46), Mirosevic, Perez, Tapia H (Norambuena 67), Pinilla.
Peru: Delgado; Jorge Soto, Galliquio, Rebosio, Hidalgo, Jayo, Zegarra, Solano (Jose Soto 81), Palacios (Farfan 75), Mendoza, Pizarro.
Referee: Aquino (Paraguay).

Caracas, 9 September 2003, 25,000

Venezuela (0) 0

Argentina (3) 3 *(Aimar 7, Crespo 25, Delgado 32)*

Venezuela: Angelucci; Gonzalez H (Vallenilla 46), Rey, Alvaravo, Rojas, Vera, Jimenez, Arango (Moreno 61), Paez, Moran (Urdaneta 46), Noriega.
Argentina: Cavallero; Vivas, Ayala, Piacente, Zanetti, Veron, Kily Gonzalez, Aimar (Heinze 63), D'Alessandro (Gonzalez L 85), Delgado (Almeyda 81), Crespo.
Referee: Vazquez (Uruguay).

La Paz, 10 September 2003, 30,000

Bolivia (2) 4 *(Baldivieso 12, Botero 28, 49, 58)*

Colombia (0) 0

Bolivia: Fernandez L (Fernandez JC 46); Paz Garcia, Pena, Sanchez O, Gatti Ribeiro, Rojas (Garcia R 74), Cristaldo, Baldivieso, Mendez, Botero, Suarez (Justinano 62).
Colombia: Cordoba O; Martinez, Cordoba I▪, Yepes, Cortes, Viafara, Vargas (Restrepo 46), Patino (Molina 46), Hernandez (Castillo 46), Angel, Aristizabal.
Referee: Oliveira (Brazil).

Manaus, 10 September 2003, 35,000

Brazil (1) 1 *(Ronaldinho 13)*

Ecuador (0) 0

Brazil: Dida; Cafu, Lucio, Roque Junior, Roberto Carlos, Emerson (Renato 62), Gilberto Silva, Ze Roberto, Ronaldinho (Kaka 68), Ronaldo, Rivaldo (Alex 90).
Ecuador: Cevallos; De la Cruz, Hurtado I, Espinoza G, Reasco, Obregon, Tenorio E, Ayovi M, Mendez, Chala, Tenorio C (Tenorio O 83).
Referee: Solozano (Venezuela).

Asuncion, 10 September 2003, 20,000

Paraguay (1) 4 *(Cardozo 27, 58, 73, Paredes 54)*

Uruguay (1) 1 *(Chevanton 24)*

Paraguay: Villar; Arce, Gamarra, Da Silva, Caceres J, Bonet, Enciso (Ortiz 90), Paredes, Santa Cruz, Cardozo, Campos (Gavilan 81).
Uruguay: Munua; Gonzalez, Sorondo, Aguiai, Regueiro (Nunez 78), Abeijon, Oliveira, Giacomazzi (Liguera 46), Chevanton, Bueno (Recoba 61), Forlan.
Referee: Ruiz (Colombia).

Buenos Aires, 15 November 2003, 30,042

Argentina (0) 3 *(D'Alessandro 56, Crespo 61, Aimar 63)*

Bolivia (0) 0

Argentina: Cavallero; Quiroga, Ayala, Samuel, Zanetti, Almeyda (Cambiasso 89), Kily Gonzalez, Aimar, D'Alessandro (Sorin 84), Crespo (Saviola 80), Delgado.
Bolivia: Fernandez L; Raldes, Sanchez O, Paz Garcia, Ricaldi, Gatti Ribeiro, Justiniano, Reyes, Suarez (Etcheverry 69), Mercado (Castillo 64), Botero (Mendez 64).
Referee: Hidalgo (Peru).

Barranquilla, 15 November 2003, 20,000

Colombia (0) 0

Venezuela (1) 1 *(Arango 8)*

Colombia: Mondragon; Vallejo, Perez, Yepes, Viveros, Lozano, Bolano (Arriaga 54), Hernandez (Patino 46), Grisales, Becerra, Angel.
Venezuela: Angelucci; Vallenilla, Hernandez, Rey, Cichero, Jimenez, Mea Vitali (Vielna 6), Paez (Gonzalez H 57), Urdaneta (Rojas 57), Arango, Noriega.
Referee: Chandia (Chile).

Asuncion, 15 November 2003, 30,000

Paraguay (1) 2 *(Santa Cruz 30, Cardozo 70)*

Ecuador (0) 1 *(Mendez 59)*

Paraguay: Villar; Arce, Caceres J, Gamarra, Caniza, Bonet (Gavilan 72), Ortiz, Paredes, Campos (Cuevas 61), Santa Cruz, Cardozo (Alvarenga 87).
Ecuador: Cevallos; De la Cruz, Hurtado I, Espinoza G, Corozo, Mendez, Tenorio E (Fernandez 63), Ambrossi (Salas 77), Gomez, Chala, Ordonez.
Referee: Paniagua (Bolivia).

Montevideo, 15 November 2003, 60,000

Uruguay (1) 2 *(Chevanton 31, Romero 48)*

Chile (1) 1 *(Melendez 20)*

Uruguay: Munua; Gonzalez, Lopez, Lago, Munoz (Romero 46), Sosa, Nunez, Liguera (Recoba 70), Chevanton, Bueno, Forlan (Hornos 46).
Chile: Tapia N; Rojas R, Olarra, Ramirez, Perez, Martel (Ormazabal 53), Nunoz, Melendez, Mark Gonzalez (Mirosevic 53), Navia (Norambuena 75), Pinilla.
Referee: Martin (Argentina).

Lima, 16 November 2003, 70,000

Peru (0) 1 *(Solano 58)*

Brazil (1) 1 *(Rivaldo 20 (pen))*

Peru: Ibanez; Jorge Soto, Galliquio, Rebosio, Hidalgo (Salas 52), Jayo, Ciurlizza, Solano, Palacios (Garcia 74), Mendoza, Pizarro.
Brazil: Dida; Cafu, Lucio, Roque Junior, Junior, Gilberto Silva, Ze Roberto, Emerson (Renato 61), Kaka (Alex 74), Rivaldo (Luis Fabiano 84), Ronaldo.
Referee: Ruiz (Colombia).

Santiago, 18 November 2003, 63,000

Chile (0) 0

Paraguay (1) 1 *(Paredes 30)*

Chile: Tapia N; Contreras, Ramirez, Olarra, Alvarez (Ormazabal 46), Marcos Gonzalez (Melendez 46), Perez, Mirosevic, Pizarro, Pinilla, Navia (Norambuena 62).
Paraguay: Villar; Arce, Caceres J, Gamarra, Caniza, Bonet (Gavilan 79), Ortiz, Paredes (Da Silva 88), Enciso, Santa Cruz, Cardozo (Alvarenga 87).
Referee: Mendez (Uruguay).

Maracaibo, 18 November 2003, 25,000

Venezuela (0) 2 *(Rey 89, Arango 90)*

Bolivia (0) 1 *(Botero 60)*

Venezuela: Angelucci; Vallenilla, Cichero, Rey, Hernandez (Rojas 61), Jimenez, Arango, Urdaneta, Paez, Moran (Rondon 59), Noriega (Moreno 52).
Bolivia: Fernandez L; Raldes (Sandy 79), Sanchez O, Paz Garcia, Reyes, Alvarez, Gatti Ribeiro, Justiniano, Suarez (Mendez 69), Mercado (Vaca 66), Botero.
Referee: Reinoso (Ecuador).

Barranquilla, 19 November 2003, 30,000

Colombia (0) 1 *(Angel 47)*

Argentina (1) 1 *(Crespo 26)*

Colombia: Cordoba O; Martinez, Cordoba I, Yepes, Viveros, Grisales, Viafara, Lozano (Bolano 20), Patino (Arriaga 46), Montoya (Becerra 71), Angel.
Argentina: Cavallero; Quiroga, Ayala, Samuel, Zanetti, Almeyda, Piacente, Kily Gonzalez, Aimar (D'Alessandro 70), Delgado (Veron 46), Crespo (Saviola 71).
Referee: Simon (Brazil).

Quito, 19 November 2003, 43,000

Ecuador (0) 0

Peru (0) 0

Ecuador: Cevallos; De la Cruz, Hurtado I, Reasco, Espinoza G, Ayovi M, Obregon (Fernandez 66), Chala (Aguinaga 79), Mendez, Tenorio C, Ordonez (Salas 46).
Peru: Ibanez; Jorge Soto, Rebosio, Galliquio, Salas, Jayo, Ciurlizza, Garcia, Palacios (Moran 53), Mendoza (Farfan 46), Pizarro.
Referee: Gonzalez (Paraguay).

Curitiba, 19 November 2003, 30,000

Brazil (2) 3 *(Kaka 19, Ronaldo 29, 87)*

Uruguay (0) 3 *(Forlan 57, 76, Gilberto Silva 79 (og))*

Brazil: Dida; Cafu, Lucio, Roque Junior, Junior, Renato (Juninho Pernambucano 79), Gilberto Silva, Ze Roberto, Kaka (Alex 72), Rivaldo (Luis Fabiano 80), Ronaldo.
Uruguay: Munua; Romero (Recoba 46), Bizera, Lopez, Lago, Sosa, Abeijon (Nunez 36), Liguera, Hornos (Chevanton 55), Zalayeta, Forlan.
Referee: Elizondo (Argentina).

Buenos Aires, 30 March 2004, 55,000

Argentina (0) 1 *(Crespo 60)*

Ecuador (0) 0

Argentina: Cavallero; Ayala, Sorin, Rodriguez C, Gonzalez L, Heinze, Gonzalez M (Tevez 46), D'Alessandro, Aimar (Riquelme 55), Delgado (Burdisso 66), Crespo.
Ecuador: Cevallos; Hurtado I, De la Cruz, Obregon, Tenorio C (Salas 73), Ayovi M, Chala (Delgado 63), Espinoza G, Reasco, Mendez, Tenorio E (Kaviedes 67).
Referee: Vazquez (Uruguay).

La Paz, 30 March 2004, 42,000

Bolivia (0) 0

Chile (1) 2 *(Villarroel 38, Mark Gonzalez 60)*

Bolivia: Fernandez L; Sanchez, Pena, Pizarro, Suarez (Gatti Ribeiro 46), Angulo, Reyes (Vaca 61), Pachi, Da Rosa, Castillo, Botero (Mendez 46).
Chile: Tapia N; Rojas R, Vargas, Olarra, Perez, Villarroel (Maldonado 55), Melendez, Mark Gonzalez, Martel (Valenzuela 74), Salas, Galaz (Pinilla 55).
Referee: Martin (Argentina).

Asuncion, 31 March 2004, 40,000

Paraguay (0) 0

Brazil (0) 0

Paraguay: Tavarelli; Arce, Caceres J (Da Silva 73), Gamarra, Bonet (Ortiz 30), Paredes, Toledo (Campos 56), Enciso, Caniza, Cardozo, Santa Cruz.
Brazil: Dida; Cafu, Lucio, Roque Junior, Roberto Carlos, Renato (Juninho Pernambucano 67), Gilberto Silva, Ze Roberto, Kaka, Ronaldinho, Ronaldo.
Referee: Ruiz (Colombia).

Lima, 31 March 2004, 29,325

Peru (0) 0

Colombia (2) 2 *(Grisales 30, Oviedo 42)*

Peru: Ibanez; Rebosio, Jorge Soto, Hidalgo (Farfan 46), Jayo, Palacios (Silva 58), Quinteros (Salas 46), Ciurlizza, Galliquio, Pizarro, Mendoza.
Colombia: Calero; Cordoba I, Yepes, Vargas, Oviedo, Murillo (Viveros 72), Perea, Ramirez (Viafara 90), Grisales (Patino 78), Bedoya, Angel.
Referee: Rezende (Brazil).

Montevideo, 31 March 2004, 40,000

Uruguay (0) 0

Venezuela (1) 3 *(Urdaneta 18, Hector Gonzalez 65, Arango 80)*

Uruguay: Munua; Lopez■, Sorondo, Rodriguez D, Liguera, Sosa, Nunez, Recoba, Chevanton (Correa 59), Hornos (Pandiani 46), Forlan (Bueno 72).
Venezuela: Angelucci; Vallenilla, Rey, Cichero, Hernandez, Jimenez, Vera, Paez (Rojas 61), Arango (Gonzalez A 83), Urdaneta (Gonzalez H 61), Rondon.
Referee: Ortube (Bolivia).

La Paz, 1 June 2004, 20,000

Bolivia (1) 2 *(Cristaldo 9, Suarez 72)*

Paraguay (1) 1 *(Cardozo 33)*

Bolivia: Fernandez L; Jauregui, Raldes, Pena■, Gatti Ribeiro (Solis 90), Cristaldo, Sanchez O, Alvarez (Suarez 60), Baldivieso, Gutierrez (Angulo 86), Botero.
Paraguay: Villa; Espinola, Lugo (Cabanas 82), Gamarra, Da Silva, Edgar Gonzalez, Ortiz, Duarte (De Los Santos 74), Enciso, Cardozo, Santa Cruz (Ramirez 63).
Referee: Resende de Freitas (Brazil).

Montevideo, 1 June 2004, 30,000

Uruguay (0) 1 *(Forlan 73)*

Peru (2) 3 *(Solano 12, Pizarro 19, Farfan 62)*

Uruguay: Munua; De Souza, Sorondo■, Lembo, Guigou (Romero 46), Sosa, Garcia, Pacheco (Forlan 46), Nunez, Chevanton, Pandiani (Dario Silva 72).
Peru: Ibanez; Galliquio, Acasiete, Rebosio (Garcia 80), Vilchez, Zegarra, Solano, Jayo, Palacios (Jose Soto 59), Pizarro (Mendoza 46), Farfan.
Referee: Selma (Chile).

San Cristobal, 1 June 2004, 30,000

Venezuela (0) 0

Chile (0) 1 *(Pinilla 84)*

Venezuela: Angelucci; Vallenilla (Gonzalez H 65), Cichero, Rey, Hernandez, Jimenez, Vielma (Gonzalez A 75), Urdaneta (Margiotta 46), Paez, Arango, Rondon.
Chile: Tapia N; Rojas R, Vargas, Olarra, Perez, Maldonado, Melendez, Mark Gonzalez (Mirosevic 59), Pizarro (Valenzuela 79), Galaz (Pinilla 46), Navia.
Referee: Torres (Paraguay).

Belo Horizonte, 2 June 2004, 48,000

Brazil (1) 3 *(Ronaldo 16 (pen), 67 (pen), 90 (pen))*

Argentina (0) 1 *(Sorin 80)*

Brazil: Dida; Cafu, Juan, Roque Junior, Roberto Carlos, Edmilson, Juninho Pernambucano (Julio Baptista 75), Ze Roberto, Kaka (Alex 75), Luis Fabiano, Ronaldo.
Argentina: Cavallero; Quiroga, Samuel, Heinze, Zanetti, Mascherano, Gonzalez L (Aimar 61), Sorin, Delgado (Rosales 36) (Saviola 61), Crespo, Kily Gonzalez.
Referee: Ruiz (Colombia).

Quito, 2 June 2004, 40,000

Ecuador (1) 2 *(Delgado 3, Salas 66)*

Colombia (0) 1 *(Oviedo 56)*

Ecuador: Espinoza J; De la Cruz, Hurtado I, Espinoza G, Ambrossi, Ayovi M (Lastra 87), Tenorio E, Mendez (Aguinaga 65), Chala, Figueroa (Salas 50), Delgado.
Colombia: Calero; Perea, Yepes, Cordoba I, Bedoya (Ferreira 78), Vargas, Ramirez, Viafara (Viveros 46), Oviedo, Valentierra (Murillo■ 70), Rey.
Referee: Baldassi (Argentina).

Quito, 5 June 2004, 40,000

Ecuador (3) 3 *(Solis 29 (og), Delgado 33, De la Cruz 40)*

Bolivia (0) 2 *(Gutierrez 58, Castillo 75)*

Ecuador: Espinoza J; De la Cruz, Hurtado I, Espinoza G, Reasco, Tenorio E, Obregon (Aguinaga 70), Ambrossi (Ayovi M 80), Chala (Mendez 66), Delgado, Salas.
Bolivia: Fernandez L; Solis (Gatti Ribeiro 46), Sanchez O, Raldes, Jauregui, Alvarez, Angulo (Galindo 46), Suarez (Castillo 67), Baldivieso, Botero, Gutierrez.
Referee: Brand (Venezuela).

Buenos Aires, 6 June 2004, 30,000

Argentina (0) 0

Paraguay (0) 0

Argentina: Abbondanzieri; Ayala, Samuel, Heinze, Gonzalez L (Rosales 69), Mascherano, Sorin, Tevez, Saviola, Crespo, Kily Gonzalez.
Paraguay: Villar; Caniza, Caceres J, Gamarra, Da Silva, Gavilan (Sarabia 90), Ortiz■, Toledo (Edgar Gonzalez 64), Enciso, Santa Cruz, Cardozo (Ramirez 84).
Referee: Simon (Brazil).

Santiago, 6 June 2004, 65,000

Chile (0) 1 *(Navia 89 (pen))*

Brazil (1) 1 *(Luis Fabiano 16)*

Chile: Tapia N; Rojas R (Alvarez 46), Fuentes, Olarra, Perez, Helo (Galaz 46), Melendez, Maldonado, Mark Gonzalez (Mirosevic 56), Pizarro, Navia.
Brazil: Dida; Cafu, Roberto Carlos, Juninho Pernambucano, Juan, Roque Junior, Edmilson, Kaka (Julio Baptista 72), Ronaldo, Luis Fabiano, Edu.
Referee: Elizondo (Argentina).

Barranquilla, 6 June 2004, 20,000

Colombia (3) 5 *(Pacheco 18, 32, Moreno 20, Restrepo 81, Herrera 86)*

Uruguay (0) 0

Colombia: Calero; Palacios, Perea, Yepes, Bedoya, Ramirez, Restrepo, Oviedo (Vargas 74), Pacheco (Ferreira 84), Moreno (Arriaga 74), Herrera.
Uruguay: Munua; Gonzalez, Lembo, De Souza (Lago 64), Romero (De Los Santos 46), Romero, Garcia, Delgado, Canobbio (Forlan 46), Recoba, Chevanton.
Referee: Carlos (Paraguay).

Lima, 6 June 2004, 45,000

Peru (0) 0

Venezuela (0) 0

Peru: Ibanez; Jorge Soto, Rebosio, Acasiete, Hidalgo (Vilchez 67), Jayo, Zegarra, Solano, Palacios (Orejuela 67), Farfan, Mendoza (Silva 79).
Venezuela: Angelucci; Vallenilla, Cichero, Rey, Hernandez, Mea Vitali, Jimenez, Urdaneta (Margiotta 79), Paez (Gonzalez H 66), Arango, Rondon (Moran 61).
Referee: Larrionda (Uruguay).

Lima, 4 September 2004, 60,000

Peru (0) 1 *(Jorge Soto 62)*

Argentina (1) 3 *(Rosales 14, Coloccini 66, Sorin 90)*

Peru: Ibanez; Salas, Acasiete, Galliquio, Vilchez, Jayo, Solano, Palacios (Olcese 76), Jorge Soto (Garcia 77), Mendoza, Farfan.
Argentina: Abbondanzieri; Coloccini, Heinze, Milito G, Zanetti, Mascherano, Kily Gonzalez■, D'Alessandro (Milito D 64), Delgado (Sorin 70), Tevez (Medina 83), Rosales.
Referee: Simon (Brazil).

Sao Paulo, 5 September 2004, 72,000

Brazil (3) 3 *(Ronaldo 1, Ronaldinho 13 (pen), Adriano 44)*

Bolivia (0) 1 *(Cristaldo 48)*

Brazil: Julio Cesar; Belletti, Edmilson, Roque Junior, Roberto Carlos, Juninho Pernambucano (Renato 60), Gilberto Silva, Edu (Robinho 72), Ronaldinho (Alex 60), Ronaldo, Adriano.
Bolivia: Fernandez L; Ribeiro (Arena 46), Alvarez, Pena, Raldes, Cristaldo, Sanchez O, Colque (Tufino 46), Gutierrez (Coimbra 76), Pizarro, Botero.
Referee: Baldassi (Argentina).

Santiago, 5 September 2004, 63,000

Chile (0) 0

Colombia (0) 0

Chile: Tapia N; Villaroel, Fuentes, Olarra, Perez■, Maldonado■, Acuna, Mirosevic (Tello 60), Pizarro (Valenzuela 60), Navia (Salas 46), Pinilla.
Colombia: Calero; Perea L, Cordoba I, Yepes, Bedoya, Vargas, Viafara■, Oviedo (Perea E 87), Hernandez (Patino■ 56), Castillo, Preciado (Murillo 65).
Referee: Mendonca (Brazil).

Asuncion, 5 September 2004, 45,000

Paraguay (0) 1 *(Gamarra 53)*

Venezuela (0) 0

Paraguay: Villar; Sarabia, Caceres J, Gamarra (Mansur 84), Da Silva, Paredes, Enciso, Gavilan (Barreto 78), Quevas, Cardozo (Ramirez 58), Santa Cruz.
Venezuela: Angelucci; Vallenilla, Rey, Cichero, Rojas, Jimenez, Vera, Paez (Rondon 68), Urdaneta (Gonzalez H 71), Arango, Castellin (Moreno 77).
Referee: Mendez (Uruguay).

Montevideo, 5 September 2004, 40,000

Uruguay (0) 1 *(Bueno 58)*

Ecuador (0) 0

Uruguay: Viera; Bizera, Montero, Rodriguez D, Diogo, Sosa, Delgado, Recoba (Perez 78), Rodriguez C (Estoyanoff 57), Dario Silva (Sanchez 25), Bueno.
Ecuador: Villafuerte; De la Cruz, Hurtado I, Espinoza, Reasco, Ayovi M, Soledispa (Quinonez 70), Mendez, Ayovi W (Valencia 75), Baldeon (Delgado 60), Tenorio C.
Referee: Hidalgo (Peru).

Buenos Aires, 9 October 2004, 60,000

Argentina (3) 4 *(Gonzalez L 6, Figueroa 33, 54, Zanetti 45)*

Uruguay (0) 2 *(Rodriguez C 63, Chevanton 86 (pen))*

Argentina: Abbondanzieri; Coloccini, Gonzalez L (Rodriguez M 68), Samuel, Heinze, Zanetti, Cambiasso, Saviola, Figueroa (Insua 81), Riquelme, Sorin.
Uruguay: Viera; Bizera (Lago 57), Lembo, Rodriguez D, Diogo, Sosa, Diego Perez (Garcia 55), Delgado, Rodriguez C, Dario Silva (Forlan 55), Chevanton.
Referee: Mendonca (Brazil).

La Paz, 9 October 2004, 30,000

Bolivia (0) 1 *(Botero 56)*

Peru (0) 0

Bolivia: Fernandez L; Arana, Sanchez O, Raldes, Ribeiro■, Garcia R, Cristaldo, Sanchez E (Tufino 86), Colque, Botero, Gutierrez (Galindo 90).
Peru: Ibanez; Rodriguez, Galliquio (La Rosa 72), Acasiete, Salas, Jorge Soto, Jayo, Garcia (Palacios 56), Ciurlizza (Carty 64), Guerrero, Farfan.
Referee: Reynoso (Ecuador).

Baranquilla, 9 October 2004, 25,000

Colombia (1) 1 *(Grisales 17)*

Paraguay (0) 1 *(Torres 78)*

Colombia: Calero; Perea L, Cordoba I, Yepes, Bedoya, Diaz (Rodriguez 81), Restrepo, Oviedo, Grisales (Moreno 67), Pacheco, Angel.
Paraguay: Villar; Caniza, Caceres J, Sarabia, Da Silva, Ortiz (Gavilan 46), Enciso, Paredes, Torres (Monges 81), Bareiro (Cuevas 60), Cardozo.
Referee: Elizondo (Argentina).

Maracaibo, 9 October 2004, 35,000

Venezuela (0) 2 *(Moran 80, 90)*

Brazil (2) 5 *(Kaka 6, 35, Ronaldo 49, 51, Adriano 75)*

Venezuela: Angelucci; Vallenilla, Rey, Cichero, Hernandez (Vielma 55), Vera (Gonzalez C 68), Jimenez, Arango, Vargas, Margiotta (Gonzalez H 46), Moran.
Brazil: Dida; Cafu, Roberto Carlos, Juninho Pernambucano (Edu 62), Roque Junior, Juan, Renato, Ze Roberto, Ronaldo (Alex 72), Ronaldinho, Kaka (Adriano 68).
Referee: Chandia (Chile).

Quito, 10 October 2004, 26,000

Ecuador (0) 2 *(Kaviedes 59, Mendez 64)*

Chile (0) 0

Ecuador: Villafuerte; De la Cruz, Hurtado I, Espinoza G, Guerron, Tenorio E, Ayovi M, Ayovi W (Salas 46), Mendez, Kaviedes (Fernandez 88), Ordonez (Ambrossi 61).
Chile: Tapia N; Rojas R, Fuentes, Olarra, Contreras, Martel (Beausejour 46), Gonzalez L, Melendez, Valenzuela (Mirosevic 58), Salas, Galaz (Quinteros 76).
Referee: Ortube (Bolivia).

La Paz, 12 October 2004, 28,000

Bolivia (0) 0

Uruguay (0) 0

Bolivia: Fernandez L; Carballo (Colque 65), Arana, Raldes, Sanchez O, Garcia (Cabrera 46), Cristaldo, Sanchez E, Alvarez (Galindo 80), Gutierrez, Botero.
Uruguay: Viera; Diogo, Rodriguez G, Pouso■, Lago, Rodriguez D, Varela, Garcia, Morales R (Chevanton 78), Sanchez (Sosa 76), Regueiro (Parodi 73).
Referee: De Freitas (Brazil).

Maceio, 13 October 2004, 30,000

Brazil (0) 0

Colombia (0) 0

Brazil: Dida; Cafu, Roberto Carlos, Magrao (Elano 59), Roque Junior, Juan, Renato, Ze Roberto (Edu 84), Ronaldo, Ronaldinho, Alex (Adriano 58).
Colombia: Calero; Perea L, Cordoba I, Yepes, Bedoya, Grisales (Leal 87), Restrepo, Diaz, Oviedo (Moreno 86), Pacheco (Viveros 77), Angel.
Referee: Larrionda (Uruguay).

Santiago, 13 October 2004, 45,000

Chile (0) 0

Argentina (0) 0

Chile: Tapia N; Rojas R (Olarra 46), Fuentes, Vargas, Contreras, Alvarez, Melendez (Mirosevic 60), Valenzuela, Valdivia (Quinteros 72), Salas, Navia.
Argentina: Abbondanzieri; Coloccini, Samuel, Heinze, Zanetti, Cambiasso, Riquelme, Sorin, Gonzalez L (Mascherano 46), Saviola (D'Alessandro 76), Figueroa (Tevez 63).
Referee: Amarilla (Paraguay).

Asuncion, 13 October 2004, 30,000

Paraguay (1) 1 *(Paredes 29)*

Peru (0) 1 *(Solano 74 (pen))*

Paraguay: Villar; Caniza J, Caceres, Manzur, Da Silva, Enciso, Paredes, Gavilan (Bareiro 83), Torres (Cuevas 53), Haedo, Cardozo (Monges 73).
Peru: Ibanez; Galliquio (Ciurlizza 46), Rebosio, Acasiete, Vargas, Solano, Jayo, Palacios, Jorge Soto, Mendoza (Guerrero 67), Farfan.
Referee: Ruiz (Colombia).

San Cristobal, 14 October 2004, 20,000

Venezuela (1) 3 *(Urdaneta 21 (pen), Moran 73, 81)*

Ecuador (1) 1 *(Ayovi M 42 (pen))*

Venezuela: Dudamel; Vallenilla (Gonzalez H 66), Rey, Cichero, Rojas, Vera, Jimenez (Paez 64), Arango, Urdaneta, Rondon (Garcia 61), Moran.
Ecuador: Villafuerte; Reasco, Hurtado I, Espinoza, Guerron, Tenorio E, Ayovi M, Ambrossi, Mendez, Kaviedes, Salas (Baldeon 72).
Referee: Lecca (Peru).

Buenos Aires, 17 November 2004, 30,000

Argentina (2) 3 *(Rey 3 (og), Riquelme 46, Saviola 65)*

Venezuela (1) 2 *(Moran 31, Vielma 72)*

Argentina: Abbondanzieri; Rodriguez G, Sorin, Zanetti, Mascherano, Milito G, Riquelme, Figueroa, Solari (Gonzalez L 65), Cambiasso (Placente 79), Delgado (Saviola 58).
Venezuela: Dudamel; Vallenilla, Rey, Cichero, Vera, Paez (Vielma 70), Jimenez (Casseres 77), Moran, Rojas, Arango, Hernandez (Urdaneta 52).
Referee: Hidalgo (Peru).

Barranquilla, 17 November 2004, 25,000

Colombia (1) 1 *(Yepes 18)*

Bolivia (0) 0

Colombia: Calero; Cordoba I, Yepes, Viveros, Oviedo (Perez 62), Angel, Pacheco (Hernandez 76), Murillo (Ferreira 70), Perea, Grisales, Restrepo.
Bolivia: Fernandez L; Pena (Arce 80), Jauregui, Alvarez, Cristaldo, Tufino (Vaca Diez 76), Coimbra (Galindo 46), Gutierrez, Raldes, Botero, Arana.
Referee: Torres (Paraguay).

Quito, 17 November 2004, 38,308

Ecuador (0) 1 *(Mendez 77)*

Brazil (0) 0

Ecuador: Villafuerte; Hurtado I, De La Cruz, Mendez, Kaviedes (Ayovi W 75), Delgado (Reasco 90), Ambrosi, Urrutia (Salas 46), Ayovi M, Espinoza G, Tenorio E.
Brazil: Dida; Cafu, Juan, Roque Junior, Renato, Roberto Carlos, Juninho Pernambucano (Dudu 74), Kaka (Adriano 81), Ronaldo, Ronaldinho, Kleberson (Ricardinho 64).
Referee: Ruiz (Colombia).

Lima, 17 November 2004, 39,752

Peru (0) 2 *(Farfan 56, Guerrero 85)*

Chile (0) 1 *(Gonzalez S 90)*

Peru: Ibanez; Acasiete■, Jorge Soto, Vargas, Solano, Jayo, Palacios, Pizarro (Guerrero 71), Farfan, Ciurlizza (Zegarra 37) (Villalta 62), Rodriguez.
Chile: Tapia N; Alvarez, Maldonado (Valdivia 75), Contreras, Valenzuela (Gonzalez L 46), Pizarro, Pinilla, Melendez■, Olarra (Gonzalez S 62), Mark Gonzalez, Fuentes.
Referee: Baldassi (Argentina).

Montevideo, 17 November 2004, 35,000

Uruguay (0) 1 *(Montero 78)*

Paraguay (0) 0

Uruguay: Viera; Lugano, Rodriguez G, Montero, Garcia, Lopez, Varela (Estoyanoff 67), Dario Silva (Morales 46), Recoba (Sanchez 70), Delgado, Chevanton.
Paraguay: Villar; Caceres J, Gamarra, Monges (Gavilan 80), Barreto (Bareiro 80), Paredes, Da Silva, Ortiz, Cardozo, Caniza, Cuevas (Ramirez 68).
Referee: Simon (Brazil).

La Paz, 26 March 2005, 35,000

Bolivia (0) 1 *(Castillo 49)*

Argentina (0) 2 *(Figueroa 58, Galletti 63)*

Bolivia: Fernandez L; Colque (Pachi 46), Sanchez O, Raldes, Alvarez L, Angulo (Cabrera 68), Pizarro, Galindo (Garcia 86), Sanchez E, Castillo, Botero.
Argentina: Abbondanzieri; Cufre, Burdisso, Milito G, Rodriguez C, Scaloni, Cambiasso, Duscher, Rodriguez M (Porzini 64), Galletti (Palacio 84), Figueroa (Zarate 73).
Referee: Larrionda (Uruguay).

Santiago, 26 March 2005, 45,000

Chile (0) 1 *(Mirosevic 47)*

Uruguay (1) 1 *(Requeiro 4)*

Chile: Tapia N; Fuentes, Rojas R, Conteras (Valdivia 46), Alvarez, Maldonado, Pizarro, Mark Gonzalez (Valenzuela 82), Mirosevic (Gonzalez S 82), Salas, Pinilla.
Uruguay: Viera; Lopez, Lugano, Monero, Rodriguez D, Diogo, Olivera (Sosa 59), Garcia, Requeiro (Sanchez 81), Forlan, Zalayeta (Morales 69).
Referee: Ruiz (Colombia).

Maracaibo, 26 March 2005, 20,000

Venezuela (0) 0

Colombia (0) 0

Venezuela: Dudamel; Hector Gonzalez, Rey, Cichero, Hernandez, Vielma, Jimenez, Maldonado, Urdaneta (Gonzalez A 65), Castellin (Gonzalez C 56), Margiotta (Noriega 74).
Colombia: Calero; Orozco, Cordoba I, Yepes, Bedoya, Restrepo, Ramirez (Vargas 72), Ferreira, Hernandez (Pacheco 73), Castillo (Herrera 86), Perea.
Referee: Simon (Brazil).

Goiania, 27 March 2005, 52,000

Brazil (0) 1 *(Kaka 74)*

Peru (0) 0

Brazil: Dida; Cafu, Roberto Carlos, Juninho Pernambucano (Robinho 46), Lucio, Juan, Emerson, Kaka (Renato 83), Ronaldo, Ronaldinho, Ze Roberto.
Peru: Ibanez; Jorge Soto, Rebosio, Rodriguez (Guadalupe 73), Vilchez, Jayo, Zegarra, Solano (Cominges 68), Palacios (Olcese 46), Farfan, Pizarro.
Referee: Amarilla (Paraguay).

Quito, 27 March 2005, 25,000

Ecuador (2) 5 *(Valencia 32, 49, Mendez 45, 47, Marlon Ayovi M 77 (pen))*

Paraguay (2) 2 *(Cardozo 9 (pen), Cabanas 14)*

Ecuador: Villafuerte; De la Cruz, Ambrossi, Espinoza, Hurtado I, Ayovi M, Tenorio E (Caicedo 78), Mendez, Valencia, Tenorio O (Salas 57), Delgado (Kaviedes 78).
Paraguay: Villar; Sarabia, Gamarra, Da Silva, Caniza, Gavilan (Cuevas 52), Ortiz, Bonet, Monges (Barreto 52), Cabanas, Cardozo.
Referee: Mendez (Uruguay).

La Paz, 29 March 2005, 15,000

Bolivia (2) 3 *(Cichero 2 (og), Castillo 25, Vaca 83)*

Venezuela (0) 1 *(Maldonado 71)*

Bolivia: Fernandez L; Jauregui, Raldes, Sanchez O, Alvarez, Pizarro, Garcia R (Vaca 19), Galindo, Sanchez E (Pachi 80), Botero, Castillo.
Venezuela: Dudamel; De Ornelas (Rondon 70), Rey, Cichero (Noriega 46), Hernandez, Fuenmayor, Gonzalez A, Gonzalez H, Vera, Urdaneta (Gonzalez C 57), Maldonado.
Referee: Lecca (Peru).

Buenos Aires, 30 March 2005, 44,000

Argentina (0) 1 *(Crespo 65)*

Colombia (0) 0

Argentina: Abbondanzieri; Zanetti, Ayala, Heinze, Sorin, Gonzalez L, Mascherano (Galletti 55), Cambiasso, Riquelme, Saviola (Palcente 79), Crespo.
Colombia: Calero; Orozco, Cordoba I, Yepes, Bedoya, Viafara, Restrepo (Pacheco 79), Vargas■, Oviedo, Hernandez (Viveros 46), Perea (Castillo 68).
Referee: Amarilla (Paraguay).

Asuncion, 30 March 2005, 35,000

Paraguay (1) 2 *(Morinigo 37, Cardozo 59)*

Chile (0) 1 *(Fuentes 72)*

Paraguay: Villar; Bonet, Caceres J, Gamarra, Da Silva, Nunez, Paredes (Gavilan 82), Ortiz, Morinigo (Barreto 60), Cabanas, Cardozo (Valdez 71).
Chile: Tapia N; Rojas R, Fuentes, Olarra, Perez (Alvarez 46), Melendez (Pizarro 53), Maldonado, Mirosevic (Gonzalez S 64), Mark Gonzalez, Salas, Pinilla.
Referee: Elizondo (Argentina).

Lima, 30 March 2005, 45,000

Peru (1) 2 *(Guerrero 1, Farfan 58)*

Ecuador (2) 2 *(De la Cruz 3, Valencia 43)*

Peru: Ibanez; Jorge Soto (Salas 60), Rebosio, Acasiete, Vargas, Jayo, Solano (Mendoza 84), Zegarra (Palacios 60), Farfan, Pizarro, Guerrero.
Ecuador: Villafuerte; De la Cruz, Espinoza G, Hurtado I, Ambrossi, Ayovi M (Caicado 71), Tenorio E, Valencia, Mendez (Ayovi W 85), Baldeon (Salas 46), Delgado.
Referee: Chandia (Chile).

Montevideo, 30 March 2005, 50,000

Uruguay (0) 1 *(Forlan 48)*

Brazil (0) 1 *(Emerson 68)*

Uruguay: Viera; Lopez, Lugano, Montero, Rodriguez D, Olivera (Chevanton 72), Garcia, Diogo (De Los Santos 86), Requeiro (Delgado 58), Forlan, Zalayeta.
Brazil: Dida; Cafu, Roberto Carlos, Ricardo Oliveira (Robinho 63), Lucio, Luisao, Emerson, Kaka, Ronaldo, Ronaldinho, Ze Roberto (Renato 69).
Referee: Baldassi (Argentina).

Santiago, 4 June 2005, 35,000

Chile (2) 3 *(Fuentes 7, 35, Salas 69)*

Bolivia (0) 1 *(Castillo 85 (pen))*

Chile: Tapia N; Gonzalez S■, Fuentes, Rojas R, Villarroel, Rojas F, Maldonado, Pizarro, Melendez (Acuna 13), Jimenez (Tello 76), Salas (Galaz 75).
Bolivia: Fernandez L; Alvarez, Raldes, Arana, Castillo, Justiniano, Gutierrez, Coimbra, Pachi (Arce 46), Jauregui (Parada 81), Garcia (Vaca 35).
Referee: Rezende (Brazil).

Barranquilla, 4 June 2005, 25,000

Colombia (1) 5 *(Rey 29, Soto 56, Angel 59, Restrepo 76, Perea E 78)*

Peru (0) 0

Colombia: Mondragon; Palacio, Perea L, Yepes (Mendoza 80), Bedoya, Viafara, Restrepo, Soto, Moreno, Angel (Perea E 65), Rey (Arzuaga 72).
Peru: Flores; Solano, Acasiete, Rebosio, Vilches (Guerrero 46), Jayo■, Juan Vargas, La Rosa, Palacios (Cominges 64), Farfan (Mendoza 64), Pizarro.
Referee: Torres (Paraguay).

Quito, 4 June 2005, 37,500

Ecuador (0) 2 *(Lara 53, Delgado 88)*

Argentina (0) 0

Ecuador: Villafuerte; Ambrossi, Espinoza G, Hurtado I, De la Cruz, Ayovi M, Tenorio E, Delgado, Valencia (Tenorio C 83), Gomez (Lara 46), Reasco (Quiroz 76).
Argentina: Franco; Zanetti, Coloccini, Samuel, Milito G (Figueroa 68), Duscher (Tevez 31), Cambiasso■, Aimar (D'Alessandro 74), Kily Gonzalez, Galletti, Maxi Rodriguez.
Referee: Selman (Chile).

Maracaibo, 4 June 2005, 30,000

Venezuela (0) 1 *(Maldonado 73)*

Uruguay (1) 1 *(Forlan 2)*

Venezuela: Dudamel; Hector Gonzalez, Rojas J, Rey, Cichero, Vera, Arango, Vielma (Urdaneta 38), Paez (Casseres 63), Moran, Maldonado.
Uruguay: Viera; Diogo■, Lopez, Lugano, Montero, Rodriguez D (De Los Santos 62), Olivera, Sosa, Requeiro (Perez 41), Forlan (Chevanton 76), Zalayeta.
Referee: Brazenas (Argentina).

Porto Alegre, 5 June 2005, 55,000

Brazil (2) 4 *(Ronaldinho 33 (pen), 42 (pen), Ze Roberto 71, Robinho 83)*

Paraguay (0) 1 *(Santa Cruz 73)*

Brazil: Dida; Belletti, Lucio■, Roque Junior, Roberto Carlos, Emerson (Gilberto Silva 76), Ze Roberto, Kaka, Ronaldinho, Robinho (Juan 84), Adriano (Ricardo Oliveira 76).
Paraguay: Villa; Caniza, Gamarra, Manzur, Da Silva, Bonet (Barreto 46), Ortiz, Paredes, Torres, Santa Cruz, Cabanas (Cuevas 64).
Referee: Broquetas (Uruguay).

Lima, 7 June 2005, 28,000

Peru (0) 0

Uruguay (0) 0

Peru: Flores; Cominges (Palacios 62), Rebosio, Mendoza, Vilchez, La Rosa (Solano 86), Villalta, Guadelupe, Farfan, Guerrero, Pizarro.
Uruguay: Viera; Rodriguez G, Lopez (Perez 31), Lugano, Rodriguez D, Oliveira, Pablo Garcia, Delgado, Chevanton (Estoyanoff 71), Zalayeta (Morales 83), Forlan.
Referee: Baldassi (Argentina).

Buenos Aires, 8 June 2005, 60,000

Argentina (3) 3 *(Crespo 4, 40, Riquelme 18)*

Brazil (0) 1 *(Roberto Carlos 71)*

Argentina: Abbondanzieri; Coloccini, Ayala, Heinze, Gonzalez L (Zanetti 70), Mascherano, Riquelme, Sorin, Kily Gonzalez, Saviola (Tevez 82), Crespo.
Brazil: Dida; Cafu, Roberto Carlos, Emerson, Juan, Roque Junior, Ronaldinho, Kaka, Adriano, Robinho (Renato 61), Ze Roberto.
Referee: Mendez (Uruguay).

Santiago, 8 June 2005, 35,000

Chile (1) 2 *(Jimenez 30, 59)*

Venezuela (0) 1 *(Moran 82)*

Chile: Tapia N; Fuentes, Rojas R, Contreras, Villarroel, Acuna, Maldonado, Rojas F, Pizarro (Gonzalez J 89), Jimenez (Valdivia 81), Galaz (Villanueva 62).
Venezuela: Dudamel; De Ornela (Vallenilla 46), Rey, Cichero, Hernandez, Jimenez, Gonzalez A (Perez 71), Urdaneta, Arango, Casseres (Gonzalez C 57), Moran.
Referee: Torres (Paraguay).

Barranquilla, 8 June 2005, 35,000

Colombia (2) 3 *(Moreno 5, 8, Arzuaga 70)*

Ecuador (0) 0

Colombia: Mondragon; Palacio, Yepes, Perea L, Benitez, Viafara, Restrepo, Soto (Vargas 36), Rey (Hurtado 66), Moreno (Arzuaga 68), Angel.
Ecuador: Villafuerte; De la Cruz, Hurtado I, Espinoza G, Reasco, Quiroz, Tenorio C, Ayovi M (Caicedo 46), Valencia (Ayovi W 54), Ambrossi (Lara 60), Delgado.
Referee: Simon (Brazil).

Asuncion, 8 June 2005, 45,000

Paraguay (2) 4 *(Gamarra 17, Santa Cruz 45, Cesar Caceres 54, Nunez 68)*

Bolivia (1) 1 *(Galindo 30)*

Paraguay: Villar; Caceres J, Cesar Caceres, Gamarra, Nunez, Ortiz, Paredes, Barreto (Gavilan 75), Cardozo (Salcedo 64), Santa Cruz, Cabanas (Cuevas 77).
Bolivia: Galerza; Alvarez, Raldes, Flores, Galindo, Jauregui, Centeno, Gutierrez L, Mojica (Vaca 78), Castillo (Arce 65), Parada (Coimbra 46).
Referee: Brand (Venezuela).

South America Table

	P	*W*	*D*	*L*	*F*	*A*	*Pts*
Argentina	15	9	4	2	27	15	31
Brazil	15	7	6	2	26	16	27
Ecuador	15	7	2	6	21	18	23
Paraguay	15	6	4	5	21	22	22
Colombia	15	5	5	5	20	12	20
Chile	15	5	5	5	17	16	20
Uruguay	15	4	6	5	19	26	18
Peru	15	3	6	6	15	21	15
Venezuela	15	4	3	8	16	23	15
Bolivia	15	4	1	10	17	30	13

OCEANIA

FIRST STAGE

Group 1
Solomon Islands 6, Tonga 0; Tahiti 2, Cook Islands 0; Solomon Islands 5, Cook Islands 0; Tahiti 0, New Caledonia, 0; Tonga 2, Cook Islands 1; Solomon Islands 2, New Caledonia 0; New Caledonia 8, Cook Islands 0; Tahiti 2, Tonga 0; New Caledonia 8, Tonga 0; Solomon Islands 1, Tahiti 1.

Group 2
Papua New Guinea 1, Vanuatu 1; Samoa 4, American Samoa 0; American Samoa 1, Vanuatu 9; Fiji 4, Papua New Guinea 2; Fiji 11, American Samoa 0; Samoa 0, Vanuatu 3; American Samoa 0, Papua New Guinea 10; Samoa 0, Fiji 4; Fiji 0, Vanuatu 3; Samoa 1, Papua New Guinea 4.
Top two from each group in the second stage joining Australia and New Zealand.

SECOND STAGE

Six qualifiers in final group; winners and runners-up advance to third stage.
Vanuatu 0, Solomon Islands 1; Tahiti 0, Fiji 0; Australia 1, New Zealand 0; New Zealand 3, Solomon Islands 0; Australia 9, Tahiti 0; Fiji 1, Vanuatu 0; Australia 6, Fiji 1; Tahiti 0, Solomon Islands 4; New Zealand 2, Vanuatu 4; New Zealand 10, Tahiti 0; Fiji 1, Solomon Islands 2; Vanuatu 0, Australia 3; Tahiti 2, Vanuatu 1; Fiji 0, New Zealand 2; Solomon Islands 2, Australia 2.

THIRD STAGE

Two qualifiers Australia and Solomon Islands play-off, the winners meet fifth placed South American team for place in finals.

ASIA

FIRST STAGE

Group 1
Jordan 1, Qatar 0; Laos 0, Iran 7; Iran 3, Qatar 1; Jordan 5, Laos 0; Iran 0, Jordan 1; Qatar 5, Laos 0; Jordan 0, Iran 2; Laos 1, Qatar 6; Laos 2, Jordan 3; Qatar 2, Iran 3.

Group 2
Palestine 1, Iraq 1; Taiwan 0, Uzbekistan 1; Palestine 8, Taiwan 0; Uzbekistan 1, Iraq 1; Uzbekistan 3, Palestine 0; Iraq 6, Taiwan 1; Palestine 0, Uzbekistan 3; Taiwan 1, Iraq 4; Iraq 1, Uzbekistan 2; Taiwan 0, Palestine 1.

Group 3
India 1, Singapore 0; Japan 1, Oman 0; India 1, Oman 5; Singapore 1, Japan 2; Japan 7, India 0; Oman 7, Singapore 0; India 0, Japan 4; Singapore 0, Oman 2; Oman 0, Japan 1; Singapore 2, India 0.

Group 4
China 1, Kuwait 0; Malaysia 1, Hong Kong 3; Hong Kong 0, China 1; Malaysia 0, Kuwait 2; China 4, Malaysia 0; Kuwait 4, Hong Kong 0; Hong Kong 0, Kuwait 2; Malaysia 0, China 1; Hong Kong 2, Malaysia 0; Kuwait 1, China 0.

Group 5
UAE 1, Thailand 0; Yemen 1, North Korea 1; North Korea 0, UAE 0; Yemen 0, Thailand 3; Thailand 1, North Korea 4; UAE 3, Yemen 0; North Korea 4, Thailand 1; Yemen 3, UAE 1; North Korea 2, Yemen 1; Thailand 3, UAE 0.

Group 6
Bahrain 2, Syria 1; Kyrgyzstan 1, Tajikistan 2; Kyrgyzstan 1, Syria 1; Tajikistan 0, Bahrain 0; Bahrain 5, Kyrgyzstan 0; Syria 3, Tajikistan 1; Kyrgyzstan 1, Bahrain 2; Tajikistan 0, Syria 1; Syria 2, Bahrain 2; Tajikistan 2, Kyrgyzstan 1.

Group 7
South Korea 2, Lebanon 0; Vietnam 4, Maldives 0; Maldives 0, South Korea 0; Vietnam 0, Lebanon 2; Lebanon 3, Maldives 0; South Korea 2, Vietnam 0; Maldives 2, Lebanon 5; Vietnam 1, South Korea 2; Lebanon 1, South Korea 1; Maldives 3, Vietnam 0.

Group 8
Saudi Arabia 3, Indonesia 0; Turkmenistan 2, Sri Lanka 0; Sri Lanka 0, Saudi Arabia 1; Turkmenistan 3, Indonesia 1; Indonesia 1, Sri Lanka 0; Saudi Arabia 3, Turkmenistan 0; Sri Lanka 2, Indonesia 2; Turkmenistan 0, Saudi Arabia 1; Indonesia 1, Saudi Arabia 3.

SECOND STAGE

Group A
South Korea 2, Kuwait 0; Uzbekistan 1, Saudi Arabia 1, Kuwait 2, Uzbekistan 1; Saudi Arabia 2, South Korea 0; Kuwait 0, Saudi Arabia 0; South Korea 2, Uzbekistan 1; Saudi Arabia 3, Kuwait 0; Uzbekistan 1, South Korea 1; Kuwait 0, South Korea 4; Saudi Arabia 3, Uzbekistan 0.

Group B
Bahrain 0, Iran 0; Japan 2, North Korea 1; Iran 2, Japan 1; North Korea 1, Bahrain 2; Japan 1, Bahrain 0; North Korea 0, Iran 2; Iran 1, North Korea 0; Bahrain 0, Japan 1; Iran 1, Bahrain 0; North Korea 0, Japan 2.

CONCACAF

FIRST STAGE

Group 1
Game 1
Grenada 5, Guyana 0; Guyana 1, Grenada 3.

Game 2
USA 3, Grenada 0; Grenada 2, USA 3.

Group 2
Game 1
Bermuda 13, Montserrat 0; Montserrat 0, Bermuda 7.

Game 2
El Salvador 2, Bermuda 1; Bermuda 2, El Salvador 2.

Group 3
Game 1
Haiti 5, Turks & Caicos Islands 0; Turks & Caicos Islands 0, Haiti 2.

Game 2
Haiti 1, Jamaica 1; Jamaica 3, Haiti 0.

Group 4
Game 1
British Virgin Islands 0, St Lucia 1; St Lucia 9, British Virgin Islands 0.

Game 2
Panama 4, St Lucia 0; St Lucia 0, Panama 3.

Group 5
Game 1
Cayman Islands 1, Cuba 2; Cuba 3, Cayman Islands 0.

Game 2
Cuba 2, Costa Rica 2; Costa Rica 1, Cuba 1.

Group 6
Game 1
Aruba 1, Surinam 2; Surinam 8, Aruba 1.

Game 2
Surinam 1, Guatemala 1; Guatemala 3, Surinam 1.

Group 7
Game 1
Antigua & Barbuda 2, Netherlands Antilles 0; Netherlands Antilles 3, Antigua & Barbuda 0.

Game 2
Netherlands Antilles 1, Honduras 2; Honduras 4, Netherlands Antilles 0.

Group 8
Canada 4, Belize 0; Belize 0, Canada 4.

Group 9
Game 1
Dominica 1, Bahamas 1; Bahamas 1, Dominica 3.

Game 2
Dominica 0, Mexico 10; Mexico 8, Dominica 0.

Group 10
Game 1
US Virgin Islands 0, St Kitts & Nevis 4; St Kitts & Nevis 7, US Virgin Islands 0.

Game 2
Barbados 0, St Kitts & Nevis 2; St Kitts & Nevis 3, Barbados 2.

Group 11
Game 1
Dominican Republic 0, Anguilla 0; Anguilla 0, Dominican Republic 6.

Game 2
Dominican Republic 0, Trinidad & Tobago 2; Trinidad & Tobago 4, Dominican Republic 0.

Group 12
Game 1
Nicaragua 2, St Vincent & the Grenadines 2; St Vincent & the Grenadines 4, Nicaragua 1.

Game two group winners to second stage.

SECOND STAGE

Group 1
El Salvador 2, Panama 1; Jamaica 1, USA 1; Jamaica 1, Panama 2; USA 2, El Salvador 0; El Salvador 0, Jamaica 3; Panama 1, USA 1; El Salvador 0, USA 2; Panama 1, Jamaica 1; Jamaica 0, El Salvador 0; USA 6, Panama 0.

Group 2
Canada 0, Guatemala 2; Costa Rica 2, Honduras 5; Canada 1, Honduras 1; Guatemala 2, Costa Rica 1; Costa Rica 1, Canada 0; Honduras 2, Guatemala 2; Costa Rica 5, Guatemala 0; Honduras 1, Canada 1; Canada 1, Costa Rica 3; Guatemala 1, Honduras 0.

Group 3
St Vincent & the Grenadines 0, Trinidad & Tobago 2; St Kitts & Nevis 1, Trinidad & Tobago 2; Trinidad & Tobago 1, Mexico 3; Mexico 7, St Vincent & the Grenadines 0; St Vincent & the Grenadines 0, Mexico 1; Trinidad & Tobago 5, St Kitts & Nevis 1; Mexico 3, Trinidad & Tobago 0; St Kitts & Nevis 0, St Vincent & the Grenadines 3.

Top two from each group to third stage.

THIRD STAGE
Costa Rica 1, Mexico 2; Panama 0, Guatemala 0; Trinidad & Tobago 1, United States 2; Costa Rica 2, Panama 1; Guatemala 5, Trinidad & Tobago 1; Mexico 2, United States 1; Panama 1, Mexico 1; Trinidad & Tobago 0, Costa Rica 0; United States 2, Guatemala 0; Guatemala 0, Mexico 2; Trinidad & Tobago 2, Panama 0; United States 3, Costa Rica 0; Costa Rica 3, Guatemala 2; Mexico 2, Trinidad & Tobago 0; Panama 0, United States 3.

Top three qualify for finals, fourth placed team play-off against fifth placed Asian team.

AFRICA

Group 1
Senegal 2, Congo 0; Zambia 1, Togo 0; Liberia 1, Mali 0; Mali 1, Zambia 1; Congo 3, Liberia 0; Togo 3, Senegal 1; Senegal 1, Zambia 0; Congo 1, Mali 0; Liberia 0, Togo 0; Zambia 1, Liberia 0; Mali 2, Senegal 2; Togo 2, Congo 0; Congo 2, Zambia 3; Togo 1, Mali 0; Liberia 0, Senegal 3; Senegal 6, Liberia 1; Zambia 2, Congo 0; Mali 1, Togo 2; Congo 0, Senegal 0; Mali 4, Liberia 1; Togo 4, Zambia 1; Senegal 2, Togo 2; Zambia 2, Mali 1; Liberia 0, Congo 2.

Group 2
Burkina Faso 1, Ghana 0; South Africa 2, Cape Verde Islands 1; Uganda 1, DR Congo 0; Ghana 3, South Africa 0; DR Congo 3, Burkina Faso 2; Cape Verde Islands 1, DR Congo 1; South Africa 2, Burkina Faso 0; Uganda 1, Ghana 1; Burkina Faso 2, Uganda 0; DR Congo 1, South Africa 0; Ghana 2, Cape Verde Islands 0; Cape Verde Islands 1, Burkina Faso 0; Uganda 0, South Africa 1; Ghana 0, DR Congo 0; Burkina Faso 1, Cape Verde Islands 2; South Africa 2, Uganda 1; DR Congo 1, Ghana 1; Cape Verde Islands 1, South Africa 2; DR Congo 4, Uganda 0; Ghana 2, Burkina Faso 1; Burkina Faso 2, DR Congo 0; South Africa 0, Ghana 2; Uganda 1, Cape Verde Islands 0.

Group 3
Cameroon 2, Benin 1; Ivory Coast 2, Libya 0; Sudan 0, Egypt 3; Liberia 0, Cameroon 0; Benin 1, Sudan 1; Egypt 1, Ivory Coast 2; Sudan 0, Libya 1; Benin 3, Egypt 3; Cameroon 2, Ivory Coast 0; Libya 4, Benin 1; Egypt 3, Cameroon 2; Ivory Coast 5, Sudan 0; Libya 2, Egypt 1; Sudan 1, Cameroon 1; Benin 0, Ivory Coast 1; Cameroon 2, Sudan 1; Egypt 4, Libya 1; Ivory Coast 3, Benin 0; Libya 0, Ivory Coast 0; Benin 1, Cameroon 4; Egypt 6, Sudan 1; Cameroon 1, Libya 0; Ivory Coast 2, Egypt 0.

Group 4
Algeria 0, Angola 0; Gabon 1, Zimbabwe 1; Nigeria 2, Rwanda 0; Rwanda 3, Gabon 1; Angola 1, Nigeria 0; Zimbabwe 1, Algeria 1; Gabon 2, Angola 2; Nigeria 1, Algeria 0; Rwanda 0, Zimbabwe 2; Zimbabwe 0, Nigeria 3; Algeria 0, Gabon 3; Angola 1, Rwanda 0; Gabon 1, Nigeria 1; Rwanda 1, Algeria 1; Angola 1, Zimbabwe 0; Nigeria 2, Gabon 0; Algeria 1, Rwanda 0; Zimbabwe 2, Angola 0; Angola 2, Algeria 1; Rwanda 1, Nigeria 1; Zimbabwe 1, Gabon 0; Gabon 3, Rwanda 0; Nigeria 1, Angola 1; Algeria 2, Zimbabwe 2.

Group 5
Malawi 1, Morocco 1; Tunisia 4, Botswana 1; Botswana 2, Malawi 0; Guinea 2, Tunisia 1; Botswana 0, Morocco 1; Malawi 1, Guinea 1; Kenya 3, Malawi 2; Morocco 1, Tunisia 1; Guinea 4, Botswana 0; Malawi 2, Tunisia 2; Botswana 2, Kenya 1; Guinea 1, Morocco 1; Kenya 2, Guinea 1; Morocco 5, Kenya 1; Kenya 1, Botswana 0; Morocco 1, Guinea 0; Tunisia 7, Malawi 0; Botswana 1, Tunisia 3; Morocco 4, Malawi 1; Guinea 1, Kenya 0; Tunisia 2, Guinea 0; Kenya 0, Morocco 0; Malawi 1, Botswana 3.

Group winners qualify for finals.

THE WORLD CUP 2006

REMAINING FIXTURES

SOUTH AMERICA

Top four qualify for finals; fifth placed team enters play-off against Oceania winners for a place in finals.

03/04.09.05 Bolivia v Ecuador
03/04.09.05 Brazil v Chile
03/04.09.05 Paraguay v Argentina
03/04.09.05 Uruguay v Colombia
03/04.09.05 Venezuela v Peru
08/09.10.05 Argentina v Peru
08/09.10.05 Bolivia v Brazil
08/09.10.05 Colombia v Chile
08/09.10.05 Ecuador v Uruguay
08/09.10.05 Venezuela v Paraguay
11/12.10.05 Brazil v Venezuela
11/12.10.05 Chile v Ecuador
11/12.10.05 Paraguay v Colombia
11/12.10.05 Peru v Bolivia
11/12.10.05 Uruguay v Argentina

EUROPE

Group winners and two best runners-up qualify for finals. Remaining six runners-up paired in two leg play-off matches, the winners of which also qualify for finals. Group runners-up ranked according to results against teams finishing in order in their respective groups.

GROUP 1
17.08.05 Macedonia v Finland
17.08.05 Romania v Andorra
03.09.05 Andorra v Finland
03.09.05 Armenia v Holland
03.09.05 Romania v Czech Republic
07.09.05 Czech Republic v Armenia
07.09.05 Finland v Macedonia
07.09.05 Holland v Andorra
08.10.05 Czech Republic v Holland
08.10.05 Finland v Romania
12.10.05 Andorra v Armenia
12.10.05 Finland v Czech Republic
12.10.05 Holland v Macedonia

GROUP 2
03.09.05 Albania v Kazakhstan
03.09.05 Georgia v Ukraine
03.09.05 Turkey v Denmark
07.09.05 Denmark v Georgia
07.09.05 Kazakhstan v Greece
07.09.05 Ukraine v Turkey
08.10.05 Denmark v Greece
08.10.05 Georgia v Kazakhstan
08.10.05 Ukraine v Albania
12.10.05 Albania v Turkey
12.10.05 Greece v Georgia
12.10.05 Kazakhstan v Denmark

GROUP 3
17.08.05 Latvia v Russia
17.08.05 Liechtenstein v Slovakia
03.09.05 Estonia v Latvia
03.09.05 Portugal v Luxembourg
03.09.05 Russia v Liechtenstein
07.09.05 Latvia v Slovakia
07.09.05 Liechtenstein v Luxembourg
07.09.05 Russia v Portugal
08.10.05 Portugal v Liechtenstein
08.10.05 Russia v Luxembourg
08.10.05 Slovakia v Estonia
12.10.05 Luxembourg v Estonia
12.10.05 Portugal v Latvia
12.10.05 Slovakia v Russia

GROUP 4
17.08.05 Faeroes v Cyprus
03.09.05 France v Faeroes
03.09.05 Switzerland v Israel
07.09.05 Cyprus v Switzerland
07.09.05 Faeroes v Israel
07.09.05 Republic of Ireland v France
08.10.05 Cyprus v Republic of Ireland
08.10.05 Switzerland v France
08.10.05 Israel v Faeroes
12.10.05 France v Cyprus
12.10.05 Republic of Ireland v Switzerland

GROUP 5
03.09.05 Moldova v Belarus
03.09.05 Scotland v Italy
03.09.05 Slovenia v Norway
07.09.05 Belarus v Italy
07.09.05 Moldova v Slovenia
07.09.05 Norway v Scotland
08.10.05 Italy v Slovenia
08.10.05 Norway v Moldova
08.10.05 Scotland v Belarus
12.10.05 Belarus v Norway
12.10.05 Italy v Moldova
12.10.05 Slovenia v Scotland

GROUP 6
03.09.05 Northern Ireland v Azerbaijan
03.09.05 Poland v Austria
03.09.05 Wales v England
07.09.05 Azerbaijan v Austria
07.09.05 Northern Ireland v England
07.09.05 Poland v Wales
08.10.05 England v Austria
08.10.05 Northern Ireland v Wales
12.10.05 Austria v Northern Ireland
12.10.05 England v Poland
12.10.05 Wales v Azerbaijan

GROUP 7
03.09.05 Bosnia v Belgium
03.09.05 Serbia-Montenegro v Lithuania
07.09.05 Belgium v San Marino
07.09.05 Lithuania v Bosnia
07.09.05 Spain v Serbia-Montenegro
08.10.05 Belgium v Spain
08.10.05 Bosnia v San Marino
08.10.05 Lithuania v Serbia-Montenegro
12.10.05 Lithuania v Belgium
12.10.05 San Marino v Spain
12.10.05 Serbia-Montenegro v Bosnia

GROUP 8
03.09.05 Hungary v Malta
03.09.05 Iceland v Croatia
03.09.05 Sweden v Bulgaria
07.09.05 Bulgaria v Iceland
07.09.05 Hungary v Sweden
07.09.05 Malta v Croatia
08.10.05 Bulgaria v Hungary
08.10.05 Croatia v Sweden
12.10.05 Hungary v Croatia
12.10.05 Malta v Bulgaria
12.10.05 Sweden v Iceland

THE WORLD CUP 1930–2002

Year	Winners	Runners-up	Venue	Attendance	Referee
1930	Uruguay 4	Argentina 2	Montevideo	90,000	Langenus (B)
1934	Italy 2 *(after extra time)*	Czechoslovakia 1	Rome	50,000	Eklind (Se)
1938	Italy 4	Hungary 2	Paris	45,000	Capdeville (F)
1950	Uruguay 2	Brazil 1	Rio de Janeiro	199,854	Reader (E)
1954	West Germany 3	Hungary 2	Berne	60,000	Ling (E)
1958	Brazil 5	Sweden 2	Stockholm	49,737	Guigue (F)
1962	Brazil 3	Czechoslovakia 1	Santiago	68,679	Latychev (USSR)
1966	England 4 *(after extra time)*	West Germany 2	Wembley	93,802	Dienst (Sw)
1970	Brazil 4	Italy 1	Mexico City	107,412	Glockner (EG)
1974	West Germany 2	Holland 1	Munich	77,833	Taylor (E)
1978	Argentina 3 *(after extra time)*	Holland 1	Buenos Aires	77,000	Gonella (I)
1982	Italy 3	West Germany 1	Madrid	90,080	Coelho (Br)
1986	Argentina 3	West Germany 2	Mexico City	114,580	Filho (Br)
1990	West Germany 1	Argentina 0	Rome	73,603	Mendez (Mex)
1994	Brazil 0 *(Brazil won 3-2 on penalties aet)*	Italy 0	Los Angeles	94,194	Puhl (H)
1998	France 3	Brazil 0	St-Denis	75,000	Belqola (Mor)
2002	Brazil 2	Germany 0	Yokohama	69,029	Collina (I)

GOALSCORING AND ATTENDANCES IN WORLD CUP FINAL ROUNDS

Venue	*Matches*	*Goals (av)*	*Attendance (av)*
1930, Uruguay	18	70 (3.9)	434,500 (24,138)
1934, Italy	17	70 (4.1)	395,000 (23,235)
1938, France	18	84 (4.6)	483,000 (26,833)
1950, Brazil	22	88 (4.0)	1,337,000 (60,772)
1954, Switzerland	26	140 (5.4)	943,000 (36,270)
1958, Sweden	35	126 (3.6)	868,000 (24,800)
1962, Chile	32	89 (2.8)	776,000 (24,250)
1966, England	32	89 (2.8)	1,614,677 (50,458)
1970, Mexico	32	95 (2.9)	1,673,975 (52,311)
1974, West Germany	38	97 (2.5)	1,774,022 (46,684)
1978, Argentina	38	102 (2.7)	1,610,215 (42,374)
1982, Spain	52	146 (2.8)	2,064,364 (38,816)
1986, Mexico	52	132 (2.5)	2,441,731 (46,956)
1990, Italy	52	115 (2.2)	2,515,168 (48,368)
1994, USA	52	141 (2.7)	3,567,415 (68,604)
1998, France	64	171 (2.6)	2,775,400 (43,366)
2002, Japan/S. Korea	64	161 (2.5)	2,705,566 (42,274)

LEADING GOALSCORERS

Year	*Player*	*Goals*
1930	Guillermo Stabile (Argentina)	8
1934	Angelo Schiavio (Italy), Oldrich Nejedly (Czechoslovakia), Edmund Conen (Germany)	4
1938	Leonidas da Silva (Brazil)	8
1950	Ademir (Brazil)	9
1954	Sandor Kocsis (Hungary)	11
1958	Just Fontaine (France)	13
1962	Valentin Ivanov (USSR), Leonel Sanchez (Chile), Garrincha, Vava (both Brazil), Florian Albert (Hungary), Drazen Jerkovic (Yugoslavia)	4
1966	Eusebio (Portugal)	9
1970	Gerd Muller (West Germany)	10
1974	Grzegorz Lato (Poland)	7
1978	Mario Kempes (Argentina)	6
1982	Paolo Rossi (Italy)	6
1986	Gary Lineker (England)	6
1990	Salvatore Schillaci (Italy)	6
1994	Oleg Salenko (Russia) Hristo Stoichkov (Bulgaria)	6
1998	Davor Suker (Croatia)	6
2002	Ronaldo (Brazil)	8

EUROPEAN FOOTBALL CHAMPIONSHIP

(formerly EUROPEAN NATIONS' CUP)

Year	*Winners*		*Runners-up*		*Venue*	*Attendance*
1960	USSR	2	Yugoslavia	1	Paris	17,966
1964	Spain	2	USSR	1	Madrid	120,000
1968	Italy After 1-1 draw	2	Yugoslavia	0	Rome	60,000 75,000
1972	West Germany	3	USSR	0	Brussels	43,437
1976	Czechoslovakia *(Czechoslovakia won on penalties)*	2	West Germany	2	Belgrade	45,000
1980	West Germany	2	Belgium	1	Rome	47,864
1984	France	2	Spain	0	Paris	48,000
1988	Holland	2	USSR	0	Munich	72,308
1992	Denmark	2	Germany	0	Gothenburg	37,800
1996	Germany *(Germany won on sudden death)*	2	Czech Republic	1	Wembley	73,611
2000	France *(France won on sudden death)*	2	Italy	1	Rotterdam	50,000
2004	Greece	1	Portugal	0	Lisbon	62,865

OLYMPIC GAMES 2004

GROUP A
Greece 2, South Korea 2
Mali 0, Mexico 0
South Korea 1, Mexico 0
Greece 0, Mali 2
South Korea 3, Mali 3
Greece 2, Mexico 3

	P	W	D	L	F	A	Pts
Mali	3	1	2	0	5	3	5
South Korea	3	1	2	0	6	5	5
Mexico	3	1	1	1	3	3	4
Greece	3	0	1	2	4	7	1

GROUP B
Paraguay 4, Japan 3
Ghana 2, Italy 2
Paraguay 1, Ghana 2
Japan 2, Italy 3
Paraguay 1, Italy 0
Japan 1, Ghana 0

	P	W	D	L	F	A	Pts
Paraguay	3	2	0	1	6	5	6
Italy	3	1	1	1	5	5	4
Ghana	3	1	1	1	4	4	4
Japan	3	1	0	2	6	7	3

GROUP C
Tunisia 1, Australia 1
Argentina 6, Serbia & Montenegro 0
Serbia & Montenegro 1, Australia 5
Argentina 2, Tunisia 0
Argentina 1, Australia 0
Serbia & Montenegro 2, Tunisia 3

	P	W	D	L	F	A	Pts
Argentina	3	3	0	0	9	0	9
Australia	3	1	1	1	6	3	4
Tunisia	3	1	1	1	4	5	4
Serbia & Montenegro	3	0	0	3	3	14	0

GROUP D
Costa Rica 0, Morocco 0
Iraq 4, Portugal 2
Costa Rica 0, Iraq 2
Morocco 1, Portugal 2
Costa Rica 4, Portugal 2
Morocco 2, Iraq 1

	P	W	D	L	F	A	Pts
Iraq	3	2	0	1	7	4	6
Costa Rica	3	1	1	1	4	4	4
Morocco	3	1	1	1	3	3	4
Portugal	3	1	0	2	6	9	3

QUARTER-FINALS
Mali 0, Italy 1
Iraq 1, Australia 0
Argentina 4, Costa Rica 0
Paraguay 3, South Korea 2

SEMI-FINALS
Italy 0, Argentina 3
Iraq 1, Paraguay 3

MATCH FOR THIRD PLACE
Italy 1, Iraq 0

FINAL (in Athens)
28 August 2004

Argentina (1) 1 Paraguay (0) 0

Argentina: Lux; Ayala, Mascherano, Rosales, Heinze, Coloccini, Tevez, D'Alessandro, Delgado (Rodriguez C 76), Kily Gonzalez, Gonzalez L.
Scorer: Tevez 18.
Paraguay: Barreto; Martinez▪, Esquivel (Gonzalez 76), Gimenez, Manzur, Gamarra, Barreto E (Cristaldo 72), Figueredo▪, Torres, Enciso (Diaz 63), Bareiro.
Attendance: 41,116
Referee: K. Vassaras (Greece).
▪ *Denotes player sent off.*

OLYMPIC FOOTBALL

Previous medallists

1896	Athens*	1 Denmark; 2 Greece
1900	Paris*	1 Great Britain; 2 France
1904	St Louis**	1 Canada; 2 USA
1908	London	1 Great Britain; 2 Denmark; 3 Holland
1912	Stockholm	1 England; 2 Denmark; 3 Holland
1920	Antwerp	1 Belgium; 2 Spain; 3 Holland
1924	Paris	1 Uruguay; 2 Switzerland; 3 Sweden
1928	Amsterdam	1 Uruguay; 2 Argentina; 3 Italy
1932	Los Angeles	no tournament
1936	Berlin	1 Italy; 2 Austria; 3 Norway
1948	London	1 Sweden; 2 Yugoslavia; 3 Denmark
1952	Helsinki	1 Hungary; 2 Yugoslavia; 3 Sweden
1956	Melbourne	1 USSR; 2 Yugoslavia; 3 Bulgaria
1960	Rome	1 Yugoslavia; 2 Denmark; 3 Hungary
1964	Tokyo	1 Hungary; 2 Czechoslovakia; 3 East Germany
1968	Mexico City	1 Hungary; 2 Bulgaria; 3 Japan
1972	Munich	1 Poland; 2 Hungary; 3 E Germany/USSR
1976	Montreal	1 East Germany; 2 Poland; 3 USSR
1980	Moscow	1 Czechoslovakia; 2 East Germany; 3 USSR
1984	Los Angeles	1 France; 2 Brazil; 3 Yugoslavia
1988	Seoul	1 USSR; 2 Brazil; 3 West Germany
1992	Barcelona	1 Spain; 2 Poland; 3 Ghana
1996	Atlanta	1 Nigeria; 2 Argentina; 3 Brazil
2000	Sydney	1. Cameroon; 2. Spain; 3. Chile
2004	Athens	1. Argentina; 2. Paraguay; 3. Italy

* No official tournament
** No official tournament but gold medal later awarded by IOC

BRITISH AND IRISH INTERNATIONAL RESULTS 1872–2005

Note: In the results that follow, WC=World Cup, EC=European Championship, UI=Umbro International Trophy. TF = Tournoi de France. For Ireland, read Northern Ireland from 1921. *After extra time.

ENGLAND v SCOTLAND

Played: 110; England won 45, Scotland won 41, Drawn 24. Goals: England 192, Scotland 169.

			E	*S*
1872	30 Nov	Glasgow	0	0
1873	8 Mar	Kennington Oval	4	2
1874	7 Mar	Glasgow	1	2
1875	6 Mar	Kennington Oval	2	2
1876	4 Mar	Glasgow	0	3
1877	3 Mar	Kennington Oval	1	3
1878	2 Mar	Glasgow	2	7
1879	5 Apr	Kennington Oval	5	4
1880	13 Mar	Glasgow	4	5
1881	12 Mar	Kennington Oval	1	6
1882	11 Mar	Glasgow	1	5
1883	10 Mar	Sheffield	2	3
1884	15 Mar	Glasgow	0	1
1885	21 Mar	Kennington Oval	1	1
1886	31 Mar	Glasgow	1	1
1887	19 Mar	Blackburn	2	3
1888	17 Mar	Glasgow	5	0
1889	13 Apr	Kennington Oval	2	3
1890	5 Apr	Glasgow	1	1
1891	6 Apr	Blackburn	2	1
1892	2 Apr	Glasgow	4	1
1893	1 Apr	Richmond	5	2
1894	7 Apr	Glasgow	2	2
1895	6 Apr	Everton	3	0
1896	4 Apr	Glasgow	1	2
1897	3 Apr	Crystal Palace	1	2
1898	2 Apr	Glasgow	3	1
1899	8 Apr	Birmingham	2	1
1900	7 Apr	Glasgow	1	4
1901	30 Mar	Crystal Palace	2	2
1902	3 Mar	Birmingham	2	2
1903	4 Apr	Sheffield	1	2
1904	9 Apr	Glasgow	1	0
1905	1 Apr	Crystal Palace	1	0
1906	7 Apr	Glasgow	1	2
1907	6 Apr	Newcastle	1	1
1908	4 Apr	Glasgow	1	1
1909	3 Apr	Crystal Palace	2	0
1910	2 Apr	Glasgow	0	2
1911	1 Apr	Everton	1	1
1912	23 Mar	Glasgow	1	1
1913	5 Apr	Chelsea	1	0
1914	14 Apr	Glasgow	1	3
1920	10 Apr	Sheffield	5	4
1921	9 Apr	Glasgow	0	3
1922	8 Apr	Aston Villa	0	1
1923	14 Apr	Glasgow	2	2
1924	12 Apr	Wembley	1	1
1925	4 Apr	Glasgow	0	2
1926	17 Apr	Manchester	0	1
1927	2 Apr	Glasgow	2	1
1928	31 Mar	Wembley	1	5
1929	13 Apr	Glasgow	0	1
1930	5 Apr	Wembley	5	2
1931	28 Mar	Glasgow	0	2
1932	9 Apr	Wembley	3	0
1933	1 Apr	Glasgow	1	2
1934	14 Apr	Wembley	3	0
1935	6 Apr	Glasgow	0	2
1936	4 Apr	Wembley	1	1
1937	17 Apr	Glasgow	1	3
1938	9 Apr	Wembley	0	1
1939	15 Apr	Glasgow	2	1
1947	12 Apr	Wembley	1	1
1948	10 Apr	Glasgow	2	0
1949	9 Apr	Wembley	1	3
WC1950	15 Apr	Glasgow	1	0
1951	14 Apr	Wembley	2	3
1952	5 Apr	Glasgow	2	1
1953	18 Apr	Wembley	2	2
WC1954	3 Apr	Glasgow	4	2
1955	2 Apr	Wembley	7	2
1956	14 Apr	Glasgow	1	1
1957	6 Apr	Wembley	2	1
1958	19 Apr	Glasgow	4	0
1959	11 Apr	Wembley	1	0
1960	9 Apr	Glasgow	1	1
1961	15 Apr	Wembley	9	3
1962	14 Apr	Glasgow	0	2
1963	6 Apr	Wembley	1	2
1964	11 Apr	Glasgow	0	1
1965	10 Apr	Wembley	2	2
1966	2 Apr	Glasgow	4	3
EC1967	15 Apr	Wembley	2	3
EC1968	24 Jan	Glasgow	1	1
1969	10 May	Wembley	4	1
1970	25 Apr	Glasgow	0	0
1971	22 May	Wembley	3	1
1972	27 May	Glasgow	1	0
1973	14 Feb	Glasgow	5	0
1973	19 May	Wembley	1	0
1974	18 May	Glasgow	0	2
1975	24 May	Wembley	5	1
1976	15 May	Glasgow	1	2
1977	4 June	Wembley	1	2
1978	20 May	Glasgow	1	0
1979	26 May	Wembley	3	1
1980	24 May	Glasgow	2	0
1981	23 May	Wembley	0	1
1982	29 May	Glasgow	1	0
1983	1 June	Wembley	2	0
1984	26 May	Glasgow	1	1
1985	25 May	Glasgow	0	1
1986	23 Apr	Wembley	2	1
1987	23 May	Glasgow	0	0
1988	21 May	Wembley	1	0
1989	27 May	Glasgow	2	0
EC1996	15 June	Wembley	2	0
EC1999	13 Nov	Glasgow	2	0
EC1999	17 Nov	Wembley	0	1

ENGLAND v WALES

Played: 98; England won 63, Wales won 14, Drawn 21. Goals: England 241, Wales 90.

			E	*W*
1879	18 Jan	Kennington Oval	2	1
1880	15 Mar	Wrexham	3	2
1881	26 Feb	Blackburn	0	1
1882	13 Mar	Wrexham	3	5
1883	3 Feb	Kennington Oval	5	0
1884	17 Mar	Wrexham	4	0

			E	*W*
1885	14 Mar	Blackburn	1	1
1886	29 Mar	Wrexham	3	1
1887	26 Feb	Kennington Oval	4	0
1888	4 Feb	Crewe	5	1
1889	23 Feb	Stoke	4	1
1890	15 Mar	Wrexham	3	1
1891	7 May	Sunderland	4	1
1892	5 Mar	Wrexham	2	0
1893	13 Mar	Stoke	6	0
1894	12 Mar	Wrexham	5	1
1895	18 Mar	Queen's Club, Kensington	1	1
1896	16 Mar	Cardiff	9	1
1897	29 Mar	Sheffield	4	0
1898	28 Mar	Wrexham	3	0
1899	20 Mar	Bristol	4	0
1900	26 Mar	Cardiff	1	1
1901	18 Mar	Newcastle	6	0
1902	3 Mar	Wrexham	0	0
1903	2 Mar	Portsmouth	2	1
1904	29 Feb	Wrexham	2	2
1905	27 Mar	Liverpool	3	1
1906	19 Mar	Cardiff	1	0
1907	18 Mar	Fulham	1	1
1908	16 Mar	Wrexham	7	1
1909	15 Mar	Nottingham	2	0
1910	14 Mar	Cardiff	1	0
1911	13 Mar	Millwall	3	0
1912	11 Mar	Wrexham	2	0
1913	17 Mar	Bristol	4	3
1914	16 Mar	Cardiff	2	0
1920	15 Mar	Highbury	1	2
1921	14 Mar	Cardiff	0	0
1922	13 Mar	Liverpool	1	0
1923	5 Mar	Cardiff	2	2
1924	3 Mar	Blackburn	1	2
1925	28 Feb	Swansea	2	1
1926	1 Mar	Crystal Palace	1	3
1927	12 Feb	Wrexham	3	3
1927	28 Nov	Burnley	1	2
1928	17 Nov	Swansea	3	2
1929	20 Nov	Chelsea	6	0
1930	22 Nov	Wrexham	4	0
1931	18 Nov	Liverpool	3	1
1932	16 Nov	Wrexham	0	0
1933	15 Nov	Newcastle	1	2

			E	*W*
1934	29 Sept	Cardiff	4	0
1936	5 Feb	Wolverhampton	1	2
1936	17 Oct	Cardiff	1	2
1937	17 Nov	Middlesbrough	2	1
1938	22 Oct	Cardiff	2	4
1946	13 Nov	Manchester	3	0
1947	18 Oct	Cardiff	3	0
1948	10 Nov	Aston Villa	1	0
WC1949	15 Oct	Cardiff	4	1
1950	15 Nov	Sunderland	4	2
1951	20 Oct	Cardiff	1	1
1952	12 Nov	Wembley	5	2
WC1953	10 Oct	Cardiff	4	1
1954	10 Nov	Wembley	3	2
1955	27 Oct	Cardiff	1	2
1956	14 Nov	Wembley	3	1
1957	19 Oct	Cardiff	4	0
1958	26 Nov	Aston Villa	2	2
1959	17 Oct	Cardiff	1	1
1960	23 Nov	Wembley	5	1
1961	14 Oct	Cardiff	1	1
1962	21 Oct	Wembley	4	0
1963	12 Oct	Cardiff	4	0
1964	18 Nov	Wembley	2	1
1965	2 Oct	Cardiff	0	0
EC1966	16 Nov	Wembley	5	1
EC1967	21 Oct	Cardiff	3	0
1969	7 May	Wembley	2	1
1970	18 Apr	Cardiff	1	1
1971	19 May	Wembley	0	0
1972	20 May	Cardiff	3	0
WC1972	15 Nov	Cardiff	1	0
WC1973	24 Jan	Wembley	1	1
1973	15 May	Wembley	3	0
1974	11 May	Cardiff	2	0
1975	21 May	Wembley	2	2
1976	24 Mar	Wrexham	2	1
1976	8 May	Cardiff	1	0
1977	31 May	Wembley	0	1
1978	3 May	Cardiff	3	1
1979	23 May	Wembley	0	0
1980	17 May	Wrexham	1	4
1981	20 May	Wembley	0	0
1982	27 Apr	Cardiff	1	0
1983	23 Feb	Wembley	2	1
1984	2 May	Wrexham	0	1
EC2004	9 Oct	Old Trafford	2	0

ENGLAND v IRELAND

Played: 97; England won 75, Ireland won 6, Drawn 16. Goals: England 323, Ireland 80.

			E	*I*
1882	18 Feb	Belfast	13	0
1883	24 Feb	Liverpool	7	0
1884	23 Feb	Belfast	8	1
1885	28 Feb	Manchester	4	0
1886	13 Mar	Belfast	6	1
1887	5 Feb	Sheffield	7	0
1888	31 Mar	Belfast	5	1
1889	2 Mar	Everton	6	1
1890	15 Mar	Belfast	9	1
1891	7 Mar	Wolverhampton	6	1
1892	5 Mar	Belfast	2	0
1893	25 Feb	Birmingham	6	1
1894	3 Mar	Belfast	2	2
1895	9 Mar	Derby	9	0
1896	7 Mar	Belfast	2	0
1897	20 Feb	Nottingham	6	0
1898	5 Mar	Belfast	3	2
1899	18 Feb	Sunderland	13	2
1900	17 Mar	Dublin	2	0
1901	9 Mar	Southampton	3	0
1902	22 Mar	Belfast	1	0

			E	*I*
1903	14 Feb	Wolverhampton	4	0
1904	12 Mar	Belfast	3	1
1905	25 Feb	Middlesbrough	1	1
1906	17 Feb	Belfast	5	0
1907	16 Feb	Everton	1	0
1908	15 Feb	Belfast	3	1
1909	13 Feb	Bradford	4	0
1910	12 Feb	Belfast	1	1
1911	11 Feb	Derby	2	1
1912	10 Feb	Dublin	6	1
1913	15 Feb	Belfast	1	2
1914	14 Feb	Middlesbrough	0	3
1919	25 Oct	Belfast	1	1
1920	23 Oct	Sunderland	2	0
1921	22 Oct	Belfast	1	1
1922	21 Oct	West Bromwich	2	0
1923	20 Oct	Belfast	1	2
1924	22 Oct	Everton	3	1
1925	24 Oct	Belfast	0	0
1926	20 Oct	Liverpool	3	3
1927	22 Oct	Belfast	0	2

			E	I
1928	22 Oct	Everton	2	1
1929	19 Oct	Belfast	3	0
1930	20 Oct	Sheffield	5	1
1931	17 Oct	Belfast	6	2
1932	17 Oct	Blackpool	1	0
1933	14 Oct	Belfast	3	0
1935	6 Feb	Everton	2	1
1935	19 Oct	Belfast	3	1
1936	18 Nov	Stoke	3	1
1937	23 Oct	Belfast	5	1
1938	16 Nov	Manchester	7	0
1946	28 Sept	Belfast	7	2
1947	5 Nov	Everton	2	2
1948	9 Oct	Belfast	6	2
WC1949	16 Nov	Manchester	9	2
1950	7 Oct	Belfast	4	1
1951	14 Nov	Aston Villa	2	0
1952	4 Oct	Belfast	2	2
WC1953	11 Nov	Everton	3	1
1954	2 Oct	Belfast	2	0
1955	2 Nov	Wembley	3	0
1956	10 Oct	Belfast	1	1
1957	6 Nov	Wembley	2	3
1958	4 Oct	Belfast	3	3
1959	18 Nov	Wembley	2	1
1960	8 Oct	Belfast	5	2
1961	22 Nov	Wembley	1	1
1962	20 Oct	Belfast	3	1
1963	20 Nov	Wembley	8	3
1964	3 Oct	Belfast	4	3
1965	10 Nov	Wembley	2	1
EC1966	20 Oct	Belfast	2	0
EC1967	22 Nov	Wembley	2	0
1969	3 May	Belfast	3	1
1970	21 Apr	Wembley	3	1
1971	15 May	Belfast	1	0
1972	23 May	Wembley	0	1
1973	12 May	Everton	2	1
1974	15 May	Wembley	1	0
1975	17 May	Belfast	0	0
1976	11 May	Wembley	4	0
1977	28 May	Belfast	2	1
1978	16 May	Wembley	1	0
EC1979	7 Feb	Wembley	4	0
1979	19 May	Belfast	2	0
EC1979	17 Oct	Belfast	5	1
1980	20 May	Wembley	1	1
1982	23 Feb	Wembley	4	0
1983	28 May	Belfast	0	0
1984	24 Apr	Wembley	1	0
WC1985	27 Feb	Belfast	1	0
WC1985	13 Nov	Wembley	0	0
EC1986	15 Oct	Wembley	3	0
EC1987	1 Apr	Belfast	2	0
EC2005	26 Mar	Old Trafford	4	0

SCOTLAND v WALES

Played: 103; Scotland won 60, Wales won 20, Drawn 23. Goals: Scotland 238, Wales 116.

			S	W
1876	25 Mar	Glasgow	4	0
1877	5 Mar	Wrexham	2	0
1878	23 Mar	Glasgow	9	0
1879	7 Apr	Wrexham	3	0
1880	3 Apr	Glasgow	5	1
1881	14 Mar	Wrexham	5	1
1882	25 Mar	Glasgow	5	0
1883	12 Mar	Wrexham	3	0
1884	29 Mar	Glasgow	4	1
1885	23 Mar	Wrexham	8	1
1886	10 Apr	Glasgow	4	1
1887	21 Mar	Wrexham	2	0
1888	10 Mar	Edinburgh	5	1
1889	15 Apr	Wrexham	0	0
1890	22 Mar	Paisley	5	0
1891	21 Mar	Wrexham	4	3
1892	26 Mar	Edinburgh	6	1
1893	18 Mar	Wrexham	8	0
1894	24 Mar	Kilmarnock	5	2
1895	23 Mar	Wrexham	2	2
1896	21 Mar	Dundee	4	0
1897	20 Mar	Wrexham	2	2
1898	19 Mar	Motherwell	5	2
1899	18 Mar	Wrexham	6	0
1900	3 Feb	Aberdeen	5	2
1901	2 Mar	Wrexham	1	1
1902	15 Mar	Greenock	5	1
1903	9 Mar	Cardiff	1	0
1904	12 Mar	Dundee	1	1
1905	6 Mar	Wrexham	1	3
1906	3 Mar	Edinburgh	0	2
1907	4 Mar	Wrexham	0	1
1908	7 Mar	Dundee	2	1
1909	1 Mar	Wrexham	2	3
1910	5 Mar	Kilmarnock	1	0
1911	6 Mar	Cardiff	2	2
1912	2 Mar	Tynecastle	1	0
1913	3 Mar	Wrexham	0	0
1914	28 Feb	Glasgow	0	0
1920	26 Feb	Cardiff	1	1
1921	12 Feb	Aberdeen	2	1
1922	4 Feb	Wrexham	1	2
1923	17 Mar	Paisley	2	0
1924	16 Feb	Cardiff	0	2
1925	14 Feb	Tynecastle	3	1
1925	31 Oct	Cardiff	3	0
1926	30 Oct	Glasgow	3	0
1927	29 Oct	Wrexham	2	2
1928	27 Oct	Glasgow	4	2
1929	26 Oct	Cardiff	4	2
1930	25 Oct	Glasgow	1	1
1931	31 Oct	Wrexham	3	2
1932	26 Oct	Edinburgh	2	5
1933	4 Oct	Cardiff	2	3
1934	21 Nov	Aberdeen	3	2
1935	5 Oct	Cardiff	1	1
1936	2 Dec	Dundee	1	2
1937	30 Oct	Cardiff	1	2
1938	9 Nov	Edinburgh	3	2
1946	19 Oct	Wrexham	1	3
1947	12 Nov	Glasgow	1	2
WC1948	23 Oct	Cardiff	3	1
1949	9 Nov	Glasgow	2	0
1950	21 Oct	Cardiff	3	1
1951	14 Nov	Glasgow	0	1
WC1952	18 Oct	Cardiff	2	1
1953	4 Nov	Glasgow	3	3
1954	16 Oct	Cardiff	1	0
1955	9 Nov	Glasgow	2	0
1956	20 Oct	Cardiff	2	2
1957	13 Nov	Glasgow	1	1
1958	18 Oct	Cardiff	3	0
1959	4 Nov	Glasgow	1	1
1960	20 Oct	Cardiff	0	2
1961	8 Nov	Glasgow	2	0
1962	20 Oct	Cardiff	3	2
1963	20 Nov	Glasgow	2	1
1964	3 Oct	Cardiff	2	3
EC1965	24 Nov	Glasgow	4	1
EC1966	22 Oct	Cardiff	1	1

			S	W
1967	22 Nov	Glasgow	3	2
1969	3 May	Wrexham	5	3
1970	22 Apr	Glasgow	0	0
1971	15 May	Cardiff	0	0
1972	24 May	Glasgow	1	0
1973	12 May	Wrexham	2	0
1974	14 May	Glasgow	2	0
1975	17 May	Cardiff	2	2
1976	6 May	Glasgow	3	1
wc1976	17 Nov	Glasgow	1	0
1977	28 May	Wrexham	0	0
wc1977	12 Oct	Liverpool	2	0
1978	17 May	Glasgow	1	1
1979	19 May	Cardiff	0	3
1980	21 May	Glasgow	1	0
1981	16 May	Swansea	0	2
1982	24 May	Glasgow	1	0
1983	28 May	Cardiff	2	0
1984	28 Feb	Glasgow	2	1
wc1985	27 Mar	Glasgow	0	1
wc1985	10 Sept	Cardiff	1	1
1997	27 May	Kilmarnock	0	1
2004	18 Feb	Cardiff	0	4

SCOTLAND v IRELAND

Played: 93; Scotland won 62, Ireland won 15, Drawn 16. Goals: Scotland 257, Ireland 81.

			S	I
1884	26 Jan	Belfast	5	0
1885	14 Mar	Glasgow	8	2
1886	20 Mar	Belfast	7	2
1887	19 Feb	Glasgow	4	1
1888	24 Mar	Belfast	10	2
1889	9 Mar	Glasgow	7	0
1890	29 Mar	Belfast	4	1
1891	28 Mar	Glasgow	2	1
1892	19 Mar	Belfast	3	2
1893	25 Mar	Glasgow	6	1
1894	31 Mar	Belfast	2	1
1895	30 Mar	Glasgow	3	1
1896	28 Mar	Belfast	3	3
1897	27 Mar	Glasgow	5	1
1898	26 Mar	Belfast	3	0
1899	25 Mar	Glasgow	9	1
1900	3 Mar	Belfast	3	0
1901	23 Feb	Glasgow	11	0
1902	1 Mar	Belfast	5	1
1902	9 Aug	Belfast	3	0
1903	21 Mar	Glasgow	0	2
1904	26 Mar	Dublin	1	1
1905	18 Mar	Glasgow	4	0
1906	17 Mar	Dublin	1	0
1907	16 Mar	Glasgow	3	0
1908	14 Mar	Dublin	5	0
1909	15 Mar	Glasgow	5	0
1910	19 Mar	Belfast	0	1
1911	18 Mar	Glasgow	2	0
1912	16 Mar	Belfast	4	1
1913	15 Mar	Dublin	2	1
1914	14 Mar	Belfast	1	1
1920	13 Mar	Glasgow	3	0
1921	26 Feb	Belfast	2	0
1922	4 Mar	Glasgow	2	1
1923	3 Mar	Belfast	1	0
1924	1 Mar	Glasgow	2	0
1925	28 Feb	Belfast	3	0
1926	27 Feb	Glasgow	4	0
1927	26 Feb	Belfast	2	0
1928	25 Feb	Glasgow	0	1
1929	23 Feb	Belfast	7	3
1930	22 Feb	Glasgow	3	1
1931	21 Feb	Belfast	0	0
1931	19 Sept	Glasgow	3	1
1932	12 Sept	Belfast	4	0
1933	16 Sept	Glasgow	1	2
1934	20 Oct	Belfast	1	2
1935	13 Nov	Edinburgh	2	1
1936	31 Oct	Belfast	3	1
1937	10 Nov	Aberdeen	1	1
1938	8 Oct	Belfast	2	0
1946	27 Nov	Glasgow	0	0
1947	4 Oct	Belfast	0	2
1948	17 Nov	Glasgow	3	2
1949	1 Oct	Belfast	8	2
1950	1 Nov	Glasgow	6	1
1951	6 Oct	Belfast	3	0
1952	5 Nov	Glasgow	1	1
1953	3 Oct	Belfast	3	1
1954	3 Nov	Glasgow	2	2
1955	8 Oct	Belfast	1	2
1956	7 Nov	Glasgow	1	0
1957	5 Oct	Belfast	1	1
1958	5 Nov	Glasgow	2	2
1959	3 Oct	Belfast	4	0
1960	9 Nov	Glasgow	5	2
1961	7 Oct	Belfast	6	1
1962	7 Nov	Glasgow	5	1
1963	12 Oct	Belfast	1	2
1964	25 Nov	Glasgow	3	2
1965	2 Oct	Belfast	2	3
1966	16 Nov	Glasgow	2	1
1967	21 Oct	Belfast	0	1
1969	6 May	Glasgow	1	1
1970	18 Apr	Belfast	1	0
1971	18 May	Glasgow	0	1
1972	20 May	Glasgow	2	0
1973	16 May	Glasgow	1	2
1974	11 May	Glasgow	0	1
1975	20 May	Glasgow	3	0
1976	8 May	Glasgow	3	0
1977	1 June	Glasgow	3	0
1978	13 May	Glasgow	1	1
1979	22 May	Glasgow	1	0
1980	17 May	Belfast	0	1
wc1981	25 Mar	Glasgow	1	1
1981	19 May	Glasgow	2	0
wc1981	14 Oct	Belfast	0	0
1982	28 Apr	Belfast	1	1
1983	24 May	Glasgow	0	0
1983	13 Dec	Belfast	0	2
1992	19 Feb	Glasgow	1	0

WALES v IRELAND

Played: 91; Wales won 42, Ireland won 27, Drawn 22. Goals: Wales 184, Ireland 129.

			W	I
1882	25 Feb	Wrexham	7	1
1883	17 Mar	Belfast	1	1
1884	9 Feb	Wrexham	6	0
1885	11 Apr	Belfast	8	2
1886	27 Feb	Wrexham	5	0
1887	12 Mar	Belfast	1	4
1888	3 Mar	Wrexham	11	0
1889	27 Apr	Belfast	3	1

			W	*I*
1890	8 Feb	Shrewsbury	5	2
1891	7 Feb	Belfast	2	7
1892	27 Feb	Bangor	1	1
1893	8 Apr	Belfast	3	4
1894	24 Feb	Swansea	4	1
1895	16 Mar	Belfast	2	2
1896	29 Feb	Wrexham	6	1
1897	6 Mar	Belfast	3	4
1898	19 Feb	Llandudno	0	1
1899	4 Mar	Belfast	0	1
1900	24 Feb	Llandudno	2	0
1901	23 Mar	Belfast	1	0
1902	22 Mar	Cardiff	0	3
1903	28 Mar	Belfast	0	2
1904	21 Mar	Bangor	0	1
1905	18 Apr	Belfast	2	2
1906	2 Apr	Wrexham	4	4
1907	23 Feb	Belfast	3	2
1908	11 Apr	Aberdare	0	1
1909	20 Mar	Belfast	3	2
1910	11 Apr	Wrexham	4	1
1911	28 Jan	Belfast	2	1
1912	13 Apr	Cardiff	2	3
1913	18 Jan	Belfast	1	0
1914	19 Jan	Wrexham	1	2
1920	14 Feb	Belfast	2	2
1921	9 Apr	Swansea	2	1
1922	4 Apr	Belfast	1	1
1923	14 Apr	Wrexham	0	3
1924	15 Mar	Belfast	1	0
1925	18 Apr	Wrexham	0	0
1926	13 Feb	Belfast	0	3
1927	9 Apr	Cardiff	2	2
1928	4 Feb	Belfast	2	1
1929	2 Feb	Wrexham	2	2
1930	1 Feb	Belfast	0	7
1931	22 Apr	Wrexham	3	2
1931	5 Dec	Belfast	0	4
1932	7 Dec	Wrexham	4	1
1933	4 Nov	Belfast	1	1
1935	27 Mar	Wrexham	3	1
1936	11 Mar	Belfast	2	3

			W	*I*
1937	17 Mar	Wrexham	4	1
1938	16 Mar	Belfast	0	1
1939	15 Mar	Wrexham	3	1
1947	16 Apr	Belfast	1	2
1948	10 Mar	Wrexham	2	0
1949	9 Mar	Belfast	2	0
WC1950	8 Mar	Wrexham	0	0
1951	7 Mar	Belfast	2	1
1952	19 Mar	Swansea	3	0
1953	15 Apr	Belfast	3	2
WC1954	31 Mar	Wrexham	1	2
1955	20 Apr	Belfast	3	2
1956	11 Apr	Cardiff	1	1
1957	10 Apr	Belfast	0	0
1958	16 Apr	Cardiff	1	1
1959	22 Apr	Belfast	1	4
1960	6 Apr	Wrexham	3	2
1961	12 Apr	Belfast	5	1
1962	11 Apr	Cardiff	4	0
1963	3 Apr	Belfast	4	1
1964	15 Apr	Cardiff	2	3
1965	31 Mar	Belfast	5	0
1966	30 Mar	Cardiff	1	4
EC1967	12 Apr	Belfast	0	0
EC1968	28 Feb	Wrexham	2	0
1969	10 May	Belfast	0	0
1970	25 Apr	Swansea	1	0
1971	22 May	Belfast	0	1
1972	27 May	Wrexham	0	0
1973	19 May	Everton	0	1
1974	18 May	Wrexham	1	0
1975	23 May	Belfast	0	1
1976	14 May	Swansea	1	0
1977	3 June	Belfast	1	1
1978	19 May	Wrexham	1	0
1979	25 May	Belfast	1	1
1980	23 May	Cardiff	0	1
1982	27 May	Wrexham	3	0
1983	31 May	Belfast	1	0
1984	22 May	Swansea	1	1
EC2004	8 Sept	Cardiff	2	2

OTHER BRITISH INTERNATIONAL RESULTS 1908–2005

ENGLAND

		v ALBANIA	*E*	*A*
WC1989	8 Mar	Tirana	2	0
WC1989	26 Apr	Wembley	5	0
WC2001	28 Mar	Tirana	3	1
WC2001	5 Sept	Newcastle	2	0

		v ARGENTINA	*E*	*A*
1951	9 May	Wembley	2	1
1953	17 May	Buenos Aires	0	0
(*abandoned after 21 mins*)				
WC1962	2 June	Rancagua	3	1
1964	6 June	Rio de Janeiro	0	1
WC1966	23 July	Wembley	1	0
1974	22 May	Wembley	2	2
1977	12 June	Buenos Aires	1	1
1980	13 May	Wembley	3	1
WC1986	22 June	Mexico City	1	2
1991	25 May	Wembley	2	2
WC1998	30 June	St Etienne	2	2
2000	23 Feb	Wembley	0	0
WC2002	7 June	Sapporo	1	0

		v AUSTRALIA	*E*	*A*
1980	31 May	Sydney	2	1
1983	11 June	Sydney	0	0
1983	15 June	Brisbane	1	0
1983	18 June	Melbourne	1	1
1991	1 June	Sydney	1	0
2003	12 Feb	West Ham	1	3

		v AUSTRIA	*E*	*A*
1908	6 June	Vienna	6	1
1908	8 June	Vienna	11	1
1909	1 June	Vienna	8	1
1930	14 May	Vienna	0	0
1932	7 Dec	Chelsea	4	3
1936	6 May	Vienna	1	2
1951	28 Nov	Wembley	2	2
1952	25 May	Vienna	3	2
WC1958	15 June	Boras	2	2
1961	27 May	Vienna	1	3
1962	4 Apr	Wembley	3	1
1965	20 Oct	Wembley	2	3
1967	27 May	Vienna	1	0
1973	26 Sept	Wembley	7	0
1979	13 June	Vienna	3	4
EC2004	4 Sept	Vienna	2	2

		v AZERBAIJAN	*E*	*A*
EC2004	13 Oct	Baku	1	0
EC2005	30 Mar	St James' Park	2	0

		v BELGIUM	*E*	*B*
1921	21 May	Brussels	2	0
1923	19 Mar	Highbury	6	1
1923	1 Nov	Antwerp	2	2
1924	8 Dec	West Bromwich	4	0
1926	24 May	Antwerp	5	3
1927	11 May	Brussels	9	1
1928	19 May	Antwerp	3	1
1929	11 May	Brussels	5	1
1931	16 May	Brussels	4	1

			E	*B*
1936	9 May	Brussels	2	3
1947	21 Sept	Brussels	5	2
1950	18 May	Brussels	4	1
1952	26 Nov	Wembley	5	0
WC1954	17 June	Basle	4	4*
1964	21 Oct	Wembley	2	2
1970	25 Feb	Brussels	3	1
EC1980	12 June	Turin	1	1
WC1990	27 June	Bologna	1	0*
1998	29 May	Casablanca	0	0
1999	10 Oct	Sunderland	2	1

		v BOHEMIA	*E*	*B*
1908	13 June	Prague	4	0

		v BRAZIL	*E*	*B*
1956	9 May	Wembley	4	2
WC1958	11 June	Gothenburg	0	0
1959	13 May	Rio de Janeiro	0	2
WC1962	10 June	Vina del Mar	1	3
1963	8 May	Wembley	1	1
1964	30 May	Rio de Janeiro	1	5
1969	12 June	Rio de Janeiro	1	2
WC1970	7 June	Guadalajara	0	1
1976	23 May	Los Angeles	0	1
1977	8 June	Rio de Janeiro	0	0
1978	19 Apr	Wembley	1	1
1981	12 May	Wembley	0	1
1984	10 June	Rio de Janeiro	2	0
1987	19 May	Wembley	1	1
1990	28 Mar	Wembley	1	0
1992	17 May	Wembley	1	1
1993	13 June	Washington	1	1
UI1995	11 June	Wembley	1	3
TF1997	10 June	Paris	0	1
2000	27 May	Wembley	1	1
WC2002	21 June	Shizuoka	1	2

		v BULGARIA	*E*	*B*
WC1962	7 June	Rancagua	0	0
1968	11 Dec	Wembley	1	1
1974	1 June	Sofia	1	0
EC1979	6 June	Sofia	3	0
EC1979	22 Nov	Wembley	2	0
1996	27 Mar	Wembley	1	0
EC1998	10 Oct	Wembley	0	0
EC1999	9 June	Sofia	1	1

		v CAMEROON	*E*	*C*
WC1990	1 July	Naples	3	2*
1991	6 Feb	Wembley	2	0
1997	15 Nov	Wembley	2	0
2002	26 May	Kobe	2	2

		v CANADA	*E*	*C*
1986	24 May	Burnaby	1	0

		v CHILE	*E*	*C*
WC1950	25 June	Rio de Janeiro	2	0
1953	24 May	Santiago	2	1
1984	17 June	Santiago	0	0
1989	23 May	Wembley	0	0
1998	11 Feb	Wembley	0	2

		v CHINA	*E*	*C*
1996	23 May	Beijing	3	0

		v CIS	*E*	*C*
1992	29 Apr	Moscow	2	2

		v COLOMBIA	*E*	*C*
1970	20 May	Bogota	4	0
1988	24 May	Wembley	1	1
1995	6 Sept	Wembley	0	0
WC1998	26 June	Lens	2	0
2005	31 May	New Jersey	3	2

		v CROATIA	*E*	*C*
1996	24 Apr	Wembley	0	0
2003	20 Aug	Ipswich	3	1
EC2004	21 June	Lisbon	4	2

		v CYPRUS	*E*	*C*
EC1975	16 Apr	Wembley	5	0
EC1975	11 May	Limassol	1	0

		v CZECHOSLOVAKIA	*E*	*C*
1934	16 May	Prague	1	2
1937	1 Dec	Tottenham	5	4
1963	29 May	Bratislava	4	2
1966	2 Nov	Wembley	0	0
WC1970	11 June	Guadalajara	1	0
1973	27 May	Prague	1	1
EC1974	30 Oct	Wembley	3	0
EC1975	30 Oct	Bratislava	1	2
1978	29 Nov	Wembley	1	0
WC1982	20 June	Bilbao	2	0
1990	25 Apr	Wembley	4	2
1992	25 Mar	Prague	2	2

		v CZECH REPUBLIC	*E*	*C*
1998	18 Nov	Wembley	2	0

		v DENMARK	*E*	*D*
1948	26 Sept	Copenhagen	0	0
1955	2 Oct	Copenhagen	5	1
WC1956	5 Dec	Wolverhampton	5	2
WC1957	15 May	Copenhagen	4	1
1966	3 July	Copenhagen	2	0
EC1978	20 Sept	Copenhagen	4	3
EC1979	12 Sept	Wembley	1	0
EC1982	22 Sept	Copenhagen	2	2
EC1983	21 Sept	Wembley	0	1
1988	14 Sept	Wembley	1	0
1989	7 June	Copenhagen	1	1
1990	15 May	Wembley	1	0
EC1992	11 June	Malmo	0	0
1994	9 Mar	Wembley	1	0
WC2002	15 June	Niigata	3	0
2004	16 Nov	Old Trafford	2	3

		v ECUADOR	*E*	*Ec*
1970	24 May	Quito	2	0

		v EGYPT	*E*	*Eg*
1986	29 Jan	Cairo	4	0
WC1990	21 June	Cagliari	1	0

		v FIFA	*E*	*FIFA*
1938	26 Oct	Highbury	3	0
1953	21 Oct	Wembley	4	4
1963	23 Oct	Wembley	2	1

		v FINLAND	*E*	*F*
1937	20 May	Helsinki	8	0
1956	20 May	Helsinki	5	1
1966	26 June	Helsinki	3	0
WC1976	13 June	Helsinki	4	1
WC1976	13 Oct	Wembley	2	1
1982	3 June	Helsinki	4	1
WC1984	17 Oct	Wembley	5	0
WC1985	22 May	Helsinki	1	1
1992	3 June	Helsinki	2	1
WC2000	11 Oct	Helsinki	0	0
WC2001	24 Mar	Liverpool	2	1

		v FRANCE	*E*	*F*
1923	10 May	Paris	4	1
1924	17 May	Paris	3	1
1925	21 May	Paris	3	2
1927	26 May	Paris	6	0
1928	17 May	Paris	5	1
1929	9 May	Paris	4	1
1931	14 May	Paris	2	5
1933	6 Dec	Tottenham	4	1
1938	26 May	Paris	4	2
1947	3 May	Highbury	3	0
1949	22 May	Paris	3	1

			E	*F*
1951	3 Oct	Highbury	2	2
1955	15 May	Paris	0	1
1957	27 Nov	Wembley	4	0
EC1962	3 Oct	Sheffield	1	1
EC1963	27 Feb	Paris	2	5
WC1966	20 July	Wembley	2	0
1969	12 Mar	Wembley	5	0
WC1982	16 June	Bilbao	3	1
1984	29 Feb	Paris	0	2
1992	19 Feb	Wembley	2	0
EC1992	14 June	Malmo	0	0
TF1997	7 June	Montpellier	1	0
1999	10 Feb	Wembley	0	2
2000	2 Sept	Paris	1	1
EC2004	13 June	Lisbon	1	2

		v GEORGIA	*E*	*G*
WC1996	9 Nov	Tbilisi	2	0
WC1997	30 Apr	Wembley	2	0

		v GERMANY	*E*	*G*
1930	10 May	Berlin	3	3
1935	4 Dec	Tottenham	3	0
1938	14 May	Berlin	6	3
1991	11 Sept	Wembley	0	1
1993	19 June	Detroit	1	2
EC1996	26 June	Wembley	1	1*
EC2000	17 June	Charleroi	1	0
WC2000	7 Oct	Wembley	0	1
WC2001	1 Sept	Munich	5	1

		v EAST GERMANY	*E*	*EG*
1963	2 June	Leipzig	2	1
1970	25 Nov	Wembley	3	1
1974	29 May	Leipzig	1	1
1984	12 Sept	Wembley	1	0

		v WEST GERMANY	*E*	*WG*
1954	1 Dec	Wembley	3	1
1956	26 May	Berlin	3	1
1965	12 May	Nuremberg	1	0
1966	23 Feb	Wembley	1	0
WC1966	30 July	Wembley	4	2*
1968	1 June	Hanover	0	1
WC1970	14 June	Leon	2	3*
EC1972	29 Apr	Wembley	1	3
EC1972	13 May	Berlin	0	0
1975	12 Mar	Wembley	2	0
1978	22 Feb	Munich	1	2
WC1982	29 June	Madrid	0	0
1982	13 Oct	Wembley	1	2
1985	12 June	Mexico City	3	0
1987	9 Sept	Dusseldorf	1	3
WC1990	4 July	Turin	1	1*

		v GREECE	*E*	*G*
EC1971	21 Apr	Wembley	3	0
EC1971	1 Dec	Piraeus	2	0
EC1982	17 Nov	Salonika	3	0
EC1983	30 Mar	Wembley	0	0
1989	8 Feb	Athens	2	1
1994	17 May	Wembley	5	0
WC2001	6 June	Athens	2	0
WC2001	6 Oct	Old Trafford	2	2

		v HOLLAND	*E*	*H*
1935	18 May	Amsterdam	1	0
1946	27 Nov	Huddersfield	8	2
1964	9 Dec	Amsterdam	1	1
1969	5 Nov	Amsterdam	1	0
1970	14 Jun	Wembley	0	0
1977	9 Feb	Wembley	0	2
1982	25 May	Wembley	2	0
1988	23 Mar	Wembley	2	2
EC1988	15 June	Dusseldorf	1	3
WC1990	16 June	Cagliari	0	0
2005	9 Feb	Villa Park	0	0
WC1993	28 Apr	Wembley	2	2
WC1993	13 Oct	Rotterdam	0	2
EC1996	18 June	Wembley	4	1
2001	15 Aug	Tottenham	0	2
2002	13 Feb	Amsterdam	1	1

		v HUNGARY	*E*	*H*
1908	10 June	Budapest	7	0
1909	29 May	Budapest	4	2
1909	31 May	Budapest	8	2
1934	10 May	Budapest	1	2
1936	2 Dec	Highbury	6	2
1953	25 Nov	Wembley	3	6
1954	23 May	Budapest	1	7
1960	22 May	Budapest	0	2
WC1962	31 May	Rancagua	1	2
1965	5 May	Wembley	1	0
1978	24 May	Wembley	4	1
WC1981	6 June	Budapest	3	1
WC1982	18 Nov	Wembley	1	0
EC1983	27 Apr	Wembley	2	0
EC1983	12 Oct	Budapest	3	0
1988	27 Apr	Budapest	0	0
1990	12 Sept	Wembley	1	0
1992	12 May	Budapest	1	0
1996	18 May	Wembley	3	0
1999	28 Apr	Budapest	1	1

		v ICELAND	*E*	*I*
1982	2 June	Reykjavik	1	1
2004	5 June	City of Manchester	6	1

		v REPUBLIC OF IRELAND	*E*	*RI*
1946	30 Sept	Dublin	1	0
1949	21 Sept	Everton	0	2
WC1957	8 May	Wembley	5	1
WC1957	19 May	Dublin	1	1
1964	24 May	Dublin	3	1
1976	8 Sept	Wembley	1	1
EC1978	25 Oct	Dublin	1	1
EC1980	6 Feb	Wembley	2	0
1985	26 Mar	Wembley	2	1
EC1988	12 June	Stuttgart	0	1
WC1990	11 June	Cagliari	1	1
EC1990	14 Nov	Dublin	1	1
EC1991	27 Mar	Wembley	1	1
1995	15 Feb	Dublin	0	1

(abandoned after 27 mins)

		v ISRAEL	*E*	*I*
1986	26 Feb	Ramat Gan	2	1
1988	17 Feb	Tel Aviv	0	0

		v ITALY	*E*	*I*
1933	13 May	Rome	1	1
1934	14 Nov	Highbury	3	2
1939	13 May	Milan	2	2
1948	16 May	Turin	4	0
1949	30 Nov	Tottenham	2	0
1952	18 May	Florence	1	1
1959	6 May	Wembley	2	2
1961	24 May	Rome	3	2
1973	14 June	Turin	0	2
1973	14 Nov	Wembley	0	1
1976	28 May	New York	3	2
WC1976	17 Nov	Rome	0	2
WC1977	16 Nov	Wembley	2	0
EC1980	15 June	Turin	0	1
1985	6 June	Mexico City	1	2
1989	15 Nov	Wembley	0	0
WC1990	7 July	Bari	1	2
WC1997	12 Feb	Wembley	0	1
TF1997	4 June	Nantes	2	0
WC1997	11 Oct	Rome	0	0
2000	15 Nov	Turin	0	1
2002	27 Mar	Leeds	1	2

		v JAPAN	*E*	*J*
UI1995	3 June	Wembley	2	1
2004	1 June	City of Manchester	1	1

		v KUWAIT	E	K
wc1982	25 June	Bilbao	1	0

		v LIECHTENSTEIN	E	L
EC2003	29 Mar	Vaduz	2	0
EC2003	10 Sept	Old Trafford	2	0

		v LUXEMBOURG	E	L
1927	21 May	Esch-sur-Alzette	5	2
wc1960	19 Oct	Luxembourg	9	0
wc1961	28 Sept	Highbury	4	1
wc1977	30 Mar	Wembley	5	0
wc1977	12 Oct	Luxembourg	2	0
EC1982	15 Dec	Wembley	9	0
EC1983	16 Nov	Luxembourg	4	0
EC1998	14 Oct	Luxembourg	3	0
EC1999	4 Sept	Wembley	6	0

		v MACEDONIA	E	M
EC2002	16 Oct	Southampton	2	2
EC2003	6 Sept	Skopje	2	1

		v MALAYSIA	E	M
1991	12 June	Kuala Lumpur	4	2

		v MALTA	E	M
EC1971	3 Feb	Valletta	1	0
EC1971	12 May	Wembley	5	0
2000	3 June	Valletta	2	1

		v MEXICO	E	M
1959	24 May	Mexico City	1	2
1961	10 May	Wembley	8	0
wc1966	16 July	Wembley	2	0
1969	1 June	Mexico City	0	0
1985	9 June	Mexico City	0	1
1986	17 May	Los Angeles	3	0
1997	29 Mar	Wembley	2	0
2001	25 May	Derby	4	0

		v MOLDOVA	E	M
wc1996	1 Sept	Chisinau	3	0
wc1997	10 Sept	Wembley	4	0

		v MOROCCO	E	M
wc1986	6 June	Monterrey	0	0
1998	27 May	Casablanca	1	0

		v NEW ZEALAND	E	NZ
1991	3 June	Auckland	1	0
1991	8 June	Wellington	2	0

		v NIGERIA	E	N
1994	16 Nov	Wembley	1	0
wc2002	12 June	Osaka	0	0

		v NORWAY	E	N
1937	14 May	Oslo	6	0
1938	9 Nov	Newcastle	4	0
1949	18 May	Oslo	4	1
1966	29 June	Oslo	6	1
wc1980	10 Sept	Wembley	4	0
wc1981	9 Sept	Oslo	1	2
wc1992	14 Oct	Wembley	1	1
wc1993	2 June	Oslo	0	2
1994	22 May	Wembley	0	0
1995	11 Oct	Oslo	0	0

		v PARAGUAY	E	P
wc1986	18 June	Mexico City	3	0
2002	17 Apr	Liverpool	4	0

		v PERU	E	P
1959	17 May	Lima	1	4
1962	20 May	Lima	4	0

		v POLAND	E	P
1966	5 Jan	Everton	1	1
1966	5 July	Chorzow	1	0
wc1973	6 June	Chorzow	0	2
wc1973	17 Oct	Wembley	1	1
wc1986	11 June	Monterrey	3	0
wc1989	3 June	Wembley	3	0
wc1989	11 Oct	Katowice	0	0
EC1990	17 Oct	Wembley	2	0
EC1991	13 Nov	Poznan	1	1
wc1993	29 May	Katowice	1	1
wc1993	8 Sept	Wembley	3	0
wc1996	9 Oct	Wembley	2	1
wc1997	31 May	Katowice	2	0
EC1999	27 Mar	Wembley	3	1
EC1999	8 Sept	Warsaw	0	0
EC2004	8 Sept	Katowice	2	1

		v PORTUGAL	E	P
1947	25 May	Lisbon	10	0
1950	14 May	Lisbon	5	3
1951	19 May	Everton	5	2
1955	22 May	Oporto	1	3
1958	7 May	Wembley	2	1
wc1961	21 May	Lisbon	1	1
wc1961	25 Oct	Wembley	2	0
1964	17 May	Lisbon	4	3
1964	4 June	São Paulo	1	1
wc1966	26 July	Wembley	2	1
1969	10 Dec	Wembley	1	0
1974	3 Apr	Lisbon	0	0
EC1974	20 Nov	Wembley	0	0
EC1975	19 Nov	Lisbon	1	1
wc1986	3 June	Monterrey	0	1
1995	12 Dec	Wembley	1	1
1998	22 Apr	Wembley	3	0
EC2000	12 June	Eindhoven	2	3
2002	7 Sept	Villa Park	1	1
2004	18 Feb	Faro	1	1
EC2004	24 June	Lisbon	2	2*

		v ROMANIA	E	R
1939	24 May	Bucharest	2	0
1968	6 Nov	Bucharest	0	0
1969	15 Jan	Wembley	1	1
wc1970	2 June	Guadalajara	1	0
wc1980	15 Oct	Bucharest	1	2
wc1981	29 April	Wembley	0	0
wc1985	1 May	Bucharest	0	0
wc1985	11 Sept	Wembley	1	1
1994	12 Oct	Wembley	1	1
wc1998	22 June	Toulouse	1	2
EC2000	20 June	Charleroi	2	3

		v SAN MARINO	E	SM
wc1992	17 Feb	Wembley	6	0
wc1993	17 Nov	Bologna	7	1

		v SAUDI ARABIA	E	SA
1988	16 Nov	Riyadh	1	1
1998	23 May	Wembley	0	0

		v SERBIA-MONTENEGRO	E	S-M
2003	3 June	Leicester	2	1

		v SLOVAKIA	E	S
EC2002	12 Oct	Bratislava	2	1
EC2003	11 June	Middlesbrough	2	1

		v SOUTH AFRICA	E	SA
1997	24 May	Old Trafford	2	1
2003	22 May	Durban	2	1

		v SOUTH KOREA	E	SK
2002	21 May	Seoguipo	1	1

		v SPAIN	E	S
1929	15 May	Madrid	3	4
1931	9 Dec	Highbury	7	1
wc1950	2 July	Rio de Janeiro	0	1
1955	18 May	Madrid	1	1
1955	30 Nov	Wembley	4	1
1960	15 May	Madrid	0	3
1960	26 Oct	Wembley	4	2
1965	8 Dec	Madrid	2	0
1967	24 May	Wembley	2	0
EC1968	3 Apr	Wembley	1	0
EC1968	8 May	Madrid	2	1
1980	26 Mar	Barcelona	2	0
EC1980	18 June	Naples	2	1
1981	25 Mar	Wembley	1	2

			E	*S*
WC1982	5 July	Madrid	0	0
1987	18 Feb	Madrid	4	2
1992	9 Sept	Santander	0	1
EC1996	22 June	Wembley	0	0
2001	28 Feb	Villa Park	3	0
2004	17 Nov	Madrid	0	1

		v SWEDEN	*E*	*S*
1923	21 May	Stockholm	4	2
1923	24 May	Stockholm	3	1
1937	17 May	Stockholm	4	0
1947	19 Nov	Highbury	4	2
1949	13 May	Stockholm	1	3
1956	16 May	Stockholm	0	0
1959	28 Oct	Wembley	2	3
1965	16 May	Gothenburg	2	1
1968	22 May	Wembley	3	1
1979	10 June	Stockholm	0	0
1986	10 Sept	Stockholm	0	1
WC1988	19 Oct	Wembley	0	0
WC1989	6 Sept	Stockholm	0	0
EC1992	17 June	Stockholm	1	2
UI1995	8 June	Leeds	3	3
EC1998	5 Sept	Stockholm	1	2
EC1999	5 June	Wembley	0	0
2001	10 Nov	Old Trafford	1	1
WC2002	2 June	Saitama	1	1
2004	31 Mar	Gothenburg	0	1

		v SWITZERLAND	*E*	*S*
1933	20 May	Berne	4	0
1938	21 May	Zurich	1	2
1947	18 May	Zurich	0	1
1948	2 Dec	Highbury	6	0
1952	28 May	Zurich	3	0
WC1954	20 June	Berne	2	0
1962	9 May	Wembley	3	1
1963	5 June	Basle	8	1
EC1971	13 Oct	Basle	3	2
EC1971	10 Nov	Wembley	1	1
1975	3 Sept	Basle	2	1
1977	7 Sept	Wembley	0	0
WC1980	19 Nov	Wembley	2	1
WC1981	30 May	Basle	1	2
1988	28 May	Lausanne	1	0
1995	15 Nov	Wembley	3	1
EC1996	8 June	Wembley	1	1
1998	25 Mar	Berne	1	1
EC2004	17 June	Coimbra	3	0

		v TUNISIA	*E*	*T*
1990	2 June	Tunis	1	1
WC1998	15 June	Marseilles	2	0

		v TURKEY	*E*	*T*
WC1984	14 Nov	Istanbul	8	0
WC1985	16 Oct	Wembley	5	0
EC1987	29 Apr	Izmir	0	0
EC1987	14 Oct	Wembley	8	0
EC1991	1 May	Izmir	1	0
EC1991	16 Oct	Wembley	1	0
WC1992	18 Nov	Wembley	4	0
WC1993	31 Mar	Izmir	2	0
EC2003	2 Apr	Sunderland	2	0
EC2003	11 Oct	Istanbul	0	0

		v UKRAINE	*E*	*U*
2000	31 May	Wembley	2	0
2004	18 Aug	St James' Park	3	0

		v URUGUAY	*E*	*U*
1953	31 May	Montevideo	1	2
WC1954	26 June	Basle	2	4
1964	6 May	Wembley	2	1
WC1966	11 July	Wembley	0	0
1969	8 June	Montevideo	2	1
1977	15 June	Montevideo	0	0
1984	13 June	Montevideo	0	2
1990	22 May	Wembley	1	2
1995	29 Mar	Wembley	0	0

		v USA	*E*	*USA*
WC1950	29 June	Belo Horizonte	0	1
1953	8 June	New York	6	3
1959	28 May	Los Angeles	8	1
1964	27 May	New York	10	0
1985	16 June	Los Angeles	5	0
1993	9 June	Foxboro	0	2
1994	7 Sept	Wembley	2	0
2005	28 May	Chicago	2	1

		v USSR	*E*	*USSR*
1958	18 May	Moscow	1	1
WC1958	8 June	Gothenburg	2	2
WC1958	17 June	Gothenburg	0	1
1958	22 Oct	Wembley	5	0
1967	6 Dec	Wembley	2	2
EC1968	8 June	Rome	2	0
1973	10 June	Moscow	2	1
1984	2 June	Wembley	0	2
1986	26 Mar	Tbilisi	1	0
EC1988	18 June	Frankfurt	1	3
1991	21 May	Wembley	3	1

		v YUGOSLAVIA	*E*	*Y*
1939	18 May	Belgrade	1	2
1950	22 Nov	Highbury	2	2
1954	16 May	Belgrade	0	1
1956	28 Nov	Wembley	3	0
1958	11 May	Belgrade	0	5
1960	11 May	Wembley	3	3
1965	9 May	Belgrade	1	1
1966	4 May	Wembley	2	0
EC1968	5 June	Florence	0	1
1972	11 Oct	Wembley	1	1
1974	5 June	Belgrade	2	2
EC1986	12 Nov	Wembley	2	0
EC1987	11 Nov	Belgrade	4	1
1989	13 Dec	Wembley	2	1

SCOTLAND

		v ARGENTINA	*S*	*A*
1977	18 June	Buenos Aires	1	1
1979	2 June	Glasgow	1	3
1990	28 Mar	Glasgow	1	0

		v AUSTRALIA	*S*	*A*
WC1985	20 Nov	Glasgow	2	0
WC1985	4 Dec	Melbourne	0	0
1996	27 Mar	Glasgow	1	0
2000	15 Nov	Glasgow	0	2

		v AUSTRIA	*S*	*A*
1931	16 May	Vienna	0	5
1933	29 Nov	Glasgow	2	2
1937	9 May	Vienna	1	1
1950	13 Dec	Glasgow	0	1
1951	27 May	Vienna	0	4
WC1954	16 June	Zurich	0	1
1955	19 May	Vienna	4	1
1956	2 May	Glasgow	1	1
1960	29 May	Vienna	1	4
1963	8 May	Glasgow	4	1
		(*abandoned after 79 mins*)		
WC1968	6 Nov	Glasgow	2	1
WC1969	5 Nov	Vienna	0	2
EC1978	20 Sept	Vienna	2	3
EC1979	17 Oct	Glasgow	1	1
1994	20 Apr	Vienna	2	1
WC1996	31 Aug	Vienna	0	0
WC1997	2 Apr	Celtic Park	2	0
2003	30 Apr	Glasgow	0	2

		v BELARUS	*S*	*B*
WC1997	8 June	Minsk	1	0
WC1997	7 Sept	Aberdeen	4	1
EC2005	8 June	Minsk	0	0

		v BELGIUM	*S*	*B*
1947	18 May	Brussels	1	2
1948	28 Apr	Glasgow	2	0
1951	20 May	Brussels	5	0
EC1971	3 Feb	Liège	0	3
EC1971	10 Nov	Aberdeen	1	0
1974	2 June	Brussels	1	2
EC1979	21 Nov	Brussels	0	2
EC1979	19 Dec	Glasgow	1	3
EC1982	15 Dec	Brussels	2	3
EC1983	12 Oct	Glasgow	1	1
EC1987	1 Apr	Brussels	1	4
EC1987	14 Oct	Glasgow	2	0
WC2001	24 Mar	Glasgow	2	2
WC2001	5 Sept	Brussels	0	2

		v BOSNIA	*S*	*B*
EC1999	4 Sept	Sarajevo	2	1
EC1999	5 Oct	Glasgow	1	0

		v BRAZIL	*S*	*B*
1966	25 June	Glasgow	1	1
1972	5 July	Rio de Janeiro	0	1
1973	30 June	Glasgow	0	1
WC1974	18 June	Frankfurt	0	0
1977	23 June	Rio de Janeiro	0	2
WC1982	18 June	Seville	1	4
1987	26 May	Glasgow	0	2
WC1990	20 June	Turin	0	1
WC1998	10 June	Saint-Denis	1	2

		v BULGARIA	*S*	*B*
1978	22 Feb	Glasgow	2	1
EC1986	10 Sept	Glasgow	0	0
EC1987	11 Nov	Sofia	1	0
EC1990	14 Nov	Sofia	1	1
EC1991	27 Mar	Glasgow	1	1

		v CANADA	*S*	*C*
1983	12 June	Vancouver	2	0
1983	16 June	Edmonton	3	0
1983	20 June	Toronto	2	0
1992	21 May	Toronto	3	1
2002	15 Oct	Easter Road	3	1

		v CHILE	*S*	*C*
1977	15 June	Santiago	4	2
1989	30 May	Glasgow	2	0

		v CIS	*S*	*C*
EC1992	18 June	Norrkoping	3	0

		v COLOMBIA	*S*	*C*
1988	17 May	Glasgow	0	0
1996	30 May	Miami	0	1
1998	23 May	New York	2	2

		v COSTA RICA	*S*	*CR*
WC1990	11 June	Genoa	0	1

		v CROATIA	*S*	*C*
WC2000	11 Oct	Zagreb	1	1
WC2001	1 Sept	Glasgow	0	0

		v CYPRUS	*S*	*C*
WC1968	17 Dec	Nicosia	5	0
WC1969	11 May	Glasgow	8	0
WC1989	8 Feb	Limassol	3	2
WC1989	26 Apr	Glasgow	2	1

		v CZECHOSLOVAKIA	*S*	*C*
1937	22 May	Prague	3	1
1937	8 Dec	Glasgow	5	0
WC1961	14 May	Bratislava	0	4
WC1961	26 Sept	Glasgow	3	2
WC1961	29 Nov	Brussels	2	4*
1972	2 July	Porto Alegre	0	0
WC1973	26 Sept	Glasgow	2	1
WC1973	17 Oct	Prague	0	1
WC1976	13 Oct	Prague	0	2
WC1977	21 Sept	Glasgow	3	1

		v CZECH REPUBLIC	*S*	*C*
EC1999	31 Mar	Glasgow	1	2
EC1999	9 June	Prague	2	3

		v DENMARK	*S*	*D*
1951	12 May	Glasgow	3	1
1952	25 May	Copenhagen	2	1
1968	16 Oct	Copenhagen	1	0
EC1970	11 Nov	Glasgow	1	0
EC1971	9 June	Copenhagen	0	1
WC1972	18 Oct	Copenhagen	4	1
WC1972	15 Nov	Glasgow	2	0
EC1975	3 Sept	Copenhagen	1	0
EC1975	29 Oct	Glasgow	3	1
WC1986	4 June	Nezahualcayotl	0	1
1996	24 Apr	Copenhagen	0	2
1998	25 Mar	Glasgow	0	1
2002	21 Aug	Glasgow	0	1
2004	28 Apr	Copenhagen	0	1

		v ECUADOR	*S*	*E*
1995	24 May	Toyama	2	1

		v EGYPT	*S*	*E*
1990	16 May	Aberdeen	1	3

		v ESTONIA	*S*	*E*
WC1993	19 May	Tallinn	3	0
WC1993	2 June	Aberdeen	3	1
WC1997	11 Feb	Monaco	0	0
WC1997	29 Mar	Kilmarnock	2	0
EC1998	10 Oct	Edinburgh	3	2
EC1999	8 Sept	Tallinn	0	0
2004	27 May	Tallinn	1	0

		v FAEROES	*S*	*F*
EC1994	12 Oct	Glasgow	5	1
EC1995	7 June	Toftir	2	0
EC1998	14 Oct	Aberdeen	2	1
EC1999	5 June	Toftir	1	1
EC2002	7 Sept	Toftir	2	2
EC2003	6 Sept	Glasgow	3	1

		v FINLAND	*S*	*F*
1954	25 May	Helsinki	2	1
WC1964	21 Oct	Glasgow	3	1
WC1965	27 May	Helsinki	2	1
1976	8 Sept	Glasgow	6	0
1992	25 Mar	Glasgow	1	1
EC1994	7 Sept	Helsinki	2	0
EC1995	6 Sept	Glasgow	1	0
1998	22 Apr	Edinburgh	1	1

		v FRANCE	*S*	*F*
1930	18 May	Paris	2	0
1932	8 May	Paris	3	1
1948	23 May	Paris	0	3
1949	27 Apr	Glasgow	2	0
1950	27 May	Paris	1	0
1951	16 May	Glasgow	1	0
WC1958	15 June	Orebro	1	2
1984	1 June	Marseilles	0	2
WC1989	8 Mar	Glasgow	2	0
WC1989	11 Oct	Paris	0	3
1997	12 Nov	St Etienne	1	2
2000	29 Mar	Glasgow	0	2
2002	27 Mar	Paris	0	5

		v GERMANY	*S*	*G*
1929	1 June	Berlin	1	1
1936	14 Oct	Glasgow	2	0
EC1992	15 June	Norrkoping	0	2
1993	24 Mar	Glasgow	0	1
1998	28 Apr	Bremen	1	0
EC2003	7 June	Glasgow	1	1
EC2003	10 Sept	Dortmund	1	2

v EAST GERMANY

			S	EG
1974	30 Oct	Glasgow	3	0
1977	7 Sept	East Berlin	0	1
EC1982	13 Oct	Glasgow	2	0
EC1983	16 Nov	Halle	1	2
1985	16 Oct	Glasgow	0	0
1990	25 Apr	Glasgow	0	1

v WEST GERMANY

			S	WG
1957	22 May	Stuttgart	3	1
1959	6 May	Glasgow	3	2
1964	12 May	Hanover	2	2
WC1969	16 Apr	Glasgow	1	1
WC1969	22 Oct	Hamburg	2	3
1973	14 Nov	Glasgow	1	1
1974	27 Mar	Frankfurt	1	2
WC1986	8 June	Queretaro	1	2

v GREECE

			S	G
EC1994	18 Dec	Athens	0	1
EC1995	16 Aug	Glasgow	1	0

v HOLLAND

			S	H
1929	4 June	Amsterdam	2	0
1938	21 May	Amsterdam	3	1
1959	27 May	Amsterdam	2	1
1966	11 May	Glasgow	0	3
1968	30 May	Amsterdam	0	0
1971	1 Dec	Rotterdam	1	2
WC1978	11 June	Mendoza	3	2
1982	23 Mar	Glasgow	2	1
1986	29 Apr	Eindhoven	0	0
EC1992	12 June	Gothenburg	0	1
1994	23 Mar	Glasgow	0	1
1994	27 May	Utrecht	1	3
EC1996	10 June	Birmingham	0	0
2000	26 Apr	Arnhem	0	0
EC2003	15 Nov	Glasgow	1	0
EC2003	19 Nov	Amsterdam	0	6

v HONG KONG XI

			S	HK
†2002	23 May	Hong Kong	4	0

†match not recognised by FIFA

v HUNGARY

			S	H
1938	7 Dec	Glasgow	3	1
1954	8 Dec	Glasgow	2	4
1955	29 May	Budapest	1	3
1958	7 May	Glasgow	1	1
1960	5 June	Budapest	3	3
1980	31 May	Budapest	1	3
1987	9 Sept	Glasgow	2	0
2004	18 Aug	Glasgow	0	3

v ICELAND

			S	I
WC1984	17 Oct	Glasgow	3	0
WC1985	28 May	Reykjavik	1	0
EC2002	12 Oct	Reykjavik	2	0
EC2003	29 Mar	Glasgow	2	1

v IRAN

			S	I
WC1978	7 June	Cordoba	1	1

v REPUBLIC OF IRELAND

			S	RI
WC1961	3 May	Glasgow	4	1
WC1961	7 May	Dublin	3	0
1963	9 June	Dublin	0	1
1969	21 Sept	Dublin	1	1
EC1986	15 Oct	Dublin	0	0
EC1987	18 Feb	Glasgow	0	1
2000	30 May	Dublin	2	1
2003	12 Feb	Glasgow	0	2

v ISRAEL

			S	I
WC1981	25 Feb	Tel Aviv	1	0
WC1981	28 Apr	Glasgow	3	1
1986	28 Jan	Tel Aviv	1	0

v ITALY

			S	I
1931	20 May	Rome	0	3
WC1965	9 Nov	Glasgow	1	0
WC1965	7 Dec	Naples	0	3
1988	22 Dec	Perugia	0	2
WC1992	18 Nov	Glasgow	0	0
WC1993	13 Oct	Rome	1	3
EC2005	26 Mar	Milan	0	2

v JAPAN

			S	J
1995	21 May	Hiroshima	0	0

v LATVIA

			S	L
WC1996	5 Oct	Riga	2	0
WC1997	11 Oct	Glasgow	2	0
WC2000	2 Sept	Riga	1	0
WC2001	6 Oct	Glasgow	2	1

v LITHUANIA

			S	L
EC1998	5 Sept	Vilnius	0	0
EC1999	9 Oct	Glasgow	3	0
EC2003	2 Apr	Kaunas	0	1
EC2003	11 Oct	Glasgow	1	0

v LUXEMBOURG

			S	L
1947	24 May	Luxembourg	6	0
EC1986	12 Nov	Glasgow	3	0
EC1987	2 Dec	Esch	0	0

v MALTA

			S	M
1988	22 Mar	Valletta	1	1
1990	28 May	Valletta	2	1
WC1993	17 Feb	Glasgow	3	0
WC1993	17 Nov	Valletta	2	0
1997	1 June	Valletta	3	2

v MOLDOVA

			S	M
EC2004	13 Oct	Chisinau	1	1
EC2005	4 June	Glasgow	2	0

v MOROCCO

			S	M
WC1998	23 June	St Etienne	0	3

v NEW ZEALAND

			S	NZ
WC1982	15 June	Malaga	5	2
2003	27 May	Tynecastle	1	1

v NIGERIA

			S	N
2002	17 Apr	Aberdeen	1	2

v NORWAY

			S	N
1929	28 May	Oslo	7	3
1954	5 May	Glasgow	1	0
1954	19 May	Oslo	1	1
1963	4 June	Bergen	3	4
1963	7 Nov	Glasgow	6	1
1974	6 June	Oslo	2	1
EC1978	25 Oct	Glasgow	3	2
EC1979	7 June	Oslo	4	0
WC1988	14 Sept	Oslo	2	1
WC1989	15 Nov	Glasgow	1	1
1992	3 June	Oslo	0	0
WC1998	16 June	Bordeaux	1	1
2003	20 Aug	Oslo	0	0
EC2004	9 Oct	Glasgow	0	1

v PARAGUAY

			S	P
WC1958	11 June	Norrkoping	2	3

v PERU

			S	P
1972	26 Apr	Glasgow	2	0
WC1978	3 June	Cordoba	1	3
1979	12 Sept	Glasgow	1	1

v POLAND

			S	P
1958	1 June	Warsaw	2	1
1960	4 June	Glasgow	2	3
WC1965	23 May	Chorzow	1	1
WC1965	13 Oct	Glasgow	1	2
1980	28 May	Poznan	0	1
1990	19 May	Glasgow	1	1
2001	25 Apr	Bydgoszcz	1	1

v PORTUGAL

			S	P
1950	21 May	Lisbon	2	2
1955	4 May	Glasgow	3	0
1959	3 June	Lisbon	0	1
1966	18 June	Glasgow	0	1
EC1971	21 Apr	Lisbon	0	2
EC1971	13 Oct	Glasgow	2	1
1975	13 May	Glasgow	1	0
EC1978	29 Nov	Lisbon	0	1

			S	*P*
EC1980	26 Mar	Glasgow	4	1
WC1980	15 Oct	Glasgow	0	0
WC1981	18 Nov	Lisbon	1	2
WC1992	14 Oct	Glasgow	0	0
WC1993	28 Apr	Lisbon	0	5
2002	20 Nov	Braga	0	2

		v ROMANIA	*S*	*R*
EC1975	1 June	Bucharest	1	1
EC1975	17 Dec	Glasgow	1	1
1986	26 Mar	Glasgow	3	0
EC1990	12 Sept	Glasgow	2	1
EC1991	16 Oct	Bucharest	0	1
2004	31 Mar	Glasgow	1	2

		v RUSSIA	*S*	*R*
EC1994	16 Nov	Glasgow	1	1
EC1995	29 Mar	Moscow	0	0

		v SAN MARINO	*S*	*SM*
EC1991	1 May	Serravalle	2	0
EC1991	13 Nov	Glasgow	4	0
EC1995	26 Apr	Serravalle	2	0
EC1995	15 Nov	Glasgow	5	0
WC2000	7 Oct	Serravalle	2	0
WC2001	28 Mar	Glasgow	4	0

		v SAUDI ARABIA	*S*	*SA*
1988	17 Feb	Riyadh	2	2

		v SLOVENIA	*S*	*SL*
EC2004	8 Sept	Glasgow	0	0

		v SOUTH AFRICA	*S*	*SA*
2002	20 May	Hong Kong	0	2

		v SOUTH KOREA	*S*	*SK*
2002	16 May	Busan	1	4

		v SPAIN	*S*	*Sp*
WC1957	8 May	Glasgow	4	2
WC1957	26 May	Madrid	1	4
1963	13 June	Madrid	6	2
1965	8 May	Glasgow	0	0
EC1974	20 Nov	Glasgow	1	2
EC1975	5 Feb	Valencia	1	1
1982	24 Feb	Valencia	0	3
WC1984	14 Nov	Glasgow	3	1
WC1985	27 Feb	Seville	0	1
1988	27 Apr	Madrid	0	0
2004	3 Sept	Valencia	1	1

Match abandoned afer 60 minutes; floodlight failure.

		v SWEDEN	*S*	*Sw*
1952	30 May	Stockholm	1	3
1953	6 May	Glasgow	1	2
1975	16 Apr	Gothenburg	1	1
1977	27 Apr	Glasgow	3	1
WC1980	10 Sept	Stockholm	1	0
WC1981	9 Sept	Glasgow	2	0
WC1990	16 June	Genoa	2	1
1995	11 Oct	Stockholm	0	2
WC1996	10 Nov	Glasgow	1	0
WC1997	30 Apr	Gothenburg	1	2
2004	17 Nov	Edinburgh	1	4

		v SWITZERLAND	*S*	*Sw*
1931	24 May	Geneva	3	2
1948	17 May	Berne	1	2
1950	26 Apr	Glasgow	3	1
WC1957	19 May	Basle	2	1
WC1957	6 Nov	Glasgow	3	2
1973	22 June	Berne	0	1
1976	7 Apr	Glasgow	1	0
EC1982	17 Nov	Berne	0	2
EC1983	30 May	Glasgow	2	2
EC1990	17 Oct	Glasgow	2	1
EC1991	11 Sept	Berne	2	2
WC1992	9 Sept	Berne	1	3
WC1993	8 Sept	Aberdeen	1	1
EC1996	18 June	Birmingham	1	0

		v TRINIDAD & TOBAGO	*S*	*T*
2004	30 May	Edinburgh	4	1

		v TURKEY	*S*	*T*
1960	8 June	Ankara	2	4

		v URUGUAY	*S*	*U*
WC1954	19 June	Basle	0	7
1962	2 May	Glasgow	2	3
1983	21 Sept	Glasgow	2	0
WC1986	13 June	Nezahualcoyotl	0	0

		v USA	*S*	*USA*
1952	30 Apr	Glasgow	6	0
1992	17 May	Denver	1	0
1996	26 May	New Britain	1	2
1998	30 May	Washington	0	0

		v USSR	*S*	*USSR*
1967	10 May	Glasgow	0	2
1971	14 June	Moscow	0	1
WC1982	22 June	Malaga	2	2
1991	6 Feb	Glasgow	0	1

		v YUGOSLAVIA	*S*	*Y*
1955	15 May	Belgrade	2	2
1956	21 Nov	Glasgow	2	0
WC1958	8 June	Vasteras	1	1
1972	29 June	Belo Horizonte	2	2
WC1974	22 June	Frankfurt	1	1
1984	12 Sept	Glasgow	6	1
WC1988	19 Oct	Glasgow	1	1
WC1989	6 Sept	Zagreb	1	3

		v ZAIRE	*S*	*Z*
WC1974	14 June	Dortmund	2	0

WALES

		v ALBANIA	*W*	*A*
EC1994	7 Sept	Cardiff	2	0
EC1995	15 Nov	Tirana	1	1

		v ARGENTINA	*W*	*A*
1992	3 June	Tokyo	0	1
2002	13 Feb	Cardiff	1	1

		v ARMENIA	*W*	*A*
WC2001	24 Mar	Erevan	2	2
WC2001	1 Sept	Cardiff	0	0

		v AUSTRIA	*W*	*A*
1954	9 May	Vienna	0	2
EC1955	23 Nov	Wrexham	1	2
EC1974	4 Sept	Vienna	1	2
1975	19 Nov	Wrexham	1	0
1992	29 Apr	Vienna	1	1
EC2005	26 Mar	Cardiff	0	2
EC2005	30 Mar	Vienna	0	1

		v AZERBAIJAN	*W*	*A*
EC2002	20 Nov	Baku	2	0
EC2003	29 Mar	Cardiff	4	0
EC2004	4 Sept	Baku	1	1

		v BELARUS	*W*	*B*
EC1998	14 Oct	Cardiff	3	2
EC1999	4 Sept	Minsk	2	1
WC2000	2 Sept	Minsk	1	2
WC2001	6 Oct	Cardiff	1	0

		v BELGIUM	*W*	*B*
1949	22 May	Liège	1	3
1949	23 Nov	Cardiff	5	1

			W	*B*
EC1990	17 Oct	Cardiff	3	1
EC1991	27 Mar	Brussels	1	1
WC1992	18 Nov	Brussels	0	2
WC1993	31 Mar	Cardiff	2	0
WC1997	29 Mar	Cardiff	1	2
WC1997	11 Oct	Brussels	2	3

v BOSNIA

			W	*B*
2003	12 Feb	Cardiff	2	2

v BRAZIL

			W	*B*
WC1958	19 June	Gothenburg	0	1
1962	12 May	Rio de Janeiro	1	3
1962	16 May	São Paulo	1	3
1966	14 May	Rio de Janeiro	1	3
1966	18 May	Belo Horizonte	0	1
1983	12 June	Cardiff	1	1
1991	11 Sept	Cardiff	1	0
1997	12 Nov	Brasilia	0	3
2000	23 May	Cardiff	0	3

v BULGARIA

			W	*B*
EC1983	27 Apr	Wrexham	1	0
EC1983	16 Nov	Sofia	0	1
EC1994	14 Dec	Cardiff	0	3
EC1995	29 Mar	Sofia	1	3

v CANADA

			W	*C*
1986	10 May	Toronto	0	2
1986	20 May	Vancouver	3	0
2004	30 May	Wrexham	1	0

v CHILE

			W	*C*
1966	22 May	Santiago	0	2

v COSTA RICA

			W	*CR*
1990	20 May	Cardiff	1	0

v CROATIA

			W	*C*
2002	21 Aug	Varazdin	1	1

v CYPRUS

			W	*C*
WC1992	14 Oct	Limassol	1	0
WC1993	13 Oct	Cardiff	2	0

v CZECHOSLOVAKIA

			W	*C*
WC1957	1 May	Cardiff	1	0
WC1957	26 May	Prague	0	2
EC1971	21 Apr	Swansea	1	3
EC1971	27 Oct	Prague	0	1
WC1977	30 Mar	Wrexham	3	0
WC1977	16 Nov	Prague	0	1
WC1980	19 Nov	Cardiff	1	0
WC1981	9 Sept	Prague	0	2
EC1987	29 Apr	Wrexham	1	1
EC1987	11 Nov	Prague	0	2
WC1993	28 Apr	Ostrava†	1	1
WC1993	8 Sept	Cardiff†	2	2

†*Czechoslovakia played as RCS (Republic of Czechs and Slovaks).*

v CZECH REPUBLIC

			W	*CR*
2002	27 Mar	Cardiff	0	0

v DENMARK

			W	*D*
WC1964	21 Oct	Copenhagen	0	1
WC1965	1 Dec	Wrexham	4	2
EC1987	9 Sept	Cardiff	1	0
EC1987	14 Oct	Copenhagen	0	1
1990	11 Sept	Copenhagen	0	1
EC1998	10 Oct	Copenhagen	2	1
EC1999	9 June	Liverpool	0	2

v ESTONIA

			W	*E*
1994	23 May	Tallinn	2	1

v FINLAND

			W	*F*
EC1971	26 May	Helsinki	1	0
EC1971	13 Oct	Swansea	3	0
EC1987	10 Sept	Helsinki	1	1
EC1987	1 Apr	Wrexham	4	0
WC1988	19 Oct	Swansea	2	2
WC1989	6 Sept	Helsinki	0	1
2000	29 Mar	Cardiff	1	2
EC2002	7 Sept	Helsinki	2	0
EC2003	10 Sept	Cardiff	1	1

v FAEROES

			W	*F*
WC1992	9 Sept	Cardiff	6	0
WC1993	6 June	Toftir	3	0

v FRANCE

			W	*F*
1933	25 May	Paris	1	1
1939	20 May	Paris	1	2
1953	14 May	Paris	1	6
1982	2 June	Toulouse	1	0

v GEORGIA

			W	*G*
EC1994	16 Nov	Tbilisi	0	5
EC1995	7 June	Cardiff	0	1

v GERMANY

			W	*G*
EC1995	26 Apr	Dusseldorf	1	1
EC1995	11 Oct	Cardiff	1	2
2002	14 May	Cardiff	1	0

v EAST GERMANY

			W	*EG*
WC1957	19 May	Leipzig	1	2
WC1957	25 Sept	Cardiff	4	1
WC1969	16 Apr	Dresden	1	2
WC1969	22 Oct	Cardiff	1	3

v WEST GERMANY

			W	*WG*
1968	8 May	Cardiff	1	1
1969	26 Mar	Frankfurt	1	1
1976	6 Oct	Cardiff	0	2
1977	14 Dec	Dortmund	1	1
EC1979	2 May	Wrexham	0	2
EC1979	17 Oct	Cologne	1	5
WC1989	31 May	Cardiff	0	0
WC1989	15 Nov	Cologne	1	2
EC1991	5 June	Cardiff	1	0
EC1991	16 Oct	Nuremberg	1	4

v GREECE

			W	*G*
WC1964	9 Dec	Athens	0	2
WC1965	17 Mar	Cardiff	4	1

v HOLLAND

			W	*H*
WC1988	14 Sept	Amsterdam	0	1
WC1989	11 Oct	Wrexham	1	2
1992	30 May	Utrecht	0	4
WC1996	5 Oct	Cardiff	1	3
WC1996	9 Nov	Eindhoven	1	7

v HUNGARY

			W	*H*
WC1958	8 June	Sanviken	1	1
WC1958	17 June	Stockholm	2	1
1961	28 May	Budapest	2	3
EC1962	7 Nov	Budapest	1	3
EC1963	20 Mar	Cardiff	1	1
EC1974	30 Oct	Cardiff	2	0
EC1975	16 Apr	Budapest	2	1
1985	16 Oct	Cardiff	0	3
2004	31 Mar	Budapest	2	1
2005	9 Feb	Cardiff	2	0

v ICELAND

			W	*I*
WC1980	2 June	Reykjavik	4	0
WC1981	14 Oct	Swansea	2	2
WC1984	12 Sept	Reykjavik	0	1
WC1984	14 Nov	Cardiff	2	1
1991	1 May	Cardiff	1	0

v IRAN

			W	*I*
1978	18 Apr	Teheran	1	0

v REPUBLIC OF IRELAND

			W	*RI*
1960	28 Sept	Dublin	3	2
1979	11 Sept	Swansea	2	1
1981	24 Feb	Dublin	3	1
1986	26 Mar	Dublin	1	0

			W	RI
1990	28 Mar	Dublin	0	1
1991	6 Feb	Wrexham	0	3
1992	19 Feb	Dublin	1	0
1993	17 Feb	Dublin	1	2
1997	11 Feb	Cardiff	0	0

		v ISRAEL	W	I
WC1958	15 Jan	Tel Aviv	2	0
WC1958	5 Feb	Cardiff	2	0
1984	10 June	Tel Aviv	0	0
1989	8 Feb	Tel Aviv	3	3

		v ITALY	W	I
1965	1 May	Florence	1	4
WC1968	23 Oct	Cardiff	0	1
WC1969	4 Nov	Rome	1	4
1988	4 June	Brescia	1	0
1996	24 Jan	Terni	0	3
EC1998	5 Sept	Liverpool	0	2
EC1999	5 June	Bologna	0	4
EC2002	16 Oct	Cardiff	2	1
EC2003	6 Sept	Milan	0	4

		v JAMAICA	W	J
1998	25 Mar	Cardiff	0	0

		v JAPAN	W	J
1992	7 June	Matsuyama	1	0

		v LATVIA	W	L
2004	18 Aug	Riga	2	0

		v KUWAIT	W	K
1977	6 Sept	Wrexham	0	0
1977	20 Sept	Kuwait	0	0

		v LUXEMBOURG	W	L
EC1974	20 Nov	Swansea	5	0
EC1975	1 May	Luxembourg	3	1
EC1990	14 Nov	Luxembourg	1	0
EC1991	13 Nov	Cardiff	1	0

		v MALTA	W	M
EC1978	25 Oct	Wrexham	7	0
EC1979	2 June	Valletta	2	0
1988	1 June	Valletta	3	2
1998	3 June	Valletta	3	0

		v MEXICO	W	M
WC1958	11 June	Stockholm	1	1
1962	22 May	Mexico City	1	2

		v MOLDOVA	W	M
EC1994	12 Oct	Kishinev	2	3
EC1995	6 Sept	Cardiff	1	0

		v NORWAY	W	N
EC1982	22 Sept	Swansea	1	0
EC1983	21 Sept	Oslo	0	0
1984	6 June	Trondheim	0	1
1985	26 Feb	Wrexham	1	1
1985	5 June	Bergen	2	4
1994	9 Mar	Cardiff	1	3
WC2000	7 Oct	Cardiff	1	1
WC2001	5 Sept	Oslo	2	3
2004	27 May	Oslo	0	0

		v POLAND	W	P
WC1973	28 Mar	Cardiff	2	0
WC1973	26 Sept	Katowice	0	3
1991	29 May	Radom	0	0
WC2000	11 Oct	Warsaw	0	0
WC2001	2 June	Cardiff	1	2
EC2004	13 Oct	Cardiff	2	3

		v PORTUGAL	W	P
1949	15 May	Lisbon	2	3
1951	12 May	Cardiff	2	1
2000	2 June	Chaves	0	3

		v QATAR	W	Q
2000	23 Feb	Doha	1	0

		v ROMANIA	W	R
EC1970	11 Nov	Cardiff	0	0
EC1971	24 Nov	Bucharest	0	2
1983	12 Oct	Wrexham	5	0
WC1992	20 May	Bucharest	1	5
WC1993	17 Nov	Cardiff	1	2

		v RUSSIA	W	R
EC2003	15 Nov	Moscow	0	0
EC2003	19 Nov	Cardiff	0	1

		v SAN MARINO	W	SM
WC1996	2 June	Serravalle	5	0
WC1996	31 Aug	Cardiff	6	0

		v SAUDI ARABIA	W	SA
1986	25 Feb	Dahran	2	1

		v SERBIA-MONTENEGRO	W	SM
EC2003	20 Aug	Belgrade	0	1
EC2003	11 Oct	Cardiff	2	3

		v SPAIN	W	S
WC1961	19 Apr	Cardiff	1	2
WC1961	18 May	Madrid	1	1
1982	24 Mar	Valencia	1	1
WC1984	17 Oct	Seville	0	3
WC1985	30 Apr	Wrexham	3	0

		v SWEDEN	W	S
WC1958	15 June	Stockholm	0	0
1988	27 Apr	Stockholm	1	4
1989	26 Apr	Wrexham	0	2
1990	25 Apr	Stockholm	2	4
1994	20 Apr	Wrexham	0	2

		v SWITZERLAND	W	S
1949	26 May	Berne	0	4
1951	16 May	Wrexham	3	2
1996	24 Apr	Lugano	0	2
EC1999	31 Mar	Zurich	0	2
EC1999	9 Oct	Wrexham	0	2

		v TUNISIA	W	T
1998	6 June	Tunis	0	4

		v TURKEY	W	T
EC1978	29 Nov	Wrexham	1	0
EC1979	21 Nov	Izmir	0	1
WC1980	15 Oct	Cardiff	4	0
WC1981	25 Mar	Ankara	1	0
WC1996	14 Dec	Cardiff	0	0
WC1997	20 Aug	Istanbul	4	6

		v REST OF UNITED KINGDOM	W	UK
1951	5 Dec	Cardiff	3	2
1969	28 July	Cardiff	0	1

		v UKRAINE	W	U
WC2001	28 Mar	Cardiff	1	1
WC2001	6 June	Kiev	1	1

		v USA	W	USA
2003	27 May	San Jose	0	2

		v URUGUAY	W	U
1986	21 Apr	Wrexham	0	0

		v USSR	W	USSR
WC1965	30 May	Moscow	1	2
WC1965	27 Oct	Cardiff	2	1
WC1981	30 May	Wrexham	0	0
WC1981	18 Nov	Tbilisi	0	3
1987	18 Feb	Swansea	0	0

		v YUGOSLAVIA	W	Y
1953	21 May	Belgrade	2	5
1954	22 Nov	Cardiff	1	3
EC1976	24 Apr	Zagreb	0	2
EC1976	22 May	Cardiff	1	1
EC1982	15 Dec	Titograd	4	4
EC1983	14 Dec	Cardiff	1	1
1988	23 Mar	Swansea	1	2

NORTHERN IRELAND

		v ALBANIA	*NI*	*A*
WC1965	7 May	Belfast	4	1
WC1965	24 Nov	Tirana	1	1
EC1982	15 Dec	Tirana	0	0
EC1983	27 Apr	Belfast	1	0
WC1992	9 Sept	Belfast	3	0
WC1993	17 Feb	Tirana	2	1
WC1996	14 Dec	Belfast	2	0
WC1997	10 Sept	Zurich	0	1

		v ALGERIA	*NI*	*A*
WC1986	3 June	Guadalajara	1	1

		v ARGENTINA	*NI*	*A*
WC1958	11 June	Halmstad	1	3

		v ARMENIA	*NI*	*A*
WC1996	5 Oct	Belfast	1	1
WC1997	30 Apr	Erevan	0	0
EC2003	29 Mar	Erevan	0	1
EC2003	10 Sept	Belfast	0	1

		v AUSTRALIA	*NI*	*A*
1980	11 June	Sydney	2	1
1980	15 June	Melbourne	1	1
1980	18 June	Adelaide	2	1

		v AUSTRIA	*NI*	*A*
WC1982	1 July	Madrid	2	2
EC1982	13 Oct	Vienna	0	2
EC1983	21 Sept	Belfast	3	1
EC1990	14 Nov	Vienna	0	0
EC1991	16 Oct	Belfast	2	1
EC1994	12 Oct	Vienna	2	1
EC1995	15 Nov	Belfast	5	3
EC2004	13 Oct	Belfast	3	3

		v AZERBAIJAN	*NI*	*A*
EC2004	9 Oct	Baku	0	0

		v BARBADOS	*NI*	*B*
2004	30 May	Waterford	1	1

		v BELGIUM	*NI*	*B*
WC1976	10 Nov	Liège	0	2
WC1977	16 Nov	Belfast	3	0
1997	11 Feb	Belfast	3	0

		v BRAZIL	*NI*	*B*
WC1986	12 June	Guadalajara	0	3

		v BULGARIA	*NI*	*B*
WC1972	18 Oct	Sofia	0	3
WC1973	26 Sept	Sheffield	0	0
EC1978	29 Nov	Sofia	2	0
EC1979	2 May	Belfast	2	0
WC2001	28 Mar	Sofia	3	4
WC2001	2 June	Belfast	0	1

		v CANADA	*NI*	*C*
1995	22 May	Edmonton	0	2
1999	27 Apr	Belfast	1	1
2005	9 Feb	Belfast	0	1

		v CHILE	*NI*	*C*
1989	26 May	Belfast	0	1
1995	25 May	Edmonton	1	2

		v COLOMBIA	*NI*	*C*
1994	4 June	Boston	0	2

		v CYPRUS	*NI*	*C*
EC1971	3 Feb	Nicosia	3	0
EC1971	21 Apr	Belfast	5	0
WC1973	14 Feb	Nicosia	0	1
WC1973	8 May	London	3	0
2002	21 Aug	Belfast	0	0

		v CZECHOSLOVAKIA	*NI*	*C*
WC1958	8 June	Halmstad	1	0
WC1958	17 June	Malmo	2	1*

**After extra time*

		v CZECH REPUBLIC	*NI*	*C*
WC2001	24 Mar	Belfast	0	1
WC2001	6 June	Teplice	1	3

		v DENMARK	*NI*	*D*
EC1978	25 Oct	Belfast	2	1
EC1979	6 June	Copenhagen	0	4
1986	26 Mar	Belfast	1	1
EC1990	17 Oct	Belfast	1	1
EC1991	13 Nov	Odense	1	2
WC1992	18 Nov	Belfast	0	1
WC1993	13 Oct	Copenhagen	0	1
WC2000	7 Oct	Belfast	1	1
WC2001	1 Sept	Copenhagen	1	1

		v ESTONIA	*NI*	*E*
2004	31 Mar	Tallinn	1	0

		v FAEROES	*NI*	*F*
EC1991	1 May	Belfast	1	1
EC1991	11 Sept	Landskrona	5	0

		v FINLAND	*NI*	*F*
WC1984	27 May	Pori	0	1
WC1984	14 Nov	Belfast	2	1
EC1998	10 Oct	Belfast	1	0
EC1998	9 Oct	Helsinki	1	4
2003	12 Feb	Belfast	0	1

		v FRANCE	*NI*	*F*
1928	21 Feb	Paris	0	4
1951	12 May	Belfast	2	2
1952	11 Nov	Paris	1	3
WC1958	19 June	Norrkoping	0	4
1982	24 Mar	Paris	0	4
WC1982	4 July	Madrid	1	4
1986	26 Feb	Paris	0	0
1988	27 Apr	Belfast	0	0
1999	18 Aug	Belfast	0	1

		v GERMANY	*NI*	*G*
1992	2 June	Bremen	1	1
1996	29 May	Belfast	1	1
WC1996	9 Nov	Nuremberg	1	1
WC1997	20 Aug	Belfast	1	3
EC1999	27 Mar	Belfast	0	3
EC1999	8 Sept	Dortmund	0	4
2005	4 June	Belfast	1	4

		v WEST GERMANY	*NI*	*WG*
WC1958	15 June	Malmo	2	2
WC1960	26 Oct	Belfast	3	4
WC1961	10 May	Hamburg	1	2
1966	7 May	Belfast	0	2
1977	27 Apr	Cologne	0	5
EC1982	17 Nov	Belfast	1	0
EC1983	16 Nov	Hamburg	1	0

		v GREECE	*NI*	*G*
WC1961	3 May	Athens	1	2
WC1961	17 Oct	Belfast	2	0
1988	17 Feb	Athens	2	3
EC2003	2 Apr	Belfast	0	2
EC2003	11 Oct	Athens	0	1

		v HOLLAND	*NI*	*H*
1962	9 May	Rotterdam	0	4
WC1965	17 Mar	Belfast	2	1
WC1965	7 Apr	Rotterdam	0	0
WC1976	13 Oct	Rotterdam	2	2
WC1977	12 Oct	Belfast	0	1

		v HONDURAS	*NI*	*H*
WC1982	21 June	Zaragoza	1	1

		v HUNGARY	*NI*	*H*
WC1988	19 Oct	Budapest	0	1
WC1989	6 Sept	Belfast	1	2
2000	26 Apr	Belfast	0	1

v ICELAND			NI	I
wc1977	11 June	Reykjavik	0	1
wc1977	21 Sept	Belfast	2	0
wc2000	11 Oct	Reykjavik	0	1
wc2001	5 Sept	Belfast	3	0

v REPUBLIC OF IRELAND			NI	RI
EC1978	20 Sept	Dublin	0	0
EC1979	21 Nov	Belfast	1	0
wc1988	14 Sept	Belfast	0	0
wc1989	11 Oct	Dublin	0	3
wc1993	31 Mar	Dublin	0	3
wc1993	17 Nov	Belfast	1	1
EC1994	16 Nov	Belfast	0	4
EC1995	29 Mar	Dublin	1	1
1999	29 May	Dublin	1	0

v ISRAEL			NI	I
1968	10 Sept	Jaffa	3	2
1976	3 Mar	Tel Aviv	1	1
wc1980	26 Mar	Tel Aviv	0	0
wc1981	18 Nov	Belfast	1	0
1984	16 Oct	Belfast	3	0
1987	18 Feb	Tel Aviv	1	1

v ITALY			NI	I
wc1957	25 Apr	Rome	0	1
1957	4 Dec	Belfast	2	2
wc1958	15 Jan	Belfast	2	1
1961	25 Apr	Bologna	2	3
1997	22 Jan	Palermo	0	2
2003	3 June	Campobasso	0	2

v LATVIA			NI	L
wc1993	2 June	Riga	2	1
wc1993	8 Sept	Belfast	2	0
EC1995	26 Apr	Riga	1	0
EC1995	7 June	Belfast	1	2

v LIECHTENSTEIN			NI	L
EC1994	20 Apr	Belfast	4	1
EC1995	11 Oct	Eschen	4	0
2002	27 Mar	Vaduz	0	0

v LITHUANIA			NI	L
wc1992	28 Apr	Belfast	2	2
wc1993	25 May	Vilnius	1	0

v LUXEMBOURG			NI	L
2000	23 Feb	Luxembourg	3	1

v MALTA			NI	M
wc1988	21 May	Belfast	3	0
wc1989	26 Apr	Valletta	2	0
2000	28 Mar	Valletta	3	0
wc2000	2 Sept	Belfast	1	0
wc2001	6 Oct	Valletta	1	0

v MEXICO			NI	M
1966	22 June	Belfast	4	1
1994	11 June	Miami	0	3

v MOLDOVA			NI	M
EC1998	18 Nov	Belfast	2	2
EC1999	31 Mar	Chisinau	0	0

v MOROCCO			NI	M
1986	23 Apr	Belfast	2	1

v NORWAY			NI	N
1922	25 May	Bergen	1	2
EC1974	4 Sept	Oslo	1	2
EC1975	29 Oct	Belfast	3	0
1990	27 Mar	Belfast	2	3
1996	27 Mar	Belfast	0	2
2001	28 Feb	Belfast	0	4
2004	18 Feb	Belfast	1	4

v POLAND			NI	P
EC1962	10 Oct	Katowice	2	0
EC1962	28 Nov	Belfast	2	0
1988	23 Mar	Belfast	1	1
1991	5 Feb	Belfast	3	1
2002	13 Feb	Limassol	1	4
EC2004	4 Sept	Belfast	0	3
EC2005	30 Mar	Warsaw	0	1

v PORTUGAL			NI	P
wc1957	16 Jan	Lisbon	1	1
wc1957	1 May	Belfast	3	0
wc1973	28 Mar	Coventry	1	1
wc1973	14 Nov	Lisbon	1	1
wc1980	19 Nov	Lisbon	0	1
wc1981	29 Apr	Belfast	1	0
EC1994	7 Sept	Belfast	1	2
EC1995	3 Sept	Lisbon	1	1
wc1997	29 Mar	Belfast	0	0
wc1997	11 Oct	Lisbon	0	1

v ROMANIA			NI	R
wc1984	12 Sept	Belfast	3	2
wc1985	16 Oct	Bucharest	1	0
1994	23 Mar	Belfast	2	0

v ST KITTS & NEVIS			NI	SK
2004	2 June	Basseterre	2	0

v SERBIA-MONTENEGRO			NI	SM
2004	28 Apr	Belfast	1	1

v SLOVAKIA			NI	S
1998	25 Mar	Belfast	1	0

v SOUTH AFRICA			NI	SA
1924	24 Sept	Belfast	1	2

v SPAIN			NI	S
1958	15 Oct	Madrid	2	6
1963	30 May	Bilbao	1	1
1963	30 Oct	Belfast	0	1
EC1970	11 Nov	Seville	0	3
EC1972	16 Feb	Hull	1	1
wc1982	25 June	Valencia	1	0
1985	27 Mar	Palma	0	0
wc1986	7 June	Guadalajara	1	2
wc1988	21 Dec	Seville	0	4
wc1989	8 Feb	Belfast	0	2
wc1992	14 Oct	Belfast	0	0
wc1993	28 Apr	Seville	1	3
1998	2 June	Santander	1	4
2002	17 Apr	Belfast	0	5
EC2002	12 Oct	Albacete	0	3
EC2003	11 June	Belfast	0	0

v SWEDEN			NI	S
EC1974	30 Oct	Solna	2	0
EC1975	3 Sept	Belfast	1	2
wc1980	15 Oct	Belfast	3	0
wc1981	3 June	Solna	0	1
1996	24 Apr	Belfast	1	2

v SWITZERLAND			NI	S
wc1964	14 Oct	Belfast	1	0
wc1964	14 Nov	Lausanne	1	2
1998	22 Apr	Belfast	1	0
2004	18 Aug	Zurich	0	0

v THAILAND			NI	T
1997	21 May	Bangkok	0	0

v TRINIDAD & TOBAGO			NI	TT
2004	6 June	Bacolet	3	0

v TURKEY			NI	T
wc1968	23 Oct	Belfast	4	1
wc1968	11 Dec	Istanbul	3	0
EC1983	30 Mar	Belfast	2	1
EC1983	12 Oct	Ankara	0	1
wc1985	1 May	Belfast	2	0
wc1985	11 Sept	Izmir	0	0
EC1986	12 Nov	Izmir	0	0
EC1987	11 Nov	Belfast	1	0
EC1998	5 Sept	Istanbul	0	3
EC1999	4 Sept	Belfast	0	3

		v UKRAINE	NI	U
WC1996	31 Aug	Belfast	0	1
WC1997	2 Apr	Kiev	1	2
EC2002	16 Oct	Belfast	0	0
EC2003	6 Sept	Donetsk	0	0

		v URUGUAY	NI	U
1964	29 Apr	Belfast	3	0
1990	18 May	Belfast	1	0

		v USSR	NI	USSR
WC1969	19 Sept	Belfast	0	0
WC1969	22 Oct	Moscow	0	2
EC1971	22 Sept	Moscow	0	1
EC1971	13 Oct	Belfast	1	1

		v YUGOSLAVIA	NI	Y
EC1975	16 Mar	Belfast	1	0
EC1975	19 Nov	Belgrade	0	1
WC1982	17 June	Zaragoza	0	0
EC1987	29 Apr	Belfast	1	2
EC1987	14 Oct	Sarajevo	0	3
EC1990	12 Sept	Belfast	0	2
EC1991	27 Mar	Belgrade	1	4
2000	16 Aug	Belfast	1	2

REPUBLIC OF IRELAND

		v ALBANIA	RI	A
WC1992	26 May	Dublin	2	0
WC1993	26 May	Tirana	2	1
EC2003	2 Apr	Tirana	0	0
EC2003	7 June	Dublin	2	1

		v ALGERIA	RI	A
1982	28 Apr	Algiers	0	2

		v ANDORRA	RI	A
WC2001	28 Mar	Barcelona	3	0
WC2001	25 Apr	Dublin	3	1

		v ARGENTINA	RI	A
1951	13 May	Dublin	0	1
†1979	29 May	Dublin	0	0
1980	16 May	Dublin	0	1
1998	22 Apr	Dublin	0	2

†*Not considered a full international.*

		v AUSTRALIA	RI	A
2003	19 Aug	Dublin	2	1

		v AUSTRIA	RI	A
1952	7 May	Vienna	0	6
1953	25 Mar	Dublin	4	0
1958	14 Mar	Vienna	1	3
1962	8 Apr	Dublin	2	3
EC1963	25 Sept	Vienna	0	0
EC1963	13 Oct	Dublin	3	2
1966	22 May	Vienna	0	1
1968	10 Nov	Dublin	2	2
EC1971	30 May	Dublin	1	4
EC1971	10 Oct	Linz	0	6
EC1995	11 June	Dublin	1	3
EC1995	6 Sept	Vienna	1	3

		v BELGIUM	RI	B
1928	12 Feb	Liège	4	2
1929	30 Apr	Dublin	4	0
1930	11 May	Brussels	3	1
WC1934	25 Feb	Dublin	4	4
1949	24 Apr	Dublin	0	2
1950	10 May	Brussels	1	5
1965	24 Mar	Dublin	0	2
1966	25 May	Liège	3	2
WC1980	15 Oct	Dublin	1	1
WC1981	25 Mar	Brussels	0	1
EC1986	10 Sept	Brussels	2	2
EC1987	29 Apr	Dublin	0	0
WC1997	29 Oct	Dublin	1	1
WC1997	16 Nov	Brussels	1	2

		v BOLIVIA	RI	B
1994	24 May	Dublin	1	0
1996	15 June	New Jersey	3	0

		v BRAZIL	RI	B
1974	5 May	Rio de Janeiro	1	2
1982	27 May	Uberlandia	0	7
1987	23 May	Dublin	1	0
2004	18 Feb	Dublin	0	0

		v BULGARIA	RI	B
WC1977	1 June	Sofia	1	2
WC1977	12 Oct	Dublin	0	0
EC1979	19 May	Sofia	0	1
EC1979	17 Oct	Dublin	3	0
WC1987	1 Apr	Sofia	1	2
WC1987	14 Oct	Dublin	2	0
2004	18 Aug	Dublin	1	1

		v CAMEROON	RI	C
WC2002	1 June	Niigata	1	1

		v CANADA	RI	C
2003	18 Nov	Dublin	3	0

		v CHILE	RI	C
1960	30 Mar	Dublin	2	0
1972	21 June	Recife	1	2
1974	12 May	Santiago	2	1
1982	22 May	Santiago	0	1
1991	22 May	Dublin	1	1

		v CHINA	RI	C
1984	3 June	Sapporo	1	0
2005	29 Mar	Dublin	1	0

		v CROATIA	RI	C
1996	2 June	Dublin	2	2
EC1998	5 Sept	Dublin	2	0
EC1999	4 Sept	Zagreb	0	1
2001	15 Aug	Dublin	2	2
2004	16 Nov	Dublin	1	0

		v CYPRUS	RI	C
WC1980	26 Mar	Nicosia	3	2
WC1980	19 Nov	Dublin	6	0
WC2001	24 Mar	Nicosia	4	0
WC2001	6 Oct	Dublin	4	0
EC2004	4 Sept	Dublin	3	0

		v CZECHOSLOVAKIA	RI	C
1938	18 May	Prague	2	2
EC1959	5 Apr	Dublin	2	0
EC1959	10 May	Bratislava	0	4
WC1961	8 Oct	Dublin	1	3
WC1961	29 Oct	Prague	1	7
EC1967	21 May	Dublin	0	2
EC1967	22 Nov	Prague	2	1
WC1969	4 May	Dublin	1	2
WC1969	7 Oct	Prague	0	3
1979	26 Sept	Prague	1	4
1981	29 Apr	Dublin	3	1
1986	27 May	Reykjavik	1	0

		v CZECH REPUBLIC	RI	C
1994	5 June	Dublin	1	3
1996	24 Apr	Prague	0	2
1998	25 Mar	Olomouc	1	2
2000	23 Feb	Dublin	3	2
2004	31 Mar	Dublin	2	1

		v DENMARK	RI	D
WC1956	3 Oct	Dublin	2	1
WC1957	2 Oct	Copenhagen	2	0
WC1968	4 Dec	Dublin	1	1
		(*abandoned after 51 mins*)		
WC1969	27 May	Copenhagen	0	2
WC1969	15 Oct	Dublin	1	1
EC1978	24 May	Copenhagen	3	3

			RI	D
EC1979	2 May	Dublin	2	0
WC1984	14 Nov	Copenhagen	0	3
WC1985	13 Nov	Dublin	1	4
WC1992	14 Oct	Copenhagen	0	0
WC1993	28 Apr	Dublin	1	1
2002	27 Mar	Dublin	3	0

		v ECUADOR	RI	E
1972	19 June	Natal	3	2

		v EGYPT	RI	E
WC1990	17 June	Palermo	0	0

		v ENGLAND	RI	E
1946	30 Sept	Dublin	0	1
1949	21 Sept	Everton	2	0
WC1957	8 May	Wembley	1	5
WC1957	19 May	Dublin	1	1
1964	24 May	Dublin	1	3
1976	8 Sept	Wembley	1	1
EC1978	25 Oct	Dublin	1	1
EC1980	6 Feb	Wembley	0	2
1985	26 Mar	Wembley	1	2
EC1988	12 June	Stuttgart	1	0
WC1990	11 June	Cagliari	1	1
EC1990	14 Nov	Dublin	1	1
EC1991	27 Mar	Wembley	1	1
1995	15 Feb	Dublin	1	0

(abandoned after 27 mins)

		v ESTONIA	RI	E
WC2000	11 Oct	Dublin	2	0
WC2001	6 June	Tallinn	2	0

		v FAEROES	RI	F
EC2004	13 Oct	Dublin	2	0
EC2005	8 June	Toftir	2	0

		v FINLAND	RI	F
WC1949	8 Sept	Dublin	3	0
WC1949	9 Oct	Helsinki	1	1
1990	16 May	Dublin	1	1
2000	15 Nov	Dublin	3	0
2002	21 Aug	Helsinki	3	0

		v FRANCE	RI	F
1937	23 May	Paris	2	0
1952	16 Nov	Dublin	1	1
WC1953	4 Oct	Dublin	3	5
WC1953	25 Nov	Paris	0	1
WC1972	15 Nov	Dublin	2	1
WC1973	19 May	Paris	1	1
WC1976	17 Nov	Paris	0	2
WC1977	30 Mar	Dublin	1	0
WC1980	28 Oct	Paris	0	2
WC1981	14 Oct	Dublin	3	2
1989	7 Feb	Dublin	0	0
EC2004	9 Oct	Paris	0	0

		v GEORGIA	RI	G
EC2003	29 Mar	Tbilisi	2	1
EC2003	11 June	Dublin	2	0

		v GERMANY	RI	G
1935	8 May	Dortmund	1	3
1936	17 Oct	Dublin	5	2
1939	23 May	Bremen	1	1
1994	29 May	Hanover	2	0
WC2002	5 June	Ibaraki	1	1

		v WEST GERMANY	RI	WG
1951	17 Oct	Dublin	3	2
1952	4 May	Cologne	0	3
1955	28 May	Hamburg	1	2
1956	25 Nov	Dublin	3	0
1960	11 May	Dusseldorf	1	0
1966	4 May	Dublin	0	4
1970	9 May	Berlin	1	2
1975	1 Mar	Dublin	1	0†
1979	22 May	Dublin	1	3
1981	21 May	Bremen	0	3†
1989	6 Sept	Dublin	1	1

†v West Germany 'B'

		v GREECE	RI	G
2000	26 Apr	Dublin	0	1
2002	20 Nov	Athens	0	0

		v HOLLAND	RI	N
1932	8 May	Amsterdam	2	0
1934	8 Apr	Amsterdam	2	5
1935	8 Dec	Dublin	3	5
1955	1 May	Dublin	1	0
1956	10 May	Rotterdam	4	1
WC1980	10 Sept	Dublin	2	1
WC1981	9 Sept	Rotterdam	2	2
EC1982	22 Sept	Rotterdam	1	2
EC1983	12 Oct	Dublin	2	3
EC1988	18 June	Gelsenkirchen	0	1
WC1990	21 June	Palermo	1	1
1994	20 Apr	Tilburg	1	0
WC1994	4 July	Orlando	0	2
EC1995	13 Dec	Liverpool	0	2
1996	4 June	Rotterdam	1	3
WC2000	2 Sept	Amsterdam	2	2
WC2001	1 Sept	Dublin	1	0
2004	5 June	Amsterdam	1	0

		v HUNGARY	RI	H
1934	15 Dec	Dublin	2	4
1936	3 May	Budapest	3	3
1936	6 Dec	Dublin	2	3
1939	19 Mar	Cork	2	2
1939	18 May	Budapest	2	2
WC1969	8 June	Dublin	1	2
WC1969	5 Nov	Budapest	0	4
WC1989	8 Mar	Budapest	0	0
WC1989	4 June	Dublin	2	0
1991	11 Sept	Gyor	2	1

		v ICELAND	RI	I
EC1962	12 Aug	Dublin	4	2
EC1962	2 Sept	Reykjavik	1	1
EC1982	13 Oct	Dublin	2	0
EC1983	21 Sept	Reykjavik	3	0
1986	25 May	Reykjavik	2	1
WC1996	10 Nov	Dublin	0	0
WC1997	6 Sept	Reykjavik	4	2

		v IRAN	RI	I
1972	18 June	Recife	2	1
WC2001	10 Nov	Dublin	2	0
WC2001	15 Nov	Tehran	0	1

		v N. IRELAND	RI	NI
EC1978	20 Sept	Dublin	0	0
EC1979	21 Nov	Belfast	0	1
WC1988	14 Sept	Belfast	0	0
WC1989	11 Oct	Dublin	3	0
WC1993	31 Mar	Dublin	3	0
WC1993	17 Nov	Belfast	1	1
EC1994	16 Nov	Belfast	4	0
EC1995	29 Mar	Dublin	1	1
1999	29 May	Dublin	0	1

		v ISRAEL	RI	I
1984	4 Apr	Tel Aviv	0	3
1985	27 May	Tel Aviv	0	0
1987	10 Nov	Dublin	5	0
EC2005	26 Mar	Tel Aviv	1	1
EC2005	4 June	Dublin	2	2

		v ITALY	RI	I
1926	21 Mar	Turin	0	3
1927	23 Apr	Dublin	1	2
EC1970	8 Dec	Rome	0	3
EC1971	10 May	Dublin	1	2
1985	5 Feb	Dublin	1	2
WC1990	30 June	Rome	0	1
1992	4 June	Foxboro	0	2
WC1994	18 June	New York	1	0

		v JAMAICA	RI	J
2004	2 June	Charlton	1	0

		v LATVIA	RI	L
WC1992	9 Sept	Dublin	4	0
WC1993	2 June	Riga	2	1
EC1994	7 Sept	Riga	3	0
EC1995	11 Oct	Dublin	2	1

		v LIECHTENSTEIN	RI	L
EC1994	12 Oct	Dublin	4	0
EC1995	3 June	Eschen	0	0
WC1996	31 Aug	Eschen	5	0
WC1997	21 May	Dublin	5	0

		v LITHUANIA	RI	L
WC1993	16 June	Vilnius	1	0
WC1993	8 Sept	Dublin	2	0
WC1997	20 Aug	Dublin	0	0
WC1997	10 Sept	Vilnius	2	1

		v LUXEMBOURG	RI	I
1936	9 May	Luxembourg	5	1
WC1953	28 Oct	Dublin	4	0
WC1954	7 Mar	Luxembourg	1	0
EC1987	28 May	Luxembourg	2	0
EC1987	9 Sept	Dublin	2	1

		v MACEDONIA	RI	M
WC1996	9 Oct	Dublin	3	0
WC1997	2 Apr	Skopje	2	3
EC1999	9 June	Dublin	1	0
EC1999	9 Oct	Skopje	1	1

		v MALTA	RI	M
EC1983	30 Mar	Valletta	1	0
EC1983	16 Nov	Dublin	8	0
WC1989	28 May	Dublin	2	0
WC1989	15 Nov	Valletta	2	0
1990	2 June	Valletta	3	0
EC1998	14 Oct	Dublin	5	0
EC1999	8 Sept	Valletta	3	2

		v MEXICO	RI	M
1984	8 Aug	Dublin	0	0
WC1994	24 June	Orlando	1	2
1996	13 June	New Jersey	2	2
1998	23 May	Dublin	0	0
2000	4 June	Chicago	2	2

		v MOROCCO	RI	M
1990	12 Sept	Dublin	1	0

		v NIGERIA	RI	N
2002	16 May	Dublin	1	2
2004	29 May	Charlton	0	3

		v NORWAY	RI	N
WC1937	10 Oct	Oslo	2	3
WC1937	7 Nov	Dublin	3	3
1950	26 Nov	Dublin	2	2
1951	30 May	Oslo	3	2
1954	8 Nov	Dublin	2	1
1955	25 May	Oslo	3	1
1960	6 Nov	Dublin	3	1
1964	13 May	Oslo	4	1
1973	6 June	Oslo	1	1
1976	24 Mar	Dublin	3	0
1978	21 May	Oslo	0	0
WC1984	17 Oct	Oslo	0	1
WC1985	1 May	Dublin	0	0
1988	1 June	Oslo	0	0
WC1994	28 June	New York	0	0
2003	30 Apr	Dublin	1	0

		v PARAGUAY	RI	P
1999	10 Feb	Dublin	2	0

		v POLAND	RI	P
1938	22 May	Warsaw	0	6
1938	13 Nov	Dublin	3	2
1958	11 May	Katowice	2	2
1958	5 Oct	Dublin	2	2
1964	10 May	Kracow	1	3
1964	25 Oct	Dublin	3	2
1968	15 May	Dublin	2	2
1968	30 Oct	Katowice	0	1
1970	6 May	Dublin	1	2
1970	23 Sept	Dublin	0	2
1973	16 May	Wroclaw	0	2
1973	21 Oct	Dublin	1	0
1976	26 May	Poznan	2	0
1977	24 Apr	Dublin	0	0
1978	12 Apr	Lodz	0	3
1981	23 May	Bydgoszcz	0	3
1984	23 May	Dublin	0	0
1986	12 Nov	Warsaw	0	1
1988	22 May	Dublin	3	1
EC1991	1 May	Dublin	0	0
EC1991	16 Oct	Poznan	3	3
2004	28 Apr	Bydgoszcz	0	0

		v PORTUGAL	RI	P
1946	16 June	Lisbon	1	3
1947	4 May	Dublin	0	2
1948	23 May	Lisbon	0	2
1949	22 May	Dublin	1	0
1972	25 June	Recife	1	2
1992	7 June	Boston	2	0
EC1995	26 Apr	Dublin	1	0
EC1995	15 Nov	Lisbon	0	3
1996	29 May	Dublin	0	1
WC2000	7 Oct	Lisbon	1	1
WC2001	2 June	Dublin	1	1
2005	9 Feb	Dublin	1	0

		v ROMANIA	RI	R
1988	23 Mar	Dublin	2	0
WC1990	25 June	Genoa	0	0*
WC1997	30 Apr	Bucharest	0	1
WC1997	11 Oct	Dublin	1	1
2004	27 May	Dublin	1	0

		v RUSSIA	RI	R
1994	23 Mar	Dublin	0	0
1996	27 Mar	Dublin	0	2
2002	13 Feb	Dublin	2	0
EC2002	7 Sept	Moscow	2	4
EC2003	6 Sept	Dublin	1	1

		v SAUDI ARABIA	RI	SA
WC2002	11 June	Yokohama	3	0

		v SCOTLAND	RI	S
WC1961	3 May	Glasgow	1	4
WC1961	7 May	Dublin	0	3
1963	9 June	Dublin	1	0
1969	21 Sept	Dublin	1	1
EC1986	15 Oct	Dublin	0	0
EC1987	18 Feb	Glasgow	1	0
2000	30 May	Dublin	1	2
2003	12 Feb	Glasgow	2	0

		v SOUTH AFRICA	RI	SA
2000	11 June	New Jersey	2	1

		v SPAIN	RI	S
1931	26 Apr	Barcelona	1	1
1931	13 Dec	Dublin	0	5
1946	23 June	Madrid	1	0
1947	2 Mar	Dublin	3	2
1948	30 May	Barcelona	1	2
1949	12 June	Dublin	1	4
1952	1 June	Madrid	0	6
1955	27 Nov	Dublin	2	2
EC1964	11 Mar	Seville	1	5
EC1964	8 Apr	Dublin	0	2
WC1965	5 May	Dublin	1	0
WC1965	27 Oct	Seville	1	4
WC1965	10 Nov	Paris	0	1
EC1966	23 Oct	Dublin	0	0
EC1966	7 Dec	Valencia	0	2

			RI	S
1977	9 Feb	Dublin	0	1
EC1982	17 Nov	Dublin	3	3
EC1983	27 Apr	Zaragoza	0	2
1985	26 May	Cork	0	0
WC1988	16 Nov	Seville	0	2
WC1989	26 Apr	Dublin	1	0
WC1992	18 Nov	Seville	0	0
WC1993	13 Oct	Dublin	1	3
WC2002	16 June	Suwon	1	1

v SWEDEN

			RI	S
WC1949	2 June	Stockholm	1	3
WC1949	13 Nov	Dublin	1	3
1959	1 Nov	Dublin	3	2
1960	18 May	Malmo	1	4
EC1970	14 Oct	Dublin	1	1
EC1970	28 Oct	Malmo	0	1
1999	28 Apr	Dublin	2	0

v SWITZERLAND

			RI	S
1935	5 May	Basle	0	1
1936	17 Mar	Dublin	1	0
1937	17 May	Berne	1	0
1938	18 Sept	Dublin	4	0
1948	5 Dec	Dublin	0	1
EC1975	11 May	Dublin	2	1
EC1975	21 May	Berne	0	1
1980	30 Apr	Dublin	2	0
WC1985	2 June	Dublin	3	0
WC1985	11 Sept	Berne	0	0
1992	25 Mar	Dublin	2	1
EC2002	16 Oct	Dublin	1	2
EC2003	11 Oct	Basle	0	2
EC2004	8 Sept	Basle	1	1

v TRINIDAD & TOBAGO

			RI	TT
1982	30 May	Port of Spain	1	2

v TUNISIA

			RI	T
1988	19 Oct	Dublin	4	0

v TURKEY

			RI	T
EC1966	16 Nov	Dublin	2	1
EC1967	22 Feb	Ankara	1	2
EC1974	20 Nov	Izmir	1	1
EC1975	29 Oct	Dublin	4	0
1976	13 Oct	Ankara	3	3
1978	5 Apr	Dublin	4	2
1990	26 May	Izmir	0	0
EC1990	17 Oct	Dublin	5	0
EC1991	13 Nov	Istanbul	3	1
EC2000	13 Nov	Dublin	1	1
EC2000	17 Nov	Bursa	0	0
2003	9 Sept	Dublin	2	2

v URUGUAY

			RI	U
1974	8 May	Montevideo	0	2
1986	23 Apr	Dublin	1	1

v USA

			RI	USA
1979	29 Oct	Dublin	3	2
1991	1 June	Boston	1	1
1992	29 Apr	Dublin	4	1
1992	30 May	Washington	1	3
1996	9 June	Boston	1	2
2000	6 June	Boston	1	1
2002	17 Apr	Dublin	2	1

v USSR

			RI	USSR
WC1972	18 Oct	Dublin	1	2
WC1973	13 May	Moscow	0	1
EC1974	30 Oct	Dublin	3	0
EC1975	18 May	Kiev	1	2
WC1984	12 Sept	Dublin	1	0
WC1985	16 Oct	Moscow	0	2
EC1988	15 June	Hanover	1	1
1990	25 Apr	Dublin	1	0

v WALES

			RI	W
1960	28 Sept	Dublin	2	3
1979	11 Sept	Swansea	1	2
1981	24 Feb	Dublin	1	3
1986	26 Mar	Dublin	0	1
1990	28 Mar	Dublin	1	0
1991	6 Feb	Wrexham	3	0
1992	19 Feb	Dublin	0	1
1993	17 Feb	Dublin	2	1
1997	11 Feb	Cardiff	0	0

v YUGOSLAVIA

			RI	Y
1955	19 Sept	Dublin	1	4
1988	27 Apr	Dublin	2	0
EC1998	18 Nov	Belgrade	0	1
EC1999	1 Sept	Dublin	2	1

OTHER BRITISH AND IRISH INTERNATIONAL MATCHES 2004–05

FRIENDLIES

St James' Park, 18 August 2004, 35,387

England (1) 3 *(Beckham 27, Owen 50, Wright-Phillips 72)*

Ukraine (0) 0

England: James; Neville G (Johnson G 46), Cole A (Carragher 60), Gerrard (Dyer 46), Terry, King, Beckham, Butt (Wright-Phillips 52), Smith (Defoe 46), Owen, Lampard (Jenas 75).
Ukraine: Shovkovskyi; Rusol, Fedorov, Yezersky, Vorobei, Tymoschuk, Shelayev, Nesmachni (Radchenko 61), Gusev (Korniytsev 61), Rotan (Zakaryluka 64), Shevchenko (Voronin 52).
Referee: M. McCurry (Scotland).

Madrid, 17 November 2004, 48,000

Spain (1) 1 *(Del Horno 10)*

England (0) 0

Spain: Casillas; Michel Salgado, Del Horno, Xavi, Juanito, Marchena (Pablo 46), Joaquin (Romero 80), Xabi Alonso (Orbaiz 69, Fernando Torres (Luque 46), Raul (Guti 46), Reyes (Angulo 53).
England: Robinson; Neville G, Cole A (Defoe 76), Butt, Terry (Upson 65), Ferdinand (Carragher 62), Beckham (Wright-Phillips 60), Lampard (Jenas 60), Rooney (Smith 42), Owen, Bridge.
Referee: G. Kasnaferis (Greece).

Villa Park, 9 February 2005, 40,705

England (0) 0

Holland (0) 0

England: Robinson; Neville G, Cole A, Gerrard (Jenas 80), Carragher, Brown, Beckham (Dyer 80), Lampard (Hargreaves 46), Rooney (Johnson A 61), Owen, Wright-Phillips (Downing 61).
Holland: Van der Sar; Kromkamp, Van Bronckhorst, Landzaat, Boulahrouz, Mathijsen, Heitinga (Van Bommel 61), Van der Vaart, Makaay, Kuijt, Castelen (Yildirim 62).
Referee: P. Frojdfeldt (Sweden).

Chicago, 28 May 2005, 45,000

USA (0) 1 *(Dempsey 79)*

England (2) 2 *(Richardson 4, 44)*

USA: Keller; Cherundolo, Vanney, Zavagnin, Pope (Bocanegra 73), Gibbs, Ralston (Convey 73), Donovan, McBride (Casey 81), Wolff, Dempsey (Simms 90).
England: James; Johnson G, Cole A (Defoe 63), Jenas, Campbell (Knight 46), Brown, Cole J, Carrick, Smith, Johnson A (Young 76), Richardson (Neville P 59).
Referee: B. Archundia (Mexico).

New Jersey, 31 May 2005, 58,000

Colombia (1) 2 *(Yepes 45, Ramirez 78)*

England (2) 3 *(Owen 36, 42, 58)*

Colombia: Mondragon; Palacio (Ramirez 72), Benitez, Viafara (Anchico 60), Perea, Yepes (Mendoza 81), Hurtado (Vargas 46), Restrepo (Diaz 72), Angel (Perea E 60), Rey, Soto.
England: James (Green 46); Neville P, Cole A (Young 85), Jenas, Johnson G, Knight, Beckham (Richardson 72), Carrick, Crouch (Smith 72), Owen (Defoe 72), Cole J.
Referee: B. Hall (USA).

Hampden Park, 18 August 2004, 15,933

Scotland (0) 0

Hungary (1) 3 *(Huszti 45 (pen), 53, Marshall 73 (og))*

Scotland: Marshall; Holt, Naysmith, Caldwell G (Thompson 46), Pressley, Webster, Fletcher (Pearson 74), Ferguson B (Severin 70), Miller (Crawford 57), McFadden, Quashie.
Hungary: Kiraly; Juhasz, Bodnar, Huszti (Bodor 87), Stark, Toth, Feher (Rosa 63), Gera (Leandro 76), Torghelle (Kovacs 25), Simek, Molnar.
Referee: L. Duhamel (France).

Valencia, 3 September 2004, 15,000

Spain (0) 1 *(Raul 57 (pen))*

Scotland (1) 1 *(Baraja 18 (og))*

Spain: Casillas; Lopez Rekarte, Del Horno, Baraja (Valeron 46), Puyol, Marchena (Helguera 57), Joaquin, Xabi Alonso, Fernando Torres (Raul 46), Tamudo (Vicente 46), Reyes.
Scotland: Gordon; Caldwell G, Naysmith, McNamara, Mackay, Webster, Quashie, Ferguson B, Crawford (Cameron 57), McFadden (Pearson 46), Fletcher (Miller 57).
Referee: S. Bre (France).
Match abandoned 60 minutes; floodlight failure.

Edinburgh, 17 November 2004, 15,071

Scotland (0) 1 *(McFadden 78 (pen))*

Sweden (1) 4 *(Allback 27, 49, Elmander 72, Berglund 73)*

Scotland: Marshall; McNaughton, Murray, Nicholson, Anderson, Webster (Hammell 53), McNamara (Severin 64), Quashie (Hughes 82), Miller (Crawford 71), Pearson.
Sweden: Hedman; Nilsson (Ostlund 62), Dorsin, Andersson, Mellberg, Lucic, Alexandersson N, Kallstrom, Allback, Berglund, Wilhelmsson (Touma 78).
Referee: J. Jara (Czech Republic).

Riga, 18 August 2004, 10,000

Latvia (0) 0

Wales (0) 2 *(Hartson 80, Bellamy 89)*

Latvia: Kolinko; Isakovs, Blagonadezhdin (Korablovs 74), Miholaps (Semyonov 61), Zemlinskis, Stepanovs, Laizans, Labanovs, Prohorenkovs (Rimkus 66), Verpakovskis, Rubins.
Wales: Jones (Crossley 46); Delaney, Thatcher, Savage (Johnson 46), Page, Melville (Collins J 24), Koumas (Robinson 89), Speed, Hartson (Taylor 84), Bellamy, Pembridge (Roberts G 69).
Referee: V. Ivanov (Russia).

Cardiff, 9 February 2005, 16,672

Wales (0) 2 *(Bellamy 63, 80)*

Hungary (0) 0

Wales: Coyne; Edwards (Weston 50), Ricketts, Fletcher, Page, Gabbidon, Partridge (Collins D 65), Davies, Earnshaw (Roberts G 75), Bellamy, Robinson (Roberts S 90).
Hungary: Kiraly; Juhasz, Hajnal (Leandro 58), Bodnar, Gyepes (Vincze 80), Dragoner, Huszti, Korsos G (Rosa 65), Gera, Torghelle, Lipcsei (Kovacs 68).
Referee: C. Richmond (Scotland).

Zurich, 18 August 2004, 4000

Switzerland (0) 0

Northern Ireland (0) 0

Switzerland: Zuberbuhler; Haas, Spycher, Vogel (Lonfat 77), Yakin M (Henchoz 46), Muller, Huggel (Magnin 46), Wicky, Yakin H, Vonlanthen (Muff 60), Cabanas (Frei 82).
Northern Ireland: Carroll; Hughes A, Capaldi, Johnson, Williams (Murdock 67), Craigan (Duff 78), Gillespie (McVeigh 51), Sonner, Healy (Hamilton 70), Smith, Elliott (Brunt 81).
Referee: N. Vollquartz (Denmark).

Windsor Park, 9 February 2005, 11,156

Northern Ireland (0) 0

Canada (1) 1 *(Occean 32)*

Northern Ireland: Taylor (Carroll 46); Baird, McCartney, Doherty (Mulryne 46), Hughes A, Murdock (Kirk 46), Gillespie (Jones S 75), Whitley, Healy, Davis, Capaldi (Craigan 79).
Canada: Sutton; Reda, Simpson, Serioux (Peters 86), McKenna (Klokowski 47), Gervais, Bernier, Imhof, De Rosario, Occean, Brennan (Hume 83).
Referee: J. Attard (Malta).

Windsor Park, 4 June 2005, 14,000

Northern Ireland (1) 1 *(Healy 15 (pen))*

Germany (1) 4 *(Asamoah 17, Ballack 62, 66 (pen), Podolski 81)*

Northern Ireland: Taylor (Ingham 77); Gillespie (McAuley 77), Craigan (Smith 77), Clyde, Baird, McCartney, Johnson, Davis, Healy (Brunt 77), Jones S (Feeney 67), Elliott (Kirk 67).
Germany: Lehmann; Owormeyela, Hitzlsperger, Ernst, Huth, Mertesacker, Schneider (Diesler 46), Ballack (Borowski 73), Asamoah (Schweinsteiger 46), Kuranyi (Podolski 46), Frings.
Referee: C. Richmond (Scotland).

Dublin, 18 August 2004, 31,887

Republic of Ireland (1) 1 *(Reid A 15)*

Bulgaria (0) 1 *(Bozhinov 70)*

Republic of Ireland: Given (Kenny 71); Finnan (Quinn 71), O'Shea, Roy Keane (Kavanagh 64), Cunningham, Doherty (Breen 46), Miller (Carr 52), Kilbane, Morrison (Macken 64), Duff, Reid A.
Bulgaria: Zdravkov; Kishishev, Stoyanov (Topuzakov 64), Yakov (Kamburov 77), Kirilov, Markov, Petrov S, Hristov (Yanev 46), Bozhinov, Berbatov (Gargorov 46), Lazarov (Manchev 56).
Referee: I. Brines (Scotland).

Dublin, 16 November 2004, 30,000

Republic of Ireland (1) 1 *(Robbie Keane 24)*

Croatia (0) 0

Republic of Ireland: Kenny (Given 80); Finnan, O'Shea, Kavanagh, Breen (Cunningham 62), Dunne, Miller, Kilbane (Quinn 80), Elliott (Barrett 84), Robbie Keane (McGeady 90), Duff.
Croatia: Butina; Tomas (Tokic 65), Simunic (Neretijak 74), Tudor (Balaban 46), Kovac R, Vranjes (Leko I 65), Srna, Kranjcar, Babic (Pranjic 59), Kovac N, Klasnic (Da Silva 59).
Referee: G. Orrason (Iceland).

Dublin, 9 February 2005, 44,100

Republic of Ireland (1) 1 *(O'Brien 21)*

Portugal (0) 0

Republic of Ireland: Given; Finnan, O'Shea, Holland, Cunningham (Dunne 60), O'Brien, Reid A, Kilbane (Kavanagh 46), Morrison, Robbie Keane (McGeady 84), Duff (Miller 69).
Portugal: Ricardo; Paulo Ferreira (Hugo Viana 46), Matias, Simao Sabrosa (Boa Morte 61), Caneira, Jorge Andrade, Tiago (Fernando Meira 46), Petit, Pauleta (Nuno Gomes 46), Deco (Ricardo Costa 46), Cristiano Ronaldo (Manuel Fernandes 70).
Referee: M. Messias (England).

Dublin, 29 March 2005, 35,222

Republic of Ireland (0) 1 *(Morrison 82)*

China (0) 0

Republic of Ireland: Kenny; Maybury, O'Shea, Kavanagh, Cunningham (O'Brien 46), Dunne, Reid A, Kilbane (Roy Keane 65), Robbie Keane (Morrison 62), Elliott (Doherty 74), Duff (Miller 46).
China: Li Leilei; Wei (Wang 46), Zhang Yongha (Zhang Yaokun 75), Li Weifeng, Ji, Sun, Hu (Zheng 86), Chen (Li Yan 38), Zhano, Shao (Du 64), Li Yi (Shi 46).
Referee: A. Casha (Malta).

CONFEDERATIONS CUP 2005

(in Germany)

GROUP A
Argentina 2, Tunisia 1
Germany 4, Australia 3
Tunisia 0, Germany 3
Australia 2, Argentina 4
Australia 0, Tunisia 2
Argentina 2, Germany 2

	P	*W*	*D*	*L*	*F*	*A*	*Pts*
Germany	3	2	1	0	9	5	7
Argentina	3	2	1	0	8	5	7
Tunisia	3	1	0	2	3	5	3
Australia	3	0	0	3	5	10	0

GROUP B
Japan 1, Mexico 2
Brazil 3, Greece 0
Greece 0, Japan 1
Mexico 1, Brazil 0
Greece 0, Mexico 0
Japan 2, Brazil 2

	P	*W*	*D*	*L*	*F*	*A*	*Pts*
Mexico	3	2	1	0	3	1	7
Brazil	3	1	1	1	5	3	4
Japan	3	1	1	1	4	4	4
Greece	3	0	1	0	0	4	1

SEMI-FINALS
Germany 2, Brazil 3
Mexico 1, Argentina 1
Argentina won 6-5 on penalties.

MATCH FOR THIRD PLACE
Germany 4, Mexico 3 (*aet.*)

FINAL (in Frankfurt)
29 June 2005

Brazil (2) 4, Argentina (0) 1

Brazil: Dida; Cicinho (Maicon 86), Ze Roberto, Emerson, Lucio, Roque Junior, Kaka (Renato 90), Robinho (Juninho Pernambucano 90), Adriano, Silva, Ronaldinho.
Scorers: Adriano 11, 63, Kaka 16, Ronaldinho 47.

Argentina: Lux; Zanetti, Sorin, Coloccini, Heinze, Placente, Bernardi, Figueroa (Tevez 72), Cambiasso (Aimar 56), Delgado (Galletti 81), Riquelme.
Scorer: Aimar 65.

Attendance: 45,591.

Referee: Michel (Slovakia).

BRITISH & IRISH INTERNATIONAL MANAGERS

England
Walter Winterbottom 1946–1962 (after period as coach); Alf Ramsey 1963–1974; Joe Mercer (caretaker) 1974; Don Revie 1974–1977; Ron Greenwood 1977–1982; Bobby Robson 1982–1990; Graham Taylor 1990–1993; Terry Venables (coach) 1994–1996; Glenn Hoddle 1996–1999; Kevin Keegan 1999–2000; Sven-Goran Eriksson from January 2001.

Northern Ireland
Peter Doherty 1951–1952; Bertie Peacock 1962–1967; Billy Bingham 1967–1971; Terry Neill 1971–1975; Dave Clements (player-manager) 1975–1976; Danny Blanchflower 1976–1979; Billy Bingham 1980–1994; Bryan Hamilton 1994–1998; Lawrie McMenemy 1998–1999; Sammy McIlroy 2000–03; Lawrie Sanchez from January 2004.

Scotland (since 1967)
Bobby Brown 1967–1971; Tommy Docherty 1971–1972; Willie Ormond 1973–1977; Ally MacLeod 1977–1978; Jock Stein 1978–1985; Alex Ferguson (caretaker) 1985–1986 Andy Roxburgh (coach) 1986–1993; Craig Brown 1993–2001; Berti Vogts 2002–04; Walter Smith from December 2004.

Wales (since 1974)
Mike Smith 1974–1979; Mike England 1980–1988; David Williams (caretaker) 1988; Terry Yorath 1988–1993; John Toshack 1994 for one match; Mike Smith 1994–1995; Bobby Gould 1995–1999; Mark Hughes 1999–2004; John Toshack from November 2004.

Republic of Ireland
Liam Tuohy 1971–1972; Johnny Giles 1973–1980 (after period as player-manager); Eoin Hand 1980–1985; Jack Charlton 1986–1996; Mick McCarthy 1996–2002; Brian Kerr from January 2003.

INTERNATIONAL APPEARANCES 1872–2005

This is a list of full international appearances by Englishmen, Irishmen, Scotsmen and Welshmen in matches against the Home Countries and against foreign nations. It does not include unofficial matches against Commonwealth and Empire countries. The year indicated refers to the season; ie 2005 is the 2004–05 season.
Explanatory code for matches played by all five countries: A represents Austria; Alb, Albania; Alg, Algeria; An, Angola; And, Andorra; Arg, Argentina; Arm, Armenia; Aus, Australia; Az, Azerbaijan; B, Bohemia; Bar, Barbados; Bel, Belgium; Bl, Belarus; Bol, Bolivia; Bos, Bosnia; Br, Brazil; Bul, Bulgaria; C,CIS; Ca, Canada; Cam, Cameroon; Ch, Chile; Chn, China; Co, Colombia; Cr, Costa Rica; Cro, Croatia; Cy, Cyprus; Cz, Czechoslovakia; CzR, Czech Republic; D, Denmark; E, England; Ec, Ecuador; Ei, Republic of Ireland; EG, East Germany; Eg, Egypt; Es, Estonia; F, France; Fa, Faeroes; Fi, Finland; G, Germany; Ge, Georgia; Gh, Ghana; Gr, Greece; H, Hungary; Hk, Hong Kong; Ho, Holland; Hon, Honduras; I, Italy; Ic, Iceland; Ir, Iran; Is, Israel; J, Japan; Jam, Jamaica; K, Kuwait; L, Luxembourg; La, Latvia; Li, Lithuania; Lie, Liechtenstein; M, Mexico; Ma, Malta; Mac, Macedonia; Mal, Malaysia; Mol, Moldova; Mor, Morocco; N, Norway; Ng, Nigeria; Ni, Northern Ireland; Nz, New Zealand; P, Portugal; Para, Paraguay; Pe, Peru; Pol, Poland; R, Romania; RCS, Republic of Czechs and Slovaks; R of E, Rest of Europe; R of UK, Rest of United Kingdom; R of W, Rest of World; Ru, Russia; S.Af, South Africa; S.Ar, Saudi Arabia; S, Scotland; Se, Sweden; Ser, Serbia-Montenegro; Sk, South Korea; Slv, Slovakia; Slo, Slovenia; Sm, San Marino; Sp, Spain; Stk, St Kitts & Nevis; Sw, Switzerland; T, Turkey; Th, Thailand; Tr, Trinidad & Tobago; Tun, Tunisia; U, Uruguay; Uk, Ukraine; US, United States of America; USSR, Soviet Union; W, Wales; WG, West Germany; Y, Yugoslavia; Z, Zaire.
As at July 2005.

ENGLAND

Abbott, W. (Everton), 1902 v W (1)
A'Court, A. (Liverpool), 1958 v Ni, Br, A, USSR; 1959 v W (5)
Adams, T. A. (Arsenal), 1987 v Sp, T, Br; 1988 v WG, T, Y, Ho, H, S, Co, Sw, Ei, Ho, USSR; 1989 v D, Se, S.Ar.; 1991 v Ei (2); 1993 v N, T, Sm, T, Ho, Pol, N; 1994 v Pol, Ho, D, Gr, N; 1995 v US, R, Ei, U; 1996 v Co, N, Sw, P, Chn, Sw, S, Ho, Sp, G; 1997 v Ge (2); 1998 v I, Ch, P, S.Ar, Tun, R, Co, Arg; 1999 v Se, F; 2000 v L, Pol, Bel, S (2), Uk, P; 2001 v F, G (66)
Adcock, H. (Leicester C), 1929 v F, Bel, Sp; 1930 v Ni, W (5)
Alcock, C. W. (Wanderers), 1875 v S (1)
Alderson, J. T. (C Palace), 1923 v F (1)
Aldridge, A. (WBA), 1888 v Ni; (with Walsall Town Swifts), 1889 v Ni (2)
Allen, A. (Stoke C) 1960 v Se, W, Ni (3)
Allen, A. (Aston Villa), 1888 v Ni (1)
Allen, C. (QPR), 1984 v Br (sub), U, Ch; (with Tottenham H), 1987 v T; 1988 v Is (5)
Allen, H. (Wolverhampton W), 1888 v S, W, Ni; 1889 v S; 1890 v S (5)
Allen, J. P. (Portsmouth), 1934 v Ni, W (2)
Allen, R. (WBA), 1952 v Sw; 1954 v Y, S; 1955 v WG, W (5)
Alsford, W. J. (Tottenham H), 1935 v S (1)
Amos, A. (Old Carthusians), 1885 v S; 1886 v W (2)
Anderson, R. D. (Old Etonians), 1879 v W (1)
Anderson, S. (Sunderland), 1962 v A, S (2)
Anderson, V. (Nottingham F), 1979 v Cz, Se; 1980 v Bul, Sp; 1981 v N, R, W, S; 1982 v Ni, Ic; 1984 v Ni; (with Arsenal), 1985 v T, Ni, Ei, R, Fi, S, M, US; 1986 v USSR, M; 1987 v Se, Ni (2), Y, Sp, T; (with Manchester U), 1988 v WG, H, Co (30)
Anderton, D. R. (Tottenham H), 1994 v D, Gr, N; 1995 v US, Ei, U, J, Se, Br; 1996 v H, Chn, Sw, S, Ho, Sp, G; 1998 v S.Ar, Mor, Tun, R, Co, Arg; 1999 v Se, Bul, L, CzR, F; 2001 v F, I (sub); 2002 v Se (sub) (30)
Angus, J. (Burnley), 1961 v A (1)
Armfield, J. C. (Blackpool), 1959 v Br, Pe, M, US; 1960 v Y, Sp, H, S; 1961 v L, P, Sp, M, I, A, W, Ni, S; 1962 v A, Sw, Pe, W, Ni, S, L, P, H, Arg, Bul, Br; 1963 v F (2), Br, EG, Sw, Ni, W, S; 1964 v R of W, W, Ni, S; 1966 v Y, Fi (43)
Armitage, G. H. (Charlton Ath), 1926 v Ni (1)
Armstrong, D. (Middlesbrough), 1980 v Aus; (with Southampton), 1983 v WG; 1984 v W (3)
Armstrong, K. (Chelsea), 1955 v S (1)
Arnold, J. (Fulham), 1933 v S (1)
Arthur, J. W. H. (Blackburn R), 1885 v S, W, Ni; 1886 v S, W; 1887 v W, Ni (7)
Ashcroft, J. (Woolwich Arsenal), 1906 v Ni, W, S (3)
Ashmore, G. S. (WBA), 1926 v Bel (1)
Ashton, C. T. (Corinthians), 1926 v Ni (1)
Ashurst, W. (Notts Co), 1923 v Se (2); 1925 v S, W, Bel (5)
Astall, G. (Birmingham C), 1956 v Fi, WG (2)
Astle, J. (WBA), 1969 v W; 1970 v S, P, Br (sub), Cz (5)
Aston, J. (Manchester U), 1949 v S, W, D, Sw, Se, N, F; 1950 v S, W, Ni, Ei, I, P, Bel, Ch, US; 1951 v Ni (17)
Athersmith, W. C. (Aston Villa), 1892 v Ni, 1897 v S, W, Ni; 1898 v S, W, Ni; 1899 v S, W, Ni; 1900 v S, W (12)
Atyeo, P. J. W. (Bristol C), 1956 v Br, Se, Sp; 1957 v D, Ei (2) (6)
Austin, S. W. (Manchester C), 1926 v Ni (1)
Bach, P. (Sunderland), 1899 v Ni (1)
Bache, J. W. (Aston Villa), 1903 v W; 1904 v W, Ni; 1905 v S; 1907 v Ni; 1910 v Ni; 1911 v S (7)
Baddeley, T. (Wolverhampton W), 1903 v S, Ni; 1904 v S, W, Ni (5)
Bagshaw, J. J. (Derby Co), 1920 v Ni (1)
Bailey, G. R. (Manchester U), 1985 v Ei, M (2)
Bailey, H. P. (Leicester Fosse), 1908 v W, A (2), H, B (5)
Bailey, M. A. (Charlton Ath), 1964 v US; 1965 v W (2)
Bailey, N. C. (Clapham Rovers), 1878 v S; 1879 v S, W; 1880 v S; 1881 v S; 1882 v S, W; 1883 v S, W; 1884 v S, W, Ni; 1885 v S, W, Ni; 1886 v S, W; 1887 v S, W (19)
Baily, E. F. (Tottenham H), 1950 v Sp; 1951 v Y, Ni, W; 1952 v A (2), Sw, W; 1953 v Ni (9)
Bain, J. (Oxford University), 1877 v S (1)
Baker, A. (Arsenal), 1928 v W (1)
Baker, B. H. (Everton), 1921 v Bel; (with Chelsea), 1926 v Ni (2)
Baker, J. H. (Hibernian), 1960 v Y, Sp, H, Ni, S; (with Arsenal) 1966 v Sp, Pol, Ni (8)
Ball, A. J. (Blackpool), 1965 v Y, WG, Se; 1966 v S, Sp, Fi, D, U, Arg, P, WG (2), Pol (2); (with Everton), 1967 v W, S, Ni, A, Cz, Sp; 1968 v W, S, USSR, Sp (2), Y, WG; 1969 v Ni, W, S, R (2), M, Br, U; 1970 v P, Co, Ec, R, Br, Cz (sub), WG, W, S, Bel; 1971 v Ma, EG, Gr, Ma (sub), Ni, S; 1972 v Sw, Gr; (with Arsenal) WG (2), S; 1973 v W (3), Y, S (2), Cz, Ni, Pol; 1974 v P (sub); 1975 v WG, Cy (2), Ni, W, S (72)
Ball, J. (Bury), 1928 v Ni (1)
Ball, M. J. (Everton), 2001 v Sp (sub) (1)
Balmer, W. (Everton), 1905 v Ni (1)
Bamber, J. (Liverpool), 1921 v W (1)
Bambridge, A. L. (Swifts), 1881 v W; 1883 v W; 1884 v Ni (3)
Bambridge, E. C. (Swifts), 1879 v S; 1880 v S; 1881 v S; 1882 v S, W, Ni; 1883 v W; 1884 v S, W, Ni; 1885 v S, W, Ni; 1886 v S, W; 1887 v S, W, Ni (18)
Bambridge, E. H. (Swifts), 1876 v S (1)
Banks, G. (Leicester C), 1963 v S, Br, Cz, EG; 1964 v W, Ni, S, R of W, U, P (2), US, Arg; 1965 v Ni, S, H, Y, WG, Se; 1966 v Ni, S, Sp, Pol (2), WG (2), Y, Fi, U, M, F, Arg, P; 1967 v Ni, W, S, Cz; (with Stoke C), 1968 v W, Ni, S, USSR (2), Sp, WG, Y; 1969 v Ni, S, R (2), F, U, Br; 1970 v W, Ni, S, Ho, Bel, Co, Ec, R, Br, Cz; 1971 v Gr, Ma (2), Ni, S; 1972 v Sw, Gr, WG (2), W, S (73)
Banks, H. E. (Millwall), 1901 v Ni (1)
Banks, T. (Bolton W), 1958 v USSR (3), Br, A; 1959 v Ni (6)
Bannister, W. (Burnley), 1901 v W; (with Bolton W), 1902 v Ni (2)
Barclay, R. (Sheffield U), 1932 v S; 1933 v Ni; 1936 v S (3)
Bardsley, D. J. (QPR), 1993 v Sp (sub), Pol (2)
Barham, M. (Norwich C), 1983 v Aus (2) (2)
Barkas, S. (Manchester C), 1936 v Bel; 1937 v S; 1938 v W, Ni, Cz (5)
Barker, J. (Derby Co), 1935 v I, Ho, S, W, Ni; 1936 v G, A, S, W, Ni; 1937 v W (11)
Barker, R. (Herts Rangers), 1872 v S (1)
Barker, R. R. (Casuals), 1895 v W (1)
Barlow, R. J. (WBA), 1955 v Ni (1)
Barmby, N. J. (Tottenham H), 1995 v U (sub), Se (sub); (with Middlesbrough), 1996 v Co, N, P, Chn, Sw (sub), Ho (sub), Sp (sub); 1997 v Mol; (with Everton), 2000 v Br (sub), Uk

(sub), Ma, G (sub), R (sub); (with Liverpool), 2001 v F, G, I, Sp; 2002 v Ho (sub), G, Alb, Gr (23)
Barnes, J. (Watford), 1983 v Ni (sub), Aus (sub), Aus (2); 1984 v D, L (sub), F (sub), S, USSR, Br, U, Ch; 1985 v EG, Fi, T, Ni, R, Fi, S, I (sub), M, WG (sub), US (sub); 1986 v R (sub), Is (sub), M (sub), Ca (sub), Arg (sub); 1987 v Se, T (sub), Br; (with Liverpool), 1988 v WG, T, Y, Is, Ho, S, Co, Sw, Ei, Ho, USSR; 1989 v Se, Gr, Alb, Pol, D; 1990 v Se, I, Br, D, U, Tun, Ei, Ho, Eg, Bel, Cam; 1991 v H, Pol, Cam, Ei, T, USSR, Arg; 1992 v Cz, Fi; 1993 v Sm, T, Ho, Pol, US, G; 1995 v US, R, Ng, U, Se; 1996 v Co (sub) (79)
Barnes, P. S. (Manchester C), 1978 v I, WG, Br, W, S, H; 1979 v D, Ei, Cz, Ni (2), S, Bul, A; (with WBA), 1980 v D, W; 1981 v Sp (sub), Br, W, Sw (sub); (with Leeds U), 1982 v N (sub), Ho (sub) (22)
Barnet, H. H. (Royal Engineers), 1882 v Ni (1)
Barrass, M. W. (Bolton W), 1952 v W, Ni; 1953 v S (3)
Barrett, A. F. (Fulham), 1930 v Ni (1)
Barrett, E. D. (Oldham Ath), 1991 v Nz; (with Aston Villa), 1993 v Br, G (3)
Barrett, J. W. (West Ham U), 1929 v Ni (1)
Barry, G. (Aston Villa), 2000 v Uk (sub), Ma (sub); 2001 v F, G (sub), Fi, I ; 2003 v S.Af (sub), Ser (sub) (8)
Barry, L. (Leicester C), 1928 v F, Bel; 1929 v F, Bel, Sp (5)
Barson, F. (Aston Villa), 1920 v W (1)
Barton, J. (Blackburn R), 1890 v Ni (1)
Barton, P. H. (Birmingham), 1921 v Bel; 1922 v Ni; 1923 v F; 1924 v Bel, S, W; 1925 v Ni (7)
Barton, W. D. (Wimbledon), 1995 v Ei; (with Newcastle U), Se, Br (sub) (3)
Bassett, W. I. (WBA), 1888 v Ni, 1889 v S, W; 1890 v S, W; 1891 v S, Ni; 1892 v S; 1893 v S, W; 1894 v S; 1895 v S, Ni; 1896 v S, W, Ni (16)
Bastard, S. R. (Upton Park), 1880 v S (1)
Bastin, C. S. (Arsenal), 1932 v W; 1933 v I, Sw; 1934 v S, Ni, W, H, Cz; 1935 v S, Ni, I; 1936 v S, W, G, A; 1937 v W, Ni; 1938 v S, G, Sw, F (21)
Batty, D. (Leeds U), 1991 v USSR (sub), Arg, Aus, Nz, Mal; 1992 v G, T, H (sub), F, Se; 1993 v N, Sm, US, Br; (with Blackburn R), 1994 v D (sub); 1995 v J, Br; (with Newcastle U), 1997 v Mol (sub), Ge, I, M, Ge, S.Af (sub), Pol (sub), F; 1998 v Mol, I, Ch, Sw (sub), P, S.Ar, Tun, R, Co (sub), Arg (sub); 1999 v Bul (sub), L; (with Leeds U), H, Se, Bul; 2000 v L, Pol (42)
Baugh, R. (Stafford Road), 1886 v Ni; (with Wolverhampton W) 1890 v Ni (2)
Bayliss, A. E. J. M. (WBA), 1891 v Ni (1)
Baynham, R. L. (Luton T), 1956 v Ni, D, Sp (3)
Beardsley, P. A. (Newcastle U), 1986 v Eg (sub), Is, USSR, M, Ca (sub), P (sub), Pol, Para, Arg; 1987 v Ni (2), Y, Sp, Br, S; (with Liverpool), 1988 v WG, T, Y, Is, Ho, H, S, Co, Sw, Ei, Ho; 1989 v D, Se, S.Ar, Gr (sub), Alb (sub+1), Pol, D; 1990 v Se, Pol, I, Br, U (sub), Tun (sub), Ei, Eg (sub), Cam (sub), WG, I; 1991 v Pol (sub), Ei (2), USSR (sub); (with Newcastle U), 1994 v D, Gr, N; 1995 v Ng, Ei, U, J, Se; 1996 v P (sub), Chn (sub) (59)
Beasant, D. J. (Chelsea), 1990 v I (sub), Y (sub) (2)
Beasley, A. (Huddersfield T), 1939 v S (1)
Beats, W. E. (Wolverhampton W), 1901 v W; 1902 v S (2)
Beattie, J. S. (Southampton), 2003 v Aus, Ser (sub); 2004 v Cro (sub), Lie, D (sub) (5)
Beattie, T. K. (Ipswich T), 1975 v Cy (2), S; 1976 v Sw, P; 1977 v Fi, I (sub), Ho; 1978 v L (sub) (9)
Beckham, D. R. J. (Manchester U), 1997 v Mol, Pol, Ge, I, Ge, S.Af (sub), Pol, I, F; 1998 v Mol, I, Cam, P, S.Ar, Bel (sub), R (sub), Co, Arg; 1999 v L, CzR, F, Pol, Se; 2000 v L, Pol, S(2), Arg, Br, Uk, Ma, P, G, R; 2001 v F, G, I, Sp, Fi, Alb, M, Gr; 2002 v Ho, G, Alb, Gr, Se, Ho, I, Se, Arg, Ng, D, Br; 2003 v Slo, Mac, Aus, Lie, T, S.Af; (with Real Madrid), 2004 v Cro, Mac, Lie, T, D, P, J, Ic, F, Sw, Cro, P; 2005 v Uk, A, Pol, W, Sp, Ho, Ni, Az, Co (81)
Becton, F. (Preston NE), 1895 v Ni; (with Liverpool), 1897 v W (2)
Bedford, H. (Blackpool), 1923 v Se; 1925 v Ni (2)
Bell, C. (Manchester C), 1968 v Se, WG; 1969 v W, Bul, F, U, Br; 1970 v Ni (sub), Ho (2), P, Br (sub), Cz, WG (sub); 1972 v Gr, WG (2), W, Ni, S; 1973 v W (3), Y, S (2), Ni, Cz, Pol; 1974 v A, Pol, I, W, Ni, S, Arg, EG, Bul, Y; 1975 v Cz, P, WG, Cy (2), Ni, S; 1976 v Sw, Cz (48)
Bennett, W. (Sheffield U), 1901 v S, W (2)
Benson, R. W. (Sheffield U), 1913 v Ni (1)
Bentley, R. T. F. (Chelsea), 1949 v Se; 1950 v S, P, Bel, Ch, USA; 1953 v W, Bel; 1955 v W, WG, Sp, P (12)
Beresford, J. (Aston Villa), 1934 v Cz (1)
Berry, A. (Oxford University), 1909 v Ni (1)
Berry, J. J. (Manchester U), 1953 v Arg, Ch, U; 1956 v Se (4)
Bestall, J. G. (Grimsby T), 1935 v Ni (1)
Betmead, H. A. (Grimsby T), 1937 v Fi (1)
Betts, M. P. (Old Harrovians), 1877 v S (1)
Betts, W. (Sheffield W), 1889 v W (1)
Beverley, J. (Blackburn R), 1884 v S, W, Ni (3)
Birkett, R. H. (Clapham Rovers), 1879 v S (1)
Birkett, R. J. E. (Middlesbrough), 1936 v Ni (1)
Birley, F. H. (Oxford University), 1874 v S; (with Wanderers), 1875 v S (2)
Birtles, G. (Nottingham F), 1980 v Arg (sub), I; 1981 v R (3)
Bishop, S. M. (Leicester C), 1927 v S, Bel, L, F (4)
Blackburn, F. (Blackburn R), 1901 v S; 1902 v Ni; 1904 v S (3)
Blackburn, G. F. (Aston Villa), 1924 v F (1)
Blenkinsop, E. (Sheffield W), 1928 v F, Bel; 1929 v S, W, Ni, F, Bel, Sp; 1930 v S, W, Ni, G, A; 1931 v S, W, Ni, F, Bel; 1932 v S, W, Ni, Sp; 1933 v S, W, Ni, A (26)
Bliss, H. (Tottenham H), 1921 v S (1)
Blissett, L. (Watford), 1983 v WG (sub), L, W, Gr (sub), H, Ni, S (sub), Aus (1+1 sub); (with AC Milan), 1984 v D (sub), H, W (sub), S, USSR (14)
Blockley, J. P. (Arsenal), 1973 v Y (1)
Bloomer, S. (Derby Co), 1895 v S, Ni; 1896 v W, Ni; 1897 v S, W, Ni; 1898 v S; 1899 v S, W, Ni; 1900 v S; 1901 v S, W; 1902 v S, W, Ni; 1904 v S; 1905 v S, W, Ni; (with Middlesbrough), 1907 v S, W (23)
Blunstone, F. (Chelsea), 1955 v W, S, F, P; 1957 v Y (5)
Bond, R. (Preston NE), 1905 v Ni, W; 1906 v S, W, Ni; (with Bradford C), 1910 v S, W, Ni (8)
Bonetti, P. P. (Chelsea), 1966 v D; 1967 v Sp, A; 1968 v Sp; 1970 v Ho, P, WG (7)
Bonsor, A. G. (Wanderers), 1873 v S; 1875 v S (2)
Booth, F. (Manchester C), 1905 v Ni (1)
Booth, T. (Blackburn R), 1898 v W; (with Everton), 1903 v S (2)
Bould, S. A. (Arsenal), 1994 v Gr, N (2)
Bowden, E. R. (Arsenal), 1935 v W, I; 1936 v W, Ni, A; 1937 v H (6)
Bower, A. G. (Corinthians), 1924 v Ni, Bel; 1925 v W, Bel; 1927 v W (5)
Bowers, J. W. (Derby Co), 1934 v S, Ni, W (3)
Bowles, S. (QPR), 1974 v P, W, Ni; 1977 v I, Ho (5)
Bowser, S. (WBA), 1920 v Ni (1)
Bowyer, L. D. (Leeds U), 2003 v P (1)
Boyer, P. J. (Norwich C), 1976 v W (1)
Boyes, W. (WBA), 1935 v Ho; (with Everton), 1939 v W, R of E (3)
Boyle, T. W. (Burnley), 1913 v Ni (1)
Brabrook, P. (Chelsea), 1958 v USSR; 1959 v Ni; 1960 v Sp (3)
Bracewell, P. W. (Everton), 1985 v WG (sub), US; 1986 v Ni (3)
Bradford, G. R. W. (Bristol R), 1956 v D (1)
Bradford, J. (Birmingham), 1924 v Ni; 1925 v Bel; 1928 v S; 1929 v Ni, W, F, Sp; 1930 v S, Ni, G, A; 1931 v W (12)
Bradley, W. (Manchester U), 1959 v I, US, M (sub) (3)
Bradshaw, F. (Sheffield W), 1908 v A (1)
Bradshaw, T. H. (Liverpool), 1897 v Ni (1)
Bradshaw, W. (Blackburn R), 1910 v W, Ni; 1912 v Ni; 1913 v W (4)
Brann, G. (Swifts), 1886 v S, W; 1891 v W (3)
Brawn, W. F. (Aston Villa), 1904 v W, Ni (2)
Bray, J. (Manchester C), 1935 v W; 1936 v S, W, Ni, G; 1937 v S (6)
Brayshaw, E. (Sheffield W), 1887 v Ni (1)
Bridge W. M. (Southampton), 2002 v Ho, I, Para, Sk (sub), Cam, Arg (sub), Ng (sub); 2003 v P (sub), Mac, Lie, T, Ser (sub); (with Chelsea), 2004 v Cro (sub), Lie, D (sub), P (sub), Ic (sub); 2005 v A, Pol, Sp (20)
Bridges, B. J. (Chelsea), 1965 v S, H, Y; 1966 v A (4)
Bridgett, A. (Sunderland), 1905 v S; 1908 v S, A (2), H, B; 1909 v Ni, W, H (2), A (11)
Brindle, T. (Darwen), 1880 v S, W (2)
Brittleton, J. T. (Sheffield W), 1912 v S, W, Ni; 1913 v S; 1914 v W (5)
Britton, C. S. (Everton), 1935 v S, W, Ni, I; 1937 v S, Ni, H, N, Se (9)
Broadbent, P. F. (Wolverhampton W), 1958 v USSR; 1959 v S, W, Ni, I, Br; 1960 v S (7)
Broadis, I. A. (Manchester C), 1952 v S, A, I; 1953 v S, Arg, Ch, U, US; (with Newcastle U), 1954 v S, H, Y, Bel, Sw, U (14)
Brockbank, J. (Cambridge University), 1872 v S (1)
Brodie, J. B. (Wolverhampton W), 1889 v S, Ni; 1891 v Ni (3)
Bromilow, T. G. (Liverpool), 1921 v W; 1922 v S, W; 1923 v Bel; 1926 v Ni (5)
Bromley-Davenport, W. E. (Oxford University), 1884 v S, W (2)

Brook, E. F. (Manchester C), 1930 v Ni; 1933 v Sw: 1934 v S, W, Ni, F, H, Cz; 1935 v S, W, Ni, I; 1936 v S, W, Ni; 1937 v H; 1938 v W, Ni (18)
Brooking, T. D. (West Ham U), 1974 v P, Arg, EG, Bul, Y; 1975 v Cz (sub), P; 1976 v P, W, Br, I, Fi; 1977 v Ei, Fi, I, Ho, Ni, W; 1978 v I, WG, W, S (sub), H; 1979 v D, Ei, Ni, W (sub), S, Bul, Se (sub), A; 1980 v D, Ni, Arg (sub), W, Ni, S, Bel, Sp; 1981 v Sw, Sp, R, H; 1982 v H, S, Fi, Sp (sub) (47)
Brooks, J. (Tottenham H), 1957 v W, Y, D (3)
Broome, F. H. (Aston Villa), 1938 v G, Sw, F; 1939 v N, I, R, Y (7)
Brown, A. (Aston Villa), 1882 v S, W, Ni (3)
Brown, A. S. (Sheffield U), 1904 v W; 1906 v Ni (2)
Brown, A. (WBA), 1971 v W (1)
Brown, G. (Huddersfield T), 1927 v S, W, Ni, Bel, L, F; 1928 v W; 1929 v S; (with Aston Villa), 1933 v W (9)
Brown, J. (Blackburn R), 1881 v W; 1882 v Ni; 1885 v S, W, Ni (5)
Brown, J. H. (Sheffield W), 1927 v S, W, Bel, L, F; 1930 v Ni (6)
Brown, K. (West Ham U), 1960 v Ni (1)
Brown, W. (West Ham U), 1924 v Bel (1)
Brown, W. M. (Manchester U), 1999 v H; 2001 v Fi (sub), Alb (sub); 2002 v Ho, Sk (sub), Cam; 2003 v Aus (sub); 2005 v Ho, US (9)
Bruton, J. (Burnley), 1928 v F, Bel; 1929 v S (3)
Bryant, W. I. (Clapton), 1925 v F (1)
Buchan, C. M. (Sunderland), 1913 v Ni; 1920 v W; 1921 v W, Bel; 1923 v F; 1924 v S (6)
Buchanan, W. S. (Clapham R), 1876 v S (1)
Buckley, F. C. (Derby Co), 1914 v Ni (1)
Bull, S. G. (Wolverhampton W), 1989 v S (sub), D (sub); 1990 v Y, Cz, D (sub), U (sub), Tun (sub), Ei (sub), Ho (sub), Eg, Bel (sub); 1991 v H, Pol (13)
Bullock, F. E. (Huddersfield T), 1921 v Ni (1)
Bullock, N. (Bury), 1923 v Bel; 1926 v W; 1927 v Ni (3)
Burgess, H. (Manchester C), 1904 v S, W, Ni; 1906 v S (4)
Burgess, H. (Sheffield W), 1931 v S, Ni, F, Bel (4)
Burnup, C. J. (Cambridge University), 1896 v S (1)
Burrows, H. (Sheffield W), 1934 v H, Cz; 1935 v Ho (3)
Burton, F. E. (Nottingham F), 1889 v Ni (1)
Bury, L. (Cambridge University), 1877 v S; (with Old Etonians), 1879 v W (2)
Butcher, T. (Ipswich T), 1980 v Aus; 1981 v Sp; 1982 v W, S, F, Cz, WG, Sp; 1983 v D, WG, L, W, Gr, H, Ni, S, Aus (3); 1984 v D, H, L, F, Ni; 1985 v EG, Fi, T, Ni, Ei, R, Fi, S, I, WG, US; 1986 v Is, USSR, S, M, Ca, P, Mor, Pol, Para, Arg; (with Rangers), 1987 v Se, Ni (2), Y, Sp, Br, S; 1988 v T, Y; 1989 v D, Se, Gr, Alb (2), Ch, S, Pol, D; 1990 v Se, Pol, I, Y, Br, Cz, D, U, Tun, Ei, Ho, Bel, Cam, WG (77)
Butler, J. D. (Arsenal), 1925 v Bel (1)
Butler, W. (Bolton W), 1924 v S (1)
Butt, N. (Manchester U), 1997 v M (sub), S.Af (sub); 1998 v Mol (sub), I (sub), Ch, Bel; 1999 v CzR, H; 2001 v I, Sp, Fi (sub), Alb, M (sub), Gr (sub); 2002 v Se, Ho (sub), I, Para, Arg, Ng, D, Br; 2003 v P, Slo, Mac (sub), Lie (sub), T; 2004 v Cro, Mac, T, D, P, Se, J (sub), Ic (sub); (with Newcastle U), 2005 v Uk, W, Az, Sp (39)
Byrne, G. (Liverpool), 1963 v S; 1966 v N (2)
Byrne, J. J. (C Palace), 1962 v Ni; (with West Ham U), 1963 v Sw; 1964 v S, U, P (2), Ei, Br, Arg; 1965 v W, S (11)
Byrne, R. W. (Manchester U), 1954 v S, H, Y, Bel, Sw, U; 1955 v S, W, Ni, WG, F, Sp, P; 1956 v S, W, Ni, Br, Se, Fi, WG, D, Sp; 1957 v S, W, Ni, Y, D (2), Ei (2); 1958 v W, Ni, F (33)

Callaghan, I. R. (Liverpool), 1966 v Fi, F; 1978 v Sw, L (4)
Calvey, J. (Nottingham F), 1902 v Ni (1)
Campbell, A. F. (Blackburn R), 1929 v W, Ni; (with Huddersfield T), 1931 v W, S, Ni; 1932 v W, Ni, Sp (8)
Campbell, S. (Tottenham H), 1996 v H (sub), S (sub); 1997 v Ge, I, Ge, S.Af (sub), Pol, F, Br; 1998 v Mol, I, Cam, Ch, P, Mor, Bel, Tun, R, Co, Arg; 1999 v Se, Bul, L, CzR, Pol, Se, Bul; 2000 v S (2), Arg, Br, Uk, Ma, P, G, R; 2001 v F, Sp, Fi, Alb; (with Arsenal), 2002 v G, Alb, Ho, I, Sk, Cam, Se, Arg, Ng, D, Br; 2003 v Mac, Aus, T; 2004 v Mac, T, J, Ic, F, Sw, Cro, P; 2005 v W, Az, US (65)
Camsell, G. H. (Middlesbrough), 1929 v F, Bel; 1930 v Ni, W; 1934 v F; 1936 v S, G, A, Bel (9)
Capes, A. J. (Stoke C), 1903 v S (1)
Carr, J. (Middlesbrough), 1920 v Ni; 1923 v W (2)
Carr, J. (Newcastle U), 1905 v Ni; 1907 v Ni (2)
Carr, W. H. (Owlerton, Sheffield), 1875 v S (1)
Carragher, J. L. (Liverpool), 1999 v H (sub); 2001 v I (sub), M (sub); 2002 v Ho, G (sub), Alb (sub), Se, Para (sub); 2003 v Ser (sub); 2004 v P (sub), Se, Ic; 2005 v Uk (sub), A (sub), Pol (sub), Sp (sub), Ho (17)
Carrick, M. (West Ham U), 2001 v M (sub); 2002 v Ho (sub) ; (with Tottenham H), 2005 v US, Col (4)
Carter, H. S. (Sunderland), 1934 v S, H; 1936 v G; 1937 v S, Ni, H; (with Derby Co), 1947 v S, W, Ni, Ei, Ho, F, Sw (13)
Carter, J. H. (WBA), 1926 v Bel; 1929 v Bel, Sp (3)
Catlin, A. E. (Sheffield W), 1937 v W, Ni, H, N, Se (5)
Chadwick, A. (Southampton), 1900 v S, W (2)
Chadwick, E. (Everton), 1891 v S, W; 1892 v S; 1893 v S; 1894 v S; 1896 v Ni; 1897 v S (7)
Chamberlain, M (Stoke C), 1983 v L (sub); 1984 v D (sub), S, USSR, Br, U, Ch; 1985 v Fi (sub) (8)
Chambers, H. (Liverpool), 1921 v S, W, Bel; 1923 v S, W, Ni, Bel; 1924 v Ni (8)
Channon, M. R. (Southampton), 1973 v Y, S (2), Ni, W, Cz, USSR, I; 1974 v A, Pol, I, P, W, Ni, S, Arg, EG, Bul, Y; 1975 v Cz, P, WG, Cy (2), Ni (sub), W, S; 1976 v Sw, Cz, P, W, Ni, S, Br, I, Fi; 1977 v Fi, I, L, Ni, W, S, Br (sub), Arg, U; (with Manchester C), 1978 v Sw (46)
Charles, G. A. (Nottingham F), 1991 v Nz, Mal (2)
Charlton, J. (Leeds U), 1965 v S, H, Y, WG, Se; 1966 v W, Ni, S, A, Sp, Pol (2), WG (2), Y, Fi, D, U, M, F, Arg, P; 1967 v W, S, Ni, Cz; 1968 v W, Sp; 1969 v W, R, F; 1970 v Ho (2), P, Cz (35)
Charlton, R. (Manchester U), 1958 v S, P, Y; 1959 v S, W, Ni, USSR, I, Br, Pe, M, US; 1960 v W, S, Se, Y, Sp, H; 1961 v Ni, W, S, L, P, Sp, M, I, A; 1962 v W, Ni, S, A, Sw, Pe, L, P, H, Arg, Bul, Br; 1963 v S, F, Br, Cz, EG, Sw; 1964 v S, W, Ni, R of W, U, P, Ei, Br, Arg, US (sub); 1965 v Ni, S, Ho; 1966 v W, Ni, S, A, Sp, WG (2), Y, Fi, N, Pol, U, M, F, Arg, P; 1967 v Ni, W, S, Cz; 1968 v W, Ni, S, USSR (2), Sp (2), Se, Y; 1969 v S, W, Ni, R (2), Bul, M, Br; 1970 v W, Ni, Ho (2), P, Co, Ec, Cz, R, Br, WG (106)
Charnley, R. O. (Blackpool), 1963 v F (1)
Charsley, C. C. (Small Heath), 1893 v Ni (1)
Chedgzoy, S. (Everton), 1920 v W; 1921 v W, S, Ni; 1922 v Ni; 1923 v S; 1924 v W; 1925 v Ni (8)
Chenery, C. J. (C Palace), 1872 v S; 1873 v S; 1874 v S (3)
Cherry, T. J. (Leeds U), 1976 v W, S (sub), Br, Fi; 1977 v Ei, I, L, Ni, S (sub), Br, Arg, U; 1978 v Sw, L, I, Br, W; 1979 v Cz, W, Se; 1980 v Ei, Arg (sub), W, Ni, S, Aus, Sp (sub) (27)
Chilton, A. (Manchester U), 1951 v Ni; 1952 v F (2)
Chippendale, H. (Blackburn R), 1894 v Ni (1)
Chivers, M. (Tottenham H), 1971 v Ma (2), Gr, Ni, S; 1972 v Sw (1+1 sub), Gr, WG (2), Ni (sub), S; 1973 v W (3), S (2), Ni, Cz, Pol, USSR, I; 1974 v A, Pol (24)
Christian, E. (Old Etonians), 1879 v S (1)
Clamp, E. (Wolverhampton W), 1958 v USSR (2), Br, A (4)
Clapton, D. R. (Arsenal), 1959 v W (1)
Clare, T. (Stoke C), 1889 v Ni; 1892 v Ni; 1893 v W; 1894 v S (4)
Clarke, A. J. (Leeds U), 1970 v Cz; 1971 v EG, Ma, Ni, W (sub), S (sub); 1973 v S (2), W, Cz, Pol, USSR, I; 1974 v A, Pol, I; 1975 v P; 1976 v Cz, P (sub) (19)
Clarke, H. A. (Tottenham H), 1954 v S (1)
Clay, T. (Tottenham H), 1920 v W; 1922 v W, S, Ni (4)
Clayton, R. (Blackburn R), 1956 v Ni, Br, Se, Fi, WG, Sp; 1957 v S, W, Ni, Y, D (2), Ei (2); 1958 v S, W, Ni, F, P, Y, USSR; 1959 v S, W, Ni, USSR, I, Br, Pe, M, US; 1960 v W, Ni, S, Se, Y (35)
Clegg, J. C. (Sheffield W), 1872 v S (1)
Clegg, W. E. (Sheffield W), 1873 v S; (with Sheffield Albion), 1879 v W (2)
Clemence, R. N. (Liverpool), 1973 v W (2); 1974 v EG, Bul, Y; 1975 v Cz, P, WG, Cy, Ni, W, S; 1976 v Sw, Cz, P, W (2), Ni, S, Br, Fi; 1977 v Ei, Fi, I, Ho, L, S, Br, Arg, U; 1978 v Sw, L, I, WG, Ni, S; 1979 v D, Ei, Ni (2), S, Bul, A (sub); 1980 v D, Bul, Ei, Arg, W, S, Bel, Sp; 1981 v R, Sp, Br, Sw, H; (with Tottenham H), 1982 v N, Ni, Fi; 1983 v L; 1984 v L (61)
Clement, D. T. (QPR), 1976 v W (sub+1), I; 1977 v I, Ho (5)
Clough, B. H. (Middlesbrough), 1960 v W, Se (2)
Clough, N. H. (Nottingham F), 1989 v Ch; 1991 v Arg (sub), Aus, Mal; 1992 v F, Cz, C (sub); 1993 v Sp, T (sub), Pol (sub), N (sub), US, Br, G (14)
Coates, R. (Burnley), 1970 v Ni; 1971 v Gr (sub); (with Tottenham H), Ma, W (4)
Cobbold, W. N. (Cambridge University), 1883 v S, Ni; 1885 v S, Ni; 1886 v S, W; (with Old Carthusians), 1887 v S, W, Ni (9)
Cock, J. G. (Huddersfield T), 1920 v Ni; (with Chelsea), v S (2)
Cockburn, H. (Manchester U), 1947 v W, Ni, Ei; 1948 v S, I; 1949 v S, Ni, D, Sw, Se; 1951 v Arg, P; 1952 v F (13)

Cohen, G. R. (Fulham), 1964 v U, P, Ei, US, Br; 1965 v W, S, Ni, Bel, H, Ho, Y, WG, Se; 1966 v W, S, Ni, A, Sp, Pol (2), WG (2), N, D, U, M, F, Arg, P; 1967 v W, S, Ni, Cz, Sp; 1968 v W, Ni (37)
Cole, A. (Manchester U), 1995 v U (sub); 1997 v I (sub); 1999 v F (sub), Pol, Se; 2000 v S (sub), Arg (sub); 2001 v F, G, Fi, Sp, Fi, Alb; 2002 v Ho, Gr (sub) (15)
Cole, A. (Arsenal), 2001 v Alb, M, Gr; 2002 v Ho, G, Alb, Gr, Sk, Se, Arg, Ng, D, Br; 2003 v P, Slo, Mac, Aus, Ser, Slo; 2004 v Cro, Mac, T, D, P, J, Ic, F, Sw, Cro, P; 2005 v Uk, A, Pol, W, Az, Sp, Ho, Ni, Az, US, Col (41)
Cole, J. J. (West Ham U), 2001 v M (sub); 2002 v Ho (sub), I (sub), Para (sub), Sk (sub), Cam, Se (sub); 2003 v P (sub), S.Af (sub), Ser (sub); (with Chelsea), 2004 v Cro (sub), Lie (sub), D, P (sub), Se (sub), J (sub), Ic (sub); 2005 v A (sub), Az (sub), Ni, Az, US, Col (23)
Colclough, H. (C Palace), 1914 v W (1)
Coleman, E. H. (Dulwich Hamlet), 1921 v W (1)
Coleman, J. (Woolwich Arsenal), 1907 v Ni (1)
Collymore, S. V. (Nottingham F), 1995 v J, Br (sub); (with Aston Villa), 1998 v Mol (sub) (3)
Common, A. (Sheffield U), 1904 v W, Ni; (with Middlesbrough), 1906 v W (3)
Compton, L. H. (Arsenal), 1951 v W, Y (2)
Conlin, J. (Bradford C), 1906 v S (1)
Connelly, J. M. (Burnley), 1960 v W, Ni, S, Se; 1962 v W, A, Sw, P; 1963 v W, F; (with Manchester U), 1965 v H, Y, Se; 1966 v W, Ni, S, A, N, D, U (20)
Cook, T. E. R. (Brighton), 1925 v W (1)
Cooper, C. T. (Nottingham F), 1995 v Se, Br (2)
Cooper, N. C. (Cambridge University), 1893 v Ni (1)
Cooper, T. (Derby Co), 1928 v Ni; 1929 v W, Ni, S, F, Bel, Sp; 1931 v F; 1932 v W, Sp; 1933 v S; 1934 v S, H, Cz; 1935 v W (15)
Cooper, T. (Leeds U), 1969 v W, S, F, M; 1970 v Ho, Bel, Co, Ec, R, Cz, Br, WG; 1971 v EG, Ma, Ni, W, S; 1972 v Sw (2); 1975 v P (20)
Coppell, S. J. (Manchester U), 1978 v I, WG, Br, W, Ni, S, H; 1979 v D, Ei, Cz, Ni (2), W (sub), S, Bul, A; 1980 v D, Ni, Ei (sub), Sp, Arg, W, S, Bel, I; 1981 v R (sub), Sw, R, Br, W, S, Sw, H; 1982 v H, S, Fi, F, Cz, K, WG; 1983 v L, Gr (42)
Copping, W. (Leeds U), 1933 v I, Sw; 1934 v S, Ni, W, F; (with Arsenal), 1935 v Ni, I; 1936 v A, Bel; 1937 v N, Se, Fi; 1938 v S, W, Ni, Cz; 1939 v W, R of E; (with Leeds U), R (20)
Corbett, B. O. (Corinthians), 1901 v W (1)
Corbett, R. (Old Malvernians), 1903 v W (1)
Corbett, W. S. (Birmingham), 1908 v A, H, B (3)
Corrigan, J. T. (Manchester C), 1976 v I (sub), Br; 1979 v W; 1980 v Ni, Aus; 1981 v W, S; 1982 v W, Ic (9)
Cottee, A. R. (West Ham U), 1987 v Se (sub), Ni (sub); 1988 v H (sub); (with Everton) 1989 v D (sub), Se (sub), Ch (sub), S (7)
Cotterill, G. H. (Cambridge University), 1891 v Ni; (with Old Brightonians), 1892 v W; 1893 v S, Ni (4)
Cottle, J. R. (Bristol C), 1909 v Ni (1)
Cowan, S. (Manchester C), 1926 v Bel; 1930 v A; 1931 v Bel (3)
Cowans, G. (Aston Villa), 1983 v W, H, Ni, S, Aus (3); (with Bari), 1986 v Eg, USSR; (with Aston Villa), 1991 v Ei (10)
Cowell, A. (Blackburn R), 1910 v Ni (1)
Cox, J. (Liverpool), 1901 v Ni; 1902 v S; 1903 v S (3)
Cox, J. D. (Derby Co), 1892 v Ni (1)
Crabtree, J. W. (Burnley), 1894 v Ni; 1895 v Ni, S; (with Aston Villa), 1896 v W, S, Ni; 1899 v S, W, Ni; 1900 v S, W, Ni; 1901 v W; 1902 v W (14)
Crawford, J. F. (Chelsea), 1931 v S (1)
Crawford, R. (Ipswich T), 1962 v Ni, A (2)
Crawshaw, T. H. (Sheffield W), 1895 v Ni; 1896 v S, W, Ni; 1897 v S, W, Ni; 1901 v Ni; 1904 v W, Ni (10)
Crayston, W. J. (Arsenal), 1936 v S, W, G, A, Bel; 1938 v W, Ni, Cz (8)
Creek, F. N. S. (Corinthians), 1923 v F (1)
Cresswell, W. (South Shields), 1921 v W; (with Sunderland), 1923 v F; 1924 v Bel; 1925 v Ni; 1926 v W; 1927 v Ni; (with Everton), 1930 v Ni (7)
Crompton, R. (Blackburn R), 1902 v S, W, Ni; 1903 v S, W; 1904 v S, W, Ni; 1906 v S, W, Ni; 1907 v S, W, Ni; 1908 v S, W, Ni, A (2), H, B; 1909 v S, W, Ni, H (2), A; 1910 v S, W; 1911 v S, W, Ni; 1912 v S, W, Ni; 1913 v S, W, Ni; 1914 v S, W, Ni (41)
Crooks, S. D. (Derby Co), 1930 v S, G, A; 1931 v S, W, Ni, F, Bel; 1932 v S, W, Ni, Sp; 1933 v Ni, W, A; 1934 v S, Ni, W, F, H, Cz; 1935 v Ni; 1936 v S, W; 1937 v W, H (26)
Crouch, P.J. (Southampton), 2005 v Co (1)
Crowe, C. (Wolverhampton W), 1963 v F (1)
Cuggy, F. (Sunderland), 1913 v Ni; 1914 v Ni (2)
Cullis, S. (Wolverhampton W), 1938 v S, W, Ni, F, Cz; 1939 v S, Ni, R of E, N, I, R, Y (12)
Cunliffe, A. (Blackburn R), 1933 v Ni, W (2)
Cunliffe, D. (Portsmouth), 1900 v Ni (1)
Cunliffe, J. N. (Everton), 1936 v Bel (1)
Cunningham, L. (WBA), 1979 v W, Se, A (sub); (with Real Madrid), 1980 v Ei, Sp (sub); 1981 v R (sub) (6)
Curle, K. (Manchester C), 1992 v C (sub), H, D (3)
Currey, E. S. (Oxford University), 1890 v S, W (2)
Currie, A. W. (Sheffield U), 1972 v Ni; 1973 v USSR, I; 1974 v A, Pol, I; 1976 v Sw; (with Leeds U), 1978 v Br, W (sub), Ni, S, H (sub); 1979 v Cz, Ni (2), W, Se (17)
Cursham, A. W. (Notts Co), 1876 v S; 1877 v S; 1878 v S; 1879 v W; 1883 v S, W (6)
Cursham, H. A. (Notts Co), 1880 v W; 1882 v S, W, Ni; 1883 v S, W, Ni; 1884 v Ni (8)

Daft, H. B. (Notts Co), 1889 v Ni; 1890 v S, W; 1891 v Ni; 1892 v Ni (5)
Daley, A. M. (Aston Villa), 1992 v Pol (sub), C, H, Br, Fi (sub), D (sub), Se (7)
Danks, T. (Nottingham F), 1885 v S (1)
Davenport, P. (Nottingham F), 1985 v Ei (sub) (1)
Davenport, J. K. (Bolton W), 1885 v W; 1890 v Ni (2)
Davis, G. (Derby Co), 1904 v W, Ni (2)
Davis, H. (Sheffield W), 1903 v S, W, Ni (3)
Davison, J. E. (Sheffield W), 1922 v W (1)
Dawson, J. (Burnley), 1922 v S, Ni (2)
Day, S. H. (Old Malvernians), 1906 v Ni, W, S (3)
Dean, W. R. (Everton), 1927 v S, W, F, Bel, L; 1928 v S, W, Ni, F, Bel; 1929 v S, W, Ni; 1931 v S; 1932 v Sp; 1933 v Ni (16)
Deane, B. C. (Sheffield U), 1991 v Nz (sub + 1); 1993 v Sp (sub) (3)
Deeley, N. V. (Wolverhampton W), 1959 v Br, Pe (2)
Defoe, J. C. (Tottenham H), 2004 v Se (sub), Ic (sub); 2005 v Uk (sub), A (sub), Pol, W, Az, Sp (sub), Ni (sub), Az (sub), US (sub), Co (sub) (12)
Devey, J. H. G. (Aston Villa), 1892 v Ni; 1894 v Ni (2)
Devonshire, A. (West Ham U), 1980 v Aus (sub), Ni; 1982 v Ho, Ic; 1983 v WG, W, Gr; 1984 v L (8)
Dewhurst, F. (Preston NE), 1886 v W, Ni; 1887 v S, W, Ni; 1888 v S, W, Ni; 1889 v W (9)
Dewhurst, G. P. (Liverpool Ramblers), 1895 v W (1)
Dickinson, J. W. (Portsmouth), 1949 v N, F; 1950 v S, W, Ei, P, Bel, Ch, US, Sp; 1951 v Ni, W, Y; 1952 v W, Ni, S, A (2), I, Sw; 1953 v W, Ni, S, Bel, Arg, Ch, U, US; 1954 v W, Ni, S, R of E, H (2), Y, Bel, Sw, U; 1955 v Sp, P; 1956 v W, Ni, S, D, Sp; 1957 v W, Y, D (48)
Dimmock, J. H. (Tottenham H), 1921 v S; 1926 v W, Bel (3)
Ditchburn, E. G. (Tottenham H), 1949 v Sw, Se; 1953 v US; 1957 v W, Y, D (6)
Dix, R. W. (Derby Co), 1939 v N (1)
Dixon, J. A. (Notts Co), 1885 v W (1)
Dixon, K. M. (Chelsea), 1985 v M (sub), WG, US; 1986 v Ni, Is, M (sub), Pol (sub); 1987 v Se (8)
Dixon, L. M. (Arsenal), 1990 v Cz; 1991 v H, Pol, Ei (2), Cam, T, Arg; 1992 v G, T, Pol, Cz (sub); 1993 v Sp, N, T, Sm, T, Ho, N, US; 1994 v Sm; 1999 v F (22)
Dobson, A. T. C. (Notts Co), 1882 v Ni; 1884 v S, W, Ni (4)
Dobson, C. F. (Notts Co), 1886 v Ni (1)
Dobson, J. M. (Burnley), 1974 v P, EG, Bul, Y; (with Everton), 1975 v Cz (5)
Doggart, A. G. (Corinthians), 1924 v Bel (1)
Dorigo, A. R. (Chelsea), 1990 v Y (sub), Cz (sub), D (sub), I; 1991 v H (sub), USSR; (with Leeds U), 1992 v G, Cz (sub), H, Br; 1993 v Sm, Pol, US, Br; 1994 v Ho (15)
Dorrell, A. R. (Aston Villa), 1925 v W, Bel, F; 1926 v Ni (4)
Douglas, B. (Blackburn R), 1958 v S, W, Ni, F, P, Y, USSR (2), Br, A; 1959 v S, USSR; 1960 v Y, H; 1961 v Ni, W, S, L, P, Sp, M, I, A; 1962 v W, Ni, S, Pe, L, P, H, Arg, Bul, Br; 1963 v S, Br, Sw (36)
Downing, S. (Middlesbrough), 2005 v Ho (sub) (1)
Downs, R. W. (Everton), 1921 v Ni (1)
Doyle, M. (Manchester C), 1976 v W, S (sub), Br, I; 1977 v Ho (5)
Drake, E. J. (Arsenal), 1935 v Ni, I; 1936 v W; 1937 v H; 1938 v F (5)
Dublin, D. (Coventry C), 1998 v Ch, Mor, Bel (sub); (with Aston Villa), 1999 v CzR (4)
Ducat, A. (Woolwich Arsenal), 1910 v S, W, Ni; (with Aston Villa), 1920 v S, W; 1921 v Ni (6)
Dunn, A. T. B. (Cambridge University), 1883 v Ni; 1884 v Ni; (with Old Etonians), 1892 v S, W (4)
Dunn, D. J. I. (Blackburn R), 2003 v P (sub) (1)

Duxbury, M. (Manchester U), 1984 v L, F, W, S, USSR, Br, U, Ch; 1985 v EG, Fi (10)
Dyer, K. C. (Newcastle U), 2000 v L, Pol (sub), Bel, Arg, Uk (sub); 2001 v F (sub), G (sub), I; 2002 v Para, Se (sub), D (sub), Br (sub); 2003 v Slo (sub), Aus, Lie, T (sub); 2004 v Cro (sub), Mac (sub), T (sub), P (sub), J (sub), Ic (sub), Sw (sub); 2005 v Uk (sub), Pol (sub), Ho (sub), Ni (sub), Az (sub) (28)

Earle, S. G. J. (Clapton), 1924 v F; (with West Ham U), 1928 v Ni (2)
Eastham, G. (Arsenal), 1963 v Br, Cz, EG; 1964 v W, Ni, S, R of W, U, P, Ei, US, Br, Arg; 1965 v H, WG, Se; 1966 v Sp, Pol, D (19)
Eastham, G. R. (Bolton W), 1935 v Ho (1)
Eckersley, W. (Blackburn R), 1950 v Sp; 1951 v S, Y, Arg, P; 1952 v A (2), Sw; 1953 v Ni, Arg, Ch, U, US; 1954 v W, Ni, R of E, H (17)
Edwards, D. (Manchester U), 1955 v S, F, Sp, P; 1956 v S, Br, Se, Fi, WG; 1957 v S, Ni, Ei (2), D (2); 1958 v W, Ni, F (18)
Edwards, J. H. (Shropshire Wanderers), 1874 v S (1)
Edwards, W. (Leeds U), 1926 v S, W; 1927 v W, Ni, S, F, Bel, L; 1928 v S, F, Bel; 1929 v S, W, Ni; 1930 v W, Ni (16)
Ehiogu, U. (Aston Villa), 1996 v Chn (sub); (with Middlesbrough), 2001 v Sp (sub); 2002 v Ho (sub), I (sub) (4)
Ellerington, W. (Southampton), 1949 v N, F (2)
Elliott, G. W. (Middlesbrough), 1913 v Ni; 1914 v Ni; 1920 v W (3)
Elliott, W. H. (Burnley), 1952 v I, A; 1953 v Ni, W, Bel (5)
Evans, R. E. (Sheffield U), 1911 v S, W, Ni; 1912 v W (4)
Ewer, F. H. (Casuals), 1924 v F; 1925 v Bel (2)

Fairclough, P. (Old Foresters), 1878 v S (1)
Fairhurst, D. (Newcastle U), 1934 v F (1)
Fantham, J. (Sheffield W), 1962 v L (1)
Fashanu, J. (Wimbledon), 1989 v Ch, S (2)
Felton, W. (Sheffield W), 1925 v F (1)
Fenton, M. (Middlesbrough), 1938 v S (1)
Fenwick, T. (QPR), 1984 v W (sub), S, USSR, Br, U, Ch; 1985 v Fi, S, M, US; 1986 v R, T, Ni, Eg, M, P, Mor, Pol, Arg; (with Tottenham H), 1988 v Is (sub) (20)
Ferdinand, L. (QPR), 1993 v Sm, Ho, N, US; 1994 v Pol, Sm; 1995 v US (sub); (with Newcastle U), 1996 v P, Bul, H; 1997 v Pol, Ge, I (sub); (with Tottenham H), 1998 v Mol, S.Ar (sub), Mor (sub), Bel (17)
Ferdinand, R. G. (West Ham U), 1998 v Cam (sub), Sw, Bel (sub); 1999 v L, CzR, F (sub), H, Se (sub); 2000 v Arg (sub); 2001 v I; (with Leeds U), Sp, Fi, Alb, M, Gr; 2002 v G, Alb, Gr, Se, Ho, Sk, Cam, Se, Arg, Ng, D, Br; (with Manchester U), 2003 v P, Aus, Lie, T, S.Af ; 2004 v Cro; 2005 v W, Az, Sp, Ni, Az (38)
Field, E. (Clapham Rovers), 1876 v S; 1881 v S (2)
Finney, T. (Preston NE), 1947 v W, Ni, Ei, Ho, F, P; 1948 v S, W, Ni, Bel, Se, I; 1949 v S, W, Ni, Se, N, F; 1950 v S, W, Ni, Ei, I, P, Bel, Ch, US, Sp; 1951 v W, S, Arg, P; 1952 v W, Ni, S, F, I, Sw, A; 1953 v W, Ni, S, Bel, Arg, Ch, U, US; 1954 v W, S, Bel, Sw, U, H, Y; 1955 v WG; 1956 v S, W, Ni, D, Sp; 1957 v S, W, Y, D (2), Ei (2); 1958 v W, S, F, P, Y, USSR (2); 1959 v Ni, USSR (76)
Fleming, H. J. (Swindon T), 1909 v S, H (2); 1910 v W, Ni; 1911 v W, Ni; 1912 v Ni; 1913 v S, W; 1914 v S (11)
Fletcher, A. (Wolverhampton W), 1889 v W; 1890 v W (2)
Flowers, R. (Wolverhampton W), 1955 v F; 1959 v S, W, I, Br, Pe, US, M (sub); 1960 v W, Ni, S, Se, Y, Sp, H; 1961 v Ni, W, S, L, P, Sp, M, I, A; 1962 v W, Ni, S, A, Sw, Pe, L, P, H, Arg, Bul, Br; 1963 v Ni, W, S, F (2), Sw; 1964 v Ei, US, P; 1965 v W, Ho, WG; 1966 v N (49)
Flowers, T. D. (Southampton), 1993 v Br; (with Blackburn R), 1994 v Gr; 1995 v Ng, U, J, Se, Br; 1996 v Chn; 1997 v I; 1998 v Sw, Mor (11)
Forman, Frank (Nottingham F), 1898 v S, Ni; 1899 v S, W, Ni; 1901 v S; 1902 v S, Ni; 1903 v W (9)
Forman, F. R. (Nottingham F), 1899 v S, W, Ni (3)
Forrest, J. H. (Blackburn R), 1884 v W; 1885 v S, W, Ni; 1886 v S, W; 1887 v S, W, Ni; 1889 v S; 1890 v Ni (11)
Fort, J. (Millwall), 1921 v Bel (1)
Foster, R. E. (Oxford University), 1900 v W; (with Corinthians), 1901 v W, Ni, S; 1902 v W (5)
Foster, S. (Brighton & HA), 1982 v Ni, Ho, K (3)
Foulke, W. J. (Sheffield U), 1897 v W (1)
Foulkes, W. A. (Manchester U), 1955 v Ni (1)
Fowler, R. B. (Liverpool), 1996 v Bul (sub), Cro, Chn (sub), Ho (sub), Sp (sub); 1997 v M; 1998 v Cam; 1999 v CzR (sub), Bul; 2000 v L, Pol, Br (sub), Uk, Ma (sub); 2001 v I (sub), Fi (sub), M, Gr; 2002 v Ho, Alb (sub), Gr, Se (sub); (with Leeds U), I (sub), Para (sub), Cam (sub), D (sub) (26)
Fox, F. S. (Millwall), 1925 v F (1)
Francis, G. C. J. (QPR), 1975 v Cz, P, W, S; 1976 v Sw, Cz, P, W, Ni, S, Br, Fi (12)
Francis, T. (Birmingham C), 1977 v Ho, L, S, Br; 1978 v Sw, L, I (sub), WG (sub), Br, W, S, H; (with Nottingham F), 1979 v Bul (sub), Se, A (sub); 1980 v Ni, Bul, Sp; 1981 v Sp, R, S (sub), Sw; (with Manchester C), 1982 v N, Ni, W, S (sub), Fi (sub), F, Cz, K, WG, Sp; (with Sampdoria), 1983 v D, Gr, H, Ni, S, Aus (3); 1984 v D, Ni, USSR; 1985 v EG (sub), T (sub), Ni (sub), R, Fi, S, I, M; 1986 v S (52)
Franklin, C. F. (Stoke C), 1947 v S, W, Ni, Ei, Ho, F, Sw, P; 1948 v S, W, Ni, Bel, Se, I; 1949 v S, W, Ni, D, Sw, N, F, Se; 1950 v W, S, Ni, Ei, I (27)
Freeman, B. C. (Everton), 1909 v S, W; (with Burnley), 1912 v S, W, Ni (5)
Froggatt, J. (Portsmouth), 1950 v Ni, I; 1951 v S; 1952 v S, A (2), I, Sw; 1953 v Ni, W, S, Bel, US (13)
Froggatt, R. (Sheffield W), 1953 v W, S, Bel, US (4)
Fry, C. B. (Corinthians), 1901 v Ni (1)
Furness, W. I. (Leeds U), 1933 v I (1)

Galley, T. (Wolverhampton W), 1937 v N, Se (2)
Gardner, A. (Tottenham H), 2004 v Se (sub) (1)
Gardner, T. (Aston Villa), 1934 v Cz; 1935 v Ho (2)
Garfield, B. (WBA), 1898 v Ni (1)
Garraty, W. (Aston Villa), 1903 v W (1)
Garrett, T. (Blackpool), 1952 v S, I; 1954 v W (3)
Gascoigne, P. J. (Tottenham H), 1989 v D (sub), S.Ar (sub), Alb (sub), Ch, S (sub); 1990 v Se (sub), Br (sub), Cz, D, U, Tun, Ei, Ho, Eg, Bel, Cam, WG; 1991 v H, Pol, Cam; (with Lazio), 1993 v N, T, Sm, T, Ho, Pol, N; 1994 v Pol, D; 1995 v J (sub), Se (sub), Br (sub); (with Rangers), 1996 v Co, Sw, P, Bul, Cro, Chn, Sw, S, Ho, Sp, G; 1997 v Mol, Pol, Ge, S.Af, Pol, I (sub), F, Br; 1998 v Mol, I, Cam; (with Middlesbrough), S.Ar (sub), Mor, Bel (57)
Gates, E. (Ipswich T), 1981 v N, R (2)
Gay, L. H. (Cambridge University), 1893 v S; (with Old Brightonians), 1894 v S, W (3)
Geary, F. (Everton), 1890 v Ni; 1891 v S (2)
Geaves, R. L. (Clapham Rovers), 1875 v S (1)
Gee, C. W. (Everton), 1932 v W, Sp; 1937 v Ni (3)
Geldard, A. (Everton), 1933 v I, Sw; 1935 v S; 1938 v Ni (4)
George, C. (Derby Co), 1977 v Ei (1)
George, W. (Aston Villa), 1902 v S, W, Ni (3)
Gerrard, S. G. (Liverpool), 2000 v Uk, G (sub); 2001 v Fi, M, Gr; 2002 v G, Alb, Gr, Ho, Para; 2003 v P, Slo, Mac, Lie, T, S.Af, Ser, Slo; 2004 v Cro, Lie, T, Se, J, Ic, F, Sw, Cro, P; 2005 v Uk, A, Pol, Ho, Ni, Az (34)
Gibbins, W. V. T. (Clapton), 1924 v F; 1925 v F (2)
Gidman, J. (Aston Villa), 1977 v L (1)
Gillard, I. T. (QPR), 1975 v WG, W; 1976 v Cz (3)
Gilliat, W. E. (Old Carthusians), 1893 v Ni (1)
Goddard, P. (West Ham U), 1982 v Ic (sub) (1)
Goodall, F. R. (Huddersfield T), 1926 v S; 1927 v S, F, Bel, L; 1928 v S, W, F, Bel; 1930 v S, G, A; 1931 v S, W, Ni, Bel; 1932 v Ni; 1933 v W, Ni, A, I, Sw; 1934 v W, Ni, F (25)
Goodall, J. (Preston NE), 1888 v S, W; 1889 v S, W; (with Derby Co), 1891 v S, W; 1892 v S; 1893 v W; 1894 v S; 1895 v S, Ni; 1896 v S, W; 1898 v W (14)
Goodhart, H. C. (Old Etonians), 1883 v S, W, Ni (3)
Goodwyn, A. G. (Royal Engineers), 1873 v S (1)
Goodyer, A. C. (Nottingham F), 1879 v S (1)
Gosling, R. C. (Old Etonians), 1892 v W; 1893 v S; 1894 v W; 1895 v W, S (5)
Gosnell, A. A. (Newcastle U), 1906 v Ni (1)
Gough, H. C. (Sheffield U), 1921 v S (1)
Goulden, L. A. (West Ham U), 1937 v Se, N; 1938 v W, Ni, Cz, G, Sw, F; 1939 v S, W, R of E, I, R, Y (14)
Graham, L. (Millwall), 1925 v S, W (2)
Graham, T. (Nottingham F), 1931 v F; 1932 v Ni (2)
Grainger, C. (Sheffield U), 1956 v Br, Se, Fi, WG; 1957 v W, Ni; (with Sunderland), 1957 v S (7)
Gray, A. A. (C Palace), 1992 v Pol (1)
Gray, M. (Sunderland), 1999 v H (sub), Se (sub), Bul (3)
Greaves, J. (Chelsea), 1959 v Pe, M, US; 1960 v W, Se, Y, Sp; 1961 v Ni, W, S, L, P, Sp, I, A; (with Tottenham H), 1962 v S, Sw, Pe, H, Arg, Bul, Br; 1963 v Ni, W, S, F (2), Br, Cz, Sw; 1964 v W, Ni, R of W, P (2), Ei, Br, U, Arg; 1965 v Ni, S, Bel, Ho, H, Y; 1966 v W, A, Y, N, D, Pol, U, M, F; 1967 v S, Sp, A (57)
Green, F. T. (Wanderers), 1876 v S (1)
Green, G. H. (Sheffield U), 1925 v F; 1926 v S, Bel, W; 1927 v W, Ni; 1928 v F, Bel (8)
Green, R. P. (Norwich C), 2005 v Co (sub) (1)

Greenhalgh, E. H. (Notts Co), 1872 v S; 1873 v S (2)
Greenhoff, B. (Manchester U), 1976 v W, Ni; 1977 v Ei, Fi, I, Ho, Ni, W, S, Br, Arg, U; 1978 v Br, W, Ni, S (sub), H (sub); (with Leeds U), 1980 v Aus (sub) (18)
Greenwood, D. H. (Blackburn R), 1882 v S, Ni (2)
Gregory, J. (QPR), 1983 v Aus (3); 1984 v D, H, W (6)
Grimsdell, A. (Tottenham H), 1920 v S, W; 1921 v S, Ni; 1923 v W, Ni (6)
Grosvenor, A. T. (Birmingham), 1934 v Ni, W, F (3)
Gunn, W. (Notts Co), 1884 v S, W (2)
Guppy, S. (Leicester C), 2000 v Bel (1)
Gurney, R. (Sunderland), 1935 v S (1)

Hacking, J. (Oldham Ath), 1929 v S, W, Ni (3)
Hadley, H. (WBA), 1903 v Ni (1)
Hagan, J. (Sheffield U), 1949 v D (1)
Haines, J. T. W. (WBA), 1949 v Sw (1)
Hall, A. E. (Aston Villa), 1910 v Ni (1)
Hall, G. W. (Tottenham H), 1934 v F; 1938 v S, W, Ni, Cz; 1939 v S, Ni, R of E, I, Y (10)
Hall, J. (Birmingham C), 1956 v S, W, Ni, Br, Se, Fi, WG, D, Sp; 1957 v S, W, Ni, Y, D (2), Ei (2) (17)
Halse, H. J. (Manchester U), 1909 v A (1)
Hammond, H. E. D. (Oxford University), 1889 v S (1)
Hampson, J. (Blackpool), 1931 v Ni, W; 1933 v A (3)
Hampton, H. (Aston Villa), 1913 v S, W; 1914 v S, W (4)
Hancocks, J. (Wolverhampton W), 1949 v Sw; 1950 v W; 1951 v Y (3)
Hapgood, E. (Arsenal), 1933 v I, Sw; 1934 v S, Ni, W, H, Cz; 1935 v S, Ni, W, I, Ho; 1936 v S, Ni, W, G, A, Bel; 1937 v Fi; 1938 v S, G, Sw, F; 1939 v S, W, Ni, R of E, N, I, Y (30)
Hardinge, H. T. W. (Sheffield U), 1910 v S (1)
Hardman, H. P. (Everton), 1905 v W; 1907 v S, Ni; 1908 v W (4)
Hardwick, G. F. M. (Middlesbrough), 1947 v S, W, Ni, Ei, Ho, F, Sw, P; 1948 v S, W, Ni, Bel, Se (13)
Hardy, H. (Stockport Co), 1925 v Bel (1)
Hardy, S. (Liverpool), 1907 v S, W, Ni; 1908 v S; 1909 v S, W, Ni, H (2), A; 1910 v S, W, Ni; 1912 v Ni; (with Aston Villa), 1913 v S; 1914 v Ni, W, S; 1920 v S, W, Ni (21)
Harford, M. G. (Luton T), 1988 v Is (sub); 1989 v D (2)
Hargreaves, F. W. (Blackburn R), 1880 v W; 1881 v W; 1882 v Ni (3)
Hargreaves, J. (Blackburn R), 1881 v S, W (2)
Hargreaves, O. (Bayern Munich) 2002 v Ho, G (sub), I (sub), Para (sub), Sk, Cam, Se, Arg; 2003 v P (sub), Slo (sub), Aus (sub), Ser (sub), Slo (sub); 2004 v Mac, Lie (sub), P (sub), Se, J (sub), Ic (sub), F (sub), Sw (sub), P (sub); 2005 v Pol (sub), W (sub), Ho (sub), Ni (sub) (26)
Harper, E. C. (Blackburn R), 1926 v S (1)
Harris, G. (Burnley), 1966 v Pol (1)
Harris, P. P. (Portsmouth), 1950 v Ei; 1954 v H (2)
Harris, S. S. (Cambridge University), 1904 v S; (with Old Westminsters), 1905 v Ni, W; 1906 v S, W, Ni (6)
Harrison, A. H. (Old Westminsters), 1893 v S, Ni (2)
Harrison, G. (Everton), 1921 v Bel; 1922 v Ni (2)
Harrow, J. H. (Chelsea), 1923 v Ni, Se (2)
Hart, E. (Leeds U), 1929 v W; 1930 v W, Ni; 1933 v S, A; 1934 v S, H, Cz (8)
Hartley, F. (Oxford C), 1923 v F (1)
Harvey, A. (Wednesbury Strollers), 1881 v W (1)
Harvey, J. C. (Everton), 1971 v Ma (1)
Hassall, H. W. (Huddersfield T), 1951 v S, Arg, P; 1952 v F; (with Bolton W), 1954 v Ni (5)
Hateley, M. (Portsmouth), 1984 v USSR (sub), Br, U, Ch; (with AC Milan), 1985 v EG (sub), Fi, Ni, Ei, Fi, S, I, M; 1986 v R, T, Eg, S, M, Ca, P, Mor, Para (sub); 1987 v T (sub), Br (sub), S; (with Monaco), 1988 v WG (sub), Ho (sub), H (sub), Co (sub), Ei (sub), Ho (sub), USSR (sub); (with Rangers), 1992 v Cz (32)
Hawkes, R. M. (Luton T), 1907 v Ni; 1908 v A (2), H, B (5)
Haworth, G. (Accrington), 1887 v Ni, W, S; 1888 v S; 1890 v S (5)
Hawtrey, J. P. (Old Etonians), 1881 v S, W (2)
Haygarth, E. B. (Swifts), 1875 v S (1)
Haynes, J. N. (Fulham), 1955 v Ni; 1956 v S, Ni, Br, Se, Fi, WG, Sp; 1957 v W, Y, D, Ei (2); 1958 v W, Ni, S, F, P, Y, USSR (3), Br, A; 1959 v S, Ni, USSR, I, Br, Pe, M, US; 1960 v Ni, Y, Sp, H; 1961 v Ni, W, S, L, P, Sp, M, I, A; 1962 v W, Ni, S, A, Sw, Pe, P, H, Arg, Bul, Br (56)
Healless, H. (Blackburn R), 1925 v Ni; 1928 v S (2)
Hector, K. J. (Derby Co), 1974 v Pol (sub), I (sub) (2)
Hedley, G. A. (Sheffield U), 1901 v Ni (1)
Hegan, K. E. (Corinthians), 1923 v Bel, F; 1924 v Ni, Bel (4)
Hellawell, M. S. (Birmingham C), 1963 v Ni, F (2)
Hendrie, L. A. (Aston Villa), 1999 v CzR (sub) (1)
Henfrey, A. G. (Cambridge University), 1891 v Ni; (with Corinthians), 1892 v W; 1895 v W; 1896 v S, W (5)
Henry, R. P. (Tottenham H), 1963 v F (1)
Heron, F. (Wanderers), 1876 v S (1)
Heron, G. H. H. (Uxbridge), 1873 v S; 1874 v S; (with Wanderers), 1875 v S; 1876 v S; 1878 v S (5)
Heskey, E. W. (Leicester C), 1999 v H (sub), Bul (sub); 2000 v Bel (sub), S (sub), Arg; (with Liverpool), Uk (sub), Ma (sub), P (sub), R (sub); 2001 v Fi, I, Sp (sub), Fi (sub), Alb (sub), M, Gr; 2002 v G, Alb, Gr, Se, Ho, I, Sk, Cam, Se, Arg, Ng, D, Br; 2003 v P, Slo, Lie, S.Af, Ser; 2004 v Cro, Mac (sub), T, D, P (sub), Se (sub); (with Birmingham C), J (sub), Ic (sub), F (sub) (43)
Hibbert, W. (Bury), 1910 v S (1)
Hibbs, H. E. (Birmingham), 1930 v S, W, A, G; 1931 v S, W, Ni; 1932 v W, Ni, Sp; 1933 v S, W, Ni, A, I, Sw; 1934 v Ni, W, F; 1935 v S, W, Ni, Ho; 1936 v G, W (25)
Hill, F. (Bolton W), 1963 v Ni, W (2)
Hill, G. A. (Manchester U), 1976 v I; 1977 v Ei (sub), Fi (sub), L; 1978 v Sw (sub), L (6)
Hill, J. H. (Burnley), 1925 v W; 1926 v S; 1927 v S, Ni, Bel, F; 1928 v Ni, W; (with Newcastle U), 1929 v F, Bel, Sp (11)
Hill, R. (Luton T), 1983 v D (sub), WG; 1986 v Eg (sub) (3)
Hill, R. H. (Millwall), 1926 v Bel (1)
Hillman, J. (Burnley), 1899 v Ni (1)
Hills, A. F. (Old Harrovians), 1879 v S (1)
Hilsdon, G. R. (Chelsea), 1907 v Ni; 1908 v S, W, Ni, A, H, B; 1909 v Ni (8)
Hinchcliffe, A. G. (Everton), 1997 v Mol, Pol, Ge; 1998 v Cam; (with Sheffield W), Sw, S.Ar; 1999 v Bul (7)
Hine, E. W. (Leicester C), 1929 v W, Ni; 1930 v W, Ni; 1932 v W, Ni (6)
Hinton, A. T. (Wolverhampton W), 1963 v F; (with Nottingham F), 1965 v W, Bel (3)
Hirst, D. E. (Sheffield W), 1991 v Aus, Nz (sub); 1992 v F (3)
Hitchens, G. A. (Aston Villa), 1961 v M, I, A; (with Inter-Milan), 1962 v Sw, Pe, H, Br (7)
Hobbis, H. H. F. (Charlton Ath), 1936 v A, Bel (2)
Hoddle, G. (Tottenham H), 1980 v Bul, W, Aus, Sp; 1981 v Sp, W, S; 1982 v N, Ni, W, Ic, Cz (sub), K; 1983 v L (sub), Ni, S; 1984 v H, L, F; 1985 v Ei (sub), S, I (sub), M, WG, US; 1986 v R, T, Ni, Is, USSR, S, M, Ca, P, Mor, Pol, Para, Arg; 1987 v Se, Ni, Y, Sp, T, S; (with Monaco), 1988 v WG, T (sub), Y (sub), Ho (sub), H (sub), Co (sub), Ei (sub), Ho, USSR (53)
Hodge, S. B. (Aston Villa), 1986 v USSR (sub), S, Ca, P (sub), Mor (sub), Pol, Para, Arg; 1987 v Se, Ni, Y; (with Tottenham H), Sp, Ni, T, S; (with Nottingham F), 1989 v D; 1990 v I (sub), Y (sub), Cz, D, U, Tun; 1991 v Cam (sub), T (sub) (24)
Hodgetts, D. (Aston Villa), 1888 v S, W, Ni; 1892 v S, Ni; 1894 v Ni (6)
Hodgkinson, A. (Sheffield U), 1957 v S, Ei (2), D; 1961 v W (5)
Hodgson, G. (Liverpool), 1931 v S, Ni, W (3)
Hodkinson, J. (Blackburn R), 1913 v W, S; 1920 v Ni (3)
Hogg, W. (Sunderland), 1902 v S, W, Ni (3)
Holdcroft, G. H. (Preston NE), 1937 v W, Ni (2)
Holden, A. D. (Bolton W), 1959 v S, I, Br, Pe, M (5)
Holden, G. H. (Wednesbury OA), 1881 v S; 1884 v S, W, Ni (4)
Holden-White, C. (Corinthians), 1888 v W, S (2)
Holford, T. (Stoke), 1903 v Ni (1)
Holley, G. H. (Sunderland), 1909 v S, W, H (2), A; 1910 v W; 1912 v S, W, Ni; 1913 v S (10)
Holliday, E. (Middlesbrough), 1960 v W, Ni, Se (3)
Hollins, J. W. (Chelsea), 1967 v Sp (1)
Holmes, R. (Preston NE), 1888 v Ni; 1891 v S; 1892 v S; 1893 v S, W; 1894 v Ni; 1895 v Ni (7)
Holt, J. (Everton), 1890 v W; 1891 v S, W; 1892 v S, Ni; 1893 v S; 1894 v S, Ni; 1895 v S; (with Reading), 1900 v Ni (10)
Hopkinson, E. (Bolton W), 1958 v W, Ni, S, F, P, Y; 1959 v S, I, Br, Pe, M, US; 1960 v W, Se (14)
Hossack, A. H. (Corinthians), 1892 v W; 1894 v W (2)
Houghton, W. E. (Aston Villa), 1931 v Ni, W, F, Bel; 1932 v S, Ni; 1933 v A (7)
Houlker, A. E. (Blackburn R), 1902 v S; (with Portsmouth), 1903 v S, W; (with Southampton), 1906 v W, Ni (5)
Howarth, R. H. (Preston NE), 1887 v Ni; 1888 v S, W; 1891 v S; (with Everton), 1894 v Ni (5)
Howe, D. (WBA), 1958 v S, W, Ni, F, P, Y, USSR (3), Br, A; 1959 v S, W, Ni, USSR, I, Br, Pe, M, US; 1960 v W, Ni, Se (23)
Howe, J. R. (Derby Co), 1948 v I; 1949 v S, Ni (3)
Howell, L. S. (Wanderers), 1873 v S (1)
Howell, R. (Sheffield U), 1895 v Ni; (with Liverpool) 1899 v S (2)

Howey, S. N. (Newcastle U), 1995 v Ng; 1996 v Co, P, Bul (4)
Hudson, A. A. (Stoke C), 1975 v WG, Cy (2)
Hudson, J. (Sheffield), 1883 v Ni (1)
Hudspeth, F. C. (Newcastle U), 1926 v Ni (1)
Hufton, A. E. (West Ham U), 1924 v Bel; 1928 v S, Ni; 1929 v F, Bel, Sp (6)
Hughes, E. W. (Liverpool), 1970 v W, Ni, S, Ho, P, Bel; 1971 v EG, Ma (2), Gr, W; 1972 v Sw, Gr, WG (2), W, Ni, S; 1973 v W (3), S (2), Pol, USSR, I; 1974 v A, Pol, I, W, Ni, S, Arg, EG, Bul, Y; 1975 v Cz, P, Cy (sub), Ni; 1977 v I, L, W, S, Br, Arg, U; 1978 v Sw, L, I, WG, Ni, S, H; 1979 v D, Ei, Ni, W, Se; (with Wolverhampton W), 1980 v Sp (sub), Ni, S (sub) (62)
Hughes, L. (Liverpool), 1950 v Ch, US, Sp (3)
Hulme, J. H. A. (Arsenal), 1927 v S, Bel, F; 1928 v S, Ni, W; 1929 v Ni, W; 1933 v S (9)
Humphreys, P. (Notts Co), 1903 v S (1)
Hunt, G. S. (Tottenham H), 1933 v I, Sw, S (3)
Hunt, Rev K. R. G. (Leyton), 1911 v S, W (2)
Hunt, R. (Liverpool), 1962 v A; 1963 v EG; 1964 v S, US, P; 1965 v W; 1966 v S, Sp, Pol (2), WG (2), Fi, N, U, M, F, Arg, P; 1967 v Ni, W, Cz, Sp, A; 1968 v W, Ni, USSR (2), Sp (2), Se, Y; 1969 v R (2) (34)
Hunt, S. (WBA), 1984 v S (sub), USSR (sub) (2)
Hunter, J. (Sheffield Heeley), 1878 v S; 1880 v S, W; 1881 v S, W; 1882 v S, W (7)
Hunter, N. (Leeds U), 1966 v WG, Y, Fi, Sp (sub); 1967 v A; 1968 v Sp, Se, Y, WG, USSR; 1969 v R, W; 1970 v Ho, WG (sub); 1971 v Ma; 1972 v WG (2), W, Ni, S; 1973 v W (2) USSR (sub); 1974 v A, Pol, Ni (sub), S; 1975 v Cz (28)
Hurst, G. C. (West Ham U), 1966 v S, WG (2), Y, Fi, D, Arg, P; 1967 v Ni, W, S, Cz, Sp, A; 1968 v W, Ni, S, Se (sub), WG, USSR (2); 1969 v Ni, S, R (2), Bul, F, M, U, Br; 1970 v W, Ni, S, Ho (1+1 sub), Bel, Co, Ec, R, Br, WG; 1971 v EG, Gr, W, S; 1972 v Sw (2), Gr, WG (49)

Ince, P. E. C. (Manchester U), 1993 v Sp, N, T (2), Ho, Pol, US, Br, G; 1994 v Pol, Ho, Sm, D, N; 1995 v R, Ei; (with Internazionale), 1996 v Bul, Cro, H, Sw, S, Ho, G; 1997 v Mol, Pol, Ge, I, M, Ge, Pol, I, F (sub), Br; (with Liverpool), 1998 v I, Cam, Ch (sub), Sw, P, Mor, Tun, R, Co, Arg; 1999 v Se, F; (with Middlesbrough), 2000 v Bel, S (2), Br, Ma (sub), P, G, R (53)
Iremonger, J. (Nottingham F), 1901 v S; 1902 v Ni (2)

Jack, D. N. B. (Bolton W), 1924 v S, W; 1928 v F, Bel; (with Arsenal), 1930 v S, G, A; 1933 v W, A (9)
Jackson, E. (Oxford University), 1891 v W (1)
James. D. B. (Liverpool), 1997 v M; (with Aston Villa), 2001 v I, Sp, M (sub); (with West Ham U), 2002 v Ho (sub + sub), I (sub), Sk (sub), Cam (sub); 2003 v P, Aus, Lie, T, S.Af, Ser, Slo; 2004 v Cro, Mac, Lie, T, D; (with Manchester C), P, Se, J, F, Sw, Cro, P; 2005 v Uk, A, US, Co (32)
Jarrett, B. G. (Cambridge University), 1876 v S; 1877 v S; 1878 v S (3)
Jefferis, F. (Everton), 1912 v S, W (2)
Jeffers, F. (Arsenal), 2003 v Aus (sub) (1)
Jenas, J. A. (Newcastle U), 2003 v Aus (sub), S.Af (sub), Ser (sub); 2004 v D (sub), P (sub), Se (sub); 2005 v Uk (sub), Az, Sp (sub), Ho (sub), US, Co (12)
Jezzard, B. A. G. (Fulham), 1954 v H; 1956 v Ni (2)
Johnson, A. (C Palace), 2005 v Ho (sub), US (2)
Johnson, D. E. (Ipswich T), 1975 v W, S; 1976 v Sw; (with Liverpool), 1980 v Ei, Arg, Ni, S, Bel (8)
Johnson, E. (Saltley College), 1880 v W; (with Stoke C), 1884 v Ni (2)
Johnson, G. M. C. (Chelsea), 2004 v D (sub); 2005 v Uk (sub), US, Co (4)
Johnson, J. A. (Stoke C), 1937 v N, Se, Fi, S, Ni (5)
Johnson, S. A. M. (Derby Co), 2001 v I (sub) (1)
Johnson, T. C. F. (Manchester C), 1926 v Bel; 1930 v W; (with Everton), 1932 v S, Sp; 1933 v Ni (5)
Johnson, W. H. (Sheffield U), 1900 v S, W, Ni; 1903 v S, W, Ni (6)
Johnston, H. (Blackpool), 1947 v S, Ho; 1951 v S; 1953 v Arg, Ch, U, US; 1954 v W, Ni, H (10)
Jones, A. (Walsall Swifts), 1882 v S, W; (with Great Lever), 1883 v S (3)
Jones, H. (Blackburn R), 1927 v S, Bel, L, F; 1928 v S, Ni (6)
Jones, H. (Nottingham F), 1923 v F (1)
Jones, M. D. (Sheffield U), 1965 v WG, Se; (with Leeds U), 1970 v Ho (3)
Jones, R. (Liverpool), 1992 v F; 1994 v Pol, Gr, N; 1995 v US, R, Ng, U (8)
Jones, W. (Bristol C), 1901 v Ni (1)
Jones, W. H. (Liverpool), 1950 v P, Bel (2)

Joy, B. (Casuals), 1936 v Bel (1)

Kail, E. I. L. (Dulwich Hamlet), 1929 v F, Bel, Sp (3)
Kay, A. H. (Everton), 1963 v Sw (1)
Kean, F. W. (Sheffield W), 1923 v S, Bel; 1924 v W; 1925 v Ni; 1926 v Ni, Bel; 1927 v L; (with Bolton W), 1929 v F, Sp (9)
Keegan, J. K. (Liverpool), 1973 v W (2); 1974 v W, Ni, Arg, EG, Bul, Y; 1975 v Cz, WG, Cy (2), Ni, S; 1976 v Sw, Cz, P, W (2), Ni, S, Br, Fi; 1977 v Ei, Fi, I, Ho, L; (with SV Hamburg), W, Br, Arg, U; 1978 v Sw, I, WG, Br, H; 1979 v D, Ei, Cz, Ni, W, S, Bul, Se, A; 1980 v D, Ni, Ei, Sp (2), Arg, Bel, I; (with Southampton), 1981 v Sp, Sw, H; 1982 v N, H, Ni, S, Fi, Sp (sub) (63)
Keen, E. R. L. (Derby Co), 1933 v A; 1937 v W, Ni, H (4)
Kelly, R. (Burnley), 1920 v S; 1921 v S, W, Ni; 1922 v S, W; 1923 v S; 1924 v Ni; 1925 v W, Ni, S; (with Sunderland), 1926 v W; (with Huddersfield T), 1927 v L; 1928 v S (14)
Kennedy, A. (Liverpool), 1984 v Ni, W (2)
Kennedy, R. (Liverpool), 1976 v W (2), Ni, S; 1977 v L, W, S, Br (sub), Arg (sub); 1978 v Sw, L; 1980 v Bul, Sp, Arg, W, Bel (sub), I (17)
Kenyon-Slaney, W. S. (Wanderers), 1873 v S (1)
Keown, M. R. (Everton), 1992 v F, Cz, C, H, Br, Fi, D, F, Se; (with Arsenal), 1993 v Ho, G (sub); 1997 v M, S.Af, I, Br; 1998 v Sw, Mor, Bel; 1999 v CzR, F, Pol, H, Se; 2000 v L, Pol, Bel, S, Arg, Br, Ma, P (sub), G, R; 2001 v F, G, Fi, M, Gr; 2002 v Ho, Gr, Para, Sk (sub), Cam (sub) (43)
Kevan, D. T. (WBA), 1957 v S; 1958 v W, Ni, S, P. Y, USSR (3), Br, A; 1959 v M, US; 1961 v M (14)
Kidd, B. (Manchester U), 1970 v Ni, Ec (sub) (2)
King, L. B. (Tottenham H), 2002 v I (sub); 2003 v Aus (sub); 2004 v P, J (sub), Ic (sub), F, Cro (sub); 2005 v Uk, A, Pol, W (sub), Az (sub) (12)
King, R. S. (Oxford University), 1882 v Ni (1)
Kingsford, R. K. (Wanderers), 1874 v S (1)
Kingsley, M. (Newcastle U), 1901 v W (1)
Kinsey, G. (Wolverhampton W), 1892 v W; 1893 v S; (with Derby Co), 1896 v W, Ni (4)
Kirchen, A. J. (Arsenal), 1937 v N, Se, Fi (3)
Kirton, W. J. (Aston Villa), 1922 v Ni (1)
Knight, A. E. (Portsmouth), 1920 v Ni (1)
Knight, Z. (Fulham), 2005 v US (sub), Co (2)
Knowles, C. (Tottenham H), 1968 v USSR, Sp, Se, WG (4)
Konchesky, P. M. (Charlton Ath), 2003 v Aus (sub) (1)

Labone, B. L. (Everton), 1963 v Ni, W, F; 1967 v Sp, A; 1968 v S, Sp, Se, Y, USSR, WG; 1969 v Ni, S, R, Bul, M, U, Br; 1970 v S, W, Bel, Co, Ec, R, Br, WG (26)
Lampard, F. J. (West Ham U), 2000 v Bel; 2001 v Sp (sub); (with Chelsea), 2002 v Ho (sub), Se (sub), Ho (sub), I, Para (sub); 2003 v Aus, S.Af (sub), Ser, Slo; 2004 v Cro (sub), Mac, Lie, T (sub), D, P, J, Ic, F, Sw, Cro, P; 2005 v Uk, A, Pol, W, Az, Sp, Ho, Ni, Az (32)
Lampard, F. R. G. (West Ham U), 1973 v Y; 1980 v Aus (2)
Langley, E. J. (Fulham), 1958 v S, P, Y (3)
Langton, R. (Blackburn R), 1947 v W, Ni, Ei, Ho, F, Sw; 1948 v Se; (with Preston NE), 1949 v D, Se; (with Bolton W), 1950 v S; 1951 v Ni (11)
Latchford, R. D. (Everton), 1978 v I, Br, W; 1979 v D, Ei, Cz (sub), Ni (2), W, S, Bul, A (12)
Latheron, E. G. (Blackburn R), 1913 v W; 1914 v Ni (2)
Lawler, C. (Liverpool), 1971 v Ma, W, S; 1972 v Sw (4)
Lawton, T. (Everton), 1939 v S, W, Ni, R of E, N, I, R, Y; (with Chelsea), 1947 v S, W, Ni, Ei, Ho, F, Sw, P; 1948 v W, Ni, Bel; (with Notts Co), 1948 v S, Se, I; 1949 v D (23)
Leach, T. (Sheffield W), 1931 v W, Ni (2)
Leake, A. (Aston Villa), 1904 v S, Ni; 1905 v S, W, Ni (5)
Lee, E. A. (Southampton), 1904 v W (1)
Lee, F. H. (Manchester C), 1969 v Ni, W, S, Bul, F, M, U; 1970 v W, Ho (2), P, Bel, Co, Ec, R, Br, WG; 1971 v EG, Gr, Ma, Ni, W, S; 1972 v Sw (2), Gr, WG (27)
Lee, J. (Derby Co), 1951 v Ni (1)
Lee, R. M. (Newcastle U), 1995 v R, Ng; 1996 v Co (sub), N, Sw, Bul (sub), H; 1997 v M, Ge, S.Af, Pol, F (sub), Br (sub); 1998 v Cam (sub), Ch, Sw, Bel, Co (sub); 1999 v Se (sub), Bul, L (sub) (21)
Lee, S. (Liverpool), 1983 v Gr, L, W, Gr, H, S, Aus; 1984 v D, H, L, F, Ni, W, Ch (sub) (14)
Leighton, J. E. (Nottingham F), 1886 v Ni (1)
Le Saux, G. P. (Blackburn R), 1994 v D, Gr, N; 1995 v US, R, Ng, Ei, U, Se, Br; 1996 v Co, P (sub); 1997 v I, M, Ge, S.Af, Pol, I, F, Br; (with Chelsea), 1998 v I, Ch (sub), P, Mor, Bel, Tun, R, Co, Arg; 1999 v Se, Bul (sub), CzR, F, Pol, Se; 2001 v G (36)
Le Tissier, M. P. (Southampton), 1994 v D (sub), Gr (sub), N (sub); 1995 v R, Ng (sub), Ei; 1997 v Mol (sub), I (8)

Lilley, H. E. (Sheffield U), 1892 v W (1)
Linacre, H. J. (Nottingham F), 1905 v W, S (2)
Lindley, T. (Cambridge University), 1886 v S, W, Ni; 1887 v S, W, Ni; 1888 v S, W, Ni; (with Nottingham F), 1889 v S; 1890 v S, W; 1891 v Ni (13)
Lindsay, A. (Liverpool), 1974 v Arg, EG, Bul, Y (4)
Lindsay, W. (Wanderers), 1877 v S (1)
Lineker, G. (Leicester C), 1984 v S (sub); 1985 v Ei, R (sub), S (sub), I (sub), WG, US; (with Everton), 1986 v R, T, Ni, Eg, USSR, Ca, P, Mor, Pol, Para, Arg; (with Barcelona), 1987 v Ni (2), Y, Sp, T, Br; 1988 v WG, T, Y, Ho, H, S, Co, Sw, Ei, Ho, USSR; 1989 v Se, S.Ar, Gr, Alb (2), Pol, D; (with Tottenham H), 1990 v Se, Pol, I, Y, Br, Cz, D, U, Tun, Ei, Ho, Eg, Bel, Cam, WG, I; 1991 v H, Pol, Ei (2), Cam, T, Arg, Aus, Nz, Mal; 1992 v G, T, Pol, F (sub), Cz (sub), C, H, Br, Fi, D, F, Se (80)
Lintott, E. H. (QPR), 1908 v S, W, Ni; (with Bradford C), 1909 v S, Ni, H (2) (7)
Lipsham, H. B. (Sheffield U), 1902 v W (1)
Little, B. (Aston Villa), 1975 v W (sub) (1)
Lloyd, L. V. (Liverpool), 1971 v W; 1972 v Sw, Ni; (with Nottingham F), 1980 v W (4)
Lockett, A. (Stoke C), 1903 v Ni (1)
Lodge, L. V. (Cambridge University), 1894 v W; 1895 v S, W; (with Corinthians), 1896 v S, Ni (5)
Lofthouse, J. M. (Blackburn R), 1885 v S, W, Ni; 1887 v S, W; (with Accrington), 1889 v Ni; (with Blackburn R), 1890 v Ni (7)
Lofthouse, N. (Bolton W), 1951 v Y; 1952 v W, Ni, S, A (2), I, Sw; 1953 v W, Ni, S, Bel, Arg, Ch, U, US; 1954 v W, Ni, R of E, Bel, U; 1955 v Ni, S, F, Sp, P; 1956 v W, S, Sp, D, Fi (sub); 1959 v W, USSR (33)
Longworth, E. (Liverpool), 1920 v S; 1921 v Bel; 1923 v S, W, Bel (5)
Lowder, A. (Wolverhampton W), 1889 v W (1)
Lowe, E. (Aston Villa), 1947 v F, Sw, P (3)
Lucas, T. (Liverpool), 1922 v Ni; 1924 v F; 1926 v Bel (3)
Luntley, E. (Nottingham F), 1880 v S, W (2)
Lyttelton, Hon. A. (Cambridge University), 1877 v S (1)
Lyttelton, Hon. E. (Cambridge University), 1878 v S (1)

McCall, J. (Preston NE), 1913 v S, W; 1914 v S; 1920 v S; 1921 v Ni (5)
McCann, G. P. (Sunderland), 2001 v Sp (sub) (1)
McDermott, T. (Liverpool), 1978 v Sw, L; 1979 v Ni, W, Se; 1980 v D, Ni (sub), Ei, Ni, S, Bel (sub), Sp; 1981 v N, R, Sw, R (sub), Br, Sw (sub), H; 1982 v N, H, W (sub), Ho, S (sub), Ic (25)
McDonald, C. A. (Burnley), 1958 v USSR (3), Br, A; 1959 v W, Ni, USSR (8)
McFarland, R. L. (Derby Co), 1971 v Gr, Ma (2), Ni, S; 1972 v Sw, Gr, WG, W, S; 1973 v W (3), Ni, S, Cz, Pol, USSR, I; 1974 v A, Pol, I, W, Ni; 1976 v Cz, S; 1977 v Ei, I (28)
McGarry, W. H. (Huddersfield T), 1954 v Sw, U; 1956 v W, D (4)
McGuinness, W. (Manchester U), 1959 v Ni, M (2)
McInroy, A. (Sunderland), 1927 v Ni (1)
McMahon, S. (Liverpool), 1988 v Is, H, Co, USSR; 1989 v D (sub); 1990 v Se, Pol, I, Y (sub), Br, Cz (sub), D, Ei (sub), Eg, Bel, I; 1991 v Ei (17)
McManaman, S. (Liverpool), 1995 v Ng (sub), U (sub), J (sub); 1996 v Co, N, Sw, P (sub), Bul, Cro, Chn, Sw, S, Ho, Sp, G; 1997 v Pol, I, M; 1998 v Cam, Sw, Mor, Co (sub); 1999 v Pol, H; (with Real Madrid), 2000 v L, Pol, Uk, Ma (sub), P; 2001 v F (sub), Fi (sub+1), Alb, Gr (sub); 2002 v G (sub), Alb (sub), Gr (sub) (37)
McNab, R. (Arsenal), 1969 v Ni, Bul, R (1+1 sub) (4)
McNeal, R. (WBA), 1914 v S, W (2)
McNeil, M. (Middlesbrough), 1961 v W, Ni, S, L, P, Sp, M, I; 1962 v L (9)
Mabbutt, G. (Tottenham H), 1983 v WG, Gr, L, W, Gr, H, Ni, S (sub); 1984 v H; 1987 v Y, Ni, T; 1988 v WG; 1992 v T, Pol, Cz (16)
Macaulay, R. H. (Cambridge University), 1881 v S (1)
Macdonald, M. (Newcastle U), 1972 v W, Ni, S (sub); 1973 v USSR (sub); 1974 v P, S (sub), Y (sub); 1975 v WG, Cy (2), Ni; 1976 v Sw (sub), Cz, P (14)
Macrae, S. (Notts Co), 1883 v S, W, Ni; 1884 v S, Ni (5)
Maddison, F. B. (Oxford University), 1872 v S (1)
Madeley, P. E. (Leeds U), 1971 v Ni; 1972 v Sw (2), Gr, WG (2), W, S; 1973 v S, Cz, Pol, USSR, I; 1974 v A, Pol, I; 1975 v Cz, P, Cy; 1976 v Cz, P, Fi; 1977 v Ei, Ho (24)
Magee, T. P. (WBA), 1923 v W, Se; 1925 v S, Bel, F (5)
Makepeace, H. (Everton), 1906 v S; 1910 v S; 1912 v S, W (4)
Male, C. G. (Arsenal), 1935 v S, Ni, I, Ho; 1936 v S, W, Ni, G, A, Bel; 1937 v S, Ni, H, N, Se, Fi; 1939 v I, R, Y (19)
Mannion, W. J. (Middlesbrough), 1947 v S, W, Ni, Ei, Ho, F, Sw, P; 1948 v W, Ni, Bel, Se, I; 1949 v N, F; 1950 v S, Ei, P, Bel, Ch, US; 1951 v Ni, W, S, Y; 1952 v F (26)
Mariner, P. (Ipswich T), 1977 v L (sub), Ni; 1978 v L, W (sub), S; 1980 v W, Ni (sub), S, Aus, I (sub), Sp (sub); 1981 v N, Sw, Sp, Sw, H; 1982 v N, H, Ho, S, Fi, F, Cz, K, WG, Sp; 1983 v D, WG, Gr, W; 1984 v D, H, L; (with Arsenal), 1985 v EG, R (35)
Marsden, J. T. (Darwen), 1891 v Ni (1)
Marsden, W. (Sheffield W), 1930 v W, S, G (3)
Marsh, R. W. (QPR), 1972 v Sw (sub); (with Manchester C), WG (sub+1), W, Ni, S; 1973 v W (2), Y (9)
Marshall, T. (Darwen), 1880 v W; 1881 v W (2)
Martin, A. (West Ham U), 1981 v Br, S (sub); 1982 v H, Fi; 1983 v Gr, L, W, Gr, H; 1984 v H, L, W; 1985 v Ni; 1986 v Is, Ca, Para; 1987 v Se (17)
Martin, H. (Sunderland), 1914 v Ni (1)
Martyn, A. N. (C Palace), 1992 v C (sub), H; 1993 v G; (with Leeds U), 1997 v S.Af; 1998 v Cam, Ch, Bel; 1999 v CzR, F (sub); 2000 v L, Pol, Bel (sub), Uk, R; 2001 v Sp (sub), M; 2002 v Ho, Gr, Se, Ho, I, Sk, Cam (23)
Marwood, B. (Arsenal), 1989 v S.Ar (sub) (1)
Maskrey, H. M. (Derby Co), 1908 v Ni (1)
Mason, C. (Wolverhampton W), 1887 v Ni; 1888 v W; 1890 v Ni (3)
Matthews, R. D. (Coventry C), 1956 v S, Br, Se, WG; 1957 v Ni (5)
Matthews, S. (Stoke C), 1935 v W, I; 1936 v G; 1937 v S; 1938 v S, W, Cz, G, Sw, F; 1939 v S, W, Ni, R of E, N, I, Y; 1947 v S; (with Blackpool), 1947 v Sw, P; 1948 v S, W, Ni, Bel, I; 1949 v S, W, Ni, D, Sw; 1950 v Sp; 1951 v Ni, S; 1954 v Ni, R of E, H, Bel, U; 1955 v Ni, W, S, F, WG, Sp, P; 1956 v W, Br; 1957 v S, W, Ni, Y, D (2), Ei (54)
Matthews, V. (Sheffield U), 1928 v F, Bel (2)
Maynard, W. J. (1st Surrey Rifles), 1872 v S; 1876 v S (2)
Meadows, J. (Manchester C), 1955 v S (1)
Medley, L. D. (Tottenham H), 1951 v Y, W; 1952 v F, A, W, Ni (6)
Meehan, T. (Chelsea), 1924 v Ni (1)
Melia, J. (Liverpool), 1963 v S, Sw (2)
Mercer, D. W. (Sheffield U), 1923 v Ni, Bel (2)
Mercer, J. (Everton), 1939 v S, Ni, I, R, Y (5)
Merrick, G. H. (Birmingham C), 1952 v Ni, S, A (2), I, Sw; 1953 v Ni, W, S, Bel, Arg, Ch, U; 1954 v W, Ni, S, R of E, H (2), Y, Bel, Sw, U (23)
Merson, P. C. (Arsenal), 1992 v G (sub), Cz, H, Br (sub), Fi (sub), D, Se (sub); 1993 v Sp (sub), N (sub), Ho (sub), Br (sub), G; 1994 v Ho, Gr; 1997 v I (sub); (with Middlesbrough), 1998 v Sw, P (sub), Bel, Arg (sub); 1999 v Se (sub); (with Aston Villa), CzR (21)
Metcalfe, V. (Huddersfield T), 1951 v Arg, P (2)
Mew, J. W. (Manchester U), 1921 v Ni (1)
Middleditch, B. (Corinthians), 1897 v Ni (1)
Milburn, J. E. T. (Newcastle U), 1949 v S, W, Ni, Sw; 1950 v W, P, Bel, Sp; 1951 v W, Arg, P; 1952 v F; 1956 v D (13)
Miller, B. G. (Burnley), 1961 v A (1)
Miller, H. S. (Charlton Ath), 1923 v Se (1)
Mills, D. J. (Leeds U), 2001 v M (sub); 2002 v Ho (sub), Se (sub), I, Para (sub), Sk, Cam (sub), Se, Arg, Ng, D, Br; 2003 v P, Aus (sub), S.Af, Ser, Slo; 2004 v Cro (sub), P (sub) (19)
Mills, G. R. (Chelsea), 1938 v W, Ni, Cz (3)
Mills, M. D. (Ipswich T), 1973 v Y; 1976 v W (2), Ni, S, Br, I (sub), Fi; 1977 v Fi (sub), I, Ni, W, S; 1978 v WG, Br, W, Ni, S, H; 1979 v D, Ei, Ni (2), S, Bul, A; 1980 v D, Ni, Sp (2); 1981 v Sw (2), H; 1982 v N, H, S, Fi, F, Cz, K, WG, Sp (42)
Milne, G. (Liverpool), 1963 v Br, Cz, EG; 1964 v W, Ni, S, R of W, U, P, Ei, Br, Arg; 1965 v Ni, Bel (14)
Milton, C. A. (Arsenal), 1952 v A (1)
Milward, A. (Everton), 1891 v S, W; 1897 v S, W (4)
Mitchell, C. (Upton Park), 1880 v W; 1881 v S; 1883 v S, W; 1885 v W (5)
Mitchell, J. F. (Manchester C), 1925 v Ni (1)
Moffat, H. (Oldham Ath), 1913 v W (1)
Molyneux, G. (Southampton), 1902 v S; 1903 v S, W, Ni (4)
Moon, W. R. (Old Westminsters), 1888 v S, W; 1889 v S, W; 1890 v S, W; 1891 v S (7)
Moore, H. T. (Notts Co), 1883 v Ni; 1885 v W (2)
Moore, J. (Derby Co), 1923 v Se (1)
Moore, R. F. (West Ham U), 1962 v Pe, H, Arg, Bul, Br; 1963 v W, Ni, S, F (2), Br, Cz, EG, Sw; 1964 v W, Ni, S, R of W, U, P (2), Ei, Br, Arg; 1965 v Ni, S, Bel, H, Y, WG, Se; 1966 v W, Ni, S, A, Sp, Pol (2), WG (2), N, D, U, M, F, Arg, P; 1967 v W, Ni, S, Cz, Sp, A; 1968 v W, Ni, S, USSR (2), Sp (2), Se, Y, WG; 1969 v Ni, W, S, R, Bul, F, M, U, Br; 1970 v W, Ni, S, Ho, P, Bel, Co, Ec, R, Br, Cz, WG; 1971 v EG, Gr,

Ma, Ni, S; 1972 v Sw (2), Gr, WG (2), W, S; 1973 v W (3), Y, S (2), Ni, Cz, Pol, USSR, I; 1974 v I (108)
Moore, W. G. B. (West Ham U), 1923 v Se (1)
Mordue, J. (Sunderland), 1912 v Ni; 1913 v Ni (2)
Morice, C. J. (Barnes), 1872 v S (1)
Morley, A. (Aston Villa), 1982 v H (sub), Ni, W, Ic; 1983 v D, Gr (6)
Morley, H. (Notts Co), 1910 v Ni (1)
Morren, T. (Sheffield U), 1898 v Ni (1)
Morris, F. (WBA), 1920 v S; 1921 v Ni (2)
Morris, J. (Derby Co), 1949 v N, F; 1950 v Ei (3)
Morris, W. W. (Wolverhampton W), 1939 v S, Ni, R (3)
Morse, H. (Notts Co), 1879 v S (1)
Mort, T. (Aston Villa), 1924 v W, F; 1926 v S (3)
Morten, A. (C Palace), 1873 v S (1)
Mortensen, S. H. (Blackpool), 1947 v P; 1948 v W, S, Ni, Bel, Se, I; 1949 v S, W, Ni, Se, N; 1950 v S, W, Ni, I, P, Bel, Ch, US, Sp; 1951 v S, Arg; 1954 v R of E, H (25)
Morton, J. R. (West Ham U), 1938 v Cz (1)
Mosforth, W. (Sheffield W), 1877 v S; (with Sheffield Albion), 1878 v S; 1879 v S, W; 1880 v S, W; (with Sheffield W), 1881 v W; 1882 v S, W (9)
Moss, F. (Arsenal), 1934 v S, H, Cz; 1935 v I (4)
Moss, F. (Aston Villa), 1922 v S, Ni; 1923 v Ni; 1924 v S, Bel (5)
Mosscrop, E. (Burnley), 1914 v S, W (2)
Mozley, B. (Derby Co), 1950 v W, Ni, Ei (3)
Mullen, J. (Wolverhampton W), 1947 v S; 1949 v N, F; 1950 v Bel (sub), Ch, US; 1954 v W, Ni, S, R of E, Y, Sw (12)
Mullery, A. P. (Tottenham H), 1965 v Ho; 1967 v Sp, A; 1968 v W, Ni, S, USSR, Sp (2), Se, Y; 1969 v Ni, S, R, Bul, F, M, U, Br; 1970 v W, Ni, S (sub), Ho (1 + 1 sub), P, Co, Ec, R, Cz, WG, Br; 1971 v Ma, EG, Gr; 1972 v Sw (35)
Murphy, D. B. (Liverpool), 2002 v Se (sub), I (sub), Para (sub), Sk; 2003 v P (sub), Aus (sub), Lie (sub); 2004 v Cro (sub), D (sub) (9)

Neal, P. G. (Liverpool), 1976 v W, I; 1977 v W, S, Br, Arg, U; 1978 v Sw, I, WG, Ni, S, H; 1979 v D, Ei, Ni (2), S, Bul, A; 1980 v D, Ni, Sp, Arg, W, Bel, I; 1981 v R, Sw, Sp, Br, H; 1982 v N, H, W, Ho, Ic, F (sub), K; 1983 v D, Gr, L, W, Gr, H, Ni, S, Aus (2); 1984 v D (50)
Needham, E. (Sheffield U), 1894 v S; 1895 v S; 1897 v S, W, Ni; 1898 v S, W; 1899 v S, W, Ni; 1900 v S, Ni; 1901 v S, W, Ni; 1902 v W (16)
Neville, G. A. (Manchester U), 1995 v J, Br; 1996 v Co, N, Sw, P, Bul, Cro, H, Chn, Sw, S, Ho, Sp; 1997 v Mol, Pol, I, Ge, Pol, I (sub), F, Br (sub); 1998 v Mol, Ch, P, S.Ar, Bel, R, Co, Arg; 1999 v Bul, Pol; 2000 v L (sub), Pol, Br, Ma, P, G, R; 2001 v G, I, Sp (sub), Fi, Alb; 2002 v Ho, G, Alb, Gr, Se, Ho, I (sub), Para; 2003 v Slo, Mac, Aus, Lie, T; 2004 v Mac, Lie, T, D, J, Ic, F, Sw, Cro, P; 2005 v Uk, A, Pol, W, Az, Sp, Ho, Ni, Az (76)
Neville, P. J. (Manchester U), 1996 v Chn; 1997 v S.Af, Pol (sub), I, F, Br; 1998 v Mol, Cam, Ch, P (sub), S.Ar (sub), Bel; 1999 v L, Pol (sub), H, Se, Bul; 2000 v L (sub), Pol (sub), Bel (sub), S (2), Arg (sub), Br, Uk, Ma, P, G, R; 2001 v Fi, Sp, M, Gr; 2002 v Se (sub), Ho (sub), I (sub), Para (sub); 2003 v S.Af, Ser, Slo; 2004 v Cro, Mac (sub), Lie (sub), D (sub), P, Se, J (sub), Ic (sub), Cro (sub), P (sub); 2005 v US (sub), Co (52)
Newton, K. R. (Blackburn R), 1966 v S, WG; 1967 v Sp, A; 1968 v W, S, Sp, Se, Y, WG; 1969 v Ni, W, S, R, Bul, M, U, Br, F; (with Everton), 1970 v Ni, S, Ho, Co, Ec, R, Cz, WG (27)
Nicholls, J. (WBA), 1954 v S, Y (2)
Nicholson, W. E. (Tottenham H), 1951 v P (1)
Nish, D. J. (Derby Co), 1973 v Ni; 1974 v P, W, Ni, S (5)
Norman, M. (Tottenham H), 1962 v Pe, H, Arg, Bul, Br; 1963 v S, F, Br, Cz, EG; 1964 v W, Ni, S, R of W, U, P (2), US, Br, Arg; 1965 v Ni, Bel, Ho (23)
Nuttall, H. (Bolton W), 1928 v W, Ni; 1929 v S (3)

Oakley, W. J. (Oxford University), 1895 v W; 1896 v S, W, Ni; (with Corinthians), 1897 v S, W, Ni; 1898 v S, W, Ni; 1900 v S, W, Ni; 1901 v S, W, Ni (16)
O'Dowd, J. P. (Chelsea), 1932 v S; 1933 v Ni, Sw (3)
O'Grady, M. (Huddersfield T), 1963 v Ni; (with Leeds U), 1969 v F (2)
Ogilvie, R. A. M. M. (Clapham R), 1874 v S (1)
Oliver, L. F. (Fulham), 1929 v Bel (1)
Olney, B. A. (Aston Villa), 1928 v F, Bel (2)
Osborne, F. R. (Fulham), 1923 v Ni, F; (with Tottenham H), 1925 v Bel; 1926 v Bel (4)
Osborne, R. (Leicester C), 1928 v W (1)
Osgood, P. L. (Chelsea), 1970 v Bel, R (sub), Cz (sub); 1974 v I (4)
Osman, R. (Ipswich T), 1980 v Aus; 1981 v Sp, R, Sw; 1982 v N, Ic; 1983 v D, Aus (3); 1984 v D (11)
Ottaway, C. J. (Oxford University), 1872 v S; 1874 v S (2)
Owen, J. R. B. (Sheffield), 1874 v S (1)
Owen, M. J. (Liverpool), 1998 v Ch, Sw, P (sub), Mor (sub), Bel (sub), Tun (sub), R (sub), Co, Arg; 1999 v Se, Bul, L, F; 2000 v L (sub), Pol (sub), Bel (sub), S (2), Br, P, G, R; 2001 v F (sub), G, Sp, Fi, Alb, M, Gr; 2002 v Ho (sub), G, Alb, I, Para, Sk, Cam, Se, Arg, Ng, D, Br; 2003 v P, Slo, Mac, Aus, Lie, T, S.Af, Ser, Slo; 2004 v Cro, Mac, Lie, P, J, Ic, F, Sw, Cro, P; (with Real Madrid), 2005 v Uk, A, Pol, W, Az, Sp, Ho, Ni, Az, Co (70)
Owen, S. W. (Luton T), 1954 v H, Y, Bel (3)

Page, L. A. (Burnley), 1927 v S, W, Bel, L, F; 1928 v W, Ni (7)
Paine, T. L. (Southampton), 1963 v Cz, EG; 1964 v W, Ni, S, R of W, U, US, P; 1965 v Ni, H, Y, WG, Se; 1966 v W, A, Y, N, M (19)
Pallister, G. A. (Middlesbrough), 1988 v H; 1989 v S.Ar; (with Manchester U), 1991 v Cam (sub), T; 1992 v G; 1993 v N, US, Br, G; 1994 v Pol, Ho, Sm, D; 1995 v US, R, Ei, U, Se; 1996 v N, Sw; 1997 v Mol, Pol (sub) (22)
Palmer, C. L. (Sheffield W), 1992 v C, H, Br, Fi (sub), D, F, Se; 1993 v Sp (sub), N (sub), T, Sm, T, Ho, Pol, N, US, Br (sub); 1994 v Ho (18)
Pantling, H. H. (Sheffield U), 1924 v Ni (1)
Paravicini, P. J. de (Cambridge University), 1883 v S, W, Ni (3)
Parker, P. A. (QPR), 1989 v Alb (sub), Ch, D; 1990 v Y, U, Ho, Eg, Bel, Cam, WG, I; 1991 v H, Pol, USSR, Aus, Nz; (with Manchester U), 1992 v G; 1994 v Ho, D (19)
Parker, S. M. (Charlton Ath), 2004 v D (sub); (with Chelsea), v Se (sub) (2)
Parker, T. R. (Southampton), 1925 v F (1)
Parkes, P. B. (QPR), 1974 v P (1)
Parkinson, J. (Liverpool), 1910 v S, W (2)
Parlour, R. (Arsenal), 1999 v Pol (sub), Se (sub), Bul (sub); 2000 v L, S (sub), Arg (sub), Br (sub); 2001 v G (sub), Fi, I (10)
Parr, P. C. (Oxford University), 1882 v W (1)
Parry, E. H. (Old Carthusians), 1879 v W; 1882 v W, S (3)
Parry, R. A. (Bolton W), 1960 v Ni, S (2)
Patchitt, B. C. A. (Corinthians), 1923 v Se (2) (2)
Pawson, F. W. (Cambridge University), 1883 v Ni; (with Swifts), 1885 v Ni (2)
Payne, J. (Luton T), 1937 v Fi (1)
Peacock, A. (Middlesbrough), 1962 v Arg, Bul; 1963 v Ni, W; (with Leeds U), 1966 v W, Ni (6)
Peacock, J. (Middlesbrough), 1929 v F, Bel, Sp (3)
Pearce, S. (Nottingham F), 1987 v Br, S; 1988 v WG (sub), Is, H; 1989 v D, Se, S.Ar, Gr, Alb (2), Ch, S, Pol, D; 1990 v Se, Pol, I, Y, Br, Cz, D, U, Tun, Ei, Ho, Eg, Bel, Cam, WG; 1991 v H, Pol, Ei (2), Cam, T, Arg, Aus, Nz (2), Mal; 1992 v T, Pol, F, Cz, Br (sub), Fi, D, F, Se; 1993 v Sp, N, T; 1994 v Pol, Sm, Gr (sub); 1995 v R (sub), J, Br; 1996 v N, Sw, P, Bul, Cro, H, Sw, S, Ho, Sp, G; 1997 v Mol, Pol, I, M, S.Af, I; (with West Ham U), 2000 v L, Pol (78)
Pearson, H. F. (WBA), 1932 v S (1)
Pearson, J. H. (Crewe Alex), 1892 v Ni (1)
Pearson, J. S. (Manchester U), 1976 v W, Ni, S, Br, Fi; 1977 v Ei, Ho (sub), W, S, Br, Arg, U; 1978 v I (sub), WG, Ni (15)
Pearson, S. C. (Manchester U), 1948 v S; 1949 v S, Ni; 1950 v Ni, I; 1951 v P; 1952 v S, I (8)
Pease, W. H. (Middlesbrough), 1927 v W (1)
Pegg, D. (Manchester U), 1957 v Ei (1)
Pejic, M. (Stoke C), 1974 v P, W, Ni, S (4)
Pelly, F. R. (Old Foresters), 1893 v Ni; 1894 v S, W (3)
Pennington, J. (WBA), 1907 v S, W; 1908 v S, W, Ni, A; 1909 v S, W, H (2), A; 1910 v S, W; 1911 v S, W, Ni; 1912 v S, W, Ni; 1913 v S, W; 1914 v S, Ni; 1920 v S, W (25)
Pentland, F. B. (Middlesbrough), 1909 v S, W, H (2), A (5)
Perry, C. (WBA), 1890 v Ni; 1891 v Ni; 1893 v W (3)
Perry, T. (WBA), 1898 v W (1)
Perry, W. (Blackpool), 1956 v Ni, S, Sp (3)
Perryman, S. (Tottenham H), 1982 v Ic (sub) (1)
Peters, M. (West Ham U), 1966 v Y, Fi, Pol, M, F, Arg, P, WG; 1967 v Ni, W, S, Cz; 1968 v W, Ni, S, USSR (2), Sp (2), Se, Y; 1969 v Ni, S, R, Bul, F, M, U, Br; 1970 v Ho (2), P (sub), Bel; (with Tottenham H), W, Ni, S, Co, Ec, R, Br, Cz, WG; 1971 v EG, Gr, Ma (2), Ni, W, S; 1972 v Sw, Gr, WG (1+1 sub), Ni (sub); 1973 v S (2), Ni, W, Cz, Pol, USSR, I; 1974 v A, Pol, I, P, S (67)
Phelan, M. C. (Manchester U), 1990 v I (sub) (1)

Phillips, K. (Sunderland), 1999 v H; 2000 v Bel, Arg (sub), Br (sub), Ma; 2001 v I (sub); 2002 v Se, Ho (sub) (8)
Phillips, L. H. (Portsmouth), 1952 v Ni; 1955 v W, WG (3)
Pickering, F. (Everton), 1964 v US; 1965 v Ni, Bel (3)
Pickering, J. (Sheffield U), 1933 v S (1)
Pickering, N. (Sunderland), 1983 v Aus (1)
Pike, T. M. (Cambridge University), 1886 v Ni (1)
Pilkington, B. (Burnley), 1955 v Ni (1)
Plant, J. (Bury), 1900 v S (1)
Platt, D. (Aston Villa), 1990 v I (sub), Y (sub), Br, D (sub), Tun (sub), Ho (sub), Eg (sub), Bel (sub), Cam, WG, I; 1991 v H, Pol, Ei (2), T, USSR, Arg, Aus, Nz (2), Mal; (with Bari), 1992 v G, T, Pol, Cz, C, Br, Fi, D, F, Se; (with Juventus), 1993 v Sp, N, T, Sm, T, Ho, Pol, N, Br (sub), G; (with Sampdoria), 1994 v Pol, Ho, Sm, D, Gr, N; 1995 v US, Ng, Ei, U, J, Se, Br; (with Arsenal), 1996 v Bul (sub), Cro, H, Sw (sub), Ho (sub), Sp, G (62)
Plum, S. L. (Charlton Ath), 1923 v F (1)
Pointer, R. (Burnley), 1962 v W, L, P (3)
Porteous, T. S. (Sunderland), 1891 v W (1)
Powell, C. G. (Charlton Ath), 2001 v Sp, Fi, M (sub); 2002 v Ho (sub+sub) (5)
Priest, A. E. (Sheffield U), 1900 v Ni (1)
Prinsep, J. F. M. (Clapham Rovers), 1879 v S (1)
Puddefoot, S. C. (Blackburn R), 1926 v S, Ni (2)
Pye, J. (Wolverhampton W), 1950 v Ei (1)
Pym, R. H. (Bolton W), 1925 v S, W; 1926 v W (3)

Quantrill, A. (Derby Co), 1920 v S, W; 1921 v W, Ni (4)
Quixall, A. (Sheffield W), 1954 v W, Ni, R of E; 1955 v Sp, P (sub) (5)

Radford, J. (Arsenal), 1969 v R; 1972 v Sw (sub) (2)
Raikes, G. B. (Oxford University), 1895 v W; 1896 v W, Ni, S (4)
Ramsey, A. E. (Southampton), 1949 v Sw; (with Tottenham H), 1950 v S, I, P, Bel, Ch, US, Sp; 1951 v S, Ni, W, Y, Arg, P; 1952 v S, W, Ni, F, A (2), I, Sw; 1953 v Ni, W, S, Bel, Arg, Ch, U, US; 1954 v R of E, H (32)
Rawlings, A. (Preston NE), 1921 v Bel (1)
Rawlings, W. E. (Southampton), 1922 v S, W (2)
Rawlinson, J. F. P. (Cambridge University), 1882 v Ni (1)
Rawson, H. E. (Royal Engineers), 1875 v S (1)
Rawson, W. S. (Oxford University), 1875 v S; 1877 v S (2)
Read, A. (Tufnell Park), 1921 v Bel (1)
Reader, J. (WBA), 1894 v Ni (1)
Reaney, P. (Leeds U), 1969 v Bul (sub); 1970 v P; 1971 v Ma (3)
Redknapp, J. F. (Liverpool), 1996 v Co, N, Sw, Chn, S (sub); 1997 v M (sub), Ge (sub), S.Af; 1999 v Se, Bul, F, Pol (sub), H (sub), Bul; 2000 v Bel, S (2) (17)
Reeves, K. (Norwich C), 1980 v Bul; (with Manchester C), Ni (2)
Regis, C. (WBA), 1982 v Ni (sub), W (sub), Ic; 1983 v WG; (with Coventry C), 1988 v T (sub) (5)
Reid, P. (Everton), 1985 v M (sub), WG, US (sub); 1986 v R, S (sub), Ca (sub), Pol, Para, Arg; 1987 v Br; 1988 v WG, Y (sub), Sw (sub) (13)
Revie, D. G. (Manchester C), 1955 v Ni, S, F; 1956 v W, D; 1957 v Ni (6)
Reynolds, J. (WBA), 1892 v S; 1893 v S, W; (with Aston Villa), 1894 v S, Ni; 1895 v S; 1897 v S, W (8)
Richards, C. H. (Nottingham F), 1898 v Ni (1)
Richards, G. H. (Derby Co), 1909 v A (1)
Richards, J. P. (Wolverhampton W), 1973 v Ni (1)
Richardson, J. R. (Newcastle U), 1933 v I, Sw (2)
Richardson, K. (Aston Villa), 1994 v Gr (1)
Richardson, K. E. (Manchester U), 2005 v US, Co (sub) (2)
Richardson, W. G. (WBA), 1935 v Ho (1)
Rickaby, S. (WBA), 1954 v Ni (1)
Ricketts, M. B. (Bolton W), 2002 v Ho (1)
Rigby, A. (Blackburn R), 1927 v S, Bel, L, F; 1928 v W (5)
Rimmer, E. J. (Sheffield W), 1930 v S, G, A; 1932 v Sp (4)
Rimmer, J. J. (Arsenal), 1976 v I (1)
Ripley, S. E. (Blackburn R), 1994 v Sm; 1998 v Mol (sub) (2)
Rix, G. (Arsenal), 1981 v N, R, Sw (sub), Br, W, S; 1982 v Ho (sub), Fi (sub), F, Cz, K, WG, Sp; 1983 v D, WG (sub), Gr (sub); 1984 v Ni (17)
Robb, G. (Tottenham H), 1954 v H (1)
Roberts, C. (Manchester U), 1905 v Ni, W, S (3)
Roberts, F. (Manchester C), 1925 v S, W, Bel, F (4)
Roberts, G. (Tottenham H), 1983 v Ni, S; 1984 v F, Ni, S, USSR (6)
Roberts, H. (Arsenal), 1931 v S (1)
Roberts, H. (Millwall), 1931 v Bel (1)
Roberts, R. (WBA), 1887 v S; 1888 v Ni; 1890 v Ni (3)
Roberts, W. T. (Preston NE), 1924 v W, Bel (2)
Robinson, J. (Sheffield W), 1937 v Fi; 1938 v G, Sw; 1939 v W (4)
Robinson, J. W. (Derby Co), 1897 v S, Ni; (with New Brighton Tower), 1898 v S, W, Ni; (with Southampton), 1899 v W, S; 1900 v S, W, Ni; 1901 v Ni (11)
Robinson, P. W. (Leeds U), 2003 v Aus (sub), S.Af (sub); 2004 v Cro (sub), D (sub); (with Tottenham H), Ic; 2005 v Pol, W, Az, Sp, Ho, Ni, Az (12)
Robson, B. (WBA), 1980 v Ei, Aus; 1981 v N, R, Sw, Sp, R, Br, W, S, Sw, H; 1982 v N; (with Manchester U), H, Ni, W, Ho, S, Fi, F, Cz, WG, Sp; 1983 v D, Gr, L, S; 1984 v H, L, F, Ni, S, USSR, Br, U, Ch; 1985 v EG, Fi, T, Ei, R, Fi, S, M, I, WG, US; 1986 v R, T, Is, M, P, Mor; 1987 v Ni (2), Sp, T, Br, S; 1988 v T, Y, Ho, H, S, Co, Sw, Ei, Ho, USSR; 1989 v D, Se, S.Ar, Gr, Alb (2), Ch, S, Pol, D; 1990 v Pol, I, Y, Cz, U, Tun, Ei, Ho; 1991 v Cam, Ei; 1992 v T (90)
Robson, R. (WBA), 1958 v F, USSR (2), Br, A; 1960 v Sp, H; 1961 v Ni, W, S, L, P, Sp, M, I; 1962 v W, Ni, Sw, L, P (20)
Rocastle, D. (Arsenal), 1989 v D, S.Ar, Gr, Alb (2), Pol (sub), D; 1990 v Se (sub), Pol, Y, D (sub); 1992 v Pol, Cz, Br (sub) (14)
Rooney, W. (Everton), 2003 v Aus (sub), Lie (sub), T, Ser (sub), Slo; 2004 v Mac, Lie, T, D, P, Se, J, Ic, F, Sw, Cro, P; (with Manchester U), 2005 v W, Az, Sp, Ho, Ni, Az (23)
Rose, W. C. (Swifts), 1884 v S, W, Ni; (with Preston NE), 1886 v Ni; (with Wolverhampton W), 1891 v Ni (5)
Rostron, T. (Darwen), 1881 v S, W (2)
Rowe, A. (Tottenham H), 1934 v F (1)
Rowley, J. F. (Manchester U), 1949 v Sw, Se, F; 1950 v Ni, I; 1952 v S (6)
Rowley, W. (Stoke C), 1889 v Ni; 1892 v Ni (2)
Royle, J. (Everton), 1971 v Ma; 1973 v Y; (with Manchester C), 1976 v Ni (sub), I; 1977 v Fi, L (6)
Ruddlesdin, H. (Sheffield W), 1904 v W, Ni; 1905 v S (3)
Ruddock, N. (Liverpool), 1995 v Ng (1)
Ruffell, J. W. (West Ham U), 1926 v S; 1927 v Ni; 1929 v S, W, Ni; 1930 v W (6)
Russell, B. B. (Royal Engineers), 1883 v W (1)
Rutherford, J. (Newcastle U), 1904 v S; 1907 v S, Ni, W; 1908 v S, Ni, W, A (2), H, B (11)

Sadler, D. (Manchester U), 1968 v Ni, USSR; 1970 v Ec (sub); 1971 v EG (4)
Sagar, C. (Bury), 1900 v Ni; 1902 v W (2)
Sagar, E. (Everton), 1936 v S, Ni, A, Bel (4)
Salako, J. A. (C Palace), 1991 v Aus (sub), Nz (sub + 1), Mal; 1992 v G (5)
Sandford, E. A. (WBA), 1933 v W (1)
Sandilands, R. R. (Old Westminsters), 1892 v W; 1893 v Ni; 1894 v W; 1895 v W; 1896 v W (5)
Sands, J. (Nottingham F), 1880 v W (1)
Sansom, K. (C Palace), 1979 v W; 1980 v Bul, Ei, Arg, W (sub), Ni, S, Bel, I; (with Arsenal), 1981 v N, R, Sw, Sp, R, Br, W, S, Sw; 1982 v Ni, W, Ho, S, Fi, F, Cz, WG, Sp; 1983 v D, WG, Gr, L, Gr, H, Ni, S; 1984 v D, H, L, F, S, USSR, Br, U, Ch; 1985 v EG, Fi, T, Ni, Ei, R, Fi, S, I, M, WG, US; 1986 v R, T, Ni, Eg, Is, USSR, S, M, Ca, P, Mor, Pol, Para, Arg; 1987 v Se, Ni (2), Y, Sp, T; 1988 v WG, T, Y, Ho, S, Co, Sw, Ei, Ho, USSR (86)
Saunders, F. E. (Swifts), 1888 v W (1)
Savage, A. H. (C Palace), 1876 v S (1)
Sayer, J. (Stoke C), 1887 v Ni (1)
Scales, J. R. (Liverpool), 1995 v J, Se (sub), Br (3)
Scattergood, E. (Derby Co), 1913 v W (1)
Schofield, J. (Stoke C), 1892 v W; 1893 v W; 1895 v Ni (3)
Scholes, P. (Manchester U), 1997 v S.Af (sub), I, Br; 1998 v Mol, Cam, P, S.Ar, Tun, R, Co, Arg; 1999 v Se, Bul, L, F (sub), Pol, Se; 2000 v Pol, S (2), Arg, Br, Uk, Ma, P, G, R; 2001 v F, G, Fi, Sp, Fi, Alb, M, Gr; 2002 v Ho, G, Alb, Gr, Se, Ho, Para, Sk, Cam, Se, Arg, Ng, D, Br; 2003 v Slo, Mac, Aus, Lie, T, S.Af, Ser, Slo; 2004 v Cro, T, P, J, Ic, F, Sw, Cro, P (66)
Scott, L. (Arsenal), 1947 v S, W, Ni, Ei, Ho, F, Sw, P; 1948 v S, W, Ni, Bel, Se, I; 1949 v W, Ni, D (17)
Scott, W. R. (Brentford), 1937 v W (1)
Seaman, D. A. (QPR), 1989 v S.Ar, D (sub); 1990 v Cz (sub); (with Arsenal), 1991 v Cam, Ei, T, Arg; 1992 v Cz, H (sub); 1994 v Pol, Ho, Sm, D, N; 1995 v US, R, Ei; 1996 v Co, N, Sw, P, Bul, Cro, H, Sw, S, Ho, Sp, G; 1997 v Mol, Pol, Ge (2), Pol, F, Br; 1998 v Mol, I, P, S.Ar, Tun, R, Co, Arg; 1999 v Se, Bul, L, F, Pol, H, Se, Bul; 2000 v Bel, S (2), Arg, Br, P, G; 2001 v F, G, Fi (2), Alb, Gr; 2002 v G, Alb, Para, Se, Arg, Ng, D, Br; 2003 v Slo, Mac (75)
Seddon, J. (Bolton W), 1923 v F, Se (2); 1924 v Bel; 1927 v W; 1929 v S (6)

Seed, J. M. (Tottenham H), 1921 v Bel: 1923 v W, Ni, Bel; 1925 v S (5)
Settle, J. (Bury), 1899 v S, W, Ni; (with Everton), 1902 v S, Ni; 1903 v Ni (6)
Sewell, J. (Sheffield W), 1952 v Ni, A, Sw; 1953 v Ni; 1954 v H (2) (6)
Sewell, W. R. (Blackburn R), 1924 v W (1)
Shackleton, L. F. (Sunderland), 1949 v W, D; 1950 v W; 1955 v W, WG (5)
Sharp, J. (Everton), 1903 v Ni; 1905 v S (2)
Sharpe, L. S. (Manchester U), 1991 v Ei (sub); 1993 v T (sub), N, US, Br, G; 1994 v Pol, Ho (8)
Shaw, G. E. (WBA), 1932 v S (1)
Shaw, G. L. (Sheffield U), 1959 v S, W, USSR, I; 1963 v W (5)
Shea, D. (Blackburn R), 1914 v W, Ni (2)
Shearer, A. (Southampton), 1992 v F, C, F; (with Blackburn R), 1993 v Sp, N, T; 1994 v Ho, D, Gr, N; 1995 v US, R, Ng, Ei, J, Se, Br; 1996 v Co, N, Sw, P, H (sub), Chn, Sw, S, Ho, Sp, G; (with Newcastle U), 1997 v Mol, Pol, I, Ge, Pol, F, Br; 1998 v Ch (sub), Sw, P, S.Ar, Tun, R, Co, Arg; 1999 v Se, Bul, L, F, Pol, H, Se, Bul; 2000 v L, Pol, Bel, S (2), Arg, Br, Uk, Ma, P, G, R (63)
Shellito, K. J. (Chelsea), 1963 v Cz (1)
Shelton A. (Notts Co), 1889 v Ni; 1890 v S, W; 1891 v S, W; 1892 v S (6)
Shelton, C. (Notts Rangers), 1888 v Ni (1)
Shepherd, A. (Bolton W), 1906 v S; (with Newcastle U), 1911 v Ni (2)
Sheringham, E. P. (Tottenham H), 1993 v Pol, N; 1995 v US, R (sub), Ng (sub), U, J (sub), Se, Br; 1996 v Co (sub), N (sub), Sw, Bul, Cro, H, Sw, S, Ho, Sp, G; 1997 v Ge, M, Ge, S.Af, Pol, I, F (sub), Br; (with Manchester U), 1998 v I, Ch, Sw (sub), P, S.Ar, Tun, R; 1999 v Se (sub), Bul (sub), Bul; 2001 v Fi, Alb (sub), M (sub); (with Tottenham H), 2002 v Gr (sub), Se (sub), I (sub), Para (sub), Sk (sub), Cam (sub), Arg (sub), Ng (sub), D (sub), Br (sub) (51)
Sherwood, T. A. (Tottenham H), 1999 v Pol, H, Se (3)
Shilton, P. L. (Leicester C), 1971 v EG, W; 1972 v Sw, Ni; 1973 v Y, S (2), Ni, W, Cz, Pol, USSR, I; 1974 v A, Pol, I, W, Ni, S, Arg; (with Stoke C), 1975 v Cy; 1977 v Ni, W; (with Nottingham F), 1978 v W, H; 1979 v Cz, Se, A; 1980 v Ni, Sp, I; 1981 v N, Sw, R; 1982 v H, Ho, S, F, Cz, K, WG, Sp; (with Southampton), 1983 v D, WG, Gr, W, Gr, H, Ni, S, Aus (3); 1984 v D, H, F, Ni, W, S, USSR, Br, U, Ch; 1985 v EG, Fi, T, Ni, R, Fi, S, I, WG; 1986 v R, T, Ni, Eg, Is, USSR, S, M, Ca, P, Mor, Pol, Para, Arg; 1987 v Se, Ni (2), Sp, Br; (with Derby Co), 1988 v WG, T, Y, Ho, S, Co, Sw, Ei, Ho; 1989 v D, Se, Gr, Alb (2), Ch, S, Pol, D; 1990 v Se, Pol, I, Y, Br, Cz, D, U, Tun, Ei, Ho, Eg, Bel, Cam, WG, I (125)
Shimwell, E. (Blackpool), 1949 v Se (1)
Shutt, G. (Stoke C), 1886 v Ni (1)
Silcock, J. (Manchester U), 1921 v S, W; 1923 v Se (3)
Sillett, R. P. (Chelsea), 1955 v F, Sp, P (3)
Simms, E. (Luton T), 1922 v Ni (1)
Simpson, J. (Blackburn R), 1911 v S, W, Ni; 1912 v S, W, Ni; 1913 v S; 1914 v W (8)
Sinclair, T. (West Ham U), 2002 v Se, I, Para (sub), Sk (sub), Cam (sub), Arg (sub), Ng, D, Br; 2003 v P (sub), S.Af; (with Manchester C), 2004 v Cro (sub) (12)
Sinton, A. (QPR), 1992 v Pol, C, H (sub), Br, F, Se; 1993 v Sp, T, Br, G; (with Sheffield W), 1994 v Ho (sub), Sm (12)
Slater, W. J. (Wolverhampton W), 1955 v W, WG; 1958 v S, P, Y, USSR (3), Br, A; 1959 v USSR; 1960 v S (12)
Smalley, T. (Wolverhampton W), 1937 v W (1)
Smart, T. (Aston Villa), 1921 v S; 1924 v S, W; 1926 v Ni; 1930 v W (5)
Smith, A. (Nottingham F), 1891 v S, W; 1893 v Ni (3)
Smith, A. (Leeds U), 2001 v M (sub), Gr (sub); 2002 v Ho (sub); 2003 v P, Slo (sub), Mac; 2004 v P (sub), Se (sub); (with Manchester U), 2005 v Uk, A, W (sub), Az (sub), Sp (sub), US, Co (sub) (15)
Smith, A. K. (Oxford University), 1872 v S (1)
Smith, A. M. (Arsenal), 1989 v S.Ar (sub), Gr, Alb (sub), Pol (sub); 1991 v T, USSR, Arg; 1992 v G, T, Pol (sub), H (sub), D, Se (sub) (13)
Smith, B. (Tottenham H), 1921 v S; 1922 v W (2)
Smith, C. E. (C Palace), 1876 v S (1)
Smith, G. O. (Oxford University), 1893 v Ni; 1894 v W, S; 1895 v W; 1896 v Ni, W, S; (with Old Carthusians), 1897 v Ni, W, S; 1898 v Ni, W, S; (with Corinthians), 1899 v Ni, W, S; 1899 v Ni, W, S; 1901 v S (20)
Smith, H. (Reading), 1905 v W, S; 1906 v W, Ni (4)
Smith, J. (WBA), 1920 v Ni; 1923 v Ni (2)
Smith, Joe (Bolton W), 1913 v Ni; 1914 v S, W; 1920 v W, Ni (5)
Smith, J. C. R. (Millwall), 1939 v Ni, N (2)
Smith, J. W. (Portsmouth), 1932 v Ni, W, Sp (3)
Smith, Leslie (Brentford), 1939 v R (1)
Smith, Lionel (Arsenal), 1951 v W; 1952 v W, Ni; 1953 v W, S, Bel (6)
Smith, R. A. (Tottenham H), 1961 v Ni, W, S, L, P, Sp; 1962 v S; 1963 v S, F, Br, Cz, EG; 1964 v W, Ni, R of W (15)
Smith, S. (Aston Villa), 1895 v S (1)
Smith, S. C. (Leicester C), 1936 v Ni (1)
Smith, T. (Birmingham C), 1960 v W, Se (2)
Smith, T. (Liverpool), 1971 v W (1)
Smith, W. H. (Huddersfield T), 1922 v W, S; 1928 v S (3)
Sorby, T. H. (Thursday Wanderers, Sheffield), 1879 v W (1)
Southgate, G. (Aston Villa), 1996 v P (sub), Bul, H (sub), Chn, Sw, S, Ho, Sp, G; 1997 v Mol, Pol, Ge, M, Ge (sub), S.Af, Pol, I, F, Br; 1998 v Mol, I, Cam, Sw, S.Ar, Mor, Tun, Arg (sub); 1999 v Se, Bul, L, Bul; 2000 v Bel, S, Arg, Uk, Ma (sub), R (sub); 2001 v F (sub), G, Fi, I, M (sub); (with Middlesbrough), 2002 v Ho (sub), Se, Ho (sub), I, Para, Sk (sub), Cam (sub); 2003 v P, Slo, Lie, S.Af, Ser, Slo; 2004 v P, Se (sub) (57)
Southworth, J. (Blackburn R), 1889 v W; 1891 v W; 1892 v S (3)
Sparks, F. J. (Herts Rangers), 1879 v S; (with Clapham Rovers), 1880 v S, W (3)
Spence, J. W. (Manchester U), 1926 v Bel; 1927 v Ni (2)
Spence, R. (Chelsea), 1936 v A, Bel (2)
Spencer, C. W. (Newcastle U), 1924 v S; 1925 v W (2)
Spencer, H. (Aston Villa), 1897 v S, W; 1900 v W; 1903 v Ni; 1905 v W, S (6)
Spiksley, F. (Sheffield W), 1893 v S, W; 1894 v S, Ni; 1896 v Ni; 1898 v S, W (7)
Spilsbury, B. W. (Cambridge University), 1885 v Ni; 1886 v Ni, S (3)
Spink, N. (Aston Villa), 1983 v Aus (sub) (1)
Spouncer, W. A. (Nottingham F), 1900 v W (1)
Springett, R. D. G. (Sheffield W), 1960 v Ni, S, Y, Sp, H; 1961 v Ni, S, L, P, Sp, M, I, A; 1962 v W, Ni, S, A, Sw, Pe, L, P, H, Arg, Bul, Br; 1963 v Ni, W, F (2), Sw; 1966 v W, A, N (33)
Sproston, B. (Leeds U), 1937 v W; 1938 v S, W, Ni, Cz, G, Sw, F; (with Tottenham H), 1939 v W, R of E; (with Manchester C), N (11)
Squire, R. T. (Cambridge University), 1886 v S, W, Ni (3)
Stanbrough, M. H. (Old Carthusians), 1895 v W (1)
Staniforth, R. (Huddersfield T), 1954 v S, H, Y, Bel, Sw, U; 1955 v W, WG (8)
Starling, R. W. (Sheffield W), 1933 v S; (with Aston Villa), 1937 v S (2)
Statham, D. (WBA), 1983 v W, Aus (2) (3)
Steele, F. C. (Stoke C), 1937 v S, W, Ni, N, Se, Fi (6)
Stein, B. (Luton T), 1984 v F (1)
Stephenson, C. (Huddersfield T), 1924 v W (1)
Stephenson, G. T. (Derby Co), 1928 v F, Bel; (with Sheffield W), 1931 v F (3)
Stephenson, J. E. (Leeds U), 1938 v S; 1939 v Ni (2)
Stepney, A. C. (Manchester U), 1968 v Se (1)
Sterland, M. (Sheffield W), 1989 v S.Ar (1)
Steven, T. M. (Everton), 1985 v Ni, Ei, R, Fi, I, US (sub); 1986 v T (sub), Eg, USSR (sub), M (sub), Pol, Para, Arg; 1987 v Se, Y (sub), Sp (sub); 1988 v T, Y, Ho, H, S, Sw, Ho, USSR; 1989 v S; (with Rangers), 1990 v Cz, Cam (sub), WG (sub), I; 1991 v Cam; (with Marseille), 1992 v G, C, Br, Fi, D, F (36)
Stevens, G. A. (Tottenham H), 1985 v Fi (sub), T (sub), Ni; 1986 v S (sub), M (sub), Mor (sub), Para (sub) (7)
Stevens, M. G. (Everton), 1985 v I, WG; 1986 v R, T, Ni, Eg, Is, S, Ca, P, Mor, Pol, Para, Arg; 1987 v Br, S; 1988 v T, Y, Is, Ho, H (sub), S, Sw, Ei, Ho, USSR; (with Rangers), 1989 v D, Se, Gr, Alb (2), S, Pol; 1990 v Se, Pol, I, Br, D, Tun, Ei, I; 1991 v USSR; 1992 v C, H, Br, Fi (46)
Stewart, J. (Sheffield W), 1907 v S, W; (with Newcastle U), 1911 v S (3)
Stewart, P. A. (Tottenham H), 1992 v G (sub), Cz (sub), C (sub) (3)
Stiles, N. P. (Manchester U), 1965 v S, H, Y, Se; 1966 v W, Ni, S, A, Sp, Pol (2), WG (2), N, D, U, M, F, Arg, P; 1967 v Ni, W, S, Cz; 1968 v USSR; 1969 v R; 1970 v Ni, S (28)
Stoker, J. (Birmingham), 1933 v W; 1934 v S, H (3)
Stone, S. B. (Nottingham F), 1996 v N (sub), Sw (sub), P, Bul, Cro, Chn (sub), Sw (sub), S (sub), Sp (sub) (9)
Storer, H. (Derby Co), 1924 v F; 1928 v Ni (2)
Storey, P. E. (Arsenal), 1971 v Gr, Ni, S; 1972 v Sw, WG, W, Ni, S; 1973 v W (3), Y, S (2), Ni, Cz, Pol, USSR, I (19)
Storey-Moore, I. (Nottingham F), 1970 v Ho (1)

Strange, A. H. (Sheffield W), 1930 v S, A, G; 1931 v S, W, Ni, F, Bel; 1932 v S, W, Ni, Sp; 1933 v S, Ni, A, I, Sw; 1934 v Ni, W, F (20)
Stratford, A. H. (Wanderers), 1874 v S (1)
Streten, B. (Luton T), 1950 v Ni (1)
Sturgess, A. (Sheffield U), 1911 v Ni; 1914 v S (2)
Summerbee, M. G. (Manchester C), 1968 v S, Sp, WG; 1972 v Sw, WG (sub), W, Ni; 1973 v USSR (sub) (8)
Sunderland, A. (Arsenal), 1980 v Aus (1)
Sutcliffe, J. W. (Bolton W), 1893 v W; 1895 v S, Ni; 1901 v S; (with Millwall), 1903 v W (5)
Sutton, C. R. (Blackburn R), 1998 v Cam (sub) (1)
Swan, P. (Sheffield W), 1960 v Y, Sp, H; 1961 v Ni, W, S, L, P, Sp, M, I, A; 1962 v W, Ni, S, A, Sw, L, P (19)
Swepstone, H. A. (Pilgrims), 1880 v S; 1882 v S, W; 1883 v S, W, Ni (6)
Swift, F. V. (Manchester C), 1947 v S, W, Ni, Ei, Ho, F, Sw, P; 1948 v S, W, Ni, Bel, Se, I; 1949 v S, W, Ni, D, N (19)

Tait, G. (Birmingham Excelsior), 1881 v W (1)
Talbot, B. (Ipswich T), 1977 v Ni (sub), S, Br, Arg, U; (with Arsenal), 1980 v Aus (6)
Tambling, R. V. (Chelsea), 1963 v W, F; 1966 v Y (3)
Tate, J. T. (Aston Villa), 1931 v F, Bel; 1933 v W (3)
Taylor, E. (Blackpool), 1954 v H (1)
Taylor, E. H. (Huddersfield T), 1923 v S, W, Ni, Bel; 1924 v S, Ni, F; 1926 v S (8)
Taylor, J. G. (Fulham), 1951 v Arg, P (2)
Taylor, P. H. (Liverpool), 1948 v W, Ni, Se (3)
Taylor, P. J. (C Palace), 1976 v W (sub+1), Ni, S (4)
Taylor, T. (Manchester U), 1953 v Arg, Ch, U; 1954 v Bel, Sw; 1956 v S, Br, Se, Fi, WG; 1957 v Ni, Y (sub), D (2), Ei (2); 1958 v W, Ni, F (19)
Temple, D. W. (Everton), 1965 v WG (1)
Terry, J. G. (Chelsea), 2003 v Ser (sub); 2004 v Cro, Mac, Lie, T, D, Se, J, Sw, Cro, P; 2005 v Uk, A, Pol, Sp, Ni, Az (17)
Thickett, H. (Sheffield U), 1899 v S, W (2)
Thomas, D. (Coventry C), 1983 v Aus (1+1 sub) (2)
Thomas, D. (QPR), 1975 v Cz (sub), P, Cy (sub+1), W, S (sub); 1976 v Cz (sub), P (sub) (8)
Thomas, G. R. (C Palace), 1991 v T, USSR, Arg, Aus, Nz (2), Mal; 1992 v Pol, F (9)
Thomas, M. L. (Arsenal), 1989 v S.Ar; 1990 v Y (2)
Thompson, A. (Celtic), 2004 v Se (1)
Thompson, P. (Liverpool), 1964 v P (2), Ei, US, Br, Arg; 1965 v Ni, W, S, Bel, Ho; 1966 v Ni; 1968 v Ni, WG; 1970 v S, Ho (sub) (16)
Thompson, P. B. (Liverpool), 1976 v W (2), Ni, S, Br, I, Fi; 1977 v Fi; 1979 v Ei (sub), Cz, Ni, S, Bul, Se (sub), A; 1980 v D, Ni, Bul, Ei, Sp (2), Arg, W, S, Bel, I; 1981 v N, R, H; 1982 v N, H, W, Ho, S, Fi, F, Cz, K, WG, Sp; 1983 v WG, Gr (42)
Thompson T. (Aston Villa), 1952 v W; (with Preston NE), 1957 v S (2)
Thomson, R. A. (Wolverhampton W), 1964 v Ni, US, P, Arg; 1965 v Bel, Ho, Ni, W (8)
Thornewell, G. (Derby Co), 1923 v Se (2); 1924 v F; 1925 v F (4)
Thornley, I. (Manchester C), 1907 v W (1)
Tilson, S. F. (Manchester C), 1934 v H, Cz; 1935 v W; 1936 v Ni (4)
Titmuss, F. (Southampton), 1922 v W; 1923 v W (2)
Todd, C. (Derby Co), 1972 v Ni; 1974 v P, W, Ni, S, Arg, EG, Bul, Y; 1975 v P (sub), WG, Cy (2), Ni, W, S; 1976 v Sw, Cz, P, Ni, S, Br, Fi; 1977 v Ei, Fi, Ho (sub), Ni (27)
Toone, G. (Notts Co), 1892 v S, W (2)
Topham, A. G. (Casuals), 1894 v W (1)
Topham, R. (Wolverhampton W), 1893 v Ni; (with Casuals) 1894 v W (2)
Towers, M. A. (Sunderland), 1976 v W, Ni (sub), I (3)
Townley, W. J. (Blackburn R), 1889 v W; 1890 v Ni (2)
Townrow, J. E. (Clapton Orient), 1925 v S; 1926 v W (2)
Tremelling, D. R. (Birmingham), 1928 v W (1)
Tresadern, J. (West Ham U), 1923 v S, Se (2)
Tueart, D. (Manchester C), 1975 v Cy (sub), Ni; 1977 v Fi, Ni, W (sub), S (sub) (6)
Tunstall, F. E. (Sheffield U), 1923 v S; 1924 v S, W, Ni, F; 1925 v Ni, S (7)
Turnbull, R. J. (Bradford), 1920 v Ni (1)
Turner, A. (Southampton), 1900 v Ni; 1901 v Ni (2)
Turner, H. (Huddersfield T), 1931 v F, Bel (2)
Turner, J. A. (Bolton W), 1893 v W; (with Stoke C) 1895 v Ni; (with Derby Co) 1898 v Ni (3)
Tweedy, G. J. (Grimsby T), 1937 v H (1)

Ufton, D. G. (Charlton Ath), 1954 v R of E (1)
Underwood A. (Stoke C), 1891 v Ni; 1892 v Ni (2)
Unsworth, D. G. (Everton), 1995 v J (1)
Upson, M. J. (Birmingham C), 2003 v S.Af (sub), Ser, Slo; 2004 v Cro (sub), Lie, D; 2005 v Sp (sub) (7)
Urwin, T. (Middlesbrough), 1923 v Se (2); 1924 v Bel; (with Newcastle U), 1926 v W (4)
Utley, G. (Barnsley), 1913 v Ni (1)

Vassell, D. (Aston Villa), 2002 v Ho, I (sub), Para, Sk, Cam, Se, Ng (sub), Br (sub); 2003 v Mac (sub), Aus (sub), T (sub), S.Af (sub), Ser (sub), Slo (sub); 2004 v T (sub), Se, J (sub), Ic (sub), F (sub), Sw (sub), Cro (sub), P (sub) (22)
Vaughton, O. H. (Aston Villa), 1882 v S, W, Ni; 1884 v S, W (5)
Veitch, C. C. M. (Newcastle U), 1906 v S, W, Ni; 1907 v S, W; 1909 v W (6)
Veitch, J. G. (Old Westminsters), 1894 v W (1)
Venables, T. F. (Chelsea), 1965 v Bel, Ho, (2)
Venison, B. (Newcastle U), 1995 v US, U (2)
Vidal, R. W. S. (Oxford University), 1873 v S (1)
Viljoen, C. (Ipswich T), 1975 v Ni, W (2)
Viollet, D. S. (Manchester U), 1960 v H; 1962 v L (2)
Von Donop (Royal Engineers), 1873 v S; 1875 v S (2)

Wace, H. (Wanderers), 1878 v S; 1879 v S, W (3)
Waddle, C. R. (Newcastle U), 1985 v Ei, R (sub), Fi (sub), S (sub), I, M (sub), WG, US; (with Tottenham H), 1986 v R, T, Ni, Is, USSR, S, M, Ca, P, Mor, Pol (sub), Arg (sub); 1987 v Se (sub), Ni (2), Y, Sp, T, Br, S; 1988 v WG, Is, H, S (sub), Co, Sw (sub), Ei, Ho (sub); 1989 v Se, S.Ar, Alb (2), Ch, S, Pol, D (sub); (with Marseille), 1990 v Se, Pol, I, Y, Br, D, U, Tun, Ei, Ho, Eg, Bel, Cam, WG, I (sub); 1991 v H (sub), Pol (sub); 1992 v T (62)
Wadsworth, S. J. (Huddersfield T), 1922 v S; 1923 v S, Bel; 1924 v S, Ni; 1925 v S, Ni; 1926 v W; 1927 v Ni (9)
Wainscoat, W. R. (Leeds U), 1929 v S (1)
Waiters, A. K. (Blackpool), 1964 v Ei, Br; 1965 v W, Bel, Ho (5)
Walden, F. I. (Tottenham H), 1914 v S; 1922 v W (2)
Walker, D. S. (Nottingham F), 1989 v D (sub), Se (sub), Gr, Alb (2), Ch, S, Pol, D; 1990 v Se, Pol, I, Y, Br, Cz, D, U, Tun, Ei, Ho, Eg, Bel, Cam, WG, I; 1991 v H, Pol, Ei (2), Cam, T, Arg, Aus, Nz (2), Mal; 1992 v T, Pol, F, Cz, C, H, Br, Fi, D, F, Se; (with Sampdoria), 1993 v Sp, N, T, Sm, T, Ho, Pol, N, US (sub), Br, G; (with Sheffield W), 1994 v Sm (59)
Walker, I. M. (Tottenham H), 1996 v H (sub), Chn (sub); 1997 v I; (with Leicester C), 2004 v Ic (sub) (4)
Walker, W. H. (Aston Villa), 1921 v Ni; 1922 v Ni, W, S; 1923 v Se (2); 1924 v S; 1925 v Ni, W, S, Bel, F; 1926 v Ni, W, S; 1927 v Ni, W; 1933 v A (18)
Wall, G. (Manchester U), 1907 v W; 1908 v Ni; 1909 v S; 1910 v W, S; 1912 v S; 1913 v Ni (7)
Wallace, C. W. (Aston Villa), 1913 v W; 1914 v Ni; 1920 v S (3)
Wallace, D. L. (Southampton), 1986 v Eg (1)
Walsh, P. (Luton T), 1983 v Aus (2 + 1 sub); 1984 v F, W (5)
Walters, A. M. (Cambridge University), 1885 v S, N; 1886 v S; 1887 v S, W; (with Old Carthusians), 1889 v S, W; 1890 v S, W (9)
Walters, K. M. (Rangers), 1991 v Nz (1)
Walters, P. M. (Oxford University), 1885 v S, Ni; (with Old Carthusians), 1886 v S, W, Ni; 1887 v S, W; 1888 v S, Ni; 1889 v S, W; 1890 v S, W (13)
Walton, N. (Blackburn R), 1890 v Ni (1)
Ward, J. T. (Blackburn Olympic), 1885 v W (1)
Ward, P. (Brighton & HA), 1980 v Aus (sub) (1)
Ward, T. V. (Derby Co), 1948 v Bel; 1949 v W (2)
Waring, T. (Aston Villa), 1931 v F, Bel; 1932 v S, W, Ni (5)
Warner, C. (Upton Park), 1878 v S (1)
Warren, B. (Derby Co), 1906 v S, W, Ni; 1907 v S, W, Ni; 1908 v S, W, Ni, A (2), H, B; (with Chelsea), 1909 v S, Ni, W, H (2), A; 1911 v S, Ni, W (22)
Waterfield, G. S. (Burnley), 1927 v W (1)
Watson, D. (Norwich C), 1984 v Br, U, Ch; 1985 v M, US (sub); 1986 v S; (with Everton), 1987 v Ni; 1988 v Is, Ho, S, Sw (sub), USSR (12)
Watson, D. V. (Sunderland), 1974 v P, S (sub), Arg, EG, Bul, Y; 1975 v Cz, P, WG, Cy (2), Ni, W, S; (with Manchester C), 1976 v Sw, Cz (sub), P; 1977 v Ho, L, Ni, W, S, Br, Arg, U; 1978 v Sw, L, I, WG, Br, W, Ni, S, H; 1979 v D, Ei, Cz, Ni (2), W, S, Bul, Se, A; (with Werder Bremen), 1980 v D; (with Southampton), Ni, Bul, Ei, Sp (2), Arg, Ni, S, Bel, I; 1981 v N, R, Sw, R, W, S, Sw, H; (with Stoke C), 1982 v Ni, Ic (65)
Watson, V. M. (West Ham U), 1923 v W, S; 1930 v S, G, A (5)
Watson, W. (Burnley), 1913 v S; 1914 v Ni; 1920 v Ni (3)

Watson, W. (Sunderland), 1950 v Ni, I; 1951 v W, Y (4)
Weaver, S. (Newcastle U), 1932 v S, 1933 v S, Ni (3)
Webb, G. W. (West Ham U), 1911 v S, W (2)
Webb, N. J. (Nottingham F), 1988 v WG (sub), T, Y, Is, Ho, S, Sw, Ei, USSR (sub); 1989 v D, Se, Gr, Alb (2), Ch, S, Pol, D; (with Manchester U), 1990 v Se, I (sub); 1992 v F, H, Br (sub), Fi, D (sub), Se (26)
Webster, M. (Middlesbrough), 1930 v S, A, G (3)
Wedlock, W. J. (Bristol C), 1907 v S, Ni, W; 1908 v S, Ni, W, A (2), H, B; 1909 v S, W, Ni, H (2), A; 1910 v S, W, Ni; 1911 v S, W, Ni; 1912 v S, W, Ni; 1914 v W (26)
Weir, D. (Bolton W), 1889 v S, Ni (2)
Welch, R. de C. (Wanderers), 1872 v S; (with Harrow Chequers), 1874 v S (2)
Weller, K. (Leicester C), 1974 v W, Ni, S, Arg (4)
Welsh, D. (Charlton Ath), 1938 v G, Sw; 1939 v R (3)
West, G. (Everton), 1969 v W, Bul, M (3)
Westwood, R. W. (Bolton W), 1935 v S, W, Ho; 1936 v Ni, G; 1937 v W (6)
Whateley, O. (Aston Villa), 1883 v S, Ni (2)
Wheeler, J. E. (Bolton W), 1955 v Ni (1)
Wheldon, G. F. (Aston Villa), 1897 v Ni; 1898 v S, W, Ni (4)
White, D. (Manchester C), 1993 v Sp (1)
White, T. A. (Everton), 1933 v I (1)
Whitehead, J. (Accrington), 1893 v W; (with Blackburn R), 1894 v Ni (2)
Whitfeld, H. (Old Etonians), 1879 v W (1)
Whitham, M. (Sheffield U), 1892 v Ni (1)
Whitworth, S. (Leicester C), 1975 v WG, Cy, Ni, W, S; 1976 v Sw, P (7)
Whymark, T. J. (Ipswich T), 1978 v L (sub) (1)
Widdowson, S. W. (Nottingham F), 1880 v S (1)
Wignall, F. (Nottingham F), 1965 v W, Ho (2)
Wilcox, J. M. (Blackburn R), 1996 v H; 1999 v F (sub); (with Leeds U), 2000 v Arg (3)
Wilkes, A. (Aston Villa), 1901 v S, W; 1902 v S, W, Ni (5)
Wilkins, R. G. (Chelsea), 1976 v I; 1977 v Ei, Fi, Ni, Br, Arg, U; 1978 v Sw (sub), L, I, WG, W, Ni, S, H; 1979 v D, Ei, Cz, Ni, W, S, Bul, Se (sub), A; (with Manchester U), 1980 v D, Ni, Bul, Sp (2), Arg, W (sub), Ni, S, Bel, I; 1981 v Sp (sub), R, Br, W, S, Sw, H (sub); 1982 v Ni, W, Ho, S, Fi, F, Cz, K, WG, Sp; 1983 v D, WG; 1984 v D, Ni, W, S, USSR, Br, U, Ch; (with AC Milan), 1985 v EG, Fi, T, Ni, Ei, R, Fi, S, I, M; 1986 v T, Ni, Is, Eg, USSR, S, M, Ca, P, Mor; 1987 v Se, Y (sub) (84)
Wilkinson, B. (Sheffield U), 1904 v S (1)
Wilkinson, L. R. (Oxford University), 1891 v W (1)
Williams, B. F. (Wolverhampton W), 1949 v F; 1950 v S, W, Ei, I, P, Bel, Ch, US, Sp; 1951 v Ni, W, S, Y, Arg, P; 1952 v W, F; 1955 v S, WG, F, Sp, P; 1956 v W (24)
Williams, O. (Clapton Orient), 1923 v W, Ni (2)
Williams, S. (Southampton), 1983 v Aus (1+1 sub); 1984 v F; 1985 v EG, Fi, T (6)
Williams, W. (WBA), 1897 v Ni; 1898 v W, Ni, S; 1899 v W, Ni (6)
Williamson, E. C. (Arsenal), 1923 v Se (2) (2)
Williamson, R. G. (Middlesbrough), 1905 v Ni; 1911 v Ni, S, W; 1912 v S, W; 1913 v Ni (7)
Willingham, C. K. (Huddersfield T), 1937 v Fi; 1938 v S, G, Sw, F; 1939 v S, W, Ni, R of E, N, I, Y (12)
Willis, A. (Tottenham H), 1952 v F (1)
Wilshaw, D. J. (Wolverhampton W), 1954 v W, Sw, U; 1955 v S, F, Sp, P; 1956 v W, Ni, Fi, WG; 1957 v Ni (12)
Wilson, C. P. (Hendon), 1884 v S, W (2)
Wilson, C. W. (Oxford University), 1879 v W; 1881 v S (2)
Wilson, G. (Sheffield W), 1921 v S, W, Bel; 1922 v S, Ni; 1923 v S, W, Ni, Bel; 1924 v W, Ni, F (12)
Wilson, G. P. (Corinthians), 1900 v S, W (2)
Wilson, R. (Huddersfield T), 1960 v S, Y, Sp, H; 1962 v W, Ni, S, A, Sw, Pe, P, H, Arg, Bul, Br; 1963 v Ni, F, Br, Cz, EG, Sw; 1964 v W, S, R of W, U, P (2), Ei, Br, Arg; (with Everton), 1965 v S, H, Y, WG, Se; 1966 v WG (sub), W, Ni, A, Sp, Pol (2), Y, Fi, D, U, M, F, Arg, P, WG; 1967 v Ni, W, S, Cz, A; 1968 v Ni, S, USSR (2), Sp (2), Y (63)
Wilson, T. (Huddersfield T), 1928 v S (1)
Winckworth, W. N. (Old Westminsters), 1892 v W; 1893 v Ni (2)
Windridge, J. E. (Chelsea), 1908 v S, W, Ni, A (2), H, B; 1909 v Ni (8)
Wingfield-Stratford, C. V. (Royal Engineers), 1877 v S (1)
Winterburn, N. (Arsenal), 1990 v I (sub); 1993 v G (sub) (2)
Wise, D. F. (Chelsea), 1991 v T, USSR, Aus (sub), Nz (2); 1994 v N; 1995 v R (sub), Ng; 1996 v Co, N, P, H (sub); 2000 v Bel (sub), Arg, Br, Ma, P (sub), G, R; 2001 v F, Fi (21)
Withe, P. (Aston Villa), 1981 v Br, W, S; 1982 v N (sub), W, Ic; 1983 v H, Ni, S; 1984 v H (sub); 1985 v T (11)
Wollaston, C. H. R. (Wanderers), 1874 v S; 1875 v S; 1877 v S; 1880 v S (4)
Wolstenholme, S. (Everton), 1904 v S; (with Blackburn R), 1905 v W, Ni (3)
Wood, H. (Wolverhampton W), 1890 v S, W; 1896 v S (3)
Wood, R. E. (Manchester U), 1955 v Ni, W; 1956 v Fi (3)
Woodcock, A. S. (Nottingham F), 1978 v Ni; 1979 v Ei (sub), Cz, Bul (sub), Se; 1980 v Ni; (with Cologne), Bul, Ei, Sp (2), Arg, Bel, I; 1981 v N, R, Sw, R, W (sub), S; 1982 v Ni (sub), Ho, Fi (sub), WG (sub), Sp; (with Arsenal), 1983 v WG (sub), Gr, L, Gr; 1984 v L, F (sub), Ni, W, S, Br, U (sub); 1985 v EG, Fi, T, Ni; 1986 v R (sub), T (sub), Is (sub) (42)
Woodgate, J. S. (Leeds U), 1999 v Bul; 2003 v P (sub), Slo, Mac; (with Newcastle U), 2004 v Se (5)
Woodger, G. (Oldham Ath), 1911 v Ni (1)
Woodhall, G. (WBA), 1888 v S, W (2)
Woodley, V. R. (Chelsea), 1937 v S, N, Se, Fi; 1938 v S, W, Ni, Cz, G, Sw, F; 1939 v S, W, Ni, R of E, N, I, R, Y (19)
Woods, C. C. E. (Norwich C), 1985 v US; 1986 v Eg (sub), Is (sub), Ca (sub); (with Rangers), 1987 v Y, Sp (sub), Ni (sub), T, S; 1988 v Is, H, Sw (sub), USSR; 1989 v D (sub); 1990 v Br (sub), D (sub); 1991 v H, Pol, Ei, USSR, Aus, Nz (2), Mal; (with Sheffield W), 1992 v G, T, Pol, F, C, Br, Fi, D, F, Se; 1993 v Sp, N, T, Sm, T, Ho, Pol, N, US (43)
Woodward, V. J. (Tottenham H), 1903 v S, W, Ni; 1904 v S, Ni; 1905 v S, W, Ni; 1907 v S; 1908 v S, W, Ni, A (2), H, B; 1909 v W, Ni, H (2), A; (with Chelsea), 1910 v Ni; 1911 v W (23)
Woosnam, M. (Manchester C), 1922 v W (1)
Worrall, F. (Portsmouth), 1935 v Ho; 1937 v Ni (2)
Worthington, F. S. (Leicester C), 1974 v Ni (sub), S, Arg, EG, Bul, Y; 1975 v Cz, P (sub) (8)
Wreford-Brown, C. (Oxford University), 1889 v Ni; (with Old Carthusians), 1894 v W; 1895 v W; 1898 v S (4)
Wright, E. G. D. (Cambridge University), 1906 v W (1)
Wright, I. E. (C Palace), 1991 v Cam, Ei (sub), USSR, Nz; (with Arsenal), 1992 v H (sub); 1993 v N, T (2), Pol (sub), N (sub), US (sub), Br, G (sub); 1994 v Pol, Ho (sub), Sm, Gr (sub), N (sub); 1995 v US (sub), R; 1997 v Ge (sub), I (sub), M (sub), S.Af, I, F, Br (sub); 1998 v Mol, I, S.Ar (sub), Mor; (with West Ham U), 1999 v L (sub), CzR (33)
Wright, J. D. (Newcastle U), 1939 v N (1)
Wright, M. (Southampton), 1984 v W; 1985 v EG, Fi, T, Ei, R, I, WG; 1986 v R, T, Ni, Eg, USSR; 1987 v Y, Ni, S; (with Derby Co), 1988 v Is, Ho (sub), Co, Sw, Ei, Ho; 1990 v Cz (sub), Tun (sub), Ho, Eg, Bel, Cam, WG, I; 1991 v H, Pol, Ei (2), Cam, USSR, Arg, Aus, Nz, Mal; (with Liverpool), 1992 v F, Fi; 1993 v Sp; 1996 v Cro, H (45)
Wright, R. I. (Ipswich T), 2000 v Ma; (with Arsenal), 2002 v Ho (sub) (2)
Wright, T. J. (Everton), 1968 v USSR; 1969 v R (2), M (sub), U, Br; 1970 v W, Ho, Bel, R (sub), Br (11)
Wright, W. A. (Wolverhampton W), 1947 v S, W, Ni, Ei, Ho, F, Sw, P; 1948 v S, W, Ni, Bel, Se, I; 1949 v S, W, Ni, D, Sw, Se, N, F; 1950 v S, W, Ni, Ei, I, P, Bel, Ch, US, Sp; 1951 v Ni, S, Arg; 1952 v W, Ni, S, F, A (2), I, Sw; 1953 v Ni, W, S, Bel, Arg, Ch, U, US; 1954 v W, Ni, S, R of E, H (2), Y, Bel, Sw, U; 1955 v W, Ni, S, WG, F, Sp, P; 1956 v Ni, W, S, Br, Se, Fi, WG, D, Sp; 1957 v S, W, Ni, Y, D (2), Ei (2); 1958 v W, Ni, S, P, Y, USSR (3), Br, A, F; 1959 v W, Ni, S, USSR, I, Br, Pe, M, US (105)
Wright-Phillips, S. C. (Manchester C), 2005 v Uk (sub), Az (sub), Sp (sub), Ho (4)
Wylie, J. G. (Wanderers), 1878 v S (1)

Yates, J. (Burnley), 1889 v Ni (1)
York, R. E. (Aston Villa), 1922 v S; 1926 v S (2)
Young, A. (Huddersfield T), 1933 v W; 1937 v S, H, N, Se; 1938 v G, Sw, F; 1939 v W (9)
Young, G. M. (Sheffield W), 1965 v W (1)
Young, L. P. (Charlton Ath), 2005 v US (sub), Co (sub) (2)
R. E. Evans also played for Wales against E, Ni, S; J. Reynolds also played for Ireland against E, W, S.

NORTHERN IRELAND

Addis, D. J. (Cliftonville), 1922 v N (1)
Aherne, T. (Belfast C), 1947 v E; 1948 v S; 1949 v W; (with Luton T), 1950 v W (4)
Alexander, T. E. (Cliftonville), 1895 v S (1)
Allan, C. (Cliftonville), 1936 v E (1)
Allen, J. (Limavady), 1887 v E (1)
Anderson, J. (Distillery), 1925 v S.Af (1)
Anderson, T. (Manchester U), 1973 v Cy, E, S, W; 1974 v Bul, P; (with Swindon T), 1975 v S (sub); 1976 v Is; 1977 v Ho, Bel, WG, E, S, W, Ic; 1978 v Ic, Ho, Bel; (with Peterborough U), S, E, W; 1979 v D (sub) (22)
Anderson, W. (Linfield), 1898 v W, E, S; (with Cliftonville), 1899 v S (4)
Andrews, W. (Glentoran), 1908 v S; (with Grimsby T), 1913 v E, S (3)
Armstrong, G. J. (Tottenham H), 1977 v WG, E, W (sub), Ic (sub); 1978 v Bel, S, E, W; 1979 v Ei, D, Bul, E, Bul, E, S, W, D; 1980 v E, Ei, Is, S, E, W, Aus (3); 1981 v Se; (with Watford), P, S, P, S, Se; 1982 v S, Is, E, F, W, Y, Hon, Sp, A, F; 1983 v A, T, Alb, S, E, W; (with Real Mallorca), 1984 v A, WG, E, W, Fi; 1985 v R, Fi, E, Sp; (with WBA), 1986 v T, R (sub), E (sub), F (sub); (with Chesterfield), D (sub), Br (sub) (63)

Baird, C. P. (Southampton), 2003 v I, Sp; 2004 v Uk, Arm, Gr, N, Es, Ser, Bar, Stk, Tr; 2005 v Az, Ca, E, Pol, G (16)
Baird, G. (Distillery), 1896 v S, E, W (3)
Baird, H. C. (Huddersfield T), 1939 v E (1)
Balfe, J. (Shelbourne), 1909 v E; 1910 v W (2)
Bambrick, J. (Linfield), 1929 v W, S, E; 1930 v W, S, E; 1932 v W; (with Chelsea), 1935 v W; 1936 v E, S; 1938 v W (11)
Banks, S. J. (Cliftonville), 1937 v W (1)
Barr, H. H. (Linfield), 1962 v E; (with Coventry C), 1963 v E, Pol (3)
Barron, J. H. (Cliftonville), 1894 v E, W, S; 1895 v S; 1896 v S; 1897 v E, W (7)
Barry, J. (Cliftonville), 1888 v W, S; 1889 v E (3)
Barry, J. (Bohemians), 1900 v S (1)
Baxter, R. A. (Distillery), 1887 v S (1)
Baxter, S. N. (Cliftonville), 1887 v W (1)
Bennett, L. V. (Dublin University), 1889 v W (1)
Best, G. (Manchester U), 1964 v W, U; 1965 v E, Ho (2), S, Sw (2), Alb; 1966 v S, E, Alb; 1967 v E; 1968 v S; 1969 v E, S, W, T; 1970 v S, E, W, USSR; 1971 v Cy (2), Sp, E, S, W; 1972 v USSR, Sp; 1973 v Bul; 1974 v P; (with Fulham), 1977 v Ho, Bel, WG; 1978 v Ic, Ho (37)
Bingham, W. L. (Sunderland), 1951 v F; 1952 v E, S, W; 1953 v E, S, F, W; 1954 v E, S, W; 1955 v E, S, W; 1956 v E, S, W; 1957 v E, S, W, P (2), I; 1958 v S, E, W, I (2), Arg, Cz (2), WG, F; (with Luton T), 1959 v E, S, W, Sp; 1960 v S, E, W; (with Everton), 1961 v E, S, WG (2), Gr, I; 1962 v E, Gr; 1963 v E, S, Pol (2), Sp; (with Port Vale), 1964 v S, E, Sp (56)
Black, K. T. (Luton T), 1988 v Fr (sub), Ma (sub); 1989 v Ei, H, Sp (2), Ch (sub); 1990 v H, N, U; 1991 v Y (2), D, A, Pol, Fa; (with Nottingham F), 1992 v Fa, A, D, S, Li, G; 1993 v Sp, D (sub), Alb, Ei (sub), Sp; 1994 v D (sub), Ei (sub), R (sub) (30)
Black, T. (Glentoran), 1901 v E (1)
Blair, H. (Portadown), 1928 v F; 1931 v S; 1932 v S; (with Swansea), 1934 v S (4)
Blair, J. (Cliftonville), 1907 v W, E, S; 1908 v E, S (5)
Blair, R. V. (Oldham Ath), 1975 v Se (sub), S (sub), W; 1976 v Se, Is (5)
Blanchflower, J. (Manchester U), 1954 v W; 1955 v E, S; 1956 v S, W; 1957 v S, E, P; 1958 v S, E, I (2) (12)
Blanchflower, R. D. (Barnsley), 1950 v S, W; 1951 v E, S; (with Aston Villa), F; 1952 v W; 1953 v E, S, W, F; 1954 v E, S, W; 1955 v E, S (with Tottenham H), W; 1956 v E, S, W; 1957 v E, S, W, I, P (2); 1958 v E, S, W, I (2), Cz (2), Arg, F, WG; 1959 v E, S, W, Sp; 1960 v E, S, W; 1961 v E, S, W, WG (2); 1962 v E, S, W, Gr, Ho; 1963 v E, S, Pol (2) (56)
Bookman, L. J. O. (Bradford C), 1914 v W; (with Luton T), 1921 v S, W; 1922 v E (4)
Bothwell, A. W. (Ards), 1926 v S, E, W; 1927 v E, W (5)
Bowler, G. C. (Hull C), 1950 v E, S, W (3)
Boyle, P. (Sheffield U), 1901 v E; 1902 v E; 1903 v S, W; 1904 v E (5)
Braithwaite, R. M. (Linfield), 1962 v W; 1963 v P, Sp; (with Middlesbrough), 1964 v W, U; 1965 v E, S, Sw (2), Ho (10)
Breen, T. (Belfast C), 1935 v E, W; 1937 v E, S; (with Manchester U), 1937 v W; 1938 v E, S; 1939 v W, S (9)
Brennan, B. (Bohemians), 1912 v W (1)
Brennan, R. A. (Luton T), 1949 v W; (with Birmingham C), 1950 v E, S, W; (with Fulham), 1951 v E (5)
Briggs, W. R. (Manchester U), 1962 v W; (with Swansea T), 1965 v Ho (2)
Brisby, D. (Distillery), 1891 v S (1)
Brolly, T. H. (Millwall), 1937 v W; 1938 v W; 1939 v E, W (4)
Brookes, E. A. (Shelbourne), 1920 v S (1)
Brotherston, N. (Blackburn R), 1980 v S, E, W, Aus (3); 1981 v Se, P; 1982 v S, Is, E, F, S, W, Hon (sub), A (sub); 1983 v A (sub), WG, Alb, T, Alb, S (sub), E (sub), W; 1984 v T; 1985 v Is (sub), T (27)
Brown, J. (Glenavon), 1921 v W; (with Tranmere R), 1924 v E, W (3)
Brown, J. (Wolverhampton W), 1935 v E, W; 1936 v E; (with Coventry C), 1937 v E, W; 1938 v S, W; (with Birmingham C), 1939 v E, S, W (10)
Brown, N. M. (Limavady), 1887 v E (1)
Brown, W. G. (Glenavon), 1926 v W (1)
Browne, F. (Cliftonville), 1887 v E, S, W; 1888 v E, S (5)
Browne, R. J. (Leeds U), 1936 v E, W; 1938 v E, W; 1939 v E, S (6)
Bruce, A. (Belfast C), 1925 v S.Af (1)
Bruce, W. (Glentoran), 1961 v S; 1967 v W (2)
Brunt, C. (Sheffield W), 2005 v Sw (sub), G (sub) (2)
Buckle, H. R. (Cliftonville), 1903 v S; (with Sunderland), 1904 v E; (with Bristol R), 1908 v W (3)
Buckle, J. (Cliftonville), 1882 v E (1)
Burnett, J. (Distillery), 1894 v E, W, S; (with Glentoran), 1895 v E, W (5)
Burnison, J. (Distillery), 1901 v E, W (2)
Burnison, S. (Distillery), 1908 v E; 1910 v E, S; (with Bradford), 1911 v E, S, W; (with Distillery), 1912 v E; 1913 v W (8)
Burns, J. (Glenavon), 1923 v E (1)
Burns, W. (Glentoran), 1925 v S.Af (1)
Butler, M. P. (Blackpool), 1939 v W (1)

Campbell, A. C. (Crusaders), 1963 v W; 1965 v Sw (2)
Campbell, D. A. (Nottingham F), 1986 v Mor (sub), Br; 1987 v E (2), T, Y; (with Charlton Ath), 1988 v Y, T (sub), Gr (sub), Pol (sub) (10)
Campbell, James (Cliftonville), 1897 v E, S, W; 1898 v E, S, W; 1899 v E; 1900 v E, S; 1901 v S, W; 1902 v S; 1903 v E; 1904 v S (14)
Campbell, John (Cliftonville), 1896 v W (1)
Campbell, J. P. (Fulham), 1951 v E, S (2)
Campbell, R. M. (Bradford C), 1982 v S, W (sub) (2)
Campbell, W. G. (Dundee), 1968 v S, E; 1969 v T; 1970 v S, W, USSR (6)
Capaldi, A. C. (Plymouth Arg), 2004 v Es, Ser, Bar, Stk, Tr; 2005 v Sw, Pol, W, Ca, E, Pol (11)
Carey, J. J. (Manchester U), 1947 v E, S, W; 1948 v E; 1949 v E, S, W (7)
Carroll, E. (Glenavon), 1925 v S (1)
Carroll, R. E. (Wigan Ath), 1997 v Th (sub); 1999 v Ei (sub); 2000 v L, Ma; 2001 v Ma, D, Ic, CzR, Bul; (with Manchester U), 2002 v Lie (sub), Sp (sub); 2003 v Fi (sub), I (sub); 2004 v Ser (sub); 2005 v Sw, A, Ca (sub) (17)
Casey, T. (Newcastle U), 1955 v W; 1956 v W; 1957 v E, S, W, I, P (2); 1958 v WG, F; (with Portsmouth), 1959 v E, Sp (12)
Caskey, W. (Derby Co), 1979 v Bul, E, Bul, E, S (sub), D (sub); 1980 v E (sub); (with Tulsa R), 1982 v F (sub) (8)
Cassidy, T. (Newcastle U), 1971 v E (sub); 1972 v USSR (sub); 1974 v Bul (sub), S, E, W; 1975 v N; 1976 v S, E, W; 1977 v WG (sub); 1980 v E, Ei (sub), Is, S, E, W, Aus (3); (with Burnley), 1981 v Se, P; 1982 v Is, Sp (sub) (24)
Caughey, M. (Linfield), 1986 v F (sub), D (sub) (2)
Chambers, R. J. (Distillery), 1921 v W; (with Bury), 1928 v E, S, W; 1929 v E, S, W; 1930 v S, W; (with Nottingham F), 1932 v E, S, W (12)
Chatton, H. A. (Partick T), 1925 v E, S; 1926 v E (3)
Christian, J. (Linfield), 1889 v S (1)
Clarke, C. J. (Bournemouth), 1986 v F, D, Mor, Alg (sub), Sp, Br; (with Southampton), 1987 v E, T, Y; 1988 v Y, T, Gr, Pol, F, Ma; 1989 v Ei, H, Sp (1+1 sub); (with QPR), Ma, Ch; 1990 v H, Ei, N; (with Portsmouth), 1991 v Y (sub), D, A, Pol, Y (sub), Fa; 1992 v Fa, D, S, G; 1993 v Alb, Sp, D (38)
Clarke, R. (Belfast C), 1901 v E, S (2)
Cleary, J. (Glentoran), 1982 v S, W; 1983 v W (sub); 1984 v T (sub); 1985 v Is (5)
Clements, D. (Coventry C), 1965 v W, Ho; 1966 v M; 1967 v S, W; 1968 v S, E; 1969 v T (2), S, W; 1970 v S, E, W, USSR (2); 1971 v Sp, E, S, W, Cy; (with Sheffield W), 1972 v

USSR (2), Sp, E, S, W; 1973 v Bul, Cy (2), P, E, S, W; (with Everton), 1974 v Bul, P, S, E, W; 1975 v N, Y, E, S, W; 1976 v Se, Y; (with New York Cosmos), E, W (48)
Clugston, J. (Cliftonville), 1888 v W; 1889 v W, S, E; 1890 v E, S; 1891 v E, W; 1892 v E, S, W; 1893 v E, S, W (14)
Clyde, M. G. (Wolverhampton W), 2005 v W, Az, G (3)
Cochrane, D. (Leeds U), 1939 v E, W; 1947 v E, S, W; 1948 v E, S, W; 1949 v S, W; 1950 v S, E (12)
Cockrane, G. (Cliftonville), 1903 v S (1)
Cochrane, G. T. (Coleraine), 1976 v N (sub); (with Burnley), 1978 v S (sub), E (sub), W (sub); 1979 v Ei (sub); (with Middlesbrough), D, Bul, E, Bul, E; 1980 v Is, E (sub), W (sub), Aus (1+2 sub); 1981 v Se (sub), P (sub), S, P, S, Se; 1982 v E (sub), F; (with Gillingham), 1984 v S, Fi (sub) (26)
Cochrane, M. (Distillery), 1898 v S, W, E; 1899 v E; 1900 v E, S, W; (with Leicester Fosse), 1901 v S (8)
Collins, F. (Celtic), 1922 v S (1)
Collins, R. (Cliftonville), 1922 v N (1)
Condy, J. (Distillery), 1882 v W; 1886 v E, S (3)
Connell, T. E. (Coleraine), 1978 v W (sub) (1)
Connor, J. (Glentoran), 1901 v S, E; (with Belfast C), 1905 v E, S, W; 1907 v E, S; 1908 v E, S; 1909 v W; 1911 v S, E, W (13)
Connor, M. J. (Brentford), 1903 v S, W; (with Fulham), 1904 v E (3)
Cook, W. (Celtic), 1933 v E, W, S; (with Everton), 1935 v E; 1936 v S, W; 1937 v E, S, W; 1938 v E, S, W; 1939 v E, S, W (15)
Cooke, S. (Belfast YMCA), 1889 v E; (with Cliftonville), 1890 v E, S (3)
Coote, A. (Norwich C), 1999 v Ca, Ei (sub); 2000 v Fi (sub), L (sub), Ma (sub), H (sub) (6)
Coulter, J. (Belfast C), 1934 v E, S, W; (with Everton), 1935 v E, S, W; 1937 v S, W; (with Grimsby T), 1938 v S, W; (with Chelmsford C), 1939 v S (11)
Cowan, J. (Newcastle U), 1970 v E (sub) (1)
Cowan, T. S. (Queen's Island), 1925 v W (1)
Coyle, F. (Coleraine), 1956 v E, S; 1957 v P; (with Nottingham F), 1958 v Arg (4)
Coyle, L. (Derry C), 1989 v Ch (sub) (1)
Coyle, R. I. (Sheffield W), 1973 v P, Cy (sub), W (sub); 1974 v Bul (sub), P (sub) (5)
Craig, A. B. (Rangers), 1908 v E, S, W; 1909 v S; (with Morton), 1912 v S, W; 1914 v E, S, W (9)
Craig, D. J. (Newcastle U), 1967 v W; 1968 v W; 1969 v T (2), E, S, W; 1970 v E, S, W, USSR; 1971 v Cy (2), Sp, S (sub); 1972 v USSR, S (sub); 1973 v Cy (2), E, S, W; 1974 v Bul, P; 1975 v N (25)
Craigan, S. J. (Partick T), 2003 v Fi (sub), Arm, Gr; (with Motherwell), 2004 v Es, Ser, Bar, Stk, Tr; 2005 v Sw, Pol, Ca (sub), G (12)
Crawford, A. (Distillery), 1889 v E, W; (with Cliftonville), 1891 v E, S, W; 1893 v E, W (7)
Croft, T. (Queen's Island), 1922 v N; 1924 v E; 1925 v S.Af (3)
Crone, R. (Distillery), 1889 v S; 1890 v E, S, W (4)
Crone, W. (Distillery), 1882 v W; 1884 v E, S, W; 1886 v E, S, W; 1887 v E; 1888 v E, W; 1889 v S; 1890 v W (12)
Crooks, W. J. (Manchester U), 1922 v W (1)
Crossan, E. (Blackburn R), 1950 v S; 1951 v E; 1955 v W (3)
Crossan, J. A. (Sparta-Rotterdam), 1960 v E; (with Sunderland), 1963 v W, P, Sp; 1964 v E, S, W, U, Sp; 1965 v E, S, Sw (2); (with Manchester C), W, Ho (2), Alb; 1966 v S, E, Alb, WG; 1967 v E, S; (with Middlesbrough), 1968 v S (24)
Crothers, C. (Distillery), 1907 v W (1)
Cumming, L. (Huddersfield T), 1929 v W, S; (with Oldham Ath), 1930 v E (3)
Cunningham, W. (Ulster), 1892 v S, E, W; 1893 v E (4)
Cunningham, W. E. (St Mirren), 1951 v W; 1953 v E; 1954 v S; 1955 v S; (with Leicester C), 1956 v E, S, W; 1957 v E, S, W, I, P (2); 1958 v S, W, I, Cz (2), Arg, WG, F; 1959 v E, S, W; 1960 v E, S, W; (with Dunfermline Ath), 1961 v W; 1962 v W, Ho (30)
Curran, S. (Belfast C), 1926 v S, W; 1928 v F, S (4)
Curran, J. J. (Glenavon), 1922 v W, N; (with Pontypridd), 1923 v E, S; (with Glenavon), 1924 v E (5)
Cush, W. W. (Glenavon), 1951 v E, S; 1954 v S, E; 1957 v W, I, P (2); (with Leeds U), 1958 v I (2), W, Cz (2), Arg, WG, F; 1959 v E, S, W, Sp; 1960 v E, S, W; (with Portadown), 1961 v WG, Gr; 1962 v Gr (26)

Dalrymple, J. (Distillery), 1922 v N (1)
Dalton, W. (YMCA), 1888 v S; (with Linfield), 1890 v S, W; 1891 v S, W; 1892 v E, S, W; 1894 v E, S, W (11)
D'Arcy, S. D. (Chelsea), 1952 v W; 1953 v E; (with Brentford), 1953 v S, W, F (5)
Darling, J. (Linfield), 1897 v E, S; 1900 v S; 1902 v E, S, W; 1903 v E, S (2), W; 1905 v E, S, W; 1906 v E, S, W; 1908 v W; 1909 v E; 1910 v E, S, W; 1912 v S (22)
Davey, H. H. (Reading), 1926 v E; 1927 v E, S; 1928 v E; (with Portsmouth), 1928 v W (5)
Davis, S. (Aston Villa), 2005 v Ca, E (sub), Pol, G (4)
Davis, T. L. (Oldham Ath), 1937 v E (1)
Davison, A. J. (Bolton W), 1996 v Se; (with Bradford C), 1997 v Th; (with Grimsby T), 1998 v G (3)
Davison, J. R. (Cliftonville), 1882 v E, W; 1883 v E, W; 1884 v E, W, S; 1885 v E (8)
Dennison, R. (Wolverhampton W), 1988 v F, Ma; 1989 v H, Sp Ch (sub); 1990 v Ei, U; 1991 v Y (2), A. Pol, Fa (sub); 1992 v Fa, A, D (sub); 1993 v Sp (sub); 1994 v Co (sub); 1997 v I (sub) (18)
Devine, A. O. (Limavady), 1886 v E, W; 1887 v W; 1888 v W (4)
Devine, J. (Glentoran), 1990 v U (sub) (1)
Dickson, D. (Coleraine), 1970 v S (sub), W; 1973 v Cy, P (4)
Dickson, T. A. (Linfield), 1957 v S (1)
Dickson, W. (Chelsea), 1951 v W, F; 1952 v E, S, W; 1953 v E, S, W, F; (with Arsenal), 1954 v E, W; 1955 v E (12)
Diffin, W. J. (Belfast C), 1931 v W (1)
Dill, A. H. (Knock), 1882 v E, W; (with Down Ath), 1883 v W; (with Cliftonville), 1884 v E, S, W; 1885 v E, S, W (9)
Doherty, I. (Belfast C), 1901 v E (1)
Doherty, J. (Portadown), 1928 v F (1)
Doherty, J. (Cliftonville), 1933 v E, W (2)
Doherty, L. (Linfield), 1985 v Is; 1988 v T (sub) (2)
Doherty, M. (Derry C), 1938 v S (1)
Doherty, P. D. (Blackpool), 1935 v E, W; 1936 v E, S; (with Manchester C), 1937 v E, W; 1938 v E, S; 1939 v E, W; (with Derby Co), 1947 v E; (with Huddersfield T), W; 1948 v E, W; 1949 v S; (with Doncaster R), 1951 v S (16)
Doherty, T. E. (Bristol C), 2003 v I, Sp; 2004 v Uk, Arm, Ser; 2005 v Az, A, Ca, E (9)
Donaghey, B. (Belfast C), 1903 v S (1)
Donaghy, M. M. (Luton T), 1980 v S, E, W; 1981 v Se, P, S (sub); 1982 v S, Is, E, F, S, W, Y, Hon, Sp, F; 1983 v A, WG, Alb, T, Alb, S, E, W; 1984 v A, T, WG, S, E, W, Fi; 1985 v R, Fi, E, Sp, T; 1986 v T, R, E, F, D, Mor, Alg, Sp, Br; 1987 v E (2), T, Is, Y; 1988 v Y, T, Gr, Pol, F, Ma; 1989 v Ei, H; (with Manchester U), Sp (2), Ma, Ch; 1990 v Ei, N; 1991 v Y (2), D, A, Pol, Fa; 1992 v Fa, A, D, S, Li, G; (with Chelsea), 1993 v Alb, Sp, D, Alb, Ei, Sp, Li, La; 1994 v La, D, Ei, R, Lie, Co, M (91)
Donnelly, L. (Distillery), 1913 v W (1)
Doran, J. F. (Brighton), 1921 v E; 1922 v E, W (3)
Dougan, A. D. (Portsmouth), 1958 v Cz; (with Blackburn R), 1960 v S; 1961 v E, W, I, Gr; (with Aston Villa), 1963 v S, Pol (2); (with Leicester C), 1966 v S, E, Alb, W, WG, M; 1967 v E, S; (with Wolverhampton W), W; 1968 v S, W; 1969 v Is, T (2), E, S, W; 1970 v USSR (2), S, E; 1971 v Sp, Cy (2), E, S, W; 1972 v USSR (2), S, E, W; 1973 v Bul, Cy (43)
Douglas, J. P. (Belfast C), 1947 v E (1)
Dowd, H. O. (Glenavon), 1974 v W; (with Sheffield W), 1975 v N (sub), Se (3)
Dowie, I. (Luton T), 1990 v N (sub), U; 1991 v Y, D, A (sub), (with West Ham U), Y, Fa; (with Southampton) 1992 v Fa, A, D (sub), S (sub), Li; 1993 v Alb (2), Ei, Sp (sub), Li, La; 1994 v La, D, Ei (sub), R (sub), Lie, Co, M (sub); 1995 v A, Ei; (with C Palace) Ei, La, Ca, Ch, La; 1996 v P; (with West Ham U), A, N, G; 1997 v Uk, Arm, G, Alb, P, Uk, Arm, Th; 1998 v Alb, P; (with QPR), Slo, Sw, Sp; 1999 v T, Fi, Mol, G, Mol, Ca, Ei; 2000 v F, T, G (59)
Duff, M. J. (Cheltenham T), 2002 v Pol (sub); 2003 v Cy (sub); 2004 v Es (sub); (with Burnley), 2005 v Sw (sub) (4)
Duggan, H. A. (Leeds U), 1930 v E; 1931 v E, W; 1933 v E; 1934 v E; 1935 v S, W; 1936 v S (8)
Dunlop, G. (Linfield), 1985 v Is; 1987 v E, Y; 1990 v Ei (4)
Dunne, J. (Sheffield U), 1928 v W; 1931 v W, E; 1932 v E, S; 1933 v E, W (7)

Eames, W. L. E. (Dublin U), 1885 v E, S, W (3)
Eglington, T. J. (Everton), 1947 v S, W; 1948 v E, S, W; 1949 v E (6)
Elder, A. R. (Burnley), 1960 v W; 1961 v S, E, W, WG (2), Gr; 1962 v E, S, Gr; 1963 v E, S, W, Pol (2), Sp; 1964 v W, U; 1965 v E, S, W, Sw (2), Ho (2), Alb; 1966 v E, S, W, M, Alb; 1967 v E, S, W; (with Stoke C), 1968 v E, W; 1969 v E (sub), S, W; 1970 v USSR (40)
Elleman, A. R. (Cliftonville), 1889 v W; 1890 v E (2)

Elliott, S. (Motherwell), 2001 v Ma, D, Ic, N (sub), CzR, Bul (2), CzR; 2002 v D (sub), Ma, Pol (sub), Lie (sub), Sp; (with Hull C), 2003 v Fi (sub), Arm (sub), I (sub); 2004 v Gr, Bar (sub), Stk, Tr; 2005 v Sw, Pol, Az, A (sub), E, Pol (sub), G (27)
Elwood, J. H. (Bradford), 1929 v W; 1930 v E (2)
Emerson, W. (Glentoran), 1920 v E, S, W; 1921 v E; 1922 v E, S; (with Burnley), 1922 v W; 1923 v E, S, W; 1924 v E (11)
English, S. (Rangers), 1933 v W, S (2)
Enright, J. (Leeds C), 1912 v S (1)

Falloon, E. (Aberdeen), 1931 v S; 1933 v S (2)
Farquharson, T. G. (Cardiff C), 1923 v S, W; 1924 v E, S, W; 1925 v E, S (7)
Farrell, P. (Distillery), 1901 v S, W (2)
Farrell, P. (Hibernian), 1938 v W (1)
Farrell, P. D. (Everton), 1947 v S, W; 1948 v E, S, W; 1949 v E, W (7)
Feeney, J. M. (Linfield), 1947 v S; (with Swansea T), 1950 v E (2)
Feeney, W. (Glentoran), 1976 v Is (1)
Feeney, W. J. (Bournemouth), 2002 v Lie, Sp; 2003 v Cy (sub); (with Luton T), 2005 v Pol (sub), G (sub) (5)
Ferguson, G. (Linfield), 1999 v Ca (sub); 2001 v N, CzR (sub), Bul (sub), CzR (sub) (5)
Ferguson, W. (Linfield), 1966 v M; 1967 v E (2)
Ferris, J. (Belfast C), 1920 v E, W; (with Chelsea), 1921 v S, E; (with Belfast C), 1928 v F, S (6)
Ferris, R. O. (Birmingham C), 1950 v S; 1951 v F; 1952 v S (3)
Fettis, A. W. (Hull C), 1992 v D, Li; 1993 v D; 1994 v M; 1995 v P, Ei, La, Ca, Ch, La; 1996 v P, Lie, A; (with Nottingham F), v N, G; 1997 v Uk, Arm (2); (with Blackburn R), 1998 v P, Slo, Sw, Sp; 1999 v T, Fi, Mol (25)
Finney, T. (Sunderland), 1975 v N, E (sub), S, W; 1976 v N, Y, S; (with Cambridge U), 1980 v E, Is, S, E, W, Aus (2) (14)
Fitzpatrick, J. C. (Bohemians), 1896 v E, S (2)
Flack, H. (Burnley), 1929 v S (1)
Fleming, J. G. (Nottingham F), 1987 v E (2), Is, Y; 1988 v T, Gr, Pol; 1989 v Ma, Ch; (with Manchester C), 1990 v H, Ei; (with Barnsley), 1991 v Y; 1992 v Li (sub), G; 1993 v Alb, Sp, D, Alb, Sp, Li, La; 1994 v La, D, Ei, R, Lie, Co, M; 1995 v P, A, Ei (31)
Forbes, G. (Limavady), 1888 v W; (with Distillery), 1891 v E, S (3)
Forde, J. T. (Ards), 1959 v Sp; 1961 v E, S, WG (4)
Foreman, T. A. (Cliftonville), 1899 v S (1)
Forsythe, J. (YMCA), 1888 v E, S (2)
Fox, W. T. (Ulster), 1887 v E, S (2)
Frame, T. (Linfield), 1925 v S.Af (1)
Fulton, R. P. (Larne), 1928 v F; (Belfast C), 1930 v W; 1931 v E, S, W; 1932 v W, E; 1933 v E, S; 1934 v E, W, S; 1935 v E, W, S; 1936 v S, W; 1937 v E, S, W; 1938 v W (21)

Gaffikin, G. (Linfield Ath), 1890 v S, W; 1891 v S, W; 1892 v E, S, W; 1893 v E, S, W; 1894 v E, S, W; 1895 v E, W (15)
Galbraith, W. (Distillery), 1890 v W (1)
Gallagher, P. (Celtic), 1920 v E, S; 1922 v S; 1923 v S, W; 1924 v S, W; 1925 v S, W, E; (with Falkirk), 1927 v S (11)
Gallogly, C. (Huddersfield T), 1951 v E, S (2)
Gara, A. (Preston NE), 1902 v E, S, W (3)
Gardiner, A. (Cliftonville), 1930 v S, W; 1931 v S; 1932 v E, S (5)
Garrett, J. (Distillery), 1925 v W (1)
Gaston, R. (Oxford U), 1969 v Is (sub) (1)
Gaukrodger, G. (Linfield), 1895 v W (1)
Gaussen, A. D. (Moyola Park), 1884 v E, S; (with Magherafelt), 1888 v E, W; 1889 v E, W (6)
Geary, J. (Glentoran), 1931 v S; 1932 v S (2)
Gibb, J. T. (Wellington Park) 1884 v S, W; 1885 v S, E, W; 1886 v S; 1887 v S, E, W; (with Cliftonville), 1889 v S (10)
Gibb, T. J. (Cliftonville), 1936 v W (1)
Gibson W. K. (Cliftonville), 1894 v S, W, E; 1895 v S; 1897 v W; 1898 v S, W, E; 1901 v S, W, E; 1902 v S, W; 1903 v S (14)
Gillespie, K. R. (Manchester U), 1995 v P, A, Ei; (with Newcastle U), Ei, La, Ca, Ch (sub), La (sub); 1996 v P, A, N, G; 1997 v Uk, Arm, Bel, P, Uk; 1998 v G, Alb, Slo, Sw; 1999 v T, Fi, Mol; (with Blackburn R), G, Mol; 2000 v F (sub), T (sub), G (sub), L, Ma, H; 2001 v Y (sub), CzR, Bul (2); 2002 v D, Ic, Pol, Lie, Sp; 2003 v Cy, Sp, Uk, Fi, Arm, Gr; (with Leicester C), 2004 v Uk, Arm, Gr, N, Ser, Bar, Stk (sub), Tr (sub); 2005 v Sw, Az (sub), A, Ca, E, Pol, G (62)
Gillespie, S. (Hertford), 1886 v E, S, W; 1887 v E, S, W (6)
Gillespie, W. (Sheffield U), 1913 v E, S; 1914 v E, W; 1920 v S, W; 1921 v E; 1922 v E, S, W; 1923 v E, S, W; 1924 v E, S, W; 1925 v E, S; 1926 v S, W; 1927 v E, W; 1928 v E; 1929 v E; 1931 v E (25)
Gillespie, W. (West Down), 1889 v W (1)
Goodall, A. L. (Derby Co), 1899 v S, W; 1900 v E, W; 1901 v E; 1902 v S; 1903 v E, W; (with Glossop), 1904 v E, W (10)
Goodbody, M. F. (Dublin University), 1889 v E; 1891 v W (2)
Gordon, H. (Linfield), 1895 v E; 1896 v E, S (3)
Gordon R. W. (Linfield), 1891 v S; 1892 v W, E, S; 1893 v E, S, W (7)
Gordon, T. (Linfield), 1894 v W; 1895 v E (2)
Gorman, W. C. (Brentford), 1947 v E, S, W; 1948 v W (4)
Gough, J. (Queen's Island), 1925 v S.Af (1)
Gowdy, J. (Glentoran), 1920 v E; (with Queen's Island), 1924 v W; (with Falkirk), 1926 v E, S; 1927 v E, S (6)
Gowdy, W. A. (Hull C), 1932 v S; (with Sheffield W), 1933 v S; (with Linfield), 1935 v E, S, W; (with Hibernian), 1936 v W (6)
Graham, W. G. L. (Doncaster R), 1951 v W, F; 1952 v E, S, W; 1953 v S, F; 1954 v E, W; 1955 v S, W; 1956 v E, S; 1959 v E (14)
Gray, P. (Luton T), 1993 v D (sub), Alb, Ei, Sp; (with Sunderland), 1994 v La, D, Ei, R, Lie (sub); 1995 v P, A, Ei, Ca, Ch (sub); 1996 v P (sub), Lie, A; (with Nancy), 1997 v Uk, Arm, G (sub); (with Luton T), 1999 v Mol (sub); (with Burnley), 2001 v Ma (sub), D (sub), Ic (sub); (with Oxford U), N (sub), CzR (sub) (26)
Greer, W. (QPR), 1909 v E, S, W (3)
Gregg, H. (Doncaster R), 1954 v W; 1957 v E, S, W, I, P (2); 1958 v E, I; (with Manchester U), 1958 v Cz, Arg, WG, F, W; 1959 v E, W; 1960 v S, E, W; 1961 v E, S; 1962 v S, Gr; 1964 v S, E (25)
Griffin, D. J. (St Johnstone), 1996 v G; 1997 v Uk, I, Bel (sub), Th; 1998 v G (sub), Alb; 1999 v Mol, Ei (sub); 2000 v L, Ma, H; (with Dundee U), 2001 v Y (sub), N (sub), CzR, Bul (2), CzR; 2002 v D, Ic, Ma, Pol; 2003 v Cy, I, Sp; 2004 v Uk, Arm, Gr; (with Stockport Co), N (29)

Hall, G. (Distillery), 1897 v E (1)
Halligan, W. (Derby Co), 1911 v W; (with Wolverhampton W), 1912 v E (2)
Hamill, M. (Manchester U), 1912 v E; 1914 v E, S; (with Belfast C), 1920 v E, S, W; (with Manchester C), 1921 v S (7)
Hamill, R. (Glentoran), 1999 v Ca (sub) (1)
Hamilton, B. (Linfield), 1969 v T; 1971 v Cy (2), E, S, W; (with Ipswich T), 1972 v USSR (1+1 sub), Sp; 1973 v Bul, Cy (2), P, E, S, W; 1974 v Bul, S, E, W; 1975 v N, Se, Y, E; 1976 v Se, N, Y; (with Everton), Is, S, E, W; 1977 v Ho, Bel, WG, E, S, W, Ic; (with Millwall), 1978 v S, E, W; 1979 v Ei (sub); (with Swindon T), Bul (2), E, S, W, D; 1980 v Aus (2 sub) (50)
Hamilton, G. (Portadown), 2003 v I (sub); 2004 v Ser (sub), Bar (sub), Stk; 2005 v Sw (sub) (5)
Hamilton, J. (Knock), 1882 v E, W (2)
Hamilton, R. (Rangers), 1928 v S; 1929 v E; 1930 v S, E; 1932 v S (5)
Hamilton, W. D. (Dublin Association), 1885 v W (1)
Hamilton, W. J. (Distillery), 1908 v W (1)
Hamilton, W. J. (Dublin Association), 1885 v W (1)
Hamilton, W. R. (QPR), 1978 v S (sub); (with Burnley), 1980 v S, E, W, Aus (2); 1981 v Se, P, S, P, S, Se; 1982 v S, Is, E, W, Y, Hon, Sp, A, F; 1983 v A, WG, Alb (2), S, E, W; 1984 v A, T, WG, S, E, W, Fi; (with Oxford U), 1985 v R, Sp; 1986 v Mor (sub), Alg, Sp (sub), Br (sub) (41)
Hampton, H. (Bradford C), 1911 v E, S, W; 1912 v E, W; 1913 v E, S, W; 1914 v E (9)
Hanna, J. (Nottingham F), 1912 v S, W (2)
Hanna, J. D. (Royal Artillery, Portsmouth), 1899 v W (1)
Hannon, D. J. (Bohemians), 1908 v E, S; 1911 v E, S; 1912 v W; 1913 v E (6)
Harkin, J. T. (Southport), 1968 v W; 1969 v T; (with Shrewsbury T), W (sub); 1970 v USSR; 1971 v Sp (5)
Harland, A. I. (Linfield), 1922 v N; 1923 v E (2)
Harris, J. (Cliftonville), 1921 v W; (with Glenavon), 1925 v S.Af (2)
Harris, V. (Shelbourne), 1906 v E; 1907 v E, W; 1908 v E, W, S; (with Everton), 1909 v E, W, S; 1910 v E, S, W; 1911 v E, S, W; 1912 v E; 1913 v E, S; 1914 v S, W (20)
Harvey, M. (Sunderland), 1961 v I; 1962 v Ho; 1963 v W, Sp; 1964 v S, E, W, U, Sp; 1965 v E, S, W, Sw (2), Ho (2), Alb; 1966 v S, E, W, M, Alb, WG; 1967 v E, S; 1968 v E, W; 1969 v Is, T (2), E; 1970 v USSR; 1971 v Cy, W (sub) (34)
Hastings, J. (Knock), 1882 v E, W; (with Ulster), 1883 v W; 1884 v E, S; 1886 v E, S (7)
Hatton, S. (Linfield), 1963 v S, Pol (2)
Hayes, W. E. (Huddersfield T), 1938 v E, S; 1939 v E, S (4)

Healy, D. J. (Manchester U), 2000 v L, Ma, H; 2001 v Y, Ma, D, Ic; (with Preston NE), N, CzR, Bul (2), CzR; 2002 v D, Ic, Ma, Pol, Lie, Sp; 2003 v Cy, Sp (sub), Uk, Fi, Arm, Gr, I, Sp; 2004 v Uk, Arm, Gr, N, Es, Ser, Bar, Stk (sub), Tr; 2005 v Sw, Pol, W, A; (with Leeds U), Ca, E, Pol, G (43)
Healy, P. J. (Coleraine), 1982 v S, W, Hon (sub); (with Glentoran), 1983 v A (sub) (4)
Hegan, D. (WBA), 1970 v USSR; (with Wolverhampton W), 1972 v USSR, E, S, W; 1973 v Bul, Cy (7)
Henderson, J. (Ulster), 1885 v E, S, W (3)
Hewison, G. (Moyola Park), 1885 v E, S (2)
Hill, C. F. (Sheffield U), 1990 v N, U; 1991 v Pol, Y; 1992 v A, D; (with Leicester C), 1995 v Ei, La; 1996 v P, Lie, A, N, Se, G; 1997 v Uk, Arm, G, Alb, P, Uk, Arm, Th; (with Trelleborg), 1998 v G, Alb, P; (with Northampton T), Slo; 1999 v T (27)
Hill, M. J. (Norwich C), 1959 v W; 1960 v W; 1961 v WG; 1962 v S; (with Everton), 1964 v S, E, Sp (7)
Hinton, E. (Fulham), 1947 v S, W; 1948 v S, E, W; (with Millwall), 1951 v W, F (7)
Holmes, S. P. (Wrexham), 2002 v Lie (sub) (1)
Hopkins, J. (Brighton), 1926 v E (1)
Horlock, K. (Swindon T), 1995 v La, Ca; 1997 v G, Alb, I; (with Manchester C), v Bel, Uk, Arm, Th; 1998 v G, Alb, P; 1999 v T, Fi, G, Mol, Ca; 2000 v F, T, G, Ma (sub); 2001 v Y, Ma, D, Ic; 2002 v D, Ic, Ma, Sp; 2003 v Cy, Sp, Uk (32)
Houston, J. (Linfield), 1912 v S, W; 1913 v W; (with Everton), 1913 v E, S; 1914 v S (6)
Houston, W. (Linfield), 1933 v W (1)
Houston, W. J. (Moyola Park), 1885 v E, S (2)
Hughes, A. W. (Newcastle U), 1998 v Slo, Sw, Sp (sub); 1999 v T, Fi, Mol (sub), Ca, Ei; 2000 v F, T, L, H; 2001 v Y, Ma, D, Ic, N, CzR, Bul, CzR; 2002 v D, Ic, Pol, Sp; 2003 v Sp, Uk, Fi, Arm, Gr, I, Sp; 2004 v Uk, Arm, Gr, N; 2005 v Sw, Pol, W, Az, A, Ca, E, Pol (43)
Hughes, M. E. (Manchester C), 1992 v D, S, Li, G; (with Strasbourg), 1993 v Alb, Sp, D, Ei, Sp, Li, La; 1994 v La, D, Ei, R, Lie, Co, M; 1995 v P, A, Ei (2) La, Ca, Ch, La; 1996 v P, Lie, A, N, G; (with West Ham U), 1997 v Uk, Arm, G, Alb, I, Uk; 1998 v G; (with Wimbledon), P, Slo, Sw, Sp; 1999 v T, Fi, Mol, G, Mol; 2000 v F, T, G, Fi, L (sub), Ma, H; 2001 v CzR, Bul (2), CzR; 2002 v D, Ic, Ma, Pol, Lie (sub); 2003 v Sp (sub), Uk; (with C Palace), 2004 v Uk, Gr, N, Ser (sub); 2005 v Pol, W (71)
Hughes, P. A. (Bury), 1987 v E, T, Is (3)
Hughes, W. (Bolton W), 1951 v W (1)
Humphries, W. M. (Ards), 1962 v W; (with Coventry C), 1962 v Ho; 1963 v E, S, W, Pol, Sp; 1964 v S, E, Sp; 1965 v S, Ho; (with Swansea T), 1965 v W, Alb (14)
Hunter, A. (Distillery), 1905 v W; 1906 v W, E, S; (with Belfast C), 1908 v W; 1909 v W, E, S (8)
Hunter, A. (Blackburn R), 1970 v USSR; 1971 v Cy (2), E, S, W; (with Ipswich T), 1972 v USSR (2), Sp, E, S, W; 1973 v Bul, Cy (2), P, E, S, W; 1974 v Bul, S, E, W; 1975 v N, Se, Y, E, S, W; 1976 v Se, N, Y, Is, S, E, W; 1977 v Ho, Bel, WG, E, S, W, Ic; 1978 v Ic, Ho, Bel; 1979 v Ei, D, S, W, D; 1980 v E, Ei (53)
Hunter, B. V. (Wrexham), 1995 v La; 1996 v P, Lie, A, Se, G; (with Reading), 1997 v Arm, G, Alb, I, Bel; 1999 v Ca, Ei; 2000 v F, T (15)
Hunter, R. J. (Cliftonville), 1884 v E, S, W (3)
Hunter, V. (Coleraine), 1962 v E; 1964 v Sp (2)

Ingham, M. G. (Sunderland), 2005 v G (sub) (1)
Irvine, R. J. (Linfield), 1962 v Ho; 1963 v E, S, W, Pol (2), Sp; (with Stoke C), 1965 v W (8)
Irvine, R. W. (Everton), 1922 v S; 1923 v E, W; 1924 v E, S; 1925 v E; 1926 v E; 1927 v E, W; 1928 v E, S; (with Portsmouth), 1929 v E; 1930 v S; (with Connah's Quay), 1931 v E; (with Derry C), 1932 v W (15)
Irvine, W. J. (Burnley), 1963 v W, Sp; 1965 v S, W, Sw, Ho (2), Alb; 1966 v S, E, W, M, Alb; 1967 v E, S; 1968 v E, W; (with Preston NE), 1969 v Is, T, E; (with Brighton & HA), 1972 v E, S, W (23)
Irving, S. J. (Dundee), 1923 v S, W; 1924 v S, E, W; 1925 v S, E, W; 1926 v S, W; (with Cardiff C), 1927 v S, E, W; 1928 v S, E, W; (with Chelsea), 1929 v E; 1931 v W (18)

Jackson, T. A. (Everton), 1969 v Is, E, S, W; 1970 v USSR (1+1 sub); (with Nottingham F), 1971 v Sp; 1972 v E, S, W; 1973 v Cy, E, S, W; 1974 v Bul, P, S (sub), E (sub), W (sub); 1975 v N (sub), Se, Y, E, S, W; (with Manchester U); 1976 v Se, N, Y; 1977 v Ho, Bel, WG, E, S, W, Ic (35)
Jamison, J. (Glentoran), 1976 v N (1)
Jenkins, I. (Chester C), 1997 v Arm, Th; 1998 v Slo; (with Dundee U), Sw, Sp; 2000 v Fi (6)
Jennings, P. A. (Watford), 1964 v W, U; (with Tottenham H), 1965 v E, S, Sw (2), Ho, Alb; 1966 v S, E, W, Alb, WG; 1967 v E, S; 1968 v S, E, W; 1969 v Is, T (2), E, S, W; 1970 v S, E, USSR (2); 1971 v Cy (2), E, S, W; 1972 v USSR, Sp, S, E, W; 1973 v Bul, Cy, P, E, S, W; 1974 v P, S, E, W; 1975 v N, Se, Y, E, S, W; 1976 v Se, N, Y, Is, S, E, W; 1977 v Ho, Bel, WG, E, S, W, Ic; (with Arsenal), 1978 v Ic, Ho, Bel; 1979 v Ei, D, Bul, E, Bul, E, S, W, D; 1980 v E, Ei, Is; 1981 v S, P, S, Se; 1982 v S, Is, E, W, Y, Hon, Sp, F; 1983 v Alb, S, E, W; 1984 v A, T, WG, S, W, Fi; 1985 v R, Fi, E, Sp, T; (with Tottenham H), 1986 v T, R, E, F, D; (with Everton), Mor; (with Tottenham H), Alg, Sp, Br (119)
Johnson, D. M. (Blackburn R), 1999 v Ei (sub); 2000 v Fi (sub), L, Ma (sub), H (sub); 2001 v Y, Ma, Ic, N (sub), Bul (sub+1), CzR; 2002 v Ma, Pol; (with Birmingham C), Lie, Sp; 2003 v Cy, Sp, Uk, Fi, Arm, Gr, I, Sp; 2004 v Uk, Arm, N, Bar, Stk (sub), Tr; 2005 v Sw, Pol, W, Az, A, E, G (37)
Johnston, H. (Portadown), 1927 v W (1)
Johnston, R. S. (Distillery), 1882 v W; 1884 v E; 1886 v E, S (4)
Johnston, R. S. (Distillery), 1905 v W (1)
Johnston, S. (Linfield), 1890 v W; 1893 v S, W; 1894 v E (4)
Johnston, W. (Oldpark), 1885 v S, W (2)
Johnston, W. C. (Glenavon), 1962 v W; (with Oldham Ath), 1966 v M (sub) (2)
Jones, J. (Linfield), 1930 v S, W; 1931 v S, W, E; 1932 v S, E; 1933 v S, E, W; 1934 v S, E, W; 1935 v S, E, W; 1936 v E, S; (with Hibernian), 1936 v W; 1937 v E, W, S; (with Glenavon), 1938 v E (23)
Jones, J. (Glenavon), 1956 v W; 1957 v E, W (3)
Jones, S. (Distillery), 1934 v E; (with Blackpool), 1934 v W (2)
Jones, S. G. (Crewe Alex), 2003 v I (sub), Sp; 2004 v Uk (sub), Arm (sub), Gr (sub), N (sub), Es, Ser (sub), Bar (sub), Stk (sub), Tr (sub); 2005 v Pol (sub), A (sub), Ca (sub), E (sub), G (16)
Jordan, T. (Linfield), 1895 v E, W (2)

Kavanagh, P. J. (Celtic), 1930 v E (1)
Keane, T. R. (Swansea T), 1949 v S (1)
Kearns, A. (Distillery), 1900 v E, S, W; 1902 v E, S, W (6)
Kee, P. V. (Oxford U), 1990 v N; 1991 v Y (2), D, A, Pol, Fa; (with Ards), 1995 v A, Ei (9)
Keith, R. M. (Newcastle U), 1958 v E, W, Cz (2), Arg, I, WG, F; 1959 v E, S, W, Sp; 1960 v S, E; 1961 v S, E, W, I, WG (2), Gr; 1962 v W, Ho (23)
Kelly, H. R. (Fulham), 1950 v E, W; (with Southampton), 1951 v E, S (4)
Kelly, J. (Glentoran), 1896 v E (1)
Kelly, J. (Derry C), 1932 v E, W; 1933 v E, W, S; 1934 v W; 1936 v E, S, W; 1937 v S, E (11)
Kelly, P. J. (Manchester C), 1921 v E (1)
Kelly, P. M. (Barnsley), 1950 v S (1)
Kennedy, A. L. (Arsenal), 1923 v W; 1925 v E (2)
Kennedy, P. H. (Watford), 1999 v Mol, G (sub); 2000 v F, T, G, Fi; 2001 v N, Bul (sub), CzR (sub); (with Wigan Ath), 2002 v D, Ic, Ma, Pol; 2003 v Cy, Fi, I, Sp; 2004 v Uk, Gr, N (20)
Kernaghan, N. (Belfast C), 1936 v W; 1937 v S; 1938 v E (3)
Kirk, A. R. (Hearts), 2000 v H; 2001 v N (sub); 2003 v Uk (sub), Fi (sub), Gr (sub); (with Boston U), 2005 v Ca (sub); (with Northampton T), E (sub), G (sub) (8)
Kirkwood, H. (Cliftonville), 1904 v W (1)
Kirwan, J. (Tottenham H), 1900 v W; 1902 v E, W; 1903 v E, S, W; 1904 v E, S, W; 1905 v E, S, W; (with Chelsea), 1906 v E, S, W; 1907 v W; (with Clyde), 1909 v S (17)

Lacey, W. (Everton), 1909 v E, S, W; 1910 v E, S, W; 1911 v E, S, W; 1912 v E; (with Liverpool), 1913 v W; 1914 v E, S, W; 1920 v E, S, W; 1921 v E, S, W; 1922 v E, S; (with New Brighton), 1925 v E (23)
Lawther, R. (Glentoran), 1888 v E, S (2)
Lawther, W. I. (Sunderland), 1960 v W; 1961 v I; (with Blackburn R), 1962 v S, Ho (4)
Leatham, J. (Belfast C), 1939 v W (1)
Ledwidge, J. J. (Shelbourne), 1906 v S, W (2)
Lemon, J. (Glentoran), 1886 v W; (with Belfast YMCA), 1888 v S; 1889 v W (3)
Lennon, N. F. (Crewe Alex), 1994 v M (sub); 1995 v Ch; 1996 v P, Lie, A; (with Leicester C), v N; 1997 v Uk, Arm, G, Alb, Bel, P, Uk, Arm, Th; 1998 v G, Alb, P, Slo, Sw, Sp; 1999 v T, Fi, Mol, G, Mol, Ei; 2000 v F, T, G, Fi, Ma, H; 2001 v D, Ic; (with Celtic), N, CzR, Bul (2); 2002 v Pol (sub) (40)
Leslie, W. (YMCA), 1887 v E (1)
Lewis, J. (Glentoran), 1899 v S, E, W; (with Distillery), 1900 v S (4)
Lockhart, H. (Russell School), 1884 v W (1)

Lockhart, N. H. (Linfield), 1947 v E; (with Coventry C), 1950 v W; 1951 v W; 1952 v W; (with Aston Villa), 1954 v S, E; 1955 v W; 1956 v W (8)
Lomas, S. M. (Manchester C), 1994 v R, Lie, Co (sub), M; 1995 v P, A; 1996 v P, Lie, A, N, Se, G; 1997 v Uk, Arm, G, Alb, I, Bel; (with West Ham U), P, Uk, Arm, Th; 1998 v Alb, P, Slo, Sw; 1999 v Mol, G, Mol, Ca; 2000 v F, T, G, L, Ma; 2001 v Ma, D, Ic; 2002 v Pol, Lie; 2003 v Sp, Uk, Fi, Arm, Gr (45)
Loyal, J. (Clarence), 1891 v S (1)
Lutton, R. J. (Wolverhampton W), 1970 v S, E; (with West Ham U), 1973 v Cy (sub), S (sub), W (sub); 1974 v P (6)
Lynas, R. (Cliftonville), 1925 v S.Af (1)
Lyner, D. R. (Glentoran), 1920 v E, W; 1922 v S, W; (with Manchester U), 1923 v E; (with Kilmarnock), 1923 v W (6)
Lytle, J. (Glentoran), 1898 W (1)

McAdams, W. J. (Manchester C), 1954 v W; 1955 v S; 1957 v E; 1958 v S, I; (with Bolton W), 1961 v E, S, W, I, WG (2), Gr; 1962 v E, Gr; (with Leeds U), Ho (15)
McAlery, J. M. (Cliftonville), 1882 v E, W (2)
McAlinden, J. (Belfast C), 1938 v S; 1939 v S; (with Portsmouth), 1947 v E; (with Southend U), 1949 v E (4)
McAllen, J. (Linfield), 1898 v E; 1899 v E, S, W; 1900 v E, S, W; 1901 v W; 1902 v S (9)
McAlpine, S. (Cliftonville), 1901 v S (1)
McArthur, A. (Distillery), 1886 v W (1)
McAuley, G. (Lincoln C), 2005 v G (sub) (1)
McAuley, J. L. (Huddersfield T), 1911 v E, W; 1912 v E, S; 1913 v E, S (6)
McAuley, P. (Belfast C), 1900 v S (1)
McBride, S. D. (Glenavon), 1991 v D (sub), Pol (sub); 1992 v Fa (sub), D (4)
McCabe, J. J. (Leeds U), 1949 v S, W; 1950 v E; 1951 v W; 1953 v W; 1954 v S (6)
McCabe, W. (Ulster), 1891 v E (1)
McCambridge, J. (Ballymena), 1930 v S, W; (with Cardiff C), 1931 v W; 1932 v E (4)
McCandless, J. (Bradford), 1912 v W; 1913 v W; 1920 v W, S; 1921 v E (5)
McCandless, W. (Linfield), 1920 v E, W; 1921 v E; (with Rangers), 1921 v W; 1922 v S; 1924 v W, S; 1925 v S; 1929 v W (9)
McCann, G. S. (West Ham U), 2002 v Ma (sub), Pol (sub), Lie; 2003 v Sp (sub), Uk (sub); (with Cheltenham T), Arm, Gr; 2004 v Arm, Es (sub) (9)
McCann, P. (Belfast C), 1910 v E, S, W; 1911 v E; (with Glentoran), 1911 v S; 1912 v E; 1913 v W (7)
McCarthy, J. D. (Port Vale), 1996 v Se; 1997 v I, Arm, Th; (with Birmingham C), 1998 v P (sub), Slo (sub), Sp; 1999 v Fi (sub), Mol (sub), G (sub), Ca, Ei; 2000 v F, T, G, Fi; 2001 v N, Bul (sub) (18)
McCartney, A. (Ulster), 1903 v S, W; (with Linfield), 1904 v S, W; (with Everton), 1905 v E, S; (with Belfast C), 1907 v E, S, W; 1908 v E, S, W; (with Glentoran), 1909 v E, S, W (15)
McCartney, G. (Sunderland), 2002 v Ic, Ma, Pol (sub), Lie, Sp; 2003 v Cy, Sp, Uk, Fi, Gr, I, Sp; 2004 v Uk, Arm, Gr, N; 2005 v W (sub), A, Ca, G (20)
McCashin, J. W. (Cliftonville), 1896 v W; 1898 v S, W; 1899 v S; 1903 v S (5)
McCavana, W. T. (Coleraine), 1955 v S; 1956 v E, S (3)
McCaw, D. (Malone), 1882 v E (1)
McCaw, J. H. (Linfield), 1927 v W; 1928 v F; 1930 v S; 1931 v E, S, W (6)
McClatchey, J. (Distillery), 1886 v E, S, W (3)
McClatchey, T. (Distillery), 1895 v S (1)
McCleary, J. W. (Cliftonville), 1955 v W (1)
McCleery, W. (Cliftonville), 1922 v N; (Linfield), 1930 v E, W; 1931 v E, S, W; 1932 v S, W; 1933 v E, W (10)
McClelland, J. (Mansfield T), 1980 v S (sub), Aus (3); 1981 v Se, S; (with Rangers), S, Se (sub); 1982 v S, W, Y, Hon, Sp, A, F; 1983 v A, WG, Alb, T, Alb, S, E, W; 1984 v A, T, WG, S, E, W, Fi; 1985 v R, Is; (with Watford), Fi, E, Sp, T; 1986 v T, F (sub); 1987 v E (2), T, Is, Y; 1988 v T, Gr, F, Ma; 1989 v Ei, H, Sp (2), Ma; (with Leeds U), 1990 v N (53)
McClelland, J. T. (Arsenal), 1961 v W, I, WG (2), Gr; (with Fulham), 1966 v M (6)
McCluggage, A. (Cliftonville), 1922 v N; (Bradford), 1924 v E; (with Burnley), 1927 v S, W; 1928 v S, E, W; 1929 v S, E, W; 1930 v W; 1931 v E, W (13)
McClure, G. (Cliftonville), 1907 v S, W; 1908 v E; (with Distillery), 1909 v E (4)
McConnell, E. (Cliftonville), 1904 v S, W; (with Glentoran), 1905 v S; (with Sunderland), 1906 v E; 1907 v E; 1908 v S, W; (with Sheffield W), 1909 v S, W; 1910 v S, W, E (12)
McConnell, P. (Doncaster R), 1928 v W; (with Southport), 1932 v E (2)
McConnell, W. G. (Bohemians), 1912 v W; 1913 v E, S; 1914 v E, S, W (6)
McConnell, W. H. (Reading), 1925 v W; 1926 v E, W; 1927 v E, S, W; 1928 v E, W (8)
McCourt, F. J. (Manchester C), 1952 v E, W; 1953 v E, S, W, F (6)
McCourt, P. J. (Rochdale), 2002 v Sp (sub) (1)
McCoy, R. K. (Coleraine), 1987 v Y (sub) (1)
McCoy, S. (Distillery), 1896 v W (1)
McCracken, E. (Barking), 1928 v F (1)
McCracken, R. (C Palace), 1921 v E; 1922 v E, S, W (4)
McCracken, R. (Linfield), 1922 v N (1)
McCracken, W. R. (Distillery), 1902 v E, W; 1903 v S, E; 1904 v E, S, W; (with Newcastle U), 1905 v E, S, W; 1907 v E; 1920 v E; 1922 v E, S, W; (with Hull C), 1923 v S (16)
McCreery, D. (Manchester U), 1976 v S (sub), E, W; 1977 v Ho, Bel, WG, E, S, W, Ic; 1978 v Ic, Ho, Bel, S, E, W; 1979 v Ei, D, Bul, E, Bul, W, D; (with QPR), 1980 v E, Ei, S (sub), E (sub), W (sub), Aus (1+1 sub); 1981 v Se (sub), P (sub); (with Tulsa R), S, P, Se; 1982 v S, Is, E (sub), F, Y, Hon, Sp, A, F; (with Newcastle U), 1983 v A; 1984 v T (sub); 1985 v R, Sp (sub); 1986 v T (sub), R, E, F, D, Alg, Sp, Br; 1987 v T, E, Y; 1988 v Y; 1989 v Sp, Ma, Ch; (with Hearts), 1990 v H, Ei, N, U (sub) (67)
McCrory, S. (Southend U), 1958 v E (1)
McCullough, K. (Belfast C), 1935 v W; 1936 v E; (with Manchester C), 1936 v S; 1937 v E, S (5)
McCullough, W. J. (Arsenal), 1961 v I; 1963 v Sp; 1964 v S, E, W, U, Sp; 1965 v E, Sw; (with Millwall), 1967 v E (10)
McCurdy, C. (Linfield), 1980 v Aus (sub) (1)
McDonald, A. (QPR), 1986 v R, E, F, D, Mor, Alg, Sp, Br; 1987 v E (2), T, Is, Y; 1988 v Y, T, Pol, F, Ma; 1989 v Ei, H, Sp, Ch; 1990 v H, Ei, U; 1991 v Y, D, A, Fa; 1992 v Fa, S, Li, G; 1993 v Alb, Sp, D, Alb, Ei, Sp, Li, La; 1994 v D, Ei; 1995 v P, A, Ei, La, Ca, Ch, La; 1996 v A (sub), N (52)
McDonald, R. (Rangers), 1930 v S; 1932 v E (2)
McDonnell, J. (Bohemians), 1911 v E, S; 1912 v W; 1913 v W (4)
McElhinney, G. M. A. (Bolton W), 1984 v WG, S, E, W, Fi; 1985 v R (6)
McEvilly, L. R. (Rochdale), 2002 v Sp (sub) (1)
McFaul, W. S. (Linfield), 1967 v E (sub); (with Newcastle U), 1970 v W; 1971 v Sp; 1972 v USSR; 1973 v Cy; 1974 v Bul (6)
McGarry, J. K. (Cliftonville), 1951 v W, F, S (3)
McGaughey, M. (Linfield), 1985 v Is (sub) (1)
McGibbon, P. C. G. (Manchester U), 1995 v Ca (sub), Ch, La; 1996 v Lie (sub); 1997 v Th; (with Wigan Ath), 1998 v Alb; 2000 v L (sub) (7)
McGrath, R. C. (Tottenham H), 1974 v S, E, W; 1975 v N; 1976 v Is (sub); 1977; (with Manchester U), Ho, Bel, WG, E, S, W, Ic; 1978 v Ic, Ho, Bel, S, E, W; 1979 v Bul (sub), E (2 sub) (21)
McGregor, S. (Glentoran), 1921 v S (1)
McGrillen, J. (Clyde), 1924 v S; (with Belfast C), 1927 v S (2)
McGuire, E. (Distillery), 1907 v S (1)
McGuire, J. (Linfield), 1928 v F (1)
McIlroy, H. (Cliftonville), 1906 v E (1)
McIlroy, J. (Burnley), 1952 v E, S, W; 1953 v E, S, W; 1954 v E, S, W; 1955 v E, S, W; 1956 v E, S, W; 1957 v E, S, W, I, P (2); 1958 v E, S, W, I (2), Cz (2), Arg, WG, F; 1959 v E, S, W, Sp; 1960 v E, S, W; 1961 v E, W, WG (2), Gr; 1962 v E, S, Gr, Ho; 1963 v E, S, Pol (2); (with Stoke C), 1963 v W; 1966 v S, E, Alb (55)
McIlroy, S. B. (Manchester U), 1972 v Sp, S (sub); 1974 v S, E, W; 1975 v N, Se, Y, E, S, W; 1976 v Se, N, Y, S, E, W; 1977 v Ho, Bel, E, S, W, Ic; 1978 v Ic, Ho, Bel, S, E, W; 1979 v Ei, D, Bul, E, Bul, E, S, W, D; 1980 v E, Ei, Is, S, E, W; 1981 v Se, P, S, P, S, Se; 1982 v S, Is; (with Stoke C), E, F, S, W, Y, Hon, Sp, A, F; 1983 v A, WG, Alb, T, Alb, S, E, W; 1984 v A, T, S, E, W, Fi; 1985 v Fi, E, T; (with Manchester C), 1986 v T, R, E, F, D, Mor, Alg, Sp, Br; 1987 v E (sub) (88)
McIlvenny, P. (Distillery), 1924 v W (1)
McIlvenny, R. (Distillery), 1890 v E; (with Ulster), 1891 v E (2)
McKeag, W. (Glentoran), 1968 v S, W (2)
McKeague, T. (Glentoran), 1925 v S.Af (1)
McKee, F. W. (Cliftonville), 1906 v S, W; (with Belfast C), 1914 v E, S, W (5)
McKelvey, H. (Glentoran), 1901 v W; 1903 v S (2)
McKenna, J. (Huddersfield), 1950 v E, S, W; 1951 v E, S, F; 1952 v E (7)
McKenzie, H. (Distillery), 1922 v N; 1923 v S (2)
McKenzie, R. (Airdrie), 1967 v W (1)
McKeown, N. (Linfield), 1892 v E, S, W; 1893 v S, W; 1894 v S, W (7)

McKie, H. (Cliftonville), 1895 v E, S, W (3)
McKinney, D. (Hull C), 1921 v S; (with Bradford C), 1924 v S (2)
McKinney, V. J. (Falkirk), 1966 v WG (1)
McKnight, A. D. (Celtic), 1988 v Y, T, Gr, Pol, F, Ma; (with West Ham U), 1989 v Ei, H, Sp (2) (10)
McKnight, J. (Preston NE), 1912 v S; (with Glentoran), 1913 v S (2)
McLaughlin, J. C. (Shrewsbury T), 1962 v E, S, W, Gr; 1963 v W; (with Swansea T), 1964 v W, U; 1965 v E, W, Sw (2); 1966 v W (12)
McLean, T. (Limavady), 1885 v S (1)
McMahon, G. J. (Tottenham H), 1995 v Ca (sub), Ch, La; 1996 v Lie, N (sub), Se, G; (with Stoke C), 1997 v Arm (sub), Alb (sub), Bel, P (sub), Uk (sub), Arm (sub), Th (sub); 1998 v G (sub), Alb (sub), P (sub) (17)
McMahon, J. (Bohemians), 1934 v S (1)
McMaster, G. (Glentoran), 1897 v E, S, W (3)
McMichael, A. (Newcastle U), 1950 v E, S; 1951 v E, S, F; 1952 v E, S, W; 1953 v E, S, W, F; 1954 v E, S, W; 1955 v E, W; 1956 v W; 1957 v E, S, W, I, P (2); 1958 v E, S, W, I (2), Cz (2), Arg, WG, F; 1959 v S, W, Sp; 1960 v E, S, W (40)
McMillan, G. (Distillery), 1903 v E; 1905 v W (2)
McMillan, S. T. (Manchester U), 1963 v E, S (2)
McMillen, W. S. (Manchester U), 1934 v E; 1935 v S; 1937 v S; (with Chesterfield), 1938 v S, W; 1939 v E, S (7)
McMordie, A. S. (Middlesbrough), 1969 v Is, T (2), E, S, W; 1970 v E, S, W, USSR; 1971 v Cy (2), E, S, W; 1972 v USSR, Sp, E, S, W; 1973 v Bul (21)
McMorran, E. J. (Belfast C), 1947 v E; (with Barnsley), 1951 v E, S, W; 1952 v E, S, W; 1953 v E, S, F; (with Doncaster R), 1953 v W; 1954 v E; 1956 v W; 1957 v I, P (15)
McMullan, D. (Liverpool), 1926 v E, W; 1927 v S (3)
McNally, B. A. (Shrewsbury T), 1986 v Mor; 1987 v T (sub); 1988 v Y, Gr, Ma (sub) (5)
McNinch, J. (Ballymena), 1931 v S; 1932 v S, W (3)
McParland, P. J. (Aston Villa), 1954 v W; 1955 v E, S; 1956 v E, S; 1957 v E, S, W, P; 1958 v E, S, W, I (2), Cz (2), Arg, WG, F; 1959 v E, S, W, Sp; 1960 v E, S, W; 1961 v E, S, W, I, WG (2), Gr; (with Wolverhampton W), 1962 v Ho (34)
McShane, J. (Cliftonville), 1899 v S; 1900 v E, S, W (4)
McVeigh, P. (Tottenham H), 1999 v Ca (sub); (with Norwich C), 2002 v Ic (sub), Pol (sub); 2003 v Sp, Uk, Fi, Arm, Gr (sub), I, Sp (sub); 2004 v Arm (sub), N (sub), Ser (sub), Bar (sub), Stk, Tr (sub); 2005 v Sw (sub), Pol (sub), W (sub), A (sub) (20)
McVicker, J. (Linfield), 1888 v E; (with Glentoran), 1889 v S (2)
McWha, W. B. R. (Knock), 1882 v E, W; (with Cliftonville), 1883 v E, W; 1884 v E; 1885 v E, W (7)
Mackie, J. (Arsenal), 1923 v W; (with Portsmouth), 1935 v S, W (3)
Madden, O. (Norwich C), 1938 v E (1)
Magee, G. (Wellington Park), 1885 v E, S, W (3)
Magill, E. J. (Arsenal), 1962 v E, S, Gr; 1963 v E, S, W, Pol (2), Sp; 1964 v E, S, W, U, Sp; 1965 v E, S, Sw (2), Ho, Alb; 1966 v S; (with Brighton & HA), E, Alb, W, WG, M (26)
Magilton, J. (Oxford U), 1991 v Pol, Y, Fa; 1992 v Fa, A, D, S, Li, G; 1993 v Alb, D, Alb, Ei, Li, La; 1994 v La, D, Ei; (with Southampton), R, Lie, Co, M; 1995 v P, A, Ei (2), Ca, Ch, La; 1996 v P, N, G; 1997 v Uk (sub), Arm (sub), Bel, P; 1998 v G; (with Sheffield W), P, Sp; (with Ipswich T), 2000 v L; 2001 v Y, Ma, D, Ic, N, CzR, Bul; 2002 v D, Ic, Ma, Pol, Lie (52)
Maginnis, H. (Linfield), 1900 v E, S, W; 1903 v S, W; 1904 v E, S, W (8)
Mahood, J. (Belfast C), 1926 v S; 1928 v E, S, W; 1929 v E, S, W; 1930 v W; (with Ballymena), 1934 v S (9)
Mannus, A. (Linfield), 2004 v Tr (sub) (1)
Manderson, R. (Rangers), 1920 v W, S; 1925 v S, E; 1926 v S (5)
Mansfield, J. (Dublin Freebooters), 1901 v E (1)
Martin, C. (Cliftonville), 1882 v E, W; 1883 v E (3)
Martin, C. (Bo'ness), 1925 v S (1)
Martin, C. J. (Glentoran), 1947 v S; (with Leeds U), 1948 v E, S, W; (with Aston Villa), 1949 v E; 1950 v W (6)
Martin, D. K. (Belfast C), 1934 v E, S, W; 1935 v S; (with Wolverhampton W), 1935 v E; 1936 v W; (with Nottingham F), 1937 v S; 1938 v E, S; 1939 v S (10)
Mathieson, A. (Luton T), 1921 v W; 1922 v E (2)
Maxwell, J. (Linfield), 1902 v W; 1903 v W, E; (with Glentoran), 1905 v W, S; (with Belfast C), 1906 v W; 1907 v S (7)
Meek, H. L. (Glentoran), 1925 v W (1)
Mehaffy, J. A. C. (Queen's Island), 1922 v W (1)
Meldon, P. A. (Dublin Freebooters), 1899 v S, W (2)
Mercer, H. V. A. (Linfield), 1908 v E (1)
Mercer, J. T. (Distillery), 1898 v E, S, W; 1899 v E; (with Linfield), 1902 v E, W; (with Distillery), 1903 v S (2), W; (with Derby Co), 1904 v E, W; 1905 v S (12)
Millar, W. (Barrow), 1932 v W; 1933 v S (2)
Miller, J. (Middlesbrough), 1929 v W, S; 1930 v E (3)
Milligan, D. (Chesterfield), 1939 v W (1)
Milne, R. G. (Linfield), 1894 v E, S, W; 1895 v E, W; 1896 v E, S, W; 1897 v E, S; 1898 v E, S, W; 1899 v E, W; 1901 v W; 1902 v E, S, W; 1903 v E, S (2); 1904 v E, S, W; 1906 v E, S, W (28)
Mitchell, E. J. (Cliftonville), 1933 v S; (with Glentoran), 1934 v W (2)
Mitchell, W. (Distillery), 1932 v E, W; 1933 v E, W; (with Chelsea), 1934 v W, S; 1935 v S, E; 1936 v S, E; 1937 v E, S, W; 1938 v E, S (15)
Molyneux, T. B. (Ligoniel), 1883 v E, W; (with Cliftonville), 1884 v E, W, S; 1885 v E, W; 1886 v E, W, S; 1888 v S (11)
Montgomery, F. J. (Coleraine), 1955 v E (1)
Moore, C. (Glentoran), 1949 v W (1)
Moore, P. (Aberdeen), 1933 v E (1)
Moore, R. (Linfield Ath), 1891 v E, S, W (3)
Moore, R. L. (Ulster), 1887 v S, W (2)
Moore, W. (Falkirk), 1923 v S (1)
Moorhead, F. W. (Dublin University), 1885 v E (1)
Moorhead, G. (Linfield), 1923 v S; 1928 v F, S; 1929 v S (4)
Moran, J. (Leeds C), 1912 v S (1)
Moreland, V. (Derby Co), 1979 v Bul (2 sub), E, S; 1980 v E, Ei (6)
Morgan, G. F. (Linfield), 1922 v N; 1923 v E; (with Nottingham F), 1924 v S; 1927 v E; 1928 v E, S, W; 1929 v E (8)
Morgan, S. (Port Vale), 1972 v Sp; 1973 v Bul (sub), P, Cy, E, S, W; (with Aston Villa), 1974 v Bul, P, S, E; 1975 v Se; 1976 v Se (sub), N, Y; (with Brighton & HA), S, W (sub); (with Sparta Rotterdam), 1979 v D (18)
Morrison, R. (Linfield Ath), 1891 v E, W (2)
Morrison, T. (Glentoran), 1895 v E, S, W; (with Burnley), 1899 v W; 1900 v W; 1902 v E, S (7)
Morrogh, D. (Bohemians), 1896 v S (1)
Morrow, S. J. (Arsenal), 1990 v U (sub); 1991 v A (sub), Pol, Y; 1992 v Fa, S (sub), G (sub); 1993 v Sp (sub), Alb, Ei; 1994 v R, Co, M (sub); 1995 v P, Ei (2), La; 1996 v P, Se; 1997 v Uk, G, Alb, I, Bel; (with QPR), P, Uk, Arm; 1998 v G, P, Slo, Sw, Sp; 1999 v T, Fi, Mol, G, Mol; 2000 v G, Fi (39)
Morrow, W. J. (Moyola Park), 1883 v E, W; 1884 v S (3)
Muir, R. (Oldpark), 1885 v S, W (2)
Mulholland, T.S. (Belfast C), 1906 v S, E (2)
Mullan, G. (Glentoran), 1983 v S, E, W, Alb (sub) (4)
Mulligan, J. (Manchester C), 1921 v S (1)
Mulryne, P. P. (Manchester U), 1997 v Bel (sub), Arm (sub), Th; 1998 v Alb (sub), Sp (sub); 1999 v T, Fi; (with Norwich C), Ca; 2001 v Y, D (sub), Bul (sub), CzR; 2002 v D, Ic, Pol, Lie; 2003 v Sp, Uk; 2004 v Uk (sub), Arm (sub), Es, Ser, Bar, Stk (sub), Tr; 2005 v Ca (sub) (26)
Murdock, C. J, (Preston NE), 2000 v L (sub), Ma, H (sub); 2001 v Y, Ma, D, Ic, N, CzR, Bul (2), CzR; 2002 v D, Ma; 2003 v Cy, Sp, Uk (sub); (with Hibernian), 2004 v Gr (sub), Bar (sub), Stk, Tr (sub); 2005 v Sw (sub), W, Az, A; (with Crewe Alex), Ca, E, Pol (28)
Murphy, J. (Bradford C), 1910 v E, S, W (3)
Murphy, N. (QPR), 1905 v E, S, W (3)
Murray, J. M. (Motherwell), 1910 v E, S; (with Sheffield W), W (3)

Napier, R. J. (Bolton W), 1966 v WG (1)
Neill, W. J. T. (Arsenal), 1961 v I, Gr, WG; 1962 v E, S, W, Gr; 1963 v E, W, Pol, Sp; 1964 v S, E, W, U, Sp; 1965 v E, S, W, Sw, Ho (2), Alb; 1966 v S, E, W, Alb, WG, M; 1967 v S, W; 1968 v S, E; 1969 v E, S, W, Is, T (2); 1970 v S, E, W, USSR (2); (with Hull C), 1971 v Cy, Sp; 1972 v USSR (2), Sp, S, E, W; 1973 v Bul, Cy (2), P, E, S, W (59)
Nelis, P. (Nottingham F), 1923 v E (1)
Nelson, S. (Arsenal), 1970 v W, E (sub); 1971 v Cy, Sp, E, S, W; 1972 v USSR (2), Sp, E, S, W; 1973 v Bul, Cy, P; 1974 v S, E; 1975 v Se, Y; 1976 v Se, N, Is, E; 1977 v Bel (sub), WG, W, Ic; 1978 v Ic, Ho, Bel; 1979 v Ei, D, Bul, E, Bul, E, S, W, D; 1980 v E, Ei, Is; 1981 v S, P, S, Se; (with Brighton & HA), 1982 v E, S, Sp (sub), A (51)
Nicholl, C. J. (Aston Villa), 1975 v Se, Y, E, S, W; 1976 v Se, N, Y, S, E, W; 1977 v W; (with Southampton), 1978 v Bel (sub), S, E, W; 1979 v Ei, Bul, E, Bul, E, W; 1980 v Ei, Is, S, E, W, Aus (3); 1981 v Se, P, S, P, S, Se; 1982 v S, Is, E, F, W, Y, Hon, Sp, A, F; 1983 v S (sub), E, W; (with Grimsby T), 1984 v A, T (51)
Nicholl, H. (Belfast C), 1902 v E, W; 1905 v E (3)

Nicholl, J. M. (Manchester U), 1976 v Is, W (sub); 1977 v Ho, Bel, E, S, W, Ic; 1978 v Ic, Ho, Bel, S, E, W; 1979 v Ei, D, Bul, E, Bul, E, S, W, D; 1980 v E, Ei, Is, S, E, W, Aus (3); 1981 v Se, P, S, P, S, Se; 1982 v S, Is, E; (with Toronto B), F, W, Y, Hon, Sp, A, F; (with Sunderland), 1983 v A, WG, Alb, T, Alb; (with Toronto B), S, E, W; 1984 v T; (with Rangers), WG, S, E; (with Toronto B), Fi; 1985 v R; (with WBA), Fi, E, Sp, T; 1986 v T, R, E, F, Alg, Sp, Br (73)
Nicholson, J. J. (Manchester U), 1961 v S, W; 1962 v E, W, Gr, Ho; 1963 v E, S, Pol (2); (with Huddersfield T), 1965 v W, Ho (2), Alb; 1966 v S, E, W, Alb, M; 1967 v S, W; 1968 v S, E, W; 1969 v S, E, W, T (2); 1970 v S, E, W, USSR (2); 1971 v Cy (2), E, S, W; 1972 v USSR (2) (41)
Nixon, R. (Linfield), 1914 v S (1)
Nolan, I. R. (Sheffield W), 1997 v Arm, G, Alb, P, Uk; 1998 v G, P; 2000 v G, Fi, L, Ma, H; (with Bradford C), 2001 v Y, Ma, Bul (2), CzR; (with Wigan Ath), 2002 v Sp (18)
Nolan-Whelan, J. V. (Dublin Freebooters), 1901 v E, W; 1902 v S, W; 1903 v S (5)

O'Boyle, G. (Dunfermline Ath), 1994 v Co (sub), M; (with St Johnstone), 1995 v P (sub), La (sub), Ca (sub), Ch (sub); 1996 v Se (sub), G (sub); 1997 v I (sub), Bel (sub); 1998 v Slo (sub), Sw (sub); 1999 v Fi (sub) (13)
O'Brien, M. T. (QPR), 1921 v S; (with Leicester C), 1922 v S, W; 1924 v S, W; (with Hull C), 1925 v S, E, W; 1926 v W; (with Derby Co), 1927 v W (10)
O'Connell, P. (Sheffield W), 1912 v E, S; (with Hull C), 1914 v E, S, W (5)
O'Doherty, A. (Coleraine), 1970 v E, W (sub) (2)
O'Driscoll, J. F. (Swansea T), 1949 v E, S, W (3)
O'Hagan, C. (Tottenham H), 1905 v S, W; 1906 v S, W, E; (with Aberdeen), 1907 v E, S, W; 1908 v S, W; 1909 v E (11)
O'Hagan, W. (St Mirren), 1920 v E, W (2)
O'Hehir, J. C. (Bohemians), 1910 v W (1)
O'Kane, W. J. (Nottingham F), 1970 v E, W, S (sub); 1971 v Sp, E, S, W; 1972 v USSR (2); 1973 v P, Cy; 1974 v Bul, P, S, E, W; 1975 v N, Se, E, S (20)
O'Mahoney, M. T. (Bristol R), 1939 v S (1)
O'Neill, C. (Motherwell), 1989 v Ch (sub); 1990 v Ei (sub); 1991 v D (3)
O'Neill, J. (Sunderland), 1962 v W (1)
O'Neill, J. P. (Leicester C), 1980 v Is, S, E, W, Aus (3); 1981 v P, S, P, S, Se; 1982 v S, Is, E, F, S, F (sub); 1983 v A, WG, Alb, T, Alb, S; 1984 v S (sub); 1985 v Is, Fi, E, Sp, T; 1986 v T, R, E, F, D, Mor, Alg, Sp, Br (39)
O'Neill, M. A. M. (Newcastle U), 1988 v Gr, Pol, F, Ma; 1989 v Ei, H, Sp (sub), Sp (sub), Ma (sub), Ch; (with Dundee U), 1990 v H (sub), Ei; 1991 v Pol; 1992 v Fa (sub), S (sub), G (sub); 1993 v Alb (sub + 1), Ei, Sp, Li, La; (with Hibernian), 1994 v Lie (sub); 1995 v A (sub), Ei; 1996 v Lie, A, N, Se; (with Coventry C), 1997 v Uk (sub), Arm (sub) (31)
O'Neill, M. H. M. (Distillery), 1972 v USSR (sub), (with Nottingham F), Sp (sub), W (sub); 1973 v P, Cy, E, S, W; 1974 v Bul, P, E (sub), W; 1975 v Se, Y, E, S; 1976 v Y (sub); 1977 v E (sub), S; 1978 v Ic, Ho, S, E, W; 1979 v Ei, D, Bul, E, Bul, D; 1980 v Ei, Is, Aus (3); 1981 v Se, P; (with Norwich C), P, S, Se; (with Manchester C), 1982 v S; (with Norwich C), E, F, S, Y, Hon, Sp, A, F; 1983 v A, WG, Alb, T, Alb, S, E; (with Notts Co), 1984 v A, T, WG, E, W, Fi; 1985 v R, Fi (64)
O'Reilly, H. (Dublin Freebooters), 1901 v S, W; 1904 v S (3)

Parke, J. (Linfield), 1964 v S; (with Hibernian), 1964 v E, Sp; (with Sunderland), 1965 v Sw, S, W, Ho (2), Alb; 1966 v WG; 1967 v E, S; 1968 v S, E (14)
Patterson, D. J. (C Palace), 1994 v Co (sub), M (sub); 1995 v Ei (sub+1), La, Ca, Ch (sub), La (sub); (with Luton T), 1996 v N (sub), Se; 1998 v Sw, Sp; (with Dundee U), 1999 v Fi, Mol, G, Mol, Ei (17)
Peacock, R. (Celtic), 1952 v S; 1953 v F; 1954 v W; 1955 v E, S; 1956 v E, S; 1957 v W, I, P; 1958 v S, E, W, I (2), Arg, Cz (2), WG; 1959 v E, S, W; 1960 v S, E; 1961 v E, S, I, WG (2), Gr; (with Coleraine), 1962 v S (31)
Peden, J. (Linfield), 1887 v S, W; 1888 v W, E; 1889 v S, E; 1890 v W, S; 1891 v W, E; 1892 v W, E; 1893 v E, S, W; (with Distillery), 1896 v W, E, S; 1897 v W, S; 1898 v W, E, S; 1899 v W (24)
Penney, S. (Brighton & HA), 1985 v Is; 1986 v T, R, E, F, D, Mor, Alg, Sp; 1987 v E, T, Is; 1988 v Pol, F, Ma; 1989 v Ei, Sp (17)
Percy, J. C. (Belfast YMCA), 1889 v W (1)
Platt, J. A. (Middlesbrough), 1976 v Is (sub); 1978 v S, E, W; 1980 v S, E, W, Aus (3); 1981 v Se, P; 1982 v F, S, W (sub), A; 1983 v A, WG, Alb, T; (with Ballymena U), 1984 v E, W (sub); (with Coleraine), 1986 v Mor (sub) (23)
Pollock, W. (Belfast C), 1928 v F (1)
Ponsonby, J. (Distillery), 1895 v S, W; 1896 v E, S, W; 1897 v E, S, W; 1899 v E (9)
Potts, R. M. C. (Cliftonville), 1883 v E, W (2)
Priestley, T. J. M. (Coleraine), 1933 v S; (with Chelsea), 1934 v E (2)
Pyper, Jas. (Cliftonville), 1897 v S, W; 1898 v S, E, W; 1899 v S; 1900 v E (7)
Pyper, John (Cliftonville), 1897 v E, S, W; 1899 v E, W; 1900 v E, W, S; 1902 v S (9)
Pyper, M. (Linfield), 1932 v W (1)

Quinn, J. M. (Blackburn R), 1985 v Is, Fi, E, Sp, T; 1986 v T, R, E, F, D (sub), Mor (sub); 1987 v E (sub), T; (with Swindon T), 1988 v Y (sub), T, Gr, Pol, F (sub), Ma; (with Leicester C), 1989 v Ei, H (sub), Sp (sub+1); (with Bradford C), Ma, Ch; 1990 v H; (with West Ham U), N; 1991 v Y (sub); (with Bournemouth), 1992 v Li; (with Reading), 1993 v Sp, D, Alb (sub), Ei (sub), La (sub); 1994 v La, D (sub), Ei, R, Lie, Co, M; 1995 v P, A (sub), La (sub); 1996 v Lie, A (sub) (46)
Quinn, S. J. (Blackpool), 1996 v Se (sub); 1997 v Alb (sub), I, Bel, P, Uk (sub), Arm, Th (sub); 1998 v G, Alb; (with WBA), Slo, Sw; 1999 v T (sub), Fi (sub), Ei; 2000 v F (sub), T (sub), G (sub), Fi, L, Ma; 2001 v Y (sub), Bul (sub), CzR (sub); 2002 v Ma (sub); (with Willem II), 2003 v Cy, Fi, Arm, Gr; 2004 v Ser, Bar, Tr; 2005 v Pol, W, Az, A; (with Sheffield W), Pol (37)

Rafferty, P. (Linfield), 1980 v E (sub) (1)
Ramsey, P. C. (Leicester C), 1984 v A, WG, S; 1985 v Is, E, Sp, T; 1986 v T, Mor; 1987 v Is, E, Y (sub); 1988 v Y; 1989 v Sp (14)
Rankine, J. (Alexander), 1883 v E, W (2)
Rattray, D. (Avoniel), 1882 v E; 1883 v E, W (3)
Rea, R. (Glentoran), 1901 v E (1)
Redmond, R. (Cliftonville), 1884 v W (1)
Reid, G. H. (Cardiff C), 1923 v S (1)
Reid, J. (Ulster), 1883 v E; 1884 v W; 1887 v S; 1889 v W; 1890 v S, W (6)
Reid, S. E. (Derby Co), 1934 v E, W; 1936 v E (3)
Reid, W. (Hearts), 1931 v E (1)
Reilly, M. M. (Portsmouth), 1900 v E; 1902 v E (2)
Renneville, W. T. J. (Leyton), 1910 v S, E, W; (with Aston Villa), 1911 v W (4)
Reynolds, J. (Distillery), 1890 v E, W; (with Ulster), 1891 v E, S, W (5)
Reynolds, R. (Bohemians), 1905 v W (1)
Rice, P. J. (Arsenal), 1969 v Is; 1970 v USSR; 1971 v E, S, W; 1972 v USSR, Sp, E, S, W; 1973 v Bul, Cy, E, S, W; 1974 v Bul, P, S, E, W; 1975 v N, Y, E, S, W; 1976 v Se, N, Y, Is, S, E, W; 1977 v Ho, Bel, WG, E, S, Ic; 1978 v Ic, Ho, Bel; 1979 v Ei, D, E (2), S, W, D; 1980 v E (49)
Roberts, F. C. (Glentoran), 1931 v S (1)
Robinson, P. (Distillery), 1920 v S; (with Blackburn R), 1921 v W (2)
Robinson, S. (Bournemouth), 1997 v Th (sub); 1999 v Mol, Ei; 2000 v L (sub), H (sub) (5)
Rogan, A. (Celtic), 1988 v Y (sub), Gr, Pol (sub); 1989 v Ei (sub), H, Sp (2), Ma (sub), Ch; 1990 v H, N (sub), U; 1991 v Y (2), D, A; (with Sunderland), 1992 v Li (sub); (with Millwall), 1997 v G (sub) (18)
Rollo, D. (Linfield), 1912 v W; 1913 v W; 1914 v W, E; (with Blackburn R), 1920 v S, W; 1921 v E, S, W; 1922 v E; 1923 v E; 1924 v S, W; 1925 v W; 1926 v E; 1927 v E (16)
Roper, E. O. (Dublin University), 1886 v W (1)
Rosbotham, A. (Cliftonville), 1887 v E, S, W; 1888 v E, S, W; 1889 v E (7)
Ross, W. E. (Newcastle U), 1969 v Is (1)
Rowland, K. (West Ham U), 1994 v La (sub); 1995 v Ca, Ch, La; 1996 v P (sub), Lie (sub), N (sub), Se, G (sub); 1997 v Uk, Arm, I (sub); 1998 v Alb; (with QPR), 1999 v T, Fi, Mol, G, Ca, Ei (19)
Rowley, R. W. M. (Southampton), 1929 v S, W; 1930 v W, E; (with Tottenham H), 1931 v W; 1932 v S (6)
Rushe, F. (Distillery),1925 v S.Af (1)
Russell, A. (Linfield), 1947 v E (1)
Russell, S. R. (Bradford C), 1930 v E, S; (with Derry C), 1932 v E (3)
Ryan, R. A. (WBA), 1950 v W (1)

Sanchez, L. P. (Wimbledon), 1987 v T (sub); 1989 v Sp, Ma (3)
Scott, E. (Liverpool), 1920 v S; 1921 v E, S, W; 1922 v E; 1925 v W; 1926 v E, S, W; 1927 v E, S, W; 1928 v E, S, W; 1929 v E, S, W; 1930 v E; 1931 v E; 1932 v W; 1933 v E, S, W; 1934 v E, S, W; (with Belfast C), 1935 v S; 1936 v E, S, W (31)

Scott, J. (Grimsby), 1958 v Cz, F (2)
Scott, J. E. (Cliftonville), 1901 v S (1)
Scott, L. J. (Dublin University), 1895 v S, W (2)
Scott, P. W. (Everton), 1975 v W; 1976 v Y; (with York C), Is, S, E (sub), W; 1978 v S, E, W; (with Aldershot), 1979 v S (sub) (10)
Scott, T. (Cliftonville), 1894 v E, S; 1895 v S, W; 1896 v S, E, W; 1897 v E, W; 1898 v E, S, W; 1900 v W (13)
Scott, W. (Linfield), 1903 v E, S, W; 1904 v E, S, W; (with Everton), 1905 v E, S; 1907 v E, S; 1908 v E, S, W; 1909 v E, S, W; 1910 v E, S; 1911 v E, S, W; 1912 v E; (with Leeds City), 1913 v E, S, W (25)
Scraggs, M. J. (Glentoran), 1921 v W; 1922 v E (2)
Seymour, H. C. (Bohemians), 1914 v W (1)
Seymour, J. (Cliftonville), 1907 v W; 1909 v W (2)
Shanks, T. (Woolwich Arsenal), 1903 v S; 1904 v W; (with Brentford), 1905 v E (3)
Sharkey, P. G. (Ipswich T), 1976 v S (1)
Sheehan, Dr G. (Bohemians), 1899 v S; 1900 v E, W (3)
Sheridan, J. (Everton), 1903 v W, E, S; 1904 v E, S; (with Stoke C), 1905 v E (6)
Sherrard, J. (Limavady), 1885 v S; 1887 v W; 1888 v W (3)
Sherrard, W. C. (Cliftonville), 1895 v E, W, S (3)
Sherry, J. J. (Bohemians), 1906 v E; 1907 v W (2)
Shields, R. J. (Southampton), 1957 v S (1)
Silo, M. (Belfast YMCA), 1888 v E (1)
Simpson, W. J. (Rangers), 1951 v W, F; 1954 v E, S; 1955 v E; 1957 v I, P; 1958 v S, E, W, I; 1959 v S (12)
Sinclair, J. (Knock), 1882 v E, W (2)
Slemin, J. C. (Bohemians), 1909 v W (1)
Sloan, A. S. (London Caledonians), 1925 v W (1)
Sloan, D. (Oxford U), 1969 v Is; 1971 v Sp (2)
Sloan, H. A. de B. (Bohemians), 1903 v E; 1904 v S; 1905 v E; 1906 v W; 1907 v E, W; 1908 v W; 1909 v S (8)
Sloan, J. W. (Arsenal), 1947 v W (1)
Sloan, T. (Manchester U), 1979 v S, W (sub), D (sub) (3)
Sloan, T. (Cardiff C), 1926 v S, W, E; 1927 v W, S; 1928 v E, W; 1929 v E; (with Linfield), 1930 v W, S; 1931 v S (11)
Small, J. M. (Clarence), 1887 v E; (with Cliftonville), 1893 v E, S, W (4)
Smith, A. W. (Glentoran), 2003 v I, Sp; 2004 v Uk (sub), Arm, Gr (sub), N, Es, Ser (sub), Bar (sub), Stk, Tr (sub); (with Preston NE), 2005 v Sw, Pol (sub), W (sub), Az (sub), Ca (sub), Pol (sub), G (sub) (18)
Smith, E. E. (Cardiff C), 1921 v S; 1923 v W, E; 1924 v E (4)
Smith, J. E. (Distillery), 1901 v S, W (2)
Smyth, R. H. (Dublin University), 1886 v W (1)
Smyth, S. (Wolverhampton W), 1948 v E, S, W; 1949 v S, W; 1950 v E, S, W; (with Stoke C), 1952 v E (9)
Smyth, W. (Distillery), 1949 v E, S; 1954 v S, E (4)
Snape, A. (Airdrie), 1920 v E (1)
Sonner, D. J. (Ipswich T), 1998 v Alb (sub); (with Sheffield W), 1999 v G (sub), Ca (sub); 2000 v L (sub), Ma (sub), H; (with Birmingham C), 2001 v N (sub); (with Nottingham F), 2004 v Es, Ser (sub), Bar, Stk, Tr (sub); (with Peterborough U), 2005 v Sw (13)
Spence, D. W. (Bury), 1975 v Y, E, S, W; 1976 v Se, Is, E, W, S (sub); (with Blackpool), 1977 v Ho (sub), WG (sub), E (sub), S (sub), W (sub), Ic (sub); 1979 v Ei, D (sub), E (sub), Bul (sub), E (sub), S, W, D; 1980 v Ei; (with Southend U), Is (sub), Aus (sub); 1981 v S (sub), Se (sub); 1982 v F (sub) (29)
Spencer, S. (Distillery), 1890 v E, S; 1892 v E, S, W; 1893 v E (6)
Spiller, E. A. (Cliftonville), 1883 v E, W; 1884 v E, W, S (5)
Stanfield, O. M. (Distillery), 1887 v E, S, W; 1888 v E, S, W; 1889 v E, S, W; 1890 v E, S; 1891 v E, S, W; 1892 v E, S, W; 1893 v E, W; 1894 v E, S, W; 1895 v E, S; 1896 v E, S, W; 1897 v E, S, W (30)
Steele, A. (Charlton Ath), 1926 v W, S; (with Fulham), 1929 v W, S (4)
Stevenson, A. E. (Rangers), 1934 v E, S, W; (with Everton), 1935 v E, S; 1936 v S, W; 1937 v E, W; 1938 v E, W; 1939 v E, S, W; 1947 v S, W; 1948 v S (17)
Stewart, A. (Glentoran), 1967 v W; 1968 v S, E; (with Derby Co), 1968 v W; 1969 v Is, T (1+1 sub) (7)
Stewart, D. C. (Hull C), 1978 v Bel (1)
Stewart, I. (QPR), 1982 v F (sub); 1983 v A, WG, Alb, T, Alb, S, E, W; 1984 v A, T, WG, S, E, W, Fi; 1985 v R, Fi, Is, E, Sp, T; (with Newcastle U), 1986 v R, E, D, Mor, Alg (sub), Sp (sub), Br; 1987 v E, Is (sub) (31)
Stewart, R. K. (St Columb's Court), 1890 v E, S, W; (with Cliftonville), 1892 v E, S, W; 1893 v E, W; 1894 v E, S, W (11)
Stewart, T. C. (Linfield), 1961 v W (1)
Swan, S. (Linfield), 1899 v S (1)

Taggart, G. P. (Barnsley), 1990 v N, U; 1991 v Y, D, A, Pol, Fa; 1992 v Fa, A, D, S, Li, G; 1993 v Alb, Sp, D, Alb, Ei, Sp, Li, La; 1994 v La, D, Ei, R, Lie, Co, M; 1995 v P (sub), A, Ei (2), Ca, Ch, La; (with Bolton W), 1997 v G, Alb, I, Bel, P, Uk, Arm; 1998 v G, P, Sp; (with Leicester C), 2000 v H; 2001 v Ma, D, Ic, N; 2003 v Sp (51)
Taggart, J. (Walsall), 1899 v W (1)
Taylor, M. S. (Fulham), 1999 v G, Mol, Ca, Ei; 2000 v F, T, G, Fi, L (sub), Ma (sub), H; 2001 v Y, N, Bul, CzR; 2002 v D, Ic, Ma, Pol, Lie, Sp; 2003 v Cy, Sp, Uk, Fi, Arm, Gr, I, Sp; 2004 v Uk, Arm, Gr, N; (with Birmingham C), Es, Ser, Bar, Stk, Tr; 2005 v Pol, W, Az, Ca, E, Pol, G (45)
Thompson, F. W. (Cliftonville), 1910 v E, S, W; (with Linfield), 1911 v W; (with Bradford C), 1911 v E; 1912 v E, W; 1913 v E, S, W; (with Clyde), 1914 v E, S (12)
Thompson, J. (Distillery), 1897 v S (1)
Thompson, R. (Queen's Island), 1928 v F (1)
Thompson, W. (Belfast Ath), 1889 v S (1)
Thunder, P. J. (Bohemians), 1911 v W (1)
Todd, S. J. (Burnley), 1966 v M (sub); 1967 v E; 1968 v W; 1969 v E, S, W; 1970 v S, USSR; (with Sheffield W), 1971 v Cy (2), Sp (sub) (11)
Toner, C. (Leyton Orient), 2003 v I (sub), Sp (sub) (2)
Toner, J. (Arsenal), 1922 v W; 1923 v W; 1924 v W, E; 1925 v E, S; (with St Johnstone), 1927 v E, S (8)
Torrans, R. (Linfield), 1893 v S (1)
Torrans, S. (Linfield), 1889 v S; 1890 v S, W; 1891 v S, W; 1892 v E, S, W; 1893 v E, S; 1894 v E, S, W; 1895 v E; 1896 v E, S, W; 1897 v E, S, W; 1898 v E, S; 1899 v E, W; 1901 v S, W (26)
Trainor, D. (Crusaders), 1967 v W (1)
Tully, C. P. (Celtic), 1949 v E; 1950 v E; 1952 v S; 1953 v E, S, W, F; 1954 v S; 1956 v E; 1959 v Sp (10)
Turner, A. (Cliftonville), 1896 v W (1)
Turner, E. (Cliftonville), 1896 v E (1)
Turner, W. (Cliftonville), 1886 v E, S; 1888 v S (3)
Twoomey, J. F. (Leeds U), 1938 v W; 1939 v E (2)

Uprichard, W. N. M. C. (Swindon T), 1952 v E, S, W; 1953 v E, S; (with Portsmouth), 1953 v W, F; 1955 v E, S, W; 1956 v E, S, W; 1958 v S, I, Cz; 1959 v S, Sp (18)

Vernon, J. (Belfast C), 1947 v E, S; (with WBA), 1947 v W; 1948 v E, S, W; 1949 v E, S, W; 1950 v E, S; 1951 v E, S, W, F; 1952 v S, E (17)

Waddell, T. M. R. (Cliftonville), 1906 v S (1)
Walker, J. (Doncaster R), 1955 v W (1)
Walker, T. (Bury), 1911 v S (1)
Walsh, D. J. (WBA), 1947 v S, W; 1948 v E, S, W; 1949 v E, S, W; 1950 v W (9)
Walsh, W. (Manchester C), 1948 v E, S, W; 1949 v E, S (5)
Waring, J. (Cliftonville), 1899 v E (1)
Warren, P. (Shelbourne), 1913 v E, S (2)
Watson, J. (Ulster), 1883 v E, W; 1886 v E, S, W; 1887 v S, W; 1889 v E, W (9)
Watson, P. (Distillery), 1971 v Cy (sub) (1)
Watson, T. (Cardiff C), 1926 v S (1)
Wattie, J. (Distillery), 1899 v E (1)
Webb, C. G. (Brighton), 1909 v S, W; 1911 v S (3)
Weir, E. (Clyde), 1939 v W (1)
Welsh, E. (Carlisle U), 1966 v W, WG, M; 1967 v W (4)
Whiteside, N. (Manchester U), 1982 v Y, Hon, Sp, A, F; 1983 v WG, Alb, T; 1984 v A, T, WG, S, E, W, Fi; 1985 v R, Fi, Is, E, Sp, T; 1986 v R, E, F, D, Mor, Alg, Sp, Br; 1987 v E (2), Is, Y; 1988 v T, Pol, F; (with Everton), 1990 v H, Ei (38)
Whiteside, T. (Distillery), 1891 v E (1)
Whitfield, E. R. (Dublin University), 1886 v W (1)
Whitley, Jeff (Manchester C), 1997 v Bel (sub), Th (sub); 1998 v Sp (sub); 2000 v Fi; 2001 v Y, D, N; (with Sunderland), 2004 v Gr, Es, Ser, Stk, Tr; 2005 v Pol, W, Az, A, Ca, E, Pol (19)
Whitley, Jim (Manchester C), 1998 v Sp; 1999 v T (sub); 2000 v Fi (sub) (3)
Williams, J. R. (Ulster), 1886 v E, S (2)
Williams, M. S. (Chesterfield), 1999 v G, Mol, Ca, Ei; (with Watford), 2000 v F, T, G, Fi, L, Ma, H (sub); (with Wimbledon), 2001 v Y, Ic (sub), N (sub), CzR, Bul, CzR; 2002 v Lie, Sp; 2003 v Cy, Fi; (with Stoke C), Arm, Gr, I (sub), Sp (sub); (with Wimbledon), 2004 v N (sub), Es, Ser, Bar, Tr; (with Milton Keynes D), 2005 v Sw, Pol, W, Az, A, Pol (36)
Williams, P. A. (WBA), 1991 v Fa (sub) (1)
Williamson, J. (Cliftonville), 1890 v E; 1892 v S; 1893 v S (3)
Willighan, T. (Burnley), 1933 v W; 1934 v S (2)
Willis, G. (Linfield), 1906 v S, W; 1907 v S; 1912 v S (4)

Wilson, D. J. (Brighton & HA), 1987 v T, Is, E (sub); (with Luton T), 1988 v Y, T, Gr, Pol, F, Ma; 1989 v Ei, H, Sp, Ma, Ch; 1990 v H, Ei, N, U; (with Sheffield W), 1991 v Y, D, A, Fa; 1992 v A (sub), S (24)
Wilson, H. (Linfield), 1925 v W, S.Af (2)
Wilson, K. J. (Ipswich T), 1987 v Is, E, Y; (with Chelsea), 1988 v Y, T, Gr (sub), Pol (sub), F (sub); 1989 v H (sub), Sp (2), Ma, Ch; 1990 v Ei (sub), N, U; 1991 v Y (2), A, Pol, Fa; 1992 v Fa, A, D, S; (with Notts Co), Li, G; 1993 v Alb, Sp, D, Sp, Li, La; 1994 v La, D, Ei, R, Lie, Co, M; (with Walsall), 1995 v Ei (sub), La (42)
Wilson, M. (Distillery), 1884 v E, S, W (3)
Wilson, R. (Cliftonville), 1888 v S (1)
Wilson, S. J. (Glenavon), 1962 v S; 1964 v S; (with Falkirk), 1964 v E, W, U, Sp; 1965 v E, Sw; (with Dundee), 1966 v W, WG; 1967 v S; 1968 v E (12)
Wilton, J. M. (St Columb's Court), 1888 v E, W; 1889 v S, E; (with Cliftonville), 1890 v E; (with St Columb's Court), 1893 v W, S (7)
Wood, T. J. (Walsall), 1996 v Lie (sub) (1)
Worthington, N. (Sheffield W), 1984 v W, Fi (sub); 1985 v Is, Sp (sub); 1986 v T, R (sub), E (sub), D, Alg, Sp; 1987 v E (2), T, Is, Y; 1988 v Y, T, Gr, Pol, F, Ma; 1989 v Ei, H, Sp, Ma; 1990 v H, Ei, U; 1991 v Y, D, A, Fa; 1992 v A, D, S, Li, G; 1993 v Alb, Sp, D, Ei, Sp, Li, La; 1994 v La, D, Ei, Lie, Co, M; (with Leeds U), 1995 v P, A, Ei (2), La, Ca (sub), Ch, La; 1996 v P, Lie, A, N, Se, G; (with Stoke C), 1997 v I, Bel (sub) (66)
Wright, J. (Cliftonville), 1906 v E, S, W; 1907 v E, S, W (6)
Wright, T. J. (Newcastle U), 1989 v Ma, Ch; 1990 v H, U; 1992 v Fa, A, S, G; 1993 v Alb, Sp, Alb, Ei, Sp, Li, La; 1994 v La; (with Nottingham F), D, Ei, R, Lie, Co, M (sub); 1997 v G, Alb, I, Bel; (with Manchester C), P, Uk; 1998 v Alb; 1999 v Ca (sub); 2000 v F (sub) (31)

Young, S. (Linfield), 1907 v E, S; 1908 v E, S; (with Airdrie), 1909 v E; 1912 v S; (with Linfield), 1914 v E, S, W (9)

SCOTLAND

Adams, J. (Hearts), 1889 v Ni; 1892 v W; 1893 v Ni (3)
Agnew, W. B. (Kilmarnock), 1907 v Ni; 1908 v W, Ni (3)
Aird, J. (Burnley), 1954 v N (2), A, U (4)
Aitken, A. (Newcastle U), 1901 v E; 1902 v E; 1903 v E, W; 1904 v E; 1905 v E, W; 1906 v E; (with Middlesbrough), 1907 v E, W; 1908 v E; (with Leicester Fosse), 1910 v E; 1911 v E, Ni (14)
Aitken, G. G. (East Fife), 1949 v E, F; 1950 v W, Ni, Sw; (with Sunderland), 1953 v W, Ni; 1954 v E (8)
Aitken, R. (Dumbarton), 1886 v E; 1888 v Ni (2)
Aitken, R. (Celtic), 1980 v Pe (sub), Bel, W (sub), E, Pol; 1983 v Bel, Ca (1+1 sub); 1984 v Bel (sub), Ni, W (sub); 1985 v E, Ic; 1986 v W, EG, Aus (2), Is, R, E, D, WG, U; 1987 v Bul, Ei (2), L, Bel, E, Br; 1988 v H, Bel, Bul, L, S.Ar, Ma, Sp, Co, E; 1989 v N, Y, I, Cy, F, Cy, E, Ch; 1990 v Y, F, N; (with Newcastle U), Arg (sub), Pol, Ma, Cr, Se, Br; (with St Mirren), 1992 v R (sub) (57)
Aitkenhead, W. A. C. (Blackburn R), 1912 v Ni (1)
Albiston, A. (Manchester U), 1982 v Ni; 1984 v U, Bel, EG, W, E; 1985 v Y, Ic, Sp (2), W; 1986 v EG, Ho, U (14)
Alexander, D. (East Stirlingshire), 1894 v W, Ni (2)
Alexander, G. (Preston NE), 2002 v Ng (sub), Sk, S.Af (sub), Hk (sub); 2003 v D (sub), Fa (sub), Ca, P, Ei, Ic, Li, Nz (sub); 2004 v Li (sub), R; 2005 v Mol, Bl (16)
Allan, D. S. (Queen's Park), 1885 v E, W; 1886 v W (3)
Allan, G. (Liverpool), 1897 v E (1)
Allan, H. (Hearts), 1902 v W (1)
Allan, J. (Queen's Park), 1887 v E, W (2)
Allan, T. (Dundee), 1974 v WG, N (2)
Ancell, R. F. D. (Newcastle U), 1937 v W, Ni (2)
Anderson, A. (Hearts), 1933 v E; 1934 v A, E, W, Ni; 1935 v E, W, Ni; 1936 v E, W, Ni; 1937 v G, E, W, Ni, A; 1938 v E, W, Ni, Cz, Ho; 1939 v W, H (23)
Anderson, F. (Clydesdale), 1874 v E (1)
Anderson, G. (Kilmarnock), 1901 v Ni (1)
Anderson, H. A. (Raith R), 1914 v W (1)
Anderson, J. (Leicester C), 1954 v Fi (1)
Anderson, K. (Queen's Park), 1896 v Ni; 1898 v E, Ni (3)
Anderson, R. (Aberdeen), 2003 v Ic (sub), Ca, P, Ei; 2005 v N, Se (6)
Anderson, W. (Queen's Park), 1882 v E; 1883 v E, W; 1884 v E; 1885 v E, W (6)
Andrews, P. (Eastern), 1875 v E (1)
Archibald, A. (Rangers), 1921 v W; 1922 v W, E; 1923 v Ni; 1924 v E, W; 1931 v E; 1932 v E (8)
Archibald, S. (Aberdeen), 1980 v P (sub); (with Tottenham H), Ni, Pol, H; 1981 v Se (sub), Is, Ni, Is, Ni, E; 1982 v Ni, P, Sp (sub), Ho, Nz (sub), Br, USSR; 1983 v EG, Sw (sub), Bel; 1984 v EG, E, F; (with Barcelona), 1985 v Sp, E, Ic (sub); 1986 v WG (27)
Armstrong, M. W. (Aberdeen), 1936 v W, Ni; 1937 v G (3)
Arnott, W. (Queen's Park), 1883 v W; 1884 v E, Ni; 1885 v E, W; 1886 v E; 1887 v E, W; 1888 v E; 1889 v E; 1890 v E; 1891 v E; 1892 v E; 1893 v E (14)
Auld, J. R. (Third Lanark), 1887 v E, W; 1889 v W (3)
Auld, R. (Celtic), 1959 v H, P; 1960 v W (3)

Baird, A. (Queen's Park), 1892 v Ni; 1894 v W (2)
Baird, D. (Hearts), 1890 v Ni; 1891 v E; 1892 v W (3)
Baird, H. (Airdrieonians), 1956 v A (1)
Baird, J. C. (Vale of Leven), 1876 v E; 1878 v W; 1880 v E (3)
Baird, S. (Rangers), 1957 v Y, Sp (2), Sw, WG; 1958 v F, Ni (7)
Baird, W. U. (St Bernard), 1897 v Ni (1)
Bannon, E. (Dundee U), 1980 v Bel; 1983 v Ni, W, E, Ca; 1984 v EG; 1986 v Is, R, E, D (sub), WG (11)
Barbour, A. (Renton), 1885 v Ni (1)
Barker, J. B. (Rangers), 1893 v W; 1894 v W (2)
Barrett, F. (Dundee), 1894 v Ni; 1895 v W (2)
Battles, B. (Celtic), 1901 v E, W, Ni (3)
Battles, B. jun. (Hearts), 1931 v W (1)
Bauld, W. (Hearts), 1950 v E, Sw, P (3)
Baxter, J. C. (Rangers), 1961 v Ni, Ei (2), Cz; 1962 v Ni, W, E, Cz (2), U; 1963 v W, Ni, E, A, N, Ei, Sp; 1964 v W, E, N, WG; 1965 v W, Ni, Fi; (with Sunderland), 1966 v P, Br, Ni, W, E, I; 1967 v W, E, USSR; 1968 v W (34)
Baxter, R. D. (Middlesbrough), 1939 v E, W, H (3)
Beattie, A. (Preston NE), 1937 v E, A, Cz; 1938 v E; 1939 v W, Ni, H (7)
Beattie, R. (Preston NE), 1939 v W (1)
Begbie, I. (Hearts), 1890 v Ni; 1891 v E; 1892 v W; 1894 v E (4)
Bell, A. (Manchester U), 1912 v Ni (1)
Bell, J. (Dumbarton), 1890 v Ni; 1892 v E; (with Everton), 1896 v E; 1897 v E; 1898 v E; (with Celtic), 1899 v E, W, Ni; 1900 v E, W (10)
Bell, M. (Hearts), 1901 v W (1)
Bell, W. J. (Leeds U), 1966 v P, Br (2)
Bennett, A. (Celtic), 1904 v W; 1907 v Ni; 1908 v W; (with Rangers), 1909 v W, Ni, E; 1910 v E, W; 1911 v E, W; 1913 v Ni (11)
Bennie, R. (Airdrieonians), 1925 v W, Ni; 1926 v Ni (3)
Bernard, P. R. J. (Oldham Ath), 1995 v J (sub), Ec (2)
Berry, D. (Queen's Park), 1894 v W; 1899 v W, Ni (3)
Berry, W. H. (Queen's Park), 1888 v E; 1889 v E; 1890 v E; 1891 v E (4)
Bett, J. (Rangers), 1982 v Ho; 1983 v Bel; (with Lokeren), 1984 v Bel, W, E, F; 1985 v Y, Ic, Sp (2), W, E, Ic; (with Aberdeen), 1986 v W, Is, Ho; 1987 v Bel; 1988 v H (sub); 1989 v Y; 1990 v F (sub), N, Arg, Eg, Ma, Cr (25)
Beveridge, W. W. (Glasgow University), 1879 v E, W; 1880 v W (3)
Black, A. (Hearts), 1938 v Cz, Ho; 1939 v H (3)
Black, D. (Hurlford), 1889 v Ni (1)
Black, E. (Metz), 1988 v H (sub), L (sub) (2)
Black, I. H. (Southampton), 1948 v E (1)
Blackburn, J. E. (Royal Engineers), 1873 v E (1)
Blacklaw, A. S. (Burnley), 1963 v N, Sp; 1966 v I (3)
Blackley, J. (Hibernian), 1974 v Cz, E, Bel, Z; 1976 v Sw; 1977 v W, Se (7)
Blair, D. (Clyde), 1929 v W, Ni; 1931 v E, A, I; 1932 v W, Ni; (with Aston Villa), 1933 v W (8)
Blair, J. (Sheffield W), 1920 v E, Ni; (with Cardiff C), 1921 v E; 1922 v E; 1923 v E, W, Ni; 1924 v W (8)
Blair, J. (Motherwell), 1934 v W (1)
Blair, J. A. (Blackpool), 1947 v W (1)
Blair, W. (Third Lanark), 1896 v W (1)
Blessington, J. (Celtic), 1894 v E, Ni; 1896 v E, Ni (4)
Blyth, J. A. (Coventry C), 1978 v Bul, W (2)
Bone, J. (Norwich C), 1972 v Y (sub); 1973 v D (2)
Booth, S. (Aberdeen), 1993 v G (sub), Es (2 subs); 1994 v Sw, Ma (sub); 1995 v Fa, Ru; 1996 v Fi, Sm, Aus (sub), US, Ho, Sw (sub); (with Borussia Dortmund), 1998 v D, Fi, Co (sub), Mor (sub); (with Twente), 2001 v Pol; 2002 v Cro, Bel (sub), La (sub) (21)

Bowie, J. (Rangers), 1920 v E, Ni (2)
Bowie, W. (Linthouse), 1891 v Ni (1)
Bowman, D. (Dundee U), 1992 v Fi, US (sub); 1993 v G, Es; 1994 v Sw, I (6)
Bowman, G. A. (Montrose), 1892 v Ni (1)
Boyd, J. M. (Newcastle U), 1934 v Ni (1)
Boyd, R. (Mossend Swifts), 1889 v Ni; 1891 v W (2)
Boyd, T. (Motherwell), 1991 v R (sub), Sw, Bul, USSR; (with Chelsea), 1992 v Sw, R; (with Celtic), Fi, Ca, N, C; 1993 v Sw, P, I, Ma, G, Es (2); 1994 v I, Ma (sub), Ho (sub), A; 1995 v Fi, Fa, Ru, Gr, Ru, Sm; 1996 v Gr, Fi, Se, Sm, Aus, D, US, Co, Ho, E, Sw; 1997 v A, La, Se, Es (2), A, Se, W, Ma, Bl; 1998 v Bl, La, F, D, Fi (sub), Co, US, Br, N, Mor; 1999 v Li, Es, Fa, CzR, G, Fa, CzR; 2001 v La, Cro, Aus, Bel, Sm (sub), Pol; 2002 v Bel (72)
Boyd, W. G. (Clyde), 1931 v I, Sw (2)
Bradshaw, T. (Bury), 1928 v E (1)
Brand, R. (Rangers), 1961 v Ni, Cz, Ei (2); 1962 v Ni, W, Cz, U (8)
Brandon, T. (Blackburn R), 1896 v E (1)
Brazil, A. (Ipswich T), 1980 v Pol (sub), H; 1982 v Sp, Ho (sub), Ni, W, E, Nz, USSR (sub); 1983 v EG, Sw; (with Tottenham H), W, E (sub) (13)
Breckenridge, T. (Hearts), 1888 v Ni (1)
Bremner, D. (Hibernian), 1976 v Sw (sub) (1)
Bremner, W. J. (Leeds U), 1965 v Sp; 1966 v E, Pol, P, Br, I (2); 1967 v W, Ni, E; 1968 v W, E; 1969 v W, E, Ni, D, A, WG, Cy (2); 1970 v Ei, WG, A; 1971 v W, E; 1972 v P, Bel, Ho, Ni, W, E, Y, Cz, Br; 1973 v D (2), E (2), Ni (sub), Sw, Br; 1974 v Cz, WG, Ni, W, E, Bel, N, Z, Br, Y; 1975 v Sp (2); 1976 v D (54)
Brennan, F. (Newcastle U), 1947 v W, Ni; 1953 v W, Ni, E; 1954 v Ni, E (7)
Breslin, B. (Hibernian), 1897 v W (1)
Brewster, G. (Everton), 1921 v E (1)
Brogan, J. (Celtic), 1971 v W, Ni, P, E (4)
Brown, A. (St Mirren), 1890 v W; 1891 v W (2)
Brown, A. (Middlesbrough), 1904 v E (1)
Brown, A. D. (East Fife), 1950 v Sw, P, F; (with Blackpool), 1952 v USA, D, Se; 1953 v W; 1954 v W, E, N (2), Fi, A, U (14)
Brown, G. C. P. (Rangers), 1931 v W; 1932 v E, W, Ni; 1933 v E; 1934 v A; 1935 v E, W; 1936 v E, W; 1937 v G, E, W, Ni, Cz; 1938 v E, W, Cz, Ho (19)
Brown, H. (Partick T), 1947 v W, Bel, L (3)
Brown, J. (Cambuslang), 1890 v W (1)
Brown, J. B. (Clyde), 1939 v W (1)
Brown, J. G. (Sheffield U), 1975 v R (1)
Brown, R. (Dumbarton), 1884 v W, Ni (2)
Brown, R. (Rangers), 1947 v Ni; 1949 v Ni; 1952 v E (3)
Brown, R. jun. (Dumbarton), 1885 v W (1)
Brown, W. D. F. (Dundee), 1958 v F; 1959 v E, W, Ni; (with Tottenham H), 1960 v W, Ni, Pol, A, H, T; 1962 v Ni, W, E, Cz; 1963 v W, Ni, E, A; 1964 v Ni, W, N; 1965 v E, Fi, Pol, Sp; 1966 v Ni, Pol, I (28)
Browning, J. (Celtic), 1914 v W (1)
Brownlie, J. (Third Lanark), 1909 v E, Ni; 1910 v E, W, Ni; 1911 v W, Ni; 1912 v W, Ni, E; 1913 v W, Ni, E; 1914 v W, Ni, E (16)
Brownlie, J. (Hibernian), 1971 v USSR; 1972 v Pe, Ni, E; 1973 v D (2); 1976 v R (7)
Bruce, D. (Vale of Leven), 1890 v W (1)
Bruce, R. F. (Middlesbrough), 1934 v A (1)
Buchan, M. M. (Aberdeen), 1972 v P (sub), Bel; (with Manchester U), W, Y, Cz, Br; 1973 v D (2), E; 1974 v WG, Ni, W, N, Br, Y; 1975 v EG, Sp, P; 1976 v D, R; 1977 v Fi, Cz, Ch, Arg, Br; 1978 v EG, W (sub), Ni, Pe, Ir, Ho; 1979 v A, N, P (34)
Buchanan, J. (Cambuslang), 1889 v Ni (1)
Buchanan, J. (Rangers), 1929 v E; 1930 v E (2)
Buchanan, P. S. (Chelsea), 1938 v Cz (1)
Buchanan, R. (Abercorn), 1891 v W (1)
Buckley, P. (Aberdeen), 1954 v N; 1955 v W, Ni (3)
Buick, A. (Hearts), 1902 v W, Ni (2)
Burchill, M. J. (Celtic), 2000 v Bos (sub), Li, E (sub + sub), F (sub), Ho (sub) (6)
Burley, C. W. (Chelsea), 1995 v J, Ec, Fa; 1996 v Gr, Se, Aus, D, US, Co (sub), Ho (sub), E (sub), Sw; 1997 v A, La, Se, Es, A, Se, Ma, Bl; (with Celtic), 1998 v Bl, La, F, Co, US (sub), Br, N, Mor; 1999 v Fa, CzR; 2000 v Bos, Es, Bos, Li, E (2); (with Derby Co), Ho, Ei; 2001 v Cro, Aus, Bel, Sm; 2002 v Cro, Bel, La; 2003 v A (46)
Burley, G. (Ipswich T), 1979 v W, Ni, E, Arg, N; 1980 v P, Ni, E (sub), Pol; 1982 v W (sub), E (11)
Burns, F. (Manchester U), 1970 v A (1)
Burns, K. (Birmingham C), 1974 v WG; 1975 v EG (sub), Sp (2); 1977 v Cz (sub), W, Se, W (sub); (with Nottingham F), 1978 v Ni (sub), W, E, Pe, Ir; 1979 v N; 1980 v Pe, A, Bel; 1981 v Is, Ni, W (20)
Burns, T. (Celtic), 1981 v Ni; 1982 v Ho (sub), W; 1983 v Bel (sub), Ni, Ca (1 + 1 sub); 1988 v E (sub) (8)
Busby, M. W. (Manchester C), 1934 v W (1)

Cairns, T. (Rangers), 1920 v W; 1922 v E; 1923 v E, W; 1924 v Ni; 1925 v W, E, Ni (8)
Calderhead, D. (Q of S Wanderers), 1889 v Ni (1)
Calderwood, C. (Tottenham H), 1995 v Ru, Sm, J, Ec, Fa; 1996 v Gr, Fi, Se, Sm, US, Co, Ho, E, Sw; 1997 v A, La, Se, Es (2), A, Se; 1998 v Bl, La, F, D, Fi, Co, US, Br, N; 1999 v Li, Es; (with Aston Villa), Fa, CzR; 2000 v Bos (1 + sub) (36)
Calderwood, R. (Cartvale), 1885 v Ni, E, W (3)
Caldow, E. (Rangers), 1957 v Sp (2), Sw, WG, E; 1958 v Ni, W, Sw, Par, H, Pol, Y, F; 1959 v E, W, Ni, WG, Ho, P; 1960 v E, W, Ni, A, H, T; 1961 v E, W, Ni, Ei (2), Cz; 1962 v Ni, W, E, Cz (2), U; 1963 v W, Ni, E (40)
Caldwell, G. (Newcastle U), 2002 v F, Ng (sub), Sk, S.Af; (with Hibernian), 2004 v R, D, Es, Tr; 2005 v H, Sp, Slo, N, Mol, I (14)
Caldwell, S. (Newcastle U), 2001 v Pol (sub); 2003 v Ei; 2004 v W, Tr (sub); (with Sunderland), 2005 v Mol, Bl (6)
Callaghan, P. (Hibernian), 1900 v Ni (1)
Callaghan, W. (Dunfermline Ath), 1970 v Ei (sub), W (2)
Cameron, C. (Hearts), 1999 v G (sub), Fa (sub); 2000 v Li (sub), F, Ei (sub); 2001 v La (sub), Sm, Cro, Aus, Sm, Pol; (with Wolverhampton W), 2002 v Cro (sub), Bel (sub), La, F; 2003 v Ei (sub), Li (sub), A (sub), G; 2004 v N, Fa, G, Li, W, R, D; 2005 v Sp (sub), Mol (28)
Cameron, J. (Rangers), 1886 v Ni (1)
Cameron, J. (Queen's Park), 1896 v Ni (1)
Cameron, J. (St Mirren), 1904 v Ni; (with Chelsea), 1909 v E (2)
Campbell, C. (Queen's Park), 1874 v E; 1876 v W; 1877 v E, W; 1878 v E; 1879 v E; 1880 v E; 1881 v E; 1882 v E, W; 1884 v E; 1885 v E; 1886 v E (13)
Campbell, H. (Renton), 1889 v W (1)
Campbell, Jas (Sheffield W), 1913 v W (1)
Campbell, J. (South Western), 1880 v W (1)
Campbell, J. (Kilmarnock), 1891 v Ni; 1892 v W (2)
Campbell, John (Celtic), 1893 v E, Ni; 1898 v E, Ni; 1900 v E, Ni; 1901 v E, W, Ni; 1902 v W, Ni; 1903 v W (12)
Campbell, John (Rangers), 1899 v E, W, Ni; 1901 v Ni (4)
Campbell, K. (Liverpool), 1920 v E, W, Ni; (with Partick T), 1921 v W, Ni; 1922 v W, Ni, E (8)
Campbell, P. (Rangers), 1878 v W; 1879 v W (2)
Campbell, P. (Morton), 1898 v W (1)
Campbell, R. (Falkirk), 1947 v Bel, L; (with Chelsea), 1950 v Sw, P, F (5)
Campbell, W. (Morton), 1947 v Ni; 1948 v E, Bel, Sw, F (5)
Canero, P. (Leicester C), 2004 v D (sub) (1)
Carabine, J. (Third Lanark), 1938 v Ho; 1939 v E, Ni (3)
Carr, W. M. (Coventry C), 1970 v Ni, W, E; 1971 v D; 1972 v Pe; 1973 v D (sub) (6)
Cassidy, J. (Celtic), 1921 v W, Ni; 1923 v Ni; 1924 v W (4)
Chalmers, S. (Celtic), 1965 v W, Fi; 1966 v P (sub), Br; 1967 v Ni (5)
Chalmers, W. (Rangers), 1885 v Ni (1)
Chalmers, W. S. (Queen's Park), 1929 v Ni (1)
Chambers, T. (Hearts), 1894 v W (1)
Chaplin, G. D. (Dundee), 1908 v W (1)
Cheyne, A. G. (Aberdeen), 1929 v E, N, G, Ho; 1930 v F (5)
Christie, A. J. (Queen's Park), 1898 v W; 1899 v E, Ni (3)
Christie, R. M. (Queen's Park), 1884 v E (1)
Clark, J. (Celtic), 1966 v Br; 1967 v W, Ni, USSR (4)
Clark, R. B. (Aberdeen), 1968 v W, Ho; 1970 v Ni; 1971 v W, Ni, E, D, P, USSR; 1972 v Bel, Ni, W, E, Cz, Br; 1973 v D, E (17)
Clarke, S. (Chelsea), 1988 v H, Bel, Bul, S.Ar, Ma; 1994 v Ho (6)
Cleland, J. (Royal Albert), 1891 v Ni (1)
Clements, R. (Leith Ath), 1891 v Ni (1)
Clunas, W. L. (Sunderland), 1924 v E; 1926 v W (2)
Collier, W. (Raith R), 1922 v W (1)
Collins, J. (Hibernian), 1988 v S.Ar; 1990 v EG, Pol (sub), Ma (sub); (with Celtic), 1991 v Sw (sub), Bul (sub); 1992 v Ni (sub), Fi; 1993 v P, Ma, G, P, Es (2); 1994 v Sw, Ho (sub), A, Ho; 1995 v Fi, Fa, Ru, Gr, Ru, Sm, Fa; 1996 v Gr, Fi, Se, Sm, Aus, D, US (sub), Co, Ho, E, Sw; (with Monaco), 1997 v A, La, Se, Es, A, Se, Ma; 1998 v Bl, La, F, Fi, Co, US, Br, N, Mor; (with Everton), 1999 v Li; 2000 v Bos, Es, Bos, E (2) (58)

Collins, R. Y. (Celtic), 1951 v W, Ni, A; 1955 v Y, A, H; 1956 v Ni, W; 1957 v E, W, Sp (2), Sw, WG; 1958 v Ni, W, Sw, H, Pol, Y, F, Par; (with Everton), 1959 v E, W, Ni, WG, Ho, P; (with Leeds U), 1965 v E, Pol, Sp (31)
Collins, T. (Hearts), 1909 v W (1)
Colman, D. (Aberdeen), 1911 v E, W, Ni; 1913 v Ni (4)
Colquhoun, E. P. (Sheffield U), 1972 v P, Ho, Pe, Y, Cz, Br; 1973 v D (2), E (9)
Colquhoun, J. (Hearts), 1988 v S.Ar (sub), Ma (sub) (2)
Combe, J. R. (Hibernian), 1948 v E, Bel, Sw (3)
Conn, A. (Hearts), 1956 v A (1)
Conn, A. (Tottenham H), 1975 v Ni (sub), E (2)
Connachan, E. D. (Dunfermline Ath), 1962 v Cz, U (2)
Connelly, G. (Celtic), 1974 v Cz, WG (2)
Connolly, J. (Everton), 1973 v Sw (1)
Connor, J. (Airdrieonians), 1886 v Ni (1)
Connor, J. (Sunderland), 1930 v F; 1932 v Ni; 1934 v E; 1935 v Ni (4)
Connor, R. (Dundee), 1986 v Ho; (with Aberdeen), 1988 v S.Ar (sub); 1989 v E; 1991 v R (4)
Cook, W. L. (Bolton W), 1934 v E; 1935 v W, Ni (3)
Cooke, C. (Dundee), 1966 v W, I; (with Chelsea), P, Br; 1968 v E, Ho; 1969 v W, Ni, A, WG (sub), Cy (2); 1970 v A; 1971 v Bel; 1975 v Sp, P (16)
Cooper, D. (Rangers), 1980 v Pe, A (sub); 1984 v W, E; 1985 v Y, Ic, Sp (2), W; 1986 v W (sub), EG, Aus (2), Ho, WG (sub), U (sub); 1987 v Bul, L, Ei, Br; (with Motherwell), 1990 v N, Eg (22)
Cormack, P. B. (Hibernian), 1966 v Br; 1969 v D (sub); 1970 v Ei, WG; (with Nottingham F), 1971 v D (sub), W, P, E; 1972 v Ho (sub) (9)
Cowan, J. (Aston Villa), 1896 v E; 1897 v E; 1898 v E (3)
Cowan, J. (Morton), 1948 v Bel, Sw; F; 1949 v E, W, F; 1950 v E, W, Ni, Sw, P, F; 1951 v E, W, Ni, A (2), D, F, Bel; 1952 v Ni, W, USA, D, Se (25)
Cowan, W. D. (Newcastle U), 1924 v E (1)
Cowie, D. (Dundee), 1953 v E, Se; 1954 v Ni, W, Fi, N, A, U; 1955 v W, Ni, A, H; 1956 v W, A; 1957 v Ni, W; 1958 v H, Pol, Y, Par (20)
Cox, C. J. (Hearts), 1948 v F (1)
Cox, S. (Rangers), 1949 v E, F; 1950 v E, F, W, Ni, Sw, P; 1951 v E, D, F, Bel, A; 1952 v Ni, W, USA, D, Se; 1953 v W, Ni, E; 1954 v W, Ni, E (24)
Craig, A. (Motherwell), 1929 v N, Ho; 1932 v E (3)
Craig, J. (Celtic), 1977 v Se (sub) (1)
Craig, J. P. (Celtic), 1968 v W (1)
Craig, T. (Rangers), 1927 v Ni; 1928 v Ni; 1929 v N, G, Ho; 1930 v Ni, E, W (8)
Craig, T. B. (Newcastle U), 1976 v Sw (1)
Crainey, S. (Celtic), 2002 v F, Ng; 2003 v D (sub), Fa; (with Southampton), 2004 v R (sub), D (6)
Crapnell, J. (Airdrieonians), 1929 v E, N, G; 1930 v F; 1931 v Ni, Sw; 1932 v E, F; 1933 v Ni (9)
Crawford, D. (St Mirren), 1894 v W, Ni; (with Rangers), 1900 v W (3)
Crawford, J. (Queen's Park), 1932 v F, Ni; 1933 v E, W, Ni (5)
Crawford, S. (Raith R), 1995 v Ec (sub); (with Dunfermline Ath), 2001 v Pol (sub); 2002 v F; 2003 v Fa (sub), Ic, Ca, P, Ei, Ic, Li, A (sub), Nz, G; 2004 v N, Fa, Li, Ho (sub), R (sub), Es (sub), Tr; (with Plymouth Arg), 2005 v H (sub), Sp, Slo (sub), Mol, Se (sub) (25)
Crerand, P. T. (Celtic), 1961 v Ei (2), Cz; 1962 v Ni, W, E, Cz (2), U; 1963 v W, Ni; (with Manchester U), 1964 v Ni; 1965 v E, Pol, Fi; 1966 v Pol (16)
Cringan, W. (Celtic), 1920 v W; 1922 v E, Ni; 1923 v W, E (5)
Crosbie, J. A. (Ayr U), 1920 v W; (with Birmingham), 1922 v E (2)
Croal, J. A. (Falkirk), 1913 v Ni; 1914 v E, W (3)
Cropley, A. J. (Hibernian), 1972 v P, Bel (2)
Cross, J. H. (Third Lanark), 1903 v Ni (1)
Cruickshank, J. (Hearts), 1964 v WG; 1970 v W, E; 1971 v D, Bel; 1976 v R (6)
Crum, J. (Celtic), 1936 v E; 1939 v Ni (2)
Cullen, M. J. (Luton T), 1956 v A (1)
Cumming, D. S. (Middlesbrough), 1938 v E (1)
Cumming, J. (Hearts), 1955 v E, H, P, Y; 1960 v E, Pol, A, H, T (9)
Cummings, G. (Partick T), 1935 v E; 1936 v W, Ni; (with Aston Villa), E; 1937 v G; 1938 v W, Ni, Cz; 1939 v E (9)
Cummings, W. (Chelsea), 2002 v Hk (sub) (1)
Cunningham, A. N. (Rangers), 1920 v Ni; 1921 v W, E; 1922 v Ni; 1923 v E, W; 1924 v E, Ni; 1926 v E, Ni; 1927 v E, W (12)
Cunningham, W. C. (Preston NE), 1954 v N (2), U, Fi, A; 1955 v W, E, H (8)
Curran, H. P. (Wolverhampton W), 1970 v A; 1971 v Ni, E, D, USSR (sub) (5)

Dailly, C. (Derby Co), 1997 v W, Ma, Bl; 1998 v Bl, La, F, D, Fi, Co, US, Br, N, Mor; (with Blackburn R), 1999 v Li; 2000 v Bos (sub), Es, Bos, Li, E (2), F, Ho, Ei; 2001 v La, Sm, Aus; (with West Ham U), Pol; 2002 v Cro, Bel, La, F, Ng, Sk, S.Af, Hk; 2003 v D, Fa, Ic, Ca, P, Ei, Ic, Li, A, Nz, G; 2004 v N, G, Li, Ho, W, R, D; 2005 v Mol (sub), Bl (55)
Dalglish, K. (Celtic), 1972 v Bel (sub), Ho; 1973 v D (1+1 sub), E (2), W, Ni, Sw, Br; 1974 v Cz (2), WG (2), Ni, W, E, Bel, N (sub), Z, Br, Y; 1975 v EG, Sp (sub+1), Se, P, W, Ni, E, R; 1976 v D (2), R, Sw, Ni, E; 1977 v Fi, Cz, W (2), Se, Ni, E, Ch, Arg, Br; (with Liverpool), 1978 v EG, Cz, W, Bul, Ni (sub), W, E, Pe, Ir, Ho; 1979 v A, N, P, W, Ni, E, Arg, N; 1980 v Pe, A, Bel (2), P, Ni, W, E, Pol, H; 1981 v Se, P, Is; 1982 v Se, Ni, P (sub), Sp, Ho, Ni, W, E, Nz, Br (sub); 1983 v Bel, Sw; 1984 v U, Bel, EG; 1985 v Y, Ic, Sp, W; 1986 v EG, Aus, R; 1987 v Bul (sub), L (102)
Davidson, C. I. (Blackburn R), 1999 v Li (sub), Es, Fa, CzR, G, Fa, CzR; 2000 v Es, Bos, Li, E, F; (with Leicester C), 2001 v La, Pol; 2002 v La; 2003 v Ic (sub), Ca (sub) (17)
Davidson, D. (Queen's Park), 1878 v W; 1879 v W; 1880 v W; 1881 v E, W (5)
Davidson, J. A. (Partick T), 1954 v N (2), A, U; 1955 v W, Ni, E, H (8)
Davidson, S. (Middlesbrough), 1921 v E (1)
Dawson, A. (Rangers), 1980 v Pol (sub), H; 1983 v Ni, Ca (2) (5)
Dawson, J. (Rangers), 1935 v Ni; 1936 v E; 1937 v G, E, W, Ni, A, Cz; 1938 v W, Ho, Ni; 1939 v E, Ni, H (14)
Deans, J. (Celtic), 1975 v EG, Sp (2)
Delaney, J. (Celtic), 1936 v W, Ni; 1937 v G, E, A, Cz; 1938 v Ni; 1939 v W, Ni; (with Manchester U), 1947 v E; 1948 v E, W, Ni (13)
Devine, A. (Falkirk), 1910 v W (1)
Devlin, P. J. (Birmingham C), 2003 v Ca, P (sub), Ei (sub), Ic (sub), Li (sub), A, Nz, G; 2004 v N (sub), Fa (10)
Dewar, G. (Dumbarton), 1888 v Ni; 1889 v E (2)
Dewar, N. (Third Lanark), 1932 v E, F; 1933 v W (3)
Dick, J. (West Ham U), 1959 v E (1)
Dickie, M. (Rangers), 1897 v Ni; 1899 v Ni; 1900 v W (3)
Dickov, P. (Manchester C), 2001 v Sm (sub), Cro (sub), Aus (sub); (with Leicester C), 2003 v Fa; 2004 v Fa, Ho (2), W; (with Blackburn R), 2005 v Slo, N (10)
Dickson, W. (Dundee Strathmore), 1888 v Ni (1)
Dickson, W. (Kilmarnock), 1970 v Ni, W, E; 1971 v D, USSR (5)
Divers, J. (Celtic), 1895 v W (1)
Divers, J. (Celtic), 1939 v Ni (1)
Dobie, R. S. (WBA), 2002 v Sk, S.Af, Hk (sub); 2003 v D (sub), Fa, P (6)
Docherty, T. H, (Preston NE), 1952 v W; 1953 v E, Se; 1954 v N (2), A, U; 1955 v W, E, H (2), A; 1957 v E, Y, Sp (2), Sw, WG; 1958 v Ni, W, E, Sw; (with Arsenal), 1959 v W, E, Ni (25)
Dodds, D. (Dundee U), 1984 v U (sub), Ni (2)
Dodds, J. (Celtic), 1914 v E, W, Ni (3)
Dodds, W. (Aberdeen), 1997 v La (sub), W, Bl (sub); 1998 v Bl (sub); (with Dundee U), 1999 v Es (sub), Fa, G, Fa, CzR; 2000 v Bos, Es, Bos, Li (sub), E (2); (with Rangers), F, Ho, Ei; 2001 v La, Sm, Aus, Bel, Sm, Pol; 2002 v Cro (sub), Bel (26)
Doig, J. E. (Arbroath), 1887 v Ni; 1889 v Ni; (with Sunderland), 1896 v E; 1899 v E; 1903 v E (5)
Donachie, W. (Manchester C), 1972 v Pe, Ni, E, Y, Cz, Br; 1973 v D, E, W, Ni; 1974 v Ni; 1976 v R, Ni, W, E; 1977 v Fi, Cz, W (2), Se, Ni, E, Ch, Arg, Br; 1978 v EG, W, Bul, W, E, Ir, Ho; 1979 v A, N, P (sub) (35)
Donaldson, A. (Bolton W), 1914 v E, Ni, W; 1920 v E, Ni; 1922 v Ni (6)
Donnachie, J. (Oldham Ath), 1913 v E; 1914 v E, Ni (3)
Donnelly, S. (Celtic), 1997 v W (sub), Ma (sub); 1998 v La (sub), F (sub), D (sub), Fi (sub), Co (sub), US (sub); 1999 v Es (sub), Fa (10)
Dougall, C. (Birmingham C), 1947 v W (1)
Dougall, J. (Preston NE), 1939 v E (1)
Dougan, R. (Hearts), 1950 v Sw (1)
Douglas, A. (Chelsea), 1911 v Ni (1)
Douglas, J. (Renfrew), 1880 v W (1)
Douglas, R. (Celtic), 2002 v Ng, S.Af, Hk; 2003 v D, Fa, Ic, P, Ic, Nz, G; 2004 v N, Fa, G, Li, Ho (2), W; 2005 v I (18)
Dowds, P. (Celtic), 1892 v Ni (1)
Downie, R. (Third Lanark), 1892 v W (1)
Doyle, D. (Celtic), 1892 v E; 1893 v W; 1894 v E; 1895 v E, Ni; 1897 v E; 1898 v E, Ni (8)
Doyle, J. (Ayr U), 1976 v R (1)

Drummond, J. (Falkirk), 1892 v Ni; (with Rangers), 1894 v Ni; 1895 v Ni, E; 1896 v E, Ni; 1897 v Ni; 1898 v E; 1900 v E; 1901 v E; 1902 v E, W, Ni; 1903 v Ni (14)
Dunbar, M. (Cartvale), 1886 v Ni (1)
Duncan, A. (Hibernian), 1975 v P (sub), W, Ni, E, R; 1976 v D (sub) (6)
Duncan, D. (Derby Co), 1933 v E, W; 1934 v A, W; 1935 v E, W; 1936 v E, W, Ni; 1937 v G, E, W, Ni; 1938 v W (14)
Duncan, D. M. (East Fife), 1948 v Bel, Sw, F (3)
Duncan, J. (Alexandra Ath), 1878 v W; 1882 v W (2)
Duncan, J. (Leicester C), 1926 v W (1)
Duncanson, J. (Rangers), 1947 v Ni (1)
Dunlop, J. (St Mirren), 1890 v W (1)
Dunlop, W. (Liverpool), 1906 v E (1)
Dunn, J. (Hibernian), 1925 v W, Ni; 1927 v Ni; 1928 v Ni, E; (with Everton), 1929 v W (6)
Durie, G. S. (Chelsea), 1988 v Bul (sub); 1989 v I (sub), Cy; 1990 v Y, EG, Eg, Se; 1991 v Sw (sub), Bul (2), USSR (sub), Sm; (with Tottenham H), 1992 v Sw, R, Sm, Ni (sub), Fi, Ca, N (sub), Ho, G; 1993 v Sw, I; 1994 v Sw, I; (with Rangers), Ho (2); 1996 v US, Ho, E, Sw; 1997 v A (sub), Se (sub), Ma (sub), Bl; 1998 v Bl, La, F, Fi (sub), Co, Br, N, Mor (43)
Durrant, I. (Rangers), 1988 v H, Bel, Ma, Sp; 1989 v N (sub); 1993 v Sw (sub), P (sub), I, P (sub); 1994 v I (sub), Ma; (with Kilmarnock), 1999 v Es, Fa (sub), G, Fa, CzR; 2000 v Bos (sub), Es, Ho (sub), Ei (sub) (20)
Dykes, J. (Hearts), 1938 v Ho; 1939 v Ni (2)

Easson, J. F. (Portsmouth), 1931 v A, Sw; 1934 v W (3)
Elliott, M. S. (Leicester C), 1998 v F (sub), D, Fi; 1999 v Li, Fa, CzR, Fa; 2000 v Ho, Ei; 2001 v La, Sm, Cro, Aus (sub), Bel, Sm; 2002 v Cro, Bel, La (18)
Ellis, J. (Mossend Swifts), 1892 v Ni (1)
Evans, A. (Aston Villa), 1982 v Ho, Ni, E, Nz (4)
Evans, R. (Celtic), 1949 v E, W, Ni, F; 1950 v W, Ni, Sw, P; 1951 v E, A; 1952 v Ni; 1953 v Se; 1954 v Ni, W, E, N, Fi; 1955 v Ni, P, Y, A, H; 1956 v E, Ni, W, A; 1957 v WG, Sp; 1958 v Ni, W, E, Sw, H, Pol, Y, Par, F; 1959 v E, WG, Ho, P; 1960 v E, Ni, W, Pol; (with Chelsea), 1960 v A, H, T (48)
Ewart, J. (Bradford C), 1921 v E (1)
Ewing, T. (Partick T), 1958 v W, E (2)

Farm, G. N. (Blackpool), 1953 v W, Ni, E, Se; 1954 v Ni, W, E; 1959 v WG, Ho, P (10)
Ferguson, B. (Rangers), 1999 v Li; 2000 v Bos, Es (sub), E (2), F, Ei; 2001 v La, Aus, Bel; 2003 v D, Fa, Ic, Ei, Ic; 2004 v N (with Blackburn R), Fa, G, Li, Ho (2); 2005 v H, Sp, Slo, N, Mol; (with Rangers), I, Mol, Bl (29)
Ferguson, D. (Rangers), 1988 v Ma, Co (sub) (2)
Ferguson, D. (Dundee U), 1992 v US (sub), Ca, Ho (sub); 1993 v G; (with Everton), 1995 v Gr; 1997 v A, Es (7)
Ferguson, I. (Rangers), 1989 v I, Cy (sub), F; 1993 v Ma (sub), Es; 1994 v Ma, A (sub), Ho (sub); 1997 v Es (sub) (9)
Ferguson, J. (Vale of Leven), 1874 v E; 1876 v E, W; 1877 v E, W; 1878 v W (6)
Ferguson, R. (Kilmarnock), 1966 v W, E, Ho, P, Br; 1967 v W, Ni (7)
Fernie, W. (Celtic), 1954 v Fi, A, U; 1955 v W, Ni; 1957 v E, Ni, W, Y; 1958 v W, Sw, Par (12)
Findlay, R. (Kilmarnock), 1898 v W (1)
Fitchie, T. T. (Woolwich Arsenal), 1905 v W; 1906 v W, Ni; (with Queen's Park), 1907 v W (4)
Flavell, R. (Airdrieonians), 1947 v Bel, L (2)
Fleck, R. (Norwich C), 1990 v Arg, Se, Br (sub); 1991 v USSR (4)
Fleming, C. (East Fife), 1954 v Ni (1)
Fleming, J. W. (Rangers), 1929 v G, Ho; 1930 v E (3)
Fleming, R. (Morton), 1886 v Ni (1)
Fletcher, D. B. (Manchester U), 2004 v N (sub), Li (sub), Ho (2), W, D, Es, Tr; 2005 v H, Sp, Slo, N, Mol (1+1), Bl (15)
Forbes, A. R. (Sheffield U), 1947 v Bel, L, E; 1948 v W, Ni; (with Arsenal), 1950 v E, P, F; 1951 v W, Ni, A; 1952 v W, D, Se (14)
Forbes, J. (Vale of Leven), 1884 v E, W, Ni; 1887 v W, E (5)
Ford, D. (Hearts), 1974 v Cz (sub), WG (sub), W (3)
Forrest, J. (Rangers), 1966 v W, I; (with Aberdeen), 1971 v Bel (sub), D, USSR (5)
Forrest, J. (Motherwell), 1958 v E (1)
Forsyth, A. (Partick T), 1972 v Y, Cz, Br; 1973 v D; (with Manchester U), E; 1975 v Sp, Ni (sub), R, EG; 1976 v D (10)
Forsyth, C. (Kilmarnock), 1964 v E; 1965 v W, Ni, Fi (4)
Forsyth, T. (Motherwell), 1971 v D; (with Rangers), 1974 v Cz; 1976 v Sw, Ni, W, E; 1977 v Fi, Se, W, Ni, E, Ch, Arg, Br; 1978 v Cz, W, Ni, W (sub), E, Pe, Ir (sub), Ho (22)
Foyers, R. (St Bernards), 1893 v W; 1894 v W (2)
Fraser, D. M. (WBA), 1968 v Ho; 1969 v Cy (2)
Fraser, J. (Moffat), 1891 v Ni (1)
Fraser, M. J. E. (Queen's Park), 1880 v W; 1882 v W, E; 1883 v W, E (5)
Fraser, J. (Dundee), 1907 v Ni (1)
Fraser, W. (Sunderland), 1955 v W, Ni (2)
Freedman, D. A. (C Palace), 2002 v La, F (2)
Fulton, W. (Abercorn), 1884 v Ni (1)
Fyfe, J. H. (Third Lanark), 1895 v W (1)

Gabriel, J. (Everton), 1961 v W; 1964 v N (sub) (2)
Gallacher, H. K. (Airdrieonians), 1924 v Ni; 1925 v E, W, Ni; 1926 v W; (with Newcastle U), 1926 v E, Ni; 1927 v E, W, Ni; 1928 v E, W; 1929 v E, W, Ni; 1930 v W, Ni, F; (with Chelsea), 1934 v E; (with Derby Co), 1935 v E (20)
Gallacher, K. W. (Dundee U), 1988 v Co, E (sub); 1989 v N, I; (with Coventry C), 1991 v Sm; 1992 v R (sub), Sm (sub), Ni (sub), N (sub), Ho (sub), G (sub), C; 1993 v Sw (sub), P; (with Blackburn R), P, Es (2); 1994 v I, Ma; 1996 v Aus (sub), D, Co (sub), Ho; 1997 v Se (sub), Es (2), A, Se, W, Ma, Bl; 1998 v Bl, La, F, Fi (sub), US, Br, N, Mor; 1999 v Li, Es, Fa, CzR; 2000 v Bos (sub); (with Newcastle U), Bos, Li (sub), E, F, Ei (sub); 2001 v Sm, Cro, Bel (sub), Sm (sub) (53)
Gallacher, P. (Sunderland), 1935 v Ni (1)
Gallacher, P. (Dundee U), 2002 v Hk (sub); 2003 v Ca, Ei (sub), Li, A; 2004 v R, D, Es (8)
Gallagher, P. (Blackburn R), 2004 v W (sub) (1)
Galloway, M. (Celtic), 1992 v R (1)
Galt, J. H. (Rangers), 1908 v W, Ni (2)
Gardiner, I. (Motherwell), 1958 v W (1)
Gardner, D. R. (Third Lanark), 1897 v W (1)
Gardner, R. (Queen's Park), 1872 v E; 1873 v E; (with Clydesdale), 1874 v E; 1875 v E; 1878 v E (5)
Gemmell, T. (St Mirren), 1955 v P, Y (2)
Gemmell, T. (Celtic), 1966 v E; 1967 v W, Ni, E, USSR; 1968 v Ni, E; 1969 v W, Ni, E, D, A, WG, Cy; 1970 v E, Ei, WG; 1971 v Bel (18)
Gemmill, A. (Derby Co), 1971 v Bel; 1972 v P, Ho, Pe, Ni, W, E; 1976 v D, R, Ni, W, E; 1977 v Fi, Cz, W (2), Ni (sub), E (sub), Ch (sub), Arg, Br; 1978 v EG (sub); (with Nottingham F), Bul, Ni, W, E (sub), Pe (sub), Ir, Ho; 1979 v A, N, P, N; (with Birmingham C), 1980 v A, P, Ni, W, E, H; 1981 v Se, P, Is, Ni (43)
Gemmill, S. (Nottingham F), 1995 v J, Ec, Fa (sub); 1996 v Sm, D (sub), US; 1997 v Es, Se (sub), W, Ma (sub), Bl (sub); 1998 v D, Fi; (with Everton), 1999 v G, Fa (sub); 2001 v Sm (sub), Pol (sub); 2002 v Cro (sub), F (sub), Ng, Sk, S.Af, Hk; 2003 v Ca, Ei (sub), A (sub) (26)
Gibb, W. (Clydesdale), 1873 v E (1)
Gibson, D. W. (Leicester C), 1963 v A, N, Ei, Sp; 1964 v Ni; 1965 v W, Fi (7)
Gibson, J. D. (Partick T), 1926 v E; 1927 v E, W, Ni; (with Aston Villa), 1928 v E, W; 1930 v W, Ni (8)
Gibson, N. (Rangers), 1895 v E, Ni; 1896 v E, Ni; 1897 v E, Ni; 1898 v E; 1899 v E, W, Ni; 1900 v E, Ni; 1901 v W; (with Partick T), 1905 v Ni (14)
Gilchrist, J. E. (Celtic), 1922 v E (1)
Gilhooley, M. (Hull C), 1922 v W (1)
Gillespie, G. (Rangers), 1880 v W; 1881 v E, W; 1882 v E; (with Queen's Park), 1886 v W; 1890 v W; 1891 v Ni (7)
Gillespie, G. T. (Liverpool), 1988 v Bel, Bul, Sp; 1989 v N, F, Ch; 1990 v Y, EG, Eg, Pol, Ma, Br (sub); 1991 v Bul (13)
Gillespie, Jas (Third Lanark), 1898 v W (1)
Gillespie, John (Queen's Park), 1896 v W (1)
Gillespie, R. (Queen's Park), 1927 v W; 1931 v W; 1932 v F; 1933 v E (4)
Gillick, T. (Everton), 1937 v A, Cz; 1939 v W, Ni, H (5)
Gilmour, J. (Dundee), 1931 v W (1)
Gilzean, A. J. (Dundee), 1964 v W, E, N, WG; 1965 v Ni, (with Tottenham H), Sp; 1966 v Ni, W, Pol, I; 1968 v W; 1969 v W, E, WG, Cy (2), A (sub); 1970 v Ni, E (sub), WG, A; 1971 v P (22)
Glass, S. (Newcastle U), 1999 v Fa (sub) (1)
Glavin, R. (Celtic), 1977 v Se (1)
Glen, A. (Aberdeen), 1956 v E, Ni (2)
Glen, R. (Renton), 1895 v W; 1896 v W; (with Hibernian), 1900 v Ni (3)
Goram, A. L. (Oldham Ath), 1986 v EG (sub), R, Ho; 1987 v Br; (with Hibernian), 1989 v Y, I; 1990 v EG, Pol, Ma; 1991 v R, Sw, Bul (2), USSR, Sm; (with Rangers), 1992 v Sw, R, Sm, Fi, N, Ho, G, C; 1993 v Sw, P, I, Ma, P; 1994 v Ho; 1995 v Fi, Fa, Ru, Gr; 1996 v Se (sub), D (sub), Co, Ho, E, Sw; 1997 v A, La, Es; 1998 v D (sub) (43)

Gordon, C. S. (Hearts), 2004 v Tr; 2005 v Sp, Slo, N, Mol, I (sub), Mol, Bl (8)
Gordon, J. E. (Rangers), 1912 v E, Ni; 1913 v E, Ni, W; 1914 v E, Ni; 1920 v W, E, Ni (10)
Gossland, J. (Rangers), 1884 v Ni (1)
Goudle, J. (Abercorn), 1884 v Ni (1)
Gough, C. R. (Dundee U), 1983 v Sw, Ni, W, E, Ca (3); 1984 v U, Bel, EG, Ni, W, E, F; 1985 v Sp, E, Ic; 1986 v W, EG, Aus, Is, R, E, D, WG, U; (with Tottenham H), 1987 v Bul, L, Ei (2), Bel, E, Br; 1988 v H; (with Rangers), S.Ar, Sp, Co, E; 1989 v Y, I, Cy, F, Cy; 1990 v F, Arg, EG, Eg, Pol, Ma, Cr; 1991 v USSR, Bul; 1992 v Sm, Ni, Ca, N, Ho, G, C; 1993 v Sw, P (61)
Gould, J. (Celtic), 2000 v Li; 2001 v Aus (2)
Gourlay, J. (Cambuslang), 1886 v Ni; 1888 v W (2)
Govan, J. (Hibernian), 1948 v E, W, Bel, Sw, F; 1949 v Ni (6)
Gow, D. R. (Rangers), 1888 v E (1)
Gow, J. J. (Queen's Park), 1885 v E (1)
Gow, J. R. (Rangers), 1888 v Ni (1)
Graham, A. (Leeds U), 1978 v EG (sub); 1979 v A (sub), N, W, Ni, E, Arg, N; 1980 v A; 1981 v W (10)
Graham, G. (Arsenal), 1972 v P, Ho, Ni, Y, Cz, Br; 1973 v D (2); (with Manchester U), E, W, Ni, Br (sub) (12)
Graham, J. (Annbank), 1884 v Ni (1)
Graham, J. A. (Arsenal), 1921 v Ni (1)
Grant, J. (Hibernian), 1959 v W, Ni (2)
Grant, P. (Celtic), 1989 v E (sub), Ch (2)
Gray, A. (Hibernian), 1903 v Ni (1)
Gray, A. D. (Bradford C), 2003 v Li (sub), Nz (sub) (2)
Gray, A. M. (Aston Villa), 1976 v R, Sw; 1977 v Fi, Cz; 1979 v A, N; (with Wolverhampton W), 1980 v P, E (sub); 1981 v Se, P, Is (sub), Ni; 1982 v Se (sub), Ni (sub); 1983 v Ni, W, E, Ca (1+1 sub); (with Everton), 1985 v Ic (20)
Gray, D. (Rangers), 1929 v W, Ni, G, Ho; 1930 v W, E, Ni; 1931 v W; 1933 v W, Ni (10)
Gray, E. (Leeds U), 1969 v E, Cy; 1970 v WG, A; 1971 v W, Ni; 1972 v Bel, Ho; 1976 v W, E; 1977 v Fi, W (12)
Gray, F. T. (Leeds U), 1976 v Sw; 1979 v N, P, W, Ni, E, Arg (sub); (with Nottingham F), 1980 v Bel (sub); 1981 v Se, P, Is, Ni, Is, W; (with Leeds U), Ni, E; 1982 v Se, Ni, P, Sp, Ho, W, Nz, Br, USSR; 1983 v EG, Sw, Bel, Sw, W, E, Ca (32)
Gray, W. (Pollokshields Ath), 1886 v E (1)
Green, A. (Blackpool), 1971 v Bel (sub), P (sub), Ni, E; (with Newcastle U), 1972 v W, E (sub) (6)
Greig, J. (Rangers), 1964 v E, WG; 1965 v W, Ni, E, Fi (2), Sp, Pol; 1966 v Ni, W, E, Pol, I (2), P, Ho, Br; 1967 v W, Ni, E; 1968 v Ni, W, E, Ho; 1969 v W, Ni, E, D, A, WG, Cy (2); 1970 v W, E, Ei, WG, A; 1971 v D, Bel, W (sub), Ni, E; 1976 v D (44)
Groves, W. (Hibernian), 1888 v W; (with Celtic), 1889 v Ni; 1890 v E (3)
Guilliland, W. (Queen's Park), 1891 v W; 1892 v Ni; 1894 v E; 1895 v E (4)
Gunn, B. (Norwich C), 1990 v Eg; 1993 v Es (2); 1994 v Sw, I, Ho (sub) (6)

Haddock, H. (Clyde), 1955 v E, H (2), P, Y; 1958 v E (6)
Haddow, D. (Rangers), 1894 v E (1)
Haffey, F. (Celtic), 1960 v E; 1961 v E (2)
Hamilton, A. (Queen's Park), 1885 v E, W; 1886 v E; 1888 v E (4)
Hamilton, A. W. (Dundee), 1962 v Cz, U, W, E; 1963 v W, Ni, E, A, N, Ei; 1964 v Ni, W, E, N, WG; 1965 v Ni, W, E, Fi (2), Pol, Sp; 1966 v Pol, Ni (24)
Hamilton, G. (Aberdeen), 1947 v Ni; 1951 v Bel, A; 1954 v N (2) (5)
Hamilton, G. (Port Glasgow Ath), 1906 v Ni (1)
Hamilton, J. (Queen's Park), 1892 v W; 1893 v E, Ni (3)
Hamilton, J. (St Mirren), 1924 v Ni (1)
Hamilton, R. C. (Rangers), 1899 v E, W, Ni; 1900 v W; 1901 v E, Ni; 1902 v W, Ni; 1903 v E; 1904 v Ni; (with Dundee), 1911 v W (11)
Hamilton, T. (Hurlford), 1891 v Ni (1)
Hamilton, T. (Rangers), 1932 v E (1)
Hamilton, W. M. (Hibernian), 1965 v Fi (1)
Hammell, S. (Motherwell), 2005 v Se (sub) (1)
Hannah, A. B. (Renton), 1888 v W (1)
Hannah, J. (Third Lanark), 1889 v W (1)
Hansen, A. D. (Liverpool), 1979 v W, Arg; 1980 v Bel, P; 1981 v Se, P, Is; 1982 v Se, Ni, P, Sp, Ni (sub), W, E, Nz, Br, USSR; 1983 v EG, Sw, Bel, Sw; 1985 v W (sub); 1986 v R (sub); 1987 v Ei (2), L (26)
Hansen, J. (Partick T), 1972 v Bel (sub), Y (sub) (2)
Harkness, J. D. (Queen's Park), 1927 v E, Ni; 1928 v E; (with Hearts), 1929 v W, E, Ni; 1930 v E, W; 1932 v W, F; 1934 v Ni, W (12)
Harper, J. M. (Aberdeen), 1973 v D (1+1 sub); (with Hibernian), 1976 v D; (with Aberdeen), 1978 v Ir (sub) (4)
Harper, W. (Hibernian), 1923 v E, Ni, W; 1924 v E, Ni, W; 1925 v E, Ni, W; (with Arsenal), 1926 v E, Ni (11)
Harris, J. (Partick T), 1921 v W, Ni (2)
Harris, N. (Newcastle U), 1924 v E (1)
Harrower, W. (Queen's Park), 1882 v E; 1884 v Ni; 1886 v W (3)
Hartford, R. A. (WBA), 1972 v Pe, W (sub), E, Y, Cz, Br; (with Manchester C), 1976 v D, R, Ni (sub); 1977 v Cz (sub), W (sub), Se, W, Ni, E, Ch, Arg, Br; 1978 v EG, Cz, W, Bul, W, E, Pe, Ir, Ho; 1979 v A, N, P, W, Ni, E, Arg, N; (with Everton), 1980 v Pe, Bel; 1981 v Ni (sub), Is, W, Ni, E; 1982 v Se; (with Manchester C), Ni, P, Sp, Ni, W, E, Br (50)
Hartley, P. J. (Hearts), 2005 v I, Mol (2)
Harvey, D. (Leeds U), 1973 v D; 1974 v Cz, WG, Ni, W, E, Bel, Z, Br, Y; 1975 v EG, Sp (2); 1976 v D (2); 1977 v Fi (sub) (16)
Hastings, A. C. (Sunderland), 1936 v Ni; 1938 v Ni (2)
Haughney, M. (Celtic), 1954 v E (1)
Hay, D. (Celtic), 1970 v Ni, W, E; 1971 v D, Bel, W, P, Ni; 1972 v P, Bel, Ho; 1973 v W, Ni, E, Sw, Br; 1974 v Cz (2), WG, Ni, W, E, Bel, N, Z, Br, Y (27)
Hay, J. (Celtic), 1905 v Ni; 1909 v Ni; 1910 v W, Ni, E; 1911 v Ni, E; (with Newcastle U), 1912 v E, W; 1914 v E, Ni (11)
Hegarty, P. (Dundee U), 1979 v W, Ni, E, Arg, N (sub); 1980 v W, E; 1983 v Ni (8)
Heggie, C. (Rangers), 1886 v Ni (1)
Henderson, G. H. (Rangers), 1904 v Ni (1)
Henderson, J. G. (Portsmouth), 1953 v Se; 1954 v Ni, E, N; 1956 v W; (with Arsenal), 1959 v W, Ni (7)
Henderson, W. (Rangers), 1963 v W, Ni, E, A, N, Ei, Sp; 1964 v W, Ni, E, N, WG; 1965 v Fi, Pol, E, Sp; 1966 v Ni, W, Pol, I, Ho; 1967 v W, Ni; 1968 v Ho; 1969 v Ni, E, Cy; 1970 v Ei; 1971 v P (29)
Hendry, E. C. J. (Blackburn R), 1993 v Es (2); 1994 v Ma, Ho, A, Ho; 1995 v Fi, Fa, Gr, Ru, Sm; 1996 v Fi, Se, Sm, Aus, D, US, Co, Ho, E, Sw; 1997 v A, Se, Es (2), A, Se; 1998 v La, D, Fi, Co, US, Br, N, Mor; (with Rangers), 1999 v Li, Es, Fa, G; 2000 v Bos, Es, Bos, E (2); (with Coventry C), F; 2001 v La, Sm, Cro, Aus (sub); (with Bolton W), Bel, Sm (51)
Hepburn, J. (Alloa Ath), 1891 v W (1)
Hepburn, R. (Ayr U), 1932 v Ni (1)
Herd, A. C. (Hearts), 1935 v Ni (1)
Herd, D. G. (Arsenal), 1959 v E, W, Ni; 1961 v Ei, Cz (5)
Herd, G. (Clyde), 1958 v E; 1960 v H, T; 1961 v W, Ni (5)
Herriot, J. (Birmingham C), 1969 v Ni, E, D, Cy (2), W (sub); 1970 v Ei (sub), WG (8)
Hewie, J. D. (Charlton Ath), 1956 v E, A; 1957 v E, Ni, W, Y, Sp (2), Sw, WG; 1958 v H, Pol, Y, F; 1959 v Ho, P; 1960 v Ni, W, Pol (19)
Higgins, A. (Kilmarnock), 1885 v Ni (1)
Higgins, A. (Newcastle U), 1910 v E, Ni; 1911 v E, Ni (4)
Highet, T. C. (Queen's Park), 1875 v E; 1876 v E, W; 1878 v E (4)
Hill, D. (Rangers), 1881 v E, W; 1882 v W (3)
Hill, D. A. (Third Lanark), 1906 v Ni (1)
Hill, F. R. (Aberdeen), 1930 v F; 1931 v W, Ni (3)
Hill, J. (Hearts), 1891 v E; 1892 v W (2)
Hogg, G (Hearts), 1896 v E, Ni (2)
Hogg, J. (Ayr U), 1922 v Ni (1)
Hogg, R. M. (Celtic), 1937 v Cz (1)
Holm, A. H. (Queen's Park), 1882 v W; 1883 v E, W (3)
Holt, D. D. (Hearts), 1963 v A, N, Ei, Sp; 1964 v WG (sub) (5)
Holt, G. J. (Kilmarnock), 2001 v La (sub), Cro (sub); (with Norwich C), 2002 v F (sub); 2004 v D, Es, Tr; 2005 v H, Slo (sub), N, Mol (10)
Holton, J. A. (Manchester U), 1973 v W, Ni, E, Sw, Br; 1974 v Cz, WG, Ni, W, E, N, Z, Br, Y; 1975 v EG (15)
Hope, R. (WBA), 1968 v Ho; 1969 v D (2)
Hopkin, D. (C Palace), 1997 v Ma, Bl; (with Leeds U), 1998 v Bl (sub), F (sub); 1999 v CzR; 2000 v Bos (2) (7)
Houliston, W. (Queen of the South), 1949 v E, Ni, F (3)
Houston, S. M. (Manchester U), 1976 v D (1)
Howden, W. (Partick T), 1905 v Ni (1)
Howe, R. (Hamilton A), 1929 v N, Ho (2)
Howie, H. (Hibernian), 1949 v W (1)
Howie, J. (Newcastle U), 1905 v E; 1906 v E; 1908 v E (3)
Howieson, J. (St Mirren), 1927 v Ni (1)
Hughes, J. (Celtic), 1965 v Pol, Sp; 1966 v Ni, I (2); 1968 v E; 1969 v A; 1970 v Ei (8)
Hughes, R. D. (Portsmouth), 2004 v Es, Tr (sub); 2005 v N, Se (sub) (4)
Hughes, W. (Sunderland), 1975 v Se (sub) (1)
Humphries, W. (Motherwell), 1952 v Se (1)

Hunter, A. (Kilmarnock), 1972 v Pe, Y; (with Celtic), 1973 v E; 1974 v Cz (4)
Hunter, J. (Dundee), 1909 v W (1)
Hunter, J. (Third Lanark), 1874 v E; (with Eastern), 1875 v E; (with Third Lanark), 1876 v E; 1877 v W (4)
Hunter, R. (St Mirren), 1890 v Ni (1)
Hunter, W. (Motherwell), 1960 v H, T; 1961 v W (3)
Husband, J. (Partick T), 1947 v W (1)
Hutchison, D. (Everton), 1999 v CzR (sub), G; 2000 v Bos, Es, Li, E (2), F, Ho, Ei; (with Sunderland), 2001 v La, Sm, Cro, Aus, Bel, Sm; (with West Ham U), 2002 v Cro, Bel, La; 2003 v Ei, Ic, Li, A; 2004 v N, Li (sub), Ho (sub) (26)
Hutchison, T. (Coventry C), 1974 v Cz (2), WG (2), Ni, W, Bel (sub), N, Z (sub), Y (sub); 1975 v EG, Sp (2), P, E (sub), R (sub); 1976 v D (17)
Hutton, J. (Aberdeen), 1923 v E, W, Ni; 1924 v Ni; 1926 v W, E, Ni; (with Blackburn R), 1927 v Ni; 1928 v W, Ni (10)
Hutton, J. (St Bernards), 1887 v Ni (1)
Hyslop, T. (Stoke C), 1896 v E; (with Rangers), 1897 v E (2)

Imlach, J. J. S. (Nottingham F), 1958 v H, Pol, Y, F (4)
Imrie, W. N. (St Johnstone), 1929 v N, G (2)
Inglis, J. (Rangers), 1883 v E, W (2)
Inglis, J. (Kilmarnock Ath), 1884 v Ni (1)
Irons, J. H. (Queen's Park), 1900 v W (1)
Irvine, B. (Aberdeen), 1991 v R; 1993 v G, Es (2); 1994 v Sw, I, Ma, A, Ho (9)

Jackson, A. (Cambuslang), 1886 v W; 1888 v Ni (2)
Jackson, A. (Aberdeen), 1925 v E, W, Ni; (with Huddersfield T), 1926 v E, W, Ni; 1927 v W, Ni; 1928 v E, W; 1929 v E, W, Ni; 1930 v E, W, Ni, F (17)
Jackson, C. (Rangers), 1975 v Se, P (sub), W; 1976 v D, R, Ni, W, E (8)
Jackson, D. (Hibernian), 1995 v Ru, Sm, J, Ec, Fa; 1996 v Gr, Fi (sub), Se (sub), Sm (sub), Aus (sub), D (sub), US; 1997 v La, Se, Es, A, Se, W, Ma, Bl; (with Celtic), 1998 v D, Fi, Co, US, Br, N; 1999 v Li, Es (sub) (28)
Jackson, J. (Partick T), 1931 v A, I, Sw; 1933 v E; (with Chelsea), 1934 v E; 1935 v E; 1936 v W, Ni (8)
Jackson, T. A. (St Mirren), 1904 v W, E, Ni; 1905 v W; 1907 v W, Ni (6)
James, A. W. (Preston NE), 1926 v W; 1928 v E; 1929 v E, Ni; (with Arsenal), 1930 v E, W, Ni; 1933 v W (8)
Jardine, A. (Rangers), 1971 v D (sub); 1972 v P, Bel, Ho; 1973 v E, Sw, Br; 1974 v Cz (2), WG (2), Ni, W, E, Bel, N, Z, Br, Y; 1975 v EG, Sp (2), Se, P, W, Ni, E; 1977 v Se (sub), Ch (sub), Br (sub); 1978 v Cz, W, Ni, Ir; 1980 v Pe, A, Bel (2) (38)
Jarvie, A. (Airdrieonians), 1971 v P (sub), Ni (sub), E (sub) (3)
Jenkinson, T. (Hearts), 1887 v Ni (1)
Jess, E. (Aberdeen), 1993 v I (sub), Ma; 1994 v Sw (sub), I, Ho (sub), A, Ho (sub); 1995 v Fi (sub); 1996 v Se (sub), Sm; (with Coventry C), US, Co (sub), E (sub); (with Aberdeen), 1998 v D (sub); 1999 v CzR, G (sub), Fa (sub), CzR (sub) (18)
Johnston, A. (Sunderland), 1999 v Es, Fa, CzR (sub), G, Fa, CzR; 2000 v Es, F (sub), Ei (sub); (with Rangers), 2001 v Sm (sub), Cro, Sm; (with Middlesbrough), 2002 v Ng (sub), Sk, S.Af, Hk; 2003 v D (sub), Fa (18)
Johnston, L. H. (Clyde), 1948 v Bel, Sw (2)
Johnston, M. (Watford), 1984 v W (sub), E (sub), F; 1985 v Y; (with Celtic), Ic, Sp (2), W; 1986 v EG; 1987 v Bul, Ei (2), L; (with Nantes), 1988 v H, Bel, L, S.Ar, Sp, Co, E; 1989 v N, Y, I, Cy, F, Cy, E, Ch (sub); (with Rangers), 1990 v F, N, EG, Pol, Ma, Cr, Se, Br; 1992 v Sw, Sm (sub) (38)
Johnston, R. (Sunderland), 1938 v Cz (1)
Johnston, W. (Rangers), 1966 v W, E, Pol, Ho; 1968 v W, E; 1969 v Ni (sub); 1970 v Ni; 1971 v D; (with WBA), 1977 v Se, W (sub), Ni, E, Ch, Arg, Br; 1978 v EG, Cz, W (2), E, Pe (22)
Johnstone, D. (Rangers), 1973 v W, Ni, E, Sw, Br; 1975 v EG (sub), Se (sub); 1976 v Sw, Ni (sub), E (sub); 1978 v Bul (sub), Ni, W; 1980 v Bel (14)
Johnstone, J. (Abercorn), 1888 v W (1)
Johnstone, J. (Celtic), 1965 v W, Fi; 1966 v E; 1967 v W, USSR; 1968 v W; 1969 v A, WG; 1970 v E, WG; 1971 v D, E; 1972 v P, Bel, Ho, Ni, E (sub); 1974 v W, E, Bel, N; 1975 v EG, Sp (23)
Johnstone, Jas (Kilmarnock), 1894 v W (1)
Johnstone, J. A. (Hearts), 1930 v W; 1933 v W, Ni (3)
Johnstone, R. (Hibernian), 1951 v E, D, F; 1952 v Ni, E; 1953 v E, Se; 1954 v W, E, N, Fi; 1955 v Ni, H; (with Manchester C), 1955 v E; 1956 v E, Ni, W (17)
Johnstone, W. (Third Lanark), 1887 v Ni; 1889 v W; 1890 v E (3)
Jordan, J. (Leeds U), 1973 v E (sub), Sw (sub), Br; 1974 v Cz (sub+1), WG (sub), Ni (sub), W, E, Bel, N, Z, Br, Y; 1975 v EG, Sp (2); 1976 v Ni, W, E; 1977 v Cz, W, Ni, E; 1978 v EG, Cz, W; (with Manchester U), Bul, Ni, E, Pe, Ir, Ho; 1979 v A, P, W (sub), Ni, E, N; 1980 v Bel, Ni (sub), W, E, Pol; 1981 v Is, W, E; (with AC Milan), 1982 v Se, Ho, W, E, USSR (52)

Kay, J. L. (Queen's Park), 1880 v E; 1882 v E, W; 1883 v E, W; 1884 v W (6)
Keillor, A. (Montrose), 1891 v W; 1892 v Ni; (with Dundee), 1894 v Ni; 1895 v W; 1896 v W; 1897 v W (6)
Keir, L. (Dumbarton), 1885 v W; 1886 v Ni; 1887 v E, W; 1888 v E (5)
Kelly, H. T. (Blackpool), 1952 v USA (1)
Kelly, J. (Renton), 1888 v E; (with Celtic), 1889 v E; 1890 v E; 1892 v E; 1893 v E, Ni; 1894 v W; 1896 v Ni (8)
Kelly, J. C. (Barnsley), 1949 v W, Ni (2)
Kelso, R. (Renton), 1885 v W, Ni; 1886 v W; 1887 v E, W; 1888 v E; (with Dundee), 1898 v Ni (7)
Kelso, T. (Dundee), 1914 v W (1)
Kennaway, J. (Celtic), 1934 v A (1)
Kennedy, A. (Eastern), 1875 v E; 1876 v E, W; (with Third Lanark), 1878 v E; 1882 v W; 1884 v W (6)
Kennedy, J. (Hibernian), 1897 v W (1)
Kennedy, J. (Celtic), 1964 v W, E, WG; 1965 v W, Ni, Fi (6)
Kennedy, J. (Celtic), 2004 v R (1)
Kennedy, S. (Aberdeen), 1978 v Bul, W, E, Pe, Ho; 1979 v A, P; 1982 v P (sub) (8)
Kennedy, S. (Partick T), 1905 v W (1)
Kennedy, S. (Rangers), 1975 v Se, P, W, Ni, E (5)
Ker, G. (Queen's Park), 1880 v E; 1881 v E, W; 1882 v W, E (5)
Ker, W. (Queen's Park), 1872 v E; 1873 v E (2)
Kerr, A. (Partick T), 1955 v A, H (2)
Kerr, B. (Newcastle U), 2003 v Nz (sub); 2004 v Es (sub); Tr (sub) (3)
Kerr, P. (Hibernian), 1924 v Ni (1)
Key, G. (Hearts), 1902 v Ni (1)
Key, W. (Queen's Park), 1907 v Ni (1)
King, A. (Hearts), 1896 v E, W; (with Celtic), 1897 v Ni; 1898 v Ni; 1899 v Ni, W (6)
King, J. (Hamilton A), 1933 v Ni; 1934 v Ni (2)
King, W. S. (Queen's Park), 1929 v W (1)
Kinloch, J. D. (Partick T), 1922 v Ni (1)
Kinnaird, A. F. (Wanderers), 1873 v E (1)
Kinnear, D. (Rangers), 1938 v Cz (1)
Kyle, K. (Sunderland), 2002 v Sk (sub), S.Af, Hk; 2003 v D, Fa, Ca (sub), P (sub), Nz ; 2004 v D (9)

Lambert, P. (Motherwell), 1995 v J, Ec (sub); (with Borussia Dortmund), 1997 v La (sub), Se (sub), A, Se, Bl; 1998 v Bl, La; (with Celtic), Fi (sub), Co, US, Br, N, Mor; 1999 v Li, CzR, G, Fa, CzR; 2000 v Bos, Li, Ho, Ei; 2001 v Bel, Sm; 2002 v Cro, Bel, F, Ng; 2003 v D, Fa, Ic, P, Ei, Ic, Li, G; 2004 v N, G (40)
Lambie, J. A. (Queen's Park), 1886 v Ni; 1887 v Ni; 1888 v E (3)
Lambie, W. A. (Queen's Park), 1892 v Ni; 1893 v W; 1894 v E; 1895 v E, Ni; 1896 v E, Ni; 1897 v E, Ni (9)
Lamont, W. (Pilgrims), 1885 v Ni (1)
Lang, A. (Dumbarton), 1880 v W (1)
Lang, J. J. (Clydesdale), 1876 v W; (with Third Lanark), 1878 v W (2)
Latta, A. (Dumbarton), 1888 v W; 1889 v E (2)
Law, D. (Huddersfield T), 1959 v W, Ni, Ho, P; 1960 v Ni, W; (with Manchester C), 1960 v E, Pol, A; 1961 v E, Ni; (with Torino), 1962 v Cz (2), E; (with Manchester U), 1963 v W, Ni, E, A, N, Ei, Sp; 1964 v W, E, N, WG; 1965 v W, Ni, E, Fi (2), Pol, Sp; 1966 v Ni, E, Pol; 1967 v W, E, USSR; 1968 v Ni; 1969 v Ni, A, WG; 1972 v Pe, Ni, W, E, Y, Cz, Br; (with Manchester C), 1974 v Cz (2), WG (2), Ni, Z (55)
Law, G. (Rangers), 1910 v E, Ni, W (3)
Law, T. (Chelsea), 1928 v E; 1930 v E (2)
Lawrence, J. (Newcastle U), 1911 v E (1)
Lawrence, T. (Liverpool), 1963 v Ei; 1969 v W, WG (3)
Lawson, D. (St Mirren), 1923 v E (1)
Leckie, R. (Queen's Park), 1872 v E (1)
Leggat, G. (Aberdeen), 1956 v E; 1957 v W; 1958 v Ni, H, Pol, Y, Par; (with Fulham), 1959 v E, W, Ni, WG, Ho; 1960 v E, Ni, W, Pol, A, H (18)
Leighton, J. (Aberdeen), 1983 v EG, Sw, Bel, Sw, W, E, Ca (2); 1984 v U, Bel, Ni, W, E, F; 1985 v Y, Ic, Sp (2), W, E, Ic; 1986 v W, EG, Aus (2), Is, D, WG, U; 1987 v Bul, Ei (2), L,

Bel, E; 1988 v H, Bel, Bul, L, S.Ar, Ma, Sp; (with Manchester U), Co, E; 1989 v N, Cy, F, Cy, E, Ch; 1990 v Y, F, N, Arg, Ma (sub, Cr, Se, Br; (with Hibernian), 1994 v Ma, A, Ho; 1995 v Gr (sub), Ru, Sm, J, Ec, Fa; 1996 v Gr, Fi, Se, Sm, Aus, D, US; 1997 v Se, Es, A, Se, W (sub), Ma, Bl; (with Aberdeen), 1998 v Bl, La, D, Fi, US, Br, N, Mor; 1999 v Li, Es (91)
Lennie, W. (Aberdeen), 1908 v W, Ni (2)
Lennox, R. (Celtic), 1967 v Ni, E, USSR; 1968 v W, L; 1969 v D, A, WG, Cy (sub); 1970 v W (sub) (10)
Leslie, L. G. (Airdrieonians), 1961 v W, Ni, Ei (2), Cz (5)
Levein, C. (Hearts), 1990 v Arg, EG, Eg (sub), Pol, Ma (sub), Se; 1992 v R, Sm; 1993 v P, G, P; 1994 v Sw, Ho; 1995 v Fi, Fa, Ru (16)
Liddell, W. (Liverpool), 1947 v W, Ni; 1948 v E, W, Ni; 1950 v E, W, P, F; 1951 v W, Ni, E, A; 1952 v W, Ni, E, USA, D, Se; 1953 v W, Ni, E; 1954 v W; 1955 v P, Y, A, H; 1956 v Ni (28)
Liddle, D. (East Fife), 1931 v A, I, Sw (3)
Lindsay, D. (St Mirren), 1903 v Ni (1)
Lindsay, J. (Dumbarton), 1880 v W; 1881 v W, E; 1884 v W, E; 1885 v W, E; 1886 v E (8)
Lindsay, J. (Renton), 1888 v E; 1893 v E, Ni (3)
Linwood, A. B. (Clyde), 1950 v W (1)
Little, R. J. (Rangers), 1953 v Se (1)
Livingstone, G. T. (Manchester C), 1906 v E; (with Rangers), 1907 v W (2)
Lochhead, A. (Third Lanark), 1889 v W (1)
Logan, J. (Ayr), 1891 v W (1)
Logan, T. (Falkirk), 1913 v Ni (1)
Logie, J. T. (Arsenal), 1953 v Ni (1)
Loney, W. (Celtic), 1910 v W, Ni (2)
Long, H. (Clyde), 1947 v Ni (1)
Longair, W. (Dundee), 1894 v Ni (1)
Lorimer, P. (Leeds U), 1970 v A (sub); 1971 v W, Ni; 1972 v Ni (sub), W, E; 1973 v D (2), E (2); 1974 v WG (sub), E, Bel, N, Z, Br, Y; 1975 v Sp (sub); 1976 v D (2), R (sub) (21)
Love, A. (Aberdeen), 1931 v A, I, Sw (3)
Low, A. (Falkirk), 1934 v Ni (1)
Low, J. (Cambuslang), 1891 v Ni (1)
Low, T. P. (Rangers), 1897 v Ni (1)
Low, W. L. (Newcastle U), 1911 v E, W; 1912 v Ni; 1920 v E, Ni (5)
Lowe, J. (St Bernards), 1887 v Ni (1)
Lundie, J. (Hibernian), 1886 v W (1)
Lyall, J. (Sheffield W), 1905 v E (1)

McAdam, J. (Third Lanark), 1880 v W (1)
McAllister, B. (Wimbledon), 1997 v W, Ma, Bl (sub) (3)
McAllister, G. (Leicester C), 1990 v EG, Pol, Ma (sub); (with Leeds U), 1991 v R, Sw, Bul, USSR (sub), Sm; 1992 v Sw (sub), Sm, Ni, Fi (sub), US, Ca, N, Ho, G, C; 1993 v Sw, P, I, Ma; 1994 v Sw, I, Ma, Ho, A, Ho; 1995 v Fi, Ru, Gr, Ru, Sm; 1996 v Gr, Fi, Se, Sm, Aus, D, US (sub), Co, Ho, E, Sw; (with Coventry C), 1997 v A, La, Es (2), A, Se, W, Ma, Bl; 1998 v Bl, La, F; 1999 v CzR (57)
McAllister, J. R. (Livingston), 2004 v Tr (1)
McArthur, D. (Celtic), 1895 v E, Ni; 1899 v W (3)
McAtee, A. (Celtic), 1913 v W (1)
McAulay, J. (Arthurlie), 1884 v Ni (1)
McAulay, J. D. (Dumbarton), 1882 v W; 1883 v E, W; 1884 v E; 1885 v E, W; 1886 v E; 1887 v E, W (9)
McAuley, R. (Rangers), 1932 v Ni, W (2)
McAvennie, F. (West Ham U), 1986 v Aus (2), D (sub), WG (sub); (with Celtic), 1988 v S.Ar (5)
McBain, E. (St Mirren), 1894 v W (1)
McBain, N. (Manchester U), 1922 v E; (with Everton), 1923 v Ni; 1924 v W (3)
McBride, J. (Celtic), 1967 v W, Ni (2)
McBride, P. (Preston NE), 1904 v E; 1906 v E; 1907 v E, W; 1908 v E; 1909 v W (6)
McCall, A. (Renton), 1888 v Ni (1)
McCall, J. (Renton), 1886 v W; 1887 v E, W; 1888 v E; 1890 v E (5)
McCall, S. M. (Everton), 1990 v Arg, EG, Eg (sub), Pol, Ma, Cr, Se, Br; 1991 v Sw, USSR, Sm; (with Rangers), 1992 v Sw, R, Sm, US, Ca, N, Ho, G, C; 1993 v Sw, P (2); 1994 v I, Ho, A (sub), Ho; 1995 v Fi (sub), Ru, Gr; 1996 v Gr, D, US (sub), Co, Ho, E, Sw; 1997 v A, La; 1998 v D (sub) (40)
McCalliog, J. (Sheffield W), 1967 v E, USSR; 1968 v Ni; 1969 v D; (with Wolverhampton W), 1971 v P (5)
McCallum, N. (Renton), 1888 v Ni (1)
McCann, N. (Hearts), 1999 v Li (sub); (with Rangers), CzR; 2000 v Bos, Es (sub), E, F (sub), Ho, Ei; 2001 v La, Sm, Aus (sub); 2002 v Cro, La, F, Ng; 2003 v Ei; (with Southampton), 2004 v Fa, G, Ho (2), R, D (sub); 2005 v I (sub) (23)
McCann, R. J. (Motherwell), 1959 v WG; 1960 v E, Ni, W; 1961 v E (5)
McCartney, W. (Hibernian), 1902 v Ni (1)
McClair, B. (Celtic), 1987 v L, Ei, E, Br (sub); (with Manchester U), 1988 v Bul, Ma (sub), Sp (sub); 1989 v N, Y, I (sub), Cy, F (sub); 1990 v N (sub), Arg (sub); 1991 v Bul (2), Sm; 1992 v Sw (sub), R, Ni, US, Ca (sub), N, Ho, G, C; 1993 v Sw, P (sub), Es (2) (30)
McClory, A. (Motherwell), 1927 v W; 1928 v Ni; 1935 v W (3)
McCloy, P. (Ayr U), 1924 v E; 1925 v E (2)
McCloy, P. (Rangers), 1973 v W, Ni, Sw, Br (4)
McCoist, A. (Rangers), 1986 v Ho; 1987 v L (sub), Ei (sub), Bel, E, Br; 1988 v H, Bel, Ma, Sp, Co, E; 1989 v Y (sub), F, Cy, E; 1990 v Y, F, N, EG (sub), Eg, Pol, Ma (sub), Cr (sub), Se (sub), Br; 1991 v R, Sw, Bul (2), USSR; 1992 v Sw, Sm, Ni, Fi (sub), US, Ca, N, Ho, G, C; 1993 v Sw, P, I, Ma, P; 1996 v Gr (sub), Fi (sub), Sm (sub), Aus, D (sub), Co, E (sub), Sw; 1997 v A, Se (sub), Es (sub), A (sub); 1998 v Bl (sub); (with Kilmarnock), 1999 v Li, Es (61)
McColl, I. M. (Rangers), 1950 v E, F; 1951 v W, Ni, Bel; 1957 v E, Ni, W, Y, Sp, Sw, WG; 1958 v Ni, E (14)
McColl, R. S. (Queen's Park), 1896 v W, Ni; 1897 v Ni; 1898 v Ni; 1899 v Ni, E, W; 1900 v E, W; 1901 v E, W; (with Newcastle U), 1902 v E; (with Queen's Park), 1908 v Ni (13)
McColl, W. (Renton), 1895 v W (1)
McCombie, A. (Sunderland), 1903 v E, W; (with Newcastle U), 1905 v E, W (4)
McCorkindale, J. (Partick T), 1891 v W (1)
McCormick, R. (Abercorn), 1886 v W (1)
McCrae, D. (St Mirren), 1929 v N, G (2)
McCreadie, E. G. (Chelsea), 1965 v E, Sp, Fi, Pol; 1966 v P, Ni, W, Pol, I; 1967 v E, USSR; 1968 v Ni, W, E, Ho; 1969 v W, Ni, E, D, A, WG, Cy (2) (23)
McCredie, A. (Rangers), 1893 v W; 1894 v E (2)
McCulloch, D. (Hearts), 1935 v W; (with Brentford), 1936 v E; 1937 v W, Ni; 1938 v Cz; (with Derby Co), 1939 v H, W (7)
McCulloch, L. (Wigan Ath), 2005 v Mol (sub), I, Mol, Bl (4)
MacDonald, A. (Rangers), 1976 v Sw (1)
McDonald, J. (Edinburgh University), 1886 v E (1)
McDonald, J. (Sunderland), 1956 v W, Ni (2)
MacDougall, E. J. (Norwich C) 1975 v Se, P, W, Ni, E; 1976 v D, R (sub) (7)
McDougall, J. (Vale of Leven), 1877 v E, W; 1878 v E; 1879 v E, W (5)
McDougall, J. (Airdrieonians), 1926 v Ni (1)
McDougall, J. (Liverpool), 1931 v I, A (2)
McFadden, J. (Motherwell), 2002 v S.Af (sub); 2003 v Ca (sub), A, Nz; (with Everton), 2004 v Fa (sub), G, Li, Ho (2), W (sub), R (sub), D, Es, Tr; 2005 v H, Sp, Slo, N, Se, Mol (sub), Bl (sub) (21)
McFadyen, W. (Motherwell), 1934 v A, W (2)
Macfarlane, A. (Dundee), 1904 v W; 1906 v W; 1908 v W; 1909 v Ni; 1911 v W (5)
Macfarlane, W. (Hearts), 1947 v L (1)
McFarlane, R. (Greenock Morton), 1896 v W (1)
McGarr, E. (Aberdeen), 1970 v Ei, A (2)
McGarvey, F. P. (Liverpool), 1979 v Ni (sub), Arg; (with Celtic), 1984 v U, Bel (sub), EG (sub), Ni, W (7)
McGeoch, A. (Dumbreck), 1876 v E, W; 1877 v E, W (4)
McGhee, J. (Hibernian), 1886 v W (1)
McGhee, M. (Aberdeen), 1983 v Ca (1+1 sub); 1984 v Ni (sub), E (4)
McGinlay, J. (Bolton W), 1994 v A, Ho; 1995 v Fa, Ru, Gr, Ru, Sm, Fa; 1996 v Se; 1997 v Se, Es (1 + sub), A (sub) (13)
McGonagle, W. (Celtic), 1933 v E; 1934 v A, E, Ni; 1935 v Ni, W (6)
McGrain, D. (Celtic), 1973 v W, Ni, E, Sw, Br; 1974 v Cz (2), WG, W (sub), E, Bel, N, Z, Br, Y; 1975 v Sp, Se, P, W, Ni, E, R; 1976 v D (2), Sw, Ni, W, E; 1977 v Fi, Cz, W (2), Se, Ni, E, Ch, Arg, Br; 1978 v EG, Cz; 1980 v Bel, P, Ni, W, E, Pol, H; 1981 v Se, P, Is, Ni, Is, W (sub), Ni, E; 1982 v Se, Sp, Ho, Ni, E, Nz, USSR (sub) (62)
McGregor, J. C. (Vale of Leven), 1877 v E, W; 1878 v E; 1880 v E (4)
McGrory, J. (Celtic), 1928 v Ni; 1931 v E; 1932 v Ni, W; 1933 v E, Ni; 1934 v Ni (7)
McGrory, J. E. (Kilmarnock), 1965 v Ni, Fi; 1966 v P (3)
McGuire, W. (Beith), 1881 v E, W (2)
McGurk, F. (Birmingham), 1934 v W (1)
McHardy, H. (Rangers), 1885 v Ni (1)
McInally, A. (Aston Villa), 1989 v Cy (sub), Ch; (with Bayern Munich), 1990 v Y (sub), F (sub), Arg, Pol (sub), Ma, Cr (8)
McInally, J. (Dundee U), 1987 v Bel, Br; 1988 v Ma (sub); 1991 v Bul (2); 1992 v US (sub), N (sub), C (sub); 1993 v G, P (10)

McInally, T. B. (Celtic), 1926 v Ni; 1927 v W (2)
McInnes, D. (WBA), 2003 v D (sub), P (sub) (2)
McInnes, T. (Cowlairs), 1889 v Ni (1)
McIntosh, W. (Third Lanark), 1905 v Ni (1)
McIntyre, A. (Vale of Leven), 1878 v E; 1882 v E (2)
McIntyre, H. (Rangers), 1880 v W (1)
McIntyre, J. (Rangers), 1884 v W (1)
MacKay, D. (Celtic), 1959 v E, WG, Ho, P; 1960 v E, Pol, A, H, T; 1961 v W, Ni; 1962 v Ni, Cz, U (sub) (14)
Mackay, D. C. (Hearts), 1957 v Sp; 1958 v F; 1959 v W, Ni; (with Tottenham H), 1959 v WG, E; 1960 v W, Ni, A, Pol, H, T; 1961 v W, Ni, E; 1963 v E, A, N; 1964 v Ni, W, N; 1966 v Ni (22)
Mackay, G. (Hearts), 1988 v Bul (sub), L (sub), S.Ar (sub), Ma (4)
Mackay, M. (Norwich C), 2004 v D, Es, Tr; 2005 v Sp, Slo (5)
McKay, J. (Blackburn R), 1924 v W (1)
McKay, R. (Newcastle U), 1928 v W (1)
McKean, R. (Rangers), 1976 v Sw (sub) (1)
McKenzie, D. (Brentford), 1938 v Ni (1)
Mackenzie, J. A. (Partick T), 1954 v W, E, N, Fi, A, U; 1955 v E, H; 1956 v A (9)
McKeown, M. (Celtic), 1889 v Ni; 1890 v E (2)
McKie, J. (East Stirling), 1898 v W (1)
McKillop, T. R. (Rangers), 1938 v Ho (1)
McKimmie, S. (Aberdeen), 1989 v E, Ch; 1990 v Arg, Eg, Cr (sub), Br; 1991 v R, Sw, Bul, Sm; 1992 v Sw, R, Ni, Fi, US, Ca (sub), N (sub), Ho, G, C; 1993 v P, Es (sub); 1994 v Sw, I, Ho, A, Ho; 1995 v Fi, Fa, Ru, Gr, Ru, Fa; 1996 v Gr, Fi, Se, D, Co, Ho, E (40)
McKinlay, D. (Liverpool), 1922 v W, Ni (2)
McKinlay, T. (Celtic), 1996 v Gr, Fi, D, Co, E, Sw; 1997 v A, La, Se, Es (sub + 1), A, Se, W, Ma, Bl; 1998 v Bl, La (sub), F (sub), US, Br (sub), Mor (sub) (22)
McKinlay, W. (Dundee U), 1994 v Ma, Ho (sub), A, Ho; 1995 v Fa (sub), Ru, Gr, Ru (sub), Sm (sub), J, Ec, Fa; 1996 v Fi (sub), Se (sub); (with Blackburn R), Sm (sub), Aus, D (sub), Ho (sub); 1997 v Se, Es (sub); 1998 v La (sub), F, D, Fi, Co (sub), US, Br (sub); 1999 v Es, Fa (29)
McKinnon, A. (Queen's Park), 1874 v E (1)
McKinnon, R. (Rangers), 1966 v W, E, I (2), Ho, Br; 1967 v W, Ni, E; 1968 v Ni, W, E, Ho; 1969 v D, A, WG, Cy; 1970 v Ni, W, E, Ei, WG, A; 1971 v D, Bel, P, USSR, D (28)
McKinnon, R. (Motherwell), 1994 v Ma; 1995 v J, Fa (3)
MacKinnon, W. (Dumbarton), 1883 v E, W; 1884 v E, W (4)
MacKinnon, W. W. (Queen's Park), 1872 v E; 1873 v E; 1874 v E; 1875 v E; 1876 v E, W; 1877 v E; 1878 v E; 1879 v E (9)
McLaren, A. (St Johnstone), 1929 v N, G, Ho; 1933 v W, Ni (5)
McLaren, A. (Preston NE), 1947 v E, Bel, L; 1948 v W (4)
McLaren, A. (Hearts), 1992 v US, Ca, N; 1993 v I, Ma, G, Es (sub + 1); 1994 v I, Ma, Ho, A; 1995 v Fi, Fa; (with Rangers), Ru, Gr, Ru, Sm, J, Ec, Fa; 1996 v Fi, Se, Sm (24)
McLaren, A. (Kilmarnock), 2001 v Pol (sub) (1)
McLaren, J. (Hibernian), 1888 v W; (with Celtic), 1889 v E; 1890 v E (3)
McLean, A. (Celtic), 1926 v W, Ni; 1927 v W, E (4)
McLean, D. (St Bernards), 1896 v W; 1897 v Ni (2)
McLean, D. (Sheffield W), 1912 v E (1)
McLean, G. (Dundee), 1968 v Ho (1)
McLean, T. (Kilmarnock), 1969 v D, Cy, W; 1970 v Ni, W; 1971 v D (6)
McLeish, A. (Aberdeen), 1980 v P, Ni, W, E, Pol, H; 1981 v Se, Is, Ni, Is, Ni, E; 1982 v Se, Sp, Ni, Br (sub); 1983 v Bel, Sw (sub), W, E, Ca (3); 1984 v U, Bel, EG, Ni, W, E, F; 1985 v Y, Ic, Sp (2), W, E, Ic; 1986 v W, EG, Aus (2), E, Ho, D; 1987 v Bel, E, Br; 1988 v Bel, Bul, L, S.Ar (sub), Ma, Sp, Co, E; 1989 v N, Y, I, Cy, F, Cy, E, Ch; 1990 v Y, F, N, Arg, EG, Eg, Cr, Se, Br; 1991 v R, Sw, USSR, Bul; 1993 v Ma (77)
McLeod, D. (Celtic), 1905 v Ni; 1906 v E, W, Ni (4)
McLeod, J. (Dumbarton), 1888 v Ni; 1889 v W; 1890 v Ni; 1892 v E; 1893 v W (5)
MacLeod, J. M. (Hibernian), 1961 v E, Ei (2), Cz (4)
MacLeod, M. (Celtic), 1985 v E (sub); 1987 v Ei, L, E, Br; (with Borussia Dortmund), 1988 v Co, E; 1989 v I, Ch; 1990 v Y, F, N (sub), Arg, EG, Pol, Se Br; (with Hibernian), 1991 v R, Sw, USSR (sub) (20)
McLeod, W. (Cowlairs), 1886 v Ni (1)
McLintock, A. (Vale of Leven), 1875 v E; 1876 v E; 1880 v E (3)
McLintock, F. (Leicester C), 1963 v N (sub), Ei, Sp; (with Arsenal), 1965 v Ni; 1967 v USSR; 1970 v Ni; 1971 v W, Ni, E (9)
McLuckie, J. S. (Manchester C), 1934 v W (1)
McMahon, A. (Celtic), 1892 v E; 1893 v E, Ni; 1894 v E; 1901 v Ni; 1902 v W (6)
McMenemy, J. (Celtic), 1905 v Ni; 1909 v Ni; 1910 v E, W; 1911 v Ni, W, E; 1912 v W; 1914 v W, Ni, E; 1920 v Ni (12)
McMenemy, J. (Motherwell), 1934 v W (1)
McMillan, I. L. (Airdrieonians), 1952 v E, USA, D; 1955 v E; 1956 v E; (with Rangers), 1961 v Cz (6)
McMillan, J. (St Bernards), 1897 v W (1)
McMillan, T. (Dumbarton), 1887 v Ni (1)
McMullan, J. (Partick T), 1920 v W; 1921 v W, Ni, E; 1924 v E, Ni; 1925 v E; 1926 v W; (with Manchester C), 1926 v E; 1927 v E, W; 1928 v E, W; 1929 v W, E, Ni (16)
McNab, A. (Morton), 1921 v E, Ni (2)
McNab, A. (Sunderland), 1937 v A; (with WBA), 1939 v E (2)
McNab, C. D. (Dundee), 1931 v E, W, A, I, Sw; 1932 v E (6)
McNab, J. S. (Liverpool), 1923 v W (1)
McNair, A. (Celtic), 1906 v W; 1907 v Ni; 1908 v E, W; 1909 v E; 1910 v W; 1912 v E, W, Ni; 1913 v E; 1914 v E, Ni; 1920 v E, W, Ni (15)
McNamara, J. (Celtic), 1997 v La (sub), Se, Es, W (sub); 1998 v D, Co, US (sub), N (sub), Mor; 2000 v Ho; 2001 v Sm; 2002 v Bel (sub), F (sub); 2003 v Ic (1+sub), Li, Nz, G (sub); 2004 v Fa, G, Li, Ho (2), W, Tr; 2005 v Sp, Slo, Se, I, Mol (30)
McNamee, D. (Livingston), 2004 v Es, Tr (sub) (2)
McNaught, W. (Raith R), 1951 v A, W, Ni; 1952 v E; 1955 v Ni (5)
McNaughton, K. (Aberdeen), 2002 v Ng; 2003 v D; 2005 v Se (3)
McNeill, W. (Celtic), 1961 v E, Ei (2), Cz; 1962 v Ni, E, Cz, U; 1963 v Ei, Sp; 1964 v W, E, WG; 1965 v E, Fi, Pol, Sp; 1966 v Ni, Pol; 1967 v USSR; 1968 v E; 1969 v Cy, W, E, Cy (sub); 1970 v WG; 1972 v Ni, W, E (29)
McNiel, H. (Queen's Park), 1874 v E; 1875 v E; 1876 v E, W; 1877 v W; 1878 v E; 1879 v E, W; 1881 v E, W (10)
McNiel, M. (Rangers), 1876 v W; 1880 v E (2)
McPhail, J. (Celtic), 1950 v W; 1951 v W, Ni, A; 1954 v Ni (5)
McPhail, R. (Airdrieonians), 1927 v E; (with Rangers), 1929 v W; 1931 v E, Ni; 1932 v W, Ni, F; 1933 v E, Ni; 1934 v A, Ni; 1935 v E; 1937 v G, E, Cz; 1938 v W, Ni (17)
McPherson, D. (Kilmarnock), 1892 v Ni (1)
McPherson, D. (Hearts), 1989 v Cy, E; 1990 v N, Ma, Cr, Se, Br; 1991 v Sw, Bul (2), USSR (sub), Sm; 1992 v Sw, R, Sm, Ni, Fi, US, Ca, N, Ho, G, C; (with Rangers), 1993 v Sw, I, Ma, P (27)
McPherson, J. (Clydesdale), 1875 v E (1)
McPherson, J. (Vale of Leven), 1879 v E, W; 1880 v E; 1881 v W; 1883 v E, W; 1884 v E; 1885 v Ni (8)
McPherson, J. (Kilmarnock), 1888 v W; (with Cowlairs), 1889 v E; 1890 v Ni, E; (with Rangers), 1892 v W; 1894 v E; 1895 v E, Ni; 1897 v Ni (9)
McPherson, J. (Hearts), 1891 v E (1)
McPherson, R. (Arthurlie), 1882 v E (1)
McQueen, G. (Leeds U), 1974 v Bel; 1975 v Sp (2), P, W, Ni, E, R; 1976 v D; 1977 v Cz, W (2), Ni, E; 1978 v EG, Cz, W; (with Manchester U), Bul, Ni, W; 1979 v A, N, P, Ni, E, N; 1980 v Pe, A, Bel; 1981 v W (30)
McQueen, M. (Leith Ath), 1890 v W; 1891 v W (2)
McRorie, D. M. (Morton), 1931 v W (1)
McSpadyen, A. (Partick T), 1939 v E, H (2)
McStay, P. (Celtic), 1984 v U, Bel, EG, Ni, W, E (sub); 1985 v Y, Ic, Sp (2), W; 1986 v EG (sub), Aus, Is, U; 1987 v Bul, Ei (1+1 sub), L (sub), Bel, E, Br; 1988 v H, Bel, Bul, L, S.Ar, Sp, Co, E; 1989 v N, Y, I, Cy, F, Cy, E, Ch; 1990 v Y, F, N, Arg, EG (sub), Eg, Pol (sub), Ma, Cr, Se (sub), Br; 1991 v R, USSR, Bul; 1992 v Sm, Fi, US, Ca, N, Ho, G, C; 1993 v Sw, P, I, Ma, P, Es (2); 1994 v I (sub), Ho; 1995 v Fi, Fa, Ru; 1996 v Aus; 1997 v Es (2), A (sub) (76)
McStay, W. (Celtic), 1921 v W, Ni; 1925 v E, Ni, W; 1926 v E, Ni, W; 1927 v E, Ni, W; 1928 v W, Ni (13)
McSwegan, G. (Hearts), 2000 v Bos (sub), Li (2)
McTavish, J. (Falkirk), 1910 v Ni (1)
McWattie, G. C. (Queen's Park), 1901 v W, Ni (2)
McWilliam, P. (Newcastle U), 1905 v E; 1906 v E; 1907 v E, W; 1909 v E, W; 1910 v E; 1911 v W (8)
Macari, L. (Celtic), 1972 v W (sub), E, Y, Cz, Br; 1973 v D; (with Manchester U), E (2), W (sub), Ni (sub); 1975 v Se, P (sub), W, E (sub), R; 1977 v Ni (sub), E (sub), Ch, Arg; 1978 v EG, W, Bul, Pe (sub), Ir (24)
Macauley, A. R. (Brentford), 1947 v E; (with Arsenal), 1948 v E, W, Ni, Bel, Sw, F (7)
Madden, J. (Celtic), 1893 v W; 1895 v W (2)
Main, F. R. (Rangers), 1938 v W (1)
Main, J. (Hibernian), 1909 v Ni (1)
Maley, W. (Celtic), 1893 v E, Ni (2)

Malpas, M. (Dundee U), 1984 v F; 1985 v E, Ic; 1986 v W, Aus (2), Is, R, E, Ho, D, WG; 1987 v Bul, Ei, Bel; 1988 v Bel, Bul, L, S.Ar, Ma; 1989 v N, Y, I, Cy, F, Cy, E, Ch; 1990 v Y, F, N, Eg, Pol, Ma, Cr, Se, Br; 1991 v R, Bul (2), USSR, Sm; 1992 v Sw, R, Sm, Ni, Fi, US, Ca (sub), N, Ho, G; 1993 v Sw, P, I (55)
Marshall, D. J. (Celtic), 2005 v H, Se (2)
Marshall, G. (Celtic), 1992 v US (1)
Marshall, H. (Celtic), 1899 v W; 1900 v Ni (2)
Marshall, J. (Third Lanark), 1885 v Ni; 1886 v W; 1887 v E, W (4)
Marshall, J. (Middlesbrough), 1921 v E, W, Ni; 1922 v E, W, Ni; (with Llanelly), 1924 v W (7)
Marshall, J. (Rangers), 1932 v E; 1933 v E; 1934 v E (3)
Marshall, R. W. (Rangers), 1892 v Ni; 1894 v Ni (2)
Martin, B. (Motherwell), 1995 v J, Ec (2)
Martin, F. (Aberdeen), 1954 v N (2), A, U; 1955 v E, H (6)
Martin, N. (Hibernian), 1965 v Fi, Pol; (with Sunderland), 1966 v I (3)
Martis, J. (Motherwell), 1961 v W (1)
Mason, J. (Third Lanark), 1949 v E, W, Ni; 1950 v Ni; 1951 v Ni, Bel, A (7)
Massie, A. (Hearts), 1932 v Ni, W, F; 1933 v Ni; 1934 v E, Ni; 1935 v E, Ni, W; 1936 v W, Ni; (with Aston Villa), 1936 v E; 1937 v G, E, W, Ni, A; 1938 v W (18)
Masson, D. S. (QPR), 1976 v Ni, W, E; 1977 v Fi, Cz, W, Ni, E, Ch, Arg, Br; 1978 v EG, Cz, W; (with Derby Co), Ni, E, Pe (17)
Mathers, D. (Partick T), 1954 v Fi (1)
Matteo, D. (Leeds U), 2001 v Aus, Bel, Sm; 2002 v Cro, Bel, F (6)
Maxwell, W. S. (Stoke C), 1898 v E (1)
May, J. (Rangers), 1906 v W, Ni; 1908 v E, Ni; 1909 v W (5)
Meechan, P. (Celtic), 1896 v Ni (1)
Meiklejohn, D. D. (Rangers), 1922 v W; 1924 v W; 1925 v W, Ni, E; 1928 v W, Ni; 1929 v E, Ni; 1930 v E, Ni; 1931 v E; 1932 v W, Ni; 1934 v A (15)
Menzies, A. (Hearts), 1906 v E (1)
Mercer, R. (Hearts), 1912 v W; 1913 v Ni (2)
Middleton, R. (Cowdenbeath), 1930 v Ni (1)
Millar, A. (Hearts), 1939 v W (1)
Millar, J. (Rangers), 1897 v E; 1898 v E, W (3)
Millar, J. (Rangers), 1963 v A, Ei (2)
Miller, C. (Dundee U), 2001 v Pol (1)
Miller, J. (St Mirren), 1931 v E, I, Sw; 1932 v F; 1934 v E (5)
Miller, K. (Rangers), 2001 v Pol (sub); (with Wolverhampton W), 2003 v Ic, Li, A (sub), G; 2004 v Li, Ho (sub + sub), W, R, Es, Tr (sub); 2005 v H, Sp (sub), N (sub), Mol (sub), Se, I, Mol, Bl (20)
Miller, P. (Dumbarton), 1882 v E; 1883 v E, W (3)
Miller, T. (Liverpool), 1920 v E; (with Manchester U), 1921 v E, Ni (3)
Miller, W. (Third Lanark), 1876 v E (1)
Miller, W. (Celtic), 1947 v E, W, Bel, L; 1948 v W, Ni (6)
Miller, W. (Aberdeen), 1975 v R; 1978 v Bul; 1980 v Bel, W, E, Pol, H; 1981 v Se, P, Is (sub), Ni, W, Ni, E; 1982 v Ni, P, Ho, Br, USSR; 1983 v EG, Sw (2), W, E, Ca (3); 1984 v U, Bel, EG, W, E, F; 1985 v Y, Ic, Sp (2), W, E, Ic; 1986 v W, EG, Aus (2), Is, R, E, Ho, D, WG, U; 1987 v Bul, E, Br; 1988 v H, L, S.Ar, Ma, Sp, Co, E; 1989 v N, Y; 1990 v Y, N (65)
Mills, W. (Aberdeen), 1936 v W, Ni; 1937 v W (3)
Milne, J. V. (Middlesbrough), 1938 v E; 1939 v E (2)
Mitchell, D. (Rangers), 1890 v Ni; 1892 v E; 1893 v E, Ni; 1894 v E (5)
Mitchell, J. (Kilmarnock), 1908 v Ni; 1910 v Ni, W (3)
Mitchell, R. C. (Newcastle U), 1951 v D, F (2)
Mochan, N. (Celtic), 1954 v N, A, U (3)
Moir, W. (Bolton W), 1950 v E (1)
Moncur, R. (Newcastle U), 1968 v Ho; 1970 v Ni, W, E, Ei; 1971 v D, Bel, W, P, Ni, E, D; 1972 v Pe, Ni, W, E (16)
Morgan, H. (St Mirren), 1898 v W; (with Liverpool), 1899 v E (2)
Morgan, W. (Burnley), 1968 v Ni; (with Manchester U), 1972 v Pe, Y, Cz, Br; 1973 v D (2), E (2), W, Ni, Sw, Br; 1974 v Cz (2), WG (2), Ni, Bel (sub), Br, Y (21)
Morris, D. (Raith R), 1923 v Ni; 1924 v E, Ni; 1925 v E, W, Ni (6)
Morris, H. (East Fife), 1950 v Ni (1)
Morrison, T. (St Mirren), 1927 v E (1)
Morton, A. L. (Queen's Park), 1920 v W, Ni; (with Rangers), 1921 v E; 1922 v E, W; 1923 v E, W, Ni; 1924 v E, W, Ni; 1925 v E, W, Ni; 1927 v E, Ni; 1928 v E, W, Ni; 1929 v E, W, Ni; 1930 v E, W, Ni; 1931 v E, W, Ni; 1932 v E, W, F (31)
Morton, H. A. (Kilmarnock), 1929 v G, Ho (2)
Mudie, J. K. (Blackpool), 1957 v W, Ni, E, Y, Sw, Sp (2), WG; 1958 v Ni, E, W, Sw, H, Pol, Y, Par, F (17)
Muir, W. (Dundee), 1907 v Ni (1)
Muirhead, T. A. (Rangers), 1922 v Ni; 1923 v E; 1924 v W; 1927 v Ni; 1928 v Ni; 1929 v W, Ni; 1930 v W (8)
Mulhall, G. (Aberdeen), 1960 v Ni; (with Sunderland), 1963 v Ni; 1964 v Ni (3)
Munro, A. D. (Hearts), 1937 v W, Ni; (with Blackpool), 1938 v Ho (3)
Munro, F. M. (Wolverhampton W), 1971 v Ni (sub), E (sub), D, USSR; 1975 v Se, W (sub), Ni, E, R (9)
Munro, I. (St Mirren), 1979 v Arg, N; 1980 v Pe, A, Bel, W, E (7)
Munro, N. (Abercorn), 1888 v W; 1889 v E (2)
Murdoch, J. (Motherwell), 1931 v Ni (1)
Murdoch, R. (Celtic), 1966 v W, E, I (2); 1967 v Ni; 1968 v Ni; 1969 v W, Ni, E, WG, Cy; 1970 v A (12)
Murphy, F. (Celtic), 1938 v Ho (1)
Murray, I. (Hibernian), 2003 v Ca (sub); 2005 v Mol (sub), Se (3)
Murray, J. (Renton), 1895 v W (1)
Murray, J. (Hearts), 1958 v E, H, Pol, Y, F (5)
Murray, J. W. (Vale of Leven), 1890 v W (1)
Murray, P. (Hibernian), 1896 v Ni; 1897 v W (2)
Murray, S. (Aberdeen), 1972 v Bel (1)
Murty, G. S. (Reading), 2004 v W (sub) (1)
Mutch, G. (Preston NE), 1938 v E (1)

Napier, C. E. (Celtic), 1932 v E; 1935 v E, W; (with Derby Co), 1937 v Ni, A (5)
Narey, D. (Dundee U), 1977 v Se (sub); 1979 v P, Ni (sub), Arg; 1980 v P, Ni, Pol, H; 1981 v W, E (sub); 1982 v Ho, W, E, Nz (sub), Br, USSR; 1983 v EG, Sw, Bel, Ni, W, E, Ca (3); 1986 v Is, R, Ho, WG, U; 1987 v Bul, E, Bel; 1989 v I, Cy (35)
Naysmith, G. A. (Hearts), 2000 v Ei; 2001 v La (sub), Sm, Cro; (with Everton), 2002 v Cro, Bel; 2003 v D, Ic, P, Ei, Ic, Li, A, Nz, G; 2004 v N, Fa, G, Li, Ho (2), W; 2005 v H, Sp, Slo, N, Mol, I (28)
Neil, R. G. (Hibernian), 1896 v W; (with Rangers), 1900 v W (2)
Neill, R. W. (Queen's Park), 1876 v W; 1877 v E, W; 1878 v W; 1880 v E (5)
Nellies, P. (Hearts), 1913 v Ni; 1914 v W (2)
Nelson, J. (Cardiff C), 1925 v W, Ni; 1928 v E; 1930 v F (4)
Nevin, P. K. F. (Chelsea), 1986 v R (sub), E (sub); 1987 v L, Ei, Bel (sub); 1988 v L; (with Everton), 1989 v Cy, E; 1991 v R (sub), Bul (sub), Sm (sub); 1992 v US, G (sub), C (sub); (with Tranmere R), 1993 v Ma, P (sub), Es; 1994 v Sw, Ma, Ho, A (sub), Ho; 1995 v Fa, Ru (sub), Sm; 1996 v Se (sub), Sm, Aus (sub) (28)
Niblo, T. D. (Aston Villa), 1904 v E (1)
Nibloe, J. (Kilmarnock), 1929 v E, N, Ho; 1930 v W; 1931 v E, Ni, A, I, Sw; 1932 v E, F (11)
Nicholas, C. (Celtic), 1983 v Sw, Ni, E, Ca (3); (with Arsenal), 1984 v Bel, F (sub); 1985 v Y (sub), Ic (sub), Sp (sub), W (sub); 1986 v Is, R (sub), E, D, U (sub); 1987 v Bul, E (sub); (with Aberdeen), 1989 v Cy (sub) (20)
Nicholson, B. (Dunfermline Ath), 2001 v Pol; 2002 v La; 2005 v Se (3)
Nicol, S. (Liverpool), 1985 v Y, Ic, Sp, W; 1986 v W, EG, Aus, E, D, WG, U; 1988 v H, Bul, S.Ar, Sp, Co, E; 1989 v N, Y, Cy, F; 1990 v Y, F; 1991 v Sw, USSR, Sm; 1992 v Sw (27)
Nisbet, J. (Ayr U), 1929 v N, G, Ho (3)
Niven, J. B. (Moffat), 1885 v Ni (1)

O'Connor, G. (Hibernian), 2002 v Ng (sub), Sk, Hk (sub); 2005 v I (sub) (4)
O'Donnell, F. (Preston NE), 1937 v E, A, Cz; 1938 v W; (with Blackpool), E, Ho (6)
O'Donnell, P. (Motherwell), 1994 v Sw (sub) (1)
Ogilvie, D. H. (Motherwell), 1934 v A (1)
O'Hare, J. (Derby Co), 1970 v W, Ni, E; 1971 v D, Bel, W, Ni; 1972 v P, Bel, Ho (sub), Pe, Ni, W (13)
O'Neil, B. (Celtic), 1996 v Aus; (with Wolfsburg), 1999 v G (sub); 2000 v Li, Ho (sub), Ei; (with Derby Co), 2001 v Aus (6)
O'Neil, J. (Hibernian), 2001 v Pol (1)
Ormond, W. E. (Hibernian), 1954 v E, N, Fi, A, U; 1959 v E (6)
O'Rourke, F. (Airdrieonians), 1907 v Ni (1)
Orr, J. (Kilmarnock), 1892 v W (1)
Orr, R. (Newcastle U), 1902 v E; 1904 v E (2)
Orr, T. (Morton), 1952 v Ni, W (2)
Orr, W. (Celtic), 1900 v Ni; 1903 v Ni; 1904 v W (3)
Orrock, R. (Falkirk), 1913 v W (1)
Oswald, J. (Third Lanark), 1889 v E; (with St Bernards), 1895 v E; (with Rangers), 1897 v W (3)

Parker, A. H. (Falkirk), 1955 v P, Y, A; 1956 v E, Ni, W, A; 1957 v Ni, W, Y; 1958 v Ni, W, E, Sw; (with Everton), Par (15)
Parlane, D. (Rangers), 1973 v W, Sw, Br; 1975 v Sp (sub), Se, P, W, Ni, E, R; 1976 v D (sub); 1977 v W (12)
Parlane, R. (Vale of Leven), 1878 v W; 1879 v E, W (3)
Paterson, G. D. (Celtic), 1939 v Ni (1)
Paterson, J. (Leicester C), 1920 v E (1)
Paterson, J. (Cowdenbeath), 1931 v A, I, Sw (3)
Paton, A. (Motherwell), 1952 v D, Se (2)
Paton, D. (St Bernards), 1896 v W (1)
Paton, M. (Dumbarton), 1883 v E; 1884 v W; 1885 v W, E; 1886 v E (5)
Paton, R. (Vale of Leven), 1879 v E, W (2)
Patrick, J. (St Mirren), 1897 v E, W (2)
Paul, H. McD. (Queen's Park), 1909 v E, W, Ni (3)
Paul, W. (Partick T), 1888 v W; 1889 v W; 1890 v W (3)
Paul, W. (Dykebar), 1891 v Ni (1)
Pearson, S. P. (Motherwell), 2004 v Ho (sub); (with Celtic), W; 2005 v H (sub), Sp (sub), N (sub), Se (6)
Pearson, T. (Newcastle U), 1947 v E, Bel (2)
Penman, A. (Dundee), 1966 v Ho (1)
Pettigrew, W. (Motherwell), 1976 v Sw, Ni, W; 1977 v W (sub), Se (5)
Phillips, J. (Queen's Park), 1877 v E, W; 1878 v W (3)
Plenderleith, J. B. (Manchester C), 1961 v Ni (1)
Porteous, W. (Hearts), 1903 v Ni (1)
Pressley, S. J. (Hearts), 2000 v F (sub), Ei (sub); 2003 v Ic, Ca, P, Ic, Li, A, Nz, G; 2004 v N, G, Li, Ho (2), R, D, Es, Tr; 2005 v H, I, Mol, Bl (23)
Pringle, C. (St Mirren), 1921 v W (1)
Provan, D. (Rangers), 1964 v Ni, N; 1966 v I (2), Ho (5)
Provan, D. (Celtic), 1980 v Bel (2 sub), P (sub), Ni (sub); 1981 v Is, W, E; 1982 v Se, P, Ni (10)
Pursell, P. (Queen's Park), 1914 v W (1)

Quashie, N. F. (Portsmouth), 2004 v Es, Tr; 2005 v H, Sp, Slo, Se; (with Southampton), I (7)
Quinn, J. (Celtic), 1905 v Ni; 1906 v Ni, W; 1908 v Ni, E; 1909 v E; 1910 v E, Ni, W; 1912 v E, W (11)
Quinn, P. (Motherwell), 1961 v E, Ei (2); 1962 v U (4)

Rae, G. (Dundee), 2001 v Pol; 2002 v La (sub); 2003 v G (sub); 2004 v N (sub), Fa (sub), G (sub), Li, Ho; (with Rangers), R (9)
Rae, J. (Third Lanark), 1889 v W; 1890 v Ni (2)
Raeside, J. S. (Third Lanark), 1906 v W (1)
Raisbeck, A. G. (Liverpool), 1900 v E; 1901 v E; 1902 v E; 1903 v E, W; 1904 v E; 1906 v E; 1907 v E (8)
Rankin, G. (Vale of Leven), 1890 v Ni; 1891 v E (2)
Rankin, R. (St Mirren), 1929 v N, G, Ho (3)
Redpath, W. (Motherwell), 1949 v W, Ni; 1951 v E, D, F, Bel, A; 1952 v Ni, E (9)
Reid, J. G. (Airdrieonians), 1914 v W; 1920 v W; 1924 v Ni (3)
Reid, R. (Brentford), 1938 v E, Ni (2)
Reid, W. (Rangers), 1911 v E, W, Ni; 1912 v Ni; 1913 v E, W, Ni; 1914 v E, Ni (9)
Reilly, L. (Hibernian), 1949 v E, W, F; 1950 v W, Ni, Sw, F; 1951 v W, E, D, F, Bel, A; 1952 v Ni, W, E, USA, D, Se; 1953 v Ni, W, E, Se; 1954 v W; 1955 v H (2), P, Y, A, E; 1956 v E, W, Ni, A; 1957 v E, Ni, W, Y (38)
Rennie, H. G. (Hearts), 1900 v E, Ni; (with Hibernian), 1901 v E; 1902 v E, Ni, W; 1903 v Ni, W; 1904 v Ni; 1905 v W; 1906 v Ni; 1908 v Ni, W (13)
Renny-Tailyour, H. W. (Royal Engineers), 1873 v E (1)
Rhind, A. (Queen's Park), 1872 v E (1)
Richmond, A. (Queen's Park), 1906 v W (1)
Richmond, J. T. (Clydesdale), 1877 v E; (with Queen's Park), 1878 v E; 1882 v W (3)
Ring, T. (Clyde), 1953 v Se; 1955 v W, Ni, E, H; 1957 v E, Sp (2), Sw, WG; 1958 v Ni, Sw (12)
Rioch, B. D. (Derby Co), 1975 v P, W, Ni, E, R; 1976 v D (2), R, Ni, W, E; 1977 v Fi, Cz, W; (with Everton), W, Ni, E, Ch, Br; 1978 v Cz; (with Derby Co), Ni, E, Pe, Ho (24)
Ritchie, A. (East Stirlingshire), 1891 v W (1)
Ritchie, H. (Hibernian), 1923 v W; 1928 v Ni (2)
Ritchie, J. (Queen's Park), 1897 v W (1)
Ritchie, P. S. (Hearts), 1999 v G (sub), CzR; 2000 v Li, E; (with Bolton W), F, Ho; (with Walsall), 2004 v W (7)
Ritchie, W. (Rangers), 1962 v U (sub) (1)
Robb, D. T. (Aberdeen), 1971 v W, E, P, D (sub), USSR (5)
Robb, W. (Rangers), 1926 v W; (with Hibernian), 1928 v W (2)
Robertson, A. (Clyde), 1955 v P, A, H; 1958 v Sw, Par (5)
Robertson, D. (Rangers), 1992 v Ni; 1994 v Sw, Ho (3)
Robertson, G. (Motherwell), 1910 v W; (with Sheffield W), 1912 v W; 1913 v E, Ni (4)
Robertson, G. (Kilmarnock), 1938 v Cz (1)
Robertson, H. (Dundee), 1962 v Cz (1)
Robertson, J. (Dundee), 1931 v A, I (2)
Robertson, J. (Hearts), 1991 v R, Sw, Bul (sub), Sm (sub); 1992 v Sm, Ni (sub), Fi; 1993 v I (sub), Ma (sub), G, Es; 1995 v J (sub), Ec, Fa (sub); 1996 v Gr (sub), Se (16)
Robertson, J. N. (Nottingham F), 1978 v Ni, W (sub), Ir; 1979 v P, N; 1980 v Pe, A, Bel (2), P; 1981 v Se, P, Is, Ni, Is, Ni, E; 1982 v Se, Ni (2), E (sub), Nz, Br, USSR; 1983 v EG, Sw; (with Derby Co), 1984 v U, Bel (28)
Robertson, J. G. (Tottenham H), 1965 v W (1)
Robertson, J. T. (Everton), 1898 v E; (with Southampton), 1899 v E; (with Rangers), 1900 v E, W; 1901 v W, Ni, E; 1902 v W, Ni, E; 1903 v E, W; 1904 v E, W, Ni; 1905 v W (16)
Robertson, P. (Dundee), 1903 v Ni (1)
Robertson, T. (Queen's Park), 1889 v Ni; 1890 v E; 1891 v W; 1892 v Ni (4)
Robertson, T. (Hearts), 1898 v Ni (1)
Robertson, W. (Dumbarton), 1887 v E, W (2)
Robinson, R. (Dundee), 1974 v WG (sub); 1975 v Se, Ni, R (sub) (4)
Ross, M. (Rangers), 2002 v Sk, S.Af, Hk; 2003 v D, Fa, Ic, Ca, P, Nz, G; 2004 v N, G (sub), Ho (sub) (13)
Rough, A. (Partick T), 1976 v Sw, Ni, W, E; 1977 v Fi, Cz, W (2), Se, Ni, E, Ch, Arg, Br; 1978 v Cz, W, Ni, E, Pe, Ir, Ho; 1979 v A, P, W, Arg, N; 1980 v Pe, A, Bel (2), P, W, E, Pol, H; 1981 v Se, P, Is, Ni, Is, W, E; 1982 v Se, Ni, Sp, Ho, W, E, Nz, Br, USSR; (with Hibernian), 1986 v W (sub), E (53)
Rougvie, D. (Aberdeen), 1984 v Ni (1)
Rowan, A. (Caledonian), 1880 v E; (with Queen's Park), 1882 v W (2)
Russell, D. (Hearts), 1895 v E, Ni; (with Celtic), 1897 v W; 1898 v Ni; 1901 v W, Ni (6)
Russell, J. (Cambuslang), 1890 v Ni (1)
Russell, W. F. (Airdrieonians), 1924 v W; 1925 v E (2)
Rutherford, E. (Rangers), 1948 v F (1)

St John, I. (Motherwell), 1959 v WG; 1960 v E, Ni, W, Pol, A; 1961 v E; (with Liverpool), 1962 v Ni, W, E, Cz (2), U; 1963 v W, Ni, E, N, Ei (sub), Sp; 1964 v Ni; 1965 v E (21)
Sawers, W. (Dundee), 1895 v W (1)
Scarff, P. (Celtic), 1931 v Ni (1)
Schaedler, E. (Hibernian), 1974 v WG (1)
Scott, A. S. (Rangers), 1957 v Ni, Y, WG; 1958 v W, Sw; 1959 v P; 1962 v Ni, W, E, Cz, U; (with Everton), 1964 v W, N; 1965 v Fi; 1966 v P, Br (16)
Scott, J. (Hibernian), 1966 v Ho (1)
Scott, J. (Dundee), 1971 v D (sub), USSR (2)
Scott, M. (Airdrieonians), 1898 v W (1)
Scott, R. (Airdrieonians), 1894 v Ni (1)
Scoular, J. (Portsmouth), 1951 v D, F, A; 1952 v E, USA, D, Se; 1953 v W, Ni (9)
Sellar, W. (Battlefield), 1885 v E; 1886 v E; 1887 v E, W; 1888 v E; (with Queen's Park), 1891 v E; 1892 v E; 1893 v E, Ni (9)
Semple, W. (Cambuslang), 1886 v W (1)
Severin, S. D. (Hearts), 2002 v La (sub), Sk (sub), S.Af (sub), Hk; 2003 v D (sub), Ic (sub), Ca (sub), P (sub); (with Aberdeen), 2005 v H (sub), Se (sub) (10)
Shankly, W. (Preston NE), 1938 v E; 1939 v E, W, Ni, H (5)
Sharp, G. M. (Everton), 1985 v Ic; 1986 v W, Aus (2 sub), Is, R, U; 1987 v Ei; 1988 v Bel (sub), Bul, L, Ma (12)
Sharp, J. (Dundee), 1904 v W; (with Woolwich Arsenal), 1907 v W, E; 1908 v E; (with Fulham), 1909 v W (5)
Shaw, D. (Hibernian), 1947 v W, Ni; 1948 v E, Bel, Sw, F; 1949 v W, Ni (8)
Shaw, F. W. (Pollokshields Ath), 1884 v E, W (2)
Shaw, J. (Rangers), 1947 v E, Bel, L; 1948 v Ni (4)
Shearer, D. (Aberdeen), 1994 v A (sub), Ho (sub); 1995 v Fi, Ru (sub), Sm, Fa; 1996 v Gr (7)
Shearer, R. (Rangers), 1961 v E, Ei (2), Cz (4)
Sillars, D. C. (Queen's Park), 1891 v Ni; 1892 v E; 1893 v W; 1894 v E; 1895 v W (5)
Simpson, J. (Third Lanark), 1895 v E, W, Ni (3)
Simpson, J. (Rangers), 1935 v E, W, Ni; 1936 v E, W, Ni; 1937 v G, E, W, Ni, A, Cz; 1938 v W, Ni (14)
Simpson, N. (Aberdeen), 1983 v Ni; 1984 v U (sub), F (sub); 1987 v E; 1988 v E (5)
Simpson, R. C. (Celtic), 1967 v E, USSR; 1968 v Ni, E; 1969 v A (5)
Sinclair, G. L. (Hearts), 1910 v Ni; 1912 v W, Ni (3)
Sinclair, J. W. E. (Leicester C), 1966 v P (1)
Skene, L. H. (Queen's Park), 1904 v W (1)

Sloan, T. (Third Lanark), 1904 v W (1)
Smellie, R. (Queen's Park), 1887 v Ni; 1888 v W; 1889 v E; 1891 v E; 1893 v E, Ni (6)
Smith, A. (Rangers), 1898 v E; 1900 v E, Ni, W; 1901 v E, Ni, W; 1902 v E, Ni, W; 1903 v E, Ni, W; 1904 v Ni; 1905 v W; 1906 v E, Ni; 1907 v W; 1911 v E, Ni (20)
Smith, D. (Aberdeen), 1966 v Ho; (with Rangers), 1968 v Ho (2)
Smith, G. (Hibernian), 1947 v E, Ni; 1948 v W, Bel, Sw, F; 1952 v E, USA; 1955 v P, Y, A, H; 1956 v E, Ni, W; 1957 v Sp (2), Sw (18)
Smith, H. G. (Hearts), 1988 v S.Ar (sub); 1992 v Ni, Ca (3)
Smith, J. (Ayr U), 1924 v E (1)
Smith, J. (Rangers), 1935 v Ni; 1938 v Ni (2)
Smith, J. (Aberdeen), 1968 v Ho (sub); (with Newcastle U), 1974 v WG, Ni (sub), W (sub) (4)
Smith, J. (Celtic), 2003 v Ei (sub), A (sub) (2)
Smith, J. E. (Celtic), 1959 v H, P (2)
Smith, Jas (Queen's Park), 1872 v E (1)
Smith, John (Mauchline), 1877 v E, W; 1879 v E, W; (with Edinburgh University), 1880 v E; (with Queen's Park), 1881 v W, E; 1883 v E, W; 1884 v E (10)
Smith, N. (Rangers), 1897 v E; 1898 v W; 1899 v E, W, Ni; 1900 v E, W, Ni; 1901 v Ni, W; 1902 v E, Ni (12)
Smith, R. (Queen's Park), 1872 v E; 1873 v E (2)
Smith, T. M. (Kilmarnock), 1934 v E; (with Preston NE), 1938 v E (2)
Somers, P. (Celtic), 1905 v E, Ni; 1907 v Ni; 1909 v W (4)
Somers, W. S. (Third Lanark), 1879 v E, W; (with Queen's Park), 1880 v W (3)
Somerville, G. (Queen's Park), 1886 v E (1)
Souness, G. J. (Middlesbrough), 1975 v EG, Sp, Se; (with Liverpool), 1978 v Bul, W, E (sub), Ho; 1979 v A, N, W, Ni, E; 1980 v Pe, A, Bel, P, Ni; 1981 v P, Is (2); 1982 v Ni, P, Sp, W, E, Nz, Br, USSR; 1983 v EG, Sw, Bel, Sw, W, E, Ca (2 + 1 sub); 1984 v U, Ni, W; (with Sampdoria), 1985 v Y, Ic, Sp (2), W, E, Ic; 1986 v EG, Aus (2), R, E, D, WG (54)
Speedie, D. R. (Chelsea), 1985 v E; 1986 v W, EG (sub), Aus, E; (with Coventry C), 1989 v Y (sub), I (sub), Cy (1+1 sub), Ch (10)
Speedie, F. (Rangers), 1903 v E, W, Ni (3)
Speirs, J. H. (Rangers), 1908 v W (1)
Spencer, J. (Chelsea), 1995 v Ru (sub), Gr (sub), Sm (sub), J; 1996 v Fi, Aus, D, US (sub), Co, Ho (sub), E, Sw (sub); 1997 v La; (with QPR), W (sub) (14)
Stanton, P. (Hibernian), 1966 v Ho; 1969 v Ni; 1970 v Ei, A; 1971 v D, Bel, P, USSR, D; 1972 v P, Bel, Ho, W; 1973 v W, Ni; 1974 v WG (16)
Stark, J. (Rangers), 1909 v E, Ni (2)
Steel, W. (Morton), 1947 v E, Bel, L; (with Derby Co), 1948 v F, E, W, Ni; 1949 v E, W, Ni, F; 1950 v E, W, Ni, Sw, P, F; (with Dundee), 1951 v W, Ni, E, A (2), D, F, Bel; 1952 v W; 1953 v W, E, Ni, Se (30)
Steele, D. M. (Huddersfield), 1923 v E, W, Ni (3)
Stein, C. (Rangers), 1969 v W, Ni, D, E, Cy (2); 1970 v A (sub), Ni (sub), W, E, Ei, WG; 1971 v D, USSR, Bel, D; 1972 v Cz (sub); (with Coventry C), 1973 v E (2 sub), W (sub), Ni (21)
Stephen, J. F. (Bradford), 1947 v W; 1948 v W (2)
Stevenson, G. (Motherwell), 1928 v W, Ni; 1930 v Ni, E, F; 1931 v E, W; 1932 v W, Ni; 1933 v Ni; 1934 v E; 1935 v Ni (12)
Stewart, A. (Queen's Park), 1888 v Ni; 1889 v W (2)
Stewart, A. (Third Lanark), 1894 v W (1)
Stewart, D. (Dumbarton), 1888 v Ni (1)
Stewart, D. (Queen's Park), 1893 v W; 1894 v Ni; 1897 v Ni (3)
Stewart, D. S. (Leeds U), 1978 v EG (1)
Stewart, G. (Hibernian), 1906 v W, E; (with Manchester C), 1907 v E, W (4)
Stewart, J. (Kilmarnock), 1977 v Ch (sub); (with Middlesbrough), 1979 v N (2)
Stewart, M. J. (Manchester U), 2002 v Ng (sub), Sk, S.Af (sub) (3)
Stewart, R. (West Ham U), 1981 v W, Ni, E; 1982 v Ni, P, W; 1984 v F; 1987 v Ei (2), L (10)
Stewart, W. G. (Queen's Park), 1898 v Ni; 1900 v Ni (2)
Stockdale, R. K. (Middlesbrough), 2002 v Ng, Sk (sub), S.Af, Hk; 2003 v D (5)
Storrier, D. (Celtic), 1899 v E, W, Ni (3)
Strachan, G. (Aberdeen), 1980 v Ni, W, E, Pol, H (sub); 1981 v Se, P; 1982 v Ni, P, Sp, Ho (sub), Nz, Br, USSR; 1983 v EG, Sw, Bel, Sw, Ni (sub), W, E, Ca (2 + 1 sub); 1984 v EG, Ni, E, F; (with Manchester U), 1985 v Sp (sub), E, Ic; 1986 v W, Aus, R, D, WG, U; 1987 v Bul, Ei (2); 1988 v H; 1989 v F (sub); (with Leeds U), 1990 v F; 1991 v USSR, Bul, Sm; 1992 v Sw, R, Ni, Fi (50)
Sturrock, P. (Dundee U), 1981 v W (sub), Ni, E (sub); 1982 v P, Ni (sub), W (sub), E (sub); 1983 v EG (sub), Sw, Bel (sub), Ca (3); 1984 v W; 1985 v Y (sub); 1986 v Is (sub), Ho, D, U; 1987 v Bel (20)
Sullivan, N. (Wimbledon), 1997 v W; 1998 v F, Co; 1999 v Fa, CzR, G, Fa, CzR; 2000 v Bos, Es, Bos, E (2), F, Ho, Ei; (with Tottenham H), 2001 v La, Sm, Cro, Bel, Sm, Pol; 2002 v Cro, Bel, La, F, Sk; 2003 v Ei (28)
Summers, W. (St Mirren), 1926 v E (1)
Symon, J. S. (Rangers), 1939 v H (1)

Tait, T. S. (Sunderland), 1911 v W (1)
Taylor, J. (Queen's Park), 1872 v E; 1873 v E; 1874 v E; 1875 v E; 1876 v E, W (6)
Taylor, J. D. (Dumbarton), 1892 v W; 1893 v W; 1894 v Ni; (with St Mirren), 1895 v Ni (4)
Taylor, W. (Hearts), 1892 v E (1)
Telfer, P. N. (Coventry C), 2000 v F (1)
Telfer, W. (Motherwell), 1933 v Ni; 1934 v Ni (2)
Telfer, W. D. (St Mirren), 1954 v W (1)
Templeton, R. (Aston Villa), 1902 v E; (with Newcastle U), 1903 v E, W; 1904 v E; (with Woolwich Arsenal), 1905 v W; (with Kilmarnock), 1908 v Ni; 1910 v E, Ni; 1912 v E, Ni; 1913 v W (11)
Thompson, S. (Dundee U), 2002 v F (sub), Ng, Hk; 2003 v D, Fa (sub), Ic, Ca; (with Rangers), Ei (sub), A, G (sub); 2004 v Fa (sub), G, R; 2005 v H (sub), N (sub), Mol (16)
Thomson, A. (Arthurlie), 1886 v Ni (1)
Thomson, A. (Third Lanark), 1889 v W (1)
Thomson, A. (Airdrieonians), 1909 v Ni (1)
Thomson, A. (Celtic), 1926 v E; 1932 v F; 1933 v W (3)
Thomson, C. (Hearts), 1904 v Ni; 1905 v E, Ni, W; 1906 v W, Ni; 1907 v E, W, Ni; 1908 v E, W, Ni; (with Sunderland), 1909 v W; 1910 v E; 1911 v Ni; 1912 v E, W; 1913 v E, W; 1914 v E, Ni (21)
Thomson, C. (Sunderland), 1937 v Cz (1)
Thomson, D. (Dundee), 1920 v W (1)
Thomson, J. (Celtic), 1930 v F; 1931 v E, W, Ni (4)
Thomson, J. J. (Queen's Park), 1872 v E; 1873 v E; 1874 v E (3)
Thomson, J. R. (Everton), 1933 v W (1)
Thomson, R. (Celtic), 1932 v W (1)
Thomson, R. W. (Falkirk), 1927 v E (1)
Thomson, S. (Rangers), 1884 v W, Ni (2)
Thomson, W. (Dumbarton), 1892 v W; 1893 v W; 1898 v Ni, W (4)
Thomson, W. (Dundee), 1896 v W (1)
Thomson, W. (St Mirren), 1980 v Ni; 1981 v Ni (sub+1) 1982 v P; 1983 v Ni, Ca; 1984 v EG (7)
Thornton, W. (Rangers), 1947 v W, Ni; 1948 v E, Ni; 1949 v F; 1952 v D, Se (7)
Toner, W. (Kilmarnock), 1959 v W, Ni (2)
Townsley, T. (Falkirk), 1926 v W (1)
Troup, A. (Dundee), 1920 v E; 1921 v W, Ni; 1922 v Ni; (with Everton), 1926 v E (5)
Turnbull, E. (Hibernian), 1948 v Bel, Sw; 1951 v A; 1958 v H, Pol, Y, Par, F (8)
Turner, T. (Arthurlie), 1884 v W (1)
Turner, W. (Pollokshields Ath), 1885 v Ni; 1886 v Ni (2)

Ure, J. F. (Dundee), 1962 v W, Cz; 1963 v W, Ni, E, A, N, Sp; (with Arsenal), 1964 v Ni, N; 1968 v Ni (11)
Urquhart, D. (Hibernian), 1934 v W (1)

Vallance, T. (Rangers), 1877 v E, W; 1878 v E; 1879 v E, W; 1881 v E, W (7)
Venters, A. (Cowdenbeath), 1934 v Ni; (with Rangers), 1936 v E; 1939 v E (3)

Waddell, T. S. (Queen's Park), 1891 v Ni; 1892 v E; 1893 v E, Ni; 1895 v E, Ni (6)
Waddell, W. (Rangers), 1947 v W; 1949 v E, W, Ni, F; 1950 v E, Ni; 1951 v E, D, F, Bel, A; 1952 v Ni, W; 1954 v Ni; 1955 v W, Ni (17)
Wales, H. M. (Motherwell), 1933 v W (1)
Walker, A. (Celtic), 1988 v Co (sub); 1995 v Fi, Fa (sub) (3)
Walker, F. (Third Lanark), 1922 v W (1)
Walker, G. (St Mirren), 1930 v F; 1931 v Ni, A, Sw (4)
Walker, J. (Hearts), 1895 v Ni; 1897 v W; 1898 v Ni; (with Rangers), 1904 v W, Ni (5)
Walker, J. (Swindon T), 1911 v E, W, Ni; 1912 v E, W, Ni; 1913 v E, W, Ni (9)
Walker, J. N. (Hearts), 1993 v G; (with Partick T), 1996 v US (sub) (2)
Walker, R. (Hearts), 1900 v E, Ni; 1901 v E, W; 1902 v E, W, Ni; 1903 v E, W, Ni; 1904 v E, W, Ni; 1905 v E, W, Ni; 1906

v Ni; 1907 v E, Ni; 1908 v E, W, Ni; 1909 v E, W; 1912 v E, W, Ni; 1913 v E, W (29)
Walker, T. (Hearts), 1935 v E, W; 1936 v E, W, Ni; 1937 v G, E, W, Ni, A, Cz; 1938 v E, W, Ni, Cz, Ho; 1939 v E, W, Ni, H (20)
Walker, W. (Clyde), 1909 v Ni; 1910 v Ni (2)
Wallace, I. A. (Coventry C), 1978 v Bul (sub); 1979 v P (sub), W (3)
Wallace, W. S. B. (Hearts), 1965 v Ni; 1966 v E, Ho; (with Celtic), 1967 v E, USSR (sub); 1968 v Ni; 1969 v E (sub) (7)
Wardhaugh, J. (Hearts), 1955 v H; 1957 v Ni (2)
Wark, J. (Ipswich T), 1979 v W, Ni, E, Arg, N (sub); 1980 v Pe, A, Bel (2); 1981 v Is, Ni; 1982 v Se, Sp, Ho, Ni, Nz, Br, USSR; 1983 v EG, Sw (2), Ni, E (sub); 1984 v U, Bel, EG; (with Liverpool), E, F; 1985 v Y (29)
Watson, A. (Queen's Park), 1881 v E, W; 1882 v E (3)
Watson, J. (Sunderland), 1903 v E, W; 1904 v E; 1905 v E; (with Middlesbrough), 1909 v E, Ni (6)
Watson, J. (Motherwell), 1948 v Ni; (with Huddersfield T), 1954 v Ni (2)
Watson, J. A. K. (Rangers), 1878 v W (1)
Watson, P. R. (Blackpool), 1934 v A (1)
Watson, R. (Motherwell), 1971 v USSR (1)
Watson, W. (Falkirk), 1898 v W (1)
Watt, F. (Kilbirnie), 1889 v W, Ni; 1890 v W; 1891 v E (4)
Watt, W. W. (Queen's Park), 1887 v Ni (1)
Waugh, W. (Hearts), 1938 v Cz (1)
Webster, A. (Hearts), 2003 v A, Nz, G; 2004 v N, Fa, W (sub), Es (sub), Tr (sub); 2005 v H, Sp, Slo, N, Mol, Se, Mol, Bl (16)
Weir, A. (Motherwell), 1959 v WG; 1960 v E, P, A, H, T (6)
Weir, D. G. (Hearts), 1997 v W, Ma (sub); 1998 v F, D (sub), Fi (sub), N (sub), Mor; 1999 v Es, Fa; (with Everton), CzR, G, Fa, CzR; 2000 v Bos, Es, Bos, Li, E (2), Ho; 2001 v La, Sm (sub), Cro, Aus, Bel, Sm, Pol (sub); 2002 v Cro, Bel, La, F, Ng, Sk, S.Af, Hk; 2003 v D, Fa; 2005 v I, Mol, Bl (40)
Weir, J. (Third Lanark), 1887 v Ni (1)
Weir, J. B. (Queen's Park), 1872 v E; 1874 v E; 1875 v E; 1878 v W (4)
Weir, P. (St Mirren), 1980 v Ni, W, Pol (sub), H; (with Aberdeen), 1983 v Sw; 1984 v Ni (6)
White, John (Albion R), 1922 v W; (with Hearts), 1923 v Ni (2)
White, J. A. (Falkirk), 1959 v WG, Ho, P; 1960 v Ni; (with Tottenham H), 1960 v W, Pol, A, T; 1961 v W; 1962 v Ni, W, E, Cz (2); 1963 v W, Ni, E; 1964 v Ni, W, E, N, WG (22)
White, W. (Bolton W), 1907 v E; 1908 v E (2)
Whitelaw, A. (Vale of Leven), 1887 v Ni; 1890 v W (2)
Whyte, D. (Celtic), 1988 v Bel (sub), L; 1989 v Ch (sub); 1992 v US (sub); (with Middlesbrough), 1993 v P, I; 1995 v J (sub), Ec; 1996 v US; 1997 v La; (with Aberdeen), 1998 v Fi; 1999 v G (sub) (12)
Wilkie, L. (Dundee), 2002 v S.Af (sub), Hk; 2003 v Ic, Ca, P, Ic, Li, A; 2004 v Fa, Ho (2) (11)
Williams, G. (Nottingham F), 2002 v Ng, Sk (sub), S.Af, Hk (sub); 2003 v P (sub) (5)
Wilson, A. (Sheffield W), 1907 v E; 1908 v E; 1912 v E; 1913 v E, W; 1914 v Ni (6)
Wilson, A. (Portsmouth), 1954 v Fi (1)
Wilson, A. N. (Dunfermline), 1920 v E, W, Ni; 1921 v E, W, Ni; (with Middlesbrough), 1922 v E, W, Ni; 1923 v E, W, Ni (12)
Wilson, D. (Queen's Park), 1900 v W (1)
Wilson, D. (Oldham Ath), 1913 v E (1)
Wilson, D. (Rangers), 1961 v E, W, Ni, Ei (2), Cz; 1962 v Ni, W, E, Cz, U; 1963 v W, E, A, N, Ei, Sp; 1964 v E, WG; 1965 v Ni, E, Fi (22)
Wilson, G. W. (Hearts), 1904 v W; 1905 v E, Ni; 1906 v W; (with Everton), 1907 v E; (with Newcastle U), 1909 v E (6)
Wilson, Hugh, (Newmilns), 1890 v W; (with Sunderland), 1897 v E; (with Third Lanark), 1902 v W; 1904 v Ni (4)
Wilson, I. A. (Leicester C), 1987 v E, Br; (with Everton), 1988 v Bel, Bul, L (5)
Wilson, J. (Vale of Leven), 1888 v W; 1889 v E; 1890 v E; 1891 v E (4)
Wilson, P. (Celtic), 1926 v Ni; 1930 v F; 1931 v Ni; 1933 v E (4)
Wilson, P. (Celtic), 1975 v Sp (sub) (1)
Wilson, R. P. (Arsenal), 1972 v P, Ho (2)
Winters, R. (Aberdeen), 1999 v G (sub) (1)
Wiseman, W. (Queen's Park), 1927 v W; 1930 v Ni (2)
Wood, G. (Everton), 1979 v Ni, E, Arg (sub); (with Arsenal), 1982 v Ni (4)
Woodburn, W. A. (Rangers), 1947 v E, Bel, L; 1948 v W, Ni; 1949 v E, F; 1950 v E, W, Ni, P, F; 1951 v E, W, Ni, A (2), D, F, Bel; 1952 v E, W, Ni, USA (24)
Wotherspoon, D. N. (Queen's Park), 1872 v E; 1873 v E (2)
Wright, K. (Hibernian), 1992 v Ni (1)
Wright, S. (Aberdeen), 1993 v G, Es (2)
Wright, T. (Sunderland), 1953 v W, Ni, E (3)
Wylie, T. G. (Rangers), 1890 v Ni (1)

Yeats, R. (Liverpool), 1965 v W; 1966 v I (2)
Yorston, B. C. (Aberdeen), 1931 v Ni (1)
Yorston, H. (Aberdeen), 1955 v W (1)
Young, A. (Everton), 1905 v E; 1907 v W (2)
Young, A. (Hearts), 1960 v E, A (sub), H, T; 1961 v W, Ni; (with Everton), Ei; 1966 v P (8)
Young, G. L. (Rangers), 1947 v E, Ni, Bel, L; 1948 v E, Ni, Bel, Sw, F; 1949 v E, W, Ni, F; 1950 v E, W, Ni, Sw, P, F; 1951 v E, W, Ni, A (2), D, F, Bel; 1952 v E, W, Ni, USA, D, Se; 1953 v W, E, Ni, Se; 1954 v Ni, W; 1955 v W, Ni, P, Y; 1956 v Ni, W, E, A; 1957 v E, Ni, W, Y, Sp, Sw (53)
Young, J. (Celtic), 1906 v Ni (1)
Younger, T. (Hibernian), 1955 v P, Y, A, H; 1956 v E, Ni, W, A; (with Liverpool), 1957 v E, Ni, W, Y, Sp (2), Sw, WG; 1958 v Ni, W, E, Sw, H, Pol, Y, Par (24)

WALES

Adams, H. (Berwyn R), 1882 v Ni, E; (with Druids), 1883 v Ni, E (4)
Aizlewood, M. (Charlton Ath), 1986 v S.Ar, Ca (2); 1987 v Fi; (with Leeds U), USSR, Fi (sub); 1988 v D (sub), Se, Ma, I; 1989 v Ho, Se (sub), WG; (with Bradford C), 1990 v Fi, WG, Ei, Cr; (with Bristol C), 1991 v D, Bel (2), L, Ei, Ic, Pol, WG; 1992 v Br, L, Ei, A, R, Ho, Arg, J; 1993 v Ei, Bel, Fa; 1994 v RCS, Cy; (with Cardiff C), 1995v Bul (39)
Allchurch, I. J. (Swansea T), 1951 v E, Ni, P, Sw; 1952 v E, S, Ni, R of UK; 1953 v S, E, Ni, F, Y; 1954 v S, E, Ni, A; 1955 v S, E, Ni, Y; 1956 v E, S, Ni, A; 1957 v E, S; 1958 v Ni, Is (2), H (2), M, Sw, Br; (with Newcastle U), 1959 v E, S, Ni; 1960 v E, S; 1961 v Ni, H, Sp (2); 1962 v E, S, Br (2), M; (with Cardiff C), 1963 v S, E, Ni, H (2); 1964 v E; 1965 v S, E, Ni, Gr, I, USSR; (with Swansea T), 1966 v USSR, E, S, D, Br (2), Ch (68)
Allchurch, L. (Swansea T), 1955 v Ni; 1956 v A; 1958 v S, Ni, EG, Is; 1959 v S; (with Sheffield U), 1962 v S, Ni, Br; 1964 v E (11)
Allen, B. W. (Coventry C), 1951 v S, E (2)
Allen, M. (Watford), 1986 v S.Ar (sub), Ca (1 + 1 sub); (with Norwich C), 1989 v Is (sub); 1990 v Ho, WG; (with Millwall), Ei, Se, Cr (sub); 1991 v L (sub), Ei (sub); 1992 v A; 1993 v Ei (sub); (with Newcastle U), 1994 v R (sub) (14)
Arridge, S. (Bootle), 1892 v S, Ni; (with Everton), 1894 v Ni; 1895 v Ni; 1896 v E; (with New Brighton Tower), 1898 v E, Ni; 1899 v E (8)
Astley, D. J. (Charlton Ath), 1931 v Ni; (with Aston Villa), 1932 v E; 1933 v E, S, Ni; 1934 v E, S; 1935 v S; 1936 v E, Ni; (with Derby Co), 1939 v E, S; (with Blackpool), F (13)
Atherton, R. W. (Hibernian), 1899 v E, Ni; 1903 v E, S, Ni; (with Middlesbrough), 1904 v E, S, Ni; 1905 v Ni (9)

Bailiff, W. E. (Llanelly), 1913 v E, S, Ni; 1920 v Ni (4)
Baker, C. W. (Cardiff C), 1958 v M; 1960 v S, Ni; 1961 v S, E, Ei; 1962 v S (7)
Baker, W. G. (Cardiff C), 1948 v Ni (1)
Bamford, T. (Wrexham), 1931 v E, S, Ni; 1932 v Ni; 1933 v F (5)
Barnard, D. S. (Barnsley), 1998 v Jam; 1999 v I, D, Bl, I, D; 2000 v Bl, Sw, Q, Fi, Br (sub), P; 2001 v Uk, Pol, Uk; 2002 v Arm (sub); (with Grimsby T), 2003 v Cro, Az; 2004 v Ser, Ru (2), N (sub) (22)
Barnes, W. (Arsenal), 1948 v E, S, Ni; 1949 v E, S, Ni; 1950 v E, S, Ni, Bel; 1951 v E, S, Ni, P; 1952 v E, S, Ni, R of UK; 1954 v E, S; 1955 v S, Y (22)
Bartley, T. (Glossop NE), 1898 v E (1)
Bastock, A. M. (Shrewsbury), 1892 v Ni (1)
Beadles, G. H. (Cardiff C), 1925 v E, S (2)
Bell, W. S. (Shrewsbury Engineers), 1881 v E, S; (with Crewe Alex), 1886 v E, S, Ni (5)
Bellamy, C. D. (Norwich C), 1998 v Jam (sub), Ma, Tun; 1999 v D (sub), Sw (sub), I, D (sub); 2000 v Br (sub), P; (with Coventry C), 2001 v Bl, Arm, Uk; (with Newcastle U), 2002

v Arm, N, Bl, Arg; 2003 v Fi (sub), I, Bos, Az; 2004 v Ser, I, Ser, N, Ca; 2005 v La, Az, Ni, E, Pol, H, A (2) (33)
Bennion, S. R. (Manchester U), 1926 v S; 1927 v S; 1928 v S, E, Ni; 1929 v S, E, Ni; 1930 v S; 1932 v Ni (10)
Berry, G. F. (Wolverhampton W), 1979 v WG; 1980 v Ei, WG (sub), T; (with Stoke C), 1983 v E (sub) (5)
Blackmore, C. G. (Manchester U), 1985 v N (sub); 1986 v S (sub), H (sub), S.Ar, Ei, U; 1987 v Fi (2), USSR, Cz; 1988 v D (2), Cz, Y, Se, Ma, I; 1989 v Ho, Fi, Is, WG; 1990 v F; Ho, WG, Cr; 1991 v Bel, L; 1992 v Ei (sub), A, R (sub), Ho, Arg, J; 1993 v Fa, Cy, Bel, RCS; 1994 v Se (sub); (with Middlesbrough), 1997 v Bel (39)
Blake, N. A. (Sheffield U), 1994 v N, Se (sub); 1995 v Alb, Mol; 1996 v G (with Bolton W), I (sub); 1998 v T; 1999 v I, D, Bl; (with Blackburn R) Sw; 2000 v Bl, Sw, Q, Fi; 2001 v Bl (sub), N, Pol (2), Uk; 2002 v N (sub); (with Wolverhampton W), CzR; 2003 v I (sub); 2004 v Ser, I (sub), Fi (sub), Ser (sub), Ru (sub + sub) (29)
Blew, H. (Wrexham), 1899 v E, S, Ni; 1902 v S, Ni; 1903 v E, S; 1904 v E, S, Ni; 1905 v S, Ni; 1906 v E, S, Ni; 1907 v S; 1908 v E, S, Ni; 1909 v E, S; 1910 v E (22)
Boden, T. (Wrexham), 1880 v E (1)
Bodin, P. J. (Swindon T), 1990 v Cr; 1991 v D, Bel, L, Ei; (with C Palace), Bel, Ic, Pol, WG; 1992 v Br, G, L (sub); (with Swindon T), Ei (sub), Ho, Arg; 1993 v Ei, Bel, RCS, Fa; 1994 v R, Se, Es (sub); 1995 v Alb (23)
Boulter, L. M. (Brentford), 1939 v Ni (1)
Bowdler, H. E. (Shrewsbury), 1893 v S (1)
Bowdler, J. C. H. (Shrewsbury), 1890 v Ni; (with Wolverhampton W), 1891 v S; 1892 v Ni; (with Shrewsbury), 1894 v E (4)
Bowen, D. L. (Arsenal), 1955 v S, Y; 1957 v Ni, Cz, EG; 1958 v E, S, Ni, EG, Is (2), H (2), M, Se, Br; 1959 v E, S, Ni (19)
Bowen, E. (Druids), 1880 v S; 1883 v S (2)
Bowen, J. P. (Swansea C), 1994 v Es; (with Birmingham C), 1997 v Ho (2)
Bowen, M. R. (Tottenham H), 1986 v Ca (2 sub); (with Norwich C), 1988 v Y (sub); 1989 v Fi (sub), Is, Se, WG (sub); 1990 v Fi (sub), Ho, WG, Se; 1992 v Br (sub), G, L, Ei, A, R, Ho (sub), J; 1993 v Fa, Cy, Bel (1 + sub), RCS (sub); 1994 v RCS, Se; 1995 v Mol, Ge, Bul (2), G, Ge; 1996 v Mol, G, Alb, Sw, Sm; (with West Ham U), 1997 v Sm, Ho (2), Ei (sub) (41)
Bowsher, S. J. (Burnley), 1929 v Ni (1)
Boyle, T. (C Palace), 1981 v Ei, S (sub) (2)
Britten, T. J. (Parkgrove), 1878 v S; (with Presteigne), 1880 v S (2)
Brookes, S. J. (Llandudno), 1900 v E, Ni (2)
Brown, A. I. (Aberdare Ath), 1926 v Ni (1)
Browning, M. T. (Bristol R), 1996 v I (sub), Sm; 1997 v Sm, Ho (with Huddersfield T), S (sub) (5)
Bryan, T. (Oswestry), 1886 v E, Ni (2)
Buckland, T. (Bangor), 1899 v E (1)
Burgess, W. A. R. (Tottenham H), 1947 v E, S, Ni; 1948 v E, S; 1949 v E, S, Ni, P, Bel, Sw; 1950 v E, S, Ni, Bel; 1951 v S, Ni, P, Sw; 1952 v E, S, Ni, R of UK; 1953 v S, E, Ni, F, Y; 1954 v S, E, Ni, A (32)
Burke, T. (Wrexham), 1883 v E; 1884 v S; 1885 v E, S, Ni; (with Newton Heath), 1887 v E, S; 1888 v S (8)
Burnett, T. B. (Ruabon), 1877 v S (1)
Burton, A. D. (Norwich C), 1963 v Ni, H; (with Newcastle U), 1964 v E; 1969 v S, E, Ni, I, EG; 1972 v Cz (9)
Butler, J. (Chirk), 1893 v E, S, Ni (3)
Butler, W. T. (Druids), 1900 v S, Ni (2)

Cartwright, L. (Coventry C), 1974 v E (sub), S, Ni; 1976 v S (sub); 1977 v WG (sub); (with Wrexham), 1978 v Ir (sub); 1979 v Ma (7)
Carty, T. See McCarthy (Wrexham).
Challen, J. B. (Corinthians), 1887 v E, S; 1888 v E; (with Wellingborough GS), 1890 v E (4)
Chapman, T. (Newtown), 1894 v E, S, Ni; 1895 v S, Ni; (with Manchester C), 1896 v E; (with Grimsby T), 1897 v E (7)
Charles, J. M. (Swansea C), 1981 v Cz, T (sub), S (sub), USSR (sub); 1982 v Ic; 1983 v N (sub), Y (sub), Bul (sub), S, Ni, Br; 1984 v Bul (sub); (with QPR), Y (sub), S; (with Oxford U), 1985 v Ic (sub), Sp, Ic; 1986 v Ei; 1987 v Fi (19)
Charles, M. (Swansea T), 1955 v Ni; 1956 v E, S, A; 1957 v E, Ni, Cz (2), EG; 1958 v E, S, EG, Is (2), H (2), M, Se, Br; 1959 v E, S; (with Arsenal), 1961 v Ni, H, Sp (2); 1962 v E, S; (with Cardiff C), 1962 v Br, Ni; 1963 v S, H (31)
Charles, W. J. (Leeds U), 1950 v Ni; 1951 v Sw; 1953 v Ni, F, Y; 1954 v E, S, Ni, A; 1955 v S, E, Ni, Y; 1956 v E, S, A, Ni; 1957 v E, S, Ni, Cz (2), EG; (with Juventus), 1958 v Is (2), H (2) M, Se; 1960 v S; 1962 v E, Br (2), M; (with Leeds U), 1963 v S; (with Cardiff C), 1964 v S; 1965 v S, USSR (38)
Clarke, R. J. (Manchester C), 1949 v E; 1950 v S, Ni, Bel; 1951 v E, S, Ni, P, Sw; 1952 v S, E, Ni, R of UK; 1953 v S, E; 1954 v E, S, Ni; 1955 v Y, S, E; 1956 v Ni (22)
Coleman, C. (C Palace), 1992 v A (sub); 1993 v Ei (sub); 1994 v N, Es; 1995 v Alb, Mol, Ge, Bul (2), G; 1996 v Mol; (with Blackburn R), I, Sw, Sm; 1997 v Sm; 1998 v Br; (with Fulham), Jam, Ma, Tun; 1999 v I, D, Bl, Sw, D; 2000 v Bl, Sw, Q, Fi; 2001 v Bl, N, Pol; 2002 v G (sub) (32)
Collier, D. J. (Grimsby T), 1921 v S (1)
Collins, D. L. (Sunderland), 2005 v H (sub) (1)
Collins, J. M. (Cardiff C), 2004 v N, Ca; 2005 v La (sub), Ni, Pol, A (6)
Collins, W. S. (Llanelly), 1931 v S (1)
Conde, C. (Chirk), 1884 v E, S, Ni (3)
Cook, F. C. (Newport Co), 1925 v E, S; (with Portsmouth), 1928 v E, S; 1930 v E, S, Ni; 1932 v E (8)
Cornforth, J. M. (Swansea C), 1995 v Bul (sub), Ge (2)
Coyne, D. (Tranmere R), 1996 v Sw; (with Grimsby T), 2002 v CzR (sub); (with Leicester C), 2004 v H (sub), N, Ca; 2005 v H, A (2) (8)
Crompton, W. (Wrexham), 1931 v E, S, Ni (3)
Cross, E. A. (Wrexham), 1876 v S; 1877 v S (2)
Crosse, K. (Druids), 1879 v S; 1881 v E, S (3)
Crossley, M. G. (Nottingham F), 1997 v Ei; 1999 v Sw (sub); 2000 v Fi; (with Middlesbrough), 2002 v Arg (sub), G; 2003 v Bos (sub); (with Fulham), 2004 v S; 2005 v La (sub) (8)
Crowe, V. H. (Aston Villa), 1959 v E, Ni; 1960 v E, Ni; 1961 v S, E, Ni, Ei, H, Sp (2); 1962 v E, S, Br, M; 1963 v H (16)
Cumner, R. H. (Arsenal), 1939 v E, S, Ni (3)
Curtis, A. (Swansea C), 1976 v E, Y (sub), S, Ni, Y (sub), E; 1977 v WG, S (sub), Ni (sub); 1978 v WG, E, S; 1979 v WG, S; (with Leeds U), E, Ni, Ma; 1980 v Ei, WG, T; (with Swansea C), 1982 v Cz, Ic, USSR, Sp, E, S, Ni; 1983 v N; 1984 v R (sub); (with Southampton), S; 1985 v Sp, N (1 + 1 sub); 1986 v H; (with Cardiff C), 1987 v USSR (35)
Curtis, E. R. (Cardiff C), 1928 v S; (with Birmingham), 1932 v S; 1934 v Ni (3)

Daniel, R. W. (Arsenal), 1951 v E, Ni, P; 1952 v E, S, Ni, R of UK; 1953 v S, E, Ni, F, Y; (with Sunderland), 1954 v E, S, Ni; 1955 v E, Ni; 1957 v S, E, Ni, Cz (21)
Darvell, S. (Oxford University), 1897 v S, Ni (2)
Davies, A. (Manchester U), 1983 v Ni, Br; 1984 v E, Ni; 1985 v Ic (2), N; (with Newcastle U), 1986 v H; (with Swansea C), 1988 v Ma, I; 1989 v Ho; (with Bradford C), 1990 v Fi, Ei (13)
Davies, A. (Wrexham), 1876 v S; 1877 v S (2)
Davies, A. (Druids), 1904 v S; (with Middlesbrough), 1905 v S (2)
Davies, A. O. (Barmouth), 1885 v Ni; 1886 v E, S; (with Swifts), 1887 v E, S; 1888 v E, Ni; (with Wrexham), 1889 v S; (with Crewe Alex), 1890 v E (9)
Davies, A. T. (Shrewsbury), 1891 v Ni (1)
Davies, C. (Charlton Ath), 1972 v R (sub) (1)
Davies, D. (Bolton W), 1904 v S, Ni; 1908 v E (sub) (3)
Davies, D. C. (Brecon), 1899 v Ni; (with Hereford); 1900 v Ni (2)
Davies, D. W. (Treharris), 1912 v Ni; (with Oldham Ath), 1913 v Ni (2)
Davies, E. Lloyd (Stoke C), 1904 v E; 1907 v E, S, Ni; (with Northampton T), 1908 v S; 1909 v Ni; 1910 v Ni; 1911 v E, S; 1912 v E, S; 1913 v E, S; 1914 v Ni, E, S (16)
Davies, E. R. (Newcastle U), 1953 v S, E; 1954 v E, S; 1958 v E, EG (6)
Davies, G. (Fulham), 1980 v T, Ic; 1982 v Sp (sub), F (sub); 1983 v E, Bul, S, Ni, Br; 1984 v R (sub), S (sub), E, Ni; 1985 v Ic; (with Manchester C), 1986 v S.Ar, Ei (16)
Davies, Rev. H. (Wrexham), 1928 v Ni (1)
Davies, Idwal (Liverpool Marine), 1923 v S (1)
Davies, J. E. (Oswestry), 1885 v E (1)
Davies, Jas (Wrexham), 1878 v S (1)
Davies, John (Wrexham), 1879 v S (1)
Davies, Jos (Newton Heath), 1888 v E, S, Ni; 1889 v S; 1890 v E; (with Wolverhampton W), 1892 v E; 1893 v E (7)
Davies, Jos (Everton), 1889 v S, Ni; (with Chirk), 1891 v Ni; (with Ardwick), v E, S; (with Sheffield U), 1895 v E, S, Ni; (with Manchester C), 1896 v E; (with Millwall), 1897 v E; (with Reading), 1900 v E (11)
Davies, J. P. (Druids), 1883 v E, Ni (2)
Davies, Ll. (Wrexham), 1907 v Ni; 1910 v Ni, S, E; (with Everton), 1911 v S, Ni; (with Wrexham), 1912 v Ni, S, E; 1913 v Ni, S, E; 1914 v Ni (13)
Davies, L. S. (Cardiff C), 1922 v E, S, Ni; 1923 v E, S, Ni; 1924 v E, S, Ni; 1925 v S, Ni; 1926 v E, Ni; 1927 v E, Ni; 1928 v S, Ni, E; 1929 v S, Ni, E; 1930 v E, S (23)
Davies, O. (Wrexham), 1890 v S (1)
Davies, R. (Wrexham), 1883 v Ni; 1884 v Ni; 1885 v Ni (3)

Davies, R. (Druids), 1885 v E (1)
Davies, R. O. (Wrexham), 1892 v Ni, E (2)
Davies, R. T. (Norwich C), 1964 v Ni; 1965 v E; 1966 v Br (2), Ch; (with Southampton), 1967 v S, E, Ni; 1968 v S, Ni, WG; 1969 v S, E, Ni, I, WG, R of UK; 1970 v E, S, Ni; 1971 v Cz, S, E, Ni; 1972 v R, E, S, N; (with Portsmouth), 1974 v E (29)
Davies, R. W. (Bolton W), 1964 v E; 1965 v E, S, Ni, D, Gr, USSR; 1966 v E, S, Ni, USSR, D, Br (2), Ch (sub); 1967 v S; (with Newcastle U), E; 1968 v S, Ni, WG; 1969 v S, E, Ni, I; 1970 v EG; 1971 v R, Cz; (with Manchester C), 1972 v E, S, Ni; (with Manchester U), 1973 v E, S (sub), Ni; (with Blackpool), 1974 v Pol (34)
Davies, S. (Tottenham H), 2001 v Uk (sub+1); 2002 v Arm, N, Bl, Arg, CzR, G; 2003 v Cro, Fi, I, Az, Bos, Az, US; 2004 v Ser, I, Fi, S; 2005 v E, Pol, H, A (2) (24)
Davies, S. I. (Manchester U), 1996 v Sw (sub) (1)
Davies, Stanley (Preston NE), 1920 v E, S, Ni; (with Everton), 1921 v E, S, Ni; (with WBA), 1922 v E, S, Ni; 1923 v S; 1925 v S, Ni; 1926 v S, E, Ni; 1927 v S; 1928 v S; (with Rotherham U), 1930 v Ni (18)
Davies, T. (Oswestry), 1886 v E (1)
Davies, T. (Druids), 1903 v E, Ni, S; 1904 v S (4)
Davies, W. (Wrexham), 1884 v Ni (1)
Davies, W. (Swansea T), 1924 v E, S, Ni; (with Cardiff C), 1925 v E, S, Ni; 1926 v E, S, Ni; 1927 v S; 1928 v Ni; (with Notts Co), 1929 v E, S, Ni; 1930 v E, S, Ni (17)
Davies, William (Wrexham), 1903 v Ni; 1905 v Ni; (with Blackburn R), 1908 v E, S; 1909 v E, S, Ni; 1911 v E, S, Ni; 1912 v Ni (11)
Davies, W. C. (C Palace), 1908 v S; (with WBA), 1909 v E; 1910 v S; (with C Palace), 1914 v E (4)
Davies, W. D. (Everton), 1975 v H, L, S, E, Ni; 1976 v Y (2), E, Ni; 1977 v WG, S (2), Cz, E, Ni; 1978 v K; (with Wrexham), S, Cz, WG, Ir, E, S, Ni; 1979 v Ma, T, WG, S, E, Ni, Ma; 1980 v Ei, WG, T, E, S, Ni, Ic; 1981 v T, Cz, Ei, T, S, E, USSR; (with Swansea C), 1982 v Cz, Ic, USSR, Sp, E, S, F; 1983 v Y (52)
Davies, W. H. (Oswestry), 1876 v S; 1877 v S; 1879 v E; 1880 v E (4)
Davis, G. (Wrexham), 1978 v Ir, E (sub), Ni (3)
Davis, W. O. (Millwall Ath), 1913 v E, S, Ni; 1914 v S, Ni (5)
Day, A. (Tottenham H), 1934 v Ni (1)
Deacy, N. (PSV Eindhoven), 1977 v Cz, S, E, Ni; 1978 v K (sub), S (sub), Cz (sub), WG, Ir, S (sub), Ni; (with Beringen), 1979 v T (12)
Dearson, D. J. (Birmingham), 1939 v S, Ni, F (3)
Delaney, M. A. (Aston Villa), 2000 v Sw, Q, Br, P; 2001 v N, Pol, Arm, Uk (2); 2002 v Arm, N, Bl, Arg, CzR, G; 2003 v Cro, Fi, I, Az; 2004 v Ser, I, Ser, Ru (2), N, Ca; 2005 v La, Az, Ni, E, Pol, A (2) (33)
Derrett, S. C. (Cardiff C), 1969 v S, WG; 1970 v I; 1971 v Fi (4)
Dewey, F. T. (Cardiff Corinthians), 1931 v E, S (2)
Dibble, A. (Luton T), 1986 v Ca (1+1 sub); (with Manchester C), 1989 v Is (3)
Doughty, J. (Druids), 1886 v S; (with Newton Heath), 1887 v S, Ni; 1888 v E, S, Ni; 1889 v S; 1890 v E (8)
Doughty, R. (Newton Heath), 1888 v S, Ni (2)
Durban, A. (Derby Co), 1966 v Br (sub); 1967 v Ni; 1968 v E, S, Ni, WG; 1969 v EG, S, E, Ni, WG; 1970 v E, S, Ni, EG, I; 1971 v R, S, E, Ni, Cz, Fi; 1972 v Fi, Cz, E, S, Ni (27)
Dwyer, P. (Cardiff C), 1978 v Ir, E, S, Ni; 1979 v T, S, E, Ni, Ma (sub); 1980 v WG (10)

Earnshaw, R. (Cardiff C), 2002 v G; 2003 v Cro, Az, Bos; 2004 v Ser (sub), I (sub), Fi, Ser, Ru (sub), S, H, N, Ca (sub); 2005 v Az (sub); (with WBA), Ni (sub), E (sub), Pol, H, A (sub) (19)
Edwards, C. (Wrexham), 1878 v S (1)
Edwards, C. N. H. (Swansea C), 1996 v Sw (sub) (1)
Edwards, G. (Birmingham C), 1947 v E, S, Ni; 1948 v E, S, Ni; (with Cardiff C), 1949 v Ni, P, Bel, Sw; 1950 v E, S (12)
Edwards, H. (Wrexham Civil Service), 1878 v S; (with Wrexham), 1880 v E, S; 1882 v E, S; 1883 v S; 1884 v Ni; 1887 v Ni (8)
Edwards, J. H. (Wanderers), 1876 v S (1)
Edwards, J. H. (Oswestry), 1895 v Ni; 1897 v E, Ni (3)
Edwards, J. H. (Aberystwyth), 1898 v Ni (1)
Edwards, L. T. (Charlton Ath), 1957 v Ni, EG (2)
Edwards, R. I. (Chester), 1978 v K (sub); 1979 v Ma, WG; (with Wrexham), 1980 v T (sub) (4)
Edwards, R. O. (Aston Villa), 2003 v Az (sub); 2004 v Ser (sub), S, H (sub), N (sub), Ca (sub); (with Wolverhampton W), 2005 v H (7)
Edwards, R. W. (Bristol C), 1998 v T (sub), Bel, Ma (sub), Tun (sub) (4)
Edwards, T. (Linfield), 1932 v S (1)

Egan, W. (Chirk), 1892 v S (1)
Ellis, B. (Motherwell), 1932 v E; 1933 v E, S; 1934 v S; 1936 v E; 1937 v S (6)
Ellis, E. (Nunhead), 1931 v S; (with Oswestry), E; 1932 v Ni (3)
Emanuel, W. J. (Bristol C), 1973 v E (sub), Ni (sub) (2)
England, H. M. (Blackburn R), 1962 v Ni, Br, M; 1963 v Ni, H; 1964 v E, S, Ni; 1965 v E, D, Gr (2), USSR, Ni, I; 1966 v E, S, Ni, USSR, D; (with Tottenham H), 1967 v S, E; 1968 v E, Ni, WG; 1969 v EG; 1970 v R of UK, EG, E, S, Ni, I; 1971 v R; 1972 v Fi, E, S, Ni; 1973 v E (3), S; 1974 v Pol; 1975 v H, L (44)
Evans, B. C. (Swansea C), 1972 v Fi, Cz; 1973 v E (2), Pol, S; (with Hereford U), 1974 v Pol (7)
Evans, D. G. (Reading), 1926 v Ni; 1927 v Ni, E; (with Huddersfield T), 1929 v S (4)
Evans, H. P. (Cardiff C), 1922 v E, S, Ni; 1924 v E, S, Ni (6)
Evans, I. (C Palace), 1976 v A, E, Y (2), E, Ni; 1977 v WG, S (2), Cz, E, Ni; 1978 v K (13)
Evans, J. (Oswestry), 1893 v Ni; 1894 v E, Ni (3)
Evans, J. (Cardiff C), 1912 v Ni; 1913 v Ni; 1914 v S; 1920 v S, Ni; 1922 v Ni; 1923 v E, Ni (8)
Evans, J. H. (Southend U), 1922 v E, S, Ni; 1923 v S (4)
Evans, Len (Aberdare Ath), 1927 v Ni; (with Cardiff C), 1931 v E, S; (with Birmingham), 1934 v Ni (4)
Evans, M. (Oswestry), 1884 v E (1)
Evans, P. S. (Brentford), 2002 v CzR (sub); (with Bradford C), Cro (sub) (2)
Evans, R. (Clapton), 1902 v Ni (1)
Evans, R. E. (Wrexham), 1906 v E, S; (with Aston Villa), Ni; 1907 v E; 1908 v E, S; (with Sheffield U), 1909 v S; 1910 v E, S, Ni (10)
Evans, R. O. (Wrexham), 1902 v Ni; 1903 v E, S, Ni; (with Blackburn R), 1908 v Ni; (with Coventry C), 1911 v E, Ni; 1912 v E, S, Ni (10)
Evans, R. S. (Swansea T), 1964 v Ni (1)
Evans, T. J. (Clapton Orient), 1927 v S; 1928 v E, S; (with Newcastle U), Ni (4)
Evans, W. (Tottenham H), 1933 v Ni; 1934 v E, S; 1935 v E; 1936 v E, Ni (6)
Evans, W. A. W. (Oxford University), 1876 v S; 1877 v S (2)
Evans, W. G. (Bootle), 1890 v E; (with Aston Villa), 1891 v E; 1892 v E (3)
Evelyn, E. C. (Crusaders), 1887 v E (1)
Eyton-Jones, J. A. (Wrexham), 1883 v Ni; 1884 v Ni, E, S (4)

Farmer, G. (Oswestry), 1885 v E, S (2)
Felgate, D. (Lincoln C), 1984 v R (sub) (1)
Finnigan, R. J. (Wrexham), 1930 v Ni (1)
Fletcher, C. N. (Bournemouth), 2004 v S (sub), H (sub), N, Ca; (with West Ham U), 2005 v H, A (2) (7)
Flynn, B. (Burnley), 1975 v L (2 sub), H (sub), S, E, Ni; 1976 v A, E, Y (2), E, Ni; 1977 v WG (sub), S (2), Cz, E, Ni; 1978 v K (2), S; (with Leeds U), Cz, WG, Ir (sub), E, S, Ni; 1979 v Ma, T, S, E, Ni, Ma; 1980 v Ei, WG, E, S, Ni, Ic; 1981 v T, Cz, Ei, T, S, E, USSR; 1982 v Cz, USSR, E, S, Ni, F; 1983 v N; (with Burnley), Y, E, Bul, S, Ni, Br; 1984 v N, R, Bul, Y, S, N, Is (66)
Ford, T. (Swansea T), 1947 v S; (with Aston Villa), 1947 v Ni; 1948 v S, Ni; 1949 v E, S, Ni, P, Bel, Sw; 1950 v E, S, Ni, Bel; 1951 v S; (with Sunderland), 1951 v E, Ni, P, Sw; 1952 v E, S, Ni, R of UK; 1953 v S, E, Ni, F, Y; (with Cardiff C), 1954 v A; 1955 v S, E, Ni, Y; 1956 v S, Ni, E, A; 1957 v S (38)
Foulkes, H. E. (WBA), 1932 v Ni (1)
Foulkes, W. I. (Newcastle U), 1952 v E, S, Ni, R of UK; 1953 v E, S, F, Y; 1954 v E, S, Ni (11)
Foulkes, W. T. (Oswestry), 1884 v Ni; 1885 v S (2)
Fowler, J. (Swansea T), 1925 v E; 1926 v E, Ni; 1927 v S; 1928 v S; 1929 v E (6)
Freestone, R. (Swansea C), 2000 v Br (1)

Gabbidon, D. L. (Cardiff C), 2002 v CzR; 2003 v Cro, Fi, I; 2004 v Ser (2), Ru (2), S, H, N, Ca; 2005 v Az, Ni, E, Pol, H, A (2) (19)
Garner, J. (Aberystwyth), 1896 v S (1)
Giggs, R. J. (Manchester U), 1992 v G (sub), L (sub), R (sub); 1993 v Fa (sub), Bel (sub + 1), RCS, Fa; 1994 v RCS, Cy, R; 1995 v Alb, Bul; 1996 v G, Alb, Sm; 1997 v Sm, T, Bel; 1998 v T, Bel; 1999 v I (2), D; 2000 v Bl, Fi; 2001 v Bl, N, Pol, Uk, Pol, Uk; 2002 v Arm, N, Arg, G; 2003 v Fi, I, Az (2); 2004 v Ser, I, Fi, Ser, Ru (2), S, Ca; 2005 v E, A (2) (51)
Giles, D. (Swansea C), 1980 v E, S, Ni, Ic; 1981 v T, Cz, T (sub), E (sub), USSR (sub); (with C Palace), 1982 v Sp (sub); 1983 v Ni (sub), Br (12)
Gillam, S. G. (Wrexham), 1889 v S (sub), Ni; (with Shrewsbury), 1890 v E, Ni; (with Clapton), 1894 v S (5)

Glascodine, G. (Wrexham), 1879 v E (1)
Glover, E. M. (Grimsby T), 1932 v S; 1934 v Ni; 1936 v S; 1937 v E, S, Ni; 1939 v Ni (7)
Godding, G. (Wrexham), 1923 v S, Ni (2)
Godfrey, B. C. (Preston NE), 1964 v Ni; 1965 v D, I (3)
Goodwin, U. (Ruthin), 1881 v E (1)
Goss, J. (Norwich C), 1991 v Ic, Pol (sub); 1992 v A; 1994 v Cy (sub), R (sub), Se; 1995 v Alb; 1996 v Sw (sub), Sm (sub) (9)
Gough, R. T. (Oswestry White Star), 1883 v S (1)
Gray, A. (Oldham Ath), 1924 v E, S, Ni; 1925 v E, S, Ni; 1926 v E, S; 1927 v S; (with Manchester C), 1928 v E, S; 1929 v E, S, Ni; (with Manchester Central), 1930 v S; (with Tranmere R), 1932 v E, S, Ni; (with Chester), 1937 v E, S, Ni; 1938 v E, S, Ni (24)
Green, A. W. (Aston Villa), 1901 v Ni; (with Notts Co), 1903 v E; 1904 v S, Ni; 1906 v Ni, E; (with Nottingham F), 1907 v E; 1908 v S (8)
Green, C. R. (Birmingham C), 1965 v USSR, I; 1966 v E, S, USSR, Br (2); 1967 v E; 1968 v E, S, Ni, WG; 1969 v S, I, Ni (sub) (15)
Green, G. H. (Charlton Ath), 1938 v Ni; 1939 v E, Ni, F (4)
Green, R. M. (Wolverhampton W), 1998 v Ma, Tun (2)
Grey, Dr W. (Druids), 1876 v S; 1878 v S (2)
Griffiths, A. T. (Wrexham), 1971 v Cz (sub); 1975 v A, H (2), L (2), E, Ni; 1976 v A, E, S, E (sub), Ni, Y (2); 1977 v WG, S (17)
Griffiths, F. J. (Blackpool), 1900 v E, S (2)
Griffiths, G. (Chirk), 1887 v Ni (1)
Griffiths, J. H. (Swansea T), 1953 v Ni (1)
Griffiths, L. (Wrexham), 1902 v S (1)
Griffiths, M. W. (Leicester C), 1947 v Ni; 1949 v P, Bel; 1950 v E, S, Bel; 1951 v E, Ni, P, Sw; 1954 v A (11)
Griffiths, P. (Chirk), 1884 v E, Ni; 1888 v E; 1890 v S, Ni; 1891 v Ni (6)
Griffiths, P. H. (Everton), 1932 v S (1)
Griffiths, T. P. (Everton), 1927 v E, Ni; 1929 v E; 1930 v E; 1931 v Ni; 1932 v Ni, S, E; (with Bolton W), 1933 v E, S, Ni; (with Middlesbrough), F; 1934 v E, S; 1935 v E, Ni; 1936 v S; (with Aston Villa), Ni; 1937 v E, S, Ni (21)

Hall, G. D. (Chelsea), 1988 v Y (sub), Ma, I; 1989 v Ho, Fi, Is; 1990 v Ei; 1991 v Ei; 1992 v A (sub) (9)
Hallam, J. (Oswestry), 1889 v E (1)
Hanford, H. (Swansea T), 1934 v Ni; 1935 v S; 1936 v E; (with Sheffield W), 1936 v Ni; 1938 v E, S; 1939 v F (7)
Harrington, A. C. (Cardiff C), 1956 v Ni; 1957 v E, S; 1958 v S, Ni, Is (2); 1961 v S, E; 1962 v E, S (11)
Harris, C. S. (Leeds U), 1976 v E, S; 1978 v WG, Ir, E, S, Ni; 1979 v Ma, T, WG, E (sub), Ma; 1980 v Ni (sub), Ic (sub); 1981 v T, Cz (sub), Ei, T, S, E, USSR; 1982 v Cz, Ic, E (sub) (24)
Harris, W. C. (Middlesbrough), 1954 v A; 1957 v EG, Cz; 1958 v E, S, EG (6)
Harrison, W. C. (Wrexham), 1899 v E; 1900 v E, S, Ni; 1901 v Ni (5)
Hartson, J. (Arsenal), 1995 v Bul, G (sub), Ge (sub); 1996 v Mol (sub), Sw; 1997 v Ho, T (sub), Ei; (with West Ham U), Bel (sub), S; 1998 v Bel, Jam, Ma, Tun; (with Wimbledon), 1999 v Sw (sub), I (sub), D; 2000 v Sw (sub); 2001 v N, Pol; (with Coventry C), Arm, Uk, Pol, Uk; (with Celtic), 2002 v N, Bl, Arg, CzR, G; 2003 v Cro, Fi, I, Az, Bos, Az; 2004 v I, Fi, Ser, Ru (2); 2005 v La, Az, Ni, E, Pol (sub), A (46)
Haworth, S. O. (Cardiff C), 1997 v S (sub); (with Coventry C), 1998 v Br, Jam (sub), Ma (sub), Tun (sub) (5)
Hayes, A. (Wrexham), 1890 v Ni; 1894 v Ni (2)
Hennessey, W. T. (Birmingham C), 1962 v Ni, Br (2); 1963 v S, E, H (2); 1964 v E, S; 1965 v S, E, D, Gr, USSR; 1966 v E, USSR; (with Nottingham F), 1966 v S, Ni, D, Br (2), Ch; 1967 v S, E; 1968 v E, S, Ni; 1969 v WG, EG, R of UK; 1970 v EG; (with Derby Co), E, S, Ni; 1972 v Fi, Cz, E, S; 1973 v E (39)
Hersee, A. M. (Bangor), 1886 v S, Ni (2)
Hersee, R. (Llandudno), 1886 v Ni (1)
Hewitt, R. (Cardiff C), 1958 v Ni, Is, Se, H, Br (5)
Hewitt, T. J. (Wrexham), 1911 v E, S, Ni; (with Chelsea), 1913 v E, S, Ni; (with South Liverpool), 1914 v E, S (8)
Heywood, D. (Druids), 1879 v E (1)
Hibbott, H. (Newtown Excelsior), 1880 v E, S; (with Newtown), 1885 v S (3)
Higham, G. G. (Oswestry), 1878 v S; 1879 v E (2)
Hill, M. R. (Ipswich T), 1972 v Cz, R (2)
Hockey, T. (Sheffield U), 1972 v Fi, R; 1973 v E (2); (with Norwich C), Pol, S, E, Ni; (with Aston Villa), 1974 v Pol (9)
Hoddinott, T. F. (Watford), 1921 v E, S (2)
Hodges, G. (Wimbledon), 1984 v N (sub), Is (sub); 1987 v USSR, Fi, Cz; (with Newcastle U), 1988 v D; (with Watford), D (sub), Cz (sub), Se, Ma (sub), I (sub); 1990 v Se, Cr; (with Sheffield U), 1992 v Br (sub), Ei (sub), A; 1996 v G (sub), I (18)
Hodgkinson, A. V. (Southampton), 1908 v Ni (1)
Holden, A. (Chester C), 1984 v Is (sub) (1)
Hole, B. G. (Cardiff C), 1963 v Ni; 1964 v Ni; 1965 v S, E, Ni, D, Gr (2), USSR, I; 1966 v E, S, Ni, USSR, D, Br (2), Ch; (with Blackburn R), 1967 v S, E, Ni; 1968 v E, S, Ni, WG; (with Aston Villa), 1969 v I, WG, EG; 1970 v I; (with Swansea C), 1971 v R (30)
Hole, W. J. (Swansea T), 1921 v Ni; 1922 v E; 1923 v E, Ni; 1928 v E, S, Ni; 1929 v E, S (9)
Hollins, D. M. (Newcastle U), 1962 v Br (sub), M; 1963 v Ni, H; 1964 v E; 1965 v Ni, Gr, I; 1966 v S, D, Br (11)
Hopkins, I. J. (Brentford), 1935 v S, Ni; 1936 v E, Ni; 1937 v E, S, Ni; 1938 v E, Ni; 1939 v E, S, Ni (12)
Hopkins, J. (Fulham), 1983 v Ni, Br; 1984 v N, R, Bul, Y, S, E, Ni, N, Is; 1985 v Ic (1 + 1 sub), N; (with C Palace), 1990 v Ho, Cr (16)
Hopkins, M. (Tottenham H), 1956 v Ni; 1957 v Ni, S, E, Cz (2), EG; 1958 v E, S, Ni, EG, Is (2), H (2), M, Se, Br; 1959 v E, S, Ni; 1960 v E, S; 1961 v Ni, H, Sp (2); 1962 v Ni, Br (2), M; 1963 v S, Ni, H (34)
Horne, B. (Portsmouth), 1988 v D (sub), Y, Se (sub), Ma, I; 1989 v Ho, Fi, Is; (with Southampton), Se, WG; 1990 v WG (sub), Ei, Se, Cr; 1991 v D, Bel (2), L, Ei, Ic, Pol, WG; 1992 v Br, G, L, Ei, A, R, Ho, Arg, J; (with Everton), 1993 v Fa, Cy, Bel, Ei, Bel, RCS, Fa; 1994 v RCS, Cy, R, N, Se, Es; 1995 v Mol, Ge, Bul, G, Ge; 1996 v Mol, G, I, Sw, Sm; (with Birmingham C), 1997 v Sm, Ho, T, Ei, Bel (59)
Howell, E. G. (Builth), 1888 v Ni; 1890 v E; 1891 v E (3)
Howells, R. G. (Cardiff C), 1954 v E, S (2)
Hugh, A. R. (Newport Co), 1930 v Ni (1)
Hughes, A. (Rhos), 1894 v E, S (2)
Hughes, A. (Chirk), 1907 v Ni (1)
Hughes, C. M. (Luton T), 1992 v Ho (sub); 1994 v N (sub), Se (sub), Es; 1996 v Alb; 1997 v Ei (sub); (with Wimbledon), 1998 v T, Bel (8)
Hughes, E. (Everton), 1899 v S, Ni; (with Tottenham H), 1901 v E, S; 1902 v Ni; 1904 v E, Ni, S; 1905 v E, Ni, S; 1906 v E, Ni; 1907 v E (14)
Hughes, E. (Wrexham), 1906 v S; (with Nottingham F), 1906 v Ni; 1908 v S, E; 1910 v Ni, E, S; 1911 v Ni, E, S; (with Wrexham), 1912 v Ni, E, S; (with Manchester C), 1913 v E, S; 1914 v Ni (16)
Hughes, F. W. (Northwich Victoria), 1882 v E, Ni; 1883 v E, Ni, S; 1884 v S (6)
Hughes, I. (Luton T), 1951 v E, Ni, P, Sw (4)
Hughes, J. (Cambridge University), 1877 v S; (with Aberystwyth), 1879 v S (2)
Hughes, J. (Liverpool), 1905 v E, S, Ni (3)
Hughes, J. I. (Blackburn R), 1935 v Ni (1)
Hughes, L. M. (Manchester U), 1984 v E, Ni; 1985 v Ic, Sp, Ic, N, S, Sp, N; 1986 v S, H, U; (with Barcelona), 1987 v USSR, Cz; 1988 v D (2), Cz, Se, Ma, I; (with Manchester U), 1989 v Ho, Fi, Is, Se, WG; 1990 v Fi, WG, Cr; 1991 v D, Bel (2), L, Ic, Pol, WG; 1992 v Br, G, L, Ei, R, Ho, Arg, J; 1993 v Fa, Cy, Bel, Ei, Bel, RCS, Fa; 1994 v RCS, Cy, N; 1995 v Ge, Bul, G, Ge; (with Chelsea), 1996 v Mol, I, Sm; 1997 v Sm, Ho, T, Ei, Bel; 1998 v T; (with Southampton), 1999 v I, D, Bl, Sw, I, D (72)
Hughes, P. W. (Bangor), 1887 v Ni; 1889 v Ni, E (3)
Hughes, W. (Bootle), 1891 v E; 1892 v S, Ni (3)
Hughes, W. A. (Blackburn R), 1949 v E, Ni, P, Bel, Sw (5)
Hughes, W. M. (Birmingham), 1938 v E, Ni, S; 1939 v E, Ni, S, F; 1947 v E, S, Ni (10)
Humphreys, J. V. (Everton), 1947 v Ni (1)
Humphreys, R. (Druids), 1888 v Ni (1)
Hunter, A. H. (FA of Wales Secretary), 1887 v Ni (1)

Jackett, K. (Watford), 1983 v N, Y, E, Bul, S; 1984 v N, R, Y, S, Ni, N, Is; 1985 v Ic, Sp, Ic, N, S, Sp, N; 1986 v S, H, S.Ar, Ei, Ca (2); 1987 v Fi (2); 1988 v D, Cz, Y, Se (31)
Jackson, W. (St Helens Rec), 1899 v Ni (1)
James, E. (Chirk), 1893 v E, Ni; 1894 v E, S, Ni; 1898 v S, E; 1899 v Ni (8)
James, E. G. (Blackpool), 1966 v Br (2), Ch; 1967 v Ni; 1968 v S; 1971 v Cz, S, E, Ni (9)
James, L. (Burnley), 1972 v Cz, R, S (sub); 1973 v E (3), Pol, S, Ni; 1974 v Pol, E, S, Ni; 1975 v A, H (2), L (2), S, E, Ni; 1976 v A; (with Derby Co), S, E, Y (2), Ni; 1977 v WG, S (2), Cz, E, Ni; 1978 v K (2); (with QPR), WG; (with Burnley), 1979 v T; (with Swansea C), 1980 v E, S, Ni, Ic; 1981 v T, Ei, T, S, E; 1982 v Cz, Ic, USSR, E (sub), S, Ni, F; (with Sunderland), 1983 v E (sub) (54)

James, R. M. (Swansea C), 1979 v Ma, WG (sub), S, E, Ni, Ma; 1980 v WG; 1982 v Cz (sub), Ic, Sp, E, S, Ni, F; 1983 v N, Y, E, Bul; (with Stoke C), 1984 v N, R, Bul, Y, S, E, Ni, N, Is; 1985 v Ic, Sp, Ic; (with QPR), N, S, Sp, N; 1986 v S, S.Ar, Ei, U, Ca (2); 1987 v Fi (2), USSR, Cz; (with Leicester C), 1988 v D (2); (with Swansea C), Y (47)
James, W. (West Ham U), 1931 v Ni; 1932 v Ni (2)
Jarrett, R. H. (Ruthin), 1889 v Ni; 1890 v S (2)
Jarvis, A. L. (Hull C), 1967 v S, E, Ni (3)
Jenkins, E. (Lovell's Ath), 1925 v E (1)
Jenkins, J. (Brighton), 1924 v Ni, E, S; 1925 v S, Ni; 1926 v E, S; 1927 v S (8)
Jenkins, R. W. (Rhyl), 1902 v Ni (1)
Jenkins, S. R. (Swansea C), 1996 v G; (with Huddersfield T), Alb, I; 1997 v Ho (sub), T, S; 1998 v T, Bel, Br, Jam; 1999 v I (sub), D; 2001 v Pol (sub), Uk (sub); 2002 v Arm, N (16)
Jenkyns, C. A. L. (Small Heath), 1892 v E, S, Ni; 1895 v E; (with Woolwich Arsenal), 1896 v S; (with Newton Heath), 1897 v Ni; (with Walsall), 1898 v S, E (8)
Jennings, W. (Bolton W), 1914 v E, S; 1920 v S; 1923 v Ni, E; 1924 v E, S, Ni; 1927 v S, Ni; 1929 v S (11)
John, R. F. (Arsenal), 1923 v S, Ni; 1925 v Ni; 1926 v E; 1927 v E; 1928 v E, Ni; 1930 v E, S; 1932 v E; 1933 v F, Ni; 1935 v Ni; 1936 v S; 1937 v E (15)
John, W. R. (Walsall), 1931 v Ni; (with Stoke C), 1933 v E, S, Ni, F; 1934 v E, S; (with Preston NE), 1935 v E, S; (with Sheffield U), 1936 v E, S, Ni; (with Swansea T), 1939 v E, S (14)
Johnson, A. J. (Nottingham F), 1999 v I, D, Bl, Sw; 2000 v Fi (sub), Br (sub), P (sub); (with WBA), 2003 v Cro, Fi, US; 2004 v I (sub), Fi (sub), Ru (2); 2005 v La (sub) (15)
Johnson, M. G. (Swansea T), 1964 v Ni (1)
Jones, A. (Port Vale), 1987 v Fi, Cz (sub); 1988 v D, (with Charlton Ath), D (sub), Cz (sub); 1990 v Hol (sub) (6)
Jones, A. F. (Oxford University), 1877 v S (1)
Jones, A. T. (Nottingham F), 1905 v E; (with Notts Co), 1906 v E (2)
Jones, Bryn (Wolverhampton W), 1935 v Ni; 1936 v E, S, Ni; 1937 v E, S, Ni; 1938 v E, S, Ni; (with Arsenal), 1939 v E, S, Ni; 1947 v S, Ni; 1948 v E; 1949 v S (17)
Jones, B. S. (Swansea T), 1963 v S, E, Ni, H (2); 1964 v S, Ni; (with Plymouth Arg), 1965 v D; (with Cardiff C), 1969 v S, E, Ni, I (sub), WG, EG, R of UK (15)
Jones, Charlie (Nottingham F), 1926 v E; 1927 v S, Ni; 1928 v E; (with Arsenal), 1930 v E, S; 1932 v E; 1933 v F (8)
Jones, Cliff (Swansea T), 1954 v A; 1956 v E, Ni, S, A; 1957 v E, S, Ni, Cz (2), EG; 1958 v EG, E, S, Is (2); (with Tottenham H), 1958 v Ni, H (2), M, Se, Br; 1959 v Ni; 1960 v E, S, Ni; 1961 v S, E, Ni, Sp, H, Ei; 1962 v E, Ni, S, Br (2), M; 1963 v S, Ni, H; 1964 v E, S, Ni; 1965 v E, S, Ni, D, Gr (2), USSR, I; 1967 v S, E; 1968 v E, S, WG; (with Fulham), 1969 v I, R of UK (59)
Jones, C. W. (Birmingham), 1935 v Ni; 1939 v F (2)
Jones, D. (Chirk), 1888 v S, Ni; (with Bolton W), 1889 v E, S, Ni; 1890 v E; 1891 v S; 1892 v Ni; 1893 v E; 1894 v E; 1895 v E; 1898 v S; (with Manchester C), 1900 v E, Ni (14)
Jones, D. E. (Norwich C), 1976 v S, E (sub); 1978 v S, Cz, WG, Ir, E; 1980 v E (8)
Jones, D. O. (Leicester C), 1934 v E, Ni; 1935 v E, S; 1936 v E, Ni; 1937 v Ni (7)
Jones, Evan (Chelsea), 1910 v S, Ni; (with Oldham Ath), 1911 v E, S; 1912 v E, S; (with Bolton W), 1914 v Ni (7)
Jones, F. R. (Bangor), 1885 v E, Ni; 1886 v S (3)
Jones, F. W. (Small Heath), 1893 v S (1)
Jones, G. P. (Wrexham), 1907 v S, Ni (2)
Jones, H. (Aberaman), 1902 v Ni (1)
Jones, Humphrey (Bangor), 1885 v E, Ni, S; 1886 v E, Ni, S; (with Queen's Park), 1887 v E; (with East Stirlingshire), 1889 v E, S; 1890 v E, S, Ni; (with Queen's Park), 1891 v E, S (14)
Jones, Ivor (Swansea T), 1920 v S, Ni; 1921 v Ni, E; 1922 v S, Ni; (with WBA), 1923 v E, Ni; 1924 v S; 1926 v Ni (10)
Jones, Jeffrey (Llandrindod Wells), 1908 v Ni; 1909 v Ni; 1910 v S (3)
Jones, J. (Druids), 1876 v S (1)
Jones, J. (Berwyn Rangers), 1883 v S, Ni; 1884 v S (3)
Jones, J. (Wrexham), 1925 v Ni (1)
Jones, J. L. (Sheffield U), 1895 v E, S, Ni; 1896 v Ni, S, E; 1897 v Ni, S, E; (with Tottenham H), 1898 v Ni, E, S; 1899 v S, Ni; 1900 v S; 1902 v E, S, Ni; 1904 v E, S, Ni (21)
Jones, J. Love (Stoke C), 1906 v S; (with Middlesbrough), 1910 v Ni (2)
Jones, J. O. (Bangor), 1901 v S, Ni (2)
Jones, J. P. (Liverpool), 1976 v A, E, S; 1977 v WG, S (2), Cz, E, Ni; 1978 v K (2), S, Cz, WG, Ir, E, S, Ni; (with Wrexham), 1979 v Ma, T, WG, S, E, Ni, Ma; 1980 v Ei, WG, T, E, S, Ni, Ic; 1981 v T, Ei, T, S, E, USSR; 1982 v Cz, Ic, USSR, Sp, E, S, Ni, F; 1983 v N; (with Chelsea), Y, E, Bul, S, Ni, Br; 1984 v N, R, Bul, Y, S, E, Ni, N, Is; 1985 v Ic, N, S, N; (with Huddersfield T), 1986 v S, H, Ei, U, Ca (2) (72)
Jones, J. T. (Stoke C), 1912 v E, S, Ni; 1913 v E, Ni; 1914 v S, Ni; 1920 v E, S, Ni; (with C Palace), 1921 v E, S; 1922 v E, S, Ni (15)
Jones, K. (Aston Villa), 1950 v S (1)
Jones, Leslie J. (Cardiff C), 1933 v F; (with Coventry C), 1935 v Ni; 1936 v S; 1937 v E, S, Ni; (with Arsenal), 1938 v E, S, Ni; 1939 v E, S (11)
Jones, M. G. (Leeds U), 2000 v Sw (sub), Q, Br, P; 2001 v Pol (sub); (with Leicester C), Arm (sub), Uk, Pol (sub); 2002 v Arm (sub), N (sub), Bl; 2003 v Bos (sub), US (13)
Jones, P. L. (Liverpool), 1997 v S (sub); (with Tranmere R), 1998 v T (sub) (2)
Jones, P. S. (Stockport Co), 1997 v S (sub); (with Southampton), 1998 v T (sub), Br, Jam, Ma; 1999 v I, D, Bl, Sw, I, D; 2000 v Bl, Sw, Q; 2001 v Bl, N, Pol, Arm, Uk, Pol, Uk; 2002 v Arm, N, Bl, Arg; 2003 v Cro, Fi, I, Az (2), US; 2004 v Ser, I, Fi, Ser, Ru (2); (with Wolverhampton W), H; 2005 v La, Az, Ni, E, Pol (43)
Jones, P. W. (Bristol R), 1971 v Fi (1)
Jones, R. (Bangor), 1887 v S; 1889 v E; (with Crewe Alex), 1890 v E (3)
Jones, R. (Leicester Fosse), 1898 v S (1)
Jones, R. (Druids), 1899 v S (1)
Jones, R. (Bangor), 1900 v S, Ni (2)
Jones, R. (Millwall), 1906 v S, Ni (2)
Jones, R. A. (Druids), 1884 v E, Ni, S; 1885 v S (4)
Jones, R. A. (Sheffield W), 1994 v Es (1)
Jones, R. S. (Everton), 1894 v Ni (1)
Jones, S. (Wrexham), 1887 v Ni; (with Chester), 1890 v S (2)
Jones, S. (Wrexham), 1893 v S, Ni; (with Burton Swifts), 1895 v S; 1896 v E, Ni; (with Druids), 1899 v E (6)
Jones, T. (Manchester U), 1926 v Ni; 1927 v E, Ni; 1930 v Ni (4)
Jones, T. D. (Aberdare), 1908 v Ni (1)
Jones, T. G. (Everton), 1938 v Ni; 1939 v E, S, Ni; 1947 v E, S; 1948 v E, S, Ni; 1949 v E, Ni, P, Bel, Sw; 1950 v E, S, Bel (17)
Jones, T. J. (Sheffield W), 1932 v Ni; 1933 v F (2)
Jones, V. P. (Wimbledon), 1995 v Bul (2), G, Ge; 1996 v Sw; 1997 v Ho, T, Ei, Bel (9)
Jones, W. E. A. (Swansea T), 1947 v E, S; (with Tottenham H), 1949 v E, S (4)
Jones, W. J. (Aberdare), 1901 v E, S; (with West Ham U), 1902 v E, S (4)
Jones, W. Lot (Manchester C), 1905 v E, Ni; 1906 v E, S, Ni; 1907 v E, S, Ni; 1908 v S; 1909 v E, S, Ni; 1910 v E; 1911 v E; 1913 v E, S; 1914 v S, Ni; (with Southend U), 1920 v E, Ni (20)
Jones, W. P. (Druids), 1889 v E, Ni; (with Wynnstay), 1890 v S, Ni (4)
Jones, W. R. (Aberystwyth), 1897 v S (1)

Keenor, F. C. (Cardiff C), 1920 v E, Ni; 1921 v E, Ni, S; 1922 v Ni; 1923 v E, Ni, S; 1924 v E, Ni, S; 1925 v E, Ni, S; 1926 v S; 1927 v E, Ni, S; 1928 v E, Ni, S; 1929 v E, Ni, S; 1930 v E, Ni, S; 1931 v E, Ni, S; (with Crewe Alex), 1933 v S (32)
Kelly, F. C. (Wrexham), 1899 v S, Ni; (with Druids), 1902 v Ni (3)
Kelsey, A. J. (Arsenal), 1954 v Ni, A; 1955 v S, Ni, Y; 1956 v E, Ni, S, A; 1957 v E, Ni, S, Cz (2), EG; 1958 v E, S, Ni, Is (2), H (2), M, Se, Br; 1959 v E, S; 1960 v E, Ni, S; 1961 v E, Ni, S, H, Sp (2); 1962 v E, S, Ni, Br (2) (41)
Kenrick, S. L. (Druids), 1876 v S; 1877 v S; (with Oswestry), 1879 v E, S; (with Shropshire Wanderers), 1881 v E (5)
Ketley, C. F. (Druids), 1882 v Ni (1)
King, J. (Swansea T), 1955 v E (1)
Kinsey, N. (Norwich C), 1951 v Ni, P, Sw; 1952 v E; (with Birmingham C), 1954 v Ni; 1956 v E, S (7)
Knill, A. R. (Swansea C), 1989 v Ho (1)
Koumas, J. (Tranmere R), 2001 v Uk (sub); 2002 v CzR; (with WBA), 2003 v Bos (sub), US; 2004 v I, Fi, Ru (2), H; 2005 v La, Az, Ni, E, Pol (14)
Krzywicki, R. L. (WBA), 1970 v EG, I; (with Huddersfield T), Ni, E, S; 1971 v R, Fi; 1972 v Cz (sub) (8)

Lambert, R. (Liverpool), 1947 v S; 1948 v E; 1949 v P, Bel, Sw (5)
Latham, G. (Liverpool), 1905 v E, S; 1906 v S; 1907 v E, S, Ni; 1908 v E; 1909 v Ni; (with Southport Central), 1910 v E; (with Cardiff C), 1913 v Ni (10)
Law, B. J. (QPR), 1990 v Se (1)
Lawrence, E. (Clapton Orient), 1930 v Ni; (with Notts Co), 1932 v S (2)

Lawrence, S. (Swansea T), 1932 v Ni; 1933 v F; 1934 v S, E, Ni; 1935 v E, S; 1936 v S (8)
Lea, A. (Wrexham), 1889 v E; 1891 v S, Ni; 1893 v Ni (4)
Lea, C. (Ipswich T), 1965 v Ni, I (2)
Leary, P. (Bangor), 1889 v Ni (1)
Leek, K. (Leicester C), 1961 v S, E, Ni, H, Sp (2); (with Newcastle U), 1962 v S; (with Birmingham C), v Br (sub), M; 1963 v E; 1965 v S, Gr; (with Northampton T), 1965 v Gr (13)
Legg, A. (Birmingham C), 1996 v Sw, Sm (sub); 1997 v Ho (sub), Ei; (with Cardiff C), 1999 v D (sub); 2001 v Arm (6)
Lever, A. R. (Leicester C), 1953 v S (1)
Lewis, B. (Chester), 1891 v Ni; (with Wrexham), 1892 v S, E, Ni; (with Middlesbrough), 1893 v S, E; (with Wrexham), 1894 v S, E, Ni; 1895 v S (10)
Lewis, D. (Arsenal), 1927 v E; 1928 v Ni; 1930 v E (3)
Lewis, D. (Swansea C), 1983 v Br (sub) (1)
Lewis, D. J. (Swansea T), 1933 v E, S (2)
Lewis, D. M. (Bangor), 1890 v Ni, S (2)
Lewis, J. (Bristol R), 1906 v E (1)
Lewis, J. (Cardiff C), 1926 v S (1)
Lewis, T. (Wrexham), 1881 v E, S (2)
Lewis, W. (Bangor), 1885 v E; 1886 v E, S; 1887 v E, S; 1888 v E; 1889 v E, Ni, S; (with Crewe Alex), 1890 v E; 1891 v E, S; (with Chester), 1892 v E, S, Ni; 1894 v E, S, Ni; 1895 v S, Ni, E; 1896 v E, S, Ni; (with Manchester C), 1897 v E, S; (with Chester), 1898 v Ni (27)
Lewis, W. L. (Swansea T), 1927 v E, Ni; 1928 v E, Ni; 1929 v S; (with Huddersfield T), 1930 v E (6)
Llewellyn, C. M. (Norwich C), 1998 v Ma (sub), Tun (sub); (with Wrexham), 2004 v N (sub), Ca (sub) (4)
Lloyd, B. W. (Wrexham), 1976 v A, E, S (3)
Lloyd, J. W. (Wrexham), 1879 v S; (with Newtown), 1885 v S (2)
Lloyd, R. A. (Ruthin), 1891 v Ni; 1895 v S (2)
Lockley, A. (Chirk), 1898 v Ni (1)
Lovell, S. (C Palace), 1982 v USSR (sub); (with Millwall), 1985 v N; 1986 v S (sub), H (sub), Ca (1+1 sub) (6)
Lowndes, S. (Newport Co), 1983 v S (sub), Br (sub); (with Millwall), 1985 v N (sub); 1986 v S.Ar (sub), Ei, U, Ca (2); (with Barnsley), 1987 v Fi (sub); 1988 v Se (sub) (10)
Lowrie, G. (Coventry C), 1948 v E, S, Ni; (with Newcastle U), 1949 v P (4)
Lucas, P. M. (Leyton Orient), 1962 v Ni, M; 1963 v S, E (4)
Lucas, W. H. (Swansea T), 1949 v S, Ni, P, Bel, Sw; 1950 v E; 1951 v E (7)
Lumberg, A. (Wrexham), 1929 v Ni; 1930 v E, S; (with Wolverhampton W), 1932 v S (4)

McCarthy, T. P. (Wrexham), 1889 v Ni (1)
McMillan, R. (Shrewsbury Engineers), 1881 v E, S (2)
Maguire, G. T. (Portsmouth), 1990 v Fi (sub), Ho, WG, Ei, Se; 1992 v Br (sub), G (7)
Mahoney, J. F. (Stoke C), 1968 v E; 1969 v EG; 1971 v Cz; 1973 v E (3), Pol, S, Ni; 1974 v Pol, E, S, Ni; 1975 v A, H (2), L (2), S, E, Ni; 1976 v A, Y (2), E, Ni; 1977 v WG, Cz, S, E, Ni; (with Middlesbrough), 1978 v K (2), S, Cz, Ir, E (sub), S, Ni; 1979 v WG, S, E, Ni, Ma; (with Swansea C), 1980 v Ei, WG, T (sub); 1982 v Ic, USSR; 1983 v Y, E (51)
Mardon, P. J. (WBA), 1996 v G (sub) (1)
Margetson, M. W. (Cardiff C), 2004 v Ca (sub) (1)
Marriott, A. (Wrexham), 1996 v Sw (sub); 1997 v S; 1998 v Bel, Br (sub), Tun (5)
Martin, T. J. (Newport Co), 1930 v Ni (1)
Marustik, C. (Swansea C), 1982 v Sp, E, S, Ni, F; 1983 v N (6)
Mates, J. (Chirk), 1891 v Ni; 1897 v E, S (3)
Matthews, R. W. (Liverpool), 1921 v Ni; (with Bristol C), 1923 v E; (with Bradford), 1926 v Ni (3)
Matthews, W. (Chester), 1905 v Ni; 1908 v E (2)
Matthias, J. S. (Brymbo), 1896 v S, Ni; (with Shrewsbury), 1897 v E, S; (with Wolverhampton W), 1899 v S (5)
Matthias, T. J. (Wrexham), 1914 v S, E; 1920 v Ni, S, E; 1921 v S, E, Ni; 1922 v S, E, Ni; 1923 v S (12)
Mays, A. W. (Wrexham), 1929 v Ni (1)
Medwin, T. C. (Swansea T), 1953 v Ni, F, Y; (with Tottenham H), 1957 v E, S, Ni, Cz (2), EG; 1958 v E, S, Ni, Is (2), H (2), M, Br; 1959 v E, S, Ni; 1960 v E, S, Ni; 1961 v S, Ei, E, Sp; 1963 v E, H (30)
Melville, A. K. (Swansea C), 1990 v WG, Ei, Se, Cr (sub); (with Oxford U), 1991 v Ic, Pol, WG; 1992 v Br, G, L, R, Ho, J (sub); 1993 v RCS, Fa (sub); (with Sunderland), 1994 v RCS (sub), R, N, Se, Es; 1995 v Alb, Mol (sub), Ge, Bul; 1996 v G, Alb, Sm; 1997 v Sm, Ho (2), T; 1998 v T; (with Fulham), 1999 v I, D; 2000 v Bl, Q, Fi, Br, P; 2001 v Bl, N, Pol, Arm, Uk, Pol, Uk; 2002 v Arm, Bl, Arg, CzR, G; 2003 v Cro, Fi, I, Az, Bos, Az, US; 2004 v Fi, Ru (2); (with West Ham U), S, H; 2005 v La, Az (65)
Meredith, S. (Chirk), 1900 v S; 1901 v S, E, Ni; (with Stoke C), 1902 v E; 1903 v Ni; 1904 v E; (with Leyton), 1907 v E (8)
Meredith, W. H. (Manchester C), 1895 v E, Ni; 1896 v E, Ni; 1897 v E, Ni, S; 1898 v E, Ni; 1899 v E; 1900 v E, Ni; 1901 v E, Ni; 1902 v E, S; 1903 v E, S, Ni; 1904 v E; 1905 v E, S; (with Manchester U), 1907 v E, S, Ni; 1908 v E, Ni; 1909 v E, S, Ni; 1910 v E, S, Ni; 1911 v E, S, Ni; 1912 v E, S, Ni; 1913 v E, S, Ni; 1914 v E, S, Ni; 1920 v E, S, Ni (48)
Mielczarek, R. (Rotherham U), 1971 v Fi (1)
Millership, H. (Rotherham Co), 1920 v E, S, Ni; 1921 v E, S, Ni (6)
Millington, A. H. (WBA), 1963 v S, E, H; (with C Palace), 1965 v E, USSR; (with Peterborough U), 1966 v Ch, Br; 1967 v E, Ni; 1968 v Ni, WG; 1969 v I, EG; (with Swansea T), 1970 v E, S, Ni; 1971 v Cz, Fi; 1972 v Fi (sub), Cz, R (21)
Mills, T. J. (Clapton Orient), 1934 v E, Ni; (with Leicester C), 1935 v E, S (4)
Mills-Roberts, R. H. (St Thomas' Hospital), 1885 v E, S, Ni; 1886 v E; 1887 v E; (with Preston NE), 1888 v E, Ni; (with Llanberis), 1892 v E (8)
Moore, G. (Cardiff C), 1960 v E, S, Ni; 1961 v Ei, Sp; (with Chelsea), 1962 v Br; 1963 v Ni, H; (with Manchester U), 1964 v S, Ni; (with Northampton T), 1966 v Ni, Ch; (with Charlton Ath), 1969 v S, E, Ni, R of UK; 1970 v E, S, Ni, I; 1971 v R (21)
Morgan, J. R. (Cambridge University), 1877 v S; (with Derby School Staff), 1879 v S; 1880 v E, S; 1881 v E, S; 1882 v E, S, Ni; 1883 v E (10)
Morgan, J. T. (Wrexham), 1905 v Ni (1)
Morgan-Owen, H. (Oxford University), 1902 v S; (with Corinthians), 1906 v E, Ni; 1907 v S (4)
Morgan-Owen, M. M. (Oxford University), 1897 v S, Ni; 1898 v E, S; 1899 v S; 1900 v E; (with Corinthians), 1901 v S, E; 1903 v S; 1906 v S, E, Ni; 1907 v E (13)
Morley, E. J. (Swansea T), 1925 v E; (with Clapton Orient), 1929 v E, S, Ni (4)
Morris, A. G. (Aberystwyth), 1896 v E, Ni, S; (with Swindon T), 1897 v E; 1898 v S; (with Nottingham F), 1899 v E, S; 1903 v E, S; 1905 v E, S; 1907 v E, S; 1908 v E; 1910 v E, S, Ni; 1911 v E, S, Ni; 1912 v E (21)
Morris, C. (Chirk), 1900 v E, S, Ni; (with Derby Co), 1901 v E, S, Ni; 1902 v E; 1903 v E, S, Ni; 1904 v Ni; 1905 v E, S, Ni; 1906 v S; 1907 v S; 1908 v E, S; 1909 v E, S, Ni; 1910 v E, S, Ni; (with Huddersfield T), 1911 v E, S, Ni (27)
Morris, E. (Chirk), 1893 v E, S, Ni (3)
Morris, H. (Sheffield U), 1894 v S; (with Manchester C), 1896 v E; (with Grimsby T), 1897 v E (3)
Morris, J. (Oswestry), 1887 v S (1)
Morris, J. (Chirk), 1898 v Ni (1)
Morris, R. (Chirk), 1900 v E, Ni; 1901 v Ni; 1902 v S; (with Shrewsbury T), 1903 v E, Ni (6)
Morris, R. (Druids), 1902 v E, S; (with Newtown), Ni; (with Liverpool), 1903 v S, Ni; 1904 v E, S, Ni; (with Leeds C), 1906 v S; (with Grimsby T), 1907 v Ni; (with Plymouth Arg), 1908 v Ni (11)
Morris, S. (Birmingham), 1937 v E, S; 1938 v E, S; 1939 v F (5)
Morris, W. (Burnley), 1947 v Ni; 1949 v E; 1952 v S, Ni, R of UK (5)
Moulsdale, J. R. B. (Corinthians), 1925 v Ni (1)
Murphy, J. P. (WBA), 1933 v F, E, Ni; 1934 v E, S; 1935 v E, S, Ni; 1936 v E, S, Ni; 1937 v S, Ni; 1938 v E, S (15)

Nardiello, D. (Coventry C), 1978 v Cz, WG (sub) (2)
Neal, J. E. (Colwyn Bay), 1931 v E, S (2)
Neilson, A. B. (Newcastle U), 1992 v Ei; 1994 v Se, Es; 1995 v Ge; (with Southampton), 1997 v Ho (5)
Newnes, J. (Nelson), 1926 v Ni (1)
Newton, L. F. (Cardiff Corinthians), 1912 v Ni (1)
Nicholas, D. S. (Stoke C), 1923 v S; (with Swansea T), 1927 v E, Ni (3)
Nicholas, P. (C Palace), 1979 v S (sub), Ni (sub), Ma; 1980 v Ei, WG, T, E, S, Ni, Ic; 1981 v T, Cz, E; (with Arsenal), T, S, E, USSR; 1982 v Cz, Ic, USSR, Sp, E, S, Ni, F; 1983 v Y, Bul, S, Ni; 1984 v N, Bul, N, Is; (with C Palace), 1985 v Sp; (with Luton T), N, S, Sp, N; 1986 v S, H, S.Ar, Ei, U, Ca (2); 1987 v Fi (2) USSR, Cz; (with Aberdeen), 1988 v D (2), Cz, Y, Se; (with Chelsea), 1989 v Ho, Fi, Is, Se, WG; 1990 v Fi, Ho, WG, Ei, Se, Cr; 1991 v D (sub), Bel, L, Ei; (with Watford), Bel, Pol, WG; 1992 v L (73)
Nicholls, J. (Newport Co), 1924 v E, Ni; (with Cardiff C), 1925 v E, S (4)
Niedzwiecki, E. A. (Chelsea), 1985 v N (sub); 1988 v D (2)
Nock, W. (Newtown), 1897 v Ni (1)

Nogan, L. M. (Watford), 1992 v A (sub); (with Reading), 1996 v Mol (2)
Norman, A. J. (Hull C), 1986 v Ei (sub), U, Ca; 1988 v Ma, I (5)
Nurse, M. T. G. (Swansea T), 1960 v E, Ni; 1961 v S, E, H, Ni, Ei, Sp (2); (with Middlesbrough), 1963 v E, H; 1964 v S (12)

O'Callaghan, E. (Tottenham H), 1929 v Ni; 1930 v S; 1932 v S, E; 1933 v Ni, S, E; 1934 v Ni, S, E; 1935 v E (11)
Oliver, A. (Blackburn R), 1905 v E; (with Bangor), S (2)
Oster, J. M. (Everton), 1998 v Bel (sub), Br, Jam; (with Sunderland), 2000 v Sw; 2003 v Bos (sub), Az, US; 2004 v Ser (sub), S, N, Ca; 2005 v Az (sub), Ni (13)
O'Sullivan, P. A. (Brighton), 1973 v S (sub); 1976 v S; 1979 v Ma (sub) (3)
Owen, D. (Oswestry), 1879 v E (1)
Owen, E. (Ruthin Grammar School), 1884 v E, Ni, S (3)
Owen, G. (Chirk), 1888 v S; (with Newton Heath), 1889 v S, Ni; (with Chirk), 1893 v Ni (4)
Owen, J. (Newton Heath), 1892 v E (1)
Owen, Trevor (Crewe Alex), 1899 v E, S (2)
Owen, T. (Oswestry), 1879 v E (1)
Owen, W. (Chirk), 1884 v E; 1885 v Ni; 1887 v E; 1888 v E; 1889 v E, Ni, S; 1890 v S, Ni; 1891 v E, S, Ni; 1892 v E, S; 1893 v S, Ni (16)
Owen, W. P. (Ruthin), 1880 v E, S; 1881 v E, S; 1882 v E, S, Ni; 1883 v E, S; 1884 v E, S, Ni (12)
Owens, J. (Wrexham), 1902 v S (1)

Page, M. E. (Birmingham C), 1971 v Fi; 1972 v S, Ni; 1973 v E (1+1 sub), Ni; 1974 v S, Ni; 1975 v H, L, S, E, Ni; 1976 v E, Y (2), E, Ni; 1977 v WG, S; 1978 v K (sub+1), WG, Ir, E, S; 1979 v Ma, WG (28)
Page, R. J. (Watford), 1997 v T, Bel, S; 1998 v T, Bel (sub), Br, I; 2000 v Bl, Sw, Q, Fi, Br, P; 2001 v Bl, N, Pol, Arm, Uk, Pol, Uk; (with Sheffield U), 2002 v N, Bl (sub), Arg, CzR, G; 2003 v Az, Bos, Az ; 2004 v Ser, I, Fi, S, H; (with Cardiff C), 2005 v La, Az, H, A (1+sub) (38)
Palmer, D. (Swansea T), 1957 v Cz; 1958 v E, EG (3)
Parris, J. E. (Bradford), 1932 v Ni (1)
Parry, B. J. (Swansea T), 1951 v S (1)
Parry, C. (Everton), 1891 v E, S; 1893 v E; 1894 v E; 1895 v E, S; (with Newtown), 1896 v E, S, Ni; 1897 v Ni; 1898 v E, S, Ni (13)
Parry, E. (Liverpool), 1922 v S; 1923 v E, Ni; 1925 v Ni; 1926 v Ni (5)
Parry, M. (Liverpool), 1901 v E, S, Ni; 1902 v E, S, Ni; 1903 v E, S; 1904 v E, Ni; 1906 v E; 1908 v E, S, Ni; 1909 v E, S (16)
Parry, P. I. (Cardiff C), 2004 v S (sub), N, Ca; 2005 v Ni (sub), Pol (sub) (5)
Parry, T. D. (Oswestry), 1900 v E, S, Ni; 1901 v E, S, Ni; 1902 v E (7)
Parry, W. (Newtown), 1895 v Ni (1)
Partridge, D. W. (Motherwell), 2005 v H, A (2)
Pascoe, C. (Swansea C), 1984 v N, Is; (with Sunderland), 1989 v Fi, Is, WG (sub); 1990 v Ho (sub), WG (sub); 1991 v Ei, Ic (sub); 1992 v Br (10)
Paul, R. (Swansea T), 1949 v E, S, Ni, P, Sw; 1950 v E, S, Ni, Bel; (with Manchester C), 1951 v S, E, Ni, P, Sw; 1952 v E, S, Ni, R of UK; 1953 v S, E, Ni, F, Y; 1954 v E, S, Ni; 1955 v S, E, Y; 1956 v E, Ni, S, A (33)
Peake, E. (Aberystwyth), 1908 v Ni; (with Liverpool), 1909 v Ni, S, E; 1910 v S, Ni; 1911 v Ni; 1912 v E; 1913 v E, Ni; 1914 v Ni (11)
Peers, E. J. (Wolverhampton W), 1914 v Ni, S, E; 1920 v E, S; 1921 v S, Ni, E; (with Port Vale), 1922 v E, S, Ni; 1923 v E (12)
Pembridge, M. A. (Luton T), 1992 v Br, Ei, R; (with Derby Co), Ho, J (sub); 1993 v Bel (sub), Ei; 1994 v N (sub); 1995 v Alb (sub), Mol, Ge (sub); (with Sheffield W), 1996 v Mol, G, Alb, Sw, Sm; 1997 v Sm, Ho (2), T, Ei, Bel, S; 1998 v Bel, Br, Jam, Ma, Tun; (with Benfica), 1999 v D (sub), Bl, Sw, I (sub), D (sub); (with Everton), 2000 v Bl, Q, Fi; 2001 v Arm, Pol, Uk; 2002 v Bl, Arg, G; 2003 v Cro, Fi, I, Bos, Az, US; 2004 v Ser; (with Fulham), I, Fi; 2005 v La, Az, E (54)
Perry, E. (Doncaster R), 1938 v E, S, Ni (3)
Perry, J. (Cardiff C), 1994 v N (1)
Phennah, E. (Civil Service), 1878 v S (1)
Phillips, C. (Wolverhampton W), 1931 v Ni; 1932 v E; 1933 v S; 1934 v E, S, Ni; 1935 v E, S, Ni; 1936 v S; (with Aston Villa), 1936 v E, Ni; 1938 v S (13)
Phillips, D. (Plymouth Arg), 1984 v E, Ni, N; (with Manchester C), 1985 v Sp, Ic, S, Sp, N; 1986 v S, H, S.Ar, Ei, U; (with Coventry C), 1987 v Fi, Cz; 1988 v D (2), Cz, Y, Se; 1989 v Se, WG; (with Norwich C), 1990 v Fi, Ho, WG, Ei, Se; 1991 v D, Bel, Ic, Pol, WG; 1992 v L, Ei, A, R, Ho (sub), Arg, J; 1993 v Fa, Cy, Bel, Ei, Bel, RCS, Fa; (with Nottingham F), 1994 v RCS, Cy, R, N, Se, Es; 1995 v Alb, Mol, Ge, Bul (2), G, Ge; 1996 v Mol (sub), Alb, I (62)
Phillips, L. (Cardiff C), 1971 v Cz, S, E, Ni; 1972 v Cz, R, S, Ni; 1973 v E; 1974 v Pol (sub), Ni; 1975 v A; (with Aston Villa), H (2), L (2), S, E, Ni; 1976 v A, E, Y (2), E, Ni; 1977 v WG, S (2), Cz, E; 1978 v K (2), S, Cz, WG, E, S; 1979 v Ma; (with Swansea C), T, WG, S, E, Ni, Ma; 1980 v Ei, WG, T, S (sub), Ni, Ic; 1981 v T, Cz, T, S, E, USSR; (with Charlton Ath), 1982 v Cz, USSR (58)
Phillips, T. J. S. (Chelsea), 1973 v E; 1974 v E; 1975 v H (sub); 1978 v K (4)
Phoenix, H. (Wrexham), 1882 v S (1)
Pipe, D. R. (Coventry C), 2003 v US (sub) (1)
Poland, G. (Wrexham), 1939 v Ni, F (2)
Pontin, K. (Cardiff C), 1980 v E (sub), S (2)
Powell, A. (Leeds U), 1947 v E, S; 1948 v E, S, Ni; (with Everton), 1949 v E; 1950 v Bel; (with Birmingham C), 1951 v S (8)
Powell, D. (Wrexham), 1968 v WG; (with Sheffield U), 1969 v S, E, Ni, I, WG; 1970 v E, S, Ni, EG; 1971 v R (11)
Powell, I. V. (QPR), 1947 v E; 1948 v E, S, Ni; (with Aston Villa), 1949 v Bel; 1950 v S, Bel; 1951 v S (8)
Powell, J. (Druids), 1878 v S; 1880 v E, S; 1882 v E, S, Ni; 1883 v E, S, Ni; (with Bolton W), 1884 v E; (with Newton Heath), 1887 v E, S; 1888 v E, S, Ni (15)
Powell, Seth (Oswestry), 1885 v S; 1886 v E, Ni; (with WBA), 1891 v E, S; 1892 v E, S (7)
Price, H. (Aston Villa), 1907 v S; (with Burton U), 1908 v Ni; (with Wrexham), 1909 v S, E, Ni (5)
Price, J. (Wrexham), 1877 v S; 1878 v S; 1879 v E; 1880 v E, S; 1881 v E, S; 1882 v S, E, Ni; 1883 v S, Ni (12)
Price, P. (Luton T), 1980 v E, S, Ni, Ic; 1981 v T, Cz, Ei, T, S, E, USSR; (with Tottenham H), 1982 v USSR, Sp, F; 1983 v N, Y, E, Bul, S, Ni; 1984 v N, R, Bul, Y, S (sub) (25)
Pring, K. D. (Rotherham U), 1966 v Ch, D; 1967 v Ni (3)
Pritchard, H. K. (Bristol C), 1985 v N (sub) (1)
Pryce-Jones, A. W. (Newtown), 1895 v E (1)
Pryce-Jones, W. E. (Cambridge University), 1887 v S; 1888 v S, E, Ni; 1890 v Ni (5)
Pugh, A. (Rhostyllen), 1889 v S (1)
Pugh, D. H. (Wrexham), 1896 v S, Ni; 1897 v S, Ni; (with Lincoln C), 1900 v S; 1901 v S, E (7)
Pugsley, J. (Charlton Ath), 1930 v Ni (1)
Pullen, W. J. (Plymouth Arg), 1926 v E (1)

Rankmore, F. E. J. (Peterborough), 1966 v Ch (sub) (1)
Ratcliffe, K. (Everton), 1981 v Cz, Ei, T, S, E, USSR; 1982 v Cz, Ic, USSR, Sp, E; 1983 v Y, E, Bul, S, Ni, Br; 1984 v N, R, Bul, Y, S, E, Ni, N, Is; 1985 v Ic, Sp, Ic, N, S, Sp; 1986 v S, H, S.Ar, U; 1987 v Fi (2), USSR, Cz; 1988 v D (2), Cz; 1989 v Fi, Is, Se, WG; 1990 v Fi; 1991 v D, Bel (2), L, Ei, Ic, Pol, WG; 1992 v Br, G; (with Cardiff C), 1993 v Bel (59)
Rea, J. C. (Aberystwyth), 1894 v Ni, S, E; 1895 v S; 1896 v S, Ni; 1897 v S, Ni; 1898 v Ni (9)
Ready, K. (QPR), 1997 v Ei; 1998 v Bel, Br, Ma, Tun (5)
Reece, G. I. (Sheffield U), 1966 v E, S, Ni, USSR; 1967 v S; 1969 v R of UK (sub); 1970 v I (sub); 1971 v S, E, Ni, Fi; 1972 v Fi, R, E (sub), S, Ni; (with Cardiff C), 1973 v E (sub), Ni; 1974 v Pol (sub), E, S, Ni; 1975 v A, H (2), L (2), S, Ni (29)
Reed, W. G. (Ipswich T), 1955 v S, Y (2)
Rees, A. (Birmingham C), 1984 v N (sub) (1)
Rees, J. M. (Luton T), 1992 v A (sub) (1)
Rees, R. R. (Coventry C), 1965 v S, E, Ni, D, Gr (2), I, R; 1966 v E, S, Ni, R, D, Br (2), Ch; 1967 v E, Ni; 1968 v E, S, Ni; (with WBA), WG; 1969 v I; (with Nottingham F), 1969 v WG, EG, S (sub), R of UK; 1970 v E, S, Ni, EG, I; 1971 v Cz, R, E (sub), Ni (sub), Fi; 1972 v Cz (sub), R (39)
Rees, W. (Cardiff C), 1949 v Ni, Bel, Sw; (with Tottenham H), 1950 v Ni (4)
Richards, A. (Barnsley), 1932 v S (1)
Richards, D. (Wolverhampton W), 1931 v Ni; 1933 v E, S, Ni; 1934 v E, S, Ni; 1935 v E, S, Ni; 1936 v S; (with Brentford), 1936 v E, Ni; 1937 v S, E; (with Birmingham), Ni; 1938 v E, S, Ni; 1939 v E, S (21)
Richards, G. (Druids), 1899 v E, S, Ni; (with Oswestry), 1903 v Ni; (with Shrewsbury), 1904 v S; 1905 v Ni (6)
Richards, R. W. (Wolverhampton W), 1920 v E, S; 1921 v Ni; 1922 v E, S; (with West Ham U), 1924 v E, S, Ni; (with Mold), 1926 v S (9)
Richards, S. V. (Cardiff C), 1947 v E (1)
Richards, W. E. (Fulham), 1933 v Ni (1)
Ricketts, S. (Swansea C), 2005 v H, A (2) (3)
Roach, J. (Oswestry), 1885 v Ni (1)

Robbins, W. W. (Cardiff C), 1931 v E, S; 1932 v Ni, E, S; (with WBA), 1933 v F, E, S, Ni; 1934 v S; 1936 v S (11)
Roberts, A. M. (QPR), 1993 v Ei (sub); 1997 v Sm (sub) (2)
Roberts, D. F. (Oxford U), 1973 v Pol, E (sub), Ni; 1974 v E, S; 1975 v A; (with Hull C), L, Ni; 1976 v S, Ni, Y; 1977 v E (sub), Ni; 1978 v K (1+1 sub), S, Ni (17)
Roberts, G. W. (Tranmere R), 2000 v Fi (sub), Br, P; 2001 v Bl; 2004 v H (sub), N (sub); 2005 v La (sub), H (sub) (8)
Roberts, I. W. (Watford), 1990 v Ho; (with Huddersfield T), 1992 v A, Arg, J; (with Leicester C), 1994 v Se; 1995 v Alb (sub), Mol; (with Norwich C), 2000 v Fi (sub), Br, P; 2001 v Bl, N (sub), Arm (sub); 2002 v Arm, Bl (sub) (15)
Roberts, Jas (Wrexham), 1913 v S, Ni (2)
Roberts, J. (Corwen), 1879 v S; 1880 v E, S; 1882 v E, S, Ni; (with Berwyn R), 1883 v E (7)
Roberts, J. (Ruthin), 1881 v S; 1882 v S (2)
Roberts, J. (Bradford C), 1906 v Ni; 1907 v Ni (2)
Roberts, J. G. (Arsenal), 1971 v S, E, Ni, Fi; 1972 v Fi, E, Ni; (with Birmingham C), 1973 v E (2), Pol, S, Ni; 1974 v Pol, E, S, Ni; 1975 v A, H, S, E; 1976 v E, S (22)
Roberts, J. H. (Bolton), 1949 v Bel (1)
Roberts, N. W. (Wrexham), 2000 v Sw (sub); (with Wigan Ath), 2003 v Az (sub), US (sub); 2004 v N (sub) (4)
Roberts, P. S. (Portsmouth), 1974 v E; 1975 v A, H, L (4)
Roberts, R. (Druids), 1884 v S; (with Bolton W), 1887 v S; 1888 v S, E; 1889 v S, E; 1890 v S; 1892 v Ni; (with Preston NE), S (9)
Roberts, R. (Wrexham), 1886 v Ni; 1887 v Ni; 1891 v Ni (3)
Roberts, R. (Rhos), 1891 v Ni; (with Crewe Alex), 1893 v E (2)
Roberts, R. L. (Chester), 1890 v Ni (1)
Roberts, S. W. (Wrexham), 2005 v H (sub) (1)
Roberts, W. (Llangollen), 1879 v E, S; 1880 v E, S; (with Berwyn R), 1881 v S; 1883 v S (6)
Roberts, W. (Rhyl), 1883 v E (1)
Roberts, W. (Wrexham), 1886 v E, S, Ni; 1887 v Ni (4)
Roberts, W. H. (Ruthin), 1882 v E, S; 1883 v E, S, Ni; (with Rhyl), 1884 v S (6)
Robinson, C. P. (Wolverhampton W), 2000 v Bl (sub), P (sub); 2001 v Arm (sub), Uk; 2002 v Arm, N, Bl (sub), Arg (sub); (with Portsmouth), 2003 v Cro, Az (1+sub), US (sub); 2004 v Ser, S (sub), H, N, Ca; (with Sunderland), 2005 v La (sub), E (sub), H, A (2) (22)
Robinson, J. R. C. (Charlton Ath), 1996 v Alb (sub), Sw, Sm; 1997 v Sm, Ho (1 + sub), Ei, S; 1998 v Bel, Br; 1999 v I, D (sub), Bl, Sw, I, D; 2000 v Bl, Sw, Q, Fi, Br, P; 2001 v Bl, N, Pol, Arm; 2002 v N (sub), Bl, Arg (sub), CzR (30)
Rodrigues, P. J. (Cardiff C), 1965 v Ni, Gr (2); 1966 v USSR, E, S, D; (with Leicester C), Ni, Br (2), Ch; 1967 v S; 1968 v E, S, Ni; 1969 v E, Ni, EG, R of UK; 1970 v E, S, Ni, EG; (with Sheffield W), 1971 v R, E, S, Cz, Ni; 1972 v Fi, Cz, R, E, Ni (sub); 1973 v E (3), Pol, S, Ni; 1974 v Pol (40)
Rogers, J. P. (Wrexham), 1896 v E, S, Ni (3)
Rogers, W. (Wrexham), 1931 v E, S (2)
Roose, L. R. (Aberystwyth), 1900 v Ni; (with London Welsh), 1901 v E, S, Ni; (with Stoke C), 1902 v E, S; 1904 v E; (with Everton), 1905 v S, E; (with Stoke C), 1906 v E, S, Ni; 1907 v E, S, Ni; (with Sunderland), 1908 v E, S; 1909 v E, S, Ni; 1910 v E, S, Ni; 1911 v S (24)
Rouse, R. V. (C Palace), 1959 v Ni (1)
Rowlands, A. C. (Tranmere R), 1914 v E (1)
Rowley, T. (Tranmere R), 1959 v Ni (1)
Rush, I. (Liverpool), 1980 v S (sub), Ni; 1981 v E (sub); 1982 v Ic (sub), USSR, E, S, Ni, F; 1983 v N, Y, E, Bul; 1984 v N, R, Bul, Y, S, E, Ni; 1985 v Ic, N, S, Sp; 1986 v S, S.Ar, Ei, U; 1987 v Fi (2), USSR, Cz; (with Juventus), 1988 v D, Cz, Y, Se, Ma, I; (with Liverpool), 1989 v Ho, Fi, Se, WG; 1990 v Fi, Ei; 1991 v D, Bel (2), L, Ei, Pol, WG; 1992 v G, L, R; 1993 v Fa, Cy, Bel (2), RCS, Fa; 1994 v RCS, Cy, R, N, Se, Es; 1995 v Alb, Ge, Bul, G, Ge; 1996 v Mol, I (73)
Russell, M. R. (Merthyr T), 1912 v S, Ni; 1914 v E; (with Plymouth Arg), 1920 v E, S, Ni; 1921 v E, S, Ni; 1922 v E, Ni; 1923 v E, S, Ni; 1924 v E, S, Ni; 1925 v E, S; 1926 v E, S; 1928 v S; 1929 v E (23)

Sabine, H. W. (Oswestry), 1887 v Ni (1)
Saunders, D. (Brighton & HA), 1986 v Ei (sub), Ca (2); 1987 v Fi, USSR (sub); (with Oxford U), 1988 v Y, Se, Ma, I (sub); 1989 v Ho (sub), Fi; (with Derby Co), Is, Se, WG; 1990 v Fi, Ho, WG, Se, Cr; 1991 v D, Bel (2), L, Ei, Ic, Pol, WG; (with Liverpool), 1992 v Br, G, Ei, R, Ho, Arg, J; 1993 v Fa; (with Aston Villa), Cy, Bel (2), RCS, Fa; 1994 v RCS, Cy, R, N (sub); 1995 v Ge, Bul (2), G, Ge; (with Galatasaray), 1996 v G, Alb, Sm; (with Nottingham F), 1997 v Sm, Ho (2), T, Bel, S; 1998 v T, Bel, Br; (with Sheffield U), Ma, Tun; 1999 v I (sub), D, Bl; (with Benfica) Sw, I, D; (with Bradford C), 2000 v Bl, Sw, Fi (sub), Br; 2001 v Arm, Uk (sub) (75)
Savage, R. W. (Crewe Alex), 1996 v Alb (sub), Sw (sub), Sm (sub); 1997 v Ei (sub), S; (with Leicester C), 1998 v T, Bel, Jam, Tun; 1999 v I (sub), D, Bl, Sw; 2000 v Sw, Fi, Br; 2001 v Bl, N, Pol (2); 2002 v Arm, N, Arg, CzR, G; (with Birmingham C), 2003 v Fi, I, Bos, Az; 2004 v Ser, I, Ru (2), S, H; 2005 v La, Az, Ni, Pol (39)
Savin, G. (Oswestry), 1878 v S (1)
Sayer, P. (Cardiff C), 1977 v Cz, S, E, Ni; 1978 v K (2), S (7)
Scrine, F. H. (Swansea T), 1950 v E, Ni (2)
Sear, C. R. (Manchester C), 1963 v E (1)
Shaw, E. G. (Oswestry), 1882 v Ni; 1884 v S, Ni (3)
Sherwood, A. T. (Cardiff C), 1947 v E, Ni; 1948 v S, Ni; 1949 v E, S, Ni, P, Sw; 1950 v E, S, Ni, Bel; 1951 v E, S, Ni, P, Sw; 1952 v E, S, Ni, R of UK; 1953 v S, E, Ni, F, Y; 1954 v E, S, Ni, A; 1955 v S, E, Y, Ni; 1956 v E, S, Ni, A; (with Newport Co), 1957 v E, S (41)
Shone, W. W. (Oswestry), 1879 v E (1)
Shortt, W. W. (Plymouth Arg), 1947 v Ni; 1950 v Ni, Bel; 1952 v E, S, Ni, R of UK; 1953 v S, E, Ni, F, Y (12)
Showers, D. (Cardiff C), 1975 v E (sub), Ni (2)
Sidlow, C. (Liverpool), 1947 v E, S; 1948 v E, S, Ni; 1949 v S; 1950 v E (7)
Sisson, H. (Wrexham Olympic), 1885 v Ni; 1886 v S, Ni (3)
Slatter, N. (Bristol R), 1983 v S; 1984 v N (sub), Is; 1985 v Ic, Sp, Ic, N, S, Sp, N; (with Oxford U), 1986 v H (sub), S.Ar, Ca (2); 1987 v Fi (sub), Cz; 1988 v D (2), Cz, Ma, I; 1989 v Is (sub) (22)
Smallman, D. P. (Wrexham), 1974 v E (sub), S (sub), Ni; (with Everton), 1975 v H (sub), E, Ni (sub); 1976 v A (7)
Southall, N. (Everton), 1982 v Ni; 1983 v N, E, Bul, S, Ni, Br; 1984 v N, R, Bul, Y, S, E, Ni, N, Is; 1985 v Ic, Sp, Ic, N, S, Sp, N; 1986 v S, H, S.Ar, Ei; 1987 v USSR, Fi, Cz; 1988 v D, Cz, Y, Se; 1989 v Ho, Fi, Se, WG; 1990 v Fi, Ho, WG, Ei, Se, Cr; 1991 v D, Bel (2), L, Ei, Ic, Pol, WG; 1992 v Br, G, L, Ei, A, R, Ho, Arg, J; 1993 v Fa, Cy, Bel, Ei, Bel, RCS, Fa; 1994 v RCS, Cy, R, N, Se, Es; 1995 v Alb, Mol, Ge, Bul (2), G, Ge; 1996 v Mol, G, Alb, I, Sm; 1997 v Sm, Ho (2), T, Bel; 1998 v T (92)
Speed, G. A. (Leeds U), 1990 v Cr (sub); 1991 v D, L (sub), Ei (sub), Ic, WG (sub); 1992 v Br, G (sub), L, Ei, R, Ho,Arg,J; 1993 v Fa, Cy, Bel, Ei, Bel, Fa (sub); 1994 v RCS (sub), Cy, R, N, Se; 1995 v Alb, Mol, Ge, Bul (2), G; 1996 v Mol, G, I, Sw (sub); (with Everton), 1997 v Sm (sub), Ho (2), T, Ei, Bel, S; 1998 v T, Br; (with Newcastle U), Jam, Ma, Tun; 1999 v I, D, Sw, I, D; 2000 v Bl, Sw, Q, Fi, Br, P; 2001 v Bl, N, Pol, Arm, Uk, Pol, Uk; 2002 v Bl, Arg, G; 2003 v Fi, I, Az, Bos, Az; 2004 v Ser, I, Fi, Ser, Ru (2), S; (with Bolton W), 2005 v La, Az, Ni, E, Pol (85)
Sprake, G. (Leeds U), 1964 v S, Ni; 1965 v S, D, Gr; 1966 v E, Ni, USSR; 1967 v S; 1968 v E, S; 1969 v S, E, Ni, WG, R of UK; 1970 v EG, I; 1971 v R, S, E, Ni; 1972 v Fi, E, S, Ni; 1973 v E (2), Pol, S, Ni; 1974 v Pol; (with Birmingham C), S, Ni; 1975 v A, H, L (37)
Stansfield, F. (Cardiff C), 1949 v S (1)
Stevenson, B. (Leeds U), 1978 v Ni; 1979 v Ma, T, S, E, Ni, Ma; 1980 v WG, T, Ic (sub); 1982 v Cz; (with Birmingham C), Sp, S, Ni, F (15)
Stevenson, N. (Swansea C), 1982 v E, S, Ni; 1983 v N (4)
Stitfall, R. F. (Cardiff C), 1953 v E; 1957 v Cz (2)
Sullivan, D. (Cardiff C), 1953 v Ni, F, Y; 1954 v Ni; 1955 v E, Ni; 1957 v E, S; 1958 v Ni, H (2), Se, Br; 1959 v S, Ni; 1960 v E, S (17)
Symons, C. J. (Portsmouth), 1992 v Ei, Ho, Arg, J; 1993 v Fa, Cy, Bel, Ei, RCS, Fa; 1994 v RCS, Cy, R; 1995 v Mol, Ge (sub), Bul, G, Ge; (with Manchester C), 1996 v Mol, G, I, Sw; 1997 v Ho (2), Ei, Bel, S; (with Fulham), 1999 v I, D, Bl, Sw; 2000 v Q (sub); 2001 v Pol; 2002 v Arm, N, Bl; (with C Palace), 2004 v S (sub) (37)

Tapscott, D. R. (Arsenal), 1954 v A; 1955 v S, E, Ni, Y; 1956 v E, Ni, S, A; 1957 v Ni, Cz, EG; (with Cardiff C), 1959 v E, Ni (14)
Taylor, G. K. (C Palace), 1996 v Alb, I (sub); (with Sheffield U), Sw; 1997 v Sm (sub), Ho (sub), Ei (sub); 1998 v Bel (sub), Jam; (with Burnley), 2002 v CzR (sub); 2003 v Cro (sub), Bos (sub), US; (with Nottingham F), 2004 v S (sub), H; 2005 v La (sub) (15)
Taylor, J. (Wrexham), 1898 v E (1)
Taylor, O. D. S. (Newtown), 1893 v S, Ni; 1894 v S, Ni (4)
Thatcher, B. D. (Leicester C), 2004 v H, N, Ca; (with Manchester C), 2005 v La, Ni, E, Pol (7)
Thomas, C. (Druids), 1899 v Ni; 1900 v S (2)
Thomas, D. A. (Swansea T), 1957 v Cz; 1958 v EG (2)
Thomas, D. S. (Fulham), 1948 v E, S, Ni; 1949 v S (4)

Thomas, E. (Cardiff Corinthians), 1925 v E (1)
Thomas, G. (Wrexham), 1885 v E, S (2)
Thomas, H. (Manchester U), 1927 v E (1)
Thomas, M. (Wrexham), 1977 v WG, S (1+1 sub), Ni (sub); 1978 v K (sub), S, Cz, Ir, E, Ni (sub); 1979 v Ma; (with Manchester U), T, WG, Ma (sub); 1980 v Ei, WG (sub), T, E, S, Ni; 1981 v Cz, S, E, USSR; (with Everton), 1982 v Cz; (with Brighton & HA), USSR (sub), Sp, E, S (sub), Ni (sub); 1983 (with Stoke C), v N, Y, E, Bul, S, Ni, Br; 1984 v R, Bul, Y; (with Chelsea), S, E; 1985 v Ic, Sp, Ic, S, Sp, N; 1986 v S; (with WBA), H, S.Ar (sub) (51)
Thomas, M. R. (Newcastle U), 1987 v Fi (1)
Thomas, R. J. (Swindon T), 1967 v Ni; 1968 v WG; 1969 v E, Ni, I, WG, R of UK; 1970 v E, S, Ni, EG, I; 1971 v S, E, Ni, R, Cz; 1972 v Fi, Cz, R, E, S, Ni; 1973 v E (3), Pol, S, Ni; 1974 v Pol; (with Derby Co), E, S, Ni; 1975 v H (2), L (2), S, E, Ni; 1976 v A, Y, E; 1977 v Cz, S, E, Ni; 1978 v K, S; (with Cardiff C), Cz (50)
Thomas, T. (Bangor), 1898 v S, Ni (2)
Thomas, W. R. (Newport Co), 1931 v E, S (2)
Thomson, D. (Druids), 1876 v S (1)
Thomson, G. F. (Druids), 1876 v S; 1877 v S (2)
Toshack, J. B. (Cardiff C), 1969 v S, E, Ni, WG, EG, R of UK; 1970 v EG, I; (with Liverpool), 1971 v S, E, Ni, Fi; 1972 v Fi, E; 1973 v E (3), Pol, S; 1975 v A, H (2), L (2), S, E; 1976 v Y (2), E; 1977 v S; 1978 v K (2), S, Cz; (with Swansea C), 1979 v WG (sub), S, E, Ni, Ma; 1980 v WG (40)
Townsend, W. (Newtown), 1887 v Ni; 1893 v Ni (2)
Trainer, H. (Wrexham), 1895 v E, S, Ni (3)
Trainer, J. (Bolton W), 1887 v S; (with Preston NE), 1888 v S; 1889 v E; 1890 v S; 1891 v S; 1892 v Ni, S; 1893 v E; 1894 v Ni, E; 1895 v Ni, E; 1896 v S; 1897 v Ni, S, E; 1898 v S, E; 1899 v Ni, S (20)
Trollope, P. J. (Derby Co), 1997 v S; 1998 v Br (sub); (with Fulham), Jam (sub), Ma, Tun; (with Coventry C), 2002 v CzR (sub); (with Northampton T), 2003 v Cro (sub), Az (sub+sub) (9)
Turner, H. G. (Charlton Ath), 1937 v E, S, Ni; 1938 v E, S, Ni; 1939 v Ni, F (8)
Turner, J. (Wrexham), 1892 v E (1)
Turner, R. E. (Wrexham), 1891 v E, Ni (2)
Turner, W. H. (Wrexham), 1887 v E, Ni; 1890 v S; 1891 v E, S (5)

Van Den Hauwe, P. W. R. (Everton), 1985 v Sp; 1986 v S, H; 1987 v USSR, Fi, Cz; 1988 v D (2), Cz, Y, I; 1989 v Fi, Se (13)
Vaughan, D. O. (Crewe Alex), 2003 v US; 2004 v H (2)
Vaughan, Jas (Druids), 1893 v E, S, Ni; 1899 v E (4)
Vaughan, John (Oswestry), 1879 v S; (with Druids), 1880 v S; 1881 v E, S; 1882 v E, S, Ni; 1883 v E, S, Ni; (with Bolton W), 1884 v E (11)
Vaughan, J. O. (Rhyl), 1885 v Ni; 1886 v Ni, E, S (4)
Vaughan, N. (Newport Co), 1983 v Y (sub), Br; 1984 v N; (with Cardiff C), R, Bul, Y, Ni (sub), N, Is; 1985 v Sp (sub) (10)
Vaughan, T. (Rhyl), 1885 v E (1)
Vearncombe, G. (Cardiff C), 1958 v EG; 1961 v Ei (2)
Vernon, T. R. (Blackburn R), 1957 v Ni, Cz (2), EG; 1958 v E, S, EG, Se; 1959 v S; (with Everton), 1960 v Ni; 1961 v S, E, Ei; 1962 v Ni, Br (2), M; 1963 v S, E, H; 1964 v E, S; (with Stoke C), 1965 v Ni, Gr, I; 1966 v E, S, Ni, USSR, D; 1967 v Ni; 1968 v E (32)
Villars, A. K. (Cardiff C), 1974 v E, S, Ni (sub) (3)
Vizard, E. T. (Bolton W), 1911 v E, S, Ni; 1912 v E, S; 1913 v S; 1914 v E, Ni; 1920 v E; 1921 v E, S, Ni; 1922 v E, S; 1923 v E, Ni; 1924 v E, S, Ni; 1926 v E, S; 1927 v S (22)

Walley, J. T. (Watford), 1971 v Cz (1)
Walsh, I. (C Palace), 1980 v Ei, T, E, S, Ic; 1981 v T, Cz, Ei, T, S, E, USSR; 1982 v Cz (sub), Ic; (with Swansea C), Sp, S (sub), Ni (sub), F (18)
Ward, D. (Bristol R), 1959 v E; (with Cardiff C), 1962 v E (2)
Ward, D. (Notts Co), 2000 v P; (with Nottingham F), 2002 v CzR; 2003 v Bos, US (sub); 2004 v S (sub) (5)
Warner, J. (Swansea T), 1937 v E; (with Manchester U), 1939 v F (2)
Warren, F. W. (Cardiff C), 1929 v Ni; (with Middlesbrough), 1931 v Ni; 1933 v F, E; (with Hearts), 1937 v Ni; 1938 v Ni (6)
Watkins, A. E. (Leicester Fosse), 1898 v E, S; (with Aston Villa), 1900 v E, S; (with Millwall), 1904 v Ni (5)
Watkins, W. M. (Stoke C), 1902 v E; 1903 v E, S; (with Aston Villa); 1904 v E, S, Ni; (with Sunderland), 1905 v E, S, Ni; (with Stoke C), 1908 v Ni (10)
Webster, C. (Manchester U), 1957 v Cz; 1958 v H, M, Br (4)
Weston, R. D. (Arsenal), 2000 v P (sub); (with Cardiff C), 2003 v Cro (sub), Az (sub), Bos; 2004 v Fi, Ser; 2005 v H (sub) (7)
Whatley, W. J. (Tottenham H), 1939 v E, S (2)
White, P. F. (London Welsh), 1896 v Ni (1)
Wilcock, A. R. (Oswestry), 1890 v Ni (1)
Wilding, J. (Wrexham Olympians), 1885 v E, S, Ni; 1886 v E, Ni; (with Bootle), 1887 v E; 1888 v S, Ni; (with Wrexham), 1892 v S (9)
Williams, A. (Reading), 1994 v Es; 1995 v Alb, Mol, G (sub), Ge; 1996 v Mol, I; (with Wolverhampton W), 1998 v Br (sub), Jam; 1999 v I, D, I; (with Reading), 2003 v US (13)
Williams, A. L. (Wrexham), 1931 v E (1)
Williams, A. P. (Southampton), 1998 v Br (sub), Ma (2)
Williams, B. (Bristol C), 1930 v Ni (1)
Williams, B. D. (Swansea T), 1928 v Ni, E; 1930 v E, S; (with Everton), 1931 v Ni; 1932 v E; 1933 v E, S, Ni; 1935 v Ni (10)
Williams, D. G. (Derby Co), 1988 v Cz, Y, Se, Ma, I; 1989 v Ho, Is, Se, WG; 1990 v Fi, Ho; (with Ipswich T), 1993 v Ei; 1996 v G (sub) (13)
Williams, D. M. (Norwich C), 1986 v S.Ar (sub), U, Ca (2); 1987 v Fi (5)
Williams, D. R. (Merthyr T), 1921 v E, S; (with Sheffield W), 1923 v S; 1926 v S; 1927 v E, Ni; (with Manchester U), 1929 v E, S (8)
Williams, E. (Crewe Alex), 1893 v E, S (2)
Williams, E. (Druids), 1901 v E, Ni, S; 1902 v E, Ni (5)
Williams, G. (Chirk), 1893 v S; 1894 v S; 1895 v E, S, Ni; 1898 v Ni (6)
Williams, G. E. (WBA), 1960 v Ni; 1961 v S, E, Ei; 1963 v Ni, H; 1964 v E, S, Ni; 1965 v S, E, Ni, D, Gr (2), USSR, I; 1966 v Ni, Br (2), Ch; 1967 v S, E, Ni; 1968 v Ni; 1969 v I (26)
Williams, G. G. (Swansea T), 1961 v Ni, H, Sp (2); 1962 v E (5)
Williams, G. J. J. (Cardiff C), 1951 v Sw (1)
Williams, G. O. (Wrexham), 1907 v Ni (1)
Williams, H. J. (Swansea), 1965 v Gr (2); 1972 v R (3)
Williams, H. T. (Newport Co), 1949 v Ni, Sw; (with Leeds U), 1950 v Ni; 1951 v S (4)
Williams, J. H. (Oswestry), 1884 v E (1)
Williams, J. J. (Wrexham), 1939 v F (1)
Williams, J. T. (Middlesbrough), 1925 v Ni (1)
Williams, J. W. (C Palace), 1912 v S, Ni (2)
Williams, R. (Newcastle U), 1935 v S, E (2)
Williams, R. P. (Caernarvon), 1886 v S (1)
Williams, S. G. (WBA), 1954 v A; 1955 v E, Ni; 1956 v E, S, A; 1958 v E, S, Ni, Is (2), H (2), M, Se, Br; 1959 v E, S, Ni; 1960 v E, S, Ni; 1961 v Ni, Ei, H, Sp (2); 1962 v E, S, Ni, Br (2), M; (with Southampton), 1963 v S, E, H (2); 1964 v E, S; 1965 v S, E, D; 1966 v D (43)
Williams, W. (Druids), 1876 v S; 1878 v S; (with Oswestry), 1879 v E, S; (with Druids), 1880 v E; 1881 v E, S; 1882 v E, S, Ni; 1883 v Ni (11)
Williams, W. (Northampton T), 1925 v S (1)
Witcomb, D. F. (WBA), 1947 v E, S; (with Sheffield W), 1947 v Ni (3)
Woosnam, A. P. (Leyton Orient), 1959 v S; (with West Ham U), E; 1960 v E, S, Ni; 1961 v S, E, Ni, Ei, Sp, H; 1962 v E, S, Ni, Br; (with Aston Villa), 1963 v Ni, H (17)
Woosnam, G. (Newtown Excelsior), 1879 v S (1)
Worthington, T. (Newtown), 1894 v S (1)
Wynn, G. A. (Wrexham), 1909 v E, S, Ni; (with Manchester C), 1910 v E; 1911 v Ni; 1912 v E, S; 1913 v E, S; 1914 v E, S (11)
Wynn, W. (Chirk), 1903 v Ni (1)

Yorath, T. C. (Leeds U), 1970 v I; 1971 v S, E, Ni; 1972 v Cz, E, S, Ni; 1973 v E, Pol, S; 1974 v Pol, E, S, Ni; 1975 v A, H (2), L (2), S; 1976 v A, E, S, Y (2), E, Ni; (with Coventry C), 1977 v WG, S (2), Cz, E, Ni; 1978 v K (2), S, Cz, WG, Ir, E, S, Ni; 1979 v T, WG, S, E, Ni; (with Tottenham H), 1980 v Ei, T, E, S, Ni, Ic; 1981 v T, Cz; (with Vancouver W), Ei, T, USSR (59)
Young, E. (Wimbledon), 1990 v Cr; (with C Palace), 1991 v D, Bel (2), L, Ei; 1992 v G, L, Ei, A; 1993 v Fa, Cy, Bel, Ei, Bel, Fa; 1994 v RCS, Cy, R, N; (with Wolverhampton W), 1996 v Alb (21)

REPUBLIC OF IRELAND

Aherne, T. (Belfast C), 1946 v P, Sp; (with Luton T), 1950 v Fi, E, Fi, Se, Bel; 1951 v N, Arg, N; 1952 v WG (2), A, Sp; 1953 v F; 1954 v F (16)
Aldridge, J. W. (Oxford U), 1986 v W, U, Ic, Cz; 1987 v Bel, S, Pol; (with Liverpool), S, Bul, Bel, Br, L; 1988 v Bul, Pol, N, E, USSR, Ho; 1989 v Ni, Tun, Sp, F (sub), H, Ma (sub), H; 1990 v WG; (with Real Sociedad), Ni, Ma, Fi (sub), T. E, Eg, Ho, R, I; 1991 v T, E (2), Pol; (with Tranmere R), 1992 v H (sub), T, W (sub), Sw (sub), US (sub), Alb, I, P (sub); 1993 v La, D, Sp, D, Alb, La, Li; 1994 v Li, Ni, CzR, I (sub), M (sub), N; 1995 v La, Ni, P, Lie; 1996 v La, P, Ho, Ru; 1997 v Mac (sub) (69)
Ambrose, P. (Shamrock R), 1955 v N, Ho; 1964 v Pol, N, E (5)
Anderson, J. (Preston NE), 1980 v Cz (sub), US (sub); 1982 v Ch, Br, Tr; (with Newcastle U), 1984 v Chn; 1986 v W, Ic, Cz; 1987 v Bul, Bel, Br, L; 1988 v R (sub), Y (sub); 1989 v Tun (16)
Andrews, P. (Bohemians), 1936 v Ho (1)
Arrigan, T. (Waterford), 1938 v N (1)

Babb, P. A. (Coventry C), 1994 v Ru, Ho, Bol, G, CzR (sub), I, M, N, Ho; (with Liverpool), 1995 v La, Lie, Ni (2), P, Lie, A; 1996 v La, P, Ho, CzR; 1997 v Ic; 1998 v Li (sub), R, Arg (sub), M; 1999 v Cro, Para (sub), Se (sub), Ni; 2000 v CzR (sub), S, M (sub), US, S.Af; (with Sunderland), 2003 v Ru (sub) (35)
Bailham, E. (Shamrock R), 1964 v E (1)
Barber, E. (Shelbourne), 1966 v Sp; (with Birmingham C), 1966 v Bel (2)
Barrett, G. (Arsenal), 2003 v Fi (sub); (with Coventry C), 2004 v Pol (sub), Ng (sub), Jam, Ho; 2005 v Cro (sub) (6)
Barry, P. (Fordsons), 1928 v Bel; 1929 v Bel (2)
Beglin, J. (Liverpool), 1984 v Chn; 1985 v M, D, I, Is, E, N, Sw; 1986 v Sw, USSR, D, W; 1987 v Bel (sub), S, Pol (15)
Bermingham, J. (Bohemians), 1929 v Bel (1)
Bermingham, P. (St James' Gate), 1935 v H (1)
Bonner, P. (Celtic), 1981 v Pol; 1982 v Alg; 1984 v Ma, Is, Chn; 1985 v I, Is, E, N; 1986 v U, Ic; 1987 v Bel (2), S (2), Pol, Bul, Br, L; 1988 v Bul, R, Y, N, E, USSR, Ho; 1989 v Sp, F, H, Sp, Ma, H; 1990 v WG, Ni, Ma, W, Fi, T, E, Eg, Ho, R, I; 1991 v Mor, T, E (2), W, Pol, US; 1992 v H, Pol, T, W, Sw, Alb, I; 1993 v La, D, Sp, W, Ni, D, Alb, La, Li; 1994 v Li, Sp, Ni, Ru, Ho, Bol, CzR, I, M, N, Ho; 1995 v Lie; 1996 v M, Bol (sub) (80)
Braddish, S. (Dundalk), 1978 v T (sub), Pol (2)
Bradshaw, P. (St James' Gate), 1939 v Sw, Pol, H (2), G (5)
Brady, F. (Fordsons), 1926 v I; 1927 v I (2)
Brady, T. R. (QPR), 1964 v A (2), Sp (2), Pol, N (6)
Brady, W. L. (Arsenal), 1975 v USSR, T, Sw, USSR, Sw, WG; 1976 v T, N, Pol; 1977 v E, T, F (2), Sp, Bul; 1978 v Bul, N; 1979 v Ni, E, D, Bul, WG; 1980 v W, Bul, E, Cy; (with Juventus), 1981 v Ho, Bel, F, Cy, Bel; 1982 v Ho, F, Ch, Br, Tr; (with Sampdoria), 1983 v Ho, Sp, Ic, Ma; 1984 v Ic, Ho, Ma, Pol, Is; (with Internazionale), 1985 v USSR, N, D, I, E, N, Sp, Sw; 1986 v Sw, USSR, D, W; (with Ascoli), 1987 v Bel, S (2), Pol; (with West Ham U), Bul, Bel, Br, L; 1988 v L, Bul; 1989 v F, H (sub), H (sub); 1990 v WG, Fi (72)
Branagan, K. G. (Bolton W), 1997 v W (1)
Breen, G. (Birmingham C), 1996 v P (sub), Cro, Ho, US, M, Bol (sub); 1997 v Lie, Mac, Ic; (with Coventry C), v Mac; 1998 v Li (sub), R, CzR, Arg, M; 1999 v Ma, Y, Para, Se, Mac; 2000 v Y, Cro, Ma, Mac, T (2), Gr, S, M, US, S.Af; 2001 v Ho, P, Es, Fi, Cy, And (2); 2002 v Cy, Ir (2), Ru (sub), US, Cam, G, S.Ar, Sp; (with West Ham U), 2003 v Fi, Ru, Sw, S, Ge, Alb, N, Alb, Ge; (with Sunderland), 2004 v Aus, Ru, T, Sw; 2005 v Bul (sub), Cro (62)
Breen, T. (Manchester U), 1937 v Sw, F; (with Shamrock R), 1947 v E, Sp, P (5)
Brennan, F. (Drumcondra), 1965 v Bel (1)
Brennan, S. A. (Manchester U), 1965 v Sp; 1966 v Sp, A, Bel; 1967 v Sp, T, Sp; 1969 v Cz, D, H; 1970 v S, Cz, D, H, Pol (sub), WG; (with Waterford), 1971 v Pol, Se, I (19)
Brown, J. (Coventry C), 1937 v Sw, F (2)
Browne, W. (Bohemians), 1964 v A, Sp, E (3)
Buckley, L. (Shamrock R), 1984 v Pol (sub); (with Waregem), 1985 v M (2)
Burke, F. (Cork Ath), 1952 v WG (1)
Burke, J. (Shamrock R), 1929 v Bel (1)
Burke, J. (Cork), 1934 v Bel (1)
Butler, P. J. (Sunderland), 2000 v CzR (1)
Butler, T. (Sunderland), 2003 v Fi, Sw (sub) (2)
Byrne, A. B. (Southampton), 1970 v D, Pol, WG; 1971 v Pol, Se (2), I (2), A; 1973 v F, USSR (sub), F, N; 1974 v Pol (14)
Byrne, D. (Shelbourne), 1929 v Bel; (with Shamrock R), 1932 v Sp; (with Coleraine), 1934 v Bel (3)
Byrne, J. (Bray Unknowns), 1928 v Bel (1)
Byrne, J. (QPR), 1985 v I, Is (sub), E (sub), Sp (sub); 1987 v S (sub), Bel (sub), Br, L (sub); 1988 v L, Bul (sub), Is, R, Y (sub), Pol (sub); (with Le Havre), 1990 v WG (sub), W, Fi, T (sub), Ma; (with Brighton & HA), 1991 v W; (with Sunderland), 1992 v T, W; (with Millwall), 1993 v W (23)
Byrne, J. (Shelbourne), 2004 v Pol (sub) (1)
Byrne, P. (Dolphin), 1931 v Sp; (with Shelbourne), 1932 v Ho; (with Drumcondra), 1934 v Ho (3)
Byrne, P. (Shamrock R), 1984 v Pol, Chn; 1985 v M; 1986 v D (sub), W (sub), U (sub), Ic (sub), Cz (8)
Byrne, S. (Bohemians), 1931 v Sp (1)

Campbell, A. (Santander), 1985 v I (sub), Is, Sp (3)
Campbell, N. (St Patrick's Ath), 1971 v A (sub); (with Fortuna Cologne), 1972 v Ir, Ec, Ch, P; 1973 v USSR, F (sub); 1975 v WG; 1976 v N; 1977 v Sp, Bul (sub) (11)
Cannon, H. (Bohemians), 1926 v I; 1928 v Bel (2)
Cantwell, N. (West Ham U), 1954 v L; 1956 v Sp, Ho; 1957 v D, WG, E (2); 1958 v D, Pol, A; 1959 v Pol, Cz (2); 1960 v Se, Ch, Se; 1961 v N; (with Manchester U), S (2); 1962 v Cz (2), A; 1963 v Ic (2), S; 1964 v A, Sp, E; 1965 v Pol, Sp; 1966 v Sp (2), A, Bel; 1967 v Sp, T (36)
Carey, B. P. (Manchester U), 1992 v US (sub); 1993 v W; (with Leicester C), 1994 v Ru (3)
Carey, J. J. (Manchester U), 1938 v N, Cz, Pol; 1939 v Sw, Pol, H (2), G; 1946 v P, Sp; 1947 v E, Sp, P; 1948 v P, Sp; 1949 v Sw, Bel, P, Se, Sp; 1950 v Fi, E, Fi, Se; 1951 v N, Arg, N; 1953 v F, A (29)
Carolan, J. (Manchester U), 1960 v Se, Ch (2)
Carr, S. (Tottenham H), 1999 v Se, Ni, Mac; 2000 v Y (sub), Cro, Ma, T (2), S, M, US, S.Af; 2001 v Ho, P, Es, And (sub), P, Es; 2003 v S, Ge, Alb, N, Alb, Ge; 2004 v Aus, Ru, T (sub), Sw, Ca, Br; (with Newcastle U), 2005 v Bul (sub), Cy, Sw, F, Fa, Is, Fa (37)
Carroll, B. (Shelbourne), 1949 v Bel; 1950 v Fi (2)
Carroll, T. R. (Ipswich T), 1968 v Pol; 1969 v Pol, A, D; 1970 v Cz, Pol, WG; 1971 v Se; (with Birmingham C), 1972 v Ir, Ec, Ch, P; 1973 v USSR (2), Pol, F, N (17)
Carsley, L. K. (Derby Co), 1998 v R, Bel (1 + sub), CzR, Arg, M; 1999 v Cro (sub), Ma (sub), Para (sub); (with Blackburn R) Ni, Mac; 2000 v Y (sub), Cro, Ma, T; 2001 v Fi (sub); (with Coventry C), 2002 v Cro, Cy (sub), Ru (sub); (with Everton), S.Ar (sub); 2003 v Fi, Gr, S (sub), Ge, Alb, N (sub), Alb (sub), Ge; 2004 v Ru (29)
Cascarino, A. G. (Gillingham), 1986 v Sw, USSR, D; (with Millwall), 1988 v Pol, N (sub), USSR (sub), Ho (sub); 1989 v Ni, Tun, Sp, F, H, Sp, Ma, H; 1990 v WG (sub), Ni, Ma; (with Aston Villa), W, Fi, T, E, Eg, Ho (sub), R (sub), I (sub); 1991 v Mor (sub),T(sub), E (2 sub), Pol (sub), Ch (sub), US; (with Celtic), 1992 v Pol, T; (with Chelsea), W, Sw, US (sub); 1993 v W, Ni (sub), D (sub), Alb (sub), La (sub); 1994 v Li (sub), Sp (sub), Ni (sub), Ru, Bol (sub), G, CzR, Ho (sub); (with Marseille), 1995 v La (sub), Ni (sub), P (sub), Lie (sub), A (sub); 1996 v A (sub), P (sub), Ho, Ru (sub), P, Cro (sub), Ho; 1997 v Lie (sub), Mac, Ic; (with Nancy), v W, Mac, R (sub), Lie (sub); 1998 v Li (sub), Ic (sub), Li, R, Bel (2); 1999 v Cro (sub), Ma (sub), Y (sub), Para (sub), Se (sub), Ni (sub), Mac (sub); 2000 v Y (sub), Cro, Mac (sub), T (1 + sub) (88)
Chandler, J. (Leeds U), 1980 v Cz (sub), US (2)
Chatton, H. A. (Shelbourne), 1931 v Sp; (with Dumbarton), 1932 v Sp; (with Cork), 1934 v Ho (3)
Clarke, C. R. (Stoke C), 2004 v Ng (sub), Jam (sub) (2)
Clarke, J. (Drogheda U), 1978 v Pol (sub) (1)
Clarke, K. (Drumcondra), 1948 v P, Sp (2)
Clarke, M. (Shamrock R), 1950 v Bel (1)
Clinton, T. J. (Everton), 1951 v N; 1954 v F, L (3)
Coad, P. (Shamrock R), 1947 v E, Sp, P; 1948 v P, Sp; 1949 v Sw, Bel, P, Se; 1951 v N (sub); 1952 v Sp (11)
Coffey, T. (Drumcondra), 1950 v Fi (1)
Colfer, M. D. (Shelbourne), 1950 v Bel; 1951 v N (2)
Colgan, N. (Hibernian), 2002 v D (sub); 2003 v S (sub), N (sub); 2004 v Aus, T, Ca (sub), Pol (sub), Ng (8)
Collins, F. (Jacobs), 1927 v I (1)
Conmy, O. M. (Peterborough U), 1965 v Bel; 1967 v Cz; 1968 v Cz, Pol; 1970 v Cz (5)
Connolly, D. J. (Watford), 1996 v P, Ho, US, M; 1997 v R, Lie; (with Feyenoord), 1998 v Li, Ic, Li, Bel (1 + sub), CzR, M; (with Wolverhampton W), 1999 v Y, Para (sub), Se, Ni (sub), Mac (sub); (with Excelsior), 2000 v T (1 + sub), CzR

(sub), Gr; 2001 v Ho (sub), Fi (sub), Cy, And; (with Feyenoord), And; (with Wimbledon), 2002 v Cro (sub), Cy, Ir, D (sub), US (sub), Ng (sub), Sp (sub); 2003 v S (sub), N, Alb; (with West Ham U), 2004 v Aus (sub), T, Sw (40)
Connolly, H. (Cork), 1937 v G (1)
Connolly, J. (Fordsons), 1926 v I (1)
Conroy, G. A. (Stoke C), 1970 v Cz, D, H, Pol, WG; 1971 v Pol, Se (2), I; 1973 v USSR, F, USSR, N; 1974 v Pol, Br, U, Ch; 1975 v T, Sw, USSR, Sw, WG (sub); 1976 v T (sub), Pol; 1977 v E, T, Pol (27)
Conway, J. P. (Fulham), 1967 v Sp, T, Sp; 1968 v Cz; 1969 v A (sub), H; 1970 v S, Cz, D, H, Pol, WG; 1971 v I, A; 1974 v U, Ch; 1975 v WG (sub); 1976 v N, Pol; (with Manchester C), 1977 v Pol (20)
Corr, P. J. (Everton), 1949 v P, Sp; 1950 v E, Se (4)
Courtney, E. (Cork U), 1946 v P (1)
Coyle, O. C. (Bolton W), 1994 v Ho (sub) (1)
Coyne, T. (Celtic), 1992 v Sw, US, Alb (sub), US (sub), I (sub), P (sub); 1993 v W (sub), La (sub); (with Tranmere R), Ni; (with Motherwell), 1994 v Ru (sub), Ho, Bol, G (sub), CzR (sub), I, M, Ho; 1995 v Lie, Ni (sub), A; 1996 v Ru (sub); 1998 v Bel (sub) (22)
Crowe, G. (Bohemians), 2003 v Gr, N (sub) (2)
Cummins, G. P. (Luton T), 1954 v L (2); 1955 v N (2), WG; 1956 v Y, Sp; 1958 v D, Pol, A; 1959 v Pol, Cz (2); 1960 v Se, Ch, WG, Se; 1961 v S (2) (19)
Cuneen, T. (Limerick), 1951 v N (1)
Cunningham, K. (Wimbledon), 1996 v CzR, P, Cro, Ho (sub), US, Bol; 1997 v Ic (sub), W, R, Lie; 1998 v Li, Ic, Li, Bel (2), CzR; 1999 v Cro, Ma, Y, Para, Se, Ni, Mac; 2000 v Y, Cro, Ma, Mac, T (2), CzR, Gr; 2001 v Cy, And; 2002 v Ir (sub), Ru, D, US (sub), Ng, G (sub), Sp (sub); (with Birmingham C), 2003 v Fi, Ru, Sw, Gr, Ge, Alb (2), Ge; 2004 v Aus, Ru, Ca, Br, CzR, Pol, R, Ng, Ho; 2005 v Bul, Cy, Sw, F, Fa, Cro (sub), P, Is, Chn, Is, Fa (68)
Curtis, D. P. (Shelbourne), 1957 v D, WG; (with Bristol C), 1957 v E (2); 1958 v D, Pol, A; (with Ipswich T), 1959 v Pol; 1960 v Se, Ch, WG, Se; 1961 v N, S; 1962 v A; 1963 v Ic; (with Exeter C), 1964 v A (17)
Cusack, S. (Limerick), 1953 v F (1)

Daish, L. S. (Cambridge U), 1992 v W, Sw (sub); (with Coventry C), 1996 v CzR (sub), Cro, M (5)
Daly, G. A. (Manchester U), 1973 v Pol (sub), N; 1974 v Br (sub), U (sub); 1975 v Sw (sub), WG; 1977 v E, T, F; (with Derby Co), F, Bul; 1978 v Bul, T, D; 1979 v Ni, E, D, Bul; 1980 v Ni, E, Cy, Sw, Arg; (with Coventry C), 1981 v WG 'B', Ho, Bel, Cy, W, Bel, Cz, Pol (sub); 1982 v Alg, Ch, Br, Tr; 1983 v Ho, Sp (sub); 1984 v Is (sub), Ma; (with Birmingham C), 1985 v M (sub), N, Sp, Sw; 1986 v Sw; (with Shrewsbury T), U, Ic (sub), Cz (sub); 1987 v S (sub) (48)
Daly, J. (Shamrock R), 1932 v Ho; 1935 v Sw (2)
Daly, M. (Wolverhampton W), 1978 v T, Pol (2)
Daly, P. (Shamrock R), 1950 v Fi (sub) (1)
Davis, T. L. (Oldham Ath), 1937 v G, H; (with Tranmere R), 1938 v Cz, Pol (4)
Deacy, E. (Aston Villa), 1982 v Alg (sub), Ch, Br, Tr (4)
Delap, R. J. (Derby Co), 1998 v CzR (sub), Arg (sub), M (sub); 2000 v T (2), Gr (sub); (with Southampton), 2002 v US; 2003 v Fi (sub), Gr (sub); 2004 v Ca (sub), CzR (sub) (11)
De Mange, K. J. P. P. (Liverpool), 1987 v Br (sub); (with Hull C), 1989 v Tun (sub) (2)
Dempsey, J. T. (Fulham), 1967 v Sp, Cz; 1968 v Cz, Pol; 1969 v Pol, A, D; (with Chelsea), 1969 v Cz, D; 1970 v H, WG; 1971 v Pol, Se (2), I; 1972 v Ir, Ec, Ch, P (19)
Dennehy, J. (Cork Hibernians), 1972 v Ec (sub), Ch; (with Nottingham F), 1973 v USSR (sub), Pol, F, N; 1974 v Pol (sub); 1975 v T (sub), WG (sub); (with Walsall), 1976 v Pol (sub); 1977 v Pol (sub) (11)
Desmond, P. (Middlesbrough), 1950 v Fi, E, Fi, Se (4)
Devine, J. (Arsenal), 1980 v Cz, Ni; 1981 v WG 'B', Cz; 1982 v Ho, Alg; 1983 v Sp, Ma; (with Norwich C), 1984 v Ic, Ho, Is; 1985 v USSR, N (13)
Doherty, G. M. T. (Luton T), 2000 v Gr (sub); (with Tottenham H), US, S.Af (sub); 2001 v Cy (sub), And (sub+1), P (sub), Es (sub); 2002 v US (sub); 2003 v Fi (sub), Ru (sub), Sw (sub), Gr, S, Ge, Alb (sub+sub), Ge; 2004 v Aus, Ru (sub), T, Ca, CzR, Pol, Ng, Jam; 2005 v Bul; (with Norwich C), Sw (sub), Chn (sub), Is (sub), Fa (sub) (31)
Donnelly, J. (Dundalk), 1935 v H, Sw, G; 1936 v Ho, Sw, H, L; 1937 v G, H; 1938 v N (10)
Donnelly, T. (Drumcondra), 1938 v N; (Shamrock R), 1939 v Sw (2)
Donovan, D. C. (Everton), 1955 v N, Ho, N, WG; 1957 v E (5)
Donovan, T. (Aston Villa), 1980 v Cz; 1981 v WG 'B'(sub) (2)
Douglas, J. (Blackburn R), 2004 v Pol (sub), Ng (sub) (2)
Dowdall, C. (Fordsons), 1928 v Bel; (with Barnsley), 1929 v Bel; (with Cork), 1931 v Sp (3)
Doyle, C. (Shelbourne), 1959 v Cz (1)
Doyle, D. (Shamrock R), 1926 v I (1)
Doyle, L. (Dolphin), 1932 v Sp (1)
Doyle, M. P. (Coventry C), 2004 v Ho (sub) (1)
Duff, D. A. (Blackburn R), 1998 v CzR, M; 1999 v Cro, Ma, Y, Para, Se (sub), Ni, Mac; 2000 v Cro, Ma (sub), T (sub + sub), S (sub); 2001 v P (sub), Es (sub), Cy (sub), And, P (sub), Es; 2002 v Cro, Ho, Ru, D, US, Ng, Cam, G, S.Ar, Sp; 2003 v Fi, Ru, Sw, Ge, Alb, N, Alb; (with Chelsea), 2004 v Aus, Ru, T, Sw, Ca, CzR; 2005 v Bul, Cy, Sw, F, Fa, Cro, P, Is, Chn, Is, Fa (54)
Duffy, B. (Shamrock R), 1950 v Bel (1)
Duggan, H. A. (Leeds U), 1927 v I; 1930 v Bel; 1936 v H, L; (with Newport Co), 1938 v N (5)
Dunne, A. P. (Manchester U), 1962 v A; 1963 v Ic, S; 1964 v A, Sp, Pol, N, E; 1965 v Pol, Sp; 1966 v Sp (2), A, Bel; 1967 v Sp, T, Sp; 1969 v Pol, D, H; 1970 v H; 1971 v Se, I, A; (with Bolton W), 1974 v Br (sub), U, Ch; 1975 v T, Sw, USSR, Sw, WG; 1976 v T (33)
Dunne, J. (Sheffield U), 1930 v Bel; (with Arsenal), 1936 v Sw, H, L; (with Southampton), 1937 v Sw, F; (with Shamrock R), 1938 v N (2), Cz, Pol; 1939 v Sw, Pol, H (2), G (15)
Dunne, J. C. (Fulham), 1971 v A (1)
Dunne, L. (Manchester C), 1935 v Sw, G (2)
Dunne, P. A. J. (Manchester U), 1965 v Sp; 1966 v Sp (2), WG; 1967 v T (5)
Dunne, R. P. (Everton), 2000 v Gr, S (sub), M; 2001 v Ho, P, Es; (with Manchester C), Fi, And, P, Es; 2002 v Cro, Ho, Ru (sub), D (sub); 2003 v Gr, S (sub), N; 2004 v Aus (sub), T (sub), Ca; 2005 v Cro, P (sub), Chn (23)
Dunne, S. (Luton T), 1953 v F, A; 1954 v F, L; 1956 v Sp, Ho; 1957 v D, WG, E; 1958 v D, Pol, A; 1959 v Pol; 1960 v WG, Se (15)
Dunne, T. (St Patrick's Ath), 1956 v Ho; 1957 v D, WG (3)
Dunning, P. (Shelbourne), 1971 v Se, I (2)
Dunphy, E. M. (York C), 1966 v Sp; (with Millwall), 1966 v WG; 1967 v T, Sp, T, Cz; 1968 v Cz, Pol; 1969 v Pol, A, D (2), H; 1970 v D, H, Pol, WG (sub); 1971 v Pol, Se (2), I (2), A (23)
Dwyer, N. M. (West Ham U), 1960 v Se, Ch, WG, Se; (with Swansea T), 1961 v W, N, S (2); 1962 v Cz (2); 1964 v Pol (sub), N, E; 1965 v Pol (14)

Eccles, P. (Shamrock R), 1986 v U (sub) (1)
Egan, R. (Dundalk), 1929 v Bel (1)
Eglington, T. J. (Shamrock R), 1946 v P, Sp; (with Everton), 1947 v E, Sp, P; 1948 v P; 1949 v Sw, P, Se; 1951 v N, Arg; 1952 v WG (2), A, Sp; 1953 v F, A; 1954 v F, L, F; 1955 v N, Ho, WG; 1956 v Sp (24)
Elliott, S. W. (Sunderland), 2005 v Cro, Chn, Fa (3)
Ellis, P. (Bohemians), 1935 v Sw, G; 1936 v Ho, Sw, L; 1937 v G, H (7)
Evans, M. J. (Southampton), 1998 v R (sub) (1)

Fagan, E. (Shamrock R), 1973 v N (sub) (1)
Fagan, F. (Manchester C), 1955 v N; 1960 v Se; (with Derby Co), 1960 v Ch, WG, Se; 1961 v W, N, S (8)
Fagan, J. (Shamrock R), 1926 v I (1)
Fairclough, M. (Dundalk), 1982 v Ch (sub), Tr (sub) (2)
Fallon, S. (Celtic), 1951 v N; 1952 v WG (2), A, Sp; 1953 v F; 1955 v N, WG (8)
Fallon, W. J. (Notts Co), 1935 v H; 1936 v H; 1937 v H, Sw, F; 1939 v Sw, Pol; (with Sheffield W), 1939 v H, G (9)
Farquharson, T. G. (Cardiff C), 1929 v Bel; 1930 v Bel; 1931 v Sp; 1932 v Sp (4)
Farrell, P. (Hibernian), 1937 v Sw, F (2)
Farrell, P. D. (Shamrock R), 1946 v P, Sp; (with Everton), 1947 v Sp, P; 1948 v P, Sp; 1949 v Sw, P (sub), Sp; 1950 v E, Fi, Se; 1951 v Arg, N; 1952 v WG (2), A, Sp; 1953 v F, A; 1954 v F (2); 1955 v N, Ho, WG; 1956 v Y, Sp; 1957 v E (28)
Farrelly, G. (Aston Villa), 1996 v P, US, Bol; (with Everton), 1998 v CzR, M; (with Bolton W), 2000 v US (6)
Feenan, J. J. (Sunderland), 1937 v Sw, F (2)
Finnan, S. (Fulham), 2000 v Gr, S; 2001 v P (sub), Es (sub), Fi, And (sub+sub); 2002 v Cro (sub), Ho (sub), Cy, Ir (2), Ru, US, Ng, Cam (sub), G, S.Ar, Sp; 2003 v Ru, Gr, N (sub); (with Liverpool), 2004 v Aus, T, Sw (sub), R, Ng, Ho; 2005 v Bul, Cy (sub), Sw, F, Fa, Cro, P, Is (36)
Finucane, A. (Limerick), 1967 v T, Cz; 1969 v Cz, D, H; 1970 v S, Cz; 1971 v Se, I (1+sub); 1972 v A (11)
Fitzgerald, F. J. (Waterford), 1955 v Ho; 1956 v Ho (2)
Fitzgerald, P. J. (Leeds U), 1961 v W, N, S; (with Chester), 1962 v Cz (2) (5)

Fitzpatrick, K. (Limerick), 1970 v Cz (1)
Fitzsimons, A. G. (Middlesbrough), 1950 v Fi, Bel; 1952 v WG (2), A, Sp; 1953 v F, A; 1954 v F, L, F; 1955 v Ho, N, WG; 1956 v Y, Sp, Ho; 1957 v D, WG, E (2); 1958 v D, Pol, A; 1959 v Pol; (with Lincoln C), 1959 v Cz (26)
Fleming, C. (Middlesbrough), 1996 v CzR (sub), P, Cro (sub), Ho (sub), US (sub), M, Bol; 1997 v Lie (sub); 1998 v R (sub), M (10)
Flood, J. J. (Shamrock R), 1926 v I; 1929 v Bel; 1930 v Bel; 1931 v Sp; 1932 v Sp (5)
Fogarty, A. (Sunderland), 1960 v WG, Se; 1961 v S; 1962 v Cz (2); 1963 v Ic (2), S (sub); 1964 v A (2); (with Hartlepools U), Sp (11)
Foley, D. J. (Watford), 2000 v S (sub), M (sub), US, S.Af; 2001 v Es (sub), Fi (6)
Foley, J. (Cork), 1934 v Bel, Ho; (with Celtic), 1935 v H, Sw, G; 1937 v G, H (7)
Foley, M. (Shelbourne), 1926 v I (1)
Foley, T. C. (Northampton T), 1964 v Sp, Pol, N; 1965 v Pol, Bel; 1966 v Sp (2), WG; 1967 v Cz (9)
Foy, T. (Shamrock R), 1938 v N; 1939 v H (2)
Fullam, J. (Preston NE), 1961 v N; (with Shamrock R), 1964 v Sp, Pol, N; 1966 v A, Bel; 1968 v Pol; 1969 v Pol, A, D; 1970 v Cz (sub) (11)
Fullam, R. (Shamrock R), 1926 v I; 1927 v I (2)

Gallagher, C. (Celtic), 1967 v T, Cz (2)
Gallagher, M. (Hibernian), 1954 v L (1)
Gallagher, P. (Falkirk), 1932 v Sp (1)
Galvin, A. (Tottenham H), 1983 v Ho, Ma; 1984 v Ho (sub), Is (sub); 1985 v M, USSR, N, D, I, N, Sp; 1986 v U, Ic, Cz; 1987 v Bel (2), S, Bul, L; (with Sheffield W), 1988 v L, Bul, R, Pol, N, E, USSR, Ho; 1989 v Sp; (with Swindon T), 1990 v WG (29)
Gannon, E. (Notts Co), 1949 v Sw; (with Sheffield W), 1949 v Bel, P, Se, Sp; 1950 v Fi; 1951 v N; 1952 v WG, A; 1954 v L, F; 1955 v N; (with Shelbourne), 1955 v N, WG (14)
Gannon, M. (Shelbourne), 1972 v A (1)
Gaskins, P. (Shamrock R), 1934 v Bel, Ho; 1935 v H, Sw, G; (with St James' Gate), 1938 v Cz, Pol (7)
Gavin, J. T. (Norwich C), 1950 v Fi (2); 1953 v F; 1954 v L; (with Tottenham H), 1955 v Ho, WG; (with Norwich C), 1957 v D (7)
Geoghegan, M. (St James' Gate), 1937 v G; 1938 v N (2)
Gibbons, A. (St Patrick's Ath), 1952 v WG; 1954 v L; 1956 v Y, Sp (4)
Gilbert, R. (Shamrock R), 1966 v WG (1)
Giles, C. (Doncaster R), 1951 v N (1)
Giles, M. J. (Manchester U), 1960 v Se, Ch; 1961 v W, N, S (2); 1962 v Cz (2), A; 1963 v Ic, S; (with Leeds U), 1964 v A (2), Sp (2), Pol, N, E; 1965 v Sp; 1966 v Sp (2), A, Bel; 1967 v Sp, T (2); 1969 v A, D, Cz; 1970 v S, Pol, WG; 1971 v I; 1973 v F, USSR; 1974 v Br, U, Ch; 1975 v USSR, T, Sw, USSR, Sw; (with WBA), 1976 v T; 1977 v E, T, F (2), Pol, Bul; (with Shamrock R), 1978 v Bul, T, Pol, N, D; 1979 v Ni, D, Bul, WG (59)
Given, S. J. J. (Blackburn R), 1996 v Ru, CzR, P, Cro, Ho, US, Bol; 1997 v Lie (2); (with Newcastle U), 1998 v Li, Ic, Li, Bel (2), CzR, Arg, M; 1999 v Cro, Ma, Y, Para, Se, Ni; 2000 v Gr, S.Af; 2001 v Fi, Cy, And (2), P, Es; 2002 v Cro, Ho, Cy, Ir (2), Ru, US, Ng, Cam, G, S.Ar, Sp; 2003 v Fi (sub), Ru, Sw, Gr, Ge, Alb, N, Alb, Ge; 2004 v Ru, Sw, Ca, Br, CzR, Pol, R, Ho; 2005 v Bul, Cy, Sw, F, Fa, Cro (sub), P, Is (2), Fa (70)
Givens, D. J. (Manchester U), 1969 v D, H; 1970 v S, Cz, D, H; (with Luton T), 1970 v Pol, WG; 1971 v Se, I (2), A; 1972 v Ir, Ec, P; (with QPR), 1973 v F, USSR, Pol, F, N; 1974 v Pol, Br, U, Ch; 1975 v USSR, T, Sw, USSR, Sw, WG; 1976 v T, N, Pol; 1977 v E, T, F (2), Sp, Bul; 1978 v Bul, N, D; (with Birmingham C), 1979 v Ni (sub), E, D, Bul, WG; 1980 v US (sub), Ni (sub), Sw, Arg; 1981 v Ho, Bel, Cy (sub), W; (with Neuchatel X), 1982 v F (sub) (56)
Glen, W. (Shamrock R), 1927 v I; 1929 v Bel; 1930 v Bel; 1932 v Sp; 1936 v Ho, Sw, H, L (8)
Glynn, D. (Drumcondra), 1952 v WG; 1955 v N (2)
Godwin, T. F. (Shamrock R), 1949 v P, Se, Sp; 1950 v Fi, E; (with Leicester C), 1950 v Fi, Se, Bel; 1951 v N; (with Bournemouth), 1956 v Ho; 1957 v E; 1958 v D, Pol (13)
Golding, J. (Shamrock R), 1928 v Bel; 1930 v Bel (2)
Goodman, J. (Wimbledon), 1997 v W, Mac, R (sub), Lie (sub) (4)
Goodwin, J. (Stockport Co), 2003 v Fi (sub) (1)
Gorman, W. C. (Bury), 1936 v Sw, H, L; 1937 v G, H; 1938 v N, Cz, Pol; 1939 v Sw, Pol; (with Brentford), H; 1947 v E, P (13)
Grace, J. (Drumcondra), 1926 v I (1)
Grealish, A. (Orient), 1976 v N, Pol; 1978 v N, D; 1979 v Ni, E, WG; (with Luton T), 1980 v W, Cz, Bul, US, Ni, E, Cy, Sw, Arg; 1981 v WG 'B', Ho, Bel, F, Cy, W, Bel, Pol; (with Brighton & HA), 1982 v Ho, Alg, Ch, Br, Tr; 1983 v Ho, Sp, Ic, Sp; 1984 v Ic, Ho; (with WBA), Pol, Chn; 1985 v M, USSR, N, D, Sp (sub), Sw; 1986 v USSR, D (45)
Gregg, E. (Bohemians), 1978 v Pol, D (sub); 1979 v E (sub), D, Bul, WG; 1980 v W, Cz (8)
Griffith, R. (Walsall), 1935 v H (1)
Grimes, A. A. (Manchester U), 1978 v T, Pol, N (sub); 1980 v Bul, US, Ni, E, Cy; 1981 v WG 'B' (sub), Cz, Pol; 1982 v Alg; 1983 v Sp (2); (with Coventry C), 1984 v Pol, Is; (with Luton T), 1988 v L, R (18)

Hale, A. (Aston Villa), 1962 v A; (with Doncaster R), 1963 v Ic; 1964 v Sp (2); (with Waterford), 1967 v Sp; 1968 v Pol (sub); 1969 v Pol, A, D; 1970 v S, Cz; 1971 v Pol (sub); 1972 v A (sub); 1974 v Pol (sub) (14)
Hamilton, T. (Shamrock R), 1959 v Cz (2) (2)
Hand, E. K. (Portsmouth), 1969 v Cz (sub); 1970 v Pol, WG; 1971 v Pol, A; 1973 v USSR, F, USSR, Pol, F; 1974 v Pol, Br, U, Ch; 1975 v T, Sw, USSR, Sw, WG; 1976 v T (20)
Harrington, W. (Cork), 1936 v Ho, Sw, H, L; 1938 v Pol (sub) (5)
Harte, I. P. (Leeds U), 1996 v Cro (sub), Ho, M, Bol; 1997 v Lie, Mac, Ic (sub), W, Mac (sub), R, Lie; 1998 v Li, Ic, Li, Bel (2), Arg, M; 1999 v Para; 2000 v Cro (sub), Ma (sub), CzR; 2001 v Ho, P, Es, Fi, Cy, And (2), P, Es; 2002 v Cro, Ho, Cy, Ir (2), Ru, D, US, Ng, Cam, G, S.Ar, Sp; 2003 v Fi, Ru, Sw, S, N; 2004 v Aus (sub), Ru (sub), T, Sw, Ca (sub), CzR, Pol ; (with Levante), 2005 v Is, Fa (58)
Hartnett, J. B. (Middlesbrough), 1949 v Sp; 1954 v L (2)
Haverty, J. (Arsenal), 1956 v Ho; 1957 v D, WG, E (2); 1958 v D, Pol, A; 1959 v Pol; 1960 v Se, Ch; 1961 v W, N, S (2); (with Blackburn R), 1962 v Cz (2); (with Millwall), 1963 v S; 1964 v A, Sp, Pol, N, E; (with Celtic), 1965 v Pol; (with Bristol R), 1965 v Sp; (with Shelbourne), 1966 v Sp (2), WG, A, Bel; 1967 v T, Sp (32)
Hayes, A. W. P. (Southampton), 1979 v D (1)
Hayes, W. E. (Huddersfield T), 1947 v E, P (2)
Hayes, W. J. (Limerick), 1949 v Bel (1)
Healey, R. (Cardiff C), 1977 v Pol; 1980 v E (sub) (2)
Healy, C. (Celtic), 2002 v Ru, D (sub), US; 2003 v Fi (sub), Sw, Gr, S (sub), N (sub), Ge; (with Sunderland), 2004 v Aus (sub), Ru, T, Sw (13)
Heighway, S. D. (Liverpool), 1971 v Pol, Se (2), I, A; 1973 v USSR; 1975 v USSR, T, USSR, WG; 1976 v T, N; 1977 v E, F (2), Sp, Bul; 1978 v Bul, N, D; 1979 v Ni, Bul; 1980 v Bul, US, Ni, E, Cy, Arg; 1981 v Bel, F, Cy, W, Bel; (with Minnesota K), 1982 v Ho (34)
Henderson, B. (Drumcondra), 1948 v P, Sp (2)
Hennessy, J. (Shelbourne), 1965 v Pol, Bel, Sp; 1966 v WG; (with St Patrick's Ath), 1969 v A (5)
Herrick, J. (Cork Hibernians), 1972 v A, Ch (sub); (with Shamrock R), 1973 v F (sub) (3)
Higgins, J. (Birmingham C), 1951 v Arg (1)
Holland, M. R. (Ipswich T), 2000 v Mac (sub), M, US, S.Af; 2001 v P (sub), Fi, Cy (sub), And (2), P (sub), Es; 2002 v Ho, Cy, Ir (2), Ru (sub), D, US (sub), Ng, Cam, G, S.Ar, Sp; 2003 v Fi (sub), Ru, Sw, Gr, S, Ge, Alb, N, Alb, Ge; (with Charlton Ath), 2004 v Aus, Ru, Sw, Ca (sub), Br, CzR, R, Ng, Jam (sub), Ho; 2005 v P, Is (sub+1) (46)
Holmes, J. (Coventry C), 1971 v A (sub); 1973 v F, USSR, Pol, F, N; 1974 v Pol, Br; 1975 v USSR, Sw; 1976 v T, N, Pol; 1977 v E, T, F, Sp; (with Tottenham H), F, Pol, Bul; 1978 v Bul, T, Pol, N, D; 1979 v Ni, E, D, Bul; (with Vancouver W), 1981 v W (30)
Horlacher, A. F. (Bohemians), 1930 v Bel; 1932 v Sp, Ho; 1934 v Ho (sub); 1935 v H;1936 v Ho, Sw (7)
Houghton, R. J. (Oxford U), 1986 v W, U, Ic, Cz; 1987 v Bel (2), S (2), Pol, L; 1988 v L, Bul; (with Liverpool), Is, Y, N, E, USSR, Ho; 1989 v Ni, Tun, Sp, F, H, Sp, Ma, H; 1990 v Ni, Ma, Fi, E, Eg, Ho, R, I; 1991 v Mor, T, E (2), Pol, Ch, US; 1992 v H, Alb, US, I, P; (with Aston Villa), 1993 v D, Sp, Ni, D, Alb, La, Li; 1994 v Li, Sp, Ni, Bol, G (sub), I, M, N, Ho; (with C Palace), 1995 v P, A; 1996 v A, CzR; 1997 v Lie, R, Lie; (with Reading), 1998 v Li, R, Bel (1 + sub) (73)
Howlett, G. (Brighton & HA), 1984 v Chn (sub) (1)
Hoy, M. (Dundalk), 1938 v N; 1939 v Sw, Pol, H (2), G (6)
Hughton, C. (Tottenham H), 1980 v US, E, Sw, Arg; 1981 v Ho, Bel, F, Cy, W, Bel, Pol; 1982 v F; 1983 v Ho, Sp, Ma, Sp; 1984 v Ic, Ho, Ma; 1985 v M (sub), USSR, N, I, Is, E, Sp; 1986 v Sw, USSR, U, Ic; 1987 v Bel, Bul; 1988 v Is, Y, Pol, N, E, USSR, Ho; 1989 v Ni, F, H, Sp, Ma, H; 1990 v W (sub), USSR (sub), Fi, T (sub), Ma; 1991 v T; (with West Ham U), Ch; 1992 v T (53)

Hurley, C. J. (Millwall), 1957 v E; (with Sunderland), 1958 v D, Pol, A; 1959 v Cz (2); 1960 v Se, Ch, WG, Se; 1961 v W, N, S (2); 1962 v Cz (2), A; 1963 v Ic (2), S; 1964 v A (2), Sp (2), Pol, N; 1965 v Sp; 1966 v WG, A, Bel; 1967 v T, Sp, T, Cz; 1968 v Cz, Pol; 1969 v Pol, D, Cz, (with Bolton W), H (40)
Hutchinson, F. (Drumcondra), 1935 v Sw, G (2)

Irwin, D. J. (Manchester U), 1991 v Mor, T, W, E, Pol, US; 1992 v H, Pol, W, US, Alb, US (sub), I; 1993 v La, D, Sp, Ni, D, Alb, La, Li; 1994 v Li, Sp, Ni, Bol, G, I, M; 1995 v La, Lie, Ni, E, Ni, P, Lie, A; 1996 v A, P, Ho, CzR; 1997 v Lie, Mac, Ic, Mac, R; 1998 v Li, Bel, Arg (sub); 1999 v Cro, Y, Para, Mac; 2000 v Y, Mac, T (2) (56)

Jordan, D. (Wolverhampton W), 1937 v Sw, F (2)
Jordan, W. (Bohemians), 1934 v Ho; 1938 v N (2)

Kavanagh, G. A. (Stoke C), 1998 v CzR (sub); 1999 v Se (sub), Ni (sub); (with Cardiff C), 2004 v Ca, Br; 2005 v Bul (sub), Cy, Sw (sub), Cro, P (sub); (with Wigan Ath), Chn, Is (sub) (12)
Kavanagh, P. J. (Celtic), 1931 v Sp; 1932 v Sp (2)
Keane, R. D. (Wolverhampton W), 1998 v CzR (sub), Arg, M; 1999 v Cro, Ma, Para, Se (sub), Ni, Mac; (with Coventry C), 2000 v Y, Ma, Mac, T, CzR, Gr, S, M, S.Af (sub); (with Internazionale), 2001 v Ho, P, Es, Fi, Cy, And, P; (with Leeds U), 2002 v Cro, Ho, Ir (2), Ru, D, US, Ng, Cam, G, S.Ar, Sp; 2003 v Fi; (with Tottenham H), Ru, Sw, Alb, N, Alb, Ge; 2004 v Aus, Sw, Ca, Br, CzR, R, Ng, Ho; 2005 v Cy, Sw, F, Fa, Cro, P, Is, Chn, Is (61)
Keane, R. M. (Nottingham F), 1991 v Ch; 1992 v H, Pol, W, Sw, Alb, US; 1993 v La, D, Sp, W, Ni, D, Alb, La, Li; (with Manchester U), 1994 v Li, Sp, Ni, Bol, G, CzR (sub), I, M, N, Ho; 1995 v Ni (2); 1996 v A, Ru; 1997 v Ic, W, Mac, R, Lie; 1998 v Li, Ic, Li; 1999 v Cro, Ma, Y, Para; 2000 v Y, T (2), CzR; 2001 v Ho, P, Es, Cy, And, P; 2002 v Cro, Ho, Cy, Ir, Ru, Ng; 2004 v R; 2005 v Bul, Sw, F, Fa, Is, Chn (sub), Fa (66)
Keane, T. R. (Swansea T), 1949 v Sw, P, Se, Sp (4)
Kearin, M. (Shamrock R), 1972 v A (1)
Kearns, F. T. (West Ham U), 1954 v L (1)
Kearns, M. (Oxford U), 1971 v Pol (sub); (with Walsall), 1974 v Pol (sub), U, Ch; 1976 v N, Pol; 1977 v E, T, F (2), Sp, Bul; 1978 v N, D; 1979 v Ni, E; (with Wolverhampton W), 1980 v US, Ni (18)
Kelly, A. T. (Sheffield U), 1993 v W (sub); 1994 v Ru (sub), G; 1995 v La, Ni, E, Ni, P, Lie, A; 1996 v A, La, P, Ho; 1997 v Mac, Ic, Mac, R; 1998 v R, Arg (sub); 1999 v Para (sub), Mac; (with Blackburn R), 2000 v Y, Cro, Ma, Mac, T, CzR, S, US; 2001 v Ho, P, Es; 2002 v Cro (sub) (34)
Kelly, D. T. (Walsall), 1988 v Is, R, Y; (with West Ham U), 1989 v Tun (sub); (with Leicester C), 1990 v USSR, Ma; 1991 v Mor, W (sub), Ch, US; 1992 v H; (with Newcastle U), I (sub), P; 1993 v Sp (sub), Ni; (with Wolverhampton W), 1994 v Ru, N (sub); 1995 v E, Ni; (with Sunderland), 1996 v La (sub); 1997 v Ic, W (sub), Mac (sub); (with Tranmere R), 1998 v Li (sub), R (sub), Bel (sub) (26)
Kelly, G. (Leeds U), 1994 v Ru, Ho, Bol (sub), G (sub), CzR, N, Ho; 1995 v La, Lie, Ni (2), P, Lie, A; 1996 v A, La, P, Ho; 1997 v W (sub), R, Lie; 1998 v Ic, Li, Bel (2), CzR, Arg, M; 2000 v Cro, Mac, CzR; 2001 v Ho (sub), Fi, Cy, And (2), P, Es; 2002 v Cro, Ho, Ir (sub+sub), Ru (sub), D, US (sub), Ng (sub), Cam, G, S.Ar, Sp; 2003 v Fi, Sw (52)
Kelly, J. (Derry C), 1932 v Ho; 1934 v Bel; 1936 v Sw, L (4)
Kelly, J. A. (Drumcondra), 1957 v WG, E; (with Preston NE), 1962 v A; 1963 v Ic (2), S; 1964 v A (2), Sp (2), Pol; 1965 v Bel; 1966 v A, Bel; 1967 v Sp (2), T, Cz; 1968 v Pol, Cz; 1969 v Pol, A, D, Cz, D, H; 1970 v S, D, H, Pol, WG; 1971 v Pol, Se (2), I (2), A; 1972 v Ir, Ec, Ch, P; 1973 v USSR, F, USSR, Pol, F, N (47)
Kelly, J. P. V. (Wolverhampton W), 1961 v W, N, S; 1962 v Cz (2) (5)
Kelly, M. J. (Portsmouth), 1988 v Y, Pol (sub); 1989 v Tun; 1991 v Mor (4)
Kelly, N. (Nottingham F), 1954 v L (1)
Kendrick, J. (Everton), 1927 v I; (with Dolphin) 1934 v Bel, Ho; 1936 v Ho (4)
Kenna, J. J. (Blackburn R), 1995 v P (sub), Lie (sub), A (sub); 1996 v La, P, Ho, Ru (sub), CzR, P, Cro, Ho, US; 1997 v Lie, Mac, Ic, R (sub), Lie; 1998 v Li, Ic, R, Bel (1 + sub), CzR, Arg; 1999 v Cro (sub), Ma; 2000 v T (sub) (27)
Kennedy, M. F. (Portsmouth), 1986 v Ic, Cz (sub) (2)
Kennedy, M. J. (Liverpool), 1996 v A, La (sub), P, Ru, CzR, Cro, Ho (sub), US (sub), M, Bol (sub); 1997 v R, Lie; 1998 v Li, Ic (sub), R, Bel (2), (with Wimbledon), M (sub); 1999 v Ma (sub), Se, Ni, Mac; (with Manchester C), 2000 v Y, Ma, Mac, CzR, S, M, US (sub), S.Af (sub); 2001 v And; (with Wolverhampton W), 2002 v Cro, Cy, Ru (sub) (34)
Kennedy, W. (St James' Gate), 1932 v Ho; 1934 v Bel, Ho (3)
Kenny, P. (Sheffield U), 2004 v CzR (sub), Jam; 2005 v Bul (sub), Cro, Chn (5)
Keogh, J. (Shamrock R), 1966 v WG (sub) (1)
Keogh, S. (Shamrock R), 1959 v Pol (1)
Kernaghan, A. N. (Middlesbrough), 1993 v La, D (2), Alb, La, Li; 1994 v Li; (with Manchester C), Sp, Ni, Bol (sub), CzR; 1995 v Lie, E; 1996 v A, P (sub), Ho (sub), Ru, P, Cro (sub), Ho, US, Bol (22)
Kiely, D. L. (Charlton Ath), 2000 v T (sub + 1), Gr (sub), M; 2002 v Ru (sub), D; 2003 v Fi, S (8)
Kiernan, F. W. (Shamrock R), 1951 v Arg, N; (with Southampton), 1952 v WG (2), A (5)
Kilbane, K. D. (WBA), 1998 v Ic, CzR (sub), Arg; 1999 v Se (sub), Mac (sub); 2000 v Y, Cro (sub), Ma, T (2); (with Sunderland), CzR, Gr, S, M (sub), US, S.Af (sub); 2001 v Ho, P, Es, Fi, Cy, And (2), P, Es; 2002 v Cro (sub), Ho, Cy, Ir (2), Ru, US, Ng, Cam, G, S.Ar, Sp; 2003 v Fi (sub), Ru, Sw, S, Ge, Alb, N, Alb, Ge; 2004 v Aus (sub); (with Everton), Ru, T, Sw, Ca (sub), Br, CzR; 2005 v Bul, Cy, Sw, F, Fa, Cro, P, Is, Chn, Is, Fa (64)
Kinnear, J. P. (Tottenham H), 1967 v T; 1968 v Cz, Pol; 1969 v A; 1970 v Cz, D, H, Pol; 1971 v Se (sub), I; 1972 v Ir, Ec, Ch, P; 1973 v USSR, F; 1974 v Pol, Br, U, Ch; 1975 v USSR, T, Sw, USSR, WG; (with Brighton & HA), 1976 v T (sub) (26)
Kinsella, J. (Shelbourne), 1928 v Bel (1)
Kinsella, M. A. (Charlton Ath), 1998 v CzR, Arg; 1999 v Cro, Ma, Y, Para, Se, Ni, Mac; 2000 v Y, Cro, Ma, Mac, T, CzR, Gr; 2001 v Ho, P, Es, Fi, Cy, And, P, Es; 2002 v Ir, D, US, Ng (sub), Cam, G, S.Ar, Sp; 2003 v Fi; (with Aston Villa), Ru, Sw, S, Ge, Alb, N, Alb, Ge (sub); 2004 v Aus, T, Sw (sub); (with WBA), CzR (sub), Pol, Ng, Jam (48)
Kinsella, O. (Shamrock R), 1932 v Ho; 1938 v N (2)
Kirkland, A. (Shamrock R), 1927 v I (1)

Lacey, W. (Shelbourne), 1927 v I; 1928 v Bel; 1930 v Bel (3)
Langan, D. (Derby Co), 1978 v T, N; 1980 v Sw, Arg; (with Birmingham C), 1981 v WG 'B', Ho, Bel, F, Cy, W, Bel, Cz, Pol; 1982 v Ho, F; (with Oxford U), 1985 v N, Sp, Sw; 1986 v W, U; 1987 v Bel, S, Pol, Br (sub), L (sub); 1988 v L (26)
Lawler, J. F. (Fulham), 1953 v A; 1954 v L, F; 1955 v N, H, N, WG; 1956 v Y (8)
Lawlor, J. C. (Drumcondra), 1949 v Bel; (with Doncaster R), 1951 v N, Arg (3)
Lawlor, M. (Shamrock R), 1971 v Pol, Se (2), I (sub); 1973 v Pol (5)
Lawrenson, M. (Preston NE), 1977 v Pol; (with Brighton), 1978 v Bul, Pol, N (sub); 1979 v Ni, E; 1980 v E, Cy, Sw; 1981 v Ho, Bel, F, Cy, Pol; (with Liverpool), 1982 v Ho, F; 1983 v Ho, Sp, Ic, Ma, Sp; 1984 v Ic, Ho, Ma, Is; 1985 v USSR, N, D, I, E, N; 1986 v Sw, USSR, D; 1987 v Bel, S; 1988 v Bul, Is (38)
Lee, A. D. (Rotherham U), 2003 v N (sub), Ge (sub); (with Cardiff C), 2004 v CzR (sub), Pol, Ng, Jam, Ho (sub); 2005 v Cy (sub) (8)
Leech, M. (Shamrock R), 1969 v Cz, D, H; 1972 v A, Ir, Ec, P; 1973 v USSR (sub) (8)
Lennon, C. (St James' Gate), 1935 v H, Sw, G (3)
Lennox, G. (Dolphin), 1931 v Sp; 1932 v Sp (2)
Lowry, D. (St Patrick's Ath), 1962 v A (sub) (1)
Lunn, R. (Dundalk), 1939 v Sw, Pol (2)
Lynch, J. (Cork Bohemians), 1934 v Bel (1)

McAlinden, J. (Portsmouth), 1946 v P, Sp (2)
McAteer, J. W. (Bolton W), 1994 v Ru, Ho (sub), Bol (sub), G, CzR (sub), I (sub), M (sub), N, Ho (sub); 1995 v La, Lie, Ni (2 sub), Lie; (with Liverpool), 1996 v La, P, Ho (sub), Ru; 1997 v Mac, Ic, W, Mac; 1998 v Ic (sub), Li, R; 1999 v Cro, Ma, Y; (with Blackburn R), Para, Se; 2000 v CzR (sub), S, M, US (sub), S.Af; 2001 v Ho, P, Es, Fi (sub), Cy; 2002 v Cro (sub), Ho; (with Sunderland), Ir (2), Ru (sub), D, Ng, Cam, S.Ar (sub); 2003 v Fi, Ru; 2004 v Br (sub) (52)
McCann, J. (Shamrock R), 1957 v WG (1)
McCarthy, J. (Bohemians), 1926 v I; 1928 v Bel; 1930 v Bel (3)
McCarthy, M. (Shamrock R), 1932 v Ho (1)
McCarthy, M. (Manchester C), 1984 v Pol, Chn; 1985 v M, D, I, Is, E, Sp, Sw; 1986 v Sw, USSR, W (sub), U, Ic, Cz; 1987 v S (2), Pol, Bul, Bel (with Celtic), Br, L; 1988 v Bul, Is, R, Y, N, E, USSR, Ho; 1989 v Ni, Tun, Sp, F, H, Sp; (with Lyon), 1990 v WG, Ni (with Millwall), W, USSR, Fi, T, E, Eg, Ho, R, I; 1991 v Mor, T, E, US; 1992 v H, T, Alb (sub), US, I, P (57)

McConville, T. (Dundalk), 1972 v A; (with Waterford), 1973 v USSR, F, USSR, Pol, F (6)
McDonagh, Jacko (Shamrock R), 1984 v Pol (sub), Ma (sub); 1985 v M (sub) (3)
McDonagh, J. (Everton), 1981 v WG 'B', W, Bel, Cz; (with Bolton W), 1982 v Ho, F, Ch, Br; 1983 v Ho, Sp, Ic, Ma, Sp; (with Notts Co), 1984 v Ic, Ho, Pol; 1985 v M, USSR, N, D, Sp, Sw; 1986 v Sw, USSR; (with Wichita Wings) D (25)
McEvoy, M. A. (Blackburn R), 1961 v S (2); 1963 v S; 1964 v A, Sp (2), Pol, N, E; 1965 v Pol, Bel, Sp; 1966 v Sp (2); 1967 v Sp, T, Cz (17)
McGeady, A. (Celtic), 2004 v Jam (sub); 2005 v Cro (sub), P (sub) (3)
McGee, P. (QPR), 1978 v T, N (sub), D (sub); 1979 v Ni, E, D (sub), Bul (sub); 1980 v Cz, Bul; (with Preston NE), US, Ni, Cy, Sw, Arg; 1981 v Bel (sub) (15)
McGoldrick, E. J. (C Palace), 1992 v Sw, US, I, P (sub); 1993 v D, W, Ni (sub), D; (with Arsenal), 1994 v Ni, Ru, Ho, CzR; 1995 v La (sub), Lie, E (15)
McGowan, D. (West Ham U), 1949 v P, Se, Sp (3)
McGowan, J. (Cork U), 1947 v Sp (1)
McGrath, M. (Blackburn R), 1958 v A; 1959 v Pol, Cz (2); 1960 v Se, WG, Se; 1961 v W; 1962 v Cz (2); 1963 v S; 1964 v A (2), E; 1965 v Pol, Bel, Sp; 1966 v Sp; (with Bradford), 1966 v WG, A, Bel; 1967 v T (22)
McGrath, P. (Manchester U), 1985 v I (sub), Is, E, N (sub), Sw (sub); 1986 v Sw (sub), D, W, Ic, Cz; 1987 v Bel (2), S (2), Pol, Bul, Br, L; 1988 v L, Bul, Y, Pol, N, E, Ho; 1989 v Ni, F, H, Sp, Ma, H; (with Aston Villa), 1990 v WG, Ma, USSR, Fi, T, E, Eg, Ho, R, I; 1991 v E (2), W, Pol, Ch (sub), US; 1992 v Pol, T, Sw, US, Alb, US, I, P; 1993 v La, Sp, Ni, D, La, Li; 1994 v Sp, Ni, G, CzR, I, M, N, Ho; 1995 v La, Ni, E, Ni, P, Lie, A; 1996 v A, La, P, Ho, Ru, CzR; (with Derby Co), 1997 v W (83)
McGuire, W. (Bohemians), 1936 v Ho (1)
McKenzie, G. (Southend U), 1938 v N (2), Cz, Pol; 1939 v Sw, Pol, H (2), G (9)
Mackey, G. (Shamrock R), 1957 v D, WG, E (3)
McLoughlin, A. F. (Swindon T), 1990 v Ma, E (sub), Eg (sub); 1991 v Mor (sub), E (sub); (with Southampton), W, Ch (sub); 1992 v H (sub), W (sub); (with Portsmouth), US (1 + sub), I (sub), P; 1993 v W; 1994 v Ni (sub), Ru, Ho (sub); 1995 v Lie (sub); 1996 v P, Cro, Ho, US, M, Bol (sub); 1997 v Lie, Mac, Ic, W, Mac; 1998 v Li (sub), Ic, Li, R, Bel, CzR (sub); 1999 v Y, Para (sub), Se, Ni (sub); 2000 v Cro, Ma (sub), Mac (42)
McLoughlin, F. (Fordsons), 1930 v Bel; (with Cork), 1932 v Sp (2)
McMillan, W. (Belfast Celtic), 1946 v P, Sp (2)
McNally, J. B. (Luton T), 1959 v Cz; 1961 v S; 1963 v Ic (3)
McPhail, S. (Leeds U), 2000 v S, US, S.Af; 2002 v Cro (sub), Cy (sub); 2003 v Fi (sub), Gr; 2004 v T (sub), Ca (sub), Ng (10)
Macken, A. (Derby Co), 1977 v Sp (1)
Macken J. P. (Manchester C), 2005 v Bul (sub) (1)
Madden, O. (Cork), 1936 v H (1)
Maguire, J. (Shamrock R), 1929 v Bel (1)
Mahon, A. J. (Tranmere R), 2000 v Gr (sub), S.Af (2)
Malone, G. (Shelbourne), 1949 v Bel (1)
Mancini, T. J. (QPR), 1974 v Pol, Br, U, Ch; (with Arsenal), 1975 v USSR (5)
Martin, C. (Bo'ness), 1927 v I (1)
Martin, C. J. (Glentoran), 1946 v P (sub), Sp; 1947 v E; (with Leeds U), 1947 v Sp; 1948 v P, Sp; (with Aston Villa), 1949 v Sw, Bel, P, Se, Sp; 1950 v Fi, E, Fi, Se, Bel; 1951 v Arg; 1952 v WG, A, Sp; 1954 v F (2), L; 1955 v N, Ho, N, WG; 1956 v Y, Sp, Ho (30)
Martin, M. P. (Bohemians), 1972 v A, Ir, Ec, Ch, P; 1973 v USSR; (with Manchester U), 1973 v USSR, Pol, F, N; 1974 v Pol, Br, U, Ch; 1975 v USSR, T, Sw, USSR, Sw, WG; (with WBA), 1976 v T, N, Pol; 1977 v E, T, F (2), Sp, Pol, Bul; (with Newcastle U), 1979 v D, Bul, WG; 1980 v W, Cz, Bul, US, Ni; 1981 v WG 'B', F, Bel, Cz; 1982 v Ho, F, Alg, Ch, Br, Tr; 1983 v Ho, Sp, Ma, Sp (52)
Maybury, A. (Leeds U), 1998 v CzR; 1999 v Ni; (with Hearts), 2004 v CzR, Pol (sub), R, Ng, Jam, Ho; 2005 v Cy (sub); (with Leicester C), Chn (10)
Meagan, M. K. (Everton), 1961 v S; 1962 v A; 1963 v Ic; 1964 v Sp; (with Huddersfield T), 1965 v Bel; 1966 v Sp (2), A, Bel; 1967 v Sp, T, Sp, T, Cz; 1968 v Cz, Pol; (with Drogheda), 1970 v S (17)
Meehan, P. (Drumcondra), 1934 v Ho (1)
Miller, L. W. P. (Celtic), 2004 v CzR (sub), Pol, R, Ng; (with Manchester U), 2005 v Bul, Fa (sub), Cro, P (sub), Chn (sub) (9)
Milligan, M. J. (Oldham Ath), 1992 v US (sub) (1)
Monahan, P. (Sligo R), 1935 v Sw, G (2)
Mooney, J. (Shamrock R), 1965 v Pol, Bel (2)
Moore, A. (Middlesbrough), 1996 v CzR, Cro (sub), Ho, M, Bol; 1997 v Lie (sub), Mac (sub), Ic (sub) (8)
Moore, P. (Shamrock R), 1931 v Sp; 1932 v Ho; (with Aberdeen), 1934 v Bel, Ho; 1935 v H, G; (with Shamrock R), 1936 v Ho; 1937 v G, H (9)
Moran, K. (Manchester U), 1980 v Sw, Arg; 1981 v WG 'B', Bel, F, Cy, W (sub), Bel, Cz, Pol; 1982 v F, Alg; 1983 v Ic; 1984 v Ic, Ho, Ma, Is; 1985 v M; 1986 v D, Ic, Cz; 1987 v Bel (2), S (2), Pol, Bul, Br, L; 1988 v L, Bul, Is, R, Y, Pol, N, E, USSR, Ho; (with Sporting Gijon), 1989 v Ni, Sp, H, Sp, Ma, H; 1990 v Ni, Ma; (with Blackburn R), W, USSR (sub), Ma, E, Eg, Ho, R, I; 1991 v T (sub), W, E, Pol, Ch, US; 1992 v Pol, US; 1993 v D, Sp, Ni, Alb; 1994 v Li, Sp, Ho, Bol (71)
Moroney, T. (West Ham U), 1948 v Sp; 1949 v P, Se, Sp; 1950 v Fi, E, Fi, Bel; 1951 v N (2); 1952 v WG; (with Evergreen U), 1954 v F (12)
Morris, C. B. (Celtic), 1988 v Is, R, Y, Pol, N, E, USSR, Ho; 1989 v Ni, Tun, Sp, F, H (1+sub); 1990 v WG, Ni, Ma (sub), W, USSR, Fi (sub), T, E, Eg, Ho, R, I; 1991 v E; 1992 v H (sub), Pol, W, Sw, US (2), P; (with Middlesbrough), 1993 v W (35)
Morrison, C. H. (C Palace), 2002 v Cro (sub), Cy (sub), Ir (sub), Ru (sub), D, US (sub), Ng (sub); (with Birmingham C), 2003 v Ru (sub), Sw (sub), S; 2004 v Aus (sub), Ru, T (sub), Sw (sub), Ca (sub), Br, CzR, Pol, R, Jam, Ho; 2005 v Bul, Cy, Sw, F, P, Is, Chn (sub), Is, Fa (30)
Moulson, C. (Lincoln C), 1936 v H, L; (with Notts Co), 1937 v H, Sw, F (5)
Moulson, G. B. (Lincoln C), 1948 v P, Sp; 1949 v Sw (3)
Mucklan, C. (Drogheda U), 1978 v Pol (1)
Muldoon, T. (Aston Villa), 1927 v I (1)
Mulligan, P. M. (Shamrock R), 1969 v Cz, D, H; 1970 v S, Cz, D; (with Chelsea), 1970 v H, Pol, WG; 1971 v Pol, Se, I; 1972 v A, Ir, Ec, Ch, P; (with C Palace), 1973 v F, USSR, Pol, F, N; 1974 v Pol, Br, U, Ch; 1975 v USSR, T, Sw, USSR, Sw; (with WBA), 1976 v T, Pol; 1977 v E, T, F (2), Pol, Bul; 1978 v Bul, N, D; 1979 v E, D, Bul (sub), WG; (with Shamrock R), 1980 v W, Cz, Bul, US (sub) (50)
Munroe, L. (Shamrock R), 1954 v L (1)
Murphy, A. (Clyde), 1956 v Y (1)
Murphy, B. (Bohemians), 1986 v U (1)
Murphy, J. (C Palace), 1980 v W, US, Cy (3)
Murphy, J. (WBA), 2004 v T (sub) (1)
Murray, T. (Dundalk), 1950 v Bel (1)

Newman, W. (Shelbourne), 1969 v D (1)
Nolan, R. (Shamrock R), 1957 v D, WG, E; 1958 v Pol; 1960 v Ch, WG, Se; 1962 v Cz (2); 1963 v Ic (10)

O'Brien, A. J. (Newcastle U), 2001 v Es (sub); 2002 v Cro (sub), Ho (sub), Ru, US; 2003 v S (sub); 2004 v Aus (sub), T, Br, Pol (sub), R, Jam, Ho; 2005 v Cy, Sw, F, Fa, P, Is, Chn (sub), Is (21)
O'Brien, F. (Philadelphia F), 1980 v Cz, E, Cy (sub) (3)
O'Brien, L. (Shamrock R), 1986 v U; (with Manchester U), 1987 v Br; 1988 v Is (sub), R (sub), Y (sub), Pol (sub); 1989 v Tun; (with Newcastle U), Sp (sub); 1992 v Sw (sub); 1993 v W; (with Tranmere R), 1994 v Ru; 1996 v Cro, Ho, US, Bol; 1997 v Mac (sub) (16)
O'Brien, M. T. (Derby Co), 1927 v I; (with Walsall), 1929 v Bel; (with Norwich C), 1930 v Bel; (with Watford), 1932 v Ho (4)
O'Brien, R. (Notts Co), 1976 v N, Pol; 1977 v Sp, Pol; 1980 v Arg (sub) (5)
O'Byrne, L. B. (Shamrock R), 1949 v Bel (1)
O'Callaghan, B. R. (Stoke C), 1979 v WG (sub); 1980 v W, US; 1981 v W; 1982 v Br, Tr (6)
O'Callaghan, K. (Ipswich T), 1981 v WG 'B', Cz, Pol; 1982 v Alg, Ch, Br, Tr (sub); 1983 v Sp, Ic (sub), Ma (sub), Sp (sub); 1984 v Ic, Ho, Ma; 1985 v M (sub), N (sub), D (sub), (with Portsmouth) E (sub); 1986 v Sw (sub), USSR (sub); 1987 v Br (21)
O'Connell, A. (Dundalk), 1967 v Sp; (with Bohemians), 1971 v Pol (sub) (2)
O'Connor, T. (Shamrock R), 1950 v Fi, E, Fi, Se (4)
O'Connor, T. (Fulham), 1968 v Cz; (with Dundalk), 1972 v A, Ir (sub), Ec (sub), Ch; (with Bohemians), 1973 v F (sub), Pol (sub) (7)
O'Driscoll, J. F. (Swansea T), 1949 v Sw, Bel, Se (3)
O'Driscoll, S. (Fulham), 1982 v Ch, Br, Tr (sub) (3)
O'Farrell, F. (West Ham U), 1952 v A; 1953 v A; 1954 v F; 1955 v Ho, N; 1956 v Y, Ho; (with Preston NE), 1958 v D; 1959 v Cz (9)

O'Flanagan, K. P. (Bohemians), 1938 v N, Cz, Pol; 1939 v Pol, H (2), G; (with Arsenal), 1947 v E, Sp, P (10)
O'Flanagan, M. (Bohemians), 1947 v E (1)
O'Hanlon, K. G. (Rotherham U), 1988 v Is (1)
O'Kane, P. (Bohemians), 1935 v H, Sw, G (3)
O'Keefe, E. (Everton), 1981 v W; (with Port Vale), 1984 v Chn; 1985 v M, USSR (sub), E (5)
O'Keefe, T. (Cork), 1934 v Bel; (with Waterford), 1938 v Cz, Pol (3)
O'Leary, D. (Arsenal), 1977 v E, F (2), Sp, Bul; 1978 v Bul, N, D; 1979 v E, Bul, WG; 1980 v W, Bul, Ni, E, Cy; 1981 v WG 'B',Ho, Cz, Pol; 1982 v Ho, F; 1983 v Ho, Ic, Sp; 1984 v Pol, Is, Chn; 1985 v USSR, N, D, Is, E (sub), N, Sp, Sw; 1986 v Sw, USSR, D, W; 1989 v Sp, Ma, H; 1990 v WG, Ni (sub), Ma, W (sub), USSR, Fi, T, Ma, R (sub); 1991 v Mor, T, E (2), Pol, Ch; 1992 v H, Pol, T, W, Sw, US, Alb, I, P; 1993 v W (68)
O'Leary, P. (Shamrock R), 1980 v Bul, US, Ni, E (sub), Cz, Arg; 1981 v Ho (7)
O'Mahoney, M. T. (Bristol R), 1938 v Cz, Pol; 1939 v Sw, Pol, H, G (6)
O'Neill, F. S. (Shamrock R), 1962 v Cz (2); 1965 v Pol, Bel, Sp; 1966 v Sp (2), WG, A; 1967 v Sp, T, Sp, T; 1969 v Pol, A, D, Cz, D (sub), H (sub); 1972 v A (20)
O'Neill, J. (Everton), 1952 v Sp; 1953 v F, A; 1954 v F, L, F; 1955 v N, Ho, N, WG; 1956 v Y, Sp; 1957 v D; 1958 v A; 1959 v Pol, Cz (2) (17)
O'Neill, J. (Preston NE), 1961 v W (1)
O'Neill, K. P. (Norwich C), 1996 v P (sub), Cro, Ho (sub), US (sub), M, Bol; 1997 v Lie, Mac (1 + sub); 1999 v Cro, Y (sub); (with Middlesbrough), Ni (sub); 2000 v Mac (sub) (13)
O'Neill, W. (Dundalk), 1936 v Ho, Sw, H, L; 1937 v G, H, Sw, F; 1938 v N; 1939 v H, G (11)
O'Regan, K. (Brighton & HA), 1984 v Ma, Pol; 1985 v M, Sp (sub) (4)
O'Reilly, J. (Brideville), 1932 v Ho; (with Aberdeen), 1934 v Bel, Ho; (with Brideville), 1936 v Ho; Sw, H, L; (with St James' Gate), 1937 v G, H, Sw, F; 1938 v N (2), Cz, Pol; 1939 v Sw, Pol, H (2), G (20)
O'Reilly, J. (Cork U), 1946 v P, Sp (2)
O'Shea, J. F. (Manchester U), 2002 v Cro (sub); 2003 v Gr, S, Ge, Alb (2), Ge; 2004 v Aus, Ru, Sw, Ca, Br, Pol, Jam; 2005 v Bul, Cy, F, Fa, Cro, P, Is, Chn, Is, Fa (24)

Peyton, G. (Fulham), 1977 v Sp (sub); 1978 v Bul, T, Pol; 1979 v D, Bul, WG; 1980 v W, Cz, Bul, E, Cy, Sw, Arg; 1981 v Ho, Bel, F, Cy; 1982 v Tr; 1985 v M (sub); 1986 v W, Cz; (with Bournemouth), 1988 v L, Pol; 1989 v Ni, Tun; 1990 v USSR, Ma; 1991 v Ch; (with Everton) 1992 v US (2), I (sub), P (33)
Peyton, N. (Shamrock R), 1957 v WG; (with Leeds U), 1960 v WG, Se (sub); 1961 v W; 1963 v Ic, S (6)
Phelan, T. (Wimbledon), 1992 v H, Pol (sub), T, W, Sw, US, I (sub), P; (with Manchester C), 1993 v La (sub), D, Sp, Ni, Alb, La, Li; 1994 v Li, Sp, Ni, Ho, Bol, G, CzR, I, M, Ho; 1995 v E; 1996 v La; (with Chelsea), Ho, Ru, P, Cro, Ho, US, M (sub), Bol; (with Everton), 1997 v W, Mac; 1998 v R; (with Fulham), 2000 v S (sub), M, US, S.Af (42)

Quinn, A. (Sheffield W), 2003 v N (sub); 2004 v Aus (sub), Jam, Ho; (with Sheffield U), 2005 v Bul (sub), Cro (sub) (6)
Quinn, B. S. (Coventry C), 2000 v Gr, M, US (sub), S.Af (sub) (4)
Quinn, N. J. (Arsenal), 1986 v Ic (sub), Cz; 1987 v Bul (sub), Br (sub); 1988 v L (sub), Bul (sub), Is, R (sub), Pol (sub), E (sub); 1989 v Tun (sub), Sp (sub), H (sub); (with Manchester C), 1990 v USSR, Ma, Eg (sub), Ho, R, I; 1991 v Mor, T, E(2) W, Pol; 1992 v H, W (sub), US, Alb, US, I (sub), P; 1993 v La, D, Sp, Ni, D, Alb, La, Li; 1994 v Li, Sp, Ni; 1995 v La, Lie, Ni, E, Ni, P, Lie, A; 1996 v A, La, P, Ru, CzR, P (sub), Cro, Ho (sub), US; (with Sunderland), 1997 v Lie; 1998 v Li, Arg; 1999 v Ma, Y, Para, Se, Ni, Mac; 2000 v Y, Cro (sub), Ma, Mac, T, CzR, S, M, US (sub), S.Af; 2001 v Ho, P, Es, P, Es; 2002 v Ho (sub), Cy, Ir, Ru (sub), G (sub), S.Ar (sub), Sp (sub) (91)

Reid, A. M. (Nottingham F), 2004 v Ca, Br, CzR, Pol, R, Jam, Ho; 2005 v Bul, Cy, Sw, F (sub), Fa; (with Tottenham H), P, Chn, Is, Fa (16)
Reid, C. (Brideville), 1931 v Sp (1)
Reid, S. J. (Millwall), 2002 v Cro, Ru, D (sub), US (sub), Ng (sub), Cam (sub), G (sub); 2003 v S, Alb (sub); (with Blackburn R), 2004 v Ru (sub), T (sub), Ca, Pol (13)
Richardson, D. J. (Shamrock R), 1972 v A (sub); (with Gillingham), 1973 v N (sub); 1980 v Cz (3)
Rigby, A. (St James' Gate), 1935 v H, Sw, G (3)
Ringstead, A. (Sheffield U), 1951 v Arg, N; 1952 v WG (2), A, Sp; 1953 v A; 1954 v F; 1955 v N; 1956 v Y, Sp, Ho; 1957 v E (2); 1958 v D, Pol, A; 1959 v Pol, Cz (2) (20)
Robinson, J. (Bohemians), 1928 v Bel; (with Dolphin), 1931 v Sp (2)
Robinson, M. (Brighton & HA), 1981 v WG 'B', F, Cy, Bel, Pol; 1982 v Ho, F, Alg, Ch; 1983 v Ho, Sp, Ic, Ma; (with Liverpool), 1984 v Ic, Ho, Is; 1985 v USSR, N; (with QPR), N, Sp, Sw; 1986 v D (sub), W, Cz (24)
Roche, P. J. (Shelbourne), 1972 v A; (with Manchester U), 1975 v USSR, T, Sw, USSR, Sw, WG; 1976 v T (8)
Rogers, E. (Blackburn R), 1968 v Cz, Pol; 1969 v Pol, A, D, Cz, D, H; 1970 v S, D, H; 1971 v I (2), A; (with Charlton Ath), 1972 v Ir, Ec, Ch, P; 1973 v USSR (19)
Rowlands, M. C. (QPR), 2004 v R (sub), Ng (sub), Jam (sub) (3)
Ryan, G. (Derby Co), 1978 v T; (with Brighton & HA), 1979 v E, WG; 1980 v W, Cy (sub), Sw, Arg (sub); 1981 v WG 'B' (sub), F (sub), Pol (sub); 1982 v Br (sub), Ho (sub), Alg (sub), Ch (sub), Tr; 1984 v Pol, Chn; 1985 v M (18)
Ryan, R. A. (WBA), 1950 v Se, Bel; 1951 v N, Arg, N; 1952 v WG (2), A, Sp; 1953 v F, A; 1954 v F, L, F; 1955 v N; (with Derby Co), 1956 v Sp (16)

Sadlier, R. T. (Millwall), 2002 v Ru (sub) (1)
Savage, D. P. T. (Millwall), 1996 v P (sub), Cro (sub), US (sub), M, Bol (5)
Saward, P. (Millwall), 1954 v L; (with Aston Villa), 1957 v E (2); 1958 v D, Pol, A; 1959 v Pol, Cz; 1960 v Se, Ch, WG, Se; 1961 v W, N; (with Huddersfield T), 1961 v S; 1962 v A; 1963 v Ic (2) (18)
Scannell, T. (Southend U), 1954 v L (1)
Scully, P. J. (Arsenal), 1989 v Tun (sub) (1)
Sheedy, K. (Everton), 1984 v Ho (sub), Ma; 1985 v D, I, Is, Sw; 1986 v Sw, D; 1987 v S, Pol; 1988 v Is, R, Pol, E (sub), USSR; 1989 v Ni, Tun, H, Sp, Ma, H; 1990 v Ni, Ma, W (sub), USSR, Fi (sub), T, E, Eg, Ho, R, I; 1991 v W, E, Pol, Ch, US; 1992 v H, Pol, T, W; (with Newcastle U), Sw (sub), Alb; 1993 v La, W (sub) (45)
Sheridan, J. J. (Leeds U), 1988 v R, Y, Pol, N (sub); 1989 v Sp; (with Sheffield W), 1990 v W, T (sub), Ma, I (sub); 1991 v Mor (sub), T, Ch, US (sub); 1992 v H; 1993 v La; 1994 v Sp (sub), Ho, Bol, G, CzR, I, M, N, Ho; 1995 v La, Lie, Ni, E, Ni, P, Lie, A; 1996 v A, Ho (34)
Slaven, B. (Middlesbrough), 1990 v W, Fi, T (sub), Ma; 1991 v W, Pol (sub); 1993 v W (7)
Sloan, J. W. (Arsenal), 1946 v P, Sp (2)
Smyth, M. (Shamrock R), 1969 v Pol (sub) (1)
Squires, J. (Shelbourne), 1934 v Ho (1)
Stapleton, F. (Arsenal), 1977 v T, F, Sp, Bul; 1978 v Bul, N, D; 1979 v Ni, E (sub), D, WG; 1980 v W, Bul, Ni, E, Cy; 1981 v WG 'B', Ho, Bel, F, Cy, Bel, Cz, Pol; (with Manchester U), 1982 v Ho, F, Alg; 1983 v Ho, Sp, Ic, Ma, Sp; 1984 v Ic, Ho, Ma, Pol, Is, Chn; 1985 v N, D, I, Is, E, N, Sw; 1986 v Sw, USSR, D, U, Ic, Cz (sub); 1987 v Bel (2), S (2), Pol, Bul, L; (with Ajax), 1988 v L, Bul, R, Y, N, E, USSR, Ho; (with Le Havre), 1989 v F, Sp, Ma; (with Blackburn R), 1990 v WG, Ma (sub) (71)
Staunton, S. (Liverpool), 1989 v Tun, Sp (2), Ma, H; 1990 v WG, Ni, Ma, W, USSR, Fi, T, Ma, E, Eg, Ho, R, I; 1991 v Mor, T, E (2), W, Pol, Ch, US; (with Aston Villa), 1992 v Pol, T, Sw, US, Alb, US, I, P; 1993 v La, Sp, Ni, D, Alb, La, Li; 1994 v Li, Sp, Ho, Bol, G, CzR, I, M, N, Ho; 1995 v La, Lie, Ni, E, Ni, P, Lie, A; 1996 v La, P, Ru; 1997 v Lie, Mac (2), W, R, Lie; 1998 v Li, Ic, Li, Bel (2), Arg; (with Liverpool), 1999 v Cro, Ma, Y, Se; 2000 v Y, Cro, Ma, Mac, CzR (sub), Gr; 2001 v Ho (sub), Fi (sub); (with Aston Villa), And (sub), P, Es; 2002 v Cro, Ho, Cy, Ir (2), Ru (sub), D, US (sub), Ng, Cam, G, S.Ar, Sp (102)
Stevenson, A. E. (Dolphin), 1932 v Ho; (with Everton), 1947 v E, Sp, P; 1948 v P, Sp; 1949 v Sw (7)
Strahan, F. (Shelbourne), 1964 v Pol, N, E; 1965 v Pol; 1966 v WG (5)
Sullivan, J. (Fordsons), 1928 v Bel (1)
Swan, M. M. G. (Drumcondra), 1960 v Se (sub) (1)
Synnott, N. (Shamrock R), 1978 v T, Pol; 1979 v Ni (3)

Taylor, T. (Waterford), 1959 v Pol (sub) (1)
Thomas, P. (Waterford), 1974 v Pol, Br (2)
Thompson, J. (Nottingham F), 2004 v Ca (sub) (1)
Townsend, A. D. (Norwich C), 1989 v F, Sp (sub), Ma (sub), H; 1990 v WG (sub), Ni, Ma, W, USSR, Fi (sub), T, Ma (sub), E, Eg, Ho, R, I; (with Chelsea), 1991 v Mor, T, E (2), W, Pol, Ch, US; 1992 v Pol, W, US, Alb, US, I; 1993 v La, D, Sp, Ni, D, Alb, La, Li; (with Aston Villa), 1994 v Li, Ni,

Ho, Bol, G, CzR, I, M, N, Ho; 1995 v La, Ni, E, Ni, P; 1996 v A, La, Ho, Ru, CzR, P; 1997 v Lie, Mac (2), Ic, R, Lie; 1998 v Li; (with Middlesbrough), Ic, Bel (2) (70)
Traynor, T. J. (Southampton), 1954 v L; 1962 v A; 1963 v Ic (2), S; 1964 v A (2), Sp (8)
Treacy, R. C. P. (WBA), 1966 v WG; 1967 v Sp, Cz; 1968 v Cz; (with Charlton Ath), 1968 v Pol; 1969 v Pol, Cz, D; 1970 v S, D, H (sub), Pol (sub), WG (sub); 1971 v Pol, Se (sub+1), I, A; (with Swindon T), 1972 v Ir, Ec, Ch, P; 1973 v USSR, F, USSR, Pol, F, N; 1974 v Pol; (with Preston NE), Br; 1975 v USSR, Sw (2), WG; 1976 v T, N (sub), Pol (sub); (with WBA), 1977 v F, Pol; (with Shamrock R), 1978 v T, Pol; 1980 v Cz (sub) (42)
Tuohy, L. (Shamrock R), 1956 v Y; 1959 v Cz (2); (with Newcastle U), 1962 v A; 1963 v Ic (2); (with Shamrock R), 1964 v A; 1965 v Bel (8)
Turner, C. J. (Southend U), 1936 v Sw; 1937 v G, H, Sw, F; 1938 v N (2); (with West Ham U), Cz, Pol; 1939 v H (10)
Turner, P. (Celtic), 1963 v S; 1964 v Sp (2)

Vernon, J. (Belfast C), 1946 v P, Sp (2)

Waddock, G. (QPR), 1980 v Sw, Arg; 1981 v W, Pol (sub); 1982 v Alg; 1983 v Ic, Ma, Sp, Ho (sub); 1984 v Ma (sub), Ic, Ho, Is; 1985 v I, Is, E, N, Sp; 1986 v USSR; (with Millwall), 1990 v USSR, T (21)
Walsh, D. J. (Linfield), 1946 v P, Sp; (with WBA), 1947 v Sp, P; 1948 v P, Sp; 1949 v Sw, P, Se, Sp; 1950 v E, Fi, Se; 1951 v N; (with Aston Villa), Arg, N; 1952 v Sp; 1953 v A; 1954 v F (2) (20)
Walsh, J. (Limerick), 1982 v Tr (1)
Walsh, M. (Blackpool), 1976 v N, Pol; 1977 v F (sub), Pol; (with Everton), 1979 v Ni (sub); (with QPR), D (sub), Bul, WG (sub); (with Porto), 1981 v Bel (sub), Cz; 1982 v Alg (sub); 1983 v Sp, Ho (sub), Sp (sub); 1984 v Ic (sub), Ma, Pol, Chn; 1985 v USSR, N (sub), D (21)
Walsh, M. (Everton), 1982 v Ch, Br, Tr; 1983 v Ic (4)
Walsh, W. (Manchester C), 1947 v E, Sp, P; 1948 v P, Sp; 1949 v Bel; 1950 v E, Se, Bel (9)
Waters, J. (Grimsby T), 1977 v T; 1980 v Ni (sub) (2)
Watters, F. (Shelbourne), 1926 v I (1)
Weir, E. (Clyde), 1939 v H (2), G (3)
Whelan, R. (St Patrick's Ath), 1964 v A, E (sub) (2)
Whelan, R. (Liverpool), 1981 v Cz (sub); 1982 v Ho (sub), F; 1983 v Ic, Ma, Sp; 1984 v Is; 1985 v USSR, N, I (sub), Is, E, N (sub), Sw (sub); 1986 v USSR (sub), W; 1987 v Bel (sub), S, Bul, Bel, Br, L; 1988 v L, Bul, Pol, N, E, USSR, Ho; 1989 v Ni, F, H, Sp, Ma; 1990 v WG, Ni, Ma, W, Ho (sub); 1991 v Mor, E; 1992 v Sw; 1993 v La, W (sub), Li (sub); 1994 v Li (sub), Sp, Ru, Ho, G (sub), N (sub); (with Southend U), 1995 v Lie, A (53)
Whelan, W. (Manchester U), 1956 v Ho; 1957 v D, E (2) (4)
White, J. J. (Bohemians), 1928 v Bel (1)
Whittaker, R. (Chelsea), 1959 v Cz (1)
Williams, J. (Shamrock R), 1938 v N (1)

BRITISH AND IRISH INTERNATIONAL GOALSCORERS SINCE 1872

Where two players with the same surname and initials have appeared for the same country, and one or both have scored, they have been distinguished by reference to the club which appears *first* against their name in the international appearances section.

ENGLAND

Player	Goals
A'Court, A.	1
Adams, T. A.	5
Adcock, H.	1
Alcock, C. W.	1
Allen, A.	3
Allen, R.	2
Amos, A.	1
Anderson, V.	2
Anderton, D. R.	7
Astall, G.	1
Athersmith, W. C.	3
Atyeo, P. J. W.	5
Bache, J. W.	4
Bailey, N. C.	2
Baily, E. F.	5
Baker, J. H.	3
Ball, A. J.	8
Bambridge, A. L.	1
Bambridge, E. C.	11
Barclay, R.	2
Barmby, N. J.	4
Barnes, J.	11
Barnes, P. S.	4
Barton, J.	1
Bassett, W. I.	8
Bastin, C. S.	12
Beardsley, P. A.	9
Beasley, A.	1
Beattie, T. K.	1
Beckham, D. R. J.	16
Becton, F.	2
Bedford, H.	1
Bell, C.	9
Bentley, R. T. F.	9
Bishop, S. M.	1
Blackburn, F.	1
Blissett, L.	3
Bloomer, S.	28
Bond, R.	2
Bonsor, A. G.	1
Bowden, E. R.	1
Bowers, J. W.	2
Bowles, S.	1
Bradford, G. R. W.	1
Bradford, J.	7
Bradley, W.	2
Bradshaw, F.	3
Brann, G.	1
Bridge, W. M.	1
Bridges, B. J.	1
Bridgett, A.	3
Brindle, T.	1
Britton, C. S.	1
Broadbent, P. F.	2
Broadis, I. A.	8
Brodie, J. B.	1
Bromley-Davenport, W.	2
Brook, E. F.	10
Brooking, T. D.	5
Brooks, J.	2
Broome, F. H.	3
Brown, A.	4
Brown, A. S.	1
Brown, G.	5
Brown, J.	3
Brown, W.	1
Buchan, C. M.	4
Bull, S. G.	4
Bullock, N.	2
Burgess, H.	4
Butcher, T.	3
Byrne, J. J.	8
Campbell, S. J.	1
Camsell, G. H.	18
Carter, H. S.	7
Carter, J. H.	4
Chadwick, E.	3
Chamberlain, M.	1
Chambers, H.	5
Channon, M. R.	21
Charlton, J.	6
Charlton, R.	49
Chenery, C. J.	1
Chivers, M.	13
Clarke, A. J.	10
Cobbold, W. N.	6
Cock, J. G.	2
Cole, A.	1
Cole, J. J.	3
Common, A.	2
Connelly, J. M.	7
Coppell, S. J.	7
Cotterill, G. H.	2
Cowans, G.	2
Crawford, R.	1
Crawshaw, T. H.	1
Crayston, W. J.	1
Creek, F. N. S.	1
Crooks, S. D.	7
Currey, E. S.	2
Currie, A. W.	3
Cursham, A. W.	2
Cursham, H. A.	5
Daft, H. B.	3
Davenport, J. K.	2
Davis, G.	1
Davis, H.	1
Day, S. H.	2
Dean, W. R.	18
Defoe, J. C.	1
Devey, J. H. G.	1
Dewhurst, F.	11
Dix, W. R.	1
Dixon, K. M.	4
Dixon, L. M.	1
Dorrell, A. R.	1
Douglas, B.	11
Drake, E. J.	6
Ducat, A.	1
Dunn, A. T. B.	2
Eastham, G.	2
Edwards, D.	5
Ehiogu, U.	1
Elliott, W. H.	3
Evans, R. E.	1
Ferdinand, L.	5
Ferdinand, R. G.	1
Finney, T.	30
Fleming, H. J.	9
Flowers, R.	10
Forman, Frank	1
Forman, Fred	3
Foster, R. E.	3
Fowler, R. B.	7
Francis, G. C. J.	3
Francis, T.	12
Freeman, B. C.	3
Froggatt, J.	2
Froggatt, R.	2
Galley, T.	1
Gascoigne, P. J.	10
Geary, F.	3
Gerrard, S. G.	6
Gibbins, W. V. T.	3
Gilliatt, W. E.	3
Goddard, P.	1
Goodall, J.	12
Goodyer, A. C.	1
Gosling, R. C.	2
Goulden, L. A.	4
Grainger, C.	3
Greaves, J.	44
Grovesnor, A. T.	2
Gunn, W.	1
Haines, J. T. W.	2
Hall, G. W.	9
Halse, H. J.	2
Hampson, J.	5
Hampton, H.	2
Hancocks, J.	2
Hardman, H. P.	1
Harris, S. S.	2
Hassall, H. W.	4
Hateley, M.	9
Haynes, J. N.	18
Hegan, K. E.	4
Henfrey, A. G.	2
Heskey, E. W.	5
Hilsdon, G. R.	14
Hine, E. W.	4
Hinton, A. T.	1
Hirst, D. E.	1
Hitchens, G. A.	5
Hobbis, H. H. F.	1
Hoddle, G.	8
Hodgetts, D.	1
Hodgson, G.	1
Holley, G. H.	8
Houghton, W. E.	5
Howell, R.	1
Hughes, E. W.	1
Hulme, J. H. A.	4
Hunt, G. S.	1
Hunt, R.	18
Hunter, N.	2
Hurst, G. C.	24
Ince, P. E. C.	2
Jack, D. N. B.	3
Jeffers, F.	1
Johnson, D. E.	6
Johnson, E.	2
Johnson, J. A.	2
Johnson, T. C. F.	5
Johnson, W. H.	1
Kail, E. I. L.	2
Kay, A. H.	1
Keegan, J. K.	21
Kelly, R.	8
Kennedy, R.	3
Kenyon-Slaney, W. S.	2
Keown, M. R.	2
Kevan, D. T.	8
Kidd, B.	1
King, L. B.	1
Kingsford, R. K.	1
Kirchen, A. J.	2
Kirton, W. J.	1
Lampard, F. J.	8
Langton, R.	1
Latchford, R. D.	5
Latherton, E. G.	1
Lawler, C.	1
Lawton, T.	22
Lee, F.	10
Lee, J.	1
Lee, R. M.	2
Lee, S.	2
Le Saux, G. P.	1
Lindley, T.	14
Lineker, G.	48
Lofthouse, J. M.	3
Lofthouse, N.	30
Hon. A. Lyttelton	1
Mabbutt, G.	1
Macdonald, M.	6
Mannion, W. J.	11
Mariner, P.	13
Marsh, R. W.	1
Matthews, S.	11
Matthews, V.	1
McCall, J.	1
McDermott, T.	3
McManaman, S.	3
Medley, L. D.	1
Melia, J.	1
Mercer, D. W.	1
Merson, P. C.	3
Milburn, J. E. T.	10
Miller, H. S.	1
Mills, G. R.	3
Milward, A.	3
Mitchell, C.	5
Moore, J.	1
Moore, R. F.	2
Moore, W. G. B.	2
Morren, T.	1
Morris, F.	1
Morris, J.	3
Mortensen, S. H.	23
Morton, J. R.	1
Mosforth, W.	3
Mullen, J.	6
Mullery, A. P.	1
Murphy, D. B	1
Neal, P. G.	5
Needham, E.	3
Nicholls, J.	1
Nicholson, W. E.	1
O'Grady, M.	3
Osborne, F. R.	3
Owen, M. J.	32
Own goals	26
Page, L. A.	1
Paine, T. L.	7
Palmer, C. L.	1
Parry, E. H.	1
Parry, R. A.	1
Pawson, F. W.	1

Payne, J. 2
Peacock, A. 3
Pearce, S. 5
Pearson, J. S. 5
Pearson, S. C. 5
Perry, W. 2
Peters, M. 20
Pickering, F. 5
Platt, D. 27
Pointer, R. 2

Quantrill, A. 1

Ramsay, A. E. 3
Revie, D. G. 4
Redknapp, J. F. 1
Reynolds, J. 3
Richardson, K. E. 2
Richardson, J. R. 2
Rigby, A. 3
Rimmer, E. J. 2
Roberts, F. 2
Roberts, H. 1
Roberts, W. T. 2
Robinson, J. 3
Robson, B. 26
Robson, R. 4
Rooney, W. 9
Rowley, J. F. 6
Royle, J. 2
Rutherford, J. 3

Sagar, C. 1
Sandilands, R. R. 3
Sansom, K. 1
Schofield, J. 1
Scholes, P. 14
Seed, J. M. 1
Settle, J. 6
Sewell, J. 3
Shackleton, L. F. 1
Sharp, J. 1
Shearer, A. 30
Shelton, A. 1
Shepherd, A. 2
Sheringham, E. P. 11
Simpson, J. 1
Smith, A. 1
Smith, A. M. 2
Smith, G. O. 11
Smith, Joe 1
Smith, J. R. 2
Smith, J. W. 4
Smith, R. 13
Smith, S. 1
Sorby, T. H. 1
Southgate, G. 2
Southworth, J. 3
Sparks, F. J. 3
Spence, J. W. 1
Spiksley, F. 5
Spilsbury, B. W. 5
Steele, F. C. 8
Stephenson, G. T. 2
Steven, T. M. 4
Stewart, J. 2
Stiles, N. P. 1
Storer, H. 1
Stone, S. B. 2
Summerbee, M. G. 1

Tambling, R. V. 1
Taylor, P. J. 2
Taylor, T. 16
Thompson, P. B. 1
Thornewell, G. 1
Tilson, S. F. 6
Townley, W. J. 2
Tueart, D. 2

Vassell, D. 6
Vaughton, O. H. 6
Veitch, J. G. 3
Violett, D. S. 1

Waddle, C. R. 6
Walker, W. H. 9
Wall, G. 2
Wallace, D. 1
Walsh, P. 1
Waring, T. 4
Warren, B. 2
Watson, D. V. 4
Watson, V. M. 4
Webb, G. W. 1
Webb, N. 4
Wedlock, W. J. 2
Weller, K. 1
Welsh, D. 1
Whateley, O. 2
Wheldon, G. F. 6
Whitfield, H. 1
Wignall, F. 2
Wilkes, A. 1
Wilkins, R. G. 3
Willingham, C. K. 1
Wilshaw, D. J. 10
Wilson, G. P. 1
Winckworth, W. N. 1
Windridge, J. E. 7
Wise, D. F. 1
Withe, P. 1
Wollaston, C. H. R. 1
Wood, H. 1
Woodcock, T. 16
Woodhall, G. 1
Woodward, V. J. 29
Worrall, F. 2
Worthington, F. S. 2
Wright, I. E. 9
Wright, M. 1
Wright, W. A. 3
Wright-Phillips, S. C. 1
Wylie, J. G. 1

Yates, J. 3

NORTHERN IRELAND

Anderson, T. 4
Armstrong, G. 12

Bambrick, J. 12
Barr, H. H. 1
Barron, H. 3
Best, G. 9
Bingham, W. L. 10
Black, K. 1
Blanchflower, D. 2
Blanchflower, J. 1
Brennan, B. 1
Brennan, R. A. 1
Brotherston, N. 3
Brown, J. 1
Browne, F. 2

Campbell, J. 1
Campbell, W. G. 1
Casey, T. 2
Caskey, W. 1
Cassidy, T. 1
Chambers, J. 3
Clarke, C. J. 13
Clements, D. 2
Cochrane, T. 1
Condy, J. 1
Connor, M. J. 1
Coulter, J. 1
Croft, T. 1
Crone, W. 1
Crossan, E. 1
Crossan, J. A. 10
Curran, S. 2
Cush, W. W. 5

Dalton, W. 4
D'Arcy, S. D. 1
Darling, J. 1
Davey, H. H. 1
Davis, T. L. 1
Dill, A. H. 1
Doherty, L. 1
Doherty, P. D. 3
Dougan, A. D. 8
Dowie, I. 12
Dunne, J. 4

Elder, A. R. 1
Elliott, S. 3
Emerson, W. 1
English, S. 1

Feeney, W 1
Ferguson, W. 1
Ferris, J. 1
Ferris, R. O. 1
Finney, T. 2

Gaffkin, J. 4
Gara, A. 3
Gaukrodger, G. 1
Gibb, J. T. 2
Gibb, T. J. 1
Gillespie, K. R. 1
Gillespie, W. 13
Goodall, A. L. 2
Griffin, D. J. 1
Gray, P. 6

Halligan, W. 1
Hamill, M. 1
Hamilton, B. 4
Hamilton, W. R. 5
Hannon, D. J. 1
Harkin, J. T. 2
Harvey, M. 3
Healy, D. J. 17
Hill, C. F. 1
Hughes, M. E. 5
Humphries, W. 1
Hunter, A. (*Distillery*) 1
Hunter, A. (*Blackburn R*) 1
Hunter, B. V. 1

Irvine, R. W. 3
Irvine, W. J. 8

Johnston, H. 2
Johnston, S. 2
Johnston, W. C. 1
Jones, S. 1
Jones, S. (*Crewe Alex*) 1
Jones, J. 1

Kelly, J. 4
Kernaghan, N. 2
Kirwan, J. 2

Lacey, W. 3
Lemon, J. 2
Lennon, N. F. 2
Lockhart, N. 3
Lomas, S. M. 3

Magilton, J. 5
Mahood, J. 2
Martin, D. K. 3
Maxwell, J. 2
McAdams, W. J. 7
McAllen, J. 1
Mcauley, J. L. 1
McCartney, G. 1
McCandless, J. 3
McCaw, J. H. 1
McClelland, J. 1
McCluggage, A. 2
McCracken, W. 1
McCrory, S. 1
McCurdy, C. 1
McDonald, A. 3
McGarry, J. K. 1
McGrath, R. C. 4
McIlroy, J. 10
McIlroy, S. B. 5
McKenzie, H 1
McKnight, J. 2
McLaughlin, J. C. 6
McMahon, G. J. 2
McMordie, A. S. 3
McMorran, E. J. 4
McParland, P. J. 10
McWha, W. B. R. 1
Meldon, J. 1
Mercer, J. T. 1
Millar, W. 1
Milligan, D. 1
Milne, R. G. 2
Molyneux, T. B. 1
Moreland, V. 1
Morgan, S. 3
Morrow, S. J. 1
Morrow, W. J. 1
Mulryne, P. P. 3
Murdock, C. J. 1
Murphy, N. 1

Neill, W. J. T. 2
Nelson, S. 1
Nicholl, C. J. 3
Nicholl, J. M. 1
Nicholson, J. J. 6

O'Boyle, G. 1
O'Hagan, C. 2
O'Kane, W. J. 1
O'Neill, J. 2
O'Neill, M. A. 4
O'Neill, M. H. 8
Own goals 6

Patterson, D. J. 1
Peacock, R. 2
Peden, J. 7
Penney, S. 2
Pyper, James 2
Pyper, John 1

Quinn, J. M. 12
Quinn, S. J. 4

Reynolds, J. 1
Rowland, K. 1
Rowley, R. W. M. 2
Rushe, F. 1

Sheridan, J. 2
Sherrard, J. 1
Sherrard, W. C. 2
Simpson, W. J. 5
Sloan, H. A. de B. 4
Smyth, S. 5
Spence, D. W. 3
Stanfield, O. M. 11
Stevenson, A. E. 5
Stewart, I. 2

Taggart, G. P. 7
Thompson, F. W. 2
Torrans, S. 1
Tully, C. P. 3
Turner, E. 1

Walker, J. 1
Walsh, D. J. 5
Welsh, E. 1
Whiteside, N. 9
Whiteside, T. 1
Whitley, Jeff 2
Williams, J. R. 1
Williams, M. S. 1
Williamson, J. 1
Wilson, D. J. 1
Wilson, K. J. 6
Wilson, S. J. 7
Wilton, J. M. 2

Young, S. 1

N.B. In 1914 Young goal should be credited to Gillespie W v Wales

SCOTLAND

Aitken, R. (*Celtic*) 1
Aitken, R. (*Dumbarton*) 1
Aitkenhead, W. A. C. 2
Alexander, D. 1
Allan, D. S. 4
Allan, J. 2
Anderson, F. 1
Anderson, W. 4
Andrews, P. 1
Archibald, A. 1
Archibald, S. 4

Baird, D. 2
Baird, J. C. 2
Baird, S. 2
Bannon, E. 1
Barbour, A. 1
Barker, J. B. 4
Battles, B. Jr 1
Bauld, W. 2
Baxter, J. C. 3
Bell, J. 5
Bennett, A. 2
Berry, D. 1
Bett, J. 1
Beveridge, W. W. 1
Black, A. 3
Black, D. 1
Bone, J. 1
Booth, S. 6
Boyd, R. 2
Boyd, T. 1
Boyd, W. G. 1
Brackenridge, T. 1
Brand, R. 8
Brazil, A. 1
Bremner, W. J. 3
Brown, A. D. 6
Buchanan, P. S. 1
Buchanan, R. 1
Buckley, P. 1
Buick, A. 2
Burley, C. W. 3
Burns, K. 1

Cairns, T. 1
Caldwell, G. 1
Calderwood, C. 1
Calderwood, R. 2
Caldow, E. 4
Cameron, C. 2
Campbell, C. 1
Campbell, John (*Celtic*) 5
Campbell, John (*Rangers*) 4
Campbell, P. 2
Campbell, R. 1
Cassidy, J. 1
Chalmers, S. 3
Chambers, T. 1
Cheyne, A. G. 4
Christie, A. J. 1
Clunas, W. L. 1
Collins, J. 12
Collins, R. Y. 10
Combe, J. R. 1
Conn, A. 1
Cooper, D. 6
Craig, J. 1
Craig, T. 1
Crawford, S. 4
Cunningham, A. N. 5
Curran, H. P. 1

Dailly, C. 5
Dalglish, K. 30
Davidson, D. 1
Davidson, J. A. 1
Delaney, J. 3
Devine, A. 1
Dewar, G. 1
Dewar, N. 4
Dickov, P. 1
Dickson, W. 4
Divers, J. 1
Dobie, R. S. 1
Docherty, T. H. 1
Dodds, D. 1
Dodds, W. 7
Donaldson, A. 1
Donnachie, J. 1
Dougall, J. 1
Drummond, J. 2
Dunbar, M. 1
Duncan, D. 7
Duncan, D. M. 1
Duncan, J. 1
Dunn, J. 2
Durie, G. S. 7

Easson, J. F. 1
Elliott, M. S. 1
Ellis, J. 1

Ferguson, B. 2
Ferguson, J. 6
Fernie, W. 1
Fitchie, T. T. 1
Flavell, R. 2
Fleming, C. 2
Fleming, J. W. 3
Fletcher, D. 2
Fraser, M. J. E. 3
Freedman, D. A. 1

Gallacher, H. K. 23
Gallacher, K. W. 9
Gallacher, P. 1
Galt, J. H. 1
Gemmell, T. (*St Mirren*) 1
Gemmell, T. (*Celtic*) 1
Gemmill, A. 8
Gemmill, S. 1
Gibb, W. 1
Gibson, D. W. 3
Gibson, J. D. 1
Gibson, N. 1
Gillespie, Jas. 3
Gillick, T. 3
Gilzean, A. J. 12
Gossland, J. 2
Goudie, J. 1
Gough, C. R. 6
Gourlay, J. 1
Graham, A. 2
Graham, G. 3
Gray, A. 6
Gray, E. 3
Gray, F. 1
Greig, J. 3
Groves, W. 4

Hamilton, G. 4
Hamilton, J. (*Queen's Park*) 3
Hamilton, R. C. 14
Harper, J. M. 2
Harrower, W. 5
Hartford, R. A. 4
Heggie, C. 5
Henderson, J. G. 1
Henderson, W. 5
Hendry, E. C. J. 3
Herd, D. G. 3
Herd, G. 1
Hewie, J. D. 2
Higgins, A. (*Newcastle U*) 1
Higgins, A. (*Kilmarnock*) 4
Highet, T. C. 1
Holt, G.J. 1
Holton, J. A. 2
Hopkin, D. 2
Houliston, W. 2
Howie, H. 1
Howie, J. 2
Hughes, J. 1
Hunter, W. 1
Hutchison, D. 6
Hutchison, T. 1
Hutton, J. 1
Hyslop, T. 1

Imrie, W. N. 1

Jackson, A. 8
Jackson, C. 1
Jackson, D. 4
James, A. W. 4
Jardine, A. 1
Jenkinson, T. 1
Jess, E. 2
Johnston, A. 2
Johnston, L. H. 1
Johnston, M. 14
Johnstone, D. 2
Johnstone, J. 4
Johnstone, Jas. 1
Johnstone, R. 9
Johnstone, W. 1
Jordan, J. 11

Kay, J. L. 5
Keillor, A. 3
Kelly, J. 1
Kelso, J. 1
Ker, G. 10
King, A. 1
King, J. 1
Kinnear, D. 1
Kyle, K. 1

Lambert, P. 1
Lambie, J. 1
Lambie, W. A. 5
Lang, J. J. 1
Law, D. 30
Leggat, G. 8
Lennie, W. 1
Lennox, R. 3
Liddell, W. 6
Lindsay, J. 6
Linwood, A. B. 1
Logan, J. 1
Lorimer, P. 4
Love, A. 1
Lowe, J. (*Cambuslang*) 1
Lowe, J. (*St Bernards*) 1

Macari, L. 5
MacDougall, E. J. 3
MacLeod, M. 1
Mackay, D. C. 4
Mackay, G. 1
MacKenzie, J. A. 1
MacKinnon, W. W. 6
Madden, J. 5
Marshall, H. 1
Marshall, J. 1
Mason, J. 4
Massie, A. 1
Masson, D. S. 5
McAdam, J. 1
McAllister, G. 5
McAulay, J. D. 1
McAvennie, F. 1
McCall, J. 1
McCall, S. M. 1
McCalliog, J. 1
McCallum, N. 1
McCann, N. 3
McClair, B. J. 2
McCoist, A. 19
McColl, R. S. 13
McCulloch, D. 3
McDougall, J. 4
McFarlane, A. 1
McFadden, J. 6
McFadyen, W. 2
McGhee, M. 2
McGinlay, J. 4
McGrory, J. 6
McGuire, W. 1
McInally, A. 3
McInnes, T. 2
McKie, J. 2
McKimmie, S. 1
McKinlay, W. 4
McKinnon, A. 1
McKinnon, R. 1
McLaren, A. 4
McLaren, J. 1
McLean, A. 1
McLean, T. 1
McLeish, A. 1
McLintock, F. 1
McMahon, A. 6
McMenemy, J. 5
McMillan, I. L. 2
McNeil, H. 5
McNeill, W. 3
McPhail, J. 3
McPhail, R. 7
McPherson, J. 8
McPherson, R. 1
McQueen, G. 5
McStay, P. 9
McSwegan, G. 1
Meiklejohn, D. D. 3
Millar, J. 2
Miller, K. 2
Miller, T. 2
Miller, W. 1
Mitchell, R. C. 1
Morgan, W. 1
Morris, D. 1
Morris, H. 3
Morton, A. L. 5
Mudie, J. K. 9
Mulhall, G. 1
Munro, A. D. 1
Munro, N. 1
Murdoch, R. 5
Murphy, F. 1
Murray, J. 1

Napier, C. E. 3
Narey, D. 1
Naysmith, G. A. 1
Neil, R. G. 2
Nevin, P. K. F. 5
Nicholas, C. 5
Nisbet, J. 2

O'Donnell, F. 2
O'Hare, J. 5
Ormond, W. E. 1
O'Rourke, F. 1
Orr, R. 1
Orr, T. 1
Oswald, J. 1
Own goals 16

Parlane, D. 1
Paul, H. McD. 2
Paul, W. 6
Pettigrew, W. 2
Provan, D. 1

Quashie, N. F. 1
Quinn, J. 7
Quinn, P. 1

Rankin, G. 2
Rankin, R. 2
Reid, W. 4
Reilly, L. 22
Renny-Tailyour, H. W. 1
Richmond, J. T. 1

Ring, T.	2
Rioch, B. D.	6
Ritchie, J.	1
Ritchie, P. S.	1
Robertson, A.	2
Robertson, J.	2
Robertson, J. N.	9
Robertson, J. T.	2
Robertson, T.	1
Robertson, W.	1
Russell, D.	1
Scott, A. S.	5
Sellar, W.	4
Sharp, G.	1
Shaw, F. W.	1
Shearer, D.	2
Simpson, J.	1
Smith, A.	5
Smith, G.	4
Smith, J.	1
Smith, John	13
Somerville, G.	1
Souness, G. J.	4
Speedie, F.	2
St John, I.	9
Steel, W.	12
Stein, C.	10
Stevenson, G.	4
Stewart, A.	1
Stewart, R.	1
Stewart, W. E.	1
Strachan, G.	5
Sturrock, P.	3
Taylor, J. D.	1
Templeton, R.	1
Thompson, S.	3
Thomson, A.	1
Thomson, C.	4
Thomson, R.	1
Thomson, W.	1
Thornton, W.	1
Waddell, T. S.	1
Waddell, W.	6
Walker, J.	2
Walker, R.	7
Walker, T.	9
Wallace, I. A.	1
Wark, J.	7
Watson, J. A. K.	1
Watt, F.	2
Watt, W. W.	1
Weir, A.	1
Weir, D.	1
Weir, J. B.	2
White, J. A.	3
Wilkie, L.	1
Wilson, A.	2
Wilson, A. N.	13
Wilson, D. (*Queen's Park*)	2
Wilson, D. (*Rangers*)	9
Wilson, H.	1
Wylie, T. G.	1
Young, A.	5

WALES

Allchurch, I. J.	23
Allen, M.	3
Astley, D. J.	12
Atherton, R. W.	2
Bamford, T.	1
Barnes, W.	1
Bellamy, C. D.	9
Blackmore, C. G.	1
Blake, N. A.	4
Bodin, P. J.	3
Boulter, L. M.	1
Bowdler, J. C. H.	3
Bowen, D. L.	1
Bowen, M.	3
Boyle, T.	1
Bryan, T.	1
Burgess, W. A. R.	1
Burke, T.	1
Butler, W. T.	1
Chapman, T.	2
Charles, J.	1
Charles, M.	6
Charles, W. J.	15
Clarke, R. J.	5
Coleman, C.	4
Collier, D. J.	1
Crosse, K.	1
Cumner, R. H.	1
Curtis, A.	6
Curtis, E. R.	3
Davies, D. W.	1
Davies, E. Lloyd	1
Davies, G.	2
Davies, L. S.	6
Davies, R. T.	9
Davies, R. W.	6
Davies, S.	5
Davies, Simon	4
Davies, W.	6
Davies, W. H.	1
Davies, William	5
Davis, W. O.	1
Deacy, N.	4
Doughty, J.	6
Doughty, R.	2
Durban, A.	2
Dwyer, P.	2
Earnshaw, R.	9
Edwards, G.	2
Edwards, R. I.	4
England, H. M.	4
Evans, I.	1
Evans, J.	1
Evans, R. E.	2
Evans, W.	1
Eyton-Jones, J. A.	1
Flynn, B.	7
Ford, T.	23
Foulkes, W. I.	1
Fowler, J.	3
Giles, D.	2
Giggs, R. J.	8
Glover, E. M.	7
Godfrey, B. C.	2
Green, A. W.	3
Griffiths, A. T.	6
Griffiths, M. W.	2
Griffiths, T. P.	3
Harris, C. S.	1
Hartson, J.	14
Hersee, R.	1
Hewitt, R.	1
Hockey, T.	1
Hodges, G.	2
Hole, W. J.	1
Hopkins, I. J.	2
Horne, B.	2
Howell, E. G.	3
Hughes, L. M.	16
James, E.	2
James, L.	10
James, R.	7
Jarrett, R. H.	3
Jenkyns, C. A.	1
Jones, A.	1
Jones, Bryn	6
Jones, B. S.	2
Jones, Cliff	16
Jones, C. W.	1
Jones, D. E.	1
Jones, Evan	1
Jones, H.	1
Jones, I.	1
Jones, J. L.	1
Jones, J. O.	1
Jones, J. P.	1
Jones, Leslie J.	1
Jones, R. A.	2
Jones, W. L.	6
Keenor, F. C.	2
Koumas, J.	1
Krzywicki, R. L.	1
Leek, K.	5
Lewis, B.	4
Lewis, D. M.	2
Lewis, W.	8
Lewis, W. L.	3
Lovell, S.	1
Lowrie, G.	2
Mahoney, J. F.	1
Mays, A. W.	1
Medwin, T. C.	6
Melville, A. K	3
Meredith, W. H.	11
Mills, T. J.	1
Moore, G.	1
Morgan, J. R.	2
Morgan-Owen, H.	1
Morgan-Owen, M. M.	2
Morris, A. G.	9
Morris, H.	2
Morris, R.	1
Morris, S.	2
Nicholas, P.	2
O'Callaghan, E.	3
O'Sullivan, P. A.	1
Owen, G.	2
Owen, W.	4
Owen, W. P.	6
Own goals	13
Palmer, D.	3
Parry, P. I.	1
Parry, T. D.	3
Paul, R.	1
Peake, E.	1
Pembridge, M.	6
Perry, E.	1
Phillips, C.	5
Phillips, D.	2
Powell, A.	1
Powell, D.	1
Price, J.	4
Price, P.	1
Pryce-Jones, W. E.	3
Pugh, D. H.	2
Reece, G. I.	2
Rees, R. R.	3
Richards, R. W.	1
Roach, J.	2
Robbins, W. W.	4
Roberts, J. (*Corwen*)	1
Roberts, Jas.	1
Roberts, P. S.	1
Roberts, R. (*Druids*)	1
Roberts, W. (*Llangollen*)	2
Roberts, W. (*Wrexham*)	1
Roberts, W. H.	1
Robinson, J. R. C.	3
Rush, I.	28
Russell, M. R.	1
Sabine, H. W.	1
Saunders, D.	22
Savage, R. W.	2
Shaw, E. G.	2
Sisson, H.	4
Slatter, N.	2
Smallman, D. P.	1
Speed, G. A.	7
Symons, C. J.	2
Tapscott, D. R.	4
Taylor, G. K.	1
Thomas, M.	4
Thomas, T.	1
Toshack, J. B.	12
Trainer, H.	2
Vaughan, John	2
Vernon, T. R.	8
Vizard, E. T.	1
Walsh, I.	7
Warren, F. W.	3
Watkins, W. M.	4
Wilding, J.	4
Williams, A.	1
Williams, D. R.	2
Williams, G. E.	1
Williams, G. G.	1
Williams, W.	1
Woosnam, A. P.	3
Wynn, G. A.	1
Yorath, T. C.	2
Young, E.	1

REPUBLIC OF IRELAND

Aldridge, J.	19
Ambrose, P.	1
Anderson, J.	1
Barrett, G.	2
Bermingham, P.	1
Bradshaw, P.	4
Brady, L.	9
Breen, G.	6
Brown, D.	1
Byrne, J. (*Bray*)	1
Byrne, J. (*QPR*)	4
Cantwell, J.	14
Carey, J.	3
Carroll, T.	1
Cascarino, A.	19
Coad, P.	3
Connolly, D. J.	9
Conroy, T.	2
Conway, J.	3
Coyne, T.	6
Cummings, G.	5
Curtis, D.	8
Daly, G.	13
Davis, T.	4
Dempsey, J.	1
Dennehy, M.	2
Doherty, G. M. T.	4
Donnelly, J.	4
Donnelly, T.	1
Duff, D. A.	6
Duffy, B.	1
Duggan, H.	1
Dunne, J.	13
Dunne, L.	1
Dunne, R. P.	4
Eglington, T.	2
Ellis, P.	2
Fagan, F.	5
Fallon, S.	2
Fallon, W.	2

Farrell, P.	3	Houghton, R.	6	McGrath, P.	8	Reid, A. M.	2
Finnan, S.	1	Hughton, C.	1	McLoughlin, A. F.	2	Reid, S. J.	2
Fitzgerald, P.	2	Hurley, C.	2	McPhail, S. J. P.	1	Ringstead, A.	7
Fitzgerald, J.	1			Mancini, T.	1	Robinson, M.	4
Fitzsimmons, A.	7	Irwin, D.	4	Martin, C.	6	Rogers, E.	5
Flood, J. J.	4			Martin, M.	4	Ryan, G.	1
Fogarty, A.	3	Jordan, D.	1	Mooney, J.	1	Ryan, R.	3
Foley, D.	2			Moore, P.	7		
Fullam, J.	1	Kavanagh, G. A.	1	Moran, K.	6	Sheedy, K.	9
Fullam, R.	1	Keane, R. D.	25	Morrison, C. H.	9	Sheridan, J.	5
		Keane, R. M.	9	Moroney, T.	1	Slaven, B.	1
Galvin, A.	1	Kelly, D.	9	Mulligan, P.	1	Sloan, W.	1
Gavin, J.	2	Kelly, G.	2			Squires, J.	1
Geoghegan, M.	2	Kelly, J.	2	O'Brien, A. J.	1	Stapleton, F.	20
Giles, J.	5	Kennedy, M.	3	O'Callaghan, K.	1	Staunton, S.	7
Givens, D.	19	Kernaghan, A. N.	1	O'Connor, T.	2	Strahan, J.	1
Glynn, D.	1	Kilbane, K. D.	5	O'Farrell, F.	2	Sullivan, J.	1
Grealish, T.	8	Kinsella, M. A.	3	O'Flanagan, K.	3		
Grimes, A. A.	1			O'Keefe, E.	1	Townsend, A. D.	7
		Lacey, W.	1	O'Leary, D. A.	1	Treacy, R.	5
Hale, A.	2	Lawrenson, M.	5	O'Neill, F.	1	Touhy, L.	4
Hand, E.	2	Leech, M.	2	O'Neill, K. P.	4		
Harte, I. P.	11			O'Reilly, J. (*Brideville*)	2	Waddock, G.	3
Haverty, J.	3	McAteer, J. W.	3	O'Reilly, J. (*Cork*)	1	Walsh, D.	5
Healy, C.	1	McCann, J.	1	O'Shea, J. F.	1	Walsh, M.	3
Holland, M. R.	5	McCarthy, M.	2	Own goals	10	Waters, J.	1
Holmes, J.	1	McEvoy, A.	6			White, J. J.	2
Horlacher, A.	2	McGee, P.	4	Quinn, N.	21	Whelan, R.	3

Jamie Carragher is brought down by Poland's Arkadiusz Glowacki during the World Cup qualifying match in Chorzow. (Empics Sports Agency Photo)

SOUTH AMERICA

COPA LIBERTADORES 2005

PRELIMINARY ROUND
Quilmes 0, Colo Colo 0
Colo Colo 2, Quilmes 2
Mineros 0, America 2
America 3, Mineros 1
Guadalajara 3, Cienciano 1
Cienciano 1, Guadalajara 5
Tacuary 2, Palmeiras 2
Palmeiras 2, Tacuary 0
At Junior 2, Oriente 1
Oriente 1, At Junior 3
LDU Quito 3, Penarol 0
Penarol 4, LDU Quito 1

GROUP 1	P	W	D	L	F	A	Pts
Indep Medellin	6	3	1	2	14	8	10
Paranaense	6	3	1	2	8	11	10
America	6	3	0	3	7	7	9
Libertad	6	2	0	4	8	11	6

GROUP 2	P	W	D	L	F	A	Pts
Santos	6	4	0	2	18	10	12
LDU Quito	6	2	2	2	7	10	8
Danubio	6	2	1	3	9	8	7
Bolivar	6	2	1	3	8	14	7

GROUP 3	P	W	D	L	F	A	Pts
Sao Paulo	6	3	3	0	16	9	12
Univ de Chile	6	2	3	1	9	9	9
Quilmes	6	1	2	3	8	11	5
The Strongest	6	1	2	3	6	10	5

GROUP 4	P	W	D	L	F	A	Pts
Cerro Porteno	6	3	3	0	10	4	12
Palmeiras	6	2	3	1	8	5	9
Santo Andre	6	2	2	2	11	6	8
Dep Tachira	6	1	0	5	3	17	3

GROUP 5	P	W	D	L	F	A	Pts
River Plate	6	5	1	0	12	5	16
At Junior	6	3	0	3	8	9	9
Olmedo	6	2	1	3	10	11	7
Nacional	6	1	0	5	7	12	3

GROUP 6	P	W	D	L	F	A	Pts
Tigres	6	3	3	0	13	5	12
Banfield	6	3	2	1	10	9	11
Alianza	6	1	2	3	4	7	5
Caracas	6	1	1	4	8	14	4

GROUP 7	P	W	D	L	F	A	Pts
Guadalajara	6	3	2	1	10	7	11
Once Caldas	6	2	3	1	6	4	9
Cobreloa	6	2	2	2	6	7	8
San Lorenzo	6	0	3	3	1	5	3

GROUP 7	P	W	D	L	F	A	Pts
Boca Juniors	6	4	1	1	14	3	13
Pachuca	6	3	1	2	8	9	10
Sporting Cristal	6	2	1	3	5	10	7
Cuenca	6	0	3	3	4	9	3

FIRST KNOCK-OUT ROUND FIRST LEG
At Junior 3, Boca Juniors 3
LDU Quito 2, River Plate 1
Banfield 3, Indep Medellin 0
Pachuca 1, Guadalajara 1
Palmeiras 0, Sao Paulo 1
Paranaense 2, Cerro Porteno 1
Once Caldas 1, Tigres 1
Univ de Chile 2, Santos 1

FIRST KNOCK-OUT ROUND SECOND LEG
Guadalajara 3, Pachuca 1
Indep Medellin 0, Banfield 2
Santos 3, Univ de Chile 0
Sao Paulo 2, Palmeiras 0
Boca Juniors 4, At Junior 0
Cerro Porteno 2, Paranaense 1
River Plate 4, LDU Quito 2
Tigres 2, Once Caldas 1

QUARTER-FINALS FIRST LEG
Paranaense 3, Santos 2
Sao Paulo 4, Tigres 0
Banfield 1, River Plate 1
Guadalajara 4, Boca Juniors 0

QUARTER-FINALS SECOND LEG
Tigres 2, Sao Paulo 1
Santos 0, Paranaense 2
River Plate 3, Banfield 2
Boca Juniors 0, Guadalajara 0

SEMI-FINALS FIRST LEG
Sao Paulo 2, River Plate 0
Paranaense 3, Guadalajara 0

SEMI-FINALS SECOND LEG
River Plate 2, Sao Paulo 3
Guadalajara 2, Paranaense 2

FINAL FIRST LEG
Paranaense 1 Sao Paulo 1

FINAL SECOND LEG
Sao Paulo v Paranaense – 14/7/05

COPA LIBERTADORES PAST WINNERS

1960 Penarol (Uruguay)
1961 Penarol
1962 Santos (Brazil)
1963 Santos
1964 Independiente (Argentina)
1965 Independiente
1966 Penarol
1967 Racing Club (Argentina)
1968 Estudiantes (Argentina)
1969 Estudiantes
1970 Estudiantes
1971 Nacional (Uruguay)
1972 Independiente
1973 Independiente
1974 Independiente
1975 Independiente
1976 Cruzeiro (Brazil)
1977 Boca Juniors (Argentina)
1978 Boca Juniors
1979 Olimpia (Paraguay)
1980 Nacional
1981 Flamengo (Brazil)
1982 Penarol
1983 Gremio Porto Alegre (Brazil)
1984 Independiente
1985 Argentinos Juniors (Argentina)
1986 River Plate (Argentina)
1987 Penarol
1988 Nacional (Uruguay)
1989 Nacional (Colombia)
1990 Olimpia
1991 Colo Colo (Chile)
1992 São Paulo (Brazil)
1993 São Paulo
1994 Velez Sarsfield (Argentina)
1995 Gremio Porto Alegre
1996 River Plate
1997 Cruzeiro
1998 Vasco da Gama
1999 Palmeiras
2000 Boca Juniors
2001 Boca Juniors
2002 Olimpia
2003 Boca Juniors
2004 Once Caldas

COPA SUDAMERICANA

FINAL FIRST LEG
Bolivar 1, Boca Juniors 0

FINAL SECOND LEG
Boca Juniors 2, Bolivar 0

COPA AMERICA 2004

GROUP A
Colombia 1, Venezuela 0
Peru 2, Bolivia 2
Colombia 1, Bolivia 0
Peru 3, Venezuela 1
Venezuela 1, Bolivia 1
Peru 2, Colombia 2

GROUP B
Uruguay 2, Mexico 2
Argentina 6, Ecuador 1
Uruguay 2, Ecuador 1
Argentina 0, Mexico 1
Mexico 2, Ecuador 1
Argentina 4, Uruguay 2

GROUP C
Paraguay 1, Costa Rica 0
Brazil 1, Chile 0
Costa Rica 1, Brazil 4
Paraguay 1, Chile 1
Chile 1, Costa Rica 2
Brazil 1, Paraguay 2

QUARTER-FINALS
Peru 0, Argentina 1
Colombia 2, Costa Rica 0
Paraguay 1, Uruguay 3
Mexico 0, Brazil 4

SEMI-FINALS
Argentina 3, Colombia 0
Brazil 1, Uruguay 1
Brazil won 5-3 on penalties.

MATCH FOR THIRD PLACE
Uruguay 2, Colombia 1

FINAL
Brazil 2, Argentina 2
Brazil won 4-2 on penalties.

COPA AMERICA PAST WINNERS

1916	Uruguay
1917	Uruguay
1919	Brazil
1920	Uruguay
1921	Argentina
1922	Brazil
1923	Uruguay
1924	Uruguay
1925	Argentina
1926	Uruguay
1927	Argentina
1929	Argentina
1935	Uruguay
1937	Argentina
1939	Peru
1941	Argentina
1942	Uruguay
1945	Argentina
1946	Argentina
1947	Argentina
1949	Brazil
1953	Paraguay
1955	Argentina
1956	Uruguay
1957	Argentina
1959	Argentina
1959	Uruguay
1963	Bolivia
1967	Uruguay
1975	Peru
1979	Paraguay
1983	Uruguay
1987	Uruguay
1989	Brazil
1991	Argentina
1993	Argentina
1995	Uruguay
1997	Brazil
1999	Brazil
2001	Colombia
2004	Brazil

CONCACAF

CONCACAF CUP OF THE CHAMPIONS 2005

FINAL FIRST LEG
Saprissa 2, UNAM 0

FINAL SECOND LEG
UNAM 2, Saprissa 1

UNCAF CUP

FINAL
Costa Rica 1, Honduras 1
Costa Rica won 7-6 on penalties.

OCEANIA

CONCACAF CUP OF THE CHAMPIONS 2005

FINAL FIRST LEG
Saprissa 2, UNAM 0

FINAL SECOND LEG
UNAM 2, Saprissa 1

NATIONS CUP

FINAL FIRST LEG
Soloman Islands 1, Australia 5

FINAL SECOND LEG
Australia 6, Soloman Islands 0

NORTH AMERICA

MLS CUP 2005

FINAL
Kansas City Wizards 2, DC United 3

ASIA

ASIA CHAMPIONS LEAGUE

FINAL FIRST LEG
Al-Ittihad 1, Seongnam 3

FINAL SECOND LEG
Seongnam 0, Al-Ittihad 5

NATIONS CUP

FINAL
China 1, Japan 3

TIGER CUP

FINAL FIRST LEG
Indonesia 1, Singapore 3

FINAL SECOND LEG
Singapore 2, Indonesia 1

GULF CUP

FINAL
Oman 1, Qatar 1
Qatar won 5-4 on penalties.

AFC CUP

FINAL FIRST LEG
Al-Wehda 2, Al-Jaish 3

FINAL SECOND LEG
Al-Jaish 0, Al-Wehda 1

ARAB CHAMPIONS LEAGUE

FINAL
CS Sfaxien 0, Ismaili 0
CS Sfaxien won 4-3 on penalties.

AFRICA

COSAFA CUP 2005

FINAL
Zambia 0, Angola 0
Angola won 5-4 on penalties.

AFRICAN CHAMPIONS LEAGUE FINAL 2005

FINAL FIRST LEG
Etoile du Sahel 2, Enyimba 1

FINAL SECOND LEG
Enyimba 2, Etoile du Sahel 1
Enyimba won 5-3 on penalties.

CAF CUP 2005

FINAL FIRST LEG
Hearts of Oak 1, Ashanti 1

FINAL SECOND LEG
Ashanti 1, Hearts of Oak 1
Hearts of Oak won 8-7 on penalties.

AFRICAN SUPER CUP 2005

FINAL
Enyimba 2, Hearts of Oak 0

UEFA UNDER-21 CHAMPIONSHIP 2004–06

GROUP 1
Romania 1, Finland 0
Macedonia 4, Armenia 0
Romania 5, Macedonia 1
Holland 0, Czech Republic 0
Armenia 0, Finland 1
Czech Republic 4, Romania 1
Finland 0, Armenia 1
Macedonia 0, Holland 2
Holland 4, Finland 1
Armenia 0, Czech Republic 4
Armenia 0, Romania 5
Macedonia 2, Czech Republic 2
Romania 2, Holland 0
Czech Republic 3, Finland 0
Holland 0, Armenia 0
Macedonia 1, Romania 0
Holland 2, Romania 0
Armenia 0, Macedonia 0
Czech Republic 2, Macedonia 0
Finland 1, Holland 2
Romania 2, Armenia 0

GROUP 2
Albania 1, Greece 1
Denmark 3, Ukraine 2
Turkey 0, Georgia 0
Kazakhstan 0, Ukraine 1
Georgia 2, Albania 1
Greece 2, Turkey 1
Albania 1, Denmark 2
Ukraine 1, Greece 0
Turkey 1, Kazakhstan 0
Kazakhstan 0, Albania 1
Ukraine 6, Georgia 0
Denmark 1, Turkey 1
Greece 5, Kazakhstan 0
Georgia 2, Denmark 4
Turkey 1, Ukraine 0
Albania 1, Ukraine 1
Greece 0, Denmark 1
Denmark 5, Kazakhstan 1
Georgia 1, Greece 1
Turkey 4, Albania 0
Georgia 0, Turkey 2
Greece 2, Albania 0
Ukraine 0, Denmark 1
Albania 0, Georgia 1
Ukraine 2, Kazakhstan 1
Turkey 0, Greece 2
Kazakhstan 2, Turkey 1
Denmark 7, Albania 0
Greece 0, Ukraine 1

GROUP 3
Slovakia 1, Luxembourg 0
Estonia 0, Luxembourg 0
Latvia 1, Portugal 2
Russia 4, Slovakia 0
Luxembourg 1, Latvia 2
Portugal 3, Estonia 0
Luxembourg 0, Russia 4
Slovakia 3, Latvia 1
Latvia 0, Estonia 0
Portugal 2, Russia 0
Russia 3, Estonia 0
Luxembourg 1, Portugal 6
Estonia 0, Slovakia 2
Latvia 2, Luxembourg 1
Slovakia 0, Portugal 1
Estonia 1, Russia 5
Portugal 2, Slovakia 1
Russia 1, Latvia 1
Luxembourg 0, Slovakia 2
Estonia 0, Portugal 5

GROUP 4
France 1, Israel 0
Republic of Ireland 3, Cyprus 0
Israel 1, Cyprus 0
Switzerland 4, Republic of Ireland 2
Israel 1, Switzerland 1
France 1, Republic of Ireland 0
Cyprus 0, France 1
Cyprus 0, Israel 1
Israel 3, Republic of Ireland 1
France 1, Switzerland 1
Israel 3, France 2
Switzerland 3, Cyprus 0
Republic of Ireland 2, Israel 2

GROUP 5
Italy 2, Norway 0
Slovenia 1, Moldova 0
Norway 2, Belarus 3
Scotland 1, Slovenia 1
Moldova 0, Italy 1
Belarus 2, Moldova 3
Scotland 0, Norway 2
Slovenia 0, Italy 3
Moldova 0, Scotland 0
Norway 0, Slovenia 0
Italy 2, Belarus 1
Italy 2, Scotland 0
Moldova 1, Norway 3
Slovenia 1, Belarus 4
Belarus 1, Slovenia 2
Scotland 0, Moldova 0
Norway 1, Italy 0
Belarus 3, Scotland 2

GROUP 6
Azerbaijan 0, Wales 1
Austria 0, England 2
Austria 3, Azerbaijan 0
Poland 1, England 3
Austria 0, Poland 3
England 2, Wales 0
Azerbaijan 0, Germany 2
Wales 2, Poland 2
Germany 2, Austria 0
Azerbaijan 0, England 0
Germany 1, Poland 1
Wales 0, Germany 4
Wales 1, Austria 0
Poland 3, Azerbaijan 0
England 2, Germany 2
Austria 2, Wales 0
England 2, Azerbaijan 0
Azerbaijan 1, Poland 1

GROUP 7
Belgium 3, Lithuania 0
San Marino 0, Serbia & Montenegro 5
Bosnia 0, Spain 2
Lithuania 2, San Marino 0
Bosnia 1, Serbia & Montenegro 3
Spain 2, Belgium 2
Serbia & Montenegro 9, San Marino 0
Lithuania 1, Spain 1
Belgium 4, Serbia & Montenegro 0
San Marino 1, Lithuania 2
Spain 14, San Marino 0
Belgium 2, Bosnia 1
Serbia & Montenegro 1, Spain 0
Bosnia 2, Lithuania 0
San Marino 0, Belgium 4
Serbia & Montenegro 1, Belgium 1
San Marino 1, Bosnia 4
Spain 2, Lithuania 0
Spain 4, Bosnia 2

GROUP 8
Iceland 3, Bulgaria 1
Croatia 1, Hungary 0
Malta 0, Sweden 1
Hungary 1, Iceland 0
Sweden 0, Croatia 2
Croatia 1, Bulgaria 0
Malta 1, Iceland 0
Sweden 2, Hungary 1
Iceland 3, Sweden 1
Bulgaria 2, Malta 1
Malta 0, Hungary 2
Bulgaria 1, Sweden 2
Croatia 2, Iceland 1
Hungary 1, Bulgaria 0
Croatia 1, Malta 0
Bulgaria 2, Croatia 1
Iceland 0, Hungary 1
Sweden 6, Malta 0
Iceland 0, Malta 0
Competition still being played.

UEFA UNDER-21 CHAMPIONSHIP PREVIOUS WINNERS

1978 Yugoslavia
1980 USSR
1982 England
1984 England
1986 Spain
1988 France
1990 USSR
1992 Italy
1994 Italy
1996 Italy
1998 Spain
2000 Italy
2002 Czech Republic
2004 Italy

UEFA UNDER-17 CHAMPIONSHIP 2005

(Finals in Italy)

GROUP A
Belarus 0, England 4
Italy 1, Turkey 0
Italy 0, Belarus 1
Turkey 3, England 2
England 0, Italy 1
Turkey 5, Belarus 1

GROUP B
Israel 0, Switzerland 3
Croatia 2, Holland 2
Switzerland 0, Holland 0
Israel 2, Croatia 4
Holland 2, Israel 1
Switzerland 2, Croatia 5

SEMI-FINALS
Italy 0, Holland 1
Croatia 1, Turkey 3

MATCH FOR THIRD PLACE
Italy 2, Croatia 1

FINAL
Turkey 2, Holland 0

WORLD YOUTH CUP 2005

(Finals in Holland)

GROUP A	P	W	D	L	F	A	Pts
Holland	3	3	0	0	6	1	9
Japan	3	0	2	1	3	4	2
Benin	3	0	2	1	2	3	2
Australia	3	0	2	1	2	5	2

GROUP B	P	W	D	L	F	A	Pts
China	3	3	0	0	9	4	9
Ukraine	3	1	1	1	7	6	4
Turkey	3	1	1	1	4	4	4
Panama	3	0	0	3	2	8	0

GROUP C	P	W	D	L	F	A	Pts
Spain	3	3	0	0	13	1	9
Morocco	3	2	0	1	7	3	6
Chile	3	1	0	2	7	8	3
Honduras	3	0	0	3	0	15	0

GROUP D	P	W	D	L	F	A	Pts
USA	3	2	1	0	2	0	7
Argentina	3	2	0	1	3	1	6
Germany	3	1	1	1	2	1	4
Egypt	3	0	0	3	0	5	0

GROUP E	P	W	D	L	F	A	Pts
Colombia	3	3	0	0	6	0	9
Syria	3	1	1	1	3	4	4
Italy	3	1	0	2	5	5	3
Canada	3	0	1	2	2	7	1

GROUP F	P	W	D	L	F	A	Pts
Brazil	3	2	1	0	3	0	7
Nigeria	3	1	1	1	4	2	4
South Korea	3	1	0	2	3	5	3
Switzerland	3	1	0	2	2	5	3

SECOND ROUND
USA 1, Italy 3
Morocco 1, Japan 0
Brazil 1, Syria 0
China 2, Germany 3
Nigeria 1, Ukraine 0
Holland 3, Chile 0
Colombia 1, Argentina 2
Spain 3, Turkey 0

QUARTER-FINALS
Morocco 2, Italy 2
Morocco won 4-2 on penalties.
Germany 1, Brazil 2
Nigeria 1, Holland 1
Nigeria won 10-9 on penalties.
Argentina 3, Spain 1

SEMI-FINALS
Brazil 1, Argentina 2
Morocco 0, Nigeria 3

MATCH FOR THIRD PLACE
Brazil 2, Morocco 1

FINAL IN UTRECHT
Argentina 2, Nigeria 1

ENGLAND UNDER-21 RESULTS 1976–2005

EC UEFA Competition for Under-21 Teams

Year	Date		Venue		
			v ALBANIA	Eng	Alb
EC1989	Mar	7	Shkroda	2	1
EC1989	April	25	Ipswich	2	0
EC2001	Mar	27	Tirana	1	0
EC2001	Sept	4	Middlesbrough	5	0
			v ANGOLA	Eng	Ang
1995	June	10	Toulon	1	0
1996	May	28	Toulon	0	2
			v ARGENTINA	Eng	Arg
1998	May	18	Toulon	0	2
2000	Feb	22	Fulham	1	0
			v AUSTRIA	Eng	Aus
1994	Oct	11	Kapfenberg	3	1
1995	Nov	14	Middlesbrough	2	1
2004	Sept	3	Krems	2	0
			v AZERBAIJAN	Eng	Az
EC2004	Oct	12	Baku	0	0
EC2005	Mar	29	Middlesbrough	2	0
			v BELGIUM	Eng	Bel
1994	June	5	Marseille	2	1
1996	May	24	Toulon	1	0
			v BRAZIL	Eng	B
1993	June	11	Toulon	0	0
1995	June	6	Toulon	0	2
1996	June	1	Toulon	1	2
			v BULGARIA	Eng	Bul
EC1979	June	5	Pernik	3	1
EC1979	Nov	20	Leicester	5	0
1989	June	5	Toulon	2	3
EC1998	Oct	9	West Ham	1	0
EC1999	June	8	Vratsa	1	0
			v CROATIA	Eng	Cro
1996	Apr	23	Sunderland	0	1
2003	Aug	19	West Ham	0	3
			v CZECHOSLOVAKIA	Eng	Cz
1990	May	28	Toulon	2	1
1992	May	26	Toulon	1	2
1993	June	9	Toulon	1	1
			v CZECH REPUBLIC	Eng	CzR
1998	Nov	17	Ipswich	0	1
			v DENMARK	Eng	Den
EC1978	Sept	19	Hvidovre	2	1
EC1979	Sept	11	Watford	1	0
EC1982	Sept	21	Hvidovre	4	1
EC1983	Sept	20	Norwich	4	1
EC1986	Mar	12	Copenhagen	1	0
EC1986	Mar	26	Manchester	1	1
1988	Sept	13	Watford	0	0
1994	Mar	8	Brentford	1	0
1999	Oct	8	Bradford	4	1
			v EAST GERMANY	Eng	EG
EC1980	April	16	Sheffield	1	2
EC1980	April	23	Jena	0	1
			v FINLAND	Eng	Fin
EC1977	May	26	Helsinki	1	0
EC1977	Oct	12	Hull	8	1
EC1984	Oct	16	Southampton	2	0
EC1985	May	21	Mikkeli	1	3
EC2000	Oct	10	Valkeakoski	2	2
EC2001	Mar	23	Barnsley	4	0
			v FRANCE	Eng	Fra
EC1984	Feb	28	Sheffield	6	1
EC1984	Mar	28	Rouen	1	0
1987	June	11	Toulon	0	2
EC1988	April	13	Besancon	2	4
EC1988	April	27	Highbury	2	2
1988	June	12	Toulon	2	4
1990	May	23	Toulon	7	3
1991	June	3	Toulon	1	0
1992	May	28	Toulon	0	0
1993	June	15	Toulon	1	0
1994	May	31	Aubagne	0	3
1995	June	10	Toulon	0	2
1998	May	14	Toulon	1	1
1999	Feb	9	Derby	2	1
			v GEORGIA	Eng	Geo
EC1996	Nov	8	Batumi	1	0
EC1997	April	29	Charlton	0	0
2000	Aug	31	Middlesbrough	6	1
			v GERMANY	Eng	Ger
1991	Sept	10	Scunthorpe	2	1
EC2000	Oct	6	Derby	1	1
EC2001	Aug	31	Frieburg	2	1
2005	Mar	25	Hull	2	2
			v GREECE	Eng	Gre
EC1982	Nov	16	Piraeus	0	1
EC1983	Mar	29	Portsmouth	2	1
1989	Feb	7	Patras	0	1
EC1997	Nov	13	Heraklion	0	2
EC1997	Dec	17	Norwich	4	2
EC2001	June	5	Athens	1	3
EC2001	Oct	5	Ewood Park	2	1
			v HOLLAND	Eng	H
EC1993	April	27	Portsmouth	3	0
EC1993	Oct	12	Utrecht	1	1
2001	Aug	14	Reading	4	0
EC2001	Nov	9	Utrecht	2	2
EC2001	Nov	13	Derby	1	0
2004	Feb	17	Hull	3	2
2005	Feb	8	Derby	1	2
			v HUNGARY	Eng	Hun
EC1981	June	5	Keszthely	2	1
EC1981	Nov	17	Nottingham	2	0
EC1983	April	26	Newcastle	1	0
EC1983	Oct	11	Nyiregyhaza	2	0
1990	Sept	11	Southampton	3	1
1992	May	12	Budapest	2	2
1999	April	27	Budapest	2	2
			v ITALY	Eng	Italy
EC1978	Mar	8	Manchester	2	1
EC1978	April	5	Rome	0	0
EC1984	April	18	Manchester	3	1
EC1984	May	2	Florence	0	1
EC1986	April	9	Pisa	0	2
EC1986	April	23	Swindon	1	1
EC1997	Feb	12	Bristol	1	0
EC1997	Oct	10	Rieti	1	0
EC2000	May	27	Bratislava	0	2
2000	Nov	14	Monza*	0	0
2002	Mar	26	Valley Parade	1	1
EC2002	May	20	Basle	1	2
2003	Feb	11	Pisa	0	1

**Abandoned 11 mins; fog.*

Year	Date		Venue		
			v ISRAEL	Eng	Isr
1985	Feb	27	Tel Aviv	2	1
			v LATVIA	Eng	Lat
1995	April	25	Riga	1	0
1995	June	7	Burnley	4	0
			v LUXEMBOURG	Eng	Lux
EC1998	Oct	13	Greven Macher	5	0
EC1999	Sept	3	Reading	5	0
			v MACEDONIA	Eng	M
EC2002	Oct	15	Reading	3	1
EC2003	Sept	5	Skopje	1	1
			v MALAYSIA	Eng	Mal
1995	June	8	Toulon	2	0
			v MEXICO	Eng	Mex
1988	June	5	Toulon	2	1
1991	May	29	Toulon	6	0
1992	May	25	Toulon	1	1
2001	May	24	Leicester	3	0

			v MOLDOVA	Eng	Mol
EC1996	Aug	31	Chisinau	2	0
EC1997	Sept	9	Wycombe	1	0

			v MOROCCO	Eng	Mor
1987	June	7	Toulon	2	0
1988	June	9	Toulon	1	0

			v NORWAY	Eng	Nor
EC1977	June	1	Bergen	2	1
EC1977	Sept	6	Brighton	6	0
1980	Sept	9	Southampton	3	0
1981	Sept	8	Drammen	0	0
EC1992	Oct	13	Peterborough	0	2
EC1993	June	1	Stavanger	1	1
1995	Oct	10	Stavanger	2	2

			v POLAND	Eng	Pol
EC1982	Mar	17	Warsaw	2	1
EC1982	April	7	West Ham	2	2
EC1989	June	2	Plymouth	2	1
EC1989	Oct	10	Jastrzebie	3	1
EC1990	Oct	16	Tottenham	0	1
EC1991	Nov	12	Pila	1	2
EC1993	May	28	Zdroj	4	1
EC1993	Sept	7	Millwall	1	2
EC1996	Oct	8	Wolverhampton	0	0
EC1997	May	30	Katowice	1	1
EC1999	Mar	26	Southampton	5	0
EC1999	Sept	7	Plock	1	3
EC2004	Sept	7	Rybnik	3	1

			v PORTUGAL	Eng	Por
1987	June	13	Toulon	0	0
1990	May	21	Toulon	0	1
1993	June	7	Toulon	2	0
1994	June	7	Toulon	2	0
EC1994	Sept	6	Leicester	0	0
1995	Sept	2	Lisbon	0	2
1996	May	30	Toulon	1	3
2000	Apr	16	Stoke	0	1
EC2002	May	22	Zurich	1	3
EC2003	Mar	28	Rio Major	2	4
EC2003	Sept	9	Everton	1	2

			v REPUBLIC OF IRELAND	Eng	RoI
1981	Feb	25	Liverpool	1	0
1985	Mar	25	Portsmouth	3	2
1989	June	9	Toulon	0	0
EC1990	Nov	13	Cork	3	0
EC1991	Mar	26	Brentford	3	0
1994	Nov	15	Newcastle	1	0
1995	Mar	27	Dublin	2	0

			v ROMANIA	Eng	Rom
EC1980	Oct	14	Ploesti	0	4
EC1981	April	28	Swindon	3	0
EC1985	April	30	Brasov	0	0
EC1985	Sept	10	Ipswich	3	0

			v RUSSIA	Eng	Rus
1994	May	30	Bandol	2	0

			v SAN MARINO	Eng	SM
EC1993	Feb	16	Luton	6	0
EC1993	Nov	17	San Marino	4	0

			v SENEGAL	Eng	Sen
1989	June	7	Toulon	6	1
1991	May	27	Toulon	2	1

			v SERBIA-MONTENEGRO	Eng	S-M
2003	June	2	Hull	3	2

			v SCOTLAND	Eng	Sco
1977	April	27	Sheffield	1	0
EC1980	Feb	12	Coventry	2	1
EC1980	Mar	4	Aberdeen	0	0
EC1982	April	19	Glasgow	1	0
EC1982	April	28	Manchester	1	1
EC1988	Feb	16	Aberdeen	1	0
EC1988	Mar	22	Nottingham	1	0
1993	June	13	Toulon	1	0

			v SLOVAKIA	Eng	Slo
EC2002	June	1	Bratislava	0	2
EC2002	Oct	11	Trnava	4	0
EC2003	June	10	Sunderland	2	0

			v SLOVENIA	Eng	Slo
2000	Feb	12	Nova Gorica	1	0

			v SOUTH AFRICA	Eng	SA
1998	May	16	Toulon	3	1

			v SPAIN	Eng	Spa
EC1984	May	17	Seville	1	0
EC1984	May	24	Sheffield	2	0
1987	Feb	18	Burgos	2	1
1992	Sept	8	Burgos	1	0
2001	Feb	27	Birmingham	0	4
2004	Nov	16	Alcala	0	1

			v SWEDEN	Eng	Swe
1979	June	9	Vasteras	2	1
1986	Sept	9	Ostersund	1	1
EC1988	Oct	18	Coventry	1	1
EC1989	Sept	5	Uppsala	0	1
EC1998	Sept	4	Sundvall	2	0
EC1999	June	4	Huddersfield	3	0
2004	Mar	30	Kristiansund	2	2

			v SWITZERLAND	Eng	Swit
EC1980	Nov	18	Ipswich	5	0
EC1981	May	31	Neuenburg	0	0
1988	May	28	Lausanne	1	1
1996	April	1	Swindon	0	0
1998	Mar	24	Brugglifeld	0	2
EC2002	May	17	Zurich	2	1

			v TURKEY	Eng	Tur
EC1984	Nov	13	Bursa	0	0
EC1985	Oct	15	Bristol	3	0
EC1987	April	28	Izmir	0	0
EC1987	Oct	13	Sheffield	1	1
EC1991	April	30	Izmir	2	2
1991	Oct	15	Reading	2	0
EC1992	Nov	17	Orient	0	1
EC1993	Mar	30	Izmir	0	0
EC2000	May	29	Bratislava	6	0
EC2003	April	1	Newcastle	1	1
EC2003	Oct	10	Istanbul	0	1

			v UKRAINE	Eng	Uk
2004	Aug	17	Middlesbrough	3	1

			v USA	Eng	USA
1989	June	11	Toulon	0	2
1994	June	2	Toulon	3	0

			v USSR	Eng	USSR
1987	June	9	Toulon	0	0
1988	June	7	Toulon	1	0
1990	May	25	Toulon	2	1
1991	May	31	Toulon	2	1

			v WALES	Eng	Wales
1976	Dec	15	Wolverhampton	0	0
1979	Feb	6	Swansea	1	0
1990	Dec	5	Tranmere	0	0
EC2004	Oct	8	Blackburn	2	0

			v WEST GERMANY	Eng	WG
EC1982	Sept	21	Sheffield	3	1
EC1982	Oct	12	Bremen	2	3
1987	Sept	8	Ludenscheid	0	2

			v YUGOSLAVIA	Eng	Yugo
EC1978	April	19	Novi Sad	1	2
EC1978	May	2	Manchester	1	1
EC1986	Nov	11	Peterborough	1	1
EC1987	Nov	10	Zemun	5	1
EC2000	Mar	29	Barcelona	3	0
2002	Sept	6	Bolton	1	1

BRITISH AND IRISH UNDER-21 TEAMS 2004–05

▪ *Denotes player sent off.*

ENGLAND UNDER-21 TEAMS 2004–05

Middlesbrough, 17 August 2004, 5658

England (2) 3 *(Cole C 13, 42, Bent 90)*

Ukraine (0) 1 *(Alyev 88)*

England: Carson; Hunt (Hoyte 46), Kilgallon, Ferdinand, Richards (Harding 46), Pennant, Milner (Bent 60), O'Neil, Downing (Reo-Coker 76), Cole C (Ashton 46), Stead (Whittingham 46).

Krems, 3 September 2004, 4500

Austria (0) 0

England (1) 2 *(Cole C 32, Bent 89)*

England: Carson; Hunt, Davenport, Ferdinand, Pennant (Hoyte 90), O'Neil, Reo-Coker, Downing (Milner 74), Stead (Bent 66), Cole C.

Rybnik, 7 September 2004, 3000

Poland (1) 1 *(Burkhartd 5)*

England (1) 3 *(Cole C 45, Bent 72 (pen), 83)*

England: Carson; Johnson G, Ferdinand (Kilgallon 38), Davenport, Baines (Hoyte 83), Pennant, O'Neil, Bentley (Bent 64), Milner, Reo-Coker, Cole C.

Blackburn, 8 October 2004, 17,500

England (0) 2 *(Milner 46, Bent 73)*

Wales (0) 0

England: Carson; Johnson G (Taylor S 84), Hunt, Davenport, Harding, Pennant (Whittingham 75), O'Neil, Milner, Downing, Cole C (Bent 19), Stead.
Wales: Price; Anthony, Duffy, Parslow, Gilbert, Fowler (Crowell 69), Pipe, Tolley, Vaughan, Birchall (Carpenter 76), Calliste.

Baku, 12 October 2004, 1500

Azerbaijan (0) 0

England (0) 0

England: Carson; Johnson G, Hunt, Davenport (Kilgallon 70), Harding, O'Neil (Downing 46), Reo-Coker▪, Whittingham, Pennant, Stead, Milner.

Alcala, 16 November 2004, 3000

Spain (0) 1 *(Fabregas 63)*

England (0) 0

England: Carson (Camp 46); Johnson G▪, Dawson (Daveport 79), Hunt (Ridgewell 79), Harding (Watson 46), Ambrose (Routledge 60), Hoyte, Whittingham, Milner (Downing 60), Cole C, Bent.

Derby, 8 February 2005, 33,184

England (0) 1 *(Lita 90)*

Holland (2) 2 *(John 19, Jager 37)*

England: Carson (Camp 46); Hoyte (Lita 64), Taylor S, Ridgewell, Baines (Welsh 46), Huddlestone, Routledge (Marney 69), Whittingham, Milner, Cole C (Stead 40), Ashton (Richardson 46).

Hull, 25 March 2005, 21,746

England (0) 2 *(Bent 50, Ashton 52)*

Germany (0) 2 *(Klessling 49, Hilbert 89)*

England: Carson; Johnson G, Hunt, Davenport, Ridgewell (Welsh 46), Milner, O'Neil (Taylor S 90), Huddlestone, Richardson (Rosenior 80), Ashton, Bent.

Middlesbrough, 29 March 2005, 19,095

England (2) 2 *(Welsh 27, Ashton 42)*

Azerbaijan (0) 0

England: Carson; Rosenior, Taylor S, Davenport, Huddlestone, Whittingham, Milner, Welsh, Richardson (Routledge 56), Ashton (Stead 67), Bent (Ambrose 81).

SCOTLAND UNDER-21 TEAMS 2004–05

Dunaujvaros, 18 August 2004, 300

Hungary (2) 4 *(Jovanczai 13, 60, Czvitkovics 39, Kanta 90)*

Scotland (1) 2 *(Boyd 43, Whittaker 89)*

Scotland: Samson (Smith 46); Wilson, Morrison, Diamond (McCunnie 75), Robertson, Hutton (Whittaker 62), Brown, Foy (Prunty 46), Sweeney (Lappin 75), Boyd, Gallagher (Riordan 65).

Alcoi, 2 September 2004, 5312

Spain (0) 3 *(Iniesta 55, Cazorla 66, Melli 73 (pen))*

Scotland (1) 1 *(O'Connor 43)*

Scotland: Smith (Turner 74); Dowie, Morrison, Diamond, Robertson, McCunnie, Whittaker, Sweeney, O'Connor (Prunty 79), Brown (Riordan 60), Clarkson!.

St Johnstone, 7 September 2004, 2768

Scotland (1) 1 *(O'Connor 11)*

Slovenia (1) 1 *(Sernier 14)*

Scotland: Smith; Dowie, Lappin, Diamond, Robertson, McCunnie (Whittaker 46), Hutton (Prunty 56), Sweeney, O'Connor, Brown, Clarkson (Riordan 46).

Cumbernauld, 8 October 2004, 3014

Scotland (0) 0

Norway (1) 2 *(Grindheim 42, Eriksen 75)*

Scotland: Smith; Dowie, Lappin, Whittaker, Robertson, Wilson, Foy (McCunnie 54), Wallace, O'Connor, Fagan (Clarkson 70), Boyd.

Chisinau, 12 October 2004, 750

Moldova (0) 0

Scotland (0) 0

Scotland: Smith; Dowie, Lappin, Whittaker, Robertson, McCunnie, Foster, Wilson, O'Connor, Clarkson (Boyd 65), Morrison.

Falkirk, 16 November 2004, 2076

Scotland (0) 1 *(McCunnie 59)*

Sweden (1) 2 *(Dahlberg 44, Runstrom 58)*

Scotland: Turner; Dowie, Morrison, Whittaker, Robertson, McCunnie, Hutton (Foster 64), Wilson, Gallagher (Sweeney 34), Lappin (Leven 46), Duffy.

Belfast, 8 February 2005, 1300

Northern Ireland (0) 2 *(Brunt 47, Morrow 59)*

Scotland (1) 1 *(Maloney 36)*

Northern Ireland: McGovern; Ward (Gault 46), Friars, Hughes, Webb, McChrystal, Gilfillan (Murtagh 86), Clingan, Braniff (Teggart 75), Shiels (Morrow 57), Brunt.
Scotland: Samson; Dowie, Brighton (Clarkson 80), Whittaker (Hutton 46), Robertson, McCunnie, Wilson, Leven (Burke 67), Morrison, Duffy, Maloney.

Pavia, 25 March 2005, 4300

Italy (0) 2 *(Bianchi 65, Rosina 71)*

Scotland (0 0

Scotland: Marshall; Dowie, Morrison, Diamond, Berra, Wilson, Whitaker, McCunnie, Maloney (Brighton 79), Riordan (Boyd 87), Brown.

Firhill, 3 June 2005

Scotland (0) 0

Moldova (0) 0

Scotland: Samson; Watt, Morrison, Collins, Robertson, Wilson (Clarkson 60), Whittaker, McCunnie, Maloney, Brown (Sweeney 65), Gallagher (Brighton 55).

Minsk, 7 June 2005, 1500

Belarus (1) 3 *(Kovel 3, Stashchaniuk 48, Afanasyev 51)*

Scotland (0) 2 *(Whittaker 57, Clarkson 86)*

Scotland: Marshall; Dowie, Morrison, Diamond, Berra, Wilson, Whittaker, McCunnie, Maloney (Brighton 79), Riordan (Boyd 87), Brown.

NORTHERN IRELAND UNDER-21 TEAMS 2004–05

Belfast, 18 August 2004, 300

Northern Ireland (0) 0

Switzerland (0) 0

Northern Ireland: Julian; Ervin, Friars, Clingan, Webb, McChrystal, Hughes, Davis, Braniff (Teggart 60), Clarke, McCourt (Shiels 46).

WALES UNDER-21 TEAMS 2004–05

Riga, 18 August 2004, 700

Latvia (0) 0

Wales (0) 0

Wales: Price (Worgan 73); Duffy (Spender 63), Gilbert, Fowler, Morgan (Anthony 63), Parslow, Fleetwood (Jones M), Fish (Davies A), Hughes, Birchall (Calliste 46), Pipe (Davies L 86).

Baku, 1 September 2004, 1000

Azerbaijan (0) 0

Wales (0) 1 *(Crowell 85)*

Wales: Price; Pipe, Gilbert, Fowler (Spender 61), Parslow, Jones S, Fleetwood (Crowell 82), Tolley, Birchall (Fish 87), Calliste, Vaughan.

Swansea, 12 October 2004, 1801

Wales (1) 2 *(Vaughan 28, Birchall 73)*

Poland (1) 2 *(Gregorek 7, Brozek 82)*

Wales: Price; Anthony, Gilbert, Fowler (Crowell 76), Parslow, Duffy, Pipe, Tolley, Calliste, Vaughan, Birchall.

Wrexham, 8 February 2005, 5005

Wales (0) 0

Germany (2) 4 *(Senesie 15, Ludwig 27, Hanke 79, Jansen 90)*

Wales: Price; Duffy (Nyatanga 54), Gilbert, Pipe, Morgan, Collins (Beevers 31), Crofts (Tolley 74), Fowler, Calliste, Vaughan, Ledley.

Merthyr, 25 March 2005, 2043

Wales (1) 1 *(Berger 19 (og))*

Austria (0) 0

Wales: Worgan; Beevers, Gilbert, Crofts, Morgan, Duffy, Pipe (Birchall 67), Davies A, Calliste (Critchell 71), Davies C (Cotterill 79), Ledley.

Neusiedl Am See, 29 March 2005, 1000

Austria (1) 2 *(Klenast 9, Samuel 80)*

Wales (0) 0

Wales: Price; Beevers, Gilbert, Crofts, Morgan, Duffy, Birchall (Crowell 81), Davies A, Calliste (Cotterill 46), Davies C, Ledley.

REPUBLIC OF IRELAND UNDER-21 TEAMS 2004–05

Drogheda, 17 August 2004

Republic of Ireland (1) 3 *(Elliott 9, Tabb 71, McCarthy 89)*

Bulgaria (0) 2 *(Rangelov 57, 81)*

Republic of Ireland: Henderson (Murphy 46); McStay, McCarthy, Fitzgerald, Capper (Kendrick 75), McGeady, Potter (Flood 66), Whelan, Kearney (Thornton 46), Doyle (Tabb 46), Elliott.

Kilkenny, 3 September 2004, 1200

Republic of Ireland (1) 3 *(Whelan 34, Fitzgerald 60, Doyle 79)*

Cyprus (0) 0

Republic of Ireland: Murphy; Kelly, McCarthy (McStay 64, Fitzgerald, Capper, McGeady, Potter (Flood 86), Whelan, Kearney, Doyle (Tabb 83), Elliott.

Berne, 7 September 2004, 2200

Switzerland (1) 4 *(Lichsteiner 3, Margairaz 49, 55, McCarthy 80 (og))*

Republic of Ireland (0) 2 *(Elliott 63, McGeady 86 (pen))*

Republic of Ireland: Henderson; Kelly, McCarthy, Fitzgerald, Capper (Thornton 78), McGeady, Potter, Whelan, Kearney (Flood 61), Doyle (Tabb 55), Elliott.

Troyes, 8 October 2004, 14,263

France (0) 1 *(Drouin 84)*

Republic of Ireland (0) 0

Republic of Ireland: Henderson; Kelly, McCarthy, Fitzgerald, Capper, Flood, Potter, Whelan, McGeady, Murphy, Tabb.

Rio Maior, 8 February 2005, 1979

Portugal (2) 2 *(Hugo Almeida 16, 31)*

Republic of Ireland (0) 0

Republic of Ireland: Henderson (Deeney), Foley, Kelly, Fitzgerald, Timlin, Whelan (O'Brien), Potter (Bell), Thornton, Flood, Quigley, Yeates (McAliskey).

Tel Aviv, 25 March 2005, 3500

Israel (2) 3 *(Azran 5, McStay 6 (og), Arbeitman 52)*

Republic of Ireland (1) 1 *(McStay 35)*

Republic of Ireland: Deeney; Foley, McStay, McShane, Paisley, Flood (Thornton 66), Whelan, Potter (O'Brien 75), McGeady, Tabb, Murphy (Doyle 64).

Longford, 3 June 2005, 2400

Republic of Ireland (0) 2 *(Murphy 65, Doyle 77)*

Israel (2) 2 *(Ohayon 3, Alberman 36)*

Republic of Ireland: Henderson; Foley, McCarthy, Fitzgerald (Paisley 46), Sheehan, Bell (Doyle 59), Potter, Whelan (O'Brien 74), McGeady, Tabb, Murphy.

BRITISH UNDER-21 APPEARANCES 1976–2005

ENGLAND

Ablett, G. (Liverpool), 1988 v F (1)
Adams, A. (Arsenal). 1985 v Ei, Fi; 1986 v D; 1987 v Se, Y (5)
Adams, N. (Everton), 1987 v Se (1)
Allen, B. (QPR), 1992 v H, M, Cz, F; 1993 v N (sub), T, P, Cz (sub) (8)
Allen, C. A. (Oxford U), 1995 v Br (sub), F (sub) (2)
Allen, C. (QPR), 1980 v EG (sub); (with C Palace), 1981 v N, R (3)
Allen, M. (QPR), 1987 v Se (sub); 1988 v Y (sub) (2)
Allen, P. (West Ham U), 1985 v Ei, R; (with Tottenham H), 1986 v R (3)
Allen, R. W. (Tottenham H), 1998 v F (sub), S.Af, Arg (sub) (3)
Ambrose, D. P. F. (Ipswich T), 2003 v I (sub); (with Newcastle U), Ser (sub); 2004 v Se (sub); 2005 v Sp, Az (sub) (5)
Ameobi, F. (Newcastle U), 2001 v Sp (sub), Fi (sub), Alb (sub), M, Gr (sub); 2002 v Ho (sub+1), Slv (sub), Sw (sub), I (sub), P (sub); 2003 v Y (sub), Slo, Mac, I, P, Ser, Slo; 2004 v Mac, P, T (19)
Anderson, V. A. (Nottingham F), 1978 v I (1)
Anderton, D. R. (Tottenham H), 1993 v Sp, Sm, Ho, Pol, N, P, Cz, Br, S, F; 1994 v Pol, Sm (12)
Andrews, I. (Leicester C), 1987 v Se (1)
Ardley, N. C. (Wimbledon), 1993 v Pol, N, P, Cz, Br, S, F, 1994 v Pol (sub), Ho, Sm (10)
Ashcroft, L. (Preston NE), 1992 v H (sub) (1)
Ashton, D. (Crewe Alex), 2004 v Ho, Se; 2005 v Uk (sub); (with Norwich C), Ho, G, Az (6)
Atherton, P. (Coventry C), 1992 v T (1)
Atkinson, B. (Sunderland), 1991 v W (sub), Sen, M, USSR (sub), F; 1992 v Pol (sub) (6)
Awford, A. T. (Portsmouth), 1993 v Sp, N, T, P, Cz, Br, S, F; 1994 v Ho (9)

Bailey, G. R. (Manchester U), 1979 v W, Bul; 1980 v D, S (2), EG; 1982 v N; 1983 v D, Gr; 1984 v H, F (2), I, Sp (14)
Baines, L.J. (Wigan Ath), 2005 v A, Pol, Ho (3)
Baker, G. E. (Southampton), 1981 v N, R (2)
Ball, M. J. (Everton), 1999 v Se, Bul, L, CzR, Pol; 2000 v L, D (sub) (7)
Barker, S. (Blackburn R), 1985 v Is (sub), Ei, R; 1986 v I (4)
Barmby, N. J. (Tottenham H), 1994 v D; 1995 v P, A (sub); (with Everton), 1998 v Sw (4)
Bannister, G. (Sheffield W), 1982 v Pol (1)
Barnes, J. (Watford), 1983 v D, Gr (2)
Barnes, P. S. (Manchester C), 1977 v W (sub), S, Fi, N; 1978 v N, Fi, I (2), Y (9)
Barrett, E. D. (Oldham Ath), 1990 v P, F, USSR, Cz (4)
Barry, G. (Aston Villa), 1999 v CzR, F, H; 2000 v Y; 2001 v Sp, Fi, Alb; 2002 v Ho, G, Alb, Gr, Ho (sub), Slv, I, P, Sw, I, P; 2003 v Y, Slo, Mac, I, P, T, Slo; 2004 v Cro, P (27)
Barton, J. (Manchester C), 2004 v Mac, P (2)
Bart-Williams, C. G. (Sheffield W), 1993 v Sp, N, T; 1994 v D, Ru, F, Bel, P; 1995 v P, A, Ei (2), La (2); (with Nottingham F), 1996 v P (sub), A (16)
Batty, D. (Leeds U), 1988 v Sw (sub); 1989 v Gr (sub), Bul, Sen, Ei, US; 1990 v Pol (7)
Bazeley, D. S. (Watford), 1992 v H (sub) (1)
Beagrie, P. (Sheffield U), 1988 v WG, T (2)
Beardsmore, R. (Manchester U), 1989 v Gr, Alb (sub), Pol, Bul, USA (5)
Beattie, J. S. (Southampton), 1999 v CzR (sub), F (sub), Pol, H; 2000 v Pol (5)
Beckham, D. R. J. (Manchester U), 1995 v Br, Mal, An, F; 1996 v P, A (sub), Bel, An, P (9)
Bent, D. A. (Ipswich T), 2003 v I (sub), Ser (sub); 2004 v T (sub), Ho (sub), Se (sub); 2005 v Uk (sub), A (sub), Pol (sub), W (sub), Sp, G, Az (12)
Bent, M. N. (C Palace), 1998 v S.Af (sub), Arg (2)
Bentley, D. M. (Arsenal), 2004 v Ho, Se; 2005 v Pol (3)
Beeston, C (Stoke C), 1988 v USSR (1)
Benjamin, T. J. (Leicester C), 2001 v M (sub) (1)
Bertschin, K. E. (Birmingham C), 1977 v S; 1978 v Y (2) (3)
Birtles, G. (Nottingham F), 1980 v Bul, EG (sub) (2)
Blackwell, D. R. (Wimbledon), 1991 v W, T, Sen (sub), M, USSR, F (6)
Blake, M. A. (Aston Villa), 1990 v F (sub), Cz (sub); 1991 v H, Pol, Ei (2), W; 1992 v Pol (8)
Blissett, L. L. (Watford), 1979 v W, Bul (sub), Se; 1980 v D (4)
Booth, A. D. (Huddersfield T), 1995 v La (2 subs); 1996 v N (3)
Bothroyd, J. (Coventry C), 2001 v M (sub) (1)
Bowyer, L. D. (Charlton Ath), 1996 v N (sub), Bel, P, Br; (with Leeds U), 1997 v Mol, I, Sw, Ge; 1998 v Mol; 1999 v F, Pol; 2000 v D, Arg (13)
Bracewell, P. (Stoke C), 1983 v D, Gr (1 + 1 sub), H; 1984 v D, H, F (2), I (2), Sp (2); 1985 v T (13)
Bradbury, L. M. (Portsmouth), 1997 v Pol; (with Manchester C), 1998 v Mol (sub), I (sub) (3)
Bramble, T. M. (Ipswich T), 2001 v Ge, G, Fi, Alb (sub), M; 2002 v Ho (sub); (with Newcastle U), 2003 v Y, Slo, Mac, P (10)
Branch, P. M. (Everton), 1997 v Pol (sub) (1)
Bradshaw, P. W. (Wolverhampton W), 1977 v W, S; 1978 v Fi, Y (4)
Breacker, T. (Luton T), 1986 v I (2) (2)
Brennan, M. (Ipswich T), 1987 v Y, Sp, T, Mor, F (5)
Bridge, W. M. (Southampton), 1999 v H (sub); 2001 v Sp; 2002 v Ho, G, Alb, Gr, Ho (2) (8)
Bridges, M. (Sunderland), 1997 v Sw (sub); 1999 v F; (with Leeds U), 2000 v D (3)
Brightwell, I. (Manchester C), 1989 v D, Alb; 1990 v Se (sub), Pol (4)
Briscoe, L. S. (Sheffield W), 1996 v Cro, Bel (sub), An, Br; 1997 v Sw (sub) (5)
Brock, K. (Oxford U), 1984 v I, Sp (2); 1986 v I (4)
Broomes, M. C. (Blackburn R), 1997 v Sw, Ge (2)
Brown, M. R. (Manchester C), 1996 v Cro, Bel, An, P (4)
Brown, W. M. (Manchester U), 1999 v Se, Bul, L, CzR, Pol, Se, Bul; 2001 v G (8)
Bull, S. G. (Wolverhampton W), 1989 v Alb (2) Pol; 1990 v Se, Pol (5)
Bullock, M. J. (Barnsley), 1998 v Gr (sub) (1)
Burrows, D. (WBA), 1989 v Se (sub); (with Liverpool), Gr, Alb (2), Pol; 1990 v Se, Pol (7)
Butcher, T. I. (Ipswich T), 1979 v Se; 1980 v D, Bul, S (2), EG (2) (7)
Butt, N. (Manchester U), 1995 v Ei (2), La; 1996 v P, A; 1997 v Ge, Pol (7)
Butters, G. (Tottenham H), 1989 v Bul, Sen (sub), Ei (sub) (3)
Butterworth, I. (Coventry C), 1985 v T, R; (with Nottingham F), 1986 v R, T, D (2), I (2) (8)
Bywater, S. (West Ham U), 2001 v M (sub), Gr; 2002 v Ho (sub), I (sub); 2003 v P, Ser (sub) (6)

Cadamarteri, D. L. (Everton), 1999 v CzR (sub); 2000 v Y (sub); 2001 v M (sub) (3)
Caesar, G. (Arsenal), 1987 v Mor, USSR (sub), F (3)
Callaghan, N. (Watford), 1983 v D, Gr (sub), H (sub); 1984 v D, H, F (2), I, Sp (9)
Camp, L.M.J. (Derby Co), 2005 v Sp (sub), Ho (sub) (2)
Campbell, A. P. (Middlesbrough), 2000 v Y, T (sub), Slo (sub); 2001 v Ge (sub) (4)
Campbell, K. J. (Arsenal), 1991 v H, T (sub); 1992 v G, T (4)
Campbell, S. (Tottenham), 1994 v D, Ru, F, US, Bel, P; 1995 v P, A, Ei; 1996 v N, A (11)
Carbon, M. P. (Derby Co), 1996 v Cro (sub); 1997 v Ge, I, Sw (4)
Carr, C. (Fulham), 1985 v Ei (sub) (1)
Carr, F. (Nottingham F), 1987 v Se, Y, Sp (sub), Mor, USSR; 1988 v WG (sub), T, Y, F (9)
Carragher, J. L. (Liverpool), 1997 v I (sub), Sw, Ge, Pol; 1998 v Mol (sub), I, Gr, Sw (sub), F, S.Af, Arg; 1999 v Se, Bul, L, CzR, F, Pol, Se, Bul; 2000 v L, Pol, D, Arg, Y, I, T, Slo (27)
Carlisle, C. J. (QPR), 2001 v Ge (sub), G (sub), Fi (sub) (3)
Carrick, M. (West Ham U), 2001 v Ge, G, Fi, I, Gr; 2002 v Gr, Ho (2), P; 2003 v Y, Slo, Mac, I, P (14)
Carson, S. P. (Leeds U), 2004 v Ho, Se; 2005 v Uk, A, Pol, W, Az, Sp; (with Liverpool), Ho, G, Az (11)

Casper, C. M. (Manchester U), 1995 v Mal (1)
Caton, T. (Manchester C), 1982 v N, H (sub), Pol (2), S; 1983 v WG (2), Gr; 1984 v D, H, F (2), I (2) (14)
Chadwick, L. H. (Manchester U), 2000 v L, D, Arg, I (sub), Slo (sub); 2001 v Ge (sub), I, Sp, Fi, Alb; 2002 v Ho, G, Alb (13)
Challis, T. M. (QPR), 1996 v An, P (2)
Chamberlain, M. (Stoke C), 1983 v Gr; 1984 v F (sub), I, Sp (4)
Chaplow, R. D. (Burnley), 2004 v Ho (sub) (1)
Chapman, L. (Stoke C), 1981 v Ei (1)
Charles, G. A. (Nottingham F), 1991 v H, W (sub), Ei; 1992 v T (4)
Chettle, S. (Nottingham F), 1988 v M, USSR, Mor, F; 1989 v D, Se, Gr, Alb (2), Bul; 1990 v Se, Pol (12)
Chopra, R, M. (Newcastle U), 2004 v Se (sub) (1)
Clark, L. R. (Newcastle U), 1992 v Cz, F; 1993 v Sp, N, T, Ho (sub), Pol (sub), Cz, Br, S; 1994 v Ho (11)
Clarke, P. M. (Everton), 2003 v Slo (sub), I, T, Ser, Slo; 2004 v Cro, Mac, P (8)
Christie, M. N. (Derby Co), 2001 v Fi (sub), Sp, Fi, Alb, M, Gr; 2002 v Ho (sub), Gr (sub), Ho, Slv, P (11)
Clegg, M. J. (Manchester U), 1998 v Fr (sub), S.Af (sub) (2)
Clemence, S. N. (Tottenham H), 1999 v Se (sub) (1)
Clough, N. (Nottingham F), 1986 v D (sub); 1987 v Se, Y, T, USSR, F (sub), P; 1988 v WG, T, Y, S (2), M, Mor, F (15)
Cole, A. A. (Arsenal), 1992 v H, Cz (sub), F (sub); (with Bristol C), 1993 v Sm; (with Newcastle U), Pol, N; 1994 v Pol, Ho (8)
Cole, A. (Arsenal), 2001 v Ge, G, Fi, I (4)
Cole, C. (Chelsea), 2003 v T (sub), Ser (sub), Slo (sub); 2004 v Cro (sub), Ho, Se; 2005 v Uk, A, Pol, W, Sp, Ho (12)
Cole, J. J. (West Ham U), 2000 v Arg (sub); 2001 v Ge, Gr; 2002 v G; 2003 v Slo, Mac, P, T (8)
Coney, D. (Fulham), 1985 v T (sub); 1986 v R; 1988 v T, WG (4)
Connor, T. (Brighton & HA), 1987 v Y (1)
Cooke, R. (Tottenham H), 1986 v D (sub) (1)
Cooke, T. J. (Manchester U), 1996 v Cro, Bel, An (sub), P (4)
Cooper, C. (Middlesbrough), 1988 v F (2), M, USSR, Mor; 1989 v D, Se, Gr (8)
Corrigan, J. T. (Manchester C), 1978 v I (2), Y (3)
Cort, C. E. R. (Wimbledon), 1999 v L (sub), CzR, H (sub), Se, Bul; 2000 v L (sub), Pol, D (sub), Arg, I, T, Slo (12)
Cottee, A. (West Ham U), 1985 v Fi (sub), Is (sub), Ei, R, Fi; 1987 v Sp, P; 1988 v WG (8)
Couzens, A. J. (Leeds U), 1995 v Mal (sub), An, F (sub) (3)
Cowans, G. S. (Aston Villa), 1979 v W, Se; 1980 v Bul, EG; 1981 v R (5)
Cox, N. J. (Aston Villa), 1993 v T, Ho, Pol, N; 1994 v Pol, Sm (6)
Cranson, I. (Ipswich T), 1985 v Fi, Is, R; 1986 v R, I (5)
Cresswell, R. P. W. (York C), 1999 v F (sub); (with Sheffield W) H (sub), Se, Bul (4)
Croft, G. (Grimsby T), 1995 v Br, Mal, An, F (4)
Crooks, G. (Stoke C), 1980 v Bul, S (2), EG (sub) (4)
Crossley, M. G. (Nottingham F), 1990 v P, USSR, Cz (3)
Crouch, P. J. (Portsmouth), 2002 v I (sub), P (sub), Sw; (with Aston Villa), 2003 v Mac (sub), P (sub) (5)
Cundy, J. V. (Chelsea), 1991 v Ei (2); 1992 v Pol (3)
Cunningham, L. (WBA), 1977 v S, Fi, N (sub); 1978 v N, Fi, I (6)
Curbishley, L. C. (Birmingham C), 1981 v Sw (1)
Curtis, J. C. K. (Manchester U), 1998 v I (sub), Gr, Sw, F, S.Af, Arg; 1999 v Se (sub), Bul, L, CzR, F, Pol (sub), H, Se (sub), Bul; 2000 v Pol (16)

Daniel, P. W. (Hull C), 1977 v S, Fi, N; 1978 v Fi, I, Y (2) (7)
Davenport, C.R.P. (Tottenham H), 2005 v A, Pol, W, Az, Sp (sub), G, Az (7)
Davies, A. J. (Middlesbrough), 2004 v T (1)
Davies, K. C. (Southampton), 1998 v Gr (sub); (with Blackburn R), 1999 v CzR; (with Southampton), 2000 v Y (sub) (3)
Davis, K. G. (Luton T), 1995 v An; 1996 v Cro (sub), P (3)
Davis, P. (Arsenal), 1982 v Pol, S; 1983 v D, Gr (1 + 1 sub), H (sub); 1987 v T; 1988 v WG, T, Y, Fr (11)
Davis, S. (Fulham), 2001 v Fi, Alb, M, Gr; 2002 v Ho, G, Al, Ho (2), P, Sw (11)
Dawson, M. R. (Nottingham F), 2003 v Slo (sub), I, P, T; 2004 v P, Se; 2005 v Sp (7)
Day, C. N. (Tottenham H), 1996 v Cro, Bel, Br; (with C Palace), 1997 v Mol, Ge, Sw (6)
D'Avray, M. (Ipswich T), 1984 v I, Sp (sub) (2)
Deehan, J. M. (Aston Villa), 1977 v N; 1978 v N, Fi, I; 1979 v Bul, Se (sub); 1980 v D (7)
Defoe, J. C. (West Ham U), 2001 v M, Gr; 2002 v Ho (sub), G (sub), Alb, Gr, Ho (2), Slv, I, P (sub), Sw, I, P; 2003 v Y, P, T, Ser, Slo; 2004 v Cro, Mac (sub), P (sub), T (23)
Dennis, M. E. (Birmingham C), 1980 v Bul; 1981 v N, R (3)
Dichio, D. S. E. (QPR), 1996 v N (sub) (1)
Dickens, A. (West Ham U), 1985 v Fi (sub) (1)
Dicks, J. (West Ham U), 1988 v Sw (sub), M, Mor, F (4)
Digby, F. (Swindon T), 1987 v Sp (sub), USSR, P; 1988 v T; 1990 v Pol (5)
Dillon, K. P. (Birmingham C), 1981 v R (1)
Dixon, K. (Chelsea), 1985 v Fi (1)
Dobson, A. (Coventry C), 1989 v Bul, Sen, Ei, US (4)
Dodd, J. R. (Southampton), 1991 v Pol, Ei, T, Sen, M, F; 1992 v G, Pol (8)
Donowa, L. (Norwich C), 1985 v Is, R (sub), Fi (sub) (3)
Dorigo, A. (Aston Villa), 1987 v Se, Sp, T, Mor, USSR, F, P; 1988 v WG, Y, S (2) (11)
Downing, S. (Middlesbrough), 2004 v Ho, Se; 2005 v Uk, A, W, Az (sub), Sp (sub) (7)
Dozzell, J. (Ipswich T), 1987 v Se, Y (sub), Sp, USSR, F, P; 1989 v Se, Gr (sub); 1990 v Se (sub) (9)
Draper, M. A. (Notts Co), 1991 v Ei (sub); 1992 v G, Pol (3)
Duberry, M. W. (Chelsea), 1997 v Mol, Pol, Ge; 1998 v Mol, Gr (5)
Dunn, D. J. I. (Blackburn R), 1999 v CzR (sub); 2000 v I (sub), T, Slo; 2001 v Ge, G, Fi, I, Sp, M, Gr; 2002 v Ho, Gr, Ho (2), Slv, P, Sw, I, P (20)
Duxbury, M. (Manchester U), 1981 v Sw (sub), Ei (sub), R (sub), Sw; 1982 v N; 1983 v WG (2) (7)
Dyer, B. A. (C Palace), 1994 v Ru, F, US, Bel, P; 1995 v P (sub); 1996 v Cro; 1997 v Mol, Ge; 1998 v Mol, Gr (10)
Dyer, K. C. (Ipswich T), 1998 v Mol, I, Gr, Sw, S.Af, Arg; 1999 v Se, Bul, CzR, Se; (with Newcastle U), 2000 v Y (11)
Dyson, P. I. (Coventry C), 1981 v N, R, Sw, Ei (4)

Eadie, D. M. (Norwich C), 1994 v F (sub), US; 1997 v Mol, Ge (2), I; 1998 v I (7)
Ebbrell, J. (Everton), 1989 v Sen, Ei, US (sub); 1990 v P, F, USSR, Cz; 1991 v H, Pol, Ei, W, T; 1992 v G, T (14)
Edghill, R. A. (Manchester C), 1994 v D, Ru; 1995 v A (3)
Ehiogu, U. (Aston Villa), 1992 v H, M, Cz, F; 1993 v Sp, N, T, Sm, T, Ho, Pol, N; 1994 v Pol, Ho, Sm (15)
Elliott, P. (Luton T), 1985 v Fi; 1986 v T, D (3)
Elliott, R. J. (Newcastle U), 1996 v P, A (2)
Elliott, S. W. (Derby Co), 1998 v F, Arg (sub) (2)
Etherington, N, (Tottenham H), 2002 v Slv (sub), I; 2003 v Y (sub) (3)
Euell, J. J. (Wimbledon), 1998 v F, Arg (sub); 1999 v Se (sub), Bul (se), Pol (sub), H (6)
Evans, R. (Chelsea), 2003 v Ser, Slo (2)

Fairclough, C. (Nottingham F), 1985 v T, Is, Ei; 1987 v Sp, T; (with Tottenham H), 1988 v Y, F (7)
Fairclough, D. (Liverpool), 1977 v W (1)
Fashanu, J. (Norwich C), 1980 v EG; 1981 v N (sub), R, Sw, Ei (sub), H; (with Nottingham F), 1982 v N, H, Pol, S; 1983 v WG (sub) (11)
Fear, P. (Wimbledon), 1994 v Ru, F, US (sub) (3)
Fenton, G. A. (Aston Villa), 1995 v Ei (1)
Fenwick, T. W. (C Palace), 1981 v N, R, Sw, Ei; (with QPR), R; 1982 v N, H, S (2); 1983 v WG (2) (11)
Ferdinand, A.J. (West Ham U), 2005 v Uk, A, Pol (3)
Ferdinand, R. G. (West Ham U), 1997 v Sw, Ge; 1998 v I, Gr; 2000 v Y (5)
Fereday, W. (QPR), 1985 v T, Ei (sub). Fi; 1986 v T (sub), I (5)
Flitcroft, G. W. (Manchester C), 1993 v Sm, Hol, N, P, Cz, Br, S, F; 1994 v Pol, Ho (10)
Flowers, T. (Southampton), 1987 v Mor, F; 1988 v WG (sub) (3)
Ford, M. (Leeds U), 1996 v Cro; 1997 v Mol (2)
Forster, N. M. (Brentford), 1995 v Br, Mal, An, F (4)
Forsyth, M. (Derby Co), 1988 v Sw (1)
Foster, S. (Brighton & HA), 1980 v EG (sub) (1)

Fowler, R. B. (Liverpool), 1994 v Sm, Ru (sub), F, US; 1995 v P, A; 1996 v P, A (8)
Froggatt, S. J. (Aston Villa), 1993 v Sp, Sm (sub) (2)
Futcher, P. (Luton T), 1977 v W, S, Fi, N; (with Manchester C), 1978 v N, Fi, I (2), Y (2); 1979 v D (11)

Gabbiadini, M. (Sunderland), 1989 v Bul, USA (2)
Gale, A. (Fulham), 1982 v Pol (1)
Gallen, K. A. (QPR), 1995 v Ei, La (2); 1996 v Cro (4)
Gardner, A. (Tottenham H), 2002 v I (sub) (1)
Gascoigne, P. (Newcastle U), 1987 v Mo, USSR, P; 1988 v WG, Y, S (2), F (2), Sw, M, USSR (sub), Mor (13)
Gayle, H. (Birmingham C), 1984 v I, Sp (2) (3)
Gernon, T. (Ipswich T), 1983 v Gr (1)
Gerrard, P. W. (Oldham Ath), 1993 v T, Ho, Pol, N, P, Cz, Br, S, F; 1994 v D, Ru; 1995 v P, A, Ei (2), La (2); 1996 v P (18)
Gerrard, S. G. (Liverpool), 2000 v L, Pol, D, Y (4)
Gibbs, N. (Watford), 1987 v Mor, USSR, F, P; 1988 v T (5)
Gibson, C. (Aston Villa), 1982 v N (1)
Gilbert, W. A. (C Palace), 1979 v W, Bul; 1980 v Bul; 1981 v N, R, Sw, R, Sw, H; 1982 v N (sub), H (11)
Goddard, P. (West Ham U), 1981 v N, Sw, Ei (sub); 1982 v N (sub), Pol, S; 1983 v WG (2) (8)
Gordon, D. (Norwich C), 1987 v T (sub), Mor (sub), F, P (4)
Gordon, D. D. (C Palace), 1994 v Ru, F, US, Bel, P; 1995 v P, A, Ei (2), La (2); 1996 v P, N (13)
Grant, A. J. (Everton), 1996 v An (sub) (1)
Grant, L. A. (Derby Co), 2003 v I (sub); 2004 v P, T, Se (sub) (4)
Granville, D. P. (Chelsea), 1997 v Ge (sub), Pol; 1998 v Mol (3)
Gray, A. (Aston Villa), 1988 v S, F (2)
Greening, J. (Manchester U), 1999 v H, Se (sub), Bul; 2000 v Pol; 2001 v Ge, G, Fi, I, Sp (sub), Fi, Alb; (with Middlesbrough), 2002 v Ho, G, Alb, Gr, Ho (sub), I, P (18)
Griffin, A. (Newcastle U), 1999 v H; 2001 v I, Sp (3)
Guppy, S. A. (Leicester C), 1998 v Sw (1)

Haigh, P. (Hull C), 1977 v N (sub) (1)
Hall, M. T. J. (Coventry C), 1997 v Pol (2), I, Sw, Ge; 1998 v Mol, Gr (2) (8)
Hall, R. A. (Southampton), 1992 v H (sub), F; 1993 v Sm, T, Ho, Pol, P, Cz, Br, S, F (11)
Hamilton, D. V. (Newcastle U), 1997 v Pol (1)
Harding, D. A. (Brighton & HA), 2005 v Uk (sub), W, Az, Sp (4)
Hardyman, P. (Portsmouth), 1985 v Ei; 1986 v D (2)
Hargreaves, O. (Bayern Munich), 2001 v Ge (sub), I, Sp (3)
Harley, J. (Chelsea), 2000 v Arg (sub), T (sub), Slo (3)
Hateley, M. (Coventry C), 1982 v Pol, S; 1983 v Gr (2), H; (with Portsmouth), 1984 v F (2), I, Sp (2) (10)
Hayes, M. (Arsenal), 1987 v Sp, T; 1988 v F (sub) (3)
Hazell, R. J. (Wolverhampton W), 1979 v D (1)
Heaney, N. A. (Arsenal), 1992 v H, M, Cz, F; 1993 v N, T (6)
Heath, A. (Stoke C), 1981 v R, Sw, H; 1982 v N, H; (with Everton), Pol, S; 1983 v WG (8)
Hendon, I. M. (Tottenham H), 1992 v H, M, Cz, F; 1993 v Sp, N, T (7)
Hendrie, L. A. (Aston Villa), 1996 v Cro (sub); 1998 v Sw (sub); 1999 v Se, Bul, L, F, Pol; 2000 v L, D, Arg, Y, I, Slo (sub) (13)
Hesford, I. (Blackpool), 1981 v Ei (sub), Pol (2), S (2); 1983 v WG (2) (7)
Heskey, E. W. I. (Leicester C), 1997 v I, Ge, Pol (2); 1998 v I, Gr (2), Sw, F, S.Af, Arg; 1999 v Se, Bul, L; 2000 v L; (with Liverpool), Y (16)
Hilaire, V. (C Palace), 1980 v Bul, S (1+1 sub), EG (2); 1981 v N, R, Sw (sub); 1982 v Pol (sub) (9)
Hill, D. R. L. (Tottenham H), 1995 v Br, Mal, An, F (4)
Hillier, D. (Arsenal), 1991 v T (1)
Hinchcliffe, A. (Manchester C), 1989 v D (1)
Hinshelwood, P. A. (C Palace), 1978 v N; 1980 v EG (2)
Hirst, D. (Sheffield W), 1988 v USSR, F; 1989 v D, Bul (sub), Sen, Ei, US (7)
Hislop, N. S. (Newcastle U), 1998 v Sw (1)
Hoddle, G. (Tottenham H), 1977 v W (sub); 1978 v Fi (sub), I (2), Y; 1979 v D, W, Bul; 1980 v S (2), EG (2) (12)
Hodge, S. (Nottingham F), 1983 v Gr (sub); 1984 v D, F, I, Sp (2); (with Aston Villa), 1986 v R, T (8)
Hodgson, D. J. (Middlesbrough), 1981 v N, R (sub), Sw, Ei; 1982 v Pol; 1983 v WG (6)
Holdsworth, D. (Watford), 1989 v Gr (sub) (1)
Holland, C. J. (Newcastle U), 1995 v La; 1996 v N (sub), A (sub), Cro, Bel, An, Br; 1997 v Mol, Pol, Sw (10)
Holland, P. (Mansfield T), 1995 v Br, Mal, An, F (4)
Holloway, D. (Sunderland), 1998 v Sw (sub) (1)
Horne, B. (Millwall), 1989 v Gr (sub), Pol, Bul, Ei, US (5)
Howe, E. J. F. (Bournemouth), 1998 v S.Af (sub), Arg (2)
Hoyte, J. R. (Arsenal), 2004 v Ho (sub), Se; 2005 v Uk (sub), A (sub), Pol (sub), Sp, Ho (7)
Hucker, P. (QPR), 1984 v I, Sp (2)
Huckerby, D. (Coventry C), 1997 v I (sub), Sw, Ge (sub), Pol (sub) (4)
Huddlestone, T. A. (Derby Co), 2005 v Ho, G, Az (3)
Hughes, S. J. (Arsenal), 1997 v I, Sw, Ge, Pol; 1998 v Mol, I, Gr, Sw (sub) (8)
Humphreys, R. J. (Sheffield W), 1997 v Pol, Ge (sub), Sw (3)
Hunt, N. B. (Bolton W), 2004 v Ho; 2005 v Uk, A, W, Az, Sp, G (7)

Impey, A. R. (QPR), 1993 v T (1)
Ince, P. (West Ham U), 1989 v Alb; 1990 v Se (2)

Jackson, M. A. (Everton), 1992 v H, M, Cz, F; 1993 v Sm (sub), T, Ho, Pol, N; 1994 v Pol (10)
Jagielka, P. N. (Sheffield U), 2003 v Ser, Slo; 2004 v Cro (sub), Mac, P, T (6)
James, D. (Watford), 1991 v Ei (2), T, Sen, M, USSR, F; 1992 v G, T, Pol (10)
James, J. C. (Luton T), 1990 v F, USSR (2)
Jansen, M. B (C Palace), 1999 v Se, Bul, L; (with Blackburn R), F (sub), Pol; 2000 v I (sub) (6)
Jeffers, F. (Everton), 2000 v L, Arg, I, T, Slo; 2001 v Ge; (with Arsenal), 2002 v Ho, G (sub), Alb; 2003 v Y, Slo, Mac, T; 2004 v Cro, Mac, P (16)
Jemson, N. B. (Nottingham F), 1991 v W (1)
Jenas, J. A. (Newcastle U), 2002 v Slo, I, P (sub); 2003 v Y, Slo, Mac, T; 2004 v Cro, T (9)
Joachim, J. K. (Leicester C), 1994 v D (sub); 1995 v P, A, Ei, Br, Mal, An, F; 1996 v N (9)
Johnson, G. M. C. (West Ham U), 2003 v T (sub), Ser (sub); (with Chelsea), 2004 v Cro, Mac, P, T, Ho; 2005 v Pol, W, Az, Sp, G (12)
Johnson, S. A. M. (Crewe Alex), 1999 v L (sub), CzR (sub), F (sub), Pol; (with Derby Co), Se, Bul; 2000 v D, Arg (sub), Y, I, T; 2001 v Fi; 2002 v Ho (sub), Alb (sub); (with Leeds U), P (15)
Johnson, T. (Notts Co), 1991 v H (sub), Ei (sub); 1992 v G, T, Pol; (with Derby Co), M, Cz (sub) (7)
Johnston, C. P. (Middlesbrough), 1981 v N, Ei (2)
Jones, D. R. (Everton), 1977 v W (1)
Jones, C. H. (Tottenham H), 1978 v Y (sub) (1)
Jones, D. F. L. (Manchester U), 2004 v Se (sub) (1)
Jones, R. (Liverpool), 1993 v Sm, Ho (2)

Keegan, G. A. (Manchester C), 1977 v W (1)
Kenny, W. (Everton), 1993 v T (1)
Keown, M. (Aston Villa), 1987 v Sp, Mor, USSR, P; 1988 v T, S, F (2) (8)
Kerslake, D. (QPR), 1986 v T (1)
Kilcline, B. (Notts C), 1983 v D, Gr (2)
Kilgallon, M. (Leeds U), 2004 v Se (sub); 2005 v Uk, Pol (sub), Az (sub) (4)
King, A. E. (Everton), 1977 v W; 1978 v Y (2)
King, L. B. (Tottenham H), 2000 v L (sub), I, T, Slo; 2001 v I, Sp (sub), Fi; 2002 v G, Alb, Gr, Ho (2) (12)
Kirkland, C. E. (Coventry C), 2001 v M; (with Liverpool), 2002 v Gr, Ho (2), P (sub); 2003 v Y, Mac; 2004 v Mac (8)
Kitson, P. (Leicester C), 1991 v Sen (sub), M, F; 1992 v Pol; (with Derby Co), M, Cz, F (7)
Knight, A. (Portsmouth), 1983 v Gr, H (2)
Knight, I. (Sheffield W), 1987 v Se (sub), Y (2)
Knight, Z. (Fulham), 2002 v Slo (sub), I (2), P (4)
Konchesky, P. M. (Charlton Ath), 2002 v Slo, P, Sw, I, P; 2003 Y, Slo, Mac, P, T, Ser, Slo; 2004 v Cro, Mac, P (15)
Kozluk, R. (Derby Co), 1998 v F, Arg (sub) (2)

Lake, P. (Manchester C), 1989 v D, Alb (2), Pol; 1990 v Pol (5)
Lampard, F. J. (West Ham U), 1998 v Gr (2), Sw, F, S.Af, Arg; 1999 v Se, Bul, L, CzR, F, Pol, Se; 2000 v L, Arg, Y, I, T, Slo (19)
Langley, T. W. (Chelsea), 1978 v I (sub) (1)

Lee, D. J. (Chelsea), 1990 v F; 1991 v H, Pol, Ei (2), T, Sen, USSR, F; 1992 v Pol (10)
Lee, R. (Charlton Ath), 1986 v I (sub); 1987 v Se (sub) (2)
Lee, S. (Liverpool), 1981 v R, Sw, H; 1982 v S; 1983 v WG (2) (6)
Le Saux, G. (Chelsea), 1990 v P, F, USSR, Cz (4)
Lescott, J. P. (Wolverhampton W), 2003 v Y (sub), I (sub) (2)
Lita, L. H. (Bristol C), 2005 v Ho (sub) (1)
Lowe, D. (Ipswich T), 1988 v F, Sw (sub) (2)
Lukic, J. (Leeds U), 1981 v N, R, Ei, R, Sw, H; 1982 v H (7)
Lund, G. (Grimsby T), 1985 v T; 1986 v R, T (3)

McCall, S. H. (Ipswich T), 1981 v Sw, H; 1982 v H, S; 1983 v WG (2) (6)
McDonald, N. (Newcastle U), 1987 v Se (sub), Sp, T; 1988 v WG, Y (sub) (5)
McEveley, J. (Blackburn R), 2003 v I (sub) (1)
McGrath, L. (Coventry C), 1986 v D (1)
MacKenzie, S. (WBA), 1982 v N, S (2) (3)
McLeary, A. (Millwall), 1988 v Sw (1)
McMahon, S. (Everton), 1981 v Ei; 1982 v Pol; 1983 v D, Gr (2); (with Aston Villa), 1984 v H (6)
McManaman, S. (Liverpool), 1991 v W, M (sub); 1993 v N, T, Sm, T; 1994 v Pol (7)
Mabbutt, G. (Bristol R), 1982 v Pol (2), S; (with Tottenham H), 1983 v D; 1984 v F; 1986 v D, I (7)
Makin, C. (Oldham Ath), 1994 v Ru (sub), F, US, Bel, P (5)
Marney, D. E. (Tottenham H), 2005 v Ho (sub) (1)
Marriott, A. (Nottingham F), 1992 v M (1)
Marsh, S. T. (Oxford U), 1998 v F (1)
Marshall, A. J. (Norwich C), 1995 v Mal, An; 1997 v Pol, I (4)
Marshall, L. K. (Norwich C), 1999 v F (sub) (1)
Martin, L. (Manchester U), 1989 v Gr (sub), Alb (sub) (2)
Martyn, N. (Bristol R), 1988 v S (sub), M, USSR, Mor, F; 1989 v D, Se, Gr, Alb (2); 1990 v Se (11)
Matteo, D. (Liverpool), 1994 v F (sub), Bel, P; 1998 v Sw (4)
Matthew, D. (Chelsea), 1990 v P, USSR (sub), Cz; 1991 v Ei, M, USSR, F; 1992 v G (sub), T (9)
May, A. (Manchester C), 1986 v I (sub) (1)
Merson, P. (Arsenal), 1989 v D, Gr, Pol (sub); 1990 v Pol (4)
Middleton, J. (Nottingham F), 1977 v Fi, N; (with Derby Co), 1978 v N (3)
Miller, A. (Arsenal), 1988 v Mor (sub); 1989 v Sen; 1991 v H, Pol (4)
Mills, D. J. (Charlton Ath), 1999 v Se, Bul (sub), L, Pol, H, Se; (with Leeds U), 2000 v L, Pol, D, Arg, Y (sub), I, T, Slo (14)
Mills, G. R. (Nottingham F), 1981 v R; 1982 v N (2)
Milner, J. P. (Leeds U), 2004 v Se (sub); (with Newcastle U), 2005 v Uk, A (sub), Pol, W, Az, Sp, Ho, G, Az (10)
Mimms, R. (Rotherham U), 1985 v Is (sub), Ei (sub); (with Everton), 1986 v I (3)
Minto, S. C. (Charlton Ath), 1991 v W; 1992 v H, M, Cz; 1993 v T; 1994 v Ho (6)
Moore, I. (Tranmere R), 1996 v Cro (sub), Bel (sub), An, P, Br; 1997 v Mol (sub); (with Nottingham F), Sw (sub) (7)
Moran, S. (Southampton), 1982 v N (sub); 1984 v F (2)
Morgan, S. (Leicester C), 1987 v Se, Y (2)
Morris, J. (Chelsea), 1997 v Pol (sub), Sw (sub), Ge (sub); 1999 v Bul (sub), L (sub), CzR; 2000 v Pol (7)
Mortimer, P. (Charlton Ath), 1989 v Sen, Ei (2)
Moses, A. P. (Barnsley), 1997 v Pol; 1998 v Gr (sub) (2)
Moses, R. M. (WBA), 1981 v N (sub), Sw, Ei, R, Sw, H; 1982 v N (sub); (with Manchester U), H (8)
Mountfield, D. (Everton), 1984 v Sp (1)
Muggleton, C. D. (Leicester C), 1990 v F (1)
Mullins, H. I. (C Palace), 1999 v Pol (sub), H, Bul (3)
Murphy, D. B. (Liverpool), 1998 v Mol, Gr (sub); 2000 v T, Slo (4)
Murray, P. (QPR), 1997 v I, Pol; 1998 v I, Gr (4)
Murray, M. W. (Wolverhampton W), 2003 v Slo, Mac (sub), I, T; 2004 v Cro (5)
Mutch, A. (Wolverhampton W), 1989 v Pol (1)
Myers. A. (Chelsea), 1995 v Br, Mal, An (sub), F (4)

Naylor, L. M. (Wolverhampton W), 2000 v Arg; 2001 v M, Gr (3)
Nethercott, S. (Tottenham), 1994 v D, Ru, F, US, Bel, P; 1995 v La (2) (8)
Neville, P. J. (Manchester U), 1995 v Br, Mal, An, F; 1996 v P, N (sub); 1997 v Ge (7)
Newell, M. (Luton T), 1986 v D (1 + 1 sub), I (1 + 1 sub) (4)
Newton, A. L. (West Ham U), 2001 v Ge (1)
Newton, E. J. I. (Chelsea), 1993 v T (sub); 1994 v Sm (2)
Newton, S. O. (Charlton Ath), 1997 v Mol, Pol, Ge (3)
Nicholls, A. (Plymouth Arg), 1994 v F (1)
Nolan, K. A. J. (Bolton W), 2003 v I (sub) (1)

Oakes, M. C. (Aston Villa), 1994 v D (sub), F (sub), US, Bel, P; 1996 v A (6)
Oakes, S. J. (Luton T), 1993 v Br (sub) (1)
Oakley, M. (Southampton), 1997 v Ge; 1998 v F, S.Af, Arg (4)
O'Brien, A. J. (Bradford C), 1999 v F (1)
O'Connor, J. (Everton), 1996 v Cro, An, Br (3)
O'Neil, G. P. (Portsmouth) 2005 v Uk, A, Pol, W, Az, G (6)
Oldfield, D. (Luton T), 1989 v Se (1)
Olney, I. A. (Aston Villa), 1990 v P, F, USSR, Cz; 1991 v H, Pol, Ei (2), T; 1992 v Pol (sub) (10)
Ord, R. J. (Sunderland), 1991 v W, M, USSR (3)
Osman, R. C. (Ipswich T), 1979 v W (sub), Se; 1980 v D, S (2), EG (2) (7)
Owen, G. A. (Manchester C), 1977 v S, Fi, N; 1978 v N, Fi, I (2), Y; 1979 v D, W; (with WBA), Bul, Se (sub); 1980 v D, S (2), EG; 1981 v Sw, R; 1982 v N (sub), H; 1983 v WG (2) (22)
Owen, M. J. (Liverpool), 1998 v Gr (1)

Painter, I. (Stoke C), 1986 v I (1)
Palmer, C. (Sheffield W), 1989 v Bul, Sen, Ei, US (4)
Parker, G. (Hull C), 1986 v I (2); (with Nottingham F), F; 1987 v Se, Y (sub), Sp (6)
Parker, P. (Fulham), 1985 v Fi, T, Is (sub), Ei, R, Fi; 1986 v T, D (8)
Parker, S. M. (Charlton Ath), 2001 v Ge (sub), G, Fi (sub), Alb (sub); 2002 v Ho (sub), G (sub), Alb, Slo, I (sub), Sw (sub), I (sub), P (sub) (12)
Parkes, P. B. F. (QPR), 1979 v D (1)
Parkin, S. (Stoke C), 1987 v Sp (sub); 1988 v WG (sub), T, S (sub), F (5)
Parlour, R. (Arsenal), 1992 v H, M, Cz, F; 1993 v Sp, N, T; 1994 v D, Ru, Bel, P; 1995 v A (12)
Parnaby, S. (Middlesbrough), 2003 v Y (sub), Ser, Slo; 2004 v Cro (4)
Peach, D. S. (Southampton), 1977 v S, Fi, N; 1978 v N, I (2) (6)
Peake, A. (Leicester C), 1982 v Pol (1)
Pearce, I. A. (Blackburn R), 1995 v Ei, La; 1996 v N (3)
Pearce, S. (Nottingham F), 1987 v Y (1)
Pennant, J. (Arsenal), 2001 v M (sub), Gr (sub); 2002 v Ho (sub), Alb (sub), Gr, Ho (2), Slv, I (sub), P (sub), Sw, I, P; 2003 v Y, P (sub), Ser, Slo; 2004 v Cro, Mac; 2005 v Uk, A, Pol, W, Az (24)
Pickering N. (Sunderland), 1983 v D (sub), Gr, H; 1984 v F (sub + 1), I (2), Sp; 1985 v Is, R, Fi; 1986 v R, T; (with Coventry C), D, I (15)
Platt, D. (Aston Villa), 1988 v M, Mor, F (3)
Plummer, C. S. (QPR), 1996 v Cro (sub), Bel, An, P (sub), Br (5)
Pollock, J. (Middlesbrough), 1995 v Ei (sub); 1996 v N, A (3)
Porter, G. (Watford), 1987 v Sp (sub), T, Mor, USSR, F, P (sub); 1988 v T (sub), Y, S (2), F, Sw (12)
Potter, G. S. (Southampton), 1997 v Mol (1)
Pressman, K. (Sheffield W), 1989 v D (sub) (1)
Proctor, M. (Middlesbrough), 1981 v Ei (sub), Sw; (with Nottingham F) 1982 v N, Pol (4)
Prutton, D. T. (Nottingham F), 2001 v Ge (sub), G (sub), Fi, Sp (sub), M, Gr (sub); 2002 v Ho (sub), G, Gr (sub), Slv (sub), I, Sw (sub), I, P; 2003 v Y, Slo, Mac; (with Southampton), I, P, T, Ser, Slo; 2004 v Cro, P, T (25)
Purse, D. J. (Birmingham C), 1998 v F. S.Af (2)

Quashie, N. F. (QPR), 1997 v Pol; 1998 v Mol, Gr, Sw (4)
Quinn, W. R. (Sheffield U), 1998 v Mol (sub), I (2)

Ramage, C. D. (Derby Co), 1991 v Pol (sub), W; 1992 v Fr (sub) (3)
Ranson, R. (Manchester C), 1980 v Bul, EG; 1981 v R (sub), R, Sw (1 + 1 sub), H, Pol (2), S (10)
Redknapp, J. F. (Liverpool), 1993 v Sm, Pol, N, P, Cz, Br, S, F; 1994 v Pol, Ho (sub), D, Ru, F, US, Bel, P; 1995 v P, A; 1998 v Sw (19)

Redmond, S. (Manchester C), 1988 v F (2), M, USSR, Mor, F; 1989 v D, Se, Gr, Alb (2), Pol; 1990 v Se, Pol (14)
Reeves, K. P. (Norwich C), 1978 v I, Y (2); 1979 v N, W, Bul, Sw; 1980 v D, S; (with Manchester C), EG (10)
Regis, C. (WBA), 1979 v D, Bul, Se; 1980 v S, EG; 1983 v D (6)
Reid, N. S. (Manchester C), 1981 v H (sub); 1982 v H, Pol (2), S (2) (6)
Reid, P. (Bolton W), 1977 v S, Fi, N; 1978 v Fi, I, Y (6)
Reo-Coker, N. S. A. (Wimbledon), 2004 v T (sub); (with West Ham U), Ho, Se; 2005 v Uk (sub), A, Pol, Az (7)
Richards, D. I. (Wolverhampton W), 1995 v Br, Mal, An, F (4)
Richards, J. P. (Wolverhampton W), 1977 v Fi, N (2)
Richards, M.L. (Ipswich T), 2005 v Uk (1)
Richardson, K. E. (Manchester U), 2005 v Ho (sub), G, Az (3)
Rideout, P. (Aston Villa), 1985 v Fi, Is, Ei (sub), R; (with Bari), 1986 v D (5)
Ridgewell, L. M. (Aston Villa), 2004 v Ho, Se; 2005 v Sp (sub), Ho, G (5)
Riggott, C. M. (Derby Co), 2001 v Sp (sub), Fi (sub), Alb, M (sub); 2002 v Ho (sub), Slv, P, Sw (8)
Ripley, S. (Middlesbrough), 1988 v USSR, F (sub); 1989 v D (sub), Se, Gr, Alb (2); 1990 v Se (8)
Ritchie, A. (Brighton & HA), 1982 v Pol (1)
Rix, G. (Arsenal), 1978 v Fi (sub), Y; 1979 v D, Se; 1980 v D (sub), Bul, S (7)
Roberts, A. J. (Millwall), 1995 v Ei, La (2); (with C Palace), 1996 v N, A (5)
Roberts, B. J. (Middlesbrough), 1997 v Sw (sub) (1)
Robins, M. G. (Manchester U), 1990 v P, F, USSR, Cz; 1991 v H (sub), Pol (6)
Robinson, P. P. (Watford), 1999 v Se, Bul; 2000 v Pol (3)
Robinson, P. W. (Leeds U), 2000 v D; 2001 v Ge, G, Fi, Sp; 2002 v Slv, I, P, Sw, I, P (11)
Robson, B. (WBA), 1979 v W, Bul (sub), Se; 1980 v D, Bul, S (2) (7)
Robson, S. (Arsenal), 1984 v I; 1985 v Fi, Is, Fi; 1986 v R, I; (with West Ham U); 1988 v S, Sw (8)
Rocastle, D. (Arsenal), 1987 v Se, Y, Sp, T; 1988 v WG, T, Y, S (2), F (2 subs), M, USSR, Mor (14)
Roche, L. P. (Manchester U), 2001 v Fi (1)
Rodger, G. (Coventry C), 1987 v USSR, F, P; 1988 v WG (4)
Rogers, A. (Nottingham F), 1998 v F, S.Af, Arg (3)
Rosario, R. (Norwich C), 1987 v T (sub), Mor, F, P (sub) (4)
Rose, M. (Arsenal), 1997 v Ge (sub), I (2)
Rosenior, L. J. (Fulham), 2005 v G (sub), Az (2)
Routledge, W. (Crystal Palace), 2005 v Sp (sub), Ho, Az (sub) (3)
Rowell, G. (Sunderland), 1977 v Fi (1)
Ruddock, N. (Southampton), 1989 v Bul (sub), Sen, Ei, US (4)
Rufus, R. R. (Charlton Ath), 1996 v Cro, Bel, An, P, Br; 1997 v I (6)
Ryan, J. (Oldham Ath), 1983 v H (1)
Ryder, S.H. (Walsall), 1995 v Br, An, F (3)

Samuel, J. (Aston Villa), 2002 v I; 2003 v Y, Slo, Mac, I, P, T (7)
Samways, V. (Tottenham H), 1988 v Sw (sub), USSR, F; 1989 v D, Se (5)
Sansom, K. G. (C Palace), 1979 v D, W, Bul, Se; 1980 v S (2), EG (2) (8)
Scimeca, R. (Aston Villa), 1996 v P; 1997 v Mol, Pol, Ge, I; 1998 v Mol, I, Gr (2) (9)
Scowcroft, J. B. (Ipswich T), 1997 v Pol, Ge (2), I (sub); 1998 v Gr (sub) (5)
Seaman, D. (Birmingham C), 1985 v Fi, T, Is, Ei, R, Fi; 1986 v R, F, D, I (10)
Sedgley, S. (Coventry C), 1987 v USSR, F (sub), P; 1988 v F; 1989 v D (sub), Se, Gr, Alb (2), Pol; (with Tottenham H), 1990 v Se (11)
Sellars, S. (Blackburn R), 1988 v S (sub), F, Sw (3)
Selley, I. (Arsenal), 1994 v Ru (sub), F (sub), US (3)
Serrant, C. (Oldham Ath), 1998 v Gr (2) (2)
Sharpe, L. (Manchester U), 1989 v Gr; 1990 v P (sub), F, USSR, Cz; 1991 v H, Pol (sub), Ei (8)
Shaw, G. R. (Aston Villa), 1981 v Ei, Sw, H; 1982 v H, S; 1983 v WG (2) (7)
Shearer, A. (Southampton), 1991 v Ei (2), W, T, Sen, M, USSR, F; 1992 v G, T, Pol (11)
Shelton, G. (Sheffield W), 1985 v Fi (1)
Sheringham, T. (Millwall), 1988 v Sw (1)
Sheron, M. N. (Manchester C), 1992 v H, F; 1993 v N (sub), T (sub), Sm, Ho, Pol, N, P, Cz, Br, S, F; 1994 v Pol (sub), Ho, Sm (16)
Sherwood, T. A. (Norwich C), 1990 v P, F, USSR, Cz (4)
Shipperley, N. J. (Chelsea), 1994 v Sm (sub); (with Southampton) 1995 v Ei, La (2); 1996 v P, N, A (7)
Sidwell, S. J. (Reading), 2003 v Ser, Slo; 2004 v Cro (sub), Mac, T (5)
Simonsen, S. P. A. (Tranmere R), 1998 v F; (with Everton), 1999 v CzR, F, Bul (4)
Simpson, P. (Manchester C), 1986 v D (sub); 1987 v Y, Mor, F, P (5)
Sims, S. (Leicester C), 1977 v W, S, Fi, N; 1978 v N, Fi, I (2), Y (2) (10)
Sinclair, T. (QPR), 1994 v Ho, Sm, D, Ru, F, US, Bel, P; 1995 v P, Ei (2), La; 1996 v P; (with West Ham U), 1998 v Sw (5)
Sinnott, L. (Watford), 1985 v Is (sub) (1)
Slade, S. A. (Tottenham H), 1996 v Bel, An, P, Br (4)
Slater, S. I. (West Ham U), 1990 v P, USSR (sub), Cz (sub) (3)
Small, B. (Aston Villa), 1993 v Sm, T, Ho, Pol, N, P, Cz, Br, S, F; 1994 v Pol, Sm (12)
Smith, A. (Leeds U), 2000 v D, Arg (sub); 2001 v G, Fi, Sp; 2002 v I, P, Sw, I, P (10)
Smith, D. (Coventry C), 1988 v M, USSR (sub), Mor; 1989 v D, Se, Alb (2), Pol; 1990 v Se, Pol (10)
Smith, M. (Sheffield W), 1981 v Ei, R, Sw, H; 1982 v Pol (sub) (5)
Smith, M. (Sunderland), 1995 v Ei (sub) (1)
Smith, T. W. (Watford), 2001 v Ge (sub) (1)
Snodin, I. (Doncaster R), 1985 v T, Is, R, Fi (4)
Statham, B. (Tottenham H), 1988 v Sw; 1989 v D (sub), Se (3)
Statham, D. J. (WBA), 1978 v Fi, 1979 v W, Bul, Se; 1980 v D; 1983 v D (6)
Stead, J. G. (Blackburn R), 2004 v Ho (sub), Se (sub); 2005 v Uk, A, W, Az, Ho (sub), Az (sub) (8)
Stein, B. (Luton T), 1984 v D, H, I (3)
Sterland, M. (Sheffield W), 1984 v D, H, F (2), I, Sp (2) (7)
Steven, T. (Everton), 1985 v Fi, T (2)
Stevens, G. (Brighton & HA), 1983 v H; (with Tottenham H), 1984 v H, F (1+1 sub), I (sub), Sp (1+1 sub); 1986 v I (8)
Stewart, J. (Leicester C), 2003 v P (sub) (1)
Stewart, P. (Manchester C), 1988 v F (1)
Stockdale, R. K. (Middlesbrough), 2001 v Ge (sub) (1)
Stuart, G. C. (Chelsea), 1990 v P (sub), F, USSR, Cz; 1991 v T (sub) (5)
Stuart, J. C. (Charlton Ath), 1996 v Bel, An, P, Br (4)
Suckling, P. (Coventry C), 1986 v D; (with Manchester C), 1987 v Se (sub), Y, Sp, T; (with C Palace), 1988 v S (2), F (2), Sw (10)
Summerbee, N.J. (Swindon T), 1993 v P (sub), S (sub), F (3)
Sunderland, A. (Wolverhampton W), 1977 v W (1)
Sutton, C. R. (Norwich), 1993 v Sp (sub), T (sub + 1), Ho, P (sub), Cz, Br, S, F; 1994 v Pol, Ho, Sm, D (13)
Swindlehurst, D. (C Palace), 1977 v W (1)
Sutch, D. (Norwich C), 1992 v H, M, Cz; 1993 v T (4)

Talbot, B. (Ipswich T), 1977 v W (1)
Taylor, M. (Blackburn R), 2001 v M (sub) (1)
Taylor, M. S. (Portsmouth), 2003 v Slo (sub), I; 2004 v T (3)
Taylor, S. J. (Arsenal), 2002 v Ho, G, Alb (3)
Taylor, S. V. (Newcastle U), 2004 v Ho, Se; 2005 v W (sub), Ho, G (sub), Az (6)
Terry, J. G. (Chelsea), 2001 v Fi, Sp, Fi, Alb, M, Gr; 2002 v Ho (3) (9)
Thatcher, B. D. (Millwall), 1996 v Cro; (with Wimbledon), 1997 v Mol, Pol; 1998 v I (4)
Thelwell, A. A. (Tottenham H), 2001 v Sp (sub) (1)
Thirlwell, P. (Sunderland), 2001 v Ge (sub) (1)
Thomas, D. (Coventry C), 1981 v Ei; 1983 v WG (2), Gr, H; (with Tottenham H), I, Sp (7)
Thomas, M. (Luton T), 1986 v T, D, I (3)
Thomas, M. (Arsenal), 1988 v Y, S, F (2), M, USSR, Mor; 1989 v Gr, Alb (2), Pol; 1990 v Se (12)
Thomas, R. E. (Watford), 1990 v P (1)
Thompson, A. (Bolton W), 1995 v La; 1996 v P (2)
Thompson, D. A. (Liverpool), 1997 v Pol (sub), Ge; 2000 v L (sub), Pol (sub), D (sub), I, T (sub) (7)
Thompson, G. L. (Coventry C), 1981 v R, Sw, H; 1982 v N, H, S (6)

Thorn, A. (Wimbledon), 1988 v WG (sub). Y, S, F, Sw (5)
Thornley, B. L. (Manchester U), 1996 v Bel, P, Br (3)
Tiler, C. (Barnsley), 1990 v P, USSR, Cz; 1991 v H, Pol, Ei (2), T, Sen, USSR, F; (with Nottingham F), 1992 v G, T (13)
Tonge, M. W. E. (Sheffield U), 2004 v Mac, Se (2)

Unsworth, D. G. (Everton), 1995 v A, Ei (2), La; 1996 v N, A (6)
Upson, M. J. (Arsenal), 1999 v Se, Bul, L, F; 2000 v L, Pol, D; 2001 v I, Sp (sub), M (sub), Gr (11)

Vassell, D. (Aston Villa), 1999 v H (sub); 2000 v Pol (sub); 2001 v Ge, G, Fi, I, Fi, Alb; 2002 v Ho, G, Gr (11)
Venison, B. (Sunderland), 1983 v D, Gr; 1985 v Fi, T, Is, Fi; 1986 v R, T, D (2) (10)
Vernazza, P. A. P. (Arsenal), 2001 v G (sub); (with Watford), M (sub) (2)
Vinnicombe, C. (Rangers), 1991 v H (sub), Pol, Ei (2), T, Sen, M, USSR (sub), F; 1992 v G, T, Pol (12)

Waddle, C. (Newcastle U), 1985 v Fi (1)
Wallace, D. (Southampton), 1983 v Gr, H; 1984 v D, H, F (2), I, Sp (sub); 1985 v Fi, T, Is; 1986 v R, D, I (14)
Wallace, Ray (Southampton), 1989 v Bul, Sen (sub), Ei; 1990 v Se (4)
Wallace, Rod (Southampton), 1989 v Bul, Ei (sub), US; 1991 v H, Pol, Ei, T, Sen, M, USSR, F (11)
Walker, D. (Nottingham F), 1985 v Fi; 1987 v Se, T; 1988 v WG, T, S (2) (7)
Walker, I. M. (Tottenham H), 1991 v W; 1992 v H, Cz, F; 1993 v Sp, N, T, Sm; 1994 v Pol (9)
Walsh, G. (Manchester U), 1988 v WG, Y (2)
Walsh, P. M. (Luton T), 1983 v D (sub), Gr (2), H (4)
Walters, K. (Aston Villa), 1984 v D (sub), H (sub); 1985 v Is, Ei, R; 1986 v R, T, D, I (sub) (9)
Ward, P. D. (Brighton & HA), 1978 v N; 1980 v EG (2)
Warhurst, P. (Oldham Ath), 1991 v H, Pol, W, Sen, M (sub), USSR, F (sub); (with Sheffield W), 1992 v G (8)
Watson, D. (Norwich C), 1984 v D, F (2), I (2), Sp (2) (7)
Watson, D. N. (Barnsley), 1994 v Ho, Sm; 1995 v Br, F; 1996 v N (5)
Watson, G. (Sheffield W), 1991 v Sen, USSR (2)
Watson, S. C. (Newcastle U), 1993 v Sp (sub), N; 1994 v Sm (sub), D; 1995 v P, A, Ei (2), La (2); 1996 v N, A (12)
Weaver, N. J. (Manchester C), 2000 v L, Pol, Arg, I, T, Slo; 2001 v I, Fi, Alb; 2002 v Slv (sub) (10)
Webb, N. (Portsmouth), 1985 v Ei; (with Nottingham F), 1986 v D (2) (3)
Welsh, J. J. (Liverpool), 2004 v Ho; 2005 v Ho (sub), G (sub), Az (4)
Whelan, P. J. (Ipswich T), 1993 v Sp, T (sub), P (3)
Whelan, N. (Leeds U), 1995 v A (sub), Ei (2)
Whittingham, P. (Aston Villa), 2004 v Ho (sub); 2005 v Uk (sub), W (sub), Az, Sp, Ho, Az (7)
Wilson, M. A. (Manchester U), 2001 v Sp, Fi (sub), Alb, M (sub); (with Middlesbrough), 2002 v Ho (sub), Alb (sub) (6)
White, D. (Manchester C), 1988 v S (2), F, USSR; 1989 v Se; 1990 v Pol (6)
Whyte, C. (Arsenal), 1982 v S (1+1 sub); 1983 v D, Gr (4)
Wicks, S. (QPR), 1982 v S (1)
Wilkins, R. C. (Chelsea), 1977 v W (1)
Wilkinson, P. (Grimsby T), 1985 v Ei, R (sub); (with Everton), 1986 v R (sub), I (4)
Williams, D. (Sunderland), 1998 v Sw (sub); 1999 v F (2)
Williams, P. (Charlton Ath), 1989 v Bul, Sen, Ei, US (sub) (4)
Williams, P. D. (Derby Co), 1991 v Sen, M, USSR; 1992 v G, T, Pol (6)
Williams, S. C. (Southampton), 1977 v S, Fi, N; 1978 v N, I (1 + 1 sub), Y (2); 1979 v D, Bul, Se (sub); 1980 v D, EG (2) (14)
Winterburn, N. (Wimbledon), 1986 v I (1)
Wise, D. (Wimbledon), 1988 v Sw (1)
Woodcook, A. S. (Nottingham F), 1978 v Fi, I (2)
Woodgate, J. S. (Leeds U), 2000 v Arg (1)
Woodhouse, C. (Sheffield U), 1999 v H, Se, Bul; 2000 v Pol (sub) (4)
Woods, C. C. E. (Nottingham F), 1979 v W (sub), Se; (with QPR), 1980 v Bul, EG; 1981 v Sw; (with Norwich C), 1984 v D (6)
Wright, A. G. (Blackburn), 1993 v Sp, N (2)
Wright, M. (Southampton), 1983 v Gr, H; 1984 v D, H (4)
Wright, R. I. (Ipswich T), 1997 v Ge, Pol; 1998 v Mol, I, Gr (2), S.Af, Arg; 1999 v Se, Bul, L, Pol, H, Se; 2000 v Y (15)
Wright, S. J. (Liverpool), 2001 v Ge (sub), G, M (sub); 2002 v Ho (sub), G, Alb, Ho, Slv, I, P (10)
Wright, W. (Everton), 1979 v D, W, Bul; 1980 v D, S (2) (6)
Wright-Phillips, S. C. (Manchester C), 2002 v I; 2003 v Y (sub), Mac (sub), I; 2004 v Mac (sub), T (6)

Yates, D. (Notts Co), 1989 v D (sub), Bul, Sen, Ei, US (5)
Young, L. P. (Tottenham H), 1999 v H; 2000 v D (sub), Arg (sub), T, Slo; (with Charlton Ath), 2002 v Ho, Gr, Ho, P (sub), Sw, I, P (12)

Zamora, R. L. (Brighton & HA), 2002 v P (sub), I (sub), P (sub); 2003 v I, Ser, Slo (sub) (6)

SCOTLAND

Aitken, R. (Celtic), 1977 v Cz, W, Sw; 1978 v Cz, W; 1979 v P, N (2); 1980 v Bel, E; 1984 v EG, Y (2); 1985 v WG, Ic, Sp (16)
Albiston, A. (Manchester U), 1977 v Cz, W, Sw; 1978 v Sw, Cz (5)
Alexander, N. (Stenhousemuir), 1997 v P; 1998 v Bl, Ei, I; (with Livingston), 1999 v Li, Es, Bel (2), CzR, G (10)
Anderson, I. (Dundee), 1997 v Co (sub), US, CzR, P; 1998 v Bl, La, Fi, D (sub), Ei (sub), Ni; 1999 v G (sub), Ei, Ni, CzR; (with Toulouse), 2000 v Bos (15)
Anderson, R. (Aberdeen), 1997 v Es, A, Se; 1998 v La (sub), Fi, Ei, I; 1999 v Es, Bel, G, Ei, Ni, CzR; 2000 v Bos, Es (15)
Anthony, M. (Celtic), 1997 v La (sub), Es (sub), Col (3)
Archdeacon, O. (Celtic), 1987 v WG (sub) (1)
Archibald, A. (Partick T), 1998 v Fi, Ei, Ni, I; 1999 v Li (5)
Archibald, S. (Aberdeen), 1980 v B, E (2), WG; (with Tottenham H), 1981 v D (5)

Bagen, D. (Kilmarnock), 1997 v Es, A (sub), Se (sub), Bl (4)
Bain, K. (Dundee), 1993 v P, I, Ma, P (4)
Baker, M. (St. Mirren), 1993 v F, M, E; 1994 v Ma, A; 1995 v Gr, M, F (sub), Sk (sub); 1996 v H (sub) (10)
Baltacha, S. S. (St Mirren), 2000 v Bos, Li (sub), F (sub) (3)
Bannon, E. J. P. (Hearts), 1979 v US; (with Chelsea), P, N (2); (with Dundee U), 1980 v Bel, WG, E (7)
Beattie, C. (Celtic), 2004 v H (sub), R, D (sub), Ei (4)
Beattie, J. (St Mirren), 1992 v D, US, P, Y (4)
Beaumont, D. (Dundee U), 1985 v Ic (1)
Bell, D. (Aberdeen), 1981 v D; 1984 v Y (2)
Bernard, P. R. J. (Oldham Ath), 1992 v R (sub), D, Se (sub), US; 1993 v Sw, P, I, Ma, P, F, Bul, M, E; 1994 v I, Ma (15)
Berra, C. (Hearts), 2005 v I (1)
Bett, J. (Rangers), 1981 v Se, D; 1982 v Se, D, I, E (2) (7)
Black, E. (Aberdeen), 1983 v EG, Sw (2), Bel; 1985 v Ic, Sp (2), Ic (8)
Blair, A. (Coventry C), 1980 v E; 1981 v Se; (with Aston Villa), 1982 v Se, D, I (5)
Bollan, G. (Dundee U), 1992 v D, G (sub), US, P, Y; 1993 v Sw, P, I, P, F, Bul, M, E; 1994 v Sw; 1995 v Gr; (with Rangers) v Ru, Sm (17)
Bonar, P. (Raith R), 1997 v A, La, Es (sub), Se (4)
Booth, S. (Aberdeen), 1991 v R (sub), Bul (sub + 1), Pol, F (sub); 1992 v Sw, R, D, Se, US, P, Y; 1993 v Ma, P (14)
Bowes, M. J. (Dunfermline Ath), 1992 v D (sub) (1)
Bowman, D. (Hearts), 1985 v WG (sub) (1)
Boyack, S. (Rangers), 1997 v Se (1)
Boyd, K. (Kilmarnock), 2003 v Bel (sub); 2004 v R (sub), D, Ei; 2005 v H, N, Mol (sub), I (sub) (8)
Boyd, T. (Motherwell), 1987 v WG, Ei (2), Bel; 1988 v Bel (5)
Brazil, A. (Hibernian), 1978 v W (1)
Brazil, A. (Ipswich T), 1979 v N; 1980 v Bel (2), E (2), WG; 1981 v Se; 1982 v Se (8)
Brebner, G. I. (Manchester U), 1997 v Col, CzR (sub), US (sub), P; 1998 v Bl, La, Fi, D; (with Reading), 1999 v Li, Es, Bel (2), CzR, G, Ei, Ni, CzR; (with Hibernian), 2000 v Bos (18)
Brighton, T. (Rangers), 2005 v Ni, I (sub), Mol (sub), Bl (4)

Broadfoot, K. (St Mirren), 2005 v Bl (1)
Brough, J. (Hearts), 1981 v D (1)
Brown, A. H. (Hibernian), 2004 v D (1)
Brown, S. (Hibernian), 2005 v H, Sp, Slv, I, Mol (5)
Browne, P. (Raith R), 1997 v A (1)
Buchan, J. (Aberdeen), 1997 v Se, Col, CzR, P; 1998 v Bl, La, Fi; 1999 v Li, Es, Bel, CzR, G, Ei (13)
Burchill, M. (Celtic), 1998 v Fi, D (sub); 1999 v Li, Es (sub), Bel (2), CzR, Ei, Ni, CzR; 2000 v Bos, Es; 2001 v La, Bel, Pol (15)
Burke, A. (Kilmarnock), 1997 v Es, A, Bl (sub); 1998 v Ei (sub) (4)
Burke, C. (Rangers), 2004 v R (sub), D (sub); 2005 v Ni (sub) (3)
Burley, G. E. (Ipswich T), 1977 v Cz, W, Sw; 1978 v Sw, Cz (5)
Burley, C. (Chelsea), 1992 v D; 1993 v Sw, P, I, P; 1994 v Sw, I (sub) (7)
Burns, H. (Rangers), 1985 v Sp, Ic (sub) (2)
Burns, T. (Celtic), 1977 v Cz, W, E; 1978 v Sw; 1982 v E (5)

Caldwell, G. (Newcastle U), 2000 v F, Ni, W; 2002 v Cro, Bel, La; 2003 v Is (sub), Ic, Gh, Bel, Ei, Ic, Li, A, G; 2004 v N, G, Li, Cro (19)
Caldwell, S. (Newcastle U), 2001 v La, Cro, Bel; 2002 v Cro (4)
Campbell, S. (Dundee), 1989 v N (sub), Y, F (3)
Campbell, S. P. (Leicester C), 1998 v Fi (sub), D, Ei, Ni (sub), I; 1999 v Li, Es, Bel (2), CzR, G, Ei, Ni, CzR (sub); 2000 v Bos (sub) (15)
Canero, P. (Kilmarnock), 2000 v F; 2001 v La (sub), Cro (sub), Bel, Pol; 2002 v La (sub); 2003 v D, Ni, Bel (sub), Ei, ic, Li, A, G; 2004 v Li, Cro (2) (17)
Carey, L. A. (Bristol C), 1998 v D (1)
Casey, J. (Celtic), 1978 v W (1)
Christie, M. (Dundee), 1992 v D, P (sub), Y (3)
Clark, R. (Aberdeen), 1977 v Cz, W, Sw (3)
Clarke, S. (St Mirren), 1984 v Bel, EG, Y; 1985 v WG, Ic, Sp (2), Ic (8)
Clarkson, D. (Motherwell), 2004 v D (sub); 2005 v Sp, Slv, N (sub), Mol, Ni (sub), Mol (sub), Bl (sub) (8)
Cleland, A. (Dundee U), 1990 v F, N (2); 1991 v R, Sw, Bul; 1992 v Sw, R, G, Se (2) (11)
Collins, J. (Hibernian), 1988 v Bel, E; 1989 v N, Y, F; 1990 v Y, F, N (8)
Collins, N. (Sunderland), 2005 v Mol, Bl (2)
Connolly, P. (Dundee U), 1991 v R (sub), Sw, Bul (3)
Connor, R. (Ayr U), 1981 v Se; 1982 v Se (2)
Cooper, D. (Clydebank), 1977 v Cz, W, Sw, E; (with Rangers), 1978 v Sw, Cz (6)
Cooper, N. (Aberdeen), 1982 v D, E (2); 1983 v Bel, EG, Sw (2); 1984 v Bel, EG, Y; 1985 v Ic, Sp, Ic (13)
Crabbe, S. (Hearts), 1990 v Y (sub), F (2)
Craig, M. (Aberdeen), 1998 v Bl, La (2)
Craig, T. (Newcastle U), 1977 v E (1)
Crainey, S. D. (Celtic), 2000 v F (sub); 2003 v Bel, Ei (sub), A, G; 2004 v N, G (7)
Crainie, D. (Celtic), 1983 v Sw (sub) (1)
Crawford, S. (Raith R), 1994 v A, Eg, P, Bel; 1995 v Fi, Ru,Gr, Ru, Sm, M, F (sub), Sk (sub), Br (sub); 1996 v Gr, Fi (sub), H (1 + sub), Sp (sub), F (sub) (19)
Creaney, G. (Celtic), 1991 v Sw, Bul (2), Pol, F; 1992 v Sw, R, G (2), Se (2) (11)
Cummings, W. (Chelsea), 2000 v F, Ni; 2001 v La, Cro, Bel, Pol; 2002 v Cro, Bel (8)

Dailly, C. (Dundee U), 1991 v R; 1992 v US, R; 1993 v Sw, P, I, Ic, P, F, Bul, M, E; 1994 v Sw, I, Ma, A, Eg, P, Bel; 1995 v Fi, Ru, Gr, Ru, Sm, M, F, Sk, Br; 1996 v Fi, Sm, H (2), Sp, F (34)
Dalglish, P. (Newcastle U), 1999 v Es, Bel, CzR; (with Norwich C), 2000 v Es (sub), Bos, Li (sub) (6)
Dargo, C. (Raith R), 1998 v Fi, Ei, Ni (sub), I; 1999 v Es, Bel (1+sub), CzR (sub), G, Ni (sub) (10)
Davidson, C. (St Johnstone), 1997 v Se, Bl (2)
Davidson, H. N. (Dundee U), 2000 v Es (sub), Li, F (3)
Dawson, A. (Rangers), 1979 v P, N (2); 1980 v B (2), E (2), WG (8)
Deas, P. A. (St Johnstone), 1992 v D (sub); 1993 v Ma (2)
Dempster, J. (Rushden & D), 2004 v H (sub) (1)
Dennis, S. (Raith R), 1992 v Sw (1)
Diamond, A. (Aberdeen), 2004 v H (sub); 2005 v H, Sp, Slv, I (5)
Dickov, P. (Arsenal), 1992 v Y; 1993 v F, M, E (4)
Dodds, D. (Dundee U), 1978 v W (1)
Dods, D. (Hibernian), 1997 v La, Es, Se (2), Bl (5)
Doig, C. R. (Nottingham F), 2000 v Ni, W; 2001 v La, Cro, Pol; 2003 v D, Is, Ni, Ic, Gh, Bel, Ei; 2004 v N (sub) (13)
Donald, G. S. (Hibernian), 1992 v US (sub), P, Y (sub) (3)
Donnelly, S. (Celtic), 1994 v Eg, P, Bel; 1995 v Fi, Gr (sub); 1996 v Gr (sub), Sm, H (2), Sp, F (11)
Dow, A. (Dundee), 1993 v Ma (sub), Ic; (with Chelsea) 1994 v I (3)
Dowie, A. J. (Rangers), 2003 v D, Is; 2004 v N (sub), H, R, D. Ei; (with Partick), 2005 v Sp, Slv, N, Mol, Se, Ni, I (14)
Duffy, D. A. (Falkirk), 2005 v Se, Ni (2)
Duffy, J. (Dundee), 1987 v Ei (1)
Duff, S. (Dundee U), 2003 v Is, Ni (sub), Ic, Gh, Bel, Ei (sub); 2004 v N, G, Cro (9)
Durie, G. S. (Chelsea), 1987 v WG, Ei, Bel; 1988 v Bel (4)
Durrant, I. (Rangers), 1987 v WG, Ei, Bel; 1988 v E (4)
Doyle, J. (Partick Th), 1981 v D, I (sub) (2)

Easton, C. (Dundee U), 1997 v Col, US, CzR, P; 1998 v Bl, Fi, D, Ei, Ni, I; 1999 v Li, Es, Bel (1+sub); 2000 v Li, F; 2001 v La (sub), Cro, Bel; 2002 v Cro, Bel (21)
Elliot, B. (Celtic), 1998 v Ni; 1999 v Li (sub) (2)
Esson, R. (Aberdeen), 2000 v Li, Ni; 2001 v La, Cro, Bel, Pol; 2002 v Bel (7)

Fagan, S. M. (Motherwell), 2005 v N (1)
Ferguson, B. (Rangers), 1997 v Col (sub), US, CzR, P; 1998 v Bl, La, Fi, D (sub), Ei, Ni, I; 1999 v Bel (12)
Ferguson, D. (Rangers), 1987 v WG, Ei, Bel; 1988 v E; 1990 v Y (5)
Ferguson, D. (Dundee U), 1992 v D, G, Se (2); 1993 v Sw, I, Ma (7)
Ferguson, D. (Manchester U), 1992 v US, P (sub), Y; 1993 v Sw, Ma (5)
Ferguson, I. (Dundee), 1983 v EG (sub), Sw (sub); 1984 v Bel (sub), EG (4)
Ferguson, I. (Clyde), 1987 v WG (sub), Ei; (with St Mirren), Ei, Bel; 1988 v Bel; (with Rangers), E (sub) (6)
Ferguson, R. (Hamilton A), 1977 v E (1)
Findlay, W. (Hibernian), 1991 v R, Pol, Bul (2), Pol (5)
Fitzpatrick, A. (St Mirren), 1977 v W (sub), Sw (sub), E; 1978 v Sw, Cz (5)
Flannigan, C. (Clydebank), 1993 v Ic (sub) (1)
Fleck, R. (Rangers), 1987 v WG (sub), Ei, Bel; (with Norwich C), 1988 v E (2); 1989 v Y (6)
Fletcher, D. B. (Manchester U), 2003 v Ic (sub); 2004 v G (sub) (2)
Foster, R. M. (Aberdeen), 2005 v Mol, Se (sub) (2)
Fotheringham, M. M. (Dundee), 2004 v R, D (sub), Ei (sub) (3)
Fowler, J. (Kilmarnock), 2002 v Cro (sub), Bel, La (3)
Foy, R. A. (Liverpool), 2004 v H, R (sub), D; 2005 v H, N (5)
Fraser, S. T. (Luton T), 2000 v Ni (sub), W; 2001 v La, Cro (4)
Freedman, D. A. (Barnet), 1995 v Ru (sub + 1), Sm, M, F, Sk, Br; (with C Palace) 1996 v Sm (sub) (8)
Fridge, L. (St Mirren), 1989 v F; 1990 v Y (2)
Fullarton, J. (St. Mirren), 1993 v F, Bul; 1994 v Ma, A, Eg, P, Bel; 1995 v M, F, Sk, Br; 1996 v Gr, Fi, H (sub + 1), Sp (sub), F (17)
Fulton, M. (St Mirren), 1980 v Bel, WG, E; 1981 v Se, D (sub) (5)
Fulton, S. (Celtic), 1991 v R, Sw, Bul, Pol, F; 1992 v G (2) (7)

Gallacher, K. (Dundee U), 1987 v WG, Ei (2), Bel (sub); 1988 v E (2); 1990 v Y (7)
Gallacher, P. (Dundee U), 1999 v Ei, Ni, CzR; 2000 v Bos, Es, Bos, F (7)
Gallagher, P. (Blackburn R), 2003 v G (sub); 2004 v N (sub), Li (sub), D; 2005 v H, Se, Mol (7)
Galloway, M. (Hearts), 1989 v F; (with Celtic), 1990 v N (2)
Gardiner, J. (Hibernian), 1993 v F (1)
Geddes, R. (Dundee), 1982 v Se, D, E (2); 1988 v E (5)
Gemmill, S. (Nottingham F), 1992 v Sw, R (sub), G (sub), Se (sub) (4)
Germaine, G. (WBA), 1997 v Se (1)
Gilles, R. (St Mirren), 1997 v A (1 + sub), La, Es (2), Se, Bl (7)
Gillespie, G. (Coventry C), 1979 v US; 1980 v E; 1981 v D; 1982 v Se, D, I (2), E (8)
Glass, S. (Aberdeen), 1995 v M, F, Sk, Br; 1996 v Gr, Fi, H, Sp; 1997 v A (2), Es (11)

Glover, L. (Nottingham F), 1988 v Bel (sub); 1989 v N; 1990 v Y (3)
Goram, A. (Oldham Ath), 1987 v Ei (1)
Gordon, C. (Hearts), 2003 v Is (sub), Gh; 2004 v N (sub), Cro (2) (5)
Gough, C. R. (Dundee U), 1983 v EG, Sw, Bel; 1984 v Y (2) (5)
Graham, D. (Rangers), 1998 v Bl (sub), La (sub), Fi (sub), D, Ei (sub), Ni, I; 1999 v Li (8)
Grant, P. (Celtic), 1985 v WG, Ic, Sp; 1987 v WG, Ei (2), Bel; 1988 v Bel, E (2) (10)
Gray S. (Celtic), 1995 v F, Sk, Br; 1996 v Gr, H, Sp, F (7)
Gray, S. (Aberdeen), 1987 v WG (1)
Gunn, B. (Aberdeen), 1984 v EG, Y (2); 1985 v WG, Ic, Sp (2), Ic; 1990 v F (9)

Hagen, D. (Rangers), 1992 v D (sub), US (sub), P, Y; 1993 v Sw (sub), P, Ic, P (8)
Hammell, S. (Motherwell), 2001 v Pol (sub); 2002 v La; 2003 v Is, Ni, Gh, Bel (sub), Ei; 2004 v N, Li, Cro (2) (11)
Hamilton, B. (St Mirren), 1989 v Y, F (sub); 1990 v F, N (4)
Hamilton, J. (Dundee) 1995 v Sm (sub), Br; 1996 v Fi (sub), Sm, H (sub), Sp (sub), F; 1997 v A, La, Es, Se; (with Hearts), Es, A, Se (14)
Handyside, P. (Grimsby T), 1993 v Ic (sub), Bul, M, E; 1995 v Ru; 1996 v Fi, Sm (7)
Hannah, D. (Dundee U), 1993 v F (sub), Bul, M; 1994 v A, Eg, P, Bel; 1995 v Fi, Ru (sub), Gr, Ru, M, F, Sk, Br; 1996 v Gr (16)
Harper, K. (Hibernian), 1995 v Ru (sub); 1996 v Fi; 1997 v A (2), La, Es, Se (7)
Hartford, R. A. (Manchester C), 1977 v Sw (1)
Hartley, P. (Millwall), 1997 v A (sub) (1)
Hegarty, P. (Dundee U), 1987 v WG, Bel; 1988 v E (2); 1990 v F, N (6)
Hendry, J. (Tottenham H), 1992 v D (sub) (1)
Hetherston, B. (St Mirren), 1997 v Es (sub) (1)
Hewitt, J. (Aberdeen), 1982 v I; 1983 v EG, Sw (2); 1984 v Bel, Y (sub) (6)
Hogg, G. (Manchester U), 1984 v Y; 1985 v WG, Ic, Sp (4)
Hood, G. (Ayr U), 1993 v F, E (sub); 1994 v A (3)
Horn, R. (Hearts), 1997 v US, CzR, P; 1998 v Bl, La, D (sub) (6)
Howie, S. (Cowdenbeath), 1993 v Ma, Ic, P; 1994 v Sw, I (5)
Hughes, R. D. (Bournemouth), 1999 v CzR, Ei, Ni, CzR; 2000 v Bos, Es; 2001 v La, Cro, Bel (9)
Hughes, S. (Rangers), 2002 v La; 2003 v D, Ic, Gh, Be, Ei (sub), Ic (sub), A; 2004 v N (sub), Li (sub), Cro (sub+sub) (12)
Hunter, G. (Hibernian), 1987 v Ei (sub); 1988 v Bel, E (3)
Hunter, P. (East Fife), 1989 v N (sub), F (sub); 1990 v F (sub) (3)
Hutton, A, (Rangers), 2004 v R, D; 2005 v H, Slv, Se, Ni (sub) (6)

James, K. F. (Falkirk), 1997 v Bl (1)
Jardine, I. (Kilmarnock), 1979 v US (1)
Jess, E. (Aberdeen), 1990 v F (sub), N (sub); 1991 v R, Sw, Bul (2), Pol, F; 1992 v Sw, R, G (2), Se (1 + 1 sub) (14)
Johnson, G. I. (Dundee U), 1992 v US, P, Y; 1993 v Sw, P, Ma (6)
Johnston, A. (Hearts), 1994 v Bel; 1995 v Ru, 1996 v Sp (3)
Johnston, F. (Falkirk), 1993 v Ic (1)
Johnston, M. (Partick Th), 1984 v EG (sub); (with Watford), Y (2) (3)
Jordan, A. J. (Bristol C), 2000 v Bos (sub), Li, F (3)
Jupp, D. A. (Fulham), 1995 v Fi, Ru (2), Sm, M, F, Sk, Br; 1997 v Se (9)

Kirkwood, D. (Hearts), 1990 v Y (1)
Kennedy, J. (Celtic), 2003 v Is (sub), Ni, Ic, Gh, Bel, Ei, Ic, Li, A, G; 2004 v N (sub), Li, Cro (2), H (15)
Kerr, B. (Newcastle U), 2003 v D, Is, Ni, Ic, Gh, Bel, Ei, Ic, Li, A, G; 2004 v Li, Cro (2) (14)
Kerr, M. (Kilmarnock), 2001 v Pol (sub) (1)
Kerr, S. (Celtic), 1993 v Bul, M, E; 1994 v Ma, A, Eg, P, Bel; 1995 v Fi, Gr (10)
Kinniburgh, W. D. (Motherwell), 2004 v R (sub) (1)
Kyle, K. (Sunderland), 2001 v La (sub), Cro (sub), Pol (sub); 2003 v Ic, Ei, Ic, Li, G; 2004 v N. G, Cro (2) (12)

Lambert, P. (St Mirren), 1991 v R, Sw, Bul (2), Pol, F; 1992 v Sw, R, G (2), Se (11)
Langfield, J. (Dundee), 2000 v W; 2002 v Cro (2)
Lappin, S. (St Mirren), 2004 v H, R, D, Ei; 2005 v H (sub), Slv, N, Mol, Se (9)
Lauchlan, J. (Kilmarnock), 1998 v Ei, Ni, I; 1999 v CzR, G, Ni, CzR; 2000 v Bos, Es, Bos, Li (11)
Lavety, B. (St. Mirren), 1993 v Ic, Bul (sub), M (sub), E; 1994 v Ma, A (sub), Eg (sub), Bel (sub); 1995 v Fi (sub) (9)
Lavin, G. (Watford), 1993 v F, Bul, M; 1994 v Ma, Eg, P, Bel (7)
Lawson, P. (Celtic), 2004 v H, R, Ei (3)
Leighton, J. (Aberdeen), 1982 v I (1)
Levein, C. (Hearts), 1985 v Sp, Ic (2)
Leven, P. (Kilmarnock), 2005 v Se (sub), Ni (2)
Liddell, A. M. (Barnsley), 1994 v Ma (sub); 1995 v Sm (sub), M (sub), F, Sk; 1996 v Gr, Fi, Sm, H (2), Sp, F (sub) (12)
Lindsey, J. (Motherwell), 1979 v US (1)
Locke, G. (Hearts), 1994 v Ma, A, Eg, P; 1995 v Fi; 1996 v Fi, H; 1997 v Es, A, Bl (10)
Love, G. (Hibernian), 1995 v Ru (1)
Lynch, S. (Celtic), 2003 v Is (sub), Ni (sub), Ic (sub), Gh (sub), Bel; (with Preston NE), Ei (sub), Li (sub), A (sub), G; 2004 v N, G, Li, Cro (sub) (13)

McAllister, G. (Leicester C), 1990 v N (1)
McAlpine, H. (Dundee U), 1983 v EG, Sw (2), Bel; 1984 v Bel (5)
McAnespie, K. (St Johnstone), 1998 v Fi (sub); 1999 v G (sub); 2000 v Ni, W (4)
McAuley, S. (St. Johnstone), 1993 v P (sub) (1)
McAvennie, F. (St Mirren), 1982 v I, E; 1985 v Is, Ei, R (5)
McBride, J. (Everton), 1981 v D (1)
McBride, J. P. (Celtic), 1998 v Ni (sub), I (sub) (2)
McCall, S. (Bradford C), 1988 v E; (with Everton), 1990 v F (2)
McCann, N. (Dundee), 1994 v A, Eg, P, Bel; 1995 v Fi, Gr (sub), Sm; 1996 v Fi, Sm (9)
McClair, B. (Celtic), 1984 v Bel (sub), EG, Y (1 + 1 sub); 1985 v WG, Ic, Sp, Ic (8)
McCluskey, G. (Celtic), 1979 v US, P; 1980 v Bel (2); 1982 v D, I (6)
McCluskey, S. (St Johnstone), 1997 v Es (2), A, Se, Col, US, CzR; 1998 v Bl, La, D, Ei (sub), Ni, I; 1999 v Li (14)
McCoist, A. (Rangers), 1984 v Bel (1)
McConnell, I. (Clyde), 1997 v A (sub) (1)
McCracken, D. (Dundee U), 2002 v La; 2004 v N, G, Li, Cro (5)
McCulloch, A. (Kilmarnock); 1981 v Se (1)
McCulloch, I. (Notts Co), 1982 v E (2)
McCulloch, L. (Motherwell), 1997 v La (sub), Es (1 + sub), Se (sub + 1), A (sub), Col (sub); 1998 v Bl (sub), Fi (sub), D, Ei, Ni; 1999 v CzR, G (14)
McCunnie, J. (Dundee U), 2001 v Pol; 2002 v Cro; 2003 v D. Is, Ni; (with Ross Co), 2004 v H, R, Ei; 2005 v H (sub), Sp, Slv, N (sub), Mol, Se, Ni, I, Mol, Bl (18)
MacDonald, J. (Rangers), 1980 v WG (sub); 1981 v Se; 1982 v Se (sub), L, I (2), E (2 sub) (8)
McDonald, C. (Falkirk), 1995 v Fi (sub), Ru, M (sub), F (sub), Br (sub) (5)
McEwan, C. (Clyde), 1997 v Col, US (sub), CzR (sub), P; (with Raith R), 1998 v Bl, La, Fi, D, Ei, Ni, I; 1999 v Li, Es (sub), Bel (2), CzR, G (sub) (17)
McEwan, D. (Livingston), 2003 v Ni (sub), Gh (sub) (2)
McFadden, J. (Motherwell), 2003 v D (sub), Is, Ni, Gh, Ei (sub), Ic, Li (7)
McFarlane, D. (Hamilton A), 1997 v Col, US (sub), P (sub) (3)
McGarry, S. (St Mirren), 1997 v US, CzR, P (sub) (3)
McGarvey, F. (St Mirren), 1977 v E; 1978 v Cz; (with Celtic), 1982 v D (3)
McGarvey, S. (Manchester U), 1982 v E (sub); 1983 v Bel, Sw; 1984 v Bel (4)
McGhee, M. (Aberdeen), 1981 v D (1)
McGinnis, G. (Dundee U), 1985 v Sp (1)
McGregor, A. (Rangers), 2003 v D (sub), Is, Bel (sub), Ei (sub), A (sub); 2004 v N (6)
McGrillen, P. (Motherwell), 1994 v Sw (sub), I (2)
McGuire, D. (Aberdeen), 2002 v Bel, La (2)
McInally, J. (Dundee U), 1989 v F (1)
McKenzie, R. (Hearts), 1997 v Es, Bl (2)
McKimmie, S. (Aberdeen), 1985 v WG, Ic (2) (3)
McKinlay, T. (Dundee), 1984 v EG (sub); 1985 v WG, Ic, Sp (2), Ic (6)

McKinlay, W. (Dundee U), 1989 v N, Y (sub), F; 1990 v Y, F, N (6)
McKinnon, R. (Dundee U), 1991 v R, Pol (sub); 1992 v G (2), Se (2) (6)
McLaren, A, (Hearts), 1989 v F; 1990 v Y, N; 1991 v Sw, Bul, Po1, F; 1992 v R, G, Se (2) (11)
McLaren, A. (Dundee U), 1993 v I, Ma (sub); 1994 v Sw, I (sub) (4)
McLaughlin, B. (Celtic), 1995 v Ru, Sm, M, Sk (sub), Br (sub); 1996 v Gr (sub), Sm (sub), H (8)
McLaughlin, J. (Morton), 1981 v D; 1982 v Se, D, I, E (2); 1983 v EG, Sw (2), Bel (10)
McLean, S. (Rangers), 2003 v D (sub), Ni (sub), Gh (sub), Bel (sub) (4)
McLeish, A. (Aberdeen), 1978 v W; 1979 v US; 1980 v Bel, E (2); 1987 v Ei (6)
MacLeod, A. (Hibernian), 1979 v P, N (2) (3)
McLeod, J. (Dundee U), 1989 v N; 1990 v F (2)
MacLeod, M. (Dumbarton), 1979 v US; (with Celtic), P (sub), N (2); 1980 v Bel (5)
McManus, T. (Hibernian), 2001 v Bel (sub), Pol (sub); 2002 v Cro, Bel, La; 2003 v D (sub), Ni (sub), Ic, Gh, A, G (sub); 2004 v N (sub), Li (sub), Cro (14)
McMillan, S. (Motherwell), 1997 v A (sub + sub), Se, Bl (4)
McNab, N. (Tottenham H), 1978 v W (1)
McNally, M. (Celtic), 1991 v Bul; 1993 v Ic (2)
McNamara, J. (Dunfermline Ath), 1994 v A, Bel; 1995 v Gr, Ru, Sm; 1996 v Gr, Fi; (with Celtic), Sm, H (2), Sp, F (12)
McNaughton, K. (Aberdeen), 2002 v La (sub) (1)
McNichol, J. (Brentford), 1979 v P, N (2); 1980 v Bel (2), WG, E (7)
McNiven, D. (Leeds U), 1977 v Cz, W (sub), Sw (sub) (3)
McNiven, S. A. (Oldham Ath), 1996 v Sm (sub) (1)
McParland, A. (Celtic), 2003 v Gh (sub) (1)
McPhee, S. (Port Vale), 2002 v La (sub) (1)
McPherson, D. (Rangers), 1984 v Bel; 1985 v Sp; (with Hearts), 1989 v N, Y (4)
McQuilken, J. (Celtic), 1993 v Bul, E (2)
McStay, P. (Celtic), 1983 v EG, Sw (2); 1984 v Y (2) (5)
McWhirter, N. (St Mirren), 1991 v Bul (sub) (1)
Main, A. (Dundee U), 1988 v E; 1989 v Y; 1990 v N (3)
Malcolm, R. (Rangers), 2001 v Pol (1)
Maloney, S. (Celtic), 2002 v Cro (sub), Bel (sub), La; 2003 v D, Is, Ni, Bel, Ei, Ic (sub), Li (sub), A; 2004 v G (sub), Li, Cro (1+sub), H; 2005 v Ni, I, Mol, Bl (20)
Malpas, M. (Dundee U), 1983 v Bel, Sw (1+1 sub); 1984 v Bel, EG, Y (2); 1985 v Sp (8)
Marshall, D. J. (Celtic), 2004 v H (sub), D; 2005 v I (3)
Marshall, S. R. (Arsenal), 1995 v Ru, Gr; 1996 v H, Sp, F (5)
Mason, G. R. (Manchester C), 1999 v Li (sub); (with Dunfermline Ath), 2002 v Bel (2)
Mathieson, D. (Queen of the South), 1997 v Col; 1998 v La; 1999 v G (sub) (3)
May, E. (Hibernian), 1989 v Y (sub), F (2)
Meldrum, C. (Kilmarnock), 1996 v F (sub); 1997 v A (2), La, Es, Se (6)
Melrose, J. (Partick Th), 1977 v Sw; 1979 v US, P, N (2); 1980 v Bel (sub), WG, E (8)
Miller, C. (Rangers), 1995 v Gr, Ru; 1996 v Gr, Sp, F; 1997 v A, La, Es (8)
Miller, J. (Aberdeen), 1987 v Ei (sub); 1988 v Bel; (with Celtic), E; 1989 v N, Y; 1990 v F, N (7)
Miller, K. (Hibernian), 2000 v F, Ni, W; (with Rangers), 2001 v Cro, Bel; 2002 v Cro, Bel (7)
Miller, W. (Aberdeen), 1978 v Sw, Cz (2)
Miller, W. (Hibernian), 1991 v R, Sw, Bul, Pol, F; 1992 v R, G (sub) (7)
Milne, K. (Hearts), 2000 v F (1)
Milne, R. (Dundee U), 1982 v Se (sub); 1984 v Bel, EG (3)
Money, I. C. (St Mirren), 1987 v Ei; 1988 v Bel; 1989 v N (3)
Montgomery, N. A. (Sheffield U), 2003 v A (sub); 2004 v Cro (sub) (2)
Morrison, S. A. (Aberdeen), 2004 v H (sub), D (sub), Ei; 2005 v H, Sp, Mol, Se, Ni, I, Mol, Bl (11)
Muir, L. (Hibernian), 1977 v Cz (sub) (1)
Murray, H. (St Mirren), 2000 v F (sub), Ni (sub), W (sub) (3)
Murray, I. (Hibernian), 2001 v Bel (sub), Pol; 2002 v Cro, Bel, La; 2003 v D, Ic, Gh, Bel, Ic, Li, G; 2004 v G, Cro (2) (15)
Murray, N. (Rangers), 1993 v P (sub), Ma, Ic, P; 1994 v Sw, I; 1995 v Fi, Ru, Gr, Sm; 1996 v Gr (sub), Fi, Sm, H (2), F (16)
Murray, R. (Bournemouth), 1993 v Ic (sub) (1)
Murray, S. (Kilmarnock), 2004 v D (sub), Ei (sub) (2)

Narey, D. (Dundee U), 1977 v Cz, Sw; 1978 v Sw, Cz (4)
Naysmith, G. (Hearts), 1997 v La, Es (1 + sub), Se, A, Col, US, CzR, P; 1998 v La, D; 1999 v Es, Bel (2), CzR, G, Ei, CzR; 2000 v Bos, Es, Bos, Li (22)
Neilson, R. (Hearts), 2000 v Ni (1)
Nevin, P. (Chelsea), 1985 v WG, Ic, Sp (2), Ic (5)
Nicholas, C. (Celtic), 1981 v Se; 1982 v Se; 1983 v EG, Sw, Bel; (with Arsenal), 1984 v Y (6)
Nicholson, B. (Rangers), 1999 v G, Ni, CzR (sub); 2000 v Bos (sub), Es, Bos, Li (7)
Nicol, S. (Ayr U), 1981 v Se; 1982 v Se, D; (with Liverpool), I (2), E (2); 1983 v EG, Sw (2), Bel; 1984 v Bel, EG, Y (14)
Nisbet, S. (Rangers), 1989 v N, Y, F; 1990 v Y, F (5)
Noble, D. J. (West Ham U), 2003 v A (sub); 2004 v N (sub) (2)
Notman, A. M. (Manchester U), 1999 v Li (sub), Es, Bel (sub+sub); 2000 v Li, F (sub), Ni, W; 2001 v La, Cro (10)

O'Brien, B. (Blackburn R), 1999 v Ei (sub), Ni (sub), CzR (sub); 2000 v Bos (sub); (with Livingston), 2003 v Is (sub), Gh (sub) (6)
O'Connor, G. (Hibernian), 2003 v D; 2004 v Cro, H, R; 2005 v Sp, Slv, N, Mol (8)
O'Donnell, P. (Motherwell), 1992 v Sw (sub), R, D, G (2), Se (1 + 1 sub); 1993 v P (8)
O'Neil, B. (Celtic), 1992 v D, G, Se (2); 1993 v Sw, P, I (7)
O'Neil, J. (Dundee U), 1991 v Bul (sub) (1)
O'Neill, M. (Clyde), 1995 v Ru (sub), F, Sk, Br; 1997 v Se (sub), Bl (sub) (6)
Orr, N. (Morton), 1978 v W (sub); 1979 v US, P, N (2); 1980 v Bel, E (7)

Parker, K. (St Johnstone), 2001 v Pol (sub) (1)
Parlane, D. (Rangers), 1977 v W (1)
Paterson, C. (Hibernian), 1981 v Se; 1982 v I (2)
Paterson, J. (Dundee U), 1997 v Col, US, CzR; 1999 v Bel (sub+sub); 2000 v Es, Bos, Li; 2002 v Cro (sub) (9)
Payne, G. (Dundee U), 1978 v Sw, Cz, W (3)
Peacock, L. A. (Carlisle U), 1997 v Bl (1)
Pearson, S. (Motherwell), 2003 v Is, Ni, Bel (sub), Ei, A, G; 2004 v N, G (8)
Pressley, S. (Rangers), 1993 v Ic, F, Bul, M, E; 1994 v Sw, I, M, A, Eg, P, Bel; 1995 v Fi; (with Coventry C), Ru (2), Sm, M, F, Sk, Br; (with Dundee U), 1996 v Gr, Sm, H (2), Sp, F (26)
Provan, D. (Kilmarnock), 1977 v Cz (sub) (1)
Prunty, B. (Aberdeen), 2004 v H, R (sub), Ei; 2005 v H (sub), Sp (sub), Slv (sub) (6)

Quinn, P. C. (Motherwell), 2004 v D (1)

Rae, A. (Millwall), 1991 v Bul (sub + 1), F (sub); 1992 v Sw, R, G (sub), Se (2) (8)
Rae, G. (Dundee), 1999 v Ei (sub), Ni, CzR; 2000 v Bos, Es, Bos (6)
Redford, I. (Rangers), 1981 v Se (sub); 1982 v Se, D, I (2), E (6)
Reid, B. (Rangers), 1991 v F; 1992 v D, US, P (4)
Reid, C. (Hibernian), 1993 v Sw, P, I (3)
Reid, M. (Celtic), 1982 v E; 1984 v Y (2)
Reid, R. (St Mirren), 1977 v W, Sw, E (3)
Reilly, A. (Wycombe W), 2004 v H (sub) (1)
Renicks, S. (Hamilton A), 1997 v Bl (1)
Rice, B. (Hibernian), 1985 v WG (1)
Richardson, L. (St Mirren), 1980 v WG, E (sub) (2)
Riordan, D. G. (Hibernian), 2004 v R; 2005 v H (sub), Sp (sub), Slv (sub), I (5)
Ritchie, A. (Morton), 1980 v Bel (1)
Ritchie, P. R. (Hearts), 1996 v H; 1997 v A (2), La, Es (2), Se (7)
Robertson, A. (Rangers) 1991 v F (1)
Robertson, C. (Rangers), 1977 v E (sub) (1)
Robertson, D. (Aberdeen), 1987 v Ei (sub); 1988 v E (2); 1989 v N, Y; 1990 v Y, N (7)
Robertson, G. A. (Nottingham F), 2004 v Ei; 2005 v H, Sp, Slv, N, Mol, Se, Ni, Mol, Bl (10)
Robertson, H. (Aberdeen), 1994 v Eg; 1995 v Fi (2)
Robertson, J. (Hearts), 1985 v WG, Ic (sub) (2)
Robertson, L. (Rangers), 1993 v F, M (sub), E (sub) (3)
Robertson, S. (St Johnstone), 1998 v Fi, Ni (2)
Roddie, A. (Aberdeen), 1992 v US, P; 1993 v Sw (sub), P, Ic (5)

Ross, T. W. (Arsenal), 1977 v W (1)
Rowson, D. (Aberdeen), 1997 v La, Es, Se (2), Bl (5)
Russell, R. (Rangers), 1978 v W; 1980 v Bel; 1984 v Y (3)

Salton, D. B. (Luton T), 1992 v D, US, P, Y; 1993 v Sw, I (6)
Samson, C. I. (Kilmarnock), 2004 v R, Ei; 2005 v H, Ni, Mol, Bl (6)
Scott, P. (St Johnstone), 1994 v A (sub), Eg (sub), P, Bel (4)
Scrimgour, D. (St Mirren), 1997 v US, CzR; 1998 v D (3)
Seaton, A. (Falkirk), 1998 v Bl (sub) (1)
Severin, S. D. (Hearts), 2000 v Es, Bos, Li (sub), F, Ni, W; 2001 v La, Bel; 2002 v Cro, Bel (10)
Shannon, R. (Dundee), 1987 v WG, Ei (2), Bel; 1988 v Bel, E (2) (7)
Sharp, G. (Everton), 1982 v E (1)
Sharp, R. (Dunfermline Ath), 1990 v N (sub); 1991 v R, Sw, Bul (4)
Sheerin, P. (Southampton), 1996 v Sm (1)
Shields, G. (Rangers), 1997 v A, La (2)
Simmons, S. (Hearts), 2003 v Gh (sub) (1)
Simpson, N. (Aberdeen), 1982 v I (2), E; 1983 v EG, Sw (2), Bel; 1984 v Bel, EG, Y; 1985 v Sp (11)
Sinclair, G. (Dumbarton), 1977 v E (1)
Skilling, M. (Kilmarnock), 1993 v Ic (sub); 1994 v I (2)
Smith, B. M. (Celtic), 1992 v G (2), US, P, Y (5)
Smith, G. (Rangers), 1978 v W (1)
Smith, G. (Rangers), 2004 v H, D (sub), Ei (sub); 2005 v H (sub), Sp, Slv, N, Mol (8)
Smith, H. G. (Hearts), 1987 v WG, Bel (2)
Sneddon, A. (Celtic), 1979 v US (1)
Soutar, D. (Dundee), 2003 v D, Ni, Ic, Bel, Ei, Ic, Li, A, G; 2004 v G, Li (11)
Speedie, D. (Chelsea), 1985 v Sp (1)
Spencer, J. (Rangers), 1991 v Sw (sub), F; 1992 v Sw (3)
Stanton, P. (Hibernian), 1977 v Cz (1)
Stark, W. (Aberdeen), 1985 v Ic (1)
Stephen, R. (Dundee), 1983 v Bel (sub) (1)
Stevens, G. (Motherwell), 1977 v E (1)
Stewart, C. (Kilmarnock), 2002 v La (1)
Stewart, J. (Kilmarnock), 1978 v Sw, Cz; (with Middlesbrough), 1979 v P (3)
Stewart, M. J. (Manchester U), 2000 v Ni; 2001 v La, Cro, Bel, Pol; 2002 v La; 2003 v D, Is, Ni, Ei (sub), Ic, Li, A; 2004 v N, G, Li, Cro (17)
Stewart, R. (Dundee U), 1979 v P, N (2); (with West Ham U), 1980 v Bel (2), E (2), WG; 1981 v D; 1982 v I (2), E (12)
Stillie, D. (Aberdeen), 1995 v Ru (2), Sm, M, F, Sk, Br; 1996 v Gr, Fi, Sm, H (2), Sp, F (14)
Strachan, G. D. (Aberdeen), 1980 v Bel (1)
Strachan, G. D. (Coventry C), 1998 v D, Ei; 1999 v Li, Es, Bel (2); 2000 v Li (7)
Sturrock, P. (Dundee U), 1977 v Cz, W, Sw, E; 1978 v Sw, Cz; 1982 v Se, I, E (9)
Sweeney, P. H. (Millwall), 2004 v H (sub), D, Ei (sub); 2005 v H, Sp, Slv, Se (sub), Mol (sub) (8)
Sweeney, S. (Clydebank), 1991 v R, Sw (sub), Bul (2), Pol; 1992 v Sw, R (7)

Tarrant, N. K. (Aston Villa), 1999 v Ni (sub); 2000 v Es (sub), Bos (sub), Li, Ni (sub) (5)
Teale, G. (Clydebank), 1997 v La (sub), Es, Bl; (with Ayr U), 1999 v CzR (sub), G (sub), Ei (sub) (6)
Telfer, P. (Luton T), 1993 v Ma, P; 1994 v Sw (3)
Thomas, K. (Hearts), 1993 v F (sub), Bul, M, E; 1994 v Sw, Ma; 1995 v Gr; 1997 v A (8)
Thompson, S. (Dundee U), 1997 v US, CzR, P; 1998 v Bl, La; 1999 v G (sub), Ei, Ni, CzR; 2000 v Bos, Es, Bos (12)
Thomson, K. (Hibernian), 2005 v Bl (sub) (1)
Thomson, W. (Partick Th), 1977 v E (sub); 1978 v W; (with St Mirren), 1979 v US, N (2); 1980 v Bel (2), E (2), WG (10)
Tolmie, J. (Morton), 1980 v Bel (sub) (1)
Tortolano, J. (Hibernian), 1987 v WG, Ei (2)
Turner, I. (Everton), 2005 v Sp (sub), Se (2)
Tweed, S. (Hibernian), 1993 v Ic; 1994 v Sw, I (3)

Wales, G. (Hearts), 2000 v F (1)
Walker, A. (Celtic), 1988 v Bel (1)
Wallace, I. (Coventry C), 1978 v Sw (1)
Wallace, R. (Celtic), 2004 v H (sub); 2005 v N (2)
Walsh, C. (Nottingham F), 1984 v EG, Sw (2), Bel; 1984 v EG (5)
Wark, J. (Ipswich T), 1977 v Cz, W, Sw; 1978 v W; 1979 v P; 1980 v E (2), WG (8)
Watson, A. (Aberdeen), 1981 v Se, D; 1982 v D, I (sub) (4)
Watson, K. (Rangers), 1977 v E; 1978 v Sw (sub) (2)
Watt, M. (Aberdeen), 1991 v R, Sw, Bul (2), Pol, F; 1992 v Sw, R, G (2), Se (2) (12)
Watt. S. M. (Chelsea), 2005 v Mol, Bl (2)
Webster, A. (Hearts), 2003 v Ic, Li (2)
Whiteford, A. (St Johnstone), 1997 v US (1)
Whittaker, S. G. (Hibernian), 2005 v H (sub), Sp, Slv (sub), N, Mol, Se, Ni, I, Mol, Bl (10)
Whyte, D. (Celtic), 1987 v Ei (2), Bel; 1988 v E (2); 1989 v N, Y; 1990 v Y, N (9)
Wilkie, L. (Dundee), 2000 v Bos, F, Ni, W; 2001 v La, Cro (6)
Will, J. A. (Arsenal), 1992 v D (sub), Y; 1993 v Ic (sub) (3)
Williams, G. (Nottingham F), 2002 v Bel (sub); 2003 v Ic, Ei, Ic, Li; 2004 v N, G, Li, Cro (9)
Wilson, M. (Dundee U), 2004 v H, R, D, Ei; 2005 v H, N, Mol, Se, Ni, I, Mol, Bl (12)
Wilson, S. (Rangers), 1999 v Es, Bel (2), G, Ei, CzR; 2000 v Bos (7)
Wilson, T. (St Mirren), 1983 v Sw (sub) (1)
Wilson, T. (Nottingham F), 1988 v E; 1989 v N, Y; 1990 v F (4)
Winnie, D. (St Mirren), 1988 v Bel (1)
Wright, P. (Aberdeen), 1989 v Y, F; (with QPR), 1990 v Y (sub) (3)
Wright, S. (Aberdeen), 1991 v Bul, Pol, F; 1992 v Sw, G (2), Se (2); 1993 v Sw, P, I, Ma; 1994 v I, Ma (14)
Wright, T. (Oldham Ath), 1987 v Bel (sub) (1)

Young, Darren (Aberdeen), 1997 v Es (sub), Se, Col, CzR (sub), P; 1998 v La (sub); 1999 v CzR (sub), G (sub) (8)
Young, Derek (Aberdeen), 2000 v W; 2001 v Cro (sub), Bel (sub), Pol; 2002 v Cro (5)

WALES

Aizlewood, M. (Luton T), 1979 v E; 1981 v Ho (2)
Anthony, B. (Cardiff C), 2005 v La (sub), E, Pol (3)

Baddeley, L. M. (Cardiff C), 1996 v Mol (sub), G (sub) (2)
Balcombe, S. (Leeds U), 1982 v F (sub) (1)
Barnhouse, D. J. (Swansea), 1995 v Mol; 1996 v Mol, Sm (3)
Bater, P. T. (Bristol R), 1977 v E, S (2)
Beevers, L. J. (Boston U), 2005 v G (sub); (with Lincoln C), A (1+1) (3)
Bellamy, C. D. (Norwich C), 1996 v Sm (sub); 1997 v Sm, T, Bel; 1998 v T, Bel, I; 1999 v I (8)
Birchall, A. S. (Arsenal), 2003 v Fi, I, Az; 2005 v La, Az, E, Pol, A (sub +1) (9)
Bird, A. (Cardiff C), 1993 v Cy (sub); 1994 v Cy (sub); 1995 v Mol, Ge (sub), Bul; 1996 v G (sub) (6)
Blackmore, C. (Manchester U), 1984 v N, Bul, Y (3)
Blake, N. (Cardiff C), 1991 v Pol (sub); 1993 v Cy, Bel, RCS; 1994 v RCS (5)
Blaney, S. D. (West Ham U), 1997 v Sm, Ho, T (3)
Bodin, P. (Cardiff C), 1983 v Y (1)
Bowen, J. P. (Swansea C), 1993 v Cy, Bel (2); 1994 v RCS, R (sub) (5)
Bowen, M. (Tottenham H), 1983 v N; 1984 v Bul, Y (3)
Boyle, T. (C Palace), 1982 v F (1)
Brace, D. P. (Wrexham), 1995 v Ge, Bul (2); 1997 v Sm Ho; 1998 v T (6)
Brough, M. (Notts Co), 2003 v As (sub); 2004 v I, Fi (3)
Brown, J. R. (Gillingham), 2003 v Fi, I, Az; 2004 v Ser, I, Fi, Ser (7)
Byrne, M. T. (Bolton W), 2003 v Az (sub) (1)

Calliste, R. T. (Manchester U), 2005 v La (sub), Az, E, Pol, G, A (1+1) (7)
Carpenter, R. E. (Burnley), 2005 v E (sub) (1)
Cegielski, W. (Wrexham), 1977 v E (sub), S (2)
Chapple, S. R. (Swansea C), 1992 v R; 1993 v Cy, Bel (2), RCS; 1994 v RCS; Bul (2) (8)

Charles, J. M. (Swansea C), 1979 v E; 1981 v Ho (2)
Clark, J. (Manchester U), 1978 v S; (with Derby Co), 1979 v E (2)
Coates, J. S. (Swansea C), 1996 v Mol, G; 1997 v Ho, T (sub); 1998 v T (sub) (5)
Coleman, C. (Swansea C), 1990 v Pol; 1991 v E, Pol (3)
Collins, J. M. (Cardiff C), 2003 v I (sub), Az (sub+1); 2004 v Ser, I, Fi (sub), Ser (7)
Cotterill D. (Bristol C), 2005 v A (sub+sub) (2)
Coyne, D. (Tranmere R), 1992 v R; 1994 v Cy (sub), R; 1995 v Mol, Ge, Bul (2) (7)
Critchell, K. A. R. (Southampton), 2005 v A (sub) (1)
Crofts, A. L. (Gillingham), 2005 v G, A (1+1) (3)
Crowell, M. T. (Wrexham), 2004 v Ser (sub); 2005 v Az (sub), E (sub), Pol (sub), A (sub) (5)
Curtis, A. T. (Swansea C), 1977 v E (1)

Davies, A. (Manchester U), 1982 v F (2), Ho; 1983 v N, Y, Bul (6)
Davies, A. R. (Southampton), 2005 v La (sub); (with Yeovil T), A (1+1) (3)
Davies, C. M. (Oxford U), 2005 v A (1+1) (2)
Davies, D. (Barry T), 1999 v D (sub) (1)
Davies, G. M. (Hereford U), 1993 v Bel, RCS; 1995 v Mol (sub), Ge, Bul (2); (with C Palace), 1996 v Mol (7)
Davies, I. C. (Norwich C), 1978 v S (sub) (1)
Davies, L. (Bangor C), 2005 v La (sub) (1)
Davies, S. (Peterborough U), 1999 v D, Bl, Sw, I, D; (with Tottenham H), 2000 v S; 2001 v Bl, N, Pol, Arm (10)
Day, R. (Manchester C), 2000 v S (sub), Ni; 2001 v Uk, Pol, Uk; 2002 v Arm, N, Bl; 2003 v Fi, I, Az; (with Mansfield T), Az; 2004 v Ser (11)
Deacy, N. (PSV Eindhoven), 1977 v S (1)
De-Vulgt, L. S. (Swansea C), 2002 v Arm (sub), Bl (2)
Dibble, A. (Cardiff C), 1983 v Bul; 1984 v N, Bul (3)
Doyle, S. C. (Preston NE), 1979 v E (sub); (with Huddersfield T), 1984 v N (2)
Duffy, R. M. (Portsmouth), 2005 v La, E, Pol, G, A (1+1) (6)
Dwyer, P. J. (Cardiff C), 1979 v E (1)

Earnshaw, R. (Cardiff C), 1999 v P (sub), I, D; 2000 v S, Ni; 2001 v Bl (sub), N, Pol (2), Uk (10)
Ebdon, M. (Everton), 1990 v Pol; 1991 v E (2)
Edwards, C. N. H. (Swansea C), 1996 v G; 1997 v Sm, Ho (2), T, Bel; 1998 v T (7)
Edwards, R. I. (Chester), 1977 v S; 1978 v W (2)
Edwards, R. W. (Bristol C), 1991 v Pol; 1992 v R; 1993 v Cy, Bel (2), RCS; 1994 v RCS, Cy, R; 1995 v Ge, Bul; 1996 v Mol, G (13)
Evans, A. (Bristol R), 1977 v E (1)
Evans, K. (Leeds U), 1999 v I (sub), D; (with Cardiff C), 2001 v N (sub), Pol (sub) (4)
Evans, P. S. (Shrewsbury T), 1996 v G (1)
Evans, S. J. (C Palace), 2001 v Bl, Arm (2)
Evans, T. (Cardiff C), 1995 v Bul (sub); 1996 v Mol, G (3)

Fish, N. (Cardiff C), 2005 v La, Az (sub) (2)
Fleetwood, S. (Cardiff C), 2005 v La, Az (2)
Folland, R. W. (Oxford U), 2000 v Ni (sub) (1)
Foster, M. G. (Tranmere R), 1993 v RCS (1)
Fowler, L. A. (Coventry C), 2003 v I; (with Huddersfield T), 2004 v Ser, I, Fi; 2005 v La, Az, E, Pol, G (9)
Freestone, R. (Chelsea), 1990 v Pol (1)

Gabbidon, D. L. (WBA), 1999 v D, P, Sw, I (sub), D; 2000 v Bl, Sw, S, Ni; (with Cardiff C), 2001 v N, Pol, Arm, Uk, Pol, Uk; 2002 v Arm, N (17)
Gale, D. (Swansea C), 1983 v Bul; 1984 v N (sub) (2)
Gall, K. A. (Bristol R), 2002 v N (sub), Bl (sub); 2003 v Fi (sub), Az; (with Yeovil T), 2004 v Ser, I, Fi, Ser (8)
Gibson, N. D. (Tranmere R), 1999 v D (sub), Bl (sub), P; 2000 v S (sub), Ni; (with Sheffield W), 2001 v Uk, Pol, Uk; 2002 v Arm, N, Bl (11)
Giggs, R. (Manchester U), 1991 v Pol (1)
Gilbert, P. (Plymouth Arg), 2005 v La, Az, E, Pol, G, A (1+1) (7)
Giles, D. C. (Cardiff C), 1977 v S; 1978 v S; (with Swansea C), 1981 v Ho; (with C Palace), 1983 v Y (4)
Giles, P. (Cardiff C), 1982 v F (2), Ho (3)
Graham, D. (Manchester U), 1991 v E (1)
Green, R. M. (Wolverhampton W), 1998 v I; 1999 v I, D, Bl, Sw, I, D; 2000 v Bl, S, Ni; 2001 v Bl, N, Pol, Arm, Uk, Pol (16)
Griffith, C. (Cardiff C), 1990 v Pol (1)
Griffiths, C. (Shrewsbury T), 1991 v Pol (sub) (1)

Hall, G. D. (Chelsea), 1990 v Pol (1)
Hartson, J. (Luton T), 1994 v Cy, R; 1995 v Mol, Ge, Bul; (with Arsenal), 1996 v G, Sm; 1997 v Sm, Ho (9)
Haworth, S. O. (Cardiff C), 1997 v Ho, T, Bel; (with Coventry C), 1998 v T, Bel; I; 1999 v I, D; (with Wigan Ath), Bl, Sw; 2000 v Bl, Sw (12)
Hillier, I. M. (Tottenham H), 2001 v Uk (sub), Pol (sub), Uk; (with Luton T), 2002 v Arm, N (5)
Hodges, G. (Wimbledon), 1983 v Y (sub), Bul (sub); 1984 v N, Bul, Y (5)
Holden, A. (Chester C), 1984 v Y (sub) (1)
Holloway, C. D. (Exeter C), 1999 v P, D (2)
Hopkins, J. (Fulham), 1982 v F (sub), Ho; 1983 v N, Y, Bul (5)
Hopkins, S. A. (Wrexham), 1999 v P (sub) (1)
Huggins, D. S. (Bristol C), 1996 v Sm (1)
Hughes, D. (Kaiserslautern), 2005 v La (1)
Hughes, D. R. (Southampton), 1994 v R (1)
Hughes, R. D. (Aston Villa), 1996 v Sm; 1997 v Sm (sub), Ho (2), T, Bel; 1998 v T, Bel, I; 1999 v I, Sw, I; (with Shrewsbury T), 2000 v Sw (13)
Hughes, I. (Bury), 1992 v R; 1993 v Cy, Bel (sub), RCS; 1994 v Cy, R; 1995 v Mol, Ge, Bul; 1996 v Mol (sub), G (11)
Hughes, L. M. (Manchester U), 1983 v N, Y; 1984 v N, Bul, Y (5)
Hughes, W. (WBA), 1977 v E, S; 1978 v S (3)

Jackett, K. (Watford), 1981 v Ho; 1982 v F (2)
James, R. M. (Swansea C), 1977 v E, S; 1978 v S (3)
Jarman, L. (Cardiff C), 1996 v Sm; 1997 v Sm, Ho (2), Bel; 1998 v T, Bel; 1999 v I, P; 2000 v Bl (10)
Jeanne, L. C. (QPR), 1999 v P (sub), Sw, I; 2000 v Bl, Sw, S, Ni; 2001 v Bl (8)
Jelleyman, G. A. (Peterborough U), 1999 v D (sub) (1)
Jenkins, L. D. (Swansea C), 1998 v T (sub); 2000 v Bl, Sw, S, Ni; 2001 v N, Pol, Arm, Uk (9)
Jenkins, S. R. (Swansea C), 1993 v Cy (sub), Bel (2)
Jones, E. P. (Blackpool), 2000 v Ni (sub) (1)
Jones, F. (Wrexham), 1981 v Ho (1)
Jones, J. A. (Swansea C); 2001 v Pol, Uk; 2002 v N (sub) (3)
Jones, L. (Cardiff C), 1982 v F (2), Ho (3)
Jones, M. A. (Wrexham), 2004 v Ser (1)
Jones, M. G. (Leeds U), 1998 v Bel; 1999 v I, D, Bl, Sw, I; 2000 v Sw (7)
Jones, P. L. (Liverpool), 1992 v R; 1993 v Cy, Bel (2), RCS; 1994 v RCS (sub), Cy, R; 1995 v Mol, Ge; 1996 v Mol, G (12)
Jones, R. (Sheffield W), 1994 v R; 1995 v Bul (2) (3)
Jones, S. J. (Swansea C), 2005 v Az (1)
Jones, V. (Bristol R), 1979 v E; 1981 v Ho (2)

Kendall, L. M. (C Palace), 2001 v N, Pol (2)
Kendall, M. (Tottenham H), 1978 v S (1)
Kenworthy, J. R. (Tranmere R), 1994 v Cy; 1995 v Mol, Bul (3)
Knott, G. R. (Tottenham H), 1996 v Sm (1)

Law, B. J. (QPR), 1990 v Pol; 1991 v E (2)
Ledley,J. C. (Cardiff C), 2005 v G, A (1+1) (3)
Letheran, G. (Leeds U), 1977 v E, S (2)
Lewis, D. (Swansea C), 1982 v F (2), Ho; 1983 v N, Y, Bul; 1984 v N, Bul, Y (9)
Lewis, J. (Cardiff C), 1983 v N (1)
Llewellyn, C. M. (Norwich C), 1998 v T (sub), Bel (sub), I; 1999 v I, D, Bl, I; 2000 v Bl, Sw, S; 2001 v N, Pol, Arm, Uk (14)
Loveridge, J. (Swansea C), 1982 v Ho; 1983 v N, Bul (3)
Low, J. D. (Bristol R), 1999 v P; (with Cardiff C), 2002 v Arm (sub), N (sub), Bl (1)
Lowndes, S. R. (Newport Co), 1979 v E; 1981 v Ho; (with Millwall), 1984 v Bul, Y (4)

McCarthy, A. J. (QPR), 1994 v RCS, Cy, R (3)
Maddy, P. (Cardiff C), 1982 v Ho; 1983 v N (sub) (2)
Margetson, M. W. (Manchester C), 1992 v R; 1993 v Cy, Bel (2), RCS; 1994 v RCS, Cy (7)
Martin, A. P. (C Palace), 1999 v D (1)
Marustik, C. (Swansea C), 1982 v F (2); 1983 v Y, Bul; 1984 v N, Bul, Y (7)
Maxwell, L. J. (Liverpool), 1999 v Sw (sub), I; 2000 v Sw (sub), S, Ni; 2001 v Bl, Pol, Arm, Uk, Pol, Uk; (with Cardiff C), 2002 v Arm, N, Bl (sub) (14)
Meaker, M. J. (QPR), 1994 v RCS (sub), R (sub) (2)

Melville, A. K. (Swansea C), 1990 v Pol; (with Oxford U), 1991 v E (2)
Micallef, C. (Cardiff C), 1982 v F, Ho; 1983 v N (3)
Morgan, A. M. (Tranmere R), 1995 v Mol, Bul; 1996 v Mol, G (4)
Morgan, C. (Wrexham), 2004 v Fi, Ser (sub); 2005 v La, G, A (1+1) (6)
Moss, D. M. (Shrewsbury T), 2003 v Fi, I, Az (2); 2004 v Ser (2) (6)
Mountain, P. D. (Cardiff C), 1997 v Ho, T (2)
Mumford, A. O. (Swansea C), 2003 v Fi, I, Az (2) (4)

Nardiello, D. (Coventry C), 1978 v S (1)
Neilson, A. B. (Newcastle U), 1993 v Cy, Bel (2), RCS; 1994 v RCS, Cy, R (7)
Nicholas, P. (C Palace), 1978 v S; 1979 v E; (with Arsenal), 1982 v F (3)
Nogan, K. (Luton T), 1990 v Pol; 1991 v E (2)
Nogan, L. (Oxford U) 1991 v E (1)
Nyatanga, L. J. (Derby Co), 2005 v G (sub) (1)

Oster, J. M. (Grimsby T), 1997 v Sm (sub), Ho (sub), T, Bel; (with Everton), 1998 v T, Bel, I; 1999 v I, Sw (9)
Owen, G. (Wrexham), 1991 v E (sub), Pol; 1992 v R; 1993 v Cy, Bel (2); 1994 v Cy, R (8)

Page, R. J. (Watford), 1995 v Mol, Ge, Bul; 1996 v Mol (4)
Parslow, D. (Cardiff C), 2005 v La, Az, E, Pol (4)
Partridge, D. W. (West Ham U), 1997 v T (1)
Pascoe, C. (Swansea C), 1983 v Bul (sub); 1984 v N (sub), Bul, Y (4)
Pejic, S. M. (Wrexham), 2003 v Fi, I, Az; 2004 v Ser, I, Fi (6)
Pembridge, M. (Luton T), 1991 v Pol (1)
Perry, J. (Cardiff C), 1990 v Pol; 1991 v E, Pol (3)
Peters, M. (Manchester C), 1992 v R; (with Norwich C), 1993 v Cy, RCS (3)
Phillips, D. (Plymouth Arg), 1984 v N, Bul, Y (3)
Phillips, G. R. (Swansea C), 2001 v Uk (sub); 2002 v Arm (sub), Bl (3)
Phillips, L. (Swansea C), 1979 v E; (with Charlton Ath), 1983 v N (2)
Pipe, D. R. (Coventry C), 2003 v As (2); 2004 v Ser, I, Fi, Ser;(with Notts Co), 2005 v La, Az, E, Pol, G, A (12)
Pontin, K. (Cardiff C), 1978 v S (1)
Powell, L. (Southampton), 1991 v Pol (sub); 1992 v R (sub); 1993 v Bel (sub); 1994 v RCS (4)
Powell, L. (Leicester C), 2004 v Ser (sub), I (sub) Fi (3)
Price, J. J. (Swansea C), 1998 v I (sub); 1999 v I (sub), D, Bl, P; 2000 v Bl, Sw (7)
Price, L. P. (Ipswich T), 2005 v La, Az, E, Pol, G, A (6)
Price, M. D. (Everton), 2001 v Uk. Pol (sub), Uk; (with Hull C), 2002 v Arm, N, Bl; 2003 v Fi, I; (with Scarborough), Az (2); 2004 v Ser, Fi, Ser (13)
Price, P. (Luton T), 1981 v Ho (1)
Pugh, D. (Doncaster R), 1982 v F (2) (2)
Pugh, S. (Wrexham), 1993 v Bel (sub + sub) (2)

Ramasut, M. W. T. (Bristol R), 1997 v Ho, Bel; 1998 v T, I (4)
Ratcliffe, K. (Everton), 1981 v Ho; 1982 v F (2)
Ready, K. (QPR), 1992 v R; 1993 v Bel (2); 1994 v RCS, Cy (5)
Rees, A. (Birmingham C), 1984 v N (1)
Rees, J. (Luton T), 1990 v Pol; 1991 v E, Pol (3)
Rees, M. R. (Millwall), 2003 v Fi (sub), Az; 2004 v Ser, I (4)
Roberts, A. (QPR), 1991 v E, Pol (2)
Roberts, C. J. (Cardiff C), 1999 v D (sub) (1)
Roberts, G. (Hull C), 1983 v Bul (1)
Roberts, G. W. (Liverpool), 1997 v Ho, T, Bel; 1998 v T, I; 1999 v I, D, Bl, P; (with Panionios), D; (with Tranmere R), 2000 v Sw (11)
Roberts, J. G. (Wrexham), 1977 v E (1)
Roberts, N. W. (Wrexham), 1999 v I (sub), P; 2000 v Sw (sub) (3)
Roberts, P. (Porthmadog), 1997 v Ho (sub) (1)
Roberts, S. I. (Swansea C), 1999 v Sw, I (sub), D; 2000 v Bl (sub), Ni; 2001 v Bl (sub), N, Pol, Arm, Uk; 2002 v Arm, N, Bl (13)
Roberts, S. W. (Wrexham), 2000 v S; 2001 v Bl, N (sub) (3)
Robinson, C. P. (Wolverhampton W), 1996 v Sm; 1997 v Sm, Ho (2), T, Bel (6)
Robinson, J. (Brighton & HA), 1992 v R; (with Charlton Ath), 1993 v Bel; 1994 v RCS, Cy, R (5)
Rowlands, A. J. R. (Manchester C), 1996 v Sm; 1997 v Sm, Ho (1 + sub), T (sub) (5)
Rush, I. (Liverpool), 1981 v Ho; 1982 v F (2)

Savage, R. W. (Crewe Alex), 1995 v Bul; 1996 v Mol, G (3)
Sayer, P. A. (Cardiff C), 1977 v E, S (2)
Searle, D. (Cardiff C), 1991 v Pol (sub); 1992 v R; 1993 v Cy, Bel (2), RCS; 1994 v RCS (6)
Slatter, D. (Chelsea), 2000 v Sw (sub), S; 2001 v Bl, N (sub), Pol (sub), Uk (sub) (6)
Slatter, N. (Bristol R), 1983 v N, Y, Bul; 1984 v N, Bul, Y (6)
Somner, M. J. (Brentford), 2004 v Ser (sub), I (2)
Speed, G. A. (Leeds U), 1990 v Pol; 1991 v E, Pol (3)
Spender, S. (Wrexham), 2005 v La (sub), Az (sub) (2)
Stevenson, N. (Swansea C), 1982 v F, Ho (2)
Stevenson, W. B. (Leeds U), 1977 v E, S; 1978 v S (3)
Stock, B. B. (Bournemouth), 2003 v Fi (sub), I (sub); 2004 v Fi, Ser (4)
Symons, K. (Portsmouth), 1991 v E, Pol (2)

Taylor, G. K. (Bristol R), 1995 v Ge, Bul (2); 1996 v Mol (4)
Thomas, D. J. (Watford), 1998 v T, Bel (2)
Thomas, J. A. (Blackburn R), 1996 v Sm; 1997 v Sm, Ho (2), T, Bel; 1998 v Bel; 1999 v D, Bl, P; 2000 v Bl (sub); 2001 v Bl, N, Pol, Arm, Uk, Pol, Uk; 2002 v Arm, N, Bl (21)
Thomas, Martin R. (Bristol R), 1979 v E; 1981 v Ho (2)
Thomas, Mickey R. (Wrexham), 1977 v E; 1978 v S (2)
Thomas, S. (Wrexham), 2001 v Pol, Uk; 2002 v Arm, N, Bl (5)
Thomas, D. G. (Leeds U), 1977 v E; 1979 v E; 1984 v N (3)
Tibbott, L. (Ipswich T), 1977 v E, S (2)
Tipton, M. J. (Oldham Ath), 1998 v I (sub); 1999 v P, Sw (sub); 2000 v Ni; 2001 v Arm (sub), Uk (sub) (6)
Tolley, J. C. (Shrewsbury T), 2001 v Pol, Uk (sub); 2003 v Fi, I, Az (2); 2004 v Ser (2); 2005 v Az, E, Pol, G (sub) (12)
Twiddy, C. (Plymouth Arg), 1995 v Mol, Ge; 1996 v G (sub) (3)

Vaughan, D. O. (Crewe Alex), 2003 v Fi, Az; 2004 v I; 2005 v Az, E, Pol, G (7)
Vaughan, N. (Newport Co), 1982 v F, Ho (2)
Valentine, R. D. (Everton), 2001 v Pol, Uk; 2002 v Arm, N, Bl; (with Darlington), 2003 v Fi, I, Az (8)

Walsh, D. (Wrexham), 2000 v S, Ni; 2001 v Bl, Arm, Uk; 2002 v Arm, N, Bl (8)
Walsh, I. P. (C Palace), 1979 v E; (with Swansea C), 1983 v Bul (2)
Walton, M. (Norwich C.), 1991 v Pol (sub) (1)
Ward, D. (Notts Co), 1996 v Mol, G (2)
Weston, R. D. (Arsenal), 2001 v Bl, N, Pol; (with Cardiff C), Arm (4)
Whitfield, P. M. (Wrexham), 2003 v Az (1)
Williams, A. P. (Southampton), 1998 v Bel, I; 1999 v I, D (sub), Bl, Sw, I; 2000 v Bl, Sw (9)
Williams, A. S. (Blackburn R), 1996 v Sm; 1997 v Sm, Ho, Bel; 1998 v T, Bel, I; 1999 v I, D, Bl, P, Sw, I, D; 2000 v Bl, Sw (16)
Williams, D. (Bristol R), 1983 v Y (1)
Williams, D. I. L. (Liverpool), 1998 v I; 1999 v D, Bl; (with Wrexham) I, D; 2000 v Bl, S, Ni; 2001 v Bl (9)
Williams, E. (Caernarfon T), 1997 v Ho (sub), T (sub) (2)
Williams, G. (Bristol R), 1983 v Y, Bul (2)
Williams, G. A. (C Palace), 2003 v I (sub), Az; 2004 v Ser, I, Ser (sub) (5)
Williams, M. (Manchester U), 2001 v Pol (sub), Uk (sub); 2002 v Bl (sub); 2003 v Fi, I, Az (sub); 2004 v Ser (sub), I (sub), Fi, Ser (10)
Williams, S. J. (Wrexham), 1995 v Mol, Ge, Bul (2) (4)
Wilmot, R. (Arsenal), 1982 v F (2), Ho; 1983 v N, Y; 1984 v Y (6)
Worgan, L. J. (Milton Keynes D), 2005 v La (sub), A (2)
Wright, A. A. (Oxford U), 1998 v Bel, I (sub); 1999 v D (sub) (3)

Young, S. (Cardiff C), 1996 v Sm; 1997 v Sm, Ho (2), Bel (sub) (5)

NORTHERN IRELAND

Bailie, N. (Linfield), l990 v Is; 1994 v R (sub) (2)
Baird, C. P. (Southampton), 2002 v G; 2003 v S, Sp, Uk, Fi, Gr (6)
Beatty, S. (Chelsea), 1990 v Is; (with Linfield), 1994 v R (2)
Black, J. (Tottenham H), 2003 v Uk (sub) (1)
Black, K. T. (Luton T), 1990 v Is (1)
Black, R. Z. (Morecambe), 2002 v G (1)
Blackledge, G. (Portadown), 1978 v Ei (1)
Blayney, A. (Southampton), 2003 v Fi (sub); 2004 v Uk, Arm, Gr (4)
Boyle, W. S. (Leeds U), 1998 v Sw (sub), S (sub); 2001 v CzR (sub), Bul (1+sub), CzR; 2002 v Ma (7)
Braniff, K. R. (Millwall), 2002 v G; 2003 v S (sub), Sp (sub), Fi, Arm (sub), Gr, Sp; 2004 v Gr (sub); 2005 v Sw, S (10)
Brotherston, N. (Blackburn R), 1978 v Ei (sub) (1)
Browne, G. (Manchester C), 2003 v S, Sp, Uk, Fi (sub), Sp (5)
Brunt, C. (Sheffield W), 2005 v S (1)
Buchanan, W. B. (Bolton W), 2002 v G (sub); 2003 v Uk (sub); (with Lisburn Distillery), 2004 v Uk, Arm, Gr (5)
Burns, L. (Port Vale), 1998 v Sw, S, Ei; 1999 v T, Fi, Mol, G, Mol, Ei; 2000 v F, T, G, Fi (13)

Campbell, S. (Ballymena U), 2003 v Sp (sub) (1)
Capaldi, A. C. (Birmingham C), 2002 v D (sub), Ic, Ma, G; 2003 v S, Sp, Uk, Fi, Arm, Gr; (with Plymouth Arg), Sp; 2004 v Uk, Arm, Gr (14)
Carlisle, W. T. (C Palace), 2000 v Fi (sub); 2001 v Ma, Ic, Bul (1+sub), CzR; 2002 v D, Ic, Ma (9)
Carroll, R. E. (Wigan Ath), 1998 v S, Ei; 1999 v T, Fi, Mol, G, Mol, Ei; 2000 v T, G, Fi (11)
Carson, S. (Rangers), 2000 v Ma; (wirh Dundee U), 2002 v D (sub) (2)
Clarke, L. (Peterborough U), 2003 v Sp (sub); 2004 v Uk (sub), Arm (sub); 2005 v Sw (4)
Clarke, R. D. J. (Portadown), 1999 v Ei (sub), S; 2000 v F (sub), S, W (sub) (5)
Clingan, S. G. (Wolverhampton W), 2003 v Arm (sub); 2004 v Uk, Arm, Gr; 2005 v Sw, S (6)
Close, B. (Middlesbrough), 2002 v Ic, Ma (sub), G; 2003 v S, Sp, Uk, Arm, Sp; 2004 v Arm, Gr (10)
Clyde, M. G. (Wolverhampton W), 2002 v G; 2003 v S, Sp, Uk, Fi (5)
Connell, T. E. (Coleraine), 1978 v Ei (sub) (1)
Coote, A. (Norwich C), 1998 v Sw (sub), S, Ei; 1999 v T, Fi,Mol, G, Mol, Ei; 2000 v F, T, G (12)
Convery, J. (Celtic), 2000 v S, W; 2001 v D, Ic (4)

Davey, H. (UCD), 2004 v Uk, Arm, Gr (3)
Davis, S. (Aston Villa), 2004 v Uk (sub), Arm (sub); 2005 v Sw (3)
Devine, D. (Omagh T), 1994 v R (1)
Devine, J. (Glentoran), 1990 v Is (1)
Dickson, H. (Wigan Ath). 2002 v Ma (1)
Dolan, J. (Millwall), 2000 v Fi, Ma, S; 2001 v Ma, D, Ic (6)
Donaghy, M. M. (Larne), 1978 v Ei (1)
Dowie, I. (Luton T), 1990 v Is (1)
Duff, S. (Cheltenham T), 2003 v Sp (1)

Elliott, S. (Glentoran), 1999 v Fi (sub), Ei, S (sub) (3)
Ervin, J. (Linfield), 2005 v Sw (1)

Feeney, L. (Linfield), 1998 v Ei (sub); 1999 v T, Fi, Mol; (with Rangers), G (sub), Ei, S; 2000 v Fi (8)
Feeney, W. (Bournemouth), 2002 v D, Ic (sub); 2003 v Fi, Arm, Gr; 2004 v Uk, Arm, Gr (8)
Ferguson, M. (Glentoran), 2000 v T (sub), Ma (sub) (2)
Fitzgerald, D. (Rangers), 1998 v Sw, S; 1999 v T (sub), Fi (4)
Friars, E. (Notts Co), 2005 v Sw, S (2)
Friars, S. M. (Liverpool), 1998 v Sw, S, Ei; (with Ipswich T), 1999 v T, Fi, Mol, G, Mol; 2000 v F, T, G, Ma, S, W; 2001 v Ma, D, Ic, CzR, Bul (2), CzR (21)

Gault, M. (Linfield), 2005 v S (sub) (1)
Gilfillan, B. J. (Gretna), 2005 v S (1)
Gillespie, K. R. (Manchester U), 1994 v R (1)
Glendinning, M. (Bangor), 1994 v R (1)
Graham, G. L. (C Palace), 1999 v S; 2000 v F, T, G, Fi (5)
Graham, R. S. (QPR), 1999 v Fi (sub), Mol, Ei (sub); 2000 v F (sub), T (sub), G (sub), Fi (sub), Ma, S, W; 2001 v Ma, D, CzR (sub), Bul (sub), CzR (sub) (15)
Gray, P. (Luton T), 1990 v Is (sub) (1)
Griffin, D. J. (St Johnstone), 1998 v S (sub), Ei; 1999 v T, Fi, G, Mol, Ei, S; 2000 v F, T (10)

Hamilton, G. (Blackburn R), 2000 v Ma (sub), S, W (sub); 2001 v Ma, D, Ic, CzR, Bul (2), CzR; (wirh Portadown), 2002 v Ic, Ma (12)
Hamilton, W. R. (Linfield), 1978 v Ei (1)
Harkin, M. P. (Wycombe W), Ma (sub), S (sub), W; 2001 v Ma (sub), D (sub), Ic, CzR, Bul (sub+1) (9)
Harvey, J. (Arsenal), 1978 v Ei (1)
Hawe, S. (Blackburn R), 2001 v Cz (1+sub) (2)
Hayes, T. (Luton T), 1978 v Ei (1)
Healy, D. J. (Manchester U), 1999 v Mol (sub), G (sub), Ei (sub), S; 2000 v F (sub), T, G, Fi (8)
Herron, C. J. (QPR), 2003 v Arm, Gr (2)
Holmes, S. (Manchester C), Ma, S, W; 2001 v Ma, D, Ic, CzR, Bul (2), CzR; (with Wrexham), 2002 v D, Ic, Ma (13)
Hughes, M. A. (Tottenham H), 2003 v Sp (sub), Uk (sub), Fi, Arm, Gr, Sp; 2004 v Uk, Arm, Gr (sub); 2005 v Sw, S (11)
Hughes, M. E. (Manchester C), 1990 v Is (sub)
Hunter, M. (Glentoran), 2002 v G (sub) (1)

Ingham, M. (Sunderland), 2001 v CzR, Bul (2), CzR (4)

Johnson, D. M. (Blackburn R), 1998 v Sw, S, Ei; 1999 v T, Fi, G, Mol, Ei; 2000 v F, T, G (11)
Johnston, B. (Cliftonville), 1978 v Ei (1)
Julian, A. A. (Brentford), 2005 v Sw (1)

Kee, P. V. (Oxford U), 1990 v Is (1)
Kelly, D. (Derry C), 2000 v Ma, W; 2001 v Ma, Ic (sub), CzR, Bul (2), CzR; 2002 v D, Ic, Ma (11)
Kelly, N. (Oldham Ath), 1990 v Is (sub) (1)
Kirk, A. (Hearts), 1999 v S; 2000 v Ma, S, W; 2001 v Ma, D, Ic (sub); 2002 v D, Ic (9)

Lennon, N. F. (Manchester C), 1990 v Is; (with Crewe Alex), 1994 v R (2)
Lyttle, G. (Celtic), 1998 v Sw, S; (with Peterborough U), 1999 v T (sub), Mol (2), S; 2000 v G, Fi (8)

Magee, J. (Bangor), 1994 v R (sub) (1)
Magilton, J. (Liverpool), 1990 v Is (1)
Matthews, N. P. (Blackpool), 1990 v Is (1)
McAreavey, P. (Swindon T), 2000 v Ma, S; 2001 v Ma, D; 2002 v D, Ic (sub), Ma (sub) (7)
McBride, J. (Glentoran), 1994 v R (sub) (1)
McCallion, E. (Coleraine), 1998 v Sw (sub) (1)
McCann, G. S. (West Ham U), 2000 v S (sub), W; 2001 v D (sub), Ic, CzR, Bul (2), CzR; 2002 v D, Ic, Ma (11)
McCann, P. (Portadown), 2003 v Sp (1)
McCann, R. (Rangers), 2002 v G (sub); (with Linfield), 2003 v S (sub) (2)
McCartney, G. (Sunderland), 2001 v D, CzR, Bul (2); 2002 v D (5)
McChrystal, M. (Derry C), 2005 v Sw, S (2)
McCourt, P. J. (Rochdale), 2002 v G; 2003 v S (sub), Sp, Uk, Fi (sub), Arm (sub), Gr (sub); 2005 v Sw (7)
McCoy, R. K. (Coleraine), 1990 v Is (1)
McCreery, D. (Manchester U), 1978 v Ei (1)
McEvilly, L. (Rochdale), 2003 v S, Sp, Uk, Fi (sub), Arm, Gr (sub); 2004 v Uk, Arm, Gr (9)
McFlynn, T. M. (QPR), 2000 v Ma (sub), W (sub); 2001 v Ma (sub), CzR (sub), Bul (sub+sub), CzR; (with Woking), 2002 v D (sub), Ic (sub); (wirh Margate), G; 2003 v S (sub), Sp (sub), Fi (sub), Arm, Gr (sub), Sp (sub); 2004 v Uk, Arm (sub), Gr (19)
McGibbon, P. C. G. (Manchester U), 1994 v R (1)
McGlinchey, B. (Manchester C), 1998 v Sw, S, Ei; (with Port Vale), 1999 v T, Fi, Mol, G, Mol, Ei, S; (with Gillingham), 2000 v F, G, T, Fi (14)
McGovern, M. (Celtic), 2005 v S (1)
McIlroy, T. (Linfield), 1994 v R (sub) (1)
McKnight, P. (Rangers), 1998 v Sw; 1999 v T (sub), Mol (sub) (3)
McMahon, G. J. (Tottenham H),1994 v R (sub) (1)
McVeigh, A. (Ayr U), 2002 v G (sub) (1)
McVeigh, P. F. (Tottenham H), 1998 v S (sub), Ei; 1999 v T, Mol, G, Mol, Ei; 2000 v F, T (sub), G (sub), Fi (11)
Melaugh, G. M. (Aston Villa), 2002 v G; 2003 v S, Sp, Uk, Fi, Arm, Gr, Sp; (with Glentoran), 2004 v Uk, Arm, Gr (11)

Millar, W. P. (Port Vale), 1990 v Is (1)
Miskelly, D. T. (Oldham Ath), 2000 v F, Ma, S, W; 2001 v Ma, D, Ic; 2002 v D, Ic, Ma (10)
Moreland, V. (Glentoran), 1978 v Ei (sub) (1)
Morgan, M, P. T. (Preston NE), 1999 v S (1)
Morris, E. J. (WBA), 2002 v G; (with Glentoran), 2003 v S, Sp, Uk, Fi, Arm, Gr, Sp (8)
Morrison, O. (Sheffield W), 2001 v Bul (sub); 2002 v Ma (sub); 2003 S, Fi; (with Sheffield U) Arm, Gr, Sp (7)
Morrow, A. (Northampton T), 2001 v D (sub) (1)
Morrow, S. (Hibernian), 2005 v S (sub) (1)
Mulryne, P. P. (Manchester U), Sw, S, Ei; (with Norwich C), 1999 v G, Mol (5)
Murray, W. (Linfield), 1978 v Ei (sub) (1)
Murtagh, C. (Hearts), 2005 v S (sub) (1)

Nicholl, J. M. (Manchester U), 1978 v Ei (1)
Nixon, C. (Glentoran), 2000 v Fi (sub) (1)

O'Hara, G. (Leeds U), 1994 v R (1)
O'Neill, M. A. M. (Hibernian), 1994 v R (1)
O'Neill, J. P. (Leicester C), 1978 v Ei (1)

Patterson, D. J. (C Palace), 1994 v R (1)

Quinn, S. J. (Blackpool), 1994 v R (1)

Robinson, S. (Tottenham H), 1994 v R (1)

Shiels, D. (Hibernian), 2005 v Sw (sub), S (2)
Simms, G. (Hartlepool U), 2001 v Bul (2), CzR; 2002 v D, Ic, Ma, G; 2003 v S, Sp, Uk, Fi, Arm, Gr, Sp (14)
Skates, G. (Blackburn R), 2000 v Ma; 2001 v Ic (sub), CzR (2) (4)
Sloan, T. (Ballymena U), 1978 v Ei (1)

Taylor, M. S. (Fulham), 1998 v Sw (1)
Toner, C. (Tottenham H), 2000 v Ma (sub), S (sub), W; 2001 v D, Ic, CzR, Bul (2), CzR; 2002 v D, Ic, Ma; (with Leyton Orient), 2003 v S, Sp, Uk, Fi, Gr (17)
Teggart, N. (Sunderland), 2005 v Sw (sub), S (sub) (2)

Ward, S. (Glentoran), 2005 v S (1)
Waterman, D. G. (Portsmouth), 1998 v Sw, S, Ei; 1999 v T, Fi, Mol, G, Mol, Ei, S (sub); 2000 v F, T, G, Fi (14)
Webb, S. M. (Ross Co), 2004 v Uk, Arm, Gr; (with St Johnstone), 2005 v Sw, S (5)
Wells, D. P. (Barry T), 1999 v S (1)
Whitley, Jeff (Manchester C), 1998 v Sw, S, Ei; 1999 v T, Fi, Mol, G, Ei, S; 2000 v F, G, T, Ma, S, W; 2001 v Ma, Ic (17)

ENGLAND NATIONAL GAME XI 2004–05

10 Nov

Italy 0
England 1 *(King)* 2000
(in Ivrea).
England: Bull (Aldershot Town); Blackburn (Morecambe), Yakubu (Barnet), King (Barnet), Perkins (Morecambe), Thurgood (Grays Athletic), Kerr (Scarborough), Sinclair (Barnet), Elding (Stevenage Borough), Hawley (Carlisle United), Bishop (York City).
Subs: Stockdale (York City), Jackson (Woking), Surey (Gravesend & Northfleet), Purdie (Hereford United), Craney (Accrington Stanley).

16 Feb

England 3 *(Thurgood, Elding, Hatch)*
Holland 0 3343
(at Woking).
England: Bull; Blackburn, Oliver (Woking), King, Moxey (Exeter City), Thurgood, Kerr, Sinclair, Elding, Hawley, Bishop.
Subs: Jalal (Woking), Bailey (Barnet), Hatch (Barnet), Grant (Carlisle United).

SCOTLAND B INTERNATIONALS (FUTURE) 2004–05

Mannheim, 7 December 2004

Germany 3 *(Auer 5, 19, Marx 50)* 4500
Scotland 0
Scotland: Soutar (McGregor); Diamond (Corrigan), Murray, McNaughton, Virgo, Malcolm (Nicholson), Wilson, Hartley, O'Connor, Smith, Lynch (McDonald).

Mattersburg, 19 April 2005

Austria 2 *(Mair 30, Morz 57)* 1000
Scotland 1 *(Beattie 84)*
Scotland: Gordon (Berra); McCunnie (Fotheringham), Webster, Watt, Murray, Smith, Severin, McDonald, Sweeney (Brown), Parkin (Maloney), Beattie.

FOOTBALL AND THE LAW

Football and the Law ended 2004–05 with a warning to all who believe that contact sports, particularly football and rugby, create a licence to commit crime on the playing field.

After Lee Bowyer and Kieron Dyer were witnessed fighting before millions of TV viewers and 52,306 St James' Park fans, the Chief Superintendent of Northumbrian Police explained that if what had happened took place in the town centre they would have been banged/locked up. In due course, Bowyer was charged with a Public Order offence which will be heard after this page appears.

About the same time a whole day conference mounted by the Crown Prosecution Service confirmed that it was considering what policy should be adopted with the police and prosecution sources to create a consistent approach to what has been a long standing problem, more often in lower league levels than the high profile professional areas where television today picks out what were unknown or unidentified criminal foul play.

During the 1980's and 1990's, the Criminal Injuries Compensation Board Annual Reports specified the misery and physical and even fatal injuries caused by unlawful tackles in both codes. The Courts have dealt with them for over a century. Different police and prosecuting authorities have discretionarily operated their decisions in different selective dimensions. Rugby in South Wales has been before the courts more frequently than elsewhere; but the latest development and warning for all involved at all levels in all games when the Criminal Division of the Court of Appeal at the end of December 2004 adjudicated on appeal from Canterbury Crown Court from a conviction against an amateur footballer who had tackled a player on the opposing team and caused a serious injury to his right leg. He was charged with inflicting grievous bodily harm, contrary to Section 20 of the Offences Against The Person Act 1861, the allegation being that the tackle which caused the injury was crushing, late, unnecessary, reckless and high.

The appellant claimed that the tackle was a fair if harsh challenge and that any injury caused was accidental.

In summing up to the jury, the judge directed that the appellant could be convicted only if the prosecution had proved that what he had done had *not* been by way of legitimate sport.

The Court of Appeal held that the concept of legitimate sport was not unhelpful in general terms, but it was insufficient and inadequate for guiding the jury to consider what is and what is not 'legitimate' within the context of a football match. Particularly the jury should have been told why it was important to determine (a) where the ball was at the time when the tackle took place and (b) whether the appellant had been going for the man or the ball.

Without being aware or being told of the Criminal Injuries Compensation Board's, decision, the Court of Appeal considered that criminal proceedings for sporting injuries should remain rare. This not only because of the high burden of proof threshold, but because of alternatives in internal disciplinary arrangements and even civil negligence claimed. There, however, the withdrawal of legal aid except in unusual circumstances an inclusive and indefinable position today which will always depend on the precise circumstances. As sport becomes more intense and aggressive, the Courts may yet be unable to avoid involvement.

EDWARD GRAYSON
Founder President, British Association for Sport and Law.

FOUR NATIONS TOURNAMENT 2005

(in the Republic of Ireland)

24 May

Republic of Ireland 0

England 1 *(Elding)* 2500

(in Cork).
England: Bull; Travis (Hereford United), Yakubu, Charnock (Northwich Victoria), Robinson (Hereford United), Bailey, Sinclair, Kerr, Elding, Campbell (Yeading), Stansfield (Hereford United).
Subs: Haslam (Halifax Town), Stanley (Hereford United), Taylor (Exeter City).

26 May

England 1 *(Mackail-Smith)*

Wales 0

(in Cork).
England: Glennon (Carlisle United); Haslam, Yakubu, Charnock, Robinson, Stanley, Southam (Dagenham & Redbridge), Kerr, Elding, Taylor, Mackail-Smith (Dagenham & Redbridge).
Subs: Bailey, Sinclair.

28 May

England 3 *(Stansfield, Kerr, Sinclair (pen))*

Scotland 2

(in Cork).
England: Glennon; Haslam, Yakubu, King, Robinson, Bailey, Sinclair, Kerr, Elding, Campbell, Stansfield.
Subs: Southam, Taylor, Mackail-Smith.

	P	*W*	*D*	*L*	*F*	*A*	*Pts*
England	3	3	0	0	5	2	9
Scotland	3	1	1	1	8	5	4
Wales	3	1	0	2	3	7	3
Republic of Ireland	3	0	1	2	2	4	1

RESULTS
24 May 2005 Scotland 5, Wales 1 *(in Cork).*
24 May 2005 Republic of Ireland 0, England 1 *(in Cork).*
26 May 2005 Republic of Ireland 1, Scotland 1 *(in Cork).*
26 May 2005 England 1, Wales 0 *(in Cork).*
28 May 2005 Republic of Ireland 1, Wales 2 *(in Cork).*
28 May 2005 Scotland 2, England 3 *(in Cork).*

FA SCHOOLS & YOUTH GAMES 2004–05

ENGLAND UNDER-20

Cahill, Ridgewell, Whittingham (Aston Villa); Flinders (Barnsley); Kilkenny (Birmingham C); Chaplow (Burnley & WBA); Samba (Cadiz); Long, Sam, Sankofa (Charlton Ath); Halford (Colchester U); Borrowdale, Routledge, Soares (Crystal Palace); Fontaine, Rosenior (Fulham); Wiseman (Hull C); Mannix, Raven, Smyth, Welsh (Liverpool); Steele (Manchester U); Croft, Onuoha, Wright-Phillips B, (Manchester C); Davies, Graham, Turnbull (Middlesbrough); Ambrose, Guy, Milner, Taylor (Newcastle U); Henderson (Norwich C); Gardner (Nottingham F); Nugent (Preston NE); Young (Reading); Francis (Sheffield U); Collins (Sheffield W); Huddlestone (Tottenham H); Ferdinand, Reo-Coker (West Ham U);

10 Oct

England 1 *(Chaplow 60)*

Holland 0 5059

(at Huddersfield).
England: Steele (Young 46); Sankofa (Collins 67), Borrowdale, Gardner, Cahill, Raven, Routledge, Kilkenny (Mannix 74), Henderson (Guy 67), Long (Chaplow 58), Smyth (Croft 80).

8 Feb

England 2 *(Onuoha, Sam)*

Russia 0

(at Charlton).
England: Steele (Turnbull); Raven (Francis), Borrowdale, Gardner, Cahill, Onuoha (Fontaine), Samba (Sam), Chaplow, Graham, Kilkenny (Long), Croft (Wright-Phillips B).

2 June

Tunisia 0

England 2 *(Ambrose, Routledge)*

(in Toulon).
England: Young; Rosenior (Wiseman), Davies (Nugent), Taylor, Ridgewell (Whittingham), Routledge, Welsh, Huddlestone, Milner, Wright-Phillips B, Ambrose.

4 June

Portugal 1

England 0

(in La Seyne).
England: Young; Taylor, Whittingham, Huddlestone, Ferdinand, Reo-Coker, Routledge, Welsh (Davies), Soares (Halford), Nugent (Henderson), Milner.

6 June

South Korea 0

England 3 *(Rosenior, Halford, Reo-Coker)*

(in La Seyne).
England: Flinders; Wiseman, Ferdinand, Davies, Ridgewell, Rosenior, Reo-Coker (Welsh), Soares (Nugent), Ambrose, Halford, Wright-Phillips B (Henderson).

8 June

France 0

England 0

(in Toulon).
England: Flinders; Ridgewell, Taylor, Davies (Wiseman), Whittingham (Rosenior), Reo-Coker, Soares, Huddlestone, Milner, Ambrose (Routledge), Halford.
France won on penalties.

10 June

Mexico 1

England 1 *(Nugent)*

(in Toulon).
England: Young (Flinders); Whittingham, Taylor, Ridgewell, Rosenior (Welsh), Huddlestone, Milner, Routledge, Halford (Nugent), Ambrose, Henderson (Wright-Phillips B).

ENGLAND UNDER-19

Smith (Arsenal); Moore (Aston Villa); Hall (Birmingham C); Barker, Taylor A (Blackburn R); Giddings (Coventry C); Holmes, Huddlestone (Derby Co); Wilson (Everton); Bowditch (Ipswich T); Lennon (Leeds U); Heaton, Jones (Manchester U); Bates, Knight, McMahon, Morrison, Taylor AD, Wheater (Middlesbrough); Martin (Milton Keynes D); Jarvis (Norwich C); Hoskins (Rotherham U); Blackstock, Cranie, Mills (Southampton); Leadbitter (Sunderland); Ifil (Tottenham H); Fryatt (Walsall); Noble (West Ham U);

9 Sept

Republic of Ireland 0

England 2 *(Morrison 39, Jarvis 85)* 3500

(in Cork).
England: Heaton (Knight); Cranie, Bates (Jarvis), Giddings (Taylor A), Huddlestone (Taylor AD), Leadbitter, Ifil, Bowditch, Morrison (Jones), Moore (Fryatt), Holmes.

6 Oct

England 1 *(Holmes 80)*

Czech Republic 1 19,968

(at Norwich).
England: Martin; Ifil, Taylor A, Leadbitter, Bates, Cranie, Morrison (Fryatt 63), Huddlestone (Jones 88), Moore (Holmes 56), Jarvis, Bowditch.

18 Nov

England 1 *(Holmes)*

France 0

(at Barnsley).
England: Martin; Ifil, Giddings (Taylor A), Huddlestone (Leadbitter), Mills, Cranie, Morrison (Lennon), Jones, Jarvis (Wilson), Bowditch (Fryatt), Holmes.

9 Feb

Belgium 1

England 1 *(Holmes)*

(in Coxyde).
England: Martin; McMahon, Taylor AD, Leadbitter (Wilson), Bates, Cranie, Morrison (Smith), Noble (Jones), Fryatt (Blackstock), Bowditch, Holmes (Barker).

26 Mar

England 1 *(Holmes)*

Denmark 0 *

(at Bury).
England: Martin; Ifil, Taylor AD, Leadbitter, Mills, Cranie, Smith (Hoskins), Jones, Blackstock (Jarvis), Bowditch (Wilson), Holmes.

28 Mar

England 1 *(Blackstock)*

Sweden 0*

(at Bury).
England: Martin; Ifil, Taylor AD, Leadbitter, Mills, Cranie, Smith (Hoskins), Jones, Jarvis, Bowditch (Blackstock), Holmes.

*UEFA Championship Qualifiers.

30 Mar

England 1 *(Leadbitter (pen))*

Moldova 0*

(at Blackpool).
England: Heaton; Ifil, Wheater, Cranie, Taylor A, Leadbitter, Hall (Smith), Wilson, Hoskins, Holmes (Blackstock), Jarvis.

ENGLAND UNDER-18

Gilbert (Arsenal); Green, Paul (Aston Villa); Denvers (Bradford C); Ashton, Walker (Charlton Ath); Smith (Chelsea); Roberts (Crewe Alex); Ainsworth, Doyle (Derby Co); James (Fulham); Clarke (Huddersfield T); Parker (Leeds U); Porter (Leicester C); Campbell, Martin (Manchester U); Wheater (Middlesbrough); Huntingdon, Walton (Newcastle U); Lewis (Norwich C); Rudd, Dyer (Southampton); Alnwick (Sunderland); Ashikodi, Noble, Reid (West Ham U);

22 Dec

England 1 *(Wheater)*

Scotland 0

(at Hartlepool).
England: Alnwick; Doyle, Ashton, Noble (Ainsworth), Wheater, Huntingdon, Paul (Roberts), Martin (Green), Campbell (Walker), James (Porter), Reid.

10 June

England 0

Norway 0

(at Port Vale).
England: Alnwick (Lewis); Parker, Rudd (Denvers), Smith, Clarke (Huntingdon), Gilbert, Roberts, Doyle, Dyer (Walton), Walker (Ashikodi), Reid (James).

ENGLAND UNDER-17

Muamba, Simpson (Arsenal); Arestidou, Garner, Jones, Woods (Blackburn R); Sissons (Bolton W); Golbourne (Bristol C); Weston (Charlton Ath); Mancienne (Chelsea); Gooding (Coventry C); Kelly, Phelan, Vaughan (Everton); Omozusi, Watts (Fulham); Knights (Ipswich T); Gardner (Leeds U); Cattermole, Hines (Middlesbrough); Holmes (Liverpool); Gamble, McGugan (Nottingham F); Law (Sheffield U); Mulvany, Walcott (Southampton); Button, Davis, Holloway, Martin, Mills, Riley (Tottenham H); Ephraim, Tomkins (West Ham U); Davies (Wolverhampton W);

3 Aug

Sweden 0

England 1 *(Ephraim)*

(in Seinajoki).
England: Arestidou; Omozusi, Hines, Mills (Watts), Golbourne, Cattermole (Mulvaney), Gardner (Simpson), Gooding (Davis), Sissons, Ephraim, Woods (Kelly).

4 Aug

Faeroes 0

England 2 *(Sissons, Law)*

(in Kauhajoki).
England: Holloway; Law, Hines, Watts, Golbourne, Mulvaney (Gooding), Kelly (Sissons), Davis (Omozusi), Ephraim, Woods (Mills), Simpson.

6 Aug

Denmark 2

England 0

(in Vaasa).
England: Arestidou; Omozusi, Hines (Watts), Mills, Golbourne, Cattermole, Gardner (Simpson), Sissons, Mulvany (Gooding), Woods (Davis), Ephraim.

8 Aug

Norway 0

England 4 *(Ephraim, Davis 2, Gooding)*

(in Korsholm).
England: Holloway; Law (Omozusi), Watts, Mills, Golbourne, Cattermole, Gooding (Mulvany), Kelly (Sissons), Davis (Woods), Simpson, Ephraim.

1 Sept

England 2 *(Weston 60, Garner 70)*

Italy 1

(at Gillingham).

England: Button; Omozusi, Golbourne, Hines, Knights (Ephraim 55), Martin (McGugan 46), Weston, Garner, Phelan (Cattermole 73), Mancienne, Walcott.

3 Sept

England 5 *(Ephraim 4, Walcott)*

Russia 1

(at Gillingham).
England: Jones; Golbourne, McGugan, Mills, Sissons, Ephraim (Garner), Weston, Cattermole, Mancienne, Walcott (Knights), Gooding (Martin).

5 Sept

England 3 *(McGugan, Weston, Garner)*

Portugal 1

(at Gillingham).
England: Button; Omozusi, Golbourne, McGugan, Hines, Knights (Sissons), Ephraim, Gooding, Garner, Phelan, Mancienne.

7 Oct

Slovenia 0

England 5 *(Garner 2, Davies 17, Walcott 39, Golbourne 55, own goal 77)*

(in Ljubljana).
England: Jones (Button); Hines, Golbourne, McGugan, Mills, Muamba, Walcott, Gooding, Garner, Davies, Knights.

17 Nov

England 0

Hungary 0

(at Preston)
England: Gamble; Omozusi (Sissons), Riley (Woods), McGugan, Mills, Tomkins (Davies), Davis (Walcott), Muamba, Garner (Ephraim), Phelan, Weston.

26 Jan
France 1
England 3 *(Hines, Garner, Walcott)*
(in Guia).
England: Button; Golbourne, Muamba, Hines, Tomkins, Walcott, Garner (Knights), Ephraim, Holmes, Davies (McGugan), Weston (Phelan).

27 Jan
Portugal 1
England 0
(in Lagos).
England: Jones; Riley, Golbourne, Hines, Walcott, Gooding, Garner, Ephraim (Knights), Davies (Phelan), Omozusi, Muamba (McGugan).

29 Jan
Norway 2
England 1 *(Phelan)*
(in Guia).
England: Button (Jones); Riley, Muamba (McGugan), Tomkins, Gooding (Phelan), Ephraim, Knights (Walcott), Holmes, Omozusi, Davies, Weston (Garner).

26 Mar
England 3 *(Weston, Walcott, Garner)*
Serbia & Montenegro 1*
(at Stoke).
England: Button; Golbourne, Hines, Mancienne, Omozusi, Davies, Weston, Walcott (Knights), Muamba, Ephraim (Phelan), Garner (Vaughan).

28 Mar
England 3 *(Vaughan, Davies, Mancienne)*
Northern Ireland 0*
(at Wolverhampton).
England: Button; Golbourne, Hines, Mancienne, Mills, Davies (Cattermole), Gooding, Weston (Garner), Vaughan, Knights, Ephraim (Phelan).

30 Mar
England 3 *(Ephraim, Walcott, Vaughan)*
Republic of Ireland 1*
(at Walsall).
England: Button; Hines, Mills, Mancienne, Golbourne, Weston (Phelan), Davies, Muamba, Walcott (Gooding), Ephraim, Garner (Vaughan).

3 May
Belarus 0
England 4+ *(Weston, Ephraim 2, Garner)*
(in Santa Croce).
England: Button; Omozusi, Mills, Mancienne, Golbourne, Weston (Muamba), Phelan, McGugan (Gooding), Ephraim, Vaughan (Garner), Knights.

5 May
Turkey 3
England 2+ *(Garner 2)*
(in Pontedera).
England: Button; Omozusi, Golbourne, Mills, Mancienne, Davies (McGugan), Muamba (Phelan), Walcott, Ephraim, Weston (Vaughan), Garner.

8 May
Italy 1
England 0+
(in Cascina).
England: Button; Omozusi, Golbourne, Mills, Mancienne, McGugan (Gooding), Phelan (Ephraim), Davies, Walcott, Weston (Vaughan), Garner.

*UEFA Championship Qualifiers
+UEFA Championship Finals

ENGLAND UNDER-16

Bowes, Randall, Rodgers (Arsenal); Collins (Aston Villa); Aluko (Birmingham C); Arestidou (Blackburn R); Wright (Charlton Ath); Cork, Sawyer (Chelsea); Richards (Derby Co); Kissock, Molyneux (Everton); Magunda (Leicester C); Putterill (Liverpool), Sturridge (Manchester C); Amos, Bellamy, Brandy, Derbyshire, Nardiello (Manchester U); Porrit, Walker (Middlesbrough); Daley (Norwich C); Thomson (Southampton); Chandler, Kay (Sunderland); Asayile, Fraser-Allen, Holloway (Tottenham H); Hales, Spence, Tomkins (West Ham U).

14 Oct
Wales 1 *(Jones 25 (pen))*
England 5* *(Magunda 11, Sturridge 37, 61, Thomson 50, Walker 54)*
(in Llanelli).
England: Amos; Collins, Molyneux, Thomson, Magunda (Bellamy 55), Walker, Brandy (Bowes 40), Asayile (Porritt 60), Sturridge, Richards (Hayles 40), Aluko.

4 Nov
Northern Ireland 1
England 3* *(Thomson 2, Bellamy)*
(in Belfast).
England: Holloway; Bellamy, Molyneux (Cork), Thomson, Rodgers, Walker, Fraser-Allen (Kay), Randall, Putterill, Derbyshire (Brandy), Porritt (Daley).

26 Nov
England 0
Scotland 0*
(at Blackpool).
England: Arestidou; Spence, Molyneux, Thomson (Richards), Rodgers (Magunda), Walker (Kissock), Hales (Nardiello), Sawyer, Sturridge, Putterill (Brandy), Aluko.

*Victory Shield

23 Mar
Japan 2
England 0
(in St Georges).
England: Arestidou; Cork, Molyneux, Thomson (Wright), Tomkins, Walker, Brandy, Nardiello (Sturridge), Aluko, Richards (Chandler), Sawyer (Kissock).

24 Mar
Portugal 3
England 3 *(Walker, Sturridge, Nardiello)*
(in Venansault).
England: Arestidou; Walker, Molyneux (Cork), Tomkins, Brandy, Chandler (Wright), Sturridge, Kissock (Thomson), Richards (Nardiello), Magunda (Sawyer), Aluko.

26 Mar
Cameroon 1
England 2 *(Nardiello, Sturridge)*
(in Chantonnay).
England: Arestidou; Walker, Cork, Thomson (Tomkins), Sturridge, Nardiello, Aluko (Brandy), Kissock (Chandler), Rodgers (Molyneux), Wright (Sawyer), Magunda.

28 Mar
Ivory Coast 0
England 2 *(Sturridge, Aluko)*
(in Montaigu).
England: Amos; Molyneux (Thomson), Tomkins, Walker, Brandy, Chandler (Wright), Nardiello (Sturridge), Rodgers, Richards (Aluko), Sawyer (Kissock), Cork.

WOMEN'S FOOTBALL 2004–05

A most accomplished Women's European Championship in England in the summer (although not in terms of success for England, the host nation, who failed to qualify from their group) was marred by what was held to be another sexist remark from a top official. After FIFA President Sepp Blatter's infamous comment last year on tight shorts to stimulate interest in the women's game, this time we had UEFA supremo Lennart Johansson (who apparently chided Blatter at the time) doing an almost about face and suggesting that in order to promote the female game financially it should encourage an image of "sweaty lovely looking girls on the pitch whilst emerging from the showers looking resplendently lovely". He later emphasised that he was not a sexist and his remarks were about advertising and had been misinterpreted. Subsequently he expressed his delight at the success of the event which had been the biggest in its 21 year history. He also particularly praised the organisation involved and said it had been the right decision to hold the games in England.

Back on the pitch Germany the current World Champions were crowned "Euro Champs" for the fourth successive time. They beat Norway 3-1 thanks to goals from Anja Mittag after 21 minutes, Renate Lingor (24) and Birgit Prinz (63). Norway scored through Dagny Mellagren (41). The Final was played at Blackburn's Ewood Park in front of a crowd figure of 21,105, a record for a European Final. Germany's Coach Tina Theune-Mayer bowed out with this victory after several successful years in charge.

Full details of the Tournament appear below.

Domestically yet again Arsenal dominated the scene completing a double of Premier League Championship and Premier League Cup. It was their seventh Championship in thirteen seasons and their eighth win in the League Cup. That victory was at the expense of Charlton the holders by a 3-0 margin at Griffin Park in March with over 2500 fans present. Two goals from skipper Fay White and one from Julie Fleeting set up their record win in the competition.

However Charlton did have some compensation because they defeated Everton (surprise 3-0 winners over Arsenal in the semi-final) in what was their third successive Women's FA Cup Final. This time in May an attendance of 8567 saw them lift the Trophy, for the first time, by virtue of a 1-0 score line thanks to a great 58th minute goal from 18-year-old Eniola Aluko who was also voted woman of the match.

In the League the Premiership saw Arsenal 7 points clear winners from Charlton with Bristol City and Liverpool relegated. The Northern Division was won by Sunderland from Wolves 6 points behind whilst Coventry go down. In the Southern Division Chelsea the winners were 8 points above Portsmouth with Ipswich relegated. To show how competitive women's football is these days, 33 teams contested the Reserve section. There are two divisions in each of the Mids/North and South areas. In M/N Division One Birmingham were the winners and the Division Two Championship went to the Doncaster Rovers Belles. The Southern Division League One saw Charlton come top and in Division Two Bristol City were champions. The Premier Reserve League Cup was won by Fulham who beat Birmingham 3-2.

There were a number of other initiatives throughout the season including the official launch in May of the Triple "F" which is Fitness and Fun through Football. This was devised by Birmingham County FA to encourage girls 15–16 who for various social or health reasons, take little or no exercise. It uses training drills set to music with "Football Dance" allowing girls to make up their own routines. Hendon Ladies released a CD/Video called "Girls are playing football" which was aired on a Sky music channel and Luton had a girls "Football Active Sports Tournament" for the 10–15-year-olds which was a great success.

Birmingham City and England colleagues Rachel Yankey and Karen Carney were presented with Awards at the 7th Annual FA Women's Football Awards held at the Sheraton Park Lane Hotel on the 10th May 2005. Left winger Rachel Yankey was named the Nationwide International Player of the Year, and 17-year-old right winger Karen Carney took the Young Player of the Year accolade. Carney graduated via the National Under-19 side into the senior squad, becoming the youngest player to be handed a debut in the seven years that Hope Powell the England Coach has been in charge. Players' Player of the Year was won by Arsenal and Scotland striker Julie Fleeting and the prolific scorer hit 24 goals in all competitions for the Gunners.

The annual awards are aimed at rewarding those people who have worked hard to raise the standards of the women's game both on and off the pitch, so the annual event is an occasion for The Football Association and its Partners to recognise the efforts invested in developing the game and taking the sport to a wider audience.

Other list of winners is as follows:

UMBRO TOP GOALSCORERS
National Division: Trudy Williams – Bristol Rovers
Northern Division: Amy McCann – Wolverhampton Wanderers
Southern Division: Emma Mead – Brighton & Hove Albion

NATIONWIDE MANAGER OF THE YEAR AWARD
Vic Akers
(The incredible Manager of the Arsenal Women's team who have had so much success under his stewardship).

NATIONWIDE CLUB OF THE YEAR AWARD
Everton

THE FA SPECIAL ACHIEVEMENT AWARD
Gill Wallworth
(A volunteer who has been involved in the administration of local Women's Football for over twenty years).

The FA National Media Award
BBC TV Sport

The FA Regional Media Award
The Lincolnshire Echo

Club Media Award
Wolves

Club Marketing Award
Leeds United

Programme of the Year
Arsenal

Fair Play Award
Three-way tie – Cardiff City, Coventry City, Sunderland
So far as media coverage is concerned the *Fair Game* Magazine continues to flourish whilst the FA Website contains a lively and informative amount of information some of which has been utilised here.

KEN GOLDMAN

WOMEN'S FOOTBALL LEAGUES

NATIONAL DIVISION

		P	W	D	L	GD	Pts
1	Arsenal LFC	18	15	3	0	44	48
2	Charlton Ath WFC	18	13	2	3	26	41
3	Everton LFC	18	11	4	3	21	37
4	Birmingham C LFC	18	9	3	6	9	30
5	Bristol R WFC	18	9	1	8	7	28
6	Leeds U LFC	18	8	2	8	–3	26
7	Fulham LFC	18	3	5	10	–21	14
8	Doncaster R Belles LFC	18	3	3	12	–28	12
9	Liverpool LFC *	18	3	2	13	–28	10
10	Bristol C WFC	18	2	3	13	–27	9

**One point deducted*

NORTHERN DIVISION

		P	W	D	L	GD	Pts
1	Sunderland AFC Ladies	22	17	2	3	40	53
2	Wolverhampton W WFC	22	14	5	3	27	47
3	Blackburn R LFC	22	10	9	3	20	39
4	Stockport Co LFC	22	7	9	6	–2	30
5	Lincoln C LFC	22	8	5	9	–5	29
6	Aston Villa LFC	22	8	4	10	–7	28
7	Middlesbrough LFC	22	6	6	10	–7	24
8	Tranmere R LFC	22	7	3	12	–7	24
9	Oldham Curzon LFC	22	6	6	10	–8	24
10	Manchester C LFC	22	7	3	12	–16	24
11	Sheffield W LFC	22	5	8	9	–14	23
12	Coventry C LFC	22	4	6	12	–21	18

SOUTHERN DIVISION

		P	W	D	L	GD	Pts
1	Chelsea LFC	22	16	4	2	47	52
2	Portsmouth LFC	22	13	5	4	16	44
3	Brighton & HA WFC	22	11	3	8	16	36
4	Crystal Palace LFC	22	10	6	6	11	36
5	AFC Wimbledon LFC	22	11	2	9	19	35
6	Millwall Lionesses LFC	22	9	8	5	4	35
7	Cardiff C LFC	22	9	7	6	11	34
8	Southampton Saints WFC	22	7	6	9	–1	27
9	Watford LFC	22	7	6	9	–2	27
10	Langford LFC	22	6	5	11	–24	23
11	Enfield T LFC	22	1	6	15	–41	9
12	Ipswich T LFC	22	2	2	18	–56	8

RESERVE SECTION

MIDLANDS/NORTH DIVISION ONE

		P	W	D	L	GD	Pts
1	Birmingham C LFC (res)	14	10	1	3	32	31
2	Everton LFC (res)	14	8	3	3	15	27
3	Leeds U LFC (res)	14	6	3	5	5	21
4	Sunderland AFC Ladies (res)	14	7	0	7	–2	21
5	Liverpool LFC (res)*	14	5	7	2	8	19
6	Aston Villa LFC (res)	14	4	4	6	–21	16
7	Stockport Co LFC (res)	14	4	1	9	–13	13
8	Wolverhampton W LFC (res)	14	1	3	10	–24	6

**Three points deducted*

MIDLANDS/NORTH DIVISION TWO

		P	W	D	L	GD	Pts
1	Doncaster R Belles (res)	14	10	2	2	27	32
2	Tranmere R LFC (res)	14	8	3	3	15	27
3	Manchester C LFC (res)	14	8	1	5	15	25
4	Coventry C LFC (res)	14	7	3	4	17	24
5	Middlesbrough LFC (res)	14	6	4	4	19	22
6	Blackburn R LFC (res)	14	3	2	9	–13	11
7	Oldham Curzon LFC (res)	14	2	3	9	–46	9
8	Lincoln C LFC (res)	14	2	2	10	–34	8

SOUTHERN DIVISION ONE

		P	W	D	L	GD	Pts
1	Charlton Ath LFC (res)	14	11	3	0	70	36
2	Fulham LFC (res)	14	11	2	1	67	35
3	Arsenal LFC (res)	14	10	3	1	77	33
4	Southampton Saints LFC (res)	14	5	1	8	–21	16
5	Watford LFC (res)	14	5	0	9	–39	15
6	Chelsea LFC (res)	14	4	1	9	–30	13
7	Portsmouth LFC (res)	14	4	0	10	–35	12
8	Millwall Lionesses LFC (res)	14	1	0	13	–89	3

SOUTHERN DIVISION TWO

		P	W	D	L	GD	Pts
1	Bristol C (res)	16	9	4	3	15	31
2	Cardiff C Bluebirds LFC (res)	16	9	4	3	15	31
3	Crystal Palace LFC (res)	16	8	5	3	17	29
4	Ipswich T LFC (res)	16	7	2	7	15	23
5	AFC Wimbledon LFC (res)	16	6	3	7	–10	21
6	Bristol R LFC (res)	16	6	2	8	2	20
7	Enfield LFC (res)	16	5	3	8	–15	18
8	Langford LFC (res)	16	5	3	8	–15	18
9	Brighton & HA LFC (res)	16	3	2	11	–24	11

NATIONAL DIVISION LEAGUE – PREVIOUS WINNERS

1992–93	Arsenal	1997–98	Everton	2002–03	Fulham
1993–94	Doncaster Belles	1998–99	Croydon	2003–04	Arsenal
1994–95	Arsenal	1999–00	Croydon		
1995–96	Croydon	2000–01	Arsenal		
1996–97	Arsenal	2001–02	Arsenal		

THE FA WOMEN'S CUP 2004–05

IN PARTNERSHIP WITH NATIONWIDE

FIRST QUALIFYING ROUND

Stockport Celtic v Gateshead Cleveland Hall
walkover for Gateshead Cleveland Hall – Stockport Celtic withdrawn
Wigan v York City 4-1
Windscale v Leeds City Vixens 1-5
Blyth Spartans v Huddersfield Town 1-3
Morley Spurs v Darwen 6-1
Bolton Wanderers v Ossett Albion 9-0
Liverpool Manweb Feds v Chew Moor Brook 11-0
Garswood Saints v Killingworth YPC 4-2
Cleator Moor Celtic v Durham City 1-1
aet; Durham City won 4-1 on penalties
Bradford City v Penrith Sapphires 5-2
Macclesfield Town v Lumley Ladies 2-3
Blyth Town v Thorpe United 4-2
South Durham Royals v Crook Town 4-2
Kirklees v Hopwood 2-1
Loughborough Dynamo v Kirkley 2-7
Stoke City v Heelands Rangers 12-0
Cosford v Rea Valley *aet* 3-2
Derby County v Barwell 8-0
Belper Town v Leicester City Women's 0-11
Colchester Town v Buxton 0-8
Valiant v Peterborough Azure 0-10
Cambridge United v Bradwell Belles 21-0
Solihull Glades v AFC Telford United Ladies 1-5
Southam United v Birmingham University 4-1
TNS Ladies v Birstall United 7-1
Colchester United v Rushcliffe Eagles 13-0
Dudley United v Stratford Town 0-5
Dynamo North London v Slough 2-2
aet; Dynamo North London won 5-3 on penalties
Dagenham & Redbridge v Maidstone Mavrix
walkover for Dagenham & Redbridge – Maidstone Mavrix withdrawn
AEI Gravesend v Wycombe Wanderers 7-0
Luton Town Belles v Brentford 5-6
Brentwood Town v Haywards Heath Town *aet* 3-2
Hampton & Richmond Borough v FC London Ladies 15-0
Haringey Borough v Chelmsford City 1-7
London Women v Hoddesdon Owls 9-0
Carterton v Clapton Orient 1-5
Panthers v Woodbridge Town 2-1
Redhill v Hitchin Town 4-0
Redbridge v Henley Town
walkover for Henley Town – Redbridge withdrawn
Thatcham Town v Eastbourne Town 6-2
Luton Borough v Hastings United
walkover for Hastings United – Luton Borough withdrawn
Woking v Hendon 7-1

Tottenham Hotspur v Banbury United 1-0
Leighton Linslade v Billericay 0-1
MK Wanderers v Viking 2-4
AFC Newbury Ladies v Morden United 7-2
Woodstock v Royston Town 1-3
Bowers & Pitsea v Dover Athletic *aet* 3-4
Saffron Walden Town v Crowborough Athletic 2-6
Aylesbury United v Abbey Rangers 8-3
Lewes v Basildon Town
walkover for Lewes – Basildon Town withdrawn
CEFI v Haywood United 3-3
aet; CEFI won 3-1 on penalties
Yeovil Town v Swindon Spitfires 9-2
Ross Town v Penzance 4-3
Madron v Reading Girls
walkover for Madron – Reading Girls withdrawn
Bath City v Launceston 7-1
Alphington v Isca Vikings 0-3
Team Bath v Newquay AFC *aet* 1-2
Aldershot Town v St Peter's 3-1
Ashdown Rovers v Southampton 11-2

SECOND QUALIFYING ROUND
Bolton Wanderers v Lumley Ladies 2-1
Leeds City Vixens v Huddersfield Town 3-0
Liverpool Manweb Feds v Garswood Saints 3-4
Bury Girls & Ladies v Barnsley 1-1
aet; Bury Girls & Ladies won 4-1 on penalties
Gateshead Cleveland Hall v Darlington RA 0-5
Wigan v Blyth Town 5-3
Kirklees v South Durham Royals 0-1
Durham City v Morley Spurs 0-6
Bradford City v Bolton Ambassadors 10-0
AFC Telford United v Derby County *aet* 2-5
Buxton v Kettering Town 2-0
Stoke City v Cosford 4-3
Cambridge United v Kirkley 7-0
Whittington v TNS Ladies 0-14
Walsall v Colchester United 2-7
Peterborough Azure v Southam United 2-1
Stratford Town v Leicester City Women's 2-7
CEFI v Woking *aet* 4-3
Crowborough Athletic v London Women 1-3
Lordswood v Chelmsford City 3-1
AFC Newbury Ladies v Brentford 2-4
Dagenham & Redbridge v Royston Town 3-0
Panthers v Brentwood Town 4-0
Lewes v Viking 3-1
Henley Town v Billericay 7-2
Dover Athletic v AEI Gravesend 0-2
Thatcham Town v Aylesbury United 2-1
Hastings United v Tottenham Hotspur 1-3
Redhill v Hampton & Richmond Borough 5-2
Dynamo North London v Clapton Orient 2-1
Yeovil Town v Buckfastleigh Rangers 7-0
Exeter City v Newquay AFC 1-7
Ross Town v Madron 8-0
AFC Bournemouth v Gloucester City 6-2
Isca Vikings v Bath City *aet* 3-6
Ashdown Rovers v Aldershot Town 3-2

FIRST ROUND
Garswood Saints v Bradford City 3-3
aet; Garswood Saints won 4-2 on penalties (reversed tie)
South Durham Royals v Manchester United 2-1
Morley Spurs v Leeds City Vixens 1-3
Chester le Street Town v Newcastle 0-1
Wigan v Blackpool Wren Rovers 0-8
Preston North End v Bury Girls & Ladies 3-0
Crewe v Scunthorpe United 4-0
Chester City v Darlington RA 2-0
Bolton Wanderers v Doncaster Parklands Rovers 2-3
Bedford Town Bells v Stoke City 4-1
Rushden & Diamonds v Long Eaton Villa 2-3
Northampton Town v Loughborough Students 3-1
Leicester City Women's v Stafford Rangers 7-0
Colchester United v TNS Ladies 2-1
Peterborough Azure v Norwich City Ladies 2-4
Buxton v Ilkeston Town 2-2
aet; Ilkeston Town won 3-0 on penalties
Shrewsbury Town v Leicester City Ladies 0-5
Cambridge United v Nottingham Forest 0-2
Lichfield Diamonds v Chesterfield 3-4
Leafield Athletic v Derby County 2-0
CEFI v Reading 6-2
Oxford City v Henley Town
walkover for Oxford City – Henley Town failed to fulfil the fixture
Lordswood v Barking 3-0
Dagenham & Redbridge v Gillingham 1-1
aet; Gillingham won 4-2 on penalties
Reading Royals v Panthers 10-1
Barnet FC Ladies v Tottenham Hotspur 3-1
Lewes v Brentford 3-2
London Women v Sophtlogic *aet* 1-3
Launton v AEI Gravesend 2-1
Leyton Orient v Queens Park Rangers 0-1
West Ham United v Dynamo North London 3-0
Redhill v Chesham United 0-5
Wembley Ladies v Thatcham Town *aet* 1-3
Cardiff City Bluebirds v AFC Bournemouth 5-1
Keynsham Town v Newquay AFC 5-2
Plymouth Argyle v Ashdown Rovers 9-1
Newton Abbot v Forest Green Rovers *aet* 1-1
aet; Newton Abbot won 5-4 on penalties (reversed tie)
Yeovil Town v Clevedon Town 1-2
Bath City v Swindon Town 0-4
bye – Ross Town

SECOND ROUND
Doncaster Parklands Rovers v Newcastle 2-4
South Durham Royals v Chester City 2-3
Preston North End v Blackpool Wren Rovers 3-3
aet; Blackpool Wren Rovers won 4-2 on penalties
Crewe v Leeds City Vixens *aet* 2-3
Chesterfield v Garswood Saints 2-1
Nottingham Forest v Leicester City Women's 6-0
Long Eaton Villa v Leicester City Ladies 0-1
Norwich City Ladies v Colchester United 4-3
Ilkeston Town v Northampton Town 0-9
Leafield Athletic v Bedford Town Bells 1-0
Thatcham Town v Queens Park Rangers 0-4
Gillingham v Reading Royals 0-3
CEFI v Lordswood 1-3
West Ham United v Chesham United 4-2
Sophtlogic v Lewes 2-1
Barnet FC Ladies v Launton 9-3
Swindon Town v Clevedon Town 2-1
Newton Abbot v Keynsham Town 1-4
Cardiff City Bluebirds v Ross Town 8-1
Oxford City v Plymouth Argyle 2-3

THIRD ROUND
Tranmere Rovers v Aston Villa 3-1
Wolverhampton Wanderers v Coventry City 5-0
Sheffield Wednesday v Lincoln City 7-1
Leafield Athletic v Chesterfield 3-2
Nottingham Forest v Leicester City Ladies 0-2
Blackburn Rovers v Newcastle 6-0
Stockport County v Chester City 2-0
Blackpool Wren Rovers v Middlesbrough 0-1
Manchester City v Sunderland AFC Ladies *aet* 1-2
Oldham Curzon v Leeds City Vixens 7-1
Lordswood v Ipswich Town 1-6
Southampton Saints v Portsmouth 0-5
West Ham United v Crystal Palace 1-0
Swindon Town v Langford 1-2
Queens Park Rangers v Enfield Town 4-1
Cardiff City Bluebirds v Plymouth Argyle 6-1
Millwall Lionesses v Keynsham Town 1-1
aet; Millwall Lionesses won 5-4 on penalties
Sophtlogic v Northampton Town 0-4
Reading Royals v Brighton & Hove Albion 3-1
Chelsea v Barnet FC Ladies 1-0
AFC Wimbledon Ladies v Norwich City Ladies 2-0
Watford v Cardiff City 5-2
tie awarded to Cardiff City – Watford removed for playing an ineligible player

FOURTH ROUND
Leafield Athletic v Northampton Town 1-1
aet; Leafield Athletic won 5-4 on penalties
Oldham Curzon v Fulham 0-1
Doncaster Rovers Belles v Birmingham City 1-9
Middlesbrough v Sheffield Wednesday 0-2
Charlton Athletic v Wolverhampton Wanderers 4-1
Cardiff City v Chelsea 3-4
Tranmere Rovers v Langford 3-1
Arsenal v AFC Wimbledon Ladies 2-0

Blackburn Rovers v Leeds United	1-4
Leicester City Ladies v West Ham United	*aet* 0-1
Queens Park Rangers v Sunderland AFC Ladies	1-3
Reading Royals v Ipswich Town	2-1
Cardiff City Bluebirds v Millwall Lionesses	4-5
Bristol City v Everton	0-6
Portsmouth v Liverpool	2-3
Bristol Rovers v Stockport County	4-0

FIFTH ROUND

Reading Royals v Chelsea	1-3
Fulham v Birmingham City	1-5
Leeds United v Arsenal	1-3
Millwall Lionesses v Tranmere Rovers	1-3
Leafield Athletic v Everton	0-2
Charlton Athletic v West Ham United	5-0
Sunderland AFC Ladies v Liverpool	2-0
Bristol Rovers v Sheffield Wednesday	6-0

SIXTH ROUND

Tranmere Rovers v Bristol Rovers	1-7
Charlton Athletic v Sunderland AFC Ladies	4-1
Birmingham City v Arsenal	0-3
Chelsea v Everton	*aet* 0-1

SEMI-FINAL

Charlton Athletic v Bristol Rovers	1-0
at Dagenham & Redbridge FC	
Everton v Arsenal	3-0
at Southport FC	

THE FA WOMEN'S CUP FINAL

Monday, 2 May 2004
(at Upton Park)

Charlton Athletic (0) 1 *(Aluko 58)*

Everton (0) 0 8567

Charlton Athletic: Cope; Hills, Coss, Stoney, Sinclair-Chambers, Murphy, Smith, Williams, Broadhurst, Aluko, Heatherson (Clarke 69).

Everton: Hill; Eason, Britton, Johnson, Unitt, Williams, McDougall, Duffy (Evans 66), Handley, Parry, Kane (J. Jones 87)

Referee: M. J. Jones (Cheshire).

THE FA WOMEN'S CUP – PREVIOUS WINNERS

Year	*Winners*	*Runners-up*	*Score*
1971	Southampton	Stewarton & Thistle	4-1
1972	Southampton	Lee's Ladies	3-2
1973	Southampton	West Horn United	2-0
1974	Foxdens	Southampton	2-1
1975	Southampton	Warminster	4-2
1976	Southampton	QPR	2-1
1977	QPR	Southampton	1-0
1978	Southampton	QPR	8-2
1979	Southampton	Lowestoft	1-0
1980	St Helens	Preston North End	1-0
1981	Southampton	St Helens	4-2
1982	Lowestoft	Cleveland Spartans	2-0
1983	Doncaster Belles	St Helens	3-2
1984	Howbury Grange	Doncaster Belles	4-2
1985	Friends of Fulham	Doncaster Belles	2-0
1986	Norwich	Doncaster Belles	4-3
1987	Doncaster Belles	St Helens	2-0
1988	Doncaster Belles	Leasowe Pacific	3-1
1989	Leasowe Pacific	Friends of Fulham	3-2
1990	Doncaster Belles	Friends of Fulham	1-0
1991	Millwall Lionesses	Doncaster Belles	1-0
1992	Doncaster Belles	Red Star Southampton	4-0
1993	Arsenal	Doncaster Belles	3-0
1994	Doncaster Belles	Knowsley United	1-0
1995	Arsenal	Liverpool	3-2
1996	Croydon	Liverpool	1-1
	Croydon won 4-2 on penalties.		
1997	Millwall Lionesses	Wembley	1-0
1998	Arsenal	Croydon	3-2
1999	Arsenal	Southampton Saints	2-0
2000	Croydon	Doncaster Belles	2-1
2001	Arsenal	Fulham	1-0
2002	Fulham	Doncaster Belles	2-1
2003	Fulham	Charlton Atheltic	3-0
2004	Arsenal	Charlton Athletic	3-0

THE FA NATIONWIDE PREMIER LEAGUE CUP 2004–05

PRELIMINARY ROUND

Blackburn Rovers v Oldham Curzon	3-2
Tranmere Rovers v Southampton Saints	2-0

FIRST ROUND

Ipswich Town v Sheffield Wednesday	0-1
Enfield Town v Fulham	1-5
Coventry City v Cardiff City	1-2
Tranmere Rovers v Millwall Lionesses	0-2
Brighton & Hove Albion v Langford	5-1
AFC Wimbledon v Birmingham City	0-7
Middlesbrough v Manchester City	1-3
Doncaster Rovers Belles v Aston Villa	1-0
Lincoln City v Everton	0-6
Blackburn Rovers v Leeds United	0-3
Portsmouth v Watford	2-3
Wolverhampton Wanderers v Bristol Rovers	0-5
Arsenal w.o. v Sunderland withdrew	
Chelsea v Bristol City	1-2
Crystal Palace v Liverpool	1-3
Charlton Athletic w.o. v Stockport County withdrew	

SECOND ROUND

Arsenal v Bristol City	4-1
Birmingham City v Millwall Lionesses	6-0
Brighton & Hove Albion v Watford	4-0
Cardiff City v Doncaster Rovers Belles	1-5
Charlton Athletic v Manchester City	6-0
Everton v Bristol Rovers	0-2
Leeds United v Fulham	2-3
Sheffield Wednesday v Liverpool	0-3

THIRD ROUND

Brighton & Hove Albion v Liverpool	2-5
Arsenal v Fulham	3-0
Charlton Athletic v Bristol Rovers	3-0
Doncaster Rovers Belles v Birmingham City	1-2

SEMI-FINALS

Liverpool v Charlton Athletic	0-3
Birmingham City v Arsenal	1-3

FINAL

Charlton Athletic v Arsenal	0-3

THE WOMEN'S PREMIER LEAGUE CUP – PREVIOUS WINNERS

Year	*Winners*	*Runners-up*	*Score*
1993	Arsenal	Knowsley	3-0
1994	Arsenal	Doncaster Belles	4-0
1995	Wimbledon	Villa Aztecs	2-0
1996	Wembley	Doncaster Belles	2-2
	Wembley won 5-3 on penalties.		
1997	Millwall Lionesses	Everton	2-1
1998	Arsenal	Croydon	3-2
1999	Arsenal	Everton	3-1
2000	Arsenal	Leeds United	5-1
2001	Arsenal	Tranmere Rovers	3-0
2002	Fulham	Birmingham City	7-1
2003	Fulham	Arsenal	1-1
	Fulham won 3-2 on penalties.		
2004	Charlton Athletic	Fulham	1-0

FIFA WOMEN'S WORLD CUP PAST WINNERS

1991 USA 2, Norway 1 (in China)
1995 Norway 2, Germany 0 (in Sweden)
1999 USA 0, China 0 (in USA)
USA won 5-4 on penalties.
2003 Germany 1, Sweden 1 (in USA)
Germany won 2-1 on sudden death.

WOMEN'S EUROPEAN CHAMPIONSHIP 2005

GROUP A MATCHES

Sunday 5 June 2005

Sweden 1 Denmark 1
Blackpool FC

England 3 Finland 2
Manchester City FC

Wednesday 8 June 2005

Denmark 2 England 1
Blackburn Rovers FC

Sweden 0 Finland 0
Blackpool FC

Saturday 11 June 2005

England 0 Sweden 1
Blackburn Rovers FC

Finland 2 Denmark 1
Blackpool FC

Group A – Table

	P	*W*	*D*	*L*	*F*	*A*	*GD*	*Pts*
Sweden	3	1	2	0	2	1	1	5
Finland	3	1	1	1	4	4	0	4
Denmark	3	1	1	1	4	4	0	4
England	3	1	0	2	4	5	–1	3

GROUP B MATCHES

Monday 6 June 2005

Germany 1 Norway 0
Warrington Wolves RFC

France 3 Italy 1
Preston North End FC

Thursday 9 June 2005

Italy 0 Germany 4
Preston North End FC

France 1 Norway 1
Warrington Wolves RFC

Sunday 12 June 2005

Germany 3 France 0
Warrington Wolves RFC

Norway 5 Italy 3
Preston North End FC

Group B – Table

	P	*W*	*D*	*L*	*F*	*A*	*GD*	*Pts*
Germany	3	3	0	0	8	0	8	9
Norway	3	1	1	1	6	5	1	4
France	3	1	1	1	4	5	–1	4
Italy	3	0	0	3	4	12	–8	0

SEMI-FINALS

Wednesday 15 June 2005

Germany 4 Finland 1
Preston North End FC

Thursday 16 June 2005

Norway 3 Sweden 2 (aet)
Warrington Wolves RFC

FINAL

Sun 19 June 2005

Germany 3 Norway 1
Blackburn Rovers FC

UEFA WOMEN'S CHAMPIONSHIP PAST WINNERS

1984 Sweden 1, 0, England 0, 1
Sweden won 4-3 on penalties.
1987 Norway 2, Sweden 1
1989 Germany 4, Norway 1
1991 Germany 3, Norway 1
1993 Norway 1, Italy 0
1995 Germany 3, Sweden 2
1997 Germany 2, Italy 0
2001 Germany 1, Sweden 0
2002 France 1, 1, England 0, 0
2005 Germany 3 Norway 1

UEFA WOMEN'S CUP PAST WINNERS

2001–02 Frankfurt 2, Umea 0
2002–03 Umea 4, 3, Fortuna Hjorring 1, 0
2003–04 Frankfurt 0, Umea 5
2004–05 Djurgaarden/Alvsjo 0, 1, Potsdam 2, 3

UEFA WOMEN'S UNDER-19 CHAMPIONSHIP PAST WINNERS

1998 Denmark 2, 2, France 3, 0
1999 Sweden
2000 Germany 4, Spain 2
2001 Germany 3, Norway 2
2002 Germany 3, France 1
2003 France 2, Norway 0

FIFA WOMEN'S UNDER-19 CHAMPIONSHIP PAST WINNERS

2002 USA 1, Canada 0 (in Canada)
2004 Germany 2, China PR 0 (in Thailand)

WOMEN'S OLYMPICS PAST WINNERS

1996 USA 2, China 1 (in Atlanta)
2000 Norway 3, USA 2 (in Sydney)
2004 Brazil 2, USA 1 *(aet.)* (in Athens)

ENGLAND WOMEN'S INTERNATIONAL APPEARANCES 2004-05

Asante, Champ, Phillip, Smith K, White (Arsenal); Barr, Bassett, Carney, Chamberlain, Fletcher, Maggs, Potter, Scott, Yankey (Birmingham C); McArthur (Bristol C); Bardsley (California State); Aluko, Chapman, Stoney, Walker (Charlton Ath); Exley (Doncaster Rovers Belles); Brown, Handley, Johnson, McDougall, Unitt, Williams (Everton); Moore (Floya); Hall (Fulham); Smith S (Leeds U); Westwood (Wolverhampton W).

19 Aug *(at Bristol Rovers).*

England 1 *(Williams 67)* **Russia 2** 1439
England: Hall; Champ, Stoney, Phillip, Unitt, Handley (Smith S 63), McDougall (Exley 63), Chapman, Williams, Yankey, Walker (Moore 46).

18 Sept *(in Heerhugowaard).*

Holland 1 England 2 *(Exley 45, Barr 63)*
England: Hall; Bassett (Scott), Stoney, Johnson, Unitt, Exley, Chapman, Williams (McDougall), Handley (Potter 78), Aluko (Barr 60), Smith S.

22 Sept *(in Tuitjenhoorn).*

Holland 0 England 1 *(Unitt 67)*
England: Chamberlain (Hall 46); Scott (Champ 46), Phillip, Johnson (Asante 46), Unitt, Exley (McArthur 46), Chapman, Williams, Aluko (Potter 46), Moore (Maggs 65), Yankey.

17 Feb *(at Milton Keynes).*

England 4 *(Williams, Handley, Barr, Carney)*
Italy 1
England: Fletcher; Scott, White, Phillip, Unitt, Handley (Carney), Williams, Chapman, Yankey (Smith), Westwood, Barr (Aluko).

9 Mar *(in Paderne).*

Northern Ireland 0
England 4 *(Carney, Exley 2, McArthur).*
England: Bardsley; Scott, Stoney, Johnson, Unitt, McArthur, Exley, Asante, Carney, Aluko, Smith S.

11 Mar *(in Faro).*

Portugal 0 England 4 *(Stoney, Yankey 2, Barr)*
England: Fletcher; Scott, Stoney, Phillip, Unitt, Westwood, Williams, Chapman, Handley (Carney), Barr, Yankey.

13 Mar *(in Lagos).*

Mexico 0 England 5 *(Williams 2, Handley, Yankey, Smith S).*
England: Fletcher; Scott (Johnson), White (Stoney), Phillip, Unitt, Handley, Williams, Chapman (McArthur), Yankey (Smith S), Westwood (Exley), Barr (Aluko).

15 Mar *(in Guia).*

China 0 England 0
England: Fletcher; Scott, Unitt, Johnson, Phillip, Handley (Carney), Williams, Chapman, Yankey, Westwood, Barr.

21 Apr *(at Tranmere).*

England 2 *(Barr, og)* **Scotland 1**
England: Fletcher; Scott, White, Phillip, Unitt, Williams, Westwood, Chapman (Asante), Handley (Carney), Barr (Aluko), Yankey.

6 May *(at Barnsley).*

England 1 *(Asante)* **Norway 1**
England: Fletcher; Scott, White, Phillip, Unitt, Williams, Westwood (Smith K), Asante, Carney (Stoney), Barr, Yankey.

26 May *(at Walsall).*

England 4 *(Unit 2, Smith K, Aluko)*
Czech Republic 1
England: Fletcher (Brown); Scott, White (Johnson), Phillip, Unitt, Chapman (Exley), Westwood (Smith K), Williams, Handley (Carney), Barr (Aluko), Yankey.

5 June *(at Manchester City).*

England 3 *(Barr, Carney, og)* **Finland 2***
England: Fletcher; Scott, Unitt, Chapman, White (Johnson), Phillip, Bardsley, Williams, Barr (Aluko), Smith K (Westwood), Yankey.

8 June *(at Blackburn).*

England 1 *(Williams (pen))* **Denmark 2***
England: Fletcher; Scott, Unitt, Chapman, White, Phillip, Carney, Williams, Barr (Aluko), Smith K (Exley), Yankey.

11 June *(at Blackburn).*

England 0 Sweden 1*
England: Brown; Scott, Unitt, Chapman, White, Phillip, Carney (Barr), Williams, Aluko, Smith K, Yankey.

*Women's Euro 2005.

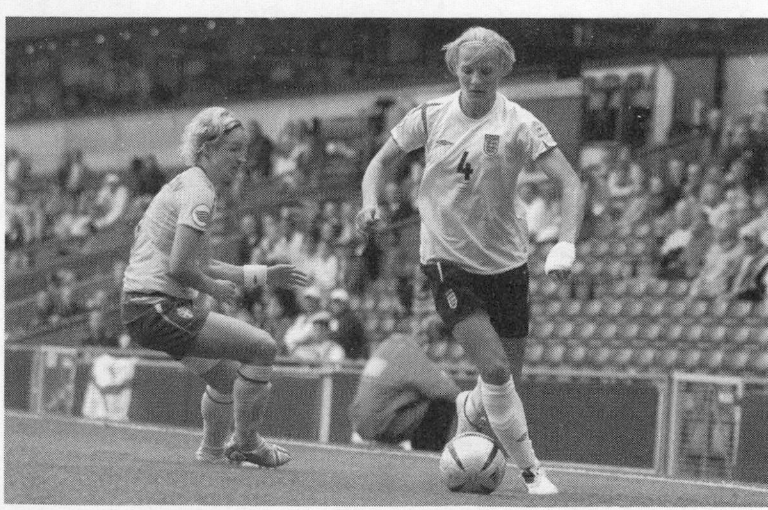

England's Katie Chapman (right) takes on Sweden's Victoria Svensson during the European Championship group match at Ewood Park. (Empics)

UNIBOND LEAGUE 2004–05

PREMIER DIVISION

			Home					Away					Total						
		P	W	D	L	F	A	W	D	L	F	A	W	D	L	F	A	GD	Pts
1	Hyde United*	42	14	6	1	42	18	11	7	3	38	25	25	13	4	80	43	37	88
2	Workington	42	13	3	5	38	15	13	4	4	35	15	26	7	9	73	30	43	85
3	Farsley Celtic	42	11	5	5	37	17	14	3	4	44	24	25	8	9	81	41	40	83
4	Whitby Town	42	14	3	4	37	24	9	8	4	28	25	23	11	8	65	49	16	80
5	Prescot Cables**	42	10	3	8	28	31	11	5	5	35	23	21	8	13	63	54	9	71
6	Burscough	42	11	3	7	57	40	10	4	7	36	34	21	7	14	93	74	19	70
7	Leek Town**	42	8	9	4	32	22	8	6	7	31	30	16	15	11	63	52	11	63
8	Witton Albion	42	10	6	5	29	22	5	11	5	27	22	15	17	10	56	44	12	62
9	Radcliffe Borough*	42	5	10	6	27	30	11	4	6	33	31	16	14	12	60	61	–1	62
10	Guiseley	42	9	7	5	40	33	7	6	8	30	31	16	13	13	70	64	6	61
11	Matlock Town	42	7	7	7	28	29	7	6	8	31	38	14	13	15	59	67	–8	55
12	Blyth Spartans	42	10	4	7	33	25	3	9	9	20	30	13	13	16	53	55	–2	52
13	Wakefield & Emley	42	9	6	6	33	24	5	4	12	27	43	14	10	18	60	67	–7	52
14	Lincoln United*	42	9	0	12	30	33	6	4	11	23	33	15	4	23	53	66	–13	49
15	Marine*	42	5	11	5	32	31	5	7	9	21	29	10	18	14	53	60	–7	48
16	Ossett Town	42	10	4	7	33	26	1	9	11	20	36	11	13	18	53	62	–9	46
17	Gateshead	42	7	9	5	36	35	4	3	14	25	49	11	12	19	61	84	–23	45
18	Frickley Athletic	42	7	6	8	25	29	3	8	10	19	28	10	14	18	44	57	–13	44
19	Bishop Auckland	42	8	3	10	34	33	3	4	14	17	41	11	7	24	51	74	–23	40
20	Bridlington Town*	42	4	10	7	21	24	3	4	14	23	42	7	14	21	44	66	–22	35
21	Bamber Bridge	42	5	4	12	23	41	4	3	14	25	51	9	7	26	48	92	–44	34
22	Spennymoor United (–24)	42	6	5	10	24	26	3	5	13	20	39	9	10	23	44	65	–21	13

**FA ruling on 4/5/05 – 3 points were awarded to Spennymoor United opponents for each unfulfilled fixture.*

DIVISION ONE

			Home					Away					Total						
		P	W	D	L	F	A	W	D	L	F	A	W	D	L	F	A	GD	Pts
1	North Ferriby United	42	14	3	4	44	20	11	5	5	39	29	25	8	9	83	49	34	83
2	Ilkeston Town	42	13	5	3	38	22	11	4	6	26	18	24	9	9	64	40	24	81
3	AFC Telford United	42	11	6	4	35	20	12	5	4	43	24	23	11	8	78	44	34	80
4	Willenhall Town	42	12	5	4	30	21	10	7	4	41	25	22	12	8	71	46	25	78
5	Kendal Town	42	12	5	4	50	26	9	3	9	39	43	21	8	13	89	69	20	71
6	Eastwood Town	42	11	5	5	43	23	9	4	8	30	31	20	9	13	73	54	19	69
7	Mossley	42	11	2	8	38	24	9	4	8	43	32	20	6	16	81	56	25	66
8	Brigg Town	42	9	8	4	34	26	6	11	4	25	20	15	19	8	59	46	13	64
9	Gresley Rovers	42	11	5	5	34	26	6	7	8	23	27	17	12	13	57	53	4	63
10	Kidsgrove Athletic	42	7	9	5	33	29	8	6	7	27	26	15	15	12	60	55	5	60
11	Woodley Sports	42	10	6	5	37	35	6	5	10	31	39	16	11	15	68	74	–6	59
12	Ossett Albion	42	7	7	7	43	41	8	6	7	40	33	15	13	14	83	74	9	58
13	Colwyn Bay	42	9	6	6	28	28	5	7	9	26	34	14	13	15	54	62	–8	55
14	Stocksbridge Park Steels*	42	8	5	8	28	26	7	4	10	30	32	15	9	18	58	58	0	51
15	Shepshed Dynamo	42	8	5	8	37	34	5	6	10	16	41	13	11	18	53	75	–22	50
16	Chorley	42	9	3	9	33	27	4	6	11	29	42	13	9	20	62	69	–7	48
17	Belper Town	42	4	7	10	26	35	9	1	11	31	31	13	8	21	57	66	–9	47
18	Spalding United	42	7	5	9	27	31	6	3	12	30	38	13	8	21	57	69	–12	47
19	Clitheroe	42	7	5	9	28	25	5	5	11	19	32	12	10	20	47	57	–10	46
20	Warrington Town	42	6	7	8	23	31	5	6	10	22	28	11	13	18	45	59	–14	46
21	Rossendale United	42	5	3	13	28	43	5	7	9	36	44	10	10	22	64	87	–23	40
22	Rocester	42	0	3	18	16	68	0	3	18	15	64	0	6	36	31	132	–101	6

**3 points deducted – breach of league rule.*

LEADING GOALSCORERS (in order of League goals)

Premier Division	*Lge*	*Cup*	*Total*
Foster (Radcliffe Borough)	26	7	33
Moseley (Witton Albion)	22	4	26
Barraclough (Matlock Town)	20	5	25
Midwood (Farsley Celtic)	18	4	22
Bett (Farsley Celtic)	18	3	21
Muller (Wakefield & Emley)	18	3	21
Tolson (Hyde United)	17	11	28
Gedman (Burscough)	17	10	27
Ward (Bamber Bridge)	16	10	26
Palmer (Bridlington Town)	16	4	20
Cohen (Workington)	16	2	18
Nazha (Frickley Athletic)	16	2	18

(Includes 10 League and 2 Cup goals for Belper Town).

LEADING GOALSCORERS (in order of League goals)

Division One	*Lge*	*Cup*	*Total*
Daniel Toronczak (Ossett Albion)	33	5	38
Gary Bradshaw (North Ferriby U)	29	7	36
Peter Knox (Eastwood Town)	19	9	28
Kenny Mayers (Kendal Town)	19	7	26
Aaron O'Conner (Gresley Rovers)	15	7	22
Andy Kinsey (Kidsgrove Ath)	14	8	22
Chris Downey (Mossley)	16	5	21
Kyle Perry (AFC Telford United)	19	1	20
Lee Ashcroft (Kendal Town)	18	2	20
Dave Foster (Kendal Town)	15	4	19
Carl Forthergill (Nth Ferriby Utd)	14	5	19
Liam Nimmo (Spalding United)	14	5	19
Calvin Davies (Colwyn Bay)	10	9	19

ATTENDANCES

Premier Division
Highest Attendances:
1301 Hyde United v Workington
899 Workington v Hyde United
804 Workington v Whitby Town

ATTENDANCES

First Division
Highest Attendances:
3774 AFC Telford United v Gresley Rovers*
3740 AFC Telford United v Ilkeston Town
2232 AFC Telford United v Willenhall Town
**First Division record.*

UNIBOND LEAGUE CHALLENGE CUP 2004–05

FIRST ROUND
AFC Telford United 1, Willenhall Town 3
Belper Town 0, Shepshed Dynamo 2
Bishop Auckland 2, Ossett Albion 1
Chorley 5, Woodley Sports 1
Colwyn Bay 1, Warrington Town 4
Kendal Town 5, Rossendale United 2
Kidsgrove Athletic 1, Eastwood Town 2
Mossley 5, Clitheroe 0
North Ferriby United 3, Brigg Town 1
Rocester 1, Gresley Rovers 3
Spalding United 1, Ilkeston Town 2
Stocksbridge Park Steels 0, Ossett Town 2

SECOND ROUND
Bamber Bridge 1, Burscough 2
Bridlington Town 2, Frickley Athletic 1
Chorley 2, Mossley 1
Eastwood Town 2, Willenhall Town 3
Farsley Celtic 3, Gateshead 2
Gresley Rovers 1, Lincoln United 2
Hyde United 3, Kendal Town 1
Leek Town 1, Matlock Town 2
Marine 2, Prescot Cables 1
North Ferriby United 4, Bishop Auckland 1
Shepshed Dynamo 1, Ilkeston Town 2
Spennymoor United 1, Ossett Town 4
Wakefield & Emley 4, Guiseley 0
Tie awarded to Guiseley; Wakefield & Emley fielded an ineligible player.
Warrington Town 3, Radcliffe Borough 4
Whitby Town 1, Blyth Spartans 0
Witton Albion 0, Workington 2

THIRD ROUND
Bridlington Town 0, Hyde United 2
Burscough 3, Radcliffe Borough 2
Farsley Celtic 3, Ossett Town 2
Guiseley 0, Matlock Town 4
North Ferriby United 2, Marine 0
Whitby Town 2, Lincoln United 1
Willenhall Town 3, Chorley 2
Workington 1, Ilkeston Town 3

FOURTH ROUND
Farsley Celtic 1, Willenhall Town 3
Matlock Town 5, Hyde United 0
North Ferriby United 1, Burscough 4
Whitby Town 3, Ilkeston Town 1

SEMI-FINALS
Matlock Town 3, Burscough 3
Matlock Town won 4-2 on penalties.
Whitby Town 2, Willenhall Town 1

FINAL
Matlock Town 2, 3, Whitby Town 2, 1

PRESIDENT'S CUP

FIRST ROUND
Blyth Spartans 2, Gresley Rovers 1
Eastwood Town 1, Leek Town 2
Frickley Athletic 1, Prescot Cables 0
Gateshead 1, Bamber Bridge 2
Kendal Town 1, Bishop Auckland 2
Shepshed Dynamo 2, Spennymoor United 3
Warrington Town 4, Mossley 3
Witton Albion 1, Wakefield & Emley 0

SECOND ROUND
Blyth Spartans 2, Witton Albion 3
Leek Town 4, Bishop Auckland 1
Spennymoor United 4, Frickley Athletic 1
Warrington Town 1, Bamber Bridge 4

SEMI-FINALS
Bamber Bridge 2, Leek Town 1
Witton Albion w.o. v Spennymoor United unable to field a team.

FINAL
Witton Albion 1, 1, Bamber Bridge 1, 2

CHAIRMAN'S CUP

FIRST ROUND
Belper Town 2, Clitheroe 2
Belper Town won 3-1 on penalties.
Ossett Albion 1, Rocester 0
Stocksbridge Park Steels 2, Colwyn Bay 1
Woodley Sports 1, Rossendale United 1
Woodley Sports won 6-5 on penalties.

SECOND ROUND
AFC Telford United 2, Stocksbridge Park Steels 1
Belper Town 0, Brigg Town 1
Ossett Albion 2, Kidsgrove Athletic 3
Woodley Sports 2, Spalding United 1

SEMI-FINALS
AFC Telford United 1, Kidsgrove Athletic 3
Brigg Town 0, Woodley Sports 2

FINAL
Woodley Sports 3, 3, Kidsgrove Athletic 3, 4

UNIBOND PREMIER LEAGUE PLAY-OFFS

SEMI-FINALS
Farsley Celtic 1, Whitby Town 0
Workington 3, Prescot Cables 1

FINAL
Workington 0, Farsley Celtic 0
Workington won 6-5 on penalties.

UNIBOND LEAGUE ONE PROMOTION PLAY-OFFS

SEMI-FINALS
AFC Telford United 1, Eastwood Town 0
Willenhall Town 0, Kendal Town 1

FINAL
AFC Telford United 2, Kendal Town 1

SOUTHERN LEAGUE 2004–05

PREMIER DIVISION

									Home								Away		Total	
		P	W	D	L	F	A	W	D	L	F	A	W	D	L	F	A	GD	Pts
1	Histon	42	13	3	5	45	26	11	3	7	48	31	24	6	12	93	57	36	78
2	Chippenham Town	42	10	5	6	39	30	12	4	5	42	25	22	9	11	81	55	26	75
3	Merthyr Tydfil	42	8	9	4	29	23	11	5	5	33	24	19	14	9	62	47	15	71
4	Hednesford Town	42	12	3	6	36	22	8	7	6	32	18	20	10	12	68	40	28	70
5	Bedford Town	42	13	5	3	39	19	6	7	8	31	33	19	12	11	70	52	18	69
6	Bath City	42	9	6	6	27	23	10	6	5	30	20	19	12	11	57	43	14	69
7	Cirencester Town	42	12	4	5	39	23	7	7	7	24	29	19	11	12	63	52	11	68
8	Tiverton Town	42	13	4	4	48	30	5	9	7	22	25	18	13	11	70	55	15	67
9	Halesowen Town	42	10	5	6	31	23	9	4	8	33	29	19	9	14	64	52	12	66
10	Aylesbury United	42	11	1	9	36	34	9	2	10	31	32	20	3	19	67	66	1	63
11	Kings Lynn	42	12	3	6	49	28	7	1	13	29	41	19	4	19	78	69	9	61
12	Chesham United	42	9	2	10	42	38	9	3	9	42	44	18	5	19	84	82	2	59
13	Grantham Town	42	12	2	7	34	24	5	5	11	23	31	17	7	18	57	55	2	58
14	Team Bath	42	9	5	7	30	35	5	7	9	24	32	14	12	16	54	68	–14	54
15	Gloucester City	42	9	7	5	40	30	3	10	8	23	31	12	17	13	63	61	2	53
16	Rugby United	42	5	9	7	18	20	8	3	10	30	38	13	12	17	48	60	–12	51
17	Banbury United	42	7	7	7	31	32	6	2	13	24	35	13	9	20	56	69	–13	48
18	Hitchin Town	42	6	5	10	24	35	7	4	10	31	42	13	9	20	55	77	–22	48
19	Hemel Hempstead Town*	42	6	6	9	30	40	5	4	12	30	48	11	10	21	60	88	–28	42
20	Dunstable Town	42	8	1	12	31	48	3	5	13	24	49	11	6	25	56	98	–42	39
21	Stamford	42	4	11	6	23	22	2	7	12	17	38	6	18	18	40	60	–20	36
22	Solihull Borough	42	5	3	13	22	39	5	1	15	23	46	10	4	28	45	85	–40	34

**Points deducted for fielding an ineligible player.*

EASTERN DIVISION

				Home			Away					Total			
		P	W	D	L	W	D	L	W	D	L	F	A	GD	Pts
1	Fisher Athletic (London)	42	15	3	3	15	3	3	30	6	6	96	41	55	96
2	East Thurrock United	42	15	5	1	10	7	4	25	12	5	92	38	54	87
3	Maldon Town	42	14	3	4	13	3	5	27	6	9	92	51	41	87
4	Uxbridge	42	16	3	2	10	4	7	26	7	9	87	37	50	85
5	Wivenhoe Town	42	12	6	3	9	5	7	21	11	10	74	49	25	74
6	Barking & East Ham United	42	11	6	4	9	4	8	20	10	12	63	37	26	70
7	Boreham Wood	42	10	3	8	9	6	6	19	9	14	80	61	19	66
8	Barton Rovers	42	12	2	7	8	2	11	20	4	18	76	72	4	64
9	Waltham Forest	42	8	4	9	8	5	8	16	9	17	68	61	7	57
10	Leighton Town	42	6	6	9	7	9	5	13	15	14	57	59	–2	54
11	Chatham Town	42	7	5	9	8	4	9	15	9	18	53	63	–10	54
12	Wingate & Finchley	42	7	5	9	8	3	10	15	8	19	60	75	–15	53
13	Arlesey Town	42	8	6	7	6	4	11	14	10	18	53	67	–14	52
14	Beaconsfield SYCOB	42	8	5	8	4	7	10	12	12	18	54	65	–11	48
15	Harlow Town	42	6	4	11	7	4	10	13	8	21	53	65	–12	47
16	Dartford	42	7	8	6	4	5	12	11	13	18	58	75	–17	46
17	Aveley	42	7	5	9	5	4	12	12	9	21	57	69	–12	45
18	Berkhamsted Town*	42	8	5	8	7	2	12	15	7	20	66	101	–35	45
19	Sittingbourne	42	6	5	10	4	7	10	10	12	20	53	70	–17	42
20	Great Wakering Rovers	42	4	6	11	5	5	11	9	11	22	45	78	–33	38
21	Erith & Belvedere*	42	5	2	14	6	5	10	11	7	24	56	92	–36	37
22	Tilbury	42	3	5	13	3	4	14	6	9	27	41	108	–67	27

** Points deducted for fielding an ineligible player.*

WESTERN DIVISION

				Home			Away					Total			
		P	W	D	L	W	D	L	W	D	L	F	A	GD	Pts
1	Mangotsfield United	42	12	5	4	12	6	3	24	11	7	89	49	40	83
2	Yate Town	42	14	2	5	10	7	4	24	9	9	83	40	43	81
3	Evesham United	42	11	6	4	12	4	5	23	10	9	66	31	35	79
4	Clevedon Town	42	11	5	5	13	1	7	24	6	12	82	49	33	78
5	Bromsgrove Rovers	42	10	7	4	9	8	4	19	15	8	60	42	18	72
6	Ashford Town (Middlesex)	42	10	5	6	7	8	6	17	13	12	63	46	17	64
7	Brackley Town	42	10	5	6	8	5	8	18	10	14	69	53	16	64
8	Paulton Rovers	42	10	4	7	8	3	10	18	7	17	62	61	1	61
9	Burnham	42	8	2	11	9	5	7	17	7	18	64	64	0	58
10	Rothwell Town	42	9	5	7	7	5	9	16	10	16	57	57	0	58
11	Thame United	42	8	4	9	9	2	10	17	6	19	58	69	–11	57
12	Corby Town	42	11	5	5	3	7	11	14	12	16	52	62	–10	54
13	Marlow	42	6	7	8	7	7	7	13	14	15	58	67	–9	53
14	Stourport Swifts	42	9	2	10	6	5	10	15	7	20	62	63	–1	52
15	Bedworth United	42	9	5	7	6	2	13	15	7	20	51	60	–9	52
16	Cinderford Town	42	8	7	6	5	5	11	13	12	17	50	64	–14	51
17	Taunton Town	42	6	5	10	8	3	10	14	8	20	66	75	–9	50
18	Sutton Coldfield Town*	42	11	4	6	5	7	9	16	11	15	54	61	–7	48
19	Swindon Supermarine	42	7	5	9	5	7	9	12	12	18	43	60	–17	48
20	Bracknell Town	42	4	8	9	6	5	10	10	13	19	53	75	–22	43
21	Oxford City	42	3	5	13	8	3	10	11	8	23	49	71	–22	41
22	Egham Town	42	4	3	14	2	1	18	6	4	32	25	97	–72	22

** Points deducted for fielding an ineligible player.*

SOUTHERN LEAGUE ATTENDANCES

Premier Average	400	Division Highest: 1920 Histon v Chippenham Town (30/4/2005)
Eastern Division Average	124	Division Highest: 463 Dartford v East Thurrock United (30/4/2005)
Western Division Average	157	Division Highest: 524 Mangotsfield United v Yate Town (26/3/2005)

SOUTHERN LEAGUE LEADING GOALSCORERS

PREMIER DIVISION

John Lawford (Chesham United)	33
Daniel Bloomfield (King's Lynn)	26
James Mudge (Tiverton Town)	26
Neil Kennedy (Histon)	25
Howard Forinton (Banbury United)	23
Andrew Bell (Hednesford Town)	21
David Gilroy (Chippenham Town)	21
Craig Steins (Merthyr Tydfil)	21
Grant Carney (Hemel Hempstead Town)	20
Christopher Dillon (Bedford Town)	20

DIVISION 1 WEST

Thomas Jacobs (Clevedon Town)	30
Darren Edwards (Yate Town)	26
David Seal (Mangotsfield United)	26
Jack Pitcher (Clevedon Town)	25
Richard Ball (Evesham United)	23
Michael Bartley (Burnham)	22
Paul Szewczyk (Bromsgrove Rovers)	19
Robert Claridge (Mangotsfield United)	18
Jermaine Clarke (Evesham United)	18
Antony Lynch (Taunton Town)	18
Damien Markman (Sutton Coldfield Town)	17

DIVISION 1 EAST

Simon Parker (Maldon Town)	35
Steven Watts (Fisher Athletic)	33
Paul Barnes (Barton Rovers)	32
Vincent John (East Thurrock United)	26
Ian Cooper (Waltham Forest)	23
Hamid Barr (Fisher Athletic)	20
Tostao Kwashi (Dartford)	19
Stafford Browne (Wivenhoe Town)	18
Dewayne Clarke (Waltham Forest)	17
Christopher Dickson (Erith & Belvedere)	17
Nicholas Rugg (Maldon Town)	17

SOUTHERN LEAGUE LEAGUE CUP 2004–05

FIRST ROUND
Boreham Wood 1, Wingate & Finchley 2
Paulton Rovers 2, Cinderford Town 1
Sutton Coldfield Town 3, Bedworth United 1
Bracknell Town 5, Berkhamsted Town 4
Bromsgrove Rovers 1, Stourport Swifts 2
Chatham Town 0, Dartford 1
Clevedon Town 3, Swindon Supermarine 1
Evesham United 2, Taunton Town 1
Leighton Town 2, Barton Rovers 0
Maldon Town 2, Wivenhoe Town 1
Marlow 0, Burnham 1
Oxford City 4, Thame United 2
Rothwell Town 1, Arlesey Town 1
Rothwell Town won 4-2 on penalties.
Sittingbourne 4, Great Wakering Rovers 1
Uxbridge 1, Beaconsfield SYCOB 0
Waltham Forest 3, Erith & Belvedere 1
Yate Town 3, Mangotsfield United 1
Barking & East Ham United 3, Tilbury 1
Ashford Town (Middlesex) 5, Egham Town 0
Aveley 1, Fisher Athletic 3
Brackley Town 3, Corby Town 0
Harlow Town 3, East Thurrock United 4

SECOND ROUND
Sutton Coldfield Town 1, Stourport Swifts 0
Barking & East Ham United 0, East Thurrock United 1
Leighton Town 3, Hemel Hempstead 0
Maldon Town 3, Sittingbourne 1
Oxford City 1, Rothwell Town 2
Waltham Forest 1, Fisher Athletic 2
Wingate & Finchley 5, Dartford 2
Yate Town 2, Evesham United 3
Brackley Town 4, Banbury United 1
Ashford Town (Middlesex) 2, Burnham 1
Clevedon Town 1, Paulton Rovers 2
Uxbridge 1, Bracknell Town 1
Bracknell Town won on penalties.

THIRD ROUND
Bedford Town 3, Dunstable Town 1
Bath City 0, Merthyr Tydfil 1
Chippenham Town 2, Cirencester 1
King's Lynn 4, Grantham Town 0
Aylesbury United 0, Bracknell Town 3
Chesham United 4, Rothwell Town 1
Gloucester City 0, Paulton Rovers 1
Tiverton Town 3, Team Bath 2
Histon 4, Leighton Town 3
Fisher Athletic 2, Ashford Town (Middlesex) 1
Hednesford Town 2, Halesowen Town 3
Sutton Coldfield Town 8, Rugby United 2
East Thurrock United 4, Hitchin Town 1
Stamford 1, Brackley Town 1
Stamford won 4-2 on penalties.
Wingate & Finchley 1, Maldon Town 4
Solihull Borough 2, Evesham United 1

FOURTH ROUND
Stamford 0, King's Lynn 1
Bedford Town 3, Solihull Borough 1
Chippenham Town 4, Tiverton Town 0
Histon 5, Fisher Athletic 1
Sutton Coldfield Town 4, Halesowen Town 0
Chesham United 2, Bracknell Town 1
Maldon Town 3, East Thurrock United 3
Maldon Town won 5-4 on penalties.
Paulton Rovers 1, Merthyr Tydfil 0

FIFTH ROUND
King's Lynn 1, Sutton Coldfield Town 0
Chesham United 0, Bedford Town 2
Paulton Rovers 3, Chippenham Town 2
Histon 3, Maldon Town 2

SEMI-FINALS
Bedford Town 4, Paulton Rovers 1
King's Lynn 2, Histon 1

FINAL FIRST LEG
Bedford Town 2, King's Lynn 2

FINAL SECOND LEG
King's Lynn 1, Bedford Town 0

2003-04 CHAMPIONSHIP MATCH

Crawley Town 2, Moor Green 0

RYMAN LEAGUE 2004–05

PREMIER DIVISION

			Home					Away					Total						
		P	*W*	*D*	*L*	*F*	*A*	*W*	*D*	*L*	*F*	*A*	*W*	*D*	*L*	*F*	*A*	*GD*	*Pts*
1	Yeading	42	12	6	3	38	23	13	5	3	36	25	25	11	6	74	48	26	86
2	Billericay Town	42	13	6	2	36	14	10	5	6	42	26	23	11	8	78	40	38	80
3	Eastleigh	42	12	7	2	44	19	10	6	5	40	30	22	13	7	84	49	35	79
4	Braintree Town	42	11	8	2	35	12	8	9	4	32	21	19	17	6	67	33	34	74
5	Leyton	42	11	3	7	36	33	10	5	6	35	24	21	8	13	71	57	14	71
6	Hampton & Richmond	42	15	4	2	37	21	6	4	11	27	32	21	8	13	64	53	11	71
7	Heybridge Swifts	42	10	4	7	43	29	8	5	8	33	36	18	9	15	76	65	11	63
8	Chelmsford City	42	11	3	7	39	32	6	8	7	24	26	17	11	14	63	58	5	62
9	Staines Town	42	6	8	7	28	28	11	1	9	31	25	17	9	16	59	53	6	60
10	Worthing	42	10	6	5	32	21	6	5	10	18	24	16	11	15	50	45	5	59
11	Hendon	42	9	4	8	21	23	8	3	10	27	37	17	7	18	48	60	–12	58
12	Salisbury City	42	9	5	7	23	23	7	4	10	37	41	16	9	17	60	64	–4	57
13	Slough Town	42	9	4	8	29	32	6	6	9	32	34	15	10	17	61	66	–5	55
14	Folkestone Invicta	42	11	4	6	33	25	3	6	12	18	28	14	10	18	51	53	–2	52
15	Windsor & Eton	42	7	8	6	24	28	5	6	10	24	34	12	14	16	48	62	–14	50
16	Harrow Borough	42	8	5	8	26	31	5	5	11	15	23	13	10	19	41	54	–13	49
17	Northwood	42	9	2	10	27	33	5	5	11	22	33	14	7	21	49	66	–17	49
18	Wealdstone	42	7	4	10	39	42	6	4	11	21	31	13	8	21	60	73	–13	47
19	Cheshunt	42	6	8	7	24	33	6	3	12	34	38	12	11	19	58	71	–13	47
20	Tonbridge Angels	42	8	3	10	30	42	3	7	11	17	31	11	10	21	47	73	–26	43
21	Dover Athletic	42	7	4	10	28	32	3	5	13	22	34	10	9	23	50	66	–16	39
22	Kingstonian	42	2	3	16	13	41	5	2	14	30	52	7	5	30	43	93	–50	26

DIVISION ONE

			Home					Away					Total						
		P	*W*	*D*	*L*	*F*	*A*	*W*	*D*	*L*	*F*	*A*	*W*	*D*	*L*	*F*	*A*	*GD*	*Pts*
1	AFC Wimbledon	42	15	5	1	52	13	14	5	2	39	20	29	10	3	91	33	58	97
2	Walton & Hersham	42	15	3	3	36	13	13	1	7	33	21	28	4	10	69	34	35	88
3	Horsham	42	12	4	5	51	26	12	2	7	39	35	24	6	12	90	61	29	78
4	Bromley	42	11	6	4	41	23	11	3	7	28	21	22	9	11	69	44	25	75
5	Metropolitan Police	42	15	4	2	43	23	7	4	10	29	28	22	8	12	72	51	21	74
6	Cray Wanderers	42	8	9	4	43	29	11	7	3	52	25	19	16	7	95	54	41	73
7	Leatherhead	42	10	6	5	34	24	10	7	4	39	31	20	13	9	73	55	18	73
8	Tooting & Mitcham	42	12	5	4	58	32	6	10	5	34	28	18	15	9	92	60	32	69
9	Whyteleafe	42	12	4	5	29	18	8	2	11	31	41	20	6	16	60	59	1	66
10	Burgess Hill Town	42	12	1	8	42	27	7	5	9	31	35	19	6	17	73	62	11	63
11	Hastings United	42	9	6	6	31	22	6	5	10	24	35	15	11	16	55	57	–2	56
12	Croydon Athletic	42	8	6	7	41	35	5	10	6	25	30	13	16	13	66	65	1	55
13	Corinthian Casuals	42	9	5	7	32	32	6	4	11	24	32	15	9	18	56	64	–8	54
14	Bashley	42	5	7	9	28	34	8	6	7	40	40	13	13	16	68	74	–6	52
15	Dulwich Hamlet	42	7	5	9	34	30	3	9	9	27	34	10	14	18	61	64	–3	44
16	Molesey	42	9	2	10	28	32	3	6	12	18	38	12	8	22	46	70	–24	44
17	Banstead Athletic	42	4	6	11	28	35	6	4	11	22	29	10	10	22	50	64	–14	40
18	Newport IOW	42	5	5	11	22	40	5	5	11	28	48	10	10	22	50	88	–38	40
19	Fleet Town	42	7	3	11	25	38	4	2	15	22	48	11	5	26	47	86	–39	38
20	Ashford Town	42	7	9	5	32	33	1	3	17	15	52	8	12	22	47	85	–38	36
21	Dorking	42	6	6	9	21	35	2	5	14	22	54	8	11	23	43	89	–46	35
22	Croydon	42	3	4	14	23	42	2	6	13	14	49	5	10	27	37	91	–54	25

DIVISION TWO

			Home					Away					Total						
		P	*W*	*D*	*L*	*F*	*A*	*W*	*D*	*L*	*F*	*A*	*W*	*D*	*L*	*F*	*A*	*GD*	*Pts*
1	Ilford	30	13	2	0	35	8	9	1	5	27	15	22	3	5	62	23	39	69
2	Enfield	30	14	1	0	43	12	7	2	6	21	21	21	3	6	64	33	31	66
3	Brook House	30	11	2	2	35	12	9	2	4	30	13	20	4	6	65	25	40	64
4	Hertford Town	30	11	3	1	42	16	6	4	5	23	24	17	7	6	65	40	25	58
5	Witham Town	30	8	2	5	39	27	8	1	6	28	26	16	3	11	67	53	14	51
6	Chertsey Town	30	8	1	6	31	27	7	5	3	24	21	15	6	9	55	48	7	51
7	Abingdon Town	30	9	4	2	39	14	4	5	6	26	28	13	9	8	65	42	23	48
8	Edgware Town	30	7	1	7	20	19	5	2	8	20	22	12	3	15	40	41	–1	39
9	Flackwell Heath	30	5	4	6	28	23	6	1	8	22	32	11	5	14	50	55	–5	38
10	Ware	30	7	4	4	23	23	2	6	7	18	32	9	10	11	41	55	–14	37
11	Chalfont St Peter	30	5	5	5	24	22	4	2	9	17	30	9	7	14	41	52	–11	34
12	Camberley Town	30	6	1	8	15	18	3	4	8	21	26	9	5	16	36	44	–8	32
13	Wembley	30	5	4	6	24	24	3	1	11	17	31	8	5	17	41	55	–14	29
14	Epsom & Ewell	30	6	1	8	24	34	2	3	10	17	30	8	4	18	41	64	–23	28
15	Kingsbury Town	30	3	2	10	17	34	2	2	11	18	42	5	4	21	35	76	–41	19
16	Clapton	30	0	5	10	6	30	3	1	11	14	52	3	6	21	20	82	–62	15

RYMAN LEAGUE PLAY OFFS 2004–05

PLAY-OFF SEMI-FINAL FOR STEP 2
Eastleigh 2, Braintree Town 0
Billericay Town 0, Leyton 2

PLAY-OFF FINAL FOR STEP 2
Eastleigh 2, Leyton 1
Horsham 1, Bromley 3

PLAY-OFF SEMI-FINAL FOR STEP 3
Bromley 1, Metropolitan Police 1
Bromley won 4-3 on penalties.
Horsham 3, Cray Wanderers 1

RYMAN LEAGUE GOALSCORERS

PREMIER DIVISION			*Lge*	*BC*
30	Carl Griffiths	Heybridge Swifts	29	1
26	James Dryden	Folkestone Invicta	24	2
25	Andy Forbes	Eastleigh	23	1
	Includes 1 play-off goal			
24	Matt Murphy	Slough Town	20	4
22	D.J. Campbell	Yeading	22	
21	Leli Bajada	Leyton	20	
	Includes 1 play-off goal			
21	Richard Jolly	Wealdstone	21	
17	Alex Revell	Braintree Town	17	
16	Dean Clark	Northwood	16	
15	Gary Ansell	Chelmsford City	12	3
15	Nathan Elder	Billericay Town	15	

DIVISION ONE			*Lge*	*BC*
32	Stephen Harper	Burgess Hill Town	29	3
30	Jamie Taylor	Horsham	29	1
	Includes 4 League goals for AFC Wimbledon and 2 play-off goals			
30	Mark Tompkins	Bromley	30	
	Includes 23 League goals for Whyteleafe and 1 League goal for Cray Wanderers			
28	John Hastings	Tooting & Mitcham United	28	
27	David Stevens	Leatherhead	23	4
26	Richard Butler	AFC Wimbledon	24	2
26	Richard Gillespie	Bashley	23	3

DIVISION TWO			*Lge*	*BC*	*AMT*
29	Kevin Cooper	Hertford Town	26	1	2
25	Kevin Hawes	Witham Town	21		4
25	Jamie Richards	Enfield	21	2	2
25	Marlon Stuart	Brook House	18	2	5

LEADING ATTENDANCES

PREMIER DIVISION
2390 Dover Athletic v Folkestone Invicta (28/3/2005)
2278 Folkestone Invicta v Dover Athletic (27/12/2004)
1547 Chelmsford City v Billericay Town (28/3/2005)

DIVISION ONE
3358 AFC Wimbledon v Cray Wanderers (23/4/2005)
2637 Tooting & Mitcham United v AFC Wimbledon (16/4/2005)
2536 Dorking v AFC Wimbledon (27/12/2004)

DIVISION TWO
428 Enfield v Hertford Town (28/3/2005)
411 Hertford Town v Enfield (27/12/2004)
250 Edgware Town v Camberley Town (21/8/2004)

AVERAGE PREMIER DIVISION ATTENDANCE
324

HIGHEST AVERAGE ATTENDANCE
Dover Athletic 713

AVERAGE DIVISION ONE ATTENDANCE
364

HIGHEST AVERAGE ATTENDANCE
AFC Wimbledon 2858

HE BRYCO CUP 2004–05

FIRST ROUND
AFC Wimbledon 2, Flackwell Heath 0
Bashley 4, Abingdon Town 0
Brook House 3, Molesey 2
Chalfont St Peter 3, Clapton 4
Chertsey Town 1, Burgess Hill Town 2
Cray Wanderers 5, Camberley Town 1
Croydon Athletic 4, Dorking 1
Dulwich Hamlet 6, Corinthian Casuals 0
Edgware Town 3, Horsham 4
Epsom & Ewell 1, Witham Town 2
Hertford Town 1, Bromley 0
Ilford 1, Kingsbury Town 2
Leatherhead 1, Newport (IW) 0
Metropolitan Police 5, Hastings United 1
Tooting & Mitcham United 2, Ashford Town 1
Walton & Hersham 7, Banstead Athletic 1
Ware 2, Enfield 3
Wembley 0, Croydon 2

SECOND ROUND
Burgess Hill Town 3, Whyteleafe 0
Clapton 0, Walton & Hersham 1
Cray Wanderers 2, Croydon 1
Dulwich Hamlet 4, Croydon Athletic 1
Fleet Town 3, Brook House 0
Horsham 1, AFC Wimbledon 2
Kingsbury Town 3, Enfield 4
Leatherhead 2, Tooting & Mitcham United 0
Metropolitan Police 2, Hertford Town 3
Witham Town 2, Bashley 3

THIRD ROUND
Billericay Town 0, Heybridge Swifts 2
Cray Wanderers 1, Burgess Hill Town 0
Dover Athletic 1, AFC Wimbledon 2
Enfield 1, Bashley 4
Fleet Town 0, Yeading 2
Folkestone Invicta 6, Kingstonian 1
Hampton & Richmond Borough 2, Dulwich Hamlet 1
Harrow Borough 0, Braintree Town 1
Hendon 3, Leatherhead 6
Hertford Town 0, Chelmsford City 1
Salisbury City 2, Leyton 0
Slough Town 1, Cheshunt 0
Walton & Hersham 2, Northwood 1
Wealdstone 3, Tonbridge Angels 0
Windsor & Eton 0, Staines Town 1
Worthing 0, Eastleigh 2

FOURTH ROUND
AFC Wimbledon 3, Cray Wanderers 2
Chelmsford City 2, Wealdstone 1
Eastleigh 1, Hampton & Richmond Borough 2
Folkestone Invicta 2, Bashley 1
Leatherhead 3, Yeading 3
Leatherhead won 4-2 on penalties.
Slough Town 3, Salisbury City 0
Staines Town 0, Heybridge Swifts 1
Walton & Hersham 0, Braintree Town 2

FIFTH ROUND
Chelmsford City 3, Leatherhead 0
Hampton & Richmond Borough 1, Braintree Town 0
Heybridge Swifts 1, Folkestone Invicta 1
Heybridge Swifts won 3-2 on penalties.
Slough Town 4, AFC Wimbledon 2

SEMI-FINAL FIRST LEG
Hampton & Richmond Borough 0, Chelmsford City 0
Heybridge Swifts 1, Slough Town 2

SEMI-FINAL SECOND LEG
Chelmsford City 0, Hampton & Richmond Borough 1
Slough Town 2, Heybridge Swifts 1

FINAL
Hampton & Richmond Borough 1, Slough Town 3

ASSOCIATE MEMBERS TROPHY

GROUP A

	P	W	D	L	F	A	GD	Pts
Enfield	6	4	2	0	19	10	9	14
Witham Town	6	2	2	2	14	17	−3	8
Hertford Town	6	2	1	3	12	10	2	7
Ware	6	1	1	4	6	14	−8	4

GROUP B

	P	W	D	L	F	A	GD	Pts
Flackwell Heath	6	5	1	0	12	5	7	16
Chalfont St Peter	6	3	0	3	10	10	0	9
Abingdon Town	6	2	2	2	8	6	2	8
Wembley	6	0	1	5	2	11	−9	1

GROUP C

	P	W	D	L	F	A	GD	Pts
Brook House	5	5	0	0	12	2	10	15
Chertsey Town	6	3	1	2	10	7	3	10
Epsom & Ewell	5	1	2	2	8	9	−1	5
Camberley Town	6	0	1	5	5	17	−12	1

GROUP D

	P	W	D	L	F	A	GD	Pts
Ilford	6	4	1	1	14	8	6	13
Edgware Town	6	4	0	2	12	6	6	12
Kingsbury Town	5	2	1	2	9	12	−3	7
Clapton	5	0	0	5	4	13	−9	0

QUARTER-FINALS
Enfield 5, Edgware Town 2
Flackwell Heath 2, Chertsey Town 0
Brook House 2, Witham Town 1
Ilford 2, Chalfont St Peter 1

SEMI-FINALS
Enfield 2, Ilford 5
Brook House 1, Flackwell Heath 2

FINAL
Ilford 2, Flackwell Heath 1

THE FA TROPHY 2004–05

IN PARTNERSHIP WITH CARLSBERG

PRELIMINARY ROUND

Clitheroe v Kendal Town	1-4
North Ferriby United v Brigg Town	3-1
Gresley Rovers v Spalding United	4-3
Warrington Town v Ossett Albion	2-3
Kidsgrove Athletic v AFC Telford United	4-2
Belper Town v Rossendale United	3-0
Woodleigh Sports v Ilkeston Town	2-0
Stocksbridge Park Steels v Chorley	3-2
Corinthian Casuals v Banstead Athletic	2-2, 4-5
Cray Wanderers v Aveley	3-1
Horsham v Uxbridge	3-2
Dartford v Leatherhead	5-2
AFC Wimbledon v Metropolitan Police	2-0
Bashley v Ashford Town	2-1
Hastings United v East Thurrock United	0-3
Great Wakering Rovers v Maldon Town	1-0
Barton Rovers v Wivenhoe Town	2-3
Burgess Hill Town v Wingate & Finchley	2-1
Berkhamsted Town v Waltham Forest	1-4
Bromley v Chatham Town	2-1
Barking & East Ham United v Fisher Athletic	2-1
Arlesey Town v Croydon Athletic	2-1
Newport (IW) v Tooting & Mitcham United	0-2
Fleet Town v Tilbury	1-1, 1-2
Erith & Belvedere v Harlow Town	0-2
Beaconsfield SYCOB v Boreham Wood	0-1
Sittingbourne v Leighton Town	2-1
Taunton Town v Marlow	2-1
Corby Town v Brackley Town	1-2
Ashford Town (Middlesex) v Evesham United	2-1
Thame United v Egham Town	4-2
Bromsgrove Rovers v Burnham	1-0
Yate Town v Swindon Supermarine	2-0

FIRST ROUND

Shepshed Dynamo v Willenhall Town	0-1
Rocester v Ossett Town	2-1
Colwyn Bay v Kendal Town	0-1
Bishop Auckland v Kidsgrove Athletic	2-3
Witton Albion v Blyth Spartans	2-3
Altrincham v Ossett Albion	6-1
Hyde United v Belper Town	4-1
Gateshead v Southport	1-1, 1-2
Mossley v Bridlington Town	2-2, 1-4
Woodleigh Sports v Barrow	0-1
Burscough v Guiseley	2-1
Droylsden v Leek Town	1-0
Bradford Park Avenue v North Ferriby United	1-1, 2-2
North Ferriby United won 3-1 on penalties.	
Stalybridge Celtic v Harrogate Town	3-2
Eastwood Town v Worksop Town	1-0
Gresley Rovers v Frickley Athletic	2-1
Vauxhall Motors v Ashton United	2-1
Bamber Bridge v Spennymoor United	0-0, 1-4
Radcliffe Borough v Stocksbridge Park Steels	4-1
Matlock Town v Lancaster City	2-2, 3-4
Alfreton Town v Runcorn FC Halton	2-0
Gainsborough Trinity v Workington	2-1
Wakefield & Emley v Farsley Celtic	2-1
Marine v Whitby Town	1-1, 1-2
Prescot Cables v Lincoln United	1-1, 3-1
Cheshunt v Braintree Town	2-1
Eastbourne Borough v Harrow Borough	3-1
Staines Town v Dover Athletic	2-0
Waltham Forest v East Thurrock United	1-1, 0-1
Hendon v AFC Wimbledon	3-0
Worthing v Whyteleafe	1-0
Wivenhoe Town v Chelmsford City	0-3
Grays Athletic v Great Wakering Rovers	5-1
Tonbridge Angels v Horsham	3-1
Maidenhead United v Bromley	3-4
Bognor Regis Town v Billericay Town	0-1
Cray Wanderers v Folkestone Invicta	2-2, 3-1
Windsor & Eton v Basingstoke Town	4-0
Walton & Hersham v Margate	3-2
Tooting & Mitcham United v Harlow Town	4-1
Leyton v Barking & East Ham United	2-1
Dulwich Hamlet v Havant & Waterlooville	1-1, 0-3
Arlesey Town v Hornchurch	0-1
Northwood v Boreham Wood	1-4
Tilbury v Lewes	1-4
Carshalton Athletic v Heybridge Swifts	4-1
Banstead Athletic v Wealdstone	2-3
Salisbury City v Thurrock	0-4
Kingstonian v Bishop's Stortford	2-3
Hampton & Richmond Borough v Sutton United	1-1, 1-4
Redbridge v Dartford	5-1
Eastleigh v St Albans City	1-2
Yeading v Croydon	6-1
Molesey v Welling United	1-2
Burgess Hill Town v Sittingbourne	1-0
Hayes v Bashley	1-0
Slough Town v Dorking	7-0
Stourport Swifts v Sutton Coldfield Town	0-1
Rothwell Town v Nuneaton Borough	2-1
Mangotsfield United v Ashford Town (Middlesex)	1-0
Chesham United v Bedworth United	1-2
Worcester City v Chippenham Town	3-0
Banbury United v Yate Town	1-1, 1-3
Hucknall Town v Bracknell Town	4-0
Hinckley United v Stafford Rangers	3-1
Paulton Rovers v Dorchester Town	2-3
Cinderford Town v Cambridge City	1-1, 1-3
Dunstable Town v Histon	2-6
Gloucester City v King's Lynn	0-2
Cirencester Town v Thame United	3-2
Team Bath v Hitchin Town	3-0
Oxford City v Brackley Town	4-1
Bromsgrove Rovers v Halesowen Town	2-1
Tiverton Town v Bath City	0-2
Bedford Town v Stamford	2-3
Rugby United v Clevedon Town	2-2, 1-0
Newport County v Kettering Town	0-4
Aylesbury United v Solihull Borough	2-1
Hemel Hempstead Town v Taunton Town	1-3
Weston-Super-Mare v Grantham Town	0-0, 0-1
Moor Green v Weymouth	1-1, 1-2
Redditch United v Merthyr Tydfil	2-1

SECOND ROUND

King's Lynn v Southport	1-3
Stalybridge Celtic v Whitby Town	0-1
Stamford v Rocester	3-1
Droylsden v Spennymoor United	2-4
Kidsgrove Athletic v Vauxhall Motors	1-2
Blyth Spartans v Sutton Coldfield Town	0-3
Gainsborough Trinity v Altrincham	1-1, 0-1
Wakefield & Emley v Redditch United	0-1
Lancaster City v Bromsgrove Rovers	1-0
Kettering Town v Burscough	1-0
Barrow v Rothwell Town	3-1
Hucknall Town v Radcliffe Borough	2-1
Kendal Town v Hyde United	1-1, 2-3
Hinckley United v Willenhall Town	1-2
North Ferriby United v Alfreton Town	1-2
Worcester City v Prescot Cables	2-1
Gresley Rovers v Bedworth United	2-0
Bridlington Town v Eastwood Town	0-0, 0-4
Bath City v Carshalton Athletic	4-2
Staines Town v Aylesbury United	2-3
Chelmsford City v Slough Town	0-1
Welling United v Sutton United	0-1
Redbridge v Weymouth	1-0
Boreham Wood v Leyton	0-1
Tooting & Mitcham United v Hayes	2-2, 1-2
Worthing v Mangotsfield United	1-0
Yeading v Billericay Town	0-4
Thurrock v Burgess Hill Town	6-1
Tonbridge Angels v Oxford City	1-1, 4-2
Eastbourne Borough v Dorchester Town	2-1
East Thurrock United v Histon	0-2
Cambridge City v Hornchurch	1-1, 4-0
Cray Wanderers v St Albans City	2-2, 2-3
Taunton Town v Hendon	0-3
Team Bath v Wealdstone	4-2
Grays Athletic v Windsor & Eton	4-1
Walton & Hersham v Cirencester Town	3-2
Lewes v Bishop's Stortford	1-4
Cheshunt v Bromley	2-1
Havant & Waterlooville v Grantham Town	2-1
Rugby United v Yate Town	0-1

THIRD ROUND

Morecambe v Sutton Coldfield Town	2-1
Southport v Hucknall Town	2-2, 0-1

Eastwood Town v Spennymoor United	3-2
Vauxhall Motors v Lancaster City	1-1, 0-3
Halifax Town v Northwich Victoria	0-1
Barrow v Scarborough	2-1
Burton Albion v York City	3-0
Hyde United v Whitby Town	3-3, 1-0
Leigh RMI v Altrincham	1-2
Hednesford Town v Worcester City	1-0
Tamworth v Gresley Rovers	5-0
Stamford v Willenhall Town	3-1
Carlisle United v Redditch United	3-1
Accrington Stanley v Hereford United	0-0, 0-4
Kettering Town v Alfreton Town	0-0, 1-2
Team Bath v Histon	1-2
Redbridge v Cambridge City	1-5
Bath City v Canvey Island	0-3
Slough Town v Hendon	4-3
Barnet v Farnborough Town	1-0
Leyton v Cheshunt	0-0, 3-0
Dagenham & Redbridge v Bishop's Stortford	1-2
Gravesend & Northfleet v Eastbourne Borough	0-0, 1-0
Forest Green Rovers v Aylesbury United	1-2
Tonbridge Angels v Walton & Hersham	1-1, 1-1
Walton & Hersham won 3-2 on penalties.	
Yate Town v Hayes	1-1, 2-7
Thurrock v Aldershot Town	1-0
Crawley Town v Worthing	3-2
Woking v Stevenage Borough	1-0
Billericay Town v Exeter City	2-2, 0-2
Sutton United v Grays Athletic	0-2
St Albans City v Havant & Waterlooville	0-1

FOURTH ROUND

Gravesend & Northfleet v Histon	2-1
Bishop's Stortford v Leyton	3-0
Grays Athletic v Havant & Waterlooville	5-0
Alfreton Town v Woking	0-3
Northwich Victoria v Hucknall Town	0-1
Altrincham v Barrow	1-0
Aylesbury United v Canvey Island	0-1
Stamford v Walton & Hersham	0-0, 3-3
Stamford won 2-0 on penalties.	
Carlisle United v Barnet	4-1
Cambridge City v Crawley Town	3-3, 2-1
Lancaster City v Morecambe	1-2
Eastwood Town v Hayes	1-0
Slough Town v Thurrock	1-0
Hereford United v Hyde United	3-0
Tamworth v Exeter City	0-3
Burton Albion v Hednesford Town	2-0

FIFTH ROUND

Gravesend & Northfleet v Slough Town	3-2
Burton Albion v Morecambe	1-0
Cambridge City v Hucknall Town	0-1
Eastwood Town v Hereford United	1-1, 2-4
Woking v Carlisle United	1-0
Altrincham v Grays Athletic	2-4
Stamford v Exeter City	0-1
Canvey Island v Bishop's Stortford	2-2, 1-2

SIXTH ROUND

Burton Albion v Woking	1-0
Hereford United v Hucknall Town	2-2, 0-1
Bishop's Stortford v Gravesend & Northfleet	1-1, 3-2
Grays Athletic v Exeter City	4-1

SEMI-FINALS (TWO LEGS)

Bishop's Stortford v Hucknall Town	1-2, 2-3
Grays Athletic v Burton Albion	5-0, 2-0

THE FA TROPHY FINAL

Sunday, 22 May 2005

(at Villa Park)

Grays Athletic (0) 1 *(Martin 64)*

Hucknall Town (0) 1 *(Bacon 77)* 8116

Grays Athletic: Bayes; Brennan, Nutter, Thurgood, Matthews, Stuart, Hooper (Carthy), Martin, Oli (Powell), Battersby (West), Cole.
Hucknall Town: Smith G; Asher, Barrick (Plummer), Palmer (Heathcote), Cooke, Timons, Smith M (Ward), Hunter, Ricketts, Bacon, Todd.

aet; Grays Athletic won 6-5 on penalties.

Referee: P. Dowd (Stoke).

THE FA TROPHY – PREVIOUS WINNERS

Year	*Winners*	*Runners-up*	*Score*
1970	Macclesfield Town	Telford United	2-0
1971	Telford United	Hillingdon Borough	3-2
1972	Stafford Rangers	Barnet	3-0
1973	Scarborough	Wigan Athletic	2-1
1974	Morecambe	Dartford	2-1
1975	Matlock Town	Scarborough	4-0
1976	Scarborough	Stafford Rangers	3-2
1977	Scarborough	Dagenham	2-1
1978	Altrincham	Leatherhead	3-1
1979	Stafford Rangers	Kettering Town	2-0
1980	Dagenham	Mossley	2-1
1981	Bishop's Stortford	Sutton United	1-0
1982	Enfield	Altrincham	1-0
1983	Telford United	Northwich Victoria	2-0
1984	Northwich Victoria	Bangor City	1-1
	Replay		2-1
1985	Wealdstone	Boston United	2-1
1986	Altrincham	Runcorn	1-0
1987	Kidderminster Harriers	Burton Albion	0-0
	Replay		2-1
1988	Enfield	Telford United	0-0
	Replay		3-2
1989	Telford United	Macclesfield Town	1-0
1990	Barrow	Leek Town	3-0
1991	Wycombe Wanderers	Kidderminster Harriers	2-1
1992	Colchester United	Witton Albion	3-1
1993	Wycombe Wanderers	Runcorn	4-1
1994	Woking	Runcorn	2-1
1995	Woking	Kidderminster Harriers	2-1
1996	Macclesfield Town	Northwich Victoria	3-1
1997	Woking	Dagenham & Redbridge	1-0
1998	Cheltenham Town	Southport	1-0
1999	Kingstonian	Forest Green Rovers	1-0
2000	Kingstonian	Kettering Town	3-2
2001	Canvey Island	Forest Green Rovers	1-0
2002	Yeovil Town	Stevenage Borough	2-0
2003	Burscough	Tamworth	2-1
2004	Hednesford Town	Canvey Island	3-2

THE FA VASE – PREVIOUS WINNERS

Year	*Winners*	*Runners-up*	*Score*
1975	Hoddesdon Town	Epsom & Ewell	2-1
1976	Billericay Town	Stamford	1-0
1977	Billericay Town	Sheffield	1-1
	Replay		2-1
1978	Blue Star	Barton Rovers	2-1
1979	Billericay Town	Almondsbury Greenway	4-1
1980	Stamford	Guisborough Town	2-0
1981	Wickham	Willenhall Town	3-2
1982	Forest Green Rovers	Rainworth MW	3-0
1983	VS Rugby	Halesowen Town	1-0
1984	Stansted	Stamford	3-2
1985	Halesowen Town	Fleetwood Town	3-1
1986	Halesowen Town	Southall	3-0
1987	St Helens Town	Warrington Town	3-2
1988	Colne Dynamoes	Emley	1-0
1989	Tamworth	Sudbury Town	1-1
	Replay		3-0
1990	Yeading	Bridlington Town	0-0
	Replay		1-0
1991	Guiseley	Gresley Rovers	4-4
	Replay		3-1
1992	Wimborne Town	Guiseley	5-3
1993	Bridlington Town	Tiverton Town	1-0
1994	Diss Town	Taunton Town	2-1
1995	Arlesey Town	Oxford City	2-1
1996	Brigg Town	Clitheroe	3-0
1997	Whitby Town	North Ferriby United	3-0
1998	Tiverton Town	Tow Law Town	1-0
1999	Tiverton Town	Bedlington Terriers	1-0
2000	Deal Town	Chippenham Town	1-0
2001	Taunton Town	Berkhamsted Town	2-1
2002	Whitley Bay	Tiptree United	1-0
2003	Brigg Town	AFC Sudbury	2-1
2004	Winchester City	AFC Sudbury	2-0

THE FA VASE 2004–05

IN PARTNERSHIP WITH CARLSBERG

FIRST QUALIFYING ROUND

Great Harwood Town v New Mills	3-2
Squires Gate v Norton & Stockton Ancients	0-1
Brodsworth MW v Oldham Town	4-3
Selby Town v Winterton Rangers	2-0
Ryton v Abbey Hey	3-2
Murton v St Helens Town	0-2
Worsbrough Bridge MW v Yorkshire Amateur	1-3
Ramsbottom United v Shotton Comrades	6-1
North Shields v Hebburn Town	4-1
West Auckland Town v Chester-le-Street Town	1-3
Paulton Victoria v Padiham	1-1, 1-2
Armthorpe Welfare v Blackpool Mechanics	2-0
Darwen v Horden CW	0-2
Wretford United v Castleton Gabriels	1-1, 3-0
Thackley v Maine Road	1-0
Atherton Collieries v Alsager Town	0-3
Loughborough Dynamo v Romulus	5-2
Pershore Town v Coventry Sphinx	2-4
Wellington v Cradley Town	0-2
Arnold Town v Deeping Rangers	2-1
Lye Town v Boston Town	0-1
Sandiacre Town v Blackstones	2-4
Holbrook MW v Coalville Town	2-1
Shifnal Town v South Normanton Athletic	2-0
Newark Town v Bromyard Town	0-1
Lincoln Moorlands v Newcastle Town	2-3
Ford Sports Daventry v Quorn	2-6
Heanor Town v Coventry Marconi	3-2
Friar Lane & Epworth v Shawbury United	2-1
West Midlands Police v Malvern Town	1-3
Oldbury United v Bolehall Swifts	4-2
Alvechurch v Stapenhill	2-0
Oxhey Jets v Bedford United & Valerio	1-0
Yaxley v Newport Pagnell Town	3-1
Needham Market v Fakenham Town	3-2
Woodbridge Town v Leiston	2-1
Welwyn Garden City v Cogenhoe United	1-5
Enfield Town v St Ives Town	2-0
Stanway Rovers v Diss Town	0-4
Long Buckby v Halstead Town	0-3
Gorleston v Ruislip Manor	0-0, 3-2
Rothwell Corinthians v Witton United	0-5
Holmer Green v Potters Bar Town	1-5
Wootton Blue Cross v Cockfosters	3-3, 2-0
Clacton Town v Henley Town	3-2
Woodford United v Norwich United	1-0
Felixstowe & Walton United v Flackwell Heath	0-2
Wisbech Town v Tiptree United	2-3
Haringey Borough v Langford	1-0
Oakwood v Herne Bay	5-2
Raynes Park Vale v AFC Totton	0-1
Petersfield Town v East Grinstead Town	0-0, 2-0
Southwick v Broadbridge Heath	3-2
Ramsgate w.o. v Withdean 2000 withdrew	
Horley Town v Chessington & Hook United	5-4
Whitchurch United v Sidlesham	1-2
Abingdon Town v Horsham YMCA	2-0
Lancing v Arundel	1-4
Hillingdon Borough v Steyning Town	6-1
Eastbourne United v Selsey	1-0
Walton Casuals v Shoreham	2-3
Haywards Heath Town v Three Bridges	1-6
Ringmer v Cove	10-0
Maidstone United v Godalming & Guildford	3-1
Tunbridge Wells v Camberley Town	3-1
Street v Melksham Town	2-0
Wellington Town v Wootton Bassett Town	4-0
Willand Rovers v Harrow Hill	4-0
Brislington v Tuffley Rovers	1-0
Fairford Town v Falmouth Town	2-0
Wadebridge Town v Corsham Town	0-2
Ottery St Mary v Hallen	1-2
Witney United v Budleigh Salterton	2-0
Larkhall Athletic v Highworth Town	2-3
Tavistock v Ilfracombe Town	7-2

SECOND QUALIFYING ROUND

Winsford United v Marske United	3-4
North Shields v Thackley	1-3
Morpeth Town v Liversedge	3-1
Chadderton v Seaham Red Star	1-5
Parkgate v Curzon Ashton	0-2
Newcastle Benfield Saints v Ramsbottom United	1-1, 1-2
Evenwood Town v Consett	1-2
Holker Old Boys v Whickham	0-1
Peterlee Newtown v Clipstone Welfare	2-1
Washington v Brandon United	4-2
Tadcaster Albion v Formby	2-1
Cammell Laird v Garforth Town	3-1
Skelmersdale United v Brodsworth MW	6-4
Pontefract Collieries v Prudhoe Town	0-3
Glasshoughton Welfare v Pickering Town	1-1, 2-3
Wretford United v South Shields	3-1
Ryton v Flixton	5-2
Northallerton Town v Crook Town	0-2
Selby Town v Alnwick Town	2-0
Thornaby v Chester-le-Street Town	3-2
Washington Nissan v Whitley Bay	1-6
Atherton LR v Horden CW	3-4
Sheffield v Rossington Main	4-1
Padiham v Maltby Main	1-2
Penrith v Norton & Stockton Ancients	2-0
Armthorpe Welfare v Esh Winning	0-1
Salford City v Willington	3-0
Goole v Guisborough Town	0-2
Jarrow Roofing Boldon CA v Nelson	5-1
Trafford v Yorkshire Amateur	2-2, 1-2
Bacup Borough v Tow Law Town	6-3
Silsden v Harrogate Railway	3-1
Shildon v Ashington	3-2
Newcastle Blue Star v Easington Colliery	0-0, 1-1
Newcastle Blue Star won 5-3 on penalties.	
Hall Road Rangers v Great Harwood Town	1-2
Eccleshill United v Alsager Town	2-1
Kennek Ryehope CA v St Helens Town	0-5
Cheadle Town v Hallam	1-1, 2-4
Harrowby United v Ibstock Welfare	2-1
Causeway United v Blidworth Welfare	1-0
Meir KA v Staveley MW	2-3
Heath Hayes v Malvern Town	1-2
Racing Club Warwick v Ludlow Town	1-2
Mickleover Sports v Shirebrook Town	5-1
Boldmere St Michaels v Biddulph Victoria	2-3
Rolls Royce Leisure v Carlton Town	0-2
Pelsall Villa v Barrow Town	2-3
Kirby Muxloe v Eccleshall	3-2
Glapwell v Dunkirk	2-1
Blackstones v Friar Lane & Epworth	1-5
Castle Vale v Westfields	3-5
Borrowash Victoria v Birstall United	0-1
Kimberley Town v Shifnal Town	3-0
Stourbridge v Coleshill Town	4-1
Quorn v Tivedale	4-1
Loughborough Dynamo v Downes Sports	3-0
Dudley Town v Leek CSOB	4-0
Chasetown v Oldbury United	0-2
Heanor Town v Wednesfield	9-0
Bourne Town v Bromyard Town	2-1
Teversal v Highgate United	1-2
St Andrews v Alvechurch	0-1
Bridgnorth Town v Brierly & Hagley	2-0
Ellistown v Long Eaton United	2-3
Boston Town v Daventry Town	7-0
Buxton v Rushall Olympic	1-0
Arnold Town v Holbeach United	0-1
Tipton Town v Anstay Nomads	6-2
Blackwell MW v Graham St Prims	4-3
Barwell v Cradley Town	4-3
Coventry Sphinx v Gornal Athletic	2-1
Norton United v Holwell Sports	1-2
Rainworth MW v Pegasus Juniors	1-0
Nettleham v Barnt Green Spartak	1-2
Nuneaton Griff v Ledbury Town	0-2
Newcastle Town v Blabey & Whetstone Athletic	4-0
Holbrook MW v Glossop North End	2-3
Sutton Town v Highfield Rangers	3-1
Oxhey Jets v Royston Town	0-1
Flackwell Heath v Bicester Town	5-0
Northampton Spencer v Godmanchester Rovers	1-3
Hadleigh United v Stotfold	0-5
Downham Town v Haverhill Rovers	1-7
Ely City v Eton Manor	0-2
Potters Bar Town v Brimsdown Rovers	1-0
Potton United v Woodbridge Town	3-1
Great Yarmouth Town v Bury Town	0-1

Kingsbury Town v Cornard United	3-1
Thetford Town v Waltham Abbey	1-4
Hullbridge Sports v North Greenford United	0-4
Colney Heath v Soham Town Rangers	0-6
Haringey Borough v London Colney	2-3
Harwich & Parkeston v Gorleston	1-0
Tring Athletic v Clacton Town	2-3
Biggleswade United v Burnham Ramblers	2-2, 1-2
Stowmarket Town v Edgware Town	2-3
Southall v Sporting Bengal United	1-3
Eynesbury Rovers v Tiptree United	2-3
Sileby Rangers removed v Stansted w.o.	
Lowestoft Town v Bugbrooke St Michaels	10-1
Haywood United v Halstead Town	1-2
Enfield Town v Chalfont St Peter	3-1
Saffron Walden Town v Kirkley	1-2
Romford v Biggleswade Town	2-0
Broxbourne Borough V&E w.o. v Greenacres (Hemel Hempstead) withdrew	
Ipswich Wanderers v Arlesey Athletic	5-0
Leverstock Green v Wootton Blue Cross	3-2
Brentwood Town v Harpenden Town	2-1
Long Melford v Raunds Town	2-0
March Town United v Needham Market	1-0
Diss Town v Cogenhoe United	4-2
Woodford United v Yaxley	1-1, 2-1
Bowers & Pitsea v Harefield United	1-3
Dereham Town v Hoddesdon Town	0-3
Southend Manor v Clapton	1-0
Mildenhall Town v Ware	5-0
Witton United v London APSA	6-2
Hanwell Town v AFC Kempston Rovers	9-0
Newmarket Town v Barkingside	1-0
Wembley v Witham Town	1-2
Andover New Street v Alton Town	0-1
Westfield v Brockenhurst	0-3
Cobham v Tunbridge Wells	1-3
Abingdon Town v Farnham Town	5-0
Three Bridges v Littlehampton Town	1-0
Maidstone United v AFC Totton	4-0
Hamble ASSC v Slade Green	0-1
Blackfield & Langley v Milton United	2-3
Erith Town v Horley Town	2-1
Mile Oak v United Services Portsmouth	3-1
Hythe Town v Whitstable Town	3-4
Chessington United v Oakwood	3-4
Abingdon United v Arundel	3-2
Bedfont v Cowes Sports	0-2
Sevenoaks Town v Deal Town	1-2
Eastbourne United v Whitehawk	0-1
Hartley Wintney v Petersfield Town	1-2
AFC Newbury v Redhill	5-2
Merstham v Wick	0-3
Wantage Town v Ramsgate	1-2
Moneyfields v Sidley United	4-1
Chipstead v Pagham	3-5
BAT Sports v Shoreham	4-0
Saltdean United v Greenwich Borough	1-2
Hailsham Town v Eastbourne Town	2-1
Sandhurst Town v Ash United	2-0
Frimley Green v Hungerford Town	2-5
Lordswood v Sidlesham	4-3
Ringmer v Fareham Town	0-2
Lymington Town v Thatcham Town	3-1
Hillingdon Borough v Southwick	6-1
Didcot Town v Carterton	2-1
Peacehaven & Telscombe v Hassocks	0-2
Westbury United v Elmore	4-3
Ringwood Town v Bodmin Town	0-3
Barnstaple Town v Dawlish Town	1-1, 1-3
Porthleven v Street	2-6
Bridgwater Town v Highworth Town	2-0
Chipping Norton Town v Saltash United	2-1
Newquay v Devizes Town	1-2
Hallen v Fairford Town	3-1
Bishop Sutton v Clevedon United	1-2
Amesbury Town v Minehead	4-1
Launceston v Almondsbury Town	6-1
Willand Rovers v Portland United	3-1
Tavistock v Brislington	0-2
Millbrook v Exmouth Town	1-2
Cullompton Rangers v Pewsey Vale	2-0
Bridport v Bemerton Heath Harlequins	2-2, 0-3
Christchurch v Penzance	3-2
Bournemouth v Hamworthy United	1-0
Shepton Mallet v Shortwood United	2-1
Slimbridge v Odd Down	2-2, 1-0
Welton Rovers v Newton Abbott	1-0
Bristol Manor Farm v Liskeard Athletic	3-4
Corsham Town v Calne Town	4-0
Chard Town v Backwell United	1-4
Downton v Wellington Town	0-1
Malmesbury Victoria v Witney United	1-2

FIRST ROUND

St Helens Town v Hallam	6-2
Eccleshill United v Esh Winning	1-4
Whitley Bay v Newcastle Blue Star	3-1
Pickering Town v Sheffield	2-1
Durham City v Maltby Main	3-1
Thornaby v Great Harwood Town	1-0
Yorkshire Amateur v Marske United	2-0
Jarrow Roofing Boldon CA v Morpeth Town	4-1
Ramsbottom United v Consett	3-0
Whickham v Dunston FB	0-2
Curzon Ashton v Washington	4-3
Shildon v Bedlington Terriers	0-1
Penrith v Salford City	0-2
Silsden v Tadcaster Albion	2-1
Guisborough Town v Bacup Borough	3-2
Wretford United v Cammell Laird	0-6
Seaham Red Star v Selby Town	2-1
Crook Town v Horden CW	1-2
Ryton v Skelmersdale United	1-3
Prudhoe Town v Thackley	0-5
Peterlee Newtown v Fleetwood Town	1-3
Carlton Town v Kirby Muxloe	4-1
Coventry Sphinx v Ludlow Town	1-1, 4-0
Stourbridge v Bourne Town	4-1
Newcastle Town v Buxton	2-0
Ledbury Town v Biddulph Victoria	4-1
Quorn v Heanor Town	3-0
Malvern Town v Staveley MW	4-1
Highgate United v Birstall United	2-0
Barwell v Glossop North End	0-2
Causeway United v Bridgnorth Town	2-0
Blackwell MW v Holbeach United	0-2
Westfields v Long Eaton United	1-2
Rainworth MW v Friar Lane & Epworth	0-1
Barrow Town v Barnt Green Spartak	2-4
Loughborough Dynamo v Harrowby United	5-3
Glapwell v Oldbury United	1-2
Alvechurch v Buckingham Town	0-0, 4-2
Sutton Town v Stratford Town	3-0
Tipton Town v Holwell Sports	1-0
Boston Town v Dudley Town	5-2
Mickleover Sports v Kimberley Town	6-1
Bury Town v Leverstock Green	4-3
Hoddesdon Town v Kirkley	2-2, 2-3
Brentwood Town v Harwich & Parkeston	0-2
Haverhill Rovers v Brook House	2-4
Edgware Town v Waltham Abbey	2-1
Hertford Town v Long Melford	2-3
North Greenford United v Stotfold	0-2
Eton Manor v March Town United	2-2, 1-1
Eton Manor won 5-4 on penalties.	
Tiptree United v Sawbridgeworth Town	2-2, 1-2
Flackwell Heath v London Colney	2-4
Lowestoft Town v Witham Town	3-1
Southend Manor v Potton United	1-2
Kingsbury Town v Romford	4-3
Mildenhall Town v Godmanchester Rovers	6-0
Hanwell Town v Ilford	3-5
Enfield v Halstead Town	2-1
St Margaretsbury v Broxbourne Borough V&E	0-2
Enfield Town v Diss Town	2-1
Potters Bar Town v Witton United	6-1
Woodford United v Stansted	2-1
Burnham Ramblers v Harefield United	0-1
Ipswich Wanderers v Sporting Bengal United	0-2
Clacton Town v Newmarket Town	3-1
Soham Town Rangers v Royston Town	5-0
Deal Town v Petersfield Town	3-1
Hassocks v Witney United	3-4
Sandhurst Town v Reading Town	1-0
Oakwood v Alton Town	2-4
Wick v VCD Athletic	1-4
Milton United v Whitehawk	2-1
Brockenhurst v Thamesmead Town	0-3
Lymington Town v Mile Oak	3-1
Fareham Town v Moneyfields	3-1
Slade Green v Abingdon Town	1-3
Ramsgate v Chichester City United	4-1
Hailsham Town v Three Bridges	0-3
Maidstone United v Whitstable Town	4-1
Cowes Sports v Hungerford Town	2-1
Erith Town v BAT Sports	3-1
Lordswood v Hillingdon Borough	1-2

Pagham v Tunbridge Wells	1-3
Greenwich Borough v Rye & Iden United	3-2
AFC Wallingford v AFC Newbury	0-7
Didcot Town v Abingdon United	1-0
Epsom & Ewell v East Preston	2-3
Cullompton Rangers v Wimborne Town	0-4
Frome Town v Hallen	2-0
Willand Rovers v Devizes Town	4-4, 1-2
Dawlish Town v Bodmin Town	0-5
Wellington Town v Chipping Norton Town	1-2
Brislington v Bishop's Cleeve	3-0
Clevedon United v Slimbridge	3-6
Amesbury Town v Bridgwater Town	0-3
Shepton Mallet v Bournemouth	0-3
Westbury United v Exmouth Town	1-3
Launceston v Welton Rovers	1-1
Tie awarded to Welton Rovers; Launceston removed for fielding a suspended player.	
Liskeard Athletic v Street	4-3
Backwell United v Corsham Town	2-1
Christchurch v Bemerton Heath Harlequins	4-0

SECOND ROUND

Colne v Congleton Town	5-0
Dunston FB v Pickering Town	2-4
Curzon Ashton v Guisborough Town	2-3
Horden CW v Salford City	1-2
Esh Winning v West Allotment Celtic	1-2
Thornaby v Billingham Town	0-2
Seaham Red Star v Durham City	2-4
Fleetwood Town v St Helens Town	2-3
Skelmersdale United v Ramsbottom United	3-0
Bedlington Terriers v Silsden	1-0
Thackley v Whitley Bay	3-1
Jarrow Roofing Boldon CA v Cammell Laird	3-1
Yorkshire Amateur v Billingham Synthonia	3-3, 0-4
Barnt Green Spartak v Studley	0-4
Malvern Town v Coventry Sphinx	4-3
Oldbury United v Friar Lane & Epworth	3-0
Loughborough Dynamo v Leamington	1-1, 0-3
Tipton Town v Newcastle Town	2-1
Stourbridge v Highgate United	5-0
Quorn v Glossop North End	1-1, 3-1
Gedling Town v Nantwich Town	3-0
Holbeach United v Alvechurch	2-1
Boston Town v Mickleover Sports	0-1
Carlton Town v Desborough Town	0-3
Oadby Town v Long Eaton United	3-1
Stone Dominoes v Causeway United	3-2
Ledbury Town v Sutton Town	2-0
Stotfold v AFC Sudbury	0-1
Long Melford v Harwich & Parkeston	3-2
St Neots Town v Potters Bar Town	3-2
Edgware Town v Potton United	1-4
Enfield Town v London Colney	2-0
Wroxham v Kirkley	4-2
Ilford v Bury Town	1-2
Woodford United v Eton Manor	2-0
Lowestoft Town v Mildenhall Town	3-2
Kingsbury Town v Broxbourne Borough V&E	3-2
Soham Town Rangers v Sporting Bengal United	5-1
Clacton Town v Harefield United	1-1, 1-3
Brook House v Sawbridgeworth Town	2-1
Enfield v Concord Rangers	5-0
Cowes Sports v Hillingdon Borough	1-2
Alton Town v Winchester City	2-6
East Preston v Didcot Town	0-4
Sandhurst Town v Milton United	3-1
Thamesmead Town v Maidstone United	2-1
AFC Newbury v North Leigh	2-1
Gosport Borough v VCD Athletic	3-2
Tunbridge Wells v Erith Town	4-3
Deal Town v Witney United	1-0
Ramsgate v Greenwich Borough	2-2, 2-0
Andover v Fareham Town	0-1
Three Bridges v Chertsey Town	4-4, 1-2
Lymington Town v Abingdon Town	0-1
Frome Town v Devizes Town	3-1
Bournemouth v Lymington & New Milton	1-3
Bitton v Christchurch	3-3, 1-0
Slimbridge v Chipping Norton Town	4-0
Bridgwater Town v Liskeard Athletic	3-3, 4-1
Backwell United v Wimborne Town	4-0
Bideford v Bodmin Town	0-1
Welton Rovers v Exmouth Town	1-2
Brislington v Torrington	3-0
St Blazey v Keynsham Town	6-0

THIRD ROUND

Oldbury United v Gedling Town	1-2
Malvern Town v Skelmersdale United	1-3
Ledbury Town v Studley	3-1
Stourbridge v Oadby Town	1-0
Salford City v West Allotment Celtic	1-2
Holbeach United v Thackley	2-4
Leamington v Bedlington Terriers	2-3
Billingham Town v St Helens Town	4-3
Quorn v Mickleover Sports	2-1
Colne v Stone Dominoes	1-1, 1-0
Guisborough Town v Jarrow Roofing Boldon CA	1-2
Billingham Synthonia v Pickering Town	2-3
Tipton Town v Durham City	2-1
Thamesmead Town v Winchester City	1-3
Abingdon Town v Desborough Town	0-2
Harefield United v AFC Sudbury	1-3
Lymington & New Milton v Wroxham	4-1
Kingsbury Town v Frome Town	1-2
Lowestoft Town v Chertsey Town	5-1
Bury Town v Tunbridge Wells	1-0
Deal Town v Fareham Town	1-0
Bodmin Town v Hillingdon Borough	5-1
St Neots Town v Soham Town Rangers	3-4
Bitton v Ramsgate	2-0
Gosport Borough v Didcot Town	0-1
Potton United v St Blazey	2-1
Enfield v Enfield Town	1-0
Backwell United v Slimbridge	2-1
Bridgwater Town v Exmouth Town	2-1
Brislington v Woodford United	1-0
Long Melford v Brook House	0-0, 0-3
AFC Newbury v Sandhurst Town	2-0
after abandoned game due to fog 2-3.	

FOURTH ROUND

Bridgwater Town v Winchester City	2-0
Didcot Town v Ledbury Town	2-0
Bury Town v Potton United	2-1
Stourbridge v Desborough Town	1-0
Bodmin Town v Colne	2-3
Billingham Town v Lymington & New Milton	1-3
Jarrow Roofing Boldon CA v Deal Town	3-0
Bitton v Bedlington Terriers	1-2
Skelmersdale United v Frome Town	0-2
Tipton Town v Gedling Town	3-0
Backwell United v Lowestoft Town	0-0, 3-0
Enfield v Brislington	1-0
AFC Newbury v Thackley	1-0
West Allotment Celtic v Soham Town Rangers	1-3
Pickering Town v Brook House	1-3
Quorn v AFC Sudbury	2-3

FIFTH ROUND

Jarrow Roofing Boldon CA v Tipton Town	1-1, 1-1
Jarrow Roofing Boldon CA won 4-2 on penalties.	
Enfield v Bedlington Terriers	0-3
Frome Town v Brook House	3-0
Bury Town v Lymington & New Milton	3-2
Colne v Didcot Town	2-3
Soham Town Rangers v AFC Newbury	0-1
Bridgwater Town v AFC Sudbury	0-4
Backwell United v Stourbridge	1-2

SIXTH ROUND

Jarrow Roofing Boldon CA v Frome Town	3-0
Bedlington Terriers v AFC Newbury	2-1
AFC Sudbury v Stourbridge	4-1
Didcot Town v Bury Town	2-1

SEMI-FINAL (TWO LEGS)

Didcot Town v Jarrow Roofing Boldon CA	1-0, 1-0
AFC Sudbury v Bedlington Terriers	2-1, 1-2
AFC Sudbury won 5-4 on penalties.	

THE FA VASE FINAL

Saturday, 14 May 2005

(at White Hart Lane, Tottenham Hotspur FC)

AFC Sudbury (0) 2 *(Wardley 65, Calver 90 (pen))*

Didcot Town (0) 3 *(Beavon 55, 89, Wardley 68 (og))* 8862

AFC Sudbury: Greygoose; Girling, Wardley, Bennett, Hyde (Hayes 78), Owen (Norfolk 64), Claydon (Banya 57), Head, Calver, Betson, Rayner.

Didcot Town: Webb; Goodall, Heapy, Campbell, Green, Parrott, Hannigan, Ward, Concannon (Jones 88), Beavon (Bianchini 90), Powell.

Referee: R. Beeby (Northamptonshire).

THE FA YOUTH CUP 2004–05

IN PARTNERSHIP WITH PEPSI

PRELIMINARY ROUND

Leigh RMI v Barrow 2-2
Barrow won 5-4 on penalties.
Burscough v Willington 5-1
Vauxhall Motors v Ossett Albion 2-2
Ossett Albion won 3-2 on penalties.
Warrington Town v Farsley Celtic 1-4
Hallam v Selby Town 2-3
Lancaster City v Carlisle United 2-7
Moor Green v Chasetown 2-1
Kimberley Town v Deeping Rangers 4-2
Nuneaton Griff v Leek Town 1-3
Barton Rovers w.o. v Wingate & Finchley withdrew
Romford v Brentwood Town 2-1
Hoddesdon Town v Bishop's Stortford 5-0
Histon v Tring Athletic 3-2
Clacton Town v Aylesbury United 1-5
Brook House v Long Buckby 3-1
Haringey Borough v Stansted 2-1
Cogenhoe United v Harlow Town 5-1
Ruislip Manor v Billericay Town 1-3
Marlow v Stotfold 0-5
Woodbridge Town v Thame United 2-3
Witham Town v Chelmsford City 3-1
Bedford Town v Sawbridgeworth Town 8-0
East Thurrock United v Hemel Hempstead Town 4-6
North Greenford United v Newport Pagnell Town 2-2
North Greenford United won 5-4 on penalties.
Reading Town v Thatcham Town 3-3
Reading Town won 3-1 on penalties.
Abingdon United withdrew v Mile Oak w.o.
Crawley Town v Erith & Belvedere 2-0
Sittingbourne withdrew v Brockenhurst w.o.
Epsom & Ewell v Thamesmead Town 2-2
Epsom & Ewell won 5-4 on penalties.
Peacehaven & Telscombe v East Grinstead Town 3-1
Dartford v Steyning Town 4-0
Walton Casuals v Bracknell Town 2-0
Fisher Athletic v Herne Bay 3-2
Malmsbury Victoria v Bridgwater Town 1-5
Wootton Bassett Town v Brislington 2-2
Wootton Bassett Town won 4-0 on penalties.
Gloucester City v Weymouth 0-2
Worcester City v Newport County 3-4
Salisbury City v Clevedon Town 9-1

FIRST QUALIFYING ROUND

Scarborough v Guisley 5-2
Halifax Town v Whitley Bay 1-2
Worksop Town v Burscough 1-4
Wakefield & Emley v Bradford Park Avenue 9-0
Goole v Frickley Athletic 0-1
Pickering Town v Ossett Albion 2-2
Ossett Albion won 5-4 on penalties.
Seaham Red Star withdrew v Wretford United w.o.
Altrincham v Southport 2-3
Stocksbridge Park Steels v Stalybridge Celtic 1-2
Carlisle United v Trafford 5-0
Radcliffe Borough v Thackley 1-3
Witton Albion v Workington 1-4
Marine v Curzon Ashton 1-0
Pontefract Collieries v Selby Town 0-3
Wrighton v North Ferriby United 2-1
Dunston FB v York City 4-0
Consett v Ossett Town 1-3
Penrith v Garforth Town 2-1
Farsley Celtic v Barrow 3-2
Morecambe v Northwich Victoria 1-3
Coleshill Town v Oadby Town 0-2
Kettering Town v Eastwood Town 1-4
Nantwich Town v Racing Club Warwick 4-2
Coventry Marconi v Leek Town 1-6
Rugby United v Matlock Town 3-0
Cradley Town v Bourne Town 1-3
Wellington v Hednesford Town 1-5
Bromyard Town v Burton Albion 0-3
Gornal Athletic v Hucknall Town 4-4
Gornal Athletic won 5-4 on penalties.
Alfreton Town v Bedworth United 7-1
Arnold Town v Belper Town 0-1
Hinckley United v Lye Town 0-1
Carlton Town v Boldmere St Michaels 2-1
Corby Town v Alvechurch 1-1
Alvechurch won 5-4 on penalties.
Lincoln United v Mickleover Sports 0-3
Castle Vale v Teversal 4-0
Glossop North End v Gresley Rovers 0-2
Tamworth w.o. v Stone Dominoes withdrew
Nuneaton Borough v Borrowash Victoria 3-3
Borrowash Victoria won 4-3 on penalties.
Newcastle Town v Ledbury Town 3-0
Malvern Town v Coventry Sphinx 1-3
Ford Sports Daventry v Stratford Town 0-2
Kimberley Town v Moor Green 1-3
Congleton Town v Sutton Coldfield Town 0-10
Redbridge v North Greenford United 4-1
Hemel Hempstead Town v Newmarket Town 5-2
Leyton v Hornchurch 1-1
Hornchurch won 7-6 on penalties.
Bugbrooke St Michaels v Hullbridge Sports 2-2
Bugbrooke St Michaels won 3-1 on penalties.
Beaconsfield SYCOB v Stotfold 10-2
Thurrock v Witham Town 3-0
Chalfont St Peter v Ware 2-3
St Albans City v Cogenhoe United 0-3
Needham Market v Chesham United 2-3
St Margaretsbury v Wealdstone 1-2
Southend Manor v Waltham Abbey 1-3
March Town United v Stevenage Borough 1-2
Hitchin Town v Thame United 1-2
Bury Town v AFC Kempston Rovers 7-0
Broxbourne Borough V&E v Histon 1-2
Leighton Town v Hampton & Richmond Borough 5-2
Uxbridge v Brook House 0-2
Concord Rangers v Northampton Spencer 0-1
Great Wakering Rovers v Boreham Wood 2-4
Burnham Ramblers v Billericay Town 1-4
Romford w.o. v Eton Manor withdrew
Yeading v Barking & East Ham United 0-3
Cheshunt w.o. v Hertford Town withdrew
Lowestoft Town v Kirkley 3-0
Aylesbury United v Heybridge Swifts 3-0
Godmanchester Rovers v King's Lynn 2-3
Wroxham v Barton Rovers 0-5
Berkhamsted Town v Grays Athletic 0-1
Hoddesdon Town v Waltham Forest 2-1
Bedford Town v Harwich & Parkeston 4-0
Barnet v Hayes 1-1
Barnet won 4-1 on penalties.
Haringey Borough v Banbury United 3-1
Diss Town v Braintree Town 4-4
Diss Town won 6-5 on penalties.
Buckingham Town v Northwood 4-3
Henley Town w.o. v Fakenham Town withdrew
Staines Town v Great Yarmouth Town 1-0
Wembley v Royston Town 3-2
Canvey Island v Cambridge City 2-1
Kingsbury Town v Enfield Town 1-4
Halstead Town v Ilford 0-4
Woking v Walton & Hersham 4-1
Burgess Hill Town v Cobham 2-1
Saltdean United v Sandhurst Town 1-3
Sevenoaks Town v Aldershot Town 0-2
Littlehampton Town v Tonbridge Angels 2-6
Whitstable Town v Winchester City 7-5
Chertsey Town v Croydon Athletic 2-4
Brockenhurst v AFC Newbury 3-1
Eastbourne Borough v Ashford Town 5-2
Peacehaven & Telscombe v Fisher Athletic 1-4
Leatherhead v Reading Town 2-4
Sutton United v Hailsham Town 6-0
Westfield v Maidenhead United 2-0
Burnham v Carterton 2-3
Three Bridges v Ramsgate 1-2
Ashford Town (Middlesex) v Molesey 6-5
Camberley Town v Chatham Town 0-1
Pagham v Fleet Town 0-2
Dover Athletic v Basingstoke Town 2-1
Corinthian Casuals v Gravesend & Northfleet 1-1
Corinthian Casuals won 9-8 on penalties.
Dulwich Hamlet v Wick 5-1
Epsom & Ewell v Horsham YMCA 3-1
Hillingdon Borough v Farnborough Town 2-6
Havant & Waterlooville v Mile Oak 6-0
Eastleigh v Whitehawk 2-1
Crawley Town v Oxford City 1-0
Horsham v Whyteleafe 0-5
Andover v Maidstone United 0-0
Andover won 6-5 on penalties.
Dartford v Folkestone Invicta 4-2
Walton Casuals v Lewes 3-5
Alton Town v Erith Town 1-6
Lewisham Borough v Chipstead 0-2
Witney United v Bemerton Heath Harlequins 2-0

Bridgwater Town v Forest Green Rovers 3-1
Chippenham Town v Bath City 1-4
Frome Town v Bristol Manor Farm 0-4
Yate Town v Newport County 0-2
Bournemouth v Calne Town 0-3
Street v Cinderford Town 1-3
Paulton Rovers v Hereford United 2-3
Salisbury City v Exeter City 1-3
Bitton v Weston-Super-Mare 0-2
Weymouth v Evesham United 3-2
Wootton Bassett Town v Mangotsfield United 2-5

SECOND QUALIFYING ROUND

Penrith v Ossett Albion 1-2
Thackley v Southport 2-0
Dunston FB v Northwich Victoria 2-3
Wretford United v Scarborough 0-1
Wrighton v Workington 4-1
Whitley Bay v Frickley Athletic 2-0
Wakefield & Emley v Selby Town 1-3
Stalybridge Celtic v Burscough 1-6
Farsley Celtic v Ossett Town 3-2
Carlisle United v Marine 5-1
Moor Green v Hednesford Town 2-3
Oadby Town v Castle Vale 3-0
Lye Town v Bourne Town 2-0
Gresley Rovers v Alfreton Town 1-2
Sutton Coldfield Town v Leek Town 5-2
Gornal Athletic v Belper Town 2-3
Coventry Sphinx v Carlton Town 3-4
Newcastle Town v Tamworth 0-4
Tie awarded to Newcastle Town; Tamworth fielded an over age player.
Rugby United v Mickleover Sports 3-3
Mickleover Sports won 5-4 on penalties.
Burton Albion v Stratford Town 1-2
Nantwich Town v Alvechurch 1-4
Eastwood Town v Borrowash Victoria 7-0
Grays Athletic v Histon 3-2
Leighton Town v Staines Town 5-2
Enfield Town v Hemel Hempstead Town 1-0
Henley Town v Cogenhoe United 2-2
Henley Town won 4-3 on penalties.
Bury Town v Stevenage Borough 0-2
Cheshunt v Hornchurch 3-5
Hoddesdon Town v King's Lynn 2-1
Ware v Bedford Town 1-0
Haringey Borough v Barnet 4-1
Thurrock v Buckingham Town 2-1
Aylesbury United v Diss Town 2-0
Wembley v Canvey Island 0-1
Tie awarded to Wembley; Canvey Island fielded an over age player.
Brook House v Wealdstone 0-2
Lowestoft Town v Beaconsfield SYCOB 1-4
Barton Rovers v Boreham Wood 0-1
Waltham Abbey v Ilford 1-1
Waltham Abbey won 5-3 on penalties.
Chesham United v Romford 4-1
Barking & East Ham United v Thame United 3-2
Bugbrooke St Michaels v Redbridge 0-7
Northampton Spencer v Billericay Town 0-2
Andover v Reading Town 1-5
Lewes v Brockenhurst 3-2
Sandhurst Town v Carterton 3-1
Ramsgate v Dover Athletic 1-1
Dover Athletic won 5-4 on penalties.
Aldershot Town v Burgess Hill Town 2-2
Burgess Hill Town won 4-3 on penalties.
Westfield v Whyteleafe 1-4
Corinthian Casuals v Chatham Town 1-2
Eastbourne Borough v Havant & Waterlooville 3-2
Woking v Croydon Athletic 2-0
Fisher Athletic v Epsom & Ewell 2-4
Erith Town v Whitstable Town 1-4
Dartford v Crawley Town 2-3
Dulwich Hamlet v Eastleigh 4-2
Fleet Town v Farnborough Town 2-4
Chipstead v Tonbridge Angels 1-3
Ashford Town (Middlesex) v Sutton United 0-10
Hereford United v Mangotsfield United 2-4
Newport County v Bath City 4-1
Exeter City v Witney United 5-0
Weston-Super-Mare v Bristol Manor Farm 5-4
Calne Town v Bridgwater Town 1-4
Weymouth v Cinderford Town 5-0

THIRD QUALIFYING ROUND

Selby Town v Thackley 1-4
Ossett Albion v Farsley Celtic 2-4
Carlisle United v Northwich Victoria 4-0
Scarborough v Whitley Bay 1-2
Wrighton v Burscough 0-2
Newcastle Town v Eastwood Town 0-5
Sutton Coldfield Town v Lye Town 1-2
Mickleover Sports v Hednesford Town 0-2
Stratford Town v Alfreton Town 0-1
Belper Town v Oadby Town 1-0
Alvechurch v Carlton Town 1-3
Barking & East Ham United v Hornchurch 4-3
Aylesbury United v Ware 1-4
Waltham Abbey v Billericay Town 2-3
Hoddesdon Town v Grays Athletic 0-2
Boreham Wood v Wembley 1-3
Leighton Town v Stevenage Borough 2-4
Henley Town v Beaconsfield SYCOB 1-0
Haringey Borough v Enfield Town 3-2
Redbridge v Chesham United 3-0
Thurrock v Wealdstone 0-2
Chatham Town v Farnborough Town 1-2
after abandoned tie 1-2.
Whyteleafe v Burgess Hill Town 4-2
Whitstable Town v Sandhurst Town 8-1
Crawley Town v Dulwich Hamlet 1-3
Woking v Reading Town 7-1
Dover Athletic v Epsom & Ewell 2-0
Sutton United v Lewes 3-1
Tonbridge Angels v Eastbourne Borough 5-1
Exeter City v Weston-Super-Mare 11-0
Weymouth v Mangotsfield United 0-0
Weymouth won 6-5 on penalties.
Newport County v Bridgwater Town 0-0
Bridgwater Town won 6-5 on penalties.

FIRST ROUND

Chester-le-Street Town v Stockport County 0-7
Barnsley v Oldham Athletic 3-1
Doncaster Rovers v Sheffield Wednesday 0-1
Scunthorpe United v Hartlepool United 1-3
Huddersfield Town v Rochdale 2-1
Bury v Wrexham 2-1
Hull City v Carlisle United 4-1
Bradford City v Burscough 2-3
Chesterfield v Thackley 1-2
Blackpool v Tranmere Rovers 2-1
Chester City v Whitley Bay 3-1
Darlington v Farsley Celtic 4-0
Carlton Town v Walsall 0-3
Boston United v Northampton Town 3-2
Hednesford Town v Grimsby Town 1-2
Belper Town v Notts County 2-3
Milton Keynes Dons v Kidderminster Harriers 2-0
Mansfield Town v Cambridge United 1-3
Rushden & Diamonds v Port Vale 1-2
Eastwood Town v Lye Town 2-3
Lincoln City v Alfreton Town 5-1
Macclesfield Town v Shrewsbury Town 0-1
Barking & East Ham United v Farnborough Town 0-2
Brentford v Henley Town 3-0
Billericay Town v Wealdstone 1-2
Redbridge v Grays Athletic 3-1
Wembley v Haringey Borough 1-2
Luton Town v Whitstable Town 8-0
Stevenage Borough v Dover Athletic 3-4
Leyton Orient v Tonbridge Angels 3-1
Wycombe Wanderers v Dulwich Hamlet 5-1
Colchester United v Whyteleafe 4-2
Southend United v Sutton United 2-2
Sutton United won 7-6 on penalties.
Ware v Woking 2-4
Swindon Town v Yeovil Town 0-2
Exeter City v Cheltenham Town 3-4
Weymouth v Bristol Rovers 1-3
Bridgwater Town v Bristol City 0-3
Cirencester Town v Oxford United 2-0
Swansea City v AFC Bournemouth 0-1

SECOND ROUND

Hull City v Notts County 3-1
Stockport County v Walsall 6-3
Boston United v Huddersfield Town 2-1
Thackley v Port Vale 0-3
Lincoln City v Shrewsbury Town 2-2
Shrewsbury Town won 4-3 on penalties.
Lye Town v Burscough 0-1
Grimsby Town v Bury 3-2
Sheffield Wednesday v Cambridge United 0-1
Milton Keynes Dons v Darlington 2-3
Barnsley v Hartlepool United 2-1
Blackpool v Chester City 4-0
Wycombe Wanderers v Dover Athletic 4-1
Bristol City v Sutton United 4-1
Farnborough Town v Wealdstone 0-2
Luton Town v Cirencester Town 2-0
Haringey Borough v Woking 0-2
Yeovil Town v Brentford 4-0

Cheltenham Town v Colchester United	0-1
Redbridge v Bristol Rovers	2-2
Redbridge won 5-4 on penalties.	
AFC Bournemouth v Leyton Orient	2-3

THIRD ROUND

Sheffield United v Millwall	3-2
Liverpool v Wealdstone	6-0
Barnsley v Boston United	4-1
Tottenham Hotspur v Nottingham Forest	1-0
Crewe Alexandra v Stockport County	4-2
Ipswich Town v Portsmouth	3-2
Newcastle United v Blackpool	2-1
Queens Park Rangers v Southampton	1-3
Cambridge United v Port Vale	0-1
Bristol City v Rotherham United	3-1
Wigan Athletic v Leeds United	1-2
Fulham v Birmingham City	2-1
Wolverhampton Wanderers v Reading	1-0
Colchester United v Chelsea	2-1
Burnley v Norwich City	1-2
Aston Villa v Wycombe Wanderers	1-0
Burscough v Preston North End	0-1
Arsenal v Crystal Palace	3-0
Manchester City v West Bromwich Albion	4-1
Manchester United v Stoke City	0-1
Sunderland v Leicester City	2-0
Gillingham v West Ham United	3-6
Redbridge v Middlesbrough	0-3
Derby County v Grimsby Town	4-0
Watford v Coventry City	1-0
Plymouth Argyle v Darlington	1-0
Bolton Wanderers v Blackburn Rovers	2-3
Woking v Brighton & Hove Albion	0-6
Hull City v Cardiff City	0-1
Yeovil Town v Luton Town	2-0
Everton v Charlton Athletic	1-0
Leyton Orient v Shrewsbury Town	2-0

FOURTH ROUND

Aston Villa v Port Vale	1-0
Yeovil Town v Everton	0-6
Manchester City v Brighton & Hove Albion	2-1
Watford v Newcastle United	1-0
Arsenal v Preston North End	2-1
Derby County v Sheffield United	3-2
Middlesbrough v Sunderland	3-0
Colchester United v Cardiff City	3-2
Wolverhampton Wanderers v Barnsley	2-1
West Ham United v Blackburn Rovers	4-1
Leeds United v Fulham	0-0
Fulham won 5-4 on penalties.	
Southampton v Norwich City	1-0
Liverpool v Tottenham Hotspur	1-1
Tottenham Hotspur won 4-2 on penalties.	
Stoke City v Ipswich Town	1-2
Leyton Orient v Bristol City	3-1
Plymouth Argyle v Crewe Alexandra	0-2

FIFTH ROUND

Ipswich Town v Aston Villa	3-1
Crewe Alexandra v Colchester United	1-2
Southampton v Arsenal	1-0
West Ham United v Leyton Orient	3-2
Wolverhampton Wanderers v Manchester City	2-0
Tottenham Hotspur v Everton	2-1
Fulham v Derby County	1-2
Watford v Middlesbrough	0-0
Watford won 4-1 on penalties.	

SIXTH ROUND

Colchester United v Ipswich Town	0-5
Watford v Tottenham Hotspur	0-2
West Ham United v Southampton	1-4
Derby County v Wolverhampton Wanderers	1-2

SEMI-FINALS (TWO LEGS)

Southampton v Wolverhampton Wanderers	1-0, 2-3
Ipswich Town v Tottenham Hotspur	2-0, 2-1

THE FA YOUTH CUP FINAL (First Leg)

Monday, 18 April 2005

Southampton (1) 2 *(McGoldrick 45 (pen), Best 62)*

Ipswich Town (0) 2 *(Lordan 48, 58)* 9902

Souhampton: McNeil; Richards, Wallis-Taylor, McGoldrick, Rudd, Cranie, James, Sparv, Walcott, Best (Condesso 82), Dyer.
Ipswich Town: Supple; Synott (Haynes 63), Krause, Garvan, Casement, Collins, Moore, Lordan, Knights (Hammond 85), Trotter (Sheringham 90), Craig.
Referee: A. Marriner (West Midlands).

THE FA YOUTH CUP FINAL (Second Leg)

Thursday, 21 April 2005

Ipswich Town (0) 1 *(Upson 118)*

Southampton (0) 0 14,889

Ipswich Town: Supple; Synott, Krause, Haynes (Sheringham 71), Casement, Collins, Moore, Lordan (Hammond 82), Knights, Trotter (Upson 105), Craig.
Southampton: McNeil; Richards, Wallis-Taylor, McGoldrick (Condesso 86), Rudd, Cranie, James, Sparv (Lallana 106), Walcott, Best, Dyer.

aet.

Referee: A. Marriner (West Midlands).

THE FA YOUTH CUP – PREVIOUS WINNERS
(Aggregate Scores)

Year	*Winners*	*Runners-up*	*Score*
1953	Manchester United	Wolverhampton W	9-3
1954	Manchester United	Wolverhampton W	5-4
1955	Manchester United	West Bromwich Albion	7-1
1956	Manchester United	Chesterfield	4-3
1957	Manchester United	West Ham United	8-2
1958	Wolverhampton W	Chelsea	7-6
1959	Blackburn Rovers	West Ham United	2-1
1960	Chelsea	Preston North End	5-2
1961	Chelsea	Everton	5-3
1962	Newcastle United	Wolverhampton W	2-1
1963	West Ham United	Liverpool	6-5
1964	Manchester United	Swindon Town	5-2
1965	Everton	Arsenal	3-2
1966	Arsenal	Sunderland	5-3
1967	Sunderland	Birmingham City	2-0
1968	Burnley	Coventry City	3-2
1969	Sunderland	West Bromwich Albion	6-3
1970	Tottenham Hotspur	Coventry City	4-3
1971	Arsenal	Cardiff City	2-0
1972	Aston Villa	Liverpool	5-2
1973	Ipswich Town	Bristol City	4-1
1974	Tottenham Hotspur	Huddersfield Town	2-1
1975	Ipswich Town	West Ham United	5-1
1976	West Bromwich Albion	Wolverhampton W	5-0
1977	Crystal Palace	Everton	1-0*
1978	Crystal Palace	Aston Villa	1-0
1979	Millwall	Manchester City	2-0
1980	Aston Villa	Manchester City	3-2
1981	West Ham United	Tottenham Hotspur	2-1
1982	Watford	Manchester United	7-6
1983	Norwich City	Everton	6-5
1984	Everton	Stoke City	4-2
1985	Newcastle United	Watford	4-1
1986	Manchester City	Manchester United	3-1
1987	Coventry City	Charlton Athletic	2-1
1988	Arsenal	Doncaster Rovers	6-1
1989	Watford	Manchester City	2-1
1990	Tottenham Hotspur	Middlesbrough	3-2
1991	Millwall	Sheffield Wednesday	3-0
1992	Manchester United	Crystal Palace	6-3
1993	Leeds United	Manchester United	4-1
1994	Arsenal	Millwall	5-3
1995	Manchester United	Tottenham Hotspur	2-2
	Manchester United won 4-3 on penalties.		
1996	Liverpool	West Ham United	4-1
1997	Leeds United	Crystal Palace	3-1
1998	Everton	Blackburn Rovers	5-3
1999	West Ham United	Coventry City	9-0
2000	Arsenal	Coventry City	5-1
2001	Arsenal	Blackburn Rovers	6-3
2002	Aston Villa	Everton	4-2
2003	Manchester United	Middlesbrough	3-1
2004	Middlesbrough	Aston Villa	4-0

* One match only

THE FA SUNDAY CUP 2004–05

IN PARTNERSHIP WITH CARLSBERG

FIRST ROUND

Hartlepool Athletic Rugby v Allerton	3-1
Hessle Rangers v AFC Brombrough	5-4
Home & Bargain v Albion Sports	0-2
Britannia v Seaburn	2-4
Bruce Ennis Square v Seaton Sluice SC	6-0
Orchard Park v Hartlepool Lion Hillcarter	2-1
Prestige Brighams v Forest Town Welfare	7-0
Rawdon v BRNESC	1-3
Western Approaches v Fairweather Green WMC	1-2
Smith & Nephew v Bolton Woods	2-1
Sandon Dock v Canada Edinburgh Park	0-1
Queens Park v Hartlepool Supporters Athletic	1-3
Oakenshaw v Hetton Lyons Cricket Club	2-4
Norcoast v Canon	3-1
Taxi Club v Harraby Catholic Seniors	7-0
Clifton v Maryport	3-1
Queensbury w.o. v Clubmoor Nalgo removed.	
Mirehouse v St Aloysius E	1-4
Dock v The Warby	3-1
Stanley Road v Fantail (MF Logistics)	0-6
Seymour KFCA v Pocklington Town	3-0
61 FC (Sunday) v Moggerhanger Sunday	2-1
Ebstree v Austin Ex Apprentices	1-3
AC Sportsman v Trooper	1-4
Longboat v Bartley Green	1-2
Celtic SC (Luton) v Wernley	5-4
Toll End v Grosvenor Park (Sunday)	4-0
St Margarets v Queensmen	5-2
Inter Volante v Crawley Green (Sunday)	7-0
Green Baize v Standens Barn	4-0
Linfield Schofields v FC Houghton Centre	2-3
Greyhound v The Cutters Friday	10-0
Shireway Sports v Lodge Cottrell	2-1
Mackadown Lane S&S v Lebeq Tavern Courage	1-2
Moat v Bardwell Wasps	4-0
Kings Head v Slade Celtic	1-5
Pioneer v St Joseph's (Luton)	2-2
St Joseph's (Luton) won 4-3 on penalties.	
AFC Hornets (Studham) v Dun Cow	1-2
Honeyfield Trailers v Coopers Kensington	1-0
Holt v Reading Irish	3-4
Richfield Rovers v Hanham Sunday	2-3
Bournemouth Electric v Sandford	3-1
Rainham Sports v CB Hounslow United	2-1
Lashings v Sutton High	1-4
Global v Quested	3-7
Freemasons Sunday v CFC Shalford	2-0
London Maccabi Lions v Ashlyn's United	1-3
Belstone v Risden Wood	4-1
Hammer v Bedfont Sunday	3-2
Cheam Sports v Hexton	0-1
VS Villa v London Colney VCH	3-2

SECOND ROUND

Hartlepool Athletic Rugby v Albion Sports	0-2
Coach & Horses withdrew v Hessle Rangers w.o.	
Clifton v Queensbury	3-1
Orchard Park v Seaburn	1-2
St Aloysius E v Bruce Ennis Square	7-4
Pablo Derby Arms v BRNESC	7-0
Fairweather Green WMC v Prestige Brighams	0-1
Smith & Nephew v Canada Edinburgh Park	1-1
Canada Edinburgh Park won 2-0 on penalties.	
Hartlepool Supporters Athletic v Nicosia	0-2
Shankhouse United v Hetton Lyons Cricket Club	0-2
Norcoast v Taxi Club	2-3
Seymour KFCA v Dock	0-1
Fantail (MF Logistics) v Travellers	8-0
Barr Point v 61 FC (Sunday)	4-3
Austin Ex Apprentices v Duke of York	0-1
Grange Athletic v Bartley Green	0-2
Casino v St Margarets	3-3
Casino won 3-1 on penalties.	
St Joseph's (Luton) w.o. v UK Flooring withdrew	
Toll End v Dun Cow	2-3
Trooper v Celtic SC (Luton)	4-1
Lewsey Social v Green Baize	4-1
Inter Volante v Shireway Sports	4-0
Lebeq Tavern Courage v FC Houghton Centre	7-3
Greyhound v VS Villa	5-1
Ashlyn's United v Moat	1-3
Slade Celtic v Belstone	5-2
Bournemouth Electric v Honeyfield Trailers	1-1
Honeyfield Trailers won 4-2 on penalties.	
Reading Irish v Hanham Sunday	3-1
Gossoms End v Rainham Sports	5-1
Sutton High v Luton Old Boys (Sunday)	5-3
Hammer v Freemasons Sunday	3-2
Quested v Hexton	4-4 (abandoned 86 minutes)
Both clubs found guilty of causing the situation and were removed from the competition; third round tie awarded to Duke of York.	

THIRD ROUND

Taxi Club v Slade Celtic	3-0
Pablo Derby Arms w.o. v Barr Point failed to fulfil fixture	
Clifton v Canada Edinburgh Park	0-2
Trooper v Hetton Lyons Cricket Club	1-2
Inter Volante v St Aloysius E	1-3
Nicosia v Fantail (MF Logistics)	0-5
Seaburn v Prestige Brighams	3-2
Albion Sports v Bartley Green	6-0
Dock v Hessle Rangers	4-1
St Joseph's (Luton) v Gossoms End	0-2
Lebeq Tavern Courage v Sutton High	7-0
Greyhound v Honeyfield Trailers	4-1
Lewsey Social v Hammer	2-0
Casino v Dun Cow	2-0
Reading Irish v Moat	2-1
Duke of York received a bye.	

FOURTH ROUND

Seaburn v Taxi Club	1-0
Pablo Derby Arms v Canada Edinburgh Park	0-1
Dock v Hetton Lyons Cricket Club	1-3
Fantail (MF Logistics) v St Aloysius E	1-2
Reading Irish v Duke of York	2-1
Gossoms End v Lebeq Tavern Courage	2-1
Albion Sports v Greyhound	4-2
Casino v Lewsey Social	5-3

FIFTH ROUND

Seaburn v Hetton Lyons Cricket Club	1-0
Canada Edinburgh Park v St Aloysius E	2-0
Reading Irish v Albion Sports	1-3
Gossoms End v Casino	2-1

SEMI-FINALS

Seaburn v Albion Sports	0-1
Canada Edinburgh Park v Gossoms End	4-0
Canada Edinburgh Park removed from the competition for fielding an ineligible player.	

FINAL

Albion Sports 2 *(Zoll 2)*
Gossoms End 3 *(Porter 2, Osborne)* *(at Liverpool FC).*

THE FA SUNDAY CUP – PREVIOUS WINNERS

Year	*Winners*	*Runners-up*	*Score*
1965	London	Staffordshire	6-2
1966	Ubique United	Aldridge Fabrications	1-0
1967	Carlton United	Stoke Works	2-0
1968	Drovers	Brook United	2-0
1969	Leigh Park	Loke United	3-1
1970	Vention United	Ubique United	1-0
1971	Beacontree United	Saltley United	2-0
1972	Newtown Unity	Springfield Colts	4-0
1973	Carlton United	Wear Valley	2-1
1974	Newtown Unity	Brentford East	3-0
1975	Fareham Town Centipedes	Players Athletic Engineers	1-0
1976	Brandon United	Evergreen	2-1
1977	Langley Park Rams Head	Newtown Unity	2-0
1978	Arras	Lion Rangers	2-1
1979	Lobster	Carlton United	3-2
1980	Fantail	Twin Foxes	1-0
1981	Fantail	Mackintosh	1-0
1982	Dingle Rail	Twin Foxes	2-1
1983	Eagle	Lee Chapel North	1-1
	Replay		2-1
1984	Lee Chapel North	Eagle	4-3
1985	Hobbies United	Avenue	2-2
	Replay		1-1
	Second Replay		2-1
1986	Avenue	Glenn Sports	1-0
1987	Lodge Cottrell	Avenue	1-0
1988	Nexday	Humbledon Plains Farm	2-0
1989	Almithak	East Levenshulme	3-1
1990	Humbledon Plains Farm	Marston Sports	2-1

THE FA SUNDAY CUP – PREVIOUS WINNERS (cont.)

1991	Nicosia	Ouzavich	3-2
1992	Theale	Marston Sports	3-2
1993	Seymour	Bedfont Sunday	1-0
1994	Ranelagh Sports	Hartlepool Lion Hotel	2-0
1995	St Joseph's (Luton)	B&A Scaffolding	2-1
1996	St Joseph's (Luton)	Croxteth & Gilmoss RBL	2-1
1997	Marston United	Northwood	1-0
1998	Olympic Star	St Joseph's (Luton)	1-1
	Olympic Star won 5-3 on penalties.		
1999	Little Paxton	St Joseph's (Luton)	2-2
	Little Paxton won 4-3 on penalties.		
2000	Prestige Brighams	Albion Sports	1-0
2001	Hartlepool Lion Hillcarter	FC Houghton Centre	0-0
	Hartlepool Lion Hillcarter won 3-2 on penalties.		
2002	Britannia	Little Paxton	2-0
2003	Duke of York	Travellers	3-1
2004	Nicosia	UK Flooring	3-1

THE FA COUNTY YOUTH CUP 2004–05

IN PARTNERSHIP WITH PEPSI

FIRST ROUND

Isle of Man v Leicestershire & Rutland	1-4
Westmoreland v West Riding	0-6
Cheshire v Derbyshire	6-0
Staffordshire v Liverpool	2-0
Lincolnshire v Shropshire	4-1
Lancashire v Sheffield & Hallamshire	0-2
Hertfordshire v Devon	2-1
Kent v Herefordshire	5-3
Oxfordshire v Sussex	3-4
Guernsey v Army	5-3
Surrey v Bedfordshire	0-2
Gloucestershire v Hampshire	1-5
Northamptonshire v Dorset	2-1
Cambridgeshire v Norfolk	4-2
Cornwall v Essex	1-5

SECOND ROUND

Manchester v East Riding	1-3
Birmingham v Cheshire	1-0
Staffordshire v Cumberland	4-1
Leicestershire & Rutland v North Riding	0-2
West Riding v Lincolnshire	1-4
Sheffield & Hallamshire v Nottinghamshire	2-2
Nottinghamshire won 6-5 on penalties.	
Durham v Northumberland	2-1
Worcestershire v Wiltshire	4-5
Guernsey v Middlesex	2-0
Cambridgeshire v Hertfordshire	2-3
Bedfordshire v Northamptonshire	1-0
London v Suffolk	1-3
Sussex v Essex	4-4
Sussex won 3-2 on penalties.	
Berks & Bucks v Jersey	2-1
Huntingdonshire v Hampshire	0-2
Kent v Somerset	2-3

THIRD ROUND

Somerset v Birmingham	0-1
Suffolk v Durham	3-2
East Riding v Nottinghamshire	3-0
Staffordshire v Lincolnshire	2-2
Staffordshire won 4-3 on penalties.	
Wiltshire v North Riding	2-1
Hertfordshire v Berks & Bucks	0-1
Hampshire v Guernsey	6-1
Sussex v Bedfordshire	3-1

FOURTH ROUND

Wiltshire v Suffolk	1-2
East Riding v Berks & Bucks	3-2
Birmingham v Hampshire	1-3
Staffordshire v Sussex	1-4

SEMI-FINALS

Suffolk v Sussex	2-0
Hampshire v East Riding	2-1

FINAL

Suffolk v Hampshire	2-1
att: 991	

THE FA COUNTY YOUTH CUP – PREVIOUS WINNERS
(Aggregate scores until 1970)

Year	*Winners*	*Runners-up*	*Score*
1945	Staffordshire	Wiltshire	3-2
1946	Berks & Bucks	Durham	4-3
1947	Durham	Essex	4-2
1948	Essex	Liverpool	5-3
1949	Liverpool	Middlesex	4-3
1950	Essex	Middlesex	4-3
1951	Middlesex	Leicestershire & Rutland	3-1
1952	Sussex	Liverpool	3-1
1953	Sheffield & Hallamshire	Hampshire	5-3
1954	Liverpool	Gloucestershire	4-1
1955	Bedfordshire	Sheffield & Hallamshire	2-0
1956	Middlesex	Staffordshire	3-2
1957	Hampshire	Cheshire	4-3
1958	Staffordshire	London	8-0
1959	Birmingham	London	7-5
1960	London	Birmingham	6-4
1961	Lancashire	Nottinghamshire	6-3
1962	Middlesex	Nottinghamshire	6-3
1963	Durham	Essex	3-2
1964	Sheffield & Hallamshire	Birmingham	1-0
1965	Northumberland	Middlesex	7-4
1966	Leicestershire & Rutland	London	6-5
1967	Northamptonshire	Hertfordshire	5-4
1968	North Riding	Devon	7-4
1969	Northumberland	Sussex	1-0
1970	Hertfordshire	Cheshire	2-1
1971	Lancashire	Gloucestershire	2-0
1972	Middlesex	Liverpool	2-0
1973	Hertfordshire	Northumberland	3-0
1974	Nottinghamshire	London	2-0
1975	Durham	Bedfordshire	2-1
1976	Northamptonshire	Surrey	7-1
1977	Liverpool	Surrey	3-0
1978	Liverpool	Kent	3-1
1979	Hertfordshire	Liverpool	4-1
1980	Liverpool	Lancashire	2-0
1981	Lancashire	East Riding	3-2
1982	Devon	Kent	0-0
	Replay		3-2
1983	London	Gloucestershire	3-0
1984	Cheshire	Manchester	2-1
1985	East Riding	Middlesex	2-1
1986	Hertfordshire	Manchester	4-0
1987	North Riding	Gloucestershire	3-1
1988	East Riding	Middlesex	1-1
	Replay		5-3
1989	Liverpool	Hertfordshire	2-1
1990	Staffordshire	Hampshire	1-1
	Replay		2-1
1991	Lancashire	Surrey	6-0
1992	Nottinghamshire	Surrey	1-0
1993	Durham	Liverpool	4-0
1994	West Riding	Sussex	3-1
1995	Liverpool	Essex	3-2
1996	Durham	Gloucestershire	1-0
1997	Cambridgeshire	Lancashire	1-0
1998	Northumberland	West Riding	2-1
1999	Durham	Sussex	1-0
2000	Birmingham	Surrey	2-1
2001	Northamptonshire	Birmingham	3-0
2002	Birmingham	Durham	2-1
2003	Northumberland	Liverpool	1-0
2004	Durham	North Riding	4-0

SCHOOLS FOOTBALL 2004–05

BOODLE & DUNTHORNE INDEPENDENT SCHOOLS FA CUP 2004–05

FIRST ROUND
Bradfield 1, Hulme GS 0
Charterhouse 1, Brentwood 2
Chigwell 2, Bolton 0
Malvern 1, Shrewsbury 4
Millfield 5, Highgate 0
QEGS, Blackburn 8, Dover College 0
Repton 3, Eton 2
St Bede's, Manchester 2, KES, Witley 0
Wellingborough 2, Haileybury 3
Westminster 4, King's School, Ely 0
Winchester 0, Ardingly 0
(aet; Winchester won 6-5 on penalties.)

SECOND ROUND
Brentwood 2, Alleyn's 4
Chigwell 1, Winchester 0
City of London 0, Bradfield 5
Dulwich College 2, St Bede's, Manchester 5
Haileybury 3, Grange 0
Hampton 8, John Lyon 1
Kimbolton 4, Forest 2
Lancing 5, Westminster 1
Oswestry 0, Millfield 3
Repton 3, Aldenham 0
QEGS Blackburn 1, King's School, Chester 1
(aet; QEGS, Blackburn won 4-3 on penalties.)
St Bede's, Hailsham 2, RGS, Newcastle 5
St Mary's College 3, Latymer Upper 2
St Edmund's, Cantab 3, Bury GS 2
Shrewsbury 3, Manchester GS 1
Wolverhampton GS 3, Birkdale 0

THIRD ROUND
Alleyn's 2, Repton 2
(aet; Repton won 4-3 on penalties.)
Bradfield 0, Millfield 2
Hampton 2, Shrewsbury 1
Kimbolton 3, Haileybury 1
RGS, Newcastle 4, QEGS, Blackburn 1
St Edmunds, Cantab 0, St Bede's, Manchester 3
St Mary's College 3, Lancing 4
Wolverhampton GS 2, Chigwell 0

FOURTH ROUND
Hampton 1, Wolverhampton GS 0
Lancing 1, Millfield 3
Repton 1, St Bede's, Manchester 0
RGS, Newcastle 5, Kimbolton 1

SEMI-FINALS
Hampton 0, Repton 0
(aet; Hampton won 4-3 on penalties.)
Millfield 2, RGS, Newcastle 1

FINAL *(at Leicester City FC)*
Millfield 3 *(Reid 2, Irish)*
Hampton 1 *(Paxton)*
Millfield: S. Cooper; S. Jenkins (K. John), K. Follett, D. Middleton, J. Cook, J. Walker, A. Turner, L. Irish, B. Middleton (S. Bird), F. Rolli (T. Crostwaite), R. Reid.
Hampton: N. Jupp; G. Hayhurst, A. Phakey, R. Campain (J. Dewhurst), A. Lightman, C. Judd, T. Gearing, C. Heritage, J. Phillips (H. Butt), R. Allen, F. Paxton.
Referee: M. Riley (Leeds).

UEFA REGIONS CUP 2005

FINAL TOURNAMENT

GROUP A
South-West Sofia 3, Brno 1
Malopolska 1, Central Slovakia 1
Central Slovakia 6, Brno 0
Malopolska 0, South-West Sofia 4
Central Slovakia 2, South-West Sofia 2
Brno 1, Malopolska 3

GROUP B
Dacia 1, Republic of Ireland 1
Vasca 4, Kahovka-Kzeso 1
Republic of Ireland 2, Kahovka-Kzeso 4
Dacia 1, Vasca 2
Republic of Ireland 3, Vasca 1
Kahovka-Kzeso 3, Dacia 1

FINAL
South-West Sofia 0, Vasca 1

VICTORY SHIELD 2004-05

Scotland 2, Northern Ireland 2
Wales 1, England 5
Scotland 0, Wales 1
Northern Ireland 1, England 3
Northern Ireland 1, Wales 0
England 0, Scotland 0

	P	*W*	*D*	*L*	*F*	*A*	*Pts*
England	3	2	1	0	8	2	7
Northern Ireland	3	1	1	1	4	5	4
Wales	3	1	0	2	2	6	3
Scotland	3	0	2	1	2	3	2

UNIVERSITY FOOTBALL 2004–05

121st UNIVERSITY MATCH

(at Cambridge United, 11 March 2005)

Oxford (0) 1 Cambridge (0) 0

Oxford: N Baker; *M Addley, M Elliot, J Hazzard, A Backhouse (P Walker), L Sullivan, *C Griffin, *J Perkins, R Tavares; *N Armstrong (V Vitale), J Forrest (M Rigby).
Substitutes not used: P McMahon (Gk). *Captain J Darby* unable to play, injury.*
Scorer: Sullivan

Cambridge: *D Heath; A Coleman (A Spanos, 35), M Clamp (N Leslie, 70), C Turnbull, N Pantelides (S Bailey, 30); J Hughes, *G Devine, S Smith, *A Mugan, *M Adams, R Payne.
Substitutes not used: M Daniels.

Referee: M Messias (Sheffield & Hallamshire).

**denotes Old Blue.*

Oxford drew one ahead with their 47th win. 28 matches have been drawn.

UNIVERSITY OF LONDON MEN'S INTER-COLLEGIATE LEAGUE

In all Leagues some games were not played and points awarded

Premier Division One	*P*	*W*	*D*	*L*	*F*	*A*	*Pts*
Queen Mary College	11	9	2	0	44	14	29
King's College	11	9	1	1	25	9	28
London School of Economics	11	7	1	3	35	14	22
University College	11	6	4	1	24	13	22
Imperial College	11	5	3	3	26	13	18
R Free, Mx & Univ Coll Hosp MS	11	4	3	4	11	19	15
London School of Economics Res	11	4	2	5	12	18	14
Royal Holloway College	11	3	4	4	22	24	13
School of Oriental & African Studies	11	2	2	7	16	47	8
Imperial College Res	11	2	1	8	17	24	7
St Bart's & R London Hosps MS	11	0	5	6	7	19	5
Imperial College Medicals	11	0	2	9	11	36	2

Premier Division Two	*P*	*W*	*D*	*L*	*F*	*A*	*Pts*
University College Res	10	7	2	1	35	15	23
Guy's, King's, St Thomas's MS	10	7	1	2	48	12	22
Imperial College 3rd	10	7	0	3	32	11	21
St George's Hospital MS	10	4	3	3	30	19	15
Royal Holloway College 3rd	10	4	2	4	27	21	14
University College 3rd	10	4	2	4	15	14	14
Royal Holloway College Res	10	3	5	2	17	23	14
Imperial College Medicals Res	10	2	4	4	19	30	10
St George's Hospital Res	10	2	1	7	12	31	7
Queen Mary College Res	10	2	1	7	15	40	7
King's College Res	10	2	1	7	15	49	7

Division 1	*P*	*W*	*D*	*L*	*F*	*A*	*Pts*
London School of Economics 3rd	22	17	2	3	52	23	53
Guy's, King's, St Thomas's MS Res	22	17	1	4	93	29	52
Royal Holloway College 4th	22	17	1	4	61	24	52
Goldsmiths' College	22	14	3	5	62	30	45
Imperial College 4th	22	8	6	8	46	40	30
University College 4th	22	9	2	11	28	45	29
University College 5th	22	9	2	11	40	59	29
Royal Veterinary College	22	8	1	13	41	51	25
R Free, Mx & Univ Coll Hosp MS Res	22	7	2	13	32	64	23
R Free, Mx & Univ Coll Hosp MS 3rd	22	5	1	16	28	52	16
Guy's, King's, St Thomas's MS 3rd	22	5	1	16	41	72	16
London School of Economics 4th	22	4	2	16	29	64	14

Division 2	*P*	*W*	*D*	*L*	*F*	*A*	*Pts*
King's College 3rd	22	16	4	2	78	29	52
Imperial College 5th	22	14	6	2	44	17	48
Royal Holloway College 5th	22	12	8	2	50	23	44
London School of Economics 5th	22	12	4	6	45	29	40
Royal School of Mines (IC)	22	10	6	6	53	50	36
King's College 6th	22	9	5	8	62	48	32
University College 7th	22	9	3	10	39	49	30
King's College 4th	22	7	6	9	43	39	27
St Bart's & R London Hosps MS Res	22	7	1	14	29	51	22
Imperial College Medicals 3rd	22	6	3	13	33	54	21
Goldsmiths' College Res	22	3	2	17	35	55	11
R Free, Mx & Univ Coll Hosp 4th	22	2	2	18	15	82	8

Division 3	*P*	*W*	*D*	*L*	*F*	*A*	*Pts*
University College 6th	22	19	1	2	130	17	58
Queen Mary College 3rd	22	16	5	1	83	21	53
London School of Economics 7th	22	17	1	4	88	31	52
Imperial College 6th	22	9	6	7	37	42	33
St Bart's & R London Hosps MS 3rd	22	8	6	8	34	32	30
Guy's, King's, St Thomas's MS 4th	22	8	6	8	36	36	30
London School of Economics 6th	22	8	4	10	46	71	28
King's College 7th	22	8	3	11	40	55	27
Queen Mary College 4th	22	7	2	13	43	58	23
King's College 5th	22	4	6	12	31	72	18
School of Slavonic & E European Studies	22	3	4	15	32	86	13
Imperial College Medicals 4th	22	2	2	18	21	100	8

Division 4	*P*	*W*	*D*	*L*	*F*	*A*	*Pts*
Royal Holloway College 6th	20	18	1	1	130	14	55
Guy's, King's, St Thomas's Hosp MS 5th	20	14	1	5	58	43	43
University of the Arts	20	12	6	2	81	40	42
School of Pharmacy	20	12	1	7	55	26	37
Royal Veterinary College Res	20	10	3	7	64	51	33
St George's Hospital MS 3rd	20	10	0	10	42	57	30
Queen Mary College 5th	20	8	0	12	51	69	24
Imperial College 7th	20	5	1	14	38	67	16
School of Oriental & African Studies Res	20	2	8	10	20	39	14
Goldsmiths' College 3rd	20	4	2	14	44	102	14
Royal School of Mines (IC) Res	20	2	3	15	16	91	9

CHALLENGE CUP
University College 2 Imperial College 1

RESERVES CHALLENGE CUP
Royal Free Res 2 Royal Holloway 4th 4

RESERVES PLATE
London School of Economics 5th 0 Imperial College 5th 2

VASE
University College 6th 3 Royal Holloway 6th 1

UNIVERSITY OF LONDON WOMEN'S INTER-COLLEGIATE LEAGUE

Premier Division	*P*	*W*	*D*	*L*	*F*	*A*	*Pts*
University College	10	10	0	0	73	15	30
Royal Holloway College	10	7	1	2	28	11	22
Guy's, King's, St. Thomas's Hosp MS	10	5	0	5	51	34	15
London School Economics	10	3	2	5	27	31	11
Imperial College	10	2	0	8	16	49	6
Queen Mary College	10	1	1	8	17	72	4

Division 1	*P*	*W*	*D*	*L*	*F*	*A*	*Pts*
King's College	10	10	0	0	53	7	30
Royal Veterinary College	10	8	0	2	28	21	24
City University	10	6	0	4	46	18	18
R Free, Mx & Univ Coll Hosp MS	10	3	1	6	13	32	10
University College Res	10	1	1	8	1	39	4
School of Oriental & African Studies	10	1	0	9	3	27	3

Division 2	*P*	*W*	*D*	*L*	*F*	*A*	*Pts*
Goldsmiths' College	6	6	0	0	34	8	18
St George's Hospital MS	6	1	0	5	17	10	3
R Free, Mx & Univ Coll Hosp MS Res	6	3	0	3	4	18	9
Guy's, King's, St Thomas's MS Res	6	2	0	4	6	25	6

WOMEN'S CHALLENGE CUP
King's College 0 University College 4

FA PREMIER RESERVE LEAGUES 2004–05

FA PREMIER RESERVE LEAGUE – NORTH SECTION

	P	W	D	L	F	A	GD	Pts
Manchester U	28	19	6	3	68	23	+45	63
Aston Villa	28	16	6	6	62	38	+24	54
Manchester C	28	16	6	6	55	32	+23	54
Blackburn R	28	11	12	5	45	28	+17	45
Birmingham C	28	12	7	9	37	36	+1	43
Wolverhampton W	28	9	9	10	32	32	0	36
Middlesbrough	28	10	6	12	41	42	−1	36
Everton	28	8	11	9	23	34	−11	35
Sunderland	28	8	9	11	38	44	−6	33
Bolton W	28	8	9	11	32	41	−9	33
WBA	28	6	13	9	29	36	−7	31
Newcastle U	28	8	7	13	30	41	−11	31
Leeds U	28	7	7	14	31	52	−21	28
Liverpool	28	6	8	14	27	47	−20	26
Nottingham F	28	5	6	17	21	45	−24	21

Highest attendance
Birmingham City v Manchester United 7822
(*at St Andrews*)

Leading Goalscorers

Moore L	Aston Villa	18
Wright-Phillips B	Manchester C	17
Rossi G	Manchester U	16
Graham D	Middlesbrough	15
Clarke L	Wolverhampton W	13
Vaz Te R	Bolton W	11
Ebanks-Blake S	Manchester U	11
Elvins R	WBA	10
Negouai C	Manchester C	9
Kyle K	Sunderland	9
Miller I	Manchester C	8
Vaughan J	Everton	7
Mellor N	Liverpool	7
Jones D	Manchester U	7
Bridges M	Sunderland	7
Agbonlahor G	Aston Villa	6
Derbyshire M	Blackburn R	6
Johnson J	Blackburn R	6
Bermingham K	Manchester C	6
Bellion D	Manchester U	6
Poole D	Manchester U	6
Craddock T	Middlesbrough	6

North Section Results 2004–2005	Aston Villa	Birmingham C	Blackburn R	Bolton W	Everton	Leeds U	Liverpool	Manchester C	Manchester U	Middlesbrough	Newcastle U	Nottingham F	Sunderland	WBA	Wolverhampton W
Aston Villa	—	4-1	0-0	2-1	0-1	2-1	4-0	3-2	4-4	4-1	3-0	3-3	1-0	0-0	1-0
Birmingham C	1-2	—	0-1	2-0	1-1	3-1	2-1	1-0	0-3	2-1	1-1	1-0	3-0	0-0	1-2
Blackburn R	2-1	2-2	—	1-1	0-0	2-1	2-2	4-1	2-2	1-2	1-1	3-0	0-1	3-1	3-0
Bolton W	1-1	1-1	1-0	—	0-1	3-4	2-1	2-2	0-3	1-3	1-2	0-0	2-4	2-0	2-3
Everton	3-1	1-2	1-3	0-0	—	1-1	1-1	0-1	0-1	2-2	1-0	0-0	0-4	0-0	2-1
Leeds U	3-2	1-1	0-0	1-2	3-0	—	1-1	0-3	0-4	0-5	2-1	2-1	2-2	1-2	1-3
Liverpool	1-6	2-0	3-3	1-2	0-1	0-1	—	0-1	0-1	2-1	1-1	0-0	1-0	4-1	0-2
Manchester C	2-0	2-1	0-2	1-0	2-2	4-1	5-0	—	2-1	1-1	5-0	2-0	3-2	3-3	1-1
Manchester U	0-0	2-3	2-1	5-0	3-1	3-0	5-2	3-1	—	2-0	1-1	2-0	4-1	2-0	3-0
Middlesbrough	0-2	0-1	2-2	1-3	0-1	1-1	1-0	1-3	3-3	—	0-2	4-1	1-0	3-1	1-0
Newcastle U	2-5	3-0	0-1	0-1	1-0	2-0	0-0	0-3	0-3	3-0	—	0-2	1-1	1-0	2-0
Nottingham F	1-2	0-1	1-4	1-3	0-1	1-0	1-2	3-1	1-0	0-4	2-1	—	0-3	0-1	0-1
Sunderland	7-5	1-3	1-1	1-1	1-1	0-2	0-0	0-0	0-4	3-1	2-1	2-1	—	0-3	2-2
WBA	0-1	1-0	2-1	0-0	1-1	0-0	3-1	1-3	1-1	1-2	3-3	2-2	0-0	—	0-0
Wolverhampton W	1-3	3-3	0-0	0-0	5-0	3-1	0-1	0-1	0-1	0-0	2-1	0-0	1-0	2-2	—

FA PREMIER RESERVE LEAGUE – SOUTH SECTION

	P	W	D	L	F	A	GD	Pts
Charlton Ath	28	18	7	3	46	21	+25	61
Southampton	28	18	4	6	68	29	+39	58
Arsenal	28	17	5	6	65	38	+27	56
Crystal P	28	16	5	7	47	22	+25	53
Tottenham H	28	13	8	7	47	35	+12	47
Chelsea	28	10	8	10	28	28	0	38
Watford	28	9	9	10	32	33	−1	36
Norwich C	28	10	4	14	24	40	−16	34
Fulham	28	8	9	11	29	35	−6	33
Derby Co	28	9	6	13	29	48	−19	33
West Ham U	28	7	9	12	33	51	−18	30
Coventry C	28	7	8	13	29	50	−21	29
Ipswich T	28	6	6	16	24	35	−11	24
Leicester C	28	5	9	14	36	49	−13	24
Portsmouth	28	5	7	16	28	51	−23	22

Highest attendance
Norwich City v Arsenal 6014 (*at Carrow Road*)

Leading Goalscorers

Lupoli A	Arsenal	19
Barnard L	Tottenham H	17
Best L	Southampton	13
Junior	Derby Co	10
Keene J	Portsmouth	9
Aliadiere J	Arsenal	8
Stokes A	Arsenal	8
Sam L	Charlton Ath	8
Freedman D	Crystal P	7
Crow D	Norwich C	7
Blackstock D	Southampton	7
Ashikodi M	West Ham U	7
Rebrov S	West Ham U	7
Stuart G	Charlton Ath	6
Andrews W	Crystal P	6
Counago P	Ipswich T	6
Jarvis R	Norwich C	6
Silva Sousa E	Tottenham H	6
Norville J	Watford	6

South Section Results 2004–2005

	Arsenal	Charlton Ath	Chelsea	Coventry C	Crystal Palace	Derby Co	Fulham	Ipswich T	Leicester C	Norwich C	Portsmouth	Southampton	Tottenham H	Watford	West Ham
Arsenal	—	2-2	3-2	4-0	2-0	3-0	1-0	2-1	1-1	4-0	4-1	1-2	2-1	3-2	4-2
Charlton Ath	3-1	—	3-0	1-0	0-4	5-2	1-0	4-0	2-0	5-0	0-0	1-0	2-1	1-1	1-0
Chelsea	0-2	0-0	—	0-0	0-2	3-0	1-1	1-1	1-0	0-2	1-0	1-1	0-0	1-0	2-1
Coventry C	3-2	1-1	0-2	—	2-1	0-1	1-1	1-0	0-0	3-1	1-1	1-4	0-5	3-4	2-4
Crystal Palace	1-1	1-0	1-0	3-0	—	3-1	1-0	1-0	1-2	0-1	8-0	2-1	1-1	1-1	1-1
Derby Co	0-2	0-0	0-0	2-1	1-4	—	3-2	1-1	2-1	2-0	1-0	1-4	0-1	0-0	0-2
Fulham	5-1	1-2	2-1	0-2	0-1	1-0	—	1-0	1-0	0-4	2-1	2-3	0-0	0-0	0-0
Ipswich T	1-2	3-0	1-4	0-1	1-2	4-0	0-1	—	0-1	1-2	1-0	0-0	1-0	0-0	1-1
Leicester C	2-4	1-2	1-1	1-2	0-1	3-3	2-2	3-2	—	3-3	1-3	1-2	1-4	1-1	3-0
Norwich C	2-1	0-0	0-1	3-0	0-1	0-3	0-1	0-0	0-1	—	1-0	1-0	0-2	1-0	1-2
Portsmouth	0-0	1-2	0-1	0-0	1-3	0-1	2-2	1-3	4-3	1-1	—	3-1	3-0	0-2	3-0
Southampton	2-2	1-2	2-0	3-1	2-1	3-1	2-2	2-0	3-1	5-0	5-1	—	3-0	3-0	3-2
Tottenham H	4-3	1-3	3-0	2-2	1-1	5-2	1-1	2-0	2-1	2-0	2-0	0-5	—	1-1	2-0
Watford	1-3	0-2	1-0	2-0	2-1	0-2	3-0	2-0	1-1	0-1	3-0	2-1	1-2	—	0-0
West Ham U	0-5	0-1	1-5	2-2	1-0	0-0	2-1	0-2	1-1	2-0	2-2	0-5	2-2	5-2	—

RESERVE LEAGUE PLAY-OFF

Charlton Athletic (0) 2 *(Sam 53 (pen), Walker 78)*

Manchester United (1) 4 *(Rossi 14, 56, 73, Jones 50)* 7102

at The Valley

Charlton Athletic: Randolph; Wilson, Gross, Fuller, Ricketts, Fish, Sam, Long, Bartlett (John), Walker, Thomas (Weston).

Manchester United: Heaton; Picken, Tierney, Pique, McShane, Fox, Eagles, Jones D, Bellion (Campbell), Rossi, Martin.

PONTIN'S RESERVE LEAGUES 2004–05

PONTIN'S HOLIDAYS LEAGUE

PREMIER DIVISION

	P	W	D	L	F	A	GD	Pts
Hull C	22	14	5	3	58	28	+30	47
Barnsley	22	12	3	7	44	30	+14	39
Sheffield W	22	11	4	7	36	28	+8	37
Sheffield U	22	9	7	6	41	34	+7	34
Stoke C	22	10	3	9	28	26	+2	33
Hartlepool U	22	8	7	7	35	33	+2	31
Tranmere R	22	9	4	9	25	26	–1	31
Preston NE	22	7	6	9	31	46	–15	27
Rotherham U	22	6	8	8	31	39	–8	26
Walsall	22	6	5	11	40	46	–6	23
Wigan Ath	22	5	6	11	21	32	–11	21
Bradford C	22	3	6	13	21	43	–22	15

DIVISION ONE WEST

	P	W	D	L	F	A	GD	Pts
Manchester U	22	14	5	3	49	28	+21	47
Carlisle U	22	13	3	6	43	36	+7	42
Blackpool	22	12	4	6	34	21	+13	40
Oldham Ath	22	12	3	7	48	34	+14	39
Bury	22	10	7	5	30	23	+7	37
Macclesfield T	22	8	7	7	31	27	+4	31
Burnley	22	5	11	6	24	21	+3	26
Chester C	22	7	3	12	25	37	–12	24
Stockport Co	22	5	7	10	28	37	–9	22
Shrewsbury T	22	5	6	11	25	31	–6	21
Rochdale	22	4	6	12	23	38	–15	18
Wrexham	22	6	0	16	27	54	–27	18

DIVISION ONE EAST

	P	W	D	L	F	A	GD	Pts
Huddersfield T	18	4	0	4	41	16	+25	42
Scunthorpe U	18	12	2	4	33	21	+12	38
Doncaster R	18	11	4	3	42	26	+16	37
Lincoln C	18	9	2	7	35	27	+8	29
York C	18	6	5	7	21	27	–6	23
Grimsby T	18	7	1	10	33	37	–4	22
Boston U	17	6	3	8	27	27	0	21
Halifax T	17	4	3	10	18	33	–15	15
Notts Co	18	4	3	11	17	36	–19	15
Darlington	18	3	3	12	14	31	–17	12

PONTIN'S HOLIDAYS COMBINATION

CENTRAL AND EAST DIVISION

	P	W	D	L	F	A	GD	Pts
Luton T	15	11	3	1	34	10	+24	36
Reading	15	9	3	3	41	16	+25	30
Millwall	15	8	5	2	28	14	+14	29
Brighton & HA	15	7	6	2	19	9	+10	27
Northampton T	15	7	6	2	20	12	+8	27
QPR	15	8	2	5	21	13	+8	26
Peterborough U	15	6	4	5	27	24	+3	22
Colchester U	15	5	4	6	35	23	+12	19
MK Dons	15	6	1	8	26	26	0	19
Crawley T	15	4	5	6	27	42	–15	17
Southend U	15	4	4	7	25	27	–2	16
Gillingham	15	3	6	6	16	22	–6	15
Oxford U	15	3	6	6	16	29	–13	15
Aldershot T	15	4	1	10	12	34	–22	13
Woking	15	3	2	10	19	41	–22	11
Stevenage B	15	1	4	10	14	38	–24	7

WALES AND WEST DIVISION

	P	W	D	L	F	A	GD	Pts
Cardiff C	16	10	2	4	34	19	+15	32
Plymouth Arg	16	9	2	5	31	24	+7	29
Cheltenham T	16	7	6	3	25	19	+6	27
Yeovil T	16	7	2	7	31	27	+4	23
Bristol C	16	7	2	7	29	27	+2	23
Bristol R	16	6	4	6	30	35	–5	22
Swindon T	16	5	2	9	29	28	+1	17
Swansea C	16	5	2	9	25	45	–20	17
Bournemouth	16	3	4	9	18	28	–10	13

FOOTBALL LEAGUE YOUTH TABLES 2004–05

DIVISION 1 NORTH	P	W	D	L	F	A	GD	Pts
Oldham Ath	9	8	1	0	24	9	+15	25
Tranmere R	9	5	3	1	13	4	+9	18
Burnley	9	4	4	1	18	9	+9	16
Port Vale	9	3	4	2	12	10	+2	13
Scunthorpe U	9	3	3	3	11	8	+3	12
Hartlepool U	9	3	2	4	15	23	–8	11
Wigan Ath	9	3	1	5	12	18	–6	10
Chesterfield	9	2	2	5	10	13	–3	8
Darlington	9	1	3	5	12	16	–4	6
Mansfield T	9	1	1	7	11	28	–17	4

DIVISION 2 NORTH	P	W	D	L	F	A	GD	Pts
Rotherham U	9	6	2	1	16	9	+7	20
Stockport Co	9	5	2	2	20	12	+8	17
Blackpool	9	4	2	3	9	6	+3	14
Bury	9	4	0	5	14	12	+2	12
Doncaster R	9	3	3	3	10	8	+2	12
Chester C	9	3	3	3	14	13	+1	12
Macclesfield T	8	3	3	2	11	10	+1	12
Grimsby T	8	3	2	3	11	14	–3	11
Hull C	9	2	2	5	10	19	–9	8
York C	9	1	1	7	8	20	–12	4

DIVISION 3 NORTH	P	W	D	L	F	A	GD	Pts
Preston NE	8	7	0	1	19	5	+14	21
Carlisle U	8	7	0	1	18	10	+8	21
Notts Co	8	4	1	3	20	15	+5	13
Shrewsbury T	8	3	1	4	14	15	–1	10
Bradford C	8	3	1	4	14	17	–3	10
Lincoln C	8	3	1	4	10	14	–4	10
Wrexham	8	3	0	5	11	16	–5	9
Rochdale	8	2	2	4	16	16	0	8
Boston U	8	0	2	6	5	19	–14	2

DIVISION 1 SOUTH	P	W	D	L	F	A	GD	Pts
Cambridge U	8	6	2	0	16	10	+6	20
AFC Bournemouth	8	4	1	3	16	14	+2	13
QPR	8	4	0	4	16	11	+5	12
WBA	8	3	2	3	13	11	+2	11
Leyton Orient	8	3	2	3	16	15	+1	11
Swindon T	8	3	2	3	11	15	–4	11
Brentford	8	3	1	4	15	15	0	10
Exeter C	8	1	4	3	10	15	–5	7
Luton T	8	1	2	5	9	16	–7	5

DIVISION 2 SOUTH	P	W	D	L	F	A	GD	Pts
Portsmouth	8	6	1	1	19	8	+11	19
Bristol R	8	6	0	2	20	14	+6	18
Colchester U	8	5	0	3	14	9	+5	15
Brighton & HA	8	4	1	3	12	8	+4	13
Rushden & D	8	3	2	3	12	9	+3	11
Walsall	8	3	2	3	14	16	–2	11
Plymouth Arg	8	2	2	4	9	14	–5	8
Yeovil T	8	1	4	3	13	17	–4	7
Oxford U	8	0	0	8	7	25	–18	0

DIVISION 3 SOUTH	P	W	D	L	F	A	GD	Pts
Northampton T	8	5	0	3	16	6	+10	15
Newport Co	8	5	0	3	15	9	+6	15
Gillingham	8	4	2	2	12	7	+5	14
Wycombe W	8	4	2	2	11	8	+3	14
Southend U	8	4	1	3	10	11	–1	13
Swansea C	8	3	2	3	11	15	–4	11
Cheltenham T	8	2	1	5	10	12	–2	7
Cirencester T	8	1	4	3	9	14	–5	7
Hereford U	8	0	4	4	5	17	–12	4

THE YOUTH ALLIANCE CUP

FIRST ROUND
Hull C 4, Lincoln C 2
Grimsby T 2, Notts Co 1
Darlington 3, Hartlepool U 2
Burnley 2, Blackpool 1
Wrexham 0, Tranmere R 2
Preston NE 2, Carlisle U 2
Preston NE won 5-3 on penalties.
Scunthorpe U 5, Chesterfield 5
Chesterfield won 5-4 on penalties.
Oldham Ath 3, Wigan Ath 3
Oldham Ath won 6-5 on penalties.
Rotherham U 3, Bradford C 1
Doncaster R 4, Mansfield T 3
Rochdale 2, York C 1
Bury 0, Stockport Co 1
Rushden & D 0, Luton T 3
Exeter C 2, Bristol R 0
Southend U 0, Leyton Orient 0
Southend U won 4-2 on penalties.
Swindon T 2, Plymouth Arg 0
Cheltenham T 4, Swansea C 2
Northampton T 1, WBA 2
Bournemouth 1, Newport Co 1
Bournemouth won 5-4 on penalties.
Cirencester T 1, Cambridge U 1
Cambridge U won 9-8 on penalties.
QPR 2, Brentford 1
Oxford U 3, Wycombe W 6
Gillingham 1, Colchester U 3
Portsmouth 2, Yeovil T 0
Byes: Brighton & HA, Boston U, Chester C, Hereford U, Macclesfield T, Port Vale, Shrewsbury T, Walsall.

SECOND ROUND
Bournemouth 4, Southend U 3
Burnley 3, Darlington 0
Cheltenham T 4, Brighton & HA 4
Cheltenham T won 7-6 on penalties.
Chester C 2, Tranmere R 4
Doncaster R 2, Boston U 0
Hull C 2, Grimsby T 2
Grimsby T won 4-2 on penalties.
Oldham Ath 2, Macclesfield T 0
Portsmouth 4, Hereford U 0
Port Vale 3, Rotherham U 2
QPR 2, Colchester U 0
Rochdale 1, Chesterfield 2
Shrewsbury T 4, Exeter C 7
Stockport Co 1, Preston NE 2
Swindon T 7, Luton T 0
Walsall 2, Wycombe W 4
WBA 2, Cambridge U 1

THIRD ROUND
Burnley 3, Tranmere R 2
Grimsby T 4, Chesterfield 0
Oldham Ath 2, Port Vale 0
Preston NE 0, Doncaster R 1
Cheltenham T 1, Bournemouth 3
QPR 1, WBA 0
Swindon T 5, Exeter C 3
Wycombe W 2, Portsmouth 1

FOURTH ROUND
Bournemouth 0, QPR 1
Swindon T 2, Wycombe W 1
Burnley 4, Doncaster R 0
Oldham Ath 3, Grimsby T 0

SEMI-FINALS
Oldham Ath 5, Burnley 5
Burnley won 4-1 on penalties.
Swindon T 3, QPR 2

FINAL
Burnley 1, Swindon T 1
Swindon T won 5-4 on penalties.

FA ACADEMY UNDER 18 LEAGUE 2004–05

GROUP A	P	W	D	L	F	A	GD	Pts
Southampton	28	23	2	3	62	25	37	71
Charlton Ath	28	14	6	8	35	28	7	48
Arsenal	28	13	3	12	45	39	6	42
Ipswich T	28	11	6	11	39	39	0	39
West Ham U	28	11	4	13	37	53	–16	37
Millwall	28	11	2	15	34	44	–10	35
Chelsea	28	8	5	15	24	33	–9	29
Crystal P	27	7	7	13	35	51	–16	28
Norwich C	28	6	7	15	26	38	–12	25
Fulham	27	4	5	18	23	54	–31	17

Crystal P v Fulham, fixture not completed.

GROUP B	P	W	D	L	F	A	GD	Pts
Coventry C	28	17	5	6	58	32	26	56
Reading	28	15	8	5	58	36	22	53
Aston Villa	28	16	4	8	55	42	13	52
Watford	28	15	6	7	46	27	19	51
Leicester C	28	13	0	15	59	52	7	39
Cardiff C	28	9	11	8	39	37	2	38
Birmingham C	28	10	6	12	44	45	–1	36
Tottenham H	28	8	11	9	41	47	–6	35
Bristol C	28	5	5	18	31	55	–24	20
Milton Keynes Dons	28	5	5	18	34	64	–30	20

GROUP C	P	W	D	L	F	A	GD	Pts
Blackburn R	28	19	4	5	57	24	33	61
Manchester U	28	17	6	5	61	41	20	57
Everton	28	14	9	5	46	34	12	51
Manchester C	28	13	10	5	66	37	29	49
Crewe Alex	28	13	6	9	53	44	9	45
Stoke C	28	10	9	9	39	46	–7	39
Wolverhampton W	28	8	13	7	38	39	–1	37
Bolton W	28	6	7	15	38	53	–15	25
Liverpool	28	5	7	16	24	52	–28	22

GROUP D	P	W	D	L	F	A	GD	Pts
Newcastle U	28	17	8	3	55	26	29	59
Sheffield W	28	15	6	7	51	33	18	51
Barnsley	28	11	8	9	41	43	–2	41
Leeds U	28	12	4	12	50	43	7	40
Sunderland	28	10	5	13	32	34	–2	35
Nottingham F	28	8	8	12	33	40	–7	32
Sheffield U	28	5	11	12	39	45	–6	26
Derby Co	28	5	9	14	28	56	–28	24
Huddersfield T	28	5	7	16	30	47	–17	22
Middlesbrough	28	4	9	15	31	58	–27	21

NON-LEAGUE TABLES 2004–05

MINERVA SPARTAN SOUTH MIDLANDS PREMIER

	P	W	D	L	F	A	GD	Pts
Potters Bar Town	38	29	5	4	95	32	63	92
Hanwell Town	38	22	10	6	91	52	39	76
Haywood United	38	19	10	9	72	48	24	67
Tring Athletic	38	18	11	9	53	43	10	65
Harefield United	38	15	17	6	48	33	15	62
Hillingdon Borough	38	18	6	14	76	55	21	60
St Margaretsbury	38	15	11	12	65	49	16	56
Welwyn Garden City	38	16	8	14	61	52	9	56
Broxbourne Borough V&E	38	15	9	14	64	63	1	54
Biggleswade Town	38	15	5	18	61	72	–11	50
London Colney	38	14	8	16	56	67	–11	50
Ruislip Manor	38	13	10	15	54	61	–7	49
Holmer Green	38	14	7	17	47	58	–11	49
Leverstock Green	38	10	15	13	62	61	1	45
Harpenden Town	38	11	11	16	43	60	–17	44
Royston Town	38	10	11	17	55	76	–21	41
Langford	38	11	6	21	56	82	–26	39
Haringey Borough	38	10	6	22	43	72	–29	36
Bedford United & Valerio	38	7	10	21	43	77	–34	31
Hoddesdon Town	38	7	6	25	49	81	–32	27

MINERVA SPARTAN SOUTH MIDLANDS DIVISION ONE

	P	W	D	L	F	A	GD	Pts
Oxhey Jets	32	25	4	3	101	28	73	79
Buckingham Athletic	32	23	3	6	65	28	37	72
Biggleswade United	32	22	3	7	110	41	69	69
New Bradwell St Peter	32	22	3	7	72	56	16	69
Colney Heath	32	18	9	5	72	40	32	63
Winslow United	32	17	5	10	80	56	24	56
Brache Sparta	32	16	5	11	68	53	15	53
Cockfosters	32	16	4	12	60	53	7	52
Kentish Town	32	12	6	14	52	58	–6	42
Arlesey Athletic	32	11	5	16	53	63	–10	38
Brimsdown Rovers	32	11	3	18	48	63	–15	36
Stony Stratford Town	32	10	6	16	51	76	–25	36
Sun Postal Sports	32	8	3	21	46	79	–33	27
Shillington	32	6	7	19	52	84	–32	25
Cranfield United	32	5	9	18	54	87	–33	24
Amersham Town	32	7	2	23	37	98	–61	23
Ampthill Town	32	2	5	25	36	94	–58	11

COMBINED COUNTIES PREMIER

	P	W	D	L	F	A	GD	Pts
Walton Casuals	46	38	4	4	134	35	99	118
North Greenford U (–3)	46	29	8	9	117	69	48	92
Chessington & Hook	46	26	13	7	117	61	56	91
Godalming & Guildford	46	28	7	11	107	59	48	91
Sandhurst Town	46	26	10	10	106	61	45	88
Bedfont	46	26	7	13	80	63	17	85
Horley Town	46	23	9	14	82	51	31	78
Chipstead	46	22	7	17	78	69	9	73
Raynes Park Vale	46	20	8	18	85	80	5	68
Westfield	46	19	9	18	68	67	1	66
Southall	46	20	6	20	75	83	–8	66
AFC Guildford	46	20	6	20	73	82	–9	66
Ash United	46	15	17	14	76	67	9	62
Colliers Wood United	46	17	10	19	89	82	7	61
Frimley Green (+3)	46	13	16	17	68	88	–20	58
Merstham	46	15	12	19	78	73	5	57
Feltham	46	16	9	21	71	83	–12	57
Cobham	46	16	7	23	56	73	–17	55
Reading Town (–6)	46	16	7	23	76	94	–18	49
Cove (+3)	46	10	11	25	60	92	–32	44
Farnham Town	46	11	7	28	48	85	–37	40
Chessington U (+3)	46	7	8	31	62	133	–71	32
Hartley Wintney	46	6	13	27	44	110	–66	31
AFC Wallingford	46	5	5	36	43	133	–90	20

COMBINED COUNTIES DIVISION ONE

	P	W	D	L	F	A	GD	Pts
Coney Hall	34	28	5	1	111	41	70	89
Bedfont Green (+3)	34	24	7	3	101	36	65	82
Bookham (+2)	34	24	3	7	99	37	62	77
Warlingham	34	21	9	4	93	32	61	72
Farleigh Rovers	34	21	4	9	84	44	40	67
Worcester Park (+3)	34	17	7	10	87	45	42	61
Crescent Rovers	34	18	6	10	70	62	8	60
Staines Lammas (+4)	34	15	6	13	74	55	19	55
Seelec Delta	34	15	5	14	86	55	31	50
Sheerwater	34	13	8	13	75	68	7	47
Monotype (–1)	34	13	4	17	62	78	–16	42
Ditton (–1)	34	8	7	19	41	71	–30	30
Merrow (+2)	34	7	6	21	49	71	–22	29
Chobham & Ottershaw (+2)	34	8	3	23	49	109	–60	29
Netherne Village (–1)	34	8	4	22	60	103	–43	27

Shottermill & Haslemere	34	6	5	23	31	94	–63	23
Hersham RBL (–7)	34	6	8	20	51	81	–30	19
Cranleigh	34	5	1	28	27	168	–141	16

EASTWAY ESSEX SENIOR

	P	W	D	L	F	A	GD	Pts
Enfield Town	28	20	6	2	62	21	41	66
Burnham Ramblers	28	21	2	5	63	34	29	65
Waltham Abbey (–1)	28	19	2	7	61	29	32	58
Barkingside	28	16	7	5	62	31	31	55
Romford	28	16	5	7	56	40	16	53
Southend Manor	28	14	5	9	51	44	7	47
Basildon United	28	14	4	10	42	31	11	46
Sawbridgeworth Town	28	11	9	8	47	36	11	42
Concord Rangers	28	12	3	13	50	44	6	39
Bowers & Pitsea	28	9	7	12	53	53	0	34
Stansted	28	7	4	17	41	74	–33	25
Eton Manor	28	6	3	19	34	62	–28	21
London APSA	28	5	4	19	33	72	–39	19
Brentwood Town	28	3	7	18	30	66	–36	16
Hullbridge Sports	28	1	4	23	22	70	–48	7

GREENE KING ESSEX INTERMEDIATE

	P	W	D	L	F	A	GD	Pts
White Ensign	22	17	2	3	66	27	39	53
Frenford Senior	22	16	2	4	47	23	24	50
Manford Way	22	15	3	4	60	26	34	48
Debden Sports	22	12	2	8	41	33	8	38
Harold Wood Athletic	22	11	2	9	44	36	8	35
Bishop's Stortford Swifts	22	9	5	8	44	36	8	32
Epping	22	7	5	10	25	39	–14	26
Takeley	22	7	4	11	30	41	–11	25
Old Chelmsfordians	22	8	0	14	34	53	–19	24
Kelvedon Hatch	22	6	2	14	26	49	–23	20
Shenfield AFC	22	4	4	14	21	44	–23	16
Rayleigh Town	22	4	1	17	24	55	–31	13

GLS FOOTBALL HELLENIC PREMIER

	P	W	D	L	F	A	GD	Pts
Highworth Town	42	30	8	4	101	33	68	98
Didcot Town (–1)	42	31	5	6	99	21	78	97
Bishops Cleeve	42	25	11	6	86	30	56	86
Slimbridge	42	26	8	8	87	48	39	86
Abingdon United	42	25	9	8	88	49	39	84
Carterton Town	42	24	8	10	72	48	24	80
North Leigh	42	24	7	11	76	46	30	79
Fairford Town	42	19	5	18	62	54	8	62
Almondsbury Town	42	16	13	13	80	59	21	61
Wantage Town	42	13	16	13	52	43	9	55
Witney United	42	15	10	17	45	52	–7	55
Tuffley Rovers	42	12	14	16	43	47	–4	50
Milton United	42	14	7	21	48	67	–19	49
Henley Town (–3)	42	14	8	20	58	79	–21	47
Shortwood United	42	13	7	22	58	77	–19	46
Pegasus Juniors	42	12	8	22	62	95	–33	44
Hungerford Town	42	11	9	22	45	66	–21	42
Ardley United	42	9	15	18	48	71	–23	42
Chipping Norton Town	42	11	7	24	39	83	–44	40
Bicester Town	42	8	4	30	38	103	–65	28
Wootton Bassett Town	42	6	9	27	30	84	–54	27
Pewsey Vale	42	6	8	28	42	104	–62	26

GLS FOOTBALL HELLENIC DIVISION ONE WEST

	P	W	D	L	F	A	GD	Pts
Shrivenham	34	25	3	6	91	36	55	78
Trowbridge Town	34	24	5	5	97	38	59	77
Kidlington	34	20	6	8	79	49	30	66
Tytherington Rocks	34	20	4	10	91	54	37	64
Easington Sports	34	18	7	9	60	38	22	61
Cheltenham Saracens	34	18	6	10	60	45	15	60
Headington Amateurs	34	17	6	11	69	44	25	57
Harrow Hill	34	16	6	12	60	44	16	54
Winterbourne United	34	15	7	12	73	53	20	52
Clanfield	34	13	7	14	55	51	4	46
Hook Norton	34	12	10	12	51	56	–5	46
Ross Town	34	11	7	16	57	54	3	40
Purton	34	9	8	17	39	61	–22	35
Cirencester United	34	7	11	16	40	63	–23	32
Quarry Nomads	34	10	1	23	61	106	–45	31
Middle Barton	34	7	4	23	36	116	–80	25
Malmesbury Victoria	34	7	3	24	33	80	–47	24
Adderbury Park	34	6	1	27	47	111	–64	19

GLS FOOTBALL HELLENIC DIVISION ONE EAST

	P	*W*	*D*	*L*	*F*	*A*	*GD*	*Pts*
Eton Wick	34	23	8	3	100	35	65	77
Kintbury Rangers	34	23	5	6	79	33	46	74
Penn & Tylers Green	34	23	3	8	94	51	43	72
Finchampstead	34	19	7	8	62	37	25	64
Binfield	34	16	8	10	54	35	19	56
Banbury United Res	34	16	8	10	66	68	–2	56
Badshot Lea	34	16	4	14	75	63	12	52
Rayners Lane	34	15	5	14	75	56	19	50
Chinnor	34	12	8	14	49	47	2	44
Hounslow Borough	34	12	7	15	61	85	–24	43
Wokingham & Emmbrook	34	13	3	18	50	66	–16	42
Letcombe	34	11	7	16	53	66	–13	40
Englefield Green Rovers	34	11	7	16	49	67	–18	40
Old Woodstock Town	34	10	9	15	50	64	–14	39
Holyport	34	9	7	18	44	91	–47	34
Prestwood	34	9	4	21	50	82	–32	31
Chalfont Wasps	34	7	7	20	50	69	–19	28
Bisley Sports	34	6	3	25	33	79	–46	21

TRAVEL FACTORY MIDLAND ALLIANCE

	P	*W*	*D*	*L*	*F*	*A*	*GD*	*Pts*
Rushall Olympic	42	27	7	8	88	44	44	88
Chasetown	42	25	6	11	78	45	33	81
Coalville	42	22	11	9	68	38	30	77
Quorn	42	21	11	10	78	52	26	74
Malvern Town	42	21	9	12	78	70	8	72
Westfields	42	18	13	11	61	48	13	67
Oadby Town	42	18	11	13	64	53	11	65
Stourbridge	42	19	7	16	85	65	20	64
Racing Club Warwick	42	19	7	16	79	68	11	64
Boldmere St Michaels	42	19	7	16	79	70	9	64
Stratford Town	42	20	4	18	71	67	4	64
Romulus	42	17	11	14	74	66	8	62
Barwell	42	17	10	15	60	60	0	61
Loughborough Dynamo	42	16	6	20	69	83	–14	54
Alvechurch	42	16	5	21	75	69	6	53
Causeway United	42	12	9	21	53	68	–15	45
Oldbury United (–3)	42	13	8	21	70	90	–20	44
Studley	42	11	11	20	55	76	–21	44
Cradley Town	42	12	7	23	59	84	–25	43
Biddulph Victoria	42	10	11	21	59	83	–24	41
Ludlow Town	42	12	5	25	55	84	–29	41
Bridgnorth Town	42	7	4	31	38	113	–75	25

MIDLAND COMBINATION

	P	*W*	*D*	*L*	*F*	*A*	*GD*	*Pts*
Leamington	42	35	4	3	132	40	92	109
Coventry Sphinx	42	28	6	8	137	73	64	90
Coventry Marconi	42	28	4	10	111	55	56	88
Bloxwich Town	42	26	7	9	91	55	36	85
Barnt Green Spartak	42	22	11	9	93	60	33	77
Southam United	42	23	5	14	84	68	16	74
Feckenham	42	19	10	13	85	78	7	67
Brocton	42	18	11	13	89	61	28	65
Coleshill Town	42	19	4	19	80	78	2	61
Castle Vale	42	19	4	19	79	77	2	61
Bolehall Swifts	42	16	9	17	67	75	–8	57
Nuneaton Griff	42	17	4	21	75	79	–4	55
Dudley Sports	42	15	10	17	64	71	–7	55
Meir KA	42	15	6	21	88	91	–3	51
Pilkington XXX	42	12	11	19	75	89	–14	47
Pershore Town	42	13	6	23	75	95	–20	45
Shifnal Town	42	12	9	21	55	82	–27	45
Highgate United	42	12	8	22	50	94	–44	44
Massey Ferguson (–3)	42	13	2	27	57	88	–31	38
Continental Star	42	10	6	26	56	108	–52	36
Alveston	42	9	5	28	59	122	–63	32
West Midlands Police	42	8	4	30	47	110	–63	28

EXPRESS & STAR WEST MIDLANDS PREMIER

	P	*W*	*D*	*L*	*F*	*A*	*GD*	*Pts*
Tipton Town	38	31	3	4	111	19	92	96
Market Drayton Town	38	23	6	9	76	47	29	75
Shawbury United	38	20	7	11	59	45	14	67
Ledbury Town	38	18	7	13	81	60	21	61
Wellington	38	18	6	14	84	65	19	60
Heath Hayes	38	18	6	14	67	54	13	60
Bromyard Town	38	16	8	14	67	62	5	56
Lye Town	38	16	8	14	63	59	4	56
Bustleholme	38	15	10	13	90	67	23	55
Gornal Athletic	38	15	9	14	55	47	8	54
Wolverhampton Casuals	38	15	9	14	67	73	–6	54
Dudley Town	38	14	11	13	64	63	1	53
Kington Town	38	13	11	14	72	90	–18	50
Smethwick Sikh Temple	38	15	4	19	60	71	–11	49
Pelsall Villa	38	13	8	17	73	86	–13	47
Tividale	38	12	10	16	56	69	–13	46
Goodrich	38	11	11	16	40	60	–20	44
Brierley & Hagley Alliance	38	7	9	22	46	86	–40	30
Coseley Town	38	6	10	22	48	96	–48	28
Wednesfield	38	4	7	27	49	109	–60	19

(Ettingshall Holy Trinity record expunged)

EVERARDS LEICESTERSHIRE SENIOR PREMIER

	P	*W*	*D*	*L*	*F*	*A*	*GD*	*Pts*
Thurnby Rangers	34	25	8	1	89	21	68	83
Holwell Sports	34	23	8	3	91	35	56	77
Ellistown	34	19	4	11	69	57	12	61
Kirby Muxloe SC	34	17	9	8	66	43	23	60
Ibstock Welfare	34	17	4	13	79	61	18	55
Rothley Imperial	34	16	6	12	60	50	10	54
Thurmaston Town	34	16	6	12	67	63	4	54
Barrow Town	34	15	6	13	66	63	3	51
Friar Lane & Epworth	34	14	8	12	77	58	19	50
Ratby Sports	34	11	11	12	61	71	–10	44
St Andrews SC	34	12	7	15	69	76	–7	43
Birstall United	34	11	9	14	53	56	–3	42
Aylestone Park OB	34	11	6	17	49	74	–25	39
Stapenhill	34	10	7	17	59	79	–20	37
Blaby & Whetstone Ath	34	10	6	18	58	69	–11	36
Highfield Rangers	34	8	5	21	42	79	–37	29
Anstey Nomads	34	7	4	23	41	96	–55	25
Downes Sports	34	4	6	24	38	83	–45	18

SYDENHAMS WESSEX DIVISION ONE

	P	*W*	*D*	*L*	*F*	*A*	*GD*	*Pts*
Lymington & New Milton	42	31	6	5	123	41	82	99
Winchester City	42	31	4	7	134	38	96	97
Thatcham Town	42	24	13	5	95	51	44	85
Gosport Borough	42	25	9	8	75	49	26	84
Andover	42	24	8	10	100	67	33	80
AFC Newbury	42	23	8	11	80	45	35	77
Wimborne Town	42	20	12	10	82	53	29	72
AFC Totton	42	19	10	13	69	59	10	67
BAT Sports	42	17	12	13	63	60	3	63
Moneyfields	42	14	14	14	62	57	5	56
Bournemouth	42	16	8	18	54	65	–11	56
VT FC	42	16	7	19	69	80	–11	55
Cowes Sports	42	16	6	20	70	69	1	54
Bemerton Heath H	42	15	6	21	64	72	–8	51
Hamworthy United	42	14	9	19	51	72	–21	51
Fareham Town (–2)	42	13	9	20	50	63	–13	46
Christchurch	42	12	8	22	64	80	–16	44
Brockenhurst	42	12	5	25	52	79	–27	41
Alton Town	42	9	10	23	50	90	–40	37
Portland United	42	8	6	28	35	104	–69	30
Hamble ASSC	42	6	7	29	36	121	–85	25
Downton	42	7	3	32	50	113	–63	24

SYDENHAMS WESSEX DIVISION TWO

	P	*W*	*D*	*L*	*F*	*A*	*GD*	*Pts*
Lymington Town	42	35	3	4	121	28	93	108
Poole Town	42	33	4	5	123	29	94	103
Locks Heath	42	24	10	8	80	44	36	82
Romsey Town	42	23	8	11	84	55	29	77
Petersfield Town	42	21	10	11	77	49	28	73
Liss Athletic	42	21	8	13	106	77	29	71
Blackfield & Langley	42	20	9	13	90	62	28	69
Stockbridge	42	19	9	14	91	71	20	66
Horndean	42	18	12	12	85	76	9	66
Alresford Town	42	20	4	18	85	74	11	64
Ringwood Town	42	20	3	19	89	84	5	63
Whitchurch United	42	17	5	20	72	77	–5	56
Shaftesbury	42	15	9	18	65	85	–20	54
Hythe & Dibden	42	15	7	20	75	105	–30	52
Amesbury Town	42	14	7	21	76	99	–23	49
Brading Town	42	13	8	21	75	84	–9	47
East Cowes Vics	42	12	9	21	71	85	–14	45
Andover New Street	42	12	6	24	45	100	–55	42
United Services Portsmouth	42	9	6	27	58	103	–45	33
Bishops Waltham Town	42	7	12	23	46	104	–58	33
Fawley	42	9	4	29	54	111	–57	31
AFC Aldermaston	42	7	3	32	50	116	–66	24

SYDENHAMS WESSEX DIVISION THREE

	P	*W*	*D*	*L*	*F*	*A*	*GD*	*Pts*
Colden Common	38	28	4	6	123	39	84	88
Hayling United	38	26	8	4	104	30	74	86
Farnborough North End	38	26	7	5	111	38	73	85
Fleetlands	38	23	6	9	115	42	73	75
Paulsgrove	38	22	7	9	93	46	47	73
Otterbourne	38	23	3	12	88	36	52	72
Overton United	38	22	6	10	88	52	36	72
Tadley Calleva (–1)	38	21	7	10	84	43	41	69
Micheldever	38	18	11	9	82	49	33	65
Clanfield	38	16	12	10	72	70	2	60
Laverstock & Ford	38	14	10	14	73	59	14	52
Netley Central Sports	38	13	7	18	71	66	5	46
Ordnance Survey	38	11	9	18	44	55	–11	42
AFC Portchester	38	11	6	21	65	83	–18	39
Hamble Club	38	9	11	18	51	86	–35	38
Verwood Town	38	8	6	24	54	95	–41	30
Fleet Spurs	38	6	11	21	59	98	–39	29
Ludgershall Sports	38	7	3	28	48	118	–70	24
QK Southampton	38	4	4	30	41	178	–137	16
Yateley Green	38	2	2	34	30	213	–183	8

(Dave Coleman and RS Basingstoke records expunged)

DORSET PREMIER

	P	W	D	L	F	A	GD	Pts
Hamworthy Recreation	32	22	6	4	95	35	60	72
Poole Borough	32	21	5	6	77	33	44	68
Dorchester Town Res (−3)	32	21	6	5	81	29	52	66
Holt United	32	18	8	6	64	32	32	62
Gillingham Town	32	17	9	6	78	38	40	60
Sherborne Town (−3)	32	18	6	8	64	49	15	57
Westland Sports	32	16	7	9	69	44	25	55
Bournemouth Sports	32	16	6	10	75	53	22	54
Blandford United	32	15	4	13	61	56	5	49
Swanage Town & Herston	32	11	9	12	47	49	−2	42
Cobham Sports	32	10	7	15	53	70	−17	37
Sturminster Newton	32	9	8	15	52	63	−11	35
Dorchester United	32	8	4	20	45	66	−21	28
Wareham Rangers	32	8	2	22	53	83	−30	26
Cranborne	32	6	6	20	43	84	−41	24
Bridport Reserves	32	5	5	22	34	62	−28	20
Stourpaine	32	2	0	30	14	159	−145	6

SCREWFIX DIRECT WESTERN PREMIER

	P	W	D	L	F	A	GD	Pts
Bideford	38	28	4	6	105	26	79	88
Corsham Town	38	25	8	5	79	33	46	83
Frome Town	38	23	7	8	78	35	43	76
Hallen	38	23	6	9	81	38	43	75
Exmouth Town	38	21	8	9	64	39	25	71
Bridgwater Town	38	22	4	12	66	46	20	70
Bristol Manor Farm	38	17	7	14	56	59	−3	58
Bitton	38	15	12	11	64	66	−2	57
Backwell United	38	14	13	11	58	46	12	55
Brislington	38	14	8	16	50	51	−1	50
Keynsham Town	38	14	7	17	39	62	−23	49
Barnstaple Town	38	15	3	20	51	68	−17	48
Odd Down	38	12	9	17	47	57	−10	45
Melksham Town	38	10	9	19	57	70	−13	39
Devizes Town	38	10	8	20	37	63	−26	38
Torrington	38	11	5	22	50	83	−33	38
Welton Rovers	38	8	12	18	59	80	−21	36
Bishop Sutton	38	9	9	20	44	71	−27	36
Bridport	38	10	4	24	52	75	−23	34
Clyst Rovers	38	3	9	26	44	113	−69	18

SCREWFIX DIRECT WESTERN DIVISION ONE

	P	W	D	L	F	A	GD	Pts
Willand Rovers	38	27	7	4	88	31	57	88
Calne Town	38	23	10	5	91	30	61	79
Radstock Town	38	24	7	7	67	38	29	79
Dawlish Town	38	20	12	6	81	42	39	72
Larkhall Athletic	38	21	8	9	65	35	30	71
Shrewton United	38	22	3	13	83	56	27	69
Street	38	17	12	9	68	46	22	63
Ilfracombe Town	38	16	11	11	72	76	−4	59
Clevedon United	38	15	7	16	61	64	−3	52
Elmore	38	14	7	17	59	67	−8	49
Weston St Johns	38	14	7	17	62	88	−26	49
Almondsbury	38	11	10	17	55	79	−24	43
Cadbury Heath	38	10	12	16	46	58	−12	42
Wellington	38	11	9	18	58	76	−18	42
Chard Town	38	11	8	19	43	63	−20	41
Westbury United	38	8	14	16	57	75	−18	38
Saltash United	38	8	11	19	61	77	−16	35
Minehead	38	8	10	20	41	64	−23	34
Biddestone	38	3	14	21	40	81	−41	23
Shepton Mallet	38	3	9	26	38	90	−52	18

FIREWATCH DEVON COUNTY

	P	W	D	L	F	A	GD	Pts
Teignmouth	40	30	5	5	106	44	62	95
Plymstock United	40	27	6	7	107	41	66	87
Dartmouth	40	25	6	9	92	52	40	81
Ivybridge Town	40	22	9	9	110	60	50	75
Vospers Oak Villa (−1)	40	23	4	13	95	61	34	72
Newton Abbot (+2)	40	20	8	12	89	52	37	70
Buckland Athletic	40	19	12	9	78	52	26	69
Dartington Sports Club	40	20	9	11	76	53	23	69
Elburton Villa	40	20	6	14	95	63	32	66
Budleigh Salterton	40	20	6	14	81	78	3	66
Newton Abbot Spurs	40	18	7	15	90	71	19	61
Ottery St Mary	40	16	9	15	70	71	−1	57
St Loyes	40	16	5	19	65	80	−15	53
Holsworthy	40	15	5	20	67	65	2	50
University of Exeter	40	13	6	21	74	85	−11	45
Cullompton Rangers	40	11	10	19	68	89	−21	43
Alphington	40	12	3	25	44	93	−49	39
Appledore	40	11	3	26	59	99	−40	36
Crediton United	40	10	5	25	52	115	−63	35
Stoke Gabriel	40	6	0	34	49	137	−88	18
Exeter Civil Service (−3)	40	1	6	33	27	133	−106	6

CARLSBERG SOUTH WESTERN

	P	W	D	L	F	A	GD	Pts
St Blazey	32	26	3	3	109	25	84	81
Bodmin Town	32	24	2	6	102	23	79	74
Millbrook	32	21	7	4	77	39	38	70
Falmouth Town	32	20	6	6	76	30	46	66
Liskeard Athletic	32	20	6	6	80	39	41	66
Truro City	32	17	4	11	66	49	17	55
Wadebridge Town	32	15	8	9	56	44	12	53
Plymouth Parkway	32	14	6	12	65	54	11	48
St Austell	32	14	3	15	69	73	−4	45
Launceston	32	12	6	14	59	62	−3	42
Newquay	32	10	6	16	48	64	−16	36
Torpoint Athletic	32	9	5	18	47	81	−34	32
Penryn Athletic	32	8	6	18	45	85	−40	30
Penzance	32	6	8	18	48	78	−30	26
Tavistock	32	4	8	20	48	88	−40	20
Callington Town	32	5	2	25	37	120	−83	17
Porthleven	32	3	2	27	30	108	−78	11

RIDGEONS EASTERN COUNTIES PREMIER

	P	W	D	L	F	A	GD	Pts
AFC Sudbury	42	31	7	4	105	30	75	100
Bury Town	42	27	9	6	83	43	40	90
Halstead Town	42	24	10	8	83	53	30	82
Lowestoft Town	42	24	8	10	94	57	37	80
Wroxham	42	22	9	11	106	59	47	75
Mildenhall Town	42	20	11	11	68	54	14	71
Soham Town Rangers	42	20	10	12	88	58	30	70
Clacton Town (−2)	42	19	13	10	79	61	18	68
Cambridge City Res	42	19	8	15	78	75	3	65
Leiston (+2)	42	16	9	17	66	74	−8	59
Harwich & Parkeston	42	17	4	21	72	85	−13	55
Diss Town	42	15	8	19	77	71	6	53
Newmarket Town	42	14	9	19	67	76	−9	51
Norwich United	42	12	11	19	50	63	−13	47
Dereham Town	42	12	10	20	69	89	−20	46
Wisbech Town	42	12	10	20	59	84	−25	46
Woodbridge Town	42	12	8	22	62	85	−23	44
Kings Lynn Reserves	42	13	5	24	58	92	−34	44
Histon Reserves (−3)	42	13	7	22	61	82	−21	43
Stowmarket Town	42	11	5	26	66	88	−22	38
Gorleston	42	8	10	24	57	113	−56	34
Great Yarmouth Town	42	7	7	28	31	87	−56	28

RIDGEONS EASTERN COUNTIES DIVISION ONE

	P	W	D	L	F	A	GD	Pts
Ipswich Wanderers	38	27	8	3	103	29	74	89
Needham Market	38	26	7	5	103	50	53	85
Kirkley	38	25	6	7	99	34	65	81
Walsham le Willows	38	24	4	10	97	49	48	76
Haverhill Rovers	38	22	10	6	77	41	36	76
Stanway Rovers	38	23	4	11	89	57	32	73
March Town United	38	21	8	9	74	54	20	71
Tiptree United	38	19	6	13	75	70	5	63
Ely City	38	17	2	19	72	66	6	53
Fakenham Town	38	15	6	17	62	78	−16	51
Cornard United	38	15	5	18	43	62	−19	50
Swaffham Town	38	14	4	20	51	86	−35	46
Long Melford	38	13	6	19	62	68	−6	45
Whitton United	38	10	10	18	51	67	−16	40
Saffron Walden Town	38	10	6	22	55	83	−28	36
Hadleigh United	38	9	7	22	46	83	−37	34
Felixstowe & Walton	38	9	6	23	46	74	−28	33
Downham Town	38	10	3	25	45	94	−49	33
Thetford Town	38	6	6	26	41	98	−57	24
Godmanchester Rovers	38	5	6	27	35	83	−48	21

GO TRAVEL KENT

	P	W	D	L	F	A	GD	Pts
Ramsgate	30	22	4	4	65	27	38	70
Herne Bay	30	19	5	6	68	41	27	62
Whitstable Town	30	16	6	8	71	44	27	54
Maidstone United	30	16	6	8	60	37	23	54
VCD Athletic	30	16	6	8	67	51	16	54
Hythe Town	30	14	5	11	46	42	4	47
Tunbridge Wells (+2)	30	12	9	9	45	49	−4	47
Thamesmead Town	30	13	5	12	63	54	9	44
Greenwich Borough	30	13	4	13	52	54	−2	43
Beckenham Town (−1)	30	11	7	12	57	54	3	39
Sevenoaks Town	30	9	6	15	47	66	−19	33
Slade Green	30	8	6	16	40	56	−16	30
Deal Town	30	8	5	17	40	62	−22	29
Sporting Bengal United	30	8	5	17	42	71	−29	29
Erith Town	30	6	5	19	33	60	−27	23
Lordswood	30	5	4	21	37	65	−28	19

BRITISH ENERGY KENT COUNTY PREMIER

	P	W	D	L	F	A	GD	Pts
Cray Valley PM	26	19	4	3	84	31	53	61
Old Roan	26	15	4	7	74	51	23	49
Sheerness East	26	15	4	7	55	36	19	49
Bromley Green	26	14	6	6	64	36	28	48
Stansfield O&BC	26	13	5	8	58	36	22	44
Lewisham Borough	26	12	8	6	40	31	9	44
Bearsted (–3)	26	13	5	8	52	42	10	41
Snodland	26	10	5	11	37	47	–10	35
Milton Athletic (–3)	26	11	2	13	53	62	–9	32
Lydd Town	26	6	9	11	45	58	–13	27
Crockenhill	26	5	10	11	43	50	–7	25
Beauwater	26	8	1	17	35	63	–28	25
Greenways	26	5	6	15	40	61	–21	21
Tenterden Town	26	1	1	24	38	114	–76	4

BADGERS SUSSEX COUNTY DIVISION ONE

	P	W	D	L	F	A	GD	Pts
Horsham YMCA	38	28	5	5	87	33	54	89
Rye & Iden United	38	23	5	10	79	50	29	74
Whitehawk	38	21	10	7	71	40	31	73
Littlehampton Town	38	21	2	15	60	53	7	65
Eastbourne United Assoc	38	18	8	12	74	61	13	62
Ringmer	38	16	12	10	55	38	17	60
Three Bridges	38	15	11	12	74	50	24	56
Hassocks (+2)	38	14	10	14	69	61	8	54
Arundel (–1)	38	15	8	15	69	57	12	52
Eastbourne Town	38	14	10	14	56	57	–1	52
East Preston	38	13	11	14	70	59	11	50
Hailsham Town	38	14	8	16	58	76	–18	50
Redhill	38	12	11	15	55	65	–10	47
Worthing United	38	11	11	16	59	61	–2	44
Sidley United	38	12	8	18	63	76	–13	44
Chichester City United	38	9	16	13	63	62	1	43
Southwick	38	11	9	18	46	63	–17	42
East Grinstead Town	38	11	8	19	48	68	–20	41
Pagham	38	8	10	20	45	98	–53	34
Sidlesham	38	6	3	29	43	116	–73	21

BADGERS SUSSEX COUNTY DIVISION TWO

	P	W	D	L	F	A	GD	Pts
Crowborough Athletic	34	23	7	4	76	42	34	76
Wick	34	21	5	8	58	31	27	68
Shoreham	34	20	7	7	80	49	31	67
St Francis Rangers	34	20	3	11	61	35	26	63
Wealden	34	19	3	12	82	47	35	60
Seaford	34	15	9	10	70	59	11	54
Westfield (+2)	34	15	7	12	51	47	4	54
Oakwood	34	15	4	15	66	63	3	49
Midhurst & Easebourne	34	14	7	13	57	60	–3	49
Crawley Down	34	15	2	17	41	52	–11	47
Mile Oak	34	13	7	14	57	61	–4	46
Broadbridge Heath	34	14	4	16	55	61	–6	46
Lancing	34	14	2	18	56	71	–15	44
Selsey (–1)	34	12	7	15	59	61	–2	42
Saltdean United	34	9	7	18	43	68	–25	34
Steyning Town	34	7	12	15	46	60	–14	33
Peacehaven & Telscombe	34	5	4	25	48	93	–45	19
Pease Pottage Village	34	5	3	26	37	83	–46	18

EAGLE BITTER UNITED COUNTIES PREMIER

	P	W	D	L	F	A	GD	Pts
Cogenhoe United	42	30	7	5	108	36	72	97
Potton United	42	30	5	7	111	42	69	95
Holbeach United	42	26	4	12	84	51	33	82
Yaxley	42	23	11	8	89	51	38	80
Harrowby United	42	21	9	12	83	60	23	72
Ford Sports Daventry	42	21	5	16	72	53	19	68
Woodford United	42	17	12	13	66	49	17	63
Long Buckby	42	19	6	17	76	83	–7	63
Stotfold	42	17	9	16	69	61	8	60
Desborough Town	42	16	11	15	60	69	–9	59
Boston Town	42	14	15	13	72	65	7	57
Deeping Rangers	42	16	9	17	66	72	–6	57
Buckingham Town	42	15	9	18	64	64	0	54
St Neots Town	42	14	11	17	67	78	–11	53
Blackstone	42	13	8	21	46	68	–22	47
Northampton Spencer	42	13	6	23	65	87	–22	45
Wootton Blue Cross	42	11	12	19	56	81	–25	45
Newport Pagnell Town	42	10	13	19	55	75	–20	43
Bourne Town	42	10	12	20	54	88	–34	42
Raunds Town	42	10	8	24	41	80	–39	38
Stewarts & Lloyds	42	10	5	27	44	86	–42	35
Daventry Town	42	9	7	26	62	111	–49	34

EAGLE BITTER UNITED COUNTIES DIVISION ONE

	P	W	D	L	F	A	GD	Pts
Sileby Rangers	34	22	5	7	95	44	51	71
Wellingborough Whitworths	34	21	8	5	70	32	38	71
St Ives Town	34	21	5	8	76	46	30	68
Eye United	34	20	5	9	83	44	39	65
Blisworth	34	19	7	8	58	46	12	64
Sleaford Town	34	17	8	9	78	48	30	59
Corby Cottingham	34	14	11	9	57	40	17	53
Rothwell Corinthians	34	16	3	15	69	56	13	51
Irchester United	34	15	4	15	52	49	3	49
Higham Town	34	14	4	16	61	75	–14	46
Eynesbury Rovers	34	12	8	14	76	66	10	44
Bugbrooke St Michael	34	12	8	14	50	59	–9	44
Thrapston Town	34	12	7	15	59	64	–5	43
Huntingdon Town	34	12	7	15	49	54	–5	43
Northampton ON Cheneks	34	9	7	18	46	67	–21	34
AFC Kempston	34	9	5	20	41	81	–40	32
Olney Town	34	4	6	24	31	78	–47	18
Burton Park Wanderers	34	1	4	29	18	120	–102	7

NORTHERN COUNTIES EAST PREMIER

	P	W	D	L	F	A	GD	Pts
Goole	38	25	4	9	87	47	40	79
Selby Town	38	23	8	7	72	43	29	77
Harrogate Railway	38	24	4	10	92	54	38	76
Sheffield	38	22	8	8	78	47	31	74
Pickering Town	38	18	13	7	62	35	27	67
Liversedge	38	17	10	11	74	62	12	61
Mickleover Sports	38	16	10	12	53	45	8	58
Thackley	38	14	13	11	57	46	11	55
Buxton	38	14	13	11	59	57	2	55
Shirebrook Town	38	14	12	12	58	50	8	54
Glasshoughton Welfare	38	13	13	12	57	55	2	52
Long Eaton United	38	15	7	16	55	54	1	52
Glapwell	38	10	15	13	57	57	0	45
Eccleshill United	38	13	6	19	69	76	–7	45
Hallam	38	11	9	18	48	71	–23	42
Arnold Town	38	9	12	17	44	62	–18	39
Brodsworth Miners Wel (–3)	38	12	4	22	58	85	–27	37
Armthorpe Welfare	38	11	3	24	44	73	–29	36
Maltby Main (–2)	38	9	8	21	41	72	–31	33
Borrowash Victoria	38	0	8	30	32	106	–74	8

NORTHERN COUNTIES EAST DIV ONE

	P	W	D	L	F	A	GD	Pts
Sutton Town	30	22	5	3	94	35	59	71
Garforth Town	30	21	4	5	65	27	38	67
Carlton Town	30	21	2	7	64	34	30	65
Lincoln Moorlands	30	16	7	7	61	39	22	55
Gedling Town	30	16	7	7	53	39	14	55
Tadcaster Albion	30	14	8	8	56	38	18	50
Yorkshire Amateur	30	10	7	13	57	55	2	37
Retford United	30	10	7	13	45	58	–13	37
Staveley MW	30	11	3	16	50	56	–6	36
Winterton Rangers	30	9	9	12	50	58	–8	36
Hall Road Rangers	30	10	3	17	35	57	–22	33
Parkgate	30	7	8	15	53	80	–27	29
Pontefract Collieries (–5)	30	8	6	16	52	67	–15	25
Rossington Main (–3)	30	6	9	15	46	64	–18	24
Worsborough Bridge	30	5	6	19	36	68	–32	21
South Normanton Ath (–3)	30	6	5	19	37	79	–42	20

ABACUS LIGHTING CENTRAL MIDLANDS SUPREME

	P	W	D	L	F	A	GD	Pts
Dunkirk	42	29	8	5	109	43	66	95
Dinnington Town	42	23	10	9	75	47	28	79
Teversal (+2)	42	23	8	11	89	63	26	79
Barton Town Old Boys	42	21	14	7	84	55	29	77
Pelican (–1)	42	22	11	9	87	52	35	76
Graham Street Prims	42	20	13	9	86	56	30	73
Holbrook Miners Wel	42	20	10	12	69	54	15	70
Gedling Miners Wel (–3)	42	20	10	12	79	66	13	67
Greenwood Meadows	42	17	11	14	54	61	–7	62
Clipstone Welfare	42	16	13	13	85	74	11	61
Sandiacre Town	42	16	9	17	64	60	4	57
Radcliffe Olympic	42	14	13	15	64	59	5	55
Appleby Frodingham	42	15	10	17	75	81	–6	55
Southwell City	42	15	6	21	81	83	–2	51
Kiveton Park	42	13	12	17	68	86	–18	51
Radford	42	10	16	16	48	57	–9	46
Blackwell Miners Wel	42	12	6	24	62	115	–53	42
Nettleham	42	10	11	21	59	98	–39	41
Heanor Town	42	10	10	22	64	68	–4	40
Rainworth Miners Wel	42	11	4	27	48	87	–39	37
Rolls Royce Leisure	42	9	8	25	48	82	–34	35
Askern Welfare (–1)	42	7	5	30	50	101	–51	25

ALBANY NORTHERN DIVISION ONE

	P	W	D	L	F	A	GD	Pts
Dunston Federation Brewery	40	28	11	1	83	25	58	95
Billingham Synthonia	40	21	12	7	71	41	30	75
Bedlington Terriers	40	20	11	9	73	40	33	71
Newcastle Benfield Saints	40	19	12	9	85	52	33	69
Whitley Bay	40	20	8	12	80	62	18	68
Durham City	40	19	6	15	67	53	14	63
Billingham Town	40	17	9	14	79	53	26	60
Chester Le Street Town	40	15	15	10	69	61	8	60
Horden CW	40	16	9	15	68	63	5	57
Ashington	40	15	10	15	75	67	8	55
Shildon	40	16	7	17	73	71	2	55
Jarrow Roofing Boldon CA	40	15	8	17	84	75	9	53
Morpeth Town	40	15	8	17	62	69	–7	53
Esh Winning	40	12	14	14	58	52	6	50
Thornaby (–3)	40	14	10	16	57	69	–12	49
Tow Law Town	40	13	4	23	53	87	–34	43
West Auckland Town	40	10	9	21	66	98	–32	39
Brandon United	40	10	9	21	67	101	–34	39
Consett	40	9	9	22	40	68	–28	36
Peterlee Newtown	40	8	7	25	53	136	–83	31
Guisborough Town (–6)	40	8	12	20	49	69	–20	30

ALBANY NORTHERN DIVISION TWO

	P	W	D	L	F	A	GD	Pts
West Allotment Celtic	38	29	5	4	121	41	80	92
Washington Nissan (–3)	38	28	5	5	121	41	80	86
Newcastle Blue Star	38	27	5	6	95	39	56	86
Prudhoe Town	38	24	7	7	91	45	46	79
Northallerton Town	38	25	4	9	87	43	44	79
Norton & Stockton Ancients (–3)	38	20	6	12	72	65	7	63
Crook Town	38	19	5	14	80	65	15	62
Penrith	38	18	7	13	80	51	29	61
Whickham	38	17	3	18	83	78	5	54
Seaham Red Star	38	15	6	17	59	67	–8	51
North Shields	38	14	8	16	55	54	1	50
Alnwick Town	38	13	9	16	65	64	1	48
South Shields (–3)	38	13	8	17	73	66	7	44
Washington	38	11	6	21	47	71	–24	39
Marske United	38	11	5	22	50	78	–28	38
Evenwood Town (–3)	38	11	5	22	52	94	–42	35
Kennek Ryhope CA	38	9	7	22	59	93	–34	34
Hebburn Town	38	8	7	23	50	94	–44	31
Easington Colliery	38	7	7	24	49	97	–48	28
Willington	38	2	3	33	24	167	–143	9

MOORE & CO SOLICITORS NORTH WEST COUNTIES DIVISION ONE

	P	W	D	L	F	A	GD	Pts
Fleetwood Town	42	31	6	5	107	42	65	99
Newcastle Town	42	28	8	6	94	51	43	92
St Helens Town	42	21	13	8	75	48	27	76
Curzon Ashton	42	23	7	12	66	45	21	76
Ramsbottom United	42	22	9	11	70	47	23	75
Skelmersdale United	42	21	11	10	94	57	37	74
Alsager Town	42	19	11	12	65	47	18	68
Maine Road	42	20	7	15	76	69	7	67
Bacup Borough	42	19	8	15	52	47	5	65
Colne	42	18	10	14	75	61	14	64
Stone Dominoes	42	17	12	13	73	64	9	63
Trafford	42	16	8	18	69	59	10	56
Glossop North End	42	15	10	17	79	75	4	55
Abbey Hey	42	16	6	20	51	69	–18	54
Atherton LR	42	14	6	22	64	82	–18	48
Nantwich Town	42	12	8	22	71	91	–20	44
Squires Gate	42	12	8	22	38	64	–26	44
Salford City	42	11	9	22	68	90	–22	42
Congleton Town	42	9	7	26	54	88	–34	34
Formby	42	8	8	26	47	99	–52	32
Atherton Collieries	42	8	7	27	57	102	–45	31
Great Harwood Town (–4)	42	8	9	25	48	96	–48	29

MOORE & CO SOLICITORS NORTH WEST COUNTIES DIVISION TWO

	P	W	D	L	F	A	GD	Pts
Cammell Laird	36	27	6	3	142	34	108	87
Silsden (–3)	36	25	5	6	93	42	51	77
Winsford United	36	23	7	6	72	28	44	76
Padiham	36	21	7	8	84	56	28	70
Norton United (–3)	36	17	12	7	63	40	23	60
Nelson	36	16	11	9	75	52	23	59
Ashton Town	36	13	8	15	61	62	–1	47
Daisy Hill	36	12	10	14	61	68	–7	46
New Mills	36	13	6	17	51	74	–23	45
Blackpool Mechanics (–3)	36	12	9	15	49	67	–18	42
Eccleshall	36	11	8	17	47	58	–11	41
Cheadle Town	36	11	7	18	47	80	–33	40
Oldham Town (–3)	36	10	12	14	54	56	–2	39
Leek CSOB	36	9	10	17	59	68	–9	37
Holker Old Boys	36	10	7	19	65	81	–16	37
Darwen (–9)	36	13	5	18	39	56	–17	35
Chadderton	36	7	7	22	40	94	–54	28
Flixton (–21)	36	14	6	16	72	79	–7	27
Castleton Gabriels	36	4	5	27	32	111	–79	17

HIGHLAND LEAGUE

		Home					Away						
	P	W	D	L	F	A	W	D	L	F	A	GD	Pts
Huntly	28	11	2	2	43	16	9	3	1	36	16	47	65
Inverurie Locos	28	10	3	1	52	14	10	0	4	29	11	56	63
Fraserburgh	28	11	1	2	44	12	8	1	5	31	23	40	59
Deveronvale	28	11	1	2	39	17	8	1	5	36	23	35	59
Buckie Thistle	28	8	1	5	24	12	8	3	3	27	14	25	52
Cove Rangers	28	8	2	4	30	20	8	2	4	29	24	15	52
Clachnacuddin	28	8	2	4	33	17	6	1	7	27	20	23	45
Keith	28	8	1	5	32	26	6	2	6	24	19	11	45
Forres Mechanics	28	4	6	4	21	16	6	3	5	28	28	5	39
Nairn County	28	8	0	6	35	26	3	3	8	19	32	–4	36
Lossiemouth	28	6	0	7	29	34	4	1	10	20	46	–31	31
Wick Academy	28	4	0	10	19	31	2	1	11	11	40	–41	19
Fort William	28	3	0	11	13	40	2	1	11	13	49	–63	16
Rothes	28	2	2	10	14	32	2	0	12	16	46	–48	14
Brora	28	0	3	11	12	47	2	2	10	14	49	–70	11

AMATEUR FOOTBALL ALLIANCE 2004–05

AFA SENIOR CUP

Sponsored by www.thesoccersite.co.uk

1st ROUND PROPER
Polytechnic 4 Wood Green Old Boys 2
Hon Artillery Companyy w/o Old Esthameians w/d
Latymer Old Boys 4* Univ of Hertfordshire 3*
Old Bealonians 4 Old Parkonians 0
Old Salopians 1 Old Bromleians 0
Alleyn Old Boys 2 Lloyds TSB Bank 3
Broomfield 3 Albanian 1
Old Owens 3 Old Westminster Citizens 2
Civil Service 6* Enfield Old Grammarians 3*
Kew Association 6 Old Minchendenians 0
BB Eagles 3 Old Cholmeleians 0
Old Aloysians † Old Actonians Association
Carshalton 3 Crouch End Vampires 1
Hampstead Heathens 2 Old Finchleians 5
Alexandra Park 2 Old Wilsonians 4
Mount Pleasant PO 2 South Bank Cuaco 7
Brent 1 Wake Green 6
Glyn Old Boys 1 Old Latymerians 0
Old Hamptonians 3 Old Wokingians 0
King's Old Boys 2* Old Vaughanians 4*
Parkfield 1 Winchmore Hill 4
Old Grammarians 4* Old Danes 3*
Norsemen 0 Old Isleworthians 2
Old Buckwellians 4 Q Mary College OB 1
Hale End Athletic 1 UCL Academicals 3
Old Camdenians 1* Old Lyonians 0*
E. Barnet O. Gramm'ns 6* Old Sedcopians 3*
Old Ignatians 1 Old Stationers 4
Old Meadonians 3 Nottsborough 0
London Welsh 0 Old Salvatorians 7
Old Salesians 1*:6p Old Brentwoods 1*:7p
Merton 7 Old Edmontonians 1

2nd ROUND PROPER
Polytechnic 3 Hon Artillery Company 0
Latymer Old Boys 1* Old Bealonians 2*
Old Salopians w/d Lloyds TSB Bank w/o
Broomfield 1 Old Owens 4
Civil Service 4 Kew Association 3
BB Eagles 1* Old Aloysians 2*
Carshalton 2*:3p Old Finchleians 2*:5p
Old Wilsonians 2 South Bank Cuaco 1
Wake Green 0*:5p Glyn Old Boys 0*:6p
Old Hamptonians 6 Old Vaughanians 1
Winchmore Hill 2 Old Grammarians 3
Old Isleworthians 5*:9p Old Buckwellians 5*:5p
UCL Academicals 2 Old Camdenians 0
E. Barnet O. Gramm'ns 1 Old Stationers 2
Old Meadonians 6 Old Salvatorians 0
Old Brentwoods 3 Merton 1

3rd ROUND PROPER
Polytechnic 2 Old Bealonians 1
Lloyds TSB Bank 4 Old Owens 10
Civil Service 2 Old Aloysians 1
Old Finchleians 2 Old Wilsonians 3
Glyn Old Boys 0 Old Hamptonians 2
Old Grammarians 6 Old Isleworthians 0
UCL Academicals 3 Old Stationers 2
Old Meadonians 5 Old Brentwoods 2

4th ROUND PROPER
Polytechnic 3 Old Owens 0
Civil Service 4 Old Wilsonians 2
Old Hamptonians 1 Old Grammarians 3
UCL Academicals 2* Old Meadonians 3*

SEMI-FINALS
Polytechnic 1*:4p Civil Service 1*:1p
Old Grammarians 0 Old Meadonians 4

FINAL
Polytechnic 0 Old Meadonians 3

† w/o, dispute following abandoned tie
p – penalties.
** after extra time*

OTHER CUP FINALS

MIDDLESEX / ESSEX SENIOR
Broomfield 1 Old Meadonians 0

SURREY / KENT SENIOR
West Wickham 1 Old Westminster Citizens 0

INTERMEDIATE
Civil Service Res 2 Old Aloysian Res 0

JUNIOR
Old Finchleians 3rd 4* Winchmore Hill 3rd 1*

MINOR
Old Stationers 4th 4 Nottsborough 4th 2

VETERANS
Malden 5* Old Salvatorians 2*

OPEN VETERANS
Port of London Authority 5 Frenford 1

GREENLAND
Old Owens 3 UCL Academicals 0

MIDDLESEX / ESSEX INTERMEDIATE
Old Actonians Ass'n Res 0*:2p Leyton County OB 0*:3p

SURREY / KENT INTERMEDIATE
Carshalton Res 1 Old Addeyans 1st 4

SENIOR NOVETS
Winchmore Hill 5th 1*:4p Albanian 5th 1*:2p

INTERMEDIATE NOVETS
Old Actonians 6th 1 Old Meadonians 6th 0

JUNIOR NOVETS
Polytechnic 8th 0 Old Parmiterians 7th 1

SATURDAY YOUTH
U-18
Bethwin 4 Hale End Athletic 0
U-17
Shaftsbury 4 Deportivo YC 1
U-16
Enfield Youth 4 St Johns Wandsworth 1
U-15
Bethwin SE 2 Forty Hill "B" 10
U-14
Shoreditch w/d Providence House w/o
U-13
Norsemen 1 Solo Youth 8
U-12
AFC Wandsworth 2 Providence House 8
U-11
Winchmore Hill 3 Broomfield PL 0

SUNDAY YOUTH
U-18
Broomfield PL 1*:2p Finchleians 1*:3p
U-17
Gladstone Rangers 1 West Essex Colts 0
U-16
Forty Hill 1 Chaseside 2
U-15
Young Parmiterians 1 Forty Hill 9
U-14
Chaseside 4 Enfield Spartans 2
U-13
Chaseside 1 Winchmore Hill 3
U-12
Winchmore Hill 1 Broomfield PL 5
U-11
Ilford Colts 4 Alexandra Park 2

ARTHUR DUNN CUP FINAL

Old Etonians 2 Old Brentwoods 1
(aet.)

ARTHURIAN LEAGUE

PREMIER DIVISION	P	W	D	L	F	A	Pts
Old Etonians	18	14	2	2	41	11	44
Old Harrovians	18	12	2	4	69	31	38
Old Carthusians	18	8	4	6	45	29	28
Old Foresters	18	8	3	7	33	29	27
Old Brentwoods*	18	8	3	7	36	36	24
Lancing Old Boys	18	7	2	9	36	39	23
Old Salopians	18	7	1	10	39	49	22
Old Reptonians*	18	7	1	10	37	46	19
Old Westminsters	18	5	4	9	25	49	19
Old Wykehamists	18	2	2	14	21	63	8

DIVISION 1	P	W	D	L	F	A	Pts
Old Bradfieldians	14	9	4	1	49	24	31
Old Chigwellians	14	7	3	4	38	24	24
Old Cholmeleians	14	7	3	4	40	32	24
Old Aldenhamians	14	6	2	6	32	38	20
Old Tonbridgians	14	5	3	6	41	32	18
Old Malvernians	14	4	2	8	17	35	14
Old Witleians*	14	4	3	7	13	23	12
Old Haberdashers*	14	2	4	8	23	45	7

DIVISION 2	P	W	D	L	F	A	Pts
Old Westminsters Res	14	9	3	2	33	21	30
Old Haileyburians	14	8	3	3	26	18	27
Old Etonians Res	14	7	3	4	30	16	24
Old Carthusians 3rd	14	4	6	4	25	22	18
Old Chigwellians Res	14	4	4	6	25	29	16
Old Foresters Res	14	4	4	6	25	32	16
Old Salopians Res	14	4	4	6	27	35	16
Old Carthusians Res	14	2	1	11	19	37	7

DIVISION 3	P	W	D	L	F	A	Pts
Old Etonians 3rd	14	12	1	1	48	14	37
Old Cholmeleians Res	14	10	0	4	35	17	30
Old Brentwoods Res	14	8	3	3	31	20	27
Old Bradfieldians Res	14	7	2	5	23	17	23
Old Aldenhamians Res	14	5	2	7	27	43	17
Lancing Old Boys Res	14	4	1	9	12	24	13
Old Malvernians Res*	14	2	2	10	21	31	5
Old Foresters 3rd*	14	2	1	11	18	49	4

DIVISION 4	P	W	D	L	F	A	Pts
Old Brentwoods 3rd	14	12	1	1	50	21	37
Old Bradfieldians 3rd	14	8	3	3	42	16	27
Old Eastbournians	14	7	3	4	34	26	24
Old Cholmeleians 3rd	14	6	1	7	25	28	19
Old Brentwoods 4th	14	5	3	6	27	33	18
Old Chigwellians 3rd	14	4	2	8	24	30	14
Old Chigwellians 4th	14	3	4	7	20	30	13
Old Foresters 4th*	14	2	1	11	22	60	–2

DIVISION 5	P	W	D	L	F	A	Pts
Old Oundelians	12	9	1	2	41	15	28
Old Berkhamstedians	12	5	3	4	23	20	18
Old Harrovians Res	12	5	2	5	27	24	17
Old Westminsters 3rd	12	4	1	7	24	35	13
Old Cholmeleians 4th*	12	3	1	8	16	37	1

** Points deducted for breach of rule*

JUNIOR LEAGUE CUP
Old Etonians 2 Lancing Old Boys 1

DERRIK MOORE VETERANS' CUP
Old Salopians 1 Old Carthusians 0

JIM DIXSON SIX-A-SIDE CUP
Old Haileyburians

LONDON FINANCIAL FOOTBALL ASSOCIATION

DIVISION 1	P	W	D	L	F	A	Pts
Dresdner Kleinwort Wasserstein	14	9	3	2	43	22	30
Marsh Res	14	8	3	3	48	35	27
Old Churchillians	14	7	3	4	43	22	24
Royal Sun Alliance	14	5	4	5	24	26	19
Chislehurst Sports	14	4	3	7	32	33	15
Marsh*	14	5	1	8	32	64	15
Mount Pleasant PO*	14	4	5	5	28	25	14
Citigroup *(Former Citigroup Res)*	14	2	2	10	27	50	8

Citigroup 1st – record expunged

DIVISION 2	P	W	D	L	F	A	Pts
NatWest Bank Res	16	12	1	3	43	25	37
NatWest Bank	16	10	2	4	59	25	32
Chislehurst Sports Res	16	10	1	5	36	21	31
Fusion All Stars	16	9	1	6	49	45	28
Zurich Eagle Star	16	8	2	6	41	32	26
Royal Bank of Scotland	16	7	4	5	40	31	25
Coutts & Co.	16	7	1	8	50	38	22
Royal Sun Alliance Res	16	2	0	14	20	75	6
Civil Service "A"*	16	0	2	14	18	64	1

Marsh 3rd – record expunged

DIVISION 3	P	W	D	L	F	A	Pts
Credit Suisse First Boston	16	11	4	1	49	15	37
NatWest Bank 3rd	16	9	4	3	49	25	31
Marsh 3rd	16	9	2	5	56	31	29
South Bank Cuaco 7th*	16	9	3	4	60	39	27
Citigroup CIB	16	7	1	8	36	34	22
R Bank of Scotland Res	16	3	4	9	31	54	13
Temple Bar*	16	4	4	8	28	51	13
Chislehurst Sports 3rd	16	2	5	9	29	57	11
Foreign & Commonwealth Office*	9	2	5	9	21	53	10

** Points deducted for breach of rule*

CHALLENGE CUP
Weirside Rangers 2 Bank of England 1

SENIOR CUP
Mount Pleasant P O 3 Royal Sun Alliance 2

JUNIOR CUP
Credit Suisse First Boston 2 Natwest Bank 1

VETERANS' CUP
HSBC 2 Bank of England 1

LONDON LEGAL LEAGUE

DIVISION I	P	W	D	L	F	A	Pts
KPMG London	18	14	3	1	68	21	45
Linklaters	18	13	3	2	46	15	42
Dechert*	18	10	4	4	41	26	33
Watson Farley & Williams	18	8	4	6	31	25	28
Slaughter & May*	18	7	5	6	32	30	25
Richards Butler	18	6	3	9	32	36	21
Clifford Chance	18	5	3	10	31	35	18
Simmons & Simmons	18	4	2	12	31	50	14
Gray's Inn*	18	4	4	10	24	39	12
Baker & McKenzie	18	2	3	13	8	67	9

DIVISION II	P	W	D	L	F	A	Pts
Stephenson Harwood	18	16	0	2	58	18	48
Macfarlanes	18	14	2	2	45	16	44
Ashurst Morris Crisp*	18	8	5	5	43	31	28
Barlow Lyde & Gilbert	18	9	1	8	47	51	28
Financial Service A	18	8	2	8	31	26	26
Allen & Overy*	18	7	3	8	39	30	23
Eversheds*	18	6	2	10	37	36	19
Norton Rose	18	5	2	11	25	56	17
CMS Cameron McKenna*	18	4	2	12	21	49	13
Freshfields Bruckhaus Deringer*	18	3	1	14	18	51	7

DIVISION III	P	W	D	L	F	A	Pts
Herbert Smith	18	14	2	2	50	22	44
Nabarro Nathanson	18	14	0	4	84	18	42
Denton Wilde Sapte	18	12	1	5	47	26	37
Pegasus	18	10	2	6	43	33	32
Farrer & Co	18	9	1	8	34	49	28
Lovells	18	7	2	9	28	37	23
BBC Post Production	18	7	0	11	38	59	21
Hammond*	18	7	2	9	23	19	20
Withers*	18	5	0	13	23	49	11
Taylor Wessing*	18	0	0	18	13	71	–4

** Points deducted for breach of rule*

LEAGUE CHALLENGE CUP
KPMG 4 Stephenson Harwood 0

WEAVERS ARMS CUP
Clifford Chance 3 Grays Inn 4

INVITATION CUP
Baker & McKenzie 3 Norton Rose 1

LONDON OLD BOYS' CUPS

SENIOR
UCL Academicals 0 Old Aloysians 3
CHALLENGE
Mill Hill Village 3 Old Edmontonians 0
INTERMEDIATE
UCL Academicals Res 2 Albanian 1
JUNIOR
UCL Academicals 3rd 3 Clapham Old Xaverians 0
MINOR
Old Actonians Assn 4th 0 Old Aloysians 4th 3
DRUMMOND
Mill Hill County OB Res 2 Mill Hill County OB 3rd 5
NEMEAN
Parkfield 6th 1* Old Meadonians 8th 2*
OLYMPIAN
Old Suttonians 8th 1 Wandsworth Borough 3rd 3
JACK PERRY VETERANS
Mill Hill Village 2*:2p Old Manorians 2*:5p
** After extra time: p – kicks from the penalty mark*

OLD BOYS' INVITATION CUPS

SENIOR
Old Owens 5 Old Finchleians 0
JUNIOR
Old Owens Res 2 Old Finchleians Res 3
MINOR
Old Parmiterians 3rd 0 Old Salesians 3rd 2
4TH XI
Old Stationers 4th 1 Old Wilsonians 4th 3
5TH XI
E. Barnet O Gramm'ns 5th 0 Old Suttonians 5th 3
6TH XI
Old Owens 6th 2 Old Suttonians 6th 1
7TH XI
Old Finchleians 8th 3 Old Finchleians 7th 2
VETERANS'
Albanian 3 Old Bromleians 1

MIDLAND AMATEUR ALLIANCE

PREMIER DIVISION	P	W	D	L	F	A	Pts
Caribbean Cavaliers	24	22	0	2	95	25	66
Ashland Rovers	24	18	2	4	86	33	56
Underwood Villa	24	16	1	7	80	42	49
Old Elizabethans	24	15	4	5	55	34	49
Steelers	24	13	2	9	77	53	41
Nottingham Trent University	24	10	2	12	67	79	32
Derbyshire Amateurs Res	24	7	7	10	65	80	28
Lady Bay	24	8	2	14	59	60	26
Wollaton 3rd	24	8	2	14	52	67	26
Bassingfield	24	7	3	14	40	68	24
Sherwood Forest	24	5	5	14	39	85	20
Beeston Old Boys Assn	24	4	6	14	43	69	18
Southwell Amateurs	24	3	4	17	37	100	13

FIRST DIVISION	P	W	D	L	F	A	Pts
Woodborough United	26	21	3	2	88	29	66
Racing Athletic	26	17	4	5	73	39	55
County NALGO	26	16	4	6	82	48	52
Old Elizabethans Res	26	16	4	6	61	45	52
PASE	26	16	3	7	59	53	51
Monty Hind Old Boys	26	12	5	9	64	50	41
Caribbean Cavaliers Res	26	12	3	11	73	52	39
Keyworth United 3rd	26	8	5	13	59	58	29
Nottinghamshire	26	8	5	13	52	60	29
Radcliffe Olympic 3rd	26	9	1	16	44	73	28
Brunts Old Boys	26	7	4	15	50	71	25
Broadmeadows	26	6	6	14	52	91	24
West Bridgford United	26	4	3	19	42	82	15
Old Bemrosians	26	3	4	19	33	81	13

SECOND DIVISION	P	W	D	L	F	A	Pts
Beaufort United	26	23	3	0	136	31	72
Clinphone	26	20	3	3	124	46	63
Wollaton 4th	26	14	2	10	100	71	44
Hickling	26	13	5	8	96	68	44
Bestwood Rovers	26	13	2	11	99	72	41
Calverton Miners Welfare 3rd	26	11	5	10	72	79	38
Ashland Rovers Res	26	11	4	11	65	74	37
Nottinghamshire 3rd	26	9	3	14	52	77	30
Old Bemrosians Res	26	9	3	14	50	86	30
EMTEC	26	6	8	12	62	81	26
Tibshelf Old Boys	26	7	5	14	60	85	26
Acorn Athletic	26	6	7	13	71	108	25
Beeston Old Boys Assn	26	5	6	15	37	79	21
Derbyshire Amateurs 3rd	26	5	4	17	57	124	19

LEAGUE SENIOR CUP
Caribbean Cavaliers 1 Ashland Rovers 0

LEAGUE INTERMEDIATE CUP
Racing Athletic 2*3 Caribbean Cavaliers Res 2*2

LEAGUE MINOR CUP
Bestwood Rovers 5 Tibshelf Old Boys 2
** After extra time*

SOUTHERN AMATEUR LEAGUE

SENIOR SECTION

DIVISION 1	P	W	D	L	F	A	Pts
Broomfield	20	12	5	3	56	38	41
Winchmore Hill	20	11	4	5	43	30	37
Old Esthameians	20	9	4	7	42	40	31
Old Salesians	20	9	4	7	26	29	31
Old Actonians Association	20	8	6	6	44	37	30
Old Owens	20	8	5	7	38	37	29
Civil Service	20	7	4	9	42	44	25
Nottsborough	20	7	3	10	23	30	24
West Wickham	20	6	4	10	28	32	22
Polytechnic	20	5	3	12	29	41	18
Norsemen	20	4	6	10	28	41	18

DIVISION 2	P	W	D	L	F	A	Pts
E Barnet OG	20	13	6	1	60	32	45
Old Lyonians	20	11	5	4	35	31	38
Alleyn Old Boys	20	9	10	1	44	21	37
Bank of England	20	8	5	7	34	29	29
Carshalton	20	8	4	8	42	37	28
HSBC	20	6	6	8	41	50	24
Weirside Rangers	20	5	7	8	31	36	22
South Bank Cuaco	20	6	3	11	28	41	21
Old Finchleians	20	6	3	11	36	57	21
Old Parkonians	20	5	3	12	30	37	18
Kew Association	20	4	6	10	26	36	18

DIVISION 3	P	W	D	L	F	A	Pts
Old Wilsonians	20	15	2	3	57	26	47
Ibis	20	11	6	3	56	28	39
BB Eagles	20	10	5	5	48	32	35
Old Westminster Citizens	20	10	3	7	48	38	33
Old Stationers	20	8	7	5	41	37	31
Merton	20	8	5	7	40	43	29
Crouch End Vampires	20	7	6	7	51	50	27
Alexandra Park	20	6	8	6	41	38	26
Southgate Olympic	20	5	3	12	28	43	18
Old Latymerians*	20	2	5	13	33	62	8
Lloyds TSB Bank	20	2	2	16	31	77	8

** Points deducted for breach of rule*

RESERVE TEAM SECTION
Division 1 – 11 teams – Won by Norsemen Res
Division 2 – 11 teams – Won by Winchmore Hill Res
Division 3 – 11 teams – Won by Merton Res

THIRD TEAM SECTION
Division 1 – 11 teams – Won by Old Actonians Assn 3rd
Division 2 – 11 teams – Won by Weirside Rangers 3rd
Division 3 – 11 teams – Won by Old Esthameians 3rd

MINOR SECTION
Division 1 – 11 teams – Won by Old Actonians Assn 4th

MINOR NORTHERN SECTION
Division 2 – 10 teams – Won by Old Stationers 4th
Division 3 – 10 teams – Won by Crouch End Vampires 5th
Division 4 – 9 teams – Won by Winchmore Hill 6th
Division 5 – 10 teams – Won by Old Actonians Assn 8th
Division 6 – 9 teams – Won by Broomfield 6th

MINOR SOUTHERN SECTION
Division 2 – 10 teams – Won by Old Wilsonians 4th
Division 3 – 11 teams – Won by South Bank Cuaco 5th
Division 4 – 11 teams – Won by Kew Association 6th
Division 5 – 11 teams – Won by Polytechnic 7th
Division 6 – 11 teams – Won by South Bank Cuaco 6th

CHALLENGE CUPS
Junior
HSBC 3rd 1 Winchmore Hill 3rd 3

Minor
Civil Service 4th 2 Nottsborough 4th 5
Senior Novets
South Bank Cuaco 5th 2 Winchmore Hill 5th 3
Intermediate Novets
Broomfield 6th 3 Old Owens 6th 2
Junior Novets
Polytechnic 8th 2 HSBC 7th 3

U-16 GIRLS CENTRE OF EXCELLENCE LEAGUE

	P	W	D	L	F	A	Pts
Arsenal	18	13	3	2	61	14	42
Fulham	18	13	2	3	56	26	41
Leyton Orient	18	11	5	2	40	19	38
Chelsea	18	9	6	3	54	27	33
Charlton Athletic	18	6	5	7	36	40	23
Colchester United	18	5	3	10	37	46	18
Watford	18	4	6	8	32	41	18
Millwall	18	5	3	10	28	43	18
Reading	18	5	3	10	21	38	18
Brighton	18	1	0	17	15	86	3

AMATEUR FOOTBALL COMBINATION

PREMIER DIVISION	P	W	D	L	F	A	Pts
Old Meadonians	18	13	3	2	47	15	42
UCL Academicals	18	12	4	2	43	20	40
Albanian	18	8	5	5	41	30	29
Parkfield	18	7	5	6	31	27	26
Old Aloysians	18	7	2	9	31	34	23
Hale End Athletic	18	5	5	8	29	35	20
Old Hamptonians	18	5	4	9	19	26	19
Latymer Old Boys	18	3	9	6	31	42	18
Old Danes	18	3	7	8	24	45	16
Old Wokingians	18	4	2	12	17	39	14

SENIOR DIVISION 1	P	W	D	L	F	A	Pts
Old Bealonians	18	12	1	5	47	16	37
Honourable Artillery Company	18	11	2	5	46	28	35
Enfield Old Grammarians	18	11	2	5	40	25	35
Southgate County	18	9	5	4	41	25	32
Glyn Old Boys	18	10	2	6	33	29	32
Old Salvatorians	18	10	1	7	39	31	31
Old Tiffinians	18	10	0	8	40	31	30
Old Ignatians	18	4	2	12	25	44	14
Old Isleworthians	18	2	2	14	18	51	8
Old Tenisonians	18	2	1	15	22	71	7

SENIOR DIVISION 2	P	W	D	L	F	A	Pts
Wood Green Old Boys	20	13	4	3	66	34	43
Old Parmiterians	20	13	3	4	57	34	42
Old Grammarians	20	12	3	5	55	28	39
Economicals	20	11	2	7	52	35	35
Old Dorkinians	20	8	5	7	29	36	29
Old Suttonians	20	7	6	7	52	43	27
Old Vaughanians	20	8	1	11	42	48	25
Old Buckwellians	20	7	3	10	33	55	24
Old Manorians	20	5	4	11	29	45	19
Queen Mary College Old Boys	20	4	2	14	22	47	14
Pegasus	20	3	5	12	28	60	14

SENIOR DIVISION 3 NORTH	P	W	D	L	F	A	Pts
Old Aloysians Res	20	16	3	1	58	26	51
Old Challoners	20	15	3	2	81	21	48
UCL Academicals Res	20	14	3	3	61	26	45
University of Hertford	20	9	2	9	46	47	29
Parkfield Res	20	8	3	9	46	43	27
Old Meadonians Res	20	9	0	11	32	43	27
Old Salvatorians Res	20	6	5	9	40	36	23
Old Minchendenians	20	6	1	13	27	63	19
Brent	20	4	6	10	37	49	18
Old Woodhouseians	20	4	2	14	42	69	14
Old Vaughanians Res	20	4	2	14	25	72	14

SENIOR DIVISION 3 SOUTH	P	W	D	L	F	A	Pts
Clapham Old Xaverians	20	15	3	2	54	23	48
Shene Old Grammarians	20	11	5	4	60	40	38
Old Sedcopians	20	11	3	6	50	34	36
Old Paulines	20	10	2	8	39	33	32
King's Old Boys	20	8	5	7	50	44	29
John Fisher Old Boys	20	8	5	7	50	52	29
Old Hamptonians Res	20	8	2	10	30	39	26
Old Reigatians	20	8	1	11	42	43	25
Hampstead Heathens	20	7	4	9	40	43	25
Centymca	20	4	2	14	36	68	14
Mickleham Old Boxhillians*	20	3	2	15	28	60	8

INTERMEDIATE DIVISION NORTH	P	W	D	L	F	A	Pts
Albanians Res	20	15	3	2	72	40	48
Hale End Athletic Res	20	14	1	5	72	42	43
UCL Academicals 3rd	20	11	2	7	65	38	35
Old Buckwellians Res	20	8	4	8	50	50	28
Egbertian	20	6	7	7	39	41	25
Old Bealonians Res	20	7	3	10	49	54	24
Old Camdenians	20	7	3	10	42	53	24
Old Parmiterians Res	20	7	2	11	44	57	23
Old Edmontonians	20	6	4	10	52	63	22
Latymer Old Boys Res	20	5	5	10	45	65	20
Old Ignatians Res	20	5	4	11	40	67	19

INTERMEDIATE DIVISION SOUTH	P	W	D	L	F	A	Pts
Wandsworth Borough	20	13	3	4	76	35	42
Old Guildfordians	20	13	3	4	58	32	42
Old Suttonians Res	20	12	1	7	31	33	37
Old Josephians	20	11	2	7	50	40	35
Witan	20	10	3	7	54	33	33
Old Thorntonians	20	7	5	8	47	45	26
H A C Res	20	8	1	11	45	53	25
Old St Mary's	20	7	3	10	42	40	24
Old Tenisonians Res	20	6	6	9	48	54	24
Sinjuns	20	5	3	12	35	73	18
Pegasus Res	20	2	3	15	21	69	9

INTERMEDIATE DIVISION WEST	P	W	D	L	F	A	Pts
Old Salvatorians 3rd	20	12	5	3	49	23	41
Fitzwilliam Old Boys	20	12	4	4	44	22	40
Old Challoners Res*	20	11	6	3	55	33	36
Old Danes Res	20	11	2	7	49	40	35
Parkfield 3rd	20	8	8	4	38	24	32
Old Manorians Res	20	8	3	9	51	45	27
Phoenix Old Boys	19	8	3	8	37	41	27
Old Meadonians 3rd	20	7	5	8	39	36	26
London Welsh	20	6	3	11	40	51	21
Old Uxonians	20	3	3	14	29	45	12
Inland Revenue*	19	2	0	17	20	91	3

** Points deducted for breach of rule*

REGIONAL
Northern
Division 1 – 10 teams – Won by Mill Hill Village
Division 2 – 11 teams – Won by Old Aloysians 4th
Division 3 – 10 teams – Won by Leyton County Old Boys Res
Division 4 – 10 teams – Won by Enfield Old Grammarians 3rd
Division 5 – 10 teams – Won by Leyton County Old Boys Res
Division 6 – 11 teams – Won by Old Aloysians 6th
Division 7 – 10 teams – Won by Albanian 5th
Division 8 – 11 teams – Won by Mill Hill County Old Boys 3rd
Division 9 – 9 teams – Won by Mill Hill Village 4th

Southern
Division 1 – 11 teams – Won by Kings Old Boys Res
Division 2 – 11 teams – Won by Centymca Res
Division 3 – 11 teams – Won by Old Suttonians 4th
Division 4 – 11 teams – Won by Old Meadonians 6th
Division 5 – 11 teams – Won by Old Tenisonians 4th
Division 6 – 11 teams – Won by Old Josephians 4th
Division 7 – 10 teams – Won by Old Tiffinians 5th
Division 8 – 10 teams – Won by Old Suttonians 8th
Division 9 – 10 teams – Won by Old Guildfordians 4th
Division 10 – 11 teams – Won by Old Bromleians 4th

Western
Division 1 – 11 teams – Won by Cardinal Manning Old Boys
Division 2 – 11 teams – Won by Old Magdalenians
Division 3 – 11 teams – Won by Old Uffingtonians Res
Division 4 – 11 teams – Won by Phoenix Old Boys 3rd
Division 5 – 11 teams – Won by Birkbeck College

IMPORTANT ADDRESSES

The Football Association: The Secretary, 25 Soho Square, London W1D 4FA. *020 7745 4545*

Scotland: David Taylor, Hampden Park, Glasgow G42 9AY. *0141 616 6000*

Northern Ireland (Irish FA): Chief Executive: Howard J. C. Wells, 20 Windsor Avenue, Belfast BT9 6EG. *028 9066 9458*

Wales: D. Collins, 3 Westgate Street, Cardiff, South Glamorgan CF10 1DP. *029 2037 2325*

Republic of Ireland B. Menton (FA of Ireland): 80 Merrion Square South, Dublin 2. *00353 16766864*

International Federation (FIFA): P. O. Box 85 8030 Zurich, Switzerland. *00 411 384 9595. Fax: 00 411 384 9696*

Union of European Football Associations: Secretary, Route de Geneve 46, Case Postale CH-1260 Nyon, Switzerland. *0041 22 994 44 44. Fax: 0041 22 994 44 88*

THE LEAGUES

The Premier League: M. Foster, 11 Connaught Place, London W2 2ET. *020 7298 1600*

The Football League: Secretary, The Football League, Unit 5, Edward VII Quay, Navigation Way, Preston, Lancashire PR2 2YF. *01772 325800. Fax 01772 325801*

Scottish Premier League: R. Mitchell, Hampden Park, Somerville Drive, Glasgow G42 9BA. *0141 646 6962*

The Scottish League: P. Donald, Hampden Park, Glasgow G42 9AY. *0141 616 6000*

The Irish League: Secretary, 96 University Street, Belfast BT7 1HE. *028 9024 2888*

Football League of Ireland: D. Crowther, 80 Merrion Square, Dublin 2. *00353 16765120*

Conference National: Riverside House, 14b High Street, Crayford, DA1 4HG. *01322 411021*

Central League: A. Williamson, The Football League, Unit 5, Edward VII Quay, Navigation Way, Preston, Lancashire PR2 2YF. *01772 325800. Fax 01772 325801*

Eastern Counties League: B. A. Badcock, 41 The Copse, Southwood, Farnborough, Hampshire GU14 0QD. *01252 387588*

Football Combination: D. A. Daughtery, 3 Eastergate, Little Common, Bexhill-on-Sea, East Sussex TN31 4NU. *01424 848061*

Hellenic League: B. King, 83 Queens Road, Carterton, Oxon OX18 3YF. *01993 212738*

Kent League: R. Vinter, Bakery House, The Street, Chilham, Canterbury, Kent CT4 8BX. *01227 730457*

Leicestershire Senior League: R. J. Holmes, 8 Huntsmans Close, Markfield, Leics LE67 9XE. *01530 243093*

Manchester League: P. Platt, 26A Stalybridge Road, Mottram Hyde, Cheshire SK14 6NE. *01457 763821*

Midland Combination: N. Harvey, 115 Millfield Road, Handsworth Wood, Birmingham B20 1ED. *0121 357 4172*

Northern Premier: R. D. Bayley, 22 Woburn Drive, Hale, Altrincham, Cheshire WA15 8LZ. *0161 980 7007*

Northern League: T. Golightly, 85 Park Road North, Chester-le-Street, Co Durham DH3 3SA. *0191 3882056*

Isthmian League: Triumph House, Station Approach, Sanderstead Road, South Croydon, Surrey CR2 0PL. *020 8409 1978. Fax: 020 7639 5726*

Southern League: D. J. Strudwick, 8 College Yard, Worcester WR1 2LA. *01905 330444*

Spartan South Midlands League: M. Mitchell, 26 Leighton Court, Dunstable, Beds LU6 1EW. *01582 667291*

United Counties League: R. Gamble, 8 Bostock Avenue, Northampton NN1 4LW. *01604 637766*

Western League: K. A. Clarke, 32 Westmead Lane, Chippenham, Wilts SN15 3HZ. *01249 464467*

West Midlands Regional League: N. R. Juggins, 14 Badger Way, Blackwell, Bromsgrove, Worcs B60 1EX. *0121 445 2953*

Northern Counties (East): B. Wood, 6 Restmore Avenue, Guiseley, Leeds LS20 9DG. *01943 874558*

Central Midlands Football League: Frank Harwood, 103 Vestry Road, Oakwood, Derby, Derbyshire DE21 2BN. *01332 832372*

Combined Counties League: Clive R. Tidey, 22 Silo Road, Farncombe, Godalming, Surrey GU7 3PA. *01483 428453*

Essex Senior League: David Walls, Bramley Cottage, 2 Birch Street, Colchester CO2 0NW. *0207 587 4139*

Lancashire Football League: Barbara Howarth, 86 Windsor Road, Great Harwood, Blackburn, Lancs BB6 7RR. *01254 886267*

Midland Football Alliance: Peter Dagger, 32 Drysdale Close, Wickhamford, Worcs WR11 6RZ. *01386 831763*

North West Counties Football League: G. J. Wilkinson, 46 Oaklands Drive, Penwortham, Preston, Lancs PR1 0XY. *01772 746312*

Wessex League: Tom Lindon, 63 Downs Road, South Wonston, Winchester, Hants SO21 3EW. *01962 884760*

South Western League: R. Rowe, 5 Alverton Gardens, Truro, Cornwall TR1 1JA. *01872 242190*

COUNTY FOOTBALL ASSOCIATIONS

Bedfordshire: P. D. Brown, Century House, Skimpot Road, Dunstable, Beds LU5 4JU. *01582 565111*

Berks and Bucks: B. G. Moore, 15a London Street, Faringdon, Oxon SN7 7HD. *01367 242099*

Birmingham County: D. Shelton, County FA Offices, Rayhall Lane, Great Barr, Birmingham B43 6JF. *0121 357 4278*

Cambridgeshire: R. K. Pawley, City Ground, Milton Road, Cambridge CB4 1FA. *01223 576770*

Cheshire: Ms M. Dunford, The Cottage, Hartford Moss Rec Centre, Winnington, Northwich CW8 4BG. *01606 871166*

Cornwall: B. Cudmore, 1 High Cross Street, St. Austell, Cornwall PL25 4AB. *01726 74080*

Cumberland: G. Turrell, 17 Oxford Street, Workington, Cumbria CA14 2AL. *01900 872310*

Derbyshire: K. Compton, No 8–9 Stadium, Business Court, Millenium Way, Pride Park, Derby DE24 8HZ *01332 361422*

Devon County: C. Davidson, County HQ, Coach Road, Newton Abbot, Devon TQ12 1EJ. *01626 332077*

Dorset County: P. Hough, County Ground, Blandford Close, Hamworthy, Poole, Dorset BH15 4BF. *01202 682375*

Durham: J. Topping, 'Codeslaw', Ferens Park, Durham DH1 1JZ. *0191 3848653*

East Riding County: D. R. Johnson, 50 Boulevard, Hull HU3 2TB. *01482 221158*

Essex County: P. Sammons, 31 Mildmay Road, Chelmsford, Essex CM2 0DN. *01245 357727*

Gloucestershire: P. Britton, Oaklands Park, Almondsbury, Bristol BS32 4AG. *01454 615888*

Guernsey: D. Dorey, Haut Regard, St. Clair Hill, St. Sampson's, Guernsey, GY2 4DT, CI. *01481 246231*

Hampshire: Neil Cassar, William Pickford House, 8 Ashwood Gardens, off Winchester Road, Southampton SO16 7PW. *023 8079 1110*

Herefordshire: J. S. Lambert, County Ground Offices, Widemarsh Common, Hereford HR4 9NA. *01432 342179*

Hertfordshire: E. King, County Ground, Baldock Road, Letchworth, Herts SG6 2EN. *01462 677622*

Huntingdonshire: M. M. Armstrong, Cromwell Chambers, 8 St Johns Street, Huntingdon, Cambs PE29 6DD. *01480 414422*

Isle of Man: Mrs A. Garrett, P.O. Box 53, The Bowl, Douglas IOM IM99 1GY. *01624 615576*

Jersey: Gill Morgan, Springfield Stadium, St Helier, Jersey JE2 4LF. *01534 500165*
Kent County: K. T. Masters, 69 Maidstone Road, Chatham, Kent ME4 6DT. *01634 843824*
Lancashire: J. Kenyon, The County Ground, Thurston Road, Leyland, Preston, Lancs PR5 1LF. *01772 624000*
Leicestershire and Rutland: P. Morrison, Holmes Park, Dog and Gun Lane, Whetstone, Leicester LE8 6FA. *0116 2867828*
Lincolnshire: J. Griffin, PO Box 26, 12 Dean Road, Lincoln LN2 4DP. *01522 524917*
Liverpool County: F. L. J. Hunter, Liverpool Soccer Centre, Walton Hall Park, Walton Hall Avenue, Liverpool L4 9XP. *0151 523 4488*
London: D. Fowkes, 6 Aldworth Grove, London SE13 6HY. *020 8690 9626*
Manchester County: John Dutton, Brantingham Road, Chorlton, Manchester M21 0TT. *0161 881 0299*
Middlesex County: P. J. Clayton, 39 Roxborough Road, Harrow, Middx HA1 1NS. *020 8424 8524*
Norfolk County: R. J. Howlett, Plantation Park, Blofield, Norwich, Norfolk, NR13 4PL. *01603 717177*
Northamptonshire: D. Payne, 2 Duncan Close, Moulton Park, Northampton NN3 6WL. *01604 670741*
North Riding County: M. Jarvis, Southlands Centre, Ormesby Road, Middlesbrough TS3 0HB. *01642 318603*
Northumberland: R. E. Maughan, Churchill Pavilion, Hartley Avenue, Whitley Bay NE26 3FA. *0191 2530656*
Nottinghamshire: M. Kilbee, 7 Clarendon Street, Nottingham NG1 5HS. *0115 9418954*
Oxfordshire: I. Mason, P.O. Box 62, Witney, Oxon OX28 1HA. *01993 778586*
Sheffield and Hallamshire: J. Hope-Gill, Clegg House, 69 Cornish Place, Cornish Street, Shalesmoor, Sheffield S6 3AF. *0114 241 4999*
Shropshire: D. Rowe, Gay Meadow, Abbey Foregate, Shrewsbury SY2 6AB. *01743 362769*
Somerset & Avon (South): Mrs H. Marchment, 30 North Road, Midsomer Norton, Radstock BA3 2QD. *01761 410280*
Staffordshire: B. J. Adshead, County Showground, Weston Road, Stafford ST18 0BD. *01785 256994*
Suffolk County: M. Head, The Buntings, Cedars Park, Stowmarket, Suffolk IP14 5GZ. *01449 616606*
Surrey County: R. Ward, 321 Kingston Road, Leatherhead, Surrey KT22 7TU. *01372 373543*
Sussex County: Ken Benham, County Office, Culver Road, Lancing, West Sussex BN15 9AX. *01903 753547*
Westmorland: P. G. Ducksbury, Unit 1, Angel Court, 21 Highgate, Kendal, Cumbria LA9 4DA. *01539 730946*
West Riding County: R. Carter, Fleet Lane, Woodlesford, Leeds LS26 8NX. *0113 2821222*
Wiltshire: M. G. Benson, Covingham Square, Covingham, Swindon SN3 5AA. *01793 525245*
Worcestershire: M. R. Leggett, Craftsman House, De Salis Drive, Hampton Lovett Industrial Estate, Droitwich WR9 0QE. *01905 827137*

OTHER USEFUL ADDRESSES

Amateur Football Alliance: M. L. Brown, 55 Islington Park Street, London N1 1QB. *020 7359 3493*
English Schools FA: Ms A. Pritchard, 1/2 Eastgate Street, Stafford ST16 2NG. *01785 51142*
Oxford University: Richard Tur, Oriel College, Oriel Square, Oxford OX1 4EW. *01865 276648*
Cambridge University: Dr J. A. Little, St Catherine's College, Cambridge CB2 1RL. *01223 334376*
Army: Major W. T. E. Thomson ASCB (MOD), Clayton Barracks, Thornhill Road, Aldershot, Hants GU11 2BG. *01252 348571/4*
Royal Air Force: Sqn Ldr R. Moorehouse, OC PACS, RAF Coltishall, Norwich. *01603 737361 ext 7306*
Royal Navy: Lt-Cdr S. Vasey, RN Sports Office, HMS Temeraire, Portsmouth, Hants PO1 2HB. *023 9272 2671*
British Universities Sports Association: G. Gregory-Jones, Chief Executive: BUSA, 8 Union Street, London SE1 1SZ. *020 7357 8555*
British Olympic Association: Church Row, Wandsworth Plain, London SW18 1EH. *0208 871 2677*
The Footbal Supporters Federation: Chairman: Ian D. Todd MBE, 8 Wyke Close, Wyke Gardens, Isleworth, Middlesex TW7 5PE. *020 8847 2905 (and fax). Mobile: 0961 558908.* National Secretary: Mike Williamson, 2 Repton Avenue, Torrishome, Morecambe, Lancs LA4 6RZ. *01524 425242, 07729 906329 (mobile).* National Administrator: Mark Agate, 'The Stadium', 14 Coombe Close, Lordswood, Chatham, Kent ME5 8NU. *01634 319461 (and fax) 07931 635637 (mobile)*
National Playing Fields Association: Col. R. Satterthwaite, O.B.E., 578b Catherine Place, London, SW1.
Professional Footballers' Association: G. Taylor, 2 Oxford Court, Bishopsgate, Off Lower Mosley Street, Manchester M2 3WQ. *0161 236 0575*
Referees' Association: A. Smith, 1 Westhill Road, Coundon, Coventry CV6 2AD. *024 7660 1701*
Women's Football Alliance: Miss K. Doyle, The Football Association, 25 Soho Square, London W1D 4FA. *020 7745 4545*
Institute of Football Management and Administration: Camkin House, 8 Charles Court, Budbrooke Road, Warwick CV34 5LZ. *01926 411884. Fax: 01926 411041*
Football Administrators Association: as above.
Commercial and Marketing Managers Association: as above.
Management Stats Association: as above.
League Managers Association: as above.
The Football Programme Directory: David Stacey, 'The Beeches', 66 Southend Road, Wickford, Essex SS11 8EN. *01268 732041 (and fax)*
England Football Supporters Association: Publicity Officer, David Stacey, 'The Beeches', 66 Southend Road, Wickford, Essex SS11 8EN. *01268 732041 (and fax)*
World Cup (1966) Association: Hon. Secretary, David Duncan, 96 Glenlea Road, Eltham, London SE9 1DZ.
The Ninety-Two Club: 104 Gilda Crescent, Whitchurch, Bristol BS14 9LD.
Scottish 38 Club: Mark Byatt, 6 Greenfields Close, Loughton, Essex IG10 3HG. *0181 508 6088*
The Football Trust: Second Floor, Walkden House, 10 Melton Street, London NW1 2EJ. *020 7388 4504*
Association of Provincial Football Supporters Clubs in London: Stephen Moon, 32 Westminster Gardens, Barking, Essex IG11 0BJ. *020 8594 2367*
World Association of Friends of English Football: Carlisle Hill, Gluck, Habichthof 2, D24939 Flensburg, Germany. *0049 461 4700222*
Football Postcard Collectors Club: PRO: Bryan Horsnell, 275 Overdown Road, Tilehurst, Reading RG31 6NX. *0118 9424448 (and fax)*
UK Programme Collectors Club: Secretary, John Litster, 46 Milton Road, Kirkcaldy, Fife KY1 1TL. *01592 268718. Fax: 01592 595069*
Programme Monthly: as above.
Scottish Football Historians Association: as above.
Phil Gould (Licensed Football Agent), c/o Whoppit Management Ltd, P. O. Box 27204, London N11 2WS. *07071 732 468. Fax: 07070 732 469*
The Scandinavian Union of Supporters of British Football: Postboks, 15 Stovner, N-0913 Oslo, Norway.
Football Writers' Association: Executive Secretary, Ken Montgomery, 6 Chase Lane, Barkingside, Essex IG6 1BH. *0208 554 2455 (and fax)*
Programme Promotions: 47 The Beeches, Lampton Road, Hounslow, Middlesex TW3 4DF.
Web: www.footballprogrammes.com

FOOTBALL CLUB CHAPLAINCY

During the final few weeks of last year, there appeared on the shelves of good bookshops a football book which added some distinction to an acclaimed, occasional series promoted by one discerning publisher. This volume contributed to the series "*The Men Who Made XYZ Football Club*", but its author declined to follow the convention of the previous titles in that series which had simply used the heading as a reason to produce a Players A–Z. Past and present players were included in this latest edition, of course, but only those considered to be of significance. Also presented were many other men – plus the occasional, welcome, lady! – and among these, at the publishers' initiative, is to be found the honorary chaplain at the club concerned.

Now, the very fact that a football book for football fans includes a chapter about a chaplain, demonstrates just what an invaluable, unique contribution to a club these fellows do make. Agreed, you'll not find any of them featuring in the speculation, scandals, gossip or chatter that so often characterise the media's football coverage, but neither do the groundsmen or physios at our clubs, and no-one doubts *their* significance.

Rather, the value of a chaplain at one particular club has been highlighted by a discerning outside party – and there is no reason to suppose that broadly the same situation is to be found at all the other clubs who have had the wisdom to make a similar appointment.

Thank you to those readers who contacted us to say how their interest was captured by the article on this page in last year's yearbook – the one describing the conversation between a club chairman and a prospective chaplain, which took place over ten years ago. An update on that is envisaged for 2006 . . .

THE REV

OFFICIAL CHAPLAINS TO FA PREMIERSHIP AND FOOTBALL LEAGUE CLUBS

Rev Steven Hawkins—Bristol R; Rev Catherine Bell—Luton T; Canon Peter Bye—Carlisle U; Rev Ken Howles—Blackburn R; Rev David Langdon—QPR; Rev Andrew Taggart—Torquay U; Rev Gary Piper—Fulham; Rev David Jeans—Sheffield W; Rev Peter Amos—Barnsley; Rev Nigel Sands—Crystal Palace; Steve Prince—Reading; Rev Graham Spencer—Leicester C; Rev Martin Short and Very Rev John Richardson—Bradford C; Rev Kevan McCormack—Ipswich T; Rev John Boyers—Manchester U; Rev Allen Bagshawe—Hull C; Rev Martin Butt—Walsall; Rev David Tully—Newcastle U; Rev Derek Cleave—Bristol C; Rev Fr Alan Poulter and Fr Gerald Courell—Tranmere R; Rev Brian Rice—Hartlepool U; Rev Matt Baker and Rev Jeffrey Heskins—Charlton Ath; Rev Ray Dupere and Mr John Graham—Watford; Rev Owen Beament—Millwall; Rev Elwin Cockett—West Ham U; Rev Michael Futens—Derby Co; Rev Mick Woodhead—Sheffield U; Rev Ken Hawkins—Birmingham C; Rev Alan Comfort—Leyton Orient; Rev Simon Stevenette and Fr Kevin Hennessey—Swindon T; Rev John Hall-Matthews—Wolverhampton W; Rev Steve Collis—Port Vale; Rev Chris Cullwick—York C; Rev Ken Baker—Aston Villa and Northampton T; Rev Mark Hirst—Burnley; Rev Tony Porter—Manchester C; Rev Richard Hayton—Gillingham; Rev Clive Andrews—Notts Co; Fr Andrew McMahon—Southampton; Rev Chris Nelson—Preston North End; Rev Henry Corbett and Rev Harry Ross—Everton; Rev Paul Brown—Wrexham; Rev Jeff Howden—Plymouth Argyle; Rev Andy Rimmer and Mr Mick Mellows—Portsmouth; Rev Alan Wright—Scunthorpe U; Rev James Booth—Southend U; Rev Philip Hearn—Kidderminster H; Rev David Ottley—Bury; Rev Simon Lawton—Crewe Alex; Rev Billy Montgomery—Stockport Co; Rev Ken Hipkiss—WBA; Canon Roger Knight—Rushden & Diamonds; Rev Glyn Davies—Swansea C; Rev Richard Longfoot—Peterborough U; Revs David Male and Vaughan Pollard—Huddersfield T; Rev Jim Pearce—Yeovil T; Rev Brian Quar—Doncaster R; Rev David Tidswell—Blackpool; Rev Philip Mason—Bolton W; Rev Ron Smith—Milton Keynes Dons; Rev Jeremy Tear—Maccesfield T; Rev Paul Welch and Fr Steve Billington—Leeds U; Rev Alan Fisher—Bournemouth; Rev Tim O'Brien—Wycombe W.

The chaplains hope that those who read this page will see the value and benefit of chaplaincy work in football and will take appropriate steps to spread the word where this is possible. They would also like to thank the editors of the Football Yearbook *for their continued support for this specialist and growing area of work.*

The following addresses may be helpful: SCORE (Sports Chaplaincy Offering Resources and Encouragement), PO Box 123, Sale, Manchester M33 4ZA and Christians in Sport, Frampton House, Victoria Road, Bicester OX26 6PB.

OBITUARIES

Povl Ahm, CBE (Born Aarhus, Denmark, 26 September 1926. Died Harpenden, Herts, 15 May 2005.) Povl Ahm was a goalkeeper who played for the Corinthian Casuals team defeated by Bishop Auckland in the 1956 FA Amateur Cup final. Away from football he was a well-known civil engineer who was involved in many high profile projects including the building of the new Coventry Cathedral.

Jack Ainscough (Born Adlington, Lancs, 26 March 1926. Died 16 December 2004.) Jack Ainscough was a defender who made seven appearances for Blackpool between 1950 and 1954 before moving on to Fleetwood, where he played over 400 games.

Andy Aitken (Born Edinburgh, 21 August 1934. Died Edinburgh, 28 February 2005.) Andy Aitken was a quick and elegant inside forward who was a member of the Hibernian team that was defeated by Clyde in the 1958 Scottish Cup final. He was later sold to West Bromwich Albion, where he spent a single season, before returning to Scotland to play for Falkirk and Raith Rovers.

Alf Arrowsmith (Born Manchester, 11 December 1942. Died May 2005.) Alf Arrowsmith spent eight years on the books of Liverpool for whom he was principally a reserve centre forward, his most regular spell of first-team football coming in the second half of the 1963–64 campaign. He later spent time with Bury and Rochdale before joining Macclesfield Town.

Frank Austin (Born Stoke-on-Trent, 6 July 1933. Died Long Eaton, Derbys, July 2004.) Frank Austin was a stylish defender who made over 300 appearances for Coventry City between 1953 and 1963. A former England Schools international, he also had a brief spell with Torquay United.

Billy Baker (Born Penrhiwceiber, Glamorgan, 3 October 1920. Died Cardiff, 6 February 2005.) Billy Baker joined Cardiff City shortly before the outbreak of war and went on to become a key figure in the team that won the Division Three South title in 1946–47. Capped once for Wales, he made over 300 appearances for the Bluebirds before concluding his career with a spell at Ipswich Town.

John Barker (Born Huddersfield, 4 July 1948. Died Scunthorpe, 14 December 2004.) John Barker made his debut for Scunthorpe as an apprentice and went on to become the club's regular left back for almost a decade, making over 300 first-team appearances. He was a near ever-present in the team that won promotion from the old Fourth Division in 1971–72.

Bernard Barnes (Born Plymouth, 25 December 1937. Died August 2004.) Bernard Barnes was briefly on the books of Plymouth Argyle. A centre forward, he scored once in four appearances in the late 1950s.

Colin Bell (Born Horsley, Derbys, 24 March 1926. Died Heanor, Derbys, 21 July 2004.) Colin Bell was a versatile player who made 79 first-team appearances for Derby County in the early 1950s.

Fred Bett (Born Scunthorpe, 5 December 1920. Died Scunthorpe, 14 April 2005.) Fred Bett was a powerful inside forward who made a few pre-war appearances for Sunderland. In the post-war period he featured for both Coventry and Lincoln City (for whom he had also appeared regularly during the hostilities) before moving into non-League football.

Roy Bicknell (Born Edlington, nr. Doncaster, 19 February 1926. Died Colchester, 31 January 2005.) Roy Bicknell was a centre half who was a product of Wolves' famous Yorkshire nursery set-up. He later played for Charlton, Bristol City, Gravesend & Northfleet and Colchester United before retiring in the mid-1950s.

Ronnie Bird (Born Birmingham, 27 December 1941. Died March 2005.) After failing to make the grade with Birmingham City, Ronnie Bird did well in spells with Bradford Park Avenue and Bury before moving on to join Cardiff City. A skilful left winger with a cannonball shot, he scored 24 goals in just over 100 appearances for the Bluebirds before concluding his senior career with a spell at Crewe.

Harold Bodle (Born Adwick-le-Street, Yorkshire, 4 October 1920. Died Bournemouth, 1 January 2005.) Harold Bodle was a scheming inside left who helped Birmingham City win the old Second Division title in 1947–48. He also played for Rotherham United, Bury, Stockport County and Accrington Stanley, making over 300 senior appearances in total. He also had a brief spell as manager of Accrington in 1959–60.

Harry Bond (Born circa 1933. Died November 2004.) Harry Bond was a well-known goalkeeper in the Irish League in the 1950s and early 1960s, gaining an Irish Cup winners' medal with Ballymena United in 1958.

George Bourne (Born Burslem, Staffs, 5 March 1931. Died 7 October 2004.) George Bourne was a solid right back who made over 100 first-team appearances for Stoke City in the early 1950s before his career was effectively ended by a broken leg.

Wilson Briggs (Born Gorebridge, Midlothian, 15 May 1942. Died February 2005.) Wilson Briggs was a defender for Aston Villa in the early 1960s, making just two appearances. He was later on the books of Falkirk, East Fife and Raith Rovers but made just a few first-team appearances in total.

Alex Brown (Born Glasgow, 15 August 1930. Died 19 June 2004.) A Scottish youth international, Alex Brown had spells with Partick Thistle and Preston early in his career but it was only when he joined Carlisle United that he experienced regular first-team football. A solid and reliable right back, he made over 100 first-team appearances for the Brunton Park club between 1958 and 1961.

Bill Brown

Bill Brown (Born Arbroath, 8 October 1931. Died Simcoe, Ontario, Canada, 30 November 2004.) Bill Brown won 28 caps for Scotland and was goalkeeper for the Tottenham Hotspur team that won a League and FA Cup double in 1960–61. He had made his name with Dundee, with whom he won a Scottish League Cup winners' medal in October 1951 and made his international debut during the 1958 World Cup finals. Bill was also a member of the Spurs team that won the FA Cup in 1961–62 and the European Cup Winners' Cup 12 months later. He also had spells with Northampton Town and Toronto Falcons before settling in Canada.

Willie Browne (Born Longford, Co Longford, Republic of Ireland, 1936. Died 14 October 2004.) Willie Browne was a versatile defender who won three full caps for the Republic of Ireland in the 1960s, also gaining16 amateur caps. At club level he played for UC Dublin and Bohemians and was voted Irish Soccer Personality of the Year in 1963.

Ron Burgess (Born Cwm, nr Ebbw Vale, 9 April 1917. Died Swansea, 14 February 2005.) Ron Burgess made his debut for Tottenham Hotspur shortly before the outbreak of war and when the game resumed normality in 1946–47 he was a regular in the line-up at left half. A key figure in the title-winning sides of 1949–51 he remained a first-team regular for both club and country until 1954, by which time he had accumulated a total of 32 full caps, plus an appearance for the Great Britain team that played the Rest of Europe in a match to celebrate the return of the Home Countries to FIFA in 1947. He was later player-coach and then manager of Swansea Town and also had a spell in charge of Watford.

Reg Burr (Died 28 May 2005.) Reg Burr was a businessman who served on the board of directors at Luton in the 1960s and then Millwall from 1975 to 1981. He later returned to the Lions and was chairman from 1986 to 1995, during which time the club moved from their historic home to a new stadium, the New Den.

Arthur Burrows (Born Stockport, 4 December 1919. Died March 2005.) Arthur Burrows was a wing half who made a handful of appearances for Stockport County and Accrington Stanley in the years either side of the war. He played for County in the famous cup tie against Doncaster in March 1946 which lasted some 203 minutes before being abandoned.

Syd Bycoft (Born Lincoln, 19 February 1912. Died 4 October 2004.) One of the toughest centre halves in the old Division Three North in the seasons either side of the war, Syd made over 500 first-team appearances for Doncaster Rovers between 1936 and 1952. He later had a short spell as manager of the club before leaving the game altogether.

Jimmy Campbell (Born Glasgow, circa 1921. Died Ayr, 1 October 2004.) Jimmy Campbell was a stylish right half who joined Clyde during the war. He was capped by Scotland in the unofficial international against Belgium in January 1946 and went on to make more than 200 senior appearances, later playing for Queen of the South and Montrose.

Dick Carey (Born Paisley, 19 November 1927. Died Renfrew, 16 December 2005.) Dick Carey was a left half who spent most of his career in Scottish Junior football. He made three appearances for Cowdenbeath in 1948–49 and the following season made one appearance for Southport during a trial period with the club.

David Carr (Born Aylesham, Kent, 31 January 1957. Died 19 June 2005.) David Carr was a skilful central defender or midfielder who began his career with Luton in the mid-1970s. The best years of his career were spent at Lincoln, for whom he made over 150 senior appearances and featured in the side that gained promotion from the old Fourth Division in 1980–81. He finished off with a season at Torquay.

Norman Chalk (Born Southampton, 28 October 1916. Died Southampton, 25 May 2005.) Norman Chalk was a centre half who made five appearances for Southampton in the seasons just before the war and subsequently enjoyed a lengthy career in the local Police Force.

Brian Clough, OBE (Born Middlesbrough, 21 March 1935. Died Derby, 20 September 2004.) Brian Clough was one of the great characters of the post-war British game and one of the most successful managers of all time. As a player he was a prolific centre forward, capable of scoring more than 40 goals a season. Quick, sharp and with a

Brian Clough

great eye for goal, he would surely have won more than two caps for England but for his outspoken views. His playing career with Middlesbrough and then Sunderland was ended by injury and he entered management. Teaming up with former colleague Peter Taylor, the pair were successful in taking Hartlepool to their first-ever promotion, but it was at Derby and then Nottingham Forest that he achieved his greatest successes. He led the Rams to the Football League title in 1971–72 and after brief spells with Brighton and Leeds he took over at the City Ground. Promotion from the old Second Division was followed by the club's first-ever Football League title in 1977–78 and two remarkable European Cup successes in 1979 and 1980. Brian remained in charge at Forest until his retirement in May 1993 and thereafter retained a great enthusiasm for the game and a willingness to speak out on the issues of the day.

Willie Cowie (Born Annathill, Lanarkshire. Died May 2005.) Willie Cowie was a traditional centre half who spent three seasons on the books of Motherwell in the late 1950s when he was mostly a reserve. He later played for Queen of the South before leaving the full-time game.

José Luis Cuciuffo (Born Córdoba, Argentina, 1 February 1961. Died Bahiá Blanco, Buenos Aires, Argentina, 11 December 2004.) José Luis Cuciuffo was a defender who won 21 caps for Argentina between 1985 and 1989, and was a member of the team that defeated West Germany 3-2 to win the 1986 World Cup final. At club level he played for Velez Sarsfeld, Boca Juniors and Nimes. He died as a result of a shooting accident whilst hunting.

George Curtis (Born West Thurrock, Essex, 3 December 1919. Died Basildon, Essex, 17 November 2004.) After making his debut shortly before the outbreak of war, George Curtis played 13 league and cup games for Arsenal before moving on to Southampton. He played almost 200 games for the Saints as an inside forward or wing half and later coached around the world, including a spell in charge of Norway's national side.

Dougie Daniels (Born Salford, Manchester, 21 August 1924. Died Salford, Manchester, 7 November 2004.) Dougie Daniels was a goalkeeper who played for Manchester City, New Brighton, Chesterfield and Accrington Stanley in the immediate post-war period. In later life he became a full-time trade union official with the AEU and served as a Labour Party member on Salford Council.

Jimmy Dawson (Born Stoneyburn, West Lothian, 21 December 1927. Died February 2005.) Jimmy Dawson was a reserve winger who made a number of appearances for Portsmouth, Leicester City and Third Lanark in the late 1940s and early 1950s.

Stuart Dimond (Born Manchester, 3 January 1920. Died Didsbury, Manchester, November 2004.) Stuart Dimond played as a forward for Manchester United and Distillery during the war, and later had a brief spell on the books of Bradford City before enjoying a lengthy career in North West non-League circles.

Willie Duff (Born Winchburgh, West Lothian, 6 February 1935. Died Edinburgh, 30 August 2004.) Willie Duff came to prominence with Hearts, gaining winners' medals in the Scottish League Cup (1954–55) and Scottish Cup (1956) before moving south to join Charlton. He went on to make over 200 Football League appearances for the Addicks, succeeding the legendary Sam Bartram as the team's regular goalkeeper. Willie remained active in the game until the mid-1970s, his career later taking him to Peterborough, Dunfermline, Raith, East Stirlingshire and Albion Rovers.

Jimmy Dunn (Born Rutherglen, nr. Glasgow, 23 October 1922. Died Leeds, 24 January 2005.) Jimmy Dunn was the regular right back for Leeds United for almost a decade from the late 1940s, making over 400 first-team appearances. A member of the team that won promotion from the old Second Division in 1955–56, he later played for Darlington.

Steve Earl (Born Scunthorpe, 31 August 1956. Died 3 November 2004.) Steve Earl was a forward with Scunthorpe United during the 1970s. He finished as the club's second-top scorer in the 1978–79 season.

George Ephgrave (Born Reading, 29 April 1918. Died Guernsey, 9 December 2004.) A tall goalkeeper who played most of his football at Southampton (38 appearances in the first two post-war seasons), George Ephgrave was also on the books of Aston Villa, Swindon, Norwich City and Watford.

George Farm (Born Slateford, Edinburgh, 13 July 1924. Died Edinburgh, 14 July 2004.) As a player George Farm was a talented goalkeeper who won ten caps for Scotland. He began his career with a brief spell at Hibernian before moving on to Blackpool where he made over 500 first-team appearances and gained an FA Cup winners' medal in the famous 'Matthews' Final' of 1954. George went on to become player-manager of Queen of the South, later having spells as manager of Raith Rovers (on two occasions) and Dunfermline Athletic. He led Dunfermline to victory in the Scottish Cup final of 1968.

Peter Firmani (Born Cape Town, South Africa, 14 February 1936. Died Johannesburg, South Africa, December 2004.) One of several South Africans to play for Charlton Athletic during the 1950s, Peter Firmani was a right back who made 31 appearances for the Addicks. He later returned to South Africa where he played for the Highlands Park and Wanderers clubs.

Bobby Flavell (Born Annathill, Lanarkshire, 1 September 1921. Died Airdrie, 18 March 2005.) Bobby Flavell was a dashing centre forward who made his name with Hearts, for whom he scored 50 goals in all competitions in the 1946–47 season. He later moved on to Airdrie before joining the mini-exodus of top players to Colombia in the early 1950s. On his return he enjoyed success with Dundee (for whom he won two Scottish League Cup winners' medals) and also played for Kilmarnock and St Mirren. He was capped twice by Scotland and was later manager of a number of clubs including Ayr, St Mirren and Albion Rovers.

Bob Forrest (Born Rossington, Yorkshire, 13 May 1931. Died Weymouth, 3 May 2005.) Bob Forrest was a powerful inside forward who made over 100 appearances for Leeds United in the 1950s. He later moved on to Notts County where he captained the side that won promotion from the old Fourth Division in 1959–60.

Johnny Frye (Born Ardrossan, Ayrshire, 27 July 1933. Died March 2005.) Johnny Frye was an outside right who began his career as understudy to Gordon Smith at Hibernian. He subsequently moved on in search of first-team football and had spells with St Mirren, Sheffield Wednesday, Tranmere Rovers, Queen of the South, Hamilton Academical and Stranraer before retiring from the game in the summer of 1967.

Stan Galley (Born Stanfree, Derbyshire, 28 April 1918. Died Chesterfield, 16 January 2005.) Stan Galley was a left back who made a handful of wartime appearances for Birmingham City and Mansfield Town, later playing for the Cresswell Colliery club.

Derek Gardener (Born circa 1926. Died December 2004.) Derek Gardener was a full back who was a member of the successful Crook Town team of the late 1950s and early 1960s. He won seven caps for England amateurs and also made a single appearance for the Great Britain Olympic team.

Jimmy Gauld (Born Aberdeen, 9 May 1929. Died Westminster, London, 9 December 2004.) Jimmy Gauld was a very talented player who came to prominence with Waterford, before his goal-scoring exploits won him a transfer to Charlton. A big burly inside forward he later played for Everton, Plymouth, Swindon, St Johnstone and Mansfield and went on to score 75 goals from 195 appearances in a career that was ended after he fractured a leg on Boxing Day 1960. Sadly he became involved in a match-fixing scandal and as a result he was banned from the game for life by the FA and also received a four-year jail sentence.

Raymond Goethals (Born Brussels, Belgium, 1921. Died Brussels, 6 December 2004.) As a player, Raymond Goethals had been a goalkeeper with Daring Brussels and Racing Brussels, however, he was much better known as a coach. He was in charge of the Belgium national team from 1968 to 1976, steering them to third place in the 1972 European Championships. He was later successful at club level winning the European Cup Winners' Cup with Anderlecht (1978) and the European Cup with Olympique Marseille (1993).

Bernard Goodall (Born Islington, London, 4 October 1937. Died 9 January 2005.) Bernard Goodall made over 100 first-team appearances for Reading between 1959 and 1963 and also had brief spells at Carlisle and Halifax. From 1995 to 1998 he was Chief Executive of Leyton Orient.

Sam Goodwin (Born Tarbolton, Ayrshire, 14 March 1943. Died 9 March 2005.) Sam Goodwin was an accomplished wing half who made over 200 first-team appearances for Airdrieonians, later having a spell with Crystal Palace. He returned to Scotland and later featured for Motherwell and Clydebank.

Jimmy Greenock (Died April 2005.) Jim Greenock was a left half who made over 200 first-team appearances for Queen of the South between 1951 and 1961.

Bob Grice (Born Sutton, St Helens, 12 April 1907. Died Oldham, 5 August 2004.) Bob Grice was a powerful defender who featured for New Brighton, Oldham Athletic and Southport in the pre-war period, making over 50 senior appearances.

Paddy Hale (Born Clevedon, Somerset, 7 April 1928. Died Weston-super-Mare, 15 July 2004.) Paddy Hale was a dependable player for Bristol Rovers throughout the 1950s. Initially a goal-scoring centre forward, he subsequently converted to a role as a centre half. Paddy was a member of the Pirates' team that reached the FA Cup quarter-finals in 1957–58.

Dennis Hall (Born Southwell, Notts, 24 December 1930. Died 19 October 2004.) Dennis Hall was principally a reserve in six years with Portsmouth, but had a little more success after moving on to Reading, for whom he made 14 appearances in the 1954–55 season.

Jimmy Harrison (Born Leicester, 12 February 1921. Died July 2004.) Jimmy Harrison was a solid full back who served Leicester City, Aston Villa and Coventry City in the immediate post-war seasons. The highlight of his career was an appearance for Leicester in the 1949 FA Cup final defeat by Wolves.

Keith Hellewell (Born Barnsley, 1 April 1944. Died 18 January 2005.) Keith Hellewell was a goalkeeper who made 12 first-team appearances for Doncaster Rovers in the early 1960s before moving to South Africa where he played for Port Elizabeth City and Wanderers.

Jackie Henderson (Born Glasgow, 17 January 1932. Died Poole, Dorset, 26 January 2005.) Jackie Henderson was a big powerful forward who made over 400 appearances in the old First Division for Portsmouth, Wolves, Arsenal and Fulham between 1951 and 1964. A regular goal-scorer, he also won seven full caps for Scotland.

John Higgins (Born Monsal Head, Derbys, 15 November 1932. Died 22 April 2005.) John Higgins was a centre half who made over 150 appearances for Bolton in the 1950s. The highlight of his career came when he appeared for Wanderers in the 1958 FA Cup final victory over Manchester United.

Glyn Hood (Born Pontypool, 12 March 1928. Died Coventry, 28 September 2004.) Glyn Hood featured at left half for West Bromwich Albion in the immediate post-war seasons. He was an important figure in the club's 1948–49 promotion campaign before his career was effectively ended by a knee injury.

Arthur Hopcroft (Born Shoeburyness, Essex, 30 November 1932. Died Kingston, Surrey, 22 November 2004.) Arthur Hopcraft was the author of 'The Football Man', a well-respected work on the game published in 1968. A journalist who wrote on football for *The Guardian* and *The Observer*, he later became a screenwriter for television.

Stan Howard (Born Chorley, Lancs, 1 July 1934. Died Preston, 19 June 2004.) Stan Howard was a versatile forward who played for Huddersfield Town, Bradford City, Barrow and Halifax Town, making over 200 first-team appearances in the 1950s and 1960s.

Bobby Howitt (Born Glasgow, 15 July 1929. Died Carluke, Lanarkshire, 31 January 2005.) A skilful and intelligent inside forward, Bobby Howitt made over 300 senior appearances for Partick Thistle, Sheffield United and Stoke City between 1949 and 1962. He was later manager of Motherwell between March 1965 and March 1973.

Billy Hughes (Born Ballymena, 9 May 1929. Died June 2005.) Billy Hughes was a creative inside forward who made 47 appearances for Bolton Wanderers between 1948 and 1953, winning a single cap for Northern Ireland. He later had a season on the books of Bournemouth.

Emlyn Hughes, OBE (Born Barrow-in-Furness, 28 August 1947. Died Sheffield, 9 November 2004.) Emlyn Hughes was one of the stars of the great Liverpool team of the 1970s. A powerful, enthusiastic defender he was a member of the team that won European titles in three consecutive years: UEFA Cup (1976) and European Cup (1977 and 1978). He made over 650 first-team appearances for the Reds and also played for Blackpool, Wolves, Rotherham (where he was player-manager) and Swansea. Emlyn was also a regular in the England line-up, winning 62 caps and captaining the side on 23 occasions. After leaving the game he enjoyed a successful career as a television presenter, notably during a lengthy spell as one of the team captains in the popular BBC programme 'A Question of Sport'.

Jack Hutchinson (Born Basford, Nottingham, 1 June 1921. Died 27 November 2004.) Jack Hutchinson was a solid full back who made over 250 first-team appearances for Nottingham Forest between 1946 and 1959. He was a member of the Forest teams that won promotion in 1950–51 and 1956–57.

Bedford Jezzard (Born Clerkenwell, London, 19 October 1927. Died 21 May 2005.) Bedford Jezzard was a goal-scoring inside forward who netted over 150 goals in some 300 appearances for Fulham between 1948 and 1957. His best haul came in 1953–54 when he netted 38 times to create a post-war record for the club. Bedford won two England caps and also gained representative honours for the Football League side. He later managed Fulham from 1958 to 1964.

Mike Johnson (Born York, 4 October 1933. Died Australia, 2004.) Mike Johnson was an outside left who played for Brighton, Fulham, Doncaster Rovers and Barrow in the late 1950s and early 1960s. He eventually emigrated to Australia where he became a successful businessman.

Brian Keating (Born Lewisham, London, 19 March 1935. Died Australia, 2005.) Brian Keating made a handful of appearances for Crewe Alexandra in the late 1950s and later featured for Crook Town when they won the FA Amateur Cup in 1959. He was an amateur throughout his career, serving in the RAF.

Bernie Kelly (Born Carfin, Lanarkshire, 21 October 1932. Died Detroit, USA, October 2004.) A powerful inside forward, Bernie Kelly scored at a prolific rate for Raith Rovers to earn a move to Leicester in the summer of 1958. However, he never really settled at Filbert Street, and after a brief spell with Nottingham Forest he returned to Scotland where he concluded his career with spells at Aberdeen, Raith (a second time) and Cowdenbeath.

Lucien Laurent (Born Saint-Maur-des-Fossés, Val-de-Marne, France, 10 December 1907. Died Besançon, France, 4 April 2005.) Lucien Laurent won ten caps for France in the 1930s. A member of the squad for the 1930 World Cup finals, he created history by scoring the first-ever goal in the competition when he netted in the 19th minute of his team's 4-1 win over Mexico.

Arthur Lever (Born Cardiff, 25 March 1920. Died 20 August 2004.) Arthur Lever joined Cardiff City during the war and went on to assist the Bluebirds to the Division Three South title in 1946–47. He was later sold to Leicester, breaking the Filbert Street club's record transfer fee, where he won a solitary cap for Wales. Arthur ended his career at Newport County before injuries led to his retirement from the game.

Micky Lill (Born Romford, Essex, 3 August 1936. Died Johannesburg, South Africa, 22 September 2004.) An England Youth international winger, Micky played for Wolves, Everton, Plymouth and Portsmouth between 1954 and 1965 without ever really establishing himself as a first-team regular. He later emigrated to South Africa where he worked as a PE teacher.

Emlyn Hughes

Charlie Livesey (Born West Ham, London, 6 February 1938. Died London, 26 February 2005.) Charlie Livesey was an extremely skilful centre or inside forward who scored over 100 goals at a rate of one every three games. After beginning his career with Southampton, he subsequently had spells with Chelsea, Gillingham, Watford, Northampton and Brighton, always impressing with his talent on the ball.

Frank Lord (Born Oldham, 13 March 1936. Died South Africa, June 2005.) A big powerful centre forward who was particularly effective in the air, Frank Lord was a prolific scorer, netting 172 Football League goals during a career that saw him play for Rochdale, Crewe, Plymouth, Stockport, Blackburn and Chesterfield. He later had a spell as manager of Hereford United and more recently had been working as a scout for Manchester United in South Africa.

Tommy Lowry (Born circa 1940. Died Lurgan, Co Armagh, 2004.) Capped by Northern Ireland at B international level, Tommy Lowry won an Irish Cup winners' medal with Ballymena United in 1958. A tall centre half, he enjoyed a spell at Falkirk in the early 1960s before playing for and then managing Glenavon.

Tim McCoy (Born Birmingham, 4 March 1921. Died 27 January 2005.) Tim McCoy was a centre half who made almost 200 Football League appearances for Portsmouth, Northampton and Brighton between 1946 and 1954.

Tommy McDonald (Born Hill of Beath, Cowdenbeath, 24 May 1930. Died Dunfermline, 24 August 2004.) A tricky winger, Tommy McDonald was understudy to the great Gordon Smith at Hibernian in the early 1950s before moving south to join Leicester. He helped the Foxes win promotion in 1956–57 and later played for Dunfermline, Raith, Queen of the South, Stirling Albion and Cowdenbeath.

Don McEvoy (Born Golcar, nr. Huddersfield, 3 December 1928. Died Halifax, 9 October 2004.) Don McEvoy made over 350 senior appearances as a powerful centre half with Huddersfield, Sheffield Wednesday, Lincoln and Barrow in the 1950s and early 1960s. He remained in the game as a manager, taking charge of a string of lower division clubs including Halifax Town, Barrow (twice), Grimsby Town and Southport.

Bill McGarry (Born Stoke-on-Trent, 10 June 1927. Died South Africa, 15 March 2005.) Bill McGarry enjoyed a successful career as a gritty hard-working right half, winning four caps for England in the 1950s when he appeared for Port Vale, Huddersfield and Bournemouth. He eventually became manager of the Cherries and also served Watford, Ipswich, Wolves and Newcastle. He led the Portman Road club to the Second Division title in 1967–68 and won the Football League Cup with Wolves in 1974.

Ally McGowan (Born Airdrie, 22 January 1930. Died 5 July 2005.) Ally McGowan was a defender who spent three seasons on the books of St Johnstone before moving south to sign for Wrexham. He went on to make almost 500 first-team appearances for the Racecourse club before injury ended his career in the mid-1960s. Ally later became the club groundsman for a number of years.

Danny McGrain (Born 27 May 1953. Died 28 August 2004.) Danny McGrain was a hard-working midfield player who made over 100 senior appearances for Clyde in the early 1970s. His career was ended by a serious head injury suffered in a game against Dundee United in February 1974.

Jackie McGrory (Born Renfrew, 15 November 1941. Died 11 October 2004.) Jackie McGrory was a commanding centre half who was a key figure for Kilmarnock throughout the 1960s, making over 450 senior appearances for the club. Jackie assisted Killie to the Scottish League title in 1964–65 and also won three full caps for Scotland.

Alec Machin (Born Hampstead, London 6 July 1920. Died Truro, 18 February 2005.) Alec Machin was a classy wing half or inside forward who played for Chelsea and Plymouth in the seasons just after the war. After suffering a broken leg in April 1949 he rarely featured for Argyle and in the summer of 1952 he moved on to Southern League club Yeovil Town.

Jim MacLaren (Born Crieff, Perthshire, 26 November 1921. Died 20 July 2004.) Jim MacLaren was one of three brothers who featured as goalkeepers during the 1950s. Jim began his career with Chester but was best-known for his performances for Carlisle United, for whom he was a regular for almost a decade. He finished his career with a spell at Berwick Rangers.

Harry McNally (Born Doncaster, 7 July 1936. Died Chester, 12 December 2004.) Harry McNally played most of his football with Skelmersdale United and later became manager of Chester between 1985 and 1992. Thereafter he scouted for a number of clubs in the North West.

Charlie Marks (Born Eccles, Kent, 21 December 1919. Died Maidstone, Kent, 25 January 2005.) Charlie Marks joined Gillingham, during the war and went on to become a regular in the line-up through to 1958, mostly featuring at right back. He made over 450 appearances for the club, including his games in the Southern League, and famously once broke the net with a penalty kick.

Alan Martin (Born Smallthorne, Staffs, 23 November 1923. Died 18 October 2004.) Alan Martin was a skilful wing half who made over 300 appearances for Port Vale and Stoke City in the period up to 1959.

Bror Mellburg (Born Ambjörnby, Sweden, 9 December 1923. Died Sollentuna, Sweden, 8 September 2004.) An old-fashioned centre forward for Sweden, Bror Mellburg was one of only three players to win World Cup medals in the 1950 (third place) and 1958 (runners-up) tournaments. At club level he played for AIK, Genoa and Toulouse.

Irvine Methley (Born Worsborough, Yorkshire, 22 September 1925. Died July 2004.) Irvine Methley was a regular in the Walsall line-up at full back in the early post-war years. He was a member of the Saddlers' team, defeated by Bournemouth in the 1945–46 Division Three South Cup final.

Rinus Michels (Born Amsterdam, 9 February 1928. Died Aalst, Belgium, 3 March 2004.) Rinus Michels was coach of both Ajax and the Netherlands international side during the 1970s and 1980s when he was credited with the invention of the concept of 'Total Football'. He led Ajax to four domestic titles and victory in the 1971 European Cup final. Rinus played for Ajax between 1946 and 1958 and won five caps for his country.

Willie Miller (Born Glasgow, 20 October 1924. Died June 2005.) Willie Miller joined Celtic in May 1942 and went on to make 123 peacetime appearances during his stay at Parkhead, winning six caps and also featuring for the Scottish League representative side. Willie later played for Clyde and Hibernian before retiring from the game in the mid-1950s.

Ray Minshull (Born Bolton, 15 July 1920. Died Southport, 15 February 2005.) Ray Minshull was a capable goalkeeper who started his career as second choice to Cyril Sidlow at Liverpool. He went on to make over 200 appearances for Southport before concluding his career with a spell at Bradford Park Avenue. Ray later became a respected coach and was Youth Development Officer at Everton for many years.

Eric Moore (Born St Helens, Lancashire, 16 July 1926. Died 5 August 2004.) Eric Moore was a full back who made almost 200 appearances for Everton in the early 1950s and was a member of the team that won the old Second Division title in 1953–54. He also played for Chesterfield and Tranmere.

Pat Morrissey (Born Enniscorthey, Co Wexford, Republic of Ireland, 23 February 1948. Died Hammersmith, London, 19 February 2005.) Pat Morrissey was a forward who made over 300 appearances during a career which saw him play for Coventry City, Torquay, Crewe, Chester, Watford, Aldershot and Swansea. He was also capped for the Republic of Ireland at under-23 level.

Bill Muir (Born Ayr, 27 August 1925. Died January 2005.) Bill Muir was a reserve winger for Queen's Park Rangers and Torquay, before switching to non-League circles with Yeovil Town.

Vic Niblett (Born Frimley, Surrey, 9 December 1924. Died Gillingham, Kent, 1 October 2004.) Capped by England Schools, Vic Niblett had brief spells with Reading and West Ham without ever establishing himself before joining Gillingham in 1951. He went on to make over 150 appearances as a commanding centre half for the Kent club, later serving the club in a number of backroom positions.

Bill Nicholson, OBE (Born Scarborough, 26 January 1919. Died Potters Bar, Herts, 23 October 2004.) Bill Nicholson was one of the all-time greats for Tottenham Hotspur, serving the club as a player and manager for almost 40 years. He arrived at White Hart Lane shortly before the war, but really came to prominence in the late 1940s as a member of the famous 'push and run' team. A talented right half, he was a member of the side that won the Second Division and then the Football League title in successive seasons (1949–51) and was capped once for England. He went on to serve the club as manager from 1958 to 1974 during which time Spurs won a League and Cup double (1960–61), the European Cup Winners' Cup (1963), UEFA Cup (1972) and both the FA Cup and Football League Cup on two more occasions.

Bobby Noble (Born Newcastle upon Tyne, 25 May 1949. Died Australia, May 2005.) Bobby Noble began his career on the books of Newcastle, but failed to make the first team at St James' Park and made his senior debut whilst on loan at Barrow. A rugged defender, he subsequently played for Bury, Colchester, Southport and Darlington before emigrating to Australia.

Danny O'Callaghan (Died 4 October 2004.) Danny O'Callaghan was a talented outside left for Shamrock Rovers in the early 1950s who won representative honours for both the League of Ireland and the Republic of Ireland at amateur international level.

David Oliphant (Born Carlisle, 29 January 1942. Died Carlisle, 4 November 2004.) David Oliphant was a skilful, hard-working wing half who made over 100 first-team appearances for Carlisle United in the early 1960s. He also had a brief spell with Queen of the South before injuries led to his retirement from the game.

Junior Omand (Born 1931. Died Glasgow, 18 January 2005.) Junior Omand was a talented inside forward who appeared in over 300 first-team games for Queen's Park and was a member of the Spiders' team that won the B Division title in 1955–56. Junior was capped at amateur international level by Scotland and later served Queen's Park as a committee member before becoming the club president.

Joe O'Neil (Born Glasgow, 15 August 1931. Died Wiltshire, 16 February 2005.) This tall forward was introduced to senior football at Aberdeen, but played more first-team football whilst on loan at Southend during his National Service. Joe later had spells with Leicester and Northampton before leaving the senior game in 1959.

Rex Osman (Born Derby, 4 April 1932. Died Ipswich, 9 June 2005.) Rex Osman spent seven years as a professional with Derby County but made only two first-team appearances as a wing half before moving into the local non-League scene.

Bertie Peacock, MBE (Born Coleraine, 29 September 1928. Died Belfast 22 July 2004.) Bertie Peacock made his name with Glentoran before joining Celtic in the summer of 1949. For the next 12 years he was a regular in the side at left half, winning a Scottish League title in 1953–54 and two Scottish Cups (1951 and 1954). Bertie was also a regular at international level for Northern Ireland, winning 31 caps and being a member of the side that reached the quarter-finals of the World Cup in 1958. He later managed both Coleraine and the Northern Ireland international team. In more recent years he had been involved in organising the Northern Ireland Milk Cup tournament.

Willie Penman (Born Kelty, Fife, 1922. Died Kirkcaldy, Fife, 31 January 2005.) Willie Penman was one of the greatest players in the history of Raith Rovers, netting at the amazing rate of 211 goals in 328 appearances. He was at his best in the 1948–49 season, scoring 58 goals and assisting the Fife club to the final of the Scottish league Cup in addition to the B Division title. He also appeared for Brechin City, Montrose and Dundee United.

Jack Pinder (Born Acomb, York, 1 December 1912. Died York, 19 August 2004.) Jack Pinder captain the England Schools team in 1927, later going on to make over 200 senior appearances for York City between 1932 and 1948. A hard-tackling full back, he later served the club as trainer.

Jack Pitt (Born Willenhall, Staffs, 20 May 1920. Died Bristol, 17 August 2004.) Jack Pitt was a one-club man who gave over 40 years service to Bristol Rovers. Although he did not appear in senior football until the age of 26, he made over 500 appearances for the Pirates, principally as a wing half. He later worked on the club's groundstaff before becoming groundsman, a post he held through to the late 1980s.

Ken Powell (Born Chester, 25 September 1924. Died Chester, 17 January 2005.) Ken Powell was a wing half who appeared for Exeter City and Bristol Rovers in the period just after the war. He was also a talented cricketer and represented Gloucestershire Seconds.

Eric Probert (Born South Kirkby, Yorkshire, 17 February 1952. Died September 2004.) As a youngster Eric Probert won England Youth honours and made his debut in top-flight football for Burnley as a 16-year-old. A hard-tackling midfield player, he never quite fulfilled his early promise although he went on to make over 200 senior appearances, also playing for Notts County and Darlington.

Ernie Pym (Born Torquay, 23 March 1935. Died 22 October 2004.) Ernie Pym was a traditional-style winger who made over 300 first-team appearances for Torquay between 1957 and 1965. He was a member of the Gulls' team that won promotion from the old Fourth Division in 1959–60.

Johnny Quigley (Born Glasgow, 28 June 1935, Died Nottingham, 30 November 2004.) A skilful inside forward with excellent ball control, Johnny Quigley was a member of the Nottingham Forest team that won the FA Cup in 1959. He remained at the City Ground until 1965, and later played for Huddersfield, Bristol City and Mansfield. Johnny subsequently became a coach, working in the Middle East for many years.

John Quinn (Born circa 1933. Died 28 August 2004.) John Quinn was a fixture at right half for Airdrieonians during the 1950s and made over 250 first-team appearances during his stay at Broomfield Park. He featured in the side that reached the semi-final of the Scottish Cup in 1954–55.

Ian Rae (Born Grangemouth, Stirlingshire, 19 January 1933. Died Sussex, July 2005.) Ian Rae played at left back for Falkirk when they defeated Kilmarnock to win the Scottish Cup in 1957. Altogether he made some 350 appearances for the Bairns between 1951 and 1966 in two periods split by a brief spell at Bristol City. Ian was capped at under-23 and B international levels and later had a spell on the books of Stenhousemuir.

Roy Rea (Born circa 1935. Died Toronto, Canada, 5 April 2005.) Roy Rea was a goalkeeper with Glenavon and Glentoran in the 1950s and early 1960s. He won a B international cap for Northern Ireland and gained winners' medals for the Irish Cup with Glenavon in 1957 and 1959, plus an Irish League title in 1956–57.

Tony Reid (Born circa 1932. Died March 2005.) Tony Reid was an outside left who made ten first-team appearances for Brechin City in the mid-1950s.

Bernard Robinson (Born Cambridge, 5 December 1911. Died November 2004.) Bernard Robinson was one of the finest wing halves in the history of Norwich City. He made over 300 first-team appearances between 1932 and 1949 and was a member of the Canaries' team that won the Division Three South title in 1933–34.

Alex Rollo (Born Dumbarton, 18 September 1926. Died Whitehaven, 5 October 2004.) Alex Rollo was a cultured left back who won a Scottish Cup winners' medal with Celtic in 1951. He later continued his career with spells at Kilmarnock and Dumbarton, before moving south of the border to join Workington. He was a regular for the Borough Park side for three seasons, featuring in the famous FA Cup third round tie against Manchester United in 1958.

Willie Roy (Born Glasgow, circa 1921. Died Aberdeen, 20 July 2004.) Willie Roy was a centre half who made almost 50 senior appearances for St Mirren, Aberdeen and Dundee in the seasons immediately after the Second world War.

Bill Shortt (Born Wrexham, 13 October 1920. Died Plymouth, 20 September 2004.) Bill Shortt was a goalkeeper who made over 100 wartime appearances for Chester before joining Plymouth in February 1946. He went on to become one of the greatest 'keepers in the history of Argyle, playing over 350 first-team games and winning 12 caps for Wales.

Cyril Sidlow (Born Colwyn Bay, 26 November 1915. Died 12 April 2005.) Although Cyril Sidlow only made a handful of peacetime appearances for Wolves, he made over 70 appearances for the club during the war, when he also appeared for Wales in 11 unofficial internationals. He was sold to Liverpool in February 1946 and was a member oif the team that won the Football League title in 1946–47 and reached the FA Cup final in 1950. Cyril also won seven full caps for his country.

Omar Sivori (Born San Nicolas, Argentina, 2 October 1935. Died Buenos Aires, Argentina, 17 February 2005.) Omar Sivori was one of the most talented footballers of the late 1950s and early 1960s, making his name with the River Plate club before joining Juventus where he formed a tremendous forward partnership with John Charles. He played at international level for both Argentina and Italy and was voted European Footballer of the Year in 1961. On retiring as a player he became a coach with River Plate and the Argentine national side.

Bill Skidmore (Born Barnsley, 15 March 1925. Died 2004.) Bill Skidmore was a powerful left back who was a regular in the Walsall line-up in the early post-war years and a penalty-kick expert.

Gordon Smith (Born Edinburgh, 25 May 1924. Died North Berwick, East Lothian, 7 August 2004.) Gordon Smith was one of the greatest players in the history of Hibernian. An outrageously talented forward, he joined the Easter Road club during the war years and scored some 300 goals in 650 appearances during his stay. A member of the 'Famous Five' strike force, he won three Scottish League titles with Hibs and was a member of the team that reached the European Cup semi-final in 1955–56. Gordon won 18 caps for Scotland and later in his career had spells with both Hearts and Dundee, gaining Scottish League winners' medals with both, thus giving him a unique hat-trick of honours, none of his clubs having been members of the Old Firm.

Billy Smyth (Born circa 1923. Died Belfast, 14 January 2005.) Billy Smyth was a goalkeeper who made over 350 appearances for Distillery in the immediate post-war period. He also won four full caps for Northern Ireland and featured regularly for the Irish League representative side.

Aubrey Southwell (Born Grantham, Lincs, 21 August 1921. Died February 2005.) Aubrey Southwell made some 350 first-team appearances for Notts County in the immediate post-war period. A dependable right back, he captained the Magpies and later had a season at Boston United before retiring from the game.

Eddie Spicer (Born Liverpool, 20 September 1922. Died Rhyl, 25 December 2004.) Eddie Spicer was a left back who made over 150 appearances for Liverpool and was a member of the team defeated by Arsenal in the 1950 FA Cup final. Injury problems eventually ended his career in the mid-1950s.

Charles Steedman (Died November 2004.) Charles Steedman took over the East Stirlingshire club with his brother Jack in the late 1950s and briefly took them into the Scottish First Division. In 1964 they controversially relocated the team under the name East Stirlingshire Clydebank and subsequently ran the Clydebank club that later emerged.

Bill Stephen (Born Methil, Fife, 24 October 1934. Died Southampton, 27 March 2005.) After a spell on the books with Aberdeen, where he failed to make the first team, Bill Stephen went on to feature for East Fife in the 1958–59 season before leaving the senior game.

Alan Stewart (Born Newcastle upon Tyne, 24 July 1922. Died Acomb, York 13 July 2004.) Alan Stewart made a handful of appearances for Huddersfield Town before joining York City in the summer of 1949. He was a regular in the line-up for the Minstermen for almost a decade, making over 200 appearances and appearing in the side that reached the FA Cup semi-final in 1955.

Nelson Stiffle (Born India, 30 July 1928. Died Brisbane, Australia, 8 April 2005.) Nelson Stiffle was a small but skilful outside right who made almost 200 first-team appearances during the 1950s for Chester, Chesterfield, Bournemouth, Exeter and Coventry. A member of the Cherries team that reached the FA Cup quarter-finals in 1955–56. He later settled in Australia where he played for the Bankstown club for a while.

Ken Suttle (Born Hammersmith, London, 25 August 1928. Died Mauritius, 25 March 2005.) Ken Suttle made three appearances as a winger for Brighton in the 1949–50 season. He was much better known as a cricketer for Sussex, making more than 30,000 first-class runs as a left-handed batsman between 1949 and 1971.

Tommy Walker (Born Lanchester, Co Durham, 14 November 1923. Died Middleton, Lancashire, 13 June 2005.) Tommy Walker was a fast and tricky right winger who made his name for Newcastle United, featuring in the team that won the FA Cup in 1951 and 1952. He later starred for Oldham Athletic and also played for Chesterfield, finishing with a career tally of 356 Football League appearances.

Ken Wallace (Born Workington, 5 January 1933. Died Westfield, nr. Workington, 24 January 2005.) Ken Wallace played in Workington's first-ever Football League match at the start of the 1951–52 season. He was a regular in the team during the campaign, but only made a handful more appearances before leaving the professional game.

Johnny Warren, MBE (Born Sydney, Australia, 17 May 1943. Died Sydney, Australia, 6 November 2004.) Johnny Warren was one of the most respected figures in the history of the game in Australia. He won 42 caps for his country between 1965 and 1974, featuring in the 1974 World Cup finals, and received many awards for his services to soccer including the MBE, the Medal of the Order of Australia and the FIFA Centennial Order of Merit.

Geoffrey Watling (Born circa 1913. Died 16 November 2004.) Geoffrey Watling was associated with Norwich City for over 50 years. Chairman of the club from 1957 to 1973 he had more recently held the post of President.

Keith Weller (Born Islington, London, 11 June 1946. Died Seattle, United States, 12 November 2004.) After beginning his career at Tottenham, Keith Weller forged a reputation as a talented striker for Millwall. At Chelsea he was a member of the team that won the European Cup Winners' Cup in 1971, but it was at Leicester where he really shone. He made almost 300 appearances for the Foxes and won four full caps for England, producing some dazzling skills. He later played in the United States, where he eventually settled in the Seattle area.

Tom Wharton, OBE (Born November 1927. Died 9 May 2005.) Tom 'Tiny' Wharton was one of the most prominent referees in the Scottish game in the post-war period. Highlights of his career included taking charge of the 1962 European Cup Winners' Cup final and some 16 international matches. He received a gold FIFA Order of Merit in 1992.

Alex Willoughby (Born Glasgow, 1944. Died East Kilbride, 13 July 2004.) Alex Willoughby was a talented forward who made over 200 appearances for Rangers and Aberdeen between 1963 and 1974, maintaining a good scoring record throughout his career.

Frank Wintle (Born Stoke-on-Trent, 20 December 1929. Died Birmingham, 4 January 2005.) Frank Wintle spent eight years on the books of Port Vale as a part-time professional, but his only first-team outing came in the 1956–57 season. He also spent a season at Crewe, where he made no senior appearances.

Charlie Withers (Born Edmonton, 6 September 1922. Died Torquay, 7 June 2005.) Charlie Withers was left back for Tottenham's famous 'push and run' side, which won back-to-back Second Division and Football League titles in 1950 and 1951. He played over 150 games for Spurs and was also capped for England B against the Netherlands in March 1952.

Les Wood (Born Helmshore, nr. Haslingden, Lancs, 20 December 1932. Died Manchester, 24 January 2005.) Les Wood was the regular goalkeeper for Barrow in 1955–56, and also had brief associations with Port Vale and Southport.

Jackie Wright (Born Tyldesley, Lancs, 11 August 1926. Died 22 June 2005.) Jackie Wright was a full back who made over 150 first-team appearances for Blackpool during the 1950s. He was also capped by England B, playing against Luxembourg in May 1950.

Ernie Yard (Born Stranraer, 3 May 1941. Died November 2004.) Ernie Yard was a powerful forward who made over 250 senior appearances in a career that spanned the period 1959 to 1969. He played for Stranraer, Kilmarnock, Partick Thistle, Bury, Crystal Palace and Reading before emigrating to live in South Africa.

Hicham Zerouali (Born Rabat, Morocco, 17 January 1977. Died Rabat, Morocco, 5 December 2004.) Hicham was a talented player who spent three years on the books of Aberdeen between 1999 and 2000, where he was extremely popular with the fans who nicknamed him 'Zero'. An international for Morocco he had returned there and was playing for FAR at the time of his tragic death, which came as a result of a car accident.

Ian Nannestad, Soccer History Magazine

THE FA BARCLAYS PREMIERSHIP AND COCA-COLA FOOTBALL LEAGUE FIXTURES 2005–06

**Sky Sports; †PremPlus pay per view*

Saturday, 6 August 2005

Coca-Cola Football League Championship

Coventry C v Norwich C
Crewe Alex v Burnley
Crystal Palace v Luton T
Derby Co v Brighton & HA
Hull C v QPR
Ipswich T v Cardiff C
Reading v Plymouth Arg
Sheffield U v Leicester C* (12.45)
Southampton v Wolverhampton W* (5.15)
Stoke C v Sheffield W
Watford v Preston NE

Coca-Cola Football League One

Barnsley v Swindon T
Blackpool v Chesterfield
Brentford v Scunthorpe U
Bristol C v Doncaster R
Gillingham v Colchester U
Hartlepool U v Bradford C
Milton Keynes Dons v Bournemouth
Nottingham F v Huddersfield T
Oldham Ath v Yeovil T
Rotherham U v Walsall
Southend U v Port Vale
Swansea C v Tranmere R

Coca-Cola Football League Two

Barnet v Bristol R
Cheltenham T v Bury
Grimsby T v Oxford U
Leyton Orient v Macclesfield T
Lincoln C v Northampton T
Peterborough U v Chester C
Rushden & D'monds v Darlington
Shrewsbury T v Rochdale
Stockport Co v Mansfield T
Torquay U v Notts Co
Wrexham v Boston U
Wycombe W v Carlisle U

Sunday, 7 August 2005

FA Community Shield

Arsenal v Chelsea* (3.00)

Coca-Cola Football League Championship

Leeds U v Millwall* (12.15)

Monday, 8 August 2005

Coca-Cola Football League Championship

Preston NE v Derby Co* (7.45)

Tuesday, 9 August 2005

Coca-Cola Football League Championship

Brighton & HA v Reading
Burnley v Sheffield U
Cardiff C v Leeds U
Leicester C v Stoke C
Luton T v Southampton
Millwall v Coventry C
Norwich C v Crewe Alex
Plymouth Arg v Watford
QPR v Ipswich T
Sheffield W v Hull C
Wolverhampton W v Crystal Palace

Coca-Cola Football League One

Bournemouth v Hartlepool U
Bradford C v Southend U
Colchester U v Swansea C
Doncaster R v Milton Keynes Dons
Huddersfield T v Bristol C
Port Vale v Gillingham
Scunthorpe U v Barnsley
Swindon T v Oldham Ath
Tranmere R v Blackpool
Walsall v Nottingham F
Yeovil T v Rotherham U

Coca-Cola Football League Two

Bristol R v Grimsby T
Bury v Leyton Orient
Carlisle U v Peterborough U
Chester C v Lincoln C
Darlington v Stockport Co
Macclesfield T v Cheltenham T
Mansfield T v Rushden & D'monds
Northampton T v Barnet
Notts Co v Wrexham
Rochdale v Wycombe W

Wednesday, 10 August 2005

Coca-Cola Football League One

Chesterfield v Brentford

Coca-Cola Football League Two

Boston U v Shrewsbury T
Oxford U v Torquay U

Friday, 12 August 2005

Coca-Cola Football League Championship

Cardiff C v Watford* (7.45)

Saturday, 13 August 2005

Barclays Premiership

Aston Villa v Bolton W
Everton v Manchester U† (12.45)
Fulham v Birmingham C
Manchester C v WBA
Middlesbrough v Liverpool† (5.15)
Portsmouth v Tottenham H
Sunderland v Charlton Ath
West Ham U v Blackburn R

Coca-Cola Football League Championship

Brighton & HA v Crewe Alex
Burnley v Coventry C
Leicester C v Ipswich T
Luton T v Leeds U
Millwall v Stoke C
Norwich C v Crystal Palace
Plymouth Arg v Derby Co
Preston NE v Reading
QPR v Sheffield U
Sheffield W v Southampton
Wolverhampton W v Hull C

Coca-Cola Football League One

Bournemouth v Bristol C
Bradford C v Milton Keynes Dons
Chesterfield v Rotherham U
Colchester U v Barnsley
Doncaster R v Hartlepool U
Huddersfield T v Swansea C
Scunthorpe U v Gillingham
Swindon T v Nottingham F
Tranmere R v Oldham Ath
Walsall v Southend U
Yeovil T v Blackpool

Coca-Cola Football League Two

Boston U v Stockport Co
Bristol R v Peterborough U
Bury v Shrewsbury T
Carlisle U v Barnet
Chester C v Grimsby T
Darlington v Leyton Orient
Macclesfield T v Rushden & D'monds
Mansfield T v Torquay U
Northampton T v Wrexham
Notts Co v Lincoln C
Oxford U v Wycombe W
Rochdale v Cheltenham T

Sunday, 14 August 2005

Barclays Premiership

Arsenal v Newcastle U* (1.30)
Wigan Ath v Chelsea* (4.00)

Monday, 15 August 2005

Coca-Cola Football League One

Port Vale v Brentford* (7.45)

Saturday, 20 August 2005

Barclays Premiership

Birmingham C v Manchester C† (5.15)
Blackburn R v Fulham
Charlton Ath v Wigan Ath
Liverpool v Sunderland
Manchester U v Aston Villa† (12.45)
Newcastle U v West Ham U
Tottenham H v Middlesbrough
WBA v Portsmouth

Coca-Cola Football League Championship
Coventry C v QPR
Crewe Alex v Leicester C
Crystal Palace v Plymouth Arg
Derby Co v Cardiff C
Hull C v Brighton & HA
Ipswich T v Sheffield W
Leeds U v Wolverhampton W
Reading v Millwall
Sheffield U v Preston NE
Southampton v Norwich C
Stoke C v Luton T
Watford v Burnley

Coca-Cola Football League One
Barnsley v Yeovil T
Blackpool v Swindon T
Brentford v Tranmere R
Bristol C v Port Vale
Gillingham v Bournemouth
Hartlepool U v Walsall
Milton Keynes Dons v Colchester U
Nottingham F v Scunthorpe U
Oldham Ath v Chesterfield
Rotherham U v Bradford C
Southend U v Huddersfield T
Swansea C v Doncaster R

Coca-Cola Football League Two
Barnet v Macclesfield T
Cheltenham T v Boston U
Grimsby T v Darlington
Leyton Orient v Rochdale
Lincoln C v Oxford U
Peterborough U v Mansfield T
Rushden & D'monds v Chester C
Shrewsbury T v Northampton T
Stockport Co v Notts Co
Torquay U v Bristol R
Wrexham v Carlisle U
Wycombe W v Bury

Sunday, 21 August 2005
Barclays Premiership
Bolton W v Everton* (1.30)
Chelsea v Arsenal* (4.00)

Tuesday, 23 August 2005
Barclays Premiership
Arsenal v Fulham
Birmingham C v Middlesbrough
Bolton W v Newcastle U
Charlton Ath v Liverpool
Portsmouth v Aston Villa
Sunderland v Manchester C

Wednesday, 24 August 2005
Barclays Premiership
Blackburn R v Tottenham H
Chelsea v WBA
Everton v West Ham U
Manchester U v Wigan Ath

Friday, 26 August 2005
Coca-Cola Football League Championship
QPR v Sheffield W* (7.45)

Saturday, 27 August 2005
Barclays Premiership
Aston Villa v Blackburn R
Fulham v Everton
Liverpool v Arsenal
Manchester C v Portsmouth
Tottenham H v Chelsea
WBA v Birmingham C† (12.15)
West Ham U v Bolton W
Wigan Ath v Sunderland

Coca-Cola Football League Championship
Burnley v Derby Co
Cardiff C v Wolverhampton W
Crystal Palace v Stoke C
Leicester C v Luton T
Millwall v Ipswich T
Norwich C v Leeds U
Plymouth Arg v Hull C
Preston NE v Brighton & HA
Sheffield U v Coventry C
Southampton v Crewe Alex
Watford v Reading* (5.15)

Coca-Cola Football League One
Barnsley v Brentford
Bradford C v Bournemouth
Bristol C v Milton Keynes Dons
Chesterfield v Tranmere R
Colchester U v Oldham Ath
Gillingham v Nottingham F
Huddersfield T v Hartlepool U
Port Vale v Doncaster R
Rotherham U v Blackpool
Scunthorpe U v Southend U
Swindon T v Yeovil T
Walsall v Swansea C

Coca-Cola Football League Two
Barnet v Grimsby T
Boston U v Mansfield T
Bury v Wrexham
Carlisle U v Northampton T
Cheltenham T v Leyton Orient
Chester C v Darlington
Notts Co v Bristol R
Oxford U v Stockport Co
Peterborough U v Torquay U
Rochdale v Macclesfield T
Rushden & D'monds v Lincoln C
Shrewsbury T v Wycombe W

Sunday, 28 August 2005
Barclays Premiership
Middlesbrough v Charlton Ath* (1.30)
Newcastle U v Manchester U* (4.00)

Monday, 29 August 2005
Coca-Cola Football League Championship
Brighton & HA v Plymouth Arg
Coventry C v Southampton
Crewe Alex v Sheffield U
Derby Co v Watford
Hull C v Leicester C
Ipswich T v Preston NE
Luton T v Millwall
Reading v Burnley
Sheffield W v Cardiff C
Stoke C v Norwich C
Wolverhampton W v QPR

Coca-Cola Football League One
Blackpool v Bradford C
Bournemouth v Walsall
Brentford v Gillingham
Doncaster R v Huddersfield T
Hartlepool U v Scunthorpe U
Milton Keynes Dons v Port Vale
Nottingham F v Bristol C
Oldham Ath v Rotherham U
Southend U v Colchester U
Swansea C v Barnsley
Tranmere R v Swindon T
Yeovil T v Chesterfield

Coca-Cola Football League Two
Bristol R v Oxford U
Darlington v Rochdale
Grimsby T v Rushden & D'monds
Leyton Orient v Shrewsbury T
Lincoln C v Carlisle U
Macclesfield T v Bury
Mansfield T v Notts Co
Northampton T v Boston U
Stockport Co v Peterborough U
Torquay U v Chester C
Wrexham v Barnet
Wycombe W v Cheltenham T

Tuesday, 30 August 2005
Coca-Cola Football League Championship
Leeds U v Crystal Palace* (7.45)

Saturday, 3 September 2005
Coca-Cola Football League One
Bournemouth v Tranmere R
Bradford C v Chesterfield
Bristol C v Colchester U* (12.05)
Doncaster R v Blackpool
Gillingham v Barnsley
Hartlepool U v Yeovil T
Huddersfield T v Scunthorpe U
Milton Keynes Dons v Swansea C
Nottingham F v Brentford
Port Vale v Rotherham U
Southend U v Oldham Ath
Walsall v Swindon T

Coca-Cola Football League Two
Bury v Carlisle U
Cheltenham T v Barnet
Chester C v Mansfield T
Darlington v Notts Co
Grimsby T v Stockport Co
Leyton Orient v Bristol R
Lincoln C v Wrexham
Macclesfield T v Boston U
Rochdale v Torquay U
Rushden & D'monds v Peterborough U
Shrewsbury T v Oxford U
Wycombe W v Northampton T

Saturday, 10 September 2005
Barclays Premiership
Birmingham C v Charlton Ath
Chelsea v Sunderland
Everton v Portsmouth
Manchester U v Manchester C
Middlesbrough v Arsenal† (5.15)
Newcastle U v Fulham
Tottenham H v Liverpool
WBA v Wigan Ath

Coca-Cola Football League Championship
Burnley v Cardiff C
Coventry C v Reading
Crystal Palace v Hull C
Leeds U v Brighton & HA
Leicester C v Sheffield W
Luton T v Wolverhampton W
Millwall v Preston NE
Norwich C v Plymouth Arg* (12.45)
Sheffield U v Ipswich T
Southampton v QPR
Stoke C v Watford

Coca-Cola Football League One
Barnsley v Nottingham F
Blackpool v Hartlepool U
Brentford v Milton Keynes Dons
Chesterfield v Bournemouth
Colchester U v Doncaster R
Oldham Ath v Huddersfield T
Rotherham U v Gillingham
Scunthorpe U v Port Vale
Swansea C v Bristol C
Swindon T v Southend U
Tranmere R v Bradford C
Yeovil T v Walsall

Coca-Cola Football League Two
Barnet v Leyton Orient
Boston U v Rochdale
Bristol R v Lincoln C
Carlisle U v Macclesfield T
Mansfield T v Darlington
Northampton T v Bury
Notts Co v Chester C
Oxford U v Rushden & D'monds
Peterborough U v Grimsby T
Stockport Co v Wycombe W
Torquay U v Shrewsbury T
Wrexham v Cheltenham T

Sunday, 11 September 2005
Coca-Cola Football League Championship
Bolton W v Blackburn R* (4.00)
Crewe Alex v Derby Co* (1.30)

Monday, 12 September 2005
West Ham U v Aston Villa* (8.00)

Tuesday, 13 September 2005
Coca-Cola Football League Championship
Brighton & HA v Sheffield U
Cardiff C v Leicester C
Hull C v Stoke C
Ipswich T v Southampton
Plymouth Arg v Crewe Alex
Preston NE v Burnley
QPR v Luton T
Reading v Crystal Palace
Sheffield W v Leeds U
Watford v Norwich C
Wolverhampton W v Millwall

Wednesday, 14 September 2005
Coca-Cola Football League Championship
Derby Co v Coventry C

Friday, 16 September 2005
Preston NE v Stoke C* (7.45)

Saturday, 17 September 2005
Barclays Premiership
Aston Villa v Tottenham H† (5.15)
Charlton Ath v Chelsea
Fulham v West Ham U
Manchester C v Bolton W
Portsmouth v Birmingham C
Sunderland v WBA
Wigan Ath v Middlesbrough

Coca-Cola Football League Championship
Brighton & HA v Coventry C
Cardiff C v Crystal Palace
Hull C v Luton T* (12.45)
Ipswich T v Norwich C
Plymouth Arg v Burnley
QPR v Leeds U
Reading v Crewe Alex
Sheffield W v Millwall
Watford v Sheffield U
Wolverhampton W v Leicester C

Coca-Cola Football League One
Bournemouth v Swindon T
Bradford C v Yeovil T
Bristol C v Blackpool
Doncaster R v Scunthorpe U
Gillingham v Oldham Ath
Hartlepool U v Swansea C
Huddersfield T v Brentford
Milton Keynes Dons v Barnsley
Nottingham F v Rotherham U
Port Vale v Colchester U
Southend U v Tranmere R
Walsall v Chesterfield

Coca-Cola Football League Two
Bury v Boston U
Cheltenham T v Carlisle U
Chester C v Bristol R
Darlington v Oxford U
Grimsby T v Torquay U
Leyton Orient v Wrexham
Lincoln C v Peterborough U
Macclesfield T v Northampton T
Rochdale v Mansfield T
Rushden & D'monds v Stockport Co
Shrewsbury T v Notts Co
Wycombe W v Barnet

Sunday, 18 September 2005
Barclays Premiership
Blackburn R v Newcastle U† (2.00)
Liverpool v Manchester U* (12.00)

Coca-Cola Football League Championship
Derby Co v Southampton* (4.00)

Monday, 19 September 2005
Barclays Premiership
Arsenal v Everton* (8.00)

Friday, 23 September 2005
Coca-Cola Football League Championship
Luton T v Sheffield W* (7.45)

Saturday, 24 September 2005
Barclays Premiership
Birmingham C v Liverpool† (12.45)
Bolton W v Portsmouth† (5.15)
Chelsea v Aston Villa
Everton v Wigan Ath
Manchester U v Blackburn R
Newcastle U v Manchester C
WBA v Charlton Ath
West Ham U v Arsenal

Coca-Cola Football League Championship
Burnley v Brighton & HA
Coventry C v Hull C
Crewe Alex v Watford
Crystal Palace v Preston NE
Leeds U v Ipswich T
Leicester C v QPR
Millwall v Cardiff C
Norwich C v Reading
Sheffield U v Derby Co
Southampton v Plymouth Arg
Stoke C v Wolverhampton W

Coca-Cola Football League One
Barnsley v Doncaster R
Blackpool v Milton Keynes Dons
Brentford v Bristol C
Chesterfield v Hartlepool U
Colchester U v Huddersfield T
Oldham Ath v Bournemouth
Rotherham U v Southend U
Scunthorpe U v Walsall
Swansea C v Nottingham F
Swindon T v Bradford C
Tranmere R v Gillingham
Yeovil T v Port Vale

Coca-Cola Football League Two
Barnet v Rochdale
Boston U v Grimsby T
Bristol R v Darlington
Carlisle U v Leyton Orient
Mansfield T v Wycombe W
Northampton T v Cheltenham T
Notts Co v Rushden & D'monds
Oxford U v Bury
Peterborough U v Shrewsbury T
Stockport Co v Chester C
Torquay U v Lincoln C
Wrexham v Macclesfield T

Sunday, 25 September 2005
Barclays Premiership
Middlesbrough v Sunderland* (4.00)

Monday, 26 September 2005
Barclays Premiership
Tottenham H v Fulham* (8.00)

Tuesday, 27 September 2005
Coca-Cola Football League Championship
Burnley v Ipswich T
Crewe Alex v Wolverhampton W
Crystal Palace v Sheffield W
Leeds U v Derby Co
Leicester C v Brighton & HA
Luton T v Preston NE
Millwall v QPR
Norwich C v Hull C
Sheffield U v Plymouth Arg
Stoke C v Cardiff C

Coca-Cola Football League One
Bournemouth v Swansea C
Bradford C v Colchester U
Bristol C v Barnsley
Doncaster R v Swindon T
Gillingham v Chesterfield
Hartlepool U v Rotherham U
Huddersfield T v Tranmere R
Milton Keynes Dons v Scunthorpe U
Nottingham F v Blackpool
Port Vale v Oldham Ath
Southend U v Yeovil T
Walsall v Brentford

Coca-Cola Football League Two
Bury v Bristol R
Cheltenham T v Peterborough U
Chester C v Carlisle U
Darlington v Boston U
Grimsby T v Notts Co
Leyton Orient v Torquay U
Lincoln C v Stockport Co
Macclesfield T v Mansfield T
Rochdale v Oxford U
Rushden & D'monds v Northampton T

Shrewsbury T v Barnet
Wycombe W v Wrexham

Wednesday, 28 September 2005
Coca-Cola Football League Championship
Coventry C v Watford
Southampton v Reading

Friday, 30 September 2005
Coca-Cola Football League Championship
Wolverhampton W v Burnley* (7.45)

Saturday, 1 October 2005
Barclays Premiership
Aston Villa v Middlesbrough
Blackburn R v WBA
Charlton Ath v Tottenham H
Fulham v Manchester U
Manchester C v Everton† (12.45)
Portsmouth v Newcastle U
Sunderland v West Ham U† (5.15)
Wigan Ath v Bolton W

Coca-Cola Football League Championship
Brighton & HA v Norwich C
Cardiff C v Luton T
Derby Co v Leicester C
Hull C v Millwall
Ipswich T v Crewe Alex
Plymouth Arg v Stoke C
Preston NE v Southampton
Reading v Sheffield U
Sheffield W v Coventry C
Watford v Leeds U

Coca-Cola Football League One
Barnsley v Oldham Ath
Brentford v Rotherham U
Bristol C v Hartlepool U
Colchester U v Chesterfield
Doncaster R v Bradford C
Gillingham v Southend U
Huddersfield T v Bournemouth
Milton Keynes Dons v Swindon T
Nottingham F v Tranmere R
Port Vale v Walsall
Scunthorpe U v Yeovil T
Swansea C v Blackpool

Coca-Cola Football League Two
Barnet v Oxford U
Boston U v Peterborough U
Bury v Lincoln C
Carlisle U v Bristol R
Cheltenham T v Torquay U
Leyton Orient v Mansfield T
Macclesfield T v Notts Co
Northampton T v Darlington
Rochdale v Rushden & D'monds
Shrewsbury T v Grimsby T
Wrexham v Stockport Co
Wycombe W v Chester C

Sunday, 2 October 2005
Barclays Premiership
Arsenal v Birmingham C* (1.30)
Liverpool v Chelsea* (4.00)

Monday, 3 October 2005
Coca-Cola Football League Championship
QPR v Crystal Palace* (7.45)

Saturday, 8 October 2005
Coca-Cola Football League One
Blackpool v Colchester U
Bournemouth v Doncaster R
Chesterfield v Bristol C
Hartlepool U v Gillingham
Oldham Ath v Brentford
Rotherham U v Barnsley
Swindon T v Port Vale
Tranmere R v Scunthorpe U
Walsall v Milton Keynes Dons
Yeovil T v Swansea C

Coca-Cola Football League Two
Bristol R v Northampton T
Chester C v Rochdale
Darlington v Macclesfield T
Grimsby T v Wycombe W
Lincoln C v Cheltenham T
Mansfield T v Shrewsbury T
Notts Co v Boston U
Oxford U v Carlisle U
Peterborough U v Wrexham
Rushden & D'monds v Bury
Stockport Co v Leyton Orient
Torquay U v Barnet

Sunday, 9 October 2005
Coca-Cola Football League One
Southend U v Nottingham F* (4.00)

Monday, 10 October 2005
Coca-Cola Football League One
Bradford C v Huddersfield T* (7.45)

Saturday, 15 October 2005
Barclays Premiership
Birmingham C v Aston Villa
Chelsea v Bolton W
Liverpool v Blackburn R
Middlesbrough v Portsmouth* (5.15)
Sunderland v Manchester U
Tottenham H v Everton
WBA v Arsenal
Wigan Ath v Newcastle U† (12.45)

Coca-Cola Football League Championship
Brighton & HA v Cardiff C
Burnley v Leeds U
Coventry C v Crystal Palace
Crewe Alex v Luton T
Derby Co v Stoke C
Norwich C v Millwall
Plymouth Arg v Sheffield W
Preston NE v QPR
Sheffield U v Wolverhampton W
Southampton v Hull C
Watford v Leicester C

Coca-Cola Football League One
Barnsley v Blackpool
Brentford v Swindon T
Bristol C v Tranmere R
Colchester U v Bournemouth
Doncaster R v Southend U
Gillingham v Yeovil T
Huddersfield T v Walsall
Milton Keynes Dons v Chesterfield
Nottingham F v Hartlepool U
Port Vale v Bradford C
Scunthorpe U v Rotherham U
Swansea C v Oldham Ath

Coca-Cola Football League Two
Barnet v Chester C
Boston U v Bristol R
Bury v Darlington
Carlisle U v Mansfield T
Cheltenham T v Grimsby T
Leyton Orient v Lincoln C
Macclesfield T v Peterborough U
Northampton T v Oxford U
Rochdale v Notts Co
Shrewsbury T v Stockport Co
Wrexham v Torquay U
Wycombe W v Rushden & D'monds

Sunday, 16 October 2005
Barclays Premiership
Manchester C v West Ham U* (4.00)

Coca-Cola Football League Championship
Reading v Ipswich T* (1.30)

Monday, 17 October 2005
Barclays Premiership
Charlton Ath v Fulham* (8.00)

Tuesday, 18 October 2005
Coca-Cola Football League Championship
Cardiff C v Preston NE
Crystal Palace v Brighton & HA
Hull C v Reading
Ipswich T v Coventry C
Leeds U v Southampton
Leicester C v Burnley
Luton T v Norwich C
Millwall v Sheffield U
QPR v Plymouth Arg
Sheffield W v Watford
Stoke C v Crewe Alex
Wolverhampton W v Derby Co

Friday, 21 October 2005
Coca-Cola Football League Championship
Leeds U v Sheffield U* (7.45)

Saturday, 22 October 2005
Barclays Premiership
Arsenal v Manchester C
Aston Villa v Wigan Ath
Blackburn R v Birmingham C* (12.45)
Bolton W v WBA
Fulham v Liverpool
Manchester U v Tottenham H
Portsmouth v Charlton Ath† (5.15)
West Ham U v Middlesbrough

Coca-Cola Football League Championship
Cardiff C v Crewe Alex
Crystal Palace v Burnley
Hull C v Derby Co
Ipswich T v Watford
Leicester C v Coventry C
Luton T v Plymouth Arg
Millwall v Southampton
QPR v Norwich C
Sheffield W v Brighton & HA
Stoke C v Reading
Wolverhampton W v Preston NE

Coca-Cola Football League One
Blackpool v Brentford
Bournemouth v Port Vale
Bradford C v Gillingham
Chesterfield v Huddersfield T
Hartlepool U v Milton Keynes Dons

Oldham Ath v Bristol C
Rotherham U v Swansea C
Southend U v Barnsley
Swindon T v Scunthorpe U
Tranmere R v Colchester U
Walsall v Doncaster R
Yeovil T v Nottingham F

Coca-Cola Football League Two
Bristol R v Wrexham
Chester C v Bury
Darlington v Cheltenham T
Grimsby T v Leyton Orient
Lincoln C v Wycombe W
Mansfield T v Barnet
Notts Co v Carlisle U
Oxford U v Boston U
Peterborough U v Rochdale
Rushden & D'monds v Shrewsbury T
Stockport Co v Northampton T
Torquay U v Macclesfield T

Sunday, 23 October 2005
Barclays Premiership
Everton v Chelsea* (4.00)
Newcastle U v Sunderland† (1.30)

Friday, 28 October 2005
Coca-Cola Football League Championship
Burnley v Hull C* (7.45)

Saturday, 29 October 2005
Barclays Premiership
Birmingham C v Everton
Charlton Ath v Bolton W
Chelsea v Blackburn R
Liverpool v West Ham U
Middlesbrough v Manchester U† (5.15)
Sunderland v Portsmouth
Tottenham H v Arsenal
Wigan Ath v Fulham† (12.45)

Coca-Cola Football League Championship
Brighton & HA v Ipswich T
Coventry C v Luton T
Crewe Alex v Crystal Palace
Derby Co v QPR
Norwich C v Sheffield W
Preston NE v Leicester C
Reading v Leeds U
Sheffield U v Cardiff C
Southampton v Stoke C
Watford v Wolverhampton W

Coca-Cola Football League One
Barnsley v Walsall
Brentford v Bournemouth
Bristol C v Southend U
Colchester U v Yeovil T
Doncaster R v Tranmere R
Gillingham v Blackpool
Huddersfield T v Swindon T
Milton Keynes Dons v Rotherham U
Nottingham F v Bradford C
Port Vale v Hartlepool U
Scunthorpe U v Oldham Ath
Swansea C v Chesterfield

Coca-Cola Football League Two
Barnet v Rushden & D'monds
Boston U v Torquay U
Bury v Notts Co
Carlisle U v Stockport Co
Cheltenham T v Mansfield T
Leyton Orient v Oxford U
Macclesfield T v Bristol R
Northampton T v Grimsby T
Rochdale v Lincoln C
Shrewsbury T v Chester C
Wrexham v Darlington
Wycombe W v Peterborough U

Sunday, 30 October 2005
Barclays Premiership
WBA v Newcastle U* (4.00)

Coca-Cola Football League Championship
Plymouth Arg v Millwall* (1.30)

Monday, 31 October 2005
Barclays Premiership
Manchester C v Aston Villa* (8.00)

Tuesday, 1 November 2005
Coca-Cola Football League Championship
Brighton & HA v Wolverhampton W
Burnley v Millwall
Crewe Alex v Leeds U
Norwich C v Cardiff C
Plymouth Arg v Leicester C
Preston NE v Hull C
Reading v Sheffield W
Sheffield U v Luton T
Watford v QPR

Wednesday, 2 November 2005
Coca-Cola Football League Championship
Coventry C v Stoke C
Derby Co v Ipswich T
Southampton v Crystal Palace

Saturday, 5 November 2005
Barclays Premiership
Arsenal v Sunderland
Aston Villa v Liverpool† (12.45)
Blackburn R v Charlton Ath
Everton v Middlesbrough
Fulham v Manchester C
Newcastle U v Birmingham C
Portsmouth v Wigan Ath* (5.15)
West Ham U v WBA

Coca-Cola Football League Championship
Cardiff C v Coventry C
Crystal Palace v Sheffield U
Hull C v Watford
Ipswich T v Plymouth Arg
Leeds U v Preston NE
Leicester C v Southampton
Luton T v Burnley
Millwall v Crewe Alex
QPR v Reading
Sheffield W v Derby Co
Stoke C v Brighton & HA
Wolverhampton W v Norwich C

Sunday, 6 November 2005
Barclays Premiership
Manchester U v Chelsea* (4.00)

Monday, 7 November 2005
Barclays Premiership
Bolton W v Tottenham H* (8.00)

Friday, 11 November 2005
Coca-Cola Football League One
Swindon T v Bristol C* (7.45)

Saturday, 12 November 2005
Coca-Cola Football League One
Bournemouth v Nottingham F
Bradford C v Barnsley
Chesterfield v Port Vale
Hartlepool U v Brentford
Oldham Ath v Doncaster R
Rotherham U v Colchester U
Southend U v Swansea C
Tranmere R v Milton Keynes Dons
Walsall v Gillingham
Yeovil T v Huddersfield T

Coca-Cola Football League Two
Bristol R v Rochdale
Chester C v Northampton T
Darlington v Wycombe W
Grimsby T v Macclesfield T
Lincoln C v Shrewsbury T
Mansfield T v Bury
Notts Co v Cheltenham T
Oxford U v Wrexham
Peterborough U v Leyton Orient
Rushden & D'monds v Boston U
Torquay U v Carlisle U

Sunday, 13 November 2005
Coca-Cola Football League One
Blackpool v Scunthorpe U* (4.00)

Coca-Cola Football League Two
Stockport Co v Barnet* (1.30)

Friday, 18 November 2005
Coca-Cola Football League Championship
Derby Co v Wolverhampton W* (7.45)

Saturday, 19 November 2005
Barclays Premiership
Charlton Ath v Manchester U
Chelsea v Newcastle U
Liverpool v Portsmouth
Manchester C v Blackburn R
Sunderland v Aston Villa
Tottenham H v West Ham U
WBA v Everton† (5.15)
Wigan Ath v Arsenal* (12.45)

Coca-Cola Football League Championship
Burnley v Leicester C
Coventry C v Ipswich T
Crewe Alex v Stoke C
Norwich C v Luton T
Plymouth Arg v QPR
Preston NE v Cardiff C
Reading v Hull C
Sheffield U v Millwall
Southampton v Leeds U
Watford v Sheffield W

Coca-Cola Football League One
Barnsley v Rotherham U
Brentford v Oldham Ath
Bristol C v Chesterfield
Colchester U v Blackpool
Doncaster R v Bournemouth
Gillingham v Hartlepool U
Huddersfield T v Bradford C
Milton Keynes Dons v Walsall
Nottingham F v Southend U

Port Vale v Swindon T
Scunthorpe U v Tranmere R
Swansea C v Yeovil T

Coca-Cola Football League Two
Barnet v Torquay U
Boston U v Notts Co
Bury v Rushden & D'monds
Carlisle U v Oxford U
Cheltenham T v Lincoln C
Leyton Orient v Stockport Co
Macclesfield T v Darlington
Northampton T v Bristol R
Rochdale v Chester C
Shrewsbury T v Mansfield T
Wrexham v Peterborough U
Wycombe W v Grimsby T

Sunday, 20 November 2005
Barclays Premiership
Middlesbrough v Fulham* (4.00)

Coca-Cola Football League Championship
Brighton & HA v Crystal Palace* (1.30)

Monday, 21 November 2005
Barclays Premiership
Birmingham C v Bolton W* (8.00)

Tuesday, 22 November 2005
Coca-Cola Football League Championship
Cardiff C v Brighton & HA
Crystal Palace v Coventry C
Hull C v Southampton
Ipswich T v Reading
Leeds U v Burnley
Leicester C v Watford
Luton T v Crewe Alex
Millwall v Norwich C
QPR v Preston NE
Sheffield W v Plymouth Arg
Stoke C v Derby Co
Wolverhampton W v Sheffield U

Saturday, 26 November 2005
Barclays Premiership
Arsenal v Blackburn R
Aston Villa v Charlton Ath
Fulham v Bolton W
Manchester C v Liverpool
Middlesbrough v WBA
Portsmouth v Chelsea† (5.15)
Sunderland v Birmingham C
Wigan Ath v Tottenham H

Coca-Cola Football League Championship
Brighton & HA v Derby Co
Burnley v Crewe Alex
Cardiff C v Ipswich T
Leicester C v Sheffield U
Luton T v Crystal Palace
Millwall v Leeds U
Norwich C v Coventry C
Plymouth Arg v Reading
Preston NE v Watford
QPR v Hull C
Sheffield W v Stoke C
Wolverhampton W v Southampton

Coca-Cola Football League One
Bournemouth v Milton Keynes Dons
Bradford C v Hartlepool U
Chesterfield v Blackpool
Colchester U v Gillingham
Doncaster R v Bristol C
Huddersfield T v Nottingham F
Port Vale v Southend U
Scunthorpe U v Brentford
Swindon T v Barnsley
Tranmere R v Swansea C
Walsall v Rotherham U
Yeovil T v Oldham Ath

Coca-Cola Football League Two
Boston U v Wrexham
Bristol R v Barnet
Bury v Cheltenham T
Carlisle U v Wycombe W
Chester C v Peterborough U
Darlington v Rushden & D'monds
Macclesfield T v Leyton Orient
Mansfield T v Stockport Co
Northampton T v Lincoln C
Notts Co v Torquay U
Oxford U v Grimsby T
Rochdale v Shrewsbury T

Sunday, 27 November 2005
Barclays Premiership
Everton v Newcastle U* (1.30)
West Ham U v Manchester U* (4.00)

Saturday, 3 December 2005
Barclays Premiership
Blackburn R v Everton
Bolton W v Arsenal
Chelsea v Middlesbrough
Liverpool v Wigan Ath
Manchester U v Portsmouth† (5.15)
Newcastle U v Aston Villa
Tottenham H v Sunderland
WBA v Fulham

Coca-Cola Football League Championship
Coventry C v Plymouth Arg
Crewe Alex v Preston NE
Crystal Palace v Millwall
Derby Co v Norwich C
Hull C v Cardiff C
Ipswich T v Wolverhampton W
Leeds U v Leicester C
Reading v Luton T
Sheffield U v Sheffield W
Southampton v Burnley
Stoke C v QPR
Watford v Brighton & HA

Sunday, 4 December 2005
Barclays Premiership
Charlton Ath v Manchester C* (4.00)

Monday, 5 December 2005
Barclays Premiership
Birmingham C v West Ham U* (8.00)

Tuesday, 6 December 2005
Coca-Cola Football League One
Barnsley v Tranmere R
Blackpool v Bournemouth
Brentford v Yeovil T
Bristol C v Bradford C
Gillingham v Doncaster R
Hartlepool U v Colchester U
Milton Keynes Dons v Huddersfield T
Nottingham F v Port Vale
Oldham Ath v Walsall
Rotherham U v Swindon T
Southend U v Chesterfield
Swansea C v Scunthorpe U

Coca-Cola Football League Two
Barnet v Bury
Cheltenham T v Oxford U
Grimsby T v Rochdale
Leyton Orient v Chester C
Lincoln C v Macclesfield T
Peterborough U v Notts Co
Rushden & D'monds v Carlisle U
Shrewsbury T v Darlington
Stockport Co v Bristol R
Torquay U v Northampton T
Wrexham v Mansfield T
Wycombe W v Boston U

Saturday, 10 December 2005
Barclays Premiership
Birmingham C v Fulham
Blackburn R v West Ham U
Bolton W v Aston Villa
Charlton Ath v Sunderland
Chelsea v Wigan Ath
Liverpool v Middlesbrough* (12,45)
Newcastle U v Arsenal† (5.15)
WBA v Manchester C

Coca-Cola Football League Championship
Coventry C v Millwall
Crewe Alex v Norwich C
Crystal Palace v Wolverhampton W
Derby Co v Preston NE
Hull C v Sheffield W
Ipswich T v QPR
Leeds U v Cardiff C
Reading v Brighton & HA
Sheffield U v Burnley
Southampton v Luton T
Stoke C v Leicester C
Watford v Plymouth Arg

Coca-Cola Football League One
Barnsley v Scunthorpe U
Blackpool v Tranmere R
Brentford v Chesterfield
Bristol C v Huddersfield T
Gillingham v Port Vale
Hartlepool U v Bournemouth
Milton Keynes Dons v Doncaster R
Nottingham F v Walsall
Oldham Ath v Swindon T
Rotherham U v Yeovil T
Southend U v Bradford C
Swansea C v Colchester U

Coca-Cola Football League Two
Barnet v Northampton T
Cheltenham T v Macclesfield T
Grimsby T v Bristol R
Leyton Orient v Bury
Lincoln C v Chester C
Peterborough U v Carlisle U
Rushden & D'monds v Mansfield T
Shrewsbury T v Boston U
Stockport Co v Darlington
Torquay U v Oxford U
Wrexham v Notts Co
Wycombe W v Rochdale

Sunday, 11 December 2005
Barclays Premiership
Manchester U v Everton* (4.00)

Monday, 12 December 2005

Barclays Premiership
Tottenham H v Portsmouth* (8.00)

Saturday, 17 December 2005

Barclays Premiership
Aston Villa v Manchester U† (12.45)
Everton v Bolton W
Fulham v Blackburn R
Manchester C v Birmingham C
Portsmouth v WBA
Sunderland v Liverpool† (5.15)
West Ham U v Newcastle U
Wigan Ath v Charlton Ath

Coca-Cola Football League Championship
Brighton & HA v Hull C
Burnley v Watford
Cardiff C v Derby Co
Leicester C v Crewe Alex
Luton T v Stoke C
Millwall v Reading
Norwich C v Southampton
Plymouth Arg v Crystal Palace
Preston NE v Sheffield U
QPR v Coventry C
Sheffield W v Ipswich T
Wolverhampton W v Leeds U

Coca-Cola Football League One
Bournemouth v Gillingham
Bradford C v Rotherham U
Chesterfield v Oldham Ath
Colchester U v Milton Keynes Dons
Doncaster R v Swansea C
Huddersfield T v Southend U
Port Vale v Bristol C
Scunthorpe U v Nottingham F
Swindon T v Blackpool
Tranmere R v Brentford
Walsall v Hartlepool U
Yeovil T v Barnsley

Coca-Cola Football League Two
Boston U v Cheltenham T
Bristol R v Torquay U
Bury v Wycombe W
Carlisle U v Wrexham
Chester C v Rushden & D'monds
Darlington v Grimsby T
Macclesfield T v Barnet
Mansfield T v Peterborough U
Northampton T v Shrewsbury T
Notts Co v Stockport Co
Oxford U v Lincoln C
Rochdale v Leyton Orient

Sunday, 18 December 2005

Barclays Premiership
Arsenal v Chelsea* (4.00)
Middlesbrough v Tottenham H* (1.30)

Monday, 26 December 2005

Barclays Premiership
Aston Villa v Everton* (5.15)
Charlton Ath v Arsenal* (12.45)
Chelsea v Fulham
Liverpool v Newcastle U† (3.00)
Manchester U v WBA
Middlesbrough v Blackburn R
Portsmouth v West Ham U
Sunderland v Bolton W
Tottenham H v Birmingham C
Wigan Ath v Manchester C

Coca-Cola Football League Championship
Brighton & HA v QPR
Burnley v Stoke C
Cardiff C v Plymouth Arg
Crewe Alex v Hull C
Derby Co v Luton T
Ipswich T v Crystal Palace
Leeds U v Coventry C
Leicester C v Millwall
Preston NE v Sheffield W
Sheffield U v Norwich C
Watford v Southampton
Wolverhampton W v Reading

Coca-Cola Football League One
Barnsley v Hartlepool U
Brentford v Swansea C
Gillingham v Bristol C
Nottingham F v Doncaster R
Oldham Ath v Bradford C
Port Vale v Blackpool
Rotherham U v Huddersfield T
Scunthorpe U v Chesterfield
Southend U v Milton Keynes Dons
Swindon T v Colchester U
Walsall v Tranmere R
Yeovil T v Bournemouth

Coca-Cola Football League Two
Barnet v Peterborough U
Bristol R v Shrewsbury T
Bury v Grimsby T
Carlisle U v Darlington
Cheltenham T v Chester C
Leyton Orient v Rushden & D'monds
Lincoln C v Boston U
Macclesfield T v Stockport Co
Northampton T v Mansfield T
Oxford U v Notts Co
Torquay U v Wycombe W
Wrexham v Rochdale

Wednesday, 28 December 2005

Barclays Premiership
Arsenal v Portsmouth
Birmingham C v Manchester U
Blackburn R v Sunderland
Bolton W v Middlesbrough
Everton v Liverpool* (8.00)
Fulham v Aston Villa
Manchester C v Chelsea
Newcastle U v Charlton Ath
WBA v Tottenham H
West Ham U v Wigan Ath

Coca-Cola Football League Championship
Coventry C v Crewe Alex
Crystal Palace v Derby Co
Hull C v Ipswich T
Luton T v Brighton & HA
Millwall v Watford
Norwich C v Burnley
Plymouth Arg v Preston NE
QPR v Cardiff C
Reading v Leicester C
Sheffield W v Wolverhampton W
Southampton v Sheffield U
Stoke C v Leeds U

Coca-Cola Football League One
Blackpool v Oldham Ath
Bournemouth v Barnsley
Bradford C v Walsall
Bristol C v Rotherham U
Chesterfield v Swindon T
Colchester U v Scunthorpe U
Doncaster R v Brentford
Hartlepool U v Southend U
Huddersfield T v Port Vale
Milton Keynes Dons v Nottingham F
Swansea C v Gillingham
Tranmere R v Yeovil T

Coca-Cola Football League Two
Boston U v Carlisle U
Chester C v Wrexham
Darlington v Barnet
Grimsby T v Lincoln C
Mansfield T v Bristol R
Notts Co v Northampton T
Peterborough U v Oxford U
Rochdale v Bury
Rushden & D'monds v Cheltenham T
Shrewsbury T v Macclesfield T
Stockport Co v Torquay U
Wycombe W v Leyton Orient

Saturday, 31 December 2005

Barclays Premiership
Aston Villa v Arsenal* (12.45)
Charlton Ath v West Ham U
Chelsea v Birmingham C
Liverpool v WBA
Manchester U v Bolton W
Middlesbrough v Manchester C
Portsmouth v Fulham
Sunderland v Everton
Tottenham H v Newcastle U
Wigan Ath v Blackburn R

Coca-Cola Football League Championship
Brighton & HA v Millwall
Burnley v Sheffield W
Cardiff C v Southampton
Crewe Alex v QPR
Derby Co v Reading
Ipswich T v Luton T
Leeds U v Hull C
Leicester C v Norwich C
Preston NE v Coventry C
Sheffield U v Stoke C
Watford v Crystal Palace
Wolverhampton W v Plymouth Arg

Coca-Cola Football League One
Barnsley v Huddersfield T
Brentford v Colchester U
Gillingham v Milton Keynes Dons
Nottingham F v Chesterfield
Oldham Ath v Hartlepool U
Port Vale v Tranmere R
Rotherham U v Doncaster R
Scunthorpe U v Bradford C
Southend U v Bournemouth
Swindon T v Swansea C
Walsall v Blackpool
Yeovil T v Bristol C

Coca-Cola Football League Two
Barnet v Boston U
Bristol R v Wycombe W
Bury v Stockport Co
Carlisle U v Rochdale
Cheltenham T v Shrewsbury T
Leyton Orient v Notts Co
Lincoln C v Darlington
Macclesfield T v Chester C
Northampton T v Peterborough U
Oxford U v Mansfield T
Torquay U v Rushden & D'monds
Wrexham v Grimsby T

Monday, 2 January 2006

Barclays Premiership

Birmingham C v Wigan Ath
Blackburn R v Portsmouth
Bolton W v Liverpool
Everton v Charlton Ath
Fulham v Sunderland
Manchester C v Tottenham H
Newcastle U v Middlesbrough
WBA v Aston Villa
West Ham U v Chelsea† (12.45)

Coca-Cola Football League Championship

Coventry C v Wolverhampton W
Crystal Palace v Leicester C
Hull C v Sheffield U
Luton T v Watford
Millwall v Derby Co
Norwich C v Preston NE
Plymouth Arg v Leeds U
QPR v Burnley
Reading v Cardiff C
Sheffield W v Crewe Alex
Southampton v Brighton & HA
Stoke C v Ipswich T

Coca-Cola Football League One

Blackpool v Southend U
Bournemouth v Scunthorpe U
Bradford C v Brentford
Bristol C v Walsall
Chesterfield v Barnsley
Colchester U v Nottingham F
Doncaster R v Yeovil T
Hartlepool U v Swindon T
Huddersfield T v Gillingham
Milton Keynes Dons v Oldham Ath
Swansea C v Port Vale
Tranmere R v Rotherham U

Coca-Cola Football League Two

Boston U v Leyton Orient
Chester C v Oxford U
Darlington v Torquay U
Grimsby T v Carlisle U
Mansfield T v Lincoln C
Notts Co v Barnet
Peterborough U v Bury
Rochdale v Northampton T
Rushden & D'monds v Bristol R
Shrewsbury T v Wrexham
Stockport Co v Cheltenham T
Wycombe W v Macclesfield T

Tuesday, 3 January 2006

Barclays Premiership

Arsenal v Manchester U* (8.00)

Saturday, 7 January 2006

Coca-Cola Football League One

Barnsley v Gillingham
Blackpool v Doncaster R
Brentford v Nottingham F
Chesterfield v Bradford C
Colchester U v Bristol C
Oldham Ath v Southend U
Rotherham U v Port Vale
Scunthorpe U v Huddersfield T
Swansea C v Milton Keynes Dons
Swindon T v Walsall
Tranmere R v Bournemouth
Yeovil T v Hartlepool U

Coca-Cola Football League Two

Barnet v Cheltenham T
Boston U v Macclesfield T
Bristol R v Leyton Orient
Carlisle U v Bury
Mansfield T v Chester C
Northampton T v Wycombe W
Notts Co v Darlington
Oxford U v Shrewsbury T
Peterborough U v Rushden & D'monds
Stockport Co v Grimsby T
Torquay U v Rochdale
Wrexham v Lincoln C

Saturday, 14 January 2006

Barclays Premiership

Arsenal v Middlesbrough
Aston Villa v West Ham U
Blackburn R v Bolton W† (5.15)
Charlton Ath v Birmingham C
Fulham v Newcastle U
Liverpool v Tottenham H
Manchester C v Manchester U* (12.45)
Portsmouth v Everton

Coca-Cola Football League Championship

Brighton & HA v Leeds U
Cardiff C v Burnley
Derby Co v Crewe Alex
Hull C v Crystal Palace
Ipswich T v Sheffield U
Plymouth Arg v Norwich C
Preston NE v Millwall
QPR v Southampton
Reading v Coventry C
Sheffield W v Leicester C
Watford v Stoke C
Wolverhampton W v Luton T

Coca-Cola Football League One

Bournemouth v Rotherham U
Bradford C v Swansea C
Bristol C v Scunthorpe U
Doncaster R v Chesterfield
Gillingham v Swindon T
Hartlepool U v Tranmere R
Huddersfield T v Blackpool
Milton Keynes Dons v Yeovil T
Nottingham F v Oldham Ath
Port Vale v Barnsley
Southend U v Brentford
Walsall v Colchester U

Coca-Cola Football League Two

Bury v Torquay U
Cheltenham T v Bristol R
Chester C v Boston U
Darlington v Peterborough U
Grimsby T v Mansfield T
Leyton Orient v Northampton T
Lincoln C v Barnet
Macclesfield T v Oxford U
Rochdale v Stockport Co
Rushden & D'monds v Wrexham
Shrewsbury T v Carlisle U
Wycombe W v Notts Co

Sunday, 15 January 2006

Barclays Premiership

Sunderland v Chelsea* (4.00)
Wigan Ath v WBA* (1.30)

Saturday, 21 January 2006

Barclays Premiership

Birmingham C v Portsmouth
Bolton W v Manchester C
Chelsea v Charlton Ath
Everton v Arsenal
Manchester U v Liverpool
Middlesbrough v Wigan Ath
Newcastle U v Blackburn R
Tottenham H v Aston Villa
WBA v Sunderland
West Ham U v Fulham

Coca-Cola Football League Championship

Burnley v Preston NE
Coventry C v Derby Co
Crewe Alex v Plymouth Arg
Crystal Palace v Reading
Leeds U v Sheffield W
Leicester C v Cardiff C
Luton T v QPR
Millwall v Wolverhampton W
Norwich C v Watford
Sheffield U v Brighton & HA
Southampton v Ipswich T
Stoke C v Hull C

Coca-Cola Football League One

Barnsley v Milton Keynes Dons
Blackpool v Bristol C
Brentford v Huddersfield T
Chesterfield v Walsall
Colchester U v Port Vale
Oldham Ath v Gillingham
Rotherham U v Nottingham F
Scunthorpe U v Doncaster R
Swansea C v Hartlepool U
Swindon T v Bournemouth
Tranmere R v Southend U
Yeovil T v Bradford C

Coca-Cola Football League Two

Barnet v Wycombe W
Boston U v Bury
Bristol R v Chester C
Carlisle U v Cheltenham T
Mansfield T v Rochdale
Northampton T v Macclesfield T
Notts Co v Shrewsbury T
Oxford U v Darlington
Peterborough U v Lincoln C
Stockport Co v Rushden & D'monds
Torquay U v Grimsby T
Wrexham v Leyton Orient

Saturday, 28 January 2006

Coca-Cola Football League One

Bournemouth v Chesterfield
Bradford C v Tranmere R
Bristol C v Swansea C
Doncaster R v Colchester U
Gillingham v Rotherham U
Hartlepool U v Blackpool
Huddersfield T v Oldham Ath
Milton Keynes Dons v Brentford
Nottingham F v Barnsley
Port Vale v Scunthorpe U
Southend U v Swindon T
Walsall v Yeovil T

Coca-Cola Football League Two

Bury v Northampton T
Cheltenham T v Wrexham
Chester C v Notts Co
Darlington v Mansfield T
Grimsby T v Peterborough U
Leyton Orient v Barnet
Lincoln C v Bristol R
Macclesfield T v Carlisle U
Rochdale v Boston U

Rushden & D'monds v Oxford U
Shrewsbury T v Torquay U
Wycombe W v Stockport Co

Tuesday, 31 January 2006

Barclays Premiership
Arsenal v West Ham U
Charlton Ath v WBA
Liverpool v Birmingham C
Portsmouth v Bolton W
Sunderland v Middlesbrough
Wigan Ath v Everton

Coca-Cola Football League Championship
Brighton & HA v Burnley
Cardiff C v Millwall
Hull C v Coventry C
Ipswich T v Leeds U
Plymouth Arg v Southampton
Preston NE v Crystal Palace
QPR v Leicester C
Reading v Norwich C
Sheffield W v Luton T
Watford v Crewe Alex
Wolverhampton W v Stoke C

Wednesday, 1 February 2006

Barclays Premiership
Aston Villa v Chelsea
Blackburn R v Manchester U
Fulham v Tottenham H
Manchester C v Newcastle U

Coca-Cola Football League Championship
Derby Co v Sheffield U

Saturday, 4 February 2006

Barclays Premiership
Birmingham C v Arsenal
Bolton W v Wigan Ath
Chelsea v Liverpool
Everton v Manchester C
Manchester U v Fulham
Middlesbrough v Aston Villa
Newcastle U v Portsmouth
Tottenham H v Charlton Ath
WBA v Blackburn R
West Ham U v Sunderland

Coca-Cola Football League Championship
Burnley v Plymouth Arg
Coventry C v Brighton & HA
Crewe Alex v Reading
Crystal Palace v Cardiff C
Leeds U v QPR
Leicester C v Wolverhampton W
Luton T v Hull C
Millwall v Sheffield W
Norwich C v Ipswich T
Sheffield U v Watford
Southampton v Derby Co
Stoke C v Preston NE

Coca-Cola Football League One
Barnsley v Bristol C
Blackpool v Nottingham F
Brentford v Walsall
Chesterfield v Gillingham
Colchester U v Bradford C
Oldham Ath v Port Vale
Rotherham U v Hartlepool U
Scunthorpe U v Milton Keynes Dons
Swansea C v Bournemouth
Swindon T v Doncaster R
Tranmere R v Huddersfield T
Yeovil T v Southend U

Coca-Cola Football League Two
Barnet v Shrewsbury T
Boston U v Darlington
Bristol R v Bury
Carlisle U v Chester C
Mansfield T v Macclesfield T
Northampton T v Rushden & D'monds
Notts Co v Grimsby T
Oxford U v Rochdale
Peterborough U v Cheltenham T
Stockport Co v Lincoln C
Torquay U v Leyton Orient
Wrexham v Wycombe W

Saturday, 11 February 2006

Barclays Premiership
Arsenal v Bolton W
Aston Villa v Newcastle U
Everton v Blackburn R
Fulham v WBA
Manchester C v Charlton Ath
Middlesbrough v Chelsea
Portsmouth v Manchester U
Sunderland v Tottenham H
West Ham U v Birmingham C
Wigan Ath v Liverpool

Coca-Cola Football League Championship
Brighton & HA v Leicester C
Cardiff C v Stoke C
Derby Co v Leeds U
Hull C v Norwich C
Ipswich T v Burnley
Plymouth Arg v Sheffield U
Preston NE v Luton T
QPR v Millwall
Reading v Southampton
Sheffield W v Crystal Palace
Watford v Coventry C
Wolverhampton W v Crewe Alex

Coca-Cola Football League One
Bournemouth v Oldham Ath
Bradford C v Swindon T
Bristol C v Brentford
Doncaster R v Barnsley
Gillingham v Tranmere R
Hartlepool U v Chesterfield
Huddersfield T v Colchester U
Milton Keynes Dons v Blackpool
Nottingham F v Swansea C
Port Vale v Yeovil T
Southend U v Rotherham U
Walsall v Scunthorpe U

Coca-Cola Football League Two
Bury v Oxford U
Cheltenham T v Northampton T
Chester C v Stockport Co
Darlington v Bristol R
Grimsby T v Boston U
Leyton Orient v Carlisle U
Lincoln C v Torquay U
Macclesfield T v Wrexham
Rochdale v Barnet
Rushden & D'monds v Notts Co
Shrewsbury T v Peterborough U
Wycombe W v Mansfield T

Tuesday, 14 February 2006

Coca-Cola Football League Championship
Burnley v Wolverhampton W
Crewe Alex v Ipswich T
Crystal Palace v QPR
Leeds U v Watford
Leicester C v Derby Co
Luton T v Cardiff C
Millwall v Hull C
Norwich C v Brighton & HA
Sheffield U v Reading
Stoke C v Plymouth Arg

Coca-Cola Football League One
Barnsley v Port Vale
Blackpool v Huddersfield T
Brentford v Southend U
Colchester U v Walsall
Oldham Ath v Nottingham F
Rotherham U v Bournemouth
Scunthorpe U v Bristol C
Swansea C v Bradford C
Swindon T v Gillingham
Tranmere R v Hartlepool U
Yeovil T v Milton Keynes Dons

Coca-Cola Football League Two
Barnet v Lincoln C
Bristol R v Cheltenham T
Carlisle U v Shrewsbury T
Mansfield T v Grimsby T
Northampton T v Leyton Orient
Notts Co v Wycombe W
Peterborough U v Darlington
Stockport Co v Rochdale
Torquay U v Bury
Wrexham v Rushden & D'monds

Wednesday, 15 February 2006

Coca-Cola Football League Championship
Coventry C v Sheffield W
Southampton v Preston NE

Coca-Cola Football League One
Chesterfield v Doncaster R

Coca-Cola Football League Two
Boston U v Chester C
Oxford U v Macclesfield T

Saturday, 18 February 2006

Coca-Cola Football League Championship
Brighton & HA v Watford
Burnley v Southampton
Cardiff C v Hull C
Leicester C v Leeds U
Luton T v Reading
Millwall v Crystal Palace
Norwich C v Derby Co
Plymouth Arg v Coventry C
Preston NE v Crewe Alex
QPR v Stoke C
Sheffield W v Sheffield U
Wolverhampton W v Ipswich T

Coca-Cola Football League One
Bournemouth v Blackpool
Bradford C v Bristol C
Chesterfield v Southend U
Colchester U v Hartlepool U
Doncaster R v Gillingham
Huddersfield T v Milton Keynes Dons
Port Vale v Nottingham F

Scunthorpe U v Swansea C
Swindon T v Rotherham U
Tranmere R v Barnsley
Walsall v Oldham Ath
Yeovil T v Brentford

Coca-Cola Football League Two
Boston U v Wycombe W
Bristol R v Stockport Co
Bury v Barnet
Carlisle U v Rushden & D'monds
Chester C v Leyton Orient
Darlington v Shrewsbury T
Macclesfield T v Lincoln C
Mansfield T v Wrexham
Northampton T v Torquay U
Notts Co v Peterborough U
Oxford U v Cheltenham T
Rochdale v Grimsby T

Saturday, 25 February 2006

Barclays Premiership
Birmingham C v Sunderland
Blackburn R v Arsenal
Bolton W v Fulham
Charlton Ath v Aston Villa
Chelsea v Portsmouth
Liverpool v Manchester C
Manchester U v West Ham U
Newcastle U v Everton
Tottenham H v Wigan Ath
WBA v Middlesbrough

Coca-Cola Football League Championship
Coventry C v Burnley
Crewe Alex v Brighton & HA
Crystal Palace v Norwich C
Derby Co v Plymouth Arg
Hull C v Wolverhampton W
Ipswich T v Leicester C
Leeds U v Luton T
Reading v Preston NE
Sheffield U v QPR
Southampton v Sheffield W
Stoke C v Millwall
Watford v Cardiff C

Coca-Cola Football League One
Barnsley v Colchester U
Blackpool v Yeovil T
Brentford v Port Vale
Bristol C v Bournemouth
Gillingham v Scunthorpe U
Hartlepool U v Doncaster R
Milton Keynes Dons v Bradford C
Nottingham F v Swindon T
Oldham Ath v Tranmere R
Rotherham U v Chesterfield
Southend U v Walsall
Swansea C v Huddersfield T

Coca-Cola Football League Two
Barnet v Carlisle U
Cheltenham T v Rochdale
Grimsby T v Chester C
Leyton Orient v Darlington
Lincoln C v Notts Co
Peterborough U v Bristol R
Rushden & D'monds v Macclesfield T
Shrewsbury T v Bury
Stockport Co v Boston U
Torquay U v Mansfield T
Wrexham v Northampton T
Wycombe W v Oxford U

Saturday, 4 March 2006

Barclays Premiership
Aston Villa v Portsmouth
Fulham v Arsenal
Liverpool v Charlton Ath
Manchester C v Sunderland
Middlesbrough v Birmingham C
Newcastle U v Bolton W
Tottenham H v Blackburn R
WBA v Chelsea
West Ham U v Everton
Wigan Ath v Manchester U

Coca-Cola Football League Championship
Burnley v Reading
Cardiff C v Sheffield W
Crystal Palace v Leeds U
Leicester C v Hull C
Millwall v Luton T
Norwich C v Stoke C
Plymouth Arg v Brighton & HA
Preston NE v Ipswich T
QPR v Wolverhampton W
Sheffield U v Crewe Alex
Southampton v Coventry C
Watford v Derby Co

Coca-Cola Football League One
Barnsley v Swansea C
Bradford C v Blackpool
Bristol C v Nottingham F
Chesterfield v Yeovil T
Colchester U v Southend U
Gillingham v Brentford
Huddersfield T v Doncaster R
Port Vale v Milton Keynes Dons
Rotherham U v Oldham Ath
Scunthorpe U v Hartlepool U
Swindon T v Tranmere R
Walsall v Bournemouth

Coca-Cola Football League Two
Barnet v Wrexham
Boston U v Northampton T
Bury v Macclesfield T
Carlisle U v Lincoln C
Cheltenham T v Wycombe W
Chester C v Torquay U
Notts Co v Mansfield T
Oxford U v Bristol R
Peterborough U v Stockport Co
Rochdale v Darlington
Rushden & D'monds v Grimsby T
Shrewsbury T v Leyton Orient

Saturday, 11 March 2006

Barclays Premiership
Arsenal v Liverpool
Birmingham C v WBA
Blackburn R v Aston Villa
Bolton W v West Ham U
Charlton Ath v Middlesbrough
Chelsea v Tottenham H
Everton v Fulham
Manchester U v Newcastle U
Portsmouth v Manchester C
Sunderland v Wigan Ath

Coca-Cola Football League Championship
Brighton & HA v Preston NE
Coventry C v Sheffield U
Crewe Alex v Southampton
Derby Co v Burnley
Hull C v Plymouth Arg
Ipswich T v Millwall
Leeds U v Norwich C
Luton T v Leicester C
Reading v Watford
Sheffield W v QPR
Stoke C v Crystal Palace
Wolverhampton W v Cardiff C

Coca-Cola Football League One
Blackpool v Rotherham U
Bournemouth v Bradford C
Brentford v Barnsley
Doncaster R v Port Vale
Hartlepool U v Huddersfield T
Milton Keynes Dons v Bristol C
Nottingham F v Gillingham
Oldham Ath v Colchester U
Southend U v Scunthorpe U
Swansea C v Walsall
Tranmere R v Chesterfield
Yeovil T v Swindon T

Coca-Cola Football League Two
Bristol R v Notts Co
Darlington v Chester C
Grimsby T v Barnet
Leyton Orient v Cheltenham T
Lincoln C v Rushden & D'monds
Macclesfield T v Rochdale
Mansfield T v Boston U
Northampton T v Carlisle U
Stockport Co v Oxford U
Torquay U v Peterborough U
Wrexham v Bury
Wycombe W v Shrewsbury T

Saturday, 18 March 2006

Barclays Premiership
Arsenal v Charlton Ath
Birmingham C v Tottenham H
Blackburn R v Middlesbrough
Bolton W v Sunderland
Everton v Aston Villa
Fulham v Chelsea
Manchester C v Wigan Ath
Newcastle U v Liverpool
WBA v Manchester U
West Ham U v Portsmouth

Coca-Cola Football League Championship
Coventry C v Leeds U
Crystal Palace v Ipswich T
Hull C v Crewe Alex
Luton T v Derby Co
Millwall v Leicester C
Norwich C v Sheffield U
Plymouth Arg v Cardiff C
QPR v Brighton & HA
Reading v Wolverhampton W
Sheffield W v Preston NE
Southampton v Watford
Stoke C v Burnley

Coca-Cola Football League One
Blackpool v Port Vale
Bournemouth v Yeovil T
Bradford C v Oldham Ath
Bristol C v Gillingham
Chesterfield v Scunthorpe U
Colchester U v Swindon T
Doncaster R v Nottingham F
Hartlepool U v Barnsley
Huddersfield T v Rotherham U
Milton Keynes Dons v Southend U
Swansea C v Brentford
Tranmere R v Walsall

Coca-Cola Football League Two
Boston U v Lincoln C
Chester C v Cheltenham T
Darlington v Carlisle U
Grimsby T v Bury
Mansfield T v Northampton T
Notts Co v Oxford U
Peterborough U v Barnet
Rochdale v Wrexham
Rushden & D'monds v Leyton Orient
Shrewsbury T v Bristol R
Stockport Co v Macclesfield T
Wycombe W v Torquay U

Saturday, 25 March 2006

Barclays Premiership
Aston Villa v Fulham
Charlton Ath v Newcastle U
Chelsea v Manchester C
Liverpool v Everton
Manchester U v Birmingham C
Middlesbrough v Bolton W
Portsmouth v Arsenal
Sunderland v Blackburn R
Tottenham H v WBA
Wigan Ath v West Ham U

Coca-Cola Football League Championship
Brighton & HA v Luton T
Burnley v Norwich C
Cardiff C v QPR
Crewe Alex v Coventry C
Derby Co v Crystal Palace
Ipswich T v Hull C
Leeds U v Stoke C
Leicester C v Reading
Preston NE v Plymouth Arg
Sheffield U v Southampton
Watford v Millwall
Wolverhampton W v Sheffield W

Coca-Cola Football League One
Barnsley v Bournemouth
Brentford v Doncaster R
Gillingham v Swansea C
Nottingham F v Milton Keynes Dons
Oldham Ath v Blackpool
Port Vale v Huddersfield T
Rotherham U v Bristol C
Scunthorpe U v Colchester U
Southend U v Hartlepool U
Swindon T v Chesterfield
Walsall v Bradford C
Yeovil T v Tranmere R

Coca-Cola Football League Two
Barnet v Darlington
Bristol R v Mansfield T
Bury v Rochdale
Carlisle U v Boston U
Cheltenham T v Rushden & D'monds
Leyton Orient v Wycombe W
Lincoln C v Grimsby T
Macclesfield T v Shrewsbury T
Northampton T v Notts Co
Oxford U v Peterborough U
Torquay U v Stockport Co
Wrexham v Chester C

Saturday, 1 April 2006

Barclays Premiership
Arsenal v Aston Villa
Birmingham C v Chelsea
Blackburn R v Wigan Ath
Bolton W v Manchester U
Everton v Sunderland
Fulham v Portsmouth
Manchester C v Middlesbrough
Newcastle U v Tottenham H
WBA v Liverpool
West Ham U v Charlton Ath

Coca-Cola Football League Championship
Coventry C v Preston NE
Crystal Palace v Watford
Hull C v Leeds U
Luton T v Ipswich T
Millwall v Brighton & HA
Norwich C v Leicester C
Plymouth Arg v Wolverhampton W
QPR v Crewe Alex
Reading v Derby Co
Sheffield W v Burnley
Southampton v Cardiff C
Stoke C v Sheffield U

Coca-Cola Football League One
Blackpool v Walsall
Bournemouth v Southend U
Bradford C v Scunthorpe U
Bristol C v Yeovil T
Chesterfield v Nottingham F
Colchester U v Brentford
Doncaster R v Rotherham U
Hartlepool U v Oldham Ath
Huddersfield T v Barnsley
Milton Keynes Dons v Gillingham
Swansea C v Swindon T
Tranmere R v Port Vale

Coca-Cola Football League Two
Boston U v Barnet
Chester C v Macclesfield T
Darlington v Lincoln C
Grimsby T v Wrexham
Mansfield T v Oxford U
Notts Co v Leyton Orient
Peterborough U v Northampton T
Rochdale v Carlisle U
Rushden & D'monds v Torquay U
Shrewsbury T v Cheltenham T
Stockport Co v Bury
Wycombe W v Bristol R

Saturday, 8 April 2006

Barclays Premiership
Aston Villa v WBA
Charlton Ath v Everton
Chelsea v West Ham U
Liverpool v Bolton W
Manchester U v Arsenal
Middlesbrough v Newcastle U
Portsmouth v Blackburn R
Sunderland v Fulham
Tottenham H v Manchester C
Wigan Ath v Birmingham C

Coca-Cola Football League Championship
Brighton & HA v Southampton
Burnley v QPR
Cardiff C v Reading
Crewe Alex v Sheffield W
Derby Co v Millwall
Ipswich T v Stoke C
Leeds U v Plymouth Arg
Leicester C v Crystal Palace
Preston NE v Norwich C
Sheffield U v Hull C
Watford v Luton T
Wolverhampton W v Coventry C

Coca-Cola Football League One
Barnsley v Chesterfield
Brentford v Bradford C
Gillingham v Huddersfield T
Nottingham F v Colchester U
Oldham Ath v Milton Keynes Dons
Port Vale v Swansea C
Rotherham U v Tranmere R
Scunthorpe U v Bournemouth
Southend U v Blackpool
Swindon T v Hartlepool U
Walsall v Bristol C
Yeovil T v Doncaster R

Coca-Cola Football League Two
Barnet v Notts Co
Bristol R v Rushden & D'monds
Bury v Peterborough U
Carlisle U v Grimsby T
Cheltenham T v Stockport Co
Leyton Orient v Boston U
Lincoln C v Mansfield T
Macclesfield T v Wycombe W
Northampton T v Rochdale
Oxford U v Chester C
Torquay U v Darlington
Wrexham v Shrewsbury T

Saturday, 15 April 2006

Barclays Premiership
Arsenal v WBA
Aston Villa v Birmingham C
Blackburn R v Liverpool
Bolton W v Chelsea
Everton v Tottenham H
Fulham v Charlton Ath
Manchester U v Sunderland
Newcastle U v Wigan Ath
Portsmouth v Middlesbrough
West Ham U v Manchester C

Coca-Cola Football League Championship
Cardiff C v Sheffield U
Crystal Palace v Crewe Alex
Hull C v Burnley
Ipswich T v Brighton & HA
Leeds U v Reading
Leicester C v Preston NE
Luton T v Coventry C
Millwall v Plymouth Arg
QPR v Derby Co
Sheffield W v Norwich C
Stoke C v Southampton
Wolverhampton W v Watford

Coca-Cola Football League One
Blackpool v Swansea C
Bournemouth v Huddersfield T
Bradford C v Doncaster R
Chesterfield v Colchester U
Hartlepool U v Bristol C
Oldham Ath v Barnsley
Rotherham U v Brentford
Southend U v Gillingham
Swindon T v Milton Keynes Dons
Tranmere R v Nottingham F
Walsall v Port Vale
Yeovil T v Scunthorpe U

Coca-Cola Football League Two
Bristol R v Carlisle U
Chester C v Wycombe W
Darlington v Northampton T
Grimsby T v Shrewsbury T
Lincoln C v Bury
Mansfield T v Leyton Orient

Notts Co v Macclesfield T
Oxford U v Barnet
Peterborough U v Boston U
Rushden & D'monds v Rochdale
Stockport Co v Wrexham
Torquay U v Cheltenham T

Monday, 17 April 2006

Barclays Premiership

Birmingham C v Blackburn R
Charlton Ath v Portsmouth
Chelsea v Everton
Liverpool v Fulham
Manchester C v Arsenal
Middlesbrough v West Ham U
Sunderland v Newcastle U
Tottenham H v Manchester U
WBA v Bolton W
Wigan Ath v Aston Villa

Coca-Cola Football League Championship

Brighton & HA v Sheffield W
Burnley v Crystal Palace
Coventry C v Leicester C
Crewe Alex v Cardiff C
Derby Co v Hull C
Norwich C v QPR
Plymouth Arg v Luton T
Preston NE v Wolverhampton W
Reading v Stoke C
Sheffield U v Leeds U
Southampton v Millwall
Watford v Ipswich T

Coca-Cola Football League One

Barnsley v Southend U
Brentford v Blackpool
Bristol C v Oldham Ath
Colchester U v Tranmere R
Doncaster R v Walsall
Gillingham v Bradford C
Huddersfield T v Chesterfield
Milton Keynes Dons v Hartlepool U
Nottingham F v Yeovil T
Port Vale v Bournemouth
Scunthorpe U v Swindon T
Swansea C v Rotherham U

Coca-Cola Football League Two

Barnet v Mansfield T
Boston U v Oxford U
Bury v Chester C
Carlisle U v Notts Co
Cheltenham T v Darlington
Leyton Orient v Grimsby T
Macclesfield T v Torquay U
Northampton T v Stockport Co
Rochdale v Peterborough U
Shrewsbury T v Rushden & D'monds
Wrexham v Bristol R
Wycombe W v Lincoln C

Saturday, 22 April 2006

Barclays Premiership

Arsenal v Tottenham H
Aston Villa v Manchester C
Blackburn R v Chelsea
Bolton W v Charlton Ath
Everton v Birmingham C
Fulham v Wigan Ath
Manchester U v Middlesbrough
Newcastle U v WBA
Portsmouth v Sunderland
West Ham U v Liverpool

Coca-Cola Football League Championship

Cardiff C v Norwich C
Crystal Palace v Southampton
Hull C v Preston NE
Ipswich T v Derby Co
Leeds U v Crewe Alex
Leicester C v Plymouth Arg
Luton T v Sheffield U
Millwall v Burnley
QPR v Watford
Sheffield W v Reading
Stoke C v Coventry C
Wolverhampton W v Brighton & HA

Coca-Cola Football League One

Blackpool v Barnsley
Bournemouth v Colchester U
Bradford C v Port Vale
Chesterfield v Milton Keynes Dons
Hartlepool U v Nottingham F
Oldham Ath v Swansea C
Rotherham U v Scunthorpe U
Southend U v Doncaster R
Swindon T v Brentford
Tranmere R v Bristol C
Walsall v Huddersfield T
Yeovil T v Gillingham

Coca-Cola Football League Two

Bristol R v Boston U
Chester C v Barnet
Darlington v Bury
Grimsby T v Cheltenham T
Lincoln C v Leyton Orient
Mansfield T v Carlisle U
Notts Co v Rochdale
Oxford U v Northampton T
Peterborough U v Macclesfield T
Rushden & D'monds v Wycombe W
Stockport Co v Shrewsbury T
Torquay U v Wrexham

Saturday, 29 April 2006

Barclays Premiership

Birmingham C v Newcastle U
Charlton Ath v Blackburn R
Chelsea v Manchester U
Liverpool v Aston Villa
Manchester C v Fulham
Middlesbrough v Everton
Sunderland v Arsenal
Tottenham H v Bolton W
WBA v West Ham U
Wigan Ath v Portsmouth

Coca-Cola Football League One

Barnsley v Bradford C
Brentford v Hartlepool U
Bristol C v Swindon T
Colchester U v Rotherham U
Doncaster R v Oldham Ath
Gillingham v Walsall
Huddersfield T v Yeovil T
Milton Keynes Dons v Tranmere R
Nottingham F v Bournemouth
Port Vale v Chesterfield
Scunthorpe U v Blackpool
Swansea C v Southend U

Coca-Cola Football League Two

Barnet v Stockport Co
Boston U v Rushden & D'monds
Bury v Mansfield T
Carlisle U v Torquay U
Cheltenham T v Notts Co
Leyton Orient v Peterborough U
Macclesfield T v Grimsby T
Northampton T v Chester C
Rochdale v Bristol R
Shrewsbury T v Lincoln C
Wrexham v Oxford U
Wycombe W v Darlington

Sunday, 30 April 2006

Coca-Cola Football League Championship

Brighton & HA v Stoke C
Burnley v Luton T
Coventry C v Cardiff C
Crewe Alex v Millwall
Derby Co v Sheffield W
Norwich C v Wolverhampton W
Plymouth Arg v Ipswich T
Preston NE v Leeds U
Reading v QPR
Sheffield U v Crystal Palace
Southampton v Leicester C
Watford v Hull C

Saturday, 6 May 2006

Coca-Cola Football League One

Blackpool v Gillingham
Bournemouth v Brentford
Bradford C v Nottingham F
Chesterfield v Swansea C
Hartlepool U v Port Vale
Oldham Ath v Scunthorpe U
Rotherham U v Milton Keynes Dons
Southend U v Bristol C
Swindon T v Huddersfield T
Tranmere R v Doncaster R
Walsall v Barnsley
Yeovil T v Colchester U

Coca-Cola Football League Two

Bristol R v Macclesfield T
Chester C v Shrewsbury T
Darlington v Wrexham
Grimsby T v Northampton T
Lincoln C v Rochdale
Mansfield T v Cheltenham T
Notts Co v Bury
Oxford U v Leyton Orient
Peterborough U v Wycombe W
Rushden & D'monds v Barnet
Stockport Co v Carlisle U
Torquay U v Boston U

Sunday, 7 May 2006

Barclays Premiership

Arsenal v Wigan Ath
Aston Villa v Sunderland
Blackburn R v Manchester C
Bolton W v Birmingham C
Everton v WBA
Fulham v Middlesbrough
Manchester U v Charlton Ath
Newcastle U v Chelsea
Portsmouth v Liverpool
West Ham U v Tottenham H

CONFERENCE NATIONAL FIXTURES 2005-06

Saturday, 13 August 2005
Accrington Stanley v Canvey Island
Aldershot T v Tamworth
Burton Alb v Grays Ath
Dagenham & Red v Southport
Forest Green v Cambridge U
Gravesend & N v Exeter C
Hereford U v Scarborough
Kidderminster H v Woking
Morecambe v Halifax T
Stevenage B v Altrincham
York C v Crawley T

Tuesday, 16 August 2005
Altrincham v Accrington Stanley
Cambridge U v Hereford U
Canvey Island v Aldershot T
Crawley T v Dagenham & Red
Exeter C v Kidderminster H
Grays Ath v Gravesend & N
Halifax T v Burton Alb
Scarborough v Morecambe
Southport v York C
Tamworth v Forest Green
Woking v Stevenage B

Saturday, 20 August 2005
Altrincham v Forest Green
Cambridge U v Accrington Stanley
Canvey Island v Gravesend & N
Crawley T v Hereford U
Exeter C v Morecambe
Grays Ath v York C
Halifax T v Aldershot T
Scarborough v Kidderminster H
Southport v Stevenage B
Tamworth v Dagenham & Red
Woking v Burton Alb

Saturday, 27 August 2005
Accrington Stanley v Exeter C
Aldershot T v Altrincham
Burton Alb v Canvey Island
Dagenham & Red v Scarborough
Forest Green v Halifax T
Gravesend & N v Cambridge U
Hereford U v Grays Ath
Kidderminster H v Southport
Morecambe v Crawley T
Stevenage B v Tamworth
York C v Woking

Monday, 29 August 2005
Altrincham v Morecambe
Cambridge U v Kidderminster H
Canvey Island v Dagenham & Red
Crawley T v Stevenage B
Exeter C v Forest Green
Grays Ath v Aldershot T
Halifax T v York C
Scarborough v Accrington Stanley
Southport v Burton Alb
Tamworth v Hereford U
Woking v Gravesend & N

Saturday, 3 September 2005
Accrington Stanley v Woking
Aldershot T v Crawley T
Burton Alb v Scarborough
Dagenham & Red v Exeter C
Forest Green v Grays Ath
Gravesend & N v Southport
Hereford U v Altrincham
Kidderminster H v Canvey Island
Morecambe v Tamworth
Stevenage B v Halifax T
York C v Cambridge U

Saturday, 10 September 2005
Altrincham v Dagenham & Red
Burton Alb v Accrington Stanley
Crawley T v Canvey Island
Exeter C v Cambridge U
Forest Green v York C
Grays Ath v Kidderminster H
Halifax T v Tamworth
Morecambe v Aldershot T
Scarborough v Gravesend & N
Stevenage B v Hereford U
Woking v Southport

Saturday, 17 September 2005
Accrington Stanley v Crawley T
Aldershot T v Stevenage B
Cambridge U v Woking
Canvey Island v Scarborough
Dagenham & Red v Burton Alb
Gravesend & N v Halifax T
Hereford U v Morecambe
Kidderminster H v Forest Green
Southport v Exeter C
Tamworth v Grays Ath
York C v Altrincham

Tuesday, 20 September 2005
Accrington Stanley v Aldershot T
Altrincham v Scarborough
Burton Alb v Morecambe
Forest Green v Crawley T
Grays Ath v Cambridge U
Hereford U v Gravesend & N
Kidderminster H v Halifax T
Southport v Tamworth
Stevenage B v Exeter C
Woking v Canvey Island
York C v Dagenham & Red

Saturday, 24 September 2005
Aldershot T v York C
Cambridge U v Altrincham
Canvey Island v Southport
Crawley T v Grays Ath
Dagenham & Red v Accrington Stanley
Exeter C v Burton Alb
Gravesend & N v Kidderminster H
Halifax T v Hereford U
Morecambe v Stevenage B
Scarborough v Forest Green
Tamworth v Woking

Tuesday, 27 September 2005
Aldershot T v Hereford U
Cambridge U v Burton Alb
Canvey Island v Stevenage B
Crawley T v Kidderminster H
Dagenham & Red v Grays Ath
Exeter C v Woking
Gravesend & N v Forest Green
Halifax T v Altrincham
Morecambe v Accrington Stanley
Scarborough v Southport
Tamworth v York C

Saturday, 1 October 2005
Accrington Stanley v Gravesend & N
Altrincham v Crawley T
Burton Alb v Aldershot T
Forest Green v Morecambe
Grays Ath v Halifax T
Hereford U v Canvey Island
Kidderminster H v Tamworth
Southport v Cambridge U
Stevenage B v Dagenham & Red
Woking v Scarborough
York C v Exeter C

Saturday, 8 October 2005
Accrington Stanley v Hereford U
Burton Alb v Stevenage B
Cambridge U v Tamworth
Canvey Island v Altrincham
Dagenham & Red v Aldershot T
Exeter C v Halifax T
Gravesend & N v York C
Kidderminster H v Morecambe
Scarborough v Crawley T
Southport v Forest Green
Woking v Grays Ath

Saturday, 15 October 2005
Aldershot T v Kidderminster H
Altrincham v Southport
Crawley T v Exeter C
Forest Green v Woking
Grays Ath v Scarborough
Halifax T v Cambridge U
Hereford U v Burton Alb
Morecambe v Dagenham & Red
Stevenage B v Accrington Stanley
Tamworth v Gravesend & N
York C v Canvey Island

Saturday, 29 October 2005
Accrington Stanley v York C
Burton Alb v Altrincham
Cambridge U v Crawley T
Canvey Island v Morecambe
Dagenham & Red v Forest Green
Exeter C v Tamworth
Gravesend & N v Stevenage B
Kidderminster H v Hereford U
Scarborough v Aldershot T
Southport v Grays Ath
Woking v Halifax T

Saturday, 12 November 2005
Aldershot T v Gravesend & N
Altrincham v Exeter C
Crawley T v Southport
Forest Green v Canvey Island
Grays Ath v Accrington Stanley
Halifax T v Dagenham & Red
Hereford U v Woking
Morecambe v Cambridge U
Stevenage B v Kidderminster H
Tamworth v Scarborough
York C v Burton Alb

Saturday, 19 November 2005
Accrington Stanley v Forest Green
Burton Alb v Crawley T

Cambridge U v Aldershot T
Canvey Island v Tamworth
Dagenham & Red v Hereford U
Exeter C v Grays Ath
Gravesend & N v Altrincham
Kidderminster H v York C
Scarborough v Stevenage B
Southport v Halifax T
Woking v Morecambe

Saturday, 26 November 2005
Accrington Stanley v Southport
Aldershot T v Forest Green
Altrincham v Tamworth
Burton Alb v Kidderminster H
Canvey Island v Cambridge U
Crawley T v Gravesend & N
Dagenham & Red v Woking
Hereford U v Exeter C
Morecambe v York C
Scarborough v Halifax T
Stevenage B v Grays Ath

Saturday, 3 December 2005
Cambridge U v Scarborough
Exeter C v Canvey Island
Forest Green v Burton Alb
Gravesend & N v Morecambe
Grays Ath v Altrincham
Halifax T v Crawley T
Kidderminster H v Dagenham & Red
Southport v Hereford U
Tamworth v Accrington Stanley
Woking v Aldershot T
York C v Stevenage B

Saturday, 10 December 2005
Accrington Stanley v Kidderminster H
Aldershot T v Southport
Altrincham v Woking
Burton Alb v Gravesend & N
Canvey Island v Halifax T
Crawley T v Tamworth
Dagenham & Red v Cambridge U
Hereford U v York C
Morecambe v Grays Ath
Scarborough v Exeter C
Stevenage B v Forest Green

Monday, 26 December 2005
Cambridge U v Stevenage B
Exeter C v Aldershot T
Forest Green v Hereford U
Gravesend & N v Dagenham & Red
Grays Ath v Canvey Island
Halifax T v Accrington Stanley
Kidderminster H v Altrincham
Southport v Morecambe
Tamworth v Burton Alb
Woking v Crawley T
York C v Scarborough

Saturday, 31 December 2005
Cambridge U v Canvey Island
Exeter C v Hereford U
Forest Green v Aldershot T
Gravesend & N v Crawley T
Grays Ath v Stevenage B
Halifax T v Scarborough
Kidderminster H v Burton Alb
Southport v Accrington Stanley
Tamworth v Altrincham
Woking v Dagenham & Red
York C v Morecambe

Monday, 2 January 2006
Accrington Stanley v Halifax T
Aldershot T v Exeter C
Altrincham v Kidderminster H
Burton Alb v Tamworth
Canvey Island v Grays Ath
Crawley T v Woking
Dagenham & Red v Gravesend & N
Hereford U v Forest Green
Morecambe v Southport
Scarborough v York C
Stevenage B v Cambridge U

Saturday, 7 January 2006
Altrincham v Stevenage B
Cambridge U v Forest Green
Canvey Island v Accrington Stanley
Crawley T v York C
Exeter C v Gravesend & N
Grays Ath v Burton Alb
Halifax T v Morecambe
Scarborough v Hereford U
Southport v Dagenham & Red
Tamworth v Aldershot T
Woking v Kidderminster H

Saturday, 21 January 2006
Accrington Stanley v Cambridge U
Aldershot T v Halifax T
Burton Alb v Woking
Dagenham & Red v Tamworth
Forest Green v Altrincham
Gravesend & N v Canvey Island
Hereford U v Crawley T
Kidderminster H v Scarborough
Morecambe v Exeter C
Stevenage B v Southport
York C v Grays Ath

Tuesday, 24 January 2006
Accrington Stanley v Altrincham
Aldershot T v Canvey Island
Burton Alb v Halifax T
Dagenham & Red v Crawley T
Forest Green v Tamworth
Gravesend & N v Grays Ath
Hereford U v Cambridge U
Kidderminster H v Exeter C
Morecambe v Scarborough
Stevenage B v Woking
York C v Southport

Saturday, 28 January 2006
Altrincham v Aldershot T
Cambridge U v Gravesend & N
Canvey Island v Burton Alb
Crawley T v Morecambe
Exeter C v Accrington Stanley
Grays Ath v Hereford U
Halifax T v Forest Green
Scarborough v Dagenham & Red
Southport v Kidderminster H
Tamworth v Stevenage B
Woking v York C

Saturday, 4 February 2006
Aldershot T v Accrington Stanley
Cambridge U v Grays Ath
Canvey Island v Woking
Crawley T v Forest Green
Dagenham & Red v York C
Exeter C v Stevenage B
Gravesend & N v Hereford U
Halifax T v Kidderminster H
Morecambe v Burton Alb
Scarborough v Altrincham
Tamworth v Southport

Saturday, 11 February 2006
Accrington Stanley v Dagenham & Red
Altrincham v Cambridge U
Burton Alb v Exeter C
Forest Green v Scarborough
Grays Ath v Crawley T
Hereford U v Halifax T
Kidderminster H v Gravesend & N
Southport v Canvey Island
Stevenage B v Morecambe
Woking v Tamworth
York C v Aldershot T

Saturday, 18 February 2006
Aldershot T v Burton Alb
Cambridge U v Southport
Canvey Island v Hereford U
Crawley T v Altrincham
Dagenham & Red v Stevenage B
Exeter C v York C
Gravesend & N v Accrington Stanley
Halifax T v Grays Ath
Morecambe v Forest Green
Scarborough v Woking
Tamworth v Kidderminster H

Tuesday, 21 February 2006
Accrington Stanley v Morecambe
Altrincham v Halifax T
Burton Alb v Cambridge U
Forest Green v Gravesend & N
Grays Ath v Dagenham & Red
Hereford U v Aldershot T
Kidderminster H v Crawley T
Southport v Scarborough
Stevenage B v Canvey Island
Woking v Exeter C
York C v Tamworth

Saturday, 25 February 2006
Accrington Stanley v Burton Alb
Aldershot T v Morecambe
Cambridge U v Exeter C
Canvey Island v Crawley T
Dagenham & Red v Altrincham
Gravesend & N v Scarborough
Hereford U v Stevenage B
Kidderminster H v Grays Ath
Southport v Woking
Tamworth v Halifax T
York C v Forest Green

Saturday, 4 March 2006
Altrincham v York C
Burton Alb v Dagenham & Red
Crawley T v Accrington Stanley
Exeter C v Southport
Forest Green v Kidderminster H
Grays Ath v Tamworth
Halifax T v Gravesend & N
Morecambe v Hereford U
Scarborough v Canvey Island
Stevenage B v Aldershot T
Woking v Cambridge U

Saturday, 11 March 2006
Aldershot T v Dagenham & Red
Altrincham v Canvey Island
Crawley T v Scarborough
Forest Green v Southport
Grays Ath v Woking
Halifax T v Exeter C
Hereford U v Accrington Stanley
Morecambe v Kidderminster H
Stevenage B v Burton Alb
Tamworth v Cambridge U
York C v Gravesend & N

Saturday, 18 March 2006
Accrington Stanley v Stevenage B
Burton Alb v Hereford U
Cambridge U v Halifax T
Canvey Island v York C
Dagenham & Red v Morecambe
Exeter C v Crawley T
Gravesend & N v Tamworth
Kidderminster H v Aldershot T
Scarborough v Grays Ath
Southport v Altrincham
Woking v Forest Green

Saturday, 25 March 2006
Aldershot T v Scarborough
Altrincham v Burton Alb
Crawley T v Cambridge U
Forest Green v Dagenham & Red
Grays Ath v Southport
Halifax T v Woking
Hereford U v Kidderminster H
Morecambe v Canvey Island
Stevenage B v Gravesend & N
Tamworth v Exeter C
York C v Accrington Stanley

Saturday, 1 April 2006
Accrington Stanley v Grays Ath
Burton Alb v York C
Cambridge U v Morecambe
Canvey Island v Forest Green
Dagenham & Red v Halifax T
Exeter C v Altrincham
Gravesend & N v Aldershot T
Kidderminster H v Stevenage B
Scarborough v Tamworth
Southport v Crawley T
Woking v Hereford U

Saturday, 8 April 2006
Aldershot T v Cambridge U
Altrincham v Gravesend & N
Crawley T v Burton Alb
Forest Green v Accrington Stanley
Grays Ath v Exeter C
Halifax T v Southport
Hereford U v Dagenham & Red
Morecambe v Woking
Stevenage B v Scarborough
Tamworth v Canvey Island
York C v Kidderminster H

Saturday, 15 April 2006
Altrincham v Hereford U
Cambridge U v York C
Canvey Island v Kidderminster H
Crawley T v Aldershot T
Exeter C v Dagenham & Red
Grays Ath v Forest Green
Halifax T v Stevenage B
Scarborough v Burton Alb
Southport v Gravesend & N
Tamworth v Morecambe
Woking v Accrington Stanley

Monday, 17 April 2006
Accrington Stanley v Scarborough
Aldershot T v Grays Ath
Burton Alb v Southport
Dagenham & Red v Canvey Island
Forest Green v Exeter C
Gravesend & N v Woking
Hereford U v Tamworth
Kidderminster H v Cambridge U
Morecambe v Altrincham
Stevenage B v Crawley T
York C v Halifax T

Saturday, 22 April 2006
Accrington Stanley v Tamworth
Aldershot T v Woking
Altrincham v Grays Ath
Burton Alb v Forest Green
Canvey Island v Exeter C
Crawley T v Halifax T
Dagenham & Red v Kidderminster H
Hereford U v Southport
Morecambe v Gravesend & N
Scarborough v Cambridge U
Stevenage B v York C

Saturday, 29 April 2006
Cambridge U v Dagenham & Red
Exeter C v Scarborough
Forest Green v Stevenage B
Gravesend & N v Burton Alb
Grays Ath v Morecambe
Halifax T v Canvey Island
Kidderminster H v Accrington Stanley
Southport v Aldershot T
Tamworth v Crawley T
Woking v Altrincham
York C v Hereford U

THE SCOTTISH PREMIER LEAGUE AND FOOTBALL LEAGUE FIXTURES 2005–06

Saturday, 30 July 2005
Bank of Scotland
Scottish Premier League
Dundee U v Aberdeen
Falkirk v Inverness CT
Hibernian v Dunfermline Ath
Kilmarnock v Hearts
Motherwell v Celtic

Sunday, 31 July 2005
Bank of Scotland
Scottish Premier League
Rangers v Livingston

Saturday, 6 August 2005
Bank of Scotland
Scottish Premier League
Aberdeen v Kilmarnock
Celtic v Dundee U
Dunfermline Ath v Motherwell
Inverness CT v Rangers
Livingston v Falkirk

Bell's Scottish First Division
Brechin C v Hamilton A
Dundee v St Mirren
Ross Co v Clyde
St Johnstone v Queen of the S
Stranraer v Airdrie U

Bell's Scottish Second Division
Alloa Ath v Peterhead
Ayr U v Dumbarton
Gretna v Forfar Ath
Morton v Raith R
Partick T v Stirling Alb

Bell's Scottish Third Division
Albion R v Arbroath
East Fife v Berwick R
East Stirlingshire v Cowdenbeath
Elgin C v Montrose
Queen's Park v Stenhousemuir

Sunday, 7 August 2005
Bank of Scotland
Scottish Premier League
Hearts v Hibernian

Saturday, 13 August 2005
Bank of Scotland
Scottish Premier League
Celtic v Falkirk
Dundee U v Hearts
Dunfermline Ath v Inverness CT
Hibernian v Livingston
Kilmarnock v Motherwell

Bell's Scottish First Division
Airdrie U v Ross Co
Clyde v Dundee
Hamilton A v St Johnstone
Queen of the S v Brechin C
St Mirren v Stranraer

Bell's Scottish Second Division
Dumbarton v Alloa Ath
Forfar Ath v Ayr U
Peterhead v Partick T
Raith R v Gretna
Stirling Alb v Morton

Bell's Scottish Third Division
Arbroath v East Fife
Berwick R v East Stirlingshire
Cowdenbeath v Queen's Park
Montrose v Albion R
Stenhousemuir v Elgin C

Sunday, 14 August 2005
Bank of Scotland
Scottish Premier League
Aberdeen v Rangers

Saturday, 20 August 2005
Bank of Scotland
Scottish Premier League
Falkirk v Hibernian
Hearts v Aberdeen
Inverness CT v Kilmarnock
Livingston v Dunfermline Ath
Motherwell v Dundee U
Rangers v Celtic

Bell's Scottish First Division
Brechin C v Airdrie U
Dundee v Queen of the S
Ross Co v Hamilton A
St Johnstone v St Mirren
Stranraer v Clyde

Bell's Scottish Second Division
Alloa Ath v Raith R
Ayr U v Peterhead
Gretna v Stirling Alb
Morton v Forfar Ath
Partick T v Dumbarton

Bell's Scottish Third Division
Albion R v Stenhousemuir
East Fife v Montrose
East Stirlingshire v Arbroath
Elgin C v Cowdenbeath
Queen's Park v Berwick R

Saturday, 27 August 2005
Bank of Scotland
Scottish Premier League
Aberdeen v Falkirk
Dundee U v Inverness CT
Hearts v Motherwell
Kilmarnock v Livingston
Rangers v Hibernian

Bell's Scottish First Division
Airdrie U v St Johnstone
Clyde v Queen of the S
Hamilton A v Dundee
Ross Co v Stranraer
St Mirren v Brechin C

Bell's Scottish Second Division
Dumbarton v Morton
Forfar Ath v Peterhead
Gretna v Ayr U
Partick T v Raith R
Stirling Alb v Alloa Ath

Bell's Scottish Third Division
Berwick R v Elgin C
East Fife v Cowdenbeath
Montrose v Arbroath
Queen's Park v Albion R
Stenhousemuir v East Stirlingshire

Sunday, 28 August 2005
Bank of Scotland
Scottish Premier League
Dunfermline Ath v Celtic

Saturday, 10 September 2005
Bank of Scotland
Scottish Premier League
Celtic v Aberdeen
Falkirk v Rangers
Hibernian v Dundee U
Inverness CT v Motherwell
Kilmarnock v Dunfermline Ath
Livingston v Hearts

Bell's Scottish First Division
Brechin C v Clyde
Dundee v Airdrie U
Queen of the S v St Mirren
St Johnstone v Ross Co
Stranraer v Hamilton A

Bell's Scottish Second Division
Alloa Ath v Forfar Ath
Ayr U v Partick T
Morton v Gretna
Peterhead v Dumbarton
Raith R v Stirling Alb

Bell's Scottish Third Division
Albion R v East Fife
Arbroath v Stenhousemuir
Cowdenbeath v Berwick R
East Stirlingshire v Montrose
Elgin C v Queen's Park

Saturday, 17 September 2005
Bank of Scotland
Scottish Premier League
Dundee U v Livingston
Dunfermline Ath v Aberdeen
Hibernian v Celtic
Inverness CT v Hearts
Motherwell v Falkirk
Rangers v Kilmarnock

Bell's Scottish First Division
Hamilton A v Airdrie U
Ross Co v Brechin C
St Johnstone v Dundee
St Mirren v Clyde
Stranraer v Queen of the S

Bell's Scottish Second Division
Forfar Ath v Dumbarton
Gretna v Partick T
Morton v Alloa Ath
Raith R v Ayr U
Stirling Alb v Peterhead

Bell's Scottish Third Division
Berwick R v Arbroath
Cowdenbeath v Montrose
Elgin C v Albion R
Queen's Park v East Stirlingshire
Stenhousemuir v East Fife

Saturday, 24 September 2005
Bank of Scotland
Scottish Premier League
Aberdeen v Livingston
Celtic v Inverness CT
Dunfermline Ath v Dundee U
Hearts v Rangers
Kilmarnock v Falkirk
Motherwell v Hibernian

Bell's Scottish First Division
Airdrie U v St Mirren
Brechin C v Stranraer
Clyde v St Johnstone
Dundee v Ross Co
Queen of the S v Hamilton A

Bell's Scottish Second Division
Alloa Ath v Gretna
Ayr U v Morton
Dumbarton v Stirling Alb
Partick T v Forfar Ath
Peterhead v Raith R

Bell's Scottish Third Division
Albion R v Berwick R
Arbroath v Cowdenbeath
East Fife v Queen's Park
East Stirlingshire v Elgin C
Montrose v Stenhousemuir

Saturday, 1 October 2005
Bank of Scotland
Scottish Premier League
Aberdeen v Motherwell
Dundee U v Kilmarnock
Falkirk v Hearts
Hibernian v Inverness CT
Livingston v Celtic
Rangers v Dunfermline Ath

Bell's Scottish First Division
Airdrie U v Clyde
Brechin C v Dundee
Hamilton A v St Mirren
Ross Co v Queen of the S
Stranraer v St Johnstone

Bell's Scottish Second Division
Alloa Ath v Partick T
Gretna v Dumbarton
Morton v Peterhead
Raith R v Forfar Ath
Stirling Alb v Ayr U

Bell's Scottish Third Division
Berwick R v Montrose
Cowdenbeath v Stenhousemuir
East Stirlingshire v Albion R
Elgin C v East Fife
Queen's Park v Arbroath

Saturday, 15 October 2005
Bank of Scotland
Scottish Premier League
Celtic v Hearts
Dundee U v Rangers
Dunfermline Ath v Falkirk
Hibernian v Kilmarnock
Inverness CT v Aberdeen
Motherwell v Livingston

Bell's Scottish First Division
Clyde v Hamilton A
Dundee v Stranraer
Queen of the S v Airdrie U
St Johnstone v Brechin C
St Mirren v Ross Co

Bell's Scottish Second Division
Ayr U v Alloa Ath
Dumbarton v Raith R
Forfar Ath v Stirling Alb
Partick T v Morton
Peterhead v Gretna

Bell's Scottish Third Division
Albion R v Cowdenbeath
Arbroath v Elgin C
East Fife v East Stirlingshire
Montrose v Queen's Park
Stenhousemuir v Berwick R

Saturday, 22 October 2005
Bank of Scotland
Scottish Premier League
Aberdeen v Hibernian
Falkirk v Dundee U
Hearts v Dunfermline Ath
Kilmarnock v Celtic
Livingston v Inverness CT
Rangers v Motherwell

Bell's Scottish First Division
Airdrie U v Stranraer
Clyde v Ross Co
Hamilton A v Brechin C
Queen of the S v St Johnstone
St Mirren v Dundee

Bell's Scottish Second Division
Dumbarton v Ayr U
Forfar Ath v Gretna
Peterhead v Alloa Ath
Raith R v Morton
Stirling Alb v Partick T

Bell's Scottish Third Division
Arbroath v Albion R
Berwick R v East Fife
Cowdenbeath v East Stirlingshire
Montrose v Elgin C
Stenhousemuir v Queen's Park

Tuesday, 25 October 2005
Bell's Scottish First Division
Brechin C v Queen of the S
Ross Co v Airdrie U
St Johnstone v Hamilton A
Stranraer v St Mirren

Bell's Scottish Second Division
Alloa Ath v Dumbarton
Gretna v Raith R
Morton v Stirling Alb
Partick T v Peterhead

Bell's Scottish Third Division
Albion R v Montrose
East Fife v Arbroath
East Stirlingshire v Berwick R
Elgin C v Stenhousemuir
Queen's Park v Cowdenbeath

Wednesday, 26 October 2005
Bank of Scotland
Scottish Premier League
Aberdeen v Dundee U
Celtic v Motherwell
Dunfermline Ath v Hibernian
Hearts v Kilmarnock

Inverness CT v Falkirk
Livingston v Rangers

Bell's Scottish First Division
Dundee v Clyde

Bell's Scottish Second Division
Ayr U v Forfar Ath

Saturday, 29 October 2005
Bank of Scotland
Scottish Premier League
Dundee U v Celtic
Falkirk v Livingston
Hibernian v Hearts
Kilmarnock v Aberdeen
Motherwell v Dunfermline Ath
Rangers v Inverness CT

Bell's Scottish First Division
Airdrie U v Dundee
Clyde v Brechin C
Hamilton A v Stranraer
Ross Co v St Johnstone
St Mirren v Queen of the S

Bell's Scottish Second Division
Dumbarton v Peterhead
Forfar Ath v Alloa Ath
Gretna v Morton
Partick T v Ayr U
Stirling Alb v Raith R

Bell's Scottish Third Division
Berwick R v Cowdenbeath
East Fife v Albion R
Montrose v East Stirlingshire
Queen's Park v Elgin C
Stenhousemuir v Arbroath

Saturday, 5 November 2005
Bank of Scotland
Scottish Premier League
Falkirk v Celtic
Hearts v Dundee U
Inverness CT v Dunfermline Ath
Livingston v Hibernian
Motherwell v Kilmarnock
Rangers v Aberdeen

Bell's Scottish First Division
Brechin C v St Mirren
Dundee v Hamilton A
Queen of the S v Clyde
St Johnstone v Airdrie U
Stranraer v Ross Co

Bell's Scottish Second Division
Alloa Ath v Stirling Alb
Ayr U v Gretna
Morton v Dumbarton
Peterhead v Forfar Ath
Raith R v Partick T

Bell's Scottish Third Division
Albion R v Queen's Park
Arbroath v Montrose
Cowdenbeath v East Fife
East Stirlingshire v Stenhousemuir
Elgin C v Berwick R

Saturday, 12 November 2005
Bell's Scottish First Division
Airdrie U v Hamilton A
Brechin C v Ross Co
Clyde v St Mirren
Dundee v St Johnstone
Queen of the S v Stranraer

Bell's Scottish Second Division
Alloa Ath v Morton
Ayr U v Raith R
Dumbarton v Forfar Ath
Partick T v Gretna
Peterhead v Stirling Alb

Bell's Scottish Third Division
Albion R v Elgin C
Arbroath v Berwick R
East Fife v Stenhousemuir
East Stirlingshire v Queen's Park
Montrose v Cowdenbeath

Saturday, 19 November 2005
Bank of Scotland
Scottish Premier League
Aberdeen v Hearts
Celtic v Rangers
Dundee U v Motherwell
Dunfermline Ath v Livingston
Hibernian v Falkirk
Kilmarnock v Inverness CT

Bell's Scottish First Division
Hamilton A v Queen of the S
Ross Co v Dundee
St Johnstone v Clyde
St Mirren v Airdrie U
Stranraer v Brechin C

Saturday, 26 November 2005
Bank of Scotland
Scottish Premier League
Celtic v Dunfermline Ath
Falkirk v Aberdeen
Hibernian v Rangers
Inverness CT v Dundee U
Livingston v Kilmarnock
Motherwell v Hearts

Bell's Scottish First Division
Clyde v Airdrie U
Dundee v Brechin C
Queen of the S v Ross Co
St Johnstone v Stranraer
St Mirren v Hamilton A

Bell's Scottish Second Division
Forfar Ath v Partick T
Gretna v Alloa Ath
Morton v Ayr U
Raith R v Peterhead
Stirling Alb v Dumbarton

Bell's Scottish Third Division
Berwick R v Albion R
Cowdenbeath v Arbroath
Elgin C v East Stirlingshire
Queen's Park v East Fife
Stenhousemuir v Montrose

Saturday, 3 December 2005
Bank of Scotland
Scottish Premier League
Aberdeen v Celtic
Dundee U v Hibernian
Dunfermline Ath v Kilmarnock
Hearts v Livingston
Motherwell v Inverness CT
Rangers v Falkirk

Bell's Scottish First Division
Airdrie U v Queen of the S
Brechin C v St Johnstone
Hamilton A v Clyde
Ross Co v St Mirren
Stranraer v Dundee

Bell's Scottish Second Division
Alloa Ath v Ayr U
Gretna v Peterhead
Morton v Partick T
Raith R v Dumbarton
Stirling Alb v Forfar Ath

Bell's Scottish Third Division
Berwick R v Stenhousemuir
Cowdenbeath v Albion R
East Stirlingshire v East Fife
Elgin C v Arbroath
Queen's Park v Montrose

Saturday, 10 December 2005
Bank of Scotland
Scottish Premier League
Aberdeen v Dunfermline Ath
Celtic v Hibernian
Falkirk v Motherwell
Hearts v Inverness CT
Kilmarnock v Rangers
Livingston v Dundee U

Bell's Scottish First Division
Brechin C v Hamilton A
Dundee v St Mirren
Ross Co v Clyde
St Johnstone v Queen of the S
Stranraer v Airdrie U

Saturday, 17 December 2005
Bank of Scotland
Scottish Premier League
Dundee U v Dunfermline Ath
Falkirk v Kilmarnock

Hibernian v Motherwell
Inverness CT v Celtic
Livingston v Aberdeen
Rangers v Hearts

Bell's Scottish First Division
Airdrie U v Brechin C
Clyde v Stranraer
Hamilton A v Ross Co
Queen of the S v Dundee
St Mirren v St Johnstone

Bell's Scottish Second Division
Ayr U v Stirling Alb
Dumbarton v Gretna
Forfar Ath v Raith R
Partick T v Alloa Ath
Peterhead v Morton

Bell's Scottish Third Division
Albion R v East Stirlingshire
Arbroath v Queen's Park
East Fife v Elgin C
Montrose v Berwick R
Stenhousemuir v Cowdenbeath

Monday, 26 December 2005
Bank of Scotland
Scottish Premier League
Celtic v Livingston
Dunfermline Ath v Rangers
Hearts v Falkirk
Inverness CT v Hibernian
Kilmarnock v Dundee U
Motherwell v Aberdeen

Bell's Scottish First Division
Brechin C v Clyde
Dundee v Airdrie U
Queen of the S v St Mirren
St Johnstone v Ross Co
Stranraer v Hamilton A

Bell's Scottish Second Division
Alloa Ath v Peterhead
Ayr U v Dumbarton
Gretna v Forfar Ath
Morton v Raith R
Partick T v Stirling Alb

Bell's Scottish Third Division
Albion R v Arbroath
East Fife v Berwick R
East Stirlingshire v Cowdenbeath
Elgin C v Montrose
Queen's Park v Stenhousemuir

Saturday, 31 December 2005
Bank of Scotland
Scottish Premier League
Aberdeen v Inverness CT
Falkirk v Dunfermline Ath
Hearts v Celtic
Kilmarnock v Hibernian
Livingston v Motherwell
Rangers v Dundee U

Bell's Scottish First Division
Airdrie U v St Johnstone
Clyde v Queen of the S
Hamilton A v Dundee
Ross Co v Stranraer
St Mirren v Brechin C

Bell's Scottish Second Division
Dumbarton v Partick T
Forfar Ath v Morton
Peterhead v Ayr U
Raith R v Alloa Ath
Stirling Alb v Gretna

Bell's Scottish Third Division
Arbroath v East Stirlingshire
Berwick R v Queen's Park
Cowdenbeath v Elgin C
Montrose v East Fife
Stenhousemuir v Albion R

Monday, 2 January 2006
Bell's Scottish First Division
Hamilton A v Airdrie U
Ross Co v Brechin C
St Johnstone v Dundee
St Mirren v Clyde
Stranraer v Queen of the S

Bell's Scottish Second Division
Dumbarton v Morton
Forfar Ath v Peterhead
Gretna v Ayr U
Partick T v Raith R
Stirling Alb v Alloa Ath

Bell's Scottish Third Division
Berwick R v Elgin C
East Fife v Cowdenbeath
Montrose v Arbroath
Queen's Park v Albion R
Stenhousemuir v East Stirlingshire

Saturday, 14 January 2006
Bank of Scotland
Scottish Premier League
Celtic v Kilmarnock
Dundee U v Falkirk
Dunfermline Ath v Hearts
Hibernian v Aberdeen
Inverness CT v Livingston
Motherwell v Rangers

Bell's Scottish First Division
Airdrie U v St Mirren
Brechin C v Stranraer
Clyde v St Johnstone
Dundee v Ross Co
Queen of the S v Hamilton A

Bell's Scottish Second Division
Alloa Ath v Forfar Ath
Ayr U v Partick T
Morton v Gretna
Peterhead v Dumbarton
Raith R v Stirling Alb

Bell's Scottish Third Division
Albion R v East Fife
Arbroath v Stenhousemuir
Cowdenbeath v Berwick R
East Stirlingshire v Montrose
Elgin C v Queen's Park

Saturday, 21 January 2006
Bank of Scotland
Scottish Premier League
Dundee U v Aberdeen
Falkirk v Inverness CT
Hibernian v Dunfermline Ath
Kilmarnock v Hearts
Motherwell v Celtic
Rangers v Livingston

Bell's Scottish First Division
Airdrie U v Clyde
Brechin C v Dundee
Hamilton A v St Mirren
Ross Co v Queen of the S
Stranraer v St Johnstone

Bell's Scottish Second Division
Forfar Ath v Dumbarton
Gretna v Partick T
Morton v Alloa Ath
Raith R v Ayr U
Stirling Alb v Peterhead

Bell's Scottish Third Division
Berwick R v Arbroath
Cowdenbeath v Montrose
Elgin C v Albion R
Queen's Park v East Stirlingshire
Stenhousemuir v East Fife

Saturday, 28 January 2006
Bank of Scotland
Scottish Premier League
Aberdeen v Kilmarnock
Celtic v Dundee U
Dunfermline Ath v Motherwell
Hearts v Hibernian
Inverness CT v Rangers
Livingston v Falkirk

Bell's Scottish First Division
Clyde v Hamilton A
Dundee v Stranraer
Queen of the S v Airdrie U
St Johnstone v Brechin C
St Mirren v Ross Co

Bell's Scottish Second Division
Alloa Ath v Gretna
Ayr U v Morton
Dumbarton v Stirling Alb
Partick T v Forfar Ath
Peterhead v Raith R

Bell's Scottish Third Division
Albion R v Berwick R
Arbroath v Cowdenbeath

East Fife v Queen's Park
East Stirlingshire v Elgin C
Montrose v Stenhousemuir

Saturday, 4 February 2006
Bell's Scottish Second Division
Alloa Ath v Partick T
Gretna v Dumbarton
Morton v Peterhead
Raith R v Forfar Ath
Stirling Alb v Ayr U

Bell's Scottish Third Division
Berwick R v Montrose
Cowdenbeath v Stenhousemuir
East Stirlingshire v Albion R
Elgin C v East Fife
Queen's Park v Arbroath

Tuesday, 7 February 2006
Bank of Scotland
Scottish Premier League
Dundee U v Hearts

Wednesday, 8 February 2006
Bank of Scotland
Scottish Premier League
Aberdeen v Rangers
Celtic v Falkirk
Dunfermline Ath v Inverness CT
Hibernian v Livingston
Kilmarnock v Motherwell

Saturday, 11 February 2006
Bank of Scotland
Scottish Premier League
Falkirk v Hibernian
Hearts v Aberdeen
Inverness CT v Kilmarnock
Livingston v Dunfermline Ath
Motherwell v Dundee U
Rangers v Celtic

Bell's Scottish First Division
Brechin C v Airdrie U
Dundee v Queen of the S
Ross Co v Hamilton A
St Johnstone v St Mirren
Stranraer v Clyde

Bell's Scottish Second Division
Ayr U v Alloa Ath
Dumbarton v Raith R
Forfar Ath v Stirling Alb
Partick T v Morton
Peterhead v Gretna

Bell's Scottish Third Division
Albion R v Cowdenbeath
Arbroath v Elgin C
East Fife v East Stirlingshire
Montrose v Queen's Park
Stenhousemuir v Berwick R

Saturday, 18 February 2006
Bank of Scotland
Scottish Premier League
Aberdeen v Falkirk
Dundee U v Inverness CT
Dunfermline Ath v Celtic
Hearts v Motherwell
Kilmarnock v Livingston
Rangers v Hibernian

Bell's Scottish First Division
Airdrie U v Ross Co
Clyde v Dundee
Hamilton A v St Johnstone
Queen of the S v Brechin C
St Mirren v Stranraer

Bell's Scottish Second Division
Dumbarton v Alloa Ath
Forfar Ath v Ayr U
Peterhead v Partick T
Raith R v Gretna
Stirling Alb v Morton

Bell's Scottish Third Division
Arbroath v East Fife
Berwick R v East Stirlingshire
Cowdenbeath v Queen's Park
Montrose v Albion R
Stenhousemuir v Elgin C

Saturday, 25 February 2006
Bell's Scottish Second Division
Alloa Ath v Raith R
Ayr U v Peterhead
Gretna v Stirling Alb
Morton v Forfar Ath
Partick T v Dumbarton

Bell's Scottish Third Division
Albion R v Stenhousemuir
East Fife v Montrose
East Stirlingshire v Arbroath
Elgin C v Cowdenbeath
Queen's Park v Berwick R

Saturday, 4 March 2006
Bank of Scotland
Scottish Premier League
Celtic v Aberdeen
Falkirk v Rangers
Hibernian v Dundee U
Inverness CT v Motherwell
Kilmarnock v Dunfermline Ath
Livingston v Hearts

Bell's Scottish First Division
Brechin C v St Mirren
Dundee v Hamilton A
Queen of the S v Clyde
St Johnstone v Airdrie U
Stranraer v Ross Co

Bell's Scottish Second Division
Alloa Ath v Stirling Alb
Ayr U v Gretna
Morton v Dumbarton
Peterhead v Forfar Ath
Raith R v Partick T

Bell's Scottish Third Division
Albion R v Queen's Park
Arbroath v Montrose
Cowdenbeath v East Fife
East Stirlingshire v Stenhousemuir
Elgin C v Berwick R

Saturday, 11 March 2006
Bank of Scotland
Scottish Premier League
Dundee U v Livingston
Dunfermline Ath v Aberdeen
Hibernian v Celtic
Inverness CT v Hearts
Motherwell v Falkirk
Rangers v Kilmarnock

Bell's Scottish First Division
Airdrie U v Dundee
Clyde v Brechin C
Hamilton A v Stranraer
Ross Co v St Johnstone
St Mirren v Queen of the S

Bell's Scottish Second Division
Dumbarton v Peterhead
Forfar Ath v Alloa Ath
Gretna v Morton
Partick T v Ayr U
Stirling Alb v Raith R

Bell's Scottish Third Division
Berwick R v Cowdenbeath
East Fife v Albion R
Montrose v East Stirlingshire
Queen's Park v Elgin C
Stenhousemuir v Arbroath

Saturday, 18 March 2006
Bank of Scotland
Scottish Premier League
Aberdeen v Livingston
Celtic v Inverness CT
Dunfermline Ath v Dundee U
Hearts v Rangers
Kilmarnock v Falkirk
Motherwell v Hibernian

Bell's Scottish First Division
Airdrie U v Hamilton A
Brechin C v Ross Co
Clyde v St Mirren
Dundee v St Johnstone
Queen of the S v Stranraer

Bell's Scottish Second Division
Alloa Ath v Morton
Ayr U v Raith R
Dumbarton v Forfar Ath
Partick T v Gretna
Peterhead v Stirling Alb

Bell's Scottish Third Division
Albion R v Elgin C
Arbroath v Berwick R
East Fife v Stenhousemuir
East Stirlingshire v Queen's Park
Montrose v Cowdenbeath

Saturday, 25 March 2006

Bank of Scotland
Scottish Premier League
Aberdeen v Motherwell
Dundee U v Kilmarnock
Falkirk v Hearts
Hibernian v Inverness CT
Livingston v Celtic
Rangers v Dunfermline Ath

Bell's Scottish First Division
Hamilton A v Queen of the S
Ross Co v Dundee
St Johnstone v Clyde
St Mirren v Airdrie U
Stranraer v Brechin C

Bell's Scottish Second Division
Forfar Ath v Partick T
Gretna v Alloa Ath
Morton v Ayr U
Raith R v Peterhead
Stirling Alb v Dumbarton

Bell's Scottish Third Division
Berwick R v Albion R
Cowdenbeath v Arbroath
Elgin C v East Stirlingshire
Queen's Park v East Fife
Stenhousemuir v Montrose

Saturday, 1 April 2006

Bank of Scotland
Scottish Premier League
Celtic v Hearts
Dundee U v Rangers
Dunfermline Ath v Falkirk
Hibernian v Kilmarnock
Inverness CT v Aberdeen
Motherwell v Livingston

Bell's Scottish First Division
Clyde v Airdrie U
Dundee v Brechin C
Queen of the S v Ross Co
St Johnstone v Stranraer
St Mirren v Hamilton A

Bell's Scottish Second Division
Ayr U v Stirling Alb
Dumbarton v Gretna
Forfar Ath v Raith R
Partick T v Alloa Ath
Peterhead v Morton

Bell's Scottish Third Division
Albion R v East Stirlingshire
Arbroath v Queen's Park
East Fife v Elgin C
Montrose v Berwick R
Stenhousemuir v Cowdenbeath

Saturday, 8 April 2006

Bank of Scotland
Scottish Premier League
Aberdeen v Hibernian
Falkirk v Dundee U
Hearts v Dunfermline Ath
Kilmarnock v Celtic
Livingston v Inverness CT
Rangers v Motherwell

Bell's Scottish First Division
Airdrie U v Queen of the S
Brechin C v St Johnstone
Hamilton A v Clyde
Ross Co v St Mirren
Stranraer v Dundee

Bell's Scottish Second Division
Alloa Ath v Ayr U
Gretna v Peterhead
Morton v Partick T
Raith R v Dumbarton
Stirling Alb v Forfar Ath

Bell's Scottish Third Division
Berwick R v Stenhousemuir
Cowdenbeath v Albion R
East Stirlingshire v East Fife
Elgin C v Arbroath
Queen's Park v Montrose

Saturday, 15 April 2006

Bell's Scottish First Division
Airdrie U v Stranraer
Clyde v Ross Co
Hamilton A v Brechin C
Queen of the S v St Johnstone
St Mirren v Dundee

Bell's Scottish Second Division
Dumbarton v Ayr U
Forfar Ath v Gretna
Peterhead v Alloa Ath
Raith R v Morton
Stirling Alb v Partick T

Bell's Scottish Third Division
Arbroath v Albion R
Berwick R v East Fife
Cowdenbeath v East Stirlingshire
Montrose v Elgin C
Stenhousemuir v Queen's Park

Saturday, 22 April 2006

Bell's Scottish First Division
Brechin C v Queen of the S
Dundee v Clyde
Ross Co v Airdrie U
St Johnstone v Hamilton A
Stranraer v St Mirren

Bell's Scottish Second Division
Alloa Ath v Dumbarton
Ayr U v Forfar Ath
Gretna v Raith R
Morton v Stirling Alb
Partick T v Peterhead

Bell's Scottish Third Division
Albion R v Montrose
East Fife v Arbroath
East Stirlingshire v Berwick R
Elgin C v Stenhousemuir
Queen's Park v Cowdenbeath

Saturday, 29 April 2006

Bell's Scottish First Division
Airdrie U v Brechin C
Clyde v Stranraer
Hamilton A v Ross Co
Queen of the S v Dundee
St Mirren v St Johnstone

Bell's Scottish Second Division
Dumbarton v Partick T
Forfar Ath v Morton
Peterhead v Ayr U
Raith R v Alloa Ath
Stirling Alb v Gretna

Bell's Scottish Third Division
Arbroath v East Stirlingshire
Berwick R v Queen's Park
Cowdenbeath v Elgin C
Montrose v East Fife
Stenhousemuir v Albion R

OTHER FIXTURES 2005–06

JULY 2005

Sat 2	UEFA Intertoto Cup 2 (1)
Sun 3	UEFA Intertoto Cup 2 (1)
Sat 9	UEFA Intertoto Cup 2 (2)
Sun 10	UEFA Intertoto Cup 2 (2)
Wed 13	UEFA Champions League 1Q (1)
Thur 14	UEFA Cup 1Q (1)
Sat 16	UEFA Intertoto Cup 3 (1)
Sun 17	UEFA Intertoto Cup 3 (1)
Wed 20	UEFA Champions League 1Q (2)
Sat 23	UEFA Intertoto Cup 3 (2)
Wed 27	UEFA Champions League 2Q (1)
	UEFA Intertoto Cup SF (1)
Thur 28	UEFA Cup 1Q (2)
Fri 29	UEFA Champions League 3Q Draw
	UEFA Cup 2Q Draw

AUGUST 2005

Wed 3	UEFA Champions League 2Q (2)
	UEFA Intertoto Cup SF (2)
Sat 6	Start of Football League
Sun 7	FA Community Shield
Tue 9	UEFA Intertoto Cup Final (1)
	UEFA Champions League 3Q (1)
Wed 10	UEFA Champions League 3Q (1)
Thur 11	UEFA Cup 2Q (1)
Sat 13	Start of FA Premier League
Tue 16	Russia v England – U/20 Friendly
Wed 17	Denmark v England – Copenhagen – Friendly
Sat 20	FA Cup EP
Tue 23	UEFA Intertoto Cup Final (2)
	UEFA Champions League 3Q (2)
Wed 24	UEFA Champions League 3Q (2)
	FL Carling Cup 1
Thur 25	UEFA Cup 2Q (2)
	UEFA Champions League Group Stage Draw
Fri 26	UEFA Super Cup
	UEFA Cup 1st Rd Draw
Sat 27	FA Cup P
Mon 29	Bank Holiday

SEPTEMBER 2005

Fri 2	Wales v England – venue tbc – U21 UEFA Qualifier
Sat 3	Wales v England – Cardiff – FIFA World Cup Qualifier
Tue 6	Germany v England – venue tbc – U21 UEFA Qualifier
Wed 7	Northern Ireland v England – Belfast – FIFA World Cup Qualifier
	England v tbc – U/19 Friendly
Sat 10	FA Cup 1Q
Sun 11	FA Women's Cup 1Q
Mon12	FA Youth Cup P**
Tue 13	UEFA Champions League Match Day 1
Wed 14	UEFA Champions League Match Day 1
Thur 15	UEFA Cup 1 (1)
Sat 17	FA Vase 1Q
Wed 21	FL Carling Cup 2
Sat 24	FA Cup 2Q
Sun 25	FA Women's Cup 2Q
Mon 26	FA Youth Cup 1Q**
Tue 27	UEFA Champions League Match Day 2
Wed 28	FA National League System Cup 1*
	UEFA Champions League Match Day 2
Thur 29	UEFA Cup 1 (2)

OCTOBER 2005

Sat 1	FA Vase 2Q
Sun 2	FA Sunday Cup 1
Tue 4	UEFA Cup Group Stage Draw
Fri 7	England v Austria venue tbc – U21 UEFA Qualifier
Sat 8	England v Austria – Manchester United FC – FIFA World Cup Qualifier
	FA Cup 3Q
Sun 9	FA County Youth Cup 1*
Mon 10	FA Youth Cup 2Q**
Tue 11	England v Poland – venue tbc – U21 UEFA Qualifier
Wed 12	England v Poland – Manchester United FC – FIFA World Cup Qualifier
Fri 14	England v Wales – U/16 Victory Shield
Sat 15	FA Trophy 1Q
Tue 18	UEFA Champions League Match Day 3
Wed 19	UEFA Champions League Match Day 3
	LDV Vans Trophy 1
Thur 20	UEFA Cup Match Day 1
Sat 22	FA Cup 4Q
Sun 23	FA Women's Cup 1P
Mon 24	FA Youth Cup 3Q**
Wed 26	FL Carling Cup 3
Sat 29	FA Vase 1P
Sun 30	FA Sunday Cup 2
	British summer time ends

NOVEMBER 2005

Tue 1	UEFA Champions League Match Day 4
Wed 2	UEFA Champions League Match Day 4
Thur 3	UEFA Cup Match Day 2
Fri 4	England v Northern Ireland – U16 Victory Shield
Sat 5	FA Cup 1P
Sun 6	FA County Youth Cup 2*
Sat 12	FA Trophy 2Q
	FA Youth Cup 1P*
	FIFA World Cup Play Off's
Sun 13	FA Women's Cup 2P
	Remembrance Sunday
Wed 16	Holland v England – Friendly
	FIFA World Cup Play Off's
	England v Switzerland – U/19 Friendly
Sat 19	FA Vase 2P
Sun 20	FA Sunday Cup 3
Tue 22	UEFA Champions League Match Day 5
Wed 23	UEFA Champions League Match Day 5
	LDV Vans Trophy 2
Thur 24	UEFA Cup Match Day 3
Fri 25	Scotland v England – U16 Victory Shield
Sat 26	FA Trophy 3Q
	FA Youth Cup 2P*
Wed 30	UEFA Cup Match Day 4 *(English Clubs seeded with a 'bye' on this date)*
	FL Carling Cup 4

DECEMBER 2005

Sat 3	FA Cup 2P
	FA National League System Cup 2*
Sun 4	FA Women's Cup 3P
Tue 6	UEFA Champions League Match Day 6
Wed 7	UEFA Champions League Match Day 6
	LDV Vans Trophy Area QF
Sat 10	FA Vase 3P
Sun 11	FA County Youth Cup 3*
Wed 14	UEFA Cup Match Day 5
Fri 16	UEFA Champions League 1st Knock-out Rd Draw
	UEFA Cup Last 32/16 Rd's Draws

Sat 17 FA Trophy 1P
FA Youth Cup 3P*
Wed 21 FL Carling Cup 5
Sat 24 Christmas Eve
Sun 25 Christmas Day
Mon 26 Boxing Day
Tue 27 Bank Holiday
Sat 31

JANUARY 2006
Sun 1 New Years Day
Mon 2 Bank Holiday
Sat 7 FA Cup 3P
Sun 8 FA Women's Cup 4P
Wed 11 FL Carling Cup SF 1
Sat 14 FA Trophy 2P
Sun 15 FA Sunday Cup 4
Sat 21 FA Vase 4P
FA Youth Cup 4P*
Wed 25 FL Carling Cup SF 2
LDV Vans Trophy Area SF
Sat 28 FA Cup 4P
Sun 29 FA County Youth Cup 4*
FA Women's Cup 5P

FEBRUARY 2006
Sat 4 FA Trophy 3P
FA Youth Cup 5P*
Sat 11 FA Vase 5P
Sun 12 FA Women's Cup 6P
Wed 15 UEFA Cup 32 (1)
LDV Vans Trophy Area Final 1
Sat 18 FA Cup 5P
FA Youth Cup 6P*
Sun 19 FA Sunday Cup 5
Tue 21 UEFA Champions League 16 (1)
Wed 22 UEFA Champions League 16 (1)
LDV Vans Trophy Area Final 2
Thur 23 UEFA Cup 32 (2)
Sat 25 FA Trophy 4P
FA National League System Cup 3*
Sun 26 FL Carling Cup Final

MARCH 2006
Wed 1 International Friendly
Sat 4 FA Vase 6P
Sun 5 FA County Youth Cup SF*
Tue 7 UEFA Champions League 16 (2)
Wed 8 UEFA Champions League 16 (2)
Thur 9 UEFA Cup 16 (1)
Sat 11 FA Youth Cup SF (1)*
Sun 12 FA Women's Cup SF
Wed 15 UEFA Cup 16 (2)
Fri 17 UEFA Champions League QF/SF Draws
UEFA Cup QF/SF Draws
Sat 18 FA Trophy SF (1)
Sun 19 FA Sunday Cup SF
Wed 22 FA Cup 6P+
Sat 25 FA Trophy SF (2)
FA Youth Cup SF (2)*

** closing date of round*
*** ties to be played in the week commencing*
+ actual dates of ties to be decided

Sun 26 British summer time begins
Tue 28 UEFA Champions League QF (1)
Wed 29 UEFA Champions League QF (1)
Thur 30 UEFA Cup QF (1)

APRIL 2006
Sat 1 FA Vase SF (1)
Sun 2 LDV Vans Trophy Final
Tue 4 UEFA Champions League QF (2)
Wed 5 UEFA Champions League QF (2)
Thur 6 UEFA Cup QF (2)
Sat 8 FA Vase SF (2)
Fri 14 Good Friday
Sat 15
Mon 17 Easter Monday
Tue 18 UEFA Champions League SF (1)
Wed 19 UEFA Champions League SF (1)
Thur 20 UEFA Cup SF (1)
Sat 22 FA Cup SF
FA National League System Cup SF*
Tue 25 UEFA Champions League SF (2)
Wed 26 UEFA Champions League SF (2)
Thur 27 UEFA Cup SF (2)
Sat 29 FA County Youth Cup Final (prov)
Sun 30 FA Sunday Cup Final (prov)
End of Football League Championship

MAY 2006
Mon 1 Bank Holiday
FA Women's Cup Final
Sat 6 FA Vase Final (prov)
FA National League System Cup Final (prov)
Play Off SF (1) – League Championship
End of FA Premier League
End of Football League 1 & 2
Sun 7 FA Vase Final (prov)
FA National League System Cup Final (prov)
Wed 10 UEFA Cup Final
Play Off SF (2) – League Championship
Sat 13 FA Cup Final
Play Off SF (1) – League 1 & 2
Sun 14 FA Trophy Final
Wed 17 UEFA Champions League Final
Play Off SF (2) – League 1 & 2
Sun 21 Play Off Final – League Championship
Sat 27 Play Off Final – League 1
Sun 28 Play Off Final – League 2
Mon 29 Bank Holiday
Wed 31 Start of close season at midnight

JUNE 2006
Fri 9 World Cup Commences
Fri 30 World Cup Quarter Finals
End of close season at midnight

JULY 2006
Sat 1 World Cup Quarter Finals
Tue 4 World Cup Semi-Finals
Wed 5 World Cup Semi-Finals
Sat 8 World Cup 3rd Place
Sun 9 World Cup Final

STOP PRESS

Gerrard U-turn and Euro treble ... Italy bound Vieira by Juve ... Jose and Sir Alex on the Dein fixture machine ... Shaun W-P £21m to Chelsea, but Lyon's Essien would cost them £32m.

Summer transfers completed and pending: **Premier Division: Arsenal:** Alexander Hleb (Stuttgart). **Aston Villa:** Aaron Hughes (Newcastle U) £1,500,000; Kevin Phillips (Southampton) £1,000,000; Patrik Berger (Portsmouth); Stuart Taylor (Arsenal). **Birmingham C:** Mikael Forssell (Chelsea) £3,000,000; Mehdi Nafti (Santander). **Blackburn R:** Craig Bellamy (Newcastle U) £5,000,000; Shefki Kuqi (Ipswich T). **Bolton W:** El-Hadji Diouf (Liverpool); Ian Walker (Leicester C). **Charlton Ath:** Darren Bent (Ipswich T) £3,000,000; Darren Ambrose (Newcastle U); Chris Powell (West Ham U); Alexei Smertin (Chelsea) Loan; Gonzalo Sorondo (Internazionale) Loan; Jonathan Spector (Manchester U) Loan. **Chelsea:** Shaun Wright-Phillips (Manchester C) £21,000,000; Asier Del Horno (Athletic Bilbao) £8,000,000; Lassana Diarra (Le Havre); Scott Sinclair (Bristol R). **Everton:** Per Kroldrup (Udinese) £5,000,000; Mikel Arteta (Real Sociedad) £2,000,000. **Fulham:** Heidar Helguson (Watford) £1,300,000; Jaroslav Drobny (Panionios); Ahmad Elrich (Pusan Icons); Niclas Jensen (B. Dortmund). **Liverpool:** Jose Reina (Villarreal) £6,000,000; Mohamed Sissoko (Valencia) £5,600,000; Antonio Barragan (Sevilla); Mark Gonzalez (Albecete); Boudewijn Zenden (Middlesbrough). **Manchester C:** Kiki Musampa (Continuing Loan). **Manchester U:** Park Ji-Sung (PSV Eindhoven) £4,000,000; Edwin Van der Sar (Fulham). **Middlesbrough:** Ayegbeni Yakubu (Portsmouth) £7,500,000; Emanuel Pogatetz (Leverkusen) £1,800,000. **Newcastle U:** Scott Parker (Chelsea) £6,500,000; Emre Belezoglu (Internazionale); Tim Krul (Den Haag). **Portsmouth:** Andy O'Brien (Newcastle U) £2,000,000; Collins Mbesuma (Kaiser Chiefs); Laurent Robert (Newcastle U) Loan; John Viafara (Once Caldas); Gregory Vignal (Liverpool). **Sunderland:** Jon Stead (Blackburn R) £1,800,000; Kelvin Davis (Ipswich T) £1,250,000; Tommy Miller (Ipswich T); Daryl Murphy (Waterford U); Nyron Nosworthy (Gillingham); Martin Woods (Leeds U). **Tottenham H:** Tom Huddlestone (Derby Co) £2,500,000; Aaron Lennon (Leeds U); Wayne Routledge (Crystal Palace); Paul Stalteri (Werder Bremen); Teemu Tainio (Auxerre). **West Bromwich Albion:** Darren Carter (Birmingham C) £1,500,000; Chris Kirkland (Liverpool) Loan; Steve Watson (Everton). **West Ham U:** Paul Konchesky (Charlton Ath) £1,500,000; Roy Carroll (Manchester U); James Collins (Cardiff C); Danny Gabbidon (Cardiff C). **Wigan Ath:** Mike Pollitt (Rotherham U) £200,000; Ryan Taylor (Tranmere R) £750,000; Pascal Chimbonda (Bastia).

Football League Championship: Brighton & HA: Jason Dodd (Southampton); Colin Kazim-Richards (Bury). **Burnley:** Wade Elliott (Bournemouth); Daniel Karbassiyoon (Arsenal); Richard Keogh (Stoke C); Gareth O'Connor (Bournemouth); Wayne Thomas (Stoke C). **Cardiff C:** Mikkel Bischoff (Manchester C); Neil Cox (Watford); Jeff Whitley (Sunderland). **Coventry C:** Richard Duffy (Portsmouth) Loan; Matt Heath (Leicester C); Clayton Ince (Crewe Alex); James Scowcroft (Ipswich T). **Crewe Alex:** Juan Ugarte (Wrexham). **Crystal Palace:** Jonathan Macken (Manchester C) £1,100,000; Jobi McAnuff (Cardiff C). **Derby Co:** Marc Edworthy (Norwich C). **Hull C:** Stephen McPhee (Beira Mar) £220,000; Keith Andrews (Wolverhampton W). **Ipswich T:** Nicky Forster (Reading); Dean McDonald (Arsenal); Sam Parkin (Swindon T). **Leeds U:** Dan Harding (Brighton & HA) Tribunal; Eddie Lewis (Preston NE); Steve Stone (Portsmouth). **Leicester C:** Rab Douglas (Celtic); Nils-Eric Johansson (Blackburn R); Momo Sylla (Celtic). **Luton T:** Rowan Vine (Portsmouth) £250,000. **Norwich C:** Matthieu Louis-Jean (Nottingham F); Peter Thorne (Cardiff C). **Plymouth Arg:** Rufus Brevett (West Ham U); Akos Buzsaki (Porto); Taribo West (Al-Arabi). **Preston NE:** Danny Dichio (Millwall) £160,000; Joe Anyinsah (Bristol C). **QPR:** Simon Royce (Charlton Ath). **Reading:** Leroy Lita (Bristol C) £1,000,000; Kevin Doyle (Cork C); Steve Hunt (Brentford); Shane Long (Cork C). **Sheffield U:** Danny Webber (Watford) £500,000; Gary Mulligan (Wolverhampton W); Lilian Nalis (Leicester C); Karl Nix (Aston Villa); Craig Short (Blackburn R). **Sheffield W:** John Hills (Gillingham). **Southampton:** Darren Powell (Crystal Palace); Dennis Wise (Millwall). **Stoke C:** Mamady Sidibe (Gillingham); Peter Sweeney (Millwall). **Watford:** Martin Devaney (Cheltenham T); Junior (Derby Co). **Wolverhampton W:** Rohan Ricketts (Tottenham H).

Football League 1: Barnsley: Paul Hayes (Scunthorpe U) Tribunal; Brian Howard (Swindon T); Richard Kell (Scunthorpe U); Daniel Nardiello (Manchester U). **Blackpool:** John Doolan (Doncaster R); Scott Vernon (Oldham Ath). **Bournemouth:** Stephen Cooke (Aston Villa). **Bradford C:** Russell Howarth (Tranmere R); Bobby Petta (Darlington); Andrew Taylor (Middlesbrough) Loan. **Brentford:** Paul Brooker (Reading); DJ Campbell (Yeading); Ricky Newman (Reading); Lloyd Owusu (Reading); Olafur Ingi Skulason (Arsenal); Sam Tillen (Chelsea). **Bristol C:** Matt Heywood (Swindon T); Alex Russell (Torquay U); Grant Smith (Swindon T); Marcus Stewart (Sunderland). **Chesterfield:** Paul Hall (Tranmere R). **Colchester U:** Chris Iwelumo (Aachen). **Doncaster R:** Sean Thornton (Sunderland) £175,000; Paul Heffernan (Bristol C) £100,000; Jan Budtz (Nordsjaelland); Phil McGuire (Aberdeen); Tonny Nielsen (Fremad); Steve Roberts (Wrexham). **Gillingham:** Tony Bullock (Dundee U). **Hartlepool U:** Chris Llewellyn (Wrexham); Michael Proctor (Rotherham U). **Huddersfield T:** Martin McIntosh (Rotherham U). **Milton Keynes Dons:** Craig Morgan (Wrexham); Aaron Wilbraham (Hull C). **Nottingham F:** Ian Breckin (Wigan Ath) £350,000; Nicky Eaden (Wigan Ath); Gary Holt (Norwich C); Gino Padula (QPR). **Oldham Ath:** Luke Beckett (Sheffield U) Loan; Richard Butler (Lincoln C); Paul Edwards (Blackpool); Terrell Forbes (Grimsby T); Andy Liddell (Sheffield U); Gareth Owen (Stoke C); Chris Porter (Bury); Rob Scott (Rotherham U); Chris Swailes (Rotherham U); Paul Warne (Rotherham U); Richard Wellens (Blackpool). **Port Vale:** Mickey Bell (Bristol C); Tony Dinning (Bristol C); Mark Innes (Chesterfield); Danny Sonner (Peterborough U). **Rotherham U:** Deon Burton (Brentford); Colin Murdock (Crewe Alex); Jon Otsemobor (Liverpool); Gregor Robertson (Nottingham F); Lee Williamson (Northampton T); David Worrell (Plymouth Arg). **Scunthorpe U:** Jim Goodwin (Stockport Co); Ritchie Ryan (Sunderland). **Swansea C:** Marc Goodfellow (Bristol C). **Swindon T:** Nicky Nicolau (Southend U); Gareth Whalley (Wigan Ath). **Tranmere R:** Sam Aiston (Shrewsbury T); Chris Greenacre (Stoke C); Steve Wilson (Macclesfield T). **Walsall:** Daniel Fox (Everton); Anthony Gerrard (Everton); Chris Westwood (Hartlepool U). **Yeovil T:** Matt Harrold (Brentford); Nathan Jones (Brighton & HA); Luke Oliver (Woking); David Poole (Manchester U).

Football League 2: Boston U: Lee Canoville (Torquay U); Ben Futcher (Lincoln C); Julian Joachim (Leeds U); Gavin Johnson (Colchester U); Stuart Talbot (Brentford); Noel Whelan (Aberdeen). **Bury:** Stuart Barlow (Stockport Co); Craig Dootson (Stalybridge C); Neil Edwards (Rochdale); John Fitzgerald (Blackburn R); Jake Sedgemore (Shrewsbury T). **Carlisle U:** Zigor Aranalde (Sheffield W); Anthony Williams (Grimsby T). **Chester C:** Scott McNiven (Mansfield T); Marcus Richardson (Yeovil T). **Darlington:** Simon Johnson (Leeds U). **Grimsby T:** Terry Barwick (Scunthorpe U); Paul Bolland (Notts Co); John Lukic (Nottingham F); Steve Mildenhall (Oldham Ath); Jermaine Palmer (Stoke C). **Leyton Orient:** Joe Dolan (Millwall); Craig Easton (Livingston); Glyn Garner (Bury); Joe Keith (Colchester U); Shane Tudor (Cambridge U). **Lincoln C:** Danny Bacon (Hucknall T); Omari Coleman (Watford); Colin Cryan (Scarborough); Dean Keates (Kidderminster H); Scott Kerr (Scarborough); Paul Mayo (Watford); Steve Robinson (Swindon T). **Macclesfield T:** Kevin Townson (Rochdale). **Mansfield T:** Adam Birchall (Arsenal); Jason Talbot (Bolton W); Matthew Tipton (Macclesfield T); Gus Uhlenbeek (Wycombe W). **Northampton T:** Chris Doig (Nottingham F); Eoin Jess (Nottingham F); Bradley Johnson (Cambridge U); Brett Johnson (Aldershot T); Ian Taylor (Derby Co). **Notts Co:** Kevin Pilkington (Mansfield T). **Oxford U:** Stuart Gray (Rushden & D); Chris Hargreaves (Brentford); Lee Mansell (Luton T); Billy Turley (Rushden & D); Chris Willmott (Northampton T). **Peterborough U:** Paul Carden (Chester C); Danny Crow (Norwich C); Lee Harrison (Leyton Orient); Dean Holden (Oldham Ath). **Rochdale:** Jon Boardman (Woking); Tommy Jaszczun (Northampton T). **Rushden & D:** Neil McCafferty (Charlton Ath); Greg Pearson (West Ham U); Dave Savage (Bristol R). **Shrewsbury T:** Jay Denny (Stoke C); Ben Herd (Watford); Neil Sorvel (Crewe Alex); Mark Stallard (Barnsley). **Stockport Co:** Rob Clare (Blackpool); Jermaine Easter (Boston U); Mark Robinson (Hereford U). **Torquay U:** Alan Connell (Bournemouth); Darren Garner (Rotherham U); Matt Villis (Plymouth Arg). **Wrexham:** Dave Bayliss (Luton T); Michael Ingham (Sunderland); Lee Roche (Burnley); Jonathan Walters (Hull C). **Wycombe W:** Will Antwi (Aldershot T); Kevin Betsy (Oldham Ath); Tommy Mooney (Oxford U); Stefan Oakes (Notts Co).

Leaving the country: Thimothee Atouba Tottenham H to Hamburg; Thomas Hitzlsperger Aston Villa to Stuttgart; Andreas Jakobsson Southampton to Helsingborg; Mateja Kezman Chelsea to Atletico Madrid £5,300,000; Christian Negouai Manchester C to Standard Liege; Mauricio Pellegrino Liverpool to Alaves; Patrick Vieira Arsenal to Juventus £13,700,000; Adam Virgo Brighton & HA to Celtic.

Add to records: Most capped: Kenny Cunningham, equals Birmingham C record; Jonatan Johansson Charlton Ath.
Youngest players: Ikechi Anya (Wycombe W); David McDermott (Walsall); Rob Norris (Boston U); Paul Turnbull (Stockport Co).
Most goals in a season: Jon Parkin (Macclesfield T).
Most goals overall: Neil Harris, equals Millwall record.